THE RISK MANAGEMENT ASSOCIATION
Serving the Financial Services Industry

ANNUAL STATEMENT STUDIES

Financial Ratio Benchmarks

2010
2011

RMA
Annual Statement Studies®
Copyright, Ordering, Licensing, and Use of Data

All of the information contained herein is obtained from sources believed to be accurate and reliable.

To **obtain permission** to copy, quote, reproduce, replicate, disseminate, or distribute the Statement Studies® data/material please fax or e-mail a brief letter stating who you are and how you intend to use the Statement Studies® data to: Statement Studies Information Products at fax number 215-446-4101 or via e-mail to studies@rmahq.org. Depending on the requested use, RMA may require a license agreement and royalty fee. A **License Agreement is required** if you wish to use or incorporate any portion of the data, in whole or in part in other products that will in turn be sold to others, such as in software oriented or derived products, scholarly publications, or training materials.

To **purchase** a copy, or additional copies, of the Statement Studies® data in book or online format, contact RMA's Customer Relations at 1-800-677-7621. Regional data presented in the same fashion as you see in this book is only available in eStatement Studies.

If you have a **question regarding the data** please reference the detailed explanatory notes provided in the Introduction section of the enclosed product. If you are unable to find the answer to your question please contact us by e-mail at: studies@rmahq.org. Be sure to include your detailed question along with your telephone number, fax number, and e-mail address.

The Risk Management Association
1801 Market Street, Suite 300
Philadelphia, PA 19103
©2010 by RMA.
ISBN# 978-1-57070-326-3

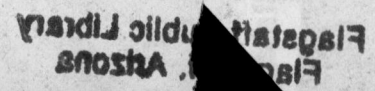

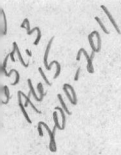

TABLE OF CONTENTS

Information on Copyright, Ordering, Licensing, and use of Data 2

List of Participating Institutions 5

Introduction to Statement Studies and Organization of Content 9

Definition of Ratios 12

Explanation of Noncontractor Balance Sheet and Income Data 21

Explanation of Contractor—Percentage-of-Completion Basis of Accounting 22

IDP Sample Report 25

NAICS Codes Appearing in the Statement Studies 29

Full Descriptions of Industries Appearing in the Statement Studies 35

	Description Index	Data Set Begins On
Agriculture, Forestry, Fishing and Hunting	35	97
Mining	36	155
Utilities	37	171
Construction—General Industries Format*	37	179
Manufacturing	40	241
Wholesale Trade	59	767
Retail Trade	64	911
Transportation and Warehousing	68	1039
Information	71	1105
Finance and Insurance	73	1145
Real Estate and Rental and Leasing	75	1203
Professional, Scientific and Technical Services	76	1245
Management of Companies and Enterprises	80	1319
Administrative and Support and Waste Management and Remediation Services	80	1325
Educational Services	82	1383
Health Care and Social Assistance	83	1401
Arts, Entertainment and Recreation	87	1481
Accommodation and Food Services	89	1513
Other Services (Except Public Administration)	90	1535
Public Administration	92	1605
Construction—Percentage of Completion Basis of Accounting*	93	1631

Supplemental Information:

Construction Financial Management Association Data 1655

Text—Key Word Index of Industries Appearing in the Statement Studies 1671

RMA's Credit & Lending Dictionary 1679

*General Industries Format means that a valid construction NAICS was assigned to the subject companies contained in the sample; however, the financial statements were prepared using a general or traditional manufacturing or service industries presentation of results versus using a percentage-of-completion method of accounting. Industries found in the percentage-of-completion presentation follow the presentation used by RMA in the past.

About RMA

Founded in 1914, The Risk Management Association is a not-for-profit, member-driven professional association whose sole purpose is to advance the use of sound risk principles in the financial services industry. RMA promotes an enterprise approach to risk management that focuses on credit risk, market risk, and operational risk.

Headquartered in Philadelphia, Pennsylvania, RMA has 3,000 institutional members that include banks of all sizes as well as nonbank financial institutions. They are represented in the association by 18,000 risk management professionals who are chapter members in financial centers throughout North America, Europe, and Asia/Pacific. Visit RMA on the Web at www.rmahq.org.

RMA ACKNOWLEDGES AND THANKS THE FOLLOWING INSTITUTIONS, CONTRIBUTORS TO THE 2010 STATEMENT STUDIES DATA SUBMISSION PROGRAM.

ALABAMA
BBVA Compass Bank
Regions Bank

ALASKA
Northrim Bank

ARKANSAS
Simmons First National Corporation

CALIFORNIA
Bank of Agriculture & Commerce
Bank of Stockton
Bank of the West
California Bank and Trust
Citizens Business Bank
East West Bank
Farmers & Merchants Bank Central
    California
First Commerce Bank
First Northern Bank of Dixon
Pacific Enterprise Bank
Security Business Bank
Tri Counties Bank
Valley Community Bank
Wells Fargo
Westamerica Bank

COLORADO
American National Bank
CoBank
Colorado Business Bank
First National Bank
First National Bank of Durango

CONNECTICUT
Chelsea Groton Savings Bank
Dime Bank
The Milford Bank
Windsor Federal Savings

DELAWARE
Christiana Bank & Trust
Delaware National Bank

FLORIDA
The Bank of Tampa
Capital City Bank

FirstCity Bank of Commerce
Seacoast National Bank

GEORGIA
The Brand Banking Company
First American Bank & Trust Co.
Georgia Bank & Trust Co.
Heritage Bank of the South
SunTrust Bank
Wachovia Corporation

HAWAII
American Savings Bank
Central Pacific Bank
Finance Factors, Ltd.
First Hawaiian Bank

IDAHO
Mountain West Bank
Washington Trust Bank

ILLINOIS
Albany Bank & Trust Company N.A.
Alpine Bank & Trust Co.
American National Bank DeKalb
    County
First Midwest Bank
Glenview State Bank
National Republic Bank of Chicago

INDIANA
2nd Source Bank
Lake City Bank
Old National Bank
STAR Financial Bank

IOWA
American Trust & Savings Bank
First National Bank
Heartland Financial USA, Inc.
Security National Bank
Wells Fargo

KANSAS
Emprise Bank
Fidelity Bank
INTRUST Bank N.A.
Midland National Bank
Silver Lake Bank

SNB Bank of Kansas
Sunflower Bank, N.A.

KENTUCKY
Central Bancshares, Inc.
Community Trust Bank, Inc.

LOUISIANA
Capital One
Jeff Davis Bank & Trust Co.
Red River Bank
South Louisiana Bank
Whitney National Bank

MAINE
The First, N.A.
Gorham Savings Bank
Kennebunk Savings Bank
Norway Savings Bank
Skowhegan Savings Bank
TD Banknorth N.A.

MARYLAND
The Bank of Glen Burnie
The Columbia Bank
Frederick County Bank
National Penn Bank
New Windsor State Bank
OBA Federal Savings Bank
Sandy Spring Bank
Susquehanna Bank

MASSACHUSETTS
Bank of Canton N.A.
BankFive N.A.
Bristol County Savings Bank
Charles River Bank
Eastern Bank
Enterprise Bank & Trust Co.
North Middlesex Savings Bank
Randolph Savings Bank
Rockland Trust Company
Sovereign Bank
United Bank

MICHIGAN
Citizens Bank
Citizens National Bank of
    Cheboygan

6

Mercantile Bank of Michigan
National Bank of Middlebury
State Bank
United Bank of Michigan

MINNESOTA

AgriBank, FCB
AgStar Financial Services
American Bank of St. Paul
BankCherokee
Beacon Bank
Citizens Independent Bank
Community Bank Corporation
Fidelity Bank
Home Federal Savings Bank
KleinBank
Merchants Bank N.A.
Peoples Bank of Commerce
Roundbank
State Bank & Trust
Stearns Bank N.A.
U.S. Bank
Western Bank

MISSISSIPPI

BancorpSouth
First Commercial Bank
Merchants & Farmers Bank
Renasant Bank
The Peoples Bank
Trustmark National Bank

MISSOURI

Cass Commercial Bank
Commerce Bank
First Banks Inc.
Hawthorn Bank
Jefferson Bank of Missouri
Missouri Bank & Trust Company
Pulaski Bank
Royal Banks of Missouri
Triad Bank

MONTANA

First Interstate Bank

NEBRASKA

First National Bank
First National Bank and Trust
First National Bank North Platte
Mutual of Omaha Bank
Union Bank & Trust Company

NEW HAMPSHIRE

Connecticut River Bank
Laconia Savings Bank
Ledyard National Bank

NEW JERSEY

The Bank
Grand Bank, N.A.
Harmony Bank
Magyar Bank
Peapack-Gladstone Bank
Skylands Community Bank
Sun National Bank
Union Center National Bank

NEW YORK

Adirondack Bank
The Adirondack Trust Company
Alliance Bank N.A.
Bank of Castile
The Bank of New York Mellon
Canandaigua National Bank
Champlain National Bank
Chemung Canal Trust Company
Citibank, N.A.
Community Bank, N.A.
HSBC Bank USA N.A.
National Union Bank of Kinderhook
NBT Bank N.A.
State Bank of Long Island
Steuben Trust Company
Suffolk County National Bank
Tioga State Bank

NORTH CAROLINA

Bank of America
Branch Banking & Trust
First Citizens Bank & Trust Co.
NewBridge Bancorp

NORTH DAKOTA

Alerus Financial N.A.
Frandsen Bank & Trust

OHIO

Fifth Third Bank
First Financial Bank
FirstMerit Bank, N.A.
Huntington National Bank
KeyBank
Liberty Savings Bank FSB
Second National Bank a Division of
   the Park National Bank

OKLAHOMA

Stillwater National Bank

OREGON

Pacific Continental Bank
People's Bank of Commerce
Washington Trust Bank
West Coast Bank

PENNSYLVANIA

AmeriServ Financial
The Bank of New York Mellon
Bryn Mawr Trust Co.
CNB Bank
Community Bank
DNB First, National Association
Dollar Bank, FSB
Fidelity Bank Pa SB
Fidelity Deposit & Discount Bank
First Columbia Bank & Trust Co.
First Commonwealth Bank
First Liberty Bank and Trust
First Niagara Bank, N.A.
Firstrust Bank
FNB Bank
FNB Corp.
Fulton Bank
Lafayette Ambassador Bank
Luzerne Bank
Mainline National Bank
National Penn Bank
Orrstown Bank
PeoplesBank a Codorus Valley
   Company
PNC Bank
Somerset Trust Company
Swineford National Bank
Univest National Bank & Trust Co.
VIST Bank
Washington Financial Bank
Woodlands Bank
York Traditions Bank

RHODE ISLAND

Citizens Financial Group
Randolph Savings Bank
The Washington Trust Company

SOUTH CAROLINA

Conway National Bank
First Citizens Bank & Trust Co.
   of South Carolina
Harbor National Bank
The South Financial Group

SOUTH DAKOTA

First National Bank South Dakota
The First National Bank in Sioux
   Falls
First Premier Bank
Home Federal Bank

TENNESSEE

First Farmers and Merchants Bank
First Tennessee Bank

TEXAS

Amarillo National Bank
American Bank of Texas
Bank of the West - El Paso
Broadway National Bank
Comerica Bank
ExtracoBanks, N.A.
First State Bank Central Texas
Frost National Bank
Southside Bank
Southwest Bank
Stillwater National Bank

UTAH

Bank of Utah
First Utah Bank
Washington Trust Bank
Zions Bancorporation

VERMONT

Community National Bank
Mascoma Savings Bank
Merchants Bank

VIRGINIA

Bank of Lancaster
First Community Bank N.A.
Freedom Bank of Virginia
Monarch Bank
StellarOne
Towne Bank
United Bank
Virginia Commerce Bank
Virginia National Bank

WASHINGTON

Bank of the Pacific
Banner Bank
Columbia State Bank
Northwest Commercial Bank
Northwest Farm Credit Services
Security State Bank
Washington Trust Bank
Whidbey Island Bank

WEST VIRGINIA

United Bank
WesBanco Bank Wheeling

WISCONSIN

Associated Bank
Badgerland Financial
Bank of Sun Prairie
The Business Bank
First Bank Financial Centre
First National Bank Fox Valley
Horicon Bank
Johnson Bank
M&I Marshall & Ilsley Bank
Oak Bank
Park Bank
TCF National Bank

Introduction to
Annual Statement Studies:
Financial Ratio Benchmarks,
2010-2011
and
General Organization of Content

The notes below will explain the presentation of *Annual Statement Studies: Financial Ratio Benchmarks,* describe how the book is organized, and answer most of your questions.

- **The Quality You Expect from RMA:** RMA is the most respected source of objective, unbiased information on issues of importance to credit risk professionals. For over 90 years, RMA's *Annual Statement Studies*® has been the industry standard for comparison financial data. Material contained in today's *Annual Statement Studies* was first published in the March 1919 issue of the *Federal Reserve Bulletin*. In the days before computers, the *Annual Statement Studies* data was recorded in pencil on yellow ledger paper! Today, it features data for over 765 industries derived <u>directly</u> from more than 200,000 statements of financial institutions' borrowers and prospects.

- **Data That Comes Straight from Original Sources:** The more than 200,000 statements used to produce the composites presented here come directly from RMA member institutions and represent the financials from their commercial customers and prospects. RMA does not know the names of the individual entities. In fact, to ensure confidentiality, company names are removed before the data is even delivered to RMA. The raw data making up each composite is not available to any third party.

- **Data Presented in Common Size:** *Annual Statement Studies: Financial Ratio Benchmarks* contains composite financial data. Balance sheet and income statement information is shown in common size format, with each item a percentage of total assets and sales. RMA computes common size statements for each individual statement in an industry group, then aggregates and averages all the figures. In some cases, because of computer rounding, the figures to the right of the decimal point do not balance exactly with the totals shown. A minus sign beside the value indicates credits and losses.

- **Includes the Most Widely Used Ratios:** Nineteen of the most widely used ratios in the financial services industry accompany the balance sheet information, including various types of liquidity, coverage, leverage, and operating ratios.

- **Organized by the NAICS for Ease of Use:** This edition is organized according to the North American Industry Classification System (NAICS), a product of the U.S. Office of Management and Budget. At the top of each page of data, you will find the NAICS.

- **Twenty Sections Outline Major Types of Businesses:** To provide further delineation, the book is divided into 20 sections outlining major lines of businesses. If you know the NAICS number you are looking for, use the NAICS-page guide provided in the front of this book. In general, the book is arranged in ascending NAICS numerical order. For your convenience, full descriptions of each NAICS are presented in this book. In addition, you will find a text-based index near the end of the book.

- **If You Do Not Know the NAICS Code You Are Looking for...** If you do not know the precise industry NAICS you are looking for, contact the Census Bureau at 1-888-75NAICS or naics@census.gov. Describe the activity of the establishment for which you need an industry code and you will receive a reply. Another source to help you assign the correct NAICS industry name and number can be found at www.census.gov/epcd/www/naics.html.

- **Can't Find the Industry You Want?** There are a number of reasons you may not find the industry you are looking for (i.e., you know you need industry xxxxxx but it is not in the product). Many times we have information on an industry, but it is not published because the sample size was too small or there were significant questions concerning the data. (For an industry to be displayed in the *Annual Statement Studies: Financial Ratio Benchmarks,* there must be at least 30 valid statements submitted to RMA.) In other instances, we simply do not have the data. Generally, most of what we receive is published.

- **Composite Data Not Shown?** When there are fewer than 10 financial statements in a particular asset or sales size category, the composite data is not shown because a sample this small is not considered representative and could be misleading. However, all the data for that industry is shown in the All Sizes column. The total number of statements for each size category is shown in bold print at the top of each column. In addition, the number of statements used in a ratio array will differ from the number of statements in a sample because certain elements of data may not be present in all financial statements. In these cases, the number of statements used is shown in parentheses to the left of the array.

- **Presentation of the Data on Each Page-Spread:** For all non-contracting spread statements, the data for a particular industry appears on both the left and right pages. The heading Current Data Sorted by Assets is in the five columns on the left side. The center section of the double-page presentation contains the Comparative Historical Data, with the All Sizes column for the current year shown under the heading 4/1/xx-3/31/xx. Comparable data from past editions of the *Annual Statement Studies: Financial Ratio Benchmarks* also appears in this section. Current Data Sorted by Sales is displayed in the five columns to the far right.

- **Companies with Less than $250 Million in Total Assets:** In our presentation, we used companies having less than $250 million in total assets—except in the case of contractors who use the percentage-of-completion method of accounting. *The section for contractors using the percentage-of-completion method of accounting contains data only sorted by revenue.* There is no upper limit placed on revenue size for any industry. Its information is found on only one page.

- **Page Headers:** The information shown at the top of each page includes the following: 1) the identity of the industry group; 2) its North American Industry Classification System (NAICS); 3) a breakdown by size categories of the types of financial statements reported; 4) the number of statements in each category; 5) the dates of the statements used; and 6) the size categories. For instance, 16 (4/1-9/30/09) means that 16 statements with fiscal dates between April 1 and September 30, 2009 make up part of the sample.

- **Page Footers:** At the bottom of each page, we have included the sum of the sales (or revenues) and total assets for all the financial statements in each size category. This data allows recasting of the common size statements into dollar amounts. To do this, divide the number at the bottom of the page by the number of statements in that size category. Then multiply the result by the percentages in the common size statement.
  Please note: The dollar amounts will be an appoximation because RMA computes the balance sheet and income statement percentages for each individual statement in an industry group, then aggregates and averages all the figures.

- **Our Thanks to CFMA:** RMA appreciates the cooperation of the Construction Financial Management Association in permitting us to reproduce excerpts from its *Construction Industry Annual Financial Survey.* This data complements the RMA contractor industry data. For more details on this data, please visit www.cfma.org.

- **Recommended for Use as General Guidelines:** RMA recommends you use *Annual Statement Studies: Financial Ratio Benchmarks* data only as general guidelines and not as absolute industry norms. There are several reasons why the data may not be fully representative of a given industry:

1. **Data Not Random**—The financial statements used in the *Annual Statement Studies: Financial Ratio Benchmarks* are not selected by any random or statistically reliable method. RMA member banks voluntarily submit the raw data they have available each year with no limitation on company size.

2. **Categorized by Primary Product Only**—Many companies have varied product lines; however, the *Annual Statement Studies: Financial Ratio Benchmarks* categorizes them by their primary product NAICS number only.

3. **Small Samples**—Some of the industry samples are small in relation to the total number of firms for a given industry. A relatively small sample can increase the chances that some composites do not fully represent an industry.

4. **Extreme Statements**—An extreme or outlier statement can occasionally be present in a sample, causing a disproportionate influence on the industry composite. This is particularly true in a relatively small sample.

5. **Operational Differences**—Companies within the same industry may differ in their method of operations, which in turn can directly influence their financial statements. Since they are included in the sample, these statements can significantly affect the composite calculations.

6. **Additional Considerations**—There are other considerations that can result in variations among different companies engaged in the same general line of business. These include different labor markets, geographical location, different accounting methods, quality of products handled, sources and methods of financing, and terms of sale.

For these reasons, RMA does not recommend using the *Annual Statement Studies: Financial Ratio Benchmarks* figures as absolute norms for a given industry. Rather, you should use the figures only as general guidelines and as a supplement to the other methods of financial analysis. RMA makes no claim regarding how representative the figures printed in this book are.

DEFINITION OF RATIOS
INTRODUCTION

On each data page, below the common-size balance sheet and income statement information, you will find a series of ratios computed from the financial statement data.

Here is how these figures are calculated for any given ratio:

1. The ratio is computed for each financial statement in the sample.

2. These values are arrayed (listed) in an order from the strongest to the weakest. In interpreting ratios, the "strongest" or "best" value is not always the largest numerical value, nor is the "weakest" always the lowest numerical value. (For certain ratios, there may be differing opinions as to what constitutes a strong or a weak value. RMA follows general banking guidelines consistent with sound credit practice to resolve this problem.)

3. The array of values is divided into four groups of equal size. The description of each ratio appearing in the *Statement Studies* provides details regarding the arraying of the values.

What Are Quartiles?

Each ratio has three points, or "cut-off values," that divide an array of values into four equal-sized groups called quartiles, as shown below. The quartiles include the upper quartile, upper-middle quartile, lower-middle quartile, and the lower quartile. The upper quartile is the cut-off value where one-quarter of the array of ratios falls between it and the strongest ratio. The median is the midpoint—that is, the middle cut-off value where half of the array falls above it and half below it. The lower quartile is the point where one-quarter of the array falls between it and the weakest ratio. In many cases, the average of two values is used to arrive at the quartile value. You will find the median and quartile values on all *Statement Studies* data pages in the order indicated in the chart below.

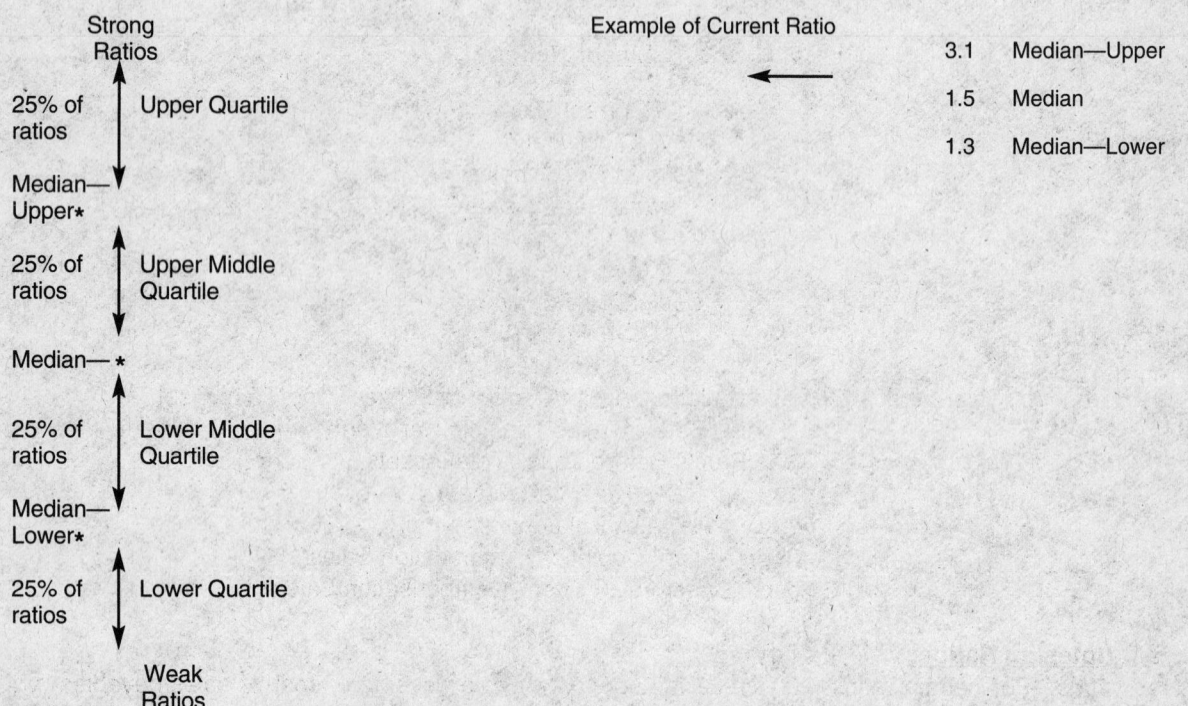

Why Use Medians/Quartiles Instead of the Average?

There are several reasons medians and quartiles are used instead of an average. Medians and quartiles eliminate the influence an "outlier" (an extremely high or low value compared to the rest of the values). They also more accurately reflect the ranges of ratio values than a straight averaging method would.

It is important to understand that the spread (range) between the upper and lower quartiles represents the middle 50% of all the companies in a sample. Therefore, ratio values greater than the upper quartile or less than the lower quartile may begin to approach "unusual" values.

Non-Conventional Values:

For some ratio values, you will occasionally see an entry that is other than a conventional number. These entries are defined as follows:

(1) <u>UND</u>—This stands for "undefined," the result of the denominator in a ratio calculation approaching zero.

(2) <u>NM</u>—This may occasionally appear as a quartile or median for the ratios sales/working capital, debt/worth, and fixed/worth. It stands for "no meaning" in cases where the dispersion is so small that any interpretation is meaningless.

(3) <u>999.8</u>—When a ratio value equals 1,000 or more, it also becomes an "unusual" value and is given the "999.8" designation. This is considered to be a close enough approximation to the actual unusually large value.

Linear versus Nonlinear Ratios:

An array that is ordered in ascending sequence or in descending sequence is linear. An array that deviates from true ascending or true descending when its values change from positive to negative (low to high positive, followed by high to low negative) is nonlinear.

A specific example of a nonlinear ratio would be the Sales/Working Capital ratio. In other words, when the Sales/Working Capital ratio is positive, then the top quartile would be represented by the *lowest positive* ratio. However, if the ratio is negative, the top quartile will be represented by the *highest negative* ratio! In a nonlinear array such as this, the median could be either positive or negative because it is whatever the middle value is in the particular array of numbers.

Nonlinear Ratios

Sales/Working Capital
Fixed/Worth
Debt/Worth

Linear Ratios

Current Ratio
Quick Ratio
Sales Receivables
Days' Receivables
Cost of Sales/Inventory
Days' Inventory
Cost of Sales/Payables
Days' Payables
EBIT/Interest
Net Profit + Deprec, Depletion, Amort/Current Maturities Long-Term Debt
% Profits Before Taxes/Tangible Net Worth
% Profits Before Taxes/Total Assets
Sales/Net Fixed Assets
Sales/Total Assets
% Depreciation, Depletion, Amortization/Sales
% Officers', Directors', Owners' Compensation/Sales

Important Notes on Ratios:

Turnover Ratios—For certain ratios (sales/receivables, cost of sales/inventory, cost of sales/payables) you will see two numbers, one in **BOLD** and one in regular type. These ratios are generally called turnover ratios. The number in **BOLD** represents **the number of days** and the number in regular type is the **number of times**. Please see the definition of sales/receivables on the following pages for a more complete description of the two types of calculations and what each means.

Inventory Presentations—**Inventory presentations** are based on fiscal year-end point-in-time balances, not averages. In addition, our data capture does not permit us to know what method of inventory accounting (LIFO or FIFO, for instance) was used.

The following ratios contained in the *Statement Studies* are grouped into five principal categories: liquidity, coverage, leverage, operating, and specific expense items.

LIQUIDITY RATIOS

Liquidity is a measure of the quality and adequacy of current assets to meet current obligations as they come due. In other words, can a firm quickly convert its assets to cash—without a loss in value—in order to meet its immediate and short-term obligations? For firms such as utilities that can readily and accurately predict their cash inflows, liquidity is not nearly as critical as it is for firms like airlines or manufacturing businesses that can have wide fluctuations in demand and revenue streams. These ratios provide a level of comfort to lenders in case of liquidation.

1. Current Ratio

How to Calculate: Divide total current assets by total current liabilities.

$$\frac{\text{Total Current Assets}}{\text{Total Current Liabilities}}$$

How to Interpret: This ratio is a rough indication of a firm's ability to service its current obligations. Generally, the higher the current ratio, the greater the "cushion" between current obligations and a firm's ability to pay them. While a stronger ratio shows that the numbers for current assets exceed those for current liabilities, the composition and quality of current assets are critical factors in the analysis of an individual firm's liquidity.

The ratio values are arrayed from the highest positive to the lowest positive.

2. Quick Ratio

How to Calculate: Add cash and equivalents to trade receivables. Then, divide by total current liabilities.

$$\frac{\text{Cash \& Equivalents + Trade Receivables (net)}}{\text{Total Current Liabilities}}$$

How to Interpret: Also known as the "acid test" ratio, this is a stricter, more conservative measure of liquidity than the current ratio. This ratio reflects the degree to which a company's current liabilities are covered by its most liquid current assets, the kind of assets that can be converted quickly to cash and at amounts close to book value. Inventory and other less liquid current assets are removed from the calculation. Generally, if the ratio produces a value that's less than 1 to 1, it implies a "dependency" on inventory or other "less" current assets to liquidate short-term debt.

The ratio values are arrayed from the highest positive to the lowest positive.

3. Sales/Receivables

How to Calculate: Divide net sales by trade receivables.

$$\frac{\text{Net Sales}}{\text{Trade Receivables (net)}}$$

Please note—In the contractor section, both accounts receivable-progress billings and accounts receivable-current retention are included in the receivables figure used in calculating the revenues/receivables and receivables/payables ratios.

How to Interpret: This ratio measures the number of times trade receivables turn over during the year. The higher the turnover of receivables, the shorter the time between sale and cash collection.

For example, a company with sales of $720,000 and receivables of $120,000 would have a sales/receivables ratio of 6.0. This means receivables turn over six times a year. If a company's receivables appear to be turning more slowly than the rest of the industry, further research is needed and the quality of the receivables should be examined closely.

Cautions—A problem with this ratio is that it compares one day's receivables, shown at statement date, to total annual sales and does not take into consideration seasonal fluctuations. An additional problem in interpretation may arise when there is a large proportion of cash sales to total sales.

When the receivables figure is zero, the quotient will be undefined (UND) and represents the best possible ratio. The ratio values are therefore arrayed starting with undefined (UND) and then from the numerically highest value to the numerically lowest value. The only time a zero will appear in the array is when the sales figure is low and the quotient rounds off to zero. By definition, this ratio cannot be negative.

4. Days' Receivables

The sales/receivables ratio will have a figure printed in bold type directly to the left of the array. This figure is the days' receivables.

How to Calculate the Days' Receivables: Divide the sales/receivables ratio into 365 (the number of days in one year).

$$\frac{365}{\text{Sales/Receivable ratio}}$$

How to Interpret the Days' Receivables: This figure expresses the average number of days that receivables are outstanding. Generally, the greater the number of days outstanding, the greater the probability of delinquencies in accounts receivable. A comparison of a company's daily receivables may indicate the extent of a company's control over credit and collections.

Please note—You should take into consideration the terms offered by a company to its customers because these may differ from terms within the industry.

For example, using the sales/receivable ratio calculated above, 365 ÷ 6 = 61 (i.e., the average receivable is collected in 61 days).

5. Cost of Sales/Inventory

How to Calculate: Divide cost of sales by inventory.

$$\frac{\text{Cost of Sales}}{\text{Inventory}}$$

How to Interpret: This ratio measures the number of times inventory is turned over during the year.

High Inventory Turnover—On the positive side, high inventory turnover can indicate greater liquidity or superior merchandising. Conversely, it can indicate a shortage of needed inventory for sales.

Low Inventory Turnover—Low inventory turnover can indicate poor liquidity, possible overstocking, or obsolescence. On the positive side, it could indicate a planned inventory buildup in the case of material shortages.

Cautions—A problem with this ratio is that it compares one day's inventory to cost of goods sold and does not take seasonal fluctuations into account. When the inventory figure is zero, the quotient will be undefined (UND) and represents the best possible ratio. The ratio values are arrayed starting with undefined (UND) and then from the numerically highest value to the numerically lowest value. The only time a zero will appear in the array is when the figure for cost of sales is very low and the quotient rounds off to zero.

Please note—For service industries, the cost of sales is included in operating expenses. In addition, please note that the data collection process does not differentiate the method of inventory valuation.

6. Days' Inventory

The days' inventory is the figure printed in bold directly to the left of the cost of sales/inventory ratio.

How to Calculate the Days' Inventory: Divide the cost of sales/inventory ratio into 365 (the number of days in one year).

$$\frac{365}{\text{Cost of Sales/Inventory ratio}}$$

How to Interpret: Dividing the inventory turnover ratio into 365 days yields the average length of time units are in inventory.

7. Cost of Sales/Payables

How to Calculate: Divide cost of sales by trade payables.

$$\frac{\text{Cost of Sales}}{\text{Trade Payables}}$$

Please note—In the contractor section, both accounts payable-trade and accounts payable-retention are included in the payables figure used in calculating the cost of revenues/payables and receivables/payables ratios.

How to Interpret: This ratio measures the number of times trade payables turn over during the year. The higher the turnover of payables, the shorter the time between purchase and payment. If a company's payables appear to be turning more slowly than the industry, then the company may be experiencing cash shortages, disputing invoices with suppliers, enjoying extended terms, or deliberately expanding its trade credit. The ratio comparison of company to industry suggests the existence of these or other possible causes. If a firm buys on 30-day terms, it is reasonable to expect this ratio to turn over in approximately 30 days.

Cautions—A problem with this ratio is that it compares one day's payables to cost of goods sold and does not take seasonal fluctuations into account. When the payables figure is zero, the quotient will be undefined (UND) and represents the best possible ratio. The ratio values are arrayed starting with undefined (UND) and then from the numerically highest to the numerically lowest value. The only time a zero will appear in the array is when the figure for cost of sales is very low and the quotient rounds off to zero.

8. Days' Payables

The days' payables is the figure printed in bold type directly to the left of the cost of sales/payables ratio.

How to Calculate the Days' Payables: Divide the cost of sales/payables ratio into 365 (the number of days in one year).

$$\frac{365}{\text{Cost of Sales/Payables ratio}}$$

How to Interpret: Division of the payables turnover ratio into 365 days yields the average length of time trade debt is outstanding.

9. Sales/Working Capital

How to Calculate: Divide net sales by net working capital (current assets less current liabilities equals net working capital).

$$\frac{\text{Net Sales}}{\text{Net Working Capital}}$$

How to Interpret: Because it reflects the ability to finance current operations, working capital is a measure of the margin of protection for current creditors. When you relate the level of sales resulting from operations to the underlying working capital, you can measure how efficiently working capital is being used.

Low ratio (close to zero)—A low ratio may indicate an inefficient use of working capital.

High ratio (high positive or high negative)—A very high ratio often signifies overtrading, which is a vulnerable position for creditors.

Please note—sales/working capital ratio is a nonlinear array. In other words, an array that is NOT ordered from highest positive to highest negative as is the case for linear arrays. The ratio values are arrayed from the lowest positive to the highest positive, to undefined (UND), and then from the highest negative to the lowest negative. If working capital is zero, the quotient is undefined (UND).

If the sales/working capital ratio is positive, then the top quartile would be represented by the *lowest positive* ratio. However, if the ratio is negative, the top quartile will be represented by the *highest negative* ratio! In a nonlinear array such as the sales/working capital ratio, the median could be either positive or negative because it is whatever the middle value is in the particular array of numbers.

Cautions—When analyzing this ratio, you need to focus on working capital, not on the sales figure. Although sales cannot be negative, working capital can be. If you have a large, positive working capital number, the ratio will be small *and* positive—which is good. Because negative working capital is bad, if you have a large, negative working capital number, the sales/working capital ratio will be small *and* negative—which is NOT good. Therefore, the lowest positive ratio is the best and the lowest negative ratio is the worst. If working capital is a small negative number, the ratio will be large, which is the best of the negatives.

COVERAGE RATIOS

Coverage ratios measure a firm's ability to service its debt. In other words, how well does the flow of a company's funds cover its short-term financial obligations? In contrast to liquidity ratios that focus on the possibility of liquidation, coverage ratios seek to provide lenders a comfort level based on the belief the firm will remain a viable enterprise.

1. Earnings Before Interest and Taxes (EBIT)/Interest

How to Calculate: Divide earnings (profit) before annual interest expense and taxes by annual interest expense.

$$\frac{\text{Earnings Before Interest \& Taxes}}{\text{Annual Interest Expense}}$$

How to Interpret: This ratio measures a firm's ability to meet interest payments. A high ratio may indicate that a borrower can easily meet the interest obligations of a loan. This ratio also indicates a firm's capacity to take on additional debt.

Please note—Only statements reporting annual interest expense were used in the calculation of this ratio. The ratio values are arrayed from the highest positive to the lowest positive and then from the lowest negative to the highest negative.

2. Net Profit + Depreciation, Depletion, Amortization/Current Maturities Long-Term Debt

How to Calculate: Add net profit to depreciation, depletion, and amortization expenses. Then, divide by the current portion of long-term debt.

$$\frac{\text{Net Profit + Depreciation, Depletion, Amortization Expenses}}{\text{Current Portion of Long-Term Debt}}$$

How to Interpret: This ratio reflects how well cash flow from operations covers current maturities. Because cash flow is the primary source of debt retirement, the ratio measures a firm's ability to service principal repayment and take on additional debt. Even though it is a mistake to believe all cash flow is available for debt service, this ratio is still a valid measure of the ability to service long-term debt.

Please note—Only data for corporations with the following items was used:

(1) Profit or loss after taxes (positive, negative, or zero).

(2) A positive figure for depreciation/depletion/amortization expenses.

(3) A positive figure for current maturities of long-term debt.

Ratio values are arrayed from the highest to the lowest positive and then from the lowest to the highest negative.

LEVERAGE RATIOS

How much protection do a company's assets provide for the debt held by its creditors? Highly leveraged firms are companies with heavy debt in relation to their net worth. These firms are more vulnerable to business downturns than those with lower debt-to-worth positions. While leverage ratios help measure this vulnerability, keep in mind that these ratios vary greatly depending on the requirements of particular industry groups.

1. Fixed/Worth

How to Calculate: Divide fixed assets (net of accumulated depreciation) by tangible net worth (net worth minus intangibles).

$$\frac{\text{Net Fixed Assets}}{\text{Tangible Net Worth}}$$

How to Interpret: This ratio measures the extent to which owner's equity (capital) has been invested in plant and equipment (fixed assets). A lower ratio indicates a proportionately smaller investment in fixed assets in relation to net worth and a better "cushion" for creditors in case of liquidation. Similarly, a higher ratio would indicate the opposite situation. The presence of a substantial number of fixed assets that are leased—and not appearing on the balance sheet—may result in a deceptively lower ratio.

18

Fixed assets may be zero, in which case the quotient is zero. If tangible net worth is zero, the quotient is undefined (UND). If tangible net worth is negative, the quotient is negative.

Please note—Like the sales/working capital ratio discussed above, this fixed/worth ratio is a nonlinear array. In other words, it is an array that is NOT ordered from highest positive to highest negative as a linear array would be. The ratio values are arrayed from the lowest positive to the highest positive, to undefined (UND), and then from the highest negative to the lowest negative.

If the Fixed/Worth ratio is positive, then the top quartile would be represented by the *lowest positive* ratio. However, if the ratio is negative, the top quartile will be represented by the *highest negative* ratio! In a nonlinear array such as this, the median could be either positive or negative because it is whatever the middle value is in the particular array of numbers.

2. Debt/Worth

How to Calculate: Divide total liabilities by tangible net worth.

$$\frac{\text{Total Liabilities}}{\text{Tangible Net Worth}}$$

How to Interpret: This ratio expresses the relationship between capital contributed by creditors and that contributed by owners. Basically, it shows how much protection the owners are providing creditors. The higher the ratio, the greater the risk being assumed by creditors. A lower ratio generally indicates greater long-term financial safety. Unlike a highly leveraged firm, a firm with a low debt/worth ratio usually has greater flexibility to borrow in the future.

Tangible net worth may be zero, in which case the ratio is undefined (UND). Tangible net worth may also be negative, which results in the quotient being negative. The ratio values are arrayed from the lowest to highest positive, to undefined, and then from the highest to lowest negative.

Please note—Like the sales/working capital ratio discussed above, this debt/worth ratio is a nonlinear array. In other words, it is an array that is NOT ordered from highest positive to highest negative as a linear array would be. The ratio values are arrayed from the lowest positive to the highest positive, to undefined (UND), and then from the highest negative to the lowest negative.

If the debt/worth ratio is positive, then the top quartile would be represented by the *lowest positive* ratio. However, if the ratio is negative, the top quartile will be represented by the *highest negative* ratio! In a nonlinear array such as this, the median could be either positive or negative because it is whatever the middle value is in the particular array of numbers.

OPERATING RATIOS

Operating ratios are designed to assist in the evaluation of management performance.

1. % Profits Before Taxes/Tangible Net Worth

How to Calculate: Divide profit before taxes by tangible net worth. Then, multiply by 100.

$$\frac{\text{Profit Before Taxes}}{\text{Tangible Net Worth}} \times 100$$

How to Interpret: This ratio expresses the rate of return on tangible capital employed. While it can serve as an indicator of management performance, you should always use it in conjunction with other ratios. Normally associated with effective management, a high return could actually point to an undercapitalized firm. Conversely, a low return that's usually viewed as an indicator of inefficient management performance could actually reflect a highly capitalized, conservatively operated business.

This ratio has been multiplied by 100 because it is shown as a percentage.

Profit before taxes may be zero, in which case the ratio is zero. Profits before taxes may be negative, resulting in negative quotients. Firms with negative tangible net worth have been omitted from the ratio arrays. Negative ratios will therefore only result in the case of negative profit before taxes. If the tangible net worth is zero, the quotient is undefined (UND). If there are fewer than 10 ratios for a particular size class, the result is not shown. The ratio values are arrayed starting with undefined (UND), then from the highest to the lowest positive values, and finally from the lowest to the highest negative values.

2. % Profits Before Taxes/Total Assets

How to Calculate: Divide profit before taxes by total assets and multiply by 100.

$$\frac{\text{Profit Before Taxes}}{\text{Total Assets}} \times 100$$

How to Interpret: This ratio expresses the pre-tax return on total assets and measures the effectiveness of management in employing the resources available to it. If a specific ratio varies considerably from the ranges found in this book, the analyst will need to examine the makeup of the assets and take a closer look at the earnings figure. A heavily depreciated plant and a large amount of intangible assets or unusual income or expense items will cause distortions of this ratio.

This ratio has been multiplied by 100 since it is shown as a percentage. If profit before taxes is zero, the quotient is zero. If profit before taxes is negative, the quotient is negative. These ratio values are arrayed from the highest to the lowest positive and then from the lowest to the highest negative.

3. Sales/Net Fixed Assets

How to Calculate: Divide net sales by net fixed assets (net of accumulated depreciation).

$$\frac{\text{Net Sales}}{\text{Net Fixed Assets}}$$

How to Interpret: This ratio is a measure of the productive use of a firm's fixed assets. Largely depreciated fixed assets or a labor-intensive operation may cause a distortion of this ratio.

If the net fixed figure is zero, the quotient is undefined (UND). The only time a zero will appear in the array will be when the net sales figure is low and the quotient rounds off to zero. These ratio values cannot be negative.

They are arrayed from undefined (UND) and then from the highest to the lowest positive values.

4. Sales/Total Assets

How to Calculate: Divide net sales by total assets.

$$\frac{\text{Net Sales}}{\text{Total Assets}}$$

How to Interpret: This ratio is a general measure of a firm's ability to generate sales in relation to total assets. It should be used only to compare firms within specific industry groups and in conjunction with other operating ratios to determine the effective employment of assets.

The only time a zero will appear in the array will be when the net sales figure is low and the quotient rounds off to zero. The ratio values cannot be negative. They are arrayed from the highest to the lowest positive values.

EXPENSE TO SALES RATIOS

The following two ratios relate specific expense items to net sales and express this relationship as a percentage. Comparisons are convenient because the item, net sales, is used as a constant. Variations in these ratios are most pronounced between capital- and labor-intensive industries.

1. % Depreciation, Depletion, Amortization/Sales

How to Calculate: Divide annual depreciation, amortization, and depletion expenses by net sales and multiply by 100.

$$\frac{\text{Depreciation, Amortization, Depletion Expenses}}{\text{Net Sales}} \times 100$$

2. % Officers', Directors', Owners' Compensation/Sales

How to Calculate: Divide annual officers', directors', owners' compensation by net sales and multiply by 100. Include total salaries, bonuses, commissions, and other monetary remuneration to all officers, directors, and/or owners of the firm during the year covered by the statement. This includes drawings of partners and proprietors.

$$\frac{\text{Officers', Directors', Owners' Compensation}}{\text{Net Sales}} \times 100$$

Only statements showing a positive figure for each of the expense categories shown above were used. The ratios are arrayed from the lowest to highest positive values.

Explanation of Noncontractor Balance Sheet and Income Data

Cash & Equivalents
All cash, marketplace, securities, and other near-cash items. Excludes sinking funds.

Trade Receivables (net)
All accounts from trade, net of allowance for doubtful accounts.

Inventory
Anything constituting inventory for the firm.

All Other Current
Any other current assets. Does not include prepaid items.

Total Current
Total of all current assets listed above.

ASSETS
Cash & Equivalents
Trade Receivables (net)
Inventory
All Other Current
Total Current
Fixed Assets (net)
Intangibles (net)
All Other Non-Current
Total

Fixed Assets (net)
All property, plant, leasehold improvements and equipment, net of accumulated depreciation or depletion.

Intangibles (net)
Intangible assets, including goodwill, trademarks, patents, catalogs, brands, copyrights, formulas, franchises, and mailing lists, net of accumulated amortization.

All Other Non-Current
Prepaid items and any other non-current assets.

Total
Total of all items listed above.

Notes Payable—Short Term
All short-term note obligations, including bank and commercial paper. Does not include trade notes payable.

Current Maturities—L/T/D
That portion of long-term obligations that is due within the next fiscal year.

Trade Payables
Open accounts due to the trade.

Income Taxes Payable
Income taxes including current portion of deferred taxes.

All Other Current
Any other current liabilities, including bank overdrafts and accrued expenses.

LIABILITIES
Notes Payable-Short Term
Cur. Mat.-L/T/D
Trade Payables
Income Taxes Payable
All Other Current
Total Current
Long-Term Debt
Deferred Taxes
All Other Non-Current
Net Worth
Total Liabilities & Net Worth

Total Current
Total of all current liabilities listed above.

Long-Term Debt
All senior debt, including bonds, debentures, bank debt, mortgages, deferred portions of long-term debt, and capital lease obligations.

Deferred Taxes
All deferred taxes.

All Other Non-Current
Any other non-current liabilities, including subordinated debt, and liability reserves.

Net Worth
Difference between Total Liabilities and Total Assets. Minority interest is included here.

Total Liabilities & Net Worth
Total of all items listed above.

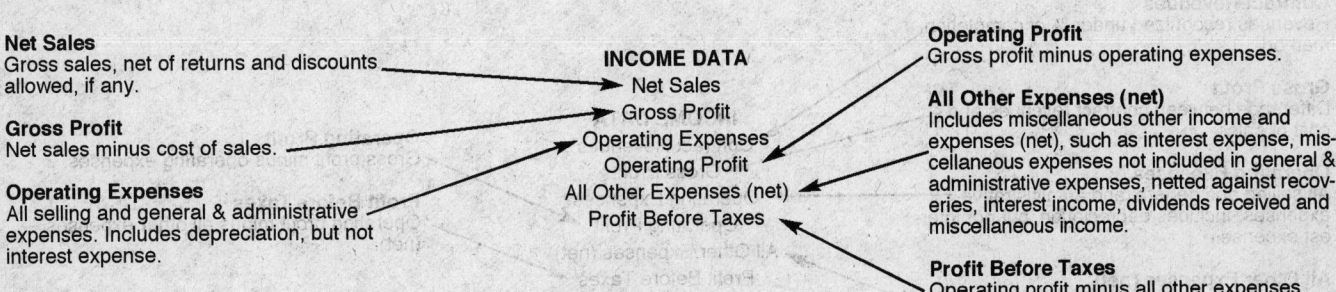

Net Sales
Gross sales, net of returns and discounts allowed, if any.

Gross Profit
Net sales minus cost of sales.

Operating Expenses
All selling and general & administrative expenses. Includes depreciation, but not interest expense.

INCOME DATA
Net Sales
Gross Profit
Operating Expenses
Operating Profit
All Other Expenses (net)
Profit Before Taxes

Operating Profit
Gross profit minus operating expenses.

All Other Expenses (net)
Includes miscellaneous other income and expenses (net), such as interest expense, miscellaneous expenses not included in general & administrative expenses, netted against recoveries, interest income, dividends received and miscellaneous income.

Profit Before Taxes
Operating profit minus all other expenses (net).

Explanation of Contractor Percentage-of-Completion Basis of Accounting Balance Sheet and Income Data

Cash & Equivalents
All cash, marketable securities, and other near-cash items. Excludes sinking funds.

Accts. Rec.-Progress Billings
Amounts billed on current contracts excluding retention.

Accts. Rec.-Current Retention
Amounts held back by customers on current contracts as retention.

All Other Current
Any other current assets. Does not include prepaid items.

Total Current
Total of all current assets listed above.

Fixed Assets (net)
All property, plant, leasehold improvements and equipment, net of accumulated depreciation or depletion.

All Other Non-Current
Prepaid items and other non-current assets.

Inventory
Costs attributable to equipment, small tools, supplies, and other deferred costs related to contracts in progress wherein a portion of the cost applies to work not yet performed.

Costs & Estimated Earnings in Excess of Billings
The difference between the total of costs and recognized estimated earnings to date and the total billings to date.

Joint Ventures & Investments
The total of investments and equity in joint ventures.

Intangibles (net)
Intangible assets, including goodwill, trademarks, patents, catalogs, brands, copyrights, formulas, franchises, and mailing lists, net of accumulated amortization.

Total
Total of all items listed above.

ASSETS
Cash & Equivalents
Accounts Receivable—Progress Billings
Accounts Receivable—Current Retention
Inventory
Costs & Estimated Earnings in Excess of Billings
All Other Current
Total Current
Fixed Assets (net)
Joint Ventures & Investments
Intangibles (net)
All Other Non-Current
Total

Notes Payable—Short Term
All short-term note obligations, including bank and commercial paper. Does not include trade notes payable.

Accounts Payable—Trade
Open accounts and note obligations due to the trade.

Accounts Payable—Retention
Amounts held back as retention in payments to subcontractors on current contracts.

Long-Term Debt
All senior debt, including bonds, debentures, bank debt, mortgages, deferred portions of long-term debt, and capital lease obligations.

Deferred Taxes
Total of all deferred taxes.

All Other Non-Current
Any other non-current liabilities, including subordinated debt, and liability reserves.

Billings in Excess of Costs & Est. Earn.
The difference between the total billings to date and the total of costs and recognized estimated earnings to date.

Income Taxes Payable
Income taxes including current portion of deferred taxes.

Current Maturities—LTD
That portion of long-term obligations that is due within the next fiscal year.

All Other Current
Any other current liabilities, including bank overdrafts and accrued expenses.

Total Current
Total of all current liabilities listed above.

Net Worth
Difference between total assets and total liabilities. Minority interest is included here.

Total Liabilities & Net Worth
Total of all items listed above.

LIABILITIES
Notes Payable—Short Term
Accounts Payable—Trade
Accounts Payable—Retention
Billings in Excess of Costs & Estimated Earnings
Income Taxes Payable
Current Maturities—LTD
All Other Current
Total Current
Long-Term Debt
Deferred Taxes
All Other Non-Current
Net Worth
Total Liabilities & Net Worth

Contract Revenues
Revenues recognized under % of completion method.

Gross Profit
Difference between contract revenues and cost of sales.

Operating Expenses
All selling and general and administrative expenses. Includes depreciation, but not interest expense.

All Other Expenses (net)
Includes miscellaneous other income and expenses (net), such as interest expense, miscellaneous expenses not included in general & administrative expenses, netted against recoveries, interest income, dividends received and miscellaneous income.

Operating Profit
Gross profit minus operating expenses.

Profit Before Taxes
Operating profit minus all other expenses (net).

INCOME DATA
Contract Revenues
Gross Profit
Operating Expenses
Operating Profit
All Other Expenses (net)
Profit Before Taxes

For further analysis, please refer to *Industry Default Probabilities and Cash Flow Measures*

If you think *Financial Ratio Benchmarks* is a valuable resource, wait until you see its companion study. Now in its eleventh year and bigger than ever, *Industry Default Probabilities and Cash Flow Measures* is a major expansion of our *Annual Statement Studies.* It brings together the power of Moody's RiskCalc® for private companies and the *Statement Studies* database to provide distribution statistics on one-year and five-year probability of default estimates by industry. The new benchmarks add substantial value to the critical analysis of cash flow for private companies.

The latest edition of *Industry Default Probabilities and Cash Flow Measures* includes many new industries, stronger statements, four years of historical data sorted by assets and sales. In short, it is more like our traditional *Statement Studies.*

Industry Default Probabilities and Cash Flow Measures includes:

• Probability of default estimates on a percentage scale, mapped to a "dot" EDF bond rating scale.
• Cash flow measures on a common-size percentage scale. Ratios include:
  - Cash from Trading
  - Cash after Operations
  - Net Cash after Operations
  - Cash after Debt Amortization
  - Debt Service P&I Coverage
  - Interest Coverage (Operating Cash)
• Change in position, normalized, year over year, for eight financial statement line items. Ratios include:
  - Change in Inventory
  - Total Current Assets (TCA)
  - Total Assets (TA)
  - Retained Earnings (RE)
  - Net Sales (NS)
  - Cost of Goods Sold (CGS)
  - Profit before Interest & Taxes (PBIT)
  - Depreciation/Depletion/Amortization (DDA)
• Trend data available for five years.
• Other ratios.
  - Sustainable Growth Rate
  - Funded Debt/EBITDA
• Data arrayed by asset and sales size.

Please see the next page for a copy of a sample report. For more information regarding the *Industry Default Probabilities and Cash Flow Measures,* **please call 1-800-677-7621!**

INDUSTRY DEFAULT PROBABILITIES AND CASH FLOW MEASURES SAMPLE REPORT

AGRICULTURE—Wheat Farming NAICS 111140

Current Data Sorted by Assets						Type of Statement	Comparative Historical Data	
2	2	7	11	4	4	Unqualified	2	13
	3	10	5		1	Reviewed	6	8
1	4	6	1			Compiled	9	14
5	9	1				Tax Returns	11	21
5	9	15	12	2	2	Other	12	33
	31 (4/1-9/30/07)		90 (10/1/07-3/31/08)				4/1/03-3/31/04	4/1/04-3/31/05
0-500M	500M-2MM	2-10MM	10-50MM	50-100MM	100-250MM	Assets Size	ALL	ALL
13	27	39	29	6	7	Number of Statements	40	89
%	%	%	%	%	%	EXPECTED DEFAULT FREQUENCY	%	%
.20	.24	.23	.19				.58	.14
.48	.73 (38)	.41	.49			Risk Calc EDF	1.16 (81)	.27
1.03	1.27	1.10	.98			(1 yr)	2.98	.86
Baa1 1.74	Baa1 1.66	Baa1 1.41	Baa1 1.38			Moodys EDF Risk Calc EDF	Ba1 5.52 A3 1.18	
Baa3 4.14	Baa3 4.14	Baa3 3.03	Baa2 2.67			Rating (see note) (5 yr)	Ba2 7.92 Baa2 2.65	
Ba2 5.97	Ba2 6.88	Ba2 5.94	Ba1 5.21				Ba3 12.23 Ba1 5.21	
%	%	%	%	%	%	CASH FLOW MEASURES	%	%
						Cash from Trading/Sales		
27.4	20.8	14.1	25.5				12.9	24.6
12.6	10.8	5.9	8.7			Cash after	4.8	6.6
4.3	3.3	.1	1.0			Operations/Sales	.3	.6
27.3	19.2	13.6	24.7				12.6	23.2
13.0	10.9	6.6	9.3			Net Cash after	4.4	6.5
4.4	1.6	.1	1.5			Operations/Sales	.5	1.1
8.1	12.7	5.0	5.3				6.3	9.3
2.9	2.4	.4	1.5			Net Cash after Debt	1.2	2.2
-.3	-4.6	-1.6	-6.8			Amortization/Sales	-4.5	-4.0
9.2	3.2	3.4	5.1				2.8	4.9
(11) 2.1	(25) 1.3	(34) 1.5	(27) 1.4			Debt Service	(34) 1.3 (81)	2.0
1.4	.0	.1	.5			P&I Coverage	.0	.2
12.0	5.8	7.2	5.6				7.0	8.8
(11) 4.1	(25) 1.9	(32) 2.7	(26) 3.1			Interest Coverage	(33) 2.5 (81)	3.3
2.1	.0	-.2	.4			(Operating Cash)	.2	.4
	41.7	70.2	53.8				36.7	16.8
	(16) 2.0	(21) 24.1	(18) 12.4			Δ Inventory	(24) 3.2 (60)	-1.1
	-7.5	2.8	-1.0				-11.4	-22.5
33.7	40.6	38.7	26.7				27.6	21.4
.0	15.9	14.7	3.4			Δ Total Current Assets	5.2	10.2
-36.0	-7.5	.2	-9.8				-10.4	-11.4
21.9	24.2	28.5	27.9				28.0	30.0
4.9	2.3	11.8	5.0			Δ Total Assets	4.8	7.9
-23.2	-5.1	1.8	-1.7				-3.1	-2.8
148.6	24.3	73.8	33.2				25.8	49.2
52.3	(26) 6.3	27.7	8.5			Δ Retained Earnings	(39) 3.4 (85)	10.3
-47.1	-3.1	8.4	6.4				-14.1	-9.8
45.8	34.0	41.2	27.0				21.6	28.2
9.5	15.3	14.5	8.1			Δ Net Sales	3.2	7.9
-3.0	-2.8	4.9	-3.3				-7.8	.0
						Δ Cost of Goods Sold		
231.5	79.6	189.7	90.0				150.6	95.7
58.1	(26) 1.2	25.5	9.3			Δ Profit before	30.8 (88)	11.5
-12.5	-32.4	-26.5	-28.5			Int. & Taxes	-28.0	-26.9
143.8	12.9	38.6	5.9				31.0	19.8
(10) -4.1	(25) -14.5	(38) 5.1	(27) -4.0			Δ Depr./Depl./Amort.	(34) 5.2 (71)	.0
-77.6	-60.0	-18.5	-10.4				-23.0	-12.6
59.0	22.1	62.3	21.4			RATIOS	38.2	26.1
-34.8	(26) 8.1	17.4	7.9			Sustainable	8.2 (87)	5.8
-64.5	.5	-3.7	2.3			Growth Rate	-.8	-2.6
.3	.3	.6	1.4				1.3	.7
.6	2.4	1.4	2.7			Funded Debt/EBITDA	3.4	3.4
3.7	7.0	3.7	7.3				7.3	6.6
23696M	71595M	494325M	1060928M	676390M	2248216M	Net Sales ($)	593939M	1930153M
2688M	30938M	203770M	681568M	448459M	1210501M	Total Assets ($)	433841M	1644466M

See Pages 00 through 00 for Explanation of Ratios and Data

M = $ thousand   MM = $ million

Note: The ratings are Moody's.edf rating (e.g. Ba1.edf) and not Moody's Investor Services Long-Term Bond Ratings. If a number of statements appears for the Risk Calc EDF (1 yr), it also applies to the (5 yr).

AGRICULTURE—Wheat Farming NAICS 111140

Comparative Historical Data | Current Data Sorted by Sales

Type of Statement	4/1/05–3/31/06	4/1/06–3/31/07	4/1/07–3/31/08	0-1MM	1-3MM	3-5MM	5-10MM	10-25MM	25MM & OVER
Unqualified	24	21	30	1	6	2	2	5	14
Reviewed	14	20	19		2	1	5	6	5
Compiled	23	27	12	2	2	1	4	3	
Tax Returns	24	35	15	3	6	4	2	2	
Other	52	46	45	10	7	4	6	10	8
	ALL	ALL	ALL	31 (4/1-9/30/07)			90 (10/1/07-3/31/08)		
Number of Statements	137	149	121	16	23	12	17	26	27

EXPECTED DEFAULT FREQUENCY

	4/1/05–3/31/06	4/1/06–3/31/07	4/1/07–3/31/08	0-1MM	1-3MM	3-5MM	5-10MM	10-25MM	25MM & OVER
Risk Calc EDF (1 yr) (%)	.17 / (126) .37 / .89	.15 / (136) .24 / .67	.24 / (119) .48 / 1.11	.28 / .71 / 1.40	.24 / .49 / 1.03	.22 / .48 / 1.12	.18 / (25) .41 / 1.20	.27 / (26) .48 / 1.16	.19 / .38 / .89
Moodys EDF Rating / Risk Calc EDF (5 yr)	A3 1.28 / Baa3 3.13 / Ba1 5.72	A2 .94 / Baa2 2.10 / Ba1 4.78	Baa1 1.61 / Baa3 3.15 / Ba2 6.02	Baa2 2.67 / Ba1 4.39 / Ba2 6.50	Baa2 2.04 / Baa2 2.67 / Ba1 5.75	Baa1 1.55 / Baa3 3.19 / Ba2 6.50	A3 1.31 / Baa3 2.99 / Ba2 6.24	Baa1 1.84 / Baa3 3.12 / Ba2 6.56	A3 1.29 / Baa2 2.43 / Ba1 5.47

CASH FLOW MEASURES (%)

	4/1/05–3/31/06	4/1/06–3/31/07	4/1/07–3/31/08	0-1MM	1-3MM	3-5MM	5-10MM	10-25MM	25MM & OVER
Cash from Trading/Sales									
Cash after Operations/Sales	16.3 / 6.7 / .6	19.1 / 8.3 / -.4	21.2 / 8.9 / 2.0	67.9 / 20.5 / 7.9	24.8 / 15.9 / 3.9	21.2 / 11.6 / -.2	15.7 / 9.6 / 1.6	14.9 / 4.5 / .0	12.1 / 4.9 / .8
Net Cash after Operations/Sales	17.3 / 7.0 / 1.0	20.4 / 8.9 / 1.6	19.3 / 9.1 / 1.6	66.7 / 23.6 / 6.7	24.2 / 17.9 / 5.8	17.9 / 8.5 / -.1	14.6 / 10.4 / 1.6	14.8 / 4.8 / -.4	12.3 / 5.7 / .9
Net Cash after Debt Amortization/Sales	8.0 / 1.9 / -2.0	7.9 / 2.3 / -5.9	6.6 / 2.2 / -2.2	21.6 / 6.0 / .6	13.9 / 2.5 / -4.7	6.7 / -1.2 / -4.8	11.5 / 4.6 / -1.2	4.6 / .2 / -6.4	4.6 / 2.5 / -.4
Debt Service P&I Coverage	7.4 / (125) 2.1 / .6	5.9 / (137) 2.0 / .3	4.2 / (110) 1.5 / .5	2.1 / (15) 1.4 / 1.0	5.0 / (21) 1.7 / .6		23.3 / 2.5 / 1.1	5.1 / (22) 1.2 / -.2	5.0 / (26) 1.7 / .7
Interest Coverage (Operating Cash)	12.2 / (118) 3.9 / .5	10.4 / (132) 4.2 / .8	6.5 / (107) 3.1 / .7	4.0 / (15) 2.1 / 1.3	5.2 / (21) 2.0 / .9	(16)	30.1 / 6.6 / .4	6.9 / (20) 2.4 / -1.3	8.8 / (26) 4.9 / 1.5
Δ Inventory	16.9 / (91) 3.0 / -13.9	30.7 / (87) 7.3 / -6.5	48.7 / (69) 10.6 / .0				72.6 / (11) 23.9 / 1.4	56.9 / (16) 5.3 / -5.1	48.5 / (24) 13.5 / 1.4
Δ Total Current Assets	34.7 / 6.8 / -12.1	40.2 / 12.9 / -2.4	32.1 / 12.5 / -6.5	37.4 / 26.6 / -25.4	18.6 / 10.7 / -27.2	39.1 / .8 / -28.8	39.4 / 13.2 / -5.1	62.0 / 10.7 / -3.3	29.7 / 10.6 / 3.0
Δ Total Assets	26.7 / 6.0 / -5.8	31.9 / 9.3 / -.5	24.4 / 7.7 / -.8	14.5 / 2.8 / -.7	34.3 / 5.1 / -1.8	28.5 / 6.3 / -4.5	42.1 / 7.3 / -7.1	22.7 / 12.2 / 1.3	24.6 / 15.2 / .1
Δ Retained Earnings	42.7 / (131) 16.2 / -2.5	40.2 / (148) 11.0 / -3.3	52.3 / (119) 11.1 / -.7	116.1 / 1.8 / -45.1	52.3 / 9.5 / -1.8	84.4 / 16.9 / -20.8	572.4 / 30.9 / -20.8	45.3 / (25) 8.6 / 7.3	41.4 / (26) 18.4 / .6
Δ Net Sales	25.9 / 7.4 / -2.4	24.9 / 8.5 / -.9	30.4 / 10.6 / 1.8	20.0 / 3.7 / -4.9	33.8 / 16.5 / -1.6	41.7 / 18.7 / 1.9	25.7 / 9.4 / -1.4	62.1 / 10.7 / 4.4	30.0 / 10.3 / 3.7
Δ Cost of Goods Sold									
Δ Profit before Int. & Taxes	102.7 / 16.3 / -27.2	94.1 / 9.9 / -27.1	102.0 / (120) 10.4 / -24.8	68.7 / (15) 1.0 / -18.2	176.0 / 11.5 / -39.8	215.7 / 54.2 / -46.4	126.9 / 41.3 / -34.2	117.7 / 26.1 / -21.4	51.9 / .1 / -14.0
Δ Depr./Depl./Amort.	19.7 / (119) -3.6 / -28.4	33.3 / (135) 1.7 / -14.8	17.9 / (111) -3.0 / -27.3	3.1 / (14) -20.9 / -69.5	17.8 / (20) .9 / -14.7	40.8 / -29.5 / -62.6	19.0 / (16) -3.7 / -18.0	25.1 / (24) 5.6 / -32.8	15.5 / (25) 1.0 / -6.9

RATIOS

	4/1/05–3/31/06	4/1/06–3/31/07	4/1/07–3/31/08	0-1MM	1-3MM	3-5MM	5-10MM	10-25MM	25MM & OVER
Sustainable Growth Rate	35.8 / (136) 5.2 / -10.9	32.1 / (147) 8.7 / -8.7	28.7 / (120) 7.9 / -3.7	18.5 / 2.5 / -46.9	15.8 / (22) 3.6 / -39.2	32.6 / 6.2 / .2	225.5 / 27.7 / -3.3	32.8 / 9.1 / -5.9	23.9 / 4.4 / -3.7
Funded Debt/EBITDA	.4 / 2.3 / 6.5	.9 / 2.3 / 5.7	.7 / 2.2 / 5.9	.8 / 2.8 / 5.4	1.3 / 5.9 / 9.0	.0 / 2.3 / 3.5	.8 / 1.3 / 6.9	.1 / 1.3 / 3.5	1.2 / 2.3 / 3.7
Net Sales ($)	4750465M	4122798M	4575150M	6832M	42569M	49530M	125607M	430732M	3919880M
Total Assets ($)	2237648M	2722141M	2577924M	11216M	130824M	44166M	108700M	439722M	1843296M

M = $ thousand   MM = $ million

Note: The ratings are Moody's.edf rating (e.g. Ba1.edf) and not Moody's Investor Services Long-Term Bond Ratings. If a number of statements appears for the Risk Calc EDF (1 yr), it also applies to the (5 yr).

NAICS CODES APPEARING IN THE STATEMENT STUDIES

NAICS Codes	Page	NAICS Codes	Page	NAICS Codes	Page
111110	98-99	238150	212-213, 1646	315222	322-323
111140	100-101	238160	214-215, 1647	315228	324-325
111150	102-103	238190	216-217	315233	326-327
111199	104-105	238210	218-219, 1648	315239	328-329
111211	106-107	238220	220-221, 1649	315299	330-331
111219	108-109	238290	222-223	315999	332-333
111310	110-111	238310	224-225, 1650	316110	334-335
111331	112-113	238320	226-227, 1651	321113	336-337
111332	114-115	238330	228-229	321114	338-339
111335	116-117	238340	230-231	321211	340-341
111411	118-119	238350	232-233	321214	342-343
111421	120-121	238390	234-235	321911	344-345
111920	122-123	238910	236-237, 1652	321912	346-347
111998	124-125	238990	238-239, 1653	321918	348-349
112111	126-127	311119	242-243	321920	350-351
112112	128-129	311211	244-245	321991	352-353
112120	130-131	311330	246-247	321992	354-355
112210	132-133	311411	248-249	321999	356-357
112310	134-135	311412	250-251	322121	358-359
112920	136-137	311421	252-253	322211	360-361
113110	138-139	311423	254-255	322212	362-363
113310	140-141	311511	256-257	322213	364-365
114111	142-143	311513	258-259	322221	366-367
114112	144-145	311520	260-261	322222	368-369
115111	146-147	311611	262-263	322223	370-371
115112	148-149	311612	264-265	322232	372-373
115114	150-151	311613	266-267	322291	374-375
115210	152-153	311615	268-269	322299	376-377
211111	156-157	311712	270-271	323110	378-379
212111	158-159	311811	272-273	323112	380-381
212312	160-161	311812	274-275	323113	382-383
212319	162-163	311821	276-277	323114	384-385
212321	164-165	311911	278-279	323116	386-387
213111	166-167	311919	280-281	323117	388-389
213112	168-169, 1632	311920	282-283	323119	390-391
221122	172-173	311930	284-285	323121	392-393
221210	174-175	311941	286-287	323122	394-395
221310	176-177	311942	288-289	324110	396-397
236115	180-181, 1633	311991	290-291	324121	398-399
236116	182-183, 1634	311999	292-293	324191	400-401
236117	184-185, 1635	312111	294-295	324199	402-403
236118	186-187, 1636	312112	296-297	325188	404-405
236210	188-189, 1637	312120	298-299	325193	406-407
236220	190-191, 1638	312130	300-301	325199	408-409
237110	192-193, 1639	313111	302-303	325211	410-411
237120	194-195	313210	304-305	325311	412-413
237130	196-197	313311	306-307	325314	414-415
237210	198-199, 1640	313320	308-309	325320	416-417
237310	200-201, 1641	314110	310-311	325411	418-419
237990	202-203, 1642	314129	312-313	325412	420-421
238110	204-205, 1643	314912	314-315	325510	422-423
238120	206-207, 1644	314999	316-317	325520	424-425
238130	208-209	315211	318-319	325611	426-427
238140	210-211, 1645	315212	320-321	325612	428-429

NAICS CODES APPEARING IN THE STATEMENT STUDIES

NAICS Codes	Page	NAICS Codes	Page	NAICS Codes	Page
325620	430-431	332612	538-539	334310	646-647
325910	432-433	332618	540-541	334412	648-649
325991	434-435	332710	542-543	334413	650-651
325998	436-437	332721	544-545	334416	652-653
326111	438-439	332722	546-547	334417	654-655
326112	440-441	332811	548-549	334419	656-657
326113	442-443	332812	550-551	334510	658-659
326121	444-445	332813	552-553	334511	660-661
326122	446-447	332911	554-555	334512	662-663
326130	448-449	332912	556-557	334513	664-665
326140	450-451	332913	558-559	334514	666-667
326160	452-453	332919	560-561	334515	668-669
326191	454-455	332991	562-563	334516	670-671
326199	456-457	332996	564-565	334519	672-673
326212	458-459	332999	566-567	335121	674-675
326220	460-461	333111	568-569	335122	676-677
326291	462-463	333112	570-571	335129	678-679
326299	464-465	333120	572-573	335311	680-681
327121	466-467	333131	574-575	335312	682-683
327215	468-469	333132	576-577	335313	684-685
327320	470-471	333220	578-579	335314	686-687
327331	472-473	333291	580-581	335931	688-689
327332	474-475	333292	582-583	335999	690-691
327390	476-477	333293	584-585	336111	692-693
327910	478-479	333294	586-587	336211	694-695
327991	480-481	333298	588-589	336212	696-697
327999	482-483	333314	590-591	336214	698-699
331111	484-485	333315	592-593	336360	700-701
331210	486-487	333319	594-595	336370	702-703
331221	488-489	333412	596-597	336399	704-705
331222	490-491	333414	598-599	336412	706-707
331314	492-493	333415	600-601	336413	708-709
331316	494-495	333511	602-603	336510	710-711
331422	496-497	333512	604-605	336611	712-713
331491	498-499	333513	606-607	336612	714-715
331492	500-501	333514	608-609	336991	716-717
331511	502-503	333515	610-611	336999	718-719
331513	504-505	333518	612-613	337110	720-721
331521	506-507	333612	614-615	337121	722-723
331522	508-509	333613	616-617	337122	724-725
331524	510-511	333911	618-619	337127	726-727
331528	512-513	333912	620-621	337211	728-729
332111	514-515	333922	622-623	337214	730-731
332116	516-517	333923	624-625	337215	732-733
332117	518-519	333924	626-627	337910	734-735
332212	520-521	333992	628-629	337920	736-737
332311	522-523	333993	630-631	339112	738-739
332312	524-525	333994	632-633	339113	740-741
332313	526-527	333999	634-635	339114	742-743
332321	528-529	334111	636-637	339115	744-745
332322	530-531	334119	638-639	339116	746-747
332323	532-533	334210	640-641	339911	748-749
332439	534-535	334220	642-643	339914	750-751
332510	536-537	334290	644-645	339920	752-753

NAICS CODES APPEARING IN THE STATEMENT STUDIES

NAICS Codes	Page	NAICS Codes	Page	NAICS Codes	Page
339932	754-755	424440	864-865	446191	974-975
339950	756-757	424450	866-867	446199	976-977
339991	758-759	424460	868-869	447110	978-979
339992	760-761	424470	870-871	447190	980-981
339994	762-763	424480	872-873	448110	982-983
339999	764-765	424490	874-875	448120	984-985
423110	768-769	424510	876-877	448140	986-987
423120	770-771	424520	878-879	448150	988-989
423130	772-773	424590	880-881	448190	990-991
423140	774-775	424610	882-883	448210	992-993
423210	776-777	424690	884-885	448310	994-995
423220	778-779	424710	886-887	451110	996-997
423310	780-781	424720	888-889	451120	998-999
423320	782-783	424810	890-891	451140	1000-1001
423330	784-785	424820	892-893	451211	1002-1003
423390	786-787	424910	894-895	452111	1004-1005
423410	788-789	424920	896-897	452990	1006-1007
423420	790-791	424930	898-899	453110	1008-1009
423430	792-793	424940	900-901	453210	1010-1011
423440	794-795	424950	902-903	453220	1012-1013
423450	796-797	424990	904-905	453310	1014-1015
423460	798-799	425110	906-907	453910	1016-1017
423490	800-801	425120	908-909	453920	1018-1019
423510	802-803	441110	912-913	453930	1020-1021
423520	804-805	441120	914-915	453991	1022-1023
423610	806-807	441210	916-917	453998	1024-1025
423620	808-809	441221	918-919	454111	1026-1027
423690	810-811	441222	920-921	454113	1028-1029
423710	812-813	441229	922-923	454210	1030-1031
423720	814-815	441310	924-925	454311	1032-1033
423730	816-817	441320	926-927	454312	1034-1035
423740	818-819	442110	928-929	454390	1036-1037
423810	820-821	442210	930-931	481111	1040-1041
423820	822-823	442299	932-933	481211	1042-1043
423830	824-825	443111	934-935	481219	1044-1045
423840	826-827	443112	936-937	482111	1046-1047
423850	828-829	443120	938-939	483113	1048-1049
423860	830-831	444110	940-941	483211	1050-1051
423910	832-833	444120	942-943	484110	1052-1053
423920	834-835	444130	944-945	484121	1054-1055
423930	836-837	444190	946-947	484122	1056-1057
423940	838-839	444210	948-949	484210	1058-1059
423990	840-841	444220	950-951	484220	1060-1061
424110	842-843	445110	952-953	484230	1062-1063
424120	844-845	445120	954-955	485310	1064-1065
424130	846-847	445210	956-957	485320	1066-1067
424210	848-849	445230	958-959	485410	1068-1069
424310	850-851	445291	960-961	485510	1070-1071
424320	852-853	445292	962-963	485999	1072-1073
424330	854-855	445299	964-965	488119	1074-1075
424340	856-857	445310	966-967	488190	1076-1077
424410	858-859	446110	968-969	488320	1078-1079
424420	860-861	446120	970-971	488330	1080-1081
424430	862-863	446130	972-973	488390	1082-1083

NAICS CODES APPEARING IN THE STATEMENT STUDIES

NAICS Codes	Page	NAICS Codes	Page	NAICS Codes	Page
488410	1084-1085	524298	1196-1197	541910	1308-1309
488490	1086-1087	525910	1198-1199	541921	1310-1311
488510	1088-1089	525990	1200-1201	541922	1312-1313
488991	1090-1091	531110	1204-1205	541940	1314-1315
488999	1092-1093	531120	1206-1207	541990	1316-1317
492110	1094-1095	531130	1208-1209	551111	1320-1321
493110	1096-1097	531190	1210-1211	551112	1322-1323
493120	1098-1099	531210	1212-1213	561110	1326-1327
493130	1100-1101	531311	1214-1215	561210	1328-1329
493190	1102-1103	531312	1216-1217	561311	1330-1331
511110	1106-1107	531390	1218-1219	561320	1332-1333
511120	1108-1109	532111	1220-1221	561330	1334-1335
511130	1110-1111	532112	1222-1223	561439	1336-1337
511140	1112-1113	532120	1224-1225	561440	1338-1339
511199	1114-1115	532210	1226-1227	561499	1340-1341
511210	1116-1117	532291	1228-1229	561510	1342-1343
512110	1118-1119	532299	1230-1231	561520	1344-1345
512131	1120-1121	532310	1232-1233	561599	1346-1347
512199	1122-1123	532411	1234-1235	561612	1348-1349
515112	1124-1125	532412	1236-1237	561621	1350-1351
515120	1126-1127	532420	1238-1239	561710	1352-1353
515210	1128-1129	532490	1240-1241	561720	1354-1355
517110	1130-1131	533110	1242-1243	561730	1356-1357
517210	1132-1133	541110	1246-1247	561740	1358-1359
517911	1134-1135	541191	1248-1249	561790	1360-1361
517919	1136-1137	541211	1250-1251	561910	1362-1363
518210	1138-1139	541214	1252-1253	561990	1364-1365
519130	1140-1141	541219	1254-1255	562111	1366-1367
519190	1142-1143	541310	1256-1257	562119	1368-1369
522210	1146-1147	541320	1258-1259	562211	1370-1371
522220	1148-1149	541330	1260-1261	562212	1372-1373
522291	1150-1151	541370	1262-1263	562219	1374-1375
522292	1152-1153	541380	1264-1265	562910	1376-1377
522294	1154-1155	541410	1266-1267	562920	1378-1379
522298	1156-1157	541430	1268-1269	562998	1380-1381
522310	1158-1159	541511	1270-1271	611110	1384-1385
522320	1160-1161	541512	1272-1273	611210	1386-1387
522390	1162-1163	541519	1274-1275	611310	1388-1389
523110	1164-1165	541611	1276-1277	611430	1390-1391
523120	1166-1167	541612	1278-1279	611519	1392-1393
523130	1168-1169	541613	1280-1281	611610	1394-1395
523140	1170-1171	541614	1282-1283	611699	1396-1397
523910	1172-1173	541618	1284-1285	611710	1398-1399
523920	1174-1175	541620	1286-1287	621111	1402-1403
523930	1176-1177	541690	1288-1289	621112	1404-1405
523991	1178-1179	541712	1290-1291	621210	1406-1407
523999	1180-1181	541720	1292-1293	621310	1408-1409
524113	1182-1183	541810	1294-1295	621320	1410-1411
524114	1184-1185	541820	1296-1297	621330	1412-1413
524126	1186-1187	541840	1298-1299	621340	1414-1415
524127	1188-1189	541850	1300-1301	621391	1416-1417
524128	1190-1191	541860	1302-1303	621399	1418-1419
524210	1192-1193	541870	1304-1305	621410	1420-1421
524292	1194-1195	541890	1306-1307	621420	1422-1423

NAICS CODES APPEARING IN THE STATEMENT STUDIES

NAICS Codes	Page	NAICS Codes	Page	NAICS Codes	Page
621491	1424-1425	811118	1540-1541		
621492	1426-1427	811121	1542-1543		
621493	1428-1429	811122	1544-1545		
621498	1430-1431	811191	1546-1547		
621511	1432-1433	811192	1548-1549		
621512	1434-1435	811198	1550-1551		
621610	1436-1437	811212	1552-1553		
621910	1438-1439	811219	1554-1555		
621991	1440-1441	811310	1556-1557		
621999	1442-1443	811412	1558-1559		
622110	1444-1445, 1446-1447	811490	1560-1561		
622210	1448-1449	812112	1562-1563		
622310	1450-1451	812210	1564-1565		
623110	1452-1453	812220	1566-1567		
623210	1454-1455	812310	1568-1569		
623220	1456-1457	812320	1570-1571		
623311	1458-1459	812331	1572-1573		
623312	1460-1461	812910	1574-1575		
623990	1462-1463	812921	1576-1577		
624110	1464-1465	812930	1578-1579		
624120	1466-1467	812990	1580-1581		
624190	1468-1469	813110	1582-1583		
624210	1470-1471	813211	1584-1585		
624221	1472-1473	813212	1586-1587		
624229	1474-1475	813219	1588-1589		
624310	1476-1477	813319	1590-1591		
624410	1478-1479	813410	1592-1593		
711110	1482-1483	813910	1594-1595		
711130	1484-1485	813920	1596-1597		
711211	1486-1487	813930	1598-1599		
711212	1488-1489	813990	1600-1601		
711310	1490-1491	814110	1602-1603		
712110	1492-1493	921110	1606-1607		
713110	1494-1495	921120	1608-1609		
713120	1496-1497	921140	1610-1611		
713210	1498-1499	921150	1612-1613		
713910	1500-1501	921190	1614-1615		
713920	1502-1503	922160	1616-1617		
713930	1504-1505	923110	1618-1619		
713940	1506-1507	923120	1620-1621		
713950	1508-1509	924110	1622-1623		
713990	1510-1511	925110	1624-1625		
721110	1514-1515	925120	1626-1627		
721120	1516-1517	926110	1628-1629		
721211	1518-1519				
721214	1520-1521				
722110	1522-1523				
722211	1524-1525				
722213	1526-1527				
722310	1528-1529				
722320	1530-1531				
722410	1532-1533				
811111	1536-1537				
811112	1538-1539				

DESCRIPTION OF INDUSTRIES INCLUDED IN THE STATEMENT STUDIES

AGRICULTURE, FORESTRY, FISHING AND HUNTING

NAICS #   **Page**

111110 **Soybean Farming.** This industry comprises establishments primarily engaged in growing soybeans and/or producing soybean seeds. 98-99

111140 **Wheat Farming.** This industry comprises establishments primarily engaged in growing wheat and/or producing wheat seeds. 100-101

111150 **Corn Farming.** This industry comprises establishments primarily engaged in growing corn (except sweet corn) and/or producing corn seeds. 102-103

111199 **All Other Grain Farming.** This U.S. industry comprises establishments primarily engaged in growing grains and/or producing grain(s) seeds (except wheat, corn, rice, and oilseed(s) and grain(s) combinations). 104-105

111211 **Potato Farming.** This U.S. industry comprises establishments primarily engaged in growing potatoes and/or producing seed potatoes (except sweet potatoes). 106-107

111219 **Other Vegetable (except Potato) and Melon Farming.** This U.S. industry comprises establishments primarily engaged in one or more of the following: (1) growing melons and/or vegetables (except potatoes; dry peas; dry beans; field, silage, or seed corn; and sugar beets); (2) producing vegetable and/or melon seeds; and (3) growing vegetable and/or melon bedding plants. 108-109

111310 **Orange Groves.** This industry comprises establishments primarily engaged in growing oranges. 110-111

111331 **Apple Orchards.** This U.S. industry comprises establishments primarily engaged in growing apples. 112-113

111332 **Grape Vineyards.** This U.S. industry comprises establishments primarily engaged in growing grapes and/or growing grapes to sun dry into raisins. 114-115

111335 **Tree Nut Farming.** This U.S. industry comprises establishments primarily engaged in growing tree nuts. 116-117

111411 **Mushroom Production.** This U.S. industry comprises establishments primarily engaged in growing mushrooms under cover in mines underground, or in other controlled environments. 118-119

111421 **Nursery and Tree Production.** This U.S. industry comprises establishments primarily engaged in (1) growing nursery products, nursery stock, shrubbery, bulbs, fruit stock, sod, and so forth, under cover or in open fields and/or (2) growing short rotation woody trees with a growth and harvest cycle of 10 years or less for pulp or tree stock. 120-121

111920 **Cotton Farming.** This industry comprises establishments primarily engaged in growing cotton. 122-123

111998 **All Other Miscellaneous Crop Farming.** This U.S. industry comprises establishments primarily engaged in one of the following: (1) growing crops (except oilseeds and/or grains; vegetables and/or melons; fruits and/or tree nuts; greenhouse, nursery and/or floriculture products; tobacco; cotton; sugarcane; hay; sugar beets; or peanuts); (2) growing a combination of crops (except a combination of oilseed(s) and grain(s); and a combination of fruit(s) and tree nut(s)) with no one crop or family of crop(s) accounting for one-half of the establishment's agricultural production (i.e., value of crops for market); or (3) gathering tea or maple sap. 124-125

112111 **Beef Cattle Ranching and Farming.** This U.S. industry comprises establishments primarily engaged in raising cattle (including cattle for dairy herd replacements). 126-127

112112 **Cattle Feedlots.** This U.S. industry comprises establishments primarily engaged in feeding cattle for fattening. 128-129

112120 **Dairy Cattle and Milk Production.** This industry comprises establishments primarily engaged in milking dairy cattle. 130-131

112210 **Hog and Pig Farming.** This industry comprises establishments primarily engaged in raising hogs and pigs. These establishments may include farming activities, such as breeding, farrowing, and the raising of weanling pigs, feeder pigs, or market size hogs. 132-133

NAICS #   **Page**

112310 **Chicken Egg Production.** This industry comprises establishments primarily engaged in raising chickens for egg production. The eggs produced may be for use as table eggs or hatching eggs. 134-135

112920 **Horses and Other Equine Production.** This industry comprises establishments primarily engaged in raising horses, mules, donkeys and other equines. 136-137

113110 **Timber Tract Operations.** This industry comprises establishments primarily engaged in the operation of timber tracts for the purpose of selling standing timber. 138-139

113310 **Logging.** This industry comprises establishments primarily engaged in one or more of the following: (1) cutting timber; (2) cutting and transporting timber; and (3) producing wood chips in the field. 140-141

114111 **Finfish Fishing.** This U.S. industry comprises establishments primarily engaged in the commercial catching or taking of finfish (e.g., bluefish, salmon, trout, tuna) from their natural habitat. 142-143

114112 **Shellfish Fishing.** This U.S. industry comprises establishments primarily engaged in the commercial catching or taking of shellfish (e.g., clams, crabs, lobsters, mussels, oysters, sea urchins, shrimp) from their natural habitat. 144-145

115111 **Cotton Ginning.** This U.S. industry comprises establishments primarily engaged in ginning cotton. 146-147

115112 **Soil Preparation, Planting, and Cultivating.** This U.S. industry comprises establishments primarily engaged in performing a soil preparation activity or crop production service, such as plowing, fertilizing, seed bed preparation, planting, cultivating, and crop protecting services. 148-149

115114 **Postharvest Crop Activities (except Cotton Ginning).** This U.S. industry comprises establishments primarily engaged in performing services on crops, subsequent to their harvest, with the intent of preparing them for market or further processing. These establishments provide postharvest activities, such as crop cleaning, sun drying, shelling, fumigating, curing, sorting, grading, packing, and cooling. 150-151

115210 **Support Activities for Animal Production.** This industry comprises establishments primarily engaged in performing support activities related to raising livestock (e.g., cattle, goats, hogs, horses, poultry, sheep). These establishments may perform one or more of the following: (1) breeding services for animals, including companion animals (e.g., cats, dogs, pet birds); (2) pedigree record services; (3) boarding horses; (4) dairy herd improvement activities; (5) livestock spraying; and (6) sheep dipping and shearing. 152-153

MINING

211111 **Crude Petroleum and Natural Gas Extraction.** This U.S. industry comprises establishments primarily engaged in (1) the exploration, development and/or the production of petroleum or natural gas from wells in which the hydrocarbons will initially flow or can be produced using normal pumping techniques or (2) the production of crude petroleum from surface shales or tar sands or from reservoirs in which the hydrocarbons are semisolids. Establishments in this industry operate oil and gas wells on their own account or for others on a contract or fee basis. 156-157

212111 **Bituminous Coal and Lignite Surface Mining.** This U.S. industry comprises establishments primarily engaged in one or more of the following: (1) surface mining of bituminous coal and lignite; (2) developing bituminous coal and lignite surface mine sites; (3) surface mining and beneficiating (e.g., cleaning, washing, screening, and sizing coal) of bituminous coal; or (4) beneficiating (e.g., cleaning, washing, screening, and sizing coal), but not mining, bituminous coal. 158-159

212312 **Crushed and Broken Limestone Mining and Quarrying.** This U.S. industry comprises (1) establishments primarily engaged in developing the mine site, mining or quarrying crushed and broken limestone (including related rocks, such as dolomite, cement rock, marl, travertine, and calcareous tufa); and (2) preparation plants primarily engaged in beneficiating limestone (e.g., grinding or pulverizing). 160-161

NAICS #   **Page**

212319 Other Crushed and Broken Stone Mining and Quarrying. This U.S. industry comprises: (1) establishments primarily engaged in developing the mine site and/or mining or quarrying crushed and broken stone (except limestone and granite); (2) preparation plants primarily engaged in beneficiating (e.g., grinding and pulverizing) stone (except limestone and granite); and (3) establishments primarily engaged in mining or quarrying bituminous limestone and bituminous sandstone. 162-163

212321 Construction Sand and Gravel Mining. This U.S. industry comprises establishments primarily engaged in one or more of the following: (1) operating commercial grade (i.e., construction) sand and gravel pits; (2) dredging for commercial grade sand and gravel; and (3) washing, screening, or otherwise preparing commercial grade sand and gravel. 164-165

213111 Drilling Oil and Gas Wells. This U.S. industry comprises establishments primarily engaged in drilling oil and gas wells for others on a contract or fee basis. This industry includes contractors that specialize in spudding in, drilling in, redrilling, and directional drilling. 166-167

213112 Support Activities for Oil and Gas Operations. This U.S. industry comprises establishments primarily engaged in performing support activities on a contract or fee basis for oil and gas operations (except site preparation and related construction activities). Services included are exploration (except geophysical surveying and mapping); excavating slush pits and cellars, well surveying; running, cutting, and pulling casings, tubes, and rods; cementing wells, shooting wells; perforating well casings; acidizing and chemically treating wells; and cleaning out, bailing, and swabbing wells. 168-169

UTILITIES

221122 Electric Power Distribution. This U.S. industry comprises electric power establishments primarily engaged in either (1) operating electric power distribution systems (i.e., consisting of lines, poles, meters, and wiring) or (2) operating as electric power brokers or agents that arrange the sale of electricity via power distribution systems operated by others. 172-173

221210 Natural Gas Distribution. This industry comprises: (1) establishments primarily engaged in operating gas distribution systems (e.g., mains, meters); (2) establishments known as gas marketers that buy gas from the well and sell it to a distribution system; (3) establishments known as gas brokers or agents that arrange the sale of gas over gas distribution systems operated by others; and (4) establishments primarily engaged in transmitting and distributing gas to final consumers. 174-175

221310 Water Supply and Irrigation Systems. This industry comprises establishments primarily engaged in operating water treatment plants and/or operating water supply systems. The water supply system may include pumping stations, aqueducts, and/or distribution mains. The water may be used for drinking, irrigation, or other uses. 176-177

CONSTRUCTION—GENERAL

236115 New Single-Family Housing Construction (except Operative Builders). This U.S. industry comprises general contractor establishments primarily respon-sible for the entire construction of new single-family housing, such as single-family detached houses and town houses or row houses where each housing unit (1) is separated from its neighbors by a ground-to-roof wall and (2) has no housing units constructed above or below. This industry includes general contractors responsible for the on-site assembly of modular and prefabricated houses. Single-family housing design-build firms and single-family construction management firms acting as general contractors are included in this industry. 180-181

236116 New Multifamily Housing Construction (except Operative Builders). This U.S. industry comprises general contractor establishments responsible for the construction of new multifamily residential housing units (e.g., high-rise, garden, and town house apartments and condominiums where each unit is not separated from its neighbors by a ground-to-roof wall). Multifamily design-build firms and multifamily housing construction management firms acting as general contractors are included in this industry. 182-183

CONSTRUCTION-GENERAL

NAICS #   **Page**

236117 New Housing Operative Builders. This U.S. industry comprises operative builders primarily responsible for the entire construction of new houses and other residential buildings, single-family and multifamily, on their own account for sale. Operative builders are also known as speculative or merchant builders. 184-185

236118 Residential Remodelers. This U.S. industry comprises establishments primarily responsible for the remodeling construction (including additions, alterations, reconstruction, maintenance and repair work) of houses and other residential buildings, single-family and multifamily. Included in this industry are remodeling general contractors, operative remodelers, remodeling design-build firms, and remodeling project construction management firms. 186-187

236210 Industrial Building Construction. This industry comprises establishments primarily responsible for the construction (including new work, additions, alterations, maintenance, and repairs) of industrial buildings (except warehouses). The construction of selected additional structures, whose production processes are similar to those for industrial buildings (e.g., incinerators, cement plants, blast furnaces, and similar nonbuilding structures), is included in this industry. Included in this industry are industrial building general contractors, industrial building operative builders, industrial building design-build firms, and industrial building construction management firms. 188-189

236220 Commercial and Institutional Building Construction. This industry comprises establishments primarily responsible for the construction (including new work, additions, alterations, maintenance, and repairs) of commercial and institutional buildings and related structures, such as stadiums, grain elevators, and indoor swimming pools. This industry includes establishments responsible for the on-site assembly of modular or prefabricated commercial and institutional buildings. Included in this industry are commercial and institutional building general contractors, commercial and institutional building operative builders, commercial and institutional building design-build firms, and commercial and institutional building project construction management firms. 190-191

237110 Water and Sewer Line and Related Structures Construction. This industry comprises establishments primarily engaged in the construction of water and sewer lines, mains, pumping stations, treatment plants and storage tanks. The work performed may include new work, reconstruction, rehabilitation, and repairs. Specialty trade contractors are included in this group if they are engaged in activities primarily related to water and sewer line and related structures construction. All structures (including buildings) that are integral parts of water and sewer networks (e.g., storage tanks, pumping stations, water treatment plants, and sewage treatment plants) are included in this industry. 192-193

237120 Oil and Gas Pipeline and Related Structures Construction. This industry comprises establishments primarily engaged in the construction of oil and gas lines, mains, refineries, and storage tanks. The work performed may include new work, reconstruction, rehabilitation, and repairs. Specialty trade contractors are included in this group if they are engaged in activities primarily related to oil and gas pipeline and related structures construction. All structures (including buildings) that are integral parts of oil and gas networks (e.g., storage tanks, pumping stations, and refineries) are included in this industry. 194-195

237130 Power and Communication Line and Related Structures Construction. This industry comprises establishments primarily engaged in the construction of power lines and towers, power plants, and radio, television, and telecommunications transmitting/receiving towers. The work performed may include new work, reconstruction, rehabilitation, and repairs. Specialty trade contractors are included in this group if they are engaged in activities primarily related to power and communication line and related structures construction. All structures (including buildings) that are integral parts of power and communication networks (e.g., transmitting towers, substations, and power plants) are included. 196-197

237210 Land Subdivision. This industry comprises establishments primarily engaged in servicing land and subdividing real property into lots, for subsequent sale to builders. Servicing of land may include excavation work for the installation of roads and utility lines. The extent of work may vary from project to project. Land subdivision precedes building activity and the subsequent building is often residential, but may also be commercial tracts and industrial parks. These establishments may do all the work themselves or subcontract the work to others. Establishments that perform only the legal subdivision of land are not included in this industry. 198-199

CONSTRUCTION-GENERAL

NAICS #   **Page**

237310 Highway, Street, and Bridge Construction. This industry comprises establishments primarily engaged in the construction of highways (including elevated), streets, roads, airport runways, public sidewalks, or bridges. The work performed may include new work, reconstruction, rehabilitation, and repairs. Specialty trade contractors are included in this group if they are engaged in activities primarily related to highway, street, and bridge construction (e.g., installing guardrails on highways). 200-201

237990 Other Heavy and Civil Engineering Construction. This industry comprises establishments primarily engaged in heavy and engineering construction projects (excluding highway, street, bridge, and distribution line construction). The work performed may include new work, reconstruction, rehabilitation, and repairs. Specialty trade contractors are included in this group if they are engaged in activities primarily related to engineering construction projects (excluding highway, street, bridge, distribution line, oil and gas structure, and utilities building and structure construction). Construction projects involving water resources (e.g., dredging and land drainage), development of marine facilities, and projects involving open space improvement (e.g., parks and trails) are included in this industry. 202-203

238110 Poured Concrete Foundation and Structure Contractors. This industry comprises establishments primarily engaged in pouring and finishing concrete foundations and structural elements. This industry also includes establishments performing grout and shotcrete work. The work performed may include new work, additions, alterations, maintenance, and repairs. 204-205

238120 Structural Steel and Precast Concrete Contractors. This industry comprises establishments primarily engaged in: (1) erecting and assembling structural parts made from steel or precast concrete (e.g., steel beams, structural steel components, and similar products of precast concrete); and/or (2) assembling and installing other steel construction products (e.g., steel rods, bars, rebar, mesh, and cages) to reinforce poured-in-place concrete. The work performed may include new work, additions, alterations, maintenance, and repairs. 206-207

238130 Framing Contractors. This industry comprises establishments primarily engaged in structural framing and sheathing using materials other than structural steel or concrete. The work performed may include new work, additions, alterations, maintenance, and repairs. 208-209

238140 Masonry Contractors. This industry comprises establishments primarily engaged in masonry work, stone setting, brick laying, and other stone work. The work performed may include new work, additions, alterations, maintenance, and repairs. 210-211

238150 Glass and Glazing Contractors. This industry comprises establishments primarily engaged in installing glass panes in prepared openings (i.e., glazing work) and other glass work for buildings. The work performed may include new work, additions, alterations, maintenance, and repairs. 212-213

238160 Roofing Contractors. This industry comprises establishments primarily engaged in roofing. This industry also includes establishments treating roofs (i.e., spraying, painting, or coating) and installing skylights. The work performed may include new work, additions, alterations, maintenance, and repairs. 214-215

238190 Other Foundation, Structure, and Building Exterior Contractors. This industry comprises establishments primarily engaged in building foundation and structure trades work (except poured concrete, structural steel, precast concrete, framing, masonry, glass and glazing, roofing, and siding). The work performed may include new work, additions, alterations, maintenance, and repairs. 216-217

238210 Electrical Contractors and Other Wiring Installation Contractors. This industry comprises establishments primarily engaged in installing and servicing electrical wiring and equipment. Electrical contractors included in this industry may include both the parts and labor when performing work. Electrical contractors may perform new work, additions, alterations, maintenance, and repairs. 218-219

238220 Plumbing, Heating, and Air-Conditioning Contractors. This industry comprises establishments primarily engaged in installing and servicing plumbing, heating, and air-conditioning equipment. Contractors in this industry may provide both parts and labor when performing work. The work performed may include new work, additions, alterations, maintenance, and repairs. 220-221

MANUFACTURING

NAICS #   **Page**

238290 **Other Building Equipment Contractors.** This industry comprises establishments primarily engaged in installing or servicing building equipment (except electrical; plumbing; heating, cooling, or ventilation equipment). The repair and maintenance of miscellaneous building equipment is included in this industry. The work performed may include new work, additions, alterations, maintenance, and repairs. 222-223

238310 **Drywall and Insulation Contractors.** This industry comprises establishments primarily engaged in drywall, plaster work, and building insulation work. Plaster work includes applying plain or ornamental plaster, and installation of lath to receive plaster. The work performed may include new work, additions, alterations, maintenance, and repairs. 224-225

238320 **Painting and Wall Covering Contractors.** This industry comprises establishments primarily engaged in interior or exterior painting or interior wall covering. The work performed may include new work, additions, alterations, maintenance, and repairs. 226-227

238330 **Flooring Contractors.** This industry comprises establishments primarily engaged in the installation of resilient floor tile, carpeting, linoleum, and hard wood flooring. The work performed may include new work, additions, alterations, maintenance, and repairs. 228-229

238340 **Tile and Terrazzo Contractors.** This industry comprises establishments primarily engaged in setting and installing ceramic tile, stone (interior only), and mosaic and/or mixing marble particles and cement to make terrazzo at the job site. The work performed may include new work, additions, alterations, maintenance, and repairs. 230-231

238350 **Finish Carpentry Contractors.** This industry comprises establishments primarily engaged in finish carpentry work. The work performed may include new work, additions, alterations, maintenance, and repairs. 232-233

238390 **Other Building Finishing Contractors.** This industry comprises establishments primarily engaged in building finishing trade work (except drywall, plaster and insulation work; painting and wall covering work; flooring work; tile and terrazzo work; and finish carpentry work). The work performed may include new work, additions, alterations, or maintenance and repairs. . . . 234-235

238910 **Site Preparation Contractors.** This industry comprises establishments primarily engaged in site preparation activities, such as excavating and grading, demolition of buildings and other structures, septic system installation, and house moving. Earth moving and land clearing for all types of sites (e.g., building, nonbuilding, mining) is included in this industry. Establishments primarily engaged in construction equipment rental with operator (except cranes) are also included. 236-237

238990 **All Other Specialty Trade Contractors.** This industry comprises establishments primarily engaged in specialized trades (except foundation, structure, and building exterior contractors; building equipment contractors; building finishing contractors; and site preparation contractors). The specialty trade work performed includes new work, additions, alterations, maintenance, and repairs. 238-239

MANUFACTURING

311119 **Other Animal Food Manufacturing.** This U.S. industry comprises establishments primarily engaged in manufacturing animal food (except dog and cat) from ingredients, such as grains, oilseed mill products, and meat products. 242-243

311211 **Flour Milling.** This U.S. industry comprises establishments primarily engaged in (1) milling flour or meal from grains (except rice) or vegetables and/or (2) milling flour and preparing flour mixes or doughs. 244-245

311330 **Confectionery Manufacturing from Purchased Chocolate.** This industry comprises establishments primarily engaged in manufacturing chocolate confectioneries from chocolate produced elsewhere. Included in this industry are establishments primarily engaged in retailing chocolate confectionery products not for immediate consumption made on the premises from chocolate made elsewhere. 246-247

311411 **Frozen Fruit, Juice, and Vegetable Manufacturing.** This U.S. industry comprises establishments primarily engaged in manufacturing frozen fruits; frozen vegetables; and frozen fruit juices, ades, drinks, cocktail mixes and concentrates. 248-249

MANUFACTURING

NAICS # **Page**

311412 Frozen Specialty Food Manufacturing. This U.S. industry comprises establishments primarily engaged in manufacturing frozen specialty foods (except seafood), such as frozen dinners, entrees, and side dishes; frozen pizza; frozen whipped topping; and frozen waffles, pancakes, and french toast. 250-251

311421 Fruit and Vegetable Canning. This U.S. industry comprises establishments primarily engaged in manufacturing canned, pickled, and brined fruits and vegetables. 252-253

311423 Dried and Dehydrated Food Manufacturing. This U.S. industry comprises establishments primarily engaged in (1) drying (including freeze-dried) and/or dehydrating fruits, vegetables, and soup mixes and bouillon and/or (2) drying and/or dehydrating ingredients and packaging them with other purchased ingredients, such as rice and dry pasta. 254-255

311511 Fluid Milk Manufacturing. This U.S. industry comprises establishments primarily engaged in (1) manufacturing processed milk products, such as pasteurized milk or cream and sour cream and/or (2) manufacturing fluid milk dairy substitutes from soybeans and other nondairy substances. 256-257

311513 Cheese Manufacturing. This U.S. industry comprises establishments primarily engaged in (1) manufacturing cheese products (except cottage cheese) from raw milk and/or processed milk products and/or (2) manufacturing cheese substitutes from soybean and other nondairy substances. 258-259

311520 Ice Cream and Frozen Dessert Manufacturing. This industry comprises establishments primarily engaged in manufacturing ice cream, frozen yogurts, frozen ices, sherbets, frozen tofu, and other frozen desserts (except bakery products). 260-261

311611 Animal (except Poultry) Slaughtering. This U.S. industry comprises establishments primarily engaged in slaughtering animals (except poultry and small game). Establishments that slaughter and prepare meats are included in this industry. 262-263

311612 Meat Processed from Carcasses. This U.S. industry comprises establishments primarily engaged in processing or preserving meat and meat byproducts (except poultry and small game) from purchased meats. This industry includes establishments primarily engaged in assembly cutting and packing of meats (i.e., boxed meats) from purchased meats. 264-265

311613 Rendering and Meat Byproduct Processing. This U.S. industry comprises establishments primarily engaged in rendering animal fat, bones, and meat scraps. 266-267

311615 Poultry Processing. This U.S. industry comprises establishments primarily engaged in (1) slaughtering poultry and small game and/or (2) preparing processed poultry and small game meat and meat byproducts. 268-269

311712 Fresh and Frozen Seafood Processing. This U.S. industry comprises establishments primarily engaged in one or more of the following: (1) eviscerating fresh fish by removing heads, fins, scales, bones, and entrails; (2) shucking and packing fresh shellfish; (3) manufacturing frozen seafood; and (4) processing fresh and frozen marine fats and oils. 270-271

311811 Retail Bakeries. This U.S. industry comprises establishments primarily engaged in retailing bread and other bakery products not for immediate consumption made on the premises from flour, not from prepared dough. 272-273

311812 Commercial Bakeries. This U.S. industry comprises establishments primarily engaged in manufacturing fresh and frozen bread and bread-type rolls and other fresh bakery (except cookies and crackers) products. 274-275

311821 Cookie and Cracker Manufacturing. This U.S. industry comprises establishments primarily engaged in manufacturing cookies, crackers, and other products, such as ice cream cones. . . 276-277

311911 Roasted Nuts and Peanut Butter Manufacturing. This U.S. industry comprises establishments primarily engaged in one or more of the following: (1) salting, roasting, drying, cooking, or canning nuts; (2) processing grains or seeds into snacks; and (3) manufacturing peanut butter. 278-279

311919 Other Snack Food Manufacturing. This U.S. industry comprises establishments primarily engaged in manufacturing snack foods (except roasted nuts and peanut butter). 280-281

311920 Coffee and Tea Manufacturing. This industry comprises establishments primarily engaged in one or more of the following: (1) roasting coffee; (2) manufacturing coffee and tea concentrates (including instant and freeze-dried); (3) blending tea; (4) manufacturing herbal tea; and (5) manufacturing coffee extracts, flavorings, and syrups. 282-283

MANUFACTURING

NAICS #   **Page**

311930 **Flavoring Syrup and Concentrate Manufacturing.** This industry comprises establishments primarily engaged in manufacturing flavoring syrup drink concentrates and related products for soda fountain use or for the manufacture of soft drinks. 284-285

311941 **Mayonnaise, Dressing, and Other Prepared Sauce Manufacturing.** This U.S. industry comprises establishments primarily engaged in manufacturing mayonnaise, salad dressing, vinegar, mustard, horseradish, soy sauce, tarter sauce, Worcestershire sauce, and other prepared sauces (except tomato-based and gravy). 286-287

311942 **Spice and Extract Manufacturing.** This U.S. industry comprises establishments primarily engaged in (1) manufacturing spices, table salt, seasonings, flavoring extracts (except coffee and meat), and natural food colorings and/or (2) manufacturing dry mix food preparations, such as salad dressing mixes, gravy and sauce mixes, frosting mixes, and other dry mix preparations. 288-289

311991 **Perishable Prepared Food Manufacturing.** This U.S. industry comprises establishments primarily engaged in manufacturing perishable prepared foods, such as salads, sandwiches, prepared meals, fresh pizza, fresh pasta, and peeled or cut vegetables. 290-291

311999 **All Other Miscellaneous Food Manufacturing.** This U.S. industry comprises establishments primarily engaged in manufacturing food (except animal food; grain and oilseed milling; sugar and confectionery products; preserved fruits, vegetables, and specialties; dairy products; meat products; seafood products; bakeries and tortillas; snack foods; coffee and tea; flavoring syrups and concentrates; seasonings and dressings; and perishable prepared food). Included in this industry are establishments primarily engaged in mixing purchased dried and/or dehydrated ingredients including those mixing purchased dried and/ or dehydrated ingredients for soup mixes and bouillon. 292-293

312111 **Soft Drink Manufacturing.** This U.S. industry comprises establishments primarily engaged in manufacturing soft drinks and artificially carbonated waters. 294-295

312112 **Bottled Water Manufacturing.** This U.S. industry comprises establishments primarily engaged in purifying and bottling water (including naturally carbonated). 296-297

312120 **Breweries.** This industry comprises establishments primarily engaged in brewing beer, ale, malt liquors, and nonalcoholic beer. 298-299

312130 **Wineries.** This industry comprises establishments primarily engaged in one or more of the following: (1) growing grapes and manufacturing wine and brandies; (2) manufacturing wine and brandies from grapes and other fruits grown elsewhere; and (3) blending wines and brandies. 300-301

313111 **Yarn Spinning Mills.** This U.S. industry comprises establishments primarily engaged in spinning yarn from any fiber and/or producing hemp yarn and further processing into rope or bags. 302-303

313210 **Broadwoven Fabric Mills.** This industry comprises establishments primarily engaged in weaving broadwoven fabrics and felts (except tire fabrics and rugs). Establishments in this industry may weave only, weave and finish, or weave, finish, and further fabricate fabric products. . . 304-305

313311 **Broadwoven Fabric Finishing Mills.** This U.S. industry comprises (1) establishments primarily engaged in finishing broadwoven fabrics, and (2) establishments of converters who buy broadwoven fabrics in the grey, have them finished on contract, and sell at wholesale. Finishing operations include bleaching, dyeing, printing (roller, screen, flock, plisse), and other mechanical finishing, such as preshrinking, shrinking, sponging, calendering, mercerizing and napping. 306-307

313320 **Fabric Coating Mills.** This industry comprises establishments primarily engaged in coating, laminating, varnishing, waxing, and rubberizing textiles and apparel. 308-309

314110 **Carpet and Rug Mills.** This industry comprises establishments primarily engaged in (1) manufacturing woven, tufted, and other carpets and rugs, such as art squares, floor mattings, needlepunch carpeting, and door mats and mattings, from textile materials or from twisted paper, grasses, reeds, sisal, jute, or rags and/or (2) finishing carpets and rugs. 310-311

314129 **Other Household Textile Product Mills.** This U.S. industry comprises establishments primarily engaged in manufacturing household textile products (except window curtains and draperies), such as bedspreads, sheets, tablecloths, towels, and shower curtains, from purchased materials. 312-313

MANUFACTURING

NAICS #   Page

314912   Canvas and Related Product Mills. This U.S. industry comprises establishments primarily engaged in manufacturing canvas and canvas-like products, such as awnings, sails, tarpaulins, and tents, from purchased fabrics.   314-315

314999   All Other Miscellaneous Textile Product Mills. This U.S. industry comprises establishments primarily engaged in manufacturing textile products (except carpets and rugs; curtains and linens; textile bags and canvas products; rope, cordage, and twine; and tire cords and tire fabrics) from purchased materials.   316-317

315211   Men's and Boys' Cut and Sew Apparel Contractors. This U.S. industry comprises establishments commonly referred to as contractors primarily engaged in (1) cutting materials owned by others for men's and boys' apparel and/or (2) sewing materials owned by others for men's and boys' apparel.   318-319

315212   Women's, Girls', and Infants' Cut and Sew Apparel Contractors. This U.S. industry comprises establishments commonly referred to as contractors primarily engaged in (1) cutting materials owned by others for women's, girls', and infants' apparel and accessories and/or (2) sewing materials owned by others for women's, girls', and infants' apparel and accessories.   320-321

315222   Men's and Boys' Cut and Sew Suit, Coat, and Overcoat Manufacturing. This U.S. industry comprises establishments primarily engaged in manufacturing men's and boys' suits, overcoats, sport coats, tuxedos, dress uniforms, and other tailored apparel (except fur and leather) from purchased fabric. Men's and boys' suit, coat, and overcoat jobbers, who perform entrepreneurial functions involved in apparel manufacture, including buying raw materials, designing and preparing samples, arranging for apparel to be made from their materials, and marketing finished apparel, are included.   322-323

315228   Men's and Boys' Cut and Sew Other Outerwear Manufacturing. This U.S. industry comprises establishments primarily engaged in manufacturing men's and boys' cut and sew outerwear from purchased fabric (except underwear, nightwear, shirts, suits, overcoats and tailored coats, separate trousers and slacks, and work clothing). Men's and boys' other outerwear jobbers, who perform entrepreneurial functions involved in apparel manufacture, including buying raw materials, designing and preparing samples, arranging for apparel to be made from their materials, and marketing finished apparel, are included. Unisex sweatpants and similar garments that are sized without specific reference to gender (i.e., adult S, M, L, XL) are also included in this industry.   324-325

315233   Women's and Girls' Cut and Sew Dress Manufacturing. This U.S. industry comprises establishments primarily engaged in manufacturing women's and girls' dresses from purchased fabric. Women's and girls' dress jobbers, who perform entrepreneurial functions involved in apparel manufacture, including buying raw materials, designing and preparing samples, arranging for apparel to be made from their materials, and marketing finished apparel, are included.   326-327

315239   Women's and Girls' Cut and Sew Other Outerwear Manufacturing. This U.S. industry comprises establishments primarily engaged in manufacturing women's and girls' cut and sew apparel from purchased fabric (except underwear, lingerie, nightwear, blouses, shirts, dresses, suits, tailored coats, tailored jackets, and skirts). Women's and girls' other outerwear clothing jobbers, who perform entrepreneurial functions involved in apparel manufacture, including buying raw materials, designing and preparing samples, arranging for apparel to be made from their materials, and marketing finished apparel, are included.   328-329

315299   All Other Cut and Sew Apparel Manufacturing. This U.S. industry comprises establishments primarily engaged in manufacturing cut and sew apparel from purchased fabric (except cut and sew apparel contractors; men's and boys' cut and sew underwear, nightwear, suits, coats, shirts, trousers, work clothing, and other outerwear; women's and girls' lingerie, blouses, shirts, dresses, suits, coats, and other outerwear; infants' apparel; and fur and leather apparel). Clothing jobbers for these products, who perform entrepreneurial functions involved in apparel manufacture, including buying raw materials, designing and preparing samples, arranging for apparel to be made from their materials, and marketing finished apparel, are included.   330-331

MANUFACTURING

NAICS #
Page

315999 **Other Apparel Accessories and Other Apparel Manufacturing.** This U.S. industry comprises establishments primarily engaged in manufacturing apparel and apparel accessories (except apparel knitting mills; cut and sew apparel contractors; cut and sew apparel; hats and caps; mittens and gloves; and men's and boys' neckwear). Jobbers for these products, who perform entrepreneurial functions involved in other apparel and accessory manufacture, including buying raw materials, designing and preparing samples, arranging for other apparel and accessories to be made from their materials, and marketing finished other apparel and accessories, are included. 332-333

316110 **Leather and Hide Tanning and Finishing.** This industry comprises establishments primarily engaged in one or more of the following: (1) tanning, currying, and finishing hides and skins; (2) having others process hides and skins on a contract basis; and (3) dyeing or dressing furs. . . . 334-335

321113 **Sawmills.** This U.S. industry comprises establishments primarily engaged in sawing dimension lumber, boards, beams, timbers, poles, ties, shingles, shakes, siding, and wood chips from logs or bolts. Sawmills may plane the rough lumber that they make with a planing machine to achieve smoothness and uniformity of size. 336-337

321114 **Wood Preservation.** This U.S. industry comprises establishments primarily engaged in (1) treating wood sawed, planed, or shaped in other establishments with creosote or other preservatives, such as chromated copper arsenate, to prevent decay and to protect against fire and insects and/or (2) sawing round wood poles, pilings, and posts and treating them with preservatives. 338-339

321211 **Hardwood Veneer and Plywood Manufacturing.** This U.S. industry comprises establishments primarily engaged in manufacturing hardwood veneer and/or hardwood plywood. 340-341

321214 **Truss Manufacturing.** This U.S. industry comprises establishments primarily engaged in manufacturing laminated or fabricated wood roof and floor trusses. 342-343

321911 **Wood Window and Door Manufacturing.** This U.S. industry comprises establishments primarily engaged in manufacturing window and door units, sash, window and door frames, and doors from wood or wood clad with metal or plastics. 344-345

321912 **Cut Stock, Resawing Lumber, and Planing.** This U.S. industry comprises establishments primarily engaged in one or more of the following: (1) manufacturing dimension lumber from purchased lumber; (2) manufacturing dimension stock (i.e., shapes) or cut stock; (3) resawing the output of sawmills; and (4) planing purchased lumber. These establishments generally use woodworking machinery, such as jointers, planers, lathes, and routers to shape wood. 346-347

321918 **Other Millwork (including Flooring).** This U.S. industry comprises establishments primarily engaged in manufacturing millwork (except wood windows, wood doors, and cut stock). . . . 348-349

321920 **Wood Container and Pallet Manufacturing.** This industry comprises establishments primarily engaged in manufacturing wood pallets, wood box shook, wood boxes, other wood containers, and wood parts for pallets and containers. 350-351

321991 **Manufactured Home (Mobile Home) Manufacturing.** This U.S. industry comprises establishments primarily engaged in making manufactured homes (i.e., mobile homes) and nonresidential mobile buildings. Manufactured homes are designed to accept permanent water, sewer, and utility connections and although equipped with wheels, they are not intended for regular highway movement. 352-353

321992 **Prefabricated Wood Building Manufacturing.** This U.S. industry comprises establishments primarily engaged in manufacturing prefabricated wood buildings and wood sections and panels for prefabricated wood buildings. 354-355

321999 **All Other Miscellaneous Wood Product Manufacturing.** This U.S. industry comprises establishments primarily engaged in manufacturing wood products (except establishments operating sawmills and preservation facilities; establishments manufacturing veneer, engineered wood products, millwork, wood containers, pallets, and wood container parts; and establishments making manufactured homes (i.e., mobile homes) and prefabricated buildings and components). 356-357

322121 **Paper (except Newsprint) Mills.** This U.S. industry comprises establishments primarily engaged in manufacturing paper (except newsprint and uncoated groundwood paper) from pulp. These establishments may manufacture or purchase pulp. In addition, the establishments may also convert the paper they make. 358-359

MANUFACTURING

NAICS #   **Page**

322211 **Corrugated and Solid Fiber Box Manufacturing.** This U.S. industry comprises establishments primarily engaged in laminating purchased paper or paperboard into corrugated or solid fiber boxes and related products, such as pads, partitions, pallets, and corrugated paper without manufacturing paperboard. These boxes are generally used for shipping. 360-361

322212 **Folding Paperboard Box Manufacturing.** This U.S. industry comprises establishments primarily engaged in converting paperboard (except corrugated) into folding paperboard boxes without manufacturing paper and paperboard. 362-363

322213 **Setup Paperboard Box Manufacturing.** This U.S. industry comprises establishments primarily engaged in converting paperboard into setup paperboard boxes (i.e., rigid-sided boxes not shipped flat) without manufacturing paperboard. 364-365

322221 **Coated and Laminated Packaging Paper Manufacturing.** This U.S. industry comprises establishments primarily engaged in performing one or more of the following activities associated with the manufacturing of packaging materials: (1) cutting and coating paper; and (2) cutting and laminating paper with other flexible materials (except plastics to plastics or foil to paper laminates). The products made in this industry are made from purchased sheet materials and may be printed in the same establishment. 366-367

322222 **Coated and Laminated Paper Manufacturing.** This U.S. industry comprises establishments primarily engaged in performing one or more of the following activities associated with making products designed for purposes other than packaging: (1) cutting and coating paper; (2) cutting and laminating paper and other flexible materials (except plastics film to plastics film); and (3) laminating aluminum and other metal foils for nonpackaging uses from purchased foils. The products made in this industry are made from purchased sheet materials and may be printed in the same establishment. 368-369

322223 **Coated Paper Bag and Pouch Manufacturing.** This U.S. industry comprises establishments primarily engaged in manufacturing bags of coated paper, of metal foil, or of laminated or coated combinations of plastics, foil, and paper, whether or not printed. 370-371

322232 **Envelope Manufacturing.** This U.S. industry comprises establishments primarily engaged in manufacturing envelopes for mailing or stationery of any material including combinations. . . 372-373

322291 **Sanitary Paper Product Manufacturing.** This U.S. industry comprises establishments primarily engaged in converting purchased sanitary paper stock or wadding into sanitary paper products, such as facial tissues and handkerchiefs, table napkins, toilet paper, towels, disposable diapers, sanitary napkins, and tampons. 374-375

322299 **All Other Converted Paper Product Manufacturing.** This U.S. industry comprises establishments primarily engaged in converting paper or paperboard into products (except containers, bags, coated and treated paper, stationery products, and sanitary paper products) or converting pulp into pulp products, such as egg cartons, food trays, and other food containers from molded pulp. 376-377

323110 **Commercial Lithographic Printing.** This U.S. industry comprises establishments primarily engaged in lithographic (i.e., offset) printing without publishing (except books, grey goods, and manifold business forms). This industry includes establishments engaged in lithographic printing on purchased stock materials, such as stationery, letterhead, invitations, labels, and similar items, on a job order basis. 378-379

323112 **Commercial Flexographic Printing.** This U.S. industry comprises establishments primarily engaged in flexographic printing without publishing (except books, grey goods, and manifold business forms). This industry includes establishments engaged in flexographic printing on purchased stock materials, such as stationery, invitations, labels, and similar items, on a job order basis. 380-381

323113 **Commercial Screen Printing.** This U.S. industry comprises establishments primarily engaged in screen printing without publishing (except books, grey goods, and manifold business forms). This industry includes establishments engaged in screen printing on purchased stock materials, such as stationery, invitations, labels, and similar items, on a job order basis. Establishments primarily engaged in printing on apparel and textile products, such as T-shirts, caps, jackets, towels, and napkins, are included in this industry. 382-383

MANUFACTURING

NAICS #   **Page**

323114   **Quick Printing.** This U.S. industry comprises establishments primarily engaged in traditional printing activities, such as short-run offset printing or prepress services, in combination with providing document photocopying service. Prepress services include receiving documents in electronic format and directly duplicating from the electronic file and formatting, colorizing, and otherwise modifying the original document to improve presentation. These establishments, known as quick printers, generally provide short-run printing and copying with fast turnaround times. **384-385**

323116   **Manifold Business Forms Printing.** This U.S. industry comprises establishments primarily engaged in printing special forms, including checkbooks, for use in the operation of a business. The forms may be in single and multiple sets, including carbonized, interleaved with carbon, or otherwise processed for multiple reproduction. **386-387**

323117   **Books Printing.** This U.S. industry comprises establishments primarily engaged in printing or printing and binding books and pamphlets without publishing. **388-389**

323119   **Other Commercial Printing.** This U.S. industry comprises establishments primarily engaged in commercial printing (except lithographic, gravure, screen, or flexographic printing) without publishing (except books, grey goods, and manifold business forms). Printing processes included in this industry are letterpress printing and engraving printing. This industry includes establishments engaged in commercial printing on purchased stock materials, such as stationery, invitations, labels, and similar items, on a job order basis. **390-391**

323121   **Tradebinding and Related Work.** This U.S. industry comprises establishments primarily engaged in one or more of the following: (1) tradebinding; (2) sample mounting; and (3) postpress services (e.g., book or paper bronzing, die-cutting, edging, embossing, folding, gilding, gluing, indexing). **392-393**

323122   **Prepress Services.** This U.S. industry comprises (1) establishments primarily engaged in prepress services, such as imagesetting or typesetting, for printers and (2) establishments primarily engaged in preparing film or plates for printing purposes. **394-395**

324110   **Petroleum Refineries.** This industry comprises establishments primarily engaged in refining crude petroleum into refined petroleum. Petroleum refining involves one or more of the following activities: (1) fractionation; (2) straight distillation of crude oil; and (3) cracking. **396-397**

324121   **Asphalt Paving Mixture and Block Manufacturing.** This U.S. industry comprises establishments primarily engaged in manufacturing asphalt and tar paving mixtures and blocks from purchased asphaltic materials. **398-399**

324191   **Petroleum Lubricating Oil and Grease Manufacturing.** This U.S. industry comprises establishments primarily engaged in blending or compounding refined petroleum to make lubricating oils and greases and/or rerefining used petroleum lubricating oils. **400-401**

324199   **All Other Petroleum and Coal Products Manufacturing.** This U.S. industry comprises establishments primarily engaged in manufacturing petroleum products (except asphalt paving, roofing, and saturated materials and lubricating oils and greases) from refined petroleum and coal products made in coke ovens not integrated with a steel mill. **402-403**

325188   **All Other Basic Inorganic Chemical Manufacturing.** This U.S. industry comprises establishments primarily engaged in manufacturing basic inorganic chemicals (except industrial gases, inorganic dyes and pigments, alkalies and chlorine, and carbon black). **404-405**

325193   **Ethyl Alcohol Manufacturing.** This U.S. industry comprises establishments primarily engaged in manufacturing nonpotable ethyl alcohol. **406-407**

325199   **All Other Basic Organic Chemical Manufacturing.** This U.S. industry comprises establishments primarily engaged in manufacturing basic organic chemical products (except aromatic petrochemicals, industrial gases, synthetic organic dyes and pigments, gum and wood chemicals, cyclic crudes and intermediates, and ethyl alcohol). **408-409**

325211   **Plastics Material and Resin Manufacturing.** This U.S. industry comprises establishments primarily engaged in (1) manufacturing resins, plastics materials, and nonvulcanizable thermoplastic elastomers and mixing and blending resins on a custom basis and/or (2) manufacturing noncustomized synthetic resins. **410-411**

325311   **Nitrogenous Fertilizer Manufacturing.** This U.S. industry comprises establishments primarily engaged in one or more of the following: (1) manufacturing nitrogenous fertilizer materials and mixing ingredients into fertilizers; (2) manufacturing fertilizers from sewage or animal waste; and (3) manufacturing nitrogenous materials and mixing them into fertilizers. **412-413**

MANUFACTURING

NAICS #   **Page**

325314 **Fertilizer (Mixing Only) Manufacturing.** This U.S. industry comprises establishments primarily
engaged in mixing ingredients made elsewhere into fertilizers.   414-415

325320 **Pesticide and Other Agricultural Chemical Manufacturing.** This industry comprises establishments primarily engaged in the formulation and preparation of agricultural and household
pest control chemicals (except fertilizers).   416-417

325411 **Medicinal and Botanical Manufacturing.** This U.S. industry comprises establishments primarily
engaged in (1) manufacturing uncompounded medicinal chemicals and their derivatives (i.e.,
generally for use by pharmaceutical preparation manufacturers) and/or (2) grading, grinding,
and milling uncompounded botanicals.   418-419

325412 **Pharmaceutical Preparation Manufacturing.** This U.S. industry comprises establishments primarily engaged in manufacturing in-vivo diagnostic substances and pharmaceutical preparations (except biological) intended for internal and external consumption in dose forms, such
as ampoules, tablets, capsules, vials, ointments, powders, solutions, and suspensions.   420-421

325510 **Paint and Coating Manufacturing.** This industry comprises establishments primarily engaged
in (1) mixing pigments, solvents, and binders into paints and other coatings, such as stains,
varnishes, lacquers, enamels, shellacs, and water repellant coatings for concrete and masonry,
and/or (2) manufacturing allied paint products, such as putties, paint and varnish removers,
paint brush cleaners, and frit.   422-423

325520 **Adhesive Manufacturing.** This industry comprises establishments primarily engaged in manufacturing adhesives, glues, and caulking compounds.   424-425

325611 **Soap and Other Detergent Manufacturing.** This U.S. industry comprises establishments primarily engaged in manufacturing and packaging soaps and other detergents, such as laundry detergents; dishwashing detergents; toothpaste gels, and tooth powders; and natural glycerin. . .   426-427

325612 **Polish and Other Sanitation Good Manufacturing.** This U.S. industry comprises establishments
primarily engaged in manufacturing and packaging polishes and specialty cleaning preparations.   428-429

325620 **Toilet Preparation Manufacturing.** This industry comprises establishments primarily engaged
in preparing, blending, compounding, and packaging toilet preparations, such as perfumes,
shaving preparations, hair preparations, face creams, lotions (including sunscreens), and other
cosmetic preparations.   430-431

325910 **Printing Ink Manufacturing.** This industry comprises establishments primarily engaged in manufacturing printing and inkjet inks and inkjet cartridges.   432-433

325991 **Custom Compounding of Purchased Resins.** This industry comprises establishments primarily
engaged in (1) custom mixing and blending plastics resins made elsewhere or (2) reformulating
plastics resins from recycled plastics products.   434-435

325998 **All Other Miscellaneous Chemical Product and Preparation Manufacturing.** This U.S. industry comprises establishments primarily engaged in manufacturing chemical products (except
basic chemicals, resins, synthetic rubber; cellulosic and noncellulosic fiber and filaments; pesticides, fertilizers, and other agricultural chemicals; pharmaceuticals and medicines; paints,
coatings and adhesives; soap, cleaning compounds, and toilet preparations; printing inks; ex-
plosives; custom compounding of purchased resins; and photographic films, papers, plates,
and chemicals).   436-437

326111 **Plastics Bag and Pouch Manufacturing.** This U.S. industry comprises establishments primarily
engaged in (1) converting plastics resins into plastics bags or (2) forming, coating or laminating
plastics film and sheet into single wall or multiwall plastics bags. Establishments in this industry
may print on the bags they manufacture.   438-439

326112 **Plastics Packaging Film and Sheet (including Laminated) Manufacturing.** This U.S. industry
comprises establishments primarily engaged in converting plastics resins into plastics packaging (flexible) film and packaging sheet.   440-441

326113 **Unlaminated Plastics Film and Sheet (except Packaging) Manufacturing.** This U.S. industry
comprises establishments primarily engaged in converting plastics resins into plastics film
and unlaminated sheet (except packaging).   442-443

326121 **Unlaminated Plastics Profile Shape Manufacturing.** This U.S. industry comprises establishments primarily engaged in converting plastics resins into nonrigid plastics profile shapes (except film, sheet and bags), such as rod, tube, and sausage casings.   444-445

MANUFACTURING

NAICS #   **Page**

326122   **Plastics Pipe and Pipe Fitting Manufacturing.** This U.S. industry comprises establishments primarily engaged in converting plastics resins into rigid plastics pipes and pipe fittings. . . .   **446-447**

326130   **Laminated Plastics Plate, Sheet (except Packaging), and Shape Manufacturing.** This industry comprises establishments primarily engaged in laminating plastics profile shapes such as plate, sheet (except packaging), and rod. The lamination process generally involves bonding or impregnating profiles with plastics resins and compressing them under heat. **448-449**

326140   **Polystyrene Foam Product Manufacturing.** This industry comprises establishments primarily engaged in manufacturing polystyrene foam products. **450-451**

326160   **Plastics Bottle Manufacturing.** This industry comprises establishments primarily engaged in manufacturing plastics bottles. **452-453**

326191   **Plastics Plumbing Fixture Manufacturing.** This U.S. industry comprises establishments primarily engaged in manufacturing plastics or fiberglass plumbing fixtures. Examples of products made by these establishments are plastics or fiberglass bathtubs, hot tubs, portable toilets, and shower stalls. **454-455**

326199   **All Other Plastics Product Manufacturing.** This U.S. industry comprises establishments primarily engaged in manufacturing plastics products (except film, sheet, bags, profile shapes, pipes, pipe fittings, laminates, foam products, bottles, plumbing fixtures, and resilient floor coverings). **456-457**

326212   **Tire Retreading.** This U.S. industry comprises establishments primarily engaged in retreading, or rebuilding tires. **458-459**

326220   **Rubber and Plastics Hoses and Belting Manufacturing.** This industry comprises establishments primarily engaged in manufacturing rubber hose and/or plastics (reinforced) hose and belting from natural and synthetic rubber and/or plastics resins. Establishments manufacturing garden hoses from purchased hose are included in this industry. **460-461**

326291   **Rubber Product Manufacturing for Mechanical Use.** This U.S. industry comprises establishments primarily engaged in molding, extruding or lathe-cutting rubber to manufacture rubber goods (except tubing) for mechanical applications. Products of this industry are generally parts for motor vehicles, machinery, and equipment. **462-463**

326299   **All Other Rubber Product Manufacturing.** This U.S. industry comprises establishments primarily engaged in manufacturing rubber products (except tires; hoses and belting; and molded, extruded, and lathecut rubber goods for mechanical applications) from natural and synthetic rubber. **464-465**

327121   **Brick and Structural Clay Tile Manufacturing.** This U.S. industry comprises establishments primarily engaged in manufacturing brick and structural clay tiles. **466-467**

327215   **Glass Product Manufacturing Made of Purchased Glass.** This U.S. industry comprises establishments primarily engaged in coating, laminating, tempering, or shaping purchased glass. . . .   **468-469**

327320   **Ready-Mix Concrete Manufacturing.** This industry comprises establishments, such as batch plants or mix plants, primarily engaged in manufacturing concrete delivered to a purchaser in a plastic and unhardened state. Ready-mix concrete manufacturing establishments may mine, quarry, or purchase sand and gravel. **470-471**

327331   **Concrete Block and Brick Manufacturing.** This U.S. industry comprises establishments primarily engaged in manufacturing concrete block and brick. **472-473**

327332   **Concrete Pipe Manufacturing.** This U.S. industry comprises establishments primarily engaged in manufacturing concrete pipe. **474-475**

327390   **Other Concrete Product Manufacturing.** This industry comprises establishments primarily engaged in manufacturing concrete products (except block, brick, and pipe). **476-477**

327910   **Abrasive Product Manufacturing.** This industry comprises establishments primarily engaged in manufacturing abrasive grinding wheels of natural or synthetic materials, abrasive-coated products, and other abrasive products. **478-479**

327991   **Cut Stone and Stone Product Manufacturing.** This U.S. industry comprises establishments primarily engaged in cutting, shaping, and finishing granite, marble, limestone, slate, and other stone for building and miscellaneous uses. Stone product manufacturing establishments may mine, quarry, or purchase stone. **480-481**

MANUFACTURING

NAICS # | **Page**

327999 **All Other Miscellaneous Nonmetallic Mineral Product Manufacturing.** This U.S. industry comprises establishments primarily engaged in manufacturing nonmetallic mineral products (except pottery, ceramics, and plumbing fixtures; clay building materials and refractories; glass and glass products; cement; readymix concrete; concrete products; lime; gypsum products; abrasive products; cut stone and stone products; ground and treated minerals and earth; and mineral wool). 482-483

331111 **Iron and Steel Mills.** This U.S. industry comprises establishments primarily engaged in one or more of the following: (1) direct reduction of iron ore; (2) manufacturing pig iron in molten or solid form; (3) converting pig iron into steel; (4) making steel; (5) making steel and manufacturing shapes (e.g., bar, plate, rod, sheet, strip, wire); and (6) making steel and forming tube and pipe. 484-485

331210 **Iron and Steel Pipe and Tube Manufacturing from Purchased Steel.** This industry comprises establishments primarily engaged in manufacturing welded, riveted, or seamless pipe and tube from purchased iron or steel. 486-487

331221 **Rolled Steel Shape Manufacturing.** This U.S. industry comprises establishments primarily engaged in rolling or drawing shapes (except wire), such as plate, sheet, strip, rod, and bar, from purchased steel. 488-489

331222 **Steel Wire Drawing.** This U.S. industry comprises establishments primarily engaged in drawing wire from purchased steel. 490-491

331314 **Secondary Smelting and Alloying of Aluminum.** This U.S. industry comprises establishments primarily engaged in (1) recovering aluminum and aluminum alloys from scrap and/or dross (i.e., secondary smelting) and making billet or ingot (except by rolling) and/or (2) manufacturing alloys, powder, paste, or flake from purchased aluminum. 492-493

331316 **Aluminum Extruded Product Manufacturing.** This U.S. industry comprises establishments primarily engaged in (1) extruding aluminum bar, pipe, and tube blooms or extruding or drawing tube from purchased aluminum; and/or (2) recovering aluminum from scrap and extruding bar, pipe, and tube blooms or drawing tube in integrated mills. 494-495

331422 **Copper Wire (except Mechanical) Drawing.** This U.S. industry comprises establishments primarily engaged in drawing or drawing and insulating communication and energy wire and cable from purchased copper or in integrated secondary smelting and wire drawing plants. 496-497

331491 **Nonferrous Metal (except Copper and Aluminum) Rolling, Drawing, and Extruding.** This U.S. industry comprises establishments primarily engaged in (1) rolling, drawing, or extruding shapes (e.g., bar, plate, sheet, strip, tube) from purchased nonferrous metals) and/or (2) recovering nonferrous metals from scrap and rolling, drawing, and/or extruding shapes (e.g., bar, plate, sheet, strip, tube) in integrated mills. 498-499

331492 **Secondary Smelting, Refining, and Alloying of Nonferrous Metal (except Copper and Aluminum).** This U.S. industry comprises establishments primarily engaged in (1) alloying purchased nonferrous metals and/or (2) recovering nonferrous metals from scrap. Establishments in this industry make primary forms (e.g., bar, billet, bloom, cake, ingot, slab, slug, wire) using smelting or refining processes. 500-501

331511 **Iron Foundries.** This U.S. industry comprises establishments primarily engaged in pouring molten pig iron or iron alloys into molds to manufacture castings, (e.g., cast iron manhole covers, cast iron pipe, cast iron skillets). Establishments in this industry purchase iron made in other establishments. 502-503

331513 **Steel Foundries (except Investment).** This U.S. industry comprises establishments primarily engaged in manufacturing steel castings (except steel investment castings). Establishments in this industry purchase steel made in other establishments. 504-505

331521 **Aluminum Die-Casting Foundries.** This U.S. industry comprises establishments primarily engaged in introducing molten aluminum, under high pressure, into molds or dies to make aluminum die-castings. Establishments in this industry purchase aluminum made in other establishments. 506-507

331522 **Nonferrous (except Aluminum) Die-Casting Foundries.** This U.S. industry comprises establishments primarily engaged in introducing molten nonferrous metal (except aluminum), under high pressure, into molds to make nonferrous metal die-castings. Establishments in this industry purchase nonferrous metals made in other establishments. 508-509

MANUFACTURING

NAICS #   **Page**

331524   **Aluminum Foundries (except Die-Casting).** This U.S. industry comprises establishments primarily engaged in pouring molten aluminum into molds to manufacture aluminum castings. Establishments in this industry purchase aluminum made in other establishments. 510-511

331528   **Other Nonferrous Foundries (except Die-Casting).** This U.S. industry comprises establishments primarily engaged in pouring molten nonferrous metals (except aluminum and copper) into molds to manufacture nonferrous castings (except aluminum die-castings, nonferrous (except aluminum) die-castings, aluminum castings, and copper castings). Establishments in this industry purchase nonferrous metals, such as nickel, lead, and zinc, made in other establishments. 512-513

332111   **Iron and Steel Forging.** This U.S. industry comprises establishments primarily engaged in manufacturing iron and steel forgings from purchased iron and steel by hammering mill shapes. Establishments making iron and steel forgings and further manufacturing (e.g., machining, assembling) a specific manufactured product are classified in the industry of the finished product. Iron and steel forging establishments may perform surface finishing operations, such as cleaning and deburring, on the forgings they manufacture. 514-515

332116   **Metal Stamping.** This U.S. industry comprises establishments primarily engaged in manufacturing unfinished metal stampings and spinning unfinished metal products (except crowns, cans, closures, automotive, and coins). Establishments making metal stampings and metal spun products and further manufacturing (e.g., machining, assembling) a specific product are classified in the industry of the finished product. Metal stamping and metal spun products establishments may perform surface finishing operations, such as cleaning and deburring, on the products they manufacture. 516-517

332117   **Powder Metallurgy Part Manufacturing.** This U.S. industry comprises establishments primarily engaged in manufacturing powder metallurgy products by compacting them in a shaped die and sintering. Establishments in this industry generally make a wide range of parts on a job or order basis. 518-519

332212   **Hand and Edge Tool Manufacturing.** This industry comprises establishments primarily engaged in manufacturing nonpowered hand and edge tools (except saws). 520-521

332311   **Prefabricated Metal Building and Component Manufacturing.** This U.S. industry comprises establishments primarily engaged in manufacturing prefabricated metal buildings, panels, and sections. 522-523

332312   **Fabricated Structural Metal Manufacturing.** This U.S. industry comprises establishments primarily engaged in fabricating structural metal products, such as concrete reinforcing bars and fabricated bar joists. 524-525

332313   **Plate Work Manufacturing.** This industry comprises establishments primarily engaged in manufacturing fabricated metal plate work by cutting, punching, bending, shaping, and welding purchased metal plate. 526-527

332321   **Metal Window and Door Manufacturing.** This U.S. industry comprises establishments primarily engaged in manufacturing metal framed windows (i.e., typically using purchased glass) and metal doors. 528-529

332322   **Sheet Metal Work Manufacturing.** This U.S. industry comprises establishments primarily engaged in manufacturing sheet metal work (except stampings). 530-531

332323   **Ornamental and Architectural Metal Work Manufacturing.** This U.S. industry comprises establishments primarily engaged in manufacturing ornamental and architectural metal work, such as staircases, metal open steel flooring, fire escapes, railings, and scaffolding. 532-533

332439   **Other Metal Container Manufacturing.** This U.S. industry comprises establishments primarily engaged in manufacturing metal (light gauge) containers (except cans). 534-535

332510   **Hardware Manufacturing.** This industry comprises establishments primarily engaged in manufacturing metal hardware, such as metal hinges, metal handles, keys, and locks (except coin-operated time locks). 536-537

332612   **Spring (Light Gauge) Manufacturing.** This U.S. industry comprises establishments primarily engaged in manufacturing light gauge springs from purchased wire or strip. 538-539

332618   **Other Fabricated Wire Product Manufacturing.** This U.S. industry comprises establishments primarily engaged in manufacturing fabricated wire products (except springs) made from purchased wire. 540-541

50

MANUFACTURING

NAICS # **Page**

332710 **Machine Shops.** This industry comprises establishments known as machine shops primarily engaged in machining metal parts on a job or order basis. Generally machine shop jobs are low volume using machine tools, such as lathes (including computer numerically controlled); automatic screw machines; and machines for boring, grinding, and milling. 542-543

332721 **Precision Turned Product Manufacturing.** This U.S. industry comprises establishments known as precision turned manufacturers primarily engaged in machining precision products of all materials on a job or order basis. Generally precision turned product jobs are large volume using machines, such as automatic screw machines, rotary transfer machines, computer numerically controlled (CNC) lathes, or turning centers. 544-545

332722 **Bolt, Nut, Screw, Rivet, and Washer Manufacturing.** This U.S. industry comprises establishments primarily engaged in manufacturing metal bolts, nuts, screws, rivets, and washers, and other industrial fasteners using machines, such as headers, threaders, and nut forming machines. 546-547

332811 **Metal Heat Treating.** This U.S. industry comprises establishments primarily engaged in heat treating, such as annealing, tempering, and brazing, metals and metal products for the trade. 548-549

332812 **Metal Coating, Engraving (except Jewelry and Silverware), and Allied Services to Manufacturers.** This U.S. industry comprises establishments primarily engaged in one or more of the following: (1) enameling, lacquering, and varnishingmetals and metal products; (2) hot dip galvanizing metals and metal products; (3) engraving, chasing, or etching metals and metal products (except jewelry; personal goods carried on or about the person, such as compacts and cigarette cases; preciousmetal products (except precious plated flatware and other plated ware); and printing plates); (4) powder coatingmetals and metal products; and (5) providing other metal surfacing services for the trade. 550-551

332813 **Electroplating, Plating, Polishing, Anodizing, and Coloring.** This U.S. industry comprises establishments primarily engaged in electroplating, plating, anodizing, coloring, buffing, polishing, cleaning, and sandblasting metals and metal products for the trade. 552-553

332911 **Industrial Valve Manufacturing.** This U.S. industry comprises establishments primarily engaged in manufacturing industrial valves and valves for water works and municipal water systems. 554-555

332912 **Fluid Power Valve and Hose Fitting Manufacturing.** This U.S. industry comprises establishments primarily engaged in manufacturing fluid power valves and hose fittings. 556-557

332913 **Plumbing Fixture Fitting and Trim Manufacturing.** This U.S. industry comprises establishments primarily engaged in manufacturing metal and plastics plumbing fixture fittings and trim, such as faucets, flush valves, and shower heads. 558-559

332919 **Other Metal Valve and Pipe Fitting Manufacturing.** This U.S. industry comprises establishments primarily engaged in manufacturing metal valves (except industrial valves, fluid power valves, fluid power hose fittings, and plumbing fixture fittings and trim). 560-561

332991 **Ball and Roller Bearing Manufacturing.** This U.S. industry comprises establishments primarily engaged in manufacturing ball and roller bearings of all materials. 562-563

332996 **Fabricated Pipe and Pipe Fitting Manufacturing.** This U.S. industry comprises establishments primarily engaged in fabricating, such as cutting, threading and bending metal pipes and pipe fittings made from purchased metal pipe. 564-565

332999 **All Other Miscellaneous Fabricated Metal Product Manufacturing.** This U.S. industry comprises establishments primarily engaged in manufacturing fabricated metal products (except forgings and stampings, cutlery and handtools, architectural and structural metals, boilers, tanks, shipping containers, hardware, spring and wire products, machine shop products, turned products, screws, nuts and bolts, metal valves, ball and roller bearings, ammunition, small arms and other ordnances, fabricated pipes and pipe fittings, industrial patterns, and enameled iron and metal sanitary ware). 566-567

333111 **Farm Machinery and Equipment Manufacturing.** This U.S. industry comprises establishments primarily engaged in manufacturing agricultural and farm machinery and equipment, and other turf and grounds care equipment, including planting, harvesting, and grass mowing equipment (except lawn and garden-type). 568-569

NAICS #   **Page**

333112   **Lawn and Garden Tractor and Home Lawn and Garden Equipment Manufacturing.** This U.S. industry comprises establishments primarily engaged in manufacturing powered lawnmowers, lawn and garden tractors, and other home lawn and garden equipment, such as tillers, shredders, and yard vacuums and blowers. **570-571**

333120   **Construction Machinery Manufacturing.** This industry comprises establishments primarily engaged in manufacturing construction machinery, surface mining machinery, and logging equipment. **572-573**

333131   **Mining Machinery and Equipment Manufacturing.** This U.S. industry comprises establishments primarily engaged in (1) manufacturing underground mining machinery and equipment, such as coal breakers, mining cars, core drills, coal cutters, rock drills and (2) manufacturing mineral beneficiating machinery and equipment used in surface or underground mines. **574-575**

333132   **Oil and Gas Field Machinery and Equipment Manufacturing.** This U.S. industry comprises establishments primarily engaged in (1) manufacturing oil and gas field machinery and equipment, such as oil and gas field drilling machinery and equipment; oil and gas field production machinery and equipment; and oil and gas field derricks and (2) manufacturing water well drilling machinery. **576-577**

333220   **Plastics and Rubber Industry Machinery Manufacturing.** This industry comprises establishments primarily engaged in manufacturing plastics and rubber products making machinery, such as plastics compression, extrusion and injection molding machinery and equipment, and tire building and recapping machinery and equipment. **578-579**

333291   **Paper Industry Machinery Manufacturing.** This U.S. industry comprises establishments primarily engaged in manufacturing paper industry machinery for making paper and paper products, such as pulp making machinery, paper and paperboard making machinery, and paper and paperboard converting machinery. **580-581**

333292   **Textile Machinery Manufacturing.** This U.S. industry comprises establishments primarily engaged in manufacturing textile machinery for making thread, yarn, and fiber. **582-583**

333293   **Printing Machinery and Equipment Manufacturing.** This U.S. industry comprises establishments primarily engaged in manufacturing printing and bookbinding machinery and equipment, such as printing presses, typesetting machinery, and bindery machinery. **584-585**

333294   **Food Product Machinery Manufacturing.** This U.S. industry comprises establishments primarily engaged in manufacturing food and beverage manufacturing-type machinery and equipment, such as dairy product plant machinery and equipment (e.g., homogenizers, pasteurizers, ice cream freezers), bakery machinery and equipment (e.g., dough mixers, bake ovens, pastry rolling machines), meat and poultry processing and preparation machinery, and other commercial food products machinery (e.g., slicers, choppers, and mixers). **586-587**

333298   **All Other Industrial Machinery Manufacturing.** This U.S. industry comprises establishments primarily engaged in manufacturing industrial machinery (except agricultural and farm-type, construction and mining machinery, sawmill and woodworking machinery, plastics and rubber making machinery, paper and paperboard making machinery, textile machinery, printing machinery and equipment, food manufacturing-type machinery, and semiconductor making machinery). **588-589**

333314   **Optical Instrument and Lens Manufacturing.** This U.S. industry comprises establishments primarily engaged in one or more of the following: (1) manufacturing optical instruments and lens, such as binoculars, microscopes (except electron, proton), telescopes, prisms, and lenses (except ophthalmic); (2) coating or polishing lenses (except ophthalmic); and (3) mounting lenses (except ophthalmic). **590-591**

333315   **Photographic and Photocopying Equipment Manufacturing.** This U.S. industry comprises establishments primarily engaged in manufacturing photographic and photocopying equipment, such as cameras (except television, video and digital) projectors , film developing equipment, photocopying equipment, and microfilm equipment. **592-593**

333319   **Other Commercial and Service Industry Machinery Manufacturing.** This U.S. industry comprises establishments primarily engaged in manufacturing commercial and service industry equipment (except automatic vending machines, commercial laundry, drycleaning and pressing machines, office machinery, optical instruments and lenses, and photographic and photocopying equipment). **594-595**

MANUFACTURING

NAICS #   **Page**

333412 **Industrial and Commercial Fan and Blower Manufacturing.** This U.S. industry comprises establishments primarily engaged in manufacturing attic fans and industrial and commercial fans and blowers, such as commercial exhaust fans and commercial ventilating fans. 596-597

333414 **Heating Equipment (except Warm Air Furnaces) Manufacturing.** This U.S. industry comprises establishments primarily engaged in manufacturing heating equipment (except electric and warm air furnaces), such as heating boilers, heating stoves, floor and wall furnaces, and wall and baseboard heating units. 598-599

333415 **Air-Conditioning and Warm Air Heating Equipment and Commercial and Industrial Refrigeration Equipment Manufacturing.** This U.S. industry comprises establishments primarily engaged in (1) manufacturing air-conditioning (except motor vehicle) and warm air furnace equipment and/or (2) manufacturing commercial and industrial refrigeration and freezer equipment. 600-601

333511 **Industrial Mold Manufacturing.** This U.S. industry comprises establishments primarily engaged in manufacturing industrial molds for casting metals or forming other materials, such as plastics, glass, or rubber. 602-603

333512 **Machine Tool (Metal Cutting Types) Manufacturing.** This U.S. industry comprises establishments primarily engaged in manufacturing metal cutting machine tools (except handtools). . . 604-605

333513 **Machine Tool (Metal Forming Types) Manufacturing.** This U.S. industry comprises establishments primarily engaged in manufacturing metal forming machine tools (except handtools), such as punching, sheering, bending, forming, pressing, forging and die-casting machines. . . 606-607

333514 **Special Die and Tool, Die Set, Jig, and Fixture Manufacturing.** This U.S. industry comprises establishments, known as tool and die shops, primarily engaged in manufacturing special tools and fixtures, such as cutting dies and jigs. 608-609

333515 **Cutting Tool and Machine Tool Accessory Manufacturing.** This U.S. industry comprises establishments primarily engaged in manufacturing accessories and attachments for metal cutting and metal forming machine tools. 610-611

333518 **Other Metalworking Machinery Manufacturing.** This U.S. industry comprises establishments primarily engaged in manufacturing metal working machinery (except industrial molds; metal cutting machine tools; metal forming machine tools; special dies and tools, die sets, jigs, and fixtures; cutting tools and machine tool accessories; and rolling mill machinery and equipment). 612-613

333612 **Speed Changer, Industrial High-Speed Drive, and Gear Manufacturing.** This U.S. industry comprises establishments primarily engaged in manufacturing gears, speed changers, and industrial high-speed drives (except hydrostatic). 614-615

333613 **Mechanical Power Transmission Equipment Manufacturing.** This U.S. industry comprises establishments primarily engaged in manufacturing mechanical power transmission equipment (except motor vehicle and aircraft), such as plain bearings, clutches (except motor vehicle and electromagnetic industrial control), couplings, joints, and drive chains. 616-617

333911 **Pump and Pumping Equipment Manufacturing.** This U.S. industry comprises establishments primarily engaged in manufacturing general purpose pumps and pumping equipment (except fluid power pumps and motors), such as reciprocating pumps, turbine pumps, centrifugal pumps, rotary pumps, diaphragm pumps, domestic water system pumps, oil well and oil field pumps and sump pumps. 618-619

333912 **Air and Gas Compressor Manufacturing.** This U.S. industry comprises establishments primarily engaged in manufacturing general purpose air and gas compressors, such as reciprocating compressors, centrifugal compressors, vacuum pumps (except laboratory), and nonagricultural spraying and dusting compressors and spray gun units. 620-621

333922 **Conveyor and Conveying Equipment Manufacturing.** This U.S. industry comprises establishments primarily engaged in manufacturing conveyors and conveying equipment, such as gravity conveyors, trolley conveyors, tow conveyors, pneumatic tube conveyors, carousel conveyors, farm conveyors, and belt conveyors. 622-623

333923 **Overhead Traveling Crane, Hoist, and Monorail System Manufacturing.** This U.S. industry comprises establishments primarily engaged in manufacturing overhead traveling cranes, hoists, and monorail systems. 624-625

MANUFACTURING

NAICS #		Page

333924 **Industrial Truck, Tractor, Trailer, and Stacker Machinery Manufacturing.** This U.S. industry comprises establishments primarily engaged in manufacturing industrial trucks, tractors, trailers, and stackers (i.e., truck-type), such as forklifts, pallet loaders and unloaders, and portable loading docks. 626-627

333992 **Welding and Soldering Equipment Manufacturing.** This U.S. industry comprises establishments primarily engaged in manufacturing welding and soldering equipment and accessories (except transformers), such as arc, resistance, gas, plasma, laser, electron beam, and ultrasonic welding equipment; welding electrodes; coated or cored welding wire; and soldering equipment (except handheld). 628-629

333993 **Packaging Machinery Manufacturing.** This U.S. industry comprises establishments primarily engaged in manufacturing packaging machinery, such as wrapping, bottling, canning, and labeling machinery. 630-631

333994 **Industrial Process Furnace and Oven Manufacturing.** This U.S. Industry comprises establishments primarily engaged in manufacturing industrial process furnaces, ovens, induction and dielectric heating equipment, and kilns (except cement, chemical, wood). 632-633

333999 **All Other Miscellaneous General Purpose Machinery Manufacturing.** This U.S. industry comprises establishments primarily engaged in manufacturing general purpose machinery (except ventilating, heating, air-conditioning, and commercial refrigeration equipment; metal working machinery; engines, turbines, and power transmission equipment; pumps and compressors; material handling equipment; power-driven handtools; welding and soldering equipment; packaging machinery; industrial process furnaces and ovens; fluid power cylinders and actuators; fluid power pumps and motors; and scales and balances). 634-635

334111 **Electronic Computer Manufacturing.** This U.S. industry comprises establishments primarily engaged in manufacturing and/or assembling electronic computers, such as mainframes, personal computers, workstations, laptops, and computer servers. Computers can be analog, digital, or hybrid. Digital computers, the most common type, are devices that do all of the following: (1) store the processing program or programs and the data immediately necessary for the execution of the program; (2) can be freely programmed in accordance with the requirements of the user; (3) perform arithmetical computations specified by the user; and (4) execute, without human intervention, a processing program that requires the computer to modify its execution by logical decision during the processing run. Analog computers are capable of simulating mathematical models and contain at least analog, control, and programming elements. The manufacture of computers includes the assembly or integration of processors, coprocessors, memory, storage, and input/output devices into a user-programmable final product. . . 636-637

334119 **Other Computer Peripheral Equipment Manufacturing.** This U.S. industry comprises establishments primarily engaged in manufacturing computer peripheral equipment (except storage devices and computer terminals). 638-639

334210 **Telephone Apparatus Manufacturing.** This industry comprises establishments primarily engaged in manufacturing wire telephone and data communications equipment. These products may be standalone or board-level components of a larger system. Examples of products made by these establishments are central office switching equipment, cordless telephones (except cellular), PBX equipment, telephones, telephone answering machines, LAN modems, multiuser modems, and other data communications equipment, such as bridges, routers, and gateways. 640-641

334220 **Radio and Television Broadcasting and Wireless Communications Equipment Manufacturing.** This industry comprises establishments primarily engaged in manufacturing radio and television broadcast and wireless communications equipment. Examples of products made by these establishments are: transmitting and receiving antennas, cable television equipment, GPS equipment, pagers, cellular phones, mobile communications equipment, and radio and television studio and broadcasting equipment. 642-643

334290 **Other Communications Equipment Manufacturing.** This industry comprises establishments primarily engaged in manufacturing communications equipment (except telephone apparatus, and radio and television broadcast, and wireless communications equipment). 644-645

MANUFACTURING

NAICS #   **Page**

334310 **Audio and Video Equipment Manufacturing.** This industry comprises establishments primarily engaged in manufacturing electronic audio and video equipment for home entertainment, motor vehicle, public address and musical instrument amplifications. Examples of products made by these establishments are video cassette recorders, televisions, stereo equipment, speaker systems, household-type video cameras, jukeboxes, and amplifiers for musical instruments and public address systems. 646-647

334412 **Bare Printed Circuit Board Manufacturing.** This U.S. industry comprises establishments primarily engaged in manufacturing bare (i.e., rigid or flexible) printed circuit boards without mounted electronic components. These establishments print, perforate, plate, screen, etch, or photoprint interconnecting pathways for electric current on laminates. 648-649

334413 **Semiconductor and Related Device Manufacturing.** This U.S. industry comprises establishments primarily engaged in manufacturing semiconductors and related solid state devices. ... 650-651

334416 **Electronic Coil, Transformer, and Other Inductor Manufacturing.** This U.S. industry comprises establishments primarily engaged in manufacturing electronic inductors, such as coils and transformers. 652-653

334417 **Electronic Connector Manufacturing.** This U.S. industry comprises establishments primarily engaged in manufacturing electronic connectors, such as coaxial, cylindrical, rack and panel, pin and sleeve, printed circuit and fiber optic. 654-655

334419 **Other Electronic Component Manufacturing.** This U.S. industry comprises establishments primarily engaged in manufacturing electronic components (except electron tubes; bare printed circuit boards; semiconductors and related devices; electronic capacitors; electronic resistors; coils, transformers and other inductors; connectors; and loaded printed circuit boards). 656-657

334510 **Electromedical and Electrotherapeutic Apparatus Manufacturing.** This U.S. industry comprises establishments primarily engaged in manufacturing electromedical and electrotherapeutic apparatus, such as magnetic resonance imaging equipment, medical ultrasound equipment, pacemakers, hearing aids, electrocardiographs, and electromedical endoscopic equipment. 658-659

334511 **Search, Detection, Navigation, Guidance, Aeronautical, and Nautical System and Instrument Manufacturing.** This U.S. industry comprises establishments primarily engaged in manufacturing search, detection, navigation, guidance, aeronautical, and nautical systems and instruments. 660-661

334512 **Automatic Environmental Control Manufacturing for Residential, Commercial, and Appliance Use.** This U.S. industry comprises establishments primarily engaged in manufacturing automatic controls and regulators for applications, such as heating, air-conditioning, refrigeration and appliances. 662-663

334513 **Instruments and Related Products Manufacturing for Measuring, Displaying, and Controlling Industrial Process Variables.** This U.S. industry comprises establishments primarily engaged in manufacturing instruments and related devices for measuring, displaying, indicating, recording, transmitting, and controlling industrial process variables. These instruments measure, display or control (monitor, analyze, and so forth) industrial process variables, such as temperature, humidity, pressure, vacuum, combustion, flow, level, viscosity, density, acidity, concentration, and rotation. 664-665

334514 **Totalizing Fluid Meter and Counting Device Manufacturing.** This U.S. industry comprises establishments primarily engaged in manufacturing totalizing (i.e., registering) fluid meters and counting devices. 666-667

334515 **Instrument Manufacturing for Measuring and Testing Electricity and Electrical Signals.** This U.S. industry comprises establishments primarily engaged in manufacturing instruments for measuring and testing the characteristics of electricity and electrical signals. 668-669

334516 **Analytical Laboratory Instrument Manufacturing.** Instruments and instrumentation systems for laboratory analysis of the chemical or physical composition or concentration of samples of solid, fluid, gaseous, or composite material. 670-671

MANUFACTURING

NAICS #   **Page**

334519 Other Measuring and Controlling Device Manufacturing. This U.S. industry comprises establishments primarily engaged in manufacturing measuring and controlling devices (except search, detection, navigation, guidance, aeronautical, and nautical instruments and systems; automatic environmental controls for residential, commercial, and appliance use; instruments for measurement, display, and control of industrial process variables; totalizing fluid meters and counting devices; instruments for measuring and testing electricity and electrical signals; analytical laboratory instruments; watches, clocks, and parts; irradiation equipment; and electromedical and electrotherapeutic apparatus). 672-673

335121 Residential Electric Lighting Fixture Manufacturing. This U.S. industry comprises establishments primarily engaged in manufacturing fixed or portable residential electric lighting fixtures and lamp shades of metal, paper, or textiles. Residential electric lighting fixtures include those for use both inside and outside the residence. 674-675

335122 Commercial, Industrial, and Institutional Electric Lighting Fixture Manufacturing. This U.S. industry comprises establishments primarily engaged in manufacturing commercial, industrial, and institutional electric lighting fixtures. 676-677

335129 Other Lighting Equipment Manufacturing. This U.S. industry comprises establishments primarily engaged in manufacturing electric lighting fixtures (except residential, commercial, industrial, institutional, and vehicular electric lighting fixtures) and nonelectric lighting equipment. 678-679

335311 Power, Distribution, and Specialty Transformer Manufacturing. This U.S. industry comprises establishments primarily engaged in manufacturing power, distribution, and specialty transformers (except electronic components). Industrial-type and consumer-type transformers in this industry vary (e.g., step up or step down) voltage but do not convert alternating to direct or direct to alternating current. 680-681

335312 Motor and Generator Manufacturing. This U.S. industry comprises establishments primarily engaged in manufacturing electric motors (except internal combustion engine starting motors), power generators (except battery charging alternators for internal combustion engines), and motor generator sets (except turbine generator set units). This industry includes establishments rewinding armatures on a factory basis. 682-683

335313 Switchgear and Switchboard Apparatus Manufacturing. This U.S. industry comprises establishments primarily engaged in manufacturing switchgear and switchboard apparatus. 684-685

335314 Relay and Industrial Control Manufacturing. This U.S. industry comprises establishments primarily engaged in manufacturing relays, motor starters and controllers, and other industrial controls and control accessories. 686-687

335931 Current-Carrying Wiring Device Manufacturing. This U.S. industry comprises establishments primarily engaged in manufacturing current-carrying wiring devices. 688-689

335999 All Other Miscellaneous Electrical Equipment and Component Manufacturing. This U.S. industry comprises establishments primarily engaged in manufacturing industrial and commercial electric apparatus and other equipment (except lighting equipment, household appliances, transformers, motors, generators, switchgear, relays, industrial controls, batteries, communication and energy wire and cable, wiring devices, and carbon and graphite products). This industry includes power converters (i.e., AC to DC and DC to AC), power supplies, surge suppressors, and similar equipment for industrial-type and consumer-type equipment. 690-691

336111 Automobile Manufacturing. This U.S. industry comprises establishments primarily engaged in (1) manufacturing complete automobiles (i.e., body and chassis or unibody) or (2) manufacturing automobile chassis only. 692-693

336211 Motor Vehicle Body Manufacturing. This U.S. industry comprises establishments primarily engaged in manufacturing truck and bus bodies and cabs and automobile bodies. The products made may be sold separately or may be assembled on purchased chassis and sold as complete vehicles. 694-695

336212 Truck Trailer Manufacturing. This U.S. industry comprises establishments primarily engaged in manufacturing truck trailers, truck trailer chassis, cargo container chassis, detachable trailer bodies, and detachable trailer chassis for sale separately. 696-697

MANUFACTURING

NAICS #   **Page**

336214 **Travel Trailer and Camper Manufacturing.** This U.S. industry comprises establishments primarily engaged in one or more of the following: (1) manufacturing travel trailers and campers designed to attach to motor vehicles; (2) manufacturing pickup coaches (i.e., campers) and caps (i.e., covers) for mounting on pickup trucks; and (3) manufacturing automobile, utility and light-truck trailers. Travel trailers do not have their own motor but are designed to be towed by a motor unit, such as an automobile or a light truck. 698-699

336360 **Motor Vehicle Seating and Interior Trim Manufacturing.** This industry comprises establishments primarily engaged in manufacturing motor vehicle seating, seats, seat frames, seat belts, and interior trimmings. 700-701

336370 **Motor Vehicle Metal Stamping.** This industry comprises establishments primarily engaged in manufacturing motor vehicle stampings, such as fenders, tops, body parts, trim, and molding. 702-703

336399 **All Other Motor Vehicle Parts Manufacturing.** This U.S. industry comprises establishments primarily engaged in manufacturing and/or rebuilding motor vehicle parts and accessories (except motor vehicle gasoline engines and engine parts, motor vehicle electrical and electronic equipment, motor vehicle steering and suspension components, motor vehicle brake systems, motor vehicle transmission and power train parts, motor vehicle seating and interior trim, motor vehicle stampings, and motor vehicle air-conditioning systems and compressors). 704-705

336412 **Aircraft Engine and Engine Parts Manufacturing.** This U.S. industry comprises establishments primarily engaged in one or more of the following: (1) manufacturing aircraft engines and engine parts; (2) developing and making prototypes of aircraft engines and engine parts; (3) aircraft propulsion system conversion (i.e., major modifications to systems); and (4) aircraft propulsion systems overhaul and rebuilding (i.e., periodic restoration of aircraft propulsion system to original design specifications). 706-707

336413 **Other Aircraft Parts and Auxiliary Equipment Manufacturing.** This U.S. industry comprises establishment primarily engaged in (1) manufacturing aircraft parts or auxiliary equipment (except engines and aircraft fluid power subassemblies) and/or (2) developing and making prototypes of aircraft parts and auxiliary equipment. Auxiliary equipment includes such items as crop dusting apparatus, armament racks, inflight refueling equipment, and external fuel tanks. 708-709

336510 **Railroad Rolling Stock Manufacturing.** This industry comprises establishments primarily engaged in one or more of the following: (1) manufacturing and/or rebuilding locomotives, locomotive frames and parts; (2) manufacturing railroad, street, and rapid transit cars and car equipment for operation on rails for freight and passenger service; and (3) manufacturing rail layers, ballast distributors, rail tamping equipment and other railway track maintenance equipment. 710-711

336611 **Ship Building and Repairing.** This U.S. industry comprises establishments primarily engaged in operating a shipyard. Shipyards are fixed facilities with drydocks and fabrication equipment capable of building a ship, defined as watercraft typically suitable or intended for other than personal or recreational use. Activities of shipyards include the construction of ships, their repair, conversion and alteration, the production of prefabricated ship and barge sections, and specialized services, such as ship scaling. 712-713

336612 **Boat Building.** This U.S. industry comprises establishments primarily engaged in building boats. Boats are defined as watercraft not built in shipyards and typically of the type suitable or intended for personal use. 714-715

336991 **Motorcycle, Bicycle, and Parts Manufacturing.** This U.S. industry comprises establishments primarily engaged in manufacturing motorcycles, bicycles, tricycles and similar equipment, and parts. 716-717

336999 **All Other Transportation Equipment Manufacturing.** This U.S. industry comprises establishments primarily engaged in manufacturing transportation equipment (except motor vehicles, motor vehicle parts, boats, ships, railroad rolling stock, aerospace products, motorcycles, bicycles, armored vehicles and tanks). 718-719

337110 **Wood Kitchen Cabinet and Countertop Manufacturing.** This industry comprises establishments primarily engaged in manufacturing wood or plastics laminated on wood kitchen cabinets, bathroom vanities, and countertops (except freestanding). The cabinets and counters may be made on a stock or custom basis. 720-721

MANUFACTURING

NAICS #   **Page**

337121   **Upholstered Household Furniture Manufacturing.** This U.S. industry comprises establishments primarily engaged in manufacturing upholstered household-type furniture. The furniture may be made on a stock or custom basis. 722-723

337122   **Nonupholstered Wood Household Furniture Manufacturing.** This U.S. industry comprises establishments primarily engaged in manufacturing nonupholstered wood household-type furniture and freestanding cabinets (except television, radio, and sewing machine cabinets). The furniture may be made on a stock or custom basis and may be assembled or unassembled (i.e., knockdown). 724-725

337127   **Institutional Furniture Manufacturing.** This U.S. industry comprises establishments primarily engaged in manufacturing institutional-type furniture (e.g., library, school, theater, and church furniture). The furniture may be made on a stock or custom basis and may be assembled or unassembled (i.e., knockdown). 726-727

337211   **Wood Office Furniture Manufacturing.** This U.S. industry comprises establishments primarily engaged in manufacturing wood office-type furniture. The furniture may be made on a stock or custom basis and may be assembled or unassembled (i.e., knockdown). 728-729

337214   **Office Furniture (except Wood) Manufacturing.** This U.S. industry comprises establishments primarily engaged in manufacturing nonwood office-type furniture. The furniture may be made on a stock or custom basis and may be assembled or unassembled (i.e., knockdown). 730-731

337215   **Showcase, Partition, Shelving, and Locker Manufacturing.** This U.S. industry comprises establishments primarily engaged in manufacturing wood and nonwood office and store fixtures, shelving, lockers, frames, partitions, and related fabricated products of wood and nonwood materials, including plastics laminated fixture tops. The products are made on a stock basis and may be assembled or unassembled (i.e., knockdown). Establishments exclusively making furniture parts (e.g., frames) are included in this industry. 732-733

337910   **Mattress Manufacturing.** This industry comprises establishments primarily engaged in manufacturing innerspring, box spring, and noninnerspring mattresses, including mattresses for waterbeds. 734-735

337920   **Blind and Shade Manufacturing.** This industry comprises establishments primarily engaged in manufacturing one or more of the following: venetian blinds, other window blinds, shades; curtain and drapery rods, poles; and/or curtain and drapery fixtures. The blinds and shades may be made on a stock or custom basis and may be made of any material. 736-737

339112   **Surgical and Medical Instrument Manufacturing.** This U.S. industry comprises establishments primarily engaged in manufacturing medical, surgical, ophthalmic, and veterinary instruments and apparatus (except electrotherapeutic, electromedical and irradiation apparatus). Examples of products made by these establishments are syringes, hypodermic needles, anesthesia apparatus, blood transfusion equipment, catheters, surgical clamps, and medical thermometers. 738-739

339113   **Surgical Appliance and Supplies Manufacturing.** This U.S. industry comprises establishments primarily engaged in manufacturing surgical appliances and supplies. Examples of products made by these establishments are orthopedic devices, prosthetic appliances, surgical dressings, crutches, surgical sutures, and personal industrial safety devices (except protective eyewear). 740-741

339114   **Dental Equipment and Supplies Manufacturing.** This U.S. industry comprises establishments primarily engaged in manufacturing dental equipment and supplies used by dental laboratories and offices of dentists, such as dental chairs, dental instrument delivery systems, dental hand instruments, and dental impression material and dental cements. 742-743

339115   **Ophthalmic Goods Manufacturing.** This U.S. industry comprises establishments primarily engaged in manufacturing ophthalmic goods. Examples of products made by these establishments are prescription eyeglasses (except manufactured in a retail setting), contact lenses, sunglasses, eyeglass frames, and reading glasses made to standard powers, and protective eyewear. 744-745

339116   **Dental Laboratories.** This U.S. industry comprises establishments primarily engaged in manufacturing dentures, crowns, bridges, and orthodontic appliances customized for individual application. 746-747

NAICS #   **Page**

339911   Jewelry (except Costume) Manufacturing. This U.S. industry comprises establishments primarily engaged in one or more of the following: (1) manufacturing, engraving, chasing, or etching precious metal solid or precious metal clad jewelry; (2) manufacturing, engraving, chasing, or etching personal goods (i.e., small articles carried on or about the person, such as compacts or cigarette cases) made of precious solid or clad metal; and (3) stamping coins.   748-749

339914   Costume Jewelry and Novelty Manufacturing. This U.S. industry comprises establishments primarily engaged in (1) manufacturing, engraving, chasing, and etching costume jewelry; and/or (2) manufacturing, engraving, chasing, or etching nonprecious metal personal goods (i.e., small articles carried on or about the person, such as compacts or cigarette cases). This industry includes establishments primarily engaged in manufacturing precious plated jewelry and precious plated personal goods.   750-751

339920   Sporting and Athletic Goods Manufacturing. This industry comprises establishments primarily engaged in manufacturing sporting and athletic goods (except apparel and footwear).   752-753

339932   Game, Toy, and Children's Vehicle Manufacturing. This U.S. industry comprises establishments primarily engaged in manufacturing games (including electronic), toys, and children's vehicles (except bicycles and metal tricycles).   754-755

339950   Sign Manufacturing. This industry comprises establishments primarily engaged in manufacturing signs and related displays of all materials (except printing paper and paperboard signs, notices, displays).   756-757

339991   Gasket, Packing, and Sealing Device Manufacturing. This U.S. industry comprises establishments primarily engaged in manufacturing gaskets, packing, and sealing devices of all materials.   758-759

339992   Musical Instrument Manufacturing. This U.S. industry comprises establishments primarily engaged in manufacturing musical instruments (except toys).   760-761

339994   Broom, Brush, and Mop Manufacturing. This U.S. industry comprises establishments primarily engaged in manufacturing brooms, mops, and brushes.   762-763

339999   All Other Miscellaneous Manufacturing. This U.S. industry comprises establishments primarily engaged in miscellaneous manufacturing (except medical equipment and supplies, jewelry and flatware, sporting and athletic goods, dolls, toys, games, office supplies (except paper), musical instruments, fasteners, buttons, needles, pins, brooms, brushes, mops, and burial caskets). . .   764-765

WHOLESALE TRADE

423110   Automobile and Other Motor Vehicle Merchant Wholesalers. This industry comprises establishments primarily engaged in the merchant wholesale distribution of new and used passenger automobiles, trucks, trailers, and other motor vehicles, such as motorcycles, motor homes, and snowmobiles.   768-769

423120   Motor Vehicle Supplies and New Parts Merchant Wholesalers. This industry comprises establishments primarily engaged in the merchant wholesale distribution of motor vehicle supplies, accessories, tools, and equipment; and new motor vehicle parts (except new tires and tubes).   770-771

423130   Tire and Tube Merchant Wholesalers. This industry comprises establishments primarily engaged in the merchant wholesale distribution of new and/or used tires and tubes for passenger and commercial vehicles.   772-773

423140   Motor Vehicle Parts (Used) Merchant Wholesalers. This industry comprises establishments primarily engaged in the merchant wholesale distribution of used motor vehicle parts (except used tires and tubes) and establishments primarily engaged in dismantling motor vehicles for the purpose of selling the parts.   774-775

423210   Furniture Merchant Wholesalers. This industry comprises establishments primarily engaged in the merchant wholesale distribution of furniture (except hospital beds, medical furniture, and drafting tables).   776-777

423220   Home Furnishing Merchant Wholesalers. This industry comprises establishments primarily engaged in the merchant wholesale distribution of home furnishings and/or housewares.   778-779

NAICS #   Page

423310   Lumber, Plywood, Millwork, and Wood Panel Merchant Wholesalers. This industry comprises establishments primarily engaged in the merchant wholesale distribution of lumber; plywood; reconstituted wood fiber products; wood fencing; doors and windows and their frames (all materials); wood roofing and siding; and/or other wood or metal millwork.   780-781

423320   Brick, Stone, and Related Construction Material Merchant Wholesalers. This industry comprises establishments primarily engaged in the merchant wholesale distribution of stone, cement, lime, construction sand, and gravel; brick; asphalt and concrete mixtures; and/or concrete, stone, and structural clay products.   782-783

423330   Roofing, Siding, and Insulation Material Merchant Wholesalers. This industry comprises establishments primarily engaged in the merchant wholesale distribution of nonwood roofing and nonwood siding and insulation materials.   784-785

423390   Other Construction Material Merchant Wholesalers. This industry comprises (1) establishments primarily engaged in the merchant wholesale distribution of manufactured homes (i.e., mobile homes) and/or prefabricated buildings and (2) establishments primarily engaged in the merchant wholesale distribution of construction materials (except lumber, plywood, millwork, wood panels, brick, stone, roofing, siding, electrical and wiring supplies, and insulation materials).   786-787

423410   Photographic Equipment and Supplies Merchant Wholesalers. This industry comprises establishments primarily engaged in the merchant wholesale distribution of photographic equipment and supplies (except office equipment).   788-789

423420   Office Equipment Merchant Wholesalers. This industry comprises establishments primarily engaged in the merchant wholesale distribution of office machines and related equipment (except computers and computer peripheral equipment).   790-791

423430   Computer and Computer Peripheral Equipment and Software Merchant Wholesalers. This industry comprises establishments primarily engaged in the merchant wholesale distribution of computers, computer peripheral equipment, loaded computer boards, and/or computer software.   792-793

423440   Other Commercial Equipment Merchant Wholesalers. This industry comprises establishments primarily engaged in the merchant wholesale distribution of commercial and related machines and equipment (except photographic equipment and supplies; office equipment; and computers and computer peripheral equipment and software) generally used in restaurants and stores.   794-795

423450   Medical, Dental, and Hospital Equipment and Supplies Merchant Wholesalers. This industry comprises establishments primarily engaged in the merchant wholesale distribution of professional medical equipment, instruments, and supplies (except ophthalmic equipment and instruments and goods used by ophthalmologists, optometrists, and opticians).   796-797

423460   Ophthalmic Goods Merchant Wholesalers. This industry comprises establishments primarily engaged in the merchant wholesale distribution of professional equipment, instruments, and/or goods sold, prescribed, or used by ophthalmologists, optometrists, and opticians.   798-799

423490   Other Professional Equipment and Supplies Merchant Wholesalers. This industry comprises establishments primarily engaged in the merchant wholesale distribution of professional equipment and supplies (except ophthalmic goods and medical, dental, and hospital equipment and supplies).   800-801

423510   Metal Service Centers and Other Metal Merchant Wholesalers. This industry comprises establishments primarily engaged in the merchant wholesale distribution of products of the primary metals industries. Service centers maintain inventory and may perform functions, such as sawing, shearing, bending, leveling, cleaning, or edging, on a custom basis as part of sales transactions.   802-803

423520   Coal and Other Mineral and Ore Merchant Wholesalers. This industry comprises establishments primarily engaged in the merchant wholesale distribution of coal, coke, metal ores, and/or nonmetallic minerals (except precious and semiprecious stones and minerals used in construction, such as sand and gravel).   804-805

WHOLESALE

NAICS # **Page**

423610 Electrical Apparatus and Equipment, Wiring Supplies, and Related Equipment Merchant Wholesalers. This industry comprises establishments primarily engaged in the merchant wholesale distribution of electrical construction materials; wiring supplies; electric light fixtures; light bulbs; and/or electrical power equipment for the generation, transmission, distribution, or control of electric energy. 806-807

423620 Electrical and Electronic Appliance, Television, and Radio Set Merchant Wholesalers. This industry comprises establishments primarily engaged in the merchant wholesale distribution of household-type electrical appliances, room air-conditioners, gas and electric clothes dryers, and/or household-type audio or video equipment. 808-809

423690 Other Electronic Parts and Equipment Merchant Wholesalers. This industry comprises establishments primarily engaged in the merchant wholesale distribution of electronic parts and equipment (except electrical apparatus and equipment, wiring supplies and construction material; and electrical appliances, television and radio sets). 810-811

423710 Hardware Merchant Wholesalers. This industry comprises establishments primarily engaged in the merchant wholesale distribution of hardware, knives, or handtools. 812-813

423720 Plumbing and Heating Equipment and Supplies (Hydronics) Merchant Wholesalers. This industry comprises establishments primarily engaged in the merchant wholesale distribution of plumbing equipment, hydronic heating equipment, house-hold- type gas appliances (except gas clothes dryers), and/or supplies. 814-815

423730 Warm Air Heating and Air-Conditioning Equipment and Supplies Merchant Wholesalers. This industry comprises establishments primarily engaged in the merchant wholesale distribution of warm air heating and air-conditioning equipment and supplies. 816-817

423740 Refrigeration Equipment and Supplies Merchant Wholesalers. This industry comprises establishments primarily engaged in the merchant wholesale distribution of refrigeration equipment (except household-type refrigerators, freezers, and air-conditioners). 818-819

423810 Construction and Mining (except Oil Well) Machinery and Equipment Merchant Wholesalers. This industry comprises establishments primarily engaged in the merchant wholesale distribution of specialized machinery, equipment, and related parts generally used in construction, mining (except oil well) and logging activities. 820-821

423820 Farm and Garden Machinery and Equipment Merchant Wholesalers. This industry comprises establishments primarily engaged in the merchant wholesale distribution of specialized machinery, equipment, and related parts generally used in agricultural, farm, and lawn and garden activities. 822-823

423830 Industrial Machinery and Equipment Merchant Wholesalers. This industry comprises establishments primarily engaged in the merchant wholesale distribution of specialized machinery, equipment, and related parts generally used in manufacturing, oil well, and warehousing activities. 824-825

423840 Industrial Supplies Merchant Wholesalers. This industry comprises establishments primarily engaged in the merchant wholesale distribution of supplies for machinery and equipment generally used in manufacturing, oil well, and warehousing activities. 826-827

423850 Service Establishment Equipment and Supplies Merchant Wholesalers. This industry comprises establishments primarily engaged in the merchant wholesale distribution of specialized equipment and supplies of the type used by service establishments (except specialized equipment and supplies used in offices, stores, hotels, restaurants, schools, health and medical facilities, photographic facilities, and specialized equipment used in transportation and construction activities). 828-829

423860 Transportation Equipment and Supplies (except Motor Vehicle) Merchant Wholesalers. This industry comprises establishments primarily engaged in the merchant wholesale distribution of transportation equipment and supplies (except marine pleasure craft and motor vehicles). 830-831

423910 Sporting and Recreational Goods and Supplies Merchant Wholesalers. This industry comprises establishments primarily engaged in the merchant wholesale distribution of sporting goods and accessories; billiard and pool supplies; sporting firearms and ammunition; and/or marine pleasure craft, equipment, and supplies. 832-833

423920 Toy and Hobby Goods and Supplies Merchant Wholesalers. This industry comprises establishments primarily engaged in the merchant wholesale distribution of games, toys, fireworks, playing cards, hobby goods and supplies, and/or related goods. 834-835

WHOLESALE

NAICS #		Page

423930 Recyclable Material Merchant Wholesalers. This industry comprises establishments primarily engaged in the merchant wholesale distribution of automotive scrap, industrial scrap, and other recyclable materials. Included in this industry are auto wreckers primarily engaged in dismantling motor vehicles for the purpose of wholesaling scrap. 836-837

423940 Jewelry, Watch, Precious Stone, and Precious Metal Merchant Wholesalers. This industry comprises establishments primarily engaged in the merchant wholesale distribution of jewelry, precious and semiprecious stones, precious metals and metal flatware, costume jewelry, watches, clocks, silverware, and/or jewelers' findings. 838-839

423990 Other Miscellaneous Durable Goods Merchant Wholesalers. This industry comprises establishments primarily engaged in the merchant wholesale distribution of durable goods (except motor vehicle and motor vehicle parts and supplies; furniture and home furnishings; lumber and other construction materials; professional and commercial equipment and supplies; metals and minerals (except petroleum); electrical goods; hardware, and plumbing and heating equipment and supplies; machinery, equipment and supplies; sporting and recreational goods and supplies; toy and hobby goods and supplies; recyclable materials; and jewelry, watches, precious stones and precious metals). 840-841

424110 Printing and Writing Paper Merchant Wholesalers. This industry comprises establishments primarily engaged in the merchant wholesale distribution of bulk printing and/or writing paper generally on rolls for further processing. 842-843

424120 Stationery and Office Supplies Merchant Wholesalers. This industry comprises establishments primarily engaged in the merchant wholesale distribution of stationery, office supplies and/or gift wrap. 844-845

424130 Industrial and Personal Service Paper Merchant Wholesalers. This industry comprises establishments primarily engaged in the merchant wholesale distribution of kraft wrapping and other coarse paper, paperboard, converted paper (except stationery and office supplies), and/or related disposable plastics products. 846-847

424210 Drugs and Druggists' Sundries Merchant Wholesalers. This industry comprises establishments primarily engaged in the merchant wholesale distribution of biological and medical products; botanical drugs and herbs; and pharmaceutical products intended for internal and external consumption in such forms as ampoules, tablets, capsules, vials, ointments, powders, solutions, and suspensions. 848-849

424310 Piece Goods, Notions, and Other Dry Goods Merchant Wholesalers. This industry comprises establishments primarily engaged in the merchant wholesale distribution of piece goods, fabrics, knitting yarns (except industrial), thread and other notions, and/or hair accessories. 850-851

424320 Men's and Boys' Clothing and Furnishings Merchant Wholesalers. This industry comprises establishments primarily engaged in the merchant wholesale distribution of men's and/or boys' clothing and furnishings. 852-853

424330 Women's, Children's, and Infants' Clothing and Accessories Merchant Wholesalers. This industry comprises establishments primarily engaged in the merchant wholesale distribution of (1) women's, children's, infants', and/or unisex clothing and accessories and/or (2) fur clothing. 854-855

424340 Footwear Merchant Wholesalers. This industry comprises establishments primarily engaged in the merchant wholesale distribution of footwear (including athletic) of leather, rubber, and other materials. 856-857

424410 General Line Grocery Merchant Wholesalers. This industry comprises establishments primarily engaged in the merchant wholesale distribution of a general line (wide range) of groceries. . . 858-859

424420 Packaged Frozen Food Merchant Wholesalers. This industry comprises establishments primarily engaged in the merchant wholesale distribution of packaged frozen foods (except dairy products). 860-861

424430 Dairy Product (except Dried or Canned) Merchant Wholesalers. This industry comprises establishments primarily engaged in the merchant wholesale distribution of dairy products (except dried or canned). 862-863

424440 Poultry and Poultry Product Merchant Wholesalers. This industry comprises establishments primarily engaged in the merchant wholesale distribution of poultry and/or poultry products (except canned and packaged frozen). 864-865

WHOLESALE

NAICS #   **Page**

424450   **Confectionery Merchant Wholesalers.** This industry comprises establishments primarily engaged in the merchant wholesale distribution of confectioneries; salted or roasted nuts; popcorn; potato, corn, and similar chips; and/or fountain fruits and syrups. 866-867

424460   **Fish and Seafood Merchant Wholesalers.** This industry comprises establishments primarily engaged in the merchant wholesale distribution of fish and seafood (except canned or packaged frozen). 868-869

424470   **Meat and Meat Product Merchant Wholesalers.** This industry comprises establishments primarily engaged in the merchant wholesale distribution of meats and meat products (except canned and packaged frozen) and/or lard. 870-871

424480   **Fresh Fruit and Vegetable Merchant Wholesalers.** This industry comprises establishments primarily engaged in the merchant wholesale distribution of fresh fruits and vegetables. . . . 872-873

424490   **Other Grocery and Related Products Merchant Wholesalers.** This industry comprises establishments primarily engaged in the merchant wholesale distribution of groceries and related products (except a general line of groceries; packaged frozen food; dairy products (except dried and canned); poultry products (except canned); confectioneries; fish and seafood (except canned); meat products (except canned); and fresh fruits and vegetables). Included in this industry are establishments primarily engaged in the bottling and merchant wholesale distribution of spring and mineral waters processed by others. 874-875

424510   **Grain and Field Bean Merchant Wholesalers.** This industry comprises establishments primarily engaged in the merchant wholesale distribution of grains, such as corn, wheat, oats, barley, and unpolished rice; dry beans; and soybeans and other inedible beans. Included in this industry are establishments primarily engaged in operating country or terminal grain elevators primarily for the purpose of wholesaling. 876-877

424520   **Livestock Merchant Wholesalers.** This industry comprises establishments primarily engaged in the merchant wholesale distribution of livestock (except horses and mules). 878-879

424590   **Other Farm Product Raw Material Merchant Wholesalers.** This industry comprises establishments primarily engaged in the merchant wholesale distribution of farm products (except grain and field beans, livestock, raw milk, live poultry, and fresh fruits and vegetables). 880-881

424610   **Plastics Materials and Basic Forms and Shapes Merchant Wholesalers.** This industry comprises establishments primarily engaged in the merchant wholesale distribution of plastics materials and resins, and unsupported plastics film, sheet, sheeting, rod, tube, and other basic forms and shapes. 882-883

424690   **Other Chemical and Allied Products Merchant Wholesalers.** This industry comprises establishments primarily engaged in the merchant wholesale distribution of chemicals and allied products (except agricultural and medicinal chemicals, paints and varnishes, fireworks, and plastics materials and basic forms and shapes). 884-885

424710   **Petroleum Bulk Stations and Terminals.** This industry comprises establishments with bulk liquid storage facilities primar-ily engaged in the merchant wholesale distribution of crude petroleum and petroleum products, including liquefied petroleum gas. 886-887

424720   **Petroleum and Petroleum Products Merchant Wholesalers (except Bulk Stations and Terminals).** This industry comprises establishments primarily engaged in the merchant wholesale distribution of petroleum and petroleum products (except from bulk liquid storage facilities). 888-889

424810   **Beer and Ale Merchant Wholesalers.** This industry comprises establishments primarily engaged in the merchant wholesale distribution of beer, ale, porter, and other fermented malt beverages. 890-891

424820   **Wine and Distilled Alcoholic Beverage Merchant Wholesalers.** This industry comprises establishments primarily engaged in the merchant wholesale distribution of wine, distilled alcoholic beverages, and/or neutral spirits and ethyl alcohol used in blended wines and distilled liquors. 892-893

424910   **Farm Supplies Merchant Wholesalers.** This industry comprises establishments primarily engaged in the merchant wholesale distribution of farm supplies, such as animal feeds, fertilizers, agricultural chemicals, pesticides, plant seeds, and plant bulbs. 894-895

RETAIL

NAICS #		Page

424920 **Book, Periodical, and Newspaper Merchant Wholesalers.** This industry comprises establishments primarily engaged in the merchant wholesale distribution of books, periodicals, and newspapers. 896-897

424930 **Flower, Nursery Stock, and Florists' Supplies Merchant Wholesalers.** This industry comprises establishments primarily engaged in the merchant wholesale distribution of flowers, florists' supplies, and/or nursery stock (except plant seeds and plant bulbs). 898-899

424940 **Tobacco and Tobacco Product Merchant Wholesalers.** This industry comprises establishments primarily engaged in the merchant wholesale distribution of tobacco products, such as cigarettes, snuff, cigars, and pipe tobacco. 900-901

424950 **Paint, Varnish, and Supplies Merchant Wholesalers.** This industry comprises establishments primarily engaged in the merchant wholesale distribution of paints, varnishes, and similar coatings; pigments; wallpaper; and supplies, such as paint brushes and rollers. 902-903

424990 **Other Miscellaneous Nondurable Goods Merchant Wholesalers.** This industry comprises establishments primarily engaged in the merchant wholesale distribution of nondurable goods (except printing and writing paper; stationery and office supplies; industrial and personal service paper; drugs and druggists' sundries; apparel, piece goods, and notions; grocery and related products; farm product raw materials; chemical and allied products; petroleum and petroleum products; beer, wine, and distilled alcoholic beverages; farm supplies; books, periodicals and newspapers; flower, nursery stock and florists' supplies; tobacco and tobacco products; and paint, varnishes, wallpaper, and supplies). 904-905

425110 **Business to Business Electronic Markets.** This industry comprises business-to-business electronic markets bringing together buyers and sellers of goods using the Internet or other electronic means and generally receiving a commission or fee for the service. Business-to-business electronic markets for durable and nondurable goods are included in this industry. 906-907

425120 **Wholesale Trade Agents and Brokers.** This industry comprises wholesale trade agents and brokers acting on behalf of buyers or sellers in the wholesale distribution of goods. Agents and brokers do not take title to the goods being sold but rather receive a commission or fee for their service. Agents and brokers for all durable and nondurable goods are included in this industry. 908-909

RETAIL TRADE

441110 **New Car Dealers.** This industry comprises establishments primarily engaged in retailing new automobiles and light trucks, such as sport utility vehicles, and passenger and cargo vans, or retailing these new vehicles in combination with activities, such as repair services, retailing used cars, and selling replacement parts and accessories. 912-913

441120 **Used Car Dealers.** This industry comprises establishments primarily engaged in retailing used automobiles and light trucks, such as sport utility vehicles, and passenger and cargo vans. . . 914-915

441210 **Recreational Vehicle Dealers.** This industry comprises establishments primarily engaged in retailing new and/or used recreational vehicles commonly referred to as RVs or retailing these new vehicles in combination with activities, such as repair services and selling replacement parts and accessories. 916-917

441221 **Motorcycle, ATV, and Personal Watercraft Dealers.** This U.S. industry comprises establishments primarily engaged in retailing new and/or used motorcycles, motor scooters, motor bikes, mopeds, off-road all-terrain vehicles, and personal watercraft, or retailing these new vehicles in combination with repair services and selling replacement parts and accessories. 918-919

441222 **Boat Dealers.** This U.S. industry comprises establishments primarily engaged in (1) retailing new and/or used boats or retailing new boats in combination with activities, such as repair services and selling replacement parts and accessories, and/or (2) retailing new and/or used outboard motors, boat trailers, marine supplies, parts, and accessories. 920-921

441229 **All Other Motor Vehicle Dealers.** This U.S. industry comprises establishments primarily engaged in retailing new and/or used utility trailers and vehicles (except automobiles, light trucks, recreational vehicles, motorcycles, boats, motor scooters, motorbikes, off-road allterrain vehicles, and personal watercraft) or retailing these new vehicles in combination with activities, such as repair services and selling replacement parts and accessories. 922-923

RETAIL

NAICS #   **Page**

441310   **Automotive Parts and Accessories Stores.** This industry comprises one or more of the follow-ing: (1) establishments known as automotive supply stores primarily engaged in retailing new, used, and/or rebuilt automotive parts and accessories; (2) automotive supply stores that are primarily engaged in both retailing automotive parts and accessories and repairing automo-biles; and (3) establishments primarily engaged in retailing and installing automo-tive acces-sories.   924-925

441320   **Tire Dealers.** This industry comprises establishments primarily engaged in retailing new and/or used tires and tubes or retailing new tires in combination with automotive repair services. . .   926-927

442110   **Furniture Stores.** This industry comprises establishments primarily engaged in retailing new furniture, such as household furniture (e.g., baby furniture box springs and mattresses) and outdoor furniture; office furniture (except those sold in combination with office supplies and equipment); and/or furniture sold in combination with major appliances, home electronics, home furnishings, or floor coverings.   928-929

442210   **Floor Covering Stores.** This industry comprises establishments primarily engaged in retailing new floor coverings, such as rugs and carpets, vinyl floor coverings, and floor tile (except ceramic or wood only); or retailing new floor coverings in combination with installation and repair services.   930-931

442299   **All Other Home Furnishings Stores.** This U.S. industry comprises establishments primarily engaged in retailing new home furnishings (except floor coverings, furniture, and window treatments).   932-933

443111   **Household Appliance Stores.** This U.S. industry comprises establishments known as appliance stores primarily engaged in retailing an array of new household appliances, such as refrigera-tors, dishwashers, ovens, irons, coffeemakers, hair dryers, electric razors, room aircondition-ers, microwave ovens, sewing machines, and vacuum cleaners, or retailing new appliances in combination with appliance repair services.   934-935

443112   **Radio, Television, and Other Electronics Stores.** This U.S. industry comprises: (1) establish-ments known as consumer electronics stores primarily engaged in retailing a general line of new consumer-type electronic products; (2) establishments specializing in retailing a single line of consumer-type electronic products (except computers); or (3) establishments primarily engaged in retailing these new electronic products in combination with repair services.   936-937

443120   **Computer and Software Stores.** This industry comprises establishments primarily engaged in retailing new computers, computer peripherals, and prepackaged computer software with-out retailing other consumer-type electronic products or office equipment, office furniture and office supplies; or retailing these new products in combination with repair and support ser-vices.   938-939

444110   **Home Centers.** This industry comprises establishments known as home centers primarily en-gaged in retailing a general line of new home repair and improvement materials and supplies, such as lumber, plumbing goods, electrical goods, tools, housewares, hardware, and lawn and garden supplies, with no one merchandise line predominating. The merchandise lines are nor-mally arranged in separate departments.   940-941

444120   **Paint and Wallpaper Stores.** This industry comprises establishments known as paint and wall-paper stores primarily engaged in retailing paint, wallpaper, and related supplies.   942-943

444130   **Hardware Stores.** This industry comprises establishments known as hardware stores primarily engaged in retailing a general line of new hardware items, such as tools and builders' hard-ware.   944-945

444190   **Other Building Material Dealers.** This industry comprises establishments (except those known as home centers, paint and wallpaper stores, and hardware stores) primarily engaged in retail-ing specialized lines of new building materials, such as lumber, fencing, glass, doors, plumb-ing fixtures and supplies, electrical supplies, prefabricated buildings and kits, and kitchen and bath cabinets and countertops to be installed.   946-947

444210   **Outdoor Power Equipment Stores.** This industry comprises establishments primarily engaged in retailing new outdoor power equipment or new outdoor power equipment in combination with activities, such as repair services and selling replacement parts.   948-949

NAICS #   **Page**

444220 Nursery, Garden Center, and Farm Supply Stores. This industry comprises establishments primarily engaged in retailing nursery and garden products, such as trees, shrubs, plants, seeds, bulbs, and sod, that are predominantly grown elsewhere. These establishments may sell a limited amount of a product they grow themselves.   950-951

445110 Supermarkets and Other Grocery (except Convenience) Stores. This industry comprises establishments generally known as supermarkets and grocery stores primarily engaged in retailing a general line of food, such as canned and frozen foods; fresh fruits and vegetables; and fresh and prepared meats, fish, and poultry. Included in this industry are delicatessen-type establishments primarily engaged in retailing a general line of food.   952-953

445120 Convenience Stores. This industry comprises establishments known as convenience stores or food marts (except those with fuel pumps) primarily engaged in retailing a limited line of goods that generally includes milk, bread, soda, and snacks.   954-955

445210 Meat Markets. This industry comprises establishments primarily engaged in retailing fresh, frozen, or cured meats and poultry. Delicatessen-type establishments primarily engaged in retailing fresh meat are included in this industry.   956-957

445230 Fruit and Vegetable Markets. This industry comprises establishments primarily engaged in retailing fresh fruits and vegetables.   958-959

445291 Baked Goods Stores. This U.S. industry comprises establishments primarily engaged in retailing baked goods not for immediate consumption and not made on the premises.   960-961

445292 Confectionery and Nut Stores. This U.S. industry comprises establishments primarily engaged in retailing candy and other confections, nuts, and popcorn not for immediate consumption and not made on the premises.   962-963

445299 All Other Specialty Food Stores. This U.S. industry comprises establishments primarily engaged in retailing miscellaneous specialty foods (except meat, fish, seafood, fruit and vegetables, confections, nuts, popcorn, and baked goods) not for immediate consumption and not made on the premises.   964-965

445310 Beer, Wine, and Liquor Stores. This industry comprises establishments primarily engaged in retailing packaged alcoholic beverages, such as ale, beer, wine, and liquor.   966-967

446110 Pharmacies and Drug Stores. This industry comprises establishments known as pharmacies and drug stores engaged in retailing prescription or nonprescription drugs and medicines. . . .   968-969

446120 Cosmetics, Beauty Supplies, and Perfume Stores. This industry comprises establishments known as cosmetic or perfume stores or beauty supply shops primarily engaged in retailing cosmetics, perfumes, toiletries, and personal grooming products.   970-971

446130 Optical Goods Stores. This industry comprises establishments primarily engaged in one or more of the following: (1) retailing and fitting prescription eyeglasses and contact lenses; (2) retailing prescription eyeglasses in combination with the grinding of lenses to order on the premises; and (3) selling nonprescription eyeglasses.   972-973

446191 Food (Health) Supplement Stores. This U.S. industry comprises establishments primarily engaged in retailing food supplement products, such as vitamins, nutrition supplements, and body enhancing supplements.   974-975

446199 All Other Health and Personal Care Stores. This U.S. industry comprises establishments primarily engaged in retailing specialized lines of health and personal care merchandise (except drugs, medicines, optical goods, cosmetics, beauty supplies, perfume, and food supplement products).   976-977

447110 Gasoline Stations with Convenience Stores. This industry comprises establishments engaged in retailing automotive fuels (e.g., diesel fuel, gasohol, gasoline) in combination with convenience store or food mart items. These establishments can either be in a convenience store (i.e., food mart) setting or a gasoline station setting. These establishments may also provide automotive repair services.   978-979

447190 Other Gasoline Stations. This industry comprises establishments known as gasoline stations (except those with convenience stores) primarily engaged in one of the following: (1) retailing automotive fuels (e.g., diesel fuel, gasohol, gasoline) or (2) retailing these fuels in combination with activities, such as providing repair services; selling automotive oils, replacement parts, and accessories; and/or providing food services.   980-981

RETAIL

NAICS #		Page

448110   **Men's Clothing Stores.** This industry comprises establishments primarily engaged in retailing a general line of new men's and boys' clothing. These establishments may provide basic alterations, such as hemming, taking in or letting out seams, or lengthening or shortening sleeves. **982-983**

448120   **Women's Clothing Stores.** This industry comprises establishments primarily engaged in retailing a general line of new women's, misses'; and juniors' clothing, including maternity wear. . . . **984-985**

448140   **Family Clothing Stores.** This industry comprises establishments primarily engaged in retailing a general line of new clothing for men, women, and children, without specializing in sales for an individual gender or age group. These establishments may provide basic alterations, such as hemming, taking in or letting out seams, or lengthening or shortening sleeves. **986-987**

448150   **Clothing Accessories Stores.** This industry comprises establishments primarily engaged in retailing single or combination lines of new clothing accessories, such as hats and caps, costume jewelry, gloves, handbags, ties, wigs, toupees, and belts. **988-989**

448190   **Other Clothing Stores.** This industry comprises establishments primarily engaged in retailing specialized lines of new clothing (except general lines of men's, women's, children's, infants', and family clothing). These establishments may provide basic alterations, such as hemming, taking in or letting out seams, or lengthening or shortening sleeves. **990-991**

448210   **Shoe Stores.** This industry comprises establishments primarily engaged in retailing all types of new footwear (except hosiery and specialty sports footwear, such as golf shoes, bowling shoes, and spiked shoes). Establishments primarily engaged in retailing new tennis shoes or sneakers are included in this industry. **992-993**

448310   **Jewelry Stores.** This industry comprises establishments primarily engaged in retailing one or more of the following items: (1) new jewelry (except costume jewelry); (2) new sterling and plated silverware; and (3) new watches and clocks. Also included are establishments retailing these new products in combination with lapidary work and/or repair services. **994-995**

451110   **Sporting Goods Stores.** This industry comprises establishments primarily engaged in retailing new sporting goods, such as bicycles and bicycle parts; camping equipment; exercise and fitness equipment; athletic uniforms; specialty sports footwear; and sporting goods, equipment, and accessories. **996-997**

451120   **Hobby, Toy, and Game Stores.** This industry comprises establishments primarily engaged in retailing new toys, games, and hobby and craft supplies (except needlecraft). **998-999**

451140   **Musical Instrument and Supplies Stores.** This industry comprises establishments primarily engaged in retailing new musical instruments, sheet music, and related supplies; or retailing these new products in combination with musical instrument repair, rental, or music instruction. . . **1000-1001**

451211   **Book Stores.** This U.S. industry comprises establishments primarily engaged in retailing new books. **1002-1003**

452111   **Department Stores (except Discount Department Stores).** This U.S. industry comprises establishments known as department stores that have separate departments for various merchandise lines, such as apparel, jewelry, home furnishings, and linens, each with separate cash registers and sales associates. Department stores in this industry generally do not have central customer checkout and cash register facilities. **1004-1005**

452990   **All Other General Merchandise Stores.** This industry comprises establishments primarily engaged in retailing new goods in general merchandise stores (except department stores, warehouse clubs, super-stores, and supercenters). These establishments retail a general line of new merchandise, such as apparel, automotive parts, dry goods, hardware, groceries, housewares or home furnishings, and other lines in limited amounts, with none of the lines predominating. **1006-1007**

453110   **Florists.** This industry comprises establishments known as florists primarily engaged in retailing cut flowers, floral arrangements, and potted plants purchased from others. These establishments usually prepare the arrangements they sell. **1008-1009**

453210   **Office Supplies and Stationery Stores.** This industry comprises establishments primarily engaged in one or more of the following: (1) retailing new stationery, school supplies, and office supplies; (2) selling a combination of new office equipment, furniture, and supplies; and (3) selling new office equipment, furniture, and supplies in combination with selling new computers. **1010-1011**

NAICS #   **Page**

453220   **Gift, Novelty, and Souvenir Stores.** This industry comprises establishments primarily engaged in retailing new gifts, novelty merchandise, souvenirs, greeting cards, seasonal and holiday decorations, and curios. 1012-1013

453310   **Used Merchandise Stores.** This industry comprises establishments primarily engaged in retailing used merchandise, antiques, and secondhand goods (except motor vehicles, such as automobiles, RVs, motorcycles, and boats; motor vehicle parts; tires; and mobile homes). . . . 1014-1015

453910   **Pet and Pet Supplies Stores.** This industry comprises establishments primarily engaged in retailing pets, pet foods, and pet supplies. 1016-1017

453920   **Art Dealers.** This industry comprises establishments primarily engaged in retailing original and limited edition art works. Included in this industry are establishments primarily engaged in displaying works of art for retail sale in art galleries. 1018-1019

453930   **Manufactured (Mobile) Home Dealers.** This industry comprises establishments primarily engaged in retailing new and/ or used manufactured homes (i.e., mobile homes), parts, and equipment. 1020-1021

453991   **Tobacco Stores.** This U.S. industry comprises establishments primarily engaged in retailing cigarettes, cigars, tobacco, pipes, and other smokers' supplies. 1022-1023

453998   **All Other Miscellaneous Store Retailers (except Tobacco Stores).** This U.S. industry comprises establishments primarily engaged in retailing specialized lines of merchandise (except motor vehicle and parts dealers; furniture and home furnishings stores; electronic and appliance stores; building material and garden equipment and supplies dealers; food and beverage stores; health and personal care stores; gasoline stations; clothing and clothing accessories stores; sporting goods, hobby, book and music stores; general merchandise stores; florists; office supplies, stationery and gift stores; used merchandise stores; pet and pet supplies stores; art dealers; manufactured home (i.e., mobile homes) dealers; and tobacco stores). This industry also includes establishments primarily engaged in retailing a general line of new and used merchandise on an auction basis. 1024-1025

454111   **Electronic Shopping.** This U.S. Industry comprises establishments engaged in retailing all types of merchandise using the Internet. 1026-1027

454113   **Mail-Order Houses.** This U.S. industry comprises establishments primarily engaged in retailing all types of merchandise using mail catalogs or television to generate clients and display merchandise. Included in this industry are establishments primarily engaged in retailing from catalog showrooms of mail-order houses as well as establishments providing a combination of Internet and mail-order sales. 1028-1029

454210   **Vending Machine Operators.** This industry comprises establishments primarily engaged in retailing merchandise through vending machines that they service. 1030-1031

454311   **Heating Oil Dealers.** This U.S. industry comprises establishments primarily engaged in retailing heating oil via direct selling. 1032-1033

454312   **Liquefied Petroleum Gas (Bottled Gas) Dealers.** This U.S. industry comprises establishments primarily engaged in retailing liquefied petroleum (LP) gas via direct selling. 1034-1035

454390   **Other Direct Selling Establishments.** This industry comprises establishments primarily engaged in retailing merchan-dise (except food for immediate consumption and fuel) via direct sale to the customer by means, such as in-house sales (i.e., party plan merchandising), truck or wagon sales, and portable stalls (i.e., street vendors). 1036-1037

TRANSPORTATION AND WAREHOUSING

481111   **Scheduled Passenger Air Transportation.** This U.S. industry comprises establishments primarily engaged in providing air transportation of passengers or passengers and freight over regular routes and on regular schedules. Establishments in this industry operate flights even if partially loaded. Scheduled air passenger carriers including commuter and helicopter carriers (except scenic and sightseeing) are included in this industry. 1040-1041

481211   **Nonscheduled Chartered Passenger Air Transportation.** This U.S. industry comprises establishments primarily engaged in providing air transportation of passengers or passengers and cargo with no regular routes and regular schedules. 1042-1043

TRANSPORTATION

NAICS #   **Page**

481219   **Other Nonscheduled Air Transportation.** This U.S. industry comprises establishments primarily engaged in providing air transportation with no regular routes and regular schedules (except nonscheduled chartered passenger and/or cargo air transportation). These establishments provide a variety of specialty air transportation or flying services based on individual customer needs using general purpose aircraft. 1044-1045

482111   **Line-Haul Railroads.** This U.S. industry comprises establishments known as line-haul railroads primarily engaged in operating railroads for the transport of passengers and/or cargo over a long distance within a rail network. These establishments provide for the intercity movement of trains between the terminals and stations on main and branch lines of a line-haul rail network (except for local switching services). 1046-1047

483113   **Coastal and Great Lakes Freight Transportation.** This U.S. industry comprises establishments primarily engaged in providing water transportation of cargo in coastal waters, on the Great Lakes System, or deep seas between ports of the United States, Puerto Rico, and United States island possessions or protectorates. Marine transportation establishments using the facilities of the St. Lawrence Seaway Authority Commission are considered to be using the Great Lakes Water Transportation System. Establishments primarily engaged in providing coastal and/or Great Lakes barge transportation services are included in this industry. 1048-1049

483211   **Inland Water Freight Transportation.** This U.S. industry comprises establishments primarily engaged in providing inland water transportation of cargo on lakes, rivers, or intracoastal waterways (except on the Great Lakes System). 1050-1051

484110   **General Freight Trucking, Local.** This industry comprises establishments primarily engaged in providing local general freight trucking. General freight establishments handle a wide variety of commodities, generally palletized and transported in a container or van trailer. Local general freight trucking establishments usually provide trucking within a metropolitan area which may cross state lines. Generally the trips are same-day return. 1052-1053

484121   **General Freight Trucking, Long-Distance, Truckload.** This U.S. industry comprises establishments primarily engaged in providing long-distance general freight truckload (TL) trucking. These long-distance general freight truckload carrier establishments provide full truck movement of freight from origin to destination. The shipment of freight on a truck is characterized as a full single load not combined with other shipments. 1054-1055

484122   **General Freight Trucking, Long-Distance, Less Than Truckload.** This U.S. industry comprises establishments primarily engaged in providing long-distance, general freight, less than truckload (LTL) trucking. LTL carriage is characterized as multiple shipments combined onto a single truck for multiple deliveries within a network. These establishments are generally characterized by the following network activities: local pickup, local sorting and terminal operations, line-haul, destination sorting and terminal operations, and local delivery. 1056-1057

484210   **Used Household and Office Goods Moving.** This industry comprises establishments primarily engaged in providing local or long-distance trucking of used household, used institutional, or used commercial furniture and equipment. Incidental packing and storage activities are often provided by these establishments. 1058-1059

484220   **Specialized Freight (except Used Goods) Trucking, Local.** This industry comprises establishments primarily engaged in providing local, specialized trucking. Local trucking establishments provide trucking within a metropolitan area that may cross state lines. Generally the trips are same-day return. 1060-1061

484230   **Specialized Freight (except Used Goods) Trucking, Long-Distance.** This industry comprises establishments primarily engaged in providing long-distance specialized trucking. These establishments provide trucking between metropolitan areas that may cross North American country borders. 1062-1063

485310   **Taxi Service.** This industry comprises establishments primarily engaged in providing passenger transportation by automobile or van, not operated over regular routes and on regular schedules. Establishments of taxicab owner/operators, taxicab fleet operators, or taxicab organizations are included in this industry. 1064-1065

485320   **Limousine Service.** This industry comprises establishments primarily engaged in providing an array of specialty and luxury passenger transportation services via limousine or luxury sedans generally on a reserved basis. These establishments do not operate over regular routes and on regular schedules. 1066-1067

TRANSPORTATION

NAICS # **Page**

485410 **School and Employee Bus Transportation.** This industry comprises establishments primarily engaged in providing buses and other motor vehicles to transport pupils to and from school or employees to and from work. 1068-1069

485510 **Charter Bus Industry.** This industry comprises establishments primarily engaged in providing buses for charter. These establishments provide bus services to meet customers' road transportation needs and generally do not operate over fixed routes and on regular schedules. . . 1070-1071

485999 **All Other Transit and Ground Passenger Transportation.** This U.S. industry comprises establishments primarily engaged in providing ground passenger transportation (except urban transit systems; interurban and rural bus transportation, taxi and/or limousine services (except shuttle services), school and employee bus transportation, charter bus services, and special needs transportation). Establishments primarily engaged in operating shuttle services and vanpools are included in this industry. Shuttle services establishments generally provide travel on regular routes and on regular schedules between hotels, airports, or other destination points. . . . 1072-1073

488119 **Other Airport Operations.** This U.S. industry comprises establishments primarily engaged in (1) operating international, national, or civil airports, or public flying fields or (2) supporting airport operations, such as rental of hangar space, and providing baggage handling and/or cargo handling services. 1074-1075

488190 **Other Support Activities for Air Transportation.** This industry comprises establishments primarily engaged in providing specialized services for air transportation (except air traffic control and other airport operations). 1076-1077

488320 **Marine Cargo Handling.** This industry comprises establishments primarily engaged in providing stevedoring and other marine cargo handling services (except warehousing). 1078-1079

488330 **Navigational Services to Shipping.** This industry comprises establishments primarily engaged in providing navigational services to shipping. Marine salvage establishments are included in this industry. 1080-1081

488390 **Other Support Activities for Water Transportation.** This industry comprises establishments primarily engaged in providing services to water transportation (except port and harbor operations; marine cargo handling services; and navigational services to shipping). 1082-1083

488410 **Motor Vehicle Towing.** This industry comprises establishments primarily engaged in towing light or heavy motor vehicles, both local and long distance. These establishments may provide incidental services, such as storage and emergency road repair services. 1084-1085

488490 **Other Support Activities for Road Transportation.** This industry comprises establishments primarily engaged in providing services (except motor vehicle towing) to road network users. . . 1086-1087

488510 **Freight Transportation Arrangement.** This industry comprises establishments primarily engaged in arranging transportation of freight between shippers and carriers. These establishments are usually known as freight forwarders, marine shipping agents, or customs brokers and offer a combination of services spanning transportation modes. 1088-1089

488991 **Packing and Crating.** This U.S. industry comprises establishments primarily engaged in packing, crating, and otherwise preparing goods for transportation. 1090-1091

488999 **All Other Support Activities for Transportation.** This U.S. industry comprises establishments primarily engaged in providing support activities to transportation (except for air transportation; rail transportation; water transportation; road transportation; freight transportation arrangement; and packing and crating). 1092-1093

492110 **Couriers and Express Delivery Services.** This industry comprises establishments primarily engaged in providing air, surface, or combined courier delivery services of parcels generally between metropolitan areas or urban centers. The establishments of this industry form a network including courier local pick-up and delivery to serve their customers' needs. 1094-1095

493110 **General Warehousing and Storage.** This industry comprises establishments primarily engaged in operating merchandise warehousing and storage facilities. These establishments generally handle goods in containers, such as boxes, barrels, and/or drums, using equipment, such as forklifts, pallets, and racks. They are not specialized in handling bulk products of any particular type, size, or quantity of goods or products. 1096-1097

FINANCE AND INSURANCE

522210 **Credit Card Issuing.** This industry comprises establishments primarily engaged in providing credit by issuing credit cards. Credit card issuance provides the funds required to purchase goods and services in return for payment of the full balance or payments on an installment basis. Credit card banks are included in this industry. 1146-1147

522220 **Sales Financing.** This industry comprises establishments primarily engaged in sales financing or sales financing in combination with leasing. Sales financing establishments are primarily engaged in lending money for the purpose of providing collateralized goods through a contractual installment sales agreement, either directly from or through arrangements with dealers. . . . 1148-1149

522291 **Consumer Lending.** This U.S. industry comprises establishments primarily engaged in making unsecured cash loans to consumers. 1150-1151

522292 **Real Estate Credit.** This U.S. industry comprises establishments primarily engaged in lending funds with real estate as collateral. 1152-1153

522294 **Secondary Market Financing.** This U.S. industry comprises establishments primarily engaged in buying, pooling, and repackaging loans for sale to others on the secondary market. 1154-1155

522298 **All Other Nondepository Credit Intermediation.** This U.S. industry comprises establishments primarily engaged in providing nondepository credit (except credit card issuing, sales financing, consumer lending, real estate credit, international trade financing, and secondary market financing). 1156-1157

522310 **Mortgage and Nonmortgage Loan Brokers.** This industry comprises establishments primarily engaged in arranging loans by bringing borrowers and lenders together on a commission or fee basis. 1158-1159

522320 **Financial Transactions Processing, Reserve, and Clearinghouse Activities.** This industry comprises establishments primarily engaged in providing one or more of the following: (1) financial transaction processing (except central bank); (2) reserve and liquidity services (except central bank); and/or (3) check or other financial instrument clearinghouse services (except central bank). 1160-1161

522390 **Other Activities Related to Credit Intermediation.** This industry comprises establishments primarily engaged in facilitating credit intermediation (except mortgage and loan brokerage; and financial transactions processing, reserve, and clearinghouse activities). 1162-1163

523110 **Investment Banking and Securities Dealing.** This industry comprises establishments primarily engaged in underwriting, originating, and/or maintaining markets for issues of securities. Investment bankers act as principals (i.e., investors who buy or sell on their own account) in firm commitment transactions or act as agents in best effort and standby commitments. This industry also includes establishments acting as principals in buying or selling securities generally on a spread basis, such as securities dealers or stock option dealers. 1164-1165

523120 **Securities Brokerage.** This industry comprises establishments primarily engaged in acting as agents (i.e., brokers) between buyers and sellers in buying or selling securities on a commission or transaction fee basis. 1166-1167

523130 **Commodity Contracts Dealing.** This industry comprises establishments primarily engaged in acting as principals (i.e., investors who buy or sell for their own account) in buying or selling spot or futures commodity contracts or options, such as precious metals, foreign currency, oil, or agricultural products, generally on a spread basis. 1168-1169

523140 **Commodity Contracts Brokerage.** This industry comprises establishments primarily engaged in acting as agents (i.e., brokers) in buying or selling spot or future commodity contracts or options on a commission or transaction fee basis. 1170-1171

523910 **Miscellaneous Intermediation.** This industry comprises establishments primarily engaged in acting as principals (except investment bankers, securities dealers, and commodity contracts dealers) in buying or selling of financial contracts generally on a spread basis. Principals are investors that buy or sell for their own account. 1172-1173

523920 **Portfolio Management.** This industry comprises establishments primarily engaged in managing the portfolio assets (i.e., funds) of others on a fee or commission basis. Establishments in this industry have the authority to make investment decisions, and they derive fees based on the size and/or overall performance of the portfolio. 1174-1175

FINANCE

NAICS #   **Page**

523930   **Investment Advice.** This industry comprises establishments primarily engaged in providing customized investment advice to clients on a fee basis, but do not have the authority to execute trades. Primary activities performed by establishments in this industry are providing financial planning advice and investment counseling to meet the goals and needs of specific clients. . . 1176-1177

523991   **Trust, Fiduciary, and Custody Activities.** This U.S. industry comprises establishments primarily engaged in providing trust, fiduciary, and custody services to others, as instructed, on a fee or contract basis, such as bank trust offices and escrow agencies (except real estate). 1178-1179

523999   **Miscellaneous Financial Investment Activities.** This U.S. industry comprises establishments primarily engaged in acting as agents and/or brokers (except securities brokerages and commodity contracts brokerages) in buying or selling financial contracts and those providing financial investment services (except securities and commodity exchanges; portfolio management; investment advice; and trust, fiduciary, and custody services) on a fee or commission basis. . . 1180-1181

524113   **Direct Life Insurance Carriers.** This U.S. industry comprises establishments primarily engaged in initially underwriting (i.e., assuming the risk and assigning premiums) annuities and life insurance policies, disability income insurance policies, and accidental death and dismemberment insurance policies. 1182-1183

524114   **Direct Health and Medical Insurance Carriers.** This U.S. industry comprises establishments primarily engaged in initially underwriting (i.e., assuming the risk and assigning premiums) health and medical insurance policies. Group hospitalization plans and HMO establishments (except those providing health care services) that provide health and medical insurance policies without providing health care services are included in this industry. 1184-1185

524126   **Direct Property and Casualty Insurance Carriers.** This U.S. industry comprises establishments primarily engaged in initially underwriting (i.e., assuming the risk and assigning premiums) insurance policies that protect policyholders against losses that may occur as a result of property damage or liability. 1186-1187

524127   **Direct Title Insurance Carriers.** This U.S. industry comprises establishments primarily engaged in initially underwriting (i.e., assuming the risk and assigning premiums) insurance policies to protect the owners of real estate or real estate creditors against loss sustained by reason of any title defect to real property. 1188-1189

524128   **Other Direct Insurance (except Life, Health, and Medical) Carriers.** This U.S. industry comprises establishments primarily engaged in initially underwriting (e.g., assuming the risk, assigning premiums) insurance policies (except life, disability income, accidental death and dismemberment, health and medical, property and casualty, and title insurance policies). 1190-1191

524210   **Insurance Agencies and Brokerages.** This industry comprises establishments primarily engaged in acting as agents (i.e., brokers) in selling annuities and insurance policies. 1192-1193

524292   **Third Party Administration of Insurance and Pension Funds.** This U.S. industry comprises establishments primarily engaged in providing third party administration services of insurance and pension funds, such as claims processing and other administrative services to insurance carriers, employee-benefit plans, and self-insurance funds. 1194-1195

524298   **All Other Insurance Related Activities.** This U.S. industry comprises establishments primarily engaged in providing insurance services on a contract or fee basis (except insurance agencies and brokerages, claims adjusting, and third party administration). Insurance advisory services and insurance ratemaking services are included in this industry. 1196-1197

525910   **Open-End Investment Funds.** This industry comprises legal entities (i.e., open-end investment funds) organized to pool assets that consist of securities or other financial instruments. Shares in these pools are offered to the public in an initial offering with additional shares offered continuously and perpetually and redeemed at a specific price determined by the net asset value. 1198-1199

525990   **Other Financial Vehicles.** This industry comprises legal entities (i.e., funds (except insurance and employee benefit funds; open-end investment funds; trusts, estates, and agency accounts; and Real Estate Investment Trusts (REITs)). 1200-1201

REAL ESTATE AND RENTAL AND LEASING

531110 **Lessors of Residential Buildings and Dwellings.** This industry comprises establishments primarily engaged in acting as lessors of buildings used as residences or dwellings, such as single-family homes, apartment buildings, and town homes. Included in this industry are owner-lessors and establishments renting real estate and then acting as lessors in subleasing it to others. The establishments in this industry may manage the property themselves or have another establishment manage it for them. 1204-1205

531120 **Lessors of Nonresidential Buildings (except Miniwarehouses).** This industry comprises establishments primarily engaged in acting as lessors of buildings (except miniwarehouses and self-storage units) that are not used as residences or dwellings. Included in this industry are: (1) owner-lessors of nonresidential buildings; (2) establishments renting real estate and then acting as lessors in subleasing it to others; and (3) establishments providing full service office space, whether on a lease or service contract basis. The establishments in this industry may manage the property themselves or have another establishment manage it for them. 1206-1207

531130 **Lessors of Miniwarehouses and Self-Storage Units.** This industry comprises establishments primarily engaged in renting or leasing space for self-storage. These establishments provide secure space (i.e., rooms, compartments, lockers, containers, or outdoor space) where clients can store and retrieve their goods. 1208-1209

531190 **Lessors of Other Real Estate Property.** This industry comprises establishments primarily engaged in acting as lessors of real estate (except buildings), such as manufactured home (i.e., mobile home) sites, vacant lots, and grazing land. 1210-1211

531210 **Offices of Real Estate Agents and Brokers.** This industry comprises establishments primarily engaged in acting as agents and/or brokers in one or more of the following: (1) selling real estate for others; (2) buying real estate for others; and (3) renting real estate for others. 1212-1213

531311 **Residential Property Managers.** This U.S. industry comprises establishments primarily engaged in managing residential real estate for others. 1214-1215

531312 **Nonresidential Property Managers.** This U.S. industry comprises establishments primarily engaged in managing nonresidential real estate for others. 1216-1217

531390 **Other Activities Related to Real Estate.** This industry comprises establishments primarily engaged in performing real estate related services (except lessors of real estate, offices of real estate agents and brokers, real estate property managers, and offices of real estate appraisers). 1218-1219

532111 **Passenger Car Rental.** This industry comprises establishments primarily engaged in renting passenger cars without drivers, generally for short periods of time. 1220-1221

532112 **Passenger Car Leasing.** This industry comprises establishments primarily engaged in leasing passenger cars without drivers, generally for long periods of time. 1222-1223

532120 **Truck, Utility Trailer, and RV (Recreational Vehicle) Rental and Leasing.** This industry comprises establishments primarily engaged in renting or leasing, without drivers, one or more of the following: trucks, truck tractors or buses: semitrailers, utility trailers, or RVs (recreational vehicles). 1224-1225

532210 **Consumer Electronics and Appliances Rental.** This industry comprises establishments primarily engaged in renting consumer electronics equipment and appliances, such as televisions, stereos, and refrigerators. Included in this industry are appliance rental centers. 1226-1227

532291 **Home Health Equipment Rental.** This U.S. industry comprises establishments primarily engaged in renting hometype health and invalid equipment, such as wheel chairs, hospital beds, oxygen tanks, walkers, and crutches. 1228-1229

532299 **All Other Consumer Goods Rental.** This U.S. industry comprises establishments primarily engaged in renting consumer goods and products (except consumer electronics and appliances; formal wear and costumes; prerecorded video tapes and discs for home electronic equipment; home health furniture and equipment; and recreational goods). Included in this industry are furniture rental centers and party rental supply centers. 1230-1231

PROFESSIONAL SERVICES

NAICS #   **Page**

532310   **General Rental Centers.** This industry comprises establishments primarily engaged in renting a range of consumer, commercial, and industrial equipment. Establishments in this industry typically operate from conveniently located facilities where they maintain inventories of goods and equipment that they rent for short periods of time. The type of equipment that establishments in this industry provide often includes, but is not limited to: audio visual equipment, contractors' and builders' tools and equipment, home repair tools, lawn and garden equipment, moving equipment and supplies, and party and banquet equipment and supplies. . . . 1232-1233

532411   **Commercial Air, Rail, and Water Transportation Equipment Rental and Leasing.** This U.S. industry comprises establishments primarily engaged in renting or leasing off-highway transportation equipment without operators, such as aircraft, railroad cars, steamships, or tugboats. . . 1234-1235

532412   **Construction, Mining, and Forestry Machinery and Equipment Rental and Leasing.** This U.S. industry comprises establishments primarily engaged in renting or leasing heavy equipment without operators that may be used for construction, mining, or forestry, such as bulldozers, earthmoving equipment, well-drilling machinery and equipment, or cranes. 1236-1237

532420   **Office Machinery and Equipment Rental and Leasing.** This industry comprises establishments primarily engaged in renting or leasing office machinery and equipment, such as computers, office furniture, duplicating machines (i.e., copiers), or facsimile machines. 1238-1239

532490   **Other Commercial and Industrial Machinery and Equipment Rental and Leasing.** This industry comprises establishments primarily engaged in renting or leasing nonconsumer-type machinery and equipment (except heavy construction, transportation, mining, and forestry machinery and equipment without operators; and office machinery and equipment). Establishments in this industry rent or lease products, such as manufacturing equipment; metalworking, telecommunications, motion picture, or theatrical machinery and equipment; institutional (i.e., public building) furniture, such as furniture for schools, theaters, or buildings; or agricultural equipment without operators. 1240-1241

533110   **Lessors of Nonfinancial Intangible Assets (except Copyrighted Works).** This industry comprises establishments primarily engaged in assigning rights to assets, such as patents, trademarks, brand names, and/or franchise agreements for which a royalty payment or licensing fee is paid to the asset holder. 1242-1243

PROFESSIONAL, SCIENTIFIC, AND TECHNICAL SERVICES

541110   **Offices of Lawyers.** This industry comprises offices of legal practitioners known as lawyers or attorneys (i.e., counselors-at-law) primarily engaged in the practice of law. Estab-lishments in this industry may provide expertise in a range or in specific areas of law, such as criminal law, corporate law, family and estate law, patent law, real estate law, or tax law. 1246-1247

541191   **Title Abstract and Settlement Offices.** This U.S. industry comprises establishments (except offices of lawyers and attorneys) primarily engaged in one or more of the following activities: (1) researching public land records to gather information relating to real estate titles; (2) preparing documents necessary for the transfer of the title, financing, and settlement; (3) conducting final real estate settlements and closings; and (4) filing legal and other documents relating to the sale of real estate. Real estate settlement offices, title abstract companies, and title search companies are included in this industry. 1248-1249

541211   **Offices of Certified Public Accountants.** This U.S. industry comprises establishments of accountants that are certified to audit the accounting records of public and private organizations and to attest to compliance with generally accepted accounting practices. Offices of certified public accountants (CPAs) may provide one or more of the following accounting services: (1) auditing financial statements; (2) designing accounting systems; (3) preparing financial statements; (4) developing budgets; and (5) providing advice on matters related to accounting. These establishments may also provide related services, such as bookkeeping, tax return preparation, and payroll processing. 1250-1251

PROFESSIONAL SERVICES

NAICS #   **Page**

541214   **Payroll Services.** This U.S. industry comprises establishments (except offices of CPAs) engaged in the following without also providing accounting, bookkeeping, or billing services: (1) collecting information on hours worked, pay rates, deductions, and other payroll- related data from their clients and (2) using that information to generate paychecks, payroll reports, and tax filings. These establishments may use data processing and tabulating techniques as part of providing their services. 1252-1253

541219   **Other Accounting Services.** This U.S. industry comprises establishments (except offices of CPAs) engaged in providing accounting services (except tax return preparation services only or payroll services only). These establishments may also provide tax return preparation or payroll services. Accountant (except CPA) offices, bookkeeper offices, and billing offices are included in this industry. 1254-1255

541310   **Architectural Services.** This industry comprises establishments primarily engaged in planning and designing residential, institutional, leisure, commercial, and industrial buildings and structures by applying knowledge of design, construction procedures, zoning regulations, building codes, and building materials. 1256-1257

541320   **Landscape Architectural Services.** This industry comprises establishments primarily engaged in planning and designing the development of land areas for projects, such as parks and other recreational areas; airports; highways; hospitals; schools; land subdivisions; and commercial, industrial, and residential areas, by applying knowledge of land characteristics, location of buildings and structures, use of land areas, and design of landscape projects. 1258-1259

541330   **Engineering Services.** This industry comprises establishments primarily engaged in applying physical laws and principles of engineering in the design, development, and utilization of machines, materials, instruments, structures, processes, and systems. The assignments undertaken by these establishments may involve any of the following activities: provision of advice, preparation of feasibility studies, preparation of preliminary and final plans and designs, provision of technical services during the construction or installation phase, inspection and evaluation of engineering projects, and related services. 1260-1261

541370   **Surveying and Mapping (except Geophysical) Services.** This industry comprises establishments primarily engaged in performing surveying and mapping services of the surface of the earth, including the sea floor. These services may include surveying and mapping of areas above or below the surface of the earth, such as the creation of view easements or segregating rights in parcels of land by creating underground utility easements. 1262-1263

541380   **Testing Laboratories.** This industry comprises establishments primarily engaged in performing physical, chemical, and other analytical testing services, such as acoustics or vibration testing, assaying, biological testing (except medical and veterinary), calibration testing, electrical and electronic testing, geotechnical testing, mechanical testing, nondestructive testing, or thermal testing. The testing may occur in a laboratory or on-site. 1264-1265

541410   **Interior Design Services.** This industry comprises establishments primarily engaged in planning, designing and administering projects in interior spaces to meet the physical and aesthetic needs of people using them, taking into consideration building codes, health and safety regulations, traffic patterns and floor planning, mechanical and electrical needs, and interior fittings and furniture. Interior designers and interior design consultants work in areas, such as hospitality design, health care design, institutional design, commercial and corporate design, and residential design. This industry also includes interior decorating consultants engaged exclusively in providing aesthetic services associated with interior spaces. 1266-1267

541430   **Graphic Design Services.** This industry comprises establishments primarily engaged in planning, designing, and managing the production of visual communication in order to convey specific messages or concepts, clarify complex information, or project visual identi-ties. These services can include the design of printed materials, packaging, advertising, signage systems, and corporate identification (logos). This industry also includes commercial artists engaged exclusively in generating drawings and illustrations requiring technical accuracy or interpretative skills. 1268-1269

541511   **Custom Computer Programming Services.** This U.S. industry comprises establishments primarily engaged in writing, modifying, testing, and supporting software to meet the needs of a particular customer. 1270-1271

PROFESSIONAL SERVICES

NAICS #   **Page**

541512 **Computer Systems Design Services.** This U.S. industry comprises establishments primarily engaged in planning and designing computer systems that integrate computer hardware, software, and communication technologies. The hardware and software components of the system may be provided by this establishment or company as part of integrated services or may be provided by third parties or vendors. These establishments often install the system and train and support users of the system. 1272-1273

541519 **Other Computer Related Services.** This U.S. industry comprises establishments primarily engaged in providing computer related services (except custom programming, systems integration design, and facilities management services). Establishments providing computer disaster recovery services or software installation services are included in this industry. 1274-1275

541611 **Administrative Management and General Management Consulting Services.** This U.S. industry comprises establishments primarily engaged in providing operating advice and assistance to businesses and other organizations on administrative management issues, such as financial planning and budgeting, equity and asset management, records management, office planning, strategic and organizational planning, site selection, new business startup, and business process improvement. This industry also includes establishments of general management consultants that provide a full range of administrative; human resource; marketing; process, physical distribution, and logistics; or other management consulting services to clients. 1276-1277

541612 **Human Resources Consulting Services.** This U.S. industry comprises establishments primarily engaged in providing advice and assistance to businesses and other organizations in one or more of the following areas: (1) human resource and personnel policies, practices, and procedures; (2) employee benefits planning, communication, and administration; (3) compensation systems planning; (4) wage and salary administration; and (5) executive search and recruitment. 1278-1279

541613 **Marketing Consulting Services.** This U.S. industry comprises establishments primarily engaged in providing operating advice and assistance to businesses and other organizations on marketing issues, such as developing marketing objectives and policies, sales forecasting, new product developing and pricing, licensing and franchise planning, and marketing planning and strategy. 1280-1281

541614 **Process, Physical Distribution, and Logistics Consulting Services.** This U.S. industry comprises establishments primarily engaged in providing operating advice and assistance to businesses and other organizations in areas, such as: (1) manufacturing operations improvement; (2) productivity improvement; (3) production planning and control; (4) quality assurance and quality control; (5) inventory management; (6) distribution networks; (7) warehouse use, operations, and utilization; (8) transportation and shipment of goods and materials; and (9) materials management and handling. 1282-1283

541618 **Other Management Consulting Services.** This U.S. industry comprises establishments primarily engaged in providing management consulting services (except administrative and general management consulting; human resources consulting; marketing consulting; or process, physical distribution, and logistics consulting). Establishments providing telecommunications or utilities management consulting services are included in this industry. 1284-1285

541620 **Environmental Consulting Services.** This industry comprises establishments primarily engaged in providing advice and assistance to businesses and other organizations on environmental issues, such as the control of environmental contamination from pollutants, toxic substances, and hazardous materials. These establishments identify problems (e.g. inspect buildings for hazardous materials), measure and evaluate risks, and recommend solutions. They employ a multidisciplined staff of scientists, engineers, and other technicians with expertise in areas, such as air and water quality, asbestos contamination, remediation, and environmental law. Establishments providing sanitation or site remediation consulting services are included in this industry. 1286-1287

541690 **Other Scientific and Technical Consulting Services.** This industry comprises establishments primarily engaged in providing advice and assistance to businesses and other organizations on scientific and technical issues (except environmental). 1288-1289

PROFESSIONAL SERVICES

NAICS #   **Page**

541712 **Reseach and Development in the Physical, Engineering, and Life Sciences (except Biotechnology).** This U.S. Industry comprises establishments primarily engaged in conducting research and experimental development (except biotechnology research and experimental development) in the physical, engineering, and life sciences, such as agriculture, electronics, environmental, biology, botany, computers, chemistry, food, fisheries, forests, geology, health, mathematics, medicine, oceanography, pharmacy, physics, veterinary and other allied subjects. . . 1290-1291

541720 **Research and Development in the Social Sciences and Humanities.** This industry comprises establishments primarily engaged in conducting research and analyses in cognitive development, sociology, psychology, language, behavior, economic, and other social science and humanities research. 1292-1293

541810 **Advertising Agencies.** This industry comprises establishments primarily engaged in creating advertising campaigns and placing such advertising in periodicals, newspapers, radio and television, or other media. These establishments are organized to provide a full range of services (i.e., through in-house capabilities or subcontracting), including advice, creative services, account management, production of advertising material, media planning, and buying (i.e., placing advertising). 1294-1295

541820 **Public Relations Agencies.** This industry comprises establishments primarily engaged in designing and implementing public relations campaigns. These campaigns are designed to promote the interests and image of their clients. Establishments providing lobbying, political consulting, or public relations consulting are included in this industry. 1296-1297

541840 **Media Representatives.** This industry comprises establishments of independent representatives primarily engaged in selling media time or space for media owners. 1298-1299

541850 **Display Advertising.** This industry comprises establishments primarily engaged in creating and designing public display advertising, campaign materials, such as printed, painted, or electronic displays, and/or placing such displays on indoor or outdoor billboards and panels, or on or within transit vehicles or facilities, shopping malls, retail (in-store) displays, and other display structures or sites. 1300-1301

541860 **Direct Mail Advertising.** This industry comprises establishments primarily engaged in (1) creating and designing advertising campaigns for the purpose of distributing advertising materials (e.g., coupons, flyers, samples) or specialties (e.g., key chains, magnets, pens with customized messages imprinted) by mail or other direct distribution; and/ or (2) preparing advertising materials or specialties for mailing or other direct distribution. These establishments may also compile, maintain, sell, and rent mailing lists. 1302-1303

541870 **Advertising Material Distribution Services.** This industry comprises establishments primarily engaged in the direct distribution or delivery of advertisements (e.g., circulars, coupons, handbills) or samples. Establishments in this industry use methods, such as delivering advertisements or samples door-to-door, placing flyers or coupons on car windshields in parking lots, or handing out samples in retail stores. 1304-1305

541890 **Other Services Related to Advertising.** This industry comprises establishments primarily engaged in providing advertising services (except advertising agency services, public relations agency services, media buying agency services, media representative services, display advertising services, direct mail advertising services, advertising material distribution services, and marketing consulting services). 1306-1307

541910 **Marketing Research and Public Opinion Polling.** This industry comprises establishments primarily engaged in systematically gathering, recording, tabulating, and presenting marketing and public opinion data. 1308-1309

541921 **Photography Studios, Portrait.** This U.S. industry comprises establishments known as portrait studios primarily engaged in providing still, video, or digital portrait photography services. . . 1310-1311

541922 **Commercial Photography.** This U.S. industry comprises establishments primarily engaged in providing commercial photography services, generally for advertising agencies, publishers, and other business and industrial users. 1312-1313

541940 **Veterinary Services.** This industry comprises establishments of licensed veterinary practitioners primarily engaged in the practice of veterinary medicine, dentistry, or surgery for animals; and establishments primarily engaged in providing testing services for licensed veterinary practitioners. 1314-1315

NAICS #   **Page**

541990   **All Other Professional, Scientific, and Technical Services.** This industry comprises establishments primarily engaged in the provision of professional, scientific, or technical services (except legal services; accounting, tax preparation, bookkeeping, and related services; architectural, engineering, and related services; specialized design services; computer systems design and related services; management, scientific, and technical consulting services; scientific research and development services; advertising and related services; market research and public opinion polling; photographic services; translation and interpretation services; and veterinary services). 1316-1317

MANAGEMENT OF COMPANIES AND ENTERPRISES

551111   **Offices of Bank Holding Companies.** This U.S. industry comprises legal entities known as bank holding companies primarily engaged in holding the securities of (or other equity interests in) companies and enterprises for the purpose of owning a controlling interest or influencing the management decisions of these firms. The holding companies in this industry do not administer, oversee, and manage other establishments of the company or enterprise whose securities they hold. 1320-1321

551112   **Offices of Other Holding Companies.** This U.S. industry comprises legal entities known as holding companies (except bank holding) primarily engaged in holding the securities of (or other equity interests in) companies and enterprises for the purpose of owning a controlling interest or influencing the management decisions of these firms. The holding companies in this industry do not administer, oversee, and manage other establishments of the company or enterprise whose securities they hold. 1322-1323

ADMINISTRATIVE AND SUPPORT AND WASTE MANAGEMENT AND REMEDIATION SERVICES

561110   **Office Administrative Services.** This industry comprises establishments primarily engaged in providing a range of day-to-day office administrative services, such as financial planning; billing and recordkeeping; personnel; and physical distribution and logistics for others on a contract or fee basis. These establishments do not provide operating staff to carry out the complete operations of a business. 1326-1327

561210   **Facilities Support Services.** This industry comprises establishments primarily engaged in providing operating staff to perform a combination of support services within a client's facilities. Establishments in this industry typically provide a combination of services, such as janitorial; maintenance; trash disposal; guard and security; mail routing; reception; laundry; and related services to support operations within facilities. These establishments provide operating staff to carry out these support activities; but, are not involved with or responsible for the core business or activities of the client. Establishments providing facilities (except computer and/or data processing) operation support services and establishments operating correctional facilities (i.e., jails) on a contract or fee basis are included in this industry. 1328-1329

561311   **Employment Placement Agencies.** This U.S. industry comprises establishments primarily engaged in listing employment vacancies and in referring or placing applicants for employment. The individuals referred or placed are not employees of the employment agencies. 1330-1331

561320   **Temporary Help Services.** This industry comprises establishments primarily engaged in supplying workers to clients' businesses for limited periods of time to supplement the working force of the client. The individuals provided are employees of the temporary help service establishment. However, these establishments do not provide direct supervision of their employees at the clients' work sites. 1332-1333

NAICS #   **Page**

561330 **Professional Employer Organizations.** This industry comprises establishments primarily engaged in providing human resources and human resource management services to client businesses. Establishments in this industry operate in a coemployment relationship with client businesses or organizations and are specialized in performing a wide range of human resource and personnel management duties, such as payroll, payroll tax, benefits administration, workers' compensation, unemployment, and human resource administration. Professional employer organizations (PEOs) are responsible for payroll, including withholding and remitting employment-related taxes, for some or all of the employees of their clients, and also serve as the employer of those employees for benefits and related purposes. 1334-1335

561439 **Other Business Service Centers (including Copy Shops).** This U.S. industry comprises (1) establishments generally known as copy centers or shops primarily engaged in providing photocopying, duplicating, blueprinting, and other document copying services, without also providing printing services (e.g., offset printing, quick printing, digital printing, prepress services) and (2) establishments (except private mail centers) engaged in providing a range of office support services (except printing services), such as document copying services, facsimile services, word processing services, on-site PC rental services, and office product sales. 1336-1337

561440 **Collection Agencies.** This industry comprises establishments primarily engaged in collecting payments for claims and remitting payments collected to their clients. 1338-1339

561499 **All Other Business Support Services.** This U.S. industry comprises establishments primarily engaged in providing business support services (except secretarial and other document preparation services; telephone answering and telemarketing services; private mail services or document copying services conducted as separate activities or in conjunction with other office support services; monetary debt collection services; credit reporting services; repossession services; and court reporting and stenotype recording services). 1340-1341

561510 **Travel Agencies.** This industry comprises establishments primarily engaged in acting as agents in selling travel, tour, and accommodation services to the general public and commercial clients. 1342-1343

561520 **Tour Operators.** This industry comprises establishments primarily engaged in arranging and assembling tours. The tours are sold through travel agencies or tour operators. Travel or wholesale tour operators are included in this industry. 1344-1345

561599 **All Other Travel Arrangement and Reservation Services.** This U.S. industry comprises establishments (except travel agencies, tour operators, and convention and visitors bureaus) primarily engaged in providing travel arrangement and reservation services. 1346-1347

561612 **Security Guards and Patrol Services.** This U.S. industry comprises establishments primarily engaged in providing guard and patrol services, such as bodyguard, guard dog, and parking security services. 1348-1349

561621 **Security Systems Services (except Locksmiths).** This U.S. industry comprises establishments primarily engaged in (1) selling security alarm systems, such as burglar and fire alarms, along with installation, repair, or monitoring services or (2) remote monitoring of electronic security alarm systems. 1350-1351

561710 **Exterminating and Pest Control Services.** This industry comprises establishments primarily engaged in exterminating and controlling birds, mosquitoes, rodents, termites, and other insects and pests (except for crop production and forestry production). Establishments providing fumigation services are included in this industry. 1352-1353

561720 **Janitorial Services.** This industry comprises establishments primarily engaged in cleaning building interiors, interiors of transportation equipment (e.g., aircraft, rail cars, ships), and/or windows. 1354-1355

561730 **Landscaping Services.** This industry comprises (1) establishments primarily engaged in providing landscape care and maintenance services and/or installing trees, shrubs, plants, lawns, or gardens and (2) establishments primarily engaged in providing these services along with the design of landscape plans and/or the construction (i.e., installation) of walkways, retaining walls, decks, fences, ponds, and similar structures. 1356-1357

561740 **Carpet and Upholstery Cleaning Services.** This industry comprises establishments primarily engaged in cleaning and dyeing used rugs, carpets, and upholstery. 1358-1359

NAICS #   **Page**

561790   **Other Services to Buildings and Dwellings.** This industry comprises establishments primarily engaged in providing services to buildings and dwellings (except exterminating and pest control; janitorial; landscaping care and maintenance; and carpet and upholstery cleaning). . . . 1360-1361

561910   **Packaging and Labeling Services.** This industry comprises establishments primarily engaged in packaging client-owned materials. The services may include labeling and/or imprinting the package. 1362-1363

561990   **All Other Support Services.** This industry comprises establishments primarily engaged in providing day-to-day business and other organizational support services (except office administrative services, facilities support services, employment services, business support services, travel arrangement and reservation services, security and investigation services, services to buildings and other structures, packaging and labeling services, and convention and trade show organizing services). 1364-1365

562111   **Solid Waste Collection.** This U.S. industry comprises establishments primarily engaged in one or more of the following: (1) collecting and/or hauling nonhazardous solid waste (i.e., garbage) within a local area; (2) operating nonhazardous solid waste transfer stations; and (3) collecting and/or hauling mixed recyclable materials within a local area. 1366-1367

562119   **Other Waste Collection.** This U.S. industry comprises establishments primarily engaged in collecting and/or hauling waste (except nonhazardous solid waste and hazardous waste) within a local area. Establishments engaged in brush or rubble removal services are included in this industry. 1368-1369

562211   **Hazardous Waste Treatment and Disposal.** This U.S. industry comprises establishments primarily engaged in (1) operating treatment and/or disposal facilities for hazardous waste or (2) the combined activity of collecting and/or hauling of hazardous waste materials within a local area and operating treatment or disposal facilities for hazardous waste. 1370-1371

562212   **Solid Waste Landfill.** This U.S. industry comprises establishments primarily engaged in (1) operating landfills for the disposal of nonhazardous solid waste or (2) the combined activity of collecting and/or hauling nonhazardous waste materials within a local area and operating landfills for the disposal of nonhazardous solid waste. 1372-1373

562219   **Other Nonhazardous Waste Treatment and Disposal.** This U.S. industry comprises establishments primarily engaged in (1) operating nonhazardous waste treatment and disposal facilities (except landfills, combustors, incinerators and sewer systems or sewage treatment facilities) or (2) the combined activity of collecting and/or hauling of nonhazardous waste materials within a local area and operating waste treatment or disposal facilities (except landfills, combustors, incinerators and sewer systems, or sewage treatment facilities). Compost dumps are included in this industry. 1374-1375

562910   **Remediation Services.** This industry comprises establishments primarily engaged in one or more of the following: (1) remediation and cleanup of contaminated buildings, mine sites, soil or ground water; (2) integrated mine reclamation activities, including demolition, soil remediation, waste water treatment, hazardous material removal, contouring land and revegitation; and (3) asbestos, lead paint and other toxic material abatement. 1376-1377

562920   **Materials Recovery Facilities.** This industry comprises establishments primarily engaged in (1) operating facilities for separating and sorting recyclable materials from nonhazardous waste streams (i.e., garbage) and/or (2) operating facilities where commingled recyclable materials, such as paper, plastics, used beverage cans, and metals are sorted into distinct categories. . . . 1378-1379

562998   **All Other Miscellaneous Waste Management Services.** This U.S. industry comprises establishments primarily engaged in providing waste management services (except waste collection, waste treatment and disposal, remediation, operation of materials recovery facilities, septic tank pumping and related services, and waste management consulting services). 1380-1381

EDUCATIONAL SERVICES

611110   **Elementary and Secondary Schools.** This industry comprises establishments primarily engaged in furnishing academic courses and associated course work that comprise a basic preparatory education. A basic preparatory education ordinarily constitutes kindergarten through 12th grade. This industry includes school boards and school districts. 1384-1385

HEALTH CARE

NAICS #   Page

611210 **Junior Colleges.** This industry comprises establishments primarily engaged in furnishing academic, or academic and technical, courses and granting associate degrees, certificates, or diplomas below the baccalaureate level. The requirement for admission to an associate or equivalent degree program is at least a high school diploma or equivalent general academic training. Instruction may be provided in diverse settings, such as the establishment's or client's training facilities, educational institutions, the workplace, or the home, and through correspondence, television, Internet, or other means. 1386-1387

611310 **Colleges, Universities, and Professional Schools.** This industry comprises establishments primarily engaged in furnishing academic courses and granting degrees at baccalaureate or graduate levels. The requirement for admission is at least a high school diploma or equivalent general academic training. Instruction may be provided in diverse settings, such as the establishment's or client's training facilities, educational institutions, the workplace, or the home, and through correspondence, television, Internet, or other means. 1388-1389

611430 **Professional and Management Development Training.** This industry comprises establishments primarily engaged in offering an array of short duration courses and seminars for management and professional development. Training for career development may be provided directly to individuals or through employers' training programs; and courses may be customized or modified to meet the special needs of customers. Instruction may be provided in diverse settings, such as the establishment's or client's training facilities, educational institutions, the workplace, or the home, and through correspondence, television, Internet, or other means. . . 1390-1391

611519 **Other Technical and Trade Schools.** This U.S. industry comprises establishments primarily engaged in offering job or career vocational or technical courses (except cosmetology and barber training, aviation and flight training, and apprenticeship training). The curriculums offered by these schools are highly structured and specialized and lead to job-specific certification. 1392-1393

611610 **Fine Arts Schools.** This industry comprises establishments primarily engaged in offering instruction in the arts, including dance, art, drama, and music. 1394-1395

611699 **All Other Miscellaneous Schools and Instruction.** This U.S. industry comprises establishments primarily engaged in offering instruction (except business, computer, management, technical, trade, fine arts, athletic, language instruction, tutoring, and automobile driving instruction). Also excluded from this industry are academic schools, colleges, and universities. 1396-1397

611710 **Educational Support Services.** This industry comprises establishments primarily engaged in providing noninstructional services that support educational processes or systems. 1398-1399

HEALTH CARE AND SOCIAL ASSISTANCE

621111 **Offices of Physicians (except Mental Health Specialists).** This U.S. industry comprises establishments of health practitioners having the degree of M.D. (Doctor of medicine) or D.O. (Doctor of osteopathy) primarily engaged in the independent practice of general or specialized medicine (except psychiatry or psychoanalysis) or surgery. These practitioners operate private or group practices in their own offices (e.g., centers, clinics) or in the facilities of others, such as hospitals or HMO medical centers. 1402-1403

621112 **Offices of Physicians, Mental Health Specialists.** This U.S. industry comprises establishments of health practitioners having the degree of M.D. (Doctor of medicine) or D.O. (Doctor of osteopathy) primarily engaged in the independent practice of psychiatry or psychoanalysis. These practitioners operate private or group practices in their own offices (e.g., centers, clinics) or in the facilities of others, such as hospitals or HMO medical centers. 1404-1405

621210 **Offices of Dentists.** This industry comprises establishments of health practitioners having the degree of D.M.D. (Doctor of dental medicine), D.D.S. (Doctor of dental surgery), or D.D.Sc. (Doctor of dental science) primarily engaged in the independent practice of general or specialized dentistry or dental surgery. These practitioners operate private or group practices in their own offices (e.g., centers, clinics) or in the facilities of others, such as hospitals or HMO medical centers. They can provide either comprehensive preventive, cosmetic, or emergency care, or specialize in a single field of dentistry. 1406-1407

NAICS #   **Page**

621310 **Offices of Chiropractors.** This industry comprises establishments of health practitioners having the degree of D.C. (Doctor of chiropractic) primarily engaged in the independent practice of chiropractic. These practitioners provide diagnostic and therapeutic treatment of neuromusculoskeletal and related disorders through the manipulation and adjustment of the spinal column and extremities, and operate private or group practices in their own offices (e.g., centers, clinics) or in the facilities of others, such as hospitals or HMO medical centers. 1408-1409

621320 **Offices of Optometrists.** This industry comprises establishments of health practitioners having the degree of O.D. (Doctor of optometry) primarily engaged in the independent practice of optometry. These practitioners provide eye examinations to determine visual acuity or the presence of vision problems and to prescribe eyeglasses, contact lenses, and eye exercises. They operate private or group practices in their own offices (e.g., centers, clinics) or in the facilities of others, such as hospitals or HMO medical centers, and may also provide the same service as opticians, such as selling and fitting prescription eyeglasses and contact lenses. . . . 1410-1411

621330 **Offices of Mental Health Practitioners (except Physicians).** This industry comprises establishments of independent mental health practitioners (except physicians) primarily engaged in (1) the diagnosis and treatment of mental, emotional, and behavioral disorders and/or (2) the diagnosis and treatment of individual or group social dysfunction brought about by such causes as mental illness, alcohol and substance abuse, physical and emotional trauma, or stress. These practitioners operate private or group practices in their own offices (e.g., centers, clinics) or in the facilities of others, such as hospitals or HMO medical centers. 1412-1413

621340 **Offices of Physical, Occupational and Speech Therapists, and Audiologists.** This industry comprises establishments of independent health practitioners primarily engaged in one of the following: (1) administering medically prescribed physical therapy treatment for patients suffering from injuries or muscle, nerve, joint, and bone disease; (2) planning and administering educational, recreational, and social activities designed to help patients or individuals with disabilities, regain physical or mental functioning or to adapt to their disabilities; and (3) diagnosing and treating speech, language, or hearing problems. These practitioners operate private or group practices in their own offices (e.g., centers, clinics) or in the facilities of others, such as hospitals or HMO medical centers. 1414-1415

621391 **Offices of Podiatrists.** This U.S. industry comprises establishments of health practitioners having the degree of D.P. (Doctor of podiatry) primarily engaged in the independent practice of podiatry. These practitioners diagnose and treat diseases and deformities of the foot and operate private or group practices in their own offices (e.g., centers, clinics) or in the facilities of others, such as hospitals or HMO medical centers. 1416-1417

621399 **Offices of All Other Miscellaneous Health Practitioners.** except physicians; dentists; chiropractors; optometrists; mental health specialists; physical, occupational, and speech therapists; audiologists; and podiatrists). These practitioners operate private or group practices in their own offices (e.g., centers, clinics) or in the facilities of others, such as hospitals or HMO medical centers. 1418-1419

621410 **Family Planning Centers.** This industry comprises establishments with medical staff primarily engaged in providing a range of family planning services on an outpatient basis, such as contraceptive services, genetic and prenatal counseling, voluntary sterilization, and therapeutic and medically indicated termination of pregnancy. 1420-1421

621420 **Outpatient Mental Health and Substance Abuse Centers.** This industry comprises establishments with medical staff primarily engaged in providing outpatient services related to the diagnosis and treatment of mental health disorders and alcohol and other substance abuse. These establishments generally treat patients who do not require inpatient treatment. They may provide a counseling staff and information regarding a wide range of mental health and substance abuse issues and/or refer patients to more extensive treatment programs, if necessary. 1422-1423

621491 **HMO Medical Centers.** This U.S. industry comprises establishments with physicians and other medical staff primarily engaged in providing a range of outpatient medical services to the health maintenance organization (HMO) subscribers with a focus generally on primary health care. These establishments are owned by the HMO. Included in this industry are HMO establishments that both provide health care services and underwrite health and medical insurance policies. 1424-1425

621492 **Kidney Dialysis Centers.** This U.S. industry comprises establishments with medical staff primarily engaged in providing outpatient kidney or renal dialysis services. 1426-1427

HEALTH CARE

NAICS #   **Page**

621493 **Freestanding Ambulatory Surgical and Emergency Centers.** This U.S. industry comprises establishments with physicians and other medical staff primarily engaged in (1) providing surgical services (e.g., orthoscopic and cataract surgery) on an outpatient basis or (2) providing emergency care services (e.g., setting broken bones, treating lacerations, or tending to patients suffering injuries as a result of accidents, trauma, or medical conditions necessitating immediate medical care) on an outpatient basis. Outpatient surgical establishments have specialized facilities, such as operating and recovery rooms, and specialized equipment, such as anesthetic or X-ray equipment. 1428-1429

621498 **All Other Outpatient Care Centers.** This U.S. industry comprises establishments with medical staff primarily engaged in providing general or specialized outpatient care (except family planning centers, outpatient mental health and substance abuse centers, HMO medical centers, kidney dialysis centers, and freestanding ambulatory surgical and emergency centers). Centers or clinics of health practitioners with different degrees from more than one industry practicing within the same establishment (i.e., Doctor of medicine and Doctor of dental medicine) are included in this industry. 1430-1431

621511 **Medical Laboratories.** This U.S. industry comprises establishments known as medical laboratories primarily engaged in providing analytic or diagnostic services, including body fluid analysis, generally to the medical profession or to the patient on referral from a health practitioner. 1432-1433

621512 **Diagnostic Imaging Centers.** This U.S. industry comprises establishments known as diagnostic imaging centers primarily engaged in producing images of the patient generally on referral from a health practitioner. 1434-1435

621610 **Home Health Care Services.** This industry comprises establishments primarily engaged in providing skilled nursing services in the home, along with a range of the following: personal care services; homemaker and companion services; physical therapy; medical social services; medications; medical equipment and supplies; counseling; 24-hour home care; occupation and vocational therapy; dietary and nutritional services; speech therapy; audiology; and high-tech care, such as intravenous therapy. 1436-1437

621910 **Ambulance Services.** This industry comprises establishments primarily engaged in providing transportation of patients by ground or air, along with medical care. These services are often provided during a medical emergency but are not restricted to emergencies. The vehicles are equipped with lifesaving equipment operated by medically trained personnel. 1438-1439

621991 **Blood and Organ Banks.** This U.S. industry comprises establishments primarily engaged in collecting, storing, and distributing blood and blood products and storing and distributing body organs. 1440-1441

621999 **All Other Miscellaneous Ambulatory Health Care Services.** This U.S. industry comprises establishments primarily engaged in providing ambulatory health care services (except offices of physicians, dentists, and other health practitioners; outpatient care centers; medical and diagnostic laboratories; home health care providers; ambulances; and blood and organ banks). . . 1442-1443

622110 **General Medical and Surgical Hospitals.** This industry comprises establishments known and licensed as general medical and surgical hospitals primarily engaged in providing diagnostic and medical treatment (both surgical and nonsurgical) to inpatients with any of a wide variety of medical conditions. These establishments maintain inpatient beds and provide patients with food services that meet their nutritional requirements. These hospitals have an organized staff of physicians and other medical staff to provide patient care services. These establishments usually provide other services, such as outpatient services, anatomical pathology services, diagnostic X-ray services, clinical labora-tory services, operating room services for a variety of procedures, and phar-macy services. 1444-1445

622110 **General Medical and Surgical Hospitals (Non-Profit).** This industry comprises establishments known and licensed as general medical and surgical hospitals primarily engaged in providing diagnostic and medical treatment (both surgical and nonsurgical) to inpatients with any of a wide variety of medical conditions. These establishments maintain inpatient beds and provide patients with food services that meet their nutritional requirements. These hospitals have an organized staff of physicians and other medical staff to provide patient care services. These establishments usually provide other services, such as outpatient services, anatomical pathology services, diagnostic X-ray services, clinical laboratory services, operating room services for a variety of procedures, and pharmacy services. 1446-1447

HEALTH CARE

NAICS #   Page

622210 Psychiatric and Substance Abuse Hospitals. This industry comprises establishments known and licensed as psychiatric and substance abuse hospitals primarily engaged in providing diagnostic, medical treatment, and monitoring services for inpatients who suffer from mental illness or substance abuse disorders. The treatment often requires an extended stay in the hospital. These establishments maintain inpatient beds and provide patients with food services that meet their nutritional requirements. They have an organized staff of physicians and other medical staff to provide patient care services. Psychiatric, psychological, and social work services are available at the facility. These hospitals usually provide other services, such as outpatient services, clinical laboratory services, diagnostic X-ray services, and electroencephalograph services. 1448-1449

622310 Specialty (except Psychiatric and Substance Abuse) Hospitals. This industry consists of establishments known and licensed as specialty hospi-tals primarily engaged in providing diagnostic and medical treatment to inpatients with a specific type of disease or medical condition (except psychiatric or substance abuse). Hospitals providing long-term care for the chronically ill and hospitals providing rehabilitation, restorative, and adjustive services to physically challenged or disabled people are included in this industry. These establishments maintain inpatient beds and provide patients with food services that meet their nutritional requirements. They have an organized staff of physicians and other medical staff to provide patient care services. These hospitals may provide other services, such as outpatient services, diagnostic X-ray services, clinical laboratory services, operating room services, physical therapy services, educational and vocational services, and psychological and social work services. 1450-1451

623110 Nursing Care Facilities. This industry comprises establishments primarily engaged in providing inpatient nursing and rehabilitative services. The care is generally provided for an extended period of time to individuals requiring nursing care. These establishments have a permanent core staff of registered or licensed practical nurses who, along with other staff, provide nursing and continuous personal care services. 1452-1453

623210 Residential Mental Retardation Facilities. This industry comprises establishments (e.g. group homes, hospitals, intermediate care facilities) primarily engaged in providing residential care services for persons diagnosed with mental retardation. These facilities may provide some health care, though the focus is on room, board, protective supervision, and counseling. . . . 1454-1455

623220 Residential Mental Health and Substance Abuse Facilities. This industry comprises establishments primarily engaged in providing residential care and treatment for patients with mental health and substance abuse illnesses. These establishments provide room, board, supervision, and counseling services. Although medical services may be available at these establishments, they are incidental to the counseling, mental rehabilitation, and support services offered. These establishments generally provide a wide range of social services in addition to counseling. . . . 1456-1457

623311 Continuing Care Retirement Communities. This U.S. industry comprises establishments primarily engaged in providing a range of residential and personal care services with on-site nursing care facilities for (1) the elderly and other persons who are unable to fully care for themselves and/or (2) the elderly and other persons who do not desire to live independently. Individuals live in a variety of residential settings with meals, housekeeping, social, leisure, and other services available to assist residents in daily living. Assistedliving facilities with on-site nursing care facilities are included in this industry. 1458-1459

623312 Homes for the Elderly. This U.S. industry comprises establishments primarily engaged in providing residential and personal care services (i.e., without on-site nursing care facilities) for (1) the elderly or other persons who are unable to fully care for themselves and/or (2) the elderly or other persons who do not desire to live independently. The care typically includes room, board, supervision, and assistance in daily living, such as housekeeping services. 1460-1461

623990 Other Residential Care Facilities. This industry comprises establishments primarily engaged in providing residential care (except residential mental retardation facilities, residential health and substance abuse facilities, continuing care retirement communities, and homes for the elderly). These establishments also provide supervision and personal care services. 1462-1463

624110 Child and Youth Services. This industry comprises establishments primarily engaged in providing nonresidential social assistance services for children and youth. These establishments provide for the welfare of children in such areas as adoption and foster care, drug prevention, life skills training, and positive social development. 1464-1465

NAICS #   **Page**

624120   Services for the Elderly and Persons with Disabilities. This industry comprises establishments primarily engaged in providing nonresidential social assistance services to improve the quality of life for the elderly, persons diagnosed with mental retardation, or persons with disabilities. These establishments provide for the welfare of these individuals in such areas as day care, nonmedical home care or homemaker services, social activities, group support, and companionship. 1466-1467

624190   Other Individual and Family Services. This industry comprises establishments primarily engaged in providing nonresidential individual and family social assistance services (except those specifically directed toward children, the elderly, persons diagnosed with mental retardation, or persons with disabilities). 1468-1469

624210   Community Food Services. This industry comprises establishments primarily engaged in the collection, preparation, and delivery of food for the needy. Establishments in this industry may also distribute clothing and blankets to the poor. These establishments may prepare and deliver meals to persons who by reason of age, disability, or illness are unable to prepare meals for themselves; collect and distribute salvageable or donated food; or prepare and provide meals at fixed or mobile locations. Food banks, meal delivery programs, and soup kitchens are included in this industry. 1470-1471

624221   Temporary Shelters. This U.S. industry comprises establishments primarily engaged in providing (1) short term emergency shelter for victims of domestic violence, sexual assault, or child abuse and/or (2) temporary residential shelter for homeless individuals or families, runaway youth, and patients and families caught in medical crises. These establishments may operate their own shelters or may subsidize housing using existing homes, apartments, hotels, or motels. 1472-1473

624229   Other Community Housing Services. This U.S. industry comprises establishments primarily engaged in providing one or more of the following community housing services: (1) transitional housing to low-income individuals and families; (2) volunteer construction or repair of lowcost housing, in partnership with the homeowner who may assist in the construction or repair work; and (3) the repair of homes for elderly or disabled homeowners. These establishments may subsidize housing using existing homes, apartments, hotels, or motels or may require a low-cost mortgage or sweat equity. These establishments may also provide low-income families with furniture and household supplies. 1474-1475

624310   Vocational Rehabilitation Services. This industry comprises (1) establishments primarily engaged in providing vocational rehabilitation or habilitation services, such as job counseling, job training, and work experience, to unemployed and underemployed persons, persons with disabilities, and persons who have a job market disadvantage because of lack of education, job skill, or experience and (2) establishments primarily engaged in providing training and employment to persons with disabilities. Vocational rehabilitation job training facilities (except schools) and sheltered workshops (i.e., work experience centers) are included in this industry. 1476-1477

624410   Child Day Care Services. This industry comprises establishments primarily engaged in providing day care of infants or children. These establishments generally care for preschool children, but may care for older children when they are not in school and may also offer prekindergarten educational programs. 1478-1479

ARTS, ENTERTAINMENT, AND RECREATION

711110   Theater Companies and Dinner Theaters. This industry comprises (1) companies, groups, or theaters primarily engaged in producing the following live theatrical presentations: musicals; operas; plays; and comedy, improvisational, mime, and puppet shows and (2) establishments, commonly known as dinner theaters, engaged in producing live theatrical productions and in providing food and beverages for consumption on the premises. Theater groups or companies may or may not operate their own theater or other facility for staging their shows. 1482-1483

711130   Musical Groups and Artists. This industry comprises (1) groups primarily engaged in producing live musical entertainment (except theatrical musical or opera productions) and (2) independent (i.e., freelance) artists primarily engaged in providing live musical entertainment. Musical groups and artists may perform in front of a live audience or in a studio, and may or may not operate their own facilities for staging their shows. 1484-1485

NAICS #   **Page**

711211   **Sports Teams and Clubs.** This U.S. industry comprises professional or semiprofessional sports teams or clubs primarily engaged in participating in live sporting events, such as baseball, basketball, football, hockey, soccer, and jai alai games, before a paying audience. These establishments may or may not operate their own arena, stadium, or other facility for presenting these events. 1486-1487

711212   **Racetracks.** This U.S. industry comprises establishments primarily engaged in operating racetracks. These establishments may also present and /or promote the events, such as auto, dog, and horse races, held in these facilities. 1488-1489

711310   **Promoters of Performing Arts, Sports, and Similar Events with Facilities.** This industry comprises establishments primarily engaged in (1) organizing, promoting, and/or managing live performing arts productions, sports events, and similar events, such as state fairs, county fairs, agricultural fairs, concerts, and festivals, held in facilities that they manage and operate and/or (2) managing and providing the staff to operate arenas, stadiums, theaters, or other related facilities for rent to other promoters. 1490-1491

712110   **Museums.** This industry comprises establishments primarily engaged in the preservation and exhibition of objects of historical, cultural, and/or educational value. 1492-1493

713110   **Amusement and Theme Parks.** This industry comprises establishments, known as amusement or theme parks, primarily engaged in operating a variety of attractions, such as mechanical rides, water rides, games, shows, theme exhibits, refreshment stands, and picnic grounds. These establishments may lease space to others on a concession basis. 1494-1495

713120   **Amusement Arcades.** This industry comprises establishments primarily engaged in operating amusement (except gambling, billiard, or pool) arcades and parlors. 1496-1497

713210   **Casinos (except Casino Hotels).** This industry comprises establishments primarily engaged in operating gambling facilities that offer table wagering games along with other gambling activities, such as slot machines and sports betting. These establishments often provide food and beverage services. Included in this industry are floating casinos (i.e., gambling cruises, riverboat casinos). 1498-1499

713910   **Golf Courses and Country Clubs.** This industry comprises (1) establishments primarily engaged in operating golf courses (except miniature) and (2) establishments primarily engaged in operating golf courses, along with dining facilities and other recreational facilities that are known as country clubs. These establishments often provide food and beverage services, equipment rental services, and golf instruction services. 1500-1501

713920   **Skiing Facilities.** This industry comprises establishments primarily engaged in (1) operating downhill, cross-country, or related skiing areas and/or (2) operating equipment, such as ski lifts and tows. These establishments often provide food and beverage services, equipment rental services, and ski instruction services. Four season resorts without accommodations are included in this industry. 1502-1503

713930   **Marinas.** This industry comprises establishments, commonly known as marinas, engaged in operating docking and/or storage facilities for pleasure craft owners, with or without one or more related activities, such as retailing fuel and marine supplies; and repairing, maintaining, or renting pleasure boats. 1504-1505

713940   **Fitness and Recreational Sports Centers.** This industry comprises establishments primarily engaged in operating fitness and recreational sports facilities featuring exercise and other active physical fitness conditioning or recreational sports activities, such as swimming, skating, or racquet sports. 1506-1507

713950   **Bowling Centers.** This industry comprises establishments engaged in operating bowling centers. These establishments often provide food and beverage services. 1508-1509

713990   **All Other Amusement and Recreation Industries.** This industry comprises establishments (except amusement parks and arcades; gambling industries; golf courses and country clubs; skiing facilities; marinas; fitness and recreational sports centers; and bowling centers) primarily engaged in providing recreational and amusement services. 1510-1511

ACCOMMODATION AND FOOD SERVICES

721110 **Hotels (except Casino Hotels) and Motels.** This industry comprises establishments primarily engaged in providing short-term lodging in facilities known as hotels, motor hotels, resort hotels, and motels. The establishments in this industry may offer food and beverage services, recreational services, conference rooms and convention services, laundry services, parking, and other services. 1514-1515

721120 **Casino Hotels.** This industry comprises establishments primarily engaged in providing short-term lodging in hotel facilities with a casino on the premises. The casino on premises includes table wagering games and may include other gambling activities, such as slot machines and sports betting. These establishments generally offer a range of services and amenities, such as food and beverage services, entertainment, valet parking, swimming pools, and conference and convention facilities. 1516-1517

721211 **RV (Recreational Vehicle) Parks and Campgrounds.** This U.S. industry comprises establishments primarily engaged in operating sites to accommodate campers and their equipment, including tents, tent trailers, travel trailers, and RVs (recreational vehicles). These establishments may provide access to facilities, such as washrooms, laundry rooms, recreation halls and playgrounds, stores, and snack bars. 1518-1519

721214 **Recreational and Vacation Camps (except Campgrounds).** This U.S. industry comprises establishments primarily engaged in operating overnight recreational camps, such as children's camps, family vacation camps, hunting and fishing camps, and outdoor adventure retreats that offer trail riding, white-water rafting, hiking, and similar activities. These establishments provide accommodation facilities, such as cabins and fixed campsites, and other amenities, such as food services, recreational facilities and equipment, and organized recreational activities. 1520-1521

722110 **Full-Service Restaurants.** This industry comprises establishments primarily engaged in providing food services to patrons who order and are served while seated (i.e. waiter/waitress service) and pay after eating. These establishments may provide this type of food services to patrons in combination with selling alcoholic beverages, providing carry out services, or presenting live nontheatrical entertainment. 1522-1523

722211 **Limited-Service Restaurants.** This U.S. industry comprises establishments primarily engaged in providing food services (except snack and nonalcoholic beverage bars) where patrons generally order or select items and pay before eating. Food and drink may be consumed on premises, taken out, or delivered to the customer's location. Some establishments in this industry may provide these food services in combination with selling alcoholic beverages. . . . 1524-1525

722213 **Snack and Nonalcoholic Beverage Bars.** This U.S. industry comprises establishments primarily engaged in (1) preparing and/or serving a specialty snack, such as ice cream, frozen yogurt, cookies, or popcorn or (2) serving nonalcoholic beverages, such as coffee, juices, or sodas for consumption on or near the premises. These establishments may carry and sell a combination of snack, nonalcoholic beverage, and other related products (e.g., coffee beans, mugs, coffee makers) but generally promote and sell a unique snack or nonalcoholic beverage. 1526-1527

722310 **Food Service Contractors.** This industry comprises establishments primarily engaged in providing food services at institutional, governmental, commercial, or industrial locations of others based on contractual arrangements with these type of organizations for a specified period of time. The establishments of this industry provide food services for the convenience of the contracting organization or the contracting organization's customers. The contractual arrangement of these establishments with contracting organizations may vary from type of facility operated (e.g., cafeteria, restaurant, fast-food eating place), revenue sharing, cost structure, to providing personnel. Management staff is always provided by the food service contractors. . . 1528-1529

722320 **Caterers.** This industry comprises establishments primarily engaged in providing single event-based food services. These establishments generally have equipment and vehicles to transport meals and snacks to events and/or prepare food at an off-premise site. Banquet halls with catering staff are included in this industry. Examples of events catered by establishments of this industry are graduation parties, wedding receptions, business or retirement luncheons, and trade shows. 1530-1531

722410 **Drinking Places (Alcoholic Beverages).** This industry comprises establishments known as bars, taverns, nightclubs, or drinking places primarily engaged in preparing and serving alcoholic beverages for immediate consumption. These establishments may also provide limited food services. 1532-1533

OTHER SERVICES (EXCEPT PUBLIC ADMINISTRATION)

811111 **General Automotive Repair.** This U.S. industry comprises establishments primarily engaged in providing (1) a wide range of mechanical and electrical repair and maintenance services for automotive vehicles, such as passenger cars, trucks, and vans, and all trailers or (2) engine repair and replacement. 1536-1537

811112 **Automotive Exhaust System Repair.** This U.S. industry comprises establishments primarily engaged in replacing or repairing exhaust systems of automotive vehicles, such as passenger cars, trucks, and vans. 1538-1539

811118 **Other Automotive Mechanical and Electrical Repair and Maintenance.** This U.S. industry comprises establishments primarily engaged in providing specialized mechanical or electrical repair and maintenance services (except engine repair and replacement, exhaust systems repair, and transmission repair) for automotive vehicles, such as passenger cars, trucks, and vans, and all trailers. 1540-1541

811121 **Automotive Body, Paint, and Interior Repair and Maintenance.** This U.S. industry comprises establishments primarily engaged in repairing or customizing automotive vehicles, such as passenger cars, trucks, and vans, and all trailer bodies and interiors; and/or painting automotive vehicles and trailer bodies. 1542-1543

811122 **Automotive Glass Replacement Shops.** This U.S. industry comprises establishments primarily engaged in replacing, repairing, and/or tinting automotive vehicle, such as passenger car, truck, and van, glass. 1544-1545

811191 **Automotive Oil Change and Lubrication Shops.** This U.S. industry comprises establishments primarily engaged in changing motor oil and lubricating the chassis of automotive vehicles, such as passenger cars, trucks, and vans. 1546-1547

811192 **Car Washes.** This U.S. industry comprises establishments primarily engaged in cleaning, washing, and/or waxing automotive vehicles, such as passenger cars, trucks, and vans, and trailers. 1548-1549

811198 **All Other Automotive Repair and Maintenance.** This U.S. industry comprises establishments primarily engaged in providing automotive repair and maintenance services (except mechanical and electrical repair and maintenance; body, paint, interior, and glass repair; motor oil change and lubrication; and car washing) for automotive vehicles, such as passenger cars, trucks, and vans, and all trailers. 1550-1551

811212 **Computer and Office Machine Repair and Maintenance.** This U.S. industry comprises establishments primarily engaged in repairing and maintaining computers and office machines without retailing new computers and office machines, such as photocopying machines; and computer terminals, storage devices, printers; and CD-ROM drives. 1552-1553

811219 **Other Electronic and Precision Equipment Repair and Maintenance.** This U.S. industry comprises establishments primarily engaged in repairing and maintaining (without retailing) electronic and precision equipment (except consumer electronics, computers and office machines, and communications equipment). Establishments in this industry repair and maintain equipment, such as medical diagnostic imaging equipment, measuring and surveying instruments, laboratory instruments, and radar and sonar equipment. 1554-1555

811310 **Commercial and Industrial Machinery and Equipment (except Automotive and Electronic) Repair and Maintenance.** This industry comprises establishments primarily engaged in the repair and maintenance of commercial and industrial machinery and equipment. Establishments in this industry either sharpen/install commercial and industrial machinery blades and saws or provide welding (e.g., automotive, general) repair services; or repair agricultural and other heavy and industrial machinery and equipment (e.g., forklifts and other materials handling equipment, machine tools, commercial refrigeration equipment, construction equipment, and mining machinery). 1556-1557

811412 **Appliance Repair and Maintenance.** This U.S. industry comprises establishments primarily engaged in repairing and servicing household appliances without retailing new appliances, such as refrigerators, stoves, washing machines, clothes dryers, and room air-conditioners. . . . 1558-1559

OTHER SERVICES

NAICS #   **Page**

811490 **Other Personal and Household Goods Repair and Maintenance.** This industry comprises establishments primarily engaged in repairing and servicing personal or household-type goods without retailing new personal and household-type goods (except home and garden equipment, appliances, furniture, and footwear and leather goods). Establishments in this industry repair items, such as garments; watches; jewelry; musical instruments; bicycles and motorcycles; motorboats, canoes, sailboats, and other recreational boats. 1560-1561

812112 **Beauty Salons.** This U.S. industry comprises establishments (except those known as barber shops or men's hair stylist shops) primarily engaged in one or more of the following: (1) cutting, trimming, shampooing, weaving, coloring, waving, or styling hair; (2) providing facials; and (3) applying makeup (except permanent makeup). 1562-1563

812210 **Funeral Homes and Funeral Services.** This industry comprises establishments primarily engaged in preparing the dead for burial or interment and conducting funerals (i.e., providing facilities for wakes, arranging transportation for the dead, selling caskets and related merchandise). Funeral homes combined with crematories are included in this industry. 1564-1565

812220 **Cemeteries and Crematories.** This industry comprises establishments primarily engaged in operating sites or structures reserved for the interment of human or animal remains and/or cremating the dead. 1566-1567

812310 **Coin-Operated Laundries and Drycleaners.** This industry comprises (1) establishments primarily engaged in operating facili-ties with coin-operated or similar self-service laundry and drycleaning equipment for customer use on the premises and (2) establishments primarily engaged in supplying and servicing coin-operated or similar self-service laundry and drycleaning equipment for customer use in places of business operated by others, such as apartments and dormitories. 1568-1569

812320 **Drycleaning and Laundry Services (except Coin-Operated).** This industry comprises establishments primarily engaged in one or more of the following: (1) providing drycleaning services (except coin-operated); (2) providing laundering services (except linen and uniform supply or coin-operated); (3) providing dropoff and pickup sites for laundries and/or drycleaners; and (4) providing specialty cleaning services for specific types of garments and other textile items (except carpets and upholstery), such as fur, leather, or suede garments; wedding gowns; hats; draperies; and pillows. These establishments may provide all, a combination of, or none of the cleaning services on the premises. 1570-1571

812331 **Linen Supply.** This U.S. industry comprises establishments primarily engaged in supplying, on a rental or contract basis, laundered items, such as table and bed linens; towels; diapers; and uniforms, gowns, or coats of the type used by doctors, nurses, barbers, beauticians, and waitresses. 1572-1573

812910 **Pet Care (except Veterinary) Services.** This industry comprises establishments primarily engaged in providing pet care services (except veterinary), such as boarding, grooming, sitting, and training pets. 1574-1575

812921 **Photofinishing Laboratories (except One-Hour).** This U.S. industry comprises establishments (except those known as "onehour" photofinishing labs) primarily engaged in developing film and/or making photographic slides, prints, and enlargements. 1576-1577

812930 **Parking Lots and Garages.** This industry comprises establishments primarily engaged in providing parking space for motor vehicles, usually on an hourly, daily, or monthly basis and/or valet parking services. 1578-1579

812990 **All Other Personal Services.** This industry comprises establishments primarily engaged in providing personal services (except personal care services, death care services, drycleaning and laundry services, pet care services, photofinishing services, or parking space and/or valet parking services). 1580-1581

813110 **Religious Organizations.** This industry comprises (1) establishments primarily engaged in operating reli-gious organizations, such as churches, religious temples, and monasteries and/or (2) establishments primarily engaged in administering an organized religion or promoting religious activities. 1582-1583

813211 **Grantmaking Foundations.** This U.S. industry comprises establishments known as grantmaking foundations or charitable trusts. Establishments in this industry award grants from trust funds based on a competitive selection process or the preferences of the foundation managers and grantors; or fund a single entity, such as a museum or university. 1584-1585

PUBLIC ADMINISTRATION

NAICS #   **Page**

813212 **Voluntary Health Organizations.** This U.S. industry comprises establishments primarily engaged in raising funds for health related research, such as disease (e.g., heart, cancer, diabetes) prevention, health education, and patient services. 1586-1587

813219 **Other Grantmaking and Giving Services.** This U.S. industry comprises establishments (except voluntary health organizations) primarily engaged in raising funds for a wide range of social welfare activities, such as educational, scientific, cultural, and health. 1588-1589

813319 **Other Social Advocacy Organizations.** This U.S. industry comprises establishments primarily engaged in social advocacy (except human rights and environmental protection, conservation, and wildlife preservation). Establishments in this industry address issues, such as peace and international understanding; community action (excluding civic organizations); or advancing social causes, such as firearms safety, drunk driving prevention, drug abuse awareness. These organizations may solicit contributions and offer memberships to support these causes. . . . 1590-1591

813410 **Civic and Social Organizations.** This industry comprises establishments primarily engaged in promoting the civic and social interests of their members. Establishments in this industry may operate bars and restaurants for their members. 1592-1593

813910 **Business Associations.** This industry comprises establishments primarily engaged in promoting the business interests of their members. These establishments may conduct research on new products and services; develop market statistics; sponsor quality and certification standards; lobby public officials; or publish newsletters, books, or periodicals for distribution to their members. 1594-1595

813920 **Professional Organizations.** This industry comprises establishments primarily engaged in promoting the professional interests of their members and the profession as a whole. These establishments may conduct research; develop statistics; sponsor quality and certi-fication standards; lobby public officials; or publish newsletters, books, or periodicals for distribution to their members. 1596-1597

813930 **Labor Unions and Similar Labor Organizations.** This industry comprises establishments primarily engaged in promoting the interests of organized labor and union employees. 1598-1599

813990 **Other Similar Organizations (except Business, Professional, Labor, and Political Organizations).** This industry comprises establishments (except religious organizations, social advocacy organizations, civic and social organizations, business associations, professional organizations, labor unions, and political organizations) primarily engaged in promoting the interest of their members. 1600-1601

814110 **Private Households.** This industry comprises private households primarily engaged in employing workers on or about the premises in activities primarily concerned with the operation of the household. These private households may employ individuals, such as cooks, maids, nannies, and butlers, and outside workers, such as gardeners, caretakers, and other maintenance workers. 1602-1603

PUBLIC ADMINISTRATION

921110 **Executive Offices.** This industry comprises government establishments serving as offices of chief executives and their advisory committees and commissions. This industry includes offices of the president, governors, and mayors, in addition to executive advisory commissions. 1606-1607

921120 **Legislative Bodies.** This industry comprises government establishments serving as legislative bodies and their advisory committees and commissions. Included in this industry are legislative bodies, such as Congress, state legislatures, and advisory and study legislative commissions. 1608-1609

921140 **Executive and Legislative Offices, Combined.** This industry comprises government establishments serving as councils and boards of commissioners or supervisors and such bodies where the chief executive (e.g., county executive or city mayor) is a member of the legislative body (e.g., county or city council) itself. 1610-1611

921150 **American Indian and Alaska Native Tribal Governments.** This industry comprises American Indian and Alaska Native governing bodies. Establishments in this industry perform legislative, judicial, and administrative functions for their American Indian and Alaska Native lands. Included in this industry are American Indian and Alaska Native councils, courts, and law enforcement bodies. 1612-1613

CONSTRUCTION-% OF COMPLETION

NAICS #   **Page**

921190   **Other General Government Support.** This industry comprises government establishments primarily engaged in providing general support for government. Such support services include personnel services, election boards, and other general government support establishments that are not classified elsewhere in public administration. 1614-1615

922160   **Fire Protection.** This industry comprises government establishments primarily engaged in fire fighting and other related fire protection activities. Government establishments providing combined fire protection and ambulance or rescue services are classified in this industry. . . 1616-1617

923110   **Administration of Education Programs.** This industry comprises government establishments primarily engaged in the central coordination, planning, supervision and administration of funds, policies, intergovernmental activities, statistical reports and data collection, and central-ized programs for educational administration. Government scholarship programs are included in this industry. 1618-1619

923120   **Administration of Public Health Programs.** This industry comprises government establish-ments primarily engaged in the planning, administration, and coordination of public health pro-grams and services, including environmental health activities, mental health, categorical health programs, health statistics, and immunization services. Government establishments primarily engaged in conducting public health-related inspections are included in this industry. 1620-1621

924110   **Administration of Air and Water Resource and Solid Waste Management Programs.** This in-dustry comprises government establishments primarily engaged in one or more of the follow-ing: (1) the administration, regulation, and enforcement of air and water resource programs; (2) the administration and regulation of solid waste management programs; (3) the adminis-tration and regulation of water and air pollution control and prevention programs; (4) the ad-ministration and regulation of flood control programs; (5) the administration and regulation of drainage development and water resource consumption programs; (6) the administration and regulation of toxic waste removal and cleanup programs; and (7) coordination of these activi-ties at intergovernmental levels. 1622-1623

925110   **Administration of Housing Programs.** This industry comprises government establishments primarily engaged in the administration and planning of housing programs. 1624-1625

925120   **Administration of Urban Planning and Community and Rural Development.** This industry comprises government establishments primarily engaged in the administration and planning of the development of urban and rural areas. Included in this industry are government zoning boards and commissions. 1626-1627

926110   **Administration of General Economic Programs.** This industry comprises government estab-lishments primarily engaged in the administration, promotion and development of economic resources, including business, industry, and tourism. Included in this industry are government establishments responsible for the development of general statistical data and analyses and promotion of the general economic well-being of the governed area. 1628-1629

CONSTRUCTION—PERCENTAGE OF COMPLETION

213112   **Support Activities for Oil and Gas Operations.** This U.S. industry comprises establishments primarily engaged in performing support activities on a contract or fee basis for oil and gas operations (except site preparation and related construction activities). Services included are exploration (except geophysical surveying and mapping); excavating slush pits and cellars, well surveying; running, cutting, and pulling casings, tubes, and rods; cementing wells, shoot-ing wells; perforating well casings; acidizing and chemically treating wells; and cleaning out, bailing, and swabbing wells. 1632

236115   **New Single-Family Housing Construction (except Operative Builders).** This U.S. industry com-prises general contractor establishments primarily responsible for the entire construction of new single-family housing, such as single-family detached houses and town houses or row houses where each housing unit (1) is separated from its neighbors by a ground-to-roof wall and (2) has no housing units constructed above or below. This industry includes general con-tractors respon-sible for the on-site assembly of modular and prefabricated houses. Single-family housing design-build firms and single-family construction management firms acting as general contractors are included in this industry. 1633

CONSTRUCTION-% OF COMPLETION

NAICS #   **Page**

236116   **New Multifamily Housing Construction (except Operative Builders).** This U.S. industry comprises general contractor establishments responsible for the construction of new multifamily residential housing units (e.g., high-rise, garden, and town house apartments and condominiums where each unit is not separated from its neighbors by a ground-to-roof wall). Multifamily design-build firms and multifamily housing construction management firms acting as general contractors are included in this industry.   1634

236117   **New Housing Operative Builders.** This U.S. industry comprises operative builders primarily responsible for the entire construction of new houses and other residential buildings, single-family and multifamily, on their own account for sale. Operative builders are also known as speculative or merchant builders.   1635

236118   **Residential Remodelers.** This U.S. industry comprises establishments primarily responsible for the remodeling construction (including additions, alterations, reconstruction, maintenance and repair work) of houses and other residential buildings, single-family and multifamily. Included in this industry are remodeling general contractors, operative remodelers, remodeling design-build firms, and remodeling project construction management firms.   1636

236210   **Industrial Building Construction.** This industry comprises establishments primarily responsible for the construction (including new work, additions, alterations, maintenance, and repairs) of industrial buildings (except warehouses). The construction of selected additional structures, whose production processes are similar to those for industrial buildings (e.g., incinerators, cement plants, blast furnaces, and similar nonbuilding structures), is included in this industry. Included in this industry are industrial building general contractors, industrial building operative builders, industrial building design-build firms, and industrial building construction management firms.   1637

236220   **Commercial and Institutional Building Construction.** This industry comprises establishments primarily responsible for the construction (including new work, additions, alterations, maintenance, and repairs) of commercial and institutional buildings and related structures, such as stadiums, grain elevators, and indoor swimming pools. This industry includes establishments responsible for the on-site assembly of modular or prefabricated commercial and institutional buildings. Included in this industry are commercial and institutional building general contractors, commercial and institutional building operative builders, commercial and institutional building design-build firms, and commercial and institutional building project construction management firms.   1638

237110   **Water and Sewer Line and Related Structures Construction.** This industry comprises establishments primarily engaged in the construction of water and sewer lines, mains, pumping stations, treatment plants and storage tanks. The work performed may include new work, reconstruction, rehabilitation, and repairs. Specialty trade contractors are included in this group if they are engaged in activities primarily related to water and sewer line and related structures construction. All structures (including buildings) that are integral parts of water and sewer networks (e.g., storage tanks, pumping stations, water treatment plants, and sewage treatment plants) are included in this industry.   1639

237210   **Land Subdivision.** This industry comprises establishments primarily engaged in servicing land and subdividing real property into lots, for subsequent sale to builders. Servicing of land may include excavation work for the installation of roads and utility lines. The extent of work may vary from project to project. Land subdivision precedes building activity and the subsequent building is often residential, but may also be commercial tracts and industrial parks. These establishments may do all the work themselves or subcontract the work to others. Establishments that perform only the legal subdivision of land are not included in this industry.   1640

237310   **Highway, Street, and Bridge Construction.** This industry comprises establishments primarily engaged in the construction of highways (including elevated), streets, roads, airport runways, public sidewalks, or bridges. The work performed may include new work, reconstruction, rehabilitation, and repairs. Specialty trade contractors are included in this group if they are engaged in activities primarily related to highway, street, and bridge construction (e.g., installing guardrails on highways).   1641

CONSTRUCTION-% OF COMPLETION

NAICS #		Page
237990	**Other Heavy and Civil Engineering Construction.** This industry comprises establishments primarily engaged in heavy and engineering construction projects (excluding highway, street, bridge, and distribution line construction). The work performed may include new work, reconstruction, rehabilitation, and repairs. Specialty trade contractors are included in this group if they are engaged in activities primarily related to engineering construction projects (excluding highway, street, bridge, distribution line, oil and gas structure, and utilities building and structure construction). Construction projects involving water resources (e.g., dredging and land drainage), development of marine facilities, and projects involving open space improvement (e.g., parks and trails) are included in this industry.	1642
238110	**Poured Concrete Foundation and Structure Contractors.** This industry comprises establishments primarily engaged in pouring and finishing concrete foundations and structural elements. This industry also includes establishments performing grout and shotcrete work. The work performed may include new work, additions, alterations, maintenance, and repairs.	1643
238120	**Structural Steel and Precast Concrete Contractors.** This industry comprises establishments primarily engaged in: (1) erecting and assembling structural parts made from steel or precast concrete (e.g., steel beams, structural steel components, and similar products of precast concrete); and/or (2) assembling and installing other steel construction products (e.g., steel rods, bars, rebar, mesh, and cages) to reinforce poured-in-place concrete. The work performed may include new work, additions, alterations, maintenance, and repairs.	1644
238140	**Masonry Contractors.** This industry comprises establishments primarily engaged in masonry work, stone setting, brick laying, and other stone work. The work performed may include new work, additions, alterations, maintenance, and repairs.	1645
238150	**Glass and Glazing Contractors.** This industry comprises establishments primarily engaged in installing glass panes in prepared openings (i.e., glazing work) and other glass work for buildings. The work performed may include new work, additions, alterations, maintenance, and repairs.	1646
238160	**Roofing Contractors.** This industry comprises establishments primarily engaged in roofing. This industry also includes establishments treating roofs (i.e., spraying, painting, or coating) and installing skylights. The work performed may include new work, additions, alterations, maintenance, and repairs.	1647
238210	**Electrical Contractors.** This industry comprises establishments primarily engaged in installing and servicing electrical wiring and equipment. Electrical contractors included in this industry may include both the parts and labor when performing work. Electrical contractors may perform new work, additions, alterations, maintenance, and repairs.	1648
238220	**Plumbing, Heating, and Air-Conditioning Contractors.** This industry comprises establishments primarily engaged in installing and servicing plumbing, heating, and air-conditioning equipment. Contractors in this industry may provide both parts and labor when performing work. The work performed may include new work, additions, alterations, maintenance, and repairs.	1649
238310	**Drywall and Insulation Contractors.** This industry comprises establishments primarily engaged in drywall, plaster work, and building insulation work. Plaster work includes applying plain or ornamental plaster, and installation of lath to receive plaster. The work performed may include new work, additions, alterations, maintenance, and repairs.	1650
238320	**Painting and Wall Covering Contractors.** This industry comprises establishments primarily engaged in interior or exterior painting or interior wall covering. The work performed may include new work, additions, alterations, maintenance, and repairs.	1651
238910	**Site Preparation Contractors.** This industry comprises establishments primarily engaged in site preparation activities, such as excavating and grading, demolition of buildings and other structures, septic system installation, and house moving. Earth moving and land clearing for all types of sites (e.g., building, nonbuilding, mining) is included in this industry. Establishments primarily engaged in construction equipment rental with operator (except cranes) are also included.	1652
238990	**All Other Specialty Trade Contractors.** This industry comprises establishments primarily engaged in specialized trades (except foundation, structure, and building exterior contractors; building equipment contractors; building finishing contractors; and site preparation contractors). The specialty trade work performed includes new work, additions, alterations, maintenance, and repairs.	1653

AGRICULTURE, FORESTRY, FISHING AND HUNTING

Current Data Sorted by Assets							Comparative Historical Data	
	2	4	2	2		**Type of Statement** Unqualified	2	4
		1	1			Reviewed	1	5
	4	2	2			Compiled	2	4
11	9	2				Tax Returns	1	3
7	7	9	1	1		Other	8	4
	12 (4/1-9/30/09)		55 (10/1/09-3/31/10)				4/1/05-3/31/06 ALL	4/1/06-3/31/07 ALL
0-500M	500M-2MM	2-10MM	10-50MM	50-100MM	100-250MM			
18	22	18	6	3		NUMBER OF STATEMENTS	14	20
%	%	%	%	%	%	**ASSETS**	%	%
28.5	11.1	8.0			DATA NOT AVAILABLE	Cash & Equivalents	5.2	11.7
3.7	12.1	19.6				Trade Receivables (net)	15.3	26.3
10.3	13.3	19.2				Inventory	21.0	15.8
5.2	2.0	4.4				All Other Current	2.6	2.0
47.7	38.5	51.3				Total Current	44.2	55.8
42.7	44.9	37.8				Fixed Assets (net)	33.6	37.1
7.0	3.9	4.7				Intangibles (net)	3.5	1.3
2.5	12.7	6.1				All Other Non-Current	18.7	5.8
100.0	100.0	100.0				Total	100.0	100.0
						LIABILITIES		
30.3	9.1	7.5				Notes Payable-Short Term	17.2	12.3
5.3	5.6	1.7				Cur. Mat.-L.T.D.	1.2	3.9
4.9	8.7	6.9				Trade Payables	11.0	12.1
.0	.0	.2				Income Taxes Payable	.4	.0
5.3	6.4	8.6				All Other Current	8.2	6.0
45.8	29.9	24.8				Total Current	38.1	34.4
56.6	32.5	27.8				Long-Term Debt	11.9	26.3
.0	.1	.7				Deferred Taxes	1.3	.2
3.5	1.7	3.2				All Other Non-Current	2.5	9.1
-6.0	35.8	43.6				Net Worth	46.3	30.0
100.0	100.0	100.0				Total Liabilties & Net Worth	100.0	100.0
						INCOME DATA		
100.0	100.0	100.0				Net Sales	100.0	100.0
						Gross Profit		
89.4	79.4	87.4				Operating Expenses	96.0	96.3
10.6	20.6	12.6				Operating Profit	4.0	3.7
3.0	12.2	5.4				All Other Expenses (net)	2.1	1.9
7.6	8.4	7.3				Profit Before Taxes	1.9	1.8
						RATIOS		
6.6	3.1	4.8					1.5	3.0
1.1	1.3	1.8				Current	1.1	1.3
.1	.4	1.4					.6	1.1
3.4	1.9	1.6					.9	2.9
.5	.7	1.2				Quick	.5	.9
.1	.1	.7					.1	.5
0 UND	**0** UND	**0** UND					**0** UND	**14** 25.3
0 UND	**0** UND	**27** 13.5				Sales/Receivables	**25** 14.4	**45** 8.1
4 82.9	**29** 12.7	**54** 6.8					**66** 5.5	**59** 6.2
						Cost of Sales/Inventory		
						Cost of Sales/Payables		
8.0	5.2	3.3					5.5	5.0
NM	21.6	8.1				Sales/Working Capital	39.0	14.7
-4.9	-4.2	15.9					-4.1	101.8
14.1	6.8	21.7					6.0	8.0
(10) 1.2	(15) 4.1	(13) 4.3				EBIT/Interest	(13) .8	(14) 2.1
-3.2	1.2	2.8					-2.7	.2
						Net Profit + Depr., Dep., Amort./Cur. Mat. L/T/D		
.2	.2	.2					.3	.5
2.0	.8	.7				Fixed/Worth	.6	1.1
-1.3	14.2	2.2					2.4	3.6
.1	.4	.7					.4	.8
7.9	2.1	1.1				Debt/Worth	1.4	2.6
-3.5	NM	3.1					3.4	3.6
109.4	30.0	21.4					22.5	49.1
(10) 33.2	(17) 10.4	(16) 10.9				% Profit Before Taxes/Tangible Net Worth	(12) -.7	(16) 14.6
8.9	-.1	6.2					-10.8	-1.2
65.4	15.4	6.6					8.7	13.1
8.9	3.8	3.7				% Profit Before Taxes/Total Assets	-.1	4.0
-1.7	.0	2.1					-2.7	-2.3
40.6	124.7	26.2					21.0	21.7
16.7	1.8	7.2				Sales/Net Fixed Assets	2.5	7.6
4.6	.6	.5					1.1	1.1
5.4	2.4	2.8					1.9	2.8
3.6	1.1	1.8				Sales/Total Assets	1.2	1.9
2.0	.3	.3					.3	.8
.7	.9	1.3					.7	.6
(13) 2.3	(18) 6.6	(15) 2.5				% Depr., Dep., Amort./Sales	(13) 2.8	(18) 2.0
13.8	19.4	10.8					10.9	6.1
						% Officers', Directors' Owners' Comp/Sales		
12532M	42272M	191496M	186347M	318412M		Net Sales ($)	172045M	404011M
3810M	22477M	103975M	111378M	221299M		Total Assets ($)	316942M	393064M

M = $ thousand MM = $ million

See Pages 9 through 22 for Explanation of Ratios and Data

Comparative Historical Data / Current Data Sorted by Sales

				Type of Statement	0-1MM	1-3MM	3-5MM	5-10MM	10-25MM	25MM & OVER
6		2	10	Unqualified	1			2	3	4
8		12	2	Reviewed				1	1	
2		1	8	Compiled	5	1		2		
5		4	22	Tax Returns	16	5	1			
17		7	25	Other	8	6	1	2	6	2
4/1/07-3/31/08 ALL		4/1/08-3/31/09 ALL	4/1/09-3/31/10 ALL		12 (4/1-9/30/09)			55 (10/1/09-3/31/10)		
38		26	67	**NUMBER OF STATEMENTS**	30	12	2	7	10	6
%		%	%	**ASSETS**	%	%	%	%	%	%
14.0		13.6	14.5	Cash & Equivalents	16.5	23.1			6.3	
16.2		24.5	12.0	Trade Receivables (net)	2.1	6.1			31.3	
18.5		12.4	14.5	Inventory	7.9	11.8			14.9	
5.9		7.6	3.8	All Other Current	1.8	7.0			4.8	
54.6		58.0	44.7	Total Current	28.2	48.0			57.4	
36.0		34.8	41.5	Fixed Assets (net)	55.2	43.1			25.1	
2.4		2.7	6.5	Intangibles (net)	9.0	.6			8.3	
7.0		4.5	7.3	All Other Non-Current	7.6	8.3			9.3	
100.0		100.0	100.0	Total	100.0	100.0			100.0	
				LIABILITIES						
12.4		4.4	14.2	Notes Payable-Short Term	18.4	17.4			8.2	
2.7		3.1	4.1	Cur. Mat.-L.T.D.	6.7	1.9			1.4	
10.1		13.0	7.2	Trade Payables	1.7	6.7			10.0	
.0		.1	.1	Income Taxes Payable	.0	.0			.3	
9.2		10.3	7.0	All Other Current	2.2	12.7			12.5	
34.4		31.0	32.6	Total Current	29.0	38.7			32.4	
31.9		18.7	37.7	Long-Term Debt	56.6	29.3			16.5	
.0		.4	.4	Deferred Taxes	.0	.0			.8	
5.7		7.0	2.5	All Other Non-Current	2.1	1.8			5.4	
27.9		42.9	26.8	Net Worth	12.2	30.2			45.0	
100.0		100.0	100.0	Total Liabilities & Net Worth	100.0	100.0			100.0	
				INCOME DATA						
100.0		100.0	100.0	Net Sales	100.0	100.0			100.0	
				Gross Profit						
91.2		95.1	85.9	Operating Expenses	75.0	92.2			95.8	
8.8		4.9	14.1	Operating Profit	25.0	7.8			4.2	
8.3		3.2	6.6	All Other Expenses (net)	13.3	1.6			1.8	
.5		1.7	7.6	Profit Before Taxes	11.7	6.2			2.3	
				RATIOS						
3.0		5.2	2.8		4.3	10.9			1.7	
1.4		1.6	1.5	Current	1.3	1.4			1.6	
1.0		1.1	.8		.2	.2			1.4	
1.4		2.1	1.6		2.7	4.0			1.5	
.9		.9	.9	Quick	.4	.8			1.2	
.2		.5	.2		.1	.1			.6	
0 UND	8	46.7	0 UND		0 UND	0 UND			18 19.9	
10 36.9	45	8.0	4 96.2	Sales/Receivables	0 UND	0 UND			37 9.8	
42 8.7	63	5.8	37 9.8		9 42.0	6 61.5			54 6.8	
				Cost of Sales/Inventory						
				Cost of Sales/Payables						
5.8		3.8	6.8		6.9	4.8			10.1	
17.1		10.5	12.3	Sales/Working Capital	15.9	30.8			12.7	
UND		94.0	-24.9		-4.4	-6.5			21.4	
5.7		8.8	8.9		9.9					
(25) 2.4	(20)	4.2	(47) 3.8	EBIT/Interest	(19) 1.5					
.9		.6	1.2		.6					
				Net Profit + Depr., Dep., Amort./Cur. Mat. L/T/D						
.1		.1	.2		.6	.1			.2	
.9		.8	1.2	Fixed/Worth	2.5	1.5			.6	
15.7		1.4	9.9		-1.6	NM			2.3	
.9		.6	.6		.2	.4			1.0	
2.1		1.2	2.1	Debt/Worth	2.7	3.7			1.9	
20.5		3.9	29.7		-3.5	NM			5.6	
48.1		35.0	36.5	% Profit Before Taxes/Tangible Net Worth	27.1				56.6	
(30) 10.4	(25)	19.1	(51) 12.0		(19) 11.6				18.1	
-1.2		-2.0	4.3		.1				6.6	
16.0		13.8	14.9	% Profit Before Taxes/Total Assets	15.3	33.6			10.5	
3.4		7.0	5.2		2.8	15.9			5.7	
-1.0		-2.4	.3		-.2	1.1			3.4	
83.2		44.8	31.1	Sales/Net Fixed Assets	14.6	124.3			41.6	
9.3		11.0	5.8		1.6	14.0			10.3	
.5		1.5	1.0		.2	1.6			6.4	
3.0		2.5	3.2	Sales/Total Assets	2.5	5.3			4.2	
1.6		2.0	1.8		.9	2.7			2.5	
.3		.9	.5		.2	1.2			1.6	
.6		.7	1.1	% Depr., Dep., Amort./Sales	1.7	.6				
(25) 1.7	(23)	2.3	(54) 4.2		(25) 8.5	(10) 7.7				
6.5		8.9	12.5		19.4	13.0				
1.9			2.6	% Officers', Directors' Owners' Comp/Sales	4.9					
(12) 4.6			(21) 5.1		(10) 6.8					
6.2			11.4		11.4					
1065309M		685004M	751059M	Net Sales ($)	14972M	20283M	7934M	50745M	163653M	493472M
473036M		596750M	462939M	Total Assets ($)	33938M	19427M	3138M	50619M	81588M	274229M

M = $ thousand   MM = $ million
See Pages 9 through 22 for Explanation of Ratios and Data

Current Data Sorted by Assets

Comparative Historical Data

						Type of Statement		
2	3	4	7	3	2	Unqualified	27	26
1	6	3	5		1	Reviewed	16	21
4	3	8	2			Compiled	25	30
9	6	6	1			Tax Returns	31	44
4	13	22	8	3	1	Other	68	63
	26 (4/1-9/30/09)		101 (10/1/09-3/31/10)				4/1/05-3/31/06	4/1/06-3/31/07
0-500M	500M-2MM	2-10MM	10-50MM	50-100MM	100-250MM		ALL	ALL
20	31	43	23	6	4	NUMBER OF STATEMENTS	167	184
%	%	%	%	%	%	ASSETS	%	%
24.6	19.6	6.9	10.1			Cash & Equivalents	14.6	13.4
6.6	16.7	16.0	15.1			Trade Receivables (net)	21.7	18.1
3.5	5.1	14.7	14.0			Inventory	19.0	15.7
9.0	5.3	3.7	2.3			All Other Current	4.6	3.2
43.7	46.7	41.3	41.4			Total Current	59.8	50.3
44.0	44.5	46.5	51.0			Fixed Assets (net)	29.2	39.5
4.1	3.1	5.6	1.5			Intangibles (net)	4.0	4.3
8.2	5.6	6.5	6.1			All Other Non-Current	7.0	5.9
100.0	100.0	100.0	100.0			Total	100.0	100.0
						LIABILITIES		
12.3	21.9	11.0	7.3			Notes Payable-Short Term	13.5	13.2
5.6	5.9	2.6	3.2			Cur. Mat.-L.T.D.	2.2	3.8
14.3	9.9	6.3	8.9			Trade Payables	12.6	8.9
.0	.5	.3	.2			Income Taxes Payable	.2	.3
27.6	16.8	8.4	6.6			All Other Current	12.6	11.4
59.9	54.9	28.6	26.3			Total Current	41.2	37.5
67.7	32.7	23.7	18.5			Long-Term Debt	22.3	23.4
.0	.0	.6	.9			Deferred Taxes	.2	.2
1.0	2.3	1.8	5.2			All Other Non-Current	4.3	5.4
-28.6	10.1	45.3	49.1			Net Worth	32.0	33.4
100.0	100.0	100.0	100.0			Total Liabilities & Net Worth	100.0	100.0
						INCOME DATA		
100.0	100.0	100.0	100.0			Net Sales	100.0	100.0
						Gross Profit		
92.0	85.5	93.7	83.4			Operating Expenses	88.5	88.8
8.0	14.5	6.3	16.6			Operating Profit	11.5	11.2
4.1	5.1	3.0	2.9			All Other Expenses (net)	3.3	3.8
3.9	9.4	3.3	13.6			Profit Before Taxes	8.2	7.4
						RATIOS		
7.5	1.9	3.1	2.5				2.8	2.3
1.1	1.1	1.6	1.4			Current	1.4	1.3
.3	.4	.9	1.0				1.0	.9
7.0	1.8	1.2	2.3				1.8	1.8
.6	.8	.7	.8			Quick	(166) .9	.8
.1	.2	.2	.5				.3	.3
0 UND	0 UND	0 UND	3 109.5				2 147.9	1 496.4
0 UND	9 41.6	22 16.9	28 12.9			Sales/Receivables	30 12.3	23 16.2
6 56.3	41 8.8	51 7.1	61 6.0				52 7.1	55 6.6
						Cost of Sales/Inventory		
						Cost of Sales/Payables		
8.2	7.2	3.9	2.4				4.8	5.7
132.9	40.9	11.6	13.7			Sales/Working Capital	12.8	18.5
-7.0	-6.0	-30.4	96.7				-233.4	-70.7
7.7	20.3	7.0	24.9				10.5	8.5
(16) 1.8	(25) 4.7	(38) 1.9	(20) 4.1			EBIT/Interest	(124) 3.6	(146) 3.4
-1.9	.8	.8	.6				1.5	1.6
						Net Profit + Depr., Dep.,	5.1	6.8
						Amort./Cur. Mat. L/T/D	(27) 2.0	(28) 1.9
							.6	1.3
.0	.2	.4	.4				.1	.3
2.9	1.4	1.2	.8			Fixed/Worth	.7	1.1
-1.4	-7.5	3.4	1.9				4.1	5.2
.7	.7	.4	.5				.7	.7
66.4	2.3	1.3	.9			Debt/Worth	2.7	2.5
-2.6	-16.8	5.8	3.2				12.6	15.1
132.2	56.2	22.0	34.0			% Profit Before Taxes/Tangible	48.8	64.1
(12) 19.5	(22) 17.5	(38) 1.8	(22) 9.9			Net Worth	(135) 23.5	(150) 23.7
-3.7	-.9	-1.9	-.5				3.5	4.2
26.1	24.5	8.0	15.4			% Profit Before Taxes/Total	15.5	15.1
4.1	6.3	1.1	5.5			Assets	5.2	6.5
-2.0	-.1	-.9	-.3				1.0	.7
UND	29.3	19.7	5.7				60.4	28.8
12.7	6.0	1.8	2.3			Sales/Net Fixed Assets	16.0	6.5
1.9	1.7	.7	.4				3.0	1.6
9.5	2.9	2.5	2.0				3.1	3.1
2.3	1.9	.8	1.0			Sales/Total Assets	1.7	1.7
1.1	.8	.5	.4				.8	.8
2.2	.8	2.0	2.1				.6	.9
(10) 4.2	(21) 2.8	(38) 5.4	6.8			% Depr., Dep., Amort./Sales	(129) 1.6	(145) 2.7
14.3	8.3	12.8	13.0				4.6	7.1
	2.2	.6					1.9	1.3
	(11) 3.0	(14) 3.0				% Officers', Directors'	(51) 3.8	(57) 2.7
	5.2	5.6				Owners' Comp/Sales	10.6	5.7
22219M	73704M	314787M	675088M	567267M	1984100M	Net Sales ($)	5054232M	4999043M
4991M	35583M	214764M	462085M	413305M	661899M	Total Assets ($)	2587005M	3126190M

© RMA 2010

M = $ thousand   MM = $ million
See Pages 9 through 22 for Explanation of Ratios and Data

Comparative Historical Data

Current Data Sorted by Sales

			Type of Statement						
35	24	21	Unqualified	4	2	2	2	3	8
24	21	16	Reviewed	1	4	3	2	1	5
16	15	17	Compiled	3	5	1	4	4	
19	26	22	Tax Returns	11	6	1	2	2	
70	53	51	Other	8	16	6	10	5	6
4/1/07-3/31/08 ALL	4/1/08-3/31/09 ALL	4/1/09-3/31/10 ALL		26 (4/1-9/30/09) 0-1MM	1-3MM	3-5MM	101 (10/1/09-3/31/10) 5-10MM	10-25MM	25MM & OVER
164	139	127	NUMBER OF STATEMENTS	27	33	13	20	15	19
%	%	%	ASSETS	%	%	%	%	%	%
12.3	12.3	13.8	Cash & Equivalents	19.4	13.6	10.4	17.6	6.0	10.9
20.5	18.0	14.5	Trade Receivables (net)	1.3	13.0	13.3	15.3	30.8	22.6
15.4	18.3	10.3	Inventory	1.2	8.2	4.6	14.8	15.1	22.4
4.3	3.5	4.8	All Other Current	6.1	5.9	.9	4.1	3.7	5.1
52.6	52.0	43.4	Total Current	28.1	40.7	29.3	51.8	55.7	61.1
35.9	35.1	46.4	Fixed Assets (net)	62.7	47.9	56.0	39.3	30.9	33.9
4.4	4.7	3.6	Intangibles (net)	3.2	4.5	3.9	.7	9.8	.8
7.1	8.2	6.6	All Other Non-Current	6.1	6.9	10.8	8.2	3.6	4.2
100.0	100.0	100.0	Total	100.0	100.0	100.0	100.0	100.0	100.0
			LIABILITIES						
15.6	13.9	12.9	Notes Payable-Short Term	4.3	25.8	11.6	7.5	13.9	8.3
3.7	2.9	4.0	Cur. Mat.-L.T.D.	5.1	5.7	3.7	2.1	3.2	2.2
10.1	11.7	9.3	Trade Payables	9.0	8.9	5.0	6.2	9.7	16.0
.5	.4	.3	Income Taxes Payable	.0	.5	.4	.1	.3	.3
8.6	8.6	13.2	All Other Current	16.5	11.9	11.5	9.4	18.7	11.6
38.5	37.5	39.6	Total Current	35.0	52.8	32.1	25.2	45.8	38.4
25.0	21.2	32.6	Long-Term Debt	83.1	21.6	16.2	17.8	15.9	19.6
.3	.4	.4	Deferred Taxes	.0	.0	.3	1.2	.9	.2
7.1	5.9	3.8	All Other Non-Current	1.2	2.3	.3	1.5	12.6	8.1
29.2	35.0	23.7	Net Worth	-19.3	23.3	51.1	54.2	24.7	33.7
100.0	100.0	100.0	Total Liabilties & Net Worth	100.0	100.0	100.0	100.0	100.0	100.0
			INCOME DATA						
100.0	100.0	100.0	Net Sales	100.0	100.0	100.0	100.0	100.0	100.0
			Gross Profit						
86.5	88.1	89.6	Operating Expenses	82.5	88.0	93.2	93.9	92.4	92.9
13.5	11.9	10.4	Operating Profit	17.5	12.0	6.8	6.1	7.6	7.1
4.6	3.6	3.5	All Other Expenses (net)	9.9	2.3	3.9	.8	1.0	1.1
8.9	8.4	6.9	Profit Before Taxes	7.6	9.7	2.9	5.3	6.6	6.0
			RATIOS						
2.4	2.3	2.6		5.7	2.3	2.0	4.2	2.2	2.1
1.4	1.4	1.3	Current	1.1	1.2	.9	2.3	1.3	1.7
1.0	.9	.7		.2	.4	.6	1.1	.9	1.2
1.8	1.7	1.9		3.7	1.2	1.3	3.5	1.6	1.8
1.0	.8	.8	Quick	.4	.6	.8	1.8	.9	.9
.1	.4	.2		.1	.1	.2	.7	.5	.3
0 999.8	2 152.3	0 UND		0 UND	0 UND	0 UND	2 230.6	21 17.1	19 19.1
28 13.1	28 13.0	19 19.2	Sales/Receivables	0 UND	1 302.4	22 16.9	31 11.9	44 8.4	34 10.6
53 6.9	47 7.8	44 8.4		4 90.2	46 7.9	38 9.7	64 5.7	64 5.7	51 7.1
			Cost of Sales/Inventory						
			Cost of Sales/Payables						
4.7	5.4	4.9		4.6	4.8	27.6	2.4	6.8	5.7
16.8	16.2	16.5	Sales/Working Capital	161.3	19.8	-32.2	6.6	15.7	13.7
-114.5	-67.8	-16.2		-4.6	-5.2	-9.5	32.1	-59.1	28.7
7.6	16.0	9.8		11.3	6.9	5.1	29.8	10.9	22.5
(133) 3.4	(111) 4.0	(109) 2.6	EBIT/Interest	(16) 3.4	(29) 2.1	(12) 1.8	(18) 4.0	3.5	2.2
1.5	1.4	.5		-.2	.9	.4	.8	1.1	-.6
5.9	8.6	2.3	Net Profit + Depr., Dep.,						
(25) 2.5	(22) 3.2	(18) 1.5	Amort./Cur. Mat. L/T/D						
.8	1.6	1.0							
.3	.2	.4		.9	.6	.6	.2	.3	.4
1.2	.8	1.2	Fixed/Worth	2.3	1.2	1.3	.7	1.1	.8
4.8	2.3	5.4		-3.9	NM	2.5	1.6	-4.0	1.9
.8	.7	.6		.4	.7	.3	.3	1.7	.9
2.5	1.9	2.0	Debt/Worth	4.4	2.3	1.1	.7	2.0	3.2
11.0	6.7	15.2		-3.6	-18.1	3.6	4.9	-10.5	6.2
53.1	48.5	32.3		26.9	33.1	5.6	70.8	49.8	36.1
(134) 20.3	(118) 16.6	(101) 8.7	% Profit Before Taxes/Tangible Net Worth	(18) -.3	(24) 9.0	(11) 2.2	9.9	(11) 25.4	(17) 11.0
6.3	4.1	-1.1		-13.9	1.5	-.5	-.6	-15.2	-9.5
15.8	15.4	12.0		20.2	10.7	2.8	12.0	12.0	14.0
6.6	5.6	2.3	% Profit Before Taxes/Total Assets	1.5	2.6	1.3	5.9	8.0	2.3
2.0	1.0	-.7		-1.6	.6	-1.7	-.4	.6	-3.8
31.0	48.0	20.8		16.8	19.5	6.5	12.6	37.4	32.4
7.7	7.6	3.7	Sales/Net Fixed Assets	1.1	3.7	1.1	3.9	15.1	6.4
2.5	2.3	.8		.2	.7	.6	1.3	3.7	2.3
3.3	3.1	2.7		1.8	2.6	1.7	2.4	3.6	3.5
1.7	2.0	1.4	Sales/Total Assets	.8	1.6	.6	1.5	2.7	2.3
.9	.8	.5		.2	.4	.4	.6	1.0	1.3
.8	.8	1.9		2.5	2.8		1.1	.7	.8
(126) 2.0	(109) 2.5	(99) 5.1	% Depr., Dep., Amort./Sales	(18) 11.9	(24) 5.6	(18) 4.4	(14) 2.6	(16) 2.3	
5.5	6.3	12.1		20.6	18.1		7.6	7.8	4.5
.8	1.3	1.6	% Officers', Directors' Owners' Comp/Sales		1.2				
(42) 3.1	(29) 3.3	(37) 3.9			(12) 3.0				
7.0	5.5	7.1			5.0				
5938124M	8189597M	3637165M	Net Sales ($)	11213M	59421M	48142M	135253M	234293M	3148843M
3618296M	3930356M	1792627M	Total Assets ($)	31698M	117185M	72947M	139603M	195695M	1235499M

M = $ thousand   MM = $ million
See Pages 9 through 22 for Explanation of Ratios and Data

Current Data Sorted by Assets | Comparative Historical Data

	0-500M	500M-2MM	2-10MM	10-50MM	50-100MM	100-250MM	Type of Statement	4/1/05-3/31/06 ALL	4/1/06-3/31/07 ALL
			2	2			Unqualified	4	7
	1		2	3		1	Reviewed	10	9
		2	4	2			Compiled		9
	5	11	10	1			Tax Returns	11	19
	3	1	8	3			Other	17	11
		8 (4/1-9/30/09)		53 (10/1/09-3/31/10)					
NUMBER OF STATEMENTS	9	14	26	11		1		42	55
	%	%	%	%	%	%	ASSETS	%	%
		4.7	5.5	4.0			Cash & Equivalents	4.1	5.4
		5.8	5.2	13.7			Trade Receivables (net)	12.0	9.2
		11.5	14.3	27.1			Inventory	16.7	18.6
		7.5	4.7	5.5			All Other Current	5.5	8.1
		29.5	29.6	50.3			Total Current	38.3	41.2
		55.0	59.9	42.7			Fixed Assets (net)	49.6	52.1
		3.9	.1	.0			Intangibles (net)	1.7	.1
		11.6	10.3	7.0			All Other Non-Current	10.5	6.5
		100.0	100.0	100.0			Total	100.0	100.0
							LIABILITIES		
		24.9	13.6	20.9			Notes Payable-Short Term	22.8	26.5
		8.3	3.5	4.3			Cur. Mat.-L.T.D.	2.1	3.7
		1.9	3.3	13.9			Trade Payables	4.3	5.7
		.0	.2	.0			Income Taxes Payable	.3	.6
		3.4	4.5	4.2			All Other Current	8.5	6.3
		38.5	25.1	43.3			Total Current	38.0	42.9
		35.2	22.6	25.0			Long-Term Debt	22.9	28.2
		.0	.6	2.0			Deferred Taxes	.5	.4
		5.0	.4	7.8			All Other Non-Current	3.9	1.6
		21.3	51.2	21.9			Net Worth	34.7	26.9
		100.0	100.0	100.0			Total Liabilities & Net Worth	100.0	100.0
							INCOME DATA		
		100.0	100.0	100.0			Net Sales	100.0	100.0
							Gross Profit		
		95.0	84.5	92.5			Operating Expenses	87.4	88.5
		5.0	15.5	7.5			Operating Profit	12.6	11.5
		1.8	6.6	4.9			All Other Expenses (net)	4.6	5.8
		3.2	8.9	2.6			Profit Before Taxes	8.0	5.7
							RATIOS		
		1.9	2.3	1.4			Current	1.7	1.8
		.7	1.3	1.1				1.0	1.1
		.1	.6	.8				.8	.3
		.8	.7	.5			Quick	1.2	.7
		.2	.2	.3				.3	.2
		.1	.0	.1				.1	.1
	0 UND	0 UND	4 81.8				Sales/Receivables	0 UND	0 UND
	0 UND	0 UND	21 17.5					24 15.0	0 UND
	26 14.1	32 11.5	37 9.8					58 6.3	41 8.9
							Cost of Sales/Inventory		
							Cost of Sales/Payables		
		9.0	4.6	6.0			Sales/Working Capital	4.6	4.6
		NM	11.5	18.8				NM	13.2
		-3.1	-3.8	-25.4				-10.8	-4.4
		4.3	8.2	8.0			EBIT/Interest	4.2	5.4
	(12) 1.2	(24) 3.0	(10) 3.7					(37) 2.0	(47) 1.9
		1.0	1.8	.8				.6	.6
							Net Profit + Depr., Dep., Amort./Cur. Mat. L/T/D		
		.9	.6	.8			Fixed/Worth	.7	.5
		2.8	1.0	1.7				1.4	1.4
		NM	1.6	4.9				6.2	5.5
		1.0	.4	2.0			Debt/Worth	.5	.6
		2.9	.8	2.6				2.4	2.3
		NM	1.9	6.9				13.0	15.0
		133.9	18.9				% Profit Before Taxes/Tangible Net Worth	34.9	30.2
	(11) 23.9	(25) 7.7						(35) 11.5	(43) 8.0
		.7	1.6					.5	.2
		11.7	8.2	8.9			% Profit Before Taxes/Total Assets	9.3	8.8
		3.1	3.9	3.4				1.4	1.8
		.1	1.0	-.4				-1.1	-1.3
		8.6	2.1	6.9			Sales/Net Fixed Assets	4.1	13.3
		2.6	.5	2.2				1.8	2.0
		1.1	.3	1.2				.7	.5
		2.2	.7	2.5			Sales/Total Assets	1.5	1.8
		1.0	.4	.9				.7	.8
		.6	.2	.6				.4	.3
		4.7	4.0	1.6			% Depr., Dep., Amort./Sales	3.0	2.8
	(13) 7.9	(23) 7.8	4.0					(37) 5.5	(44) 6.4
		12.9	19.6	10.8				14.2	13.3
							% Officers', Directors' Owners' Comp/Sales		2.2
								(11)	3.0
									27.8
Net Sales ($)	17505M	23526M	74749M	406444M		172457M		251921M	325337M
Total Assets ($)	3463M	15656M	121507M	245500M		194459M		326399M	357582M

Note: Columns 50-100MM and 100-250MM marked "DATA NOT AVAILABLE."

© RMA 2010

M = $ thousand　　MM = $ million
See Pages 9 through 22 for Explanation of Ratios and Data

Comparative Historical Data   Current Data Sorted by Sales

			Type of Statement						
8	4	4	Unqualified	2					2
7	11	7	Reviewed	2					4
6	11	8	Compiled		1	5	1	1	
22	29	27	Tax Returns	13	11	1	2		
7	16	15	Other	1	8	2	1	3	
4/1/07-3/31/08	4/1/08-3/31/09	4/1/09-3/31/10		8 (4/1-9/30/09)		53 (10/1/09-3/31/10)			
ALL	ALL	ALL		0-1MM	1-3MM	3-5MM	5-10MM	10-25MM	25MM & OVER
50	71	61	**NUMBER OF STATEMENTS**	18	20	8	4	5	6
%	%	%	**ASSETS**	%	%	%	%	%	%
4.9	7.1	8.9	Cash & Equivalents	1.5	14.5				
7.0	10.7	7.0	Trade Receivables (net)	.6	1.9				
16.8	16.7	15.8	Inventory	11.9	6.4				
6.4	4.1	5.2	All Other Current	2.6	7.6				
35.1	38.6	37.0	Total Current	16.6	30.4				
54.0	52.3	51.1	Fixed Assets (net)	66.3	55.5				
2.0	1.9	1.2	Intangibles (net)	.0	2.7				
9.0	7.2	10.7	All Other Non-Current	17.1	11.4				
100.0	100.0	100.0	Total	100.0	100.0				
			LIABILITIES						
17.3	21.5	21.7	Notes Payable-Short Term	11.4	35.9				
6.4	7.3	4.3	Cur. Mat.-L.T.D.	4.5	5.3				
4.7	3.8	4.5	Trade Payables	.6	1.9				
.1	.0	.1	Income Taxes Payable	.1	.0				
8.6	9.5	4.4	All Other Current	3.5	1.3				
37.1	42.0	34.9	Total Current	20.0	44.4				
29.0	32.9	26.6	Long-Term Debt	30.8	34.3				
.4	.2	.6	Deferred Taxes	.0	.0				
2.5	3.3	2.7	All Other Non-Current	1.2	4.8				
31.0	21.7	35.2	Net Worth	48.1	16.5				
100.0	100.0	100.0	Total Liabilities & Net Worth	100.0	100.0				
			INCOME DATA						
100.0	100.0	100.0	Net Sales	100.0	100.0				
			Gross Profit						
93.4	85.0	88.7	Operating Expenses	83.3	88.9				
6.6	15.0	11.3	Operating Profit	16.7	11.1				
2.3	3.4	5.0	All Other Expenses (net)	8.8	5.3				
4.3	11.6	6.3	Profit Before Taxes	7.9	5.8				
			RATIOS						
2.0	1.7	1.8	Current	2.1	1.5				
1.1	1.2	1.1		.8	.9				
.6	.3	.4		.1	.2				
.6	1.1	.8	Quick	.5	.7				
.2	.3	.3		.1	.2				
.1	.1			.0	.0				
0 UND	0 UND	0 UND	Sales/Receivables	0 UND	0 UND				
0 UND	2 217.9	0 UND		0 UND	0 UND				
19 18.7	40 9.1	31 11.9		0 UND	13 27.7				
			Cost of Sales/Inventory						
			Cost of Sales/Payables						
4.6	4.2	5.6	Sales/Working Capital	4.6	7.1				
20.9	25.7	20.6		NM	-27.1				
-9.3	-7.2	-4.0		-2.9	-3.2				
4.2	7.3	7.0	EBIT/Interest	4.7	4.6				
(46) 2.2	(66) 3.1	(54) 2.9		(15) 2.0	(18) 2.5				
1.1	1.3	1.0		1.0	1.0				
			Net Profit + Depr., Dep., Amort./Cur. Mat. L/T/D						
.8	.8	.6	Fixed/Worth	.9	.7				
1.3	1.8	1.3		1.3	1.6				
NM	90.5	3.4		4.5	NM				
.6	1.0	.6	Debt/Worth	.2	.9				
1.9	2.3	1.7		.8	2.0				
NM	-739.0	5.6		4.6	-9.0				
24.2	50.7	26.8	% Profit Before Taxes/Tangible Net Worth	16.3	18.4				
(38) 8.8	(53) 18.7	(52) 11.2		(17) 1.9	(13) 4.3				
3.0	3.5	.8		.0	.5				
9.9	15.4	10.8	% Profit Before Taxes/Total Assets	6.4	15.4				
4.4	5.2	4.1		1.1	2.7				
.4	.6	.1		.0	.1				
6.1	7.1	6.6	Sales/Net Fixed Assets	2.0	10.0				
1.9	2.1	1.9		.4	1.2				
.5	.5	.4		.2	.4				
2.3	2.7	2.2	Sales/Total Assets	1.0	2.2				
.9	.9	.8		.3	.7				
.4	.4	.3		.2	.2				
2.1	1.6	2.7	% Depr., Dep., Amort./Sales	6.8	4.1				
(47) 5.6	(58) 6.6	(54) 6.8		13.5	(15) 7.9				
11.7	15.0	16.4		24.8	19.5				
1.5	2.2	.7	% Officers', Directors' Owners' Comp/Sales						
(13) 4.1	(20) 3.6	(16) 2.1							
6.5	5.0	3.7							
764427M	768872M	694681M	Net Sales ($)	11034M	31814M	33358M	30944M	79050M	508481M
657420M	820588M	580585M	Total Assets ($)	39184M	71389M	40540M	16575M	74451M	338446M

M = $ thousand   MM = $ million
See Pages 9 through 22 for Explanation of Ratios and Data

Current Data Sorted by Assets   Comparative Historical Data

0-500M	500M-2MM	2-10MM	10-50MM	50-100MM	100-250MM	Type of Statement	4/1/05-3/31/06 ALL	4/1/06-3/31/07 ALL
	3	3	6	2	3	Unqualified	9	9
	1	4	5	2		Reviewed	4	3
	3	11	5			Compiled	12	22
8	12	11	1	2	1	Tax Returns	13	25
1	6	7	7		2	Other	23	25
	18 (4/1-9/30/09)		88 (10/1/09-3/31/10)					
9	25	36	24	6	6	NUMBER OF STATEMENTS	61	84
%	%	%	%	%	%	**ASSETS**	%	%
	6.1	3.7	7.2			Cash & Equivalents	5.3	6.6
	6.4	16.4	9.9			Trade Receivables (net)	9.8	7.3
	20.9	15.9	28.2			Inventory	25.1	17.2
	4.0	2.8	4.5			All Other Current	4.1	8.6
	37.4	38.8	49.8			Total Current	44.4	39.7
	49.9	49.6	43.2			Fixed Assets (net)	43.8	48.1
	1.7	.2	.7			Intangibles (net)	1.9	1.1
	11.0	11.3	6.3			All Other Non-Current	10.0	11.1
	100.0	100.0	100.0			Total	100.0	100.0
						LIABILITIES		
	25.6	15.4	22.2			Notes Payable-Short Term	28.8	35.4
	5.5	5.7	2.2			Cur. Mat.-L.T.D.	5.1	2.1
	2.9	7.9	8.2			Trade Payables	7.6	5.9
	.2	.1	.2			Income Taxes Payable	.2	.2
	6.4	5.2	7.8			All Other Current	9.1	9.0
	40.5	34.3	40.4			Total Current	50.8	52.5
	27.0	29.7	21.1			Long-Term Debt	34.4	22.1
	.0	.0	.5			Deferred Taxes	.4	.1
	2.8	2.3	.4			All Other Non-Current	.7	3.2
	29.6	33.6	37.6			Net Worth	13.8	22.0
	100.0	100.0	100.0			Total Liabilities & Net Worth	100.0	100.0
						INCOME DATA		
	100.0	100.0	100.0			Net Sales	100.0	100.0
						Gross Profit		
	92.0	89.8	90.3			Operating Expenses	90.7	88.3
	8.0	10.2	9.7			Operating Profit	9.3	11.7
	.2	4.8	1.2			All Other Expenses (net)	1.5	3.2
	7.8	5.4	8.5			Profit Before Taxes	7.8	8.5
						RATIOS		
	3.9	1.8	1.5				1.5	1.4
	1.1	1.2	1.2			Current	1.1	1.0
	.2	.6	1.1				.4	.7
	1.5	1.1	.7				.7	.7
	.4	.4	.4			Quick	.3	.2
	.1	.0	.1				.1	.1
	0 UND	0 UND	12 29.3				0 UND	0 UND
	1 474.3	8 44.9	32 11.5			Sales/Receivables	3 116.5	0 UND
	11 33.4	62 5.9	46 7.9				24 15.2	23 16.2
						Cost of Sales/Inventory		
						Cost of Sales/Payables		
	10.5	3.4	3.3				10.7	9.4
	259.9	9.0	11.2			Sales/Working Capital	26.5	-321.1
	-7.2	-8.8	61.9				-8.2	-5.9
	9.3	9.4	6.0				8.3	5.4
	(22) 2.5	(32) 1.9	3.0			EBIT/Interest	(55) 2.9	(73) 2.3
	1.0	.6	1.8				.8	.4
						Net Profit + Depr., Dep., Amort./Cur. Mat. L/T/D		
	.3	.7	.7				.5	.7
	1.5	1.2	1.1			Fixed/Worth	1.4	1.3
	NM	4.3	1.5				31.1	2.6
	.4	.5	.9				1.0	.7
	2.1	1.6	2.2			Debt/Worth	2.9	2.1
	NM	10.1	2.9				-33.0	13.1
	32.5	28.0	30.9				42.6	31.6
	(19) 8.3	(30) 5.8	13.0			% Profit Before Taxes/Tangible Net Worth	(45) 16.9	(70) 10.4
	.0	-.5	4.5				2.5	.0
	12.1	11.2	7.9				16.8	9.1
	4.5	2.5	4.5			% Profit Before Taxes/Total Assets	5.7	4.3
	.2	-.7	1.9				-.7	-1.1
	30.0	5.1	10.6				15.0	12.1
	4.0	1.1	2.6			Sales/Net Fixed Assets	4.3	2.5
	1.2	.4	.6				1.8	.7
	2.9	1.5	1.7				3.1	2.4
	1.8	.6	.9			Sales/Total Assets	1.4	1.1
	.9	.3	.4				.8	.4
	1.1	3.1	1.3				1.2	1.5
	(23) 5.5	(33) 12.5	(21) 2.5			% Depr., Dep., Amort./Sales	(46) 4.0	(64) 6.2
	13.5	17.0	4.4				9.3	9.8
	1.3	1.4					1.5	1.6
	(12) 2.1	(13) 4.2				% Officers', Directors' Owners' Comp/Sales	(17) 3.2	(17) 4.2
	4.3	9.8					8.8	8.8
8673M	80369M	252632M	842492M	933953M	2223941M	Net Sales ($)	2582515M	1001840M
3009M	27824M	170424M	509413M	404813M	1072354M	Total Assets ($)	1094924M	595848M

M = $ thousand   MM = $ million
See Pages 9 through 22 for Explanation of Ratios and Data

Comparative Historical Data | | Current Data Sorted by Sales

			Type of Statement						
10	11	17	Unqualified		2	1	1	4	9
11	11	12	Reviewed		2		2	4	4
12	21	19	Compiled	1	6	2	5	3	2
25	36	35	Tax Returns	16	14	1	1		3
24	19	23	Other	2	7	4	3	3	4
4/1/07-3/31/08	4/1/08-3/31/09	4/1/09-3/31/10		18 (4/1-9/30/09)			88 (10/1/09-3/31/10)		
ALL	ALL	ALL		0-1MM	1-3MM	3-5MM	5-10MM	10-25MM	25MM & OVER
82	98	106	NUMBER OF STATEMENTS	19	31	8	12	14	22
%	%	%	ASSETS	%	%	%	%	%	%
7.6	5.7	9.9	Cash & Equivalents	11.7	5.1		4.7	6.3	22.6
7.6	9.9	11.1	Trade Receivables (net)	.2	7.3		11.3	18.2	19.0
17.5	16.4	19.1	Inventory	5.6	12.9		33.6	27.6	23.0
9.8	8.2	3.8	All Other Current	.4	2.6		4.9	6.6	6.3
42.6	40.2	43.9	Total Current	17.9	27.8		54.5	58.7	70.9
41.6	47.2	43.8	Fixed Assets (net)	57.5	59.1		38.9	33.3	21.7
1.1	.6	1.2	Intangibles (net)	.1	1.8		.7	.4	1.0
14.7	12.0	11.0	All Other Non-Current	24.6	11.3		5.9	7.5	6.4
100.0	100.0	100.0	Total	100.0	100.0		100.0	100.0	100.0
			LIABILITIES						
31.4	24.2	21.1	Notes Payable-Short Term	15.7	27.6		15.3	24.6	15.5
8.4	11.0	8.6	Cur. Mat.-L.T.D.	8.0	7.9		2.1	2.6	18.7
7.1	5.4	6.7	Trade Payables	.0	3.6		3.9	11.1	15.8
.3	.2	.2	Income Taxes Payable	.0	.4		.0	.1	.1
7.1	8.6	8.0	All Other Current	.7	6.1		18.1	7.4	13.6
54.3	49.4	44.5	Total Current	24.4	45.6		39.5	45.8	63.7
26.3	26.8	24.9	Long-Term Debt	30.9	34.9		23.2	18.4	10.6
.1	.2	.3	Deferred Taxes	.0	.0		.0	.6	.7
4.1	3.8	1.8	All Other Non-Current	1.0	2.6		2.0	.9	.9
15.2	19.7	28.5	Net Worth	43.6	16.9		35.3	34.2	24.1
100.0	100.0	100.0	Total Liabilities & Net Worth	100.0	100.0		100.0	100.0	100.0
			INCOME DATA						
100.0	100.0	100.0	Net Sales	100.0	100.0		100.0	100.0	100.0
			Gross Profit						
86.6	88.0	90.7	Operating Expenses	87.5	89.4		96.1	92.3	92.4
13.4	12.0	9.3	Operating Profit	12.5	10.6		3.9	7.7	7.6
3.8	3.2	1.9	All Other Expenses (net)	3.2	3.3		-.6	1.8	.0
9.6	8.8	7.4	Profit Before Taxes	9.3	7.3		4.5	5.9	7.6
			RATIOS						
2.1	1.6	1.8		4.0	1.7		2.8	1.6	1.6
1.1	1.1	1.2	Current	1.1	1.0		1.5	1.2	1.3
.4	.3	.8		.2	.1		.7	1.1	1.1
.9	.6	1.0		2.8	1.0		1.1	.8	1.2
.3 (96)	.2	.4	Quick	.4	.2		.5	.5	.5
.1	.0	.1		.1	.1		.1	.2	.4
0 UND	0 UND	0 UND		0 UND	0 UND		1 258.7	19 19.1	7 55.8
1 598.5	2 218.7	9 40.2	Sales/Receivables	0 UND	1 474.3		11 33.4	34 10.8	18 20.3
19 18.9	27 13.7	35 10.4		0 UND	33 11.1		52 7.1	47 7.7	33 11.0
			Cost of Sales/Inventory						
			Cost of Sales/Payables						
4.0	6.6	4.3		2.5	2.9		4.0	7.5	9.8
34.8	62.3	20.4	Sales/Working Capital	40.0	80.4		9.5	8.6	22.0
-5.0	-4.2	-28.6		-2.4	-3.4		-41.0	87.8	106.9
5.4	5.7	7.1		21.0	5.2		7.0	13.1	8.9
(71) 2.7	(92) 3.0	(95) 2.8	EBIT/Interest	(14) 4.0	(30) 2.0	(11) 1.8	3.3	(18) 3.7	
1.4	1.1	1.3		.9	.4		-.7	2.4	1.8
		6.3	Net Profit + Depr., Dep.,						
	(13)	3.9	Amort./Cur. Mat. L/T/D						
		2.2							
.5	.7	.6		.6	.9		.3	.4	.3
1.0	1.5	1.1	Fixed/Worth	1.4	1.7		.9	.8	.6
11.7	13.1	3.1		7.1	-5.5		33.7	1.8	1.3
.8	1.1	.8		.4	.6		.6	1.2	1.3
3.0	2.9	2.0	Debt/Worth	1.0	2.1		1.3	2.5	2.2
128.6	87.4	7.5		45.4	-9.3		143.6	3.9	4.1
37.5	58.6	34.2	% Profit Before Taxes/Tangible	55.1	14.9		24.5	45.1	47.7
(64) 15.4	(78) 22.1	(89) 12.9	Net Worth	(16) 7.1	(21) 7.4	(11) 5.7	25.1	(20) 19.9	
2.4	6.1	2.4		-.2	-.4		1.0	9.9	9.1
15.3	12.0	13.7	% Profit Before Taxes/Total	14.0	9.5		11.4	19.0	17.0
4.7	5.7	4.6	Assets	4.2	4.1		2.3	5.1	6.3
.8	.5	.9		-.2	-.8		-6.6	3.4	2.5
17.4	11.7	13.0		4.0	3.0		19.7	13.2	86.0
3.9	3.1	3.1	Sales/Net Fixed Assets	.6	1.3		8.9	6.8	11.5
1.0	.7	.8		.3	.6		1.2	1.7	5.3
2.6	2.4	2.7		1.2	1.8		4.1	3.0	4.3
1.3	1.2	1.2	Sales/Total Assets	.6	.7		1.9	1.3	2.6
.6	.6	.5		.2	.4		.6	.6	1.5
1.6	2.2	1.3		4.5	8.2		1.1	.9	.4
(61) 5.0	(83) 6.7	(89) 4.2	% Depr., Dep., Amort./Sales	(16) 13.7	(27) 12.5	(11) 1.8	(12) 2.8	(17) 1.4	
9.8	14.4	13.0		29.3	16.5		5.7	4.3	2.4
1.7	1.1	1.4	% Officers', Directors'				1.4		
(20) 3.8	(31) 1.6	(37) 3.7	Owners' Comp/Sales		(17) 3.0				
6.1	3.1	5.8			4.9				
1283224M	4659895M	4342060M	Net Sales ($)	10243M	55486M	30860M	88008M	254279M	3903184M
792676M	1245167M	2187837M	Total Assets ($)	37257M	102130M	55946M	89288M	247358M	1655858M

© RMA 2010

M = $ thousand   MM = $ million
See Pages 9 through 22 for Explanation of Ratios and Data

Current Data Sorted by Assets | Comparative Historical Data

0-500M	500M-2MM	2-10MM	10-50MM	50-100MM	100-250MM	Type of Statement	4/1/05-3/31/06 ALL	4/1/06-3/31/07 ALL
		1	3	2	2	Unqualified	5	8
	3	4	8	1		Reviewed	4	7
	13	2	7			Compiled	15	20
2	13	7			1	Tax Returns	8	8
	1	5	8			Other	12	23
	13 (4/1-9/30/09)		58 (10/1/09-3/31/10)					
2	17	19	26	4	3	**NUMBER OF STATEMENTS**	44	66
%	%	%	%	%	%	**ASSETS**	%	%
	7.9	14.9	4.1			Cash & Equivalents	5.1	6.4
	8.8	10.5	15.0			Trade Receivables (net)	9.6	10.5
	8.8	6.0	19.6			Inventory	17.5	15.5
	8.3	5.7	4.6			All Other Current	3.5	4.3
	33.8	37.0	43.3			Total Current	35.6	36.7
	48.5	53.7	42.7			Fixed Assets (net)	52.1	47.3
	4.5	2.0	.6			Intangibles (net)	.6	3.4
	13.2	7.2	13.8			All Other Non-Current	11.7	12.7
	100.0	100.0	100.0			Total	100.0	100.0
						LIABILITIES		
	29.2	20.9	15.0			Notes Payable-Short Term	23.1	18.9
	13.9	4.5	4.5			Cur. Mat.-L.T.D.	8.8	10.5
	3.6	8.5	6.0			Trade Payables	3.7	4.3
	.5	.5	.4			Income Taxes Payable	.8	1.0
	3.0	11.1	5.2			All Other Current	5.0	5.9
	50.1	45.5	31.0			Total Current	41.4	40.5
	37.6	32.7	24.9			Long-Term Debt	29.9	36.0
	.8	.2	.1			Deferred Taxes	.5	.2
	6.2	3.2	2.3			All Other Non-Current	1.4	4.7
	5.3	18.4	41.8			Net Worth	26.9	18.7
	100.0	100.0	100.0			Total Liabilities & Net Worth	100.0	100.0
						INCOME DATA		
	100.0	100.0	100.0			Net Sales	100.0	100.0
						Gross Profit		
	96.7	89.2	89.1			Operating Expenses	89.2	87.7
	3.3	10.8	10.9			Operating Profit	10.8	12.3
	-.5	4.3	4.3			All Other Expenses (net)	4.7	2.5
	3.8	6.5	6.6			Profit Before Taxes	6.1	9.8
						RATIOS		
	6.0	2.0	2.3				1.4	1.7
	.8	1.0	1.5			Current	.9	1.1
	.1	.2	1.0				.4	.5
	3.7	1.7	1.0				.8	.8
	.3	.6	.5			Quick	.2	.3
	.0	.1	.2				.0	.1
0 UND	0 UND	13 28.0					0 UND	0 UND
0 UND	1 595.2	33 11.1				Sales/Receivables	16 23.1	16 23.0
45 8.0	21 17.6	64 5.7					71 5.1	60 6.1
						Cost of Sales/Inventory		
						Cost of Sales/Payables		
	4.8	4.9	2.5				6.3	4.2
	-35.3	55.8	9.0			Sales/Working Capital	-102.8	61.1
	-3.2	-3.5	501.6				-4.6	-5.9
	19.3	8.8	8.5				6.7	7.9
	(15) 3.0	(17) 3.2	(23) 3.1			EBIT/Interest	(36) 2.5	(55) 3.1
	.6	1.4	-.5				.4	1.6
						Net Profit + Depr., Dep., Amort./Cur. Mat. L/T/D		5.8
							(11)	3.3
								1.3
	.5	1.6	.6				.7	.8
	2.2	3.2	1.0			Fixed/Worth	1.3	1.5
	-2.2	17.5	2.5				7.0	9.8
	.8	2.2	.8				.8	.9
	3.8	5.7	1.3			Debt/Worth	1.9	2.0
	-2.2	20.3	4.2				7.9	21.2
	22.8	62.9	24.2				29.0	36.3
	(11) 8.2	(15) 34.2	9.0			% Profit Before Taxes/Tangible Net Worth	(36) 5.2	(52) 17.0
	2.5	.8	-14.6				-1.6	6.7
	10.3	12.3	11.6				8.9	13.7
	2.8	6.6	5.0			% Profit Before Taxes/Total Assets	1.7	5.9
	-1.9	.1	-3.4				-1.5	1.2
	19.0	2.8	4.1				4.0	5.2
	2.9	2.1	2.1			Sales/Net Fixed Assets	2.3	2.7
	1.9	1.1	.9				1.2	1.2
	2.8	1.8	1.6				1.9	1.8
	1.5	1.0	.7			Sales/Total Assets	1.1	1.1
	1.0	.6	.4				.5	.5
	2.3	2.1	3.1				4.0	3.5
	(15) 6.3	(18) 5.3	(25) 5.6			% Depr., Dep., Amort./Sales	(40) 6.1	(53) 5.2
	9.7	9.9	7.7				7.9	7.7
						% Officers', Directors' Owners' Comp/Sales		1.4
							(16)	3.2
								6.4
1909M	32135M	131192M	1011708M	313884M	205643M	Net Sales ($)	779955M	1349823M
650M	19463M	89356M	675923M	307178M	417049M	Total Assets ($)	610146M	1263850M

M = $ thousand   MM = $ million
See Pages 9 through 22 for Explanation of Ratios and Data

Comparative Historical Data | Current Data Sorted by Sales

4/1/07-3/31/08 ALL	4/1/08-3/31/09 ALL	4/1/09-3/31/10 ALL	Type of Statement	0-1MM	1-3MM	3-5MM	5-10MM	10-25MM	25MM & OVER
6	6	8	Unqualified					1	7
14	19	13	Reviewed		1	1	2	3	6
15	23	12	Compiled		4		1	4	1
7	6	23	Tax Returns	2	15	3	1	1	1
19	16	15	Other	3	3		3	3	5
					13 (4/1-9/30/09)		58 (10/1/09-3/31/10)		
61	70	71	**NUMBER OF STATEMENTS**	5	23	4	7	12	20
%	%	%	**ASSETS**	%	%	%	%	%	%
9.4	5.5	8.1	Cash & Equivalents		10.6			8.0	5.5
12.7	11.9	11.3	Trade Receivables (net)		6.7			10.7	19.8
13.2	17.8	13.3	Inventory		7.3			13.3	22.4
4.7	5.3	5.9	All Other Current		6.9			11.0	4.5
40.0	40.5	38.7	Total Current		31.5			42.9	52.3
40.0	44.4	48.6	Fixed Assets (net)		52.5			50.0	37.0
3.8	3.8	2.1	Intangibles (net)		3.4			.6	3.2
16.1	11.4	10.6	All Other Non-Current		12.5			6.4	7.5
100.0	100.0	100.0	Total		100.0			100.0	100.0
			LIABILITIES						
16.2	17.4	21.4	Notes Payable-Short Term		26.0			18.9	17.1
9.7	6.2	6.5	Cur. Mat.-L.T.D.		13.1			5.3	3.7
7.0	4.3	5.8	Trade Payables		1.0			8.7	10.0
.3	.6	.4	Income Taxes Payable		.5			.1	.4
7.2	8.9	6.1	All Other Current		5.3			6.8	7.8
40.4	37.4	40.2	Total Current		46.0			39.8	39.0
27.8	26.9	31.6	Long-Term Debt		42.7			21.8	24.4
.5	.5	.3	Deferred Taxes		.0			.0	.1
5.1	3.6	3.2	All Other Non-Current		4.9			1.3	2.2
26.2	31.7	24.7	Net Worth		6.3			37.1	34.4
100.0	100.0	100.0	Total Liabilties & Net Worth		100.0			100.0	100.0
			INCOME DATA						
100.0	100.0	100.0	Net Sales		100.0			100.0	100.0
			Gross Profit						
86.1	86.1	90.9	Operating Expenses		90.8			97.1	91.3
13.9	13.9	9.1	Operating Profit		9.2			2.9	8.7
4.3	3.7	2.4	All Other Expenses (net)		1.7			4.6	-.2
9.6	10.2	6.6	Profit Before Taxes		7.4			-1.7	8.9
			RATIOS						
2.9	2.4	2.3			4.9			2.6	1.9
1.2	1.2	1.2	Current		.7			1.3	1.3
.9	.6	.7			.1			.8	1.0
1.8	1.2	1.5			2.2			.6	.9
.7	.3	.5	Quick		.2			.4	.6
.1	.1	.1			.0			.2	.4
0 UND	0 UND	0 UND		0 UND				9 39.2	31 12.0
23 16.1	28 12.9	21 17.6	Sales/Receivables	0 UND				31 11.9	38 9.6
49 7.4	56 6.5	58 6.3		16 22.9				65 5.7	77 4.8
			Cost of Sales/Inventory						
			Cost of Sales/Payables						
4.6	2.9	3.5			4.9			3.1	3.4
16.1	12.9	14.9	Sales/Working Capital		-6.3			10.8	9.0
-12.9	-9.8	-6.3			-2.9			NM	282.9
10.7	6.9	9.3			5.1			9.0	16.4
(50) 2.1	(61) 3.6	(64) 3.3	EBIT/Interest	(20) 2.8			(11) 1.1	(19) 5.3
1.3	1.5	.7			.5			-1.5	3.0
2.9	4.2	5.8	Net Profit + Depr., Dep.,						
(10) 1.5	(17) 2.7	(16) 3.1	Amort./Cur. Mat. L/T/D						
-.4	1.4	.0							
.3	.7	.7			.7			.8	.6
1.2	1.3	1.9	Fixed/Worth		3.0			1.4	1.5
5.2	3.7	4.7			-3.7			7.5	2.7
.4	.7	1.1			1.5			.7	1.2
1.8	1.8	2.7	Debt/Worth		5.3			1.3	2.5
18.7	20.4	9.3			-2.8			16.6	6.0
36.8	54.6	40.8	% Profit Before Taxes/Tangible		22.8			57.4	50.0
(52) 10.0	(59) 18.5	(60) 15.1	Net Worth	(15) 7.5			4.5	(19) 31.6
5.3	4.5	-2.9			.8			-22.7	10.2
9.0	13.9	11.4	% Profit Before Taxes/Total		8.6			17.8	13.7
4.5	5.6	5.9	Assets		2.8			1.6	9.3
1.4	1.4	-1.1			.1			-7.8	2.2
7.9	5.6	4.1			4.2			3.8	7.1
2.9	2.2	2.2	Sales/Net Fixed Assets		2.8			2.1	3.1
1.1	1.1	1.1			1.1			.9	1.5
1.8	1.9	1.8			1.8			1.8	2.1
1.0	.9	1.0	Sales/Total Assets		1.1			1.2	.9
.5	.5	.5			.6			.4	.6
2.7	3.2	3.1			5.0			5.2	2.8
(51) 5.0	(63) 5.0	(65) 5.6	% Depr., Dep., Amort./Sales	(20) 7.4			5.8	(18) 4.1
7.9	7.5	9.3			12.6			7.4	5.4
		1.1	% Officers', Directors'						
	(13) 4.5	(19) 2.1	Owners' Comp/Sales						
	7.5	5.4							
1487510M	1762945M	1696471M	Net Sales ($)	3104M	43844M	14476M	51324M	171805M	1411918M
1264892M	1862901M	1509619M	Total Assets ($)	8464M	85259M	13684M	79822M	229048M	1093342M

M = $ thousand   MM = $ million
See Pages 9 through 22 for Explanation of Ratios and Data

Current Data Sorted by Assets

Comparative Historical Data

						Type of Statement		
		1	5	6	6	Unqualified	16	7
		4	12	3		Reviewed	19	11
	5	10	6			Compiled	18	15
4	9	5	1			Tax Returns	13	12
	7	15	11	7	1	Other	28	39
	30 (4/1-9/30/09)		88 (10/1/09-3/31/10)				4/1/05-3/31/06	4/1/06-3/31/07
0-500M	500M-2MM	2-10MM	10-50MM	50-100MM	100-250MM		ALL	ALL
4	21	35	35	16	7	NUMBER OF STATEMENTS	94	84
%	%	%	%	%	%	ASSETS	%	%
	14.5	10.6	8.6	6.2		Cash & Equivalents	8.5	7.0
	10.8	23.8	18.0	13.1		Trade Receivables (net)	18.4	17.5
	6.1	9.4	18.7	20.7		Inventory	13.3	15.4
	2.7	5.0	6.0	7.6		All Other Current	4.1	6.6
	34.1	48.8	51.3	47.6		Total Current	44.3	46.5
	55.0	38.1	35.9	32.5		Fixed Assets (net)	39.0	40.7
	.1	2.6	.7	2.8		Intangibles (net)	.8	1.7
	10.7	10.6	12.1	17.1		All Other Non-Current	15.9	11.1
	100.0	100.0	100.0	100.0		Total	100.0	100.0
						LIABILITIES		
	14.4	15.6	13.5	8.8		Notes Payable-Short Term	18.7	17.1
	5.7	2.9	2.9	1.0		Cur. Mat.-L.T.D.	3.2	2.5
	6.2	12.8	11.9	8.1		Trade Payables	11.2	9.8
	.1	.0	.5	.1		Income Taxes Payable	.5	.4
	34.6	16.5	7.3	8.4		All Other Current	10.3	6.5
	61.0	47.9	36.2	26.3		Total Current	44.0	36.3
	40.6	28.6	13.5	11.9		Long-Term Debt	22.4	19.5
	.0	.7	1.3	1.3		Deferred Taxes	1.2	.6
	22.9	5.1	3.9	3.3		All Other Non-Current	6.1	3.7
	-24.5	17.7	45.1	57.3		Net Worth	26.4	39.9
	100.0	100.0	100.0	100.0		Total Liabilties & Net Worth	100.0	100.0
						INCOME DATA		
	100.0	100.0	100.0	100.0		Net Sales	100.0	100.0
						Gross Profit		
	94.6	92.2	95.2	90.0		Operating Expenses	92.4	93.0
	5.4	7.8	4.8	10.0		Operating Profit	7.6	7.0
	4.1	3.0	.7	-1.6		All Other Expenses (net)	2.0	1.3
	1.3	4.8	4.1	11.6		Profit Before Taxes	5.6	5.6
						RATIOS		
	6.7	2.2	3.9	2.7			1.9	2.7
	.5	1.4	1.7	1.9		Current	1.2	1.2
	.2	.6	1.1	1.2			.7	.9
	3.8	1.5	2.0	1.4			1.4	1.2
	.5	.7	.9	.8		Quick	.7	.5
	.0	.2	.4	.2			.2	.2
0	UND	0 950.6	11 32.2	27 13.7			0 UND	0 999.8
0	UND	28 13.1	32 11.2	40 9.1		Sales/Receivables	28 12.9	27 13.5
11	32.9	44 8.2	55 6.6	62 5.9			43 8.5	47 7.8
						Cost of Sales/Inventory		
						Cost of Sales/Payables		
	20.0	5.8	4.2	3.6			7.5	6.2
	-25.9	23.8	7.5	6.6		Sales/Working Capital	28.9	21.5
	-6.6	-12.1	51.7	23.2			-26.8	-51.8
	6.5	10.7	9.7	28.3			13.5	11.8
(16)	2.2	(30) 3.7	(32) 3.9	(13) 3.2		EBIT/Interest	(80) 3.2	(72) 3.0
	.0	.9	1.2	-.8			.9	.4
			28.7			Net Profit + Depr., Dep.,	7.7	7.7
		(11) 9.3				Amort./Cur. Mat. L/T/D	(19) 2.3	(14) 2.9
		1.5					.9	1.7
	.6	.5	.3	.4			.5	.5
	53.7	1.3	.7	.6		Fixed/Worth	1.0	.9
	-1.0	-7.7	1.7	1.1			2.9	1.9
	1.4	1.1	.5	.3			.5	.5
	52.8	2.5	1.1	.5		Debt/Worth	1.6	1.4
	-3.0	-9.1	4.7	2.4			6.1	4.6
	127.5	31.9	28.2	30.1		% Profit Before Taxes/Tangible	34.3	50.0
(11)	24.7	(24) 13.4	(32) 11.9	10.2		Net Worth	(83) 12.7	(75) 15.1
	6.9	6.4	1.8	-1.0			.6	-.2
	18.3	15.7	11.1	18.3		% Profit Before Taxes/Total	14.6	21.6
	2.6	6.2	3.8	7.0		Assets	4.8	4.2
	-14.0	.9	.6	-.4			.0	-1.9
	15.4	19.5	15.7	8.4			16.3	11.1
	9.0	6.3	4.8	4.0		Sales/Net Fixed Assets	5.3	5.1
	3.1	2.8	2.4	1.9			2.8	2.5
	6.0	3.5	2.5	1.7			3.7	3.3
	3.6	2.1	1.5	1.2		Sales/Total Assets	1.9	2.0
	2.3	1.3	1.0	.5			1.2	1.2
	1.1	.9	1.3	2.0			1.3	1.8
(17)	3.6	(28) 1.9	(34) 2.2	(15) 3.1		% Depr., Dep., Amort./Sales	(80) 3.0	(69) 3.0
	7.6	5.1	5.2	4.0			5.0	4.7
		1.0	1.2			% Officers', Directors'	.7	1.1
	(12)	1.7	(13) 1.8			Owners' Comp/Sales	(25) 1.7	(23) 3.0
		3.4	3.3					5.0
6714M	90980M	442576M	1453637M	1392092M	1610251M	Net Sales ($)	3086065M	2138147M
1107M	22164M	163015M	731893M	1184241M	1133285M	Total Assets ($)	1811315M	1437164M

M = $ thousand   MM = $ million
See Pages 9 through 22 for Explanation of Ratios and Data

Comparative Historical Data | | | Current Data Sorted by Sales

Comparative Historical Data				Current Data Sorted by Sales					
			Type of Statement						
12	13	18	Unqualified					3	15
11	24	19	Reviewed				2	8	9
13	20	21	Compiled				6	5	4
12	15	19	Tax Returns	2	2	2	4		2
32	31	41	Other	4	5	4	4	8	15
4/1/07-3/31/08	4/1/08-3/31/09	4/1/09-3/31/10				9	8		
ALL	ALL	ALL				30 (4/1-9/30/09)		88 (10/1/09-3/31/10)	
				0-1MM	1-3MM	3-5MM	5-10MM	10-25MM	25MM & OVER
80	103	118	**NUMBER OF STATEMENTS**	6	8	15	20	24	45
%	%	%	**ASSETS**	%	%	%	%	%	%
8.8	7.8	9.7	Cash & Equivalents			7.7	7.4	14.5	9.1
17.4	16.9	17.0	Trade Receivables (net)			20.1	8.8	22.5	21.4
14.5	16.2	13.2	Inventory			10.1	9.9	10.1	19.9
5.8	6.1	5.8	All Other Current			8.9	1.6	5.2	8.0
46.4	47.0	45.6	Total Current			46.8	27.6	52.3	58.4
39.3	38.5	40.5	Fixed Assets (net)			37.0	49.7	31.6	32.6
1.8	3.1	1.4	Intangibles (net)			.2	3.4	.7	1.6
12.5	11.5	12.5	All Other Non-Current			16.0	19.3	15.4	7.3
100.0	100.0	100.0	Total			100.0	100.0	100.0	100.0
			LIABILITIES						
17.7	15.7	13.8	Notes Payable-Short Term			16.0	18.5	14.3	10.3
3.1	4.2	3.0	Cur. Mat.-L.T.D.			6.2	2.4	3.9	1.8
11.7	11.6	10.3	Trade Payables			6.7	2.6	14.1	15.7
.4	.5	.3	Income Taxes Payable			.1	.0	.7	.3
9.8	12.7	16.4	All Other Current			38.6	21.4	3.3	11.5
42.7	44.6	43.7	Total Current			67.6	44.9	36.4	39.6
16.9	20.8	26.4	Long-Term Debt			51.2	25.3	16.2	13.9
.7	.8	1.0	Deferred Taxes			.0	2.6	1.1	.8
5.4	5.2	8.6	All Other Non-Current			3.2	7.5	8.7	1.6
34.3	28.6	20.3	Net Worth			-22.0	19.7	37.5	44.1
100.0	100.0	100.0	Total Liabilties & Net Worth			100.0	100.0	100.0	100.0
			INCOME DATA						
100.0	100.0	100.0	Net Sales			100.0	100.0	100.0	100.0
			Gross Profit						
94.2	95.0	93.8	Operating Expenses			91.0	89.7	97.2	96.2
5.8	5.0	6.2	Operating Profit			9.0	10.3	2.8	3.8
1.5	1.8	1.7	All Other Expenses (net)			2.7	.1	1.4	-.6
4.4	3.2	4.5	Profit Before Taxes			6.3	10.2	1.4	4.4
			RATIOS						
2.3	2.4	2.6				2.3	4.8	2.3	2.7
1.3	1.2	1.5	Current			1.5	1.3	1.3	1.7
.8	.8	.8				.4	.1	.9	1.2
1.4	1.2	1.6				1.2	2.6	2.0	1.4
.6	.5	.7	Quick			.7	.5	.8	.8
.2	.3	.3				.0	.0	.4	.4
0 999.8	1 254.7	1 426.3		0 UND	0 UND	12 29.9	25 14.7		
24 15.5	29 12.4	28 13.1	Sales/Receivables	9 41.8	1 495.2	31 11.9	35 10.5		
46 7.9	51 7.1	49 7.4		90 4.1	37 9.8	51 7.1	53 6.8		
			Cost of Sales/Inventory						
			Cost of Sales/Payables						
5.7	6.0	5.0				3.2	6.8	5.2	4.2
19.7	18.9	13.6	Sales/Working Capital			9.6	24.6	13.6	7.5
-38.1	-26.4	-25.2				-13.0	-6.3	-51.2	31.8
15.5	7.6	9.6				11.4	12.0	6.2	13.9
(70) 5.0	(90) 3.3	(102) 3.6	EBIT/Interest	(12) 5.8	(18) 3.0	(21) 2.4	(41) 4.7		
1.2	.6	.5				.9	1.1	-.2	2.3
19.0	3.9	11.6	Net Profit + Depr., Dep.,						11.4
(13) 4.4	(23) 2.1	(27) 3.6	Amort./Cur. Mat. L/T/D					(16)	5.3
1.2	1.3	1.5							2.8
.4	.4	.5				.1	.6	.4	.5
.8	1.0	1.1	Fixed/Worth			.8	2.0	.8	.7
2.6	2.6	NM				-.9	-1.7	2.5	1.6
.6	.6	.6				.8	.8	.6	.5
1.2	1.5	1.9	Debt/Worth			2.1	2.9	1.6	1.1
3.7	10.4	NM				-2.1	-3.9	6.3	4.9
30.7	37.3	33.2	% Profit Before Taxes/Tangible			17.8	25.8	32.6	
(69) 15.2	(81) 10.6	(89) 12.9	Net Worth		(13) 8.3	(21) 9.3	(40) 16.0		
2.2	.1	2.3				2.2	-.8	5.5	
14.7	13.1	15.3	% Profit Before Taxes/Total			25.7	18.0	8.0	15.5
5.4	3.9	4.7	Assets			5.0	5.9	2.7	6.8
-.5	-.2	-.4				-7.3	.6	-.9	2.0
12.7	13.5	14.4				57.6	10.3	20.3	17.5
4.8	7.2	4.9	Sales/Net Fixed Assets			12.0	4.5	6.5	5.1
2.3	3.1	2.4				3.4	1.9	2.9	2.8
2.9	3.3	3.3				3.7	3.3	3.5	3.0
1.8	1.9	1.7	Sales/Total Assets			3.1	1.9	1.9	1.7
1.1	1.1	1.1				1.4	1.3	1.1	1.3
1.4	1.4	1.2				1.3	1.0	1.0	1.3
(64) 2.9	(94) 2.6	(104) 2.4	% Depr., Dep., Amort./Sales	(11) 2.3	(16) 3.3	(22) 2.0	(42) 2.2		
4.9	4.3	5.2				6.5	4.8	6.8	3.6
1.2	1.0	1.5	% Officers', Directors'						1.5
(20) 2.1	(32) 2.4	(38) 1.9	Owners' Comp/Sales					(15)	2.2
4.6	6.3	3.8							3.6
2953240M	4110465M	4996250M	Net Sales ($)	3031M	15994M	59944M	135758M	383084M	4398439M
1924935M	2490137M	3235705M	Total Assets ($)	25385M	9248M	40506M	165688M	285132M	2709746M

M = $ thousand   MM = $ million
See Pages 9 through 22 for Explanation of Ratios and Data

Current Data Sorted by Assets

Comparative Historical Data

0-500M	500M-2MM	2-10MM	10-50MM	50-100MM	100-250MM	Type of Statement	4/1/05-3/31/06 ALL	4/1/06-3/31/07 ALL
1	1	2	1	2	8	Unqualified	13	5
	1	1	3		1	Reviewed	6	2
1	2	6	4			Compiled	7	13
4	8	3	1			Tax Returns	7	7
1	5	7	4	1	1	Other	10	6
	24 (4/1-9/30/09)		43 (10/1/09-3/31/10)					
6	16	19	13	3	10	NUMBER OF STATEMENTS	43	33
%	%	%	%	%	%	ASSETS	%	%
	13.2	7.2	10.2		17.3	Cash & Equivalents	15.1	14.9
	5.7	14.6	10.9		9.9	Trade Receivables (net)	9.4	6.1
	8.6	5.3	6.8		11.9	Inventory	10.2	5.6
	13.4	3.7	.9		1.6	All Other Current	2.6	4.3
	40.9	30.8	28.8		40.7	Total Current	37.2	31.0
	48.0	53.6	49.5		45.7	Fixed Assets (net)	49.4	51.3
	1.3	.2	2.9		1.2	Intangibles (net)	4.5	.6
	9.9	15.4	18.9		12.4	All Other Non-Current	8.9	17.1
	100.0	100.0	100.0		100.0	Total	100.0	100.0
						LIABILITIES		
	23.1	8.8	6.2		9.2	Notes Payable-Short Term	11.2	11.2
	4.2	2.8	1.9		2.0	Cur. Mat.-L.T.D.	5.4	3.1
	2.6	11.8	11.5		10.3	Trade Payables	5.5	3.3
	.0	.0	.0		.0	Income Taxes Payable	.5	.1
	4.3	10.1	6.8		3.9	All Other Current	11.9	8.0
	34.3	33.4	26.4		25.5	Total Current	34.5	25.8
	27.4	33.6	26.9		21.3	Long-Term Debt	32.9	52.8
	.1	.0	1.7		2.8	Deferred Taxes	.7	.0
	3.2	6.5	1.8		4.4	All Other Non-Current	3.6	5.2
	35.0	26.5	43.1		46.0	Net Worth	28.4	16.2
	100.0	100.0	100.0		100.0	Total Liabilties & Net Worth	100.0	100.0
						INCOME DATA		
	100.0	100.0	100.0		100.0	Net Sales	100.0	100.0
						Gross Profit		
	98.3	86.9	89.8		94.3	Operating Expenses	89.4	86.9
	1.7	13.1	10.2		5.7	Operating Profit	10.6	13.1
	3.0	3.6	9.0		3.5	All Other Expenses (net)	2.6	1.9
	-1.3	9.5	1.2		2.2	Profit Before Taxes	8.0	11.2
						RATIOS		
	2.8	4.8	1.9		2.5		2.4	3.3
	1.2	.9	1.2		1.7	Current	1.7	1.2
	.2	.1	.6		1.2		.6	.6
	1.5	1.5	1.7		1.3		1.9	2.2
	.7	.5	.7		.9	Quick	.6	.6
	.1	.0	.4		.5		.3	.2
0 UND	0 UND	0 UND		7 53.7			0 UND	0 UND
0 UND	17 21.0	33 11.1		30 12.3		Sales/Receivables	9 40.2	7 55.0
0 UND	38 9.5	80 4.6		60 6.1			39 9.4	69 5.3
						Cost of Sales/Inventory		
						Cost of Sales/Payables		
	2.7	2.6	2.6		2.4		3.1	3.6
	63.7	-145.6	19.4		4.1	Sales/Working Capital	9.7	99.4
	-4.1	-2.2	-11.5		11.7		-6.3	-6.1
	8.4	23.5	56.3		7.1		7.3	6.7
	(14) 1.5	3.0	(11) 3.3		1.2	EBIT/Interest	(36) 3.6	(28) 2.8
	-3.1	1.5	.8		.5		1.2	1.3
						Net Profit + Depr., Dep., Amort./Cur. Mat. L/T/D		
	.6	.4	.6		.7		.8	.8
	1.6	1.3	1.0		1.1	Fixed/Worth	1.3	1.8
	NM	-12.5	2.2		5.3		9.7	UND
	.6	.4	.2		.6		.7	.8
	2.2	4.1	.9		1.0	Debt/Worth	1.5	2.3
	NM	-13.9	7.3		6.5		20.3	UND
	35.8	65.7	11.2			% Profit Before Taxes/Tangible Net Worth	36.2	58.4
	(12) 3.0	(13) 41.4	(12) 1.9				(35) 12.8	(25) 29.6
	-9.4	11.5	-6.0				.8	4.6
	9.5	18.0	6.6		3.9	% Profit Before Taxes/Total Assets	14.0	15.1
	.3	5.2	.5		.0		4.4	5.4
	-6.2	1.6	-2.7		-1.1		.0	1.1
	13.0	8.3	9.2		1.5	Sales/Net Fixed Assets	7.4	5.6
	3.7	2.4	.9		.8		1.8	1.2
	.9	1.0	.3		.6		.5	.5
	1.5	1.7	1.4		.7	Sales/Total Assets	2.4	1.6
	.8	1.1	.4		.4		.9	.5
	.5	.4	.3		.3		.3	.3
	1.6	.6	4.3			% Depr., Dep., Amort./Sales	2.3	5.3
	(14) 6.3	(15) 3.5	(12) 7.6				(37) 6.1	(26) 7.5
	11.9	5.7	15.4				12.4	11.8
						% Officers', Directors' Owners' Comp/Sales		
15818M	43296M	136625M	236853M	142770M	1056829M	Net Sales ($)	910241M	359568M
1445M	20753M	90807M	309936M	260770M	1759617M	Total Assets ($)	1261290M	756157M

M = $ thousand   MM = $ million
See Pages 9 through 22 for Explanation of Ratios and Data

Comparative Historical Data | Current Data Sorted by Sales

			Type of Statement						
9	14	13	Unqualified				2		11
6	5	6	Reviewed			1	4		1
10	11	13	Compiled	3	3	2	2	2	1
10	11	16	Tax Returns	8	5	3			
6	7	19	Other	4	5	2	2	3	3
4/1/07-3/31/08 ALL	4/1/08-3/31/09 ALL	4/1/09-3/31/10 ALL		0-1MM	24 (4/1-9/30/09) 1-3MM	3-5MM	43 (10/1/09-3/31/10) 5-10MM	10-25MM	25MM & OVER
41	48	67	**NUMBER OF STATEMENTS**	15	13	7	5	11	16
%	%	%	**ASSETS**	%	%	%	%	%	%
18.9	12.8	13.8	Cash & Equivalents	12.8	19.2			20.1	12.9
4.3	7.3	9.3	Trade Receivables (net)	2.5	11.3			12.3	15.5
9.1	8.5	7.9	Inventory	1.3	9.1			4.4	19.0
1.3	1.6	6.9	All Other Current	17.2	2.7			1.5	2.0
33.6	30.1	37.9	Total Current	33.9	42.2			38.4	49.4
50.1	53.6	46.2	Fixed Assets (net)	51.8	32.5			37.8	38.9
1.2	.9	1.1	Intangibles (net)	.4	.0			.2	1.1
15.2	15.3	14.7	All Other Non-Current	13.9	25.2			23.6	10.6
100.0	100.0	100.0	Total	100.0	100.0			100.0	100.0
			LIABILITIES						
5.9	7.3	11.9	Notes Payable-Short Term	1.4	30.5			2.4	13.1
2.8	2.9	4.1	Cur. Mat.-L.T.D.	11.4	1.3			1.4	2.1
4.7	6.1	8.0	Trade Payables	2.3	2.9			13.3	15.1
.3	.5	.0	Income Taxes Payable	.0	.0			.0	.0
10.9	4.9	8.1	All Other Current	3.6	5.4			18.3	5.6
24.6	21.8	32.0	Total Current	18.8	40.1			35.3	36.0
29.8	30.4	29.8	Long-Term Debt	39.4	33.7			30.5	17.1
1.1	1.6	.8	Deferred Taxes	1.4	.0			.1	2.1
4.9	4.1	3.6	All Other Non-Current	11.2	.4			1.1	3.4
39.6	42.2	33.7	Net Worth	29.1	25.8			32.9	41.4
100.0	100.0	100.0	Total Liabilties & Net Worth	100.0	100.0			100.0	100.0
			INCOME DATA						
100.0	100.0	100.0	Net Sales	100.0	100.0			100.0	100.0
			Gross Profit						
80.4	88.1	91.1	Operating Expenses	84.9	96.0			95.1	94.8
19.6	11.9	8.9	Operating Profit	15.1	4.0			4.9	5.2
3.4	4.3	4.7	All Other Expenses (net)	8.9	1.0			9.4	2.6
16.2	7.6	4.2	Profit Before Taxes	6.2	3.0			-4.5	2.5
			RATIOS						
3.4	3.2	2.6		21.5	9.3			2.1	1.7
1.8	1.2	1.2	Current	4.0	1.2			1.2	1.4
1.0	.6	.6		.4	.1			.9	1.1
2.4	2.2	1.7		12.4	8.6			1.7	1.2
1.1	.7	.7	Quick	1.7	.9			.9	.6
.4	.3	.2		.2	.1			.5	.5
0 UND	0 UND	0 UND		0 UND	0 UND			0 UND	23 15.9
0 UND	4 90.3	2 151.2	Sales/Receivables	0 UND	0 UND			2 151.2	36 10.1
18 19.7	36 10.3	41 9.0		0 UND	78 4.7			99 3.7	43 8.5
			Cost of Sales/Inventory						
			Cost of Sales/Payables						
3.4	2.5	2.6		1.1	1.4			3.0	2.7
12.4	18.1	19.4	Sales/Working Capital	11.1	8.3			69.9	7.4
-512.6	-11.9	-13.9		-3.4	-3.8			-145.6	59.6
20.7	10.5	10.9		5.4	23.5				4.3
(35) 5.6	(38) 2.6	(59) 2.6	EBIT/Interest	(12) 1.4	(11) 2.1				2.4
2.1	1.1	-.5		-.8	-3.1				.6
		17.3	Net Profit + Depr., Dep., Amort./Cur. Mat. L/T/D						
	(11) 8.4								
		1.6							
.6	.7	.4		.1	.2			.2	.5
1.1	1.2	1.1	Fixed/Worth	1.1	1.0			.6	.9
5.9	4.6	4.4		2.0	-2.3			2.9	1.7
.3	.4	.4		.2	.5			.1	.7
1.2	1.2	1.5	Debt/Worth	.8	1.5			2.8	1.4
8.2	5.3	11.6		-13.9	-7.0			11.5	2.6
33.8	22.2	40.6	% Profit Before Taxes/Tangible Net Worth	28.5					28.7
(34) 17.5	(43) 5.8	(52) 5.9		(11) .7					(15) 3.6
5.2	.6	-1.8		-6.8					-1.9
16.4	12.1	10.8	% Profit Before Taxes/Total Assets	5.2	35.9			18.0	4.4
9.1	2.9	3.2		1.4	1.6			5.2	2.3
2.2	.0	-1.5		-2.9	-5.6			-7.3	-.7
6.4	3.7	14.6	Sales/Net Fixed Assets	4.6	24.0			23.0	24.8
1.5	1.3	1.8		1.0	7.4			2.8	1.3
.6	.5	.8		.2	1.0			.8	.7
1.5	1.3	1.6	Sales/Total Assets	1.0	1.4			4.1	2.0
.6	.7	.8		.3	.9			1.3	.6
.4	.3	.4		.2	.7			.4	.4
1.6	2.4	1.9	% Depr., Dep., Amort./Sales	1.8					2.3
(37) 5.7	(44) 6.1	(53) 5.0		(11) 8.7					(13) 6.2
9.3	12.3	9.5		19.1					8.7
			% Officers', Directors' Owners' Comp/Sales						
947315M	1503199M	1632191M	Net Sales ($)	7484M	26101M	24258M	30916M	178958M	1364474M
1375214M	2113556M	2443328M	Total Assets ($)	48089M	34554M	32630M	40828M	294004M	1993223M

© RMA 2010   **M = $ thousand   MM = $ million**
See Pages 9 through 22 for Explanation of Ratios and Data

Current Data Sorted by Assets

Comparative Historical Data

Type of Statement	0-500M	500M-2MM	2-10MM	10-50MM	50-100MM	100-250MM		4/1/05-3/31/06 ALL	4/1/06-3/31/07 ALL
Unqualified	1				1			1	4
Reviewed		1		2				3	7
Compiled		1	3	4	1			8	12
Tax Returns	2	5						4	10
Other		1	1	4				14	6
	6 (4/1-9/30/09)			21 (10/1/09-3/31/10)					
NUMBER OF STATEMENTS	3	8	4	10	2			30	39
	%	%	%	%	%	%		%	%
ASSETS									
Cash & Equivalents				3.1				3.8	7.5
Trade Receivables (net)				12.0				9.9	9.2
Inventory				27.2				17.4	19.3
All Other Current				1.3				5.7	5.0
Total Current				43.6				36.8	41.0
Fixed Assets (net)				50.5				53.9	47.1
Intangibles (net)				.1				.2	.2
All Other Non-Current				5.8				9.0	11.6
Total				100.0				100.0	100.0
LIABILITIES									
Notes Payable-Short Term				16.8				16.4	12.6
Cur. Mat.-L.T.D.				3.9				2.9	6.5
Trade Payables				4.8				7.7	5.0
Income Taxes Payable				.1				.1	.0
All Other Current				4.6				10.4	12.9
Total Current				30.3				37.3	37.0
Long-Term Debt				30.2				22.2	37.6
Deferred Taxes				2.2				.3	.2
All Other Non-Current				.5				.7	3.5
Net Worth				36.8				39.5	21.6
Total Liabilties & Net Worth				100.0				100.0	100.0
INCOME DATA									
Net Sales				100.0				100.0	100.0
Gross Profit									
Operating Expenses				88.4				91.1	84.3
Operating Profit				11.6				8.9	15.7
All Other Expenses (net)				2.8				1.7	3.4
Profit Before Taxes				8.8				7.2	12.3
RATIOS									
Current				1.9				3.4	2.5
				1.5				1.6	1.3
				.9				.6	.9
Quick				.8				2.0	1.3
				.4				.5 (38)	.6
				.1				.0	.1
Sales/Receivables			1	300.2				0 UND	0 UND
			47	7.7				14 25.8	11 34.0
			92	4.0				41 8.8	45 8.2
Cost of Sales/Inventory									
Cost of Sales/Payables									
Sales/Working Capital				3.4				2.4	3.5
				6.4				15.1	25.2
				-14.5				-9.5	-21.5
EBIT/Interest				6.6				5.5	9.0
				2.3				(27) 2.1	(35) 4.3
				.7				.1	1.6
Net Profit + Depr., Dep., Amort./Cur. Mat. L/T/D									
Fixed/Worth				.8				.7	.8
				1.2				1.2	1.4
				3.0				4.5	4.2
Debt/Worth				.9				.5	.6
				1.7				1.1	1.9
				3.4				8.5	8.2
% Profit Before Taxes/Tangible Net Worth								27.5	44.5
								(26) 6.8	(31) 31.8
								-1.7	13.9
% Profit Before Taxes/Total Assets				15.5				9.4	21.7
				4.5				1.8	14.3
				-.7				-1.4	3.9
Sales/Net Fixed Assets				2.1				3.3	6.0
				1.7				1.9	1.9
				1.2				.9	1.1
Sales/Total Assets				1.0				1.7	1.9
				.8				.9	1.0
				.7				.6	.6
% Depr., Dep., Amort./Sales				4.6				3.6	3.2
				6.0				(28) 5.8	(34) 5.0
				7.5				7.9	6.6
% Officers', Directors' Owners' Comp/Sales									
Net Sales ($)	1759M	17703M	19672M	228343M	179171M			2121737M	556097M
Total Assets ($)	1040M	10499M	17269M	287412M	145339M			600128M	516871M

M = $ thousand   MM = $ million

See Pages 9 through 22 for Explanation of Ratios and Data

Comparative Historical Data   Current Data Sorted by Sales

Comparative Historical Data			Type of Statement	Current Data Sorted by Sales					
3	7	2	Unqualified		1				1
8	5	3	Reviewed		1		1	1	
11	15	9	Compiled		1	1	2	2	3
1	3	7	Tax Returns		2	1			
7	5	6	Other	4	2			2	2
4/1/07-3/31/08 ALL	4/1/08-3/31/09 ALL	4/1/09-3/31/10 ALL		1	6 (4/1-9/30/09)		21 (10/1/09-3/31/10)		
				0-1MM	1-3MM	3-5MM	5-10MM	10-25MM	25MM & OVER
30	35	27	NUMBER OF STATEMENTS	5	6	2	3	5	6
%	%	%	ASSETS	%	%	%	%	%	%
6.4	6.8	7.7	Cash & Equivalents						
9.8	11.8	10.4	Trade Receivables (net)						
20.4	28.1	18.0	Inventory						
2.6	2.8	2.8	All Other Current						
39.3	49.5	38.9	Total Current						
54.8	46.6	55.1	Fixed Assets (net)						
.2	.7	.9	Intangibles (net)						
5.6	3.2	5.2	All Other Non-Current						
100.0	100.0	100.0	Total						
			LIABILITIES						
17.1	18.9	19.9	Notes Payable-Short Term						
4.5	2.7	2.9	Cur. Mat.-L.T.D.						
4.8	6.1	4.4	Trade Payables						
.1	.0	.0	Income Taxes Payable						
2.7	6.1	5.4	All Other Current						
29.2	33.8	32.7	Total Current						
26.0	25.4	29.1	Long-Term Debt						
.3	.3	.8	Deferred Taxes						
1.2	.7	9.6	All Other Non-Current						
43.3	39.8	27.8	Net Worth						
100.0	100.0	100.0	Total Liabilties & Net Worth						
			INCOME DATA						
100.0	100.0	100.0	Net Sales						
			Gross Profit						
88.0	86.4	95.4	Operating Expenses						
12.0	13.6	4.6	Operating Profit						
2.5	2.5	2.0	All Other Expenses (net)						
9.5	11.1	2.7	Profit Before Taxes						
			RATIOS						
2.1	3.3	1.6	Current						
1.4	1.5	1.2							
1.0	1.1	.7							
1.2	1.1	1.1	Quick						
.4	.6	.5							
.0	.0	.2							
0 UND	0 UND	0 999.8	Sales/Receivables						
14 26.3	16 23.1	27 13.6							
45 8.2	59 6.2	52 7.1							
			Cost of Sales/Inventory						
			Cost of Sales/Payables						
3.7	3.0	5.0	Sales/Working Capital						
12.5	6.4	25.5							
NM	38.5	-12.3							
6.1	9.4	5.6	EBIT/Interest						
(29) 3.9	(32) 3.4	(25) 2.3							
1.1	1.6	.6							
			Net Profit + Depr., Dep., Amort./Cur. Mat. L/T/D						
1.1	.9	.8	Fixed/Worth						
1.3	1.2	1.6							
2.2	3.0	4.2							
.4	.8	.8	Debt/Worth						
1.8	1.7	2.2							
3.2	4.1	4.8							
35.9	51.0	28.0	% Profit Before Taxes/Tangible Net Worth						
22.1 (34)	19.2 (22)	12.8							
.7	1.6	.8							
16.7	16.4	12.6	% Profit Before Taxes/Total Assets						
8.5	8.1	3.2							
.6	1.5	-1.7							
2.5	4.1	3.8	Sales/Net Fixed Assets						
1.6	1.8	2.0							
1.1	1.2	1.2							
1.5	1.3	2.1	Sales/Total Assets						
.9	.8	.9							
.7	.6	.7							
3.2	3.6	4.1	% Depr., Dep., Amort./Sales						
(25) 5.1	(29) 4.6	(25) 5.8							
8.5	6.4	7.6							
			% Officers', Directors' Owners' Comp/Sales						
741511M	726160M	446648M	Net Sales ($)	2572M	14365M	8317M	22519M	86698M	312177M
830751M	725391M	461559M	Total Assets ($)	4023M	16699M	2422M	16257M	112975M	309183M

M = $ thousand   MM = $ million
See Pages 9 through 22 for Explanation of Ratios and Data

Current Data Sorted by Assets   Comparative Historical Data

Type of Statement	0-500M	500M-2MM	2-10MM	10-50MM	50-100MM	100-250MM	4/1/05-3/31/06 ALL	4/1/06-3/31/07 ALL
Unqualified		1	8	1	1	1	4	10
Reviewed	2	4	9	3	3		16	13
Compiled		12	8	3	1		12	11
Tax Returns	6	5	24	2	3		19	19
Other	3			11		2	33	26
		10 (4/1-9/30/09)		103 (10/1/09-3/31/10)				
NUMBER OF STATEMENTS	11	22	49	20	8	3	84	79
	%	%	%	%	%	%	%	%
ASSETS								
Cash & Equivalents	21.0	5.8	9.9	4.4			10.3	7.5
Trade Receivables (net)	.1	7.9	8.1	9.5			10.1	11.1
Inventory	14.6	8.0	8.4	10.6			5.6	10.5
All Other Current	2.5	7.9	6.7	7.6			5.0	4.8
Total Current	38.2	29.6	33.1	32.1			31.1	34.0
Fixed Assets (net)	52.2	67.0	53.7	59.3			57.8	55.2
Intangibles (net)	.2	.3	1.0	3.5			.9	1.9
All Other Non-Current	9.4	3.0	12.2	5.1			10.2	8.9
Total	100.0	100.0	100.0	100.0			100.0	100.0
LIABILITIES								
Notes Payable-Short Term	44.6	14.2	10.3	10.5			11.8	13.1
Cur. Mat.-L.T.D.	3.4	2.6	3.2	3.1			3.6	2.8
Trade Payables	.3	4.4	2.2	2.6			2.8	3.8
Income Taxes Payable	.1	.0	.1	.0			.0	.0
All Other Current	3.7	4.4	4.3	5.0			2.5	3.9
Total Current	52.2	25.6	20.1	21.2			20.6	23.5
Long-Term Debt	50.2	63.7	40.8	40.7			43.1	39.0
Deferred Taxes	.6	.0	.1	.8			.0	.2
All Other Non-Current	3.0	6.8	9.5	4.8			7.2	4.7
Net Worth	-5.9	3.9	29.4	32.4			29.0	32.7
Total Liabilities & Net Worth	100.0	100.0	100.0	100.0			100.0	100.0
INCOME DATA								
Net Sales	100.0	100.0	100.0	100.0			100.0	100.0
Gross Profit								
Operating Expenses	86.1	76.3	84.4	85.2			83.5	90.4
Operating Profit	13.9	23.7	15.6	14.8			16.5	9.6
All Other Expenses (net)	6.7	10.9	8.1	9.3			5.8	5.8
Profit Before Taxes	7.2	12.8	7.5	5.4			10.8	3.8
RATIOS								
Current	2.5	6.1	6.2	4.1			5.4	4.1
	.8	1.1	2.3	2.1			2.2	2.0
	.2	.2	.9	1.1			.7	.8
Quick	2.5	2.1	4.1	1.5			4.3	2.3
	.2	.3	.8	.9			1.1	.9
	.1	.0	.1	.3			.2	.2
Sales/Receivables	0 UND	0 UND	0 UND	16 23.5			0 UND	0 UND
	0 UND	0 UND	17 22.1	39 9.5			20 18.6	32 11.3
	0 UND	7 53.5	70 5.2	121 3.0			108 3.4	120 3.0
Cost of Sales/Inventory								
Cost of Sales/Payables								
Sales/Working Capital	13.6	4.1	1.5	1.6			2.2	1.9
	-35.3	NM	4.7	3.4			5.7	5.7
	-4.0	-3.7	-12.9	26.0			-28.1	-17.0
EBIT/Interest		5.5	10.2	7.1			6.4	4.7
		(19) 2.6	(40) 3.9	(13) 1.8			(64) 1.8	(62) 1.9
		1.1	.6	-1.6			.6	.5
Net Profit + Depr., Dep., Amort./Cur. Mat. L/T/D							9.8	5.1
							(11) 7.0	(15) 1.8
							3.3	.5
Fixed/Worth	.2	1.1	.7	.7			.7	.6
	1.5	2.5	1.5	1.5			1.6	1.2
	-1.7	-2.2	41.7	NM			5.3	10.0
Debt/Worth	.4	.6	.5	.3			.4	.5
	6.0	4.2	1.7	1.4			1.6	1.7
	-3.2	-3.5	60.9	NM			8.7	13.4
% Profit Before Taxes/Tangible Net Worth		47.2	38.8	16.2			31.5	20.4
	(15)	5.4 (38)	14.3 (15)	4.1		(69)	16.6 (62)	6.5
		-3.5	-2.1	-1.2			-.3	-7.8
% Profit Before Taxes/Total Assets	61.4	12.8	12.7	5.1			13.7	12.2
	7.4	6.2	4.1	1.3			2.9	1.8
	.0	-.1	-1.8	-5.2			-1.8	-3.5
Sales/Net Fixed Assets	15.9	2.2	2.2	1.9			3.7	4.8
	9.4	1.3	.8	.6			1.2	.9
	2.1	.6	.4	.3			.6	.6
Sales/Total Assets	7.2	1.3	.7	.7			1.2	1.0
	2.1	.7	.5	.4			.6	.6
	1.1	.4	.2	.2			.4	.4
% Depr., Dep., Amort./Sales		3.8	2.8	3.8			3.8	3.6
	(18)	7.2 (41)	7.4 (17)	6.0		(68)	7.3 (68)	7.2
		10.4	13.7	12.1			16.2	13.9
% Officers', Directors' Owners' Comp/Sales							3.7	3.2
						(19)	6.0 (19)	7.5
							8.2	9.8
Net Sales ($)	10337M	24336M	156908M	296983M	353054M	381886M	1019113M	1046827M
Total Assets ($)	3022M	27254M	239014M	392818M	560531M	412153M	1614507M	1375487M

M = $ thousand   MM = $ million
See Pages 9 through 22 for Explanation of Ratios and Data

Comparative Historical Data | Current Data Sorted by Sales

			Type of Statement						
5	3	3	Unqualified		1		2		
4	17	15	Reviewed		5	1	2	4	3
15	11	18	Compiled	8	8		2		
21	30	29	Tax Returns	12	9	2	4	1	1
33	32	48	Other	12	20	5	1	6	4
4/1/07-3/31/08 ALL	4/1/08-3/31/09 ALL	4/1/09-3/31/10 ALL		0-1MM	1-3MM	3-5MM	5-10MM	10-25MM	25MM & OVER
				32	10 (4/1-9/30/09)		103 (10/1/09-3/31/10)		
78	93	113	NUMBER OF STATEMENTS	32	43	8	11	11	8
%	%	%	**ASSETS**	%	%	%	%	%	%
6.8	7.9	8.7	Cash & Equivalents	11.5	7.1		9.3	4.8	
9.4	8.8	7.7	Trade Receivables (net)	2.7	8.7		11.8	8.4	
9.9	9.8	9.3	Inventory	6.9	11.0		8.1	7.2	
4.2	7.4	6.3	All Other Current	5.3	4.5		13.3	12.4	
30.3	33.8	32.1	Total Current	26.4	31.3		42.4	32.9	
55.9	53.5	57.7	Fixed Assets (net)	63.0	59.8		52.3	43.6	
2.5	1.2	1.6	Intangibles (net)	1.3	.8		4.6	.3	
11.4	11.4	8.7	All Other Non-Current	9.3	8.1		.7	23.2	
100.0	100.0	100.0	Total	100.0	100.0		100.0	100.0	
			LIABILITIES						
14.1	13.0	13.8	Notes Payable-Short Term	12.6	17.7		16.0	8.7	
2.7	2.7	2.9	Cur. Mat.-L.T.D.	2.4	3.7		2.9	3.0	
3.5	3.4	3.0	Trade Payables	.9	3.5		4.4	3.0	
.1	.0	.1	Income Taxes Payable	.0	.0		.0	.4	
9.0	6.4	4.0	All Other Current	2.3	3.9		5.8	11.3	
29.4	25.6	23.8	Total Current	18.3	28.8		29.1	26.4	
41.7	42.3	44.7	Long-Term Debt	47.5	50.6		44.3	26.2	
.2	.6	.3	Deferred Taxes	.2	.1		.3	1.5	
7.8	8.6	6.7	All Other Non-Current	4.8	9.5		5.8	5.5	
20.9	22.9	24.5	Net Worth	29.2	11.1		20.6	40.5	
100.0	100.0	100.0	Total Liabilities & Net Worth	100.0	100.0		100.0	100.0	
			INCOME DATA						
100.0	100.0	100.0	Net Sales	100.0	100.0		100.0	100.0	
			Gross Profit						
90.4	90.8	83.5	Operating Expenses	79.1	82.5		89.2	91.3	
9.6	9.2	16.5	Operating Profit	20.9	17.5		10.8	8.7	
5.2	7.2	8.0	All Other Expenses (net)	15.0	6.8		4.3	1.7	
4.4	2.0	8.6	Profit Before Taxes	5.9	10.6		6.6	6.9	
			RATIOS						
3.3	4.3	5.2		7.0	5.2		5.2	2.6	
1.6	1.5	1.9	Current	1.3	1.8		2.9	1.4	
.4	.6	.8		.3	.8		.9	1.1	
1.8	2.2	2.7		4.7	2.6		2.8	1.3	
.6	(92) .7	.7	Quick	.3	.8		1.1	.6	
.1	.1	.1		.1	.1		.4	.4	
0 UND	0 UND	0 UND		0 UND			16 23.2	0 UND	
11 32.6	10 36.2	9 42.5	Sales/Receivables	0 UND	15 24.8		46 7.9	23 16.2	
76 4.8	72 5.1	73 5.0		5 71.7	114 3.2		74 4.9	108 3.4	
			Cost of Sales/Inventory						
			Cost of Sales/Payables						
2.6	2.4	1.9		1.4	1.8		1.6	4.7	
10.1	14.2	5.8	Sales/Working Capital	18.3	5.6		2.6	11.0	
-6.0	-7.5	-11.6		-2.6	-10.5		-12.7	66.4	
3.7	4.4	9.5		5.6	7.4		14.0		
(61) 1.4	(68) 1.5	(89) 3.3	EBIT/Interest	(18) 1.1	(38) 3.2		(10) 4.1		
.3	-.3	1.0		.5	.5		1.6		
	4.3	9.7	Net Profit + Depr., Dep.,						
	(16) 2.1	(17) 3.4	Amort./Cur. Mat. L/T/D						
	-.1	1.8							
.8	.9	.7		1.1	.8		.9	.2	
1.7	1.5	1.5	Fixed/Worth	1.5	2.2		8.2	1.1	
-14.2	-8.5	41.7		4.7	-2.6		-1.8	4.0	
.5	.6	.5		.5	.4		.5	.5	
1.9	2.5	1.7	Debt/Worth	1.9	2.1		9.1	1.7	
-19.2	-12.9	NM		6.0	-4.3		-5.9	5.3	
17.3	24.7	30.0	% Profit Before Taxes/Tangible	49.3	38.5			25.5	
(55) 6.5	(64) 4.0	(85) 9.6	Net Worth	(27) 2.4	(27) 9.3			(10) 12.9	
-10.3	-7.5	-.2		-3.5	-.1			1.1	
9.9	7.1	11.1	% Profit Before Taxes/Total	8.4	13.2		9.5	15.1	
2.5	.5	3.6	Assets	.3	4.9		4.3	3.1	
-2.7	-4.8	-.5		-1.6	-1.8		.4	.4	
3.4	6.4	2.6		2.2	2.1		2.5	19.2	
1.2	1.2	.9	Sales/Net Fixed Assets	.6	.8		1.6	2.1	
.7	.5	.4		.2	.4		.8	.5	
1.1	1.1	1.1		1.1	.9		.8	1.7	
.6	.6	.6	Sales/Total Assets	.4	.5		.7	1.2	
.4	.3	.3		.1	.3		.5	.4	
3.8	3.5	3.5		5.6	2.0		2.5	.9	
(68) 6.9	(79) 8.6	(93) 6.7	% Depr., Dep., Amort./Sales	(23) 8.6	(34) 7.4		(10) 5.3	4.1	
13.4	14.7	11.6		20.5	12.0		10.0	10.9	
1.8	1.3	1.7	% Officers', Directors'						
(14) 2.9	(20) 4.0	(23) 4.9	Owners' Comp/Sales						
7.4	6.4	8.7							
1155100M	1028417M	1223504M	Net Sales ($)	18221M	76508M	30854M	77145M	182825M	837951M
1346911M	1190133M	1634792M	Total Assets ($)	81732M	259407M	65234M	230011M	291063M	707345M

M = $ thousand   MM = $ million
See Pages 9 through 22 for Explanation of Ratios and Data

Current Data Sorted by Assets

Comparative Historical Data

Type of Statement		
Unqualified	1	2
Reviewed	5	1
Compiled	6	5
Tax Returns	7	3
Other	3	5

	3 2	1 2 5 5 8 (4/1-9/30/09)	3 7 2 9	2 3 7	1 1 1				4/1/05- 3/31/06	4/1/06- 3/31/07
	0-500M	500M-2MM	2-10MM	10-50MM 47 (10/1/09-3/31/10)	50-100MM	100-250MM			ALL	ALL
	5	13	21	12	4		NUMBER OF STATEMENTS		22	16
%	%	%	%	%	%				%	%
		9.4	6.5	6.2		D	Cash & Equivalents		9.2	12.7
		15.9	17.6	21.1		A	Trade Receivables (net)		12.9	9.9
		11.9	10.5	15.8		T	Inventory		11.5	14.7
		2.1	6.9	1.6		A	All Other Current		6.2	4.3
		39.3	41.5	44.8			Total Current		39.8	41.6
		49.8	47.9	47.6		N	Fixed Assets (net)		53.6	52.9
		.9	1.2	.1		O	Intangibles (net)		.1	.1
		9.9	9.4	7.5		T	All Other Non-Current		6.6	5.4
		100.0	100.0	100.0			Total		100.0	100.0
						A	**LIABILITIES**			
		23.4	18.3	11.4		V	Notes Payable-Short Term		14.9	18.4
		3.2	4.1	1.2		A	Cur. Mat.-L.T.D.		1.9	2.2
		2.7	6.8	9.6		I	Trade Payables		5.5	2.7
		.0	.4	.0		L	Income Taxes Payable		.8	.6
		2.3	3.8	4.9		A	All Other Current		11.9	4.9
		31.6	33.5	27.0		B	Total Current		35.0	28.8
		32.8	33.4	29.8		L	Long-Term Debt		32.6	31.4
		.0	.0	1.4		E	Deferred Taxes		1.0	1.4
		2.0	8.4	2.9			All Other Non-Current		9.7	3.6
		33.6	24.7	38.9			Net Worth		21.7	34.9
		100.0	100.0	100.0			Total Liabilties & Net Worth		100.0	100.0
							INCOME DATA			
		100.0	100.0	100.0			Net Sales		100.0	100.0
							Gross Profit			
		85.0	90.8	86.4			Operating Expenses		74.5	83.1
		15.0	9.2	13.6			Operating Profit		25.5	16.9
		2.8	4.8	4.0			All Other Expenses (net)		2.2	4.1
		12.1	4.4	9.6			Profit Before Taxes		23.3	12.8
							RATIOS			
		3.0	2.3	2.8					3.1	5.6
		1.4	1.2	2.1			Current		1.7	2.1
		.6	.8	1.1					.2	1.1
		2.3	1.4	1.8					2.5	5.2
		.5	.7	1.3			Quick		.5	.7
		.2	.2	.6					.1	.3
	0 UND	0 UND	0 UND	26 14.0				0 UND	0 UND	
	0 UND	0 UND	37 9.9	58 6.3			Sales/Receivables	25 14.4	35 10.4	
	86 4.3		285 1.3	172 2.1				121 3.0	74 4.9	
							Cost of Sales/Inventory			
							Cost of Sales/Payables			
		3.0	3.5	1.9					3.1	1.8
		30.2	6.4	6.9			Sales/Working Capital		9.1	8.4
		-31.5	-17.9	22.8					-29.3	27.3
		15.6	5.2	3.6					19.7	23.5
	(12) 3.9	(19) 2.6	(11) 2.3			EBIT/Interest	(20) 8.4	(15) 4.6	
		1.5	.1	1.2					3.5	1.4
							Net Profit + Depr., Dep., Amort./Cur. Mat. L/T/D			
		1.0	1.0	.7					.8	.5
		1.2	1.7	1.1			Fixed/Worth		1.3	1.0
		4.1	11.7	3.1					NM	1.9
		.6	1.2	.6					1.3	.9
		2.7	3.4	2.0			Debt/Worth		4.0	1.3
		4.2	NM	5.4					NM	3.4
		52.0	31.5	80.4			% Profit Before Taxes/Tangible Net Worth		104.8	55.4
	(11) 7.8	(16) 7.1	5.4				(17) 50.6	(14) 23.9	
		3.3	-1.1	.8					14.0	8.0
		20.4	9.2	11.6			% Profit Before Taxes/Total Assets		51.0	29.6
		7.5	1.3	2.6					15.2	6.8
		1.7	-4.5	.6					.9	1.7
		10.3	3.4	10.7			Sales/Net Fixed Assets		6.9	5.1
		3.6	1.4	1.1					2.2	2.1
		1.0	.7	.4					.6	.8
		2.5	1.4	1.7			Sales/Total Assets		1.9	1.3
		1.1	.5	.4					.9	.9
		.6	.4	.3					.5	.6
		2.5	3.0	1.4			% Depr., Dep., Amort./Sales		2.4	2.0
	(11) 5.5	(17) 10.9	(10) 6.7				(19) 3.9	4.7	
		13.7	18.3	13.1					7.6	9.8
							% Officers', Directors' Owners' Comp/Sales			
	2673M	26081M	133678M	269440M	357870M		Net Sales ($)		392850M	251230M
	1438M	16656M	110632M	281926M	302196M		Total Assets ($)		386544M	300571M

© RMA 2010

M = $ thousand   MM = $ million
See Pages 9 through 22 for Explanation of Ratios and Data

Comparative Historical Data

Current Data Sorted by Sales

07-08 ALL	08-09 ALL	09-10 ALL	Type of Statement	0-1MM	1-3MM	3-5MM	5-10MM	10-25MM	25MM & OVER
2	11	4	Unqualified		1			1	2
2	11	7	Reviewed		2	2			2
6	10	10	Compiled		4	2	2		
3	8	10	Tax Returns	5	4	1		2	
5	21	24	Other	8	5	3		4	4
4/1/07-3/31/08	4/1/08-3/31/09	4/1/09-3/31/10		*8 (4/1-9/30/09)*		*47 (10/1/09-3/31/10)*			
				0-1MM	1-3MM	3-5MM	5-10MM	10-25MM	25MM & OVER
18	61	55	NUMBER OF STATEMENTS	13	16	8	3	7	8
%	%	%	ASSETS	%	%	%	%	%	%
5.8	7.6	7.3	Cash & Equivalents	4.5	9.9				
9.8	16.3	15.9	Trade Receivables (net)	10.5	22.0				
19.4	9.8	11.8	Inventory	2.6	9.3				
6.5	5.1	5.3	All Other Current	3.3	2.9				
41.4	38.8	40.3	Total Current	21.0	44.1				
47.6	47.7	48.7	Fixed Assets (net)	64.4	39.3				
.2	.3	.7	Intangibles (net)	.3	2.2				
10.8	13.1	10.2	All Other Non-Current	14.3	14.4				
100.0	100.0	100.0	Total	100.0	100.0				
			LIABILITIES						
26.6	23.6	18.3	Notes Payable-Short Term	20.5	21.7				
3.0	1.3	3.5	Cur. Mat.-L.T.D.	6.7	3.9				
5.4	4.3	6.3	Trade Payables	.6	2.7				
.6	.7	.2	Income Taxes Payable	.0	.0				
11.8	2.9	6.4	All Other Current	8.6	2.8				
47.5	32.7	34.7	Total Current	36.5	31.1				
21.4	25.3	33.4	Long-Term Debt	42.0	43.5				
.7	2.2	.3	Deferred Taxes	.0	.0				
5.0	1.8	5.7	All Other Non-Current	7.1	6.4				
25.4	38.0	25.9	Net Worth	14.4	18.9				
100.0	100.0	100.0	Total Liabilities & Net Worth	100.0	100.0				
			INCOME DATA						
100.0	100.0	100.0	Net Sales	100.0	100.0				
			Gross Profit						
91.1	84.6	88.7	Operating Expenses	78.8	88.2				
8.9	15.4	11.3	Operating Profit	21.2	11.8				
6.1	3.4	3.9	All Other Expenses (net)	6.4	5.0				
2.7	12.1	7.4	Profit Before Taxes	14.7	6.7				
			RATIOS						
4.2	3.2	2.6		1.6	5.0				
1.2	1.6	1.3	Current	.8	1.4				
.4	1.0	.7		.0	.7				
3.7	2.9	1.8		1.6	4.7				
.3	1.0	.7	Quick	.1	1.0				
.1	.3	.2		.0	.4				
0 UND	0 UND	0 UND		0 UND	0 UND				
9 42.7	36 10.2	29 12.6	Sales/Receivables	0 UND	40 9.2				
38 9.6	203 1.8	95 3.8		61 6.0	323 1.1				
			Cost of Sales/Inventory						
			Cost of Sales/Payables						
4.6	2.2	3.6		16.8	1.6				
25.8	6.1	8.9	Sales/Working Capital	-14.7	5.5				
-1.3	369.1	-21.8		-3.5	-41.1				
2.0	15.9	5.9		17.3	4.6				
(15) 1.2	(56) 2.9	(50) 2.6	EBIT/Interest	(10) 5.4	(15) 1.6				
-.5	.0	.8		-.1	.8				
	12.1	3.9	Net Profit + Depr., Dep.,						
	(12) 5.1	(15) 2.9	Amort./Cur. Mat. L/T/D						
	3.5	1.5							
.5	.6	1.0		1.1	.9				
1.6	1.0	1.2	Fixed/Worth	1.2	2.3				
-6.3	2.7	3.6		NM	-23.4				
.9	.4	1.2		.9	1.6				
3.6	1.2	2.3	Debt/Worth	3.4	3.9				
-10.2	7.1	9.0		NM	-37.6				
23.5	30.7	35.0		129.0	52.0				
(13) 5.5	(51) 11.6	(46) 7.4	% Profit Before Taxes/Tangible Net Worth	(10) 14.6	(11) 7.5				
-5.1	-2.3	.3		-5.5	-1.8				
3.6	19.9	11.5		20.8	10.9				
2.2	5.3	3.8	% Profit Before Taxes/Total Assets	5.7	2.9				
-2.9	-3.0	-.5		-7.9	-1.1				
9.7	5.2	5.3		3.5	5.2				
2.3	1.6	2.0	Sales/Net Fixed Assets	.7	2.1				
.8	.7	.7		.4	1.4				
2.5	1.8	2.0		1.5	2.0				
1.1	.7	.7	Sales/Total Assets	.5	.7				
.5	.4	.4		.3	.4				
1.5	2.5	2.6			5.5				
(17) 3.1	(49) 5.2	(44) 9.2	% Depr., Dep., Amort./Sales		(15) 11.5				
6.7	10.7	13.7			17.5				
	1.7		% Officers', Directors' Owners' Comp/Sales						
	(10) 5.1								
	10.2								
571060M	982100M	789742M	Net Sales ($)	8985M	30790M	33478M	21227M	97028M	598234M
353557M	1146874M	712848M	Total Assets ($)	26218M	46608M	53860M	98097M	156312M	331753M

M = $ thousand   MM = $ million
See Pages 9 through 22 for Explanation of Ratios and Data

Current Data Sorted by Assets							Comparative Historical Data	
						Type of Statement		
			1	1		Unqualified	3	2
		3	4			Reviewed	6	6
3	6	10	6			Compiled	10	12
2	1	1				Tax Returns	11	7
1		7	3	2		Other	4	12
12 (4/1-9/30/09)			39 (10/1/09-3/31/10)				**4/1/05-3/31/06**	**4/1/06-3/31/07**
0-500M	**500M-2MM**	**2-10MM**	**10-50MM**	**50-100MM**	**100-250MM**		**ALL**	**ALL**
6	7	21	14	3		**NUMBER OF STATEMENTS**	34	39
%	%	%	%	%	%	**ASSETS**	%	%
		2.6	.7		DATA NOT AVAILABLE	Cash & Equivalents	3.3	2.1
		29.2	11.6			Trade Receivables (net)	20.3	25.9
		18.0	17.7			Inventory	11.6	13.7
		.6	1.6			All Other Current	2.5	3.0
		50.3	31.6			Total Current	37.6	44.7
		39.4	64.1			Fixed Assets (net)	49.0	44.6
		2.6	.9			Intangibles (net)	1.1	3.0
		7.6	3.4			All Other Non-Current	12.3	7.7
		100.0	100.0			Total	100.0	100.0
						LIABILITIES		
		12.9	7.2			Notes Payable-Short Term	7.7	8.1
		5.6	5.8			Cur. Mat.-L.T.D.	16.3	10.8
		16.6	11.1			Trade Payables	12.9	18.6
		.9	.0			Income Taxes Payable	.4	.2
		4.2	2.2			All Other Current	6.8	6.9
		40.2	26.2			Total Current	44.2	44.6
		36.0	48.7			Long-Term Debt	37.8	28.9
		.0	3.3			Deferred Taxes	1.0	.7
		.5	1.9			All Other Non-Current	4.7	5.6
		23.2	19.9			Net Worth	12.3	20.1
		100.0	100.0			Total Liabilties & Net Worth	100.0	100.0
						INCOME DATA		
		100.0	100.0			Net Sales	100.0	100.0
						Gross Profit		
		94.7	86.8			Operating Expenses	98.8	95.8
		5.3	13.2			Operating Profit	1.2	4.2
		3.7	7.7			All Other Expenses (net)	.9	.5
		1.6	5.4			Profit Before Taxes	.3	3.6
						RATIOS		
		1.8	3.4				1.8	1.5
		1.4	1.3			Current	1.1	1.1
		.8	.6				.5	.8
		1.3	1.0				1.0	.9
		.6	.5			Quick	.5	.7
		.4	.1				.0	.2
		22 16.2	**1** 266.0				**0** UND	**13** 27.3
		36 10.1	**30** 12.2			Sales/Receivables	**24** 15.4	**35** 10.3
		52 7.0	**47** 7.7				**36** 10.2	**46** 7.9
						Cost of Sales/Inventory		
						Cost of Sales/Payables		
		10.5	8.2				19.1	11.3
		20.5	20.9			Sales/Working Capital	90.8	57.5
		-37.5	-5.4				-19.7	-27.7
		7.2	2.9				5.5	3.2
		(20) 1.5	(12) 2.0			EBIT/Interest	(30) 2.5	(34) 1.1
		-2.9	1.1				-.5	.2
						Net Profit + Depr., Dep., Amort./Cur. Mat. L/T/D		
		.7	1.2				.8	.9
		1.2	4.4			Fixed/Worth	1.4	1.6
		NM	NM				6.8	11.0
		1.3	2.1				1.5	1.8
		2.3	6.2			Debt/Worth	2.5	4.2
		NM	NM				9.1	21.4
		33.6	32.2				36.4	31.0
		(16) 19.7	(11) 15.6			% Profit Before Taxes/Tangible Net Worth	(27) 14.7	(31) 2.5
		-9.4	.4				5.8	-17.3
		8.9	6.0				12.8	7.9
		1.9	3.1			% Profit Before Taxes/Total Assets	3.7	.4
		-4.5	-.1				-2.8	-3.1
		16.7	3.2				17.9	13.7
		7.4	1.6			Sales/Net Fixed Assets	9.4	7.5
		2.6	1.1				4.0	2.9
		4.1	1.9				7.8	6.2
		2.7	1.0			Sales/Total Assets	3.4	2.9
		1.0	.5				2.0	1.2
		1.1	1.9				1.2	1.3
		(20) 2.3	4.9			% Depr., Dep., Amort./Sales	(29) 2.4	(35) 2.5
		5.8	7.9				3.6	4.9
		1.0					1.3	.9
		(10) 1.3				% Officers', Directors' Owners' Comp/Sales	(17) 1.9	(14) 1.6
		2.4					5.3	1.8
30873M	**31761M**	**255112M**	**399106M**	**280626M**		Net Sales ($)	**666853M**	**787452M**
1784M	**7691M**	**98484M**	**301162M**	**193791M**		Total Assets ($)	**267000M**	**382728M**

M = $ thousand MM = $ million

See Pages 9 through 22 for Explanation of Ratios and Data

Comparative Historical Data | Current Data Sorted by Sales

4/1/07-3/31/08 ALL	4/1/08-3/31/09 ALL	4/1/09-3/31/10 ALL	Type of Statement	0-1MM	1-3MM	3-5MM	5-10MM	10-25MM	25MM & OVER
3	1	2	Unqualified						2
6	3	7	Reviewed		1	1		4	1
13	12	25	Compiled	1	4	4	3	11	2
9	2	4	Tax Returns	2	2				
8	3	13	Other	1	1	2	2	3	4
				12 (4/1-9/30/09)			**39 (10/1/09-3/31/10)**		
39	21	51	NUMBER OF STATEMENTS	4	8	7	5	18	9
%	%	%	**ASSETS**	%	%	%	%	%	%
5.7	1.8	3.9	Cash & Equivalents					2.6	
23.9	22.5	18.3	Trade Receivables (net)					26.4	
14.3	15.0	16.3	Inventory					16.1	
.6	1.0	1.2	All Other Current					.9	
44.5	40.3	39.7	Total Current					46.0	
43.1	51.0	50.5	Fixed Assets (net)					46.7	
2.2	2.2	1.5	Intangibles (net)					.7	
10.2	6.5	8.4	All Other Non-Current					6.6	
100.0	100.0	100.0	Total					100.0	
			LIABILITIES						
13.6	11.0	14.3	Notes Payable-Short Term					13.9	
8.2	8.9	4.8	Cur. Mat.-L.T.D.					4.1	
20.8	15.7	14.3	Trade Payables					16.3	
.2	.3	.4	Income Taxes Payable					.3	
6.6	2.4	6.1	All Other Current					5.0	
49.4	38.3	39.9	Total Current					39.7	
37.3	37.5	43.2	Long-Term Debt					27.3	
.4	.4	.9	Deferred Taxes					1.3	
1.5	.1	1.6	All Other Non-Current					3.0	
11.4	23.6	14.4	Net Worth					28.7	
100.0	100.0	100.0	Total Liabilities & Net Worth					100.0	
			INCOME DATA						
100.0	100.0	100.0	Net Sales					100.0	
			Gross Profit						
98.2	97.8	93.9	Operating Expenses					96.4	
1.8	2.2	6.1	Operating Profit					3.6	
1.6	1.7	4.0	All Other Expenses (net)					1.6	
.2	.5	2.1	Profit Before Taxes					2.0	
			RATIOS						
1.6	2.1	1.9	Current					1.6	
1.1	1.1	.9						1.2	
.5	.6	.5						.7	
1.0	1.0	1.0	Quick					1.0	
.5	.7	.5						.7	
.3	.3	.2						.4	
2 148.4	20 17.8	0 UND	Sales/Receivables					21 17.3	
29 12.4	33 10.9	25 14.8						30 12.1	
37 9.8	37 9.9	42 8.8						46 8.0	
			Cost of Sales/Inventory						
			Cost of Sales/Payables						
21.4	14.0	11.4	Sales/Working Capital					11.1	
170.0	65.0	-247.5						28.3	
-22.2	-12.7	-14.9						-66.1	
6.9	8.6	7.3	EBIT/Interest					8.5	
(36) 1.2	1.0	(48) 2.2						2.0	
-.1	-.6	.4						-3.9	
			Net Profit + Depr., Dep., Amort./Cur. Mat. L/T/D						
.8	.6	1.0	Fixed/Worth					.7	
1.7	1.8	3.2						1.3	
16.6	-43.6	-6.0						4.7	
1.4	1.1	1.7	Debt/Worth					1.2	
4.8	4.0	4.6						2.5	
247.6	-59.6	-26.9						5.3	
47.0	26.8	33.3	% Profit Before Taxes/Tangible Net Worth					38.2	
(30) 7.0	(15) 17.2	(35) 16.1						(16) 18.5	
-9.7	-11.2	-6.2						-8.7	
12.1	9.1	10.7	% Profit Before Taxes/Total Assets					16.2	
.5	.2	3.3						5.0	
-3.4	-8.3	-2.1						-4.4	
21.0	8.6	14.4	Sales/Net Fixed Assets					36.3	
9.0	4.4	3.8						7.9	
4.2	2.1	1.9						1.8	
6.3	3.1	4.1	Sales/Total Assets					4.3	
3.7	2.3	2.2						2.8	
2.1	1.4	1.0						1.4	
.6	1.2	1.7	% Depr., Dep., Amort./Sales					.9	
(35) 1.8	(19) 1.7	(50) 2.9						(17) 1.9	
4.0	6.1	6.7						5.1	
.7	1.2	1.0	% Officers', Directors' Owners' Comp/Sales						
(14) 1.5		(19) 1.3							
2.9		2.4							
615247M	429662M	997478M	Net Sales ($)	2686M	14592M	27477M	37921M	289325M	625477M
245030M	215262M	602912M	Total Assets ($)	5527M	36251M	24266M	34767M	158560M	343541M

M = $ thousand   MM = $ million
See Pages 9 through 22 for Explanation of Ratios and Data

Current Data Sorted by Assets   **Comparative Historical Data**

	0-500M	500M-2MM	2-10MM	10-50MM	50-100MM	100-250MM	Type of Statement	15	17
			2	9	10	6	Unqualified	15	17
		1	14	15		3	Reviewed	23	25
	5	15	17	6	1	1	Compiled	26	33
	12	8	2		4	3	Tax Returns	26	25
	7	9	22	20	3	3	Other	45	56
		43 (4/1-9/30/09)		149 (10/1/09-3/31/10)				4/1/05-3/31/06 ALL	4/1/06-3/31/07 ALL
NUMBER OF STATEMENTS	24	33	57	50	15	13		135	156
	%	%	%	%	%	%	ASSETS	%	%
	12.1	8.8	4.0	2.6	2.8	.9	Cash & Equivalents	7.6	8.2
	9.4	12.0	14.1	9.5	7.8	10.8	Trade Receivables (net)	12.4	12.7
	14.8	27.2	32.3	41.6	46.1	41.0	Inventory	26.5	26.1
	5.6	3.4	1.9	3.1	.6	1.1	All Other Current	2.5	2.5
	41.9	51.5	52.4	56.8	57.3	53.8	Total Current	49.1	49.5
	44.7	39.3	38.4	33.1	35.1	33.7	Fixed Assets (net)	39.7	41.4
	4.5	4.3	.7	2.8	3.0	8.9	Intangibles (net)	2.5	2.0
	9.0	4.9	8.6	7.3	4.6	3.5	All Other Non-Current	8.8	7.0
	100.0	100.0	100.0	100.0	100.0	100.0	Total	100.0	100.0
							LIABILITIES		
	40.1	19.4	16.3	14.7	13.7	14.7	Notes Payable-Short Term	15.1	16.4
	2.2	3.2	3.3	3.7	8.8	5.3	Cur. Mat.-L.T.D.	3.8	3.3
	8.6	9.0	11.5	10.0	13.6	8.0	Trade Payables	8.0	8.5
	.0	.2	1.1	1.6	2.8	1.1	Income Taxes Payable	1.0	1.2
	6.3	16.6	3.9	9.3	2.9	3.1	All Other Current	7.0	10.0
	57.2	48.4	36.0	39.4	42.0	32.2	Total Current	34.8	39.3
	50.4	27.7	23.6	24.7	19.3	23.6	Long-Term Debt	27.7	23.7
	.0	.8	.8	.8	1.8	1.7	Deferred Taxes	.7	.9
	25.5	.9	3.7	4.9	1.4	1.2	All Other Non-Current	9.0	7.5
	-33.1	22.3	35.8	30.2	35.5	41.2	Net Worth	27.7	28.7
	100.0	100.0	100.0	100.0	100.0	100.0	Total Liabilities & Net Worth	100.0	100.0
							INCOME DATA		
	100.0	100.0	100.0	100.0	100.0	100.0	Net Sales	100.0	100.0
	50.4	43.8	36.5	41.0	30.3	34.4	Gross Profit	42.3	42.9
	52.4	42.8	33.3	37.7	28.0	27.6	Operating Expenses	36.8	37.2
	-2.0	1.0	3.2	3.3	2.4	6.8	Operating Profit	5.5	5.7
	1.7	2.1	5.1	2.1	4.2	3.4	All Other Expenses (net)	1.3	2.0
	-3.7	-1.0	-1.9	1.2	-1.8	3.4	Profit Before Taxes	4.2	3.7
							RATIOS		
	2.3	3.8	3.8	2.5	1.8	3.4	Current	4.0	3.2
	1.0	1.1	1.4	1.6	1.4	1.6		1.4	1.5
	.3	.6	.8	1.1	1.1	1.2		1.0	.9
	1.2	1.2	1.3	.6	.5	.7	Quick	1.5	1.5
	.3	.4	.5	.3	.2	.4		.5	.5
	.0	.1	.2	.2	.1	.2		.2	.2
	0 UND	1 401.7	10 35.6	10 36.4	19 19.0	23 15.7	Sales/Receivables	1 343.1	2 156.7
	4 85.6	10 35.7	26 14.2	26 14.2	35 10.5	45 8.1		17 21.1	17 21.3
	11 33.7	35 10.3	47 7.8	55 6.7	62 5.9	54 6.7		40 9.1	47 7.8
	0 UND	0 UND	0 UND	130 2.8	102 3.6	93 3.9	Cost of Sales/Inventory	0 UND	0 748.1
	17 21.2	41 8.8	89 4.1	220 1.7	288 1.3	208 1.8		75 4.9	59 6.1
	63 5.8	135 2.7	276 1.3	387 .9	564 .6	487 .7		165 2.2	196 1.9
	0 UND	0 UND	0 UND	20 18.5	56 6.5	18 20.1	Cost of Sales/Payables	2 146.8	0 UND
	6 61.5	18 20.6	18 20.5	40 9.0	75 4.9	41 8.8		16 23.4	18 19.9
	34 10.9	48 7.5	69 5.3	76 4.8	85 4.3	74 4.9		46 7.9	48 7.6
	13.5	5.2	3.1	2.2	3.0	1.9	Sales/Working Capital	5.0	3.9
	NM	58.5	9.6	8.0	5.5	8.9		16.3	11.1
	-5.1	-12.0	-26.5	51.0	18.4	20.2		-90.1	-112.9
	2.8	10.3	6.7	4.4	4.9	5.0	EBIT/Interest	8.1	6.8
	(23) .8	(28) 2.2	(50) 1.7	(48) 2.0	1.5	(12) 2.6		(125) 2.7	(145) 2.5
	-4.4	-2.0	-.5	-.1	-2.1	1.0		.7	.7
			7.4	3.1			Net Profit + Depr., Dep., Amort./Cur. Mat. L/T/D	5.8	3.7
		(18) 2.8	(22) 2.2					(28) 2.1	(29) 2.1
		1.3	1.5					1.4	1.1
	.5	.5	.4	.3	.5	.5	Fixed/Worth	.5	.6
	UND	1.5	1.3	1.3	.7			1.1	1.1
	-.6	-42.8	2.5	3.4	5.3	1.6		4.8	4.7
	.9	.7	.9	.9	1.2	.8	Debt/Worth	.6	.6
	UND	1.8	2.4	2.6	1.9	1.8		1.8	1.6
	-2.3	-32.3	3.7	5.7	7.7	3.6		13.2	8.8
	75.4	45.8	35.4	31.6	19.5	19.6	% Profit Before Taxes/Tangible Net Worth	36.0	35.5
	(12) 17.2	(22) 13.1	(54) 2.9	(44) 6.4	11.7	(12) 8.7		(110) 13.4	(131) 15.8
	-6.9	-9.3	-10.1	-4.1	-15.4	.5		2.0	1.3
	15.3	12.4	9.8	8.1	7.2	5.4	% Profit Before Taxes/Total Assets	13.6	11.6
	-.5	3.4	.5	2.8	2.1	1.7		4.5	5.1
	-22.3	-8.8	-3.7	-1.7	-5.1	.2		-1.3	-1.3
	42.2	27.8	8.3	7.3	3.8	5.8	Sales/Net Fixed Assets	11.1	10.0
	8.2	6.3	4.4	3.6	1.9	2.4		6.1	4.8
	2.9	3.1	2.3	1.7	1.3	1.7		3.3	2.7
	5.6	3.5	2.6	1.5	1.0	1.1	Sales/Total Assets	3.0	2.9
	3.7	2.0	1.4	.9	.8	1.0		1.8	1.8
	1.5	1.1	.9	.6	.5	.6		1.0	.9
	1.3	1.2	2.1	1.5	2.4	2.9	% Depr., Dep., Amort./Sales	1.6	1.6
	(23) 2.5	(27) 3.9	(50) 3.9	(47) 3.1	4.8	(11) 4.6		(116) 2.9	(141) 3.1
	5.4	6.0	5.9	4.2	7.4	5.9		4.3	4.8
	4.7	2.5	1.8				% Officers', Directors' Owners' Comp/Sales	1.4	1.9
	(15) 8.9	(18) 3.1	(16) 2.3					(61) 3.1	(63) 2.8
	13.7	5.2	7.3					8.8	7.9
	25918M	91710M	525364M	1255458M	892821M	1913791M	Net Sales ($)	4175213M	3904061M
	6717M	35014M	299680M	1038057M	1004063M	2305557M	Total Assets ($)	1983995M	2340671M

© RMA 2010

M = $ thousand   MM = $ million
See Pages 9 through 22 for Explanation of Ratios and Data

Comparative Historical Data | Current Data Sorted by Sales

			Type of Statement						
18	22	27	Unqualified				4	4	19
27	33	33	Reviewed		1	4	9	12	7
28	37	44	Compiled	5	11	9	11	6	2
27	23	23	Tax Returns	10	6	3	3		1
58	80	65	Other	12	10	4	8	14	17
4/1/07-3/31/08 ALL	4/1/08-3/31/09 ALL	4/1/09-3/31/10 ALL		43 (4/1-9/30/09)			149 (10/1/09-3/31/10)		
				0-1MM	1-3MM	3-5MM	5-10MM	10-25MM	25MM & OVER
158	195	192	NUMBER OF STATEMENTS	27	28	20	35	36	46
%	%	%	ASSETS	%	%	%	%	%	%
6.8	5.7	5.2	Cash & Equivalents	7.5	5.4	8.2	5.6	5.0	2.3
12.2	13.1	11.2	Trade Receivables (net)	6.5	11.3	12.0	14.8	12.1	10.2
30.9	33.6	33.3	Inventory	18.5	31.4	35.0	34.7	34.1	40.8
2.3	3.2	2.8	All Other Current	3.2	5.2	.5	1.9	2.3	3.1
52.2	55.6	52.5	Total Current	35.8	53.4	55.7	57.0	53.5	56.4
39.2	34.3	37.4	Fixed Assets (net)	50.1	35.8	35.1	32.6	37.4	35.4
1.6	2.1	3.1	Intangibles (net)	3.2	5.2	2.9	.5	3.2	3.6
7.0	7.9	7.0	All Other Non-Current	11.0	5.6	6.4	9.9	5.9	4.5
100.0	100.0	100.0	Total	100.0	100.0	100.0	100.0	100.0	100.0
			LIABILITIES						
16.3	20.9	19.1	Notes Payable-Short Term	16.2	39.6	14.6	12.5	17.7	16.4
3.7	4.0	3.8	Cur. Mat.-L.T.D.	3.7	3.2	2.3	3.1	3.9	5.3
11.4	10.3	10.2	Trade Payables	4.8	8.0	10.5	8.9	12.6	13.8
1.2	.8	1.1	Income Taxes Payable	.0	.3	.9	1.7	.2	2.4
8.9	8.9	7.7	All Other Current	6.8	5.3	20.8	4.1	10.2	4.6
41.5	45.0	41.9	Total Current	31.4	56.5	49.1	30.4	44.6	42.6
28.7	22.9	27.6	Long-Term Debt	58.3	26.8	24.9	21.7	23.0	19.4
.9	.9	.9	Deferred Taxes	.0	1.5	.1	.7	.9	1.4
7.7	7.0	5.9	All Other Non-Current	11.5	15.9	1.5	1.6	4.1	3.1
21.2	24.2	23.8	Net Worth	-1.2	-.6	24.5	45.6	27.3	33.5
100.0	100.0	100.0	Total Liabilities & Net Worth	100.0	100.0	100.0	100.0	100.0	100.0
			INCOME DATA						
100.0	100.0	100.0	Net Sales	100.0	100.0	100.0	100.0	100.0	100.0
38.2	39.7	40.0	Gross Profit	56.7	39.8	43.6	33.1	40.2	34.1
34.2	37.5	37.7	Operating Expenses	50.4	43.5	42.1	33.0	35.1	30.3
4.0	2.2	2.4	Operating Profit	6.3	-3.7	1.5	.1	5.0	3.8
2.3	2.4	3.2	All Other Expenses (net)	11.2	1.5	2.0	1.2	1.9	2.5
1.7	-.2	-.8	Profit Before Taxes	-4.9	-5.2	-.5	-1.1	3.1	1.3
			RATIOS						
2.9	3.0	2.4	Current	2.3	4.2	3.6	4.1	2.0	1.8
1.5	1.4	1.4		1.0	1.4	1.6	2.0	1.2	1.5
1.0	.8	.8		.2	.5	.7	1.2	.8	1.1
1.0	1.0	.8	Quick	.7	1.2	1.1	1.5	.8	.5
.4	(193) .4	.4		.2	.3	.3	.6	.4	.2
.2	.2	.1		.1	.1	.2	.2	.1	.1
2 218.0	13 29.2	8 47.5	Sales/Receivables	0 UND	1 405.2	8 46.2	10 35.7	13 27.9	10 35.4
19 18.9	27 13.5	21 17.7		6 65.1	10 37.1	20 18.3	34 10.8	24 15.1	25 14.7
47 7.8	49 7.4	47 7.7		35 10.6	46 7.9	41 9.0	64 5.7	40 9.2	52 7.0
10 36.5	28 13.2	28 13.1	Cost of Sales/Inventory	0 UND	0 UND	14 26.6	37 9.7	49 7.4	89 4.1
85 4.3	112 3.3	107 3.4		43 8.5	47 7.8	92 4.0	147 2.5	192 1.9	158 2.3
234 1.6	358 1.0	297 1.2		339 1.1	198 1.8	299 1.2	325 1.1	270 1.4	273 1.3
0 999.8	7 53.2	4 86.9	Cost of Sales/Payables	0 UND	0 UND	3 129.3	3 106.2	8 47.5	23 16.0
25 14.6	29 12.5	28 13.0		3 112.0	13 29.0	26 14.0	26 13.9	34 10.6	42 8.7
55 6.6	64 5.7	68 5.4		43 8.5	35 10.5	61 6.0	64 5.7	82 4.5	78 4.7
4.2	2.8	3.3	Sales/Working Capital	4.7	4.9	2.4	2.3	5.7	3.8
11.0	9.6	10.7		166.7	20.9	13.6	6.0	16.5	9.1
-82.7	-27.3	-22.4		-3.1	-8.1	-22.2	26.8	-20.4	34.0
4.0	4.3	5.3	EBIT/Interest	2.6	7.6	11.0	3.8	7.0	6.3
(150) 1.8	(183) 1.7	(176) 1.6		(22) .9	(27) -.8	(17) 1.1	(33) 1.4	(33) 2.5	(44) 2.7
.4	-.6	-.8		-1.2	-6.5	-1.4	-.3	1.1	.8
3.7	2.7	4.4	Net Profit + Depr., Dep., Amort./Cur. Mat. L/T/D				3.3	5.0	6.5
(41) 1.8	(42) 1.4	(54) 2.4					(13) 2.1	(16) 1.9	(21) 2.6
.7	-.7	1.4					.3	1.5	1.6
.5	.4	.4	Fixed/Worth	1.2	.3	.5	.3	.4	.6
1.2	1.0	1.3		141.0	.7	1.4	.6	1.3	1.2
4.9	3.8	5.2		-.8	-1.2	6.7	1.6	3.4	4.3
1.0	.8	.9	Debt/Worth	1.2	.8	.7	.4	1.3	1.1
2.7	2.1	2.3		260.0	3.1	2.4	1.2	2.3	2.1
9.8	10.3	8.9		-4.2	-3.3	20.8	3.2	-6.4	7.6
26.4	22.3	29.9	% Profit Before Taxes/Tangible Net Worth	26.2	21.9	43.8	14.7	38.2	31.2
(129) 11.6	(162) 7.6	(159) 7.0		(16) -1.0	(18) -2.2	(16) -.3	1.4	(31) 18.1	(43) 16.0
.3	-4.9	-7.9		-8.4	-31.2	-13.3	-9.1	3.7	2.7
8.8	7.4	8.7	% Profit Before Taxes/Total Assets	7.5	8.7	13.6	4.4	10.5	8.6
3.8	1.9	1.9		-.4	-4.2	-.7	.4	4.8	4.9
-2.1	-3.9	-3.9		-5.1	-30.5	-5.3	-5.0	-.3	-.5
10.3	10.9	10.0	Sales/Net Fixed Assets	6.3	20.9	16.3	7.7	10.2	7.1
4.6	4.6	4.4		2.8	6.0	6.2	4.4	3.7	3.8
2.5	2.4	2.1		.8	3.1	2.9	2.0	1.6	2.2
2.7	2.3	2.6	Sales/Total Assets	2.2	3.5	3.4	2.6	2.3	2.3
1.6	1.3	1.2		1.2	2.2	1.7	1.0	1.2	1.1
.9	.7	.8		.5	.8	.9	.6	.6	.9
1.9	1.7	1.9	% Depr., Dep., Amort./Sales	2.9	1.4	1.9	2.5	1.7	1.5
(143) 2.9	(168) 3.2	(173) 3.5		(25) 6.0	(26) 2.7	(14) 4.1	(32) 3.6	(33) 3.8	(43) 3.0
4.7	5.0	5.5		11.5	5.3	5.8	5.0	5.1	4.8
1.9	2.0	2.1	% Officers', Directors' Owners' Comp/Sales		2.8		1.9		
(59) 2.8	(60) 3.5	(56) 3.1			(19) 4.9		(15) 2.3		
7.9	9.3	8.4			7.6		7.7		
3254239M	4651251M	4705062M	Net Sales ($)	14553M	48580M	77499M	249762M	617193M	3697475M
3128917M	4790815M	4689088M	Total Assets ($)	30373M	39679M	85785M	270853M	822119M	3440279M

© RMA 2010

M = $ thousand   MM = $ million
See Pages 9 through 22 for Explanation of Ratios and Data

Current Data Sorted by Assets   **Comparative Historical Data**

0-500M	500M-2MM	2-10MM	10-50MM	50-100MM	100-250MM	Type of Statement	4/1/05-3/31/06 ALL	4/1/06-3/31/07 ALL
	8	3				Unqualified	8	5
1	6	5				Reviewed	5	4
2	3	3	3			Compiled	15	16
7		7	2			Tax Returns	5	10
4		3				Other	11	10
	3 (4/1-9/30/09)		54 (10/1/09-3/31/10)					
14	17	21	5			**NUMBER OF STATEMENTS**	44	45
%	%	%	%	%	%	**ASSETS**	%	%
20.8	12.0	8.2				Cash & Equivalents	9.8	11.6
.0	4.3	12.1				Trade Receivables (net)	12.0	11.3
3.5	9.0	9.4				Inventory	16.9	10.4
5.0	.9	5.5				All Other Current	2.9	7.9
29.2	26.2	35.2				Total Current	41.6	41.2
38.1	61.3	57.8				Fixed Assets (net)	45.8	50.0
6.3	.4	.3				Intangibles (net)	.4	1.0
26.3	12.1	6.7				All Other Non-Current	12.3	7.8
100.0	100.0	100.0				Total	100.0	100.0
						LIABILITIES		
35.5	19.4	13.8				Notes Payable-Short Term	25.9	40.9
2.2	12.3	6.5				Cur. Mat.-L.T.D.	5.1	10.0
.0	1.2	2.0				Trade Payables	6.4	3.1
.0	.2	.0				Income Taxes Payable	.1	.4
39.8	21.8	10.8				All Other Current	7.9	8.0
77.5	54.8	33.1				Total Current	45.4	62.5
9.1	42.3	27.7				Long-Term Debt	22.7	24.8
.0	.0	.0				Deferred Taxes	.1	.2
.1	.7	9.6				All Other Non-Current	2.5	.7
13.3	2.2	29.6				Net Worth	29.3	11.8
100.0	100.0	100.0				Total Liabilities & Net Worth	100.0	100.0
						INCOME DATA		
100.0	100.0	100.0				Net Sales	100.0	100.0
						Gross Profit		
70.3	92.9	91.4				Operating Expenses	89.0	90.3
29.7	7.1	8.6				Operating Profit	11.0	9.7
9.5	4.4	1.0				All Other Expenses (net)	1.1	4.3
20.1	2.7	7.6				Profit Before Taxes	9.9	5.4
						RATIOS		
2.3	1.1	2.8				Current	2.3	1.4
1.0	.6	1.6					1.3	1.0
.2	.2	.6					.4	.5
2.3	.8	1.3				Quick	1.3	1.0
.8	.3	1.0					.5	.6
.0	.1	.3					.0	.1
0 UND	0 UND	0 UND				Sales/Receivables	0 UND	0 UND
0 UND	0 UND	21 17.5					11 31.8	0 UND
0 UND	1 513.1	109 3.4					43 8.5	58 6.3
						Cost of Sales/Inventory		
						Cost of Sales/Payables		
23.1	57.3	3.4				Sales/Working Capital	7.1	10.2
UND	-7.8	5.9					36.2	194.5
-5.6	-3.4	-6.0					-4.9	-2.8
	6.0	10.0				EBIT/Interest	18.4	4.5
(13)	1.8	2.7					(40) 5.7	(41) 1.8
	-.2	.5					1.9	-.5
						Net Profit + Depr., Dep., Amort./Cur. Mat. L/T/D		
.0	.9	1.0				Fixed/Worth	.4	.7
.9	6.5	1.4					1.1	1.3
UND	-4.9	NM					3.0	3.6
.1	.7	.6				Debt/Worth	.6	.6
.9	8.0	1.2					1.2	1.7
UND	-6.3	NM					6.5	11.9
266.7		24.3				% Profit Before Taxes/Tangible Net Worth	45.1	31.7
(11) 38.9		(16) 9.5					(37) 21.6	(36) 8.4
12.3		1.0					9.4	-7.1
107.2	15.2	13.4				% Profit Before Taxes/Total Assets	19.9	11.8
21.5	6.7	2.7					9.3	2.4
-.2	-3.7	-1.1					3.0	-2.7
UND	5.5	2.9				Sales/Net Fixed Assets	9.9	7.7
13.3	1.9	1.3					2.6	2.2
4.5	1.2	.5					1.2	1.0
5.0	2.0	1.3				Sales/Total Assets	2.6	2.1
3.1	1.1	.7					1.4	1.2
1.5	.7	.4					.6	.5
	4.8	2.5				% Depr., Dep., Amort./Sales	1.2	2.7
	(15) 9.7	(19) 6.5					(35) 3.0	(38) 6.1
	15.5	14.5					7.1	11.0
						% Officers', Directors' Owners' Comp/Sales	2.1	
							(10) 7.4	
							10.8	
11560M	26194M	88366M	29449M			Net Sales ($)	860967M	664656M
3052M	17511M	104413M	101680M			Total Assets ($)	506672M	445090M

(Columns 50-100MM and 100-250MM: DATA NOT AVAILABLE)

M = $ thousand   MM = $ million
See Pages 9 through 22 for Explanation of Ratios and Data

Comparative Historical Data | | | | Current Data Sorted by Sales

4/1/07-3/31/08 ALL	4/1/08-3/31/09 ALL	4/1/09-3/31/10 ALL	Type of Statement	0-1MM	1-3MM	3-5MM	5-10MM	10-25MM	25MM & OVER
			Unqualified			2		1	
2	2	3	Reviewed		3	3		1	
7	15	9	Compiled	8	4		2	1	
10	16	15	Tax Returns	8	6	5	2		
14	17	20	Other	5	4	1	1		
13	12	10			3 (4/1-9/30/09)		54 (10/1/09-3/31/10)		
46	62	57	NUMBER OF STATEMENTS	21	17	11	5	3	
%	%	%	ASSETS	%	%	%	%	%	%
12.3	12.4	11.8	Cash & Equivalents	15.1	7.7	16.1			D
12.9	12.6	7.0	Trade Receivables (net)	.6	6.0	8.0			A
7.4	12.0	9.1	Inventory	4.1	5.6	10.4			T
5.6	4.0	3.7	All Other Current	1.5	4.9	5.4			A
38.2	41.0	31.5	Total Current	21.4	24.2	39.9			
53.0	50.0	53.5	Fixed Assets (net)	55.2	66.1	48.2			N
1.0	.6	1.8	Intangibles (net)	3.1	.0	2.8			O
7.8	8.4	13.2	All Other Non-Current	20.2	9.7	9.1			T
100.0	100.0	100.0	Total	100.0	100.0	100.0			
			LIABILITIES						A
36.1	28.2	21.7	Notes Payable-Short Term	15.0	13.9	39.7			V
19.0	11.8	6.9	Cur. Mat.-L.T.D.	4.3	5.8	16.9			A
5.3	2.0	1.3	Trade Payables	.5	1.1	1.3			I
.0	.0	.1	Income Taxes Payable	.0	.2	.0			L
5.4	5.1	20.4	All Other Current	10.0	12.6	65.6			A
65.8	47.1	50.4	Total Current	29.8	33.6	123.5			B
30.7	28.5	26.6	Long-Term Debt	17.9	43.5	30.0			L
.1	.0	.0	Deferred Taxes	.0	.0	.0			E
2.1	3.5	4.0	All Other Non-Current	3.2	1.2	.5			
1.3	20.9	19.0	Net Worth	49.1	21.7	-54.1			
100.0	100.0	100.0	Total Liabilties & Net Worth	100.0	100.0	100.0			
			INCOME DATA						
100.0	100.0	100.0	Net Sales	100.0	100.0	100.0			
			Gross Profit						
93.5	89.4	85.9	Operating Expenses	85.4	82.9	87.7			
6.5	10.6	14.1	Operating Profit	14.6	17.1	12.3			
3.2	2.2	4.3	All Other Expenses (net)	7.9	4.5	-1.2			
3.3	8.4	9.8	Profit Before Taxes	6.7	12.5	13.5			
			RATIOS						
1.6	3.2	2.1		2.7	1.9	1.6			
1.0	1.6	1.1	Current	.5	1.0	1.0			
.4	.7	.3		.2	.6	.2			
1.1	2.5	1.3		2.3	1.3	1.1			
.5	.8	.6	Quick	.5	.7	.2			
.2	.2	.1		.1	.1	.1			
0 UND	0 UND	0 UND		0 UND	0 UND	0 999.8			
8 43.9	2 222.4	0 UND	Sales/Receivables	0 UND	0 UND	8 48.0			
95 3.8	87 4.2	43 8.5		0 UND	66 5.6	41 8.9			
			Cost of Sales/Inventory						
			Cost of Sales/Payables						
9.3	3.4	5.2		15.5	6.4	4.7			
681.5	11.1	150.5	Sales/Working Capital	-70.0	999.8	150.5			
-3.2	-6.7	-5.5		-3.1	-7.8	-3.0			
4.7	7.0	7.8		3.5	7.1	12.3			
(40) 1.0	(60) 3.0	(46) 2.2	EBIT/Interest	(13) 1.2	(14) 2.7	2.3			
-2.1	1.1	.8		-2.0	.6	1.0			
			Net Profit + Depr., Dep., Amort./Cur. Mat. L/T/D						
.7	.7	.8		.2	1.3	1.0			
1.6	1.3	1.3	Fixed/Worth	1.0	2.3	1.4			
-14.2	7.9	-11.8		1.9	-5.5	-1.1			
.8	.7	.6		.1	.7	.7			
3.1	2.1	1.6	Debt/Worth	.8	2.0	5.7			
-9.7	UND	-11.8		3.0	-9.0	-2.2			
22.5	34.7	38.5		31.6	74.9				
(32) 3.5	(48) 15.8	(41) 12.0	% Profit Before Taxes/Tangible Net Worth	(17) 11.7	(11) 21.5				
-6.2	2.1	1.8		1.2	6.0				
12.6	15.8	16.8		15.9	24.8	28.5			
.0	4.3	5.8	% Profit Before Taxes/Total Assets	1.5	9.7	6.7			
-4.8	.2	-.5		-5.5	-1.0	.0			
5.2	13.6	9.2		18.6	2.4	6.0			
1.9	2.1	2.1	Sales/Net Fixed Assets	1.9	1.6	2.2			
.9	.9	.9		.5	.6	1.1			
1.8	1.9	1.8		1.8	2.0	3.3			
1.1	1.1	1.1	Sales/Total Assets	.8	1.1	1.2			
.5	.5	.5		.4	.5	.7			
2.8	3.6	3.1		3.1	8.3	4.7			
(35) 6.2	(50) 5.9	(45) 7.4	% Depr., Dep., Amort./Sales	(14) 6.2	(13) 13.7	(10) 7.0			
9.7	14.1	14.9		34.4	15.4	11.4			
	3.5								
	(11) 7.2		% Officers', Directors' Owners' Comp/Sales						
	10.8								
496764M	637995M	155569M	Net Sales ($)	12284M	29055M	41282M	32741M	40207M	
358832M	630295M	226656M	Total Assets ($)	33601M	46075M	52596M	64712M	29672M	

© RMA 2010

M = $ thousand   MM = $ million
See Pages 9 through 22 for Explanation of Ratios and Data

Current Data Sorted by Assets   Comparative Historical Data

						Type of Statement		
	2	8	7	2	2	Unqualified	6	13
1	5	15	16	4		Reviewed	36	30
4	12	33	12	2	2	Compiled	58	58
26	45	28	8			Tax Returns	68	88
7	15	34	18	1	1	Other	109	83
	54 (4/1-9/30/09)		256 (10/1/09-3/31/10)				4/1/05-3/31/06 ALL	4/1/06-3/31/07 ALL
0-500M	500M-2MM	2-10MM	10-50MM	50-100MM	100-250MM			
38	79	118	61	9	5	NUMBER OF STATEMENTS	277	272
%	%	%	%	%	%	ASSETS	%	%
27.1	11.9	4.8	6.7			Cash & Equivalents	8.5	8.1
1.9	5.5	9.9	13.9			Trade Receivables (net)	10.7	11.3
6.4	9.2	12.0	20.0			Inventory	13.3	11.4
1.6	5.1	4.9	5.6			All Other Current	5.5	5.2
37.0	31.6	31.6	46.1			Total Current	38.0	36.0
50.5	57.9	55.5	44.9			Fixed Assets (net)	48.6	52.8
.5	2.7	1.6	.3			Intangibles (net)	1.0	1.2
12.0	7.8	11.3	8.7			All Other Non-Current	12.4	10.0
100.0	100.0	100.0	100.0			Total	100.0	100.0
						LIABILITIES		
61.3	16.9	14.3	18.5			Notes Payable-Short Term	24.9	22.8
7.7	7.4	3.2	2.9			Cur. Mat.-L.T.D.	4.1	4.7
3.0	3.2	4.2	5.2			Trade Payables	6.5	4.8
.0	.3	.4	1.1			Income Taxes Payable	.2	.4
25.8	5.2	5.4	5.6			All Other Current	7.2	8.2
97.7	33.1	27.5	33.2			Total Current	42.9	40.9
51.9	36.6	27.7	20.5			Long-Term Debt	29.6	27.4
.0	.0	.6	.9			Deferred Taxes	.5	.4
5.9	8.8	6.9	2.2			All Other Non-Current	6.4	5.2
-55.5	21.5	37.4	43.2			Net Worth	20.6	26.1
100.0	100.0	100.0	100.0			Total Liabilities & Net Worth	100.0	100.0
						INCOME DATA		
100.0	100.0	100.0	100.0			Net Sales	100.0	100.0
						Gross Profit		
86.9	90.6	88.0	89.6			Operating Expenses	92.0	90.7
13.1	9.4	12.0	10.4			Operating Profit	8.0	9.3
2.1	3.2	4.1	3.0			All Other Expenses (net)	2.9	3.2
11.0	6.2	7.9	7.4			Profit Before Taxes	5.1	6.1
						RATIOS		
2.1	1.8	2.6	1.9			Current	1.9	1.9
.5	.7	1.2	1.3				1.1	1.1
.1	.1	.5	1.0				.5	.4
2.1	.9	1.3	1.0			Quick	1.0	1.1
.3	.3	(117) .4	.5				.4 (271)	.4
.1	.1	.1	.3				.1	.1
0 UND	0 UND	0 UND	11 31.9			Sales/Receivables	0 UND	0 UND
0 UND	0 UND	8 43.8	33 11.2				13 28.8	4 87.4
0 UND	15 23.7	47 7.7	75 4.9				43 8.4	48 7.6
						Cost of Sales/Inventory		
						Cost of Sales/Payables		
21.9	8.6	3.7	3.3			Sales/Working Capital	5.2	7.2
-22.6	-25.1	26.4	12.6				56.2	54.0
-5.4	-4.3	-8.8	-540.2				-7.2	-5.8
10.8	8.5	10.1	9.5			EBIT/Interest	5.5	5.0
(28) 3.3	(73) 2.7	(103) 3.1	(56) 3.2				(248) 2.4	(245) 2.4
.8	.9	.7	1.0				1.0	.7
	7.9	6.0	4.1			Net Profit + Depr., Dep., Amort./Cur. Mat. L/T/D	3.5	4.3
	(12) 3.4	(22) 2.4	(16) .9				(34) 2.3	(38) 2.1
	1.8	1.4	-.2				1.3	.9
.4	.9	.7	.6			Fixed/Worth	.6	.7
3.8	2.0	1.2	1.1				1.4	1.4
-2.1	19.4	3.6	1.5				8.5	6.5
1.2	.8	.5	.6			Debt/Worth	.7	.6
8.7	2.0	1.2	1.4				1.8	1.7
-2.1	99.4	5.9	2.9				81.3	16.3
125.2	77.4	25.9	27.6			% Profit Before Taxes/Tangible Net Worth	20.9	28.5
(21) 45.5	(61) 15.3	(103) 10.9	(58) 10.3				(212) 8.3	(217) 12.9
18.5	.6	-.1	.0				1.7	.5
65.8	22.2	12.6	9.9			% Profit Before Taxes/Total Assets	10.3	11.0
8.7	5.9	4.2	5.1				3.2	4.0
-3.3	-.2	-.4	-.4				-.1	-.6
43.8	7.3	4.6	7.1			Sales/Net Fixed Assets	8.5	7.1
5.7	2.2	1.4	2.3				2.2	2.3
2.2	1.1	.5	.9				.9	.9
6.7	2.5	1.6	1.8			Sales/Total Assets	2.2	2.2
3.2	1.4	.7	.8				1.0	1.1
1.6	.8	.4	.4				.5	.5
1.7	4.1	2.3	1.9			% Depr., Dep., Amort./Sales	2.5	2.8
(19) 4.3	(64) 8.3	(97) 6.7	(51) 4.8				(240) 6.1	(225) 6.0
11.3	15.5	10.1	8.3				10.4	10.0
3.1	2.0	1.2	.4			% Officers', Directors' Owners' Comp/Sales	1.2	1.3
(13) 5.7	(34) 2.8	(30) 2.6	(10) 1.6				(71) 3.0	(84) 3.3
8.6	6.6	4.8	5.3				7.4	5.4
33685M	156822M	653562M	1439117M	313973M	1433191M	Net Sales ($)	2510402M	3520128M
10047M	90644M	557013M	1176660M	638959M	764994M	Total Assets ($)	2425968M	2996729M

Comparative Historical Data | | | Current Data Sorted by Sales

			Type of Statement						
18	26	21	Unqualified	2	1	2		4	12
35	46	41	Reviewed	4	6	4	9	7	11
65	68	65	Compiled	5	26	6	16	7	5
82	91	107	Tax Returns	37	43	13	10	2	2
76	81	76	Other	17	22	11	14	6	6
4/1/07-3/31/08 ALL	4/1/08-3/31/09 ALL	4/1/09-3/31/10 ALL		54 (4/1-9/30/09)			256 (10/1/09-3/31/10)		
				0-1MM	1-3MM	3-5MM	5-10MM	10-25MM	25MM & OVER
276	312	310	NUMBER OF STATEMENTS	65	98	36	49	26	36
%	%	%	ASSETS	%	%	%	%	%	%
8.0	8.3	9.8	Cash & Equivalents	14.0	8.7	10.1	8.9	4.4	9.9
9.2	8.9	8.8	Trade Receivables (net)	3.3	5.1	9.7	11.8	14.3	19.8
13.1	13.3	12.1	Inventory	4.0	9.2	17.7	12.7	22.2	21.1
6.4	6.7	5.0	All Other Current	3.1	4.1	4.6	4.4	6.4	10.6
36.8	37.2	35.7	Total Current	24.4	27.2	42.1	37.8	47.3	61.4
52.1	50.9	52.9	Fixed Assets (net)	66.7	59.5	46.1	47.6	41.3	32.5
2.5	1.0	1.5	Intangibles (net)	1.1	1.5	2.8	1.4	1.1	.9
8.6	11.0	10.0	All Other Non-Current	7.7	11.8	9.0	13.2	10.3	5.3
100.0	100.0	100.0	Total	100.0	100.0	100.0	100.0	100.0	100.0
			LIABILITIES						
24.4	22.6	21.3	Notes Payable-Short Term	20.7	26.2	14.7	17.2	24.1	19.2
6.3	5.5	4.7	Cur. Mat.-L.T.D.	7.3	5.9	1.6	3.3	2.7	3.2
5.5	5.0	4.0	Trade Payables	2.5	1.5	5.5	3.7	6.2	11.1
.5	.4	.5	Income Taxes Payable	.0	.4	.2	.6	1.7	.6
8.7	6.9	8.1	All Other Current	10.0	9.6	6.4	2.0	8.5	10.7
45.3	40.4	38.6	Total Current	40.6	43.6	28.5	26.8	43.1	44.6
30.8	28.8	30.8	Long-Term Debt	35.9	43.5	20.2	25.0	19.8	13.7
.5	.5	.5	Deferred Taxes	.0	.3	.5	.7	.5	1.3
4.3	4.6	6.4	All Other Non-Current	8.4	7.1	5.6	5.8	3.3	4.5
19.1	25.7	23.7	Net Worth	15.2	5.4	45.2	41.7	33.3	35.9
100.0	100.0	100.0	Total Liabilities & Net Worth	100.0	100.0	100.0	100.0	100.0	100.0
			INCOME DATA						
100.0	100.0	100.0	Net Sales	100.0	100.0	100.0	100.0	100.0	100.0
			Gross Profit						
88.9	90.4	88.9	Operating Expenses	78.4	91.2	92.8	89.2	91.5	95.1
11.1	9.6	11.1	Operating Profit	21.6	8.8	7.2	10.8	8.5	4.9
3.2	3.1	3.3	All Other Expenses (net)	10.0	2.7	1.3	.5	.9	.7
7.9	6.5	7.8	Profit Before Taxes	11.6	6.1	5.9	10.3	7.6	4.2
			RATIOS						
1.9	2.1	2.3		2.0	2.4	3.5	2.3	2.1	2.2
1.1	1.1	1.1	Current	.7	.8	1.4	1.2	1.4	1.3
.3	.4	.4		.2	.1	.7	.9	1.0	1.0
1.0	1.0	1.3		1.6	.9	1.5	1.4	.8	1.2
.3	.4 (309)	.4	Quick	.3 (97)	.2	.7	.6	.6	.6
.1	.1	.1		.1	.1	.2	.2	.3	.4

0	UND	0	UND	0	UND			0 UND	0 UND	0 UND	0 UND	3	129.4	15	23.9
5	75.0	8	44.7	3	132.0	Sales/Receivables		0 UND	0 UND	9 38.7	20 18.0	36	10.0	29	12.5
35	10.4	42	8.7	40	9.2			2 205.2	21 17.3	52 7.0	54 6.8	72	5.1	51	7.2

			Cost of Sales/Inventory						
			Cost of Sales/Payables						

4.5	4.4	4.7	Sales/Working Capital	9.0	5.1	2.5	4.5	4.7	5.0
51.5	27.0	32.7		-25.8	-22.6	11.4	17.2	10.4	11.7
-5.4	-6.9	-8.8		-2.6	-4.3	-39.0	-77.3	NM	71.4
6.1	7.1	9.4		11.4	5.4	11.6	16.4	10.3	9.7
(249) 2.8	(281) 2.6	(273) 3.1	EBIT/Interest	(46) 1.7	(88) 2.2	(33) 2.6	(47) 5.7	(25) 4.8	(34) 3.8
1.1	.9	.9		.1	.6	-.6	2.3	2.5	1.0
5.2	5.5	6.0				7.0		8.6	6.0
(39) 2.3	(56) 2.9	(55) 2.3	Net Profit + Depr., Dep., Amort./Cur. Mat. L/T/D		(17) 2.3		(10) 4.9	(11) 3.3
1.4	1.3	.9				1.1		1.9	.5
.7	.7	.7		1.1	.9	.4	.5	.4	.4
1.5	1.3	1.3	Fixed/Worth	2.2	1.5	1.1	1.0	1.0	.8
17.6	4.5	4.3		7.2	-6.2	2.7	2.6	1.9	1.4
.7	.7	.6		.6	.6	.4	.4	.7	.8
2.2	1.7	1.7	Debt/Worth	2.2	1.8	1.2	1.2	1.5	1.9
34.1	7.3	6.8		14.3	-8.5	4.5	3.7	2.1	4.1
41.0	34.3	33.8		59.6	31.3	82.8	32.2	34.9	29.4
(221) 17.4	(259) 12.1	(257) 13.5	% Profit Before Taxes/Tangible Net Worth	(53) 7.1	(68) 9.1	(34) 10.5	(44) 15.4	(25) 22.4	(33) 16.6
4.3	1.0	.6		-3.3	.2	-1.9	4.5	6.4	1.4
15.0	12.1	14.2		16.8	11.7	17.3	18.3	16.6	10.8
5.8	4.2	4.9	% Profit Before Taxes/Total Assets	2.6	3.6	4.5	8.3	7.9	5.6
.4	-.3	-.4		-2.3	-1.4	-1.6	2.2	3.1	-.4
7.1	6.9	7.7		2.2	4.9	12.3	6.5	13.2	22.5
2.6	2.2	2.1	Sales/Net Fixed Assets	1.0	1.7	2.2	2.1	3.6	7.6
1.0	.9	.9		.2	.8	1.1	1.1	1.8	3.1
2.2	2.1	2.2		1.5	1.9	2.6	2.0	2.1	3.0
1.3	1.0	1.1	Sales/Total Assets	.6	1.0	1.2	1.1	1.3	2.2
.5	.5	.5		.2	.4	.6	.6	.7	1.2
2.5	3.1	2.8		4.1	5.2	2.4	2.2	2.8	1.4
(241) 5.7	(269) 6.2	(243) 6.6	% Depr., Dep., Amort./Sales	(46) 11.0	(80) 8.6	(27) 4.0	(37) 6.2	(22) 4.4	(31) 1.9
11.1	11.2	10.7		26.9	11.8	9.5	10.1	6.3	4.8
1.6	2.0	1.8		2.0	2.5	1.9	1.5		
(58) 3.3	(83) 3.3	(87) 3.1	% Officers', Directors' Owners' Comp/Sales	(12) 7.0	(39) 3.6	(10) 2.4	(15) 1.8		
7.2	6.4	6.3		10.4	6.5	4.6	6.3		
3275098M	3863180M	4030350M	Net Sales ($)	31402M	177669M	138335M	365348M	410896M	2906700M
3026334M	3928484M	3238317M	Total Assets ($)	117256M	290755M	151462M	545009M	447641M	1686194M

M = $ thousand   MM = $ million
See Pages 9 through 22 for Explanation of Ratios and Data

	Current Data Sorted by Assets							Comparative Historical Data	
			3	2	1		Type of Statement		
		2	2	8		1	Unqualified	10	10
		4	9	10			Reviewed	18	20
	5	23	13	2			Compiled	21	30
	18	9	12	7			Tax Returns	24	39
	1				2		Other	33	31
		14 (4/1-9/30/09)		120 (10/1/09-3/31/10)				4/1/05-3/31/06	4/1/06-3/31/07
	0-500M	500M-2MM	2-10MM	10-50MM	50-100MM	100-250MM		ALL	ALL
	24	38	39	29	3	1	NUMBER OF STATEMENTS	106	130
	%	%	%	%	%	%	ASSETS	%	%
	18.0	8.7	5.7	4.2			Cash & Equivalents	7.7	8.4
	6.5	3.9	6.3	5.3			Trade Receivables (net)	7.6	6.5
	19.2	22.0	29.2	35.9			Inventory	31.4	29.7
	13.8	5.7	3.2	1.8			All Other Current	5.3	4.9
	57.4	40.3	44.3	47.2			Total Current	52.0	49.6
	36.0	47.7	45.8	37.2			Fixed Assets (net)	39.8	41.7
	2.4	2.4	1.1	1.1			Intangibles (net)	.5	.3
	4.2	9.6	8.8	14.6			All Other Non-Current	7.7	8.4
	100.0	100.0	100.0	100.0			Total	100.0	100.0
							LIABILITIES		
	107.8	31.3	23.7	27.8			Notes Payable-Short Term	26.8	29.4
	8.3	5.8	1.9	1.5			Cur. Mat.-L.T.D.	2.7	3.1
	.8	1.6	2.4	3.5			Trade Payables	3.2	2.9
	.0	.1	.4	.1			Income Taxes Payable	.7	.3
	6.8	5.2	5.9	3.5			All Other Current	8.6	7.6
	123.6	44.0	34.3	36.4			Total Current	42.0	43.3
	16.2	24.8	19.4	15.8			Long-Term Debt	24.9	22.7
	.0	.0	1.7	.2			Deferred Taxes	.4	.4
	12.3	5.3	1.7	1.3			All Other Non-Current	4.6	4.2
	-52.2	26.0	42.9	46.3			Net Worth	28.1	29.4
	100.0	100.0	100.0	100.0			Total Liabilties & Net Worth	100.0	100.0
							INCOME DATA		
	100.0	100.0	100.0	100.0			Net Sales	100.0	100.0
							Gross Profit		
	98.6	97.6	92.4	93.3			Operating Expenses	90.7	92.2
	1.4	2.4	7.6	6.7			Operating Profit	9.3	7.8
	5.8	1.5	2.8	-1.2			All Other Expenses (net)	3.3	3.8
	-4.4	.9	4.9	7.9			Profit Before Taxes	6.1	4.0
							RATIOS		
	1.4	2.1	2.1	2.2				1.8	2.4
	.7	1.0	1.2	1.3			Current	1.2	1.2
	.2	.2	.9	1.0				.8	.6
	.6	.9	.6	.9				.8	.7
	.1	.2	(37) .2	.2			Quick	(103) .2	(128) .2
	.0	.0	.0	.0				.0	.1
	0 UND	0 UND	0 UND	0 UND				0 UND	0 UND
	0 UND	0 UND	0 UND	13 27.6			Sales/Receivables	1 582.9	0 UND
	0 UND	3 134.5	21 17.3	47 7.8				16 23.2	15 23.7
							Cost of Sales/Inventory		
							Cost of Sales/Payables		
	42.7	4.7	3.6	2.6				4.3	3.5
	-23.2	103.2	33.3	6.0			Sales/Working Capital	29.0	62.0
	-3.2	-2.7	-12.6	88.7				-9.4	-6.8
	5.0	4.2	4.6	3.7				6.0	3.6
	(21) -.3	(37) .5	(35) 2.3	(26) 1.0			EBIT/Interest	(89) 1.8	(110) 1.7
	-5.2	-1.1	.6	-2.9				.9	.1
								22.3	10.0
							Net Profit + Depr., Dep., Amort./Cur. Mat. L/T/D	(12) 4.2	(14) 4.6
								1.9	1.8
	.4	.5	.5	.3				.4	.3
	NM	1.5	1.1	.7			Fixed/Worth	.8	1.1
	-.5	-3.6	2.2	1.2				2.7	3.4
	1.8	.4	.6	.7				.6	.8
	-6.2	2.2	1.1	1.4			Debt/Worth	1.8	2.0
	-2.2	-6.8	2.8	1.9				6.8	9.2
	85.4	36.6	12.6	7.3				23.7	24.7
	(11) 6.3	(26) 6.7	(36) 3.9	(28) .6			% Profit Before Taxes/Tangible Net Worth	(87) 8.9	(109) 6.5
	-7.8	-7.5	-1.2	-12.5				.3	-1.1
	23.8	10.7	5.1	4.0				11.9	8.1
	-4.2	.0	2.1	.1			% Profit Before Taxes/Total Assets	2.8	2.4
	-30.4	-4.6	-.8	-6.7				-.1	-1.5
	151.5	10.3	9.2	9.1				17.7	23.1
	18.5	2.1	1.5	2.4			Sales/Net Fixed Assets	3.7	3.1
	2.9	.7	.6	.6				1.1	.7
	8.2	2.0	1.5	1.4				1.9	1.8
	2.4	.8	.8	.7			Sales/Total Assets	1.1	1.1
	1.5	.5	.3	.2				.6	.5
	.9	1.6	2.0	.4				.8	.8
	(18) 6.2	(31) 4.5	(34) 6.8	(27) 1.4			% Depr., Dep., Amort./Sales	(90) 2.2	(103) 3.9
	23.5	15.1	13.7	9.2				6.8	10.5
	1.7	.8	.7					.6	.5
	(11) 3.2	(15) 2.6	(13) 1.3				% Officers', Directors' Owners' Comp/Sales	(21) 1.7	(29) 1.5
	6.2	6.4	3.6					5.1	5.6
	29509M	125224M	321162M	575814M	123909M	36230M	Net Sales ($)	2357448M	3335504M
	5450M	42163M	176753M	630151M	176607M	212040M	Total Assets ($)	985571M	1635775M

M = $ thousand   MM = $ million
See Pages 9 through 22 for Explanation of Ratios and Data

Comparative Historical Data | Current Data Sorted by Sales

	4/1/07-3/31/08 ALL	4/1/08-3/31/09 ALL	4/1/09-3/31/10 ALL		14 (4/1-9/30/09)			120 (10/1/09-3/31/10)	
Type of Statement				0-1MM	1-3MM	3-5MM	5-10MM	10-25MM	25MM & OVER
Unqualified	7	6	6		2		1		3
Reviewed	15	17	13		3	3	3	1	3
Compiled	32	33	28	7	5	3	2	5	6
Tax Returns	36	44	56	35	9	6	1	3	2
Other	39	47	31	10	6	6	1	6	2
NUMBER OF STATEMENTS	129	147	134	52	25	18	8	15	16
ASSETS	%	%	%	%	%	%	%	%	%
Cash & Equivalents	10.1	7.0	8.3	11.1	7.8	7.5		6.0	5.9
Trade Receivables (net)	5.7	7.1	5.6	3.9	6.0	2.6		9.3	11.0
Inventory	25.1	27.0	26.7	16.6	18.3	31.5		41.9	34.4
All Other Current	4.5	6.4	5.6	8.7	3.0	4.4		1.1	6.7
Total Current	45.4	47.5	46.1	40.4	35.1	46.0		58.3	58.0
Fixed Assets (net)	46.7	44.9	42.3	52.2	50.5	37.4		26.9	27.5
Intangibles (net)	.8	.1	1.7	3.4	.0	1.0		.0	1.8
All Other Non-Current	7.0	7.5	9.9	3.9	14.4	15.6		14.7	12.7
Total	100.0	100.0	100.0	100.0	100.0	100.0		100.0	100.0
LIABILITIES									
Notes Payable-Short Term	28.7	25.8	41.7	58.1	34.9	22.4		35.2	27.2
Cur. Mat.-L.T.D.	4.0	4.9	4.0	5.7	6.7	1.8		.9	1.3
Trade Payables	4.1	2.5	2.2	.4	1.3	3.3		2.9	6.9
Income Taxes Payable	.3	.7	.1	.0	.0	.8		.0	.0
All Other Current	4.5	7.2	5.7	2.4	2.9	12.0		10.3	8.2
Total Current	41.8	41.1	53.6	66.7	45.9	40.3		49.3	43.6
Long-Term Debt	20.2	21.0	19.5	20.6	29.6	16.1		5.7	19.7
Deferred Taxes	.2	.4	.5	.0	1.4	.2		1.8	.0
All Other Non-Current	4.4	5.4	4.5	6.4	6.7	2.4		1.3	2.5
Net Worth	33.5	32.1	21.7	6.2	16.4	41.0		41.9	34.3
Total Liabilties & Net Worth	100.0	100.0	100.0	100.0	100.0	100.0		100.0	100.0
INCOME DATA									
Net Sales	100.0	100.0	100.0	100.0	100.0	100.0		100.0	100.0
Gross Profit									
Operating Expenses	91.0	94.4	95.4	93.0	94.3	93.5		96.4	101.8
Operating Profit	9.0	5.6	4.6	7.0	5.7	6.5		3.6	-1.8
All Other Expenses (net)	4.0	2.9	2.2	5.7	.8	-1.4		.7	.4
Profit Before Taxes	5.0	2.8	2.4	1.2	4.9	7.9		2.9	-2.1
RATIOS									
Current	2.3	2.2	1.8	1.6	2.5	2.1		2.1	1.9
	1.2	1.1	1.1	.9	1.2	1.1		1.4	1.3
	.7	.7	.7	.3	.6	.8		1.0	.8
Quick	.8	.7	.7	.8	1.1	.6		.4	.9
	(128) .2	.2	(132) .2	.1	.4	(17) .1	(14)	.2	.2
	.0	.0	.0	.0	.1	.0		.1	.1
Sales/Receivables	0 UND	0 UND	0 UND	0 UND	0 UND	0 UND		0 UND	2 231.8
	0 UND	0 UND	0 UND	0 UND	4 101.3	0 UND		13 27.6	4 100.5
	15 24.3	18 20.2	19 19.3	0 UND	33 11.1	1 473.2		28 13.0	32 11.4
Cost of Sales/Inventory									
Cost of Sales/Payables									
Sales/Working Capital	4.0	4.1	4.3	3.9	2.3	4.2		5.1	5.0
	21.9	27.1	40.3	-52.3	10.1	88.6		7.9	38.6
	-12.2	-6.2	-8.3	-2.4	-4.6	-7.1		96.4	NM
EBIT/Interest	4.6	3.2	4.5	3.6	3.3	5.3		25.0	3.4
	(112) 1.8	(124) 1.7	(122) 1.1	(44) -.1	(23) 1.3	(17) 2.5		3.2	(15) 1.0
	.9	.0	-1.2	-2.5	.4	-1.7		-.1	-1.2
Net Profit + Depr., Dep., Amort./Cur. Mat. L/T/D	6.6	5.2	8.0						
	(11) 3.6	(16) 1.0	(15) 2.3						
	1.0	-2.6	.8						
Fixed/Worth	.5	.5	.4	.9	.7	.3		.1	.1
	1.3	1.1	1.1	1.7	1.2	.6		.6	.8
	4.2	2.9	3.4	-1.4	NM	2.0		1.0	2.1
Debt/Worth	.6	.6	.7	.6	.7	.4		.7	.8
	1.5	1.7	1.7	2.2	1.1	1.6		1.2	2.0
	9.1	6.4	8.9	-3.6	-8.6	3.7		2.6	4.3
% Profit Before Taxes/Tangible Net Worth	20.7	16.4	18.3	13.9	15.2	28.6		32.5	13.8
	(107) 7.4	(121) 3.8	(105) 2.7	(34) 2.0	(18) 3.0	(17) 4.5	(14)	3.1	(14) -1.6
	1.0	-3.5	-6.4	-6.1	-.3	-7.1		-10.0	-18.6
% Profit Before Taxes/Total Assets	7.3	5.9	5.9	6.2	3.3	5.9		23.5	5.4
	2.6	1.5	.7	-.9	.8	2.7		3.3	-.9
	-.3	-3.0	-5.1	-5.8	-1.6	-3.7		-2.1	-8.8
Sales/Net Fixed Assets	14.2	12.5	16.4	6.2	4.5	19.3		284.0	38.3
	2.1	2.7	2.6	2.0	1.1	3.6		10.0	11.8
	.7	.7	.8	.5	.4	1.5		2.1	5.8
Sales/Total Assets	1.9	1.9	1.9	1.7	1.6	1.8		6.6	5.9
	1.0	.8	1.0	.5	.5	1.2		1.4	1.7
	.5	.4	.4	.3	.2	.6		.8	.8
% Depr., Dep., Amort./Sales	1.0	1.0	1.0	3.7	1.6	1.1		.3	.3
	(104) 3.7	(122) 4.7	(113) 4.5	(41) 11.8	(20) 8.1	(17) 4.6	(13)	1.4	(15) .4
	10.6	11.1	13.0	25.1	15.6	9.3		4.0	1.4
% Officers', Directors' Owners' Comp/Sales	.9	.7	.8	1.8					
	(32) 1.9	(39) 2.1	(42) 2.0	(20) 4.1					
	6.4	5.5	4.6	8.3					
Net Sales ($)	2505764M	1588660M	1211848M	27198M	48152M	69138M	54425M	227940M	784995M
Total Assets ($)	1790535M	1307862M	1243164M	85406M	199921M	84524M	73326M	177922M	622065M

Current Data Sorted by Assets | Comparative Historical Data

Type of Statement	0-500M	500M-2MM	2-10MM	10-50MM	50-100MM	100-250MM		4/1/05-3/31/06 ALL	4/1/06-3/31/07 ALL
Unqualified		1	2	16	11	10		47	39
Reviewed	1	3	18	21	8	1		34	41
Compiled	5	8	13	8	2			29	36
Tax Returns	2	8	3	2				13	22
Other		6	22	14	10	3		59	63
		52 (4/1-9/30/09)		146 (10/1/09-3/31/10)					
NUMBER OF STATEMENTS	8	26	58	61	31	14		182	201
	%	%	%	%	%	%		%	%
ASSETS									
Cash & Equivalents		5.1	4.3	4.8	2.8	.7		4.9	4.2
Trade Receivables (net)		14.5	17.8	16.2	14.7	7.2		12.8	15.8
Inventory		28.5	44.5	38.5	45.3	62.3		39.8	42.3
All Other Current		2.5	6.7	7.6	6.8	4.0		9.9	7.6
Total Current		50.6	73.2	67.0	69.6	74.2		67.4	69.8
Fixed Assets (net)		33.5	21.6	20.9	24.9	21.9		23.2	21.0
Intangibles (net)		.6	.3	.0	.1	.0		.5	.3
All Other Non-Current		15.3	4.9	12.0	5.3	3.9		8.9	8.9
Total		100.0	100.0	100.0	100.0	100.0		100.0	100.0
LIABILITIES									
Notes Payable-Short Term		32.0	43.4	36.5	34.8	45.1		37.1	35.6
Cur. Mat.-L.T.D.		5.3	1.9	1.6	1.0	1.6		2.1	1.8
Trade Payables		8.2	5.8	6.6	4.5	6.1		6.3	5.5
Income Taxes Payable		.1	.2	.2	.2	.2		.3	.4
All Other Current		8.8	7.8	5.9	5.9	7.2		8.4	7.2
Total Current		54.3	59.2	50.8	46.3	60.2		54.2	50.5
Long-Term Debt		41.2	9.1	11.1	10.9	12.1		11.7	12.3
Deferred Taxes		.1	.0	1.1	.1	.6		.3	.3
All Other Non-Current		2.6	4.8	3.3	2.9	1.8		4.7	3.3
Net Worth		1.8	26.9	33.7	39.8	25.3		29.0	33.6
Total Liabilties & Net Worth		100.0	100.0	100.0	100.0	100.0		100.0	100.0
INCOME DATA									
Net Sales		100.0	100.0	100.0	100.0	100.0		100.0	100.0
Gross Profit									
Operating Expenses		90.7	100.1	95.3	99.1	101.0		94.6	94.5
Operating Profit		9.3	-.1	4.7	.9	-1.0		5.4	5.5
All Other Expenses (net)		4.1	.9	2.4	-.4	.0		2.2	2.3
Profit Before Taxes		5.3	-1.0	2.3	1.3	-1.0		3.2	3.2
RATIOS									
Current		2.3	1.6	1.6	2.2	1.3		1.8	1.8
		1.1	1.2	1.2	1.4	1.2		1.3	1.3
		.3	1.0	1.1	1.1	1.2		1.1	1.1
Quick		1.2	.6	.7	.7	.2		.6	.6
		.2	(57) .3	(60) .3	.3	.2	.1	(180) .3	(200) .3
		.0	.1	.1	.1	.0		.1	.1
Sales/Receivables		0 UND	1 668.0	8 44.8	9 38.8	5 78.6		3 146.0	1 281.3
		12 29.4	18 19.9	21 17.4	19 18.9	21 17.7		17 21.8	17 21.4
		35 10.4	48 7.6	48 7.5	73 5.0	41 8.9		42 8.6	54 6.7
Cost of Sales/Inventory									
Cost of Sales/Payables									
Sales/Working Capital		7.6	5.3	4.7	4.0	7.9		5.1	4.6
		67.0	16.1	10.0	7.3	10.2		10.1	9.0
		-5.9	-778.0	29.0	17.9	12.2		50.2	36.0
EBIT/Interest		5.9	5.5	5.8	5.4	2.8		5.5	4.3
	(24) 1.7	(57) 1.5	(59) 1.8	(29) 2.6	1.4		(167) 2.2	(186) 1.8	
		-1.1	-1.1	-.3	-.6	.9		1.0	.7
Net Profit + Depr., Dep., Amort./Cur. Mat. L/T/D								4.1	5.7
								(28) 2.3	(29) 2.2
								.7	1.3
Fixed/Worth		.2	.1	.2	.2	.3		.3	.2
		2.0	.5	.6	.5	.7		.6	.5
		-3.4	1.3	1.3	1.2	1.7		1.3	1.3
Debt/Worth		.8	1.2	.8	.8	2.1		1.0	1.0
		10.9	2.6	2.5	1.8	2.9		2.3	2.3
		-5.2	5.1	5.4	3.4	4.0		5.0	4.6
% Profit Before Taxes/Tangible Net Worth		29.0	26.3	23.2	23.0	9.6		20.5	21.2
	(16) 15.2	(54) 4.7	(57) 8.6	(30) 4.8	1.5		(165) 8.7	(190) 8.5	
		2.6	-14.5	-4.4	-7.0	-3.0		-.1	-1.0
% Profit Before Taxes/Total Assets		11.5	7.3	6.0	8.5	2.9		6.9	7.8
		1.9	1.0	1.7	2.9	.4		2.5	2.3
		-11.8	-5.9	-1.6	-3.3	-.4		-.5	-.5
Sales/Net Fixed Assets		19.8	151.6	30.4	16.7	20.5		26.9	29.1
		9.5	12.9	9.9	12.0	7.5		8.3	9.5
		2.6	3.4	4.1	6.8	3.8		4.2	5.1
Sales/Total Assets		3.4	2.8	2.3	2.0	1.7		2.2	2.0
		2.0	1.8	1.4	1.5	1.4		1.5	1.5
		.7	1.0	.8	.8	1.0		.9	1.0
% Depr., Dep., Amort./Sales		.9	.4	.7	.8	.7		.8	.8
	(18) 2.8	(47) 1.5	(57) 1.3	(25) 1.5	(13) 1.4		(163) 1.7	(170) 1.5	
		8.4	3.3	2.1	2.5	3.1		3.1	2.6
% Officers', Directors' Owners' Comp/Sales		.6	.5	.3				.6	.4
	(10) 2.0	(13) 1.8	(13) .6				(43) 1.2	(49) 1.5	
		3.8	5.6	3.0				3.7	3.8
Net Sales ($)	29724M	76291M	1341928M	1999288M	3659853M	2534100M		7535831M	9238645M
Total Assets ($)	2202M	28652M	307359M	1302508M	2243012M	1900483M		4675648M	6043572M

M = $ thousand   MM = $ million
See Pages 9 through 22 for Explanation of Ratios and Data

Comparative Historical Data | Current Data Sorted by Sales

Hist 4/1/07-3/31/08 ALL	Hist 4/1/08-3/31/09 ALL	Hist 4/1/09-3/31/10 ALL	Type of Statement	0-1MM	1-3MM	3-5MM	5-10MM	10-25MM	25MM & OVER
34	38	40	Unqualified		1			5	34
49	47	51	Reviewed	2	1	1	11	16	20
27	39	32	Compiled	3	3	5	7	8	6
15	16	18	Tax Returns	6	7	1	3	1	
72	80	57	Other	5	9	3	11	6	23
				52 (4/1-9/30/09)			146 (10/1/09-3/31/10)		
197	220	198	NUMBER OF STATEMENTS	16	21	10	32	36	83
%	%	%	ASSETS	%	%	%	%	%	%
4.3	5.4	4.8	Cash & Equivalents	15.0	3.9	2.1	4.0	3.8	4.1
16.5	16.6	15.7	Trade Receivables (net)	17.2	10.0	20.6	12.9	19.9	15.6
43.6	41.3	40.5	Inventory	9.3	34.9	35.1	41.5	41.4	47.8
6.5	6.6	6.0	All Other Current	1.6	1.4	7.7	5.9	7.7	7.1
70.9	69.9	67.0	Total Current	43.1	50.2	65.5	64.3	72.8	74.6
21.0	21.8	24.2	Fixed Assets (net)	42.0	31.4	31.8	26.4	18.4	19.7
.3	.3	.2	Intangibles (net)	1.0	.0	.0	.4	.0	.1
7.8	8.0	8.6	All Other Non-Current	13.8	18.3	2.7	8.8	8.8	5.7
100.0	100.0	100.0	Total	100.0	100.0	100.0	100.0	100.0	100.0
			LIABILITIES						
39.8	36.2	38.8	Notes Payable-Short Term	38.2	38.3	24.6	46.8	40.5	37.0
1.4	1.4	2.0	Cur. Mat.-L.T.D.	2.2	3.2	6.3	2.5	1.2	1.3
5.8	5.8	6.3	Trade Payables	8.2	1.7	8.3	4.1	8.0	6.9
.3	.2	.2	Income Taxes Payable	.1	.0	.0	.4	.2	.1
6.8	6.4	6.9	All Other Current	8.7	2.8	4.7	8.6	4.8	8.0
54.0	50.0	54.1	Total Current	57.4	46.0	43.9	62.4	54.8	53.4
12.1	13.5	14.9	Long-Term Debt	39.1	27.9	21.7	13.2	8.8	9.4
.5	.4	.4	Deferred Taxes	.0	1.0	.0	.5	.1	.5
4.2	3.1	4.4	All Other Non-Current	10.8	5.4	.0	8.3	2.8	2.7
29.4	33.0	26.1	Net Worth	-7.3	19.6	34.4	15.7	33.5	34.0
100.0	100.0	100.0	Total Liabilities & Net Worth	100.0	100.0	100.0	100.0	100.0	100.0
			INCOME DATA						
100.0	100.0	100.0	Net Sales	100.0	100.0	100.0	100.0	100.0	100.0
			Gross Profit						
94.8	95.7	97.1	Operating Expenses	81.7	91.8	101.6	100.8	98.1	99.0
5.2	4.3	2.9	Operating Profit	18.3	8.2	-1.6	-.8	1.9	1.0
3.3	2.4	1.6	All Other Expenses (net)	5.7	5.3	2.2	1.2	1.5	-.1
2.0	1.9	1.3	Profit Before Taxes	12.6	2.9	-3.8	-2.1	.5	1.1
			RATIOS						
1.9 1.3 1.1	2.0 1.3 1.1	1.7 1.2 1.0	Current	2.8 1.0 .1	1.3 1.0 .6	2.7 1.4 1.0	2.4 1.1 .9	1.7 1.2 1.1	1.6 1.3 1.2
.7 .3 .1	.8 .3 .1	.7 .2 .1	Quick	2.8 .5 .0	.3 .1 .0	1.2 .1 .0	.7 .1 .1	.6 .3 .1	.7 .2 .1
2 188.8 19 18.8 50 7.3	1 282.6 16 22.7 53 6.9	4 102.4 17 21.0 45 8.2	Sales/Receivables	0 UND 6 62.0 107 3.4	0 UND 0 929.0 28 13.2	0 UND 8 44.7 33 11.2	0 UND 19 18.8 48 7.6	6 62.2 29 12.5 60 6.1	7 49.1 20 18.7 40 9.1
			Cost of Sales/Inventory						
			Cost of Sales/Payables						
4.2 10.1 43.2	4.0 10.5 27.7	5.2 11.3 156.8	Sales/Working Capital	2.7 54.5 -1.2	7.2 65.1 -6.3	3.8 15.5 NM	5.0 35.7 -48.8	5.4 11.3 128.6	6.2 9.9 18.7
3.7 (185) 1.6 .6	4.5 (205) 1.5 -.1	5.5 (190) 1.6 -.5	EBIT/Interest	10.6 (14) 1.8 -.5	1.9 (19) 1.0 -4.7		8.6 2.2 -2.0	6.8 1.5 -.3	5.7 (80) 2.3 .3
11.3 (30) 2.4 .8	11.7 (20) 3.3 -.5	6.5 (19) 1.8 .2	Net Profit + Depr., Dep., Amort./Cur. Mat. L/T/D					6.1 (13) 1.8 1.1	
.2 .5 1.4	.1 .6 1.3	.2 .6 1.4	Fixed/Worth	.2 2.1 -2.6	.0 1.2 -20.0	.1 .6 2.6	.1 .7 3.6	.1 .4 1.2	.2 .5 1.1
1.0 2.6 5.5	.8 2.3 5.8	1.0 2.5 5.4	Debt/Worth	1.1 4.7 -4.0	1.1 4.6 -48.3	.7 2.0 3.7	.5 3.0 7.4	1.1 2.4 4.8	1.3 2.4 4.1
20.0 (178) 7.9 -3.2	25.9 (197) 5.8 -5.4	22.4 (176) 5.8 -7.0	% Profit Before Taxes/Tangible Net Worth	24.4 (11) 3.6 -45.5	22.6 (15) .0 -9.4	(27)	20.8 6.5 -18.5	25.5 (33) 8.8 -8.4	24.4 (81) 6.5 -4.0
6.3 2.3 -1.3	9.1 1.7 -3.3	6.8 1.5 -3.2	% Profit Before Taxes/Total Assets	14.4 3.0 -3.7	2.2 .0 -9.5	4.0 -.4 -12.1	6.8 2.0 -10.6	7.6 2.0 -2.9	7.8 2.1 -1.2
29.6 9.9 5.2	36.3 10.7 4.8	29.0 10.5 3.8	Sales/Net Fixed Assets	6.3 3.2 .8	18.3 2.9 1.0	313.0 12.3 1.5	53.1 14.9 2.9	77.0 13.3 4.5	25.3 12.5 6.8
2.2 1.5 1.0	2.3 1.6 1.0	2.3 1.6 .9	Sales/Total Assets	1.7 .7 .2	2.0 .7 .2	4.0 2.2 .7	2.9 1.6 1.1	2.3 1.6 .9	2.4 1.8 1.3
.7 (164) 1.4 2.5	.7 (175) 1.4 2.4	.7 (167) 1.5 3.1	% Depr., Dep., Amort./Sales	4.1 (12) 6.2 11.3	.9 (16) 3.3 8.6	(27)	.7 (30) 1.5 3.9	.6 (75) 1.7 2.6	.7 1.2 1.6
.4 (45) 1.3 3.7	.3 (46) .8 2.2	.4 (44) 1.0 3.7	% Officers', Directors' Owners' Comp/Sales					(15)	.2 2.0
8389083M 5536584M	10754155M 6575425M	9641184M 5784216M	Net Sales ($) Total Assets ($)	7590M 18855M	38812M 114594M	39795M 30496M	245486M 214439M	602773M 543859M	8706728M 4861973M

M = $ thousand   MM = $ million
See Pages 9 through 22 for Explanation of Ratios and Data

AGRICULTURE—Dairy Cattle and Milk Production NAICS 112120

Current Data Sorted by Assets

Comparative Historical Data

0-500M	500M-2MM	2-10MM	10-50MM	50-100MM	100-250MM		4/1/05-3/31/06 ALL	4/1/06-3/31/07 ALL
		2	5	1	9	Type of Statement — Unqualified	5	9
1	10	125	190	23	5	Reviewed	279	256
	8	66	28	1		Compiled	77	64
4	19	20	1			Tax Returns	21	31
1	7	28	24	5	3	Other	44	50
	40 (4/1-9/30/09)			546 (10/1/09-3/31/10)				
6	44	241	248	30	17	**NUMBER OF STATEMENTS**	426	410
%	%	%	%	%	%	**ASSETS**	%	%
	3.5	1.6	.9	1.7	1.8	Cash & Equivalents	1.2	1.9
	5.7	5.2	5.3	5.5	10.1	Trade Receivables (net)	8.2	6.6
	12.1	10.9	11.7	8.7	12.2	Inventory	12.9	13.4
	1.4	2.7	2.9	1.4	2.3	All Other Current	2.5	2.5
	22.7	20.3	20.9	17.4	26.4	Total Current	24.8	24.4
	66.3	67.5	66.8	69.0	60.3	Fixed Assets (net)	64.7	64.8
	.8	1.2	.7	1.0	4.0	Intangibles (net)	1.1	1.2
	10.2	11.0	11.6	12.7	9.2	All Other Non-Current	9.4	9.7
	100.0	100.0	100.0	100.0	100.0	Total	100.0	100.0
						LIABILITIES		
	25.7	14.8	13.3	11.6	10.0	Notes Payable-Short Term	14.4	15.9
	5.8	6.5	5.9	5.7	3.0	Cur. Mat.-L.T.D.	5.2	5.3
	5.1	5.0	3.7	5.1	4.4	Trade Payables	3.2	4.3
	.0	.0	.1	.0	.0	Income Taxes Payable	.1	.0
	5.2	3.2	2.6	1.7	5.7	All Other Current	2.8	2.9
	41.8	29.5	25.7	24.1	23.1	Total Current	25.7	28.4
	74.5	47.6	44.1	52.2	37.6	Long-Term Debt	41.9	44.0
	.0	.1	.2	.3	.4	Deferred Taxes	.1	.2
	8.4	5.8	3.1	.6	3.6	All Other Non-Current	2.8	3.4
	-24.7	17.1	26.9	22.9	35.2	Net Worth	29.4	24.0
	100.0	100.0	100.0	100.0	100.0	Total Liabilities & Net Worth	100.0	100.0
						INCOME DATA		
	100.0	100.0	100.0	100.0	100.0	Net Sales	100.0	100.0
						Gross Profit		
	108.1	108.3	113.1	109.2	96.8	Operating Expenses	87.0	97.8
	-8.1	-8.3	-13.1	-9.2	3.2	Operating Profit	13.0	2.2
	4.7	8.0	7.0	9.7	4.8	All Other Expenses (net)	5.6	7.1
	-12.7	-16.3	-20.1	-18.9	-1.7	Profit Before Taxes	7.4	-4.9
						RATIOS		
	2.1	1.1	1.1	1.9	1.8	Current	1.4	1.3
	.7	.7	.8	.8	1.3		.9	.8
	.3	.4	.6	.5	.9		.6	.6
	.7	.3	.4	.7	.9	Quick	.6	.5
	.2	.2	.2	.3	.6		.3	.2
	.1	.1	.1	.1	.3		.2	.1
0 UND	12 29.4	21 17.1	22 16.7	27 13.7		Sales/Receivables	16 23.4	16 23.3
0 UND	23 16.2	28 12.8	32 11.5	41 9.0			28 12.9	23 15.9
24 15.1	38 9.5	42 8.7	54 6.8	73 5.0			52 7.0	36 10.1
						Cost of Sales/Inventory		
						Cost of Sales/Payables		
	16.4	26.7	20.5	6.2	6.3	Sales/Working Capital	12.6	15.3
	-26.0	-8.4	-15.6	-11.9	16.6		-71.1	-17.6
	-5.1	-3.4	-4.5	-3.1	NM		-8.9	-6.6
	.8	-.6	-.7	.5	4.1	EBIT/Interest	4.5	1.4
	(40) -1.6	(222) -2.8	(242) -2.6	(15) -1.9	1.4		(415) 2.6	(395) .3
	-6.3	-7.8	-5.4	-4.0	-1.0		1.3	-.9
		2.9				Net Profit + Depr., Dep., Amort./Cur. Mat. L/T/D	4.2	3.9
		(12) .1					(23) 2.2	(24) 1.6
		-2.9					1.5	.4
	1.8	1.6	1.4	2.1	1.3	Fixed/Worth	1.3	1.4
	6.8	3.0	2.7	3.8	2.2		2.1	2.6
	-1.4	172.3	5.1	6.5	3.3		3.9	6.3
	1.8	1.6	1.3	2.3	1.0	Debt/Worth	1.2	1.4
	8.4	3.3	3.0	3.6	2.0		2.1	2.8
	-4.1	215.1	6.2	8.2	3.7		4.3	7.4
	2.4	-5.8	-10.8	-1.4	13.9	% Profit Before Taxes/Tangible Net Worth	28.6	6.7
	(25) -23.6	(184) -31.8	(218) -30.1	(28) -28.3	.4		(388) 15.5	(356) -6.6
	-60.2	-86.5	-63.7	-88.0	-17.9		5.0	-26.3
	.0	-3.2	-4.5	-1.0	4.5	% Profit Before Taxes/Total Assets	9.3	1.8
	-14.6	-11.0	-9.5	-7.7	.2		5.0	-2.6
	-28.7	-19.8	-14.1	-13.8	-5.5		1.1	-8.1
	3.8	1.3	1.0	.9	2.4	Sales/Net Fixed Assets	1.6	1.5
	2.0	.9	.7	.6	.7		1.0	1.0
	1.0	.6	.6	.4	.6		.8	.7
	2.3	.8	.6	.6	1.3	Sales/Total Assets	.9	.9
	1.0	.6	.5	.4	.5		.7	.6
	.8	.5	.4	.3	.3		.5	.5
	4.4	9.1	9.6	5.7	5.3	% Depr., Dep., Amort./Sales	6.9	8.2
	(38) 10.1	(230) 12.4	(240) 12.8	(28) 13.2	(13) 11.6		(416) 9.7	(390) 11.3
	14.7	16.4	16.9	18.1	17.0		12.6	14.6
	1.4	1.2	.6			% Officers', Directors' Owners' Comp/Sales	.7	.8
	(13) 2.3	(60) 2.0	(58) .9				(128) 1.4	(126) 1.7
	7.4	3.6	1.8				3.2	3.5
5619M	85887M	1040306M	2762133M	1246015M	3003206M	Net Sales ($)	4546514M	4840161M
1862M	53592M	1437162M	5300618M	2174447M	2537872M	Total Assets ($)	5848813M	6144693M

M = $ thousand   MM = $ million
See Pages 9 through 22 for Explanation of Ratios and Data

Comparative Historical Data / Current Data Sorted by Sales

6	13	17	Type of Statement			1		4	12
257	365	354	Unqualified / Reviewed	8	48	59	127	86	26
80	106	103	Compiled	6	27	29	29	11	1
51	47	44	Tax Returns	7	20	10	7		
52	61	68	Other	8	14	13	13	9	11
4/1/07-3/31/08 ALL	4/1/08-3/31/09 ALL	4/1/09-3/31/10 ALL		40 (4/1-9/30/09)		546 (10/1/09-3/31/10)			
				0-1MM	1-3MM	3-5MM	5-10MM	10-25MM	25MM & OVER
446	592	586	**NUMBER OF STATEMENTS**	29	109	112	176	110	50
%	%	%	**ASSETS**	%	%	%	%	%	%
1.9	1.4	1.6	Cash & Equivalents	1.5	2.6	1.6	1.1	1.0	2.1
8.6	7.0	5.5	Trade Receivables (net)	1.2	4.3	5.3	5.4	6.0	10.5
14.1	15.4	11.1	Inventory	3.2	10.3	10.4	12.1	12.7	12.3
4.0	3.0	2.6	All Other Current	4.7	2.0	1.4	3.3	3.1	1.9
28.6	26.9	20.8	Total Current	10.7	19.2	18.6	21.9	22.9	26.9
60.3	61.1	67.0	Fixed Assets (net)	80.9	67.2	68.8	65.8	65.1	62.8
1.5	.6	1.0	Intangibles (net)	.2	1.8	.5	1.1	.6	1.3
9.6	11.5	11.2	All Other Non-Current	8.1	11.8	12.1	11.2	11.4	8.9
100.0	100.0	100.0	Total	100.0	100.0	100.0	100.0	100.0	100.0
			LIABILITIES						
14.5	15.8	14.8	Notes Payable-Short Term	5.3	19.8	14.2	13.8	16.6	10.1
4.9	5.0	6.1	Cur. Mat.-L.T.D.	3.4	6.8	6.3	5.9	7.0	4.9
3.5	4.4	4.4	Trade Payables	2.3	3.6	4.7	4.7	3.7	7.4
.1	.0	.0	Income Taxes Payable	.0	.0	.0	.1	.0	.1
3.4	3.1	3.1	All Other Current	1.5	2.5	3.2	1.9	5.0	5.6
26.4	28.4	28.5	Total Current	12.5	32.8	28.4	26.3	32.2	28.1
40.6	38.8	48.7	Long-Term Debt	80.9	54.1	50.2	44.2	43.4	42.3
.2	.2	.2	Deferred Taxes	.0	.2	.2	.1	.1	.4
5.2	3.9	4.4	All Other Non-Current	4.6	7.5	4.8	3.2	3.6	2.8
27.7	28.8	18.2	Net Worth	2.0	5.3	16.4	26.2	20.7	26.4
100.0	100.0	100.0	Total Liabilities & Net Worth	100.0	100.0	100.0	100.0	100.0	100.0
			INCOME DATA						
100.0	100.0	100.0	Net Sales	100.0	100.0	100.0	100.0	100.0	100.0
			Gross Profit						
81.8	92.1	110.1	Operating Expenses	74.3	110.2	111.9	115.1	111.3	106.0
18.2	7.9	-10.1	Operating Profit	25.7	-10.2	-11.9	-15.1	-11.3	-6.0
6.6	5.1	7.3	All Other Expenses (net)	23.2	6.9	6.7	6.6	6.3	5.0
11.5	2.8	-17.4	Profit Before Taxes	2.5	-17.1	-18.6	-21.7	-17.6	-11.0
			RATIOS						
1.7	1.5	1.2	Current	1.0	1.3	1.0	1.2	1.1	1.7
1.1	1.0	.8		.4	.7	.7	.8	.8	1.1
.8	.7	.5		.2	.4	.4	.6	.5	.6
.7	.5	.4	Quick	.3	.4	.4	.4	.4	.7
(444) .3	(588) .2	.2		.1	.2	.2	.2	.2	.4
.2	.1	.1		.1	.1	.1	.1	.1	.2
17 21.2	13 27.2	18 20.1	Sales/Receivables	0 UND	0 UND	18 20.0	21 17.6	21 17.5	20 17.9
30 12.3	22 16.4	24 14.9		0 UND	22 16.4	24 15.4	26 14.0	27 13.8	27 13.4
47 7.7	37 10.0	40 9.1		13 28.3	41 9.0	40 9.2	39 9.4	52 7.0	42 8.7
			Cost of Sales/Inventory						
			Cost of Sales/Payables						
6.9	7.8	19.4	Sales/Working Capital	NM	14.7	170.2	20.6	14.6	8.5
49.9	-210.0	-11.4		-5.8	-7.6	-8.7	-12.8	-12.2	29.1
-13.5	-8.4	-4.1		-3.0	-3.6	-3.4	-5.0	-3.7	-7.5
5.3	3.5	-.4	EBIT/Interest	1.0	.8	-.6	-1.1	-.5	3.0
(426) 3.4	(573) 1.6	(555) -2.5		(16) -.7	(103) -1.9	(108) -2.9	(172) -3.1	(108) -2.6	(48) -.8
1.8	.2	-5.8		-2.2	-6.7	-6.5	-7.1	-5.5	-2.9
3.9	3.0	2.6	Net Profit + Depr., Dep., Amort./Cur. Mat. L/T/D						
(17) 2.1	(29) 1.3	(26) .2							
.4	.6	-1.0							
1.2	1.2	1.5	Fixed/Worth	1.8	1.6	1.6	1.4	1.5	1.8
2.1	2.0	2.9		3.1	3.5	3.5	2.8	2.8	2.7
4.8	3.9	9.8		NM	-7.3	NM	6.2	5.1	5.2
1.2	1.2	1.5	Debt/Worth	1.9	1.5	1.5	1.3	1.7	1.9
2.3	2.2	3.3		2.7	4.6	3.3	3.2	3.3	3.0
5.8	5.0	13.5		NM	-11.0	NM	7.2	7.2	7.0
51.2	17.2	-6.0	% Profit Before Taxes/Tangible Net Worth	11.1	-3.7	-10.7	-13.2	-9.1	8.6
(400) 30.7	(536) 6.9	(474) -29.1		(22) 1.6	(73) -18.8	(84) -34.7	(153) -39.1	(95) -30.8	(47) -15.4
12.8	-5.0	-71.1		-25.1	-58.5	-85.5	-88.5	-61.5	-38.1
15.3	6.2	-3.1	% Profit Before Taxes/Total Assets	2.8	-1.4	-4.7	-5.7	-4.4	2.9
9.0	1.8	-10.0		.0	-9.2	-11.1	-12.0	-9.3	-3.8
2.4	-2.1	-16.4		-10.7	-22.1	-16.7	-18.1	-14.2	-10.2
2.1	1.9	1.3	Sales/Net Fixed Assets	.6	1.6	1.2	1.3	1.1	3.0
1.2	1.2	.8		.3	.9	.9	.8	.8	.8
.9	.8	.6		.1	.5	.6	.6	.6	.6
1.0	1.0	.7	Sales/Total Assets	.4	.9	.7	.7	.7	1.4
.8	.7	.5		.3	.6	.6	.6	.5	.6
.6	.5	.4		.1	.4	.4	.4	.4	.4
5.9	6.5	9.0	% Depr., Dep., Amort./Sales	10.0	9.8	9.6	9.1	8.7	4.0
(422) 8.5	(559) 8.9	(555) 12.5		(24) 15.4	(102) 13.3	(108) 12.3	(172) 12.2	(106) 13.3	(43) 10.2
11.6	12.2	16.4		22.6	17.6	16.6	15.4	17.9	14.3
.5	.6	.7	% Officers', Directors' Owners' Comp/Sales		1.6	1.2	.6	.4	
(113) 1.0	(153) 1.2	(137) 1.5			(23) 2.1	(32) 2.3	(50) .9	(21) .9	
2.5	2.6	2.9			4.6	3.9	1.8	2.7	
5023836M	10964876M	8143166M	Net Sales ($)	14085M	216828M	444717M	1240511M	1586306M	4640719M
7351873M	11314558M	11505553M	Total Assets ($)	70550M	460715M	894402M	2333505M	3415545M	4330836M

© RMA 2010

M = $ thousand   MM = $ million
See Pages 9 through 22 for Explanation of Ratios and Data

Current Data Sorted by Assets   Comparative Historical Data

Type of Statement	0-500M	500M-2MM	2-10MM	10-50MM	50-100MM	100-250MM		4/1/05-3/31/06 ALL	4/1/06-3/31/07 ALL
Unqualified			1	3	3	2		15	21
Reviewed			3	4	1			3	8
Compiled		5	4	4				5	12
Tax Returns	4	4	8	2				14	14
Other	4	4	11	3	4	1		21	33
	8 (4/1-9/30/09)		63 (10/1/09-3/31/10)						
NUMBER OF STATEMENTS	4	13	27	16	8	3		58	88

	0-500M	500M-2MM	2-10MM	10-50MM	50-100MM	100-250MM		4/1/05-3/31/06 ALL	4/1/06-3/31/07 ALL
	%	%	%	%	%	%	**ASSETS**	%	%
		8.3	2.0	1.9			Cash & Equivalents	3.2	3.2
		9.1	5.6	8.1			Trade Receivables (net)	6.7	8.7
		18.9	30.2	36.3			Inventory	25.2	33.6
		1.3	1.7	1.1			All Other Current	5.6	5.0
		37.5	39.5	47.4			Total Current	40.8	50.5
		51.2	51.8	43.9			Fixed Assets (net)	50.7	43.3
		4.3	1.3	3.6			Intangibles (net)	.5	.3
		6.9	7.3	5.0			All Other Non-Current	8.1	5.9
		100.0	100.0	100.0			Total	100.0	100.0
							LIABILITIES		
		47.6	27.3	18.4			Notes Payable-Short Term	19.7	18.3
		5.5	6.8	4.9			Cur. Mat.-L.T.D.	7.0	3.4
		16.6	7.3	5.4			Trade Payables	5.2	7.6
		.0	.3	.2			Income Taxes Payable	.0	.1
		5.7	4.6	4.4			All Other Current	4.8	7.1
		75.5	46.4	33.5			Total Current	36.7	36.5
		41.1	54.1	31.1			Long-Term Debt	36.5	28.3
		.0	.8	.3			Deferred Taxes	.0	.5
		5.1	4.0	6.5			All Other Non-Current	7.5	5.1
		-21.6	-5.2	28.6			Net Worth	19.3	29.6
		100.0	100.0	100.0			Total Liabilties & Net Worth	100.0	100.0
							INCOME DATA		
		100.0	100.0	100.0			Net Sales	100.0	100.0
							Gross Profit		
		98.7	103.6	105.1			Operating Expenses	85.0	94.4
		1.3	-3.6	-5.1			Operating Profit	15.0	5.6
		2.5	3.4	1.7			All Other Expenses (net)	3.5	1.8
		-1.2	-7.0	-6.8			Profit Before Taxes	11.4	3.8
							RATIOS		
		3.2	1.2	2.1				2.4	2.4
		.6	.9	1.5			Current	1.3	1.6
		.1	.5	1.1				.5	1.0
		.6	.4	.7				.6	.6
		.2	.1	.2			Quick	(55) .2 (87) .3	
		.1	.0	.1				.1	.1
	0 UND	0 UND	8 46.2					0 UND	0 UND
	5 70.6	4 100.3	15 24.0				Sales/Receivables	0 999.8 7 54.2	
	16 23.1	19 19.4	27 13.5					16 22.2 26 14.1	
							Cost of Sales/Inventory		
							Cost of Sales/Payables		
		18.8	18.8	4.5				4.7	4.3
		-14.8	-21.1	7.6			Sales/Working Capital	17.4	9.2
		-3.9	-7.2	20.8				-12.5	72.0
		3.4	1.6	3.6				10.0	9.5
		(11) 1.1	(25) .8	(15) -.1			EBIT/Interest	(55) 4.2 (84) 3.3	
		-5.6	-7.1	-16.4				2.4	.8
							Net Profit + Depr., Dep., Amort./Cur. Mat. L/T/D		
		.4	1.1	1.0				.8	.3
		4.1	3.4	1.6			Fixed/Worth	1.3	1.1
		-4.8	-1.6	NM				6.6	3.0
		1.6	1.9	.8				.8	.7
		3.9	11.9	2.7			Debt/Worth	1.7	1.9
		-5.8	-4.0	NM				7.9	5.9
			23.0	16.3				72.0	29.7
		(17) .0	(12) -16.6				% Profit Before Taxes/Tangible Net Worth	(46) 40.6 (78) 16.4	
		-84.1	-95.4					14.3	2.8
		10.1	2.0	8.6				25.1	13.5
		.4	-1.2	-6.3			% Profit Before Taxes/Total Assets	12.7	6.4
		-18.1	-24.6	-24.4				4.0	-.4
		140.5	28.9	4.8				8.6	12.3
		6.2	2.5	2.9			Sales/Net Fixed Assets	3.0	3.2
		.9	1.0	1.2				1.1	1.4
		3.4	2.2	1.6				1.9	1.9
		2.0	1.2	1.3			Sales/Total Assets	1.3	1.2
		.7	.6	.6				.7	.7
		1.0	2.4	3.1				1.6	2.1
		(10) 2.1	(21) 10.1	(15) 4.0			% Depr., Dep., Amort./Sales	(50) 4.8 (72) 4.3	
		25.1	18.6	9.0				15.2	8.9
									.6
							% Officers', Directors' Owners' Comp/Sales	(18) 1.7	
									5.0
	3042M	42460M	174689M	408603M	723531M	657213M	Net Sales ($)	1410368M	2607019M
	1351M	15816M	137416M	332885M	557989M	504440M	Total Assets ($)	1021404M	2057350M

M = $ thousand   MM = $ million
See Pages 9 through 22 for Explanation of Ratios and Data

Comparative Historical Data | | | | Current Data Sorted by Sales

4/1/07-3/31/08 ALL	4/1/08-3/31/09 ALL	4/1/09-3/31/10 ALL	Type of Statement	0-1MM	1-3MM	3-5MM	5-10MM	10-25MM	25MM & OVER
9	13	9	Unqualified					2	7
9	12	8	Reviewed					5	3
11	4	13	Compiled	1	2	1	5	3	1
20	23	18	Tax Returns	6	3	6	8	4	
36	28	23	Other	2	3	6	1	4	7
				8 (4/1-9/30/09)			63 (10/1/09-3/31/10)		
85	80	71	NUMBER OF STATEMENTS	9	11	3	17	13	18
%	%	%	ASSETS	%	%	%	%	%	%
2.8	4.9	3.8	Cash & Equivalents	8.4			2.3	2.2	4.4
9.1	3.2	6.1	Trade Receivables (net)	5.2			6.5	7.4	7.5
29.3	27.4	30.3	Inventory	12.6			34.3	42.0	40.9
3.7	3.3	2.5	All Other Current	3.3			1.1	1.1	5.5
44.8	38.8	42.8	Total Current	29.4			44.3	52.8	58.3
44.2	49.5	48.8	Fixed Assets (net)	54.8			47.8	39.9	33.3
.4	.3	2.1	Intangibles (net)	.2			1.3	4.4	3.2
10.5	11.5	6.3	All Other Non-Current	15.5			6.6	3.0	5.1
100.0	100.0	100.0	Total	100.0			100.0	100.0	100.0
			LIABILITIES						
17.6	16.9	28.4	Notes Payable-Short Term	11.8			26.4	64.9	29.6
5.0	4.0	5.2	Cur. Mat.-L.T.D.	4.8			8.3	4.7	2.9
5.8	3.8	8.0	Trade Payables	4.4			6.6	19.2	7.1
.1	.1	.2	Income Taxes Payable	.0			.5	.3	.0
4.6	6.6	4.3	All Other Current	4.7			5.1	6.4	3.0
33.2	31.3	46.2	Total Current	25.7			46.9	95.6	42.6
35.6	40.0	40.8	Long-Term Debt	31.8			52.4	30.1	25.9
.4	.1	.4	Deferred Taxes	.8			.7	.4	.2
4.5	4.2	4.7	All Other Non-Current	5.7			2.9	7.6	6.6
26.2	24.4	8.0	Net Worth	36.1			-2.8	-33.7	24.8
100.0	100.0	100.0	Total Liabilties & Net Worth	100.0			100.0	100.0	100.0
			INCOME DATA						
100.0	100.0	100.0	Net Sales	100.0			100.0	100.0	100.0
			Gross Profit						
97.2	97.0	102.9	Operating Expenses	100.8			105.5	107.1	106.9
2.8	3.0	-2.9	Operating Profit	-.8			-5.5	-7.1	-6.9
2.1	3.4	2.4	All Other Expenses (net)	.4			1.8	.7	1.0
.7	-.4	-5.3	Profit Before Taxes	-1.2			-7.3	-7.8	-7.8
			RATIOS						
2.3	2.1	1.6	Current	2.7			1.4	1.9	1.8
1.3	1.3	1.2		1.2			1.1	1.3	1.3
.8	.8	.6		.6			.6	.8	1.2
.6	.6	.5	Quick	.9			.3	.2	.5
(83) .2	(79) .2	.2		.6			.1	.1	.2
.1	.1	.1		.1			.1	.0	.1
0 UND	0 UND	0 UND	Sales/Receivables	0 UND				4 102.7	5 76.1
7 49.0	4 100.2	7 53.8		0 UND			15 24.2	10 36.8	8 48.7
26 13.9	18 20.5	19 19.4		36 10.2			22 16.4	15 23.8	24 15.2
			Cost of Sales/Inventory						
			Cost of Sales/Payables						
4.6	4.8	7.6	Sales/Working Capital	16.0			8.1	6.7	5.6
15.8	15.5	27.8		69.3			38.2	27.8	10.5
-19.2	-21.6	-13.6		-15.6			-9.5	-10.6	19.7
5.6	3.6	1.9	EBIT/Interest	3.1			1.9	1.6	.9
(80) 1.3	(72) .4	(63) -.1		(10) 1.2		(15) .9		-4.0	(17) -4.1
-1.2	-3.6	-6.4		-1.2			-7.1	-9.8	-6.1
			Net Profit + Depr., Dep., Amort./Cur. Mat. L/T/D						
.5	.8	.9	Fixed/Worth	.2			.8	1.3	.9
1.1	1.4	1.8		1.1			1.4	2.7	1.6
3.3	5.0	-7.1		4.6			-1.6	-5.0	NM
.9	.8	1.3	Debt/Worth	.3			1.0	2.3	1.3
1.7	2.2	3.6		1.9			8.4	10.6	3.4
6.6	12.4	-18.3		3.9			-4.3	-10.8	NM
21.1	15.2	16.1	% Profit Before Taxes/Tangible Net Worth	10.7			119.0		12.4
(76) 6.6	(68) .0	(51) -1.0		(10) .4		(11) .0			(14) -23.9
-15.5	-35.8	-55.9		-34.4			-112.3		-78.0
8.6	5.6	3.0	% Profit Before Taxes/Total Assets	7.2			4.1	1.4	2.7
1.0	-.6	-1.5		.4			-1.2	-12.3	-8.8
-6.6	-12.4	-20.5		-7.9			-29.2	-26.8	-22.6
13.0	6.5	8.6	Sales/Net Fixed Assets	10.7			39.1	19.1	8.6
3.1	2.3	3.1		2.6			3.4	3.0	4.3
1.6	1.1	1.2		.8			1.2	1.7	2.8
2.0	1.7	2.1	Sales/Total Assets	2.2			2.3	2.4	1.7
1.2	1.2	1.3		1.3			1.8	1.5	1.4
.8	.8	.7		.5			.6	.9	1.1
1.8	2.6	2.2	% Depr., Dep., Amort./Sales				1.9	3.1	2.2
(62) 4.1	(64) 6.0	(59) 5.0					(14) 7.3	(11) 5.3	(15) 2.7
11.2	18.8	11.9					13.5	8.0	4.0
.5	.7	.6	% Officers', Directors' Owners' Comp/Sales						
(17) 1.3	(14) 1.7	(15) 1.5							
4.5	5.0	5.5							
2739630M	2029348M	2009538M	Net Sales ($)	6511M	21482M	11123M	100924M	222507M	1646991M
1961762M	1808970M	1549897M	Total Assets ($)	17166M	24668M	15168M	100380M	179472M	1213043M

© RMA 2010

M = $ thousand   MM = $ million
See Pages 9 through 22 for Explanation of Ratios and Data

Current Data Sorted by Assets   Comparative Historical Data

0-500M	500M-2MM	2-10MM	10-50MM	50-100MM	100-250MM	Type of Statement	4/1/05-3/31/06 ALL	4/1/06-3/31/07 ALL
			4	9	1	Unqualified	21	18
	1		4	2		Reviewed	5	7
	1	3	1	1		Compiled	8	6
1	6	3	1			Tax Returns	4	6
1		6	6		2	Other	14	12
		9 (4/1-9/30/09)	44 (10/1/09-3/31/10)					
2	8	12	16	12	3	NUMBER OF STATEMENTS	52	49
%	%	%	%	%	%	ASSETS	%	%
		3.9	8.1	7.9		Cash & Equivalents	9.4	8.3
		24.8	15.5	13.0		Trade Receivables (net)	15.5	11.6
		19.5	18.0	21.7		Inventory	14.6	15.9
		3.7	1.1	2.9		All Other Current	4.9	3.4
		51.8	42.7	45.5		Total Current	44.4	39.2
		39.6	48.2	45.1		Fixed Assets (net)	46.4	52.7
		1.5	.6	2.3		Intangibles (net)	1.2	1.8
		7.2	8.5	7.1		All Other Non-Current	8.0	6.4
		100.0	100.0	100.0		Total	100.0	100.0
						LIABILITIES		
		3.2	5.1	5.1		Notes Payable-Short Term	9.1	10.8
		4.0	2.3	3.2		Cur. Mat.-L.T.D.	3.1	5.2
		20.7	11.8	7.7		Trade Payables	9.6	9.9
		1.0	.4	1.0		Income Taxes Payable	1.3	.2
		2.4	8.8	5.9		All Other Current	6.0	3.9
		31.2	28.4	22.8		Total Current	29.1	30.0
		17.0	21.0	17.8		Long-Term Debt	20.9	30.4
		.4	.8	4.0		Deferred Taxes	.8	1.0
		1.4	1.0	3.0		All Other Non-Current	5.9	4.1
		50.1	48.8	52.3		Net Worth	43.3	34.5
		100.0	100.0	100.0		Total Liabilities & Net Worth	100.0	100.0
						INCOME DATA		
		100.0	100.0	100.0		Net Sales	100.0	100.0
						Gross Profit		
		92.6	94.3	96.0		Operating Expenses	99.5	98.9
		7.4	5.7	4.0		Operating Profit	.5	1.1
		2.1	-.4	.3		All Other Expenses (net)	.9	3.2
		5.3	6.1	3.8		Profit Before Taxes	-.4	-2.1
						RATIOS		
		3.9	2.8	2.6			2.5	2.3
		1.2	2.2	2.0		Current	1.5	1.4
		.5	.8	1.3			1.0	.8
		2.1	1.5	1.4			1.7	1.5
		.7	1.1	.9		Quick	.8	.6
		.5	.3	.4			.5	.3
		0 UND	15 24.4	20 18.6			19 19.7	15 23.7
		23 15.6	24 15.4	32 11.3		Sales/Receivables	27 13.3	28 13.2
		32 11.3	29 12.5	39 9.4			37 10.0	40 9.1
						Cost of Sales/Inventory		
						Cost of Sales/Payables		
		4.6	5.6	5.4			6.4	6.5
		43.6	8.2	6.9		Sales/Working Capital	12.3	15.1
		-48.3	NM	8.8			181.2	-17.5
			67.8	13.7			4.6	2.5
			6.6	(10) 3.0		EBIT/Interest	(46) -.3	(40) .9
			2.1	1.7			-4.9	-1.3
							5.6	2.6
						Net Profit + Depr., Dep., Amort./Cur. Mat. L/T/D	(14) 1.9	(13) 1.2
							-.3	.1
		.2	.4	.6			.4	1.0
		.6	.8	.9		Fixed/Worth	1.2	1.6
		3.3	2.0	2.0			2.4	4.1
		.1	.3	.4			.5	1.0
		1.5	1.1	1.3		Debt/Worth	1.7	2.2
		22.9	1.5	2.4			3.5	5.2
		24.3	29.0	18.6			15.7	15.9
		13.3	(15) 12.2	7.1		% Profit Before Taxes/Tangible Net Worth	(50) -2.2	(43) 2.1
		-10.2	7.6	1.0			-31.7	-24.4
		19.1	12.6	11.3			9.1	6.0
		2.8	6.7	3.2		% Profit Before Taxes/Total Assets	-.6	-.2
		-.6	4.0	.3			-13.6	-6.0
		34.8	10.8	6.1			11.0	5.0
		11.4	3.4	3.3		Sales/Net Fixed Assets	3.5	2.4
		1.6	1.5	1.9			1.5	1.5
		4.6	2.6	1.9			2.5	2.1
		3.3	1.6	1.6		Sales/Total Assets	1.6	1.3
		1.1	.9	1.0			.9	.8
		1.0	1.2	2.0			2.0	2.4
		(11) 3.3	(13) 2.5	(10) 4.5		% Depr., Dep., Amort./Sales	(43) 4.0	(43) 5.8
		11.9	8.5	7.3			9.3	11.6
						% Officers', Directors' Owners' Comp/Sales		
757M	30167M	212718M	720161M	1465314M	549174M	Net Sales ($)	2580487M	1965652M
210M	11116M	67770M	375858M	928019M	401815M	Total Assets ($)	2028421M	1672456M

© RMA 2010

M = $ thousand   MM = $ million
See Pages 9 through 22 for Explanation of Ratios and Data

Comparative Historical Data | Current Data Sorted by Sales

Type of Statement

4/1/07-3/31/08 ALL	4/1/08-3/31/09 ALL	4/1/09-3/31/10 ALL	Type of Statement	0-1MM	1-3MM	3-5MM	5-10MM	10-25MM	25MM & OVER
10	14	14	Unqualified		1			2	11
4	6	7	Reviewed				1	1	5
5	5	5	Compiled	1		1		2	1
7	11	12	Tax Returns	4	1		3	2	1
15	8	15	Other	1	1			3	10
					9 (4/1-9/30/09)			44 (10/1/09-3/31/10)	

Main Data

4/1/07-3/31/08 ALL	4/1/08-3/31/09 ALL	4/1/09-3/31/10 ALL		0-1MM	1-3MM	3-5MM	5-10MM	10-25MM	25MM & OVER
41	44	53	**NUMBER OF STATEMENTS**	6	4	1	4	10	28
%	%	%	**ASSETS**	%	%	%	%	%	%
12.6	17.5	9.8	Cash & Equivalents					3.8	8.7
17.2	14.0	14.1	Trade Receivables (net)					12.5	20.8
17.3	16.7	16.9	Inventory					24.7	19.6
3.3	2.7	1.9	All Other Current					.9	2.2
50.3	51.0	42.6	Total Current					41.9	51.3
42.6	43.0	48.8	Fixed Assets (net)					50.9	40.3
2.6	1.3	1.5	Intangibles (net)					.7	1.7
4.5	4.8	7.1	All Other Non-Current					6.6	6.7
100.0	100.0	100.0	Total					100.0	100.0
			LIABILITIES						
8.2	6.9	5.1	Notes Payable-Short Term					4.5	4.4
4.3	5.6	3.9	Cur. Mat.-L.T.D.					1.0	2.9
11.2	10.5	10.3	Trade Payables					3.5	17.5
.8	.7	.6	Income Taxes Payable					.0	.6
10.9	10.2	5.3	All Other Current					8.3	5.5
35.5	33.9	25.1	Total Current					17.3	30.9
21.6	23.7	25.0	Long-Term Debt					18.0	15.9
.4	1.0	1.3	Deferred Taxes					.5	2.2
1.4	2.0	7.8	All Other Non-Current					.6	2.1
41.1	39.5	40.8	Net Worth					63.6	48.8
100.0	100.0	100.0	Total Liabilties & Net Worth					100.0	100.0
			INCOME DATA						
100.0	100.0	100.0	Net Sales					100.0	100.0
			Gross Profit						
88.0	86.8	93.0	Operating Expenses					94.9	95.1
12.0	13.2	7.0	Operating Profit					5.1	4.9
1.8	2.5	1.5	All Other Expenses (net)					-.2	.2
10.2	10.7	5.5	Profit Before Taxes					5.3	4.7
			RATIOS						
3.3	3.8	3.0	Current					9.6	2.7
1.3	1.8	2.0						2.5	2.2
.8	1.1	.9						.2	1.2
1.9	2.0	1.5	Quick					3.3	1.4
.7	1.0	.9						.8	1.1
.4	.5	.4						.2	.6
22 16.8	0 UND	0 UND	Sales/Receivables					0 UND	18 19.8
30 12.4	21 17.6	23 15.9						21 17.5	28 12.9
36 10.1	26 13.8	31 11.9						35 10.5	35 10.5
			Cost of Sales/Inventory						
			Cost of Sales/Payables						
5.4	5.0	5.6	Sales/Working Capital					3.5	5.7
14.2	10.1	9.1						8.3	7.3
-23.2	168.2	-120.6						-58.1	32.5
14.1	32.7	29.0	EBIT/Interest						64.7
(33) 5.7	(35) 10.2	(41) 4.2							(25) 4.2
2.4	1.9	1.8							2.0
		5.0	Net Profit + Depr., Dep., Amort./Cur. Mat. L/T/D						
		(10) 1.9							
		1.1							
.5	.4	.5	Fixed/Worth					.2	.4
.9	.8	1.0						.9	.7
3.5	2.0	2.5						1.8	2.0
.7	.3	.3	Debt/Worth					.1	.3
2.4	1.1	1.2						.8	1.1
5.0	4.5	2.9						1.4	2.6
69.6	65.0	24.3	% Profit Before Taxes/Tangible Net Worth					26.2	18.6
(38) 45.2	(40) 41.0	(48) 13.3						18.8	(27) 12.2
16.6	10.5	5.5						-1.9	5.8
31.5	41.4	13.9	% Profit Before Taxes/Total Assets					21.3	12.8
12.3	14.7	6.5						8.8	5.7
4.5	1.8	1.3						-.3	2.2
13.3	14.5	10.4	Sales/Net Fixed Assets					17.8	11.2
4.6	5.0	3.5						3.3	4.5
2.7	2.3	1.6						1.6	2.5
2.5	2.9	3.1	Sales/Total Assets					3.8	3.1
1.8	1.8	1.6						1.8	1.8
1.4	1.2	1.0						.8	1.2
1.5	1.5	1.9	% Depr., Dep., Amort./Sales						1.4
(35) 2.7	(34) 3.6	(44) 4.5							(22) 2.4
6.1	8.8	10.1							5.3
		.8	% Officers', Directors' Owners' Comp/Sales						
		(10) 1.5							
		2.5							
2306692M	3274193M	2978291M	Net Sales ($)	2887M	8891M	4312M	30662M	179227M	2752312M
1330454M	1773839M	1784788M	Total Assets ($)	7307M	45221M	1470M	10736M	136377M	1583677M

M = $ thousand   MM = $ million
See Pages 9 through 22 for Explanation of Ratios and Data

Current Data Sorted by Assets   Comparative Historical Data

Type of Statement

	0-500M	500M-2MM	2-10MM	10-50MM	50-100MM	100-250MM		4/1/05-3/31/06 ALL	4/1/06-3/31/07 ALL
Unqualified									2
Reviewed		1						1	
Compiled	1	1	2	1				5	1
Tax Returns	2	3	2	1				11	10
Other	1	4	6	2				8	9
	4 (4/1-9/30/09)			23 (10/1/09-3/31/10)					
NUMBER OF STATEMENTS	4	9	10	4				25	22

Note: Columns **50-100MM** and **100-250MM** show "DATA NOT AVAILABLE."

	0-500M %	500M-2MM %	2-10MM %	10-50MM %	50-100MM %	100-250MM %	Item	4/1/05-3/31/06 ALL %	4/1/06-3/31/07 ALL %
							ASSETS		
			10.9				Cash & Equivalents	27.4	20.1
			11.9				Trade Receivables (net)	5.3	11.6
			5.8				Inventory	6.3	8.0
			10.3				All Other Current	3.5	5.0
			39.0				Total Current	42.5	44.6
			49.8				Fixed Assets (net)	44.3	38.5
			.9				Intangibles (net)	.7	1.1
			10.3				All Other Non-Current	12.4	15.9
			100.0				Total	100.0	100.0
							LIABILITIES		
			16.8				Notes Payable-Short Term	27.6	31.9
			8.8				Cur. Mat.-L.T.D.	2.1	3.5
			3.1				Trade Payables	4.2	16.6
			.0				Income Taxes Payable	.1	.0
			22.0				All Other Current	16.2	17.2
			50.7				Total Current	50.1	69.3
			46.5				Long-Term Debt	23.9	29.2
			.0				Deferred Taxes	.0	.0
			6.7				All Other Non-Current	9.1	13.0
			-3.8				Net Worth	16.9	-11.5
			100.0				Total Liabilities & Net Worth	100.0	100.0
							INCOME DATA		
			100.0				Net Sales	100.0	100.0
							Gross Profit		
			90.7				Operating Expenses	87.8	95.4
			9.3				Operating Profit	12.2	4.6
			3.2				All Other Expenses (net)	2.7	6.0
			6.0				Profit Before Taxes	9.6	-1.4
							RATIOS		
			2.9				Current	1.8	2.0
			1.3					.9	.8
			.3					.3	.3
			1.2				Quick	1.7	1.9
			.7					.5	.7
			.3					.1	.1
		0	UND				Sales/Receivables	0 UND	0 UND
		36	10.1					0 999.8	15 24.1
		139	2.6					4 93.9	62 5.9
							Cost of Sales/Inventory		
							Cost of Sales/Payables		
			3.8				Sales/Working Capital	7.6	2.8
			44.4					-72.0	-509.1
			-.6					-3.3	-1.7
							EBIT/Interest	22.6	16.9
								(21) 1.5	(18) 1.9
								-1.3	-1.0
							Net Profit + Depr., Dep., Amort./Cur. Mat. L/T/D		
			1.8				Fixed/Worth	.3	.1
			NM					1.3	2.2
			-6.0					-5.9	-.7
			2.0				Debt/Worth	.4	1.1
			NM					5.5	2.8
			-9.7					-9.2	-2.4
							% Profit Before Taxes/Tangible Net Worth	100.2	60.5
								(16) 20.6	(13) 14.4
								-12.2	-9.9
			21.6				% Profit Before Taxes/Total Assets	38.0	14.5
			6.3					2.1	-.7
			-9.1					-5.6	-11.3
			5.2				Sales/Net Fixed Assets	39.4	48.0
			1.5					4.4	6.6
			.6					1.2	2.0
			1.2				Sales/Total Assets	2.3	2.6
			.6					1.2	1.3
			.3					.6	.7
							% Depr., Dep., Amort./Sales	1.4	.9
								(21) 4.1	(16) 2.5
								19.5	7.7
							% Officers', Directors' Owners' Comp/Sales		
3362M	13805M	38857M	74809M				Net Sales ($)	195835M	113989M
226M	9533M	44577M	94457M				Total Assets ($)	215118M	140808M

M = $ thousand   MM = $ million
See Pages 9 through 22 for Explanation of Ratios and Data

Comparative Historical Data | Current Data Sorted by Sales

			Type of Statement						
1		1	Unqualified	1					
1	1	2	Reviewed		1	1		1	
4	3	5	Compiled	2	1		1	1	
10	8	7	Tax Returns	4	2		1	1	
5	11	12	Other	2	5	2			1
4/1/07-3/31/08 ALL	4/1/08-3/31/09 ALL	4/1/09-3/31/10 ALL		4 (4/1-9/30/09)			23 (10/1/09-3/31/10)		
				0-1MM	1-3MM	3-5MM	5-10MM	10-25MM	25MM & OVER
21	23	27	NUMBER OF STATEMENTS	9	9	3	2	3	1
%	%	%	**ASSETS**	%	%	%	%	%	%
18.5	12.9	16.3	Cash & Equivalents						
15.5	17.8	7.3	Trade Receivables (net)						
7.1	2.0	5.2	Inventory						
2.1	2.0	5.4	All Other Current						
43.1	34.7	34.2	Total Current						
41.0	49.2	48.7	Fixed Assets (net)						
3.3	.1	2.3	Intangibles (net)						
12.7	16.1	14.8	All Other Non-Current						
100.0	100.0	100.0	Total						
			LIABILITIES						
9.2	30.3	16.4	Notes Payable-Short Term						
13.0	4.4	7.1	Cur. Mat.-L.T.D.						
7.7	21.5	8.0	Trade Payables						
.0	.1	.0	Income Taxes Payable						
20.5	35.4	15.5	All Other Current						
50.4	91.7	47.0	Total Current						
34.7	25.7	43.7	Long-Term Debt						
.0	.2	.0	Deferred Taxes						
15.0	12.8	4.9	All Other Non-Current						
-.1	-30.4	4.5	Net Worth						
100.0	100.0	100.0	Total Liabilities & Net Worth						
			INCOME DATA						
100.0	100.0	100.0	Net Sales						
			Gross Profit						
91.0	103.2	93.0	Operating Expenses						
9.0	-3.2	7.0	Operating Profit						
3.6	3.4	2.2	All Other Expenses (net)						
5.4	-6.7	4.8	Profit Before Taxes						
			RATIOS						
5.4	1.2	3.0	Current						
1.2	.4	.7							
.3	.1	.2							
5.4	1.1	1.6	Quick						
.5	.3	.5							
.1	.1	.2							
0 UND	0 UND	0 UND	Sales/Receivables						
17 20.9	23 16.1	1 725.0							
67 5.5	89 4.1	43 8.4							
			Cost of Sales/Inventory						
			Cost of Sales/Payables						
5.6	13.2	4.4	Sales/Working Capital						
45.0	-15.4	-73.8							
-3.5	-1.9	-1.6							
11.3	3.1	4.8	EBIT/Interest						
(15) 1.6	(21) 1.0	(25) 1.3							
.9	-6.2	-4.0							
			Net Profit + Depr., Dep., Amort./Cur. Mat. L/T/D						
.1	.6	.5	Fixed/Worth						
1.8	2.8	4.0							
-1.2	-.5	-1.7							
.2	1.1	.8	Debt/Worth						
2.6	3.5	16.3							
-6.0	-2.3	-4.1							
45.6	18.0	71.8	% Profit Before Taxes/Tangible Net Worth						
(15) 3.2	(14) -.8	(16) 3.0							
-1.0	-30.7	-29.7							
14.7	8.5	17.6	% Profit Before Taxes/Total Assets						
1.7	.2	1.6							
-1.4	-11.9	-10.7							
42.0	14.4	36.2	Sales/Net Fixed Assets						
4.0	4.8	2.1							
1.5	1.3	.7							
2.4	3.0	2.5	Sales/Total Assets						
1.2	1.4	1.0							
.6	.5	.5							
1.1	3.7	3.0	% Depr., Dep., Amort./Sales						
(15) 4.8	(15) 5.8	(15) 7.1							
21.4	24.2	22.8							
		1.7	% Officers', Directors' Owners' Comp/Sales						
	(12)	5.4							
		10.6							
110004M	134532M	130833M	Net Sales ($)	5750M	18142M	10659M	12803M	44089M	39390M
132623M	169222M	148793M	Total Assets ($)	13086M	19321M	11177M	16781M	52760M	35668M

M = $ thousand   MM = $ million
See Pages 9 through 22 for Explanation of Ratios and Data

Current Data Sorted by Assets   Comparative Historical Data

						Type of Statement		
		3	8	3	4	Unqualified	9	17
	1	7	6		1	Reviewed	16	11
1	7	7	4			Compiled	22	16
8	10	7				Tax Returns	22	15
4	7	7	17	3		Other	32	42
	21 (4/1-9/30/09)		93 (10/1/09-3/31/10)				4/1/05-3/31/06 ALL	4/1/06-3/31/07 ALL
0-500M	500M-2MM	2-10MM	10-50MM	50-100MM	100-250MM	NUMBER OF STATEMENTS	101	101
13	25	30	35	6	5			
%	%	%	%	%	%	ASSETS	%	%
9.5	10.5	5.6	5.3			Cash & Equivalents	8.6	9.7
12.5	13.9	10.7	5.1			Trade Receivables (net)	10.2	10.2
11.2	30.6	14.5	16.6			Inventory	22.8	15.2
.0	3.4	4.7	4.4			All Other Current	4.8	4.7
33.2	58.5	35.4	31.5			Total Current	46.4	39.9
46.9	25.4	46.1	52.8			Fixed Assets (net)	41.1	44.3
1.1	2.8	1.0	1.9			Intangibles (net)	.9	.4
18.4	13.4	17.5	13.9			All Other Non-Current	11.6	15.4
100.0	100.0	100.0	100.0			Total	100.0	100.0
						LIABILITIES		
20.9	16.4	18.8	14.4			Notes Payable-Short Term	17.3	14.8
14.6	8.8	10.6	2.8			Cur. Mat.-L.T.D.	6.8	7.3
4.2	6.6	4.6	1.9			Trade Payables	5.3	7.2
.0	.0	.0	.1			Income Taxes Payable	.2	.1
27.0	9.7	7.6	3.7			All Other Current	8.3	8.5
66.6	41.5	41.7	22.9			Total Current	37.8	37.9
70.1	16.1	20.0	31.8			Long-Term Debt	28.9	32.0
.0	.0	.2	1.4			Deferred Taxes	.1	.3
.0	11.3	5.1	4.7			All Other Non-Current	1.9	3.6
-37.1	31.1	33.0	39.2			Net Worth	31.2	26.2
100.0	100.0	100.0	100.0			Total Liabilties & Net Worth	100.0	100.0
						INCOME DATA		
100.0	100.0	100.0	100.0			Net Sales	100.0	100.0
						Gross Profit		
94.7	97.1	98.0	87.9			Operating Expenses	84.7	84.9
5.3	2.9	2.0	12.1			Operating Profit	15.3	15.1
2.6	1.9	1.9	4.6			All Other Expenses (net)	3.7	5.7
2.8	1.0	.1	7.6			Profit Before Taxes	11.6	9.4
						RATIOS		
1.0	6.2	1.9	2.6				2.5	2.7
.2	1.4	.9	1.1			Current	1.2	1.1
.1	.6	.4	.5				.7	.5
.8	2.9	1.2	.7				1.2	1.3
.2	.6	.3	.3			Quick	.4	.5
.1	.2	.2	.1				.1	.2
0 UND	0 UND	4 82.2	6 61.0				0 UND	0 UND
0 UND	10 37.7	10 37.4	12 31.0			Sales/Receivables	8 43.2	9 39.6
7 52.9	20 18.6	25 14.5	22 16.5				26 14.0	23 16.2
						Cost of Sales/Inventory		
						Cost of Sales/Payables		
UND	8.7	8.2	2.3				7.1	5.6
-13.2	15.7	-184.7	16.0			Sales/Working Capital	23.2	46.2
-4.2	-12.2	-11.4	-4.3				-12.1	-11.2
4.6	9.9	3.5	4.6				7.8	6.9
(12) 2.3	1.0	(26) .4	(26) 1.9			EBIT/Interest	(91) 3.5	(85) 2.1
-.4	-.5	-1.8	-.4				1.7	.8
								21.5
						Net Profit + Depr., Dep., Amort./Cur. Mat. L/T/D	(11) 6.8	
								.9
3.5	.1	.6	.4				.3	.3
UND	.7	2.0	1.5			Fixed/Worth	1.2	1.1
-1.6	6.8	3.0	3.7				3.3	3.7
3.6	.6	1.1	.7				.8	.8
UND	1.9	2.9	2.3			Debt/Worth	2.3	2.0
-3.3	127.2	6.2	3.8				6.2	8.3
	41.1	27.3	12.1			% Profit Before Taxes/Tangible Net Worth	41.4	46.6
(20) 9.0	(27) -.7	(33) 1.6				(89) 22.6	(88) 12.6
	-10.8	-11.1	-9.6				5.2	-.9
9.1	19.7	3.6	7.0			% Profit Before Taxes/Total Assets	18.4	13.9
2.5	-.1	-.6	.5				8.5	5.3
-7.1	-3.9	-6.2	-2.5				1.8	-.4
52.0	133.1	20.5	5.2				19.5	18.5
6.8	13.8	6.1	.8			Sales/Net Fixed Assets	7.4	4.6
1.8	4.8	1.5	.2				1.3	1.1
3.6	4.5	4.6	1.1				3.6	3.4
2.0	2.7	2.8	.5			Sales/Total Assets	1.7	1.2
1.0	1.2	.5	.2				.5	.4
	.2	.7	1.2				.9	1.3
(16) 1.2	(28) 2.3	(30) 7.6			% Depr., Dep., Amort./Sales	(83) 2.3	(79) 3.6
	4.7	6.2	11.2				6.9	10.2
	1.2						1.5	1.0
(11) 1.7					% Officers', Directors' Owners' Comp/Sales	(29) 2.6	(28) 2.8
7.2							6.5	6.1
16066M	101896M	336621M	557775M	349641M	460117M	Net Sales ($)	2049263M	1909258M
3642M	29736M	148562M	732016M	442992M	826295M	Total Assets ($)	1888009M	1945321M

M = $ thousand   MM = $ million
See Pages 9 through 22 for Explanation of Ratios and Data

Comparative Historical Data | Current Data Sorted by Sales

	4/1/07-3/31/08 ALL	4/1/08-3/31/09 ALL	4/1/09-3/31/10 ALL	0-1MM	1-3MM	3-5MM	5-10MM	10-25MM	25MM & OVER
Type of Statement				21 (4/1-9/30/09)			93 (10/1/09-3/31/10)		
Unqualified	15	15	18	1	2	1	2	7	5
Reviewed	11	17	15		4	1	2	6	2
Compiled	12	23	19	1	3	4	4	5	2
Tax Returns	18	18	24	9	5	2	3	4	1
Other	27	32	38	8	10	2		4	4
NUMBER OF STATEMENTS	83	105	114	19	24	10	16	31	14
ASSETS	%	%	%	%	%	%	%	%	%
Cash & Equivalents	6.4	8.3	6.7	8.3	6.9	10.5	5.4	5.5	5.4
Trade Receivables (net)	8.8	7.5	9.5	7.4	3.7	17.5	10.6	10.8	12.2
Inventory	18.4	17.0	18.0	12.5	10.8	19.9	29.8	21.4	15.8
All Other Current	4.4	3.8	3.5	.0	6.9	1.8	.8	3.2	7.6
Total Current	37.9	36.5	37.7	28.2	28.4	49.7	46.6	40.9	41.0
Fixed Assets (net)	46.8	45.5	45.0	50.9	57.4	41.4	40.5	38.4	37.6
Intangibles (net)	1.2	1.1	1.6	.9	.0	7.0	2.9	1.0	1.3
All Other Non-Current	14.1	16.9	15.6	19.8	14.2	1.8	10.1	19.6	20.1
Total	100.0	100.0	100.0	100.0	100.0	100.0	100.0	100.0	100.0
LIABILITIES									
Notes Payable-Short Term	16.4	20.5	15.7	28.6	7.4	13.7	10.3	19.5	11.8
Cur. Mat.-L.T.D.	6.8	4.8	7.5	4.7	15.3	8.6	10.5	3.1	3.5
Trade Payables	5.3	4.3	3.9	2.9	2.2	3.1	5.9	5.2	3.5
Income Taxes Payable	.3	.0	.1	.0	.1	.0	.0	.0	.3
All Other Current	5.6	8.3	8.5	10.4	15.2	6.6	3.0	7.2	4.8
Total Current	34.4	38.0	35.7	46.6	40.2	32.1	29.6	35.1	23.9
Long-Term Debt	30.0	33.3	31.6	47.6	36.7	14.3	21.9	26.6	35.5
Deferred Taxes	.6	.4	.6	.0	.3	.0	2.3	.4	.6
All Other Non-Current	7.3	3.7	5.7	.3	10.0	17.4	3.6	4.4	2.3
Net Worth	27.7	24.7	26.5	5.3	12.8	36.2	42.6	33.6	37.6
Total Liabilities & Net Worth	100.0	100.0	100.0	100.0	100.0	100.0	100.0	100.0	100.0
INCOME DATA									
Net Sales	100.0	100.0	100.0	100.0	100.0	100.0	100.0	100.0	100.0
Gross Profit									
Operating Expenses	88.4	89.6	94.1	83.7	91.5	90.3	98.9	99.7	97.8
Operating Profit	11.6	10.4	5.9	16.3	8.5	9.7	1.1	.3	2.2
All Other Expenses (net)	4.0	6.0	3.0	11.7	3.3	.8	.0	1.5	-.9
Profit Before Taxes	7.7	4.5	2.9	4.6	5.2	8.9	1.2	-1.2	3.1
RATIOS									
Current	2.9	2.9	2.8	1.0	20.3	3.8	3.9	3.3	2.6
	1.1	1.2	1.1	.3	.7	1.7	1.1	1.4	1.5
	.6	.5	.5	.0	.2	.3	.7	.8	1.1
Quick	1.3	1.5	1.3	.6	1.6	2.7	2.5	1.2	1.1
	.4	.4	.4	.2	.2	.8	.5	.3	.6
	.1	.1	.2	.0	.2	.2	.2	.2	.4
Sales/Receivables	0 UND	1 384.6	0 UND	0 UND	0 UND	7 54.1	6 56.6	9 38.8	14 26.2
	10 37.3	9 41.3	11 33.4	0 UND	0 UND	15 24.6	9 42.4	16 23.0	24 15.3
	22 16.7	22 16.9	24 15.2	11 32.9	17 21.5	23 15.9	22 16.2	27 13.6	40 9.1
Cost of Sales/Inventory									
Cost of Sales/Payables									
Sales/Working Capital	6.5	4.7	5.8	UND	3.4	5.9	9.1	5.0	4.3
	52.7	63.8	35.0	-6.3	-41.4	12.9	NM	12.0	14.3
	-11.5	-11.5	-8.3	-2.0	-2.2	-8.1	-12.0	-19.2	57.3
EBIT/Interest	(69) 4.3	(86) 3.3	(99) 4.5	(11) 2.5	(20) 3.5		10.0	(30) 4.1	4.8
	2.0	1.2	1.3	1.9	1.0		1.1	.7	2.6
	1.0	-.6	-.9	-.9	-.1		-1.9	-1.3	.1
Net Profit + Depr., Dep., Amort./Cur. Mat. L/T/D	(16) 4.7	(16) 6.1	(15) 4.7						
	1.3	1.2	1.2						
	.4	.4	-.7						
Fixed/Worth	.6	.4	.5	1.9	.8	.5	.4	.4	.3
	1.4	1.4	1.7	5.6	1.6	.9	1.3	1.4	1.2
	3.9	4.8	5.3	-3.1	7.7	9.1	6.9	2.6	4.8
Debt/Worth	1.0	.9	1.0	2.2	.4	1.5	.5	1.3	.9
	2.2	2.2	2.3	12.8	1.9	2.5	1.1	2.8	1.7
	10.5	11.0	8.4	-6.9	12.2	10.5	7.8	4.8	7.6
% Profit Before Taxes/Tangible Net Worth	(74) 35.5	(88) 25.6	(98) 26.5	(13) 302.6	(19) 23.3		(15) 37.7	(29) 19.2	(13) 25.5
	13.2	5.5	2.6	6.3	2.1		4.9	-1.4	10.4
	.5	-4.5	-8.4	-.1	-8.5		-11.1	-10.8	-7.2
% Profit Before Taxes/Total Assets	6.7	7.0	7.3	2.5	7.4	15.8	16.0	4.8	10.8
	3.4	1.1	.6	.1	.7	2.0	.4	-.5	4.9
	.0	-3.5	-3.0	-1.3	-3.5	-4.5	-4.8	-2.9	-2.5
Sales/Net Fixed Assets	23.3	18.2	15.6	19.6	6.4	25.3	108.5	19.2	7.4
	3.0	3.3	3.6	2.0	1.8	10.2	4.8	8.7	4.8
	.7	.4	.8	.1	.3	.6	1.9	2.0	1.5
Sales/Total Assets	3.5	3.6	3.2	1.3	1.7	4.5	7.4	4.6	2.6
	1.0	1.0	1.2	.7	.8	2.7	2.8	1.5	1.6
	.3	.3	.4	.0	.2	.3	.7	.6	.7
% Depr., Dep., Amort./Sales	(74) 1.2	(93) .8	(93) 1.0	(13) 2.6	(18) -1.9		(13) 2.3	(30) .5	(11) .5
	4.4	3.5	4.3	13.2	5.2		5.9	1.7	1.3
	10.4	10.1	11.4	16.2	23.4		8.6	9.3	6.2
% Officers', Directors' Owners' Comp/Sales	(18) 1.2	(24) 1.0	(23) 1.2						
	2.0	1.7	1.7						
	5.2	2.9	4.3						
Net Sales ($)	1527490M	2148210M	1822116M	7621M	48950M	39510M	116492M	529026M	1080517M
Total Assets ($)	1957947M	2586946M	2183243M	79335M	152526M	63665M	123535M	771313M	992869M

M = $ thousand   MM = $ million
See Pages 9 through 22 for Explanation of Ratios and Data

AGRICULTURE—Logging NAICS 113310

Current Data Sorted by Assets **Comparative Historical Data**

						Type of Statement		
						Unqualified	10	13
						Reviewed	27	21
						Compiled	34	34
						Tax Returns	38	40
						Other	21	27
	28 (4/1-9/30/09)			94 (10/1/09-3/31/10)			4/1/05-3/31/06	4/1/06-3/31/07
0-500M	500M-2MM	2-10MM	10-50MM	50-100MM	100-250MM		ALL	ALL
16	48	45	12		1	**NUMBER OF STATEMENTS**	130	135
%	%	%	%	%	%	**ASSETS**	%	%
19.8	12.6	11.9	23.5			Cash & Equivalents	9.6	10.3
6.2	10.0	12.1	4.5			Trade Receivables (net)	9.8	9.9
6.1	11.9	16.7	9.6			Inventory	16.1	16.6
5.0	6.7	3.3	1.7			All Other Current	2.9	3.6
37.2	41.2	44.1	39.3			Total Current	38.5	40.4
52.1	50.5	44.1	46.4			Fixed Assets (net)	52.2	50.1
.5	1.0	3.9	.2			Intangibles (net)	1.0	1.7
10.1	7.3	7.9	14.1			All Other Non-Current	8.3	7.8
100.0	100.0	100.0	100.0			Total	100.0	100.0
						LIABILITIES		
7.3	13.1	12.8	5.1			Notes Payable-Short Term	15.4	18.5
9.5	9.0	9.6	3.3			Cur. Mat.-L.T.D.	8.7	8.6
9.0	4.5	6.1	2.3			Trade Payables	6.0	6.2
.0	.0	.2	.0			Income Taxes Payable	.2	.3
7.5	7.0	6.2	16.2			All Other Current	5.4	4.7
33.3	33.6	34.9	26.9			Total Current	35.7	38.4
57.6	35.9	26.2	29.4			Long-Term Debt	33.3	32.7
.4	.2	1.4	.4			Deferred Taxes	.9	.8
21.5	1.2	2.1	1.4			All Other Non-Current	3.3	4.2
-12.8	29.1	35.4	41.8			Net Worth	26.8	24.0
100.0	100.0	100.0	100.0			Total Liabilties & Net Worth	100.0	100.0
						INCOME DATA		
100.0	100.0	100.0	100.0			Net Sales	100.0	100.0
48.6	45.6	28.7	41.4			Gross Profit	36.3	35.9
42.9	43.3	28.2	36.1			Operating Expenses	33.0	32.2
5.8	2.2	.5	5.3			Operating Profit	3.3	3.6
.2	.8	.2	-.1			All Other Expenses (net)	1.4	1.1
5.6	1.4	.3	5.4			Profit Before Taxes	1.9	2.5
						RATIOS		
5.4	3.1	2.4	4.2				2.7	1.9
.8	1.3	1.4	1.4			Current	1.0	1.1
.2	.7	.6	.5				.5	.4
3.1	1.5	1.8	2.5				1.7	1.4
.5	.6	(44) .6	.8			Quick	(128) .5	(134) .5
.2	.3	.2	.4				.2	.2
0 UND	0 UND	2 152.9	0 UND				0 UND	0 UND
0 UND	9 39.3	13 28.4	9 39.0			Sales/Receivables	10 36.0	10 36.6
4 100.0	20 18.6	41 8.9	25 14.5				22 16.9	22 16.2
0 UND	0 UND	0 UND	2 161.7				0 UND	0 UND
0 UND	0 UND	26 14.2	8 46.5			Cost of Sales/Inventory	9 38.8	15 24.5
0 UND	39 9.4	56 6.5	81 4.5				67 5.4	62 5.9
0 UND	0 UND	2 164.5	0 772.5				0 UND	0 UND
0 UND	4 93.7	8 44.2	9 38.4			Cost of Sales/Payables	8 46.5	9 45.5
14 26.1	21 17.1	25 14.4	42 8.6				17 22.0	24 15.1
8.3	9.1	6.1	3.2				9.7	9.9
-152.7	41.6	23.0	14.0			Sales/Working Capital	339.3	113.2
-16.3	-13.0	-14.8	-8.6				-14.5	-13.4
4.0	5.9	4.3	23.1				5.5	5.4
(12) 2.6	(44) 1.7	(43) 1.5	(11) 2.9			EBIT/Interest	(118) 2.6	(129) 1.8
-1.7	.2	-.1	1.4				1.2	.9
						Net Profit + Depr., Dep.,	2.8	4.3
						Amort./Cur. Mat. L/T/D	(22) 1.2	(21) 2.0
							.8	1.2
.9	.6	.8	.3				.6	.7
4.6	1.6	1.2	.8			Fixed/Worth	1.8	1.8
-.8	14.8	16.1	3.4				11.0	8.5
1.9	.7	.5	.1				1.0	.8
5.7	2.2	2.3	2.1			Debt/Worth	2.8	3.4
-2.0	16.4	19.3	8.1				20.0	20.6
186.0	46.8	21.8	22.4				43.3	41.4
(10) 50.6	(39) 8.0	(37) 7.5	(11) 15.2			% Profit Before Taxes/Tangible Net Worth	(106) 18.0	(113) 9.7
7.9	-9.0	-1.5	3.8				4.5	.6
31.1	8.0	9.6	12.7				12.4	13.1
13.9	2.3	1.6	3.0			% Profit Before Taxes/Total Assets	4.7	3.6
-9.4	-2.9	-2.0	.8				.6	-.2
85.3	16.5	15.5	11.9				11.1	11.4
6.5	5.4	5.1	2.1			Sales/Net Fixed Assets	4.3	4.5
3.1	2.8	3.2	.9				2.4	2.2
9.5	3.6	2.9	1.8				3.5	3.5
3.6	2.3	2.2	.7			Sales/Total Assets	2.1	2.1
2.1	1.7	1.6	.3				1.3	1.4
.8	1.7	2.5	2.0				2.1	2.8
(14) 8.2	(40) 5.8	(42) 5.0	(11) 10.9			% Depr., Dep., Amort./Sales	(116) 6.4	(114) 6.9
10.8	11.8	10.7	11.9				11.1	11.7
3.3	1.6	.7					2.0	1.8
(11) 9.2	(25) 3.1	(16) 2.0				% Officers', Directors' Owners' Comp/Sales	(55) 3.9	(56) 3.3
13.2	6.3	3.8					7.2	5.5
30099M	152343M	462743M	315450M		149622M	Net Sales ($)	2868419M	1805721M
4522M	58781M	197884M	271083M		178967M	Total Assets ($)	1220349M	1255678M

M = $ thousand   MM = $ million
See Pages 9 through 22 for Explanation of Ratios and Data

Comparative Historical Data / Current Data Sorted by Sales

	Type of Statement								
				0-1MM	**1-3MM**	**3-5MM**	**5-10MM**	**10-25MM**	**25MM & OVER**
Unqualified				1					1
Reviewed					4		4	10	1
Compiled					7	13	10	5	2
Tax Returns				8	14	5	9	3	
Other					5	10	6	3	1
	7	5	2						
	19	16	19						
	32	17	37						
	37	36	39						
	32	28	25						
	4/1/07-3/31/08 ALL	4/1/08-3/31/09 ALL	4/1/09-3/31/10 ALL	__28 (4/1-9/30/09)__		___94 (10/1/09-3/31/10)___			

Label	4/1/07-3/31/08 ALL	4/1/08-3/31/09 ALL	4/1/09-3/31/10 ALL	0-1MM	1-3MM	3-5MM	5-10MM	10-25MM	25MM & OVER
NUMBER OF STATEMENTS	127	102	122	9	30	28	29	21	5
ASSETS	%	%	%	%	%	%	%	%	%
Cash & Equivalents	9.7	10.5	14.3		16.7	12.7	10.5	8.7	
Trade Receivables (net)	8.3	9.7	9.8		6.2	10.7	11.4	10.4	
Inventory	14.3	13.4	12.6		6.1	11.8	18.5	17.3	
All Other Current	3.9	3.3	4.7		8.9	2.8	4.9	3.5	
Total Current	36.1	36.9	41.4		38.0	37.9	45.2	39.9	
Fixed Assets (net)	53.1	51.7	48.1		54.3	51.5	45.9	41.4	
Intangibles (net)	1.6	3.2	1.9		1.0	2.1	.3	5.4	
All Other Non-Current	9.1	8.1	8.5		6.7	8.6	8.5	13.2	
Total	100.0	100.0	100.0		100.0	100.0	100.0	100.0	
LIABILITIES									
Notes Payable-Short Term	12.9	14.1	11.4		7.6	14.6	13.9	12.7	
Cur. Mat.-L.T.D.	11.5	10.3	8.7		8.3	11.8	9.9	7.1	
Trade Payables	6.7	5.1	5.5		6.1	4.0	6.9	4.7	
Income Taxes Payable	.2	.0	.1		.0	.0	.0	.3	
All Other Current	3.8	7.6	7.7		7.0	10.3	9.2	6.8	
Total Current	35.1	37.2	33.4		29.1	40.8	40.0	31.7	
Long-Term Debt	38.3	32.9	34.5		38.6	31.9	30.6	28.6	
Deferred Taxes	.6	.5	.7		.3	.0	1.3	1.6	
All Other Non-Current	3.6	4.6	4.2		8.8	.9	1.8	2.2	
Net Worth	22.4	24.8	27.2		23.2	26.4	26.3	35.9	
Total Liabilties & Net Worth	100.0	100.0	100.0		100.0	100.0	100.0	100.0	
INCOME DATA									
Net Sales	100.0	100.0	100.0		100.0	100.0	100.0	100.0	
Gross Profit	37.0	36.0	39.2		44.8	44.7	36.5	20.1	
Operating Expenses	34.5	34.5	36.8		41.8	40.4	37.0	18.1	
Operating Profit	2.5	1.5	2.5		2.9	4.3	-.5	2.0	
All Other Expenses (net)	1.0	.7	.5		.9	.5	-.1	.2	
Profit Before Taxes	1.5	.7	2.0		2.0	3.7	-.4	1.8	
RATIOS									
Current	2.1	2.5	2.5		3.4	2.4	2.3	2.4	
Current	1.0	1.1	1.3		1.2	.9	1.0	1.5	
Current	.4	.5	.5		.7	.4	.5	.6	
Quick	1.3	1.5	1.8		1.6	1.2	.9	1.9	
Quick	(126) .5	(100) .5	(121) .6		.7	.6	(28) .4	.4	
Quick	.2	.2	.2		.2	.2	.2	.2	
Sales/Receivables	0 UND	0 UND	0 UND		0 UND	0 UND	0 UND	3 126.0	
Sales/Receivables	8 48.0	6 56.3	9 39.3		8 46.6	10 38.0	13 29.1	11 33.4	
Sales/Receivables	20 18.1	15 23.9	25 14.9		21 17.5	29 12.7	23 15.6	31 11.7	
Cost of Sales/Inventory	0 UND	0 UND	0 UND		0 UND	0 UND	0 UND	1 423.9	
Cost of Sales/Inventory	8 43.4	5 76.1	6 57.3		0 UND	17 21.9	9 42.7	26 14.2	
Cost of Sales/Inventory	58 6.3	43 8.5	43 8.6		22 16.4	40 9.1	58 6.3	70 5.2	
Cost of Sales/Payables	0 849.0	0 940.2	0 UND		0 UND	0 UND	0 UND	3 127.9	
Cost of Sales/Payables	8 47.9	6 56.4	7 55.2		10 35.5	3 118.7	6 56.7	8 44.2	
Cost of Sales/Payables	26 14.1	19 19.6	23 15.8		26 13.8	17 21.1	25 14.4	21 17.5	
Sales/Working Capital	12.9	10.8	7.0		4.6	11.1	8.9	7.9	
Sales/Working Capital	295.8	83.4	41.6		UND	NM	-193.7	21.6	
Sales/Working Capital	-13.9	-13.0	-14.4		-17.5	-7.3	-12.8	-24.8	
EBIT/Interest	4.2	5.4	4.3		5.5	6.9	3.7	3.4	
EBIT/Interest	(119) 1.7	(96) 1.9	(111) 1.7		(27) 2.2	(27) 1.9	(27) 1.1	(20) 1.9	
EBIT/Interest	-.2	-.9	.1		.3	.8	-1.9	1.0	
Net Profit + Depr., Dep., Amort./Cur. Mat. L/T/D	3.2	4.2	2.9						
Net Profit + Depr., Dep., Amort./Cur. Mat. L/T/D	(23) 1.7	(13) 1.9	(17) 1.7						
Net Profit + Depr., Dep., Amort./Cur. Mat. L/T/D	.8	.9	.7						
Fixed/Worth	.8	.7	.6		.7	.5	1.0	.7	
Fixed/Worth	3.0	1.7	1.9		1.9	2.0	2.7	1.1	
Fixed/Worth	21.0	NM	13.5		5.5	12.7	68.1	12.5	
Debt/Worth	1.1	.7	.6		.5	.7	.9	.5	
Debt/Worth	3.9	2.1	2.7		2.1	4.1	3.6	1.9	
Debt/Worth	39.3	NM	22.2		6.2	13.5	94.3	16.0	
% Profit Before Taxes/Tangible Net Worth	33.3	32.0	29.8		26.8	62.0	24.6	13.3	
% Profit Before Taxes/Tangible Net Worth	(98) 12.8	(77) 10.8	(98) 9.6		(25) 8.5	(23) 11.2	(23) 7.5	(17) 9.6	
% Profit Before Taxes/Tangible Net Worth	.6	-3.7	-2.3		-3.1	-2.7	-8.3	1.4	
% Profit Before Taxes/Total Assets	10.0	11.4	11.5		15.5	14.4	7.4	9.9	
% Profit Before Taxes/Total Assets	3.7	3.6	2.7		3.8	4.5	.6	2.4	
% Profit Before Taxes/Total Assets	-5.7	-7.4	-1.8		-1.4	-1.1	-9.9	.0	
Sales/Net Fixed Assets	10.8	8.9	17.6		8.0	21.6	23.4	19.6	
Sales/Net Fixed Assets	4.4	5.1	4.9		4.3	5.6	5.1	5.6	
Sales/Net Fixed Assets	2.4	2.6	2.7		2.8	2.9	2.2	3.2	
Sales/Total Assets	3.3	3.5	3.1		3.0	3.6	3.1	4.1	
Sales/Total Assets	2.3	2.4	2.2		2.0	2.4	2.2	2.3	
Sales/Total Assets	1.6	1.6	1.6		1.6	1.8	1.5	1.7	
% Depr., Dep., Amort./Sales	2.7	2.4	2.1		1.4	3.3	2.3	1.1	
% Depr., Dep., Amort./Sales	(112) 8.3	(82) 7.1	(108) 5.8		(27) 8.3	(21) 7.6	(28) 5.4	(19) 4.6	
% Depr., Dep., Amort./Sales	11.8	12.7	11.3		13.9	13.5	11.8	7.7	
% Officers', Directors' Owners' Comp/Sales	1.8	1.5	1.7		1.8	1.8	.9		
% Officers', Directors' Owners' Comp/Sales	(63) 3.5	(51) 2.1	(57) 3.2		(19) 4.5	(13) 2.3	(10) 2.3		
% Officers', Directors' Owners' Comp/Sales	5.4	4.0	6.4		8.2	5.6	3.4		
Net Sales ($)	1687253M	1119120M	1110257M	5921M	52482M	110633M	197246M	320703M	423272M
Total Assets ($)	865255M	564898M	711237M	7485M	28712M	73628M	149469M	170884M	281059M

AGRICULTURE—Finfish Fishing NAICS 114111

Current Data Sorted by Assets | Comparative Historical Data

Type of Statement

Type of Statement	0-500M	500M-2MM	2-10MM	10-50MM	50-100MM	100-250MM	4/1/05-3/31/06 ALL	4/1/06-3/31/07 ALL
Unqualified				7	2		8	9
Reviewed		1	1	1	1		3	2
Compiled	4		3	1			7	3
Tax Returns	4	10					6	7
Other	3	3	7	8	1	2	21	21

Periods: 5 (4/1-9/30/09) · 54 (10/1/09-3/31/10)

	0-500M	500M-2MM	2-10MM	10-50MM	50-100MM	100-250MM	4/1/05-3/31/06 ALL	4/1/06-3/31/07 ALL
NUMBER OF STATEMENTS	11	14	11	17	4	2	45	42
	%	%	%	%	%	%	%	%
ASSETS								
Cash & Equivalents	14.8	18.3	19.2	8.1			10.2	11.1
Trade Receivables (net)	.0	.8	5.1	7.1			9.7	7.8
Inventory	.0	1.5	8.2	14.9			8.6	10.4
All Other Current	.0	.6	.9	3.3			7.2	4.2
Total Current	14.9	21.2	33.3	33.4			35.6	33.4
Fixed Assets (net)	24.3	37.9	37.0	41.3			50.0	42.3
Intangibles (net)	28.9	23.1	20.0	14.3			6.9	12.3
All Other Non-Current	31.9	17.9	9.7	11.0			7.4	12.0
Total	100.0	100.0	100.0	100.0			100.0	100.0
LIABILITIES								
Notes Payable-Short Term	112.4	13.8	.7	7.2			6.5	7.4
Cur. Mat.-L.T.D.	9.8	10.0	5.2	3.4			5.3	4.3
Trade Payables	1.2	1.8	4.8	3.6			6.9	8.2
Income Taxes Payable	.0	.0	.3	.1			.5	.3
All Other Current	9.5	5.9	5.5	7.6			7.3	5.3
Total Current	132.9	31.6	16.6	21.9			26.6	25.5
Long-Term Debt	47.9	61.6	41.6	28.4			37.2	41.1
Deferred Taxes	.0	.0	.4	.9			.2	.3
All Other Non-Current	.0	4.5	2.1	2.1			1.6	5.2
Net Worth	-80.8	2.2	39.3	46.7			34.4	27.8
Total Liabilities & Net Worth	100.0	100.0	100.0	100.0			100.0	100.0
INCOME DATA								
Net Sales	100.0	100.0	100.0	100.0			100.0	100.0
Gross Profit								
Operating Expenses	90.6	88.9	76.9	85.7			88.5	83.9
Operating Profit	9.4	11.1	23.1	14.3			11.5	16.1
All Other Expenses (net)	5.8	3.7	3.4	3.4			1.3	1.9
Profit Before Taxes	3.6	7.4	19.7	10.9			10.3	14.2
RATIOS								
Current	.5	2.5	3.2	2.1			2.9	2.6
	.0	1.2	2.3	1.4			1.3	1.5
	.0	.0	.7	1.1			.7	.7
Quick	.5	2.4	3.2	1.6			1.7	1.7
	.0	.8	2.0	.6			.7	.8
	.0	.0	.4	.3			.3	.5
Sales/Receivables	0 UND	0 UND	0 UND	0 UND			0 999.8	0 UND
	0 UND	0 UND	4 93.0	20 18.0			11 33.5	8 44.3
	0 UND	0 UND	18 20.7	32 11.5			27 13.7	28 13.2
Cost of Sales/Inventory								
Cost of Sales/Payables								
Sales/Working Capital	-35.7	8.1	3.0	4.4			6.9	5.3
	-2.1	39.8	8.4	9.6			20.0	14.1
	-1.4	-2.8	-36.1	44.3			-35.9	-27.0
EBIT/Interest		11.8	55.4	14.2			15.1	14.6
		3.7	(10) 9.1	3.8			5.8	4.6
		.4	3.9	.9			1.5	2.2
Net Profit + Depr., Dep., Amort./Cur. Mat. L/T/D								
Fixed/Worth	.0	1.0	.6	.5			.7	.7
	.0	-1.1	3.9	1.6			1.7	1.8
	-8.9	-.5	-1.1	3.1			6.9	-3.9
Debt/Worth	52.5	NM	.4	.6			.6	.9
	-2.2	-2.7	3.8	1.6			3.4	2.8
	-1.3	-2.0	-2.7	7.6			9.7	-16.2
% Profit Before Taxes/Tangible Net Worth				30.8			98.0	77.5
				(15) 14.2			(38) 48.6	(30) 36.3
				-.4			9.9	8.8
% Profit Before Taxes/Total Assets	24.1	33.5	32.0	8.4			31.2	27.5
	-8.2	7.0	18.4	4.5			12.3	10.7
	-25.7	-7.1	10.3	-.2			2.5	2.8
Sales/Net Fixed Assets	UND	52.4	9.7	7.9			6.2	8.8
	UND	3.9	4.0	3.0			3.7	4.8
	2.3	1.4	1.2	1.6			1.9	2.2
Sales/Total Assets	5.1	1.9	2.2	1.8			2.6	2.9
	2.7	1.1	.9	1.1			1.6	1.5
	1.0	.7	.8	.3			1.0	.8
% Depr., Dep., Amort./Sales		.8		3.6			3.1	2.0
	(11)	6.9		(15) 5.4			(42) 5.2	(36) 3.8
		15.8		8.1			8.7	8.7
% Officers', Directors' Owners' Comp/Sales								.5
								(13) 1.5
								6.0
Net Sales ($)	18026M	22476M	79407M	472142M	439110M	408555M	1265028M	1199565M
Total Assets ($)	1960M	14241M	47047M	383901M	318684M	355190M	743899M	971806M

M = $ thousand   MM = $ million
See Pages 9 through 22 for Explanation of Ratios and Data

Comparative Historical Data | | | | ## Current Data Sorted by Sales | | | | | |

			Type of Statement						
9	6	9	Unqualified			1	1	2	5
6	2	4	Reviewed		1	1			2
4	6	8	Compiled	4	4				
5	10	14	Tax Returns	10	3		1		
21	33	24	Other	4	3	4	3	4	7
4/1/07-3/31/08 ALL	4/1/08-3/31/09 ALL	4/1/09-3/31/10 ALL		5 (4/1-9/30/09)		54 (10/1/09-3/31/10)			
				0-1MM	1-3MM	3-5MM	5-10MM	10-25MM	25MM & OVER
45	57	59	**NUMBER OF STATEMENTS**	18	10	6	5	6	14
%	%	%	**ASSETS**	%	%	%	%	%	%
14.7	14.8	13.6	Cash & Equivalents	8.8	21.8				8.7
10.7	8.7	4.5	Trade Receivables (net)	.0	4.4				12.3
10.8	8.8	7.6	Inventory	1.1	.0				21.1
3.4	5.8	1.9	All Other Current	.2	.7				4.1
39.5	38.0	27.6	Total Current	10.1	26.9				46.2
34.5	35.7	36.0	Fixed Assets (net)	36.2	30.8				36.7
12.9	15.4	20.2	Intangibles (net)	26.5	34.7				8.7
13.1	10.9	16.2	All Other Non-Current	27.1	7.6				8.3
100.0	100.0	100.0	Total	100.0	100.0				100.0
			LIABILITIES						
6.0	10.4	27.7	Notes Payable-Short Term	79.4	.0				13.9
4.2	13.5	6.6	Cur. Mat.-L.T.D.	9.0	8.9				2.7
4.7	5.9	3.5	Trade Payables	1.4	2.4				7.5
.2	.2	.1	Income Taxes Payable	.0	.0				.1
4.8	14.5	6.7	All Other Current	6.5	5.9				8.8
19.9	44.5	44.5	Total Current	96.2	17.2				33.0
34.5	46.1	42.5	Long-Term Debt	55.1	49.6				22.0
.4	.5	.4	Deferred Taxes	.0	.1				1.1
5.3	2.2	2.7	All Other Non-Current	.0	4.1				3.8
39.9	6.7	9.7	Net Worth	-51.4	29.1				40.1
100.0	100.0	100.0	Total Liabilities & Net Worth	100.0	100.0				100.0
			INCOME DATA						
100.0	100.0	100.0	Net Sales	100.0	100.0				100.0
			Gross Profit						
85.9	86.4	86.4	Operating Expenses	90.8	79.7				91.7
14.1	13.6	13.6	Operating Profit	9.2	20.3				8.3
2.2	3.6	3.9	All Other Expenses (net)	5.5	5.2				2.3
11.9	10.0	9.6	Profit Before Taxes	3.7	15.0				6.1
			RATIOS						
4.8	3.3	2.3		.7	6.4				2.6
1.9	1.7	1.3	Current	.0	2.2				1.4
1.1	1.0	.3		.0	.6				.9
2.4	2.4	1.8		.4	6.1				2.2
1.3	1.1	.5	Quick	.0	2.1				.4
.7	.3	.2		.0	.6				.2
0 UND	0 UND	0 UND		0 UND	0 UND				10 36.7
14 27.0	13 28.2	0 UND	Sales/Receivables	0 UND	0 UND				23 15.6
37 9.8	39 9.5	20 18.0		0 UND	20 18.6				46 8.0
			Cost of Sales/Inventory						
			Cost of Sales/Payables						
4.7	4.2	5.9		NM	3.0				5.2
9.1	10.5	20.9	Sales/Working Capital	-2.6	5.7				17.0
30.9	-650.6	-4.9		-1.5	-17.8				NM
11.3	10.8	11.7		4.6					14.7
(43) 4.2	(51) 5.6	(54) 4.0	EBIT/Interest	(15) .1				(13)	6.6
2.3	2.0	.7		-2.0					1.2
			Net Profit + Depr., Dep., Amort./Cur. Mat. L/T/D						
.5	.5	.5		.0	.8				.4
1.4	1.5	1.7	Fixed/Worth	2.0	-.8				1.3
3.7	-1.5	-1.2		-.9	-.4				2.9
.7	.7	.8		NM	.6				.6
2.2	2.1	9.2	Debt/Worth	-2.4	-4.9				2.3
21.6	-5.9	-2.4		-1.6	-1.8				9.7
80.6	60.9	55.6	% Profit Before Taxes/Tangible Net Worth						55.8
(36) 40.2	(39) 31.1	(33) 26.9						(13)	28.4
15.2	8.0	1.7							7.1
26.4	28.7	18.5	% Profit Before Taxes/Total Assets	12.1	30.8				10.5
9.3	9.2	5.9		-4.1	11.0				8.0
2.8	1.6	-.9		-21.8	1.8				1.0
10.0	10.7	19.6		UND	5.8				13.3
4.3	4.4	3.8	Sales/Net Fixed Assets	5.3	3.2				3.9
2.0	2.1	1.6		1.4	1.5				2.5
2.3	2.6	2.2		2.7	1.6				2.4
1.2	1.2	1.1	Sales/Total Assets	1.1	.9				1.5
.8	.7	.7		.6	.7				.8
2.8	1.8	2.4	% Depr., Dep., Amort./Sales						2.2
(37) 4.3	(47) 4.6	(44) 5.6						(13)	3.9
9.0	7.5	11.7							6.4
1.3	2.0		% Officers', Directors' Owners' Comp/Sales						
(16) 2.6	(11) 4.4								
5.7	7.7								
1236803M	1439570M	1439716M	Net Sales ($)	8131M	22363M	25531M	31319M	105672M	1246700M
978190M	1213677M	1121023M	Total Assets ($)	8250M	34452M	72399M	41882M	84602M	879438M

M = $ thousand   MM = $ million
See Pages 9 through 22 for Explanation of Ratios and Data

Current Data Sorted by Assets / Comparative Historical Data

0-500M	500M-2MM	2-10MM	10-50MM	50-100MM	100-250MM	Type of Statement	4/1/05-3/31/06 ALL	4/1/06-3/31/07 ALL
			1			Unqualified	3	
	1		3	1		Reviewed	5	7
	3	4	1			Compiled	9	7
5	10	5				Tax Returns	13	11
2	1	6	1			Other	10	12
	6 (4/1-9/30/09)		38 (10/1/09-3/31/10)					
7	15	15	6	1		NUMBER OF STATEMENTS	40	37
%	%	%	%	%	%	**ASSETS**	%	%
	14.9	10.6			D	Cash & Equivalents	15.1	22.1
	11.4	8.7			A	Trade Receivables (net)	10.9	14.1
	3.0	4.1			T	Inventory	8.2	6.4
	.1	4.6			A	All Other Current	2.8	3.1
	29.4	28.0				Total Current	37.0	45.7
	22.3	43.4			N	Fixed Assets (net)	46.3	42.5
	32.8	14.2			O	Intangibles (net)	7.7	4.0
	15.5	14.5			T	All Other Non-Current	9.0	7.8
	100.0	100.0				Total	100.0	100.0
					A	**LIABILITIES**		
	6.3	5.6			V	Notes Payable-Short Term	9.0	9.0
	6.9	3.2			A	Cur. Mat.-L.T.D.	2.9	3.1
	8.8	6.6			I	Trade Payables	6.9	8.3
	.0	.0			L	Income Taxes Payable	.0	.2
	2.8	4.4			A	All Other Current	7.5	19.9
	24.8	19.8			B	Total Current	26.4	40.5
	49.2	47.0			L	Long-Term Debt	34.4	20.3
	.0	.0			E	Deferred Taxes	.1	.4
	21.3	3.2				All Other Non-Current	1.3	4.2
	4.7	30.0				Net Worth	37.8	34.6
	100.0	100.0				Total Liabilties & Net Worth	100.0	100.0
						INCOME DATA		
	100.0	100.0				Net Sales	100.0	100.0
						Gross Profit		
	84.9	84.6				Operating Expenses	90.3	92.5
	15.1	15.4				Operating Profit	9.7	7.5
	5.6	4.4				All Other Expenses (net)	2.9	3.8
	9.5	11.0				Profit Before Taxes	6.8	3.7
						RATIOS		
	2.1	2.6					2.4	3.3
	1.0	1.3				Current	1.5	1.7
	.1	.7					1.0	.9
	2.1	1.9					2.0	2.9
	1.0	.8				Quick	1.0	1.2
	.1	.4					.5	.5
	0 UND	0 UND					0 UND	0 UND
	0 UND	1 259.1				Sales/Receivables	0 966.1	0 UND
	12 30.9	26 14.2					28 13.1	25 14.8
						Cost of Sales/Inventory		
						Cost of Sales/Payables		
	11.1	4.0					7.1	6.1
	999.8	21.5				Sales/Working Capital	28.1	21.3
	-3.9	-44.9					-277.4	-61.1
	15.5	30.9					13.4	7.9
	(13) 2.5	6.1				EBIT/Interest	(37) 3.4	(32) 4.0
	1.2	.5					1.7	1.6
						Net Profit + Depr., Dep., Amort./Cur. Mat. L/T/D		
	.0	.8					.9	.5
	.6	1.0				Fixed/Worth	1.3	.9
	-1.5	-.7					6.3	2.2
	.9	.4					.8	.8
	12.5	2.6				Debt/Worth	1.9	1.6
	-1.2	-4.2					27.5	4.4
							125.3	78.4
						% Profit Before Taxes/Tangible Net Worth	(33) 26.6	(33) 33.8
							5.5	6.7
	32.6	18.3					26.2	25.5
	8.8	5.2				% Profit Before Taxes/Total Assets	7.9	9.4
	1.8	-4.5					2.5	2.3
	566.5	9.2					25.9	35.8
	18.5	4.6				Sales/Net Fixed Assets	4.7	8.0
	6.1	1.8					1.5	1.7
	2.8	2.4					4.0	5.0
	1.3	1.1				Sales/Total Assets	1.8	2.1
	.9	.6					.7	.8
		1.9					.8	.7
		(14) 6.0				% Depr., Dep., Amort./Sales	(29) 3.8	(30) 3.9
		20.3					6.9	8.0
							1.3	.7
						% Officers', Directors' Owners' Comp/Sales	(17) 3.2	(17) 1.7
							7.9	6.7
6417M	51151M	88160M	91253M	43416M		Net Sales ($)	1992771M	264969M
1746M	16427M	61930M	145011M	51667M		Total Assets ($)	731205M	144898M

M = $ thousand MM = $ million

See Pages 9 through 22 for Explanation of Ratios and Data

Comparative Historical Data | | Current Data Sorted by Sales

4/1/07-3/31/08 ALL	4/1/08-3/31/09 ALL	4/1/09-3/31/10 ALL	Type of Statement	0-1MM	1-3MM	3-5MM	5-10MM	10-25MM	25MM & OVER
1	1	1	Unqualified					1	2
4	6	5	Reviewed					2	
12	5	8	Compiled	3	1	1	1	2	
20	21	20	Tax Returns	4	14		1	2	
11	10	10	Other	1	2	2	4	1	
					6 (4/1-9/30/09)		38 (10/1/09-3/31/10)		
48	43	44	NUMBER OF STATEMENTS	8	17	3	6	8	2
%	%	%	ASSETS	%	%	%	%	%	%
14.7	13.6	14.2	Cash & Equivalents		18.2				
7.2	5.3	7.6	Trade Receivables (net)		1.9				
5.4	6.4	4.8	Inventory		2.5				
4.5	1.4	1.8	All Other Current		1.2				
31.8	26.8	28.4	Total Current		23.7				
42.5	44.7	32.8	Fixed Assets (net)		20.9				
15.2	18.7	23.4	Intangibles (net)		25.9				
10.5	9.8	15.5	All Other Non-Current		29.5				
100.0	100.0	100.0	Total		100.0				
			LIABILITIES						
7.4	8.4	9.8	Notes Payable-Short Term		11.3				
17.2	4.2	4.8	Cur. Mat.-L.T.D.		4.9				
5.1	4.3	5.9	Trade Payables		1.9				
.0	.3	.0	Income Taxes Payable		.0				
21.8	6.6	6.0	All Other Current		10.3				
51.5	23.8	26.4	Total Current		28.3				
36.4	38.8	50.4	Long-Term Debt		61.7				
2.0	.3	.4	Deferred Taxes		.0				
10.9	11.3	8.6	All Other Non-Current		18.8				
-.8	25.8	14.2	Net Worth		-8.7				
100.0	100.0	100.0	Total Liabilties & Net Worth		100.0				
			INCOME DATA						
100.0	100.0	100.0	Net Sales		100.0				
			Gross Profit						
86.2	91.2	84.7	Operating Expenses		87.7				
13.8	8.8	15.3	Operating Profit		12.3				
3.4	2.3	4.7	All Other Expenses (net)		5.4				
10.4	6.5	10.7	Profit Before Taxes		6.9				
			RATIOS						
3.6	2.4	2.2	Current		4.3				
1.4	1.1	1.2			.9				
.2	.2	.3			.1				
2.2	1.4	1.9	Quick		2.6				
1.1	.6	.7			.9				
.1	.1	.3			.1				
0 UND	0 UND	0 UND	Sales/Receivables		0 UND				
0 UND	0 UND	0 UND			0 UND				
20 18.0	25 14.5	18 20.6			0 UND				
			Cost of Sales/Inventory						
			Cost of Sales/Payables						
8.4	7.9	9.0	Sales/Working Capital		8.1				
24.1	172.8	46.4			-193.7				
-25.6	-11.2	-10.4			-7.3				
8.5	7.2	12.1	EBIT/Interest		7.7				
(43) 3.0	(38) 2.6	(38) 3.6			(14) 2.5				
.7	.5	.9			.8				
			Net Profit + Depr., Dep., Amort./Cur. Mat. L/T/D						
.7	.9	.3	Fixed/Worth		.2				
1.5	1.7	1.0			1.1				
49.7	-5.6	-2.8			-.2				
1.0	.5	.7	Debt/Worth		1.0				
4.2	3.9	4.0			-9.8				
-2.8	-2.7	-2.2			-1.2				
95.7	49.4	77.0	% Profit Before Taxes/Tangible Net Worth						
(31) 38.0	(29) 11.1	(26) 29.9							
8.4	-5.4	7.2							
25.8	18.9	32.6	% Profit Before Taxes/Total Assets		38.1				
7.3	4.7	8.0			8.8				
.8	-1.4	.9			1.2				
26.6	9.5	50.6	Sales/Net Fixed Assets		151.8				
7.2	2.9	8.7			9.6				
2.3	1.5	1.9			3.8				
3.6	2.3	2.7	Sales/Total Assets		2.8				
1.8	1.1	1.1			1.1				
.9	.7	.6			.7				
.9	4.4	2.0	% Depr., Dep., Amort./Sales		3.0				
(39) 4.9	(33) 8.0	(32) 4.3			(11) 6.0				
8.4	12.9	10.6			19.7				
.5	2.9	1.6	% Officers', Directors' Owners' Comp/Sales						
(12) 1.9	(16) 4.6	(17) 3.6							
8.4	10.5	8.6							
401652M	203517M	280397M	Net Sales ($)	5038M	24829M	11267M	43460M	123818M	71985M
148873M	188036M	276781M	Total Assets ($)	14554M	22690M	9099M	59996M	106028M	64414M

M = $ thousand   MM = $ million
See Pages 9 through 22 for Explanation of Ratios and Data

Current Data Sorted by Assets							Comparative Historical Data	
0-500M	500M-2MM	2-10MM	10-50MM	50-100MM	100-250MM	**Type of Statement**	4/1/05-3/31/06 ALL	4/1/06-3/31/07 ALL
	6	16	1	1	1	Unqualified	30	25
	2	11	2			Reviewed	8	10
	2	4	1			Compiled	9	4
6	5	3	1			Tax Returns	6	6
6	4	5	3			Other	4	3
	33 (4/1-9/30/09)		47 (10/1/09-3/31/10)					
12	19	39	8	1	1	**NUMBER OF STATEMENTS**	57	48
%	%	%	%	%	%	**ASSETS**	%	%
15.1	12.8	14.5				Cash & Equivalents	10.3	10.5
5.3	12.4	13.9				Trade Receivables (net)	13.3	15.1
.0	12.4	15.1				Inventory	12.3	12.4
3.2	5.4	1.3				All Other Current	7.8	5.8
23.6	43.0	44.9				Total Current	43.7	43.8
67.9	41.7	43.7				Fixed Assets (net)	46.7	45.9
.6	.9	.9				Intangibles (net)	.3	.4
7.8	14.4	10.5				All Other Non-Current	9.3	9.9
100.0	100.0	100.0				Total	100.0	100.0
						LIABILITIES		
12.7	5.4	6.9				Notes Payable-Short Term	10.7	8.8
17.2	3.3	5.3				Cur. Mat.-L.T.D.	4.0	4.0
.8	8.6	6.4				Trade Payables	8.2	6.0
.0	.1	.0				Income Taxes Payable	.2	.3
14.4	15.5	18.4				All Other Current	15.8	10.1
45.1	33.0	37.0				Total Current	38.9	29.3
30.8	26.9	14.0				Long-Term Debt	26.1	17.8
.0	.0	.1				Deferred Taxes	.4	.2
26.8	.4	1.3				All Other Non-Current	1.6	1.1
-2.7	39.8	47.6				Net Worth	33.1	51.6
100.0	100.0	100.0				Total Liabilties & Net Worth	100.0	100.0
						INCOME DATA		
100.0	100.0	100.0				Net Sales	100.0	100.0
						Gross Profit		
84.2	90.1	89.4				Operating Expenses	88.5	88.5
15.8	9.9	10.6				Operating Profit	11.5	11.5
4.3	1.6	.4				All Other Expenses (net)	.1	.0
11.5	8.3	10.2				Profit Before Taxes	11.4	11.5
						RATIOS		
58.3	3.1	2.1				Current	2.1	2.8
1.2	1.6	1.4					1.3	1.5
.1	.7	.9					.9	1.1
44.3	2.0	1.5				Quick	1.3	1.3
1.2	.9	.8					.6	.9
.0	.1	.5					.3	.5
0 UND	0 UND	6 59.0				Sales/Receivables	5 69.1	8 43.3
1 618.6	5 79.0	23 15.7					20 18.6	23 15.9
15 24.1	33 11.2	56 6.6					52 7.1	50 7.3
						Cost of Sales/Inventory		
						Cost of Sales/Payables		
10.0	4.4	5.2				Sales/Working Capital	4.5	4.4
NM	9.1	11.1					10.2	10.1
-3.9	-9.1	-86.3					-68.6	60.8
	9.9	20.8				EBIT/Interest	32.4	24.3
(14)	2.8	(33) 9.8					(54) 8.5	(46) 5.2
	.4	-1.4					2.2	1.9
						Net Profit + Depr., Dep., Amort./Cur. Mat. L/T/D	5.3	10.5
							(13) 2.5	(14) 3.3
							1.4	2.1
.7	.3	.5				Fixed/Worth	.6	.5
2.0	.8	.8					.9	.8
-1.3	6.6	1.1					1.6	1.3
.3	.5	.2				Debt/Worth	.5	.4
2.4	1.1	1.0					1.1	.8
-3.4	7.3	3.1					2.9	1.8
	81.0	45.8				% Profit Before Taxes/Tangible Net Worth	51.6	50.3
(17)	19.8	(35) 19.9					(53) 23.2	(46) 18.6
	-3.0	-1.8					6.2	4.8
17.7	27.4	17.6				% Profit Before Taxes/Total Assets	24.1	24.9
3.5	7.5	9.6					8.3	6.8
-3.7	-2.1	-2.3					2.6	2.4
7.9	11.8	8.5				Sales/Net Fixed Assets	6.4	7.4
3.0	4.3	2.2					2.9	3.1
.7	2.6	1.2					1.5	1.6
4.0	3.0	2.2				Sales/Total Assets	2.3	2.2
2.0	1.7	1.1					1.2	1.3
.6	.8	.6					.8	.8
	2.8	2.5				% Depr., Dep., Amort./Sales	2.0	2.7
(16)	5.6	(35) 5.8					(54) 4.2	4.7
	12.7	12.7					6.7	9.5
						% Officers', Directors' Owners' Comp/Sales	1.2	
							(10) 2.5	
							9.8	
13917M	52743M	610998M	147797M	4297M	760195M	Net Sales ($)	754694M	281880M
4429M	23706M	193974M	136741M	67391M	187797M	Total Assets ($)	611171M	209436M

M = $ thousand   MM = $ million
See Pages 9 through 22 for Explanation of Ratios and Data

Comparative Historical Data   Current Data Sorted by Sales

Hist 1	Hist 2	Hist 3	Type of Statement	0-1MM	1-3MM	3-5MM	5-10MM	10-25MM	25MM & OVER
22	20	25	Unqualified	2	8	7	1	5	2
7	8	15	Reviewed	1	1	7	1	5	
7	7	7	Compiled	1	4		1	1	
7	7	15	Tax Returns	4	2	6	1		2
2	4	18	Other	5	6	1	1	4	1
4/1/07-3/31/08 ALL	4/1/08-3/31/09 ALL	4/1/09-3/31/10 ALL		33 (4/1-9/30/09)			47 (10/1/09-3/31/10)		
45	46	80	NUMBER OF STATEMENTS	13	21	21	5	15	5
%	%	%	ASSETS	%	%	%	%	%	%
8.9	11.3	12.7	Cash & Equivalents	14.6	12.5	10.7		11.4	
14.6	16.1	14.5	Trade Receivables (net)	2.9	17.0	12.3		16.4	
11.4	12.7	12.6	Inventory	.1	11.5	9.5		19.5	
4.9	3.8	2.5	All Other Current	.2	5.3	2.7		1.6	
39.8	43.9	42.3	Total Current	17.7	46.3	35.2		49.0	
50.0	44.1	45.9	Fixed Assets (net)	60.7	45.5	55.4		37.7	
.3	.1	.7	Intangibles (net)	.4	.3	1.3		.3	
9.9	11.9	11.0	All Other Non-Current	21.2	7.8	8.2		12.9	
100.0	100.0	100.0	Total	100.0	100.0	100.0		100.0	
			LIABILITIES						
10.5	9.9	9.0	Notes Payable-Short Term	11.1	6.7	9.1		10.4	
5.2	6.0	6.3	Cur. Mat.-L.T.D.	3.1	2.8	17.6		2.1	
5.0	8.5	7.3	Trade Payables	1.6	7.9	5.1		9.1	
.2	.1	.1	Income Taxes Payable	.0	.1	.0		.2	
9.2	9.8	15.9	All Other Current	14.8	9.5	9.8		18.7	
30.2	34.4	38.5	Total Current	30.7	27.0	41.6		40.4	
22.9	19.1	21.0	Long-Term Debt	37.0	16.6	25.9		11.2	
.2	.1	.1	Deferred Taxes	.0	.0	.1		.4	
1.3	2.1	5.3	All Other Non-Current	.2	15.6	.4		1.7	
45.4	44.3	35.2	Net Worth	32.1	40.8	32.0		46.3	
100.0	100.0	100.0	Total Liabilities & Net Worth	100.0	100.0	100.0		100.0	
			INCOME DATA						
100.0	100.0	100.0	Net Sales	100.0	100.0	100.0		100.0	
			Gross Profit						
86.2	87.8	89.0	Operating Expenses	83.4	88.1	90.0		94.4	
13.8	12.2	11.0	Operating Profit	16.6	11.9	10.0		5.6	
.7	-.6	1.5	All Other Expenses (net)	5.5	1.3	2.0		-1.8	
13.0	12.8	9.4	Profit Before Taxes	11.1	10.5	8.0		7.4	
			RATIOS						
2.4	2.3	2.5	Current	3.3	4.1	1.9		1.5	
1.2	1.3	1.3		.6	1.8	1.3		1.3	
1.0	1.0	.7		.1	1.1	.7		.9	
1.7	1.5	1.9	Quick	3.3	3.3	1.5		1.4	
1.0	.9	.8		.6	1.2	.6		.7	
.3	.6	.2		.0	.2	.1		.2	
7 52.5	2 208.6	1 249.4	Sales/Receivables	0 UND	1 724.4	1 446.0		8 47.8	
21 17.4	23 15.9	20 18.5		3 105.7	39 9.4	14 26.8		21 17.1	
56 6.5	69 5.3	44 8.3		19 19.3	89 4.1	45 8.0		41 8.8	
			Cost of Sales/Inventory						
			Cost of Sales/Payables						
4.3	4.8	5.2	Sales/Working Capital	5.5	3.1	5.4		12.2	
12.0	13.9	13.2		-13.2	6.8	17.0		34.2	
-179.6	-412.2	-23.4		-1.5	NM	-19.1		-29.5	
29.4	22.7	16.6	EBIT/Interest		15.5	13.7		23.5	
(39) 3.5	(38) 4.6	(61) 3.0		(17) 2.7	(16) 3.6			(12) 10.3	
1.4	-.6	.5			-2.8	-.1		2.6	
12.4		4.7	Net Profit + Depr., Dep., Amort./Cur. Mat. L/T/D						
(13) 3.6		(10) 1.8							
1.7		.4							
.5	.4	.5	Fixed/Worth	.9	.4	.6		.4	
1.0	.9	.9		1.4	.8	.9		.9	
1.4	1.3	2.3		NM	3.1	4.0		2.2	
.4	.4	.4	Debt/Worth	.4	.4	.2		.6	
1.0	.9	1.1		1.0	.6	1.0		1.2	
2.0	3.2	5.1		NM	4.8	4.5		3.1	
56.9	49.3	38.5	% Profit Before Taxes/Tangible Net Worth	25.1	75.0	26.3		43.8	
(42) 15.6	(43) 14.4	(69) 15.8		(10) 2.8	(19) 15.8	(17) 15.5		19.9	
2.8	1.1	-.8		-2.6	-5.0	8.4		10.8	
25.1	29.2	16.8	% Profit Before Taxes/Total Assets	16.8	31.3	15.9		16.5	
6.1	6.2	6.7		.3	5.5	7.5		9.4	
1.4	-4.5	-1.9		-.9	-4.4	-.7		3.5	
8.6	7.7	8.7	Sales/Net Fixed Assets	2.1	6.9	6.3		19.5	
2.0	2.8	3.0		.8	2.9	1.9		6.4	
1.4	1.2	1.2		.4	1.1	1.2		2.7	
1.9	1.9	2.8	Sales/Total Assets	1.1	2.4	2.2		3.8	
1.1	1.1	1.3		.6	1.1	.9		2.2	
.7	.7	.6		.2	.5	.6		1.3	
2.3	2.2	2.4	% Depr., Dep., Amort./Sales	4.1	3.6	2.5		1.6	
(44) 5.3	(45) 4.2	(67) 5.0		(10) 15.2	(16) 8.6	(19) 5.6		(13) 2.7	
10.1	9.2	10.0		23.7	16.4	7.9		5.6	
		.8	% Officers', Directors' Owners' Comp/Sales						
	(13)	2.3							
		7.8							
230058M	337202M	1589947M	Net Sales ($)	6541M	43270M	76981M	41530M	230582M	1191043M
299748M	301384M	614038M	Total Assets ($)	10989M	55372M	148648M	36075M	132121M	230833M

© RMA 2010

M = $ thousand   MM = $ million
See Pages 9 through 22 for Explanation of Ratios and Data

Current Data Sorted by Assets   Comparative Historical Data

0-500M	500M-2MM	2-10MM	10-50MM	50-100MM	100-250MM	Type of Statement	4/1/05-3/31/06 ALL	4/1/06-3/31/07 ALL
		1	3		2	Unqualified	11	8
	2	6	1	1		Reviewed	5	7
1	6	10	1			Compiled	11	17
8	8	1			1	Tax Returns	17	28
2	5	3	3	3		Other	9	6
	17 (4/1-9/30/09)		52 (10/1/09-3/31/10)					
11	22	21	8	4	3	**NUMBER OF STATEMENTS**	53	66
%	%	%	%	%	%	**ASSETS**	%	%
29.5	19.1	10.3				Cash & Equivalents	12.0	13.3
.3	10.7	16.1				Trade Receivables (net)	14.3	16.2
2.1	9.9	17.7				Inventory	14.9	14.0
2.5	1.7	4.8				All Other Current	3.9	5.3
34.4	41.4	48.9				Total Current	45.2	48.8
55.7	40.5	39.5				Fixed Assets (net)	44.4	39.0
.1	2.8	1.0				Intangibles (net)	2.2	2.9
9.8	15.3	10.6				All Other Non-Current	8.2	9.4
100.0	100.0	100.0				Total	100.0	100.0
						LIABILITIES		
23.8	16.5	12.9				Notes Payable-Short Term	12.0	16.8
5.6	5.8	4.3				Cur. Mat.-L.T.D.	5.6	5.7
1.0	3.6	5.2				Trade Payables	7.0	10.8
.3	.1	.0				Income Taxes Payable	.2	.2
10.1	11.7	5.5				All Other Current	7.5	8.0
40.7	37.7	28.0				Total Current	32.4	41.6
51.7	33.9	19.3				Long-Term Debt	25.5	23.8
.0	.1	.1				Deferred Taxes	.4	.3
.6	2.0	2.2				All Other Non-Current	4.4	7.2
7.0	26.3	50.4				Net Worth	37.5	27.1
100.0	100.0	100.0				Total Liabilities & Net Worth	100.0	100.0
						INCOME DATA		
100.0	100.0	100.0				Net Sales	100.0	100.0
						Gross Profit		
90.9	92.9	87.8				Operating Expenses	97.4	95.5
9.1	7.1	12.2				Operating Profit	2.6	4.5
1.9	4.1	1.6				All Other Expenses (net)	.1	1.1
7.2	3.0	10.5				Profit Before Taxes	2.6	3.4
						RATIOS		
1.9	3.4	4.3					3.2	3.6
.3	1.3	1.9				Current	1.5	1.1
.1	.7	.9					1.0	.7
1.8	3.1	3.2					2.6	2.0
.3	1.0	.9				Quick	.8	.7
.1	.2	.2					.4	.3
0 UND	0 UND	4 83.0					1 696.2	1 439.6
0 UND	9 41.5	20 18.2				Sales/Receivables	26 13.9	17 21.4
0 UND	35 10.4	41 8.8					54 6.8	46 7.9
						Cost of Sales/Inventory		
						Cost of Sales/Payables		
21.0	4.8	3.3					5.2	6.8
-39.9	21.9	7.5				Sales/Working Capital	14.2	38.8
-5.4	-32.0	NM					-230.1	-15.5
	20.7	24.7					5.2	8.9
	(19) 2.3	(19) 6.7				EBIT/Interest	(47) 1.6	(60) 3.0
	.0	3.6					.1	1.2
						Net Profit + Depr., Dep.,	5.6	15.2
						Amort./Cur. Mat. L/T/D	(12) 1.8	(10) 5.1
							.8	2.3
.6	.5	.3					.6	.4
3.0	.9	.5				Fixed/Worth	1.5	2.1
-2.1	2.4	2.3					4.3	11.5
1.2	.4	.2					.6	.8
6.1	1.7	1.1				Debt/Worth	2.1	4.0
-3.4	4.1	3.3					7.9	32.4
	41.7	37.7				% Profit Before Taxes/Tangible	39.8	71.5
	(21) 15.9	(20) 24.9				Net Worth	(49) 12.2	(54) 28.7
	.9	10.6					-7.4	6.8
54.5	14.5	16.6				% Profit Before Taxes/Total	9.8	17.4
9.6	4.8	11.5				Assets	3.1	7.5
-1.7	-.6	3.3					-2.2	.9
24.2	11.2	17.6					9.9	19.3
9.3	6.7	5.5				Sales/Net Fixed Assets	5.9	7.6
3.1	2.8	1.3					2.7	3.7
10.3	3.7	2.4					2.6	3.2
4.0	2.0	1.5				Sales/Total Assets	1.9	2.2
2.1	1.3	.9					1.3	1.5
	2.4	1.5					2.6	1.7
	(17) 5.4	(18) 6.8				% Depr., Dep., Amort./Sales	(46) 4.6	(57) 3.9
	12.9	11.9					7.1	7.2
	1.4						2.1	2.5
	(12) 4.3					% Officers', Directors'	(22) 6.9	(29) 5.0
	9.2					Owners' Comp/Sales	14.6	8.8
10892M	67005M	172722M	181145M	318007M	850583M	Net Sales ($)	1239572M	1011066M
2417M	21097M	102309M	189971M	254361M	501153M	Total Assets ($)	566282M	582563M

M = $ thousand   MM = $ million
See Pages 9 through 22 for Explanation of Ratios and Data

Comparative Historical Data / Current Data Sorted by Sales

Hist 1	Hist 2	Hist 3	Type of Statement	0-1MM	1-3MM	3-5MM	5-10MM	10-25MM	25MM & OVER
7	7	7	Unqualified		2			2	3
7	7	10	Reviewed		3			3	1
21	16	18	Compiled	6	3		3	3	4
22	12	18	Tax Returns	6	5	2	1	3	1
14	10	16	Other	3	3	2	1	3	4
4/1/07-3/31/08 ALL	4/1/08-3/31/09 ALL	4/1/09-3/31/10 ALL		17 (4/1-9/30/09)			52 (10/1/09-3/31/10)		
71	52	69	NUMBER OF STATEMENTS	15	16	6	8	15	9
%	%	%	ASSETS	%	%	%	%	%	%
12.3	13.6	16.1	Cash & Equivalents	19.4	19.3			17.4	
14.9	18.8	11.3	Trade Receivables (net)	5.7	9.9			10.2	
12.7	18.5	13.7	Inventory	1.7	10.4			19.7	
4.0	4.7	3.3	All Other Current	1.6	2.3			4.1	
43.8	55.7	44.4	Total Current	28.4	42.0			51.4	
46.3	35.3	39.8	Fixed Assets (net)	50.2	48.9			35.9	
2.8	1.1	2.1	Intangibles (net)	5.1	.1			.0	
7.1	7.9	13.7	All Other Non-Current	16.4	9.1			12.6	
100.0	100.0	100.0	Total	100.0	100.0			100.0	
			LIABILITIES						
17.8	12.2	15.5	Notes Payable-Short Term	15.5	12.3			16.0	
6.9	5.2	5.3	Cur. Mat.-L.T.D.	6.3	7.0			4.0	
9.1	9.9	4.5	Trade Payables	1.0	4.9			5.0	
.2	.2	.4	Income Taxes Payable	.2	.1			.7	
8.4	10.2	8.5	All Other Current	7.2	14.5			6.9	
42.5	37.7	34.1	Total Current	30.2	38.9			32.6	
29.0	24.9	28.8	Long-Term Debt	50.1	34.2			15.5	
.1	.5	.2	Deferred Taxes	.0	.2			.1	
3.8	2.1	2.2	All Other Non-Current	1.2	4.6			2.0	
24.6	34.8	34.7	Net Worth	18.6	22.2			49.8	
100.0	100.0	100.0	Total Liabilities & Net Worth	100.0	100.0			100.0	
			INCOME DATA						
100.0	100.0	100.0	Net Sales	100.0	100.0			100.0	
			Gross Profit						
95.0	92.8	90.2	Operating Expenses	78.4	94.8			92.4	
5.0	7.2	9.8	Operating Profit	21.6	5.2			7.6	
.9	-.1	2.0	All Other Expenses (net)	9.3	.8			-.6	
4.0	7.4	7.7	Profit Before Taxes	12.2	4.4			8.2	
			RATIOS						
2.2	3.0	2.6	Current	3.3	2.6			2.7	
1.2	1.6	1.4	Current	1.3	1.3			1.4	
.6	1.0	.6	Current	.2	.2			1.1	
1.7	1.6	2.2	Quick	3.3	2.1			1.9	
.6	.8	.7	Quick	.3	.7			.7	
.3	.3	.2	Quick	.1	.1			.2	
0 732.8	4 89.8	0 UND	Sales/Receivables	0 UND	0 UND			9 41.7	
19 19.2	27 13.5	15 23.9	Sales/Receivables	0 UND	9 41.5			18 20.1	
45 8.1	62 5.9	41 8.9	Sales/Receivables	9 41.2	39 9.3			42 8.6	
			Cost of Sales/Inventory						
			Cost of Sales/Payables						
8.3	4.7	4.8	Sales/Working Capital	3.4	7.2			5.1	
37.8	13.1	15.6	Sales/Working Capital	29.3	27.2			7.5	
-17.9	426.9	-38.7	Sales/Working Capital	-5.4	-10.8			76.8	
9.0	11.0	21.4	EBIT/Interest	4.4	9.5			113.3	
(66) 2.7	(47) 4.5	(62) 4.6	EBIT/Interest	(13) 1.8	(13) 2.4		(14)	7.6	
.7	2.0	1.7	EBIT/Interest	1.3	-.8			2.8	
11.0		6.6	Net Profit + Depr., Dep., Amort./Cur. Mat. L/T/D						
(15) 2.0	(16)	3.3	Net Profit + Depr., Dep., Amort./Cur. Mat. L/T/D						
.8		1.7	Net Profit + Depr., Dep., Amort./Cur. Mat. L/T/D						
.6	.4	.3	Fixed/Worth	.4	.5			.4	
1.8	.8	.7	Fixed/Worth	1.8	1.1			.5	
90.0	2.2	2.7	Fixed/Worth	-2.1	3.2			1.5	
.6	.7	.4	Debt/Worth	1.2	.3			.4	
4.4	2.0	1.6	Debt/Worth	2.3	1.5			1.5	
140.5	5.2	3.8	Debt/Worth	-7.0	5.0			1.9	
69.8	62.3	42.5	% Profit Before Taxes/Tangible Net Worth	113.6	27.7			53.4	
(55) 16.8	(49) 29.9	(62) 21.1	% Profit Before Taxes/Tangible Net Worth	(11) 16.3	(15) 10.5			33.8	
1.3	10.5	6.4	% Profit Before Taxes/Tangible Net Worth	2.1	.9			7.8	
13.0	22.7	16.8	% Profit Before Taxes/Total Assets	13.0	14.1			25.9	
5.0	8.8	8.1	% Profit Before Taxes/Total Assets	4.9	4.9			12.2	
-1.3	2.5	1.7	% Profit Before Taxes/Total Assets	.3	-1.2			7.5	
13.2	18.4	14.4	Sales/Net Fixed Assets	8.0	10.0			19.8	
4.9	6.8	8.6	Sales/Net Fixed Assets	3.1	5.2			11.3	
2.4	3.5	2.6	Sales/Net Fixed Assets	1.1	2.4			2.3	
3.6	3.1	2.8	Sales/Total Assets	3.3	3.2			3.2	
1.9	1.9	1.7	Sales/Total Assets	1.4	2.0			1.6	
1.2	1.4	1.1	Sales/Total Assets	.5	1.3			1.1	
1.8	1.5	1.6	% Depr., Dep., Amort./Sales	8.3	3.1			1.3	
(68) 4.9	(44) 3.6	(54) 4.8	% Depr., Dep., Amort./Sales	(10) 13.3	(13) 7.3			2.4	
11.1	10.2	10.4	% Depr., Dep., Amort./Sales	18.6	12.6			7.2	
1.6	.9	1.3	% Officers', Directors' Owners' Comp/Sales						
(27) 4.9	(21) 1.7	(22) 4.6	% Officers', Directors' Owners' Comp/Sales						
9.4	6.8	10.5	% Officers', Directors' Owners' Comp/Sales						
684447M	1384893M	1600354M	Net Sales ($)	8374M	28909M	20396M	57801M	225079M	1259795M
395444M	771715M	1071308M	Total Assets ($)	11440M	22338M	12039M	28822M	168975M	827694M

© RMA 2010

M = $ thousand   MM = $ million
See Pages 9 through 22 for Explanation of Ratios and Data

Current Data Sorted by Assets   Comparative Historical Data

Type of Statement	0-500M	500M-2MM	2-10MM	10-50MM	50-100MM	100-250MM		4/1/05-3/31/06 ALL	4/1/06-3/31/07 ALL
Unqualified			11	31	4	9		41	61
Reviewed	1		21	23	5	1		46	53
Compiled		9	13	11				32	41
Tax Returns	5	11	3		12			12	19
Other	5	11	20	17	11	8		77	55
	92 (4/1-9/30/09)			138 (10/1/09-3/31/10)					
NUMBER OF STATEMENTS	11	31	68	82	20	18		208	229
ASSETS	%	%	%	%	%	%		%	%
Cash & Equivalents	23.9	10.6	10.3	7.9	4.2	5.5		7.7	7.4
Trade Receivables (net)	18.0	19.0	21.4	19.4	12.9	17.1		19.4	21.5
Inventory	6.9	7.6	17.5	20.9	28.2	31.6		19.1	21.4
All Other Current	3.1	5.7	5.4	5.7	6.1	4.8		6.0	6.2
Total Current	51.9	43.0	54.7	54.0	51.4	58.9		52.1	56.4
Fixed Assets (net)	41.5	42.9	37.7	37.8	34.7	34.5		39.8	34.4
Intangibles (net)	.0	3.0	1.6	.8	3.4	1.3		1.6	1.2
All Other Non-Current	6.6	11.0	6.0	7.4	10.5	5.3		6.6	8.1
Total	100.0	100.0	100.0	100.0	100.0	100.0		100.0	100.0
LIABILITIES									
Notes Payable-Short Term	17.3	6.9	11.2	12.1	12.5	13.0		14.7	15.3
Cur. Mat.-L.T.D.	6.2	5.2	4.5	3.2	5.0	2.7		5.0	3.2
Trade Payables	2.0	7.7	17.7	15.0	10.9	17.8		14.2	17.0
Income Taxes Payable	.0	.1	.3	.2	.1	.2		.3	.1
All Other Current	2.4	11.6	8.4	11.1	11.9	10.8		10.9	10.3
Total Current	27.9	31.5	42.0	41.5	40.5	44.4		45.1	45.9
Long-Term Debt	27.7	25.2	21.5	17.4	19.3	16.4		22.7	19.5
Deferred Taxes	.0	.2	.7	.7	.6	.8		.6	.7
All Other Non-Current	.0	4.7	3.0	2.8	1.7	4.0		3.2	3.8
Net Worth	44.4	38.4	32.8	37.5	37.9	34.3		28.4	30.1
Total Liabilities & Net Worth	100.0	100.0	100.0	100.0	100.0	100.0		100.0	100.0
INCOME DATA									
Net Sales	100.0	100.0	100.0	100.0	100.0	100.0		100.0	100.0
Gross Profit									
Operating Expenses	86.5	88.0	94.3	90.9	93.6	93.6		92.7	93.2
Operating Profit	13.5	12.0	5.7	9.1	6.4	6.4		7.3	6.8
All Other Expenses (net)	3.0	3.3	1.6	1.2	1.2	1.1		1.8	1.1
Profit Before Taxes	10.5	8.7	4.1	7.9	5.3	5.2		5.5	5.6
RATIOS									
Current	8.0	2.0	1.9	1.6	1.6	1.5		1.7	1.8
	1.5	1.3	1.3	1.3	1.4	1.2		1.2	1.2
	.3	.6	1.0	1.0	1.0	1.1		1.0	1.0
Quick	4.7	1.6	1.3	1.0	.8	.7		1.1	1.0
	1.1	1.0	(67) .9	.6	.4	.5		.6	.6
	.3	.2	.4	.3	.2	.4		.3	.4
Sales/Receivables	0 UND	0 UND	7 50.4	23 15.6	11 32.1	22 16.7		7 52.0	14 26.1
	18 20.8	12 29.4	33 10.9	36 10.1	32 11.3	30 12.4		29 12.4	32 11.5
	42 8.7	40 9.2	52 7.0	52 7.1	50 7.2	62 5.9		47 7.7	54 6.7
Cost of Sales/Inventory									
Cost of Sales/Payables									
Sales/Working Capital	6.0	5.4	6.0	5.5	4.8	6.8		7.5	6.6
	45.6	102.9	19.0	13.6	13.6	12.9		21.4	17.3
	-4.6	-39.3	NM	NM	85.0	44.8		-128.3	NM
EBIT/Interest	16.0	27.9	7.7	16.6	8.8	12.1		7.9	7.5
	(10) 4.5	(27) 4.0	(66) 3.4	(78) 4.9	4.2	3.9		(193) 3.5	(215) 2.9
	-9.0	.6	1.0	1.4	2.0	1.8		1.3	1.3
Net Profit + Depr., Dep., Amort./Cur. Mat. L/T/D			7.5	21.3				3.9	9.1
			(21) 2.5	(31) 5.1				(59) 2.4	(71) 3.2
			.8	1.8				1.7	1.3
Fixed/Worth	.5	.1	.5	.4	.4	.7		.6	.5
	.6	1.1	.9	1.0	.9	1.0		1.2	.9
	6.1	4.1	2.3	2.0	1.7	1.7		2.7	1.7
Debt/Worth	.5	.4	.9	.9	1.1	1.5		1.0	1.1
	.9	1.0	2.1	1.6	1.8	1.9		2.2	2.0
	5.4	7.5	6.0	3.0	4.1	3.0		8.9	4.7
% Profit Before Taxes/Tangible Net Worth		61.3	34.7	36.9	29.3	27.2		42.8	32.8
	(25) 10.0	(62) 15.7	(76) 18.4	(19) 25.0	(17) 16.8			(181) 19.9	(212) 17.6
		-9.0	1.4	5.4	6.5	8.2		6.2	4.8
% Profit Before Taxes/Total Assets	38.5	18.7	11.4	12.7	11.1	11.3		12.9	12.4
	20.9	5.4	5.6	6.3	5.3	5.7		5.9	5.3
	-5.4	-5.4	.2	1.2	2.3	2.2		1.0	.8
Sales/Net Fixed Assets	63.2	64.2	13.0	13.1	18.9	9.4		13.5	14.5
	7.4	7.5	6.7	5.0	6.8	7.0		6.1	7.0
	1.4	2.4	1.8	1.7	1.2	2.6		2.4	3.0
Sales/Total Assets	9.7	5.9	2.9	2.5	2.0	2.3		3.4	3.0
	4.1	1.7	1.8	1.4	1.1	1.8		1.9	1.8
	1.2	.9	1.0	.8	.9	1.1		1.1	1.0
% Depr., Dep., Amort./Sales		2.1	1.1	1.2	1.3	1.1		1.2	1.0
	(24) 4.2	(62) 2.3	(78) 2.1	(17) 2.4	(14) 1.4			(184) 2.4	(209) 1.9
		10.5	4.3	6.3	5.8	1.7		5.5	4.2
% Officers', Directors' Owners' Comp/Sales			1.2	.5				1.0	1.1
		(16) 1.9	(16) 1.9					(46) 2.1	(53) 2.1
			4.2	1.9				4.6	4.3
Net Sales ($)	13076M	114927M	842676M	3355706M	1870745M	5604964M		8840560M	10279836M
Total Assets ($)	3137M	37733M	393466M	1991848M	1348815M	2937775M		4349892M	5184469M

© RMA 2010

M = $ thousand   MM = $ million
See Pages 9 through 22 for Explanation of Ratios and Data

Comparative Historical Data				Current Data Sorted by Sales					
			Type of Statement						
47	48	55	Unqualified				3	17	35
55	55	51	Reviewed		2	1	9	17	22
49	42	33	Compiled	5	5	3	7	9	4
11	18	19	Tax Returns	4	7	3	3	2	
58	73	72	Other	6	10	7	4	16	29
4/1/07-3/31/08 ALL	4/1/08-3/31/09 ALL	4/1/09-3/31/10 ALL		92 (4/1-9/30/09)			138 (10/1/09-3/31/10)		
				0-1MM	1-3MM	3-5MM	5-10MM	10-25MM	25MM & OVER
220	236	230	**NUMBER OF STATEMENTS**	15	24	14	26	61	90
%	%	%	**ASSETS**	%	%	%	%	%	%
8.8	8.6	9.3	Cash & Equivalents	16.0	10.5	7.5	11.5	9.0	7.6
19.0	20.3	19.2	Trade Receivables (net)	16.3	14.1	8.3	24.7	20.4	20.2
20.5	19.8	18.9	Inventory	5.5	7.5	6.8	18.9	18.0	26.7
6.1	5.8	5.5	All Other Current	3.1	4.6	9.8	4.9	6.8	4.7
54.3	54.5	52.8	Total Current	40.9	36.7	32.3	60.0	54.2	59.2
36.7	36.7	38.1	Fixed Assets (net)	43.0	50.6	65.0	34.4	35.3	32.7
1.1	1.3	1.6	Intangibles (net)	4.0	1.4	.4	.3	2.1	1.4
7.8	7.4	7.5	All Other Non-Current	12.0	11.2	2.3	5.4	8.4	6.7
100.0	100.0	100.0	Total	100.0	100.0	100.0	100.0	100.0	100.0
			LIABILITIES						
14.5	12.4	11.5	Notes Payable-Short Term	6.3	9.9	6.9	14.7	12.1	12.2
3.6	4.3	4.1	Cur. Mat.-L.T.D.	8.1	4.4	7.0	4.3	3.2	3.5
13.4	14.5	14.1	Trade Payables	5.4	3.4	5.7	13.6	17.9	17.2
.2	.3	.2	Income Taxes Payable	.0	.1	.0	.0	.4	.2
11.3	10.6	10.0	All Other Current	7.2	9.9	10.3	8.5	9.6	11.1
43.0	42.0	39.8	Total Current	26.9	27.6	29.9	41.1	43.2	44.1
18.9	17.7	20.3	Long-Term Debt	29.6	36.1	29.5	21.4	15.3	16.0
.7	.6	.6	Deferred Taxes	.0	.3	.0	1.2	.9	.6
2.8	3.6	3.0	All Other Non-Current	1.3	6.1	4.6	2.6	3.0	2.3
34.6	36.0	36.3	Net Worth	42.1	29.8	35.9	33.7	37.7	37.0
100.0	100.0	100.0	Total Liabilties & Net Worth	100.0	100.0	100.0	100.0	100.0	100.0
			INCOME DATA						
100.0	100.0	100.0	Net Sales	100.0	100.0	100.0	100.0	100.0	100.0
			Gross Profit						
92.6	91.0	91.8	Operating Expenses	76.3	85.9	92.6	95.0	92.7	94.2
7.4	9.0	8.2	Operating Profit	23.7	14.1	7.4	5.0	7.3	5.8
1.8	1.4	1.6	All Other Expenses (net)	8.5	3.0	2.5	1.5	.7	.7
5.6	7.6	6.6	Profit Before Taxes	15.1	11.1	4.9	3.5	6.6	5.1
			RATIOS						
1.8	1.8	1.8	Current	2.0	3.8	2.4	2.5	1.6	1.7
1.2	1.3	1.3		1.2	1.1	1.3	1.4	1.3	1.4
1.0	1.0	1.0		.4	.4	.6	1.0	1.0	1.1
1.1	1.1	1.2	Quick	1.9	2.8	1.5	1.4	1.0	.9
.6	(235) .6	(229) .6		.4	(23) 1.0	.7	1.0	.7	.5
.3	.3	.3		.1	.2	.1	.6	.3	.3
12 31.5	12 31.4	11 32.4	Sales/Receivables	0 UND	0 UND	0 UND	16 22.4	16 23.1	22 16.7
30 12.2	30 12.0	32 11.3		32 11.3	8 43.6	4 99.9	41 9.0	36 10.3	31 12.0
52 7.1	60 6.1	50 7.2		123 3.0	41 8.8	43 8.5	81 4.5	61 6.0	47 7.8
			Cost of Sales/Inventory						
			Cost of Sales/Payables						
6.4	6.7	5.9	Sales/Working Capital	2.3	3.5	7.8	5.9	6.7	6.8
19.1	19.1	15.7		11.0	52.4	86.0	12.5	20.3	12.9
-499.5	-228.5	-174.6		-4.6	-6.6	-36.8	-445.6	152.8	63.1
7.0	12.5	11.4	EBIT/Interest	27.5	14.8	2.4	6.7	16.3	10.9
(209) 3.1	(225) 3.5	(219) 4.1		(12) 4.2	(23) 2.1	(13) 1.3	3.6	(58) 5.5	(87) 4.4
1.3	1.7	1.4		-3.5	.6	-.6	1.3	1.6	2.0
7.8	8.8	9.5	Net Profit + Depr., Dep., Amort./Cur. Mat. L/T/D					9.8	12.9
(75) 3.7	(82) 3.6	(73) 3.4						(23) 5.1	(35) 3.3
1.1	1.3	1.4						1.9	1.8
.5	.5	.5	Fixed/Worth	.0	.5	1.3	.5	.5	.4
1.0	.9	1.0		1.1	2.0	1.9	.9	.9	.9
2.0	1.8	2.0		6.1	NM	5.2	2.4	1.6	1.6
.9	.9	.9	Debt/Worth	.8	.4	.7	.6	.9	1.1
2.0	1.8	1.7		1.3	2.4	2.3	1.8	1.7	1.7
4.8	4.6	3.6		5.4	NM	17.5	34.0	3.1	2.8
36.4	40.8	35.6	% Profit Before Taxes/Tangible Net Worth	60.4	41.4	33.1	34.5	37.9	33.8
(201) 18.5	(215) 20.1	(208) 16.7		(13) 9.9	(18) 5.9	3.2	(22) 15.1	(57) 20.8	(84) 16.0
5.3	7.9	4.6		-18.5	-9.5	-13.1	5.7	9.5	6.5
11.9	13.4	12.2	% Profit Before Taxes/Total Assets	33.4	19.8	6.5	9.3	13.9	11.9
5.5	6.3	5.8		3.3	5.0	1.0	6.6	8.2	5.8
1.0	1.4	.9		-5.4	-4.4	-3.7	.6	1.1	2.2
14.5	17.3	14.2	Sales/Net Fixed Assets	147.0	5.3	7.0	22.1	13.0	16.0
6.5	6.3	6.1		4.4	2.3	2.3	9.0	6.2	8.6
2.3	2.2	1.9		.6	.6	1.3	1.9	1.9	4.1
2.9	3.0	2.7	Sales/Total Assets	1.3	1.9	5.3	2.9	2.7	3.0
1.7	1.7	1.6		.4	1.1	1.5	1.4	1.3	2.1
1.0	.9	.9		.3	.4	.7	.8	.9	1.2
1.1	.9	1.2	% Depr., Dep., Amort./Sales	5.6	2.5	.7	1.1	1.2	1.0
(200) 2.1	(208) 2.0	(204) 2.3		(11) 7.8	(21) 6.6	(13) 7.1	(24) 2.4	(56) 2.5	(79) 1.6
4.7	6.1	5.8		27.2	17.4	7.9	5.3	5.5	2.8
.8	1.0	.8	% Officers', Directors' Owners' Comp/Sales					.8	.4
(41) 1.2	(43) 1.3	(44) 1.5						(14) 1.5	(12) 1.0
3.0	3.1	4.1						5.4	1.7
8374995M	11506260M	11802094M	Net Sales ($)	7006M	45376M	59087M	193157M	988495M	10508973M
5006363M	5797190M	6712774M	Total Assets ($)	17098M	77200M	55254M	173801M	840903M	5548518M

M = $ thousand   MM = $ million
See Pages 9 through 22 for Explanation of Ratios and Data

Current Data Sorted by Assets

Comparative Historical Data

							Type of Statement		
			3	4	3	2	Unqualified	13	14
	2		4	2			Reviewed	6	7
4	10		9				Compiled	11	15
16	9		5	1			Tax Returns	14	28
3	10		12	4	1	2	Other	14	11
	16 (4/1-9/30/09)			90 (10/1/09-3/31/10)				4/1/05-3/31/06	4/1/06-3/31/07
0-500M	500M-2MM	2-10MM		10-50MM	50-100MM	100-250MM		ALL	ALL
23	31	33		11	4	4	NUMBER OF STATEMENTS	58	75
%	%	%		%	%	%	ASSETS	%	%
21.5	8.7	7.4		8.6			Cash & Equivalents	14.9	11.0
9.2	14.0	30.1		13.0			Trade Receivables (net)	18.7	19.5
10.4	21.1	15.5		25.9			Inventory	17.6	16.4
3.8	.6	3.1		3.6			All Other Current	3.8	2.9
44.7	44.4	56.2		51.1			Total Current	55.0	49.8
28.5	42.7	33.1		42.2			Fixed Assets (net)	33.9	36.3
5.1	6.5	4.3		3.0			Intangibles (net)	2.8	3.4
21.6	6.5	6.4		3.7			All Other Non-Current	8.3	10.4
100.0	100.0	100.0		100.0			Total	100.0	100.0
							LIABILITIES		
45.4	10.9	17.6		9.2			Notes Payable-Short Term	11.4	13.3
10.6	6.1	1.8		1.2			Cur. Mat.-L.T.D.	1.8	3.6
15.4	11.1	17.1		9.9			Trade Payables	12.2	10.9
.3	.0	.2		.0			Income Taxes Payable	.4	.2
20.3	6.6	6.4		7.2			All Other Current	10.5	13.9
91.9	34.7	43.1		27.5			Total Current	36.3	42.0
45.5	33.5	19.0		11.8			Long-Term Debt	19.3	24.5
.0	.0	.6		.2			Deferred Taxes	.4	.2
5.6	4.7	1.1		1.3			All Other Non-Current	5.5	4.1
-43.0	27.1	36.2		59.2			Net Worth	38.5	29.1
100.0	100.0	100.0		100.0			Total Liabilities & Net Worth	100.0	100.0
							INCOME DATA		
100.0	100.0	100.0		100.0			Net Sales	100.0	100.0
							Gross Profit		
97.3	95.6	93.2		91.4			Operating Expenses	92.3	92.6
2.7	4.4	6.8		8.6			Operating Profit	7.7	7.4
1.2	2.1	.5		-2.3			All Other Expenses (net)	1.1	2.0
1.5	2.3	6.3		10.9			Profit Before Taxes	6.6	5.4
							RATIOS		
1.4	3.9	1.8		3.1				4.0	2.8
.7	1.5	1.3		2.0			Current	1.6	1.3
.1	.3	1.1		1.5				1.0	.6
1.3	1.6	1.4		1.3				2.4	1.6
.3	.6	.7		.7			Quick	.9	.8
.1	.2	.4		.4				.4	.3
0 UND	2 242.3	16 23.3		19 19.0				1 267.1	2 200.1
0 UND	9 40.3	34 10.6		24 15.2			Sales/Receivables	21 17.1	23 16.1
10 36.5	33 11.2	55 6.7		44 8.4				42 8.6	50 7.3
							Cost of Sales/Inventory		
							Cost of Sales/Payables		
76.7	7.2	8.3		4.7				5.3	5.4
-32.6	50.0	32.7		5.8			Sales/Working Capital	12.9	26.1
-7.4	-16.9	590.9		24.0				-130.3	-13.4
9.5	7.6	10.3		355.3				15.9	8.0
(18) 2.0	(27) 1.6	(26) 3.5		(10) 49.2			EBIT/Interest	(44) 4.8	(60) 3.1
-4.0	-.2	1.4		2.9				1.3	1.6
							Net Profit + Depr., Dep., Amort./Cur. Mat. L/T/D		
.2	.2	.2		.3				.2	.3
1.6	1.2	.6		.6			Fixed/Worth	.5	.8
-.3	3.0	1.7		.9				2.0	3.5
.7	1.1	1.0		.3				.4	.5
18.4	2.4	2.1		.6			Debt/Worth	1.2	2.4
-1.9	7.0	4.0		1.1				4.6	10.2
338.1	61.2	42.0		24.5				32.2	49.9
(13) 57.4	(24) 10.1	(30) 11.9		(10) 11.5			% Profit Before Taxes/Tangible Net Worth	(51) 20.8	(63) 18.6
-6.7	-8.7	2.0		3.2				2.2	4.5
44.3	18.0	11.7		15.6				14.8	11.6
6.9	3.7	4.0		6.5			% Profit Before Taxes/Total Assets	7.5	6.3
-4.6	-2.2	1.0		4.1				.9	1.4
67.0	64.1	36.8		10.2				31.4	27.4
35.3	8.1	8.9		4.5			Sales/Net Fixed Assets	9.8	6.6
15.6	2.1	2.5		.9				3.0	2.5
12.4	3.8	4.9		2.5				4.0	3.1
6.0	2.5	2.3		1.6			Sales/Total Assets	2.2	2.1
3.7	1.2	.8		.6				1.2	.9
.5	.5	.7		1.6				1.4	1.1
(15) 1.7	(23) 1.9	(23) 2.0		(10) 4.2			% Depr., Dep., Amort./Sales	(49) 3.1	(63) 2.7
2.4	6.5	4.2		4.9				5.6	5.5
5.0	1.6	.8						2.2	1.7
(13) 8.2	(19) 2.5	(14) 2.1					% Officers', Directors' Owners' Comp/Sales	(19) 4.4	(35) 3.8
19.8	6.9	5.5						13.5	12.4
37672M	102723M	586613M		441567M	647289M	769402M	Net Sales ($)	1837641M	1892459M
4201M	34306M	142266M		248256M	283952M	626848M	Total Assets ($)	977870M	954633M

© RMA 2010

M = $ thousand   MM = $ million
See Pages 9 through 22 for Explanation of Ratios and Data

Comparative Historical Data | Current Data Sorted by Sales

	14	13	12	Type of Statement	0-1MM	1-3MM	3-5MM	5-10MM	10-25MM	25MM & OVER
	14	13	12	Unqualified			2		3	7
	9	9	8	Reviewed		2		1	3	2
	13	11	23	Compiled	2	10	3	3	2	3
	22	24	31	Tax Returns	12	7	2	5	5	
	22	28	32	Other	8	6	4	4	4	6
	4/1/07-3/31/08 ALL	4/1/08-3/31/09 ALL	4/1/09-3/31/10 ALL		16 (4/1-9/30/09)			90 (10/1/09-3/31/10)		
	80	85	106	NUMBER OF STATEMENTS	22	25	11	13	17	18
	%	%	%	ASSETS	%	%	%	%	%	%
	11.8	9.5	10.6	Cash & Equivalents	14.3	9.2	9.7	16.7	11.0	3.8
	19.6	16.0	18.9	Trade Receivables (net)	6.1	12.3	22.9	23.9	26.9	30.2
	14.7	17.8	17.0	Inventory	9.7	20.4	6.2	22.8	17.3	23.4
	3.5	3.3	2.8	All Other Current	1.8	2.4	.2	2.7	4.1	4.8
	49.6	46.7	49.3	Total Current	31.9	44.3	39.1	66.1	59.2	62.2
	37.6	39.3	34.9	Fixed Assets (net)	44.2	35.6	49.9	27.1	33.2	20.4
	3.1	5.9	5.9	Intangibles (net)	7.4	9.8	.1	2.5	2.7	8.0
	9.6	8.1	9.9	All Other Non-Current	16.6	10.3	10.9	4.3	4.8	9.5
	100.0	100.0	100.0	Total	100.0	100.0	100.0	100.0	100.0	100.0
				LIABILITIES						
	11.4	12.5	19.9	Notes Payable-Short Term	21.3	15.1	13.2	50.8	12.9	13.3
	2.2	3.9	4.8	Cur. Mat.-L.T.D.	13.2	4.8	2.7	2.9	.9	1.2
	13.1	11.0	13.5	Trade Payables	11.6	11.4	7.1	20.9	10.3	20.2
	.2	.2	.2	Income Taxes Payable	.3	.0	.0	.1	.3	.2
	11.3	11.7	9.7	All Other Current	16.1	9.1	9.6	5.3	9.1	6.3
	38.1	39.2	48.0	Total Current	62.5	40.4	32.6	79.9	33.5	41.1
	21.6	28.3	28.1	Long-Term Debt	64.4	31.3	20.3	17.4	11.8	7.0
	.4	.4	.4	Deferred Taxes	.0	.0	.0	.4	.5	1.6
	4.3	3.8	3.4	All Other Non-Current	3.8	4.6	7.0	1.4	.7	3.3
	35.6	28.2	20.1	Net Worth	-30.7	23.8	40.1	.9	53.5	47.1
	100.0	100.0	100.0	Total Liabilities & Net Worth	100.0	100.0	100.0	100.0	100.0	100.0
				INCOME DATA						
	100.0	100.0	100.0	Net Sales	100.0	100.0	100.0	100.0	100.0	100.0
				Gross Profit						
	89.7	90.7	94.2	Operating Expenses	93.8	92.7	88.1	96.0	97.8	95.8
	10.3	9.3	5.8	Operating Profit	6.2	7.3	11.9	4.0	2.2	4.2
	2.2	3.7	.8	All Other Expenses (net)	2.8	2.0	-1.1	.3	-1.0	-.3
	8.1	5.6	5.0	Profit Before Taxes	3.3	5.3	13.0	3.7	3.2	4.5
				RATIOS						
	2.8	2.2	2.0		.8	2.7	4.4	2.1	3.1	1.8
	1.5	1.3	1.4	Current	.2	1.4	1.1	1.6	1.8	1.6
	1.0	.7	.4		.1	.4	.4	1.3	1.3	1.3
	1.6	1.3	1.4		.6	1.4	4.4	1.9	2.3	1.2
	.9	.7	.7	Quick	.2	.5	.6	.7	1.4	.9
	.4	.3	.2		.1	.2	.4	.4	.6	.6
	7 / 53.5	1 / 275.2	3 / 120.9		0 / UND	0 / UND	9 / 40.3	7 / 52.8	7 / 53.6	17 / 22.0
	26 / 13.9	21 / 17.4	19 / 19.0	Sales/Receivables	0 / UND	13 / 27.3	32 / 11.4	27 / 13.5	34 / 10.6	24 / 15.5
	47 / 7.7	41 / 8.9	40 / 9.2		14 / 26.1	42 / 8.8	43 / 8.5	48 / 7.6	45 / 8.1	45 / 8.2
				Cost of Sales/Inventory						
				Cost of Sales/Payables						
	4.7	5.9	7.2		-185.6	5.8	8.5	5.6	6.4	6.9
	15.2	27.5	34.2	Sales/Working Capital	-14.7	50.0	135.4	15.2	21.8	16.3
	-160.1	-18.8	-17.5		-2.9	-15.4	-10.2	60.7	45.0	51.0
	12.1	16.8	12.5		3.0	13.3		8.2	33.5	32.6
	(62) 3.6	(69) 3.1	(88) 3.3	EBIT/Interest	(14) .8	(22) 2.2		(11) 2.3	4.6	(17) 5.9
	1.3	.9	.8		-5.0	-.4		1.4	1.3	2.5
		10.7		Net Profit + Depr., Dep., Amort./Cur. Mat. L/T/D						
		(10) 4.8								
		.8								
	.3	.3	.3		.1	.2	.6	.2	.3	.3
	.8	.9	.7	Fixed/Worth	UND	1.1	1.6	.5	.6	.5
	2.0	6.4	3.5		-1.3	15.7	2.4	1.4	1.3	.9
	.5	.7	.7		.7	1.2	1.1	.7	.4	.6
	1.4	1.9	2.1	Debt/Worth	-4.4	3.6	1.9	2.1	1.1	1.8
	4.4	12.0	11.7		-2.5	-9.6	2.8	3.0	2.2	4.2
	35.3	49.2	48.5		64.1	82.1	99.0	21.8	32.5	50.4
	(71) 14.8	(70) 13.1	(84) 10.7	% Profit Before Taxes/Tangible Net Worth	(10) 6.8	(18) 8.4	36.1	(11) 11.1	7.0	(17) 20.4
	4.8	.5	.4		-8.3	-11.9	2.7	2.0	1.5	-1.0
	14.7	18.7	17.8		17.5	19.8	27.4	16.0	12.9	16.3
	5.7	4.3	4.4	% Profit Before Taxes/Total Assets	2.0	4.1	13.5	6.6	2.5	6.5
	1.0	-.3	-.4		-8.1	-2.0	.9	1.7	.7	-.1
	16.4	21.5	44.1		57.0	146.6	9.1	69.8	25.0	53.9
	5.4	6.0	10.3	Sales/Net Fixed Assets	11.3	7.9	8.1	29.0	8.9	18.4
	2.5	1.7	4.2		.9	1.8	1.3	9.0	5.0	4.8
	2.7	3.2	4.7		5.0	3.1	4.3	6.6	5.7	6.5
	1.7	1.7	2.5	Sales/Total Assets	2.4	1.7	3.4	3.3	2.4	3.1
	.7	.6	1.4		.7	.7	.8	2.0	1.8	1.6
	1.4	1.4	.7		1.7	.5		.5	.8	.5
	(63) 2.9	(71) 3.0	(78) 1.9	% Depr., Dep., Amort./Sales	(13) 2.4	(17) 2.9		(11) .8	(16) 2.5	(14) 1.5
	6.2	6.3	4.5		9.6	5.4		1.7	4.5	3.6
	1.0	1.5	1.8			2.9				
	(27) 3.6	(31) 3.1	(47) 4.8	% Officers', Directors' Owners' Comp/Sales		(16) 5.3				
	13.4	8.0	9.1			9.2				
	2130115M	2571115M	2585266M	Net Sales ($)	11313M	47073M	42508M	100292M	255057M	2129023M
	1580938M	1344095M	1339829M	Total Assets ($)	12081M	42459M	132927M	46117M	131016M	975229M

M = $ thousand   MM = $ million
See Pages 9 through 22 for Explanation of Ratios and Data

MINING

Current Data Sorted by Assets   Comparative Historical Data

						Type of Statement		
		7	17	14	23	Unqualified	55	65
	1	4	3	1		Reviewed	17	11
1	4	5	4	1		Compiled	9	19
3	7	6				Tax Returns	8	12
2	15	25	30	13	22	Other	97	122
							4/1/05- 3/31/06	4/1/06- 3/31/07
	24 (4/1-9/30/09)		184 (10/1/09-3/31/10)				ALL	ALL
0-500M	500M-2MM	2-10MM	10-50MM	50-100MM	100-250MM	NUMBER OF STATEMENTS	186	229
6	27	47	54	29	45			
%	%	%	%	%	%	ASSETS	%	%
	11.0	16.2	7.6	10.1	6.2	Cash & Equivalents	11.0	11.3
	24.0	15.0	7.3	6.3	5.3	Trade Receivables (net)	15.9	12.3
	5.2	1.5	3.2	3.5	1.0	Inventory	2.7	1.5
	10.3	9.1	4.0	4.8	4.1	All Other Current	3.1	4.8
	50.5	41.8	22.1	24.7	16.6	Total Current	32.7	29.9
	38.1	37.3	68.0	61.6	71.1	Fixed Assets (net)	55.2	58.6
	1.6	2.8	3.2	1.7	2.2	Intangibles (net)	1.0	1.1
	9.8	18.1	6.7	12.1	10.1	All Other Non-Current	11.1	10.4
	100.0	100.0	100.0	100.0	100.0	Total	100.0	100.0
						LIABILITIES		
	5.5	10.1	4.0	.9	1.2	Notes Payable-Short Term	5.5	6.7
	2.4	4.7	5.2	2.2	1.9	Cur. Mat.-L.T.D.	2.5	2.6
	11.9	9.5	6.6	6.1	4.4	Trade Payables	12.1	11.0
	.0	.0	.1	.2	.1	Income Taxes Payable	.1	.1
	11.7	8.6	6.2	4.6	6.3	All Other Current	6.9	7.1
	31.6	32.8	22.1	14.0	13.9	Total Current	27.0	27.5
	52.6	19.6	22.2	28.9	38.1	Long-Term Debt	20.2	21.7
	.0	.1	1.2	1.9	.9	Deferred Taxes	.8	1.6
	3.7	7.2	6.8	6.2	8.8	All Other Non-Current	5.4	4.5
	12.1	40.3	47.8	49.0	38.3	Net Worth	46.6	44.8
	100.0	100.0	100.0	100.0	100.0	Total Liabilities & Net Worth	100.0	100.0
						INCOME DATA		
	100.0	100.0	100.0	100.0	100.0	Net Sales	100.0	100.0
	49.1	54.8	51.7	54.6	63.3	Gross Profit	57.9	59.4
	37.0	40.2	42.0	44.2	52.6	Operating Expenses	29.3	32.4
	12.1	14.6	9.7	10.3	10.7	Operating Profit	28.6	27.0
	3.8	.8	5.0	7.1	8.0	All Other Expenses (net)	3.8	2.0
	8.3	13.9	4.8	3.2	2.7	Profit Before Taxes	24.9	25.0
						RATIOS		
	2.9	3.9	3.1	3.3	2.5		3.0	2.2
	1.2	1.2	1.3	1.5	1.5	Current	1.3	1.2
	.8	.7	.6	.9	.8		.7	.6
	2.4	3.3	2.4	2.8	1.6		2.5	1.9
	.9	.8	1.0	.9	.8	Quick	1.1	.9
	.4	.4	.4	.5	.6		.5	.4
	0 UND	0 UND	13 27.8	23 16.2	34 10.9		5 74.3	8 47.0
	17 21.5	22 16.7	37 9.9	46 7.9	44 8.2	Sales/Receivables	44 8.4	37 9.8
	69 5.3	66 5.5	57 6.4	89 4.1	63 5.8		79 4.6	62 5.9
	0 UND	0 UND	0 UND	0 UND	0 UND		0 UND	0 UND
	0 UND	0 UND	0 UND	0 UND	0 UND	Cost of Sales/Inventory	0 UND	0 UND
	8 44.3	3 108.4	23 16.1	22 16.8	29 12.5		4 101.4	2 203.5
	5 74.7	0 UND	9 40.6	17 21.0	28 12.8		6 56.6	15 24.4
	24 15.2	22 16.6	35 10.5	53 6.9	62 5.9	Cost of Sales/Payables	52 7.0	72 5.1
	46 7.9	96 3.8	80 4.6	221 1.7	147 2.5		206 1.8	197 1.9
	4.9	2.7	4.8	2.1	4.3		7.0	6.4
	46.1	15.2	17.2	11.2	10.6	Sales/Working Capital	21.2	30.6
	-16.6	-9.3	-8.8	-397.6	-16.4		-13.3	-10.6
	18.0	17.8	18.1	5.1	4.7		27.2	44.8
	(19) 5.0	(36) 5.2	(48) 3.0	(25) 1.4	(42) 1.7	EBIT/Interest	(149) 9.8	(183) 9.1
	-.5	1.3	-1.1	-2.8	-.7		3.2	2.9
			112.4				100.0	373.2
		(12) 7.6				Net Profit + Depr., Dep., Amort./Cur. Mat. L/T/D	(20) 3.6	(28) 35.8
		.1					2.3	2.7
	.2	.2	.9	.8	1.5		.5	.7
	.8	.6	1.6	1.7	2.1	Fixed/Worth	1.2	1.3
	5.8	1.6	2.1	3.1	4.2		2.3	2.8
	.2	.3	.4	.2	.8		.4	.4
	2.0	.9	1.1	1.2	1.4	Debt/Worth	1.2	1.1
	21.8	2.5	2.5	4.3	5.6		3.5	3.8
	45.7	47.4	29.8	13.4	15.3	% Profit Before Taxes/Tangible Net Worth	56.8	58.9
	(21) 15.6	(43) 10.7	(49) 12.4	(28) -.1	(41) 1.4		(171) 37.6	(208) 33.1
	2.2	1.1	-3.8	-5.2	-15.5		13.5	16.8
	25.0	24.8	13.7	6.2	6.4	% Profit Before Taxes/Total Assets	27.8	29.0
	10.0	6.5	3.7	.0	.8		12.5	14.4
	-.6	.5	-2.4	-3.1	-4.2		4.0	5.1
	22.3	15.9	2.1	2.2	.9		6.3	3.4
	4.7	3.0	.7	.5	.4	Sales/Net Fixed Assets	1.5	1.1
	1.9	1.2	.3	.3	.2		.6	.5
	3.5	1.6	1.0	.6	.5		2.1	1.4
	1.7	.8	.5	.3	.3	Sales/Total Assets	.7	.7
	.7	.4	.2	.2	.2		.4	.3
	1.1	3.6	7.3	6.7	21.0		2.4	4.2
	(14) 12.4	(33) 8.2	(49) 17.2	(23) 25.9	(11) 23.8	% Depr., Dep., Amort./Sales	(133) 8.1	(163) 8.6
	18.6	14.9	32.3	37.0	36.1		16.0	17.9
							1.2	.7
						% Officers', Directors' Owners' Comp/Sales	(25) 3.0	(19) 3.0
							4.2	5.1
	4189M	100276M	555764M	1265104M	1592530M	3627784M	Net Sales ($)	7188216M	9850729M
	1329M	36496M	251824M	1400556M	2108797M	7852377M	Total Assets ($)	7887246M	10591730M

M = $ thousand   MM = $ million
See Pages 9 through 22 for Explanation of Ratios and Data

Comparative Historical Data

Current Data Sorted by Sales

			Type of Statement						
57	59	61	Unqualified		3	4	7	19	28
7	12	9	Reviewed			1	3		5
14	16	15	Compiled	3	3	3	3	1	2
14	16	16	Tax Returns	3	8	3	1	1	
105	112	107	Other	10	15	11	13	22	36
4/1/07-3/31/08 ALL	4/1/08-3/31/09 ALL	4/1/09-3/31/10 ALL		0-1MM	24 (4/1-9/30/09) 1-3MM	3-5MM	184 (10/1/09-3/31/10) 5-10MM	10-25MM	25MM & OVER
197	215	208	NUMBER OF STATEMENTS	16	29	22	27	43	71
%	%	%	ASSETS	%	%	%	%	%	%
10.2	10.3	10.5	Cash & Equivalents	9.0	15.6	14.4	9.0	10.5	8.1
15.4	12.3	11.2	Trade Receivables (net)	16.3	11.2	12.0	12.8	11.7	8.8
1.8	2.2	2.6	Inventory	3.0	2.3	2.7	1.0	.9	4.2
4.0	5.5	6.0	All Other Current	9.3	11.0	2.3	4.6	5.4	5.2
31.3	30.3	30.2	Total Current	37.7	40.1	31.3	27.4	28.5	26.3
56.2	59.1	56.3	Fixed Assets (net)	41.7	48.6	49.1	59.3	61.8	60.3
2.0	1.8	2.4	Intangibles (net)	2.5	.8	1.5	2.8	3.1	2.7
10.5	8.8	11.1	All Other Non-Current	18.1	10.5	18.0	10.5	6.6	10.7
100.0	100.0	100.0	Total	100.0	100.0	100.0	100.0	100.0	100.0
			LIABILITIES						
6.8	6.3	5.0	Notes Payable-Short Term	11.9	8.6	7.1	4.6	4.0	2.2
3.2	3.4	3.5	Cur. Mat.-L.T.D.	2.2	1.8	3.6	2.6	7.4	2.3
10.7	10.0	7.6	Trade Payables	3.0	11.9	5.1	4.6	9.7	7.5
.4	.1	.1	Income Taxes Payable	.0	.0	.0	.0	.1	.2
7.4	6.9	7.4	All Other Current	17.4	9.8	4.7	4.0	4.9	7.9
28.4	26.8	23.6	Total Current	34.4	32.2	20.5	15.7	26.0	20.1
25.0	23.6	29.8	Long-Term Debt	19.2	37.1	26.1	25.2	35.0	28.9
.9	.9	.8	Deferred Taxes	.0	.0	.2	.5	1.3	1.3
7.6	4.9	6.6	All Other Non-Current	.5	2.3	8.4	2.5	4.7	12.0
38.1	43.8	39.2	Net Worth	45.9	28.5	44.8	56.1	33.0	37.7
100.0	100.0	100.0	Total Liabilities & Net Worth	100.0	100.0	100.0	100.0	100.0	100.0
			INCOME DATA						
100.0	100.0	100.0	Net Sales	100.0	100.0	100.0	100.0	100.0	100.0
57.0	59.7	54.8	Gross Profit	59.8	60.6	62.5	58.8	51.0	49.8
33.4	35.1	43.5	Operating Expenses	52.2	43.2	56.3	40.8	39.3	41.4
23.6	24.7	11.3	Operating Profit	7.6	17.4	6.2	18.0	11.7	8.4
4.4	4.6	4.8	All Other Expenses (net)	2.9	3.6	2.7	6.7	6.3	4.7
19.2	20.1	6.5	Profit Before Taxes	4.7	13.9	3.4	11.3	5.4	3.7
			RATIOS						
2.7	3.0	3.0	Current	1.4	3.6	5.8	8.4	2.2	2.4
1.2	1.4	1.3		1.1	1.3	2.8	2.6	1.1	1.3
.7	.6	.8		.4	.7	.4	.8	.7	.9
1.9	2.2	2.1	Quick	1.2	2.7	5.7	6.5	1.9	1.5
1.0	.9	.9		.8	.7	1.6	2.4	1.0	.8
.5	.4	.4		.1	.4	.3	.6	.5	.6
13 27.5 / 7 50.6 / 11 32.7			Sales/Receivables	0 UND	0 UND	0 UND	15 24.5	27 13.3	20 17.9
42 8.8 / 23 15.7 / 40 9.2				20 17.9	24 15.5	23 16.1	39 9.2	54 6.8	39 9.3
76 4.8 / 47 7.8 / 63 5.8				64 5.7	76 4.8	66 5.5	60 6.1	81 4.5	50 7.3
0 UND / 0 UND / 0 UND			Cost of Sales/Inventory	0 UND	0 UND	0 UND	0 UND	0 UND	0 UND
0 UND / 0 UND / 0 UND				0 UND	0 UND	4 96.1	18 20.5	8 44.3	0 999.8
3 146.0 / 2 241.5 / 18 20.2				0 UND	0 UND	18 20.5	8 44.3	17 21.3	25 14.6
12 30.5 / 9 39.0 / 7 53.9			Cost of Sales/Payables	0 UND	0 UND	1 316.4	3 140.9	24 14.9	14 25.4
56 6.5 / 46 8.0 / 36 10.1				16 22.2	24 15.4	31 12.0	20 18.0	71 5.1	34 10.8
184 2.0 / 211 1.7 / 100 3.7				44 8.3	165 2.2	67 5.4	71 5.1	184 2.0	87 4.2
6.6	5.8	4.5	Sales/Working Capital	7.1	1.9	2.7	3.0	8.8	5.1
22.1	22.7	14.7		NM	13.8	4.7	7.0	36.8	11.4
-9.6	-15.7	-15.2		-5.2	-8.1	-8.5	-29.6	-9.6	-27.2
21.3	29.7	9.7	EBIT/Interest	16.9	15.0	16.9	21.2	8.1	7.5
(161) 4.8	(174) 7.7	(174) 2.5		(14) .9	(21) 2.5	(16) 3.1	(22) 3.4	(37) 2.5	(64) 2.5
1.5	1.8	-.6		-10.8	.4	-1.2	-.2	-2.5	.5
82.2	107.4	37.0	Net Profit + Depr., Dep., Amort./Cur. Mat. L/T/D						
(21) 8.3	(12) 11.5	(20) 2.0							
3.0	3.5	.3							
.7	.7	.6	Fixed/Worth	.1	.4	.2	.5	1.0	1.0
1.2	1.4	1.4		.8	.8	.9	1.0	1.7	1.8
3.3	3.0	2.6		2.4	2.1	1.9	2.1	3.6	3.9
.4	.4	.4	Debt/Worth	.2	.1	.6	.3	.6	.7
1.3	1.1	1.2		1.8	1.0	1.0	.6	1.2	1.6
5.3	4.7	3.6		4.5	5.5	1.3	1.7	3.6	5.3
55.6	58.0	22.9	% Profit Before Taxes/Tangible Net Worth	21.4	21.5	46.8	33.6	18.9	25.3
(172) 22.9	(189) 23.2	(188) 6.2		(15) 2.3	(25) 9.1	(20) 6.2	(26) 6.1	(37) 6.8	(65) 6.9
8.1	6.5	-4.0		-7.6	-.4	-4.8	-3.0	-4.8	-3.8
22.1	25.1	12.0	% Profit Before Taxes/Total Assets	16.7	20.6	29.4	16.9	10.4	9.2
8.1	10.3	2.8		-.7	3.9	5.1	2.4	2.2	3.5
1.9	2.4	-2.4		-5.7	-1.1	-3.0	-1.6	-3.2	-1.5
4.3	6.5	5.9	Sales/Net Fixed Assets	6.9	5.5	11.0	6.7	2.3	5.0
1.3	1.3	1.1		3.9	2.1	2.8	.6	.8	.9
.4	.4	.4		1.1	.4	.2	.3	.3	.4
1.5	1.8	1.4	Sales/Total Assets	2.2	1.2	1.6	1.2	1.3	1.5
.6	.7	.5		.6	.5	.8	.4	.4	.5
.3	.3	.3		.3	.3	.2	.2	.2	.3
2.6	3.1	4.8	% Depr., Dep., Amort./Sales	5.7	7.4	3.6	15.8	9.6	1.2
(135) 8.9	(142) 9.9	(135) 14.1		(11) 18.3	(19) 9.0	(14) 8.0	(21) 28.3	(39) 21.8	(31) 4.8
19.8	20.6	27.5		20.6	17.7	18.7	42.7	34.4	15.8
1.4	1.1	2.5	% Officers', Directors' Owners' Comp/Sales						
(23) 4.4	(32) 4.3	(24) 5.9							
7.5	8.9	12.2							
12816137M	9792082M	7145647M	Net Sales ($)	10248M	55437M	88303M	193439M	729285M	6068935M
10808083M	11145386M	11651379M	Total Assets ($)	23627M	134614M	220991M	692167M	2155723M	8424257M

© RMA 2010

M = $ thousand   MM = $ million
See Pages 9 through 22 for Explanation of Ratios and Data

	Current Data Sorted by Assets						Comparative Historical Data	
Type of Statement								
				10	6	14		
		1		3			15	18
		4		1			5	8
		4					8	16
	2	1	2	5	9	18	6	5
			13 (4/1-9/30/09)	74 (10/1/09-3/31/10)		7	29	27
	0-500M	500M-2MM	2-10MM	10-50MM	50-100MM	100-250MM	4/1/05-3/31/06 ALL	4/1/06-3/31/07 ALL
Unqualified				10	6	14	15	18
Reviewed			1	3			5	8
Compiled			4	1			8	16
Tax Returns			4				6	5
Other	2	3	5	9	18	7	29	27
NUMBER OF STATEMENTS	2	3	14	23	24	21	63	74
	%	%	%	%	%	%	%	%
ASSETS								
Cash & Equivalents			18.7	11.5	11.9	5.7	10.7	10.0
Trade Receivables (net)			19.9	16.5	11.2	7.7	18.9	14.5
Inventory			5.9	9.0	7.5	4.7	7.4	6.1
All Other Current			4.6	1.7	1.8	2.5	2.8	5.0
Total Current			49.1	38.7	32.4	20.6	39.8	35.5
Fixed Assets (net)			39.4	48.1	43.3	60.8	40.1	47.4
Intangibles (net)			.4	1.1	8.0	3.8	5.0	3.6
All Other Non-Current			11.2	12.2	16.3	14.8	15.1	13.6
Total			100.0	100.0	100.0	100.0	100.0	100.0
LIABILITIES								
Notes Payable-Short Term			12.8	4.6	2.3	1.6	4.7	7.7
Cur. Mat.-L.T.D.			7.9	7.8	4.1	4.3	6.7	6.7
Trade Payables			11.3	9.7	7.7	7.3	15.6	11.3
Income Taxes Payable			.0	.1	.3	.7	.3	.1
All Other Current			14.8	10.5	8.6	7.3	9.6	13.7
Total Current			46.8	32.7	23.1	21.2	36.9	39.4
Long-Term Debt			29.1	21.1	13.7	23.2	26.5	29.5
Deferred Taxes			.0	1.1	.3	1.4	.2	.7
All Other Non-Current			.1	15.1	16.0	20.8	7.8	7.9
Net Worth			24.1	30.1	46.9	33.5	28.7	22.5
Total Liabilities & Net Worth			100.0	100.0	100.0	100.0	100.0	100.0
INCOME DATA								
Net Sales			100.0	100.0	100.0	100.0	100.0	100.0
Gross Profit			24.0	24.8	30.5	21.4	27.9	26.4
Operating Expenses			16.5	8.9	16.4	12.5	19.8	20.1
Operating Profit			7.5	15.8	14.1	8.9	8.0	6.3
All Other Expenses (net)			2.4	3.0	1.5	2.3	.9	1.8
Profit Before Taxes			5.1	12.9	12.6	6.6	7.1	4.5
RATIOS								
Current			1.8	2.1	2.3	1.4	2.0	1.8
			1.1	1.2	1.4	1.0	1.2	1.1
			.7	.7	1.1	.6	.7	.6
Quick			1.1	1.9	1.8	1.1	1.4	1.3
			.9	.9	.9	.5	.9	.7
			.3	.5	.5	.3	.5	.3
Sales/Receivables			13 29.1	16 23.4	17 20.9	16 22.1	19 19.2	13 29.0
			28 12.9	29 12.8	29 12.8	22 16.2	26 14.1	23 15.8
			56 6.5	43 8.4	40 9.2	32 11.3	42 8.6	39 9.3
Cost of Sales/Inventory			0 UND	7 53.5	14 25.7	12 31.0	0 999.8	0 UND
			1 509.3	14 25.6	25 14.7	14 26.7	12 30.9	5 75.6
			14 26.4	46 8.0	42 8.7	30 12.1	39 9.3	27 13.4
Cost of Sales/Payables			11 32.3	15 23.7	17 21.2	19 19.2	19 19.4	13 27.8
			17 22.0	22 16.6	22 16.6	31 11.9	27 13.3	22 16.7
			33 11.0	35 10.3	35 10.3	44 8.3	47 7.8	39 9.3
Sales/Working Capital			6.1	4.6	5.9	17.4	11.0	13.1
			173.4	45.0	11.6	616.0	58.1	75.1
			-26.0	-12.2	117.1	-11.8	-15.1	-9.9
EBIT/Interest			15.1	38.7	27.9	30.5	14.5	11.6
			(13) 4.4	(21) 14.7	(23) 10.6	5.6	(57) 4.2	(68) 3.9
			1.3	6.2	1.6	1.1	1.0	.7
Net Profit + Depr., Dep., Amort./Cur. Mat. L/T/D							6.2	6.6
							(13) 2.3	(14) 1.3
							1.1	.9
Fixed/Worth			.5	.7	.6	1.0	.6	.7
			2.2	1.5	1.0	2.5	1.6	1.8
			3.4	7.2	2.4	9.0	9.9	20.5
Debt/Worth			2.2	.9	.3	.9	1.1	.8
			3.2	1.9	1.5	2.5	2.9	2.6
			26.8	10.9	3.7	10.8	65.5	81.3
% Profit Before Taxes/Tangible Net Worth			102.6	94.0	63.1	58.9	81.5	105.7
			(12) 36.7	(19) 40.2	(22) 34.4	(18) 26.8	(50) 28.4	(61) 28.1
			5.3	24.1	7.9	2.9	-1.4	6.6
% Profit Before Taxes/Total Assets			23.2	29.7	18.2	16.9	23.3	24.0
			7.1	17.8	12.6	6.4	9.0	7.6
			-.6	8.9	1.1	-.1	.1	.0
Sales/Net Fixed Assets			28.5	5.5	4.6	3.5	13.0	9.2
			4.1	3.6	2.3	2.0	3.7	3.1
			2.2	2.1	1.6	1.0	2.2	1.8
Sales/Total Assets			3.1	2.4	1.5	1.6	2.8	2.7
			1.8	1.6	1.1	.9	1.7	1.5
			1.1	1.1	.8	.7	1.0	1.0
% Depr., Dep., Amort./Sales			1.3	3.0	3.5		1.6	2.8
			(13) 7.1	(20) 4.9	(21) 6.0		(52) 4.9	(56) 4.9
			11.4	8.0	8.9		7.7	9.8
% Officers', Directors', Owners' Comp/Sales							1.0	1.3
							(13) 1.8	(11) 4.1
Net Sales ($)	8965M	11780M	183614M	1229349M	2407451M	3979474M	4224387M	4038302M
Total Assets ($)	545M	2758M	76472M	657168M	1717116M	3468582M	2738474M	2788313M

M = $ thousand   MM = $ million
See Pages 9 through 22 for Explanation of Ratios and Data

Comparative Historical Data | **Current Data Sorted by Sales**

4/1/07-3/31/08 ALL	4/1/08-3/31/09 ALL	4/1/09-3/31/10 ALL	Type of Statement	0-1MM	1-3MM	3-5MM	5-10MM	10-25MM	25MM & OVER
20	28	30	Unqualified					4	26
5	9	4	Reviewed				1	1	2
11	4	5	Compiled		1		1	1	2
4	11	7	Tax Returns			2	4	1	
28	43	41	Other		2	4		2	33
					13 (4/1-9/30/09)		74 (10/1/09-3/31/10)		
68	95	87	NUMBER OF STATEMENTS		3	6	6	9	63
%	%	%	**ASSETS**	%	%	%	%	%	%
10.9	11.6	12.8	Cash & Equivalents	DATA NOT AVAILABLE					9.4
16.7	19.8	14.1	Trade Receivables (net)						14.4
3.9	6.4	6.5	Inventory						7.0
4.5	2.3	2.5	All Other Current						2.1
36.0	40.1	35.9	Total Current						33.0
44.3	45.1	46.9	Fixed Assets (net)						48.6
3.9	3.4	3.5	Intangibles (net)						4.5
15.9	11.4	13.7	All Other Non-Current						13.9
100.0	100.0	100.0	Total						100.0
			LIABILITIES						
5.3	4.3	4.3	Notes Payable-Short Term						3.3
6.0	6.1	6.1	Cur. Mat.-L.T.D.						4.9
14.3	15.8	9.9	Trade Payables						9.3
.1	.1	.3	Income Taxes Payable						.4
12.7	16.1	9.8	All Other Current						10.3
38.4	42.4	30.4	Total Current						28.3
26.5	22.6	20.8	Long-Term Debt						18.9
.6	.4	.7	Deferred Taxes						.9
7.8	7.8	14.4	All Other Non-Current						16.5
26.7	26.7	33.8	Net Worth						35.4
100.0	100.0	100.0	Total Liabilties & Net Worth						100.0
			INCOME DATA						
100.0	100.0	100.0	Net Sales						100.0
24.3	25.7	26.4	Gross Profit						23.3
19.3	18.7	14.2	Operating Expenses						12.0
5.0	7.0	12.2	Operating Profit						11.3
1.1	.7	2.1	All Other Expenses (net)						1.7
3.9	6.4	10.2	Profit Before Taxes						9.6
			RATIOS						
1.8	1.7	2.0							1.7
1.0	1.2	1.1	Current						1.1
.6	.6	.8							.8
1.4	1.5	1.5							1.4
.8	.8	.8	Quick						.8
.3	.4	.4							.4
10 37.1	14 25.7	16 22.8							17 21.5
22 16.8	27 13.4	26 13.9	Sales/Receivables						29 12.7
37 9.8	40 9.0	40 9.2							40 9.1
0 UND	0 UND	2 187.6							11 31.9
3 117.7	6 56.2	14 26.1	Cost of Sales/Inventory						16 22.8
20 18.4	23 15.8	35 10.5							35 10.5
15 25.1	14 26.3	16 22.4							17 21.8
26 14.2	26 14.2	23 16.2	Cost of Sales/Payables						21 17.0
43 8.4	48 7.6	38 9.5							35 10.3
9.6	8.7	7.9							9.7
195.3	40.1	47.0	Sales/Working Capital						47.0
-21.9	-12.5	-25.4							-22.0
13.3	13.6	30.2							32.0
(60) 2.2	(83) 5.2	(81) 10.6	EBIT/Interest						(60) 10.9
.3	1.0	1.8							1.6
2.9	8.6	8.7							13.7
(12) 1.6	(17) 2.3	(15) 2.3	Net Profit + Depr., Dep., Amort./Cur. Mat. L/T/D						(11) 3.8
.9	.8	.8							.8
.6	.7	.7							.7
1.8	1.6	1.5	Fixed/Worth						1.5
8.0	6.3	4.3							6.0
.6	.9	.9							.9
2.5	2.4	2.3	Debt/Worth						2.0
91.5	12.2	10.9							7.1
66.6	64.1	79.4							79.9
(55) 20.5	(77) 32.5	(73) 33.5	% Profit Before Taxes/Tangible Net Worth						(55) 34.6
-7.2	3.3	12.6							10.1
14.9	25.9	23.5							26.3
3.6	8.7	13.9	% Profit Before Taxes/Total Assets						13.8
-3.2	.1	1.5							2.0
9.6	11.0	5.5							4.9
3.4	3.7	3.0	Sales/Net Fixed Assets						2.7
1.9	1.9	1.6							1.5
3.2	2.8	2.1							2.0
1.6	1.6	1.3	Sales/Total Assets						1.3
.9	1.0	.9							.9
2.0	1.6	2.7							3.1
(52) 4.8	(75) 4.6	(62) 5.7	% Depr., Dep., Amort./Sales						(41) 4.9
7.8	7.5	8.4							7.4
	.6								
	(11) 1.5		% Officers', Directors' Owners' Comp/Sales						
	5.9								
4657346M	8426836M	7820633M	Net Sales ($)		5630M	22846M	42088M	159332M	7590737M
3161034M	5129130M	5922641M	Total Assets ($)		15092M	81017M	20097M	192372M	5614063M

M = $ thousand MM = $ million

See Pages 9 through 22 for Explanation of Ratios and Data

Current Data Sorted by Assets   **Comparative Historical Data**

Type of Statement	0-500M	500M-2MM	2-10MM	10-50MM	50-100MM	100-250MM		ALL 4/1/05-3/31/06	ALL 4/1/06-3/31/07
Unqualified				8	4	3		19	22
Reviewed		1	6	6				7	11
Compiled		2	4	2				7	8
Tax Returns	2	2	3	2				4	4
Other			12	14	3	3		42	26
		7 (4/1-9/30/09)		70 (10/1/09-3/31/10)					
NUMBER OF STATEMENTS	2	5	25	32	7	6		79	71
	%	%	%	%	%	%		%	%
ASSETS									
Cash & Equivalents			6.6	10.2				11.5	9.9
Trade Receivables (net)			14.2	11.9				16.1	16.4
Inventory			15.9	17.1				11.1	11.1
All Other Current			1.1	1.5				3.9	2.4
Total Current			37.7	40.8				42.7	39.9
Fixed Assets (net)			53.1	49.9				43.4	49.0
Intangibles (net)			3.4	2.6				5.1	4.6
All Other Non-Current			5.9	6.8				8.9	6.5
Total			100.0	100.0				100.0	100.0
LIABILITIES									
Notes Payable-Short Term			7.4	4.2				4.1	3.5
Cur. Mat.-L.T.D.			5.9	3.5				3.2	4.0
Trade Payables			8.0	5.1				7.2	8.0
Income Taxes Payable			.1	.2				.2	.2
All Other Current			3.6	4.9				8.0	8.3
Total Current			24.9	17.8				22.6	24.0
Long-Term Debt			28.6	20.6				25.7	26.5
Deferred Taxes			.6	.8				1.5	1.0
All Other Non-Current			3.3	6.5				4.3	4.1
Net Worth			42.5	54.3				45.9	44.4
Total Liabilities & Net Worth			100.0	100.0				100.0	100.0
INCOME DATA									
Net Sales			100.0	100.0				100.0	100.0
Gross Profit			39.6	25.8				29.3	29.9
Operating Expenses			30.5	15.8				19.6	16.7
Operating Profit			9.1	10.0				9.7	13.2
All Other Expenses (net)			2.4	1.9				2.0	2.1
Profit Before Taxes			6.7	8.1				7.7	11.1
RATIOS									
Current			2.9	6.5				3.6	3.3
			1.4	2.4				1.8	1.7
			.8	1.3				1.3	1.2
Quick			2.1	3.8				2.5	2.2
			1.0	1.2				1.2	1.1
			.3	.6				.6	.7
Sales/Receivables			23 15.6	30 12.0				29 12.5	29 12.7
			39 9.2	40 9.1				43 8.5	41 8.9
			48 7.5	51 7.2				55 6.6	52 7.0
Cost of Sales/Inventory			1 533.9	29 12.6				21 17.4	18 20.8
			58 6.3	74 4.9				51 7.1	40 9.2
			103 3.6	154 2.4				97 3.8	72 5.1
Cost of Sales/Payables			14 26.9	13 27.6				15 23.8	17 21.4
			25 14.4	29 12.6				23 15.7	26 13.9
			63 5.8	41 9.0				38 9.5	38 9.7
Sales/Working Capital			3.5	2.2				3.1	3.6
			11.6	6.0				6.5	10.4
			-23.7	14.4				15.1	32.7
EBIT/Interest			9.5	14.5				15.4	21.9
			(23) 4.8	(30) 5.4				(67) 3.5	(59) 6.4
			2.1	1.3				1.2	2.7
Net Profit + Depr., Dep., Amort./Cur. Mat. L/T/D								9.2	7.4
								(18) 3.8	(12) 2.7
								1.7	1.5
Fixed/Worth			.7	.6				.5	.7
			1.8	1.0				1.0	1.1
			2.8	1.5				2.8	2.3
Debt/Worth			.4	.4				.3	.4
			1.4	.9				1.1	1.3
			3.1	1.7				4.0	3.8
% Profit Before Taxes/Tangible Net Worth			36.8	30.2				30.3	53.3
			(23) 20.9	(31) 10.3				(68) 13.1	(64) 22.5
			3.9	2.4				4.5	13.1
% Profit Before Taxes/Total Assets			13.0	13.0				11.3	17.9
			5.4	4.5				6.9	8.8
			2.3	.9				.6	4.9
Sales/Net Fixed Assets			6.3	3.0				4.3	3.9
			2.0	1.7				2.3	2.1
			1.3	.9				1.3	1.4
Sales/Total Assets			1.9	1.2				1.4	1.6
			1.3	.8				1.0	1.0
			.7	.6				.7	.8
% Depr., Dep., Amort./Sales			3.5	5.0				3.5	3.5
			(22) 7.5	(31) 9.3				(69) 6.6	(62) 5.8
			11.8	11.9				10.8	9.3
% Officers', Directors' Owners' Comp/Sales								1.5	1.7
								(15) 3.5	(11) 3.0
								5.6	15.5
Net Sales ($)	2203M	7637M	163563M	650601M	451054M	678712M		1837997M	2086664M
Total Assets ($)	542M	6744M	123002M	729275M	566830M	788213M		2366983M	2367110M

M = $ thousand   MM = $ million
See Pages 9 through 22 for Explanation of Ratios and Data

Comparative Historical Data | Current Data Sorted by Sales

H: 4/1/07-3/31/08 ALL	H: 4/1/08-3/31/09 ALL	H: 4/1/09-3/31/10 ALL	Type of Statement	0-1MM	1-3MM	3-5MM	5-10MM	10-25MM	25MM & OVER
23	14	15	Unqualified				1	3	11
10	7	13	Reviewed	1	1	3	2	5	1
7	11	8	Compiled	1	1	1	2	3	
9	9	9	Tax Returns	1	3	2	2	1	
29	26	32	Other	1	3	3	4	13	8
				7 (4/1-9/30/09)			70 (10/1/09-3/31/10)		
78	67	77	NUMBER OF STATEMENTS	4	8	9	11	25	20
%	%	%	ASSETS	%	%	%	%	%	%
9.0	10.7	8.2	Cash & Equivalents				10.7	10.2	4.8
12.9	14.8	12.1	Trade Receivables (net)				14.4	11.1	9.7
13.8	14.9	15.2	Inventory				16.3	12.8	14.5
2.2	2.2	1.8	All Other Current				1.4	2.3	2.4
37.9	42.5	37.3	Total Current				42.7	36.4	31.4
52.4	48.4	52.6	Fixed Assets (net)				47.8	55.6	53.3
3.6	3.1	3.3	Intangibles (net)				1.1	1.0	7.4
6.1	6.0	6.8	All Other Non-Current				8.4	6.9	7.9
100.0	100.0	100.0	Total				100.0	100.0	100.0
			LIABILITIES						
5.0	6.3	12.7	Notes Payable-Short Term				7.2	4.0	4.5
4.4	5.8	4.4	Cur. Mat.-L.T.D.				5.2	4.6	3.3
7.8	6.5	6.7	Trade Payables				7.6	5.0	6.7
.2	.0	.1	Income Taxes Payable				.0	.0	.2
5.1	7.5	4.1	All Other Current				3.4	4.8	4.9
22.6	26.2	28.0	Total Current				23.4	18.5	19.6
25.5	28.2	24.4	Long-Term Debt				20.0	22.1	22.6
1.4	.9	1.0	Deferred Taxes				.1	1.1	2.3
4.8	3.4	5.2	All Other Non-Current				1.8	5.8	5.4
45.7	41.4	41.3	Net Worth				54.7	52.5	50.0
100.0	100.0	100.0	Total Liabilities & Net Worth				100.0	100.0	100.0
			INCOME DATA						
100.0	100.0	100.0	Net Sales				100.0	100.0	100.0
34.2	29.6	33.0	Gross Profit				34.6	28.8	22.5
23.8	23.8	23.7	Operating Expenses				24.5	17.9	13.0
10.4	5.9	9.3	Operating Profit				10.1	10.9	9.4
2.9	1.0	2.1	All Other Expenses (net)				.8	2.0	1.7
7.5	4.8	7.2	Profit Before Taxes				9.3	8.9	7.7
			RATIOS						
3.4	3.6	4.3	Current				8.0	5.2	3.1
2.1	1.9	2.2					2.8	2.4	2.0
1.2	1.1	1.1					.7	1.1	1.2
2.1	2.4	2.1	Quick				2.9	3.0	1.7
1.0	1.0	1.1					1.9	1.1	1.1
.5	.5	.4					.3	.6	.5
24 15.4	21 17.7	27 13.7	Sales/Receivables	24 15.2	32 11.4	27 13.7			
35 10.4	30 12.2	38 9.5		44 8.3	39 9.2	30 12.1			
44 8.2	44 8.3	46 7.9		52 7.0	54 6.8	42 8.8			
22 16.9	7 50.7	16 22.7	Cost of Sales/Inventory	11 34.0	25 14.5	28 12.9			
50 7.3	40 9.0	61 6.0		82 4.4	61 6.0	42 8.8			
96 3.8	82 4.4	118 3.1		105 3.5	112 3.3	112 3.3			
17 22.0	14 26.4	14 25.3	Cost of Sales/Payables	17 21.3	13 29.0	16 22.4			
26 13.8	21 17.4	27 13.4		25 14.4	27 13.4	26 13.9			
43 8.4	33 11.2	46 7.9		41 8.9	38 9.5	31 11.6			
4.0	4.1	3.2	Sales/Working Capital				2.0	2.4	4.8
6.9	9.5	6.7					4.8	6.2	8.1
72.5	51.9	54.5					-14.9	509.5	16.2
9.5	8.8	11.1	EBIT/Interest				14.4	13.9	14.6
(68) 4.0	(60) 2.8	(70) 3.6					(10) 6.4	(24) 6.2	(17) 3.9
1.8	.9	1.7					2.8	2.1	1.8
6.8	15.2	11.4	Net Profit + Depr., Dep., Amort./Cur. Mat. L/T/D						
(15) 3.7	(16) 4.1	(14) 3.3							
1.5	2.1	1.4							
.8	.7	.7	Fixed/Worth				.4	.8	.8
1.3	1.1	1.1					1.0	1.1	1.1
2.2	2.8	2.0					2.1	1.7	2.1
.5	.6	.4	Debt/Worth				.3	.4	.4
1.3	1.5	1.1					1.1	.9	1.2
3.3	3.8	2.7					2.9	1.6	3.7
38.9	34.8	30.7	% Profit Before Taxes/Tangible Net Worth				36.8	28.0	37.1
(71) 17.0	(59) 13.1	(71) 13.3					20.9	13.0	(18) 12.3
8.7	2.0	3.9					13.3	5.5	5.0
13.1	14.4	10.8	% Profit Before Taxes/Total Assets				15.5	13.0	10.2
7.7	6.1	5.2					9.8	5.3	5.6
2.7	.4	1.9					4.3	3.6	2.4
3.7	5.2	3.1	Sales/Net Fixed Assets				3.7	3.0	2.4
2.1	2.7	1.8					3.0	1.6	1.8
1.3	1.5	1.0					1.7	.9	1.2
1.6	2.0	1.4	Sales/Total Assets				1.7	1.3	1.2
1.1	1.2	.9					1.0	.8	.9
.8	.8	.6					.9	.6	.7
3.9	4.0	4.5	% Depr., Dep., Amort./Sales				4.5	4.5	3.2
(68) 6.5	(60) 6.2	(68) 8.0					5.9	(23) 8.8	(15) 5.7
10.7	9.6	11.8					10.4	10.9	8.6
1.1	1.6	2.2	% Officers', Directors' Owners' Comp/Sales						
(16) 1.5	(22) 3.1	(21) 4.7							
7.3	8.7	9.4							
3066362M	1738397M	1953770M	Net Sales ($)	3236M	12390M	34758M	84518M	404183M	1414685M
3134426M	1667753M	2214606M	Total Assets ($)	4512M	27237M	39460M	80405M	523610M	1539382M

© RMA 2010   M = $ thousand   MM = $ million
See Pages 9 through 22 for Explanation of Ratios and Data

Current Data Sorted by Assets | | | | | | | Comparative Historical Data

0-500M	500M-2MM	2-10MM	10-50MM	50-100MM	100-250MM	Type of Statement	4/1/05-3/31/06 ALL	4/1/06-3/31/07 ALL
			7	2	2	Unqualified	7	9
		3	5	1	1	Reviewed	12	9
		6	3			Compiled	1	5
1	2		1			Tax Returns	2	4
3	3	7	8	1	1	Other	18	27
							40	54
4	5	16	24	4	4	**NUMBER OF STATEMENTS**	40	54
%	%	%	%	%	%	**ASSETS**	%	%
		10.7	11.3			Cash & Equivalents	6.4	8.2
		10.2	12.9			Trade Receivables (net)	15.2	13.8
		15.2	12.5			Inventory	15.7	16.1
		.9	2.9			All Other Current	3.3	4.4
		37.1	39.5			Total Current	40.7	42.4
		49.3	49.4			Fixed Assets (net)	49.1	48.5
		3.7	4.5			Intangibles (net)	2.4	2.6
		10.0	6.6			All Other Non-Current	7.8	6.5
		100.0	100.0			Total	100.0	100.0
						LIABILITIES		
		7.2	4.5			Notes Payable-Short Term	5.6	6.1
		7.1	4.8			Cur. Mat.-L.T.D.	7.2	5.4
		8.3	5.2			Trade Payables	8.8	8.4
		.0	.2			Income Taxes Payable	.1	.2
		2.7	5.1			All Other Current	3.4	4.4
		25.3	19.7			Total Current	25.1	24.5
		23.4	16.4			Long-Term Debt	18.1	27.5
		.5	1.4			Deferred Taxes	1.2	.7
		11.6	3.1			All Other Non-Current	5.8	6.5
		39.1	59.4			Net Worth	49.8	40.9
		100.0	100.0			Total Liabilities & Net Worth	100.0	100.0
						INCOME DATA		
		100.0	100.0			Net Sales	100.0	100.0
		22.7	28.9			Gross Profit	24.6	31.9
		18.1	19.0			Operating Expenses	16.6	21.5
		4.5	9.9			Operating Profit	8.0	10.4
		2.8	1.6			All Other Expenses (net)	.8	1.8
		1.7	8.3			Profit Before Taxes	7.2	8.6
						RATIOS		
		3.1	6.5			Current	3.1	2.7
		1.2	2.7				1.6	1.7
		.9	1.1				1.0	1.3
		1.6	4.5			Quick	1.6	1.6
		.9	1.6				.8	1.0
		.4	.6				.5	.5
		11　32.0	29　12.4			Sales/Receivables	28　13.2	14　25.2
		33　11.1	39　9.4				41　9.0	35　10.5
		47　7.7	67　5.5				54　6.8	52　7.0
		22　16.6	20　17.9			Cost of Sales/Inventory	20　18.0	16　22.5
		72　5.0	67　5.5				45　8.1	43　8.4
		95　3.9	106　3.5				91　4.0	85　4.3
		18　19.9	8　43.2			Cost of Sales/Payables	12　31.2	14　26.5
		25　14.8	21　17.0				23　15.6	22　16.3
		43　8.5	34　10.7				44　8.2	42　8.6
		4.0	2.3			Sales/Working Capital	3.9	4.6
		15.9	5.0				8.8	9.4
		NM	25.1				137.1	19.6
		11.0	56.1			EBIT/Interest	15.3	13.6
		(14)　1.5	(21)　4.8				(37)　4.3	(51)　4.6
		-1.3	1.2				1.1	1.8
						Net Profit + Depr., Dep., Amort./Cur. Mat. L/T/D	12.5	17.2
							(14)　3.1	(10)　4.5
							1.5	3.0
		.6	.4			Fixed/Worth	.6	.7
		1.5	.8				1.0	1.1
		26.4	1.6				2.5	2.5
		.4	.1			Debt/Worth	.3	.5
		1.3	.4				1.0	1.2
		49.5	2.5				3.7	3.3
		30.4	24.1			% Profit Before Taxes/Tangible Net Worth	28.5	62.8
		(13)　12.7	(22)　18.6				(39)　17.4	(47)　25.8
		.0	2.6				2.7	10.0
		14.6	17.2			% Profit Before Taxes/Total Assets	14.8	20.2
		3.8	7.4				6.0	9.5
		-5.5	1.5				.3	2.3
		5.8	3.3			Sales/Net Fixed Assets	5.7	5.8
		2.1	2.4				2.7	3.3
		1.6	1.0				1.7	1.9
		1.4	1.3			Sales/Total Assets	1.8	2.2
		1.1	.9				1.3	1.4
		.8	.6				.8	.9
		2.6	4.5			% Depr., Dep., Amort./Sales	2.8	2.4
		(15)　8.4	(23)　8.0				(38)　5.2	(44)　5.4
		12.2	14.4				8.9	8.3
						% Officers', Directors' Owners' Comp/Sales	1.5	
							(11)　3.0	
							4.9	
3289M	10783M	95469M	570734M	197147M	704968M	Net Sales ($)	1052293M	1757024M
1144M	4229M	83879M	576565M	290872M	624785M	Total Assets ($)	1006782M	1370223M

M = $ thousand   MM = $ million
See Pages 9 through 22 for Explanation of Ratios and Data

Comparative Historical Data   Current Data Sorted by Sales

Type of Statement	10	12	11					1	2	8
Unqualified	10	12	11					1	2	8
Reviewed	13	10	10		1			3	2	4
Compiled	8	10	9		3	3		1	2	
Tax Returns	4	2	4		1	1		1		
Other	28	30	23	1	3	3		3	5	5
	4/1/07-3/31/08	4/1/08-3/31/09	4/1/09-3/31/10			4 (4/1-9/30/09)			53 (10/1/09-3/31/10)	
	ALL	ALL	ALL	0-1MM	1-3MM	3-5MM	5-10MM	10-25MM	25MM & OVER	
NUMBER OF STATEMENTS	63	64	57	5	8	7	9	11	17	

	%	%	%	%	%	%	%	%	%
ASSETS									
Cash & Equivalents	6.8	7.2	8.5					10.6	9.1
Trade Receivables (net)	13.4	14.5	15.3					14.7	15.2
Inventory	9.9	13.9	14.2					17.1	16.1
All Other Current	5.2	1.2	2.4					3.1	3.0
Total Current	35.3	36.9	40.4					45.5	43.3
Fixed Assets (net)	48.8	48.6	48.4					36.6	49.8
Intangibles (net)	6.7	6.7	4.8					8.4	1.9
All Other Non-Current	9.2	7.8	6.4					9.4	5.0
Total	100.0	100.0	100.0					100.0	100.0
LIABILITIES									
Notes Payable-Short Term	5.3	5.5	4.9					5.7	2.8
Cur. Mat.-L.T.D.	7.2	5.2	5.1					3.8	2.9
Trade Payables	8.2	7.4	9.8					6.8	5.3
Income Taxes Payable	.3	.2	.1					.0	.3
All Other Current	5.4	4.7	5.4					4.8	3.9
Total Current	26.4	22.9	25.3					21.1	15.2
Long-Term Debt	30.8	28.1	28.2					11.2	16.0
Deferred Taxes	.8	.7	.9					.4	2.2
All Other Non-Current	5.5	7.7	8.1					5.4	3.2
Net Worth	36.4	40.6	37.5					62.0	63.4
Total Liabilties & Net Worth	100.0	100.0	100.0					100.0	100.0
INCOME DATA									
Net Sales	100.0	100.0	100.0					100.0	100.0
Gross Profit	29.4	25.6	31.9					26.8	28.6
Operating Expenses	18.1	18.8	24.6					15.8	17.5
Operating Profit	11.3	6.8	7.3					11.1	11.1
All Other Expenses (net)	3.3	2.1	2.3					.4	1.2
Profit Before Taxes	8.1	4.7	5.0					10.6	9.9
RATIOS									
Current	3.1	4.1	4.4					4.1	5.5
	1.5	1.7	2.1					2.7	2.7
	.8	.9	1.0					1.4	2.1
Quick	1.6	1.8	2.0					2.2	3.4
	.9	.9	.9					1.4	1.8
	.4	.4	.6					.9	.7
Sales/Receivables	22 16.7	21 17.0	26 13.9					33 11.1	37 10.0
	38 9.5	37 9.9	39 9.4					50 7.3	41 8.9
	51 7.2	51 7.2	52 7.1					69 5.3	76 4.8
Cost of Sales/Inventory	13 28.0	14 25.4	20 18.6					22 16.7	20 18.2
	47 7.8	51 7.2	71 5.2					95 3.9	53 6.9
	75 4.8	89 4.1	115 3.2					120 3.0	131 2.8
Cost of Sales/Payables	14 26.5	10 36.8	14 26.8					14 26.6	13 28.4
	22 16.8	19 19.3	23 15.9					25 14.7	16 23.3
	40 9.0	33 11.2	47 7.7					44 8.2	24 14.9
Sales/Working Capital	5.1	4.4	2.9					2.1	2.7
	8.5	10.0	6.7					4.4	4.0
	-14.2	-73.7	NM					15.6	7.0
EBIT/Interest	7.2	6.6	11.5						60.2
	(57) 3.1	(55) 2.7	(51) 2.1						9.8
	1.0	-.6	-.3						1.2
Net Profit + Depr., Dep., Amort./Cur. Mat. L/T/D	9.0	8.6	15.1						
	(21) 3.1	(12) 2.4	(16) 4.7						
	1.3	.7	1.4						
Fixed/Worth	.7	.7	.6					.4	.6
	1.5	1.3	1.1					.8	.8
	8.8	4.8	4.0					1.2	1.3
Debt/Worth	.5	.4	.3					.1	.3
	1.9	1.5	1.0					1.0	.5
	21.6	6.5	12.2					2.6	1.4
% Profit Before Taxes/Tangible Net Worth	37.2	30.7	23.5					23.5	23.2
	(51) 22.0	(55) 16.3	(47) 12.3					19.6	10.6
	12.3	-6.0	1.6					11.9	2.5
% Profit Before Taxes/Total Assets	11.5	14.2	14.7					17.3	18.3
	7.8	6.6	3.2					11.6	7.6
	.3	-3.8	-2.5					2.3	.8
Sales/Net Fixed Assets	3.9	4.1	3.8					3.9	3.2
	2.2	2.5	2.4					3.1	2.4
	1.3	1.5	1.2					2.1	1.7
Sales/Total Assets	1.6	1.6	1.4					1.2	1.4
	1.0	1.2	1.0					.9	1.1
	.7	.7	.7					.8	.9
% Depr., Dep., Amort./Sales	4.1	3.7	4.0					3.7	2.6
	(59) 6.8	(56) 7.4	(48) 7.7					8.0	(15) 4.5
	10.9	10.8	12.2					14.4	8.7
% Officers', Directors' Owners' Comp/Sales	1.3	1.5							
	(10) 2.0	(10) 2.1							
	3.4	4.2							
Net Sales ($)	1595412M	1937836M	1582390M	2289M	17574M	26968M	71062M	178877M	1285620M
Total Assets ($)	1707801M	1668728M	1581474M	2126M	25684M	27558M	113030M	195753M	1217323M

© RMA 2010

M = $ thousand   MM = $ million
See Pages 9 through 22 for Explanation of Ratios and Data

	Current Data Sorted by Assets							Comparative Historical Data	
			4	15	9	2	Type of Statement		
1	1		14	13	1		Unqualified	28	34
3	2		16	6	1		Reviewed	36	40
7	10		14				Compiled	33	38
1	13		20	19	2	2	Tax Returns	25	21
							Other	56	47
	22 (4/1-9/30/09)			154 (10/1/09-3/31/10)				4/1/05-3/31/06	4/1/06-3/31/07
0-500M	500M-2MM		2-10MM	10-50MM	50-100MM	100-250MM		ALL	ALL
12	26		68	53	13	4	NUMBER OF STATEMENTS	178	180
%	%		%	%	%	%	ASSETS	%	%
24.1	8.9		10.0	11.6	14.7		Cash & Equivalents	10.7	11.3
8.4	12.9		14.0	13.9	19.1		Trade Receivables (net)	17.7	18.5
7.9	16.1		8.4	8.9	5.9		Inventory	8.9	9.2
13.4	4.7		2.3	2.2	1.9		All Other Current	3.1	2.4
53.8	42.6		34.8	36.7	41.7		Total Current	40.3	41.4
32.2	44.3		54.1	48.9	36.7		Fixed Assets (net)	50.9	49.4
.2	6.9		3.3	2.2	12.2		Intangibles (net)	1.5	2.7
13.7	6.2		7.8	12.3	9.5		All Other Non-Current	7.3	6.4
100.0	100.0		100.0	100.0	100.0		Total	100.0	100.0
							LIABILITIES		
.9	10.0		6.4	3.0	2.4		Notes Payable-Short Term	5.0	5.9
10.2	7.6		8.0	5.2	3.2		Cur. Mat.-L.T.D.	5.7	5.6
9.5	6.4		6.9	5.1	11.2		Trade Payables	8.3	8.1
.0	.0		.2	.2	.1		Income Taxes Payable	.3	.3
17.2	9.6		5.0	5.7	5.5		All Other Current	6.3	6.1
37.8	33.6		26.5	19.3	22.4		Total Current	25.6	26.0
67.9	18.5		32.3	18.6	24.9		Long-Term Debt	26.2	26.8
.0	.6		.3	.5	.6		Deferred Taxes	.6	.8
1.5	4.8		5.2	6.3	10.0		All Other Non-Current	7.1	7.1
-7.1	42.6		35.7	55.4	42.1		Net Worth	40.5	39.3
100.0	100.0		100.0	100.0	100.0		Total Liabilties & Net Worth	100.0	100.0
							INCOME DATA		
100.0	100.0		100.0	100.0	100.0		Net Sales	100.0	100.0
52.1	53.0		32.5	23.8	30.7		Gross Profit	33.8	33.6
47.1	47.0		30.4	21.8	24.7		Operating Expenses	25.7	22.8
5.0	6.0		2.2	2.0	6.1		Operating Profit	8.1	10.8
2.0	2.1		2.9	.8	3.0		All Other Expenses (net)	1.3	1.3
3.0	4.0		-.7	1.2	3.1		Profit Before Taxes	6.9	9.5
							RATIOS		
10.8	5.4		2.3	4.2	3.6			2.9	3.0
1.5	1.8		1.3	1.9	1.4		Current	1.7	1.7
.5	.8		.7	1.1	1.3			1.1	1.1
6.4	2.1		1.6	2.4	2.1			2.2	2.1
.8	.7		.7	1.3	1.4		Quick	(177) 1.1	(179) 1.2
.1	.3		.4	.7	.9			.6	.6
0 UND	11 32.9		24 15.3	33 11.0	36 10.3			28 13.2	28 12.9
3 110.2	42 8.7		36 10.0	46 7.9	49 7.5		Sales/Receivables	43 8.4	42 8.8
22 16.7	59 6.2		54 6.8	68 5.4	74 4.9			61 6.0	55 6.6
0 UND	0 UND		0 UND	13 27.7	7 49.0			0 UND	0 999.8
0 UND	26 14.0		19 19.1	35 10.5	48 7.7		Cost of Sales/Inventory	20 18.0	20 18.7
31 11.8	207 1.8		75 4.9	87 4.2	69 5.3			66 5.5	62 5.8
0 UND	1 327.1		11 32.6	12 29.7	14 26.0			12 29.8	13 28.0
7 51.1	26 14.2		26 13.9	20 18.5	34 10.8		Cost of Sales/Payables	23 15.7	25 14.8
27 13.7	58 6.2		60 6.1	45 8.1	61 6.0			39 9.4	41 9.0
3.3	2.3		5.7	2.7	2.1			5.0	4.4
5.3	9.8		11.9	5.1	7.9		Sales/Working Capital	11.2	10.1
-6.6	-29.3		-10.5	40.1	24.1			78.6	84.4
	16.8		8.7	8.7				12.0	15.2
	(22) 1.8		(60) 1.8	(48) 1.8			EBIT/Interest	(162) 3.9	(163) 4.6
	-.8		.1	-.5				1.7	1.5
			6.3	3.9				4.8	4.7
	(10) 1.7		(14) 1.8				Net Profit + Depr., Dep., Amort./Cur. Mat. L/T/D	(40) 2.1	(42) 1.9
	.4			1.4				1.3	1.2
.2	.5		.8	.5	.7			.7	.7
1.2	1.1		1.8	1.1	1.1		Fixed/Worth	1.2	1.2
NM	22.1		7.1	1.6	NM			2.2	3.0
.4	.4		.7	.3	.8			.5	.5
2.3	1.5		1.6	.7	1.3		Debt/Worth	1.4	1.4
NM	29.4		9.0	2.1	NM			3.2	4.4
	30.2		20.1	17.2	26.9			38.2	48.1
	(21) 5.9		(55) .8	(51) 1.7	(10) 13.5		% Profit Before Taxes/Tangible Net Worth	(163) 15.8	(153) 24.3
	-11.6		-15.1	-4.0	5.0			5.0	6.7
12.9	15.1		10.3	6.5	7.7			17.0	22.3
2.3	1.8		.6	.9	4.9		% Profit Before Taxes/Total Assets	6.8	9.4
-15.8	-3.8		-4.4	-2.4	1.4			1.7	1.9
35.8	5.8		4.1	3.8	5.7			4.8	5.1
8.6	2.7		2.3	1.8	1.7		Sales/Net Fixed Assets	2.5	2.7
4.5	1.4		.9	.8	.9			1.4	1.7
2.6	2.1		1.7	1.2	1.5			2.0	1.9
1.6	1.2		1.0	.9	.6		Sales/Total Assets	1.3	1.4
1.3	.6		.5	.5	.4			.8	.8
	4.3		4.4	4.4	4.1			4.0	4.5
	(21) 9.0		(63) 10.9	(47) 6.6	(12) 7.1		% Depr., Dep., Amort./Sales	(160) 7.4	(159) 6.8
	12.8		20.8	15.7	13.5			11.7	11.5
	2.2		1.4					1.1	1.8
	(10) 6.1		(24) 2.4				% Officers', Directors' Owners' Comp/Sales	(52) 2.3	(59) 2.7
	10.9		7.0					5.7	6.4
5514M	42508M		390526M	1154399M	1139879M	701051M	Net Sales ($)	3487517M	4415077M
2927M	31221M		340633M	1156903M	958719M	733831M	Total Assets ($)	2836729M	3437926M

M = $ thousand   MM = $ million
See Pages 9 through 22 for Explanation of Ratios and Data

Comparative Historical Data · Current Data Sorted by Sales

				Type of Statement						
	33	29	30	Unqualified		1	2	4	7	16
	47	41	30	Reviewed	2	6	3	4	9	6
	28	27	28	Compiled	3	6	5	8	4	2
	26	28	31	Tax Returns	11	9	5	3	3	
	69	61	57	Other	7	15	5	10	15	5
	4/1/07-3/31/08 ALL	4/1/08-3/31/09 ALL	4/1/09-3/31/10 ALL		0-1MM	1-3MM (22, 4/1-9/30/09)	3-5MM	5-10MM	10-25MM (154, 10/1/09-3/31/10)	25MM & OVER
	203	186	176	NUMBER OF STATEMENTS	23	37	20	29	38	29
	%	%	%	ASSETS	%	%	%	%	%	%
	10.7	9.2	11.7	Cash & Equivalents	11.6	11.1	3.9	12.5	15.7	11.8
	16.2	16.4	13.7	Trade Receivables (net)	9.0	7.7	13.8	13.5	17.5	20.5
	8.5	9.3	9.5	Inventory	15.6	11.9	10.0	5.2	6.2	10.0
	3.0	2.4	3.4	All Other Current	8.7	2.1	2.4	2.6	2.9	2.7
	38.4	37.3	38.3	Total Current	44.9	32.9	30.1	33.8	42.3	45.0
	50.6	50.6	48.1	Fixed Assets (net)	42.7	55.1	53.9	53.1	42.3	42.3
	2.6	3.4	4.0	Intangibles (net)	3.7	4.9	3.1	3.0	5.5	3.0
	8.5	8.6	9.5	All Other Non-Current	8.7	7.1	12.9	10.1	9.8	9.6
	100.0	100.0	100.0	Total	100.0	100.0	100.0	100.0	100.0	100.0
				LIABILITIES						
	5.8	6.3	5.1	Notes Payable-Short Term	5.5	6.0	8.9	4.5	4.7	2.1
	7.0	7.4	6.9	Cur. Mat.-L.T.D.	7.7	6.8	12.1	6.2	4.8	6.1
	6.6	7.5	6.7	Trade Payables	5.7	5.3	8.9	5.9	5.7	9.9
	.6	.3	.2	Income Taxes Payable	.0	.0	.3	.0	.3	.4
	6.3	7.7	6.8	All Other Current	6.6	10.9	5.5	4.2	6.2	6.1
	26.3	29.3	25.7	Total Current	25.5	29.0	35.8	20.9	21.6	24.7
	25.7	31.0	27.4	Long-Term Debt	49.0	34.0	33.2	20.0	18.0	17.8
	1.0	.5	.5	Deferred Taxes	.6	.1	.5	.2	.5	1.0
	5.4	5.3	5.7	All Other Non-Current	5.7	3.1	1.7	5.1	8.1	9.2
	41.6	33.9	40.7	Net Worth	19.2	33.9	28.9	53.8	51.7	47.2
	100.0	100.0	100.0	Total Liabilities & Net Worth	100.0	100.0	100.0	100.0	100.0	100.0
				INCOME DATA						
	100.0	100.0	100.0	Net Sales	100.0	100.0	100.0	100.0	100.0	100.0
	34.3	30.7	34.2	Gross Profit	64.2	36.9	26.3	32.7	27.6	22.2
	24.9	27.0	30.8	Operating Expenses	58.2	35.3	26.8	31.0	24.2	14.5
	9.4	3.8	3.4	Operating Profit	6.0	1.6	-.4	1.7	3.5	7.7
	2.2	2.3	2.1	All Other Expenses (net)	4.7	3.9	.9	.4	1.3	1.1
	7.3	1.5	1.3	Profit Before Taxes	1.2	-2.3	-1.3	1.3	2.1	6.6
				RATIOS						
	2.9	2.6	3.6	Current	14.9	3.7	1.7	2.6	4.5	3.6
	1.7	1.4	1.7		1.9	1.3	.9	1.5	2.2	1.9
	.9	.8	.9		1.1	.6	.5	.8	1.3	1.2
	2.1	1.8	2.1	Quick	3.6	1.7	1.0	1.8	3.4	2.2
	1.0	(185) 1.0	1.0		.8	.8	.4	1.3	1.4	1.2
	.5	.5	.5		.3	.3	.2	.5	.9	.8
	25 14.5	25 14.8	26 13.8	Sales/Receivables	0 UND	19 19.5	20 18.3	28 13.1	31 11.9	32 11.3
	40 9.2	40 9.1	41 8.9		21 17.6	42 8.6	47 7.7	36 10.0	42 8.7	43 8.4
	55 6.7	60 6.1	59 6.1		90 4.0	52 7.1	70 5.2	50 7.3	67 5.5	68 5.4
	0 UND	0 UND	0 UND	Cost of Sales/Inventory	0 UND	0 UND	1 430.5	1 281.0	0 UND	12 31.6
	20 18.1	19 18.9	31 11.9		32 11.4	53 6.9	36 10.1	17 21.0	17 21.1	36 10.3
	60 6.1	67 5.5	89 4.1		608 .6	141 2.6	86 4.3	63 5.8	72 5.1	51 7.2
	12 31.6	9 40.4	11 34.2	Cost of Sales/Payables	0 UND	8 44.8	12 30.0	13 28.5	9 40.0	14 25.8
	20 18.2	19 18.8	24 15.5		19 19.5	24 15.3	33 10.9	24 15.4	19 19.0	27 13.3
	37 9.9	43 8.5	51 7.1		130 2.8	76 4.8	57 6.4	45 8.2	41 8.8	46 7.9
	4.6	4.8	3.1	Sales/Working Capital	1.3	3.1	8.3	4.9	3.1	2.6
	11.1	13.1	8.5		3.7	12.0	-73.6	10.4	5.1	8.5
	-75.3	-19.6	-39.8		23.5	-8.6	-4.9	-20.5	12.5	35.1
	11.2	6.2	9.9	EBIT/Interest	17.7	11.3	4.8	8.5	13.5	13.2
	(177) 3.0	(169) 2.0	(152) 1.9		(17) 1.1	(31) .9	1.6	(24) 1.2	(34) 4.4	(26) 4.9
	1.2	.1	-.3		-2.0	-.7	-.4	-3.3	.1	1.5
	3.4	3.0	3.9	Net Profit + Depr., Dep., Amort./Cur. Mat. L/T/D					23.8	9.8
	(36) 2.0	(28) 1.9	(33) 1.9						(10) 3.0	(11) 3.2
	1.0	.4	1.0						1.4	1.6
	.7	.8	.6	Fixed/Worth	.7	.6	.7	.6	.5	.5
	1.2	1.5	1.2		1.5	2.0	1.8	1.1	1.0	.9
	2.8	4.9	3.0		15.2	NM	4.9	2.4	1.8	1.6
	.5	.7	.5	Debt/Worth	.6	.5	.8	.4	.3	.5
	1.1	1.7	1.3		2.1	1.6	2.2	.9	.9	1.1
	4.3	8.8	4.3		17.8	NM	6.9	2.4	2.1	2.4
	37.8	29.0	20.6	% Profit Before Taxes/Tangible Net Worth	21.4	18.8	20.4	18.4	21.6	23.4
	(175) 16.7	(152) 9.6	(149) 3.8		(19) .5	(28) -.4	(17) .9	(26) -2.2	(32) 6.1	(27) 11.8
	3.4	-2.2	-7.8		-25.0	-18.5	-25.8	-9.2	-1.1	5.7
	16.5	11.8	9.7	% Profit Before Taxes/Total Assets	7.9	8.7	7.2	14.8	13.4	10.3
	6.4	2.9	1.9		.3	-.8	1.2	1.7	3.2	6.2
	.3	-2.4	-3.4		-7.0	-6.5	-2.7	-4.5	-.9	1.1
	4.7	5.2	4.5	Sales/Net Fixed Assets	5.7	4.3	2.9	4.2	5.6	5.5
	2.7	2.6	2.3		1.8	1.1	2.2	2.2	2.8	2.9
	1.4	1.2	1.0		.7	.7	.8	.8	1.5	1.8
	1.9	1.9	1.6	Sales/Total Assets	1.5	1.4	1.5	1.9	1.7	2.0
	1.2	1.3	1.0		.7	.8	1.1	1.1	1.1	1.2
	.8	.7	.6		.3	.4	.5	.6	.8	.7
	4.3	4.0	4.5	% Depr., Dep., Amort./Sales	8.8	3.8	7.3	4.7	4.0	4.1
	(181) 7.4	(167) 7.7	(155) 8.4		(17) 12.5	(34) 12.3	(18) 10.7	(26) 10.4	(34) 6.3	(26) 4.9
	12.6	13.1	16.4		21.8	21.7	18.0	17.2	14.2	9.1
	1.9	1.4	1.5	% Officers', Directors' Owners' Comp/Sales		1.5				
	(62) 3.4	(57) 3.5	(45) 3.2			(10) 3.3				
	6.7	6.6	8.2			10.8				
	4411726M	3706324M	3433877M	Net Sales ($)	9958M	73341M	77117M	206142M	619236M	2448083M
	3710540M	3312624M	3224234M	Total Assets ($)	22585M	138164M	102943M	269361M	776090M	1915091M

Current Data Sorted by Assets / Comparative Historical Data

Type of Statement	0-500M	500M-2MM	2-10MM	10-50MM	50-100MM	100-250MM	4/1/05-3/31/06 ALL	4/1/06-3/31/07 ALL
Unqualified	1		2	2	7	6	4	9
Reviewed		5	3	5			8	11
Compiled	2	4	3	1		1	7	10
Tax Returns	5	9	5				9	10
Other	2	14	15	22	8	3	36	38

11 (4/1-9/30/09)   114 (10/1/09-3/31/10)

	0-500M	500M-2MM	2-10MM	10-50MM	50-100MM	100-250MM	4/1/05-3/31/06 ALL	4/1/06-3/31/07 ALL
NUMBER OF STATEMENTS	10	32	28	30	16	9	64	78
	%	%	%	%	%	%	%	%
ASSETS								
Cash & Equivalents	8.1	11.7	15.2	7.1	8.9		11.7	13.1
Trade Receivables (net)	20.5	22.7	16.8	21.1	12.5		19.1	20.9
Inventory	6.9	6.8	9.8	7.8	7.2		3.0	4.3
All Other Current	2.9	1.3	5.5	5.8	1.7		2.3	3.3
Total Current	38.5	42.6	47.3	41.9	30.4		36.2	41.6
Fixed Assets (net)	55.4	46.4	45.0	45.6	55.5		49.6	47.6
Intangibles (net)	5.6	3.6	.9	5.4	8.6		2.9	1.6
All Other Non-Current	.6	7.3	6.8	7.0	5.5		11.4	9.2
Total	100.0	100.0	100.0	100.0	100.0		100.0	100.0
LIABILITIES								
Notes Payable-Short Term	16.7	4.6	6.0	3.4	3.8		5.2	5.5
Cur. Mat.-L.T.D.	30.1	5.0	5.1	5.1	5.9		5.8	4.0
Trade Payables	10.0	10.8	7.1	10.5	5.2		7.6	8.9
Income Taxes Payable	.1	.0	.3	.2	.1		.3	.4
All Other Current	8.1	6.4	7.3	9.8	8.0		11.3	11.1
Total Current	64.9	26.7	25.8	29.0	22.9		30.2	29.9
Long-Term Debt	65.0	33.4	22.6	16.3	19.7		19.2	23.0
Deferred Taxes	.0	.4	.3	1.6	2.6		1.4	.3
All Other Non-Current	37.4	3.6	7.1	6.4	5.6		3.8	9.9
Net Worth	-67.5	35.9	44.2	46.8	49.1		45.4	36.8
Total Liabilities & Net Worth	100.0	100.0	100.0	100.0	100.0		100.0	100.0
INCOME DATA								
Net Sales	100.0	100.0	100.0	100.0	100.0		100.0	100.0
Gross Profit								
Operating Expenses	92.1	96.3	85.6	96.2	92.4		82.4	80.5
Operating Profit	7.9	3.7	14.4	3.8	7.6		17.6	19.5
All Other Expenses (net)	3.0	1.2	1.5	1.9	3.1		1.2	1.8
Profit Before Taxes	4.9	2.6	12.8	1.9	4.5		16.4	17.7
RATIOS								
Current	4.6	5.9	3.1	2.3	1.9		2.1	2.6
	.8	2.0	1.8	1.3	1.0		1.4	1.6
	.3	.6	1.2	.7	.8		.6	.8
Quick	2.7	5.3	2.4	1.5	1.6		1.9	2.3
	.5	1.4	1.1	1.0	.8		1.1	1.2
	.2	.6	.6	.5	.5		.5	.7
Sales/Receivables	0 UND	16 23.2	33 11.1	19 19.0	40 9.2		13 29.2	23 16.2
	30 12.2	42 8.7	43 8.4	48 7.6	59 6.2		54 6.7	46 8.0
	48 7.5	71 5.1	59 6.2	77 4.7	78 4.7		84 4.4	67 5.4
Cost of Sales/Inventory								
Cost of Sales/Payables								
Sales/Working Capital	35.8	5.2	2.5	4.4	5.8		5.9	7.2
	NM	10.2	8.0	17.7	-86.2		14.7	12.5
	-4.2	-21.0	32.7	-17.1	-15.9		-20.4	-25.4
EBIT/Interest		13.3	18.1	10.4	8.8		25.8	28.9
		(25) 1.8	(19) 5.9	(29) 1.5	4.4		(55) 8.5	(69) 10.1
		.0	-.5	-1.2	-.3		2.7	4.0
Net Profit + Depr., Dep., Amort./Cur. Mat. L/T/D							6.6	11.2
							(10) 2.6	(12) 6.5
							1.8	4.8
Fixed/Worth	2.2	.5	.4	.4	.7		.7	.4
	-4.1	1.4	.8	1.6	1.9		1.2	1.1
	-.2	19.4	2.3	2.8	2.6		3.0	3.1
Debt/Worth	3.1	.3	.5	.4	.7		.5	.4
	-5.7	1.4	1.1	1.5	1.3		1.1	1.2
	-1.4	45.5	2.6	3.9	2.8		4.1	4.6
% Profit Before Taxes/Tangible Net Worth		64.9	64.1	38.9	30.8		67.9	86.8
		(26) 9.6	(26) 24.5	(28) 5.1	(15) 8.6		(60) 41.0	(72) 49.5
		.6	-.6	-12.7	-13.9		18.1	23.6
% Profit Before Taxes/Total Assets	78.3	14.1	32.9	10.6	12.4		32.3	31.5
	8.3	4.3	13.2	1.8	3.8		16.8	14.5
	-14.8	-5.1	-.3	-4.8	-2.9		5.6	7.4
Sales/Net Fixed Assets	24.9	12.5	8.7	8.9	2.6		7.3	8.6
	5.4	3.5	2.6	2.7	1.1		2.8	3.7
	2.6	2.2	1.3	1.0	.6		1.4	1.5
Sales/Total Assets	8.8	2.7	2.5	1.6	1.0		2.1	2.4
	2.4	1.8	1.1	1.2	.7		1.4	1.6
	1.3	.8	.8		.4		.7	1.0
% Depr., Dep., Amort./Sales		2.7	1.8	5.3	7.8		2.7	2.5
		(21) 4.5	(22) 8.9	(23) 9.1	(14) 12.5		(52) 7.0	(58) 5.7
		13.3	12.9	13.6	16.2		10.9	9.6
% Officers', Directors', Owners' Comp/Sales		2.6					2.0	.7
		(13) 5.9					(22) 4.6	(22) 2.7
		10.6					12.7	6.1
Net Sales ($)	14800M	72781M	181029M	986113M	878115M	973856M	1201374M	2274329M
Total Assets ($)	2663M	36686M	132099M	676575M	1072031M	1571028M	1216817M	1606205M

M = $ thousand   MM = $ million
See Pages 9 through 22 for Explanation of Ratios and Data

Comparative Historical Data / Current Data Sorted by Sales

	4/1/07-3/31/08 ALL	4/1/08-3/31/09 ALL	4/1/09-3/31/10 ALL	0-1MM	1-3MM	3-5MM	5-10MM	10-25MM	25MM & OVER
Type of Statement									
Unqualified	19	18	18	1	1			4	12
Reviewed	12	13	13		4	3	2	4	
Compiled	18	8	11	3	3	1	3		1
Tax Returns	7	16	19	6	3	4	6		
Other	51	72	64	6	13	5	9	8	23
				11 (4/1-9/30/09)			114 (10/1/09-3/31/10)		
NUMBER OF STATEMENTS	107	127	125	16	24	13	20	16	36
	%	%	%	%	%	%	%	%	%
ASSETS									
Cash & Equivalents	12.0	9.8	10.5	12.3	12.3	12.7	11.3	7.3	8.8
Trade Receivables (net)	17.7	17.5	18.5	22.1	13.5	22.8	14.1	27.6	17.0
Inventory	3.7	4.3	7.6	3.5	5.2	7.6	9.4	7.0	10.4
All Other Current	3.5	3.1	3.7	.4	1.6	5.1	9.2	1.2	3.9
Total Current	36.9	34.6	40.3	38.3	32.6	48.3	44.0	43.1	40.1
Fixed Assets (net)	52.0	53.0	48.2	54.2	54.3	40.3	48.8	52.9	42.0
Intangibles (net)	4.9	4.0	5.0	3.5	5.0	.4	1.6	.6	11.0
All Other Non-Current	6.2	8.4	6.5	4.0	8.1	11.1	5.6	3.4	6.9
Total	100.0	100.0	100.0	100.0	100.0	100.0	100.0	100.0	100.0
LIABILITIES									
Notes Payable-Short Term	6.5	7.5	5.2	12.3	6.2	4.0	3.2	4.2	3.2
Cur. Mat.-L.T.D.	5.7	6.1	8.2	17.2	6.4	5.3	6.0	5.5	8.7
Trade Payables	7.9	9.7	8.7	9.8	6.6	5.3	11.9	8.5	9.2
Income Taxes Payable	.3	.2	.1	.1	.1	.0	.1	.2	.2
All Other Current	8.8	8.3	7.6	9.9	3.2	5.9	7.1	5.8	11.2
Total Current	29.2	31.8	29.8	49.2	22.5	20.6	28.4	24.2	32.6
Long-Term Debt	22.5	25.5	26.7	60.5	32.1	20.4	25.8	12.2	17.2
Deferred Taxes	.9	.7	1.1	.0	.8	.0	.7	1.9	1.9
All Other Non-Current	5.9	4.2	8.1	21.9	4.3	8.6	4.0	9.3	6.1
Net Worth	41.6	37.8	34.4	-31.6	40.3	50.4	41.2	52.5	42.1
Total Liabilities & Net Worth	100.0	100.0	100.0	100.0	100.0	100.0	100.0	100.0	100.0
INCOME DATA									
Net Sales	100.0	100.0	100.0	100.0	100.0	100.0	100.0	100.0	100.0
Gross Profit									
Operating Expenses	84.9	85.1	92.5	96.1	93.6	92.9	86.2	95.2	92.4
Operating Profit	15.1	14.9	7.5	3.9	6.4	7.1	13.8	4.8	7.6
All Other Expenses (net)	1.9	3.2	2.2	4.0	1.9	-1.2	2.9	1.1	2.8
Profit Before Taxes	13.2	11.8	5.3	-.2	4.5	8.3	10.9	3.7	4.8
RATIOS									
Current	2.2	2.0	2.8	2.6	3.7	6.5	2.5	2.8	2.0
	1.3	1.1	1.3	1.1	2.0	1.9	1.7	1.3	1.1
	.7	.6	.8	.5	.5	1.3	.6	1.0	.8
Quick	1.9	1.7	2.1	2.1	2.8	6.3	1.6	2.6	1.3
	1.1	.8	.9	.9	1.5	1.4	.8	1.1	.8
	.6	.5	.5	.4	.5	.8	.5	.8	.5
Sales/Receivables	19 19.3	12 31.1	25 14.8	35 10.5	0 UND	18 20.2	10 35.1	33 11.0	30 12.1
	49 7.4	38 9.7	44 8.3	46 8.0	35 10.4	40 9.2	40 9.1	58 6.3	48 7.6
	71 5.1	63 5.8	70 5.2	85 4.3	64 5.7	63 5.8	71 5.1	106 3.4	70 5.2
Cost of Sales/Inventory									
Cost of Sales/Payables									
Sales/Working Capital	5.6	6.1	5.1	2.1	5.2	4.6	3.6	6.6	5.3
	17.7	86.8	15.5	53.2	10.5	10.5	10.1	14.1	35.7
	-11.5	-8.7	-18.6	-4.8	-13.9	23.8	-24.4	NM	-15.9
EBIT/Interest	17.3	19.0	9.6	2.8	4.4	26.1	15.9	71.2	11.5
	(93) 6.8	(113) 5.2	(106) 2.1	(13) -.3	(18) 1.4	(10) 6.0	(15) 6.7	6.5	(34) 2.9
	2.2	1.7	-.5	-6.5	-.9	1.5	-1.4	-1.2	-.5
Net Profit + Depr., Dep., Amort./Cur. Mat. L/T/D	18.6	6.1	4.6						
	(19) 9.3	(22) 2.6	(21) 2.4						
	2.1	2.0	1.4						
Fixed/Worth	.8	.7	.6	.6	.8	.3	.3	.4	.7
	1.3	1.4	1.4	16.9	1.6	.9	.9	1.1	1.6
	3.4	4.0	3.4	-.7	3.9	2.0	3.1	1.9	3.0
Debt/Worth	.6	.6	.6	.5	.4	.3	.6	.4	.8
	1.7	1.4	1.4	33.0	1.3	.9	1.1	1.0	1.6
	6.7	4.8	5.8	-1.8	14.9	2.6	3.3	2.0	6.9
% Profit Before Taxes/Tangible Net Worth	77.8	65.8	47.8		53.3	122.1	78.0	36.8	42.7
	(90) 42.0	(109) 30.5	(107) 10.7	(19) 9.0	10.2	(18) 17.5	7.5	(32) 11.5	
	18.5	6.4	-5.1		.7	.1	-8.1	-8.6	-16.3
% Profit Before Taxes/Total Assets	25.6	25.0	14.6	12.8	14.2	43.6	34.5	17.6	13.9
	12.5	10.4	5.4	.2	4.9	8.0	9.6	5.0	4.8
	3.9	.6	-4.4	-12.3	-6.6	.1	-3.6	-4.3	-4.5
Sales/Net Fixed Assets	5.4	6.8	8.1	4.7	5.5	13.7	14.8	9.3	9.9
	2.4	2.7	2.7	2.2	2.6	6.7	2.3	2.7	2.2
	1.2	1.2	1.1	.4	1.5	2.1	.7	.5	1.0
Sales/Total Assets	2.0	2.1	2.2	2.0	2.4	2.8	2.5	2.9	1.6
	1.3	1.4	1.1	.7	1.2	1.8	.8	1.4	1.0
	.6	.7	.6	.2	.8	1.1	.6	.4	.7
% Depr., Dep., Amort./Sales	3.0	3.9	3.7	3.0	3.5	2.8	4.2	1.8	4.7
	(86) 7.0	(103) 8.0	(89) 9.1	(10) 11.7	(17) 8.9	(10) 4.9	(15) 9.1	(15) 10.0	(22) 10.4
	11.8	14.3	13.6	16.6	19.3	8.3	15.3	13.6	13.3
% Officers', Directors' Owners' Comp/Sales	1.4	1.4	1.1						
	(25) 2.8	(30) 4.3	(30) 4.6						
	5.9	8.7	10.6						
Net Sales ($)	3104123M	3264442M	3106694M	7593M	43459M	48966M	147937M	287012M	2571727M
Total Assets ($)	3036347M	3181116M	3491082M	13908M	41525M	36103M	189682M	414167M	2795697M

M = $ thousand   MM = $ million
See Pages 9 through 22 for Explanation of Ratios and Data

Current Data Sorted by Assets | Comparative Historical Data

Type of Statement	0-500M	500M-2MM	2-10MM	10-50MM	50-100MM	100-250MM	4/1/05-3/31/06 ALL	4/1/06-3/31/07 ALL
Unqualified		2	13	27	17	21	64	59
Reviewed		3	14	18	1	1	22	24
Compiled	1	11	17	7	2	1	44	41
Tax Returns	6	17	7	2			15	21
Other	6	21	49	79	30	41	129	145
		60 (4/1-9/30/09)		350 (10/1/09-3/31/10)				
NUMBER OF STATEMENTS	13	54	100	132	49	62	274	290

ASSETS	%	%	%	%	%	%	%	%
Cash & Equivalents	25.1	13.3	14.9	9.5	6.6	5.3	9.1	10.0
Trade Receivables (net)	18.7	25.2	25.8	20.5	17.1	12.3	31.5	28.4
Inventory	4.6	3.9	6.4	7.7	8.8	6.3	7.4	6.6
All Other Current	5.5	3.6	2.8	3.5	2.0	5.1	4.2	5.6
Total Current	54.0	46.1	49.9	41.2	34.5	28.9	52.2	50.6
Fixed Assets (net)	42.7	40.8	38.0	42.4	49.5	53.9	38.6	39.7
Intangibles (net)	.0	2.6	3.8	8.1	12.4	14.2	3.9	4.0
All Other Non-Current	3.2	10.5	8.3	8.3	3.6	3.0	5.2	5.6
Total	100.0	100.0	100.0	100.0	100.0	100.0	100.0	100.0

LIABILITIES								
Notes Payable-Short Term	18.6	11.6	6.2	6.9	4.3	4.9	8.2	8.9
Cur. Mat.-L.T.D.	7.7	4.9	5.1	4.7	7.5	4.2	4.7	3.4
Trade Payables	17.4	11.2	9.3	9.7	9.5	5.2	13.9	11.2
Income Taxes Payable	.0	.1	.3	.4	.2	.3	.7	.7
All Other Current	17.5	5.0	13.6	9.5	4.5	5.1	8.5	9.9
Total Current	61.2	32.7	34.4	32.2	26.0	19.7	36.1	34.0
Long-Term Debt	16.3	27.2	21.9	16.3	23.7	26.2	21.5	17.8
Deferred Taxes	1.9	.1	.6	1.2	.9	3.4	1.1	.9
All Other Non-Current	1.8	8.0	9.6	5.1	4.3	6.9	4.2	3.6
Net Worth	18.7	32.0	33.5	45.2	45.1	43.8	37.1	43.7
Total Liabilities & Net Worth	100.0	100.0	100.0	100.0	100.0	100.0	100.0	100.0

INCOME DATA								
Net Sales	100.0	100.0	100.0	100.0	100.0	100.0	100.0	100.0
Gross Profit								
Operating Expenses	102.9	92.7	93.3	91.9	90.2	88.9	84.8	83.8
Operating Profit	-2.9	7.3	6.7	8.1	9.8	11.1	15.2	16.2
All Other Expenses (net)	1.1	1.3	2.0	2.6	3.6	5.5	2.5	2.1
Profit Before Taxes	-4.0	6.0	4.7	5.5	6.1	5.7	12.7	14.1

RATIOS								
Current	4.2	3.5	2.8	2.6	2.2	2.5	2.3	2.7
	1.0	1.6	1.5	1.4	1.2	1.7	1.4	1.6
	.3	.8	.8	.8	.9	1.0	1.0	1.0
Quick	1.7	2.6	2.2	1.8	1.5	1.6	1.9	2.0
	.7	1.3	1.2	1.0	1.0	.9	1.1	1.2
	.3	.5	.5	.5	.6	.6	.7	.7
Sales/Receivables	0 UND	0 UND	23 15.8	29 12.6	46 8.0	45 8.2	41 8.9	35 10.4
	0 UND	39 9.3	40 9.2	49 7.4	60 6.1	57 6.4	62 5.9	58 6.2
	27 13.5	65 5.6	70 5.2	66 5.6	76 4.8	80 4.6	84 4.3	83 4.4
Cost of Sales/Inventory								
Cost of Sales/Payables								
Sales/Working Capital	11.3	7.6	5.9	5.9	3.7	4.0	5.3	5.3
	-130.3	20.3	17.0	12.5	17.0	8.3	13.0	10.8
	-4.6	-21.0	-16.3	-11.6	-151.5	NM	238.2	222.5
EBIT/Interest		17.6	17.7	16.5	6.0	4.0	23.2	30.7
		(46) 5.4	(87) 3.6	(117) 5.1	(42) 2.4	(54) 1.8	(238) 8.6	(241) 9.6
		-.4	.3	.8	-.5	.2	3.1	3.1
Net Profit + Depr., Dep., Amort./Cur. Mat. L/T/D			11.3	4.5	4.3	1.8	6.0	10.1
			(17) 3.8	(39) 2.2	(14) 2.1	(11) 1.3	(54) 2.8	(66) 3.4
			1.3	1.2	.6	.4	1.5	1.3
Fixed/Worth	.1	.4	.2	.6	1.1	1.0	.5	.4
	2.0	1.0	.8	1.3	1.8	1.7	1.0	.9
	NM	8.1	3.7	2.5	5.0	5.1	2.4	2.0
Debt/Worth	.6	.6	.7	.6	.7	.8	.8	.6
	4.7	2.3	1.6	1.6	1.9	1.9	1.9	1.5
	NM	20.5	8.0	3.2	9.8	7.2	5.3	3.5
% Profit Before Taxes/Tangible Net Worth	119.4	97.7	45.3	45.4	39.4	20.9	69.1	69.8
	(10) 16.1	(43) 56.4	(85) 19.7	(115) 18.6	(39) 11.9	(54) 8.3	(241) 41.5	(268) 43.8
	-87.9	2.7	.9	2.1	-6.6	-4.5	18.5	17.4
% Profit Before Taxes/Total Assets	45.7	28.8	20.5	17.2	11.9	6.0	25.8	30.0
	-13.3	6.4	6.4	7.7	2.3	1.3	13.3	15.4
	-38.2	-3.1	-1.3	.1	-3.3	-2.4	5.6	4.9
Sales/Net Fixed Assets	180.9	23.6	22.5	8.2	4.4	2.0	16.6	14.9
	11.9	6.3	6.6	3.8	1.5	1.3	5.3	4.8
	4.4	2.0	1.8	1.8	.9	.7	2.0	2.1
Sales/Total Assets	5.9	3.8	3.0	2.1	1.2	.9	2.7	2.7
	5.0	2.2	1.9	1.4	.9	.7	1.7	1.7
	2.0	1.1	1.1	.9	.5	.4	1.0	.9
% Depr., Dep., Amort./Sales		2.0	.9	2.2	3.4	4.4	1.5	1.5
		(36) 5.3	(81) 3.8	(117) 5.7	(41) 9.2	(24) 8.8	(222) 3.9	(227) 3.7
		15.2	9.9	11.9	14.9	12.6	7.1	6.4
% Officers', Directors' Owners' Comp/Sales		1.6	1.5	.7			1.4	1.3
		(29) 4.7	(25) 2.5	(19) 2.4			(58) 3.9	(62) 3.1
		9.3	5.0	9.1			9.7	11.5
Net Sales ($)	13894M	168652M	1125028M	5028985M	3774105M	7380403M	11854338M	12171108M
Total Assets ($)	2677M	66447M	506695M	3171580M	3481054M	10126089M	7741562M	9428953M

M = $ thousand   MM = $ million
See Pages 9 through 22 for Explanation of Ratios and Data

Comparative Historical Data | Current Data Sorted by Sales

			Type of Statement	0-1MM	1-3MM	3-5MM	5-10MM	10-25MM	25MM & OVER
79	86	80	Unqualified	1	1	2	7	15	54
27	34	36	Reviewed	2	1	5	7	13	8
40	45	36	Compiled	1	6	8	10	6	5
27	19	32	Tax Returns	5	12	7	4	1	3
177	195	226	Other	9	24	11	19	47	116
4/1/07-3/31/08 ALL	4/1/08-3/31/09 ALL	4/1/09-3/31/10 ALL		60 (4/1-9/30/09)			350 (10/1/09-3/31/10)		
350	379	410	NUMBER OF STATEMENTS	18	44	33	47	82	186
%	%	%	ASSETS	%	%	%	%	%	%
10.1	8.6	10.8	Cash & Equivalents	18.9	15.1	7.9	18.0	10.3	8.0
28.1	27.3	20.7	Trade Receivables (net)	9.9	16.6	22.5	25.5	20.2	21.4
7.2	7.7	6.7	Inventory	.6	5.6	5.3	4.0	4.6	9.4
5.5	5.1	3.5	All Other Current	6.4	2.4	1.2	3.8	3.2	3.9
50.9	48.7	41.7	Total Current	35.9	39.7	36.9	51.4	38.3	42.7
39.2	40.0	43.7	Fixed Assets (net)	56.3	43.8	52.9	36.3	43.4	42.9
4.7	5.2	7.5	Intangibles (net)	2.9	2.2	1.3	3.0	10.1	10.3
5.2	6.1	7.1	All Other Non-Current	4.8	14.3	8.9	9.3	8.2	4.2
100.0	100.0	100.0	Total	100.0	100.0	100.0	100.0	100.0	100.0
			LIABILITIES						
8.2	7.6	7.1	Notes Payable-Short Term	12.2	11.8	8.4	10.2	5.1	5.4
4.8	4.8	5.2	Cur. Mat.-L.T.D.	7.5	5.7	4.6	4.7	4.9	5.2
10.7	11.4	9.6	Trade Payables	3.8	13.0	8.9	9.3	8.7	10.0
.7	.6	.3	Income Taxes Payable	.0	.1	.5	.2	.2	.4
10.0	8.5	8.9	All Other Current	18.2	4.5	9.3	13.9	8.4	7.9
34.3	32.9	31.1	Total Current	41.8	35.0	31.7	38.2	27.3	28.9
20.6	20.0	21.5	Long-Term Debt	31.5	30.4	26.1	19.4	16.6	20.2
1.0	1.0	1.2	Deferred Taxes	1.7	.0	.3	.9	1.1	1.8
4.5	4.2	6.7	All Other Non-Current	10.0	8.7	4.8	4.6	9.4	5.5
39.6	41.9	39.5	Net Worth	14.8	25.9	37.1	36.9	45.6	43.6
100.0	100.0	100.0	Total Liabilities & Net Worth	100.0	100.0	100.0	100.0	100.0	100.0
			INCOME DATA						
100.0	100.0	100.0	Net Sales	100.0	100.0	100.0	100.0	100.0	100.0
			Gross Profit						
86.7	87.4	92.0	Operating Expenses	94.5	90.2	93.4	94.6	91.1	91.8
13.3	12.6	8.0	Operating Profit	5.5	9.8	6.6	5.4	8.9	8.2
1.7	1.8	2.8	All Other Expenses (net)	4.1	3.2	3.6	1.6	2.5	2.8
11.6	10.8	5.2	Profit Before Taxes	1.4	6.6	3.0	3.8	6.4	5.4
			RATIOS						
2.7	2.6	2.6	Current	3.7	2.7	2.8	2.7	2.5	2.6
1.5	1.6	1.4		.9	1.0	1.3	1.4	1.4	1.6
1.0	1.0	.8		.1	.4	.5	.8	.9	1.1
2.1	1.9	2.0	Quick	2.1	2.2	2.0	2.4	1.9	1.9
1.1 (378)	1.1	1.1		.6	.7	1.0	1.2	1.1	1.1
.6	.7	.5		.1	.3	.4	.6	.6	.6
34 10.7	31 11.8	28 13.2	Sales/Receivables	0 UND	0 UND	7 52.2	21 17.0	27 13.7	35 10.3
56 6.6	54 6.8	49 7.4		13 28.7	34 10.8	43 8.4	41 8.8	53 6.8	51 7.1
72 5.1	79 4.6	69 5.3		79 4.6	66 5.5	66 5.5	73 5.0	66 5.5	71 5.2
			Cost of Sales/Inventory						
			Cost of Sales/Payables						
5.2	5.1	5.3	Sales/Working Capital	3.8	5.5	7.8	6.0	5.9	4.5
13.5	11.3	13.8		NM	NM	30.5	12.1	14.5	11.3
-272.5	-363.3	-18.7		-3.1	-7.7	-7.4	-18.2	-69.7	104.7
24.6	23.9	12.7	EBIT/Interest	28.8	11.8	12.2	16.5	11.6	13.4
(313) 8.1	(332) 7.7	(354) 3.3		(11) -.4	(38) 4.0	(28) 2.5	(42) 2.5	(72) 3.6	(163) 3.5
2.9	2.5	.1		-2.0	.2	-.7	-.5	-1.4	.9
13.2	10.2	4.9	Net Profit + Depr., Dep., Amort./Cur. Mat. L/T/D					5.6	4.5
(77) 4.2	(88) 3.4	(84) 2.3						(22) 1.8	(49) 2.3
1.4	1.6	1.2						.9	1.3
.4	.4	.5	Fixed/Worth	.7	.4	.5	.3	.6	.6
1.1	1.1	1.4		11.3	1.3	1.6	.8	1.2	1.4
2.3	2.9	4.0		-2.7	NM	4.4	2.4	3.1	3.6
.7	.7	.7	Debt/Worth	.6	.7	.8	.6	.6	.7
1.6	1.7	1.8		20.2	4.1	1.6	1.4	1.7	1.7
4.3	4.2	6.1		-6.8	NM	4.5	3.7	5.0	4.3
78.7	69.8	45.5	% Profit Before Taxes/Tangible Net Worth	125.4	93.0	47.1	75.6	33.6	40.7
(311) 44.7	(341) 36.2	(346) 15.8		(11) .0	(33) 24.7	(29) 7.7	(42) 23.1	(70) 15.7	(161) 15.5
22.4	12.8	-2.3		-16.8	3.4	-9.7	-7.8	-4.2	.1
28.6	26.7	16.4	% Profit Before Taxes/Total Assets	8.7	20.1	15.8	29.7	14.8	15.1
15.5	12.4	4.7		-.4	3.6	3.7	6.1	6.3	4.9
5.2	3.5	-1.9		-13.7	-2.3	-4.4	-2.7	-2.5	-.7
17.3	16.7	12.6	Sales/Net Fixed Assets	7.2	17.1	6.9	21.4	10.4	8.3
5.1	4.2	3.0		1.7	4.7	2.9	9.9	2.5	2.9
2.1	1.8	1.4		.9	1.4	.8	1.8	1.5	1.4
2.7	2.6	2.3	Sales/Total Assets	2.0	2.4	2.3	3.1	2.1	2.1
1.7	1.6	1.3		.8	1.2	1.7	2.0	1.4	1.1
1.0	.9	.7		.5	.5	.5	1.1	.7	.7
1.1	1.1	2.0	% Depr., Dep., Amort./Sales		4.7	4.9	.9	2.7	1.4
(276) 3.4	(297) 3.9	(303) 5.7			(27) 9.7	(27) 7.8	(37) 4.2	(75) 7.4	(129) 4.4
7.3	8.0	12.5			22.7	21.7	11.5	15.2	9.5
1.0	1.6	1.3	% Officers', Directors' Owners' Comp/Sales		2.8	1.3	2.0	2.7	1.1
(77) 2.4	(66) 3.1	(88) 3.4			(17) 4.3	(14) 3.1	(15) 5.5	(16) 2.1	(18) 1.1
6.5	7.0	8.5			9.9	5.7	8.1	4.0	2.9
19467672M	22856599M	17491067M	Net Sales ($)	10186M	81689M	134802M	334959M	1361734M	15567697M
11894206M	14725459M	17354542M	Total Assets ($)	22769M	112869M	181410M	248033M	1808656M	14980805M

© RMA 2010

M = $ thousand   MM = $ million
See Pages 9 through 22 for Explanation of Ratios and Data

UTILITIES

Current Data Sorted by Assets   Comparative Historical Data

0-500M	500M-2MM	2-10MM	10-50MM	50-100MM	100-250MM	Type of Statement	4/1/05-3/31/06 ALL	4/1/06-3/31/07 ALL
3	4	26	141	164	123	Unqualified	273	343
4	6				1	Reviewed	25	19
1	1	3	1			Compiled	14	7
2		2				Tax Returns	4	5
	5	17	17	11	23	Other	73	39
	145 (4/1-9/30/09)		410 (10/1/09-3/31/10)					
6	14	54	159	175	147	NUMBER OF STATEMENTS	389	413
%	%	%	%	%	%	ASSETS	%	%
	22.1	11.8	7.0	4.6	4.6	Cash & Equivalents	7.3	7.8
	21.4	19.7	9.7	5.8	5.5	Trade Receivables (net)	12.8	10.0
	6.5	5.0	2.5	2.1	1.4	Inventory	2.4	2.3
	3.8	6.1	2.0	1.8	2.3	All Other Current	3.2	2.7
	53.8	42.6	21.2	14.4	13.8	Total Current	25.6	22.8
	30.7	40.0	65.2	71.6	71.0	Fixed Assets (net)	61.3	63.3
	.4	6.4	1.4	1.4	2.3	Intangibles (net)	2.6	2.0
	15.1	11.0	12.2	12.7	12.9	All Other Non-Current	10.6	11.9
	100.0	100.0	100.0	100.0	100.0	Total	100.0	100.0
						LIABILITIES		
	6.3	10.8	2.2	2.0	2.5	Notes Payable-Short Term	2.7	2.7
	28.9	3.8	2.1	2.1	2.0	Cur. Mat.-L.T.D.	2.5	2.2
	10.3	10.2	6.1	4.3	4.3	Trade Payables	9.0	6.5
	.1	.5	.5	.3	.2	Income Taxes Payable	.4	.4
	10.8	11.5	4.7	3.9	3.8	All Other Current	5.9	5.4
	56.5	36.7	15.6	12.6	12.9	Total Current	20.4	17.3
	32.0	22.9	32.9	40.7	44.6	Long-Term Debt	36.4	36.3
	.0	.9	.3	.1	.7	Deferred Taxes	.7	.9
	10.7	5.4	3.6	3.5	5.9	All Other Non-Current	3.8	5.2
	.8	34.1	47.6	43.2	35.9	Net Worth	38.7	40.3
	100.0	100.0	100.0	100.0	100.0	Total Liabilities & Net Worth	100.0	100.0
						INCOME DATA		
	100.0	100.0	100.0	100.0	100.0	Net Sales	100.0	100.0
						Gross Profit		
	84.1	89.5	91.7	91.8	90.9	Operating Expenses	89.4	90.2
	15.9	10.5	8.3	8.2	9.1	Operating Profit	10.6	9.8
	4.9	2.6	2.0	2.0	2.9	All Other Expenses (net)	4.0	2.9
	11.0	7.9	6.3	6.3	6.2	Profit Before Taxes	6.6	7.0
						RATIOS		
	2.0	2.2	1.9	1.7	1.3	Current	1.8	1.8
	1.4	1.4	1.3	1.1	1.0		1.2	1.2
	.4	.7	1.0	.7	.7		.9	.8
	1.8	1.8	1.4	1.3	1.0	Quick	1.5	1.4
	.9	.8	1.0	.7	.7		.9	.9
	.2	.4	.7	.4	.4		.6	.6
	11 33.1	22 16.8	29 12.5	26 14.3	22 16.6	Sales/Receivables	27 13.6	26 13.8
	32 11.4	35 10.3	40 9.1	34 10.8	31 11.9		37 10.0	36 10.2
	50 7.3	51 7.1	50 7.3	45 8.2	45 8.1		50 7.3	47 7.8
						Cost of Sales/Inventory		
						Cost of Sales/Payables		
	6.7	6.9	6.7	10.2	16.5	Sales/Working Capital	7.9	7.4
	9.6	15.7	22.1	50.5	-190.3		23.1	33.7
	-7.4	-9.8	-116.7	-14.4	-11.9		-36.8	-20.5
		15.5	4.0	3.1	2.9	EBIT/Interest	4.3	3.8
		(47) 3.7	(152) 2.5	(171) 2.4	(141) 2.1		(355) 2.4	(384) 2.4
		.5	1.9	1.8	1.7		1.7	1.6
		13.4	6.5	7.6	6.8	Net Profit + Depr., Dep., Amort./Cur. Mat. L/T/D	5.2	6.8
		(10) 1.4	(21) 2.5	(17) 3.9	(13) 2.7		(47) 2.7	(57) 3.3
		.6	1.6	3.0	2.2		1.5	2.2
	.0	.3	1.0	1.4	1.7	Fixed/Worth	1.0	1.2
	.6	1.0	1.6	1.8	2.1		1.7	1.8
	NM	2.9	2.2	2.4	2.8		2.6	2.5
	.8	.7	.6	1.0	1.4	Debt/Worth	.9	.9
	1.9	2.0	1.3	1.4	1.9		1.6	1.6
	NM	5.5	1.9	2.0	2.7		2.6	2.4
	43.2	48.0	10.8	10.2	10.9	% Profit Before Taxes/Tangible Net Worth	14.1	13.2
	(11) 34.7	(49) 18.0	(157) 6.4	(167) 7.6	(143) 7.7		(368) 7.2	(399) 7.5
	-13.9	4.9	4.4	5.5	4.9		4.2	4.7
	25.8	17.5	4.4	4.3	4.0	% Profit Before Taxes/Total Assets	4.8	4.9
	5.5	4.9	3.1	3.1	2.6		2.9	3.1
	.0	-.2	1.9	2.0	1.6		1.5	1.7
	195.0	42.4	1.0	.8	.9	Sales/Net Fixed Assets	1.7	1.2
	13.1	3.5	.7	.6	.6		.7	.7
	1.3	.7	.5	.5	.5		.5	.5
	3.1	3.2	.7	.6	.6	Sales/Total Assets	.9	.8
	1.3	1.0	.5	.5	.5		.5	.5
	.6	.5	.4	.4	.4		.4	.4
	1.2	1.8	5.1	5.3	5.3	% Depr., Dep., Amort./Sales	4.6	4.6
	(11) 5.6	(47) 5.7	(156) 6.8	(174) 6.7	(137) 6.8		(360) 6.3	(386) 6.3
	14.8	10.0	8.8	8.4	9.2		8.8	8.6
						% Officers', Directors' Owners' Comp/Sales	1.7	2.0
							(28) 4.5	(19) 3.2
							9.7	5.6
3023M	34213M	604857M	3984380M	7185214M	12367129M	Net Sales ($)	19397955M	18744209M
1248M	16586M	332684M	4877137M	12709690M	22754847M	Total Assets ($)	25547502M	28033672M

M = $ thousand   MM = $ million
See Pages 9 through 22 for Explanation of Ratios and Data

Comparative Historical Data

Current Data Sorted by Sales

				Type of Statement						
	308	158	461	Unqualified	8	7	11	34	120	281
	12	11	11	Reviewed	1	3		2	3	2
	9	5	6	Compiled	1	2	1			2
	4	4	4	Tax Returns	2			1	1	
	58	54	73	Other	2	4	5	10	13	39
	4/1/07- 3/31/08	4/1/08- 3/31/09	4/1/09- 3/31/10			145 (4/1-9/30/09)			410 (10/1/09-3/31/10)	
	ALL	ALL	ALL		0-1MM	1-3MM	3-5MM	5-10MM	10-25MM	25MM & OVER
	391	232	555	NUMBER OF STATEMENTS	14	16	17	47	137	324
	%	%	%	ASSETS	%	%	%	%	%	%
	6.9	9.0	6.5	Cash & Equivalents	13.1	6.6	10.0	8.5	5.8	6.0
	9.7	13.5	8.7	Trade Receivables (net)	6.8	8.7	7.0	13.2	8.3	8.3
	2.6	3.0	2.5	Inventory	10.0	2.1	2.4	3.6	1.7	2.4
	2.2	4.0	2.5	All Other Current	1.2	1.8	3.7	4.0	2.4	2.3
	21.3	29.5	20.1	Total Current	31.1	19.2	23.1	29.3	18.1	19.0
	64.7	55.7	65.1	Fixed Assets (net)	54.1	47.9	65.9	58.4	67.1	66.6
	2.2	2.1	2.3	Intangibles (net)	8.0	12.7	1.3	1.4	2.2	1.7
	11.8	12.6	12.5	All Other Non-Current	7.3	20.2	9.8	10.8	12.5	12.7
	100.0	100.0	100.0	Total	100.0	100.0	100.0	100.0	100.0	100.0
				LIABILITIES						
	2.5	3.1	3.2	Notes Payable-Short Term	5.9	21.4	5.6	2.4	2.4	2.6
	2.9	4.1	3.0	Cur. Mat.-L.T.D.	27.6	5.6	6.5	2.3	2.6	1.9
	6.6	8.3	5.5	Trade Payables	2.8	5.4	3.3	6.3	4.5	6.1
	.4	.4	.3	Income Taxes Payable	.0	.0	.4	.8	.3	.3
	5.2	6.8	5.0	All Other Current	4.8	7.7	2.8	5.9	3.9	5.3
	17.6	22.6	17.1	Total Current	41.1	40.2	18.5	17.7	13.8	16.1
	37.1	33.4	38.3	Long-Term Debt	30.1	74.3	28.3	34.3	36.8	38.6
	.7	1.3	.4	Deferred Taxes	.0	1.6	1.5	.6	.2	.4
	5.2	7.4	4.5	All Other Non-Current	2.4	17.6	2.4	4.0	2.5	5.0
	39.4	35.4	39.7	Net Worth	26.4	-33.6	49.2	43.4	46.8	39.9
	100.0	100.0	100.0	Total Liabilities & Net Worth	100.0	100.0	100.0	100.0	100.0	100.0
				INCOME DATA						
	100.0	100.0	100.0	Net Sales	100.0	100.0	100.0	100.0	100.0	100.0
				Gross Profit						
	89.1	89.2	90.9	Operating Expenses	78.1	79.9	90.9	92.0	91.1	91.8
	10.9	10.8	9.1	Operating Profit	21.9	20.1	9.1	8.0	8.9	8.2
	2.8	3.2	2.4	All Other Expenses (net)	5.8	6.2	3.6	2.4	2.6	1.9
	8.1	7.6	6.7	Profit Before Taxes	16.1	13.9	5.4	5.6	6.3	6.3
				RATIOS						
	1.7	1.9	1.7		2.6	1.2	2.6	2.7	1.8	1.5
	1.1	1.3	1.2	Current	1.4	.9	1.4	1.5	1.3	1.1
	.8	.9	.8		.3	.5	.7	.9	.9	.7
	1.3	1.5	1.3		2.2	.8	2.0	1.9	1.5	1.2
	.8	.9	.8	Quick	.4	.6	.8	.9	1.0	.7
	.5	.6	.5		.1	.4	.4	.5	.6	.6
26	14.3	26 14.0	26 14.3		0 UND	16 22.7	26 13.9	30 12.2	29 12.6	23 15.6
36	10.2	36 10.2	35 10.3	Sales/Receivables	30 12.0	36 10.2	35 10.4	44 8.3	41 8.9	33 11.2
46	7.9	53 6.9	47 7.8		37 10.0	44 8.3	49 7.4	60 6.1	52 7.1	44 8.2
				Cost of Sales/Inventory						
				Cost of Sales/Payables						
	8.9	7.6	8.7		4.9	14.5	4.2	3.8	8.0	13.3
	46.0	20.1	37.1	Sales/Working Capital	7.7	-27.4	8.4	7.9	21.9	82.7
	-18.4	-31.4	-20.0		-3.8	-3.9	-9.1	-33.9	-96.8	-16.1
	4.0	5.4	3.5			9.4	5.5	3.7	3.4	3.4
(358)	2.4	(205) 3.0	(523) 2.3	EBIT/Interest	(14)	(16) 2.6	(38) 3.0	(132) 2.5	(314) 2.3	2.3
	1.7	1.9	1.8			.3	.7	1.7	1.9	1.8
	7.0	7.3	5.8						4.7	9.6
(52)	3.7	(47) 2.7	(62) 2.9	Net Profit + Depr., Dep., Amort./Cur. Mat. L/T/D				(16) 3.5	(30) 3.6	
	1.5	1.4	1.6						1.8	2.5
	1.1	.8	1.2		.8	1.3	.9	.7	1.1	1.3
	1.8	1.5	1.8	Fixed/Worth	3.5	3.4	1.8	1.7	1.6	1.9
	2.5	2.5	2.5		NM	-.2	2.1	2.6	2.2	2.6
	.9	.7	1.0		.6	1.6	.5	.5	.8	1.1
	1.6	1.6	1.5	Debt/Worth	4.2	3.3	1.4	1.7	1.4	1.6
	2.4	3.1	2.4		NM	-1.4	2.1	3.1	1.9	2.4
	13.0	23.2	12.0		43.2	36.0	14.6	16.4	10.1	12.1
(372)	8.3	(213) 8.8	(531) 7.7	% Profit Before Taxes/Tangible Net Worth	(11) 28.3	(11) 11.2	5.7	(44) 8.1	(135) 7.0	(313) 7.7
	5.1	4.4	5.0		15.8	5.4	-3.9	4.3	5.0	5.1
	5.1	7.2	4.6		17.8	13.6	4.8	6.4	4.3	4.5
	3.4	3.5	3.1	% Profit Before Taxes/Total Assets	5.2	4.1	3.0	2.9	3.1	3.0
	1.8	1.3	1.9		3.4	.2	-1.7	1.5	2.0	1.9
	1.1	4.4	1.1		12.1	10.7	.8	1.5	.9	1.1
	.7	1.0	.7	Sales/Net Fixed Assets	1.2	.7	.7	.6	.6	.7
	.5	.6	.5		.5	.5	.5	.5	.5	.6
	.8	1.3	.7		1.7	1.1	.5	.9	.6	.7
	.5	.7	.5	Sales/Total Assets	.6	.5	.4	.4	.4	.5
	.4	.4	.4		.3	.3	.4	.3	.4	.4
	4.7	3.0	5.1		2.3	1.5	7.7	6.5	5.6	4.7
(372)	6.4	(212) 5.8	(531) 6.7	% Depr., Dep., Amort./Sales	8.2	6.4	(16) 10.3	(43) 8.5	(134) 7.4	(308) 6.1
	8.3	8.3	8.7		15.7	16.5	12.8	12.9	9.0	7.8
	2.6	3.6	1.7							
(20)	4.2	(20) 5.1	(17) 4.4	% Officers', Directors' Owners' Comp/Sales						
	5.4	9.1	6.8							
	18663848M	14267877M	24178816M	Net Sales ($)	8163M	30101M	66487M	347029M	2344493M	21382543M
	28108211M	15783151M	40692192M	Total Assets ($)	17959M	72760M	169540M	947784M	5448416M	34035733M

M = $ thousand   MM = $ million
See Pages 9 through 22 for Explanation of Ratios and Data

Current Data Sorted by Assets | | | | | | | Comparative Historical Data

						Type of Statement		
	1	7	18	9	12	Unqualified	43	75
	1	5	8	1		Reviewed	17	18
3	4	7				Compiled	17	21
2		2		2		Tax Returns	5	15
4	7	10	13	8	15	Other	47	49
	41 (4/1-9/30/09)		98 (10/1/09-3/31/10)				4/1/05-3/31/06	4/1/06-3/31/07
0-500M	500M-2MM	2-10MM	10-50MM	50-100MM	100-250MM		ALL	ALL
7	15	31	41	18	27	NUMBER OF STATEMENTS	129	178
%	%	%	%	%	%	ASSETS	%	%
	23.2	17.0	10.5	12.5	5.8	Cash & Equivalents	9.5	10.1
	19.8	24.3	23.7	12.9	10.7	Trade Receivables (net)	25.8	21.1
	5.2	8.0	9.0	3.7	3.3	Inventory	9.7	10.3
	1.7	2.7	2.1	4.0	5.7	All Other Current	4.1	3.1
	49.8	52.0	45.3	33.2	25.5	Total Current	49.2	44.6
	32.4	37.3	44.5	57.5	60.5	Fixed Assets (net)	40.5	42.4
	12.4	2.0	3.2	3.1	6.1	Intangibles (net)	4.4	5.1
	5.4	8.7	7.0	6.2	7.9	All Other Non-Current	5.9	7.9
	100.0	100.0	100.0	100.0	100.0	Total	100.0	100.0
						LIABILITIES		
	5.8	6.6	8.8	2.8	2.9	Notes Payable-Short Term	10.8	7.1
	5.1	2.2	2.1	.9	4.4	Cur. Mat.-L.T.D.	3.1	3.4
	22.1	21.7	19.2	9.0	9.1	Trade Payables	22.4	17.3
	.9	.0	.6	.0	.4	Income Taxes Payable	.7	.3
	7.1	6.7	7.8	13.3	6.9	All Other Current	7.4	9.9
	41.0	37.2	38.5	26.0	23.7	Total Current	44.4	37.9
	25.0	14.7	13.3	23.4	20.3	Long-Term Debt	20.1	24.1
	.4	1.9	2.6	2.1	3.8	Deferred Taxes	1.8	2.1
	10.6	4.2	4.7	3.0	4.8	All Other Non-Current	4.3	4.6
	22.9	42.1	40.9	45.6	47.6	Net Worth	29.3	31.3
	100.0	100.0	100.0	100.0	100.0	Total Liabilities & Net Worth	100.0	100.0
						INCOME DATA		
	100.0	100.0	100.0	100.0	100.0	Net Sales	100.0	100.0
						Gross Profit		
	89.9	91.9	93.9	76.2	88.5	Operating Expenses	93.5	92.6
	10.1	8.1	6.1	23.8	11.5	Operating Profit	6.5	7.4
	3.0	1.6	.5	6.6	4.8	All Other Expenses (net)	1.2	2.0
	7.1	6.4	5.5	17.1	6.8	Profit Before Taxes	5.3	5.3
						RATIOS		
	4.7	2.2	1.8	1.9	1.8		1.6	1.8
	1.0	1.3	1.2	1.2	1.0	Current	1.2	1.2
	.8	1.0	1.0	.5	.6		.8	.9
	4.5	1.4	1.3	1.3	.9		1.2	1.2
	1.0	1.1	1.0	.6	.6	Quick	.9	.8
	.3	.7	.8	.2	.4		.4	.5
	13 28.4	9 39.2	14 26.4	10 37.1	18 20.0		17 21.3	15 24.3
	27 13.7	15 24.6	26 14.2	36 10.1	27 13.4	Sales/Receivables	27 13.6	28 13.0
	43 8.5	35 10.3	56 6.5	48 7.5	45 8.1		52 7.0	46 8.0
						Cost of Sales/Inventory		
						Cost of Sales/Payables		
	6.5	9.9	8.3	6.1	10.0		8.4	10.8
	446.3	44.3	22.6	66.5	104.3	Sales/Working Capital	38.2	53.1
	-17.0	-669.7	245.5	-5.5	-10.3		-48.4	-33.8
	13.6	24.9	18.3	10.9	6.8		11.0	7.4
	(10) 5.0	(26) 6.1	(33) 6.7	(15) 5.9	(24) 4.9	EBIT/Interest	(116) 3.7	(151) 3.2
	.5	.5	1.5	2.9	2.3		1.8	1.6
			9.2				6.9	6.2
		(10)	5.2			Net Profit + Depr., Dep., Amort./Cur. Mat. L/T/D	(30) 2.1	(37) 2.9
			2.0				1.4	1.8
	.3	.3	.5	.5	1.0		.4	.5
	1.9	.9	1.1	1.3	1.7	Fixed/Worth	1.3	1.5
	-3.6	1.4	1.8	2.7	2.3		3.5	3.8
	2.2	.9	.6	.6	.5		1.0	.9
	3.4	1.7	1.4	1.6	1.6	Debt/Worth	2.5	2.5
	-6.2	2.7	4.1	2.5	2.1		9.8	7.4
	437.3	37.4	42.7	23.0	28.5		49.2	43.9
	(10) 41.7	(30) 25.2	(39) 9.7	14.0	(26) 15.0	% Profit Before Taxes/Tangible Net Worth	(113) 14.9	(152) 15.4
	11.0	4.7	4.1	6.5	5.5		4.7	6.5
	22.9	16.0	10.6	8.2	7.9		11.9	10.2
	6.6	8.2	5.0	5.8	5.2	% Profit Before Taxes/Total Assets	5.1	4.9
	-2.4	2.1	.9	3.2	2.8		1.7	1.0
	52.7	160.3	50.6	10.7	2.5		59.9	39.3
	9.9	21.3	3.0	.7	.9	Sales/Net Fixed Assets	6.3	3.8
	3.4	2.1	1.0	.2	.6		1.6	1.3
	4.8	6.8	3.1	1.4	1.0		5.0	3.8
	2.3	3.6	1.6	.4	.6	Sales/Total Assets	2.0	1.6
	.9	1.6	.7	.2	.4		.9	.8
	1.0	.1	.6	3.9	4.5		.6	1.2
	(10) 3.8	(27) .9	(39) 3.5	(17) 7.1	(18) 6.9	% Depr., Dep., Amort./Sales	(106) 3.3	(151) 3.6
	6.4	5.7	5.4	16.7	12.6		5.5	5.4
							.4	.6
		(23)		(26)		% Officers', Directors' Owners' Comp/Sales	1.2	1.0
							2.6	1.7
11080M	54674M	825482M	2083734M	3027357M	5247507M	Net Sales ($)	15200514M	20540237M
1463M	18587M	173800M	979356M	1342459M	4320027M	Total Assets ($)	6225734M	7960914M

M = $ thousand   MM = $ million
See Pages 9 through 22 for Explanation of Ratios and Data

Comparative Historical Data | Current Data Sorted by Sales

4/1/07-3/31/08 ALL	4/1/08-3/31/09 ALL	4/1/09-3/31/10 ALL	Type of Statement	0-1MM	1-3MM	3-5MM	5-10MM	10-25MM	25MM & OVER
62	50	47	Unqualified	1	5		3	11	27
16	17	15	Reviewed		1		1	4	9
17	10	14	Compiled		1	4		4	3
6	7	6	Tax Returns	2	1		1	2	
50	58	57	Other	5	3	2	6	12	29
					41 (4/1-9/30/09)			98 (10/1/09-3/31/10)	
151	142	139	**NUMBER OF STATEMENTS**	8	13	6	11	33	68
%	%	%	**ASSETS**	%	%	%	%	%	%
10.9	9.7	13.0	Cash & Equivalents		19.0		18.1	9.1	11.8
22.5	22.4	19.6	Trade Receivables (net)		7.9		15.0	14.2	25.4
7.9	7.9	6.6	Inventory		5.5		5.3	10.1	6.1
3.8	3.8	3.1	All Other Current		.8		1.3	2.3	4.4
45.0	43.8	42.4	Total Current		33.2		39.7	35.7	47.7
44.3	43.5	46.2	Fixed Assets (net)		52.3		52.3	53.8	39.4
4.3	4.0	4.3	Intangibles (net)		12.2		1.0	2.0	4.9
6.3	8.7	7.1	All Other Non-Current		2.3		7.0	8.6	8.1
100.0	100.0	100.0	Total		100.0		100.0	100.0	100.0
			LIABILITIES						
8.0	7.4	5.8	Notes Payable-Short Term		1.1		1.3	9.8	6.0
1.9	3.5	2.8	Cur. Mat.-L.T.D.		2.2		4.7	1.2	2.5
16.2	17.7	16.6	Trade Payables		8.5		23.8	12.1	20.5
.3	.4	.4	Income Taxes Payable		.1		1.0	.1	.3
7.5	8.3	8.8	All Other Current		9.7		4.5	7.3	9.3
34.0	37.3	34.4	Total Current		21.6		35.3	30.5	38.7
23.4	19.2	17.8	Long-Term Debt		26.2		13.3	18.1	14.0
1.7	1.8	2.2	Deferred Taxes		1.1		5.0	1.9	2.5
4.1	4.0	4.8	All Other Non-Current		8.9		7.8	3.2	4.6
36.8	37.8	40.8	Net Worth		42.3		38.7	46.3	40.2
100.0	100.0	100.0	Total Liabilities & Net Worth		100.0		100.0	100.0	100.0
			INCOME DATA						
100.0	100.0	100.0	Net Sales		100.0		100.0	100.0	100.0
			Gross Profit						
89.4	89.9	89.4	Operating Expenses		75.3		92.1	85.2	93.4
10.6	10.1	10.6	Operating Profit		24.7		7.9	14.8	6.6
3.0	2.1	2.6	All Other Expenses (net)		3.8		2.7	4.2	1.4
7.6	8.0	7.9	Profit Before Taxes		20.8		5.3	10.5	5.2
			RATIOS						
2.0	1.7	1.8			4.2		2.2	2.0	1.6
1.3	1.2	1.2	Current		1.6		1.3	1.2	1.2
1.0	.9	.8			.6		1.0	.5	.9
1.5	1.2	1.3			4.0		1.4	1.3	1.2
(150) 1.0	.9	.9	Quick		1.4		1.0	.9	.9
.6	.5	.5			.4		.5	.2	.6
15 23.9	14 25.2	13 28.4		0 UND		18 19.8	12 31.5	14 25.5	
31 11.9	29 12.8	26 13.9	Sales/Receivables	12 29.7		32 11.5	26 14.2	26 13.8	
50 7.3	47 7.8	45 8.1		29 12.4		53 6.8	52 7.1	46 7.9	
			Cost of Sales/Inventory						
			Cost of Sales/Payables						
7.3	13.1	8.8			4.9		6.6	7.2	11.1
23.5	43.9	44.3	Sales/Working Capital		41.9		13.0	30.9	52.7
999.8	-48.7	-40.0			-10.4		-605.6	-6.1	-214.9
7.0	7.0	12.0						10.9	19.7
(129) 4.0	(119) 4.2	(112) 5.3	EBIT/Interest				(30) 5.5	(57) 5.4	
1.9	2.3	2.0						2.1	1.8
9.5	8.6	8.3	Net Profit + Depr., Dep.,						9.3
(43) 3.5	(28) 3.1	(27) 3.4	Amort./Cur. Mat. L/T/D					(17) 4.2	
1.6	1.9	1.6							1.5
.7	.7	.5			.7		.4	.7	.2
1.3	1.2	1.1	Fixed/Worth		1.5		1.0	1.2	1.0
2.8	2.6	2.3			2.6		2.3	2.3	1.9
.9	1.0	.7			.4		.5	.5	1.0
2.3	2.0	1.7	Debt/Worth		2.6		1.4	1.5	1.8
5.3	4.0	3.4			4.1		7.4	2.2	3.6
39.4	35.5	37.8			217.6		60.2	19.4	36.6
(137) 16.0	(132) 17.7	(129) 17.8	% Profit Before Taxes/Tangible Net Worth	(11) 29.3		(10) 21.9	(32) 10.9	(65) 20.0	
7.4	8.1	5.8			17.2		2.7	5.1	7.0
11.9	8.9	12.2			46.3		15.9	9.3	11.8
5.2	5.2	6.4	% Profit Before Taxes/Total Assets		9.1		6.2	4.9	6.6
2.1	2.8	1.8			4.9		2.1	2.1	1.3
32.6	40.4	52.7			14.4		32.7	9.2	200.2
2.9	3.4	2.9	Sales/Net Fixed Assets		3.4		1.4	1.2	14.2
1.0	1.0	.8			.3		.4	.6	1.0
4.2	4.6	3.7			3.0		3.3	3.0	4.5
1.5	1.6	1.6	Sales/Total Assets		.9		.8	.7	2.6
.6	.7	.5			.3		.4	.3	.7
.9	.7	.6			1.2			3.4	.1
(129) 3.7	(123) 3.0	(114) 4.2	% Depr., Dep., Amort./Sales	(11) 5.7			(30) 5.5	(55) 1.3	
6.4	5.2	7.1			14.3			12.0	4.9
	.6	.4	.9	% Officers', Directors'					.4
(20) 1.5	(26) 1.4	(24) 2.1	Owners' Comp/Sales					(12) 1.4	
2.5	3.5	2.9							2.4
20177920M	19888544M	11249834M	Net Sales ($)	3447M	29822M	23688M	84124M	559238M	10549515M
6681617M	6714545M	6835692M	Total Assets ($)	6020M	68012M	7735M	268511M	1189731M	5295683M

M = $ thousand   MM = $ million
See Pages 9 through 22 for Explanation of Ratios and Data

UTILITIES—Water Supply and Irrigation Systems   NAICS 221310

	Current Data Sorted by Assets							Comparative Historical Data	
Type of Statement									
Unqualified	1	3	29	53	13	14		105	114
Reviewed	1	5	7	1				13	18
Compiled		5	6			1		21	16
Tax Returns	10	6	6	1		1		17	15
Other	6	16	10	18	2	3		48	58
		60 (4/1-9/30/09)			158 (10/1/09-3/31/10)			4/1/05-3/31/06	4/1/06-3/31/07
	0-500M	500M-2MM	2-10MM	10-50MM	50-100MM	100-250MM		ALL	ALL
NUMBER OF STATEMENTS	18	35	58	73	15	19		204	221
ASSETS	%	%	%	%	%	%		%	%
Cash & Equivalents	24.9	8.6	10.7	7.2	4.9	3.5		9.0	9.2
Trade Receivables (net)	14.9	17.5	9.8	4.7	2.1	1.3		7.5	7.8
Inventory	3.7	7.7	5.3	1.3	.4	.3		4.0	4.2
All Other Current	1.2	1.2	2.9	1.1	.7	1.7		2.1	2.2
Total Current	44.8	35.1	28.7	14.3	8.2	6.7		22.7	23.4
Fixed Assets (net)	41.4	52.2	63.5	74.3	84.4	83.5		69.4	68.6
Intangibles (net)	4.5	2.9	2.4	2.5	1.2	2.4		1.4	1.8
All Other Non-Current	9.2	9.7	5.4	8.9	6.1	7.4		6.6	6.2
Total	100.0	100.0	100.0	100.0	100.0	100.0		100.0	100.0
LIABILITIES									
Notes Payable-Short Term	7.0	10.0	2.0	1.7	.2	2.4		4.2	4.1
Cur. Mat.-L.T.D.	8.4	3.2	3.9	2.4	.9	1.0		2.6	2.7
Trade Payables	7.1	11.6	3.5	3.1	1.5	.8		4.1	4.3
Income Taxes Payable	.0	.1	.1	.1	.1	.0		.2	.2
All Other Current	30.8	14.7	4.0	4.2	3.0	2.1		5.2	4.3
Total Current	53.4	39.4	13.6	11.5	5.6	6.4		16.2	15.6
Long-Term Debt	37.2	21.1	25.5	32.5	30.7	36.1		28.6	32.0
Deferred Taxes	.1	.3	.2	.7	.2	3.0		.8	.9
All Other Non-Current	6.5	6.5	2.6	9.6	4.7	13.8		10.0	9.7
Net Worth	2.8	32.7	58.1	45.7	58.8	40.7		44.4	41.8
Total Liabilities & Net Worth	100.0	100.0	100.0	100.0	100.0	100.0		100.0	100.0
INCOME DATA									
Net Sales	100.0	100.0	100.0	100.0	100.0	100.0		100.0	100.0
Gross Profit									
Operating Expenses	94.6	96.1	90.1	81.6	83.9	81.1		81.5	80.7
Operating Profit	5.4	3.9	9.9	18.4	16.1	18.9		18.5	19.3
All Other Expenses (net)	3.1	1.9	3.5	7.6	7.4	5.7		6.3	6.0
Profit Before Taxes	2.3	2.0	6.5	10.7	8.8	13.3		12.2	13.3
RATIOS									
Current	2.5	2.2	5.7	3.5	4.1	2.0		3.0	3.4
	1.3	1.1	2.3	1.5	1.8	1.1		1.6	1.6
	.4	.7	1.1	.7	1.0	.6		.8	.9
Quick	2.2	1.9	4.7	2.9	3.4	1.0		2.5	2.9
	1.1	.8	1.8	1.1	1.3	.6		(203) 1.1	1.3
	.1	.3	.7	.4	.4	.4		.5	.5
Sales/Receivables	0 UND	5 75.5	20 18.6	20 18.2	27 13.3	24 15.1		19 19.1	20 17.9
	0 UND	31 11.8	30 12.0	31 11.9	36 10.2	33 11.0		33 10.9	34 10.7
	37 9.7	55 6.7	42 8.6	43 8.6	53 6.9	37 9.8		49 7.5	49 7.4
Cost of Sales/Inventory									
Cost of Sales/Payables									
Sales/Working Capital	7.3	10.6	1.8	2.5	2.4	4.8		3.0	2.4
	58.7	89.8	4.4	8.2	5.0	33.2		9.7	8.9
	-6.0	-18.0	115.5	-13.4	-175.5	-16.7		-17.2	-52.0
EBIT/Interest	6.9	4.1	6.4	6.6	4.7	5.2		4.8	5.7
	(13) 2.0	(30) 2.2	(53) 2.8	(62) 2.3	(12) 1.8	(18) 2.8		(174) 2.6	(186) 3.0
	-2.3	-.3	1.1	1.0	.7	1.8		1.4	1.5
Net Profit + Depr., Dep., Amort./Cur. Mat. L/T/D			4.1					7.4	10.5
			(17) 2.3					(47) 3.5	(44) 4.0
			1.3					1.8	2.1
Fixed/Worth	.3	.5	.9	1.0	1.0	1.3		1.0	1.0
	2.1	1.2	1.2	1.6	1.4	2.9		1.6	1.6
	-.7	3.3	2.2	3.0	2.3	3.6		3.1	3.3
Debt/Worth	1.0	.5	.3	.6	.3	.5		.5	.5
	6.9	2.4	.6	1.2	.6	2.2		1.2	1.3
	-2.6	4.2	1.6	3.4	1.7	3.4		3.0	3.6
% Profit Before Taxes/Tangible Net Worth	107.7	26.2	12.8	12.4	5.1	13.1		13.9	16.6
	(11) 36.5	(29) 5.4	(54) 4.7	(70) 3.5	1.6	(18) 9.9		(187) 6.0	(203) 8.3
	-14.2	-3.3	.1	-.1	-.2	2.1		1.7	2.4
% Profit Before Taxes/Total Assets	25.2	9.3	6.4	3.9	3.6	3.9		5.3	6.7
	1.5	2.5	3.2	1.5	1.4	2.4		2.8	3.0
	-14.8	-3.2	.1	.0	-.2	.8		.7	1.1
Sales/Net Fixed Assets	54.4	14.1	4.6	.4	.2	.3		.9	.9
	4.8	3.8	.4	.2	.2	.2		.3	.3
	1.1	.8	.2	.2	.1	.1		.2	.2
Sales/Total Assets	4.7	2.8	.9	.3	.2	.2		.6	.6
	1.8	1.9	.3	.2	.1	.2		.2	.2
	.8	.5	.2	.1	.1	.1		.1	.2
% Depr., Dep., Amort./Sales	1.5	1.6	6.3	10.3	15.5	12.0		6.9	7.7
	(14) 6.7	(25) 6.3	(54) 13.1	(71) 16.1	20.1	(18) 14.9		(198) 12.0	(209) 12.5
	16.7	11.6	20.1	23.2	25.2	23.6		18.8	18.9
% Officers', Directors' Owners' Comp/Sales			(10) 3.1					1.6	1.9
			7.2					(27) 3.0	(31) 3.7
			8.9					6.7	5.7
Net Sales ($)	15133M	86573M	224535M	590151M	160977M	1055399M		1254483M	1708226M
Total Assets ($)	3746M	44434M	304185M	1554759M	1030813M	3380503M		5781659M	6334368M

M = $ thousand   MM = $ million
See Pages 9 through 22 for Explanation of Ratios and Data

Comparative Historical Data | Current Data Sorted by Sales

			Type of Statement						
99	92	113	Unqualified	12	41	17	23	11	9
11	17	14	Reviewed	3	2	2	3	3	1
11	17	12	Compiled	2	4	1	2	2	1
21	30	24	Tax Returns	11	6	2	3	1	1
55	57	55	Other	15	14	6	8	6	6
4/1/07-3/31/08 ALL	4/1/08-3/31/09 ALL	4/1/09-3/31/10 ALL		60 (4/1-9/30/09)			158 (10/1/09-3/31/10)		
				0-1MM	1-3MM	3-5MM	5-10MM	10-25MM	25MM & OVER
197	213	218	NUMBER OF STATEMENTS	43	67	28	39	23	18
%	%	%	ASSETS	%	%	%	%	%	%
9.6	8.3	9.3	Cash & Equivalents	11.0	12.2	8.2	6.4	6.7	6.3
10.7	10.0	8.5	Trade Receivables (net)	8.0	5.1	9.2	10.9	12.8	10.2
5.0	4.5	3.5	Inventory	.6	2.1	4.1	5.3	8.5	3.8
3.2	2.2	1.6	All Other Current	1.3	1.6	.8	2.2	1.9	2.4
28.5	25.0	22.9	Total Current	20.9	21.0	22.4	24.8	29.8	22.7
62.6	63.3	66.7	Fixed Assets (net)	70.6	69.4	65.9	62.5	62.1	63.5
2.3	2.2	2.6	Intangibles (net)	2.5	1.5	4.8	3.0	.8	5.0
6.5	9.6	7.8	All Other Non-Current	6.0	8.1	6.9	9.7	7.2	8.9
100.0	100.0	100.0	Total	100.0	100.0	100.0	100.0	100.0	100.0
			LIABILITIES						
3.8	4.0	3.5	Notes Payable-Short Term	4.6	2.6	2.3	5.5	3.0	2.4
3.4	3.8	3.2	Cur. Mat.-L.T.D.	3.7	2.9	2.8	4.3	2.1	2.7
5.9	5.7	4.6	Trade Payables	3.7	3.0	3.8	7.3	7.3	4.6
.1	.3	.1	Income Taxes Payable	.0	.0	.0	.1	.3	.1
6.7	8.3	7.8	All Other Current	21.0	3.4	6.4	4.5	4.9	5.3
19.9	22.1	19.2	Total Current	33.1	11.9	15.4	21.7	17.7	15.2
34.2	29.7	29.4	Long-Term Debt	34.0	32.5	25.6	27.1	19.6	30.1
.6	.8	.6	Deferred Taxes	.3	.0	1.0	.2	1.1	3.1
8.6	7.3	7.0	All Other Non-Current	6.0	4.7	7.8	8.8	6.5	13.1
36.6	40.1	43.8	Net Worth	26.6	50.8	50.1	42.2	55.1	38.5
100.0	100.0	100.0	Total Liabilties & Net Worth	100.0	100.0	100.0	100.0	100.0	100.0
			INCOME DATA						
100.0	100.0	100.0	Net Sales	100.0	100.0	100.0	100.0	100.0	100.0
			Gross Profit						
86.0	85.6	87.4	Operating Expenses	91.0	86.6	82.9	89.7	90.2	80.3
14.0	14.4	12.6	Operating Profit	9.0	13.4	17.1	10.3	9.8	19.7
4.7	6.2	5.0	All Other Expenses (net)	7.4	5.0	5.0	4.0	2.2	5.3
9.3	8.2	7.6	Profit Before Taxes	1.6	8.4	12.2	6.3	7.6	14.3
			RATIOS						
2.9	3.0	3.5		2.6	4.9	3.4	2.3	4.7	2.1
1.5	1.3	1.5	Current	1.3	2.2	1.8	1.2	1.8	1.3
.9	.7	.7		.3	1.1	.8	.7	.5	.6
2.3	2.4	2.7		2.6	4.7	2.4	1.5	3.3	1.2
1.1	1.1	1.1	Quick	1.2	1.8	1.4	.9	.9	.8
.6	.4	.5		.1	.8	.6	.6	.4	.4
23 15.7	17 21.1	16 22.6		1 425.5	11 32.0	13 28.5	21 17.1	25 14.6	24 15.3
34 10.6	32 11.2	31 12.0	Sales/Receivables	26 14.2	29 12.6	30 12.1	36 10.3	33 11.2	31 11.8
52 7.1	48 7.6	44 8.4		40 9.2	39 9.4	43 8.5	51 7.1	56 6.5	38 9.7
			Cost of Sales/Inventory						
			Cost of Sales/Payables						
2.8	3.8	3.0		2.4	1.5	3.7	4.4	2.3	5.6
9.6	12.1	10.5	Sales/Working Capital	10.4	6.0	9.2	28.1	11.3	17.1
-51.9	-11.2	-19.0		-2.2	94.3	-26.7	-24.8	-12.8	-15.7
5.0	6.9	5.7		3.1	5.2	3.7	6.7	10.3	10.6
(159) 2.5	(175) 2.8	(188) 2.4	EBIT/Interest	(34) 1.7	(57) 2.4	(25) 2.3	(33) 1.8	(21) 3.0	3.2
1.2	1.5	1.0		-.4	1.3	.9	.8	.9	2.4
5.7	8.8	8.4	Net Profit + Depr., Dep.,					17.6	
(29) 3.1	(35) 4.5	(38) 2.8	Amort./Cur. Mat. L/T/D				(11) 8.1		
1.2	1.8	1.3						1.4	
1.0	.9	1.0		1.1	1.0	1.0	.9	.5	.9
1.7	1.4	1.4	Fixed/Worth	2.1	1.3	1.4	1.5	1.3	2.9
4.6	3.1	3.0		5.3	2.2	2.7	4.7	2.3	3.9
.6	.5	.5		.4	.4	.5	.6	.3	.7
1.9	1.2	1.1	Debt/Worth	1.9	1.0	1.1	1.5	.6	2.2
5.8	3.9	3.1		15.6	2.1	2.5	6.7	2.0	4.0
17.4	17.5	13.4	% Profit Before Taxes/Tangible	24.3	10.7	13.0	19.7	12.3	26.1
(171) 6.7	(185) 5.4	(197) 4.4	Net Worth	(34) 3.0	(63) 4.4	(25) 3.8	(35) 2.4	4.4	(17) 12.3
.6	.8	.0		-1.5	.4	-.2	-.9	-.4	8.1
6.2	6.7	6.0	% Profit Before Taxes/Total	6.0	5.2	6.6	6.5	7.3	11.2
2.5	2.2	2.1	Assets	.3	2.1	1.9	1.4	2.9	3.5
.2	.3	.0		-3.1	.4	-.2	-.2	-.3	2.2
4.1	4.2	3.1		1.1	1.9	3.9	7.0	6.7	7.6
.4	.4	.3	Sales/Net Fixed Assets	.3	.3	.3	.4	.4	.3
.2	.2	.2		.2	.2	.2	.2	.2	.2
1.5	1.6	1.0		.8	1.0	1.8	1.7	1.5	2.0
.3	.3	.3	Sales/Total Assets	.3	.3	.3	.3	.3	.2
.2	.2	.2		.2	.1	.2	.1	.2	.2
4.1	5.1	8.2		4.3	10.2	6.4	6.4	3.5	5.3
(181) 12.4	(199) 12.6	(197) 14.1	% Depr., Dep., Amort./Sales	(36) 15.8	(56) 15.9	14.0	(38) 11.4	(22) 12.6	(17) 11.4
18.6	19.5	21.4		25.3	23.4	18.6	20.6	22.3	14.9
1.2	1.6	2.7	% Officers', Directors'		2.6				
(32) 2.6	(39) 3.3	(28) 7.5	Owners' Comp/Sales	(12) 7.1					
6.1	5.7	10.1			8.2				
2487855M	4606446M	2132768M	Net Sales ($)	21070M	124311M	108233M	278709M	346705M	1253740M
5937739M	6585724M	6318440M	Total Assets ($)	122461M	535838M	422181M	1256791M	1394744M	2586425M

M = $ thousand   MM = $ million
See Pages 9 through 22 for Explanation of Ratios and Data

CONSTRUCTION—GENERAL
INDUSTRIES FORMAT*

Current Data Sorted by Assets | Comparative Historical Data

Type of Statement	0-500M	500M-2MM	2-10MM	10-50MM	50-100MM	100-250MM	4/1/05-3/31/06 ALL	4/1/06-3/31/07 ALL
Unqualified		5	17	26	17	13	157	154
Reviewed	6	41	89	49	7		282	311
Compiled	25	67	104	36	1	6	487	493
Tax Returns	213	329	297	54	5		1399	1520
Other	81	160	307	145	28	13	1101	1215
		179 (4/1-9/30/09)		1,962 (10/1/09-3/31/10)				
NUMBER OF STATEMENTS	325	602	814	310	58	32	3426	3693

	%	%	%	%	%	%	%	%
ASSETS								
Cash & Equivalents	20.2	10.1	8.3	7.3	5.7	9.0	11.6	9.5
Trade Receivables (net)	14.4	11.2	8.8	4.0	3.6	8.9	7.3	7.0
Inventory	25.6	46.5	56.8	65.3	61.0	49.2	55.8	58.3
All Other Current	4.8	4.2	4.9	2.9	2.3	3.5	5.2	5.5
Total Current	65.1	71.9	78.7	79.6	72.6	70.6	79.8	80.4
Fixed Assets (net)	21.6	18.1	13.0	11.6	12.4	18.9	12.2	12.3
Intangibles (net)	1.3	.3	.8	.8	2.3	.3	1.0	.8
All Other Non-Current	11.9	9.6	7.4	8.0	12.8	10.2	6.9	6.6
Total	100.0	100.0	100.0	100.0	100.0	100.0	100.0	100.0
LIABILITIES								
Notes Payable-Short Term	34.7	29.7	34.4	42.9	36.6	39.2	40.9	41.3
Cur. Mat.-L.T.D.	5.9	5.2	4.6	3.7	3.6	4.7	3.1	4.2
Trade Payables	11.8	8.5	7.6	4.9	6.8	5.0	7.9	8.0
Income Taxes Payable	.0	.2	.2	.1	.0	.4	.2	.1
All Other Current	21.1	14.3	13.3	10.2	8.4	6.8	12.4	11.8
Total Current	73.6	57.9	60.1	61.9	55.4	56.1	64.5	65.5
Long-Term Debt	16.9	17.4	14.5	10.2	16.5	14.4	13.5	13.7
Deferred Taxes	.0	.1	.0	.0	.0	.1	.0	.0
All Other Non-Current	13.1	4.1	3.3	4.3	2.5	10.4	4.3	3.6
Net Worth	-3.7	20.5	22.0	23.6	25.6	19.1	17.7	17.2
Total Liabilities & Net Worth	100.0	100.0	100.0	100.0	100.0	100.0	100.0	100.0
INCOME DATA								
Net Sales	100.0	100.0	100.0	100.0	100.0	100.0	100.0	100.0
Gross Profit	26.1	20.7	15.7	11.9	13.7	19.6	19.2	18.6
Operating Expenses	24.4	18.6	15.1	14.8	15.3	20.2	12.7	12.8
Operating Profit	1.7	2.1	.6	-2.9	-1.6	-.6	6.5	5.8
All Other Expenses (net)	.9	2.1	2.1	2.4	2.2	3.9	.7	1.1
Profit Before Taxes	.8	.0	-1.5	-5.3	-3.8	-4.5	5.8	4.7

RATIOS (values shown as upper / median / lower quartile; counts in parentheses)

Ratio	0-500M	500M-2MM	2-10MM	10-50MM	50-100MM	100-250MM	4/1/05-3/31/06 ALL	4/1/06-3/31/07 ALL
Current	2.7 / 1.2 / .6	2.4 / 1.2 / .9	1.9 / 1.2 / 1.0	1.9 / 1.3 / 1.0	2.0 / 1.3 / 1.1	1.7 / 1.5 / .9	1.8 / 1.2 / 1.0	1.7 / 1.2 / 1.0
Quick	1.5 / (324) .5 / .1	1.0 / (601) .2 / .0	.6 / .1 / .0	.2 / (309) .1 / .0	.3 / .1 / .0	.8 / .1 / .0	.6 / (3414) .1 / .0	.5 / (3673) .1 / .0
Sales/Receivables	0 UND / 0 UND / 17 21.2	0 UND / 0 UND / 21 17.7	0 UND / 0 999.8 / 18 20.7	0 UND / 1 293.4 / 5 66.8	0 UND / / 17 21.9	0 999.8 / 4 101.1 / 21 17.5	0 UND / 0 UND / 6 61.1	0 UND / 0 UND / 6 64.4
Cost of Sales/Inventory	0 UND / 0 UND / 67 5.5	0 UND / 104 3.5 / 306 1.2	43 8.5 / 244 1.5 / 565 .6	163 2.2 / 366 1.0 / 732 .5	94 3.9 / 292 1.3 / 528 .7	0 UND / 288 1.3 / 608 .6	3 131.6 / 152 2.4 / 304 1.2	6 60.0 / 189 1.9 / 376 1.0
Cost of Sales/Payables	0 UND / 1 528.0 / 20 18.7	0 UND / 6 65.3 / 25 14.6	0 999.8 / 11 32.8 / 32 11.5	5 76.9 / 13 28.6 / 23 15.9	6 56.8 / 17 21.5 / 29 12.6	11 33.7 / 25 14.3 / 51 7.1	0 UND / 9 40.7 / 25 14.7	0 UND / 9 42.7 / 26 14.1
Sales/Working Capital	8.4 / 64.7 / -15.5	3.9 / 16.2 / -25.7	2.6 / 8.2 / 186.8	1.8 / 6.1 / NM	2.6 / 5.3 / 29.3	2.5 / 5.2 / -14.6	5.5 / 15.0 / 999.8	5.0 / 14.5 / 705.0
EBIT/Interest	11.0 / (240) 2.3 / -1.6	7.2 / (443) 1.7 / -1.5	6.4 / (610) 1.5 / -1.5	3.6 / (234) 1.0 / -2.5	5.3 / (48) 1.0 / -1.5	2.0 / (27) .5 / -1.2	23.0 / (2524) 6.0 / 1.9	17.4 / (2730) 4.5 / 1.4
Net Profit + Depr., Dep., Amort./Cur. Mat. L/T/D		7.0 / (15) 1.2 / .0	4.5 / (41) 1.1 / .0	13.5 / (13) -.1 / -12.0			7.5 / (166) 2.6 / .9	6.7 / (133) 2.6 / .5
Fixed/Worth	.0 / .8 / -2.0	.0 / .3 / 5.8	.0 / .2 / 1.8	.0 / .2 / 1.2	.0 / .1 / 1.1	.0 / .2 / 2.9	.0 / .2 / 1.5	.0 / .2 / 1.6
Debt/Worth	.9 / 8.3 / -4.7	1.3 / 4.2 / 111.4	1.7 / 4.6 / 23.2	1.7 / 3.7 / 14.7	1.1 / 3.0 / 5.1	1.8 / 4.5 / 10.6	2.3 / 6.4 / 26.6	2.4 / 6.7 / 30.2
% Profit Before Taxes/Tangible Net Worth	119.4 / (203) 38.3 / .0	39.0 / (466) 9.8 / -7.6	28.2 / (681) 7.4 / -9.8	18.4 / (271) 2.7 / -20.1	17.6 / (51) 1.7 / -17.5	8.8 / (26) -4.7 / -20.9	97.3 / (2924) 47.8 / 18.0	88.3 / (3136) 40.8 / 11.8
% Profit Before Taxes/Total Assets	32.5 / 4.5 / -12.1	8.6 / 1.4 / -4.3	5.2 / .9 / -3.1	3.9 / .2 / -4.5	7.0 / .2 / -7.2	3.4 / -1.0 / -5.9	15.3 / 6.8 / 1.6	13.0 / 4.9 / .8
Sales/Net Fixed Assets	UND / 54.1 / 11.8	404.0 / 50.0 / 6.8	296.4 / 49.0 / 7.7	181.7 / 35.3 / 5.0	173.6 / 69.5 / 8.1	144.6 / 28.2 / 7.8	579.0 / 87.3 / 20.0	541.4 / 82.2 / 17.9
Sales/Total Assets	7.4 / 3.9 / 2.0	3.1 / 1.6 / .8	1.9 / 1.0 / .5	1.3 / .8 / .4	1.4 / .9 / .6	1.5 / .6 / .4	2.8 / 1.7 / 1.0	2.6 / 1.5 / .8
% Depr., Dep., Amort./Sales	.5 / (157) 1.3 / 3.6	.3 / (348) .8 / 2.2	.2 / (492) .6 / 1.4	.2 / (183) .5 / 1.1	.2 / (29) .4 / .9	.3 / (20) .8 / 1.5	.2 / (1923) .4 / 1.0	.2 / (2013) .4 / 1.0
% Officers', Directors' Owners' Comp/Sales	3.0 / (158) 5.3 / 10.7	1.9 / (306) 3.5 / 5.9	1.0 / (338) 2.2 / 4.0	.6 / (93) 1.4 /	.3 / (12) .8 /		1.2 / (1533) 2.6 / 4.9	1.3 / (1666) 2.5 / 5.1
Net Sales ($)	367647M	1425375M	5020886M	6338813M	6207293M	8171584M	68446685M	64147870M
Total Assets ($)	77129M	679834M	3731159M	6933339M	4159136M	5143068M	38874576M	45232760M

M = $ thousand   MM = $ million
See Pages 9 through 22 for Explanation of Ratios and Data

Comparative Historical Data / Current Data Sorted by Sales

Right-side groupings: **25 (4/1-9/30/09)** and **163 (10/1/09-3/31/10)**

	4/1/07-3/31/08 ALL	4/1/08-3/31/09 ALL	4/1/09-3/31/10 ALL	0-1MM	1-3MM	3-5MM	5-10MM	10-25MM	25MM & OVER
Type of Statement									
Unqualified	28	19	33		2		5	6	20
Reviewed	45	30	33	5	5	6	2	15	5
Compiled	30	17	13	3	4	2	1	1	2
Tax Returns	64	47	45	13	10	10	6	6	
Other	90	78	64	13	12	1	13	12	13
NUMBER OF STATEMENTS	257	191	188	29	33	19	27	40	40
ASSETS	%	%	%	%	%	%	%	%	%
Cash & Equivalents	13.8	14.3	17.8	10.5	16.4	10.8	16.2	19.8	26.7
Trade Receivables (net)	22.5	22.4	25.5	9.6	11.1	23.9	26.9	33.3	41.1
Inventory	28.0	26.4	22.6	38.4	38.6	33.9	20.2	10.9	6.0
All Other Current	7.9	7.2	9.0	13.4	2.8	9.0	13.8	9.0	7.9
Total Current	72.1	70.3	75.0	71.9	68.8	77.7	77.0	73.0	81.7
Fixed Assets (net)	17.2	18.3	13.3	21.4	16.9	17.4	9.2	11.0	7.6
Intangibles (net)	1.3	1.8	1.1	.2	2.4	1.5	.0	.8	1.5
All Other Non-Current	9.5	9.6	10.6	6.5	11.9	3.4	13.7	15.1	9.2
Total	100.0	100.0	100.0	100.0	100.0	100.0	100.0	100.0	100.0
LIABILITIES									
Notes Payable-Short Term	20.2	20.0	17.6	30.7	23.9	17.9	20.2	14.8	3.8
Cur. Mat.-L.T.D.	6.8	2.5	2.6	5.7	1.2	5.9	1.0	2.3	1.5
Trade Payables	16.7	18.4	20.1	11.6	8.0	15.1	16.2	25.9	35.4
Income Taxes Payable	.6	.2	.3	.0	.1	.1	.4	.8	.3
All Other Current	13.4	14.7	14.1	18.9	13.8	21.5	15.7	7.6	12.9
Total Current	57.6	55.8	54.8	66.8	47.0	60.4	53.5	51.5	53.8
Long-Term Debt	14.8	16.8	11.0	13.3	21.0	19.9	5.6	5.1	6.3
Deferred Taxes	.1	.1	.2	.0	.0	.8	.0	.2	.2
All Other Non-Current	2.6	3.4	3.8	10.5	.8	.9	5.4	2.1	3.3
Net Worth	24.9	23.9	30.3	9.3	31.1	18.0	35.4	41.1	36.4
Total Liabilities & Net Worth	100.0	100.0	100.0	100.0	100.0	100.0	100.0	100.0	100.0
INCOME DATA									
Net Sales	100.0	100.0	100.0	100.0	100.0	100.0	100.0	100.0	100.0
Gross Profit	18.9	20.6	19.6	34.2	25.8	14.6	16.6	14.7	13.2
Operating Expenses	14.6	17.2	15.9	29.9	20.6	13.1	12.3	13.5	7.9
Operating Profit	4.3	3.4	3.7	4.4	5.2	1.5	4.3	1.2	5.3
All Other Expenses (net)	.5	1.3	1.1	4.3	1.4	-.4	.1	-.1	1.3
Profit Before Taxes	3.8	2.1	2.6	.1	3.8	1.9	4.2	1.3	3.9
RATIOS									
Current	2.0	1.9	2.2	3.4	3.3	1.8	3.0	2.1	1.8
	1.3	1.3	1.4	1.1	1.2	1.2	1.6	1.4	1.5
	1.0	1.0	1.1	.7	1.0	1.0	1.1	1.1	1.3
Quick	1.3	1.2	1.4	.7	1.1	1.1	1.9	1.8	1.6
	.8	.7 (186)	1.0	(28) .1	(32) .3	.8	.8	1.2	1.3
	.1	.1	.2	.1	.1	.1	.1	.8	1.1
Sales/Receivables	0 UND	0 UND	0 930.5	0 UND	0 UND	0 UND	0 999.8	12 30.8	31 11.6
	16 23.5	19 18.9	33 11.1	2 192.3	2 222.1	26 14.2	21 17.6	40 9.1	47 7.7
	55 6.6	49 7.5	62 5.9	50 7.3	40 9.0	63 5.8	74 5.0	84 4.3	59 6.2
Cost of Sales/Inventory	0 UND	0 UND	0 UND	0 UND	0 UND	0 UND	0 UND	0 UND	0 UND
	0 999.8	0 UND	0 UND	14 26.3	117 3.1	13 28.0	0 UND	0 UND	0 UND
	228 1.6	308 1.2	161 2.3	841 .4	408 .9	222 1.6	107 3.4	9 41.5	0 UND
Cost of Sales/Payables	2 185.6	2 154.7	8 45.3	0 UND	0 UND	3 126.5	1 384.8	17 21.3	29 12.7
	17 21.9	24 15.0	31 11.8	45 8.1	20 18.6	13 27.7	9 40.7	34 10.6	45 8.1
	40 9.2	48 7.6	58 6.3	136 2.7	47 7.8	40 9.1	27 13.5	68 5.4	59 6.2
Sales/Working Capital	5.7	5.6	5.0	1.0	2.1	8.2	3.8	6.8	6.2
	18.9	16.0	12.1	19.9	9.2	19.7	7.6	10.8	13.0
	-144.9	-999.8	71.1	-2.8	-416.8	-72.6	56.2	42.1	18.3
EBIT/Interest	15.2	31.1	27.6	5.3	9.6	17.5	27.6	35.0	135.3
	(184) 3.4	(134) 5.6	(135) 3.9	(17) 1.9	(23) 1.8	(16) 3.4	(19) 8.3	(32) 8.3	(28) 16.1
	.8	.0	.2	-2.5	-.7	1.1	-2.8	.1	2.2
Net Profit + Depr., Dep., Amort./Cur. Mat. L/T/D	22.1	14.8	32.6					13.6	
	(20) 4.1	(16) 5.0	(21) 5.7					(10) 5.3	
	.7	.6	2.4					3.1	
Fixed/Worth	.1	.0	.0	.0	.0	.1	.0	.0	.0
	.3	.2	.1	.7	.1	.5	.1	.2	.1
	2.0	1.1	.8	-6.1	.9	4.1	3.0	.5	.2
Debt/Worth	1.2	1.4	1.0	1.4	1.0	1.9	.6	.9	1.1
	3.4	3.4	2.1	14.6	3.9	6.3	1.5	1.8	1.8
	14.4	11.5	9.4	-12.3	7.3	43.3	19.6	3.0	2.8
% Profit Before Taxes/Tangible Net Worth	68.0	51.7	38.8	70.0	31.5	45.5	48.1	37.0	41.4
	(220) 26.5	(171) 22.7	(162) 14.8	(19) 25.0	(28) 7.3	(15) 7.8	(23) 9.0	(39) 24.1	(38) 22.1
	1.7	-2.3	1.8	-1.3	-2.2	1.4	-9.8	3.0	5.9
% Profit Before Taxes/Total Assets	16.9	12.8	10.2	8.4	5.0	9.4	16.6	16.5	14.0
	5.1	4.0	3.8	.5	1.3	3.2	3.9	6.8	6.5
	-.1	-1.7	-.4	-4.7	-1.6	.6	-1.1	.0	1.9
Sales/Net Fixed Assets	258.3	395.1	305.9	UND	669.9	81.9	999.8	118.3	323.1
	52.6	52.5	60.2	22.0	22.4	28.2	124.5	60.4	126.7
	8.2	5.5	13.4	1.8	6.2	12.1	16.3	19.4	44.1
Sales/Total Assets	3.7	3.7	3.4	1.4	2.3	3.6	4.2	3.4	4.0
	2.0	1.8	2.0	.5	1.5	2.0	1.9	2.5	3.0
	.9	.6	.9	.2	.7	1.1	1.0	1.4	2.1
% Depr., Dep., Amort./Sales	.2	.2	.2		.6	.4	.1	.2	.2
	(164) .5	(117) .6	(111) .6		(19) 2.2	(14) .7	(14) .3	(31) .5	(24) .3
	1.2	1.7	1.4		3.6	1.0	1.1	.9	.9
% Officers', Directors' Owners' Comp/Sales	1.3	1.1	1.3	2.2		1.1		.8	
	(92) 2.5	(64) 2.5	(60) 2.7	(11) 6.6		(11) 2.7		(15) 1.3	
	4.8	7.6	6.0	11.8		6.8		1.6	
Net Sales ($)	6650354M	4877904M	6868698M	16853M	68485M	74988M	194288M	618352M	5895732M
Total Assets ($)	3995736M	2899208M	2499353M	62036M	133392M	56302M	231257M	499645M	1516721M

M = $ thousand   MM = $ million
See Pages 9 through 22 for Explanation of Ratios and Data

Current Data Sorted by Assets　　　　　Comparative Historical Data

	0-500M	500M-2MM	2-10MM	10-50MM	50-100MM	100-250MM		4/1/05-3/31/06 ALL	4/1/06-3/31/07 ALL
Type of Statement									
Unqualified	1	1	4	9	6	6		26	32
Reviewed		5	9	14	1			35	54
Compiled	3	6	12	7		1		29	64
Tax Returns	29	30	30	6	1	1		62	110
Other	6	11	45	31	7	8		81	153
		30 (4/1-9/30/09)		259 (10/1/09-3/31/10)					
NUMBER OF STATEMENTS	39	53	100	67	15	15		233	413
	%	%	%	%	%	%		%	%
ASSETS									
Cash & Equivalents	12.2	6.7	4.8	10.0	22.4	8.6		11.6	8.5
Trade Receivables (net)	8.7	12.0	5.1	6.1	12.9	6.2		15.1	8.2
Inventory	38.3	44.7	62.6	53.9	38.3	56.2		44.5	56.6
All Other Current	1.6	7.1	3.3	4.6	6.0	4.5		5.9	6.7
Total Current	60.8	70.5	75.8	74.6	79.6	75.4		77.0	80.0
Fixed Assets (net)	25.5	15.6	16.3	12.9	7.6	9.3		15.4	12.6
Intangibles (net)	.2	1.9	1.4	.5	.7	.1		1.6	.8
All Other Non-Current	13.5	12.0	6.5	11.9	12.0	15.2		6.0	6.5
Total	100.0	100.0	100.0	100.0	100.0	100.0		100.0	100.0
LIABILITIES									
Notes Payable-Short Term	42.3	28.2	40.9	26.8	13.4	24.6		28.3	38.7
Cur. Mat.-L.T.D.	5.0	3.6	1.3	4.3	18.4	1.4		3.5	3.2
Trade Payables	5.4	13.0	5.8	6.5	12.0	10.8		14.5	8.6
Income Taxes Payable	.0	.0	.1	.1	.3	.0		.5	.2
All Other Current	19.5	13.0	11.5	13.0	14.7	5.0		14.3	12.6
Total Current	72.3	57.8	59.6	50.7	58.6	41.7		61.0	63.4
Long-Term Debt	28.9	18.4	12.9	14.9	4.8	21.8		13.7	12.2
Deferred Taxes	.0	.0	.0	.1	.3	.0		.1	.2
All Other Non-Current	4.4	7.9	5.6	5.6	6.5	10.2		4.1	4.3
Net Worth	-5.6	15.9	21.9	28.8	29.8	26.2		21.1	19.9
Total Liabilites & Net Worth	100.0	100.0	100.0	100.0	100.0	100.0		100.0	100.0
INCOME DATA									
Net Sales	100.0	100.0	100.0	100.0	100.0	100.0		100.0	100.0
Gross Profit	23.8	15.2	13.8	14.2	10.8	19.5		21.2	19.9
Operating Expenses	22.1	15.8	13.6	15.4	11.8	20.4		14.2	13.2
Operating Profit	1.8	-.7	.1	-1.2	-1.0	-.8		7.0	6.7
All Other Expenses (net)	1.9	.5	3.6	2.1	-.6	5.0		.7	.9
Profit Before Taxes	-.2	-1.2	-3.5	-3.3	-.4	-5.8		6.3	5.8
RATIOS									
Current	1.7	2.5	1.9	2.2	2.1	5.2		1.9	1.7
	1.0	1.3	1.3	1.5	1.4	1.5		1.2	1.2
	.3	.9	1.0	1.1	1.2	1.2		1.0	1.0
Quick	1.1	.9	.2	.7	1.5	1.0		1.0	.5
	(37) .3	(52) .1	.1	.2	1.1	.2		.2 (411)	.1
	.0	.0	.0	.1	.1	.1		.1	.0
Sales/Receivables	0 UND	0 UND	0 UND	0 UND	0 UND	0 UND		0 UND	0 UND
	0 UND	0 994.0	0 UND	1 271.6	6 62.0	4 91.9		2 237.1	0 999.8
	2 150.3	33 11.2	5 73.0	15 24.7	53 6.9	19 19.2		29 12.6	9 39.6
Cost of Sales/Inventory	0 UND	0 UND	161 2.3	34 10.7	1 399.2	167 2.2		0 UND	8 46.2
	16 22.7	122 3.0	351 1.0	248 1.5	52 7.0	554 .7		98 3.7	212 1.7
	83 4.4	240 1.5	707 .5	412 .9	432 .8	741 .5		291 1.3	392 .9
Cost of Sales/Payables	0 UND	0 UND	1 535.5	7 53.3	14 26.0	20 17.8		3 131.5	0 973.5
	0 UND	14 26.7	7 49.9	17 21.9	23 16.0	41 9.0		17 22.1	11 33.5
	2 194.1	33 11.0	27 13.5	29 12.4	46 7.9	56 6.6		39 9.4	29 12.8
Sales/Working Capital	11.6	3.4	1.7	2.2	2.7	1.3		5.0	4.5
	-53.5	20.9	5.6	5.1	6.3	2.6		13.7	12.4
	-8.4	-31.5	NM	26.2	13.2	16.1		212.4	82.2
EBIT/Interest	21.1	7.3	1.8	2.4	27.8	7.6		33.6	21.0
	(31) 2.2	(41) 1.2	(75) .1	(48) 1.0	(13) 8.4	(13) .4		(177) 9.7	(319) 5.2
	-1.0	-.5	-2.6	-2.1	-2.6	-1.5		2.7	1.5
Net Profit + Depr., Dep., Amort./Cur. Mat. L/T/D								12.0	10.4
								(15) 7.2	(18) 4.6
								2.5	1.4
Fixed/Worth	.0	.0	.0	.0	.0	.0		.1	.0
	.9	.4	.4	.1	.2	.1		.3	.1
	-3.2	NM	3.6	.7	.5	.6		1.1	1.2
Debt/Worth	1.3	1.6	2.0	1.1	.9	2.0		1.9	2.3
	20.7	8.4	4.6	3.0	1.8	2.4		4.8	5.4
	-4.6	-22.2	67.4	11.5	3.0	7.6		13.7	18.8
% Profit Before Taxes/Tangible Net Worth	155.5	50.3	12.6	17.6	27.7	12.5		93.3	84.6
	(22) 69.3	(38) 13.1	(79) 1.8	(59) 5.1	(14) 10.2	(14) -3.7		(209) 42.2	(367) 43.3
	-3.6	-14.7	-20.2	-6.1	-1.7	-37.2		18.1	13.3
% Profit Before Taxes/Total Assets	39.4	9.3	2.6	5.2	8.3	3.1		17.9	14.5
	3.5	.1	-.5	.5	2.5	-1.9		7.4	6.0
	-5.0	-3.3	-5.7	-4.6	-6.8	-10.4		2.8	1.0
Sales/Net Fixed Assets	267.0	231.8	337.6	189.2	460.6	143.5		222.8	263.0
	59.7	37.4	43.4	51.9	63.1	86.3		48.7	73.1
	7.3	10.1	3.6	9.0	20.1	4.3		9.8	17.0
Sales/Total Assets	6.5	2.9	1.5	1.5	1.8	1.6		3.4	2.5
	4.0	1.7	.7	.9	1.0	.6		1.8	1.4
	1.0	.9	.4	.6	.7	.3		1.0	.8
% Depr., Dep., Amort./Sales	.5	.3	.2	.2		.3		.2	.2
	(24) 1.2	(35) .9	(52) .4	(38) .6		(10) 1.0		(154) .4	(246) .4
	3.1	2.1	1.2	1.3		2.1		1.0	1.0
% Officers', Directors' Owners' Comp/Sales	2.2	1.1	.7					1.5	1.3
	(17) 4.1	(24) 1.8	(38) 2.4					(90) 3.1	(163) 2.4
	9.5	4.2	4.6					6.0	6.3
Net Sales ($)	42017M	141153M	563485M	1595041M	1503771M	2854706M		8659160M	11295282M
Total Assets ($)	10316M	66034M	525601M	1548476M	996443M	2701226M		5509249M	8729070M

© RMA 2010

M = $ thousand　　MM = $ million
See Pages 9 through 22 for Explanation of Ratios and Data

Comparative Historical Data   Current Data Sorted by Sales

4/1/07-3/31/08 ALL	4/1/08-3/31/09 ALL	4/1/09-3/31/10 ALL	Type of Statement	30 (4/1-9/30/09)			259 (10/1/09-3/31/10)		
				0-1MM	1-3MM	3-5MM	5-10MM	10-25MM	25MM & OVER
29	25	26	Unqualified	1	3	4	6	8	18
36	38	30	Reviewed		7	3	6	8	8
49	26	29	Compiled	4	7	3	6	7	2
126	97	96	Tax Returns	34	38	11	6	6	1
144	133	108	Other	15	20	12	15	23	23
384	319	289	**NUMBER OF STATEMENTS**	54	68	30	33	52	52
%	%	%	**ASSETS**	%	%	%	%	%	%
6.9	9.5	8.4	Cash & Equivalents	5.9	6.8	4.8	8.3	6.9	17.1
7.3	6.3	7.5	Trade Receivables (net)	2.9	6.8	4.1	10.5	11.1	9.9
61.3	57.4	52.4	Inventory	46.7	54.5	62.3	52.9	56.2	46.0
4.6	3.7	4.3	All Other Current	3.6	2.8	4.4	8.3	3.1	5.4
80.2	76.9	72.7	Total Current	59.0	70.9	75.7	79.9	77.4	78.4
12.2	14.6	15.8	Fixed Assets (net)	27.1	17.8	17.5	11.2	11.2	8.1
.6	.3	1.0	Intangibles (net)	.2	1.7	3.4	1.1	.4	.2
7.0	8.2	10.4	All Other Non-Current	13.7	9.6	3.4	7.8	11.0	13.3
100.0	100.0	100.0	Total	100.0	100.0	100.0	100.0	100.0	100.0
			LIABILITIES						
42.4	39.3	33.2	Notes Payable-Short Term	37.4	33.0	50.0	33.5	31.4	21.1
3.6	4.1	3.8	Cur. Mat.-L.T.D.	3.4	3.2	3.0	2.9	3.7	6.2
6.8	6.4	7.8	Trade Payables	1.1	7.6	7.9	11.3	8.8	11.9
.1	.0	.1	Income Taxes Payable	.0	.0	.1	.1	.0	.2
9.8	10.8	13.0	All Other Current	14.5	17.3	4.4	16.5	9.2	12.5
62.8	60.7	57.9	Total Current	56.4	61.1	65.4	64.3	53.1	51.9
12.6	13.2	16.6	Long-Term Debt	26.4	21.1	12.8	12.0	12.2	9.9
.0	.1	.1	Deferred Taxes	.0	.0	.0	.1	.1	.1
4.3	4.9	6.1	All Other Non-Current	5.2	6.5	7.0	5.6	6.2	6.3
20.2	21.1	19.3	Net Worth	12.0	11.3	14.8	18.0	28.4	31.8
100.0	100.0	100.0	Total Liabilities & Net Worth	100.0	100.0	100.0	100.0	100.0	100.0
			INCOME DATA						
100.0	100.0	100.0	Net Sales	100.0	100.0	100.0	100.0	100.0	100.0
18.9	16.8	15.6	Gross Profit	23.4	16.0	12.9	10.2	12.7	14.9
13.4	15.3	15.8	Operating Expenses	22.9	14.9	13.2	12.6	14.6	14.6
5.5	1.4	-.2	Operating Profit	.5	1.2	-.3	-2.3	-1.8	.3
1.7	2.3	2.3	All Other Expenses (net)	4.5	2.0	2.8	1.9	1.2	1.4
3.7	-.8	-2.5	Profit Before Taxes	-4.0	-.9	-3.1	-4.2	-3.1	-1.1
			RATIOS						
1.7	1.9	2.0		4.6	1.9	1.7	1.7	1.9	2.2
1.2	1.2	1.3	Current	1.2	1.2	1.2	1.3	1.4	1.5
1.0	1.0	.9		.5	.9	.9	.9	1.1	1.2
.4	.5	.7		.4	.4	.2	.5	.6	1.2
.1 (316)	.1 (286)	.1	Quick	(52) .1	(67) .1	.1	.1	.2	.4
.0	.0	.0		.0	.0	.0	.0	.1	.1
0 UND	0 UND	0 UND		0 UND	0 UND	0 UND	0 UND	0 UND	0 UND
0 999.8	0 999.8	0 999.8	Sales/Receivables	0 UND	0 UND	0 UND	0 999.8	3 116.7	3 128.1
10 36.2	8 47.5	12 30.5		0 UND	6 58.3	15 24.0	17 21.4	25 14.7	30 12.2
33 11.1	2 176.5	4 99.2		0 UND	16 23.4	119 3.1	0 UND	48 7.7	1 340.1
235 1.6	245 1.5	209 1.7	Cost of Sales/Inventory	236 1.5	192 1.9	256 1.4	215 1.7	209 1.7	199 1.8
466 .8	525 .7	494 .7		1461 .2	550 .7	614 .6	369 1.0	338 1.1	409 .9
0 996.0	1 350.2	0 999.8		0 UND	0 UND	0 UND	6 64.8	6 63.9	11 33.3
10 37.4	9 39.7	10 37.3	Cost of Sales/Payables	0 UND	7 48.8	7 54.7	17 21.9	13 27.6	23 16.1
27 13.5	26 14.0	29 12.7		8 44.6	31 11.6	28 13.1	33 11.2	23 15.6	44 8.4
3.6	2.5	2.3		.8	3.3	2.5	3.3	2.4	2.3
9.7	8.8	9.4	Sales/Working Capital	11.6	32.0	5.3	15.6	6.8	6.5
71.1	440.2	-40.9		-4.2	-16.7	-26.0	-24.6	26.3	17.4
11.2	5.1	5.1		3.1	7.2	5.5	3.7	2.2	19.9
(287) 2.8	(235) 1.5	(221) .8	EBIT/Interest	(36) .4	(55) 1.0	(24) .6	(22) -.5	(43) 1.2	(41) 2.5
.7	-1.0	-1.8		-1.3	-2.0	-.8	-2.4	-4.4	-1.1
17.9	22.5	5.6	Net Profit + Depr., Dep.,						
(22) 3.1	(12) 4.5	(16) 1.2	Amort./Cur. Mat. L/T/D						
.0	.4	-.1							
.0	.0	.0		.0	.0	.1	.0	.0	.0
.1	.2	.2	Fixed/Worth	.8	.6	.5	.4	.2	.1
1.2	1.9	2.8		-6.5	20.5	-9.2	2.8	.5	.3
2.3	1.6	1.4		1.5	1.6	2.9	1.5	1.1	1.2
5.6	4.3	3.9	Debt/Worth	8.1	7.2	7.1	4.7	3.1	2.1
18.2	15.8	83.4		-12.9	-39.4	-67.7	NM	13.3	3.6
52.4	30.0	28.0	% Profit Before Taxes/Tangible	15.8	48.6	37.2	38.0	19.7	26.7
(332) 20.6	(269) 7.6	(226) 5.3	Net Worth	(34) .6	(48) 8.7	(22) 1.0	(25) 6.0	(47) 5.1	(50) 9.1
2.4	-6.5	-12.5		-7.2	-16.0	-28.4	-21.0	-6.6	-8.6
8.7	5.7	5.4	% Profit Before Taxes/Total	2.3	7.5	5.3	5.9	3.3	6.9
2.9	1.0	.3	Assets	-1.1	.2	.3	-1.5	1.0	2.4
-.4	-3.1	-5.0		-3.5	-5.4	-5.2	-7.3	-6.4	-3.8
289.2	314.8	220.3		UND	152.9	195.8	UND	213.9	164.6
77.3	58.8	47.3	Sales/Net Fixed Assets	17.9	34.3	31.1	83.9	49.7	87.5
14.8	9.6	6.2		2.0	7.2	3.6	8.6	10.1	18.5
2.1	2.0	2.2		1.4	2.6	2.3	2.6	2.0	2.2
1.2	1.1	1.0	Sales/Total Assets	.5	1.1	1.1	1.2	1.2	1.5
.7	.6	.5		.2	.5	.5	.7	.7	.6
.2	.2	.3		.7	.3	.2	.3	.2	.1
(221) .5	(172) .5	(167) .7	% Depr., Dep., Amort./Sales	(27) 1.6	(41) .6	(18) .7	(17) .7	(30) .5	(34) .4
1.1	1.6	1.5		8.3	1.8	1.2	1.4	1.3	1.1
1.1	1.1	.9		2.9	1.1	1.0	1.0	.7	.5
(162) 2.1	(103) 2.2	(92) 2.4	% Officers', Directors' Owners' Comp/Sales	(16) 6.2	(24) 3.5	(14) 2.5	(14) 1.4	(14) 1.9	(10) .9
4.3	3.9	5.1		12.0	5.6	3.9	2.7	4.1	2.3
8061190M	5965667M	6700173M	Net Sales ($)	28275M	131066M	111314M	234100M	808231M	5387187M
6884569M	5457664M	5848096M	Total Assets ($)	114222M	242020M	154076M	270194M	763377M	4304207M

Current Data Sorted by Assets   Comparative Historical Data

						Type of Statement		
		2	4		1	Unqualified	8	1
1	8	2	2			Reviewed	23	11
5	4	5	1			Compiled	25	9
20	6	7		1		Tax Returns	54	37
12	14	7	2	1	1	Other	44	25
	8 (4/1-9/30/09)		98 (10/1/09-3/31/10)				4/1/05-3/31/06 ALL	4/1/06-3/31/07 ALL
0-500M	500M-2MM	2-10MM	10-50MM	50-100MM	100-250MM	NUMBER OF STATEMENTS	154	83
38	32	23	9	2	2			
%	%	%	%	%	%	ASSETS	%	%
20.8	13.9	10.8				Cash & Equivalents	12.0	16.1
17.9	37.6	33.6				Trade Receivables (net)	12.0	19.0
11.1	3.2	16.2				Inventory	46.6	21.3
12.2	8.9	8.9				All Other Current	4.8	7.5
61.9	63.7	69.5				Total Current	75.4	64.0
26.1	22.9	19.6				Fixed Assets (net)	16.8	23.2
3.6	3.7	5.6				Intangibles (net)	.9	2.8
8.3	9.7	5.2				All Other Non-Current	6.9	10.0
100.0	100.0	100.0				Total	100.0	100.0
						LIABILITIES		
23.1	12.5	12.7				Notes Payable-Short Term	35.6	17.7
2.2	3.4	7.0				Cur. Mat.-L.T.D.	3.0	8.2
17.6	13.8	12.8				Trade Payables	10.0	21.3
.0	.2	.7				Income Taxes Payable	.1	.2
25.1	13.4	16.8				All Other Current	17.2	13.6
68.0	43.3	50.0				Total Current	65.9	60.9
29.3	13.5	12.7				Long-Term Debt	15.0	14.0
.0	.0	.2				Deferred Taxes	.2	.1
17.7	7.1	12.6				All Other Non-Current	4.3	6.6
-15.1	36.0	24.4				Net Worth	14.5	18.5
100.0	100.0	100.0				Total Liabilties & Net Worth	100.0	100.0
						INCOME DATA		
100.0	100.0	100.0				Net Sales	100.0	100.0
34.3	32.1	27.9				Gross Profit	19.5	29.3
32.8	27.8	24.5				Operating Expenses	15.4	26.0
1.5	4.4	3.4				Operating Profit	4.1	3.2
.6	.4	.2				All Other Expenses (net)	.6	.4
.9	3.9	3.2				Profit Before Taxes	3.5	2.8
						RATIOS		
2.6	3.1	2.2					1.6	2.4
1.3	1.7	1.2				Current	1.1	1.2
.7	.9	1.0					.9	.8
1.8	2.2	1.8					.8	1.7
.8	1.5	1.0				Quick	.2	.7
.2	.4	.4					.0	.1
0 UND	8 43.2	26 14.3					0 UND	0 UND
0 UND	30 12.1	49 7.4				Sales/Receivables	0 999.8	8 47.4
24 15.4	63 5.8	84 4.4					18 20.3	31 11.6
0 UND	0 UND	0 UND					0 UND	0 UND
0 UND	0 UND	0 UND				Cost of Sales/Inventory	96 3.8	0 UND
19 19.0	0 UND	41 9.0					228 1.6	59 6.2
0 UND	5 70.3	8 47.4					0 UND	1 483.0
9 42.4	16 22.8	20 18.0				Cost of Sales/Payables	9 41.9	14 27.0
27 13.3	26 14.2	46 8.0					26 14.0	30 12.1
12.3	6.8	4.9					6.9	9.1
36.5	15.4	18.4				Sales/Working Capital	21.9	49.7
-27.6	-38.4	170.4					-77.2	-25.2
6.0	31.9	9.9					18.6	12.2
(26) 2.1	(29) 5.7	(16) 2.4				EBIT/Interest	(121) 5.1	(59) 4.5
-4.0	-.6	.9					1.1	1.1
						Net Profit + Depr., Dep., Amort./Cur. Mat. L/T/D		
.1	.2	.1					.1	.2
1.7	.4	.9				Fixed/Worth	.4	.7
-1.1	22.3	4.1					4.3	6.0
1.3	.5	.8					1.9	.9
NM	1.7	3.6				Debt/Worth	6.3	3.6
-3.8	558.4	52.2					212.5	22.5
87.7	98.9	70.1					89.0	100.0
(19) 25.6	(25) 36.6	(18) 39.6				% Profit Before Taxes/Tangible Net Worth	(121) 40.1	(67) 34.6
-16.5	9.4	.5					8.1	8.7
25.2	37.3	16.0					18.0	19.2
6.5	13.1	6.0				% Profit Before Taxes/Total Assets	5.5	7.6
-8.2	-2.4	.6					.5	.0
173.7	55.1	67.2					245.1	79.5
37.2	15.7	16.9				Sales/Net Fixed Assets	52.0	28.9
8.0	11.9	5.3					13.0	14.4
7.9	4.8	3.5					4.2	5.1
5.4	3.7	2.7				Sales/Total Assets	2.1	3.2
3.1	2.8	1.4					1.3	1.3
.8	.8	.7					.2	.3
(24) 1.3	(22) 1.3	(18) 1.2				% Depr., Dep., Amort./Sales	(108) .5	(56) .8
1.9	2.3	2.3					1.0	1.5
5.1	4.0	2.0					1.9	2.6
(25) 6.1	(12) 5.7	(12) 3.1				% Officers', Directors' Owners' Comp/Sales	(82) 3.0	(49) 4.0
9.8	8.5	5.2					5.9	7.2
68651M	133122M	182343M	619691M	836807M	1308309M	Net Sales ($)	5402360M	1141863M
9383M	36093M	71582M	240363M	145217M	351220M	Total Assets ($)	1894690M	411056M

© RMA 2010

M = $ thousand   MM = $ million
See Pages 9 through 22 for Explanation of Ratios and Data

Comparative Historical Data   Current Data Sorted by Sales

			Type of Statement			8 (4/1-9/30/09)	98 (10/1/09-3/31/10)			
	2	7	Unqualified				1	2	4
10	18	13	Reviewed	1	1	3	5	1	2
9	17	15	Compiled	2	5	3	4		1
39	48	34	Tax Returns	11	12	4	3	3	1
28	32	37	Other	6	11	6	7	3	4
4/1/07-3/31/08 ALL	4/1/08-3/31/09 ALL	4/1/09-3/31/10 ALL		0-1MM	1-3MM	3-5MM	5-10MM	10-25MM	25MM & OVER
86	117	106	**NUMBER OF STATEMENTS**	20	29	16	20	9	12
%	%	%	**ASSETS**	%	%	%	%	%	%
15.7	14.9	16.5	Cash & Equivalents	8.7	21.7	12.5	18.1		22.1
26.5	28.5	28.5	Trade Receivables (net)	18.8	19.8	37.3	42.9		29.9
14.6	10.7	9.5	Inventory	18.9	9.4	8.2	2.6		8.9
10.1	6.8	10.4	All Other Current	15.1	8.6	12.9	4.9		12.3
66.8	60.9	65.0	Total Current	61.5	59.6	71.0	68.4		73.1
21.6	26.4	21.4	Fixed Assets (net)	29.8	22.7	15.8	24.9		7.2
3.4	2.6	6.1	Intangibles (net)	1.2	7.5	4.8	1.4		15.7
8.3	10.1	7.5	All Other Non-Current	7.5	10.2	8.4	5.3		4.0
100.0	100.0	100.0	Total	100.0	100.0	100.0	100.0		100.0
			LIABILITIES						
17.4	19.5	17.3	Notes Payable-Short Term	26.1	15.1	17.2	9.2		20.9
6.1	4.4	4.2	Cur. Mat.-L.T.D.	7.1	1.6	3.3	5.1		6.7
16.1	24.8	14.6	Trade Payables	9.1	19.8	12.0	14.2		11.5
.4	.3	.2	Income Taxes Payable	.0	.3	.4	.3		.0
16.4	20.3	21.4	All Other Current	11.6	15.3	10.7	37.4		40.2
56.4	69.3	57.7	Total Current	53.9	52.1	43.7	66.2		79.4
18.7	23.7	20.0	Long-Term Debt	22.5	31.5	9.3	12.7		23.1
.1	.1	.1	Deferred Taxes	.0	.0	.0	.2		.0
7.0	7.2	11.5	All Other Non-Current	19.5	11.7	5.1	7.4		2.5
17.9	-.2	10.7	Net Worth	3.9	4.6	41.9	13.6		-5.0
100.0	100.0	100.0	Total Liabilities & Net Worth	100.0	100.0	100.0	100.0		100.0
			INCOME DATA						
100.0	100.0	100.0	Net Sales	100.0	100.0	100.0	100.0		100.0
28.8	29.5	32.1	Gross Profit	34.3	30.9	36.6	27.9		32.8
23.7	25.5	29.4	Operating Expenses	34.5	27.3	30.9	25.2		30.5
5.0	4.0	2.7	Operating Profit	-.2	3.6	5.7	2.8		2.2
1.1	1.2	.6	All Other Expenses (net)	.9	.2	.6	.1		2.1
3.9	2.8	2.1	Profit Before Taxes	-1.1	3.4	5.0	2.6		.1
			RATIOS						
2.2	2.0	2.6		3.3	4.5	3.1	2.6		2.4
1.3	1.2	1.4	Current	1.4	1.3	1.6	1.5		1.3
.9	.8	.8		.7	.8	1.0	.9		1.0
1.6	1.8	1.8		1.4	2.1	1.7	2.4		1.3
.9	.9	.9	Quick	.8	.8	1.3	1.5		1.0
.4	.3	.4		.1	.3	.5	.8		.7
0 UND	0 UND	0 UND		0 UND	0 UND	18 20.8	23 16.0		10 35.7
17 21.4	19 19.4	25 14.7	Sales/Receivables	0 UND	7 52.1	45 8.1	37 10.0		40 9.2
46 7.9	47 7.7	51 7.1		41 9.0	28 13.0	93 3.9	58 6.3		100 3.6
0 UND	0 UND	0 UND		0 UND	0 UND	0 UND	0 UND		0 UND
0 UND	0 UND	0 UND	Cost of Sales/Inventory	0 UND	0 UND	0 UND	0 UND		3 114.3
18 20.7	9 38.6	9 40.8		33 11.0	14 25.7	1 257.6	2 221.3		27 13.3
0 UND	1 365.8	1 546.5		0 UND	0 UND	6 65.1	10 36.5		12 30.3
16 23.0	15 25.0	14 25.5	Cost of Sales/Payables	0 UND	10 38.0	22 16.4	16 23.2		23 15.8
36 10.2	35 10.4	32 11.2		37 9.9	20 17.9	59 6.2	25 14.5		46 8.0
8.3	9.4	7.8		5.4	8.1	8.5	7.7		3.7
27.1	30.4	20.4	Sales/Working Capital	14.7	28.1	12.6	22.3		16.9
-47.5	-40.4	-41.0		-10.8	-35.5	645.7	NM		173.6
18.5	13.0	10.9		4.4	6.8	31.1	27.3		
(69) 5.9	(97) 4.4	(81) 2.9	EBIT/Interest	(13) .3	(20) 3.2	(14) 9.8	(18) 2.6		
1.1	1.4	-1.2		-4.7	.3	2.7	-7.0		
8.6	16.2		Net Profit + Depr., Dep.,						
(10) 2.7	(16) 2.7		Amort./Cur. Mat. L/T/D						
.2	.6								
.2	.1	.2		.0	.2	.0	.2		.1
.5	.8	.8	Fixed/Worth	.9	1.7	.3	.7		.3
12.8	UND	-2.4		-2.1	-1.2	3.4	NM		-.2
.9	1.2	.8		.9	1.1	.4	.6		.9
3.8	3.4	3.4	Debt/Worth	7.1	4.5	1.6	2.3		4.5
60.7	-37.9	-7.7		-5.7	-5.2	8.3	NM		-2.3
86.8	68.0	81.9	% Profit Before Taxes/Tangible	96.0	86.9	67.6	70.2		
(67) 31.6	(85) 29.5	(69) 34.6	Net Worth	(12) 21.4	(16) 37.7	(13) 31.9	(15) 31.0		
8.8	4.7	4.3		-11.7	-15.2	20.1	.9		
26.6	22.6	22.6	% Profit Before Taxes/Total	19.2	30.0	28.3	23.9		18.6
7.5	7.2	6.7	Assets	1.3	10.9	13.1	4.4		6.0
1.3	.8	-2.5		-12.8	-1.9	5.8	-13.3		-13.8
124.4	98.2	81.1		UND	87.7	336.0	64.6		91.1
32.1	25.7	28.3	Sales/Net Fixed Assets	6.8	32.2	24.7	27.6		66.8
10.9	8.0	12.0		4.9	14.5	11.0	12.2		31.2
5.5	6.9	5.6		3.8	7.2	4.0	6.5		5.6
3.5	3.3	3.5	Sales/Total Assets	2.5	4.6	3.2	3.9		2.7
1.5	2.0	2.1		1.4	2.9	1.8	3.3		1.5
.5	.5	.5		1.5	.6		.5		
(58) 1.1	(86) 1.1	(73) 1.2	% Depr., Dep., Amort./Sales	(12) 2.2	(20) 1.3		(18) 1.1		
2.0	2.3	2.1		3.7	2.0		2.0		
2.3	2.3	3.0	% Officers', Directors'	4.4	4.9				
(52) 3.5	(69) 3.9	(53) 5.5	Owners' Comp/Sales	(10) 5.7	(18) 6.5				
9.0	6.2	8.5		11.4	9.1				
871204M	1885023M	3148923M	Net Sales ($)	11525M	53506M	62993M	139340M	140152M	2741407M
426249M	488971M	853858M	Total Assets ($)	8000M	18321M	28446M	33911M	49751M	715429M

© RMA 2010

M = $ thousand   MM = $ million
See Pages 9 through 22 for Explanation of Ratios and Data

Current Data Sorted by Assets   Comparative Historical Data

0-500M	500M-2MM	2-10MM	10-50MM	50-100MM	100-250MM	Type of Statement	4/1/05-3/31/06 ALL	4/1/06-3/31/07 ALL
	11	55	84	23	15	Unqualified	195	218
7	60	143	25	2	1	Reviewed	201	224
15	18	15	3			Compiled	32	34
37	48	43	2		1	Tax Returns	67	99
16	42	67	55	5	11	Other	152	154
138 (4/1-9/30/09)			666 (10/1/09-3/31/10)					
75	179	323	169	30	28	**NUMBER OF STATEMENTS**	647	729
%	%	%	%	%	%	**ASSETS**	%	%
23.9	19.9	23.1	24.1	29.8	18.7	Cash & Equivalents	19.1	19.0
20.0	34.4	37.9	41.8	32.4	39.8	Trade Receivables (net)	46.0	45.0
7.5	6.1	5.5	4.2	.4	4.3	Inventory	3.2	4.1
8.2	7.2	6.9	6.5	7.9	6.6	All Other Current	9.5	9.6
59.6	67.6	73.5	76.7	70.5	69.4	Total Current	77.8	77.7
25.8	21.1	17.0	14.9	19.7	21.3	Fixed Assets (net)	14.8	14.6
1.2	1.2	.9	1.1	2.7	3.0	Intangibles (net)	.9	1.0
13.4	10.1	8.7	7.3	7.1	6.2	All Other Non-Current	6.5	6.8
100.0	100.0	100.0	100.0	100.0	100.0	Total	100.0	100.0
						LIABILITIES		
32.0	11.1	5.9	3.8	1.8	5.2	Notes Payable-Short Term	6.7	7.3
4.3	3.9	2.6	2.2	1.4	3.1	Cur. Mat.-L.T.D.	2.4	3.0
12.8	20.6	24.8	31.3	21.5	26.8	Trade Payables	33.5	31.1
.0	.7	.5	.2	.2	.4	Income Taxes Payable	.4	.4
20.3	15.0	14.4	17.8	25.2	21.2	All Other Current	14.3	18.3
69.4	51.3	48.3	55.3	50.2	56.7	Total Current	57.2	60.0
19.7	11.8	8.7	7.1	8.0	14.2	Long-Term Debt	7.4	8.0
.0	.3	.3	.3	.1	.0	Deferred Taxes	.3	.3
12.7	2.6	1.3	2.1	2.6	10.2	All Other Non-Current	3.0	2.1
-1.7	33.9	41.4	35.2	39.1	18.8	Net Worth	32.1	29.5
100.0	100.0	100.0	100.0	100.0	100.0	Total Liabilities & Net Worth	100.0	100.0
						INCOME DATA		
100.0	100.0	100.0	100.0	100.0	100.0	Net Sales	100.0	100.0
32.2	23.3	18.1	14.3	13.5	17.2	Gross Profit	15.0	16.5
31.5	22.2	15.7	11.1	9.1	13.7	Operating Expenses	12.0	12.6
.7	1.1	2.4	3.2	4.4	3.5	Operating Profit	2.9	4.0
.9	.5	.2	.5	.0	1.7	All Other Expenses (net)	.0	.0
-.2	.6	2.2	2.7	4.5	1.8	Profit Before Taxes	2.9	4.0
						RATIOS		
4.0	2.3	2.1	1.8	1.7	1.7		1.8	1.7
1.2	1.5	1.5	1.4	1.4	1.3	Current	1.3	1.3
.5	.9	1.2	1.1	1.2	1.1		1.1	1.1
2.8	2.1	1.8	1.5	1.5	1.3		1.6	1.4
.8	1.2	1.3	1.2	1.3	1.1	Quick	1.2	1.1
.2	.7	.9	1.0	.9	.9	(646)	.9	.9
0 UND	18 20.4	32 11.6	38 9.5	37 9.8	41 8.8		36 10.0 / 35 10.3	
1 253.0	34 10.6	50 7.3	57 6.4	53 6.9	55 6.6	Sales/Receivables	55 6.7 / 54 6.8	
26 14.2	54 6.8	73 5.0	74 5.0	79 4.6	68 5.4		73 5.0 / 72 5.1	
0 UND	0 UND	0 UND	0 UND	0 UND	0 UND		0 UND / 0 UND	
0 UND	0 UND	0 UND	0 UND	0 UND	1 427.4	Cost of Sales/Inventory	0 UND / 0 UND	
2 227.6	0 876.2	1 706.9	1 442.5	1 720.8	12 29.3		0 999.8 / 0 972.9	
0 UND	7 54.2	20 18.2	23 15.6	22 16.6	21 17.0		23 15.7 / 20 18.6	
2 196.0	24 15.4	36 10.0	44 8.4	32 11.3	41 8.9	Cost of Sales/Payables	41 8.8 / 39 9.4	
21 17.5	45 8.2	58 6.3	70 5.2	57 6.4	56 6.5		62 5.9 / 58 6.3	
11.9	7.0	6.0	7.1	7.1	7.8		8.4	8.7
98.4	16.4	10.7	14.2	12.0	17.2	Sales/Working Capital	17.0	17.7
-18.0	-64.4	24.9	34.3	30.9	43.6		37.2	42.3
32.4	22.2	27.7	60.1	324.2	52.5		32.9	39.8
(49) 3.7	(136) 2.2	(246) 6.3	(132) 15.8	(25) 19.8	(24) 6.8	EBIT/Interest	(503) 8.1 / (587) 9.7	
-3.8	-3.6	.7	1.4	4.0	3.0		2.5	3.1
	3.2	10.5	26.1				8.2	14.8
	(28) 1.3	(63) 2.5	(43) 6.6			Net Profit + Depr., Dep., Amort./Cur. Mat. L/T/D	(134) 3.2 / (156) 4.8	
	-.1	1.0	1.5				1.2	1.9
.1	.1	.1	.1	.1	.2		.1	.1
.4	.4	.3	.2	.3	.5	Fixed/Worth	.3	.3
-3.3	1.8	.6	.6	.8	1.2		.7	.8
.4	.7	.9	1.1	.9	1.9		1.1	1.3
2.9	1.6	1.6	2.3	2.2	3.1	Debt/Worth	2.4	2.5
-5.3	6.5	2.7	4.2	3.3	5.7		5.1	5.4
94.0	41.3	34.5	35.8	51.9	54.7		45.6	62.2
(48) 38.7	(151) 11.6	(310) 11.2	(161) 15.2	(23) 26.2	(23) 21.6	% Profit Before Taxes/Tangible Net Worth	(597) 21.6 / (670) 32.7	
-2.4	-7.7	.0	2.6	12.4	13.5		7.0	11.0
30.4	14.2	13.0	11.4	12.7	11.2		13.5	17.4
10.8	2.2	4.2	4.4	6.9	5.9	% Profit Before Taxes/Total Assets	5.8	8.1
-12.6	-7.2	-.4	.6	2.4	3.2		1.8	2.3
401.0	63.9	97.4	98.9	82.4	72.2		103.0	123.5
41.4	25.7	26.9	39.9	25.1	47.8	Sales/Net Fixed Assets	40.2	41.7
12.7	7.4	9.3	12.8	5.4	3.3		14.7	14.9
10.2	4.5	3.6	3.6	3.5	3.4		4.0	4.1
6.6	3.1	2.5	2.6	2.3	2.7	Sales/Total Assets	3.1	3.0
2.9	1.9	1.7	1.9	1.3	1.3		2.3	2.2
.4	.6	.4	.2	.3	.3		.2	.2
(42) 1.0	(146) 1.1	(268) .8	(147) .5	(27) .6	(20) .5	% Depr., Dep., Amort./Sales	(556) .5 / (621) .6	
3.1	2.6	2.3	1.5	3.1	2.2		1.3	1.5
3.5	2.2	1.4	.6				1.0	1.0
(38) 7.6	(98) 4.2	(130) 2.6	(41) 1.4			% Officers', Directors' Owners' Comp/Sales	(255) 2.0 / (275) 2.2	
10.1	6.8	4.3	2.4				3.8	4.3
117811M	707675M	4206995M	9780658M	4998329M	11734678M	Net Sales ($)	23391822M	31762449M
17935M	212964M	1606096M	3682291M	2178763M	4310987M	Total Assets ($)	7964001M	10745251M

Comparative Historical Data / Current Data Sorted by Sales

	4/1/07-3/31/08 ALL	4/1/08-3/31/09 ALL	4/1/09-3/31/10 ALL	Type of Statement	0-1MM	1-3MM	3-5MM	5-10MM	10-25MM	25MM & OVER
	172	129	188	Unqualified	1	5	5	16	39	122
	170	175	238	Reviewed	4	25	28	65	78	38
	24	39	51	Compiled	10	13	10	8	9	1
	84	98	131	Tax Returns	26	38	25	24	14	4
	147	139	196	Other	15	31	21	29	37	63
					138 (4/1-9/30/09)			666 (10/1/09-3/31/10)		
NUMBER OF STATEMENTS	597	580	804		56	112	89	142	177	228
ASSETS	%	%	%		%	%	%	%	%	%
Cash & Equivalents	18.7	19.9	22.8		16.7	18.8	21.2	21.2	24.0	26.9
Trade Receivables (net)	40.3	39.0	36.1		15.8	24.2	28.8	38.4	40.7	45.0
Inventory	6.7	5.5	5.3		16.1	11.3	7.4	3.6	3.5	1.4
All Other Current	9.6	8.0	7.1		6.8	6.5	6.9	6.8	8.4	6.6
Total Current	75.3	72.4	71.3		55.4	60.7	64.3	70.0	76.5	79.9
Fixed Assets (net)	16.9	18.8	18.5		30.5	26.2	23.8	19.5	15.0	12.0
Intangibles (net)	1.1	1.0	1.2		1.1	.4	1.2	1.8	.8	1.5
All Other Non-Current	6.7	7.8	9.0		13.1	12.7	10.8	8.8	7.6	6.7
Total	100.0	100.0	100.0		100.0	100.0	100.0	100.0	100.0	100.0
LIABILITIES										
Notes Payable-Short Term	7.2	7.3	8.9		32.3	16.2	11.8	8.4	4.7	1.8
Cur. Mat.-L.T.D.	3.1	3.3	2.9		4.9	3.8	4.5	3.1	2.5	1.7
Trade Payables	27.4	26.6	24.1		9.4	13.6	18.1	23.6	27.1	33.0
Income Taxes Payable	.5	.5	.4		.0	.6	.4	.8	.4	.3
All Other Current	17.9	18.1	16.4		16.5	17.9	15.4	12.3	14.0	20.6
Total Current	56.2	55.8	52.8		63.2	52.1	50.2	48.3	48.7	57.4
Long-Term Debt	8.7	11.0	10.2		23.0	20.9	11.3	9.9	6.8	4.4
Deferred Taxes	.4	.2	.3		.1	.3	.2	.5	.2	.2
All Other Non-Current	3.1	2.0	3.2		13.6	3.9	3.7	.8	1.7	2.7
Net Worth	31.6	31.0	33.5		.2	22.8	34.6	40.5	42.5	35.2
Total Liabilties & Net Worth	100.0	100.0	100.0		100.0	100.0	100.0	100.0	100.0	100.0
INCOME DATA										
Net Sales	100.0	100.0	100.0		100.0	100.0	100.0	100.0	100.0	100.0
Gross Profit	17.6	18.7	19.6		36.5	27.9	24.8	18.2	17.2	12.0
Operating Expenses	13.5	15.1	17.3		32.5	28.2	24.0	16.1	14.3	8.8
Operating Profit	4.2	3.6	2.2		3.9	-.4	.8	2.1	2.9	3.2
All Other Expenses (net)	.0	.5	.4		3.5	.7	.2	.4	.1	-.1
Profit Before Taxes	4.2	3.1	1.8		.4	-1.0	.6	1.7	2.8	3.3
RATIOS										
Current	1.9	1.9	2.1		3.7	3.3	2.3	2.1	2.2	1.7
	1.3	1.3	1.4		1.0	1.6	1.4	1.6	1.5	1.4
	1.1	1.1	1.1		.4	.7	.9	1.1	1.2	1.2
Quick	1.5	1.6	1.7		1.1	2.3	2.1	1.8	1.9	1.5
	(596) 1.1	1.1	1.2		.5	1.1	1.1	1.3	1.3	1.3
	.8	.8	.8		.1	.7	.5	.9	1.0	1.0
Sales/Receivables	28 13.0	27 13.5	25 14.6		0 UND	0 UND	18 20.2	31 11.7	36 10.2	38 9.5
	50 7.2	48 7.7	45 8.1		9 41.0	27 13.7	36 10.1	46 7.9	48 7.6	56 6.5
	72 5.1	71 5.2	68 5.4		28 13.2	65 5.6	60 6.1	73 5.0	71 5.1	70 5.2
Cost of Sales/Inventory	0 UND	0 UND	0 UND		0 UND	0 UND	0 UND	0 UND	0 UND	0 UND
	0 UND	0 UND	0 UND		0 UND	0 UND	0 UND	0 UND	0 UND	0 UND
	1 357.3	1 305.2	1 484.9		128 2.8	6 65.6	2 197.3	0 999.4	0 822.7	0 814.2
Cost of Sales/Payables	16 22.6	17 21.7	16 23.1		0 UND	0 999.8	5 67.2	19 19.2	20 18.3	23 15.6
	37 9.9	34 10.8	32 11.4		3 129.4	21 17.2	23 15.9	32 11.5	36 10.1	39 9.4
	59 6.2	55 6.7	56 6.5		43 8.6	43 8.4	60 6.1	48 7.7	58 6.3	59 6.2
Sales/Working Capital	7.5	7.9	7.0		3.9	5.9	7.2	5.8	6.9	8.3
	16.2	17.0	13.6		UND	13.6	18.1	11.5	10.9	14.9
	48.2	75.3	52.2		-4.1	-13.5	-26.9	36.5	21.2	30.4
EBIT/Interest	49.8	35.4	38.3		5.4	24.9	9.1	23.8	41.1	77.8
	(476) 11.5	(463) 8.0	(612) 6.3		(33) 1.0	(82) 2.5	(66) 1.7	(118) 3.4	(134) 8.7	(179) 22.1
	3.2	1.6	.6		-3.5	-2.9	-4.7	-1.3	1.1	4.7
Net Profit + Depr., Dep., Amort./Cur. Mat. L/T/D	14.4	13.5	10.8			1.8	3.2	10.9	11.7	30.5
	(125) 5.2	(114) 4.3	(152) 3.1			(13) .5	(10) 1.5	(37) 2.2	(34) 3.5	(56) 5.8
	2.1	1.4	.8			-8.1	-5.8	.6	1.6	1.9
Fixed/Worth	.1	.1	.1		.1	.1	.2	.1	.1	.1
	.3	.4	.3		1.2	.4	.5	.4	.2	.2
	.8	.9	.9		-5.8	12.2	2.2	1.0	.5	.5
Debt/Worth	1.1	1.1	.9		.8	.5	.7	.8	.8	1.1
	2.3	2.4	1.8		5.9	1.8	1.7	1.5	1.5	2.1
	4.9	5.4	4.2		-7.8	58.8	5.7	4.0	2.6	3.6
% Profit Before Taxes/Tangible Net Worth	60.5	52.8	39.5		41.3	59.7	38.1	35.2	35.7	43.2
	(558) 32.3	(525) 23.0	(723) 14.3		(36) 11.7	(85) 10.1	(76) 6.5	(134) 11.0	(172) 15.2	(220) 19.6
	12.9	6.2	.3		-7.2	-9.7	-8.6	-5.3	1.9	5.6
% Profit Before Taxes/Total Assets	18.9	17.4	13.3		12.6	19.1	11.1	12.8	14.2	12.7
	9.7	6.8	4.4		.2	2.4	2.0	4.1	5.5	5.6
	3.0	.9	-.7		-5.7	-9.4	-7.6	-2.3	.6	1.7
Sales/Net Fixed Assets	94.4	105.9	92.8		176.9	61.2	61.6	64.8	99.2	116.7
	35.1	35.6	30.6		12.5	16.4	16.8	26.7	34.7	53.9
	12.2	9.5	9.6		2.1	5.8	5.4	9.2	12.7	17.2
Sales/Total Assets	4.0	3.9	3.9		3.0	4.5	4.2	3.9	3.8	3.9
	3.0	2.9	2.7		1.3	2.3	2.4	2.6	2.9	3.0
	2.1	1.9	1.8		.5	1.1	1.7	1.8	2.1	2.2
% Depr., Dep., Amort./Sales	.3	.3	.4		.9	.8	.6	.4	.4	.2
	(496) .7	(473) .7	(650) .8		(34) 2.5	(75) 1.6	(74) 1.4	(120) 1.1	(146) .7	(201) .5
	1.7	2.0	2.3		6.5	5.3	3.5	2.5	1.5	1.1
% Officers', Directors' Owners' Comp/Sales	1.0	1.0	1.5		5.8	3.4	2.3	1.5	1.2	.5
	(221) 2.1	(211) 2.7	(315) 3.1		(23) 8.9	(52) 5.4	(46) 4.0	(67) 2.7	(79) 2.1	(48) 1.5
	4.0	4.5	5.5		17.2	9.7	5.8	4.8	3.3	2.6
Net Sales ($)	30603987M	23063911M	31546146M		31341M	200523M	344703M	1032168M	2804823M	27132588M
Total Assets ($)	10619952M	8899647M	12009036M		44299M	181381M	183995M	570181M	1445531M	9583649M

M = $ thousand   MM = $ million
See Pages 9 through 22 for Explanation of Ratios and Data

Current Data Sorted by Assets | Comparative Historical Data

0-500M	500M-2MM	2-10MM	10-50MM	50-100MM	100-250MM	Type of Statement	4/1/05-3/31/06 ALL	4/1/06-3/31/07 ALL
6	21	152	181	43	34	Unqualified	368	462
21	163	360	69	4		Reviewed	442	504
19	25	33	6	2	1	Compiled	87	94
41	60	42	8		3	Tax Returns	106	157
22	80	158	91	23	16	Other	284	322
	290 (4/1-9/30/09)			1,394 (10/1/09-3/31/10)				
109	349	745	355	72	54	NUMBER OF STATEMENTS	1287	1539

0-500M %	500M-2MM %	2-10MM %	10-50MM %	50-100MM %	100-250MM %	ASSETS	%	%
26.2	22.1	26.2	28.4	27.0	27.4	Cash & Equivalents	19.1	19.2
32.0	37.7	41.9	40.9	40.9	42.0	Trade Receivables (net)	46.9	46.6
2.7	4.7	2.3	1.7	1.4	1.8	Inventory	3.9	4.0
5.3	8.8	8.7	9.0	7.1	8.8	All Other Current	9.5	9.3
66.3	73.4	79.2	80.0	76.5	80.0	Total Current	79.3	79.1
23.5	17.1	12.9	13.4	15.5	12.7	Fixed Assets (net)	13.7	14.1
2.5	1.3	1.5	1.4	2.0	.3	Intangibles (net)	1.0	1.1
7.7	8.2	6.4	5.2	6.0	7.0	All Other Non-Current	6.0	5.7
100.0	100.0	100.0	100.0	100.0	100.0	Total	100.0	100.0
						LIABILITIES		
27.6	8.8	4.4	2.6	1.7	1.7	Notes Payable-Short Term	6.5	6.6
3.9	2.2	2.0	1.7	1.2	.9	Cur. Mat.-L.T.D.	1.9	2.2
20.0	23.9	31.2	33.2	36.2	32.4	Trade Payables	33.9	33.6
.1	.8	.6	.2	.1	.2	Income Taxes Payable	.6	.5
17.1	11.1	13.6	18.9	19.8	26.8	All Other Current	17.0	17.9
68.8	46.8	51.9	56.6	58.9	62.1	Total Current	59.9	60.9
12.9	7.3	5.3	7.6	9.0	8.3	Long-Term Debt	7.9	7.9
.2	.4	.4	.2	.3	.2	Deferred Taxes	.3	.3
4.6	2.7	1.6	2.0	1.9	3.0	All Other Non-Current	3.0	2.8
13.4	42.7	40.8	33.5	29.9	26.4	Net Worth	28.9	28.2
100.0	100.0	100.0	100.0	100.0	100.0	Total Liabilities & Net Worth	100.0	100.0
						INCOME DATA		
100.0	100.0	100.0	100.0	100.0	100.0	Net Sales	100.0	100.0
26.4	20.7	15.6	14.2	12.9	10.2	Gross Profit	15.3	16.7
26.4	19.5	13.3	10.8	10.4	7.2	Operating Expenses	12.1	12.6
.0	1.2	2.3	3.4	2.5	3.0	Operating Profit	3.3	4.1
.3	.1	.3	.6	.8	-.3	All Other Expenses (net)	.3	.3
-.3	1.1	2.0	2.8	1.7	3.3	Profit Before Taxes	3.0	3.9
						RATIOS		
3.2	2.8	2.1	1.7	1.5	1.4	Current	1.7	1.6
1.4	1.8	1.5	1.4	1.3	1.3		1.3	1.3
.7	1.1	1.2	1.2	1.2	1.2		1.1	1.1
3.1	2.4	1.8	1.5	1.4	1.3	Quick	1.4	1.4
1.2	1.4	1.3	1.2	1.2	1.2		(1286) 1.1	(1538) 1.1
.5	.8	1.0	1.0	1.1	1.0		.9	.9
0 UND	21 17.5	31 11.6	37 9.8	39 9.4	44 8.2	Sales/Receivables	36 10.2	34 10.7
22 16.8	38 9.7	50 7.3	53 6.9	57 6.4	58 6.3		55 6.6	54 6.7
51 7.2	65 5.6	70 5.2	69 5.3	76 4.8	68 5.4		75 4.9	75 4.9
0 UND	0 UND	0 UND	0 UND	0 UND	0 UND	Cost of Sales/Inventory	0 UND	0 UND
0 UND	0 UND	0 UND	0 UND	0 UND	0 UND		0 UND	0 UND
0 UND	1 391.0	0 UND	0 UND	0 999.8	0 999.8		0 999.8	0 999.8
0 UND	13 28.5	25 14.6	32 11.6	40 9.2	34 10.8	Cost of Sales/Payables	24 15.0	22 16.8
11 33.2	27 13.6	41 9.0	47 7.8	57 6.4	48 7.6		42 8.7	42 8.7
35 10.6	48 7.5	61 6.0	65 5.6	72 5.1	56 6.5		62 5.9	62 5.9
11.2	6.0	6.4	7.2	9.2	11.0	Sales/Working Capital	9.0	9.3
37.3	13.4	11.4	13.4	14.4	18.3		17.0	18.3
-18.7	46.0	28.9	25.1	29.0	34.0		37.6	41.1
9.4	24.4	38.7	56.2	76.2	83.8	EBIT/Interest	37.7	45.1
(75) 2.4	(256) 4.3	(556) 8.1	(252) 10.4	(53) 31.8	(43) 26.0		(1017) 10.6	(1190) 11.3
-9.3	-4.5	1.0	1.8	1.7	7.0		3.1	3.3
	7.1	10.5	31.3	19.3	85.0	Net Profit + Depr., Dep., Amort./Cur. Mat. L/T/D	13.2	13.9
	(58) 3.8	(160) 4.3	(79) 6.4	(17) 5.8	(12) 8.9		(284) 3.9	(320) 5.2
	-.2	.8	1.2	1.7	3.2		1.7	1.8
.1	.1	.1	.1	.1	.1	Fixed/Worth	.1	.1
.6	.3	.2	.2	.2	.2		.3	.3
-2.6	.9	.5	.5	.5	.6		.7	.7
.5	.5	.8	1.3	1.6	2.0	Debt/Worth	1.3	1.3
2.6	1.0	1.6	2.2	3.0	3.1		2.7	2.7
-7.2	3.7	3.0	3.8	5.0	4.3		5.5	5.3
51.5	43.6	31.9	36.7	46.1	56.9	% Profit Before Taxes/Tangible Net Worth	49.9	58.9
(71) 15.9	(317) 11.6	(719) 11.7	(344) 15.9	(69) 25.9	(53) 27.3		(1204) 23.5	(1426) 31.9
-16.9	-8.5	.6	4.8	7.3	16.8		8.1	11.6
28.2	15.5	12.0	10.6	11.0	13.8	% Profit Before Taxes/Total Assets	13.5	18.0
5.1	4.3	4.2	4.6	5.3	8.1		6.1	8.4
-14.7	-7.4	.1	1.2	1.4	3.9		2.0	2.7
144.3	94.3	108.0	160.9	142.6	121.9	Sales/Net Fixed Assets	128.1	139.3
37.3	30.5	43.7	59.3	47.2	56.3		50.4	49.3
11.7	11.9	18.1	15.7	12.2	20.5		19.0	18.1
7.8	4.8	3.9	3.6	3.5	3.5	Sales/Total Assets	4.1	4.2
4.6	3.3	3.0	2.9	2.6	3.0		3.2	3.2
2.8	2.1	2.2	1.9	1.8	2.5		2.3	2.3
.5	.4	.3	.2	.2	.2	% Depr., Dep., Amort./Sales	.2	.2
(70) 1.1	(282) .9	(649) .6	(317) .4	(65) .5	(40) .3		(1112) .4	(1292) .5
2.2	2.1	1.2	1.1	1.2	.5		1.1	1.2
3.0	2.1	1.1	.6			% Officers', Directors' Owners' Comp/Sales	1.1	1.0
(61) 5.3	(173) 3.9	(303) 2.0	(80) 1.3				(507) 2.2	(588) 2.1
8.7	8.7	3.7	2.8				4.1	3.8
173942M	1611846M	11243838M	21039132M	13520767M	32924246M	Net Sales ($)	50327344M	73775968M
30043M	441023M	3667827M	7361518M	5234097M	8346077M	Total Assets ($)	17213635M	24703208M

Comparative Historical Data | Current Data Sorted by Sales

Hist 1	Hist 2	Hist 3	Type of Statement	0-1MM	1-3MM	3-5MM	5-10MM	10-25MM	25MM & OVER
419	510	437	Unqualified	4	9	12	35	96	281
527	682	617	Reviewed	9	69	79	147	216	97
81	83	86	Compiled	10	22	14	18	12	10
142	215	154	Tax Returns	21	48	19	36	20	10
339	436	390	Other	18	51	31	71	95	124
4/1/07-3/31/08 ALL	4/1/08-3/31/09 ALL	4/1/09-3/31/10 ALL		290 (4/1-9/30/09)			1,394 (10/1/09-3/31/10)		
1508	1926	1684	**NUMBER OF STATEMENTS**	62	199	155	307	439	522
%	%	%	**ASSETS**	%	%	%	%	%	%
20.9	23.4	25.9	Cash & Equivalents	23.1	19.1	22.5	23.9	28.4	28.9
45.8	43.9	40.2	Trade Receivables (net)	23.0	29.3	36.4	40.5	42.8	45.1
3.9	3.3	2.7	Inventory	5.1	7.5	4.1	3.1	1.2	1.1
9.0	9.0	8.5	All Other Current	4.9	7.4	9.4	8.2	8.8	9.1
79.6	79.6	77.2	Total Current	56.0	63.2	72.4	75.6	81.1	84.3
13.8	13.1	14.7	Fixed Assets (net)	33.1	23.5	18.3	15.9	12.0	9.5
1.1	.8	1.5	Intangibles (net)	2.6	2.6	1.0	1.6	1.3	1.1
5.5	6.4	6.6	All Other Non-Current	8.3	10.7	8.2	6.8	5.6	5.1
100.0	100.0	100.0	Total	100.0	100.0	100.0	100.0	100.0	100.0
			LIABILITIES						
6.0	6.0	6.2	Notes Payable-Short Term	15.3	17.3	8.6	6.1	4.4	1.9
2.1	2.0	2.0	Cur. Mat.-L.T.D.	3.4	4.4	2.1	2.3	1.5	1.2
32.2	32.3	29.7	Trade Payables	15.1	19.0	20.1	26.3	32.6	37.8
.6	.5	.5	Income Taxes Payable	.1	.5	.9	.8	.6	.2
18.6	17.7	15.1	All Other Current	17.1	9.3	13.6	11.1	14.1	20.8
59.5	58.5	53.5	Total Current	50.9	50.4	45.2	46.6	53.2	61.9
7.2	6.6	6.9	Long-Term Debt	16.1	15.3	6.6	7.1	5.2	4.1
.3	.3	.3	Deferred Taxes	.0	.5	.5	.4	.4	.2
2.2	2.9	2.2	All Other Non-Current	2.9	4.5	1.9	2.2	1.6	1.9
30.8	31.7	37.0	Net Worth	30.0	29.4	45.8	43.8	39.7	31.8
100.0	100.0	100.0	Total Liabilities & Net Worth	100.0	100.0	100.0	100.0	100.0	100.0
			INCOME DATA						
100.0	100.0	100.0	Net Sales	100.0	100.0	100.0	100.0	100.0	100.0
16.2	16.5	16.8	Gross Profit	35.0	27.1	22.0	18.4	14.3	10.3
12.2	13.0	14.6	Operating Expenses	32.2	27.0	18.8	15.9	11.7	8.1
4.0	3.5	2.2	Operating Profit	2.7	.0	3.2	2.5	2.6	2.2
.2	.3	.3	All Other Expenses (net)	2.8	1.5	.5	.1	.1	-.1
3.8	3.2	1.9	Profit Before Taxes	.0	-1.4	2.7	2.4	2.5	2.3
			RATIOS						
1.7	1.8	2.1	Current	3.2	3.1	3.0	2.4	2.1	1.6
1.3	1.3	1.5		1.3	1.6	1.7	1.7	1.6	1.3
1.1	1.1	1.2		.6	.8	1.1	1.2	1.2	1.2
1.5	1.6	1.8	Quick	2.9	2.4	2.7	2.1	1.9	1.5
(1506) 1.2	1.2	1.3		1.0	1.1	1.4	1.4	1.4	1.2
.9	.9	1.0		.4	.8	.8	1.0	1.1	1.0
35 10.5	32 11.4	29 12.5	Sales/Receivables	0 UND	16 22.2	21 17.0	28 12.8	30 12.1	36 10.1
53 6.9	50 7.2	48 7.6		28 13.0	37 9.9	43 8.5	49 7.5	48 7.6	52 7.1
72 5.0	70 5.2	68 5.4		68 5.4	72 5.1	73 5.0	73 5.0	66 5.6	66 5.5
0 UND	0 UND	0 UND	Cost of Sales/Inventory	0 UND	0 UND	0 UND	0 UND	0 UND	0 UND
0 UND	0 UND	0 UND		0 UND	0 UND	0 UND	0 UND	0 UND	0 UND
0 999.8	0 UND	0 UND		0 UND	4 87.0	1 335.9	0 UND	0 UND	0 UND
22 16.8	21 17.3	21 17.6	Cost of Sales/Payables	0 UND	9 42.4	13 29.0	19 19.2	23 15.7	32 11.4
42 8.8	41 9.0	39 9.3		13 29.0	34 10.8	26 14.2	35 10.5	38 9.6	47 7.8
62 5.9	61 6.0	59 6.2		53 6.8	67 5.4	49 7.5	57 6.4	59 6.2	61 6.0
9.0	8.5	6.7	Sales/Working Capital	5.6	4.8	5.1	5.7	6.6	9.5
17.2	17.1	13.2		26.0	13.7	10.6	10.2	11.5	15.3
36.8	41.3	32.2		-6.7	-18.8	87.5	26.2	26.5	28.9
58.4	61.0	39.6	EBIT/Interest	6.8	8.5	30.9	26.8	51.0	82.8
(1169) 13.9	(1449) 12.3	(1235) 7.8		(41) 2.2	(147) 1.0	(113) 7.1	(230) 7.4	(327) 9.3	(377) 17.0
3.4	2.2	.5		-3.5	-9.7	.6	-1.2	1.3	2.8
18.1	17.8	12.6	Net Profit + Depr., Dep., Amort./Cur. Mat. L/T/D		4.3	8.5	6.7	11.4	27.4
(319) 5.5	(380) 6.3	(333) 4.4		(29)	1.3	(22) 4.2	(59) 2.6	(100) 5.8	(122) 6.4
2.2	2.0	.9			-1.7	1.3	.2	1.2	1.3
.1	.1	.1	Fixed/Worth	.1	.1	.1	.1	.1	.1
.3	.2	.2		1.0	.4	.3	.2	.2	.2
.7	.6	.6		5.6	11.5	1.0	.7	.5	.4
1.3	1.1	.8	Debt/Worth	.6	.5	.4	.6	.8	1.4
2.6	2.3	1.8		2.2	1.4	1.0	1.3	1.6	2.4
5.3	4.8	3.8		10.1	48.0	3.7	2.7	3.0	4.0
61.6	53.1	38.3	% Profit Before Taxes/Tangible Net Worth	27.2	30.1	46.0	37.4	35.5	41.3
(1415) 33.0	(1801) 26.4	(1573) 14.3		(54) 4.4	(151) 3.8	(143) 11.6	(293) 12.1	(421) 13.3	(511) 18.9
12.1	7.0	1.2		-26.8	-14.3	-2.5	-.8	2.0	5.4
17.3	16.4	12.9	% Profit Before Taxes/Total Assets	11.4	11.4	17.7	13.8	13.7	11.5
8.8	7.2	4.6		1.8	.8	5.1	4.7	4.9	5.5
2.6	1.8	.1		-8.8	-13.1	-3.2	-.6	.5	1.4
131.4	138.1	116.5	Sales/Net Fixed Assets	65.2	54.7	83.3	80.2	133.5	160.1
49.4	55.7	44.2		9.3	20.2	29.0	36.6	53.0	70.7
18.7	19.2	15.4		3.9	6.2	10.5	13.3	21.2	31.8
4.1	4.3	4.1	Sales/Total Assets	3.7	3.8	4.0	4.0	4.3	4.1
3.2	3.3	3.0		2.1	2.3	2.8	2.8	3.1	3.3
2.4	2.3	2.1		.8	1.4	2.0	2.0	2.3	2.6
.2	.2	.3	% Depr., Dep., Amort./Sales	1.1	.7	.5	.4	.2	.2
(1295) .4	(1610) .5	(1423) .6		(39) 3.1	(150) 1.5	(118) 1.0	(262) .8	(386) .5	(468) .3
1.0	1.1	1.4		8.4	2.7	2.1	1.5	1.1	.6
1.1	1.0	1.2	% Officers', Directors' Owners' Comp/Sales	3.8	2.9	2.0	1.4	.9	.6
(570) 2.1	(722) 2.2	(629) 2.5		(25) 6.4	(100) 4.8	(74) 3.4	(151) 2.7	(172) 1.8	(107) 1.2
3.8	4.1	4.7		9.7	8.0	5.4	4.6	3.4	2.3
92185632M	102254767M	80513771M	Net Sales ($)	38758M	390558M	613899M	2239986M	7074778M	70155792M
26275257M	33527574M	25080585M	Total Assets ($)	84673M	338598M	311639M	1091865M	2904894M	20348916M

Current Data Sorted by Assets | Comparative Historical Data

0-500M	500M-2MM	2-10MM	10-50MM	50-100MM	100-250MM	Type of Statement	4/1/05-3/31/06 ALL	4/1/06-3/31/07 ALL
	1	52	50	7	9	Unqualified	116	123
1	35	103	22		1	Reviewed	107	147
3	8	10	1			Compiled	17	32
10	16	15	1			Tax Returns	25	33
3	25	55	41	5	4	Other	84	89
	88 (4/1-9/30/09)		390 (10/1/09-3/31/10)					
17	85	235	115	12	14	**NUMBER OF STATEMENTS**	349	424

ASSETS (%)

0-500M	500M-2MM	2-10MM	10-50MM	50-100MM	100-250MM		Hist	Hist
%	%	%	%	%	%		%	%
10.1	13.7	16.3	20.8	26.0	22.8	Cash & Equivalents	14.9	14.4
17.3	29.7	32.6	33.5	26.0	21.5	Trade Receivables (net)	38.0	36.4
13.9	3.0	4.3	2.4	4.5	1.7	Inventory	3.3	2.6
3.6	5.9	7.8	8.0	4.1	10.0	All Other Current	7.9	7.4
44.9	52.3	61.0	64.7	60.6	56.1	Total Current	64.1	60.8
39.0	36.5	30.5	27.8	23.4	28.7	Fixed Assets (net)	28.9	32.8
.1	2.7	1.1	1.8	8.0	7.1	Intangibles (net)	1.3	1.5
16.0	8.4	7.5	5.8	8.1	8.1	All Other Non-Current	5.7	4.8
100.0	100.0	100.0	100.0	100.0	100.0	Total	100.0	100.0

LIABILITIES

0-500M	500M-2MM	2-10MM	10-50MM	50-100MM	100-250MM		Hist	Hist
11.1	8.2	5.6	4.1	.6	2.8	Notes Payable-Short Term	6.5	6.0
10.8	6.5	5.8	4.9	1.7	6.7	Cur. Mat.-L.T.D.	5.2	5.8
7.8	15.3	16.1	18.2	9.4	11.5	Trade Payables	18.4	17.2
.1	.8	.5	.6	.5	.7	Income Taxes Payable	.7	.9
23.9	6.9	8.3	10.8	20.4	17.5	All Other Current	12.2	11.4
53.7	37.8	36.2	38.7	32.7	39.2	Total Current	43.2	41.4
41.3	22.6	13.2	12.4	5.5	26.1	Long-Term Debt	12.2	15.4
.0	.5	1.1	.8	.7	.6	Deferred Taxes	.8	.8
4.6	3.6	2.6	2.2	4.3	1.5	All Other Non-Current	3.2	2.4
.4	35.5	46.8	46.0	56.8	32.6	Net Worth	40.6	39.9
100.0	100.0	100.0	100.0	100.0	100.0	Total Liabilities & Net Worth	100.0	100.0

INCOME DATA

0-500M	500M-2MM	2-10MM	10-50MM	50-100MM	100-250MM		Hist	Hist
100.0	100.0	100.0	100.0	100.0	100.0	Net Sales	100.0	100.0
56.1	37.0	21.2	16.9	20.3	27.3	Gross Profit	22.5	23.8
52.6	33.9	18.8	14.4	14.8	20.4	Operating Expenses	17.5	18.2
3.5	3.1	2.4	2.5	5.4	6.9	Operating Profit	5.0	5.6
.9	.7	.1	.0	-.4	.5	All Other Expenses (net)	.1	.3
2.6	2.4	2.3	2.5	5.9	6.4	Profit Before Taxes	4.9	5.3

RATIOS

0-500M	500M-2MM	2-10MM	10-50MM	50-100MM	100-250MM		Hist	Hist
1.9	2.4	2.6	2.4	3.0	2.0	Current	2.1	2.1
1.0	1.5	1.7	1.7	1.8	1.4		1.5	1.4
.4	.9	1.2	1.2	1.7	1.3		1.2	1.2
1.4	2.0	2.3	2.1	2.6	1.6	Quick	1.9	1.8
.4	1.2	1.4	1.4	1.6	1.1		1.2	1.2
.1	.6	.9	.9	.9	.9		.9	.9
0 UND	18 19.9	37 10.0	46 7.9	45 8.0	34 10.8	Sales/Receivables	43 8.5	40 9.2
22 16.9	44 8.3	56 6.5	65 5.6	54 6.7	46 7.9		60 6.1	58 6.3
39 9.5	65 5.6	73 5.0	85 4.3	58 6.3	60 6.1		82 4.5	78 4.7
0 UND	0 UND	0 UND	0 UND	0 UND	0 UND	Cost of Sales/Inventory	0 UND	0 UND
3 136.0	0 UND	0 UND	0 UND	1 464.6	0 UND		0 UND	0 UND
73 5.0	7 48.9	5 76.7	7 53.2	10 36.2	2 229.1		5 75.1	3 116.0
0 UND	9 39.0	15 24.5	24 15.4	18 20.1	13 27.4	Cost of Sales/Payables	18 20.7	18 20.7
10 37.1	24 15.0	31 11.7	37 9.8	22 16.5	22 16.6		33 11.1	31 11.9
38 9.6	51 7.1	50 7.3	54 6.8	26 14.1	47 7.8		50 7.2	48 7.6
25.9	6.4	5.4	4.1	5.3	5.8	Sales/Working Capital	6.0	6.8
364.0	19.5	10.0	7.8	9.1	10.7		11.5	12.8
-13.9	-35.2	25.4	22.6	12.1	16.0		28.7	33.4
25.5	10.4	16.2	22.1		40.5	EBIT/Interest	20.0	21.4
(16) 2.7	(76) 1.5	(218) 4.5	(98) 7.3		(11) 4.1		(316) 7.2	(394) 6.9
.7	-2.3	.4	1.1		1.7		2.2	2.6
	12.8	3.7	8.7			Net Profit + Depr., Dep., Amort./Cur. Mat. L/T/D	5.3	5.3
	(17) 1.4	(74) 1.8	(40) 4.1				(108) 2.4	(135) 2.6
	.4	1.2	1.4				1.2	1.6
1.0	.4	.3	.3	.2	.2	Fixed/Worth	.3	.4
4.9	1.1	.6	.6	.5	.4		.6	.7
-1.3	4.7	1.2	1.2	.8	1.5		1.3	1.4
1.7	.6	.6	.7	.3	.7	Debt/Worth	.7	.8
11.8	2.0	1.1	1.1	.7	1.6		1.4	1.6
-3.9	13.1	2.1	2.4	1.4	2.1		2.7	2.7
171.7	21.6	30.5	30.9	46.9	49.7	% Profit Before Taxes/Tangible Net Worth	39.7	49.4
(10) 33.7	(71) 3.5	(224) 11.0	(111) 15.6	20.1	(13) 20.2		(326) 19.9	(406) 26.1
8.6	-18.8	.7	1.1	6.5	14.3		6.4	9.2
29.7	11.4	12.0	14.8	16.1	20.8	% Profit Before Taxes/Total Assets	16.6	19.0
9.2	1.8	4.4	6.3	5.8	8.7		7.8	9.3
-1.7	-6.8	-.1	.1	2.1	4.3		1.9	3.1
40.4	21.9	13.3	17.6	22.3	19.4	Sales/Net Fixed Assets	17.7	15.2
7.8	8.2	7.3	8.5	5.7	6.7		8.7	7.9
5.3	4.0	4.4	4.3	4.2	2.7		4.9	4.7
6.2	3.5	2.8	2.4	3.1	2.2	Sales/Total Assets	2.8	2.9
3.8	2.5	2.1	1.8	1.6	1.6		2.2	2.2
1.9	1.7	1.6	1.4	1.0	1.0		1.7	1.7
1.8	2.2	2.0	1.3	.7		% Depr., Dep., Amort./Sales	1.6	1.8
(11) 4.8	(71) 4.4	(211) 3.9	(101) 3.1	(11) 2.7			(312) 3.0	(386) 3.1
9.6	8.6	5.8	5.8	7.7			4.8	5.3
6.3	2.8	1.4	.8			% Officers', Directors' Owners' Comp/Sales	1.4	1.3
(13) 7.8	(46) 4.7	(107) 2.6	(39) 1.5				(138) 3.3	(202) 2.9
18.3	8.5	4.5	3.3				5.8	5.8
15830M	265313M	2402951M	4389439M	1795996M	3094931M	Net Sales ($)	9996443M	11220441M
4382M	101617M	1150750M	2402836M	875446M	1995753M	Total Assets ($)	4682840M	5140310M

M = $ thousand   MM = $ million
See Pages 9 through 22 for Explanation of Ratios and Data

Comparative Historical Data | Current Data Sorted by Sales

4/1/07-3/31/08 ALL	4/1/08-3/31/09 ALL	4/1/09-3/31/10 ALL	Type of Statement	0-1MM	1-3MM	3-5MM	5-10MM	10-25MM	25MM & OVER
117	115	119	Unqualified	1	2	9	14	34	59
151	168	162	Reviewed		19	25	49	58	11
22	34	22	Compiled	4	6	3	4	5	
36	37	42	Tax Returns	10	17	3	9	2	1
110	111	133	Other	5	15	17	23	34	39
				88 (4/1-9/30/09)			390 (10/1/09-3/31/10)		
ALL	**ALL**	**ALL**							
436	465	478	**NUMBER OF STATEMENTS**	20	59	57	99	133	110
%	%	%	**ASSETS**	%	%	%	%	%	%
13.4	15.3	17.1	Cash & Equivalents	7.1	16.0	16.2	13.9	18.1	21.7
35.6	32.8	31.2	Trade Receivables (net)	12.8	21.8	28.6	35.3	33.5	34.7
3.0	3.9	3.9	Inventory	21.6	4.2	4.5	2.9	2.8	2.4
8.5	7.6	7.3	All Other Current	.7	5.6	7.3	6.8	8.6	8.4
60.6	59.6	59.6	Total Current	42.2	47.7	56.6	58.9	63.1	67.2
31.7	32.3	31.0	Fixed Assets (net)	37.8	41.2	30.7	32.6	30.4	23.6
1.7	1.7	1.9	Intangibles (net)	.4	3.0	2.7	1.0	.9	3.0
6.0	6.4	7.6	All Other Non-Current	19.6	8.2	10.0	7.5	5.6	6.2
100.0	100.0	100.0	Total	100.0	100.0	100.0	100.0	100.0	100.0
			LIABILITIES						
6.7	5.3	5.7	Notes Payable-Short Term	8.9	8.2	6.9	8.3	3.6	3.2
5.8	5.5	5.8	Cur. Mat.-L.T.D.	10.9	7.0	6.2	6.0	5.6	4.1
16.4	15.6	15.9	Trade Payables	6.1	13.3	12.9	15.2	18.2	18.3
1.0	.8	.6	Income Taxes Payable	.7	.7	.7	.6	.5	.5
12.4	10.7	9.8	All Other Current	27.5	6.9	7.0	6.1	8.6	14.4
42.3	38.0	37.7	Total Current	54.1	36.1	33.6	36.1	36.6	40.5
15.6	14.9	15.9	Long-Term Debt	43.0	31.9	14.3	12.2	11.9	11.3
.8	.9	.9	Deferred Taxes	.4	.4	.9	.9	1.5	.4
2.9	3.0	2.8	All Other Non-Current	4.4	2.3	6.1	2.5	1.7	2.4
38.5	43.3	42.8	Net Worth	-1.8	29.3	45.0	48.3	48.3	45.4
100.0	100.0	100.0	Total Liabilities & Net Worth	100.0	100.0	100.0	100.0	100.0	100.0
			INCOME DATA						
100.0	100.0	100.0	Net Sales	100.0	100.0	100.0	100.0	100.0	100.0
24.1	24.0	24.3	Gross Profit	57.9	39.5	23.7	22.6	20.7	16.4
18.9	20.5	21.6	Operating Expenses	51.7	37.2	25.1	20.5	16.4	13.1
5.2	3.5	2.8	Operating Profit	6.2	2.3	-1.4	2.1	4.4	3.3
.3	.4	.2	All Other Expenses (net)	1.9	.8	-.3	-.1	.4	-.1
4.8	3.1	2.6	Profit Before Taxes	4.3	1.5	-1.1	2.3	4.0	3.4
			RATIOS						
2.0	2.4	2.5		2.0	2.2	3.0	2.4	2.9	2.2
1.5	1.6	1.6	Current	.7	1.3	1.7	1.7	1.7	1.7
1.1	1.2	1.1		.4	.8	1.1	1.1	1.2	1.3
1.7	2.0	2.1		.9	1.9	2.5	2.3	2.6	1.8
1.2	1.3	1.3	Quick	.3	1.1	1.4	1.3	1.4	1.4
.9	.9	.9		.1	.6	.7	.8	.9	1.0
41 8.9	36 10.0	35 10.5		0 UND	14 26.1	31 11.6	45 8.1	35 10.5	44 8.3
58 6.3	54 6.8	55 6.7	Sales/Receivables	21 17.5	47 7.7	48 7.5	60 6.0	54 6.7	58 6.3
80 4.6	75 4.9	74 4.9		36 10.0	72 5.0	69 5.3	81 4.5	75 4.9	76 4.8
0 UND	0 UND	0 UND		0 UND	0 UND	0 UND	0 UND	0 UND	0 UND
0 UND	0 UND	0 UND	Cost of Sales/Inventory	7 55.9	0 UND	0 UND	0 UND	0 UND	0 UND
4 95.3	6 64.9	6 59.6		145 2.5	6 65.3	6 57.8	7 53.2	4 93.6	3 126.6
18 19.8	16 22.2	16 22.8		0 UND	12 29.3	11 34.1	15 24.5	18 20.7	20 18.2
33 11.2	27 13.5	31 11.8	Cost of Sales/Payables	0 UND	34 10.9	23 15.9	31 11.8	31 11.6	32 11.5
51 7.2	47 7.7	51 7.2		48 7.5	73 5.0	50 7.3	48 7.6	49 7.4	47 7.7
6.5	5.9	5.6		12.4	6.5	4.6	5.1	5.2	5.8
11.6	11.0	10.0	Sales/Working Capital	-48.7	19.8	7.8	9.3	10.0	8.6
36.0	28.5	37.6		-4.4	-29.3	276.3	46.8	24.9	15.2
19.4	23.5	18.3		5.8	7.2	8.1	10.7	29.2	36.3
(396) 6.2	(428) 4.8	(428) 4.4	EBIT/Interest	(17) 2.3	(58) 2.4	(48) 1.3	(94) 3.4	(122) 6.5	(89) 8.7
1.6	.5	.4		-.4	.2	-5.8	-1.2	1.1	2.6
4.9	5.7	6.7			6.4	8.8	3.7	4.8	11.3
(144) 2.5	(153) 2.5	(137) 2.2	Net Profit + Depr., Dep., Amort./Cur. Mat. L/T/D		(11) 2.6	(13) 1.5	(31) 1.7	(45) 2.0	(35) 5.9
1.2	1.2	1.2			.4	.7	1.1	1.3	1.6
.4	.3	.3		.7	.5	.3	.4	.2	.2
.7	.7	.7	Fixed/Worth	3.7	1.4	.7	.6	.6	.5
1.5	1.4	1.4		-1.4	16.0	1.7	1.4	1.2	.9
.8	.7	.6		1.9	.8	.6	.5	.5	.7
1.4	1.3	1.2	Debt/Worth	NM	2.0	1.1	1.0	1.2	1.1
2.8	2.4	2.7		-4.3	21.9	3.2	2.1	2.1	2.1
45.0	36.9	30.7		54.5	21.6	17.2	27.6	33.4	34.3
(410) 21.2	(440) 14.8	(441) 11.8	% Profit Before Taxes/Tangible Net Worth	(10) 8.5	(47) 6.2	(52) 1.8	(96) 7.9	(128) 15.8	(108) 19.5
6.2	-1.2	.1		-22.6	-7.2	-32.7	-7.3	3.6	4.7
16.9	15.8	13.8		17.5	11.1	8.7	10.3	18.4	15.1
8.6	6.2	4.7	% Profit Before Taxes/Total Assets	2.3	2.9	.8	3.7	6.8	7.4
2.1	-.9	-.6		-3.0	-1.9	-13.0	-3.8	.4	2.2
15.2	15.7	17.0		85.2	11.4	13.1	11.2	19.1	22.0
7.7	7.4	7.9	Sales/Net Fixed Assets	7.5	4.7	7.5	6.4	8.6	10.9
4.6	3.9	4.2		1.8	2.5	4.6	4.4	4.3	4.8
2.7	2.8	2.8		4.2	2.6	3.0	2.7	2.9	2.7
2.2	2.1	2.0	Sales/Total Assets	1.7	1.7	2.0	2.1	2.1	2.0
1.6	1.5	1.5		1.2	1.2	1.6	1.6	1.6	1.6
1.8	1.9	1.8		1.8	2.8	2.3	2.2	1.5	1.0
(382) 3.3	(423) 3.6	(414) 3.6	% Depr., Dep., Amort./Sales	(11) 4.8	(49) 5.9	(52) 3.8	(92) 4.3	(119) 3.4	(91) 2.3
5.1	5.7	5.9		12.6	9.7	7.1	6.5	5.6	4.0
1.5	1.3	1.4		5.9	2.9	1.9	1.9	1.3	.7
(188) 3.2	(195) 2.9	(212) 2.9	% Officers', Directors' Owners' Comp/Sales	(12) 11.5	(41) 5.2	(24) 4.2	(46) 2.9	(54) 2.0	(35) 1.2
5.9	5.6	6.1		18.3	8.0	7.6	6.0	3.2	3.6
13900791M	13785628M	11964460M	Net Sales ($)	13149M	121917M	227483M	715848M	2052668M	8833395M
6839536M	6528201M	6530784M	Total Assets ($)	14830M	95298M	131835M	406820M	1113716M	4768285M

Current Data Sorted by Assets   **Comparative Historical Data**

Type of Statement	0-500M	500M-2MM	2-10MM	10-50MM	50-100MM	100-250MM		4/1/05-3/31/06 ALL	4/1/06-3/31/07 ALL
Unqualified	1		4	11	4	5		20	22
Reviewed		1	7	6				10	10
Compiled	1	3	8					2	12
Tax Returns		1	3					7	3
Other		5	6	11	6	11		18	21
		20 (4/1-9/30/09)			74 (10/1/09-3/31/10)				
NUMBER OF STATEMENTS	2	10	28	28	10	16		57	68
	%	%	%	%	%	%		%	%
ASSETS									
Cash & Equivalents		10.4	18.3	12.5	22.0	11.4		12.9	11.8
Trade Receivables (net)		24.0	33.7	20.9	18.6	16.9		31.9	36.6
Inventory		4.1	3.5	4.2	7.7	5.6		4.5	4.6
All Other Current		2.0	6.8	5.8	6.4	7.1		6.8	8.0
Total Current		40.4	62.3	43.4	54.7	41.0		56.1	61.0
Fixed Assets (net)		54.2	30.1	40.5	28.1	34.2		31.9	30.3
Intangibles (net)		.1	3.6	9.0	8.1	15.8		4.0	4.1
All Other Non-Current		5.3	4.1	7.1	9.1	9.0		8.1	4.5
Total		100.0	100.0	100.0	100.0	100.0		100.0	100.0
LIABILITIES									
Notes Payable-Short Term		.0	10.7	4.3	6.8	2.0		9.8	10.5
Cur. Mat.-L.T.D.		4.6	5.2	4.1	4.3	2.9		5.2	5.0
Trade Payables		17.4	15.6	7.7	9.2	9.7		14.0	16.9
Income Taxes Payable		.1	1.0	1.2	.7	.5		1.4	1.2
All Other Current		11.5	12.0	6.5	8.1	9.5		12.3	14.2
Total Current		33.7	44.5	23.9	29.0	24.7		42.7	47.7
Long-Term Debt		41.1	18.0	15.0	12.5	21.5		16.2	19.2
Deferred Taxes		.9	1.0	1.1	5.3	4.0		1.3	1.0
All Other Non-Current		3.8	3.7	4.0	2.1	2.7		5.0	3.9
Net Worth		20.5	32.9	56.0	51.1	47.2		35.0	28.2
Total Liabilities & Net Worth		100.0	100.0	100.0	100.0	100.0		100.0	100.0
INCOME DATA									
Net Sales		100.0	100.0	100.0	100.0	100.0		100.0	100.0
Gross Profit									
Operating Expenses		87.9	97.5	92.1	92.0	90.6		91.5	93.2
Operating Profit		12.1	2.5	7.9	8.0	9.4		8.5	6.8
All Other Expenses (net)		7.1	1.6	1.6	2.5	5.3		1.6	.7
Profit Before Taxes		5.0	.9	6.3	5.5	4.1		6.9	6.0
RATIOS									
Current		1.8	2.6	2.8	7.7	2.5		2.1	2.0
		1.0	1.4	1.6	1.4	1.9		1.4	1.5
		.6	.9	1.4	.9	1.2		1.0	1.1
Quick		1.5	2.5	2.8	6.9	2.0		1.8	1.7
		.7	1.1	1.3	1.1	1.2		1.1	1.1
		.6	.6	.8	.5	.8		.7	.8
Sales/Receivables	2 205.3	27 13.6	35 10.4	19 19.7	37 10.0			34 10.6	35 10.5
	26 13.9	41 8.8	47 7.8	44 8.3	43 8.5			54 6.7	59 6.2
	43 8.6	50 7.3	55 6.6	73 5.0	66 5.5			74 5.0	79 4.6
Cost of Sales/Inventory									
Cost of Sales/Payables									
Sales/Working Capital		9.7	11.0	3.6	3.8	4.6		7.9	7.0
		NM	16.8	9.7	10.2	8.7		15.4	12.6
		-23.2	NM	20.4	-48.4	17.2		NM	54.6
EBIT/Interest			11.8	27.2	160.7	13.7		25.4	24.9
			(25) 3.2	(26) 8.1	7.8	(15) 5.0		(48) 5.2	(58) 8.7
			.1	.5	3.0	-.7		2.2	1.9
Net Profit + Depr., Dep., Amort./Cur. Mat. L/T/D			20.6	8.4				10.2	7.8
			(10) 4.1	(11) 1.8				(18) 2.8	(22) 3.7
			1.2	.9				1.6	1.9
Fixed/Worth		.6	.4	.5	.1	.4		.4	.4
		2.4	.9	1.0	.7	1.0		.8	.8
		-40.0	2.3	2.7	2.6	2.5		3.1	1.7
Debt/Worth		.9	.7	.2	.4	.7		.8	.8
		1.8	2.5	.9	1.6	2.1		2.2	2.1
		-43.8	5.1	4.5	4.3	3.3		4.4	3.7
% Profit Before Taxes/Tangible Net Worth			48.9	33.5	47.8	41.9		70.1	76.3
			(23) 18.9	(26) 10.0	30.2	(14) 11.1		(53) 30.0	(60) 47.7
			4.8	-27.2	-4.5	-49.5		13.2	17.7
% Profit Before Taxes/Total Assets		46.2	14.8	22.6	20.7	10.9		21.3	33.1
		18.0	5.0	4.4	13.0	5.8		9.3	14.6
		-.9	-1.2	-3.3	3.2	-5.8		3.3	4.1
Sales/Net Fixed Assets		23.5	25.1	7.2	68.4	14.0		24.0	30.2
		7.7	9.8	4.0	6.2	5.4		9.1	9.6
		3.6	5.6	2.0	4.0	2.2		4.7	4.5
Sales/Total Assets		5.5	5.8	2.3	2.1	1.8		3.2	3.4
		3.6	2.7	1.3	1.8	1.1		2.3	2.2
		2.8	1.5	.8	1.1	.6		1.5	1.6
% Depr., Dep., Amort./Sales			.8	3.5		.5		.7	.7
			(26) 2.4	(24) 4.6		(11) 2.8		(50) 2.2	(57) 2.0
			5.9	6.5		6.0		5.2	3.8
% Officers', Directors', Owners' Comp/Sales			.8					1.4	.8
			(11) 2.2					(19) 3.5	(21) 1.4
			17.6					8.0	3.9
Net Sales ($)	1520M	40123M	598354M	1133554M	1282391M	3106433M		4869011M	3413120M
Total Assets ($)	497M	11105M	137886M	686279M	796918M	2532583M		1674534M	1653302M

© RMA 2010

M = $ thousand   MM = $ million
See Pages 9 through 22 for Explanation of Ratios and Data

Comparative Historical Data   **Current Data Sorted by Sales**

4/1/07-3/31/08 ALL	4/1/08-3/31/09 ALL	4/1/09-3/31/10 ALL	Type of Statement	0-1MM	1-3MM	3-5MM	5-10MM	10-25MM	25MM & OVER
32	21	25	Unqualified	1			4	2	18
15	12	14	Reviewed			1	3	5	5
9	10	12	Compiled	1	1	2	2	5	1
6	8	4	Tax Returns	1			1	1	1
37	32	39	Other		2	4	4	5	24
					20 (4/1-9/30/09)		74 (10/1/09-3/31/10)		
99	83	94	**NUMBER OF STATEMENTS**	3	3	7	14	18	49
%	%	%	**ASSETS**	%	%	%	%	%	%
12.3	15.5	15.0	Cash & Equivalents				17.1	15.6	15.7
32.5	30.8	24.5	Trade Receivables (net)				23.5	29.0	22.9
5.3	3.6	4.5	Inventory				5.8	3.2	4.6
6.6	5.9	5.9	All Other Current				3.6	11.8	5.5
56.7	55.8	49.9	Total Current				50.0	59.6	48.7
34.5	35.5	35.9	Fixed Assets (net)				32.4	28.7	35.3
3.6	3.4	7.3	Intangibles (net)				10.9	3.7	9.0
5.2	5.3	6.8	All Other Non-Current				6.7	8.0	7.0
100.0	100.0	100.0	Total				100.0	100.0	100.0
			LIABILITIES						
8.2	6.6	6.0	Notes Payable-Short Term				6.9	9.7	4.4
6.3	5.4	4.3	Cur. Mat.-L.T.D.				6.6	4.1	3.8
11.4	12.0	11.8	Trade Payables				9.7	13.7	10.2
.5	.7	.8	Income Taxes Payable				.4	2.7	.5
11.0	12.1	10.1	All Other Current				8.8	10.8	9.4
37.5	36.7	33.1	Total Current				32.4	41.1	28.4
18.4	18.6	19.4	Long-Term Debt				21.2	12.9	15.5
1.2	1.0	2.0	Deferred Taxes				.7	2.1	2.6
2.2	3.6	3.4	All Other Non-Current				8.2	3.7	1.9
40.8	40.1	42.1	Net Worth				37.4	40.2	51.6
100.0	100.0	100.0	Total Liabilities & Net Worth				100.0	100.0	100.0
			INCOME DATA						
100.0	100.0	100.0	Net Sales				100.0	100.0	100.0
			Gross Profit						
87.4	90.5	93.5	Operating Expenses				96.1	99.5	91.1
12.6	9.5	6.5	Operating Profit				3.9	.5	8.9
1.6	1.3	2.9	All Other Expenses (net)				4.0	.0	2.6
11.0	8.2	3.6	Profit Before Taxes				-.1	.5	6.3
			RATIOS						
2.6	2.4	2.5	Current				2.5	2.2	3.0
1.5	1.5	1.5					1.6	1.5	1.7
1.1	.9	1.0					1.0	1.1	1.1
2.3	2.1	2.1	Quick				2.2	2.1	2.7
1.2	1.3	1.1					1.0	1.3	1.2
.8	.8	.7					.6	.6	.8
34 10.8	26 14.1	28 13.2	Sales/Receivables				31 11.8	28 13.2	28 13.2
52 7.0	47 7.8	42 8.6					43 8.5	44 8.3	41 9.0
68 5.3	66 5.5	57 6.4					92 4.0	51 7.2	55 6.6
			Cost of Sales/Inventory						
			Cost of Sales/Payables						
6.4	6.8	5.4	Sales/Working Capital				3.0	7.3	5.4
10.4	12.5	13.1					6.5	13.5	11.3
47.4	-47.6	NM					NM	NM	97.5
32.4	41.1	22.5	EBIT/Interest				7.6	31.7	30.2
(89) 9.7	(78) 10.3	(86) 5.5					(12) 1.6	3.2	(45) 7.3
3.4	2.3	.6					-5.8	-2.9	2.6
4.5	7.0	9.1	Net Profit + Depr., Dep., Amort./Cur. Mat. L/T/D						13.2
(26) 2.4	(23) 3.2	(29) 2.8						(16)	3.1
1.3	1.7	1.1							1.0
.4	.2	.4	Fixed/Worth				.4	.3	.4
.8	.9	1.0					1.4	.8	.9
2.1	2.0	2.7					-9.3	2.6	1.9
.6	.6	.6	Debt/Worth				1.0	.5	.4
1.5	1.5	1.9					2.1	1.7	1.7
3.7	3.1	4.5					-14.3	8.2	3.3
76.4	79.9	44.7	% Profit Before Taxes/Tangible Net Worth				19.4	66.8	45.6
(87) 41.7	(74) 40.7	(81) 15.7					(10) -10.9	(16) 13.2	(46) 20.9
18.1	13.1	.2					-62.8	-19.6	4.8
31.5	33.7	18.9	% Profit Before Taxes/Total Assets				9.4	13.0	22.6
13.7	14.1	5.5					5.3	3.8	7.8
5.8	4.2	-1.3					-20.8	-15.3	3.3
21.3	28.4	13.5	Sales/Net Fixed Assets				12.7	20.1	17.4
7.7	7.7	6.6					6.9	9.2	5.9
3.8	3.5	3.0					2.4	3.6	3.4
2.9	3.3	3.1	Sales/Total Assets				2.8	3.7	2.9
2.3	2.5	1.7					1.5	2.3	1.8
1.4	1.6	1.1					.7	1.1	1.1
.7	.7	1.1	% Depr., Dep., Amort./Sales				2.1	1.3	.8
(86) 1.7	(65) 2.5	(78) 3.5					(12) 4.9	(17) 3.5	(40) 2.6
4.3	6.7	6.1					22.2	4.9	5.5
.9	1.1	.7	% Officers', Directors' Owners' Comp/Sales						.2
(29) 2.3	(23) 2.2	(23) 1.9							(10) 2.5
4.9	5.5	10.8							11.2
7356188M	4550801M	6162375M	Net Sales ($)	938M	5821M	29291M	96672M	291554M	5738099M
3572069M	2306040M	4165268M	Total Assets ($)	2485M	13735M	14650M	111412M	169911M	3853075M

M = $ thousand   MM = $ million
See Pages 9 through 22 for Explanation of Ratios and Data

Current Data Sorted by Assets   Comparative Historical Data

	0-500M	500M-2MM	2-10MM	10-50MM	50-100MM	100-250MM		4/1/05-3/31/06 ALL	4/1/06-3/31/07 ALL
Type of Statement									
Unqualified		1	7	9	4	5		13	15
Reviewed	1	3	21	6				7	16
Compiled			9	7	1			1	2
Tax Returns	1	5	2					2	3
Other	3	11	10	9	2	2		7	20
		23 (4/1-9/30/09)		96 (10/1/09-3/31/10)					
NUMBER OF STATEMENTS	5	29	47	25	6	7		30	56
	%	%	%	%	%	%		%	%
ASSETS									
Cash & Equivalents		11.3	11.7	11.9				16.9	15.7
Trade Receivables (net)		31.4	44.5	33.8				36.3	36.9
Inventory		7.1	3.5	3.0				2.2	3.5
All Other Current		8.5	6.3	12.3				8.4	9.4
Total Current		58.3	66.0	61.0				63.8	65.5
Fixed Assets (net)		37.3	27.3	28.4				30.1	28.6
Intangibles (net)		.1	1.4	5.4				1.8	1.2
All Other Non-Current		4.3	5.2	5.2				4.3	4.7
Total		100.0	100.0	100.0				100.0	100.0
LIABILITIES									
Notes Payable-Short Term		13.1	9.2	5.7				8.5	10.1
Cur. Mat.-L.T.D.		8.6	3.6	4.8				4.6	5.6
Trade Payables		12.4	18.1	18.1				17.4	18.2
Income Taxes Payable		.2	.7	.4				.7	.3
All Other Current		12.6	11.1	9.8				11.1	12.3
Total Current		46.8	42.7	38.8				42.3	46.5
Long-Term Debt		17.6	11.5	11.6				16.3	12.6
Deferred Taxes		.0	.4	.6				.8	.3
All Other Non-Current		5.9	5.5	1.8				2.8	2.2
Net Worth		29.7	39.9	47.3				37.8	38.4
Total Liabilities & Net Worth		100.0	100.0	100.0				100.0	100.0
INCOME DATA									
Net Sales		100.0	100.0	100.0				100.0	100.0
Gross Profit		31.4	26.6	21.6				26.2	23.6
Operating Expenses		31.5	20.2	19.3				21.6	18.4
Operating Profit		-.1	6.4	2.4				4.6	5.2
All Other Expenses (net)		.5	.4	.8				1.0	.2
Profit Before Taxes		-.6	6.0	1.5				3.6	5.0
RATIOS									
Current		2.3	2.4	2.2				2.2	2.3
		1.2	1.6	1.7				1.3	1.5
		.8	1.1	1.1				1.1	1.1
Quick		2.0	2.2	1.6				1.6	2.0
		1.1	1.4	1.2				1.2	1.1
		.4	.9	.8				.7	.8
Sales/Receivables	7	50.5	44 8.4	45 8.1				43 8.6	40 9.0
	41	9.0	62 5.9	58 6.3				63 5.8	54 6.8
	62	5.9	74 4.9	93 3.9				74 4.9	67 5.5
Cost of Sales/Inventory	0	UND	0 UND	0 UND				0 UND	0 UND
	0	UND	0 UND	1 336.1				0 UND	0 UND
	25	14.6	9 41.4	9 39.0				2 228.5	6 57.9
Cost of Sales/Payables	2	152.6	12 29.9	23 16.1				13 28.7	17 21.2
	13	28.0	30 12.3	42 8.7				31 11.9	29 12.5
	37	9.8	49 7.4	55 6.6				61 6.0	42 8.7
Sales/Working Capital		8.2	5.1	3.9				5.4	6.7
		22.7	10.2	8.1				18.4	13.1
		-22.1	55.6	38.8				68.5	55.8
EBIT/Interest		11.5	42.0	12.7				29.3	15.8
	(27)	1.2	(42) 9.9	(23) 7.2				(26) 6.0	(49) 5.1
		-2.3	2.0	1.5				1.0	1.3
Net Profit + Depr., Dep., Amort./Cur. Mat. L/T/D				6.4					13.1
				(11) 1.8					(15) 5.2
				-2.3					1.8
Fixed/Worth		.6	.3	.3				.3	.4
		1.1	.5	.7				.6	.7
		3.6	1.0	1.4				2.5	1.5
Debt/Worth		.9	.6	.7				.8	.8
		2.3	1.4	1.3				2.0	1.8
		8.2	3.2	2.5				4.2	4.2
% Profit Before Taxes/Tangible Net Worth		55.3	66.2	31.5				56.7	74.6
	(23)	4.5	(42) 27.5	(24) 19.2				(27) 26.3	(52) 38.3
		-10.4	1.9	1.1				-.7	6.1
% Profit Before Taxes/Total Assets		28.7	26.6	10.9				20.9	25.0
		.5	11.7	7.8				7.7	11.9
		-8.6	1.9	.7				-.6	1.0
Sales/Net Fixed Assets		19.5	35.1	26.3				21.8	20.7
		11.6	10.0	7.3				8.6	8.5
		3.9	5.5	4.0				4.2	5.2
Sales/Total Assets		3.6	3.4	2.6				2.7	3.5
		3.1	2.6	1.8				2.1	2.5
		1.9	1.7	1.4				1.6	1.8
% Depr., Dep., Amort./Sales		1.2	1.1	1.8				.9	1.2
	(21)	2.8	(38) 2.1	3.2				(27) 1.9	(47) 2.7
		6.7	5.5	5.2				3.7	5.0
% Officers', Directors', Owners' Comp/Sales		2.0	.7						1.8
	(10)	3.0	(11) 2.0						(19) 5.6
		6.9	4.3						8.3
Net Sales ($)	8146M	106993M	621641M	998255M	812578M	1495753M		1095244M	1625071M
Total Assets ($)	1366M	35185M	227540M	538727M	418396M	947372M		661389M	691458M

M = $ thousand   MM = $ million
See Pages 9 through 22 for Explanation of Ratios and Data

Comparative Historical Data / Current Data Sorted by Sales

			Type of Statement						
76	60	49	Unqualified	6	7	2	12	13	9
51	60	51	Reviewed	10	7	5	11	12	6
105	94	69	Compiled	32	16	9	6	6	
352	293	263	Tax Returns	160	66	18	14	5	
384	398	313	Other	155	75	29	25	14	15
4/1/07-3/31/08 ALL	4/1/08-3/31/09 ALL	4/1/09-3/31/10 ALL		0-1MM	1-3MM	3-5MM	5-10MM	10-25MM	25MM & OVER
					61 (4/1-9/30/09)		684 (10/1/09-3/31/10)		
968	905	745	NUMBER OF STATEMENTS	363	171	63	68	50	30
%	%	%	ASSETS	%	%	%	%	%	%
6.7	6.9	7.5	Cash & Equivalents	5.5	8.2	11.6	8.4	9.8	13.6
4.5	4.5	4.5	Trade Receivables (net)	2.5	3.8	7.5	6.2	10.0	12.4
38.7	36.9	31.5	Inventory	30.5	33.1	37.2	32.4	24.6	32.0
5.1	3.7	4.3	All Other Current	4.0	3.5	3.2	7.3	6.2	4.8
55.0	52.1	47.8	Total Current	42.5	48.5	59.5	54.4	50.6	62.8
30.2	34.1	36.4	Fixed Assets (net)	40.9	36.0	22.7	35.3	33.1	21.9
1.1	1.2	1.8	Intangibles (net)	1.9	1.6	2.5	1.3	.6	3.0
13.6	12.6	14.0	All Other Non-Current	14.7	13.9	15.3	9.1	15.7	12.4
100.0	100.0	100.0	Total	100.0	100.0	100.0	100.0	100.0	100.0
			LIABILITIES						
19.8	18.0	18.0	Notes Payable-Short Term	17.9	17.8	23.2	19.4	9.8	19.7
4.7	3.4	4.4	Cur. Mat.-L.T.D.	3.8	4.1	4.4	4.5	8.6	12.4
3.5	4.6	3.5	Trade Payables	1.7	3.5	3.6	6.3	7.9	11.1
.1	.1	.1	Income Taxes Payable	.0	.0	.1	.2	.7	.3
10.3	11.8	12.1	All Other Current	12.8	13.7	11.8	9.2	7.8	9.7
38.4	37.8	38.1	Total Current	36.1	39.2	43.3	39.5	34.8	46.3
31.4	35.1	34.3	Long-Term Debt	36.3	38.1	32.3	24.5	33.0	18.2
.1	.1	.0	Deferred Taxes	.0	.0	.0	.3	.1	.0
4.4	3.5	3.8	All Other Non-Current	3.7	4.6	1.8	3.5	4.8	2.9
25.8	23.5	23.8	Net Worth	23.8	18.1	22.7	32.2	27.2	32.5
100.0	100.0	100.0	Total Liabilities & Net Worth	100.0	100.0	100.0	100.0	100.0	100.0
			INCOME DATA						
100.0	100.0	100.0	Net Sales	100.0	100.0	100.0	100.0	100.0	100.0
			Gross Profit						
82.4	83.9	82.4	Operating Expenses	75.1	85.3	90.3	90.8	95.2	97.3
17.6	16.1	17.6	Operating Profit	24.9	14.7	9.7	9.2	4.8	2.7
8.3	10.3	11.8	All Other Expenses (net)	16.7	9.7	5.4	5.8	5.1	3.1
9.3	5.8	5.8	Profit Before Taxes	8.3	5.0	4.3	3.4	-.3	-.4
			RATIOS						
4.0	3.6	3.0		3.0	3.7	3.3	2.6	2.9	2.6
1.3	1.3	1.3	Current	1.1	1.4	1.4	1.3	1.4	1.5
.7	.6	.5		.3	.6	.8	.9	.9	1.1
1.0	.9	1.1		1.0	1.4	1.4	1.1	1.4	1.3
(963) .2	(904) .2	(744) .2	Quick	.1	(170) .2	.5	.2	.5	.5
.0	.0	.0		.0	.0	.1	.1	.1	.1
0 UND	0 UND	0 UND		0 UND	0 UND	0 UND	0 UND	1 543.1	1 303.1
0 UND	0 UND	0 UND	Sales/Receivables	0 UND	0 UND	0 UND	3 137.6	14 25.8	9 40.4
10 37.2	12 31.4	13 27.6		1 355.0	15 24.3	24 15.3	23 15.6	45 8.2	44 8.3
			Cost of Sales/Inventory						
			Cost of Sales/Payables						
1.3	.9	1.0		.6	1.4	1.5	1.7	1.8	4.2
7.2	8.5	8.5	Sales/Working Capital	11.9	7.6	10.3	8.5	5.9	7.6
-8.1	-5.6	-3.6		-1.9	-4.4	-11.7	-9.0	-20.7	38.9
8.2	6.2	5.2		5.1	4.7	3.9	6.5	5.7	15.7
(565) 2.5	(480) 2.1	(401) 1.7	EBIT/Interest	(142) 1.7	(102) 1.8	(41) 1.6	(53) 1.5	(37) 1.2	(26) 1.2
.6	-.1	-.9		-.5	-1.0	-3.3	-2.3	-2.9	-4.6
3.8	4.3	8.7	Net Profit + Depr., Dep.,						
(25) 1.0	(22) 1.2	(24) 1.8	Amort./Cur. Mat. L/T/D						
-.1	.2	.7							
.0	.0	.0		.0	.0	.0	.1	.2	.0
.4	.7	.9	Fixed/Worth	1.1	1.2	.1	1.0	.7	.5
3.6	4.9	6.3		8.9	28.5	3.8	3.0	2.0	1.3
1.1	1.2	1.2		1.2	1.5	.9	.8	.7	1.0
3.8	3.7	3.4	Debt/Worth	3.6	4.8	4.1	2.4	2.6	2.8
19.7	30.2	35.2		58.7	999.8	44.0	10.1	9.0	5.5
43.9	25.1	22.3		20.7	30.1	24.2	22.6	11.2	30.1
(806) 11.8	(733) 5.6	(594) 3.7	% Profit Before Taxes/Tangible Net Worth	(282) 4.0	(130) 6.0	(51) 2.9	(61) 2.1	(44) 2.2	(26) .6
-.2	-4.6	-5.4		-2.3	-3.2	-18.5	-13.0	-11.4	-32.6
8.8	5.4	4.5		3.7	5.5	5.2	6.4	4.3	11.7
2.2	1.0	.8	% Profit Before Taxes/Total Assets	.7	1.4	.8	.7	.6	1.0
-.9	-1.6	-2.1		-1.5	-2.0	-3.9	-3.3	-3.6	-9.4
999.8	999.8	265.7		UND	144.2	999.8	63.0	25.1	156.1
10.0	6.6	2.9	Sales/Net Fixed Assets	.7	2.7	28.7	4.0	3.9	9.5
.6	.4	.2		.1	.4	1.5	.7	.4	3.0
1.0	.8	.6		.3	.7	1.2	1.3	1.1	2.9
.4	.3	.2	Sales/Total Assets	.1	.3	.5	.5	.4	1.2
.2	.1	.1		.1	.2	.2	.2	.2	.5
.5	.7	1.2		4.3	1.3	.5	.6	.7	.3
(503) 2.4	(446) 4.6	(404) 5.7	% Depr., Dep., Amort./Sales	(155) 15.6	(105) 4.4	(33) 1.3	(51) 2.2	(39) 3.3	(21) 1.0
11.9	15.6	16.4		25.0	12.8	7.2	7.7	9.9	5.5
1.5	1.6	1.4		2.1	1.8	1.4	1.2		
(164) 4.1	(152) 3.8	(91) 3.0	% Officers', Directors' Owners' Comp/Sales	(27) 4.0	(22) 3.2	(18) 2.4	(13) 2.6		
9.0	8.2	6.8		9.7	5.0	7.8	4.8		
10960909M	10713760M	5060144M	Net Sales ($)	146475M	322301M	241303M	482937M	785936M	3081192M
18481255M	14235730M	10918647M	Total Assets ($)	1176974M	1509505M	937046M	1811037M	2577491M	2906594M

M = $ thousand   MM = $ million
See Pages 9 through 22 for Explanation of Ratios and Data

	Current Data Sorted by Assets						Comparative Historical Data	
Type of Statement								
Unqualified		10	119	184	58	37	395	405
Reviewed	7	39	130	56	5		158	224
Compiled	5	17	16	6	1		42	44
Tax Returns	13	21	11	1			43	44
Other	8	23	83	115	22	21	195	171
		186 (4/1-9/30/09)		822 (10/1/09-3/31/10)			4/1/05-3/31/06	4/1/06-3/31/07
	0-500M	500M-2MM	2-10MM	10-50MM	50-100MM	100-250MM	ALL	ALL
NUMBER OF STATEMENTS	33	110	359	362	86	58	833	888
	%	%	%	%	%	%	%	%
ASSETS								
Cash & Equivalents	21.6	17.8	18.1	21.4	24.9	20.1	15.7	16.3
Trade Receivables (net)	21.3	27.4	31.4	26.4	21.3	19.2	32.0	32.3
Inventory	3.4	3.5	3.3	4.4	3.8	5.7	4.0	3.5
All Other Current	1.5	5.6	7.5	7.3	7.9	9.7	7.6	6.8
Total Current	47.8	54.3	60.2	59.6	57.9	54.7	59.3	59.0
Fixed Assets (net)	42.4	37.0	33.0	32.9	30.8	33.1	33.1	33.9
Intangibles (net)	3.8	1.3	.9	.8	2.5	4.6	1.0	1.2
All Other Non-Current	6.0	7.4	5.9	6.8	8.8	7.6	6.6	5.9
Total	100.0	100.0	100.0	100.0	100.0	100.0	100.0	100.0
LIABILITIES								
Notes Payable-Short Term	26.5	8.3	4.6	3.3	.9	3.3	4.8	5.1
Cur. Mat.-L.T.D.	14.6	5.5	5.3	4.8	3.4	3.1	5.6	5.4
Trade Payables	9.3	11.4	16.9	15.1	14.0	11.9	17.6	15.8
Income Taxes Payable	.3	.5	.6	.4	.5	.3	.6	.7
All Other Current	14.4	7.5	8.2	11.7	14.9	18.9	10.8	11.0
Total Current	65.0	33.2	35.5	35.1	33.8	37.5	39.3	38.0
Long-Term Debt	45.7	14.8	13.6	13.6	13.1	12.7	15.5	15.3
Deferred Taxes	.2	1.0	1.3	1.2	1.5	1.1	1.2	1.2
All Other Non-Current	7.4	6.1	1.6	2.3	2.2	3.5	3.2	3.0
Net Worth	-18.3	44.8	48.0	47.7	49.4	45.2	40.7	42.5
Total Liabilties & Net Worth	100.0	100.0	100.0	100.0	100.0	100.0	100.0	100.0
INCOME DATA								
Net Sales	100.0	100.0	100.0	100.0	100.0	100.0	100.0	100.0
Gross Profit	37.1	30.2	19.2	15.1	14.1	14.5	18.5	20.1
Operating Expenses	37.0	27.0	16.3	10.6	8.6	9.2	14.5	14.3
Operating Profit	.1	3.2	2.9	4.5	5.4	5.4	3.9	5.8
All Other Expenses (net)	1.4	.4	.3	.4	-.1	-.2	.0	.1
Profit Before Taxes	-1.2	2.8	2.6	4.1	5.5	5.6	3.9	5.7
RATIOS								
Current	1.9	3.3	2.9	2.4	2.2	1.8	2.2	2.2
	.6	1.7	1.7	1.7	1.6	1.4	1.5	1.5
	.3	1.1	1.2	1.3	1.3	1.2	1.2	1.2
Quick	1.6	2.8	2.4	2.0	1.8	1.3	1.8	1.8
	.6	1.4	1.4	1.4	1.4	1.1	1.3	1.3
	.3	.9	.9	.9	1.0	.7	.9	.9
Sales/Receivables	0 UND	16 22.7	30 12.3	31 11.9	28 13.1	31 11.6	32 11.3	31 11.6
	14 25.7	39 9.3	48 7.6	47 7.8	44 8.4	45 8.0	50 7.4	52 7.1
	38 9.7	61 6.0	70 5.2	68 5.3	65 5.6	60 6.1	73 5.0	71 5.1
Cost of Sales/Inventory	0 UND	0 UND	0 UND	0 UND	0 UND	4 98.4	0 UND	0 UND
	0 UND	0 UND	0 UND	2 229.7	3 127.1	12 29.8	1 538.5	0 883.1
	0 UND	2 162.6	6 61.7	12 31.6	10 35.1	27 13.3	10 35.7	8 43.2
Cost of Sales/Payables	0 UND	5 80.6	13 28.7	19 18.9	21 17.4	20 18.7	16 22.6	15 23.6
	3 113.0	14 26.1	27 13.7	30 12.1	30 12.1	30 12.0	29 12.5	28 13.0
	13 28.2	39 9.3	48 7.6	45 8.2	43 8.4	43 8.4	47 7.8	44 8.3
Sales/Working Capital	11.7	5.7	5.2	5.0	5.0	5.8	6.3	6.4
	-80.9	11.2	9.7	8.7	8.3	10.3	11.9	11.3
	-8.6	57.3	25.6	16.2	18.2	20.0	25.9	27.5
EBIT/Interest	6.9	11.5	18.4	24.8	65.0	34.7	17.0	22.1
	(27) 2.0	(90) 4.1	(326) 5.2	(329) 6.5	(81) 14.9	(54) 10.3	(770) 6.0	(826) 6.9
	-5.3	1.1	.9	1.5	-4.5	3.4	2.0	2.6
Net Profit + Depr., Dep., Amort./Cur. Mat. L/T/D		3.3	5.9	5.6	12.9	7.8	4.3	5.7
		(24) 1.0	(119) 2.6	(128) 2.3	(45) 3.2	(19) 3.5	(287) 2.2	(299) 2.7
		-.1	1.2	1.2	1.9	1.5	1.3	1.6
Fixed/Worth	.6	.3	.3	.4	.4	.5	.4	.4
	4.7	.7	.7	.7	.6	.8	.8	.8
	-.5	1.5	1.2	1.2	1.0	1.3	1.3	1.4
Debt/Worth	1.1	.4	.5	.6	.6	.9	.7	.8
	6.8	.8	1.1	1.1	1.1	1.6	1.5	1.4
	-2.4	3.3	2.1	2.1	1.9	2.2	2.8	2.5
% Profit Before Taxes/Tangible Net Worth	63.5	37.8	28.0	29.9	32.4	30.2	38.3	46.0
	(18) 4.8	(97) 12.0	(350) 12.6	(355) 15.8	(85) 19.1	15.1	(792) 17.7	(856) 24.4
	-33.9	.5	.7	2.7	9.9	10.6	5.2	10.0
% Profit Before Taxes/Total Assets	25.6	15.5	14.5	13.2	15.2	10.2	14.5	19.1
	4.1	5.5	5.4	6.5	9.5	6.1	6.6	9.6
	-19.7	.1	-.1	1.1	3.7	2.7	1.8	3.7
Sales/Net Fixed Assets	42.9	15.6	13.9	11.1	9.0	9.7	13.5	13.0
	14.1	7.8	7.7	6.1	5.9	4.9	7.6	7.5
	5.7	3.8	4.2	3.8	4.1	3.0	4.4	4.5
Sales/Total Assets	8.5	3.5	2.8	2.5	2.2	2.0	3.0	2.9
	4.0	2.6	2.3	1.9	1.7	1.6	2.2	2.2
	2.1	1.3	1.7	1.4	1.4	1.2	1.7	1.7
% Depr., Dep., Amort./Sales	2.1	2.0	1.8	2.1		1.2	1.8	1.8
	(23) 5.5	(87) 3.9	(332) 3.4	(335) 3.5	(78) 3.2	(34) 2.0	(742) 3.2	(802) 2.9
	9.1	7.2	5.5	5.2	4.6	3.7	4.6	4.5
% Officers', Directors' Owners' Comp/Sales	5.0	2.3	1.5	.7	1.0		1.3	1.2
	(20) 9.5	(61) 4.2	(143) 2.5	(89) 1.5	(14) 2.1		(280) 2.5	(302) 2.4
	15.4	8.1	4.9	2.9	4.7		4.2	4.8
Net Sales ($)	40660M	353377M	4369145M	16333108M	10757393M	15050385M	36337043M	40273744M
Total Assets ($)	8401M	135842M	1841086M	8295972M	6102084M	9655274M	17903441M	20003568M

M = $ thousand   MM = $ million
See Pages 9 through 22 for Explanation of Ratios and Data

Comparative Historical Data / Current Data Sorted by Sales

Hist 4/1/07-3/31/08 ALL	Hist 4/1/08-3/31/09 ALL	Hist 4/1/09-3/31/10 ALL	Type of Statement	0-1MM	1-3MM	3-5MM	5-10MM	10-25MM	25MM & OVER
380	418	408	Unqualified		6	10	41	95	256
207	223	237	Reviewed	5	29	26	64	71	42
35	40	45	Compiled	7	12	3	12	8	3
43	41	46	Tax Returns	12	8	12	10	3	1
197	241	272	Other	6	19	17	26	69	135
					186 (4/1-9/30/09)		822 (10/1/09-3/31/10)		
862	963	1008	NUMBER OF STATEMENTS	30	74	68	153	246	437
%	%	%	**ASSETS**	%	%	%	%	%	%
17.9	18.6	20.1	Cash & Equivalents	21.7	20.2	18.1	16.2	19.6	21.9
30.5	30.0	27.3	Trade Receivables (net)	17.9	22.4	28.4	28.4	29.6	26.9
3.5	3.9	3.9	Inventory	6.1	4.6	2.3	3.2	3.7	4.2
6.7	7.6	7.2	All Other Current	3.5	3.0	7.1	7.9	7.5	7.8
58.7	60.0	58.4	Total Current	49.2	50.1	55.8	55.7	60.3	60.7
34.3	33.1	33.5	Fixed Assets (net)	37.4	40.2	34.2	37.1	31.9	31.6
.9	1.2	1.3	Intangibles (net)	6.1	.9	1.1	1.6	.5	1.5
6.1	5.6	6.7	All Other Non-Current	7.3	8.7	8.9	5.7	7.3	6.1
100.0	100.0	100.0	Total	100.0	100.0	100.0	100.0	100.0	100.0
			LIABILITIES						
4.3	4.7	4.9	Notes Payable-Short Term	15.0	12.2	6.5	5.9	4.3	2.6
5.4	5.0	5.1	Cur. Mat.-L.T.D.	9.6	8.0	4.9	5.8	4.9	4.2
15.2	15.7	14.9	Trade Payables	4.8	8.4	14.6	13.9	17.3	15.7
.6	.4	.5	Income Taxes Payable	.3	.4	.5	.5	.5	.4
12.0	11.3	10.8	All Other Current	11.2	5.7	6.8	8.8	8.7	14.0
37.5	36.9	36.1	Total Current	40.9	34.6	33.4	34.9	35.7	37.0
16.0	14.9	14.7	Long-Term Debt	31.0	25.2	13.9	15.8	13.3	12.3
1.1	1.1	1.2	Deferred Taxes	.5	1.0	1.2	1.2	1.3	1.2
2.3	2.6	2.7	All Other Non-Current	12.1	6.3	1.8	1.9	2.0	2.3
43.1	44.4	45.4	Net Worth	15.5	32.9	49.7	46.2	47.7	47.2
100.0	100.0	100.0	Total Liabilities & Net Worth	100.0	100.0	100.0	100.0	100.0	100.0
			INCOME DATA						
100.0	100.0	100.0	Net Sales	100.0	100.0	100.0	100.0	100.0	100.0
20.5	18.0	18.8	Gross Profit	39.0	32.2	26.3	23.5	16.1	13.9
14.1	13.6	15.1	Operating Expenses	33.0	32.1	24.2	19.7	12.4	9.4
6.4	4.4	3.8	Operating Profit	6.0	.1	2.1	3.8	3.7	4.5
.3	.3	.3	All Other Expenses (net)	2.2	.5	.1	.2	.6	.0
6.1	4.1	3.5	Profit Before Taxes	3.8	-.3	2.0	3.6	3.1	4.5
			RATIOS						
2.2	2.4	2.5	Current	6.0	4.0	3.8	2.9	2.6	2.2
1.6	1.6	1.7		1.4	1.6	2.0	1.7	1.7	1.6
1.2	1.2	1.2		.5	.9	1.1	1.1	1.3	1.3
1.8	2.0	2.1	Quick	3.3	3.5	3.5	2.4	2.1	1.8
1.3	1.3	1.3		1.1	1.3	1.6	1.4	1.4	1.3
.9	.9	.9		.4	.6	.7	.8	1.0	1.0
32 11.3	28 13.0	28 13.1	Sales/Receivables	0 UND	11 32.2	16 22.5	26 14.2	32 11.6	30 12.2
49 7.5	47 7.8	46 8.0		38 9.7	39 9.3	46 8.0	43 8.5	49 7.5	46 8.0
70 5.2	68 5.4	67 5.5		68 5.4	69 5.3	70 5.2	72 5.1	67 5.5	65 5.6
0 UND	0 UND	0 UND	Cost of Sales/Inventory	0 UND	0 UND	0 UND	0 UND	0 UND	0 UND
0 784.4	1 661.9	0 755.6		0 UND	0 UND	0 UND	0 UND	0 UND	3 131.9
8 47.2	9 41.3	10 38.0		7 55.6	3 105.9	2 158.1	7 54.6	9 38.6	12 29.9
15 23.6	14 25.3	14 25.3	Cost of Sales/Payables	0 UND	4 92.6	8 44.5	11 34.6	16 22.6	20 18.5
29 12.7	28 13.1	28 13.2		11 31.8	12 30.8	21 17.0	25 14.6	31 11.8	29 12.6
43 8.5	44 8.3	44 8.3		37 9.8	46 7.9	50 7.3	45 8.2	50 7.4	42 8.7
6.1	5.8	5.3	Sales/Working Capital	2.4	3.4	5.0	5.5	4.9	5.8
10.7	10.1	9.5		13.6	10.6	7.8	10.3	9.3	9.6
24.3	23.3	24.5		-8.2	-71.3	135.9	59.7	20.3	18.1
21.2	22.5	22.6	EBIT/Interest	8.5	5.8	10.6	18.9	20.2	35.3
(780) 7.2	(881) 6.1	(907) 5.8		(21) 3.5	(60) 1.5	(55) 2.3	(144) 5.5	(221) 5.5	(406) 8.5
2.9	1.8	1.4		-3.1	-3.1	-.9	.9	1.3	2.5
6.0	5.5	5.9	Net Profit + Depr., Dep., Amort./Cur. Mat. L/T/D		3.4	2.2	4.7	4.3	8.3
(288) 2.6	(316) 2.4	(339) 2.5			(18) .2	(16) 1.2	(47) 2.0	(85) 2.6	(171) 2.9
1.6	1.4	1.2			-7.5	.1	1.2	1.3	1.6
.4	.4	.4	Fixed/Worth	.4	.4	.2	.4	.3	.4
.8	.7	.7		1.5	.9	.6	.7	.7	.7
1.3	1.3	1.2		-.5	2.7	1.3	1.4	1.1	1.1
.7	.6	.6	Debt/Worth	.5	.4	.3	.5	.6	.7
1.3	1.3	1.1		2.6	1.2	1.0	1.0	1.1	1.2
2.5	2.4	2.2		-3.0	7.9	3.0	2.1	2.1	2.1
46.1	36.4	30.1	% Profit Before Taxes/Tangible Net Worth	41.7	20.4	21.6	38.2	27.0	31.2
(840) 26.3	(926) 17.2	(963) 14.8		(19) 20.4	(60) 6.4	(67) 3.2	(144) 12.8	(241) 13.8	(432) 18.0
11.3	5.1	2.4		2.9	-10.6	-7.3	.8	2.7	5.0
19.1	15.4	14.3	% Profit Before Taxes/Total Assets	15.6	11.3	11.4	16.7	12.8	15.0
10.1	7.2	6.2		5.5	1.6	1.4	6.0	6.1	7.3
4.3	1.7	.9		-8.9	-8.5	-3.1	.1	.9	2.1
12.0	14.4	12.9	Sales/Net Fixed Assets	17.4	12.4	20.5	12.3	13.2	12.4
6.9	7.5	6.8		4.9	5.6	7.0	7.0	7.1	6.7
4.1	4.1	3.9		1.6	2.8	4.1	3.6	4.3	4.3
2.8	2.9	2.7	Sales/Total Assets	3.8	3.0	3.1	2.8	2.7	2.6
2.1	2.2	2.0		1.0	1.6	1.9	2.2	2.1	2.0
1.6	1.7	1.5		.5	.9	1.4	1.5	1.5	1.6
1.9	1.8	1.9	% Depr., Dep., Amort./Sales	2.4	3.3	1.8	2.3	1.7	1.8
(774) 3.2	(870) 3.0	(889) 3.4		(24) 7.5	(59) 5.1	(55) 3.9	(141) 3.8	(228) 3.1	(382) 3.2
4.8	4.8	5.2		17.1	9.9	6.5	5.8	4.9	4.5
1.3	1.0	1.3	% Officers', Directors' Owners' Comp/Sales	5.7	2.6	2.7	1.6	1.1	.7
(254) 2.6	(306) 2.1	(332) 2.1		(13) 10.0	(40) 6.7	(39) 4.7	(60) 3.0	(92) 1.9	(88) 1.5
5.0	4.2	5.1		17.2	9.9	7.1	4.8	2.9	2.9
42180404M	51292388M	46904068M	Net Sales ($)	18299M	141978M	262697M	1105897M	4081835M	41293362M
22228306M	25842125M	26038659M	Total Assets ($)	20792M	137245M	168981M	594862M	2235152M	22881627M

Current Data Sorted by Assets

Comparative Historical Data

Type of Statement	0-500M	500M-2MM	2-10MM	10-50MM	50-100MM	100-250MM		4/1/05-3/31/06 ALL	4/1/06-3/31/07 ALL
Unqualified		1	29	42	18	10		81	93
Reviewed	2	19	69	29	3			104	102
Compiled	4	10	8	2				26	24
Tax Returns	12	16	13					40	47
Other	6	12	26	33	14	9		94	71
		77 (4/1-9/30/09)		310 (10/1/09-3/31/10)					
NUMBER OF STATEMENTS	24	58	145	106	35	19		345	337
	%	%	%	%	%	%		%	%
ASSETS									
Cash & Equivalents	12.0	13.9	17.5	20.1	18.9	26.8		13.6	13.7
Trade Receivables (net)	24.9	28.7	31.9	28.9	34.0	29.2		38.1	35.9
Inventory	9.9	6.3	2.8	2.6	3.7	5.5		6.1	4.8
All Other Current	3.5	4.5	7.1	8.3	11.1	6.8		8.0	7.1
Total Current	50.3	53.5	59.3	59.9	67.6	68.3		65.7	61.5
Fixed Assets (net)	34.5	37.9	32.6	32.5	24.0	24.6		27.7	31.6
Intangibles (net)	2.1	2.2	1.7	1.9	1.4	2.1		.9	1.1
All Other Non-Current	13.1	6.4	6.4	5.7	7.0	5.0		5.7	5.8
Total	100.0	100.0	100.0	100.0	100.0	100.0		100.0	100.0
LIABILITIES									
Notes Payable-Short Term	23.8	10.3	6.5	3.4	3.6	1.1		9.5	8.9
Cur. Mat.-L.T.D.	5.1	5.6	6.3	4.8	3.4	2.3		4.5	5.0
Trade Payables	10.4	11.9	16.5	16.3	16.0	15.8		18.6	17.1
Income Taxes Payable	.4	.2	.7	.2	.9	.5		.8	1.0
All Other Current	10.4	7.9	9.5	15.0	22.7	25.1		13.6	14.1
Total Current	50.0	35.9	39.6	39.6	46.6	44.8		47.0	46.1
Long-Term Debt	22.0	20.3	12.7	15.4	10.3	12.1		14.0	17.3
Deferred Taxes	.0	.8	.6	1.4	1.2	.5		.8	.9
All Other Non-Current	15.2	6.4	2.3	2.5	3.1	2.3		3.4	1.7
Net Worth	12.7	36.7	44.8	41.2	38.8	40.3		34.9	33.9
Total Liabilties & Net Worth	100.0	100.0	100.0	100.0	100.0	100.0		100.0	100.0
INCOME DATA									
Net Sales	100.0	100.0	100.0	100.0	100.0	100.0		100.0	100.0
Gross Profit	41.6	31.0	20.9	20.3	16.9	17.3		23.0	25.4
Operating Expenses	47.3	30.2	19.7	15.8	11.8	9.2		18.2	19.4
Operating Profit	-5.7	.7	1.3	4.5	5.2	8.1		4.8	6.0
All Other Expenses (net)	.8	.9	.3	.6	.3	.5		.5	.6
Profit Before Taxes	-6.5	-.1	.9	3.9	4.9	7.6		4.3	5.4
RATIOS									
Current	2.2	2.6	2.5	2.2	1.6	1.8		2.0	2.0
	1.5	1.7	1.6	1.5	1.4	1.6		1.4	1.4
	.4	.9	1.1	1.1	1.2	1.2		1.1	1.1
Quick	1.6	2.3	2.1	1.7	1.4	1.6		1.6	1.8
	(23) .8	1.3	1.3	1.2	1.1	1.4		1.1 (336)	1.2
	.3	.5	.8	.8	1.0	.9		.8	.7
Sales/Receivables	0 UND	10 35.0	38 9.6	37 9.8	47 7.8	48 7.6		39 9.2	37 9.9
	17 21.7	40 9.2	55 6.6	55 6.7	61 6.0	59 6.2		63 5.8	56 6.5
	51 7.2	63 5.8	75 4.8	76 4.8	78 4.7	82 4.5		85 4.3	79 4.6
Cost of Sales/Inventory	0 UND	0 UND	0 UND	0 UND	0 UND	0 UND		0 UND	0 UND
	0 UND	0 UND	0 UND	0 UND	0 UND	2 184.3		0 UND	0 UND
	20 18.2	18 20.4	6 57.8	8 45.9	14 25.3	14 26.6		8 44.6	4 86.5
Cost of Sales/Payables	1 675.2	6 59.4	15 24.7	19 19.7	19 19.2	17 21.4		18 20.6	14 25.6
	8 45.0	17 21.5	27 13.4	37 9.8	28 12.9	33 11.2		37 10.0	32 11.5
	38 9.7	45 8.1	45 8.2	52 7.0	46 7.9	47 7.8		56 6.5	51 7.1
Sales/Working Capital	6.5	5.9	5.0	4.8	6.2	4.2		6.6	7.0
	43.9	12.4	10.6	9.1	9.6	7.9		12.5	12.8
	-7.6	-39.6	39.4	50.9	17.5	17.6		57.7	99.9
EBIT/Interest	3.6	6.3	17.0	30.4	52.5	68.2		17.2	19.5
	(21) .5	(55) 1.7	(133) 4.0	(101) 5.5	(30) 8.2	(18) 16.0		(312) 5.5	(308) 5.5
	-7.6	-3.6	.1	1.4	2.6	1.9		1.7	2.5
Net Profit + Depr., Dep., Amort./Cur. Mat. L/T/D		16.2	4.7	10.2	11.0			4.4	6.2
		(10) 1.2	(42) 1.7	(41) 3.0	(21) 4.7			(101) 2.4	(110) 2.6
		.0	1.1	.8	1.6			1.2	1.3
Fixed/Worth	.4	.4	.3	.3	.2	.3		.3	.3
	1.2	1.1	.7	.7	.6	.6		.7	.7
	-2.5	11.8	1.4	1.7	.7	1.1		1.6	1.6
Debt/Worth	.7	.6	.6	.8	1.0	1.3		1.0	.9
	11.1	1.6	1.4	1.6	1.6	1.5		2.0	1.8
	-5.9	16.3	2.6	2.8	2.9	2.3		4.1	3.4
% Profit Before Taxes/Tangible Net Worth	47.9	41.7	28.0	38.0	35.6	59.2		45.5	54.2
	(14) -.1	(46) 5.8	(138) 9.1	(101) 17.1	21.2	26.6		(324) 23.3	(312) 27.9
	-67.5	-10.4	-4.1	2.6	7.2	7.2		7.7	11.2
% Profit Before Taxes/Total Assets	7.5	10.5	13.3	15.6	11.9	18.9		15.3	19.3
	-4.1	1.7	4.1	5.7	7.0	11.0		7.3	9.7
	-45.0	-11.4	-3.9	1.0	1.7	2.9		1.9	3.3
Sales/Net Fixed Assets	34.3	17.2	18.1	14.8	27.2	18.4		27.0	27.0
	12.1	6.8	7.6	6.7	9.0	8.2		10.4	9.5
	5.4	3.3	3.7	3.5	4.4	4.4		4.7	4.3
Sales/Total Assets	4.9	3.2	2.7	2.5	2.4	2.1		3.0	3.1
	3.3	2.3	2.0	1.9	1.8	2.0		2.2	2.3
	1.9	1.5	1.4	1.2	1.4	1.0		1.6	1.6
% Depr., Dep., Amort./Sales	1.2	1.9	1.3	1.4	1.2	.8		1.0	1.0
	(19) 3.4	(48) 3.6	(132) 3.1	(97) 3.4	(32) 3.7	(14) 1.2		(305) 2.5	(292) 2.6
	11.0	8.6	6.7	5.8	5.4	2.4		4.7	5.4
% Officers', Directors' Owners' Comp/Sales	6.0	2.9	1.3	.6				1.4	1.3
	(17) 10.4	(33) 4.8	(59) 2.7	(26) 1.5				(120) 2.5	(126) 3.2
	19.7	9.1	5.8	4.5				4.6	5.6
Net Sales ($)	27968M	168135M	1520203M	4124911M	4718402M	5095886M		14213692M	13828851M
Total Assets ($)	6581M	63284M	716799M	2153673M	2414588M	2860313M		6305883M	6619354M

Comparative Historical Data | | Current Data Sorted by Sales

			Type of Statement						
87	90	100	Unqualified		2	5	12	22	59
119	115	122	Reviewed	5	15	13	31	32	26
22	25	24	Compiled		10	5	4	4	1
27	44	41	Tax Returns	10	16	3	8	4	
91	114	100	Other	5	11	7	15	14	48
4/1/07-3/31/08 ALL	4/1/08-3/31/09 ALL	4/1/09-3/31/10 ALL		0-1MM	77 (4/1-9/30/09) 1-3MM	3-5MM	5-10MM	310 (10/1/09-3/31/10) 10-25MM	25MM & OVER
346	388	387	**NUMBER OF STATEMENTS**	20	54	33	70	76	134
%	%	%	**ASSETS**	%	%	%	%	%	%
14.6	15.8	17.9	Cash & Equivalents	8.6	17.1	15.0	17.6	17.3	20.9
33.6	33.2	30.2	Trade Receivables (net)	25.8	21.1	29.0	32.9	29.4	33.9
4.2	4.0	3.9	Inventory	9.6	6.3	3.2	3.0	3.4	3.0
7.2	7.1	7.2	All Other Current	3.1	5.1	3.5	6.7	7.9	4.3
59.6	60.0	59.2	Total Current	47.0	49.7	50.7	60.3	58.0	67.1
34.1	32.0	32.3	Fixed Assets (net)	40.0	41.6	30.5	33.1	34.1	26.4
1.3	1.6	1.9	Intangibles (net)	5.2	.6	3.7	1.5	1.7	1.7
5.1	6.4	6.6	All Other Non-Current	7.7	8.1	15.0	5.1	6.2	4.8
100.0	100.0	100.0	Total	100.0	100.0	100.0	100.0	100.0	100.0
			LIABILITIES						
6.6	6.4	6.8	Notes Payable-Short Term	26.4	9.7	10.4	6.1	4.9	3.2
5.4	6.6	5.2	Cur. Mat.-L.T.D.	4.7	7.1	5.0	7.2	5.2	3.7
16.1	16.0	15.3	Trade Payables	8.4	11.5	11.9	13.9	16.6	18.7
1.1	.6	.5	Income Taxes Payable	.5	.3	.1	.6	.7	.4
12.7	12.6	12.8	All Other Current	3.8	7.8	9.9	8.0	12.1	19.7
41.8	42.2	40.6	Total Current	43.9	36.5	37.3	35.8	39.5	45.6
17.3	16.3	14.9	Long-Term Debt	33.4	19.7	16.5	12.8	14.0	11.4
.8	.8	.9	Deferred Taxes	1.3	.2	.8	.6	1.5	.9
2.1	2.2	3.8	All Other Non-Current	16.9	4.3	3.8	2.6	3.3	2.6
38.0	38.6	39.8	Net Worth	4.5	39.2	41.7	48.2	41.7	39.4
100.0	100.0	100.0	Total Liabilities & Net Worth	100.0	100.0	100.0	100.0	100.0	100.0
			INCOME DATA						
100.0	100.0	100.0	Net Sales	100.0	100.0	100.0	100.0	100.0	100.0
26.8	24.6	23.0	Gross Profit	42.0	33.3	22.1	24.9	18.9	17.6
20.8	20.1	20.7	Operating Expenses	49.2	33.1	22.0	23.4	16.1	12.2
6.0	4.4	2.3	Operating Profit	-7.2	.2	.0	1.4	2.8	5.4
.7	.6	.5	All Other Expenses (net)	2.2	1.0	-.1	.4	.2	.5
5.4	3.8	1.8	Profit Before Taxes	-9.4	-.8	.1	1.1	2.6	4.9
			RATIOS						
2.0	2.0	2.2	Current	2.0	2.5	3.0	2.8	2.3	1.8
1.4	1.5	1.5		1.1	1.6	1.5	1.6	1.6	1.4
1.1	1.1	1.1		.5	.9	.8	1.2	1.1	1.2
1.7	1.8	1.9	Quick	1.7	2.1	2.8	2.3	2.1	1.6
1.2	1.2	(386) 1.2		(19) .8	1.1	1.2	1.4	1.3	1.2
.8	.8	.7		.3	.5	.6	1.0	.7	.9
37 9.9	37 9.9	35 10.5	Sales/Receivables	2 162.5	5 68.5	32 11.2	45 8.1	30 12.0	40 9.1
60 6.1	54 6.8	54 6.8		38 9.7	36 10.1	58 6.3	57 6.4	50 7.3	56 6.5
82 4.5	73 5.0	75 4.9		107 3.4	63 5.8	87 4.2	83 4.4	75 4.9	75 4.8
0 UND	0 UND	0 UND	Cost of Sales/Inventory	0 UND	0 UND	0 UND	0 UND	0 UND	0 UND
0 UND	0 UND	0 UND		0 UND	0 UND	0 UND	0 UND	0 UND	0 UND
5 75.0	6 60.8	8 45.4		39 9.3	8 44.3	15 24.4	6 58.4	8 46.0	8 46.6
16 23.4	14 26.2	14 25.6	Cost of Sales/Payables	0 UND	5 72.8	10 37.2	11 34.3	17 21.1	20 18.2
33 11.0	30 12.3	27 13.3		23 15.8	16 22.2	26 13.8	22 16.5	29 12.4	33 10.9
54 6.8	48 7.5	47 7.8		74 4.9	51 7.2	56 6.5	45 8.1	41 9.0	47 7.7
6.5	6.5	5.2	Sales/Working Capital	3.7	5.6	4.9	4.5	4.8	5.9
12.1	12.1	10.5		21.1	15.9	14.7	8.5	9.0	10.5
52.2	71.5	51.9		-7.6	-34.7	-17.0	22.1	118.1	24.1
20.6	18.3	20.6	EBIT/Interest	1.1	5.7	6.4	11.5	37.7	41.0
(321) 5.7	(347) 4.8	(358) 4.0		(18) -.3	(51) 1.7	(31) 1.8	(62) 4.1	(71) 4.0	(125) 9.5
2.1	1.4	.6		-5.6	-3.6	-4.1	-2.0	1.5	2.7
5.7	5.9	8.4	Net Profit + Depr., Dep., Amort./Cur. Mat. L/T/D		1.6		4.4	3.0	14.2
(115) 2.6	(120) 2.3	(123) 2.4			(10) 1.2		(17) 1.7	(25) 1.5	(61) 5.9
1.2	1.1	1.1			.1		.7	.9	2.2
.4	.4	.3	Fixed/Worth	.6	.5	.2	.3	.3	.3
.7	.8	.7		19.1	1.0	.6	.7	.8	.6
1.7	1.7	1.6		-2.4	3.5	1.5	1.3	1.6	1.1
.9	.8	.7	Debt/Worth	1.1	.6	.7	.5	.6	1.0
1.7	1.7	1.5		78.1	1.4	1.3	1.1	1.4	1.6
3.4	3.5	2.9		-4.1	4.6	3.1	2.3	2.8	2.6
51.7	43.7	34.4	% Profit Before Taxes/Tangible Net Worth	3.6	24.4	24.3	29.2	27.3	44.9
(330) 26.7	(360) 23.9	(353) 13.4		(11) -1.4	(46) 2.1	(29) 10.3	(67) 7.4	(70) 10.6	(130) 23.9
8.2	2.4	.2		-36.6	-23.6	-14.9	-13.0	2.1	7.6
17.8	17.7	13.4	% Profit Before Taxes/Total Assets	.5	7.7	13.7	12.7	13.9	17.1
9.2	7.8	4.8		-4.1	.8	3.1	3.8	4.8	9.1
2.4	.7	-1.5		-19.1	-12.3	-10.7	-5.3	.8	2.9
18.5	19.9	18.2	Sales/Net Fixed Assets	10.8	13.7	21.3	15.3	19.4	22.1
7.3	7.8	7.4		4.3	4.9	6.7	6.2	7.5	8.8
3.5	3.9	3.8		1.7	2.8	3.3	3.7	3.2	4.4
2.8	2.9	2.6	Sales/Total Assets	2.1	3.1	2.6	2.5	2.7	2.7
2.0	2.1	2.0		1.3	1.9	2.0	1.9	2.0	2.1
1.4	1.5	1.4		1.1	1.4	1.1	1.3	1.6	1.6
1.3	1.2	1.3	% Depr., Dep., Amort./Sales	1.9	2.2	1.2	1.6	1.4	1.1
(314) 2.9	(331) 2.9	(342) 3.2		(15) 9.1	(43) 4.7	(31) 3.6	(64) 4.7	(71) 2.7	(118) 2.2
5.5	6.3	6.3		13.2	9.4	9.0	7.0	5.6	4.8
1.2	1.3	1.6	% Officers', Directors' Owners' Comp/Sales	4.8	3.6		.8	1.1	.7
(118) 2.5	(126) 3.0	(141) 3.6		(13) 7.8	(37) 5.5		(34) 2.9	(26) 2.2	(22) 1.7
5.0	6.0	6.7		23.3	10.1			4.2	3.5
12918545M	16171289M	15655505M	Net Sales ($)	10532M	106103M	131462M	518451M	1259494M	13629463M
6687852M	8089219M	8215238M	Total Assets ($)	10784M	65587M	100778M	349028M	750523M	6938538M

Current Data Sorted by Assets   Comparative Historical Data

0-500M	500M-2MM	2-10MM	10-50MM	50-100MM	100-250MM	Type of Statement	4/1/05-3/31/06 ALL	4/1/06-3/31/07 ALL
	1	25	10	5	1	Unqualified	58	63
5	32	53	20	1		Reviewed	117	126
16	25	11		1		Compiled	56	56
37	33	16			2	Tax Returns	69	77
14	54	61	17	5	1	Other	120	137
	71 (4/1-9/30/09)		375 (10/1/09-3/31/10)					
72	145	166	47	12	4	NUMBER OF STATEMENTS	420	459
%	%	%	%	%	%	ASSETS	%	%
20.3	14.7	13.4	18.6	18.4		Cash & Equivalents	11.4	11.4
24.6	35.0	39.9	35.8	30.3		Trade Receivables (net)	39.2	39.1
4.0	5.0	2.9	2.3	6.7		Inventory	3.1	3.1
4.9	5.6	7.3	9.4	4.2		All Other Current	5.1	5.5
53.7	60.3	63.6	66.1	59.7		Total Current	58.8	59.1
35.7	28.3	28.0	27.0	29.0		Fixed Assets (net)	33.1	33.0
2.1	2.5	3.2	.8	4.0		Intangibles (net)	2.1	1.7
8.4	9.0	5.2	6.1	7.3		All Other Non-Current	6.0	6.3
100.0	100.0	100.0	100.0	100.0		Total	100.0	100.0
						LIABILITIES		
34.2	13.1	7.3	3.8	3.9		Notes Payable-Short Term	7.9	8.0
7.0	5.0	4.7	6.1	3.0		Cur. Mat.-L.T.D.	6.2	5.1
14.7	17.1	15.8	15.1	17.6		Trade Payables	19.2	17.8
.0	.5	.5	.3	.8		Income Taxes Payable	.5	.4
13.4	9.0	10.5	17.1	14.9		All Other Current	9.3	9.9
69.4	44.7	38.8	42.5	40.1		Total Current	43.1	41.3
29.0	18.7	15.0	12.9	13.5		Long-Term Debt	22.3	19.7
.2	.4	.5	1.1	1.6		Deferred Taxes	1.0	.6
9.3	4.4	4.6	1.6	4.7		All Other Non-Current	3.6	4.1
-7.8	31.7	41.1	41.9	40.0		Net Worth	30.0	34.2
100.0	100.0	100.0	100.0	100.0		Total Liabilities & Net Worth	100.0	100.0
						INCOME DATA		
100.0	100.0	100.0	100.0	100.0		Net Sales	100.0	100.0
40.4	27.6	21.5	18.3	23.1		Gross Profit	27.8	29.2
38.7	27.7	21.8	16.4	17.7		Operating Expenses	22.1	23.4
1.8	-.1	-.4	1.9	5.4		Operating Profit	5.7	5.7
1.3	.5	.7	.9	.6		All Other Expenses (net)	.6	.5
.5	-.6	-1.0	1.1	4.8		Profit Before Taxes	5.1	5.2
						RATIOS		
2.2	2.5	2.6	2.3	2.0		Current	2.2	2.3
1.0	1.4	1.6	1.6	1.4			1.4	1.5
.4	.8	1.2	1.1	1.2			1.1	1.0
2.0	2.1	2.4	1.9	1.5		Quick	1.9	1.9
.8	1.1	1.3	1.3	1.1		(419)	1.2	1.3
.2	.6	.9	.8	.9			.8	.8
0 UND	27 13.6	44 8.4	43 8.4	47 7.7		Sales/Receivables	30 12.1	29 12.5
8 43.7	44 8.2	60 6.1	58 6.2	57 6.4			51 7.2	50 7.3
40 9.0	74 5.0	83 4.4	75 4.9	68 5.4			75 4.9	76 4.8
0 UND	0 UND	0 UND	0 UND	0 UND		Cost of Sales/Inventory	0 UND	0 UND
0 UND	0 UND	0 UND	0 UND	10 38.0			0 UND	0 UND
0 UND	5 73.3	4 81.5	10 37.5	32 11.3			5 73.1	5 76.4
0 UND	9 41.0	16 23.0	16 22.9	24 14.9		Cost of Sales/Payables	12 29.8	10 35.8
4 102.7	28 12.8	29 12.6	30 12.3	32 11.5			26 14.0	28 13.3
20 18.6	51 7.1	49 7.5	40 9.0	52 7.1			44 8.3	46 8.0
17.4	6.8	5.5	4.6	5.0		Sales/Working Capital	7.6	7.6
-227.5	15.0	9.7	9.4	14.5			16.0	17.0
-12.6	-22.7	39.1	48.5	29.0			135.3	386.0
9.0	8.5	9.9	14.5			EBIT/Interest	18.5	20.8
(59) 1.3	(131) 1.3	(146) 1.7	(37) 2.4				(386) 5.6	(418) 6.8
-4.5	-4.8	-2.9	-.5				2.1	2.0
	2.3	7.3	9.1			Net Profit + Depr., Dep.,	4.9	4.4
(13) .3	(38) 2.2	(16) 3.4				Amort./Cur. Mat. L/T/D	(106) 2.2	(101) 2.2
	-1.0	1.0	1.3				1.1	1.3
.2	.3	.2	.2	.4		Fixed/Worth	.4	.3
3.4	.8	.5	.5	.6			.9	.8
-1.2	3.7	1.5	1.3	2.6			2.4	2.3
.6	.7	.6	.7	1.3		Debt/Worth	.9	.7
24.6	1.7	1.4	1.6	2.0			2.0	1.8
-3.0	19.3	3.4	3.6	4.2			6.1	4.8
198.3	37.3	24.8	30.2	36.4		% Profit Before Taxes/Tangible Net Worth	62.0	64.8
(44) 40.8	(117) 7.1	(148) 6.5	(46) 9.1	26.1			(365) 28.5	(409) 35.6
2.3	-29.2	-12.0	-5.5	18.0			13.9	12.9
32.6	11.8	10.6	13.0	10.9		% Profit Before Taxes/Total Assets	24.4	25.5
4.6	.8	1.2	3.1	8.4			9.4	11.5
-19.1	-11.7	-6.1	-3.3	5.0			3.1	3.4
65.9	31.7	33.3	21.8	19.8		Sales/Net Fixed Assets	25.6	27.9
17.9	11.0	10.8	11.8	7.2			11.1	11.2
6.4	5.0	4.6	4.4	3.4			5.4	5.4
8.2	3.5	3.1	2.9	3.1		Sales/Total Assets	3.9	3.9
5.6	2.6	2.2	2.0	1.7			2.8	2.8
2.9	1.7	1.5	1.5	1.5			2.0	2.1
.6	1.2	1.1	.6	1.2		% Depr., Dep., Amort./Sales	1.3	1.2
(50) 2.6	(106) 2.4	(147) 2.4	(40) 1.9	(11) 3.3			(363) 2.5	(384) 2.4
4.9	4.5	5.3	4.4	6.0			4.5	4.8
2.6	2.8	1.8	.7			% Officers', Directors' Owners' Comp/Sales	1.7	1.6
(39) 5.6	(75) 4.3	(75) 3.7	(10) 1.2				(195) 3.1	(201) 3.1
11.2	7.2	6.2	2.3				6.1	6.4
89760M	469722M	1967141M	1775829M	1809112M	2298328M	Net Sales ($)	10119761M	12541854M
17241M	171584M	818483M	838029M	855876M	746460M	Total Assets ($)	4185729M	4247805M

M = $ thousand   MM = $ million
See Pages 9 through 22 for Explanation of Ratios and Data

Comparative Historical Data — Current Data Sorted by Sales

	4/1/07-3/31/08 ALL	4/1/08-3/31/09 ALL	4/1/09-3/31/10 ALL	0-1MM	1-3MM	3-5MM	5-10MM	10-25MM	25MM & OVER
					71 (4/1-9/30/09)		375 (10/1/09-3/31/10)		
Type of Statement									
Unqualified	57	69	42		1		8	15	18
Reviewed	112	122	111	5	15	22	22	30	17
Compiled	45	53	53	9	22	9	10	2	1
Tax Returns	75	90	88	25	26	16	13	5	3
Other	132	157	152	16	32	25	30	32	17
NUMBER OF STATEMENTS	421	491	446	55	96	72	83	84	56
ASSETS	%	%	%	%	%	%	%	%	%
Cash & Equivalents	12.3	12.6	15.6	19.5	14.8	11.5	15.3	17.1	16.3
Trade Receivables (net)	39.6	37.4	34.9	22.5	27.1	37.9	36.4	43.9	41.2
Inventory	2.6	3.0	3.8	6.7	4.4	4.2	3.5	2.3	2.4
All Other Current	5.2	6.3	6.5	2.7	7.1	6.8	5.4	8.0	8.1
Total Current	59.7	59.3	60.8	51.4	53.4	60.4	60.6	71.1	68.0
Fixed Assets (net)	32.8	32.1	29.5	32.8	35.1	30.4	29.7	23.4	24.1
Intangibles (net)	2.0	2.4	2.5	6.6	1.8	3.7	2.3	.5	1.7
All Other Non-Current	5.5	6.2	7.2	9.2	9.7	5.5	7.4	4.9	6.1
Total	100.0	100.0	100.0	100.0	100.0	100.0	100.0	100.0	100.0
LIABILITIES									
Notes Payable-Short Term	7.4	8.9	13.0	27.3	21.3	9.7	6.7	8.7	5.0
Cur. Mat.-L.T.D.	5.5	5.2	5.2	5.8	4.5	7.6	5.4	4.9	2.9
Trade Payables	17.0	17.2	16.0	14.9	12.0	16.6	17.3	17.8	18.6
Income Taxes Payable	.4	.5	.4	.0	.6	.5	.4	.3	.5
All Other Current	10.0	11.4	11.3	8.8	13.5	9.2	8.1	10.3	19.2
Total Current	40.4	43.2	46.0	56.9	51.9	43.7	37.8	42.0	46.2
Long-Term Debt	19.6	20.8	18.4	35.2	17.5	18.9	20.4	11.4	10.0
Deferred Taxes	.6	.7	.5	.0	.6	.4	.7	.5	.9
All Other Non-Current	3.0	5.2	4.9	8.8	3.7	4.8	6.7	3.5	3.1
Net Worth	36.5	30.0	30.2	-.9	26.4	32.3	34.3	42.5	39.7
Total Liabilities & Net Worth	100.0	100.0	100.0	100.0	100.0	100.0	100.0	100.0	100.0
INCOME DATA									
Net Sales	100.0	100.0	100.0	100.0	100.0	100.0	100.0	100.0	100.0
Gross Profit	27.1	25.4	26.4	46.4	30.8	22.6	23.8	19.0	18.9
Operating Expenses	21.6	22.6	25.9	45.8	30.9	24.6	23.5	17.6	15.7
Operating Profit	5.5	2.8	.5	.6	-.1	-1.9	.3	1.4	3.3
All Other Expenses (net)	.5	.7	.7	2.9	.7	.4	.3	.3	.4
Profit Before Taxes	5.0	2.1	-.2	-2.3	-.8	-2.3	.0	1.1	2.9
RATIOS									
Current	2.5	2.5	2.4	3.0	2.0	3.2	3.0	3.0	2.0
	1.5	1.5	1.4	1.0	1.1	1.3	1.6	1.7	1.6
	1.0	1.0	.9	.6	.7	.9	1.2	1.2	1.2
Quick	2.2	2.2	2.1	2.4	1.7	2.6	2.2	2.5	1.7
	(420) 1.3	1.3	1.2	.8	.9	1.1	1.3	1.5	1.3
	.8	.7	.7	.3	.4	.7	.9	.9	.9
Sales/Receivables	34 10.9	29 12.4	30 12.1	0 UND	11 33.4	32 11.4	32 11.3	43 8.4	43 8.4
	53 6.9	50 7.3	52 7.0	25 14.5	39 9.4	56 6.5	55 6.6	59 6.2	58 6.3
	75 4.9	73 5.0	73 5.0	59 6.2	64 5.7	84 4.3	71 5.2	77 4.7	70 5.2
Cost of Sales/Inventory	0 UND	0 UND	0 UND	0 UND	0 UND	0 UND	0 UND	0 UND	0 UND
	0 UND	0 UND	0 UND	0 UND	0 UND	0 UND	0 UND	0 UND	0 UND
	3 119.6	5 70.4	5 71.6	4 97.5	2 207.4	6 64.0	9 39.7	6 58.5	7 53.3
Cost of Sales/Payables	11 33.8	12 31.2	10 36.4	0 UND	5 73.1	9 40.3	15 24.8	16 23.2	16 22.4
	25 14.8	25 14.8	25 14.5	8 46.2	20 18.6	27 13.3	29 12.4	28 13.0	27 13.5
	44 8.2	47 7.8	45 8.1	59 6.2	43 8.4	53 6.8	48 7.7	44 8.3	38 9.5
Sales/Working Capital	6.9	7.0	6.3	7.1	8.2	5.8	5.7	5.7	7.1
	13.9	14.7	13.3	UND	48.9	18.3	10.4	8.9	10.5
	230.4	-188.6	-68.2	-10.4	-12.3	-99.2	73.0	35.8	29.6
EBIT/Interest	20.2	13.1	9.7	8.1	6.7	4.4	14.3	11.3	26.6
	(366) 5.4	(437) 3.3	(386) 1.6	(44) .1	(86) .8	(64) 1.0	(73) 1.7	(71) 2.9	(48) 6.1
	1.4	-.5	-2.9	-4.4	-4.9	-6.9	-2.4	-1.8	.8
Net Profit + Depr., Dep., Amort./Cur. Mat. L/T/D	5.3	5.3	6.7			1.8	6.2	8.2	6.8
	(91) 2.5	(107) 1.9	(76) 2.1		(10) -.9	(17) 1.1	(20) 3.1	(21) 3.7	
	1.2	1.0	.7		-4.2	.9	1.6	1.4	
Fixed/Worth	.3	.3	.2	.2	.3	.3	.1	.2	.3
	.7	.8	.7	1.7	1.1	.7	.7	.4	.5
	2.0	3.0	2.5	-1.9	19.7	2.6	2.6	1.0	1.0
Debt/Worth	.7	.8	.7	.3	.7	.6	.6	.5	.8
	1.7	1.9	1.6	13.6	2.2	1.6	1.7	1.5	1.5
	4.0	6.2	8.7	-2.9	NM	30.2	4.8	2.8	3.3
% Profit Before Taxes/Tangible Net Worth	61.3	46.4	34.9	55.0	44.9	28.1	37.5	25.9	33.7
	(379) 31.8	(415) 17.5	(370) 10.2	(35) 16.5	(72) 2.9	(59) 3.1	(69) 8.5	(81) 10.5	(54) 20.4
	8.8	.1	-11.6	-7.1	-32.3	-42.1	-10.8	-8.4	1.2
% Profit Before Taxes/Total Assets	24.2	17.1	12.2	16.8	12.0	9.2	11.5	12.1	14.2
	10.8	5.1	1.6	-.8	.2	.1	1.2	4.2	5.2
	2.3	-2.5	-9.1	-13.5	-15.2	-19.8	-9.4	-3.8	.5
Sales/Net Fixed Assets	27.2	27.0	33.8	104.1	29.7	24.5	38.3	33.0	35.4
	11.2	12.0	11.4	9.0	9.2	11.0	11.0	13.1	16.3
	5.3	4.9	5.1	3.7	3.8	5.8	5.5	6.2	7.7
Sales/Total Assets	3.8	3.9	3.6	5.8	3.7	3.3	3.4	3.4	3.6
	2.7	2.6	2.5	2.5	2.4	2.5	2.4	2.5	2.9
	2.0	1.8	1.7	.9	1.6	1.7	1.7	1.8	1.8
% Depr., Dep., Amort./Sales	1.0	1.1	1.1	1.1	1.3	1.3	1.1	.9	.7
	(352) 2.3	(409) 2.5	(354) 2.4	(34) 4.6	(71) 2.7	(58) 2.9	(71) 2.8	(74) 2.1	(46) 1.4
	4.8	4.6	4.9	14.7	7.3	4.9	6.6	3.1	3.2
% Officers', Directors' Owners' Comp/Sales	1.5	1.5	2.2	3.9	2.8	3.5	1.7	1.4	.7
	(189) 3.0	(212) 3.3	(201) 4.1	(25) 7.3	(54) 4.3	(36) 4.6	(38) 4.6	(34) 2.2	(14) 1.6
	5.4	5.7	7.2	16.5	7.1	7.8	5.9	4.4	4.7
Net Sales ($)	9276272M	11330601M	8409892M	30597M	189084M	276248M	573749M	1372495M	5967719M
Total Assets ($)	3922963M	4635720M	3447673M	27079M	102248M	130397M	297151M	621878M	2268920M

M = $ thousand   MM = $ million
See Pages 9 through 22 for Explanation of Ratios and Data

Current Data Sorted by Assets | Comparative Historical Data

Type of Statement	0-500M	500M-2MM	2-10MM	10-50MM	50-100MM	100-250MM	4/1/05-3/31/06 ALL	4/1/06-3/31/07 ALL
Unqualified			12	16	2	2	33	53
Reviewed	2	8	43	9	1		42	58
Compiled	6	13	3	1			16	25
Tax Returns	12	14	6		1		15	35
Other	5	9	27	11	1	3	51	46
		42 (4/1-9/30/09)		165 (10/1/09-3/31/10)				
NUMBER OF STATEMENTS	25	44	91	37	5	5	157	217
ASSETS	%	%	%	%	%	%	%	%
Cash & Equivalents	15.1	15.7	14.2	20.4			9.3	11.6
Trade Receivables (net)	24.5	34.0	42.9	35.7			50.0	47.9
Inventory	3.9	8.6	5.6	5.0			3.9	5.1
All Other Current	10.8	7.5	8.5	10.2			9.5	8.3
Total Current	54.3	65.7	71.2	71.4			72.7	72.8
Fixed Assets (net)	32.2	25.9	20.4	24.0			21.7	20.2
Intangibles (net)	5.4	3.2	.7	1.8			1.4	1.2
All Other Non-Current	8.1	5.2	7.7	2.8			4.2	5.8
Total	100.0	100.0	100.0	100.0			100.0	100.0
LIABILITIES								
Notes Payable-Short Term	37.8	10.4	8.1	5.1			10.4	10.5
Cur. Mat.-L.T.D.	6.3	3.4	2.9	2.5			2.8	3.2
Trade Payables	16.4	15.0	15.7	13.9			17.7	15.7
Income Taxes Payable	.7	.2	.8	.1			.6	.6
All Other Current	37.9	12.0	11.5	18.9			14.1	16.8
Total Current	99.2	40.9	39.1	40.5			45.6	46.9
Long-Term Debt	23.6	12.5	8.5	10.5			13.0	14.3
Deferred Taxes	.1	.2	.9	.7			.6	.5
All Other Non-Current	6.0	13.5	4.3	3.2			3.9	2.7
Net Worth	-28.8	32.9	47.2	45.0			36.8	35.6
Total Liabilties & Net Worth	100.0	100.0	100.0	100.0			100.0	100.0
INCOME DATA								
Net Sales	100.0	100.0	100.0	100.0			100.0	100.0
Gross Profit	36.2	33.4	22.1	22.2			21.5	24.4
Operating Expenses	35.1	34.9	20.7	16.2			16.3	18.4
Operating Profit	1.2	-1.5	1.5	6.0			5.2	6.0
All Other Expenses (net)	.9	.1	.0	.3			.6	.7
Profit Before Taxes	.3	-1.6	1.4	5.8			4.6	5.3
RATIOS								
Current	1.5	2.8	2.6	2.3			2.3	2.5
	.7	1.8	1.8	1.7			1.5	1.5
	.2	1.1	1.3	1.4			1.2	1.2
Quick	1.1	2.2	2.2	2.0			1.9	2.0
	.3	1.2	1.5	1.4			1.2	1.3
	.2	.7	1.1	1.0			1.0	.9
Sales/Receivables	0 UND	27 13.6	54 6.8	57 6.4			52 7.0	47 7.8
	10 37.9	46 8.0	66 5.5	71 5.1			73 5.0	68 5.4
	41 9.0	71 5.1	92 4.0	86 4.2			96 3.8	91 4.0
Cost of Sales/Inventory	0 UND	0 UND	0 UND	0 UND			0 UND	0 UND
	0 UND	0 UND	2 228.7	6 60.8			0 UND	0 UND
	2 168.8	17 22.1	21 17.4	22 16.7			8 44.5	12 29.7
Cost of Sales/Payables	0 UND	1 290.6	15 24.7	18 19.9			15 24.2	11 32.8
	8 47.3	12 29.6	26 14.2	28 13.1			27 13.7	25 14.6
	17 21.0	44 8.2	46 8.0	44 8.3			48 7.5	44 4.0
Sales/Working Capital	35.3	5.0	4.1	3.6			5.7	5.8
	-39.7	10.7	7.1	6.6			10.2	10.5
	-4.9	71.7	13.9	14.0			21.2	21.7
EBIT/Interest	6.1	7.2	19.9	39.8			18.3	27.3
	(22) 3.1	(37) 3.0	(82) 5.3	(35) 5.7			(148) 5.6	(188) 6.2
	-5.6	-4.5	-.9	2.3			2.0	2.4
Net Profit + Depr., Dep., Amort./Cur. Mat. L/T/D			9.1	18.1			9.1	9.0
		(36) 3.6		(15) 5.1			(51) 3.1	(59) 4.2
			.4	1.4			1.8	2.2
Fixed/Worth	.8	.2	.1	.2			.2	.2
	15.4	.6	.3	.4			.5	.4
	-.3	2.2	.7	1.0			1.0	1.1
Debt/Worth	1.5	.5	.6	.7			.8	.8
	46.7	1.6	1.0	1.3			1.9	1.8
	-2.1	6.3	2.1	2.5			3.7	3.9
% Profit Before Taxes/Tangible Net Worth	999.8	41.8	26.0	48.6			59.5	63.9
	(14) 72.5	(36) 9.9	(88) 9.8	(35) 14.4			(146) 27.3	(199) 35.7
	-24.9	-5.2	-6.2	7.9			8.2	12.7
% Profit Before Taxes/Total Assets	30.5	9.0	12.5	13.5			20.0	21.7
	10.6	2.7	3.9	8.0			8.1	11.8
	-32.8	-10.4	-3.9	2.1			2.2	3.3
Sales/Net Fixed Assets	55.5	55.7	35.9	22.0			35.1	44.4
	20.3	18.5	13.7	11.3			14.7	19.7
	10.1	5.0	6.0	4.3			8.1	7.6
Sales/Total Assets	6.9	3.6	2.9	2.5			3.1	3.3
	5.0	2.4	2.2	1.8			2.5	2.6
	2.9	1.9	1.5	1.3			1.9	2.0
% Depr., Dep., Amort./Sales	.7	.7	.7	.9			.6	.7
	(19) 2.3	(32) 2.5	(85) 1.7	(36) 1.5			(146) 1.1	(187) 1.1
	4.5	4.7	3.3	3.2			2.1	2.6
% Officers', Directors' Owners' Comp/Sales	4.1	3.0	2.1	2.2			1.3	1.8
	(10) 11.4	(22) 4.9	(38) 3.1	(10) 3.7			(61) 2.4	(87) 3.3
	17.4	7.2	7.7	6.6			3.6	5.9
Net Sales ($)	38345M	154058M	992509M	1480768M	1892046M	1700536M	4666144M	6538115M
Total Assets ($)	6309M	53545M	452692M	817804M	337163M	820325M	2295996M	2829812M

© RMA 2010

M = $ thousand   MM = $ million
See Pages 9 through 22 for Explanation of Ratios and Data

Comparative Historical Data / Current Data Sorted by Sales

4/1/07-3/31/08 ALL	4/1/08-3/31/09 ALL	4/1/09-3/31/10 ALL	Type of Statement	0-1MM	1-3MM	3-5MM	5-10MM	10-25MM	25MM & OVER
35	39	32	Unqualified				5	8	19
50	57	63	Reviewed		6	7	19	25	6
15	16	23	Compiled	6	7	7	1	1	1
18	24	33	Tax Returns	5	12	7	6	2	1
43	42	56	Other	1	8	5	16	15	11
					42 (4/1-9/30/09)		165 (10/1/09-3/31/10)		
161	178	207	NUMBER OF STATEMENTS	12	33	26	47	51	38
%	%	%	ASSETS	%	%	%	%	%	%
11.0	12.6	16.0	Cash & Equivalents	16.3	11.2	18.0	13.3	17.1	20.4
49.9	43.9	37.0	Trade Receivables (net)	19.8	28.9	29.6	46.4	40.6	38.0
6.2	7.2	5.9	Inventory	1.6	9.7	7.1	6.3	3.6	5.7
8.8	8.5	8.7	All Other Current	7.3	7.3	8.9	10.5	7.5	9.6
75.9	72.3	67.6	Total Current	45.1	57.2	63.6	76.5	68.7	73.8
18.9	21.5	24.0	Fixed Assets (net)	34.8	31.2	29.0	18.0	22.2	21.0
1.2	1.3	2.2	Intangibles (net)	10.2	2.9	2.6	.6	1.6	1.5
4.0	4.9	6.2	All Other Non-Current	9.9	8.8	4.9	4.9	7.5	3.6
100.0	100.0	100.0	Total	100.0	100.0	100.0	100.0	100.0	100.0
			LIABILITIES						
8.0	11.3	11.4	Notes Payable-Short Term	45.1	20.7	7.0	9.6	6.7	4.2
2.5	2.9	3.5	Cur. Mat.-L.T.D.	7.4	3.9	3.2	4.1	2.4	3.0
18.6	15.3	15.3	Trade Payables	8.7	13.4	15.5	18.8	14.7	15.6
.7	.6	.5	Income Taxes Payable	1.5	.1	.4	.7	.6	.2
18.0	14.6	16.7	All Other Current	29.7	22.3	14.5	10.1	13.6	21.4
47.8	44.6	47.4	Total Current	92.4	60.3	40.7	43.3	38.0	44.3
9.9	10.4	12.0	Long-Term Debt	30.0	18.2	13.7	5.9	9.6	10.4
.4	.7	.6	Deferred Taxes	.6	.5	.7	.6	.5	.8
2.5	5.3	6.1	All Other Non-Current	2.8	16.7	3.1	5.0	4.6	3.3
39.4	39.0	33.9	Net Worth	-25.8	4.3	41.8	45.1	47.3	41.2
100.0	100.0	100.0	Total Liabilities & Net Worth	100.0	100.0	100.0	100.0	100.0	100.0
			INCOME DATA						
100.0	100.0	100.0	Net Sales	100.0	100.0	100.0	100.0	100.0	100.0
23.6	23.4	26.5	Gross Profit	41.3	33.9	34.3	20.1	23.4	22.1
16.9	17.6	24.7	Operating Expenses	47.5	35.9	32.0	20.8	17.9	16.8
6.7	5.9	1.8	Operating Profit	-6.2	-1.9	2.3	-.7	5.5	5.3
.5	.4	.3	All Other Expenses (net)	1.5	.4	.1	.1	-.3	.8
6.2	5.4	1.5	Profit Before Taxes	-7.7	-2.3	2.2	-.7	5.8	4.4
			RATIOS						
2.5	2.5	2.5	Current	1.4	2.6	3.1	3.0	2.5	2.2
1.6	1.6	1.7		.7	1.1	1.7	1.9	1.8	1.6
1.2	1.3	1.2		.2	.7	1.2	1.3	1.3	1.3
1.9	2.0	2.1	Quick	1.2	1.4	2.3	2.4	2.1	1.8
(160) 1.3	1.4	1.3		.4	.8	1.2	1.6	1.5	1.4
1.0	1.0	.8		.2	.4	.6	1.0	1.0	1.0
46 7.9	43 8.5	38 9.6	Sales/Receivables	0 UND	14 26.7	4 85.5	54 6.8	53 6.8	51 7.2
69 5.3	66 5.5	62 5.9		9 41.3	40 9.1	50 7.3	68 5.3	64 5.7	66 5.5
88 4.1	87 4.2	84 4.3		70 5.2	68 5.4	75 4.9	98 3.7	87 4.2	83 4.4
0 UND	0 UND	0 UND	Cost of Sales/Inventory	0 UND	0 UND	0 UND	0 UND	0 UND	0 UND
1 367.5	0 999.8	1 365.4		0 UND	0 UND	0 UND	1 365.4	1 719.2	6 64.0
15 24.9	14 25.7	19 19.6		13 27.3	31 11.9	37 9.8	13 27.3	11 33.0	21 17.3
14 26.0	9 39.4	10 36.4	Cost of Sales/Payables	0 UND	2 220.4	1 402.4	11 34.4	16 23.3	16 22.4
27 13.5	23 16.2	23 15.6		3 132.5	10 36.4	25 14.6	24 15.2	26 14.2	27 13.4
45 8.2	40 9.2	44 8.3		11 34.3	39 9.3	59 6.2	57 6.4	39 9.3	43 8.4
5.3	5.4	4.8	Sales/Working Capital	12.2	4.5	5.1	4.6	4.1	4.5
10.0	8.6	8.8		-34.4	47.3	10.3	7.0	8.4	8.2
25.4	19.5	33.5		-4.5	-25.6	36.8	25.6	18.0	11.9
28.6	36.5	18.4	EBIT/Interest	4.9	5.7	31.8	11.7	29.7	43.9
(149) 8.3	(162) 9.4	(185) 4.0		(11) -.3	(29) 3.0	(20) 2.8	(43) 2.7	(46) 10.7	(36) 5.5
3.3	2.3	-.3		-9.4	-5.2	-.8	-4.2	3.3	1.7
12.6	11.9	9.0	Net Profit + Depr., Dep., Amort./Cur. Mat. L/T/D				8.8	9.5	10.0
(42) 5.4	(50) 4.7	(59) 4.1				(14) 1.5	(23) 5.2	(16) 4.4	
2.8	1.8	1.1					-1.1	3.0	1.2
.2	.1	.2	Fixed/Worth	.7	.5	.1	.1	.1	.2
.4	.4	.5		NM	1.4	.5	.3	.3	.4
.8	1.0	1.2		-.2	-7.9	1.4	.7	.9	.8
.7	.6	.6	Debt/Worth	1.2	.6	.4	.5	.6	.7
1.7	1.4	1.3		NM	4.2	1.6	1.1	.9	1.4
3.5	3.0	4.2		-1.8	-14.9	4.3	3.1	2.1	2.7
64.1	61.1	39.2	% Profit Before Taxes/Tangible Net Worth		57.7	40.1	20.4	38.8	40.5
(153) 33.2	(165) 30.1	(182) 13.1		(24) 10.6	(23) 9.8	(44) 5.2	(50) 14.6	(35) 15.6	
16.8	10.7	.1			-7.5	-11.1	-13.2	6.7	6.2
25.6	22.6	13.6	% Profit Before Taxes/Total Assets	25.0	13.0	14.7	8.6	20.1	13.1
12.2	11.3	5.1		-7.6	2.0	3.2	2.4	8.1	5.7
5.1	2.9	-2.7		-39.2	-16.0	-4.0	-5.4	2.9	1.6
44.0	43.3	35.9	Sales/Net Fixed Assets	81.7	25.6	40.9	46.2	27.8	27.5
22.8	20.4	14.5		8.9	13.4	13.6	21.7	15.3	13.7
9.8	7.6	5.8		3.7	3.8	4.6	9.7	5.5	5.8
3.5	3.4	3.2	Sales/Total Assets	6.1	4.8	3.3	3.2	2.6	2.8
2.7	2.6	2.2		2.9	2.4	2.2	2.5	2.2	2.1
2.1	1.9	1.6		1.5	1.6	1.6	1.9	1.5	1.5
.5	.6	.8	% Depr., Dep., Amort./Sales		1.9	.8	.5	.9	.7
(140) 1.0	(154) 1.1	(179) 1.8		(24) 4.1	(23) 2.7	(42) 1.5	(48) 1.8	(35) 1.2	
2.0	2.4	3.7			5.6	5.2	2.4	3.2	2.4
1.5	1.3	2.3	% Officers', Directors' Owners' Comp/Sales		3.5	2.5	.9	2.1	
(63) 2.9	(73) 2.4	(81) 4.0		(17) 6.0	(12) 5.6	(18) 3.1	(21) 3.6		
6.1	5.0	8.0			10.3	7.5	4.3	11.2	
5766299M	6655704M	6258262M	Net Sales ($)	6038M	59584M	106801M	349285M	790303M	4946251M
2259480M	3051311M	2487838M	Total Assets ($)	5013M	29227M	54286M	150885M	430140M	1818287M

© RMA 2010

M = $ thousand   MM = $ million
See Pages 9 through 22 for Explanation of Ratios and Data

CONSTRUCTION-GENERAL—Framing Contractors NAICS 238130

Current Data Sorted by Assets — **Comparative Historical Data**

0-500M	500M-2MM	2-10MM	10-50MM	50-100MM	100-250MM		4/1/05-3/31/06 ALL	4/1/06-3/31/07 ALL
						Type of Statement		
						Unqualified	3	3
	5	16	1			Reviewed	10	11
3	7	1				Compiled	6	11
11	8	2				Tax Returns	9	17
4	8	5	1			Other	14	28
	13 (4/1-9/30/09)		59 (10/1/09-3/31/10)					
18	28	24	2			**NUMBER OF STATEMENTS**	42	70
%	%	%	%	%	%	**ASSETS**	%	%
22.8	15.5	20.3		D	D	Cash & Equivalents	16.9	17.8
32.3	41.8	39.5		A	A	Trade Receivables (net)	40.5	32.5
4.4	10.1	3.8		T	T	Inventory	11.0	9.7
.4	9.0	11.0		A	A	All Other Current	6.3	7.8
59.8	76.5	74.6				Total Current	74.7	67.9
21.0	13.8	14.7		N	N	Fixed Assets (net)	16.1	20.7
8.5	2.1	4.1		O	O	Intangibles (net)	3.5	4.5
10.6	7.7	6.7		T	T	All Other Non-Current	5.7	6.8
100.0	100.0	100.0				Total	100.0	100.0
				A	A	**LIABILITIES**		
37.2	7.8	9.2		V	V	Notes Payable-Short Term	13.9	14.5
5.2	7.0	1.3		A	A	Cur. Mat.-L.T.D.	3.6	4.5
22.0	20.3	19.0		I	I	Trade Payables	20.3	15.5
.0	.0	.9		L	L	Income Taxes Payable	.6	.2
26.9	12.9	17.8		A	A	All Other Current	20.3	17.5
91.2	48.0	48.2		B	B	Total Current	58.8	52.2
25.3	14.6	7.6		L	L	Long-Term Debt	12.7	13.7
.0	.2	.6		E	E	Deferred Taxes	.2	.1
18.3	1.1	.8				All Other Non-Current	3.9	6.3
-34.8	36.1	42.8				Net Worth	24.4	27.6
100.0	100.0	100.0				Total Liabilities & Net Worth	100.0	100.0
						INCOME DATA		
100.0	100.0	100.0				Net Sales	100.0	100.0
41.6	26.7	19.8				Gross Profit	21.8	33.8
39.0	25.3	16.3				Operating Expenses	21.4	30.5
2.6	1.5	3.5				Operating Profit	.4	3.2
.5	.5	.4				All Other Expenses (net)	.2	.4
2.2	.9	3.0				Profit Before Taxes	.1	2.8
						RATIOS		
1.3	3.4	3.2					2.4	2.7
.8	1.6	1.8				Current	1.3	1.6
.3	.9	1.1					.9	.9
1.1	3.0	2.6					1.6	2.1
.8	1.1	1.3				Quick	1.2	1.1
.3	.7	.7					.6	.6
0 UND	28 13.0	36 10.1					14 25.6	12 31.2
2 175.6	45 8.1	55 6.6				Sales/Receivables	37 9.8	31 11.9
54 6.7	51 7.1	74 4.9					74 5.0	50 7.4
0 UND	0 UND	0 UND					0 UND	0 UND
0 UND	0 UND	0 UND				Cost of Sales/Inventory	0 UND	1 658.2
20 17.9	21 17.7	7 50.7					27 13.6	31 11.8
0 UND	7 52.8	7 51.6					1 304.0	6 62.5
1 437.3	20 17.9	20 18.1				Cost of Sales/Payables	22 16.5	18 20.6
44 8.4	32 11.2	43 8.6					51 7.1	36 10.2
15.1	4.6	4.6					8.6	8.2
-96.5	16.9	9.4				Sales/Working Capital	25.5	15.4
-9.4	NM	78.3					-83.8	-76.7
7.4	8.4	35.5					19.9	25.8
(12) 1.3	(25) 1.2	(19) 4.4				EBIT/Interest	(33) 3.1	(61) 6.6
-5.0	-3.5	-2.1					-.4	2.1
						Net Profit + Depr., Dep., Amort./Cur. Mat. L/T/D		
.3	.1	.1					.1	.1
UND	.4	.2				Fixed/Worth	.3	.4
-.2	2.4	1.0					-4.3	6.2
1.9	.5	.5					1.0	.6
UND	2.5	1.2				Debt/Worth	2.9	1.4
-1.5	14.6	8.7					-52.5	25.6
	71.9	28.6					81.5	76.1
	(24) 4.8	(21) 15.4				% Profit Before Taxes/Tangible Net Worth	(31) 30.3	(54) 38.6
	-16.3	1.9					.3	16.2
40.3	20.8	22.1					18.9	30.2
8.4	1.3	4.6				% Profit Before Taxes/Total Assets	7.4	10.5
-17.0	-10.2	.3					-2.3	3.6
130.2	76.5	77.7					207.7	74.7
31.1	35.0	29.7				Sales/Net Fixed Assets	41.6	33.8
14.3	24.8	15.1					16.0	13.3
13.0	4.9	3.3					6.3	5.6
5.4	3.6	2.5				Sales/Total Assets	3.5	3.5
2.9	2.7	1.9					2.5	2.5
1.2	.4	.5					.2	.4
(10) 1.7	(24) .8	(19) 1.1				% Depr., Dep., Amort./Sales	(29) .8	(52) .8
2.5	1.3	2.4					1.7	1.6
6.7	2.7	1.5					1.3	1.8
(10) 8.8	(18) 4.8	(14) 2.4				% Officers', Directors' Owners' Comp/Sales	(17) 2.4	(39) 3.1
13.3	7.7	5.3					6.4	7.6
18067M	133920M	304715M	45579M			Net Sales ($)	824268M	3360458M
3200M	33101M	119711M	28731M			Total Assets ($)	238650M	1021317M

Note: Columns 50-100MM and 100-250MM: "DATA NOT AVAILABLE".

M = $ thousand   MM = $ million
See Pages 9 through 22 for Explanation of Ratios and Data

Comparative Historical Data | Current Data Sorted by Sales

Type of Statement

Type of Statement	4/1/07-3/31/08	4/1/08-3/31/09	4/1/09-3/31/10	0-1MM	1-3MM	3-5MM	5-10MM	10-25MM	25MM & OVER
Unqualified	4	2							
Reviewed	11	24	22	2	1	2	7	11	1
Compiled	6	19	11	2	2	3	3	1	
Tax Returns	18	26	21	8	7	2	2	2	
Other	31	27	18	3	4	4	4	4	

Current data periods: 13 (4/1-9/30/09) — 0-1MM, 1-3MM, 3-5MM columns; 59 (10/1/09-3/31/10) — 5-10MM, 10-25MM, 25MM & OVER columns.

	4/1/07-3/31/08 ALL	4/1/08-3/31/09 ALL	4/1/09-3/31/10 ALL	0-1MM	1-3MM	3-5MM	5-10MM	10-25MM	25MM & OVER
NUMBER OF STATEMENTS	70	98	72	13	14	11	15	18	1
	%	%	%	%	%	%	%	%	%
ASSETS									
Cash & Equivalents	12.2	16.3	19.2	23.4	14.2	16.2	16.3	25.0	
Trade Receivables (net)	38.7	37.2	38.7	36.1	30.9	43.1	45.0	38.2	
Inventory	13.1	9.6	6.5	6.1	9.1	14.8	.8	4.5	
All Other Current	8.6	7.7	7.6	.3	6.7	11.3	7.0	11.1	
Total Current	72.6	70.8	72.0	65.9	60.9	85.4	69.1	78.8	
Fixed Assets (net)	18.4	18.3	15.7	16.0	25.2	8.1	14.9	13.6	
Intangibles (net)	4.2	2.9	4.3	7.7	5.2	.2	5.7	2.6	
All Other Non-Current	4.7	8.1	8.0	10.3	8.8	6.3	10.3	5.0	
Total	100.0	100.0	100.0	100.0	100.0	100.0	100.0	100.0	
LIABILITIES									
Notes Payable-Short Term	11.7	10.6	15.4	37.3	19.0	8.8	9.3	6.6	
Cur. Mat.-L.T.D.	3.9	3.0	4.5	.8	10.7	10.2	1.1	1.8	
Trade Payables	21.1	22.0	20.4	16.2	21.8	22.6	20.5	21.2	
Income Taxes Payable	.2	.2	.3	.0	.0	.0	.3	1.0	
All Other Current	14.8	21.2	17.9	30.1	10.4	14.0	13.1	21.5	
Total Current	51.7	57.0	58.5	84.4	62.0	55.7	44.3	52.1	
Long-Term Debt	14.4	15.0	14.6	18.2	31.0	11.6	9.7	5.6	
Deferred Taxes	.1	.2	.3	.0	.0	.0	.6	.6	
All Other Non-Current	5.8	4.3	5.3	18.5	6.7	2.6	.3	.6	
Net Worth	28.0	23.5	21.3	-21.2	.2	30.2	45.0	41.1	
Total Liabilties & Net Worth	100.0	100.0	100.0	100.0	100.0	100.0	100.0	100.0	
INCOME DATA									
Net Sales	100.0	100.0	100.0	100.0	100.0	100.0	100.0	100.0	
Gross Profit	29.7	28.0	27.8	42.3	34.1	24.2	20.3	21.1	
Operating Expenses	25.1	25.9	25.8	38.7	33.8	22.4	18.3	18.3	
Operating Profit	4.5	2.1	2.0	3.7	.3	1.8	2.0	2.8	
All Other Expenses (net)	.9	.0	.3	.5	.8	.7	.7	-.6	
Profit Before Taxes	3.7	2.0	1.7	3.2	-.5	1.1	1.3	3.4	
RATIOS									
Current	2.3	2.5	3.0	1.8	2.2	5.6	3.2	2.8	
	1.6	1.6	1.4	1.0	1.1	1.6	1.9	1.8	
	1.1	.9	.9	.3	.6	.9	.9	1.2	
Quick	1.8	2.0	2.3	1.5	1.9	3.1	2.7	2.5	
	1.1	1.2	1.1	1.0	.7	1.1	1.7	1.2	
	.6	.5	.7	.3	.2	.6	.7	.8	
Sales/Receivables	21 17.5	16 23.0	16 22.8	0 UND	0 UND	29 12.6	37 9.8	27 13.4	
	47 7.7	33 11.2	47 7.8	15 24.1	35 10.5	50 7.4	47 7.8	52 7.0	
	66 5.6	64 5.7	62 5.8	57 6.4	51 7.2	97 3.8	64 5.7	65 5.7	
Cost of Sales/Inventory	0 UND	0 UND	0 UND	0 UND	0 UND	0 UND	0 UND	0 UND	
	0 780.5	0 UND	0 UND	0 UND	0 UND	18 20.0	0 UND	0 UND	
	28 13.0	15 23.8	19 19.1	25 14.7	7 52.8	47 7.7	0 UND	15 24.3	
Cost of Sales/Payables	13 28.6	9 39.6	5 77.8	0 UND	1 291.1	7 53.7	5 80.2	9 40.2	
	29 12.4	19 19.1	20 18.1	8 45.0	19 19.0	13 29.1	23 16.2	20 18.1	
	54 6.8	38 9.7	34 10.8	42 8.8	33 11.1	51 7.2	33 11.1	51 7.2	
Sales/Working Capital	7.3	7.1	5.1	8.3	4.1	4.5	8.5	4.6	
	11.4	13.5	15.6	UND	NM	10.4	17.2	9.7	
	53.5	-57.7	-43.5	-7.6	-13.9	-35.8	-40.9	50.2	
EBIT/Interest	12.6	18.7	7.8		7.7		41.4	24.4	
	(67) 4.5	(85) 5.6	(58) 1.4		(13) -.1		(14) 1.4	(13) 5.2	
	1.4	.7	-3.6		-2.1		-23.8	-.4	
Net Profit + Depr., Dep., Amort./Cur. Mat. L/T/D	22.6								
	(12) 2.4								
	.3								
Fixed/Worth	.1	.1	.1	.3	.1	.1	.1	.0	
	.4	.3	.4	2.9	2.2	.3	.4	.3	
	UND	6.5	4.4	-.2	-.6	2.5	2.7	.9	
Debt/Worth	.8	.7	.7	1.8	.9	.8	.5	.8	
	2.1	1.5	2.0	7.3	4.2	2.2	.9	1.4	
	-264.1	NM	25.0	-2.4	-3.8	23.2	16.9	3.8	
% Profit Before Taxes/Tangible Net Worth	57.0	58.6	45.0				54.5	39.1	
	(52) 24.8	(74) 19.9	(56) 10.7			(13) 6.0	(17) 26.9		
	9.2	1.6	-10.8				-51.2	3.7	
% Profit Before Taxes/Total Assets	21.2	21.4	22.6	73.5	13.7	14.9	21.3	23.2	
	9.2	7.1	3.8	6.7	.2	.7	1.9	10.0	
	2.4	-2.0	-7.6	-8.3	-13.9	-10.8	-11.2	.7	
Sales/Net Fixed Assets	70.1	90.0	76.5	96.2	53.9	263.2	75.1	121.9	
	30.8	31.5	33.6	30.2	29.7	35.5	34.5	34.1	
	12.2	14.7	15.8	8.9	15.0	27.6	18.6	14.6	
Sales/Total Assets	4.4	5.4	4.9	9.8	7.3	3.7	6.3	4.5	
	3.2	3.4	3.2	4.3	3.7	3.3	4.2	2.9	
	2.1	2.2	2.3	2.8	2.2	2.5	2.0	2.2	
% Depr., Dep., Amort./Sales	.4	.7	.5		.8		.3	.5	
	(49) .8	(73) 1.1	(54) 1.0	(12) 1.2		(13) .8	(13) .8		
	1.6	1.9	2.0		2.7		2.2	1.4	
% Officers', Directors' Owners' Comp/Sales	1.8	2.2	2.0		3.0				
	(35) 3.5	(50) 4.7	(42) 5.0	(11) 4.7					
	5.9	6.7	8.7		9.0				
Net Sales ($)	2117209M	984730M	502281M	7512M	29936M	41488M	113396M	284838M	25111M
Total Assets ($)	684479M	373768M	184743M	2060M	9057M	14594M	40171M	105868M	12993M

Current Data Sorted by Assets							Comparative Historical Data	
						Type of Statement		
	3	9	7			Unqualified	29	27
	21	50	2			Reviewed	84	107
6	10	4				Compiled	34	39
25	15	4				Tax Returns	49	45
3	15	22	8		2	Other	69	60
32 (4/1-9/30/09)			174 (10/1/09-3/31/10)				**4/1/05-3/31/06 ALL**	**4/1/06-3/31/07 ALL**
0-500M	**500M-2MM**	**2-10MM**	**10-50MM**	**50-100MM**	**100-250MM**			
34	64	89	17		2	**NUMBER OF STATEMENTS**	265	278
%	%	%	%	%	%	**ASSETS**	%	%
22.9	13.8	16.6	15.2	**DATA NOT AVAILABLE**		Cash & Equivalents	12.6	14.2
19.2	41.2	46.2	50.1			Trade Receivables (net)	48.5	44.2
7.7	6.7	2.1	5.2			Inventory	3.6	4.7
12.0	6.3	8.1	7.1			All Other Current	6.9	7.2
61.7	68.1	73.0	77.6			Total Current	71.6	70.2
24.0	20.8	18.7	12.4			Fixed Assets (net)	21.5	21.8
1.4	3.7	1.8	.7			Intangibles (net)	1.1	1.5
12.9	7.4	6.5	9.3			All Other Non-Current	5.8	6.5
100.0	100.0	100.0	100.0			Total	100.0	100.0
						LIABILITIES		
17.9	17.4	6.3	6.4			Notes Payable-Short Term	13.5	10.0
6.8	2.3	2.7	2.0			Cur. Mat.-L.T.D.	5.3	3.1
11.0	13.5	11.7	15.2			Trade Payables	17.7	14.8
.0	1.2	.7	.3			Income Taxes Payable	.7	.9
9.5	6.5	14.4	23.4			All Other Current	15.1	14.7
45.2	40.9	35.8	47.3			Total Current	52.3	43.4
29.4	11.6	6.7	5.3			Long-Term Debt	14.1	14.4
.0	.3	.5	.8			Deferred Taxes	.5	.4
5.8	9.0	1.9	2.2			All Other Non-Current	4.6	4.0
19.5	38.1	55.0	44.4			Net Worth	28.5	37.8
100.0	100.0	100.0	100.0			Total Liabilties & Net Worth	100.0	100.0
						INCOME DATA		
100.0	100.0	100.0	100.0			Net Sales	100.0	100.0
46.4	27.3	21.0	18.5			Gross Profit	26.9	26.7
44.6	26.2	19.5	14.3			Operating Expenses	22.6	20.4
1.7	1.1	1.5	4.2			Operating Profit	4.3	6.3
.5	.5	.1	.1			All Other Expenses (net)	.2	.7
1.2	.6	1.4	4.1			Profit Before Taxes	4.1	5.6
						RATIOS		
4.4	3.9	3.9	2.1				2.4	2.9
1.4	1.9	1.9	1.7			Current	1.6	1.7
.8	1.1	1.4	1.3				1.1	1.2
3.0	3.3	3.2	1.9				2.1	2.6
1.0	1.3	1.6	1.5			Quick	1.4	1.4
.2	.9	1.2	1.1				.9	1.0
0 UND	**33** 11.1	**52** 7.0	**67** 5.5				**36** 10.0	**32** 11.3
11 32.8	**53** 6.8	**70** 5.2	**85** 4.3			Sales/Receivables	**67** 5.4	**61** 6.0
48 7.7	**78** 4.7	**90** 4.0	**109** 3.3				**89** 4.1	**81** 4.5
0 UND	**0** UND	**0** UND	**0** UND				**0** UND	**0** UND
0 UND	**0** UND	**0** UND	**0** 999.8			Cost of Sales/Inventory	**0** UND	**0** UND
4 97.8	**6** 56.5	**2** 204.4	**5** 77.5				**3** 121.8	**3** 133.2
0 UND	**8** 44.7	**10** 36.6	**17** 21.2				**12** 31.1	**9** 40.4
4 84.1	**15** 24.0	**19** 19.4	**22** 16.6			Cost of Sales/Payables	**23** 16.0	**20** 18.1
54 6.7	**30** 12.3	**34** 10.9	**42** 8.7				**42** 8.7	**36** 10.2
6.6	5.2	4.1	5.1				6.1	5.3
28.1	11.3	7.3	8.5			Sales/Working Capital	10.7	10.1
-60.0	103.0	14.2	12.1				49.0	35.2
17.4	15.0	20.6	43.6				22.2	28.9
(28) 3.1	(57) 2.3	(73) 4.2	(16) 9.2			EBIT/Interest	(234) 6.3	(245) 8.6
-1.9	-3.0	-3.5	2.9				1.5	2.2
	6.5	12.3					8.3	11.3
	(11) 4.0	(23) 3.1				Net Profit + Depr., Dep., Amort./Cur. Mat. L/T/D	(51) 2.7	(62) 4.6
	1.1	1.4					1.1	2.1
.2	.2	.1	.1				.2	.2
.8	.5	.2	.2			Fixed/Worth	.4	.4
UND	2.2	.7	.4				1.3	.9
.5	.5	.4	.6				.8	.6
3.6	1.2	.8	1.5			Debt/Worth	1.6	1.3
-8.3	10.6	1.5	2.4				5.3	3.7
142.1	39.5	27.7	47.0				66.0	64.2
(24) 13.3	(51) 8.6	(87) 11.0	19.4			% Profit Before Taxes/Tangible Net Worth	(233) 27.4	(254) 29.4
-9.6	-2.8	-3.4	5.9				8.3	11.0
30.9	14.2	12.9	17.5				26.4	30.1
5.5	3.2	4.3	8.6			% Profit Before Taxes/Total Assets	9.5	11.8
-7.9	-5.6	-2.8	2.9				1.5	2.9
40.3	36.9	36.8	38.2				40.5	43.4
20.3	21.3	19.6	23.3			Sales/Net Fixed Assets	21.4	21.7
10.2	9.4	9.5	16.0				11.9	10.8
6.0	3.7	2.9	2.8				4.2	3.8
3.9	2.8	2.3	2.2			Sales/Total Assets	2.9	2.9
2.2	2.0	1.7	1.6				2.2	2.2
.7	1.1	.8	.6				.8	.7
(27) 1.3	(53) 1.8	(78) 1.4	(15) 1.1			% Depr., Dep., Amort./Sales	(224) 1.5	(235) 1.3
3.2	3.1	2.7	2.6				2.5	2.5
5.8	3.5	2.3					1.9	1.5
(29) 9.9	(38) 5.3	(48) 5.0				% Officers', Directors' Owners' Comp/Sales	(144) 3.4	(153) 3.8
13.1	10.8	8.0					6.1	6.4
42224M	**197654M**	**1025912M**	**698435M**		**745063M**	Net Sales ($)	**4830600M**	**4801454M**
9862M	**69659M**	**429433M**	**347608M**		**257013M**	Total Assets ($)	**1366063M**	**1910177M**

M = $ thousand MM = $ million

See Pages 9 through 22 for Explanation of Ratios and Data

Comparative Historical Data / Current Data Sorted by Sales

	4/1/07-3/31/08 ALL	4/1/08-3/31/09 ALL	4/1/09-3/31/10 ALL	0-1MM	1-3MM	3-5MM	5-10MM	10-25MM	25MM & OVER
Type of Statement									
Unqualified	31	27	19		1	1	4	6	7
Reviewed	85	88	73		13	16	19	22	3
Compiled	32	21	20	2	9	4	2	2	1
Tax Returns	38	35	44	16	18	7	3		
Other	72	67	50	3	6	8	12	8	13
					32 (4/1-9/30/09)		174 (10/1/09-3/31/10)		
NUMBER OF STATEMENTS	258	238	206	21	47	36	40	38	24
ASSETS	%	%	%	%	%	%	%	%	%
Cash & Equivalents	14.2	13.7	16.8	14.6	16.8	17.3	15.5	20.2	14.9
Trade Receivables (net)	47.0	46.2	40.2	19.9	30.1	45.5	40.5	54.2	46.9
Inventory	4.3	4.9	4.7	10.7	7.2	3.7	1.9	3.2	2.8
All Other Current	7.1	7.5	8.0	14.7	6.8	5.7	9.1	6.2	9.3
Total Current	72.7	72.4	69.7	59.9	60.9	72.3	67.0	83.8	73.9
Fixed Assets (net)	18.6	18.3	19.7	22.4	25.5	20.3	20.9	12.3	15.0
Intangibles (net)	.9	1.8	2.5	1.2	4.7	1.3	2.7	1.0	3.5
All Other Non-Current	7.9	7.5	8.0	16.6	8.9	6.2	9.4	2.9	7.5
Total	100.0	100.0	100.0	100.0	100.0	100.0	100.0	100.0	100.0
LIABILITIES									
Notes Payable-Short Term	10.0	11.0	11.6	18.9	19.1	11.1	7.7	6.6	6.1
Cur. Mat.-L.T.D.	3.0	3.0	3.1	3.7	4.9	3.1	2.8	1.5	2.2
Trade Payables	16.6	16.3	12.3	13.5	9.4	13.9	11.2	13.0	15.6
Income Taxes Payable	1.1	.7	.7	.1	1.1	.7	1.1	.4	.3
All Other Current	15.2	15.8	11.8	2.7	9.7	9.7	8.7	20.0	19.1
Total Current	45.8	46.9	39.6	38.9	44.2	38.5	31.6	41.5	43.3
Long-Term Debt	11.3	11.7	12.1	37.3	17.9	6.6	5.7	5.0	9.3
Deferred Taxes	.4	.3	.4	.0	.1	.5	1.0	.2	.6
All Other Non-Current	4.4	4.9	4.8	8.9	8.2	5.7	1.8	2.5	1.6
Net Worth	38.2	36.3	43.1	14.8	29.7	48.7	60.0	50.8	45.1
Total Liabilties & Net Worth	100.0	100.0	100.0	100.0	100.0	100.0	100.0	100.0	100.0
INCOME DATA									
Net Sales	100.0	100.0	100.0	100.0	100.0	100.0	100.0	100.0	100.0
Gross Profit	26.3	23.4	26.9	47.1	32.8	26.9	21.2	20.5	17.7
Operating Expenses	20.5	20.4	25.3	45.7	33.9	24.6	19.1	17.2	14.8
Operating Profit	5.8	3.0	1.6	1.4	-1.1	2.2	2.1	3.2	3.0
All Other Expenses (net)	.4	.6	.3	1.8	.1	.4	.0	.2	.3
Profit Before Taxes	5.4	2.4	1.3	-.5	-1.2	1.8	2.1	3.0	2.6
RATIOS									
Current	2.6	2.7	3.6	10.7	2.6	3.6	4.5	3.9	2.3
	1.6	1.7	1.8	1.6	1.4	2.1	2.0	1.9	1.7
	1.2	1.2	1.2	.8	.9	1.1	1.4	1.4	1.3
Quick	2.3	2.3	3.1	4.2	2.3	3.5	4.1	3.1	2.0
	(257) 1.4	1.3	1.6	1.0	1.2	1.8	1.7	1.7	1.5
	1.0	1.0	1.0	.2	.4	1.0	1.1	1.3	1.0
Sales/Receivables	**40** 9.1	**41** 9.0	**33** 10.9	**0** UND	**10** 36.9	**34** 10.7	**41** 8.9	**61** 6.0	**51** 7.2
	64 5.7	**64** 5.7	**61** 5.9	**28** 12.9	**50** 7.4	**55** 6.6	**58** 6.3	**75** 4.9	**74** 4.9
	88 4.2	**92** 4.0	**84** 4.3	**60** 6.1	**77** 4.7	**83** 4.4	**88** 4.2	**102** 3.6	**98** 3.7
Cost of Sales/Inventory	**0** UND	**0** UND	**0** UND	**0** UND	**0** UND	**0** UND	**0** UND	**0** UND	**0** UND
	0 UND	**0** UND	**0** UND	**0** UND	**0** UND	**0** UND	**0** UND	**0** UND	**0** 999.8
	4 95.3	**3** 138.3	**3** 111.2	**8** 43.3	**7** 54.4	**7** 55.6	**2** 203.2	**2** 227.1	**3** 119.6
Cost of Sales/Payables	**11** 32.4	**9** 42.2	**7** 49.2	**1** 332.5	**1** 298.5	**7** 51.1	**6** 63.0	**12** 31.7	**14** 25.7
	20 18.5	**22** 17.0	**17** 22.0	**6** 56.3	**11** 32.1	**16** 22.4	**15** 24.2	**21** 17.5	**22** 16.9
	39 9.3	**37** 9.8	**33** 11.1	**77** 4.7	**25** 14.4	**35** 10.3	**32** 11.5	**33** 10.9	**33** 11.1
Sales/Working Capital	5.6	5.1	4.9	4.1	5.5	4.7	4.2	4.2	6.5
	10.8	10.2	8.5	15.2	15.6	13.0	7.5	7.0	8.9
	33.7	25.8	31.1	-17.3	-71.9	55.4	15.4	10.8	12.3
EBIT/Interest	30.9	21.7	17.8	5.8	14.0	17.4	16.6	80.4	56.7
	(219) 6.4	(211) 5.1	(176) 4.5	(18) 1.4	(43) 1.9	(30) 3.5	(35) 3.9	(28) 10.9	(22) 8.1
	1.9	-.2	-1.4	-1.4	-6.5	-.8	-5.6	2.6	.8
Net Profit + Depr., Dep., Amort./Cur. Mat. L/T/D	8.9	7.8	8.1					22.8	
	(50) 3.8	(39) 4.0	(42) 3.8					(10) 7.8	
	1.7	1.3	1.4					2.0	
Fixed/Worth	.2	.2	.2	.2	.2	.2	.1	.1	.2
	.3	.3	.3	.8	.8	.4	.2	.2	.2
	1.0	.9	1.0	UND	9.1	1.3	.7	.4	.5
Debt/Worth	.6	.6	.4	.6	.6	.4	.3	.3	.6
	1.4	1.4	1.1	3.3	1.5	.9	.6	1.1	1.4
	4.0	4.1	3.0	-5.7	-13.1	7.0	1.2	1.6	2.6
% Profit Before Taxes/Tangible Net Worth	64.5	51.5	38.9	110.9	40.7	58.4	27.7	39.1	53.8
	(238) 29.4	(211) 15.2	(180) 11.0	(14) 10.4	(34) 5.1	(33) 12.6	(39) 9.3	(37) 11.8	(23) 19.4
	10.0	.4	-2.9	-8.2	-24.0	1.9	-17.6	2.4	-.1
% Profit Before Taxes/Total Assets	23.6	19.0	14.6	15.3	12.4	18.8	14.5	13.7	18.7
	10.5	6.9	4.3	.2	3.1	3.8	4.1	6.3	7.0
	2.6	-1.6	-3.8	-9.2	-11.6	-2.4	-6.9	2.0	-.1
Sales/Net Fixed Assets	45.0	41.9	37.4	37.6	30.6	36.7	36.0	47.3	38.5
	20.9	21.7	20.3	13.6	15.5	21.3	19.1	28.3	23.8
	11.1	12.3	9.9	7.1	6.8	9.7	10.2	15.8	15.4
Sales/Total Assets	3.6	3.7	3.5	3.8	4.7	3.7	3.0	3.0	3.5
	2.7	2.7	2.5	2.2	2.6	2.8	2.4	2.6	2.6
	2.2	2.1	1.9	1.6	1.7	2.0	1.9	2.0	2.0
% Depr., Dep., Amort./Sales	.7	.6	.8	1.0	.9	1.1	.7	.7	.7
	(212) 1.3	(192) 1.3	(174) 1.5	(15) 2.2	(41) 1.8	(31) 1.8	(35) 1.5	(32) 1.1	(20) 1.1
	2.3	2.1	2.9	5.1	3.2	3.7	3.0	2.0	3.3
% Officers', Directors' Owners' Comp/Sales	1.8	2.0	3.2	7.4	4.5	3.4	2.3	1.6	
	(138) 3.6	(120) 3.9	(121) 5.8	(17) 11.2	(31) 6.7	(21) 5.1	(21) 3.8	(24) 4.5	
	6.7	6.3	10.3	20.2	11.9	7.5	6.7	8.6	
Net Sales ($)	**4099025M**	**4830181M**	**2709288M**	**12379M**	**95283M**	**136026M**	**291424M**	**566647M**	**1607529M**
Total Assets ($)	**1664492M**	**1964403M**	**1113575M**	**7022M**	**41364M**	**57416M**	**124603M**	**245895M**	**637275M**

M = $ thousand MM = $ million

See Pages 9 through 22 for Explanation of Ratios and Data

Current Data Sorted by Assets

Comparative Historical Data

						Type of Statement		
	1	3	4	2		Unqualified	8	6
	15	45	4			Reviewed	44	41
4	10	6				Compiled	13	23
10	6	2	1			Tax Returns	14	18
4	10	8	5			Other	29	32
	30 (4/1-9/30/09)		110 (10/1/09-3/31/10)				4/1/05-3/31/06	4/1/06-3/31/07
0-500M	500M-2MM	2-10MM	10-50MM	50-100MM	100-250MM		ALL	ALL
18	42	64	14	2		NUMBER OF STATEMENTS	108	120
%	%	%	%	%	%	ASSETS	%	%
20.8	12.0	18.8	24.2			Cash & Equivalents	9.4	10.8
25.4	48.4	44.8	42.4			Trade Receivables (net)	51.8	48.9
13.9	10.6	7.0	4.2			Inventory	11.8	11.4
2.3	4.2	10.9	5.8			All Other Current	5.0	6.2
62.5	75.2	81.6	76.5			Total Current	78.1	77.2
22.8	18.1	11.7	20.2			Fixed Assets (net)	13.8	14.2
3.8	1.2	2.5	1.6			Intangibles (net)	1.9	1.6
10.9	5.6	4.2	1.7			All Other Non-Current	6.2	7.0
100.0	100.0	100.0	100.0			Total	100.0	100.0
						LIABILITIES		
19.7	21.8	9.0	4.4			Notes Payable-Short Term	13.0	11.4
3.3	2.5	1.9	2.4			Cur. Mat.-L.T.D.	2.4	3.0
9.4	21.2	16.1	13.8			Trade Payables	22.3	21.3
.1	.2	.7	.5			Income Taxes Payable	.8	.7
16.7	14.1	16.0	24.7			All Other Current	13.0	16.0
49.2	59.8	43.7	45.9			Total Current	51.5	52.4
15.2	10.8	6.0	10.9			Long-Term Debt	8.6	7.0
.0	.8	.2	.0			Deferred Taxes	.3	.2
16.4	6.7	4.5	1.4			All Other Non-Current	4.9	4.8
19.2	21.9	45.7	41.9			Net Worth	34.7	35.5
100.0	100.0	100.0	100.0			Total Liabilities & Net Worth	100.0	100.0
						INCOME DATA		
100.0	100.0	100.0	100.0			Net Sales	100.0	100.0
47.3	30.1	28.4	22.5			Gross Profit	29.7	30.1
41.0	30.8	22.8	13.3			Operating Expenses	25.6	25.1
6.3	-.8	5.6	9.2			Operating Profit	4.1	5.0
.9	.7	.3	.2			All Other Expenses (net)	.4	.6
5.4	-1.4	5.3	9.0			Profit Before Taxes	3.7	4.4
						RATIOS		
4.5	2.3	2.7	2.0				2.1	2.2
1.5	1.3	1.8	1.5			Current	1.5	1.5
.6	.9	1.4	1.4				1.2	1.2
3.3	1.9	2.3	1.8				1.7	1.7
1.2	1.3	1.4	1.4			Quick	1.2	1.2
.3	.6	1.0	1.2				.8	.8
0 UND	33 10.9	45 8.0	56 6.5				39 9.4	39 9.4
17 21.5	56 6.6	58 6.3	71 5.2			Sales/Receivables	62 5.9	63 5.8
35 10.4	75 4.9	80 4.6	89 4.1				88 4.1	84 4.4
0 UND	0 UND	0 UND	0 UND				1 363.2	1 482.3
5 74.0	9 41.4	2 203.2	2 187.7			Cost of Sales/Inventory	11 34.6	13 27.2
30 12.1	32 11.5	16 22.5	9 38.9				30 12.1	33 11.0
0 UND	13 29.2	13 27.8	16 22.1				20 17.9	18 20.4
13 27.9	30 12.4	24 15.3	24 15.2			Cost of Sales/Payables	35 10.6	36 10.2
23 16.1	57 6.4	43 8.5	29 12.6				55 6.6	53 6.9
7.9	6.5	5.1	4.9				7.1	6.3
22.3	18.9	7.7	9.0			Sales/Working Capital	11.3	10.0
-74.4	-75.1	12.5	10.8				26.2	27.2
35.5	8.2	42.0	200.8				17.1	15.9
(15) 3.2	(36) 1.5	(58) 9.1	(12) 19.2			EBIT/Interest	(98) 6.2	(106) 5.9
-1.9	-2.8	2.5	7.5				2.2	2.4
		7.1				Net Profit + Depr., Dep.,	9.4	11.7
	(16) 2.0					Amort./Cur. Mat. L/T/D	(35) 3.4	(36) 3.7
		1.1					2.0	1.7
.1	.1	.1	.1				.2	.1
.3	.4	.2	.3			Fixed/Worth	.3	.3
-2.0	1.2	.6	.9				.8	.7
.3	.9	.6	1.1				1.0	.9
1.9	2.1	1.4	1.6			Debt/Worth	2.0	2.0
-3.4	7.1	2.5	1.9				4.4	4.6
42.4	35.7	49.6	55.9			% Profit Before Taxes/Tangible	58.4	73.6
(10) 22.2	(34) 7.3	(61) 17.3	39.8			Net Worth	(99) 33.2	(117) 34.6
-12.4	-3.5	4.4	28.6				7.6	11.3
33.6	11.2	23.4	24.0			% Profit Before Taxes/Total	17.6	22.3
10.9	1.8	7.3	14.0			Assets	8.6	9.5
-5.6	-8.9	2.1	7.4				2.2	3.0
123.1	67.0	52.2	55.4				66.3	72.8
43.5	28.0	33.1	19.4			Sales/Net Fixed Assets	30.7	35.0
15.8	11.5	19.7	4.5				17.2	18.2
10.2	4.0	3.4	2.7				3.9	3.9
5.5	3.1	2.8	2.2			Sales/Total Assets	2.9	3.0
3.7	2.4	2.3	1.8				2.4	2.3
.2	.1	.5	.4				.5	.4
(13) 1.1	(37) 1.2	(58) .9	.7			% Depr., Dep., Amort./Sales	(95) .9	(104) .8
1.5	1.9	1.5	1.6				1.5	1.4
7.8	2.5	2.5					2.1	2.3
(14) 9.1	(28) 3.7	(27) 3.6				% Officers', Directors' Owners' Comp/Sales	(61) 3.8	(63) 3.6
14.8	6.8	5.6					7.3	6.6
27582M	147884M	779461M	523147M	274697M		Net Sales ($)	1176774M	2064617M
4689M	47361M	288783M	234617M	133295M		Total Assets ($)	469992M	748620M

Columns 50-100MM and 100-250MM: DATA NOT AVAILABLE

M = $ thousand   MM = $ million
See Pages 9 through 22 for Explanation of Ratios and Data

Comparative Historical Data

Current Data Sorted by Sales

						Type of Statement						
	7		12		10	Unqualified		1			3	6
	48		69		64	Reviewed		5	7	23	26	3
	13		14		20	Compiled	2	8	3	6	1	
	24		23		19	Tax Returns	3	11	2	1	1	1
	34		44		27	Other	1	11	1	5	1	4
	4/1/07-3/31/08		4/1/08-3/31/09		4/1/09-3/31/10			30 (4/1-9/30/09)		110 (10/1/09-3/31/10)		
	ALL		ALL		ALL		0-1MM	1-3MM	3-5MM	5-10MM	10-25MM	25MM & OVER
	126		162		140	NUMBER OF STATEMENTS	6	36	13	35	36	14
	%		%		%	ASSETS	%	%	%	%	%	%
	12.2		15.0		17.5	Cash & Equivalents		13.3	15.2	15.4	22.1	23.5
	50.3		47.9		43.1	Trade Receivables (net)		41.4	43.0	46.8	42.7	47.2
	11.0		7.8		8.6	Inventory		11.5	15.8	7.6	5.2	3.9
	5.9		7.3		7.4	All Other Current		3.4	4.9	8.1	12.3	8.2
	79.4		78.1		76.6	Total Current		69.7	78.9	77.9	82.4	82.9
	15.2		15.9		16.0	Fixed Assets (net)		19.4	17.9	14.2	13.3	12.6
	1.5		2.5		2.2	Intangibles (net)		1.1	.4	4.0	1.0	1.2
	3.9		3.6		5.3	All Other Non-Current		9.8	2.8	3.9	3.4	3.3
	100.0		100.0		100.0	Total		100.0	100.0	100.0	100.0	100.0
						LIABILITIES						
	9.7		11.4		13.7	Notes Payable-Short Term		20.6	23.5	14.5	6.2	5.0
	2.7		3.8		2.4	Cur. Mat.-L.T.D.		3.0	2.4	2.4	1.8	2.2
	19.7		18.5		16.6	Trade Payables		16.0	21.7	15.8	16.3	19.1
	.9		1.0		.4	Income Taxes Payable		.4	.1	.8	.4	.5
	18.2		18.6		16.5	All Other Current		16.9	15.6	9.9	20.0	25.5
	51.2		53.3		49.6	Total Current		56.8	63.2	43.4	44.6	52.2
	10.7		8.9		9.2	Long-Term Debt		13.2	8.7	7.1	7.6	6.3
	.2		.3		.3	Deferred Taxes		.7	.9	.3	.1	.0
	4.3		4.8		6.3	All Other Non-Current		9.9	8.0	3.7	4.7	1.1
	33.7		32.7		34.5	Net Worth		19.3	19.2	45.7	43.0	40.4
	100.0		100.0		100.0	Total Liabilties & Net Worth		100.0	100.0	100.0	100.0	100.0
						INCOME DATA						
	100.0		100.0		100.0	Net Sales		100.0	100.0	100.0	100.0	100.0
	29.9		31.0		30.6	Gross Profit		35.5	31.0	29.6	26.9	20.7
	24.5		24.7		26.5	Operating Expenses		35.0	26.6	25.6	20.0	12.9
	5.4		6.2		4.1	Operating Profit		.5	4.4	4.0	6.9	7.8
	.6		.5		.5	All Other Expenses (net)		1.0	.1	.3	.3	.1
	4.8		5.7		3.7	Profit Before Taxes		-.5	4.4	3.7	6.6	7.7
						RATIOS						
	2.3		2.4		2.6			4.0	2.1	2.8	2.5	1.8
	1.6		1.5		1.6	Current		1.3	1.7	1.7	1.8	1.5
	1.2		1.2		1.3			.8	.9	1.3	1.4	1.4
	2.0		2.1		2.1			2.8	1.8	2.2	2.3	1.7
	1.3		1.3		1.3	Quick		1.2	1.4	1.3	1.4	1.3
	.8		.9		.9			.5	.4	1.1	.9	1.0
39	9.5	42	8.7	36	10.2		25 14.3	24 15.0	41 8.8	43 8.5	50 7.3
64	5.7	64	5.7	54	6.7	Sales/Receivables	46 7.9	59 6.2	53 6.9	56 6.5	66 5.6
89	4.1	86	4.2	78	4.7		77 4.7	90 4.1	75 4.9	84 4.3	84 4.3
0	999.8	0	UND	0	UND		0 UND	0 UND	0 UND	0 UND	0 UND
8	44.4	3	110.8	3	104.7	Cost of Sales/Inventory	8 45.8	9 39.5	3 104.4	0 783.0	2 198.6
31	11.8	16	23.3	18	20.1		40 9.2	35 10.3	13 29.1	16 22.5	6 59.7
18	20.4	16	23.0	12	29.4		5 78.5	11 34.7	10 35.6	13 27.8	19 19.2
33	11.0	29	12.6	24	15.0	Cost of Sales/Payables	19 19.6	32 11.3	23 15.7	23 15.9	25 14.6
47	7.8	44	8.4	44	8.3		46 7.9	62 5.8	37 9.9	43 8.5	50 7.2
	6.1		5.4		5.5			5.5	5.4	5.5	5.3	6.0
	9.4		10.6		10.0	Sales/Working Capital		28.9	10.6	11.0	7.8	9.3
	25.4		20.5		21.6			-41.3	NM	19.3	10.8	12.4
	24.9		41.9		32.3			9.4	9.6	29.8	49.2	336.7
(114)	7.3	(146)	12.9	(123)	6.5	EBIT/Interest	(30) 2.7	(12) 2.4	(32) 5.9	(31) 11.7	(13) 19.8
	3.1		2.1		1.4			-2.4	.6	1.8	3.6	8.0
	19.9		18.4		13.8					3.3		
(35)	6.0	(45)	6.9	(30)	3.6	Net Profit + Depr., Dep., Amort./Cur. Mat. L/T/D			(10) 1.3		
	2.5		2.1		1.6					.3		
	.1		.1		.1			.1	.2	.1	.1	.1
	.3		.3		.3	Fixed/Worth		.4	.3	.3	.2	.2
	.8		.8		.7			2.1	NM	.7	.6	.7
	.9		.7		.7			.5	.9	.5	.7	1.1
	2.0		1.8		1.6	Debt/Worth		1.8	2.3	1.5	1.4	1.8
	4.3		3.7		3.7			-6.9	NM	3.2	2.3	2.5
	61.2		77.6		44.8			35.3	19.9	48.6	53.8	55.9
(115)	33.5	(146)	35.6	(121)	17.3	% Profit Before Taxes/Tangible Net Worth	(26) 7.3	(10) 10.2	(33) 11.2	(35) 25.8	41.8
	14.2		12.1		4.0			1.4	2.8	1.4	10.5	31.4
	20.1		28.3		19.2			13.4	17.6	19.7	24.6	24.5
	9.1		12.8		7.2	% Profit Before Taxes/Total Assets		2.9	3.0	5.5	11.5	13.5
	4.2		2.5		1.3			-12.3	.4	.9	4.5	9.3
	63.7		67.0		62.8			74.5	72.5	38.0	89.0	60.8
	31.8		32.4		32.8	Sales/Net Fixed Assets		28.0	33.9	26.5	39.5	35.3
	14.4		16.2		15.8			12.7	12.9	19.3	12.8	15.2
	3.7		4.0		3.9			4.5	4.9	3.5	3.3	2.8
	2.8		2.9		2.9	Sales/Total Assets		3.4	3.0	3.0	2.6	2.6
	2.2		2.2		2.2			2.1	2.2	2.5	2.1	2.2
	.4		.4		.5			.3		.6	.3	.3
(102)	.7	(139)	.7	(124)	1.0	% Depr., Dep., Amort./Sales	(29) 1.3		(34) 1.2	(34) .7	(13) .5
	1.3		1.2		1.6			2.1		1.6	1.4	1.0
	2.2		1.7		2.5			3.5	2.2	2.3	2.7	
(72)	3.6	(87)	2.9	(80)	3.8	% Officers', Directors' Owners' Comp/Sales	(24) 6.0	(10) 3.7	(17) 3.0	(15) 3.6	
	6.2		5.0		7.8			10.4	6.1	4.0	7.1	
	4162631M		3571529M		1752771M	Net Sales ($)	4439M	75970M	53825M	249911M	578605M	790021M
	1359390M		1308931M		708745M	Total Assets ($)	1683M	26809M	22992M	85305M	240451M	331505M

M = $ thousand   MM = $ million
See Pages 9 through 22 for Explanation of Ratios and Data

Current Data Sorted by Assets   Comparative Historical Data

	0-500M	500M-2MM	2-10MM	10-50MM	50-100MM	100-250MM	Type of Statement	4/1/05-3/31/06 ALL	4/1/06-3/31/07 ALL
		4	13	9	1	1	Unqualified	35	31
	5	42	85	10			Reviewed	145	180
	12	16	7	2			Compiled	45	49
	29	19	13	1			Tax Returns	46	48
	12	38	37	12	2	1	Other	111	92
		62 (4/1-9/30/09)		309 (10/1/09-3/31/10)					
NUMBER OF STATEMENTS	58	119	155	34	3	2	**NUMBER OF STATEMENTS**	382	400
	%	%	%	%	%	%	**ASSETS**	%	%
	19.6	15.4	16.0	14.0			Cash & Equivalents	11.1	12.3
	25.1	39.2	45.5	42.0			Trade Receivables (net)	46.4	44.1
	7.7	10.1	5.1	8.8			Inventory	8.6	7.3
	5.5	7.4	8.7	9.3			All Other Current	8.7	8.0
	57.8	72.0	75.3	74.1			Total Current	74.9	71.8
	29.9	16.9	15.4	17.0			Fixed Assets (net)	16.9	17.9
	2.0	2.8	1.9	2.6			Intangibles (net)	1.6	2.7
	10.2	8.3	7.3	6.3			All Other Non-Current	6.6	7.6
	100.0	100.0	100.0	100.0			Total	100.0	100.0
							LIABILITIES		
	17.5	13.2	7.9	10.1			Notes Payable-Short Term	10.9	11.0
	10.4	3.2	2.3	1.9			Cur. Mat.-L.T.D.	3.4	3.7
	21.1	19.6	18.1	15.2			Trade Payables	21.5	19.5
	.5	.3	.5	.1			Income Taxes Payable	.7	.8
	13.3	12.2	14.4	19.1			All Other Current	13.3	14.3
	62.7	48.5	43.1	46.4			Total Current	49.8	49.3
	28.3	10.9	6.4	5.5			Long-Term Debt	12.7	12.6
	.0	.6	.4	.2			Deferred Taxes	.4	.4
	8.6	2.5	2.4	2.6			All Other Non-Current	4.2	4.7
	.3	37.5	47.7	45.2			Net Worth	32.9	32.8
	100.0	100.0	100.0	100.0			Total Liabilities & Net Worth	100.0	100.0
							INCOME DATA		
	100.0	100.0	100.0	100.0			Net Sales	100.0	100.0
	38.7	29.5	23.8	23.5			Gross Profit	28.1	28.7
	38.2	27.7	21.1	20.2			Operating Expenses	24.3	23.6
	.6	1.8	2.7	3.3			Operating Profit	3.8	5.1
	.4	.3	.1	.4			All Other Expenses (net)	.6	.4
	.1	1.5	2.7	2.9			Profit Before Taxes	3.2	4.7
							RATIOS		
	2.2	3.0	3.0	1.9			Current	2.3	2.2
	1.3	1.6	1.7	1.5				1.5	1.5
	.4	1.1	1.3	1.3				1.2	1.2
	1.6	1.8	2.4	1.6			Quick	1.7	1.9
	.9	1.3	1.4	1.1				1.2 (399)	1.2
	.4	.8	1.0	.9				.8	.8
	0 UND	23 16.0	42 8.6	49 7.4			Sales/Receivables	33 11.0	31 11.7
	10 37.6	42 8.8	59 6.1	72 5.1				57 6.4	52 7.0
	35 10.5	62 5.9	82 4.4	89 4.1				80 4.6	74 4.9
	0 UND	1 336.8	0 UND	1 278.4			Cost of Sales/Inventory	0 999.8	0 UND
	0 774.9	10 38.2	4 92.0	8 45.0				6 57.6	5 72.6
	14 25.6	22 16.3	13 28.8	24 15.1				19 18.9	16 23.2
	0 UND	12 30.0	17 21.9	20 18.2			Cost of Sales/Payables	16 22.2	13 27.1
	12 30.1	25 14.9	28 13.1	31 11.9				31 11.7	25 14.8
	34 10.6	40 9.2	45 8.2	47 7.7				51 7.2	42 8.7
	12.7	6.7	5.1	5.6			Sales/Working Capital	7.2	7.1
	75.5	14.2	8.5	10.2				11.9	12.8
	-22.5	98.5	15.6	16.0				31.1	39.3
	17.6	19.9	28.7	25.4			EBIT/Interest	18.5	21.7
	(49) 1.2	(105) 3.4	(139) 4.6	(32) 4.9				(330) 6.0	(358) 5.0
	-8.8	-2.5	.0	1.8				2.0	1.8
		7.0	6.0	6.4			Net Profit + Depr., Dep., Amort./Cur. Mat. L/T/D	11.0	8.2
		(25) 2.3	(39) 2.7	(14) 2.5				(89) 3.6	(103) 3.2
		-.6	-.6	.1				1.4	1.3
	.2	.2	.2	.1			Fixed/Worth	.2	.2
	1.1	.4	.3	.3				.4	.4
	-2.4	1.6	.5	.6				.9	1.2
	1.0	.6	.5	1.0			Debt/Worth	.8	.8
	4.1	1.4	1.2	1.4				1.9	1.7
	-5.3	4.6	2.3	2.1				4.3	4.5
	125.5	56.0	37.8	36.7			% Profit Before Taxes/Tangible Net Worth	56.6	64.3
	(37) 34.2	(99) 12.6	(149) 12.4	12.8				(337) 25.3	(354) 24.5
	-25.6	-5.1	-.3	3.7				7.8	8.8
	39.3	24.0	16.1	17.5			% Profit Before Taxes/Total Assets	18.6	22.0
	5.4	4.8	5.2	3.9				9.0	9.3
	-21.9	-4.6	-.7	1.1				1.9	2.5
	52.0	46.4	39.5	35.2			Sales/Net Fixed Assets	46.0	48.1
	30.1	24.6	23.4	20.0				25.4	25.1
	12.7	14.9	12.9	10.3				15.1	14.3
	8.1	4.6	3.4	2.8			Sales/Total Assets	4.2	4.3
	5.1	3.4	2.7	2.2				3.1	3.1
	3.4	2.7	2.1	1.7				2.3	2.4
	.6	.7	.8	.7			% Depr., Dep., Amort./Sales	.7	.7
	(41) 1.4	(101) 1.4	(141) 1.4	(32) 1.1				(314) 1.2	(337) 1.2
	2.4	2.2	1.9	2.5				1.9	1.9
	3.4	2.1	2.0	.5			% Officers', Directors' Owners' Comp/Sales	2.3	2.0
	(39) 6.5	(67) 3.9	(78) 3.6	(10) 2.4				(188) 3.7	(201) 3.5
	10.1	7.0	5.1	5.6				6.0	6.5
	101262M	521987M	1873107M	1781451M	457248M	576673M	Net Sales ($)	4873217M	7253522M
	15570M	140203M	674155M	727689M	231498M	309944M	Total Assets ($)	1868893M	2058356M

M = $ thousand   MM = $ million
See Pages 9 through 22 for Explanation of Ratios and Data

Comparative Historical Data | Current Data Sorted by Sales

			Type of Statement						
30	34	28	Unqualified	1	1	1	5	11	9
140	141	142	Reviewed	2	17	27	46	42	8
33	46	37	Compiled	3	12	10	5	4	3
51	52	62	Tax Returns	13	19	8	12	8	2
90	116	102	Other	5	22	11	25	23	16
4/1/07-3/31/08	4/1/08-3/31/09	4/1/09-3/31/10			62 (4/1-9/30/09)			309 (10/1/09-3/31/10)	
ALL	ALL	ALL		0-1MM	1-3MM	3-5MM	5-10MM	10-25MM	25MM & OVER
344	389	371	NUMBER OF STATEMENTS	24	71	57	93	88	38
%	%	%	ASSETS	%	%	%	%	%	%
13.9	13.5	16.1	Cash & Equivalents	19.5	18.6	14.0	16.0	15.4	14.6
44.8	43.9	39.8	Trade Receivables (net)	20.2	30.3	42.5	42.5	46.2	44.6
7.0	7.0	7.6	Inventory	9.7	8.7	8.7	6.5	5.8	8.8
8.9	8.4	7.8	All Other Current	9.3	5.2	7.1	7.8	8.8	10.6
74.6	72.7	71.3	Total Current	58.7	62.7	72.3	72.9	76.2	78.6
16.1	17.8	18.2	Fixed Assets (net)	25.2	23.4	18.1	16.2	16.8	12.7
2.1	2.4	2.4	Intangibles (net)	4.2	3.8	1.0	2.2	1.2	4.2
7.2	7.1	8.0	All Other Non-Current	11.9	10.1	8.5	8.7	5.7	4.5
100.0	100.0	100.0	Total	100.0	100.0	100.0	100.0	100.0	100.0
			LIABILITIES						
9.8	10.1	11.3	Notes Payable-Short Term	17.3	13.2	13.1	10.9	9.1	7.3
3.1	4.1	3.8	Cur. Mat.-L.T.D.	12.7	5.5	3.1	2.6	2.7	1.7
19.4	19.5	18.8	Trade Payables	10.5	19.1	19.4	21.5	17.8	18.3
.5	.5	.4	Income Taxes Payable	.0	.6	.3	.6	.2	.3
15.6	16.7	14.0	All Other Current	9.4	14.5	10.3	12.6	16.1	20.0
48.3	50.9	48.2	Total Current	49.9	52.8	46.1	48.1	45.9	47.5
11.7	11.1	11.2	Long-Term Debt	25.3	21.4	9.1	7.8	7.2	4.4
.3	.3	.4	Deferred Taxes	.0	.6	.5	.4	.3	.4
4.7	5.3	3.5	All Other Non-Current	15.8	3.6	2.0	3.4	1.5	2.6
34.9	32.4	36.7	Net Worth	9.1	21.6	42.3	40.4	45.1	45.1
100.0	100.0	100.0	Total Liabilties & Net Worth	100.0	100.0	100.0	100.0	100.0	100.0
			INCOME DATA						
100.0	100.0	100.0	Net Sales	100.0	100.0	100.0	100.0	100.0	100.0
28.3	26.9	27.9	Gross Profit	40.2	35.0	28.5	24.8	24.2	22.4
23.5	22.9	25.8	Operating Expenses	39.4	35.1	26.5	22.3	21.0	18.4
4.8	4.0	2.1	Operating Profit	.7	-.2	2.0	2.6	3.2	4.0
.4	.4	.2	All Other Expenses (net)	.9	.3	.1	.2	.2	.1
4.4	3.6	1.9	Profit Before Taxes	-.2	-.5	1.9	2.4	3.0	3.9
			RATIOS						
2.4	2.2	2.7		3.5	3.2	3.2	2.5	2.6	1.9
1.6	1.5	1.6	Current	1.5	1.6	1.7	1.6	1.6	1.6
1.2	1.1	1.2		.7	.8	1.1	1.2	1.4	1.3
1.9	1.8	1.9		1.8	2.3	2.3	2.1	2.1	1.6
1.3	1.2	1.3	Quick	1.0	1.3	1.2	1.4	1.3	1.2
.9	.8	.8		.3	.6	.9	.9	1.0	.9

										Sales/Receivables											

						Sales/Receivables						
31	11.7	30	12.2	25	14.6		0	UND	12	29.7	26	14.3	29	12.7	39	9.4	44	8.3
52	7.1	51	7.1	49	7.4	Sales/Receivables	12	30.6	34	10.6	46	7.9	53	6.8	59	6.2	61	6.0
73	5.0	73	5.0	71	5.1		45	8.1	56	6.6	70	5.2	71	5.1	81	4.5	77	4.7
0	UND	0	UND	0	UND		0	UND	0	UND	2	178.6	0	UND	0	UND	1	413.3
5	81.0	4	82.2	5	67.9	Cost of Sales/Inventory	0	UND	0	64.6	9	39.7	4	94.6	6	63.5	8	45.6
14	25.7	14	26.0	17	22.0		37	9.9	32	11.6	20	18.7	13	28.1	12	29.2	20	18.1
13	28.7	14	27.0	14	26.6		0	UND	9	42.6	12	30.0	14	26.6	17	21.8	20	18.1
25	14.6	26	14.2	26	14.1	Cost of Sales/Payables	8	43.2	28	12.9	23	16.2	28	13.2	27	13.8	29	12.6
40	9.1	40	9.1	42	8.8		35	10.3	50	7.2	35	10.3	44	8.4	42	8.7	44	8.3
	6.9		7.3		6.0			6.6		6.4		5.8		6.2		5.4		6.2
	12.2		12.9		11.9	Sales/Working Capital		20.5		26.6		16.2		11.9		9.9		11.8
	30.7		42.1		48.2			-50.8		-24.1		52.7		32.5		16.7		17.3
	28.8		22.6		21.4			12.1		6.7		21.1		20.3		33.7		27.1
(317)	7.0	(354)	7.0	(330)	3.7	EBIT/Interest	(21)	-2.2	(63)	.9	(50)	3.0	(79)	7.0	(82)	6.2	(35)	10.0
	2.2		2.1		-1.3			-13.0		-10.0		-1.3		1.2		1.1		1.8
	6.7		8.4		6.3	Net Profit + Depr., Dep.,						8.8		5.9		8.4		10.6
(75)	3.0	(77)	3.2	(85)	2.3	Amort./Cur. Mat. L/T/D			(14)	1.2	(20)	2.6	(26)	2.5	(15)	3.7
	1.7		1.4		-.4					-.6		.5		-.8		1.5
	.2		.2		.2			.1		.2		.1		.2		.2		.1
	.4		.4		.4	Fixed/Worth		.6		.7		.4		.4		.3		.3
	1.0		1.1		.9			-1.8		-6.1		1.4		.7		.6		.6
	.8		.7		.6			.5		.5		.4		.6		.7		.8
	1.6		1.6		1.4	Debt/Worth		3.6		2.2		1.1		1.3		1.3		1.6
	4.0		3.8		3.4			-3.5		-12.7		3.8		3.3		2.1		2.2
	58.3		50.2		48.6	% Profit Before Taxes/Tangible		55.6		56.0		45.3		51.3		38.4		63.8
(307)	30.4	(337)	21.3	(324)	13.6	Net Worth	(15)	.0	(51)	4.7	(51)	8.4	(83)	18.1	(86)	14.9		23.4
	9.3		6.3		-.5			-63.8		-15.4		-2.0		1.3		2.2		4.3
	24.0		21.0		19.8	% Profit Before Taxes/Total		26.1		14.6		15.9		22.4		18.5		27.7
	10.7		7.9		4.5	Assets		-5.5		1.3		3.2		7.1		5.8		8.2
	2.6		1.8		-2.3			-30.0		-14.3		-2.7		.0		.6		1.1
	53.6		56.8		45.5			48.6		31.4		51.4		47.7		49.4		44.1
	27.7		26.1		23.9	Sales/Net Fixed Assets		24.4		21.2		25.7		24.8		24.0		26.9
	15.1		14.6		12.9			9.7		11.1		12.7		14.1		13.7		16.4
	4.2		4.1		4.2			5.0		4.9		5.3		4.1		3.8		3.5
	3.2		3.2		3.0	Sales/Total Assets		3.1		3.0		3.4		3.0		2.9		2.6
	2.4		2.4		2.3			2.5		2.2		2.5		2.3		2.3		2.0
	.6		.6		.7			1.0		.8		.7		.6		.7		.6
(281)	1.1	(326)	1.1	(319)	1.4	% Depr., Dep., Amort./Sales	(17)	1.6	(57)	1.6	(48)	1.4	(80)	1.4	(83)	1.2	(34)	1.0
	1.7		1.7		2.0			2.6		2.8		2.3		1.9		1.9		1.8
	2.0		2.0		2.2	% Officers', Directors'		5.2		2.8		2.4		2.1		1.6		.9
(173)	3.3	(190)	3.3	(194)	4.0	Owners' Comp/Sales	(15)	10.1	(44)	4.9	(35)	4.0	(48)	3.7	(42)	3.3	(10)	2.6
	6.9		6.0		7.0			14.7		9.7		6.5		5.4		5.1		3.8
4524187M		5839019M		5311728M		Net Sales ($)	14894M		147825M		231415M		657522M		1358436M		2901636M
1686472M		2250632M		2099059M		Total Assets ($)	5732M		57139M		81872M		228268M		509266M		1216782M

© RMA 2010

M = $ thousand   MM = $ million
See Pages 9 through 22 for Explanation of Ratios and Data

Current Data Sorted by Assets — **Comparative Historical Data**

Type of Statement	0-500M	500M-2MM	2-10MM	10-50MM	50-100MM	100-250MM		4/1/05-3/31/06 ALL	4/1/06-3/31/07 ALL
Unqualified		1	3	4		1		3	6
Reviewed		5	11	5				13	6
Compiled	3	4	5					13	5
Tax Returns	13	6		1				23	7
Other	4	12	5	2				17	9
		15 (4/1-9/30/09)		70 (10/1/09-3/31/10)					
NUMBER OF STATEMENTS	20	28	24	12		1		69	33

ASSETS	0-500M %	500M-2MM %	2-10MM %	10-50MM %	50-100MM %	100-250MM %		ALL %	ALL %
Cash & Equivalents	11.5	12.3	11.8	23.0				9.5	9.8
Trade Receivables (net)	24.3	36.0	41.0	35.1				41.9	37.2
Inventory	2.5	3.2	7.3	4.4				8.5	10.1
All Other Current	4.5	11.2	7.0	5.4				6.5	3.5
Total Current	42.8	62.7	67.2	67.9				66.4	60.5
Fixed Assets (net)	50.9	23.1	21.5	23.5				21.1	24.7
Intangibles (net)	2.9	3.0	.9	.5				4.9	5.4
All Other Non-Current	3.4	11.2	10.5	8.1				7.6	9.4
Total	100.0	100.0	100.0	100.0				100.0	100.0
LIABILITIES									
Notes Payable-Short Term	13.3	11.0	13.4	10.4				14.9	8.4
Cur. Mat.-L.T.D.	12.0	7.7	3.6	2.2				4.4	2.9
Trade Payables	13.2	14.1	18.4	21.2				17.7	17.0
Income Taxes Payable	.0	.2	.1	.2				.7	.7
All Other Current	6.6	17.5	15.4	23.8				13.6	14.9
Total Current	45.2	50.5	50.8	57.9				51.5	43.9
Long-Term Debt	47.9	18.7	10.6	6.3				16.9	20.0
Deferred Taxes	.8	.1	.8	.0				.2	.4
All Other Non-Current	17.2	14.8	3.8	21.7				5.3	6.5
Net Worth	-11.0	16.1	34.0	14.1				26.2	29.2
Total Liabilities & Net Worth	100.0	100.0	100.0	100.0				100.0	100.0
INCOME DATA									
Net Sales	100.0	100.0	100.0	100.0				100.0	100.0
Gross Profit	56.4	26.0	24.1	21.2				33.0	35.0
Operating Expenses	48.6	24.5	23.6	16.8				27.2	29.8
Operating Profit	7.8	1.5	.5	4.4				5.8	5.1
All Other Expenses (net)	1.4	.6	.0	.2				.5	1.1
Profit Before Taxes	6.4	1.0	.5	4.2				5.3	4.0

(Columns 50-100MM and 100-250MM: DATA NOT AVAILABLE)

RATIOS	0-500M	500M-2MM	2-10MM	10-50MM	50-100MM	100-250MM		ALL	ALL
Current	2.3	2.1	2.0	2.5				2.3	2.3
	1.0	1.5	1.3	2.0				1.4	1.6
	.7	.9	1.0	1.3				1.0	1.1
Quick	1.8	2.0	1.6	2.0				1.9	2.0
	.9	1.0	1.1	1.7				(68) 1.1	1.2
	.5	.4	.6	1.2				.7	.7
Sales/Receivables	0 UND	22 16.6	27 13.4	38 9.7				28 13.1	22 16.8
	16 22.7	37 9.9	63 5.8	61 6.0				55 6.6	39 9.5
	46 7.9	54 6.7	90 4.0	80 4.6				72 5.1	76 4.8
Cost of Sales/Inventory	0 UND	0 UND	0 UND	0 UND				0 UND	0 UND
	0 UND	0 UND	3 126.6	1 684.6				0 UND	3 126.0
	6 62.6	9 38.9	28 13.0	10 35.3				17 21.5	17 21.1
Cost of Sales/Payables	0 UND	5 72.7	13 27.6	6 58.4				10 37.5	9 40.9
	8 43.2	15 25.0	26 13.9	24 15.0				28 12.8	24 15.3
	31 11.9	25 14.5	54 6.7	78 4.7				48 7.6	39 9.3
Sales/Working Capital	8.4	7.1	5.4	4.6				9.2	8.1
	-829.9	22.5	17.9	7.0				19.0	12.0
	-20.2	-30.9	183.6	12.9				NM	44.7
EBIT/Interest	7.5	13.0	5.5					23.2	14.6
	(19) 2.3	(25) 1.9	(21) 2.1					(58) 5.3	(28) 3.9
	-2.2	-1.0	-1.4					2.4	1.4
Net Profit + Depr., Dep., Amort./Cur. Mat. L/T/D			5.7					5.7	
			(10) 1.4					(11) 2.7	
			1.0					1.3	
Fixed/Worth	3.1	.2	.2	.1				.2	.3
	NM	.8	.6	.4				.7	.8
	-1.0	-3.0	1.3	.7				4.6	2.7
Debt/Worth	3.3	1.0	1.2	.3				1.2	1.0
	NM	3.0	2.1	1.0				3.4	2.7
	-2.9	-7.7	3.7	2.9				32.2	9.0
% Profit Before Taxes/Tangible Net Worth	107.2	56.1	22.2	42.3				99.9	74.4
	(10) 42.5	(19) 32.4	6.8	(11) 10.6				(54) 44.0	(28) 38.7
	-19.4	-1.1	-26.3	1.8				11.4	17.5
% Profit Before Taxes/Total Assets	41.0	17.5	9.6	15.6				27.3	24.4
	8.0	7.7	2.3	6.3				10.5	9.8
	-14.4	-8.6	-7.8	2.2				4.6	.7
Sales/Net Fixed Assets	18.3	29.4	29.0	27.8				55.5	35.9
	11.2	19.0	14.9	11.2				18.0	13.3
	4.6	7.4	7.1	6.6				9.7	7.0
Sales/Total Assets	5.6	4.9	3.2	3.2				4.3	4.4
	3.7	2.9	2.6	2.4				3.2	2.8
	2.7	1.9	2.0	1.7				2.3	2.2
% Depr., Dep., Amort./Sales	.9	.9	.7	.4				.8	1.1
	(15) 2.4	(23) 2.8	(19) 2.3	(10) 1.8				(53) 1.5	(25) 2.2
	5.6	4.5	3.4	3.5				3.4	3.8
% Officers', Directors' Owners' Comp/Sales	4.2							2.0	2.7
	(14) 7.6							(35) 4.3	(17) 4.9
	13.2							6.2	8.4
Net Sales ($)	18718M	96583M	284726M	941276M		176925M		716938M	634528M
Total Assets ($)	5036M	27578M	110051M	281683M		113229M		237823M	211349M

M = $ thousand   MM = $ million
See Pages 9 through 22 for Explanation of Ratios and Data

Comparative Historical Data | Current Data Sorted by Sales

Type of Statement

	4/1/07-3/31/08 ALL	4/1/08-3/31/09 ALL	4/1/09-3/31/10 ALL	Type of Statement	0-1MM	1-3MM	3-5MM	5-10MM	10-25MM	25MM & OVER
	6	10	9	Unqualified		1	1		1	6
	11	14	21	Reviewed	1	1	4	5	5	5
	8	12	12	Compiled			6	4	2	
	15	23	20	Tax Returns	9	9	1			1
	13	14	23	Other	3	5	1	10	3	1
						15 (4/1-9/30/09)			70 (10/1/09-3/31/10)	
NUMBER OF STATEMENTS	53	73	85		13	22	7	19	11	13

ASSETS (%)

Account	4/1/07-3/31/08	4/1/08-3/31/09	4/1/09-3/31/10	0-1MM	1-3MM	3-5MM	5-10MM	10-25MM	25MM & OVER
Cash & Equivalents	11.3	15.0	13.6	13.7	8.9		13.9	12.9	18.8
Trade Receivables (net)	39.0	37.7	34.4	16.1	30.9		46.1	31.8	44.8
Inventory	8.9	7.0	4.3	3.2	2.2		7.6	4.9	3.2
All Other Current	4.3	7.6	7.6	4.2	9.7		7.6	6.8	5.1
Total Current	63.5	67.4	59.9	37.2	51.7		75.1	56.3	72.0
Fixed Assets (net)	24.0	22.9	29.2	50.4	35.9		16.5	29.8	20.9
Intangibles (net)	3.6	3.5	2.0	4.4	2.1		1.1	.0	.5
All Other Non-Current	8.8	6.2	8.9	8.0	10.4		7.2	13.9	6.6
Total	100.0	100.0	100.0	100.0	100.0		100.0	100.0	100.0

LIABILITIES

Account	4/1/07-3/31/08	4/1/08-3/31/09	4/1/09-3/31/10	0-1MM	1-3MM	3-5MM	5-10MM	10-25MM	25MM & OVER
Notes Payable-Short Term	7.3	9.6	12.0	12.9	13.9		12.0	9.7	10.6
Cur. Mat.-L.T.D.	4.3	8.0	6.7	12.5	8.4		6.4	4.1	2.1
Trade Payables	15.2	18.3	16.0	9.0	12.3		18.1	17.9	26.9
Income Taxes Payable	.7	.5	.1	.0	.3		.0	.1	.2
All Other Current	18.8	12.9	15.1	8.4	11.1		17.8	15.4	26.2
Total Current	46.4	49.2	50.0	42.7	45.9		54.4	47.2	65.9
Long-Term Debt	17.8	17.5	21.4	47.5	32.3		11.8	11.7	6.6
Deferred Taxes	.2	.3	.5	.0	.7		.0	1.7	.3
All Other Non-Current	5.9	8.1	13.0	14.7	16.7		4.3	.9	19.8
Net Worth	29.8	24.9	15.1	-4.9	4.4		29.5	38.5	7.4
Total Liabilities & Net Worth	100.0	100.0	100.0	100.0	100.0		100.0	100.0	100.0

INCOME DATA

Account	4/1/07-3/31/08	4/1/08-3/31/09	4/1/09-3/31/10	0-1MM	1-3MM	3-5MM	5-10MM	10-25MM	25MM & OVER
Net Sales	100.0	100.0	100.0	100.0	100.0		100.0	100.0	100.0
Gross Profit	35.4	31.9	31.8	61.5	34.3		24.2	21.7	20.6
Operating Expenses	30.2	27.7	28.6	52.4	33.3		21.0	23.4	15.3
Operating Profit	5.2	4.2	3.2	9.1	1.0		3.2	-1.8	5.3
All Other Expenses (net)	.4	.3	.6	1.4	.9		.2	.7	.9
Profit Before Taxes	4.8	3.9	2.6	7.8	.2		3.0	-2.5	4.4

RATIOS

Ratio	4/1/07-3/31/08	4/1/08-3/31/09	4/1/09-3/31/10	0-1MM	1-3MM	3-5MM	5-10MM	10-25MM	25MM & OVER
Current	2.3	2.1	2.1	2.5	2.0		2.1	1.6	2.4
	1.3	1.4	1.4	1.0	.9		1.6	1.3	1.8
	1.0	1.0	.9	.6	.7		1.0	1.0	1.2
Quick	1.6	1.7	2.0	2.2	1.8		2.0	1.4	2.0
	1.1	1.2	1.1	.7	.8		1.4	1.1	1.6
	.7	.7	.6	.4	.4		.6	.6	1.1
Sales/Receivables	28 13.1	23 16.0	17 21.8	0 UND	14 26.7		18 20.7	26 13.9	53 6.9
	51 7.2	44 8.3	46 7.9	7 50.8	37 9.9		41 8.9	46 7.9	62 5.9
	80 4.5	72 5.1	67 5.5	59 6.2	53 6.8		70 5.2	72 5.1	81 4.5
Cost of Sales/Inventory	0 UND	0 UND	0 UND	0 UND	0 UND		0 UND	0 UND	0 UND
	1 461.0	0 UND	1 435.0	0 UND	0 UND		3 134.6	1 386.0	0 999.8
	28 13.2	13 27.6	10 35.6	9 42.3	6 59.0		38 9.6	26 14.1	4 95.6
Cost of Sales/Payables	10 36.7	8 47.6	5 70.6	0 UND	3 136.2		5 73.9	17 21.1	8 43.0
	26 14.1	19 18.8	19 18.8	8 45.5	10 35.0		19 18.8	30 12.2	28 12.9
	52 7.1	48 7.6	41 8.8	21 17.7	26 14.3		42 8.7	50 7.4	77 4.8
Sales/Working Capital	5.9	7.4	5.8	5.2	9.6		5.3	6.1	5.9
	18.9	18.5	20.8	UND	-242.5		12.9	20.8	9.3
	121.0	173.8	-90.9	-22.7	-15.0		-151.0	200.1	35.8
EBIT/Interest	39.7	11.5	11.1	7.8	6.7		40.6	5.5	41.7
	(47) 7.0	(63) 5.9	(75) 2.7	(11) 2.0	(21) 2.2		(15) 2.1	1.8	(11) 19.2
	1.5	1.6	-.9	-2.2	-4.6		-.4	-9.8	5.5
Net Profit + Depr., Dep., Amort./Cur. Mat. L/T/D	5.5	6.4	7.2						
	(11) 1.9	(17) 3.8	(18) 3.1						
	1.8	1.7	1.1						
Fixed/Worth	.3	.2	.3	2.4	.6		.1	.3	.2
	.9	.6	.8	63.5	5.0		.4	.7	.3
	6.0	1.6	25.3	-1.1	-1.5		1.4	1.4	.6
Debt/Worth	1.1	1.0	1.1	7.5	1.6		.7	1.1	.6
	2.3	2.2	2.6	112.0	14.9		1.5	1.3	1.5
	10.0	10.1	78.0	-2.9	-5.1		8.9	2.6	3.6
% Profit Before Taxes/Tangible Net Worth	72.4	79.8	48.1		90.2		50.6	11.2	58.7
	(44) 41.6	(61) 30.5	(65) 12.1		(14) 9.7		(16) 18.5	4.6	(12) 17.6
	20.9	5.7	.3		-13.0		2.4	-82.0	5.6
% Profit Before Taxes/Total Assets	26.0	20.7	15.9	37.2	12.3		19.5	3.7	15.6
	14.1	9.4	3.7	3.4	3.0		7.3	2.1	7.3
	1.6	1.3	-3.0	-19.2	-9.6		-3.0	-12.3	3.1
Sales/Net Fixed Assets	48.3	38.6	27.0	23.1	17.5		48.3	16.4	83.1
	13.9	20.3	12.8	10.2	11.6		24.1	8.7	12.7
	8.5	9.2	6.6	3.1	4.8		12.7	5.2	8.5
Sales/Total Assets	3.7	4.7	4.0	5.6	4.0		6.2	3.0	3.7
	2.8	3.1	2.8	2.9	3.1		2.8	2.7	2.8
	1.9	2.1	1.9	1.1	1.9		2.3	1.6	1.8
% Depr., Dep., Amort./Sales	.8	.7	.9	.9	2.4		.6		.2
	(45) 1.9	(56) 1.9	(67) 2.4	(10) 2.0	(19) 4.0		(12) .9		(11) 1.6
	3.3	3.1	4.0	5.4	5.6		3.0		3.1
% Officers', Directors' Owners' Comp/Sales	1.9	2.0	2.2		3.3				
	(23) 4.5	(40) 3.3	(36) 5.7		(10) 7.2				
	11.9	6.3	9.6		10.3				
Net Sales ($)	1050839M	1352128M	1518228M	6793M	37779M	26393M	136280M	162606M	1148377M
Total Assets ($)	626142M	637650M	537577M	3284M	13321M	12593M	55421M	81512M	371446M

© RMA 2010

M = $ thousand   MM = $ million
See Pages 9 through 22 for Explanation of Ratios and Data

	Current Data Sorted by Assets							Comparative Historical Data	

Type of Statement

Type of Statement	0-500M	500M-2MM	2-10MM	10-50MM	50-100MM	100-250MM	4/1/05-3/31/06 ALL	4/1/06-3/31/07 ALL
Unqualified	2	7	66	92	21	6	170	194
Reviewed	10	143	264	50			383	451
Compiled	32	58	22	3			85	133
Tax Returns	100	87	19	1	2	1	120	186
Other	48	112	113	63	13	3	276	299
	270 (4/1-9/30/09)			1,068 (10/1/09-3/31/10)			1034	1263
NUMBER OF STATEMENTS	192	407	484	209	36	10	1034	1263

ASSETS

ASSETS	0-500M %	500M-2MM %	2-10MM %	10-50MM %	50-100MM %	100-250MM %	ALL %	ALL %
Cash & Equivalents	20.9	15.5	18.5	20.4	15.6	24.0	12.0	12.4
Trade Receivables (net)	28.6	44.8	48.4	48.2	40.8	43.1	51.0	51.2
Inventory	9.8	8.0	3.9	2.8	4.3	2.4	5.7	5.6
All Other Current	5.4	6.3	9.4	9.5	7.1	10.0	9.2	8.6
Total Current	64.8	74.6	80.2	80.8	67.9	79.6	77.8	77.9
Fixed Assets (net)	25.0	16.5	13.8	12.9	14.3	8.4	15.3	15.1
Intangibles (net)	3.5	2.2	1.5	1.6	11.2	8.8	1.5	1.6
All Other Non-Current	6.7	6.7	4.5	4.6	6.7	3.2	5.4	5.4
Total	100.0	100.0	100.0	100.0	100.0	100.0	100.0	100.0

LIABILITIES

LIABILITIES	0-500M	500M-2MM	2-10MM	10-50MM	50-100MM	100-250MM	ALL	ALL
Notes Payable-Short Term	26.8	11.8	6.5	4.3	2.4	.7	12.2	11.7
Cur. Mat.-L.T.D.	9.1	3.0	2.3	2.3	3.1	2.7	2.9	3.1
Trade Payables	16.0	17.9	17.3	15.3	12.9	15.6	20.1	19.7
Income Taxes Payable	.1	.6	.7	.5	.3	.7	.7	.8
All Other Current	19.8	11.7	16.5	23.7	26.4	35.0	16.1	17.0
Total Current	71.8	44.9	43.3	46.1	45.2	54.7	51.9	52.4
Long-Term Debt	21.7	8.7	6.2	4.6	18.2	8.0	9.7	10.3
Deferred Taxes	.1	.5	.6	.5	.3	.5	.4	.4
All Other Non-Current	5.5	4.2	3.1	2.5	11.4	1.0	4.6	4.3
Net Worth	.9	41.8	46.8	46.3	25.0	35.9	33.3	32.6
Total Liabilities & Net Worth	100.0	100.0	100.0	100.0	100.0	100.0	100.0	100.0

INCOME DATA

INCOME DATA	0-500M	500M-2MM	2-10MM	10-50MM	50-100MM	100-250MM	ALL	ALL
Net Sales	100.0	100.0	100.0	100.0	100.0	100.0	100.0	100.0
Gross Profit	42.1	30.5	23.3	19.2	24.1	23.8	25.2	25.7
Operating Expenses	40.7	29.3	19.2	13.9	18.1	19.3	21.3	21.2
Operating Profit	1.4	1.3	4.1	5.2	6.0	4.4	3.9	4.5
All Other Expenses (net)	.5	.3	.4	.4	1.4	-.6	.4	.5
Profit Before Taxes	.8	.9	3.7	4.8	4.6	5.0	3.5	4.0

RATIOS

RATIOS	0-500M	500M-2MM	2-10MM	10-50MM	50-100MM	100-250MM	ALL	ALL
Current	3.2	3.1	3.0	2.3	2.1	2.0	2.3	2.3
	1.3	1.8	1.8	1.8	1.5	1.5	1.6	1.6
	.6	1.1	1.3	1.4	1.2	1.2	1.2	1.2
Quick	2.6	2.6	2.5	2.0	1.8	1.8	1.9	1.9
	1.0	1.4	1.6	1.5	1.3	1.2	1.3	1.3
	.4	.8	1.1	1.1	.9	1.1	.9	1.0
Sales/Receivables	0 UND	35 10.5	47 7.8	57 6.4	45 8.1	57 6.4	46 7.9	43 8.6
	22 16.5	52 7.1	65 5.6	73 5.0	68 5.4	70 5.2	66 5.5	64 5.7
	51 7.2	74 4.9	84 4.3	85 4.3	77 4.7	90 4.0	86 4.3	85 4.3
Cost of Sales/Inventory	0 UND	0 UND	0 UND	0 UND	0 UND	0 UND	0 UND	0 UND
	0 UND	4 101.7	1 275.6	1 446.1	1 587.1	0 UND	2 211.7	1 245.1
	21 17.5	19 18.8	7 50.6	4 84.4	16 23.1	4 97.2	12 30.8	10 35.8
Cost of Sales/Payables	0 UND	12 29.4	14 25.8	17 21.2	17 20.9	19 19.2	17 21.3	16 22.9
	10 35.3	24 15.1	25 14.6	25 14.6	26 14.1	29 12.8	29 12.4	28 13.1
	35 10.3	43 8.4	41 9.0	37 9.7	34 10.7	45 8.0	45 8.1	43 8.5
Sales/Working Capital	9.8	5.6	4.6	4.9	6.4	5.1	6.3	6.5
	44.8	11.3	7.9	7.3	10.5	7.5	10.6	11.1
	-14.5	36.0	14.9	11.3	20.7	21.6	23.0	25.0
EBIT/Interest	12.1	15.5	45.3	47.7	69.6		19.8	22.5
	(154) 2.0	(339) 2.8	(404) 8.1	(172) 13.7	(30) 11.5		(911) 6.1	(1136) 7.1
	-3.6	-2.6	1.3	3.9	.7		1.8	2.1
Net Profit + Depr., Dep., Amort./Cur. Mat. L/T/D		4.9	8.4	21.9	13.6		7.2	12.5
		(70) 1.7	(150) 2.8	(67) 5.0	(12) 10.2		(261) 3.0	(303) 4.4
		.3	.8	2.0	3.7		1.4	1.8
Fixed/Worth	.2	.1	.1	.1	.1	.1	.1	.1
	.9	.3	.2	.2	.3	.2	.3	.3
	-.8	.9	.5	.4	-1.1	.3	.8	.8
Debt/Worth	.7	.5	.6	.7	1.0	1.1	.8	.8
	4.2	1.2	1.2	1.2	2.1	1.6	1.7	1.8
	-4.4	4.3	2.4	2.0	7.8	4.4	3.7	3.6
% Profit Before Taxes/Tangible Net Worth	94.6	44.5	37.6	37.7	58.6		43.0	53.3
	(122) 21.0	(364) 9.7	(466) 15.3	(207) 23.4	(29) 31.8		(932) 19.4	(1122) 26.3
	-10.9	-9.7	3.5	8.2	21.3		5.5	8.6
% Profit Before Taxes/Total Assets	32.5	15.9	17.4	18.0	17.6	17.4	16.9	20.3
	4.5	3.0	5.8	8.2	11.0	8.6	7.1	9.3
	-13.8	-7.4	1.1	3.5	3.3	1.0	1.7	2.4
Sales/Net Fixed Assets	98.8	60.7	60.6	62.2	54.6	100.5	58.3	64.7
	29.9	25.3	30.1	32.6	31.2	27.4	29.0	31.7
	14.8	12.2	14.6	14.6	10.3	22.2	14.9	16.3
Sales/Total Assets	8.1	4.1	3.4	3.1	3.2	2.6	3.6	3.8
	4.4	3.1	2.7	2.5	2.3	2.3	2.9	3.0
	3.0	2.4	2.1	1.9	1.7	1.8	2.3	2.4
% Depr., Dep., Amort./Sales	.9	.6	.6	.5	.5		.5	.5
	(117) 1.5	(319) 1.3	(426) .9	(187) .8	(30) .7		(894) 1.0	(1066) .9
	2.5	2.2	1.6	1.5	1.5		1.7	1.6
% Officers', Directors' Owners' Comp/Sales	5.0	2.9	1.8	.7			1.9	1.9
	(118) 8.1	(243) 5.0	(207) 3.3	(53) 1.4			(486) 3.4	(644) 3.6
	12.6	7.8	5.6	3.1			6.5	6.8
Net Sales ($)	233376M	1533126M	6354788M	10781634M	6500929M	3853345M	25525914M	31577882M
Total Assets ($)	45877M	468223M	2284531M	4376179M	2488472M	1649995M	7630230M	9614893M

M = $ thousand   MM = $ million
See Pages 9 through 22 for Explanation of Ratios and Data

Comparative Historical Data / Current Data Sorted by Sales

Hist 1	Hist 2	Hist 3	Type of Statement	0-1MM	1-3MM	3-5MM	5-10MM	10-25MM	25MM & OVER
166	193	194	Unqualified	1	2	8	21	43	119
391	462	467	Reviewed	9	48	75	128	152	55
105	109	115	Compiled	17	44	23	19	8	4
175	191	210	Tax Returns	55	76	37	26	12	4
283	337	352	Other	28	84	42	51	63	84
4/1/07-3/31/08 ALL	4/1/08-3/31/09 ALL	4/1/09-3/31/10 ALL		270 (4/1-9/30/09)			1,068 (10/1/09-3/31/10)		
1120	1292	1338	NUMBER OF STATEMENTS	110	254	185	245	278	266
%	%	%	ASSETS	%	%	%	%	%	%
13.9	15.3	18.2	Cash & Equivalents	17.2	17.3	18.5	17.0	20.1	18.3
50.9	49.2	44.2	Trade Receivables (net)	25.5	37.1	43.3	48.7	49.0	50.1
5.4	5.4	5.8	Inventory	10.6	8.5	8.5	5.0	3.2	2.8
8.1	7.8	7.8	All Other Current	6.2	6.3	6.0	8.0	9.8	9.1
78.4	77.7	76.1	Total Current	59.6	69.3	76.3	78.7	82.1	80.4
14.8	15.1	16.1	Fixed Assets (net)	27.7	19.8	16.4	15.1	12.8	11.7
1.6	1.9	2.3	Intangibles (net)	4.3	3.6	1.8	1.4	1.0	3.0
5.1	5.3	5.5	All Other Non-Current	8.3	7.4	5.4	4.9	4.1	4.9
100.0	100.0	100.0	Total	100.0	100.0	100.0	100.0	100.0	100.0
			LIABILITIES						
10.6	10.2	10.5	Notes Payable-Short Term	23.5	19.2	9.1	9.1	5.7	4.2
3.0	3.3	3.5	Cur. Mat.-L.T.D.	9.7	3.6	4.6	2.7	2.1	2.3
19.1	18.0	16.9	Trade Payables	13.5	16.2	18.0	17.4	18.1	16.2
.7	.6	.5	Income Taxes Payable	.2	.4	.6	.8	.6	.5
17.7	18.0	17.0	All Other Current	17.6	13.9	12.2	13.9	18.6	24.3
51.1	50.1	48.5	Total Current	64.4	53.3	44.6	44.0	45.1	47.5
10.1	9.7	9.3	Long-Term Debt	21.4	14.6	8.2	6.6	5.5	6.4
.4	.4	.5	Deferred Taxes	.1	.3	.6	.7	.3	.5
3.9	3.7	3.9	All Other Non-Current	7.1	3.6	4.4	4.0	2.2	3.9
34.5	36.1	37.9	Net Worth	6.9	28.1	42.2	44.6	46.9	41.7
100.0	100.0	100.0	Total Liabilities & Net Worth	100.0	100.0	100.0	100.0	100.0	100.0
			INCOME DATA						
100.0	100.0	100.0	Net Sales	100.0	100.0	100.0	100.0	100.0	100.0
26.7	26.6	27.6	Gross Profit	46.8	34.3	30.9	25.2	21.5	19.6
21.8	22.2	24.5	Operating Expenses	44.5	33.8	27.6	22.9	16.9	14.7
4.9	4.3	3.1	Operating Profit	2.3	.5	3.3	2.3	4.6	4.9
.4	.5	.4	All Other Expenses (net)	1.8	.4	.4	.2	.1	.4
4.5	3.8	2.7	Profit Before Taxes	.5	.1	3.0	2.1	4.5	4.4
			RATIOS						
2.3	2.4	2.9	Current	3.8	3.1	3.4	3.1	2.9	2.2
1.6	1.6	1.7		1.2	1.7	1.8	1.8	1.8	1.7
1.2	1.2	1.2		.6	1.0	1.1	1.3	1.3	1.4
2.0	2.0	2.4	Quick	2.6	2.6	2.8	2.7	2.4	1.9
1.3 (1291)	1.4	1.4		.8	1.3	1.4	1.6	1.5	1.4
1.0	1.0	1.0		.3	.7	.9	1.0	1.1	1.1
44 8.4	41 8.8	37 9.8	Sales/Receivables	0 UND	21 17.3	33 10.9	41 8.8	45 8.1	52 7.0
64 5.7	61 6.0	59 6.2		26 14.1	46 8.0	53 6.9	59 6.2	64 5.7	68 5.3
82 4.4	81 4.5	79 4.6		62 5.9	74 4.9	73 5.0	81 4.5	81 4.5	82 4.4
0 UND	0 UND	0 UND	Cost of Sales/Inventory	0 UND	0 UND	0 UND	0 UND	0 UND	0 UND
2 229.7	2 322.8	2 248.9		0 UND	4 102.3	5 73.2	2 206.2	1 312.3	1 483.7
10 35.1	8 43.0	10 35.5		29 12.6	25 14.8	17 21.9	9 42.0	6 63.5	4 81.7
15 23.9	13 27.4	12 29.5	Cost of Sales/Payables	0 UND	4 87.4	13 28.0	13 29.1	15 24.6	17 22.1
27 13.5	24 15.0	24 15.5		14 25.2	23 16.1	24 15.4	24 14.9	25 14.5	24 15.3
41 8.9	40 9.1	40 9.2		43 8.5	42 8.6	47 7.7	39 9.4	40 9.2	36 10.2
6.4	6.5	5.4	Sales/Working Capital	6.1	5.6	5.1	4.8	5.3	5.4
10.7	10.6	9.5		44.2	12.3	9.5	8.7	8.5	8.8
21.8	22.1	24.3		-10.7	133.6	38.4	17.7	14.9	14.2
27.3	32.0	30.1	EBIT/Interest	9.7	13.8	19.7	25.8	50.6	57.7
(979) 8.1	(1123) 7.8	(1107) 6.1		(86) .9	(209) 1.8	(147) 5.2	(205) 4.5	(235) 9.8	(225) 13.8
2.5	2.0	.3		-3.8	-7.7	-.5	.1	2.6	4.0
13.2	11.4	8.5	Net Profit + Depr., Dep., Amort./Cur. Mat. L/T/D		4.8	5.1	5.9	10.5	22.0
(269) 4.6	(317) 4.2	(310) 2.8			(31) .9	(38) 2.1	(59) 1.7	(85) 3.2	(93) 5.2
1.9	1.4	.9			-2.5	.6	.1	1.8	2.2
.1	.1	.1	Fixed/Worth	.2	.1	.1	.1	.1	.1
.3	.3	.3		1.6	.5	.3	.3	.2	.2
.8	.7	.8		-.9	1.8	.9	.6	.5	.4
.9	.8	.6	Debt/Worth	.6	.5	.5	.5	.6	.9
1.7	1.6	1.3		5.3	1.6	1.1	1.3	1.1	1.4
3.7	3.7	3.4		-4.1	8.6	3.3	3.1	2.4	2.2
60.3	55.2	43.4	% Profit Before Taxes/Tangible Net Worth	63.7	44.4	55.5	33.2	45.8	45.5
(1005) 29.9	(1154) 26.0	(1197) 16.6		(68) 12.4	(208) 8.9	(166) 16.9	(229) 9.6	(271) 17.6	(255) 26.6
11.4	8.6	2.1		-16.8	-25.0	.8	-1.1	5.8	9.8
22.4	21.0	18.4	% Profit Before Taxes/Total Assets	23.5	18.8	17.3	15.0	19.1	18.8
10.4	9.5	5.6		1.2	2.2	5.4	3.8	7.5	9.3
3.5	2.1	-.7		-14.9	-14.0	-1.3	-.6	2.3	3.6
67.2	67.3	63.4	Sales/Net Fixed Assets	55.9	58.0	71.2	59.5	70.5	67.0
32.8	32.1	29.0		19.6	22.9	25.5	27.0	35.0	35.6
16.0	16.1	14.2		6.6	11.3	13.5	14.5	16.6	16.7
3.9	3.9	3.7	Sales/Total Assets	4.8	4.3	4.1	3.9	3.5	3.4
3.0	3.1	2.9		3.0	3.0	2.9	2.9	2.9	2.7
2.4	2.4	2.2		1.8	2.1	2.3	2.3	2.2	2.1
.5	.5	.5	% Depr., Dep., Amort./Sales	.9	.9	.5	.5	.5	.4
(920) .8	(1059) .9	(1087) 1.0		(72) 1.8	(172) 1.6	(153) 1.2	(207) 1.1	(245) .8	(238) .7
1.6	1.7	1.8		3.5	2.6	2.0	1.8	1.4	1.2
1.9	2.1	2.4	% Officers', Directors' Owners' Comp/Sales	6.5	4.4	2.7	2.2	1.4	.7
(548) 3.5	(629) 4.0	(631) 4.5		(61) 10.5	(158) 6.4	(107) 4.2	(120) 3.8	(126) 2.8	(59) 1.5
6.9	7.2	7.9		16.5	9.0	7.2	5.5	4.7	3.5
27003138M	30381016M	29257198M	Net Sales ($)	70662M	473567M	751798M	1733142M	4382955M	21845074M
9919711M	11552286M	11313277M	Total Assets ($)	37707M	185609M	272092M	672475M	1745599M	8399795M

Current Data Sorted by Assets | Comparative Historical Data

						Type of Statement		
1	1	46	53	13	7	Unqualified	133	148
8	97	256	46			Reviewed	340	375
28	60	29	4			Compiled	136	150
115	95	32	7		2	Tax Returns	169	225
58	107	105	67	7	6	Other	293	243
	239 (4/1-9/30/09)		1,011 (10/1/09-3/31/10)				4/1/05-3/31/06	4/1/06-3/31/07
0-500M	500M-2MM	2-10MM	10-50MM	50-100MM	100-250MM		ALL	ALL
210	360	468	177	20	15	NUMBER OF STATEMENTS	1071	1141
%	%	%	%	%	%	ASSETS	%	%
19.1	14.3	17.3	24.4	22.6	11.7	Cash & Equivalents	12.1	14.1
27.0	40.9	48.2	43.3	43.2	20.6	Trade Receivables (net)	48.5	46.6
10.0	9.6	5.3	4.2	4.4	7.4	Inventory	8.3	7.6
3.5	6.3	7.8	8.9	7.5	4.0	All Other Current	7.6	7.2
59.6	71.0	78.5	80.8	77.7	43.6	Total Current	76.4	75.4
28.4	19.1	14.4	10.8	15.1	10.9	Fixed Assets (net)	15.8	16.4
2.3	3.1	1.8	3.9	3.2	40.9	Intangibles (net)	2.1	2.7
9.7	6.8	5.3	4.4	3.9	4.6	All Other Non-Current	5.7	5.5
100.0	100.0	100.0	100.0	100.0	100.0	Total	100.0	100.0
						LIABILITIES		
21.9	10.4	7.1	3.9	5.4	15.8	Notes Payable-Short Term	11.2	8.9
7.4	3.1	2.1	2.5	2.0	1.4	Cur. Mat.-L.T.D.	3.1	2.8
19.1	20.0	20.8	18.4	17.4	12.6	Trade Payables	23.5	21.8
.4	.2	.7	.2	.3	.3	Income Taxes Payable	.7	.7
17.7	12.1	16.4	25.8	31.9	17.8	All Other Current	15.8	17.8
66.4	46.0	47.1	50.9	56.9	48.0	Total Current	54.3	52.0
27.2	13.3	7.0	6.3	8.8	35.1	Long-Term Debt	12.0	12.4
.0	.3	.4	.2	.1	1.2	Deferred Taxes	.4	.3
12.7	5.8	3.0	3.9	4.6	26.4	All Other Non-Current	4.8	3.6
-6.3	34.7	42.5	38.7	29.6	-10.7	Net Worth	28.5	31.8
100.0	100.0	100.0	100.0	100.0	100.0	Total Liabilties & Net Worth	100.0	100.0
						INCOME DATA		
100.0	100.0	100.0	100.0	100.0	100.0	Net Sales	100.0	100.0
42.2	32.6	23.3	21.4	20.0	34.4	Gross Profit	26.5	28.3
39.1	30.6	20.2	16.4	15.7	29.9	Operating Expenses	23.4	23.5
3.0	2.0	3.1	5.0	4.3	4.5	Operating Profit	3.2	4.8
.6	.5	.1	.2	.4	2.8	All Other Expenses (net)	.2	.4
2.4	1.5	3.0	4.8	3.9	1.7	Profit Before Taxes	2.9	4.4
						RATIOS		
2.4	2.8	2.4	2.2	1.7	1.4		2.1	2.1
1.1	1.7	1.6	1.6	1.3	1.3	Current	1.5	1.5
.6	1.1	1.3	1.3	1.1	.6		1.2	1.2
2.0	2.2	1.9	1.8	1.6	1.3		1.7	1.8
.8	1.3	1.3	1.4	1.2	.7	Quick	1.2 (1139)	1.2
.3	.8	1.0	1.1	.9	.2		.8	.9
0 UND	28 13.2	42 8.7	45 8.2	55 6.6	7 50.5		35 10.3	31 11.7
17 21.2	42 8.6	61 6.0	62 5.8	71 5.1	20 18.4	Sales/Receivables	57 6.3	56 6.5
42 8.6	64 5.7	80 4.5	84 4.3	79 4.6	55 6.7		80 4.6	79 4.6
0 UND	0 999.8	0 999.8	0 UND	0 957.5	0 UND		0 UND	0 UND
2 184.8	8 43.8	4 101.0	3 138.7	2 151.4	14 26.8	Cost of Sales/Inventory	4 84.0	4 93.7
18 20.2	25 14.6	14 27.0	10 35.4	7 53.7	16 23.4		16 22.8	15 24.3
0 UND	14 25.4	18 20.7	18 20.2	22 16.8	9 39.2		20 18.7	17 21.7
15 23.8	27 13.6	30 12.0	28 13.3	28 13.2	31 11.8	Cost of Sales/Payables	32 11.5	29 12.5
42 8.7	42 8.7	45 8.2	44 8.3	37 9.8	46 7.9		50 7.3	47 7.8
11.8	6.1	5.7	5.1	7.5	11.5		7.7	7.6
103.3	12.6	10.2	8.9	14.8	27.2	Sales/Working Capital	13.3	13.2
-22.0	56.8	19.1	14.2	28.7	-18.4		35.8	36.5
8.5	11.0	31.5	71.8	63.6	2.6		19.0	22.7
(161) 2.0	(307) 3.1	(407) 6.7	(149) 17.6	31.1	(13) 1.1	EBIT/Interest	(962) 6.2	(993) 7.7
-1.0	-.9	1.6	4.5	3.5	.3		1.8	2.4
	4.6	8.0	24.5				7.8	11.1
(57)	1.6 (133)	3.6 (54)	7.9			Net Profit + Depr., Dep., Amort./Cur. Mat. L/T/D	(256) 2.7 (245)	3.9
	-.6	1.4	2.8				1.3	1.8
.2	.2	.1	.1	.1	.6		.2	.1
1.9	.5	.3	.2	.4	-.1	Fixed/Worth	.4	.4
-.8	2.0	.6	.5	.8	-.1		1.1	1.1
1.1	.6	.8	.9	1.0	4.9		1.1	.9
7.9	1.5	1.5	1.6	2.5	-1.6	Debt/Worth	2.1	2.1
-3.6	8.5	2.8	2.9	3.4	-1.3		5.6	5.0
99.8	48.0	39.7	43.9	48.9			54.8	64.2
(117) 34.1	(289) 15.9	(454) 17.2	(165) 25.1	(18) 37.1		% Profit Before Taxes/Tangible Net Worth	(932) 26.0	(1005) 32.9
-4.7	.3	2.6	10.9	17.6			7.0	11.5
28.3	18.0	16.3	16.1	18.0	10.3		17.8	22.0
4.6	5.1	6.3	9.7	9.7	2.1	% Profit Before Taxes/Total Assets	7.5	9.9
-9.1	-3.3	1.0	3.8	2.6	-4.9		1.7	3.2
77.9	47.5	53.0	76.4	49.3	49.6		59.5	63.3
28.6	23.5	30.8	34.7	25.8	27.3	Sales/Net Fixed Assets	30.5	31.4
13.0	12.0	15.4	18.2	10.6	23.4		16.9	16.6
7.7	4.2	3.5	3.2	3.2	2.8		4.1	4.3
4.8	3.3	2.9	2.5	2.6	2.5	Sales/Total Assets	3.2	3.2
3.2	2.5	2.3	1.9	2.0	1.8		2.5	2.5
.7	.7	.5	.3	.4			.5	.5
(136) 1.6	(294) 1.3	(410) 1.0	(150) .6	(19) .7		% Depr., Dep., Amort./Sales	(906) 1.0	(950) .9
2.8	2.3	1.5	1.1	1.3			1.7	1.6
3.8	2.5	1.7	1.0				1.7	1.9
(136) 6.6	(215) 4.4	(231) 2.9	(55) 2.0			% Officers', Directors' Owners' Comp/Sales	(584) 3.6	(595) 4.0
12.0	7.6	5.7	3.4				6.1	6.5
289981M	1451550M	6408880M	9883751M	3874253M	7103385M	Net Sales ($)	29702232M	35204942M
51797M	410766M	2179951M	3449426M	1448579M	2367936M	Total Assets ($)	7361791M	9600015M

© RMA 2010

M = $ thousand   MM = $ million
See Pages 9 through 22 for Explanation of Ratios and Data

Comparative Historical Data / Current Data Sorted by Sales

			Type of Statement						
139	143	121	Unqualified	1			12	36	72
344	407	407	Reviewed	4	34	42	121	152	54
109	121	121	Compiled	11	38	30	27	10	5
235	277	251	Tax Returns	60	91	43	28	22	7
275	296	350	Other	31	69	41	68	62	79
4/1/07-3/31/08 ALL	4/1/08-3/31/09 ALL	4/1/09-3/31/10 ALL		239 (4/1-9/30/09)			1,011 (10/1/09-3/31/10)		
				0-1MM	1-3MM	3-5MM	5-10MM	10-25MM	25MM & OVER
1102	1244	1250	NUMBER OF STATEMENTS	107	232	156	256	282	217
%	%	%	ASSETS	%	%	%	%	%	%
14.6	15.6	17.7	Cash & Equivalents	18.6	17.0	14.0	17.3	18.7	20.1
45.5	44.7	41.4	Trade Receivables (net)	24.6	34.1	39.8	44.1	48.9	45.9
7.3	7.0	7.2	Inventory	9.3	10.4	9.0	7.1	5.0	4.4
6.8	6.9	6.7	All Other Current	3.7	4.5	5.7	8.1	7.2	9.2
74.2	74.2	73.1	Total Current	56.1	65.9	68.4	76.7	79.7	79.6
18.0	16.6	17.6	Fixed Assets (net)	29.7	23.4	21.8	15.7	12.3	11.4
2.2	2.7	3.0	Intangibles (net)	3.0	3.0	3.2	1.5	3.1	4.7
5.6	6.5	6.3	All Other Non-Current	11.2	7.6	6.6	6.1	5.0	4.4
100.0	100.0	100.0	Total	100.0	100.0	100.0	100.0	100.0	100.0
			LIABILITIES						
9.3	10.0	10.2	Notes Payable-Short Term	22.0	14.6	12.0	8.1	6.7	5.3
3.4	3.4	3.3	Cur. Mat.-L.T.D.	5.3	4.7	4.4	3.0	1.9	2.2
21.0	21.0	19.8	Trade Payables	17.7	17.4	20.0	20.0	21.9	20.3
.7	.6	.4	Income Taxes Payable	.8	.1	.4	.6	.6	.2
17.6	17.1	17.0	All Other Current	20.4	10.9	14.2	13.9	17.9	26.3
52.0	52.1	50.7	Total Current	66.2	47.7	51.0	45.7	49.0	54.3
14.0	12.7	12.5	Long-Term Debt	28.2	18.9	15.8	9.1	5.7	8.2
.3	.3	.3	Deferred Taxes	.0	.2	.3	.3	.4	.3
4.3	4.6	5.9	All Other Non-Current	11.8	10.3	5.1	2.1	4.4	5.1
29.3	30.3	30.7	Net Worth	-6.2	22.9	27.9	42.8	40.6	32.1
100.0	100.0	100.0	Total Liabilities & Net Worth	100.0	100.0	100.0	100.0	100.0	100.0
			INCOME DATA						
100.0	100.0	100.0	Net Sales	100.0	100.0	100.0	100.0	100.0	100.0
29.1	28.0	28.9	Gross Profit	49.4	35.4	30.3	26.6	22.9	21.7
24.8	24.1	25.9	Operating Expenses	45.2	34.0	27.9	24.2	18.9	17.3
4.3	3.9	3.1	Operating Profit	4.2	1.3	2.5	2.4	4.0	4.4
.4	.4	.4	All Other Expenses (net)	.9	.5	.3	.2	.3	.3
4.0	3.6	2.7	Profit Before Taxes	3.3	.8	2.2	2.2	3.7	4.1
			RATIOS						
2.1	2.2	2.4	Current	3.6	3.2	2.4	2.5	2.3	1.9
1.5	1.5	1.6		1.4	1.5	1.4	1.7	1.6	1.5
1.2	1.2	1.2		.6	.9	1.0	1.3	1.3	1.3
1.8	1.8	2.0	Quick	3.1	2.5	1.9	2.1	2.0	1.6
(1101) 1.2	1.2	1.3		1.0	1.2	1.1	1.4	1.3	1.3
.9	.9	.9		.3	.6	.7	1.0	1.0	1.0
30 12.0	30 12.1	30 12.1	Sales/Receivables	0 UND	17 21.2	26 14.1	33 10.9	41 8.8	42 8.7
54 6.8	53 6.9	50 7.3		22 16.6	37 9.8	45 8.1	51 7.2	59 6.1	60 6.1
77 4.7	76 4.8	72 5.1		48 7.6	57 6.4	76 4.8	73 5.0	77 4.7	77 4.7
0 UND	0 UND	0 UND	Cost of Sales/Inventory	0 UND	0 UND	0 UND	0 UND	0 UND	0 999.8
4 102.8	3 108.6	4 88.7		0 UND	8 45.0	7 53.1	5 69.2	3 109.4	2 149.1
16 22.7	14 25.5	16 22.8		33 11.0	25 14.6	24 15.3	17 20.9	12 30.2	10 35.8
16 22.6	14 25.3	15 25.1	Cost of Sales/Payables	0 UND	8 43.4	13 28.1	15 24.3	19 19.4	20 18.7
29 12.6	28 13.0	27 13.7		16 23.3	24 15.0	26 14.2	28 13.2	30 12.2	28 12.9
46 7.9	45 8.1	43 8.4		48 7.6	43 8.6	48 7.7	41 9.0	44 8.3	43 8.4
7.3	7.2	6.1	Sales/Working Capital	8.3	5.7	6.1	5.9	5.9	6.7
13.1	13.1	11.9		32.6	17.1	15.6	10.6	10.6	11.0
37.2	42.0	34.3		-12.3	-106.9	150.4	20.5	21.2	17.6
26.6	27.7	24.4	EBIT/Interest	7.1	8.6	9.4	21.8	44.3	63.3
(971) 7.7	(1102) 6.4	(1057) 5.3		(78) 1.3	(188) 2.0	(140) 3.1	(218) 4.8	(245) 8.9	(188) 15.9
2.1	1.6	.8		-1.1	-1.9	-.7	-1.1	2.1	4.0
8.6	9.6	10.6	Net Profit + Depr., Dep., Amort./Cur. Mat. L/T/D		5.2	4.7	6.0	7.6	22.7
(228) 4.3	(265) 3.5	(258) 3.7			(18) 1.2	(27) 1.1	(65) 2.3	(80) 3.7	(68) 9.8
2.1	1.2	1.0			.8	-.4	-.3	1.6	3.6
.2	.2	.1	Fixed/Worth	.2	.2	.2	.1	.1	.1
.4	.4	.4		1.2	.7	.8	.3	.3	.2
1.2	1.2	1.2		-.8	-9.3	18.8	.7	.6	.5
.9	.9	.8	Debt/Worth	.8	.6	.7	.6	.8	1.1
2.1	1.9	1.7		3.3	2.6	2.2	1.2	1.6	1.8
5.3	5.0	4.7		-3.8	-24.8	103.1	3.0	3.1	3.1
62.0	56.2	47.2	% Profit Before Taxes/Tangible Net Worth	73.9	41.8	66.0	38.9	46.2	50.1
(950) 30.2	(1069) 27.3	(1048) 19.0		(61) 34.1	(167) 15.7	(119) 16.6	(239) 13.2	(266) 20.7	(196) 27.4
12.0	7.5	2.7		-3.1	-5.2	1.5	-4.6	5.5	11.4
21.3	21.0	18.1	% Profit Before Taxes/Total Assets	27.6	17.6	19.8	18.2	16.1	17.7
9.7	8.7	6.4		2.2	4.1	5.5	5.0	7.2	9.6
3.0	1.6	.0		-9.1	-7.3	-2.2	-2.0	1.9	3.4
56.9	58.9	57.8	Sales/Net Fixed Assets	85.3	42.8	40.5	52.5	62.2	79.8
28.5	30.6	28.7		18.9	20.8	23.0	28.7	35.6	38.3
15.3	16.7	14.2		7.7	10.4	10.7	15.5	19.4	20.5
4.3	4.3	4.1	Sales/Total Assets	6.1	4.6	4.4	4.1	3.8	3.6
3.2	3.1	3.1		3.8	3.2	3.1	3.2	3.1	2.9
2.5	2.5	2.3		2.3	2.3	2.4	2.4	2.4	2.2
.4	.5	.5	% Depr., Dep., Amort./Sales	.9	.9	.8	.7	.4	.3
(905) 1.0	(1041) .9	(1016) 1.1		(64) 2.0	(173) 1.8	(135) 1.3	(218) 1.1	(241) .8	(185) .6
1.7	1.7	1.8		3.8	2.8	2.1	1.7	1.3	1.1
2.1	2.0	2.0	% Officers', Directors', Owners' Comp/Sales	4.9	3.1	2.5	1.9	1.4	1.0
(569) 4.1	(685) 3.8	(645) 3.9		(67) 9.9	(144) 5.6	(86) 3.9	(142) 3.5	(143) 2.7	(63) 2.2
7.2	6.7	7.4		15.6	8.3	6.4	6.3	5.8	3.5
30744019M	28993465M	29011800M	Net Sales ($)	61149M	452663M	602157M	1893661M	4643183M	21358987M
8777716M	10095051M	9908455M	Total Assets ($)	21153M	159003M	217072M	672773M	1701181M	7137273M

Current Data Sorted by Assets							Comparative Historical Data	

						Type of Statement		
	1	14	12		3	Unqualified	22	25
2	14	44	9			Reviewed	34	59
5	13	9				Compiled	28	31
23	14	8	1			Tax Returns	17	37
9	18	19	9		2	Other	45	47
	32 (4/1-9/30/09)		198 (10/1/09-3/31/10)				4/1/05-3/31/06 ALL	4/1/06-3/31/07 ALL
0-500M	500M-2MM	2-10MM	10-50MM	50-100MM	100-250MM			
39	60	94	31	1	5	NUMBER OF STATEMENTS	146	199
%	%	%	%	%	%	ASSETS	%	%
15.1	11.6	15.0	17.2			Cash & Equivalents	12.2	12.9
30.4	41.2	38.0	34.0			Trade Receivables (net)	43.1	41.1
12.0	12.0	9.1	7.9			Inventory	10.5	10.7
2.4	4.6	6.8	6.2			All Other Current	6.2	6.5
59.9	69.4	68.8	65.4			Total Current	72.0	71.3
26.9	20.9	21.1	22.7			Fixed Assets (net)	19.8	19.8
5.6	3.0	2.7	6.0			Intangibles (net)	3.4	2.5
7.6	6.7	7.4	6.0			All Other Non-Current	4.8	6.4
100.0	100.0	100.0	100.0			Total	100.0	100.0
						LIABILITIES		
37.5	12.6	9.1	3.1			Notes Payable-Short Term	13.6	12.4
19.3	2.8	3.6	3.8			Cur. Mat.-L.T.D.	4.2	3.4
22.0	18.0	16.4	11.1			Trade Payables	17.1	16.6
.6	.4	.5	.1			Income Taxes Payable	.6	.3
14.9	12.0	14.2	17.2			All Other Current	16.9	15.6
94.4	45.8	43.8	35.4			Total Current	52.2	48.4
31.4	14.1	10.9	8.2			Long-Term Debt	17.2	13.2
.0	.5	.2	1.2			Deferred Taxes	.4	.5
10.4	4.5	2.2	10.1			All Other Non-Current	3.3	7.0
-36.2	35.1	42.9	45.2			Net Worth	26.9	31.0
100.0	100.0	100.0	100.0			Total Liabilities & Net Worth	100.0	100.0
						INCOME DATA		
100.0	100.0	100.0	100.0			Net Sales	100.0	100.0
42.9	36.4	27.3	24.5			Gross Profit	31.2	29.8
40.7	36.1	24.9	21.3			Operating Expenses	27.0	24.9
2.2	.4	2.4	3.2			Operating Profit	4.2	4.9
.5	.2	.5	.7			All Other Expenses (net)	.8	.4
1.7	.2	1.9	2.5			Profit Before Taxes	3.4	4.5
						RATIOS		
2.0	3.1	2.5	3.1			Current	2.2	2.6
1.1	1.8	1.7	2.0				1.5	1.5
.4	1.0	1.1	1.3				1.1	1.1
1.5	2.6	2.2	2.6			Quick	1.8	2.2
1.0	1.3	1.2	1.5				1.1	1.3
.2	.7	.8	.9				.7	.7
0 UND	34 10.6	40 9.2	42 8.7			Sales/Receivables	30 12.1	30 12.0
22 16.8	49 7.4	55 6.6	56 6.5				56 6.5	54 6.8
55 6.7	74 5.0	72 5.1	72 5.1				83 4.4	77 4.7
0 UND	0 UND	0 UND	0 UND			Cost of Sales/Inventory	0 UND	0 UND
0 UND	4 87.4	7 53.0	5 68.5				5 72.5	4 88.4
34 10.8	35 10.5	30 12.3	29 12.7				24 14.9	22 16.5
0 UND	10 38.0	14 27.0	10 35.1			Cost of Sales/Payables	11 34.0	10 36.0
17 21.6	29 12.4	24 15.4	20 17.8				24 15.0	21 17.6
36 10.0	53 6.9	41 8.8	40 9.0				46 7.9	36 10.1
20.0	5.9	5.2	4.1			Sales/Working Capital	6.9	6.2
135.3	8.6	9.9	6.5				13.0	12.0
-8.9	NM	53.6	28.4				73.1	94.9
10.8	7.6	28.6	61.5			EBIT/Interest	24.3	21.4
(32) 2.1	(50) 2.2	(85) 4.2	(27) 3.9				(132) 5.2	(166) 5.2
-.7	-3.7	.3	1.2				1.8	2.0
	23.8					Net Profit + Depr., Dep., Amort./Cur. Mat. L/T/D	7.6	6.3
	(16) 5.3						(36) 2.0	(35) 2.6
	2.0						1.0	1.7
.1	.2	.2	.1			Fixed/Worth	.2	.2
1.3	.5	.3	.4				.5	.4
-1.1	3.7	1.1	1.3				2.1	1.4
1.1	.5	.5	.6			Debt/Worth	.9	.7
46.8	1.4	1.6	1.0				2.3	1.7
-2.1	14.6	3.2	2.2				13.2	5.8
75.1	34.7	32.1	34.0			% Profit Before Taxes/Tangible Net Worth	62.5	53.8
(20) 42.7	(48) 5.7	(85) 15.9	(29) 11.0				(120) 31.9	(171) 29.9
-12.7	-16.9	.0	.7				12.0	11.6
28.4	11.2	15.2	12.2			% Profit Before Taxes/Total Assets	21.3	20.2
6.8	2.8	4.8	4.7				9.3	10.2
-10.4	-9.5	-.7	.3				1.6	2.5
244.5	44.4	44.2	42.4			Sales/Net Fixed Assets	53.3	46.0
28.9	23.6	16.0	14.3				24.0	23.9
11.8	10.3	8.6	4.0				10.6	10.8
9.7	4.0	3.4	3.0			Sales/Total Assets	3.9	3.8
4.1	3.3	2.5	2.3				3.1	2.9
2.7	2.0	1.8	1.3				2.2	2.1
.4	.8	.5	.7			% Depr., Dep., Amort./Sales	.5	.6
(24) 1.8	(45) 1.3	(87) 1.4	(30) 2.4				(123) 1.0	(166) 1.1
3.5	2.4	2.8	3.6				2.3	2.5
3.6	4.1	1.8				% Officers', Directors' Owners' Comp/Sales	2.6	2.0
(23) 7.0	(26) 6.4	(46) 3.5	(10) 1.9				(64) 4.7	(98) 4.1
12.5	9.8	6.1	3.4				7.9	7.5
51113M	205166M	1019760M	1360619M	198823M	1027029M	Net Sales ($)	3263332M	3101099M
8623M	67972M	414936M	615164M	55752M	898972M	Total Assets ($)	1541697M	1334880M

© RMA 2010

M = $ thousand   MM = $ million
See Pages 9 through 22 for Explanation of Ratios and Data

Comparative Historical Data

Current Data Sorted by Sales

			Type of Statement						
23	21	31	Unqualified	1		2	4	11	13
51	61	69	Reviewed	1	9	8	22	22	7
34	23	27	Compiled	3	10	4	7	2	1
36	34	46	Tax Returns	13	15	6	8	3	1
55	58	57	Other	5	16	7	10	8	11
4/1/07-3/31/08 ALL	4/1/08-3/31/09 ALL	4/1/09-3/31/10 ALL		0-1MM	32 (4/1-9/30/09) 1-3MM	3-5MM	198 (10/1/09-3/31/10) 5-10MM	10-25MM	25MM & OVER
199	197	230	**NUMBER OF STATEMENTS**	23	50	27	51	46	33
%	%	%	**ASSETS**	%	%	%	%	%	%
13.2	12.2	14.2	Cash & Equivalents	13.1	12.7	11.7	13.6	16.3	17.3
39.9	41.8	36.6	Trade Receivables (net)	30.5	31.3	39.4	37.7	42.8	36.5
10.5	10.3	10.3	Inventory	17.3	12.9	6.1	11.5	7.2	7.4
5.1	6.5	5.2	All Other Current	3.8	3.6	4.1	5.2	7.3	6.9
68.7	70.9	66.4	Total Current	64.7	60.4	61.4	68.0	73.7	68.1
21.3	19.3	22.8	Fixed Assets (net)	24.4	26.2	30.6	19.0	17.1	24.2
3.0	2.9	3.7	Intangibles (net)	7.5	4.5	1.3	4.7	3.1	1.0
7.1	6.9	7.1	All Other Non-Current	3.4	8.9	6.8	8.3	6.1	6.6
100.0	100.0	100.0	Total	100.0	100.0	100.0	100.0	100.0	100.0
			LIABILITIES						
11.4	13.1	13.8	Notes Payable-Short Term	52.7	14.2	11.9	10.2	7.4	1.9
3.4	3.1	6.1	Cur. Mat.-L.T.D.	4.8	15.1	3.0	4.6	2.6	3.0
15.5	17.9	16.8	Trade Payables	27.2	15.4	18.1	14.9	16.3	14.3
.7	.3	.4	Income Taxes Payable	.0	1.0	.1	.4	.6	.1
12.8	16.6	14.1	All Other Current	16.1	12.1	10.5	11.8	16.5	18.7
43.9	51.0	51.2	Total Current	100.7	57.8	43.5	42.0	43.4	38.0
15.8	12.6	15.1	Long-Term Debt	31.4	21.4	17.7	11.1	7.5	9.0
.7	.5	.4	Deferred Taxes	.0	.4	.3	.1	.8	.6
5.7	5.4	5.4	All Other Non-Current	9.6	7.0	.9	3.5	2.8	10.3
34.0	30.5	27.9	Net Worth	-41.7	13.4	37.6	43.3	45.5	42.2
100.0	100.0	100.0	Total Liabilties & Net Worth	100.0	100.0	100.0	100.0	100.0	100.0
			INCOME DATA						
100.0	100.0	100.0	Net Sales	100.0	100.0	100.0	100.0	100.0	100.0
31.4	31.9	32.0	Gross Profit	44.7	40.7	29.4	30.0	26.5	22.8
26.2	26.9	29.8	Operating Expenses	41.4	40.8	31.5	27.7	21.8	18.5
5.2	5.0	2.2	Operating Profit	3.3	-.1	-2.1	2.4	4.7	4.3
.8	.5	.5	All Other Expenses (net)	.6	.5	.4	.4	.4	.6
4.4	4.5	1.7	Profit Before Taxes	2.8	-.6	-2.5	1.9	4.4	3.7
			RATIOS						
2.5	2.4	2.7		2.3	3.7	2.8	2.7	2.7	2.9
1.6	1.6	1.7	Current	1.1	1.3	1.8	1.7	1.9	2.0
1.2	1.2	1.1		.3	.8	.8	1.1	1.3	1.3
2.0	1.9	2.2		1.1	2.3	2.4	2.2	2.5	2.5
(198) 1.3	1.2	1.2	Quick	.8	1.0	1.3	1.2	1.4	1.4
.9	.9	.7		.2	.5	.5	.7	1.0	.9
32 11.4	31 11.8	30 12.1		9 40.3	22 17.0	34 10.8	37 9.8	46 7.9	42 8.7
53 7.0	52 7.1	51 7.1	Sales/Receivables	25 14.4	39 9.5	55 6.7	52 7.0	58 6.3	54 6.7
69 5.3	74 5.0	70 5.2		70 5.2	73 5.0	76 4.8	69 5.3	75 4.9	65 5.6
0 UND	0 UND	0 UND		0 UND	0 UND	0 UND	0 UND	0 UND	0 UND
5 67.0	3 109.8	6 65.2	Cost of Sales/Inventory	21 17.0	6 65.0	2 183.2	14 27.0	3 143.1	2 160.2
26 14.0	31 11.8	33 11.2		50 7.3	49 7.5	23 16.0	33 10.9	17 21.2	32 11.4
11 33.8	11 32.0	10 37.2		8 46.5	5 79.4	9 42.1	10 38.0	14 25.3	12 29.3
21 17.6	25 14.7	24 15.3	Cost of Sales/Payables	27 13.5	30 12.0	23 15.5	23 15.6	21 17.2	21 17.7
35 10.4	44 8.4	41 8.8		73 7.6	48 7.6	65 5.6	43 8.5	38 9.7	37 9.8
5.7	6.1	5.4		9.3	5.2	6.4	6.6	4.8	5.2
11.2	10.2	10.6	Sales/Working Capital	58.6	47.3	21.2	9.3	9.2	7.3
39.9	44.8	332.1		-4.5	-26.1	-15.5	85.2	18.5	22.0
15.2	23.7	17.9		6.8	10.7	3.8	22.7	58.1	71.0
(166) 4.9	(172) 6.0	(200) 3.7	EBIT/Interest	(19) 1.6	(43) 1.5	(21) .4	(46) 4.0	(41) 9.2	(30) 9.0
1.9	1.8	-.4		-.5	-2.9	-4.8	-.2	1.6	1.9
8.7	17.7	9.8	Net Profit + Depr., Dep., Amort./Cur. Mat. L/T/D					20.5	5.8
(42) 4.1	(37) 4.4	(34) 3.0						(13) 5.9	(10) 3.1
1.8	1.7	1.3						1.5	2.2
.2	.1	.2		.1	.2	.2	.2	.1	.2
.4	.4	.4	Fixed/Worth	1.6	.8	.5	.3	.2	.4
1.4	1.5	2.1		-.2	-10.3	4.0	2.0	.9	1.2
.9	.9	.6		1.6	.7	.4	.5	.7	.5
1.9	1.7	1.6	Debt/Worth	-24.4	2.6	2.0	1.2	1.4	1.0
4.9	5.0	5.9		-1.7	-186.8	4.5	6.0	2.2	2.2
55.9	53.6	35.7	% Profit Before Taxes/Tangible Net Worth	72.5	27.0	32.3	39.7	36.2	35.1
(179) 23.6	(172) 26.9	(188) 12.0		(10) 13.9	(37) 5.1	(22) -2.0	(43) 15.9	(44) 17.3	(32) 13.0
11.9	11.1	-3.3		-18.3	-17.1	-31.1	-12.7	3.3	2.0
19.8	20.3	14.7	% Profit Before Taxes/Total Assets	15.8	11.8	11.5	14.6	17.1	16.0
8.2	9.3	4.8		5.4	2.3	-1.9	4.6	8.6	6.8
2.9	2.7	-3.2		-10.4	-8.6	-14.1	-6.4	1.4	1.0
58.0	64.3	46.6	Sales/Net Fixed Assets	244.5	44.1	46.6	38.4	79.2	50.3
21.8	28.1	19.9		24.0	21.4	12.2	16.1	28.7	17.2
8.0	10.4	8.5		10.0	9.0	5.9	9.4	10.5	3.5
4.1	3.9	3.7	Sales/Total Assets	4.1	4.3	3.6	3.6	3.7	3.3
2.9	3.0	2.8		3.1	2.7	2.5	2.6	3.0	2.7
2.0	2.2	1.9		1.9	1.8	1.9	1.9	1.8	1.3
.6	.5	.7		.6	.8	.8	1.0	.3	.5
(163) 1.4	(158) 1.1	(189) 1.5	% Depr., Dep., Amort./Sales	(12) 2.7	(38) 1.9	(23) 1.2	(43) 1.7	(44) 1.1	(29) 1.2
2.7	2.3	2.9		6.0	4.0	4.1	2.5	2.8	3.0
2.5	2.0	2.2	% Officers', Directors' Owners' Comp/Sales	4.2	2.6	3.7	1.7	1.7	
(95) 4.5	(92) 4.0	(105) 4.7		(11) 10.7	(27) 5.6	(15) 5.8	(22) 3.5	(21) 3.1	
7.7	7.2	7.7		17.0	7.9	8.8	6.4	5.6	
4440884M	3546219M	3862510M	Net Sales ($)	13580M	104514M	105470M	371106M	671977M	2595863M
1637261M	1571294M	2061419M	Total Assets ($)	12122M	42931M	53373M	196400M	283440M	1473153M

M = $ thousand   MM = $ million
See Pages 9 through 22 for Explanation of Ratios and Data

CONSTRUCTION-GENERAL—Drywall and Insulation Contractors   NAICS 238310

Current Data Sorted by Assets   **Comparative Historical Data**

0-500M	500M-2MM	2-10MM	10-50MM	50-100MM	100-250MM	Type of Statement	4/1/05-3/31/06 ALL	4/1/06-3/31/07 ALL
1	2	17	22	4	2	Unqualified	37	42
6	32	75	18			Reviewed	116	110
4	21	7	1			Compiled	58	66
29	21	11	1			Tax Returns	47	60
20	27	26	15	1	2	Other	85	75
	77 (4/1-9/30/09)		288 (10/1/09-3/31/10)					
60	103	136	57	5	4	**NUMBER OF STATEMENTS**	343	353
%	%	%	%	%	%	**ASSETS**	%	%
17.4	13.6	16.4	20.4			Cash & Equivalents	9.4	9.8
37.8	46.4	49.1	45.7			Trade Receivables (net)	55.5	54.6
5.5	7.0	5.0	3.2			Inventory	5.8	6.2
6.2	5.8	10.5	8.1			All Other Current	7.1	7.9
67.0	72.8	81.0	77.4			Total Current	77.8	78.4
22.2	18.1	10.0	10.8			Fixed Assets (net)	14.1	14.2
4.4	2.2	1.8	4.0			Intangibles (net)	1.9	1.4
6.5	7.0	7.2	7.8			All Other Non-Current	6.3	6.0
100.0	100.0	100.0	100.0			Total	100.0	100.0
						LIABILITIES		
55.3	13.3	9.5	5.8			Notes Payable-Short Term	15.6	14.0
3.2	2.6	1.8	1.3			Cur. Mat.-L.T.D.	3.2	2.9
15.4	15.6	13.4	12.5			Trade Payables	17.9	17.8
.1	.6	.6	.2			Income Taxes Payable	.5	.8
19.9	9.7	17.8	20.4			All Other Current	15.2	17.5
93.9	41.8	43.1	40.1			Total Current	52.4	53.0
25.3	10.3	7.0	6.3			Long-Term Debt	10.0	9.2
.0	.3	.7	.4			Deferred Taxes	.4	.3
6.7	3.5	3.3	4.7			All Other Non-Current	3.6	4.4
-25.9	44.1	45.9	48.5			Net Worth	33.6	33.0
100.0	100.0	100.0	100.0			Total Liabilities & Net Worth	100.0	100.0
						INCOME DATA		
100.0	100.0	100.0	100.0			Net Sales	100.0	100.0
36.9	26.5	22.0	20.1			Gross Profit	22.0	24.9
36.9	27.3	18.7	15.3			Operating Expenses	18.2	19.9
.0	-.9	3.2	4.7			Operating Profit	3.8	5.0
.5	1.0	.4	-.2			All Other Expenses (net)	.3	.3
-.5	-1.8	2.8	4.9			Profit Before Taxes	3.4	4.6
						RATIOS		
1.8	3.8	3.5	3.0				2.4	2.3
.9	1.8	2.0	1.8			Current	1.6	1.6
.4	1.1	1.4	1.5				1.2	1.1
1.6	3.3	2.9	2.5				2.1	1.9
.8	1.5	1.6	1.7			Quick	1.3	1.3
.3	.9	1.1	1.2				.9	.8
0 UND	37 9.9	48 7.6	57 6.4				41 8.9	39 9.4
33 11.1	57 6.4	61 6.0	71 5.1			Sales/Receivables	61 6.0	65 5.6
61 6.0	78 4.7	78 4.7	89 4.1				84 4.3	85 4.3
0 UND	0 UND	0 UND	0 UND				0 UND	0 UND
0 UND	2 162.1	1 340.0	2 190.3			Cost of Sales/Inventory	2 195.3	2 224.9
5 69.6	18 20.4	9 38.7	6 60.6				10 37.8	10 34.9
0 UND	8 44.5	10 37.1	11 32.1				11 31.8	10 35.2
9 42.7	18 20.4	18 20.0	20 17.9			Cost of Sales/Payables	19 18.7	20 18.7
33 11.0	36 10.1	28 13.1	31 11.9				31 11.8	34 10.7
10.9	5.5	4.5	4.3				6.9	7.1
-143.3	10.2	7.3	6.2			Sales/Working Capital	12.1	11.6
-13.9	34.9	13.8	10.7				38.9	41.7
12.1	9.7	39.4	65.5				19.3	29.6
(50) 2.5	(93) 1.8	(117) 6.6	(48) 10.9			EBIT/Interest	(313) 5.7	(320) 6.5
-5.5	-4.4	2.0	1.7				2.1	2.1
	2.2	16.9	40.0				9.9	12.0
	(14) .8	(34) 3.9	(13) 12.8			Net Profit + Depr., Dep., Amort./Cur. Mat. L/T/D	(81) 3.4	(78) 4.4
	-1.7	1.0	1.3				1.1	1.8
.1	.2	.1	.0				.1	.1
3.1	.4	.2	.2			Fixed/Worth	.3	.3
-.7	1.1	.5	.4				.9	1.0
1.3	.4	.5	.6				.9	.9
UND	1.3	.9	1.2			Debt/Worth	1.9	1.8
-2.2	4.8	2.8	1.8				5.1	4.5
168.1	28.1	35.2	40.3				59.0	65.3
(31) 57.1	(90) 3.9	(128) 14.0	(55) 19.9			% Profit Before Taxes/Tangible Net Worth	(302) 25.9	(314) 31.6
-18.2	-21.7	3.3	7.1				9.5	12.9
34.1	11.0	16.6	20.3				20.8	24.3
4.7	1.1	6.0	10.1			% Profit Before Taxes/Total Assets	7.6	10.7
-24.7	-11.7	.8	2.5				1.9	2.6
108.0	59.2	101.1	107.0				87.9	97.2
44.5	26.2	48.5	40.7			Sales/Net Fixed Assets	39.6	41.4
16.5	11.9	24.0	18.2				19.7	21.7
7.5	3.7	3.5	3.1				4.4	4.4
4.4	2.9	2.8	2.4			Sales/Total Assets	3.4	3.4
3.2	2.3	2.1	1.9				2.6	2.6
.5	.6	.3	.2				.3	.3
(29) .9	(92) 1.1	(121) .7	(52) .4			% Depr., Dep., Amort./Sales	(280) .7	(287) .7
2.1	1.8	1.1	1.1				1.3	1.1
3.2	2.9	2.2	1.1				1.8	1.8
(39) 7.2	(58) 5.3	(65) 4.1	(22) 1.6			% Officers', Directors' Owners' Comp/Sales	(180) 3.5	(177) 3.3
10.7	8.0	7.2	2.6				5.8	6.8
84715M	351548M	1771913M	2724579M	786363M	883102M	Net Sales ($)	5916581M	7937407M
14024M	111657M	636350M	1156311M	387006M	755556M	Total Assets ($)	1951022M	2349514M

© RMA 2010   M = $ thousand   MM = $ million
See Pages 9 through 22 for Explanation of Ratios and Data

Comparative Historical Data | Current Data Sorted by Sales

	4/1/07-3/31/08 ALL	4/1/08-3/31/09 ALL	4/1/09-3/31/10 ALL	77 (4/1-9/30/09) 0-1MM	1-3MM	3-5MM	288 (10/1/09-3/31/10) 5-10MM	10-25MM	25MM & OVER
Type of Statement									
Unqualified	38	41	48	1		3	2	14	28
Reviewed	90	123	131	3	14	21	35	37	21
Compiled	45	41	33	1	16	6	5	5	
Tax Returns	47	67	62	17	23	6	6	9	1
Other	87	101	91	11	23	10	13	17	17
NUMBER OF STATEMENTS	307	373	365	33	76	46	61	82	67
	%	%	%	%	%	%	%	%	%
ASSETS									
Cash & Equivalents	13.0	14.1	16.4	18.3	13.8	11.4	18.6	17.7	18.4
Trade Receivables (net)	54.2	51.5	45.6	37.4	39.9	50.6	45.8	47.0	50.7
Inventory	5.1	6.0	5.4	7.2	8.6	6.9	3.7	3.6	3.2
All Other Current	7.7	6.8	8.1	6.5	4.6	7.3	12.6	8.9	8.1
Total Current	80.1	78.4	75.4	69.5	67.0	76.3	80.7	77.3	80.4
Fixed Assets (net)	12.5	12.7	14.4	22.8	21.8	14.5	11.5	9.8	10.0
Intangibles (net)	1.4	1.4	3.1	4.7	2.7	2.0	2.4	3.4	4.0
All Other Non-Current	6.0	7.5	7.0	3.1	8.6	7.2	5.4	9.5	5.5
Total	100.0	100.0	100.0	100.0	100.0	100.0	100.0	100.0	100.0
LIABILITIES									
Notes Payable-Short Term	12.3	14.2	17.4	59.0	23.5	16.6	10.3	10.2	5.7
Cur. Mat.-L.T.D.	2.5	3.0	2.2	1.3	3.5	2.6	1.8	2.0	1.4
Trade Payables	14.1	14.9	14.1	13.3	14.2	17.4	14.4	12.8	13.3
Income Taxes Payable	.6	.5	.4	.0	.5	.3	.6	.7	.2
All Other Current	18.2	18.5	16.3	9.5	16.8	10.6	14.4	17.9	22.7
Total Current	47.8	51.1	50.4	83.1	58.5	47.4	41.5	43.6	43.3
Long-Term Debt	7.8	7.7	11.1	25.1	16.9	10.4	6.2	7.2	7.4
Deferred Taxes	.3	.2	.4	.0	.2	.5	.2	1.0	.2
All Other Non-Current	4.3	4.2	4.3	3.1	7.3	2.7	2.0	3.7	5.5
Net Worth	39.8	36.8	33.8	-11.3	17.1	39.0	50.1	44.5	43.5
Total Liabilities & Net Worth	100.0	100.0	100.0	100.0	100.0	100.0	100.0	100.0	100.0
INCOME DATA									
Net Sales	100.0	100.0	100.0	100.0	100.0	100.0	100.0	100.0	100.0
Gross Profit	25.7	26.1	25.5	42.6	31.1	22.4	24.0	20.1	20.7
Operating Expenses	19.9	22.4	23.7	43.0	31.0	24.6	20.5	17.6	15.6
Operating Profit	5.8	3.7	1.8	-.4	.0	-2.2	3.6	2.4	5.1
All Other Expenses (net)	.2	.4	.6	1.5	1.0	.4	.2	.1	.6
Profit Before Taxes	5.6	3.3	1.2	-1.9	-1.0	-2.6	3.3	2.3	4.5
RATIOS									
Current	2.8	2.5	3.1	2.3	3.2	2.6	3.9	3.3	2.8
	1.8	1.7	1.8	.9	1.5	1.8	2.2	2.0	1.8
	1.3	1.2	1.2	.5	1.0	1.0	1.4	1.3	1.5
Quick	2.3	2.3	2.5	1.9	2.4	2.6	3.6	2.6	2.4
	1.5	1.4	1.5	.8	1.2	1.5	1.5	1.6	1.6
	1.0	.9	.9	.3	.6	.8	1.0	1.1	1.2
Sales/Receivables	43 8.5	41 8.9	39 9.3	0 UND	17 20.9	35 10.3	39 9.4	48 7.6	56 6.5
	66 5.5	62 5.9	60 6.1	46 7.9	47 7.8	61 6.0	59 6.2	62 5.8	68 5.4
	84 4.3	82 4.4	78 4.7	79 4.6	76 4.8	83 4.4	74 4.9	79 4.6	82 4.5
Cost of Sales/Inventory	0 UND	0 UND	0 UND	0 UND	0 UND	0 UND	0 UND	0 UND	0 UND
	1 298.2	1 398.5	1 345.3	0 UND	1 509.6	2 214.1	2 162.1	1 396.9	2 194.4
	9 40.0	10 38.2	9 39.1	18 20.6	21 17.4	18 19.7	7 53.8	7 55.5	6 61.9
Cost of Sales/Payables	9 41.9	9 41.9	9 40.9	0 UND	3 116.2	7 51.1	10 35.0	9 39.8	13 27.3
	18 20.7	18 20.6	17 21.3	11 32.2	14 26.4	18 18.9	18 20.7	15 24.9	22 16.9
	29 12.8	32 11.5	32 11.5	39 9.5	32 11.5	33 10.9	29 12.4	25 14.5	32 11.6
Sales/Working Capital	5.8	6.1	5.3	8.1	5.7	5.6	4.0	5.1	4.7
	9.1	9.7	8.7	-163.8	13.5	10.2	6.9	7.5	7.6
	19.5	32.3	29.0	-17.7	495.8	-786.7	13.7	14.7	10.5
EBIT/Interest	27.8	25.5	20.9	4.1	11.8	8.2	41.2	21.2	130.7
	(267) 8.4	(324) 6.7	(317) 5.1	(28) 1.0	(63) 2.5	(43) 1.2	(54) 9.3	(70) 6.3	(59) 17.8
	2.0	1.3	-.4	-6.0	-4.0	-14.2	2.4	1.9	1.9
Net Profit + Depr., Dep., Amort./Cur. Mat. L/T/D	17.6	17.8	15.4				1.4	31.0	38.1
	(69) 5.4	(72) 4.4	(66) 3.0		(11) .1		(24) 5.6	(15) 4.0	
	1.2	.9	.5				-1.3	2.6	.9
Fixed/Worth	.1	.1	.1	.2	.1	.1	.1	.1	.1
	.2	.2	.2	1.8	.5	.3	.2	.1	.2
	.6	.6	.9	-.6	NM	1.0	.5	.4	.5
Debt/Worth	.6	.7	.6	1.1	.6	.6	.3	.5	.7
	1.4	1.5	1.3	8.0	1.8	1.4	.7	1.2	1.2
	3.1	3.8	5.5	-2.3	-14.7	6.8	3.5	2.5	2.2
% Profit Before Taxes/Tangible Net Worth	63.9	51.3	38.5	91.0	38.5	20.6	43.0	28.1	43.1
	(287) 33.0	(334) 23.7	(310) 13.4	(20) 5.0	(55) 7.2	(39) 4.2	(57) 14.7	(77) 14.1	(62) 23.9
	9.8	4.8	.1	-33.9	-17.4	-28.6	1.6	5.0	8.5
% Profit Before Taxes/Total Assets	27.2	19.7	17.7	23.7	20.5	8.9	17.9	15.2	22.6
	13.2	8.6	4.8	.0	1.2	1.3	9.3	5.7	9.6
	3.8	.7	-2.8	-23.6	-11.6	-20.2	.7	1.3	2.6
Sales/Net Fixed Assets	99.5	109.8	77.8	56.9	68.4	69.5	63.7	103.7	110.5
	46.4	40.8	37.2	26.8	27.8	29.6	33.5	60.0	40.7
	21.7	19.4	17.2	10.5	11.7	16.9	23.3	26.3	17.9
Sales/Total Assets	4.0	4.2	3.8	4.7	4.4	4.2	3.6	3.8	3.2
	3.2	3.1	2.9	3.3	2.9	3.2	2.9	2.8	2.8
	2.5	2.4	2.2	1.8	2.2	2.2	2.3	2.1	2.2
% Depr., Dep., Amort./Sales	.3	.3	.4	.9	.6	.5	.5	.3	.3
	(241) .6	(297) .7	(300) .8	(15) 1.8	(55) 1.2	(44) .9	(54) .9	(71) .6	(61) .4
	1.1	1.4	1.4	2.8	2.1	1.7	1.3	1.0	.8
% Officers', Directors' Owners' Comp/Sales	1.9	2.1	2.2	4.4	4.0	2.2	2.3	2.0	1.4
	(157) 3.2	(203) 4.1	(184) 4.4	(24) 9.7	(45) 6.2	(25) 3.0	(24) 4.0	(45) 3.0	(21) 1.4
	7.0	7.3	8.0	11.4	8.3	7.4	5.4	5.9	3.6
Net Sales ($)	5783832M	7181181M	6602220M	18812M	150696M	179475M	460038M	1276980M	4516219M
Total Assets ($)	2048015M	2891712M	3060904M	7425M	55691M	66819M	174231M	564469M	2192269M

Current Data Sorted by Assets | **Comparative Historical Data**

0-500M	500M-2MM	2-10MM	10-50MM	50-100MM	100-250MM	Type of Statement	4/1/05-3/31/06 ALL	4/1/06-3/31/07 ALL
	6	9	4			Unqualified	18	23
3	21	37	4			Reviewed	50	70
11	15	5				Compiled	20	31
20	7	5			1	Tax Returns	31	40
12	17	19	3		1	Other	52	30
	37 (4/1-9/30/09)		163 (10/1/09-3/31/10)					
46	66	75	11		2	NUMBER OF STATEMENTS	171	194
%	%	%	%	%	%	**ASSETS**	%	%
16.3	14.7	18.5	13.8	DATA NOT AVAILABLE		Cash & Equivalents	13.3	14.2
33.6	50.7	45.9	41.8			Trade Receivables (net)	45.6	45.1
3.6	2.7	1.9	2.2			Inventory	4.0	2.5
4.6	5.0	12.6	13.5			All Other Current	6.3	9.6
58.0	73.2	79.0	71.3			Total Current	69.2	71.4
29.1	18.3	15.2	19.5			Fixed Assets (net)	21.8	20.2
.8	1.7	.9	5.3			Intangibles (net)	2.0	1.7
12.1	6.8	4.9	3.9			All Other Non-Current	7.1	6.7
100.0	100.0	100.0	100.0			Total	100.0	100.0
						LIABILITIES		
39.6	9.3	8.7	10.1			Notes Payable-Short Term	10.1	11.9
5.8	3.1	1.6	1.1			Cur. Mat.-L.T.D.	3.5	2.9
14.4	15.4	9.7	6.5			Trade Payables	12.9	14.0
.0	.7	.8	.2			Income Taxes Payable	.6	.6
17.8	11.8	15.5	13.3			All Other Current	13.8	14.1
77.6	40.3	36.2	31.2			Total Current	40.8	43.6
17.5	8.6	5.1	6.0			Long-Term Debt	13.5	13.8
.0	.5	.8	.0			Deferred Taxes	.2	.3
21.2	5.2	.9	2.6			All Other Non-Current	2.7	1.5
-16.4	45.3	57.0	60.2			Net Worth	42.7	40.8
100.0	100.0	100.0	100.0			Total Liabilties & Net Worth	100.0	100.0
						INCOME DATA		
100.0	100.0	100.0	100.0			Net Sales	100.0	100.0
45.6	31.5	26.6	18.6			Gross Profit	32.4	32.7
45.8	30.4	20.8	16.2			Operating Expenses	27.1	27.0
-.2	1.1	5.8	2.3			Operating Profit	5.3	5.7
.1	.6	.5	.6			All Other Expenses (net)	.7	.5
-.2	.5	5.3	1.8			Profit Before Taxes	4.6	5.2
						RATIOS		
2.1	3.8	3.6	3.8				3.0	3.2
1.0	2.2	2.1	2.3			Current	1.7	1.7
.6	1.1	1.5	1.6				1.2	1.2
1.5	3.7	3.4	3.8				2.3	2.6
.9	1.8	1.7	1.7			Quick	1.4	(193) 1.6
.3	1.1	1.2	1.1				1.0	.9
0 UND	32 11.3	46 8.0	41 8.8				35 10.6	29 12.5
24 15.0	55 6.6	68 5.4	75 4.9			Sales/Receivables	63 5.8	58 6.3
53 6.9	80 4.5	88 4.1	95 3.8				89 4.1	86 4.2
0 UND	0 UND	0 UND	0 UND				0 UND	0 UND
0 UND	0 UND	0 UND	1 597.8			Cost of Sales/Inventory	0 UND	0 UND
2 153.8	1 476.1	1 465.2	13 27.5				4 102.3	3 137.2
0 UND	9 40.0	8 46.3	8 47.7				8 44.0	7 49.8
6 60.0	16 23.5	16 23.3	15 25.0			Cost of Sales/Payables	19 18.9	20 18.4
30 12.3	33 10.9	25 14.7	18 19.9				36 10.2	36 10.1
11.9	5.2	4.0	4.3				5.4	5.6
UND	8.9	5.9	5.5			Sales/Working Capital	8.6	9.1
-16.0	41.0	11.9	7.5				40.5	31.6
6.4	15.2	47.5	49.2				19.8	22.9
(37) .1	(54) 2.6	(65) 7.6	(10) 12.2			EBIT/Interest	(147) 4.8	(169) 8.0
-11.3	-1.8	.8	-14.2				1.5	2.3
	12.4	16.9					6.4	12.2
	(15) 2.9	(18) 3.8				Net Profit + Depr., Dep., Amort./Cur. Mat. L/T/D	(27) 3.5	(32) 5.2
	1.5	.2					1.8	2.2
.2	.1	.1	.2				.1	.1
1.3	.4	.2	.4			Fixed/Worth	.4	.4
-1.4	.8	.4	.5				1.0	.8
1.0	.3	.3	.3				.5	.5
8.6	.9	.8	.7			Debt/Worth	1.1	1.3
-3.7	3.8	1.3	1.4				3.7	3.8
55.8	36.9	32.6	32.3				50.8	55.7
(25) 15.0	(61) 7.7	(74) 14.9	18.6			% Profit Before Taxes/Tangible Net Worth	(156) 19.0	(171) 24.7
-20.5	-12.3	.3	-19.2				3.9	9.6
25.3	18.9	20.0	12.3				22.3	25.7
3.3	3.4	6.8	10.6			% Profit Before Taxes/Total Assets	7.4	11.2
-23.5	-4.0	-.2	-11.5				1.2	3.1
99.1	66.9	43.2	36.0				56.3	69.5
27.2	22.8	25.3	12.2			Sales/Net Fixed Assets	22.5	24.2
13.7	12.1	12.3	6.0				9.1	11.3
8.6	3.9	3.1	2.5				3.8	4.0
5.8	3.1	2.5	2.1			Sales/Total Assets	2.9	3.0
3.4	2.2	2.0	1.7				2.0	2.2
.9	.8	.5	.7				.5	.5
(33) 1.5	(55) 1.5	(68) 1.1	(10) 1.2			% Depr., Dep., Amort./Sales	(141) 1.2	(159) 1.2
2.4	2.8	2.1	1.7				2.3	2.1
6.7	3.5	2.5					2.8	2.3
(29) 9.6	(32) 5.8	(46) 4.3				% Officers', Directors' Owners' Comp/Sales	(91) 5.7	(107) 4.6
15.6	9.6	6.9					9.9	8.8
67932M	241996M	838415M	320023M		1553868M	Net Sales ($)	1480198M	1929034M
10868M	70561M	330610M	145233M		331294M	Total Assets ($)	603255M	808167M

M = $ thousand MM = $ million

See Pages 9 through 22 for Explanation of Ratios and Data

Comparative Historical Data

Current Data Sorted by Sales

			Type of Statement						
21	22	19	Unqualified		3	3	3	7	3
37	73	65	Reviewed	1	11	8	22	21	2
27	31	31	Compiled	7	11	2	8	3	
34	42	33	Tax Returns	5	19	4	2	2	1
47	43	52	Other	6	12	14	7	9	4
4/1/07-3/31/08 ALL	4/1/08-3/31/09 ALL	4/1/09-3/31/10 ALL		37 (4/1-9/30/09)			163 (10/1/09-3/31/10)		
				0-1MM	1-3MM	3-5MM	5-10MM	10-25MM	25MM & OVER
166	211	200	NUMBER OF STATEMENTS	19	56	31	42	42	10
%	%	%	ASSETS	%	%	%	%	%	%
12.5	14.1	16.5	Cash & Equivalents	26.2	14.7	15.4	18.0	13.8	16.6
44.8	45.7	44.0	Trade Receivables (net)	29.4	39.1	50.7	45.3	51.6	40.5
2.3	3.1	2.6	Inventory	6.4	3.3	1.3	2.2	1.5	1.1
9.3	10.0	8.4	All Other Current	4.7	4.7	9.2	9.7	11.5	15.2
68.9	73.0	71.5	Total Current	66.8	61.9	76.6	75.2	78.4	73.4
22.6	18.6	19.7	Fixed Assets (net)	22.8	27.3	14.1	18.0	15.1	14.7
2.2	2.0	1.8	Intangibles (net)	1.6	1.3	2.5	.4	1.7	9.1
6.3	6.4	7.1	All Other Non-Current	8.7	9.6	6.8	6.4	4.9	2.8
100.0	100.0	100.0	Total	100.0	100.0	100.0	100.0	100.0	100.0
			LIABILITIES						
17.2	13.7	16.3	Notes Payable-Short Term	22.1	30.2	8.6	8.9	8.7	13.3
4.0	4.8	3.5	Cur. Mat.-L.T.D.	2.3	5.1	4.5	1.7	1.4	9.7
13.9	13.1	12.4	Trade Payables	8.8	14.3	15.7	11.3	11.2	8.3
.6	.7	.6	Income Taxes Payable	.0	.1	1.1	1.6	.1	.2
12.4	16.8	14.7	All Other Current	13.6	16.0	11.8	12.9	17.2	14.8
48.2	49.2	47.4	Total Current	46.8	65.7	41.8	36.3	38.6	46.3
16.1	11.2	9.4	Long-Term Debt	15.1	14.7	6.5	7.0	4.6	8.6
.5	.4	.5	Deferred Taxes	.0	.4	1.6	.3	.1	.0
7.7	5.3	7.5	All Other Non-Current	24.1	9.8	7.4	3.0	1.0	10.9
27.5	33.9	35.2	Net Worth	14.1	9.4	42.7	53.3	55.8	34.2
100.0	100.0	100.0	Total Liabilties & Net Worth	100.0	100.0	100.0	100.0	100.0	100.0
			INCOME DATA						
100.0	100.0	100.0	Net Sales	100.0	100.0	100.0	100.0	100.0	100.0
31.3	31.9	32.2	Gross Profit	50.1	37.4	30.9	30.4	22.1	21.9
26.0	26.8	29.5	Operating Expenses	51.4	38.2	26.4	24.6	18.1	17.3
5.4	5.1	2.7	Operating Profit	-1.3	-.8	4.5	5.8	4.0	4.6
.4	.6	.4	All Other Expenses (net)	.0	.5	.8	.3	.2	.8
4.9	4.5	2.2	Profit Before Taxes	-1.3	-1.3	3.7	5.5	3.8	3.8
			RATIOS						
2.7	2.9	3.6		4.7	3.6	3.2	3.8	3.3	3.1
1.8	1.8	1.9	Current	2.1	1.1	2.0	2.2	2.0	2.2
1.1	1.2	1.2		1.0	.7	1.3	1.5	1.5	1.4
2.2	2.6	3.1		4.1	3.4	3.2	3.2	2.9	2.8
1.5	1.4	1.5	Quick	1.5	1.0	1.4	2.0	1.7	1.5
.9	.9	.9		.6	.6	1.1	1.2	1.1	1.0
25 14.4	32 11.4	28 12.9		0 UND	15 24.3	33 10.9	40 9.0	45 8.2	0 UND
58 6.3	57 6.4	55 6.6	Sales/Receivables	44 8.3	39 9.3	53 6.9	60 6.0	59 6.2	52 7.0
77 4.7	80 4.6	81 4.5		70 5.2	73 5.0	85 4.3	85 4.3	89 4.1	83 4.4
0 UND	0 UND	0 UND		0 UND	0 UND	0 UND	0 UND	0 UND	0 UND
0 UND	0 UND	0 UND	Cost of Sales/Inventory	0 UND	0 UND	0 UND	0 UND	0 UND	0 UND
3 133.4	1 336.0	1 248.5		18 20.6	2 176.5	2 159.9	0 999.8	1 273.4	2 189.5
6 57.7	7 51.4	6 61.1		0 UND	1 355.7	8 48.0	9 42.3	9 41.6	6 61.0
19 24.9	15 24.9	14 25.3	Cost of Sales/Payables	3 121.6	13 29.0	20 17.9	15 24.9	18 20.6	10 37.0
35 10.4	30 12.1	28 13.1		35 10.4	35 10.4	41 8.9	29 12.5	24 15.2	16 22.5
6.0	5.6	5.0		6.5	5.1	6.6	4.4	4.7	5.0
10.6	10.3	9.0	Sales/Working Capital	11.4	48.7	10.4	7.1	6.1	7.9
51.3	34.3	39.9		UND	-24.8	16.9	14.1	11.2	16.1
26.4	25.5	23.7		1.7	7.3	35.2	23.7	54.1	
(149) 7.8	(184) 8.0	(168) 4.4	EBIT/Interest	(13) -3.0	(45) 1.3	(29) 6.9	(37) 6.8	(35) 6.0	
2.3	2.0	-1.8		-15.4	-7.4	2.6	.9	.8	
8.6	8.3	13.4					14.5	7.4	
(28) 5.0	(44) 3.5	(37) 2.9	Net Profit + Depr., Dep., Amort./Cur. Mat. L/T/D			(11) 6.7	(11) 2.9		
1.1	1.7	.6				1.8	1.2		
.1	.1	.1		.1	.2	.1	.1	.1	.2
.4	.4	.3	Fixed/Worth	.4	.8	.3	.3	.2	.2
1.1	1.0	1.0		1.5	-6.4	.7	.7	.4	3.0
.6	.6	.4		.3	.4	.4	.4	.4	.4
1.4	1.4	1.0	Debt/Worth	1.8	3.6	1.0	.9	.8	.8
4.0	4.2	3.1		-13.6	-15.3	2.5	1.8	1.3	13.7
58.7	60.0	35.7		50.2	27.0	45.5	36.2	27.7	
(141) 26.3	(188) 25.0	(172) 14.1	% Profit Before Taxes/Tangible Net Worth	(14) 15.8	(38) 3.0	(28) 19.7	(41) 10.2	15.5	
10.0	9.0	-2.5		-36.9	-39.8	6.4	-.3	1.2	
31.1	27.7	19.8		27.5	13.3	25.1	21.3	14.3	38.6
12.2	9.0	5.4	% Profit Before Taxes/Total Assets	3.2	.1	14.3	4.8	6.7	7.7
3.7	2.8	-4.7		-28.9	-21.4	3.1	-.8	.1	-11.4
64.1	79.2	58.2		113.8	55.0	102.7	36.4	65.8	51.2
23.9	27.6	24.0	Sales/Net Fixed Assets	17.2	22.2	30.1	21.0	35.1	33.8
11.8	13.3	12.2		10.2	10.0	17.7	13.7	12.1	15.2
4.2	4.4	4.4		5.9	6.6	5.1	3.6	3.7	4.3
3.3	3.3	3.0	Sales/Total Assets	3.2	3.4	3.0	2.7	2.8	3.0
2.4	2.4	2.1		2.3	2.0	1.8	2.1	2.1	2.3
.6	.5	.8		1.4	1.0	.6	.8	.5	
(140) 1.0	(167) .9	(166) 1.3	% Depr., Dep., Amort./Sales	(13) 2.2	(45) 1.5	(25) 1.4	(38) 1.2	(38) .8	
1.9	1.7	2.3		3.8	3.1	2.1	2.1	2.0	
2.6	2.3	3.1			4.8	2.4	3.0	2.4	
(99) 4.8	(105) 4.6	(113) 5.8	% Officers', Directors' Owners' Comp/Sales		(33) 7.3	(20) 7.1	(23) 5.6	(22) 3.9	
8.5	8.8	10.7			14.1	11.7	7.3	4.7	
1615756M	2593286M	3022234M	Net Sales ($)	9844M	106671M	122271M	277699M	657926M	1847823M
548628M	724646M	888566M	Total Assets ($)	3763M	36174M	48441M	110506M	253897M	435785M

© RMA 2010

M = $ thousand   MM = $ million
See Pages 9 through 22 for Explanation of Ratios and Data

Current Data Sorted by Assets

Comparative Historical Data

						Type of Statement		
1	17	2	1			Unqualified	9	8
5	18	38	4			Reviewed	48	57
23	16	4				Compiled	27	27
8	22	2			1	Tax Returns	25	20
		24	6			Other	49	56
	23 (4/1-9/30/09)		169 (10/1/09-3/31/10)				4/1/05-3/31/06 ALL	4/1/06-3/31/07 ALL
0-500M	500M-2MM	2-10MM	10-50MM	50-100MM	100-250MM	NUMBER OF STATEMENTS		
37	73	70	11		1		158	168
%	%	%	%	%	%	ASSETS	%	%
17.4	11.7	9.1	5.3			Cash & Equivalents	7.1	9.0
29.6	47.3	53.8	51.4			Trade Receivables (net)	51.1	49.3
13.5	12.4	13.1	18.1			Inventory	12.9	15.9
8.3	3.5	8.5	10.0			All Other Current	6.9	5.1
68.9	74.9	84.4	84.8			Total Current	78.1	79.3
23.3	14.0	11.2	6.4			Fixed Assets (net)	14.9	15.3
2.7	3.6	1.0	5.5			Intangibles (net)	2.1	1.2
5.1	7.5	3.4	3.3			All Other Non-Current	4.9	4.2
100.0	100.0	100.0	100.0			Total	100.0	100.0
						LIABILITIES		
35.9	13.5	16.3	15.4			Notes Payable-Short Term	16.9	16.9
3.4	2.8	1.7	1.7			Cur. Mat.-L.T.D.	2.4	2.8
28.0	16.8	16.1	14.3			Trade Payables	19.0	17.4
.0	.0	.8	.0			Income Taxes Payable	.7	.4
36.2	11.5	11.4	23.2			All Other Current	11.1	13.9
103.4	44.6	46.3	54.6			Total Current	50.1	51.6
22.3	10.8	6.8	1.3			Long-Term Debt	10.4	11.3
.0	.0	.4	.1			Deferred Taxes	.3	.2
17.8	3.6	2.9	4.4			All Other Non-Current	4.3	3.2
-43.5	41.0	43.7	39.5			Net Worth	35.0	33.8
100.0	100.0	100.0	100.0			Total Liabilities & Net Worth	100.0	100.0
						INCOME DATA		
100.0	100.0	100.0	100.0			Net Sales	100.0	100.0
35.4	30.5	24.8	23.2			Gross Profit	28.3	27.5
34.6	29.9	22.5	20.6			Operating Expenses	23.5	23.5
.9	.6	2.3	2.6			Operating Profit	4.8	3.9
.4	-.1	.2	-.1			All Other Expenses (net)	.4	.5
.5	.7	2.1	2.7			Profit Before Taxes	4.4	3.5
						RATIOS		
2.2	3.5	2.6	2.8				2.6	2.4
.9	1.8	1.9	1.5			Current	1.5	1.6
.4	1.1	1.5	1.2				1.1	1.2
1.5	2.7	2.1	2.2				1.9	1.8
.6	1.4	1.4	.9			Quick	1.1	1.2
.2	.8	1.0	.6				.8	.8
0 UND	34 10.7	47 7.8	43 8.5				37 9.8	30 12.1
11 33.0	55 6.6	68 5.4	64 5.7			Sales/Receivables	54 6.7	49 7.4
39 9.3	85 4.3	83 4.4	90 4.1				75 4.8	74 4.9
0 UND	0 999.8	3 117.6	1 621.8				1 652.3	2 178.4
1 288.5	10 38.1	14 26.2	12 30.8			Cost of Sales/Inventory	9 38.8	13 28.9
18 20.7	37 9.9	27 13.4	37 9.9				29 12.8	27 13.5
1 415.5	7 49.8	13 27.2	18 19.9				12 29.4	10 35.1
11 33.0	19 19.0	22 16.3	25 14.5			Cost of Sales/Payables	23 16.1	21 17.4
26 14.2	43 8.5	33 11.1	33 11.0				38 9.6	34 10.7
17.6	5.3	5.6	5.4				7.5	7.1
-192.4	12.7	7.4	8.1			Sales/Working Capital	12.4	12.2
-8.7	32.9	13.9	15.7				45.0	34.0
5.1	12.4	15.9	28.7				17.2	17.1
(27) 1.2	(65) 2.3	(63) 4.0	(10) 6.4			EBIT/Interest	(139) 6.6	(151) 4.2
-2.7	-2.4	1.2	3.0				3.0	1.7
		13.8					14.8	13.0
	(15)	2.3				Net Profit + Depr., Dep., Amort./Cur. Mat. L/T/D	(29) 6.0	(35) 4.0
		1.5					2.5	1.2
.1	.1	.1	.1				.1	.1
.7	.4	.2	.1			Fixed/Worth	.3	.3
-.5	.9	.5	.4				.9	.9
.8	.5	.6	.7				.9	.8
9.1	1.4	1.4	2.2			Debt/Worth	1.9	1.7
-1.9	5.4	2.7	5.9				5.1	3.9
137.2	36.2	34.2	31.8				81.3	62.0
(21) 48.1	(66) 9.7	(69) 15.3	(10) 17.5			% Profit Before Taxes/Tangible Net Worth	(143) 38.7	(152) 28.0
.0	-25.9	1.1	5.8				14.4	11.5
33.3	13.3	18.1	13.0				25.6	24.1
1.0	3.1	4.8	6.0			% Profit Before Taxes/Total Assets	12.6	9.4
-26.3	-9.8	.3	3.2				4.2	2.0
158.1	84.8	118.6	136.0				101.3	91.9
52.0	32.4	61.4	74.8			Sales/Net Fixed Assets	48.7	42.4
19.4	15.3	21.3	24.8				17.7	18.5
11.3	3.8	3.7	3.5				4.7	4.9
6.0	3.0	3.0	2.6			Sales/Total Assets	3.6	3.6
3.8	2.5	2.5	2.3				2.7	2.7
.3	.4	.3					.2	.3
(23) .6	(54) .9	(59) .6				% Depr., Dep., Amort./Sales	(124) .5	(127) .5
1.6	2.0	1.4					1.1	1.0
4.6	2.1	1.5					2.0	1.7
(23) 8.6	(43) 3.6	(26) 3.5				% Officers', Directors', Owners' Comp/Sales	(70) 3.9	(79) 3.2
12.5	6.8	4.6					6.5	5.2
49533M	274115M	1041875M	458953M		1117446M	Net Sales ($)	4405279M	3329597M
8054M	85792M	319474M	161534M		115059M	Total Assets ($)	1374365M	871630M

M = $ thousand   MM = $ million

See Pages 9 through 22 for Explanation of Ratios and Data

Comparative Historical Data | Current Data Sorted by Sales

Type of Statement

11	7	3	Unqualified	1	7	6	16	2	1
50	59	60	Reviewed					22	8
25	26	27	Compiled	3	7	13	3	1	1
30	40	42	Tax Returns	14	13	10	1	3	1
64	52	60	Other	2	17	7	11	13	10

4/1/07-3/31/08 ALL	4/1/08-3/31/09 ALL	4/1/09-3/31/10 ALL		23 (4/1-9/30/09)			169 (10/1/09-3/31/10)		
				0-1MM	1-3MM	3-5MM	5-10MM	10-25MM	25MM & OVER
180	184	192	NUMBER OF STATEMENTS	20	44	36	31	41	20
%	%	%	**ASSETS**	%	%	%	%	%	%
10.3	10.7	11.5	Cash & Equivalents	19.3	10.8	13.9	8.0	10.9	7.4
49.5	48.7	46.2	Trade Receivables (net)	17.0	46.1	43.4	58.7	50.2	53.7
12.8	13.3	13.1	Inventory	12.4	15.0	11.6	8.6	16.1	13.4
6.9	6.6	7.1	All Other Current	7.5	4.7	4.4	7.9	7.6	14.4
79.4	79.3	77.9	Total Current	56.2	76.6	73.2	83.1	84.7	88.9
14.1	14.1	14.3	Fixed Assets (net)	31.2	14.7	16.1	11.6	10.3	5.4
1.9	3.2	2.6	Intangibles (net)	4.0	1.5	4.0	2.4	1.7	2.9
4.5	3.4	5.2	All Other Non-Current	8.6	7.1	6.7	2.8	3.3	2.9
100.0	100.0	100.0	Total	100.0	100.0	100.0	100.0	100.0	100.0
			LIABILITIES						
18.4	19.5	20.7	Notes Payable-Short Term	35.7	24.0	11.7	17.0	13.6	34.9
3.4	2.4	2.4	Cur. Mat.-L.T.D.	1.8	3.7	2.7	2.0	2.1	1.4
18.2	18.1	18.4	Trade Payables	24.4	22.6	14.6	17.1	16.1	17.1
.3	.3	.3	Income Taxes Payable	.0	.0	.0	1.5	.2	.3
13.9	13.1	16.8	All Other Current	15.8	29.3	13.8	9.1	14.6	12.3
54.3	53.4	58.7	Total Current	77.8	79.7	42.9	46.6	46.5	66.0
10.5	11.4	11.5	Long-Term Debt	32.6	13.5	10.9	5.7	5.4	8.1
.2	.4	.1	Deferred Taxes	.0	.0	.0	.7	.1	.1
3.8	4.1	6.1	All Other Non-Current	20.9	7.1	4.8	3.0	2.2	4.4
31.1	30.7	23.6	Net Worth	-31.3	-.2	41.4	44.0	45.8	21.4
100.0	100.0	100.0	Total Liabilties & Net Worth	100.0	100.0	100.0	100.0	100.0	100.0
			INCOME DATA						
100.0	100.0	100.0	Net Sales	100.0	100.0	100.0	100.0	100.0	100.0
27.3	26.3	29.1	Gross Profit	43.7	32.9	28.7	22.9	25.3	24.4
22.8	24.2	27.7	Operating Expenses	40.1	33.1	28.5	21.7	22.6	21.3
4.5	2.1	1.4	Operating Profit	3.6	-.2	.2	1.2	2.6	3.1
.6	.6	.1	All Other Expenses (net)	.6	-.3	.2	.4	.0	.1
3.9	1.5	1.3	Profit Before Taxes	3.0	.1	.0	.8	2.6	3.0
			RATIOS						
2.2 / 1.6 / 1.2	2.4 / 1.6 / 1.1	2.8 / 1.6 / 1.1	Current	3.1 / 1.0 / .3	3.2 / 1.4 / .6	3.4 / 1.9 / 1.1	2.4 / 1.7 / 1.4	2.7 / 1.9 / 1.4	3.4 / 1.6 / 1.2
1.9 / 1.2 / .2	1.8 / (183) 1.1 / .8	2.1 / 1.3 / .8	Quick	1.4 / .6 / .2	2.1 / 1.2 / .4	2.5 / 1.4 / .8	2.2 / 1.4 / .8	2.2 / 1.4 / .9	2.2 / 1.2 / .8
30 12.2 / 55 6.6 / 81 4.5	33 10.9 / 52 7.0 / 76 4.8	31 11.8 / 54 6.8 / 78 4.7	Sales/Receivables	0 UND / 6 58.4 / 45 8.2	21 17.5 / 50 7.3 / 88 4.2	31 11.7 / 53 6.9 / 71 5.2	55 6.6 / 69 5.3 / 97 3.8	39 9.4 / 59 6.2 / 75 4.8	40 9.2 / 57 6.4 / 78 4.7
0 UND / 7 52.2 / 24 15.2	1 658.2 / 10 35.9 / 28 13.3	0 999.8 / 10 37.5 / 28 13.1	Cost of Sales/Inventory	0 UND / 5 76.6 / 34 10.8	0 UND / 10 37.5 / 42 8.7	0 UND / 10 36.9 / 29 12.4	1 344.7 / 7 53.5 / 24 15.4	5 68.2 / 19 19.2 / 25 14.5	1 568.5 / 10 38.3 / 26 14.3
12 30.8 / 22 16.8 / 35 10.5	12 30.2 / 21 17.6 / 33 11.2	9 39.6 / 20 18.3 / 34 10.8	Cost of Sales/Payables	0 UND / 14 25.8 / 30 12.0	5 74.7 / 12 29.8 / 44 8.3	5 80.8 / 19 19.6 / 34 10.8	15 23.6 / 26 14.3 / 41 8.9	13 29.0 / 22 16.5 / 33 11.0	13 27.5 / 21 17.5 / 29 12.5
7.6 / 13.8 / 34.6	7.1 / 11.2 / 33.8	5.8 / 11.5 / 55.5	Sales/Working Capital	15.2 / UND / -6.6	4.8 / 20.2 / -22.8	5.8 / 13.2 / 69.8	5.9 / 7.9 / 14.2	5.8 / 8.1 / 14.3	5.4 / 9.9 / 38.4
15.1 / (160) 4.5 / 2.2	12.8 / (166) 2.9 / .4	12.0 / (166) 2.4 / -.8	EBIT/Interest	4.7 / (12) .4 / -2.0	9.8 / (39) 1.6 / -6.3	5.1 / (31) 2.0 / -2.8	8.5 / (30) 2.6 / .9	30.8 / (37) 7.9 / .9	15.2 / (17) 4.9 / 2.4
21.6 / (29) 6.1 / 2.6	9.3 / (25) 3.8 / 1.3	11.7 / (28) 2.3 / .4	Net Profit + Depr., Dep., Amort./Cur. Mat. L/T/D						
.1 / .3 / .8	.1 / .3 / 1.0	.1 / .3 / .8	Fixed/Worth	.1 / 2.8 / -.5	.1 / .3 / NM	.1 / .5 / 1.0	.1 / .2 / .6	.1 / .2 / .4	.1 / .4 / .4
.9 / 1.8 / 4.7	.9 / 2.0 / 5.8	.6 / 1.7 / 5.9	Debt/Worth	.6 / 2.6 / -1.9	.7 / 2.0 / -2.9	.6 / 2.2 / 5.6	.5 / 1.7 / 3.3	.6 / 1.1 / 2.4	.6 / 2.1 / 5.8
66.4 / (160) 33.6 / 12.6	47.2 / (156) 19.4 / .8	40.2 / (166) 13.3 / -.3	% Profit Before Taxes/Tangible Net Worth	285.7 / (14) 14.0 / -2.6	44.6 / (30) 16.6 / -9.1	37.8 / (33) 9.2 / -24.8	22.7 / (30) 7.1 / -5.6	42.6 / 25.3 / .5	42.2 / (18) 16.6 / 6.0
21.1 / 10.2 / 3.9	15.1 / 4.7 / -1.3	16.7 / 3.6 / -3.5	% Profit Before Taxes/Total Assets	44.5 / 2.1 / -8.8	16.1 / 2.8 / -19.2	12.1 / 2.5 / -13.1	7.6 / 3.2 / -1.1	19.9 / 7.6 / .3	25.1 / 7.1 / 2.8
100.7 / 43.5 / 18.4	151.9 / 44.2 / 19.2	113.6 / 44.1 / 17.9	Sales/Net Fixed Assets	94.6 / 35.0 / 8.8	164.6 / 37.8 / 15.2	99.0 / 37.8 / 14.5	91.9 / 43.0 / 17.5	108.3 / 63.4 / 23.5	166.5 / 90.6 / 45.0
4.9 / 3.4 / 2.7	4.7 / 3.4 / 2.7	4.3 / 3.2 / 2.5	Sales/Total Assets	10.8 / 4.3 / 1.8	5.6 / 3.2 / 2.3	3.9 / 3.1 / 2.6	3.4 / 2.9 / 2.5	4.0 / 3.2 / 2.7	4.1 / 3.5 / 2.7
.3 / (135) .6 / 1.3	.3 / (147) .6 / 1.3	.3 / (144) .7 / 1.6	% Depr., Dep., Amort./Sales	.4 / (12) 1.4 / 2.1	.3 / (28) 1.2 / 2.1	.4 / (28) .8 / 2.1	.3 / (28) .6 / 1.2	.4 / (34) .8 / 1.3	.3 / (14) .4 / .6
2.2 / (87) 3.9 / 6.1	1.9 / (90) 3.1 / 5.7	2.0 / (96) 4.6 / 7.6	% Officers', Directors' Owners' Comp/Sales	5.6 / (11) 11.1 / 14.0	1.4 / (26) 5.7 / 8.6	2.3 / (23) 5.6 / 8.0	2.9 / (17) 3.6 / 5.1	1.5 / (14) 2.1 / 3.4	
4147738M	2238505M	2941922M	Net Sales ($)	11317M	87891M	141547M	214165M	604408M	1882594M
1007376M	729133M	689913M	Total Assets ($)	4011M	29566M	48083M	78299M	196410M	333544M

M = $ thousand   MM = $ million
See Pages 9 through 22 for Explanation of Ratios and Data

Current Data Sorted by Assets   **Comparative Historical Data**

Type of Statement	0-500M	500M-2MM	2-10MM	10-50MM	50-100MM	100-250MM		4/1/05-3/31/06 ALL	4/1/06-3/31/07 ALL
Unqualified		4	4	1				5	3
Reviewed		6	9	3				17	20
Compiled	14	10	2	2				9	7
Tax Returns	6	9	1		1	1		21	22
Other		8 (4/1-9/30/09)	13	78 (10/1/09-3/31/10)				14	30
NUMBER OF STATEMENTS	20	29	29	6	1	1		66	82
	%	%	%	%	%	%	**ASSETS**	%	%
	12.6	14.8	12.7				Cash & Equivalents	10.0	12.4
	19.4	28.7	35.7				Trade Receivables (net)	34.9	38.7
	18.1	12.2	16.8				Inventory	16.8	11.3
	2.8	3.3	7.6				All Other Current	2.5	7.8
	53.0	59.0	72.8				Total Current	64.3	70.2
	34.5	25.4	16.6				Fixed Assets (net)	26.3	21.9
	.1	3.0	1.7				Intangibles (net)	.2	1.4
	12.5	12.5	8.8				All Other Non-Current	9.3	6.6
	100.0	100.0	100.0				Total	100.0	100.0
							LIABILITIES		
	25.3	16.3	9.7				Notes Payable-Short Term	12.3	11.8
	3.3	4.3	1.9				Cur. Mat.-L.T.D.	2.5	2.5
	21.9	20.6	12.9				Trade Payables	18.4	15.6
	.0	.2	.7				Income Taxes Payable	.3	.8
	17.3	7.3	15.4				All Other Current	10.6	16.1
	67.7	48.8	40.6				Total Current	44.1	46.8
	47.7	9.9	10.5				Long-Term Debt	15.5	17.7
	.0	.3	.0				Deferred Taxes	.2	.1
	5.8	9.3	2.5				All Other Non-Current	5.3	4.0
	-21.2	31.7	46.4				Net Worth	34.9	31.4
	100.0	100.0	100.0				Total Liabilities & Net Worth	100.0	100.0
							INCOME DATA		
	100.0	100.0	100.0				Net Sales	100.0	100.0
	46.4	32.3	24.9				Gross Profit	33.8	33.7
	45.5	31.8	23.4				Operating Expenses	27.9	28.4
	1.0	.5	1.5				Operating Profit	5.9	5.3
	1.4	.8	.2				All Other Expenses (net)	.5	.8
	-.4	-.3	1.3				Profit Before Taxes	5.4	4.4
							RATIOS		
	2.9	2.7	3.1					2.3	2.3
	.7	1.4	1.6				Current	1.4	1.5
	.4	.7	1.3					1.1	1.1
	2.3	2.3	2.8					1.8	1.9
	.4	1.0	1.1				Quick	.9	1.1
	.1	.4	.6					.6	.7
	0 UND	11 34.6	43 8.4					20 17.9	21 17.1
	8 43.0	39 9.4	62 5.9				Sales/Receivables	37 9.9	39 9.4
	24 14.9	65 5.6	76 4.8					63 5.8	79 4.6
	0 UND	0 UND	4 90.5					0 UND	0 UND
	5 72.5	6 65.7	11 32.5				Cost of Sales/Inventory	8 46.1	5 73.9
	42 8.7	34 10.9	62 5.9					71 5.1	27 13.7
	0 UND	15 24.0	15 24.3					5 78.0	6 58.4
	20 18.5	39 9.3	25 14.5				Cost of Sales/Payables	28 12.8	23 16.2
	49 7.5	61 6.0	39 9.3					53 6.9	43 8.5
	9.5	7.1	4.5					8.4	6.6
	-99.7	15.9	6.6				Sales/Working Capital	16.0	13.7
	-7.0	-18.8	13.5					55.9	34.9
	2.0	7.7	7.2					36.6	19.1
(16)	-.5	(24) 1.7	(24) 3.6				EBIT/Interest	(60) 6.9	(71) 5.8
	-3.8	-5.5	-.9					3.0	2.2
							Net Profit + Depr., Dep., Amort./Cur. Mat. L/T/D	6.3	
								(10) 3.7	
								1.7	
	.2	.3	.1					.2	.1
	7.8	.5	.3				Fixed/Worth	.6	.4
	-.6	2.9	1.0					2.3	1.8
	1.3	.5	.5					.9	.8
	NM	1.6	1.4				Debt/Worth	2.2	1.9
	-2.7	44.6	2.9					5.1	6.6
	25.1	35.5	27.4					74.3	85.8
(10)	-3.1	(24) 8.2	(28) 8.1				% Profit Before Taxes/Tangible Net Worth	(60) 37.0	(70) 40.2
	-350.0	-13.1	-5.6					16.7	17.5
	11.3	12.8	11.5					23.3	28.7
	-2.6	1.7	4.5				% Profit Before Taxes/Total Assets	11.6	14.3
	-13.0	-8.3	-2.2					5.6	3.2
	66.5	40.8	46.4					38.5	66.1
	15.7	15.4	17.4				Sales/Net Fixed Assets	14.1	27.9
	5.4	8.1	7.4					6.7	12.8
	6.3	3.6	2.6					3.9	4.9
	4.6	2.7	2.2				Sales/Total Assets	3.1	3.1
	2.7	2.0	1.6					2.2	2.2
	1.0	.8	.6					.7	.4
(15)	2.7	(25) 1.7	(23) 1.4				% Depr., Dep., Amort./Sales	(53) 1.1	(60) .8
	4.9	3.4	2.4					1.9	1.6
	6.0	2.1	1.5					1.8	2.1
(13)	7.8	(15) 7.0	(13) 3.0				% Officers', Directors' Owners' Comp/Sales	(38) 3.7	(34) 3.3
	14.4	9.6	3.6					7.3	6.0
	23427M	97452M	250819M	258029M	125378M	440002M	Net Sales ($)	866250M	1359761M
	5160M	34614M	116420M	114765M	58574M	111006M	Total Assets ($)	417983M	411351M

M = $ thousand   MM = $ million
See Pages 9 through 22 for Explanation of Ratios and Data

Comparative Historical Data   **Current Data Sorted by Sales**

				Type of Statement	0-1MM	1-3MM	3-5MM	5-10MM	10-25MM	25MM & OVER
	2	2	5	Unqualified			1		3	1
	27	26	16	Reviewed		2	1	8	3	2
	7	13	8	Compiled		1	5	1	1	
	25	21	25	Tax Returns	6	13	4	1	1	
	28	22	32	Other	6	8	2	10	1	5
	4/1/07-3/31/08 ALL	4/1/08-3/31/09 ALL	4/1/09-3/31/10 ALL		\<8 (4/1-9/30/09)\>			\<78 (10/1/09-3/31/10)\>		
	89	84	86	**NUMBER OF STATEMENTS**	12	25	12	20	9	8
	%	%	%	**ASSETS**	%	%	%	%	%	%
	9.5	13.0	13.4	Cash & Equivalents	10.4	13.1	17.9	15.1		
	40.3	42.9	29.5	Trade Receivables (net)	10.2	29.2	30.7	32.8		
	15.0	14.6	15.6	Inventory	15.6	18.7	8.7	16.3		
	6.4	5.0	4.8	All Other Current	3.1	2.8	2.7	8.4		
	71.3	75.5	63.3	Total Current	39.4	63.7	59.9	72.7		
	21.2	18.4	23.7	Fixed Assets (net)	36.4	25.5	26.5	17.0		
	.7	.3	1.6	Intangibles (net)	2.7	1.1	3.3	2.0		
	6.9	5.8	11.3	All Other Non-Current	21.4	9.6	10.3	8.4		
	100.0	100.0	100.0	Total	100.0	100.0	100.0	100.0		
				LIABILITIES						
	18.4	19.0	16.1	Notes Payable-Short Term	19.1	25.9	8.1	8.9		
	2.7	4.2	2.9	Cur. Mat.-L.T.D.	2.7	2.7	7.4	1.1		
	19.9	16.2	17.7	Trade Payables	26.0	15.0	15.5	22.4		
	.2	.9	.3	Income Taxes Payable	.0	.6	.1	.4		
	10.4	12.4	13.2	All Other Current	20.6	12.7	7.4	11.9		
	51.6	52.7	50.2	Total Current	68.4	56.9	38.4	44.6		
	16.8	15.8	18.7	Long-Term Debt	62.7	14.4	13.6	10.8		
	.1	.1	.1	Deferred Taxes	.0	.3	.2	.0		
	7.5	4.7	5.4	All Other Non-Current	5.5	10.0	4.6	4.0		
	24.0	26.7	25.6	Net Worth	-36.7	18.4	43.2	40.6		
	100.0	100.0	100.0	Total Liabilities & Net Worth	100.0	100.0	100.0	100.0		
				INCOME DATA						
	100.0	100.0	100.0	Net Sales	100.0	100.0	100.0	100.0		
	32.4	33.3	34.2	Gross Profit	47.7	36.4	31.7	26.5		
	27.9	30.8	32.3	Operating Expenses	45.2	37.9	29.6	23.9		
	4.5	2.5	1.8	Operating Profit	2.5	-1.5	2.2	2.6		
	.5	.7	.8	All Other Expenses (net)	1.6	1.1	.4	.2		
	4.0	1.8	1.0	Profit Before Taxes	.9	-2.6	1.8	2.4		
				RATIOS						
	2.5	2.4	2.9		1.6	3.6	2.9	2.6		
	1.5	1.7	1.5	Current	.7	1.2	1.7	1.4		
	1.1	1.1	.7		.2	.6	.9	1.3		
	2.1	1.9	2.3		.9	3.1	2.8	1.6		
	1.0	1.2	1.0	Quick	.3	.6	1.5	1.0		
	.5	.7	.4		.1	.3	.4	.6		
	20 18.2	28 12.9	10 37.0		1 589.1	0 UND	8 43.5	32 11.4		
	49 7.4	51 7.2	42 8.8	Sales/Receivables	9 40.3	39 9.4	45 8.2	56 6.6		
	74 5.0	80 4.6	69 5.3		21 17.2	68 5.4	72 5.0	66 5.6		
	0 UND	0 UND	0 UND		0 UND	0 UND	0 UND	5 74.8		
	8 47.8	9 42.4	9 39.7	Cost of Sales/Inventory	21 17.8	30 12.2	0 UND	14 25.8		
	44 8.3	51 7.1	46 7.9		41 8.9	69 5.3	4 95.7	43 8.4		
	10 35.6	9 38.5	14 27.0		18 20.0	0 UND	0 758.8	21 17.8		
	26 14.0	27 13.4	27 13.4	Cost of Sales/Payables	34 10.9	25 14.3	21 17.7	35 10.5		
	55 6.6	45 8.2	54 6.7		49 7.5	59 6.2	59 6.2	63 5.8		
	5.6	5.9	5.4		29.0	4.7	6.7	4.7		
	12.8	10.9	12.7	Sales/Working Capital	-16.1	29.4	13.4	10.0		
	64.4	93.9	-24.3		-4.6	-15.5	NM	24.2		
	20.0	14.2	8.0			1.8	8.3	14.3		
(78)	4.0	(73) 3.4	(71) 1.9	EBIT/Interest	(21) -2.3	(11) 3.4	(16) 4.4			
	1.5	-.3	-4.3		-6.3	-.8	1.0			
		4.5	6.9							
		(15) 2.4	(11) 3.2	Net Profit + Depr., Dep., Amort./Cur. Mat. L/T/D						
		1.0	.5							
	.1	.1	.2		.9	.3	.2	.1		
	.6	.3	.5	Fixed/Worth	-2.0	1.4	.5	.3		
	2.1	1.3	4.4		-.2	UND	.9	1.1		
	.7	.6	.5		4.4	.5	.6	.5		
	2.2	1.3	1.7	Debt/Worth	-4.3	3.7	1.6	1.5		
	7.2	10.1	12.6		-2.5	UND	2.3	6.8		
	54.1	40.6	32.8		18.2	26.6	37.4			
(74)	25.6	(69) 22.4	(70) 10.6	% Profit Before Taxes/Tangible Net Worth	(19) -3.6	(11) 5.8	(19) 13.3			
	8.0	4.3	-9.1		-90.3	-8.9	2.0			
	21.6	23.9	12.6		1.1	10.2	15.3	13.6		
	7.4	7.3	1.8	% Profit Before Taxes/Total Assets	-1.9	-4.4	4.5	4.9		
	.8	-2.5	-7.0		-10.4	-23.6	-2.0	1.6		
	53.6	51.5	47.5		45.2	60.8	40.7	44.8		
	22.1	28.9	15.9	Sales/Net Fixed Assets	8.9	10.1	16.1	19.6		
	8.6	11.6	7.2		4.0	4.9	10.1	12.3		
	3.9	4.1	3.8		5.6	4.1	4.8	3.2		
	2.8	3.0	2.6	Sales/Total Assets	4.1	2.7	2.7	2.4		
	2.1	2.4	1.8		1.4	1.5	2.4	1.8		
	.6	.5	.8		1.3	.7	.8	.7		
(67)	1.1	(70) 1.0	(68) 1.7	% Depr., Dep., Amort./Sales	(10) 3.5	(18) 1.7	(11) 2.1	(15) 1.5		
	2.3	1.7	2.9		4.9	4.3	2.8	2.7		
	1.6	2.4	2.3			7.1		1.3		
(45)	3.0	(38) 4.3	(45) 6.0	% Officers', Directors' Owners' Comp/Sales	(14) 9.4		(10) 3.2			
	5.8	7.2	8.8			11.6		4.5		
	695582M	1219897M	1195107M	Net Sales ($)	8157M	49761M	43406M	134953M	126154M	832676M
	268752M	310646M	440539M	Total Assets ($)	4405M	24431M	15168M	57037M	58494M	281004M

Current Data Sorted by Assets   **Comparative Historical Data**

0-500M	500M-2MM	2-10MM	10-50MM	50-100MM	100-250MM	Type of Statement	4/1/05-3/31/06 ALL	4/1/06-3/31/07 ALL
1	8	2	2		1	Unqualified	7	5
2	21	3				Reviewed	29	40
4	9	2				Compiled	21	22
12	7	2			1	Tax Returns	39	35
8	12	3	2			Other	39	41
	15 (4/1-9/30/09)		87 (10/1/09-3/31/10)					
27	36	30	7		2	**NUMBER OF STATEMENTS**	135	143
%	%	%	%	%	%	**ASSETS**	%	%
19.2	17.6	13.3				Cash & Equivalents	11.5	11.4
27.4	32.6	46.5				Trade Receivables (net)	38.4	37.1
12.2	9.7	7.4				Inventory	15.0	13.9
7.0	5.3	7.2				All Other Current	6.2	5.8
65.9	65.3	74.4				Total Current	71.0	68.2
28.0	23.0	16.6				Fixed Assets (net)	21.0	22.0
1.9	5.9	4.6				Intangibles (net)	1.0	1.7
4.2	5.8	4.5				All Other Non-Current	7.0	8.1
100.0	100.0	100.0				Total	100.0	100.0
						LIABILITIES		
31.2	12.0	10.5				Notes Payable-Short Term	13.0	10.6
1.6	4.7	2.4				Cur. Mat.-L.T.D.	4.9	3.8
19.2	20.0	12.7				Trade Payables	18.4	17.1
.0	.3	.1				Income Taxes Payable	.2	.2
11.1	13.1	15.1				All Other Current	16.1	15.8
63.1	50.0	40.8				Total Current	52.6	47.6
25.8	15.7	5.8				Long-Term Debt	16.8	17.5
.0	.2	.1				Deferred Taxes	.1	.2
23.0	10.0	2.1				All Other Non-Current	5.6	3.5
-11.9	24.2	51.2				Net Worth	25.0	31.3
100.0	100.0	100.0				Total Liabilties & Net Worth	100.0	100.0
						INCOME DATA		
100.0	100.0	100.0				Net Sales	100.0	100.0
40.8	34.7	23.6				Gross Profit	31.7	31.6
41.7	33.9	20.3				Operating Expenses	26.7	26.4
-.8	.8	3.3				Operating Profit	5.0	5.2
.1	.7	.3				All Other Expenses (net)	.7	.7
-1.0	.2	3.1				Profit Before Taxes	4.3	4.5
						RATIOS		
4.6	2.8	3.4					2.4	2.9
1.0	1.5	1.8				Current	1.5	1.4
.7	.8	1.4					1.0	1.1
3.2	2.6	2.5					1.7	1.9
.8	1.0	1.3				Quick	1.1	1.0
.4	.6	1.0					.7	.6
1 701.0	20 18.0	53 6.9					22 16.4	16 23.3
17 21.6	38 9.7	70 5.2				Sales/Receivables	42 8.7	38 9.7
34 10.8	78 4.7	90 4.1					65 5.6	64 5.7
0 UND	0 UND	0 UND					0 UND	0 UND
7 51.7	11 33.7	7 52.7				Cost of Sales/Inventory	12 30.7	9 41.6
27 13.5	38 9.6	20 18.7					42 8.8	39 9.3
0 UND	14 26.2	12 31.0					6 61.7	6 65.5
12 30.3	32 11.3	23 15.8				Cost of Sales/Payables	23 16.2	21 17.2
36 10.1	48 7.7	42 8.7					39 9.2	42 8.7
6.5	4.8	4.7					7.1	6.8
131.1	11.9	7.4				Sales/Working Capital	15.6	17.2
-15.6	-37.9	14.2					-135.6	195.9
3.3	7.1	17.2					20.5	22.9
(21) -2.7	(31) 1.4	(26) 7.5				EBIT/Interest	(123) 7.0	(122) 6.0
-8.3	-1.6	.3					1.6	1.5
		7.3					10.9	5.7
	(10) 2.2					Net Profit + Depr., Dep., Amort./Cur. Mat. L/T/D	(15) 4.8	(22) 3.2
		-.3					1.4	1.9
.3	.3	.1					.2	.2
22.1	1.5	.2				Fixed/Worth	.5	.6
-.9	-10.1	.6					4.0	2.0
1.7	1.2	.4					.9	.7
-116.0	3.3	1.3				Debt/Worth	3.3	2.7
-3.2	-26.2	2.0					13.3	9.2
118.8	51.7	41.2					90.3	88.8
(13) .0	(26) 3.3	8.8				% Profit Before Taxes/Tangible Net Worth	(109) 39.2	(122) 36.2
-23.4	-11.1	.2					17.3	14.6
7.5	9.7	17.3					26.6	29.3
-3.9	.6	5.4				% Profit Before Taxes/Total Assets	11.4	12.4
-29.1	-5.1	.1					2.8	1.6
64.9	37.3	67.3					49.2	77.2
24.4	12.8	22.2				Sales/Net Fixed Assets	23.5	22.1
9.8	7.4	9.3					12.6	9.8
7.8	4.0	3.0					4.6	4.5
4.8	2.7	2.4				Sales/Total Assets	3.2	3.2
1.9	1.8	1.8					2.3	2.4
1.0	.8	.7					.5	.5
(19) 1.5	(28) 1.7	(28) 1.2				% Depr., Dep., Amort./Sales	(113) 1.2	(110) 1.0
2.5	2.9	1.7					2.3	2.2
4.2	2.8	2.1					2.0	2.0
(15) 8.2	(19) 5.7	(18) 3.2				% Officers', Directors' Owners' Comp/Sales	(81) 3.9	(73) 4.5
13.5	8.4	5.6					6.3	8.4
25210M	119564M	327529M	379855M		418161M	Net Sales ($)	2215898M	1973594M
6095M	38822M	129300M	190296M		331454M	Total Assets ($)	652642M	729575M

(Columns 10-50MM, 50-100MM, 100-250MM for percentage and ratio rows: DATA NOT AVAILABLE)

M = $ thousand   MM = $ million
See Pages 9 through 22 for Explanation of Ratios and Data

Comparative Historical Data   Current Data Sorted by Sales

			Type of Statement						
8	8	6	Unqualified		1			2	3
39	17	34	Reviewed	2	4	6	7	12	3
14	13	15	Compiled	4	4	3	3	1	
26	27	22	Tax Returns	8	10		1	2	1
32	29	25	Other	6	13	2	2		2
4/1/07-3/31/08 ALL	4/1/08-3/31/09 ALL	4/1/09-3/31/10 ALL		15 (4/1-9/30/09)		87 (10/1/09-3/31/10)			
				0-1MM	1-3MM	3-5MM	5-10MM	10-25MM	25MM & OVER
119	94	102	NUMBER OF STATEMENTS	20	32	11	13	17	9
%	%	%	ASSETS	%	%	%	%	%	%
15.0	16.1	17.0	Cash & Equivalents	23.6	11.4	15.8	26.8	11.7	
35.5	38.1	35.7	Trade Receivables (net)	22.9	34.1	40.3	34.5	47.8	
11.6	8.7	9.3	Inventory	11.3	10.6	6.2	8.7	9.0	
6.1	5.4	6.2	All Other Current	3.4	8.2	5.4	6.8	7.2	
68.2	68.3	68.3	Total Current	61.2	64.3	67.7	76.9	75.7	
21.1	24.2	23.3	Fixed Assets (net)	32.6	22.5	25.3	17.4	14.8	
3.2	3.1	3.9	Intangibles (net)	2.5	7.4	1.5	.1	5.5	
7.5	4.4	4.6	All Other Non-Current	3.7	5.8	5.5	5.7	4.1	
100.0	100.0	100.0	Total	100.0	100.0	100.0	100.0	100.0	
			LIABILITIES						
12.2	16.8	16.1	Notes Payable-Short Term	31.7	18.9	13.4	9.0	5.0	
4.3	3.9	2.9	Cur. Mat.-L.T.D.	1.4	3.9	4.5	4.0	1.9	
16.7	17.8	17.2	Trade Payables	14.6	18.6	18.7	21.1	13.6	
.2	.1	.2	Income Taxes Payable	.0	.0	.0	.8	.1	
15.4	20.0	13.3	All Other Current	13.9	7.9	2.7	22.2	20.1	
48.8	58.8	49.6	Total Current	61.6	49.3	39.4	57.0	40.7	
18.3	16.6	15.1	Long-Term Debt	30.0	17.0	7.4	11.1	6.5	
.1	.0	.2	Deferred Taxes	.0	.0	.0	.5	.1	
6.3	12.3	10.3	All Other Non-Current	25.6	10.5	16.2	.4	1.1	
26.4	12.3	24.8	Net Worth	-17.3	23.2	36.9	30.9	51.6	
100.0	100.0	100.0	Total Liabilities & Net Worth	100.0	100.0	100.0	100.0	100.0	
			INCOME DATA						
100.0	100.0	100.0	Net Sales	100.0	100.0	100.0	100.0	100.0	
32.9	32.1	32.5	Gross Profit	37.9	37.5	32.2	26.3	24.2	
28.5	29.7	30.2	Operating Expenses	40.2	35.8	28.7	26.9	19.8	
4.4	2.5	2.4	Operating Profit	-2.2	1.7	3.6	-.6	4.4	
1.0	.7	.5	All Other Expenses (net)	.0	.8	.9	.2	-.1	
3.4	1.8	1.9	Profit Before Taxes	-2.2	.8	2.7	-.8	4.4	
			RATIOS						
2.5	2.1	3.4		4.7	3.4	8.4	3.3	3.5	
1.5	1.3	1.6	Current	1.2	1.5	1.7	1.3	2.0	
1.0	.9	.8		.6	.8	.9	.7	1.5	
1.8	1.7	2.6		3.0	1.9	7.0	3.2	2.7	
1.1	1.1	1.1	Quick	.8	1.0	1.1	1.0	1.4	
.7	.6	.6		.3	.5	.8	.5	1.1	
22 16.5	22 16.8	20 18.5		0 UND	19 18.8	46 7.9	12 31.2	50 7.3	
44 8.3	43 8.5	45 8.1	Sales/Receivables	16 23.5	37 9.8	65 5.6	44 8.2	64 5.7	
61 6.0	72 5.1	75 4.9		40 9.1	82 4.5	82 4.5	65 5.6	76 4.8	
0 UND	0 UND	0 UND		0 UND	0 UND	0 UND	0 UND	0 UND	
8 44.3	1 297.5	7 55.7	Cost of Sales/Inventory	0 UND	14 26.7	1 322.4	4 89.0	11 34.1	
41 9.0	21 17.1	28 13.0		67 5.5	38 9.6	19 18.7	22 16.4	18 20.7	
8 48.5	8 47.9	6 56.5		0 UND	8 43.6	14 26.4	4 90.8	11 34.0	
23 16.0	24 15.0	24 15.0	Cost of Sales/Payables	13 27.7	32 11.3	44 8.3	20 17.9	19 19.5	
48 7.6	43 8.5	44 8.3		37 10.0	57 6.4	46 8.0	34 10.8	31 11.6	
7.7	7.6	5.3		5.2	5.9	2.9	6.4	4.9	
16.0	23.5	9.9	Sales/Working Capital	39.3	11.8	8.2	14.2	7.2	
320.7	-30.5	-40.0		-14.5	-21.0	-41.7	-23.7	12.3	
17.8	23.7	12.6		4.1	3.5		5.3	20.5	
(109) 4.1	(84) 5.4	(86) 2.2	EBIT/Interest	(15) -2.7	(29) 1.2		(10) .7	(15) 12.5	
1.3	.1	-2.3		-6.0	-3.0		-7.3	4.4	
9.7	34.9	5.9	Net Profit + Depr., Dep.,						
(22) 1.8	(12) 4.5	(22) 2.2	Amort./Cur. Mat. L/T/D						
.7	1.7	-.1							
.2	.3	.2		.3	.2	.2	.1	.1	
.6	.7	.6	Fixed/Worth	12.1	1.6	1.0	.6	.2	
5.1	UND	8.4		-1.1	-2.7	2.0	2.5	.6	
.9	1.1	.8		1.9	1.3	.6	.8	.4	
2.2	3.9	2.0	Debt/Worth	NM	3.0	1.2	2.0	1.3	
94.4	UND	165.8		-2.5	-11.3	5.8	12.0	1.8	
78.7	83.2	50.7		70.2	50.7	37.1	68.0	82.3	
(95) 24.9	(71) 24.6	(78) 10.1	% Profit Before Taxes/Tangible Net Worth	(10) -5.6	(21) 8.7	(10) 3.8	(11) -5.7	16.0	
8.0	1.7	-5.8		-21.5	-12.8	.4	-16.7	2.3	
20.3	19.5	12.4		3.4	9.7	11.7	12.7	18.8	
7.0	7.2	1.2	% Profit Before Taxes/Total Assets	-3.7	.4	1.6	-3.1	11.0	
.6	-1.9	-4.9		-24.2	-11.3	-1.3	-10.7	1.1	
63.1	65.4	52.2		44.1	46.4	29.2	99.0	61.0	
19.9	20.7	19.5	Sales/Net Fixed Assets	14.2	17.6	10.0	36.9	30.8	
8.9	9.5	7.7		3.5	7.8	7.3	8.4	12.3	
4.8	4.7	4.2		7.1	4.9	3.7	6.1	3.7	
3.1	3.0	2.7	Sales/Total Assets	2.4	2.7	2.0	3.2	2.7	
2.2	2.5	1.9		1.3	1.6	1.5	2.5	2.1	
.6	.6	.7		1.1	1.0	1.0	.4	.5	
(92) 1.2	(76) 1.1	(84) 1.2	% Depr., Dep., Amort./Sales	(13) 1.3	(25) 1.7	(10) 2.1	(11) 1.2	(16) 1.0	
2.4	2.3	2.5		2.9	3.1	3.1	2.8	1.4	
2.4	2.7	2.4			2.9			1.6	
(56) 4.1	(48) 4.3	(54) 5.0	% Officers', Directors' Owners' Comp/Sales	(21) 5.7			(11) 2.2		
6.4	6.7	8.5		10.0				5.9	
2053904M	1427638M	1270319M	Net Sales ($)	10582M	62980M	41701M	95249M	252290M	807517M
891497M	475566M	695967M	Total Assets ($)	5083M	27886M	21757M	28330M	96280M	516631M

M = $ thousand   MM = $ million
See Pages 9 through 22 for Explanation of Ratios and Data

Current Data Sorted by Assets

Comparative Historical Data

0-500M	500M-2MM	2-10MM	10-50MM	50-100MM	100-250MM	Type of Statement	4/1/05-3/31/06 ALL	4/1/06-3/31/07 ALL
	10	19	4			Unqualified	5	7
1	4	2	2			Reviewed	14	24
10	6		1			Compiled	3	4
4		11	1			Tax Returns	4	8
	17 (4/1-9/30/09)		1	66 (10/1/09-3/31/10)	2	Other	4	15
15	**26**	**32**	**8**	**2**		**NUMBER OF STATEMENTS**	**30**	**58**
%	%	%	%	%	%	**ASSETS**	%	%
13.9	14.8	12.7				Cash & Equivalents	9.3	10.1
24.2	39.8	47.7				Trade Receivables (net)	47.5	42.1
4.0	7.1	9.8				Inventory	9.8	9.7
1.4	7.1	6.3				All Other Current	9.1	5.5
43.4	68.8	76.4				Total Current	75.7	67.4
33.8	20.0	13.0				Fixed Assets (net)	15.9	24.2
13.9	2.0	4.4		DATA NOT AVAILABLE		Intangibles (net)	3.0	2.8
9.2	9.1	6.2				All Other Non-Current	5.3	5.6
100.0	100.0	100.0				Total	100.0	100.0
						LIABILITIES		
16.6	10.9	8.0				Notes Payable-Short Term	15.8	14.6
4.7	6.8	2.9				Cur. Mat.-L.T.D.	13.0	3.6
12.4	18.8	19.1				Trade Payables	22.2	18.3
.0	.1	.8				Income Taxes Payable	.4	.9
12.8	8.5	13.7				All Other Current	13.6	11.8
46.5	45.2	44.6				Total Current	65.1	49.2
29.5	15.1	8.9				Long-Term Debt	16.0	16.9
.0	.6	.5				Deferred Taxes	.8	.9
39.6	2.7	9.3				All Other Non-Current	4.4	4.0
-15.5	36.4	36.8				Net Worth	13.7	29.0
100.0	100.0	100.0				Total Liabilities & Net Worth	100.0	100.0
						INCOME DATA		
100.0	100.0	100.0				Net Sales	100.0	100.0
45.2	32.0	25.2				Gross Profit	28.3	32.9
41.8	28.4	20.8				Operating Expenses	24.1	28.4
3.4	3.6	4.4				Operating Profit	4.1	4.5
.4	.5	.5				All Other Expenses (net)	.6	.6
3.0	3.0	3.9				Profit Before Taxes	3.5	4.0
						RATIOS		
3.4	3.0	2.1					2.3	2.0
.9	1.7	1.6				Current	1.7	1.5
.3	.9	1.4					1.4	1.1
3.2	2.8	1.8					1.9	1.7
.8	1.0	1.3				Quick	1.4	1.2
.3	.7	1.1					.9	.7
0 UND	23 16.1	41 9.0					41 9.0	29 12.4
10 36.7	41 9.0	68 5.4				Sales/Receivables	60 6.1	62 5.9
42 8.6	64 5.7	82 4.4					94 3.9	92 4.0
0 UND	0 UND	0 UND					1 583.4	0 UND
2 160.7	3 127.4	2 177.0				Cost of Sales/Inventory	7 55.1	7 52.1
10 37.8	19 19.5	21 17.3					23 15.6	27 13.7
0 UND	5 81.1	12 29.7					16 23.2	16 22.8
7 50.4	23 16.1	28 12.9				Cost of Sales/Payables	35 10.5	32 11.5
34 10.7	66 5.6	42 8.7					49 7.4	56 6.6
15.5	6.0	5.1					5.5	6.1
-81.8	12.1	9.4				Sales/Working Capital	10.6	10.5
-12.3	-38.1	12.4					17.3	56.8
7.7	22.0	15.6					22.5	12.9
(12) 1.5	6.5	(26) 6.8				EBIT/Interest	(26) 9.4	(53) 3.8
-1.3	1.6	.4					2.8	2.0
								7.7
						Net Profit + Depr., Dep., Amort./Cur. Mat. L/T/D		(18) 4.1
								1.6
.6	.2	.1					.1	.2
276.0	.4	.3				Fixed/Worth	.3	.6
-.3	2.9	.8					1.1	1.7
1.1	.7	1.1					.8	1.1
-162.0	2.0	1.9				Debt/Worth	1.3	2.5
-2.4	7.6	5.8					4.9	7.8
	79.3	59.9					45.6	64.8
	(22) 30.6	(28) 24.3				% Profit Before Taxes/Tangible Net Worth	(26) 21.5	(50) 17.5
	2.8	6.0					5.0	8.7
43.0	21.1	17.6					17.6	17.2
.6	11.4	7.3				% Profit Before Taxes/Total Assets	8.2	6.0
-12.9	.5	-.9					2.1	2.4
56.8	45.9	127.7					84.1	40.0
22.9	16.3	30.2				Sales/Net Fixed Assets	27.5	17.2
8.4	9.9	11.9					12.6	7.6
5.4	5.0	3.4					3.9	3.4
4.3	3.1	2.7				Sales/Total Assets	3.0	2.5
3.1	1.9	2.0					2.0	1.8
.9	.8	.4					.6	.6
(11) 1.3	(21) 1.7	(21) 1.0				% Depr., Dep., Amort./Sales	(23) 1.0	(47) 1.3
4.3	3.9	1.7					2.1	1.9
	3.9	1.9					2.4	2.9
	(17) 6.4	(13) 2.8				% Officers', Directors' Owners' Comp/Sales	(16) 3.8	(31) 5.1
	9.4	4.0					7.9	7.9
16273M	106353M	362470M	368650M	329914M		Net Sales ($)	1634802M	529811M
3827M	28367M	138479M	195986M	148060M		Total Assets ($)	340442M	239956M

M = $ thousand   MM = $ million
See Pages 9 through 22 for Explanation of Ratios and Data

Comparative Historical Data | | | | Current Data Sorted by Sales

4/1/07-3/31/08 ALL	4/1/08-3/31/09 ALL	4/1/09-3/31/10 ALL	Type of Statement	0-1MM	1-3MM	3-5MM	5-10MM	10-25MM	25MM & OVER
4	5	4	Unqualified		2	6	1	16	3
16	23	31	Reviewed				7		
10	11	8	Compiled		4	2		1	1
12	25	16	Tax Returns	5	6	2	1	2	
17	25	24	Other	2	8	2	2	7	3
				17 (4/1-9/30/09)			66 (10/1/09-3/31/10)		
59	89	83	**NUMBER OF STATEMENTS**	7	20	12	11	26	7
%	%	%	**ASSETS**	%	%	%	%	%	%
9.0	10.5	14.0	Cash & Equivalents		9.3	15.4	19.4	15.2	
40.5	44.8	39.9	Trade Receivables (net)		34.7	31.5	39.1	55.4	
9.9	8.7	7.7	Inventory		8.2	10.6	8.7	6.2	
9.7	9.3	5.7	All Other Current		3.9	10.8	4.3	6.2	
69.0	73.4	67.3	Total Current		56.1	68.3	71.6	83.0	
20.8	17.6	18.9	Fixed Assets (net)		20.6	24.7	13.4	11.1	
2.6	4.2	5.6	Intangibles (net)		9.6	2.1	9.1	1.1	
7.5	4.8	8.3	All Other Non-Current		13.7	4.9	5.9	4.8	
100.0	100.0	100.0	Total		100.0	100.0	100.0	100.0	
			LIABILITIES						
13.9	13.9	10.8	Notes Payable-Short Term		12.3	10.9	8.8	6.2	
3.4	3.6	4.4	Cur. Mat.-L.T.D.		5.7	3.7	8.8	2.6	
23.3	21.8	16.8	Trade Payables		20.9	13.7	9.3	23.8	
.3	.5	.4	Income Taxes Payable		.1	.0	.8	.7	
14.0	13.6	13.0	All Other Current		10.8	9.4	14.7	15.4	
55.0	53.4	45.3	Total Current		49.7	37.8	42.4	48.7	
26.0	14.9	15.1	Long-Term Debt		25.3	14.8	13.3	6.9	
.1	.1	.4	Deferred Taxes		.7	.0	.2	.5	
1.7	5.1	12.0	All Other Non-Current		31.0	9.7	4.8	6.0	
17.2	26.4	27.2	Net Worth		-6.7	37.8	39.3	37.8	
100.0	100.0	100.0	Total Liabilities & Net Worth		100.0	100.0	100.0	100.0	
			INCOME DATA						
100.0	100.0	100.0	Net Sales		100.0	100.0	100.0	100.0	
28.7	30.5	31.2	Gross Profit		34.1	35.3	20.9	25.3	
25.1	27.2	26.9	Operating Expenses		32.7	27.6	18.2	20.6	
3.5	3.3	4.3	Operating Profit		1.4	7.7	2.8	4.7	
.7	.9	.5	All Other Expenses (net)		.5	.4	.6	.2	
2.9	2.4	3.8	Profit Before Taxes		.9	7.3	2.2	4.5	
			RATIOS						
1.9	2.1	2.2	Current		2.0	5.2	2.2	2.3	
1.4	1.5	1.6			1.0	1.8	1.8	1.6	
1.1	1.1	1.1			.8	1.2	1.2	1.4	
1.5	1.7	1.8	Quick		1.4	4.6	2.1	2.1	
1.1	(88) 1.1	1.2			.9	1.3	1.2	1.4	
.6	.7	.8			.6	.6	.9	.9	
23 16.1	19 19.1	27 13.5	Sales/Receivables	30 12.1	5 72.7	35 10.4	41 9.0		
48 7.7	52 7.0	50 7.3		41 8.9	24 15.3	50 7.3	68 5.4		
81 4.5	95 3.9	74 5.0		58 6.3	60 6.1	103 3.5	81 4.5		
0 UND	0 UND	0 UND	Cost of Sales/Inventory	0 UND	1 251.6	0 UND	0 UND		
3 120.3	2 206.3	4 101.9		10 38.1	10 35.7	1 328.3	1 577.9		
27 13.4	16 22.6	16 22.6		33 11.2	31 11.9	8 46.5	15 23.6		
14 25.5	12 29.3	7 54.4	Cost of Sales/Payables	11 32.3	2 146.0	0 UND	18 20.0		
31 11.9	33 11.0	24 14.9		37 9.8	17 21.0	14 26.5	30 12.3		
54 6.7	55 6.6	42 8.7		72 5.1	43 8.5	32 11.3	42 8.6		
8.1	6.2	6.0	Sales/Working Capital		9.5	5.3	4.2	6.1	
14.3	10.7	10.6			-199.8	7.9	9.8	9.8	
57.6	59.7	156.8			-20.7	30.9	16.6	13.3	
11.8	19.2	17.4	EBIT/Interest		12.1	45.9	12.4	19.2	
(56) 3.6	(73) 4.8	(73) 6.5		(19) 2.1	5.9	(10) 5.1	(20) 9.8		
.6	1.7	.6			-1.0	2.0	-1.9	3.1	
	17.2	32.7	Net Profit + Depr., Dep., Amort./Cur. Mat. L/T/D						
	(15) 10.9	(16) 2.4							
	4.0	.9							
.2	.1	.2	Fixed/Worth		.3	.3	.2	.1	
.6	.4	.4			3.0	.6	.4	.2	
2.7	2.1	2.8			-.6	NM	1.0	.6	
1.2	1.2	1.0	Debt/Worth		1.4	.6	.9	1.1	
2.6	2.8	2.6			6.2	2.0	1.7	1.9	
13.9	8.4	10.8			-4.0	NM	9.7	4.9	
48.7	52.6	65.2	% Profit Before Taxes/Tangible Net Worth		76.6			59.5	
(50) 24.4	(72) 29.1	(66) 24.8		(12) 14.8			(25) 34.0		
11.4	3.9	4.8			-20.0			14.3	
18.6	19.7	20.2	% Profit Before Taxes/Total Assets		19.0	28.6	16.3	22.6	
6.8	7.3	8.7			2.2	10.3	8.8	9.7	
-.3	.7	-1.7			-14.2	1.0	-5.3	4.5	
52.4	100.2	53.8	Sales/Net Fixed Assets		45.2	27.6	36.2	163.3	
20.8	32.4	18.8			14.7	14.1	18.5	43.9	
8.9	13.0	10.3			9.8	8.7	11.9	14.4	
4.4	4.3	4.2	Sales/Total Assets		4.6	4.4	3.1	3.8	
2.8	3.0	2.9			2.7	3.4	2.0	3.2	
2.2	2.0	1.9			1.7	1.7	1.4	2.3	
.7	.4	.7	% Depr., Dep., Amort./Sales		.9		.7	.2	
(43) 1.1	(67) 1.0	(62) 1.2		(14) 2.8		(10) 1.0	(17) 1.0		
2.6	2.3	2.4			4.5		1.7	1.7	
2.1	2.1	2.8	% Officers', Directors' Owners' Comp/Sales			3.5		1.7	
(35) 3.1	(51) 3.4	(38) 4.2			(10) 4.2		(11) 2.6		
6.0	7.7	7.2				9.4		4.2	
858498M	1852524M	1183660M	Net Sales ($)	3623M	36007M	46331M	80829M	372385M	644485M
272958M	695198M	514719M	Total Assets ($)	971M	14443M	18920M	47324M	131598M	301463M

© RMA 2010   M = $ thousand   MM = $ million
See Pages 9 through 22 for Explanation of Ratios and Data

Current Data Sorted by Assets

Comparative Historical Data

						Type of Statement		
3	4	48	82	14	7	Unqualified	130	138
8	99	189	36		1	Reviewed	206	258
20	46	27	3			Compiled	83	76
98	81	42	7		1	Tax Returns	92	124
30	78	116	62	10	2	Other	165	165
	179 (4/1-9/30/09)		935 (10/1/09-3/31/10)				4/1/05-3/31/06	4/1/06-3/31/07
0-500M	500M-2MM	2-10MM	10-50MM	50-100MM	100-250MM		ALL	ALL
159	308	422	190	24	11	NUMBER OF STATEMENTS	676	761
%	%	%	%	%	%	ASSETS	%	%
18.3	11.7	11.3	13.7	15.2	22.1	Cash & Equivalents	11.1	10.5
23.0	28.7	32.9	30.4	23.4	23.9	Trade Receivables (net)	32.8	31.7
6.5	6.4	3.7	4.1	4.2	11.1	Inventory	1.9	3.4
3.4	5.0	7.5	6.9	6.7	4.7	All Other Current	6.1	6.2
51.1	51.8	55.4	55.1	49.6	61.7	Total Current	52.0	51.8
36.8	37.5	35.1	36.4	38.7	27.7	Fixed Assets (net)	40.3	41.6
2.8	2.7	1.6	1.8	2.6	5.4	Intangibles (net)	1.1	1.0
9.2	7.9	7.9	6.7	9.2	5.3	All Other Non-Current	6.6	5.6
100.0	100.0	100.0	100.0	100.0	100.0	Total	100.0	100.0
						LIABILITIES		
19.9	12.6	7.6	5.9	2.4	5.6	Notes Payable-Short Term	7.0	8.1
12.2	6.6	6.4	5.9	5.6	2.6	Cur. Mat.-L.T.D.	6.5	7.6
14.5	14.5	15.4	14.4	12.6	7.8	Trade Payables	14.9	14.7
.0	.1	.5	.4	.3	.2	Income Taxes Payable	.6	.5
30.5	9.2	9.7	9.9	13.9	12.3	All Other Current	10.6	10.6
77.1	43.0	39.7	36.6	34.7	28.4	Total Current	39.6	41.6
31.2	21.7	15.8	16.7	16.4	20.8	Long-Term Debt	23.4	24.0
.0	.3	1.0	1.0	2.1	2.9	Deferred Taxes	1.0	1.0
12.5	4.1	2.2	2.6	1.7	1.3	All Other Non-Current	3.6	2.5
-20.9	30.9	41.3	43.2	45.0	46.6	Net Worth	32.4	30.9
100.0	100.0	100.0	100.0	100.0	100.0	Total Liabilties & Net Worth	100.0	100.0
						INCOME DATA		
100.0	100.0	100.0	100.0	100.0	100.0	Net Sales	100.0	100.0
43.9	35.1	23.8	19.6	19.6	25.3	Gross Profit	28.8	29.8
43.2	33.5	22.4	16.4	15.9	19.6	Operating Expenses	23.3	23.4
.7	1.6	1.5	3.2	3.8	5.7	Operating Profit	5.5	6.4
1.0	1.0	.6	.9	1.0	.5	All Other Expenses (net)	.8	.9
-.3	.6	.9	2.3	2.7	5.2	Profit Before Taxes	4.7	5.5
						RATIOS		
2.0	2.3	2.3	2.2	2.1	4.8		2.1	2.0
1.0	1.3	1.4	1.4	1.5	2.2	Current	1.4	1.3
.4	.7	1.0	1.1	1.2	1.1		1.0	1.0
1.6	2.0	1.8	1.8	1.8	3.4		1.8	1.7
(158) .7	(306) 1.0	1.2	1.1	1.1	1.4	Quick	(675) 1.2	1.1
.3	.5	.7	.8	.8	.7		.8	.7
0 UND	20 18.5	41 8.9	48 7.5	40 9.0	37 10.0		34 10.8	34 10.6
16 22.4	42 8.7	62 5.9	65 5.6	71 5.2	66 5.6	Sales/Receivables	58 6.3	55 6.6
41 8.9	67 5.5	84 4.3	84 4.3	83 4.4	80 4.5		85 4.3	76 4.8
0 UND	0 UND	0 UND	0 UND	0 UND	0 UND		0 UND	0 UND
0 UND	0 UND	0 UND	0 825.4	6 60.3	7 54.1	Cost of Sales/Inventory	0 UND	0 UND
5 76.1	14 25.2	10 37.7	13 29.1	19 18.8	38 9.6		1 298.3	2 156.2
0 UND	7 52.6	17 21.1	22 16.9	21 17.2	16 22.2		12 29.8	11 32.1
7 50.8	20 18.0	30 12.2	35 10.5	32 11.5	24 15.4	Cost of Sales/Payables	29 12.5	28 12.9
34 10.8	46 8.0	53 6.8	54 6.7	47 7.8	38 9.6		50 7.3	50 7.4
14.6	6.7	5.8	5.2	4.2	3.6		7.4	7.9
-192.8	22.9	11.8	11.6	8.2	8.1	Sales/Working Capital	15.0	18.9
-9.3	-17.7	-999.8	43.9	28.1	18.1		-329.4	-193.3
6.5	7.4	9.9	8.8	13.0	21.0		12.7	13.5
(115) 1.7	(274) 2.0	(387) 2.3	(171) 2.2	3.5	(10) 7.4	EBIT/Interest	(621) 5.1	(704) 4.6
-3.9	-1.5	-1.0	-.3	1.7	2.2		2.0	1.7
	4.3	3.4	4.9	3.2			3.8	3.9
(39) 1.6	(124) 1.7	(63) 1.7	(13) 2.2		Net Profit + Depr., Dep., Amort./Cur. Mat. L/T/D	(197) 2.0	(189) 2.0
.4	.7	.9	1.5			1.2	1.2
.5	.4	.4	.5	.4	.3		.6	.6
3.4	1.1	.9	.8	1.0	.9	Fixed/Worth	1.0	1.2
-.7	4.6	1.6	1.6	2.2	1.6		2.2	2.5
1.4	.6	.6	.7	.6	.6		.9	.9
14.7	1.9	1.5	1.5	1.4	1.8	Debt/Worth	1.8	2.0
-2.7	11.9	2.9	2.8	2.7	3.1		4.1	4.7
97.8	35.0	26.1	27.2	16.8	31.5		46.9	59.8
(87) 26.6	(251) 9.9	(387) 7.9	(185) 6.7	(23) 8.8	(10) 16.7	% Profit Before Taxes/Tangible Net Worth	(609) 21.4	(679) 29.0
-16.0	-6.9	-4.1	-4.0	.2	8.4		7.0	10.1
23.3	11.4	10.2	9.6	9.7	16.5		17.0	20.7
3.7	3.3	3.0	2.2	3.0	6.1	% Profit Before Taxes/Total Assets	7.6	9.2
-14.4	-6.0	-3.4	-2.2	.3	2.5		2.0	2.2
82.7	21.8	15.2	9.4	7.7	11.8		11.2	11.2
15.1	6.7	5.2	4.6	4.5	4.7	Sales/Net Fixed Assets	5.5	5.6
4.5	3.3	2.8	2.7	2.2	3.3		3.2	3.3
6.5	3.0	2.5	2.1	1.7	2.3		2.7	2.8
3.7	2.2	1.8	1.6	1.4	1.6	Sales/Total Assets	2.1	2.1
2.0	1.5	1.2	1.1	.9	1.1		1.5	1.5
1.1	1.8	1.8	2.8	3.6			2.8	2.1
(103) 3.2	(248) 4.8	(384) 4.4	(171) 5.1	(22) 5.3		% Depr., Dep., Amort./Sales	(596) 4.8	(668) 4.3
8.0	9.4	8.4	8.2	6.6			7.4	7.4
4.2	2.6	1.7	.8				1.6	1.6
(80) 7.0	(158) 4.2	(176) 2.9	(50) 1.8			% Officers', Directors' Owners' Comp/Sales	(292) 3.3	(341) 3.5
10.0	7.5	4.9	3.4				6.1	6.1
171239M	892330M	3813353M	6900455M	2294422M	3444381M	Net Sales ($)	15637433M	18046954M
40085M	367831M	2004664M	3926339M	1603387M	1713914M	Total Assets ($)	6887334M	9076734M

M = $ thousand   MM = $ million
See Pages 9 through 22 for Explanation of Ratios and Data

Comparative Historical Data			Type of Statement	Current Data Sorted by Sales					
140	153	158	Unqualified	3	2	5	23	50	75
281	281	333	Reviewed	15	70	57	93	76	22
79	72	96	Compiled	20	37	16	15	8	
114	175	229	Tax Returns	73	67	39	32	12	6
209	268	298	Other	35	62	42	50	57	52
4/1/07-3/31/08 ALL	4/1/08-3/31/09 ALL	4/1/09-3/31/10 ALL		179 (4/1-9/30/09)			935 (10/1/09-3/31/10)		
				0-1MM	1-3MM	3-5MM	5-10MM	10-25MM	25MM & OVER
823	949	1114	NUMBER OF STATEMENTS	146	238	159	213	203	155
%	%	%	**ASSETS**	%	%	%	%	%	%
11.8	13.1	13.0	Cash & Equivalents	16.4	10.9	13.9	11.4	12.9	14.6
30.1	30.4	29.6	Trade Receivables (net)	16.3	26.5	33.0	32.9	32.8	34.8
3.5	4.1	5.0	Inventory	7.9	5.1	6.6	3.2	4.1	4.0
6.4	5.2	6.1	All Other Current	3.5	4.8	5.0	6.7	8.2	7.8
51.9	52.9	53.7	Total Current	44.0	47.4	58.6	54.2	58.1	61.2
41.6	39.5	36.2	Fixed Assets (net)	44.1	39.5	32.6	35.8	33.8	31.1
1.0	1.5	2.2	Intangibles (net)	3.4	3.3	2.1	1.8	.5	2.3
5.6	6.1	7.9	All Other Non-Current	8.5	9.8	6.7	8.3	7.6	5.4
100.0	100.0	100.0	Total	100.0	100.0	100.0	100.0	100.0	100.0
			LIABILITIES						
7.5	8.5	10.3	Notes Payable-Short Term	16.9	14.2	10.9	7.7	7.6	5.0
7.2	6.9	7.1	Cur. Mat.-L.T.D.	10.6	8.3	6.4	6.8	5.7	5.2
15.0	13.5	14.7	Trade Payables	9.2	14.1	16.5	15.2	16.1	16.4
.6	.5	.3	Income Taxes Payable	.0	.1	.2	.6	.6	.3
9.9	10.0	12.7	All Other Current	29.4	11.0	7.7	8.8	10.1	13.4
40.2	39.4	45.2	Total Current	66.2	47.7	41.6	39.1	40.0	40.3
24.0	22.2	19.8	Long-Term Debt	31.2	24.4	18.1	17.9	14.2	13.9
1.0	.7	.7	Deferred Taxes	.2	.4	.6	1.1	.7	1.2
2.4	3.1	4.2	All Other Non-Current	12.0	4.1	3.4	3.3	2.1	2.2
32.3	34.6	30.0	Net Worth	-9.7	23.3	36.3	38.6	43.1	42.4
100.0	100.0	100.0	Total Liabilities & Net Worth	100.0	100.0	100.0	100.0	100.0	100.0
			INCOME DATA						
100.0	100.0	100.0	Net Sales	100.0	100.0	100.0	100.0	100.0	100.0
28.6	28.2	29.0	Gross Profit	47.2	36.9	29.1	22.4	22.2	17.7
23.2	24.8	27.2	Operating Expenses	46.2	35.8	27.4	21.6	19.4	14.0
5.4	3.3	1.8	Operating Profit	1.0	1.1	1.7	.8	2.8	3.7
.9	.8	.8	All Other Expenses (net)	1.9	1.0	.5	.6	.5	.5
4.5	2.5	1.0	Profit Before Taxes	-.9	.1	1.2	.3	2.3	3.2
			RATIOS						
2.0	2.3	2.2	Current	2.4	2.0	2.5	2.4	2.4	2.1
1.3	1.4	1.4		.9	1.2	1.5	1.4	1.4	1.5
1.0	1.0	.9		.4	.6	1.0	.9	1.1	1.2
1.7	2.0	1.8	Quick	1.9	1.7	2.1	2.0	1.8	1.7
(821) 1.1	(948) 1.2	(1111) 1.1		(145) .6	(236) .9	1.2	1.2	1.2	1.2
.7	.7	.6		.2	.5	.6	.7	.7	.9
30 12.0	27 13.3	28 12.9	Sales/Receivables	0 UND	17 21.0	29 12.6	37 9.8	41 8.9	46 7.9
53 6.9	52 7.1	53 7.0		18 20.3	41 8.9	51 7.2	59 6.2	60 6.1	65 5.7
78 4.7	76 4.8	77 4.7		60 6.1	70 5.2	85 4.3	80 4.6	78 4.7	81 4.5
0 UND	0 UND	0 UND	Cost of Sales/Inventory	0 UND	0 UND	0 UND	0 UND	0 UND	0 UND
0 UND	0 UND	0 UND		0 UND	0 UND	1 532.8	0 UND	0 999.8	0 999.8
3 120.0	5 78.1	11 33.9		7 50.9	7 50.4	16 22.8	8 46.8	15 24.5	10 35.0
12 31.1	9 39.5	12 31.2	Cost of Sales/Payables	0 UND	5 70.4	14 25.4	13 28.0	21 17.7	21 17.4
29 12.6	25 14.6	25 14.4		8 45.6	19 18.9	28 13.1	26 13.8	32 11.4	32 11.6
51 7.2	45 8.1	49 7.4		43 8.5	48 7.5	53 6.9	52 7.0	49 7.5	49 7.5
7.5	6.6	6.1	Sales/Working Capital	5.6	7.8	6.0	5.5	6.2	5.7
19.0	15.2	16.2		-100.9	39.8	12.2	12.2	13.5	10.3
-135.8	-376.3	-37.3		-5.3	-12.7	UND	-86.6	108.5	28.6
11.7	11.1	8.5	EBIT/Interest	5.3	4.6	11.1	7.9	15.0	14.9
(747) 4.1	(854) 3.1	(981) 2.2		(110) 1.1	(204) 1.6	(140) 2.5	(198) 2.6	(186) 2.9	(143) 3.2
1.3	-.1	-1.0		-5.0	-2.0	-1.4	-1.2	-.7	1.2
4.4	3.6	3.6	Net Profit + Depr., Dep., Amort./Cur. Mat. L/T/D	3.8	3.3	2.6	3.5	3.7	6.4
(211) 2.2	(232) 1.8	(248) 1.7		(10) 1.4	(29) 1.2	(23) 1.6	(62) 2.1	(61) 1.4	(63) 2.3
1.2	.8	.7		.3	.3	.4	.6	.6	1.4
.6	.5	.4	Fixed/Worth	.6	.5	.3	.4	.3	.4
1.2	1.0	1.0		2.2	1.2	1.0	.9	.9	.7
2.4	2.3	2.4		-2.2	19.7	2.4	1.9	1.6	1.3
.9	.7	.7	Debt/Worth	.9	.7	.6	.6	.7	.8
1.9	1.6	1.7		6.7	2.2	1.5	1.5	1.5	1.6
4.1	3.9	5.2		-4.1	51.9	6.3	3.4	2.6	2.7
48.9	37.7	29.6	% Profit Before Taxes/Tangible Net Worth	70.0	30.8	30.6	25.0	29.0	28.6
(738) 23.4	(841) 15.2	(943) 8.9		(88) 12.9	(183) 6.7	(137) 9.5	(186) 7.2	(199) 9.7	(150) 10.1
7.5	.3	-4.2		-6.6	-21.4	-3.5	-6.8	-4.2	1.7
17.1	14.7	11.5	% Profit Before Taxes/Total Assets	14.7	11.5	12.6	10.0	11.4	12.0
7.9	5.0	3.1		.5	2.3	3.8	3.1	3.6	3.5
1.5	-2.4	-4.3		-12.0	-9.4	-2.6	-4.7	-2.8	.5
10.5	14.0	18.4	Sales/Net Fixed Assets	23.3	22.8	21.4	16.0	18.4	12.9
5.0	5.7	6.0		4.4	5.8	6.6	6.1	5.6	7.0
2.9	3.0	3.1		1.8	2.4	3.7	3.2	3.2	3.9
2.6	2.9	2.9	Sales/Total Assets	3.4	3.2	3.0	2.8	2.6	2.6
1.9	2.1	2.0		1.7	2.1	2.2	2.0	2.0	1.8
1.5	1.4	1.3		.9	1.2	1.5	1.3	1.4	1.5
2.4	2.2	1.9	% Depr., Dep., Amort./Sales	2.0	2.5	1.5	1.9	1.6	2.1
(724) 4.9	(808) 4.5	(933) 4.7		(98) 6.8	(188) 6.3	(130) 4.2	(195) 4.2	(187) 4.0	(135) 4.1
8.4	8.3	8.5		16.9	10.7	8.1	7.3	8.1	6.1
1.5	1.8	2.0	% Officers', Directors' Owners' Comp/Sales	6.3	2.9	2.0	1.6	1.3	.8
(317) 3.1	(394) 3.6	(472) 3.5		(67) 6.3	(107) 5.1	(84) 3.2	(95) 2.8	(81) 2.5	(38) 1.8
6.1	6.6	7.1		13.9	8.0	4.8	4.5	4.7	3.5
16860067M	18204788M	17516180M	Net Sales ($)	83979M	461854M	642647M	1556994M	3167352M	11603354M
9149097M	10069535M	9656220M	Total Assets ($)	69191M	313078M	356438M	958203M	1857455M	6101855M

M = $ thousand   MM = $ million
See Pages 9 through 22 for Explanation of Ratios and Data

Current Data Sorted by Assets

Comparative Historical Data

0-500M	500M-2MM	2-10MM	10-50MM	50-100MM	100-250MM	Type of Statement	4/1/05-3/31/06 ALL	4/1/06-3/31/07 ALL
3	5	36	44	19	5	Unqualified	100	122
6	65	156	35	1	1	Reviewed	236	276
28	48	37	5			Compiled	135	149
120	108	44	10		1	Tax Returns	207	254
51	97	127	46	6	5	Other	306	294
	155 (4/1-9/30/09)			954 (10/1/09-3/31/10)				
208	323	400	140	26	12	NUMBER OF STATEMENTS	984	1095
%	%	%	%	%	%	**ASSETS**	%	%
21.2	12.8	13.2	17.2	15.5	17.0	Cash & Equivalents	12.5	13.2
22.3	34.4	38.4	32.0	28.9	21.6	Trade Receivables (net)	38.6	36.0
9.0	10.8	5.9	3.7	5.5	3.4	Inventory	8.0	8.5
4.5	4.9	7.2	7.5	9.5	8.4	All Other Current	5.6	5.9
57.0	62.8	64.7	60.4	59.4	50.4	Total Current	64.7	63.6
31.2	26.2	26.4	28.2	27.9	32.2	Fixed Assets (net)	25.9	27.1
3.5	3.1	1.7	5.6	4.8	7.1	Intangibles (net)	3.0	2.5
8.3	7.9	7.2	5.8	7.8	10.3	All Other Non-Current	6.4	6.8
100.0	100.0	100.0	100.0	100.0	100.0	Total	100.0	100.0
						LIABILITIES		
21.8	12.4	8.6	5.2	4.9	.5	Notes Payable-Short Term	11.3	11.8
7.8	4.4	4.5	4.7	8.2	3.9	Cur. Mat.-L.T.D.	4.5	4.3
17.1	16.7	17.1	13.6	11.8	11.0	Trade Payables	17.6	16.4
.1	.4	.4	.2	.8	.3	Income Taxes Payable	.5	.6
18.1	9.8	12.9	14.7	18.1	11.7	All Other Current	12.8	13.3
64.9	43.7	43.6	38.5	43.7	27.5	Total Current	46.8	46.4
29.1	17.9	12.7	13.7	12.4	24.2	Long-Term Debt	17.1	17.4
.0	.4	.6	.8	.6	1.6	Deferred Taxes	.4	.5
8.6	3.1	3.8	2.1	1.8	7.0	All Other Non-Current	4.2	4.0
-2.6	34.9	39.4	44.9	41.5	39.7	Net Worth	31.6	31.6
100.0	100.0	100.0	100.0	100.0	100.0	Total Liabilities & Net Worth	100.0	100.0
						INCOME DATA		
100.0	100.0	100.0	100.0	100.0	100.0	Net Sales	100.0	100.0
42.1	36.0	28.4	25.3	18.1	34.6	Gross Profit	32.9	33.0
40.5	32.6	25.0	20.4	11.6	21.2	Operating Expenses	27.3	27.8
1.5	3.4	3.4	4.9	6.5	13.4	Operating Profit	5.6	5.1
.7	.9	.4	1.0	.9	8.0	All Other Expenses (net)	.6	.8
.8	2.5	3.0	3.9	5.6	5.5	Profit Before Taxes	5.0	4.4
						RATIOS		
2.7	2.9	2.3	2.6	1.8	2.7	Current	2.3	2.4
1.0	1.7	1.5	1.6	1.4	1.7		1.5	1.5
.5	1.0	1.1	1.1	1.1	1.4		1.1	1.1
2.1	2.3	1.9	2.1	1.7	2.0	Quick	1.9	1.9
.7	1.2	1.2	1.3	1.0	1.4		(983) 1.2	1.2
.2	.6	.8	.8	.4			.7	.7
0 UND	21 17.6	37 9.8	37 9.7	43 8.5	32 11.5	Sales/Receivables	24 15.3	19 19.5
10 37.0	39 9.4	55 6.7	63 5.8	55 6.6	45 8.1		51 7.1	44 8.2
32 11.4	64 5.7	79 4.6	80 4.6	84 4.3	93 3.9		79 4.6	71 5.2
0 UND	0 UND	0 UND	0 UND	0 UND	0 UND	Cost of Sales/Inventory	0 UND	0 UND
0 UND	4 101.1	0 778.3	0 999.8	2 170.8	1 532.3		1 562.9	1 632.0
11 33.0	28 13.0	15 25.1	10 34.9	11 32.1	24 15.2		19 19.6	18 20.7
0 UND	7 54.5	15 24.5	13 27.4	18 20.8	7 50.3	Cost of Sales/Payables	11 33.9	7 49.9
8 47.2	21 17.2	30 12.2	25 14.8	27 13.5	16 22.9		26 14.1	23 15.6
34 10.8	42 8.7	52 7.1	46 8.0	41 9.0	40 9.1		49 7.5	44 8.3
12.7	6.3	6.7	4.5	5.5	3.0	Sales/Working Capital	6.9	7.5
NM	13.1	12.7	9.3	9.6	8.0		13.4	15.2
-13.2	-144.3	38.7	60.2	60.1	12.9		63.2	118.3
10.5	14.7	16.1	26.5	109.0	176.5	EBIT/Interest	18.0	19.3
(170) 2.3	(288) 3.5	(355) 4.4	(115) 4.8	(22) 10.8	(11) 4.7		(868) 6.0	(976) 5.7
-2.5	.3	.0	.7	1.8	.7		1.8	1.7
	4.0	4.8	11.9			Net Profit + Depr., Dep., Amort./Cur. Mat. L/T/D	6.9	6.4
	(42) 1.8	(114) 1.9	(39) 3.2				(194) 3.0	(205) 2.7
	.4	.6	1.2				1.2	1.2
.2	.2	.2	.2	.1	.1	Fixed/Worth	.2	.2
1.5	.6	.6	.5	.4	.6		.6	.7
-2.1	3.1	1.3	1.8	1.2	6.0		2.0	2.1
.7	.6	.7	.7	1.1	.6	Debt/Worth	.9	.8
4.3	1.6	1.5	1.6	1.5	1.6		1.9	1.8
-4.9	10.6	3.1	3.2	2.6	6.3		5.7	6.1
100.6	54.1	42.3	38.0	54.8	32.8	% Profit Before Taxes/Tangible Net Worth	71.7	71.9
(130) 24.0	(268) 16.4	(371) 15.0	(132) 15.0	(25) 16.8	(10) 19.2		(849) 32.8	(942) 32.5
-9.0	-.6	1.2	-.3	6.7	.2		9.6	10.0
33.1	19.7	16.7	16.4	11.8	19.9	% Profit Before Taxes/Total Assets	23.0	24.0
4.4	5.7	5.4	5.3	5.2	6.6		10.3	10.4
-14.7	-1.6	-1.0	-.4	1.7	-.7		1.9	1.9
108.9	37.3	28.8	35.1	43.4	23.2	Sales/Net Fixed Assets	41.5	42.4
23.8	16.7	13.2	9.0	10.1	7.1		16.4	16.8
9.2	6.7	5.0	3.3	3.1	.7		7.1	7.1
8.5	4.1	3.2	2.5	2.2	2.0	Sales/Total Assets	4.1	4.3
4.8	2.9	2.4	1.8	1.6	1.2		2.9	3.0
3.1	2.1	1.7	1.2	.9	.5		1.9	2.1
.7	.9	.9	.9	.7	.5	% Depr., Dep., Amort./Sales	.7	.7
(141) 2.2	(259) 1.9	(357) 1.9	(119) 2.1	(23) 1.7			(800) 1.6	(899) 1.7
4.3	3.8	4.2	4.7	5.0			3.5	3.6
4.0	2.8	1.6	1.2			% Officers', Directors' Owners' Comp/Sales	2.0	2.2
(133) 6.9	(194) 4.3	(182) 2.9	(53) 1.8				(465) 4.0	(548) 4.4
11.9	7.5	5.4	3.4				7.1	7.0
320792M	1188007M	4607181M	5318368M	2767902M	2910165M	Net Sales ($)	18112652M	24332386M
52426M	361950M	1829149M	2660854M	1806497M	2153818M	Total Assets ($)	6010292M	7998529M

M = $ thousand   MM = $ million
See Pages 9 through 22 for Explanation of Ratios and Data

Comparative Historical Data				Current Data Sorted by Sales					
			Type of Statement						
103	113	112	Unqualified	3	1	4	12	34	58
255	275	264	Reviewed	6	32	42	67	90	27
135	132	118	Compiled	9	48	16	20	20	5
225	241	283	Tax Returns	65	90	56	31	34	7
303	320	332	Other	31	68	47	76	62	48
4/1/07-3/31/08 ALL	4/1/08-3/31/09 ALL	4/1/09-3/31/10 ALL		155 (4/1-9/30/09)			954 (10/1/09-3/31/10)		
				0-1MM	1-3MM	3-5MM	5-10MM	10-25MM	25MM & OVER
1021	1081	1109	**NUMBER OF STATEMENTS**	114	239	165	206	240	145
%	%	%	**ASSETS**	%	%	%	%	%	%
12.4	13.9	15.2	Cash & Equivalents	18.0	17.2	13.9	12.0	13.8	18.1
35.6	34.2	33.0	Trade Receivables (net)	15.6	28.5	34.3	37.1	39.1	36.5
8.3	8.4	7.6	Inventory	9.8	9.6	8.8	6.3	6.3	5.1
6.4	6.4	6.1	All Other Current	5.0	3.4	5.6	7.2	7.5	8.5
62.7	62.9	61.9	Total Current	48.4	58.6	62.5	62.5	66.7	68.1
26.9	26.9	27.6	Fixed Assets (net)	36.4	29.8	26.1	28.5	25.1	21.4
2.8	2.8	3.1	Intangibles (net)	6.3	2.7	3.0	1.5	2.0	5.3
7.6	7.4	7.5	All Other Non-Current	8.8	8.9	8.3	7.5	6.1	5.2
100.0	100.0	100.0	Total	100.0	100.0	100.0	100.0	100.0	100.0
			LIABILITIES						
11.6	12.0	11.6	Notes Payable-Short Term	20.2	17.1	10.3	9.3	9.0	4.9
5.0	4.6	5.2	Cur. Mat.-L.T.D.	9.3	4.6	5.8	4.3	4.8	4.2
15.6	15.5	16.4	Trade Payables	12.4	14.5	14.4	19.0	18.4	17.6
.6	.6	.3	Income Taxes Payable	.2	.1	.6	.3	.4	.3
13.6	13.5	13.3	All Other Current	16.2	12.1	11.0	10.7	13.6	19.0
46.5	46.1	46.8	Total Current	58.2	48.4	42.2	43.7	46.2	46.0
17.9	17.3	17.5	Long-Term Debt	36.1	20.8	17.0	14.4	12.8	10.3
.3	.4	.5	Deferred Taxes	.1	.3	.6	.5	.7	.6
4.5	3.9	4.2	All Other Non-Current	7.6	4.6	2.2	5.7	2.1	4.9
30.8	32.2	31.0	Net Worth	-2.0	25.9	38.0	35.8	38.2	38.3
100.0	100.0	100.0	Total Liabilities & Net Worth	100.0	100.0	100.0	100.0	100.0	100.0
			INCOME DATA						
100.0	100.0	100.0	Net Sales	100.0	100.0	100.0	100.0	100.0	100.0
33.4	33.1	32.6	Gross Profit	46.1	40.8	33.2	29.6	26.6	21.9
27.6	28.4	29.2	Operating Expenses	44.8	37.8	29.2	26.5	23.2	16.3
5.8	4.7	3.4	Operating Profit	1.3	3.0	3.9	3.1	3.4	5.6
.8	.6	.8	All Other Expenses (net)	1.7	.9	.4	.4	.5	1.1
5.0	4.1	2.7	Profit Before Taxes	-.4	2.1	3.5	2.8	2.9	4.6
			RATIOS						
2.4	2.5	2.6	Current	2.4	3.5	3.0	2.5	2.2	2.2
1.5	1.5	1.5		1.0	1.6	1.6	1.5	1.5	1.5
1.0	1.0	1.0		.4	.8	1.0	1.1	1.1	1.2
1.9	2.0	2.1	Quick	1.7	2.6	2.5	2.2	1.8	1.8
(1020) 1.2	(1080) 1.2	1.2		.6	1.1	1.1	1.2	1.2	1.2
.7	.7	.6		.2	.5	.7	.8	.8	.8
20 18.1	19 18.9	21 17.6	Sales/Receivables	0 UND	9 40.5	19 19.5	33 11.2	37 9.8	34 10.7
47 7.8	43 8.4	44 8.3		13 28.7	32 11.3	43 8.6	48 7.6	54 6.8	55 6.7
72 5.1	71 5.2	70 5.2		37 9.9	59 6.2	70 5.2	80 4.6	77 4.8	76 4.8
0 UND	0 UND	0 UND	Cost of Sales/Inventory	0 UND	0 UND	0 UND	0 UND	0 UND	0 UND
0 999.8	1 325.3	0 844.0		0 UND	0 UND	2 151.9	0 779.1	1 291.7	0 999.8
17 21.1	21 17.1	17 21.2		24 15.1	26 14.1	25 14.9	14 26.7	15 23.9	9 39.9
8 44.7	8 44.1	9 39.8	Cost of Sales/Payables	0 UND	2 208.0	6 59.0	12 29.9	17 22.1	15 23.7
23 16.1	22 16.5	23 15.7		11 33.3	18 19.9	19 19.5	29 12.7	28 12.8	26 14.1
43 8.6	40 9.1	44 8.3		56 6.6	38 9.7	39 9.3	52 7.0	46 8.0	44 8.2
6.8	6.6	6.5	Sales/Working Capital	10.3	6.2	6.1	6.3	7.1	5.8
14.2	14.1	14.1		UND	15.1	14.0	13.0	13.7	10.9
750.2	158.7	-148.5		-7.9	-30.5	-148.5	55.8	62.6	31.1
19.6	18.5	14.8	EBIT/Interest	4.5	11.2	17.0	12.2	17.4	82.4
(902) 5.2	(936) 5.0	(961) 3.7		(88) .2	(209) 2.6	(144) 5.0	(184) 3.1	(215) 5.0	(121) 11.6
1.6	1.1	.0		-5.6	-.5	1.2	-.2	.4	1.4
12.2	9.2	4.9	Net Profit + Depr., Dep., Amort./Cur. Mat. L/T/D		3.0	3.9	3.7	5.1	11.9
(189) 3.5	(222) 3.1	(217) 1.9			(23) .8	(25) 1.9	(45) 1.4	(79) 2.2	(39) 4.0
1.4	1.4	.7			-.9	.6	.3	.8	1.4
.2	.2	.2	Fixed/Worth	.3	.2	.2	.2	.2	.1
.6	.6	.6		1.8	.8	.7	.6	.5	.4
2.2	2.0	2.3		-2.4	5.1	2.0	1.7	1.4	1.0
.8	.7	.7	Debt/Worth	.8	.6	.6	.6	.7	.8
1.8	1.7	1.7		6.7	1.8	1.3	1.4	1.6	1.7
6.0	5.7	6.7		-4.2	13.9	7.1	3.4	3.5	2.9
70.2	58.7	49.0	% Profit Before Taxes/Tangible Net Worth	67.6	55.4	49.3	43.6	43.8	47.6
(870) 34.5	(915) 27.0	(936) 16.1		(68) 11.4	(189) 11.8	(140) 16.5	(182) 14.0	(223) 16.1	(134) 23.2
10.3	6.5	-.1		-38.7	-7.3	3.7	-1.1	.4	4.9
26.0	23.0	19.3	% Profit Before Taxes/Total Assets	18.2	23.1	20.9	14.7	20.5	18.9
10.3	8.5	5.3		.0	3.8	7.1	4.7	5.9	8.4
2.1	.7	-1.6		-25.3	-3.7	.7	-1.5	-.7	1.2
41.5	44.8	38.7	Sales/Net Fixed Assets	39.4	39.7	39.3	33.3	30.8	63.5
16.8	17.0	15.0		8.8	17.0	17.1	12.8	15.5	21.5
6.6	6.1	5.8		4.0	6.4	6.4	5.3	6.3	6.6
4.2	4.1	3.8	Sales/Total Assets	5.1	4.6	4.3	3.5	3.5	3.3
2.8	2.8	2.6		2.5	3.1	2.8	2.5	2.6	2.3
1.9	1.9	1.8		1.5	2.0	2.0	1.7	1.8	1.7
.7	.7	.8	% Depr., Dep., Amort./Sales	2.0	.8	.9	.8	.8	.4
(816) 1.7	(869) 1.8	(907) 2.0		(76) 4.2	(187) 2.3	(126) 2.4	(177) 1.8	(222) 1.8	(119) 1.2
3.7	3.9	4.2		9.9	4.5	4.5	4.0	3.1	3.3
2.0	2.1	2.2	% Officers', Directors' Owners' Comp/Sales	5.1	3.6	2.4	2.3	1.3	.9
(496) 4.0	(524) 4.1	(567) 4.1		(68) 7.7	(151) 5.6	(102) 4.1	(94) 3.7	(112) 2.2	(40) 1.6
7.1	6.9	7.5		14.6	8.6	6.8	5.8	4.4	3.3
15704369M	17198724M	17112415M	Net Sales ($)	62541M	461360M	654043M	1453577M	3639587M	10841307M
6451664M	7943967M	8864694M	Total Assets ($)	32574M	201100M	289960M	701982M	1705901M	5933177M

© RMA 2010

M = $ thousand   MM = $ million

See Pages 9 through 22 for Explanation of Ratios and Data

MANUFACTURING

MANUFACTURING

MANUFACTURING—Other Animal Food Manufacturing NAICS 311119

Current Data Sorted by Assets						Type of Statement	Comparative Historical Data	
	1	10	18	9	3	Unqualified	30	52
	3	11	8			Reviewed	9	16
	7	5	1			Compiled	18	16
2	8	5	1			Tax Returns	7	10
2	6	13	20	1	5	Other	36	39
	45 (4/1-9/30/09)		94 (10/1/09-3/31/10)				4/1/05-3/31/06 ALL	4/1/06-3/31/07 ALL
0-500M	500M-2MM	2-10MM	10-50MM	50-100MM	100-250MM	NUMBER OF STATEMENTS		
4	25	44	48	10	8		100	133
%	%	%	%	%	%	ASSETS	%	%
	11.6	8.1	6.1	9.0		Cash & Equivalents	9.5	6.6
	33.4	28.8	24.0	19.1		Trade Receivables (net)	23.0	25.3
	22.5	22.2	25.1	24.6		Inventory	20.0	23.4
	2.8	4.9	3.6	1.4		All Other Current	3.5	2.9
	70.3	63.9	58.8	54.1		Total Current	56.1	58.2
	22.6	30.7	28.7	32.7		Fixed Assets (net)	36.0	31.8
	.5	1.1	3.1	4.9		Intangibles (net)	2.2	2.5
	6.6	4.2	9.4	8.3		All Other Non-Current	5.6	7.5
	100.0	100.0	100.0	100.0		Total	100.0	100.0
						LIABILITIES		
	13.8	15.4	12.0	3.3		Notes Payable-Short Term	9.8	13.0
	2.2	4.5	2.4	1.5		Cur. Mat.-L.T.D.	4.0	3.1
	19.0	17.7	14.5	13.1		Trade Payables	16.4	15.9
	.1	.1	.1	.1		Income Taxes Payable	.2	.2
	6.1	11.5	9.6	9.9		All Other Current	9.0	8.3
	41.2	49.1	38.6	27.9		Total Current	39.5	40.6
	22.5	17.2	13.7	9.9		Long-Term Debt	19.5	15.5
	.1	.2	.0	.0		Deferred Taxes	.6	.6
	2.6	2.5	5.4	3.6		All Other Non-Current	2.5	3.8
	33.6	30.9	42.2	58.7		Net Worth	37.9	39.5
	100.0	100.0	100.0	100.0		Total Liabilities & Net Worth	100.0	100.0
						INCOME DATA		
	100.0	100.0	100.0	100.0		Net Sales	100.0	100.0
	31.3	17.6	19.9	23.5		Gross Profit	23.2	23.8
	25.9	15.1	12.7	16.7		Operating Expenses	18.9	19.3
	5.3	2.5	7.2	6.7		Operating Profit	4.3	4.5
	-.1	.1	1.2	-.4		All Other Expenses (net)	1.2	1.1
	5.4	2.5	6.0	7.2		Profit Before Taxes	3.1	3.4
						RATIOS		
	3.7	1.8	2.8	3.0			2.2	2.2
	1.7	1.3	1.4	2.1		Current	1.6	1.4
	1.2	1.0	1.1	1.1			1.1	1.1
	2.2	1.1	1.2	1.5			1.4	1.3
	.9	.7	.8	1.0		Quick	.8	.7
	.6	.4	.5	.6			.5	.5
	27 13.6	14 26.5	19 18.9	21 17.0			17 21.2	19 19.7
	36 10.2	31 11.6	33 11.1	25 14.5		Sales/Receivables	26 14.0	29 12.6
	41 8.9	46 7.9	41 8.8	32 11.3			38 9.7	41 8.8
	13 28.4	11 33.3	17 21.6	18 20.5			17 21.2	18 20.3
	29 12.8	29 12.4	39 9.4	35 10.3		Cost of Sales/Inventory	27 13.6	35 10.6
	57 6.4	51 7.2	70 5.2	84 4.4			45 8.1	62 5.9
	10 37.1	12 31.1	14 26.6	17 21.4			14 25.2	13 27.8
	20 17.9	21 17.6	20 18.5	25 14.6		Cost of Sales/Payables	22 16.9	23 15.8
	51 7.2	34 10.7	28 12.9	29 12.5			32 11.4	36 10.3
	6.4	10.3	7.5	5.4			8.5	9.5
	13.5	24.4	17.4	9.6		Sales/Working Capital	17.2	17.0
	69.2	NM	57.4	315.2			65.1	109.2
	25.5	13.1	17.0	30.5			14.5	10.8
	(24) 5.3	(42) 4.6	(39) 4.0	16.4		EBIT/Interest	(90) 5.2	(123) 4.4
	1.9	1.6	.5	6.3			1.9	1.8
		6.4					7.8	12.3
		(12) 2.7				Net Profit + Depr., Dep., Amort./Cur. Mat. L/T/D	(23) 3.2	(34) 3.5
		1.1					1.1	1.5
	.1	.4	.3	.4			.4	.5
	.5	.7	1.0	.6		Fixed/Worth	.8	.8
	1.8	2.8	1.8	.9			1.5	1.8
	.6	1.1	.4	.5			.6	.6
	2.2	2.6	1.8	.8		Debt/Worth	1.5	1.4
	7.1	6.3	4.5	1.3			3.0	3.7
	72.4	60.5	52.2	46.8			34.7	35.0
	(22) 42.7	(42) 23.9	(45) 23.5	31.6		% Profit Before Taxes/Tangible Net Worth	(95) 19.6	(119) 20.2
	11.0	5.4	5.8	9.6			7.2	7.5
	31.2	16.7	19.1	26.4			15.7	14.4
	12.8	8.0	11.2	21.0		% Profit Before Taxes/Total Assets	8.2	7.2
	3.2	-.1	-.4	3.8			2.2	2.6
	48.1	34.2	22.3	11.7			21.3	25.7
	24.6	16.1	12.7	9.3		Sales/Net Fixed Assets	8.9	9.7
	9.4	6.3	6.0	4.7			3.8	5.2
	5.0	4.2	3.6	4.2			3.8	3.8
	3.6	3.3	2.5	3.2		Sales/Total Assets	2.7	2.8
	2.6	2.1	1.9	1.5			1.9	1.9
	.9	.7	.7	1.0			1.0	1.1
	(17) 1.1	(41) 1.5	(43) 1.3	1.5		% Depr., Dep., Amort./Sales	(88) 1.9	(119) 1.6
	2.1	3.1	2.1	4.9			3.5	2.6
		.8					1.4	.6
		(11) 1.1				% Officers', Directors', Owners' Comp/Sales	(25) 2.0	(32) 2.1
		3.8					3.7	3.8
2355M	110928M	752742M	3516708M	2300049M	2922554M	Net Sales ($)	4926501M	10276492M
540M	29221M	237219M	1127515M	742646M	1535638M	Total Assets ($)	2100235M	3770994M

© RMA 2010

M = $ thousand   MM = $ million
See Pages 9 through 22 for Explanation of Ratios and Data

Comparative Historical Data | Current Data Sorted by Sales

			Type of Statement						
19	22	18	Unqualified	1			1		16
5	6	5	Reviewed		1	1	1	2	1
4	5	6	Compiled			3		1	2
3	4	4	Tax Returns		1		2	2	
15	20	16	Other	1	1		1	4	11
4/1/07-3/31/08	4/1/08-3/31/09	4/1/09-3/31/10		25 (4/1-9/30/09)			24 (10/1/09-3/31/10)		
ALL	ALL	ALL		0-1MM	1-3MM	3-5MM	5-10MM	10-25MM	25MM & OVER
46	57	49	**NUMBER OF STATEMENTS**	2	2	5	4	8	28
%	%	%	**ASSETS**	%	%	%	%	%	%
5.8	4.9	7.5	Cash & Equivalents						3.0
19.5	20.7	20.1	Trade Receivables (net)						20.1
25.8	29.9	26.9	Inventory						27.3
4.4	3.3	3.1	All Other Current						3.5
55.5	58.8	57.6	Total Current						53.9
37.7	32.2	33.2	Fixed Assets (net)						36.1
2.1	3.2	2.6	Intangibles (net)						3.5
4.7	5.9	6.7	All Other Non-Current						6.5
100.0	100.0	100.0	Total						100.0
			LIABILITIES						
13.7	15.6	13.3	Notes Payable-Short Term						14.2
3.0	3.5	3.5	Cur. Mat.-L.T.D.						1.9
12.8	14.1	11.1	Trade Payables						11.4
.2	.3	.3	Income Taxes Payable						.5
6.0	7.4	7.0	All Other Current						6.3
35.8	40.8	35.2	Total Current						34.4
18.8	19.1	17.5	Long-Term Debt						16.2
1.6	1.3	1.2	Deferred Taxes						1.9
3.8	4.4	3.9	All Other Non-Current						3.8
40.1	34.4	42.2	Net Worth						43.8
100.0	100.0	100.0	Total Liabilties & Net Worth						100.0
			INCOME DATA						
100.0	100.0	100.0	Net Sales						100.0
20.0	20.0	22.3	Gross Profit						16.7
14.6	15.6	15.9	Operating Expenses						10.8
5.4	4.5	6.4	Operating Profit						5.9
1.2	1.0	1.6	All Other Expenses (net)						1.1
4.2	3.4	4.8	Profit Before Taxes						4.8
			RATIOS						
2.1	1.8	2.5							2.2
1.5	1.4	1.6	Current						1.6
1.2	1.2	1.2							1.3
1.1	.9	1.4							.9
.7	.6	.7	Quick						.6
.4	.4	.5							.5
26 14.2	25 14.9	22 16.5						24	15.1
35 10.4	31 11.7	28 12.9	Sales/Receivables					28	12.8
44 8.3	38 9.7	36 10.2						38	9.7
36 10.2	34 10.8	33 11.2						35	10.5
57 6.4	52 7.0	47 7.8	Cost of Sales/Inventory					50	7.4
77 4.7	88 4.1	65 5.6						65	5.6
11 34.6	9 41.9	9 39.1						10	38.2
22 16.5	23 16.1	16 23.0	Cost of Sales/Payables					16	22.2
38 9.6	34 10.8	32 11.5						35	10.5
7.0	9.1	7.3							7.5
12.2	13.1	12.1	Sales/Working Capital						12.1
23.4	36.7	19.0							19.3
11.4	7.4	25.6							16.8
3.7	(56) 3.7	5.6	EBIT/Interest						5.9
1.8	1.1	1.7							3.5
7.6	10.9	8.4	Net Profit + Depr., Dep.,						9.5
(12) 2.5	(21) 4.2	(19) 4.7	Amort./Cur. Mat. L/T/D					(15)	5.6
1.6	1.9	1.9							3.9
.5	.5	.3							.5
1.1	1.0	.9	Fixed/Worth						1.0
1.8	1.8	1.6							1.6
.9	1.1	.8							1.0
1.6	2.2	1.7	Debt/Worth						1.4
3.6	4.0	3.1							2.6
29.1	39.2	45.0	% Profit Before Taxes/Tangible						45.0
(53) 18.7	(48) 22.7	30.0	Net Worth						35.3
8.2	6.2	13.5							20.3
12.3	13.7	22.4	% Profit Before Taxes/Total						20.9
6.3	8.6	11.8	Assets						11.9
2.5	.8	2.6							7.8
11.5	15.3	13.0							11.1
6.8	8.3	8.7	Sales/Net Fixed Assets						5.9
3.0	3.9	4.5							4.3
2.9	2.9	3.1							3.0
1.8	2.2	2.4	Sales/Total Assets						2.3
1.5	1.7	1.9							2.1
1.0	1.2	1.1							1.1
(41) 2.2	(53) 2.0	(43) 1.8	% Depr., Dep., Amort./Sales					(25)	1.9
3.3	2.8	2.6							2.5
			% Officers', Directors' Owners' Comp/Sales						
5007981M	7591347M	6269175M	Net Sales ($)	1415M	3088M	19766M	29221M	118843M	6096842M
2784036M	3724441M	2653058M	Total Assets ($)	1322M	2037M	10433M	6640M	48536M	2584090M

© RMA 2010

M = $ thousand   MM = $ million
See Pages 9 through 22 for Explanation of Ratios and Data

Current Data Sorted by Assets   Comparative Historical Data

Type of Statement

0-500M	500M-2MM	2-10MM	10-50MM	50-100MM	100-250MM	Type of Statement	4/1/05-3/31/06 ALL	4/1/06-3/31/07 ALL
		3	13	1		Unqualified	15	15
1	3	6	4			Reviewed	8	12
2	2	5				Compiled	14	12
2	5	1	1			Tax Returns	4	1
2	5	6	1	2	1	Other	25	27
	27 (4/1-9/30/09)		41 (10/1/09-3/31/10)					
7	15	21	21	3	1	NUMBER OF STATEMENTS	66	67

0-500M %	500M-2MM %	2-10MM %	10-50MM %	50-100MM %	100-250MM %		4/1/05-3/31/06 %	4/1/06-3/31/07 %
						ASSETS		
	10.5	12.6	3.6			Cash & Equivalents	8.3	8.3
	20.7	14.0	13.9			Trade Receivables (net)	16.4	16.1
	26.7	28.5	32.4			Inventory	33.2	33.3
	.2	3.0	2.1			All Other Current	2.2	2.2
	58.1	58.2	51.9			Total Current	60.1	59.8
	29.1	33.9	39.0			Fixed Assets (net)	30.5	30.7
	2.0	3.4	5.0			Intangibles (net)	5.2	4.4
	10.8	4.6	4.0			All Other Non-Current	4.2	5.0
	100.0	100.0	100.0			Total	100.0	100.0
						LIABILITIES		
	21.3	8.4	10.1			Notes Payable-Short Term	18.8	13.3
	4.6	2.4	3.4			Cur. Mat.-L.T.D.	3.1	2.9
	13.3	10.1	11.6			Trade Payables	12.8	12.7
	.2	.6	.1			Income Taxes Payable	.3	.5
	5.7	11.5	7.8			All Other Current	9.3	8.3
	45.0	33.0	33.0			Total Current	44.3	37.6
	27.8	15.4	14.2			Long-Term Debt	19.0	14.9
	.1	.8	.8			Deferred Taxes	.6	1.0
	5.2	9.0	10.6			All Other Non-Current	3.5	7.3
	21.8	41.8	41.4			Net Worth	32.7	39.1
	100.0	100.0	100.0			Total Liabilities & Net Worth	100.0	100.0
						INCOME DATA		
	100.0	100.0	100.0			Net Sales	100.0	100.0
	47.4	36.6	23.0			Gross Profit	33.5	31.6
	43.1	33.4	22.9			Operating Expenses	29.9	27.3
	4.3	3.2	.1			Operating Profit	3.5	4.3
	1.3	.9	.6			All Other Expenses (net)	1.3	1.3
	3.0	2.4	-.5			Profit Before Taxes	2.2	3.0
						RATIOS		
	2.0	3.1	2.1			Current	3.0	2.9
	1.4	1.8	1.5				1.8	1.7
	.7	1.3	1.2				1.1	1.1
	1.5	1.9	.9			Quick	1.3	1.4
	.5	.8	.5				.7	.6
	.3	.3	.2				.3	.4
	13 27.3	9 40.8	13 28.6			Sales/Receivables	12 29.5	10 34.9
	19 19.1	18 20.4	25 14.4				21 17.5	23 15.7
	32 11.3	37 9.9	42 8.7				40 9.1	42 8.8
	36 10.1	37 9.9	56 6.5			Cost of Sales/Inventory	46 8.0	50 7.3
	54 6.7	60 6.1	70 5.2				78 4.7	72 5.0
	106 3.4	106 3.4	108 3.4				110 3.3	111 3.3
	9 42.1	14 26.8	20 18.2			Cost of Sales/Payables	13 27.9	13 27.7
	26 14.1	21 17.4	26 14.2				25 14.7	21 17.3
	55 6.7	34 10.8	39 9.3				39 9.3	44 8.4
	8.0	4.8	6.7			Sales/Working Capital	5.1	6.0
	21.0	10.3	13.4				11.7	10.8
	-14.0	16.8	19.2				55.4	85.5
	7.9	5.0	16.2			EBIT/Interest	13.8	10.0
	(14) 1.6	(19) 1.8	2.6				(62) 3.1	(62) 3.2
	1.2	-11.2	-1.4				.1	1.3
			12.0			Net Profit + Depr., Dep., Amort./Cur. Mat. L/T/D	11.0	10.3
		(11) 3.0	3.0				(13) 2.7	(20) 5.0
			1.0				1.7	1.3
	.4	.4	.6			Fixed/Worth	.4	.4
	2.2	.7	.9				.9	.8
	UND	2.6	2.6				2.4	1.6
	2.1	.5	.6			Debt/Worth	.6	.6
	6.1	1.3	1.2				1.3	1.7
	UND	UND	4.2				8.4	4.9
	347.5	31.4	26.6			% Profit Before Taxes/Tangible Net Worth	37.5	37.6
	(12) 23.9	(17) 7.1	(17) 12.1				(56) 13.9	(60) 18.2
	4.6	-11.5	-6.7				1.0	4.8
	8.5	15.6	12.9			% Profit Before Taxes/Total Assets	16.0	13.3
	5.3	1.9	2.0				5.4	6.6
	.6	-4.7	-5.3				-2.1	1.3
	16.3	12.8	9.1			Sales/Net Fixed Assets	13.5	14.0
	8.6	8.2	5.2				8.4	8.5
	4.7	4.4	2.7				4.5	5.2
	3.3	3.1	2.4			Sales/Total Assets	3.2	3.0
	2.1	2.1	1.9				2.2	2.4
	1.6	1.8	1.4				1.7	1.7
	1.9	1.5	1.7			% Depr., Dep., Amort./Sales	1.3	1.4
	(14) 2.5	(18) 3.0	(20) 2.6				(53) 2.2	(58) 2.3
	3.7	4.8	4.1				3.3	3.3
						% Officers', Directors' Owners' Comp/Sales	2.1	1.8
							(21) 4.7	(17) 2.6
							7.2	6.4
8151M	47190M	247035M	1011906M	320729M	259984M	Net Sales ($)	3028375M	3132833M
1824M	18082M	103247M	513238M	232980M	156531M	Total Assets ($)	1455126M	1492357M

© RMA 2010

M = $ thousand   MM = $ million
See Pages 9 through 22 for Explanation of Ratios and Data

Comparative Historical Data   Current Data Sorted by Sales

4/1/07-3/31/08 ALL	4/1/08-3/31/09 ALL	4/1/09-3/31/10 ALL	Type of Statement	0-1MM	1-3MM	3-5MM	5-10MM	10-25MM	25MM & OVE
16	14	17	Unqualified			1	1	5	10
13	17	14	Reviewed		3	1	1	5	4
12	11	9	Compiled	1	2	3	1	2	
7	6	9	Tax Returns	2	3	1	3		
28	31	19	Other		5	2	1	4	7
				27 (4/1-9/30/09)			41 (10/1/09-3/31/10)		
76	**79**	**68**	**NUMBER OF STATEMENTS**	**3**	**13**	**8**	**7**	**16**	**21**
%	%	%	**ASSETS**	%	%	%	%	%	%
9.5	10.2	9.3	Cash & Equivalents		7.9			6.9	5.5
15.0	14.7	15.5	Trade Receivables (net)		23.7			15.7	14.5
31.8	30.7	29.2	Inventory		34.1			27.9	29.4
2.6	2.3	2.4	All Other Current		3.2			1.9	2.9
58.9	57.9	56.5	Total Current		68.8			52.4	52.3
29.0	31.7	33.0	Fixed Assets (net)		24.8			34.3	39.8
5.9	5.4	5.0	Intangibles (net)		1.3			7.3	4.1
6.2	5.0	5.5	All Other Non-Current		5.0			6.0	3.8
100.0	100.0	100.0	Total		100.0			100.0	100.0
			LIABILITIES						
15.3	9.6	12.1	Notes Payable-Short Term		27.1			13.5	6.6
3.5	3.0	4.5	Cur. Mat.-L.T.D.		8.4			2.2	3.3
11.0	11.8	11.1	Trade Payables		13.0			11.5	11.3
.3	.2	.3	Income Taxes Payable		.0			.7	.1
7.4	8.5	8.1	All Other Current		6.6			10.6	9.0
37.5	33.3	36.1	Total Current		55.0			38.3	30.4
18.2	18.2	18.5	Long-Term Debt		23.6			13.5	13.0
.6	.5	.7	Deferred Taxes		.2			.9	1.4
6.1	4.7	8.4	All Other Non-Current		5.3			16.7	4.1
37.6	43.3	36.3	Net Worth		15.9			30.6	51.1
100.0	100.0	100.0	Total Liabilties & Net Worth		100.0			100.0	100.0
			INCOME DATA						
100.0	100.0	100.0	Net Sales		100.0			100.0	100.0
34.8	36.1	35.8	Gross Profit		44.6			29.3	23.7
30.1	33.4	33.9	Operating Expenses		42.8			28.4	20.5
4.7	2.7	2.0	Operating Profit		1.9			.9	3.2
2.3	1.9	1.0	All Other Expenses (net)		1.4			2.2	1.0
2.4	.9	1.0	Profit Before Taxes		.4			-1.3	2.2
			RATIOS						
3.3 / 1.7 / 1.2	3.3 / 1.8 / 1.2	2.6 / 1.6 / 1.1	Current		2.3 / 1.2 / .7			2.3 / 1.5 / 1.2	2.5 / 1.6 / 1.3
1.4 / .7 / .4	1.7 / .8 / .3	1.4 / .7 / .3	Quick		.9 / .4 / .4			1.0 / .6 / .4	1.1 / .7 / .4
10 35.3 / 21 17.2 / 36 10.2	11 33.3 / 24 15.0 / 32 11.5	12 30.9 / 20 18.5 / 32 11.4	Sales/Receivables	0 UND / 17 21.9 / 58 6.3				12 29.9 / 21 17.3 / 38 9.7	13 27.2 / 26 14.1 / 34 10.7
44 8.3 / 65 5.6 / 108 3.4	47 7.8 / 69 5.3 / 102 3.6	39 9.3 / 63 5.8 / 109 3.4	Cost of Sales/Inventory	43 8.5 / 54 6.7 / 137 2.7				33 11.2 / 58 6.3 / 87 4.2	44 8.2 / 63 5.8 / 97 3.8
13 28.3 / 24 15.2 / 39 9.4	11 34.5 / 26 14.3 / 40 9.0	13 27.7 / 24 15.1 / 39 9.3	Cost of Sales/Payables	0 UND / 27 13.5 / 57 6.4				15 24.6 / 27 13.3 / 46 8.0	18 20.6 / 25 14.7 / 35 10.5
5.7 / 10.7 / 21.9	5.1 / 9.0 / 26.5	6.6 / 12.2 / 29.1	Sales/Working Capital		9.0 / 32.7 / -12.7			8.9 / 13.9 / 27.2	6.1 / 11.1 / 18.6
9.3 / (70) 2.4 / .7	6.7 / (72) 1.6 / -.6	12.6 / (64) 1.8 / .0	EBIT/Interest		3.6 / (12) 1.2 / -.1			1.8 / (15) .7 / -1.7	17.0 / 11.2 / 1.7
11.6 / (20) 3.4 / 1.3	3.9 / (20) 1.5 / .5	7.1 / (20) 2.8 / 1.1	Net Profit + Depr., Dep., Amort./Cur. Mat. L/T/D						12.0 / (11) 3.0 / 1.0
.4 / .8 / 1.9	.4 / .8 / 3.3	.4 / 1.1 / 4.8	Fixed/Worth		.5 / 3.5 / -6.6			.5 / 1.5 / UND	.5 / .8 / 1.5
.7 / 1.7 / 11.4	.4 / 1.6 / 7.6	.5 / 1.9 / UND	Debt/Worth		1.7 / 11.3 / -27.8			.9 / 2.6 / UND	.5 / 1.0 / 2.2
46.5 / (63) 16.0 / 2.6	25.8 / (68) 9.0 / -4.1	27.7 / (52) 11.7 / -5.3	% Profit Before Taxes/Tangible Net Worth					14.9 / (12) -1.2 / -14.5	28.1 / (19) 13.5 / 3.5
13.1 / 5.5 / -1.4	9.9 / 2.9 / -4.4	12.1 / 2.6 / -3.6	% Profit Before Taxes/Total Assets		6.3 / .6 / -8.7			1.9 / -1.8 / -8.0	12.9 / 6.8 / 1.1
15.5 / 8.2 / 4.5	12.9 / 7.5 / 4.6	12.4 / 7.4 / 4.1	Sales/Net Fixed Assets		240.9 / 10.3 / 5.1			22.7 / 6.0 / 3.9	7.9 / 5.6 / 3.3
2.8 / 2.0 / 1.5	3.0 / 2.1 / 1.5	3.0 / 2.1 / 1.6	Sales/Total Assets		5.2 / 2.6 / 1.8			2.9 / 2.0 / 1.7	2.7 / 2.2 / 1.5
1.6 / (67) 2.2 / 3.4	1.2 / (71) 2.3 / 3.6	1.8 / (58) 2.7 / 4.3	% Depr., Dep., Amort./Sales					1.4 / (13) 2.3 / 5.5	2.0 / 2.8 / 4.3
3.0 / (19) 6.4 / 8.8	2.0 / (24) 4.1 / 7.2	2.1 / (21) 4.4 / 7.2	% Officers', Directors' Owners' Comp/Sales						
2237951M	2285137M	1894995M	Net Sales ($)	1595M	24258M	31846M	50262M	251461M	1535573M
1365568M	1230427M	1025902M	Total Assets ($)	982M	10400M	16673M	37145M	129925M	830777M

    M = $ thousand   MM = $ million
See Pages 9 through 22 for Explanation of Ratios and Data

MANUFACTURING—Frozen Fruit, Juice, and Vegetable Manufacturing   NAICS 311411

Current Data Sorted by Assets							Comparative Historical Data	
						Type of Statement		
			10	3	9	Unqualified	20	24
		5	9	3		Reviewed	7	10
	1	1	1			Compiled	4	4
2	4	2				Tax Returns	2	7
	1	1	9	2	3	Other	21	15
	20 (4/1-9/30/09)		47 (10/1/09-3/31/10)				4/1/05-3/31/06 ALL	4/1/06-3/31/07 ALL
0-500M	500M-2MM	2-10MM	10-50MM	50-100MM	100-250MM			
3	6	9	29	8	12	**NUMBER OF STATEMENTS**	54	60
%	%	%	%	%	%	**ASSETS**	%	%
			4.1		5.6	Cash & Equivalents	4.3	3.2
			17.5		14.5	Trade Receivables (net)	20.6	19.6
			40.8		29.0	Inventory	33.9	34.7
			2.4		2.1	All Other Current	1.6	2.6
			64.8		51.2	Total Current	60.3	60.1
			27.9		32.9	Fixed Assets (net)	29.5	31.8
			3.1		6.5	Intangibles (net)	3.7	5.1
			4.2		9.4	All Other Non-Current	6.6	3.0
			100.0		100.0	Total	100.0	100.0
						LIABILITIES		
			16.2		7.7	Notes Payable-Short Term	14.7	14.8
			4.1		3.6	Cur. Mat.-L.T.D.	3.1	3.5
			14.8		11.4	Trade Payables	15.1	13.3
			.0		.3	Income Taxes Payable	.1	.3
			4.6		11.3	All Other Current	10.0	11.4
			39.8		34.2	Total Current	42.9	43.3
			17.0		18.1	Long-Term Debt	18.3	17.0
			.5		1.6	Deferred Taxes	.5	.6
			5.9		4.6	All Other Non-Current	4.7	6.0
			36.8		41.5	Net Worth	33.6	33.1
			100.0		100.0	Total Liabilities & Net Worth	100.0	100.0
						INCOME DATA		
			100.0		100.0	Net Sales	100.0	100.0
			16.9		17.8	Gross Profit	20.0	19.0
			11.5		10.6	Operating Expenses	15.4	14.7
			5.4		7.3	Operating Profit	4.6	4.2
			1.6		1.5	All Other Expenses (net)	2.0	2.0
			3.7		5.8	Profit Before Taxes	2.6	2.2
						RATIOS		
			3.1		2.1		1.9	1.8
			1.5		1.6	Current	1.5	1.4
			1.2		1.0		1.0	1.1
			1.2		.8		.9	.8
			.5		.7	Quick	.5	.5
			.3		.4		.3	.3
			25 14.6		22 16.7		28 13.1	28 13.2
			35 10.5		29 12.6	Sales/Receivables	34 10.9	36 10.1
			42 8.6		44 8.2		51 7.1	47 7.7
			58 6.2		33 11.2		43 8.4	54 6.7
			119 3.1		88 4.1	Cost of Sales/Inventory	95 3.8	100 3.7
			156 2.3		173 2.1		176 2.1	153 2.4
			19 18.8		11 34.0		14 26.3	17 21.2
			32 11.2		26 13.9	Cost of Sales/Payables	27 13.6	27 13.5
			42 8.7		50 7.3		43 8.4	50 7.3
			4.2		3.9		6.1	4.8
			8.2		8.9	Sales/Working Capital	14.0	10.7
			16.3		NM		79.9	71.2
			9.2		11.6		5.4	4.8
			2.8		(11) 4.3	EBIT/Interest	(50) 2.3	(56) 2.4
			1.7		1.5		.9	1.2
						Net Profit + Depr., Dep., Amort./Cur. Mat. L/T/D		7.7
							(13) 3.9	
								2.3
			.4		.4		.6	.5
			.9		1.0	Fixed/Worth	1.0	1.2
			1.9		1.9		2.4	2.2
			1.0		.6		1.2	1.1
			2.4		1.7	Debt/Worth	2.7	2.4
			4.1		2.7		5.3	7.0
			39.7		34.4	% Profit Before Taxes/Tangible Net Worth	32.2	40.1
			(28) 16.3		(10) 14.3		(49) 16.7	(53) 15.8
			7.7		4.9		.9	4.2
			13.0		12.4	% Profit Before Taxes/Total Assets	8.9	9.6
			5.0		7.0		4.2	3.8
			2.6		1.9		-.1	.8
			8.5		9.1		13.0	10.2
			6.4		5.0	Sales/Net Fixed Assets	5.8	4.9
			3.2		1.9		3.0	3.3
			2.1		1.8		2.9	2.2
			1.4		1.4	Sales/Total Assets	1.6	1.5
			1.2		.9		1.0	1.2
			1.8			% Depr., Dep., Amort./Sales	1.2	1.4
			(26) 2.4				(42) 2.9	(56) 2.5
			3.6				5.3	4.0
						% Officers', Directors' Owners' Comp/Sales		1.7
								(10) 3.3
								9.8
5784M	33030M	97725M	1448057M	952456M	2896778M	Net Sales ($)	4476171M	3989410M
1033M	8642M	48198M	798708M	625720M	1867529M	Total Assets ($)	2653797M	2937348M

M = $ thousand   MM = $ million
See Pages 9 through 22 for Explanation of Ratios and Data

Comparative Historical Data / Current Data Sorted by Sales

H (4/1/07-3/31/08)	H (4/1/08-3/31/09)	H (4/1/09-3/31/10)	Type of Statement	0-1MM	1-3MM	3-5MM	5-10MM	10-25MM	25MM & OVER
24	31	23	Unqualified	1				7	22
10	16	17	Reviewed		1				9
2	2	3	Compiled			2			1
1	4	8	Tax Returns	4	1	2	1		
17	14	16	Other			2	2	2	12
ALL	ALL	ALL		20 (4/1-9/30/09)			47 (10/1/09-3/31/10)		
54	67	67	**NUMBER OF STATEMENTS**	1	4	2	6	10	44
%	%	%	**ASSETS**	%	%	%	%	%	%
4.3	3.3	4.8	Cash & Equivalents					3.9	3.9
18.1	16.5	17.5	Trade Receivables (net)					15.7	17.3
38.8	39.2	35.9	Inventory					31.9	38.7
3.4	3.6	2.7	All Other Current					2.7	3.0
64.6	62.5	61.0	Total Current					54.2	62.9
30.4	29.6	30.8	Fixed Assets (net)					34.8	29.1
1.8	4.2	3.1	Intangibles (net)					5.4	2.7
3.2	3.7	5.1	All Other Non-Current					5.7	5.3
100.0	100.0	100.0	Total					100.0	100.0
			LIABILITIES						
19.2	19.4	16.0	Notes Payable-Short Term					13.8	16.1
2.6	2.7	4.9	Cur. Mat.-L.T.D.					5.2	3.6
13.0	15.9	14.2	Trade Payables					12.5	12.9
.3	.2	.3	Income Taxes Payable					.1	.1
9.3	8.8	7.1	All Other Current					6.3	8.1
44.3	47.0	42.6	Total Current					37.8	40.8
15.5	15.8	18.2	Long-Term Debt					25.6	16.3
1.1	.6	.7	Deferred Taxes					.5	.9
4.7	7.6	7.8	All Other Non-Current					11.2	5.2
34.3	29.0	30.7	Net Worth					24.8	36.8
100.0	100.0	100.0	Total Liabilities & Net Worth					100.0	100.0
			INCOME DATA						
100.0	100.0	100.0	Net Sales					100.0	100.0
18.7	20.7	20.1	Gross Profit					21.1	16.5
12.5	14.7	14.9	Operating Expenses					15.6	10.9
6.2	6.1	5.2	Operating Profit					5.5	5.6
1.7	1.9	1.4	All Other Expenses (net)					2.1	1.4
4.5	4.2	3.9	Profit Before Taxes					3.4	4.1
			RATIOS						
2.1	1.7	2.0	Current					2.5	2.1
1.4	1.3	1.4						1.4	1.5
1.1	1.1	1.1						.9	1.1
.8	.6	1.0	Quick					1.4	1.0
.4	.4	.5						.6	.5
.3	.2	.3						.2	.3
25 14.9	26 13.8	23 16.1	Sales/Receivables					26 14.1	24 15.2
32 11.4	34 10.7	32 11.4						33 11.2	33 11.1
51 7.2	43 8.4	42 8.6						37 10.0	44 8.4
64 5.7	50 7.3	37 9.8	Cost of Sales/Inventory					47 7.8	70 5.2
99 3.7	107 3.4	89 4.1						56 6.5	111 3.3
154 2.4	167 2.2	164 2.2						162 2.3	167 2.2
20 18.3	20 18.2	15 25.1	Cost of Sales/Payables					15 24.4	15 24.9
27 13.5	38 9.7	31 11.7						23 15.9	32 11.4
47 7.7	56 6.6	47 7.8						37 9.8	46 7.9
5.5	5.2	5.7	Sales/Working Capital					6.6	3.7
10.3	12.2	10.6						10.0	8.3
21.5	61.3	47.3						-83.9	19.8
8.2	8.0	10.6	EBIT/Interest					3.9	10.5
(53) 2.5	(65) 2.4	(66) 3.2						2.3	(43) 3.6
1.3	1.3	1.5						1.5	1.7
9.1	4.6	3.6	Net Profit + Depr., Dep., Amort./Cur. Mat. L/T/D						4.2
(19) 5.0	(18) 2.1	(21) 1.6						(14) 1.4	
1.5	1.4	1.2							.9
.5	.6	.5	Fixed/Worth					1.6	.4
1.0	1.1	1.0						2.0	.9
1.8	2.3	2.0						7.8	1.7
1.0	1.4	1.0	Debt/Worth					3.1	1.0
2.2	2.7	2.4						5.3	1.8
5.1	5.3	9.7						20.4	3.6
41.2	41.6	55.7	% Profit Before Taxes/Tangible Net Worth						38.5
(50) 24.4	(57) 16.2	(58) 16.6						(40) 14.3	
9.6	5.9	6.6							6.1
15.3	11.2	13.8	% Profit Before Taxes/Total Assets					12.2	13.7
4.8	4.6	5.3						5.4	5.5
1.2	.8	1.5						2.3	1.8
12.1	9.8	10.7	Sales/Net Fixed Assets					6.4	9.4
5.1	5.4	6.3						5.5	6.4
3.6	3.3	2.8						2.6	2.9
2.2	2.1	2.9	Sales/Total Assets					2.5	1.9
1.7	1.5	1.5						1.5	1.4
1.3	1.1	1.1						1.1	1.1
1.2	1.6	1.6	% Depr., Dep., Amort./Sales					2.8	1.6
(50) 2.3	(62) 2.4	(59) 2.5						(37) 3.5	2.3
3.1	3.6	3.8						4.4	3.4
			% Officers', Directors' Owners' Comp/Sales						
5443186M	4954708M	5433830M	Net Sales ($)	359M	10753M	7849M	43277M	158397M	5213195M
3190763M	3360152M	3349830M	Total Assets ($)	292M	4977M	4813M	17855M	108080M	3213813M

© RMA 2010

M = $ thousand   MM = $ million

See Pages 9 through 22 for Explanation of Ratios and Data

Current Data Sorted by Assets

Comparative Historical Data

0-500M	500M-2MM	2-10MM	10-50MM	50-100MM	100-250MM	Type of Statement	4/1/05-3/31/06 ALL	4/1/06-3/31/07 ALL
		2	11	5	2	Unqualified	13	16
	1	4	9	1		Reviewed	14	11
		3	3			Compiled	7	5
	2	3				Tax Returns	3	6
1	1	9	17	4	2	Other	23	29
	16 (4/1-9/30/09)		64 (10/1/09-3/31/10)					
0-500M	500M-2MM	2-10MM	10-50MM	50-100MM	100-250MM			
1	4	21	40	10	4	NUMBER OF STATEMENTS	60	67
%	%	%	%	%	%	ASSETS	%	%
		11.6	6.6	.2		Cash & Equivalents	9.8	5.7
		20.6	18.6	21.5		Trade Receivables (net)	18.6	22.6
		16.6	20.5	19.3		Inventory	17.8	20.3
		1.1	1.5	3.1		All Other Current	1.4	2.2
		49.8	47.2	44.2		Total Current	47.6	50.9
		41.2	33.3	40.3		Fixed Assets (net)	38.2	36.7
		5.2	13.6	11.3		Intangibles (net)	8.5	5.9
		3.8	5.9	4.3		All Other Non-Current	5.7	6.5
		100.0	100.0	100.0		Total	100.0	100.0
						LIABILITIES		
		4.4	9.0	3.5		Notes Payable-Short Term	10.5	11.0
		2.2	3.8	3.4		Cur. Mat.-L.T.D.	4.9	4.0
		18.5	12.2	12.0		Trade Payables	15.7	16.5
		.4	.1	.7		Income Taxes Payable	.3	.2
		14.6	10.2	6.1		All Other Current	6.9	9.3
		40.1	35.4	25.7		Total Current	38.1	41.0
		25.1	19.4	19.2		Long-Term Debt	21.2	18.5
		.1	1.2	.5		Deferred Taxes	.6	.7
		1.9	4.4	2.1		All Other Non-Current	7.1	7.9
		32.8	39.6	52.5		Net Worth	32.9	31.9
		100.0	100.0	100.0		Total Liabilities & Net Worth	100.0	100.0
						INCOME DATA		
		100.0	100.0	100.0		Net Sales	100.0	100.0
		29.8	25.2	15.4		Gross Profit	31.3	28.2
		26.1	18.9	10.4		Operating Expenses	27.4	24.1
		3.7	6.3	5.0		Operating Profit	3.9	4.1
		1.8	1.2	.4		All Other Expenses (net)	1.9	1.5
		1.9	5.1	4.6		Profit Before Taxes	2.0	2.7
						RATIOS		
		2.8	2.1	2.1			1.9	1.8
		1.9	1.4	1.9		Current	1.2	1.2
		.9	.9	1.3			1.0	.9
		1.9	1.2	1.1			1.1	1.0
		1.0	.7	.8		Quick	.8	.7
		.5		.6			.5	.4
		17 21.4	19 18.9	23 15.7			20 18.6	20 18.0
		24 15.2	24 14.9	33 11.0		Sales/Receivables	27 13.5	29 12.4
		39 9.4	32 11.4	45 8.0			35 10.6	35 10.4
		22 16.7	24 15.0	15 24.2			23 15.8	26 14.1
		35 10.6	36 10.2	29 12.5		Cost of Sales/Inventory	36 10.3	38 9.7
		44 8.4	57 6.4	56 6.5			50 7.3	59 6.2
		20 18.3	15 25.1	18 20.5			20 18.5	19 19.2
		24 15.5	27 13.6	19 19.0		Cost of Sales/Payables	30 12.2	28 13.1
		37 9.9	35 10.3	24 15.2			43 8.6	39 9.3
		8.1	8.9	8.4			10.0	11.5
		14.2	21.6	12.3		Sales/Working Capital	29.6	30.3
		-35.6	-59.0	27.3			-189.8	-43.9
		31.6	11.0	21.3			9.8	10.1
		(20) 3.1	(36) 4.4	10.5		EBIT/Interest	(57) 3.9	(62) 4.8
		1.0	1.7	2.9			.5	1.4
			5.2				4.9	5.5
			(12) 2.3			Net Profit + Depr., Dep., Amort./Cur. Mat. L/T/D	(21) 1.4	(21) 2.5
			1.0				.7	1.9
		.6	.6	.8			.8	.6
		1.2	1.2	1.0		Fixed/Worth	1.2	1.1
		NM	3.1	1.3			3.2	2.4
		.5	1.0	.8			.9	1.0
		1.6	2.1	1.6		Debt/Worth	1.9	1.9
		NM	12.5	2.0			6.2	6.5
		57.5	55.8	70.6			35.2	46.9
	(16)	26.4	(33) 25.5	50.6		% Profit Before Taxes/Tangible Net Worth	(48) 19.8	(56) 24.2
		13.4	6.3	7.3			5.7	11.7
		17.5	16.3	23.1			11.9	14.0
		6.6	7.0	18.4		% Profit Before Taxes/Total Assets	5.4	8.5
		.6	3.0	2.7			-1.7	1.7
		13.0	24.6	11.5			12.3	17.9
		7.1	8.0	6.8		Sales/Net Fixed Assets	6.0	7.3
		3.5	4.1	2.7			3.7	3.8
		3.4	3.1	4.1			3.2	3.6
		2.5	2.5	2.3		Sales/Total Assets	2.3	2.5
		1.9	1.5	1.1			1.5	1.9
		1.4	1.5	1.1			1.5	1.2
	(16)	2.3	(30) 2.3	2.3		% Depr., Dep., Amort./Sales	(50) 2.6	(54) 2.0
		4.9	3.8	5.5			4.2	3.0
							2.3	
						% Officers', Directors' Owners' Comp/Sales	(12) 3.5	
							7.7	
1777M	14156M	294885M	2172675M	1869121M	1087626M	Net Sales ($)	3032328M	3242060M
338M	4144M	105633M	984574M	789126M	588634M	Total Assets ($)	1451355M	1470407M

M = $ thousand   MM = $ million
See Pages 9 through 22 for Explanation of Ratios and Data

Comparative Historical Data | Current Data Sorted by Sales

	4/1/07-3/31/08 ALL	4/1/08-3/31/09 ALL	4/1/09-3/31/10 ALL	0-1MM	1-3MM	3-5MM	5-10MM	10-25MM	25MM & OVER
Type of Statement									
Unqualified	20	21	20					3	17
Reviewed	11	14	15		1		1	5	8
Compiled	4	6	6			2	2	1	3
Tax Returns	4	3	5	2		3			
Other	27	33	34	2	1	1		8	22
				16 (4/1-9/30/09)			64 (10/1/09-3/31/10)		
NUMBER OF STATEMENTS	66	77	80		4	4	5	17	50
	%	%	%	%	%	%	%	%	%
ASSETS									
Cash & Equivalents	6.2	6.4	7.1	D				12.2	6.1
Trade Receivables (net)	17.6	18.7	19.4	A				20.6	18.5
Inventory	20.5	18.8	19.8	T				20.0	20.2
All Other Current	2.6	1.8	1.6	A				1.4	2.0
Total Current	46.9	45.7	47.9					54.3	46.8
Fixed Assets (net)	40.9	40.8	37.2	N				35.4	34.8
Intangibles (net)	8.0	9.0	10.1	O				5.5	13.1
All Other Non-Current	4.1	4.5	4.9	T				4.9	5.2
Total	100.0	100.0	100.0					100.0	100.0
LIABILITIES				A					
Notes Payable-Short Term	10.3	10.8	7.6	V				4.1	7.7
Cur. Mat.-L.T.D.	3.7	4.9	3.5	A				3.0	4.2
Trade Payables	16.0	14.7	14.1	I				20.0	12.1
Income Taxes Payable	.2	.2	.2	L				.4	.2
All Other Current	8.9	7.9	11.6	A				10.1	8.9
Total Current	39.1	38.5	37.1	B				37.5	33.1
Long-Term Debt	23.7	21.0	22.1	L				17.6	19.4
Deferred Taxes	.8	.8	.8	E				.2	1.3
All Other Non-Current	9.2	8.9	3.8					1.8	3.8
Net Worth	27.3	30.9	36.2					42.8	42.4
Total Liabilities & Net Worth	100.0	100.0	100.0					100.0	100.0
INCOME DATA									
Net Sales	100.0	100.0	100.0					100.0	100.0
Gross Profit	26.8	24.9	25.4					25.7	23.2
Operating Expenses	23.2	21.8	20.2					19.4	17.0
Operating Profit	3.6	3.1	5.2					6.3	6.2
All Other Expenses (net)	1.5	1.2	1.2					1.3	1.0
Profit Before Taxes	2.1	1.9	4.0					4.9	5.2
RATIOS									
Current	2.1	2.0	2.2					2.6	2.0
	1.2	1.1	1.5					1.9	1.4
	.8	.8	.9					1.0	1.0
Quick	1.2	1.0	1.2					1.5	1.2
	.5	.6	.7					1.0	.7
	.4	.4	.5					.5	.4
Sales/Receivables	19 19.3	21 17.4	19 19.6					17 21.0	19 19.1
	24 15.5	25 14.6	25 14.8					24 15.2	24 14.9
	32 11.3	32 11.3	34 10.7					34 10.9	33 10.9
Cost of Sales/Inventory	23 15.9	22 16.8	24 15.0					26 14.1	22 16.3
	37 9.9	35 10.5	35 10.3					36 10.3	34 10.7
	63 5.8	45 8.1	54 6.7					59 6.2	53 6.9
Cost of Sales/Payables	18 19.8	17 21.9	16 23.3					20 18.2	15 24.8
	28 12.9	24 15.0	23 16.1					25 14.6	20 18.1
	41 8.9	37 10.0	33 11.1					36 10.2	33 11.2
Sales/Working Capital	9.4	10.6	8.7					7.0	9.0
	33.3	46.8	16.7					11.5	19.8
	-29.4	-37.5	-69.6					NM	NM
EBIT/Interest	7.5	6.1	15.3					31.6	16.3
	(63) 2.9	(71) 3.0	(75) 5.0					(16) 9.1	(46) 6.4
	1.0	1.0	1.7					1.8	2.2
Net Profit + Depr., Dep., Amort./Cur. Mat. L/T/D	9.0	5.2	5.4						4.7
	(20) 4.0	(23) 3.2	(23) 2.4					(18) 2.4	2.4
	1.3	1.4	1.7						1.1
Fixed/Worth	.7	.8	.6					.4	.6
	2.0	1.8	1.2					.7	1.2
	279.6	3.6	2.8					2.4	2.0
Debt/Worth	.9	.9	.9					.4	1.0
	3.2	2.7	2.0					1.0	1.9
	296.8	8.5	7.7					5.0	7.4
% Profit Before Taxes/Tangible Net Worth	40.4	36.4	57.9					59.9	63.1
	(51) 18.0	(62) 22.2	(67) 32.9					(16) 33.6	(43) 39.6
	5.3	6.7	12.4					14.7	10.1
% Profit Before Taxes/Total Assets	10.7	9.6	17.8					21.8	19.4
	5.7	4.6	8.1					12.1	9.7
	.1	.3	2.5					2.8	3.4
Sales/Net Fixed Assets	11.8	12.7	14.2					15.5	16.4
	6.2	6.4	7.1					7.1	7.8
	3.4	3.3	3.8					4.0	3.9
Sales/Total Assets	3.1	3.3	3.3					3.4	3.2
	2.5	2.3	2.5					2.5	2.5
	1.7	1.7	1.6					2.2	1.5
% Depr., Dep., Amort./Sales	1.4	1.4	1.4					1.1	1.5
	(56) 2.4	(65) 2.3	(63) 2.3					(14) 1.7	(38) 2.3
	3.4	3.5	4.0					3.8	3.7
% Officers', Directors' Owners' Comp/Sales	.9		1.7						
	(14) 2.5		(16) 3.2						
	5.0		3.8						
Net Sales ($)	3971702M	5300375M	5440240M		8076M	15327M	38771M	327660M	5050406M
Total Assets ($)	1792125M	2403785M	2472449M		4712M	8233M	18998M	144816M	2295690M

© RMA 2010

M = $ thousand   MM = $ million
See Pages 9 through 22 for Explanation of Ratios and Data

Current Data Sorted by Assets

Comparative Historical Data

0-500M	500M-2MM	2-10MM	10-50MM	50-100MM	100-250MM	Type of Statement	4/1/05-3/31/06 ALL	4/1/06-3/31/07 ALL
1		1	12	6	6	Unqualified	27	29
	1	3	8	1		Reviewed	15	17
		3	2			Compiled	6	4
1	4	1				Tax Returns	4	6
2		6	13	7	7	Other	24	29
	30 (4/1-9/30/09)		55 (10/1/09-3/31/10)					
2	7	14	35	14	13	NUMBER OF STATEMENTS	76	85
%	%	%	%	%	%	**ASSETS**	%	%
		10.3	3.2	2.4	2.1	Cash & Equivalents	4.6	4.1
		19.2	16.1	13.7	15.4	Trade Receivables (net)	17.2	17.1
		31.4	36.8	38.9	38.9	Inventory	36.2	35.9
		4.9	2.2	2.5	3.0	All Other Current	2.6	2.7
		65.8	58.2	57.4	59.4	Total Current	60.6	59.9
		24.1	36.3	28.9	33.8	Fixed Assets (net)	32.6	30.6
		4.9	3.0	4.3	.3	Intangibles (net)	2.1	4.1
		5.1	2.5	9.3	6.4	All Other Non-Current	4.7	5.3
		100.0	100.0	100.0	100.0	Total	100.0	100.0
						LIABILITIES		
		8.5	14.5	16.6	6.0	Notes Payable-Short Term	14.8	14.7
		1.4	2.4	4.9	1.9	Cur. Mat.-L.T.D.	2.5	3.0
		21.1	11.8	10.6	13.7	Trade Payables	17.7	16.4
		.7	.1	.3	.3	Income Taxes Payable	.3	.1
		10.3	9.2	5.6	7.2	All Other Current	6.2	7.7
		42.0	38.1	38.0	29.0	Total Current	41.6	42.0
		14.0	19.1	14.4	20.2	Long-Term Debt	18.2	16.9
		.0	.9	.5	1.0	Deferred Taxes	.7	.4
		5.9	2.6	10.8	3.8	All Other Non-Current	4.7	6.7
		38.0	39.3	36.3	46.0	Net Worth	34.7	34.1
		100.0	100.0	100.0	100.0	Total Liabilities & Net Worth	100.0	100.0
						INCOME DATA		
		100.0	100.0	100.0	100.0	Net Sales	100.0	100.0
		24.1	23.6	24.1	17.6	Gross Profit	20.2	20.9
		20.5	15.8	14.6	10.1	Operating Expenses	17.6	17.2
		3.6	7.8	9.4	7.5	Operating Profit	2.6	3.7
		.4	1.0	2.9	1.3	All Other Expenses (net)	1.2	1.5
		3.2	6.8	6.6	6.2	Profit Before Taxes	1.5	2.2
						RATIOS		
		3.3	2.1	1.9	2.7		2.1	2.2
		1.7	1.5	1.5	1.9	Current	1.6	1.5
		1.2	1.1	1.1	1.6		1.2	1.1
		1.5	.6	.6	.9		.7	.7
		.7	.4	.3	.6	Quick	.5	.5
		.4	.4	.3	.4		.3	.3
	18	19.8	22 16.9	27 13.4	22 16.3		23 16.1	21 17.0
	25	14.7	29 12.6	32 11.4	26 14.0	Sales/Receivables	30 12.1	27 13.4
	34	10.6	43 8.6	38 9.6	35 10.4		37 10.0	37 9.9
	33	11.1	57 6.4	75 4.9	60 6.1		47 7.7	44 8.3
	46	8.0	80 4.5	140 2.6	78 4.7	Cost of Sales/Inventory	90 4.0	83 4.4
	91	4.0	161 2.3	197 1.9	135 2.7		139 2.6	138 2.6
	18	19.8	13 28.5	21 17.2	20 18.4		16 22.4	14 26.5
	25	14.5	22 16.4	31 11.8	22 16.3	Cost of Sales/Payables	36 10.2	27 13.5
	43	8.6	41 8.8	37 9.8	38 9.5		56 6.6	42 8.7
		6.5	5.5	4.8	4.5		4.9	5.4
		8.4	11.0	12.0	6.5	Sales/Working Capital	8.9	12.3
		NM	34.8	42.9	8.4		40.3	60.0
		17.1	16.2	9.9	17.6		6.9	7.7
		5.0	(32) 4.3	4.8	7.3	EBIT/Interest	(75) 2.5	(79) 2.1
		1.6	1.9	2.3	3.0		1.0	.8
			10.8	10.5			6.5	8.3
			(12) 3.6	(10) 4.6		Net Profit + Depr., Dep., Amort./Cur. Mat. L/T/D	(31) 2.7	(35) 3.3
			1.8	2.2			1.3	1.4
		.2	.6	.5	.6		.7	.5
		.8	1.1	.8	.8	Fixed/Worth	1.0	1.0
		3.2	1.8	NM	1.0		1.8	2.0
		.7	.8	1.0	1.0		1.1	.9
		1.5	1.8	1.5	1.1	Debt/Worth	2.0	2.0
		7.6	4.1	NM	1.7		3.4	4.9
		43.9	44.4	33.3	35.3		28.0	29.9
	(12)	24.2	(32) 23.6	(11) 27.1	22.7	% Profit Before Taxes/Tangible Net Worth	(67) 14.8	(72) 12.7
		2.3	15.6	6.5	16.8		6.1	2.6
		23.4	16.8	14.8	17.3		9.1	12.7
		6.1	9.9	9.9	10.8	% Profit Before Taxes/Total Assets	4.8	3.8
		-.5	3.7	2.0	7.1		.1	-1.5
		50.5	10.0	7.9	7.8		12.2	14.0
		11.6	4.7	4.9	5.8	Sales/Net Fixed Assets	5.0	6.6
		5.1	3.0	3.3	3.8		3.8	4.1
		4.0	2.9	2.0	2.1		2.4	2.8
		2.8	1.6	1.4	2.0	Sales/Total Assets	1.9	2.0
		1.8	1.2	1.0	1.6		1.3	1.5
		.7	1.3	1.2			1.0	1.1
	(11)	1.5	(34) 2.1	(13) 2.7		% Depr., Dep., Amort./Sales	(68) 2.4	(74) 2.2
		2.7	3.1	3.7			4.0	3.3
							1.2	.6
						% Officers', Directors' Owners' Comp/Sales	(13) 2.0	(17) 1.5
							6.0	3.9
2175M	39396M	213993M	1767452M	1474521M	3750439M	Net Sales ($)	6851121M	5945920M
531M	8862M	71221M	913235M	988817M	1935474M	Total Assets ($)	3845896M	3453768M

M = $ thousand   MM = $ million
See Pages 9 through 22 for Explanation of Ratios and Data

Comparative Historical Data / Current Data Sorted by Sales

				Type of Statement						
30		40	26	Unqualified	1			1	2	22
14		15	13	Reviewed				1	5	7
6		6	5	Compiled			1		3	1
8		6	6	Tax Returns		4	1		2	
22		39	35	Other		4	2	2	4	26
4/1/07-		4/1/08-	4/1/09-			30 (4/1-9/30/09)			55 (10/1/09-3/31/10)	
3/31/08		3/31/09	3/31/10		0-1MM	1-3MM	3-5MM	5-10MM	10-25MM	25MM & OVER
ALL		ALL	ALL							
80		106	85	NUMBER OF STATEMENTS	1	5	3	4	16	56
%		%	%	ASSETS	%	%	%	%	%	%
4.8		5.0	5.5	Cash & Equivalents					13.2	2.3
18.4		16.4	17.2	Trade Receivables (net)					14.9	16.4
38.1		36.2	36.4	Inventory					28.8	38.6
2.9		3.0	2.7	All Other Current					2.2	3.3
64.2		60.6	61.8	Total Current					59.1	60.5
30.3		31.5	30.7	Fixed Assets (net)					35.0	32.0
2.1		3.6	3.1	Intangibles (net)					4.3	2.3
3.4		4.4	4.4	All Other Non-Current					1.6	5.2
100.0		100.0	100.0	Total					100.0	100.0
				LIABILITIES						
16.9		14.2	13.3	Notes Payable-Short Term					6.9	13.1
3.6		3.2	2.3	Cur. Mat.-L.T.D.					2.0	2.7
15.9		14.4	13.3	Trade Payables					14.7	13.1
.1		.1	.3	Income Taxes Payable					.6	.2
6.4		6.8	8.3	All Other Current					5.9	8.8
42.9		38.6	37.6	Total Current					30.1	37.8
17.2		16.3	16.7	Long-Term Debt					15.7	17.4
.4		.7	.6	Deferred Taxes					.3	.8
11.4		6.9	5.4	All Other Non-Current					7.2	5.1
28.1		37.5	39.6	Net Worth					46.8	38.9
100.0		100.0	100.0	Total Liabilities & Net Worth					100.0	100.0
				INCOME DATA						
100.0		100.0	100.0	Net Sales					100.0	100.0
22.8		23.4	22.6	Gross Profit					25.5	21.1
17.3		18.1	15.2	Operating Expenses					17.1	13.8
5.5		5.3	7.4	Operating Profit					8.4	7.3
1.5		1.4	1.2	All Other Expenses (net)					.3	1.5
4.1		3.9	6.2	Profit Before Taxes					8.1	5.7
				RATIOS						
2.1		2.4	2.4						3.5	2.1
1.5		1.6	1.7	Current					1.7	1.6
1.1		1.1	1.2						1.2	1.2
.9		.8	.9						1.8	.7
.5		.5	.5	Quick					.8	.4
.3		.4	.4						.4	.3

							Sales/Receivables						
22	16.3	20	18.3	22	16.3							18	20.6	23	15.9
28	12.9	28	13.0	28	12.9							24	15.2	29	12.8
38	9.7	34	10.7	37	9.7							33	11.1	37	9.7

							Cost of Sales/Inventory						
43	8.6	47	7.7	51	7.2							15	25.1	57	6.4
84	4.4	84	4.4	82	4.4							44	8.3	90	4.1
144	2.5	122	3.0	156	2.3							95	3.9	155	2.4

							Cost of Sales/Payables						
18	20.5	15	23.9	16	22.4							15	24.2	17	22.1
30	12.1	28	12.8	24	15.5							22	16.3	26	13.9
45	8.2	40	9.0	38	9.6							37	9.7	39	9.3

						Sales/Working Capital					
5.6		5.6		5.1						5.9	5.0
11.3		10.6		8.2						10.2	8.6
42.1		40.0		27.5						40.9	24.3

							EBIT/Interest						
	8.9		9.7		15.9								18.6		11.1
(76)	2.9	(100)	3.3	(80)	4.8							(15)	8.3	(54)	4.7
	1.4		1.7		2.5								3.7		2.5

							Net Profit + Depr., Dep., Amort./Cur. Mat. L/T/D						
	9.8		8.5		9.7										10.6
(36)	3.5	(43)	4.2	(32)	4.6									(26)	5.4
	1.3		1.1		2.6										2.7

						Fixed/Worth					
.4		.4		.5						.4	.6
.9		.9		.8						.9	.8
1.6		1.9		1.5						2.0	1.3

						Debt/Worth					
1.1		.8		.8						.6	.9
2.1		1.7		1.3						1.0	1.4
3.6		5.1		3.0						3.5	2.8

							% Profit Before Taxes/Tangible Net Worth						
	33.4		35.6		37.6								48.3		35.8
(68)	20.1	(93)	22.1	(76)	24.2							(15)	32.5	(50)	25.6
	8.7		10.6		15.4								19.7		14.4

						% Profit Before Taxes/Total Assets					
13.2		13.6		17.3						24.8	15.9
5.9		7.3		9.9						14.6	9.6
1.5		1.7		3.7						5.2	3.7

						Sales/Net Fixed Assets					
14.4		14.0		13.2						26.9	9.9
7.4		7.4		5.8						9.1	5.6
4.6		4.1		3.6						2.9	3.7

						Sales/Total Assets					
3.2		2.7		2.8						4.0	2.7
2.1		1.9		1.9						2.8	1.8
1.5		1.5		1.4						1.1	1.4

							% Depr., Dep., Amort./Sales						
	.9		1.1		1.1								.7		1.2
(72)	1.9	(91)	2.0	(73)	2.0							(14)	2.2	(50)	2.0
	3.2		3.2		3.1								4.8		3.0

						% Officers', Directors' Owners' Comp/Sales					
	.8		1.2		.7						
(16)	2.2	(25)	2.1	(20)	2.0						
	3.9		5.0		3.8						

6516618M		10249819M	7247976M	Net Sales ($)	449M	8720M	13658M	35963M	251968M	6937218M
3646516M		5234612M	3918140M	Total Assets ($)	296M	3947M	6532M	31797M	156301M	3719267M

M = $ thousand   MM = $ million
See Pages 9 through 22 for Explanation of Ratios and Data

	Current Data Sorted by Assets						Comparative Historical Data	

0-500M	500M-2MM	2-10MM	10-50MM	50-100MM	100-250MM	Type of Statement	4/1/05-3/31/06 ALL	4/1/06-3/31/07 ALL
		2	5	3	4	Unqualified	12	10
	2	5	2		1	Reviewed	7	9
		2	1			Compiled	2	5
2		1	1			Tax Returns	1	3
	1	3	8	3	1	Other	9	11
	17 (4/1-9/30/09)		27 (10/1/09-3/31/10)					
2	3	10	17	6	6	NUMBER OF STATEMENTS	31	38
%	%	%	%	%	%	ASSETS	%	%
		3.2	4.9			Cash & Equivalents	6.5	5.8
		26.0	16.9			Trade Receivables (net)	18.0	20.2
		47.7	38.6			Inventory	38.0	35.0
		2.1	2.3			All Other Current	2.2	2.3
		79.0	62.7			Total Current	64.8	63.3
		18.6	19.8			Fixed Assets (net)	26.5	25.7
		.1	5.2			Intangibles (net)	1.8	4.2
		2.2	12.3			All Other Non-Current	6.9	6.7
		100.0	100.0			Total	100.0	100.0
						LIABILITIES		
		17.9	16.1			Notes Payable-Short Term	18.4	12.1
		3.5	1.3			Cur. Mat.-L.T.D.	1.9	2.4
		21.3	13.0			Trade Payables	18.2	20.0
		.2	.6			Income Taxes Payable	.2	.4
		11.0	6.2			All Other Current	4.8	7.2
		53.7	37.3			Total Current	43.5	42.0
		20.0	9.7			Long-Term Debt	14.9	17.1
		.3	.2			Deferred Taxes	.5	.5
		6.8	4.5			All Other Non-Current	9.8	6.0
		19.1	48.4			Net Worth	31.3	34.4
		100.0	100.0			Total Liabilities & Net Worth	100.0	100.0
						INCOME DATA		
		100.0	100.0			Net Sales	100.0	100.0
		37.3	18.8			Gross Profit	27.7	32.1
		27.1	14.3			Operating Expenses	24.1	23.9
		10.3	4.5			Operating Profit	3.5	8.2
		.8	2.2			All Other Expenses (net)	3.2	2.6
		9.5	2.3			Profit Before Taxes	.4	5.6
						RATIOS		
		2.0	3.3				2.5	2.1
		1.4	1.3			Current	1.5	1.8
		1.1	1.2				1.1	1.2
		.8	1.0				.8	1.1
		.5	.7			Quick	.5	.6
		.4	.3				.3	.4
		21 17.2	28 12.9				31 11.9	23 16.2
		34 10.7	37 9.9			Sales/Receivables	36 10.1	37 10.0
		43 8.4	53 6.8				45 8.2	48 7.6
		38 9.5	66 5.5				89 4.1	51 7.1
		108 3.4	126 2.9			Cost of Sales/Inventory	124 3.0	77 4.7
		212 1.7	159 2.3				169 2.2	119 3.1
		18 20.2	14 26.5				19 19.1	18 19.9
		27 13.6	30 12.1			Cost of Sales/Payables	51 7.2	31 11.7
		149 2.4	50 7.2				100 3.7	80 4.5
		7.5	3.1				4.8	5.6
		14.4	8.3			Sales/Working Capital	7.4	9.3
		NM	16.3				24.9	18.8
		76.8	24.5				4.2	7.3
		8.9	(16) 5.7			EBIT/Interest	1.7	(37) 4.4
		3.1	1.3				-1.0	2.1
							21.8	13.2
						Net Profit + Depr., Dep., Amort./Cur. Mat. L/T/D	(13) 3.5	(10) 3.2
							-1.2	1.4
		.2	.1				.5	.5
		.4	.4			Fixed/Worth	.8	1.0
		NM	1.0				12.6	1.9
		1.3	.7				1.2	1.0
		2.6	1.4			Debt/Worth	2.3	2.3
		NM	2.4				24.3	10.6
			27.3				29.3	31.7
			11.1			% Profit Before Taxes/Tangible Net Worth	(24) 10.5	(34) 17.3
			3.2				.9	7.8
		42.3	14.2				6.2	15.0
		21.8	6.0			% Profit Before Taxes/Total Assets	1.6	6.3
		6.3	.8				-3.5	2.3
		34.8	49.6				16.2	23.6
		23.7	10.2			Sales/Net Fixed Assets	5.3	9.7
		13.2	3.3				4.0	4.9
		4.0	1.9				2.1	2.7
		2.8	1.4			Sales/Total Assets	1.5	2.0
		1.9	1.1				1.2	1.4
			.3				1.0	.9
			(15) 1.4			% Depr., Dep., Amort./Sales	(30) 2.0	(35) 1.7
			3.4				3.5	2.5
						% Officers', Directors' Owners' Comp/Sales		
1613M	13206M	133366M	617453M	507851M	1730113M	Net Sales ($)	1652625M	1674071M
475M	4355M	50798M	401733M	402851M	947897M	Total Assets ($)	1275277M	968178M

M = $ thousand   MM = $ million
See Pages 9 through 22 for Explanation of Ratios and Data

Comparative Historical Data | Current Data Sorted by Sales

			Type of Statement						
13	14	14	Unqualified					4	10
4	7	8	Reviewed					4	4
6	4	3	Compiled		1		1	1	
1	2	3	Tax Returns		1		1		
17	19	16	Other	1	1	2		3	10
4/1/07-3/31/08 ALL	4/1/08-3/31/09 ALL	4/1/09-3/31/10 ALL		0-1MM	17 (4/1-9/30/09) 1-3MM	3-5MM	5-10MM	27 (10/1/09-3/31/10) 10-25MM	25MM & OVER
41	46	44	**NUMBER OF STATEMENTS**	1	3	2	2	12	24
%	%	%	**ASSETS**	%	%	%	%	%	%
6.3	4.4	5.3	Cash & Equivalents					4.5	3.8
20.7	20.2	19.3	Trade Receivables (net)					21.1	17.6
36.4	34.8	41.7	Inventory					45.4	40.9
3.1	3.0	2.0	All Other Current					1.6	2.5
66.5	62.4	68.2	Total Current					72.6	64.8
23.0	23.5	21.2	Fixed Assets (net)					22.5	21.0
4.0	5.7	3.1	Intangibles (net)					1.4	3.6
6.5	8.3	7.5	All Other Non-Current					3.5	10.6
100.0	100.0	100.0	Total					100.0	100.0
			LIABILITIES						
17.5	16.3	15.3	Notes Payable-Short Term					19.7	13.1
2.9	2.8	2.6	Cur. Mat.-L.T.D.					3.2	2.2
17.6	14.3	16.6	Trade Payables					17.2	19.1
.2	.4	.5	Income Taxes Payable					.2	.5
7.4	5.7	6.0	All Other Current					7.6	6.3
45.6	39.5	41.0	Total Current					48.0	41.2
12.6	14.6	14.2	Long-Term Debt					16.2	14.1
.5	.4	.4	Deferred Taxes					.4	.2
6.6	4.8	4.6	All Other Non-Current					6.5	4.3
34.7	40.8	39.8	Net Worth					28.9	40.2
100.0	100.0	100.0	Total Liabilities & Net Worth					100.0	100.0
			INCOME DATA						
100.0	100.0	100.0	Net Sales					100.0	100.0
28.8	28.3	26.4	Gross Profit					32.0	24.2
21.9	20.6	20.7	Operating Expenses					22.3	17.8
6.9	7.7	5.8	Operating Profit					9.7	6.4
1.5	.3	1.3	All Other Expenses (net)					.7	1.4
5.3	7.4	4.5	Profit Before Taxes					9.0	4.9
			RATIOS						
2.3	2.8	2.3						2.3	2.2
1.5	1.5	1.5	Current					1.4	1.5
1.2	1.2	1.2						1.1	1.2
1.0	1.1	1.0						.8	1.0
.5	.6	.5	Quick					.5	.6
.3	.4	.3						.5	.2
22 16.9	24 15.4	28 12.9						24 15.4	29 12.7
36 10.1	34 10.6	36 10.0	Sales/Receivables					36 10.1	35 10.4
47 7.8	44 8.3	42 8.7						39 9.4	40 9.1
54 6.7	46 7.9	58 6.3						34 10.7	64 5.7
90 4.1	86 4.2	129 2.8	Cost of Sales/Inventory					142 2.6	111 3.3
209 1.7	123 3.0	177 2.1						175 2.1	171 2.1
20 18.5	15 25.0	17 21.9						17 21.9	20 18.3
29 12.7	22 16.3	28 13.0	Cost of Sales/Payables					24 15.5	43 8.5
62 5.9	51 7.2	83 4.4						63 5.8	90 4.1
5.0	5.1	4.5						5.1	5.9
7.4	8.9	8.8	Sales/Working Capital					8.6	9.4
18.5	34.4	16.9						53.3	14.1
10.8	14.0	33.1						38.3	33.1
(39) 3.3	(43) 6.4	(43) 5.5	EBIT/Interest					6.7	(23) 5.0
1.2	3.0	1.7						2.6	1.7
16.3	30.2	10.6	Net Profit + Depr., Dep.,						
(12) 3.9	(14) 6.6	(15) 3.2	Amort./Cur. Mat. L/T/D						
1.7	3.1	1.8							
.4	.3	.2						.2	.3
.7	.7	.5	Fixed/Worth					.6	.5
1.4	1.2	1.0						2.4	1.3
1.1	.7	.8						.8	.9
2.4	1.9	2.1	Debt/Worth					1.9	2.3
4.1	3.4	2.9						4.3	2.7
53.2	46.0	51.3	% Profit Before Taxes/Tangible					97.9	35.6
(37) 20.8	(42) 28.7	(42) 17.8	Net Worth					(10) 41.4	16.8
1.3	14.3	5.1						11.1	5.8
15.0	20.6	27.5	% Profit Before Taxes/Total					39.2	17.5
7.2	9.4	8.2	Assets					13.7	6.7
.5	5.3	1.4						4.6	1.6
23.8	26.0	28.3						35.9	20.6
8.7	8.7	10.9	Sales/Net Fixed Assets					23.7	8.7
5.9	5.5	4.1						3.9	4.1
2.7	2.9	2.3						3.6	2.2
1.7	1.9	1.9	Sales/Total Assets					2.0	1.8
1.4	1.4	1.2						1.4	1.2
1.0	.9	.8						.6	.6
(35) 1.6	(41) 1.6	(38) 1.6	% Depr., Dep., Amort./Sales					1.3	(20) 1.6
2.2	2.5	2.9						3.4	2.8
	.9		% Officers', Directors'						
	(10) 2.9		Owners' Comp/Sales						
	7.8								
2885947M	3898603M	3003602M	Net Sales ($)	178M	5968M	7926M	14488M	181881M	2793161M
1703587M	1997420M	1808109M	Total Assets ($)	90M	5128M	21357M	15447M	101635M	1664452M

M = $ thousand   MM = $ million
See Pages 9 through 22 for Explanation of Ratios and Data

Current Data Sorted by Assets   Comparative Historical Data

Type of Statement	0-500M	500M-2MM	2-10MM	10-50MM	50-100MM	100-250MM		4/1/05-3/31/06 ALL	4/1/06-3/31/07 ALL
Unqualified	1			13	5	3		24	30
Reviewed			4	4	1			7	8
Compiled		1	2					6	4
Tax Returns		5	1					3	3
Other			4	16	5	3		22	19
	15 (4/1-9/30/09)			53 (10/1/09-3/31/10)					
NUMBER OF STATEMENTS	1	6	11	33	11	6		62	64

	0-500M %	500M-2MM %	2-10MM %	10-50MM %	50-100MM %	100-250MM %		ALL %	ALL %
ASSETS									
Cash & Equivalents			9.1	8.2	9.6			6.1	7.1
Trade Receivables (net)			28.4	26.6	16.8			25.5	26.2
Inventory			24.3	9.4	9.6			12.8	13.1
All Other Current			.7	3.3	4.8			4.3	3.0
Total Current			62.5	47.6	40.9			48.7	49.4
Fixed Assets (net)			33.1	42.1	45.2			41.5	39.3
Intangibles (net)			2.5	1.9	3.1			2.6	3.0
All Other Non-Current			1.9	8.5	10.8			7.1	8.3
Total			100.0	100.0	100.0			100.0	100.0
LIABILITIES									
Notes Payable-Short Term			10.1	3.8	1.8			6.1	7.2
Cur. Mat.-L.T.D.			3.2	3.8	2.1			2.9	3.5
Trade Payables			22.7	22.0	13.8			21.3	20.8
Income Taxes Payable			.2	.0	.1			.2	.3
All Other Current			6.2	7.6	9.0			10.8	10.2
Total Current			42.3	37.2	26.8			41.3	42.0
Long-Term Debt			23.1	14.1	16.6			14.4	18.1
Deferred Taxes			.4	1.0	2.3			.8	.7
All Other Non-Current			3.3	2.5	4.4			5.7	3.9
Net Worth			30.9	45.1	50.0			37.8	35.3
Total Liabilities & Net Worth			100.0	100.0	100.0			100.0	100.0
INCOME DATA									
Net Sales			100.0	100.0	100.0			100.0	100.0
Gross Profit			32.9	22.3	29.9			19.6	22.3
Operating Expenses			31.4	20.5	26.7			17.7	19.4
Operating Profit			1.5	1.8	3.3			1.9	2.9
All Other Expenses (net)			.8	-.1	-.4			.7	1.0
Profit Before Taxes			.7	1.9	3.7			1.2	1.9

RATIOS	0-500M	500M-2MM	2-10MM	10-50MM	50-100MM	100-250MM		ALL	ALL
Current			2.6	1.7	2.0			1.8	1.6
			1.5	1.3	1.7			1.2	1.1
			.9	1.0	1.0			1.0	.9
Quick			1.6	1.3	1.1			1.2	1.1
			1.1	1.0	.8			.8	.7
			.6	.7	.7			.4	.5
Sales/Receivables	18	20.5	23 16.1	17 20.9				18 20.4	22 16.6
	25	14.6	28 13.0	21 17.5				27 13.6	27 13.5
	27	13.4	35 10.5	28 13.0				33 11.0	34 10.6
Cost of Sales/Inventory	11	32.4	9 41.9	9 39.1				7 52.3	9 39.1
	30	12.0	11 32.3	17 21.9				13 29.1	14 25.7
	61	6.0	18 20.0	77 4.7				20 18.4	28 13.2
Cost of Sales/Payables	12	31.1	22 16.8	17 21.7				17 21.4	19 19.4
	25	14.8	28 13.2	32 11.5				25 14.6	26 14.2
	57	6.4	38 9.6	49 7.5				32 11.4	33 11.1
Sales/Working Capital			7.3	15.6	10.5			13.6	19.4
			16.2	34.9	16.0			61.4	42.5
			-118.0	NM	271.3			-143.4	-148.2
EBIT/Interest			20.9	38.7				8.4	9.2
			3.0	(31) 3.7				(54) 2.6	(55) 3.3
			1.7	1.4				.6	1.3
Net Profit + Depr., Dep., Amort./Cur. Mat. L/T/D				11.8				4.1	5.0
				(13) 3.5				(18) 1.9	(20) 2.0
				2.0				1.2	1.3
Fixed/Worth			.6	.7	.6			.6	.7
			.8	.9	.8			1.1	1.2
			1.8	1.7	2.0			2.3	2.3
Debt/Worth			.4	.6	.7			.6	1.1
			2.3	1.3	.8			1.6	1.8
			5.5	2.6	1.8			5.1	4.4
% Profit Before Taxes/Tangible Net Worth			31.3	33.1	29.6			26.9	36.3
		(10)	18.7	(32) 15.9	14.7			(57) 11.8	(59) 13.2
			1.5	1.4	11.9			-.8	4.1
% Profit Before Taxes/Total Assets			21.6	14.3	9.0			7.8	13.1
			3.5	5.7	8.1			3.2	4.4
			1.5	.6	5.9			-.7	1.6
Sales/Net Fixed Assets			45.1	15.4	11.9			22.9	13.7
			9.1	6.2	5.7			6.9	7.9
			5.9	5.2	2.0			4.8	5.0
Sales/Total Assets			6.1	4.2	3.9			5.4	4.5
			3.0	3.2	2.8			3.1	3.1
			2.4	2.6	.9			2.3	2.2
% Depr., Dep., Amort./Sales			.7	1.1	1.2			.8	1.3
			(30) 2.2	(10) 2.0	2.9			(57) 2.1	(58) 1.8
			3.5	2.8	4.1			3.6	3.1
% Officers', Directors' Owners' Comp/Sales									
Net Sales ($)	1380M	26417M	224194M	3195043M	2189566M	4257816M		10473655M	9533880M
Total Assets ($)	300M	8004M	53465M	913762M	878682M	1103182M		2951686M	3100664M

© RMA 2010

M = $ thousand   MM = $ million

See Pages 9 through 22 for Explanation of Ratios and Data

Comparative Historical Data   Current Data Sorted by Sales

Type of Statement / Number of Statements

4/1/07-3/31/08	4/1/08-3/31/09	4/1/09-3/31/10	Type of Statement	0-1MM	1-3MM	3-5MM	5-10MM	10-25MM	25MM & OVER
26	19	22	Unqualified			1		1	20
5	4	9	Reviewed		1			2	6
6	4	3	Compiled				1	2	
2	1	6	Tax Returns				1		1
21	29	28	Other	1	1	2	1	2	23
ALL	ALL	ALL		15 (4/1-9/30/09)			53 (10/1/09-3/31/10)		
60	57	68	NUMBER OF STATEMENTS	1	3	4	3	7	50

Assets / Liabilities / Income Data / Ratios

4/1/07-3/31/08	4/1/08-3/31/09	4/1/09-3/31/10		0-1MM	1-3MM	3-5MM	5-10MM	10-25MM	25MM & OVER
%	%	%	**ASSETS**	%	%	%	%	%	%
4.9	7.3	8.6	Cash & Equivalents						8.1
30.4	27.6	24.5	Trade Receivables (net)						27.1
13.1	12.7	13.5	Inventory						10.8
3.4	2.9	2.7	All Other Current						3.4
51.8	50.5	49.2	Total Current						49.4
39.3	42.1	38.7	Fixed Assets (net)						39.5
1.9	1.8	3.3	Intangibles (net)						3.7
7.0	5.6	8.8	All Other Non-Current						7.3
100.0	100.0	100.0	Total						100.0
			LIABILITIES						
7.9	7.4	5.5	Notes Payable-Short Term						4.7
3.4	3.0	3.0	Cur. Mat.-L.T.D.						3.1
24.9	20.1	20.4	Trade Payables						21.1
.1	.1	.1	Income Taxes Payable						.0
10.6	9.3	7.8	All Other Current						8.6
46.9	39.9	36.8	Total Current						37.5
16.1	15.7	18.1	Long-Term Debt						14.8
.6	.8	1.0	Deferred Taxes						1.3
3.0	4.7	3.6	All Other Non-Current						3.3
33.5	39.0	40.4	Net Worth						43.1
100.0	100.0	100.0	Total Liabilities & Net Worth						100.0
			INCOME DATA						
100.0	100.0	100.0	Net Sales						100.0
20.6	23.5	26.0	Gross Profit						22.4
19.0	20.4	23.5	Operating Expenses						19.1
1.5	3.1	2.4	Operating Profit						3.3
.8	.5	.2	All Other Expenses (net)						.1
.7	2.7	2.3	Profit Before Taxes						3.2
			RATIOS						
1.6	1.9	1.8							1.8
1.1	1.2	1.3	Current						1.3
1.0	1.0	1.0							1.0
1.1	1.3	1.2							1.2
.8	.9	.9	Quick						.9
.6	.6	.6							.7
22 16.4	18 19.8	21 17.5						22	16.2
28 13.2	24 15.5	26 14.2	Sales/Receivables					26	14.0
35 10.3	29 12.4	32 11.3						33	11.2
10 37.7	8 47.3	9 39.1						9	41.0
13 28.6	12 30.1	15 25.1	Cost of Sales/Inventory					13	29.0
22 16.6	21 17.6	30 12.1						19	19.3
21 17.2	13 27.3	18 20.6						18	20.4
26 14.2	21 17.3	27 13.7	Cost of Sales/Payables					27	13.7
35 10.5	27 13.4	38 9.6						35	10.5
23.5	14.0	11.8							15.3
50.4	57.5	28.7	Sales/Working Capital						32.4
-220.0	NM	501.6							304.3
7.7	15.0	21.1							21.8
(55) 1.6	(53) 7.3	(63) 5.5	EBIT/Interest					(46)	5.4
-.2	1.7	2.0							2.1
5.3	10.8	9.8	Net Profit + Depr., Dep.,						9.4
(17) 1.8	(18) 2.8	(26) 3.8	Amort./Cur. Mat. L/T/D					(22)	3.5
1.2	1.6	2.6							2.5
.6	.6	.6							.7
1.2	.8	.9	Fixed/Worth						.9
2.7	2.2	1.7							1.9
1.1	.8	.7							.7
1.8	1.5	1.3	Debt/Worth						1.3
5.7	5.3	3.9							3.7
32.0	37.1	34.3	% Profit Before Taxes/Tangible						38.0
(56) 8.7	(55) 17.1	(64) 19.9	Net Worth					(48)	21.1
-6.7	5.8	6.9							7.5
8.2	12.5	14.1	% Profit Before Taxes/Total						13.3
1.8	7.3	7.2	Assets						7.3
-2.2	1.5	2.3							2.2
21.5	18.7	16.7							16.4
8.0	8.3	6.7	Sales/Net Fixed Assets						7.2
5.2	5.0	5.2							5.4
4.9	5.0	4.3							4.6
3.6	3.4	3.1	Sales/Total Assets						3.3
2.6	2.6	2.4							2.7
.9	.9	1.1							1.1
(57) 1.7	(49) 1.5	(61) 1.9	% Depr., Dep., Amort./Sales					(45)	1.9
2.7	2.5	3.0							2.9
		.6	% Officers', Directors'						
	(14) 1.6		Owners' Comp/Sales						
		2.8							
10208956M	11186658M	9894416M	Net Sales ($)	393M	6709M	17133M	24841M	99797M	9745543M
2956734M	2969915M	2957395M	Total Assets ($)	780M	4391M	20346M	5444M	49103M	2877331M

M = $ thousand   MM = $ million
See Pages 9 through 22 for Explanation of Ratios and Data

Current Data Sorted by Assets   Comparative Historical Data

0-500M	500M-2MM	2-10MM	10-50MM	50-100MM	100-250MM	Type of Statement		
1		4	10	5	6	Unqualified	24	29
	1	3	6	1		Reviewed	12	15
	1	6				Compiled	5	5
	1	3	1			Tax Returns	2	4
1	2	12	11	1	5	Other	26	22

0-500M	500M-2MM	2-10MM	10-50MM	50-100MM	100-250MM		4/1/05-3/31/06 ALL	4/1/06-3/31/07 ALL
		19 (4/1-9/30/09)	62 (10/1/09-3/31/10)					
2	5	28	28	7	11	**NUMBER OF STATEMENTS**	69	75
%	%	%	%	%	%	**ASSETS**	%	%
		9.5	7.3		3.9	Cash & Equivalents	5.3	6.6
		23.5	19.0		17.7	Trade Receivables (net)	22.0	21.5
		24.2	22.6		30.0	Inventory	24.1	23.6
		2.8	1.6		3.9	All Other Current	1.8	1.8
		59.9	50.5		55.4	Total Current	53.2	53.6
		32.1	40.9		32.1	Fixed Assets (net)	39.9	39.2
		.4	2.7		8.8	Intangibles (net)	1.8	2.9
		7.6	5.9		3.7	All Other Non-Current	5.1	4.2
		100.0	100.0		100.0	Total	100.0	100.0
						LIABILITIES		
		9.8	10.7		7.6	Notes Payable-Short Term	10.6	9.8
		2.7	4.3		2.5	Cur. Mat.-L.T.D.	2.6	3.5
		21.9	13.7		13.1	Trade Payables	16.5	15.8
		.0	.5		.1	Income Taxes Payable	.1	.1
		5.7	9.6		11.1	All Other Current	6.6	6.4
		40.1	38.7		34.4	Total Current	36.5	35.6
		17.5	18.5		23.1	Long-Term Debt	19.7	21.3
		.8	.7		2.0	Deferred Taxes	.8	.8
		5.1	4.7		6.6	All Other Non-Current	4.2	3.0
		36.5	37.5		33.9	Net Worth	38.8	39.2
		100.0	100.0		100.0	Total Liabilties & Net Worth	100.0	100.0
						INCOME DATA		
		100.0	100.0		100.0	Net Sales	100.0	100.0
		20.0	17.1		13.9	Gross Profit	14.9	16.5
		14.0	11.7		8.8	Operating Expenses	11.5	12.7
		6.0	5.5		5.1	Operating Profit	3.4	3.8
		1.1	1.0		.8	All Other Expenses (net)	.7	.9
		4.8	4.5		4.3	Profit Before Taxes	2.7	2.9
						RATIOS		
		2.1	2.5		2.4		2.1	2.2
		1.6	1.2		1.7	Current	1.6	1.6
		1.3	1.0		1.5		1.0	1.1
		1.2	1.3		.9		1.3	1.2
		.9	.7		.6	Quick	.7	.8
		.5	.3		.4		.4	.5
		23 15.7	22 16.9		19 19.2		20 18.6	22 16.8
		28 12.9	27 13.6		27 13.4	Sales/Receivables	26 14.2	28 13.2
		41 9.0	31 11.8		30 12.1		34 10.9	34 10.7
		10 35.0	13 28.6		26 13.8		16 22.7	17 21.3
		26 13.9	41 8.8		42 8.6	Cost of Sales/Inventory	29 12.6	31 11.7
		65 5.6	62 5.9		66 5.5		54 6.7	58 6.3
		21 17.6	14 25.6		9 39.8		16 22.3	16 22.9
		29 12.5	23 15.7		20 18.1	Cost of Sales/Payables	22 16.8	24 15.0
		44 8.4	32 11.5		27 13.7		29 12.4	31 11.7
		8.5	7.0		7.2		10.4	9.0
		14.9	54.6		14.4	Sales/Working Capital	24.9	20.7
		27.6	-434.7		16.6		310.3	82.1
		42.5	24.7		24.7		10.1	9.4
		(26) 6.4	8.7		7.7	EBIT/Interest	(63) 4.0	(71) 3.2
		2.3	3.7		2.0		1.8	1.3
		11.1				Net Profit + Depr., Dep.,	9.4	7.5
		(10) 3.6				Amort./Cur. Mat. L/T/D	(19) 3.3	(25) 2.2
		1.6					2.0	1.6
		.3	.6		.7		.6	.7
		.7	1.2		.8	Fixed/Worth	1.0	1.1
		2.4	2.0		2.2		2.2	2.2
		.7	.7		.6		1.0	.7
		1.9	2.1		1.3	Debt/Worth	1.8	1.5
		3.8	3.4		10.3		3.7	4.0
		64.2	44.1			% Profit Before Taxes/Tangible	35.7	30.1
		(26) 33.3	(26) 23.2			Net Worth	(67) 16.1	(68) 13.7
		11.0	7.7				5.6	4.4
		20.8	17.1		19.5	% Profit Before Taxes/Total	10.8	12.7
		11.5	10.3		12.4	Assets	5.4	5.5
		4.1	2.9		1.4		1.8	1.4
		16.4	11.0		18.9		15.5	13.6
		10.3	5.5		7.2	Sales/Net Fixed Assets	7.9	7.0
		4.7	4.1		4.7		4.2	4.0
		4.2	3.6		3.1		3.9	3.8
		2.7	2.7		2.6	Sales/Total Assets	3.1	2.7
		1.9	1.7		2.0		1.9	2.1
		1.2	1.3				1.0	1.3
		(25) 1.6	(27) 2.4			% Depr., Dep., Amort./Sales	(59) 1.5	(67) 1.7
		2.0	3.5				2.1	2.4
			.6				.6	.8
		(10) 1.3				% Officers', Directors' Owners' Comp/Sales	(18) 1.5	(22) 2.0
		1.9					2.4	4.0
349M	31579M	507274M	1695985M	897862M	4246080M	Net Sales ($)	9030883M	8285815M
92M	8619M	153061M	639506M	556555M	1682650M	Total Assets ($)	3244404M	3065936M

M = $ thousand   MM = $ million
See Pages 9 through 22 for Explanation of Ratios and Data

Comparative Historical Data | Current Data Sorted by Sales

	4/1/07-3/31/08 ALL	4/1/08-3/31/09 ALL	4/1/09-3/31/10 ALL	0-1MM	1-3MM	3-5MM	5-10MM	10-25MM	25MM & OVER
Type of Statement				19 (4/1-9/30/09)			62 (10/1/09-3/31/10)		
Unqualified	33	26	26	1			1	4	20
Reviewed	11	10	11				1	3	7
Compiled	4	5	7		1	1	3	1	1
Tax Returns	4	7	5		1	1	1		2
Other	23	39	32	1		2	3	10	16
NUMBER OF STATEMENTS	75	87	81	2	2	4	9	18	46
ASSETS	%	%	%	%	%	%	%	%	%
Cash & Equivalents	5.7	7.7	7.7					8.5	8.0
Trade Receivables (net)	23.5	21.7	20.0					23.1	19.8
Inventory	25.6	23.6	24.7					23.3	22.3
All Other Current	1.7	1.7	2.3					2.6	2.6
Total Current	56.5	54.7	54.8					57.6	52.6
Fixed Assets (net)	37.0	36.6	35.1					37.2	36.0
Intangibles (net)	2.4	3.3	3.0					.3	4.9
All Other Non-Current	4.1	5.4	7.1					5.0	6.5
Total	100.0	100.0	100.0					100.0	100.0
LIABILITIES									
Notes Payable-Short Term	13.1	9.3	10.3					10.3	8.2
Cur. Mat.-L.T.D.	2.9	2.9	3.2					3.0	3.5
Trade Payables	18.1	18.1	16.5					18.5	16.1
Income Taxes Payable	.2	.2	.2					.1	.3
All Other Current	9.4	5.9	7.9					5.4	9.2
Total Current	43.6	36.4	38.0					37.2	37.2
Long-Term Debt	18.4	19.5	18.6					16.0	20.1
Deferred Taxes	.8	.8	.9					1.3	.9
All Other Non-Current	3.7	3.8	4.8					2.7	5.3
Net Worth	33.6	39.5	37.7					42.9	36.5
Total Liabilities & Net Worth	100.0	100.0	100.0					100.0	100.0
INCOME DATA									
Net Sales	100.0	100.0	100.0					100.0	100.0
Gross Profit	14.5	17.5	18.9					15.1	16.8
Operating Expenses	11.9	12.9	13.3					10.3	11.8
Operating Profit	2.6	4.6	5.6					4.7	5.0
All Other Expenses (net)	.6	1.0	1.0					.5	.7
Profit Before Taxes	2.0	3.6	4.7					4.2	4.3
RATIOS									
Current	2.1	2.3	2.4					2.6	2.4
	1.4	1.6	1.6					1.6	1.7
	1.0	1.1	1.1					1.4	1.0
Quick	1.2	1.4	1.3					1.3	1.3
	.7	.7	.7					.8	.7
	.4	.4	.4					.4	.4
Sales/Receivables	20 18.0	19 19.6	21 17.3					24 14.9	19 19.2
	26 13.9	25 14.4	27 13.4					29 12.6	26 14.2
	35 10.5	33 10.9	31 11.7					40 9.1	30 12.2
Cost of Sales/Inventory	18 20.5	15 23.7	16 23.5					13 28.3	14 25.9
	30 12.1	27 13.3	36 10.2					30 12.2	33 11.0
	59 6.1	62 5.9	64 5.7					74 4.9	58 6.3
Cost of Sales/Payables	19 19.4	15 24.4	17 21.6					17 20.9	13 28.8
	24 15.0	21 17.6	26 14.0					25 14.6	24 15.3
	31 11.6	33 11.2	37 9.9					38 9.5	33 11.1
Sales/Working Capital	9.6	9.1	7.1					9.0	7.2
	19.8	17.5	15.6					11.3	16.4
	653.8	74.9	100.4					26.0	NM
EBIT/Interest	7.2	15.3	22.9					10.7	52.0
	(70) 3.0	(80) 5.0	(78) 6.6					(17) 6.0	8.5
	1.5	1.8	2.3					2.3	2.1
Net Profit + Depr., Dep., Amort./Cur. Mat. L/T/D	9.4	8.7	8.9						9.4
	(25) 3.7	(31) 2.7	(24) 3.6						(13) 4.3
	1.4	1.4	1.5						1.3
Fixed/Worth	.7	.6	.4					.6	.5
	1.0	1.0	.9					1.0	.8
	1.9	2.0	1.9					1.6	1.9
Debt/Worth	.9	.7	.7					.5	.7
	1.9	1.7	1.6					1.8	1.5
	3.5	3.2	3.6					3.9	2.7
% Profit Before Taxes/Tangible Net Worth	32.6	45.7	47.4					53.3	45.8
	(68) 19.3	(82) 20.4	(74) 27.5					20.9	(41) 29.0
	4.1	9.1	11.3					4.2	10.4
% Profit Before Taxes/Total Assets	9.0	15.9	19.5					18.4	19.5
	4.9	7.6	10.9					8.9	11.0
	1.0	1.9	3.5					3.6	2.2
Sales/Net Fixed Assets	13.9	14.5	14.8					14.7	14.9
	8.9	7.8	6.5					8.0	6.9
	4.3	4.6	4.3					4.3	4.3
Sales/Total Assets	3.9	4.0	3.7					3.9	3.8
	3.0	2.9	2.6					2.7	2.7
	2.0	2.0	1.8					1.9	1.9
% Depr., Dep., Amort./Sales	1.2	1.0	1.2					1.3	1.1
	(65) 1.5	(77) 1.5	(72) 1.8					(17) 1.9	(41) 1.6
	2.5	2.6	2.6					2.6	2.6
% Officers', Directors' Owners' Comp/Sales	.6	.4	.7						.6
	(23) 1.7	(23) 1.4	(21) 1.4						(13) 1.2
	3.0	2.6	2.2						1.8
Net Sales ($)	9494272M	10976140M	7379129M	349M	4754M	17495M	69022M	343006M	6944503M
Total Assets ($)	3437821M	3767444M	3040483M	92M	5394M	8844M	43376M	141706M	2841071M

© RMA 2010

M = $ thousand   MM = $ million
See Pages 9 through 22 for Explanation of Ratios and Data

Current Data Sorted by Assets   Comparative Historical Data

			4		1	Type of Statement		
	1	2				Unqualified	7	5
		1				Reviewed		3
2	1	2				Compiled	4	1
	1		7			Tax Returns	1	8
	6 (4/1-9/30/09)		18 (10/1/09-3/31/10)			Other	13	15
							4/1/05-3/31/06	4/1/06-3/31/07
0-500M	500M-2MM	2-10MM	10-50MM	50-100MM	100-250MM		ALL	ALL
2	3	5	11	2	1	NUMBER OF STATEMENTS	25	32
%	%	%	%	%	%	ASSETS	%	%
			7.5			Cash & Equivalents	9.1	4.6
			11.2			Trade Receivables (net)	14.9	12.5
			19.9			Inventory	21.7	17.2
			2.7			All Other Current	2.3	2.1
			41.4			Total Current	48.0	36.5
			36.8			Fixed Assets (net)	40.6	46.3
			12.6			Intangibles (net)	4.0	11.1
			9.3			All Other Non-Current	7.4	6.1
			100.0			Total	100.0	100.0
						LIABILITIES		
			11.7			Notes Payable-Short Term	12.1	10.1
			2.4			Cur. Mat.-L.T.D.	3.8	5.5
			9.3			Trade Payables	14.3	13.0
			.0			Income Taxes Payable	.0	.0
			5.0			All Other Current	5.5	15.3
			28.4			Total Current	35.7	43.9
			20.7			Long-Term Debt	26.3	28.3
			1.2			Deferred Taxes	1.2	.9
			8.7			All Other Non-Current	3.5	7.2
			41.1			Net Worth	33.3	19.7
			100.0			Total Liabilities & Net Worth	100.0	100.0
						INCOME DATA		
			100.0			Net Sales	100.0	100.0
			34.6			Gross Profit	30.6	34.0
			30.9			Operating Expenses	27.0	32.2
			3.8			Operating Profit	3.6	1.7
			3.2			All Other Expenses (net)	1.7	1.9
			.5			Profit Before Taxes	1.9	-.2
						RATIOS		
			4.3				1.7	1.8
			1.5			Current	1.4	1.0
			.9				1.0	.7
			3.0				1.2	.8
			.6			Quick	(24) .6	.6
			.4				.4	.2
		15	24.4				13 27.9	8 44.8
		20	18.0			Sales/Receivables	19 19.6	19 19.0
		36	10.1				27 13.4	31 11.9
		55	6.6				23 16.1	14 25.5
		60	6.1			Cost of Sales/Inventory	45 8.0	33 11.2
		91	4.0				71 5.2	66 5.5
		19	19.4				19 19.5	17 21.6
		23	15.9			Cost of Sales/Payables	28 13.0	25 14.5
		28	12.9				42 8.6	41 8.9
			4.4				11.8	11.5
			16.5			Sales/Working Capital	25.8	342.0
			-87.9				NM	-15.9
			8.9				6.8	5.8
			1.3			EBIT/Interest	(22) 1.3	(28) 1.5
			1.1				-.3	-.4
						Net Profit + Depr., Dep.,	3.6	6.5
						Amort./Cur. Mat. L/T/D	(10) 1.8	(10) 2.9
							.7	.4
			.6				.5	1.2
			1.3			Fixed/Worth	1.8	3.5
			6.3				6.5	-5.2
			.9				.9	1.8
			1.4			Debt/Worth	3.2	4.5
			9.0				8.8	-16.4
						% Profit Before Taxes/Tangible	38.0	42.8
						Net Worth	(21) 11.4	(23) 7.9
							-2.2	-22.8
			18.0			% Profit Before Taxes/Total	16.6	8.3
			2.1			Assets	1.9	1.9
			.1				-5.2	-6.2
			12.4				10.1	9.8
			8.2			Sales/Net Fixed Assets	5.4	6.0
			2.5				3.7	3.0
			2.1				3.6	3.1
			1.6			Sales/Total Assets	1.9	2.1
			1.2				1.6	1.3
			1.2				1.4	1.3
		(10)	2.0			% Depr., Dep., Amort./Sales	(23) 2.4	(29) 3.1
			7.2				3.6	4.8
								2.4
						% Officers', Directors'		(11) 3.3
						Owners' Comp/Sales		4.4
684M	3771M	98682M	389404M	179155M	243498M	Net Sales ($)	1209368M	1414717M
510M	3128M	23231M	232406M	131616M	104851M	Total Assets ($)	594539M	686431M

M = $ thousand   MM = $ million
See Pages 9 through 22 for Explanation of Ratios and Data

Comparative Historical Data | Current Data Sorted by Sales

	4/1/07-3/31/08 ALL	4/1/08-3/31/09 ALL	4/1/09-3/31/10 ALL	0-1MM	1-3MM	3-5MM	5-10MM	10-25MM	25MM & OVER
Type of Statement				6 (4/1-9/30/09)			18 (10/1/09-3/31/10)		
Unqualified	8	8	5						4
Reviewed	2	3	3		1			1	4
Compiled	3	5	1				1		1
Tax Returns	3	2	3					1	1
Other	13	11	12	3	1		2	4	4
NUMBER OF STATEMENTS	29	29	24	3	2		3	6	10
ASSETS	%	%	%	%	%	%	%	%	%
Cash & Equivalents	5.9	7.1	9.4						6.6
Trade Receivables (net)	11.4	11.6	12.1						18.3
Inventory	21.1	23.2	21.5						24.5
All Other Current	3.5	1.5	2.6						1.5
Total Current	41.9	43.4	45.7						51.0
Fixed Assets (net)	38.4	37.9	32.2						25.3
Intangibles (net)	13.8	11.9	15.6						17.1
All Other Non-Current	5.9	6.8	6.6						6.7
Total	100.0	100.0	100.0						100.0
LIABILITIES									
Notes Payable-Short Term	18.5	14.9	8.4						13.1
Cur. Mat.-L.T.D.	3.7	3.5	2.9						1.7
Trade Payables	13.7	10.7	12.0						14.2
Income Taxes Payable	.0	.1	.0						.0
All Other Current	3.5	20.4	7.1						8.5
Total Current	39.4	49.6	30.3						37.4
Long-Term Debt	22.4	22.2	28.4						15.2
Deferred Taxes	1.0	.8	.6						1.3
All Other Non-Current	7.2	7.0	7.4						11.6
Net Worth	30.0	20.4	33.3						34.4
Total Liabilities & Net Worth	100.0	100.0	100.0						100.0
INCOME DATA									
Net Sales	100.0	100.0	100.0						100.0
Gross Profit	36.7	38.6	42.4						27.1
Operating Expenses	35.4	36.2	36.3						18.4
Operating Profit	1.4	2.4	6.1						8.7
All Other Expenses (net)	2.5	1.5	3.0						3.6
Profit Before Taxes	-1.2	.9	3.1						5.1
RATIOS									
Current	1.9	2.2	2.7						1.6
	1.4	1.2	1.4						1.4
	.6	.8	.8						1.0
Quick	.8	1.1	1.3						1.1
	.4	.5	.6						.5
	.2	.3	.4						.3
Sales/Receivables	10 36.7	14 25.9	13 28.3						17 21.4
	20 17.9	20 18.7	19 19.4						22 16.6
	27 13.5	30 12.3	29 12.7						30 12.0
Cost of Sales/Inventory	30 12.2	37 9.8	36 10.2						39 9.4
	50 7.3	65 5.6	57 6.4						57 6.4
	77 4.8	90 4.1	90 4.0						60 6.1
Cost of Sales/Payables	18 20.5	17 21.9	16 22.3						19 19.6
	29 12.7	25 14.5	24 15.2						28 12.9
	43 8.4	35 10.5	37 9.8						40 9.1
Sales/Working Capital	11.0	8.4	5.0						10.6
	18.0	28.9	17.8						21.7
	-11.3	-17.8	-50.7						-87.5
EBIT/Interest	3.1	12.8	8.9						40.1
	(28) .4	(27) 1.5	(23) 3.2						3.3
	-1.4	-.4	.7						1.2
Net Profit + Depr., Dep., Amort./Cur. Mat. L/T/D	2.7	7.6							
	(11) .8	(10) 1.8							
	-1.7	-.5							
Fixed/Worth	.7	.6	.5						.6
	2.1	1.5	1.3						1.9
	-1.4	NM	-5.4						-3.6
Debt/Worth	1.4	.8	.7						.8
	2.3	1.6	1.6						5.7
	-6.9	NM	-15.8						-9.8
% Profit Before Taxes/Tangible Net Worth	30.1	44.9	47.0						
	(19) 9.6	(22) 12.8	(17) 27.4						
	-15.5	-4.9	2.6						
% Profit Before Taxes/Total Assets	6.3	15.8	22.1						25.4
	-2.8	2.1	4.5						8.7
	-9.0	-5.0	-1.3						1.6
Sales/Net Fixed Assets	15.2	10.2	19.5						21.8
	9.4	6.5	11.1						9.8
	3.0	3.5	4.9						6.5
Sales/Total Assets	3.0	3.0	3.2						2.8
	1.9	2.0	2.0						2.2
	1.4	1.2	1.1						1.9
% Depr., Dep., Amort./Sales	1.2	1.5	1.2						
	(24) 2.0	(24) 2.0	(20) 2.0						
	4.8	3.6	5.3						
% Officers', Directors' Owners' Comp/Sales									
Net Sales ($)	1131306M	1168840M	915194M	1270M	3185M		24653M	96800M	789286M
Total Assets ($)	738061M	663460M	495742M	1205M	2433M		32329M	59507M	400268M

For the ASSETS, LIABILITIES, INCOME DATA and RATIOS columns 0-1MM through 10-25MM: "DATA NOT AVAILABLE."

M = $ thousand   MM = $ million
See Pages 9 through 22 for Explanation of Ratios and Data

Current Data Sorted by Assets   Comparative Historical Data

						Type of Statement		
			3	11	4	1 Unqualified	21	36
1	3	10	3	1		Reviewed	16	16
	5	7	3			Compiled	19	14
1	1	3				Tax Returns	4	2
	5	7	11	6		Other	27	36
	8 (4/1-9/30/09)		78 (10/1/09-3/31/10)				4/1/05-3/31/06	4/1/06-3/31/07
0-500M	500M-2MM	2-10MM	10-50MM	50-100MM	100-250MM		ALL	ALL
2	14	30	28	11	1	NUMBER OF STATEMENTS	87	104
%	%	%	%	%	%	ASSETS	%	%
	9.2	6.3	16.9	3.9		Cash & Equivalents	8.2	7.3
	32.3	22.3	21.9	22.3		Trade Receivables (net)	22.9	24.2
	15.5	21.8	16.7	22.3		Inventory	21.7	22.3
	.4	4.0	2.9	1.4		All Other Current	2.1	2.3
	57.4	54.4	58.4	49.9		Total Current	54.9	56.1
	36.0	38.9	32.4	40.8		Fixed Assets (net)	35.0	33.3
	1.3	1.9	5.0	6.4		Intangibles (net)	1.8	3.1
	5.3	4.7	4.3	2.8		All Other Non-Current	8.3	7.6
	100.0	100.0	100.0	100.0		Total	100.0	100.0
						LIABILITIES		
	14.6	13.4	5.8	12.2		Notes Payable-Short Term	14.1	11.9
	6.6	3.0	2.1	1.6		Cur. Mat.-L.T.D.	2.6	2.4
	10.3	13.1	8.6	9.1		Trade Payables	11.2	12.1
	.1	.1	.0	.0		Income Taxes Payable	.2	.2
	6.1	6.1	9.2	12.3		All Other Current	7.3	7.2
	37.6	35.7	25.7	35.3		Total Current	35.3	34.0
	16.5	23.6	15.3	23.8		Long-Term Debt	17.7	17.2
	.1	.3	.4	.0		Deferred Taxes	.7	.6
	17.2	3.8	3.8	1.2		All Other Non-Current	4.6	8.1
	28.5	36.5	54.8	39.8		Net Worth	41.7	40.1
	100.0	100.0	100.0	100.0		Total Liabilities & Net Worth	100.0	100.0
						INCOME DATA		
	100.0	100.0	100.0	100.0		Net Sales	100.0	100.0
	25.6	24.6	19.3	17.4		Gross Profit	20.3	16.8
	26.0	24.6	13.5	14.7		Operating Expenses	17.1	14.0
	-.4	.1	5.8	2.7		Operating Profit	3.2	2.7
	-.3	-.3	.4	1.0		All Other Expenses (net)	.4	.5
	-.1	.4	5.4	1.7		Profit Before Taxes	2.8	2.3
						RATIOS		
	2.9	2.6	4.1	1.8			2.7	2.6
	1.8	1.2	2.3	1.4		Current	1.5	1.7
	.8	1.0	1.5	1.3			1.1	1.2
	2.1	1.7	3.6	1.1			1.5	1.5
	1.5	.8	1.7	.8		Quick	.8	.8
	.5	.4	.5	.5			.5	.6
	14 25.4	15 23.9	13 28.5	18 20.7			15 24.9	14 25.2
	19 18.7	21 17.0	20 17.9	21 17.8		Sales/Receivables	20 18.0	21 17.7
	30 12.3	42 8.6	31 11.9	27 13.6			27 13.8	27 13.4
	7 51.3	10 38.1	10 34.9	11 34.0			11 33.5	13 29.0
	13 27.8	21 17.1	20 18.4	15 24.0		Cost of Sales/Inventory	24 15.5	21 17.1
	28 13.0	47 7.7	28 12.9	41 8.9			44 8.3	37 9.8
	3 126.9	7 54.3	4 83.2	5 76.4			6 61.0	5 66.4
	8 43.6	16 22.8	8 45.0	9 39.0		Cost of Sales/Payables	12 31.0	11 32.8
	20 18.4	29 12.6	14 25.5	16 22.8			20 18.0	19 19.7
	12.8	9.9	7.2	13.2			10.4	10.6
	34.4	58.9	14.4	31.2		Sales/Working Capital	23.7	20.9
	-40.4	-391.4	30.3	51.1			96.2	57.5
	5.7	18.8	17.5	4.5			5.9	8.5
	(13) 2.0	(27) 2.8	(26) 8.1	2.8		EBIT/Interest	(78) 2.1	(91) 3.3
	-10.1	-1.6	3.2	1.3			.8	1.0
						Net Profit + Depr., Dep.,	9.4	5.6
						Amort./Cur. Mat. L/T/D	(28) 2.9	(21) 2.7
							1.6	1.7
	.4	.3	.3	.7			.4	.4
	1.2	1.7	.6	1.2		Fixed/Worth	.8	.9
	NM	5.3	1.2	3.1			2.1	2.1
	.7	.5	.5	.7			.7	.8
	2.0	2.6	.8	2.4		Debt/Worth	1.7	1.6
	NM	9.9	2.1	5.3			3.6	4.4
	40.3	21.5	48.0	16.9		% Profit Before Taxes/Tangible	28.5	42.3
	(11) 14.2	(27) 13.2	(26) 20.6	(10) 9.3		Net Worth	(83) 10.2	(95) 16.7
	-57.0	-4.7	7.9	1.7			1.9	1.6
	10.2	10.9	23.4	8.8		% Profit Before Taxes/Total	12.5	14.6
	4.3	4.1	9.3	4.8		Assets	3.0	6.1
	-16.1	-1.8	3.2	.5			.2	.5
	39.8	75.9	31.1	14.9			23.8	31.5
	10.8	8.5	10.5	12.6		Sales/Net Fixed Assets	11.3	12.8
	4.2	3.3	6.3	7.5			5.5	5.6
	8.1	5.7	5.6	6.1			5.4	6.0
	4.3	2.9	3.8	3.4		Sales/Total Assets	3.5	3.8
	2.0	1.2	2.4	3.0			2.3	2.4
	.5	.2	.5	1.1			.5	.5
	(12) 1.0	(28) 1.7	(25) 1.0	1.9		% Depr., Dep., Amort./Sales	(82) 1.0	(89) 1.3
	3.2	3.8	2.0	2.1			2.2	2.0
	1.5	.7					.7	.5
	(10) 2.8	(13) 1.6				% Officers', Directors' Owners' Comp/Sales	(31) 2.1	(29) 1.6
	8.1	3.9					4.4	3.8
680M	106360M	545812M	2370269M	2804910M	723632M	Net Sales ($)	7864918M	10990937M
372M	18532M	140754M	630165M	724452M	206054M	Total Assets ($)	2432228M	3417256M

M = $ thousand   MM = $ million
See Pages 9 through 22 for Explanation of Ratios and Data

Comparative Historical Data | Current Data Sorted by Sales

			Type of Statement						
23	24	19	Unqualified					3	16
12	16	18	Reviewed	1	2	1	2	4	8
11	9	15	Compiled		3	2	4	3	3
7	4	5	Tax Returns	1	1	2	1	2	
35	30	29	Other	2	1	2		2	21
4/1/07-3/31/08	4/1/08-3/31/09	4/1/09-3/31/10		8 (4/1-9/30/09)			78 (10/1/09-3/31/10)		
ALL	ALL	ALL		0-1MM	1-3MM	3-5MM	5-10MM	10-25MM	25MM & OVER
88	83	86	**NUMBER OF STATEMENTS**	4	7	6	9	12	48
%	%	%	**ASSETS**	%	%	%	%	%	%
7.3	6.7	10.1	Cash & Equivalents					9.6	8.8
22.9	26.2	23.4	Trade Receivables (net)					18.9	27.8
23.1	23.6	19.1	Inventory					23.3	20.4
2.2	2.1	2.7	All Other Current					1.6	4.2
55.5	58.5	55.3	Total Current					53.4	61.2
33.0	33.7	36.8	Fixed Assets (net)					32.6	32.7
4.2	3.5	3.3	Intangibles (net)					9.2	3.0
7.3	4.2	4.5	All Other Non-Current					4.9	3.0
100.0	100.0	100.0	Total					100.0	100.0
			LIABILITIES						
12.7	10.3	10.7	Notes Payable-Short Term					12.3	11.9
3.0	4.0	3.0	Cur. Mat.-L.T.D.					3.8	2.2
12.3	13.3	10.4	Trade Payables					11.0	11.8
.2	.2	.1	Income Taxes Payable					.3	.0
7.2	8.4	7.8	All Other Current					6.1	9.8
35.3	36.4	32.0	Total Current					33.4	35.7
20.3	19.2	19.5	Long-Term Debt					15.4	16.6
.4	.3	.3	Deferred Taxes					.6	.3
7.7	8.4	6.3	All Other Non-Current					10.7	1.9
36.3	35.7	41.9	Net Worth					39.9	45.4
100.0	100.0	100.0	Total Liabilties & Net Worth					100.0	100.0
			INCOME DATA						
100.0	100.0	100.0	Net Sales					100.0	100.0
19.1	16.1	22.5	Gross Profit					19.2	15.9
16.6	14.0	20.3	Operating Expenses					16.3	12.8
2.5	2.2	2.2	Operating Profit					2.9	3.1
.8	.5	.1	All Other Expenses (net)					.4	.4
1.7	1.7	2.1	Profit Before Taxes					2.5	2.6
			RATIOS						
2.4	2.3	3.3						2.7	3.1
1.6	1.7	1.7	Current					1.9	1.6
1.1	1.1	1.1						.9	1.2
1.5	1.5	2.0						1.8	2.0
.8	.9	1.0	Quick					1.1	1.0
.5	.6	.5						.3	.6
15 24.5	15 24.2	14 25.8	Sales/Receivables					13 27.8	13 27.4
19 18.9	20 18.2	21 17.8						18 20.1	20 18.1
26 14.2	25 14.3	29 12.7						24 15.0	27 13.7
13 27.9	12 29.6	10 36.6	Cost of Sales/Inventory					15 24.4	10 36.4
25 14.7	22 16.8	19 19.1						21 17.1	18 20.7
40 9.1	40 9.1	38 9.5						48 7.6	27 13.4
6 65.6	6 62.5	5 76.5	Cost of Sales/Payables					4 82.0	5 74.1
11 33.1	10 35.6	10 37.7						6 60.0	9 39.6
19 19.7	17 21.7	20 18.1						19 19.6	16 22.5
11.0	11.6	9.1	Sales/Working Capital					11.4	11.6
23.1	24.2	23.6						26.7	25.6
66.5	93.9	113.6						NM	51.2
6.2	12.1	13.0	EBIT/Interest					7.3	18.9
(79) 2.7	(77) 4.4	(79) 3.4						3.9	(45) 4.0
1.0	1.0	.0						1.8	1.2
4.0	8.5	4.9	Net Profit + Depr., Dep.,						5.2
(15) 2.9	(18) 2.0	(17) 2.4	Amort./Cur. Mat. L/T/D					(11)	3.0
1.6	.6	1.7							1.9
.3	.4	.4	Fixed/Worth					.4	.5
1.0	.9	.9						1.7	.7
6.4	2.1	2.9						2.7	1.9
.8	.6	.5	Debt/Worth					1.4	.6
1.8	1.4	1.7						2.6	1.4
11.6	4.5	4.9						4.6	2.7
45.1	44.3	32.6	% Profit Before Taxes/Tangible					20.7	42.0
(74) 18.8	(73) 15.4	(76) 14.3	Net Worth					(11) 14.0	(43) 17.5
4.4	3.4	1.7						4.4	4.3
11.5	16.4	13.7	% Profit Before Taxes/Total					15.5	20.2
5.8	5.9	5.4	Assets					4.1	7.0
.5	.5	-1.1						2.3	.5
43.4	35.5	28.2	Sales/Net Fixed Assets					47.8	36.8
12.8	12.1	10.4						8.5	14.1
5.8	6.3	4.4						5.1	7.9
5.7	5.8	5.7	Sales/Total Assets					5.6	6.1
3.7	3.8	3.4						3.2	4.2
2.3	2.6	2.0						1.8	3.1
.4	.5	.5	% Depr., Dep., Amort./Sales					.4	.5
(76) 1.2	(77) 1.1	(78) 1.5						(10) 1.5	(45) 1.0
2.2	1.9	2.6						2.9	2.0
1.0	.9	1.0	% Officers', Directors'						
(26) 1.9	(26) 1.7	(29) 1.9	Owners' Comp/Sales						
3.6	4.2	4.8							
8975077M	8487439M	6551663M	Net Sales ($)	2120M	14290M	21662M	66346M	199452M	6247793M
2708863M	2324899M	1720329M	Total Assets ($)	3921M	15746M	27577M	21990M	75780M	1575315M

© RMA 2010

M = $ thousand   MM = $ million
See Pages 9 through 22 for Explanation of Ratios and Data

MANUFACTURING—Meat Processed from Carcasses NAICS 311612

Current Data Sorted by Assets **Comparative Historical Data**

Type of Statement

Type of Statement	0-500M	500M-2MM	2-10MM	10-50MM	50-100MM	100-250MM	4/1/05-3/31/06 ALL	4/1/06-3/31/07 ALL
Unqualified	1		4	13	7	8	30	36
Reviewed		1	16	10	2		25	30
Compiled	1	8	9	7			25	27
Tax Returns	2	5	2	1			8	4
Other	1	3	16	19	11	3	54	54
		21 (4/1-9/30/09)		129 (10/1/09-3/31/10)				
NUMBER OF STATEMENTS	5	17	47	50	20	11	142	151

Main Table

	0-500M	500M-2MM	2-10MM	10-50MM	50-100MM	100-250MM	4/1/05-3/31/06 ALL	4/1/06-3/31/07 ALL
	%	%	%	%	%	%	%	%
ASSETS								
Cash & Equivalents		11.8	10.6	9.3	3.0	4.3	7.1	7.4
Trade Receivables (net)		23.1	24.9	19.4	18.3	14.1	24.9	24.6
Inventory		20.8	22.2	24.1	29.6	23.9	20.6	21.5
All Other Current		1.1	3.3	3.2	3.2	1.1	4.2	2.4
Total Current		56.7	61.1	56.0	54.2	43.5	56.8	55.9
Fixed Assets (net)		30.9	29.8	34.6	37.2	44.9	33.5	34.7
Intangibles (net)		3.9	3.3	3.8	5.1	6.2	3.8	3.7
All Other Non-Current		8.5	5.8	5.7	3.6	5.4	5.9	5.6
Total		100.0	100.0	100.0	100.0	100.0	100.0	100.0
LIABILITIES								
Notes Payable-Short Term		13.8	10.5	10.2	8.6	4.5	9.8	11.0
Cur. Mat.-L.T.D.		2.3	2.3	3.2	4.9	8.4	4.0	2.9
Trade Payables		16.1	15.2	10.9	13.1	12.0	14.7	13.8
Income Taxes Payable		.1	.1	.1	.0	.0	.2	.1
All Other Current		2.7	7.0	10.0	7.7	7.0	9.8	8.6
Total Current		35.1	35.1	34.4	34.3	31.9	38.6	36.3
Long-Term Debt		8.7	15.6	19.0	24.1	27.1	18.0	19.6
Deferred Taxes		.7	.1	.9	.7	.7	.5	.5
All Other Non-Current		6.6	7.7	5.2	6.5	6.9	5.8	6.0
Net Worth		48.8	41.5	40.5	34.4	33.4	37.2	37.6
Total Liabilities & Net Worth		100.0	100.0	100.0	100.0	100.0	100.0	100.0
INCOME DATA								
Net Sales		100.0	100.0	100.0	100.0	100.0	100.0	100.0
Gross Profit		25.7	23.4	21.7	15.5	18.6	20.8	19.6
Operating Expenses		25.0	20.0	16.8	12.2	11.6	17.4	15.7
Operating Profit		.7	3.3	4.9	3.3	7.0	3.4	4.0
All Other Expenses (net)		.9	.4	.7	1.6	.6	.6	.8
Profit Before Taxes		-.2	3.0	4.2	1.7	6.4	2.8	3.2
RATIOS								
Current		4.8	3.4	2.9	2.2	2.1	2.5	2.6
		2.0	1.6	1.7	1.4	1.6	1.5	1.5
		.9	1.2	1.1	1.2	1.1	1.2	1.1
Quick		3.5	1.5	1.8	.9	1.1	1.5	1.7
		1.1	.9	.9	.7	.9	.8	.8
		.5	.6	.5	.4	.3	.5	.5
Sales/Receivables		15 24.8	15 23.7	16 22.6	18 20.1	10 36.5	16 23.0	15 23.9
		20 18.6	21 17.4	20 18.1	26 14.3	14 25.6	23 16.2	21 17.0
		29 12.7	26 14.0	25 14.4	28 13.0	22 16.8	30 12.3	27 13.6
Cost of Sales/Inventory		10 35.3	15 24.1	16 22.7	27 13.4	14 25.2	14 25.9	14 26.1
		31 11.8	24 15.1	30 12.3	42 8.6	29 12.7	24 15.1	24 15.4
		49 7.4	37 9.9	54 6.8	75 4.9	55 6.6	39 9.3	39 9.4
Cost of Sales/Payables		5 77.9	9 40.6	7 48.9	10 37.5	10 37.0	8 47.2	8 47.9
		15 24.6	15 24.7	12 31.3	20 18.0	15 23.9	13 27.3	13 27.9
		30 12.2	27 13.7	20 18.7	33 11.0	27 13.7	24 14.9	20 18.1
Sales/Working Capital		9.9	8.8	6.9	7.4	10.7	10.4	10.3
		15.5	18.5	16.4	23.3	24.3	22.9	23.9
		-68.2	57.8	60.8	34.3	157.3	59.8	131.4
EBIT/Interest		21.0	12.2	20.5	8.8	14.9	13.5	9.9
		(15) 3.0	(41) 4.0	(48) 8.8	3.3	7.1	(126) 3.2	(144) 3.9
		1.0	2.2	2.9	1.1	2.4	1.4	1.6
Net Profit + Depr., Dep., Amort./Cur. Mat. L/T/D			8.7	12.2			6.9	8.6
			(15) 3.4	(13) 4.0			(41) 3.1	(44) 2.8
			2.2	1.9			1.7	1.1
Fixed/Worth		.3	.3	.6	.4	.8	.5	.5
		.4	.6	.8	1.1	1.3	.9	1.0
		2.2	1.8	2.1	3.0	2.8	2.2	2.0
Debt/Worth		.2	.5	.7	.8	1.1	.9	.9
		.8	2.0	1.4	2.0	2.5	1.9	2.0
		3.6	4.1	6.4	5.2	5.0	5.7	4.6
% Profit Before Taxes/Tangible Net Worth		27.8	42.2	56.9	31.7	112.8	40.1	39.6
		(15) 12.2	(44) 23.0	(47) 25.9	(16) 17.9	(10) 37.7	(126) 22.7	(138) 20.3
		5.2	13.2	11.6	3.4	20.5	6.3	7.1
% Profit Before Taxes/Total Assets		11.2	18.0	18.6	10.9	34.2	14.2	14.5
		5.7	9.0	10.1	4.2	17.4	5.7	7.0
		.5	2.6	3.4	.6	5.6	.8	1.8
Sales/Net Fixed Assets		27.2	59.1	19.9	12.2	12.1	31.7	28.6
		9.6	13.7	9.8	7.0	7.6	10.3	11.3
		6.7	6.2	5.7	4.4	6.1	5.7	5.1
Sales/Total Assets		4.8	5.4	3.8	4.2	4.6	5.1	6.1
		3.1	4.0	2.9	2.3	3.8	3.3	3.6
		2.4	2.5	2.0	1.5	2.6	2.4	2.2
% Depr., Dep., Amort./Sales		.8	.7	.9	1.2		.7	.6
		(15) 1.1	(44) 1.3	(46) 1.6	2.2		(131) 1.3	(137) 1.4
		1.8	2.3	2.5	3.6		2.3	2.8
% Officers', Directors' Owners' Comp/Sales		1.6	1.0	.8			.9	.7
		(11) 2.7	(22) 2.4	(12) 1.5			(46) 1.5	(53) 1.4
		11.4	3.1	4.2			4.6	4.2
Net Sales ($)	5784M	79015M	1081138M	4118005M	4255579M	6762070M	12395410M	12860938M
Total Assets ($)	1238M	22534M	245244M	1312087M	1393317M	1973468M	3685111M	3896543M

M = $ thousand   MM = $ million
See Pages 9 through 22 for Explanation of Ratios and Data

Comparative Historical Data   Current Data Sorted by Sales

			Type of Statement	0-1MM	1-3MM	3-5MM	5-10MM	10-25MM	25MM & OVER
36	30	33	Unqualified		1	1		2	29
25	30	29	Reviewed				3	7	19
17	27	25	Compiled		6	2	2	7	8
10	9	10	Tax Returns	1	2		4	3	
65	57	53	Other	1	1	2	8	8	35
4/1/07-3/31/08	4/1/08-3/31/09	4/1/09-3/31/10			21 (4/1-9/30/09)		129 (10/1/09-3/31/10)		
ALL	ALL	ALL							
153	153	150	NUMBER OF STATEMENTS	2	10	5	15	27	91
%	%	%	**ASSETS**	%	%	%	%	%	%
8.1	8.5	9.7	Cash & Equivalents		16.1		13.1	12.9	6.3
24.2	22.4	20.5	Trade Receivables (net)		17.1		19.3	18.0	22.7
22.2	24.4	23.7	Inventory		18.8		15.1	18.8	26.9
3.3	2.6	2.7	All Other Current		1.0		7.2	4.9	1.7
57.8	57.9	56.6	Total Current		52.9		54.7	54.6	57.7
33.9	33.3	33.7	Fixed Assets (net)		39.3		31.7	36.3	33.0
3.4	3.6	4.0	Intangibles (net)		2.7		5.4	4.3	4.0
5.0	5.2	5.7	All Other Non-Current		5.1		8.2	4.8	5.4
100.0	100.0	100.0	Total		100.0		100.0	100.0	100.0
			LIABILITIES						
10.9	10.7	10.2	Notes Payable-Short Term		11.7		8.6	5.2	11.5
3.1	3.9	3.4	Cur. Mat.-L.T.D.		2.1		2.7	2.2	4.0
13.8	12.3	13.2	Trade Payables		13.8		13.5	15.1	13.0
.1	.1	.1	Income Taxes Payable		.2		.0	.1	.1
8.3	7.4	8.3	All Other Current		14.2		5.7	7.7	8.4
36.3	34.3	35.2	Total Current		42.0		30.4	30.4	37.0
17.8	18.3	18.1	Long-Term Debt		17.6		11.3	21.4	19.1
.4	.3	.6	Deferred Taxes		.0		.5	.1	.7
6.9	6.2	6.3	All Other Non-Current		3.6		11.5	6.0	5.8
38.6	40.8	39.8	Net Worth		36.8		46.3	42.1	37.5
100.0	100.0	100.0	Total Liabilities & Net Worth		100.0		100.0	100.0	100.0
			INCOME DATA						
100.0	100.0	100.0	Net Sales		100.0		100.0	100.0	100.0
19.4	21.4	22.6	Gross Profit		38.5		28.9	25.9	17.4
16.6	18.1	18.8	Operating Expenses		35.5		23.0	22.7	13.3
2.7	3.3	3.9	Operating Profit		3.1		6.0	3.1	4.2
.7	.7	.7	All Other Expenses (net)		1.0		.6	.3	.9
2.1	2.6	3.2	Profit Before Taxes		2.1		5.4	2.8	3.3
			RATIOS						
2.9	2.9	2.8			6.0		5.0	2.8	2.7
1.6	1.8	1.6	Current		1.6		2.4	1.6	1.5
1.1	1.2	1.2			1.0		1.3	1.3	1.1
1.6	1.6	1.6			4.9		4.4	1.5	1.3
.9	1.0	.9	Quick		1.1		1.1	.8	.8
.5	.6	.5			.5		.4	.4	.5
15 24.6	14 25.3	15 23.9		0 UND	18 20.1		17 21.7	13 28.1	16 23.0
19 19.0	20 18.5	20 18.1	Sales/Receivables	18 20.1	20 17.8		20 17.8	20 18.6	21 17.4
27 13.4	26 14.0	26 14.1		32 11.6	24 15.0		24 15.0	25 14.8	26 14.2
12 29.4	15 23.9	16 22.7		18 19.9	11 34.4		11 34.4	19 19.1	16 22.6
20 17.9	29 12.8	29 12.5	Cost of Sales/Inventory	32 11.5	24 15.1		24 15.1	32 11.3	29 12.7
41 8.9	51 7.2	50 7.3		49 7.5	34 10.6		34 10.6	46 7.9	55 6.7
8 47.3	7 52.8	8 44.2		0 UND	7 51.6		7 51.6	14 26.5	8 45.4
13 28.3	12 31.5	14 26.2	Cost of Sales/Payables	22 16.6	18 20.8		18 20.8	25 14.6	12 29.5
21 17.7	21 17.8	27 13.6		31 11.8	33 11.2		33 11.2	29 12.7	19 19.5
10.4	7.9	8.1			6.5		4.8	7.7	9.5
20.6	16.7	18.6	Sales/Working Capital		26.0		16.8	16.6	21.6
63.6	52.0	58.0			NM		42.1	40.4	65.7
(139) 7.6	(146) 9.8	(139) 13.7					(12) 21.0	(25) 14.1	(88) 14.6
3.5	3.4	5.3	EBIT/Interest				5.4	4.5	6.4
1.3	.8	1.9					2.2	.7	2.0
(37) 6.6	(38) 6.6	(41) 6.0	Net Profit + Depr., Dep.,					(10) 10.4	(27) 6.5
3.5	2.4	2.9	Amort./Cur. Mat. L/T/D					3.1	2.9
1.7	1.0	1.8						1.7	1.8
.4	.5	.4			.2		.3	.3	.5
.9	.8	.9	Fixed/Worth		1.3		.7	.9	.9
2.2	2.0	2.1			NM		1.6	2.0	2.1
.8	.8	.6			.2		.2	.7	.8
1.7	1.7	1.7	Debt/Worth		1.0		.8	1.7	1.9
4.8	4.2	4.7			NM		2.8	3.7	5.3
35.0	37.7	42.2	% Profit Before Taxes/Tangible				(13) 38.2	(25) 43.6	(83) 44.6
(142) 14.4	(140) 14.3	(136) 22.5	Net Worth				25.0	21.9	24.2
5.5	1.2	9.8					14.2	1.1	10.4
11.5	13.2	17.4	% Profit Before Taxes/Total		11.5		19.9	10.6	16.7
5.3	5.3	9.1	Assets		4.9		11.5	6.5	9.2
1.6	-.2	2.6			3.2		.2	.2	2.7
31.9	23.3	22.5			30.1		15.5	25.7	21.0
11.5	10.6	10.0	Sales/Net Fixed Assets		14.9		9.6	8.7	10.4
4.9	5.6	5.8			4.5		5.4	3.1	6.3
5.7	5.2	4.6			4.2		4.5	4.5	5.2
3.4	3.3	3.1	Sales/Total Assets		3.5		2.9	3.0	3.3
2.2	2.2	2.2			2.2		2.1	2.1	2.4
.6	.8	.8			.7		.8	.8	.7
(139) 1.3	(137) 1.5	(135) 1.5	% Depr., Dep., Amort./Sales		1.3		(14) 1.5	(26) 1.9	(81) 1.5
2.5	2.2	2.4			2.1		2.0	2.6	2.3
.6	1.0	.9	% Officers', Directors',					2.2	.4
(53) 1.8	(44) 2.1	(50) 2.3	Owners' Comp/Sales				(12) 2.8	(20) .9	
4.2	4.8	3.7						5.7	2.3
16838085M	14382364M	16301591M	Net Sales ($)	1489M	19670M	20782M	107515M	434209M	15717926M
4771745M	4237719M	4947888M	Total Assets ($)	727M	7836M	18582M	48269M	213729M	4658745M

M = $ thousand   MM = $ million
See Pages 9 through 22 for Explanation of Ratios and Data

Current Data Sorted by Assets

Comparative Historical Data

						Type of Statement		
			2	1	5	Unqualified	11	5
						Reviewed	2	3
1	1	2				Compiled	4	2
1	1					Tax Returns	2	1
		3	2	2	2	Other	13	5
	3 (4/1-9/30/09)		20 (10/1/09-3/31/10)				4/1/05-3/31/06	4/1/06-3/31/07
0-500M	500M-2MM	2-10MM	10-50MM	50-100MM	100-250MM		ALL	ALL
2	2	5	4	3	7	NUMBER OF STATEMENTS	32	16
%	%	%	%	%	%	ASSETS	%	%
						Cash & Equivalents	9.4	7.3
						Trade Receivables (net)	16.8	16.0
						Inventory	15.2	20.7
						All Other Current	2.9	3.2
						Total Current	44.2	47.3
						Fixed Assets (net)	48.0	48.3
						Intangibles (net)	1.3	.4
						All Other Non-Current	6.5	4.1
						Total	100.0	100.0
						LIABILITIES		
						Notes Payable-Short Term	6.2	13.7
						Cur. Mat.-L.T.D.	3.2	4.7
						Trade Payables	8.5	6.4
						Income Taxes Payable	.2	.3
						All Other Current	6.5	8.1
						Total Current	24.5	33.2
						Long-Term Debt	19.8	25.4
						Deferred Taxes	.5	.1
						All Other Non-Current	3.2	2.2
						Net Worth	51.9	39.1
						Total Liabilties & Net Worth	100.0	100.0
						INCOME DATA		
						Net Sales	100.0	100.0
						Gross Profit	31.1	29.1
						Operating Expenses	21.7	20.6
						Operating Profit	9.3	8.5
						All Other Expenses (net)	1.0	2.2
						Profit Before Taxes	8.4	6.3
						RATIOS		
						Current	3.4	2.6
							1.6	1.7
							1.1	1.1
						Quick	2.0	1.0
							.9	.6
							.6	.4
						Sales/Receivables	18 19.8	15 23.9
							25 14.5	25 14.5
							32 11.5	30 12.2
						Cost of Sales/Inventory	13 27.2	16 23.0
							22 16.6	28 13.2
							41 9.0	78 4.7
						Cost of Sales/Payables	9 41.6	6 60.5
							15 23.6	11 33.0
							23 16.1	21 17.2
						Sales/Working Capital	9.3	8.4
							12.8	14.1
							117.6	116.6
						EBIT/Interest	33.1	15.9
							(31) 5.8	4.3
							2.4	3.5
						Net Profit + Depr., Dep., Amort./Cur. Mat. L/T/D	5.7	
							(11) 3.0	
							1.1	
						Fixed/Worth	.6	.7
							.9	1.2
							1.8	2.2
						Debt/Worth	.4	.6
							1.2	1.0
							2.1	2.9
						% Profit Before Taxes/Tangible Net Worth	44.4	65.6
							22.2	(15) 28.8
							10.1	5.9
						% Profit Before Taxes/Total Assets	28.5	31.3
							10.5	8.6
							4.2	3.1
						Sales/Net Fixed Assets	10.0	10.8
							5.2	4.9
							2.4	2.7
						Sales/Total Assets	3.8	3.3
							2.3	2.7
							1.3	1.7
						% Depr., Dep., Amort./Sales	1.5	.9
							(25) 2.5	(11) 2.6
							3.7	3.8
						% Officers', Directors' Owners' Comp/Sales		
6952M	4071M	111096M	256339M	519145M	2422952M	Net Sales ($)	2878901M	1335437M
822M	1777M	38659M	78059M	201197M	1239711M	Total Assets ($)	1533086M	677410M

M = $ thousand   MM = $ million
See Pages 9 through 22 for Explanation of Ratios and Data

Comparative Historical Data   Current Data Sorted by Sales

				Type of Statement							
	7		7	8	Unqualified						8
	1		1		Reviewed						
	5		2	4	Compiled		2		1		2
	3		3	2	Tax Returns		1		1	1	
	13		10	9	Other						7
	4/1/07-		4/1/08-	4/1/09-			3 (4/1-9/30/09)		20 (10/1/09-3/31/10)		
	3/31/08		3/31/09	3/31/10							
	ALL		ALL	ALL		0-1MM	1-3MM	3-5MM	5-10MM	10-25MM	25MM & OVER
	29		23	23	NUMBER OF STATEMENTS		3		2	1	17
	%		%	%	ASSETS	%	%	%	%	%	%
	12.0		9.7	11.7	Cash & Equivalents						10.1
	20.2		21.0	18.7	Trade Receivables (net)	D	D				18.6
	13.2		16.2	13.6	Inventory	A	A				12.6
	2.4		1.8	3.1	All Other Current	T	T				3.1
	47.9		48.6	47.1	Total Current	A	A				44.4
	43.4		43.4	47.2	Fixed Assets (net)						48.3
	3.3		2.4	2.5	Intangibles (net)	N	N				3.3
	5.5		5.5	3.2	All Other Non-Current	O	O				4.0
	100.0		100.0	100.0	Total	T	T				100.0
					LIABILITIES	A	A				
	6.7		8.5	3.9	Notes Payable-Short Term	V	V				5.2
	2.9		2.1	3.0	Cur. Mat.-L.T.D.	A	A				2.2
	5.8		8.3	10.6	Trade Payables	I	I				7.2
	.4		.0	.0	Income Taxes Payable	L	L				.0
	7.9		9.8	9.8	All Other Current	A	A				7.3
	23.7		28.7	27.4	Total Current	B	B				21.8
	15.8		16.5	17.0	Long-Term Debt	L	L				15.1
	1.0		.1	.5	Deferred Taxes	E	E				.7
	7.5		4.9	8.2	All Other Non-Current						8.2
	52.0		49.8	46.8	Net Worth						54.2
	100.0		100.0	100.0	Total Liabilties & Net Worth						100.0
					INCOME DATA						
	100.0		100.0	100.0	Net Sales						100.0
	31.0		24.5	28.3	Gross Profit						26.7
	22.1		16.1	21.0	Operating Expenses						18.7
	8.9		8.4	7.3	Operating Profit						8.1
	.9		.5	1.0	All Other Expenses (net)						1.0
	8.0		7.8	6.3	Profit Before Taxes						7.1
					RATIOS						
	3.2		4.0	3.4							3.8
	2.0		2.0	2.1	Current						2.2
	1.5		1.1	1.2							1.5
	1.7		3.2	2.2							2.5
	1.4		1.5	1.3	Quick						1.6
	1.0		.5	.6							.6
19	19.1	16	23.5	17 20.9						19	19.3
31	11.7	24	15.4	24 15.1	Sales/Receivables					27	13.5
38	9.5	29	12.6	36 10.1						37	10.0
13	28.2	12	30.0	11 34.1						10	36.6
20	18.3	22	16.6	27 13.3	Cost of Sales/Inventory					26	14.3
47	7.8	33	11.2	37 9.9						36	10.2
5	69.5	6	56.9	11 34.7						10	36.1
10	36.7	13	29.1	16 22.5	Cost of Sales/Payables					12	30.6
18	20.8	15	23.8	24 15.0						19	18.9
	7.9		6.8	5.7							6.3
	11.4		14.2	10.5	Sales/Working Capital						9.7
	15.1		60.6	55.7							44.0
	19.4		61.0	22.4							40.8
(26)	6.2	(22)	19.0	(20) 9.3	EBIT/Interest					(14)	10.2
	2.7		2.6	1.9							4.7
	17.6				Net Profit + Depr., Dep.,						
(10)	7.9				Amort./Cur. Mat. L/T/D						
	1.2										
	.6		.6	.6							.6
	.9		1.0	1.2	Fixed/Worth						1.1
	1.5		1.5	1.4							1.4
	.5		.6	.6							.5
	1.0		1.1	1.0	Debt/Worth						1.0
	1.6		2.1	1.7							1.5
	47.2		62.0	44.6							50.1
(28)	29.4		37.1	(22) 29.7	% Profit Before Taxes/Tangible Net Worth						34.9
	11.8		14.6	8.6							15.2
	22.9		34.2	27.3							29.3
	11.8		16.7	11.1	% Profit Before Taxes/Total Assets						13.8
	5.0		2.3	2.0							7.4
	15.8		12.6	13.5							10.4
	5.5		6.5	6.3	Sales/Net Fixed Assets						5.1
	2.7		3.6	2.2							2.3
	3.3		3.7	3.8							3.8
	2.7		2.9	2.6	Sales/Total Assets						2.6
	1.4		2.0	1.5							1.4
	1.1		1.4	1.4							1.5
(25)	1.9	(17)	1.8	(18) 2.3	% Depr., Dep., Amort./Sales					(12)	2.9
	4.4		3.5	4.2							4.3
					% Officers', Directors' Owners' Comp/Sales						
	2972362M		3970055M	3320555M	Net Sales ($)		5585M		12189M	11719M	3291062M
	1597521M		1614437M	1560225M	Total Assets ($)		2119M		9937M	4696M	1543473M

M = $ thousand   MM = $ million
See Pages 9 through 22 for Explanation of Ratios and Data

Current Data Sorted by Assets   Comparative Historical Data

Type of Statement

Type of Statement	0-500M	500M-2MM	2-10MM	10-50MM	50-100MM	100-250MM	4/1/05-3/31/06 ALL	4/1/06-3/31/07 ALL
Unqualified				8	9	10	14	32
Reviewed	1		6	4	2		8	13
Compiled			1					1
Tax Returns			3				2	1
Other			2			2	22	22

Periods: 18 (4/1-9/30/09); 39 (10/1/09-3/31/10)

	0-500M	500M-2MM	2-10MM	10-50MM	50-100MM	100-250MM	4/1/05-3/31/06 ALL	4/1/06-3/31/07 ALL
NUMBER OF STATEMENTS	1	1	12	16	16	12	46	69

Note: Columns 0-500M and 500M-2MM — DATA NOT AVAILABLE.

ASSETS (%)

	2-10MM	10-50MM	50-100MM	100-250MM	4/1/05-3/31/06 ALL	4/1/06-3/31/07 ALL
Cash & Equivalents	7.3	2.4	4.9	6.5	6.4	4.6
Trade Receivables (net)	26.8	19.3	15.1	15.6	19.0	16.5
Inventory	15.7	27.3	21.0	26.0	21.0	22.8
All Other Current	1.9	.4	2.9	3.8	1.9	1.9
Total Current	51.6	49.4	43.9	51.9	48.4	45.8
Fixed Assets (net)	40.8	42.4	47.3	40.7	44.2	45.9
Intangibles (net)	.9	2.3	2.2	5.1	2.2	2.3
All Other Non-Current	6.6	5.9	6.5	2.3	5.2	6.0
Total	100.0	100.0	100.0	100.0	100.0	100.0

LIABILITIES

	2-10MM	10-50MM	50-100MM	100-250MM	4/1/05-3/31/06 ALL	4/1/06-3/31/07 ALL
Notes Payable-Short Term	6.5	22.3	5.6	7.1	7.6	7.9
Cur. Mat.-L.T.D.	5.0	3.2	3.4	7.1	3.9	4.4
Trade Payables	16.1	15.2	8.4	12.4	13.6	11.5
Income Taxes Payable	.1	.1	.1	2.1	.1	.2
All Other Current	7.8	7.5	6.0	12.8	9.4	10.0
Total Current	35.5	48.3	23.5	41.5	34.6	34.0
Long-Term Debt	20.9	14.9	18.6	19.0	19.6	25.1
Deferred Taxes	.0	1.0	1.7	1.3	1.5	1.2
All Other Non-Current	4.4	.8	4.1	5.4	3.1	2.3
Net Worth	39.1	35.0	52.0	32.8	41.2	37.4
Total Liabilities & Net Worth	100.0	100.0	100.0	100.0	100.0	100.0

INCOME DATA

	2-10MM	10-50MM	50-100MM	100-250MM	4/1/05-3/31/06 ALL	4/1/06-3/31/07 ALL
Net Sales	100.0	100.0	100.0	100.0	100.0	100.0
Gross Profit	21.5	20.3	12.9	9.7	20.5	20.1
Operating Expenses	13.2	16.3	8.8	6.4	15.9	18.2
Operating Profit	8.3	4.0	4.1	3.4	4.6	1.9
All Other Expenses (net)	.4	.2	.7	.7	.6	.7
Profit Before Taxes	7.9	3.8	3.4	2.7	3.9	1.2

RATIOS

	2-10MM	10-50MM	50-100MM	100-250MM	4/1/05-3/31/06 ALL	4/1/06-3/31/07 ALL
Current	1.9	1.7	2.5	2.5	2.2	2.4
	1.4	1.1	2.0	1.1	1.5	1.4
	1.1	.8	1.4	.9	1.0	1.0
Quick	1.2	.9	1.3	1.2	1.2	1.0
	.9	.4	.8	.5	.7	.6
	.7	.2	.5	.3	.4	.4
Sales/Receivables	15 24.5	15 24.1	20 18.7	12 31.6	14 25.2	18 20.3
	20 18.0	17 21.1	23 16.1	18 20.3	20 17.8	20 17.9
	25 14.8	28 13.2	38 9.5	19 19.1	29 12.4	27 13.8
Cost of Sales/Inventory	6 64.8	27 13.3	28 12.8	19 19.5	21 17.1	23 16.1
	13 28.6	33 11.0	43 8.5	37 10.0	32 11.3	35 10.4
	26 14.0	101 3.6	55 6.7	56 6.6	46 8.0	67 5.5
Cost of Sales/Payables	7 49.7	8 45.3	11 33.6	11 33.1	14 26.7	12 31.5
	16 22.2	17 21.4	14 25.4	16 22.3	18 20.8	18 20.7
	26 13.9	33 11.0	21 17.3	22 16.6	22 16.7	24 15.5
Sales/Working Capital	20.1	21.8	7.6	7.7	9.9	8.7
	30.8	41.4	10.9	361.1	18.4	21.8
	122.3	-23.0	16.2	-122.3	379.3	-378.0
EBIT/Interest	25.7	13.1	17.7	11.2	18.8	7.7
	(11) 5.1	(14) 3.6	4.9	2.5	(42) 7.5	(64) 1.7
	1.6	2.5	1.7	1.6	2.2	-.6
Net Profit + Depr., Dep., Amort./Cur. Mat. L/T/D					6.3	2.9
					(14) 4.6	(23) 1.5
					2.7	.3
Fixed/Worth	.6	.9	.6	.9	.7	.8
	1.4	1.3	.9	1.9	1.0	1.2
	2.9	2.0	1.5	4.2	1.9	3.7
Debt/Worth	.6	.7	.5	.8	.7	.8
	2.0	1.8	1.0	3.3	1.2	1.7
	5.1	7.4	1.7	12.1	3.0	4.6
% Profit Before Taxes/Tangible Net Worth	86.8	56.1	26.1	59.8	41.3	33.9
	53.3	(15) 24.8	13.7	(10) 13.2	(44) 21.1	(64) 6.0
	20.7	5.6	5.6	2.8	9.6	-11.0
% Profit Before Taxes/Total Assets	36.4	20.2	11.6	15.2	14.4	11.3
	13.4	6.7	5.4	6.4	9.2	2.2
	2.5	2.5	2.2	1.8	2.2	-3.3
Sales/Net Fixed Assets	19.8	10.5	7.3	10.1	9.0	10.0
	11.5	6.3	5.4	7.6	5.8	5.5
	6.3	4.5	2.7	5.2	3.7	3.6
Sales/Total Assets	6.2	4.5	2.7	4.0	3.3	3.3
	4.9	2.7	2.3	2.8	2.5	2.3
	2.6	2.2	1.5	2.1	2.1	1.7
% Depr., Dep., Amort./Sales	.4	.9	2.2		1.4	1.5
	1.4	(15) 1.7	(14) 3.6		(40) 2.2	(56) 2.7
	2.8	2.7	4.6		3.1	3.6
% Officers', Directors' Owners' Comp/Sales						

	500M-2MM	2-10MM	10-50MM	50-100MM	100-250MM	4/1/05-3/31/06 ALL	4/1/06-3/31/07 ALL
Net Sales ($)	5820M	370717M	1257674M	2395352M	5967606M	6614034M	9623771M
Total Assets ($)	629M	67931M	397123M	1104500M	1998529M	2532002M	4174988M

M = $ thousand   MM = $ million
See Pages 9 through 22 for Explanation of Ratios and Data

Comparative Historical Data | | | Current Data Sorted by Sales

			Type of Statement	0-1MM	1-3MM	3-5MM	5-10MM	10-25MM	25MM & OVER
20	22	22	Unqualified				1	4	17
13	15	19	Reviewed		1		2	6	10
6	5	5	Compiled					5	
3	7	9	Tax Returns	1	3		2	3	
39	31	35	Other	1	1		4	8	21
4/1/07-3/31/08	4/1/08-3/31/09	4/1/09-3/31/10			20 (4/1-9/30/09)			70 (10/1/09-3/31/10)	
ALL	ALL	ALL		0-1MM	1-3MM	3-5MM	5-10MM	10-25MM	25MM & OVER
81	80	90	**NUMBER OF STATEMENTS**	2	5		9	26	48
%	%	%	**ASSETS**	%	%	%	%	%	%
7.6	7.3	7.8	Cash & Equivalents					10.5	5.2
22.0	23.1	21.0	Trade Receivables (net)					24.6	18.8
27.4	35.4	28.8	Inventory					26.6	32.4
4.1	2.2	3.7	All Other Current					4.1	2.9
61.1	67.9	61.1	Total Current					65.7	59.3
29.3	25.7	30.0	Fixed Assets (net)					26.6	32.5
2.6	1.1	3.5	Intangibles (net)					3.1	3.0
7.0	5.3	5.3	All Other Non-Current					4.5	5.1
100.0	100.0	100.0	Total					100.0	100.0
			LIABILITIES						
18.6	23.1	16.5	Notes Payable-Short Term					18.1	17.7
3.9	2.9	4.4	Cur. Mat.-L.T.D.					3.5	4.9
13.1	16.5	13.4	Trade Payables					17.4	10.8
.1	.2	.2	Income Taxes Payable					.2	.3
7.5	8.8	7.9	All Other Current					6.2	9.1
43.3	51.5	42.4	Total Current					45.4	42.7
13.6	11.1	12.9	Long-Term Debt					13.7	13.0
.2	.4	.9	Deferred Taxes					.3	1.4
4.8	4.5	5.5	All Other Non-Current					4.0	5.9
38.1	32.6	38.2	Net Worth					36.6	37.0
100.0	100.0	100.0	Total Liabilities & Net Worth					100.0	100.0
			INCOME DATA						
100.0	100.0	100.0	Net Sales					100.0	100.0
22.4	18.7	18.9	Gross Profit					18.9	16.6
17.6	15.3	16.6	Operating Expenses					17.4	13.5
4.8	3.4	2.3	Operating Profit					1.4	3.2
.2	.9	.1	All Other Expenses (net)					-.4	.7
4.6	2.5	2.2	Profit Before Taxes					1.8	2.5
			RATIOS						
2.1	1.9	2.3						2.9	2.2
1.4	1.3	1.5	Current					1.2	1.5
1.1	1.0	1.1						.9	1.2
1.1	1.0	1.0						1.1	.8
.6	.5	.7	Quick					.7	.6
.4	.3	.4						.5	.4
17 21.9	18 20.7	20 17.8					18 20.0	25 14.6	
29 12.5	30 12.4	30 12.3	Sales/Receivables				24 15.2	32 11.6	
36 10.3	37 9.8	37 9.9					31 11.7	39 9.4	
21 17.7	28 13.0	20 18.6					18 20.9	39 9.4	
46 8.0	58 6.3	46 7.9	Cost of Sales/Inventory				34 10.6	57 6.4	
80 4.6	95 3.8	92 4.0					64 5.7	118 3.1	
10 37.7	10 37.4	9 42.5					9 38.5	10 38.0	
18 20.6	20 18.5	17 21.4	Cost of Sales/Payables				20 18.5	15 23.6	
30 12.3	33 11.2	31 11.7					35 10.5	27 13.5	
7.9	8.7	6.5						8.1	6.7
15.3	19.6	14.2	Sales/Working Capital					25.3	13.2
68.9	256.3	69.7						-62.3	30.5
6.4	5.8	8.0						5.6	9.7
(79) 3.0	(76) 2.5	(88) 3.0	EBIT/Interest					2.9	3.6
1.8	1.1	1.1						1.3	1.0
12.4	9.1	17.0							17.0
(20) 4.2	(24) 4.8	(27) 4.4	Net Profit + Depr., Dep., Amort./Cur. Mat. L/T/D					(21) 3.8	
1.8	2.5	1.3							1.4
.3	.2	.4						.3	.4
.7	.7	.8	Fixed/Worth					.7	.8
1.5	1.8	2.1						3.1	1.9
.9	.9	.8						.8	.9
1.7	2.1	1.6	Debt/Worth					1.8	1.8
4.8	6.4	4.4						8.6	3.9
35.7	36.3	38.9						41.6	36.2
(76) 19.2	(70) 20.2	(79) 16.9	% Profit Before Taxes/Tangible Net Worth				(23) 18.6	(44) 18.0	
6.6	4.0	1.0						2.0	2.4
11.4	11.0	10.4						9.9	13.3
6.2	4.4	4.2	% Profit Before Taxes/Total Assets					4.9	4.0
2.2	.6	.3						.8	.0
44.2	69.8	44.3						45.8	28.2
9.0	14.7	10.6	Sales/Net Fixed Assets					15.6	7.9
4.6	5.5	3.8						7.7	3.5
3.7	3.8	3.5						5.0	3.1
2.5	2.8	2.4	Sales/Total Assets					3.4	2.1
1.8	2.0	1.5						2.6	1.5
.7	.4	.7						.7	.6
(70) 1.3	(69) 1.1	(80) 1.5	% Depr., Dep., Amort./Sales				(25) 1.5	(43) 1.5	
2.3	2.0	2.7						2.4	2.9
.5	1.0	.8						1.3	
(21) 1.8	(21) 2.9	(25) 2.0	% Officers', Directors' Owners' Comp/Sales				(13) 2.4		
3.1	4.0	3.5						4.5	
6270274M	6301777M	6699831M	Net Sales ($)	785M	10441M		69398M	434636M	6184571M
3038572M	2882641M	3475089M	Total Assets ($)	339M	7279M		48197M	155737M	3263537M

(Columns 0-1MM, 1-3MM, 3-5MM, 5-10MM under the ASSETS/LIABILITIES/INCOME/RATIOS sections marked: DATA NOT AVAILABLE)

M = $ thousand   MM = $ million
See Pages 9 through 22 for Explanation of Ratios and Data

Current Data Sorted by Assets

Comparative Historical Data

	0-500M	500M-2MM	2-10MM	10-50MM	50-100MM	100-250MM	Type of Statement		4/1/05-3/31/06 ALL	4/1/06-3/31/07 ALL
		1	3	2	2		Unqualified		4	4
		1	7	1			Reviewed		5	6
	17	23	24	5			Compiled		57	71
	22	11	2				Tax Returns		41	53
	8	7	19	7			Other		43	54
		18 (4/1-9/30/09)		144 (10/1/09-3/31/10)						
	47	43	55	15	2		NUMBER OF STATEMENTS		150	188
	%	%	%	%	%	%	ASSETS		%	%
	17.1	12.6	9.5	12.7			Cash & Equivalents		10.7	9.9
	5.0	7.0	7.5	6.5		D	Trade Receivables (net)		4.8	5.5
	6.8	3.8	5.2	5.4		A	Inventory		3.6	4.2
	.7	2.4	3.8	.7		T	All Other Current		2.9	2.0
	29.7	25.8	26.0	25.2		A	Total Current		22.0	21.5
	41.8	42.1	45.6	48.4			Fixed Assets (net)		47.3	46.6
	18.7	21.4	17.0	19.4		N	Intangibles (net)		16.6	19.7
	9.8	10.7	11.4	7.0		O	All Other Non-Current		14.0	12.2
	100.0	100.0	100.0	100.0		T	Total		100.0	100.0
							LIABILITIES			
	4.4	5.1	3.9	3.0		A	Notes Payable-Short Term		2.7	2.8
	8.5	7.2	6.6	6.6		V	Cur. Mat.-L.T.D.		8.0	5.7
	6.5	8.6	7.0	6.2		A	Trade Payables		5.5	5.3
	.1	.0	.2	.5		I	Income Taxes Payable		.0	.1
	44.7	11.6	7.8	7.9		L	All Other Current		14.6	15.7
	64.2	32.5	25.5	24.3		A	Total Current		30.8	29.6
	32.3	37.9	37.0	31.8		B	Long-Term Debt		37.6	39.2
	.0	.0	.0	.1		L	Deferred Taxes		.1	.1
	17.5	10.0	8.8	6.3		E	All Other Non-Current		11.9	10.5
	-14.0	19.6	28.6	37.5			Net Worth		19.6	20.7
	100.0	100.0	100.0	100.0			Total Liabilties & Net Worth		100.0	100.0
							INCOME DATA			
	100.0	100.0	100.0	100.0			Net Sales		100.0	100.0
	50.9	45.2	41.2	43.9			Gross Profit		46.3	45.3
	44.9	40.9	33.6	32.9			Operating Expenses		39.8	38.2
	6.1	4.3	7.6	11.0			Operating Profit		6.4	7.2
	1.9	1.3	1.3	1.8			All Other Expenses (net)		1.4	1.4
	4.1	3.0	6.3	9.2			Profit Before Taxes		5.1	5.8
							RATIOS			
	1.8	1.5	1.8	1.9					1.6	1.5
	.5	.8	.8	1.2			Current		.9	.8
	.2	.3	.3	.4					.3	.3
	1.4	1.1	1.1	1.8					1.1	1.2
	.4	.4	.6	.8			Quick		.6 (187)	.6
	.1	.1	.2	.3					.2	.2

0	UND	0	UND	0	787.2	1	643.8					0	UND	0	UND

								Ratio				
0 UND	0 UND	0 787.2	1 643.8		Sales/Receivables	0 UND	0 UND
0 UND	0 999.8	3 125.5	18 20.7			1 419.4	1 373.1
2 170.3	8 47.3	16 23.2	23 16.1			7 50.8	8 47.6
2 228.0	2 164.4	2 149.6	4 91.8		Cost of Sales/Inventory	2 171.7	2 151.0
5 78.7	3 111.4	4 81.6	9 38.9			4 90.7	4 89.3
12 29.8	11 31.8	10 37.6	39 9.3			12 30.9	10 37.2
1 653.0	1 315.0	2 161.8	8 46.3		Cost of Sales/Payables	2 220.0	0 822.0
5 77.8	9 39.6	8 45.1	21 17.7			8 44.7	5 77.2
15 24.5	23 15.7	23 15.8	37 10.0			23 15.7	18 20.0
28.0	27.7	15.6	12.8		Sales/Working Capital	31.1	37.2
-22.4	-32.9	-103.0	44.1			-96.3	-64.5
-6.4	-11.1	-11.4	-13.0			-14.4	-14.0
11.8	12.2	10.8	19.8		EBIT/Interest	11.5	12.0
(39) 3.1	(42) 3.6	4.7	5.5			(139) 4.0 (165)	4.9
.6	1.3	2.6	3.5			1.5	1.7
					Net Profit + Depr., Dep., Amort./Cur. Mat. L/T/D	6.0	
						(14) 2.9	
						1.2	
.7	1.1	1.2	.9		Fixed/Worth	1.3	1.1
-4.6	4.7	5.0	1.8			4.5	4.1
-.5	-.9	-18.1	-1.7			-1.8	-1.8
1.7	1.4	1.8	1.2		Debt/Worth	1.4	1.3
-8.2	5.0	7.9	1.6			8.6	7.8
-1.7	-2.3	-21.3	-4.7			-4.0	-3.4
148.1	88.6	172.9	76.4		% Profit Before Taxes/Tangible Net Worth	128.9	149.7
(19) 66.5	(23) 37.7	(38) 75.7	(10) 45.4			(90) 53.7 (108)	62.0
15.3	20.7	19.6	20.1			17.1	29.5
40.0	21.2	18.8	25.6		% Profit Before Taxes/Total Assets	25.9	29.9
11.5	8.6	12.9	13.8			9.5	15.9
-1.5	1.0	5.7	9.2			2.1	3.3
35.0	12.7	8.0	7.4		Sales/Net Fixed Assets	8.9	9.7
11.3	7.5	5.4	5.6			5.8	6.4
4.9	4.8	2.9	2.3			2.9	3.5
5.7	4.1	3.2	2.5		Sales/Total Assets	3.3	3.8
3.9	2.9	2.2	1.8			2.3	2.6
2.6	2.0	1.5	1.2			1.4	1.6
1.6	1.9	2.6	2.8		% Depr., Dep., Amort./Sales	2.6	2.1
(33) 2.7	(40) 3.4	(53) 3.9	(14) 3.7			(137) 3.6 (173)	3.3
4.4	4.4	5.2	4.8			6.0	5.1
1.8	2.4	1.4			% Officers', Directors' Owners' Comp/Sales	2.2	1.6
(19) 4.6	(18) 3.7	(22) 2.5				(102) 3.9 (104)	3.1
8.6	4.9	4.2				6.7	5.1
52501M	156303M	633836M	706166M	290454M		Net Sales ($)		1058011M	2002374M
12018M	47584M	271288M	325117M	147090M		Total Assets ($)		665941M	946085M

© RMA 2010

M = $ thousand   MM = $ million
See Pages 9 through 22 for Explanation of Ratios and Data

Comparative Historical Data | Current Data Sorted by Sales

4/1/07-3/31/08 ALL	4/1/08-3/31/09 ALL	4/1/09-3/31/10 ALL	Type of Statement	0-1MM	1-3MM	3-5MM	5-10MM	10-25MM	25MM & OVER
7	5	8	Unqualified		1		1	2	4
15	8	9	Reviewed			1	3	2	3
118	101	69	Compiled	10	16	10	21	9	3
41	43	35	Tax Returns	17	10	6	1	1	3
45	31	41	Other	7	5	7	5	7	7
					18 (4/1-9/30/09)			144 (10/1/09-3/31/10)	
226	188	162	**NUMBER OF STATEMENTS**	34	32	24	32	23	17
%	%	%	**ASSETS**	%	%	%	%	%	%
9.0	9.8	12.8	Cash & Equivalents	15.4	12.7	12.5	9.9	14.4	11.3
3.6	5.3	6.6	Trade Receivables (net)	4.4	5.8	3.7	6.4	10.1	12.1
2.7	4.3	5.3	Inventory	3.6	7.4	4.6	2.4	7.6	7.8
2.2	2.3	2.2	All Other Current	.6	2.1	2.1	3.7	4.0	.8
17.4	21.6	26.9	Total Current	24.0	28.0	23.0	22.4	36.1	32.0
45.5	45.0	43.9	Fixed Assets (net)	45.6	38.8	48.7	48.8	37.4	43.2
24.3	21.3	18.7	Intangibles (net)	19.3	25.0	17.5	15.9	15.6	16.7
12.7	12.1	10.5	All Other Non-Current	11.0	8.2	10.8	12.9	11.0	8.0
100.0	100.0	100.0	Total	100.0	100.0	100.0	100.0	100.0	100.0
			LIABILITIES						
1.8	3.1	4.2	Notes Payable-Short Term	2.5	7.2	2.5	3.8	4.9	4.3
6.7	6.1	7.3	Cur. Mat.-L.T.D.	7.0	8.4	8.4	6.9	6.6	5.6
5.0	6.5	7.3	Trade Payables	4.5	7.9	5.0	7.3	10.2	10.7
.1	.1	.1	Income Taxes Payable	.0	.1	.0	.1	.3	.5
12.6	18.7	19.7	All Other Current	46.3	24.0	10.2	7.9	7.6	10.4
26.2	34.5	38.6	Total Current	60.3	47.7	26.2	26.1	29.6	31.4
46.1	35.8	35.2	Long-Term Debt	32.3	43.9	34.9	42.3	28.3	20.9
.1	.0	.0	Deferred Taxes	.0	.0	.0	.0	.0	.2
14.5	14.4	11.4	All Other Non-Current	19.2	13.7	10.0	7.1	5.9	9.6
13.1	15.2	14.7	Net Worth	-11.8	-5.3	29.0	24.5	36.2	37.9
100.0	100.0	100.0	Total Liabilities & Net Worth	100.0	100.0	100.0	100.0	100.0	100.0
			INCOME DATA						
100.0	100.0	100.0	Net Sales	100.0	100.0	100.0	100.0	100.0	100.0
40.1	43.9	45.3	Gross Profit	53.4	45.8	41.6	42.5	45.2	38.8
35.1	39.6	38.7	Operating Expenses	48.0	41.6	34.1	35.4	36.9	29.9
5.0	4.4	6.6	Operating Profit	5.5	4.2	7.5	7.1	8.3	8.9
1.9	1.5	1.5	All Other Expenses (net)	2.8	1.2	1.5	1.4	.4	1.3
3.0	2.9	5.1	Profit Before Taxes	2.6	3.0	6.0	5.7	7.9	7.6
			RATIOS						
1.5	1.6	1.6	Current	1.3	1.5	2.1	1.7	1.7	1.7
.6	.6	.8		.5	.4	1.0	.6	1.2	1.0
.3	.2	.3		.1	.2	.3	.1	.8	.4
1.2	1.3	1.1	Quick	1.0	.9	1.8	1.2	1.1	1.3
(225) .4	(187) .4	.5		.4	.3	.7	.3	.8	.7
.1	.1	.1		.0	.1	.2	.1	.6	.3
0 UND	0 UND	0 UND	Sales/Receivables	0 UND	0 UND	0 UND	0 950.3	0 999.8	2 217.2
1 521.4	1 675.0	1 468.9		0 UND	0 999.8	0 867.2	1 398.0	10 37.6	18 20.3
5 77.9	8 47.6	13 27.2		1 271.2	10 38.2	10 38.3	4 87.6	25 14.8	24 14.9
2 171.9	2 160.8	2 154.4	Cost of Sales/Inventory	2 153.9	2 191.1	2 176.4	2 199.7	3 109.4	6 61.2
3 104.6	4 89.2	4 81.5		5 73.9	4 102.3	3 108.1	3 123.6	5 66.5	9 38.9
6 62.1	10 36.8	12 31.4		11 31.9	13 27.9	11 33.3	5 76.3	10 38.2	28 12.8
1 260.7	1 571.6	1 258.9	Cost of Sales/Payables	0 UND	1 398.5	1 381.3	1 250.7	8 48.4	13 27.8
6 58.3	7 54.2	9 42.4		5 70.8	6 57.6	3 104.8	8 47.7	14 27.0	24 14.9
18 20.1	16 23.1	23 15.8		13 27.8	29 12.6	14 25.6	22 16.4	35 10.4	32 11.5
42.0	40.2	22.5	Sales/Working Capital	669.7	87.1	12.0	23.6	15.0	15.8
-34.1	-36.8	-38.1		-18.8	-19.3	NM	-35.6	52.6	-762.1
-10.0	-9.2	-11.3		-5.8	-7.4	-20.6	-10.2	-65.2	-12.9
7.0	7.3	11.9	EBIT/Interest	7.0	15.8	12.7	7.3	27.8	28.4
(205) 2.6	(168) 2.6	(153) 4.4		(28) 1.9	(30) 2.2	(23) 3.9	4.5	7.0	5.5
.7	.5	1.7		.2	.0	2.2	2.9	4.1	2.2
4.3		6.0	Net Profit + Depr., Dep., Amort./Cur. Mat. L/T/D						
(12) 1.2		(23) 2.5							
.8		1.4							
1.8	1.2	1.1	Fixed/Worth	.8	4.0	.9	2.2	.7	.7
-11.1	7.4	7.6		NM	-1.3	3.6	5.3	1.8	1.3
-.8	-1.4	-1.4		-.4	-.3	-3.4	-4.0	19.0	-18.3
2.1	1.7	1.4	Debt/Worth	1.4	4.7	1.0	2.0	1.3	1.0
-17.0	17.9	19.7		-9.4	-3.7	3.8	9.8	2.5	1.5
-2.3	-2.9	-3.4		-1.7	-1.7	-5.8	-6.4	35.3	-24.2
102.4	91.6	122.3	% Profit Before Taxes/Tangible Net Worth	156.2		94.0	153.0	129.6	80.6
(101) 54.8	(103) 43.8	(92) 54.3		(16) 56.4		(17) 50.7	(20) 60.5	(18) 84.9	(12) 47.6
16.9	10.0	20.7		.6		14.2	23.9	19.0	22.0
19.8	18.8	25.3	% Profit Before Taxes/Total Assets	30.8	31.2	21.6	17.6	27.5	34.3
6.5	6.8	11.4		5.7	9.1	14.3	10.4	14.9	16.4
-1.5	-2.6	2.5		-6.2	-3.1	3.6	6.4	7.4	6.7
8.8	10.5	13.5	Sales/Net Fixed Assets	21.4	16.8	10.1	9.8	18.2	8.4
5.4	6.1	6.8		8.1	7.5	5.0	6.1	6.9	6.9
3.0	3.3	3.7		3.2	5.4	3.4	3.1	3.7	4.6
3.3	3.5	4.0	Sales/Total Assets	4.2	4.2	4.0	3.9	3.8	4.1
2.1	2.4	2.6		2.8	2.7	2.8	2.4	2.6	2.5
1.4	1.6	1.7		1.8	1.9	1.5	1.5	1.7	1.8
2.3	2.0	2.2	% Depr., Dep., Amort./Sales	1.7	2.0	1.7	2.7	2.4	1.8
(212) 3.9	(164) 3.7	(142) 3.6		(22) 3.2	(28) 4.1	(22) 3.0	(31) 3.9	(22) 3.9	2.9
5.7	5.6	4.6		4.6	5.3	4.3	4.9	4.5	5.0
1.8	1.7	1.7	% Officers', Directors' Owners' Comp/Sales		1.7	2.0	1.3		
(112) 3.5	(106) 3.4	(65) 3.5			(13) 3.8	(12) 3.4	(18) 2.6		
6.7	5.7	5.7			6.7	6.3	4.4		
2565633M	2097482M	1839260M	Net Sales ($)	20641M	59870M	96593M	231781M	358006M	1072369M
1535478M	936112M	803097M	Total Assets ($)	8757M	30322M	42970M	112727M	149181M	459140M

M = $ thousand   MM = $ million
See Pages 9 through 22 for Explanation of Ratios and Data

	Current Data Sorted by Assets							Comparative Historical Data	

			5	22	8	6	Type of Statement		
		3	32	16			Unqualified	25	40
	1	10	9	1	1		Reviewed	26	32
	8	9	4	2		1	Compiled	17	30
	3	11	19	19	4	6	Tax Returns	18	23
		38 (4/1-9/30/09)			162 (10/1/09-3/31/10)		Other	75	71
								4/1/05-3/31/06	4/1/06-3/31/07
	0-500M	500M-2MM	2-10MM	10-50MM	50-100MM	100-250MM		ALL	ALL
	12	33	69	60	13	13	NUMBER OF STATEMENTS	161	196
	%	%	%	%	%	%	ASSETS	%	%
	11.3	14.6	9.4	11.6	9.1	6.5	Cash & Equivalents	9.8	10.2
	16.2	21.9	20.3	14.4	15.1	13.5	Trade Receivables (net)	18.5	17.6
	14.8	9.7	12.9	9.3	6.4	9.1	Inventory	10.2	10.1
	1.4	4.5	2.9	2.3	2.4	5.6	All Other Current	2.8	2.1
	43.7	50.6	45.5	37.6	33.1	34.8	Total Current	41.3	39.9
	40.3	33.0	46.2	48.8	49.1	45.4	Fixed Assets (net)	45.8	49.2
	5.3	9.2	4.3	5.7	7.3	8.7	Intangibles (net)	3.6	4.5
	10.7	7.2	4.0	7.9	10.5	11.1	All Other Non-Current	9.3	6.3
	100.0	100.0	100.0	100.0	100.0	100.0	Total	100.0	100.0
							LIABILITIES		
	3.6	13.5	4.7	5.2	3.8	4.1	Notes Payable-Short Term	5.8	5.1
	17.5	2.4	5.0	4.4	4.0	4.9	Cur. Mat.-L.T.D.	4.8	5.7
	16.3	15.3	16.1	8.9	9.5	10.3	Trade Payables	14.3	14.1
	.0	.1	.3	.4	.1	.4	Income Taxes Payable	.2	.2
	10.3	7.5	6.6	6.9	9.7	10.0	All Other Current	10.0	9.1
	47.8	38.8	32.6	25.8	27.2	29.8	Total Current	35.1	34.2
	25.7	23.6	25.6	25.7	25.5	30.1	Long-Term Debt	26.4	26.1
	.0	.0	.6	.8	1.8	.9	Deferred Taxes	.8	.6
	2.6	9.3	6.5	4.3	7.7	25.1	All Other Non-Current	7.3	10.2
	23.9	28.3	34.6	43.3	37.8	14.1	Net Worth	30.3	28.9
	100.0	100.0	100.0	100.0	100.0	100.0	Total Liabilties & Net Worth	100.0	100.0
							INCOME DATA		
	100.0	100.0	100.0	100.0	100.0	100.0	Net Sales	100.0	100.0
	47.1	41.9	36.3	33.8	35.9	31.4	Gross Profit	36.4	33.2
	47.9	36.6	30.2	25.8	27.8	27.5	Operating Expenses	32.0	29.0
	-.8	5.3	6.1	8.1	8.1	3.9	Operating Profit	4.5	4.2
	.3	.8	1.1	.8	1.2	.8	All Other Expenses (net)	.9	1.4
	-1.1	4.5	5.0	7.3	6.9	3.2	Profit Before Taxes	3.6	2.9
							RATIOS		
	4.1	2.5	1.9	2.4	1.6	2.3		1.9	1.9
	.9	1.5	1.3	1.4	1.4	1.1	Current	1.4	1.3
	.6	1.1	1.0	.9	1.0	.8		.8	.8
	2.5	1.9	1.3	1.8	1.2	1.0		1.3	1.3
	.8	1.1	.8	.9	.9	.6	Quick	.9	.8
	.3	.7	.6	.5	.7	.4		.5	.5

													Sales/Receivables				
1	339.6	5	68.8	18	20.6	17	21.2	21	17.3	23	16.0			16	22.3	18	20.5
5	78.3	20	18.1	26	14.2	23	15.9	23	15.6	26	13.8	Sales/Receivables		25	14.5	25	14.6
22	16.3	37	9.9	33	11.0	31	11.9	27	13.3	34	10.6			33	11.0	34	10.7
2	161.7	6	57.4	11	34.3	11	32.9	10	35.7	16	22.8			11	34.5	9	40.3
12	31.6	12	29.3	20	18.1	19	19.2	15	24.3	23	16.0	Cost of Sales/Inventory		17	21.0	19	19.7
52	7.0	27	13.3	30	12.0	27	13.5	22	16.2	60	6.1			27	13.3	28	13.1
3	110.3	12	31.5	17	22.1	13	28.3	18	20.1	23	16.1			16	22.5	16	22.4
20	17.9	25	14.4	26	14.1	22	16.5	24	14.6	27	13.3	Cost of Sales/Payables		28	13.0	27	13.5
35	10.4	37	9.8	37	9.8	29	12.4	29	12.5	30	12.1			41	9.0	43	8.5

								Comparative	
	35.7	9.4	11.2	9.1	13.9	19.1	Sales/Working Capital	12.1	13.0
	-271.8	20.8	29.2	20.5	27.3	82.3		25.8	32.1
	-21.3	92.0	-251.2	-66.7	218.2	-19.3		-36.1	-28.5
	6.0	9.9	14.1	21.7	11.0	42.5		9.1	10.3
(10)	.4	(30) 4.6	(65) 4.8	(53) 6.5	(12) 6.1	4.1	EBIT/Interest	(141) 3.8	(181) 3.1
	-2.2	1.4	1.8	2.7	3.5	-.3		1.2	.8
			4.6	5.3			Net Profit + Depr., Dep.,	5.4	4.6
		(22) 3.0	(25) 2.8				Amort./Cur. Mat. L/T/D	(43) 2.9	(52) 2.7
			1.8	1.8				1.2	1.4
	.6	.4	.7	.9	.9	1.0		.7	.8
	1.3	1.2	1.7	1.6	1.9	4.2	Fixed/Worth	1.4	1.7
	-1.8	-3.0	3.9	3.3	3.7	-1.4		3.9	4.9
	.4	.8	1.1	.7	1.1	.8		.9	.9
	1.5	2.7	2.1	1.4	2.2	5.4	Debt/Worth	2.1	2.0
	-8.1	-10.2	5.9	4.5	4.6	-4.3		7.5	6.5
		76.5	79.6	67.3	48.4		% Profit Before Taxes/Tangible	44.8	48.4
	(24) 35.5	(62) 31.1	(56) 36.7	(11) 27.0			Net Worth	(133) 22.3	(157) 20.3
		4.1	9.5	18.0	16.9			5.5	3.8
	24.9	24.3	18.0	23.8	18.8	9.0	% Profit Before Taxes/Total	17.2	15.4
	-2.4	6.5	8.7	13.4	13.5	7.9	Assets	7.1	6.4
	-10.5	2.0	3.6	5.0	4.9	-1.8		.9	-.3
	31.6	29.0	11.8	7.4	7.0	5.2		10.9	9.3
	15.9	10.9	5.7	4.5	5.0	3.1	Sales/Net Fixed Assets	5.4	5.1
	5.5	5.2	3.4	3.2	3.5	2.2		3.2	2.9
	6.9	4.6	4.1	2.8	3.1	2.1		3.4	3.4
	3.8	3.4	2.6	2.2	2.1	1.3	Sales/Total Assets	2.4	2.3
	2.8	2.0	2.0	1.5	1.7	.9		1.8	1.7
	.8	.7	1.5	2.4	2.4			1.5	2.0
(10)	1.8	(27) 2.1	(68) 2.9	(56) 3.1	(11) 3.3		% Depr., Dep., Amort./Sales	(149) 2.6	(179) 2.9
	3.2	3.1	4.4	4.6	4.6			4.1	4.2
		2.7	1.2	.4			% Officers', Directors'	2.2	2.3
	(23) 4.4	(29) 2.9	(14) .9				Owners' Comp/Sales	(58) 4.1	(64) 3.9
		4.9	5.2	1.7				7.6	6.2
	16594M	134137M	1051145M	3224039M	2158294M	3206103M	Net Sales ($)	5890654M	7706075M
	3518M	38503M	367055M	1462160M	979537M	1818644M	Total Assets ($)	2754881M	3842862M

© RMA 2010

M = $ thousand   MM = $ million
See Pages 9 through 22 for Explanation of Ratios and Data

Comparative Historical Data / Current Data Sorted by Sales

	4/1/07-3/31/08 ALL	4/1/08-3/31/09 ALL	4/1/09-3/31/10 ALL	0-1MM	1-3MM	3-5MM	5-10MM	10-25MM	25MM & OVER
Type of Statement									
Unqualified	42	49	41			1	1	3	36
Reviewed	34	35	51			2	7	24	18
Compiled	23	25	22		4	6	7	2	3
Tax Returns	27	23	24	2	12	1	4	2	3
Other	67	70	62	4	4	5	6	17	26
				38 (4/1-9/30/09)		162 (10/1/09-3/31/10)			
NUMBER OF STATEMENTS	193	202	200	6	20	15	25	48	86
ASSETS	%	%	%	%	%	%	%	%	%
Cash & Equivalents	9.8	7.5	10.8		7.4	11.4	11.2	11.9	10.0
Trade Receivables (net)	17.0	18.3	17.8		20.8	16.4	21.3	19.0	16.7
Inventory	10.2	11.6	10.7		12.0	8.7	12.6	10.4	10.8
All Other Current	2.2	2.5	3.0		3.7	5.0	1.7	4.2	2.4
Total Current	39.3	39.8	42.4		43.9	41.4	46.8	45.4	39.9
Fixed Assets (net)	48.4	48.2	44.6		31.2	45.4	43.4	44.2	47.3
Intangibles (net)	4.3	4.6	6.1		13.4	8.6	5.6	4.7	5.1
All Other Non-Current	8.0	7.4	7.0		11.4	4.5	4.2	5.6	7.7
Total	100.0	100.0	100.0		100.0	100.0	100.0	100.0	100.0
LIABILITIES									
Notes Payable-Short Term	5.1	8.3	6.2		10.6	3.1	6.2	4.5	5.3
Cur. Mat.-L.T.D.	5.7	4.2	5.1		9.4	5.8	3.7	5.0	4.5
Trade Payables	14.8	14.5	13.0		14.4	10.4	16.0	14.9	11.6
Income Taxes Payable	.2	.1	.2		.0	.1	.1	.4	.3
All Other Current	8.6	8.7	7.5		6.2	9.4	8.0	5.7	8.5
Total Current	34.4	35.8	31.9		40.6	28.8	34.1	30.5	30.1
Long-Term Debt	28.0	27.6	25.6		24.5	37.4	28.0	22.2	25.1
Deferred Taxes	.7	.6	.6		.0	.2	.3	.5	1.1
All Other Non-Current	10.2	8.6	7.4		9.4	6.8	7.3	5.4	8.6
Net Worth	26.7	27.4	34.4		25.5	26.8	30.3	41.4	35.0
Total Liabilties & Net Worth	100.0	100.0	100.0		100.0	100.0	100.0	100.0	100.0
INCOME DATA									
Net Sales	100.0	100.0	100.0		100.0	100.0	100.0	100.0	100.0
Gross Profit	36.5	31.8	36.8		41.2	43.7	36.4	38.7	32.0
Operating Expenses	32.1	28.7	30.7		36.5	38.8	33.4	30.5	25.3
Operating Profit	4.5	3.0	6.1		4.6	4.9	3.0	8.2	6.7
All Other Expenses (net)	1.2	1.1	.9		1.1	1.7	.7	.8	.9
Profit Before Taxes	3.3	1.9	5.3		3.5	3.2	2.3	7.4	5.8
RATIOS									
Current	2.0	1.9	2.3		2.6	2.4	1.8	2.5	1.9
	1.2	1.2	1.4		1.6	1.5	1.2	1.5	1.2
	.9	.7	1.0		.7	1.3	.8	1.0	1.0
Quick	1.3	1.2	1.5		2.3	1.3	1.1	2.2	1.2
	.8	.7	.9		1.4	1.0	.8	.9	.8
	.5	.4	.5		.7	.6	.5	.5	.5
Sales/Receivables	16 22.7	16 22.2	16 22.1		6 58.6	6 61.1	17 21.3	18 20.4	19 18.8
	25 14.9	24 15.3	23 15.7		17 22.0	18 19.9	26 13.8	26 14.2	23 15.7
	34 10.6	31 11.9	32 11.5		38 9.7	31 11.9	36 10.1	34 10.8	29 12.4
Cost of Sales/Inventory	10 37.7	9 42.0	10 36.9		7 53.6	8 44.0	6 61.3	11 33.1	12 31.1
	19 19.7	18 19.8	19 19.6		12 30.3	11 32.3	15 24.3	19 19.7	19 18.7
	31 11.6	30 12.2	30 12.4		27 13.7	30 12.2	29 12.5	30 12.3	26 14.1
Cost of Sales/Payables	16 23.2	14 25.5	15 24.2		3 110.8	2 194.7	14 25.3	20 17.8	15 23.9
	27 13.3	25 14.7	25 14.7		20 18.5	14 26.2	24 15.1	31 11.8	25 14.7
	43 8.4	38 9.6	34 10.7		38 9.5	29 12.7	40 9.0	39 9.3	29 12.8
Sales/Working Capital	12.0	14.0	10.9		8.3	9.5	11.9	8.6	12.2
	38.4	60.3	30.8		28.4	24.3	54.1	21.3	33.5
	-49.6	-24.2	-164.8		-57.9	42.7	-44.0	-215.4	-169.7
EBIT/Interest	8.7	6.9	13.6		7.3	5.4	11.9	22.1	19.8
	(177) 2.9	(190) 2.4	(183) 4.9		(18) 4.3	(14) 3.3	(40) 2.7	6.4	(82) 5.7
	.9	.3	2.1		.9	.8	.8	3.9	2.6
Net Profit + Depr., Dep., Amort./Cur. Mat. L/T/D	5.6	3.5	4.9					5.5	4.5
	(53) 2.4	(58) 2.2	(61) 2.9				(16)	3.2	(34) 2.9
	1.2	.7	2.0					2.4	1.9
Fixed/Worth	.8	.9	.7		.6	.5	.4	.6	.9
	1.7	1.8	1.6		1.3	2.5	1.6	1.4	1.6
	6.6	16.3	4.6		-1.4	45.0	6.9	3.0	4.4
Debt/Worth	1.1	1.1	.9		.9	.7	1.6	.7	.9
	2.1	2.3	1.9		4.1	2.4	2.7	1.6	1.7
	12.4	24.7	7.6		-5.4	79.0	11.2	4.0	6.2
% Profit Before Taxes/Tangible Net Worth	43.5	43.0	66.5		81.9	75.1	45.9	79.8	60.2
	(155) 20.1	(159) 15.7	(170) 31.3		(13) 36.6	(12) 13.6	(21) 20.6	(45) 40.2	(75) 32.3
	3.7	4.4	10.1		.2	-1.4	-24.5	17.5	11.2
% Profit Before Taxes/Total Assets	14.2	11.8	20.5		18.6	15.1	12.3	25.5	22.3
	5.4	4.6	9.1		7.4	4.9	4.5	12.9	9.5
	.2	-1.9	3.1		.0	-.9	-1.8	8.0	3.8
Sales/Net Fixed Assets	10.4	10.5	11.4		23.3	38.0	27.2	13.2	8.4
	5.3	5.2	5.4		12.5	4.7	8.8	5.7	5.2
	2.9	3.2	3.4		5.2	1.8	3.1	3.4	3.5
Sales/Total Assets	3.6	3.9	3.6		4.3	3.9	4.4	4.0	3.2
	2.5	2.6	2.5		2.9	2.3	3.1	2.4	2.4
	1.6	1.8	1.7		1.8	1.3	2.0	1.6	1.7
% Depr., Dep., Amort./Sales	1.9	1.6	1.7		.7	1.7	1.3	1.5	2.3
	(170) 2.7	(179) 2.9	(177) 2.9		(18) 2.1	(22) 3.0	(45) 3.1	(73) 2.8	3.0
	4.8	4.4	4.3		2.9	4.0	5.7	4.3	4.4
% Officers', Directors' Owners' Comp/Sales	1.4	1.1	1.2		2.7	3.4	3.0	1.0	.8
	(63) 3.5	(67) 2.8	(74) 3.2		(11) 4.6	(11) 5.7	(14) 4.4	(14) 1.3	(22) 1.2
	5.7	5.0	5.5		6.4	10.3	5.5	3.2	3.4
Net Sales ($)	7751334M	9704262M	9790312M	2549M	36612M	58889M	180531M	761017M	8750714M
Total Assets ($)	3794262M	4459660M	4669417M	1873M	14669M	32655M	77208M	366101M	4176911M

Current Data Sorted by Assets   Comparative Historical Data

0-500M	500M-2MM	2-10MM	10-50MM	50-100MM	100-250MM	Type of Statement	4/1/05-3/31/06 ALL	4/1/06-3/31/07 ALL
		2	2	1		Unqualified	8	5
		4				Reviewed	1	6
1	1	1	1			Compiled	5	6
3	3	3	5		3	Tax Returns		2
			22 (10/1/09-3/31/10)			Other	10	8
4 (4/1-9/30/09)								
1	4	10	7	1	3	NUMBER OF STATEMENTS	24	27
%	%	%	%	%	%	ASSETS	%	%
		13.0				Cash & Equivalents	10.3	7.1
		21.3				Trade Receivables (net)	20.9	18.7
		18.2				Inventory	13.4	14.2
		.7				All Other Current	.5	1.9
		53.3				Total Current	45.2	41.9
		35.1				Fixed Assets (net)	34.0	38.9
		7.4				Intangibles (net)	11.8	11.6
		4.2				All Other Non-Current	9.0	7.5
		100.0				Total	100.0	100.0
						LIABILITIES		
		5.2				Notes Payable-Short Term	14.2	13.2
		2.6				Cur. Mat.-L.T.D.	4.2	4.3
		11.9				Trade Payables	12.4	12.7
		.0				Income Taxes Payable	.5	.1
		10.5				All Other Current	7.2	7.8
		30.2				Total Current	38.6	38.0
		12.8				Long-Term Debt	17.2	24.8
		.0				Deferred Taxes	.9	.6
		.4				All Other Non-Current	2.5	5.5
		56.6				Net Worth	40.8	31.0
		100.0				Total Liabilities & Net Worth	100.0	100.0
						INCOME DATA		
		100.0				Net Sales	100.0	100.0
		40.9				Gross Profit	31.3	32.7
		30.1				Operating Expenses	25.7	27.8
		10.9				Operating Profit	5.6	5.0
		.9				All Other Expenses (net)	.5	1.6
		10.0				Profit Before Taxes	5.1	3.4
						RATIOS		
		2.7				Current	2.5	1.9
		1.8					1.1	1.3
		1.4					.9	.7
		1.9				Quick	1.7	1.2
		1.3					.8	.8
		.9					.5	.4
		23 16.1				Sales/Receivables	24 15.0	22 16.7
		26 14.1					31 11.9	28 13.0
		32 11.4					39 9.3	41 9.0
		13 28.3				Cost of Sales/Inventory	21 17.6	19 18.8
		30 12.1					29 12.4	36 10.2
		56 6.6					51 7.1	51 7.2
		20 18.3				Cost of Sales/Payables	15 23.9	22 16.9
		24 15.3					22 16.6	28 12.9
		29 12.5					42 8.6	43 8.5
		7.8				Sales/Working Capital	10.8	8.8
		15.4					33.8	22.9
		23.5					-40.2	-17.6
						EBIT/Interest	10.4	6.2
							(21) 1.9	(23) 1.4
							.7	.5
						Net Profit + Depr., Dep., Amort./Cur. Mat. L/T/D		
		.4				Fixed/Worth	.4	.7
		.8					.8	1.2
		1.2					2.6	4.1
		.2				Debt/Worth	.8	.8
		.8					1.5	2.3
		3.2					5.8	327.3
						% Profit Before Taxes/Tangible Net Worth	36.0	49.8
							(19) 7.2	(21) 10.4
							-6.0	-2.1
		44.3				% Profit Before Taxes/Total Assets	17.8	16.3
		20.5					6.8	2.8
		2.0					-.2	-1.3
		36.4				Sales/Net Fixed Assets	22.9	12.2
		6.8					5.9	5.6
		4.6					3.7	3.4
		3.8				Sales/Total Assets	3.4	3.0
		2.5					2.2	2.1
		2.3					1.4	1.5
						% Depr., Dep., Amort./Sales	1.1	1.6
							(20) 2.7	(24) 2.7
							4.1	3.5
						% Officers', Directors' Owners' Comp/Sales		
1496M	24526M	109106M	176857M	85977M	1195370M	Net Sales ($)	1340467M	1433029M
253M	6155M	37523M	167287M	52085M	364629M	Total Assets ($)	654661M	757365M

M = $ thousand   MM = $ million
See Pages 9 through 22 for Explanation of Ratios and Data

Comparative Historical Data | Current Data Sorted by Sales

Right-side columns group: 4 (4/1-9/30/09) covers 0-1MM, 1-3MM, 3-5MM; 22 (10/1/09-3/31/10) covers 5-10MM, 10-25MM, 25MM & OVER. For ASSETS and LIABILITIES percentage data, only the 10-25MM column is populated ("DATA NOT AVAILABLE" for the other size columns).

Item	4/1/07-3/31/08 ALL	4/1/08-3/31/09 ALL	4/1/09-3/31/10 ALL	0-1MM	1-3MM	3-5MM	5-10MM	10-25MM	25MM & OVER
Type of Statement									
Unqualified	5	8	3					1	2
Reviewed	4	1	2			1		1	
Compiled	3	6	4				3	1	
Tax Returns		3	3			1	1	1	
Other	9	12	14		1		3	6	4
NUMBER OF STATEMENTS	21	30	26		1	2	7	10	6
	%	%	%	%	%	%	%	%	%
ASSETS									
Cash & Equivalents	6.6	13.6	10.7					15.4	
Trade Receivables (net)	19.8	18.5	18.0					16.3	
Inventory	17.3	18.9	16.5					15.5	
All Other Current	1.1	3.5	.8					.5	
Total Current	44.8	54.6	45.9					47.6	
Fixed Assets (net)	38.4	36.5	40.7					36.2	
Intangibles (net)	12.3	4.2	9.9					14.0	
All Other Non-Current	4.5	4.6	3.5					2.1	
Total	100.0	100.0	100.0					100.0	
LIABILITIES									
Notes Payable-Short Term	10.8	3.7	4.2					.5	
Cur. Mat.-L.T.D.	2.8	5.6	3.5					1.5	
Trade Payables	13.7	16.3	13.6					14.9	
Income Taxes Payable	.1	.0	.0					.0	
All Other Current	7.9	10.7	7.7					9.2	
Total Current	35.4	36.3	29.0					26.1	
Long-Term Debt	18.9	22.0	19.4					19.7	
Deferred Taxes	.8	.8	.3					.8	
All Other Non-Current	10.7	4.1	3.5					5.3	
Net Worth	34.2	37.0	47.8					48.1	
Total Liabilties & Net Worth	100.0	100.0	100.0					100.0	
INCOME DATA									
Net Sales	100.0	100.0	100.0					100.0	
Gross Profit	28.6	33.5	34.2					39.8	
Operating Expenses	22.3	27.1	25.8					27.7	
Operating Profit	6.2	6.5	8.4					12.0	
All Other Expenses (net)	.9	1.0	.3					.8	
Profit Before Taxes	5.4	5.5	8.1					11.2	
RATIOS									
Current	1.8 / 1.3 / .9	3.8 / 1.9 / .9	2.2 / 1.6 / 1.2					2.4 / 2.1 / 1.4	
Quick	1.2 / .7 / .4	2.1 / 1.2 / .4	1.6 / 1.0 / .6					1.7 / 1.2 / .9	
Sales/Receivables	24 14.9 / 29 12.4 / 38 9.6	18 20.4 / 25 14.6 / 33 11.2	18 20.0 / 26 14.0 / 31 11.7					18 19.9 / 27 13.4 / 37 9.8	
Cost of Sales/Inventory	23 16.2 / 42 8.6 / 55 6.6	18 20.0 / 30 12.0 / 59 6.2	20 18.6 / 34 10.8 / 52 7.0					30 12.3 / 50 7.2 / 55 6.7	
Cost of Sales/Payables	17 21.8 / 30 12.3 / 38 9.5	17 22.0 / 22 16.7 / 37 9.8	20 17.9 / 26 14.0 / 34 10.7					26 13.9 / 30 12.0 / 43 8.5	
Sales/Working Capital	8.7 / 23.4 / -39.0	7.1 / 13.8 / -182.5	8.4 / 19.3 / 36.3					7.2 / 10.1 / 22.3	
EBIT/Interest	(20) 14.3 / 4.0 / 1.4	(23) 17.3 / 4.4 / 2.0	(24) 17.7 / 7.8 / 1.7						
Net Profit + Depr., Dep., Amort./Cur. Mat. L/T/D									
Fixed/Worth	.5 / 1.1 / 2.0	.4 / .7 / 3.7	.6 / 1.1 / 2.7					.2 / .7 / NM	
Debt/Worth	.8 / 1.4 / NM	.5 / 1.1 / 5.0	.8 / 1.4 / 4.0					.5 / 1.4 / NM	
% Profit Before Taxes/Tangible Net Worth	(16) 47.2 / 25.5 / 7.0	(24) 62.0 / 29.1 / 8.6	(23) 77.1 / 24.4 / 2.6						
% Profit Before Taxes/Total Assets	15.8 / 9.5 / 2.0	27.0 / 14.8 / 1.7	28.0 / 11.3 / 1.3					28.0 / 9.6 / 1.3	
Sales/Net Fixed Assets	12.3 / 6.7 / 3.0	23.8 / 7.5 / 3.9	12.3 / 6.7 / 4.2					58.8 / 4.9 / 2.0	
Sales/Total Assets	3.0 / 2.4 / 1.4	4.0 / 2.8 / 1.8	3.6 / 2.5 / 1.6					3.8 / 1.9 / .8	
% Depr., Dep., Amort./Sales	(19) 1.5 / 2.6 / 4.3	(26) 1.0 / 2.1 / 3.5	(22) 1.9 / 2.4 / 4.6						
% Officers', Directors' Owners' Comp/Sales			(12) 2.2 / 3.5 / 14.9						
Net Sales ($)	1517108M	1311106M	1593332M		1496M	8013M	50175M	156956M	1376692M
Total Assets ($)	681787M	443329M	627932M		253M	2836M	18584M	117604M	488655M

M = $ thousand   MM = $ million
See Pages 9 through 22 for Explanation of Ratios and Data

Current Data Sorted by Assets   Comparative Historical Data

0-500M	500M-2MM	2-10MM	10-50MM	50-100MM	100-250MM	Type of Statement	4/1/05-3/31/06 ALL	4/1/06-3/31/07 ALL
		2	4	1		Unqualified	9	7
		5	2			Reviewed	5	4
	3	2	1		1	Compiled	1	2
1						Tax Returns	1	2
1	1	1	10	1		Other	4	3
		8 (4/1-9/30/09)		28 (10/1/09-3/31/10)				
2	4	10	17	2	1	**NUMBER OF STATEMENTS**	20	18
%	%	%	%	%	%	**ASSETS**	%	%
		4.6	2.8			Cash & Equivalents	7.2	5.5
		26.3	24.8			Trade Receivables (net)	26.3	23.2
		29.8	31.5			Inventory	30.2	35.4
		5.3	3.4			All Other Current	3.1	4.9
		65.9	62.5			Total Current	66.8	69.0
		21.3	28.2			Fixed Assets (net)	25.5	24.2
		1.8	7.5			Intangibles (net)	1.8	1.6
		10.9	1.8			All Other Non-Current	5.9	5.3
		100.0	100.0			Total	100.0	100.0
						LIABILITIES		
		22.1	17.8			Notes Payable-Short Term	14.3	12.8
		2.3	2.0			Cur. Mat.-L.T.D.	2.3	1.2
		18.0	19.6			Trade Payables	20.5	21.7
		2.0	.2			Income Taxes Payable	.1	.0
		9.9	5.6			All Other Current	7.7	9.1
		54.2	45.2			Total Current	44.9	44.8
		7.0	17.9			Long-Term Debt	11.5	13.4
		1.0	.2			Deferred Taxes	.7	.5
		6.3	1.8			All Other Non-Current	5.5	7.0
		31.6	35.0			Net Worth	37.4	34.3
		100.0	100.0			Total Liabilities & Net Worth	100.0	100.0
						INCOME DATA		
		100.0	100.0			Net Sales	100.0	100.0
		24.9	21.7			Gross Profit	20.7	18.6
		15.6	15.4			Operating Expenses	13.0	15.7
		9.2	6.3			Operating Profit	7.7	3.0
		1.4	1.0			All Other Expenses (net)	4.5	.6
		7.9	5.3			Profit Before Taxes	3.2	2.4
						RATIOS		
		2.1	1.8			Current	2.2	2.4
		1.4	1.4				1.4	1.6
		.9	1.1				1.1	1.2
		1.3	.8			Quick	1.1	1.0
		.6	.6				.7	.5
		.4	.5				.5	.4
		24 15.4	33 10.9			Sales/Receivables	31 11.7	23 16.1
		31 11.6	37 9.8				37 10.0	33 11.0
		47 7.8	52 7.1				47 7.8	43 8.5
		23 16.1	45 8.1			Cost of Sales/Inventory	37 10.0	29 12.4
		46 7.9	59 6.2				45 8.2	61 6.0
		72 5.1	90 4.1				86 4.2	92 3.9
		11 34.0	25 14.6			Cost of Sales/Payables	10 35.2	16 22.9
		18 20.2	35 10.4				20 17.9	28 13.2
		45 8.2	52 7.0				65 5.6	46 7.9
		12.1	8.9			Sales/Working Capital	8.2	7.1
		19.6	12.8				16.4	9.6
		-34.3	30.8				35.4	18.3
			9.5			EBIT/Interest	7.6	8.1
			(15) 5.2				(19) 4.2	(17) 3.8
			3.6				2.5	1.2
						Net Profit + Depr., Dep., Amort./Cur. Mat. L/T/D		
		.2	.5			Fixed/Worth	.3	.3
		.7	.9				.9	.8
		1.0	3.1				1.5	1.5
		.9	1.4			Debt/Worth	1.0	1.1
		1.7	3.3				2.3	2.1
		4.6	8.5				3.5	5.3
			86.4			% Profit Before Taxes/Tangible Net Worth	46.2	50.1
			(15) 38.3				(19) 31.1	(16) 26.9
			24.7				15.3	8.8
		28.5	19.8			% Profit Before Taxes/Total Assets	11.8	10.9
		8.7	8.3				9.1	7.1
		.9	4.5				2.2	-.8
		24.1	24.7			Sales/Net Fixed Assets	27.2	23.6
		15.8	10.5				9.7	13.8
		7.1	4.3				5.1	6.6
		4.2	3.2			Sales/Total Assets	3.1	3.4
		3.2	2.4				2.8	2.9
		1.6	1.6				1.5	1.8
		.9	.9			% Depr., Dep., Amort./Sales	.7	.8
		1.4	(15) 1.3				1.3	(17) 1.0
		2.1	2.0				2.6	1.7
						% Officers', Directors' Owners' Comp/Sales		
744M	12735M	176605M	1054715M	208022M	170902M	Net Sales ($)	1662297M	840280M
516M	3348M	51668M	458799M	129022M	178588M	Total Assets ($)	675830M	387151M

M = $ thousand   MM = $ million
See Pages 9 through 22 for Explanation of Ratios and Data

Comparative Historical Data | Current Data Sorted by Sales

Type of Statement

			Type of Statement	0-1MM	1-3MM	3-5MM	5-10MM	10-25MM	25MM & OVER
4	5	7	Unqualified	1				1	5
6	5	7	Reviewed			1		2	4
4	3	7	Compiled		1	1	1	2	2
	1	1	Tax Returns	1					
4	10	14	Other	1	1			2	10
4/1/07-3/31/08 ALL	4/1/08-3/31/09 ALL	4/1/09-3/31/10 ALL		8 (4/1-9/30/09)			28 (10/1/09-3/31/10)		
18	24	36	NUMBER OF STATEMENTS	3	2	2	1	7	21

Assets (%)

C1	C2	C3	ASSETS	0-1MM	1-3MM	3-5MM	5-10MM	10-25MM	25MM & OVER
6.6	5.0	6.4	Cash & Equivalents						2.8
24.2	30.6	23.4	Trade Receivables (net)						25.7
34.9	33.4	27.6	Inventory						33.6
4.2	1.4	5.3	All Other Current						6.3
69.8	70.5	62.7	Total Current						68.5
21.6	18.4	27.7	Fixed Assets (net)						23.2
1.0	3.9	4.8	Intangibles (net)						5.9
7.5	7.2	4.8	All Other Non-Current						2.4
100.0	100.0	100.0	Total						100.0

Liabilities

C1	C2	C3	LIABILITIES						25MM & OVER
14.6	19.8	17.6	Notes Payable-Short Term						16.6
1.1	1.8	1.8	Cur. Mat.-L.T.D.						2.3
22.0	21.4	17.2	Trade Payables						18.9
.0	.2	.6	Income Taxes Payable						.6
10.1	9.4	9.5	All Other Current						9.3
47.8	52.7	46.7	Total Current						47.6
7.4	8.1	14.1	Long-Term Debt						15.5
.1	.1	.4	Deferred Taxes						.2
3.6	3.5	5.6	All Other Non-Current						3.5
41.1	35.7	33.2	Net Worth						33.2
100.0	100.0	100.0	Total Liabilities & Net Worth						100.0

Income Data

C1	C2	C3	INCOME DATA						25MM & OVER
100.0	100.0	100.0	Net Sales						100.0
23.0	25.0	28.3	Gross Profit						19.9
15.1	17.0	20.6	Operating Expenses						14.2
7.9	8.0	7.7	Operating Profit						5.7
.9	.9	.6	All Other Expenses (net)						.8
7.0	7.1	7.1	Profit Before Taxes						4.9

Ratios

C1	C2	C3	RATIOS						25MM & OVER
2.1	1.8	2.1	Current						1.9
1.4	1.5	1.4							1.4
1.2	1.0	1.1							1.1
.7	1.3	1.1	Quick						.8
.6	.6	.6							.6
.5	.5	.5							.5
24 15.4	27 13.7	22 16.8	Sales/Receivables						31 11.9
35 10.4	37 9.8	35 10.4							36 10.1
41 8.8	53 6.9	50 7.2							49 7.4
32 11.4	27 13.5	24 15.1	Cost of Sales/Inventory						34 10.7
58 6.3	47 7.8	52 7.0							59 6.2
117 3.1	85 4.3	83 4.4							90 4.1
16 22.2	15 24.7	17 22.0	Cost of Sales/Payables						17 21.8
30 12.2	28 13.1	28 13.1							28 13.0
58 6.2	60 6.1	43 8.5							43 8.6
5.5	6.6	8.3	Sales/Working Capital						8.4
12.1	10.9	16.4							14.5
36.9	183.2	57.1							30.9
11.1	38.1	10.1	EBIT/Interest						9.8
5.9	(23) 5.7	(31) 5.3						(17)	5.3
2.3	2.1	3.6							3.6
			Net Profit + Depr., Dep., Amort./Cur. Mat. L/T/D						
.3	.3	.4	Fixed/Worth						.4
.5	.5	.7							.8
.9	1.2	3.2							3.1
.9	1.1	1.2	Debt/Worth						1.4
1.4	1.8	2.5							3.2
2.8	8.5	8.6							8.5
64.3	61.9	62.7	% Profit Before Taxes/Tangible Net Worth						87.5
19.8	(20) 39.8	(31) 36.3						(18)	37.3
3.9	12.4	16.6							19.4
14.6	25.6	20.0	% Profit Before Taxes/Total Assets						20.6
5.3	7.4	8.2							7.6
2.2	1.7	4.7							3.4
23.8	36.5	23.6	Sales/Net Fixed Assets						27.1
18.0	20.2	13.0							15.2
8.0	10.2	4.2							5.5
3.8	4.2	3.4	Sales/Total Assets						3.4
2.6	3.0	2.5							2.5
1.8	1.8	1.6							1.6
.9	1.1	1.0	% Depr., Dep., Amort./Sales						.9
(15) 1.2	(20) 1.4	(31) 1.4						(18)	1.2
1.8	1.9	2.3							1.8
		.5	% Officers', Directors' Owners' Comp/Sales						
	(11)	1.4							
		3.4							
1745480M	1142073M	1623723M	Net Sales ($)	1107M	3214M	7821M	5228M	118388M	1487965M
837947M	545620M	821941M	Total Assets ($)	2808M	1202M	3845M	1600M	63480M	749006M

M = $ thousand   MM = $ million
See Pages 9 through 22 for Explanation of Ratios and Data

Current Data Sorted by Assets   **Comparative Historical Data**

Type of Statement

	0-500M	500M-2MM	2-10MM	10-50MM	50-100MM	100-250MM		23 4/1/05-3/31/06 ALL	27 4/1/06-3/31/07 ALL
Unqualified		1	10	11	5	4		10	12
Reviewed		6	4	4				8	8
Compiled	2	6	1	2				3	8
Tax Returns								3	6
Other	1	5	4	14	3	4		23	27
		28 (4/1-9/30/09)		59 (10/1/09-3/31/10)					
NUMBER OF STATEMENTS	3	18	19	31	8	8		47	61

ASSETS (%)

	0-500M	500M-2MM	2-10MM	10-50MM	50-100MM	100-250MM	ASSETS	4/1/05-3/31/06 ALL	4/1/06-3/31/07 ALL
		7.2	7.1	10.0			Cash & Equivalents	5.5	5.5
		23.6	25.1	18.6			Trade Receivables (net)	19.2	20.1
		19.4	22.7	21.7			Inventory	18.2	19.8
		1.9	2.3	1.8			All Other Current	2.7	1.2
		52.2	57.1	52.0			Total Current	45.7	46.6
		28.2	35.9	39.8			Fixed Assets (net)	43.2	37.8
		5.5	2.3	2.3			Intangibles (net)	5.4	7.3
		14.1	4.7	5.9			All Other Non-Current	5.7	8.3
		100.0	100.0	100.0			Total	100.0	100.0

LIABILITIES

	0-500M	500M-2MM	2-10MM	10-50MM	50-100MM	100-250MM	LIABILITIES	4/1/05-3/31/06 ALL	4/1/06-3/31/07 ALL
		7.1	7.7	13.0			Notes Payable-Short Term	11.9	8.4
		4.8	3.8	2.2			Cur. Mat.-L.T.D.	3.9	4.5
		18.8	15.8	12.1			Trade Payables	13.5	14.3
		.0	.8	.9			Income Taxes Payable	.3	.3
		15.9	7.1	6.7			All Other Current	9.5	10.0
		46.5	35.3	34.8			Total Current	39.0	37.5
		43.7	26.2	14.0			Long-Term Debt	22.5	24.8
		.3	1.5	.8			Deferred Taxes	1.0	.9
		23.3	12.8	4.5			All Other Non-Current	5.9	12.1
		-13.9	24.2	45.9			Net Worth	31.6	24.6
		100.0	100.0	100.0			Total Liabilities & Net Worth	100.0	100.0

INCOME DATA

	0-500M	500M-2MM	2-10MM	10-50MM	50-100MM	100-250MM	INCOME DATA	4/1/05-3/31/06 ALL	4/1/06-3/31/07 ALL
		100.0	100.0	100.0			Net Sales	100.0	100.0
		27.6	32.1	29.2			Gross Profit	31.1	28.8
		30.2	26.0	21.7			Operating Expenses	30.0	25.3
		-2.6	6.1	7.5			Operating Profit	1.1	3.5
		1.1	1.3	.0			All Other Expenses (net)	1.3	1.3
		-3.7	4.8	7.5			Profit Before Taxes	-.2	2.2

RATIOS

	0-500M	500M-2MM	2-10MM	10-50MM	50-100MM	100-250MM	RATIOS	4/1/05-3/31/06 ALL	4/1/06-3/31/07 ALL
		2.5	2.4	3.3				1.7	2.1
		1.6	1.7	1.3			Current	1.1	1.2
		.7	1.3	1.1				.9	.9
		1.7	1.5	2.0				.9	1.1
		.8	1.0	.8			Quick	.6	.6
		.3	.6	.4				.5	.5
		19 18.9	25 14.7	22 16.3				25 14.4	23 15.9
		26 14.2	32 11.3	28 12.9			Sales/Receivables	32 11.5	31 11.8
		49 7.5	38 9.5	36 10.1				38 9.6	37 9.9
		18 19.7	23 16.0	28 13.1				21 17.4	22 16.4
		39 9.3	42 8.8	43 8.5			Cost of Sales/Inventory	33 11.2	35 10.3
		60 6.1	59 6.2	63 5.8				50 7.3	56 6.5
		13 27.8	18 20.7	13 27.1				15 24.9	17 21.9
		25 14.6	25 14.3	26 14.1			Cost of Sales/Payables	25 14.5	27 13.6
		62 5.9	49 7.5	32 11.5				46 8.0	38 9.7
		10.0	7.3	5.0				9.3	10.2
		24.7	13.3	22.2			Sales/Working Capital	41.9	44.0
		-8.9	67.2	54.3				-52.2	-34.6
		5.8	14.7	16.8				5.1	6.9
		(17) 2.5	(18) 3.8	(26) 8.5			EBIT/Interest	(43) 1.7	(57) 2.2
		-3.3	2.3	2.8				-.4	.5
			7.7	11.6				4.4	4.5
			(11) 5.1	(12) 5.1			Net Profit + Depr., Dep., Amort./Cur. Mat. L/T/D	(16) 2.6	(24) 2.0
			1.9	2.1				1.7	1.2
		.5	.6	.6				.7	.7
		3.5	.9	1.0			Fixed/Worth	1.3	1.6
		-.4	-3.7	1.8				7.1	NM
		1.4	1.0	.5				.7	.8
		NM	2.1	1.5			Debt/Worth	2.0	3.0
		-2.6	-9.0	2.6				13.6	NM
			68.5	41.7				26.3	47.4
			(13) 34.2	(29) 25.1			% Profit Before Taxes/Tangible Net Worth	(38) 8.1	(46) 14.5
			11.5	14.7				-.9	-.2
		21.8	26.8	20.3				6.8	10.3
		1.7	14.7	9.3			% Profit Before Taxes/Total Assets	2.0	3.9
		-19.7	4.1	3.8				-4.5	-1.9
		25.0	25.0	9.6				8.8	11.2
		9.1	7.2	6.3			Sales/Net Fixed Assets	5.2	6.1
		5.5	4.6	4.0				3.7	3.8
		3.2	4.2	3.2				3.0	3.1
		2.3	2.5	2.3			Sales/Total Assets	2.0	2.3
		1.7	2.3	1.4				1.5	1.7
		2.0	1.2	1.2				1.7	1.2
		(15) 2.9	(17) 1.4	1.9			% Depr., Dep., Amort./Sales	(41) 2.7	(52) 2.4
		5.4	2.2	2.9				4.8	3.8
								1.4	1.4
							% Officers', Directors' Owners' Comp/Sales	(15) 2.1	(21) 3.0
								8.6	6.0
4755M	72923M	322794M	1823886M	888224M	1971954M		Net Sales ($)	2190354M	2627276M
925M	23329M	86951M	775564M	596108M	1098086M		Total Assets ($)	1055089M	1296723M

M = $ thousand   MM = $ million
See Pages 9 through 22 for Explanation of Ratios and Data

Comparative Historical Data | Current Data Sorted by Sales

	4/1/07-3/31/08 ALL	4/1/08-3/31/09 ALL	4/1/09-3/31/10 ALL	Type of Statement	0-1MM	1-3MM	3-5MM	5-10MM	10-25MM	25MM & OVER
	14	13	20	Unqualified			1		2	18
	10	14	15	Reviewed			1	5	5	4
	5	5	12	Compiled			5	3	3	
	4	10	9	Tax Returns	1	2	4	1	1	
	23	39	31	Other	3	2		1	4	20
					1	2				
					3	2	1			

Periods (current): 28 (4/1-9/30/09) covers 0-1MM / 1-3MM / 3-5MM; 59 (10/1/09-3/31/10) covers 5-10MM / 10-25MM / 25MM & OVER

	4/1/07-3/31/08 ALL	4/1/08-3/31/09 ALL	4/1/09-3/31/10 ALL		0-1MM	1-3MM	3-5MM	5-10MM	10-25MM	25MM & OVER
NUMBER OF STATEMENTS	56	81	87		4	5	11	10	15	42
	%	%	%	**ASSETS**	%	%	%	%	%	%
	4.3	6.2	7.6	Cash & Equivalents			9.6	11.8	11.8	5.4
	20.1	21.4	20.3	Trade Receivables (net)			21.6	18.3	22.9	18.9
	18.4	21.6	20.2	Inventory			26.2	16.0	21.5	20.5
	1.9	3.0	1.8	All Other Current			2.7	2.0	1.7	1.9
	44.7	52.1	49.9	Total Current			60.1	48.1	57.8	46.7
	40.1	36.5	36.2	Fixed Assets (net)			20.4	44.0	34.8	38.4
	6.4	6.1	7.4	Intangibles (net)			6.3	5.1	1.3	10.4
	8.8	5.3	6.5	All Other Non-Current			13.2	2.7	6.1	4.6
	100.0	100.0	100.0	Total			100.0	100.0	100.0	100.0
				LIABILITIES						
	10.9	10.0	9.3	Notes Payable-Short Term			10.2	2.5	8.1	11.6
	5.7	4.8	3.6	Cur. Mat.-L.T.D.			3.8	5.5	2.9	2.7
	16.1	18.2	14.8	Trade Payables			17.9	8.2	19.1	12.9
	.2	.1	.6	Income Taxes Payable			.0	.0	.7	.9
	6.2	10.2	8.8	All Other Current			7.7	5.7	6.0	7.8
	39.1	43.3	37.1	Total Current			39.6	21.9	36.8	36.0
	27.3	20.4	25.1	Long-Term Debt			39.6	37.6	18.0	15.5
	1.1	.7	1.1	Deferred Taxes			.0	.0	2.6	1.3
	7.1	8.3	10.6	All Other Non-Current			8.5	11.6	7.9	5.5
	25.4	27.3	26.1	Net Worth			12.3	28.8	34.7	41.7
	100.0	100.0	100.0	Total Liabilities & Net Worth			100.0	100.0	100.0	100.0
				INCOME DATA						
	100.0	100.0	100.0	Net Sales			100.0	100.0	100.0	100.0
	31.9	27.4	29.8	Gross Profit			31.0	41.5	31.4	26.3
	29.1	24.7	24.6	Operating Expenses			31.9	29.4	25.7	20.2
	2.8	2.7	5.2	Operating Profit			-.8	12.0	5.7	6.1
	1.9	1.1	1.2	All Other Expenses (net)			1.3	.8	.9	1.1
	.9	1.6	4.0	Profit Before Taxes			-2.2	11.2	4.8	5.0
				RATIOS						
	1.7	2.1	2.4				2.8	3.5	2.7	1.5
	1.1	1.3	1.3	Current			1.6	2.5	1.7	1.2
	.9	.9	1.0				1.0	1.2	1.3	1.0
	1.1	1.1	1.4				1.8	1.8	2.2	.9
	.6	.7	.7	Quick			.8	1.1	.9	.6
	.4	.4	.5				.3	.8	.5	.5
	25 14.7	21 17.1	22 16.3		18 20.4		23 15.9	25 14.7	24 15.2	
	32 11.3	31 11.9	30 12.3	Sales/Receivables	20 18.3		37 9.8	31 11.6	29 12.6	
	39 9.4	37 10.0	37 9.8		48 7.6		42 8.7	34 10.8	33 11.1	
	23 16.1	19 18.8	25 14.3		38 9.5		33 11.1	20 18.4	27 13.7	
	36 10.1	34 10.9	37 9.9	Cost of Sales/Inventory	44 8.3		50 7.3	34 10.6	35 10.4	
	59 6.1	48 7.6	58 6.3		77 4.8		71 5.1	59 6.2	49 7.5	
	22 16.6	16 22.7	15 24.2		13 27.7		15 24.7	22 16.9	14 26.3	
	35 10.5	29 12.4	25 14.6	Cost of Sales/Payables	19 18.9		25 14.9	27 13.7	24 14.9	
	50 7.3	39 9.4	39 9.3		61 6.0		32 11.3	52 7.1	32 11.4	
	9.5	10.4	8.0				10.8	3.7	7.1	11.9
	51.2	36.8	26.7	Sales/Working Capital			14.0	6.8	12.5	47.0
	-34.1	-40.9	-207.4				-180.9	NM	26.9	-260.3
	4.4	6.2	11.6				9.3		18.8	11.3
	(52) 1.9	(71) 2.6	(79) 3.8	EBIT/Interest			(10) 4.2		5.8	(37) 5.2
	.4	.5	1.5				-.3		2.3	1.5
	5.1	6.6	11.0						14.6	11.8
	(24) 2.4	(31) 3.2	(35) 4.5	Net Profit + Depr., Dep., Amort./Cur. Mat. L/T/D					(10) 5.1	(19) 5.1
	1.1	.9	1.9						1.7	1.9
	.7	.7	.6				.3	.7	.5	.8
	2.1	1.3	1.3	Fixed/Worth			1.1	2.1	.8	1.2
	-231.6	-17.8	-60.9				-1.7	-4.2	2.0	2.8
	1.2	1.0	1.1				1.0	.8	.7	1.0
	3.0	2.4	2.3	Debt/Worth			12.9	2.6	2.1	1.8
	-262.1	-24.6	-56.1				-3.9	-10.0	5.1	3.8
	37.3	51.9	50.0						37.0	58.5
	(41) 15.6	(59) 20.1	(63) 25.8	% Profit Before Taxes/Tangible Net Worth					(13) 13.9	(35) 28.3
	.5	3.3	11.7						11.5	17.3
	9.3	12.3	19.7				25.0	26.4	19.7	20.9
	3.3	4.3	7.9	% Profit Before Taxes/Total Assets			10.3	9.2	4.6	9.2
	-2.1	-1.0	1.7				2.0	5.1	3.2	1.7
	10.3	16.6	13.5				26.2	8.0	26.8	10.3
	5.1	7.5	6.3	Sales/Net Fixed Assets			15.4	4.6	7.2	6.4
	3.3	3.9	4.0				5.6	1.7	4.1	3.9
	2.8	3.6	3.2				4.5	2.6	4.2	3.2
	2.2	2.6	2.3	Sales/Total Assets			2.7	1.6	2.5	2.3
	1.6	1.8	1.6				1.9	.6	1.9	1.7
	1.5	1.4	1.3					1.4	1.2	1.2
	(52) 2.6	(69) 2.3	(75) 2.2	% Depr., Dep., Amort./Sales				(14) 2.2	(36) 1.4	1.9
	4.1	3.4	3.0					2.7	3.5	2.9
	1.8	1.6	1.9							
	(16) 3.3	(19) 3.5	(21) 3.1	% Officers', Directors' Owners' Comp/Sales						
	7.3	4.6	5.2							
	2677418M	4561088M	5084536M	Net Sales ($)	2794M	11688M	42666M	71515M	256184M	4699689M
	1343476M	2017545M	2580963M	Total Assets ($)	1767M	5312M	16236M	63342M	115950M	2378356M

© RMA 2010   M = $ thousand   MM = $ million
See Pages 9 through 22 for Explanation of Ratios and Data

Current Data Sorted by Assets | Comparative Historical Data

0-500M	500M-2MM	2-10MM	10-50MM	50-100MM	100-250MM	Type of Statement	4/1/05-3/31/06 ALL	4/1/06-3/31/07 ALL
			4	2	4	Unqualified	9	7
	1	4	3			Reviewed	13	11
	1	5	2			Compiled	5	4
3	5	1				Tax Returns	2	4
4	3	8	2	6	1	Other	23	25
	11 (4/1-9/30/09)		48 (10/1/09-3/31/10)					
7	10	18	11	8	5	NUMBER OF STATEMENTS	52	51
%	%	%	%	%	%	**ASSETS**	%	%
	8.5	6.6	8.1			Cash & Equivalents	3.7	6.1
	22.5	22.9	21.2			Trade Receivables (net)	22.8	21.5
	21.9	27.1	30.3			Inventory	25.2	23.9
	3.2	1.6	3.0			All Other Current	2.2	1.7
	56.1	58.2	62.5			Total Current	53.9	53.2
	31.9	31.7	27.0			Fixed Assets (net)	31.9	32.9
	7.6	3.2	6.4			Intangibles (net)	7.2	5.9
	4.4	6.9	4.1			All Other Non-Current	7.0	8.0
	100.0	100.0	100.0			Total	100.0	100.0
						LIABILITIES		
	6.3	8.0	5.3			Notes Payable-Short Term	13.8	15.4
	7.4	6.6	3.5			Cur. Mat.-L.T.D.	3.6	5.1
	17.9	19.7	10.9			Trade Payables	20.3	15.5
	.0	.1	.2			Income Taxes Payable	.2	.2
	8.8	9.4	7.5			All Other Current	9.0	15.5
	40.4	43.6	27.4			Total Current	47.0	51.7
	29.9	13.1	16.3			Long-Term Debt	21.5	19.7
	.0	.0	1.0			Deferred Taxes	.9	1.0
	6.6	3.1	9.9			All Other Non-Current	4.2	4.3
	23.1	40.1	45.4			Net Worth	26.4	23.2
	100.0	100.0	100.0			Total Liabilities & Net Worth	100.0	100.0
						INCOME DATA		
	100.0	100.0	100.0			Net Sales	100.0	100.0
	44.5	40.7	33.2			Gross Profit	36.5	42.4
	44.5	36.5	28.1			Operating Expenses	33.4	38.0
	.0	4.2	5.2			Operating Profit	3.1	4.4
	1.0	.5	1.2			All Other Expenses (net)	1.2	2.3
	-1.1	3.6	4.0			Profit Before Taxes	1.9	2.1
						RATIOS		
	2.5	2.3	3.2				1.7	1.8
	1.7	1.3	2.2			Current	1.2	1.3
	.5	1.0	1.2				.9	1.0
	1.5	1.1	1.8				.8	1.0
	.8	.6	1.2			Quick	.6	.6
	.2	.4	.5				.4	.4
21 17.1	23 15.8	22 16.3					23 16.2	22 16.5
27 13.6	26 13.9	31 11.9				Sales/Receivables	36 10.2	31 11.6
30 12.3	34 10.7	46 7.9					46 7.9	40 9.2
30 12.2	46 8.0	37 9.9					39 9.4	35 10.3
39 9.4	55 6.6	64 5.7				Cost of Sales/Inventory	63 6.6	58 6.3
54 6.8	74 5.0	103 3.6					80 4.6	82 4.5
17 21.8	24 15.1	16 22.8					35 10.6	18 20.1
33 11.1	41 8.9	27 13.4				Cost of Sales/Payables	42 8.7	38 9.7
62 5.8	60 6.1	32 11.5					63 5.8	59 6.2
	6.9	7.4	5.0				9.3	10.3
	15.1	22.5	7.5			Sales/Working Capital	28.7	19.5
	-8.0	NM	16.1				-49.3	183.4
	8.0	16.8					7.1	5.0
	1.4	(17) 7.8				EBIT/Interest	(45) 3.1	2.8
	-4.7	3.5					.9	.9
							5.8	6.8
						Net Profit + Depr., Dep., Amort./Cur. Mat. L/T/D	(15) 2.2	(15) 1.9
							1.1	1.4
	.4	.6	.2				.6	.6
	1.0	1.2	.5			Fixed/Worth	1.2	1.1
	-4.5	2.2	6.4				6.1	3.8
	.9	.7	.4				1.2	1.2
	1.7	2.5	.8			Debt/Worth	3.0	2.1
	-13.4	5.3	14.0				8.2	5.4
		57.7					31.5	33.4
		30.5				% Profit Before Taxes/Tangible Net Worth	(40) 13.3	(43) 13.5
		14.9					5.5	.9
	19.7	14.1	15.4				9.0	12.8
	.9	9.0	11.9			% Profit Before Taxes/Total Assets	4.6	4.9
	-16.7	5.8	3.1				-.3	-.2
	25.3	16.1	33.5				14.0	16.9
	9.2	10.0	13.0			Sales/Net Fixed Assets	8.7	8.7
	4.7	6.2	5.6				5.8	5.0
	4.1	3.5	3.2				3.3	3.1
	2.8	3.0	2.3			Sales/Total Assets	2.4	2.4
	1.6	2.1	1.5				1.8	1.8
		1.7					1.4	1.4
	(14)	2.9				% Depr., Dep., Amort./Sales	(43) 2.7	(44) 2.8
		3.6					4.0	4.7
							.9	2.3
						% Officers', Directors' Owners' Comp/Sales	(19) 3.3	(16) 4.3
							7.9	6.5
6813M	30366M	279878M	622510M	886625M	1352939M	Net Sales ($)	2783220M	1583095M
1649M	11519M	92568M	237164M	563206M	768934M	Total Assets ($)	1226670M	660508M

M = $ thousand   MM = $ million
See Pages 9 through 22 for Explanation of Ratios and Data

Comparative Historical Data

Current Data Sorted by Sales

			Type of Statement						
9	6	10	Unqualified						10
3	6	8	Reviewed		1		1	4	2
7	10	8	Compiled				2	3	2
6	7	9	Tax Returns		4	2	1		
15	19	24	Other	2	1			5	9
				2	4	2	1		
4/1/07-3/31/08	4/1/08-3/31/09	4/1/09-3/31/10			11 (4/1-9/30/09)		48 (10/1/09-3/31/10)		
ALL	ALL	ALL		0-1MM	1-3MM	3-5MM	5-10MM	10-25MM	25MM & OVER
40	48	59	NUMBER OF STATEMENTS	4	9	3	8	12	23
%	%	%	ASSETS	%	%	%	%	%	%
7.3	5.5	7.7	Cash & Equivalents					6.0	8.8
21.7	20.4	21.1	Trade Receivables (net)					19.8	19.5
22.3	24.9	25.2	Inventory					26.5	25.1
2.4	3.7	2.3	All Other Current					2.0	3.0
53.7	54.5	56.3	Total Current					54.3	56.4
30.3	30.8	30.6	Fixed Assets (net)					27.7	29.0
6.3	7.5	8.1	Intangibles (net)					8.3	10.3
9.7	7.2	4.9	All Other Non-Current					9.6	4.3
100.0	100.0	100.0	Total					100.0	100.0
			LIABILITIES						
17.3	10.0	7.0	Notes Payable-Short Term					7.6	4.3
5.4	3.9	5.1	Cur. Mat.-L.T.D.					5.9	3.1
19.1	18.2	15.0	Trade Payables					16.7	10.5
.1	.1	.1	Income Taxes Payable					.0	.2
7.5	6.1	10.4	All Other Current					5.2	9.2
49.5	38.4	37.6	Total Current					35.4	27.3
20.1	25.7	21.2	Long-Term Debt					14.6	17.8
.5	.6	.4	Deferred Taxes					.6	.5
3.5	5.5	6.4	All Other Non-Current					6.1	5.4
26.4	29.8	34.4	Net Worth					43.2	48.9
100.0	100.0	100.0	Total Liabilities & Net Worth					100.0	100.0
			INCOME DATA						
100.0	100.0	100.0	Net Sales					100.0	100.0
39.9	39.6	39.0	Gross Profit					40.0	34.8
36.0	38.3	35.7	Operating Expenses					36.5	28.6
3.9	1.3	3.3	Operating Profit					3.5	6.1
1.2	.8	.7	All Other Expenses (net)					.7	.3
2.7	.4	2.6	Profit Before Taxes					2.8	5.8
			RATIOS						
2.0	2.2	2.9						2.2	3.2
1.2	1.4	2.1	Current					1.9	2.2
.8	.9	1.1						1.1	1.6
1.1	1.0	1.5						1.6	1.6
.6	.6	1.0	Quick					.6	1.1
.4	.4	.5						.4	.8
23 15.9	19 18.7	22 16.5						22 16.3	20 17.8
29 12.4	28 13.2	27 13.6	Sales/Receivables					26 13.9	30 12.1
37 9.8	34 10.9	36 10.2						33 11.0	38 9.6
31 11.9	33 11.2	37 10.0						41 8.9	46 7.9
50 7.3	51 7.2	53 6.9	Cost of Sales/Inventory					55 6.6	53 6.8
90 4.1	72 5.1	79 4.6						69 5.3	80 4.5
23 15.7	21 17.8	20 18.5						11 32.7	16 22.4
36 10.0	32 11.6	31 11.6	Cost of Sales/Payables					38 9.7	27 13.4
64 5.7	56 6.5	48 7.6						58 6.3	34 10.8
8.3	7.5	5.6						6.3	5.0
22.1	14.8	11.7	Sales/Working Capital					13.6	7.4
-21.9	-49.2	83.9						101.6	13.8
6.0	5.9	15.6						9.2	67.0
(34) 2.8	(44) 2.1	(50) 4.6	EBIT/Interest					3.8 (17)	9.9
.1	.1	1.8						2.5	4.1
	8.0	7.4	Net Profit + Depr., Dep.,						
(11) 1.9	(10) 4.1		Amort./Cur. Mat. L/T/D						
	1.3	2.7							
.3	.4	.3						.4	.3
1.3	1.2	1.0	Fixed/Worth					1.1	.8
NM	3.9	6.4						2.1	4.3
1.0	1.2	-.7						.5	.3
3.2	2.6	1.2	Debt/Worth					1.6	1.1
NM	9.9	17.9						8.0	14.0
43.7	25.1	47.2						55.5	45.1
(30) 21.9	(41) 15.3	(46) 25.1	% Profit Before Taxes/Tangible Net Worth				(10) 26.7		25.9 (19)
7.9	-6.6	13.1						10.0	17.9
13.6	10.3	14.4						11.5	15.4
6.0	4.2	8.4	% Profit Before Taxes/Total Assets					7.0	11.9
-3.9	-1.2	3.1						2.6	3.1
24.9	25.9	24.2						36.2	20.7
10.3	9.0	8.5	Sales/Net Fixed Assets					11.4	7.8
5.5	5.1	5.0						6.4	5.2
3.3	3.4	3.6						3.5	3.0
2.5	2.6	2.4	Sales/Total Assets					2.9	2.3
1.7	2.1	1.6						2.1	1.5
1.4	1.1	1.3							.8
(27) 2.6	(36) 2.5	(46) 2.5	% Depr., Dep., Amort./Sales					(16) 1.7	
4.4	3.3	3.7							3.2
2.6	1.8	2.4							
(16) 3.4	(17) 5.0	(19) 3.6	% Officers', Directors' Owners' Comp/Sales						
11.9	9.6	6.4							
1756113M	2481365M	3179131M	Net Sales ($)	880M	19005M	11452M	62136M	206491M	2879167M
874716M	1053172M	1675040M	Total Assets ($)	567M	7543M	3665M	38095M	84436M	1540734M

© RMA 2010

M = $ thousand   MM = $ million
See Pages 9 through 22 for Explanation of Ratios and Data

Current Data Sorted by Assets   —   Comparative Historical Data

Type of Statement

	0-500M	500M-2MM	2-10MM	10-50MM	50-100MM	100-250MM	Type of Statement	4/1/05-3/31/06 ALL	4/1/06-3/31/07 ALL
			1	5	2	1	Unqualified	12	5
		1	4	4			Reviewed	10	10
			3	2			Compiled	7	6
				1			Tax Returns		1
			6	6	2	1	Other	15	9
		8 (4/1-9/30/09)		31 (10/1/09-3/31/10)					
		1	14	18	4	2	NUMBER OF STATEMENTS	44	31

Assets / Liabilities / Income (%)

0-500M	500M-2MM	2-10MM	10-50MM	50-100MM	100-250MM		4/1/05-3/31/06 ALL	4/1/06-3/31/07 ALL
%	%	%	%	%	%	**ASSETS**	%	%
		14.0	12.5			Cash & Equivalents	8.9	6.7
		23.8	21.6			Trade Receivables (net)	22.3	25.8
		27.7	25.4			Inventory	27.3	27.2
		3.2	3.2			All Other Current	3.1	2.5
		68.8	62.6			Total Current	61.7	62.2
		23.6	29.7			Fixed Assets (net)	25.3	26.8
		4.3	4.3			Intangibles (net)	4.8	6.7
		3.3	3.3			All Other Non-Current	8.3	4.3
		100.0	100.0			Total	100.0	100.0
						LIABILITIES		
		6.7	5.8			Notes Payable-Short Term	10.6	8.5
		3.4	2.9			Cur. Mat.-L.T.D.	2.5	2.4
		13.6	9.7			Trade Payables	14.1	17.3
		.1	.9			Income Taxes Payable	.1	.9
		5.4	9.7			All Other Current	7.2	8.2
		29.1	29.0			Total Current	34.6	37.3
		5.5	9.8			Long-Term Debt	8.7	12.0
		.2	.8			Deferred Taxes	1.0	1.0
		1.2	3.9			All Other Non-Current	4.7	6.3
		63.9	56.5			Net Worth	51.0	43.4
		100.0	100.0			Total Liabilities & Net Worth	100.0	100.0
						INCOME DATA		
		100.0	100.0			Net Sales	100.0	100.0
		38.3	35.1			Gross Profit	30.6	31.4
		29.7	26.0			Operating Expenses	22.4	23.7
		8.6	9.1			Operating Profit	8.2	7.7
		-.1	.7			All Other Expenses (net)	1.3	1.3
		8.7	8.4			Profit Before Taxes	6.9	6.4

(0-500M and 500M-2MM columns marked "DATA NOT AVAILABLE")

Ratios

2-10MM	10-50MM		4/1/05-3/31/06 ALL	4/1/06-3/31/07 ALL
4.6	3.0	Current	3.3	2.7
2.6	2.4		1.9	1.6
1.5	1.8		1.1	1.2
2.4	1.8	Quick	2.1	1.4
1.7	1.2		.7	.9
.6	.9		.5	.6
27 13.7	32 11.2	Sales/Receivables	28 13.0	28 13.2
29 12.5	39 9.5		37 9.9	37 10.0
39 9.4	44 8.3		44 8.3	46 7.9
36 10.1	43 8.5	Cost of Sales/Inventory	41 8.9	37 9.8
59 6.2	56 6.5		60 6.1	59 6.2
112 3.3	86 4.2		91 4.0	83 4.4
20 18.3	17 21.6	Cost of Sales/Payables	18 20.0	26 14.2
29 12.7	28 13.3		31 11.9	35 10.5
37 10.0	37 9.9		44 8.4	48 7.6
5.6	4.2	Sales/Working Capital	4.0	6.4
6.9	6.1		8.1	13.8
12.5	10.4		31.7	23.3
116.9	27.7	EBIT/Interest	28.8	18.0
(12) 34.2	(16) 10.9		(36) 5.9	(29) 5.0
10.3	7.4		1.9	2.2
		Net Profit + Depr., Dep., Amort./Cur. Mat. L/T/D	6.8	6.0
			(17) 4.4	(14) 3.1
			2.3	1.7
.2	.3	Fixed/Worth	.2	.2
.4	.6		.5	.8
.6	.9		.9	1.4
.3	.4	Debt/Worth	.4	.7
.7	.6		.9	1.7
1.0	1.2		2.6	3.0
41.6	39.8	% Profit Before Taxes/Tangible Net Worth	50.8	60.6
32.9	(16) 24.5		(42) 18.5	(30) 36.4
17.2	12.4		3.4	15.7
27.9	26.5	% Profit Before Taxes/Total Assets	19.0	22.3
17.8	13.6		9.5	11.3
12.5	6.5		2.2	4.4
20.8	10.4	Sales/Net Fixed Assets	20.7	22.6
12.7	6.6		9.3	11.3
10.0	5.7		5.1	5.4
3.3	2.6	Sales/Total Assets	3.0	3.4
2.8	1.9		1.9	2.4
2.1	1.4		1.4	1.7
.8	1.8	% Depr., Dep., Amort./Sales	.6	1.0
(11) 1.7	2.0		(39) 2.2	(28) 1.6
4.6	3.2		3.3	2.4
		% Officers', Directors' Owners' Comp/Sales		

Dollar Data

0-500M	500M-2MM	2-10MM	10-50MM	50-100MM	100-250MM		4/1/05-3/31/06 ALL	4/1/06-3/31/07 ALL
	8872M	219845M	788413M	434593M	169074M	Net Sales ($)	1364510M	846261M
	1931M	77069M	407053M	307933M	281079M	Total Assets ($)	913026M	444037M

M = $ thousand   MM = $ million
See Pages 9 through 22 for Explanation of Ratios and Data

Comparative Historical Data | Current Data Sorted by Sales

			Type of Statement	0-1MM	1-3MM	3-5MM	5-10MM	10-25MM	25MM & OVER
7	7	9	Unqualified					2	7
9	11	8	Reviewed					2	5
7	5	6	Compiled	1	2			3	1
1		1	Tax Returns	2					1
20	12	15	Other				2	5	8
4/1/07-3/31/08 ALL	4/1/08-3/31/09 ALL	4/1/09-3/31/10 ALL				8 (4/1-9/30/09)		31 (10/1/09-3/31/10)	
44	35	39	**NUMBER OF STATEMENTS**				5	12	22
%	%	%	**ASSETS**	%	%	%	%	%	%
6.6	8.1	12.1	Cash & Equivalents					14.2	11.8
18.6	20.7	22.2	Trade Receivables (net)					22.0	22.3
24.9	27.8	26.8	Inventory					27.8	26.1
3.7	2.6	3.6	All Other Current					3.1	3.5
53.9	59.2	64.8	Total Current					67.2	63.7
31.2	29.5	26.9	Fixed Assets (net)					19.9	29.6
8.5	5.0	4.5	Intangibles (net)					9.8	2.3
6.4	6.2	3.8	All Other Non-Current					3.1	4.4
100.0	100.0	100.0	Total					100.0	100.0
			LIABILITIES						
8.9	10.9	7.0	Notes Payable-Short Term					6.8	6.7
3.6	3.2	3.2	Cur. Mat.-L.T.D.					2.3	2.3
15.0	15.4	11.7	Trade Payables					11.1	11.7
.3	.4	.5	Income Taxes Payable					.0	.8
6.7	6.5	7.4	All Other Current					5.3	8.9
34.5	36.4	29.7	Total Current					25.5	30.4
17.7	11.1	8.4	Long-Term Debt					4.8	9.3
1.3	.9	.5	Deferred Taxes					.0	.8
5.9	3.6	3.1	All Other Non-Current					2.4	3.7
40.6	48.1	58.3	Net Worth					67.4	55.7
100.0	100.0	100.0	Total Liabilities & Net Worth					100.0	100.0
			INCOME DATA						
100.0	100.0	100.0	Net Sales					100.0	100.0
34.5	31.4	35.5	Gross Profit					38.3	33.5
28.0	24.3	26.1	Operating Expenses					29.8	22.6
6.6	7.2	9.4	Operating Profit					8.5	10.8
1.3	.9	.5	All Other Expenses (net)					.4	.8
5.3	6.3	8.9	Profit Before Taxes					8.1	10.1
			RATIOS						
2.9	2.7	3.1	Current					5.6	3.1
1.4	1.6	2.4						2.8	2.2
1.1	1.3	1.7						1.7	1.8
1.3	1.7	1.9	Quick					2.3	1.8
.7	.9	1.3						1.7	1.3
.4	.5	.7						.7	.7
25 14.8	26 14.3	28 12.8	Sales/Receivables					28 13.1	35 10.4
33 11.1	36 10.1	38 9.6						33 11.2	41 8.9
44 8.3	48 7.6	44 8.3						41 9.0	47 7.7
43 8.6	39 9.3	43 8.4	Cost of Sales/Inventory					48 7.5	45 8.2
61 5.9	70 5.2	66 5.6						59 6.2	68 5.3
100 3.6	107 3.4	116 3.2						114 3.2	121 3.0
24 15.0	20 17.9	21 17.3	Cost of Sales/Payables					18 20.3	22 16.9
40 9.0	31 11.8	28 12.9						28 12.9	29 12.4
54 6.8	47 7.8	36 10.2						35 10.4	37 9.9
4.7	5.4	4.0	Sales/Working Capital					4.2	3.5
16.4	10.3	6.5						6.1	4.8
61.1	24.6	10.6						10.2	9.1
12.4	14.6	43.5	EBIT/Interest					129.9	33.8
(41) 3.6	(32) 6.2	(35) 13.1						(11) 21.9	(19) 12.9
1.8	2.8	7.4						8.9	7.4
5.8	8.2	11.9	Net Profit + Depr., Dep.,						10.7
(19) 2.7	(12) 4.2	(16) 4.9	Amort./Cur. Mat. L/T/D						(11) 5.2
1.3	2.7	2.6							3.1
.4	.3	.3	Fixed/Worth					.2	.3
.7	.7	.5						.3	.6
2.7	1.3	.8						.5	.8
.8	.6	.4	Debt/Worth					.3	.5
1.6	1.3	.7						.4	.6
4.9	2.6	1.3						1.1	1.2
56.2	54.3	38.7	% Profit Before Taxes/Tangible					38.8	39.4
(40) 21.0	27.3	(37) 24.0	Net Worth					(11) 32.7	(21) 22.1
7.3	13.8	15.6						17.1	15.7
17.8	18.1	24.6	% Profit Before Taxes/Total					23.0	26.5
8.2	10.2	14.4	Assets					17.4	13.6
3.2	6.6	8.5						8.0	8.6
14.6	21.5	14.3	Sales/Net Fixed Assets					21.1	11.9
6.6	8.7	8.7						10.7	7.1
4.0	4.3	5.8						6.9	4.5
2.9	2.8	3.0	Sales/Total Assets					3.2	2.6
1.8	2.1	2.0						2.1	1.7
1.4	1.6	1.4						1.7	1.3
1.2	1.3	1.3	% Depr., Dep., Amort./Sales					1.1	1.5
(41) 1.9	(31) 1.7	(36) 1.9						(11) 1.9	2.0
3.5	3.3	3.3						4.6	3.2
		1.1	% Officers', Directors'						
		(10) 2.0	Owners' Comp/Sales						
		3.9							
1621104M	1139553M	1620797M	Net Sales ($)				40777M	200808M	1379212M
1015134M	655016M	1075065M	Total Assets ($)				13779M	93065M	968221M

Note: For the 0-1MM, 1-3MM, and 3-5MM sales categories, the Assets and Liabilities sections read vertically: "DATA NOT AVAILABLE".

MANUFACTURING—Mayonnaise, Dressing, and Other Prepared Sauce Manufacturing NAICS 311941

	Current Data Sorted by Assets						Comparative Historical Data	

Type of Statement

0-500M	500M-2MM	2-10MM	10-50MM	50-100MM	100-250MM		4/1/05-3/31/06 ALL	4/1/06-3/31/07 ALL
		1	2	2	2	Unqualified	7	6
	1	3	2			Reviewed	7	7
	1	4	1			Compiled	3	5
2	2					Tax Returns	2	3
	1	4	6			Other	8	10
		6 (4/1-9/30/09)	28 (10/1/09-3/31/10)					
2	5	12	11	2	2	**NUMBER OF STATEMENTS**	27	31
%	%	%	%	%	%	**ASSETS**	%	%
		7.9	9.7			Cash & Equivalents	6.8	3.8
		21.9	19.3			Trade Receivables (net)	20.2	18.3
		34.1	20.8			Inventory	24.6	26.2
		1.6	1.3			All Other Current	1.5	1.6
		65.5	51.1			Total Current	53.2	49.9
		30.4	28.7			Fixed Assets (net)	35.7	40.0
		2.4	15.5			Intangibles (net)	3.9	7.0
		1.7	4.7			All Other Non-Current	7.2	3.2
		100.0	100.0			Total	100.0	100.0
						LIABILITIES		
		13.1	8.5			Notes Payable-Short Term	11.7	13.1
		3.2	2.7			Cur. Mat.-L.T.D.	3.5	3.2
		22.4	8.9			Trade Payables	15.2	12.2
		.9	.4			Income Taxes Payable	.3	.2
		13.2	7.9			All Other Current	7.3	7.6
		52.8	28.5			Total Current	38.0	36.4
		10.8	26.1			Long-Term Debt	16.0	22.7
		.3	.5			Deferred Taxes	.7	1.3
		3.6	9.5			All Other Non-Current	6.2	8.6
		32.5	35.4			Net Worth	39.1	31.0
		100.0	100.0			Total Liabilities & Net Worth	100.0	100.0
						INCOME DATA		
		100.0	100.0			Net Sales	100.0	100.0
		26.5	26.7			Gross Profit	25.5	29.2
		24.5	22.3			Operating Expenses	21.8	24.8
		2.0	4.3			Operating Profit	3.7	4.4
		.5	.7			All Other Expenses (net)	1.0	2.1
		1.6	3.6			Profit Before Taxes	2.7	2.3
						RATIOS		
		2.7	2.4			Current	1.9	2.5
		1.2	1.9				1.5	1.4
		.8	1.3				1.2	1.1
		1.8	1.7			Quick	1.0	1.3
		.4	1.0				.7	.7
		.3	.5				.5	.4
		21 17.3	26 13.8			Sales/Receivables	19 18.8	25 14.9
		28 13.0	33 11.0				26 14.0	32 11.4
		33 10.9	39 9.3				39 9.3	43 8.5
		37 9.9	30 12.4			Cost of Sales/Inventory	30 12.0	40 9.2
		51 7.2	43 8.5				47 7.8	65 5.7
		78 4.7	57 6.4				78 4.7	98 3.7
		17 21.5	14 25.8			Cost of Sales/Payables	15 24.2	13 27.2
		30 12.1	19 18.8				27 13.3	27 13.5
		71 5.1	27 13.3				37 10.0	39 9.4
		6.1	5.7			Sales/Working Capital	10.1	7.1
		20.5	11.3				14.1	16.4
		-32.6	17.1				38.5	56.6
		32.6	20.0			EBIT/Interest	14.7	6.2
		10.6	5.1				(26) 3.9	(29) 2.1
		2.6	2.0				1.2	1.3
						Net Profit + Depr., Dep., Amort./Cur. Mat. L/T/D	6.5	2.4
							(12) 2.9	(11) 1.9
							.9	.6
		.5	.4			Fixed/Worth	.6	1.0
		1.0	1.1				1.1	1.5
		1.9	2.5				1.7	4.5
		.8	.7			Debt/Worth	1.0	1.2
		2.3	2.7				1.9	2.0
		3.8	3.3				3.1	8.2
		66.9				% Profit Before Taxes/Tangible Net Worth	31.5	26.2
		(11) 32.5					(25) 18.8	(25) 11.3
		11.9					2.2	2.4
		20.3	16.6			% Profit Before Taxes/Total Assets	15.2	9.2
		7.9	6.2				6.0	3.7
		2.9	4.1				2.0	.7
		11.3	26.9			Sales/Net Fixed Assets	16.0	11.4
		9.2	7.5				6.9	6.3
		8.0	3.1				4.9	2.0
		3.7	3.1			Sales/Total Assets	3.3	3.0
		3.1	2.0				2.3	1.9
		1.9	1.3				2.1	1.0
		1.0	.8			% Depr., Dep., Amort./Sales	1.2	1.2
		(11) 1.5	1.7				(24) 2.2	(30) 2.3
		2.7	4.2				3.4	4.2
						% Officers', Directors', Owners' Comp/Sales		
1902M	20549M	194816M	532709M	232389M	846002M	Net Sales ($)	1308831M	1347150M
317M	4025M	68174M	256430M	145470M	370424M	Total Assets ($)	564477M	746142M

M = $ thousand   MM = $ million
See Pages 9 through 22 for Explanation of Ratios and Data

Comparative Historical Data | Current Data Sorted by Sales

08	09	10	Type of Statement	0-1MM	1-3MM	3-5MM	5-10MM	10-25MM	25MM & OVER
4	8	7	Unqualified					1	6
9	10	6	Reviewed			1		3	2
2	5	6	Compiled			2	1	3	
2	2	4	Tax Returns	1	3				
10	11	11	Other				2	4	5
4/1/07-3/31/08 ALL	4/1/08-3/31/09 ALL	4/1/09-3/31/10 ALL			6 (4/1-9/30/09)			28 (10/1/09-3/31/10)	
27	36	34	NUMBER OF STATEMENTS	1	3	3	3	11	13
%	%	%	**ASSETS**	%	%	%	%	%	%
8.6	6.8	10.3	Cash & Equivalents					12.7	7.3
16.8	21.3	20.0	Trade Receivables (net)					20.9	21.4
23.8	22.6	29.3	Inventory					25.3	24.7
2.1	1.0	1.2	All Other Current					1.1	1.6
51.4	51.8	60.7	Total Current					60.0	55.1
36.2	36.8	28.8	Fixed Assets (net)					33.1	31.7
5.9	4.3	6.2	Intangibles (net)					5.1	6.5
6.6	7.1	4.3	All Other Non-Current					1.7	6.7
100.0	100.0	100.0	Total					100.0	100.0
			LIABILITIES						
12.3	13.7	10.6	Notes Payable-Short Term					10.8	7.2
3.7	4.2	2.6	Cur. Mat.-L.T.D.					3.7	2.9
12.5	15.0	16.2	Trade Payables					21.1	12.3
.9	.5	.7	Income Taxes Payable					1.1	.3
5.9	8.2	19.5	All Other Current					6.4	13.4
35.2	41.5	49.6	Total Current					43.2	36.1
19.4	19.0	15.0	Long-Term Debt					14.2	18.1
.5	.4	.3	Deferred Taxes					.8	.0
3.9	10.4	6.1	All Other Non-Current					5.0	10.2
41.0	28.7	29.0	Net Worth					36.9	35.6
100.0	100.0	100.0	Total Liabilties & Net Worth					100.0	100.0
			INCOME DATA						
100.0	100.0	100.0	Net Sales					100.0	100.0
25.6	27.5	30.2	Gross Profit					26.2	28.7
20.0	23.0	25.9	Operating Expenses					23.7	21.8
5.6	4.5	4.3	Operating Profit					2.5	6.9
1.2	1.3	.5	All Other Expenses (net)					.7	.3
4.4	3.2	3.8	Profit Before Taxes					1.9	6.6
			RATIOS						
2.1	1.9	2.6	Current					4.1	2.3
1.5	1.3	1.7						1.2	1.9
1.1	1.0	1.0						.9	1.2
1.1	1.1	1.7	Quick					2.3	1.6
.7	.6	.8						.6	1.0
.4	.4	.4						.4	.5
23 15.8	24 15.3	21 17.8	Sales/Receivables					24 15.0	27 13.6
30 12.1	30 12.4	28 13.0						28 13.1	33 11.0
36 10.2	38 9.5	35 10.4						34 10.9	40 9.2
33 11.1	31 12.0	30 12.0	Cost of Sales/Inventory					27 13.3	30 12.1
49 7.5	43 8.6	47 7.7						39 9.3	43 8.5
90 4.0	61 6.0	76 4.8						57 6.4	86 4.3
18 19.9	16 23.0	16 23.0	Cost of Sales/Payables					12 30.8	16 23.1
25 14.6	29 12.5	24 15.2						24 15.5	24 15.3
32 11.3	35 10.4	41 8.9						55 6.6	33 11.2
6.8	9.2	7.5	Sales/Working Capital					5.5	7.4
14.5	26.8	13.0						26.2	11.3
50.2	282.0	-761.3						-36.5	24.9
6.0	5.9	24.4	EBIT/Interest					36.0	22.3
3.6 (35)	3.1 (33)	10.2						11.1	8.0
1.6	1.8	4.1						2.1	4.7
4.7	5.5	9.5	Net Profit + Depr., Dep., Amort./Cur. Mat. L/T/D						
2.3 (14)	1.6 (13)	3.5 (14)							
1.1	1.2	2.2							
.6	.8	.5	Fixed/Worth					.5	.5
1.2	1.3	1.0						1.2	1.0
3.4	5.4	2.2						2.0	1.9
.8	1.1	.6	Debt/Worth					.4	.7
1.5	2.2	2.1						2.4	1.2
5.7	12.5	3.8						3.8	3.3
41.3	66.9	70.6	% Profit Before Taxes/Tangible Net Worth						69.9
14.8 (24)	18.0 (30)	27.2 (30)							(12) 29.9
2.6	6.6	13.4							11.8
8.6	11.6	20.9	% Profit Before Taxes/Total Assets					20.8	20.0
5.5	5.4	9.7						8.5	10.9
2.7	2.7	4.3						4.4	4.6
9.8	11.4	25.5	Sales/Net Fixed Assets					11.3	22.2
6.8	7.7	8.9						8.9	8.2
3.3	3.4	5.1						4.3	3.9
2.8	3.5	3.7	Sales/Total Assets					3.7	3.2
2.1	2.5	2.7						3.0	2.4
1.2	1.6	1.6						1.9	1.6
1.9	1.1	.8	% Depr., Dep., Amort./Sales					1.0	1.1
3.1 (25)	2.7 (33)	1.5 (29)						1.5	(12) 2.0
4.3	3.6	3.3						3.6	3.7
			% Officers', Directors' Owners' Comp/Sales						
1694387M	1963688M	1828367M	Net Sales ($)	83M	6380M	11796M	27567M	187383M	1595158M
918695M	867253M	844840M	Total Assets ($)	57M	1629M	4005M	30183M	75381M	733585M

M = $ thousand   MM = $ million
See Pages 9 through 22 for Explanation of Ratios and Data

MANUFACTURING—Spice and Extract Manufacturing NAICS 311942

Current Data Sorted by Assets							Comparative Historical Data	
		1	2	1	1	**Type of Statement**		
		2	2			Unqualified	7	9
	2	1				Reviewed	2	4
	1	2				Compiled	2	5
		7	4	1	1	Tax Returns		2
	7 (4/1-9/30/09)		21 (10/1/09-3/31/10)			Other	11	17
							4/1/05-	4/1/06-
							3/31/06	3/31/07
0-500M	500M-2MM	2-10MM	10-50MM	50-100MM	100-250MM		ALL	ALL
3		13	8	2	2	**NUMBER OF STATEMENTS**	22	37
%	%	%	%	%	%	**ASSETS**	%	%
		9.1				Cash & Equivalents	9.8	6.8
		22.1				Trade Receivables (net)	20.3	22.3
		27.9				Inventory	24.6	28.7
		2.8				All Other Current	5.1	3.6
		62.0				Total Current	59.7	61.4
		29.5				Fixed Assets (net)	23.3	27.9
		2.2				Intangibles (net)	5.9	2.9
		6.4				All Other Non-Current	11.1	7.9
		100.0				Total	100.0	100.0
						LIABILITIES		
		13.3				Notes Payable-Short Term	12.8	10.0
		2.0				Cur. Mat.-L.T.D.	3.0	1.7
		15.1				Trade Payables	10.9	10.9
		1.9				Income Taxes Payable	.1	.1
		3.7				All Other Current	13.3	10.1
		36.0				Total Current	40.0	32.8
		5.3				Long-Term Debt	8.4	20.1
		.0				Deferred Taxes	.4	.3
		10.5				All Other Non-Current	11.2	8.3
		48.2				Net Worth	40.0	38.5
		100.0				Total Liabilties & Net Worth	100.0	100.0
						INCOME DATA		
		100.0				Net Sales	100.0	100.0
		30.2				Gross Profit	32.6	32.6
		26.3				Operating Expenses	25.5	25.2
		3.9				Operating Profit	7.1	7.4
		.5				All Other Expenses (net)	.0	.6
		3.4				Profit Before Taxes	7.1	6.8
						RATIOS		
		3.3					2.2	3.3
		1.7				Current	1.4	2.0
		1.2					1.2	1.2
		1.9					1.2	1.5
		.8				Quick	.9	.7
		.4					.4	.5
	22	16.6					21	17.0	27	13.3
	30	12.3				Sales/Receivables	37	9.9	39	9.4
	46	7.9					50	7.3	50	7.3
	53	6.9					39	9.3	47	7.8
	60	6.0				Cost of Sales/Inventory	56	6.5	63	5.8
	90	4.1					101	3.6	110	3.3
	26	14.1					20	18.1	18	20.5
	31	11.8				Cost of Sales/Payables	33	11.2	30	12.2
	36	10.1					49	7.4	44	8.3
		5.5					5.7	4.8
		12.5				Sales/Working Capital	11.3	8.3
		24.8					29.0	29.2
		69.2					16.4	16.0
		7.8				EBIT/Interest	(21)	9.5	(35)	5.1
		2.2					3.9	1.1
						Net Profit + Depr., Dep.,		8.8
						Amort./Cur. Mat. L/T/D	(10)	4.9
								1.9
		.4					.2	.1
		.6				Fixed/Worth	.6	.6
		.8					1.8	1.2
		.7					.8	.5
		1.1				Debt/Worth	1.2	1.1
		2.5					5.7	3.8
		35.8				% Profit Before Taxes/Tangible	42.5	61.1
		19.8				Net Worth	(19)	30.2	(33)	17.0
		10.0					10.2	5.5
		23.0				% Profit Before Taxes/Total	20.9	20.0
		11.5				Assets	8.7	7.4
		2.5					4.7	.7
		17.6					24.5	33.1
		12.4				Sales/Net Fixed Assets	10.9	12.3
		6.0					3.9	3.2
		3.3					2.4	2.9
		2.2				Sales/Total Assets	1.9	1.8
		1.5					1.3	1.4
		1.1					.9	1.1
	(11)	2.5				% Depr., Dep., Amort./Sales	1.9	(31)	2.1
		4.7					3.0	3.4
						% Officers', Directors'		2.1
						Owners' Comp/Sales	(10)	2.5
								7.9
15078M	136110M	319003M	140148M	600797M		Net Sales ($)	881821M	1113986M
4441M	65259M	173290M	133617M	270775M		Total Assets ($)	546708M	797527M

Note: Column "0-500M" region marked "DATA NOT AVAILABLE".

© RMA 2010

M = $ thousand   MM = $ million
See Pages 9 through 22 for Explanation of Ratios and Data

Comparative Historical Data / Current Data Sorted by Sales

Type of Statement							7 (4/1-9/30/09)		21 (10/1/09-3/31/10)		
					0-1MM	1-3MM	3-5MM	5-10MM	10-25MM	25MM & OVER
Unqualified	7	6	5							
Reviewed	5	3	4						1	4
Compiled	5	3	3					1	3	1
Tax Returns		3	3			1	1	2		
Other	14	11	13							

	4/1/07-3/31/08 ALL	4/1/08-3/31/09 ALL	4/1/09-3/31/10 ALL	0-1MM	1-3MM	3-5MM	5-10MM	10-25MM	25MM & OVER
NUMBER OF STATEMENTS	31	26	28		1	2	7	9	9
	%	%	%	%	%	%	%	%	%
ASSETS									
Cash & Equivalents	6.1	6.6	8.6						
Trade Receivables (net)	18.9	17.6	19.4	D					
Inventory	26.0	32.9	33.8	A					
All Other Current	4.8	1.5	2.5	T					
Total Current	55.9	58.6	64.4	A					
Fixed Assets (net)	37.1	33.0	28.4						
Intangibles (net)	3.0	3.2	2.5	N					
All Other Non-Current	4.0	5.2	4.7	O					
Total	100.0	100.0	100.0	T					
LIABILITIES									
Notes Payable-Short Term	8.1	11.3	9.7	A					
Cur. Mat.-L.T.D.	4.6	1.5	4.3	V					
Trade Payables	12.2	15.0	12.6	A					
Income Taxes Payable	.1	.4	1.0	I					
All Other Current	9.6	7.8	6.3	L					
Total Current	34.6	36.0	33.9	A					
Long-Term Debt	18.5	15.6	13.7	B					
Deferred Taxes	.4	.6	.4	L					
All Other Non-Current	4.8	13.9	7.8	E					
Net Worth	41.8	33.9	44.3						
Total Liabilities & Net Worth	100.0	100.0	100.0						
INCOME DATA									
Net Sales	100.0	100.0	100.0						
Gross Profit	30.8	26.7	30.3						
Operating Expenses	23.1	23.4	25.1						
Operating Profit	7.6	3.3	5.2						
All Other Expenses (net)	1.3	1.6	.6						
Profit Before Taxes	6.3	1.7	4.6						
RATIOS									
Current	2.4	2.8	3.7						
	1.5	1.5	2.2						
	1.2	1.2	1.5						
Quick	1.1	1.1	1.7						
	.8	.7	.9						
	.5	.5	.5						
Sales/Receivables	23 15.7	22 16.7	21 17.5						
	33 10.9	33 11.0	29 12.4						
	44 8.3	39 9.3	42 8.6						
Cost of Sales/Inventory	36 10.2	53 6.9	55 6.7						
	55 6.6	79 4.6	85 4.3						
	93 3.9	100 3.7	106 3.5						
Cost of Sales/Payables	18 20.0	25 14.6	21 17.1						
	28 12.9	35 10.3	29 12.5						
	52 7.0	44 8.3	37 9.7						
Sales/Working Capital	5.4	5.0	4.2						
	11.5	8.6	6.9						
	23.4	19.7	13.8						
EBIT/Interest	8.8	10.1	20.4						
	3.6	(25) 2.2	7.0						
	1.5	.5	2.2						
Net Profit + Depr., Dep., Amort./Cur. Mat. L/T/D									
Fixed/Worth	.3	.4	.4						
	.9	.8	.6						
	2.2	1.6	1.0						
Debt/Worth	.7	.9	.6						
	1.2	1.6	1.3						
	2.9	3.4	3.8						
% Profit Before Taxes/Tangible Net Worth	50.2	46.8	44.9						
	(28) 21.8	(22) 12.0	(26) 18.5						
	3.3	-2.2	10.1						
% Profit Before Taxes/Total Assets	16.7	9.5	23.1						
	7.6	3.0	9.5						
	1.2	-1.0	2.9						
Sales/Net Fixed Assets	13.7	11.5	17.3						
	3.6	6.1	10.1						
	2.5	3.4	5.2						
Sales/Total Assets	2.7	2.5	2.8						
	1.7	1.6	2.1						
	1.3	1.3	1.3						
% Depr., Dep., Amort./Sales	1.0	1.3	1.2						
	(27) 3.0	(24) 2.2	(23) 2.0						
	3.8	3.5	3.1						
% Officers', Directors', Owners' Comp/Sales									
Net Sales ($)	1121823M	929724M	1211136M		2826M	8488M	54536M	149176M	996110M
Total Assets ($)	820683M	689274M	647382M		1048M	4818M	26236M	91658M	523622M

M = $ thousand   MM = $ million
See Pages 9 through 22 for Explanation of Ratios and Data

Current Data Sorted by Assets							Comparative Historical Data	
		1	3	1	4	Type of Statement		
		1	1			Unqualified	7	5
1	2	3				Reviewed	1	3
1	1	1				Compiled	2	3
	2	4				Tax Returns	1	
	4 (4/1-9/30/09)		2	3	2	Other	3	6
			29 (10/1/09-3/31/10)				4/1/05- 3/31/06	4/1/06- 3/31/07
0-500M	500M-2MM	2-10MM	10-50MM	50-100MM	100-250MM		ALL	ALL
2	5	10	6	4	6	NUMBER OF STATEMENTS	14	17
%	%	%	%	%	%	ASSETS	%	%
		13.4				Cash & Equivalents	2.4	5.5
		18.4				Trade Receivables (net)	25.4	24.0
		15.1				Inventory	22.1	15.9
		.3				All Other Current	2.2	4.3
		47.3				Total Current	52.1	49.7
		35.9				Fixed Assets (net)	39.1	37.6
		13.2				Intangibles (net)	6.2	9.2
		3.6				All Other Non-Current	2.6	3.5
		100.0				Total	100.0	100.0
						LIABILITIES		
		6.6				Notes Payable-Short Term	7.4	7.6
		3.1				Cur. Mat.-L.T.D.	4.4	4.1
		19.1				Trade Payables	21.8	18.3
		.3				Income Taxes Payable	.0	.0
		12.3				All Other Current	8.2	11.7
		41.3				Total Current	41.8	41.8
		19.3				Long-Term Debt	29.1	17.4
		.0				Deferred Taxes	1.1	.5
		8.4				All Other Non-Current	15.0	6.5
		31.1				Net Worth	13.1	33.9
		100.0				Total Liabilities & Net Worth	100.0	100.0
						INCOME DATA		
		100.0				Net Sales	100.0	100.0
		28.4				Gross Profit	25.3	26.1
		21.6				Operating Expenses	22.9	22.7
		6.8				Operating Profit	2.4	3.4
		.8				All Other Expenses (net)	.8	1.0
		6.0				Profit Before Taxes	1.6	2.4
						RATIOS		
		3.2					1.7	1.9
		1.1				Current	1.1	1.2
		.7					.9	.9
		2.3					.9	1.1
		.7				Quick	.5	.8
		.5					.5	.5
	17	21.6					20 18.6	21 17.4
	20	18.0				Sales/Receivables	26 13.8	32 11.5
	30	12.3					37 9.8	45 8.0
	9	39.6					12 31.5	12 30.8
	14	26.9				Cost of Sales/Inventory	33 11.1	28 13.1
	28	12.9					45 8.1	46 7.9
	21	17.2					24 15.0	21 17.3
	33	10.9				Cost of Sales/Payables	31 11.6	29 12.6
	47	7.8					40 9.1	43 8.6
		9.8					15.9	9.1
		127.9				Sales/Working Capital	45.5	52.4
		-38.1					-93.4	-61.0
							5.8	7.3
						EBIT/Interest	(13) 2.2	(16) 3.5
							.9	1.3
						Net Profit + Depr., Dep., Amort./Cur. Mat. L/T/D		
		.5					1.1	.7
		1.8				Fixed/Worth	1.9	1.6
		-15.4					-5.5	3.0
		.5					1.6	.9
		3.8				Debt/Worth	3.4	1.9
		-20.8					-9.6	11.0
							37.8	61.0
						% Profit Before Taxes/Tangible Net Worth	(10) 20.1	(15) 27.6
							-7.5	4.0
		18.0					9.2	10.6
		12.2				% Profit Before Taxes/Total Assets	5.0	6.3
		6.9					-2.0	1.3
		14.5					10.8	14.6
		7.4				Sales/Net Fixed Assets	6.3	6.7
		4.1					5.6	4.3
		4.5					4.5	3.7
		2.3				Sales/Total Assets	2.8	2.5
		1.8					2.4	1.9
							1.7	1.1
						% Depr., Dep., Amort./Sales	(11) 2.0	(15) 2.1
							2.7	3.1
						% Officers', Directors' Owners' Comp/Sales		
23483M	11580M	140635M	433860M	802561M	2647659M	Net Sales ($)	1763926M	2232583M
520M	4203M	52764M	197056M	301973M	891957M	Total Assets ($)	568087M	740718M

M = $ thousand   MM = $ million
See Pages 9 through 22 for Explanation of Ratios and Data

Comparative Historical Data				Current Data Sorted by Sales					

				Type of Statement	0-1MM	1-3MM	3-5MM	5-10MM	10-25MM	25MM & OVER
5	7	9	Unqualified					2		7
3	5	2	Reviewed				1			1
2	4	6	Compiled		2	1	2			1
	2	3	Tax Returns			1				2
10	9	13	Other	1	1			4		7
					4 (4/1-9/30/09)			29 (10/1/09-3/31/10)		
10 4/1/07-3/31/08 ALL	9 4/1/08-3/31/09 ALL	13 4/1/09-3/31/10 ALL								
20	27	33	**NUMBER OF STATEMENTS**	1	3	3	2	8		16
%	%	%	**ASSETS**	%	%	%	%	%		%
11.0	6.2	10.6	Cash & Equivalents							8.1
17.4	18.4	18.9	Trade Receivables (net)							21.0
14.0	17.5	15.0	Inventory							15.0
3.2	1.5	1.4	All Other Current							2.1
45.7	43.6	45.8	Total Current							46.2
35.5	40.8	40.0	Fixed Assets (net)							42.2
14.5	9.9	8.8	Intangibles (net)							6.9
4.3	5.7	5.4	All Other Non-Current							4.7
100.0	100.0	100.0	Total							100.0
			LIABILITIES							
5.4	8.0	6.6	Notes Payable-Short Term							3.4
3.1	3.6	3.1	Cur. Mat.-L.T.D.							4.3
19.4	20.6	20.0	Trade Payables							20.8
.0	.1	.2	Income Taxes Payable							.3
15.8	9.7	9.0	All Other Current							10.3
43.8	42.0	39.0	Total Current							39.0
23.0	29.4	23.7	Long-Term Debt							25.6
.1	.9	.6	Deferred Taxes							1.2
2.9	3.1	9.4	All Other Non-Current							7.6
30.1	24.6	27.4	Net Worth							26.6
100.0	100.0	100.0	Total Liabilities & Net Worth							100.0
			INCOME DATA							
100.0	100.0	100.0	Net Sales							100.0
25.7	27.9	26.0	Gross Profit							20.7
24.4	26.9	22.9	Operating Expenses							17.3
1.3	1.0	3.1	Operating Profit							3.4
1.3	1.3	1.4	All Other Expenses (net)							1.1
.1	-.4	1.7	Profit Before Taxes							2.3
			RATIOS							
2.1	2.4	2.5								1.7
1.0	.9	1.1	Current							1.0
.7	.8	.8								.8
1.3	1.0	1.6								1.1
.6	.6	.6	Quick							.6
.4	.4	.4								.4
20 18.1	19 19.4	19 19.3								21 17.1
24 15.0	23 15.8	25 14.6	Sales/Receivables							25 14.5
31 11.7	29 12.4	31 11.8								32 11.4
17 21.8	15 24.8	10 35.9								12 29.7
24 15.2	31 11.9	17 21.0	Cost of Sales/Inventory							18 20.8
43 8.4	57 6.4	42 8.7								36 10.1
23 15.8	20 18.1	20 18.7								21 17.0
30 12.3	32 11.5	30 12.1	Cost of Sales/Payables							29 12.4
43 8.5	45 8.2	49 7.5								41 9.0
14.0	11.4	11.9								13.0
NM	-46.2	93.5	Sales/Working Capital							153.7
-17.6	-23.4	-32.4								-36.5
5.0	5.2	13.2								6.0
(16) 1.4	2.4	(30) 4.7	EBIT/Interest							4.2
-.8	.6	1.3								1.0
	8.2	12.1	Net Profit + Depr., Dep., Amort./Cur. Mat. L/T/D							
(13)	4.1	(10) 6.2								
	1.5	1.2								
1.0	1.3	.7								1.3
1.9	2.9	1.7	Fixed/Worth							1.8
NM	-4.6	-9.0								-7.7
1.3	1.4	1.2								1.7
3.3	5.3	3.2	Debt/Worth							3.6
NM	-20.6	-20.7								-17.7
58.0	31.7	74.4								63.5
(15) 7.0	(18) 15.7	(23) 52.8	% Profit Before Taxes/Tangible Net Worth						(11)	52.8
-10.1	2.6	11.0								28.2
5.5	8.7	14.3								13.5
2.7	4.4	9.5	% Profit Before Taxes/Total Assets							9.4
-13.6	-2.0	2.6								-.2
13.1	10.6	10.3								9.4
6.5	6.1	6.9	Sales/Net Fixed Assets							6.7
4.4	4.0	4.4								4.8
3.2	3.5	3.6								3.1
2.3	2.3	2.6	Sales/Total Assets							2.6
2.1	1.9	2.1								2.3
1.4	1.3	1.2								1.6
(15) 2.5	(23) 2.7	(27) 2.6	% Depr., Dep., Amort./Sales						(13)	2.4
3.8	4.4	3.4								3.0
			% Officers', Directors' Owners' Comp/Sales							
2767852M	3218909M	4059778M	Net Sales ($)	654M	5873M	10548M	12326M	142128M		3888249M
1050667M	1256857M	1448473M	Total Assets ($)	975M	1768M	8377M	5468M	70834M		1361051M

© RMA 2010

M = $ thousand   MM = $ million

See Pages 9 through 22 for Explanation of Ratios and Data

Current Data Sorted by Assets | Comparative Historical Data

Type of Statement	0-500M	500M-2MM	2-10MM	10-50MM	50-100MM	100-250MM	4/1/05-3/31/06 ALL	4/1/06-3/31/07 ALL
Unqualified	1		6	31	11	7	55	55
Reviewed		1	22	13	1		43	41
Compiled	1	8	8	2	1		30	27
Tax Returns	9	13	11			1	20	14
Other	4	15	25	39	4	10	90	77
		48 (4/1-9/30/09)		196 (10/1/09-3/31/10)				
NUMBER OF STATEMENTS	15	37	72	85	17	18	238	214
ASSETS	%	%	%	%	%	%	%	%
Cash & Equivalents	11.7	6.7	7.6	6.1	7.9	8.0	7.1	8.0
Trade Receivables (net)	19.1	20.9	25.5	21.4	12.2	15.1	22.2	22.2
Inventory	18.1	27.5	29.0	27.4	20.2	25.0	24.8	24.3
All Other Current	6.1	.9	2.3	2.2	3.9	3.7	1.9	1.9
Total Current	55.0	56.1	64.3	57.1	44.2	51.8	56.1	56.4
Fixed Assets (net)	24.2	31.8	23.7	34.7	42.1	33.2	32.0	32.1
Intangibles (net)	11.6	4.5	6.7	3.6	4.6	6.6	4.5	4.0
All Other Non-Current	9.2	7.7	5.3	4.6	9.2	8.5	7.4	7.5
Total	100.0	100.0	100.0	100.0	100.0	100.0	100.0	100.0
LIABILITIES								
Notes Payable-Short Term	17.0	8.5	10.6	11.1	6.1	6.1	11.4	11.5
Cur. Mat.-L.T.D.	.1	7.4	4.5	4.1	3.7	2.2	4.1	4.7
Trade Payables	19.3	17.4	17.6	16.0	10.2	8.4	18.5	17.5
Income Taxes Payable	.0	.1	.6	.4	.1	.7	.4	.4
All Other Current	7.0	13.7	9.7	7.9	6.1	13.5	8.3	7.9
Total Current	43.4	47.2	43.1	39.4	26.3	31.0	42.6	41.8
Long-Term Debt	38.1	21.5	15.5	19.4	22.0	17.8	18.1	19.4
Deferred Taxes	.0	.0	.5	.5	2.1	1.1	.5	.5
All Other Non-Current	21.7	12.5	6.5	6.4	5.6	2.4	7.7	7.5
Net Worth	-3.3	18.7	34.4	34.2	44.0	47.8	31.1	30.7
Total Liabilities & Net Worth	100.0	100.0	100.0	100.0	100.0	100.0	100.0	100.0
INCOME DATA								
Net Sales	100.0	100.0	100.0	100.0	100.0	100.0	100.0	100.0
Gross Profit	41.9	37.3	28.2	27.6	35.7	26.7	29.6	31.0
Operating Expenses	39.3	33.0	22.7	20.4	27.1	19.3	25.7	26.5
Operating Profit	2.6	4.3	5.5	7.3	8.7	7.4	4.0	4.4
All Other Expenses (net)	.8	.8	.6	1.1	.7	.9	1.0	1.3
Profit Before Taxes	1.8	3.5	4.9	6.2	8.0	6.5	2.9	3.1
RATIOS								
Current	3.5	2.8	2.2	1.9	2.4	3.2	2.2	2.2
	1.3	1.5	1.5	1.4	1.4	1.7	1.4	1.4
	.8	.9	1.1	1.1	1.2	1.2	1.0	1.0
Quick	2.1	1.4	1.4	.9	.9	1.4	1.1	1.2
	.8	.5	.7	.7	.7	.7	.7	.6
	.2	.4	.4	.5	.4	.4	.4	.4
Sales/Receivables	0 UND	11 33.5	23 15.9	23 16.0	19 18.8	16 22.8	20 17.9	20 18.0
	3 108.1	21 17.0	30 12.3	30 12.1	25 14.3	28 13.1	30 12.3	29 12.6
	25 14.4	33 11.0	38 9.7	41 8.9	31 11.6	46 8.0	40 9.2	38 9.5
Cost of Sales/Inventory	7 51.9	11 33.8	26 14.3	28 13.2	39 9.5	41 9.0	18 19.9	21 17.5
	21 17.3	41 8.9	47 7.7	46 8.0	79 4.6	62 5.9	41 8.8	44 8.3
	30 12.3	79 4.6	73 5.0	75 4.9	108 3.4	95 3.8	81 4.5	82 4.5
Cost of Sales/Payables	5 72.6	3 144.6	14 25.9	18 20.1	20 18.4	10 38.1	18 20.0	19 19.7
	26 13.9	21 17.7	26 14.1	29 12.7	33 11.1	23 16.1	31 11.8	30 12.0
	44 8.3	42 8.7	39 9.3	43 8.4	49 7.4	41 8.9	45 8.1	45 8.1
Sales/Working Capital	9.8	8.5	6.3	7.9	6.0	6.1	8.3	8.5
	45.0	16.8	20.2	18.9	13.8	10.7	19.6	19.6
	-76.5	-73.1	114.9	42.6	23.9	26.4	-314.3	-175.0
EBIT/Interest		8.8	14.9	14.7	64.6	23.7	9.3	8.7
		(35) 3.2	(64) 4.6	(83) 6.0	4.9	(17) 12.3	(218) 3.5	(194) 3.1
		-1.1	2.3	2.7	3.1	3.9	1.1	1.3
Net Profit + Depr., Dep., Amort./Cur. Mat. L/T/D			5.0	10.8	25.4		7.4	11.2
			(16) 2.9	(40) 5.6	(13) 3.2		(80) 3.3	(68) 3.3
			1.8	2.2	2.3		1.4	1.4
Fixed/Worth	.0	.5	.2	.5	.6	.5	.4	.4
	.9	2.5	.6	1.0	1.4	.8	.9	1.2
	-.8	-3.5	2.5	2.4	2.6	2.1	2.3	3.3
Debt/Worth	1.4	1.0	.8	1.0	.6	.7	1.1	.9
	9.0	3.1	1.9	2.2	1.6	1.4	2.2	2.3
	-3.4	-11.7	10.7	4.8	3.5	3.7	5.8	9.4
% Profit Before Taxes/Tangible Net Worth	120.5	74.0	60.9	61.7	39.9	52.8	46.5	45.0
	(10) 17.0	(27) 30.5	(59) 31.3	(76) 36.8	28.9	22.3	(205) 20.9	(180) 21.9
	-28.6	-2.9	10.7	18.6	22.9	9.2	4.8	8.0
% Profit Before Taxes/Total Assets	19.1	15.5	17.2	22.0	22.0	19.5	14.7	16.1
	7.9	7.7	8.6	11.5	8.7	10.6	5.3	6.6
	-4.5	-6.3	4.2	4.3	4.8	4.5	.5	1.0
Sales/Net Fixed Assets	999.8	38.9	45.7	19.8	6.8	13.6	22.7	22.6
	17.5	15.7	17.7	8.7	4.0	8.0	9.5	7.8
	8.8	4.9	6.6	4.0	2.6	4.0	4.7	4.7
Sales/Total Assets	6.8	5.5	4.1	3.2	2.2	2.9	3.8	3.7
	5.1	3.1	3.0	2.4	1.7	1.7	2.5	2.4
	1.7	1.7	1.9	2.0	1.3	1.4	1.6	1.7
% Depr., Dep., Amort./Sales		1.0	.7	.9	1.1	1.4	.9	1.0
		(29) 1.9	(64) 1.4	(74) 1.4	(16) 2.4	(14) 1.6	(196) 1.8	(182) 1.9
		4.8	2.5	2.7	4.2	1.9	3.2	3.2
% Officers', Directors' Owners' Comp/Sales	2.0	1.5	2.0	.7			1.2	1.6
	(12) 5.9	(17) 3.8	(24) 3.2	(16) 1.5			(80) 2.3	(57) 2.7
	8.7	7.0	5.5	2.9			5.3	5.6
Net Sales ($)	21440M	165079M	1055861M	5787055M	2169986M	6363668M	13116433M	9402031M
Total Assets ($)	4018M	44626M	336025M	2153528M	1226798M	2734473M	5216492M	3858784M

M = $ thousand   MM = $ million
See Pages 9 through 22 for Explanation of Ratios and Data

Comparative Historical Data / Current Data Sorted by Sales

				Type of Statement						
				Unqualified	1		1	1	3	50
				Reviewed			2	4	16	15
				Compiled		3	5	5	5	2
				Tax Returns	6	12	6	5	3	2
				Other	3	5	8	8	20	53
	4/1/07-3/31/08 ALL	4/1/08-3/31/09 ALL	4/1/09-3/31/10 ALL		48 (4/1-9/30/09)			196 (10/1/09-3/31/10)		
					0-1MM	1-3MM	3-5MM	5-10MM	10-25MM	25MM & OVER
NUMBER OF STATEMENTS	207	245	244		10	20	22	23	47	122
ASSETS	%	%	%		%	%	%	%	%	%
Cash & Equivalents	7.8	7.6	7.2		6.2	9.5	11.3	6.5	6.9	6.5
Trade Receivables (net)	21.9	22.3	21.3		21.1	11.8	18.0	25.9	26.8	20.5
Inventory	24.5	24.6	26.6		9.3	26.9	22.5	31.3	30.3	26.4
All Other Current	3.0	2.5	2.5		8.5	.6	.8	1.8	2.8	2.6
Total Current	57.2	57.0	57.7		45.2	48.8	52.7	65.5	66.8	56.0
Fixed Assets (net)	31.0	31.9	30.8		37.8	29.8	23.4	26.9	26.2	34.2
Intangibles (net)	5.6	4.7	5.4		11.5	7.3	15.1	5.7	2.3	4.0
All Other Non-Current	6.2	6.4	6.1		5.5	14.1	8.9	1.9	4.7	5.8
Total	100.0	100.0	100.0		100.0	100.0	100.0	100.0	100.0	100.0
LIABILITIES										
Notes Payable-Short Term	10.4	12.1	10.2		8.6	10.6	6.7	11.9	13.8	9.2
Cur. Mat.-L.T.D.	4.7	4.0	4.3		.6	8.0	4.5	6.2	3.6	3.9
Trade Payables	18.2	17.6	15.9		13.0	13.0	16.3	20.1	18.8	14.7
Income Taxes Payable	.3	.3	.4		.0	.0	.3	.1	.8	.4
All Other Current	8.3	7.9	9.5		15.8	3.4	10.7	6.7	13.8	8.7
Total Current	41.9	41.9	40.4		37.9	34.9	38.5	45.0	50.8	37.0
Long-Term Debt	24.1	19.5	19.8		66.9	15.6	17.3	21.4	13.5	19.2
Deferred Taxes	.5	.4	.6		.0	.1	.0	.4	.7	.8
All Other Non-Current	7.6	8.7	8.0		18.5	17.2	1.8	15.3	6.0	6.1
Net Worth	25.9	29.5	31.3		-23.3	32.2	42.4	17.8	29.1	37.0
Total Liabilities & Net Worth	100.0	100.0	100.0		100.0	100.0	100.0	100.0	100.0	100.0
INCOME DATA										
Net Sales	100.0	100.0	100.0		100.0	100.0	100.0	100.0	100.0	100.0
Gross Profit	28.5	28.5	30.7		50.5	39.2	34.0	31.1	28.8	27.6
Operating Expenses	24.1	23.7	24.5		46.4	35.2	27.6	26.3	23.7	20.4
Operating Profit	4.4	4.8	6.1		4.1	4.0	6.5	4.8	5.2	7.2
All Other Expenses (net)	1.6	1.2	.8		2.3	.5	.3	.7	.9	.9
Profit Before Taxes	2.8	3.6	5.3		1.8	3.5	6.2	4.2	4.3	6.3
RATIOS										
Current	2.1	2.1	2.2		6.5	4.5	2.6	3.2	1.9	2.0
	1.4	1.4	1.5		2.0	1.6	1.5	1.4	1.2	1.5
	1.0	1.1	1.1		.9	1.0	.7	.9	1.0	1.2
Quick	1.1	1.3	1.2		2.8	2.2	1.6	1.6	1.0	1.0
	.7	.7	.7		1.1	.7	.6	.6	.6	.7
	.5	.4	.4		.2	.3	.4	.4	.4	.4
Sales/Receivables	21 17.0	20 18.3	20 18.1		0 UND	2 183.5	15 24.9	21 17.7	23 16.2	21 17.4
	29 12.4	28 12.9	27 13.4		31 11.9	13 28.2	26 14.0	30 12.4	31 11.6	28 13.2
	37 9.8	37 9.8	38 9.7		77 4.7	25 14.5	44 8.4	37 9.8	42 8.7	36 10.2
Cost of Sales/Inventory	23 15.8	23 16.0	26 13.9		0 UND	20 17.9	9 39.3	37 9.8	21 17.7	28 12.9
	45 8.1	42 8.6	46 8.0		38 9.6	47 7.8	38 9.6	47 7.7	47 7.7	46 8.0
	82 4.4	78 4.7	78 4.7		78 4.7	84 4.3	85 4.3	64 5.7	85 4.3	79 4.6
Cost of Sales/Payables	17 21.1	15 24.1	15 24.2		0 UND	2 172.5	15 24.7	18 20.4	17 21.6	16 23.5
	32 11.5	27 13.6	27 13.5		8 48.6	19 19.0	30 12.1	26 14.2	29 12.8	27 13.3
	51 7.2	40 9.2	43 8.5		74 4.9	36 10.2	45 8.1	38 9.5	55 6.7	40 9.1
Sales/Working Capital	8.4	8.3	7.0		2.8	6.8	4.9	6.0	8.9	7.2
	17.9	18.2	18.0		9.6	18.9	30.3	13.5	21.0	18.0
	227.0	127.1	116.0		NM	NM	-13.9	-89.9	140.5	42.4
EBIT/Interest	8.6	9.8	14.7			9.7	18.8	14.9	8.2	21.9
	(189) 2.8	(224) 3.6	(224) 5.1			(17) 3.2	(17) 6.4	(22) 3.6	(43) 3.9	(118) 6.8
	1.1	1.1	2.2			-2.3	2.1	1.6	2.0	3.1
Net Profit + Depr., Dep., Amort./Cur. Mat. L/T/D	8.8	8.1	10.9						5.0	14.0
	(63) 4.4	(71) 3.0	(80) 4.5						(14) 3.6	(61) 5.5
	1.5	1.3	2.2						1.7	2.4
Fixed/Worth	.5	.5	.4		.7	.2	.2	.2	.3	.5
	1.2	1.1	.9		1.7	1.1	.5	1.3	.9	1.0
	3.3	3.2	3.2		-.2	NM	NM	-4.0	2.3	2.5
Debt/Worth	1.0	.9	.9		1.3	.7	.5	1.7	.9	.9
	2.8	2.3	2.1		8.7	2.8	1.2	4.7	2.1	1.9
	9.7	7.6	7.6		-1.8	NM	NM	-8.8	5.0	4.9
% Profit Before Taxes/Tangible Net Worth	51.3	53.6	60.0			50.0	50.4	74.0	57.4	62.5
	(166) 29.4	(208) 22.7	(207) 29.5			(15) -2.9	(17) 30.0	(15) 45.1	(42) 29.6	(112) 32.2
	7.9	7.1	11.5			-28.6	10.5	4.8	10.8	17.7
% Profit Before Taxes/Total Assets	16.4	15.6	18.4		10.1	15.6	16.6	15.7	16.1	23.8
	7.1	6.4	9.8		6.5	8.3	8.3	8.3	10.6	11.3
	.2	.7	3.4		-7.6	-4.9	2.6	1.3	2.0	4.6
Sales/Net Fixed Assets	19.8	24.9	25.5		UND	50.8	59.5	38.4	43.5	17.9
	9.3	10.2	10.2		7.7	10.9	12.7	18.0	17.2	8.6
	4.8	4.6	4.9		.6	5.7	4.9	6.6	6.0	4.1
Sales/Total Assets	3.4	3.8	3.9		1.8	5.6	4.2	4.5	4.7	3.5
	2.5	2.6	2.6		1.0	2.9	1.9	3.1	3.2	2.4
	1.7	1.8	1.7		.5	1.6	1.3	2.4	2.2	1.8
% Depr., Dep., Amort./Sales	.9	.8	.9			.6	1.0	.9	.7	1.0
	(171) 1.8	(204) 1.7	(206) 1.5			(15) 1.5	(17) 1.5	(18) 2.0	(43) 1.2	(106) 1.5
	3.3	2.9	2.8			5.0	4.1	4.2	2.8	2.4
% Officers', Directors' Owners' Comp/Sales	1.6	1.2	1.4			1.9		1.0	2.0	.7
	(57) 2.6	(61) 2.3	(77) 2.7			(14) 3.1		(12) 2.7	(13) 2.8	(24) 1.3
	5.9	4.6	5.8			6.4		7.0	5.3	2.3
Net Sales ($)	10977839M	16767927M	15563089M		4949M	36912M	86028M	168577M	768167M	14498456M
Total Assets ($)	4560094M	7383356M	6499468M		6904M	16072M	50227M	64908M	331594M	6029763M

M = $ thousand   MM = $ million
See Pages 9 through 22 for Explanation of Ratios and Data

Current Data Sorted by Assets | Comparative Historical Data

Type of Statement

Type of Statement	0-500M	500M-2MM	2-10MM	10-50MM	50-100MM	100-250MM	4/1/05-3/31/06 ALL	4/1/06-3/31/07 ALL
Unqualified			2	19	8	7	37	40
Reviewed		3	3	5			12	11
Compiled			5				3	2
Tax Returns	1	3		1			2	5
Other	2	2	8	17	4	8	28	35
			14 (4/1-9/30/09)	84 (10/1/09-3/31/10)				
NUMBER OF STATEMENTS	3	8	18	42	12	15	82	93

Assets, Liabilities, Income Data (%)

	0-500M	500M-2MM	2-10MM	10-50MM	50-100MM	100-250MM	4/1/05-3/31/06 ALL	4/1/06-3/31/07 ALL
ASSETS	%	%	%	%	%	%	%	%
Cash & Equivalents			7.9	11.8	3.2	5.4	9.5	6.8
Trade Receivables (net)			17.8	14.7	16.6	10.7	16.7	18.8
Inventory			17.0	13.9	12.3	11.3	17.7	16.3
All Other Current			2.7	2.8	2.1	4.4	3.1	2.3
Total Current			45.4	43.2	34.1	31.7	47.0	44.2
Fixed Assets (net)			32.9	35.5	27.7	27.9	34.5	35.1
Intangibles (net)			11.3	9.6	29.9	23.7	11.1	10.8
All Other Non-Current			10.3	11.7	8.2	16.7	7.4	9.9
Total			100.0	100.0	100.0	100.0	100.0	100.0
LIABILITIES								
Notes Payable-Short Term			5.3	2.4	2.8	2.7	5.1	7.9
Cur. Mat.-L.T.D.			5.0	4.4	3.5	1.7	4.6	2.6
Trade Payables			11.4	13.2	9.9	7.6	14.1	16.8
Income Taxes Payable			.1	.1	.3	.5	.2	.1
All Other Current			5.9	10.5	11.3	7.2	8.3	8.3
Total Current			27.7	30.6	27.8	19.7	32.4	35.7
Long-Term Debt			20.6	14.5	23.7	18.1	25.3	24.8
Deferred Taxes			.5	1.1	1.3	2.5	1.1	.9
All Other Non-Current			4.8	6.3	11.6	2.9	6.5	5.8
Net Worth			46.4	47.5	35.6	56.8	34.7	32.8
Total Liabilities & Net Worth			100.0	100.0	100.0	100.0	100.0	100.0
INCOME DATA								
Net Sales			100.0	100.0	100.0	100.0	100.0	100.0
Gross Profit			34.6	25.6	41.4	24.1	31.7	32.5
Operating Expenses			29.2	20.6	29.6	19.5	27.3	29.6
Operating Profit			5.5	5.0	11.8	4.6	4.3	3.0
All Other Expenses (net)			.6	.8	2.9	-.3	.7	1.0
Profit Before Taxes			4.9	4.2	8.8	4.9	3.6	2.0

Ratios

	0-500M	500M-2MM	2-10MM	10-50MM	50-100MM	100-250MM	4/1/05-3/31/06 ALL	4/1/06-3/31/07 ALL
Current			3.6	2.9	1.5	3.0	2.3	2.2
			2.0	1.8	1.2	1.2	1.5	1.3
			.9	1.1	1.0	.9	1.1	.9
Quick			2.5	1.9	1.0	2.1	1.6	1.4
			1.1	(41) 1.3	.7	.9	.8	.8
			.5	.4	.6	.3	.5	.4
Sales/Receivables			20 18.2	16 23.5	20 17.9	19 19.3	19 18.9	24 15.4
			27 13.6	24 15.2	26 14.1	28 12.9	30 12.3	28 13.2
			34 10.7	28 12.9	28 13.3	33 11.1	34 10.7	37 9.8
Cost of Sales/Inventory			13 27.3	18 20.8	21 17.5	18 20.7	19 19.3	18 20.0
			26 13.9	26 13.8	23 15.6	25 14.8	29 12.4	30 12.1
			77 4.8	33 11.1	64 5.7	40 9.1	50 7.3	48 7.6
Cost of Sales/Payables			10 36.9	13 28.1	11 33.6	11 33.8	14 25.3	16 23.2
			19 19.2	25 14.7	25 14.3	17 21.9	30 12.1	27 13.7
			33 11.1	30 12.0	36 10.1	39 9.4	46 8.0	49 7.4
Sales/Working Capital			6.2	7.6	15.3	6.6	7.6	11.1
			15.5	11.9	47.2	41.7	19.8	24.3
			-47.2	203.7	NM	-73.1	79.5	-104.4
EBIT/Interest			13.4	29.0	10.2	516.6	20.2	10.8
		(15) 1.8	(38) 6.7	7.0	(13) 6.1		(77) 3.2	(87) 3.1
			1.1	2.0	1.5	3.2	1.4	.8
Net Profit + Depr., Dep., Amort./Cur. Mat. L/T/D				8.0			7.2	12.6
			(12) 3.8				(19) 4.0	(20) 4.6
				1.2			2.2	1.7
Fixed/Worth			.4	.4	1.0	.5	.5	.6
			.9	.8	3.6	.9	1.0	1.4
			-112.2	2.9	-1.3	14.1	10.2	-33.1
Debt/Worth			.3	.3	1.6	.7	.6	.6
			1.2	1.1	9.3	1.2	1.6	2.4
			-182.5	3.7	-4.2	25.6	12.0	-44.5
% Profit Before Taxes/Tangible Net Worth			41.5	38.7		26.4	37.9	33.9
		(13) 9.0	(37) 19.5		(12) 12.6		(63) 20.6	(66) 19.1
			.5	6.1		3.1	6.7	2.9
% Profit Before Taxes/Total Assets			25.6	13.8	14.2	11.6	12.8	13.7
			4.4	9.9	6.3	4.3	7.1	6.2
			-.1	2.1	2.6	1.2	1.0	-.4
Sales/Net Fixed Assets			26.5	12.9	14.5	7.9	14.0	14.8
			5.5	7.5	8.7	6.7	7.0	7.3
			3.7	4.5	7.3	5.0	3.9	4.0
Sales/Total Assets			3.0	3.0	3.0	2.0	3.2	3.2
			2.3	2.2	2.3	1.6	2.2	2.2
			1.6	1.7	1.6	1.1	1.5	1.5
% Depr., Dep., Amort./Sales			2.9	1.8	1.6		1.8	1.6
		(15) 3.6	(38) 2.5	3.0			(66) 3.0	(73) 3.0
			7.0	4.0	4.1		4.2	4.5
% Officers', Directors' Owners' Comp/Sales							.9	1.0
							(10) 1.8	(12) 2.0
							5.3	5.0
Net Sales ($)	2819M	32418M	231885M	2650763M	2300208M	3804304M	7298572M	8531733M
Total Assets ($)	1051M	10083M	99342M	1067939M	938099M	2331653M	3371353M	4001980M

M = $ thousand   MM = $ million
See Pages 9 through 22 for Explanation of Ratios and Data

Comparative Historical Data | Current Data Sorted by Sales

Period groupings (Current Data): **14 (4/1-9/30/09)** covers 0-1MM, 1-3MM, 3-5MM; **84 (10/1/09-3/31/10)** covers 5-10MM, 10-25MM, 25MM & OVER.

4/1/07-3/31/08 ALL	4/1/08-3/31/09 ALL	4/1/09-3/31/10 ALL	Type of Statement	0-1MM	1-3MM	3-5MM	5-10MM	10-25MM	25MM & OVER
25	41	36	Unqualified				1	3	32
8	8	8	Reviewed					3	5
1	4	8	Compiled		2			2	4
	6	5	Tax Returns		1	3	1		
42	35	41	Other	1	3		3	10	24
76	94	98	**NUMBER OF STATEMENTS**	1	6	3	9	17	62
%	%	%	**ASSETS**	%	%	%	%	%	%
7.8	7.3	8.8	Cash & Equivalents					10.7	8.7
18.4	16.1	16.4	Trade Receivables (net)					17.5	14.5
15.2	15.8	15.4	Inventory					16.7	13.8
2.8	3.3	2.7	All Other Current					2.4	3.3
44.3	42.5	43.2	Total Current					47.3	40.3
32.1	33.4	31.8	Fixed Assets (net)					32.1	32.1
14.4	13.1	14.0	Intangibles (net)					11.1	15.4
9.3	10.9	10.9	All Other Non-Current					9.5	12.2
100.0	100.0	100.0	Total					100.0	100.0
			LIABILITIES						
5.7	6.2	4.6	Notes Payable-Short Term					3.9	2.5
2.3	3.5	4.4	Cur. Mat.-L.T.D.					4.4	3.6
13.7	13.2	14.2	Trade Payables					10.8	11.9
.1	.3	.2	Income Taxes Payable					.1	.2
6.6	10.0	9.6	All Other Current					10.0	9.7
28.4	33.1	33.0	Total Current					29.2	27.9
22.2	21.1	18.1	Long-Term Debt					13.7	16.9
1.3	1.0	1.1	Deferred Taxes					.2	1.6
5.9	6.9	6.0	All Other Non-Current					2.8	6.9
42.3	38.0	41.8	Net Worth					54.1	46.7
100.0	100.0	100.0	Total Liabilities & Net Worth					100.0	100.0
			INCOME DATA						
100.0	100.0	100.0	Net Sales					100.0	100.0
35.4	33.3	29.4	Gross Profit					37.4	26.5
29.3	29.1	24.3	Operating Expenses					28.8	20.5
6.1	4.2	5.1	Operating Profit					8.6	6.0
1.2	.8	.8	All Other Expenses (net)					2.6	.4
4.9	3.4	4.4	Profit Before Taxes					6.0	5.6
			RATIOS						
2.6	2.4	2.7	Current					3.2	2.8
1.5	1.4	1.5						2.0	1.5
1.1	.9	.9						1.2	1.0
1.5	1.4	1.8	Quick					2.2	1.9
1.0	.8	(97) 1.0						1.2	(61) .9
.6	.4	.4						.6	.4
23 15.8	20 18.0	19 19.5	Sales/Receivables					19 18.9	19 19.4
28 13.1	26 14.0	25 14.3						27 13.7	25 14.4
35 10.6	32 11.3	30 12.0						33 10.9	28 12.9
19 19.2	20 18.2	18 20.8	Cost of Sales/Inventory					15 24.2	18 20.8
28 13.2	28 12.9	26 14.0						27 13.5	25 14.8
46 7.9	50 7.4	44 8.3						53 6.8	34 10.8
15 25.0	14 25.5	13 27.8	Cost of Sales/Payables					16 22.7	11 32.3
30 12.1	23 15.9	24 15.2						21 17.7	23 15.5
50 7.3	42 8.7	37 9.9						33 11.0	33 11.1
6.7	7.7	7.9	Sales/Working Capital					7.1	8.3
15.1	22.8	17.6						11.3	22.0
63.7	-38.8	-122.0						32.8	-392.8
14.8	17.4	22.9	EBIT/Interest					18.3	30.3
(70) 4.5	(83) 3.6	(87) 5.1						(14) 4.8	(57) 7.0
1.4	1.0	1.4						.9	2.6
13.5	9.0	10.8	Net Profit + Depr., Dep., Amort./Cur. Mat. L/T/D						11.3
(17) 2.1	(28) 2.9	(28) 3.8							(22) 5.7
1.2	1.3	1.6							1.7
.4	.4	.5	Fixed/Worth					.3	.5
1.0	1.3	1.0						.8	.9
6.7	11.2	16.3						NM	5.7
.6	.7	.5	Debt/Worth					.3	.5
1.5	2.2	1.3						.6	1.3
21.0	18.5	91.0						NM	10.4
48.4	45.6	41.8	% Profit Before Taxes/Tangible Net Worth					47.0	41.8
(59) 27.2	(72) 17.3	(75) 19.5						(13) 18.5	(51) 19.5
8.1	1.1	4.7						5.4	5.1
13.3	14.6	14.0	% Profit Before Taxes/Total Assets					27.1	13.5
7.3	5.5	6.7						9.8	8.1
1.0	-.1	1.1						.1	2.6
14.7	12.4	13.5	Sales/Net Fixed Assets					23.2	12.0
8.1	7.5	7.8						5.3	7.8
4.7	4.7	5.2						3.8	5.9
3.0	3.0	3.0	Sales/Total Assets					3.0	3.0
2.0	2.2	2.2						2.4	2.1
1.4	1.4	1.6						1.5	1.6
1.5	1.7	1.8	% Depr., Dep., Amort./Sales					2.0	1.7
(60) 2.7	(82) 2.8	(82) 2.9						(14) 3.1	(53) 2.8
4.6	4.3	4.1						4.1	4.0
	1.1	.8	% Officers', Directors' Owners' Comp/Sales						
(13)	2.4	(15) .9							
	8.1	2.2							
8855232M	8086978M	9022397M	Net Sales ($)	448M	11941M	11891M	65700M	296430M	8635987M
4300349M	4004243M	4448167M	Total Assets ($)	341M	7259M	3519M	74009M	159963M	4203076M

M = $ thousand   MM = $ million
See Pages 9 through 22 for Explanation of Ratios and Data

Current Data Sorted by Assets | Comparative Historical Data

0-500M	500M-2MM	2-10MM	10-50MM	50-100MM	100-250MM	Type of Statement	4/1/05-3/31/06 ALL	4/1/06-3/31/07 ALL
		1	6	2	5	Unqualified	7	9
		2	2			Reviewed	7	10
		4	1			Compiled	8	6
2	6	1				Tax Returns	5	2
3		7	3		1	Other	12	20
		3 (4/1-9/30/09)	43 (10/1/09-3/31/10)					
2	9	15	12	3	5	NUMBER OF STATEMENTS	39	47
%	%	%	%	%	%	**ASSETS**	%	%
		2.2	7.9			Cash & Equivalents	5.7	3.9
		15.3	20.0			Trade Receivables (net)	22.8	17.6
		16.7	20.9			Inventory	21.7	15.8
		2.0	2.3			All Other Current	2.4	2.8
		36.2	51.1			Total Current	52.6	40.1
		46.9	40.3			Fixed Assets (net)	35.0	45.1
		13.3	4.1			Intangibles (net)	5.3	9.8
		3.7	4.5			All Other Non-Current	7.1	5.0
		100.0	100.0			Total	100.0	100.0
						LIABILITIES		
		13.3	9.1			Notes Payable-Short Term	12.4	9.9
		3.7	4.3			Cur. Mat.-L.T.D.	4.6	6.5
		9.9	11.3			Trade Payables	12.7	11.0
		.1	.0			Income Taxes Payable	.2	.2
		9.7	10.1			All Other Current	8.5	10.2
		36.8	34.8			Total Current	38.4	37.8
		24.2	25.9			Long-Term Debt	16.8	33.8
		.2	.1			Deferred Taxes	.3	.4
		6.9	29.6			All Other Non-Current	8.0	8.2
		32.0	9.5			Net Worth	36.5	19.9
		100.0	100.0			Total Liabilities & Net Worth	100.0	100.0
						INCOME DATA		
		100.0	100.0			Net Sales	100.0	100.0
		40.2	33.1			Gross Profit	39.1	39.0
		36.2	26.6			Operating Expenses	34.8	33.8
		4.1	6.4			Operating Profit	4.3	5.1
		1.2	2.9			All Other Expenses (net)	1.2	2.5
		2.9	3.5			Profit Before Taxes	3.1	2.6
						RATIOS		
		1.9	2.4				2.5	1.8
		.8	1.8			Current	1.5	1.2
		.5	.8				.8	.9
		.8	1.4				1.2	1.0
		.5	.8			Quick	.8	.7
		.2	.5				.5	.4
		24 15.4	25 14.6				19 18.8	21 17.7
		27 13.6	33 10.9			Sales/Receivables	32 11.5	32 11.5
		37 9.8	61 6.0				44 8.4	40 9.1
		22 16.6	37 9.8				14 26.7	16 22.2
		31 11.7	48 7.6			Cost of Sales/Inventory	34 10.6	32 11.5
		52 7.0	99 3.7				91 4.0	61 5.9
		17 22.0	14 26.7				13 28.1	14 26.4
		28 12.9	34 10.6			Cost of Sales/Payables	22 16.7	26 14.0
		46 7.9	42 8.7				37 9.8	43 8.5
		9.2	4.7				7.2	9.9
		-30.4	9.5			Sales/Working Capital	16.8	32.0
		-8.7	NM				-54.3	-26.0
		12.4	8.0				5.8	5.7
		2.7	(10) 4.5			EBIT/Interest	(36) 2.8	(43) 1.9
		1.8	2.0				1.1	1.0
						Net Profit + Depr., Dep.,		2.7
						Amort./Cur. Mat. L/T/D	(10) 1.2	1.2
								.3
		.9	.2				.2	1.1
		3.1	1.7			Fixed/Worth	.8	2.7
		-12.1	NM				4.3	-3.3
		1.4	.9				.6	1.4
		5.7	2.8			Debt/Worth	3.2	5.3
		-17.5	NM				7.6	-9.0
		52.8				% Profit Before Taxes/Tangible	41.8	62.2
	(11)	35.1				Net Worth	(34) 25.9	(30) 25.1
		4.4					1.8	8.7
		9.0	13.1			% Profit Before Taxes/Total	13.5	13.5
		6.1	8.7			Assets	5.2	3.9
		2.9	2.6				.2	.2
		7.3	13.0				50.1	10.1
		3.6	4.7			Sales/Net Fixed Assets	7.4	3.9
		2.5	1.8				2.8	2.2
		1.9	2.4				3.7	2.7
		1.6	1.3			Sales/Total Assets	2.2	1.9
		1.3	1.1				1.4	1.0
		4.4	1.5				1.2	1.9
	(11)	5.5	(11) 6.1			% Depr., Dep., Amort./Sales	(32) 4.8	(41) 4.8
		10.8	8.6				7.6	7.6
						% Officers', Directors'	1.0	.6
						Owners' Comp/Sales	(14) 2.7	(10) 2.2
							4.8	3.6
1332M	27725M	155583M	472534M	122163M	990086M	Net Sales ($)	1097550M	1717103M
563M	10383M	82446M	290064M	191137M	794707M	Total Assets ($)	623460M	1093823M

M = $ thousand   MM = $ million
See Pages 9 through 22 for Explanation of Ratios and Data

Comparative Historical Data | Current Data Sorted by Sales

			Type of Statement						
9	9	14	Unqualified					5	9
9	7	4	Reviewed			1	1	3	
4	8	5	Compiled				1	2	1
3	7	9	Tax Returns	1	5	1	1	1	
13	14	14	Other	1	2	1	3	3	4
4/1/07-3/31/08 ALL	4/1/08-3/31/09 ALL	4/1/09-3/31/10 ALL		0-1MM	1-3MM	3-5MM	5-10MM	10-25MM	25MM & QVE
					3 (4/1-9/30/09)		43 (10/1/09-3/31/10)		
38	45	46	NUMBER OF STATEMENTS	2	7	3	6	14	14
%	%	%	ASSETS	%	%	%	%	%	%
7.4	5.9	6.4	Cash & Equivalents					5.3	5.4
16.9	15.9	17.5	Trade Receivables (net)					18.3	18.2
18.3	14.9	15.0	Inventory					18.9	17.5
3.1	1.3	2.4	All Other Current					1.7	2.4
45.8	38.0	41.3	Total Current					44.2	43.5
44.1	49.0	44.7	Fixed Assets (net)					39.5	42.5
5.3	7.6	10.6	Intangibles (net)					10.1	12.6
4.8	5.4	3.4	All Other Non-Current					6.2	1.5
100.0	100.0	100.0	Total					100.0	100.0
			LIABILITIES						
8.9	6.8	7.5	Notes Payable-Short Term					10.5	7.0
8.8	6.8	5.5	Cur. Mat.-L.T.D.					3.7	5.6
12.8	10.0	10.5	Trade Payables					10.8	10.2
.7	.1	.1	Income Taxes Payable					.1	.0
9.1	15.9	14.3	All Other Current					9.0	13.2
40.2	39.6	37.8	Total Current					34.1	36.1
27.9	32.4	27.5	Long-Term Debt					21.5	20.0
.5	.4	.6	Deferred Taxes					.5	1.1
7.4	11.1	14.6	All Other Non-Current					8.1	28.3
24.1	16.5	19.6	Net Worth					35.8	14.4
100.0	100.0	100.0	Total Liabilties & Net Worth					100.0	100.0
			INCOME DATA						
100.0	100.0	100.0	Net Sales					100.0	100.0
38.5	40.9	40.9	Gross Profit					37.2	25.9
31.4	36.1	34.8	Operating Expenses					31.9	19.2
7.1	4.9	6.1	Operating Profit					5.2	6.7
2.1	2.4	2.9	All Other Expenses (net)					2.4	4.1
5.0	2.5	3.2	Profit Before Taxes					2.9	2.6
			RATIOS						
2.5	2.1	2.2						2.1	2.3
1.1	1.2	1.4	Current					1.3	1.8
.6	.6	.6						.7	1.1
1.1	1.1	1.2						1.0	1.3
.6	.6	.8	Quick					.7	1.1
.4	.4	.4						.5	.6
20 18.1	23 16.2	23 15.6						24 15.5	24 15.1
29 12.4	27 13.7	29 12.6	Sales/Receivables					29 12.7	30 12.2
35 10.4	39 9.3	39 9.4						38 9.7	44 8.3
25 14.9	21 17.7	23 15.6						21 17.0	33 11.0
44 8.3	40 9.2	38 9.5	Cost of Sales/Inventory					45 8.0	45 8.1
58 6.3	55 6.6	57 6.4						67 5.4	64 5.7
14 25.8	14 26.7	12 30.3						10 35.4	11 32.4
30 12.2	31 11.6	28 13.1	Cost of Sales/Payables					19 19.1	24 15.0
50 7.3	43 8.6	43 8.5						37 9.8	34 10.8
9.7	9.7	7.4						4.5	7.3
46.0	30.1	17.1	Sales/Working Capital					23.0	9.6
-16.1	-11.4	-10.7						-14.4	NM
4.4	3.9	7.6						11.3	6.3
(34) 1.7	(43) 2.2	(42) 2.7	EBIT/Interest					(13) 2.8	(12) 3.6
.4	-.2	1.4						1.8	1.0
2.4		2.3							
(10) 1.4	(10) 2.0		Net Profit + Depr., Dep., Amort./Cur. Mat. L/T/D						
.7		1.8							
.6	1.1	1.0						.1	.9
1.8	3.9	2.8	Fixed/Worth					2.2	2.0
-4.9	-9.5	-4.9						NM	-6.7
.6	1.8	1.4						1.3	1.3
2.2	4.3	3.3	Debt/Worth					2.6	2.6
-8.2	-23.1	-9.6						NM	-9.9
31.0	39.3	52.8						42.9	
(27) 16.0	(32) 15.3	(31) 29.5	% Profit Before Taxes/Tangible Net Worth					(11) 35.1	
7.6	-11.7	5.8						14.5	
11.6	8.2	10.2						12.7	12.3
3.5	3.2	5.6	% Profit Before Taxes/Total Assets					6.2	7.9
-2.4	-4.4	-.1						2.2	-2.2
9.4	7.6	7.6						33.8	10.6
4.8	3.1	3.6	Sales/Net Fixed Assets					5.7	3.7
2.6	1.3	1.9						1.8	1.5
3.3	2.4	2.4						3.1	2.6
2.2	1.4	1.5	Sales/Total Assets					1.6	1.4
1.0	.9	1.1						1.0	.7
1.7	3.3	3.0							1.8
(32) 5.1	(40) 5.7	(37) 6.2	% Depr., Dep., Amort./Sales						(12) 4.8
7.2	9.3	8.9							6.7
			% Officers', Directors' Owners' Comp/Sales						
1458772M	1596643M	1769423M	Net Sales ($)	1068M	9426M	14562M	42226M	237107M	1465034M
945395M	1119287M	1369300M	Total Assets ($)	960M	7060M	7037M	31019M	208761M	1114463M

© RMA 2010   M = $ thousand   MM = $ million
See Pages 9 through 22 for Explanation of Ratios and Data

Current Data Sorted by Assets   Comparative Historical Data

Type of Statement	0-500M	500M-2MM	2-10MM	10-50MM	50-100MM	100-250MM		4/1/05-3/31/06 ALL	4/1/06-3/31/07 ALL
Unqualified		1	6	6	3	1		9	11
Reviewed		2	1	7				4	6
Compiled		3	3	1				5	5
Tax Returns			2					2	2
Other	2	7	9	12	4	4		24	23
		5 (4/1-9/30/09)		69 (10/1/09-3/31/10)					
NUMBER OF STATEMENTS	2	13	21	26	7	5		44	47
ASSETS	%	%	%	%	%	%		%	%
Cash & Equivalents		17.4	6.4	9.5				10.2	7.8
Trade Receivables (net)		15.2	11.9	8.1				11.5	8.3
Inventory		24.9	15.5	11.9				15.1	13.9
All Other Current		2.4	2.5	3.5				3.2	5.6
Total Current		60.0	36.3	33.0				40.0	35.6
Fixed Assets (net)		34.4	54.7	60.8				48.7	50.0
Intangibles (net)		2.6	4.8	3.0				7.1	8.3
All Other Non-Current		2.9	4.2	3.3				4.3	6.1
Total		100.0	100.0	100.0				100.0	100.0
LIABILITIES									
Notes Payable-Short Term		4.3	5.1	1.2				3.8	4.4
Cur. Mat.-L.T.D.		4.5	4.5	5.4				3.6	3.2
Trade Payables		14.0	12.4	6.2				10.7	10.9
Income Taxes Payable		.0	.1	.4				.4	.1
All Other Current		12.0	7.9	7.9				8.4	9.5
Total Current		34.8	30.1	21.0				27.0	28.0
Long-Term Debt		44.2	33.9	26.2				29.6	31.1
Deferred Taxes		.0	1.6	.7				1.5	1.7
All Other Non-Current		3.9	1.4	4.9				8.0	3.0
Net Worth		17.1	33.0	47.2				33.8	36.3
Total Liabilties & Net Worth		100.0	100.0	100.0				100.0	100.0
INCOME DATA									
Net Sales		100.0	100.0	100.0				100.0	100.0
Gross Profit		47.7	43.6	35.8				34.9	41.0
Operating Expenses		43.6	36.0	22.9				26.3	33.7
Operating Profit		4.1	7.5	12.9				8.6	7.3
All Other Expenses (net)		.4	1.0	1.6				.9	1.5
Profit Before Taxes		3.7	6.5	11.3				7.7	5.8
RATIOS									
Current		3.0	1.8	1.9				2.4	2.0
		1.9	1.4	1.6				1.4	1.1
		1.1	.8	1.0				1.0	.9
Quick		1.7	.9	1.3				1.3	1.0
		.9	.5	.9				.8	.6
		.3	.3	.4				.5	.3
Sales/Receivables	1 488.5	6 56.6	11 33.6					9 42.5	3 117.8
	21 17.3	22 16.8	22 16.7					22 16.3	22 16.6
	36 10.2	33 10.9	28 12.8					36 10.0	35 10.5
Cost of Sales/Inventory	26 14.1	37 9.9	32 11.4					25 14.9	29 12.4
	59 6.2	60 6.1	42 8.6					42 8.7	47 7.8
	77 4.7	74 4.9	58 6.3					67 5.5	79 4.6
Cost of Sales/Payables	0 UND	22 16.5	12 30.0					11 32.4	11 33.1
	32 11.3	44 8.3	18 20.4					26 14.2	35 10.3
	61 6.0	61 6.0	29 12.5					43 8.5	61 6.0
Sales/Working Capital		6.2	10.2	7.9				6.0	8.5
		9.6	15.2	18.4				22.4	65.7
		NM	-34.5	202.5				-999.8	-159.8
EBIT/Interest		9.2	12.6	20.7				10.8	8.8
	(10) 4.1	5.0	(25) 8.8					(39) 4.2	(43) 3.8
	-1.0	2.3	3.4					1.1	1.6
Net Profit + Depr., Dep., Amort./Cur. Mat. L/T/D				5.9				5.8	4.1
			(10) 3.3					(10) 3.0	(15) 3.1
			2.1					1.8	2.0
Fixed/Worth		.4	.9	.9				.7	.7
		1.2	1.8	1.6				2.0	1.6
		NM	4.1	2.4				UND	3.3
Debt/Worth		1.0	1.4	.8				.6	.9
		1.8	1.9	1.2				1.4	1.5
		NM	5.6	2.7				UND	4.7
% Profit Before Taxes/Tangible Net Worth		96.4	111.2	54.5				85.7	51.1
	(10) 36.4	(17) 41.9	30.5					(34) 33.0	(41) 18.0
	-15.5	10.1	14.0					8.8	7.3
% Profit Before Taxes/Total Assets		23.4	23.6	25.6				21.1	14.7
		16.2	10.8	14.5				9.9	7.4
		.1	2.8	5.7				1.0	1.1
Sales/Net Fixed Assets		75.1	5.8	4.2				8.9	8.6
		10.5	3.5	2.2				3.1	2.7
		4.0	2.1	1.4				1.6	1.7
Sales/Total Assets		3.6	2.6	2.3				2.5	2.5
		3.0	2.1	1.4				1.5	1.5
		1.7	1.4	1.1				.9	.9
% Depr., Dep., Amort./Sales			2.6	2.6				2.6	2.6
		(20)	4.0	(25) 4.6				(39) 3.7	(42) 4.0
			6.3	8.4				6.5	5.2
% Officers', Directors' Owners' Comp/Sales								.6	
								(11) 3.7	
								4.8	
Net Sales ($)	1837M	56623M	180179M	1154758M	940218M	1666449M		1856364M	1794047M
Total Assets ($)	378M	16665M	94408M	715261M	523328M	839656M		1522670M	1447007M

M = $ thousand   MM = $ million
See Pages 9 through 22 for Explanation of Ratios and Data

Comparative Historical Data   Current Data Sorted by Sales

			Type of Statement						
12	13	16	Unqualified				2	5	8
4	6	9	Reviewed		1		3	3	4
4	6	6	Compiled		2		2	2	
7	12	7	Tax Returns		1		3		
19	31	36	Other	1	2	2	2		
				1	4	1	7	5	18
4/1/07-	4/1/08-	4/1/09-				5 (4/1-9/30/09)		69 (10/1/09-3/31/10)	
3/31/08	3/31/09	3/31/10							
ALL	ALL	ALL		0-1MM	1-3MM	3-5MM	5-10MM	10-25MM	25MM & OVER
46	68	74	**NUMBER OF STATEMENTS**	2	7	6	14	15	30
%	%	%	**ASSETS**	%	%	%	%	%	%
9.5	6.7	8.7	Cash & Equivalents				5.1	9.5	7.7
9.6	12.5	10.6	Trade Receivables (net)				13.6	9.5	10.1
14.2	16.2	16.0	Inventory				22.7	16.0	12.1
4.1	4.2	4.0	All Other Current				5.3	.4	6.9
37.4	39.6	39.3	Total Current				46.8	35.4	36.9
51.6	50.9	49.1	Fixed Assets (net)				49.7	58.4	43.8
6.2	5.9	8.2	Intangibles (net)				1.7	2.6	15.5
4.7	3.5	3.4	All Other Non-Current				1.7	3.6	3.8
100.0	100.0	100.0	Total				100.0	100.0	100.0
			LIABILITIES						
5.0	5.6	3.8	Notes Payable-Short Term				5.1	3.2	3.7
5.0	3.8	5.6	Cur. Mat.-L.T.D.				3.2	6.2	6.4
12.2	11.3	9.7	Trade Payables				13.2	7.7	8.7
.2	.1	.2	Income Taxes Payable				.0	.1	.5
13.5	12.5	10.3	All Other Current				12.5	7.5	11.5
35.9	33.2	29.5	Total Current				34.0	24.6	30.7
32.8	29.8	33.3	Long-Term Debt				35.1	30.2	25.8
1.0	1.1	.8	Deferred Taxes				1.1	.9	.5
3.1	6.4	6.3	All Other Non-Current				.3	.4	7.8
27.2	29.5	30.0	Net Worth				29.5	43.8	35.1
100.0	100.0	100.0	Total Liabilties & Net Worth				100.0	100.0	100.0
			INCOME DATA						
100.0	100.0	100.0	Net Sales				100.0	100.0	100.0
39.9	39.6	39.3	Gross Profit				37.5	43.2	30.9
31.2	33.4	30.3	Operating Expenses				30.2	32.1	19.5
8.6	6.2	9.0	Operating Profit				7.3	11.1	11.4
1.5	1.5	1.3	All Other Expenses (net)				1.2	1.5	1.2
7.1	4.7	7.8	Profit Before Taxes				6.2	9.6	10.1
			RATIOS						
1.7	2.1	1.9					2.2	1.8	1.8
1.1	1.1	1.4	Current				1.7	1.5	1.2
.8	.8	.9					.9	1.1	.9
1.0	1.1	1.1					1.0	1.2	1.1
.7	.5	.5	Quick				.5	.8	.5
.3	.3	.3					.3	.4	.4
5 72.0	9 39.7	4 82.6		14 25.7	3 108.9	7 53.7			
21 17.6	23 15.7	21 17.3	Sales/Receivables	21 17.3	23 16.0	20 17.9			
29 12.6	35 10.4	30 12.2		31 11.9	26 13.9	32 11.6			
25 14.7	32 11.3	24 15.3		46 7.9	28 12.9	17 21.2			
48 7.6	51 7.1	47 7.7	Cost of Sales/Inventory	62 5.9	48 7.6	36 10.1			
71 5.2	84 4.3	67 5.5		72 5.1	60 6.1	49 7.4			
16 23.2	18 20.1	15 23.8		18 20.2	15 23.8	12 30.0			
34 10.6	34 10.7	25 14.6	Cost of Sales/Payables	29 12.8	25 14.6	18 20.8			
53 6.8	51 7.1	44 8.3		53 6.9	37 9.9	37 9.9			
10.9	8.5	9.0					9.5	9.6	8.4
57.9	41.7	19.7	Sales/Working Capital				11.5	27.0	52.9
-23.1	-27.9	-51.5					-42.1	91.6	-48.4
15.2	11.3	13.1					11.2	13.9	20.1
(41) 5.8	(61) 3.0	(69) 5.5	EBIT/Interest	(12) 5.4			7.8	(28) 6.7	
1.3	1.3	2.4					2.8	3.3	3.8
7.3	6.7	5.8	Net Profit + Depr., Dep.,						21.7
(11) 3.1	(18) 3.5	(19) 3.2	Amort./Cur. Mat. L/T/D					(10) 4.4	
2.0	1.5	1.8							2.1
1.0	.9	.9					1.2	.9	.8
1.7	1.9	1.8	Fixed/Worth				1.9	1.8	1.7
5.0	4.4	3.2					NM	3.2	3.1
.9	1.0	1.0					1.4	.9	.9
2.4	2.1	1.7	Debt/Worth				2.5	1.5	1.5
6.6	5.4	3.6					NM	2.8	3.0
66.2	44.0	70.3	% Profit Before Taxes/Tangible				174.0	74.9	56.3
(36) 36.3	(55) 18.1	(59) 37.0	Net Worth	(11) 46.3	(14) 27.8	(24) 39.1			
11.5	3.2	11.1					11.1	13.2	14.9
22.5	15.3	22.2	% Profit Before Taxes/Total				25.7	24.3	23.5
11.2	5.4	12.8	Assets				11.5	12.3	16.0
2.5	.7	4.2					4.1	4.3	7.2
9.7	7.3	9.0					11.2	7.0	12.8
3.5	3.2	3.8	Sales/Net Fixed Assets				4.1	2.5	4.4
1.6	1.7	2.1					2.4	1.6	1.7
2.3	2.6	2.7					3.3	2.5	2.7
1.4	1.7	1.8	Sales/Total Assets				2.4	1.4	1.9
1.0	1.2	1.3					1.4	1.3	1.1
2.7	2.4	2.0					2.0	3.1	1.6
(39) 4.1	(61) 4.3	(65) 3.7	% Depr., Dep., Amort./Sales	(12) 3.7	(14) 4.3	(27) 2.7			
5.8	6.2	7.0					5.5	8.7	5.9
.4	1.7	.8	% Officers', Directors'						
(10) 2.3	(16) 2.6	(16) 2.8	Owners' Comp/Sales						
5.6	3.6	5.2							
1789978M	2628678M	4000064M	Net Sales ($)	768M	13604M	22702M	94267M	257261M	3611462M
1266627M	1894533M	2189696M	Total Assets ($)	1061M	7390M	19572M	50127M	202401M	1909145M

    M = $ thousand   MM = $ million
See Pages 9 through 22 for Explanation of Ratios and Data

MANUFACTURING—Wineries NAICS 312130

| Current Data Sorted by Assets | | | | | | | Comparative Historical Data | |

						Type of Statement		
1		3	7	7	6	Unqualified	22	27
	3	10	26	5	2	Reviewed	27	21
		9	2	1	1	Compiled	8	5
5	9	7			1	Tax Returns	13	12
6	13	40	20	10	2	Other	40	52
	29 (4/1-9/30/09)		167 (10/1/09-3/31/10)				4/1/05-3/31/06	4/1/06-3/31/07
0-500M	500M-2MM	2-10MM	10-50MM	50-100MM	100-250MM		ALL	ALL
12	25	69	55	23	12	NUMBER OF STATEMENTS	110	117
%	%	%	%	%	%	ASSETS	%	%
9.1	6.6	2.6	2.5	2.1	5.1	Cash & Equivalents	6.4	5.0
19.3	6.3	7.5	7.4	9.8	9.0	Trade Receivables (net)	10.8	9.0
42.3	62.9	49.7	43.1	37.6	36.0	Inventory	40.6	41.7
5.8	.4	1.6	1.8	3.0	4.1	All Other Current	1.9	2.4
76.5	76.1	61.5	54.8	52.6	54.4	Total Current	59.7	58.1
18.8	21.7	35.1	37.7	40.4	30.0	Fixed Assets (net)	33.8	35.0
.5	1.1	1.2	3.4	4.5	7.6	Intangibles (net)	2.3	2.4
4.2	1.1	2.2	4.1	2.5	8.1	All Other Non-Current	4.2	4.5
100.0	100.0	100.0	100.0	100.0	100.0	Total	100.0	100.0
						LIABILITIES		
33.4	17.0	14.7	18.3	11.6	4.4	Notes Payable-Short Term	12.4	12.1
1.7	.8	1.7	2.4	1.4	1.9	Cur. Mat.-L.T.D.	2.0	2.4
23.9	9.8	8.5	6.1	7.5	4.4	Trade Payables	8.5	7.8
.0	.0	.0	.2	.3	.1	Income Taxes Payable	.2	.2
12.6	5.1	6.9	4.0	7.8	5.3	All Other Current	7.4	7.1
71.7	32.7	31.8	30.8	28.6	16.1	Total Current	30.4	29.7
7.8	22.9	21.4	25.7	21.3	20.9	Long-Term Debt	18.9	19.6
.0	.0	.2	.4	1.3	.5	Deferred Taxes	.6	.6
14.5	16.5	9.7	4.4	5.8	2.3	All Other Non-Current	7.4	6.7
6.1	27.9	36.8	38.6	42.9	60.2	Net Worth	42.7	43.4
100.0	100.0	100.0	100.0	100.0	100.0	Total Liabilties & Net Worth	100.0	100.0
						INCOME DATA		
100.0	100.0	100.0	100.0	100.0	100.0	Net Sales	100.0	100.0
52.1	55.6	46.0	44.2	40.1	45.3	Gross Profit	47.0	48.6
49.4	48.5	40.8	35.1	25.0	26.3	Operating Expenses	33.3	35.7
2.7	7.1	5.3	9.1	15.0	19.0	Operating Profit	13.7	12.9
-.1	4.2	5.1	6.3	3.9	7.1	All Other Expenses (net)	3.9	3.6
2.8	2.9	.2	2.8	11.1	11.9	Profit Before Taxes	9.8	9.3
						RATIOS		
1.8	8.3	3.5	3.2	3.0	8.0		3.8	4.1
1.1	3.1	2.0	2.1	2.0	3.1	Current	2.3	2.2
.9	1.4	1.5	1.2	1.5	1.9		1.3	1.4
.6	1.4	.6	.7	.7	1.7		1.1	.9
.3	.5	.2	.3	.5	.7	Quick	(109) .5	.4
.1	.1	.1	.1	.2	.5		.3	.2
0	814.4	8	43.4	9	42.1	25	14.3	34	10.7	19	19.3		15	23.9	13	27.9
9	41.7	23	16.2	25	14.8	37	9.9	38	9.5	40	9.1	Sales/Receivables	41	8.8	31	11.7
38	9.6	43	8.4	50	7.3	53	6.9	56	6.5	74	4.9		59	6.1	51	7.2
26	13.9	401	.9	296	1.2	329	1.1	225	1.6	255	1.4		212	1.7	218	1.7
308	1.2	678	.5	597	.6	533	.7	382	1.0	369	1.0	Cost of Sales/Inventory	363	1.0	401	.9
439	.8	1150	.3	877	.4	925	.4	1014	.4	506	.7		601	.6	697	.5
0	UND	7	54.4	16	22.5	22	16.5	25	14.9	8	47.6		22	16.7	15	24.3
48	7.7	69	5.3	57	6.4	48	7.6	55	6.6	31	12.0	Cost of Sales/Payables	52	7.1	45	8.1
109	3.3	195	1.9	142	2.6	105	3.5	87	4.2	69	5.3		89	4.1	101	3.6
5.5	1.7	1.4	1.3	1.7	1.2		1.7	1.7
42.2	2.5	2.3	2.3	2.9	2.1	Sales/Working Capital	2.7	2.8
-57.4	3.5	5.6	5.7	8.0	4.1		8.7	6.2
	5.3	4.7	10.7	14.0	28.1		10.0	7.3
(23) 1.7	(62) 1.7	(49) 2.4	3.1	(10) 9.7		EBIT/Interest	(101) 3.7	(101) 3.2
.5	.2	.4	1.7	4.2			1.4	1.3
		10.0	5.8				7.2	9.5
	(11) 2.1	(15) 1.7				Net Profit + Depr., Dep., Amort./Cur. Mat. L/T/D	(34) 3.8	(40) 5.0
	.4	.2					1.7	1.7
.2	.2	.3	.6	.4	.2		.3	.3
.6	.4	.8	1.1	1.1	.6	Fixed/Worth	.8	.8
-.6	3.4	2.5	2.4	1.5	1.4		1.9	1.7
.8	1.3	.9	.7	.8	.3		.5	.5
5.5	2.9	1.9	2.0	1.2	.7	Debt/Worth	1.2	1.3
-9.2	5.8	3.8	3.9	2.3	1.6		3.4	2.8
	22.2	17.1	20.5	22.5	36.7		33.0	30.5
(22) 9.6	(62) 4.4	(52) 8.4	(21) 9.8	(11) 25.2		% Profit Before Taxes/Tangible Net Worth	(101) 20.3	(106) 18.8
-7.2	-5.8	-2.9	1.9	2.9			7.1	5.7
22.3	10.5	6.5	7.8	8.4	16.3		13.7	12.7
8.8	2.9	1.9	2.6	3.3	11.7	% Profit Before Taxes/Total Assets	6.5	6.4
-14.1	-1.2	-1.7	-1.6	1.4	1.3		1.1	1.1
76.0	12.3	7.0	3.5	3.0	3.9		8.9	6.1
12.5	7.0	2.6	1.6	1.5	2.7	Sales/Net Fixed Assets	2.4	2.7
5.1	2.6	.9	.5	.9	1.2		1.3	1.3
3.6	1.2	1.1	.8	1.1	.8		1.2	1.2
1.7	.8	.6	.6	.6	.7	Sales/Total Assets	.8	.8
1.0	.5	.4	.3	.3	.5		.5	.5
	2.6	1.4	2.8	2.3	1.8		3.0	2.9
(16) 7.0	(54) 4.8	(46) 7.9	(22) 4.6	(10) 5.4		% Depr., Dep., Amort./Sales	(93) 4.5	(102) 5.2
11.9	9.7	13.5	7.2	8.0			6.9	7.9
		1.3					1.3	2.9
(12) 5.3				% Officers', Directors' Owners' Comp/Sales	(20) 3.8	(20) 10.6
		12.5					7.4	16.7
7482M	29240M	240369M	880699M	1400810M	1363219M	Net Sales ($)	2246631M	2976115M
3538M	28586M	319206M	1371634M	1635000M	1871830M	Total Assets ($)	2533249M	3533833M

M = $ thousand   MM = $ million
See Pages 9 through 22 for Explanation of Ratios and Data

Comparative Historical Data | | Current Data Sorted by Sales

4/1/07-3/31/08 ALL	4/1/08-3/31/09 ALL	4/1/09-3/31/10 ALL	Type of Statement	0-1MM	1-3MM	3-5MM	5-10MM	10-25MM	25MM & OVER
					29 (4/1-9/30/09)		167 (10/1/09-3/31/10)		
23	22	24	Unqualified		1		4	2	17
28	51	43	Reviewed		9	3	9	15	7
4	14	16	Compiled	2	8	3		1	2
17	23	22	Tax Returns	7	9	3	2		1
63	90	91	Other	17	24	15	11	13	11
135	200	196	**NUMBER OF STATEMENTS**	26	51	24	26	31	38
%	%	%	**ASSETS**	%	%	%	%	%	%
3.5	2.8	3.6	Cash & Equivalents	4.2	3.7	5.3	3.4	2.2	3.3
7.4	8.4	8.4	Trade Receivables (net)	6.4	6.5	7.0	12.5	6.1	12.3
39.9	45.2	46.8	Inventory	55.8	50.0	47.3	49.4	37.8	41.8
2.9	2.4	2.1	All Other Current	2.2	1.0	2.9	2.5	1.7	3.0
53.7	58.8	60.9	Total Current	68.6	61.1	62.5	67.8	47.9	60.3
38.1	34.1	33.4	Fixed Assets (net)	28.7	34.9	36.1	24.9	42.4	31.5
3.9	2.9	2.5	Intangibles (net)	.5	1.7	.5	3.0	6.3	2.9
4.3	4.3	3.1	All Other Non-Current	2.1	2.3	.8	4.3	3.4	5.4
100.0	100.0	100.0	Total	100.0	100.0	100.0	100.0	100.0	100.0
			LIABILITIES						
13.4	15.4	16.1	Notes Payable-Short Term	27.1	15.6	10.0	21.2	15.7	10.1
2.6	2.5	1.8	Cur. Mat.-L.T.D.	1.2	1.4	2.8	1.7	2.5	1.5
7.0	8.7	8.6	Trade Payables	11.9	8.1	5.4	15.5	4.5	7.6
.2	.1	.1	Income Taxes Payable	.0	.0	.0	.2	.2	.2
6.6	7.2	6.2	All Other Current	8.0	5.5	8.0	5.3	4.0	7.2
29.9	33.9	32.8	Total Current	48.1	30.5	26.2	44.1	26.8	26.7
23.3	22.3	21.9	Long-Term Debt	23.2	21.3	23.9	18.6	26.3	19.3
.5	.3	.4	Deferred Taxes	.0	.0	.1	1.1	.8	.5
4.1	6.7	8.5	All Other Non-Current	16.8	11.2	7.5	8.8	3.0	4.1
42.2	36.8	36.4	Net Worth	11.9	36.9	42.4	27.4	43.2	49.5
100.0	100.0	100.0	Total Liabilities & Net Worth	100.0	100.0	100.0	100.0	100.0	100.0
			INCOME DATA						
100.0	100.0	100.0	Net Sales	100.0	100.0	100.0	100.0	100.0	100.0
50.4	51.1	46.4	Gross Profit	55.8	50.6	43.8	41.0	49.0	37.3
36.6	38.6	38.0	Operating Expenses	50.6	45.5	40.0	33.1	35.9	23.0
13.8	12.5	8.4	Operating Profit	5.2	5.2	3.8	7.9	13.1	14.3
3.6	4.6	5.0	All Other Expenses (net)	5.0	6.8	3.8	4.8	5.5	3.0
10.1	8.0	3.4	Profit Before Taxes	.2	-1.6	.0	3.1	7.6	11.4
			RATIOS						
3.6	3.2	3.6	Current	2.4	4.8	4.8	2.8	3.4	3.3
1.9	1.9	2.0		1.5	2.1	2.3	1.7	1.8	2.3
1.4	1.3	1.3		1.1	1.5	1.7	1.3	1.2	1.6
.7	.7	.7	Quick	.4	.7	1.1	.7	.7	1.2
.3	.3	.3		.1	.3	.2	.4	.3	.6
.2	.1	.1		.1	.1	.0	.1	.2	.3
16 22.9	12 29.9	15 25.0	Sales/Receivables	5 72.8	10 35.2	2 158.4	21 17.0	27 13.4	29 12.4
32 11.5	33 11.1	34 10.8		23 15.6	22 16.8	14 25.7	43 8.5	38 9.6	40 9.2
49 7.5	51 7.1	52 7.0		45 8.1	41 9.0	48 7.5	59 6.2	55 6.7	57 6.4
254 1.4	272 1.3	292 1.3	Cost of Sales/Inventory	379 1.0	451 .8	248 1.5	191 1.9	329 1.1	193 1.9
384 1.0	490 .7	510 .7		912 .4	697 .5	519 .7	330 1.1	516 .7	350 1.0
693 .5	830 .4	894 .4		1365 .3	1127 .3	881 .4	561 .7	925 .4	493 .7
16 23.3	19 19.3	18 20.6	Cost of Sales/Payables	8 44.1	16 22.6	13 28.0	39 9.3	22 16.5	19 19.6
40 9.2	55 6.6	54 6.7		66 5.5	64 5.7	29 12.6	61 6.0	57 6.4	44 8.4
94 3.9	97 3.8	111 3.3		218 1.7	150 2.4	70 5.2	145 2.5	102 3.6	68 5.4
1.7	1.6	1.4	Sales/Working Capital	1.4	1.1	1.4	1.7	1.7	1.9
3.2	2.9	2.5		2.7	1.9	2.2	4.3	2.3	3.1
6.9	7.3	6.0		30.2	3.7	4.0	10.1	6.9	5.8
8.7	8.9	7.6	EBIT/Interest	1.9	3.4	14.9	6.5	11.9	31.4
(125) 3.7	(182) 3.0	(174) 2.4		(21) .3	(42) 1.5	(21) 3.5	(24) 3.2	(29) 2.8	(37) 6.5
1.4	1.2	.5		-3.3	.1	-1.8	.5	1.1	3.0
11.7	13.6	10.0	Net Profit + Depr., Dep., Amort./Cur. Mat. L/T/D						18.2
(43) 6.2	(56) 4.5	(41) 2.5							(13) 10.0
1.8	1.7	.6							3.8
.5	.3	.3	Fixed/Worth	.2	.3	.2	.3	.6	.2
.9	.9	.9		1.2	.8	.7	1.0	1.1	.7
2.1	2.0	2.3		18.1	2.5	1.9	3.8	2.4	1.3
.7	.7	.7	Debt/Worth	1.3	1.0	.4	1.0	.6	.5
1.3	1.7	1.8		3.3	2.0	1.4	2.5	1.6	1.0
3.9	4.3	3.9		25.5	3.7	3.0	8.0	3.9	2.0
34.6	34.4	21.8	% Profit Before Taxes/Tangible Net Worth	22.7	17.7	17.0	26.1	20.5	32.7
(122) 19.4	(178) 14.6	(175) 8.9		(21) -.1	(46) 3.4	(22) 8.7	(21) 10.6	(29) 9.9	(36) 21.1
5.3	2.6	-3.1		-28.9	-9.9	-3.5	-5.1	2.9	6.5
14.8	13.2	8.5	% Profit Before Taxes/Total Assets	6.8	6.1	11.2	7.1	7.6	16.0
7.1	3.9	2.8		-.3	1.9	3.5	3.4	2.9	5.9
1.1	.3	-1.5		-7.0	-2.1	-2.8	-2.3	.8	1.9
4.9	8.7	7.8	Sales/Net Fixed Assets	12.0	7.1	11.1	32.1	2.6	8.0
2.1	2.1	2.5		4.3	2.6	2.2	3.7	1.2	2.7
1.0	1.1	.9		1.0	.6	.8	1.6	.5	1.2
1.1	1.0	1.1	Sales/Total Assets	.9	.9	1.4	1.4	.7	1.2
.7	.7	.6		.7	.5	.6	.8	.4	.8
.5	.4	.4		.4	.4	.4	.6	.3	.6
3.1	2.3	2.1	% Depr., Dep., Amort./Sales	3.4	2.6	1.3	.5	4.2	2.0
(113) 5.3	(158) 4.4	(156) 5.3		(15) 7.7	(41) 7.1	(19) 4.9	(20) 2.8	(26) 9.4	(35) 4.3
7.4	8.1	10.4		12.0	14.2	8.9	7.5	13.5	7.0
3.8	2.2	2.2	% Officers', Directors' Owners' Comp/Sales		4.2				
(24) 7.4	(32) 7.7	(26) 5.3			(13) 6.0				
11.8	10.2	11.0			11.4				
3566142M	4015482M	3921819M	Net Sales ($)	12813M	91694M	93857M	189827M	470844M	3062784M
4160761M	5212880M	5229794M	Total Assets ($)	27183M	207121M	210841M	276388M	1181723M	3326538M

M = $ thousand   MM = $ million
See Pages 9 through 22 for Explanation of Ratios and Data

Current Data Sorted by Assets   **Comparative Historical Data**

Type of Statement

0-500M	500M-2MM	2-10MM	10-50MM	50-100MM	100-250MM	Type of Statement	4/1/05-3/31/06 ALL	4/1/06-3/31/07 ALL
		1	7	3		Unqualified	16	14
	2	2	7			Reviewed	4	6
	2	2				Compiled	3	1
		2	1			Tax Returns	1	2
1	2	5	2		3	Other	17	15
1	6	7	20	5	3	NUMBER OF STATEMENTS	41	38

Periods: 11 (4/1-9/30/09) covers 0-500M / 500M-2MM / 2-10MM; 31 (10/1/09-3/31/10) covers 10-50MM / 50-100MM / 100-250MM.

Main Data (values shown for 10-50MM column and historical ALL columns)

10-50MM %	Item	4/1/05-3/31/06 ALL %	4/1/06-3/31/07 ALL %
	ASSETS		
6.7	Cash & Equivalents	4.2	5.9
22.8	Trade Receivables (net)	22.6	20.7
28.8	Inventory	25.1	29.7
1.1	All Other Current	2.5	4.2
59.4	Total Current	54.5	60.5
28.8	Fixed Assets (net)	32.6	29.3
2.7	Intangibles (net)	2.5	3.3
9.1	All Other Non-Current	10.4	7.0
100.0	Total	100.0	100.0
	LIABILITIES		
5.7	Notes Payable-Short Term	7.2	8.9
2.7	Cur. Mat.-L.T.D.	2.9	3.7
13.0	Trade Payables	15.5	14.5
.1	Income Taxes Payable	.3	.1
7.5	All Other Current	7.6	5.8
29.0	Total Current	33.5	33.0
8.4	Long-Term Debt	18.4	18.8
1.8	Deferred Taxes	1.1	.8
6.7	All Other Non-Current	7.2	4.5
54.2	Net Worth	39.8	42.9
100.0	Total Liabilities & Net Worth	100.0	100.0
	INCOME DATA		
100.0	Net Sales	100.0	100.0
12.4	Gross Profit	13.8	17.8
11.4	Operating Expenses	11.3	14.1
1.0	Operating Profit	2.5	3.7
-.2	All Other Expenses (net)	.9	1.2
1.2	Profit Before Taxes	1.6	2.5

Ratios

10-50MM	Ratio	4/1/05-3/31/06 ALL	4/1/06-3/31/07 ALL
3.6	Current	3.0	3.7
2.1		1.7	1.7
1.3		1.0	1.1
1.8	Quick	1.5	1.3
1.0		.8	.8
.5		.6	.4
33 11.1	Sales/Receivables	26 14.0	21 17.3
47 7.8		42 8.7	39 9.3
56 6.5		51 7.2	51 7.1
39 9.5	Cost of Sales/Inventory	29 12.4	35 10.3
59 6.2		49 7.5	59 6.2
92 4.0		75 4.9	86 4.2
13 28.7	Cost of Sales/Payables	17 21.1	14 25.9
30 12.0		30 12.1	22 16.8
34 10.6		44 8.4	45 8.0
3.3	Sales/Working Capital	4.4	4.3
6.1		7.7	7.8
16.3		357.6	25.0
9.3	EBIT/Interest	7.8	3.9
(17) 2.8		(40) 2.6	(34) 2.0
1.3		.8	1.1
	Net Profit + Depr., Dep., Amort./Cur. Mat. L/T/D	5.8	4.0
		(13) 3.9	(10) 2.4
		1.7	.9
.2	Fixed/Worth	.4	.3
.5		.8	.6
1.3		1.9	1.4
.4	Debt/Worth	.7	.5
.9		1.5	1.5
1.8		5.4	4.5
12.0	% Profit Before Taxes/Tangible Net Worth	23.3	14.9
4.0		(38) 10.2	(34) 5.3
.2		.2	1.3
5.5	% Profit Before Taxes/Total Assets	10.3	8.2
1.6		4.6	2.6
.1		-.6	.3
18.2	Sales/Net Fixed Assets	12.5	25.1
6.7		5.9	7.9
3.1		3.2	3.5
2.2	Sales/Total Assets	2.5	2.7
1.6		1.8	2.0
1.3		1.3	1.6
1.5	% Depr., Dep., Amort./Sales	1.3	.8
(18) 3.3		(38) 2.8	(33) 2.2
5.0		5.7	3.6
	% Officers', Directors' Owners' Comp/Sales	2.2	
		(12) 3.3	
		5.7	

Net Sales / Total Assets ($)

	0-500M	500M-2MM	2-10MM	10-50MM	50-100MM	100-250MM		4/1/05-3/31/06 ALL	4/1/06-3/31/07 ALL
Net Sales ($)	3M	14027M	99312M	870085M	493732M	781481M		2250800M	2675853M
Total Assets ($)	6M	7395M	40806M	492341M	301028M	405316M		1373135M	1386452M

Comparative Historical Data | Current Data Sorted by Sales

				Type of Statement	0-1MM	1-3MM	3-5MM	5-10MM	10-25MM	25MM & OVER
	9	13	11	Unqualified						11
	6	9	11	Reviewed		1	1	1	3	5
	1	6	4	Compiled		2		1	1	1
	2	2	3	Tax Returns				1	1	1
	13	15	13	Other	1	1	1		3	7
	4/1/07-3/31/08 ALL	4/1/08-3/31/09 ALL	4/1/09-3/31/10 ALL			11 (4/1-9/30/09)		31 (10/1/09-3/31/10)		
NUMBER OF STATEMENTS	31	45	42		1	4	2	3	8	24
	%	%	%	**ASSETS**	%	%	%	%	%	%
	6.7	5.3	7.3	Cash & Equivalents						3.6
	27.9	23.1	24.2	Trade Receivables (net)						24.8
	30.8	31.7	29.4	Inventory						30.4
	2.9	1.9	2.6	All Other Current						4.1
	68.2	61.9	63.5	Total Current						62.9
	23.7	28.0	25.3	Fixed Assets (net)						25.9
	2.3	.8	3.2	Intangibles (net)						2.5
	5.7	9.4	8.0	All Other Non-Current						8.6
	100.0	100.0	100.0	Total						100.0
				LIABILITIES						
	8.6	8.2	6.9	Notes Payable-Short Term						8.0
	2.6	4.6	1.8	Cur. Mat.-L.T.D.						2.1
	14.4	10.9	12.9	Trade Payables						14.2
	.2	.1	.3	Income Taxes Payable						.5
	5.6	12.6	9.1	All Other Current						5.8
	31.4	36.4	31.1	Total Current						30.8
	12.4	14.7	13.9	Long-Term Debt						14.2
	.8	1.4	1.2	Deferred Taxes						1.9
	6.8	5.4	4.8	All Other Non-Current						6.2
	48.6	42.0	49.0	Net Worth						46.9
	100.0	100.0	100.0	Total Liabilties & Net Worth						100.0
				INCOME DATA						
	100.0	100.0	100.0	Net Sales						100.0
	17.6	16.7	17.3	Gross Profit						11.0
	14.8	16.0	15.0	Operating Expenses						9.7
	2.8	.7	2.2	Operating Profit						1.3
	-.1	.2	1.0	All Other Expenses (net)						.6
	2.9	.6	1.2	Profit Before Taxes						.7
				RATIOS						
	4.1	3.3	3.7							3.6
	2.1	2.1	2.4	Current						2.4
	1.5	1.4	1.5							1.4
	1.8	1.6	1.8							1.4
	1.3	1.0	1.1	Quick						1.0
	.7	.5	.6							.6
	36 10.2	32 11.2	32 11.3	Sales/Receivables						38 9.6
	50 7.3	41 8.9	46 7.9							48 7.6
	67 5.5	55 6.7	57 6.4							56 6.5
	38 9.7	38 9.5	39 9.5	Cost of Sales/Inventory						36 10.1
	57 6.3	66 5.5	64 5.7							56 6.5
	96 3.8	102 3.6	95 3.8							94 3.9
	17 21.5	14 25.7	14 25.2	Cost of Sales/Payables						15 23.8
	26 14.1	21 17.8	28 13.2							31 11.8
	38 9.5	30 12.0	36 10.2							35 10.3
	3.7	4.2	3.5	Sales/Working Capital						3.7
	6.6	6.9	5.5							5.8
	10.4	20.8	11.2							14.8
	9.0	5.2	6.9	EBIT/Interest						5.3
	(28) 2.8	(41) 2.3	(36) 1.8						(23)	2.4
	1.0	.5	.6							.9
	5.4	6.9	7.5	Net Profit + Depr., Dep.,						6.4
	(10) 3.0	(16) 2.0	(12) 3.4	Amort./Cur. Mat. L/T/D					(10)	3.4
	1.1	.5	.9							1.4
	.2	.3	.2	Fixed/Worth						.2
	.5	.5	.4							.4
	.9	1.5	1.0							1.3
	.4	.5	.4	Debt/Worth						.7
	.9	1.2	.9							1.0
	3.8	3.3	2.0							2.1
	29.0	22.3	11.5	% Profit Before Taxes/Tangible						11.0
	(28) 8.0	(41) 3.7	(38) 2.9	Net Worth						3.2
	.0	-2.0	-2.4							-.3
	12.2	7.5	5.8	% Profit Before Taxes/Total						4.9
	6.2	2.1	1.2	Assets						1.5
	.0	-3.2	-.8							-.1
	24.8	19.6	22.3	Sales/Net Fixed Assets						18.2
	10.6	6.8	8.2							8.1
	4.7	4.1	3.9							4.0
	2.7	2.6	2.4	Sales/Total Assets						2.2
	2.1	1.9	1.8							1.7
	1.7	1.3	1.3							1.5
	.7	1.0	1.0	% Depr., Dep., Amort./Sales						1.1
	(26) 1.4	(41) 2.3	(36) 2.4						(22)	2.3
	2.8	4.1	4.1							3.7
		1.7	1.8	% Officers', Directors'						
		(13) 4.0	(14) 3.6	Owners' Comp/Sales						
		7.9	6.0							
	2565520M	3595307M	2258640M	Net Sales ($)	3M	7520M	6507M	19053M	145825M	2079732M
	1269797M	1738984M	1246892M	Total Assets ($)	6M	4512M	2883M	12833M	96663M	1129995M

M = $ thousand   MM = $ million
See Pages 9 through 22 for Explanation of Ratios and Data

MANUFACTURING—Broadwoven Fabric Mills   NAICS 313210

Current Data Sorted by Assets								Comparative Historical Data

Type of Statement

0-500M	500M-2MM	2-10MM	10-50MM	50-100MM	100-250MM		4/1/05-3/31/06 ALL	4/1/06-3/31/07 ALL
		2	8	2	3	Unqualified	15	20
	1	5	7			Reviewed	17	18
2	5	7	1			Compiled	8	3
1	5	3	1			Tax Returns	1	7
1	3	7	11	3	2	Other	27	25
	12 (4/1-9/30/09)		68 (10/1/09-3/31/10)					
4	14	24	28	5	5	**NUMBER OF STATEMENTS**	68	73
%	%	%	%	%	%	**ASSETS**	%	%
	9.0	9.0	10.2			Cash & Equivalents	4.1	5.9
	35.5	25.8	21.5			Trade Receivables (net)	25.0	25.4
	33.3	31.2	28.4			Inventory	33.1	30.1
	.8	2.1	2.6			All Other Current	2.5	3.0
	78.5	68.2	62.6			Total Current	64.7	64.4
	14.0	26.8	21.8			Fixed Assets (net)	26.3	26.2
	4.4	2.4	10.4			Intangibles (net)	4.0	2.9
	3.1	2.7	5.2			All Other Non-Current	5.0	6.5
	100.0	100.0	100.0			Total	100.0	100.0
						LIABILITIES		
	6.7	12.3	6.7			Notes Payable-Short Term	10.7	18.0
	1.9	3.2	8.7			Cur. Mat.-L.T.D.	3.6	3.5
	23.8	15.3	11.3			Trade Payables	14.6	14.3
	.0	.5	.1			Income Taxes Payable	.1	.3
	5.5	7.4	6.7			All Other Current	7.9	7.2
	37.9	38.6	33.5			Total Current	36.8	43.3
	17.1	20.3	16.4			Long-Term Debt	13.3	14.2
	.0	.4	1.0			Deferred Taxes	.4	.4
	7.6	2.8	10.6			All Other Non-Current	9.7	8.6
	37.4	37.8	38.5			Net Worth	39.8	33.4
	100.0	100.0	100.0			Total Liabilities & Net Worth	100.0	100.0
						INCOME DATA		
	100.0	100.0	100.0			Net Sales	100.0	100.0
	24.6	26.9	22.2			Gross Profit	23.5	23.9
	23.7	24.4	18.9			Operating Expenses	21.2	21.8
	.9	2.5	3.4			Operating Profit	2.3	2.2
	-.2	.3	2.5			All Other Expenses (net)	.9	1.4
	1.2	2.2	.8			Profit Before Taxes	1.4	.8
						RATIOS		
	3.9	3.1	5.2				3.2	2.3
	2.0	1.7	2.8			Current	2.0	1.7
	1.7	1.3	1.3				1.4	1.3
	2.3	1.6	2.6				1.5	1.3
	1.3	.9	1.3			Quick	.8	.8
	.5	.5	.4				.5	.5
	25 14.7	33 11.0	33 11.0				33 10.9	31 11.8
	36 10.2	49 7.4	46 7.9			Sales/Receivables	41 8.8	45 8.1
	57 6.4	52 7.0	64 5.7				52 7.0	61 6.0
	9 39.6	30 12.3	41 8.8				45 8.1	41 8.9
	43 8.5	75 4.9	86 4.2			Cost of Sales/Inventory	71 5.2	66 5.5
	117 3.1	120 3.0	121 3.0				108 3.4	115 3.2
	24 15.0	26 14.3	17 22.0				17 20.9	17 21.0
	33 11.0	33 11.2	30 12.3			Cost of Sales/Payables	25 14.3	29 12.4
	43 8.6	48 7.6	39 9.3				40 9.2	42 8.8
	4.4	4.4	2.8				4.6	5.6
	8.2	8.4	5.0			Sales/Working Capital	6.7	7.9
	16.0	17.6	15.1				16.4	19.7
	94.8	6.5	18.2				9.0	6.0
	(11) 18.5	2.4	(24) 3.0			EBIT/Interest	(60) 2.5	(65) 2.5
	.3	1.1	.4				-.4	.2
							14.7	3.7
						Net Profit + Depr., Dep., Amort./Cur. Mat. L/T/D	(16) 3.1	(19) 1.8
							.9	1.4
	.1	.2	.2				.2	.3
	.3	.4	.5			Fixed/Worth	.6	.7
	NM	2.0	1.5				1.5	1.4
	.6	.7	.4				.6	.8
	1.3	1.9	1.1			Debt/Worth	1.8	1.5
	NM	4.2	3.9				5.5	6.3
	52.4	36.6	19.1				27.1	29.4
	(11) 15.5	(21) 7.5	(22) 9.6			% Profit Before Taxes/Tangible Net Worth	(59) 7.3	(64) 8.2
	-5.4	-.7	.4				-1.2	-5.4
	32.8	10.1	9.0				12.6	11.9
	12.0	3.4	4.0			% Profit Before Taxes/Total Assets	3.9	3.4
	-3.3	.5	-4.3				-.7	-2.8
	223.2	28.5	27.4				34.6	28.7
	39.0	15.3	7.8			Sales/Net Fixed Assets	10.8	9.4
	9.7	3.3	4.4				4.3	4.5
	4.9	2.7	2.2				2.7	2.7
	3.2	2.0	1.7			Sales/Total Assets	2.2	2.1
	2.3	1.2	1.2				1.6	1.4
		.8	1.5				.7	.8
		(22) 1.5	(22) 3.1			% Depr., Dep., Amort./Sales	(51) 2.3	(58) 1.8
		5.3	4.3				3.6	3.2
							1.4	1.9
						% Officers', Directors' Owners' Comp/Sales	(17) 2.6	(22) 3.2
							6.0	7.8
9025M	58185M	267856M	1098076M	642807M	1642932M	Net Sales ($)	3829870M	4784154M
944M	15858M	129119M	648000M	377906M	803269M	Total Assets ($)	1925185M	2249117M

© RMA 2010

M = $ thousand   MM = $ million
See Pages 9 through 22 for Explanation of Ratios and Data

Comparative Historical Data | Current Data Sorted by Sales

			Type of Statement						
16	21	15	Unqualified				1	7	8
17	18	13	Reviewed	1	1	1	3	6	4
5	8	15	Compiled	3	2	3	4	5	2
11	9	10	Tax Returns	2	2	4	1		
26	28	27	Other	1	2	2	4	4	14
4/1/07-3/31/08 ALL	4/1/08-3/31/09 ALL	4/1/09-3/31/10 ALL		1	12 (4/1-9/30/09)	2	68 (10/1/09-3/31/10)		
				0-1MM	1-3MM	3-5MM	5-10MM	10-25MM	25MM & OVER
75	84	80	NUMBER OF STATEMENTS	2	8	7	12	23	28
%	%	%	ASSETS	%	%	%	%	%	%
7.5	6.9	9.9	Cash & Equivalents				14.2	10.0	9.6
26.7	23.9	25.1	Trade Receivables (net)				25.5	23.4	22.8
29.7	31.1	29.5	Inventory				25.8	36.7	28.7
2.6	1.8	1.9	All Other Current				.5	4.0	1.5
66.5	63.7	66.4	Total Current				66.0	74.1	62.6
22.5	22.8	22.2	Fixed Assets (net)				23.6	18.6	19.5
4.6	5.3	5.6	Intangibles (net)				4.2	3.2	9.5
6.5	8.2	5.8	All Other Non-Current				6.1	4.1	8.5
100.0	100.0	100.0	Total				100.0	100.0	100.0
			LIABILITIES						
11.3	11.5	8.2	Notes Payable-Short Term				13.2	9.9	4.9
4.4	5.2	5.2	Cur. Mat.-L.T.D.				3.0	4.2	7.1
17.3	14.2	15.0	Trade Payables				11.8	16.5	12.8
.2	.3	1.4	Income Taxes Payable				7.5	.1	.3
9.1	9.9	7.3	All Other Current				5.7	7.0	6.1
42.3	41.1	37.0	Total Current				41.1	37.6	31.2
16.7	14.0	17.0	Long-Term Debt				22.0	12.9	11.3
.7	.5	.6	Deferred Taxes				.0	.8	.8
9.2	6.6	7.1	All Other Non-Current				1.4	11.5	6.1
31.2	37.9	38.3	Net Worth				35.4	37.3	50.5
100.0	100.0	100.0	Total Liabilties & Net Worth				100.0	100.0	100.0
			INCOME DATA						
100.0	100.0	100.0	Net Sales				100.0	100.0	100.0
24.2	22.8	24.5	Gross Profit				30.7	24.8	20.1
20.5	21.3	21.6	Operating Expenses				26.9	20.7	16.3
3.7	1.5	3.0	Operating Profit				3.7	4.1	3.8
1.0	1.3	1.2	All Other Expenses (net)				1.3	1.7	1.2
2.7	.3	1.8	Profit Before Taxes				2.5	2.4	2.6
			RATIOS						
3.4	3.0	3.7					3.5	3.4	4.9
1.8	1.7	2.0	Current				1.9	2.1	2.2
1.3	1.2	1.3					1.3	1.3	1.5
1.8	1.6	2.0					1.9	1.8	2.7
1.0	.8	1.0	Quick				.8	1.0	1.0
.5	.5	.5					.6	.5	.7

31	11.9	26	13.9	29	12.8		25	14.8	33	11.0	31	11.9
44	8.3	42	8.7	45	8.2	Sales/Receivables	36	10.1	50	7.3	41	8.9
57	6.4	58	6.3	56	6.5		55	6.6	58	6.3	53	6.9
42	8.7	40	9.1	32	11.3		7	54.1	42	8.7	40	9.0
65	5.6	61	6.0	65	5.6	Cost of Sales/Inventory	33	10.9	88	4.2	61	6.0
99	3.7	96	3.8	114	3.2		141	2.6	125	2.9	98	3.7
19	19.2	16	23.3	18	20.0		13	27.6	20	18.2	13	27.7
29	12.5	24	15.4	31	11.8	Cost of Sales/Payables	27	13.7	30	12.3	32	11.5
43	8.4	38	9.6	42	8.6		43	8.4	43	8.5	39	9.3

4.8	5.3	4.2	Sales/Working Capital				4.5	3.2	3.7
7.5	8.4	7.2					8.0	5.1	6.3
18.2	23.4	15.2					39.4	13.7	10.9

	11.4		11.2		12.3	EBIT/Interest		11.6		22.6	11.2
(66)	2.3	(79)	2.4	(73)	3.5			4.5	(21)	6.4	(26) 2.7
	.8		.0		.5			1.9		1.9	-.6

	5.6		5.2		5.1	Net Profit + Depr., Dep., Amort./Cur. Mat. L/T/D				
(19)	1.5	(24)	1.1	(19)	2.6					
	.8		-.2		.4					

.3	.2	.2	Fixed/Worth				.1	.1	.2
.5	.5	.5					.7	.2	.5
1.6	1.4	1.5					1.9	.6	1.1
.7	.8	.6	Debt/Worth				.8	.5	.4
1.7	1.5	1.3					2.7	1.1	.9
7.9	3.9	4.3					7.3	2.2	3.2

	42.8		32.1		32.3	% Profit Before Taxes/Tangible Net Worth		78.5		33.1	23.2
(61)	12.9	(74)	9.4	(66)	10.3		(10)	11.6	(21)	10.9	(24) 9.4
	-.9		-9.1		-.5			1.3		1.8	-4.8

15.1	10.0	12.7	% Profit Before Taxes/Total Assets				32.9	12.7	10.4
4.6	3.6	4.3					7.2	4.2	3.1
-.7	-4.0	-1.5					1.5	-5.0	-5.0
32.7	26.1	32.5	Sales/Net Fixed Assets				94.3	116.5	22.0
12.0	12.0	11.7					23.0	14.8	9.3
5.0	5.5	5.4					3.5	4.1	6.7
2.7	2.8	2.7	Sales/Total Assets				4.3	2.4	2.4
2.1	2.0	2.0					2.5	1.8	1.9
1.6	1.4	1.4					1.3	1.1	1.5

	.9		.7		.8	% Depr., Dep., Amort./Sales				.6	1.0
(64)	2.1	(72)	1.7	(64)	2.3				(22)	1.3	(23) 2.8
	3.0		3.3		4.3					4.3	3.5

	1.6		1.4		1.6	% Officers', Directors' Owners' Comp/Sales				
(20)	3.6	(21)	3.9	(19)	4.2					
	6.6		6.9		7.0					

3944848M	3431212M	3718881M	Net Sales ($)	1384M	15839M	28495M	87848M	362876M	3222439M
1957269M	1962002M	1975096M	Total Assets ($)	1101M	8488M	15874M	49340M	242936M	1657357M

M = $ thousand   MM = $ million
See Pages 9 through 22 for Explanation of Ratios and Data

Current Data Sorted by Assets   Comparative Historical Data

0-500M	500M-2MM	2-10MM	10-50MM	50-100MM	100-250MM	Type of Statement	4/1/05-3/31/06 ALL	4/1/06-3/31/07 ALL
		2	5	1	1	Unqualified	11	13
		9	1			Reviewed	12	13
	2	3				Compiled	9	10
	1	1				Tax Returns	10	5
1		5	8	2		Other	15	16
	10 (4/1-9/30/09)		32 (10/1/09-3/31/10)					
1	3	20	14	3	1	NUMBER OF STATEMENTS	57	57
%	%	%	%	%	%	**ASSETS**	%	%
		2.4	6.6			Cash & Equivalents	7.9	8.3
		20.7	28.6			Trade Receivables (net)	27.4	27.1
		33.6	40.2			Inventory	33.6	30.0
		.5	.9			All Other Current	3.2	1.4
		57.1	76.3			Total Current	72.2	66.9
		27.2	14.2			Fixed Assets (net)	21.3	23.6
		4.6	.8			Intangibles (net)	1.4	3.0
		11.0	8.7			All Other Non-Current	5.1	6.4
		100.0	100.0			Total	100.0	100.0
						LIABILITIES		
		11.8	18.6			Notes Payable-Short Term	19.1	16.1
		3.7	2.8			Cur. Mat.-L.T.D.	4.0	2.1
		17.0	17.4			Trade Payables	16.3	17.1
		.0	.8			Income Taxes Payable	.4	.4
		12.9	6.4			All Other Current	8.6	9.1
		45.5	46.0			Total Current	48.4	44.8
		8.7	6.7			Long-Term Debt	17.9	15.0
		.1	.4			Deferred Taxes	.4	.1
		3.5	2.1			All Other Non-Current	7.5	5.4
		42.2	44.8			Net Worth	25.9	34.7
		100.0	100.0			Total Liabilties & Net Worth	100.0	100.0
						INCOME DATA		
		100.0	100.0			Net Sales	100.0	100.0
		26.3	20.0			Gross Profit	28.4	28.8
		23.8	16.3			Operating Expenses	25.5	25.9
		2.5	3.7			Operating Profit	2.9	2.9
		.6	1.5			All Other Expenses (net)	1.4	1.4
		1.9	2.1			Profit Before Taxes	1.5	1.5
						RATIOS		
		2.2	2.3			Current	2.5	2.6
		1.3	1.6				1.6	1.7
		.8	1.2				1.2	1.2
		.9	1.5			Quick	1.5	1.4
		.5	.6				.8	1.0
		.2	.4				.4	.5
		9 39.9	38 9.7			Sales/Receivables	28 13.1	29 12.5
		34 10.7	51 7.1				43 8.5	39 9.2
		50 7.2	67 5.5				56 6.5	56 6.6
		41 8.8	45 8.0			Cost of Sales/Inventory	36 10.2	31 11.6
		77 4.8	98 3.7				64 5.7	67 5.5
		123 3.0	150 2.4				99 3.7	94 3.9
		15 24.0	21 17.6			Cost of Sales/Payables	15 23.9	19 19.4
		31 11.8	37 10.0				27 13.3	31 11.9
		48 7.6	51 7.2				47 7.8	48 7.6
		7.9	4.9			Sales/Working Capital	4.3	4.8
		16.9	7.1				8.7	9.0
		-29.0	12.4				31.6	22.4
		5.6	11.8			EBIT/Interest	8.0	9.3
		(19) 3.7	(13) 2.5				(56) 2.1	(54) 2.1
		1.4	1.0				1.0	.1
						Net Profit + Depr., Dep., Amort./Cur. Mat. L/T/D	7.6	3.6
							(18) 3.3	(15) 1.8
							.2	.0
		.3	.1			Fixed/Worth	.1	.2
		.7	.2				.5	.6
		1.9	.8				2.4	1.4
		.5	.9			Debt/Worth	1.0	.7
		2.2	1.2				2.1	1.6
		5.7	3.4				6.0	4.3
		44.0	17.1			% Profit Before Taxes/Tangible Net Worth	29.7	45.3
		(19) 13.2	6.5				(46) 4.5	(50) 7.3
		1.9	.4				-.4	-.9
		11.2	7.7			% Profit Before Taxes/Total Assets	16.7	16.8
		3.6	3.3				1.7	2.8
		.9	.1				-.1	-2.5
		62.1	64.6			Sales/Net Fixed Assets	61.2	40.9
		15.4	17.4				20.5	12.9
		2.7	5.0				6.2	6.6
		3.1	3.0			Sales/Total Assets	3.4	3.1
		2.2	1.7				2.3	2.0
		1.4	1.5				1.7	1.7
		.5	.6			% Depr., Dep., Amort./Sales	.4	.5
		(16) 1.0	(13) 1.2				(47) 1.1	(49) 1.4
		4.3	2.6				1.9	3.1
						% Officers', Directors' Owners' Comp/Sales	2.2	1.9
							(25) 3.3	(20) 3.8
							6.3	5.8
1678M	15619M	213972M	624103M	473394M	242015M	Net Sales ($)	2214797M	2498430M
194M	2753M	87774M	298459M	235452M	138368M	Total Assets ($)	1131912M	1131078M

M = $ thousand   MM = $ million
See Pages 9 through 22 for Explanation of Ratios and Data

Comparative Historical Data   Current Data Sorted by Sales

4/1/07-3/31/08 ALL	4/1/08-3/31/09 ALL	4/1/09-3/31/10 ALL	Type of Statement	0-1MM	1-3MM	3-5MM	5-10MM	10-25MM	25MM & OVER
12	8	9	Unqualified					1	8
14	10	10	Reviewed				3	5	1
10	7	5	Compiled		1	3	3		
4	4	2	Tax Returns		1	1	1		
11	15	16	Other		1	1	2	3	9
					10 (4/1-9/30/09)		32 (10/1/09-3/31/10)		
51	44	42	**NUMBER OF STATEMENTS**	3	3	9	9		18
%	%	%	**ASSETS**	%	%	%	%	%	%
5.8	7.2	6.8	Cash & Equivalents						4.6
24.5	24.6	25.7	Trade Receivables (net)						30.4
36.3	33.2	33.1	Inventory						39.5
2.8	2.2	.7	All Other Current						1.1
69.3	67.2	66.3	Total Current						75.6
22.4	22.3	21.8	Fixed Assets (net)						16.8
1.1	4.0	3.0	Intangibles (net)						.9
7.3	6.6	8.9	All Other Non-Current						6.7
100.0	100.0	100.0	Total						100.0
			LIABILITIES						
26.1	20.0	11.9	Notes Payable-Short Term						15.4
4.7	5.9	4.6	Cur. Mat.-L.T.D.						3.8
18.4	16.6	17.2	Trade Payables						19.1
.3	.4	.3	Income Taxes Payable						.7
12.4	7.5	9.9	All Other Current						8.4
61.9	50.4	43.9	Total Current						47.4
8.0	9.6	8.6	Long-Term Debt						7.1
.6	.1	.2	Deferred Taxes						.4
9.6	3.5	2.7	All Other Non-Current						2.8
19.9	36.5	44.6	Net Worth						42.3
100.0	100.0	100.0	Total Liabilties & Net Worth						100.0
			INCOME DATA						
100.0	100.0	100.0	Net Sales						100.0
25.9	24.6	25.7	Gross Profit						20.9
24.1	22.5	22.7	Operating Expenses						16.8
1.8	2.2	3.0	Operating Profit						4.1
1.8	1.3	1.0	All Other Expenses (net)						1.7
.0	.9	2.0	Profit Before Taxes						2.4

(Middle columns 0-1MM through 10-25MM for Assets/Liabilities/Income: DATA NOT AVAILABLE)

4/1/07-3/31/08	4/1/08-3/31/09	4/1/09-3/31/10	RATIOS	25MM & OVER
2.6	2.4	2.5	Current	2.5
1.4	1.5	1.6		1.7
1.1	1.1	1.2		1.2
1.2	1.2	1.5	Quick	1.5
.6	.7	.6		.6
.3	.3	.4		.4
24 15.0	25 14.6	26 14.2	Sales/Receivables	40 9.2
40 9.2	36 10.1	45 8.1		51 7.1
58 6.3	56 6.5	57 6.5		67 5.5
45 8.1	27 13.5	43 8.6	Cost of Sales/Inventory	45 8.0
77 4.7	63 5.8	69 5.3		69 5.3
113 3.2	117 3.1	125 2.9		136 2.7
16 22.9	18 19.9	16 22.5	Cost of Sales/Payables	25 14.5
31 11.6	29 12.6	33 11.0		36 10.0
43 8.5	50 7.3	50 7.4		42 8.7
5.2	5.5	5.8	Sales/Working Capital	4.5
10.5	9.9	11.4		7.1
35.0	48.8	25.6		13.3
4.8	7.7	10.3	EBIT/Interest	11.8
(50) 1.6	(42) 1.8	(38) 3.3		(17) 3.0
-.9	.9	1.2		1.0
1.9	7.5	14.7	Net Profit + Depr., Dep., Amort./Cur. Mat. L/T/D	
(12) .9	(11) 1.0	(10) 2.6		
-10.6	-.3	-.3		
.2	.1	.1	Fixed/Worth	.1
.5	.5	.5		.4
1.5	1.4	.9		.9
.7	.9	.6	Debt/Worth	.6
2.1	1.8	1.6		1.2
6.5	4.0	3.0		3.4
25.4	20.8	23.2	% Profit Before Taxes/Tangible Net Worth	24.4
(42) 6.4	(41) 5.1	(41) 8.2		11.4
-2.3	-4.8	1.4		.4
9.3	8.0	9.5	% Profit Before Taxes/Total Assets	9.9
2.0	1.7	3.9		4.3
-4.7	-.5	.9		.1
52.3	270.5	54.1	Sales/Net Fixed Assets	41.7
16.2	19.6	16.8		17.4
7.8	5.9	4.9		6.9
3.1	3.5	3.1	Sales/Total Assets	3.1
2.3	2.0	1.9		1.9
1.7	1.6	1.6		1.7
.4	.3	.5	% Depr., Dep., Amort./Sales	.6
(43) 1.0	(33) 1.2	(35) 1.2		(16) 1.2
2.1	3.0	2.8		2.3
1.3	1.3	1.2	% Officers', Directors' Owners' Comp/Sales	
(21) 2.8	(18) 3.4	(14) 2.6		
7.6	5.4	4.6		

4/1/07-3/31/08	4/1/08-3/31/09	4/1/09-3/31/10		1-3MM	3-5MM	5-10MM	10-25MM	25MM & OVER
2069198M	1458822M	1570781M	Net Sales ($)	5428M	13514M	61634M	124573M	1365632M
1002626M	755675M	763000M	Total Assets ($)	3647M	8963M	30318M	58296M	661776M

M = $ thousand   MM = $ million
See Pages 9 through 22 for Explanation of Ratios and Data

MANUFACTURING—Fabric Coating Mills NAICS 313320

Current Data Sorted by Assets							Comparative Historical Data	

0-500M	500M-2MM	2-10MM	10-50MM	50-100MM	100-250MM	Type of Statement	4/1/05-3/31/06 ALL	4/1/06-3/31/07 ALL
	5	2	4	3		Unqualified	9	10
		7				Reviewed	14	8
		2				Compiled	3	4
						Tax Returns	3	1
	3	3	6	3		Other	15	20
	4 (4/1-9/30/09)		34 (10/1/09-3/31/10)					
	8	14	10	6		NUMBER OF STATEMENTS	44	43
%	%	%	%	%	%	**ASSETS**	%	%
		10.9	11.9			Cash & Equivalents	5.5	5.6
		26.2	20.1			Trade Receivables (net)	27.3	25.9
D		26.4	19.6		D	Inventory	29.2	30.5
A		2.7	2.2		A	All Other Current	1.5	-1.3
T		66.2	53.8		T	Total Current	63.4	63.2
A		27.7	28.6		A	Fixed Assets (net)	28.0	26.7
		1.1	13.8			Intangibles (net)	3.7	4.1
N		5.0	3.7		N	All Other Non-Current	4.9	6.0
O		100.0	100.0		O	Total	100.0	100.0
T					T	**LIABILITIES**		
		14.7	9.0			Notes Payable-Short Term	11.9	10.9
A		7.2	5.9		A	Cur. Mat.-L.T.D.	2.5	3.1
V		17.0	12.8		V	Trade Payables	20.1	13.7
A		.1	.1		A	Income Taxes Payable	.1	.2
I		6.2	4.5		I	All Other Current	9.5	7.8
L		45.2	32.3		L	Total Current	44.1	35.7
A		20.9	14.2		A	Long-Term Debt	14.5	9.7
B		.2	1.6		B	Deferred Taxes	.5	.7
L		1.6	5.9		L	All Other Non-Current	18.2	9.3
E		32.1	46.1		E	Net Worth	22.8	44.5
		100.0	100.0			Total Liabilties & Net Worth	100.0	100.0
						INCOME DATA		
		100.0	100.0			Net Sales	100.0	100.0
		25.7	22.3			Gross Profit	21.9	27.4
		25.0	17.9			Operating Expenses	20.6	21.0
		.7	4.4			Operating Profit	1.3	6.4
		1.2	1.4			All Other Expenses (net)	.6	1.1
		-.4	3.0			Profit Before Taxes	.7	5.3
						RATIOS		
		2.2	3.6				2.2	2.8
		1.6	1.4			Current	1.5	1.7
		1.1	.9				1.1	1.2
		1.4	2.3				1.2	1.3
		.9	.6			Quick	.7	.8
		.5	.4				.4	.6
		25 14.7	40 9.1				35 10.4	37 9.9
		31 11.6	49 7.5			Sales/Receivables	43 8.5	44 8.4
		54 6.7	54 6.7				52 7.0	57 6.4
		21 17.5	40 9.2				38 9.6	46 7.9
		39 9.4	50 7.2			Cost of Sales/Inventory	61 6.0	70 5.2
		83 4.4	65 5.6				85 4.3	102 3.6
		19 19.7	23 16.1				25 14.7	16 22.5
		28 13.1	34 10.7			Cost of Sales/Payables	37 9.8	32 11.6
		38 9.6	56 6.5				51 7.1	40 9.1
		5.7	3.7				5.9	5.0
		10.8	11.0			Sales/Working Capital	13.2	8.0
		66.2	-29.9				65.2	20.7
		11.3					8.5	16.5
		4.7				EBIT/Interest	(39) 2.6	(41) 3.8
		2.0					-.1	1.4
							4.4	14.8
						Net Profit + Depr., Dep., Amort./Cur. Mat. L/T/D	(15) 2.4	(17) 3.7
							2.1	.8
		.1	.3				.4	.2
		.6	1.5			Fixed/Worth	.7	.6
		2.4	-2.7				2.2	1.2
		.5	.5				.8	.6
		1.3	2.8			Debt/Worth	1.6	1.5
		4.0	-10.6				6.4	3.1
		50.5					30.8	48.5
	(13)	25.8				% Profit Before Taxes/Tangible Net Worth	(37) 18.0	(41) 18.3
		10.9					7.6	3.9
		19.5	15.0				11.8	18.7
		9.4	7.5			% Profit Before Taxes/Total Assets	4.9	7.0
		3.0	.5				2.3	.7
		59.4	10.7				18.0	26.4
		11.0	7.3			Sales/Net Fixed Assets	7.8	6.3
		5.0	3.0				4.6	4.5
		3.6	1.9				3.1	2.7
		2.5	1.7			Sales/Total Assets	2.1	2.0
		1.9	1.2				1.7	1.4
		.2					1.2	1.0
	(12)	1.8				% Depr., Dep., Amort./Sales	(38) 2.2	(39) 2.2
		3.8					3.6	3.8
							1.6	1.4
						% Officers', Directors' Owners' Comp/Sales	(12) 2.6	(12) 2.1
							3.7	6.2
	18942M	185372M	401899M	785057M		Net Sales ($)	1079274M	1826173M
	8154M	67739M	248624M	500341M		Total Assets ($)	569228M	884897M

© RMA 2010

M = $ thousand   MM = $ million
See Pages 9 through 22 for Explanation of Ratios and Data

Comparative Historical Data   Current Data Sorted by Sales

			Type of Statement						
12	13	9	Unqualified		4		2	4	5
6	7	12	Reviewed					4	
3	1	2	Compiled					2	
			Tax Returns						
			Other	1	2	2	1		
14	13	15			4 (4/1-9/30/09)		34 (10/1/09-3/31/10)		
4/1/07-	4/1/08-	4/1/09-		0-1MM	1-3MM	3-5MM	5-10MM	10-25MM	25MM & OVER
3/31/08	3/31/09	3/31/10							
ALL	ALL	ALL							
35	34	38	**NUMBER OF STATEMENTS**	1	6	2	3	13	13
%	%	%	**ASSETS**	%	%	%	%	%	%
4.6	7.4	10.1	Cash & Equivalents					11.5	11.8
25.4	21.9	25.5	Trade Receivables (net)					22.5	23.5
31.4	28.2	24.2	Inventory					23.4	21.7
2.8	2.4	2.4	All Other Current					2.8	2.6
64.2	60.0	62.2	Total Current					60.1	59.6
23.9	24.5	28.2	Fixed Assets (net)					32.7	29.7
6.6	8.0	4.4	Intangibles (net)					4.1	8.1
5.3	7.5	5.1	All Other Non-Current					3.1	2.7
100.0	100.0	100.0	Total					100.0	100.0
			LIABILITIES						
8.8	14.1	9.6	Notes Payable-Short Term					12.3	7.6
4.1	4.2	5.5	Cur. Mat.-L.T.D.					6.9	4.9
17.7	15.1	13.6	Trade Payables					15.1	12.6
.3	.2	.2	Income Taxes Payable					.2	.3
6.8	5.8	9.0	All Other Current					5.3	8.5
37.7	39.4	37.9	Total Current					39.8	33.9
13.6	12.5	16.3	Long-Term Debt					23.3	14.4
1.0	1.0	.6	Deferred Taxes					1.2	.2
3.8	6.7	4.7	All Other Non-Current					1.7	8.9
43.9	40.3	40.5	Net Worth					34.0	42.5
100.0	100.0	100.0	Total Liabilities & Net Worth					100.0	100.0
			INCOME DATA						
100.0	100.0	100.0	Net Sales					100.0	100.0
22.8	22.4	28.1	Gross Profit					28.7	23.5
17.9	18.8	24.1	Operating Expenses					26.3	16.6
4.9	3.6	4.0	Operating Profit					2.3	6.8
1.4	1.3	1.0	All Other Expenses (net)					1.5	.6
3.5	2.3	3.0	Profit Before Taxes					.8	6.2
			RATIOS						
2.8	2.5	2.7						2.8	3.0
1.7	1.6	1.8	Current					1.3	2.1
1.2	1.0	1.1						.9	1.1
1.5	1.2	1.8						1.7	1.9
.7	.7	.9	Quick					.8	1.2
.5	.5	.6						.4	.6

							Sales/Receivables				
35	10.5	31	11.6	29	12.5			27	13.5	35	10.4
48	7.6	41	9.0	47	7.7	Sales/Receivables		44	8.4	52	7.0
55	6.7	49	7.4	55	6.6			49	7.5	57	6.4
48	7.5	41	8.9	36	10.2			30	12.3	43	8.6
71	5.1	62	5.8	53	6.9	Cost of Sales/Inventory		43	8.6	63	5.8
107	3.4	89	4.1	85	4.3			69	5.3	74	4.9
21	17.7	17	21.6	13	27.7			26	14.0	13	28.2
35	10.4	30	12.1	32	11.5	Cost of Sales/Payables		32	11.5	32	11.6
48	7.6	41	8.9	45	8.1			44	8.2	42	8.8

4.3		5.4		4.6			5.1	4.0
7.1		10.2		8.7	Sales/Working Capital		12.5	8.6
20.3		NM		43.7			-48.6	29.4
	11.8		9.3		12.3		9.6	28.5
(32)	3.4	(30)	3.5	(36)	5.4	EBIT/Interest	(12) 6.9	(12) 6.8
	1.6		1.1		2.3		2.8	2.7
	13.2		8.4		3.5	Net Profit + Depr., Dep.,		
(13)	2.8	(12)	2.7	(11)	2.6	Amort./Cur. Mat. L/T/D		
	1.3		1.7		2.0			
	.2		.4		.3		.2	.4
	.6		.8		.7	Fixed/Worth	.7	.9
	2.2		2.7		2.2		56.0	5.5
	.6		.7		.6		.6	.6
	1.5		1.6		1.1	Debt/Worth	1.0	1.0
	5.0		7.0		5.4		175.2	16.0
	27.6		22.4		45.4	% Profit Before Taxes/Tangible	53.7	57.2
(32)	14.8	(29)	11.5	(33)	23.7	Net Worth	(11) 31.7	(11) 35.2
	6.9		2.6		9.8		15.5	12.1
	12.6		10.4		16.9	% Profit Before Taxes/Total	17.6	17.7
	6.3		3.1		8.2	Assets	11.4	9.5
	1.8		-1.6		3.3		5.6	3.5
	17.0		13.7		18.6		15.4	9.6
	9.2		7.3		7.3	Sales/Net Fixed Assets	7.5	7.1
	5.2		4.7		4.2		3.7	3.8
	2.6		2.5		2.8		2.9	2.1
	2.0		2.0		1.9	Sales/Total Assets	2.1	1.9
	1.5		1.5		1.5		1.6	1.3
	.9		1.4		.9		1.1	1.7
(31)	1.6	(28)	2.5	(30)	2.3	% Depr., Dep., Amort./Sales	(10) 2.4	(10) 3.3
	3.2		3.9		4.0		3.9	4.7
	1.3				1.2	% Officers', Directors'		
(11)	1.8			(12)	4.6	Owners' Comp/Sales		
	4.7				13.8			

1649704M	1868814M	1391270M	Net Sales ($)	611M	14710M	8040M	26871M	209974M	1131064M
833553M	937999M	824858M	Total Assets ($)	503M	5687M	6038M	11066M	117844M	683720M

M = $ thousand   MM = $ million
See Pages 9 through 22 for Explanation of Ratios and Data

		Current Data Sorted by Assets					Comparative Historical Data	
		2	8	4	1	Type of Statement Unqualified	11	16
		3	6	1	1	Reviewed	13	7
1	1	6	1	1		Compiled	12	10
2	1	1				Tax Returns	4	6
1	2	8	8	2	1	Other	23	18
	14 (4/1-9/30/09)		48 (10/1/09-3/31/10)				4/1/05-3/31/06 ALL	4/1/06-3/31/07 ALL
0-500M	500M-2MM	2-10MM	10-50MM	50-100MM	100-250MM	NUMBER OF STATEMENTS	63	57
4	4	20	23	8	3			
%	%	%	%	%	%	ASSETS	%	%
		11.9	9.8			Cash & Equivalents	6.1	7.6
		22.2	18.5			Trade Receivables (net)	27.9	29.7
		29.4	36.0			Inventory	34.5	31.6
		1.6	3.6			All Other Current	2.5	2.1
		65.1	67.9			Total Current	71.0	71.0
		23.8	24.5			Fixed Assets (net)	23.6	22.6
		2.7	2.0			Intangibles (net)	2.2	2.0
		8.4	5.6			All Other Non-Current	3.1	4.5
		100.0	100.0			Total	100.0	100.0
						LIABILITIES		
		4.9	6.5			Notes Payable-Short Term	10.2	14.1
		3.7	2.8			Cur. Mat.-L.T.D.	5.6	3.0
		20.1	16.0			Trade Payables	23.0	24.5
		.5	.2			Income Taxes Payable	.1	.5
		10.9	11.3			All Other Current	14.6	17.0
		40.1	36.8			Total Current	53.4	59.2
		14.8	11.1			Long-Term Debt	15.5	17.9
		.4	.6			Deferred Taxes	.6	.4
		.5	4.4			All Other Non-Current	2.8	1.6
		44.1	47.1			Net Worth	27.8	20.9
		100.0	100.0			Total Liabilities & Net Worth	100.0	100.0
						INCOME DATA		
		100.0	100.0			Net Sales	100.0	100.0
		31.4	27.0			Gross Profit	29.2	28.0
		26.1	22.1			Operating Expenses	25.2	23.6
		5.3	4.9			Operating Profit	4.0	4.4
		.9	.4			All Other Expenses (net)	.8	1.4
		4.4	4.4			Profit Before Taxes	3.2	3.0
						RATIOS		
		2.5	2.4				2.6	2.6
		1.7	1.9			Current	1.6	1.6
		1.1	1.6				1.0	1.0
		1.5	1.3				1.4	1.3
		.9	.7			Quick	(62) .7	.7
		.4	.4				.4	.4
		28 13.2	16 23.0				24 15.4	25 14.6
		37 9.9	38 9.6			Sales/Receivables	37 9.8	38 9.6
		50 7.4	46 8.0				55 6.7	58 6.3
		20 18.4	74 5.0				36 10.3	25 14.9
		55 6.7	98 3.7			Cost of Sales/Inventory	72 5.0	74 5.0
		185 2.0	130 2.8				102 3.6	98 3.7
		16 23.1	32 11.6				26 14.2	24 15.0
		32 11.4	37 9.9			Cost of Sales/Payables	39 9.4	41 8.9
		62 5.9	43 8.4				63 5.8	58 6.3
		5.1	3.8				4.8	5.8
		7.8	6.5			Sales/Working Capital	9.5	9.5
		23.3	10.2				999.8	112.8
		26.9	14.2				7.4	8.1
		(17) 5.7	(20) 4.0			EBIT/Interest	(60) 3.2	(53) 3.1
		.8	1.2				1.6	.7
						Net Profit + Depr., Dep., Amort./Cur. Mat. L/T/D	5.2	6.9
							(14) 1.5	(12) 2.4
							.4	.6
		.1	.2				.3	.2
		.5	.4			Fixed/Worth	.7	.6
		1.5	1.1				2.1	2.1
		.7	.5				.9	.9
		1.3	1.3			Debt/Worth	1.8	2.0
		2.9	1.9				7.5	8.0
		49.8	22.9				35.0	45.7
		(19) 9.4	(22) 16.6			% Profit Before Taxes/Tangible Net Worth	(54) 16.7	(47) 15.7
		3.2	4.4				6.5	4.7
		20.3	11.4				12.3	16.8
		7.9	6.6			% Profit Before Taxes/Total Assets	5.1	5.5
		.4	.1				1.0	-1.0
		58.9	24.7				34.4	27.7
		14.5	6.2			Sales/Net Fixed Assets	13.6	12.9
		3.5	3.7				6.5	5.4
		2.9	2.3				3.2	3.4
		2.2	1.7			Sales/Total Assets	2.5	2.2
		1.2	1.4				1.8	1.6
		.4	1.5				.7	.9
		(14) 1.3	(20) 2.7			% Depr., Dep., Amort./Sales	(56) 1.6	(45) 1.8
		3.6	3.9				2.9	2.7
							.8	1.6
						% Officers', Directors' Owners' Comp/Sales	(21) 2.6	(16) 4.2
							9.0	7.2
5599M	20964M	261340M	1039066M	969402M	823704M	Net Sales ($)	1513391M	2232697M
1248M	5673M	110784M	582067M	629218M	470791M	Total Assets ($)	738722M	1241633M

© RMA 2010

M = $ thousand   MM = $ million
See Pages 9 through 22 for Explanation of Ratios and Data

Comparative Historical Data | Current Data Sorted by Sales

			Type of Statement	0-1MM	1-3MM	3-5MM	5-10MM	10-25MM	25MM & OVE
13	11	15	Unqualified					2	13
10	12	11	Reviewed		2			3	6
10	5	10	Compiled		3			3	3
5	6	4	Tax Returns		2		1	1	3
17	25	22	Other	1	2	1	4	6	9
4/1/07-3/31/08 ALL	4/1/08-3/31/09 ALL	4/1/09-3/31/10 ALL			14 (4/1-9/30/09)		48 (10/1/09-3/31/10)		
55	59	62	**NUMBER OF STATEMENTS**	1	7	3	5	15	31
%	%	%	**ASSETS**	%	%	%	%	%	%
3.6	4.8	8.7	Cash & Equivalents					12.4	9.3
24.2	23.2	19.7	Trade Receivables (net)					19.8	20.3
33.4	34.6	33.2	Inventory					30.0	35.2
1.8	2.6	2.8	All Other Current					5.3	3.0
62.9	65.2	64.5	Total Current					67.4	67.7
27.0	24.9	24.8	Fixed Assets (net)					22.6	23.6
3.8	3.5	2.5	Intangibles (net)					4.1	2.2
6.3	6.5	8.1	All Other Non-Current					5.9	6.5
100.0	100.0	100.0	Total					100.0	100.0
			LIABILITIES						
11.6	11.4	7.1	Notes Payable-Short Term					6.0	5.8
3.4	4.0	2.5	Cur. Mat.-L.T.D.					2.0	2.3
25.1	24.4	19.2	Trade Payables					22.1	15.8
.0	.1	.2	Income Taxes Payable					.4	.2
11.8	11.9	11.0	All Other Current					12.2	9.9
51.9	51.8	40.1	Total Current					42.8	34.0
19.9	19.2	19.4	Long-Term Debt					35.9	10.0
.5	.2	.4	Deferred Taxes					.2	.5
1.0	4.3	4.9	All Other Non-Current					2.6	6.5
26.6	24.5	35.2	Net Worth					18.4	49.0
100.0	100.0	100.0	Total Liabilities & Net Worth					100.0	100.0
			INCOME DATA						
100.0	100.0	100.0	Net Sales					100.0	100.0
28.9	28.1	30.4	Gross Profit					30.3	28.3
25.3	25.2	26.4	Operating Expenses					26.5	24.4
3.5	3.0	4.0	Operating Profit					3.8	3.9
1.4	1.9	.7	All Other Expenses (net)					.5	.4
2.2	1.1	3.3	Profit Before Taxes					3.4	3.5
			RATIOS						
1.9	2.3	2.5	Current					3.0	3.0
1.4	1.7	1.8						1.7	2.0
1.0	1.2	1.3						1.2	1.6
.9	1.2	1.3	Quick					2.0	1.5
.6	.6	.7						.6	.8
.3	.3	.4						.3	.5
20 18.6	23 15.9	21 17.4	Sales/Receivables					21 17.5	23 15.8
35 10.4	34 10.6	37 9.9						30 12.4	38 9.6
49 7.5	48 7.6	48 7.7						41 8.9	51 7.1
29 12.7	42 8.7	41 8.9	Cost of Sales/Inventory					22 16.5	69 5.3
77 4.7	92 4.0	83 4.4						57 6.4	92 4.0
130 2.8	135 2.7	137 2.7						119 3.1	137 2.7
26 14.0	21 17.5	23 15.8	Cost of Sales/Payables					14 26.8	31 11.7
43 8.6	33 11.1	37 9.7						27 13.4	37 9.7
61 6.0	68 5.4	56 6.5						56 6.5	44 8.2
7.8	5.9	4.3	Sales/Working Capital					5.0	3.8
12.1	8.4	6.6						7.5	6.2
304.2	21.3	13.6						18.7	7.7
4.7	7.7	15.6	EBIT/Interest					48.8	18.2
(53) 2.5	(56) 2.0	(56) 4.0						(11) 2.8	(29) 5.3
1.1	-.4	.8						-2.7	2.0
3.5	15.5	7.3	Net Profit + Depr., Dep., Amort./Cur. Mat. L/T/D						
(11) 2.7	(11) 5.7	(12) 2.7							
.9	2.2	.6							
.4	.2	.2	Fixed/Worth					.1	.2
.8	.7	.5						.5	.4
2.1	1.8	1.2						1.4	1.0
1.0	.8	.6	Debt/Worth					.5	.6
2.6	1.8	1.3						1.4	1.1
6.4	5.9	2.7						7.2	1.9
34.6	26.6	25.8	% Profit Before Taxes/Tangible Net Worth					25.5	25.2
(45) 11.7	(50) 11.7	(56) 12.6						(13) 9.2	(30) 14.3
1.5	3.3	2.0						-8.4	5.1
9.1	9.4	13.9	% Profit Before Taxes/Total Assets					21.4	12.8
4.5	3.0	5.9						4.8	6.6
.2	-1.9	.1						-5.9	2.2
19.9	34.7	27.5	Sales/Net Fixed Assets					47.4	24.7
8.8	10.8	8.9						13.5	7.3
4.6	4.3	4.1						4.9	4.1
3.3	3.1	2.8	Sales/Total Assets					3.0	2.5
2.2	1.9	1.9						2.7	1.8
1.6	1.5	1.3						1.4	1.3
.8	1.1	1.1	% Depr., Dep., Amort./Sales					1.2	1.5
(50) 1.7	(53) 2.4	(49) 2.4						(11) 1.6	(26) 2.6
3.3	3.8	3.5						2.7	3.4
.3	1.0	2.1	% Officers', Directors' Owners' Comp/Sales						
(15) 2.2	(16) 2.1	(13) 3.0							
3.4	2.6	4.4							
1760213M	2469296M	3120075M	Net Sales ($)	827M	14661M	11549M	34171M	274590M	2784277M
969152M	1421178M	1799781M	Total Assets ($)	259M	10105M	9409M	19605M	141742M	1618661M

M = $ thousand   MM = $ million
See Pages 9 through 22 for Explanation of Ratios and Data

Current Data Sorted by Assets   Comparative Historical Data

		2	3	1		Type of Statement		
	1	8	4			Unqualified	14	10
		2	2			Reviewed	12	12
2	1					Compiled	9	5
	4	9	6	1	1	Tax Returns	4	5
	7 (4/1-9/30/09)		40 (10/1/09-3/31/10)			Other	17	15

0-500M	500M-2MM	2-10MM	10-50MM	50-100MM	100-250MM		ALL 4/1/05-3/31/06	ALL 4/1/06-3/31/07
2	6	21	15	2	1	NUMBER OF STATEMENTS	56	47
%	%	%	%	%	%	**ASSETS**	%	%
		12.0	6.9			Cash & Equivalents	9.0	7.7
		27.8	30.5			Trade Receivables (net)	28.6	21.1
		34.2	32.3			Inventory	33.9	40.1
		2.5	2.0			All Other Current	1.6	2.7
		76.5	71.7			Total Current	73.1	71.7
		12.0	19.2			Fixed Assets (net)	17.9	16.7
		5.0	4.0			Intangibles (net)	2.5	5.6
		6.4	5.1			All Other Non-Current	6.5	6.0
		100.0	100.0			Total	100.0	100.0
						LIABILITIES		
		10.3	17.9			Notes Payable-Short Term	13.4	12.6
		4.1	1.6			Cur. Mat.-L.T.D.	3.3	2.8
		16.1	14.5			Trade Payables	17.9	20.2
		.0	.1			Income Taxes Payable	.2	.2
		10.0	6.9			All Other Current	11.2	10.6
		40.5	40.8			Total Current	46.0	46.4
		7.2	18.0			Long-Term Debt	10.6	8.1
		.2	.0			Deferred Taxes	.5	.7
		6.0	9.1			All Other Non-Current	4.7	5.7
		46.0	32.1			Net Worth	38.2	39.1
		100.0	100.0			Total Liabilities & Net Worth	100.0	100.0
						INCOME DATA		
		100.0	100.0			Net Sales	100.0	100.0
		29.5	27.3			Gross Profit	31.2	32.7
		25.5	26.5			Operating Expenses	26.6	28.2
		4.0	.8			Operating Profit	4.6	4.5
		-.2	1.2			All Other Expenses (net)	.7	1.1
		4.1	-.4			Profit Before Taxes	3.9	3.4
						RATIOS		
		3.5	2.5			Current	2.8	2.4
		1.6	1.5				1.7	1.5
		1.3	1.3				1.1	1.1
		1.8	1.4			Quick	1.7	1.1
		.8	.8				.9	.6
		.6	.5				.5	.4
		28 13.2	45 8.1			Sales/Receivables	20 18.7	19 19.0
		39 9.5	54 6.7				41 8.9	36 10.2
		60 6.1	76 4.8				58 6.3	49 7.4
		45 8.1	55 6.6			Cost of Sales/Inventory	33 11.0	52 7.0
		75 4.9	78 4.7				65 5.6	82 4.5
		121 3.0	112 3.3				102 3.6	136 2.7
		13 28.0	16 22.7			Cost of Sales/Payables	16 23.5	24 15.2
		21 17.0	21 17.1				31 11.7	41 8.9
		52 7.1	64 5.7				45 8.2	52 7.0
		4.9	5.0			Sales/Working Capital	5.1	4.6
		7.4	8.3				8.9	8.1
		11.3	11.8				35.8	36.7
		8.0	8.6			EBIT/Interest	11.4	13.8
		(16) 2.1	(14) 2.8				(49) 3.5	(39) 3.5
		.5	.4				1.7	.9
						Net Profit + Depr., Dep.,	4.2	8.4
						Amort./Cur. Mat. L/T/D	(18) 1.4	(13) 2.6
							.3	1.7
		.1	.1			Fixed/Worth	.1	.1
		.2	.5				.3	.4
		.6	1.3				.8	.9
		.5	1.2			Debt/Worth	.5	.7
		1.6	1.7				1.2	1.9
		3.6	9.5				6.0	7.5
		41.3	30.2			% Profit Before Taxes/Tangible Net Worth	49.7	56.9
		(19) 11.1	(12) 10.4				(50) 21.4	(40) 18.8
		3.1	-21.6				7.6	4.8
		9.3	10.7			% Profit Before Taxes/Total Assets	15.9	16.3
		4.3	2.1				7.3	6.6
		.0	-2.3				2.1	1.5
		107.5	82.7			Sales/Net Fixed Assets	76.3	50.5
		22.7	19.0				30.9	18.8
		12.4	5.1				8.0	8.9
		3.0	2.2			Sales/Total Assets	3.6	3.1
		2.3	2.0				2.8	2.1
		1.6	1.2				1.9	1.7
		.2				% Depr., Dep., Amort./Sales	.4	.7
		(18) 1.0					(47) 1.0	(39) 1.4
		2.0					1.7	2.4
		1.1				% Officers', Directors' Owners' Comp/Sales	2.2	1.6
		(10) 3.3					(17) 3.0	(12) 4.1
		4.5					5.7	10.2
2069M	22315M	261895M	801772M	161318M	214787M	Net Sales ($)	1779364M	2289091M
473M	8296M	112132M	390648M	126904M	110032M	Total Assets ($)	783335M	1269172M

M = $ thousand   MM = $ million
See Pages 9 through 22 for Explanation of Ratios and Data

Comparative Historical Data | Current Data Sorted by Sales

Type of Statement	4/1/07-3/31/08 ALL	4/1/08-3/31/09 ALL	4/1/09-3/31/10 ALL		0-1MM	1-3MM	3-5MM	5-10MM	10-25MM	25MM & OVER
Unqualified	11	9	6						1	4
Reviewed	17	10	13			1		3	7	2
Compiled	2	3	4					1	2	1
Tax Returns	5	6	3		1	1	1			
Other	13	13	21			3	4	1	7	6
						7 (4/1-9/30/09)			40 (10/1/09-3/31/10)	
NUMBER OF STATEMENTS	48	41	47		1	5	5	6	17	13
	%	%	%	**ASSETS**	%	%	%	%	%	%
Cash & Equivalents	8.3	9.2	9.6						8.4	7.4
Trade Receivables (net)	25.2	20.2	28.8						26.1	36.3
Inventory	42.1	35.6	31.3						31.3	31.7
All Other Current	1.7	1.9	2.3						1.6	1.9
Total Current	77.2	66.9	72.0						67.4	77.3
Fixed Assets (net)	15.7	22.1	16.2						18.7	9.6
Intangibles (net)	2.2	3.9	5.7						5.0	11.6
All Other Non-Current	4.9	7.1	6.1						9.0	1.5
Total	100.0	100.0	100.0						100.0	100.0
				LIABILITIES						
Notes Payable-Short Term	16.4	14.6	12.7						11.2	17.4
Cur. Mat.-L.T.D.	2.5	7.6	2.5						4.8	1.0
Trade Payables	16.2	17.1	16.2						17.7	16.7
Income Taxes Payable	.2	.8	.1						.0	.1
All Other Current	10.0	10.1	13.1						10.5	6.6
Total Current	45.4	50.2	44.6						44.1	41.9
Long-Term Debt	7.9	11.7	12.2						7.9	17.2
Deferred Taxes	.4	.3	.1						.0	.0
All Other Non-Current	3.6	4.8	8.4						12.1	3.7
Net Worth	42.7	33.1	34.7						35.9	37.2
Total Liabilities & Net Worth	100.0	100.0	100.0						100.0	100.0
				INCOME DATA						
Net Sales	100.0	100.0	100.0						100.0	100.0
Gross Profit	31.2	33.8	32.3						26.6	24.0
Operating Expenses	28.6	33.2	30.6						24.7	21.6
Operating Profit	2.6	.6	1.7						1.8	2.4
All Other Expenses (net)	.6	1.4	.6						-.8	2.0
Profit Before Taxes	2.0	-.8	1.1						2.6	.4
				RATIOS						
Current	2.9	2.9	2.5						2.1	4.6
	1.6	1.4	1.5						1.4	1.5
	1.2	1.0	1.2						1.3	1.3
Quick	1.3	1.2	1.4						1.2	2.4
	.7	.6	.8						.8	.8
	.5	.3	.5						.5	.6
Sales/Receivables	31 — 11.7	16 — 22.4	28 — 12.8						26 — 14.2	48 — 7.5
	42 — 8.7	31 — 11.7	41 — 8.8						39 — 9.2	61 — 6.0
	49 — 7.5	47 — 7.8	66 — 5.5						59 — 6.1	79 — 4.6
Cost of Sales/Inventory	56 — 6.5	37 — 10.0	43 — 8.4						42 — 8.7	54 — 6.8
	94 — 3.9	80 — 4.5	69 — 5.3						66 — 5.5	73 — 5.0
	136 — 2.7	152 — 2.4	112 — 3.3						93 — 3.9	99 — 3.7
Cost of Sales/Payables	15 — 24.3	16 — 23.4	16 — 23.5						16 — 22.4	12 — 30.1
	31 — 11.6	28 — 13.0	25 — 14.4						21 — 17.0	33 — 10.9
	53 — 6.9	49 — 7.4	59 — 6.2						65 — 5.6	61 — 5.9
Sales/Working Capital	4.7	4.6	5.0						6.5	4.5
	7.3	10.8	8.7						8.7	8.3
	15.7	NM	14.9						12.1	13.3
EBIT/Interest	7.2	8.3	8.2						8.2	10.0
	(43) 2.7	(40) 1.6	(37) 3.1						(15) 4.1	(12) 4.5
	1.1	-1.1	.8						-1.6	.7
Net Profit + Depr., Dep., Amort./Cur. Mat. L/T/D			4.6							
			(13) 2.6							
			.2							
Fixed/Worth	.1	.1	.1						.1	.1
	.3	.6	.3						.4	.3
	.8	1.7	1.5						1.4	NM
Debt/Worth	.5	.6	1.0						1.2	1.2
	1.8	1.6	1.7						2.1	1.7
	4.1	3.6	14.6						10.0	NM
% Profit Before Taxes/Tangible Net Worth	37.3	35.3	28.7						21.8	37.2
	(46) 11.0	(35) 11.5	(38) 9.4						(14) 13.2	(10) 18.4
	.2	-5.3	.7						4.7	-5.9
% Profit Before Taxes/Total Assets	12.3	9.9	8.1						8.3	13.0
	4.2	1.5	3.8						4.3	2.1
	.3	-9.9	-1.0						-.6	-2.3
Sales/Net Fixed Assets	82.9	71.9	110.9						118.8	262.2
	15.2	16.2	30.8						19.2	54.3
	7.4	5.7	7.2						5.2	14.0
Sales/Total Assets	2.8	2.8	2.9						3.1	2.6
	2.0	2.1	2.1						2.2	2.0
	1.6	1.7	1.6						1.5	1.8
% Depr., Dep., Amort./Sales	.4	.7	.5						.1	
	(40) 1.0	(29) 1.5	(31) 1.2						(14) 1.2	
	2.0	3.1	2.9						3.0	
% Officers', Directors' Owners' Comp/Sales	1.4	1.6	2.3							
	(19) 2.6	(17) 3.9	(16) 4.0							
	4.4	8.5	8.2							
Net Sales ($)	2308432M	1606865M	1464156M		985M	11394M	20444M	47804M	275650M	1107879M
Total Assets ($)	1216139M	751359M	748485M		129M	65221M	9185M	21706M	140201M	512043M

M = $ thousand   MM = $ million
See Pages 9 through 22 for Explanation of Ratios and Data

Current Data Sorted by Assets   **Comparative Historical Data**

0-500M	500M-2MM	2-10MM	10-50MM	50-100MM	100-250MM		4/1/05-3/31/06 ALL	4/1/06-3/31/07 ALL
						Type of Statement		
		1	2	2		Unqualified	6	6
1	1	8	1			Reviewed	11	12
2	2	3				Compiled	15	10
2	5	1				Tax Returns	7	9
1	2	9	4			Other	12	17
	7 (4/1-9/30/09)		40 (10/1/09-3/31/10)					
6	10	22	7	2		**NUMBER OF STATEMENTS**	51	54
%	%	%	%	%	%	**ASSETS**	%	%
	8.6	9.8				Cash & Equivalents	6.2	8.0
	16.5	24.1				Trade Receivables (net)	26.2	26.2
	34.4	33.8				Inventory	33.5	31.8
	.5	3.2				All Other Current	2.2	2.1
	60.0	71.0				Total Current	68.2	68.1
	24.8	20.3				Fixed Assets (net)	22.6	22.1
	.1	.8				Intangibles (net)	3.5	2.5
	15.1	7.9				All Other Non-Current	5.6	7.2
	100.0	100.0				Total	100.0	100.0
						LIABILITIES		
	11.8	13.8				Notes Payable-Short Term	14.7	12.1
	1.5	1.0				Cur. Mat.-L.T.D.	2.2	2.9
	18.5	10.2				Trade Payables	14.4	14.4
	.0	.3				Income Taxes Payable	.1	.1
	2.7	10.0				All Other Current	9.9	10.2
	34.5	35.2				Total Current	41.3	39.7
	20.2	8.0				Long-Term Debt	16.5	13.6
	.0	.2				Deferred Taxes	.1	.1
	1.5	1.8				All Other Non-Current	11.9	5.0
	43.9	54.7				Net Worth	30.2	41.6
	100.0	100.0				Total Liabilties & Net Worth	100.0	100.0
						INCOME DATA		
	100.0	100.0				Net Sales	100.0	100.0
	42.5	32.5				Gross Profit	34.4	32.0
	43.7	28.4				Operating Expenses	29.1	27.6
	-1.2	4.1				Operating Profit	5.3	4.4
	2.3	.8				All Other Expenses (net)	.3	.7
	-3.5	3.4				Profit Before Taxes	5.0	3.7
						RATIOS		
	4.6	3.8					3.0	3.5
	1.7	2.2				Current	1.8	1.8
	1.1	1.5					1.3	1.3
	1.6	2.3					1.5	1.5
	.9	1.0				Quick	.8	.8
	.4	.4					.5	.6
	0 UND	28 13.0					23 15.9	27 13.3
	27 13.5	33 10.9				Sales/Receivables	37 10.0	39 9.5
	39 9.3	62 5.9					53 6.9	47 7.8
	50 7.4	48 7.6					46 7.9	38 9.6
	99 3.7	79 4.6				Cost of Sales/Inventory	71 5.1	58 6.3
	162 2.3	149 2.5					120 3.0	124 2.9
	7 51.7	13 27.4					14 26.7	17 22.1
	33 11.0	22 16.4				Cost of Sales/Payables	27 13.4	25 14.9
	68 5.3	37 9.8					53 6.9	38 9.5
	4.9	4.0					5.2	4.7
	10.0	5.6				Sales/Working Capital	9.4	8.7
	NM	12.3					20.7	19.4
		22.9					13.6	10.0
		(19) 3.1				EBIT/Interest	(48) 4.1	(48) 3.5
		1.6					1.6	1.4
							7.9	5.3
						Net Profit + Depr., Dep., Amort./Cur. Mat. L/T/D	(13) 4.2	(12) 2.7
							2.0	1.3
	.1	.1					.2	.2
	.2	.3				Fixed/Worth	.6	.5
	1.4	1.0					1.5	1.2
	.5	.3					.7	.5
	1.4	.8				Debt/Worth	1.5	1.4
	4.3	1.9					3.9	3.7
	43.9	27.7					55.4	41.3
	-9.8	(21) 16.7				% Profit Before Taxes/Tangible Net Worth	(43) 23.8	(49) 18.1
	-26.3	4.2					6.5	3.9
	18.9	11.8					22.4	16.2
	-1.6	7.2				% Profit Before Taxes/Total Assets	7.2	8.4
	-12.8	.5					2.2	1.3
	377.4	35.0					36.7	41.5
	24.5	14.6				Sales/Net Fixed Assets	13.9	13.1
	7.4	5.8					7.2	7.9
	2.9	2.5					3.2	3.2
	2.2	2.1				Sales/Total Assets	2.4	2.4
	1.7	1.7					1.9	1.9
		.8					.8	.8
		(19) 1.6				% Depr., Dep., Amort./Sales	(43) 1.4	(46) 1.5
		2.6					2.4	2.4
							2.5	2.4
						% Officers', Directors' Owners' Comp/Sales	(26) 5.1	(24) 3.1
							8.5	8.0
3774M	25750M	218127M	250487M	149969M		Net Sales ($)	695393M	918564M
1231M	10032M	106699M	133383M	155735M		Total Assets ($)	316387M	454840M

(Center region across the current-data columns 10-50MM / 50-100MM / 100-250MM reads: DATA NOT AVAILABLE*)*

Comparative Historical Data / Current Data Sorted by Sales

4/1/07-3/31/08 ALL	4/1/08-3/31/09 ALL	4/1/09-3/31/10 ALL	Type of Statement	0-1MM	1-3MM	3-5MM	5-10MM	10-25MM	25MM & OVER
9	5	5	Unqualified				4	3	2
10	9	11	Reviewed	1	1		4	5	
13	11	7	Compiled	2	2	2	2	1	
8	12	8	Tax Returns	3	3		7	3	
10	12	16	Other	1		1	7	3	4
				7 (4/1-9/30/09)			40 (10/1/09-3/31/10)		
50	49	47	NUMBER OF STATEMENTS	7	6	3	13	12	6
%	%	%	ASSETS	%	%	%	%	%	%
6.2	7.8	8.2	Cash & Equivalents				9.1	7.0	
24.2	22.6	21.7	Trade Receivables (net)				23.7	24.8	
30.9	32.3	31.3	Inventory				34.0	29.9	
4.4	3.3	3.0	All Other Current				3.5	2.5	
65.8	66.1	64.1	Total Current				70.3	64.2	
21.4	21.3	23.6	Fixed Assets (net)				21.3	21.0	
5.0	2.4	2.2	Intangibles (net)				.3	4.3	
7.8	10.2	10.0	All Other Non-Current				8.1	10.6	
100.0	100.0	100.0	Total				100.0	100.0	
			LIABILITIES						
11.4	11.9	11.2	Notes Payable-Short Term				12.8	10.9	
2.3	2.6	2.2	Cur. Mat.-L.T.D.				1.0	1.7	
14.0	12.2	12.0	Trade Payables				11.1	11.7	
.1	.3	.1	Income Taxes Payable				.3	.2	
10.5	9.9	10.3	All Other Current				7.8	12.6	
38.3	36.9	35.8	Total Current				33.0	37.0	
12.8	14.6	10.6	Long-Term Debt				8.4	8.9	
.1	.2	.1	Deferred Taxes				.4	.1	
12.4	8.8	7.7	All Other Non-Current				.8	2.7	
36.3	39.4	46.0	Net Worth				57.3	51.3	
100.0	100.0	100.0	Total Liabilities & Net Worth				100.0	100.0	
			INCOME DATA						
100.0	100.0	100.0	Net Sales				100.0	100.0	
32.9	36.1	34.6	Gross Profit				33.2	34.1	
29.3	31.3	31.8	Operating Expenses				29.0	26.5	
3.7	4.8	2.8	Operating Profit				4.2	7.6	
.9	1.3	1.1	All Other Expenses (net)				.9	.8	
2.8	3.5	1.7	Profit Before Taxes				3.3	6.7	
			RATIOS						
3.7 / 1.7 / 1.3	3.7 / 2.0 / 1.2	2.9 / 1.8 / 1.3	Current				4.1 / 2.4 / 1.5	3.5 / 1.6 / 1.2	
1.5 / .7 / .5	1.6 / .9 / .5	1.7 / .9 / .5	Quick				2.4 / .9 / .5	2.1 / .9 / .4	
26 13.8 / 34 10.6 / 41 8.9	19 19.5 / 32 11.3 / 49 7.5	27 13.6 / 34 10.7 / 50 7.3	Sales/Receivables				29 12.6 / 34 10.7 / 52 7.0	29 12.7 / 35 10.5 / 74 5.0	
40 9.1 / 63 5.8 / 110 3.3	49 7.5 / 79 4.6 / 115 3.2	48 7.6 / 82 4.4 / 140 2.6	Cost of Sales/Inventory				45 8.0 / 101 3.6 / 172 2.1	49 7.4 / 67 5.5 / 117 3.1	
14 25.3 / 23 15.6 / 34 10.6	12 31.6 / 20 18.1 / 41 8.9	12 29.3 / 24 15.2 / 39 9.4	Cost of Sales/Payables				13 27.5 / 23 15.6 / 33 11.1	16 22.6 / 30 12.0 / 52 7.1	
5.2 / 10.7 / 24.3	4.6 / 9.6 / 21.1	4.8 / 7.6 / 18.4	Sales/Working Capital				3.7 / 5.0 / 11.1	5.3 / 7.4 / 20.7	
8.2 / (46) 2.5 / 1.3	11.7 / (46) 3.6 / 1.3	12.9 / (40) 2.7 / -1.8	EBIT/Interest				33.6 / (11) 6.5 / 2.6	29.3 / (11) 3.4 / 1.6	
5.1 / (10) 2.2 / 1.1	7.2 / (11) 3.4 / 1.1		Net Profit + Depr., Dep., Amort./Cur. Mat. L/T/D						
.2 / .6 / 1.5	.1 / .4 / 1.0	.1 / .3 / 1.2	Fixed/Worth				.1 / .3 / 1.1	.1 / .4 / 1.2	
.6 / 1.8 / 6.1	.5 / 1.5 / 3.8	.5 / .9 / 2.3	Debt/Worth				.3 / .5 / 2.1	.4 / 1.2 / 2.2	
46.3 / (44) 10.1 / -2.6	42.0 / (45) 13.5 / 2.3	27.7 / (45) 12.9 / -3.8	% Profit Before Taxes/Tangible Net Worth				27.0 / 12.9 / 3.7	31.3 / (11) 21.9 / 4.4	
12.8 / 4.7 / .2	13.5 / 7.8 / .5	11.2 / 5.2 / -2.9	% Profit Before Taxes/Total Assets				10.9 / 6.7 / 2.2	16.5 / 10.1 / 1.1	
34.1 / 13.4 / 8.4	38.0 / 15.0 / 8.5	31.3 / 12.7 / 5.4	Sales/Net Fixed Assets				46.2 / 10.0 / 5.1	36.4 / 11.3 / 3.8	
3.3 / 2.4 / 1.9	3.2 / 2.4 / 1.8	2.7 / 2.1 / 1.7	Sales/Total Assets				2.8 / 2.1 / 1.5	2.5 / 2.0 / 1.5	
.7 / (43) 1.4 / 2.4	.8 / (37) 1.3 / 2.8	.9 / (39) 1.8 / 3.6	% Depr., Dep., Amort./Sales				.8 / (11) 1.6 / 2.7	1.1 / (10) 1.8 / 4.5	
2.8 / (23) 3.9 / 9.1	2.0 / (28) 4.4 / 6.1	1.7 / (20) 3.0 / 5.6	% Officers', Directors' Owners' Comp/Sales						
797005M	898968M	648107M	Net Sales ($)	3831M	11703M	13062M	99601M	179165M	340745M
423914M	488411M	407080M	Total Assets ($)	2273M	5164M	4895M	52001M	134896M	207851M

M = $ thousand   MM = $ million
See Pages 9 through 22 for Explanation of Ratios and Data

MANUFACTURING—All Other Miscellaneous Textile Product Mills   NAICS 314999

Current Data Sorted by Assets **Comparative Historical Data**

0-500M	500M-2MM	2-10MM	10-50MM	50-100MM	100-250MM		ALL 4/1/05-3/31/06	ALL 4/1/06-3/31/07
						Type of Statement		
		6	11	2	2	Unqualified	30	31
	1	11	7			Reviewed	19	24
3	5	8	1			Compiled	27	33
3	6	7				Tax Returns	11	14
2	13	15	15	3	4	Other	67	45
	22 (4/1-9/30/09)		103 (10/1/09-3/31/10)					
8	25	47	34	5	6	**NUMBER OF STATEMENTS**	154	147
%	%	%	%	%	%	**ASSETS**	%	%
	9.1	7.4	6.1			Cash & Equivalents	6.6	7.1
	26.9	24.4	20.6			Trade Receivables (net)	25.1	25.6
	31.3	37.1	31.8			Inventory	29.0	30.2
	1.1	1.2	5.1			All Other Current	2.2	2.4
	68.4	70.2	63.5			Total Current	62.9	65.2
	21.3	20.8	24.4			Fixed Assets (net)	25.4	23.8
	2.2	2.6	8.1			Intangibles (net)	6.7	4.0
	8.1	6.4	3.9			All Other Non-Current	5.1	7.0
	100.0	100.0	100.0			Total	100.0	100.0
						LIABILITIES		
	14.1	14.3	9.4			Notes Payable-Short Term	13.6	14.2
	3.4	3.4	6.3			Cur. Mat.-L.T.D.	3.6	4.2
	16.2	20.1	12.4			Trade Payables	16.3	15.5
	.0	.2	.2			Income Taxes Payable	.4	.4
	6.7	8.8	8.5			All Other Current	9.3	11.0
	40.4	46.7	36.7			Total Current	43.2	45.2
	20.8	11.1	10.9			Long-Term Debt	17.4	17.6
	.1	.1	1.4			Deferred Taxes	.5	.5
	5.1	5.0	6.5			All Other Non-Current	9.7	9.7
	33.6	37.1	44.5			Net Worth	29.3	27.0
	100.0	100.0	100.0			Total Liabilties & Net Worth	100.0	100.0
						INCOME DATA		
	100.0	100.0	100.0			Net Sales	100.0	100.0
	38.7	26.5	25.1			Gross Profit	32.6	32.0
	36.8	23.2	20.6			Operating Expenses	27.8	26.9
	1.8	3.3	4.5			Operating Profit	4.8	5.1
	.5	1.1	1.0			All Other Expenses (net)	1.7	1.2
	1.3	2.2	3.5			Profit Before Taxes	3.0	3.9
						RATIOS		
	2.9	2.5	3.3				2.5	2.6
	1.7	1.5	2.1			Current	1.5	1.7
	1.1	1.0	1.2				1.1	1.1
	2.2	1.0	1.4				1.3	1.4
	.8	.7	1.1			Quick	(146) .8	.8
	.4	.5	.4				.5	.5
22 16.7	21 17.1	29 12.6				Sales/Receivables	30 12.2	30 12.3
31 11.6	39 9.4	50 7.3					41 8.9	41 9.0
44 8.3	53 6.8	60 6.1					60 6.0	53 6.9
20 17.9	50 7.3	47 7.8				Cost of Sales/Inventory	37 10.0	38 9.5
55 6.7	70 5.2	73 5.0					65 5.6	69 5.3
163 2.2	124 2.9	122 3.0					116 3.2	105 3.5
10 36.3	19 19.2	15 24.6				Cost of Sales/Payables	19 19.5	19 19.5
22 16.8	34 10.7	26 13.9					35 10.5	29 12.7
88 4.1	53 6.9	43 8.5					55 6.6	46 7.9
	5.4	5.0	3.6				5.4	5.5
	10.3	7.8	6.3			Sales/Working Capital	9.2	9.3
	84.5	179.6	35.7				47.9	41.5
	25.8	5.3	8.9				9.2	7.5
	(20) 1.6	(46) 2.9	(32) 4.6			EBIT/Interest	(139) 3.0	(136) 2.9
	-1.0	.7	1.5				1.2	1.2
		3.8	10.7			Net Profit + Depr., Dep.,	9.7	10.0
		(10) 2.1	(15) 2.5			Amort./Cur. Mat. L/T/D	(32) 2.6	(38) 2.4
		-.4	1.6				1.4	1.1
	.1	.2	.3				.3	.3
	.4	.5	.6			Fixed/Worth	.7	.6
	5.5	1.8	1.4				1.8	1.6
	.7	.8	.5				.9	.7
	1.8	1.8	1.4			Debt/Worth	2.1	1.8
	10.9	6.3	3.3				6.5	5.9
	60.1	35.1	40.5			% Profit Before Taxes/Tangible	35.1	40.6
	(22) 9.7	(43) 14.8	(28) 13.4			Net Worth	(130) 16.7	(124) 18.5
	-11.5	1.1	2.1				5.5	3.7
	27.8	12.0	12.9			% Profit Before Taxes/Total	14.9	14.4
	3.1	3.7	3.9			Assets	5.9	6.6
	-3.1	-.3	-.1				.6	.6
	39.6	44.2	14.4				34.7	27.6
	22.7	18.9	8.8			Sales/Net Fixed Assets	12.1	12.2
	8.2	7.8	5.0				5.8	5.8
	3.8	3.1	2.2				3.0	3.0
	2.9	2.4	1.7			Sales/Total Assets	2.1	2.2
	1.7	1.8	1.3				1.4	1.6
	.7	.5	1.2				.9	.9
	(19) 1.8	(41) 1.1	(28) 1.7			% Depr., Dep., Amort./Sales	(129) 1.9	(128) 1.7
	2.6	2.7	3.3				3.4	2.9
	2.3	1.5				% Officers', Directors'	2.0	2.1
	(10) 8.6	(23) 2.8				Owners' Comp/Sales	(47) 3.8	(52) 4.4
	11.4	4.3					7.9	8.6
11419M	77080M	495387M	1601714M	635815M	1228580M	Net Sales ($)	5735449M	5415430M
1730M	27389M	214406M	773159M	377303M	887061M	Total Assets ($)	2914111M	3030487M

© RMA 2010

M = $ thousand   MM = $ million
See Pages 9 through 22 for Explanation of Ratios and Data

Comparative Historical Data | | Current Data Sorted by Sales

Type of Statement	07-08	08-09	09-10	0-1MM	1-3MM	3-5MM	5-10MM	10-25MM	25MM & OVER
Unqualified	26	23	21		1	1	2	6	11
Reviewed	23	26	19		1	1	4	10	4
Compiled	20	15	17	1	5	4	2	4	1
Tax Returns	12	14	16	2	5	3	4	2	
Other	57	47	52	1	6	7	8	10	20
	4/1/07-3/31/08 ALL	4/1/08-3/31/09 ALL	4/1/09-3/31/10 ALL		22 (4/1-9/30/09)		103 (10/1/09-3/31/10)		
NUMBER OF STATEMENTS	138	125	125	4	18	15	20	32	36
ASSETS	%	%	%	%	%	%	%	%	%
Cash & Equivalents	6.2	7.3	7.1		7.2	4.7	8.3	8.3	5.9
Trade Receivables (net)	24.6	22.7	24.3		28.5	23.6	27.3	23.8	20.9
Inventory	32.8	33.7	33.0		34.7	26.1	36.1	35.1	31.8
All Other Current	2.0	2.3	2.3		.6	.4	1.5	2.1	4.8
Total Current	65.6	66.0	66.6		71.0	54.8	73.2	69.3	63.4
Fixed Assets (net)	22.6	23.4	23.1		21.6	36.1	17.9	19.6	25.6
Intangibles (net)	4.8	5.3	4.6		2.3	1.4	4.9	5.8	6.3
All Other Non-Current	7.1	5.2	5.6		5.1	7.7	4.0	5.3	4.7
Total	100.0	100.0	100.0		100.0	100.0	100.0	100.0	100.0
LIABILITIES									
Notes Payable-Short Term	13.7	12.9	13.3		20.1	12.8	13.7	13.1	9.4
Cur. Mat.-L.T.D.	3.6	3.7	4.4		6.6	2.2	4.8	4.0	4.8
Trade Payables	14.5	14.7	17.9		21.4	14.3	18.4	19.9	13.3
Income Taxes Payable	.3	.2	.3		.0	.0	.2	.2	.4
All Other Current	11.6	9.5	8.2		7.3	10.6	8.3	7.8	8.3
Total Current	43.7	41.0	44.1		55.4	39.8	45.5	45.0	36.2
Long-Term Debt	14.6	14.8	16.5		33.8	28.6	9.8	9.7	11.6
Deferred Taxes	.3	.5	.6		.1	.1	.0	.3	1.8
All Other Non-Current	6.7	7.8	8.3		29.0	.8	4.2	5.1	7.1
Net Worth	34.7	35.9	30.5		-18.3	30.7	40.5	40.0	43.3
Total Liabilities & Net Worth	100.0	100.0	100.0		100.0	100.0	100.0	100.0	100.0
INCOME DATA									
Net Sales	100.0	100.0	100.0		100.0	100.0	100.0	100.0	100.0
Gross Profit	30.5	28.5	28.4		38.2	37.7	26.6	26.2	21.5
Operating Expenses	25.2	25.1	25.3		40.3	33.4	23.8	21.3	18.3
Operating Profit	5.4	3.3	3.0		-2.1	4.2	2.9	4.9	3.3
All Other Expenses (net)	1.5	1.6	1.0		.9	1.6	.2	.2	1.9
Profit Before Taxes	3.8	1.7	2.1		-3.0	2.6	2.7	4.7	1.4
RATIOS									
Current	2.5	2.7	2.7		4.5	2.2	2.4	2.9	3.2
	1.7	1.7	1.6		1.8	1.2	1.7	1.6	2.1
	1.3	1.2	1.1		1.0	.9	1.2	1.1	1.3
Quick	1.2	1.2	1.3		2.9	1.0	1.2	1.2	1.6
	.9	.7	.7		.7	.7	.8	.7	1.0
	.5	.5	.5		.3	.4	.5	.4	.5
Sales/Receivables	30 12.1	26 13.9	24 15.2		21 17.1	22 16.5	25 14.4	18 20.3	30 12.0
	40 9.1	37 9.9	39 9.4		33 10.9	33 11.2	42 8.7	40 9.1	45 8.1
	57 6.4	50 7.3	54 6.7		44 8.3	44 8.3	56 6.5	58 6.3	57 6.4
Cost of Sales/Inventory	46 7.9	46 7.9	36 10.2		29 12.8	19 19.4	37 9.9	50 7.3	46 7.9
	77 4.8	86 4.3	67 5.4		81 4.5	44 8.4	66 5.5	68 5.4	68 5.3
	120 3.0	131 2.8	120 3.0		189 1.9	127 2.9	123 3.0	121 3.0	96 3.8
Cost of Sales/Payables	17 22.0	16 23.1	17 21.4		7 50.8	16 23.3	13 27.9	18 20.5	18 20.7
	32 11.5	32 11.5	30 12.3		22 16.4	38 9.7	32 11.5	30 12.1	29 12.5
	47 7.8	47 7.8	49 7.5		86 4.2	50 7.3	53 6.9	48 7.7	42 8.6
Sales/Working Capital	4.8	4.6	4.7		3.7	6.8	5.2	4.8	3.9
	8.3	7.2	7.8		9.1	31.4	8.2	7.9	6.5
	17.1	34.9	86.6		286.9	-25.3	24.5	73.1	13.5
EBIT/Interest	8.0	7.2	8.3		2.0	20.1	8.6	7.4	9.0
	(123) 2.7	(114) 2.3	(116) 3.0		(15) -1.2	(14) 1.6	2.8	(30) 3.9	(34) 5.1
	1.3	.7	-.2		-7.2	-.5	1.4	1.9	-.2
Net Profit + Depr., Dep., Amort./Cur. Mat. L/T/D	10.7	4.5	5.2					2.5	12.1
	(31) 2.4	(31) 1.5	(32) 2.1					(10) 1.8	(16) 3.5
	1.1	.3	.0					1.2	.2
Fixed/Worth	.2	.2	.2		.1	.1	.2	.2	.3
	.6	.7	.6		.8	.6	.4	.6	.5
	1.7	1.4	1.8		-1.0	5.2	3.6	1.3	1.4
Debt/Worth	.7	.7	.7		.7	.7	.9	.8	.5
	1.8	1.6	1.8		9.1	1.7	1.4	1.8	1.2
	5.6	4.8	7.2		-3.8	6.1	7.3	6.1	2.8
% Profit Before Taxes/Tangible Net Worth	45.9	27.5	39.6		41.7	37.5	49.0	50.6	31.1
	(117) 18.1	(108) 9.1	(105) 14.8		(12) -3.8	(13) 13.4	(17) 11.8	(31) 24.5	(29) 15.7
	5.6	.1	1.0		-19.7	-7.3	1.8	9.0	.9
% Profit Before Taxes/Total Assets	15.5	10.3	13.0		15.1	20.5	14.3	12.1	11.4
	6.2	3.9	3.9		-2.9	4.0	3.5	4.3	3.7
	.8	-.9	-1.6		-20.7	-1.2	1.0	3.1	-5.4
Sales/Net Fixed Assets	29.4	29.2	37.5		41.7	38.3	48.5	36.9	17.0
	12.7	12.2	13.1		19.9	12.2	20.8	16.2	9.2
	6.1	5.1	7.0		8.6	5.0	8.8	7.9	4.9
Sales/Total Assets	2.8	2.8	3.1		3.9	3.9	3.1	3.1	2.2
	2.1	2.1	2.2		2.6	2.5	2.5	2.3	1.8
	1.5	1.5	1.6		1.5	1.6	1.7	1.5	1.6
% Depr., Dep., Amort./Sales	.8	1.0	.7		1.0	.5	.3	.5	1.2
	(122) 1.6	(103) 1.7	(104) 1.5		(16) 1.7	(13) 1.2	(16) 1.5	(29) 1.3	(28) 1.9
	2.7	2.7	2.8		2.7	2.9	2.8	2.2	3.7
% Officers', Directors' Owners' Comp/Sales	2.7	1.5	1.5				1.5	1.3	
	(39) 3.7	(34) 3.3	(44) 3.6				(11) 2.6	(11) 2.8	
	6.1	5.7	5.6				3.6	5.3	
Net Sales ($)	5854754M	4273886M	4049995M	2648M	34905M	59576M	146343M	500620M	3305903M
Total Assets ($)	3175787M	2389455M	2281048M	1381M	16685M	32652M	78283M	267072M	1884975M

M = $ thousand   MM = $ million
See Pages 9 through 22 for Explanation of Ratios and Data

Current Data Sorted by Assets   Comparative Historical Data

						Type of Statement		
		3	7	2	2	Unqualified	16	16
	4	3	9			Reviewed	14	15
	3	4				Compiled	10	5
3	3	1				Tax Returns	1	7
1	2	8	2	4		Other	6	9
	8 (4/1-9/30/09)		53 (10/1/09-3/31/10)				4/1/05-3/31/06	4/1/06-3/31/07
0-500M	500M-2MM	2-10MM	10-50MM	50-100MM	100-250MM		ALL	ALL
4	12	19	18	6	2	NUMBER OF STATEMENTS	47	52
%	%	%	%	%	%	ASSETS	%	%
	10.9	16.7	8.6			Cash & Equivalents	9.4	8.6
	33.3	29.0	33.8			Trade Receivables (net)	29.9	29.6
	41.5	28.9	38.5			Inventory	40.1	40.2
	.2	2.9	.9			All Other Current	3.9	2.5
	86.0	77.6	81.9			Total Current	83.3	80.9
	4.6	12.6	10.5			Fixed Assets (net)	7.9	10.6
	.1	1.6	3.1			Intangibles (net)	4.9	3.0
	9.4	8.2	4.6			All Other Non-Current	3.9	5.5
	100.0	100.0	100.0			Total	100.0	100.0
						LIABILITIES		
	9.8	15.8	16.4			Notes Payable-Short Term	13.3	17.2
	2.9	1.9	1.6			Cur. Mat.-L.T.D.	2.7	1.5
	17.6	16.3	16.6			Trade Payables	15.8	15.1
	.0	.1	.1			Income Taxes Payable	.6	.5
	5.4	9.2	8.7			All Other Current	8.9	8.2
	35.6	43.3	43.4			Total Current	41.3	42.5
	6.9	4.1	7.9			Long-Term Debt	8.4	7.6
	.0	.0	.1			Deferred Taxes	.3	.0
	3.1	3.5	1.5			All Other Non-Current	6.6	5.4
	54.3	49.1	47.1			Net Worth	43.4	44.4
	100.0	100.0	100.0			Total Liabilities & Net Worth	100.0	100.0
						INCOME DATA		
	100.0	100.0	100.0			Net Sales	100.0	100.0
	31.3	34.8	30.7			Gross Profit	33.2	28.6
	26.6	30.4	27.0			Operating Expenses	28.6	25.8
	4.7	4.5	3.7			Operating Profit	4.6	2.8
	1.2	1.2	.3			All Other Expenses (net)	.8	.6
	3.5	3.2	3.4			Profit Before Taxes	3.8	2.2
						RATIOS		
	4.1	6.2	2.7				3.5	4.1
	2.5	2.1	1.9			Current	2.0	1.8
	1.6	1.3	1.4				1.4	1.3
	2.2	4.4	1.9				1.6	2.2
	1.4	1.3	.9			Quick	.9	.7
	.8	.5	.5				.5	.5

35	10.3	18	20.4	38	9.7			Sales/Receivables	24	15.1	26	14.0
41	8.9	42	8.7	61	6.0				46	7.9	43	8.6
51	7.1	74	4.9	80	4.6				61	6.0	64	5.7
49	7.5	23	15.8	56	6.5			Cost of Sales/Inventory	52	7.1	52	7.0
82	4.5	58	6.3	100	3.7				94	3.9	107	3.4
101	3.6	201	1.8	170	2.1				169	2.2	136	2.7
13	27.7	8	44.7	12	31.2			Cost of Sales/Payables	21	17.7	21	17.8
20	18.2	33	11.0	43	8.6				30	12.3	30	12.0
37	9.9	58	6.3	75	4.9				50	7.3	47	7.7

	4.0		2.2		3.2			Sales/Working Capital	4.0	3.5
	5.5		6.0		5.4				6.1	7.6
	11.9		12.4		8.0				9.0	16.0
	15.6		28.2		23.7			EBIT/Interest	17.2	6.8
(11)	5.0	(15)	6.0		4.6				(38) 2.7	(47) 2.4
	1.3		1.0		.8				1.3	.7
								Net Profit + Depr., Dep., Amort./Cur. Mat. L/T/D		
	.0		.0		.0			Fixed/Worth	.0	.0
	.0		.1		.1				.1	.2
	.2		.4		.4				.5	.5
	.4		.2		.6			Debt/Worth	.6	.3
	.7		1.0		1.1				1.3	1.3
	1.1		2.8		1.7				3.0	3.7
	36.3		25.5		29.3			% Profit Before Taxes/Tangible Net Worth	31.1	29.2
(11)	8.0	(18)	8.3	(17)	15.9				(41) 12.4	(48) 9.4
	1.8		-.9		1.4				4.6	-6.1
	19.9		14.5		13.6			% Profit Before Taxes/Total Assets	15.5	12.1
	5.0		2.2		7.0				6.3	3.9
	1.1		-1.8		-.6				1.7	-3.0
	999.8		307.8		324.2			Sales/Net Fixed Assets	128.2	105.2
	160.0		25.5		29.5				35.4	35.1
	92.9		9.7		11.3				18.8	17.1
	3.6		3.2		2.4			Sales/Total Assets	3.1	3.0
	2.7		2.5		1.8				2.2	2.3
	2.5		1.5		1.5				1.7	1.6
			.2		.3			% Depr., Dep., Amort./Sales	.3	.3
		(17)	.7	(16)	1.2				(39) .8	(45) .7
			.9		2.1				1.4	1.3
								% Officers', Directors' Owners' Comp/Sales	2.0	.7
									(22) 2.9	(25) 2.3
									7.3	5.5

4021M	45916M	197692M	744063M	827674M	547173M	Net Sales ($)	1750168M	1794083M
1051M	13987M	87680M	388967M	415055M	291861M	Total Assets ($)	843558M	865337M

M = $ thousand   MM = $ million
See Pages 9 through 22 for Explanation of Ratios and Data

Comparative Historical Data

Current Data Sorted by Sales

			Type of Statement						
17	18	14	Unqualified				1	4	9
14	16	16	Reviewed		1	4	2	2	7
6	2	7	Compiled	1	1		4	1	
2	1	7	Tax Returns	3	2	1	1		
16	17	17	Other		3	2		6	6
4/1/07-	4/1/08-	4/1/09-			8 (4/1-9/30/09)		53 (10/1/09-3/31/10)		
3/31/08	3/31/09	3/31/10		0-1MM	1-3MM	3-5MM	5-10MM	10-25MM	25MM & OVER
ALL	ALL	ALL							
55	54	61	NUMBER OF STATEMENTS	4	7	7	8	13	22
%	%	%	ASSETS	%	%	%	%	%	%
10.5	9.8	13.0	Cash & Equivalents					10.4	13.7
25.9	32.6	31.3	Trade Receivables (net)					27.2	30.9
35.9	34.7	33.3	Inventory					31.2	34.2
4.9	3.8	2.0	All Other Current					2.7	2.7
77.2	80.9	79.6	Total Current					71.5	81.5
12.7	10.7	10.5	Fixed Assets (net)					14.8	9.8
4.3	1.9	1.9	Intangibles (net)					5.3	1.8
5.9	6.5	8.1	All Other Non-Current					8.4	6.9
100.0	100.0	100.0	Total					100.0	100.0
			LIABILITIES						
13.8	15.8	12.2	Notes Payable-Short Term					12.2	12.7
2.8	4.1	3.8	Cur. Mat.-L.T.D.					3.1	1.6
14.5	16.4	17.6	Trade Payables					27.8	16.1
.6	.2	.1	Income Taxes Payable					.0	.2
8.3	9.5	9.3	All Other Current					10.3	8.7
39.9	46.0	43.1	Total Current					53.4	39.2
11.1	6.7	6.3	Long-Term Debt					12.8	4.2
.2	.1	.2	Deferred Taxes					.2	.3
3.5	5.1	3.9	All Other Non-Current					.3	1.9
45.3	41.9	46.6	Net Worth					33.3	54.4
100.0	100.0	100.0	Total Liabilities & Net Worth					100.0	100.0
			INCOME DATA						
100.0	100.0	100.0	Net Sales					100.0	100.0
31.8	32.5	32.8	Gross Profit					30.5	27.9
29.2	28.0	28.3	Operating Expenses					28.1	23.4
2.5	4.5	4.5	Operating Profit					2.4	4.5
.4	.4	.7	All Other Expenses (net)					.8	-.2
2.1	4.1	3.8	Profit Before Taxes					1.6	4.6
			RATIOS						
4.6	2.6	4.2						2.1	4.5
1.9	1.9	2.0	Current					1.5	2.1
1.5	1.4	1.3						1.0	1.4
1.9	1.5	2.6						1.4	3.0
1.0	.9	1.0	Quick					.7	1.1
.5	.5	.6						.4	.6

												Sales/Receivables												
19	19.0	28	13.2	29	12.6	Sales/Receivables				23	16.1	30	12.0
38	9.6	48	7.6	46	8.0					41	8.8	61	5.9
54	6.7	74	5.0	67	5.5					55	6.6	78	4.7
40	9.2	49	7.4	43	8.4	Cost of Sales/Inventory				40	9.1	52	7.0
89	4.1	89	4.1	84	4.3					58	6.3	87	4.2
188	1.9	133	2.8	132	2.8					132	2.8	105	3.5
16	23.2	18	20.7	12	31.4	Cost of Sales/Payables				35	10.4	11	34.3
25	14.7	29	12.4	33	11.0					66	5.5	38	9.6
42	8.6	52	7.0	66	5.5					80	4.6	59	6.2

3.2		3.9		3.2	Sales/Working Capital					6.1	2.9
4.8		6.1		5.5						7.7	5.0
15.4		11.5		12.9						NM	7.7
9.0		12.5		24.3	EBIT/Interest					24.2	25.4
(47) 2.7	(48)	3.5	(52)	5.0					(12)	3.5	(20) 6.3
-.2		1.3		1.3						-.9	1.9
		14.8			Net Profit + Depr., Dep., Amort./Cur. Mat. L/T/D						
	(14)	3.9									
		.7									
.1		.0		.0	Fixed/Worth					.0	.1
.2		.1		.1						.3	.1
.7		.5		.4						.6	.5
.4		.6		.4	Debt/Worth					.9	.3
1.4		1.4		1.0						1.7	1.0
3.7		3.4		2.3						2.8	2.2
34.9		36.5		35.9	% Profit Before Taxes/Tangible Net Worth					36.8	33.9
(49) 10.8	(51)	16.8	(56)	16.2					(11)	9.5	18.2
-8.5		3.7		.9						-7.4	6.8
16.3		16.4		15.0	% Profit Before Taxes/Total Assets					13.4	15.5
5.2		5.8		6.6						.1	8.6
-2.4		1.3		.1						-4.5	2.1
101.6		183.1		257.3	Sales/Net Fixed Assets					389.8	51.4
26.2		39.1		35.8						18.0	24.4
14.1		14.2		12.8						8.1	15.8
3.0		2.9		3.1	Sales/Total Assets					3.3	2.6
2.2		2.2		2.3						2.6	2.0
1.5		1.7		1.6						1.8	1.5
.4		.3		.3	% Depr., Dep., Amort./Sales					.2	.3
(41) .9	(46)	.7	(51)	.7					(12)	.5	(21) .9
1.7		1.0		1.3						1.9	1.6
2.0		2.5		2.6	% Officers', Directors' Owners' Comp/Sales						
(20) 5.0	(18)	4.0	(23)	4.6							
11.3		5.9		7.2							

2223090M	3108503M	2366539M	Net Sales ($)	2863M	15469M	24669M	58723M	212000M	2052815M
1086770M	1452377M	1198601M	Total Assets ($)	3679M	6645M	21771M	21539M	103984M	1040983M

M = $ thousand   MM = $ million
See Pages 9 through 22 for Explanation of Ratios and Data

Current Data Sorted by Assets   **Comparative Historical Data**

0-500M	500M-2MM	2-10MM	10-50MM	50-100MM	100-250MM	Type of Statement	15	14
	2	2	11	4	1	Unqualified	15	14
		1	2		1	Reviewed	4	9
		2				Compiled	1	1
1		2				Tax Returns	2	3
1	1	4	2		4	Other	7	5
	9 (4/1-9/30/09)		32 (10/1/09-3/31/10)				4/1/05-3/31/06 ALL	4/1/06-3/31/07 ALL
2	3	11	15	4	6	**NUMBER OF STATEMENTS**	29	32
%	%	%	%	%	%	**ASSETS**	%	%
		21.6	9.0			Cash & Equivalents	6.5	13.6
		30.1	35.4			Trade Receivables (net)	28.5	28.3
		34.3	32.6			Inventory	36.7	32.8
		2.8	4.1			All Other Current	8.0	7.3
		88.8	81.2			Total Current	79.6	82.0
		4.9	10.5			Fixed Assets (net)	10.7	8.3
		2.0	3.0			Intangibles (net)	.4	4.0
		4.2	5.4			All Other Non-Current	9.3	5.8
		100.0	100.0			Total	100.0	100.0
						LIABILITIES		
		31.4	17.2			Notes Payable-Short Term	21.6	22.3
		.3	3.3			Cur. Mat.-L.T.D.	4.5	5.2
		24.2	21.2			Trade Payables	14.5	14.6
		.0	.2			Income Taxes Payable	.5	.3
		12.7	37.3			All Other Current	8.7	9.3
		68.6	79.2			Total Current	49.7	51.6
		1.1	3.1			Long-Term Debt	8.3	15.3
		.0	.0			Deferred Taxes	.7	.2
		11.5	26.6			All Other Non-Current	9.8	8.1
		18.8	-9.0			Net Worth	31.5	24.6
		100.0	100.0			Total Liabilities & Net Worth	100.0	100.0
						INCOME DATA		
		100.0	100.0			Net Sales	100.0	100.0
		30.7	33.6			Gross Profit	34.1	34.6
		28.5	30.7			Operating Expenses	31.6	29.9
		2.2	2.9			Operating Profit	2.5	4.6
		.9	2.1			All Other Expenses (net)	.9	.8
		1.4	.8			Profit Before Taxes	1.7	3.8
						RATIOS		
		2.3	2.3			Current	3.3	3.6
		1.5	1.8				1.6	2.1
		.8	1.1				1.2	1.4
		1.7	1.6			Quick	1.4	1.9
		.8	.9				(28) .8	.9
		.4	.4				.4	.5
		25 14.6	26 14.1			Sales/Receivables	18 20.0	23 16.1
		40 9.1	41 8.9				38 9.7	43 8.5
		48 7.6	70 5.2				53 6.9	54 6.8
		16 22.9	33 11.2			Cost of Sales/Inventory	42 8.6	35 10.3
		34 10.6	52 7.0				60 6.1	66 5.6
		88 4.1	79 4.6				113 3.2	113 3.2
		26 14.0	17 21.0			Cost of Sales/Payables	13 27.2	19 19.0
		41 8.9	27 13.7				25 14.3	25 14.4
		50 7.2	62 5.9				42 8.7	37 10.0
		6.4	4.5			Sales/Working Capital	4.6	3.8
		10.9	11.6				8.5	6.4
		-24.5	53.5				31.8	11.2
		13.1	23.9			EBIT/Interest	9.8	7.7
		5.9	2.0				(25) 2.0	(26) 3.2
		1.0	.7				1.1	1.0
						Net Profit + Depr., Dep., Amort./Cur. Mat. L/T/D		
		.0	.0			Fixed/Worth	.1	.0
		.2	.2				.2	.1
		.4	-.2				.9	1.4
		1.1	.7			Debt/Worth	.7	.5
		4.0	2.1				2.1	1.0
		25.2	-13.1				5.1	4.7
			83.6			% Profit Before Taxes/Tangible Net Worth	46.7	52.5
		(10)	32.0				(25) 10.5	(25) 14.9
			2.0				1.7	7.6
		9.2	20.9			% Profit Before Taxes/Total Assets	13.3	20.9
		7.5	4.1				2.9	9.5
		.0	-5.3				.2	1.4
		167.2	138.5			Sales/Net Fixed Assets	131.6	118.8
		57.7	51.6				64.2	49.7
		40.4	27.4				16.6	18.5
		4.4	3.3			Sales/Total Assets	3.7	3.5
		3.8	2.8				3.0	2.7
		2.2	2.3				1.8	1.5
			.2			% Depr., Dep., Amort./Sales	.3	.3
		(13)	.7				(23) .4	(27) .4
			.9				1.1	1.0
						% Officers', Directors' Owners' Comp/Sales	.6	1.5
							(12) 2.7	(14) 3.0
							3.8	5.7
4457M	13175M	202756M	1063320M	764925M	1420999M	Net Sales ($)	2658383M	3186908M
669M	4358M	57309M	355970M	314736M	949331M	Total Assets ($)	996030M	1444254M

Comparative Historical Data   Current Data Sorted by Sales

Type of Statement	4/1/07-3/31/08 ALL	4/1/08-3/31/09 ALL	4/1/09-3/31/10 ALL	0-1MM	1-3MM	3-5MM	5-10MM	10-25MM	25MM & OVER
Unqualified	14	18	18						18
Reviewed	2	6	6				1	2	3
Compiled	1	1	2					1	
Tax Returns	1	2	3			1		2	
Other	11	11	12	1	2	1	1	2	6
				9 (4/1-9/30/09)			32 (10/1/09-3/31/10)		
NUMBER OF STATEMENTS	29	38	41	1	2	2	2	7	27
ASSETS	%	%	%	%	%	%	%	%	%
Cash & Equivalents	11.1	10.2	15.3						9.4
Trade Receivables (net)	29.5	27.7	29.9						32.1
Inventory	34.8	36.5	28.7						28.7
All Other Current	4.5	5.4	3.3						4.3
Total Current	79.9	79.8	77.1						74.6
Fixed Assets (net)	9.7	9.4	11.0						11.3
Intangibles (net)	5.9	5.0	6.9						8.8
All Other Non-Current	4.5	5.7	5.0						5.3
Total	100.0	100.0	100.0						100.0
LIABILITIES									
Notes Payable-Short Term	13.1	15.5	18.1						19.7
Cur. Mat.-L.T.D.	5.7	1.9	2.5						3.7
Trade Payables	12.3	19.0	17.7						16.2
Income Taxes Payable	.6	.4	.1						.1
All Other Current	10.7	12.9	20.6						27.8
Total Current	42.4	49.7	59.1						67.5
Long-Term Debt	9.5	5.8	4.8						6.6
Deferred Taxes	.3	.2	.2						.3
All Other Non-Current	13.7	16.6	16.9						20.0
Net Worth	34.1	27.6	18.9						5.6
Total Liabilities & Net Worth	100.0	100.0	100.0						100.0
INCOME DATA									
Net Sales	100.0	100.0	100.0						100.0
Gross Profit	36.8	34.9	32.8						35.3
Operating Expenses	30.2	30.8	28.8						31.3
Operating Profit	6.6	4.1	4.0						3.9
All Other Expenses (net)	1.2	1.2	1.7						2.3
Profit Before Taxes	5.4	2.9	2.3						1.7
RATIOS									
Current	3.4	3.9	2.8						2.4
	2.1	1.9	1.8						1.8
	1.4	1.2	1.1						.9
Quick	1.8	1.6	1.7						1.7
	1.0	.8	1.0						.9
	.5	.3	.5						.4
Sales/Receivables	21 17.2	7 50.8	22 16.6						24 15.3
	47 7.8	36 10.1	41 8.9						42 8.6
	65 5.6	53 6.8	64 5.7						67 5.5
Cost of Sales/Inventory	52 7.0	43 8.5	29 12.5						32 11.3
	66 5.5	58 6.3	43 8.4						57 6.4
	133 2.7	120 3.0	88 4.1						92 4.0
Cost of Sales/Payables	16 22.9	15 24.3	17 21.4						17 21.0
	27 13.6	22 16.8	28 13.3						22 16.2
	37 9.8	42 8.8	47 7.8						46 8.0
Sales/Working Capital	3.8	4.1	4.6						4.7
	6.3	9.9	9.5						10.9
	15.6	36.7	38.0						-28.3
EBIT/Interest	(27) 7.5	(33) 7.7	(37) 10.4						(25) 8.0
	4.3	3.5	2.1						2.0
	1.9	.8	1.0						-.1
Net Profit + Depr., Dep., Amort./Cur. Mat. L/T/D			(10) 47.9						
			2.5						
			-24.6						
Fixed/Worth	.1	.1	.1						.1
	.1	.1	.2						.4
	NM	-7.5	NM						-.6
Debt/Worth	.5	.5	.7						.8
	1.7	1.8	2.1						4.3
	NM	-8.4	-20.5						-5.3
% Profit Before Taxes/Tangible Net Worth	(22) 54.3	(27) 53.8	(30) 70.0						(17) 89.4
	30.3	31.3	32.0						36.8
	6.4	14.0	6.8						5.3
% Profit Before Taxes/Total Assets	21.7	21.6	12.6						12.4
	11.6	9.0	5.8						4.5
	3.6	-.7	.3						-3.0
Sales/Net Fixed Assets	152.5	176.5	149.3						151.1
	38.9	53.5	51.6						49.1
	12.1	19.6	13.7						8.7
Sales/Total Assets	3.0	4.2	3.6						3.3
	2.4	2.8	2.7						2.5
	2.0	2.1	2.0						2.0
% Depr., Dep., Amort./Sales	(23) .3	(31) .2	(32) .2						(22) .3
	.5	.7	.5						.8
	.9	1.0	1.5						1.6
% Officers', Directors' Owners' Comp/Sales			1.8						
		(12) 3.8	(15) 2.7						
		6.2	5.0						
Net Sales ($)	4323863M	4350563M	3469632M	864M	4216M	6603M	10803M	118212M	3328934M
Total Assets ($)	2081015M	1839155M	1682373M	317M	4217M	2853M	2379M	39934M	1632673M

M = $ thousand   MM = $ million
See Pages 9 through 22 for Explanation of Ratios and Data

MANUFACTURING—Men's and Boys' Cut and Sew Suit, Coat, and Overcoat Manufacturing   NAICS 315222

	Current Data Sorted by Assets							Comparative Historical Data			

		2				3		Type of Statement			
		2						Unqualified		6	10
			1					Reviewed		6	6
	1	1						Compiled		1	1
	1	3	3	3	1			Tax Returns		5	6
	7 (4/1-9/30/09)		14 (10/1/09-3/31/10)					Other		7	6
										4/1/05- 3/31/06	4/1/06- 3/31/07
0-500M	500M-2MM	2-10MM	10-50MM	50-100MM	100-250MM					ALL	ALL
	2	8	4	3	4			NUMBER OF STATEMENTS		25	29
%	%	%	%	%	%			ASSETS		%	%

							ASSETS			
							Cash & Equivalents		5.8	5.0
							Trade Receivables (net)		23.4	32.3
							Inventory		44.0	34.4
							All Other Current		2.5	5.1
							Total Current		75.7	76.8
							Fixed Assets (net)		9.2	13.2
							Intangibles (net)		6.2	3.0
							All Other Non-Current		9.0	7.0
							Total		100.0	100.0
							LIABILITIES			
							Notes Payable-Short Term		14.5	12.6
							Cur. Mat.-L.T.D.		4.5	4.6
							Trade Payables		15.9	17.2
							Income Taxes Payable		.4	.2
							All Other Current		5.3	8.1
							Total Current		40.5	42.7
							Long-Term Debt		22.5	12.7
							Deferred Taxes		.5	.4
							All Other Non-Current		3.3	2.1
							Net Worth		33.2	42.1
							Total Liabilities & Net Worth		100.0	100.0
							INCOME DATA			
							Net Sales		100.0	100.0
							Gross Profit		36.0	37.8
							Operating Expenses		30.8	30.7
							Operating Profit		5.2	7.1
							All Other Expenses (net)		.9	1.7
							Profit Before Taxes		4.3	5.4

(Left-hand columns: DATA NOT AVAILABLE)

RATIOS			
		3.2	2.8
Current		1.9	1.8
		1.4	1.3
		1.2	1.6
Quick		.6	.8
		.4	.5

Sales/Receivables	2	156.3	16	22.3
	38	9.5	53	6.8
	69	5.3	68	5.3
Cost of Sales/Inventory	60	6.1	43	8.4
	101	3.6	73	5.0
	124	3.0	124	3.0
Cost of Sales/Payables	17	21.4	16	22.5
	27	13.3	36	10.1
	47	7.8	55	6.7
Sales/Working Capital		4.1		4.2
		6.5		7.1
		12.3		13.4
EBIT/Interest		9.7		6.1
	(24)	3.7	(26)	3.1
		1.1		1.6
Net Profit + Depr., Dep., Amort./Cur. Mat. L/T/D				30.0
			(12)	6.2
				2.0
Fixed/Worth		.1		.1
		.3		.2
		.6		.3
Debt/Worth		.9		.8
		1.1		1.4
		4.0		3.0
% Profit Before Taxes/Tangible Net Worth		40.8		30.6
	(23)	18.5	(27)	17.0
		3.3		5.8
% Profit Before Taxes/Total Assets		19.4		12.8
		6.1		6.1
		.3		2.3
Sales/Net Fixed Assets		151.8		67.0
		38.1		30.1
		17.4		15.8
Sales/Total Assets		3.0		3.2
		2.6		2.4
		1.6		1.8
% Depr., Dep., Amort./Sales		.3		.3
	(20)	.9	(23)	1.0
		1.6		1.3
% Officers', Directors' Owners' Comp/Sales				1.6
			(16)	3.0
				7.2

10687M	111813M	139484M	507497M	1433109M		Net Sales ($)		1461156M	2882887M
2094M	40128M	73316M	243901M	601236M		Total Assets ($)		674493M	1346708M

M = $ thousand   MM = $ million
See Pages 9 through 22 for Explanation of Ratios and Data

Comparative Historical Data

Current Data Sorted by Sales

4/1/07-3/31/08 ALL	4/1/08-3/31/09 ALL	4/1/09-3/31/10 ALL	Type of Statement	0-1MM	1-3MM	3-5MM	5-10MM	10-25MM	25MM & OVER
11	9	5	Unqualified					1	4
6	4	2	Reviewed					2	
2	1	1	Compiled						
2	2	2	Tax Returns				1	1	
5	6	11	Other				1	1	6
				1	1		3	6	10
	7 (4/1-9/30/09)					14 (10/1/09-3/31/10)			
26	22	21	**NUMBER OF STATEMENTS**	1	1		3	6	10
%	%	%	**ASSETS**	%	%	%	%	%	%
8.2	4.7	5.5	Cash & Equivalents						3.4
28.1	25.9	26.8	Trade Receivables (net)						29.5
40.0	44.7	38.1	Inventory						27.2
4.6	2.8	3.1	All Other Current	D					4.4
80.9	78.2	73.6	Total Current	A					64.4
8.4	10.3	9.1	Fixed Assets (net)	T					12.0
3.8	3.9	5.7	Intangibles (net)	A					8.0
6.9	7.6	11.6	All Other Non-Current	N O T					15.7
100.0	100.0	100.0	Total						100.0
			LIABILITIES	A V A I L A B L E					
11.0	15.2	15.6	Notes Payable-Short Term						4.5
4.1	2.7	11.0	Cur. Mat.-L.T.D.						4.6
14.4	14.8	15.4	Trade Payables						14.5
.2	.3	.8	Income Taxes Payable						1.5
12.5	9.3	13.6	All Other Current						12.7
42.2	42.3	56.4	Total Current						37.7
7.1	13.4	10.7	Long-Term Debt						15.9
.4	.5	.1	Deferred Taxes						.2
1.4	1.5	3.4	All Other Non-Current						3.4
48.9	42.3	29.4	Net Worth						42.7
100.0	100.0	100.0	Total Liabilities & Net Worth						100.0
			INCOME DATA						
100.0	100.0	100.0	Net Sales						100.0
33.9	34.0	31.7	Gross Profit						26.4
29.2	29.7	27.6	Operating Expenses						22.3
4.7	4.2	4.1	Operating Profit						4.1
.9	1.3	1.9	All Other Expenses (net)						2.3
3.8	3.0	2.2	Profit Before Taxes						1.7
			RATIOS						
2.8	2.6	2.7							2.9
2.2	1.9	1.7	Current						1.9
1.3	1.3	.8							.9
1.3	1.1	1.4							1.5
1.0	.7	1.0	Quick						1.0
.4	.5	.3							.3
21 17.1	18 19.9	12 31.6	Sales/Receivables						17 21.7
38 9.5	39 9.4	36 10.2							40 9.2
49 7.5	67 5.5	84 4.4							82 4.4
54 6.7	76 4.8	43 8.6	Cost of Sales/Inventory						36 10.3
75 4.8	106 3.4	92 4.0							61 6.0
117 3.1	147 2.5	144 2.5							93 3.9
14 26.8	14 26.7	19 18.7	Cost of Sales/Payables						20 18.5
26 13.8	30 12.0	24 15.1							22 16.7
43 8.5	61 5.9	57 6.4							34 10.6
4.7	4.6	4.6	Sales/Working Capital						5.5
6.6	6.6	6.5							8.0
11.8	15.8	-30.7							-32.7
16.9	7.3	6.1	EBIT/Interest						5.8
(23) 2.6	(20) 2.0	(19) 3.4							3.4
1.3	1.2	.9							.4
			Net Profit + Depr., Dep., Amort./Cur. Mat. L/T/D						
.1	.1	.0	Fixed/Worth						.1
.2	.2	.1							.2
.3	.3	1.7							NM
.5	.9	.8	Debt/Worth						.7
1.0	1.5	1.6							1.5
2.6	2.2	165.3							NM
29.0	32.5	29.3	% Profit Before Taxes/Tangible Net Worth						
(25) 15.9	(20) 10.3	(17) 18.5							
4.0	3.5	3.3							
15.5	12.1	10.8	% Profit Before Taxes/Total Assets						12.1
6.6	2.7	3.3							8.9
1.8	.9	-1.1							-3.2
100.9	62.5	156.7	Sales/Net Fixed Assets						38.9
35.4	33.7	34.5							27.8
19.1	19.4	12.0							10.4
3.4	3.1	3.0	Sales/Total Assets						2.8
2.6	2.6	2.3							2.3
2.0	1.8	2.0							2.1
.2	.6	.2	% Depr., Dep., Amort./Sales						
(24) .8	(19) 1.0	(16) .8							
1.3	1.1	1.3							
			% Officers', Directors' Owners' Comp/Sales						
2945119M	2913883M	2202590M	Net Sales ($)	735M	1565M		23960M	96021M	2080309M
1463784M	1250094M	960675M	Total Assets ($)	5083M	793M		7622M	45542M	901635M

M = $ thousand   MM = $ million
See Pages 9 through 22 for Explanation of Ratios and Data

Current Data Sorted by Assets

Comparative Historical Data

	0-500M	500M-2MM	2-10MM	10-50MM	50-100MM	100-250MM	Type of Statement	4/1/05-3/31/06 ALL	4/1/06-3/31/07 ALL
			2	3	2	2	Unqualified	10	14
	1	3	3				Reviewed	12	11
	1						Compiled	8	2
	1		1				Tax Returns	2	2
	1	2		1	3	2	Other	18	10
		4 (4/1-9/30/09)		24 (10/1/09-3/31/10)					
		4	8	7	5	4	NUMBER OF STATEMENTS	50	39
	%	%	%	%	%	%	ASSETS	%	%
							Cash & Equivalents	7.2	4.1
							Trade Receivables (net)	28.4	28.2
							Inventory	41.5	41.1
							All Other Current	2.8	5.0
							Total Current	79.9	78.4
							Fixed Assets (net)	11.5	10.4
							Intangibles (net)	3.0	3.7
							All Other Non-Current	5.7	7.5
							Total	100.0	100.0
							LIABILITIES		
							Notes Payable-Short Term	19.6	20.2
							Cur. Mat.-L.T.D.	1.5	2.0
							Trade Payables	12.8	13.3
							Income Taxes Payable	.2	.4
							All Other Current	5.3	9.0
							Total Current	39.3	44.9
							Long-Term Debt	5.4	9.3
							Deferred Taxes	.1	.2
							All Other Non-Current	14.8	16.3
							Net Worth	40.4	29.3
							Total Liabilities & Net Worth	100.0	100.0
							INCOME DATA		
							Net Sales	100.0	100.0
							Gross Profit	32.4	33.7
							Operating Expenses	29.8	30.3
							Operating Profit	2.6	3.4
							All Other Expenses (net)	1.6	2.5
							Profit Before Taxes	1.0	.9

(Left columns: DATA NOT AVAILABLE)

RATIOS

Ratio	4/1/05-3/31/06 ALL	4/1/06-3/31/07 ALL
Current	4.7	2.6
	2.3	1.9
	1.7	1.3
Quick	2.1	1.4
	1.0	.8
	.4	.3
Sales/Receivables	33 11.1	29 12.7
	49 7.4	49 7.4
	66 5.5	69 5.3
Cost of Sales/Inventory	62 5.9	71 5.2
	120 3.0	127 2.9
	174 2.1	151 2.4
Cost of Sales/Payables	14 25.3	16 22.9
	25 14.8	29 12.7
	43 8.5	39 9.5
Sales/Working Capital	2.7	3.9
	4.4	5.8
	7.6	10.8
EBIT/Interest	8.8	4.9
	(43) 1.7	(37) 1.6
	1.0	.8
Net Profit + Depr., Dep., Amort./Cur. Mat. L/T/D	7.0	3.2
	(11) 2.1	(11) 1.5
	1.0	.3
Fixed/Worth	.1	.1
	.2	.2
	.6	.7
Debt/Worth	.4	1.1
	1.3	1.9
	4.0	5.5
% Profit Before Taxes/Tangible Net Worth	27.8	41.6
	(43) 13.2	(33) 10.0
	1.7	-.6
% Profit Before Taxes/Total Assets	12.7	17.3
	4.1	2.7
	.1	-.3
Sales/Net Fixed Assets	73.7	77.0
	23.6	23.3
	12.3	12.3
Sales/Total Assets	2.5	2.7
	1.9	1.9
	1.6	1.5
% Depr., Dep., Amort./Sales	.5	.4
	(41) 1.3	(34) 1.1
	2.0	2.2
% Officers', Directors' Owners' Comp/Sales	2.0	1.6
	(22) 4.1	(17) 3.0
	6.6	7.6

	0-500M	500M-2MM	2-10MM	10-50MM	50-100MM	100-250MM		4/1/05-3/31/06 ALL	4/1/06-3/31/07 ALL
		12314M	105383M	449625M	811860M	764180M	Net Sales ($)	1598556M	1665392M
		4612M	51986M	175659M	388050M	454777M	Total Assets ($)	913978M	951365M

M = $ thousand   MM = $ million
See Pages 9 through 22 for Explanation of Ratios and Data

Comparative Historical Data | Current Data Sorted by Sales

10	9	9	Type of Statement						
10	9	9	Unqualified					2	7
9	11	7	Reviewed					3	2
3	2	1	Compiled	1		2	1		
2	1	2	Tax Returns					1	2
13	15	9	Other			1		1	5
4/1/07-3/31/08	4/1/08-3/31/09	4/1/09-3/31/10			4 (4/1-9/30/09)			24 (10/1/09-3/31/10)	
ALL	ALL	ALL		0-1MM	1-3MM	3-5MM	5-10MM	10-25MM	25MM & OVER
37	38	28	**NUMBER OF STATEMENTS**	1	2	2	1	8	14
%	%	%	**ASSETS**	%	%	%	%	%	%
5.0	4.6	4.2	Cash & Equivalents						4.0
26.3	26.1	24.5	Trade Receivables (net)						26.9
44.6	43.4	44.0	Inventory						39.4
4.3	3.9	3.5	All Other Current						5.0
80.2	78.0	76.2	Total Current						75.2
9.3	10.6	10.2	Fixed Assets (net)						11.5
6.3	5.7	8.3	Intangibles (net)						9.2
4.3	5.7	5.3	All Other Non-Current						4.1
100.0	100.0	100.0	Total						100.0
			LIABILITIES						
21.5	24.6	15.6	Notes Payable-Short Term						14.0
2.0	.6	1.7	Cur. Mat.-L.T.D.						1.5
12.8	11.2	17.9	Trade Payables						15.4
.6	.1	.7	Income Taxes Payable						1.4
7.1	8.9	8.2	All Other Current						11.1
43.9	45.4	44.1	Total Current						43.4
10.3	10.7	17.1	Long-Term Debt						23.2
.4	.4	.5	Deferred Taxes						1.0
8.8	5.4	8.4	All Other Non-Current						9.4
36.6	38.1	29.9	Net Worth						23.1
100.0	100.0	100.0	Total Liabilities & Net Worth						100.0
			INCOME DATA						
100.0	100.0	100.0	Net Sales						100.0
30.8	31.8	32.3	Gross Profit						32.3
28.4	31.0	30.4	Operating Expenses						27.7
2.4	.8	2.0	Operating Profit						4.7
2.1	2.4	2.7	All Other Expenses (net)						2.6
.4	-1.6	-.8	Profit Before Taxes						2.1
			RATIOS						
2.8	3.0	3.1							2.4
2.1	1.7	2.1	Current						1.9
1.4	1.3	1.4							1.5
1.1	1.1	1.4							1.5
.8	.8	.8	Quick						.8
.4	.4	.3							.3
31 11.7	30 12.2	16 23.1							11 33.0
49 7.5	39 9.3	42 8.8	Sales/Receivables						48 7.7
70 5.2	67 5.4	54 6.7							53 6.8
85 4.3	81 4.5	62 5.9							45 8.2
138 2.6	124 3.0	115 3.2	Cost of Sales/Inventory						80 4.6
164 2.2	191 1.9	193 1.9							151 2.4
17 21.6	15 24.8	19 18.9							18 20.4
29 12.4	26 14.1	32 11.3	Cost of Sales/Payables						32 11.3
42 8.7	41 9.0	44 8.4							45 8.2
3.5	3.6	4.5							4.9
4.7	5.0	5.8	Sales/Working Capital						7.0
7.8	12.0	11.7							11.9
5.4	4.7	7.5							12.4
(34) 2.4	(36) 1.5	1.3	EBIT/Interest						2.1
-.3	-1.7	-2.0							1.1
			Net Profit + Depr., Dep., Amort./Cur. Mat. L/T/D						
.1	.1	.1							.1
.2	.3	.3	Fixed/Worth						.6
.6	.7	1.8							NM
.6	.9	.9							1.4
1.4	2.2	2.1	Debt/Worth						2.8
3.4	4.4	13.4							NM
30.3	24.1	36.5							80.1
(32) 5.4	(34) 3.7	(23) 4.8	% Profit Before Taxes/Tangible Net Worth					(11) 28.1	
-4.9	-34.6	-18.2							2.3
7.0	7.5	13.5							25.6
3.1	1.0	1.4	% Profit Before Taxes/Total Assets						6.0
-3.8	-9.1	-8.6							.1
84.9	51.8	87.2							95.0
25.9	24.3	29.9	Sales/Net Fixed Assets						22.9
13.3	14.0	11.8							11.8
2.4	2.3	3.0							3.1
1.9	1.9	2.0	Sales/Total Assets						2.2
1.4	1.3	1.6							1.9
.4	.5	.4							.4
(34) .8	(31) .7	(21) 1.0	% Depr., Dep., Amort./Sales					(10) 1.1	
1.9	1.7	2.0							2.6
1.7	2.1								
(12) 3.4	(15) 5.7		% Officers', Directors' Owners' Comp/Sales						
5.2	7.0								
2141627M	1726394M	2143362M	Net Sales ($)	934M	4526M	6525M	5875M	130636M	1994866M
1425075M	1073779M	1075084M	Total Assets ($)	682M	3379M	8370M	1022M	86800M	974831M

© RMA 2010

M = $ thousand   MM = $ million

See Pages 9 through 22 for Explanation of Ratios and Data

MANUFACTURING—Women's and Girls' Cut and Sew Dress Manufacturing NAICS 315233

Current Data Sorted by Assets | **Comparative Historical Data**

						Type of Statement		
			1	2	1	Unqualified	6	6
		2	4	1		Reviewed	7	15
	2					Compiled	1	1
1		1	4		1	Tax Returns	1	2
	6 (4/1-9/30/09)	1	14 (10/1/09-3/31/10)			Other	10	8
							4/1/05-3/31/06	4/1/06-3/31/07
0-500M	500M-2MM	2-10MM	10-50MM	50-100MM	100-250MM		ALL	ALL
1	2	3	9	3	2	NUMBER OF STATEMENTS	25	32
%	%	%	%	%	%	ASSETS	%	%
						Cash & Equivalents	4.4	5.8
						Trade Receivables (net)	33.9	34.7
						Inventory	32.4	34.6
						All Other Current	3.0	3.0
						Total Current	73.7	78.2
						Fixed Assets (net)	11.4	12.5
						Intangibles (net)	4.9	3.0
						All Other Non-Current	10.0	6.3
						Total	100.0	100.0
						LIABILITIES		
						Notes Payable-Short Term	22.4	18.3
						Cur. Mat.-L.T.D.	2.0	.9
						Trade Payables	23.0	27.1
						Income Taxes Payable	.3	.2
						All Other Current	10.1	15.1
						Total Current	57.8	61.6
						Long-Term Debt	3.9	4.3
						Deferred Taxes	.4	.2
						All Other Non-Current	1.9	4.2
						Net Worth	35.9	29.8
						Total Liabilities & Net Worth	100.0	100.0
						INCOME DATA		
						Net Sales	100.0	100.0
						Gross Profit	37.8	41.3
						Operating Expenses	35.4	38.3
						Operating Profit	2.4	3.0
						All Other Expenses (net)	.1	.7
						Profit Before Taxes	2.3	2.3
						RATIOS		
						Current	1.5 / 1.3 / 1.1	1.8 / 1.5 / 1.2
						Quick	.8 / .6 / .5	1.1 / .8 / .5
						Sales/Receivables	39 9.3 / 54 6.7 / 63 5.8	24 15.2 / 42 8.8 / 58 6.3
						Cost of Sales/Inventory	51 7.2 / 75 4.9 / 129 2.8	44 8.2 / 62 5.9 / 111 3.3
						Cost of Sales/Payables	26 14.2 / 46 7.9 / 88 4.1	24 15.0 / 39 9.3 / 82 4.4
						Sales/Working Capital	9.4 / 17.5 / 183.7	8.7 / 12.8 / 27.3
						EBIT/Interest	7.0 / 2.7 / .3 (28)	6.7 / 4.2 / 2.0
						Net Profit + Depr., Dep., Amort./Cur. Mat. L/T/D		
						Fixed/Worth	.1 / .2 / .8	.1 / .2 / 1.1
						Debt/Worth	1.1 / 2.2 / 4.3	1.0 / 2.2 / 5.3
						% Profit Before Taxes/Tangible Net Worth	44.8 / 10.4 / -1.5 (24)	43.1 / 26.5 / 13.0 (28)
						% Profit Before Taxes/Total Assets	14.2 / 2.4 / -1.8	14.5 / 6.0 / 3.2
						Sales/Net Fixed Assets	119.0 / 33.3 / 15.5	163.5 / 38.9 / 21.3
						Sales/Total Assets	3.6 / 2.3 / 1.5	4.4 / 3.3 / 2.4
						% Depr., Dep., Amort./Sales	.3 / .6 / 1.4 (19)	.2 / .7 / 1.1 (23)
						% Officers', Directors' Owners' Comp/Sales	2.2 / 3.3 / 7.5 (14)	1.5 / 2.8 / 6.3 (16)
679M	5559M	91422M	535323M	423072M	580177M	Net Sales ($)	931063M	1371162M
392M	2237M	22423M	173396M	176201M	273866M	Total Assets ($)	385362M	500709M

M = $ thousand   MM = $ million
See Pages 9 through 22 for Explanation of Ratios and Data

Comparative Historical Data   **Current Data Sorted by Sales**

			Type of Statement						
4	2	4	Unqualified						4
9	9	7	Reviewed						7
		2	Compiled						
1	1	1	Tax Returns	1	1	1		1	
11	12	6	Other	1				1	5
4/1/07-3/31/08 ALL	4/1/08-3/31/09 ALL	4/1/09-3/31/10 ALL		0-1MM	6 (4/1-9/30/09) 1-3MM	3-5MM	14 (10/1/09-3/31/10) 5-10MM	10-25MM	25MM & OVER
25	24	20	**NUMBER OF STATEMENTS**	1	1	1		1	16
%	%	%	**ASSETS**	%	%	%		%	%
6.0	11.7	14.7	Cash & Equivalents						14.4
28.6	22.7	30.8	Trade Receivables (net)				D		30.5
35.3	37.2	32.8	Inventory				A		31.9
2.6	4.6	2.9	All Other Current				T		3.6
72.5	76.2	81.3	Total Current				A		80.4
15.2	16.1	11.4	Fixed Assets (net)						10.8
4.8	2.7	3.2	Intangibles (net)				N		4.0
7.5	5.0	4.1	All Other Non-Current				O		4.8
100.0	100.0	100.0	Total				T		100.0
			LIABILITIES						
27.2	16.5	14.5	Notes Payable-Short Term				A		12.6
3.3	3.2	1.7	Cur. Mat.-L.T.D.				V		1.3
16.4	21.1	20.4	Trade Payables				A		20.9
.4	.6	.2	Income Taxes Payable				I		.2
9.6	12.3	10.8	All Other Current				L		11.6
56.9	53.7	47.6	Total Current				A		46.6
4.8	8.8	12.4	Long-Term Debt				B		14.8
.0	.0	.0	Deferred Taxes				L		.0
3.9	9.1	8.4	All Other Non-Current				E		9.0
34.3	28.4	31.5	Net Worth						29.6
100.0	100.0	100.0	Total Liabilities & Net Worth						100.0
			INCOME DATA						
100.0	100.0	100.0	Net Sales						100.0
40.2	39.4	36.4	Gross Profit						36.0
35.8	36.2	31.8	Operating Expenses						31.5
4.4	3.2	4.7	Operating Profit						4.5
1.1	1.2	.8	All Other Expenses (net)						.9
3.3	2.0	3.8	Profit Before Taxes						3.6
			RATIOS						
1.9	2.0	3.1							2.5
1.4	1.5	1.5	Current						1.5
1.2	1.2	1.3							1.3
1.1	1.0	2.1							1.5
.7	.7	.9	Quick						.9
.2	.2	.6							.6
20 18.5	6 63.9	15 24.4	Sales/Receivables					15	24.4
35 10.4	25 14.3	38 9.6						38	9.6
55 6.6	35 10.3	64 5.7						64	5.7
48 7.6	35 10.4	37 9.8	Cost of Sales/Inventory					37	9.8
75 4.9	74 5.0	74 4.9						66	5.6
116 3.2	93 3.9	117 3.1						114	3.2
23 16.0	13 28.6	21 17.5	Cost of Sales/Payables					21	17.2
30 12.1	35 10.6	29 12.5						29	12.5
40 9.1	59 6.2	55 6.6						55	6.6
8.0	7.8	4.7	Sales/Working Capital						6.4
12.5	13.0	8.5							8.5
24.6	37.8	19.0							18.1
7.4	11.4	16.9	EBIT/Interest						18.0
(23) 2.2	(22) 2.9	(16) 3.1						(14)	3.1
1.3	.3	1.4							1.4
			Net Profit + Depr., Dep., Amort./Cur. Mat. L/T/D						
.1	.1	.0	Fixed/Worth						.0
.3	.4	.2							.2
1.1	2.0	1.8							1.8
.8	1.0	.6	Debt/Worth						.7
1.8	2.8	2.8							2.8
6.0	7.1	6.9							6.6
38.8	58.8	50.8	% Profit Before Taxes/Tangible Net Worth						52.8
(22) 28.6	(20) 24.1	(16) 20.5						(13)	25.3
8.0	4.0	6.0							9.5
16.6	12.6	17.1	% Profit Before Taxes/Total Assets						17.9
7.3	8.2	9.0							8.5
2.0	-5.5	2.5							2.5
77.8	169.9	284.5	Sales/Net Fixed Assets						284.5
29.7	21.9	27.7							27.7
12.8	12.6	13.1							13.1
3.7	4.5	3.8	Sales/Total Assets						3.8
2.9	3.0	2.7							2.7
2.1	2.5	1.8							1.9
.2	.2	.2	% Depr., Dep., Amort./Sales						.2
(22) .6	(21) .7	(16) .8						(14)	.7
1.4	1.9	1.6							1.2
			% Officers', Directors' Owners' Comp/Sales						
1774475M	1095148M	1636232M	Net Sales ($)	679M	2036M	3523M	15000M	10-25MM	1614994M
658449M	417247M	648515M	Total Assets ($)	392M	1217M	1020M	4862M		641024M

M = $ thousand   MM = $ million
See Pages 9 through 22 for Explanation of Ratios and Data

Current Data Sorted by Assets   ## Comparative Historical Data

Current size columns: **14 (4/1-9/30/09)** and **37 (10/1/09-3/31/10)**

	0-500M	500M-2MM	2-10MM	10-50MM	50-100MM	100-250MM		4/1/05-3/31/06 ALL	4/1/06-3/31/07 ALL
Type of Statement									
Unqualified		1	1	9	4	1		6	12
Reviewed		1	9	4				9	12
Compiled		1						3	2
Tax Returns	1							5	2
Other		3	5	9	1	1		12	10
NUMBER OF STATEMENTS	1	6	15	22	5	2		35	38
	%	%	%	%	%	%		%	%
ASSETS									
Cash & Equivalents			11.8	19.3				13.1	9.5
Trade Receivables (net)			29.7	23.9				25.9	29.4
Inventory			36.2	28.0				38.9	37.5
All Other Current			7.7	5.4				1.3	2.9
Total Current			85.3	76.6				79.2	79.2
Fixed Assets (net)			5.6	9.0				11.9	10.2
Intangibles (net)			4.5	5.3				4.0	5.0
All Other Non-Current			4.6	9.1				4.9	5.5
Total			100.0	100.0				100.0	100.0
LIABILITIES									
Notes Payable-Short Term			20.8	6.5				13.1	15.6
Cur. Mat.-L.T.D.			2.1	5.5				2.2	3.6
Trade Payables			22.2	20.2				14.3	12.3
Income Taxes Payable			.1	1.4				.2	.3
All Other Current			9.9	10.9				16.5	10.6
Total Current			55.1	44.5				46.2	42.3
Long-Term Debt			10.4	3.5				7.9	10.5
Deferred Taxes			.0	.0				.1	.3
All Other Non-Current			24.9	5.2				5.6	6.6
Net Worth			9.6	46.8				40.1	40.3
Total Liabilities & Net Worth			100.0	100.0				100.0	100.0
INCOME DATA									
Net Sales			100.0	100.0				100.0	100.0
Gross Profit			34.4	34.6				35.2	34.1
Operating Expenses			30.7	27.8				30.7	30.6
Operating Profit			3.7	6.7				4.5	3.4
All Other Expenses (net)			.8	1.4				.9	2.1
Profit Before Taxes			2.9	5.4				3.5	1.4
RATIOS									
			2.8	3.1				2.7	2.7
Current			1.9	2.0				1.7	1.8
			1.1	1.5				1.1	1.4
			1.6	1.6				1.4	1.4
Quick			.8	.9				.8	.9
			.5	.7				.4	.5
			17 21.1	12 30.9				12 31.7	24 15.5
Sales/Receivables			34 10.7	40 9.1				33 11.1	36 10.1
			52 7.0	67 5.5				62 5.9	62 5.9
			35 10.4	31 11.7				39 9.3	46 8.0
Cost of Sales/Inventory			58 6.3	58 6.3				76 4.8	76 4.8
			103 3.5	85 4.3				110 3.3	123 3.0
			18 20.1	13 27.5				12 29.2	14 26.1
Cost of Sales/Payables			23 15.8	37 9.9				25 14.8	23 15.8
			43 8.5	53 6.9				40 9.1	36 10.0
			4.5	4.5				4.7	4.5
Sales/Working Capital			7.8	7.1				9.7	7.1
			24.7	16.1				30.4	12.7
			10.0	20.8				13.5	7.0
EBIT/Interest			(13) 2.2	(18) 5.1				(32) 3.8	(36) 2.4
			1.1	2.0				1.2	1.3
Net Profit + Depr., Dep., Amort./Cur. Mat. L/T/D									
			.0	.0				.1	.1
Fixed/Worth			.1	.1				.2	.1
			1.0	.6				.9	.6
			1.1	.5				.6	.6
Debt/Worth			1.7	1.3				1.4	1.5
			6.5	4.3				4.8	5.7
			69.2	64.0				41.3	24.7
% Profit Before Taxes/Tangible Net Worth			(13) 21.8	(20) 31.4				(31) 16.4	(31) 13.3
			.8	.5				-3.3	2.7
			26.2	22.0				20.8	14.0
% Profit Before Taxes/Total Assets			8.8	11.2				9.1	5.7
			.2	.7				-.5	.6
			166.3	254.9				179.2	121.0
Sales/Net Fixed Assets			80.5	53.0				47.4	54.8
			35.0	14.1				20.0	18.6
			4.4	3.1				4.0	3.6
Sales/Total Assets			3.4	2.5				3.0	2.6
			2.1	1.7				2.0	1.8
				.2				.2	.3
% Depr., Dep., Amort./Sales				(18) .4				(29) .5	(30) .5
				.8				1.3	1.4
								1.0	.8
% Officers', Directors' Owners' Comp/Sales								(16) 2.7	(13) 1.6
								8.4	6.1
Net Sales ($)	516M	21467M	304757M	1409742M	771047M	366636M		1748013M	1991533M
Total Assets ($)	281M	5960M	88288M	584211M	330748M	391885M		904799M	1124043M

M = $ thousand   MM = $ million
See Pages 9 through 22 for Explanation of Ratios and Data

Comparative Historical Data | | | | Current Data Sorted by Sales

08	09	10	Type of Statement	0-1MM	1-3MM	3-5MM	5-10MM	10-25MM	25MM & OVER
9	13	16	Unqualified				1	1	14
9	9	14	Reviewed		3			6	5
3	1	1	Compiled		1				
1	6	1	Tax Returns						
11	12	19	Other	1	1	1	2	1	14
4/1/07-3/31/08 ALL	4/1/08-3/31/09 ALL	4/1/09-3/31/10 ALL			14 (4/1-9/30/09)		37 (10/1/09-3/31/10)		
33	41	51	**NUMBER OF STATEMENTS**	1	3	4	2	8	33
%	%	%	**ASSETS**	%	%	%	%	%	%
11.5	9.3	16.0	Cash & Equivalents						15.0
30.3	29.9	28.2	Trade Receivables (net)						26.2
37.1	38.4	30.4	Inventory						30.6
4.1	4.9	5.0	All Other Current						4.4
83.0	82.5	79.6	Total Current						76.1
10.7	8.0	7.2	Fixed Assets (net)						8.5
1.6	5.4	6.9	Intangibles (net)						8.0
4.7	4.1	6.2	All Other Non-Current						7.5
100.0	100.0	100.0	Total						100.0
			LIABILITIES						
18.9	21.7	12.0	Notes Payable-Short Term						11.2
1.9	2.3	3.4	Cur. Mat.-L.T.D.						4.4
10.6	12.0	19.7	Trade Payables						20.6
.1	.0	.7	Income Taxes Payable						1.0
11.1	8.3	10.5	All Other Current						8.9
42.6	44.4	46.2	Total Current						46.2
7.3	10.6	7.6	Long-Term Debt						7.5
.2	.0	.1	Deferred Taxes						.2
7.8	6.2	11.2	All Other Non-Current						4.1
42.1	38.8	35.0	Net Worth						42.1
100.0	100.0	100.0	Total Liabilities & Net Worth						100.0
			INCOME DATA						
100.0	100.0	100.0	Net Sales						100.0
38.7	37.7	35.4	Gross Profit						33.0
35.8	32.7	30.3	Operating Expenses						26.5
2.8	5.0	5.1	Operating Profit						6.6
.9	2.0	1.3	All Other Expenses (net)						1.8
1.9	3.0	3.8	Profit Before Taxes						4.8
			RATIOS						
2.7	2.7	2.8							2.6
1.7	2.0	1.9	Current						1.8
1.5	1.5	1.5							1.3
1.4	1.9	1.6							1.5
.9	.7	.9	Quick						.9
.5	.3	.7							.7
14 26.6	11 34.3	17 21.1						15	24.1
36 10.1	37 9.8	41 9.0	Sales/Receivables					41	9.0
65 5.6	69 5.3	61 6.0						60	6.1
41 8.8	48 7.6	33 11.0						32	11.4
77 4.7	74 4.9	55 6.6	Cost of Sales/Inventory					55	6.7
146 2.5	153 2.4	87 4.2						87	4.2
13 27.9	9 41.2	17 21.2						18	20.3
23 15.6	26 13.8	32 11.5	Cost of Sales/Payables					34	10.8
43 8.5	49 7.5	48 7.6						48	7.6
4.3	4.4	4.0							5.1
6.5	6.3	7.7	Sales/Working Capital						8.0
12.2	12.1	14.7							21.1
10.0	15.6	12.4							11.4
(29) 2.3	(37) 2.8	(42) 3.0	EBIT/Interest					(28)	4.0
1.1	1.3	1.5							2.1
		291.3							310.1
	(11)	12.2	Net Profit + Depr., Dep., Amort./Cur. Mat. L/T/D					(10)	6.8
		.4							.4
.1	.0	.0							.0
.2	.1	.1	Fixed/Worth						.2
.6	1.0	.6							.6
.6	.7	.7							.6
1.4	1.3	1.5	Debt/Worth						1.5
3.1	11.0	6.3							6.6
40.6	36.9	53.1							67.3
(30) 9.2	(34) 13.9	(44) 21.8	% Profit Before Taxes/Tangible Net Worth					(28)	24.7
.8	4.2	1.5							8.4
17.2	16.3	18.4							21.6
3.5	5.5	6.4	% Profit Before Taxes/Total Assets						9.1
.2	.7	1.2							4.3
67.5	283.9	209.7							188.0
32.8	52.7	63.4	Sales/Net Fixed Assets						54.5
16.7	22.5	27.4							31.2
3.3	3.4	3.7							3.4
2.7	2.6	2.6	Sales/Total Assets						2.6
1.8	2.0	1.8							1.8
.3	.2	.2							.2
(29) .6	(29) .5	(34) .4	% Depr., Dep., Amort./Sales					(27)	.4
1.4	1.3	.7							.7
.9	1.1	.8							.6
(14) 2.2	(20) 1.9	(21) 2.4	% Officers', Directors' Owners' Comp/Sales					(11)	1.8
7.1	5.3	4.1							2.7
1852577M	2178863M	2874165M	Net Sales ($)	516M	7129M	14929M	14007M	133401M	2704183M
797386M	952776M	1401373M	Total Assets ($)	281M	3187M	8791M	3997M	60483M	1324634M

M = $ thousand   MM = $ million
See Pages 9 through 22 for Explanation of Ratios and Data

Current Data Sorted by Assets   Comparative Historical Data

0-500M	500M-2MM	2-10MM	10-50MM	50-100MM	100-250MM	Type of Statement	4/1/05-3/31/06 ALL	4/1/06-3/31/07 ALL
	1	4	7	3	3	Unqualified	9	14
	2	7	3			Reviewed	4	9
	4	2	1			Compiled	5	8
1	6	1				Tax Returns	2	2
1	3	3	3	2	1	Other	9	12
	10 (4/1-9/30/09)		48 (10/1/09-3/31/10)					
2	16	17	14	5	4	**NUMBER OF STATEMENTS**	29	45
%	%	%	%	%	%	**ASSETS**	%	%
	3.8	11.8	12.5			Cash & Equivalents	10.1	10.1
	26.3	24.7	32.3			Trade Receivables (net)	22.8	23.7
	45.5	38.2	37.1			Inventory	39.1	38.8
	.3	4.3	2.2			All Other Current	2.0	4.5
	75.9	78.9	84.1			Total Current	73.9	77.1
	16.0	10.1	9.9			Fixed Assets (net)	17.9	12.6
	.4	.5	3.1			Intangibles (net)	4.2	5.8
	7.7	10.6	2.9			All Other Non-Current	3.9	4.4
	100.0	100.0	100.0			Total	100.0	100.0
						LIABILITIES		
	14.8	16.4	14.2			Notes Payable-Short Term	17.3	16.3
	3.7	2.7	.8			Cur. Mat.-L.T.D.	4.0	1.6
	19.0	19.9	13.4			Trade Payables	19.5	15.4
	.0	.1	.1			Income Taxes Payable	.3	.1
	7.0	17.6	8.8			All Other Current	7.2	9.1
	44.5	56.8	37.3			Total Current	48.4	42.6
	17.2	6.5	2.4			Long-Term Debt	23.7	11.1
	.1	.2	.2			Deferred Taxes	.3	.3
	2.3	12.1	.9			All Other Non-Current	6.7	2.3
	35.9	24.4	59.2			Net Worth	20.9	43.8
	100.0	100.0	100.0			Total Liabilities & Net Worth	100.0	100.0
						INCOME DATA		
	100.0	100.0	100.0			Net Sales	100.0	100.0
	36.8	27.3	33.6			Gross Profit	34.9	34.1
	33.3	25.6	24.4			Operating Expenses	31.5	28.9
	3.5	1.7	9.1			Operating Profit	3.3	5.2
	1.3	.8	.7			All Other Expenses (net)	1.5	1.2
	2.2	1.0	8.4			Profit Before Taxes	1.8	4.0
						RATIOS		
	4.4	2.6	4.4				3.6	4.1
	1.6	1.4	2.5			Current	1.5	1.8
	1.0	1.0	1.5				1.1	1.3
	1.5	1.3	2.3				1.6	1.8
	.7	.6	1.6			Quick	.7	.9
	.4	.3	.5				.4	.4
31	11.6	14 26.3	21 17.1				20 18.2	24 14.9
41	8.9	28 13.2	45 8.2			Sales/Receivables	36 10.2	36 10.1
48	7.5	40 9.2	65 5.6				55 6.7	56 6.6
55	6.6	40 9.2	39 9.4				53 6.9	48 7.6
110	3.3	53 6.8	74 4.9			Cost of Sales/Inventory	85 4.3	124 2.9
210	1.7	97 3.8	152 2.4				179 2.0	178 2.0
19	19.4	8 48.4	14 25.5				22 16.3	17 22.1
29	12.7	26 14.2	25 14.8			Cost of Sales/Payables	41 8.8	31 11.8
41	8.9	56 6.6	50 7.2				68 5.4	48 7.7
	4.9	4.8	2.6				3.5	3.3
	6.3	20.2	6.8			Sales/Working Capital	10.6	6.5
	NM	523.5	9.5				39.1	17.9
	30.3	13.5	106.1				6.1	9.3
	4.5	(15) 2.3	(12) 9.0			EBIT/Interest	(28) 3.0	(44) 4.0
	-.6	.6	4.4				.8	1.2
								17.1
						Net Profit + Depr., Dep., Amort./Cur. Mat. L/T/D	(13)	3.4
								.1
	.0	.0	.1				.2	.1
	.2	.3	.1			Fixed/Worth	.4	.2
	1.7	.5	.3				2.1	.8
	.6	.6	.3				.6	.5
	1.4	1.9	1.0			Debt/Worth	2.3	1.1
	2.6	5.4	1.5				5.9	5.4
	32.7	31.1	55.0			% Profit Before Taxes/Tangible	26.4	40.0
(13)	16.1	(14) 19.0	35.0			Net Worth	(26) 7.7	(39) 14.3
	-3.3	4.2	20.6				.0	1.2
	17.7	12.3	31.0			% Profit Before Taxes/Total	7.5	17.3
	6.0	3.0	20.5			Assets	3.2	4.2
	-3.7	-3.8	9.1				-.3	.7
	170.3	260.6	96.3				34.0	50.5
	49.4	41.2	51.4			Sales/Net Fixed Assets	16.8	23.2
	10.2	14.7	9.2				7.0	9.7
	3.2	3.9	3.0				2.9	2.9
	2.2	3.1	2.1			Sales/Total Assets	2.2	2.1
	1.7	2.5	1.7				1.5	1.5
	.2	.1	.3				.6	.4
(10)	.9	(13) .4	(12) .9			% Depr., Dep., Amort./Sales	(28) 1.6	(39) .7
	1.7	1.6	2.1				2.3	1.9
	2.0						2.1	1.4
(11)	3.4					% Officers', Directors' Owners' Comp/Sales	(11) 4.5	(15) 3.3
	4.9						10.4	5.4
971M	53599M	292083M	641138M	461500M	828342M	Net Sales ($)	758602M	1936880M
446M	21053M	85559M	234325M	338178M	709244M	Total Assets ($)	467607M	1183287M

M = $ thousand   MM = $ million

See Pages 9 through 22 for Explanation of Ratios and Data

Comparative Historical Data | Current Data Sorted by Sales

			Type of Statement	0-1MM	1-3MM	3-5MM	5-10MM	10-25MM	25MM & OVER
10	13	18	Unqualified		1			4	13
11	17	12	Reviewed		3	2		6	1
5	5	7	Compiled		1	3	1		2
5	11	8	Tax Returns	1	3	2	1	1	
15	18	13	Other	2	1	1	1	1	6
4/1/07-3/31/08 ALL	4/1/08-3/31/09 ALL	4/1/09-3/31/10 ALL		10 (4/1-9/30/09)			48 (10/1/09-3/31/10)		
46	64	58	NUMBER OF STATEMENTS	3	5	8	8	12	22
%	%	%	ASSETS	%	%	%	%	%	%
6.9	9.3	10.4	Cash & Equivalents					10.5	16.3
22.4	24.6	25.2	Trade Receivables (net)					24.7	26.0
40.2	38.7	38.0	Inventory					45.6	29.6
4.3	5.4	2.6	All Other Current					3.2	3.2
73.9	78.0	76.2	Total Current					83.9	75.0
13.7	13.6	11.9	Fixed Assets (net)					12.3	8.5
7.0	2.4	4.7	Intangibles (net)					.1	10.0
5.4	6.1	7.2	All Other Non-Current					3.6	6.5
100.0	100.0	100.0	Total					100.0	100.0
			LIABILITIES						
16.9	13.6	14.7	Notes Payable-Short Term					13.1	10.3
1.5	3.0	2.1	Cur. Mat.-L.T.D.					4.4	.4
15.9	17.6	16.3	Trade Payables					15.4	13.6
.2	.3	.1	Income Taxes Payable					.1	.1
6.7	9.2	10.4	All Other Current					10.1	11.0
41.2	43.6	43.6	Total Current					43.1	35.4
11.6	11.2	8.0	Long-Term Debt					.9	8.2
.3	.1	.5	Deferred Taxes					.4	1.0
4.2	5.8	5.8	All Other Non-Current					2.2	8.2
42.7	39.2	42.1	Net Worth					53.3	47.2
100.0	100.0	100.0	Total Liabilities & Net Worth					100.0	100.0
			INCOME DATA						
100.0	100.0	100.0	Net Sales					100.0	100.0
31.4	34.6	34.1	Gross Profit					30.1	36.0
26.9	28.9	28.4	Operating Expenses					27.3	26.6
4.5	5.7	5.6	Operating Profit					2.8	9.4
1.4	.8	.8	All Other Expenses (net)					.8	.5
3.1	4.9	4.8	Profit Before Taxes					2.0	8.9
			RATIOS						
4.3	4.6	3.9	Current					4.9	4.7
1.8	1.7	1.8						2.0	2.9
1.3	1.2	1.3						1.3	1.4
1.4	2.1	1.7	Quick					2.2	2.6
.6	.6	1.0						.6	1.6
.4	.4	.4						.4	.9
23 15.6	13 27.4	20 17.8	Sales/Receivables					22 16.5	20 18.1
40 9.2	35 10.5	37 9.8						33 11.1	43 8.5
56 6.5	51 7.1	49 7.4						48 7.7	57 6.4
58 6.3	51 7.2	49 7.4	Cost of Sales/Inventory					50 7.3	39 9.4
109 3.4	83 4.4	88 4.1						97 3.8	85 4.3
176 2.1	155 2.3	133 2.8						139 2.6	112 3.3
18 20.8	12 31.0	16 22.2	Cost of Sales/Payables					18 20.5	18 19.7
25 14.4	23 16.0	28 12.9						26 14.1	29 12.6
48 7.7	36 10.1	40 9.2						33 11.0	41 8.8
3.4	3.6	3.4	Sales/Working Capital					2.7	2.6
6.3	7.1	6.4						5.6	6.1
17.0	15.0	16.0						26.0	12.4
7.1	15.6	21.9	EBIT/Interest					9.2	30.8
(43) 2.5	(53) 3.8	(51) 5.5					(10) 2.3	(18) 11.4
1.1	.1	1.7						-3.7	6.6
11.5	22.0		Net Profit + Depr., Dep.,						
(10) 5.2	(10) 4.5		Amort./Cur. Mat. L/T/D						
1.3	1.1								
.1	.1	.1	Fixed/Worth					.1	.1
.2	.2	.2						.2	.1
.7	1.0	.5						.5	.3
.4	.3	.4	Debt/Worth					.2	.3
1.5	1.4	1.3						.8	1.4
4.6	5.4	2.9						2.6	1.8
35.4	66.2	38.1	% Profit Before Taxes/Tangible					33.8	56.5
(38) 7.6	(55) 18.4	(49) 24.1	Net Worth				(11) 13.9	(20) 34.6
.2	2.9	5.3						-6.1	20.1
11.6	22.9	20.6	% Profit Before Taxes/Total					15.8	28.3
4.7	7.2	9.9	Assets					6.4	16.1
.1	-2.3	.7						-4.0	4.4
63.9	99.3	101.9	Sales/Net Fixed Assets					95.6	82.2
18.8	23.0	34.9						14.7	36.1
9.0	9.5	11.7						10.0	13.6
3.0	3.1	3.4	Sales/Total Assets					3.6	3.5
2.1	2.3	2.2						2.5	2.1
1.5	1.7	1.6						1.9	1.4
.4	.3	.3	% Depr., Dep., Amort./Sales					.4	.4
(36) 1.2	(47) .7	(42) .9					(11) 1.2	(16) .8
1.8	1.9	1.6						1.7	1.6
1.2	1.5	1.7	% Officers', Directors'						
(14) 2.6	(27) 4.0	(27) 3.8	Owners' Comp/Sales						
4.7	6.0	5.3							
2824384M	3564311M	2277633M	Net Sales ($)	1783M	9485M	30219M	54761M	210304M	1971081M
1669346M	1840882M	1388805M	Total Assets ($)	1264M	5446M	14706M	17543M	97193M	1252653M

© RMA 2010

M = $ thousand   MM = $ million
See Pages 9 through 22 for Explanation of Ratios and Data

Current Data Sorted by Assets   Comparative Historical Data

Type of Statement	0-500M	500M-2MM	2-10MM	10-50MM	50-100MM	100-250MM	4/1/05-3/31/06 ALL	4/1/06-3/31/07 ALL
Unqualified			8	21	7	5	32	31
Reviewed		1	14	8			35	27
Compiled	1	7	9	1			16	19
Tax Returns	5	20	3				18	23
Other	4	14	18	13	5	5	59	41
		32 (4/1-9/30/09)		137 (10/1/09-3/31/10)				
NUMBER OF STATEMENTS	10	42	52	43	12	10	160	141
ASSETS	%	%	%	%	%	%	%	%
Cash & Equivalents	10.1	13.4	6.8	12.4	11.2	9.3	8.5	9.0
Trade Receivables (net)	27.5	25.2	25.6	27.0	23.1	22.0	29.2	29.4
Inventory	33.0	36.1	39.0	35.3	33.2	30.2	33.7	34.1
All Other Current	1.1	2.1	2.2	3.5	3.2	3.4	3.1	2.3
Total Current	71.6	76.7	73.6	78.2	70.7	64.8	74.4	74.8
Fixed Assets (net)	18.6	10.8	15.1	10.5	10.6	13.1	13.7	14.5
Intangibles (net)	5.0	5.7	3.9	5.9	10.6	13.9	5.0	5.1
All Other Non-Current	4.8	6.8	7.5	5.4	8.1	8.2	6.8	5.6
Total	100.0	100.0	100.0	100.0	100.0	100.0	100.0	100.0
LIABILITIES								
Notes Payable-Short Term	24.9	23.8	21.2	17.3	12.4	5.0	17.6	16.4
Cur. Mat.-L.T.D.	6.2	2.9	2.8	2.1	.4	1.2	2.9	3.2
Trade Payables	22.3	19.7	15.9	15.7	10.3	7.8	14.8	15.8
Income Taxes Payable	.0	.0	.0	.4	.4	2.6	.2	.3
All Other Current	32.8	8.1	7.8	7.2	6.4	6.7	12.4	11.1
Total Current	86.1	54.4	47.7	42.6	29.9	23.4	47.9	46.7
Long-Term Debt	15.8	19.4	12.1	6.3	10.8	23.6	12.0	12.7
Deferred Taxes	.0	.0	.2	.2	.7	2.0	.1	.2
All Other Non-Current	25.1	9.9	2.2	6.7	6.9	15.3	7.0	8.2
Net Worth	-27.1	16.2	37.8	44.3	51.8	35.6	33.0	32.2
Total Liabilties & Net Worth	100.0	100.0	100.0	100.0	100.0	100.0	100.0	100.0
INCOME DATA								
Net Sales	100.0	100.0	100.0	100.0	100.0	100.0	100.0	100.0
Gross Profit	56.3	42.7	33.8	36.7	29.1	39.9	36.1	34.8
Operating Expenses	50.5	41.4	30.0	29.6	24.1	32.4	31.7	29.2
Operating Profit	5.7	1.4	3.8	7.1	5.0	7.5	4.4	5.6
All Other Expenses (net)	1.4	1.5	1.0	1.1	.3	2.5	1.2	1.4
Profit Before Taxes	4.3	-.1	2.8	6.0	4.7	5.0	3.2	4.2
RATIOS								
Current	2.6	3.7	2.5	3.6	4.6	6.4	2.4	2.6
	1.1	1.8	1.6	1.7	3.5	3.2	1.7	1.6
	.4	1.0	1.2	1.3	1.5	1.5	1.2	1.2
Quick	.6	1.9	1.4	1.6	2.5	3.2	1.5	1.5
	.4	.9	.8	.8	1.4	1.6	.8	.9
	.4	.4	.4	.4	.8	.6	.4	.5
Sales/Receivables	6 64.2	22 16.8	22 16.5	30 12.3	43 8.6	34 10.8	29 12.6	29 12.7
	14 26.2	34 10.7	38 9.6	41 8.8	47 7.7	51 7.1	46 8.0	42 8.7
	39 9.4	49 7.5	48 7.6	61 6.0	68 5.3	59 6.2	60 6.0	54 6.8
Cost of Sales/Inventory	0 UND	31 11.9	36 10.1	61 6.0	74 4.9	79 4.6	34 10.8	25 14.7
	74 4.9	91 4.0	92 4.0	102 3.6	105 3.5	115 3.2	82 4.5	78 4.7
	209 1.7	144 2.5	150 2.4	150 2.4	164 2.2	151 2.4	141 2.6	142 2.6
Cost of Sales/Payables	15 23.8	13 27.1	18 20.2	22 17.0	26 14.3	5 80.4	16 22.8	15 24.5
	26 13.8	36 10.3	27 13.4	33 11.2	30 12.0	26 14.2	30 12.0	28 13.2
	79 4.6	60 6.0	41 8.9	57 6.4	38 9.5	40 9.0	46 7.9	50 7.4
Sales/Working Capital	12.3	3.5	5.1	4.3	2.1	2.8	4.3	5.2
	NM	9.1	8.2	6.1	3.2	4.3	8.9	9.6
	-25.1	NM	26.7	15.2	9.8	8.6	30.1	19.8
EBIT/Interest		6.7	19.6	17.3	24.4		7.8	9.2
		(40) 2.7	(46) 2.3	(37) 7.1	(11) 3.0		(142) 3.0	(126) 3.2
		.1	.7	1.3	1.8		1.1	1.2
Net Profit + Depr., Dep., Amort./Cur. Mat. L/T/D			6.5	40.0			9.8	39.4
			(10) 4.9	(11) 10.1			(24) 4.1	(25) 5.3
			.7	1.2			1.2	1.2
Fixed/Worth	.1	.1	.1	.1	.1	.2	.1	.1
	2.1	.3	.3	.2	.2	.4	.4	.3
	-.1	-1.2	1.6	.7	.8	-.3	1.5	1.8
Debt/Worth	2.9	.8	.5	.6	.4	.3	.8	.8
	12.9	4.2	1.7	1.4	.8	1.4	2.3	2.0
	-3.8	-7.6	5.8	3.0	4.3	-4.1	-6.8	7.8
% Profit Before Taxes/Tangible Net Worth		35.2	35.9	55.5	42.9		41.2	53.5
		(29) 9.7	(44) 15.8	(39) 24.1	(11) 7.2		(136) 18.5	(118) 25.6
		-7.4	3.3	6.8	2.4		3.7	6.8
% Profit Before Taxes/Total Assets	32.2	13.3	17.0	23.6	15.5	18.3	13.5	18.9
	13.3	3.3	3.2	10.0	3.2	9.1	6.0	7.6
	2.4	-4.0	-.2	1.0	.8	2.7	.7	1.0
Sales/Net Fixed Assets	UND	88.6	86.3	69.8	44.8	27.7	59.1	57.9
	79.8	40.3	26.7	27.2	15.0	11.8	25.8	22.8
	20.3	23.0	14.2	11.6	8.9	9.5	11.4	10.5
Sales/Total Assets	9.1	3.7	2.9	3.0	2.2	2.0	3.2	3.6
	5.7	2.3	2.3	2.1	1.5	1.7	2.2	2.6
	2.9	1.7	1.5	1.5	1.1	1.4	1.6	1.6
% Depr., Dep., Amort./Sales		.2	.5	.4	.6		.5	.5
		(27) .5	(38) 1.2	(37) .9	(10) 1.8		(128) 1.0	(115) 1.2
		1.8	3.0	1.6	2.2		1.9	1.9
% Officers', Directors' Owners' Comp/Sales		2.4	1.1				2.2	2.4
		(31) 3.4	(15) 4.1				(60) 4.7	(52) 4.3
		5.3	5.8				7.8	6.9
Net Sales ($)	9262M	129741M	643849M	2025708M	1368485M	2344963M	5741050M	6210307M
Total Assets ($)	2029M	46050M	262701M	921320M	875447M	1440405M	3046626M	3104416M

M = $ thousand   MM = $ million
See Pages 9 through 22 for Explanation of Ratios and Data

Comparative Historical Data / Current Data Sorted by Sales

4/1/07-3/31/08 ALL	4/1/08-3/31/09 ALL	4/1/09-3/31/10 ALL	Type of Statement	0-1MM	1-3MM	3-5MM	5-10MM	10-25MM	25MM & OVER
27	45	41	Unqualified		1		3	10	28
37	31	23	Reviewed		5		5	9	8
12	19	18	Compiled	1		1	6	4	1
23	22	28	Tax Returns	4	20	3			1
50	56	59	Other	4	10	5	10	8	22
					32 (4/1-9/30/09)		137 (10/1/09-3/31/10)		
149	173	169	NUMBER OF STATEMENTS	9	36	9	24	31	60
%	%	%	**ASSETS**	%	%	%	%	%	%
8.2	7.7	10.5	Cash & Equivalents		11.9		7.3	11.7	10.6
27.8	26.6	25.6	Trade Receivables (net)		24.3		27.5	24.3	26.4
35.4	36.5	36.0	Inventory		36.9		37.7	34.1	36.2
3.6	3.6	2.6	All Other Current		2.5		1.9	4.3	2.5
74.9	74.4	74.7	Total Current		75.6		74.4	74.3	75.8
12.9	14.5	12.6	Fixed Assets (net)		12.8		16.5	11.1	11.1
5.1	4.5	6.0	Intangibles (net)		5.2		2.7	8.4	6.6
7.0	6.6	6.7	All Other Non-Current		6.4		6.4	6.2	6.5
100.0	100.0	100.0	Total		100.0		100.0	100.0	100.0
			LIABILITIES						
17.2	19.7	19.5	Notes Payable-Short Term		16.0		28.0	17.5	15.1
3.1	1.9	2.6	Cur. Mat.-L.T.D.		4.6		1.5	3.3	1.7
17.8	16.1	16.3	Trade Payables		18.5		10.0	19.5	14.5
.4	.2	.3	Income Taxes Payable		.0		.0	.1	.8
8.0	8.3	9.0	All Other Current		10.7		6.5	5.9	7.7
46.4	46.2	47.7	Total Current		49.7		46.1	46.1	39.7
11.0	11.6	13.2	Long-Term Debt		18.3		11.8	9.8	9.6
.2	.2	.3	Deferred Taxes		.1		.0	.2	.6
7.4	11.4	7.7	All Other Non-Current		12.1		1.3	5.3	6.9
35.0	30.6	31.1	Net Worth		19.7		40.7	38.7	43.2
100.0	100.0	100.0	Total Liabilities & Net Worth		100.0		100.0	100.0	100.0
			INCOME DATA						
100.0	100.0	100.0	Net Sales		100.0		100.0	100.0	100.0
37.5	36.5	38.1	Gross Profit		46.0		37.2	30.6	34.9
32.0	32.1	33.7	Operating Expenses		43.8		33.8	25.5	28.7
5.5	4.4	4.5	Operating Profit		2.2		3.4	5.1	6.1
1.5	1.1	1.2	All Other Expenses (net)		1.7		.7	.9	1.1
4.0	3.3	3.2	Profit Before Taxes		.5		2.7	4.2	5.0
			RATIOS						
2.7 / 1.6 / 1.2	2.7 / 1.6 / 1.2	3.4 / 1.7 / 1.2	Current		4.0 / 2.0 / 1.0		3.0 / 1.5 / 1.2	2.8 / 1.7 / 1.1	3.8 / 2.1 / 1.3
1.4 / .8 / .4	1.3 / .7 / .4	1.8 / .8 / .4	Quick		1.9 / .8 / .3		2.0 / .8 / .4	1.6 / .7 / .4	1.9 / 1.0 / .6
(28) 13.0 / (41) 8.9 / (60) 6.1	(23) 15.8 / (38) 9.6 / (54) 6.7	(25) 14.9 / (39) 9.4 / (56) 6.5	Sales/Receivables		(14) 26.4 / (32) 11.5 / (49) 7.4		(31) 11.9 / (38) 9.5 / (48) 7.6	(23) 15.8 / (39) 9.4 / (52) 7.0	(29) 12.5 / (43) 8.4 / (61) 6.0
(43) 8.5 / (92) 4.0 / (157) 2.3	(42) 8.6 / (92) 4.0 / (141) 2.6	(46) 7.9 / (96) 3.8 / (150) 2.4	Cost of Sales/Inventory		(33) 10.9 / (101) 3.6 / (180) 2.0		(29) 12.4 / (93) 3.9 / (179) 2.0	(36) 10.1 / (83) 4.4 / (124) 2.9	(60) 6.0 / (103) 3.5 / (150) 2.4
(15) 23.6 / (30) 12.2 / (57) 6.4	(16) 22.6 / (29) 12.5 / (48) 7.6	(18) 20.1 / (31) 11.8 / (49) 7.4	Cost of Sales/Payables		(16) 23.2 / (35) 10.5 / (78) 4.7		(15) 24.3 / (27) 13.8 / (37) 9.9	(14) 25.7 / (34) 10.6 / (56) 6.5	(19) 18.9 / (31) 11.8 / (46) 8.0
4.3 / 7.8 / 21.8	4.8 / 8.7 / 23.5	4.2 / 7.2 / 24.0	Sales/Working Capital		3.4 / 6.8 / 280.8		4.9 / 8.1 / 24.8	5.1 / 7.4 / 28.5	3.4 / 6.0 / 11.7
(137) 15.4 / 3.8 / 1.4	(161) 10.8 / 2.5 / 1.0	(152) 16.2 / 3.4 /	EBIT/Interest		(35) 5.8 / 3.3 / .2		(22) 24.0 / 2.8 / .7	(27) 11.5 / 2.3 / .3	(53) 26.2 / 7.1 / 1.7
(25) 54.7 / 6.7 / 1.8	(39) 10.1 / 3.2 / .1	(32) 12.0 / 4.9 / .8	Net Profit + Depr., Dep., Amort./Cur. Mat. L/T/D						(17) 12.8 / 2.7 / .7
.1 / .3 / 1.5	.1 / .4 / 1.4	.1 / .3 / 2.5	Fixed/Worth		.1 / .3 / NM		.1 / .4 / 1.6	.1 / .3 / 57.7	.1 / .2 / .6
.6 / 1.7 / 6.6	.9 / 2.0 / 5.7	.6 / 2.0 / 13.9	Debt/Worth		1.2 / 4.0 / -9.9		.3 / 2.0 / 5.7	.5 / 2.5 / 417.7	.6 / 1.3 / 2.6
(128) 63.5 / 21.1 / 6.4	(146) 44.6 / 16.2 / 2.5	(136) 46.6 / 20.9 / 3.9	% Profit Before Taxes/Tangible Net Worth		(26) 55.7 / 12.3 / -.8		(22) 49.0 / 8.4 / -.3	(24) 39.0 / 23.5 / 4.6	(53) 51.9 / 22.0 / 7.0
20.5 / 6.7 / 1.8	16.5 / 4.5 / .3	18.5 / 4.9 / .0	% Profit Before Taxes/Total Assets		14.2 / 3.2 / -2.5		18.9 / 4.3 / -.4	16.6 / 4.8 / .2	19.9 / 7.8 / 1.8
66.1 / 25.9 / 11.4	60.9 / 24.1 / 10.3	80.7 / 29.8 / 13.1	Sales/Net Fixed Assets		108.7 / 40.3 / 20.7		81.3 / 23.4 / 14.4	92.8 / 32.0 / 13.6	65.8 / 24.4 / 10.5
3.0 / 2.2 / 1.5	3.5 / 2.2 / 1.7	3.1 / 2.2 / 1.5	Sales/Total Assets		3.7 / 2.3 / 1.7		3.0 / 2.1 / 1.5	2.8 / 2.2 / 1.6	3.1 / 2.0 / 1.5
(114) .5 / 1.1 / 2.1	(141) .5 / 1.0 / 2.1	(125) .4 / 1.0 / 2.1	% Depr., Dep., Amort./Sales		(24) .2 / .5 / 2.3		(18) .6 / 1.3 / 3.0	(19) .3 / 1.4 / 2.1	(53) .4 / 1.1 / 2.1
(54) 1.6 / 3.2 / 5.9	(63) 1.8 / 3.0 / 5.4	(64) 2.2 / 3.3 / 6.1	% Officers', Directors' Owners' Comp/Sales		(25) 2.6 / 3.5 / 5.8				(11) .7 / 2.4 / 6.5
6692843M	8733115M	6522008M	Net Sales ($)	5524M	75807M	35752M	167325M	507233M	5730367M
3389562M	4283343M	3547952M	Total Assets ($)	3965M	37631M	15956M	93403M	247939M	3149058M

© RMA 2010

M = $ thousand   MM = $ million
See Pages 9 through 22 for Explanation of Ratios and Data

Current Data Sorted by Assets   Comparative Historical Data

0-500M	500M-2MM	2-10MM	10-50MM	50-100MM	100-250MM	Type of Statement				
		5	3	2	1	Unqualified		7		6
		3	2			Reviewed		17		8
1	2	1	1			Compiled		7		5
	5					Tax Returns		2		1
2	3		3	2	1	Other		13		20
	8 (4/1-9/30/09)		29 (10/1/09-3/31/10)					4/1/05-3/31/06		4/1/06-3/31/07
0-500M	500M-2MM	2-10MM	10-50MM	50-100MM	100-250MM			ALL		ALL
3	10	9	9	4	2	NUMBER OF STATEMENTS		46		40
%	%	%	%	%	%	ASSETS		%		%
	12.7					Cash & Equivalents		9.1		6.9
	34.0					Trade Receivables (net)		28.0		28.0
	31.0					Inventory		29.6		31.7
	1.3					All Other Current		2.8		4.4
	79.0					Total Current		69.5		71.0
	9.0					Fixed Assets (net)		20.9		17.6
	4.7					Intangibles (net)		5.8		6.9
	7.3					All Other Non-Current		3.8		4.4
	100.0					Total		100.0		100.0
						LIABILITIES				
	16.9					Notes Payable-Short Term		14.1		14.1
	3.0					Cur. Mat.-L.T.D.		2.5		2.5
	16.3					Trade Payables		16.7		16.6
	.7					Income Taxes Payable		.1		.2
	7.7					All Other Current		10.5		10.5
	44.6					Total Current		43.9		44.0
	12.2					Long-Term Debt		12.5		12.3
	.1					Deferred Taxes		.2		.2
	1.4					All Other Non-Current		5.3		8.0
	41.7					Net Worth		38.1		35.5
	100.0					Total Liabilities & Net Worth		100.0		100.0
						INCOME DATA				
	100.0					Net Sales		100.0		100.0
	32.4					Gross Profit		26.4		25.4
	28.4					Operating Expenses		21.8		20.3
	3.9					Operating Profit		4.6		5.0
	.9					All Other Expenses (net)		.9		1.6
	3.0					Profit Before Taxes		3.7		3.4
						RATIOS				
	2.5							3.0		2.3
	1.9					Current		1.6		1.7
	1.3							1.0		1.2
	1.7							1.8		1.2
	1.0					Quick		.9		.8
	.8							.5		.4
22	16.8						24	15.2	25	14.8
39	9.3					Sales/Receivables	43	8.5	38	9.6
65	5.7						59	6.2	54	6.7
33	11.0						20	18.7	34	10.6
45	8.0					Cost of Sales/Inventory	60	6.1	64	5.7
73	5.0						124	3.0	106	3.4
2	230.5						10	37.5	12	30.5
27	13.3					Cost of Sales/Payables	24	14.9	28	13.1
54	6.7						46	7.9	50	7.3
	5.2							5.0		4.8
	10.7					Sales/Working Capital		14.3		9.6
	16.4							UND		30.8
	9.2							14.0		11.2
	3.2					EBIT/Interest	(39)	2.9	(37)	2.9
	1.5							1.2		1.1
						Net Profit + Depr., Dep.,				5.8
						Amort./Cur. Mat. L/T/D			(11)	1.8
										.7
	.0							.1		.1
	.1					Fixed/Worth		.7		.4
	.8							2.0		1.8
	.7							.7		1.0
	1.3					Debt/Worth		2.3		1.9
	5.7							13.9		7.2
	93.4					% Profit Before Taxes/Tangible		64.8		60.5
	19.9					Net Worth	(40)	15.0	(33)	16.4
	12.6							-.1		3.4
	11.8					% Profit Before Taxes/Total		14.6		16.6
	6.4					Assets		4.7		7.3
	1.9							.6		.1
	999.8							104.3		83.4
	54.6					Sales/Net Fixed Assets		14.1		14.0
	14.3							7.6		8.9
	3.8							3.6		3.2
	2.9					Sales/Total Assets		2.5		2.3
	2.6							1.5		1.3
								.5		.5
						% Depr., Dep., Amort./Sales	(40)	1.7	(36)	1.1
								3.3		2.7
								2.3		1.4
						% Officers', Directors'	(18)	5.2	(13)	2.9
						Owners' Comp/Sales		9.2		6.1
1518M	35460M	124738M	507569M	469572M	598104M	Net Sales ($)		1961188M		1660296M
261M	11529M	61657M	193893M	308667M	389214M	Total Assets ($)		995846M		795609M

M = $ thousand   MM = $ million
See Pages 9 through 22 for Explanation of Ratios and Data

Comparative Historical Data | | | Current Data Sorted by Sales

Type of Statement

	4/1/07-3/31/08 ALL	4/1/08-3/31/09 ALL	4/1/09-3/31/10 ALL	Type of Statement	0-1MM	1-3MM	3-5MM	5-10MM	10-25MM	25MM & OVER
	6	8	11	Unqualified				1	4	6
	7	7	5	Reviewed		2		2		3
	4	3	5	Compiled			1	1	1	1
	4	6	5	Tax Returns		2	2	1		
	12	13	11	Other	2	1	1			6
						8 (4/1-9/30/09)			29 (10/1/09-3/31/10)	
NUMBER OF STATEMENTS	33	37	37		2	5	4	5	5	16

	%	%	%	ASSETS	%	%	%	%	%	%
	9.5	8.5	10.3	Cash & Equivalents						10.2
	30.6	21.4	29.4	Trade Receivables (net)						28.3
	31.0	37.1	33.2	Inventory						31.5
	2.7	2.5	2.3	All Other Current						3.8
	73.8	69.4	75.2	Total Current						73.8
	13.7	15.8	12.7	Fixed Assets (net)						12.2
	9.9	9.4	6.3	Intangibles (net)						6.4
	2.6	5.4	5.8	All Other Non-Current						7.6
	100.0	100.0	100.0	Total						100.0

LIABILITIES

				LIABILITIES						
	11.7	20.7	23.4	Notes Payable-Short Term						15.9
	2.2	4.2	5.5	Cur. Mat.-L.T.D.						8.0
	16.8	16.5	14.9	Trade Payables						17.6
	.2	.0	.3	Income Taxes Payable						.2
	5.4	8.6	7.8	All Other Current						9.2
	36.4	50.1	51.9	Total Current						50.9
	12.3	14.4	12.2	Long-Term Debt						7.3
	.6	.9	.3	Deferred Taxes						.2
	8.1	6.6	4.5	All Other Non-Current						5.8
	42.6	28.0	31.0	Net Worth						35.7
	100.0	100.0	100.0	Total Liabilties & Net Worth						100.0

INCOME DATA

				INCOME DATA						
	100.0	100.0	100.0	Net Sales						100.0
	25.3	29.4	31.3	Gross Profit						28.6
	19.5	28.2	29.4	Operating Expenses						27.4
	5.8	1.2	1.8	Operating Profit						1.2
	1.4	1.0	.9	All Other Expenses (net)						.5
	4.4	.3	.9	Profit Before Taxes						.7

RATIOS

	4/1/07-3/31/08	4/1/08-3/31/09	4/1/09-3/31/10	RATIOS						25MM & OVER
	3.0	2.3	2.3	Current						2.3
	2.0	1.5	1.5							1.3
	1.4	1.2	1.1							1.1
	1.5	1.5	1.3	Quick						1.3
	1.1	.7	.9							.7
	.7	.3	.5							.5
	26 14.1	24 15.4	31 11.7	Sales/Receivables						32 11.4
	40 9.2	33 11.0	40 9.1							50 7.4
	53 6.9	50 7.3	62 5.9							60 6.1
	27 13.4	69 5.3	41 8.9	Cost of Sales/Inventory						46 7.9
	63 5.8	103 3.5	68 5.3							72 5.1
	89 4.1	124 3.0	114 3.2							111 3.3
	11 34.0	17 21.7	13 27.4	Cost of Sales/Payables						18 20.2
	23 16.0	31 12.0	30 12.2							35 10.4
	40 9.2	56 6.5	52 7.0							51 7.1
	4.9	4.5	4.8	Sales/Working Capital						4.3
	8.0	10.4	11.3							12.0
	13.3	17.2	33.5							23.3
	12.0	6.3	5.6	EBIT/Interest						7.8
	(29) 3.1	(34) 1.5	(34) 2.5						(15)	3.3
	1.0	.0	.7							.7
				Net Profit + Depr., Dep., Amort./Cur. Mat. L/T/D						
	.1	.1	.1	Fixed/Worth						.1
	.4	.6	.3							.3
	1.2	NM	2.5							1.5
	.6	.7	.8	Debt/Worth						.9
	1.8	3.9	2.5							2.5
	5.7	NM	13.8							6.8
	53.6	28.5	48.6	% Profit Before Taxes/Tangible Net Worth						50.1
	(27) 21.8	(28) 6.6	(33) 17.8						(15)	17.8
	-.4	-.5	3.9							-22.9
	23.1	7.7	7.8	% Profit Before Taxes/Total Assets						14.1
	6.4	2.7	3.4							4.6
	.9	-1.6	-1.9							-10.2
	68.4	61.1	106.3	Sales/Net Fixed Assets						96.9
	18.4	20.2	26.4							26.5
	10.8	8.7	10.9							11.0
	3.5	2.9	3.4	Sales/Total Assets						3.2
	2.6	2.1	2.3							2.1
	1.6	1.4	1.8							1.4
	.4	.5	.5	% Depr., Dep., Amort./Sales						.6
	(29) 1.4	(33) 1.0	(27) 1.2						(13)	1.1
	2.3	2.0	2.0							2.1
	2.0	1.6	3.0	% Officers', Directors' Owners' Comp/Sales						
	(11) 3.2	(12) 4.7	(14) 4.7							
	12.4	6.6	12.3							
	1564717M	1250868M	1736961M	Net Sales ($)	369M	8293M	16961M	33330M	68344M	1609664M
	711329M	792987M	965221M	Total Assets ($)	68M	3738M	5013M	23873M	33911M	898618M

M = $ thousand   MM = $ million
See Pages 9 through 22 for Explanation of Ratios and Data

Current Data Sorted by Assets   Comparative Historical Data

Type of Statement	0-500M	500M-2MM	2-10MM	10-50MM	50-100MM	100-250MM		4/1/05-3/31/06 ALL	4/1/06-3/31/07 ALL
Unqualified	2	2	1	21	5	5		64	64
Reviewed		7	11	15		1		54	56
Compiled	1	9	10	3				45	43
Tax Returns	12	9	6	1				28	26
Other		2	18	33	8	4		87	90
	44 (4/1-9/30/09)			142 (10/1/09-3/31/10)					
NUMBER OF STATEMENTS	15	29	46	73	13	10		278	279
ASSETS	%	%	%	%	%	%		%	%
Cash & Equivalents	11.4	7.1	5.4	4.5	9.4	8.3		4.9	3.8
Trade Receivables (net)	18.3	17.3	12.4	9.8	5.1	4.0		12.6	12.8
Inventory	20.7	28.0	28.5	25.3	14.7	8.4		29.3	27.8
All Other Current	.2	1.7	2.8	4.2	4.3	.7		3.5	3.8
Total Current	50.5	54.0	49.2	43.9	33.5	21.3		50.2	48.3
Fixed Assets (net)	37.3	38.9	40.3	43.5	38.7	61.6		41.0	41.5
Intangibles (net)	5.1	.2	1.9	1.1	.2	1.2		1.0	1.3
All Other Non-Current	8.2	6.8	8.6	11.6	27.6	16.0		7.7	8.9
Total	100.0	100.0	100.0	100.0	100.0	100.0		100.0	100.0
LIABILITIES									
Notes Payable-Short Term	17.8	22.6	18.7	10.8	5.6	1.2		14.8	13.2
Cur. Mat.-L.T.D.	9.5	7.6	8.4	5.5	2.5	4.9		4.6	5.6
Trade Payables	8.9	8.4	4.6	5.8	2.7	2.4		6.7	7.0
Income Taxes Payable	.0	.1	.1	.0	.2	.1		.2	.2
All Other Current	7.9	4.2	5.9	5.6	4.4	3.0		6.8	7.6
Total Current	44.2	42.8	37.7	27.7	15.4	11.6		33.1	33.6
Long-Term Debt	37.1	35.1	26.7	21.2	19.2	49.9		20.5	24.4
Deferred Taxes	.0	.0	.5	.7	.3	2.0		.6	.6
All Other Non-Current	9.3	7.6	3.0	6.6	9.6	1.1		5.8	5.8
Net Worth	8.7	14.4	32.1	43.7	55.4	35.3		39.9	35.5
Total Liabilities & Net Worth	100.0	100.0	100.0	100.0	100.0	100.0		100.0	100.0
INCOME DATA									
Net Sales	100.0	100.0	100.0	100.0	100.0	100.0		100.0	100.0
Gross Profit	33.6	27.4	17.9	10.3	16.4	18.1		21.3	18.2
Operating Expenses	33.9	29.9	20.3	14.6	18.0	16.9		16.7	15.9
Operating Profit	-.3	-2.5	-2.5	-4.3	-1.6	1.2		4.6	2.4
All Other Expenses (net)	-.3	1.6	1.2	.5	6.6	2.7		.7	1.1
Profit Before Taxes	.0	-4.1	-3.7	-4.9	-8.2	-1.5		3.9	1.2
RATIOS									
Current	3.3	2.9	2.5	2.9	8.5	2.5		2.9	2.6
	1.4	1.7	1.3	1.9	2.9	2.0		1.6	1.5
	.6	.6	.9	1.0	1.1	.6		1.1	1.0
Quick	3.2	1.7	1.1	1.1	4.0	1.4		1.0	.9
	.4	.7	.5	.6	.6	.7		.5 (277)	.5
	.3	.3	.2	.2	.2	.3		.3	.3
Sales/Receivables	2 218.7	10 35.9	12 31.5	14 26.1	6 59.8	17 22.0		13 28.7	12 30.4
	16 23.4	23 16.0	23 15.8	20 17.9	18 19.8	21 17.8		18 20.0	18 20.0
	34 10.8	40 9.1	33 11.0	29 12.8	31 11.9	33 11.0		26 14.1	28 12.9
Cost of Sales/Inventory	3 109.6	27 13.5	41 8.9	39 9.4	23 15.9	21 17.4		34 10.9	30 12.3
	14 26.6	64 5.7	70 5.2	61 6.0	57 6.5	58 6.3		56 6.5	54 6.8
	57 6.4	112 3.3	124 2.9	102 3.6	106 3.5	76 4.8		92 4.0	93 3.9
Cost of Sales/Payables	0 UND	4 88.1	5 75.3	6 65.6	6 66.2	8 47.7		6 66.2	6 66.2
	4 90.0	6 57.8	8 44.8	11 32.2	12 30.1	17 21.2		12 31.7	10 35.3
	20 18.7	19 19.3	15 23.9	22 16.4	21 17.0	33 11.2		18 20.8	17 20.9
Sales/Working Capital	7.5	5.8	5.0	4.2	2.3	3.5		5.8	5.9
	19.5	12.5	15.3	8.3	6.5	9.1		13.0	12.8
	-6.6	-10.7	-33.9	-237.2	NM	-10.5		130.6	148.2
EBIT/Interest	11.8	2.8	2.3	2.5	.9			8.6	4.9
	(12) 3.1	(28) -.8	(44) .0	(69) -.2	(12) -1.4			(264) 3.5	(268) 1.8
	-.7	-3.4	-2.9	-3.9	-8.9			1.2	.4
Net Profit + Depr., Dep., Amort./Cur. Mat. L/T/D			2.2	3.0				4.2	4.1
		(11) 1.0	(22) 1.5					(75) 2.4	(78) 2.3
		-.1	.6					1.2	.7
Fixed/Worth	.3	.4	.6	.5	.2	1.1		.5	.5
	2.7	2.0	1.4	.9	.6	1.5		1.0	1.0
	-1.4	UND	3.0	2.0	1.6	9.5		2.0	2.1
Debt/Worth	.7	.9	1.0	.5	.4	1.1		.6	.7
	11.0	3.0	2.5	1.1	.5	1.9		1.4	1.5
	-4.0	UND	4.9	3.5	1.8	10.6		3.2	3.4
% Profit Before Taxes/Tangible Net Worth		32.6	13.5	9.3	1.6	19.3		33.8	20.8
	(22) -4.6	(41) -6.4	(66) -5.0	(12) -6.0	-2.5			(256) 16.2	(250) 10.2
	-37.6	-35.1	-18.7	-16.2	-9.2			3.9	-2.1
% Profit Before Taxes/Total Assets	19.5	5.7	3.2	4.0	-.1	.9		14.6	9.9
	9.1	-4.6	-4.3	-3.1	-5.7	-.8		6.2	3.0
	-7.3	-14.3	-12.0	-11.2	-11.6	-3.4		1.0	-1.8
Sales/Net Fixed Assets	49.7	13.8	6.1	6.4	5.7	1.6		9.6	8.2
	7.2	5.7	4.0	3.7	2.9	1.2		5.5	5.4
	3.2	3.4	2.5	1.8	1.4	.5		3.0	2.9
Sales/Total Assets	4.4	4.1	2.2	1.9	1.3	.8		2.8	2.6
	3.1	1.9	1.6	1.3	.9	.6		1.9	2.0
	2.0	1.4	.9	.9	.6	.4		1.3	1.3
% Depr., Dep., Amort./Sales	.5	1.6	2.6	2.7	3.7			1.5	1.8
	(11) 3.2	(26) 3.8	4.2	(70) 5.0	(12) 5.0			(257) 2.8	(260) 2.9
	9.2	5.3	8.0	7.7	8.9			4.8	4.9
% Officers', Directors' Owners' Comp/Sales		1.3	1.2	2.1				1.5	1.3
	(19) 2.1	(18) 1.9	(11) 3.0					(82) 2.4	(76) 2.3
	5.6	2.5	3.9					4.6	3.9
Net Sales ($)	12130M	76028M	421816M	2698573M	829286M	986751M		9813605M	11441195M
Total Assets ($)	3612M	32256M	253232M	1708518M	963864M	1749018M		5706390M	7067325M

M = $ thousand   MM = $ million
See Pages 9 through 22 for Explanation of Ratios and Data

Comparative Historical Data | Current Data Sorted by Sales

	4/1/07-3/31/08 ALL	4/1/08-3/31/09 ALL	4/1/09-3/31/10 ALL	Type of Statement	0-1MM	1-3MM	3-5MM	5-10MM	10-25MM	25MM & OVER
	46	33	36	Unqualified	2	2			10	22
	46	39	34	Reviewed	1	2	6	7	10	8
	35	27	23	Compiled	1	7	6	3	5	1
	23	25	28	Tax Returns	10	10	3	3	2	
	88	77	65	Other		5	3	7	18	32
					44 (4/1-9/30/09)			142 (10/1/09-3/31/10)		
	238	201	186	**NUMBER OF STATEMENTS**	14	26	18	20	45	63
	%	%	%	**ASSETS**	%	%	%	%	%	%
	6.2	5.5	6.2	Cash & Equivalents	11.4	4.2	10.2	9.7	3.2	5.9
	11.1	9.2	11.6	Trade Receivables (net)	15.7	12.0	15.9	10.9	10.3	10.5
	27.0	25.9	24.5	Inventory	25.2	26.5	19.3	29.5	26.1	22.3
	3.6	2.5	3.0	All Other Current	.2	3.3	1.1	1.0	4.6	3.5
	47.9	43.1	45.4	Total Current	52.5	46.0	46.5	51.1	44.3	42.2
	41.9	45.4	42.1	Fixed Assets (net)	32.8	45.0	45.8	31.9	44.7	43.3
	1.5	1.3	1.4	Intangibles (net)	5.4	2.7	1.0	.2	1.4	.5
	8.8	10.2	11.2	All Other Non-Current	10.5	6.3	6.7	16.8	9.6	14.0
	100.0	100.0	100.0	Total	100.0	100.0	100.0	100.0	100.0	100.0
				LIABILITIES						
	14.0	13.5	14.3	Notes Payable-Short Term	18.3	21.0	15.6	16.1	13.8	10.0
	4.6	6.1	6.6	Cur. Mat.-L.T.D.	9.2	4.9	5.9	13.4	6.4	5.0
	6.5	5.7	5.8	Trade Payables	6.9	4.7	9.2	4.5	4.9	6.0
	.1	.1	.1	Income Taxes Payable	.0	.0	.3	.0	.1	.1
	5.2	7.9	5.4	All Other Current	8.2	3.0	5.0	3.9	7.7	4.8
	30.3	33.2	32.2	Total Current	42.7	33.6	36.0	38.0	32.8	25.8
	22.5	26.1	27.4	Long-Term Debt	40.8	45.4	21.7	20.9	20.5	25.7
	.7	.6	.5	Deferred Taxes	.0	.2	.1	.4	1.0	.6
	6.1	4.8	6.0	All Other Non-Current	1.4	15.2	2.0	2.6	6.7	5.0
	40.4	35.4	33.8	Net Worth	14.4	5.7	40.2	38.1	38.9	42.9
	100.0	100.0	100.0	Total Liabilities & Net Worth	100.0	100.0	100.0	100.0	100.0	100.0
				INCOME DATA						
	100.0	100.0	100.0	Net Sales	100.0	100.0	100.0	100.0	100.0	100.0
	17.6	19.7	17.6	Gross Profit	38.7	27.9	17.3	14.8	10.6	14.5
	16.2	19.2	20.3	Operating Expenses	38.7	32.3	19.5	16.8	16.6	15.3
	1.4	.5	-2.8	Operating Profit	.0	-4.4	-2.3	-2.0	-6.0	-.8
	1.3	1.4	1.3	All Other Expenses (net)	.7	2.1	.0	1.3	.7	2.0
	.1	-.9	-4.1	Profit Before Taxes	-.7	-6.6	-2.3	-3.3	-6.8	-2.8
				RATIOS						
	3.2	3.3	3.0	Current	4.0	2.8	3.7	2.9	2.7	3.0
	1.7	1.4	1.6		2.3	1.6	1.6	1.2	1.7	1.6
	1.1	.8	.9		.6	.6	.7	.9	1.0	.9
	1.1	1.1	1.3	Quick	3.6	1.2	2.0	2.1	1.0	1.3
	.5	.4	.6		.8	.5	.8	.4	.5	.7
	.2	.2	.2		.3	.3	.3	.2	.2	.3
	10 34.8	10 35.5	12 31.5	Sales/Receivables	0 UND	7 51.1	10 35.8	11 31.8	15 24.9	15 25.1
	17 21.5	16 23.3	20 17.9		28 13.0	12 31.1	23 15.8	19 19.4	24 15.4	20 17.9
	27 13.3	25 14.7	31 11.9		51 7.1	26 14.3	38 9.7	31 11.6	38 9.7	30 12.2
	34 10.7	31 11.7	33 11.2	Cost of Sales/Inventory	0 UND	25 14.4	12 30.0	29 12.6	43 8.5	36 10.1
	58 6.3	60 6.1	60 6.1		49 7.5	73 5.0	37 10.0	64 5.7	79 4.6	49 7.4
	93 3.9	100 3.6	107 3.4		169 2.2	115 3.2	99 3.7	122 3.0	119 3.1	85 4.3
	5 72.1	4 97.0	5 75.2	Cost of Sales/Payables	0 UND	1 244.2	5 66.5	3 112.6	6 64.7	8 47.8
	11 33.0	9 41.1	10 36.9		4 92.3	5 69.0	9 39.4	6 61.8	10 35.8	13 29.1
	19 19.0	19 19.6	19 19.3		15 24.9	13 27.9	16 22.3	17 21.7	22 16.7	23 16.1
	5.0	6.2	4.7	Sales/Working Capital	4.2	6.0	6.2	4.3	3.9	4.9
	9.5	16.4	10.8		9.1	15.0	17.1	15.1	7.8	9.2
	66.0	-31.1	-39.5		-6.0	-10.7	-12.1	-262.4	-159.4	-50.7
	2.9	2.8	2.5	EBIT/Interest	(11) 8.2	2.3	(15) 2.9	2.3	(41) 3.0	(61) 2.2
	(224) 1.0	(187) .8	(174) .0		1.2	-.3	-1.5	.0	.5	.2
	-.8	-1.7	-3.0		-1.0	-2.6	-3.6	-4.6	-6.3	-2.5
	4.0	2.3	2.5	Net Profit + Depr., Dep., Amort./Cur. Mat. L/T/D					2.4	2.7
	(61) 1.6	(56) 1.0	(42) 1.4						(13) 1.2	(18) 1.6
	.6	.1	.5						-1.8	1.0
	.5	.6	.5	Fixed/Worth	.3	.5	.3	.5	.5	.5
	1.0	1.3	1.3		3.7	3.0	2.1	.9	1.3	1.0
	2.0	3.7	3.3		-1.1	-4.2	3.3	1.9	3.6	1.8
	.6	.7	.6	Debt/Worth	.5	1.6	.5	.8	.5	.6
	1.5	1.7	1.7		6.4	6.3	2.4	2.3	1.2	1.2
	3.3	5.8	5.5		-3.6	-6.3	5.7	3.5	4.4	2.8
	14.5	14.7	12.6	% Profit Before Taxes/Tangible Net Worth		16.2	34.4	10.2	8.6	12.3
	(219) 1.3	(174) .3	(160) -4.5			(18) -4.6	(17) -9.6	(18) -17.0	(39) 1.7	(59) -3.6
	-14.5	-11.8	-18.5			-36.1	-49.9	-51.8	-20.4	-12.9
	5.9	4.3	3.8	% Profit Before Taxes/Total Assets	17.7	3.2	9.3	3.5	3.6	3.6
	.1	-.9	-3.1		.2	-4.6	-6.3	-3.7	-3.1	-2.0
	-5.2	-5.9	-11.4		-7.7	-14.7	-10.7	-14.3	-16.3	-6.1
	8.2	8.6	6.9	Sales/Net Fixed Assets	22.6	7.2	13.1	6.0	6.0	7.0
	4.6	4.0	4.0		7.1	4.4	3.5	4.6	2.8	3.3
	2.5	2.3	1.9		2.7	2.4	2.5	3.7	1.6	1.6
	2.5	2.6	2.2	Sales/Total Assets	3.1	3.5	4.5	2.5	1.6	2.2
	1.6	1.7	1.4		2.0	1.6	1.8	1.4	1.2	1.4
	1.1	1.1	.9		.7	1.1	1.0	.9	.9	.8
	1.7	2.3	2.6	% Depr., Dep., Amort./Sales	(12) 1.2	(23) 1.5	(16) 3.3	(43) 2.8	(58) 2.4	2.9
	(218) 3.7	(182) 4.0	(172) 4.6		3.4	4.5	6.9	3.8	4.3	4.7
	5.9	6.2	7.7		9.3	9.9	10.2	5.6	7.7	6.8
	1.3	1.4	1.7	% Officers', Directors' Owners' Comp/Sales		(16) .6	(10) 1.6	(10) 1.2		
	(67) 2.3	(57) 2.6	(57) 2.4			2.1	2.2	2.1		
	4.1	4.3	3.9			3.9	3.0	3.1		
	9010451M	6149687M	5024584M	Net Sales ($)	6863M	54540M	72242M	147068M	725171M	4018700M
	6407328M	4779369M	4710500M	Total Assets ($)	4790M	41915M	49096M	140320M	660580M	3813799M

© RMA 2010

M = $ thousand   MM = $ million
See Pages 9 through 22 for Explanation of Ratios and Data

Current Data Sorted by Assets   Comparative Historical Data

							Type of Statement			
		5	6	2	1		Unqualified		16	15
		5	2				Reviewed		10	15
	4	1	1				Compiled		3	3
1	1	1					Tax Returns		3	
1	1	4	9		7		Other		13	11
	14 (4/1-9/30/09)		38 (10/1/09-3/31/10)						4/1/05-3/31/06	4/1/06-3/31/07
0-500M	500M-2MM	2-10MM	10-50MM	50-100MM	100-250MM				ALL	ALL
2	6	16	18	2	8		NUMBER OF STATEMENTS		45	44
%	%	%	%	%	%		ASSETS		%	%
		11.1	9.8				Cash & Equivalents		4.6	6.0
		15.6	16.5				Trade Receivables (net)		22.2	18.7
		33.5	31.4				Inventory		36.8	39.5
		2.6	4.8				All Other Current		2.4	2.1
		62.8	62.5				Total Current		66.1	66.4
		28.1	29.4				Fixed Assets (net)		26.9	26.2
		3.4	1.3				Intangibles (net)		.9	1.0
		5.8	6.8				All Other Non-Current		6.2	6.5
		100.0	100.0				Total		100.0	100.0
							LIABILITIES			
		8.7	10.3				Notes Payable-Short Term		15.4	17.8
		2.1	3.3				Cur. Mat.-L.T.D.		5.0	3.8
		8.3	7.7				Trade Payables		10.4	9.5
		.0	.4				Income Taxes Payable		.2	.2
		5.0	6.8				All Other Current		6.6	7.2
		24.2	28.5				Total Current		37.7	38.6
		12.1	16.2				Long-Term Debt		12.9	11.5
		.1	.2				Deferred Taxes		.7	.7
		1.5	.7				All Other Non-Current		3.7	1.2
		62.2	54.3				Net Worth		45.1	48.0
		100.0	100.0				Total Liabilities & Net Worth		100.0	100.0
							INCOME DATA			
		100.0	100.0				Net Sales		100.0	100.0
		19.6	14.7				Gross Profit		20.6	17.1
		13.8	11.1				Operating Expenses		15.3	11.1
		5.9	3.6				Operating Profit		5.3	6.0
		.0	.4				All Other Expenses (net)		1.0	1.4
		5.8	3.2				Profit Before Taxes		4.3	4.6
							RATIOS			
		4.5	3.8						2.7	2.6
		3.2	2.1				Current		1.6	1.7
		1.5	1.4						1.2	1.3
		1.4	1.9						1.1	.9
		1.2	.7				Quick		.6	.6
		.8	.5						.4	.4
	13	27.8	15	23.7			Sales/Receivables	15	25.0	16	23.0
	17	21.0	22	16.7				23	16.0	20	17.8
	25	14.7	38	9.6				37	9.9	33	10.9
	27	13.3	36	10.1			Cost of Sales/Inventory	25	14.9	31	11.9
	53	6.9	53	6.9				56	6.6	58	6.3
	88	4.2	79	4.6				75	4.8	70	5.2
	7	53.1	8	48.3			Cost of Sales/Payables	8	43.3	5	66.9
	9	39.1	12	31.2				13	27.1	10	36.7
	15	23.6	21	17.7				20	18.2	21	17.7
		4.1	4.4				Sales/Working Capital		7.3	6.5
		6.9	7.5						11.2	11.1
		14.8	17.9						29.4	26.3
		23.2	31.3				EBIT/Interest		13.3	10.4
	(14)	11.7	(15)	6.5				(41)	6.1	(41)	4.8
		2.3	.4						2.2	2.0
							Net Profit + Depr., Dep., Amort./Cur. Mat. L/T/D		5.1	11.7
								(13)	2.6	(16)	2.8
									1.0	1.3
		.2	.2				Fixed/Worth		.3	.4
		.4	.6						.5	.5
		1.0	1.5						.9	.9
		.3	.4				Debt/Worth		.6	.7
		.5	.9						1.3	1.3
		1.2	2.0						2.5	2.3
		29.3	23.4				% Profit Before Taxes/Tangible Net Worth		63.9	45.9
		16.4	11.9					(44)	29.1	24.1
		5.8	-.4						15.2	12.1
		17.0	13.7				% Profit Before Taxes/Total Assets		19.4	19.0
		8.3	8.3						13.1	10.7
		2.5	.8						5.1	3.8
		17.6	24.9				Sales/Net Fixed Assets		26.2	22.9
		13.8	7.8						15.2	13.9
		5.5	4.9						8.4	8.2
		3.3	3.0				Sales/Total Assets		4.5	3.9
		2.4	2.3						3.5	3.3
		1.8	1.6						2.0	2.0
		.9	.5				% Depr., Dep., Amort./Sales		.5	.7
		1.7	(15)	1.3				(40)	1.1	(41)	1.2
		3.2	2.3						2.0	2.2
							% Officers', Directors' Owners' Comp/Sales		.4	
								(13)	1.0	
									1.5	
925M	37575M	298961M	915509M	230157M	2162288M		Net Sales ($)		2847190M	3020973M
618M	7674M	85663M	402550M	146259M	1406361M		Total Assets ($)		1038912M	1280276M

M = $ thousand   MM = $ million
See Pages 9 through 22 for Explanation of Ratios and Data

Comparative Historical Data   Current Data Sorted by Sales

			Type of Statement	0-1MM	1-3MM	3-5MM	5-10MM	10-25MM	25MM & OVER
22	14	14	Unqualified				1	3	9
11	10	7	Reviewed				3	2	2
1	4	6	Compiled			1	2	1	1
2	2	3	Tax Returns	1					1
15	15	22	Other	1	1			4	16
				2					
4/1/07- 3/31/08	4/1/08- 3/31/09	4/1/09- 3/31/10		0-1MM	14 (4/1-9/30/09) 1-3MM	3-5MM	38 (10/1/09-3/31/10) 5-10MM	10-25MM	25MM & OVER
ALL	ALL	ALL							
51	45	52	**NUMBER OF STATEMENTS**	4	1	2	6	10	29
%	%	%	**ASSETS**	%	%	%	%	%	%
5.2	7.1	9.2	Cash & Equivalents					12.9	9.6
19.4	17.2	15.7	Trade Receivables (net)					13.3	16.0
38.2	37.0	32.2	Inventory					36.1	31.6
2.0	2.6	3.1	All Other Current					3.5	3.5
64.8	63.9	60.2	Total Current					65.7	60.7
28.1	26.3	29.5	Fixed Assets (net)					27.8	28.2
.9	3.5	3.3	Intangibles (net)					.3	2.7
6.2	6.3	7.0	All Other Non-Current					6.2	8.3
100.0	100.0	100.0	Total					100.0	100.0
			LIABILITIES						
17.3	15.8	10.5	Notes Payable-Short Term					12.5	10.8
4.1	2.8	2.5	Cur. Mat.-L.T.D.					2.4	2.8
8.2	8.0	7.6	Trade Payables					8.3	7.8
.3	.1	.2	Income Taxes Payable					.0	.3
6.3	6.0	7.5	All Other Current					4.6	6.7
36.2	32.7	28.2	Total Current					27.9	28.4
17.4	15.5	17.1	Long-Term Debt					11.5	17.1
.5	.4	.1	Deferred Taxes					.0	.2
1.3	.7	1.8	All Other Non-Current					2.2	1.4
44.6	50.6	52.7	Net Worth					58.3	52.9
100.0	100.0	100.0	Total Liabilities & Net Worth					100.0	100.0
			INCOME DATA						
100.0	100.0	100.0	Net Sales					100.0	100.0
17.4	17.8	16.1	Gross Profit					18.0	13.8
12.2	13.5	12.7	Operating Expenses					12.9	10.2
5.1	4.3	3.3	Operating Profit					5.2	3.7
.9	1.0	.2	All Other Expenses (net)					.2	.1
4.2	3.3	3.1	Profit Before Taxes					4.9	3.5
			RATIOS						
3.4	3.6	4.5						4.3	4.4
1.7	1.8	2.2	Current					2.8	2.1
1.4	1.4	1.5						1.5	1.5
1.4	1.3	1.6						1.8	2.2
.6	.7	.9	Quick					1.0	.7
.4	.4	.5						.2	.5
17 21.4	12 31.0	16 22.2						14 26.3	18 20.0
25 14.4	24 14.9	24 15.4	Sales/Receivables					18 20.6	25 14.4
33 11.0	32 11.3	35 10.5						32 11.4	34 10.6
40 9.2	37 9.8	39 9.3						48 7.6	38 9.6
64 5.7	66 5.5	57 6.4	Cost of Sales/Inventory					62 5.9	53 6.8
83 4.4	88 4.1	89 4.1						89 4.1	87 4.2
6 62.5	6 66.1	8 47.9						9 41.8	7 50.8
11 33.2	10 36.1	11 32.0	Cost of Sales/Payables					14 26.4	11 32.2
18 20.0	19 18.9	20 18.7						29 12.6	20 18.5
5.1	6.2	4.1						4.0	4.3
10.4	8.0	6.1	Sales/Working Capital					7.1	5.9
15.9	19.1	15.1						10.8	14.3
9.5	12.2	15.7							11.3
(49) 5.1	(42) 3.2	(46) 5.0	EBIT/Interest					(26)	5.4
1.4	1.0	1.2							2.6
6.9	13.5	13.3							9.2
(14) 3.9	(15) 2.1	(15) 6.1	Net Profit + Depr., Dep., Amort./Cur. Mat. L/T/D					(10)	6.1
1.4	.2	4.2							3.7
.4	.3	.3						.2	.4
.6	.5	.5	Fixed/Worth					.5	.5
.8	1.0	1.0						.9	.9
.8	.6	.4						.3	.5
1.2	1.0	.9	Debt/Worth					.8	1.0
2.1	2.5	1.7						1.1	1.8
40.9	31.0	23.9	% Profit Before Taxes/Tangible Net Worth					24.5	24.3
(48) 24.4	16.9	(50) 10.7						17.8	11.1
4.3	-.2	4.1						6.9	7.0
17.9	16.1	11.8	% Profit Before Taxes/Total Assets					15.3	11.8
9.3	5.7	7.0						8.3	7.5
1.6	-.1	.5						4.3	3.1
19.8	26.4	17.6						18.1	19.5
11.8	10.0	7.3	Sales/Net Fixed Assets					11.8	6.2
7.3	5.9	5.0						4.6	5.2
3.4	3.4	2.7						2.8	3.1
2.7	2.2	2.1	Sales/Total Assets					2.3	2.2
1.8	1.9	1.5						1.8	1.4
.8	1.1	.9							.5
(47) 1.4	(39) 1.7	(44) 1.7	% Depr., Dep., Amort./Sales					(23)	1.4
2.2	2.7	2.4							2.3
		.4							
	(13) .8		% Officers', Directors' Owners' Comp/Sales						
		2.7							
3564301M	3269146M	3645415M	Net Sales ($)	1480M	2304M	8251M	40830M	179320M	3413230M
1750364M	1710228M	2049125M	Total Assets ($)	1867M	1748M	5151M	17049M	81812M	1941498M

Current Data Sorted by Assets   Comparative Historical Data

0-500M	500M-2MM	2-10MM	10-50MM	50-100MM	100-250MM	Type of Statement	4/1/05-3/31/06 ALL	4/1/06-3/31/07 ALL
		3	6	2	1	Unqualified	20	18
	2	3	1			Reviewed	19	17
	5	3				Compiled	7	8
5	4	3	1			Tax Returns	11	16
1	5	11	12	4	3	Other	29	36
		12 (4/1-9/30/09)	63 (10/1/09-3/31/10)					
6	16	23	20	6	4	**NUMBER OF STATEMENTS**	86	95
%	%	%	%	%	%	**ASSETS**	%	%
	8.0	9.1	4.6			Cash & Equivalents	5.6	5.0
	22.8	23.9	17.6			Trade Receivables (net)	22.2	21.6
	37.3	34.4	32.6			Inventory	31.2	31.0
	3.7	3.2	4.9			All Other Current	3.5	2.1
	71.9	70.6	59.7			Total Current	62.4	59.6
	23.3	23.0	29.0			Fixed Assets (net)	29.3	30.4
	.8	2.6	.4			Intangibles (net)	1.6	3.0
	4.0	3.7	10.9			All Other Non-Current	6.7	7.0
	100.0	100.0	100.0			Total	100.0	100.0
						LIABILITIES		
	18.6	19.5	14.6			Notes Payable-Short Term	15.3	15.2
	4.3	3.3	2.7			Cur. Mat.-L.T.D.	4.7	3.9
	9.4	11.8	6.6			Trade Payables	10.7	11.0
	.0	.0	.3			Income Taxes Payable	.2	.2
	9.9	7.0	3.5			All Other Current	6.5	6.5
	42.2	41.5	27.7			Total Current	37.4	36.7
	17.6	11.9	13.9			Long-Term Debt	18.9	19.7
	.0	.1	1.3			Deferred Taxes	.6	.6
	15.6	4.7	2.1			All Other Non-Current	5.8	4.6
	24.6	41.8	55.0			Net Worth	37.3	38.4
	100.0	100.0	100.0			Total Liabilities & Net Worth	100.0	100.0
						INCOME DATA		
	100.0	100.0	100.0			Net Sales	100.0	100.0
	24.6	19.3	16.7			Gross Profit	21.7	22.3
	25.2	20.6	18.7			Operating Expenses	18.0	17.5
	-.6	-1.4	-2.0			Operating Profit	3.7	4.8
	1.8	.8	1.3			All Other Expenses (net)	.7	1.0
	-2.5	-2.2	-3.3			Profit Before Taxes	3.0	3.7
						RATIOS		
	2.9	4.0	6.7				3.0	2.9
	1.5	1.7	2.2			Current	1.8	1.5
	1.2	1.1	1.6				1.2	1.2
	1.4	2.1	2.1				1.5	1.4
	.6	.7	1.0			Quick	.8	.7
	.4	.4	.4				.4	.4
	28 12.8	33 11.0	25 14.4				21 17.5	23 16.2
	40 9.2	41 9.0	40 9.1			Sales/Receivables	36 10.0	32 11.3
	46 8.0	58 6.3	67 5.5				54 6.7	48 7.6
	50 7.3	14 25.4	68 5.4				36 10.1	34 10.6
	76 4.8	63 5.8	147 2.5			Cost of Sales/Inventory	55 6.6	63 5.8
	150 2.4	118 3.1	173 2.1				118 3.1	106 3.4
	8 46.7	13 28.1	8 46.7				11 32.8	10 36.9
	25 14.9	19 19.4	11 34.1			Cost of Sales/Payables	18 20.1	18 20.0
	36 10.0	38 9.6	16 22.3				29 12.6	32 11.3
	5.2	3.7	1.7				4.5	5.9
	7.2	8.8	3.4			Sales/Working Capital	8.7	11.4
	11.2	18.1	6.9				27.3	37.1
	2.3	1.8	6.4				10.9	6.9
	(15) 1.3	(21) .8	(18) 1.9			EBIT/Interest	(82) 4.0	(90) 3.1
	-6.0	-3.8	-1.0				.9	.9
						Net Profit + Depr., Dep.,	5.1	6.1
						Amort./Cur. Mat. L/T/D	(28) 2.5	(28) 3.1
							.6	1.5
	.3	.3	.2				.3	.4
	1.0	.4	.4			Fixed/Worth	.7	.8
	4.9	1.3	1.0				1.6	2.1
	1.2	.4	.3				.6	.7
	2.4	1.7	.8			Debt/Worth	1.3	2.0
	26.4	4.9	1.5				4.6	5.2
	13.6	16.0	6.8			% Profit Before Taxes/Tangible	41.7	37.5
	(13) 2.3	(20) -1.1	(18) -1.0			Net Worth	(78) 14.1	(84) 14.7
	-76.9	-9.8	-6.3				3.4	1.2
	3.1	3.1	5.9			% Profit Before Taxes/Total	14.0	14.1
	.6	-.4	-.4			Assets	6.1	6.1
	-19.2	-5.7	-2.8				.5	.1
	31.2	30.8	6.4				18.8	20.5
	11.9	12.2	4.0			Sales/Net Fixed Assets	7.9	6.7
	6.0	3.8	3.0				4.1	3.8
	2.7	2.8	1.9				3.2	2.7
	2.2	1.9	1.1			Sales/Total Assets	2.0	1.9
	1.7	1.1	.7				1.3	1.5
	.8	.7	1.0				1.0	1.2
	(15) 2.6	(18) 2.1	(18) 2.2			% Depr., Dep., Amort./Sales	(73) 1.9	(87) 2.0
	3.2	5.0	4.0				3.7	3.6
							.6	1.4
						% Officers', Directors'	(18) 2.4	(28) 2.5
						Owners' Comp/Sales	4.3	3.8
5407M	39602M	208367M	598513M	644734M	873633M	Net Sales ($)	3142989M	3288004M
1562M	17483M	118100M	490786M	458454M	492306M	Total Assets ($)	1793388M	1681705M

© RMA 2010

M = $ thousand   MM = $ million

See Pages 9 through 22 for Explanation of Ratios and Data

Comparative Historical Data | Current Data Sorted by Sales

Type of Statement	4/1/07-3/31/08 ALL	4/1/08-3/31/09 ALL	4/1/09-3/31/10 ALL	0-1MM	1-3MM	3-5MM	5-10MM	10-25MM	25MM & OVER
Unqualified	10	12	12		1	2	2	5	5
Reviewed	12	9	6				1	1	1
Compiled	3	13	8		4		3	1	1
Tax Returns	9	10	13	4	5	1	1	1	1
Other	37	31	36	2	4	4	3	12	11
				12 (4/1-9/30/09)			63 (10/1/09-3/31/10)		
NUMBER OF STATEMENTS	71	75	75	6	14	7	10	20	18
ASSETS	%	%	%	%	%	%	%	%	%
Cash & Equivalents	5.7	5.7	7.4		4.6		8.8	4.1	6.3
Trade Receivables (net)	24.2	20.9	19.0		20.5		24.6	20.0	18.3
Inventory	32.0	35.2	32.3		42.9		22.2	43.3	23.5
All Other Current	2.6	2.8	4.0		4.2		1.5	2.4	7.2
Total Current	64.5	64.5	62.7		72.3		57.0	69.8	55.3
Fixed Assets (net)	27.7	27.0	27.2		22.2		31.8	22.3	28.9
Intangibles (net)	2.0	1.5	2.3		1.5		.3	2.8	4.5
All Other Non-Current	5.8	7.1	7.8		3.9		10.9	5.1	11.4
Total	100.0	100.0	100.0		100.0		100.0	100.0	100.0
LIABILITIES									
Notes Payable-Short Term	14.2	19.6	17.3		24.2		12.9	21.9	11.1
Cur. Mat.-L.T.D.	2.8	4.4	4.5		5.0		3.3	1.6	8.1
Trade Payables	11.0	11.5	10.0		18.1		7.9	9.7	7.5
Income Taxes Payable	.2	.0	.1		.0		.0	.0	.3
All Other Current	5.6	4.8	5.9		3.5		7.2	5.6	4.4
Total Current	33.8	40.4	37.8		50.8		31.3	38.8	31.4
Long-Term Debt	16.9	16.1	16.1		23.7		14.0	11.6	13.9
Deferred Taxes	.6	.3	.4		.0		.0	1.0	.5
All Other Non-Current	6.0	4.4	6.7		13.3		.1	2.5	6.6
Net Worth	42.7	38.7	39.0		12.3		54.6	46.1	47.6
Total Liabilities & Net Worth	100.0	100.0	100.0		100.0		100.0	100.0	100.0
INCOME DATA									
Net Sales	100.0	100.0	100.0		100.0		100.0	100.0	100.0
Gross Profit	20.6	22.5	20.4		26.9		18.1	17.6	14.5
Operating Expenses	17.5	21.1	23.0		29.1		21.0	18.2	16.5
Operating Profit	3.0	1.5	-2.6		-2.2		-2.9	-.5	-1.9
All Other Expenses (net)	.9	1.3	1.1		1.6		.6	1.3	.4
Profit Before Taxes	2.2	.2	-3.7		-3.9		-3.5	-1.8	-2.4
RATIOS									
Current	3.8	3.4	3.4		2.3		3.6	5.5	4.1
	1.8	1.7	1.8		1.6		1.7	1.9	2.0
	1.4	1.1	1.2		1.3		1.2	1.2	1.3
Quick	1.8	1.3	1.4		1.3		2.3	1.1	1.6
	.9	.6	.6		.6		.9	.6	.9
	.5	.3	.4		.3		.6	.4	.4
Sales/Receivables	24 15.2	21 17.7	25 14.6		26 14.3		27 13.7	27 13.4	25 14.9
	35 10.3	32 11.5	37 9.9		38 9.6		40 9.2	42 8.7	32 11.4
	46 8.0	46 8.0	52 7.1		50 7.2		68 5.3	57 6.5	47 7.7
Cost of Sales/Inventory	34 10.7	38 9.6	48 7.7		60 6.1	20 18.1	86 4.2	45 8.2	
	67 5.4	69 5.3	80 4.6		79 4.6	54 6.8	143 2.5	58 6.3	
	105 3.5	135 2.7	155 2.4		142 2.6	71 5.2	173 2.1	100 3.6	
Cost of Sales/Payables	10 36.9	6 57.6	9 40.9		13 28.5		9 39.0	9 40.7	10 37.2
	17 21.4	17 22.1	14 25.5		31 11.6		15 24.2	13 28.0	12 31.2
	29 12.7	32 11.5	33 11.1		43 8.6		23 15.9	25 14.5	27 13.6
Sales/Working Capital	4.2	3.9	3.1		4.8		3.5	2.3	2.9
	8.2	9.1	6.7		7.2		6.9	4.9	6.7
	15.8	22.2	13.9		13.5		42.4	13.1	12.6
EBIT/Interest	8.5	6.0	2.9		2.3			3.8	3.5
	(68) 3.0	(68) 1.7	(69) .6	(13) -.5			(18) 1.3	(17) 1.1
	.0	-1.3	-3.8		-6.7			-1.0	-2.4
Net Profit + Depr., Dep., Amort./Cur. Mat. L/T/D	4.8	2.6	3.1						
	(21) 1.7	(17) 2.0	(10) 1.7						
	.1	-2.2	1.0						
Fixed/Worth	.3	.3	.3		.2		.1	.3	.3
	.6	.7	.7		.9		.5	.4	.7
	1.1	1.6	1.5		-4.8		1.0	1.1	2.6
Debt/Worth	.6	.5	.5		1.9		.3	.4	.5
	1.3	1.7	1.5		4.7		.9	1.1	1.3
	3.9	5.0	6.0		-13.9		1.5	3.8	6.1
% Profit Before Taxes/Tangible Net Worth	29.7	20.0	6.3		8.3			11.0	5.2
	(68) 11.1	(69) 5.3	(63) -2.4	(10) -4.3			(18) 4.0	(16) -1.5
	-10.6	-13.8	-14.0		-55.4			-5.0	-34.6
% Profit Before Taxes/Total Assets	12.1	11.1	3.5		2.0		20.1	3.7	3.9
	3.6	1.8	-2.1		-2.7		-4.0	1.0	-.1
	-3.8	-9.7	-9.8		-22.7		-13.8	-2.8	-8.2
Sales/Net Fixed Assets	17.0	19.6	13.7		38.7		31.0	30.0	6.6
	8.6	8.7	6.1		14.8		6.3	9.4	5.3
	4.0	4.2	3.8		7.4		3.3	3.0	3.8
Sales/Total Assets	2.9	3.0	2.4		2.9		3.1	2.3	2.1
	2.2	2.1	1.8		2.2		1.9	1.5	1.7
	1.4	1.2	1.1		1.7		1.0	.9	1.0
% Depr., Dep., Amort./Sales	1.1	.9	1.2		.9			.5	1.5
	(64) 2.2	(68) 2.3	(64) 2.2	(12) 2.4			(17) 2.0	(15) 2.0
	3.8	4.1	3.8		3.1			3.3	4.4
% Officers', Directors' Owners' Comp/Sales	.8	1.8	1.9						
	(21) 2.5	(18) 3.3	(15) 4.9						
	4.8	4.7	8.3						
Net Sales ($)	3591248M	2228767M	2370256M	3214M	29729M	27178M	78190M	336730M	1895215M
Total Assets ($)	1844858M	1392535M	1578691M	3086M	14362M	24326M	55205M	287237M	1194475M

Current Data Sorted by Assets   Comparative Historical Data

0-500M	500M-2MM	2-10MM	10-50MM	50-100MM	100-250MM	Type of Statement	4/1/05-3/31/06 ALL	4/1/06-3/31/07 ALL
1		1	2			Unqualified	11	8
	2	13	1			Reviewed	21	21
	1	5				Compiled	21	26
4	2	1				Tax Returns	8	13
3	8	12	4			Other	23	34
	6 (4/1-9/30/09)		54 (10/1/09-3/31/10)					
8	13	32	7			NUMBER OF STATEMENTS	84	102
%	%	%	%	%	%	**ASSETS**	%	%
	8.1	12.4				Cash & Equivalents	7.6	10.6
	17.5	20.8				Trade Receivables (net)	28.2	24.3
	26.4	20.7				Inventory	22.8	23.0
	2.5	4.9				All Other Current	2.3	2.1
	54.5	58.7	DATA	DATA		Total Current	61.0	60.0
	32.8	34.0	NOT	NOT		Fixed Assets (net)	29.1	30.3
	7.7	1.2	AVAILABLE	AVAILABLE		Intangibles (net)	4.8	3.5
	4.9	6.0				All Other Non-Current	5.2	6.3
	100.0	100.0				Total	100.0	100.0
						LIABILITIES		
	10.0	10.9				Notes Payable-Short Term	10.9	12.0
	3.8	4.7				Cur. Mat.-L.T.D.	3.8	4.2
	9.3	6.8				Trade Payables	12.6	10.0
	.0	.1				Income Taxes Payable	.1	.2
	3.8	6.3				All Other Current	11.3	9.5
	26.9	28.7				Total Current	38.8	36.0
	24.2	12.9				Long-Term Debt	17.0	17.0
	.2	.4				Deferred Taxes	.5	.3
	32.5	10.9				All Other Non-Current	7.3	4.8
	16.2	47.2				Net Worth	36.4	41.8
	100.0	100.0				Total Liabilties & Net Worth	100.0	100.0
						INCOME DATA		
	100.0	100.0				Net Sales	100.0	100.0
	33.2	28.1				Gross Profit	26.8	30.3
	34.2	32.8				Operating Expenses	20.8	25.5
	-1.0	-4.7				Operating Profit	6.1	4.8
	1.1	1.0				All Other Expenses (net)	.6	.5
	-2.1	-5.7				Profit Before Taxes	5.5	4.3
						RATIOS		
	9.0	6.1					2.7	3.6
	1.7	2.1				Current	1.6	1.7
	1.0	1.3					1.1	1.2
	4.0	4.2					1.6	2.1
	.8	1.1				Quick	.9	1.1
	.4	.7					.5	.6
13 28.7		26 14.2					22 16.9	19 19.7
28 13.0		34 10.8				Sales/Receivables	33 11.1	27 13.4
36 10.1		49 7.5					48 7.7	39 9.3
35 10.6		41 9.0					25 14.7	25 14.8
53 6.9		54 6.8				Cost of Sales/Inventory	35 10.4	38 9.6
91 4.0		69 5.3					51 7.2	58 6.3
4 83.4		7 48.8					7 50.3	5 78.7
11 32.5		16 22.6				Cost of Sales/Payables	13 27.7	9 38.9
34 10.6		20 18.0					30 12.2	20 18.3
	5.2	3.4					7.0	6.1
	7.1	7.5				Sales/Working Capital	13.0	10.6
	NM	11.6					63.1	39.7
	5.4	1.1					15.7	11.9
	(12) 1.1	(30) -1.3				EBIT/Interest	(79) 5.6	(95) 4.3
	-4.6	-12.2					2.5	1.4
						Net Profit + Depr., Dep.,	5.3	3.5
						Amort./Cur. Mat. L/T/D	(17) 3.1	(14) 2.3
							.9	1.8
	.8	.5					.3	.4
	2.1	.7				Fixed/Worth	.7	.7
	NM	1.3					2.4	1.5
	1.3	.5					.7	.5
	3.4	1.0				Debt/Worth	1.6	1.4
	NM	2.1					7.8	3.6
	72.9	2.5				% Profit Before Taxes/Tangible	70.3	52.8
	(10) 4.1	(29) -7.6				Net Worth	(71) 35.9	(90) 27.4
	-7.9	-40.2					14.1	9.8
	14.5	.2				% Profit Before Taxes/Total	25.7	22.6
	.7	-7.2				Assets	12.4	8.3
	-24.4	-27.2					3.9	2.1
	39.1	12.1					23.4	25.1
	5.9	6.7				Sales/Net Fixed Assets	10.6	11.4
	5.1	3.6					6.7	5.6
	3.1	2.6					3.6	3.9
	2.4	2.0				Sales/Total Assets	2.9	2.8
	1.5	1.4					2.3	2.1
	.4	2.9					.9	1.1
	(11) 1.5	(30) 3.6				% Depr., Dep., Amort./Sales	(76) 1.6	(91) 2.0
	6.2	4.7					2.7	3.5
		2.0				% Officers', Directors'	1.6	1.5
	(15)	2.7				Owners' Comp/Sales	(29) 2.9	(33) 2.8
		4.3					5.1	5.9
7712M	36202M	331787M	209954M			Net Sales ($)	1669779M	1802993M
2832M	16240M	163257M	126132M			Total Assets ($)	692949M	640692M

M = $ thousand   MM = $ million
See Pages 9 through 22 for Explanation of Ratios and Data

Comparative Historical Data | | | Current Data Sorted by Sales

4/1/07-3/31/08 ALL	4/1/08-3/31/09 ALL	4/1/09-3/31/10 ALL	Type of Statement	0-1MM	1-3MM	3-5MM	5-10MM	10-25MM	25MM & OVER
9	5	4	Unqualified		1			1	2
22	15	16	Reviewed		1	4	6	5	
23	20	6	Compiled			1	3	2	
13	12	7	Tax Returns	1	5	1			
24	19	27	Other	3	5	5	3	10	1
				__0-1MM__	6 (4/1-9/30/09)		54 (10/1/09-3/31/10)		25MM & OVER
91	**71**	**60**	**NUMBER OF STATEMENTS**	**4**	**12**	**11**	**12**	**18**	**3**
%	%	%	**ASSETS**	%	%	%	%	%	%
8.7	10.4	9.7	Cash & Equivalents		5.4	14.7	16.4	6.5	
22.0	20.3	19.8	Trade Receivables (net)		19.9	14.9	16.2	25.4	
23.2	21.0	22.4	Inventory		26.6	23.4	17.7	22.1	
4.5	5.0	3.5	All Other Current		1.2	5.7	1.7	5.9	
58.4	56.7	55.4	Total Current		53.3	58.7	52.2	59.9	
31.2	31.9	35.2	Fixed Assets (net)		33.6	37.7	39.2	30.2	
4.8	4.0	3.2	Intangibles (net)		8.6	.1	3.0	.1	
5.6	7.4	6.2	All Other Non-Current		4.5	3.4	5.7	9.7	
100.0	100.0	100.0	Total		100.0	100.0	100.0	100.0	
			LIABILITIES						
11.0	11.1	12.7	Notes Payable-Short Term		20.9	9.0	6.4	11.4	
4.8	6.3	5.1	Cur. Mat.-L.T.D.		3.2	4.1	7.9	2.5	
7.8	7.9	8.3	Trade Payables		12.5	6.1	4.3	9.0	
.1	.0	.1	Income Taxes Payable		.0	.0	.0	.1	
9.5	9.3	8.4	All Other Current		6.1	3.2	7.7	6.8	
33.2	34.6	34.6	Total Current		42.7	22.4	26.3	29.8	
20.1	17.3	20.0	Long-Term Debt		17.4	27.4	14.7	13.8	
.2	.3	.4	Deferred Taxes		.2	.3	.7	.5	
7.4	11.5	14.3	All Other Non-Current		28.1	16.3	4.5	15.8	
39.1	36.4	30.7	Net Worth		11.6	33.6	53.8	40.1	
100.0	100.0	100.0	Total Liabilities & Net Worth		100.0	100.0	100.0	100.0	
			INCOME DATA						
100.0	100.0	100.0	Net Sales		100.0	100.0	100.0	100.0	
27.9	26.1	30.5	Gross Profit		31.2	36.2	28.7	24.7	
28.9	31.6	35.0	Operating Expenses		37.3	39.4	28.1	33.1	
-1.0	-5.5	-4.5	Operating Profit		-6.1	-3.2	.6	-8.3	
1.1	.9	1.4	All Other Expenses (net)		.4	.8	1.0	1.1	
-2.1	-6.4	-5.9	Profit Before Taxes		-6.5	-4.0	-.4	-9.4	
			RATIOS						
5.0	5.0	5.1			2.1	11.2	6.6	4.2	
2.1	2.2	1.7	Current		1.2	5.0	2.7	1.8	
1.2	1.1	1.1			.7	1.2	1.3	1.4	
2.5	2.5	2.9			.8	6.9	4.4	2.0	
1.0	1.1	.9	Quick		.5	3.1	1.5	1.0	
.6	.6	.5			.4	.5	.7	.7	
18 20.5	17 21.5	23 15.6			16 23.0	12 31.7	21 17.3	31 11.9	
28 12.9	28 13.1	32 11.6	Sales/Receivables		24 15.4	29 12.8	30 12.1	39 9.3	
40 9.1	40 9.0	44 8.2			47 7.7	35 10.4	43 8.6	52 7.0	
31 11.9	28 12.9	34 10.7			30 12.2	35 10.4	34 10.9	44 8.2	
39 9.3	41 8.8	53 6.9	Cost of Sales/Inventory		56 6.5	53 6.9	54 6.7	50 7.4	
62 5.9	60 6.1	77 4.8			81 4.5	100 3.6	63 5.8	66 5.5	
5 73.3	5 80.5	8 47.6			4 82.0	5 68.7	6 63.2	9 40.1	
9 39.1	10 37.9	14 26.3	Cost of Sales/Payables		11 33.3	11 32.3	12 30.3	17 21.2	
16 22.2	18 20.3	24 15.4			50 7.4	25 14.7	20 18.5	25 14.5	
5.1	4.5	4.7			6.6	3.1	3.2	4.9	
9.6	8.0	9.0	Sales/Working Capital		59.4	3.8	5.4	8.8	
35.6	123.1	93.8			-20.0	22.0	29.1	13.0	
5.2	2.7	3.3			1.2	5.3	7.8	.2	
(85) 1.1	(66) -1.4	(55) -1.2	EBIT/Interest	(11) -4.8		1.0	1.4	(15) -4.1	
-3.6	-6.7	-9.6			-17.8	-10.6	-1.3	-11.7	
3.9			Net Profit + Depr., Dep.,						
(14) 1.4			Amort./Cur. Mat. L/T/D						
-.9									
.4	.4	.5			1.1	.4	.4	.4	
.8	.8	1.1	Fixed/Worth		5.9	.9	.7	.7	
1.5	1.5	4.5			-.6	2.1	1.7	1.8	
.4	.4	.6			1.3	.3	.4	.5	
1.5	1.2	1.5	Debt/Worth		12.2	.9	.9	1.2	
3.2	3.7	12.2			-2.8	3.7	1.6	4.0	
25.4	5.4	4.7	% Profit Before Taxes/Tangible		18.5	11.0		-3.4	
(76) 4.7	(62) -13.5	(48) -6.5	Net Worth		(10) .2	2.4		(15) -24.6	
-21.4	-39.7	-41.2			-22.6	-27.3		-99.4	
9.7	1.4	2.2	% Profit Before Taxes/Total		22.3	3.6	8.2	-2.1	
-.2	-7.8	-7.9	Assets		-15.2	.0	1.2	-16.1	
-15.7	-25.5	-28.4			-65.3	-22.0	-7.3	-32.9	
15.2	14.7	12.3			24.2	11.9	10.0	12.5	
9.1	8.2	6.2	Sales/Net Fixed Assets		10.1	5.6	4.3	8.5	
5.6	5.0	3.9			4.5	2.2	2.6	5.2	
3.4	3.1	2.9			3.7	2.9	2.7	2.7	
2.6	2.2	2.1	Sales/Total Assets		2.3	2.0	1.6	2.1	
2.0	1.8	1.4			1.4	1.2	1.3	1.6	
1.5	2.0	1.6			.8	2.3	2.9	2.5	
(84) 2.6	(65) 2.8	(54) 3.7	% Depr., Dep., Amort./Sales	(11) 4.5		(10) 4.2	4.0	(16) 3.5	
4.1	4.4	5.7			6.4	5.9	7.2	4.1	
1.6	1.1	2.0	% Officers', Directors'						
(33) 2.7	(27) 3.4	(22) 3.3	Owners' Comp/Sales						
4.9	6.7	6.4							
1277536M	1034004M	585655M	Net Sales ($)	2813M	19929M	43755M	90624M	284199M	144335M
574349M	519959M	308461M	Total Assets ($)	1440M	10002M	25371M	54292M	142785M	74571M

M = $ thousand   MM = $ million
See Pages 9 through 22 for Explanation of Ratios and Data

Current Data Sorted by Assets   ## Comparative Historical Data

0-500M	500M-2MM	2-10MM	10-50MM	50-100MM	100-250MM	Type of Statement		
	1	2	6	2	1	Unqualified	21	23
1	8	17	8	1		Reviewed	42	44
3	11	8	2	1		Compiled	29	40
14	26	5	1			Tax Returns	25	28
8	14	15	13	1	6	Other	75	79
	25 (4/1-9/30/09)		150 (10/1/09-3/31/10)				4/1/05-3/31/06 ALL	4/1/06-3/31/07 ALL
0-500M	500M-2MM	2-10MM	10-50MM	50-100MM	100-250MM			
26	60	47	30	5	7	NUMBER OF STATEMENTS	192	214
%	%	%	%	%	%	ASSETS	%	%
7.2	9.4	6.9	9.0			Cash & Equivalents	7.0	6.2
29.2	30.7	25.1	14.3			Trade Receivables (net)	31.6	28.1
20.1	25.1	24.9	25.4			Inventory	24.8	26.3
2.0	3.3	3.0	1.6			All Other Current	2.3	2.7
58.5	68.5	60.0	50.3			Total Current	65.8	63.3
30.6	23.6	31.5	37.0			Fixed Assets (net)	27.1	28.5
2.5	2.1	1.6	7.5			Intangibles (net)	2.5	3.5
8.3	5.8	6.9	5.2			All Other Non-Current	4.6	4.7
100.0	100.0	100.0	100.0			Total	100.0	100.0
						LIABILITIES		
20.8	15.6	14.7	12.2			Notes Payable-Short Term	12.1	13.3
6.5	4.9	4.2	5.8			Cur. Mat.-L.T.D.	4.6	3.7
28.5	16.7	8.7	7.2			Trade Payables	14.0	13.0
.0	.2	.2	.3			Income Taxes Payable	.2	.3
16.7	13.2	7.7	6.4			All Other Current	10.0	10.3
72.5	50.7	35.6	31.9			Total Current	40.9	40.5
40.2	19.1	18.5	19.1			Long-Term Debt	18.6	18.2
.0	.3	.4	.7			Deferred Taxes	.4	.5
3.2	15.5	4.8	9.5			All Other Non-Current	8.8	9.9
-16.0	14.4	40.8	38.8			Net Worth	31.2	30.9
100.0	100.0	100.0	100.0			Total Liabilities & Net Worth	100.0	100.0
						INCOME DATA		
100.0	100.0	100.0	100.0			Net Sales	100.0	100.0
30.5	29.4	23.7	22.4			Gross Profit	29.4	27.6
34.5	31.7	23.7	22.4			Operating Expenses	24.8	23.2
-4.0	-2.4	.1	.0			Operating Profit	4.6	4.4
1.5	.5	1.2	1.0			All Other Expenses (net)	.9	1.4
-5.5	-2.9	-1.1	-1.0			Profit Before Taxes	3.7	2.9
						RATIOS		
2.0	3.1	3.0	2.8			Current	2.6	2.5
1.1	1.6	1.8	1.5				1.8	1.6
.6	.9	1.1	1.1				1.3	1.1
1.1	1.7	1.6	1.2			Quick	1.6	1.4
(25) .7	.8	.9	.7				1.0	.9
.4	.4	.4	.3				.6	.5
7 52.9	21 17.3	29 12.5	19 18.9			Sales/Receivables	23 15.7	22 16.9
23 15.9	42 8.7	42 8.7	27 13.6				36 10.2	35 10.3
48 7.5	54 6.8	58 6.3	41 8.8				55 6.7	52 7.0
7 48.7	19 19.4	28 12.8	37 10.0			Cost of Sales/Inventory	23 16.2	22 16.7
17 21.9	44 8.2	54 6.7	68 5.4				40 9.2	46 8.0
49 7.5	80 4.6	86 4.3	111 3.3				67 5.5	73 5.0
13 28.8	10 36.0	9 39.5	11 33.2			Cost of Sales/Payables	9 38.7	9 38.9
24 15.5	26 14.0	15 24.8	15 24.5				18 20.0	18 20.7
46 7.9	49 7.5	28 13.1	27 13.5				32 11.3	32 11.5
7.2	5.0	5.0	5.9			Sales/Working Capital	6.4	6.4
NM	11.1	8.1	12.4				11.8	11.6
-14.8	-43.6	64.7	281.0				26.1	58.5
4.4	4.3	4.9	3.7			EBIT/Interest	10.1	8.0
(24) -.7	(55) -.7	(45) 1.1	(29) 1.5				(176) 3.8	(197) 3.1
-8.4	-5.4	-2.2	-.9				1.3	1.1
		6.7				Net Profit + Depr., Dep., Amort./Cur. Mat. L/T/D	6.2	7.5
	(10) 1.4						(36) 2.1	(43) 3.1
		.3					1.3	1.4
.3	.3	.4	.5			Fixed/Worth	.3	.3
3.7	2.3	.7	1.1				.8	.9
-.8	-1.7	2.7	2.7				2.1	3.5
1.1	1.0	.6	.7			Debt/Worth	.9	.9
14.6	6.5	1.4	1.6				2.0	2.0
-3.1	-6.6	3.8	3.9				6.9	7.7
16.6	29.9	21.4	19.1			% Profit Before Taxes/Tangible Net Worth	51.9	52.2
(14) -23.9	(39) 1.6	(41) 1.5	(26) 4.4				(160) 20.6	(179) 19.8
-49.5	-13.0	-20.6	-7.9				7.5	5.4
7.9	6.2	8.5	5.1			% Profit Before Taxes/Total Assets	16.8	15.9
-10.3	-.6	.3	1.9				7.3	6.9
-27.3	-13.0	-7.6	-4.9				1.5	.7
46.5	23.0	16.0	9.9			Sales/Net Fixed Assets	27.6	26.2
15.2	12.0	8.2	3.9				14.0	10.9
6.7	6.4	4.2	2.9				6.7	5.4
6.3	3.4	2.6	2.4			Sales/Total Assets	3.9	3.7
4.1	2.6	2.1	1.6				2.9	2.7
2.6	1.9	1.7	1.1				2.1	2.0
.9	.8	1.3				% Depr., Dep., Amort./Sales	.9	1.0
(20) 2.1	(48) 2.0	(44) 2.3	(28) 3.1				(165) 1.6	(194) 1.7
4.5	2.9	3.9	5.8				2.4	3.0
3.5	3.6	1.2				% Officers', Directors' Owners' Comp/Sales	2.0	1.2
(13) 4.6	(32) 5.0	(16) 2.2					(70) 4.2	(79) 2.8
11.6	8.2	5.1					7.1	6.3
31044M	181813M	447416M	1004453M	515266M	1432354M	Net Sales ($)	5617722M	6498583M
7074M	70523M	205034M	561245M	289554M	949258M	Total Assets ($)	2260399M	2760365M

M = $ thousand   MM = $ million
See Pages 9 through 22 for Explanation of Ratios and Data

Comparative Historical Data | Current Data Sorted by Sales

			Type of Statement						
			Unqualified		1	1	1	1	8
19	17	12	Reviewed	1	6	6	5	15	2
54	46	35	Compiled	3	9	3	4	4	2
29	34	25	Tax Returns	4	29	5	7	1	2
23	27	46	Other	8	7	9	7	9	17
70	59	57				25 (4/1-9/30/09)		150 (10/1/09-3/31/10)	
4/1/07-3/31/08	4/1/08-3/31/09	4/1/09-3/31/10		0-1MM	1-3MM	3-5MM	5-10MM	10-25MM	25MM & OVER
ALL	ALL	ALL							
195	183	175	**NUMBER OF STATEMENTS**	16	52	24	24	30	29
%	%	%	**ASSETS**	%	%	%	%	%	%
8.3	8.5	8.2	Cash & Equivalents	5.6	7.8	8.5	9.7	9.0	7.8
25.9	24.6	24.9	Trade Receivables (net)	28.2	26.7	28.6	33.3	20.7	14.4
26.1	24.7	24.5	Inventory	19.2	21.1	32.0	20.7	27.5	27.2
2.8	3.0	2.9	All Other Current	3.6	2.5	3.8	2.2	2.6	3.3
63.0	60.8	60.4	Total Current	56.5	58.0	72.9	65.9	59.8	52.7
28.2	29.7	30.1	Fixed Assets (net)	33.1	31.6	22.2	27.4	29.5	35.4
2.8	3.8	3.0	Intangibles (net)	1.1	3.4	.3	1.2	4.6	5.2
5.9	5.7	6.5	All Other Non-Current	9.3	7.0	4.6	5.5	6.0	6.7
100.0	100.0	100.0	Total	100.0	100.0	100.0	100.0	100.0	100.0
			LIABILITIES						
12.1	15.3	14.9	Notes Payable-Short Term	20.3	15.8	22.5	11.9	12.4	9.1
3.5	3.7	5.0	Cur. Mat.-L.T.D.	1.0	7.1	4.1	4.4	3.6	6.0
12.7	12.6	14.0	Trade Payables	23.7	18.4	16.1	12.5	6.7	7.6
.2	.1	.2	Income Taxes Payable	.0	.3	.1	.1	.2	.3
11.8	9.7	11.3	All Other Current	6.6	13.3	15.4	11.6	6.8	11.2
40.2	41.3	45.3	Total Current	51.6	54.8	58.1	40.4	29.7	34.3
16.1	19.5	21.8	Long-Term Debt	46.4	25.3	18.1	15.8	14.8	17.6
.3	.3	.4	Deferred Taxes	.0	.2	.3	.4	.4	1.1
8.8	9.5	9.0	All Other Non-Current	17.0	10.0	7.6	8.6	4.5	9.0
34.6	29.4	23.5	Net Worth	-14.9	9.7	16.0	34.8	50.6	38.0
100.0	100.0	100.0	Total Liabilities & Net Worth	100.0	100.0	100.0	100.0	100.0	100.0
			INCOME DATA						
100.0	100.0	100.0	Net Sales	100.0	100.0	100.0	100.0	100.0	100.0
27.9	27.1	26.0	Gross Profit	31.7	32.1	17.9	27.3	20.8	23.2
24.4	26.5	27.7	Operating Expenses	37.8	34.9	22.9	24.9	19.0	24.3
3.5	.6	-1.6	Operating Profit	-6.2	-2.8	-5.0	2.5	1.7	-1.1
1.2	1.2	1.0	All Other Expenses (net)	1.4	1.4	1.0	.2	.3	1.5
2.3	-.6	-2.7	Profit Before Taxes	-7.6	-4.3	-6.0	2.3	1.5	-2.6
			RATIOS						
3.1	3.0	2.6		5.9	2.4	2.6	2.6	4.4	2.5
1.6	1.6	1.5	Current	1.8	1.1	1.3	1.6	1.9	1.5
1.1	1.0	1.0		.7	.7	.8	1.1	1.2	1.3
1.6	1.7	1.5		2.2	1.5	1.2	2.0	1.7	1.0
.8	.9 (174)	.8	Quick	(15) 1.1	.7	.6	.9	.9	.7
.5	.4	.4		.6	.3	.3	.7	.4	.3
21 17.2	19 18.9	21 17.4		8 46.6	11 33.2	32 11.5	32 11.3	21 17.7	23 15.9
32 11.5	33 11.1	33 10.9	Sales/Receivables	29 12.7	35 10.5	41 8.8	46 7.9	29 12.5	27 13.8
45 8.1	49 7.5	51 7.1		60 6.8	54 6.8	55 6.7	57 6.4	46 8.0	33 11.0
27 13.6	19 18.7	20 18.2		13 28.2	12 30.2	21 17.3	18 20.3	41 8.9	42 8.8
50 7.3	47 7.7	51 7.2	Cost of Sales/Inventory	28 13.1	40 9.1	46 8.0	43 8.6	55 6.6	68 5.4
73 5.0	81 4.5	84 4.3		72 5.0	73 5.0	121 3.0	61 6.0	90 4.1	94 3.9
10 37.4	8 47.2	10 36.0		9 40.6	14 25.2	7 55.2	10 38.2	10 38.1	12 29.7
18 20.8	17 21.8	18 19.9	Cost of Sales/Payables	23 15.9	25 14.7	22 16.6	20 18.3	13 28.2	17 21.9
33 11.2	34 10.8	37 9.9		50 7.3	47 7.7	50 7.3	36 10.1	16 22.5	24 15.4
5.9	5.7	5.6		5.0	5.6	4.1	6.2	4.7	6.0
10.9	12.8	11.7	Sales/Working Capital	7.0	42.2	15.9	11.7	7.9	10.7
97.9	108.3	-136.6		-20.1	-13.2	-23.0	32.7	22.2	21.8
7.7	6.8	3.9		.0	5.9	2.2	10.8	4.0	3.1
(180) 2.6	(173) 1.7	(163) .6	EBIT/Interest	(13) -3.0	(50) .5	(22) -1.8	(23) 2.0	(28) 1.5	(27) -.2
.6	-1.4	-4.4		-6.1	-6.9	-8.1	-.7	-1.2	-5.0
3.6	3.6	3.7	Net Profit + Depr., Dep.,						
(40) 2.2	(33) 2.2	(23) 2.1	Amort./Cur. Mat. L/T/D						
.6	-1.6	.3							
.3	.4	.3		.3	.4	.2	.4	.3	.5
.8	1.0	1.0	Fixed/Worth	NM	2.7	.9	1.0	.7	1.0
2.6	4.5	-27.7		-.5	-1.7	-1.2	2.7	1.2	2.7
.6	.8	.8		.7	1.4	.4	.8	.5	.6
2.0	2.1	2.1	Debt/Worth	NM	6.5	3.1	2.0	1.0	1.3
6.2	9.8	-59.8		-2.6	-7.4	-7.3	5.6	2.4	3.5
44.7	39.7	18.7	% Profit Before Taxes/Tangible		26.0	20.6	59.6	16.7	19.1
(164) 15.7	(149) 8.6	(131) .8	Net Worth	(32) .3	(16) -2.4	(23) 6.2	(28) 3.6	(24) -6.5	
3.5	-10.3	-21.0			-37.4	-23.2	-13.0	-9.0	-25.5
13.1	11.4	5.0	% Profit Before Taxes/Total	-4.9	7.9	2.1	17.0	8.9	5.2
5.3	2.2	-1.0	Assets	-14.7	-1.0	-5.1	1.5	1.6	-6.2
-1.3	-9.0	-11.1		-26.6	-18.0	-26.3	-4.0	-3.6	-10.3
24.0	19.6	18.1		12.4	21.5	27.9	53.4	16.1	10.5
10.6	10.2	9.4	Sales/Net Fixed Assets	6.4	10.9	13.3	9.4	7.7	5.1
5.5	5.1	4.4		4.7	6.0	6.3	4.6	3.8	3.0
3.6	3.5	3.2		3.2	4.2	3.4	3.3	2.6	2.5
2.6	2.5	2.2	Sales/Total Assets	2.4	2.6	2.2	2.5	2.0	1.6
1.8	1.6	1.6		1.8	1.7	1.7	2.1	1.5	1.2
1.0	1.1	1.2		2.4	.9	1.3	.8	1.3	2.0
(170) 1.8	(158) 1.9	(143) 2.3	% Depr., Dep., Amort./Sales	(12) 4.2	(43) 2.2	(19) 2.2	(22) 1.7	(29) 2.0	(18) 3.0
2.9	3.0	3.7		8.0	3.3	4.3	3.3	4.0	5.5
2.2	1.9	2.1			3.6		1.4		
(75) 4.8	(70) 4.9	(63) 4.2	% Officers', Directors' Owners' Comp/Sales		(29) 5.0		(14)		
7.0	8.0	8.3			8.5		5.6		
6246532M	4702492M	3612346M	Net Sales ($)	10075M	108607M	91286M	162702M	501479M	2738197M
2922596M	2414806M	2082688M	Total Assets ($)	4994M	51929M	52605M	70478M	264114M	1638568M

M = $ thousand   MM = $ million
See Pages 9 through 22 for Explanation of Ratios and Data

Current Data Sorted by Assets / Comparative Historical Data

0-500M	500M-2MM	2-10MM	10-50MM	50-100MM	100-250MM	Type of Statement	4/1/05-3/31/06 ALL	4/1/06-3/31/07 ALL
	1		8			Unqualified	15	14
	1	5	6			Reviewed	14	11
2	4	6	1			Compiled	6	21
2		2				Tax Returns	17	10
1	3	6	10	3		Other	23	19
13 (4/1-9/30/09)			48 (10/1/09-3/31/10)					
5	9	19	25	3		NUMBER OF STATEMENTS	75	75
%	%	%	%	%	%	**ASSETS**	%	%
		3.9	5.8		DATA NOT AVAILABLE	Cash & Equivalents	5.8	5.6
		12.5	11.2			Trade Receivables (net)	16.6	19.9
		39.9	35.7			Inventory	31.3	34.2
		1.3	2.3			All Other Current	2.5	1.3
		57.6	55.0			Total Current	56.3	61.0
		30.8	32.5			Fixed Assets (net)	33.0	31.7
		1.4	2.6			Intangibles (net)	2.3	1.7
		10.2	9.8			All Other Non-Current	8.4	5.7
		100.0	100.0			Total	100.0	100.0
						LIABILITIES		
		17.2	19.4			Notes Payable-Short Term	17.7	20.7
		5.9	5.3			Cur. Mat.-L.T.D.	4.9	3.6
		8.6	7.7			Trade Payables	10.2	10.6
		.2	.0			Income Taxes Payable	.1	.0
		7.0	6.8			All Other Current	9.4	7.7
		38.9	39.2			Total Current	42.2	42.7
		12.6	17.5			Long-Term Debt	22.0	16.7
		.2	1.3			Deferred Taxes	.4	.1
		6.6	2.5			All Other Non-Current	6.2	2.5
		41.7	39.6			Net Worth	29.2	38.0
		100.0	100.0			Total Liabilties & Net Worth	100.0	100.0
						INCOME DATA		
		100.0	100.0			Net Sales	100.0	100.0
		13.8	15.5			Gross Profit	23.0	20.6
		17.0	17.8			Operating Expenses	18.7	16.6
		-3.2	-2.3			Operating Profit	4.3	4.0
		.9	.7			All Other Expenses (net)	1.9	1.6
		-4.1	-3.1			Profit Before Taxes	2.4	2.4
						RATIOS		
		2.9	1.8				2.1	2.5
		1.7	1.4			Current	1.3	1.5
		1.2	1.1				1.0	1.1
		.8	.6				1.0	1.2
		.4	.4			Quick	.5	.5
		.2	.3				.3	.3
		14 25.3	**13** 27.9				**13** 27.6	**12** 30.2
		22 16.9	**27** 13.7			Sales/Receivables	**21** 17.7	**21** 17.1
		30 12.4	**37** 9.8				**32** 11.3	**34** 10.6
		52 7.0	**55** 6.6				**36** 10.1	**31** 11.7
		81 4.5	**87** 4.2			Cost of Sales/Inventory	**53** 6.9	**55** 6.7
		132 2.8	**149** 2.4				**96** 3.8	**90** 4.0
		6 64.3	**9** 39.0				**7** 55.7	**5** 68.7
		13 28.6	**16** 23.1			Cost of Sales/Payables	**12** 30.5	**12** 31.7
		21 17.7	**45** 8.1				**28** 13.2	**26** 14.0
		3.7	5.3				7.5	6.0
		7.1	9.1			Sales/Working Capital	18.9	17.1
		24.5	33.8				-72.8	67.3
		2.6	3.2				6.0	6.6
		(18) .5	-.4			EBIT/Interest	(72) 2.5	(71) 2.8
		-6.8	-2.7				.6	1.2
			1.8				4.2	
			(11) 1.2			Net Profit + Depr., Dep., Amort./Cur. Mat. L/T/D	(18) 2.4	
			-.1				1.7	
		.2	.5				.5	.3
		.6	.8			Fixed/Worth	1.0	.8
		1.5	1.7				2.2	1.7
		.8	.8				1.1	.9
		1.5	1.4			Debt/Worth	2.1	2.1
		4.0	5.1				7.5	3.7
		8.4	12.0				40.0	36.9
		(17) -11.3	(23) -4.5			% Profit Before Taxes/Tangible Net Worth	(65) 26.2	(72) 16.6
		-31.5	-14.2				5.1	3.2
		3.1	4.2				13.8	13.3
		-.7	-2.7			% Profit Before Taxes/Total Assets	3.2	5.4
		-13.4	-6.3				.0	1.0
		20.5	11.2				14.4	24.5
		4.5	5.7			Sales/Net Fixed Assets	7.5	8.0
		3.2	2.9				4.5	4.3
		2.4	2.3				3.3	3.8
		1.5	1.8			Sales/Total Assets	2.3	2.3
		1.0	1.0				1.6	1.6
		1.5	1.9				1.6	.9
		(17) 3.8	(24) 3.8			% Depr., Dep., Amort./Sales	(64) 2.6	(63) 1.8
		5.1	4.7				4.2	4.1
							.8	1.2
						% Officers', Directors' Owners' Comp/Sales	(21) 1.6	(29) 2.5
							4.2	4.3
6668M	29715M	170502M	800358M	302904M		Net Sales ($)	2038987M	3955106M
1716M	10921M	96604M	539319M	272209M		Total Assets ($)	1099218M	1188995M

M = $ thousand MM = $ million

See Pages 9 through 22 for Explanation of Ratios and Data

Comparative Historical Data

Current Data Sorted by Sales

4/1/07-3/31/08 ALL	4/1/08-3/31/09 ALL	4/1/09-3/31/10 ALL	Type of Statement	0-1MM	1-3MM	3-5MM	5-10MM	10-25MM	25MM & OVER
16	6	9	Unqualified	1				2	6
14	7	12	Reviewed				6	3	3
18	18	13	Compiled	2	3	3	2	2	1
7	5	4	Tax Returns	1	1	1		1	
24	17	23	Other	1	2	1	3	6	10
					13 (4/1-9/30/09)			48 (10/1/09-3/31/10)	
79	53	61	**NUMBER OF STATEMENTS**	5	6	5	11	14	20
%	%	%	**ASSETS**	%	%	%	%	%	%
5.9	9.1	6.6	Cash & Equivalents				5.7	5.8	3.4
13.6	14.5	12.1	Trade Receivables (net)				10.5	14.1	11.0
35.0	35.2	34.6	Inventory				41.7	39.4	36.2
2.1	1.7	2.2	All Other Current				2.9	1.8	2.2
56.6	60.5	55.6	Total Current				60.8	61.1	52.8
34.8	30.6	34.7	Fixed Assets (net)				23.8	30.5	35.7
2.1	1.1	1.7	Intangibles (net)				2.0	1.9	2.6
6.5	7.8	8.1	All Other Non-Current				13.3	6.5	8.9
100.0	100.0	100.0	Total				100.0	100.0	100.0
			LIABILITIES						
17.3	18.8	16.9	Notes Payable-Short Term				22.6	19.8	15.2
4.0	4.7	6.3	Cur. Mat.-L.T.D.				7.2	4.1	5.5
8.6	8.8	8.3	Trade Payables				3.6	13.3	7.8
.1	.1	.1	Income Taxes Payable				.3	.0	.0
6.8	6.7	6.8	All Other Current				9.1	4.5	7.7
36.7	39.1	38.4	Total Current				42.9	41.7	36.3
21.0	24.4	19.2	Long-Term Debt				9.3	14.2	16.4
.2	.1	.6	Deferred Taxes				.4	1.6	.6
3.2	7.7	-5.0	All Other Non-Current				2.3	4.4	5.4
38.8	28.7	36.8	Net Worth				45.2	38.0	41.4
100.0	100.0	100.0	Total Liabilities & Net Worth				100.0	100.0	100.0
			INCOME DATA						
100.0	100.0	100.0	Net Sales				100.0	100.0	100.0
20.7	21.2	17.2	Gross Profit				7.5	17.0	13.8
17.9	19.0	18.8	Operating Expenses				12.9	19.3	14.4
2.8	2.2	-1.6	Operating Profit				-5.4	-2.3	-.6
1.9	2.5	1.0	All Other Expenses (net)				-.2	-.1	1.7
.9	-.3	-2.6	Profit Before Taxes				-5.2	-2.2	-2.3
			RATIOS						
2.3	2.7	2.1	Current				2.0	1.8	2.0
1.4	1.5	1.7					1.8	1.6	1.4
1.0	1.1	1.1					1.2	1.1	1.1
.8	1.1	.8	Quick				.8	.8	.6
(78) .4	.5	.4					.3	.4	.4
.2	.2	.3					.2	.3	.2
10 35.7	10 37.6	12 30.4	Sales/Receivables	19 19.7	15 24.0	11 32.5			
17 21.8	20 18.5	23 15.9		22 16.9	27 13.5	26 13.9			
28 13.0	34 10.6	30 12.2		25 14.4	34 10.7	30 12.3			
33 11.1	32 11.5	43 8.6	Cost of Sales/Inventory	57 6.4	55 6.7	53 6.9			
60 6.1	63 5.8	79 4.6		99 3.7	113 3.2	76 4.8			
122 3.0	123 3.0	130 2.8		138 2.6	187 2.0	110 3.3			
7 54.0	4 82.9	7 49.4	Cost of Sales/Payables	3 118.2	13 27.8	8 45.0			
12 29.3	12 31.6	13 28.6		7 49.8	26 13.8	11 31.8			
26 14.1	26 14.0	30 12.0		13 27.4	47 7.8	34 10.6			
6.1	4.8	4.7	Sales/Working Capital				3.3	3.9	6.7
11.6	8.9	8.9					8.9	8.6	12.0
95.7	36.9	37.9					24.5	23.3	47.5
7.1	4.3	2.6	EBIT/Interest				2.5	5.8	2.7
(76) 2.7	(50) 1.5	(59) .0					.0	.4	-.4
.3	-1.4	-2.9					-14.2	-3.4	-1.9
2.4		4.5	Net Profit + Depr., Dep., Amort./Cur. Mat. L/T/D						
(16) 1.9		(18) 1.3							
1.1		.5							
.3	.3	.4	Fixed/Worth				.0	.4	.4
.8	.9	.8					.6	.7	1.0
2.0	4.7	2.6					1.4	2.1	1.9
.6	.9	.6	Debt/Worth				.8	.8	.6
1.7	2.2	1.5					1.4	1.4	1.6
5.2	24.7	5.8					2.4	7.1	4.8
28.8	13.6	12.3	% Profit Before Taxes/Tangible Net Worth				6.9	24.9	11.4
(71) 9.6	(41) 5.5	(52) -1.8		(10) -15.3	(12) 3.5	(19) -4.5			
-1.7	-6.3	-17.4					-65.5	-25.7	-14.2
9.0	6.3	4.0	% Profit Before Taxes/Total Assets				3.2	7.1	3.2
3.4	1.3	-1.1					-4.5	-.2	-2.5
-3.7	-5.5	-7.8					-20.3	-9.5	-5.2
22.1	32.5	16.5	Sales/Net Fixed Assets				34.6	26.0	9.0
6.9	7.2	5.0					5.8	7.1	5.0
3.0	3.1	3.1					3.4	2.8	3.3
3.0	2.9	2.7	Sales/Total Assets				2.4	3.5	2.4
2.2	1.9	1.7					1.5	1.8	1.8
1.4	1.3	1.0					.9	.9	1.3
.9	1.0	1.9	% Depr., Dep., Amort./Sales				.3	1.2	1.9
(72) 2.2	(43) 2.1	(55) 3.8					3.0	(12) 3.9	(19) 3.8
3.8	4.4	5.0					5.3	6.6	4.3
.7	1.3	1.5	% Officers', Directors' Owners' Comp/Sales						
(25) 2.3	(28) 4.5	(19) 4.2							
5.8	7.0	8.5							
4158455M	1084026M	1310147M	Net Sales ($)	3169M	10846M	19071M	81354M	223345M	972362M
1528780M	554769M	920769M	Total Assets ($)	5727M	3475M	12518M	89503M	173722M	635824M

© RMA 2010   M = $ thousand   MM = $ million
See Pages 9 through 22 for Explanation of Ratios and Data

Current Data Sorted by Assets   **Comparative Historical Data**

Type of Statement	0-500M	500M-2MM	2-10MM	10-50MM	50-100MM	100-250MM		4/1/05-3/31/06 ALL	4/1/06-3/31/07 ALL
Unqualified			2	5				13	15
Reviewed	1	2	14	4				17	26
Compiled	3	4	9	3				17	22
Tax Returns	8	13	3	8				16	16
Other	5	11	8	4	4			22	28
	17 (4/1-9/30/09)			86 (10/1/09-3/31/10)					
NUMBER OF STATEMENTS	17	30	36	16	4			85	107
	%	%	%	%	%	%		%	%
ASSETS									
Cash & Equivalents	11.0	8.0	5.0	10.1				6.0	6.6
Trade Receivables (net)	24.0	27.0	24.7	14.7				28.5	25.3
Inventory	18.3	22.2	29.6	34.7				25.6	26.1
All Other Current	6.1	2.2	2.9	3.2				1.8	2.8
Total Current	59.3	59.4	62.3	62.8				61.9	60.9
Fixed Assets (net)	30.4	27.7	26.7	23.8				29.4	30.3
Intangibles (net)	2.3	6.3	2.4	4.5				3.1	3.0
All Other Non-Current	8.0	6.6	8.6	8.9				5.7	5.9
Total	100.0	100.0	100.0	100.0				100.0	100.0
LIABILITIES									
Notes Payable-Short Term	25.1	10.8	17.5	12.6				11.8	12.9
Cur. Mat.-L.T.D.	10.9	8.2	3.8	2.5				7.2	5.2
Trade Payables	20.0	15.6	13.6	7.9				12.2	11.5
Income Taxes Payable	.0	.0	.3	.2				.4	.4
All Other Current	11.8	7.6	8.5	5.3				10.7	9.5
Total Current	67.9	42.1	43.7	28.5				42.4	39.5
Long-Term Debt	41.0	24.1	20.2	10.2				19.1	22.1
Deferred Taxes	.0	.2	.1	.7				.3	.3
All Other Non-Current	14.7	16.1	8.2	2.6				5.8	6.2
Net Worth	-23.5	17.4	27.9	58.0				32.4	31.9
Total Liabilities & Net Worth	100.0	100.0	100.0	100.0				100.0	100.0
INCOME DATA									
Net Sales	100.0	100.0	100.0	100.0				100.0	100.0
Gross Profit	38.0	35.2	21.0	21.3				29.0	27.5
Operating Expenses	40.1	34.9	22.8	20.3				25.5	22.3
Operating Profit	-2.0	.4	-1.8	1.1				3.5	5.2
All Other Expenses (net)	1.3	2.9	1.0	.1				1.1	1.3
Profit Before Taxes	-3.3	-2.6	-2.7	1.0				2.5	4.0

(Columns 50-100MM and 100-250MM for percentage data: DATA NOT AVAILABLE)

RATIOS

Ratio	0-500M	500M-2MM	2-10MM	10-50MM		4/1/05-3/31/06 ALL	4/1/06-3/31/07 ALL
Current	2.1 / 1.2 / .7	3.6 / 1.7 / .7	2.2 / 1.4 / 1.0	6.2 / 2.8 / 1.3		2.8 / 1.4 / 1.1	2.5 / 1.4 / 1.2
Quick	1.2 / .7 / .3	1.9 / .8 / .3	1.6 / .7 / .4	2.0 / 1.1 / .5		1.4 / .9 / .4	1.1 / .9 / .4
Sales/Receivables	9 42.9 / 22 16.5 / 54 6.7	20 18.2 / 36 10.2 / 57 6.5	27 13.4 / 36 10.0 / 48 7.6	23 15.6 / 32 11.4 / 49 7.4		22 16.7 / 35 10.5 / 55 6.6	17 21.1 / 29 12.7 / 52 7.0
Cost of Sales/Inventory	3 119.0 / 21 17.7 / 47 7.8	12 30.2 / 40 9.1 / 88 4.1	27 13.6 / 57 6.4 / 115 3.2	70 5.2 / 107 3.4 / 148 2.5		23 15.8 / 50 7.3 / 84 4.4	24 15.2 / 40 9.1 / 81 4.5
Cost of Sales/Payables	3 125.5 / 36 10.0 / 54 6.7	10 36.4 / 23 16.0 / 50 7.3	13 28.6 / 24 15.0 / 40 9.1	8 43.7 / 12 31.4 / 19 19.2		9 39.1 / 20 18.2 / 36 10.2	8 43.8 / 19 19.6 / 32 11.3
Sales/Working Capital	7.8 / 27.2 / -19.4	5.5 / 12.6 / -14.0	5.9 / 13.2 / 61.6	2.7 / 3.9 / 11.7		6.2 / 14.5 / 37.1	6.2 / 14.4 / 37.3
EBIT/Interest	3.3 / (16) .9 / -6.3	3.9 / (26) .5 / -3.4	4.7 / (31) 1.1 / -4.1	10.0 / (15) 1.3 / -3.3		10.1 / (78) 3.5 / .8	8.0 / (100) 2.6 / .9
Net Profit + Depr., Dep., Amort./Cur. Mat. L/T/D						5.8 / (16) 2.2 / 1.6	2.7 / (18) 1.6 / .4
Fixed/Worth	.6 / -2.6 / -.4	.4 / .7 / -18.9	.4 / 1.0 / 755.9	.3 / .5 / .8		.4 / .8 / 4.4	.4 / .9 / 2.8
Debt/Worth	1.9 / -7.4 / -2.0	.7 / 3.0 / -28.6	.9 / 2.6 / 768.7	.3 / .7 / 1.9		.9 / 1.7 / 23.2	.8 / 2.4 / 7.3
% Profit Before Taxes/Tangible Net Worth		25.7 / (21) 2.0 / -71.6	25.2 / (28) 2.9 / -22.6	14.3 / (15) 3.5 / -3.4		52.4 / (68) 33.6 / 11.3	43.3 / (90) 19.3 / 1.0
% Profit Before Taxes/Total Assets	17.7 / .5 / -30.6	9.1 / -1.7 / -15.6	5.9 / .3 / -9.7	9.0 / .5 / -4.8		20.1 / 9.2 / -.6	15.4 / 6.5 / -.3
Sales/Net Fixed Assets	23.6 / 15.6 / 7.5	20.5 / 11.9 / 6.3	17.4 / 8.0 / 5.5	14.6 / 5.6 / 4.4		19.5 / 12.0 / 5.6	18.9 / 10.3 / 4.3
Sales/Total Assets	5.4 / 4.2 / 2.0	3.5 / 2.5 / 1.8	2.9 / 2.0 / 1.5	2.1 / 1.4 / 1.2		3.4 / 2.5 / 2.1	3.3 / 2.4 / 1.8
% Depr., Dep., Amort./Sales	2.1 / (13) 2.9 / 4.5	1.5 / (25) 2.2 / 4.2	.9 / (34) 2.3 / 3.7	1.6 / (15) 2.7 / 3.1		1.2 / (79) 2.1 / 3.2	1.2 / (92) 1.8 / 3.0
% Officers', Directors' Owners' Comp/Sales	3.5 / (12) 6.9 / 9.2	2.4 / (23) 3.7 / 6.1	.8 / (12) 2.7 / 4.2			2.1 / (32) 3.1 / 5.8	1.6 / (45) 2.8 / 6.5

	0-500M	500M-2MM	2-10MM	10-50MM	50-100MM		4/1/05-3/31/06 ALL	4/1/06-3/31/07 ALL
Net Sales ($)	21183M	93974M	356534M	583009M	303715M		1539828M	2816654M
Total Assets ($)	5450M	36496M	159647M	354431M	280101M		699388M	1289901M

M = $ thousand   MM = $ million
See Pages 9 through 22 for Explanation of Ratios and Data

Comparative Historical Data

Current Data Sorted by Sales

Type of Statement	4/1/07-3/31/08 ALL	4/1/08-3/31/09 ALL	4/1/09-3/31/10 ALL	0-1MM	1-3MM	3-5MM	5-10MM	10-25MM	25MM & OVER
Unqualified	10	7	7				1	2	4
Reviewed	22	25	21	1	4	1	10	8	1
Compiled	20	18	19	1		6	5	1	2
Tax Returns	19	29	24	6	11	5	2		
Other	41	48	32	2	11	2	6	3	8
				17 (4/1-9/30/09)			86 (10/1/09-3/31/10)		
NUMBER OF STATEMENTS	112	127	103	10	26	14	24	14	15
ASSETS	%	%	%	%	%	%	%	%	%
Cash & Equivalents	5.7	6.7	7.5	5.8	12.6	4.8	5.0	4.4	9.3
Trade Receivables (net)	27.9	26.0	23.2	16.4	28.3	21.7	23.7	27.1	15.9
Inventory	22.7	25.9	26.2	23.4	19.2	21.6	28.6	39.1	28.4
All Other Current	2.9	2.5	3.3	1.4	2.7	6.8	2.4	3.4	4.0
Total Current	59.2	61.2	60.3	47.1	62.9	54.9	59.7	74.0	57.6
Fixed Assets (net)	31.3	28.7	27.9	35.3	26.2	36.6	27.6	17.3	27.8
Intangibles (net)	3.2	3.6	4.2	7.8	5.1	2.4	1.7	1.9	7.8
All Other Non-Current	6.3	6.5	7.7	9.8	5.8	6.1	10.9	6.8	6.8
Total	100.0	100.0	100.0	100.0	100.0	100.0	100.0	100.0	100.0
LIABILITIES									
Notes Payable-Short Term	13.2	17.5	15.5	9.3	15.2	21.3	18.2	17.5	8.8
Cur. Mat.-L.T.D.	6.1	5.6	5.9	19.1	7.0	5.3	3.8	2.7	2.4
Trade Payables	11.7	14.0	14.1	10.8	19.4	13.0	14.1	15.6	6.4
Income Taxes Payable	.2	.2	.1	.0	.0	.0	.4	.0	.2
All Other Current	11.9	8.7	8.2	10.4	8.8	8.8	7.8	6.9	7.0
Total Current	43.2	46.1	43.8	49.5	50.4	48.4	44.3	42.7	24.8
Long-Term Debt	23.6	18.4	24.1	45.6	34.4	18.4	14.1	18.4	18.5
Deferred Taxes	.3	.4	.2	.0	.1	.0	.3	.0	.7
All Other Non-Current	6.5	6.6	10.7	6.4	17.2	22.5	6.1	4.4	4.5
Net Worth	26.4	28.5	21.2	-1.5	-2.2	10.6	35.3	34.5	51.5
Total Liabilities & Net Worth	100.0	100.0	100.0	100.0	100.0	100.0	100.0	100.0	100.0
INCOME DATA									
Net Sales	100.0	100.0	100.0	100.0	100.0	100.0	100.0	100.0	100.0
Gross Profit	27.3	26.1	27.8	40.8	36.1	33.5	18.2	23.0	19.2
Operating Expenses	23.8	25.5	28.5	44.4	35.5	35.0	22.2	20.1	17.5
Operating Profit	3.5	.7	-.7	-3.6	.6	-1.5	-4.0	2.9	1.7
All Other Expenses (net)	2.0	1.1	1.6	2.4	3.1	.4	.6	1.2	1.3
Profit Before Taxes	1.6	-.5	-2.3	-6.0	-2.5	-2.0	-4.6	1.7	.4
RATIOS									
Current	2.2	2.3	3.0	2.6	2.6	2.7	2.8	2.7	4.6
	1.4	1.5	1.6	1.8	1.5	1.2	1.4	1.6	2.7
	1.1	1.0	1.0	.7	.7	.7	1.0	1.3	1.6
Quick	1.3	1.4	1.6	1.1	1.9	1.7	1.8	1.4	2.1
	(111) .8	.7	.8	.9	.8	.5	.6	.7	1.0
	.5	.4	.4	.3	.4	.2	.3	.4	.6
Sales/Receivables	23 16.0	18 20.3	21 17.2	14 25.7	18 20.5	16 23.5	27 13.7	26 14.1	23 15.7
	37 9.8	29 12.8	36 10.2	25 14.5	39 9.5	24 14.9	39 9.4	35 10.5	36 10.0
	56 6.5	49 7.5	53 6.9	52 7.0	61 5.9	49 7.4	57 6.4	41 8.8	53 6.8
Cost of Sales/Inventory	17 21.2	14 26.1	15 24.3	28 13.1	4 82.2	8 43.5	27 13.6	40 9.1	41 8.9
	46 7.9	45 8.1	50 7.2	47 7.8	23 15.9	47 7.8	51 7.1	80 4.6	87 4.2
	92 4.2	87 4.2	115 3.2	99 3.7	101 3.6	103 3.5	115 3.2	137 2.7	124 2.9
Cost of Sales/Payables	10 37.7	9 40.6	10 36.5	0 UND	15 24.3	9 39.8	8 46.1	9 40.1	9 41.4
	19 18.9	20 18.2	20 18.0	27 13.7	27 13.5	16 22.2	28 12.9	21 17.3	18 19.9
	35 10.5	31 11.9	42 8.8	56 6.5	62 5.9	22 16.5	42 8.7	30 12.0	21 17.5
Sales/Working Capital	7.3	7.0	4.5	6.1	4.7	6.7	6.3	4.8	3.1
	13.9	13.3	11.2	12.7	12.3	32.1	15.7	10.1	4.5
	224.8	-196.0	119.2	-21.4	-28.9	-12.4	205.9	20.2	12.3
EBIT/Interest	5.5	5.5	3.9	3.8	2.6	4.5	.2	10.7	9.3
	(105) 2.3	(116) 1.4	(92) 1.1	-1.8	(22) 1.1	(13) 2.4	(19) -3.3	(13) 8.0	1.3
	.2	-1.2	-3.9	-5.2	-1.7	-2.8	-8.1	1.9	-2.3
Net Profit + Depr., Dep., Amort./Cur. Mat. L/T/D	2.4	1.9	3.3						
	(16) 1.8	(20) .6	(19) 1.0						
	.9	-.1	-.3						
Fixed/Worth	.5	.4	.4	.8	.5	.4	.3	.3	.3
	1.1	.9	.9	15.1	1.7	13.1	.8	.5	.5
	3.6	2.6	-15.0	-.7	-.4	-14.9	5.3	4.3	3.5
Debt/Worth	1.1	1.0	.7	.9	1.7	.8	.5	.9	.4
	2.8	2.3	2.5	27.3	6.7	16.4	1.4	1.7	.9
	10.8	8.8	-30.0	-6.0	-2.2	-24.2	10.1	65.2	6.2
% Profit Before Taxes/Tangible Net Worth	55.1	35.0	24.4		25.7		2.5	81.7	12.8
	(93) 13.9	(108) 7.0	(74) 1.3		(15) 2.0		(19) -17.9	(12) 15.7	(13) 3.5
	.0	-20.2	-30.6		-57.9		-38.5	2.0	-10.8
% Profit Before Taxes/Total Assets	11.8	10.0	7.6	10.1	10.2	7.2	-.7	20.8	6.3
	4.0	1.4	.3	-6.0	.5	2.0	-7.5	8.0	.7
	-3.9	-7.4	-10.8	-26.0	-13.3	-4.7	-17.3	-.1	-8.5
Sales/Net Fixed Assets	16.1	21.4	19.0	14.3	19.7	17.7	13.5	46.5	15.7
	8.6	10.3	8.4	8.6	14.6	8.2	7.1	19.7	5.4
	4.0	6.0	5.3	2.7	5.6	2.8	5.6	6.9	2.7
Sales/Total Assets	3.2	3.5	3.4	4.2	3.9	3.6	3.0	3.5	2.2
	2.2	2.6	2.2	2.0	2.5	2.2	2.3	3.0	1.4
	1.7	1.9	1.4	1.3	1.6	1.4	1.5	1.8	1.1
% Depr., Dep., Amort./Sales	1.4	1.0	1.6		2.1	1.0	1.7	.4	1.5
	(86) 2.1	(111) 1.9	(90) 2.5		(21) 3.1	(12) 1.9	(21) 2.6	(13) .9	(14) 2.8
	3.3	3.5	4.0		4.6	3.6	4.4	2.0	4.7
% Officers', Directors' Owners' Comp/Sales	1.5	1.6	2.0		2.1	2.2			
	(41) 3.2	(54) 3.3	(51) 3.7		(20) 3.7	(10) 3.9			
	5.2	5.5	6.1		6.7	5.5			
Net Sales ($)	2561267M	2302769M	1358415M	6285M	53473M	56683M	168508M	253951M	819515M
Total Assets ($)	1512582M	1072040M	836125M	3108M	25998M	36062M	95178M	106212M	569567M

© RMA 2010

M = $ thousand   MM = $ million
See Pages 9 through 22 for Explanation of Ratios and Data

Current Data Sorted by Assets							Comparative Historical Data	

0-500M	500M-2MM	2-10MM	10-50MM	50-100MM	100-250MM	Type of Statement	4/1/05-3/31/06 ALL	4/1/06-3/31/07 ALL
	2	18	3	1	1	Unqualified	8	12
	5	14	7			Reviewed	38	53
1	12	6	1			Compiled	29	45
3	24	6	2			Tax Returns	18	29
1	15	19	7	1	1	Other	55	64
	23 (4/1-9/30/09)		121 (10/1/09-3/31/10)					
5	58	57	20	2	2	NUMBER OF STATEMENTS	148	203
%	%	%	%	%	%	ASSETS	%	%
	8.0	8.6	8.6			Cash & Equivalents	6.1	6.7
	30.3	25.3	19.0			Trade Receivables (net)	29.3	30.2
	24.0	23.8	18.6			Inventory	23.3	23.7
	1.5	2.8	2.0			All Other Current	1.8	2.7
	63.7	60.5	48.2			Total Current	60.5	63.3
	27.9	30.5	27.2			Fixed Assets (net)	33.0	29.6
	2.3	2.6	17.8			Intangibles (net)	1.4	2.7
	6.0	6.4	6.8			All Other Non-Current	5.2	4.3
	100.0	100.0	100.0			Total	100.0	100.0
						LIABILITIES		
	20.2	12.8	11.7			Notes Payable-Short Term	13.0	12.4
	4.8	4.0	5.5			Cur. Mat.-L.T.D.	4.7	4.5
	16.1	11.2	7.8			Trade Payables	14.5	13.4
	.1	.1	.0			Income Taxes Payable	.2	.2
	5.9	7.2	3.7			All Other Current	7.8	7.1
	47.1	35.3	28.7			Total Current	40.3	37.6
	19.8	15.8	21.7			Long-Term Debt	20.2	18.5
	.0	.1	.4			Deferred Taxes	.3	.2
	5.9	5.3	5.7			All Other Non-Current	4.6	5.5
	27.1	43.4	43.6			Net Worth	34.6	38.2
	100.0	100.0	100.0			Total Liabilities & Net Worth	100.0	100.0
						INCOME DATA		
	100.0	100.0	100.0			Net Sales	100.0	100.0
	30.9	24.8	27.1			Gross Profit	25.1	25.4
	29.0	21.8	21.9			Operating Expenses	20.9	20.6
	1.8	3.0	5.2			Operating Profit	4.2	4.8
	.7	.0	2.9			All Other Expenses (net)	.7	.7
	1.1	3.0	2.3			Profit Before Taxes	3.5	4.2
						RATIOS		
	2.8	3.6	2.4				2.4	2.8
	1.6	1.6	1.4			Current	1.4	1.6
	.9	1.1	1.1				1.1	1.2
	1.8	2.3	1.3				1.3	1.5
	.9	.8	.7			Quick	.8	.9
	.5	.5	.5				.5	.6
	24 15.4	25 14.5	29 12.5				24 15.1	25 14.7
	32 11.3	34 10.8	41 9.0			Sales/Receivables	32 11.4	33 11.1
	43 8.5	48 7.6	48 7.6				41 8.9	43 8.6
	19 18.8	28 13.3	32 11.6				17 21.3	16 22.3
	30 12.1	45 8.1	54 6.8			Cost of Sales/Inventory	33 11.0	32 11.4
	59 6.2	74 5.0	98 3.7				52 7.1	54 6.7
	8 46.1	9 40.6	13 28.3				9 41.1	10 37.2
	21 17.7	17 22.0	22 16.9			Cost of Sales/Payables	18 19.8	17 21.8
	39 9.2	36 10.0	42 8.6				31 11.6	28 13.2
	7.3	5.0	6.8				8.9	7.8
	12.7	10.0	12.5			Sales/Working Capital	17.9	15.5
	-61.2	55.4	54.4				47.8	49.6
	4.6	8.5	3.8				9.2	9.8
	(53) 1.3	(56) 4.0	(19) 2.3			EBIT/Interest	(142) 3.6	(193) 3.7
	-1.1	1.4	1.3				1.7	2.1
						Net Profit + Depr., Dep., Amort./Cur. Mat. L/T/D	3.6	3.7
							(36) 2.4	(45) 2.3
							1.5	1.5
	.3	.2	.4				.5	.4
	1.2	.7	1.4			Fixed/Worth	1.0	.8
	6.1	1.5	4.9				2.0	1.5
	.8	.5	1.1				.9	.8
	2.2	1.8	2.0			Debt/Worth	2.0	1.8
	NM	3.4	8.0				4.3	3.7
	22.6	40.5	30.0				48.3	46.4
	(44) 9.7	(53) 16.5	(16) 13.8			% Profit Before Taxes/Tangible Net Worth	(137) 19.7	(183) 23.8
	-9.9	2.7	5.1				7.2	9.2
	9.0	13.5	7.0				16.3	18.5
	1.2	4.6	4.0			% Profit Before Taxes/Total Assets	7.2	8.9
	-6.9	.7	1.7				2.0	2.9
	33.8	22.4	24.0				22.2	27.0
	12.6	11.2	8.2			Sales/Net Fixed Assets	10.9	12.3
	6.9	4.8	3.2				5.8	6.6
	4.0	3.5	2.4				4.3	4.1
	3.1	2.4	1.5			Sales/Total Assets	3.2	3.2
	2.4	1.6	1.1				2.2	2.2
	.8	1.6	.9				1.1	.9
	(49) 2.4	(53) 2.3	2.4			% Depr., Dep., Amort./Sales	(133) 2.0	(185) 1.7
	3.4	4.3	5.6				3.1	2.8
	2.2	1.6					1.0	1.6
	(35) 4.5	(20) 2.6				% Officers', Directors' Owners' Comp/Sales	(55) 2.2	(86) 2.6
	7.1	4.2					4.3	4.9
5173M	228420M	626141M	868545M	265919M	294327M	Net Sales ($)	2886868M	5325076M
1646M	69086M	274254M	464996M	155190M	309167M	Total Assets ($)	1187817M	2064807M

M = $ thousand   MM = $ million
See Pages 9 through 22 for Explanation of Ratios and Data

Comparative Historical Data | Current Data Sorted by Sales

Type of Statement

4/1/07-3/31/08 ALL	4/1/08-3/31/09 ALL	4/1/09-3/31/10 ALL	Type of Statement	0-1MM	1-3MM	3-5MM	5-10MM	10-25MM	25MM & OVER
10	7	7	Unqualified			2			5
42	28	30	Reviewed		1	5	10	9	5
28	28	28	Compiled	1	4	4	11	7	1
33	38	35	Tax Returns	2	14	4	10	4	1
63	54	44	Other	1	6	10	6	12	9
				23 (4/1-9/30/09)		121 (10/1/09-3/31/10)			
176	155	144	NUMBER OF STATEMENTS	4	25	25	37	32	21

ASSETS

4/1/07-3/31/08	4/1/08-3/31/09	4/1/09-3/31/10		0-1MM	1-3MM	3-5MM	5-10MM	10-25MM	25MM & OVER
%	%	%		%	%	%	%	%	%
6.8	8.6	8.5	Cash & Equivalents		8.6	8.6	8.1	11.3	2.1
27.2	24.9	26.1	Trade Receivables (net)		28.1	28.9	22.3	28.9	25.1
23.5	25.3	22.7	Inventory		20.9	21.9	25.4	26.5	17.7
2.7	1.3	2.1	All Other Current		1.4	1.6	2.7	1.8	3.5
60.2	60.1	59.4	Total Current		59.0	61.0	58.5	68.5	48.4
31.3	30.0	29.3	Fixed Assets (net)		29.4	30.3	30.6	26.0	26.3
3.0	3.0	4.6	Intangibles (net)		3.9	.2	3.4	1.6	18.0
5.5	6.9	6.7	All Other Non-Current		7.8	8.5	7.5	3.9	7.3
100.0	100.0	100.0	Total		100.0	100.0	100.0	100.0	100.0

LIABILITIES

4/1/07-3/31/08	4/1/08-3/31/09	4/1/09-3/31/10		0-1MM	1-3MM	3-5MM	5-10MM	10-25MM	25MM & OVER
14.2	15.9	15.7	Notes Payable-Short Term		15.9	16.4	18.8	13.0	13.9
4.3	4.6	4.5	Cur. Mat.-L.T.D.		3.9	5.9	5.2	2.8	5.5
13.1	12.7	12.4	Trade Payables		15.5	14.3	11.6	13.1	8.8
.3	.1	.2	Income Taxes Payable		.0	.1	.1	.1	.1
8.0	5.3	6.2	All Other Current		7.7	7.9	6.4	4.1	6.1
39.8	38.6	39.0	Total Current		43.0	44.7	42.1	33.3	34.3
19.9	19.0	19.2	Long-Term Debt		16.0	17.8	22.3	13.7	16.7
.3	.2	.1	Deferred Taxes		.1	.0	.3	.0	.2
4.1	7.9	5.6	All Other Non-Current		8.8	5.5	3.7	4.9	6.2
35.9	34.4	36.0	Net Worth		32.1	32.0	31.5	48.2	42.6
100.0	100.0	100.0	Total Liabilities & Net Worth		100.0	100.0	100.0	100.0	100.0

INCOME DATA

4/1/07-3/31/08	4/1/08-3/31/09	4/1/09-3/31/10		0-1MM	1-3MM	3-5MM	5-10MM	10-25MM	25MM & OVER
100.0	100.0	100.0	Net Sales		100.0	100.0	100.0	100.0	100.0
25.7	24.1	28.3	Gross Profit		36.4	32.0	24.5	21.9	26.8
22.2	21.1	25.1	Operating Expenses		35.0	31.4	21.8	18.1	21.6
3.5	3.1	3.2	Operating Profit		1.4	.6	2.7	3.8	5.2
.9	.6	.8	All Other Expenses (net)		-.1	.6	.8	.4	2.0
2.6	2.5	2.4	Profit Before Taxes		1.6	.0	2.0	3.4	3.2

RATIOS

4/1/07-3/31/08	4/1/08-3/31/09	4/1/09-3/31/10		0-1MM	1-3MM	3-5MM	5-10MM	10-25MM	25MM & OVER
2.8 / 1.7 / 1.1	2.9 / 1.7 / 1.1	3.0 / 1.6 / 1.1	Current		3.7 / 1.8 / 1.0	2.3 / 1.6 / .9	3.8 / 1.4 / 1.0	4.7 / 2.0 / 1.2	1.8 / 1.5 / 1.0
1.8 / .9 / .5	1.7 / .9 / .5	2.0 / .8 / .5	Quick		3.0 / 1.0 / .4	1.4 / .9 / .5	1.7 / .7 / .5	3.2 / .9 / .6	1.3 / .7 / .4
23 15.9 / 32 11.5 / 40 9.2	19 18.8 / 29 12.4 / 39 9.3	25 14.5 / 34 10.8 / 44 8.3	Sales/Receivables		26 14.3 / 35 10.3 / 44 8.4	23 16.0 / 31 11.8 / 44 8.3	21 17.3 / 31 11.8 / 40 9.1	28 13.0 / 34 10.6 / 47 7.7	31 11.9 / 41 9.0 / 47 7.8
18 20.4 / 37 9.9 / 55 6.6	19 18.9 / 34 10.6 / 57 6.4	24 15.4 / 43 8.5 / 74 4.9	Cost of Sales/Inventory		11 33.3 / 31 11.8 / 75 4.9	21 17.6 / 31 11.8 / 50 7.3	25 14.4 / 43 8.6 / 77 4.8	25 14.5 / 47 7.8 / 75 4.9	20 17.9 / 50 7.3 / 67 5.4
9 41.7 / 17 21.9 / 31 11.9	6 58.0 / 15 25.0 / 28 12.9	9 39.3 / 19 19.5 / 37 9.9	Cost of Sales/Payables		7 52.6 / 26 14.0 / 41 9.0	8 44.1 / 17 21.5 / 39 9.3	9 39.9 / 19 19.5 / 40 9.0	8 48.3 / 17 21.7 / 34 10.8	12 30.0 / 19 19.6 / 30 12.0
7.1 / 13.2 / 59.4	8.0 / 13.8 / 52.8	6.3 / 12.3 / 130.8	Sales/Working Capital		4.6 / 10.6 / NM	8.5 / 19.2 / -49.4	4.5 / 15.8 / -628.7	5.0 / 8.4 / 26.0	8.8 / 13.1 / NM
8.4 / (164) 2.7 / 1.1	8.8 / (143) 3.0 / 1.1	6.4 / (137) 2.3 / .9	EBIT/Interest		5.5 / (21) 2.0 / .1	4.4 / (24) 1.3 / -3.7	5.9 / (36) 1.6 / -.8	8.9 / (31) 5.0 / 2.1	11.7 / 3.0 / 1.5
9.1 / (38) 2.5 / 1.6	3.1 / (26) 2.0 / .7	5.6 / (19) 2.6 / 1.5	Net Profit + Depr., Dep., Amort./Cur. Mat. L/T/D						
.4 / .9 / 1.9	.3 / .8 / 2.0	.3 / .8 / 3.0	Fixed/Worth		.3 / .9 / 1.9	.4 / 1.4 / 4.8	.4 / 1.0 / NM	.1 / .6 / 1.1	.4 / .9 / NM
.7 / 2.0 / 3.9	.7 / 1.7 / 4.1	.7 / 1.9 / 7.4	Debt/Worth		.5 / 1.4 / 11.0	.5 / 1.9 / 16.2	.5 / 2.6 / NM	.5 / 1.4 / 2.9	1.0 / 1.6 / NM
42.5 / (156) 18.8 / 3.4	35.4 / (135) 14.1 / 2.6	35.8 / (120) 13.2 / .4	% Profit Before Taxes/Tangible Net Worth		40.0 / (20) 7.3 / -7.0	21.7 / (22) 7.3 / -15.6	48.6 / (28) 9.3 / -3.6	34.7 / (31) 16.6 / 4.4	31.0 / (16) 19.1 / 9.0
18.1 / 5.4 / .5	13.4 / 5.4 / -.3	10.6 / 3.8 / -.1	% Profit Before Taxes/Total Assets		13.5 / 2.7 / -2.4	7.3 / .5 / -10.6	9.1 / 2.2 / -1.8	14.1 / 7.5 / 2.2	10.3 / 4.9 / 1.8
25.2 / 11.5 / 5.9	26.9 / 13.3 / 5.1	26.5 / 11.5 / 4.9	Sales/Net Fixed Assets		27.3 / 11.9 / 4.4	26.0 / 10.5 / 6.0	23.1 / 8.4 / 4.8	28.3 / 15.0 / 5.7	27.1 / 9.4 / 3.5
4.0 / 3.0 / 2.0	4.4 / 3.0 / 2.1	3.6 / 2.6 / 1.7	Sales/Total Assets		3.5 / 2.8 / 2.0	4.1 / 3.1 / 2.3	3.6 / 2.5 / 1.6	3.8 / 2.9 / 1.7	3.4 / 1.9 / 1.2
1.1 / (154) 2.0 / 3.2	.9 / (139) 1.9 / 3.2	1.4 / (129) 2.4 / 4.3	% Depr., Dep., Amort./Sales		1.1 / (21) 3.0 / 5.9	1.5 / (22) 2.6 / 3.2	1.5 / (34) 2.6 / 5.1	1.5 / (29) 2.2 / 3.1	.5 / (20) 2.0 / 4.3
1.5 / (73) 2.5 / 4.5	1.5 / (77) 2.8 / 4.9	1.7 / (62) 3.0 / 5.9	% Officers', Directors' Owners' Comp/Sales		4.2 / (17) 6.1 / 9.7	1.5 / (12) 3.2 / 5.6	2.0 / (17) 2.3 / 4.8	.7 / (10) 2.7 / 3.9	
3673773M	2721399M	2288525M	Net Sales ($)	1442M	50466M	104668M	251044M	452644M	1428261M
1866817M	1248999M	1274339M	Total Assets ($)	2052M	28000M	37552M	135073M	208329M	863333M

M = $ thousand   MM = $ million
See Pages 9 through 22 for Explanation of Ratios and Data

Current Data Sorted by Assets							Comparative Historical Data	

Type of Statement

0-500M	500M-2MM	2-10MM	10-50MM	50-100MM	100-250MM		4/1/05-3/31/06 ALL	4/1/06-3/31/07 ALL
		2	2	4	2	Unqualified	13	11
1		7	3			Reviewed	4	3
1	3	2	2			Compiled	8	7
						Tax Returns	3	4
	2	3	6			Other	20	17
		7 (4/1-9/30/09)	33 (10/1/09-3/31/10)					
2	5	14	13	4	2	NUMBER OF STATEMENTS	48	42
%	%	%	%	%	%		%	%

ASSETS

0-500M	500M-2MM	2-10MM	10-50MM	50-100MM	100-250MM		4/1/05-3/31/06 ALL	4/1/06-3/31/07 ALL
		14.7	17.3			Cash & Equivalents	12.3	17.1
		14.1	10.3			Trade Receivables (net)	21.4	12.4
		23.3	24.2			Inventory	27.6	25.6
		.3	2.6			All Other Current	2.4	3.0
		52.4	54.5			Total Current	63.6	58.0
		35.2	32.5			Fixed Assets (net)	27.0	29.9
		3.6	3.8			Intangibles (net)	4.0	5.7
		8.8	9.3			All Other Non-Current	5.3	6.4
		100.0	100.0			Total	100.0	100.0

LIABILITIES

0-500M	500M-2MM	2-10MM	10-50MM	50-100MM	100-250MM		4/1/05-3/31/06 ALL	4/1/06-3/31/07 ALL
		11.1	8.2			Notes Payable-Short Term	17.0	17.6
		3.9	2.3			Cur. Mat.-L.T.D.	1.3	1.2
		8.7	5.6			Trade Payables	14.4	10.0
		.0	.2			Income Taxes Payable	.1	.2
		15.2	10.4			All Other Current	16.3	17.6
		38.8	26.7			Total Current	49.0	46.5
		25.3	27.9			Long-Term Debt	12.7	7.8
		.0	.5			Deferred Taxes	.6	1.0
		7.8	5.4			All Other Non-Current	3.2	3.9
		28.1	39.5			Net Worth	34.5	40.7
		100.0	100.0			Total Liabilities & Net Worth	100.0	100.0

INCOME DATA

0-500M	500M-2MM	2-10MM	10-50MM	50-100MM	100-250MM		4/1/05-3/31/06 ALL	4/1/06-3/31/07 ALL
		100.0	100.0			Net Sales	100.0	100.0
		21.4	17.6			Gross Profit	25.3	26.2
		25.4	19.0			Operating Expenses	18.1	18.6
		-4.0	-1.4			Operating Profit	7.1	7.5
		1.1	1.9			All Other Expenses (net)	1.0	1.3
		-5.1	-3.3			Profit Before Taxes	6.2	6.2

RATIOS

0-500M	500M-2MM	2-10MM	10-50MM	50-100MM	100-250MM		4/1/05-3/31/06 ALL	4/1/06-3/31/07 ALL
		2.8	4.0			Current	2.2	2.1
		1.2	2.4				1.4	1.4
		1.0	1.5				1.0	.7
		1.7	3.3			Quick	1.3	1.2
		.6	1.2				.7	.6
		.4	.5				.3	.2
		7 55.3	15 24.6			Sales/Receivables	12 29.9	4 85.0
		17 21.2	27 13.8				23 15.7	11 33.7
		41 8.8	30 12.3				48 7.6	21 17.2
		21 17.5	21 17.3			Cost of Sales/Inventory	17 22.0	17 21.2
		64 5.7	50 7.3				39 9.3	34 10.6
		85 4.3	112 3.3				64 5.7	49 7.5
		6 57.2	4 93.8			Cost of Sales/Payables	5 70.4	7 56.0
		9 39.0	7 51.6				15 24.2	10 37.9
		29 12.4	14 25.9				32 11.5	15 24.5
		5.3	2.4			Sales/Working Capital	6.9	8.3
		29.6	4.7				14.2	14.5
		NM	18.5				84.5	-36.4
		5.0	10.1			EBIT/Interest	11.3	25.8
		1.3	(12) 4.7				(38) 4.6	(34) 3.8
		-5.5	-1.9				2.5	-1.2
						Net Profit + Depr., Dep., Amort./Cur. Mat. L/T/D		
		.4	.2			Fixed/Worth	.2	.2
		.9	.5				.5	.6
		NM	1.9				2.3	2.7
		.9	.5			Debt/Worth	.8	.6
		2.5	.9				2.2	1.4
		NM	1.7				7.4	5.5
		7.4	20.4			% Profit Before Taxes/Tangible Net Worth	69.7	69.5
		(11) 1.7	(12) 10.8				(45) 25.9	(36) 27.0
		-104.1	-4.7				11.7	5.2
		4.2	8.6			% Profit Before Taxes/Total Assets	20.5	21.9
		.7	4.0				9.7	8.2
		-16.5	-12.3				3.5	1.3
		14.4	10.2			Sales/Net Fixed Assets	34.3	28.7
		5.7	7.0				14.6	12.8
		3.1	2.6				5.8	5.7
		2.5	2.0			Sales/Total Assets	4.0	3.7
		1.7	1.5				2.2	2.5
		1.2	1.2				1.3	1.2
		.8	1.0			% Depr., Dep., Amort./Sales	.5	.4
		(13) 1.4	(11) 2.1				(44) .9	(39) 1.0
		3.2	3.3				1.7	2.0
						% Officers', Directors' Owners' Comp/Sales	.7	.6
							(12) 1.3	(11) 1.7
							3.3	3.5
2393M	11649M	124260M	385513M	338234M	282288M	Net Sales ($)	2274109M	2476962M
357M	5497M	73673M	276669M	287213M	400461M	Total Assets ($)	1253919M	1373299M

M = $ thousand   MM = $ million
See Pages 9 through 22 for Explanation of Ratios and Data

Comparative Historical Data / Current Data Sorted by Sales

4/1/07-3/31/08 ALL	4/1/08-3/31/09 ALL	4/1/09-3/31/10 ALL		0-1MM	1-3MM	3-5MM	5-10MM	10-25MM	25MM & OVER
			Type of Statement						
13	13	10	Unqualified			1		2	7
3	11	11	Reviewed	1		1	6	1	2
9	7	8	Compiled		4		1	2	1
2	2		Tax Returns						
9	11	11	Other		2		1	3	5
				7 (4/1-9/30/09)			33 (10/1/09-3/31/10)		
36	44	40	**NUMBER OF STATEMENTS**	1	6	2	8	8	15
%	%	%	**ASSETS**	%	%	%	%	%	%
19.0	13.8	16.8	Cash & Equivalents						19.9
15.7	14.8	13.3	Trade Receivables (net)						7.9
26.5	25.6	25.1	Inventory						23.6
1.7	4.0	3.7	All Other Current						4.0
62.9	58.2	58.9	Total Current						55.5
25.1	29.5	29.2	Fixed Assets (net)						30.2
6.2	3.6	3.3	Intangibles (net)						5.5
5.7	8.7	8.6	All Other Non-Current						8.8
100.0	100.0	100.0	Total						100.0
			LIABILITIES						
12.6	12.9	9.4	Notes Payable-Short Term						6.6
1.4	2.2	3.0	Cur. Mat.-L.T.D.						2.1
7.6	7.4	9.2	Trade Payables						5.6
.3	.3	.1	Income Taxes Payable						.2
17.5	14.2	13.3	All Other Current						11.8
39.4	37.0	35.0	Total Current						26.3
12.3	19.4	26.6	Long-Term Debt						22.2
.6	.2	.4	Deferred Taxes						1.1
1.9	2.5	6.3	All Other Non-Current						6.6
45.8	40.8	31.7	Net Worth						43.8
100.0	100.0	100.0	Total Liabilities & Net Worth						100.0
			INCOME DATA						
100.0	100.0	100.0	Net Sales						100.0
23.6	24.9	17.5	Gross Profit						13.0
19.1	22.5	22.1	Operating Expenses						18.6
4.5	2.5	-4.6	Operating Profit						-5.7
.5	1.3	1.0	All Other Expenses (net)						1.8
4.0	1.1	-5.6	Profit Before Taxes						-7.5
			RATIOS						
2.4 / 1.6 / 1.3	2.8 / 1.6 / 1.1	3.5 / 1.8 / 1.1	Current						3.5 / 2.4 / 1.7
1.5 / .8 / .3	1.9 / .7 / .3	2.4 / .8 / .4	Quick						2.6 / .9 / .6
9 39.3 / 21 17.7 / 32 11.5	9 39.5 / 22 16.8 / 34 10.7	11 32.1 / 25 14.3 / 33 11.0	Sales/Receivables						12 29.6 / 17 21.5 / 28 13.2
21 17.3 / 36 10.2 / 64 5.7	30 12.0 / 44 8.4 / 74 4.9	24 15.3 / 53 6.8 / 104 3.5	Cost of Sales/Inventory						18 20.8 / 52 7.0 / 114 3.2
6 65.2 / 11 33.7 / 17 21.7	5 69.6 / 11 34.4 / 27 13.6	5 74.7 / 10 35.9 / 24 15.2	Cost of Sales/Payables						4 84.2 / 7 49.2 / 19 19.5
6.3 / 10.9 / 30.8	4.4 / 10.9 / 49.1	3.4 / 6.7 / 33.4	Sales/Working Capital						1.8 / 4.0 / 17.9
17.1 / (30) 4.1 / -.3	7.5 / (36) 2.1 / -1.0	4.8 / (36) 1.1 / -9.9	EBIT/Interest						7.4 / (13) -1.8 / -38.1
			Net Profit + Depr., Dep., Amort./Cur. Mat. L/T/D						
.1 / .5 / 2.1	.2 / .5 / 3.0	.3 / .6 / 4.6	Fixed/Worth						.3 / .5 / .6
.5 / 1.2 / 4.9	.5 / 1.6 / 4.8	.7 / 1.0 / 7.2	Debt/Worth						.5 / .9 / 1.2
57.9 / (31) 14.1 / -1.8	27.2 / (37) 6.3 / -3.9	11.7 / (32) 1.3 / -16.6	% Profit Before Taxes/Tangible Net Worth						12.0 / (14) -5.5 / -23.6
25.2 / 9.9 / -1.6	8.9 / 3.0 / -4.6	5.9 / -.3 / -15.4	% Profit Before Taxes/Total Assets						6.2 / -4.8 / -19.5
38.2 / 10.7 / 5.6	37.3 / 8.2 / 4.5	15.2 / 6.6 / 3.2	Sales/Net Fixed Assets						9.6 / 6.1 / 3.1
3.1 / 2.6 / 1.3	2.9 / 2.0 / 1.2	2.5 / 1.6 / 1.1	Sales/Total Assets						2.0 / 1.5 / 1.0
.4 / (29) .9 / 1.6	.4 / (40) 1.1 / 1.9	.9 / (32) 1.8 / 2.7	% Depr., Dep., Amort./Sales						1.0 / (12) 1.9 / 3.1
			% Officers', Directors' Owners' Comp/Sales						
1890802M	2324096M	1144337M	Net Sales ($)	22M	14020M	7924M	51773M	122902M	947696M
1029272M	1699091M	1043870M	Total Assets ($)	8M	5846M	4624M	38706M	113765M	880921M

M = $ thousand   MM = $ million
See Pages 9 through 22 for Explanation of Ratios and Data

Current Data Sorted by Assets   Comparative Historical Data

0-500M	500M-2MM	2-10MM	10-50MM	50-100MM	100-250MM	Type of Statement	4/1/05-3/31/06 ALL	4/1/06-3/31/07 ALL
		1	2	4		Unqualified	14	16
		2	10	3		Reviewed	19	20
		2	1			Compiled	11	10
2		1	3			Tax Returns	3	9
		1	7	6		Other	25	23
4 (4/1-9/30/09)		41 (10/1/09-3/31/10)						
2	7	23	13			NUMBER OF STATEMENTS	72	78
%	%	%	%	%	%	**ASSETS**	%	%
		9.4	10.1			Cash & Equivalents	12.5	9.0
		16.0	15.1	D A T A	D A T A	Trade Receivables (net)	17.8	18.4
		18.7	24.2			Inventory	23.7	27.5
		1.7	5.3	N O T	N O T	All Other Current	5.0	3.5
		45.8	54.6			Total Current	58.9	58.4
		38.6	31.4	A V A I L A B L E	A V A I L A B L E	Fixed Assets (net)	29.9	30.8
		5.7	8.0			Intangibles (net)	5.8	3.9
		9.8	6.1			All Other Non-Current	5.4	6.9
		100.0	100.0			Total	100.0	100.0
						LIABILITIES		
		13.6	14.9			Notes Payable-Short Term	9.0	11.5
		3.5	2.8			Cur. Mat.-L.T.D.	2.7	4.2
		9.9	10.2			Trade Payables	10.1	10.2
		.0	.1			Income Taxes Payable	.5	.1
		22.6	13.2			All Other Current	18.9	18.1
		49.5	41.2			Total Current	41.3	44.1
		17.8	21.0			Long-Term Debt	17.2	16.5
		.3	1.4			Deferred Taxes	.3	.3
		3.5	11.1			All Other Non-Current	4.1	5.1
		28.8	25.3			Net Worth	37.1	34.0
		100.0	100.0			Total Liabilities & Net Worth	100.0	100.0
						INCOME DATA		
		100.0	100.0			Net Sales	100.0	100.0
		26.7	26.4			Gross Profit	27.5	28.8
		33.7	26.8			Operating Expenses	21.7	24.6
		-7.0	-.3			Operating Profit	5.8	4.1
		2.2	2.0			All Other Expenses (net)	.8	.7
		-9.2	-2.3			Profit Before Taxes	5.0	3.4
						RATIOS		
		2.1	2.7				2.2	2.0
		1.1	1.7			Current	1.5	1.4
		.8	.8				1.1	1.0
		1.3	1.8				1.4	1.2
		.5	.4			Quick	(71) .7	.7
		.3	.2				.4	.3
	10	35.8	7 54.5				6 61.9	7 53.1
	33	11.1	14 26.9			Sales/Receivables	17 20.9	18 19.8
	62	5.9	48 7.7				48 7.7	36 10.1
	27	13.5	23 15.9				27 13.7	24 15.0
	74	4.9	33 11.0			Cost of Sales/Inventory	46 7.9	43 8.4
	114	3.2	94 3.9				79 4.6	81 4.5
	13	28.2	7 52.5				10 35.2	9 39.2
	27	13.6	25 14.5			Cost of Sales/Payables	20 18.6	15 24.6
	54	6.7	41 9.0				31 11.9	30 12.3
		5.8	6.0				6.7	8.2
		30.0	9.7			Sales/Working Capital	17.7	20.4
		-9.1	-16.4				67.2	83.0
		3.3	8.1				12.3	8.1
	(19)	-2.1	1.4			EBIT/Interest	(69) 4.9	(75) 3.5
		-4.1	-1.2				2.7	1.4
						Net Profit + Depr., Dep.,	9.3	8.3
	(19)					Amort./Cur. Mat. L/T/D	4.5	(20) 3.5
							1.0	1.2
		.6	.5				.5	.4
		1.0	.7			Fixed/Worth	1.0	.9
		3.7	3.7				2.6	2.4
		.8	.9				.8	.8
		1.9	2.1			Debt/Worth	2.3	2.1
		7.3	20.8				5.6	5.3
		5.3	40.8			% Profit Before Taxes/Tangible	63.3	53.4
	(19)	-16.7	(11) 24.0			Net Worth	(62) 30.3	(65) 32.4
		-48.1	-.5				8.3	8.0
		3.3	9.6			% Profit Before Taxes/Total	16.7	17.3
		-7.5	2.7			Assets	9.2	6.7
		-14.0	-7.1				3.3	1.2
		10.0	29.6				14.7	17.8
		4.3	7.2			Sales/Net Fixed Assets	8.8	9.5
		2.0	3.6				4.5	5.1
		2.3	3.0				2.9	3.5
		1.2	1.8			Sales/Total Assets	2.3	2.6
		.8	.9				1.8	2.0
		1.7	1.7				1.0	1.0
	(18)	3.3	2.4			% Depr., Dep., Amort./Sales	(63) 1.6	(72) 1.8
		4.9	3.8				2.5	2.7
						% Officers', Directors'	1.2	2.0
						Owners' Comp/Sales	(12) 2.2	(22) 3.7
							4.6	5.6
2118M	23111M	205170M	562700M			Net Sales ($)	2196855M	2134652M
665M	10515M	137036M	276696M			Total Assets ($)	1057350M	864966M

Comparative Historical Data | Current Data Sorted by Sales

			Type of Statement			4 (4/1-9/30/09)		41 (10/1/09-3/31/10)		
				0-1MM	1-3MM	3-5MM	5-10MM	10-25MM	25MM & OVER	
23	5	7	Unqualified			2		1	4	
16	15	15	Reviewed		2	4	3	4	2	
13	11	3	Compiled			3				
6	5	6	Tax Returns	1	2	1	1	1		
29	34	14	Other		2	3	1	4	4	
4/1/07-3/31/08 ALL	4/1/08-3/31/09 ALL	4/1/09-3/31/10 ALL								
87	70	45	**NUMBER OF STATEMENTS**	1	6	13	5	10	10	

4/1/07-3/31/08 ALL	4/1/08-3/31/09 ALL	4/1/09-3/31/10 ALL		0-1MM	1-3MM	3-5MM	5-10MM	10-25MM	25MM & OVER
%	%	%	**ASSETS**	%	%	%	%	%	%
11.2	12.5	8.4	Cash & Equivalents			7.2		10.3	10.1
16.1	19.3	17.2	Trade Receivables (net)			18.7		23.5	18.7
26.3	27.1	24.5	Inventory			25.5		14.3	29.0
3.7	4.1	2.5	All Other Current			.6		2.0	6.4
57.3	63.1	52.6	Total Current			52.0		50.1	64.2
29.5	27.8	32.9	Fixed Assets (net)			32.2		35.3	27.5
5.3	3.2	6.1	Intangibles (net)			7.0		7.9	3.3
7.9	5.9	8.4	All Other Non-Current			8.7		6.7	4.9
100.0	100.0	100.0	Total			100.0		100.0	100.0
			LIABILITIES						
11.0	13.2	16.2	Notes Payable-Short Term			19.0		12.4	12.3
4.4	4.3	3.1	Cur. Mat.-L.T.D.			3.0		3.8	3.6
9.5	9.5	10.0	Trade Payables			11.2		12.6	13.3
.0	.0	.1	Income Taxes Payable			.0		.1	.0
18.7	17.8	19.5	All Other Current			30.4		13.5	13.4
43.6	44.9	48.9	Total Current			63.5		42.4	42.6
17.8	15.1	18.1	Long-Term Debt			16.0		15.7	20.1
.4	.2	.6	Deferred Taxes			.2		1.2	.8
4.4	3.0	5.0	All Other Non-Current			5.6		1.0	13.7
33.8	36.8	27.4	Net Worth			14.6		39.7	22.8
100.0	100.0	100.0	Total Liabilities & Net Worth			100.0		100.0	100.0
			INCOME DATA						
100.0	100.0	100.0	Net Sales			100.0		100.0	100.0
27.5	26.4	28.1	Gross Profit			28.0		24.2	25.2
24.4	25.8	31.9	Operating Expenses			36.3		28.3	23.4
3.1	.6	-3.9	Operating Profit			-8.3		-4.1	1.8
1.0	1.0	1.8	All Other Expenses (net)			2.5		1.7	1.7
2.1	-.4	-5.6	Profit Before Taxes			-10.8		-5.8	.1
			RATIOS						
2.0	2.2	1.9	Current			1.7		2.2	3.7
1.4	1.3	1.2				1.2		1.0	1.7
1.0	1.0	.8				.4		.8	1.2
1.0	1.3	1.0	Quick			1.0		1.9	2.3
.6	.7	.5				.5		.6	.7
.3	.3	.2				.2		.4	.2
9 38.4	6 64.3	9 38.5	Sales/Receivables			9 38.7		11 33.6	6 57.0
21 17.2	22 16.7	29 12.6				44 8.3		48 7.6	18 20.3
36 10.1	46 8.0	55 6.6				65 5.6		55 6.6	36 6.6
27 13.4	31 11.9	27 13.5	Cost of Sales/Inventory			42 8.6		4 88.5	19 19.2
52 7.0	46 7.9	74 4.9				86 4.2		28 13.2	33 11.2
91 4.0	85 4.3	114 3.2				166 2.2		79 4.6	111 3.3
9 41.6	5 67.3	9 40.1	Cost of Sales/Payables			16 22.6		10 35.9	7 52.0
15 24.7	13 27.8	25 14.5				30 12.1		31 11.9	20 18.1
27 13.4	28 13.2	38 9.6				72 5.1		54 6.7	31 11.7
7.4	6.9	6.8	Sales/Working Capital			6.8		5.7	5.8
14.7	14.7	18.9				18.9		NM	9.0
695.5	254.0	-15.6				-3.8		-15.7	NM
6.5	17.8	6.7	EBIT/Interest			8.6		8.0	12.2
(78) 2.7	(63) 1.4	(41) .7				(11) -1.4		-5.4	2.6
-1.1	-2.8	-3.8				-3.7		-10.9	1.2
3.8		4.5	Net Profit + Depr., Dep.,						
(22) .9		(12) 2.2	Amort./Cur. Mat. L/T/D						
-.2		-3.2							
.4	.3	.4	Fixed/Worth			.4		.6	.4
1.1	.9	.9				1.0		1.2	.6
3.6	2.5	3.7				9.8		NM	1.9
.8	.8	1.0	Debt/Worth			1.3		.7	.6
2.3	2.2	2.1				4.0		2.0	1.3
8.7	7.9	14.4				12.4		NM	16.0
41.2	34.6	22.4	% Profit Before Taxes/Tangible			10.2			
(73) 12.5	(64) 5.9	(37) 1.4	Net Worth			(11) -18.0			
-7.0	-38.8	-28.2				-53.2			
10.0	10.4	5.2	% Profit Before Taxes/Total			4.4		7.0	9.3
3.4	1.5	-.6	Assets			-8.7		-4.6	2.7
-5.8	-8.4	-13.7				-15.9		-15.0	.3
16.0	28.9	13.2	Sales/Net Fixed Assets			15.8		8.4	30.5
8.5	9.7	5.8				5.3		6.2	9.8
5.2	4.4	2.7				2.3		4.0	5.0
3.2	3.0	2.6	Sales/Total Assets			2.0		2.6	3.1
2.4	2.3	1.6				1.3		1.9	2.8
1.6	1.6	.9				.8		1.1	1.8
1.1	1.0	1.7	% Depr., Dep., Amort./Sales						1.5
(77) 1.7	(53) 1.5	(37) 2.8							1.9
2.7	3.1	4.3							2.9
1.6		1.8	% Officers', Directors'						
(13) 2.2	(17) 2.6		Owners' Comp/Sales						
3.1		4.7							
2635592M	1769760M	793099M	Net Sales ($)	663M	13085M	50137M	33477M	160932M	534805M
1348181M	817904M	424912M	Total Assets ($)	264M	9939M	47356M	42600M	98239M	226514M

M = $ thousand   MM = $ million
See Pages 9 through 22 for Explanation of Ratios and Data

Current Data Sorted by Assets | **Comparative Historical Data**

Type of Statement	0-500M	500M-2MM	2-10MM	10-50MM	50-100MM	100-250MM		4/1/05-3/31/06 ALL	4/1/06-3/31/07 ALL
Unqualified	1		4	13	1	1		34	28
Reviewed	1	7	29	7				52	48
Compiled		9	13	1		1		37	30
Tax Returns	15	23	8	1				39	31
Other	6	11	30	19	5	1		68	67
		45 (4/1-9/30/09)		162 (10/1/09-3/31/10)					
NUMBER OF STATEMENTS	23	50	84	41	6	3		230	204
ASSETS	%	%	%	%	%	%		%	%
Cash & Equivalents	16.6	9.9	8.4	6.7				6.7	6.6
Trade Receivables (net)	22.7	24.6	16.6	14.5				23.7	24.5
Inventory	23.5	24.8	33.0	32.9				28.0	30.1
All Other Current	1.1	2.9	1.7	3.7				2.7	1.9
Total Current	63.9	62.1	59.7	58.0				61.0	63.0
Fixed Assets (net)	27.3	25.5	31.9	29.3				28.6	27.8
Intangibles (net)	5.8	3.4	2.6	5.0				4.0	3.2
All Other Non-Current	3.0	9.0	5.8	7.7				6.4	5.9
Total	100.0	100.0	100.0	100.0				100.0	100.0
LIABILITIES									
Notes Payable-Short Term	19.4	18.2	17.3	12.7				16.1	14.4
Cur. Mat.-L.T.D.	11.3	4.0	4.6	5.0				3.8	4.4
Trade Payables	16.2	14.4	10.8	7.9				12.7	12.5
Income Taxes Payable	.0	.4	.2	.1				.2	.3
All Other Current	14.2	5.6	8.1	6.5				6.8	9.2
Total Current	61.2	42.7	41.0	32.2				39.6	40.8
Long-Term Debt	19.7	22.5	18.7	17.2				20.5	18.6
Deferred Taxes	.0	.0	.3	.4				.4	.3
All Other Non-Current	25.3	6.1	4.9	9.2				4.5	6.5
Net Worth	-6.2	28.6	35.1	41.1				35.1	33.8
Total Liabilities & Net Worth	100.0	100.0	100.0	100.0				100.0	100.0
INCOME DATA									
Net Sales	100.0	100.0	100.0	100.0				100.0	100.0
Gross Profit	47.0	35.1	21.8	23.9				29.1	29.1
Operating Expenses	47.5	32.3	20.1	19.6				24.4	23.5
Operating Profit	-.5	2.8	1.7	4.3				4.6	5.6
All Other Expenses (net)	.4	.8	1.4	1.8				1.1	1.4
Profit Before Taxes	-.9	2.0	.3	2.5				3.6	4.3
RATIOS									
Current	4.4	4.1	2.6	2.4				2.7	2.9
	1.6	1.7	1.4	1.8				1.5	1.6
	.5	1.1	1.0	1.3				1.1	1.1
Quick	2.0	1.9	1.2	1.2				1.4	1.6
	1.1	1.1	.5	.5				.7	.8
	.2	.4	.3	.3				.4	.4
Sales/Receivables	0 UND	15 24.1	16 23.5	22 16.8				20 17.8	19 19.4
	10 36.5	30 12.2	23 15.9	35 10.5				32 11.5	32 11.5
	35 10.4	53 6.9	42 8.8	44 8.4				44 8.3	45 8.0
Cost of Sales/Inventory	0 UND	11 34.2	35 10.5	54 6.8				26 14.1	28 12.9
	26 13.8	39 9.3	71 5.1	114 3.2				55 6.6	56 6.5
	64 5.7	109 3.3	138 2.6	174 2.1				97 3.8	105 3.5
Cost of Sales/Payables	0 UND	10 36.8	11 33.5	17 21.8				10 36.2	10 36.7
	4 86.6	21 17.3	23 15.7	21 17.4				20 18.3	22 16.7
	44 8.2	38 9.7	38 9.6	34 10.6				34 10.6	38 9.7
Sales/Working Capital	9.0	5.4	4.9	4.0				6.8	5.9
	47.5	11.4	10.5	6.2				12.7	10.1
	-15.8	82.0	-74.3	14.4				38.0	36.4
EBIT/Interest	3.6	8.7	5.2	5.9				8.7	7.7
	(18) -.2	(42) 3.2	(80) 1.9	(38) 2.7				(216) 3.3	(185) 3.6
	-8.0	.5	-1.1	1.3				1.2	1.6
Net Profit + Depr., Dep., Amort./Cur. Mat. L/T/D			3.2	3.1				4.0	4.0
		(20) 1.5	(12) 2.3					(59) 1.9	(48) 2.6
			.5	1.0				1.2	1.4
Fixed/Worth	.1	.2	.4	.3				.3	.3
	.9	.7	.8	.7				.8	.7
	-2.4	6.2	2.5	2.1				2.4	1.6
Debt/Worth	.6	1.0	1.0	.8				.7	.9
	14.1	3.0	2.2	1.8				2.2	2.0
	-3.0	23.1	5.4	3.3				5.4	4.4
% Profit Before Taxes/Tangible Net Worth	42.8	46.8	30.8	29.8				41.9	49.8
	(13) .0	(41) 16.9	(75) 5.1	(38) 9.9				(199) 23.6	(180) 27.8
	-68.1	-3.3	-29.1	1.6				3.6	10.7
% Profit Before Taxes/Total Assets	16.3	13.7	8.3	8.9				16.9	17.1
	-2.6	4.8	1.9	3.3				5.7	8.6
	-57.0	-4.1	-6.2	.6				.5	2.3
Sales/Net Fixed Assets	468.0	33.3	14.7	11.1				25.1	26.0
	48.6	11.8	7.0	6.3				9.4	10.9
	8.7	5.0	3.7	2.7				4.6	5.0
Sales/Total Assets	7.9	3.3	2.5	2.1				3.6	3.3
	5.1	2.5	1.9	1.5				2.3	2.4
	3.5	1.5	1.4	.9				1.6	1.7
% Depr., Dep., Amort./Sales	.6	.5	1.3	1.4				1.0	.9
	(15) 1.3	(38) 1.7	(77) 3.0	(37) 2.5				(208) 1.9	(174) 1.8
	5.2	3.3	5.0	5.8				3.3	3.1
% Officers', Directors' Owners' Comp/Sales	4.8	3.8	1.5					1.7	2.0
	(13) 6.0	(32) 5.5	(25) 2.6					(87) 3.4	(75) 3.6
	16.4	7.2	4.9					5.8	6.6
Net Sales ($)	22915M	149563M	852094M	1322118M	624308M	330155M		6523388M	5661468M
Total Assets ($)	4500M	56899M	428627M	836642M	465081M	441689M		3244188M	2614028M

M = $ thousand   MM = $ million
See Pages 9 through 22 for Explanation of Ratios and Data

Comparative Historical Data / Current Data Sorted by Sales

H (4/1/07-3/31/08 ALL)	H (4/1/08-3/31/09 ALL)	H (4/1/09-3/31/10 ALL)	Type of Statement	0-1MM	1-3MM	3-5MM	5-10MM	10-25MM	25MM & OVER
26	24	20	Unqualified	1			4	4	11
47	42	44	Reviewed	1	2	4	14	19	4
23	34	24	Compiled	2	4	6	7	4	1
40	37	47	Tax Returns	10	22	5	8	2	
65	59	72	Other	2	16	9	13	16	16
				45 (4/1-9/30/09)			162 (10/1/09-3/31/10)		
201	196	207	NUMBER OF STATEMENTS	16	44	24	46	45	32
%	%	%	ASSETS	%	%	%	%	%	%
7.7	7.2	9.1	Cash & Equivalents	17.9	7.8	9.2	8.1	9.8	7.2
22.2	21.0	18.6	Trade Receivables (net)	15.3	21.0	18.3	21.0	17.9	14.5
29.8	30.3	29.8	Inventory	19.2	27.0	36.3	31.3	29.4	32.6
2.2	2.5	2.3	All Other Current	.9	2.1	1.9	2.4	2.7	2.7
61.9	61.0	59.8	Total Current	53.4	57.9	65.7	62.8	59.8	57.1
28.7	31.4	30.0	Fixed Assets (net)	39.3	28.2	26.4	28.3	28.6	35.3
3.1	2.6	3.5	Intangibles (net)	.9	6.0	2.7	3.0	4.5	1.3
6.2	5.0	6.6	All Other Non-Current	6.4	7.9	5.3	5.9	7.1	6.2
100.0	100.0	100.0	Total	100.0	100.0	100.0	100.0	100.0	100.0
			LIABILITIES						
16.6	15.3	16.5	Notes Payable-Short Term	16.1	20.5	18.3	18.3	13.4	11.7
3.5	4.2	5.2	Cur. Mat.-L.T.D.	15.9	3.6	3.9	5.4	4.9	2.9
11.1	10.8	11.5	Trade Payables	14.2	12.7	13.9	12.0	9.8	8.2
.2	.3	.2	Income Taxes Payable	.1	.0	.4	.3	.1	.2
9.6	7.8	7.7	All Other Current	4.0	11.6	6.5	4.1	9.7	7.3
41.0	38.5	41.0	Total Current	50.3	48.5	43.0	40.2	37.9	30.3
19.7	18.5	19.2	Long-Term Debt	30.5	21.6	25.7	17.8	14.0	15.0
.3	.4	.2	Deferred Taxes	.0	.1	.0	.2	.5	.2
5.9	7.1	8.1	All Other Non-Current	7.7	14.1	5.6	9.5	3.5	6.7
33.1	35.5	31.4	Net Worth	11.6	15.7	25.7	32.3	44.2	47.8
100.0	100.0	100.0	Total Liabilities & Net Worth	100.0	100.0	100.0	100.0	100.0	100.0
			INCOME DATA						
100.0	100.0	100.0	Net Sales	100.0	100.0	100.0	100.0	100.0	100.0
29.3	27.9	28.4	Gross Profit	44.7	39.9	24.7	22.2	24.4	21.4
25.1	24.8	25.9	Operating Expenses	43.1	38.3	24.0	20.7	20.0	17.4
4.2	3.0	2.5	Operating Profit	1.6	1.6	.7	1.5	4.4	3.9
1.5	1.4	1.2	All Other Expenses (net)	.0	1.2	1.6	1.6	1.3	.9
2.7	1.6	1.3	Profit Before Taxes	1.6	.4	-.8	.0	3.2	3.0
			RATIOS						
2.8	2.8	3.1	Current	5.2	3.9	2.3	3.2	2.8	3.4
1.6	1.6	1.6		1.5	1.6	1.4	1.5	1.6	1.8
1.2	1.1	1.0		.5	.7	1.0	1.1	1.1	1.4
1.6	1.3	1.4	Quick	3.5	1.5	1.2	1.3	1.5	1.4
.7	.7	.6		.9	1.0	.4	.6	.7	.7
.4	.3	.3		.2	.2	.3	.3	.3	.3
16 22.4	16 23.1	15 24.0	Sales/Receivables	0 UND	11 33.0	15 23.6	19 19.3	17 21.3	16 22.9
29 12.6	27 13.4	27 13.5		16 22.3	21 17.7	26 14.0	32 11.3	30 12.3	28 13.0
48 7.6	41 8.8	44 8.3		49 7.5	50 7.3	43 8.4	46 7.9	44 8.4	37 9.9
24 15.0	28 13.0	29 12.6	Cost of Sales/Inventory	0 UND	11 32.1	28 12.9	29 12.5	38 9.7	35 10.4
55 6.6	62 5.9	63 5.8		21 17.3	60 6.1	80 4.6	69 5.3	62 5.9	77 4.7
113 3.2	110 3.3	133 2.7		62 5.9	137 2.7	154 2.4	146 2.5	114 3.2	147 2.5
9 42.8	8 45.9	10 34.9	Cost of Sales/Payables	0 UND	4 82.6	11 32.5	12 30.3	12 29.7	14 26.9
20 18.3	19 19.1	21 17.3		2 153.2	21 17.3	38 9.6	24 15.5	21 17.1	19 19.6
35 10.5	34 10.6	37 9.9		43 8.4	38 9.5	55 6.6	33 11.1	36 10.3	28 13.2
6.0	5.6	4.9	Sales/Working Capital	8.0	5.3	4.6	4.4	4.9	4.4
9.7	10.6	10.0		64.5	11.9	14.6	9.3	8.0	7.6
26.0	41.4	186.8		-13.3	-19.5	NM	NM	30.0	18.0
7.8	6.1	6.4	EBIT/Interest	3.5	8.1	6.7	4.6	7.8	8.3
(186) 2.3	(181) 2.4	(187) 2.3		(12) .7	(37) 2.8	(23) 1.3	(40) 2.2	(43) 2.3	2.9
.7	-.1	-.3		-6.5	-.6	-2.3	.0	.9	.7
5.4	4.1	3.3	Net Profit + Depr., Dep., Amort./Cur. Mat. L/T/D						8.0
(44) 2.8	(45) 1.9	(45) 1.3						(13)	2.3
.8	.5	.5							1.0
.4	.3	.3	Fixed/Worth	.4	.2	.4	.3	.3	.4
.7	.7	.7		1.1	1.1	1.2	.7	.6	.6
2.3	1.5	2.5		UND	28.8	3.2	2.3	1.9	1.4
.8	.8	.8	Debt/Worth	.6	1.0	1.3	1.0	.5	.6
1.9	1.6	1.9		4.5	3.3	4.5	1.8	1.9	1.0
5.7	3.9	8.3		-5.7	-491.8	10.4	5.3	3.5	2.2
39.2	29.9	33.1	% Profit Before Taxes/Tangible Net Worth	23.0	47.5	57.2	25.4	33.4	30.6
(170) 16.4	(175) 11.2	(176) 9.2		(10) 1.1	(32) 13.3	(22) 15.3	(38) 7.8	(43) 9.6	(31) 9.2
2.2	-2.3	-5.4		-43.4	-24.0	-50.3	-8.9	-.4	-1.8
16.7	10.8	10.3	% Profit Before Taxes/Total Assets	9.1	11.1	13.9	8.3	9.9	15.1
4.8	3.1	2.9		-.4	4.8	1.0	2.7	2.7	4.6
-.3	-2.7	-4.5		-25.8	-14.7	-12.1	-6.9	-1.0	-.1
24.2	20.2	23.8	Sales/Net Fixed Assets	49.8	49.3	23.1	21.8	14.8	9.4
9.2	8.9	7.7		7.9	11.5	10.9	7.1	7.5	6.0
4.9	4.0	3.9		2.4	4.3	4.3	3.4	4.3	3.3
3.2	3.0	3.0	Sales/Total Assets	6.7	3.9	3.1	2.8	2.4	2.5
2.2	2.2	1.9		3.0	2.2	2.1	1.9	1.7	1.8
1.6	1.5	1.3		1.2	1.4	1.1	1.2	1.5	.9
1.1	1.1	1.1	% Depr., Dep., Amort./Sales	2.2	.7	1.1	1.1	1.4	
(160) 2.2	(170) 2.5	(175) 2.5		(11) 3.2	(33) 2.0	(21) 2.7	(39) 2.8	(40) 2.1	(31) 2.5
3.5	4.3	4.9		8.1	6.7	4.1	7.4	4.4	4.1
2.0	1.8	2.6	% Officers', Directors' Owners' Comp/Sales		4.6	2.4	2.6	1.0	
(77) 4.2	(73) 3.1	(77) 4.5			(24) 6.8	(14) 3.8	(16) 3.7	(13) 1.8	
6.6	5.9	6.9			9.7	6.3	5.7	3.0	
4635025M	3670976M	3301153M	Net Sales ($)	8341M	82657M	100152M	339696M	719852M	2050455M
2689599M	2289005M	2233438M	Total Assets ($)	4941M	44677M	60353M	239718M	526596M	1357153M

© RMA 2010

M = $ thousand   MM = $ million
See Pages 9 through 22 for Explanation of Ratios and Data

Current Data Sorted by Assets | Comparative Historical Data

0-500M	500M-2MM	2-10MM	10-50MM	50-100MM	100-250MM		4/1/05-3/31/06 ALL	4/1/06-3/31/07 ALL
						Type of Statement	24	19
		3	14	2	4	Unqualified	24	19
	1	9	2		1	Reviewed	9	12
	1	2				Compiled	4	6
2	1					Tax Returns	3	5
1	5	7	17	2	11	Other	30	28
	10 (4/1-9/30/09)		75 (10/1/09-3/31/10)					
3	8	21	33	4	16	NUMBER OF STATEMENTS	70	70
%	%	%	%	%	%		%	%
						ASSETS		
		6.4	1.9		5.5	Cash & Equivalents	7.0	5.9
		29.2	23.4		20.3	Trade Receivables (net)	25.2	26.1
		25.3	24.3		17.2	Inventory	22.1	21.6
		1.1	3.4		2.0	All Other Current	2.3	1.3
		62.0	53.0		45.0	Total Current	56.6	54.9
		29.4	36.9		43.0	Fixed Assets (net)	36.0	36.9
		1.3	2.0		6.2	Intangibles (net)	2.0	2.6
		7.3	8.1		5.7	All Other Non-Current	5.4	5.6
		100.0	100.0		100.0	Total	100.0	100.0
						LIABILITIES		
		15.3	10.0		.5	Notes Payable-Short Term	10.9	11.0
		3.4	4.7		5.6	Cur. Mat.-L.T.D.	2.9	4.9
		18.4	17.3		14.7	Trade Payables	17.5	15.9
		.1	.8		.3	Income Taxes Payable	.2	.1
		12.6	15.9		5.3	All Other Current	8.4	5.8
		49.9	48.9		26.3	Total Current	40.0	37.7
		23.3	20.9		24.5	Long-Term Debt	19.9	18.8
		.9	.5		2.9	Deferred Taxes	1.0	1.2
		3.3	4.9		5.1	All Other Non-Current	3.9	4.6
		22.6	24.8		41.2	Net Worth	35.3	37.7
		100.0	100.0		100.0	Total Liabilities & Net Worth	100.0	100.0
						INCOME DATA		
		100.0	100.0		100.0	Net Sales	100.0	100.0
		19.8	18.6		21.5	Gross Profit	19.5	20.6
		18.3	12.7		12.4	Operating Expenses	15.8	15.3
		1.4	5.9		9.1	Operating Profit	3.7	5.3
		.9	1.3		.5	All Other Expenses (net)	.9	1.0
		.5	4.7		8.6	Profit Before Taxes	2.8	4.3
						RATIOS		
		2.6	1.6		2.9		1.9	2.3
		1.4	1.1		1.9	Current	1.5	1.5
		.8	.9		1.1		1.0	.9
		1.7	.7		1.6		1.2	1.3
		.9	.5		.9	Quick	.8	.8
		.5	.4		.6		.5	.5
		27 13.7	26 14.3		29 12.7		31 11.8	31 11.7
		40 9.1	33 11.2		36 10.2	Sales/Receivables	37 9.9	40 9.2
		48 7.6	43 8.5		46 8.0		47 7.8	52 7.0
		19 18.8	29 12.6		34 10.9		23 16.2	25 14.4
		41 8.9	36 10.1		47 7.7	Cost of Sales/Inventory	41 8.9	44 8.3
		71 5.1	60 6.1		73 5.0		59 6.2	65 5.6
		15 24.6	22 16.7		22 16.4		21 17.4	20 18.6
		29 12.4	29 12.6		30 12.1	Cost of Sales/Payables	30 12.0	33 11.1
		41 9.0	38 9.7		55 6.7		42 8.7	43 8.5
		7.2	11.7		4.5		7.8	7.0
		24.3	45.1		7.1	Sales/Working Capital	15.1	12.1
		-23.2	-94.0		92.0		202.0	-76.9
		5.1	14.6		15.5		5.6	9.4
		1.8	(32) 5.6		7.2	EBIT/Interest	(62) 3.0	(62) 3.6
		-.3	.8		3.6		1.3	1.4
							5.7	3.8
						Net Profit + Depr., Dep., Amort./Cur. Mat. L/T/D	(24) 2.7	(16) 3.1
							1.3	1.7
		.5	.5		.6		.5	.4
		1.5	1.3		1.1	Fixed/Worth	1.0	1.0
		3.3	2.2		2.3		2.0	2.5
		.8	1.4		.6		1.0	.8
		3.0	2.0		2.5	Debt/Worth	1.9	1.6
		10.3	5.9		6.7		4.3	4.5
		37.3	51.1		61.5		44.7	47.5
	(17) 7.9		(28) 30.2		(14) 30.2	% Profit Before Taxes/Tangible Net Worth	(63) 15.3	(62) 24.2
		-4.0	-4.6		20.1		4.7	5.3
		8.4	17.9		16.0		11.2	16.9
		1.6	10.1		11.0	% Profit Before Taxes/Total Assets	5.7	7.1
		-4.7	1.0		4.4		.9	1.7
		23.0	10.5		6.4		25.6	15.8
		11.6	7.1		3.2	Sales/Net Fixed Assets	6.1	6.8
		4.5	3.6		1.8		3.0	2.8
		3.6	3.3		2.0		3.0	2.9
		2.5	2.3		1.4	Sales/Total Assets	2.3	2.2
		1.9	1.8		1.0		1.5	1.4
		.9	1.3		2.2		.6	1.1
		1.3	(27) 2.2		(15) 3.7	% Depr., Dep., Amort./Sales	(53) 1.8	(61) 2.3
		4.5	3.9		5.2		4.4	4.2
							1.4	1.3
						% Officers', Directors' Owners' Comp/Sales	(14) 3.3	(15) 1.9
							5.2	3.8
6041M	34097M	282236M	2074185M	389051M	4276412M	Net Sales ($)	6523031M	4387691M
1249M	10763M	103420M	848310M	300973M	2252596M	Total Assets ($)	3438327M	2491360M

M = $ thousand   MM = $ million
See Pages 9 through 22 for Explanation of Ratios and Data

Comparative Historical Data

Current Data Sorted by Sales

				Type of Statement						
18		22	23	Unqualified		1	1	2	19	
8		10	13	Reviewed	1		1	8	3	
2		6	3	Compiled		1		2		
3		6	3	Tax Returns	1		1			
32		29	43	Other	3		4	4	29	
4/1/07-3/31/08 ALL		4/1/08-3/31/09 ALL	4/1/09-3/31/10 ALL		1	10 (4/1-9/30/09)		75 (10/1/09-3/31/10)		
					0-1MM	1-3MM	3-5MM	5-10MM	10-25MM	25MM & OVE
63		73	85	**NUMBER OF STATEMENTS**	1	5	5	7	16	51
%		%	%	**ASSETS**	%	%	%	%	%	%
5.0		5.0	4.7	Cash & Equivalents					4.6	3.2
22.3		23.4	24.8	Trade Receivables (net)					26.9	23.4
24.1		24.4	23.5	Inventory					22.1	23.4
3.0		2.3	2.5	All Other Current					.5	3.0
54.4		55.0	55.5	Total Current					54.1	52.9
36.6		36.3	35.2	Fixed Assets (net)					34.9	37.8
2.6		3.0	2.4	Intangibles (net)					1.1	3.0
6.3		5.6	6.9	All Other Non-Current					9.8	6.2
100.0		100.0	100.0	Total					100.0	100.0
				LIABILITIES						
10.2		11.3	10.3	Notes Payable-Short Term					12.3	7.0
3.8		4.3	4.0	Cur. Mat.-L.T.D.					4.1	4.7
18.1		17.4	17.6	Trade Payables					15.5	17.6
.1		.2	.4	Income Taxes Payable					.1	.6
6.5		5.1	12.5	All Other Current					10.5	12.9
38.7		38.2	44.9	Total Current					42.4	42.9
23.9		26.0	20.8	Long-Term Debt					19.9	24.4
.8		.9	1.1	Deferred Taxes					1.2	1.5
6.5		7.1	5.3	All Other Non-Current					3.1	6.0
30.1		27.6	27.8	Net Worth					33.4	25.2
100.0		100.0	100.0	Total Liabilties & Net Worth					100.0	100.0
				INCOME DATA						
100.0		100.0	100.0	Net Sales					100.0	100.0
21.3		20.5	21.7	Gross Profit					18.9	18.6
18.4		16.7	15.8	Operating Expenses					13.6	12.5
2.9		3.8	6.0	Operating Profit					5.3	6.0
1.4		1.6	.9	All Other Expenses (net)					1.1	1.0
1.5		2.2	5.1	Profit Before Taxes					4.2	5.0
				RATIOS						
2.4		2.3	2.2	Current					2.0	2.2
1.4		1.4	1.4						1.4	1.3
1.1		1.0	1.0						.8	1.0
1.2		1.2	1.2	Quick					1.4	1.0
.6		.7	.7						.9	.6
.4		.4	.5						.4	.5

									Sales/Receivables								
28	13.0	23	16.0	27	13.8	Sales/Receivables							19	19.2	27	13.6
34	10.7	30	12.3	35	10.3								39	9.5	34	10.6
43	8.5	39	9.4	45	8.2								50	7.3	45	8.2
30	12.2	26	14.3	27	13.6	Cost of Sales/Inventory							24	15.3	30	12.3
45	8.2	39	9.3	43	8.5								45	8.1	45	8.1
68	5.4	58	6.3	65	5.6								59	6.2	65	5.6
20	18.4	20	18.6	21	17.2	Cost of Sales/Payables							14	25.6	22	16.4
30	12.1	26	14.0	29	12.4								26	14.0	31	11.8
47	7.8	38	9.6	40	9.1								38	9.7	41	9.0

6.3		8.0	6.9	Sales/Working Capital				7.4	6.2
13.5		25.5	17.7					18.7	19.2
76.4		265.3	NM					-21.9	183.3
4.8		6.9	8.0	EBIT/Interest				5.8	13.9
(59) 2.0		(66) 2.6	(80) 3.9				(50)	4.4	4.6
.8		1.0	.7					1.5	1.7
2.8		3.5	4.8	Net Profit + Depr., Dep., Amort./Cur. Mat. L/T/D					4.4
(19) 1.5		(21) 1.6	(23) 2.5				(16)		2.1
.4		.7	1.3						1.3
.8		.4	.5	Fixed/Worth				.4	.6
1.2		1.4	1.2					1.1	1.2
3.6		10.9	3.3					2.7	2.4
1.4		.8	.8	Debt/Worth				.6	1.2
2.8		3.1	2.4					1.8	2.5
4.4		19.3	9.3					9.8	9.1
32.8		33.2	48.4	% Profit Before Taxes/Tangible Net Worth				56.5	60.9
(54) 13.0		(59) 18.0	(70) 24.2				(13)	8.9	(43) 31.8
-.2		2.7	4.6					-.3	18.5
10.0		9.9	14.1	% Profit Before Taxes/Total Assets				13.7	15.7
4.5		4.9	7.2					6.3	10.1
-.9		-.2	.5					.6	2.8
12.8		16.5	19.4	Sales/Net Fixed Assets				17.9	10.9
7.6		7.0	6.4					6.2	6.1
3.3		3.8	3.0					3.4	3.0
3.3		3.6	3.2	Sales/Total Assets				3.8	3.1
2.2		2.2	2.2					2.1	2.2
1.4		1.5	1.5					1.4	1.4
1.3		1.1	1.1	% Depr., Dep., Amort./Sales				1.1	1.3
(53) 2.1		(64) 2.1	(75) 2.2				(15)	2.0	(44) 2.3
3.6		3.5	4.4					4.6	3.9
1.5		.7		% Officers', Directors' Owners' Comp/Sales					
(13) 2.5		(15) 1.5							
4.4		3.2							

4586589M		5866224M	7062022M	Net Sales ($)	234M	11303M	20123M	49364M	263068M	6717930M
2588737M		2808766M	3517311M	Total Assets ($)	471M	5502M	9819M	17557M	145219M	3338743M

M = $ thousand   MM = $ million
See Pages 9 through 22 for Explanation of Ratios and Data

Current Data Sorted by Assets   **Comparative Historical Data**

Type of Statement

	0-500M	500M-2MM	2-10MM	10-50MM	50-100MM	100-250MM		ALL	ALL
Unqualified			7	21	2	2		51	45
Reviewed		8	41	21	3			64	67
Compiled	2	7	14	2				23	24
Tax Returns	3	5	6					11	22
Other	3	6	24	30	5	4		78	60

		43 (4/1-9/30/09)		173 (10/1/09-3/31/10)				4/1/05-3/31/06	4/1/06-3/31/07
NUMBER OF STATEMENTS	8	26	92	74	10	6		227	218

	0-500M	500M-2MM	2-10MM	10-50MM	50-100MM	100-250MM		ALL	ALL
	%	%	%	%	%	%	**ASSETS**	%	%
		9.9	8.2	5.1	4.7		Cash & Equivalents	6.0	6.2
		36.6	28.0	24.1	18.8		Trade Receivables (net)	28.7	29.4
		16.5	16.0	15.5	15.5		Inventory	16.5	15.8
		.4	1.5	2.6	1.9		All Other Current	2.1	1.9
		63.5	53.7	47.2	41.0		Total Current	53.2	53.2
		24.4	36.0	40.9	45.9		Fixed Assets (net)	36.6	35.3
		3.4	3.4	3.2	9.2		Intangibles (net)	4.0	4.0
		8.7	6.9	8.7	3.9		All Other Non-Current	6.2	7.4
		100.0	100.0	100.0	100.0		Total	100.0	100.0
							LIABILITIES		
		10.9	8.0	9.3	4.6		Notes Payable-Short Term	10.1	9.4
		4.4	5.0	6.5	2.9		Cur. Mat.-L.T.D.	5.1	5.1
		22.6	18.2	15.5	7.9		Trade Payables	17.1	16.9
		.3	.1	.3	.6		Income Taxes Payable	.2	.2
		4.0	5.3	6.9	7.9		All Other Current	7.5	7.8
		42.3	36.5	38.6	23.9		Total Current	40.1	39.4
		17.2	18.7	21.3	21.1		Long-Term Debt	19.4	18.7
		.4	.8	.9	2.9		Deferred Taxes	1.1	.9
		11.2	6.8	5.5	4.2		All Other Non-Current	5.6	6.8
		29.0	37.2	33.7	47.9		Net Worth	33.8	34.2
		100.0	100.0	100.0	100.0		Total Liabilities & Net Worth	100.0	100.0
							INCOME DATA		
		100.0	100.0	100.0	100.0		Net Sales	100.0	100.0
		28.1	24.5	21.4	21.6		Gross Profit	25.6	26.0
		29.3	22.0	18.4	16.9		Operating Expenses	22.1	21.7
		-1.3	2.5	2.9	4.8		Operating Profit	3.4	4.4
		.6	.5	.4	3.6		All Other Expenses (net)	1.1	.8
		-1.9	2.0	2.5	1.2		Profit Before Taxes	2.3	3.6
							RATIOS		
		2.5	2.5	1.9	2.4			2.2	2.1
		1.4	1.4	1.2	1.7		Current	1.4	1.4
		1.0	1.0	1.0	1.3			1.0	1.0
		1.9	1.7	1.1	1.5			1.5	1.4
		1.1	.9	.7	1.1		Quick	.9	.9
		.7	.6	.5	.7			.6	.6
32		11.3 33	11.1 31	11.7 33	11.1			32 11.4	33 11.1
40		9.1 38	9.5 38	9.6 40	9.2		Sales/Receivables	40 9.2	40 9.1
48		7.5 44	8.3 47	7.7 48	7.6			46 7.9	48 7.7
11		33.2 18	20.1 20	17.8 33	11.0			19 18.9	18 20.3
18		20.6 27	13.3 31	11.8 44	8.3		Cost of Sales/Inventory	30 12.0	29 12.6
38		9.5 39	9.3 43	8.5 59	6.2			44 8.3	41 8.9
13		27.9 16	23.4 16	22.3 9	39.5			17 21.5	16 23.2
35		10.3 28	12.9 29	12.5 17	22.0		Cost of Sales/Payables	27 13.3	27 13.6
48		7.6 45	8.1 46	8.0 36	10.2			43 8.5	46 8.0
		8.6	6.8	9.3	6.8			8.6	9.5
		15.8	18.9	35.3	10.5		Sales/Working Capital	17.6	18.8
		147.7	NM	-111.1	NM			-239.7	991.1
		5.4	6.5	10.2	9.3			9.6	7.4
	(23)	.6 (86)	3.3	4.5	4.3		EBIT/Interest	(216) 3.0	(206) 3.6
		-4.1	1.3	1.6	.7			1.2	1.8
			2.9	4.5				2.9	4.9
		(23)	2.2 (34)	2.3			Net Profit + Depr., Dep., Amort./Cur. Mat. L/T/D	(72) 1.6	(79) 2.4
			1.3	1.3				1.0	1.6
		.3	.6	.7	.8			.6	.6
		.8	1.1	1.3	1.1		Fixed/Worth	1.2	1.1
		NM	1.9	2.9	1.7			3.7	2.7
		.6	.9	1.0	1.0			.8	.8
		1.8	1.9	1.7	1.1		Debt/Worth	2.0	2.1
		NM	4.1	5.8	1.8			6.4	6.0
		8.0	28.3	35.6				36.6	37.7
	(20)	2.1 (84)	12.7 (66)	17.3			% Profit Before Taxes/Tangible Net Worth	(190) 15.6	(193) 21.9
		-27.0	2.6	4.2				3.5	9.6
		3.7	9.9	10.4	13.2			12.1	12.1
		-1.2	4.4	4.8	4.7		% Profit Before Taxes/Total Assets	5.0	6.9
		-12.7	.2	1.5	-.2			.5	2.4
		44.5	14.5	9.8	4.7			15.4	15.0
		17.5	8.4	4.9	3.9		Sales/Net Fixed Assets	6.3	7.0
		7.6	3.9	3.9	3.1			4.0	4.2
		3.6	3.0	2.9	1.9			3.1	3.2
		3.1	2.5	2.1	1.8		Sales/Total Assets	2.4	2.5
		2.6	2.0	1.7	1.1			1.9	1.9
		.5	1.8	1.6	2.6			1.6	1.6
	(22)	1.6 (83)	2.7 (72)	2.3	3.6		% Depr., Dep., Amort./Sales	(208) 2.5	(202) 2.6
		3.1	3.8	3.6	6.5			3.8	3.8
		3.7	1.6	.9				1.8	1.8
	(16)	7.0 (31)	2.4 (17)	1.6			% Officers', Directors' Owners' Comp/Sales	(78) 3.4	(74) 3.0
		10.1	4.7	3.4				5.7	6.0
13393M	110616M	1258141M	3640354M	1108434M	1270139M		Net Sales ($)	7250281M	7066993M
2566M	34652M	506401M	1678569M	669650M	862722M		Total Assets ($)	3577212M	3425928M

M = $ thousand   MM = $ million
See Pages 9 through 22 for Explanation of Ratios and Data

Comparative Historical Data | Current Data Sorted by Sales

4/1/07-3/31/08 ALL	4/1/08-3/31/09 ALL	4/1/09-3/31/10 ALL		0-1MM	1-3MM	3-5MM	5-10MM	10-25MM	25MM & OVER
			Type of Statement						
39	26	32	Unqualified			1	5	26	
64	77	73	Reviewed		2	4	13	31	23
22	22	25	Compiled		3	6	9	4	3
13	15	14	Tax Returns	1	3	2	5	3	
80	87	72	Other	1	4	4	10	18	35
				43 (4/1-9/30/09)			**173 (10/1/09-3/31/10)**		
218	227	216	**NUMBER OF STATEMENTS**	2	12	16	38	61	87
%	%	%	**ASSETS**	%	%	%	%	%	%
6.0	6.5	6.9	Cash & Equivalents		5.8	7.8	9.9	7.9	4.8
28.7	26.1	28.0	Trade Receivables (net)		43.9	31.8	27.9	26.3	25.9
16.6	16.4	15.9	Inventory		17.7	12.0	13.8	16.7	16.3
1.9	1.7	1.8	All Other Current		.8	.2	1.1	1.5	2.6
53.3	50.7	52.5	Total Current		68.2	51.9	52.7	52.4	49.6
33.8	36.3	36.0	Fixed Assets (net)		27.3	31.1	36.0	36.4	38.4
5.7	4.8	4.3	Intangibles (net)		2.0	5.6	3.9	4.0	4.6
7.2	8.2	7.3	All Other Non-Current		2.5	11.5	7.4	7.2	7.4
100.0	100.0	100.0	Total		100.0	100.0	100.0	100.0	100.0
			LIABILITIES						
9.9	11.6	9.0	Notes Payable-Short Term		15.9	12.7	4.5	8.4	9.9
4.5	5.0	5.2	Cur. Mat.-L.T.D.		4.0	2.9	6.5	4.0	6.0
17.7	17.4	18.0	Trade Payables		33.9	20.8	17.8	17.3	15.3
.2	.1	.2	Income Taxes Payable		.7	.1	.1	.1	.4
7.2	5.9	5.8	All Other Current		5.9	3.4	5.4	4.8	7.2
39.5	40.0	38.3	Total Current		60.2	39.8	34.4	34.6	38.8
20.9	21.6	19.9	Long-Term Debt		28.0	13.2	22.6	18.7	19.4
1.1	.9	.9	Deferred Taxes		.0	.6	.6	.7	1.5
6.0	4.8	7.3	All Other Non-Current		9.9	15.2	7.3	5.9	5.1
32.5	32.7	33.6	Net Worth		1.8	31.1	35.0	40.1	35.3
100.0	100.0	100.0	Total Liabilties & Net Worth		100.0	100.0	100.0	100.0	100.0
			INCOME DATA						
100.0	100.0	100.0	Net Sales		100.0	100.0	100.0	100.0	100.0
25.4	22.8	24.0	Gross Profit		40.7	28.0	24.2	24.6	20.6
21.1	20.1	21.8	Operating Expenses		41.9	28.0	23.3	21.7	17.3
4.3	2.7	2.2	Operating Profit		-1.2	.0	.9	2.9	3.3
1.2	.7	.6	All Other Expenses (net)		.7	.8	.0	.6	.8
3.0	2.0	1.6	Profit Before Taxes		-2.0	-.8	.9	2.3	2.5
			RATIOS						
2.2	2.1	2.3	Current		1.9	2.0	2.5	3.0	1.9
1.4	1.3	1.3			1.0	1.2	1.5	1.5	1.3
1.0	1.0	1.0			.8	.9	1.0	1.1	1.0
1.4	1.3	1.5	Quick		1.2	1.5	2.0	2.2	1.2
.9	.8	.9			.8	.9	1.1	.9	.8
.6	.6	.6			.6	.6	.6	.6	.5
33 11.1	27 13.6	32 11.3	Sales/Receivables		32 11.4	38 9.6	31 11.6	33 11.1	32 11.5
39 9.5	35 10.4	39 9.3			46 8.0	40 9.1	39 9.4	38 9.6	39 9.3
45 8.1	42 8.7	47 7.8			51 7.2	47 7.8	48 7.6	43 8.5	48 7.7
17 21.3	17 21.2	18 20.1	Cost of Sales/Inventory		5 79.0	11 32.2	18 20.6	18 20.1	21 17.3
27 13.7	26 14.0	28 12.9			17 21.4	16 23.0	27 13.3	29 12.8	33 11.0
40 9.0	39 9.4	42 8.6			53 6.9	39 9.5	39 9.3	41 8.8	43 8.5
18 20.8	15 24.4	16 22.6	Cost of Sales/Payables		32 11.5	28 12.8	16 22.9	12 30.4	16 22.2
28 13.2	25 14.8	30 12.3			48 7.6	39 9.4	28 12.9	28 13.0	25 14.4
44 8.3	39 9.4	46 8.0			74 4.9	45 8.0	45 8.2	46 8.0	39 9.4
9.1	9.8	7.4	Sales/Working Capital		7.4	11.7	6.8	6.3	7.9
18.9	25.6	20.7			NM	27.4	13.8	18.7	23.0
NM	-428.0	-302.6			-21.8	-52.0	196.8	154.4	-331.3
7.1	6.4	7.6	EBIT/Interest		12.3	2.6	5.3	6.4	10.2
(209) 3.5	(218) 2.7	(206) 2.8			.1	(15) 1.6	(35) 2.4	(56) 3.0	4.9
1.6	1.0	1.0			-3.3	-3.1	-1.0	1.5	1.7
5.5	3.4	4.5	Net Profit + Depr., Dep., Amort./Cur. Mat. L/T/D						3.0	5.3
(80) 2.5	(85) 1.8	(71) 2.3						(17) 2.1	(42) 2.7
1.3	.9	1.3						1.2	1.4
.6	.6	.6	Fixed/Worth		.2	.3	.6	.5	.7
1.2	1.4	1.1			4.1	.9	1.3	1.1	1.2
2.8	3.9	2.8			-2.2	3.6	3.3	1.7	2.5
.9	1.0	.9	Debt/Worth		3.4	.9	.8	.8	1.0
2.1	2.1	1.9			21.5	1.6	2.2	1.9	1.7
7.0	7.0	5.9			-7.4	5.5	11.4	3.3	6.5
34.2	30.0	31.1	% Profit Before Taxes/Tangible Net Worth			4.4	31.7	24.1	38.2
(183) 19.0	(185) 11.5	(185) 12.2			(14) -.2	(32) 5.8	(56) 11.4	(76) 17.8	
6.9	2.0	2.6			-21.9	-.7	2.8	5.8	
12.9	8.4	9.3	% Profit Before Taxes/Total Assets		9.6	2.2	7.3	9.8	10.9
6.5	3.8	3.8			-2.5	.3	2.5	4.2	5.4
2.1	.0	-.5			-15.8	-11.3	-2.5	.9	1.8
17.1	15.5	15.0	Sales/Net Fixed Assets		55.6	41.8	18.0	12.8	11.9
8.0	7.7	7.3			25.3	12.6	7.9	7.0	4.9
4.3	4.4	4.0			6.0	4.3	3.7	4.0	4.0
3.4	3.4	3.1	Sales/Total Assets		5.6	3.3	3.2	2.9	2.9
2.5	2.5	2.4			3.4	3.0	2.5	2.3	2.2
2.0	2.0	1.8			2.3	1.8	1.8	2.0	1.8
1.3	1.4	1.6	% Depr., Dep., Amort./Sales		.2	.5	2.3	1.3	1.7
(200) 2.3	(209) 2.3	(199) 2.5			(11) 1.7	(15) 1.8	(32) 3.6	(57) 2.4	(83) 2.5
3.2	3.4	3.7			2.7	4.4	4.8	3.1	3.5
1.4	1.1	1.6	% Officers', Directors' Owners' Comp/Sales				2.3	1.6	.9
(77) 2.7	(70) 2.9	(69) 3.2					(14) 5.8	(21) 2.4	(17) 1.6
6.5	5.8	6.3					7.4	4.3	3.2
7785557M	8162256M	7401077M	Net Sales ($)	1036M	24199M	66567M	259942M	1011150M	6038183M
4055056M	3789712M	3754560M	Total Assets ($)	301M	7937M	29470M	132701M	477228M	3106923M

M = $ thousand   MM = $ million
See Pages 9 through 22 for Explanation of Ratios and Data

Current Data Sorted by Assets

Comparative Historical Data

0-500M	500M-2MM	2-10MM	10-50MM	50-100MM	100-250MM		4/1/05-3/31/06 ALL	4/1/06-3/31/07 ALL
		1	9	2		**Type of Statement** Unqualified	11	15
1	3	10	4			Reviewed	17	17
	2	1	1			Compiled	4	4
	2	2				Tax Returns	1	3
1	2	5	15	3	2	Other	31	18
	12 (4/1-9/30/09)		54 (10/1/09-3/31/10)					
2	9	19	29	5	2	**NUMBER OF STATEMENTS**	64	57
%	%	%	%	%	%	**ASSETS**	%	%
		5.4	3.0			Cash & Equivalents	5.0	5.8
		19.8	22.7			Trade Receivables (net)	23.3	24.9
		23.1	21.3			Inventory	22.1	19.5
		3.0	2.9			All Other Current	2.2	1.9
		51.3	49.9			Total Current	52.6	52.2
		44.3	44.2			Fixed Assets (net)	38.0	39.0
		2.1	1.8			Intangibles (net)	4.1	3.9
		2.4	4.1			All Other Non-Current	5.3	5.0
		100.0	100.0			Total	100.0	100.0
						LIABILITIES		
		10.2	12.8			Notes Payable-Short Term	12.4	8.9
		7.1	4.8			Cur. Mat.-L.T.D.	6.0	4.9
		12.1	13.8			Trade Payables	15.0	13.9
		.2	.1			Income Taxes Payable	.2	.1
		4.7	7.4			All Other Current	6.1	7.3
		34.2	38.9			Total Current	39.7	35.1
		25.3	22.4			Long-Term Debt	21.3	18.6
		.9	1.3			Deferred Taxes	1.1	.7
		4.9	3.5			All Other Non-Current	3.1	5.3
		34.6	34.0			Net Worth	34.7	40.4
		100.0	100.0			Total Liabilities & Net Worth	100.0	100.0
						INCOME DATA		
		100.0	100.0			Net Sales	100.0	100.0
		25.3	20.7			Gross Profit	22.9	21.5
		20.7	16.0			Operating Expenses	19.1	17.2
		4.6	4.7			Operating Profit	3.8	4.4
		1.0	1.3			All Other Expenses (net)	1.4	1.2
		3.6	3.4			Profit Before Taxes	2.3	3.2
						RATIOS		
		2.8	1.8			Current	2.1	2.3
		1.4	1.3				1.3	1.5
		1.1	1.0				1.1	1.1
		1.4	.9			Quick	1.2	1.4
		1.0	.7				.7	.8
		.6	.4				.4	.5
		28 13.2	31 12.0			Sales/Receivables	30 12.2	33 11.1
		38 9.7	43 8.5				41 9.0	39 9.3
		46 7.9	52 7.0				51 7.1	51 7.2
		28 13.0	34 10.7			Cost of Sales/Inventory	29 12.6	27 13.3
		59 6.2	52 7.1				49 7.4	43 8.5
		80 4.5	65 5.6				75 4.9	65 5.6
		15 23.6	22 16.2			Cost of Sales/Payables	15 24.1	13 28.2
		26 14.3	30 12.2				27 13.4	23 16.0
		46 8.0	41 8.9				47 7.8	35 10.5
		6.0	7.9			Sales/Working Capital	8.5	7.2
		19.1	20.0				17.6	12.7
		29.9	-534.6				407.3	73.9
		5.3	7.5			EBIT/Interest	5.4	6.0
		(18) 2.6	3.5				(60) 2.6	(52) 3.1
		1.3	2.2				.5	1.6
			5.7			Net Profit + Depr., Dep., Amort./Cur. Mat. L/T/D	3.3	3.7
			(16) 2.9				(24) 1.6	(18) 1.9
			1.4				1.0	1.5
		.8	.8			Fixed/Worth	.5	.7
		1.4	1.3				1.3	1.2
		2.7	2.9				2.3	2.0
		.9	.8			Debt/Worth	1.1	.9
		2.6	1.9				2.0	1.5
		5.0	4.9				3.8	5.0
		43.2	32.8			% Profit Before Taxes/Tangible Net Worth	37.3	33.9
		(17) 19.4	(25) 18.3				(57) 13.3	(53) 18.6
		.6	14.2				2.2	6.0
		11.3	10.6			% Profit Before Taxes/Total Assets	13.0	12.3
		8.5	5.6				4.6	6.0
		1.1	3.7				-1.4	2.1
		6.6	6.4			Sales/Net Fixed Assets	9.7	9.4
		4.4	4.0				5.7	4.9
		3.9	3.1				3.3	3.2
		2.4	2.4			Sales/Total Assets	2.6	2.4
		2.0	1.9				2.0	2.1
		1.6	1.5				1.5	1.5
		2.7	1.9			% Depr., Dep., Amort./Sales	1.8	2.1
		(18) 3.3	(25) 3.4				(58) 3.0	(46) 3.6
		4.9	5.3				4.4	4.9
						% Officers', Directors' Owners' Comp/Sales	1.9	1.8
							(14) 2.3	(16) 2.5
							4.2	3.4
170M	27993M	235361M	1275843M	581600M	355137M	Net Sales ($)	2155007M	1625428M
95M	9581M	121005M	675541M	323706M	355747M	Total Assets ($)	1196636M	905079M

M = $ thousand   MM = $ million
See Pages 9 through 22 for Explanation of Ratios and Data

Comparative Historical Data | Current Data Sorted by Sales

Type of Statement	14	14	12					1	11
Unqualified	14	14	12					1	11
Reviewed	11	14	18	1	2		4	8	3
Compiled	7	4	4	1	1		1		1
Tax Returns	3	4	4		1	1	1		
Other	26	27	28	1		2	1	5	19
	4/1/07-3/31/08 ALL	4/1/08-3/31/09 ALL	4/1/09-3/31/10 ALL	12 (4/1-9/30/09)			54 (10/1/09-3/31/10)		
				0-1MM	1-3MM	3-5MM	5-10MM	10-25MM	25MM & OVER
NUMBER OF STATEMENTS	61	63	66	3	4	3	8	14	34
	%	%	%	%	%	%	%	%	%
ASSETS									
Cash & Equivalents	6.3	5.1	4.9					4.6	3.8
Trade Receivables (net)	23.8	21.0	21.4					18.5	21.3
Inventory	21.7	21.4	21.9					24.3	20.3
All Other Current	1.1	1.1	2.9					3.5	3.5
Total Current	53.0	48.5	51.1					50.9	49.0
Fixed Assets (net)	40.2	42.1	41.1					44.3	41.9
Intangibles (net)	3.4	4.3	2.9					2.0	4.3
All Other Non-Current	3.4	5.1	4.9					2.8	4.7
Total	100.0	100.0	100.0					100.0	100.0
LIABILITIES									
Notes Payable-Short Term	8.0	9.3	10.5					11.0	11.4
Cur. Mat.-L.T.D.	5.8	5.6	5.5					5.2	4.6
Trade Payables	12.9	11.9	13.1					14.6	13.5
Income Taxes Payable	.0	.0	.1					.2	.1
All Other Current	6.2	5.4	5.8					8.1	6.2
Total Current	32.8	32.1	35.1					39.1	36.0
Long-Term Debt	22.5	24.6	25.6					20.3	19.8
Deferred Taxes	.8	.7	.8					.8	1.1
All Other Non-Current	5.6	3.6	5.4					6.8	3.6
Net Worth	38.1	38.9	33.0					33.0	39.5
Total Liabilities & Net Worth	100.0	100.0	100.0					100.0	100.0
INCOME DATA									
Net Sales	100.0	100.0	100.0					100.0	100.0
Gross Profit	22.2	23.2	24.1					21.7	20.6
Operating Expenses	18.0	18.3	20.0					16.8	16.2
Operating Profit	4.2	4.9	4.1					5.0	4.4
All Other Expenses (net)	1.8	1.5	1.2					1.1	1.2
Profit Before Taxes	2.4	3.4	2.9					3.8	3.2
RATIOS									
Current	2.4	3.0	2.4					2.3	1.9
	1.6	1.5	1.4					1.3	1.3
	1.1	1.1	1.1					1.1	1.0
Quick	1.3	1.4	1.2					1.2	.9
	.8	.8	.7					.7	.7
	.5	.5	.5					.4	.4
Sales/Receivables	29 12.6	28 12.8	29 12.5					25 14.5	29 12.5
	36 10.1	35 10.3	38 9.7					33 11.0	40 9.1
	46 8.0	43 8.5	47 7.8					44 8.3	52 7.0
Cost of Sales/Inventory	31 11.7	28 13.0	38 9.7					41 8.8	36 10.2
	49 7.5	54 6.7	52 7.0					60 6.1	51 7.2
	71 5.2	70 5.2	68 5.3					78 4.7	60 6.1
Cost of Sales/Payables	14 25.7	15 24.6	16 23.3					16 23.4	22 16.9
	23 15.8	24 14.9	29 12.6					30 12.0	30 12.1
	35 10.3	33 11.0	44 8.3					47 7.8	42 8.6
Sales/Working Capital	5.8	5.1	6.2					6.2	6.7
	17.3	12.9	16.4					24.5	18.5
	65.8	65.4	39.7					41.5	NM
EBIT/Interest	6.9	8.5	6.7					6.6	12.0
	(57) 2.8	(60) 2.7	(64) 3.2					4.3	3.4
	1.4	.9	1.3					1.0	1.9
Net Profit + Depr., Dep., Amort./Cur. Mat. L/T/D	4.4	5.9	3.8						3.8
	(27) 2.2	(26) 2.1	(27) 2.4					(20)	2.8
	1.1	.9	1.2						1.3
Fixed/Worth	.7	.7	.7					.8	.6
	1.2	1.3	1.3					1.2	1.1
	2.6	3.9	2.8					2.3	2.3
Debt/Worth	.9	.7	.8					.9	.8
	1.9	2.0	2.0					2.3	1.8
	4.8	6.3	5.0					5.1	3.8
% Profit Before Taxes/Tangible Net Worth	37.4	28.5	34.4					44.9	31.0
	(55) 17.1	(56) 15.7	(57) 18.3					(12) 28.1	(30) 18.3
	6.0	-1.4	1.1					-10.4	5.3
% Profit Before Taxes/Total Assets	11.4	12.6	11.4					11.5	11.0
	4.8	5.6	6.1					9.7	5.8
	1.6	-.3	2.0					-.1	2.7
Sales/Net Fixed Assets	8.1	7.5	7.3					6.6	6.7
	5.0	4.9	4.5					4.2	4.4
	3.2	3.2	3.2					2.8	3.2
Sales/Total Assets	2.6	2.5	2.5					2.4	2.4
	2.0	1.9	1.9					2.0	1.9
	1.6	1.5	1.6					1.7	1.6
% Depr., Dep., Amort./Sales	2.3	1.9	2.2					2.0	2.3
	(55) 3.5	(58) 3.3	(60) 3.3					(13) 3.2	(29) 3.4
	5.4	4.7	4.5					4.4	5.3
% Officers', Directors' Owners' Comp/Sales	.9	.8	.8						
	(13) 2.3	(13) 1.3	(11) 3.5						
	3.2	2.4	6.3						
Net Sales ($)	1913250M	2022448M	2476104M	617M	8514M	12364M	56118M	224225M	2174266M
Total Assets ($)	1014068M	1113274M	1485675M	598M	3595M	5167M	32805M	115170M	1328340M

M = $ thousand   MM = $ million
See Pages 9 through 22 for Explanation of Ratios and Data

Current Data Sorted by Assets   **Comparative Historical Data**

0-500M	500M-2MM	2-10MM	10-50MM	50-100MM	100-250MM	Type of Statement	4/1/05-3/31/06 ALL	4/1/06-3/31/07 ALL
						Unqualified	13	19
		5				Reviewed	19	19
	2	1	3			Compiled	2	3
		2	5			Tax Returns	2	3
	2	9	6	1		Other	21	12
	6 (4/1-9/30/09)		30 (10/1/09-3/31/10)			NUMBER OF STATEMENTS	57	56
	4	17	14	1				
%	%	%	%	%	%	**ASSETS**	%	%
D		5.0	8.9		D	Cash & Equivalents	5.4	6.4
A		27.3	21.7		A	Trade Receivables (net)	25.8	25.7
T		22.7	14.8		T	Inventory	18.1	18.4
A		2.5	5.6		A	All Other Current	1.4	1.3
		57.5	50.9			Total Current	50.8	51.8
N		36.6	42.6		N	Fixed Assets (net)	39.0	36.9
O		2.1	1.9		O	Intangibles (net)	4.1	4.9
T		3.7	4.6		T	All Other Non-Current	6.2	6.3
		100.0	100.0			Total	100.0	100.0
A					A	**LIABILITIES**		
V		11.0	6.3		V	Notes Payable-Short Term	8.6	7.0
A		6.5	3.6		A	Cur. Mat.-L.T.D.	5.6	8.0
I		12.2	10.2		I	Trade Payables	15.1	14.8
L		.1	.0		L	Income Taxes Payable	.3	.2
A		7.2	4.3		A	All Other Current	5.8	6.8
B		37.1	24.5		B	Total Current	35.3	36.9
L		25.0	24.4		L	Long-Term Debt	24.6	21.1
E		.0	1.2		E	Deferred Taxes	.8	1.1
		2.0	2.5			All Other Non-Current	4.6	5.4
		35.9	47.4			Net Worth	34.7	35.5
		100.0	100.0			Total Liabilities & Net Worth	100.0	100.0
						INCOME DATA		
		100.0	100.0			Net Sales	100.0	100.0
		26.3	20.6			Gross Profit	24.4	23.4
		23.1	15.7			Operating Expenses	21.0	17.9
		3.2	4.8			Operating Profit	3.4	5.5
		1.0	1.2			All Other Expenses (net)	1.0	1.6
		2.2	3.6			Profit Before Taxes	2.4	3.8
						RATIOS		
		2.2	3.5				2.2	2.6
		1.5	2.2			Current	1.4	1.3
		1.1	1.5				1.0	1.0
		1.6	2.1				1.4	1.7
		.7	1.5			Quick	.8	.8
		.5	.7				.6	.5
		32 11.2	31 11.7				32 11.3	30 12.4
		41 8.9	36 10.3			Sales/Receivables	44 8.3	38 9.6
		51 7.2	46 7.9				49 7.4	48 7.6
		30 12.4	20 18.3				20 18.0	19 18.9
		46 8.0	24 15.0			Cost of Sales/Inventory	34 10.7	32 11.5
		66 5.6	38 9.7				52 7.1	53 6.9
		14 26.4	13 28.8				17 21.3	15 24.3
		27 13.4	22 16.5			Cost of Sales/Payables	27 13.4	25 14.9
		30 12.0	29 12.8				40 9.2	40 9.0
		5.1	5.4				7.2	6.9
		17.2	8.2			Sales/Working Capital	15.8	21.2
		44.3	13.0				696.1	NM
		7.7	8.8				5.1	6.8
	(16)	5.1	(13) 4.3			EBIT/Interest	(54) 3.0	(53) 3.1
		.8	2.0				1.7	1.9
							2.9	4.6
						Net Profit + Depr., Dep., Amort./Cur. Mat. L/T/D	(18) 1.5	(20) 1.7
							1.1	1.2
		.4	.6				.8	.6
		.9	1.2			Fixed/Worth	1.4	1.3
		1.4	1.7				3.0	3.5
		1.1	.8				1.2	.9
		1.7	1.5			Debt/Worth	2.5	2.0
		3.5	2.1				5.4	6.3
		34.6	29.5			% Profit Before Taxes/Tangible Net Worth	45.0	44.0
	(15)	16.5	17.2				(51) 18.1	(49) 17.8
		3.7	6.1				4.2	8.7
		12.6	14.2			% Profit Before Taxes/Total Assets	11.3	13.1
		4.6	8.8				4.9	5.9
		-.4	2.2				1.3	2.5
		12.6	7.7				10.6	13.1
		7.4	4.4			Sales/Net Fixed Assets	5.4	6.1
		4.7	3.7				3.6	3.8
		2.9	2.2				2.7	3.0
		2.3	2.0			Sales/Total Assets	2.1	2.4
		2.0	1.9				1.7	1.6
		1.2	2.2				2.1	1.8
	(16)	3.2	3.1			% Depr., Dep., Amort./Sales	(51) 3.3	(51) 2.9
		4.0	4.3				4.8	4.3
							1.3	1.5
						% Officers', Directors' Owners' Comp/Sales	(22) 2.7	(19) 2.5
							5.6	5.7
	23599M	196951M	673538M	210639M		Net Sales ($)	1798041M	1784381M
	4793M	85660M	341398M	96191M		Total Assets ($)	918778M	897916M

© RMA 2010

M = $ thousand   MM = $ million
See Pages 9 through 22 for Explanation of Ratios and Data

Comparative Historical Data   ## Current Data Sorted by Sales

Middle size-range columns (0-1MM, 1-3MM, 3-5MM, 5-10MM, 10-25MM) are marked "DATA NOT AVAILABLE" in the source for the Assets/Liabilities/Income/Ratio sections; where values exist they are shown.

4/1/07-3/31/08 ALL	4/1/08-3/31/09 ALL	4/1/09-3/31/10 ALL	Item	0-1MM	1-3MM 6 (4/1-9/30/09)	3-5MM	5-10MM 30 (10/1/09-3/31/10)	10-25MM	25MM & OVER
			Type of Statement						
14	10	3	Unqualified						3
23	16	10	Reviewed				1	4	5
1	3	3	Compiled		1		2		
1	2	2	Tax Returns		1		1		
15	16	18	Other	1			5	5	7
54	47	36	**NUMBER OF STATEMENTS**	1	2		9	9	15
%	%	%	**ASSETS**	%	%	%	%	%	%
5.7	5.6	6.8	Cash & Equivalents						8.3
24.0	26.5	26.8	Trade Receivables (net)						22.5
19.2	20.3	20.0	Inventory						14.5
1.4	1.9	3.5	All Other Current						5.3
50.3	54.4	57.1	Total Current						50.6
39.5	36.2	37.4	Fixed Assets (net)						43.1
4.0	4.1	1.7	Intangibles (net)						1.8
6.3	5.3	3.8	All Other Non-Current						4.5
100.0	100.0	100.0	Total						100.0
			LIABILITIES						
7.9	8.8	8.5	Notes Payable-Short Term						6.3
5.6	6.6	5.0	Cur. Mat.-L.T.D.						3.5
12.9	17.1	13.5	Trade Payables						10.0
.7	.0	.1	Income Taxes Payable						.1
5.4	8.7	5.9	All Other Current						4.8
32.5	41.2	33.1	Total Current						24.7
22.5	20.6	23.1	Long-Term Debt						23.0
1.2	1.1	.7	Deferred Taxes						1.8
2.5	5.2	2.0	All Other Non-Current						2.5
41.3	31.8	41.0	Net Worth						48.0
100.0	100.0	100.0	Total Liabilities & Net Worth						100.0
			INCOME DATA						
100.0	100.0	100.0	Net Sales						100.0
24.1	20.6	23.7	Gross Profit						20.8
17.2	17.6	19.9	Operating Expenses						16.1
6.9	3.0	3.8	Operating Profit						4.7
1.5	1.7	1.1	All Other Expenses (net)						1.2
5.4	1.3	2.7	Profit Before Taxes						3.5
			RATIOS						
2.4	2.4	2.7	Current						3.4
1.6	1.6	1.7							2.0
1.1	.9	1.3							1.6
1.5	1.5	1.8	Quick						2.0
.9	.9	1.1							1.4
.5	.5	.6							.8
28 12.9	28 13.1	31 11.6	Sales/Receivables						31 11.6
37 9.9	36 10.1	39 9.4							36 10.1
47 7.8	47 7.8	47 7.8							55 6.7
22 16.7	22 16.3	22 16.4	Cost of Sales/Inventory						20 17.9
31 11.7	31 11.8	34 10.8							24 15.3
57 6.4	48 7.7	52 7.1							35 10.3
14 25.5	14 26.6	14 26.1	Cost of Sales/Payables						13 28.2
23 15.9	25 14.3	22 16.4							21 17.2
40 9.2	39 9.3	30 12.1							28 12.9
6.7	6.9	5.6	Sales/Working Capital						5.7
14.0	15.3	11.9							8.6
43.6	-85.4	28.9							12.8
11.3	8.3	7.5	EBIT/Interest						8.5
(52) 4.2	(46) 3.9	(33) 4.2						(14)	5.3
1.8	1.0	1.0							2.3
6.1	2.8	4.0	Net Profit + Depr., Dep., Amort./Cur. Mat. L/T/D						
(27) 1.9	(17) 1.5	(12) 2.9							
.9	.3	1.4							
.6	.7	.5	Fixed/Worth						.6
1.1	1.3	1.0							1.2
2.0	1.7	1.6							1.7
.7	.8	.8	Debt/Worth						.8
1.7	2.2	1.6							1.5
3.3	4.0	2.3							2.1
39.4	39.7	34.2	% Profit Before Taxes/Tangible Net Worth						27.7
(49) 23.8	(43) 14.8	(33) 15.9							15.9
7.6	6.6	4.5							6.4
15.5	12.4	12.9	% Profit Before Taxes/Total Assets						13.2
7.4	6.0	5.8							8.4
2.2	-1.5	1.0							2.7
8.8	13.6	11.6	Sales/Net Fixed Assets						7.4
5.4	6.1	5.9							4.4
3.6	3.8	4.0							3.8
2.8	3.0	2.8	Sales/Total Assets						2.2
2.1	2.5	2.2							2.0
1.7	1.8	2.0							1.9
1.8	1.5	1.4	% Depr., Dep., Amort./Sales						2.2
(52) 2.7	(42) 2.8	(33) 2.5						(14)	3.1
3.8	3.7	4.0							4.3
1.0	1.6	.8	% Officers', Directors' Owners' Comp/Sales						
(19) 2.1	(17) 2.4	(17) 1.9							
2.7	6.5	3.0							
1992769M	1678317M	1104727M	Net Sales ($)		2154M	8588M	70058M	139750M	884177M
983798M	812598M	528042M	Total Assets ($)		925M	3778M	33018M	52732M	437589M

MANUFACTURING—Coated and Laminated Packaging Paper Manufacturing NAICS 322221

| Current Data Sorted by Assets | | | | | | | Comparative Historical Data | |

0-500M	500M-2MM	2-10MM	10-50MM	50-100MM	100-250MM	Type of Statement	4/1/05-3/31/06 ALL	4/1/06-3/31/07 ALL
	1	4	12	4	4	Unqualified	23	24
	3	8	6			Reviewed	22	19
1	1	7	1			Compiled	11	13
1	5	3				Tax Returns	5	8
1	2	9	15	3	5	Other	37	37
	16 (4/1-9/30/09)		80 (10/1/09-3/31/10)					
3	12	31	34	7	9	NUMBER OF STATEMENTS	98	101
%	%	%	%	%	%	ASSETS	%	%
	5.9	5.9	8.1			Cash & Equivalents	5.7	5.7
	20.1	27.1	19.8			Trade Receivables (net)	29.9	26.0
	29.1	23.8	20.5			Inventory	26.4	25.0
	9.1	1.1	1.6			All Other Current	2.3	1.9
	64.3	57.8	50.0			Total Current	64.3	58.6
	25.3	31.6	40.5			Fixed Assets (net)	27.0	32.7
	6.1	5.9	5.4			Intangibles (net)	4.2	3.7
	4.3	4.7	4.0			All Other Non-Current	4.4	5.1
	100.0	100.0	100.0			Total	100.0	100.0
						LIABILITIES		
	19.0	8.8	11.8			Notes Payable-Short Term	14.7	11.5
	3.4	4.3	4.7			Cur. Mat.-L.T.D.	4.5	3.4
	13.7	15.2	12.1			Trade Payables	19.5	18.7
	.0	.3	.2			Income Taxes Payable	.2	.3
	2.9	4.0	7.3			All Other Current	6.1	7.0
	39.0	32.5	36.2			Total Current	45.1	41.0
	31.6	19.0	19.5			Long-Term Debt	14.8	18.0
	.6	.8	.8			Deferred Taxes	.8	.7
	8.2	6.2	6.8			All Other Non-Current	6.1	6.3
	20.7	41.4	36.7			Net Worth	33.2	34.0
	100.0	100.0	100.0			Total Liabilties & Net Worth	100.0	100.0
						INCOME DATA		
	100.0	100.0	100.0			Net Sales	100.0	100.0
	36.1	26.0	23.6			Gross Profit	23.3	24.4
	33.1	20.4	17.6			Operating Expenses	18.7	19.0
	3.0	5.7	5.9			Operating Profit	4.6	5.4
	3.6	1.8	1.2			All Other Expenses (net)	1.0	1.3
	-.7	3.8	4.7			Profit Before Taxes	3.6	4.1
						RATIOS		
	6.3	2.3	2.8				2.4	2.4
	1.9	1.6	1.4			Current	1.5	1.6
	.9	1.2	1.0				1.0	1.1
	3.1	1.5	1.7				1.4	1.2
	.5	.8	.7			Quick	.8	.8
	.3	.6	.5				.5	.6
1 327.7		32 11.5	29 12.5				33 11.0	32 11.5
28 13.0		39 9.3	38 9.7			Sales/Receivables	40 9.2	38 9.5
44 8.3		45 8.1	46 7.9				49 7.5	47 7.8
22 16.9		29 12.7	37 9.9				31 11.9	33 11.2
35 10.6		49 7.4	47 7.7			Cost of Sales/Inventory	46 7.9	47 7.7
80 4.5		74 4.9	67 5.4				65 5.6	66 5.5
0 UND		17 21.7	16 22.8				20 18.5	18 19.9
19 18.9		27 13.3	24 15.0			Cost of Sales/Payables	31 11.8	32 11.4
37 9.8		39 9.4	47 7.7				49 7.5	47 7.8
		6.0	7.8	4.8			6.2	6.5
		19.2	10.3	11.5		Sales/Working Capital	13.7	10.9
		NM	21.0	-161.3			122.6	70.3
		25.9	6.4	11.9			11.0	7.4
	(10) 3.1	(28) 3.0	(33) 5.9			EBIT/Interest	(90) 4.3	(93) 3.4
		-1.1	1.6	1.1			1.7	1.4
			7.8				3.5	5.9
			(13) 2.4			Net Profit + Depr., Dep., Amort./Cur. Mat. L/T/D	(28) 2.6	(29) 3.4
			.8				1.0	1.5
		.2	.3	.8			.3	.5
		1.1	.7	1.2		Fixed/Worth	.8	.8
		-3.1	2.0	2.6			2.5	2.6
		.8	.9	.8			.7	.8
		7.9	1.4	1.8		Debt/Worth	1.9	2.0
		-6.4	3.1	3.9			6.3	5.2
			42.8	35.6			42.0	47.1
		(29) 15.6	(29) 20.7			% Profit Before Taxes/Tangible Net Worth	(82) 24.1	(87) 20.3
			4.1	1.2			11.2	7.5
		21.0	13.8	16.1			15.7	13.3
		10.8	6.3	6.7		% Profit Before Taxes/Total Assets	7.1	7.9
		-6.8	1.7	.2			2.0	1.7
		35.6	22.7	7.4			20.3	14.1
		12.7	9.3	4.6		Sales/Net Fixed Assets	10.2	7.4
		10.1	3.5	2.7			5.3	4.4
		4.0	3.6	2.4			3.2	3.0
		2.7	2.7	1.7		Sales/Total Assets	2.4	2.3
		1.9	1.8	1.4			1.8	1.7
			1.0	2.8			1.0	1.5
		(26) 2.5	(30) 4.2			% Depr., Dep., Amort./Sales	(83) 1.9	(89) 2.3
			3.4	5.3			3.2	3.6
			1.3				2.1	2.7
		(10) 3.4				% Officers', Directors' Owners' Comp/Sales	(23) 2.9	(27) 4.2
							5.5	6.9
3990M	52361M	383450M	1486180M	912258M	2049505M	Net Sales ($)	4885389M	4283533M
730M	15650M	157644M	840345M	599144M	1427476M	Total Assets ($)	2389107M	2144179M

M = $ thousand   MM = $ million
See Pages 9 through 22 for Explanation of Ratios and Data

Comparative Historical Data | | | Current Data Sorted by Sales

4/1/07-3/31/08 ALL	4/1/08-3/31/09 ALL	4/1/09-3/31/10 ALL	Type of Statement	0-1MM	1-3MM	3-5MM	5-10MM	10-25MM	25MM & OVER
19	24	25	Unqualified		1	1		5	18
13	14	17	Reviewed		1	1	2	9	4
5	6	10	Compiled		1	1	1	6	1
10	6	9	Tax Returns	1	3	1	1	3	
38	54	35	Other	1	1		8	6	19
					16 (4/1-9/30/09)		**80 (10/1/09-3/31/10)**		
85	104	96	**NUMBER OF STATEMENTS**	2	7	4	12	29	42
%	%	%	**ASSETS**	%	%	%	%	%	%
5.9	6.2	7.1	Cash & Equivalents				7.5	7.2	6.6
27.2	24.0	21.8	Trade Receivables (net)				25.8	25.1	18.2
23.5	23.8	22.4	Inventory				23.7	24.0	20.5
1.3	2.0	2.5	All Other Current				1.1	4.8	1.6
57.9	56.0	53.9	Total Current				58.2	61.1	46.9
34.5	32.8	32.6	Fixed Assets (net)				33.3	29.5	36.4
4.1	6.8	8.6	Intangibles (net)				5.3	5.1	11.5
3.6	4.4	5.0	All Other Non-Current				3.2	4.3	5.2
100.0	100.0	100.0	Total				100.0	100.0	100.0
			LIABILITIES						
13.2	11.6	10.6	Notes Payable-Short Term				10.7	12.1	8.1
5.0	4.3	4.6	Cur. Mat.-L.T.D.				5.2	3.8	4.7
18.9	15.7	13.1	Trade Payables				15.6	14.5	11.0
.2	.2	.2	Income Taxes Payable				.5	.1	.3
6.1	5.2	5.5	All Other Current				4.5	4.6	7.4
43.4	37.0	34.0	Total Current				36.4	35.1	31.6
22.9	19.7	21.1	Long-Term Debt				21.4	16.0	21.7
.5	.5	.8	Deferred Taxes				.8	.5	1.1
6.3	5.7	7.0	All Other Non-Current				3.9	5.6	8.6
27.0	37.0	37.0	Net Worth				37.5	42.8	37.1
100.0	100.0	100.0	Total Liabilities & Net Worth				100.0	100.0	100.0
			INCOME DATA						
100.0	100.0	100.0	Net Sales				100.0	100.0	100.0
25.3	24.9	25.4	Gross Profit				29.5	25.6	21.8
20.7	20.2	20.1	Operating Expenses				20.9	21.8	15.8
4.6	4.8	5.3	Operating Profit				8.6	3.8	6.0
1.5	1.3	1.9	All Other Expenses (net)				3.0	.9	1.8
3.0	3.5	3.4	Profit Before Taxes				5.6	2.9	4.2
			RATIOS						
2.2	2.5	3.1	Current				2.2	3.2	3.7
1.4	1.6	1.6					1.4	1.8	1.4
1.0	1.1	1.1					1.2	1.3	1.0
1.2	1.5	1.7	Quick				1.4	1.6	1.7
.7	.8	.8					.8	.8	.7
.5	.5	.5					.5	.6	.4
31 11.7	27 13.4	28 13.2	Sales/Receivables				26 13.8	28 12.8	29 12.8
40 9.0	36 10.0	39 9.3					41 8.9	39 9.3	37 9.9
47 7.7	46 8.0	46 8.0					51 7.2	44 8.3	46 7.9
33 10.9	31 11.9	33 11.0	Cost of Sales/Inventory				21 17.7	36 10.1	39 9.4
48 7.6	50 7.3	49 7.4					40 9.1	48 7.6	51 7.1
67 5.4	67 5.4	72 5.0					88 4.2	78 4.7	69 5.3
21 17.6	14 25.9	16 23.4	Cost of Sales/Payables				21 17.2	12 29.5	17 21.3
29 12.4	24 14.9	26 14.0					33 11.1	26 14.2	26 14.0
45 8.2	43 8.5	39 9.4					41 8.9	38 9.5	37 9.9
7.0	6.4	6.7	Sales/Working Capital				7.6	6.8	5.2
15.0	12.0	10.9					12.3	10.3	12.4
999.8	88.7	33.7					36.0	18.4	-794.7
6.3	8.2	10.5	EBIT/Interest				9.0	9.7	10.5
(82) 3.6	(95) 3.7	(86) 3.8			(10) 4.6			(27) 3.5	(37) 4.7
1.6	1.4	1.5					.3	1.6	1.8
5.6	5.8	4.3	Net Profit + Depr., Dep., Amort./Cur. Mat. L/T/D						4.5
(26) 3.7	(25) 2.4	(19) 2.4						(13) 2.5	
1.8	1.9	.8							.8
.6	.5	.4	Fixed/Worth				.3	.3	.8
1.1	1.0	1.1					1.2	.6	1.6
2.9	2.5	3.2					2.5	1.2	NM
1.3	.9	.8	Debt/Worth				.9	.7	.8
2.4	2.0	2.2					1.8	1.4	2.5
6.9	6.0	9.0					3.1	3.4	NM
51.3	40.1	43.4	% Profit Before Taxes/Tangible Net Worth				56.1	37.4	45.1
(72) 25.7	(87) 16.6	(77) 20.7			(11) 30.9			(26) 15.1	(32) 25.2
11.7	6.1	3.4					6.1	1.9	1.9
13.5	14.7	14.9	% Profit Before Taxes/Total Assets				18.6	14.0	16.1
7.7	7.2	6.7					8.5	6.5	7.5
3.0	1.5	1.4					-.4	1.4	1.0
14.4	13.3	12.7	Sales/Net Fixed Assets				26.3	28.0	7.8
7.0	7.6	6.6					10.7	9.3	4.8
4.0	3.8	3.4					3.7	5.5	3.2
3.2	3.1	3.0	Sales/Total Assets				3.3	3.9	2.4
2.4	2.2	1.9					2.6	2.5	1.6
1.7	1.6	1.4					1.8	1.6	1.3
1.5	1.6	1.6	% Depr., Dep., Amort./Sales				.9	1.4	2.0
(75) 2.6	(93) 2.7	(79) 2.9			(11) 1.9			(23) 2.6	(38) 3.2
3.8	3.4	4.2					4.2	4.1	4.3
2.7	1.0	1.2	% Officers', Directors' Owners' Comp/Sales					1.2	
(25) 4.0	(27) 2.3	(23) 3.5						(12) 4.2	
9.7	4.1	7.0						6.8	
4068703M	6506244M	4887744M	Net Sales ($)	1141M	14723M	17148M	89366M	461410M	4303956M
2116773M	3378912M	3040989M	Total Assets ($)	805M	9251M	8634M	84067M	210237M	2727995M

M = $ thousand   MM = $ million
See Pages 9 through 22 for Explanation of Ratios and Data

Current Data Sorted by Assets   **Comparative Historical Data**

	0-500M	500M-2MM	2-10MM	10-50MM	50-100MM	100-250MM		4/1/05-3/31/06 ALL	4/1/06-3/31/07 ALL
Type of Statement									
Unqualified	1	1	1	10	2	6		19	19
Reviewed			18	3				17	24
Compiled		3	6					11	9
Tax Returns	1	4	1					7	4
Other		3	8	16	1	3		29	28
		18 (4/1-9/30/09)		70 (10/1/09-3/31/10)					
NUMBER OF STATEMENTS	2	11	34	29	3	9		83	84
	%	%	%	%	%	%		%	%
ASSETS									
Cash & Equivalents		5.3	6.1	5.7				5.2	6.0
Trade Receivables (net)		28.2	27.8	24.0				29.3	26.8
Inventory		17.1	25.7	25.7				25.7	26.2
All Other Current		4.0	1.7	4.1				1.5	1.9
Total Current		54.5	61.3	59.5				61.7	60.9
Fixed Assets (net)		22.6	30.0	31.0				28.6	29.4
Intangibles (net)		17.1	5.5	4.3				3.4	4.5
All Other Non-Current		5.8	3.2	5.2				6.4	5.2
Total		100.0	100.0	100.0				100.0	100.0
LIABILITIES									
Notes Payable-Short Term		14.5	12.6	11.7				14.1	12.2
Cur. Mat.-L.T.D.		4.4	3.8	4.4				4.6	3.5
Trade Payables		19.4	16.7	14.6				16.0	14.9
Income Taxes Payable		.1	.2	.1				.2	.3
All Other Current		7.3	8.8	11.2				7.2	10.6
Total Current		45.8	42.0	41.9				42.1	41.5
Long-Term Debt		12.7	12.8	15.2				18.0	15.7
Deferred Taxes		.0	.5	.8				.7	.6
All Other Non-Current		7.2	8.2	5.2				8.3	9.2
Net Worth		34.3	36.4	37.0				30.9	33.0
Total Liabilities & Net Worth		100.0	100.0	100.0				100.0	100.0
INCOME DATA									
Net Sales		100.0	100.0	100.0				100.0	100.0
Gross Profit		40.3	27.2	21.2				28.1	28.2
Operating Expenses		43.9	25.0	19.0				23.0	24.5
Operating Profit		-3.6	2.2	2.2				5.1	3.7
All Other Expenses (net)		.8	1.0	.8				1.9	1.5
Profit Before Taxes		-4.5	1.2	1.4				3.2	2.2
RATIOS									
Current		2.1	2.0	3.1				2.5	2.4
		1.5	1.4	1.7				1.4	1.5
		.9	1.0	1.0				1.2	1.1
Quick		1.6	1.3	1.4				1.2	1.4
		.8	.8	.7				.8	.8
		.4	.4	.4				.6	.5
Sales/Receivables		26 14.0	36 10.2	33 11.0				36 10.1	32 11.4
		43 8.5	41 8.9	42 8.6				43 8.6	40 9.2
		51 7.2	48 7.5	50 7.3				54 6.7	49 7.5
Cost of Sales/Inventory		23 15.7	31 11.9	41 9.0				29 12.6	30 12.1
		36 10.3	50 7.2	50 7.3				48 7.7	52 7.1
		43 8.6	76 4.8	72 5.1				77 4.8	82 4.5
Cost of Sales/Payables		31 11.7	20 17.9	16 22.8				15 24.6	14 26.4
		45 8.1	35 10.4	22 16.5				33 11.0	32 11.3
		85 4.3	55 6.6	55 6.6				52 7.1	49 7.5
Sales/Working Capital		9.7	6.1	5.3				7.0	5.8
		20.9	13.6	7.9				12.9	11.2
		-71.5	NM	NM				38.6	38.3
EBIT/Interest		7.1	6.0	8.3				6.1	7.4
		.6	(32) 1.9	(28) 1.9				(76) 2.5	(74) 3.0
		-53.3	-1.3	-1.1				1.4	1.3
Net Profit + Depr., Dep., Amort./Cur. Mat. L/T/D			7.5	8.5				3.2	5.3
			(10) 2.1	(12) 1.5				(26) 2.6	(23) 2.6
			.0	-2.1				1.1	1.5
Fixed/Worth		.4	.3	.5				.3	.4
		1.0	1.2	.9				.8	.8
		-.3	4.3	4.5				5.1	3.5
Debt/Worth		.5	.9	.5				.8	.7
		3.7	2.0	2.4				2.0	1.6
		-3.6	8.9	7.8				30.2	10.4
% Profit Before Taxes/Tangible Net Worth			36.3	42.5				41.2	45.1
			(28) 10.9	(24) 8.4				(66) 18.2	(69) 15.6
			-6.0	-3.6				6.9	5.4
% Profit Before Taxes/Total Assets		12.7	10.1	7.0				12.6	15.4
		-2.3	2.5	1.8				5.1	5.5
		-20.6	-4.2	-5.5				1.5	1.4
Sales/Net Fixed Assets		64.7	13.6	11.0				20.5	17.8
		11.7	8.5	7.1				9.2	8.8
		8.1	4.7	4.7				4.7	4.8
Sales/Total Assets		3.7	2.7	2.6				3.1	3.1
		2.1	2.2	2.0				2.4	2.3
		1.6	1.8	1.7				1.6	1.6
% Depr., Dep., Amort./Sales		.9	.7	1.7				.9	1.3
		(10) 2.7	(30) 2.3	(27) 2.7				(73) 2.3	(75) 2.1
		5.5	3.1	4.2				3.6	3.3
% Officers', Directors' Owners' Comp/Sales			1.6					2.1	1.8
			(12) 2.4					(27) 3.8	(23) 2.6
			4.9					6.7	5.3
Net Sales ($)	2963M	30189M	419010M	1388949M	187571M	2042519M		3085352M	3517265M
Total Assets ($)	576M	12415M	185852M	667174M	167297M	1440501M		1564882M	1954458M

M = $ thousand   MM = $ million
See Pages 9 through 22 for Explanation of Ratios and Data

Comparative Historical Data

Current Data Sorted by Sales

			Type of Statement						
11	16	21	Unqualified	1	1			2	17
19	15	21	Reviewed			2	6	11	2
11	8	9	Compiled	1	1	2	1	4	
9	3	6	Tax Returns			3	2	1	
26	28	31	Other		3		3	1	
4/1/07-3/31/08	4/1/08-3/31/09	4/1/09-3/31/10		0-1MM	1-3MM	3-5MM	5-10MM	10-25MM	25MM & OVE
ALL	ALL	ALL				18 (4/1-9/30/09)		70 (10/1/09-3/31/10)	
76	70	88	**NUMBER OF STATEMENTS**	2	8	7	12	25	34
%	%	%	**ASSETS**	%	%	%	%	%	%
5.0	4.7	5.3	Cash & Equivalents				7.2	7.6	3.4
28.3	26.2	25.1	Trade Receivables (net)				29.2	27.4	21.3
25.4	26.0	24.2	Inventory				19.0	26.7	23.6
2.4	2.0	2.8	All Other Current				1.2	3.5	2.8
61.1	58.9	57.5	Total Current				56.6	65.3	51.2
27.7	29.7	29.5	Fixed Assets (net)				31.2	26.9	33.9
5.0	4.8	7.9	Intangibles (net)				9.3	4.0	8.2
6.2	6.5	5.1	All Other Non-Current				2.8	3.8	6.7
100.0	100.0	100.0	Total				100.0	100.0	100.0
			LIABILITIES						
10.5	12.5	11.2	Notes Payable-Short Term				12.1	10.4	9.0
6.3	3.0	4.3	Cur. Mat.-L.T.D.				3.2	3.1	5.6
19.5	15.1	15.3	Trade Payables				15.8	15.3	13.3
.3	.2	.1	Income Taxes Payable				.2	.2	.1
9.8	7.1	9.8	All Other Current				6.3	9.6	11.2
46.3	37.8	40.7	Total Current				37.6	38.5	39.2
21.3	16.4	15.1	Long-Term Debt				10.6	13.3	17.7
.5	.4	.7	Deferred Taxes				.3	.9	1.1
6.9	5.3	7.1	All Other Non-Current				11.8	6.1	6.2
25.0	40.0	36.4	Net Worth				39.6	41.2	35.8
100.0	100.0	100.0	Total Liabilities & Net Worth				100.0	100.0	100.0
			INCOME DATA						
100.0	100.0	100.0	Net Sales				100.0	100.0	100.0
28.9	25.0	25.3	Gross Profit				29.2	24.3	19.5
24.5	21.5	23.7	Operating Expenses				26.5	22.4	16.0
4.4	3.5	1.5	Operating Profit				2.8	1.9	3.5
1.7	1.2	1.0	All Other Expenses (net)				.7	.7	1.5
2.7	2.3	.5	Profit Before Taxes				2.0	1.2	2.1
			RATIOS						
2.3	2.5	2.2	Current				2.1	3.2	2.2
1.4	1.7	1.5					1.5	1.8	1.4
1.0	1.0	1.0					1.2	1.2	.9
1.4	1.5	1.3	Quick				1.6	1.8	1.2
.7	.8	.7					1.0	.8	.6
.5	.5	.4					.6	.5	.4
32 11.2	30 12.0	32 11.4	Sales/Receivables				30 12.0	39 9.5	30 12.1
41 9.0	38 9.7	41 9.0					43 8.6	42 8.8	39 9.4
51 7.1	44 8.3	50 7.4					49 7.4	50 7.3	49 7.5
28 13.1	32 11.3	34 10.8	Cost of Sales/Inventory				23 15.9	40 9.2	38 9.7
48 7.6	44 8.3	48 7.6					35 10.3	53 6.8	49 7.4
76 4.8	72 5.1	72 5.1					53 6.8	84 4.4	73 5.0
23 15.5	16 23.1	18 19.8	Cost of Sales/Payables				16 22.8	18 20.0	18 20.3
36 10.2	28 13.0	31 11.6					40 9.2	25 14.7	26 14.0
55 6.6	41 8.8	53 6.8					50 7.4	51 7.1	39 9.3
6.7	6.6	6.0	Sales/Working Capital				8.8	5.1	5.6
14.8	10.5	13.0					14.4	8.3	15.3
-291.0	365.7	NM					38.2	25.9	-119.4
	7.3		7.9		5.3	EBIT/Interest				12.2	7.2	5.0
(68) 2.8	(65) 2.1	(82) 1.8	EBIT/Interest			(11) 3.2	(24) 1.9	(32) 1.9
.8	.6	-1.1					.3	-1.3	.5
5.3	4.3	3.8	Net Profit + Depr., Dep., Amort./Cur. Mat. L/T/D					8.1	3.4
(30) 2.7	(20) 1.6	(27) 1.8					(13) 2.0	(11) 1.4
.9	1.1	-.1						-.1	-.4
.4	.4	.5	Fixed/Worth				.3	.3	.6
.9	.8	1.2					1.0	1.1	1.3
30.8	2.2	5.3					NM	1.4	NM
.9	.6	.8	Debt/Worth				.9	.8	.8
2.3	1.6	2.5					1.3	2.0	2.8
81.7	6.4	12.3					NM	3.1	NM
30.5	30.5	34.1	% Profit Before Taxes/Tangible Net Worth					21.1	44.2
(59) 15.4	(63) 9.2	(70) 6.8					(24) 6.0	(26) 10.2
4.4	-3.9	-7.5						-6.3	.2
11.8	12.1	7.3	% Profit Before Taxes/Total Assets				12.3	6.2	7.3
5.3	3.1	1.9					8.4	2.2	3.8
.0	-.8	-4.8					-2.8	-2.8	-1.6
18.6	14.2	13.2	Sales/Net Fixed Assets				20.1	11.7	8.1
10.5	8.4	7.3					8.5	8.7	5.4
5.3	5.1	4.7					4.3	4.9	3.6
3.2	3.2	2.6	Sales/Total Assets				3.1	2.6	2.6
2.5	2.5	2.0					2.3	2.1	1.9
1.7	1.6	1.6					1.5	1.9	1.4
1.1	1.1	1.2	% Depr., Dep., Amort./Sales					1.3	1.8
(71) 1.8	(65) 1.7	(79) 2.7					(22) 2.4	(32) 2.9
3.3	3.5	3.9						3.2	4.3
1.8	2.2	1.5	% Officers', Directors' Owners' Comp/Sales						
(23) 4.2	(17) 4.4	(22) 2.4							
7.3	7.6	5.8							
2461810M	2569110M	4071201M	Net Sales ($)	1209M	16110M	28652M	91215M	449069M	3484946M
1403135M	1298922M	2473815M	Total Assets ($)	1426M	9583M	13419M	46129M	226906M	2176352M

M = $ thousand   MM = $ million
See Pages 9 through 22 for Explanation of Ratios and Data

MANUFACTURING—Coated Paper Bag and Pouch Manufacturing NAICS 322223

| Current Data Sorted by Assets | | | | | | | Comparative Historical Data | |

0-500M	500M-2MM	2-10MM	10-50MM	50-100MM	100-250MM	Type of Statement	4/1/05-3/31/06 ALL	4/1/06-3/31/07 ALL
		2	10	1	1	Unqualified	18	12
		9	3			Reviewed	18	18
	1	7				Compiled	6	6
	4	2	1			Tax Returns	5	4
	2	5	5	1	3	Other	27	22
	11 (4/1-9/30/09)		46 (10/1/09-3/31/10)					
	7	25	19	2	4	NUMBER OF STATEMENTS	74	62

Columns 0-500M and 500M-2MM: **DATA NOT AVAILABLE**

2-10MM %	10-50MM %		ASSETS	4/1/05-3/31/06 ALL %	4/1/06-3/31/07 ALL %
4.9	4.9		Cash & Equivalents	6.4	5.6
29.4	22.9		Trade Receivables (net)	29.0	27.2
21.9	24.1		Inventory	24.3	26.5
1.5	2.2		All Other Current	1.3	1.8
57.7	54.1		Total Current	61.1	61.1
31.1	30.4		Fixed Assets (net)	29.1	29.1
3.1	9.4		Intangibles (net)	3.0	3.3
8.1	6.0		All Other Non-Current	6.9	6.5
100.0	100.0		Total	100.0	100.0
			LIABILITIES		
14.5	13.5		Notes Payable-Short Term	13.9	13.4
7.7	4.5		Cur. Mat.-L.T.D.	4.9	3.7
20.4	16.5		Trade Payables	21.0	20.6
.3	.9		Income Taxes Payable	.2	.3
9.8	7.2		All Other Current	8.2	6.6
52.7	42.6		Total Current	48.1	44.6
18.3	17.0		Long-Term Debt	20.9	16.5
.9	.7		Deferred Taxes	.7	1.1
6.7	2.6		All Other Non-Current	3.6	3.2
21.4	37.0		Net Worth	26.7	34.6
100.0	100.0		Total Liabilties & Net Worth	100.0	100.0
			INCOME DATA		
100.0	100.0		Net Sales	100.0	100.0
25.9	25.7		Gross Profit	20.6	22.3
22.2	20.0		Operating Expenses	16.8	18.0
3.7	5.7		Operating Profit	3.8	4.3
.8	1.1		All Other Expenses (net)	1.9	1.3
2.9	4.6		Profit Before Taxes	2.0	3.0
			RATIOS		
1.8	2.1		Current	1.7	2.5
1.2	1.3			1.2	1.4
.9	.8			.9	1.0
1.1	1.4		Quick	1.1	1.2
.8	.6			.6	.7
.5	.5			.4	.5
34 10.8	37 9.9		Sales/Receivables	33 10.9	30 12.0
40 9.0	46 7.9			41 8.8	39 9.5
52 7.0	61 5.9			50 7.4	47 7.7
22 16.3	38 9.6		Cost of Sales/Inventory	30 12.2	33 11.0
48 7.6	51 7.1			48 7.6	48 7.6
73 5.0	91 4.0			71 5.2	70 5.2
20 18.0	20 18.0		Cost of Sales/Payables	25 14.5	21 17.0
31 11.7	37 10.0			38 9.7	39 9.4
72 5.1	52 7.1			57 6.4	43 8.5
8.5	4.9		Sales/Working Capital	8.2	7.1
19.5	19.1			21.9	13.5
-91.8	-18.8			-39.2	-290.8
13.4	12.9		EBIT/Interest	5.9	9.4
(21) 4.7	5.0			(67) 3.0	(61) 3.2
1.9	1.1			1.4	1.5
5.5			Net Profit + Depr., Dep., Amort./Cur. Mat. L/T/D	2.3	5.4
(11) 2.7				(19) 1.8	(26) 1.9
1.6				1.2	1.3
.3	.4		Fixed/Worth	.4	.4
.9	1.5			1.2	.9
-9.4	5.2			3.8	2.8
1.1	.9		Debt/Worth	1.4	1.3
3.2	3.0			2.7	1.9
-11.3	8.6			10.3	4.8
42.0	69.2		% Profit Before Taxes/Tangible Net Worth	34.3	48.4
(17) 19.3	(17) 12.3			(63) 21.0	(55) 18.1
12.9	.8			6.2	6.0
14.1	13.8		% Profit Before Taxes/Total Assets	10.0	12.5
7.5	7.6			5.3	5.5
2.8	.3			1.2	1.3
34.5	13.0		Sales/Net Fixed Assets	18.3	16.9
9.4	7.7			7.9	7.8
4.0	4.3			4.8	5.1
3.2	2.8		Sales/Total Assets	2.8	3.1
2.1	2.1			2.3	2.4
1.7	1.4			1.6	1.8
1.3	1.7		% Depr., Dep., Amort./Sales	1.4	1.1
(23) 3.9	(18) 2.1			(66) 2.2	(56) 2.0
4.9	4.3			3.3	3.2
1.3			% Officers', Directors' Owners' Comp/Sales	1.7	1.7
(10) 1.8				(25) 2.5	(20) 2.4
2.9				4.5	5.0

0-500M	500M-2MM	2-10MM	10-50MM	50-100MM	100-250MM		4/1/05-3/31/06	4/1/06-3/31/07
	31919M	280648M	907998M	287220M	1175625M	Net Sales ($)	3000070M	2628684M
	8171M	125301M	484875M	129469M	653024M	Total Assets ($)	1542599M	1327811M

M = $ thousand   MM = $ million
See Pages 9 through 22 for Explanation of Ratios and Data

Comparative Historical Data | Current Data Sorted by Sales

			Type of Statement						
15	20	14	Unqualified					2	12
14	15	12	Reviewed				3	7	2
5	7	8	Compiled	1	1		2	4	
2	2	7	Tax Returns	1	2		3	1	1
16	19	16	Other	1			3	3	9
4/1/07- 3/31/08	4/1/08- 3/31/09	4/1/09- 3/31/10			11 (4/1-9/30/09)			46 (10/1/09-3/31/10)	
ALL	ALL	ALL		0-1MM	1-3MM	3-5MM	5-10MM	10-25MM	25MM & OVE
52	63	57	NUMBER OF STATEMENTS	1	3	1	11	17	24
%	%	%	ASSETS	%	%	%	%	%	%
6.0	4.7	5.2	Cash & Equivalents				6.9	4.2	5.2
28.2	24.9	27.8	Trade Receivables (net)				39.7	27.1	22.8
26.8	25.2	23.3	Inventory				19.1	25.1	23.7
1.3	4.5	1.6	All Other Current				.8	1.1	1.9
62.3	59.3	57.7	Total Current				66.4	57.5	53.6
28.9	31.9	30.3	Fixed Assets (net)				21.9	33.8	34.4
2.6	3.9	5.4	Intangibles (net)				5.9	4.0	6.5
6.2	4.8	6.6	All Other Non-Current				5.8	4.8	5.5
100.0	100.0	100.0	Total				100.0	100.0	100.0
			LIABILITIES						
15.6	15.1	13.2	Notes Payable-Short Term				10.8	14.4	12.2
4.0	7.1	5.7	Cur. Mat.-L.T.D.				14.3	3.7	4.3
20.8	16.8	19.4	Trade Payables				29.5	20.4	15.8
.4	.4	.7	Income Taxes Payable				.2	.3	1.3
7.0	9.0	8.2	All Other Current				13.6	8.3	7.2
47.9	48.3	47.2	Total Current				68.4	47.2	40.7
26.0	15.4	18.7	Long-Term Debt				17.6	22.2	16.5
1.0	1.0	1.0	Deferred Taxes				.4	1.1	1.3
4.3	5.2	7.4	All Other Non-Current				4.9	6.7	2.1
20.9	30.1	25.8	Net Worth				8.8	22.9	39.3
100.0	100.0	100.0	Total Liabilties & Net Worth				100.0	100.0	100.0
			INCOME DATA						
100.0	100.0	100.0	Net Sales				100.0	100.0	100.0
23.8	20.4	26.1	Gross Profit				29.3	25.3	23.7
20.0	17.2	22.1	Operating Expenses				27.3	20.4	18.1
3.8	3.2	3.9	Operating Profit				2.0	4.9	5.6
1.5	1.3	1.0	All Other Expenses (net)				.3	1.1	1.2
2.3	2.0	3.0	Profit Before Taxes				1.7	3.8	4.4
			RATIOS						
1.9	1.7	1.9					1.6	1.9	2.0
1.3	1.3	1.3	Current				1.0	1.5	1.3
1.0	.9	.9					.5	1.0	1.0
1.0	.9	1.1					1.1	.9	1.3
.6	.6	.7	Quick				.8	.8	.7
.5	.4	.5					.3	.5	.5
34 10.7	30 12.0	32 11.3					31 11.8	30 12.1	34 10.7
41 8.9	37 9.9	41 8.8	Sales/Receivables				38 9.5	40 9.0	44 8.2
51 7.1	46 8.0	52 7.0					61 5.9	47 7.7	58 6.3
41 8.9	31 11.8	28 12.9					18 19.8	27 13.3	41 8.8
55 6.6	53 6.9	48 7.6	Cost of Sales/Inventory				26 14.2	52 7.0	51 7.1
73 5.0	69 5.3	73 5.0					31 11.6	77 4.7	76 4.8
16 22.8	20 18.5	19 19.2					21 17.2	15 23.8	22 16.9
34 10.7	31 11.6	32 11.5	Cost of Sales/Payables				43 8.4	24 15.1	33 11.0
56 6.5	37 9.8	58 6.3					70 5.2	60 6.1	49 7.4
6.4	8.3	7.9					10.7	7.9	6.4
13.7	25.1	19.1	Sales/Working Capital				-324.3	12.6	17.9
-187.1	-47.1	-91.8					-5.1	-138.9	NM
6.3	5.3	12.4						13.4	15.0
(48) 2.5	(62) 3.0	(53) 5.0	EBIT/Interest					5.8	5.1
1.5	.9	1.8						2.0	1.7
4.7	3.9	5.2	Net Profit + Depr., Dep.,						5.3
(21) 2.5	(32) 2.1	(24) 2.6	Amort./Cur. Mat. L/T/D					(11) 1.3	
1.8	1.2	1.2							.9
.4	.4	.3					.1	.4	.5
1.2	1.3	1.1	Fixed/Worth				.9	1.1	1.3
3.2	3.9	5.1					-3.5	NM	2.6
1.4	1.1	1.0					1.2	1.1	.9
3.2	3.0	2.5	Debt/Worth				-13.7	1.5	2.4
8.3	10.7	14.9					-4.9	NM	3.6
32.5	29.4	37.5	% Profit Before Taxes/Tangible					42.0	53.0
(44) 21.1	(52) 16.8	(44) 16.0	Net Worth					(13) 22.0	(23) 14.4
5.9	2.8	6.5						13.6	4.4
9.5	9.1	12.9	% Profit Before Taxes/Total				12.9	17.2	13.6
4.7	4.6	7.5	Assets				8.6	8.8	6.7
1.4	-.3	2.5					2.0	3.4	2.4
20.8	13.5	19.4					60.2	25.9	9.9
8.6	8.7	8.6	Sales/Net Fixed Assets				22.3	6.0	7.7
4.9	5.3	4.0					4.6	3.8	3.6
3.0	2.9	3.0					4.9	3.4	2.7
2.3	2.3	2.1	Sales/Total Assets				2.8	2.2	2.1
1.8	1.9	1.5					2.0	1.7	1.5
1.0	1.3	1.3						1.1	1.6
(47) 1.7	(59) 2.1	(50) 2.9	% Depr., Dep., Amort./Sales					3.7	(21) 2.0
2.9	3.7	4.8						5.2	4.5
1.4	1.9	1.6	% Officers', Directors'						
(13) 2.3	(20) 2.3	(17) 2.3	Owners' Comp/Sales						
5.1	3.4	5.7							
2704115M	3594568M	2683410M	Net Sales ($)	923M	8064M	3607M	79839M	232713M	2358264M
1319824M	1693785M	1400840M	Total Assets ($)	591M	5875M	2531M	30004M	104494M	1257345M

M = $ thousand   MM = $ million
See Pages 9 through 22 for Explanation of Ratios and Data

Current Data Sorted by Assets						Type of Statement	Comparative Historical Data	
		2	4	2		Unqualified	13	9
	1	10	2			Reviewed	7	9
		2				Compiled	2	5
		1				Tax Returns	2	2
2	2	5	6		1	Other	12	13
	11 (4/1-9/30/09)		29 (10/1/09-3/31/10)				4/1/05-3/31/06	4/1/06-3/31/07
0-500M	500M-2MM	2-10MM	10-50MM	50-100MM	100-250MM		ALL	ALL
2	3	20	12	2	1	NUMBER OF STATEMENTS	36	38
%	%	%	%	%	%	ASSETS	%	%
		7.3	2.8			Cash & Equivalents	4.3	6.0
		33.9	30.3			Trade Receivables (net)	34.2	30.2
		15.9	21.3			Inventory	16.0	15.1
		2.4	1.0			All Other Current	1.7	2.4
		59.5	55.5			Total Current	56.2	53.7
		34.8	38.4			Fixed Assets (net)	38.5	39.9
		2.4	2.2			Intangibles (net)	1.7	1.6
		3.3	3.8			All Other Non-Current	3.6	4.8
		100.0	100.0			Total	100.0	100.0
						LIABILITIES		
		12.1	11.2			Notes Payable-Short Term	15.8	11.2
		5.4	5.6			Cur. Mat.-L.T.D.	5.3	5.2
		20.7	13.0			Trade Payables	16.2	13.4
		.0	.0			Income Taxes Payable	.2	.2
		5.3	9.5			All Other Current	9.1	7.9
		43.5	39.3			Total Current	46.7	37.9
		16.0	37.3			Long-Term Debt	28.9	25.1
		1.1	1.1			Deferred Taxes	.5	.8
		1.6	6.6			All Other Non-Current	4.9	4.4
		37.8	15.6			Net Worth	19.1	31.9
		100.0	100.0			Total Liabilities & Net Worth	100.0	100.0
						INCOME DATA		
		100.0	100.0			Net Sales	100.0	100.0
		24.8	18.8			Gross Profit	22.5	26.2
		23.0	15.7			Operating Expenses	18.9	21.2
		1.8	3.1			Operating Profit	3.5	5.0
		.4	1.8			All Other Expenses (net)	1.0	.6
		1.4	1.4			Profit Before Taxes	2.5	4.3
						RATIOS		
		2.1	2.8				1.5	2.8
		1.5	1.3			Current	1.2	1.3
		1.0	1.0				.9	1.0
		1.5	1.6				1.1	1.8
		.9	.8			Quick	.8	1.0
		.7	.6				.6	.6
	35	10.6	43	8.5		Sales/Receivables	44	8.3	42	8.8
	49	7.4	52	7.0			49	7.5	48	7.5
	59	6.2	58	6.3			56	6.6	52	7.0
	13	27.6	24	15.1		Cost of Sales/Inventory	16	23.0	17	21.3
	27	13.8	41	8.8			27	13.3	29	12.4
	44	8.4	66	5.5			36	10.1	43	8.5
	19	18.9	17	21.3		Cost of Sales/Payables	21	17.8	14	26.6
	34	10.6	23	15.6			25	14.8	26	14.2
	51	7.2	44	8.2			34	10.7	37	10.0
		8.3	6.4			Sales/Working Capital	12.6	6.4
		14.4	18.7				30.1	19.5
		-297.2	NM				NM	NM
		5.9	3.1			EBIT/Interest	4.9	7.4
	(19)	1.8	1.8				(35) 2.8	(34) 2.8
		-1.4	.8				1.0	1.1
						Net Profit + Depr., Dep., Amort./Cur. Mat. L/T/D	3.0	4.0
							(12) 2.0	(10) 2.2
							.8	1.2
		.4	1.5			Fixed/Worth	1.0	.8
		1.0	2.1				1.6	1.2
		1.6	NM				5.6	3.8
		.7	2.1			Debt/Worth	1.4	.9
		1.7	6.4				3.3	1.9
		3.0	NM				8.9	7.1
		22.2				% Profit Before Taxes/Tangible Net Worth	26.0	32.2
	(18)	5.8					(30) 13.6	(32) 16.2
		-10.6					-.9	5.2
		6.7	7.4			% Profit Before Taxes/Total Assets	8.9	13.1
		1.9	2.0				5.1	6.3
		-4.9	-2.3				.0	.7
		16.5	11.6			Sales/Net Fixed Assets	13.3	9.1
		7.3	5.4				6.4	5.1
		4.7	3.2				3.8	3.5
		3.1	2.8			Sales/Total Assets	3.0	2.7
		2.8	2.2				2.4	2.1
		1.9	1.4				1.8	1.8
		1.4	2.1			% Depr., Dep., Amort./Sales	1.5	2.2
	(17)	2.1	(11)	2.5			(35) 2.6	(37) 2.9
		3.3	4.7				3.6	3.6
						% Officers', Directors' Owners' Comp/Sales	2.2	2.7
							(12) 2.9	(10) 6.4
							5.1	7.3
1993M	8025M	252360M	486103M	371310M	676237M	Net Sales ($)	1224564M	1201691M
634M	3471M	99974M	224882M	144233M	231769M	Total Assets ($)	506769M	606659M

M = $ thousand   MM = $ million
See Pages 9 through 22 for Explanation of Ratios and Data

Comparative Historical Data | Current Data Sorted by Sales

Type of Statement

	07-08	08-09	09-10	0-1MM	1-3MM	3-5MM	5-10MM	10-25MM	25MM & OVER
Unqualified	11	9	8			2		6	1
Reviewed	8	7	13		2	4		6	1
Compiled	3	5	2			1		1	
Tax Returns	1	8	5	1		1			
Other					1			6	6
	4/1/07-3/31/08 ALL	4/1/08-3/31/09 ALL	4/1/09-3/31/10 ALL	0-1MM	11 (4/1-9/30/09) 1-3MM	3-5MM	5-10MM	29 (10/1/09-3/31/10) 10-25MM	25MM & OVER
NUMBER OF STATEMENTS	34	39	40	1	3	3	5	15	13
	%	%	%	%	%	%	%	%	%
ASSETS									
Cash & Equivalents	7.4	5.0	6.5					9.5	3.8
Trade Receivables (net)	28.4	35.6	33.8					27.6	34.3
Inventory	16.9	17.0	18.3					16.6	20.5
All Other Current	1.0	2.4	1.8					2.3	1.7
Total Current	53.7	60.0	60.4					56.0	60.3
Fixed Assets (net)	39.4	33.0	34.2					39.0	35.4
Intangibles (net)	2.2	2.2	2.3					1.7	2.0
All Other Non-Current	4.6	4.8	3.1					3.3	2.4
Total	100.0	100.0	100.0					100.0	100.0
LIABILITIES									
Notes Payable-Short Term	7.8	15.2	16.7					11.2	14.0
Cur. Mat.-L.T.D.	5.9	6.4	4.7					5.5	6.0
Trade Payables	15.0	21.9	24.0					17.6	16.5
Income Taxes Payable	.0	.0	.0					.0	.0
All Other Current	8.1	9.4	10.4					7.8	9.3
Total Current	36.9	53.0	55.8					42.1	45.8
Long-Term Debt	32.1	26.2	28.1					19.2	31.2
Deferred Taxes	.5	.5	.9					1.3	.2
All Other Non-Current	6.0	9.9	7.0					2.8	9.6
Net Worth	24.5	10.3	8.2					34.5	13.1
Total Liabilities & Net Worth	100.0	100.0	100.0					100.0	100.0
INCOME DATA									
Net Sales	100.0	100.0	100.0					100.0	100.0
Gross Profit	24.6	23.1	22.4					26.4	15.9
Operating Expenses	19.6	21.6	21.1					21.0	14.4
Operating Profit	4.9	1.5	1.3					5.3	1.5
All Other Expenses (net)	1.2	1.5	.8					1.8	1.4
Profit Before Taxes	3.7	.0	.5					3.5	.1
RATIOS									
Current	1.9	2.1	2.1					2.2	2.4
	1.3	1.3	1.3					1.3	1.2
	1.0	.9	.9					.9	.9
Quick	1.2	1.4	1.5					1.6	1.4
	.9	.8	.8					.8	.7
	.7	.6	.6					.5	.6
Sales/Receivables	36 10.2	36 10.2	40 9.0					34 10.7	42 8.8
	42 8.6	45 8.2	49 7.4					51 7.2	48 7.7
	51 7.1	50 7.3	58 6.3					58 6.3	52 7.0
Cost of Sales/Inventory	21 17.6	17 22.0	16 22.5					16 22.6	22 16.5
	32 11.5	23 15.7	33 10.9					32 11.2	35 10.4
	51 7.2	44 8.3	53 6.9					58 6.3	45 8.1
Cost of Sales/Payables	19 19.2	18 20.6	19 19.2					19 19.2	17 21.1
	26 14.1	26 14.3	28 12.9					34 10.7	22 16.6
	39 9.3	36 10.0	51 7.2					54 6.7	37 9.9
Sales/Working Capital	7.6	8.7	8.2					8.2	8.1
	19.5	18.1	23.0					12.1	26.5
	975.7	-92.6	-54.4					-57.4	-516.4
EBIT/Interest	5.9	1.8	3.1					9.3	3.2
	(33) 3.1	(33) 1.3	(37) 1.6					2.6	1.5
	1.1	.2	-1.3					1.2	-2.0
Net Profit + Depr., Dep., Amort./Cur. Mat. L/T/D	4.6	3.1							
	(10) 2.6	(10) 1.3							
	1.7	1.0							
Fixed/Worth	.7	.7	.6					.7	1.3
	1.2	1.8	1.6					1.1	2.7
	-236.7	6.0	NM					2.2	-2.0
Debt/Worth	1.2	1.3	1.3					.9	2.0
	2.7	3.8	2.7					1.7	6.1
	-475.7	19.2	NM					6.8	-9.6
% Profit Before Taxes/Tangible Net Worth	41.8	16.2	22.2					43.2	
	(25) 24.6	(31) 3.4	(30) 5.8					(14) 15.9	
	14.7	-13.7	-12.5					.1	
% Profit Before Taxes/Total Assets	13.0	3.5	6.4					12.9	7.4
	5.5	1.1	1.7					3.4	1.7
	.6	-2.8	-4.4					.7	-5.8
Sales/Net Fixed Assets	10.8	16.1	14.1					10.6	10.7
	6.0	9.6	8.6					6.1	9.3
	3.7	4.1	4.6					3.2	5.4
Sales/Total Assets	2.8	3.5	2.9					2.8	2.9
	2.2	2.9	2.5					2.1	2.6
	1.8	2.2	1.9					1.9	2.3
% Depr., Dep., Amort./Sales	2.1	1.5	1.7					1.5	1.9
	(32) 2.8	(34) 2.3	(33) 2.3					(14) 2.1	(11) 2.3
	4.3	3.8	3.4					3.3	4.6
% Officers', Directors', Owners' Comp/Sales		2.6	1.9						
		(13) 5.1	(12) 4.2						
		7.1	7.9						
Net Sales ($)	1206123M	1250840M	1796028M	788M	5524M	11717M	39286M	209808M	1528905M
Total Assets ($)	554736M	517883M	704963M	392M	2626M	5433M	14460M	105598M	576454M

M = $ thousand   MM = $ million
See Pages 9 through 22 for Explanation of Ratios and Data

Current Data Sorted by Assets							Comparative Historical Data	
	1	1	3	3	6	**Type of Statement** Unqualified	13	13
		3	1			Reviewed	3	3
	2	1	3			Compiled	4	3
						Tax Returns	1	2
	1		3	4	2	Other	3	7
	5 (4/1-9/30/09)		29 (10/1/09-3/31/10)				**4/1/05-3/31/06 ALL**	**4/1/06-3/31/07 ALL**
0-500M	**500M-2MM**	**2-10MM**	**10-50MM**	**50-100MM**	**100-250MM**			
	4	5	10	7	8	**NUMBER OF STATEMENTS**	24	28
%	%	%	%	%	%	**ASSETS**	%	%
DATA NOT AVAILABLE			4.9			Cash & Equivalents	9.4	8.4
			23.6			Trade Receivables (net)	24.6	23.1
			22.4			Inventory	21.1	20.6
			2.0			All Other Current	2.7	1.6
			52.8			Total Current	57.8	53.8
			35.0			Fixed Assets (net)	33.3	35.4
			6.8			Intangibles (net)	2.9	6.9
			5.4			All Other Non-Current	6.0	3.9
			100.0			Total	100.0	100.0
						LIABILITIES		
			7.0			Notes Payable-Short Term	7.3	8.1
			7.0			Cur. Mat.-L.T.D.	2.4	2.2
			15.9			Trade Payables	17.4	17.6
			.0			Income Taxes Payable	.0	.2
			5.1			All Other Current	10.5	6.9
			35.0			Total Current	37.6	34.9
			21.0			Long-Term Debt	21.1	21.9
			.0			Deferred Taxes	.9	1.5
			.4			All Other Non-Current	6.0	1.8
			43.6			Net Worth	34.4	39.9
			100.0			Total Liabilities & Net Worth	100.0	100.0
						INCOME DATA		
			100.0			Net Sales	100.0	100.0
			21.6			Gross Profit	23.5	22.2
			12.4			Operating Expenses	15.6	14.4
			9.3			Operating Profit	7.9	7.8
			.7			All Other Expenses (net)	1.4	1.4
			8.5			Profit Before Taxes	6.5	6.4
						RATIOS		
			2.0				2.2	2.4
			1.4			Current	1.5	1.7
			1.1				1.2	1.1
			1.4				1.7	1.5
			.6			Quick	.7	.8
			.5				.5	.5
			30 12.3				**29** 12.5	**29** 12.6
			33 11.1			Sales/Receivables	**35** 10.4	**34** 10.6
			45 8.1				**44** 8.4	**45** 8.1
			22 16.9				**34** 10.8	**26** 13.9
			45 8.2			Cost of Sales/Inventory	**47** 7.8	**49** 7.5
			79 4.6				**57** 6.4	**66** 5.5
			17 21.9				**21** 17.8	**24** 14.9
			24 15.0			Cost of Sales/Payables	**33** 11.0	**37** 9.9
			51 7.1				**51** 7.2	**48** 7.6
			9.3				8.3	6.8
			14.4			Sales/Working Capital	12.8	9.7
			36.1				34.2	64.3
			17.9				13.8	9.7
			9.6			EBIT/Interest	(22) 3.5	(24) 4.6
			4.6				.6	2.4
						Net Profit + Depr., Dep., Amort./Cur. Mat. L/T/D		
			.6				.2	.4
			.8			Fixed/Worth	1.4	1.1
			1.5				3.3	2.5
			1.2				.7	.9
			1.8			Debt/Worth	2.6	2.0
			2.4				4.8	3.6
			59.7				68.5	53.3
			46.6			% Profit Before Taxes/Tangible Net Worth	(19) 38.7	(24) 36.4
			35.6				8.2	11.6
			25.2				22.3	17.3
			15.0			% Profit Before Taxes/Total Assets	5.2	9.0
			8.1				-2.0	4.0
			13.3				49.4	40.3
			7.3			Sales/Net Fixed Assets	6.5	4.5
			4.1				3.5	3.0
			3.1				2.9	2.7
			2.2			Sales/Total Assets	2.1	2.0
			1.7				1.7	1.5
			1.8				.7	.5
			2.2			% Depr., Dep., Amort./Sales	(16) 2.5	(21) 2.1
			4.0				3.5	3.7
						% Officers', Directors' Owners' Comp/Sales		
	8923M	**72917M**	**674942M**	**1006430M**	**1636848M**	Net Sales ($)	**2226819M**	**2604322M**
	4533M	**25322M**	**286659M**	**474304M**	**1317613M**	Total Assets ($)	**1218022M**	**1633511M**

M = $ thousand MM = $ million

See Pages 9 through 22 for Explanation of Ratios and Data

Comparative Historical Data | | | Current Data Sorted by Sales

4/1/07-3/31/08 ALL	4/1/08-3/31/09 ALL	4/1/09-3/31/10 ALL	Type of Statement	0-1MM	1-3MM	3-5MM	5-10MM	10-25MM	25MM & OVE
15	12	14	Unqualified			1		1	12
4	6	4	Reviewed					2	1
4	5	6	Compiled	1	1			2	2
	2		Tax Returns						
9	7	10	Other			1			9
				5 (4/1-9/30/09)			**29 (10/1/09-3/31/10)**		
32	32	34	NUMBER OF STATEMENTS	1	2	2		5	24
%	%	%	**ASSETS**	%	%	%	%	%	%
7.9	7.7	5.2	Cash & Equivalents						3.4
23.4	24.8	20.9	Trade Receivables (net)						18.0
21.7	23.4	19.9	Inventory						19.8
5.7	5.7	4.3	All Other Current						3.1
58.7	61.6	50.4	Total Current						44.2
31.6	34.4	39.5	Fixed Assets (net)						44.6
2.5	.9	6.1	Intangibles (net)						8.3
7.3	3.1	4.1	All Other Non-Current						2.9
100.0	100.0	100.0	Total						100.0
			LIABILITIES			DATA NOT AVAILABLE			
8.6	9.1	6.4	Notes Payable-Short Term						5.0
3.2	3.2	4.0	Cur. Mat.-L.T.D.						4.7
14.7	16.4	14.4	Trade Payables						13.6
.1	.1	.1	Income Taxes Payable						.0
7.9	7.4	7.1	All Other Current						7.2
34.5	36.2	32.0	Total Current						30.5
23.2	20.2	22.5	Long-Term Debt						26.4
1.2	1.1	1.2	Deferred Taxes						1.7
2.0	1.9	2.3	All Other Non-Current						2.6
39.2	40.7	42.0	Net Worth						38.9
100.0	100.0	100.0	Total Liabilties & Net Worth						100.0
			INCOME DATA						
100.0	100.0	100.0	Net Sales						100.0
25.1	23.5	25.0	Gross Profit						21.7
18.5	17.6	14.0	Operating Expenses						12.1
6.5	6.0	11.0	Operating Profit						9.6
.9	1.1	1.4	All Other Expenses (net)						1.4
5.7	4.9	9.6	Profit Before Taxes						8.1
			RATIOS						
3.2	2.4	2.2							2.2
1.9	1.5	1.7	Current						1.8
1.2	1.2	1.1							1.1
1.7	1.4	1.3							1.2
.8	.8	.8	Quick						.7
.4	.5	.5							.4
30 12.3	27 13.5	26 14.0							25 14.4
33 10.9	33 11.0	32 11.3	Sales/Receivables						30 12.2
45 8.2	42 8.8	45 8.2							38 9.6
26 14.1	28 13.3	29 12.5							32 11.4
49 7.5	53 6.9	48 7.6	Cost of Sales/Inventory						48 7.6
62 5.9	84 4.3	75 4.8							72 5.0
26 13.9	20 18.2	19 19.1							22 16.6
33 11.1	31 11.7	35 10.4	Cost of Sales/Payables						33 11.0
48 7.5	54 6.7	46 8.0							46 8.0
4.4	6.1	6.7							7.4
9.0	11.5	12.5	Sales/Working Capital						12.5
20.6	22.0	36.1							43.3
9.3	10.3	18.0							14.2
(30) 4.6	(27) 6.6	(31) 10.5	EBIT/Interest						(23) 8.8
2.5	2.0	4.0							3.3
			Net Profit + Depr., Dep., Amort./Cur. Mat. L/T/D						
.2	.2	.6							.7
.8	.9	1.0	Fixed/Worth						1.4
2.0	1.7	2.4							2.6
.8	.7	.8							1.2
2.0	1.8	1.7	Debt/Worth						2.0
3.4	3.9	3.2							3.2
44.5	68.8	60.8							60.4
(30) 34.6	28.5	(32) 46.6	% Profit Before Taxes/Tangible Net Worth						(22) 43.0
10.0	9.5	26.2							26.8
14.1	20.5	21.1							17.9
8.6	10.7	12.5	% Profit Before Taxes/Total Assets						12.5
4.9	3.7	7.7							6.7
21.0	43.1	15.4							8.9
7.1	7.1	5.7	Sales/Net Fixed Assets						4.5
4.3	3.4	2.7							2.2
2.3	2.8	3.0							2.7
2.1	2.2	2.1	Sales/Total Assets						2.1
1.4	1.4	1.0							.9
1.0	.9	1.3							1.8
(24) 1.7	(22) 2.0	(29) 2.5	% Depr., Dep., Amort./Sales						(20) 2.8
3.5	3.8	4.2							4.1
			% Officers', Directors' Owners' Comp/Sales						
3392173M	2601282M	3400060M	Net Sales ($)	874M	3609M	9208M		83765M	3302604M
1792171M	1475813M	2108431M	Total Assets ($)	693M	2255M	5736M		39298M	2060449M

© RMA 2010

M = $ thousand   MM = $ million
See Pages 9 through 22 for Explanation of Ratios and Data

Current Data Sorted by Assets   Comparative Historical Data

0-500M	500M-2MM	2-10MM	10-50MM	50-100MM	100-250MM	Type of Statement	4/1/05-3/31/06 ALL	4/1/06-3/31/07 ALL
		3	14	8	5	Unqualified	21	31
		15	2			Reviewed	21	23
1	1	7				Compiled	12	12
3	2	4				Tax Returns	7	5
3	3	19	16	6	1	Other	41	35
	18 (4/1-9/30/09)		95 (10/1/09-3/31/10)					
7	6	48	32	14	6	NUMBER OF STATEMENTS	102	106
%	%	%	%	%	%	**ASSETS**	%	%
		8.1	6.6	2.0		Cash & Equivalents	6.8	4.7
		27.1	22.5	18.8		Trade Receivables (net)	27.4	25.4
		26.8	24.0	26.4		Inventory	23.3	26.0
		1.1	3.8	1.2		All Other Current	1.3	1.7
		63.1	57.0	48.4		Total Current	58.8	57.8
		26.4	33.5	36.4		Fixed Assets (net)	29.3	33.1
		5.4	4.6	12.7		Intangibles (net)	4.1	3.2
		5.1	4.9	2.4		All Other Non-Current	7.7	5.9
		100.0	100.0	100.0		Total	100.0	100.0
						LIABILITIES		
		10.8	10.0	12.8		Notes Payable-Short Term	12.3	12.2
		5.5	3.9	4.8		Cur. Mat.-L.T.D.	3.9	4.4
		19.8	13.0	12.0		Trade Payables	16.2	15.9
		.1	.0	.1		Income Taxes Payable	.2	.2
		6.0	8.8	8.6		All Other Current	7.6	8.8
		42.3	35.7	38.2		Total Current	40.2	41.5
		18.4	15.0	21.3		Long-Term Debt	16.1	17.6
		.5	.7	.3		Deferred Taxes	.4	.5
		7.4	6.1	4.9		All Other Non-Current	5.2	6.7
		31.4	42.5	35.2		Net Worth	38.1	33.6
		100.0	100.0	100.0		Total Liabilities & Net Worth	100.0	100.0
						INCOME DATA		
		100.0	100.0	100.0		Net Sales	100.0	100.0
		23.8	22.8	20.2		Gross Profit	25.0	23.1
		20.6	17.8	14.1		Operating Expenses	20.6	19.0
		3.2	5.0	6.1		Operating Profit	4.4	4.2
		1.3	1.7	1.6		All Other Expenses (net)	1.0	1.3
		1.9	3.2	4.5		Profit Before Taxes	3.5	2.9
						RATIOS		
		2.6	2.6	1.7		Current	2.2	2.1
		1.6	1.9	1.3			1.4	1.3
		1.1	1.0	.9			1.0	1.0
		1.5	1.3	.9		Quick	1.3	1.1
		.8	.8	.5			.8	.7
		.5	.6	.3			.6	.5
		28 12.9	34 10.8	27 13.8		Sales/Receivables	33 10.9	30 12.4
		42 8.7	40 9.1	34 10.7			40 9.0	38 9.6
		49 7.5	48 7.7	43 8.4			53 6.9	47 7.7
		26 13.8	30 12.0	35 10.5		Cost of Sales/Inventory	30 12.3	29 12.7
		48 7.6	44 8.3	49 7.4			45 8.1	48 7.6
		74 5.0	80 4.6	82 4.5			75 4.9	77 4.8
		19 18.9	18 20.0	20 18.3		Cost of Sales/Payables	20 18.6	17 21.3
		33 11.1	26 13.9	26 14.3			33 11.1	28 12.9
		43 8.4	40 9.1	32 11.4			44 8.3	43 8.4
		5.8	5.9	8.5		Sales/Working Capital	6.2	7.4
		11.2	8.6	22.5			15.2	16.6
		43.7	288.0	-752.8			999.8	-418.6
		10.6	9.1	7.6		EBIT/Interest	7.6	6.0
		(47) 5.0	(28) 5.3	3.1			(93) 3.3	(100) 2.7
		1.8	.5	2.3			1.6	1.4
						Net Profit + Depr., Dep.,	4.4	2.8
						Amort./Cur. Mat. L/T/D	(25) 2.6 / (35) 2.1	
							1.2	.8
		.2	.3	.6		Fixed/Worth	.4	.4
		.7	.9	1.5			.8	.9
		2.5	2.2	4.3			1.8	3.3
		.7	.6	1.4		Debt/Worth	.7	.7
		2.4	1.2	3.0			1.9	1.9
		6.7	5.1	6.5			4.9	5.5
		43.2	42.1	103.2		% Profit Before Taxes/Tangible	36.5	33.4
		(40) 22.7	(30) 23.3	(13) 29.6		Net Worth	(93) 14.7	(91) 16.4
		7.3	7.3	13.3			4.2	6.0
		14.1	15.1	15.2		% Profit Before Taxes/Total	13.2	12.0
		7.2	6.9	6.6		Assets	3.8	5.3
		2.1	.8	4.3			1.4	1.4
		48.1	17.4	12.8		Sales/Net Fixed Assets	21.5	15.1
		12.9	8.4	8.8			8.0	9.4
		4.6	3.5	2.5			4.6	4.2
		3.0	2.8	2.4		Sales/Total Assets	3.1	3.3
		2.1	2.0	2.1			2.2	2.2
		1.6	1.4	1.5			1.6	1.6
		1.0	1.1	1.1		% Depr., Dep., Amort./Sales	.9	1.3
		(42) 2.2	(30) 2.1	(11) 2.0			(93) 2.0	(102) 2.1
		3.6	7.9	3.9			3.4	3.6
		1.3				% Officers', Directors'	1.2	.9
		(16) 4.0				Owners' Comp/Sales	(31) 3.0	(26) 1.5
		7.5					7.3	4.2
8348M	22378M	540154M	1649295M	2077528M	1285788M	Net Sales ($)	3596421M	4500073M
1991M	7028M	235089M	801531M	1027189M	747429M	Total Assets ($)	1915372M	2207989M

M = $ thousand   MM = $ million
See Pages 9 through 22 for Explanation of Ratios and Data

Comparative Historical Data | Current Data Sorted by Sales

	4/1/07-3/31/08 ALL	4/1/08-3/31/09 ALL	4/1/09-3/31/10 ALL	0-1MM	1-3MM	3-5MM	5-10MM	10-25MM	25MM & OVER
Type of Statement									
Unqualified	30	31	30		1		1	5	24
Reviewed	24	17	17		1		4	7	3
Compiled	10	11	9		1		4	2	
Tax Returns	4	6	9	1	1	1	2	2	2
Other	36	52	48	1	3	1	2	6	14
					5				18
				18 (4/1-9/30/09)			95 (10/1/09-3/31/10)		
NUMBER OF STATEMENTS	104	117	113	2	10	9	17	30	45
ASSETS	%	%	%	%	%	%	%	%	%
Cash & Equivalents	5.3	4.4	7.5		11.2		5.6	10.7	5.1
Trade Receivables (net)	23.7	23.7	27.0		46.4		20.5	25.7	23.9
Inventory	23.5	28.4	24.6		17.1		23.2	23.9	26.0
All Other Current	1.6	2.1	1.8		.0		4.7	1.6	1.5
Total Current	54.0	58.6	60.8		74.7		54.0	61.9	56.5
Fixed Assets (net)	35.4	30.9	29.0		18.8		33.6	28.1	32.8
Intangibles (net)	4.5	5.1	5.8		4.1		7.1	4.0	6.7
All Other Non-Current	6.1	5.4	4.4		2.3		5.2	6.1	4.0
Total	100.0	100.0	100.0		100.0		100.0	100.0	100.0
LIABILITIES									
Notes Payable-Short Term	11.0	14.5	10.5		1.9		14.3	8.5	9.3
Cur. Mat.-L.T.D.	4.4	4.6	4.3		1.4		8.5	4.4	4.0
Trade Payables	13.5	15.6	17.1		33.6		10.8	17.6	13.7
Income Taxes Payable	.1	.0	.1		.0		.0	.2	.1
All Other Current	7.7	8.8	7.8		7.0		3.7	5.5	9.3
Total Current	36.7	43.5	39.8		43.9		37.4	36.2	36.4
Long-Term Debt	20.3	17.2	17.3		19.6		27.2	13.4	17.9
Deferred Taxes	.4	.5	.5		.0		.1	.8	.7
All Other Non-Current	3.1	5.0	5.9		1.5		12.7	5.9	4.2
Net Worth	39.5	33.7	36.5		35.0		22.6	43.8	40.8
Total Liabilities & Net Worth	100.0	100.0	100.0		100.0		100.0	100.0	100.0
INCOME DATA									
Net Sales	100.0	100.0	100.0		100.0		100.0	100.0	100.0
Gross Profit	24.9	23.3	23.7		28.4		24.3	25.0	21.4
Operating Expenses	19.7	20.4	19.2		28.1		22.5	19.1	15.4
Operating Profit	5.2	2.9	4.5		.2		1.8	5.9	6.0
All Other Expenses (net)	1.4	1.0	1.4		.7		1.9	1.3	1.3
Profit Before Taxes	3.8	1.9	3.1		-.4		-.1	4.6	4.6
RATIOS									
Current	2.3	2.2	2.5		18.5		2.4	2.7	2.2
	1.4	1.4	1.7		1.8		1.3	2.3	1.7
	1.0	1.1	1.1		.9		.9	1.2	1.1
Quick	1.2	1.0	1.4		7.9		1.1	1.9	1.1
	.8	.7	.8		1.6		.7	1.1	.8
	.5	.4	.5		.7		.5	.6	.5
Sales/Receivables	30 12.0	30 12.3	30 12.0		28 13.0		29 12.8	28 12.9	33 11.0
	38 9.7	37 9.8	40 9.1		46 8.0		42 8.6	40 9.2	39 9.5
	48 7.6	51 7.1	48 7.5		59 6.2		47 7.7	48 7.6	48 7.7
Cost of Sales/Inventory	31 11.7	33 11.0	27 13.7		4 89.7		23 15.7	34 10.8	38 9.7
	49 7.4	55 6.7	44 8.2		12 31.0		44 8.3	48 7.6	45 8.1
	69 5.3	82 4.4	76 4.8		21 17.3		85 4.3	69 5.3	80 4.6
Cost of Sales/Payables	16 22.7	16 22.9	19 18.9		7 49.6		14 25.4	19 19.0	21 17.4
	25 14.4	29 12.8	29 12.7		36 10.3		21 17.6	32 11.4	27 13.8
	41 9.0	46 7.9	44 8.3		58 6.3		46 8.0	42 8.6	34 10.6
Sales/Working Capital	6.9	7.0	6.2		5.8		5.1	5.7	6.3
	13.7	15.3	10.1		12.3		15.2	7.5	8.9
	NM	134.1	54.4		NM		-36.9	21.9	54.4
EBIT/Interest	8.6	5.1	9.3				6.5	16.2	9.0
	(96) 3.6	(108) 1.9	(102) 3.9				(16) 2.5	5.7	(40) 3.9
	1.6	.3	1.8				.2	1.8	2.0
Net Profit + Depr., Dep., Amort./Cur. Mat. L/T/D	6.0	5.3	6.3						6.1
	(27) 2.4	(28) 1.7	(24) 3.3						(14) 3.8
	1.2	.3	1.7						2.2
Fixed/Worth	.6	.4	.3		.0		.3	.2	.5
	.9	1.0	.8		.1		2.5	.6	.9
	2.9	3.0	2.5		7.6		-3.7	1.5	2.8
Debt/Worth	.7	.8	.7		.2		1.0	.6	.7
	1.6	2.3	2.1		1.3		4.4	1.3	1.7
	5.3	6.5	5.5		NM		-10.5	4.5	4.1
% Profit Before Taxes/Tangible Net Worth	49.1	39.3	47.6				32.7	43.7	52.0
	(92) 20.1	(98) 14.3	(100) 24.9		(11) 12.3		(29) 22.2	(43) 26.2	
	9.5	1.1	8.7		3.4		4.1	9.0	
% Profit Before Taxes/Total Assets	16.0	10.1	15.5		37.9		10.2	18.9	15.5
	6.6	3.2	7.2		14.3		5.5	9.1	7.4
	2.7	-2.0	2.7		-4.7		-3.3	2.6	3.8
Sales/Net Fixed Assets	13.2	16.3	30.6		UND		26.7	20.1	14.8
	7.0	8.6	10.5		77.1		9.7	9.2	8.3
	3.7	4.0	4.1		12.5		2.4	4.4	3.7
Sales/Total Assets	3.0	3.1	3.0		4.8		2.8	3.1	2.8
	2.1	2.1	2.2		3.7		1.7	2.3	2.2
	1.6	1.5	1.5		1.5		1.2	1.7	1.6
% Depr., Dep., Amort./Sales	1.2	1.0	1.1				1.8	.7	1.1
	(92) 2.4	(104) 1.7	(94) 2.2				(15) 3.3	(28) 2.2	(38) 2.1
	3.4	3.4	4.8				8.9	3.3	4.6
% Officers', Directors' Owners' Comp/Sales	1.2	1.2	1.9					1.3	
	(22) 1.7	(21) 2.3	(26) 2.9					(11) 2.5	
	4.2	4.4	6.0					8.2	
Net Sales ($)	4915119M	6509702M	5583491M	1117M	19108M	36112M	119485M	495345M	4912324M
Total Assets ($)	2567214M	3468812M	2820257M	373M	13090M	20017M	89291M	269893M	2427593M

© RMA 2010   M = $ thousand   MM = $ million
See Pages 9 through 22 for Explanation of Ratios and Data

MANUFACTURING—Commercial Lithographic Printing NAICS 323110

Current Data Sorted by Assets							Comparative Historical Data	

Type of Statement

0-500M	500M-2MM	2-10MM	10-50MM	50-100MM	100-250MM	Type of Statement		
1		20	42	7	2	Unqualified	92	92
	23	76	36	1		Reviewed	175	179
5	36	36	2	1		Compiled	96	103
36	54	30	2	1		Tax Returns	96	85
22	55	100	59	8	3	Other	252	240
	115 (4/1-9/30/09)		543 (10/1/09-3/31/10)				4/1/05-3/31/06 ALL	4/1/06-3/31/07 ALL
64	168	262	141	18	5	NUMBER OF STATEMENTS	711	699

Assets / Liabilities / Income Data

0-500M %	500M-2MM %	2-10MM %	10-50MM %	50-100MM %	100-250MM %		ALL %	ALL %
						ASSETS		
12.2	9.8	8.7	8.3	3.9		Cash & Equivalents	7.4	7.7
35.5	28.1	26.7	22.7	23.9		Trade Receivables (net)	30.2	29.9
8.2	10.6	9.8	9.9	6.0		Inventory	9.6	10.2
1.6	2.4	2.2	2.1	3.3		All Other Current	1.8	1.9
57.4	50.9	47.3	43.0	37.1		Total Current	49.1	49.8
28.1	36.1	42.8	47.2	43.8		Fixed Assets (net)	41.3	40.9
6.9	5.4	4.1	5.9	13.4		Intangibles (net)	3.8	3.9
7.6	7.7	5.8	3.9	5.7		All Other Non-Current	5.9	5.4
100.0	100.0	100.0	100.0	100.0		Total	100.0	100.0
						LIABILITIES		
18.6	11.8	8.9	5.6	4.9		Notes Payable-Short Term	9.3	9.2
10.3	7.9	7.4	7.0	10.3		Cur. Mat.-L.T.D.	7.3	7.3
22.1	17.9	14.2	11.2	10.5		Trade Payables	15.3	15.4
.1	.2	.1	.3	.0		Income Taxes Payable	.1	.1
19.0	8.8	8.1	7.2	7.6		All Other Current	7.9	8.1
70.0	46.5	38.7	31.4	33.4		Total Current	40.0	40.0
57.3	34.2	25.3	26.5	25.8		Long-Term Debt	29.8	28.2
.0	.3	.9	1.1	2.3		Deferred Taxes	.8	.8
10.7	5.6	3.6	4.7	5.7		All Other Non-Current	5.7	5.2
-37.9	13.3	31.5	36.4	32.7		Net Worth	23.7	25.7
100.0	100.0	100.0	100.0	100.0		Total Liabilities & Net Worth	100.0	100.0
						INCOME DATA		
100.0	100.0	100.0	100.0	100.0		Net Sales	100.0	100.0
50.3	43.4	32.0	26.4	26.5		Gross Profit	34.4	34.5
49.0	43.3	31.2	23.2	25.6		Operating Expenses	30.6	30.3
1.3	.1	.9	3.2	1.0		Operating Profit	3.7	4.2
1.0	1.8	1.4	2.0	4.0		All Other Expenses (net)	1.3	1.4
.3	-1.6	-.5	1.2	-3.1		Profit Before Taxes	2.4	2.8

Ratios

0-500M	500M-2MM	2-10MM	10-50MM	50-100MM	100-250MM		ALL	ALL
3.1	2.0	2.0	2.3	2.6		Current	2.0	1.9
1.2	1.1	1.2	1.4	1.1			1.2	1.3
.5	.7	.9	1.0	.8			.9	.9
2.5	1.5	1.6	1.8	1.9		Quick	1.5	1.5
1.0	.9	.9	1.0	.9			.9	1.0
.4	.5	.6	.6	.5			.7	.7
17 21.4	28 13.2	35 10.4	38 9.7	41 8.8		Sales/Receivables	36 10.1	37 9.7
29 12.8	38 9.6	47 7.7	49 7.4	50 7.3			48 7.6	48 7.7
40 9.2	48 7.6	58 6.3	63 5.8	66 5.5			59 6.2	58 6.3
0 UND	5 74.4	11 33.5	14 26.2	12 30.0		Cost of Sales/Inventory	10 37.0	10 35.5
10 37.5	16 22.3	21 17.6	23 16.1	21 17.3			19 18.9	19 19.0
21 17.0	37 9.9	37 10.0	40 9.2	32 11.3			32 11.4	34 10.8
12 31.5	21 17.3	19 19.6	20 18.6	20 18.1		Cost of Sales/Payables	19 18.8	19 18.9
25 14.4	39 9.3	34 10.7	27 13.4	31 11.8			31 11.6	31 11.9
53 6.9	62 5.8	52 7.0	42 8.8	49 7.5			49 7.4	49 7.4
12.1	9.7	7.6	5.6	7.9		Sales/Working Capital	9.1	9.5
39.3	53.1	25.7	14.3	37.0			23.6	24.1
-20.5	-17.8	-28.5	-133.1	-15.2			-58.7	-97.4
3.8	3.6	4.0	3.9	2.6		EBIT/Interest	5.7	5.7
(52) 1.0	(156) .8	(251) 1.2	(138) 1.6	(17) -.3			(673) 2.5	(655) 2.6
-3.1	-1.7	-1.5	.2	-.9			1.0	1.3
	1.5	2.3	2.4	1.4		Net Profit + Depr., Dep., Amort./Cur. Mat. L/T/D	2.7	3.1
	(23) .4	(76) 1.3	(55) 1.5	(10) .5			(223) 1.6	(209) 1.7
	-.2	.3	1.0	.2			.8	1.0
.4	.7	.9	.8	.8		Fixed/Worth	.8	.8
UND	2.8	1.6	1.6	2.4			1.8	1.7
-.4	-2.5	4.1	3.4	-2.8			6.5	5.8
1.4	1.4	1.1	.9	1.6		Debt/Worth	1.3	1.2
-12.4	6.7	2.4	2.1	2.9			2.9	3.0
-1.9	-5.9	9.6	5.1	-7.3			13.8	11.0
49.6	40.3	24.7	21.6	11.1		% Profit Before Taxes/Tangible Net Worth	37.2	45.5
(30) 1.8	(103) 3.7	(224) 3.7	(125) 7.5	(12) -13.5			(578) 15.7	(565) 19.2
-35.3	-22.6	-14.6	-4.4	-21.6			2.5	6.6
25.9	6.5	7.4	6.9	5.8		% Profit Before Taxes/Total Assets	10.8	12.3
.2	-.9	.6	1.6	-4.2			4.2	5.2
-17.7	-10.3	-6.5	-2.5	-9.5			.0	1.2
83.4	18.2	8.4	5.2	6.2		Sales/Net Fixed Assets	9.7	10.2
19.8	8.3	4.6	3.5	3.3			5.0	5.5
6.8	4.2	2.9	2.2	2.0			3.2	3.4
6.3	3.5	2.5	2.0	1.7		Sales/Total Assets	2.8	2.9
3.9	2.6	1.9	1.5	1.3			2.1	2.2
2.9	1.8	1.4	1.2	1.1			1.6	1.7
1.1	1.9	3.0	3.7	5.3		% Depr., Dep., Amort./Sales	2.8	2.6
(45) 3.0	(134) 4.0	(249) 4.6	(136) 5.1	(15) 6.9			(653) 4.4	(647) 4.2
5.9	7.7	7.1	7.2	8.6			6.1	5.9
5.7	3.6	2.1	1.3			% Officers', Directors' Owners' Comp/Sales	2.6	2.3
(43) 8.4	(103) 6.0	(114) 3.5	(34) 2.7				(318) 4.6	(294) 4.0
13.9	9.9	5.7	4.1				7.5	7.2
66868M	531482M	2530559M	4688723M	1814529M	866318M	Net Sales ($)	13326449M	12671043M
14955M	201807M	1295433M	2871786M	1179824M	769415M	Total Assets ($)	7189044M	6914461M

M = $ thousand   MM = $ million
See Pages 9 through 22 for Explanation of Ratios and Data

Comparative Historical Data / Current Data Sorted by Sales

	4/1/07-3/31/08 ALL	4/1/08-3/31/09 ALL	4/1/09-3/31/10 ALL	0-1MM	1-3MM	3-5MM	5-10MM	10-25MM	25MM & OVER
Type of Statement					115 (4/1-9/30/09)			543 (10/1/09-3/31/10)	
Unqualified	85	73	72	1			8	23	40
Reviewed	158	142	136	1	11	9	44	53	18
Compiled	94	102	80	5	24	16	27	6	2
Tax Returns	75	107	123	24	44	30	15	8	2
Other	253	232	247	12	45	32	54	52	52
NUMBER OF STATEMENTS	665	656	658	43	124	87	148	142	114
	%	%	%	%	%	%	%	%	%
ASSETS									
Cash & Equivalents	8.6	8.3	9.0	8.0	9.5	12.8	9.5	7.3	7.7
Trade Receivables (net)	28.5	27.6	26.9	29.8	24.6	28.9	26.3	29.4	24.5
Inventory	9.9	10.3	9.8	8.8	8.9	9.1	9.7	10.6	10.6
All Other Current	2.3	1.8	2.2	4.5	2.0	1.7	2.1	1.7	2.9
Total Current	49.2	47.9	48.0	51.1	45.1	52.5	47.5	49.0	45.7
Fixed Assets (net)	41.1	41.7	40.6	29.8	39.8	37.8	42.5	42.0	43.4
Intangibles (net)	4.4	4.1	5.5	10.4	6.1	3.8	3.9	5.0	6.7
All Other Non-Current	5.3	6.2	6.0	8.8	9.0	5.9	6.1	4.0	4.2
Total	100.0	100.0	100.0	100.0	100.0	100.0	100.0	100.0	100.0
LIABILITIES									
Notes Payable-Short Term	8.8	8.8	9.7	18.6	11.3	11.3	9.0	8.9	5.4
Cur. Mat.-L.T.D.	7.4	7.1	7.8	8.9	8.9	7.4	7.7	7.2	7.2
Trade Payables	14.7	14.5	15.1	20.6	15.9	15.2	15.6	15.0	11.6
Income Taxes Payable	.2	.2	.2	.1	.1	.1	.2	.2	.3
All Other Current	8.2	7.8	9.2	18.0	9.3	10.6	7.9	7.0	9.0
Total Current	39.2	38.4	42.0	66.1	45.5	44.6	40.4	38.4	33.5
Long-Term Debt	28.6	31.0	31.0	58.9	42.1	31.8	25.2	24.4	23.2
Deferred Taxes	.6	.9	.8	.0	.3	.4	.9	1.1	1.2
All Other Non-Current	4.0	4.7	5.1	10.1	6.2	6.0	3.0	3.9	5.3
Net Worth	27.6	25.1	21.2	-35.1	5.9	17.3	30.4	32.1	36.7
Total Liabilities & Net Worth	100.0	100.0	100.0	100.0	100.0	100.0	100.0	100.0	100.0
INCOME DATA									
Net Sales	100.0	100.0	100.0	100.0	100.0	100.0	100.0	100.0	100.0
Gross Profit	35.5	34.5	35.2	54.7	44.0	41.9	32.8	28.3	24.8
Operating Expenses	31.1	31.8	34.0	52.6	44.5	41.9	32.7	25.3	22.3
Operating Profit	4.3	2.7	1.2	2.1	-.5	.0	.2	3.0	2.6
All Other Expenses (net)	1.4	1.4	1.6	1.5	2.3	1.5	1.0	1.6	2.0
Profit Before Taxes	2.9	1.3	-.5	.6	-2.8	-1.4	-.9	1.4	.6
RATIOS									
Current	2.0	2.1	2.2	3.0	1.9	2.7	2.1	2.0	2.2
	1.4	1.3	1.2	1.0	1.1	1.3	1.2	1.3	1.5
	.9	.9	.8	.5	.6	.7	.8	.9	1.0
Quick	1.6	1.6	1.7	2.0	1.7	2.3	1.6	1.6	1.7
	1.0	.9	.9	.7	.9	1.0	.9	.9	.9
	.7	.6	.6	.4	.4	.5	.6	.6	.7
Sales/Receivables	36 10.2	33 11.2	32 11.5	17 21.8	25 14.5	31 11.8	33 11.2	40 9.1	37 9.7
	45 8.1	42 8.7	43 8.5	30 12.4	33 11.0	41 8.8	44 8.4	51 7.1	49 7.4
	58 6.3	54 6.7	56 6.6	46 7.9	47 7.8	52 7.0	53 6.8	62 5.9	62 5.8
Cost of Sales/Inventory	10 35.1	10 37.3	9 40.3	2 225.7	3 134.5	8 43.3	9 38.8	12 30.9	14 25.5
	20 18.5	18 19.9	19 18.8	16 22.7	13 27.9	17 21.7	20 18.2	22 16.9	23 16.0
	34 10.8	35 10.6	36 10.0	55 6.6	36 10.1	34 10.8	34 10.8	38 9.7	39 9.4
Cost of Sales/Payables	19 18.9	18 19.9	19 19.4	16 23.1	18 19.9	17 21.1	19 19.2	21 17.4	18 20.0
	31 11.9	29 12.4	32 11.3	36 10.2	36 10.2	33 11.2	34 10.8	32 11.5	27 13.7
	49 7.4	46 8.0	52 7.0	78 4.7	66 5.5	53 6.9	54 6.8	47 7.8	41 8.9
Sales/Working Capital	7.9	8.6	7.9	9.3	12.2	6.6	7.7	8.2	6.7
	19.1	24.5	28.9	401.0	67.9	27.6	35.0	21.6	15.7
	-74.7	-60.1	-24.7	-10.7	-17.1	-17.8	-25.5	-46.3	-135.5
EBIT/Interest	5.8	4.4	3.7	3.1	2.3	4.6	3.7	4.6	4.6
	(627) 2.4	(629) 1.8	(619) 1.2	(34) .9	(114) .5	(80) .2	(142) 1.0	(139) 1.6	(110) 1.9
	1.0	-.1	-1.4	-2.2	-2.3	-1.9	-2.3	-.1	-.4
Net Profit + Depr., Dep., Amort./Cur. Mat. L/T/D	2.9	2.7	2.1		1.9	.8	1.6	2.4	2.5
	(198) 1.8	(193) 1.4	(164) 1.3		(15) .6	(13) .3	(41) .7	(50) 1.5	(45) 1.5
	1.0	.7	.3		.0	-1.3	.2	.8	.5
Fixed/Worth	.8	.8	.8	.2	.8	.7	.9	.8	.7
	1.6	1.8	1.9	UND	4.0	2.5	1.7	1.6	1.5
	5.6	8.2	27.4	-.4	-2.5	-6.2	4.0	3.3	4.0
Debt/Worth	1.2	1.2	1.1	.6	1.9	.9	1.2	1.0	.9
	2.5	2.7	2.9	-13.2	8.7	5.3	2.1	2.4	2.0
	10.5	17.2	UND	-1.9	-5.0	-10.6	9.9	6.6	6.4
% Profit Before Taxes/Tangible Net Worth	41.4	32.6	24.9	40.5	18.9	43.4	17.3	29.5	22.7
	(544) 18.0	(517) 11.3	(496) 4.6	(20) .4	(73) 1.1	(60) .2	(124) .1	(123) 11.7	(96) 7.6
	2.8	-3.8	-14.3	-18.5	-44.1	-27.9	-21.1	-3.4	-6.1
% Profit Before Taxes/Total Assets	12.6	9.9	7.4	23.0	4.0	9.5	5.7	8.2	8.1
	5.0	3.0	.6	.2	-3.2	-2.7	-.2	1.7	2.7
	.2	-2.9	-7.2	-11.4	-13.7	-10.6	-8.2	-3.2	-3.9
Sales/Net Fixed Assets	9.9	10.8	11.1	50.3	15.5	19.4	10.3	8.7	6.4
	5.3	5.2	4.9	14.9	6.1	6.0	4.9	4.6	3.8
	3.2	3.1	2.9	3.9	3.1	3.8	2.8	2.9	2.6
Sales/Total Assets	2.8	2.9	2.8	6.0	3.6	3.0	2.7	2.4	2.2
	2.1	2.2	2.0	2.9	2.2	2.3	2.0	2.0	1.7
	1.6	1.5	1.4	1.6	1.4	1.6	1.4	1.4	1.3
% Depr., Dep., Amort./Sales	2.7	2.6	2.7	1.5	2.5	2.0	2.9	2.8	3.5
	(609) 4.2	(587) 4.2	(579) 4.7	(31) 3.4	(99) 5.3	(73) 4.0	(141) 4.8	(134) 4.3	(101) 5.0
	5.9	6.5	7.3	8.5	8.0	7.4	7.4	6.7	6.7
% Officers', Directors' Owners' Comp/Sales	2.3	2.4	2.7	6.0	4.6	3.5	1.9	2.0	1.2
	(290) 4.2	(261) 4.3	(296) 4.7	(26) 10.1	(77) 6.6	(53) 5.6	(69) 3.2	(52) 3.2	(19) 2.3
	7.8	7.9	8.3	15.8	10.1	10.1	5.3	5.3	3.8
Net Sales ($)	12928855M	11811712M	10498479M	22648M	241550M	345760M	1066837M	2241999M	6579685M
Total Assets ($)	7176700M	6414191M	6333220M	12177M	137795M	172174M	611493M	1292506M	4107075M

Current Data Sorted by Assets　　　　　　Comparative Historical Data

0-500M	500M-2MM	2-10MM	10-50MM	50-100MM	100-250MM	Type of Statement	4/1/05-3/31/06 ALL	4/1/06-3/31/07 ALL
		2	7	1	1	Unqualified	7	11
	1	15	3			Reviewed	15	19
1	3	1				Compiled	7	15
4	5	1				Tax Returns	8	10
3	8	7	4			Other	10	35
	8 (4/1-9/30/09)		59 (10/1/09-3/31/10)					
8	17	26	14	1	1	NUMBER OF STATEMENTS	47	90
%	%	%	%	%	%	**ASSETS**	%	%
	22.1	6.4	5.9			Cash & Equivalents	7.4	8.8
	25.3	24.1	20.2			Trade Receivables (net)	29.2	27.3
	11.4	13.0	14.1			Inventory	12.8	13.0
	.1	1.9	.6			All Other Current	1.1	1.8
	59.0	45.3	40.8			Total Current	50.5	50.8
	26.2	39.0	35.5			Fixed Assets (net)	35.2	37.9
	9.5	7.0	14.9			Intangibles (net)	7.3	6.6
	5.3	8.7	8.8			All Other Non-Current	7.0	4.7
	100.0	100.0	100.0			Total	100.0	100.0
						LIABILITIES		
	5.7	8.5	7.8			Notes Payable-Short Term	8.6	10.2
	2.5	3.9	7.4			Cur. Mat.-L.T.D.	7.9	5.7
	9.8	10.5	9.9			Trade Payables	15.4	15.2
	.0	.0	.0			Income Taxes Payable	.1	.1
	11.7	5.9	6.8			All Other Current	9.1	8.3
	29.7	28.8	31.9			Total Current	41.0	39.5
	24.4	20.1	25.7			Long-Term Debt	26.7	24.5
	.1	.8	.5			Deferred Taxes	.8	.7
	13.3	9.5	5.9			All Other Non-Current	5.5	5.1
	32.5	40.8	36.1			Net Worth	26.0	30.2
	100.0	100.0	100.0			Total Liabilities & Net Worth	100.0	100.0
						INCOME DATA		
	100.0	100.0	100.0			Net Sales	100.0	100.0
	50.4	32.5	30.0			Gross Profit	34.4	35.8
	47.0	29.5	23.5			Operating Expenses	29.1	30.8
	3.4	3.1	6.5			Operating Profit	5.3	5.0
	1.0	1.4	2.2			All Other Expenses (net)	1.9	1.3
	2.3	1.6	4.3			Profit Before Taxes	3.4	3.7
						RATIOS		
	7.9	2.2	2.1			Current	2.1	2.0
	2.2	1.9	1.2				1.4	1.3
	1.1	1.0	.7				1.0	1.0
	6.1	1.8	1.3			Quick	1.4	1.5
	1.5	1.0	.8				1.0	1.0
	.9	.6	.4				.6	.6
23	16.2	35 10.5	35 10.3			Sales/Receivables	39 9.3	32 11.3
35	10.5	48 7.7	40 9.1				46 7.9	41 8.8
41	8.8	58 6.3	51 7.1				60 6.1	52 7.0
0	UND	18 20.8	22 16.6			Cost of Sales/Inventory	11 34.4	11 34.3
13	29.1	37 9.8	36 10.1				26 14.2	29 12.6
55	6.7	58 6.3	45 8.2				47 7.7	46 8.0
11	34.0	16 23.5	13 27.4			Cost of Sales/Payables	20 18.2	19 19.3
22	16.5	28 13.1	23 15.7				30 12.3	30 12.3
35	10.5	54 6.8	32 11.4				47 7.7	45 8.1
	4.5	7.2	9.7			Sales/Working Capital	9.1	9.2
	10.6	8.5	29.4				12.7	20.1
	150.7	156.1	-8.2				-88.3	458.8
	6.1	5.9	9.8			EBIT/Interest	5.2	7.3
(14)	2.7	2.2	3.4				2.5	(86) 3.3
	-4.8	-.4	1.9				1.7	1.3
						Net Profit + Depr., Dep., Amort./Cur. Mat. L/T/D	2.5	7.5
							(15) 1.6	(26) 2.1
							1.4	1.3
	.2	.6	.7			Fixed/Worth	.7	.8
	2.9	.9	2.3				1.3	1.3
	-3.7	4.5	5.1				8.1	5.0
	.3	.6	.6			Debt/Worth	1.0	1.0
	4.1	1.2	3.6				2.1	2.3
	-9.1	4.7	13.3				12.4	10.9
	64.8	39.1	71.8			% Profit Before Taxes/Tangible Net Worth	42.4	42.4
(10)	22.0	(23) 17.1	(12) 24.4				(38) 15.9	(74) 21.0
	1.7	-1.4	5.5				7.1	5.9
	21.5	12.6	10.6			% Profit Before Taxes/Total Assets	9.6	13.3
	6.0	3.1	6.8				4.0	6.7
	-6.5	-1.0	3.3				2.2	1.1
	32.6	8.2	7.4			Sales/Net Fixed Assets	14.4	14.6
	20.2	4.4	5.2				7.5	6.7
	5.2	2.8	3.7				3.8	3.4
	3.8	2.4	2.3			Sales/Total Assets	2.7	3.0
	3.0	1.8	1.8				2.2	2.2
	1.7	1.1	1.1				1.7	1.7
	.5	2.7	3.8			% Depr., Dep., Amort./Sales	2.3	2.3
(15)	1.5	(22) 4.1	(13) 4.7				(44) 3.7	(82) 3.5
	6.3	5.3	6.6				5.4	5.1
	4.0					% Officers', Directors' Owners' Comp/Sales	1.6	1.4
(11)	7.6						(17) 4.5	(37) 3.1
	11.4						9.9	7.9
11867M	51042M	262326M	405260M	56788M	141258M	Net Sales ($)	758866M	2080788M
2580M	19512M	154526M	235959M	52628M	101022M	Total Assets ($)	404473M	1151547M

M = $ thousand　　MM = $ million
See Pages 9 through 22 for Explanation of Ratios and Data

Comparative Historical Data / Current Data Sorted by Sales

Historical date columns: 4/1/07-3/31/08 ALL | 4/1/08-3/31/09 ALL | 4/1/09-3/31/10 ALL
Current data groupings: 8 (4/1-9/30/09) covers 0-1MM and 1-3MM; 59 (10/1/09-3/31/10) covers 3-5MM, 5-10MM, 10-25MM, 25MM & OVER

4/1/07-3/31/08 ALL	4/1/08-3/31/09 ALL	4/1/09-3/31/10 ALL		0-1MM	1-3MM	3-5MM	5-10MM	10-25MM	25MM & OVER
			Type of Statement						
8	11	11	Unqualified			1		4	6
19	18	19	Reviewed			1	8	7	3
14	6	5	Compiled		3	1		1	
10	7	10	Tax Returns	1	6	2	1		
24	38	22	Other	3	5	6	3	2	3
75	80	67	**NUMBER OF STATEMENTS**	4	14	11	12	14	12
%	%	%	**ASSETS**	%	%	%	%	%	%
6.8	7.9	11.6	Cash & Equivalents		26.5	9.6	8.5	5.9	6.4
27.0	25.3	24.4	Trade Receivables (net)		21.6	22.9	26.0	26.2	23.4
12.8	15.4	11.7	Inventory		7.6	10.6	10.5	16.4	15.8
1.3	2.8	1.0	All Other Current		.0	.9	.4	2.6	.9
47.9	51.4	48.6	Total Current		55.7	44.0	45.4	51.1	46.4
40.5	39.6	33.3	Fixed Assets (net)		28.3	35.2	33.6	35.4	38.6
8.0	4.9	10.1	Intangibles (net)		5.6	11.9	6.8	10.3	9.6
3.5	4.1	8.0	All Other Non-Current		10.5	8.8	14.2	3.2	5.4
100.0	100.0	100.0	Total		100.0	100.0	100.0	100.0	100.0
			LIABILITIES						
10.8	13.6	9.6	Notes Payable-Short Term		10.3	10.3	6.7	10.1	9.4
6.0	5.5	5.0	Cur. Mat.-L.T.D.		2.5	2.3	4.4	6.4	10.8
12.1	14.1	10.6	Trade Payables		10.0	10.2	9.8	10.9	11.4
.1	.0	.0	Income Taxes Payable		.0	.0	.0	.0	.1
11.1	6.4	7.3	All Other Current		7.7	8.6	5.4	6.2	6.3
40.0	39.6	32.5	Total Current		30.6	31.4	26.2	33.6	38.1
24.6	21.1	21.8	Long-Term Debt		29.6	22.1	20.5	12.4	30.1
.4	.5	.4	Deferred Taxes		.1	.0	.2	1.2	.5
7.0	13.8	13.3	All Other Non-Current		12.4	7.8	4.1	14.1	2.8
28.0	25.0	31.9	Net Worth		27.2	38.7	49.1	38.7	28.5
100.0	100.0	100.0	Total Liabilities & Net Worth		100.0	100.0	100.0	100.0	100.0
			INCOME DATA						
100.0	100.0	100.0	Net Sales		100.0	100.0	100.0	100.0	100.0
37.7	32.8	38.8	Gross Profit		43.1	53.7	39.8	27.7	23.7
33.1	30.2	35.2	Operating Expenses		40.7	46.0	35.2	24.2	19.6
4.7	2.6	3.6	Operating Profit		2.4	7.7	4.6	3.5	4.1
2.1	1.8	2.3	All Other Expenses (net)		1.0	1.5	1.4	1.5	7.0
2.6	.8	1.3	Profit Before Taxes		1.4	6.2	3.3	2.0	-2.9
			RATIOS						
2.3	2.5	2.7	Current		7.4	3.9	2.4	2.0	2.4
1.4	1.4	1.4			2.0	1.6	1.6	1.9	1.2
.9	1.0	.9			.8	.7	1.0	1.1	1.0
1.5	1.5	2.0	Quick		6.4	3.2	2.1	1.5	1.6
.9	.8	1.0			1.1	1.5	1.2	1.0	.8
.6	.6	.6			.7	.4	.7	.6	.6
32 11.5	29 12.6	34 10.6	Sales/Receivables	24 14.9	18 20.8	35 10.5	34 10.7	37 9.8	
40 9.1	39 9.3	41 9.0		38 9.6	39 9.3	43 8.5	48 7.6	47 7.8	
53 6.9	51 7.2	51 7.2		42 8.7	47 7.7	57 6.4	53 6.9	52 7.0	
12 31.6	20 18.3	12 29.4	Cost of Sales/Inventory	0 UND	10 37.6	11 31.9	21 17.4	23 15.8	
30 12.0	37 9.9	26 14.1		12 31.1	27 13.5	21 17.3	39 9.3	37 10.0	
50 7.3	54 6.7	46 7.9		33 10.9	74 4.9	46 8.0	49 7.5	44 8.3	
17 21.1	18 20.1	14 25.9	Cost of Sales/Payables	7 50.0	18 20.8	13 28.8	16 23.5	17 21.0	
25 14.4	26 13.9	26 14.0		21 17.5	39 9.3	25 14.5	24 15.0	23 15.7	
40 9.1	40 9.1	39 9.3		34 10.6	60 6.1	47 7.8	32 11.5	31 11.9	
8.0	7.9	6.7	Sales/Working Capital		4.2	6.2	5.5	7.6	9.9
18.3	20.1	17.1			9.9	14.2	16.5	9.5	29.4
-47.3	424.1	-86.6			-16.9	-17.1	NM	114.8	NM
4.2	4.5	6.8	EBIT/Interest		3.3		5.2	11.3	10.9
(74) 2.3	(74) 2.3	(60) 2.4			(11) -1.1		2.4	(11) 4.0	2.8
.7	-.2	-1.1			-5.4		1.6	.9	-2.0
4.5	7.5	2.1	Net Profit + Depr., Dep., Amort./Cur. Mat. L/T/D						
(17) 2.3	(23) 1.7	(16) 1.3							
1.0	1.1	-.2							
.8	.8	.5	Fixed/Worth		.1	.7	.2	.7	.9
1.7	1.6	1.4			3.2	4.3	.7	.8	2.9
8.5	4.6	-10.8			-.8	-20.8	1.9	NM	NM
1.0	.9	.5	Debt/Worth		.4	.3	.4	.6	1.0
2.3	2.3	2.3			3.2	4.1	1.2	1.4	5.3
19.2	9.6	-46.2			-3.6	-96.0	3.0	NM	NM
30.8	26.8	40.9	% Profit Before Taxes/Tangible Net Worth				29.9	39.1	
(60) 17.3	(66) 11.3	(48) 22.8					(11) 8.2	(11) 22.2	
1.3	-5.4	3.6					3.3	13.0	
9.6	9.9	12.5	% Profit Before Taxes/Total Assets		43.1	23.8	17.0	13.0	9.9
3.9	4.1	5.2			3.4	5.2	5.2	6.1	6.6
-1.3	-5.8	-1.1			-10.8	-4.7	1.5	.5	-12.5
11.6	11.9	18.2	Sales/Net Fixed Assets		42.7	22.2	23.0	8.2	6.0
5.0	5.6	5.6			19.2	4.9	5.2	5.4	5.0
3.2	3.7	4.1			4.5	2.7	3.8	4.4	3.6
2.8	2.9	3.0	Sales/Total Assets		3.4	4.0	2.5	2.7	2.4
2.0	2.1	2.1			2.6	2.6	1.8	2.0	2.0
1.5	1.7	1.4			1.1	1.1	1.1	1.4	1.5
2.6	2.1	2.6	% Depr., Dep., Amort./Sales		.5	.9	2.0	3.1	3.7
(67) 3.8	(72) 3.8	(58) 4.0			(11) 1.9	6.0	(10) 2.8	(12) 4.4	4.0
5.3	5.0	6.1			6.3	8.2	4.6	5.4	7.5
2.0	2.8	2.8	% Officers', Directors', Owners' Comp/Sales						
(34) 5.1	(29) 5.1	(30) 5.7							
8.3	6.3	8.4							
1272915M	1631019M	928541M	Net Sales ($)	2977M	25248M	42755M	82740M	218996M	555825M
856460M	869119M	566227M	Total Assets ($)	1196M	19281M	35801M	55351M	113001M	341597M

M = $ thousand   MM = $ million
See Pages 9 through 22 for Explanation of Ratios and Data

Current Data Sorted by Assets   **Comparative Historical Data**

0-500M	500M-2MM	2-10MM	10-50MM	50-100MM	100-250MM	Type of Statement	4/1/05-3/31/06 ALL	4/1/06-3/31/07 ALL
1	5	3	5	1	1	Unqualified	11	10
4	9	16	7			Reviewed	23	23
3	8	4				Compiled	16	17
11	12	2				Tax Returns	6	10
	21 (4/1-9/30/09)	9	88 (10/1/09-3/31/10)			Other	22	31
19	34	34	20	1	1	**NUMBER OF STATEMENTS**	78	91
%	%	%	%	%	%	**ASSETS**	%	%
17.9	6.0	9.0	9.8			Cash & Equivalents	9.2	7.5
27.9	32.2	26.7	25.7			Trade Receivables (net)	29.5	30.2
11.4	20.8	16.3	23.5			Inventory	19.3	17.9
3.5	1.8	4.4	1.8			All Other Current	1.9	3.1
60.7	60.8	56.4	60.6			Total Current	60.0	58.7
26.0	30.0	30.3	27.6			Fixed Assets (net)	31.2	29.9
2.7	7.7	7.0	5.9			Intangibles (net)	4.3	5.7
10.5	1.6	6.2	5.9			All Other Non-Current	4.6	5.7
100.0	100.0	100.0	100.0			Total	100.0	100.0
						LIABILITIES		
11.4	9.6	10.7	6.2			Notes Payable-Short Term	13.5	15.6
5.8	6.0	4.2	4.5			Cur. Mat.-L.T.D.	5.9	4.5
19.5	15.7	12.6	12.3			Trade Payables	16.8	15.0
.0	.1	.1	.0			Income Taxes Payable	.1	.2
16.8	8.2	9.3	7.3			All Other Current	10.2	12.5
53.5	39.5	36.8	30.4			Total Current	46.5	47.8
38.0	18.9	22.7	11.2			Long-Term Debt	25.2	19.7
.2	.5	.3	.0			Deferred Taxes	.5	.2
10.6	9.0	4.2	3.1			All Other Non-Current	7.3	4.0
-2.3	32.1	36.0	55.3			Net Worth	20.6	28.3
100.0	100.0	100.0	100.0			Total Liabilities & Net Worth	100.0	100.0
						INCOME DATA		
100.0	100.0	100.0	100.0			Net Sales	100.0	100.0
49.1	44.0	36.0	26.9			Gross Profit	39.4	39.3
44.6	45.0	33.2	24.8			Operating Expenses	34.6	32.4
4.5	-1.1	2.9	2.1			Operating Profit	4.8	6.9
1.2	1.3	2.0	.1			All Other Expenses (net)	1.6	1.4
3.3	-2.4	.8	2.1			Profit Before Taxes	3.2	5.5
						RATIOS		
2.7	2.3	2.3	3.8				2.5	2.1
1.2	1.4	1.6	2.3			Current	1.4	1.4
.6	1.1	1.0	1.3				1.1	1.0
2.6	1.7	1.5	2.6				1.6	1.5
.8	.9	1.0	1.7			Quick	.9	.8
.3	.5	.5	.5				.6	.6
9 38.9	31 11.7	28 13.0	32 11.4				31 11.9	31 12.0
20 18.3	40 9.0	49 7.5	50 7.4			Sales/Receivables	44 8.3	46 8.0
39 9.4	54 6.8	66 5.5	64 5.7				52 7.1	58 6.3
0 UND	8 48.3	18 20.2	29 12.7				14 25.5	17 22.1
6 59.5	38 9.5	45 8.2	54 6.8			Cost of Sales/Inventory	42 8.8	39 9.3
69 5.3	97 3.8	63 5.8	99 3.7				90 4.0	68 5.4
11 32.9	19 19.0	20 18.7	14 25.4				19 18.8	17 22.0
23 15.8	35 10.4	33 11.0	31 11.7			Cost of Sales/Payables	32 11.4	32 11.2
43 8.5	54 6.8	40 9.1	34 10.6				49 7.4	47 7.8
9.1	7.2	5.7	4.0				6.1	6.5
75.2	14.9	9.9	6.0			Sales/Working Capital	13.5	16.9
-43.9	47.4	NM	13.2				46.9	999.8
14.2	1.7	6.2	7.9				10.5	10.0
(14) 3.7	(29) -.2	1.9	(18) 2.7			EBIT/Interest	(75) 3.2	(86) 3.9
-.1	-4.1	-2.0	.9				1.4	1.1
			7.5				5.0	3.5
			(10) 3.5			Net Profit + Depr., Dep., Amort./Cur. Mat. L/T/D	(22) 2.4	(23) 1.8
			.9				1.4	1.2
.2	.4	.3	.3				.6	.6
2.6	1.1	1.3	.6			Fixed/Worth	1.3	1.0
-.5	NM	2.9	1.2				12.3	5.9
1.1	.7	1.1	.4				1.0	.9
5.6	2.5	1.9	.9			Debt/Worth	2.6	2.1
-4.5	NM	10.2	2.6				21.9	15.0
77.7	29.3	31.4	16.9				45.5	53.2
(10) 65.0	(26) .7	(28) 7.8	6.2			% Profit Before Taxes/Tangible Net Worth	(62) 21.3	(73) 23.8
43.7	-27.9	-11.6	-.8				10.4	3.6
40.7	6.9	8.8	7.6				14.1	18.4
21.6	-2.2	1.4	2.5			% Profit Before Taxes/Total Assets	6.6	8.0
-3.1	-11.9	-6.4	-.4				.8	.2
98.8	26.0	25.0	21.0				19.3	18.7
17.8	11.7	9.0	6.1			Sales/Net Fixed Assets	9.7	8.9
12.3	5.3	3.4	3.8				5.1	5.0
6.0	3.0	2.3	2.3				3.1	3.2
4.0	2.3	1.9	1.9			Sales/Total Assets	2.5	2.3
3.5	1.8	1.6	1.2				1.7	1.7
.8	1.1	1.5	1.1				1.5	1.3
(13) 1.9	(28) 2.8	(31) 2.7	(19) 2.7			% Depr., Dep., Amort./Sales	(72) 2.6	(73) 2.2
2.7	4.2	5.3	4.7				4.7	3.8
	3.3	2.5					3.4	3.3
	(15) 6.8	(16) 5.0				% Officers', Directors' Owners' Comp/Sales	(33) 6.8	(36) 5.9
	9.5	7.0					11.0	10.1
21379M	110092M	296992M	908757M	166741M	179456M	Net Sales ($)	1190912M	2028397M
4619M	38984M	146179M	463616M	97078M	121879M	Total Assets ($)	678772M	980974M

M = $ thousand   MM = $ million
See Pages 9 through 22 for Explanation of Ratios and Data

Comparative Historical Data | **Current Data Sorted by Sales**

Type of Statement

4/1/07-3/31/08 ALL	4/1/08-3/31/09 ALL	4/1/09-3/31/10 ALL	Type of Statement	0-1MM	1-3MM	3-5MM	5-10MM	10-25MM	25MM & OVER
6	12	10	Unqualified				2	2	6
24	25	29	Reviewed		2	3	12	6	6
15	19	17	Compiled	4	8	4	1		
15	23	13	Tax Returns	2	5	4	2		
36	36	40	Other	6	10	8	5	5	6
					21 (4/1-9/30/09)		88 (10/1/09-3/31/10)		
96	115	109	NUMBER OF STATEMENTS	12	25	19	22	13	18

Assets / Liabilities / Income Data (%)

4/1/07-3/31/08 ALL	4/1/08-3/31/09 ALL	4/1/09-3/31/10 ALL		0-1MM	1-3MM	3-5MM	5-10MM	10-25MM	25MM & OVER
%	%	%	**ASSETS**	%	%	%	%	%	%
8.2	7.5	9.8	Cash & Equivalents	13.0	11.6	7.8	9.8	8.5	8.3
29.8	29.2	28.3	Trade Receivables (net)	24.4	28.3	25.4	32.3	30.3	27.7
18.8	18.4	18.4	Inventory	12.3	12.1	28.0	17.2	10.6	28.0
3.5	1.9	3.0	All Other Current	3.4	1.7	2.0	2.3	9.5	1.5
60.3	57.0	59.5	Total Current	53.0	53.7	63.3	61.7	58.9	65.5
31.3	32.3	28.9	Fixed Assets (net)	31.5	33.7	25.1	28.7	31.2	23.1
3.2	5.3	6.2	Intangibles (net)	5.9	7.7	7.2	4.4	6.4	5.1
5.3	5.3	5.5	All Other Non-Current	9.6	4.9	4.5	5.1	3.4	6.4
100.0	100.0	100.0	Total	100.0	100.0	100.0	100.0	100.0	100.0
			LIABILITIES						
13.9	16.8	9.4	Notes Payable-Short Term	13.8	8.7	10.0	9.2	12.3	5.1
4.5	5.1	5.3	Cur. Mat.-L.T.D.	9.2	5.4	6.4	3.1	2.3	6.5
14.9	16.6	14.7	Trade Payables	18.8	14.7	15.8	14.4	10.3	14.5
.5	.1	.1	Income Taxes Payable	.0	.0	.0	.0	.3	.0
9.1	9.6	10.0	All Other Current	9.0	12.2	7.9	9.9	10.9	9.2
42.9	48.2	39.6	Total Current	50.7	41.0	40.3	36.6	36.3	35.3
20.9	20.1	21.7	Long-Term Debt	32.6	35.7	20.2	15.4	19.4	5.8
.2	.3	.3	Deferred Taxes	.0	.8	.0	.3	.1	.0
3.2	6.3	6.5	All Other Non-Current	15.3	10.5	4.2	3.0	5.6	2.7
32.9	25.2	31.9	Net Worth	1.4	11.9	35.3	44.6	38.7	56.2
100.0	100.0	100.0	Total Liabilities & Net Worth	100.0	100.0	100.0	100.0	100.0	100.0
			INCOME DATA						
100.0	100.0	100.0	Net Sales	100.0	100.0	100.0	100.0	100.0	100.0
37.7	38.4	38.7	Gross Profit	58.5	45.8	33.6	39.3	32.1	25.1
33.1	36.5	37.0	Operating Expenses	54.3	45.7	34.9	35.1	28.9	23.8
4.6	1.9	1.7	Operating Profit	4.2	.1	-1.3	4.3	3.2	1.2
1.2	1.4	1.2	All Other Expenses (net)	2.1	1.7	2.3	.8	-.2	.6
3.4	.5	.5	Profit Before Taxes	2.1	-1.6	-3.5	3.5	3.4	.6

Ratios

4/1/07-3/31/08 ALL	4/1/08-3/31/09 ALL	4/1/09-3/31/10 ALL		0-1MM	1-3MM	3-5MM	5-10MM	10-25MM	25MM & OVER
2.8	1.9	2.6	Current	2.2	2.5	2.7	2.7	2.8	3.9
1.5	1.3	1.5		1.3	1.5	1.4	1.9	1.5	2.2
1.0	.8	1.1		.6	.9	1.1	1.4	1.3	1.1
1.8	1.4	1.9	Quick	1.7	2.2	1.7	2.2	1.9	2.8
.9	.8	1.0		.8	.9	.8	1.2	1.1	1.5
.6	.5	.5		.3	.4	.4	.8	.6	.5
28 13.1	27 13.7	28 13.0	Sales/Receivables	14 25.2	22 16.8	26 14.0	32 11.5	36 10.1	31 11.6
40 9.1	39 9.3	41 8.9		24 15.3	34 10.7	37 9.9	53 6.9	52 7.0	46 8.0
53 6.9	56 6.5	57 6.4		59 6.2	45 8.2	45 8.2	69 5.3	65 5.6	54 6.8
13 27.9	11 34.0	10 38.2	Cost of Sales/Inventory	0 UND	4 92.1	25 14.7	12 30.0	5 71.2	32 11.5
29 12.4	33 11.2	41 8.9		29 12.6	11 32.5	52 7.0	45 8.2	27 13.6	58 6.3
68 5.4	66 5.5	77 4.7		111 3.3	54 6.8	97 3.8	63 5.8	37 9.8	104 3.5
16 23.1	16 22.5	17 21.1	Cost of Sales/Payables	13 28.8	13 27.9	21 17.5	16 23.0	20 18.6	16 22.7
26 14.0	31 11.7	32 11.5		43 8.4	28 12.9	33 10.9	32 11.6	33 11.1	25 14.4
43 8.5	55 6.7	43 8.5		71 5.1	46 7.9	40 9.2	44 8.3	39 9.3	36 10.1
6.1	8.5	5.9	Sales/Working Capital	9.3	7.3	7.1	5.9	5.1	4.2
12.1	19.9	12.1		68.2	30.7	13.5	7.8	7.4	6.8
999.8	-30.3	99.3		-9.5	-50.7	84.7	26.5	23.1	77.9
7.2	5.0	5.5	EBIT/Interest		4.7	1.5	12.7	10.4	11.4
(85) 3.0	(105) 1.6	(97) 1.5			(21) .2	(18) -2.2	(21) 3.4	2.2	(16) 1.8
1.2	.1	-2.2			-3.8	-8.2	1.0	-.1	-9.9
8.6	3.2	5.4	Net Profit + Depr., Dep., Amort./Cur. Mat. L/T/D						
(21) 3.8	(22) 1.5	(21) 1.6							
1.0	.8	.5							
.4	.5	.3	Fixed/Worth	.4	.7	.3	.2	.3	.2
.9	1.5	1.0		NM	3.1	1.1	1.1	.9	.5
2.2	11.3	4.0		-1.1	-.5	4.9	2.0	1.6	.9
.6	1.3	.8	Debt/Worth	1.4	.7	.8	.6	1.3	.2
1.9	3.4	2.0		NM	5.6	2.5	1.4	2.2	.9
9.0	27.5	18.6		-6.1	-3.7	21.5	3.3	2.9	2.9
40.7	33.4	36.8	% Profit Before Taxes/Tangible Net Worth		57.6	5.5	35.0	44.0	16.9
(83) 19.1	(89) 11.5	(86) 6.5			(14) 32.7	(15) -9.5	(21) 9.4	(12) 6.9	2.5
7.3	-4.2	-8.5			-22.6	-42.7	.0	.5	-7.6
15.5	11.0	11.0	% Profit Before Taxes/Total Assets	23.2	23.7	1.5	12.4	12.3	6.6
6.5	2.9	1.7		5.5	6.6	-4.5	3.5	3.7	1.2
1.2	-2.8	-6.5		-3.9	-14.1	-17.3	.7	-.5	-5.9
19.6	18.1	27.1	Sales/Net Fixed Assets	97.7	32.7	17.5	35.1	16.5	28.1
9.2	8.7	11.5		10.0	13.3	11.5	9.4	5.2	16.3
5.3	4.4	4.4		3.6	5.2	5.8	3.4	3.6	5.2
3.4	3.3	3.4	Sales/Total Assets	4.1	4.6	3.0	2.9	2.2	3.1
2.4	2.5	2.1		2.3	3.0	2.3	2.0	1.8	2.1
1.8	1.8	1.6		1.2	1.8	1.8	1.6	1.3	1.4
1.5	1.6	1.3	% Depr., Dep., Amort./Sales		.9	1.4	1.5	1.2	1.2
(85) 2.5	(105) 2.9	(92) 2.6			(21) 2.6	(16) 3.0	(19) 2.7	(12) 3.6	(17) 1.7
4.4	4.4	4.5			4.8	3.9	4.9	6.4	3.9
2.6	3.2	3.3	% Officers', Directors' Owners' Comp/Sales		6.3		2.5		
(49) 5.7	(65) 5.1	(46) 5.7			(13) 9.5		(12) 4.1		
11.1	9.8	9.5			11.6		6.9		
1987536M	2245588M	1683417M	Net Sales ($)	7689M	45772M	75712M	151304M	193179M	1209761M
946612M	999021M	872355M	Total Assets ($)	3540M	18043M	37836M	72010M	117929M	622997M

© RMA 2010

M = $ thousand   MM = $ million
See Pages 9 through 22 for Explanation of Ratios and Data

Current Data Sorted by Assets | Comparative Historical Data

			4			Type of Statement		7	8
1	4	8	3			Unqualified			
3	6	6				Reviewed		25	19
3	9	3				Compiled		19	13
7	10	8	5	1		Tax Returns		14	24
	20 (4/1-9/30/09)		61 (10/1/09-3/31/10)			Other		32	26
								4/1/05-	4/1/06-
								3/31/06	3/31/07
0-500M	500M-2MM	2-10MM	10-50MM	50-100MM	100-250MM			ALL	ALL
14	29	25	12	1		NUMBER OF STATEMENTS		97	90
%	%	%	%	%	%	ASSETS		%	%
7.4	9.1	6.1	4.3		D	Cash & Equivalents		6.3	7.6
25.8	32.6	24.9	28.6		A	Trade Receivables (net)		28.4	27.3
9.1	10.3	8.3	9.9		T	Inventory		9.8	10.4
.1	.3	1.1	.9		A	All Other Current		.9	1.1
42.4	52.3	40.4	43.7			Total Current		45.4	46.4
30.6	36.0	44.1	44.9		N	Fixed Assets (net)		39.9	38.9
16.2	4.2	7.1	6.4		O	Intangibles (net)		6.3	5.8
10.8	7.5	8.4	5.0		T	All Other Non-Current		8.4	8.9
100.0	100.0	100.0	100.0			Total		100.0	100.0
					A	LIABILITIES			
15.4	8.8	13.5	3.2		V	Notes Payable-Short Term		11.1	9.4
5.4	9.3	8.7	10.5		A	Cur. Mat.-L.T.D.		8.0	8.2
19.8	16.3	13.2	12.0		I	Trade Payables		14.3	13.4
.1	.0	.1	.0		L	Income Taxes Payable		.1	.0
7.4	8.4	10.3	8.4		A	All Other Current		7.3	7.3
48.0	42.7	45.8	34.1		B	Total Current		40.8	38.4
42.4	34.7	28.8	24.6		L	Long-Term Debt		30.3	32.1
.0	.5	.6	1.3		E	Deferred Taxes		.5	.5
7.1	4.3	3.1	7.6			All Other Non-Current		3.7	4.7
2.5	17.8	21.7	32.5			Net Worth		24.6	24.4
100.0	100.0	100.0	100.0			Total Liabilities & Net Worth		100.0	100.0
						INCOME DATA			
100.0	100.0	100.0	100.0			Net Sales		100.0	100.0
						Gross Profit			
99.8	97.0	98.2	96.7			Operating Expenses		93.2	93.9
.2	3.0	1.8	3.3			Operating Profit		6.8	6.1
1.1	2.7	2.1	1.5			All Other Expenses (net)		1.8	1.4
-.9	.3	-.3	1.9			Profit Before Taxes		5.0	4.7
						RATIOS			
1.9	1.9	1.2	1.6					1.8	2.0
1.0	1.2	.9	1.3			Current		1.1	1.2
.6	.8	.7	1.1					.8	.8
1.7	1.5	.9	1.3					1.4	1.5
.8	1.0	.7	.9			Quick		.8	.9
.4	.7	.6	.9					.6	.6
18 20.1	29 12.7	37 9.8	38 9.5				33 11.0	27 13.5
24 14.9	39 9.3	45 8.2	53 6.8			Sales/Receivables	44 8.2	42 8.7
40 9.2	53 6.9	56 6.5	74 5.0				58 6.2	51 7.1
						Cost of Sales/Inventory			
						Cost of Sales/Payables			
19.2	10.2	32.1	12.9					12.2	9.4
NM	28.7	-29.6	20.9			Sales/Working Capital		54.7	37.2
-10.5	-38.5	-13.3	63.8					-22.1	-31.6
3.0	3.4	1.7	4.5					6.0	6.2
(11) -.6	(26) 1.0	-.5	2.1			EBIT/Interest	(91) 2.6	(83) 2.4
-3.0	-3.3	-2.2	.1					1.3	1.0
						Net Profit + Depr., Dep.,		2.3	3.6
						Amort./Cur. Mat. L/T/D	(28) 1.8	(22) 1.6
								1.0	1.0
.7	.5	.9	.9					.7	.7
-1.6	3.6	4.4	1.8			Fixed/Worth		2.0	1.7
-.4	-6.7	NM	4.4					8.5	NM
1.3	1.1	2.0	1.2					1.2	1.2
-8.2	6.2	5.0	2.2			Debt/Worth		3.2	2.5
-2.1	-11.8	NM	6.0					13.8	NM
	53.7	16.2	26.8			% Profit Before Taxes/Tangible		41.9	44.0
(20) 5.1	(19) -21.8	(10) 13.5			Net Worth	(75) 20.4	(68) 22.5
	-11.6	-31.9	-4.6					6.2	1.0
15.9	6.1	2.5	9.0			% Profit Before Taxes/Total		11.9	15.7
-2.7	.1	-4.4	3.7			Assets		5.6	5.0
-13.9	-9.7	-8.6	-3.0					.6	.0
36.3	15.2	10.2	5.3					10.9	13.3
14.2	6.8	3.5	4.1			Sales/Net Fixed Assets		5.4	6.1
4.5	4.2	2.4	2.9					3.2	3.8
4.5	3.6	2.4	2.4					2.9	3.4
3.0	2.6	1.7	1.7			Sales/Total Assets		2.2	2.4
2.2	2.0	1.3	1.3					1.5	1.8
	2.5	3.6	3.3					2.7	2.8
(25) 4.2	6.2	(11) 5.3			% Depr., Dep., Amort./Sales	(85) 4.1	(80) 4.0
	7.3	8.0	6.2					6.6	5.6
	2.3	2.3						2.8	2.5
(17) 3.2	(12) 4.5				% Officers', Directors'	(52) 5.5	(46) 4.5
	5.4	9.5				Owners' Comp/Sales		8.1	8.8
10200M	88470M	170443M	499478M	70341M		Net Sales ($)		971343M	963014M
3412M	34605M	99753M	267458M	75000M		Total Assets ($)		559580M	490946M

M = $ thousand   MM = $ million
See Pages 9 through 22 for Explanation of Ratios and Data

Comparative Historical Data / Current Data Sorted by Sales

			Type of Statement	0-1MM	1-3MM	3-5MM	5-10MM	10-25MM	25MM & OVER
8	3	4	Unqualified	1	2	3	5	1	3
20	18	16	Reviewed	4	4	3	3	3	2
16	15	15	Compiled	3	8	4		1	
26	23	15	Tax Returns	5	7	5	7		5
29	30	31	Other					2	
4/1/07-3/31/08	4/1/08-3/31/09	4/1/09-3/31/10			20 (4/1-9/30/09)		61 (10/1/09-3/31/10)		
ALL	ALL	ALL							
99	89	81	NUMBER OF STATEMENTS	13	21	15	15	7	10
%	%	%	ASSETS	%	%	%	%	%	%
7.6	6.6	7.1	Cash & Equivalents	7.6	11.1	6.8	5.5		3.0
28.2	27.6	28.1	Trade Receivables (net)	18.1	23.0	33.4	35.7		27.3
9.6	8.4	9.3	Inventory	9.2	8.2	7.8	10.2		10.8
.8	2.0	.6	All Other Current	.1	.2	.5	.9		1.0
46.3	44.7	45.2	Total Current	35.0	42.5	48.5	52.4		42.1
40.4	43.0	38.6	Fixed Assets (net)	37.1	38.5	42.5	36.7		41.6
6.3	5.7	8.2	Intangibles (net)	15.9	8.9	4.6	3.3		12.4
7.0	6.7	7.9	All Other Non-Current	11.9	10.2	4.4	7.6		3.9
100.0	100.0	100.0	Total	100.0	100.0	100.0	100.0		100.0
			LIABILITIES						
11.6	10.8	10.4	Notes Payable-Short Term	10.2	10.3	9.4	14.6		3.8
7.7	7.8	8.6	Cur. Mat.-L.T.D.	4.9	10.0	7.6	9.1		4.7
14.3	14.2	15.1	Trade Payables	16.2	11.8	17.1	17.9		10.1
.1	.0	.0	Income Taxes Payable	.1	.0	.0	.0		.0
7.6	8.7	8.8	All Other Current	7.5	10.3	5.3	10.0		9.5
41.2	41.4	42.9	Total Current	38.9	42.4	39.4	51.6		28.1
33.9	36.2	32.7	Long-Term Debt	46.3	37.7	30.1	29.3		25.2
.3	.5	.6	Deferred Taxes	.0	.0	1.2	.8		1.5
6.0	5.9	5.1	All Other Non-Current	5.1	4.0	4.7	3.8		8.8
18.6	16.0	18.8	Net Worth	9.6	15.8	24.6	14.5		36.4
100.0	100.0	100.0	Total Liabilities & Net Worth	100.0	100.0	100.0	100.0		100.0
			INCOME DATA						
100.0	100.0	100.0	Net Sales	100.0	100.0	100.0	100.0		100.0
			Gross Profit						
96.2	95.5	97.8	Operating Expenses	94.0	97.0	98.8	100.6		95.3
3.8	4.5	2.2	Operating Profit	6.0	3.0	1.2	-.6		4.7
1.6	2.6	2.1	All Other Expenses (net)	4.7	1.5	1.9	1.2		1.7
2.2	1.9	.1	Profit Before Taxes	1.3	1.5	-.7	-1.7		3.0
			RATIOS						
2.2	1.7	1.6		1.9	2.0	2.4	1.6		2.3
1.2	1.1	1.1	Current	1.0	.9	1.1	.9		1.3
.8	.8	.7		.5	.7	.9	.8		1.2
1.8	1.4	1.3		1.8	1.5	1.6	1.1		1.2
1.0	.9	.9	Quick	.6	.7	1.0	.7		1.0
.6	.6	.6		.1	.5	.6	.6		.9
27 13.3	24 15.5	29 12.4		14 25.4	23 15.8	33 11.2	43 8.5		35 10.5
40 9.1	36 10.1	40 9.2	Sales/Receivables	20 18.5	32 11.2	44 8.3	51 7.1		43 8.5
52 7.1	51 7.2	54 6.8		33 11.2	49 7.4	49 7.5	64 5.7		72 5.1
			Cost of Sales/Inventory						
			Cost of Sales/Payables						
9.6	13.0	13.0		16.0	6.4	9.7	13.8		11.5
42.1	43.6	67.2	Sales/Working Capital	711.0	-59.5	60.0	-74.9		17.9
-25.4	-24.1	-18.6		-6.9	-12.4	-62.1	-23.1		38.1
4.2	4.5	3.0			5.7	1.7	2.7		9.5
(93) 1.9	(84) 1.8	(75) .6	EBIT/Interest		(20) .9	(14) .4	.5		2.9
.4	-1.0	-2.1			-4.4	-2.3	-1.3		1.6
2.4	2.5	1.5							
(14) 1.6	(20) 1.6	(15) .9	Net Profit + Depr., Dep., Amort./Cur. Mat. L/T/D						
.8	1.0	.1							
.8	1.0	.8		.7	.7	.7	.8		.8
1.9	2.5	3.4	Fixed/Worth	11.2	14.1	2.8	4.4		1.8
-4.3	-9.7	-4.0		-.4	-1.6	-9.1	-6.7		NM
1.7	1.3	1.3		1.1	.9	1.6	1.3		1.1
3.8	4.2	5.0	Debt/Worth	10.3	17.9	3.9	5.0		2.2
-9.4	-38.6	-10.8		-2.0	-8.1	-24.1	-12.4		NM
42.5	41.4	18.5			17.4	50.3	16.2		
(68) 17.8	(64) 14.0	(55) .4	% Profit Before Taxes/Tangible Net Worth		(12) -1.2	(11) .7	(11) -8.2		
1.4	-5.5	-25.9			-30.5	-24.3	-31.8		
13.7	10.7	6.1		9.5	8.0	4.2	4.2		9.9
3.4	3.0	-1.5	% Profit Before Taxes/Total Assets	.0	-.1	-1.9	-1.7		5.5
-1.0	-6.8	-8.5		-12.1	-11.0	-8.4	-8.7		1.9
15.5	12.8	13.8		21.6	15.2	11.3	13.5		7.1
6.6	6.4	5.4	Sales/Net Fixed Assets	11.0	6.8	5.3	7.6		4.8
3.7	3.4	3.2		3.5	3.2	2.6	3.5		3.2
3.4	3.6	3.1		3.6	3.4	3.8	3.1		2.4
2.4	2.4	2.2	Sales/Total Assets	2.6	2.6	2.3	2.4		1.9
1.7	1.6	1.5		1.7	1.1	1.7	1.6		1.2
2.4	2.9	2.9		1.9	3.5	3.9	2.1		
(84) 3.8	(77) 4.3	(71) 4.8	% Depr., Dep., Amort./Sales	(10) 2.8	(17) 4.5	(13) 4.9	4.3		
6.4	6.5	7.0		5.2	8.8	8.9	6.8		
3.0	2.6	2.2				2.4	2.3		
(50) 5.3	(50) 4.2	(39) 4.0	% Officers', Directors' Owners' Comp/Sales		(13) 3.6	(10) 4.2			
8.2	8.3	9.4			11.8	6.0			
1228207M	951117M	838932M	Net Sales ($)	7735M	42282M	59617M	104948M	107355M	516995M
629616M	510663M	480228M	Total Assets ($)	4656M	34660M	27741M	49018M	58959M	305194M

M = $ thousand   MM = $ million
See Pages 9 through 22 for Explanation of Ratios and Data

Current Data Sorted by Assets   Comparative Historical Data

0-500M	500M-2MM	2-10MM	10-50MM	50-100MM	100-250MM	Type of Statement	4/1/05-3/31/06 ALL	4/1/06-3/31/07 ALL
			4			Unqualified	13	6
		6	2			Reviewed	11	14
1	3					Compiled	3	5
2	2					Tax Returns		8
2	2	2	4		1	Other	17	15
	10 (4/1-9/30/09)		21 (10/1/09-3/31/10)					
							ALL	ALL
5	7	8	10		1	**NUMBER OF STATEMENTS**	44	48
%	%	%	%	%	%	**ASSETS**	%	%
			12.8			Cash & Equivalents	7.4	7.5
			33.5	D		Trade Receivables (net)	35.6	34.3
			10.8	A		Inventory	14.6	15.8
			3.1	T		All Other Current	3.2	1.1
			60.2	A		Total Current	60.9	58.8
			21.3			Fixed Assets (net)	27.2	25.1
			12.8	N		Intangibles (net)	5.3	9.4
			5.8	O		All Other Non-Current	6.7	6.7
			100.0	T		Total	100.0	100.0
						LIABILITIES		
			2.8	A		Notes Payable-Short Term	10.2	11.9
			2.7	V		Cur. Mat.-L.T.D.	3.9	4.1
			16.6	A		Trade Payables	19.7	18.8
			.1	I		Income Taxes Payable	.2	.2
			13.9	L		All Other Current	10.6	10.3
			36.1	A		Total Current	44.7	45.3
			17.8	B		Long-Term Debt	17.1	14.0
			.4	L		Deferred Taxes	.5	.6
			.9	E		All Other Non-Current	3.7	4.0
			44.7			Net Worth	34.0	36.1
			100.0			Total Liabilities & Net Worth	100.0	100.0
						INCOME DATA		
			100.0			Net Sales	100.0	100.0
			28.6			Gross Profit	29.9	34.9
			23.5			Operating Expenses	25.7	30.7
			5.1			Operating Profit	4.2	4.2
			.4			All Other Expenses (net)	.5	.7
			4.7			Profit Before Taxes	3.6	3.5
						RATIOS		
			2.8			Current	2.1	2.2
			1.7				1.4	1.6
			1.1				1.0	1.0
			2.1			Quick	1.5	1.6
			1.3				1.0	1.0
			.8				.5	.6
		35	10.4			Sales/Receivables	33 11.1	32 11.5
		41	9.0				45 8.1	42 8.8
		53	6.8				60 6.0	56 6.6
		15	24.3			Cost of Sales/Inventory	12 30.8	12 30.8
		18	20.3				25 14.3	23 15.7
		24	15.0				45 8.1	45 8.2
		16	23.0			Cost of Sales/Payables	19 19.4	18 20.5
		26	13.8				28 12.9	31 11.7
		46	8.0				50 7.3	52 7.1
			6.2			Sales/Working Capital	8.3	7.6
			10.1				19.9	12.2
			49.7				-208.4	451.4
						EBIT/Interest	15.1	8.3
							(37) 4.3	(40) 3.2
							1.0	1.2
						Net Profit + Depr., Dep., Amort./Cur. Mat. L/T/D	12.0	10.5
							(12) 3.8	(11) 4.0
							.4	.5
			.2			Fixed/Worth	.3	.3
			.4				1.1	.7
			1.4				9.5	6.7
			.6			Debt/Worth	.7	.6
			1.1				2.1	2.1
			3.1				22.6	12.5
						% Profit Before Taxes/Tangible Net Worth	34.0	28.7
							(34) 22.3	(37) 13.6
							16.7	5.0
			19.8			% Profit Before Taxes/Total Assets	15.7	13.1
			5.6				6.1	6.0
			2.5				1.2	.5
			48.1			Sales/Net Fixed Assets	23.4	27.1
			13.6				10.9	11.6
			6.1				6.8	6.3
			3.4			Sales/Total Assets	3.3	3.4
			2.4				2.7	2.6
			2.1				2.0	2.0
						% Depr., Dep., Amort./Sales	1.6	1.5
							(33) 2.1	(40) 2.5
							3.6	3.4
						% Officers', Directors' Owners' Comp/Sales		1.9
								(14) 3.4
								7.5
8956M	22477M	83484M	490132M		138802M	Net Sales ($)	1112757M	1218487M
1589M	9642M	45916M	175490M		133322M	Total Assets ($)	482610M	722521M

(Left columns under 50-100MM marked: DATA NOT AVAILABLE)

© RMA 2010

M = $ thousand   MM = $ million
See Pages 9 through 22 for Explanation of Ratios and Data

Comparative Historical Data

	4/1/07-3/31/08 ALL	4/1/08-3/31/09 ALL	4/1/09-3/31/10 ALL
Type of Statement			
Unqualified	8	6	4
Reviewed	13	13	11
Compiled	4	3	3
Tax Returns	2	3	2
Other	11	11	11
NUMBER OF STATEMENTS	38	36	31
	%	%	%
ASSETS			
Cash & Equivalents	12.4	13.0	8.7
Trade Receivables (net)	33.3	30.6	30.4
Inventory	12.2	16.3	13.1
All Other Current	2.9	2.1	1.8
Total Current	60.8	61.9	54.0
Fixed Assets (net)	25.7	25.4	29.3
Intangibles (net)	7.0	7.2	10.8
All Other Non-Current	6.4	5.5	5.9
Total	100.0	100.0	100.0
LIABILITIES			
Notes Payable-Short Term	9.6	6.6	8.6
Cur. Mat.-L.T.D.	4.9	3.6	5.1
Trade Payables	13.8	14.0	15.3
Income Taxes Payable	.0	.0	.1
All Other Current	10.8	11.6	10.2
Total Current	39.2	35.8	39.4
Long-Term Debt	13.0	17.1	21.1
Deferred Taxes	.6	.6	.5
All Other Non-Current	5.7	5.7	5.6
Net Worth	41.6	40.7	33.4
Total Liabilties & Net Worth	100.0	100.0	100.0
INCOME DATA			
Net Sales	100.0	100.0	100.0
Gross Profit	36.8	32.0	32.4
Operating Expenses	31.5	30.0	30.7
Operating Profit	5.3	2.0	1.7
All Other Expenses (net)	.7	1.2	.6
Profit Before Taxes	4.6	.8	1.2
RATIOS			
Current	2.5	2.4	1.8
	1.8	1.8	1.4
	1.1	1.1	1.0
Quick	1.8	1.9	1.4
	1.1	1.1	1.1
	.7	.7	.6
Sales/Receivables	33 11.2	29 12.7	31 11.8
	39 9.4	36 10.1	40 9.2
	53 6.8	51 7.2	53 6.9
Cost of Sales/Inventory	13 28.8	12 30.1	13 28.3
	21 17.4	25 14.4	21 17.5
	35 10.5	51 7.1	41 8.9
Cost of Sales/Payables	14 25.8	11 34.3	16 23.3
	22 16.7	20 17.8	24 15.4
	41 8.9	53 6.9	42 8.7
Sales/Working Capital	6.6	7.1	7.1
	11.4	12.6	24.1
	NM	65.7	-763.9
EBIT/Interest	11.9	7.4	7.1
	(34) 6.0	(29) 2.1	(29) 1.6
	1.6	.1	-1.3
Net Profit + Depr., Dep., Amort./Cur. Mat. L/T/D			
Fixed/Worth	.3	.2	.3
	.7	.6	1.3
	1.9	2.1	UND
Debt/Worth	.6	.5	.9
	1.8	1.6	1.9
	3.7	10.6	UND
% Profit Before Taxes/Tangible Net Worth	46.0	35.6	30.4
	(33) 23.4	(30) 14.9	(24) 8.0
	11.8	1.9	-6.8
% Profit Before Taxes/Total Assets	18.6	15.0	11.3
	10.6	4.2	2.9
	4.1	-.5	-4.0
Sales/Net Fixed Assets	21.8	36.0	30.2
	11.3	13.5	8.8
	6.6	6.5	4.8
Sales/Total Assets	3.4	3.8	4.2
	2.5	2.9	2.4
	2.2	2.1	1.7
% Depr., Dep., Amort./Sales	1.0	.9	1.4
	(33) 2.5	(30) 1.6	(28) 3.2
	3.7	3.3	4.4
% Officers', Directors' Owners' Comp/Sales	2.0	1.7	
	(12) 5.5	(10) 3.7	
	10.6	10.6	
Net Sales ($)	1018476M	1039612M	743851M
Total Assets ($)	601975M	556896M	365959M

Current Data Sorted by Sales

Type of Statement	0-1MM	1-3MM	3-5MM	5-10MM	10-25MM	25MM & OVER
Unqualified					1	3
Reviewed		2	1	3	4	1
Compiled		1	2			
Tax Returns	1	1				
Other	1	2	1	1	1	5
	10 (4/1-9/30/09)			21 (10/1/09-3/31/10)		
NUMBER OF STATEMENTS	2	6	4	4	6	9
	%	%	%	%	%	%
Net Sales ($)	1162M	13557M	16714M	33083M	97237M	582098M
Total Assets ($)	303M	5178M	5750M	22054M	58974M	273700M

M = $ thousand   MM = $ million
See Pages 9 through 22 for Explanation of Ratios and Data

Current Data Sorted by Assets   Comparative Historical Data

0-500M	500M-2MM	2-10MM	10-50MM	50-100MM	100-250MM	Type of Statement	4/1/05-3/31/06 ALL	4/1/06-3/31/07 ALL
		1	3	1	1	Unqualified	11	8
		3	4			Reviewed	9	10
	1					Compiled	2	2
1						Tax Returns	2	3
2	1	1	7		1	Other	7	13
	4 (4/1-9/30/09)		23 (10/1/09-3/31/10)					
3	2	5	14	1	2	**NUMBER OF STATEMENTS**	31	36
%	%	%	%	%	%		%	%
						ASSETS		
			12.3			Cash & Equivalents	9.5	8.5
			23.0			Trade Receivables (net)	28.7	29.5
			8.5			Inventory	13.7	12.6
			2.0			All Other Current	1.3	1.1
			45.8			Total Current	53.1	51.8
			43.5			Fixed Assets (net)	35.8	38.1
			2.4			Intangibles (net)	3.1	4.4
			8.3			All Other Non-Current	8.0	5.7
			100.0			Total	100.0	100.0
						LIABILITIES		
			2.1			Notes Payable-Short Term	7.7	7.4
			5.8			Cur. Mat.-L.T.D.	4.0	4.1
			8.4			Trade Payables	13.5	14.0
			.0			Income Taxes Payable	.0	.2
			7.9			All Other Current	6.6	9.6
			24.1			Total Current	31.9	35.4
			13.8			Long-Term Debt	31.9	18.0
			2.5			Deferred Taxes	2.0	1.1
			13.5			All Other Non-Current	4.7	3.4
			46.0			Net Worth	29.6	42.2
			100.0			Total Liabilities & Net Worth	100.0	100.0
						INCOME DATA		
			100.0			Net Sales	100.0	100.0
			20.4			Gross Profit	30.2	29.8
			18.8			Operating Expenses	25.8	23.0
			1.6			Operating Profit	4.3	6.8
			.5			All Other Expenses (net)	1.1	.9
			1.1			Profit Before Taxes	3.2	5.9
						RATIOS		
			4.0			Current	2.5	2.3
			2.6				1.9	1.7
			1.2				1.2	1.2
			3.2			Quick	2.0	1.8
			2.0				1.5	1.2
			.9				.8	.8
			41 8.9			Sales/Receivables	47 7.8	40 9.1
			56 6.5				55 6.7	52 7.0
			63 5.8				68 5.4	67 5.4
			12 30.4			Cost of Sales/Inventory	16 23.2	12 30.6
			19 19.7				26 14.2	26 13.8
			32 11.3				48 7.6	42 8.8
			17 20.9			Cost of Sales/Payables	21 17.6	19 18.8
			21 17.3				25 14.5	25 14.4
			33 11.2				57 6.4	47 7.7
			4.3			Sales/Working Capital	6.2	5.7
			6.0				8.3	9.9
			NM				21.0	44.7
			1.2			EBIT/Interest	(29) 5.7	(31) 8.5
			(10) -2.4				2.9	2.9
			-10.0				1.4	1.4
						Net Profit + Depr., Dep., Amort./Cur. Mat. L/T/D	(10) 4.5	
							2.5	
							1.4	
			.6			Fixed/Worth	.6	.6
			.7				.9	1.0
			2.0				2.0	3.8
			.3			Debt/Worth	.6	.6
			.6				1.0	1.3
			6.2				4.2	8.2
			22.4			% Profit Before Taxes/Tangible Net Worth	(27) 28.3	(33) 36.4
			(13) -1.7				8.8	17.1
			-16.9				2.3	4.8
			6.3			% Profit Before Taxes/Total Assets	10.2	14.9
			-1.3				4.1	6.3
			-7.4				.5	2.1
			6.4			Sales/Net Fixed Assets	7.5	11.6
			3.6				4.8	3.9
			3.0				3.3	3.0
			2.0			Sales/Total Assets	2.2	2.7
			1.6				1.7	1.7
			1.2				1.4	1.4
			4.4			% Depr., Dep., Amort./Sales	(26) 3.0	(29) 2.2
			(12) 5.2				4.6	4.3
			6.3				6.4	5.6
						% Officers', Directors' Owners' Comp/Sales		
2281M	6759M	74154M	549772M	115338M	500608M	Net Sales ($)	1165605M	1256727M
812M	2086M	31588M	343826M	61552M	416331M	Total Assets ($)	744119M	807596M

M = $ thousand   MM = $ million
See Pages 9 through 22 for Explanation of Ratios and Data

Comparative Historical Data   Current Data Sorted by Sales

				Type of Statement						
	5	6	6	Unqualified				1		5
	10	7	7	Reviewed				1	4	2
	1		1	Compiled		1				
	4	5	1	Tax Returns	1					
	12	15	12	Other	2		1	1	3	5
	4/1/07-3/31/08 ALL	4/1/08-3/31/09 ALL	4/1/09-3/31/10 ALL		0-1MM	1-3MM	4 (4/1-9/30/09) 3-5MM	5-10MM	23 (10/1/09-3/31/10) 10-25MM	25MM & OVER
	32	33	27	**NUMBER OF STATEMENTS**	3	1	1	3	7	12
	%	%	%	**ASSETS**	%	%	%	%	%	%
	8.5	5.8	8.7	Cash & Equivalents						8.1
	31.6	31.8	24.3	Trade Receivables (net)						25.1
	10.4	10.7	11.7	Inventory						10.2
	1.0	1.7	2.3	All Other Current						2.1
	51.5	50.0	47.0	Total Current						45.4
	36.6	35.3	41.0	Fixed Assets (net)						41.1
	4.4	6.5	4.5	Intangibles (net)						4.2
	7.5	8.2	7.5	All Other Non-Current						9.3
	100.0	100.0	100.0	Total						100.0
				LIABILITIES						
	7.8	5.7	4.3	Notes Payable-Short Term						2.2
	5.6	5.2	6.6	Cur. Mat.-L.T.D.						6.3
	14.4	12.3	9.1	Trade Payables						7.6
	.1	.0	.1	Income Taxes Payable						.1
	6.8	8.2	7.7	All Other Current						11.5
	34.7	31.4	27.8	Total Current						27.8
	21.4	20.0	20.9	Long-Term Debt						9.0
	.9	1.2	1.4	Deferred Taxes						1.5
	9.4	5.2	11.5	All Other Non-Current						16.0
	33.6	42.2	38.5	Net Worth						45.7
	100.0	100.0	100.0	Total Liabilties & Net Worth						100.0
				INCOME DATA						
	100.0	100.0	100.0	Net Sales						100.0
	29.2	29.1	30.8	Gross Profit						20.9
	25.2	26.2	26.6	Operating Expenses						20.4
	4.0	2.9	4.2	Operating Profit						.5
	.8	.5	1.1	All Other Expenses (net)						1.2
	3.2	2.4	3.2	Profit Before Taxes						-.6
				RATIOS						
	2.9	2.9	2.8	Current						2.8
	1.8	1.8	2.2							2.4
	1.0	1.1	1.0							1.0
	2.1	1.9	2.3	Quick						2.2
	1.1	1.1	1.3							1.3
	.8	.9	.7							.7
	41 8.9	44 8.4	36 10.2	Sales/Receivables						44 8.2
	52 7.0	55 6.7	44 8.3							56 6.5
	66 5.5	67 5.5	58 6.2							65 5.6
	7 49.2	6 63.6	10 37.5	Cost of Sales/Inventory						16 22.5
	16 23.2	21 17.3	19 19.4							22 16.6
	36 10.1	39 9.5	44 8.3							36 10.2
	19 19.0	14 25.4	19 19.5	Cost of Sales/Payables						17 21.1
	23 15.6	21 17.6	22 16.6							21 17.7
	35 10.5	36 10.0	31 11.6							24 15.0
	5.6	5.6	5.0	Sales/Working Capital						5.0
	15.2	8.8	6.5							5.7
	NM	64.2	232.0							NM
	9.8	6.0	6.1	EBIT/Interest						12.1
	(29) 1.9	(29) 1.5	(22) 1.5						(10)	-1.7
	.5	.1	-3.0							-5.9
				Net Profit + Depr., Dep., Amort./Cur. Mat. L/T/D						
	.5	.5	.6	Fixed/Worth						.7
	.9	.8	.7							.7
	2.8	1.5	2.5							2.1
	.5	.9	.3	Debt/Worth						.3
	1.4	1.2	1.0							.5
	5.3	4.1	5.1							4.6
	29.2	22.9	37.7	% Profit Before Taxes/Tangible Net Worth						9.2
	(26) 7.6	(31) 7.4	(24) 10.9						(11)	-1.7
	.0	-3.3	-3.7							-13.0
	8.7	9.5	7.9	% Profit Before Taxes/Total Assets						6.0
	3.0	1.4	4.7							-1.3
	-2.8	-2.0	-1.6							-7.0
	14.0	11.6	7.6	Sales/Net Fixed Assets						5.8
	5.1	5.3	4.0							3.5
	3.0	2.9	3.1							2.9
	2.5	2.5	2.3	Sales/Total Assets						1.8
	1.9	1.8	1.8							1.6
	1.5	1.3	1.4							1.3
	2.6	2.6	3.6	% Depr., Dep., Amort./Sales						
	(29) 3.9	(28) 4.5	(22) 4.8							
	5.3	5.5	6.1							
				% Officers', Directors' Owners' Comp/Sales						
	1088548M	1175119M	1248912M	Net Sales ($)	2281M	1934M	4825M	27607M	132818M	1079447M
	620387M	781849M	856195M	Total Assets ($)	812M	1105M	981M	12837M	86455M	754005M

M = $ thousand   MM = $ million
See Pages 9 through 22 for Explanation of Ratios and Data

Current Data Sorted by Assets   Comparative Historical Data

							Type of Statement		
1	2	15	25	3	1		Unqualified	45	59
	8	39	21				Reviewed	75	88
8	26	16	1				Compiled	69	62
20	17	8					Tax Returns	55	63
14	31	50	28	4	3		Other	144	123
	63 (4/1-9/30/09)		278 (10/1/09-3/31/10)					4/1/05-3/31/06	4/1/06-3/31/07
0-500M	500M-2MM	2-10MM	10-50MM	50-100MM	100-250MM			ALL	ALL
43	84	128	75	7	4		NUMBER OF STATEMENTS	388	395
%	%	%	%	%	%		ASSETS	%	%
19.6	10.4	9.3	7.3				Cash & Equivalents	8.2	9.2
29.3	26.5	27.8	23.0				Trade-Receivables (net)	30.8	28.4
11.3	11.0	13.3	12.4				Inventory	11.6	11.8
4.3	3.8	3.0	2.8				All Other Current	2.2	1.8
64.5	51.7	53.5	45.6				Total Current	52.9	51.2
27.5	34.5	37.6	44.4				Fixed Assets (net)	36.5	37.1
2.2	7.0	4.3	6.0				Intangibles (net)	4.6	4.5
5.8	6.8	4.6	4.0				All Other Non-Current	6.0	7.1
100.0	100.0	100.0	100.0				Total	100.0	100.0
							LIABILITIES		
21.8	13.1	9.4	7.8				Notes Payable-Short Term	10.5	9.7
3.4	6.8	8.0	6.6				Cur. Mat.-L.T.D.	6.3	6.6
18.0	19.5	16.1	11.6				Trade Payables	16.7	15.2
.6	.1	.0	.2				Income Taxes Payable	.3	.2
30.2	10.2	8.3	8.5				All Other Current	8.8	9.5
74.0	49.8	41.9	34.7				Total Current	42.6	41.1
31.9	26.7	21.8	25.7				Long-Term Debt	26.4	26.7
.2	.5	.8	.9				Deferred Taxes	.7	.8
11.5	6.6	6.8	7.7				All Other Non-Current	8.0	5.2
-17.6	16.4	28.7	30.9				Net Worth	22.3	26.2
100.0	100.0	100.0	100.0				Total Liabilities & Net Worth	100.0	100.0
							INCOME DATA		
100.0	100.0	100.0	100.0				Net Sales	100.0	100.0
48.8	44.1	32.2	26.0				Gross Profit	35.4	37.4
48.8	42.6	30.7	23.5				Operating Expenses	31.5	32.3
.0	1.5	1.5	2.5				Operating Profit	4.0	5.1
.9	1.5	1.2	1.5				All Other Expenses (net)	1.3	1.6
-.9	.1	.4	1.0				Profit Before Taxes	2.6	3.5
							RATIOS		
2.6	1.6	2.1	1.8					2.0	2.0
1.2	1.1	1.3	1.3				Current	1.3	1.3
.6	.7	.8	.9					.9	.9
1.8	1.2	1.6	1.2					1.5	1.6
.9	.7	.9	.9				Quick	.9	.9
.4	.4	.6	.6					.6	.6
17 21.9	23 15.9	35 10.5	36 10.1					35 10.4	32 11.3
27 13.7	33 11.0	47 7.8	46 7.9				Sales/Receivables	46 7.9	44 8.3
43 8.5	46 7.9	59 6.2	58 6.3					59 6.2	57 6.4
0 UND	3 115.8	9 40.0	14 25.4					9 41.1	9 38.9
10 38.3	16 22.5	25 14.4	26 14.1				Cost of Sales/Inventory	22 16.5	24 15.1
53 6.9	39 9.4	43 8.4	47 7.8					40 9.1	43 8.4
5 74.0	18 20.1	20 18.0	17 21.1					22 16.9	18 20.1
18 20.5	45 8.1	32 11.4	30 12.3				Cost of Sales/Payables	34 10.8	32 11.3
43 8.5	72 5.1	55 6.7	42 8.6					51 7.2	52 7.0
10.2	13.7	8.0	8.5					8.1	8.9
64.1	60.2	19.1	21.8				Sales/Working Capital	20.1	21.8
-13.5	-12.4	-25.4	-74.8					-75.4	-52.6
3.8	3.1	4.5	4.7					7.3	7.0
(30) .3	(75) 1.2	(123) 1.3	(73) 1.7				EBIT/Interest	(364) 2.8	(362) 2.6
-1.7	-.8	-1.0	.0					1.0	1.0
	3.2	2.4	2.4					3.6	3.4
	(11) 1.4	(29) 1.1	(36) 1.4				Net Profit + Depr., Dep., Amort./Cur. Mat. L/T/D	(93) 1.9	(106) 1.7
	.3	.2	1.2					1.2	1.1
.1	.7	.7	.8					.7	.6
2.1	2.7	1.3	1.4				Fixed/Worth	1.6	1.5
-.6	-3.0	10.4	5.4					15.2	6.0
.9	2.0	1.0	1.0					1.1	1.0
12.4	4.9	2.2	2.7				Debt/Worth	2.8	2.6
-2.8	-8.7	19.5	9.3					42.1	16.3
134.1	65.3	22.9	25.6				% Profit Before Taxes/Tangible Net Worth	44.1	55.5
(24) 19.9	(54) 7.7	(101) 7.3	(62) 7.2					(301) 21.9	(316) 22.5
-6.5	-14.3	-14.4	-7.9					7.3	5.1
22.7	8.1	7.5	7.8				% Profit Before Taxes/Total Assets	12.5	14.6
-.4	.7	.7	2.1					5.6	5.9
-15.7	-9.3	-4.3	-3.7					-.1	.0
110.6	18.1	11.8	6.4					12.8	15.2
17.7	8.0	5.6	3.7				Sales/Net Fixed Assets	6.7	6.4
6.1	3.8	3.2	2.5					3.9	3.7
6.4	3.6	2.8	2.1					3.1	3.1
3.8	2.6	2.1	1.7				Sales/Total Assets	2.3	2.2
2.4	1.6	1.7	1.4					1.7	1.7
1.4	2.3	2.6	3.5					2.1	1.9
(29) 2.5	(67) 3.6	(113) 4.3	(71) 5.3				% Depr., Dep., Amort./Sales	(352) 3.6	(352) 3.5
6.6	5.8	6.3	6.9					5.1	5.5
5.8	3.2	2.5	1.3					2.6	2.7
(25) 10.0	(48) 5.8	(44) 3.6	(14) 1.9				% Officers', Directors' Owners' Comp/Sales	(170) 4.4	(180) 5.1
12.5	8.2	6.1	3.7					7.6	8.6
57766M	256556M	1303504M	2914664M	577504M	634800M		Net Sales ($)	7310791M	8541113M
10630M	95236M	591911M	1626340M	433119M	478455M		Total Assets ($)	3668290M	4604592M

M = $ thousand   MM = $ million
See Pages 9 through 22 for Explanation of Ratios and Data

Comparative Historical Data | Current Data Sorted by Sales

Type of Statement									
	48	43	47	Unqualified	1	2	1	5	13	25
	74	75	68	Reviewed	1	5	5	22	18	17
	52	45	51	Compiled	7	20	11	6	6	1
	45	52	45	Tax Returns	14	15	6	8	2	
	140	133	130	Other	11	24	14	25	30	26

	4/1/07-3/31/08 ALL	4/1/08-3/31/09 ALL	4/1/09-3/31/10 ALL		63 (4/1-9/30/09)			278 (10/1/09-3/31/10)		
					0-1MM	1-3MM	3-5MM	5-10MM	10-25MM	25MM & OVER
NUMBER OF STATEMENTS	359	348	341		34	66	37	66	69	69
	%	%	%	**ASSETS**	%	%	%	%	%	%
	8.0	7.9	10.3	Cash & Equivalents	15.8	10.2	8.3	11.4	9.9	8.0
	28.3	26.6	26.4	Trade Receivables (net)	23.0	25.0	31.2	27.9	27.4	24.5
	11.8	12.5	12.1	Inventory	10.7	9.6	12.1	14.1	11.9	13.6
	1.9	1.9	3.3	All Other Current	5.9	4.4	1.6	3.2	2.7	2.8
	49.9	48.8	52.2	Total Current	55.3	49.2	53.3	56.6	51.9	48.9
	38.0	37.8	37.1	Fixed Assets (net)	32.5	35.5	36.3	36.3	39.0	40.3
	5.3	6.2	5.5	Intangibles (net)	5.5	8.9	1.7	3.3	4.9	7.2
	6.8	7.2	5.2	All Other Non-Current	6.8	6.4	8.7	3.7	4.3	3.7
	100.0	100.0	100.0	Total	100.0	100.0	100.0	100.0	100.0	100.0
				LIABILITIES						
	9.6	11.4	11.3	Notes Payable-Short Term	25.0	10.9	12.9	10.5	9.3	7.0
	6.6	6.8	7.0	Cur. Mat.-L.T.D.	4.9	6.3	6.9	8.1	7.3	7.3
	16.0	14.6	16.0	Trade Payables	14.7	19.4	15.2	17.8	14.8	13.3
	.1	.1	.2	Income Taxes Payable	.1	.5	.0	.0	.0	.2
	8.5	9.5	11.5	All Other Current	27.4	7.3	12.6	13.5	7.8	8.7
	40.8	42.5	46.0	Total Current	72.1	44.3	47.6	50.0	39.3	36.6
	26.7	27.4	25.2	Long-Term Debt	28.8	33.5	20.5	24.3	21.2	23.0
	.7	.6	.7	Deferred Taxes	.5	.5	.5	.8	.7	1.1
	5.5	6.4	7.6	All Other Non-Current	14.3	6.5	5.6	5.9	7.0	8.6
	26.2	23.1	20.5	Net Worth	-15.7	15.2	25.7	19.0	31.7	30.6
	100.0	100.0	100.0	Total Liabilties & Net Worth	100.0	100.0	100.0	100.0	100.0	100.0
				INCOME DATA						
	100.0	100.0	100.0	Net Sales	100.0	100.0	100.0	100.0	100.0	100.0
	35.2	36.9	35.6	Gross Profit	51.7	45.6	38.1	34.0	28.4	25.4
	31.0	34.2	34.1	Operating Expenses	52.2	43.9	37.8	33.4	25.8	22.5
	4.2	2.8	1.5	Operating Profit	-.5	1.7	.3	.7	2.6	2.8
	1.3	1.4	1.4	All Other Expenses (net)	1.9	1.3	.7	1.2	1.2	1.7
	2.9	1.3	.2	Profit Before Taxes	-2.4	.3	-.4	-.6	1.4	1.1
				RATIOS						
	2.0	1.9	1.9	Current	2.0	1.7	1.6	2.2	2.1	1.9
	1.3	1.2	1.2		.9	1.0	1.1	1.4	1.3	1.3
	.9	.9	.8		.5	.7	.7	.9	.9	1.0
	1.4	1.3	1.3	Quick	1.6	1.4	1.2	1.6	1.7	1.2
	.9	.9	.8		.6	.8	.8	.9	.9	.9
	.6	.6	.5		.2	.5	.5	.6	.6	.7
34	10.8	30	12.1	29	12.7	Sales/Receivables	13	27.8	24	15.3	33	11.0	33	11.1	34	10.7	36	10.1

Sales/Receivables (full detail):

	Hist. 1	Hist. 2	Hist. 3	0-1MM	1-3MM	3-5MM	5-10MM	10-25MM	25MM & OVER
Sales/Receivables	34 10.8	30 12.1	29 12.7	13 27.8	24 15.3	33 11.0	33 11.1	34 10.7	36 10.1
	45 8.2	42 8.8	42 8.8	27 13.8	33 11.0	43 8.6	42 8.8	48 7.6	48 7.7
	58 6.3	53 6.9	56 6.5	45 8.1	50 7.4	61 6.0	57 6.4	58 6.3	58 6.3
Cost of Sales/Inventory	11 34.7	11 33.3	8 44.0	0 UND	4 89.5	3 129.3	13 29.1	11 32.9	18 20.8
	24 15.1	23 16.2	21 17.5	12 30.4	14 26.1	11 33.4	25 19.1	22 16.4	26 14.0
	43 8.6	45 8.1	44 8.3	68 5.4	34 10.8	49 7.4	40 9.1	41 8.9	52 7.0
Cost of Sales/Payables	20 18.2	19 18.9	17 21.4	8 47.7	18 20.1	18 20.6	15 24.9	18 20.4	17 21.1
	32 11.4	31 11.6	31 11.9	27 13.7	43 8.5	33 11.2	33 10.9	29 12.6	29 12.5
	54 6.7	52 7.0	53 6.9	60 6.1	76 4.8	65 5.7	56 6.6	41 9.0	44 8.3
Sales/Working Capital	8.4	9.4	9.1	10.2	13.9	11.6	8.0	9.1	7.7
	20.3	26.2	28.3	UND	NM	46.5	19.1	17.4	15.6
	-37.6	-33.5	-21.2	-9.0	-12.0	-13.4	-32.7	-31.9	NM
EBIT/Interest	5.6	5.4	4.3	3.3	3.0	3.9	3.2	5.9	7.8
	(332) 2.4	(319) 1.6	(312) 1.4	(23) .5	(61) .3	(33) .9	(64) .8	(66) 1.8	(65) 1.9
	.8	-.2	-.9	-1.7	-1.0	-2.1	-1.0	-.1	-.2
Net Profit + Depr., Dep., Amort./Cur. Mat. L/T/D	3.5	2.8	2.5				2.4	2.9	2.9
	(103) 1.9	(99) 1.5	(84) 1.4				(12) 1.1	(21) 1.4	(34) 1.5
	1.1	.8	.3				.1	.3	.8
Fixed/Worth	.7	.6	.7	.1	.9	.4	.7	.8	.6
	1.5	1.6	1.6	2.6	5.6	1.5	1.4	1.3	1.8
	7.4	UND	-24.7	-1.1	-1.4	NM	NM	6.9	4.6
Debt/Worth	1.2	1.1	1.1	1.0	2.0	1.3	1.2	.9	1.1
	2.5	2.9	3.0	9.3	14.8	2.9	2.7	2.3	2.6
	13.2	UND	-36.2	-2.7	-6.9	NM	NM	16.7	10.7
% Profit Before Taxes/Tangible Net Worth	43.1	33.2	34.6	56.1	92.7	49.5	20.3	26.2	32.3
	(279) 18.5	(261) 10.3	(247) 7.2	(20) 2.7	(39) 23.8	(28) 7.3	(50) .6	(56) 9.2	(54) 10.6
	2.9	-3.5	-11.5	-17.0	-21.7	-8.1	-24.9	-6.1	-6.5
% Profit Before Taxes/Total Assets	12.1	9.9	8.2	12.2	9.3	8.8	6.5	8.3	9.6
	4.9	2.3	1.2	-.2	-1.5	.1	-.9	3.1	2.7
	-.8	-4.1	-6.6	-15.2	-9.7	-9.0	-5.1	-1.9	-4.2
Sales/Net Fixed Assets	12.3	13.9	15.5	108.6	18.3	16.3	15.1	11.7	8.6
	5.6	5.9	5.9	8.6	6.5	6.5	7.1	5.6	4.3
	3.2	3.5	3.2	3.3	3.2	3.6	3.3	3.2	2.9
Sales/Total Assets	2.8	2.9	3.0	5.0	3.6	3.5	2.9	2.8	2.3
	2.1	2.1	2.1	2.4	2.3	2.3	2.4	2.1	1.8
	1.5	1.5	1.5	1.2	1.4	1.7	1.7	1.6	1.5
% Depr., Dep., Amort./Sales	2.4	2.1	2.4	2.4	2.3	2.2	2.6	2.4	3.0
	(314) 3.9	(299) 4.0	(288) 4.2	(23) 4.0	(51) 4.0	(31) 4.0	(60) 4.4	(61) 4.0	(62) 4.8
	5.9	5.9	6.6	9.8	7.3	7.4	6.2	6.0	6.4
% Officers', Directors' Owners' Comp/Sales	2.6	2.7	2.6	6.9	3.4	2.2	2.1	2.2	1.0
	(132) 4.7	(128) 4.8	(132) 4.8	(17) 10.0	(38) 6.7	(19) 4.4	(28) 4.1	(17) 3.4	(13) 1.6
	7.1	7.3	8.7	12.5	10.8	7.4	6.2	6.0	2.6
Net Sales ($)	9631928M	7610589M	5744794M	20031M	133562M	147872M	479907M	1108265M	3855157M
Total Assets ($)	5410876M	4485526M	3235691M	10776M	71995M	68154M	223237M	591145M	2270384M

M = $ thousand   MM = $ million
See Pages 9 through 22 for Explanation of Ratios and Data

MANUFACTURING—Tradebinding and Related Work   NAICS 323121

Current Data Sorted by Assets | | | | | | | **Comparative Historical Data**

0-500M	500M-2MM	2-10MM	10-50MM	50-100MM	100-250MM	Type of Statement	4/1/05-3/31/06 ALL	4/1/06-3/31/07 ALL
		1	1			Unqualified	3	3
		6	3			Reviewed	15	19
2	1	2				Compiled	9	12
2	3					Tax Returns	6	5
1	1	7	2			Other	17	8
	5 (4/1-9/30/09)		29 (10/1/09-3/31/10)					
5	7	16	6			**NUMBER OF STATEMENTS**	50	47
%	%	%	%	%	%	**ASSETS**	%	%
		9.2		D	D	Cash & Equivalents	7.5	7.2
		24.7		A	A	Trade Receivables (net)	29.2	26.5
		8.2		T	T	Inventory	11.9	12.3
		1.2		A	A	All Other Current	1.6	1.3
		43.2				Total Current	50.2	47.2
		49.6		N	N	Fixed Assets (net)	36.3	41.0
		2.3		O	O	Intangibles (net)	7.2	5.4
		4.9		T	T	All Other Non-Current	6.3	6.4
		100.0				Total	100.0	100.0
				A	A	**LIABILITIES**		
		9.1		V	V	Notes Payable-Short Term	11.2	8.5
		6.7		A	A	Cur. Mat.-L.T.D.	5.7	6.4
		7.4		I	I	Trade Payables	10.4	9.3
		.1		L	L	Income Taxes Payable	.4	.4
		8.5		A	A	All Other Current	8.0	9.6
		31.7		B	B	Total Current	35.7	34.2
		33.7		L	L	Long-Term Debt	19.5	26.6
		.4		E	E	Deferred Taxes	1.4	2.1
		32.6				All Other Non-Current	10.1	11.0
		1.6				Net Worth	33.3	26.1
		100.0				Total Liabilties & Net Worth	100.0	100.0
						INCOME DATA		
		100.0				Net Sales	100.0	100.0
		31.1				Gross Profit	36.1	34.1
		28.5				Operating Expenses	31.7	30.0
		2.6				Operating Profit	4.4	4.1
		3.7				All Other Expenses (net)	1.4	1.8
		-1.1				Profit Before Taxes	3.0	2.3
						RATIOS		
		2.4					2.2	2.5
		1.3				Current	1.3	1.4
		.8					1.0	1.0
		1.7					1.7	2.1
		1.0				Quick	1.0	1.1
		.6					.7	.7
		37 9.8					35 10.5	39 9.4
		48 7.6				Sales/Receivables	51 7.2	46 7.9
		65 5.6					60 6.1	61 6.0
		4 87.7					2 214.8	0 UND
		14 26.1				Cost of Sales/Inventory	17 21.6	9 41.8
		33 10.9					41 8.9	38 9.7
		10 34.9					13 27.4	11 33.0
		17 22.0				Cost of Sales/Payables	21 17.4	20 18.4
		26 14.1					36 10.2	35 10.5
		7.5					6.9	6.7
		18.9				Sales/Working Capital	13.6	19.5
		-21.4					-377.1	788.8
		2.8					6.2	5.5
		1.5				EBIT/Interest	(47) 1.6	(46) 1.9
		-.1					.5	.8
							3.4	4.4
						Net Profit + Depr., Dep., Amort./Cur. Mat. L/T/D	(16) 1.1	(11) 2.0
							.5	1.6
		.9					.6	.8
		1.7				Fixed/Worth	1.2	1.7
		9.1					4.4	4.5
		1.3					.8	1.3
		2.9				Debt/Worth	2.3	2.4
		13.7					10.5	7.5
		21.5					34.2	33.0
	(13)	1.3				% Profit Before Taxes/Tangible Net Worth	(40) 9.6	(38) 14.6
		-21.1					.4	.6
		6.1					10.1	14.4
		1.2				% Profit Before Taxes/Total Assets	1.8	3.8
		-2.6					-1.9	-.6
		6.5					13.5	11.0
		3.4				Sales/Net Fixed Assets	7.6	5.7
		2.4					3.4	2.8
		2.5					2.6	2.8
		1.8				Sales/Total Assets	2.0	2.2
		1.3					1.4	1.3
		1.8					2.2	1.9
		3.6				% Depr., Dep., Amort./Sales	(46) 3.9	(46) 3.5
		8.5					6.3	7.2
							2.8	2.8
						% Officers', Directors' Owners' Comp/Sales	(17) 5.9	(23) 5.5
							11.5	7.6
3394M	25581M	156118M	143026M			Net Sales ($)	528893M	462804M
960M	9656M	85726M	111923M			Total Assets ($)	301136M	257348M

(Columns 50-100MM and 100-250MM: DATA NOT AVAILABLE)

Comparative Historical Data   **Current Data Sorted by Sales**

Type of Statement

4/1/07-3/31/08	4/1/08-3/31/09	4/1/09-3/31/10	Type of Statement	0-1MM	1-3MM	3-5MM	5-10MM	10-25MM	25MM & OVER
1	1	3	Unqualified				1	1	1
15	17	10	Reviewed	1	1	1	3	5	
12	7	5	Compiled	1	1	2		1	
4	3	5	Tax Returns	2	2	1			
14	13	11	Other		1	2	4	1	2
ALL	ALL	ALL		5 (4/1-9/30/09)			29 (10/1/09-3/31/10)		
46	41	34	NUMBER OF STATEMENTS	4	5	6	8	8	3

%	%	%		%	%	%	%	%	%
			ASSETS						
10.9	6.6	8.4	Cash & Equivalents						
24.9	24.9	28.2	Trade Receivables (net)						
7.8	6.7	9.2	Inventory						
1.3	1.2	1.0	All Other Current						
45.0	39.3	46.8	Total Current						
43.5	44.7	39.9	Fixed Assets (net)						
5.0	9.1	7.0	Intangibles (net)						
6.5	6.9	6.3	All Other Non-Current						
100.0	100.0	100.0	Total						
			LIABILITIES						
7.7	11.6	12.0	Notes Payable-Short Term						
8.1	6.5	7.0	Cur. Mat.-L.T.D.						
7.5	9.6	9.3	Trade Payables						
.2	.3	.2	Income Taxes Payable						
7.6	9.7	10.0	All Other Current						
31.1	37.7	38.5	Total Current						
27.5	29.1	30.3	Long-Term Debt						
1.0	.6	.2	Deferred Taxes						
14.2	19.7	20.6	All Other Non-Current						
26.3	12.9	10.4	Net Worth						
100.0	100.0	100.0	Total Liabilties & Net Worth						
			INCOME DATA						
100.0	100.0	100.0	Net Sales						
36.3	32.0	36.2	Gross Profit						
30.3	29.2	34.0	Operating Expenses						
6.0	2.8	2.2	Operating Profit						
1.3	.8	2.0	All Other Expenses (net)						
4.7	2.0	.2	Profit Before Taxes						
			RATIOS						
2.2	2.1	2.5	Current						
1.4	1.3	1.3							
1.0	.8	.8							
2.1	1.8	2.0	Quick						
1.2	1.0	1.0							
.7	.6	.7							
36 10.1	35 10.5	34 10.8	Sales/Receivables						
46 8.0	40 9.1	52 7.0							
64 5.7	54 6.7	68 5.4							
0 UND	0 UND	0 UND	Cost of Sales/Inventory						
6 59.1	9 41.3	10 37.2							
31 11.6	25 14.7	30 12.4							
8 47.6	10 37.1	8 46.6	Cost of Sales/Payables						
16 23.2	16 23.5	17 21.0							
25 14.7	24 15.2	31 12.0							
6.9	8.0	6.3	Sales/Working Capital						
14.6	26.3	22.2							
-195.5	-22.2	-24.6							
4.9	5.0	4.3	EBIT/Interest						
(45) 3.0	1.8	1.7							
1.3	1.0	-.6							
3.0	2.0		Net Profit + Depr., Dep., Amort./Cur. Mat. L/T/D						
(15) 2.1	(11) 1.5								
1.1	.6								
.8	1.0	.9	Fixed/Worth						
1.3	2.1	1.7							
4.9	NM	-2.8							
.9	1.1	1.3	Debt/Worth						
2.3	3.4	2.8							
7.5	NM	-6.8							
37.2	27.2	22.1	% Profit Before Taxes/Tangible Net Worth						
(40) 22.3	(31) 14.4	(24) 1.6							
6.0	3.2	-18.3							
11.9	10.0	9.1	% Profit Before Taxes/Total Assets						
6.7	2.9	2.1							
1.7	.0	-5.4							
8.0	8.4	18.4	Sales/Net Fixed Assets						
4.3	6.0	6.1							
2.8	2.5	2.6							
2.5	2.8	2.8	Sales/Total Assets						
1.9	1.8	1.8							
1.2	1.5	1.3							
2.7	2.5	1.6	% Depr., Dep., Amort./Sales						
(45) 4.6	(38) 4.5	(29) 4.1							
6.7	6.4	9.1							
3.3	2.6	2.6	% Officers', Directors' Owners' Comp/Sales						
(28) 5.8	(20) 4.7	(18) 3.9							
10.9	8.9	9.9							
339577M	427670M	328119M	Net Sales ($)	1972M	9511M	22795M	60434M	130912M	102495M
204720M	257344M	208265M	Total Assets ($)	513M	6316M	13911M	40301M	79183M	68041M

M = $ thousand   MM = $ million
See Pages 9 through 22 for Explanation of Ratios and Data

MANUFACTURING—Prepress Services NAICS 323122

Current Data Sorted by Assets

Comparative Historical Data

					Type of Statement		
					Unqualified	7	6
1	1				Reviewed	10	9
1	9	2			Compiled	8	6
3					Tax Returns	3	2
1	1	1			Other	20	8
1	5	2				4/1/05-	4/1/06-
8 (4/1-9/30/09)		21 (10/1/09-3/31/10)				3/31/06	3/31/07

0-500M	500M-2MM	2-10MM	10-50MM	50-100MM	100-250MM		ALL	ALL
2	7	16	4			NUMBER OF STATEMENTS	48	31
%	%	%	%	%	%	**ASSETS**	%	%
		10.2	D	D		Cash & Equivalents	11.9	11.1
		34.9	A	A		Trade Receivables (net)	32.0	32.5
		12.7	T	T		Inventory	10.1	9.2
		1.5	A	A		All Other Current	1.7	1.4
		59.3				Total Current	55.6	54.2
		31.6	N	N		Fixed Assets (net)	33.3	38.0
		.6	O	O		Intangibles (net)	4.3	3.6
		8.5	T	T		All Other Non-Current	6.8	4.3
		100.0				Total	100.0	100.0
			A	A	**LIABILITIES**			
		6.0	V	V		Notes Payable-Short Term	7.5	6.5
		9.6	A	A		Cur. Mat.-L.T.D.	5.1	5.7
		14.7	I	I		Trade Payables	12.9	9.9
		.2	L	L		Income Taxes Payable	.3	.1
		8.4	A	A		All Other Current	10.7	7.9
		38.9	B	B		Total Current	36.5	30.2
		15.9	L	L		Long-Term Debt	19.2	22.1
		.3	E	E		Deferred Taxes	.4	.5
		2.8				All Other Non-Current	7.0	2.1
		42.1				Net Worth	36.8	45.2
		100.0				Total Liabilities & Net Worth	100.0	100.0
					INCOME DATA			
		100.0				Net Sales	100.0	100.0
		30.7				Gross Profit	40.9	37.7
		27.4				Operating Expenses	34.2	32.7
		3.3				Operating Profit	6.6	5.0
		.6				All Other Expenses (net)	1.0	1.2
		2.7				Profit Before Taxes	5.7	3.8
					RATIOS			
		3.3					2.8	3.6
		1.5				Current	1.7	1.8
		.9					1.1	1.0
		2.7					2.3	2.9
		1.1				Quick	1.3	1.7
		.6					.8	.8
	39	9.3					39 9.3	43 8.5
	50	7.3				Sales/Receivables	51 7.1	59 6.2
	64	5.7					67 5.5	82 4.4
	14	25.3					15 24.9	12 30.4
	28	13.1				Cost of Sales/Inventory	23 15.9	23 16.0
	41	9.0					43 8.6	40 9.2
	11	32.1					16 22.5	10 35.6
	30	12.3				Cost of Sales/Payables	35 10.4	23 15.8
	39	9.3					52 7.0	44 8.4
		5.1					5.4	3.6
		13.7				Sales/Working Capital	10.6	9.1
		NM					54.7	-292.9
		12.2					13.3	16.9
	(15)	6.2				EBIT/Interest	(44) 4.4	(28) 3.6
		.9					1.7	.4
							3.5	
					Net Profit + Depr., Dep., Amort./Cur. Mat. L/T/D	(10) 2.0	
						1.1	
		.3					.3	.3
		.7				Fixed/Worth	.9	.9
		1.9					4.0	3.1
		.5					.5	.3
		1.3				Debt/Worth	1.9	1.1
		4.2					8.7	5.1
		27.7					48.3	40.2
	(14)	14.0				% Profit Before Taxes/Tangible Net Worth	(41) 25.7	(28) 19.3
		-.1					8.3	-3.7
		12.9					18.9	17.1
		6.0				% Profit Before Taxes/Total Assets	8.3	6.2
		-.2					2.5	-1.9
		16.5					12.3	10.5
		10.2				Sales/Net Fixed Assets	6.0	5.5
		3.5					4.3	3.1
		2.8					2.7	2.2
		2.4				Sales/Total Assets	2.0	1.8
		1.8					1.5	1.2
		2.6					2.6	2.9
	(15)	4.1				% Depr., Dep., Amort./Sales	(43) 3.7	(29) 4.6
		6.6					4.8	6.1
							3.4	4.4
					% Officers', Directors' Owners' Comp/Sales	(24) 6.9	(14) 6.7
						11.0	12.2
2425M	13989M	176674M	188359M			Net Sales ($)	1428342M	312783M
646M	6202M	76818M	95258M			Total Assets ($)	961229M	186002M

M = $ thousand   MM = $ million
See Pages 9 through 22 for Explanation of Ratios and Data

Comparative Historical Data

Current Data Sorted by Sales

Type of Statement					0-1MM	1-3MM	3-5MM	5-10MM	10-25MM	25MM & OVER
Unqualified	5	3	2			1	1			
Reviewed	10	11	12			1	1	6	3	2
Compiled	1	6	3			3				
Tax Returns	1	2	3			2	1			
Other	15	13	9		1		2		3	2
	4/1/07-3/31/08 ALL	4/1/08-3/31/09 ALL	4/1/09-3/31/10 ALL		1	8 (4/1-9/30/09)		21 (10/1/09-3/31/10)		
NUMBER OF STATEMENTS	32	35	29		1	7	5	6	6	4

	%	%	%	ASSETS	%	%	%	%	%	%
	12.6	9.3	11.3	Cash & Equivalents						
	31.2	31.2	32.8	Trade Receivables (net)						
	8.6	8.6	12.1	Inventory						
	1.1	1.5	4.6	All Other Current						
	53.4	50.5	60.8	Total Current						
	32.7	34.5	30.9	Fixed Assets (net)						
	4.8	6.1	1.3	Intangibles (net)						
	9.1	8.9	7.0	All Other Non-Current						
	100.0	100.0	100.0	Total						

LIABILITIES

	Period 1	Period 2	Period 3							
Notes Payable-Short Term	3.7	6.6	13.1							
Cur. Mat.-L.T.D.	6.0	11.8	8.7							
Trade Payables	12.3	13.9	15.2							
Income Taxes Payable	.0	.0	.2							
All Other Current	11.0	8.1	7.3							
Total Current	33.0	40.5	44.5							
Long-Term Debt	14.0	24.3	21.6							
Deferred Taxes	.4	.4	.4							
All Other Non-Current	5.3	4.8	2.9							
Net Worth	47.4	30.1	30.5							
Total Liabilities & Net Worth	100.0	100.0	100.0							

INCOME DATA

	Period 1	Period 2	Period 3							
Net Sales	100.0	100.0	100.0							
Gross Profit	38.8	33.3	35.6							
Operating Expenses	35.4	31.3	31.5							
Operating Profit	3.4	2.0	4.2							
All Other Expenses (net)	1.4	1.3	.9							
Profit Before Taxes	2.1	.7	3.3							

RATIOS

	Period 1	Period 2	Period 3
Current	3.8 / 1.6 / 1.0	2.9 / 1.4 / .8	3.3 / 1.5 / .9
Quick	3.3 / 1.2 / .9	2.2 / .9 / .6	2.6 / 1.0 / .6
Sales/Receivables	37 9.8 / 45 8.1 / 75 4.8	38 9.5 / 47 7.8 / 60 6.1	36 10.1 / 48 7.6 / 62 5.9
Cost of Sales/Inventory	14 26.9 / 20 18.0 / 33 11.0	9 39.1 / 20 18.5 / 28 13.0	15 24.9 / 28 13.1 / 39 9.4
Cost of Sales/Payables	15 23.6 / 26 14.0 / 49 7.5	13 28.7 / 26 13.8 / 45 8.1	12 30.0 / 27 13.6 / 52 7.1
Sales/Working Capital	2.8 / 14.6 / NM	5.5 / 15.8 / -35.9	5.3 / 12.7 / NM
EBIT/Interest	9.2 / (28) 2.5 / .6	5.4 / (33) 1.6 / -.1	8.6 / (26) 2.3 / -.9
Net Profit + Depr., Dep., Amort./Cur. Mat. L/T/D			
Fixed/Worth	.3 / .8 / 1.7	.4 / 1.5 / 3.2	.3 / 1.3 / 13.2
Debt/Worth	.3 / 1.2 / 7.1	.8 / 2.7 / 20.3	.5 / 2.2 / 26.7
% Profit Before Taxes/Tangible Net Worth	34.9 / (27) 5.9 / -.6	52.2 / (29) 6.1 / -10.6	29.7 / (23) 18.3 / -10.8
% Profit Before Taxes/Total Assets	15.2 / 5.7 / -.7	8.5 / 1.2 / -4.1	13.6 / 4.8 / -6.0
Sales/Net Fixed Assets	11.1 / 6.9 / 4.3	13.4 / 7.2 / 3.8	20.7 / 9.2 / 3.9
Sales/Total Assets	2.6 / 2.2 / 1.2	2.8 / 2.1 / 1.8	2.9 / 2.4 / 1.8
% Depr., Dep., Amort./Sales	2.7 / (29) 4.0 / 5.9	2.5 / (29) 4.3 / 6.0	2.6 / (24) 4.5 / 6.1
% Officers', Directors' Owners' Comp/Sales	2.0 / (13) 4.6 / 11.7	2.1 / (14) 4.3 / 8.1	

	Period 1	Period 2	Period 3		0-1MM	1-3MM	3-5MM	5-10MM	10-25MM	25MM & OVER
Net Sales ($)	436726M	497009M	381447M		828M	12203M	20091M	49806M	110160M	188359M
Total Assets ($)	223032M	236523M	178924M		168M	5959M	11366M	23263M	42910M	95258M

M = $ thousand   MM = $ million
See Pages 9 through 22 for Explanation of Ratios and Data

MANUFACTURING—Petroleum Refineries NAICS 324110

| Current Data Sorted by Assets | | | | | | | Comparative Historical Data | |

Type of Statement

0-500M	500M-2MM	2-10MM	10-50MM	50-100MM	100-250MM	Type of Statement	4/1/05-3/31/06 ALL	4/1/06-3/31/07 ALL
		1	2	4	5	Unqualified	18	10
		5	1	1		Reviewed	6	4
		3				Compiled	3	5
						Tax Returns	1	1
2	2	6	5	2	4	Other	20	24
2	10 (4/1-9/30/09)		33 (10/1/09-3/31/10)					
0-500M	500M-2MM	2-10MM	10-50MM	50-100MM	100-250MM		ALL	ALL
2	2	15	8	7	9	NUMBER OF STATEMENTS	48	44
%	%	%	%	%	%		%	%

ASSETS

2-10MM		4/1/05-3/31/06 ALL	4/1/06-3/31/07 ALL
8.3	Cash & Equivalents	13.4	10.9
31.9	Trade Receivables (net)	24.4	27.5
17.6	Inventory	13.9	15.4
1.4	All Other Current	3.7	3.1
59.2	Total Current	55.4	56.9
31.6	Fixed Assets (net)	34.0	35.5
1.0	Intangibles (net)	2.8	2.5
8.1	All Other Non-Current	7.8	5.1
100.0	Total	100.0	100.0

LIABILITIES

2-10MM		4/1/05-3/31/06 ALL	4/1/06-3/31/07 ALL
7.1	Notes Payable-Short Term	2.5	4.0
5.1	Cur. Mat.-L.T.D.	2.6	3.6
23.6	Trade Payables	23.1	20.6
.3	Income Taxes Payable	.7	.4
6.9	All Other Current	9.6	7.6
43.0	Total Current	38.5	36.2
12.5	Long-Term Debt	17.6	18.8
.9	Deferred Taxes	1.3	1.1
5.6	All Other Non-Current	4.4	5.7
38.1	Net Worth	38.2	38.3
100.0	Total Liabilities & Net Worth	100.0	100.0

INCOME DATA

2-10MM		4/1/05-3/31/06 ALL	4/1/06-3/31/07 ALL
100.0	Net Sales	100.0	100.0
25.2	Gross Profit	20.5	19.4
19.3	Operating Expenses	13.6	11.6
5.9	Operating Profit	6.9	7.8
.3	All Other Expenses (net)	1.2	1.1
5.5	Profit Before Taxes	5.7	6.7

RATIOS

2-10MM		4/1/05-3/31/06 ALL	4/1/06-3/31/07 ALL
2.4	Current	2.1	2.4
1.3		1.4	1.6
.9		1.1	1.2
2.1	Quick	1.5	1.5
1.0		1.0	1.1
.5		.7	.6
16 22.4	Sales/Receivables	15 24.2	15 25.0
30 12.0		19 19.2	22 16.5
67 5.5		37 9.9	30 12.0
5 77.3	Cost of Sales/Inventory	6 56.2	5 69.5
15 24.8		16 22.5	15 24.9
55 6.6		29 12.5	27 13.3
13 27.4	Cost of Sales/Payables	15 23.8	11 34.5
25 14.6		26 13.9	19 18.9
35 10.5		37 9.8	29 12.4
6.2	Sales/Working Capital	9.4	9.7
46.8		19.3	16.0
-42.5		198.5	62.2
19.3	EBIT/Interest	30.9	33.6
(11) 2.1		(38) 7.9	(38) 7.1
1.0		3.3	2.2
	Net Profit + Depr., Dep., Amort./Cur. Mat. L/T/D	87.2	80.7
		(15) 10.1	(11) 8.5
		3.2	1.1
.2	Fixed/Worth	.3	.4
.8		.8	.9
2.9		1.7	2.3
.4	Debt/Worth	.7	.7
1.0		1.3	1.6
4.4		3.0	3.4
61.6	% Profit Before Taxes/Tangible Net Worth	64.7	71.2
(13) 22.2		(43) 32.6	(38) 40.7
1.4		14.8	14.1
15.6	% Profit Before Taxes/Total Assets	24.6	24.8
3.5		14.5	14.0
.6		5.5	2.8
82.0	Sales/Net Fixed Assets	27.8	47.3
8.8		13.0	18.6
5.7		5.2	3.4
6.7	Sales/Total Assets	4.8	5.4
3.0		3.4	4.0
1.7		1.7	1.6
.6	% Depr., Dep., Amort./Sales	.5	.5
(11) 1.2		(46) .9	(40) .8
1.5		2.8	3.2
	% Officers', Directors' Owners' Comp/Sales		

0-500M	500M-2MM	2-10MM	10-50MM	50-100MM	100-250MM		4/1/05-3/31/06 ALL	4/1/06-3/31/07 ALL
4729M	6365M	268274M	836198M	1412936M	6166898M	Net Sales ($)	9057471M	9398206M
541M	2371M	63687M	193121M	519248M	1426518M	Total Assets ($)	2680101M	2098657M

© RMA 2010

M = $ thousand   MM = $ million
See Pages 9 through 22 for Explanation of Ratios and Data

Comparative Historical Data   Current Data Sorted by Sales

4/1/07-3/31/08 ALL	4/1/08-3/31/09 ALL	4/1/09-3/31/10 ALL	Type of Statement	0-1MM	1-3MM	3-5MM	5-10MM	10-25MM	25MM & OVER
						10 (4/1-9/30/09)			33 (10/1/09-3/31/10)
8	15	12	Unqualified						12
8	8	7	Reviewed				3	2	2
3	5	3	Compiled			1			
3	3		Tax Returns						
22	15	21	Other	2		2	2	3	12
44	46	43	**NUMBER OF STATEMENTS**	2		3	5	7	26
%	%	%	**ASSETS**	%	%	%	%	%	%
15.9	13.2	13.0	Cash & Equivalents			D			15.5
24.3	24.5	23.4	Trade Receivables (net)			A			21.2
21.7	17.4	17.8	Inventory			T			17.4
2.2	6.0	3.0	All Other Current			A			4.3
64.1	61.0	57.1	Total Current						58.4
29.7	30.3	32.2	Fixed Assets (net)			N			32.8
1.0	2.8	2.0	Intangibles (net)			O			2.7
5.3	5.9	8.7	All Other Non-Current			T			6.1
100.0	100.0	100.0	Total						100.0
			LIABILITIES			A			
3.5	5.7	5.4	Notes Payable-Short Term			V			6.2
2.5	2.5	2.7	Cur. Mat.-L.T.D.			A			1.5
24.6	19.3	20.9	Trade Payables			I			22.7
.7	.8	.5	Income Taxes Payable			L			.7
9.2	14.2	14.7	All Other Current			A			9.6
40.5	42.5	44.1	Total Current			B			40.7
9.5	14.5	8.5	Long-Term Debt			L			7.5
.5	1.4	1.2	Deferred Taxes			E			1.7
4.4	6.0	4.5	All Other Non-Current						5.6
45.1	35.7	41.6	Net Worth						44.5
100.0	100.0	100.0	Total Liabilities & Net Worth						100.0
			INCOME DATA						
100.0	100.0	100.0	Net Sales						100.0
19.8	14.8	17.2	Gross Profit						13.1
14.1	10.1	13.5	Operating Expenses						9.8
5.7	4.7	3.7	Operating Profit						3.3
.9	-.1	-.3	All Other Expenses (net)						-.5
4.8	4.8	4.1	Profit Before Taxes						3.8
			RATIOS						
2.4	2.7	2.4	Current						3.1
1.8	1.6	1.3							1.3
1.3	1.1	1.0							1.1
1.6	2.1	1.8	Quick						1.9
1.1	.9	1.0							1.0
.7	.5	.5							.7
16 23.4	9 40.7	14 26.2	Sales/Receivables						14 26.2
22 16.3	17 21.1	23 16.2							19 19.2
35 10.3	31 11.7	40 9.1							28 13.1
10 37.1	3 126.2	5 71.4	Cost of Sales/Inventory						7 48.7
24 15.3	10 36.5	15 24.8							15 24.9
47 7.8	32 11.5	36 10.2							35 10.4
14 26.5	8 44.0	13 28.4	Cost of Sales/Payables						13 29.1
25 14.8	13 27.5	21 17.3							23 16.0
38 9.7	25 14.6	32 11.3							32 11.5
7.4	7.5	6.2	Sales/Working Capital						5.9
14.9	19.6	31.5							29.5
38.3	121.3	999.8							131.1
49.1	22.1	39.2	EBIT/Interest						41.4
(38) 12.4	(38) 7.0	(35) 7.5							(22) 13.6
1.9	2.9	1.5							2.2
14.5	21.6		Net Profit + Depr., Dep.,						
(11) 8.1	(14) 4.2		Amort./Cur. Mat. L/T/D						
2.0	1.2								
.2	.3	.3	Fixed/Worth						.3
.6	.9	.8							.8
1.1	1.6	1.8							1.5
.6	.7	.4	Debt/Worth						.4
1.0	1.4	1.0							1.0
2.1	5.2	6.4							3.8
64.4	51.6	38.1	% Profit Before Taxes/Tangible						25.4
(42) 27.2	(41) 34.8	(39) 17.9	Net Worth						(24) 17.1
10.5	15.7	2.5							9.2
30.4	25.1	14.7	% Profit Before Taxes/Total						15.1
14.4	11.6	8.1	Assets						9.9
3.3	3.6	.8							1.1
40.0	34.1	24.7	Sales/Net Fixed Assets						22.8
20.9	13.9	10.9							12.9
7.3	7.4	5.5							5.9
4.8	6.2	5.4	Sales/Total Assets						6.6
3.7	3.8	3.3							3.4
2.0	2.3	1.5							2.5
.5	.5	.6	% Depr., Dep., Amort./Sales						.8
(40) .8	(40) .9	(36) 1.1							(23) 1.0
1.7	2.0	2.4							2.1
			% Officers', Directors' Owners' Comp/Sales						
9702187M	15063251M	8695400M	Net Sales ($)	1151M		13032M	32143M	116354M	8532720M
2355480M	2542304M	2205486M	Total Assets ($)	1715M		6717M	13280M	44728M	2139046M

M = $ thousand   MM = $ million
See Pages 9 through 22 for Explanation of Ratios and Data

Current Data Sorted by Assets | Comparative Historical Data

							Type of Statement		
	1	6	15	7	3		Unqualified	26	31
	6	12	8	1			Reviewed	21	14
1	2	6					Compiled	13	15
4	2	6			1		Tax Returns	2	8
3	5	17	10	5	2		Other	22	23
	27 (4/1-9/30/09)		96 (10/1/09-3/31/10)					4/1/05-3/31/06	4/1/06-3/31/07
0-500M	500M-2MM	2-10MM	10-50MM	50-100MM	100-250MM		NUMBER OF STATEMENTS	ALL	ALL
8	16	47	33	13	6			84	91
%	%	%	%	%	%		ASSETS	%	%
	10.3	15.1	16.3	9.5			Cash & Equivalents	10.2	12.8
	40.5	26.6	22.7	15.0			Trade Receivables (net)	24.4	26.9
	9.2	9.8	12.6	15.7			Inventory	8.5	10.0
	6.1	3.2	5.9	4.4			All Other Current	5.5	4.8
	66.1	54.8	57.6	44.6			Total Current	48.8	54.6
	27.7	34.0	33.7	44.0			Fixed Assets (net)	38.2	34.6
	1.0	1.5	.4	6.7			Intangibles (net)	4.1	3.0
	5.3	9.7	8.3	4.8			All Other Non-Current	8.9	7.8
	100.0	100.0	100.0	100.0			Total	100.0	100.0
							LIABILITIES		
	7.3	5.3	5.4	3.4			Notes Payable-Short Term	5.5	5.3
	3.1	3.8	3.5	2.9			Cur. Mat.-L.T.D.	4.4	4.7
	20.3	15.0	12.0	10.6			Trade Payables	15.2	15.3
	.4	.2	.2	1.0			Income Taxes Payable	.2	.2
	8.8	7.0	4.7	4.1			All Other Current	12.2	8.6
	40.0	31.3	25.8	21.9			Total Current	37.5	34.1
	12.9	11.6	18.3	18.9			Long-Term Debt	20.7	16.2
	.2	.2	.8	2.4			Deferred Taxes	.5	.5
	11.4	2.9	2.0	6.2			All Other Non-Current	4.3	5.7
	35.5	54.0	53.1	50.5			Net Worth	36.9	43.5
	100.0	100.0	100.0	100.0			Total Liabilties & Net Worth	100.0	100.0
							INCOME DATA		
	100.0	100.0	100.0	100.0			Net Sales	100.0	100.0
	27.0	25.6	18.0	21.1			Gross Profit	20.4	20.5
	22.8	18.8	14.2	12.6			Operating Expenses	16.9	15.4
	4.2	6.8	3.7	8.4			Operating Profit	3.5	5.1
	.3	.6	.3	.7			All Other Expenses (net)	.8	.7
	3.9	6.2	3.4	7.8			Profit Before Taxes	2.7	4.4
							RATIOS		
	2.9	5.2	3.9	2.8				2.6	3.1
	2.0	1.8	2.4	2.3			Current	1.3	1.7
	1.2	1.0	1.4	1.3				1.0	1.1
	2.6	3.3	3.5	1.7				1.9	2.6
	1.3	1.3	1.4	1.2			Quick	1.0 (90)	1.2
	.8	1.0	.9	.6				.7	.7
26 14.2	30 12.3	29 12.7	14 25.7				Sales/Receivables	23 15.8	20 18.6
40 9.0	36 10.1	40 9.2	49 7.4					40 9.0	37 9.8
88 4.2	55 6.6	86 4.3	67 5.5					59 6.2	54 6.8
0 UND	2 164.6	7 54.4	24 15.4				Cost of Sales/Inventory	0 999.8	2 166.9
6 66.2	13 27.7	21 17.5	44 8.2					13 27.2	14 26.2
31 11.8	38 9.6	48 7.6	61 6.0					25 14.6	33 11.1
13 29.0	11 34.7	10 35.5	17 21.1				Cost of Sales/Payables	14 26.2	11 33.1
38 9.7	24 15.4	22 16.5	34 10.8					26 13.9	23 16.1
52 7.0	41 8.9	50 7.3	43 8.5					44 8.2	41 9.0
	4.3	4.6	2.7	4.2			Sales/Working Capital	6.6	5.9
	11.2	12.4	6.9	4.9				20.4	13.5
	42.7	240.4	17.2	29.1				572.6	97.4
	17.9	37.7	27.9	25.3				9.0	17.8
(14) 7.3	(40) 10.8	(30) 5.8	4.0				EBIT/Interest	(76) 3.4	(85) 4.9
-1.6	2.7	1.8	3.3					1.1	2.0
			11.0				Net Profit + Depr., Dep., Amort./Cur. Mat. L/T/D	4.9	14.4
		(14) 5.2						(27) 2.1	(24) 3.2
		2.9						1.3	1.5
	.4	.2	.4	.5			Fixed/Worth	.5	.4
	.9	.7	.8	.9				1.1	.9
	30.1	1.3	1.4	1.6				3.2	2.3
	.4	.3	.3	.6			Debt/Worth	.5	.4
	1.2	.9	.9	1.0				2.0	1.3
	233.8	2.6	2.5	2.1				5.1	3.8
	117.9	43.7	35.7	33.5			% Profit Before Taxes/Tangible Net Worth	34.0	51.3
(13) 22.7	(46) 21.3	(32) 20.0	(12) 16.7					(75) 14.3	(81) 28.3
-6.9	8.7	5.1	10.2					2.4	12.3
	25.0	23.4	17.4	12.0			% Profit Before Taxes/Total Assets	10.7	21.3
	8.2	9.9	11.0	7.6				5.1	10.8
	-7.9	1.7	2.1	4.0				.2	3.5
	34.8	17.8	9.4	7.0			Sales/Net Fixed Assets	12.3	14.7
	9.2	8.0	6.0	3.7				6.1	6.4
	5.7	3.7	3.0	1.9				3.8	3.6
	4.8	2.9	2.6	2.0			Sales/Total Assets	2.9	3.1
	2.3	2.5	1.9	1.4				2.3	2.2
	1.5	1.6	1.0	.9				1.7	1.8
	2.5	1.6	1.7	2.2			% Depr., Dep., Amort./Sales	1.5	1.9
(12) 3.4	(42) 2.2	(32) 2.9	(12) 3.5					(76) 2.7	(81) 2.8
6.5	4.5	4.6	4.5					4.5	4.6
		2.3					% Officers', Directors' Owners' Comp/Sales	1.7	1.0
	(18) 2.9							(26) 3.0	(27) 3.2
	4.5							6.0	4.8
6865M	58932M	535879M	1660277M	1436229M	2083143M		Net Sales ($)	3097679M	3591215M
2195M	21345M	236661M	762352M	877382M	913101M		Total Assets ($)	1710990M	1804075M

M = $ thousand   MM = $ million
See Pages 9 through 22 for Explanation of Ratios and Data

Comparative Historical Data | | | Current Data Sorted by Sales

				Type of Statement						
34		27	32	Unqualified			2	3	7	20
23		28	27	Reviewed		5	2	4	9	7
7		10	9	Compiled	1	1	1	3	3	
6		11	13	Tax Returns	3	1	3	4	1	1
31		37	42	Other	3	3	4	6	11	15
4/1/07-3/31/08 ALL		4/1/08-3/31/09 ALL	4/1/09-3/31/10 ALL			27 (4/1-9/30/09)		96 (10/1/09-3/31/10)		
					0-1MM	1-3MM	3-5MM	5-10MM	10-25MM	25MM & OVER
101		113	123	NUMBER OF STATEMENTS	7	10	12	20	31	43
%		%	%	ASSETS	%	%	%	%	%	%
12.2		11.3	14.9	Cash & Equivalents		6.7	18.5	10.1	15.3	15.3
26.4		25.6	25.5	Trade Receivables (net)		40.4	21.1	26.5	28.1	20.4
9.2		11.3	11.5	Inventory		8.1	18.7	11.0	8.8	12.7
3.9		4.4	4.4	All Other Current		3.8	2.7	5.7	4.5	5.0
51.7		52.6	56.3	Total Current		58.9	61.0	53.3	56.8	53.4
36.8		38.8	33.7	Fixed Assets (net)		25.7	29.0	31.7	34.9	37.5
2.7		3.3	2.0	Intangibles (net)		.0	.5	3.3	.5	3.6
8.9		5.3	8.0	All Other Non-Current		15.4	9.5	11.6	7.7	5.6
100.0		100.0	100.0	Total		100.0	100.0	100.0	100.0	100.0
				LIABILITIES						
7.6		6.3	5.9	Notes Payable-Short Term		16.3	4.8	8.3	4.9	3.2
5.7		6.1	3.5	Cur. Mat.-L.T.D.		1.7	2.5	4.4	3.4	3.8
13.9		14.0	14.0	Trade Payables		18.3	10.9	16.4	16.2	12.0
.3		.1	.3	Income Taxes Payable		.0	.5	.2	.2	.4
6.9		6.1	8.2	All Other Current		34.4	7.8	5.8	4.3	5.9
34.5		32.6	32.0	Total Current		70.7	26.6	35.1	29.1	25.5
18.4		20.1	14.0	Long-Term Debt		10.7	10.6	18.5	11.2	15.7
.7		.6	.7	Deferred Taxes		.0	.3	.0	.6	1.5
4.9		4.3	4.3	All Other Non-Current		11.6	8.5	5.5	.9	2.9
41.6		42.5	48.9	Net Worth		7.0	54.0	40.9	58.1	54.4
100.0		100.0	100.0	Total Liabilities & Net Worth		100.0	100.0	100.0	100.0	100.0
				INCOME DATA						
100.0		100.0	100.0	Net Sales		100.0	100.0	100.0	100.0	100.0
21.1		19.0	23.9	Gross Profit		36.0	27.7	22.8	21.6	20.3
14.7		15.7	17.9	Operating Expenses		27.2	28.4	18.4	14.9	12.8
6.4		3.4	6.0	Operating Profit		8.8	-.7	4.4	6.6	7.4
.4		1.0	.5	All Other Expenses (net)		1.6	.3	.9	.4	.3
5.9		2.3	5.5	Profit Before Taxes		7.2	-1.0	3.5	6.2	7.1
				RATIOS						
2.9		2.5	4.0			3.4	13.3	2.3	5.9	3.4
1.8		1.6	2.0	Current		1.3	2.9	1.5	2.4	2.1
1.2		1.2	1.2			.5	1.6	1.1	1.1	1.3
2.1		2.1	2.9			3.2	12.2	1.4	5.6	2.2
(100) 1.4		1.2	1.4	Quick		.8	2.3	1.0	1.8	1.2
.8		.6	.8			.3	1.1	.8	.7	.7
26 14.3	22	16.5	26 14.0		41 8.9	18 20.3	25 14.7	32 11.2	24 15.0	
39 9.3	35	10.3	38 9.5	Sales/Receivables	74 5.0	30 12.3	36 10.0	38 9.6	37 9.8	
57 6.4	52	7.0	60 6.0		242 1.5	41 8.6	86 4.2	55 6.6	59 6.2	
2 191.2	3	124.2	4 81.3		5 69.5	0 UND	0 UND	4 96.0	11 32.6	
13 27.7	16	22.5	22 16.9	Cost of Sales/Inventory	25 14.6	25 14.7	27 13.7	9 38.9	24 15.2	
28 13.0	33	10.9	44 8.3		43 8.5	137 2.7	43 8.4	28 12.9	48 7.7	
14 25.6	11	32.8	12 30.3		3 117.8	4 83.4	17 21.0	10 35.2	14 25.4	
22 16.7	21	17.0	24 15.4	Cost of Sales/Payables	52 7.1	13 27.5	27 13.8	24 15.0	25 14.4	
40 9.2	43	8.5	44 8.3		68 5.3	27 13.8	52 7.0	42 8.7	35 10.4	
6.5		7.0	4.1			3.6	2.4	9.2	3.6	4.3
10.7		16.0	8.8	Sales/Working Capital		10.8	6.3	15.4	7.0	7.5
34.9		45.2	31.7			-7.4	16.1	50.1	48.7	27.1
21.6		13.0	26.2			16.2	20.2	61.1	26.1	
(95) 6.6	(104)	4.1	(107) 7.4	EBIT/Interest	(10) 1.0	(17) 7.4	(28) 8.5	(40) 7.2		
2.3		.7	2.8			-7.3	1.0	2.8	3.5	
8.6		6.2	8.8							8.0
(40) 4.0	(35)	2.8	(32) 4.2	Net Profit + Depr., Dep., Amort./Cur. Mat. L/T/D					(19)	4.3
1.9		1.2	2.6							3.0
.4		.5	.3			.2	.2	.4	.2	.4
.8		.9	.7	Fixed/Worth		.8	.4	1.1	.6	.9
1.6		2.0	1.4			-.6	1.3	4.1	1.2	1.5
.4		.6	.3			.5	.3	.6	.3	.4
1.2		1.4	.9	Debt/Worth		1.8	.5	1.4	.6	1.0
2.8		3.3	2.6			-3.2	5.6	12.7	1.5	2.0
66.7		40.6	44.0			25.3	69.2	38.3	41.3	
(90) 26.9	(99)	17.7	(115) 20.2	% Profit Before Taxes/Tangible Net Worth	7.1	(18) 19.1	(30) 19.7	(42) 20.7		
13.1		2.7	6.1			-61.4	4.8	5.3	14.7	
24.7		15.7	20.0			33.2	15.4	30.9	20.0	17.6
11.7		8.0	9.8	% Profit Before Taxes/Total Assets		6.4	3.9	9.5	9.9	11.0
4.5		-.2	2.0			-4.2	-12.6	-.7	1.6	5.9
12.5		13.0	13.4			86.5	16.9	30.9	13.9	9.2
6.7		6.6	7.1	Sales/Net Fixed Assets		7.6	7.3	9.3	7.4	6.9
3.6		3.4	3.6			4.2	3.7	2.6	3.7	3.4
3.0		3.2	2.9			2.4	3.8	2.6	3.1	2.7
2.2		2.3	2.2	Sales/Total Assets		1.5	1.8	2.4	2.5	1.8
1.6		1.5	1.4			.7	.7	1.5	1.7	1.3
1.8		1.6	1.7			1.6	1.2	1.7	2.0	
(93) 2.9	(108)	2.9	(109) 2.8	% Depr., Dep., Amort./Sales	(11) 3.4	(17) 2.3	(29) 2.6	(40) 2.9		
4.8		4.3	4.5			7.0	7.8	4.3	4.2	
1.2		1.3	2.2						2.8	
(27) 2.8	(29)	2.7	(33) 3.4	% Officers', Directors' Owners' Comp/Sales			(10) 3.5			
5.6		4.5	5.3						4.5	
3989466M		4876816M	5781325M	Net Sales ($)	5100M	15896M	52535M	141271M	495384M	5071139M
1913896M		2209285M	2813036M	Total Assets ($)	3228M	11750M	44969M	114804M	255713M	2382572M

M = $ thousand   MM = $ million
See Pages 9 through 22 for Explanation of Ratios and Data

Current Data Sorted by Assets   Comparative Historical Data

0-500M	500M-2MM	2-10MM	10-50MM	50-100MM	100-250MM	Type of Statement	ALL 4/1/05-3/31/06	ALL 4/1/06-3/31/07
		2	5	2	2	Unqualified	13	10
	1	3	3			Reviewed	13	11
	3	4				Compiled	3	4
						Tax Returns	2	3
	5	6	13	2	2	Other	24	20
	11 (4/1-9/30/09)		42 (10/1/09-3/31/10)					
	9	15	21	4	4	NUMBER OF STATEMENTS	55	48
%	%	%	%	%	%		%	%
						ASSETS		
		11.2	12.2			Cash & Equivalents	11.1	8.0
		37.4	20.4			Trade Receivables (net)	29.2	30.3
		25.4	29.5			Inventory	24.1	28.3
		1.9	5.8			All Other Current	1.9	1.9
		76.0	67.9			Total Current	66.2	68.5
		19.7	25.3			Fixed Assets (net)	23.5	21.2
		1.4	3.1			Intangibles (net)	4.8	5.8
		2.9	3.7			All Other Non-Current	5.6	4.4
		100.0	100.0			Total	100.0	100.0
						LIABILITIES		
		13.2	11.2			Notes Payable-Short Term	9.2	8.9
		2.1	2.5			Cur. Mat.-L.T.D.	3.4	3.5
		17.1	10.9			Trade Payables	19.2	19.7
		.1	.2			Income Taxes Payable	.5	.4
		7.2	6.1			All Other Current	7.4	9.6
		39.6	30.9			Total Current	39.8	42.1
		6.0	11.6			Long-Term Debt	13.5	12.7
		.5	.7			Deferred Taxes	.9	.7
		2.5	9.7			All Other Non-Current	8.3	7.2
		51.4	47.1			Net Worth	37.5	37.4
		100.0	100.0			Total Liabilities & Net Worth	100.0	100.0
						INCOME DATA		
		100.0	100.0			Net Sales	100.0	100.0
		32.0	31.5			Gross Profit	31.7	32.9
		26.4	25.4			Operating Expenses	26.6	27.6
		5.6	6.1			Operating Profit	5.0	5.3
		.5	.7			All Other Expenses (net)	.7	1.0
		5.2	5.4			Profit Before Taxes	4.3	4.3
						RATIOS		
		3.5	5.1				2.4	2.9
		2.1	2.5			Current	1.6	1.9
		1.3	1.6				1.2	1.1
		2.4	2.7				1.4	1.4
		1.4	.9			Quick	.9	1.0
		.7	.5				.5	.6
		32 11.4	27 13.5				34 10.7	36 10.2
		46 7.9	37 9.9			Sales/Receivables	44 8.3	47 7.8
		62 5.9	44 8.2				52 7.0	55 6.7
		23 16.1	48 7.7				27 13.7	42 8.8
		32 11.4	78 4.7			Cost of Sales/Inventory	48 7.6	66 5.6
		63 5.8	91 4.0				78 4.7	93 3.9
		17 22.0	18 20.2				26 13.9	21 17.3
		27 13.5	23 16.2			Cost of Sales/Payables	32 11.5	37 9.9
		47 7.7	36 10.0				46 7.9	47 7.8
		4.4	3.4				5.5	4.2
		11.1	5.6			Sales/Working Capital	10.5	9.4
		23.6	16.2				44.9	53.2
		119.8	15.6				8.1	13.2
		(14) 8.5	(20) 7.6			EBIT/Interest	(49) 3.8	(43) 4.0
		4.3	.8				1.6	2.0
						Net Profit + Depr., Dep.,	7.3	9.4
						Amort./Cur. Mat. L/T/D	(15) 3.1	(18) 4.9
							1.3	1.6
		.1	.2				.3	.3
		.3	.3			Fixed/Worth	.6	.5
		.8	1.4				1.9	1.9
		.3	.5				.8	.8
		.8	1.0			Debt/Worth	2.1	1.7
		2.5	2.2				5.6	4.3
		85.2	45.9				52.7	51.4
		(14) 25.3	(20) 25.4			% Profit Before Taxes/Tangible Net Worth	(50) 18.2	(42) 23.2
		6.0	3.6				4.1	13.0
		24.6	22.5				16.7	17.1
		8.8	10.4			% Profit Before Taxes/Total Assets	5.4	7.1
		3.8	-2.2				2.3	2.6
		40.7	21.3				25.1	32.1
		16.8	13.3			Sales/Net Fixed Assets	12.7	14.7
		8.7	6.0				7.1	6.4
		4.7	2.8				3.5	3.4
		3.0	2.1			Sales/Total Assets	2.2	2.2
		1.9	1.7				1.6	1.6
		.3	1.1				.7	.5
		1.0	(18) 1.4			% Depr., Dep., Amort./Sales	(51) 1.7	(44) 1.3
		1.4	2.4				2.4	2.4
							1.6	1.6
						% Officers', Directors' Owners' Comp/Sales	(14) 2.8	(15) 3.9
							5.9	9.0
	32035M	257517M	1339970M	367121M	1147367M	Net Sales ($)	3024968M	2662930M
	9718M	79721M	577951M	257001M	502919M	Total Assets ($)	1402577M	1241700M

(Left columns 0-500M and 500M-2MM: DATA NOT AVAILABLE)

M = $ thousand   MM = $ million
See Pages 9 through 22 for Explanation of Ratios and Data

Comparative Historical Data   Current Data Sorted by Sales

Type of Statement

4/1/07-3/31/08 ALL	4/1/08-3/31/09 ALL	4/1/09-3/31/10 ALL	Type of Statement	0-1MM	1-3MM	3-5MM	5-10MM	10-25MM	25MM & OVER
11	10	11	Unqualified				1	1	9
8	13	7	Reviewed		2		2	2	3
4	3	7	Compiled				1	3	1
3	3		Tax Returns						
22	23	28	Other		3	1	2	6	16
					11 (4/1-9/30/09)		42 (10/1/09-3/31/10)		
48	52	53	NUMBER OF STATEMENTS		5	1	6	12	29

(For size columns 0-1MM through 5-10MM the percentage columns are marked "DATA NOT AVAILABLE".)

ASSETS (%)

07-08	08-09	09-10	Assets	10-25MM	25MM & OVER
8.1	6.7	11.0	Cash & Equivalents	8.6	11.0
29.0	25.6	27.6	Trade Receivables (net)	32.7	24.7
27.9	34.0	28.8	Inventory	19.0	28.8
3.6	2.7	4.2	All Other Current	4.5	5.5
68.6	69.0	71.7	Total Current	64.8	70.0
23.2	22.1	22.3	Fixed Assets (net)	30.4	22.7
4.1	3.5	2.5	Intangibles (net)	1.5	3.8
4.1	5.3	3.5	All Other Non-Current	3.2	3.5
100.0	100.0	100.0	Total	100.0	100.0

LIABILITIES (%)

07-08	08-09	09-10	Liabilities	10-25MM	25MM & OVER
10.4	12.9	14.9	Notes Payable-Short Term	14.5	11.2
3.6	3.5	2.5	Cur. Mat.-L.T.D.	2.9	2.9
20.8	15.9	15.6	Trade Payables	14.2	13.0
.9	.4	.2	Income Taxes Payable	.0	.2
6.5	7.6	7.5	All Other Current	5.4	7.2
42.2	40.3	40.6	Total Current	37.0	34.5
12.8	14.0	8.3	Long-Term Debt	10.8	9.2
.9	.7	.6	Deferred Taxes	.7	.8
3.5	7.6	5.8	All Other Non-Current	4.5	7.5
40.6	37.3	44.6	Net Worth	47.0	48.0
100.0	100.0	100.0	Total Liabilities & Net Worth	100.0	100.0

INCOME DATA (%)

07-08	08-09	09-10	Income Data	10-25MM	25MM & OVER
100.0	100.0	100.0	Net Sales	100.0	100.0
29.6	30.1	31.8	Gross Profit	29.9	30.6
23.9	24.8	27.0	Operating Expenses	25.6	23.0
5.7	5.3	4.8	Operating Profit	4.3	7.6
.6	.9	.6	All Other Expenses (net)	.5	.6
5.1	4.5	4.2	Profit Before Taxes	3.8	7.0

RATIOS

Values listed as upper quartile / median / lower quartile. For turnover ratios the leading number is days.

07-08	08-09	09-10	Ratio	10-25MM	25MM & OVER
2.5 / 1.7 / 1.2	3.1 / 1.7 / 1.2	3.5 / 2.0 / 1.3	Current	3.7 / 2.0 / 1.0	3.3 / 2.0 / 1.4
1.4 / 1.0 / .6	1.4 / .9 / .5	2.5 / 1.0 / .6	Quick	2.3 / 1.3 / .5	2.4 / 1.0 / .6
27 13.3 / 41 9.0 / 51 7.2	22 16.4 / 34 10.6 / 49 7.5	29 12.7 / 42 8.7 / 52 7.0	Sales/Receivables	29 12.6 / 45 8.0 / 59 6.1	28 13.0 / 40 9.1 / 50 7.3
35 10.4 / 61 6.0 / 84 4.3	38 9.5 / 61 6.0 / 103 3.5	34 10.7 / 57 6.4 / 89 4.1	Cost of Sales/Inventory	21 17.2 / 30 12.1 / 48 7.7	45 8.0 / 68 5.4 / 89 4.1
20 18.3 / 32 11.4 / 50 7.4	13 27.6 / 26 14.1 / 37 9.9	17 21.4 / 27 13.5 / 39 9.3	Cost of Sales/Payables	15 24.1 / 22 16.5 / 45 8.2	18 20.8 / 25 14.4 / 38 9.7
5.6 / 10.7 / 25.9	5.3 / 10.6 / 31.8	3.6 / 7.0 / 19.8	Sales/Working Capital	4.7 / 12.7 / NM	3.6 / 7.0 / 14.4
11.8 / (44) 4.0 / 1.6	11.5 / (49) 2.7 / 1.2	21.4 / (50) 8.6 / 3.1	EBIT/Interest	42.9 / 4.9 / 3.0	25.6 / (28) 14.0 / 4.2
11.1 / (19) 3.4 / .9	9.2 / (20) 4.0 / 1.1	13.0 / (17) 5.5 / 2.4	Net Profit + Depr., Dep., Amort./Cur. Mat. L/T/D		9.4 / (11) 4.0 / 2.1
.3 / .5 / 1.2	.3 / .6 / 1.3	.2 / .4 / 1.2	Fixed/Worth	.3 / .7 / 2.7	.2 / .4 / 1.1
.7 / 2.0 / 3.3	.7 / 1.8 / 3.3	.4 / 1.1 / 2.4	Debt/Worth	.4 / 1.0 / 3.3	.6 / 1.1 / 2.1
61.4 / (45) 27.4 / 9.1	38.4 / (45) 11.5 / 3.0	47.4 / (50) 25.1 / 6.0	% Profit Before Taxes/Tangible Net Worth	73.0 / (11) 18.9 / 2.4	49.5 / (28) 35.5 / 16.9
19.1 / 9.2 / 2.1	14.6 / 4.5 / 1.1	22.1 / 9.5 / 2.6	% Profit Before Taxes/Total Assets	20.1 / 6.6 / 2.9	22.5 / 17.1 / 5.3
20.7 / 11.5 / 6.6	27.3 / 13.2 / 7.6	25.5 / 14.3 / 7.8	Sales/Net Fixed Assets	24.0 / 12.1 / 3.9	21.3 / 10.5 / 6.5
3.4 / 2.5 / 1.9	3.4 / 2.8 / 1.9	3.1 / 2.5 / 1.8	Sales/Total Assets	4.0 / 2.8 / 1.8	2.8 / 2.4 / 1.7
.7 / (38) 1.3 / 2.1	.6 / (46) 1.3 / 2.7	.6 / (49) 1.3 / 1.9	% Depr., Dep., Amort./Sales	.3 / 1.3 / 2.0	1.1 / (26) 1.3 / 2.6
1.6 / (14) 3.1 / 5.0	2.7 / (13) 3.2 / 6.4	1.4 / (12) 2.6 / 14.2	% Officers', Directors' Owners' Comp/Sales		
2758432M	3622616M	3144010M	Net Sales ($)	179589M	2907681M
1147234M	1434220M	1427310M	Total Assets ($)	77135M	1328083M

Net Sales ($) — additional size columns: 1-3MM 8616M, 3-5MM 3452M, 5-10MM 44672M
Total Assets ($) — additional size columns: 1-3MM 4058M, 3-5MM 776M, 5-10MM 17258M

M = $ thousand   MM = $ million
See Pages 9 through 22 for Explanation of Ratios and Data

MANUFACTURING—All Other Petroleum and Coal Products Manufacturing NAICS 324199

	Current Data Sorted by Assets							Comparative Historical Data	

			2	6	4	2	Type of Statement		
		1					Unqualified	6	8
	2	3					Reviewed	3	3
	2	1					Compiled	3	3
		6	4	1	1		Tax Returns	3	
	5 (4/1-9/30/09)		30 (10/1/09-3/31/10)				Other	11	14
0-500M	500M-2MM	2-10MM	10-50MM	50-100MM	100-250MM			4/1/05-3/31/06 ALL	4/1/06-3/31/07 ALL
	4	13	10	5	3	NUMBER OF STATEMENTS		23	31
%	%	%	%	%	%	ASSETS		%	%
		18.7	10.3			Cash & Equivalents		6.8	12.8
		27.7	20.3			Trade Receivables (net)		31.9	28.7
		22.0	17.7			Inventory		19.3	18.3
		2.0	1.6			All Other Current		4.5	4.3
		70.4	50.0			Total Current		62.4	64.1
		19.6	36.1			Fixed Assets (net)		26.9	29.0
		3.9	10.0			Intangibles (net)		3.8	1.6
		6.1	4.0			All Other Non-Current		6.9	5.2
		100.0	100.0			Total		100.0	100.0
						LIABILITIES			
		20.0	6.7			Notes Payable-Short Term		5.5	9.7
		1.3	4.2			Cur. Mat.-L.T.D.		4.6	2.2
		15.9	14.1			Trade Payables		15.8	20.6
		.2	.2			Income Taxes Payable		.9	.3
		8.4	8.1			All Other Current		7.4	7.1
		45.8	33.3			Total Current		34.2	39.9
		15.4	17.8			Long-Term Debt		18.4	20.3
		.3	.3			Deferred Taxes		1.5	.4
		4.5	1.1			All Other Non-Current		7.4	2.6
		33.9	47.5			Net Worth		38.5	36.9
		100.0	100.0			Total Liabilties & Net Worth		100.0	100.0
						INCOME DATA			
		100.0	100.0			Net Sales		100.0	100.0
		24.0	39.6			Gross Profit		22.9	25.0
		20.4	33.3			Operating Expenses		13.3	15.4
		3.6	6.3			Operating Profit		9.6	9.6
		.1	1.8			All Other Expenses (net)		.6	.8
		3.5	4.4			Profit Before Taxes		8.9	8.8
						RATIOS			
		3.9	3.6					3.1	3.5
		1.6	1.2			Current		1.9	1.6
		.9	1.0					1.4	1.1
		2.9	1.6					1.9	2.7
		.7	1.0			Quick		1.1	1.0
		.5	.6					.8	.5
		11 32.0	23 15.6					26 14.0	22 16.4
		38 9.5	38 9.6			Sales/Receivables		43 8.4	35 10.4
		62 5.9	51 7.1					67 5.4	59 6.2
		29 12.4	0 UND					24 15.4	4 86.5
		37 10.0	41 8.8			Cost of Sales/Inventory		46 8.0	29 12.8
		63 5.8	75 4.9					69 5.3	53 6.9
		10 35.1	21 17.6					12 29.8	7 54.0
		27 13.6	43 8.5			Cost of Sales/Payables		25 14.4	21 17.0
		33 11.2	111 3.3					49 7.4	39 9.3
		3.5	5.6					4.9	5.2
		6.5	15.3			Sales/Working Capital		7.6	15.4
		-106.6	NM					27.0	343.2
		35.4	91.4					55.9	23.6
	(10)	7.2	3.0			EBIT/Interest		(22) 12.8	(26) 8.1
		-.2	-1.7					2.6	2.8
								40.3	
						Net Profit + Depr., Dep., Amort./Cur. Mat. L/T/D		(10) 7.4	
								2.3	
		.1	.5					.3	.4
		.7	.8			Fixed/Worth		.8	.5
		-2.6	3.5					1.5	2.4
		.4	.5					.8	1.0
		2.1	2.2			Debt/Worth		2.1	1.8
		-31.0	4.3					5.7	5.7
								77.5	68.9
						% Profit Before Taxes/Tangible Net Worth		(22) 30.8	(28) 47.3
								13.6	19.4
		29.3	24.9					24.8	21.7
		7.3	6.1			% Profit Before Taxes/Total Assets		12.1	10.5
		-3.9	-4.4					3.3	3.1
		68.7	13.7					31.1	25.1
		17.1	6.3			Sales/Net Fixed Assets		8.3	9.4
		7.5	2.5					4.2	4.3
		4.2	2.3					3.3	4.0
		2.2	1.7			Sales/Total Assets		2.2	2.8
		1.9	1.2					1.3	1.7
		1.6						.6	.7
		3.2				% Depr., Dep., Amort./Sales		(18) 1.7	(25) 1.2
		6.6						3.7	2.9
						% Officers', Directors' Owners' Comp/Sales			
	10266M	207592M	416205M	557445M	160630M	Net Sales ($)		2559386M	2242903M
	4492M	70282M	243796M	366451M	335159M	Total Assets ($)		1079498M	582144M

M = $ thousand   MM = $ million
See Pages 9 through 22 for Explanation of Ratios and Data

Comparative Historical Data

Current Data Sorted by Sales

						Type of Statement						
	8		8		14	Unqualified				3		11
	1		5		1	Reviewed				1		
	8		4		5	Compiled		1	3	1		
	5		2		3	Tax Returns		2				1
	11		12		12	Other		1	1	1	4	5
	4/1/07-		4/1/08-		4/1/09-			5 (4/1-9/30/09)		30 (10/1/09-3/31/10)		
	3/31/08		3/31/09		3/31/10		0-1MM	1-3MM	3-5MM	5-10MM	10-25MM	25MM & OVER
	ALL		ALL		ALL							
	33		31		35	NUMBER OF STATEMENTS	4	4	4	1	9	17
	%		%		%	ASSETS	%	%	%	%	%	%
	12.1		14.0		12.6	Cash & Equivalents						8.0
	24.3		24.8		20.8	Trade Receivables (net)						18.0
	16.3		12.4		17.2	Inventory	D A T A					12.6
	6.6		3.2		1.6	All Other Current						1.6
	59.2		54.4		52.1	Total Current						40.2
	27.6		36.1		35.5	Fixed Assets (net)	N O T					43.7
	4.5		3.0		6.4	Intangibles (net)						11.5
	8.6		6.5		5.9	All Other Non-Current						4.5
	100.0		100.0		100.0	Total	A V A					100.0
						LIABILITIES	I L					
	16.6		10.0		11.4	Notes Payable-Short Term	A					4.1
	2.8		5.4		2.8	Cur. Mat.-L.T.D.	B					3.3
	20.5		16.3		11.6	Trade Payables	L E					11.9
	.2		.1		.2	Income Taxes Payable						.1
	7.0		7.6		7.4	All Other Current						8.2
	47.0		39.4		33.4	Total Current						27.6
	16.2		16.5		22.9	Long-Term Debt						26.4
	.2		.3		.4	Deferred Taxes						.5
	3.0		4.3		2.7	All Other Non-Current						1.7
	33.6		39.5		40.6	Net Worth						43.8
	100.0		100.0		100.0	Total Liabilties & Net Worth						100.0
						INCOME DATA						
	100.0		100.0		100.0	Net Sales						100.0
	28.1		25.6		29.3	Gross Profit						32.0
	20.9		20.1		24.3	Operating Expenses						25.1
	7.2		5.6		5.0	Operating Profit						6.9
	.7		.3		1.5	All Other Expenses (net)						1.6
	6.6		5.2		3.5	Profit Before Taxes						5.2
						RATIOS						
	2.8		3.5		3.5							3.3
	1.3		1.5		1.6	Current						1.3
	1.0		.8		1.0							1.0
	1.4		2.3		2.4							2.1
	.8		1.1		1.1	Quick						1.1
	.4		.5		.6							.6
11	34.2	10	35.1	16	22.2	Sales/Receivables					15	25.1
29	12.7	28	12.9	38	9.5						38	9.6
42	8.7	44	8.3	60	6.1						50	7.3
1	639.7	1	253.1	19	18.9	Cost of Sales/Inventory					5	74.4
15	24.5	9	39.1	37	10.0						25	14.4
50	7.4	44	8.2	65	5.6						51	7.1
12	29.3	6	61.1	10	36.8	Cost of Sales/Payables					13	29.2
26	13.9	15	24.2	27	13.7						27	13.7
40	9.1	40	9.1	34	10.8						43	8.5
	6.9		5.9		4.8	Sales/Working Capital						5.8
	53.8		56.0		7.4							17.1
	-931.8		-119.0		168.5							179.6
	13.6		10.7		9.2	EBIT/Interest						8.5
(30)	2.2	(29)	3.9	(32)	3.0						(16)	3.2
	1.0		1.1		.1							1.2
						Net Profit + Depr., Dep., Amort./Cur. Mat. L/T/D						
	.2		.4		.5	Fixed/Worth						.7
	.8		.9		1.0							1.4
	12.1		3.2		4.2							NM
	.5		.7		.5	Debt/Worth						.5
	2.2		1.7		2.1							2.5
	26.9		5.8		8.5							NM
	70.4		59.1		57.3	% Profit Before Taxes/Tangible Net Worth						47.8
(27)	25.8	(28)	24.2	(28)	19.4						(13)	20.9
	7.5		2.1		-1.9							2.5
	25.8		18.0		14.8	% Profit Before Taxes/Total Assets						13.1
	6.5		10.9		4.6							6.0
	.3		.4		-1.3							1.5
	54.4		47.9		18.2	Sales/Net Fixed Assets						13.4
	16.4		10.8		7.2							5.7
	5.8		4.3		2.2							1.5
	5.2		8.2		2.5	Sales/Total Assets						2.4
	3.2		2.9		1.9							1.7
	1.8		1.9		1.1							1.0
	.4		.5		1.3	% Depr., Dep., Amort./Sales						1.9
(25)	1.3	(26)	1.1	(29)	2.5						(15)	3.1
	2.0		2.3		4.9							5.0
	.9				.5	% Officers', Directors' Owners' Comp/Sales						
(10)	5.6			(10)	2.6							
	12.1				10.0							
	3135675M		3905331M		1352138M	Net Sales ($)		8941M	16362M	7068M	160376M	1159391M
	934268M		1363269M		1020180M	Total Assets ($)		8144M	10094M	3639M	181017M	817286M

M = $ thousand   MM = $ million
See Pages 9 through 22 for Explanation of Ratios and Data

Current Data Sorted by Assets   **Comparative Historical Data**

Type of Statement

0-500M	500M-2MM	2-10MM	10-50MM	50-100MM	100-250MM		4/1/05-3/31/06 ALL	4/1/06-3/31/07 ALL
1		2	21	4	3	Unqualified	24	34
1	1	10	8			Reviewed	19	27
1		5	2			Compiled	11	9
2	3	1	2			Tax Returns	5	7
2	5	17	15	2	6	Other	31	31
							4/1/05-3/31/06	4/1/06-3/31/07
7	9	35	48	6	9	**NUMBER OF STATEMENTS**	90	108
%	%	%	%	%	%	**ASSETS**	%	%
		9.8	9.0			Cash & Equivalents	7.3	7.0
		28.7	22.9			Trade Receivables (net)	28.2	25.3
		23.5	21.4			Inventory	19.8	21.0
		1.4	2.3			All Other Current	2.3	2.7
		63.6	55.6			Total Current	57.6	56.0
		17.8	35.3			Fixed Assets (net)	32.0	35.0
		7.6	2.6			Intangibles (net)	4.1	4.0
		11.0	6.5			All Other Non-Current	6.3	5.0
		100.0	100.0			Total	100.0	100.0
						LIABILITIES		
		11.7	5.3			Notes Payable-Short Term	9.7	7.2
		1.9	6.0			Cur. Mat.-L.T.D.	3.2	3.8
		18.5	13.2			Trade Payables	16.5	15.1
		.4	.4			Income Taxes Payable	.1	.4
		16.5	7.2			All Other Current	7.0	9.6
		49.1	32.0			Total Current	36.6	36.0
		12.6	15.8			Long-Term Debt	15.6	21.8
		.3	1.0			Deferred Taxes	1.0	1.0
		2.9	4.0			All Other Non-Current	3.9	6.5
		35.1	47.1			Net Worth	43.0	34.7
		100.0	100.0			Total Liabilities & Net Worth	100.0	100.0
						INCOME DATA		
		100.0	100.0			Net Sales	100.0	100.0
		31.3	33.2			Gross Profit	33.3	32.8
		24.7	24.0			Operating Expenses	26.0	24.8
		6.6	9.1			Operating Profit	7.4	8.0
		.7	1.2			All Other Expenses (net)	1.3	2.1
		5.9	7.9			Profit Before Taxes	6.0	5.9
						RATIOS		
		1.8	2.8				2.7	2.5
		1.4	1.9			Current	1.7	1.7
		1.1	1.2				1.1	1.2
		1.1	1.7				1.6	1.5
		.7	1.1			Quick	1.0	.9
		.5	.7				.7	.6
		(32) 11.5	(36) 10.1				(36) 10.1	(32) 11.4
		(42) 8.6	(43) 8.4			Sales/Receivables	(47) 7.7	(41) 8.8
		(51) 7.2	(48) 7.6				(61) 6.0	(57) 6.4
		(37) 10.0	(32) 11.4				(24) 15.0	(28) 12.8
		(54) 6.7	(57) 6.4			Cost of Sales/Inventory	(45) 8.0	(52) 7.1
		(96) 3.8	(109) 3.4				(88) 4.2	(73) 5.0
		(18) 20.7	(23) 15.9				(22) 16.6	(19) 19.4
		(29) 12.8	(34) 10.7			Cost of Sales/Payables	(39) 9.3	(33) 11.0
		(46) 8.0	(51) 7.2				(58) 6.3	(55) 6.6
		6.8	4.3				5.6	6.1
		15.7	8.5			Sales/Working Capital	9.4	10.2
		55.9	25.6				62.3	31.5
		11.2	18.2				20.6	15.8
		(34) 6.3	(45) 7.5			EBIT/Interest	(80) 6.9	(104) 5.5
		3.0	2.6				2.1	1.7
			6.3				5.2	7.7
			(21) 2.9			Net Profit + Depr., Dep., Amort./Cur. Mat. L/T/D	(22) 2.7	(31) 4.7
			1.7				1.4	2.2
		.1	.4				.3	.4
		.7	.9			Fixed/Worth	.8	1.0
		1.5	1.5				1.8	3.3
		1.2	.5				.6	.8
		2.8	1.3			Debt/Worth	1.3	1.9
		4.1	3.6				3.6	6.5
		54.2	56.9				44.2	55.3
		(31) 28.1	(47) 28.5			% Profit Before Taxes/Tangible Net Worth	(82) 21.7	(92) 24.2
		8.2	11.5				8.6	10.3
		20.4	19.4				19.5	19.3
		8.4	11.0			% Profit Before Taxes/Total Assets	9.2	9.5
		2.7	3.8				2.3	1.8
		122.9	10.1				22.2	16.8
		12.7	5.6			Sales/Net Fixed Assets	6.1	5.7
		5.7	2.9				3.1	2.9
		3.2	2.5				3.2	2.8
		2.3	1.9			Sales/Total Assets	1.8	1.9
		1.5	1.2				1.2	1.3
		.2	1.0				1.3	1.2
		(31) 1.6	(46) 3.3			% Depr., Dep., Amort./Sales	(73) 3.0	(87) 2.8
		3.1	5.5				5.1	4.7
		.4					1.7	1.5
		(12) 1.6				% Officers', Directors' Owners' Comp/Sales	(22) 2.7	(19) 2.7
		4.3					5.8	6.5
2680M	27987M	533384M	1765234M	562729M	1499217M	Net Sales ($)	4242876M	6652495M
1415M	12891M	195448M	926806M	453255M	1405409M	Total Assets ($)	3144846M	4542220M

M = $ thousand   MM = $ million
See Pages 9 through 22 for Explanation of Ratios and Data

Comparative Historical Data   Current Data Sorted by Sales

			Type of Statement						
22	21	31	Unqualified	1	1		1	6	22
23	26	20	Reviewed	1		1	4	11	3
3	8	8	Compiled	1			2	3	2
4	2	8	Tax Returns	2	1	2	1		2
38	55	47	Other	3	2	3	5	17	17
4/1/07-3/31/08 ALL	4/1/08-3/31/09 ALL	4/1/09-3/31/10 ALL		0-1MM	1-3MM 19 (4/1-9/30/09)	3-5MM	5-10MM	10-25MM 95 (10/1/09-3/31/10)	25MM & OVER
90	112	114	NUMBER OF STATEMENTS	8	4	6	13	37	46
%	%	%	ASSETS	%	%	%	%	%	%
6.7	6.4	9.9	Cash & Equivalents				10.7	4.5	11.7
25.2	24.3	24.0	Trade Receivables (net)				19.6	22.5	26.8
24.1	24.4	22.4	Inventory				24.3	24.2	20.1
2.7	1.7	2.0	All Other Current				.5	2.5	2.2
58.7	56.8	58.3	Total Current				55.2	53.6	60.8
31.6	31.2	28.7	Fixed Assets (net)				17.8	34.6	30.3
5.0	6.1	5.0	Intangibles (net)				10.2	5.0	3.8
4.7	5.9	7.9	All Other Non-Current				16.8	6.8	5.1
100.0	100.0	100.0	Total				100.0	100.0	100.0
			LIABILITIES						
8.3	9.2	9.1	Notes Payable-Short Term				9.5	10.7	4.2
3.4	4.2	3.7	Cur. Mat.-L.T.D.				2.6	5.2	3.5
15.0	15.0	15.9	Trade Payables				10.3	13.8	16.5
.4	.3	.4	Income Taxes Payable				.1	.5	.5
10.3	7.5	9.8	All Other Current				15.7	6.3	11.6
37.3	36.2	38.8	Total Current				38.2	36.4	36.2
19.3	19.7	14.8	Long-Term Debt				14.8	16.7	12.6
.9	1.4	.9	Deferred Taxes				.4	1.1	1.0
3.9	3.1	7.7	All Other Non-Current				.9	3.7	5.6
38.5	39.5	37.7	Net Worth				45.8	42.1	44.5
100.0	100.0	100.0	Total Liabilities & Net Worth				100.0	100.0	100.0
			INCOME DATA						
100.0	100.0	100.0	Net Sales				100.0	100.0	100.0
30.0	28.5	32.8	Gross Profit				38.6	32.4	29.3
21.0	22.5	24.4	Operating Expenses				28.0	26.8	19.3
9.0	6.1	8.4	Operating Profit				10.6	5.6	10.0
1.5	1.1	1.0	All Other Expenses (net)				.8	1.5	.9
7.6	4.9	7.4	Profit Before Taxes				9.8	4.1	9.1
			RATIOS						
2.5	2.3	2.5					2.0	2.4	2.7
1.6	1.7	1.7	Current				1.6	1.4	1.9
1.2	1.1	1.2					1.0	1.1	1.4
1.5	1.4	1.6					1.3	1.1	1.8
1.0	.9	1.0	Quick				.7	.8	1.2
.6	.6	.6					.6	.5	.7
35 10.5	30 12.2	35 10.4					44 8.3	34 10.7	35 10.4
46 7.9	40 9.0	44 8.3	Sales/Receivables				49 7.5	41 9.0	45 8.2
59 6.2	49 7.4	53 6.9					54 6.7	49 7.5	53 6.8
30 12.3	28 12.8	39 9.4					49 7.4	42 8.7	30 12.3
50 7.3	59 6.2	62 5.8	Cost of Sales/Inventory				81 4.5	61 6.0	48 7.6
89 4.1	100 3.7	113 3.2					148 2.5	113 3.2	88 4.2
22 16.7	23 16.2	22 16.3					11 31.8	21 17.1	23 16.1
33 11.0	31 11.6	34 10.7	Cost of Sales/Payables				30 12.2	35 10.4	33 11.0
51 7.1	46 7.9	52 7.1					62 5.9	53 6.9	44 8.3
5.4	5.7	4.6					5.1	5.1	4.2
9.8	11.0	10.4	Sales/Working Capital				10.2	13.6	7.9
26.4	27.2	27.1					NM	45.3	19.8
14.7	14.9	14.2					9.9	9.3	31.1
(81) 4.8	(107) 5.1	(104) 6.7	EBIT/Interest				5.4	(36) 5.1	(42) 10.0
1.4	1.6	2.4					3.7	2.2	3.6
5.8	7.7	9.3						2.9	8.2
(30) 3.0	(37) 3.5	(36) 3.0	Net Profit + Depr., Dep., Amort./Cur. Mat. L/T/D					(10) 2.0	(19) 3.5
1.4	1.9	1.8						.2	2.0
.4	.3	.3					.2	.6	.3
.9	1.0	.8	Fixed/Worth				.5	.9	.8
3.0	2.0	1.6					1.9	1.7	1.2
.7	.8	.6					.6	.8	.5
1.6	1.7	1.6	Debt/Worth				1.6	1.7	1.4
7.0	4.9	4.1					3.2	4.0	3.8
62.5	54.2	52.3					54.2	47.7	56.9
(82) 26.7	(100) 26.0	(102) 28.3	% Profit Before Taxes/Tangible Net Worth			(11)	22.5	(35) 21.3	(43) 30.4
10.7	7.4	8.1					6.7	6.3	13.5
19.0	16.2	18.9					19.3	14.6	20.4
10.4	8.1	9.9	% Profit Before Taxes/Total Assets				9.2	7.0	13.0
2.0	1.4	2.4					4.2	2.5	4.2
19.2	18.1	18.9					28.2	14.3	16.7
5.2	6.5	6.6	Sales/Net Fixed Assets				7.2	5.9	5.8
3.7	3.1	3.3					4.8	2.4	3.3
2.7	3.2	2.6					2.2	2.8	2.9
1.7	1.9	1.8	Sales/Total Assets				1.1	1.8	1.9
1.4	1.2	1.1					.9	1.2	1.2
1.2	1.1	.8					1.7	1.0	.7
(77) 2.4	(102) 2.2	(99) 2.5	% Depr., Dep., Amort./Sales			(11)	2.6	(35) 2.3	(43) 2.1
4.6	4.3	5.0					3.3	6.3	4.7
1.8	1.2	.9							
(22) 3.3	(25) 3.8	(24) 2.1	% Officers', Directors' Owners' Comp/Sales						
6.4	6.3	8.4							
4773369M	6643890M	4391231M	Net Sales ($)	3409M	8791M	22801M	91244M	639413M	3625573M
3290871M	4166481M	2995224M	Total Assets ($)	2000M	9929M	9510M	74052M	430586M	2469147M

M = $ thousand   MM = $ million
See Pages 9 through 22 for Explanation of Ratios and Data

Current Data Sorted by Assets | Comparative Historical Data

0-500M	500M-2MM	2-10MM	10-50MM	50-100MM	100-250MM		4/1/05-3/31/06 ALL	4/1/06-3/31/07 ALL
	12 (4/1-9/30/09)		31 (10/1/09-3/31/10)			**Type of Statement**		
			5	11	16	Unqualified	8	16
						Reviewed		
			1			Compiled	3	
						Tax Returns		
				7	3	Other	6	3
			6	18	19	**NUMBER OF STATEMENTS**	17	19
%	%	%	%	%	%	**ASSETS**	%	%
D	D	D		9.2	5.3	Cash & Equivalents	11.0	16.5
A	A	A		7.4	4.2	Trade Receivables (net)	15.2	8.0
T	T	T		8.2	6.0	Inventory	10.2	7.8
A	A	A		.9	1.4	All Other Current	1.4	3.9
				25.6	16.8	Total Current	37.8	36.2
N	N	N		71.9	77.3	Fixed Assets (net)	57.1	53.2
O	O	O		.6	.6	Intangibles (net)	1.1	1.2
T	T	T		1.9	5.2	All Other Non-Current	3.9	9.4
				100.0	100.0	Total	100.0	100.0
A	A	A				**LIABILITIES**		
V	V	V		.6	2.6	Notes Payable-Short Term	4.5	1.1
A	A	A		8.5	4.5	Cur. Mat.-L.T.D.	2.9	4.0
I	I	I		6.8	2.5	Trade Payables	11.6	6.5
L	L	L		.0	.0	Income Taxes Payable	.0	.0
A	A	A		5.5	3.3	All Other Current	6.9	4.6
B	B	B		21.4	12.8	Total Current	25.9	16.1
L	L	L		26.4	42.8	Long-Term Debt	18.7	16.8
E	E	E		.0	.0	Deferred Taxes	.2	.2
				.9	2.5	All Other Non-Current	6.3	2.1
				51.3	41.8	Net Worth	48.9	64.7
				100.0	100.0	Total Liabilities & Net Worth	100.0	100.0
						INCOME DATA		
				100.0	100.0	Net Sales	100.0	100.0
				15.3	16.2	Gross Profit	25.9	36.6
				11.3	15.9	Operating Expenses	12.4	9.6
				4.1	.3	Operating Profit	13.5	27.1
				1.6	2.1	All Other Expenses (net)	-.4	.4
				2.5	-1.8	Profit Before Taxes	13.9	26.7
						RATIOS		
				2.1	1.8		3.5	3.5
				1.5	1.2	Current	1.7	2.8
				.9	.9		1.3	1.7
				1.3	1.3		2.7	2.5
				.9	.8	Quick	1.2	1.9
				.5	.4		.8	1.3
				10 36.2	12 30.5		13 28.0	14 26.0
				14 26.6	16 23.3	Sales/Receivables	19 19.0	19 19.0
				19 19.1	19 19.0		25 14.6	30 12.4
				12 31.3	15 24.8		13 28.0	13 27.5
				17 21.0	25 14.4	Cost of Sales/Inventory	15 23.8	21 17.6
				36 10.1	41 9.0		29 12.7	36 10.2
				6 57.8	4 85.4		6 64.1	12 29.7
				14 25.8	8 45.9	Cost of Sales/Payables	14 26.0	19 19.0
				29 12.4	24 15.5		25 14.5	36 10.0
				10.0	11.7		6.0	5.7
				21.6	24.2	Sales/Working Capital	15.5	7.8
				-95.1	-93.2		30.8	9.5
				6.0	3.6		12.7	29.8
				(17) 2.9	1.1	EBIT/Interest	10.9	18.9
				1.1	-1.0		5.6	9.4
						Net Profit + Depr., Dep., Amort./Cur. Mat. L/T/D		
				1.1	1.8		1.0	.6
				1.5	2.0	Fixed/Worth	1.3	.7
				2.0	2.3		1.9	1.1
				.6	1.3		.6	.3
				.9	1.4	Debt/Worth	.7	.5
				2.0	2.0		1.8	1.0
				19.5	12.9		47.1	77.8
				9.1	.6	% Profit Before Taxes/Tangible Net Worth	(16) 38.8	51.7
				-.6	-16.7		29.7	28.6
				7.9	6.3		29.9	47.6
				2.8	.3	% Profit Before Taxes/Total Assets	23.6	40.5
				-.4	-5.7		13.5	21.3
				2.0	1.7		19.7	2.8
				1.8	1.3	Sales/Net Fixed Assets	2.1	2.2
				1.4	1.0		1.5	1.8
				1.6	1.2		2.7	1.4
				1.2	1.0	Sales/Total Assets	1.5	1.2
				1.2	.8		1.0	.8
				4.5	3.6		1.0	2.2
				(16) 5.8	(14) 4.6	% Depr., Dep., Amort./Sales	(16) 4.5	(17) 3.4
				6.2	4.9		6.0	5.2
						% Officers', Directors' Owners' Comp/Sales		
			303010M	2818983M	2843779M	Net Sales ($)	1557908M	1552293M
			204411M	1440578M	2870827M	Total Assets ($)	958540M	1250435M

M = $ thousand   MM = $ million
See Pages 9 through 22 for Explanation of Ratios and Data

Comparative Historical Data   ## Current Data Sorted by Sales

16	25	32	Type of Statement						32
			Unqualified						
			Reviewed						
1		1	Compiled					1	
			Tax Returns						
6	11	10	Other						10
4/1/07- 3/31/08 ALL	4/1/08- 3/31/09 ALL	4/1/09- 3/31/10 ALL		0-1MM	12 (4/1-9/30/09) 1-3MM	3-5MM	5-10MM	31 (10/1/09-3/31/10) 10-25MM	25MM & OVER
23	36	43	NUMBER OF STATEMENTS					1	42
%	%	%	**ASSETS**	%	%	%	%	%	%
7.4	7.8	7.7	Cash & Equivalents						7.6
6.4	5.5	6.2	Trade Receivables (net)	D	D	D	D		6.2
7.3	6.8	8.1	Inventory	A	A	A	A		8.0
3.6	2.0	1.2	All Other Current	T	T	T	T		1.2
24.6	22.1	23.1	Total Current	A	A	A	A		23.0
71.0	72.6	71.1	Fixed Assets (net)						72.5
.5	.6	.6	Intangibles (net)	N	N	N	N		.6
3.9	4.6	5.3	All Other Non-Current	O	O	O	O		3.9
100.0	100.0	100.0	Total	T	T	T	T		100.0
			LIABILITIES	A	A	A	A		
1.6	2.5	2.6	Notes Payable-Short Term	V	V	V	V		2.6
4.3	7.9	5.9	Cur. Mat.-L.T.D.	A	A	A	A		6.0
5.3	6.2	5.0	Trade Payables	I	I	I	I		4.9
.0	.0	.0	Income Taxes Payable	L	L	L	L		.0
3.7	3.4	4.1	All Other Current	A	A	A	A		4.1
14.8	20.0	17.5	Total Current	B	B	B	B		17.8
32.8	34.1	33.5	Long-Term Debt	L	L	L	L		34.3
.1	.0	.0	Deferred Taxes	E	E	E	E		.0
.7	1.0	1.6	All Other Non-Current						1.5
51.7	44.9	47.4	Net Worth						46.4
100.0	100.0	100.0	Total Liabilties & Net Worth						100.0
			INCOME DATA						
100.0	100.0	100.0	Net Sales						100.0
21.5	9.7	14.4	Gross Profit						14.4
13.5	10.3	13.2	Operating Expenses						13.4
7.9	-.6	1.2	Operating Profit						1.0
.4	2.6	1.8	All Other Expenses (net)						1.9
7.5	-3.1	-.6	Profit Before Taxes						-.9
			RATIOS						
2.6	2.4	2.0							1.9
1.5	1.2	1.5	Current						1.5
1.0	1.0	1.1							1.1
1.6	1.1	1.3							1.3
.8	.8	.9	Quick						.9
.5	.3	.5							.5
17 21.5	8 45.5	11 33.7	Sales/Receivables						11 33.9
25 14.8	12 29.4	15 24.8							15 24.4
51 7.1	21 17.6	19 19.0							19 18.7
17 22.1	13 28.7	13 27.2	Cost of Sales/Inventory						13 27.5
31 11.7	20 18.7	22 16.6							21 17.1
52 7.0	30 12.2	41 9.0							39 9.4
13 27.3	8 48.0	5 73.2	Cost of Sales/Payables						5 73.5
26 14.0	12 30.9	11 33.6							10 36.8
36 10.1	21 17.5	26 14.0							26 14.2
6.0	11.7	10.4	Sales/Working Capital						10.5
9.7	29.9	20.9							21.8
82.2	757.8	149.2							NM
13.2	2.2	4.5	EBIT/Interest						4.0
6.9	(35) .6	(42) 1.8						(41) 1.7	
2.0	-2.3	-.5							-.7
			Net Profit + Depr., Dep., Amort./Cur. Mat. L/T/D						
1.1	1.1	1.1	Fixed/Worth						1.2
1.5	1.9	1.8							1.8
2.0	2.8	2.1							2.1
.6	.8	.7	Debt/Worth						.8
.9	1.5	1.4							1.4
1.5	2.3	2.0							2.0
36.0	9.4	17.6	% Profit Before Taxes/Tangible Net Worth						17.7
17.5	-2.4	2.1							1.7
6.6	-20.4	-13.5							-14.3
20.9	3.7	7.4	% Profit Before Taxes/Total Assets						7.3
6.2	-.9	1.1							.8
2.4	-6.5	-4.2							-4.6
2.1	2.4	2.0	Sales/Net Fixed Assets						2.0
1.2	1.8	1.6							1.5
.6	1.1	1.3							1.2
1.3	1.7	1.5	Sales/Total Assets						1.5
.9	1.4	1.2							1.2
.5	.9	1.0							1.0
2.4	2.6	3.6	% Depr., Dep., Amort./Sales						3.8
(19) 3.8	(33) 3.7	(36) 4.8						(35) 4.8	
5.7	4.5	6.1							6.1
			% Officers', Directors' Owners' Comp/Sales						
1726104M	7730578M	5965772M	Net Sales ($)					24820M	5940952M
2093096M	3984549M	4515816M	Total Assets ($)					26871M	4488945M

© RMA 2010

M = $ thousand   MM = $ million

See Pages 9 through 22 for Explanation of Ratios and Data

Current Data Sorted by Assets   Comparative Historical Data

0-500M	500M-2MM	2-10MM	10-50MM	50-100MM	100-250MM		4/1/05-3/31/06 ALL	4/1/06-3/31/07 ALL
						Type of Statement		
		3	23	26	20	Unqualified	34	54
1		15	7			Reviewed	19	19
	3	5	3	1		Compiled	5	9
2	1	3				Tax Returns	2	2
2		7	27	8	6	Other	34	36
		26 (4/1-9/30/09)		137 (10/1/09-3/31/10)				
5	4	33	60	35	26	**NUMBER OF STATEMENTS**	94	120
%	%	%	%	%	%	**ASSETS**	%	%
		11.1	8.1	8.5	7.0	Cash & Equivalents	6.8	9.9
		27.2	19.8	9.3	8.4	Trade Receivables (net)	24.8	23.0
		27.5	19.1	11.2	9.5	Inventory	19.3	18.2
		1.4	4.1	2.3	2.0	All Other Current	3.8	3.7
		67.2	51.1	31.2	26.9	Total Current	54.7	54.8
		23.9	35.5	62.8	64.6	Fixed Assets (net)	36.4	35.4
		4.0	5.7	2.0	4.5	Intangibles (net)	3.2	4.3
		4.8	7.7	3.9	4.0	All Other Non-Current	5.8	5.4
		100.0	100.0	100.0	100.0	Total	100.0	100.0
						LIABILITIES		
		13.1	5.4	1.5	3.3	Notes Payable-Short Term	6.7	8.2
		3.4	3.0	5.0	6.5	Cur. Mat.-L.T.D.	3.2	2.9
		20.4	11.3	6.5	5.6	Trade Payables	14.5	12.7
		.2	.2	.0	.2	Income Taxes Payable	.2	.4
		5.2	7.0	5.2	3.5	All Other Current	8.3	7.5
		42.3	26.8	18.3	19.1	Total Current	32.9	31.7
		14.8	14.6	23.2	32.5	Long-Term Debt	18.2	17.3
		.3	1.0	.4	.6	Deferred Taxes	.6	.9
		5.0	6.5	4.5	5.7	All Other Non-Current	5.5	6.1
		37.6	51.2	53.5	42.1	Net Worth	42.9	44.0
		100.0	100.0	100.0	100.0	Total Liabilities & Net Worth	100.0	100.0
						INCOME DATA		
		100.0	100.0	100.0	100.0	Net Sales	100.0	100.0
		29.3	25.8	12.9	12.5	Gross Profit	30.6	34.0
		27.2	20.8	8.6	8.1	Operating Expenses	21.8	20.5
		2.1	5.0	4.4	4.4	Operating Profit	8.8	13.4
		.6	1.0	2.0	2.3	All Other Expenses (net)	.6	.6
		1.5	4.0	2.4	2.1	Profit Before Taxes	8.2	12.8
						RATIOS		
		2.3	2.9	2.5	1.8		2.5	2.9
		1.8	2.0	1.7	1.4	Current	1.7	1.9
		1.1	1.3	1.2	1.2		1.3	1.2
		1.3	1.7	1.3	1.1		1.6	1.8
		.9	1.0	1.0	.7	Quick	1.0	1.1
		.5	.6	.7	.6		.7	.7
		32 11.5	38 9.6	14 26.2	11 33.7		26 13.9	24 15.1
		39 9.4	47 7.7	19 19.6	19 19.2	Sales/Receivables	45 8.1	43 8.6
		52 7.0	59 6.2	30 12.2	31 11.6		57 6.4	58 6.3
		32 11.5	34 10.8	15 24.9	15 24.0		23 15.7	28 12.9
		49 7.5	58 6.3	36 10.2	25 14.6	Cost of Sales/Inventory	47 7.8	46 7.9
		81 4.5	81 4.5	61 6.0	43 8.5		75 4.9	68 5.4
		25 14.5	23 16.1	7 56.1	7 53.6		19 19.5	17 21.1
		37 9.9	32 11.4	18 19.8	13 27.7	Cost of Sales/Payables	30 12.0	30 12.1
		54 6.8	52 7.0	35 10.3	28 13.1		52 7.0	47 7.8
		6.1	3.8	5.1	8.2		5.0	4.6
		8.8	6.4	10.7	17.0	Sales/Working Capital	9.3	8.0
		93.0	19.5	46.8	65.6		22.0	26.5
		16.1	14.3	8.3	7.2		16.7	27.1
		(32) 5.0	(56) 5.7	(34) 4.5	2.4	EBIT/Interest	(87) 6.4	(117) 8.9
		1.9	.6	.8	.5		2.2	2.3
			14.1			Net Profit + Depr., Dep.,	14.6	17.2
			(25) 2.9			Amort./Cur. Mat. L/T/D	(23) 3.7	(38) 4.7
			1.3				1.8	1.9
		.2	.2	.9	1.2		.4	.4
		.5	.7	1.2	1.8	Fixed/Worth	1.0	.9
		2.9	1.5	2.2	2.8		1.9	1.7
		.8	.4	.4	.8		.5	.5
		2.4	.9	.7	1.2	Debt/Worth	1.2	1.5
		6.5	2.5	2.6	2.5		3.3	3.7
		81.0	39.8	17.8	15.0	% Profit Before Taxes/Tangible	46.7	63.7
		(31) 26.4	(56) 15.2	(22) 11.0	8.2	Net Worth	(85) 32.5	(107) 36.0
		6.9	-2.7	-12.9	-4.6		8.1	17.3
		15.1	15.9	9.3	8.0	% Profit Before Taxes/Total	23.6	31.7
		5.7	6.5	6.3	4.2	Assets	9.6	12.9
		1.4	-1.9	-4.3	-1.7		1.9	4.8
		72.7	14.7	2.6	3.5		14.5	16.9
		12.3	5.7	2.0	1.7	Sales/Net Fixed Assets	5.6	6.5
		4.1	2.4	1.5	1.2		2.6	2.4
		3.4	2.1	1.5	1.5		2.5	2.4
		2.3	1.5	1.3	1.1	Sales/Total Assets	1.9	1.6
		1.5	1.0	1.2	.9		1.3	1.2
		.5	1.2	3.3	3.5		1.1	1.1
		(30) 1.7	(52) 2.5	(32) 4.9	(22) 3.9	% Depr., Dep., Amort./Sales	(83) 2.4	(106) 2.3
		3.6	7.0	6.3	5.0		4.5	4.1
		1.2	1.0				2.0	1.8
		(15) 2.7	(11) 2.4			% Officers', Directors' Owners' Comp/Sales	(19) 3.1	(25) 2.8
		6.5	5.1				7.6	4.5
13897M	13948M	393127M	2349559M	3572727M	4623487M	Net Sales ($)	4345231M	6914720M
1085M	5321M	166193M	1552672M	2723837M	3784052M	Total Assets ($)	3158857M	5062886M

M = $ thousand   MM = $ million
See Pages 9 through 22 for Explanation of Ratios and Data

Comparative Historical Data   Current Data Sorted by Sales

			Type of Statement	0-1MM	1-3MM	3-5MM	5-10MM	10-25MM	25MM & OVER
67	64	72	Unqualified				1	7	64
15	18	23	Reviewed		2	1	7	9	4
4	8	12	Compiled		2	1	2	4	3
3	2	6	Tax Returns		2	1	1	2	
37	47	50	Other	2	2		4	9	33
4/1/07-3/31/08	4/1/08-3/31/09	4/1/09-3/31/10			26 (4/1-9/30/09)			137 (10/1/09-3/31/10)	
ALL	ALL	ALL							
126	139	163	**NUMBER OF STATEMENTS**	2	8	3	15	31	104
%	%	%	**ASSETS**	%	%	%	%	%	%
6.9	6.7	8.8	Cash & Equivalents				6.6	10.6	8.5
17.8	18.8	18.0	Trade Receivables (net)				17.8	24.0	15.5
16.9	17.4	17.2	Inventory				21.3	22.9	15.1
3.7	2.6	2.6	All Other Current				3.5	3.5	2.5
45.4	45.5	46.6	Total Current				49.2	61.0	41.6
42.0	41.4	42.8	Fixed Assets (net)				31.9	30.4	49.5
6.7	7.6	4.9	Intangibles (net)				10.3	3.9	3.5
5.9	5.5	5.7	All Other Non-Current				8.6	4.8	5.4
100.0	100.0	100.0	Total				100.0	100.0	100.0
			LIABILITIES						
7.2	7.6	5.9	Notes Payable-Short Term				13.4	8.0	4.0
3.6	3.8	4.1	Cur. Mat.-L.T.D.				2.1	3.2	4.3
11.7	12.0	12.2	Trade Payables				11.8	18.7	9.2
.2	.2	.2	Income Taxes Payable				.0	.5	.1
7.2	7.9	6.6	All Other Current				10.7	4.2	6.2
30.0	31.5	28.8	Total Current				38.1	34.5	23.8
20.3	18.1	19.4	Long-Term Debt				15.9	14.8	20.8
.7	.5	.6	Deferred Taxes				.7	1.0	.6
4.7	5.3	5.3	All Other Non-Current				4.6	7.2	5.0
44.3	44.6	45.9	Net Worth				40.8	42.5	49.8
100.0	100.0	100.0	Total Liabilities & Net Worth				100.0	100.0	100.0
			INCOME DATA						
100.0	100.0	100.0	Net Sales				100.0	100.0	100.0
27.9	19.9	22.3	Gross Profit				40.1	26.7	17.4
18.4	16.1	18.3	Operating Expenses				38.1	22.7	12.4
9.5	3.9	4.0	Operating Profit				2.0	4.0	5.0
1.6	1.5	1.3	All Other Expenses (net)				2.0	.5	1.4
7.9	2.4	2.8	Profit Before Taxes				.0	3.5	3.5
			RATIOS						
2.5	2.3	2.5	Current				1.8	2.3	2.5
1.6	1.7	1.7					1.5	1.9	1.8
1.1	1.1	1.2					.9	1.3	1.2
1.3	1.4	1.4	Quick				.9	1.4	1.5
.8	.9	.9					.7	1.0	1.0
.5	.5	.6					.4	.7	.6
22 17.0	18 20.7	19 19.3	Sales/Receivables				32 11.5	35 10.3	16 23.2
37 9.8	34 10.6	37 9.8					41 9.0	42 8.6	30 12.3
51 7.2	51 7.1	51 7.1					62 5.8	54 6.8	50 7.3
28 12.9	19 19.2	24 15.1	Cost of Sales/Inventory				26 14.3	32 11.5	20 18.4
45 8.1	38 9.6	43 8.5					53 6.9	60 6.1	39 9.4
66 5.5	63 5.8	70 5.2					157 2.3	85 4.3	62 5.9
16 22.3	12 30.9	15 25.1	Cost of Sales/Payables				23 16.0	25 14.4	10 36.4
31 11.9	23 15.6	28 13.0					45 8.1	32 11.4	24 15.5
47 7.7	45 8.1	47 7.8					62 5.9	59 6.2	39 9.5
5.4	5.7	4.9	Sales/Working Capital				3.5	5.9	4.7
10.2	13.9	9.9					8.9	6.9	10.8
39.9	77.1	30.4					-109.5	17.2	28.6
18.1	13.6	10.8	EBIT/Interest				2.7	16.7	12.3
(117) 5.4	(131) 3.3	(153) 4.7					(12) 1.9	(29) 5.7	(102) 5.1
2.3	-.4	.7					-3.0	.7	1.0
23.8	11.5	9.7	Net Profit + Depr., Dep.,						34.5
(37) 3.6	(39) 3.3	(42) 3.7	Amort./Cur. Mat. L/T/D					(26) 4.6	
1.6	.4	1.6							2.1
.5	.4	.4	Fixed/Worth				.4	.1	.5
1.1	1.2	1.0					1.5	.7	1.0
2.0	2.1	2.2					2.2	2.8	1.8
.6	.6	.5	Debt/Worth				.8	.5	.5
1.1	1.3	1.1					2.7	1.3	.9
2.8	3.3	3.4					5.5	4.1	2.5
44.4	31.1	29.1	% Profit Before Taxes/Tangible				52.4	47.1	27.7
(106) 27.6	(121) 11.7	(149) 13.1	Net Worth			(14) 12.2	(28) 21.3	(99) 12.4	
14.0	-5.1	-1.0					-4.8	.1	-1.4
19.5	14.4	11.3	% Profit Before Taxes/Total				6.5	11.9	12.0
10.6	5.0	6.2	Assets				2.2	5.7	6.9
3.7	-3.0	-.8					-3.5	-.8	-.4
11.7	13.7	13.9	Sales/Net Fixed Assets				41.6	35.6	6.9
4.4	4.8	3.5					6.7	10.1	2.6
2.1	2.3	1.8					3.5	2.5	1.7
2.1	2.4	2.1	Sales/Total Assets				2.5	2.8	2.0
1.5	1.6	1.4					1.8	1.9	1.4
1.0	1.3	1.1					.6	1.0	1.1
1.2	1.0	1.4	% Depr., Dep., Amort./Sales				1.9	.9	1.9
(110) 2.8	(119) 2.5	(139) 3.6				(11) 2.7	(29) 1.9	(92) 3.8	
4.4	4.0	5.7					4.1	7.2	5.6
1.5	1.2	1.0	% Officers', Directors'						1.0
(22) 2.8	(19) 2.9	(34) 2.4	Owners' Comp/Sales					(15) 1.4	
5.6	4.6	5.2							3.2
8975523M	12180578M	10966745M	Net Sales ($)	1430M	19502M	13000M	116425M	531215M	10285173M
7164486M	7724999M	8233160M	Total Assets ($)	568M	18767M	7626M	136666M	385942M	7683591M

M = $ thousand   MM = $ million
See Pages 9 through 22 for Explanation of Ratios and Data

Current Data Sorted by Assets   **Comparative Historical Data**

						Type of Statement		
1	1	7	24	8	12	Unqualified	49	54
1	4	21	14	2		Reviewed	32	40
3	5	6	2		1	Compiled	29	21
4	6	4	2			Tax Returns	12	10
3	7	33	32	4	8	Other	98	93
	36 (4/1-9/30/09)		178 (10/1/09-3/31/10)				4/1/05-3/31/06	4/1/06-3/31/07
0-500M	500M-2MM	2-10MM	10-50MM	50-100MM	100-250MM		ALL	ALL
11	23	71	74	14	21	NUMBER OF STATEMENTS	220	218
%	%	%	%	%	%	ASSETS	%	%
8.5	12.7	8.5	4.8	11.1	3.9	Cash & Equivalents	5.9	6.5
16.0	26.7	26.7	27.4	20.0	24.7	Trade Receivables (net)	30.1	27.2
27.8	29.4	24.3	25.1	19.4	20.5	Inventory	23.8	23.2
8.6	.7	3.9	2.1	2.3	2.1	All Other Current	2.4	2.5
60.8	69.6	63.4	59.4	52.8	51.2	Total Current	62.2	59.5
28.0	25.2	27.7	28.6	39.4	35.9	Fixed Assets (net)	30.3	31.1
4.5	1.7	3.8	6.1	3.1	10.5	Intangibles (net)	3.3	5.0
6.7	3.5	5.1	5.9	4.7	2.4	All Other Non-Current	4.2	4.4
100.0	100.0	100.0	100.0	100.0	100.0	Total	100.0	100.0
						LIABILITIES		
41.5	12.4	12.5	13.7	8.9	4.9	Notes Payable-Short Term	12.6	11.6
5.4	4.4	3.7	3.6	3.1	3.4	Cur. Mat.-L.T.D.	3.9	3.5
21.4	16.9	15.7	17.7	15.3	15.9	Trade Payables	18.3	17.2
.0	.3	.3	.4	.1	.2	Income Taxes Payable	.2	.2
6.1	8.5	6.4	7.3	5.3	5.3	All Other Current	9.4	8.0
74.5	42.6	38.6	42.6	32.7	29.6	Total Current	44.5	40.6
12.9	11.9	13.6	14.2	16.0	24.4	Long-Term Debt	16.7	19.6
.0	.2	.2	.8	1.1	2.5	Deferred Taxes	.8	.7
46.0	11.9	2.7	5.3	6.3	6.9	All Other Non-Current	9.4	7.2
-33.6	33.4	44.9	37.1	44.0	36.5	Net Worth	28.6	32.0
100.0	100.0	100.0	100.0	100.0	100.0	Total Liabilties & Net Worth	100.0	100.0
						INCOME DATA		
100.0	100.0	100.0	100.0	100.0	100.0	Net Sales	100.0	100.0
39.5	40.4	26.4	20.8	19.2	17.5	Gross Profit	25.9	25.2
41.6	37.2	21.7	16.8	12.7	11.6	Operating Expenses	21.1	19.2
-2.1	3.2	4.6	4.0	6.5	5.9	Operating Profit	4.8	6.0
.8	.6	.8	.8	1.4	3.1	All Other Expenses (net)	1.4	1.6
-2.9	2.6	3.9	3.2	5.1	2.8	Profit Before Taxes	3.4	4.4
						RATIOS		
3.3	3.0	3.2	1.9	2.9	2.0		2.3	2.2
1.3	1.6	1.7	1.3	1.8	1.8	Current	1.5	1.5
.5	1.0	1.1	1.0	1.1	1.3		1.1	1.1
1.0	1.8	2.1	1.2	1.7	1.4		1.4	1.4
.4	.7	.9	.6	1.2	.9	Quick	.8	.9
.1	.5	.4	.5	.5	.7		.6	.5
5 78.4	33 11.2	34 10.7	39 9.3	35 10.4	48 7.6		38 9.7	33 10.9
28 13.0	40 9.1	46 7.9	49 7.4	45 8.1	55 6.6	Sales/Receivables	48 7.6	44 8.3
36 10.2	54 6.8	53 6.9	59 6.2	54 6.8	68 5.4		57 6.4	54 6.7
6 56.8	36 10.0	36 10.2	40 9.2	21 17.1	37 9.9		30 12.3	27 13.7
41 8.9	64 5.7	55 6.7	54 6.7	53 6.9	55 6.6	Cost of Sales/Inventory	51 7.1	48 7.6
120 3.0	107 3.4	82 4.4	87 4.2	81 4.5	74 4.9		72 5.1	73 5.0
20 18.0	21 17.6	18 20.3	24 15.3	21 17.3	34 10.7		22 16.9	20 17.8
42 8.8	31 11.8	31 11.9	36 10.1	46 8.0	39 9.3	Cost of Sales/Payables	35 10.3	33 11.1
63 5.8	72 5.1	47 7.7	49 7.5	55 6.6	49 7.4		50 7.2	46 7.9
9.1	4.6	4.1	7.0	3.9	5.4		6.5	6.6
41.1	12.6	9.4	15.7	7.8	7.7	Sales/Working Capital	13.0	11.7
-4.6	-88.2	40.6	196.2	49.4	12.7		74.1	57.0
	5.7	18.5	7.4	23.1	12.7		8.5	10.5
	(19) 2.2	(63) 5.3	(71) 3.7	6.8	3.8	EBIT/Interest	(198) 3.5	(197) 3.8
	-.1	1.1	1.4	1.8	.6		1.1	1.5
		3.5	4.5				7.1	8.4
		(15) 1.8	(17) 2.8			Net Profit + Depr., Dep., Amort./Cur. Mat. L/T/D	(65) 2.3	(57) 3.5
		.7	1.4				1.2	1.9
.3	.1	.2	.3	.7	.6		.4	.5
.7	.6	.6	.9	.8	1.5	Fixed/Worth	1.0	1.1
5.3	5.7	1.7	1.9	2.1	20.0		2.2	3.5
1.5	.4	.6	.9	.5	.9		1.0	.9
2.0	1.1	1.4	2.2	1.2	2.9	Debt/Worth	2.0	2.3
-1.7	30.9	4.1	8.7	3.8	37.1		5.6	8.2
	36.3	30.7	46.5	30.0	48.8		48.8	48.6
	(18) 12.8	(63) 19.6	(68) 21.9	(13) 13.6	(17) 10.2	% Profit Before Taxes/Tangible Net Worth	(188) 20.2	(187) 25.7
	-4.0	5.7	6.8	5.2	.1		2.5	11.7
28.6	11.3	14.1	10.5	15.8	12.0		15.5	16.1
6.7	3.3	9.1	5.5	5.0	4.8	% Profit Before Taxes/Total Assets	6.1	8.5
-49.5	-2.7	.4	.6	1.1	-1.5		.0	2.1
95.7	46.0	20.5	16.6	5.6	6.0		18.3	16.2
9.2	16.9	7.9	6.5	4.1	4.4	Sales/Net Fixed Assets	7.5	7.6
4.3	5.8	5.1	3.3	3.2	2.9		4.3	4.0
3.7	3.2	2.7	2.6	1.9	2.1		2.8	2.9
2.6	2.4	2.1	1.8	1.6	1.6	Sales/Total Assets	2.2	2.1
1.8	1.5	1.6	1.3	1.4	.8		1.6	1.6
	.7	1.1	1.2	2.6	.6		.9	1.0
	(18) 1.8	(62) 2.4	(68) 2.6	(13) 3.2	(12) 1.9	% Depr., Dep., Amort./Sales	(193) 2.4	(193) 2.1
	4.0	4.3	5.0	3.9	4.4		3.8	3.7
	4.2	1.6	1.1				1.8	1.3
	(12) 5.6	(21) 3.3	(16) 2.1			% Officers', Directors' Owners' Comp/Sales	(56) 4.0	(65) 3.5
	10.4	6.2	3.3				7.3	5.9
12678M	78791M	851437M	3127618M	1679625M	5533336M	Net Sales ($)	7663320M	10495362M
2418M	31169M	390937M	1628722M	1007525M	3647215M	Total Assets ($)	3941088M	5145470M

Comparative Historical Data

Current Data Sorted by Sales

			Type of Statement						
48	50	52	Unqualified	1	1	1	1	10	40
38	45	42	Reviewed	1	1	4	9	16	11
16	18	17	Compiled	1	4	4	2	4	2
14	12	16	Tax Returns	4	3	2	2	4	1
95	104	87	Other	4	5	3	11	32	32
4/1/07-3/31/08 ALL	4/1/08-3/31/09 ALL	4/1/09-3/31/10 ALL		36 (4/1-9/30/09)			178 (10/1/09-3/31/10)		
				0-1MM	1-3MM	3-5MM	5-10MM	10-25MM	25MM & OVER
211	229	214	**NUMBER OF STATEMENTS**	10	13	14	25	66	86
%	%	%	**ASSETS**	%	%	%	%	%	%
6.5	7.0	7.4	Cash & Equivalents	8.1	17.2	9.3	8.5	6.8	5.6
28.4	26.0	25.8	Trade Receivables (net)	17.5	25.1	19.4	24.6	26.3	27.8
23.0	23.7	24.6	Inventory	23.3	29.8	22.2	26.6	25.3	23.3
3.1	2.8	2.9	All Other Current	2.8	1.4	2.8	7.5	2.5	2.1
61.0	59.4	60.7	Total Current	51.6	73.5	53.7	67.1	60.9	58.8
29.7	29.8	29.3	Fixed Assets (net)	34.9	21.8	30.4	26.9	29.2	30.4
5.1	5.7	5.0	Intangibles (net)	6.1	1.8	5.0	2.9	5.3	5.8
4.2	5.1	5.0	All Other Non-Current	7.4	2.9	10.9	3.1	4.6	4.9
100.0	100.0	100.0	Total	100.0	100.0	100.0	100.0	100.0	100.0
			LIABILITIES						
11.9	11.3	13.4	Notes Payable-Short Term	44.9	16.0	11.9	13.2	10.7	11.8
3.4	4.2	3.8	Cur. Mat.-L.T.D.	9.6	.8	3.7	3.7	4.1	3.3
18.8	16.8	16.8	Trade Payables	21.0	19.1	8.4	14.9	15.8	18.6
.4	.6	.3	Income Taxes Payable	.0	.0	.0	.2	.3	.4
6.4	8.5	6.7	All Other Current	4.6	11.5	6.0	7.5	6.9	6.1
41.0	41.3	41.0	Total Current	80.1	47.4	30.0	39.5	37.8	40.2
18.1	16.5	14.8	Long-Term Debt	21.2	6.4	20.0	12.9	12.3	16.9
.4	.7	.7	Deferred Taxes	.0	.4	.0	.3	.6	1.1
4.8	8.8	7.5	All Other Non-Current	50.6	6.3	1.6	9.4	3.1	6.4
35.8	32.8	36.0	Net Worth	-52.2	39.6	48.4	38.0	46.3	35.3
100.0	100.0	100.0	Total Liabilities & Net Worth	100.0	100.0	100.0	100.0	100.0	100.0
			INCOME DATA						
100.0	100.0	100.0	Net Sales	100.0	100.0	100.0	100.0	100.0	100.0
24.2	21.8	25.3	Gross Profit	49.3	42.0	32.9	25.5	25.4	18.6
18.9	18.3	21.1	Operating Expenses	53.2	37.2	30.3	20.8	21.7	13.1
5.3	3.5	4.2	Operating Profit	-4.0	4.7	2.6	4.7	3.6	5.5
1.3	1.8	1.0	All Other Expenses (net)	1.5	-.3	1.2	1.5	.7	1.3
4.1	1.7	3.1	Profit Before Taxes	-5.5	5.0	1.4	3.3	2.9	4.2
			RATIOS						
2.4	2.6	2.5		2.0	2.4	3.9	4.8	3.0	2.0
1.5	1.4	1.6	Current	.6	1.7	1.9	1.6	1.6	1.5
1.1	1.0	1.1		.4	.9	1.1	1.1	1.1	1.1
1.3	1.4	1.5		.6	1.7	2.4	2.1	1.7	1.3
.9	.8	.8	Quick	.4	.7	.8	.7	.9	.8
.6	.5	.5		.1	.4	.4	.4	.5	.6
36 10.2	30 12.1	36 10.1		22 16.7	15 23.8	32 11.4	34 10.9	34 10.7	41 9.0
45 8.1	38 9.7	47 7.8	Sales/Receivables	34 10.6	41 8.9	40 9.1	48 7.7	46 7.9	49 7.4
59 6.2	51 7.2	57 6.5		53 6.9	53 6.9	56 6.6	52 7.0	57 6.5	59 6.2
32 11.6	29 12.4	36 10.0		0 UND	41 9.0	22 16.6	49 7.5	36 10.0	34 10.9
51 7.2	52 7.1	55 6.6	Cost of Sales/Inventory	49 7.4	76 4.8	85 4.3	62 5.9	54 6.7	52 7.0
70 5.2	73 5.0	83 4.4		135 2.7	143 2.6	121 3.0	88 4.2	82 4.5	76 4.8
23 15.8	16 22.6	22 16.3		27 13.4	27 13.5	10 38.3	21 17.4	18 20.3	26 13.8
37 9.9	28 12.9	36 10.0	Cost of Sales/Payables	44 8.3	48 7.7	24 15.4	37 9.9	34 10.6	37 9.9
51 7.2	45 8.1	49 7.4		165 2.2	106 3.4	30 12.0	47 7.7	51 7.1	48 7.6
5.5	5.9	5.4		7.8	4.0	3.4	3.7	4.8	6.4
10.8	13.0	11.8	Sales/Working Capital	-7.8	14.9	6.3	11.4	10.0	12.5
48.3	87.6	77.2		-3.3	-54.4	NM	56.1	42.1	60.0
10.1	8.6	11.1			24.0	13.1	18.2	10.9	10.9
(199) 3.4	(209) 2.7	(196) 4.0	EBIT/Interest	(11) 2.8	(13) 1.7	(20) 2.2	(59) 4.7	(85) 4.1	
1.4	.5	1.0			-.1	-3.1	.1	1.5	1.9
9.0	7.6	5.3	Net Profit + Depr., Dep.,					4.5	7.4
(57) 4.0	(62) 2.6	(48) 2.4	Amort./Cur. Mat. L/T/D				(17) 1.5	(26) 3.4	
1.4	1.0	.8						.9	1.3
.3	.3	.3		.4	.1	.1	.2	.2	.5
.8	.8	.7	Fixed/Worth	3.9	.4	.7	.6	.6	1.1
2.3	2.7	2.1		-3.4	2.0	1.9	2.4	1.6	2.1
.9	.9	.6		1.9	.6	.3	.3	.6	1.0
2.0	2.4	1.9	Debt/Worth	8.6	1.1	1.7	2.0	1.1	2.3
6.7	6.6	5.8		-1.6	16.8	3.1	5.7	3.5	8.7
44.6	36.7	40.0	% Profit Before Taxes/Tangible		112.3	20.8	30.3	35.3	49.9
(182) 23.7	(195) 13.3	(187) 18.4	Net Worth	(11) 7.6	(12) 13.0	(21) 13.6	(61) 19.8	(76) 20.3	
7.3	.0	5.3			-3.5	-14.3	-8.5	4.7	8.4
15.4	10.8	12.6	% Profit Before Taxes/Total	6.8	29.1	10.4	15.3	14.0	12.1
6.2	4.5	5.5	Assets	-2.8	3.3	3.8	3.0	8.0	5.5
1.3	-1.1	.0		-51.4	-2.5	-6.0	-3.4	.3	1.5
15.9	21.4	18.7		144.8	44.9	23.3	33.6	18.8	16.0
7.1	7.4	6.5	Sales/Net Fixed Assets	4.9	16.9	8.1	8.8	6.8	5.8
4.2	4.1	4.2		3.3	5.8	2.9	4.9	4.2	3.6
2.8	2.9	2.7		2.6	3.1	2.2	2.8	2.6	2.7
2.2	2.1	1.9	Sales/Total Assets	1.8	2.4	1.8	1.9	2.1	1.9
1.5	1.5	1.4		1.4	1.3	1.1	1.5	1.4	1.3
1.1	1.2	1.1			.3	2.1	1.2	1.1	1.2
(183) 2.2	(193) 2.2	(181) 2.5	% Depr., Dep., Amort./Sales	(10) 1.1	(12) 3.5	(22) 3.4	(60) 2.4	(71) 2.3	
3.7	4.0	4.5			3.2	5.1	4.6	4.8	3.9
1.4	1.8	1.7	% Officers', Directors'					1.4	.9
(50) 4.1	(53) 3.4	(57) 3.7	Owners' Comp/Sales				(24) 2.7	(10) 2.1	
8.5	6.0	8.0						5.4	3.9
11212450M	15610292M	11283485M	Net Sales ($)	4520M	27893M	52401M	183435M	1070719M	9944517M
6311043M	7691781M	6707986M	Total Assets ($)	3753M	16334M	39797M	96341M	832157M	5719604M

M = $ thousand   MM = $ million
See Pages 9 through 22 for Explanation of Ratios and Data

Current Data Sorted by Assets   Comparative Historical Data

0-500M	500M-2MM	2-10MM	10-50MM	50-100MM	100-250MM	Type of Statement	4/1/05-3/31/06 ALL	4/1/06-3/31/07 ALL
	1	1	3	8	4	1 — Unqualified	14	15
1	2	6	4			Reviewed	7	6
	2	2				Compiled	3	6
	1	2				Tax Returns	6	6
1	2	3	3		1	Other	14	16
		13 (4/1-9/30/09)	34 (10/1/09-3/31/10)					
2	8	16	15	4	2	**NUMBER OF STATEMENTS**	44	49
%	%	%	%	%	%	**ASSETS**	%	%
		6.9	8.8			Cash & Equivalents	5.4	6.2
		23.5	22.3			Trade Receivables (net)	25.2	23.9
		32.4	30.0			Inventory	31.9	31.1
		.1	3.7			All Other Current	1.3	1.7
		62.9	64.7			Total Current	63.8	62.9
		27.8	25.4			Fixed Assets (net)	27.6	27.8
		.7	6.2			Intangibles (net)	2.9	3.8
		8.6	3.7			All Other Non-Current	5.7	5.5
		100.0	100.0			Total	100.0	100.0
						LIABILITIES		
		13.9	10.9			Notes Payable-Short Term	13.4	16.0
		4.3	3.4			Cur. Mat.-L.T.D.	3.8	3.1
		17.3	14.2			Trade Payables	23.7	22.1
		.0	1.0			Income Taxes Payable	.2	.2
		5.4	7.8			All Other Current	12.4	10.2
		41.0	37.4			Total Current	53.5	51.6
		12.8	10.8			Long-Term Debt	17.3	17.5
		1.0	1.1			Deferred Taxes	.7	.7
		2.4	3.5			All Other Non-Current	4.1	5.5
		42.8	47.2			Net Worth	24.3	24.8
		100.0	100.0			Total Liabilities & Net Worth	100.0	100.0
						INCOME DATA		
		100.0	100.0			Net Sales	100.0	100.0
		33.4	29.5			Gross Profit	26.1	27.9
		26.3	23.4			Operating Expenses	21.4	24.2
		7.1	6.1			Operating Profit	4.7	3.7
		2.9	.5			All Other Expenses (net)	1.2	3.1
		4.2	5.6			Profit Before Taxes	3.5	.6
						RATIOS		
		2.3	2.7				1.6	1.8
		1.7	1.7			Current	1.2	1.2
		1.1	1.2				1.0	.9
		.9	1.3				.8	.8
		.7	.9			Quick	.6	.5
		.5	.6				.4	.4
		19 19.7	18 20.1				21 17.5	26 14.2
		27 13.7	31 11.8			Sales/Receivables	34 10.7	34 10.6
		54 6.8	63 5.8				52 7.0	47 7.7
		53 6.9	40 9.0				41 8.9	42 8.8
		102 3.6	85 4.3			Cost of Sales/Inventory	66 5.6	69 5.3
		133 2.7	126 2.9				115 3.2	123 3.0
		19 19.4	13 29.0				27 13.4	27 13.5
		32 11.5	39 9.4			Cost of Sales/Payables	39 9.3	42 8.7
		73 5.0	61 6.0				56 6.5	76 4.8
		6.4	5.7				8.2	7.8
		10.6	7.9			Sales/Working Capital	21.4	18.5
		55.6	22.4				142.2	-62.1
		5.7	51.4				6.3	3.8
	(15)	2.6	5.9			EBIT/Interest	(45) 2.9	1.5
		1.7	1.7				1.5	-.9
							4.9	8.6
		(12)				Net Profit + Depr., Dep., Amort./Cur. Mat. L/T/D	(12) 2.5	(11) 2.9
							.7	1.0
		.3	.4				.7	.6
		.7	.5			Fixed/Worth	1.0	1.0
		1.2	1.2				1.3	5.8
		.7	.5				1.2	1.3
		1.4	1.1			Debt/Worth	2.4	3.7
		3.0	4.0				7.7	22.4
		32.5	42.5			% Profit Before Taxes/Tangible Net Worth	29.3	36.4
		(15) 12.9	(12) 22.5				(36) 15.6	(39) 7.7
		4.5	6.6				7.8	.9
		15.5	14.1			% Profit Before Taxes/Total Assets	10.3	8.4
		3.8	6.7				4.2	2.5
		2.1	2.5				1.6	-.2
		21.2	13.2				19.8	25.9
		12.9	8.7			Sales/Net Fixed Assets	9.2	9.9
		4.7	6.0				5.7	3.2
		2.9	2.6				3.2	3.4
		2.0	2.0			Sales/Total Assets	2.4	1.9
		1.3	1.7				1.6	1.4
		.9	1.0				.9	.7
		1.3	(13) 1.6			% Depr., Dep., Amort./Sales	(36) 1.5	(43) 1.7
		2.8	2.7				2.5	3.3
							1.7	3.4
						% Officers', Directors' Owners' Comp/Sales	(13) 3.7	(11) 5.3
							7.5	10.2
951M	19753M	133833M	785578M	711397M	952589M	Net Sales ($)	2370489M	1507598M
269M	9202M	66365M	336364M	284638M	412278M	Total Assets ($)	970480M	531778M

M = $ thousand   MM = $ million
See Pages 9 through 22 for Explanation of Ratios and Data

Comparative Historical Data | Current Data Sorted by Sales

	4/1/07-3/31/08 ALL	4/1/08-3/31/09 ALL	4/1/09-3/31/10 ALL	Type of Statement	0-1MM	1-3MM	3-5MM	5-10MM	10-25MM	25MM & OVER
	13	15	17	Unqualified	1	1		3	3	12
	9	8	13	Reviewed	1		2	5	3	2
	4	3	4	Compiled		2		2		
	6	6	3	Tax Returns		1		2		
	11	19	10	Other	2			4		4
						13 (4/1-9/30/09)			34 (10/1/09-3/31/10)	
	43	51	47	NUMBER OF STATEMENTS	4	4	2	13	6	18
	%	%	%	**ASSETS**	%	%	%	%	%	%
	6.9	6.7	8.5	Cash & Equivalents				6.5		10.9
	24.8	23.4	25.4	Trade Receivables (net)				24.8		24.5
	31.3	32.9	31.4	Inventory				35.2		26.5
	4.8	2.8	1.6	All Other Current				.2		2.7
	67.8	65.8	66.9	Total Current				66.6		64.6
	26.7	26.6	25.4	Fixed Assets (net)				24.6		25.5
	1.8	3.0	2.8	Intangibles (net)				.8		5.8
	3.8	4.5	5.0	All Other Non-Current				8.0		4.1
	100.0	100.0	100.0	Total				100.0		100.0
				LIABILITIES						
	15.8	20.2	16.0	Notes Payable-Short Term				12.0		7.4
	4.2	5.1	3.5	Cur. Mat.-L.T.D.				3.3		3.5
	19.2	20.7	18.5	Trade Payables				24.4		18.5
	.5	.6	.5	Income Taxes Payable				.0		1.0
	9.1	6.2	7.9	All Other Current				4.9		6.6
	48.8	52.7	46.4	Total Current				44.7		37.0
	22.0	18.6	13.5	Long-Term Debt				8.1		12.9
	.8	.4	.9	Deferred Taxes				1.0		1.1
	5.4	5.8	2.5	All Other Non-Current				2.9		3.5
	23.0	22.5	36.7	Net Worth				43.3		45.4
	100.0	100.0	100.0	Total Liabilties & Net Worth				100.0		100.0
				INCOME DATA						
	100.0	100.0	100.0	Net Sales				100.0		100.0
	27.5	29.2	30.8	Gross Profit				33.3		23.8
	23.1	23.2	23.9	Operating Expenses				29.2		18.3
	4.4	6.0	6.9	Operating Profit				4.1		5.4
	2.4	1.9	1.6	All Other Expenses (net)				2.3		.5
	1.9	4.1	5.3	Profit Before Taxes				1.8		5.0
				RATIOS						
	2.1	2.2	2.4	Current				2.2		2.5
	1.3	1.3	1.7					1.7		1.9
	1.1	1.1	1.2					1.1		1.2
	1.1	.9	1.3	Quick				.9		1.3
	.7	.7	.7					.7		1.0
	.4	.3	.5					.5		.6
	27 13.7	26 14.0	18 20.0	Sales/Receivables				19 19.3		20 18.4
	36 10.2	38 9.5	30 12.3					27 13.6		30 12.3
	54 6.7	48 7.6	62 5.9					50 7.3		70 5.2
	42 8.6	44 8.4	44 8.3	Cost of Sales/Inventory				65 5.6		35 10.5
	66 5.5	77 4.8	84 4.3					111 3.3		60 6.1
	103 3.5	105 3.5	123 3.0					129 2.8		89 4.1
	20 18.6	19 19.3	21 17.3	Cost of Sales/Payables				20 18.5		25 14.8
	42 8.7	35 10.5	36 10.1					57 6.4		39 9.3
	67 5.4	52 7.1	71 5.2					96 3.8		65 5.6
	7.0	7.8	6.0	Sales/Working Capital				6.2		5.9
	10.5	15.0	8.8					8.6		8.3
	48.4	59.0	22.4					60.5		21.5
	6.6	8.0	10.7	EBIT/Interest				6.1		15.1
	(38) 1.9	(46) 3.9	(44) 4.3					2.0		6.1
	.8	1.5	1.7					1.3		1.8
	8.1	24.6	5.6	Net Profit + Depr., Dep., Amort./Cur. Mat. L/T/D						
	(10) 2.1	(11) 11.0	(14) 2.1							
	1.2	2.1	1.2							
	.6	.5	.4	Fixed/Worth				.3		.4
	1.1	.8	.6					.6		.5
	3.7	4.8	1.2					1.1		1.1
	1.2	1.3	.6	Debt/Worth				.7		.5
	4.1	2.7	1.4					1.2		1.5
	15.8	34.3	3.8					3.4		3.4
	52.1	48.7	37.2	% Profit Before Taxes/Tangible Net Worth				52.2		33.3
	(36) 20.6	(41) 28.0	(40) 20.3					10.1	(15) 21.0	
	4.5	9.4	8.5					1.6		6.7
	11.5	16.2	15.6	% Profit Before Taxes/Total Assets				16.2		12.7
	2.9	6.9	6.7					3.7		6.8
	-.6	2.9	2.5					.6		2.5
	23.2	17.4	17.3	Sales/Net Fixed Assets				25.7		12.9
	12.3	10.6	9.5					13.6		8.8
	6.0	6.5	5.9					4.8		6.4
	3.1	3.1	2.8	Sales/Total Assets				2.9		2.7
	2.2	2.1	2.1					2.1		2.3
	1.7	1.7	1.6					1.4		1.6
	.6	.9	.9	% Depr., Dep., Amort./Sales				1.2		.9
	(37) 1.7	(42) 1.8	(39) 1.4					(12) 1.3	(15) 1.3	
	3.0	2.9	2.7					2.7		2.7
	3.4	1.4	3.2	% Officers', Directors' Owners' Comp/Sales				2.7		
	(12) 4.6	(14) 3.8	(15) 4.5					(10) 3.4		
	6.6	6.1	6.8					4.8		
	2075756M	2268082M	2604101M	Net Sales ($)	1966M	7012M	7133M	89470M	115225M	2383295M
	833880M	990805M	1109116M	Total Assets ($)	4088M	4619M	2716M	46964M	52689M	998040M

MANUFACTURING—Fertilizer (Mixing Only) Manufacturing NAICS 325314

	Current Data Sorted by Assets							Comparative Historical Data	
Type of Statement	0-500M	500M-2MM	2-10MM	10-50MM	50-100MM	100-250MM			
Unqualified			1	7	5			5	6
Reviewed			2					1	4
Compiled			3		1			1	1
Tax Returns	1	1	2	2		1		1	2
Other	1	3	3	2	1			12	14
		11 (4/1-9/30/09)		25 (10/1/09-3/31/10)				4/1/05-3/31/06 ALL	4/1/06-3/31/07 ALL
NUMBER OF STATEMENTS	2	4	11	11	7	1		20	27
	%	%	%	%	%	%	**ASSETS**	%	%
			9.4	10.1			Cash & Equivalents	3.7	6.6
			19.8	20.0			Trade Receivables (net)	28.6	21.1
			21.8	31.4			Inventory	24.7	25.0
			3.2	3.7			All Other Current	2.5	2.5
			54.1	65.2			Total Current	59.5	55.2
			38.8	30.6			Fixed Assets (net)	33.8	37.8
			1.6	.6			Intangibles (net)	.3	.7
			5.6	3.5			All Other Non-Current	6.4	6.3
			100.0	100.0			Total	100.0	100.0
							LIABILITIES		
			10.9	18.2			Notes Payable-Short Term	9.4	9.4
			4.0	5.3			Cur. Mat.-L.T.D.	4.9	5.3
			12.5	16.3			Trade Payables	16.2	20.7
			.0	.1			Income Taxes Payable	.0	.2
			15.4	12.7			All Other Current	10.3	12.0
			42.8	52.7			Total Current	40.8	47.6
			18.6	17.3			Long-Term Debt	21.4	21.1
			2.2	.1			Deferred Taxes	1.3	.9
			4.4	5.9			All Other Non-Current	3.3	1.6
			31.9	24.0			Net Worth	33.2	28.8
			100.0	100.0			Total Liabilties & Net Worth	100.0	100.0
							INCOME DATA		
			100.0	100.0			Net Sales	100.0	100.0
			37.1	23.5			Gross Profit	34.5	28.2
			32.0	21.6			Operating Expenses	31.5	25.0
			5.1	2.0			Operating Profit	3.0	3.1
			.4	-.5			All Other Expenses (net)	2.4	1.7
			4.7	2.5			Profit Before Taxes	.6	1.4
							RATIOS		
			2.3	1.5				2.3	1.6
			1.3	1.2			Current	1.4	1.3
			.8	1.0				1.2	1.0
			1.4	.9				1.3	.8
			.7	.5			Quick	.9	.6
			.4	.4				.5	.3
		15	25.1	17	21.1			28	13.1	18	20.6
		28	13.0	30	12.0		Sales/Receivables	48	7.6	32	11.3
		77	4.7	39	9.4			76	4.8	57	6.4
		15	24.7	43	8.4			35	10.4	36	10.0
		65	5.6	73	5.0		Cost of Sales/Inventory	76	4.8	72	5.1
		103	3.6	107	3.4			102	3.6	111	3.3
		14	26.6	22	16.9			24	15.1	24	15.2
		17	21.8	26	13.9		Cost of Sales/Payables	34	10.7	38	9.6
		72	5.1	39	9.3			66	5.5	62	5.9
			5.9	8.9				5.2	11.6
			20.9	12.7			Sales/Working Capital	13.0	16.2
			-18.2	158.3				21.1	-265.9
			10.2	15.1				9.0	3.8
			3.4	4.3			EBIT/Interest	(18) 2.3	(26) 1.9
			2.1	1.6				1.2	1.3
							Net Profit + Depr., Dep., Amort./Cur. Mat. L/T/D		
			.6	.8				.3	.6
			1.5	1.3			Fixed/Worth	.9	1.0
			3.9	2.8				1.6	2.3
			1.1	1.8				.9	1.3
			1.5	3.8			Debt/Worth	2.7	2.6
			20.1	7.7				5.7	11.5
				106.9				36.7	39.3
			(10)	47.5			% Profit Before Taxes/Tangible Net Worth	(18) 14.1	(24) 17.3
				14.9				1.7	3.0
			14.9	14.6				12.8	10.0
			9.5	12.7			% Profit Before Taxes/Total Assets	4.1	3.6
			4.2	2.8				.4	.9
			12.3	16.4				11.8	12.7
			6.0	6.2			Sales/Net Fixed Assets	6.6	4.9
			3.2	5.1				3.0	2.5
			3.0	3.4				2.8	3.2
			2.0	2.0			Sales/Total Assets	1.8	1.7
			1.4	1.6				1.4	1.2
			.7	.8				1.8	1.5
			2.4	2.4			% Depr., Dep., Amort./Sales	(17) 2.9	(25) 2.6
			7.5	3.3				7.6	6.3
							% Officers', Directors' Owners' Comp/Sales		
	2660M	9582M	110438M	597220M	1239149M	233122M	Net Sales ($)	1173683M	1786856M
	317M	4938M	45829M	237585M	526072M	237692M	Total Assets ($)	465894M	681148M

M = $ thousand   MM = $ million
See Pages 9 through 22 for Explanation of Ratios and Data

Comparative Historical Data | Current Data Sorted by Sales

			Type of Statement	0-1MM	1-3MM	3-5MM	5-10MM	10-25MM	25MM & OVER
5	7	13	Unqualified		1				12
3	2	2	Reviewed					2	
6	6	6	Compiled		2		1	1	1
4	2	8	Tax Returns			2	1	1	1
12	11	7	Other	3		1	1	2	4
4/1/07-3/31/08 ALL	4/1/08-3/31/09 ALL	4/1/09-3/31/10 ALL		0-1MM	11 (4/1-9/30/09) 1-3MM	3-5MM	25 (10/1/09-3/31/10) 5-10MM	10-25MM	25MM & OVER
30	28	36	NUMBER OF STATEMENTS	3	3	3	3	6	18

07-08 %	08-09 %	09-10 %	ASSETS	0-1MM %	1-3MM %	3-5MM %	5-10MM %	10-25MM %	25MM&OVER %
7.7	6.3	8.4	Cash & Equivalents						8.7
24.0	23.3	21.7	Trade Receivables (net)						25.9
26.8	28.8	24.1	Inventory						27.2
1.8	2.4	3.2	All Other Current						4.4
60.3	60.9	57.3	Total Current						66.2
33.5	31.8	34.5	Fixed Assets (net)						27.8
1.3	.9	3.8	Intangibles (net)						2.2
4.9	6.4	4.4	All Other Non-Current						3.9
100.0	100.0	100.0	Total						100.0
			LIABILITIES						
15.6	17.8	13.0	Notes Payable-Short Term						18.0
3.1	3.2	5.2	Cur. Mat.-L.T.D.						2.4
16.9	20.1	12.9	Trade Payables						16.1
.3	.2	.2	Income Taxes Payable						.3
10.7	10.0	11.6	All Other Current						10.6
46.7	51.2	42.9	Total Current						47.4
16.4	21.8	19.4	Long-Term Debt						17.8
.6	.7	.8	Deferred Taxes						.4
4.1	4.1	5.6	All Other Non-Current						7.9
32.2	22.2	31.3	Net Worth						26.6
100.0	100.0	100.0	Total Liabilities & Net Worth						100.0
			INCOME DATA						
100.0	100.0	100.0	Net Sales						100.0
27.5	27.9	30.8	Gross Profit						22.9
22.4	21.9	27.3	Operating Expenses						20.4
5.0	6.0	3.6	Operating Profit						2.5
.6	1.5	.1	All Other Expenses (net)						1.1
4.5	4.5	3.5	Profit Before Taxes						1.4

RATIOS

07-08	08-09	09-10	Ratio	25MM & OVER
1.7	1.4	2.1	Current	1.9
1.2	1.2	1.3		1.4
.9	1.0	1.0		1.1
1.1	.8	1.1	Quick	1.1
.6	.6	.7		.6
.4	.3	.4		.4
19 / 19.3	20 / 18.6	17 / 21.4	Sales/Receivables	26 / 14.0
32 / 11.3	33 / 11.1	30 / 12.0		34 / 10.6
58 / 6.3	59 / 6.2	49 / 7.5		44 / 8.3
40 / 9.2	37 / 9.9	21 / 17.6	Cost of Sales/Inventory	30 / 12.3
60 / 6.1	76 / 4.8	55 / 6.6		62 / 5.9
92 / 4.0	97 / 3.8	92 / 4.0		96 / 3.8
19 / 18.9	24 / 15.0	14 / 25.7	Cost of Sales/Payables	20 / 18.0
35 / 10.6	40 / 9.2	22 / 16.3		26 / 14.1
52 / 7.1	60 / 6.1	49 / 7.5		41 / 8.9
8.3	14.5	7.6	Sales/Working Capital	7.1
23.4	23.7	18.2		11.2
-44.9	-194.8	-241.8		88.7
8.1	9.1	9.5	EBIT/Interest	10.5
3.4	(27) 5.6	(35) 3.7		3.3
1.8	1.4	1.0		-1.5
			Net Profit + Depr., Dep., Amort./Cur. Mat. L/T/D	
.6	.4	.6	Fixed/Worth	.6
.9	1.2	1.3		1.0
2.6	2.8	3.7		2.5
1.2	1.6	1.2	Debt/Worth	1.9
3.4	4.0	3.9		3.9
7.2	7.1	12.8		5.9
67.1	64.7	61.1	% Profit Before Taxes/Tangible Net Worth	61.1
(27) 28.3	(25) 48.4	(33) 29.9		(17) 34.8
20.4	16.1	3.1		-27.0
19.7	16.0	14.8	% Profit Before Taxes/Total Assets	14.5
9.1	7.4	8.4		5.1
2.5	1.0	.5		-9.6
14.6	15.1	18.1	Sales/Net Fixed Assets	20.7
6.9	8.3	6.7		9.1
4.2	3.4	3.3		4.7
2.9	2.9	3.3	Sales/Total Assets	3.4
1.8	1.7	2.0		2.0
1.6	1.5	1.5		1.5
1.1	.9	.8	% Depr., Dep., Amort./Sales	.8
(29) 2.0	(25) 2.0	(34) 2.1		(17) 1.5
2.9	5.7	3.9		2.9
			% Officers', Directors' Owners' Comp/Sales	

07-08	08-09	09-10		0-1MM	1-3MM	3-5MM	5-10MM	10-25MM	25MM&OVER
1207091M	2959133M	2192171M	Net Sales ($)	1624M	7667M	13111M	20156M	96560M	2053053M
501770M	1109573M	1052433M	Total Assets ($)	1998M	5274M	5346M	12047M	36792M	990976M

M = $ thousand   MM = $ million
See Pages 9 through 22 for Explanation of Ratios and Data

Current Data Sorted by Assets | **Comparative Historical Data**

		3	10	6	2	Type of Statement		
						Unqualified	18	21
		3	4		1	Reviewed	6	4
	2	2	1			Compiled	2	3
		1				Tax Returns	2	1
3	3	2	4		1	Other	18	14
	11 (4/1-9/30/09)		37 (10/1/09-3/31/10)				4/1/05-3/31/06 ALL	4/1/06-3/31/07 ALL
0-500M	500M-2MM	2-10MM	10-50MM	50-100MM	100-250MM	NUMBER OF STATEMENTS		
3	5	11	19	6	4		46	43
%	%	%	%	%	%	**ASSETS**	%	%
		18.4	9.4			Cash & Equivalents	9.8	9.6
		26.5	16.0			Trade Receivables (net)	22.6	24.5
		24.8	30.1			Inventory	30.5	27.1
		.5	8.6			All Other Current	3.9	4.4
		70.2	64.1			Total Current	66.8	65.6
		20.5	23.3			Fixed Assets (net)	22.6	20.8
		4.3	10.1			Intangibles (net)	5.0	8.1
		5.0	2.4			All Other Non-Current	5.6	5.5
		100.0	100.0			Total	100.0	100.0
						LIABILITIES		
		10.3	6.9			Notes Payable-Short Term	17.7	14.9
		2.9	2.9			Cur. Mat.-L.T.D.	3.2	1.6
		16.4	14.2			Trade Payables	11.7	10.8
		.0	.7			Income Taxes Payable	.4	.5
		8.8	15.1			All Other Current	11.9	12.1
		38.3	39.8			Total Current	44.8	39.9
		12.5	14.0			Long-Term Debt	11.8	11.0
		.0	.6			Deferred Taxes	1.2	.7
		1.5	11.7			All Other Non-Current	3.8	5.1
		47.7	33.9			Net Worth	38.5	43.3
		100.0	100.0			Total Liabilities & Net Worth	100.0	100.0
						INCOME DATA		
		100.0	100.0			Net Sales	100.0	100.0
		39.5	33.8			Gross Profit	31.6	36.7
		34.1	27.5			Operating Expenses	25.3	29.1
		5.4	6.3			Operating Profit	6.2	7.6
		-.4	1.7			All Other Expenses (net)	1.7	1.4
		5.9	4.5			Profit Before Taxes	4.6	6.2
						RATIOS		
		5.0	2.8				3.0	2.7
		1.6	1.6			Current	1.5	1.5
		1.0	1.1				1.1	1.3
		3.8	1.0				1.4	1.4
		1.1	.6			Quick	.8	.8
		.6	.3				.5	.5
		21 17.2	14 26.3				27 13.4	36 10.3
		42 8.7	34 10.8			Sales/Receivables	50 7.4	51 7.1
		57 6.4	45 8.1				66 5.5	70 5.2
		45 8.1	68 5.4				54 6.8	56 6.5
		94 3.9	79 4.6			Cost of Sales/Inventory	88 4.2	86 4.2
		128 2.9	130 2.8				136 2.7	138 2.6
		14 25.3	14 25.9				20 18.5	17 21.6
		45 8.2	33 11.2			Cost of Sales/Payables	36 10.1	34 10.7
		79 4.6	79 4.6				48 7.6	58 6.2
		3.1	4.8				3.8	3.6
		9.6	8.7			Sales/Working Capital	7.6	6.3
		-136.7	35.7				33.5	18.2
			33.3				15.7	13.2
			(18) 5.8			EBIT/Interest	(39) 4.0	(40) 4.6
			2.4				1.4	1.6
							19.7	16.6
						Net Profit + Depr., Dep., Amort./Cur. Mat. L/T/D	(11) 2.7	(15) 6.0
							1.2	2.0
		.1	.3				.2	.2
		.4	.9			Fixed/Worth	.6	.7
		1.6	3.6				2.2	1.4
		.3	.6				.7	.6
		1.5	2.8			Debt/Worth	2.0	2.0
		4.8	20.8				6.3	4.0
		39.6	58.3				43.9	43.6
		(10) 30.4	(15) 37.5			% Profit Before Taxes/Tangible Net Worth	(39) 19.3	(42) 18.4
		16.6	24.9				7.2	7.7
		14.0	19.9				10.7	13.1
		9.0	11.1			% Profit Before Taxes/Total Assets	6.4	7.7
		3.7	4.0				2.5	2.0
		26.8	23.4				25.4	27.3
		12.2	12.8			Sales/Net Fixed Assets	9.9	9.7
		5.3	5.4				4.2	5.0
		2.1	2.8				2.6	2.3
		1.7	1.9			Sales/Total Assets	1.6	1.7
		1.4	1.6				1.2	1.1
		1.0	.7				1.3	1.1
		(10) 1.7	(18) 1.7			% Depr., Dep., Amort./Sales	(35) 1.9	(36) 2.2
		2.7	3.1				3.2	2.9
						% Officers', Directors' Owners' Comp/Sales		
6673M	23331M	129790M	967862M	536557M	1013094M	Net Sales ($)	3999517M	1310681M
918M	6954M	67398M	397524M	451379M	551988M	Total Assets ($)	1861134M	841984M

M = $ thousand   MM = $ million
See Pages 9 through 22 for Explanation of Ratios and Data

Comparative Historical Data | **Current Data Sorted by Sales**

			Type of Statement	0-1MM	1-3MM	3-5MM	5-10MM	10-25MM	25MM & OVER
13	17	21	Unqualified				1	3	16
5	10	8	Reviewed				1	1	6
3	4	5	Compiled		1		1	2	1
3	5	1	Tax Returns					1	
9	13	13	Other	2		4	2	1	4
4/1/07-3/31/08	4/1/08-3/31/09	4/1/09-3/31/10			11 (4/1-9/30/09)			37 (10/1/09-3/31/10)	
ALL	ALL	ALL							
33	49	48	NUMBER OF STATEMENTS	2	1	5	5	8	27
%	%	%	ASSETS	%	%	%	%	%	%
9.7	13.4	15.4	Cash & Equivalents						14.2
23.9	22.1	21.2	Trade Receivables (net)						18.4
35.6	36.3	29.4	Inventory						30.5
2.7	3.5	4.5	All Other Current						5.0
71.8	75.3	70.5	Total Current						68.1
15.9	18.2	19.9	Fixed Assets (net)						21.7
8.3	3.2	6.6	Intangibles (net)						7.0
4.0	3.3	3.0	All Other Non-Current						3.2
100.0	100.0	100.0	Total						100.0
			LIABILITIES						
12.9	17.6	8.4	Notes Payable-Short Term						5.7
4.6	3.9	2.4	Cur. Mat.-L.T.D.						2.5
17.1	15.5	15.7	Trade Payables						16.2
.8	.3	.7	Income Taxes Payable						.9
9.1	10.7	12.5	All Other Current						16.4
44.4	48.1	39.7	Total Current						41.6
13.4	14.8	14.4	Long-Term Debt						13.8
.4	.4	.4	Deferred Taxes						.6
4.1	3.0	9.1	All Other Non-Current						5.9
37.7	33.7	36.4	Net Worth						38.0
100.0	100.0	100.0	Total Liabilties & Net Worth						100.0
			INCOME DATA						
100.0	100.0	100.0	Net Sales						100.0
32.3	30.9	35.0	Gross Profit						30.3
23.7	26.2	27.6	Operating Expenses						24.3
8.5	4.8	7.4	Operating Profit						6.0
1.7	1.4	.8	All Other Expenses (net)						1.1
6.9	3.3	6.5	Profit Before Taxes						5.0
			RATIOS						
2.3	2.6	3.2	Current						2.8
1.8	1.4	1.8							1.8
1.2	1.2	1.2							1.1
1.3	1.7	2.1	Quick						2.0
.7	(48) .6	1.0							.9
.4	.3	.4							.4
28 12.9	21 17.1	21 17.6	Sales/Receivables						20 18.3
44 8.2	34 10.8	36 10.3							36 10.2
71 5.2	49 7.5	46 7.9							47 7.8
74 5.0	61 5.9	54 6.8	Cost of Sales/Inventory						67 5.4
115 3.2	99 3.7	80 4.6							79 4.6
162 2.3	140 2.6	129 2.8							130 2.8
23 15.9	22 16.3	14 25.6	Cost of Sales/Payables						18 20.4
44 8.4	34 10.8	42 8.7							48 7.5
56 6.5	52 7.0	65 5.7							79 4.6
4.7	4.1	4.1	Sales/Working Capital						4.1
7.0	10.8	7.5							6.6
14.3	27.0	21.8							23.9
19.4	17.1	19.8	EBIT/Interest						25.6
(29) 6.3	(45) 5.8	(42) 7.5						(24)	7.1
1.9	1.6	3.3							2.9
	13.4	14.0	Net Profit + Depr., Dep., Amort./Cur. Mat. L/T/D						
	(12) 6.0	(13) 8.4							
	1.9	3.0							
.1	.1	.2	Fixed/Worth						.2
.4	.4	.5							.5
1.6	1.5	2.3							2.2
.8	.9	.5	Debt/Worth						.6
1.8	2.4	2.0							2.1
10.6	6.3	10.9							10.2
51.2	46.2	58.0	% Profit Before Taxes/Tangible Net Worth						67.9
(29) 26.9	(43) 26.1	(40) 35.3						(24)	36.1
13.8	9.7	19.9							19.9
14.8	14.9	27.5	% Profit Before Taxes/Total Assets						19.9
10.6	8.6	12.1							9.0
3.1	2.2	5.2							4.0
44.9	34.6	34.0	Sales/Net Fixed Assets						19.5
12.9	13.7	12.5							9.6
6.2	5.8	5.6							5.4
2.4	3.0	2.8	Sales/Total Assets						2.7
1.5	1.9	1.8							1.8
1.3	1.5	1.5							1.4
.8	.8	.9	% Depr., Dep., Amort./Sales						.8
(27) 1.8	(43) 1.5	(41) 1.7						(26)	1.7
2.8	2.7	3.1							3.2
	1.2	1.0	% Officers', Directors' Owners' Comp/Sales						
	(14) 3.7	(11) 1.9							
	6.4	7.2							
1646637M	2910263M	2677307M	Net Sales ($)	1816M	2101M	20608M	39341M	137271M	2476170M
1072428M	1376819M	1476161M	Total Assets ($)	463M	1386M	8610M	16601M	78908M	1370193M

© RMA 2010

M = $ thousand   MM = $ million
See Pages 9 through 22 for Explanation of Ratios and Data

Current Data Sorted by Assets   Comparative Historical Data

0-500M	500M-2MM	2-10MM	10-50MM	50-100MM	100-250MM	Type of Statement	4/1/05-3/31/06 ALL	4/1/06-3/31/07 ALL
		4	14	4	5	Unqualified	27	23
		6	5			Reviewed	8	4
	1	1	2		1	Compiled	5	7
1	4	4	1		1	Tax Returns	7	3
	3	10	10	6	4	Other	25	28
	16 (4/1-9/30/09)		70 (10/1/09-3/31/10)					
1	8	25	32	10	10	NUMBER OF STATEMENTS	72	65
%	%	%	%	%	%	ASSETS	%	%
		8.1	10.9	23.5	14.7	Cash & Equivalents	10.8	12.9
		20.8	17.1	14.4	11.2	Trade Receivables (net)	21.2	22.8
		31.4	24.5	20.4	20.7	Inventory	25.5	25.9
		2.8	2.9	2.6	4.8	All Other Current	3.7	3.0
		63.1	55.4	61.0	51.4	Total Current	61.2	64.6
		22.0	25.3	20.6	25.0	Fixed Assets (net)	25.5	25.0
		7.5	13.4	13.8	13.1	Intangibles (net)	7.7	6.9
		7.4	5.9	4.6	10.6	All Other Non-Current	5.6	3.5
		100.0	100.0	100.0	100.0	Total	100.0	100.0
						LIABILITIES		
		7.4	7.1	8.4	3.4	Notes Payable-Short Term	9.1	8.9
		2.1	3.2	2.4	1.2	Cur. Mat.-L.T.D.	3.5	5.4
		24.8	11.4	5.6	6.8	Trade Payables	14.4	14.7
		.6	.4	.6	.7	Income Taxes Payable	.5	.8
		7.7	12.6	16.5	14.5	All Other Current	14.0	10.5
		42.5	34.7	33.5	26.6	Total Current	41.6	40.3
		13.3	16.7	19.8	5.8	Long-Term Debt	12.7	11.8
		.2	.3	.8	4.1	Deferred Taxes	.7	.9
		16.8	7.4	8.7	4.6	All Other Non-Current	9.0	8.0
		27.2	41.0	37.3	58.8	Net Worth	36.1	39.1
		100.0	100.0	100.0	100.0	Total Liabilties & Net Worth	100.0	100.0
						INCOME DATA		
		100.0	100.0	100.0	100.0	Net Sales	100.0	100.0
		40.6	47.7	62.1	51.6	Gross Profit	44.8	45.0
		36.8	38.7	41.8	41.1	Operating Expenses	39.5	38.0
		3.9	9.0	20.2	10.5	Operating Profit	5.3	6.9
		.7	2.2	2.4	.4	All Other Expenses (net)	1.6	1.6
		3.2	6.8	17.9	10.1	Profit Before Taxes	3.7	5.4
						RATIOS		
		2.4	2.5	2.4	2.8		2.3	2.7
		1.4	1.7	2.0	1.7	Current	1.6	1.6
		1.1	1.3	1.6	1.4		1.0	1.3
		1.2	1.4	1.8	1.4		1.2	1.3
		.6	.6	1.0	.8	Quick	.8	.8
		.3	.4	.7	.6		.6	.5
	16	23.1	25 14.8	7 55.2	11 33.9		27 13.7	28 13.1
	29	12.7	39 9.2	45 8.1	29 12.7	Sales/Receivables	38 9.7	39 9.3
	45	8.1	48 7.6	56 6.5	42 8.6		56 6.5	58 6.3
	53	6.9	79 4.6	80 4.6	73 5.0		56 6.5	59 6.2
	87	4.2	109 3.4	112 3.3	134 2.7	Cost of Sales/Inventory	88 4.2	90 4.0
	117	3.1	150 2.4	193 1.9	156 2.3		134 2.7	143 2.5
	27	13.3	31 12.0	14 26.4	26 14.0		23 15.6	30 12.1
	53	6.9	43 8.5	31 11.7	37 9.8	Cost of Sales/Payables	38 9.5	42 8.7
	71	5.1	75 4.8	63 5.8	47 7.8		55 6.7	61 5.9
		6.3	4.4	3.0	4.3		5.0	4.6
		8.9	8.9	5.2	8.3	Sales/Working Capital	11.4	8.5
		124.1	18.7	9.7	12.6		62.8	16.2
		35.8	19.4	67.9			21.7	18.1
	(22)	8.9	(29) 8.0	20.1		EBIT/Interest	(65) 6.9	(59) 2.8
		2.1	2.5	3.6			1.5	1.0
			26.9			Net Profit + Depr., Dep.,	11.2	5.9
			(14) 9.8			Amort./Cur. Mat. L/T/D	(25) 3.1	(17) 2.4
			1.9				1.3	1.4
		.2	.4	.3	.4		.3	.3
		1.1	.9	.7	.5	Fixed/Worth	.6	.7
		4.3	2.4	2.6	NM		2.4	1.5
		.5	1.0	1.5	.5		.7	.7
		3.3	1.7	3.7	.7	Debt/Worth	1.8	1.6
		9.0	5.0	13.7	NM		6.5	6.5
		93.1	72.9			% Profit Before Taxes/Tangible	59.2	57.2
	(20)	41.1	(28) 36.1			Net Worth	(62) 24.6	(58) 25.2
		3.6	20.9				8.3	.3
		25.7	22.4	51.5	20.8	% Profit Before Taxes/Total	19.1	19.2
		9.0	10.3	21.7	11.7	Assets	7.7	7.7
		.7	3.6	4.0	3.6		.8	.1
		40.8	18.3	37.8	11.0		20.2	21.6
		14.5	7.8	7.0	6.5	Sales/Net Fixed Assets	11.5	12.3
		4.9	3.6	3.4	3.3		5.7	3.6
		3.0	2.4	2.2	2.3		3.1	2.7
		2.3	1.6	1.6	1.5	Sales/Total Assets	1.9	2.0
		1.3	1.1	.7	1.0		1.3	1.1
		1.1	1.4				1.0	1.2
	(20)	2.0	(29) 2.3			% Depr., Dep., Amort./Sales	(58) 2.0	(58) 2.0
		3.0	4.2				3.8	3.5
						% Officers', Directors'	2.2	2.3
						Owners' Comp/Sales	(12) 5.0	(15) 3.4
							7.3	5.1
310M	31525M	310906M	1403396M	1105243M	2452592M	Net Sales ($)	3253069M	3075447M
234M	10990M	131359M	788510M	708637M	1566006M	Total Assets ($)	1929802M	1687579M

M = $ thousand   MM = $ million
See Pages 9 through 22 for Explanation of Ratios and Data

Comparative Historical Data | | | Current Data Sorted by Sales

17	26	27	Type of Statement					9	18
17	26	27	Unqualified		1		2	9	18
4	11	11	Reviewed		1			4	4
6	4	5	Compiled		1			2	2
6	3	10	Tax Returns	1.	2	1	1	2	1
33	35	33	Other		2	3	5	6	19
4/1/07-3/31/08	4/1/08-3/31/09	4/1/09-3/31/10			16 (4/1-9/30/09)		70 (10/1/09-3/31/10)		
ALL	ALL	ALL		0-1MM	1-3MM	3-5MM	5-10MM	10-25MM	25MM & OVER
66	79	86	**NUMBER OF STATEMENTS**	1	5	5	8	23	44
%	%	%	**ASSETS**	%	%	%	%	%	%
10.3	10.8	12.5	Cash & Equivalents					8.1	14.5
18.8	18.4	17.8	Trade Receivables (net)					21.4	15.0
25.6	27.7	25.7	Inventory					25.7	25.8
3.7	4.3	2.8	All Other Current					1.8	4.0
58.4	61.3	58.8	Total Current					56.9	59.3
27.2	23.4	23.7	Fixed Assets (net)					26.1	23.1
8.4	9.8	11.3	Intangibles (net)					12.3	11.1
6.0	5.6	6.2	All Other Non-Current					4.7	6.5
100.0	100.0	100.0	Total					100.0	100.0
			LIABILITIES						
7.9	8.6	6.4	Notes Payable-Short Term					5.2	7.7
2.4	5.0	2.6	Cur. Mat.-L.T.D.					4.1	1.7
13.6	13.6	14.6	Trade Payables					19.4	11.4
.5	.4	.5	Income Taxes Payable					.6	.5
12.1	11.9	10.9	All Other Current					9.9	13.7
36.4	39.4	35.0	Total Current					39.1	35.1
14.5	11.4	16.1	Long-Term Debt					15.9	12.8
.4	.7	.8	Deferred Taxes					.4	1.1
11.9	4.0	10.3	All Other Non-Current					11.3	10.7
36.8	44.5	37.9	Net Worth					33.2	40.3
100.0	100.0	100.0	Total Liabilties & Net Worth					100.0	100.0
			INCOME DATA						
100.0	100.0	100.0	Net Sales					100.0	100.0
45.6	49.0	48.5	Gross Profit					45.4	49.8
37.7	43.6	39.4	Operating Expenses					36.2	39.6
7.9	5.4	9.0	Operating Profit					9.2	10.3
1.5	1.5	1.5	All Other Expenses (net)					1.1	1.3
6.4	3.9	7.5	Profit Before Taxes					8.1	9.0
			RATIOS						
2.8	3.2	2.6	Current					2.5	2.3
1.8	1.7	1.7						1.6	1.8
1.1	1.2	1.3						1.1	1.3
1.5	1.4	1.4	Quick					1.4	1.3
.8	.8	.7						.8	.7
.5	.5	.4						.6	.4
20 18.4	23 15.7	19 18.7	Sales/Receivables					23 16.1	14 25.7
35 10.3	37 9.8	34 10.7						39 9.4	33 11.2
49 7.5	48 7.6	48 7.5						53 6.9	48 7.6
68 5.4	72 5.1	59 6.2	Cost of Sales/Inventory					70 5.2	69 5.3
89 4.1	98 3.7	102 3.6						95 3.8	103 3.6
142 2.6	147 2.5	149 2.4						139 2.6	150 2.4
23 15.7	21 17.6	28 13.1	Cost of Sales/Payables					28 13.1	28 12.9
40 9.0	44 8.4	43 8.4						57 6.4	40 9.1
57 6.4	66 5.5	65 5.6						74 4.9	55 6.7
4.6	4.6	4.5	Sales/Working Capital					4.4	4.6
8.7	7.6	8.2						8.8	8.0
44.9	21.6	22.0						110.3	16.9
17.7	25.8	38.7	EBIT/Interest					22.8	42.0
(57) 5.0	(70) 7.7	(76) 8.9						(22) 8.4	(40) 9.5
1.8	2.1	2.6						2.8	2.2
17.1	17.9	18.2	Net Profit + Depr., Dep., Amort./Cur. Mat. L/T/D						34.6
(17) 5.7	(28) 6.1	(26) 4.8						(20)	6.3
2.1	2.3	1.5							1.6
.4	.3	.3	Fixed/Worth					.3	.3
.8	.6	.8						1.2	.6
2.2	1.5	2.5						3.8	2.1
.8	.5	.7	Debt/Worth					1.1	.7
1.8	1.3	1.9						2.1	1.6
12.1	4.4	5.7						12.3	5.3
68.0	46.0	90.8	% Profit Before Taxes/Tangible Net Worth					82.7	81.6
(53) 26.2	(69) 22.2	(72) 42.9						(19) 39.1	(38) 47.2
15.0	5.1	16.0						18.5	20.9
20.5	17.5	24.1	% Profit Before Taxes/Total Assets					24.1	26.9
8.5	6.4	10.0						8.6	12.0
3.6	1.3	2.9						4.6	2.9
21.2	24.5	26.4	Sales/Net Fixed Assets					29.4	16.8
9.1	11.0	9.6						8.9	7.8
3.7	4.7	4.0						3.3	4.5
2.7	2.7	2.7	Sales/Total Assets					2.8	2.5
1.9	1.9	1.8						1.7	1.8
1.3	1.3	1.2						1.1	1.2
1.0	1.2	1.3	% Depr., Dep., Amort./Sales					1.7	1.3
(55) 2.0	(67) 2.2	(71) 2.2						(21) 2.9	(37) 2.0
3.2	3.0	3.7						4.6	2.7
1.3	1.3	1.4	% Officers', Directors' Owners' Comp/Sales						
(17) 4.0	(15) 2.3	(19) 2.9							
7.6	3.9	4.6							
4156857M	5790794M	5303972M	Net Sales ($)	310M	10082M	22293M	58430M	389193M	4823664M
2284541M	3128958M	3205736M	Total Assets ($)	234M	6275M	12177M	41924M	283057M	2862069M

© RMA 2010

M = $ thousand   MM = $ million
See Pages 9 through 22 for Explanation of Ratios and Data

Current Data Sorted by Assets   Comparative Historical Data

0-500M	500M-2MM	2-10MM	10-50MM	50-100MM	100-250MM	Type of Statement	4/1/05-3/31/06 ALL	4/1/06-3/31/07 ALL
		5	19	4	18	Unqualified	44	51
	2	15	10			Reviewed	20	15
	4	6	2	1		Compiled	12	11
2	4	11				Tax Returns	5	7
2	7	23	36	9	23	Other	61	65
	36 (4/1-9/30/09)		167 (10/1/09-3/31/10)					
4	17	60	67	14	41	**NUMBER OF STATEMENTS**	142	149
%	%	%	%	%	%	**ASSETS**	%	%
	13.0	12.1	14.6	20.1	13.4	Cash & Equivalents	12.4	11.3
	24.4	28.1	21.4	19.8	14.9	Trade Receivables (net)	21.8	22.8
	33.0	18.5	21.2	15.7	13.3	Inventory	20.8	20.4
	2.9	3.4	2.8	3.8	3.7	All Other Current	3.1	3.2
	73.2	62.2	60.0	59.4	45.3	Total Current	58.1	57.7
	13.4	27.8	26.5	23.9	22.9	Fixed Assets (net)	24.6	24.0
	7.3	4.1	10.3	11.8	24.7	Intangibles (net)	9.1	9.4
	6.1	5.9	3.1	4.9	7.1	All Other Non-Current	8.2	9.0
	100.0	100.0	100.0	100.0	100.0	Total	100.0	100.0
						LIABILITIES		
	7.9	8.8	5.3	5.5	3.1	Notes Payable-Short Term	6.7	8.5
	5.1	2.7	4.4	1.8	3.8	Cur. Mat.-L.T.D.	4.0	2.5
	17.5	15.4	11.2	14.6	6.4	Trade Payables	14.7	13.6
	.0	.4	.5	.1	.3	Income Taxes Payable	.3	.4
	11.7	15.4	11.9	14.4	9.3	All Other Current	11.3	12.0
	42.1	42.6	33.3	36.4	23.0	Total Current	37.0	37.0
	20.1	13.4	14.9	17.3	15.8	Long-Term Debt	16.4	17.0
	.0	.5	.8	1.0	1.2	Deferred Taxes	.6	.8
	.1	6.9	5.4	3.4	7.8	All Other Non-Current	7.4	7.8
	37.6	36.6	45.6	41.8	52.3	Net Worth	38.6	37.4
	100.0	100.0	100.0	100.0	100.0	Total Liabilties & Net Worth	100.0	100.0
						INCOME DATA		
	100.0	100.0	100.0	100.0	100.0	Net Sales	100.0	100.0
	38.3	40.6	40.9	46.0	48.2	Gross Profit	44.3	46.3
	34.5	35.7	34.1	36.2	38.0	Operating Expenses	37.6	39.5
	3.9	4.9	6.8	9.8	10.3	Operating Profit	6.7	6.8
	3.1	.7	1.5	1.0	3.5	All Other Expenses (net)	.8	1.2
	.8	4.2	5.4	8.8	6.8	Profit Before Taxes	5.9	5.6
						RATIOS		
	4.5	3.6	2.9	3.0	3.1	Current	2.7	2.8
	1.8	1.6	1.8	1.9	1.8		1.8	1.8
	1.1	1.1	1.3	.9	1.4		1.1	1.2
	2.5	2.6	1.7	2.2	1.7	Quick	1.6	1.7
	.7	1.0	1.1	.9	1.0		1.0	.9
	.5	.6	.6	.5	.8		.5	.6
	21 17.0	28 12.8	31 11.6	30 12.1	45 8.1	Sales/Receivables	34 10.7	33 11.1
	35 10.3	37 9.8	42 8.7	44 8.2	54 6.8		46 7.9	47 7.7
	45 8.2	56 6.5	60 6.1	60 6.1	69 5.3		58 6.3	71 5.1
	32 11.4	19 19.3	49 7.5	36 10.0	76 4.8	Cost of Sales/Inventory	41 9.0	55 6.7
	62 5.9	49 7.4	78 4.7	72 5.1	109 3.4		84 4.4	96 3.8
	85 4.3	97 3.8	130 2.8	118 3.1	140 2.6		129 2.8	133 2.7
	18 20.1	18 20.8	24 15.1	22 16.2	29 12.6	Cost of Sales/Payables	24 15.5	25 14.9
	25 14.8	29 12.4	36 10.1	47 7.8	45 8.2		42 8.6	43 8.4
	43 8.5	47 7.7	57 6.4	64 5.7	76 4.8		81 4.5	82 4.5
	5.9	4.8	2.9	2.7	2.6	Sales/Working Capital	4.0	3.7
	11.5	12.2	6.2	6.0	4.6		7.3	6.3
	52.8	35.3	14.0	-79.1	13.5		34.9	29.9
	9.2	17.5	21.1	26.2	12.3	EBIT/Interest	19.1	21.2
	(12) 3.5	(47) 5.4	(56) 4.3	3.9	(37) 3.4		(120) 6.1	(139) 5.5
	-.3	1.7	1.4	2.8	1.1		1.1	1.5
		11.2	2.4		17.9	Net Profit + Depr., Dep.,	8.2	12.4
	(11) 4.9	(24) 1.6		(17) 2.5		Amort./Cur. Mat. L/T/D	(44) 2.5	(45) 3.9
	.8	.5		1.5			.7	1.7
	.2	.2	.2	.2	.3	Fixed/Worth	.3	.3
	.5	.6	.7	1.3	.7		.8	.7
	4.4	2.5	2.1	2.8	NM		2.3	2.9
	.6	.5	.6	.5	.5	Debt/Worth	.7	.5
	3.0	2.1	1.4	1.9	1.5		1.6	1.5
	15.3	6.6	4.4	14.5	NM		6.6	12.8
	61.4	65.0	55.2	77.5	32.6	% Profit Before Taxes/Tangible	66.7	53.8
	(14) 22.8	(54) 25.9	(58) 21.9	(12) 23.1	(31) 15.6	Net Worth	(118) 25.3	(117) 24.7
	-6.4	7.0	5.2	13.3	-4.1		4.6	8.7
	17.1	21.7	16.5	16.3	10.1	% Profit Before Taxes/Total	20.6	17.3
	7.6	9.6	6.9	8.5	7.7	Assets	8.9	7.8
	-4.3	2.1	1.6	4.3	1.8		-.3	1.3
	91.5	37.1	25.6	44.4	7.7	Sales/Net Fixed Assets	20.2	19.7
	35.0	9.7	9.3	9.8	5.1		7.4	7.0
	12.1	3.7	2.5	2.6	3.0		4.1	3.6
	4.0	3.0	2.3	1.8	1.2	Sales/Total Assets	2.3	2.2
	3.0	2.0	1.4	1.3	.8		1.6	1.5
	2.4	1.5	.9	.9	.6		1.0	.9
	.6	1.0	1.1	1.3	2.8	% Depr., Dep., Amort./Sales	1.1	1.0
	(15) 1.0	(50) 2.6	(54) 2.3	(12) 3.3	(29) 4.0		(118) 2.3	(132) 2.3
	1.7	4.2	4.9	5.3	6.4		3.8	4.4
		2.1				% Officers', Directors'	1.5	2.3
	(16)	4.0				Owners' Comp/Sales	(34) 3.3	(31) 4.0
		8.3					10.4	7.3
12388M	67288M	770045M	2683435M	1615642M	5928966M	Net Sales ($)	6667726M	7545077M
1312M	21609M	342246M	1637586M	899456M	6191532M	Total Assets ($)	5246150M	6625316M

M = $ thousand   MM = $ million
See Pages 9 through 22 for Explanation of Ratios and Data

Comparative Historical Data   Current Data Sorted by Sales

4/1/07-3/31/08 ALL	4/1/08-3/31/09 ALL	4/1/09-3/31/10 ALL	Type of Statement	0-1MM	1-3MM	3-5MM	5-10MM	10-25MM	25MM & OVR
					36 (4/1-9/30/09)		167 (10/1/09-3/31/10)		
43	49	46	Unqualified	1		1	2	7	36
22	27	27	Reviewed			1	3	13	9
10	11	13	Compiled		3	1	2	5	2
7	18	17	Tax Returns		4	1	2	5	4
76	78	100	Other		3	5	11	28	53
158	183	203	**NUMBER OF STATEMENTS**	1	10	12	23	57	100
%	%	%	**ASSETS**	%	%	%	%	%	%
13.1	13.2	14.0	Cash & Equivalents		15.8	21.2	10.7	10.9	15.5
22.4	21.6	22.0	Trade Receivables (net)		17.8	15.3	22.4	25.6	21.1
21.7	19.8	19.8	Inventory		27.6	25.6	20.9	21.0	17.4
2.8	3.2	3.2	All Other Current		2.1	.4	4.9	4.0	2.8
60.0	57.8	59.0	Total Current		63.2	62.5	59.0	61.5	56.8
24.1	23.6	24.9	Fixed Assets (net)		26.9	28.5	21.3	29.2	22.8
8.7	11.4	11.0	Intangibles (net)		5.6	.3	13.1	6.1	15.3
7.2	7.2	5.1	All Other Non-Current		4.3	8.7	6.7	3.2	5.1
100.0	100.0	100.0	Total		100.0	100.0	100.0	100.0	100.0
			LIABILITIES						
8.0	6.4	6.2	Notes Payable-Short Term		9.2	11.7	7.0	5.8	5.4
3.0	3.3	3.6	Cur. Mat.-L.T.D.		5.1	4.1	3.6	3.1	3.7
12.5	12.9	12.1	Trade Payables		10.0	12.2	11.5	13.8	11.6
.4	.3	.3	Income Taxes Payable		.0	.0	.6	.3	.4
11.4	12.3	12.4	All Other Current		8.8	12.7	17.2	14.0	10.7
35.2	35.2	34.7	Total Current		33.1	40.7	39.8	37.0	31.9
18.4	16.4	15.5	Long-Term Debt		28.0	4.7	22.6	13.9	14.9
.8	.9	.7	Deferred Taxes		.0	.3	.1	.9	.9
6.2	6.6	5.7	All Other Non-Current		3.6	3.6	8.9	6.8	4.9
39.3	40.9	43.4	Net Worth		35.4	50.7	28.6	41.4	47.4
100.0	100.0	100.0	Total Liabilities & Net Worth		100.0	100.0	100.0	100.0	100.0
			INCOME DATA						
100.0	100.0	100.0	Net Sales		100.0	100.0	100.0	100.0	100.0
43.5	45.6	42.1	Gross Profit		45.7	29.2	43.7	42.0	42.6
36.1	38.2	35.2	Operating Expenses		43.9	31.0	38.6	33.7	34.6
7.4	7.4	6.9	Operating Profit		1.8	-1.7	5.1	8.4	8.0
1.0	1.4	1.7	All Other Expenses (net)		.9	.2	3.1	1.2	2.0
6.5	6.0	5.2	Profit Before Taxes		.9	-2.0	1.9	7.1	6.0
			RATIOS						
3.0	3.1	3.1	Current		7.1	14.3	4.3	2.9	3.0
1.8	1.8	1.8			1.7	1.4	2.3	1.7	1.9
1.2	1.3	1.2			.6	.8	1.2	1.2	1.2
1.7	1.8	1.9	Quick		3.6	9.9	2.2	1.8	1.7
1.0	1.0	1.0			.6	.7	1.0	.9	1.1
.6	.6	.6			.3	.3	.7	.6	.8
32 11.3	31 11.8	30 12.2	Sales/Receivables		10 35.3	15 23.7	29 12.7	28 13.1	34 10.8
45 8.2	42 8.6	43 8.5			36 10.0	29 12.5	37 9.9	40 9.1	51 7.2
58 6.3	57 6.4	59 6.2			46 7.9	42 8.7	55 6.6	57 6.4	65 5.6
44 8.2	43 8.6	40 9.0	Cost of Sales/Inventory		41 9.0	24 15.3	41 9.0	33 11.0	47 7.8
87 4.2	86 4.2	74 4.9			63 5.8	41 8.9	54 6.8	92 4.0	77 4.7
124 3.0	135 2.7	119 3.1			76 4.8	104 3.5	79 4.6	146 2.5	125 2.9
23 15.9	21 17.6	20 18.6	Cost of Sales/Payables		7 50.1	10 36.5	18 20.0	21 17.6	25 14.6
38 9.7	34 10.7	36 10.1			29 12.6	24 15.5	28 13.2	34 10.7	40 9.1
62 5.9	68 5.4	57 6.4			39 9.3	40 9.1	47 7.7	56 6.5	65 5.6
3.6	3.6	3.5	Sales/Working Capital		4.8	3.8	3.9	3.7	3.0
6.9	7.4	7.2			14.2	41.2	10.1	8.4	5.8
22.1	24.9	22.7			-7.0	-88.7	31.8	20.6	17.2
14.9	14.1	17.1	EBIT/Interest				7.9	17.5	21.8
(135) 4.2	(155) 4.7	(168) 4.2					(18) 2.4	(45) 4.9	(91) 4.3
1.2	.8	1.6					-3.5	2.0	1.7
13.3	10.1	6.1	Net Profit + Depr., Dep., Amort./Cur. Mat. L/T/D					7.1	7.6
(46) 2.5	(59) 3.3	(57) 1.9						(16) 3.5	(38) 1.9
1.0	.9	.7						1.0	.7
.3	.3	.2	Fixed/Worth		.1	.2	.1	.3	.2
.7	.7	.7			1.0	.3	.7	.8	.7
2.4	1.8	2.4			7.8	1.8	28.8	1.7	2.7
.6	.5	.6	Debt/Worth		.8	.2	.6	.6	.6
1.5	1.7	1.6			3.7	.9	2.8	1.7	1.4
5.2	7.1	6.8			11.4	10.1	39.6	6.0	7.5
59.4	57.5	52.7	% Profit Before Taxes/Tangible Net Worth			32.3	72.1	62.2	47.5
(131) 17.0	(151) 18.3	(173) 23.1			(11) 8.0	(18) 19.6	(51) 26.7	(83) 21.1	
1.8	.9	6.2				-23.8	8.2	7.4	6.4
20.7	21.2	16.3	% Profit Before Taxes/Total Assets		40.3	18.4	12.4	23.5	14.7
7.7	6.8	7.6			9.9	5.0	7.0	7.6	7.8
-.4	-.5	2.1			-12.4	-7.4	2.1	2.3	2.6
26.7	27.9	30.0	Sales/Net Fixed Assets		110.4	137.5	79.5	22.4	21.8
9.2	8.0	8.3			27.5	18.0	22.4	6.5	7.9
3.5	3.5	3.2			3.4	3.0	3.2	3.1	3.1
2.6	2.5	2.6	Sales/Total Assets		3.5	4.1	3.0	2.6	2.0
1.7	1.5	1.5			2.6	2.6	2.0	1.7	1.3
1.1	1.1	.9			.8	1.0	1.4	1.0	.8
1.0	1.4	1.1	% Depr., Dep., Amort./Sales				.9	1.1	1.5
(131) 2.2	(157) 2.6	(161) 2.6				(20) 2.1	(43) 2.7	(80) 3.0	
4.3	4.3	4.7					3.1	5.0	4.8
1.6	1.9	1.6	% Officers', Directors' Owners' Comp/Sales					1.6	.9
(40) 4.0	(45) 4.0	(36) 3.0					(13) 3.8	(12) 1.7	
9.6	8.8	5.6						6.5	2.9
8356015M	10435939M	11077764M	Net Sales ($)	756M	21459M	48098M	166247M	969502M	9871702M
5951400M	7667393M	9093741M	Total Assets ($)	618M	12403M	32943M	100224M	778939M	8168614M

M = $ thousand   MM = $ million
See Pages 9 through 22 for Explanation of Ratios and Data

Current Data Sorted by Assets   Comparative Historical Data

0-500M	500M-2MM	2-10MM	10-50MM	50-100MM	100-250MM	Type of Statement	24	23
		2	7	4	2	Unqualified	24	23
	3	20	9		1	Reviewed	18	33
	3	11	2			Compiled	19	17
3	14	1				Tax Returns	10	11
1	16	15	18	5	3	Other	37	34
23 (4/1-9/30/09)			117 (10/1/09-3/31/10)				4/1/05-3/31/06 ALL	4/1/06-3/31/07 ALL
4	36	49	36	9	6	NUMBER OF STATEMENTS	108	118

ASSETS

0-500M	500M-2MM	2-10MM	10-50MM	50-100MM	100-250MM		ALL	ALL
%	%	%	%	%	%		%	%
	9.7	8.2	8.9			Cash & Equivalents	8.0	8.5
	28.8	23.2	22.3			Trade Receivables (net)	27.0	26.7
	27.2	31.0	21.8			Inventory	25.7	26.1
	3.5	1.8	2.6			All Other Current	2.5	2.6
	69.1	64.3	55.6			Total Current	63.1	63.8
	19.4	23.6	26.8			Fixed Assets (net)	24.0	21.5
	3.1	6.2	10.5			Intangibles (net)	5.6	7.9
	8.4	5.9	7.1			All Other Non-Current	7.3	6.8
	100.0	100.0	100.0			Total	100.0	100.0

LIABILITIES

0-500M	500M-2MM	2-10MM	10-50MM	50-100MM	100-250MM		ALL	ALL
	13.7	10.8	7.4			Notes Payable-Short Term	10.3	9.4
	5.4	3.6	5.0			Cur. Mat.-L.T.D.	3.1	3.7
	17.2	13.4	12.8			Trade Payables	16.4	14.4
	.1	.1	.1			Income Taxes Payable	.2	.3
	7.8	7.7	7.2			All Other Current	8.1	10.0
	44.1	35.6	32.5			Total Current	38.1	37.8
	16.3	9.4	12.1			Long-Term Debt	14.6	18.4
	.0	.1	1.0			Deferred Taxes	.2	.4
	14.7	7.8	8.3			All Other Non-Current	7.7	6.8
	24.8	47.1	46.1			Net Worth	39.4	36.7
	100.0	100.0	100.0			Total Liabilities & Net Worth	100.0	100.0

INCOME DATA

0-500M	500M-2MM	2-10MM	10-50MM	50-100MM	100-250MM		ALL	ALL
	100.0	100.0	100.0			Net Sales	100.0	100.0
	37.3	34.2	34.8			Gross Profit	32.4	34.0
	34.8	29.9	29.7			Operating Expenses	28.2	28.3
	2.5	4.2	5.1			Operating Profit	4.3	5.6
	.5	.7	1.2			All Other Expenses (net)	1.0	1.4
	2.0	3.5	3.9			Profit Before Taxes	3.3	4.2

RATIOS

0-500M	500M-2MM	2-10MM	10-50MM	50-100MM	100-250MM		ALL	ALL
	3.8	3.2	2.8			Current	2.7	3.2
	2.0	1.7	2.1				1.9	1.9
	.9	1.2	1.3				1.2	1.2
	2.3	1.7	1.8			Quick	1.6	1.8
	1.2	.7	1.1				1.0	1.0
	.5	.5	.6				.6	.7
	23 15.9	32 11.3	34 10.7			Sales/Receivables	33 11.0	32 11.5
	36 10.0	39 9.4	46 7.9				46 7.9	41 8.8
	48 7.5	50 7.4	58 6.3				57 6.4	53 6.9
	13 27.4	58 6.3	54 6.8			Cost of Sales/Inventory	44 8.3	40 9.0
	57 6.4	92 4.0	70 5.2				71 5.1	67 5.4
	86 4.2	102 3.6	104 3.5				93 3.9	94 3.9
	13 28.6	19 18.7	20 17.8			Cost of Sales/Payables	25 14.9	20 18.4
	24 14.9	30 12.1	35 10.5				38 9.7	31 11.7
	58 6.3	43 8.5	47 7.7				53 6.9	45 8.1
	3.6	4.7	4.2			Sales/Working Capital	5.1	4.7
	7.4	7.9	6.1				8.0	8.8
	-143.8	17.6	15.8				18.1	23.2
	10.1	10.0	11.4			EBIT/Interest	8.9	14.5
	(32) 2.5	(45) 3.6	(33) 4.5				(100) 3.5	(111) 5.5
	-.8	1.0	1.3				1.0	1.8
		5.7	8.4			Net Profit + Depr., Dep., Amort./Cur. Mat. L/T/D	4.2	16.8
		(12) 1.5	(18) 3.6				(28) 2.2	(34) 4.2
		1.2	2.6				1.3	1.2
	.1	.3	.3			Fixed/Worth	.3	.3
	.3	.5	.5				.7	.6
	6.0	1.4	3.9				1.8	2.9
	.5	.5	.5			Debt/Worth	.7	.6
	1.3	1.1	1.4				1.9	1.7
	69.6	4.6	7.9				5.2	5.8
	47.1	21.1	23.0			% Profit Before Taxes/Tangible Net Worth	37.8	52.3
	(29) 15.8	(43) 9.5	(30) 10.8				(98) 17.0	(101) 22.0
	-2.5	1.0	3.1				5.8	11.1
	17.4	11.6	9.7			% Profit Before Taxes/Total Assets	12.8	16.6
	3.7	4.1	4.8				5.8	7.9
	-5.6	.3	.9				.3	3.0
	66.7	22.8	16.5			Sales/Net Fixed Assets	19.4	23.9
	29.5	11.3	7.9				9.7	11.5
	9.8	5.9	4.5				5.2	6.6
	3.5	2.7	2.3			Sales/Total Assets	2.8	3.0
	2.7	2.0	1.5				2.2	2.3
	1.9	1.5	1.2				1.6	1.6
	.3	.8	1.1			% Depr., Dep., Amort./Sales	1.3	1.0
	(30) .9	(45) 1.4	(35) 1.9				(96) 1.7	(101) 1.7
	1.9	2.7	2.8				2.5	2.6
	2.6	2.0				% Officers', Directors' Owners' Comp/Sales	1.1	1.1
	(24) 5.6	(18) 4.7					(31) 2.6	(32) 3.1
	9.1	6.3					5.8	6.4
4483M	113022M	471492M	1425067M	1046184M	1062413M	Net Sales ($)	3835442M	3708307M
819M	41780M	223296M	814377M	705324M	784195M	Total Assets ($)	2141925M	1858871M

Comparative Historical Data | | | | Current Data Sorted by Sales

			Type of Statement						
22	17	15	Unqualified		1	4	10	3	11
27	26	33	Reviewed	1	2	3	8	11	7
21	18	16	Compiled	2	5	10	1	1	2
12	12	18	Tax Returns		11	8	4	15	18
45	74	58	Other	1					
4/1/07-3/31/08 ALL	4/1/08-3/31/09 ALL	4/1/09-3/31/10 ALL		2	23 (4/1-9/30/09)		117 (10/1/09-3/31/10)		
				0-1MM	1-3MM	3-5MM	5-10MM	10-25MM	25MM & OVER
127	147	140	NUMBER OF STATEMENTS	3	19	25	24	31	38
%	%	%	ASSETS	%	%	%	%	%	%
8.6	7.0	9.4	Cash & Equivalents		7.7	8.7	10.8	9.2	10.2
27.5	24.8	24.4	Trade Receivables (net)		26.0	25.3	23.2	24.4	22.1
25.7	26.7	25.0	Inventory		18.0	32.3	27.7	26.1	21.3
2.1	2.6	3.0	All Other Current		5.8	.8	2.2	1.8	4.7
63.9	61.1	61.8	Total Current		57.7	67.1	63.9	61.5	58.3
19.5	22.2	24.2	Fixed Assets (net)		29.9	22.7	22.9	21.7	25.2
7.5	8.2	7.1	Intangibles (net)		3.0	4.8	6.9	9.1	9.5
9.1	8.6	6.9	All Other Non-Current		9.5	5.3	6.3	7.7	7.0
100.0	100.0	100.0	Total		100.0	100.0	100.0	100.0	100.0
			LIABILITIES						
11.3	12.1	9.5	Notes Payable-Short Term		16.6	11.6	8.1	7.7	6.6
3.3	3.3	4.5	Cur. Mat.-L.T.D.		9.9	2.2	3.1	6.2	3.2
17.3	15.4	13.9	Trade Payables		13.2	16.8	12.1	13.4	12.9
.3	.1	.2	Income Taxes Payable		.0	.1	.0	.1	.4
7.6	8.0	7.9	All Other Current		6.4	9.2	7.5	8.0	8.4
39.7	38.9	35.9	Total Current		46.1	39.9	30.8	35.4	31.5
15.2	14.3	13.0	Long-Term Debt		15.3	15.9	10.6	10.3	14.3
.4	.4	.5	Deferred Taxes		.0	.0	.3	.5	1.3
6.4	10.9	9.5	All Other Non-Current		2.8	18.4	4.7	9.1	9.5
38.2	35.5	41.0	Net Worth		35.8	25.7	53.7	44.8	43.4
100.0	100.0	100.0	Total Liabilities & Net Worth		100.0	100.0	100.0	100.0	100.0
			INCOME DATA						
100.0	100.0	100.0	Net Sales		100.0	100.0	100.0	100.0	100.0
35.4	32.7	35.6	Gross Profit		40.8	38.3	32.9	35.2	33.1
29.7	27.3	31.7	Operating Expenses		38.0	35.9	26.7	32.1	28.0
5.7	5.3	3.9	Operating Profit		2.8	2.4	6.2	3.1	5.0
1.1	1.4	1.0	All Other Expenses (net)		1.0	.4	1.0	.4	1.7
4.6	3.9	3.0	Profit Before Taxes		1.8	2.0	5.2	2.6	3.4
			RATIOS						
3.4	2.9	3.3	Current		3.8	3.8	3.9	2.9	2.9
2.0	1.8	1.8			1.7	1.8	1.7	1.7	2.2
1.2	1.1	1.2			.5	1.0	1.5	1.1	1.5
1.7	1.6	1.9	Quick		2.0	2.2	2.3	2.0	1.7
1.0	.9	.9			.7	.8	.7	.8	1.1
.6	.5	.6			.3	.5	.6	.5	.8
30 12.1	28 13.1	31 12.0	Sales/Receivables	23 16.0	28 12.9	36 10.3	33 11.1	32 11.5	
43 8.5	40 9.1	41 8.9		37 9.9	35 10.5	48 7.6	43 8.4	46 8.0	
55 6.7	52 7.1	51 7.1		51 7.1	43 8.5	54 6.7	55 6.7	56 6.6	
39 9.3	37 9.8	43 8.4	Cost of Sales/Inventory	1 589.5	50 7.3	56 6.5	44 8.3	49 7.5	
65 5.6	63 5.8	68 5.4		24 15.3	66 5.5	91 4.0	80 4.6	61 5.9	
90 4.1	90 4.0	99 3.7		138 2.6	97 3.8	100 3.7	104 3.5	84 4.4	
20 18.3	17 21.2	18 20.2	Cost of Sales/Payables	7 52.3	16 22.2	19 19.5	20 18.5	21 17.8	
36 10.2	29 12.6	30 12.2		20 18.1	32 11.3	30 12.4	32 11.6	31 11.8	
53 6.8	47 7.8	47 7.8		58 6.3	57 6.3	42 8.7	45 8.1	47 7.8	
4.8	5.0	4.3	Sales/Working Capital		3.5	5.3	3.7	4.6	4.4
8.3	8.6	7.3			14.2	8.0	7.3	8.2	6.1
30.7	43.5	19.2			-25.5	-279.6	11.9	51.0	11.3
13.4	9.8	11.3	EBIT/Interest	10.9	6.6	11.1	11.4	16.1	
(117) 4.4	(129) 2.7	(127) 3.6		(16) 3.1	(24) 1.8	(22) 4.5	(28) 4.5	(36) 4.1	
1.7	.9	-.1		-1.7	-1.5	1.7	-.3	1.3	
6.0	6.7	8.7	Net Profit + Depr., Dep., Amort./Cur. Mat. L/T/D						16.9
(35) 2.9	(36) 2.1	(42) 3.2						(21)	5.1
1.6	1.1	1.2							2.8
.2	.2	.2	Fixed/Worth		.1	.2	.2	.2	.4
.5	.7	.5			.6	.4	.4	.5	.5
1.6	2.7	2.3			10.8	4.6	1.2	2.8	1.3
.5	.7	.5	Debt/Worth		.2	.7	.4	.5	.6
1.8	2.0	1.2			.9	1.4	.9	1.1	1.4
6.7	8.9	5.1			105.2	5.2	2.8	7.5	5.2
48.5	43.6	28.8	% Profit Before Taxes/Tangible Net Worth	31.2	47.0	27.6	20.0	26.2	
(104) 20.6	(120) 17.4	(118) 11.3		(15) 15.8	(22) 3.9	(22) 9.5	(25) 10.8	(32) 13.6	
8.4	1.3	1.6		1.6	-7.6	2.4	.8	2.9	
16.7	12.8	12.4	% Profit Before Taxes/Total Assets		18.4	12.4	12.8	8.9	12.8
7.9	5.5	4.4			5.9	1.3	4.1	5.9	5.2
1.8	-.1	-.2			-12.3	-5.2	1.2	-2.5	1.1
31.8	28.3	24.8	Sales/Net Fixed Assets		48.9	33.1	22.8	22.7	14.3
12.2	11.7	10.9			27.0	18.1	11.6	10.6	7.2
7.3	5.7	4.9			3.0	6.9	5.4	4.7	4.6
3.0	3.1	2.9	Sales/Total Assets		3.2	3.5	2.4	2.7	2.4
2.3	2.3	2.0			2.0	2.8	1.8	1.9	1.8
1.5	1.6	1.4			1.5	1.5	1.5	1.2	1.2
.8	1.0	.9	% Depr., Dep., Amort./Sales		.3	.6	.7	.9	1.3
(116) 1.5	(125) 1.7	(126) 1.6			(14) 1.1	(23) 1.2	(23) 1.3	(29) 1.6	(35) 2.1
2.3	2.5	2.7			3.8	2.6	2.8	2.2	2.8
1.7	2.5	2.0	% Officers', Directors' Owners' Comp/Sales		7.5	2.3			
(39) 4.1	(41) 4.2	(52) 4.9			(11) 8.9	(17) 4.7			
7.2	7.0	7.9			15.3	5.8			
3603763M	4529226M	4122661M	Net Sales ($)	1831M	37115M	98859M	170852M	479399M	3334605M
2159134M	2686336M	2569791M	Total Assets ($)	904M	18478M	52259M	95423M	279869M	2122858M

© RMA 2010
M = $ thousand   MM = $ million
See Pages 9 through 22 for Explanation of Ratios and Data

Current Data Sorted by Assets   Comparative Historical Data

Type of Statement

0-500M	500M-2MM	2-10MM	10-50MM	50-100MM	100-250MM		4/1/05-3/31/06 ALL	4/1/06-3/31/07 ALL
1			14	1		Unqualified	29	24
	3	11	3	1		Reviewed	28	19
	1	3				Compiled	5	8
	2	3				Tax Returns	4	6
	2	12	13	1	4	Other	35	39
12 (4/1-9/30/09)			63 (10/1/09-3/31/10)					
1	8	29	30	3	4	**NUMBER OF STATEMENTS**	101	96
%	%	%	%	%	%	**ASSETS**	%	%

ASSETS

0-500M	500M-2MM	2-10MM	10-50MM	50-100MM	100-250MM		101 ALL	96 ALL
		5.4	4.5			Cash & Equivalents	7.4	6.2
		28.5	24.8			Trade Receivables (net)	28.7	29.1
		28.2	25.7			Inventory	25.2	25.1
		4.0	3.0			All Other Current	2.2	2.4
		66.1	58.0			Total Current	63.6	62.9
		18.2	25.4			Fixed Assets (net)	23.4	25.2
		4.5	8.0			Intangibles (net)	6.8	5.4
		11.3	8.6			All Other Non-Current	6.3	6.5
		100.0	100.0			Total	100.0	100.0

LIABILITIES

0-500M	500M-2MM	2-10MM	10-50MM	50-100MM	100-250MM		101 ALL	96 ALL
		11.4	8.1			Notes Payable-Short Term	8.9	11.3
		4.3	4.3			Cur. Mat.-L.T.D.	3.9	3.2
		18.1	12.1			Trade Payables	16.3	15.8
		.0	.7			Income Taxes Payable	.3	.2
		8.0	8.5			All Other Current	8.2	11.2
		41.8	33.7			Total Current	37.5	41.8
		8.6	19.7			Long-Term Debt	13.4	14.0
		.7	1.6			Deferred Taxes	1.0	.8
		11.5	5.9			All Other Non-Current	6.0	8.9
		37.5	39.1			Net Worth	42.1	34.5
		100.0	100.0			Total Liabilities & Net Worth	100.0	100.0

INCOME DATA

0-500M	500M-2MM	2-10MM	10-50MM	50-100MM	100-250MM		101 ALL	96 ALL
		100.0	100.0			Net Sales	100.0	100.0
		35.3	27.1			Gross Profit	32.1	31.4
		32.1	22.2			Operating Expenses	27.4	26.8
		3.3	4.9			Operating Profit	4.7	4.6
		.7	1.0			All Other Expenses (net)	1.0	1.5
		2.6	3.9			Profit Before Taxes	3.7	3.2

RATIOS

0-500M	500M-2MM	2-10MM	10-50MM	50-100MM	100-250MM		101 ALL	96 ALL
		2.5	2.4			Current	2.7	2.6
		1.8	1.9				1.8	1.6
		1.2	1.1				1.2	1.1
		1.6	1.3			Quick	1.6	1.6
		.8	.8				.9	.9
		.5	.6				.6	.6
		(37) 9.7	(43) 8.5			Sales/Receivables	(38) 9.7	(35) 10.3
		44 8.2	49 7.5				44 8.3	42 8.6
		52 7.1	53 6.9				55 6.6	55 6.7
		50 7.4	48 7.7			Cost of Sales/Inventory	40 9.1	39 9.5
		68 5.4	65 5.6				55 6.6	49 7.4
		99 3.7	95 3.8				82 4.4	79 4.6
		26 13.9	24 15.0			Cost of Sales/Payables	28 13.0	21 17.2
		36 10.0	32 11.4				36 10.2	35 10.6
		52 7.0	43 8.5				49 7.5	50 7.3
		5.8	5.5			Sales/Working Capital	5.8	6.4
		8.5	7.0				8.7	10.5
		38.0	41.7				20.2	45.5
		12.3	14.7			EBIT/Interest	14.0	11.0
		(27) 3.8	3.6				(90) 4.8	(87) 4.9
		-.6	1.9				1.3	2.0
			7.6			Net Profit + Depr., Dep., Amort./Cur. Mat. L/T/D	5.1	13.9
			(16) 2.8				(45) 2.5	(38) 4.6
			1.7				1.1	1.3
		.1	.3			Fixed/Worth	.3	.3
		.5	1.0				.6	.8
		1.4	1.8				1.3	2.1
		.7	1.0			Debt/Worth	.7	.9
		1.6	2.1				1.6	1.7
		3.0	4.2				3.2	4.5
		41.3	35.1			% Profit Before Taxes/Tangible Net Worth	40.3	46.6
		(25) 15.5	(29) 19.3				(89) 18.4	(82) 26.8
		-4.6	7.4				3.5	9.1
		15.7	13.2			% Profit Before Taxes/Total Assets	15.5	16.9
		7.1	5.6				6.5	9.7
		-3.7	3.0				1.0	2.1
		41.4	16.1			Sales/Net Fixed Assets	23.7	19.4
		16.6	8.9				10.3	11.3
		7.6	5.5				5.9	6.0
		2.8	2.2			Sales/Total Assets	2.8	3.1
		2.3	1.8				2.2	2.4
		1.7	1.6				1.7	1.8
		.5	1.3			% Depr., Dep., Amort./Sales	.9	.9
		(24) 1.1	(26) 1.9				(85) 1.7	(85) 1.6
		2.1	2.5				2.5	2.6
		2.6				% Officers', Directors' Owners' Comp/Sales	2.9	1.9
		(11) 7.8					(24) 4.0	(25) 3.3
		11.8					10.6	7.5
16M	28930M	295732M	1235510M	350591M	687712M	Net Sales ($)	3463685M	3903138M
43M	10359M	135693M	647739M	202979M	637376M	Total Assets ($)	1893389M	2075274M

M = $ thousand   MM = $ million
See Pages 9 through 22 for Explanation of Ratios and Data

Comparative Historical Data

Current Data Sorted by Sales

17	15	16	Type of Statement — Unqualified	1				2	13
15	21	18	Reviewed		1	4	4	6	3
9	9	4	Compiled				2	2	
7	7	5	Tax Returns			2	2	1	
35	29	32	Other		2	2	4	9	15
4/1/07-3/31/08 ALL	4/1/08-3/31/09 ALL	4/1/09-3/31/10 ALL		0-1MM	1-3MM 12 (4/1-9/30/09)	3-5MM	5-10MM	10-25MM 63 (10/1/09-3/31/10)	25MM & OV
83	81	75	NUMBER OF STATEMENTS	1	3	8	12	20	31
%	%	%	ASSETS	%	%	%	%	%	%
9.2	9.9	6.2	Cash & Equivalents				3.3	8.0	4.7
27.7	25.1	25.9	Trade Receivables (net)				27.5	30.8	23.5
26.8	27.9	26.3	Inventory				32.3	30.3	22.0
2.0	1.8	3.0	All Other Current				2.7	3.5	2.8
65.8	64.7	61.3	Total Current				65.9	72.6	53.0
20.6	22.1	21.4	Fixed Assets (net)				15.0	21.6	27.0
6.2	5.8	8.9	Intangibles (net)				4.3	1.1	12.5
7.4	7.4	8.3	All Other Non-Current				14.8	4.7	7.5
100.0	100.0	100.0	Total				100.0	100.0	100.0
			LIABILITIES						
10.2	10.8	9.3	Notes Payable-Short Term				14.3	9.9	7.5
3.4	3.8	4.1	Cur. Mat.-L.T.D.				6.2	3.6	4.0
15.4	15.2	14.3	Trade Payables				20.5	16.6	11.9
.2	.0	.4	Income Taxes Payable				.0	.1	.8
8.5	7.4	7.6	All Other Current				5.4	9.2	8.4
37.7	37.1	35.7	Total Current				46.4	39.4	32.5
10.7	13.6	14.5	Long-Term Debt				12.1	7.9	19.2
.5	.7	1.1	Deferred Taxes				.3	1.3	1.6
11.6	6.4	8.8	All Other Non-Current				14.4	7.3	4.8
39.5	42.2	39.8	Net Worth				26.8	44.1	41.9
100.0	100.0	100.0	Total Liabilities & Net Worth				100.0	100.0	100.0
			INCOME DATA						
100.0	100.0	100.0	Net Sales				100.0	100.0	100.0
33.8	29.2	32.8	Gross Profit				35.1	30.7	29.1
28.3	25.0	27.3	Operating Expenses				33.7	25.9	22.5
5.5	4.3	5.5	Operating Profit				1.4	4.8	6.6
1.3	.8	1.1	All Other Expenses (net)				.7	.6	1.2
4.2	3.4	4.4	Profit Before Taxes				.6	4.2	5.3
			RATIOS						
3.1	3.1	2.7	Current				2.4	2.7	2.4
1.8	1.8	1.9					1.6	2.2	1.8
1.1	1.2	1.3					1.1	1.4	1.1
1.8	2.1	1.5	Quick				1.3	1.7	1.3
1.0	.9	.9					.7	1.1	.8
.5	.5	.6					.5	.6	.6
33 11.2	30 12.4	39 9.4	Sales/Receivables				27 13.5	43 8.5	40 9.1
43 8.5	39 9.4	47 7.8					44 8.2	47 7.8	49 7.5
53 6.9	49 7.5	52 7.0					49 7.5	55 6.7	53 6.9
44 8.3	39 9.3	50 7.3	Cost of Sales/Inventory				49 7.4	50 7.4	47 7.8
60 6.1	57 6.5	67 5.4					66 5.5	69 5.3	60 6.0
83 4.4	84 4.4	97 3.8					116 3.1	96 3.8	83 4.4
22 16.7	17 21.6	25 14.5	Cost of Sales/Payables				27 13.7	24 15.1	27 13.6
33 10.9	27 13.3	32 11.4					42 8.7	31 11.8	32 11.4
48 7.6	46 7.9	45 8.1					59 6.2	42 8.8	43 8.6
5.1	4.7	5.4	Sales/Working Capital				7.1	4.3	5.6
8.5	8.0	7.2					9.9	6.2	7.8
30.0	20.9	22.4					124.3	14.2	49.1
9.4	10.7	12.3	EBIT/Interest				6.9	13.6	16.8
(71) 4.2	(69) 3.5	(70) 3.8					3.8	(18) 4.1	(30) 3.7
1.7	.8	1.5					-.7	1.0	1.9
5.0	6.9	7.6	Net Profit + Depr., Dep., Amort./Cur. Mat. L/T/D						8.0
(29) 2.8	(28) 1.5	(24) 2.8							(15) 2.9
1.0	.1	1.3							1.2
.2	.1	.2	Fixed/Worth				.1	.1	.5
.4	.5	.7					.6	.4	1.0
1.7	1.7	1.6					NM	1.2	2.0
.8	.7	.8	Debt/Worth				1.1	.6	1.0
1.9	1.4	1.9					1.6	1.2	2.4
4.7	3.8	4.9					NM	2.1	4.9
60.0	45.5	41.6	% Profit Before Taxes/Tangible Net Worth					40.3	43.6
(75) 21.5	(73) 17.0	(68) 20.6						(19) 13.5	(30) 24.1
8.2	2.5	5.5						7.6	8.6
15.0	16.2	14.9	% Profit Before Taxes/Total Assets				14.4	16.5	14.8
7.7	6.1	6.1					5.4	6.3	6.0
2.0	.1	1.9					-6.4	1.1	3.1
42.6	30.2	23.6	Sales/Net Fixed Assets				39.3	24.1	11.7
14.3	11.4	10.9					27.3	14.3	7.2
6.7	6.6	6.0					7.7	5.4	4.4
3.1	2.9	2.5	Sales/Total Assets				3.3	2.8	2.2
2.3	2.3	2.0					2.5	2.1	1.7
1.7	1.8	1.6					1.9	1.7	1.4
.4	.7	.8	% Depr., Dep., Amort./Sales				.5	.5	1.4
(72) 1.1	(70) 1.5	(61) 1.7					(10) 1.5	(15) 1.4	(26) 2.0
2.0	2.5	2.5					3.5	2.0	3.0
2.8	2.1	3.0	% Officers', Directors' Owners' Comp/Sales						
(21) 9.0	(20) 5.4	(20) 6.1							
14.4	8.7	8.6							
2969444M	2984928M	2598491M	Net Sales ($)	16M	6211M	30772M	83709M	322679M	2155104M
1560080M	1484127M	1634189M	Total Assets ($)	43M	2650M	20965M	37526M	153068M	1419937M

M = $ thousand   MM = $ million
See Pages 9 through 22 for Explanation of Ratios and Data

MANUFACTURING—Soap and Other Detergent Manufacturing NAICS 325611

Current Data Sorted by Assets							Comparative Historical Data		
			2	3		1	**Type of Statement**		
		1	7	1			Unqualified	9	12
		2	2	1			Reviewed	7	12
3		4	6				Compiled	6	6
1		8	8	7	2		Tax Returns	4	4
							Other	17	21
	6 (4/1-9/30/09)			53 (10/1/09-3/31/10)				4/1/05-3/31/06	4/1/06-3/31/07
0-500M	500M-2MM	2-10MM	10-50MM	50-100MM	100-250MM			ALL	ALL
4	15	25	12	2	1		NUMBER OF STATEMENTS	43	55
%	%	%	%	%	%			%	%
							ASSETS		
	14.3	7.8	3.1				Cash & Equivalents	4.2	6.4
	24.1	28.8	23.3				Trade Receivables (net)	28.4	25.9
	30.6	25.4	24.1				Inventory	27.6	28.8
	3.7	2.2	1.8				All Other Current	1.6	2.3
	72.7	64.2	52.3				Total Current	61.8	63.4
	15.1	21.3	27.4				Fixed Assets (net)	22.2	22.8
	4.6	5.9	15.1				Intangibles (net)	10.4	6.6
	7.6	8.5	5.2				All Other Non-Current	5.6	7.1
	100.0	100.0	100.0				Total	100.0	100.0
							LIABILITIES		
	24.1	7.5	9.6				Notes Payable-Short Term	14.4	12.4
	3.3	5.4	4.9				Cur. Mat.-L.T.D.	3.9	3.7
	19.3	15.0	11.9				Trade Payables	17.7	17.5
	.0	.2	.2				Income Taxes Payable	.3	.1
	16.2	7.0	10.2				All Other Current	9.6	8.8
	62.9	35.2	36.8				Total Current	45.9	42.5
	12.9	13.4	15.7				Long-Term Debt	15.4	15.7
	.0	.4	.4				Deferred Taxes	.5	.5
	1.8	1.9	10.2				All Other Non-Current	8.3	7.0
	22.3	49.0	37.0				Net Worth	29.5	34.3
	100.0	100.0	100.0				Total Liabilities & Net Worth	100.0	100.0
							INCOME DATA		
	100.0	100.0	100.0				Net Sales	100.0	100.0
	47.8	41.5	34.8				Gross Profit	32.4	37.5
	39.4	32.8	26.1				Operating Expenses	27.7	32.1
	8.3	8.6	8.7				Operating Profit	4.7	5.4
	1.5	.7	.2				All Other Expenses (net)	1.3	1.4
	6.8	8.0	8.5				Profit Before Taxes	3.4	4.0
							RATIOS		
	3.7	3.0	1.9					2.3	2.3
	1.6	2.1	1.7				Current	1.2	1.5
	.7	1.3	1.0					1.1	1.0
	2.3	2.0	1.1					1.2	1.2
	.8	1.0	.7				Quick	.7	.7
	.4	.6	.5					.5	.4
26	13.9	32 11.3	35 10.3					32 11.5	28 12.9
33	11.1	41 8.9	41 8.9				Sales/Receivables	42 8.8	39 9.4
40	9.1	54 6.7	51 7.2					55 6.7	45 8.1
39	9.4	39 9.4	40 9.0					36 10.0	41 8.9
68	5.4	73 5.0	67 5.5				Cost of Sales/Inventory	64 5.7	65 5.6
118	3.1	117 3.1	80 4.6					87 4.2	96 3.8
17	21.2	22 16.7	16 23.4					22 16.6	28 13.1
41	8.9	37 9.8	29 12.6				Cost of Sales/Payables	36 10.3	40 9.0
68	5.3	57 6.4	58 6.3					58 6.2	61 6.0
	6.3	3.7	8.0					8.1	5.9
	11.0	8.0	12.5				Sales/Working Capital	22.3	12.2
	-10.3	20.0	NM					95.8	-219.6
	9.8	26.4	17.4					8.9	14.9
	(11) 3.1	(22) 6.0	11.8				EBIT/Interest	(39) 2.1	(51) 3.9
	.3	2.5	4.1					.0	1.0
							Net Profit + Depr., Dep., Amort./Cur. Mat. L/T/D	4.9	8.5
								(10) 1.5	(13) 2.2
								.9	.4
	.1	.1	.6					.3	.2
	.4	.4	1.4				Fixed/Worth	.9	.7
	-4.8	1.0	NM					2.5	2.9
	.5	.7	1.2					1.0	.8
	2.5	1.3	2.3				Debt/Worth	2.2	1.6
	-20.3	2.6	NM					7.4	13.2
	134.2	61.6					% Profit Before Taxes/Tangible Net Worth	46.8	50.0
	(11) 35.6	19.6						(34) 23.2	(45) 30.1
	9.7	7.8						3.5	7.4
	19.6	21.5	26.8				% Profit Before Taxes/Total Assets	15.3	18.6
	4.9	8.6	13.2					3.5	9.0
	-2.5	3.1	9.1					-2.0	.4
	91.9	31.4	12.3				Sales/Net Fixed Assets	40.8	27.1
	42.7	17.7	9.1					12.8	11.8
	14.6	6.3	6.1					5.1	6.2
	3.6	2.7	2.6				Sales/Total Assets	3.4	3.1
	2.7	2.2	2.3					2.3	2.4
	2.0	1.4	1.5					1.7	1.7
	.4	1.0	1.2				% Depr., Dep., Amort./Sales	1.2	.9
	(10) 2.1	(20) 1.6	(11) 2.2					(34) 1.9	(46) 1.6
	2.9	2.0	4.3					4.4	2.5
		1.3					% Officers', Directors' Owners' Comp/Sales	1.4	3.1
		(12) 3.1						(13) 4.5	(17) 4.2
		4.7						6.1	6.5
1862M	44216M	242519M	616471M	415917M	158440M		Net Sales ($)	1020370M	1513028M
997M	15902M	107464M	289064M	153919M	170632M		Total Assets ($)	676033M	755644M

M = $ thousand   MM = $ million
See Pages 9 through 22 for Explanation of Ratios and Data

Comparative Historical Data   **Current Data Sorted by Sales**

4/1/07-3/31/08 ALL	4/1/08-3/31/09 ALL	4/1/09-3/31/10 ALL	Type of Statement	0-1MM	1-3MM	3-5MM	5-10MM	10-25MM	25MM & OVER
7	10	6	Unqualified					1	5
10	7	9	Reviewed			1	3	4	1
3	5	5	Compiled		2		1	2	
5	10	13	Tax Returns	3	5	1	3	1	
18	22	26	Other	1	6	4	4	3	8
					6 (4/1-9/30/09)		53 (10/1/09-3/31/10)		
43	54	59	NUMBER OF STATEMENTS	4	13	6	11	11	14
%	%	%	**ASSETS**	%	%	%	%	%	%
7.2	5.6	8.0	Cash & Equivalents		7.2		16.4	6.3	2.5
28.8	24.5	25.7	Trade Receivables (net)		23.0		28.9	28.4	26.3
28.7	29.6	26.4	Inventory		23.9		26.0	27.4	25.7
2.3	3.0	2.4	All Other Current		1.3		2.3	3.0	1.5
67.1	62.7	62.5	Total Current		55.4		73.6	65.1	56.0
20.6	21.4	22.8	Fixed Assets (net)		21.7		15.5	23.3	28.0
6.5	11.9	7.3	Intangibles (net)		9.7		5.7	6.4	11.3
5.9	4.0	7.4	All Other Non-Current		13.2		5.2	5.1	4.7
100.0	100.0	100.0	Total		100.0		100.0	100.0	100.0
			LIABILITIES						
13.6	14.3	11.8	Notes Payable-Short Term		23.1		5.4	11.9	10.2
3.0	3.8	7.1	Cur. Mat.-L.T.D.		4.9		5.9	4.8	12.4
18.7	17.4	15.0	Trade Payables		17.1		14.4	17.3	14.6
.1	.2	.1	Income Taxes Payable		.0		.2	.3	.2
8.1	8.2	10.1	All Other Current		21.8		3.7	4.0	9.6
43.6	43.9	44.2	Total Current		67.0		29.6	38.3	47.1
12.5	17.0	15.6	Long-Term Debt		18.2		15.0	12.7	11.1
.3	.2	.6	Deferred Taxes		.0		.1	1.1	1.5
6.2	3.2	3.9	All Other Non-Current		.5		.3	4.2	8.6
37.4	35.6	35.7	Net Worth		14.2		55.0	43.6	31.7
100.0	100.0	100.0	Total Liabilities & Net Worth		100.0		100.0	100.0	100.0
			INCOME DATA						
100.0	100.0	100.0	Net Sales		100.0		100.0	100.0	100.0
33.3	35.7	42.2	Gross Profit		49.5		46.0	36.8	28.0
28.4	31.1	34.4	Operating Expenses		40.7		34.1	30.7	21.8
5.0	4.7	7.7	Operating Profit		8.8		11.8	6.1	6.2
1.4	2.0	1.0	All Other Expenses (net)		1.9		.5	.1	1.2
3.5	2.7	6.8	Profit Before Taxes		6.9		11.4	6.0	5.0
			RATIOS						
2.7	2.6	2.8	Current		2.6		3.7	1.8	2.0
1.6	1.4	1.8			1.6		2.7	1.5	1.4
1.1	1.1	1.0			.6		2.1	1.3	.9
1.4	1.5	1.9	Quick		1.3		3.2	1.7	1.1
.8	.7	.9			.8		1.8	.9	.6
.5	.4	.5			.3		.6	.7	.4
35 10.3	25 14.8	31 11.9	Sales/Receivables		27 13.8		31 11.9	34 10.8	34 10.6
43 8.5	33 11.1	40 9.2			38 9.7		45 8.1	41 8.8	41 8.9
54 6.8	41 8.9	50 7.3			45 8.2		65 5.7	50 7.3	51 7.1
40 9.2	37 9.8	39 9.4	Cost of Sales/Inventory		32 11.6		53 6.8	34 10.9	32 11.4
60 6.0	61 6.0	68 5.3			76 4.8		81 4.5	39 9.3	51 7.1
89 4.1	89 4.1	113 3.2			134 2.7		117 3.1	102 3.6	78 4.7
26 14.2	19 19.1	21 17.5	Cost of Sales/Payables		23 15.8		30 12.0	21 17.8	16 22.2
40 9.1	37 9.8	36 10.0			41 8.9		50 7.3	44 8.4	30 12.0
65 5.6	48 7.7	59 6.2			74 4.9		63 5.8	50 7.4	44 8.2
5.0	6.1	4.4	Sales/Working Capital		8.5		3.7	6.9	8.5
9.5	15.3	10.0			11.0		4.2	12.4	17.8
45.0	40.6	-999.8			-6.9		8.8	24.3	-33.6
10.4	12.0	17.4	EBIT/Interest		8.6				16.3
(38) 3.7	(49) 3.5	(52) 4.9			(12) 2.9				9.7
1.1	.3	2.5			1.5				2.9
		4.4	Net Profit + Depr., Dep.,						
	(15) 1.8		Amort./Cur. Mat. L/T/D						
		1.1							
.2	.2	.2	Fixed/Worth		.2		.0	.2	.5
.5	.7	.6			1.4		.2	.4	1.2
2.0	2.9	2.4			-2.6		.9	1.1	NM
.6	.9	.9	Debt/Worth		1.8		.3	.9	1.0
2.0	2.4	2.0			3.8		1.2	2.1	2.6
7.7	6.6	4.3			-12.6		1.9	3.1	NM
45.8	48.4	79.0	% Profit Before Taxes/Tangible				89.2	54.0	91.5
(35) 16.6	(43) 17.9	(50) 30.0	Net Worth				19.6	(10) 28.3	(11) 49.1
4.6	1.4	8.8					7.8	17.0	17.7
19.0	17.4	22.1	% Profit Before Taxes/Total		13.6		31.8	19.6	25.9
5.4	5.3	8.6	Assets		3.8		8.6	10.1	10.5
.6	-2.1	3.3			-.9		4.0	8.0	5.3
53.7	36.6	33.7	Sales/Net Fixed Assets		57.3		252.0	69.0	13.2
14.6	13.8	14.6			20.0		16.2	17.7	9.1
5.2	6.9	6.3			4.6		6.4	6.0	5.8
3.3	3.6	2.9	Sales/Total Assets		2.9		2.4	3.0	2.9
2.2	2.5	2.2			2.0		2.0	2.4	2.4
1.6	1.7	1.7			1.1		1.5	2.1	1.8
.8	1.0	1.1	% Depr., Dep., Amort./Sales		1.0				1.2
(36) 1.3	(44) 1.8	(46) 1.9			(10) 2.1			(13) 2.2	
2.0	2.9	3.1			3.4				3.3
2.7	3.3	1.7	% Officers', Directors'						
(13) 5.0	(15) 5.3	(24) 3.5	Owners' Comp/Sales						
6.0	7.6	6.0							
1441986M	1867735M	1479425M	Net Sales ($)	1862M	27583M	22934M	80363M	156011M	1190672M
906557M	919395M	737978M	Total Assets ($)	997M	16986M	10617M	40129M	77786M	591463M

© RMA 2010   M = $ thousand   MM = $ million
See Pages 9 through 22 for Explanation of Ratios and Data

Current Data Sorted by Assets							Comparative Historical Data	

0-500M	500M-2MM	2-10MM	10-50MM	50-100MM	100-250MM	Type of Statement		
			9	4	1	Unqualified	17	15
		12	6	2		Reviewed	19	14
1	1	4		1		Compiled	9	10
3	3	1				Tax Returns	3	8
2	4	3	8		1	Other	22	21
	9 (4/1-9/30/09)		58 (10/1/09-3/31/10)				4/1/05-3/31/06 ALL	4/1/06-3/31/07 ALL
6	9	20	23	8	1	NUMBER OF STATEMENTS	70	68
%	%	%	%	%	%	ASSETS	%	%
		4.2	10.9			Cash & Equivalents	7.6	7.0
		32.4	25.2			Trade Receivables (net)	30.7	31.7
		28.2	27.0			Inventory	25.7	27.2
		2.1	2.5			All Other Current	2.4	3.5
		66.8	65.5			Total Current	66.4	69.4
		15.9	23.0			Fixed Assets (net)	21.4	18.4
		5.6	6.0			Intangibles (net)	6.0	6.2
		11.7	5.5			All Other Non-Current	6.1	6.0
		100.0	100.0			Total	100.0	100.0
						LIABILITIES		
		15.8	10.2			Notes Payable-Short Term	14.3	13.3
		2.8	2.6			Cur. Mat.-L.T.D.	2.8	3.0
		18.3	14.0			Trade Payables	19.4	19.2
		.1	.2			Income Taxes Payable	.2	.2
		9.2	9.2			All Other Current	7.3	9.5
		46.1	36.3			Total Current	44.0	45.2
		7.8	11.4			Long-Term Debt	12.1	15.6
		.5	.5			Deferred Taxes	.2	.4
		4.5	1.5			All Other Non-Current	5.0	6.6
		41.0	50.2			Net Worth	38.7	32.3
		100.0	100.0			Total Liabilities & Net Worth	100.0	100.0
						INCOME DATA		
		100.0	100.0			Net Sales	100.0	100.0
		39.1	36.7			Gross Profit	38.6	39.1
		34.1	27.2			Operating Expenses	33.3	33.7
		5.0	9.5			Operating Profit	5.3	5.4
		.5	1.0			All Other Expenses (net)	.7	1.1
		4.5	8.6			Profit Before Taxes	4.6	4.3
						RATIOS		
		2.4	2.7				2.6	2.8
		1.5	1.7			Current	1.6	1.7
		1.1	1.4				1.1	1.1
		1.4	1.8				1.6	1.5
		.7	.9			Quick	.9	.9
		.5	.6				.5	.5
		31 11.6	33 10.9				39 9.4	36 10.2
		37 9.8	41 8.9			Sales/Receivables	44 8.2	41 8.9
		45 8.1	45 8.1				52 7.0	50 7.3
		47 7.8	38 9.6				39 9.4	45 8.2
		57 6.4	66 5.5			Cost of Sales/Inventory	59 6.2	59 6.2
		71 5.2	91 4.0				87 4.2	94 3.9
		21 17.0	23 15.6				28 13.2	23 15.6
		35 10.3	32 11.5			Cost of Sales/Payables	38 9.5	34 10.8
		52 7.1	47 7.7				53 6.9	59 6.2
		7.7	4.4				6.1	5.6
		14.4	7.5			Sales/Working Capital	10.2	9.1
		51.4	20.9				47.6	24.4
		11.8	49.5				10.1	11.0
	(19)	3.9	10.8			EBIT/Interest	(60) 3.4	(60) 3.6
		2.3	6.5				.4	1.7
			18.4				4.8	11.4
		(10)	5.1			Net Profit + Depr., Dep., Amort./Cur. Mat. L/T/D	(16) 2.7	(19) 3.0
			2.8				1.4	2.0
		.2	.3				.2	.2
		.4	.5			Fixed/Worth	.7	.6
		1.7	1.0				1.9	NM
		.7	.6				.6	.7
		1.9	1.1			Debt/Worth	2.1	1.8
		5.6	2.5				6.9	NM
		53.7	53.7				50.5	54.0
	(18)	22.3	(22) 35.1			% Profit Before Taxes/Tangible Net Worth	(61) 23.9	(51) 25.6
		9.7	18.2				4.5	7.6
		17.4	28.2				17.3	16.5
		7.9	11.7			% Profit Before Taxes/Total Assets	6.4	6.0
		2.8	6.8				.5	2.7
		53.4	21.9				30.6	34.6
		19.9	10.0			Sales/Net Fixed Assets	15.5	14.7
		15.0	7.0				7.4	8.5
		3.8	2.8				2.9	3.1
		2.9	2.3			Sales/Total Assets	2.3	2.6
		2.3	1.5				1.8	2.0
		.7	1.2				.8	.7
	(18)	1.2	(22) 1.5			% Depr., Dep., Amort./Sales	(60) 1.3	(60) 1.5
		1.5	2.5				2.2	2.6
							1.8	2.3
						% Officers', Directors' Owners' Comp/Sales	(22) 3.8	(22) 4.2
							6.2	6.4
7113M	22637M	310524M	1143952M	895894M	501032M	Net Sales ($)	1812454M	2025244M
1965M	8279M	109684M	467753M	551604M	249618M	Total Assets ($)	831976M	902318M

M = $ thousand   MM = $ million
See Pages 9 through 22 for Explanation of Ratios and Data

Comparative Historical Data   Current Data Sorted by Sales

4/1/07-3/31/08 ALL	4/1/08-3/31/09 ALL	4/1/09-3/31/10 ALL	Type of Statement	0-1MM	1-3MM	3-5MM	5-10MM	10-25MM	25MM & OVER
18	17	14	Unqualified					3	11
13	17	21	Reviewed		1		4	9	8
7	8	7	Compiled		2	1	1	3	1
8	2	7	Tax Returns	2	2	2	1		
16	21	18	Other	3	3				
					9 (4/1-9/30/09)			58 (10/1/09-3/31/10)	
62	65	67	**NUMBER OF STATEMENTS**	5	6	3	6	20	27
%	%	%	**ASSETS**	%	%	%	%	%	%
9.2	9.3	9.8	Cash & Equivalents					7.8	11.1
31.0	27.3	28.5	Trade Receivables (net)					27.4	28.7
26.0	28.6	25.2	Inventory					26.7	25.9
2.5	2.1	2.0	All Other Current					1.7	2.6
68.7	67.2	65.5	Total Current					63.6	68.3
21.4	21.2	18.6	Fixed Assets (net)					20.2	19.8
4.7	5.3	7.4	Intangibles (net)					4.9	5.6
5.3	6.3	8.5	All Other Non-Current					11.3	6.3
100.0	100.0	100.0	Total					100.0	100.0
			LIABILITIES						
9.9	11.9	10.9	Notes Payable-Short Term					13.3	10.2
3.1	3.4	2.3	Cur. Mat.-L.T.D.					2.7	2.6
19.4	18.0	16.3	Trade Payables					14.3	14.9
.5	.2	.1	Income Taxes Payable					.1	.2
8.7	8.3	8.0	All Other Current					10.4	9.2
41.6	41.7	37.7	Total Current					40.7	37.1
13.4	15.7	12.5	Long-Term Debt					6.7	10.8
.6	.3	.3	Deferred Taxes					.4	.5
2.9	10.0	13.8	All Other Non-Current					3.2	2.2
41.5	32.2	35.6	Net Worth					49.0	49.4
100.0	100.0	100.0	Total Liabilities & Net Worth					100.0	100.0
			INCOME DATA						
100.0	100.0	100.0	Net Sales					100.0	100.0
40.5	35.7	37.9	Gross Profit					40.3	32.1
34.8	32.2	32.1	Operating Expenses					34.9	24.8
5.7	3.5	5.8	Operating Profit					5.5	7.3
.7	1.1	.9	All Other Expenses (net)					.3	.3
5.0	2.5	4.9	Profit Before Taxes					5.2	7.0
			RATIOS						
2.9	2.5	2.7	Current					2.7	2.5
1.8	1.8	1.8						1.7	1.8
1.3	1.2	1.3						1.2	1.4
1.5	1.5	1.8	Quick					1.5	1.8
1.0	.8	1.0						.9	1.0
.7	.6	.6						.5	.7
33 11.0	29 12.4	34 10.8	Sales/Receivables					32 11.3	35 10.5
40 9.0	39 9.3	41 8.9						39 9.5	41 8.9
47 7.8	48 7.7	47 7.7						48 7.6	47 7.7
42 8.7	43 8.6	41 8.8	Cost of Sales/Inventory					49 7.5	38 9.6
60 6.1	67 5.5	63 5.8						61 6.0	64 5.7
79 4.6	91 4.0	84 4.3						84 4.4	81 4.5
22 16.4	21 17.7	19 19.1	Cost of Sales/Payables					22 16.3	23 15.6
35 10.5	35 10.6	35 10.3						36 10.1	26 13.8
51 7.2	53 6.9	50 7.2						41 8.8	45 8.1
5.7	5.6	5.6	Sales/Working Capital					5.9	4.0
9.0	9.1	8.0						11.9	8.0
23.0	28.1	22.2						20.6	20.9
7.6	13.0	12.3	EBIT/Interest					29.9	16.9
(54) 4.5	(57) 4.8	(59) 7.7						6.8	(24) 10.7
2.1	-.2	2.6						2.3	4.0
6.8	7.1	8.5	Net Profit + Depr., Dep., Amort./Cur. Mat. L/T/D						10.7
(23) 3.3	(19) 2.4	(20) 3.7							(14) 4.6
1.8	1.0	1.1							1.3
.2	.2	.2	Fixed/Worth					.2	.3
.5	.5	.5						.4	.5
1.0	1.2	1.0						1.2	.7
.6	.6	.7	Debt/Worth					.5	.6
1.3	1.3	1.6						.9	1.7
3.7	3.2	4.4						4.2	2.5
45.2	41.6	46.3	% Profit Before Taxes/Tangible Net Worth					37.5	50.9
(57) 26.5	(56) 14.8	(58) 24.3						(19) 20.0	(26) 28.8
9.4	-1.3	9.5						8.0	10.1
18.7	16.4	24.5	% Profit Before Taxes/Total Assets					17.0	25.4
7.7	6.3	9.8						8.5	10.7
3.3	-2.3	2.8						2.8	5.2
36.5	35.1	30.4	Sales/Net Fixed Assets					29.4	19.3
12.5	14.7	16.6						17.5	9.5
8.1	8.9	9.1						7.9	7.2
3.4	3.1	3.1	Sales/Total Assets					3.3	3.0
2.5	2.6	2.4						2.3	2.3
2.0	1.8	1.7						1.6	1.8
.8	.9	1.1	% Depr., Dep., Amort./Sales					1.0	1.2
(52) 1.4	(58) 1.4	(57) 1.4						(18) 1.5	(26) 1.3
2.3	2.1	2.2						2.4	1.9
1.7	1.0	1.7	% Officers', Directors' Owners' Comp/Sales						
(19) 3.1	(15) 2.8	(22) 3.2							
3.9	4.1	8.2							
3090790M	2804520M	2881152M	Net Sales ($)	2619M	10352M	11097M	48316M	348348M	2460420M
1384852M	1266703M	1388903M	Total Assets ($)	2522M	4246M	2464M	21259M	179204M	1179208M

© RMA 2010   M = $ thousand   MM = $ million
See Pages 9 through 22 for Explanation of Ratios and Data

Current Data Sorted by Assets   Comparative Historical Data

0-500M	500M-2MM	2-10MM	10-50MM	50-100MM	100-250MM	Type of Statement	4/1/05-3/31/06 ALL	4/1/06-3/31/07 ALL
		5	11	4	6	Unqualified	21	17
	2	8	12			Reviewed	10	16
	2	3				Compiled	10	7
		3				Tax Returns	1	2
3	5	11	14	4	1	Other	36	38
11 (4/1-9/30/09)			83 (10/1/09-3/31/10)					
3	9	30	37	8	7	NUMBER OF STATEMENTS	78	80
%	%	%	%	%	%	**ASSETS**	%	%
		11.0	5.2			Cash & Equivalents	9.3	8.7
		30.6	24.3			Trade Receivables (net)	27.8	25.8
		29.8	31.7			Inventory	32.3	30.2
		3.8	4.7			All Other Current	1.8	2.5
		75.1	65.9			Total Current	71.2	67.2
		17.2	17.9			Fixed Assets (net)	17.6	21.3
		4.2	12.4			Intangibles (net)	4.6	4.0
		3.5	3.8			All Other Non-Current	6.6	7.5
		100.0	100.0			Total	100.0	100.0
						LIABILITIES		
		12.0	12.3			Notes Payable-Short Term	13.1	12.7
		4.0	2.6			Cur. Mat.-L.T.D.	2.7	2.4
		21.5	16.5			Trade Payables	21.2	19.1
		.3	.3			Income Taxes Payable	.4	.2
		8.3	8.0			All Other Current	8.2	12.9
		46.0	39.7			Total Current	45.7	47.3
		9.5	10.4			Long-Term Debt	13.8	11.7
		.4	.2			Deferred Taxes	.5	.1
		3.7	4.9			All Other Non-Current	7.6	6.0
		40.3	44.8			Net Worth	32.4	34.9
		100.0	100.0			Total Liabilities & Net Worth	100.0	100.0
						INCOME DATA		
		100.0	100.0			Net Sales	100.0	100.0
		40.0	35.3			Gross Profit	38.7	39.4
		35.0	27.9			Operating Expenses	30.7	34.8
		5.0	7.3			Operating Profit	8.0	4.6
		1.1	1.3			All Other Expenses (net)	1.1	1.5
		3.9	6.1			Profit Before Taxes	6.9	3.1
						RATIOS		
		2.9	2.5				2.6	2.4
		1.5	1.7			Current	1.7	1.5
		1.2	1.3				1.2	1.1
		1.5	1.0				1.4	1.2
		.9	.8			Quick	.9	.8
		.5	.5				.5	.4
		32 11.2	32 11.2				37 9.8	30 12.1
		43 8.4	43 8.5			Sales/Receivables	45 8.2	47 7.7
		59 6.1	57 6.4				61 6.0	63 5.8
		54 6.8	61 6.0				50 7.3	53 6.9
		74 4.9	95 3.8			Cost of Sales/Inventory	85 4.3	83 4.4
		117 3.1	144 2.5				151 2.4	136 2.7
		31 11.7	25 14.7				28 13.3	26 13.8
		48 7.6	44 8.4			Cost of Sales/Payables	44 8.3	45 8.0
		73 5.0	78 4.7				73 5.0	75 4.9
		5.2	4.8				4.0	5.0
		10.6	7.1			Sales/Working Capital	7.6	8.1
		26.0	16.2				20.8	33.5
		41.1	17.8				19.0	14.0
		(27) 5.5	(35) 6.0			EBIT/Interest	(68) 5.0	(73) 3.2
		2.0	2.5				1.8	.1
			17.3				5.0	8.2
			(11) 5.0			Net Profit + Depr., Dep., Amort./Cur. Mat. L/T/D	(19) 2.6	(20) 2.9
			2.5				.8	1.0
		.1	.2				.1	.2
		.6	.5			Fixed/Worth	.4	.5
		1.2	1.2				1.1	2.0
		1.1	.9				.7	.7
		2.3	2.0			Debt/Worth	1.6	1.8
		3.7	4.8				4.2	5.8
		48.8	62.1				56.1	54.8
		(29) 22.4	(31) 36.2			% Profit Before Taxes/Tangible Net Worth	(69) 27.9	(71) 21.6
		-3.1	17.5				9.8	-1.6
		14.7	19.5				21.5	18.1
		8.1	10.5			% Profit Before Taxes/Total Assets	8.4	8.2
		-.3	3.5				2.4	-2.0
		72.8	26.0				42.0	31.7
		17.3	14.1			Sales/Net Fixed Assets	15.6	13.8
		6.9	7.4				7.8	5.8
		3.5	2.6				2.9	2.8
		2.5	1.9			Sales/Total Assets	2.1	2.1
		1.5	1.4				1.5	1.4
		.7	.8				.7	.6
		(27) 1.7	(32) 1.8			% Depr., Dep., Amort./Sales	(65) 1.4	(67) 1.8
		3.2	2.4				2.4	2.8
		1.1					1.8	1.6
		(10) 3.7				% Officers', Directors' Owners' Comp/Sales	(21) 2.8	(28) 2.5
		8.9					9.0	5.1
1084M	31426M	399092M	1678024M	910464M	1203658M	Net Sales ($)	3226220M	3131027M
679M	13354M	166160M	880678M	632436M	949681M	Total Assets ($)	1618160M	1723217M

M = $ thousand   MM = $ million
See Pages 9 through 22 for Explanation of Ratios and Data

Comparative Historical Data   ·   Current Data Sorted by Sales

	4/1/07-3/31/08 ALL	4/1/08-3/31/09 ALL	4/1/09-3/31/10 ALL		0-1MM	1-3MM	3-5MM	5-10MM	10-25MM	25MM & OVER
Type of Statement								**11 (4/1-9/30/09)**	**83 (10/1/09-3/31/10)**	
Unqualified	20	25	26				1	1	5	20
Reviewed	23	15	22			1		3	8	10
Compiled	9	9	5			1		2	1	
Tax Returns	2	4	3					1	2	
Other	36	36	38		3	4	4	2	9	16
NUMBER OF STATEMENTS	90	89	94		3	6	5	9	25	46
	%	%	%	**ASSETS**	%	%	%	%	%	%
Cash & Equivalents	8.6	7.9	7.0						9.3	4.8
Trade Receivables (net)	26.5	24.6	25.9						30.2	25.4
Inventory	29.8	30.1	30.2						30.1	29.6
All Other Current	3.3	3.1	4.3						3.3	6.1
Total Current	68.1	65.7	67.4						73.0	65.8
Fixed Assets (net)	16.2	17.4	16.3						16.8	15.0
Intangibles (net)	8.6	11.5	10.4						7.3	14.1
All Other Non-Current	7.1	5.4	5.9						2.9	5.1
Total	100.0	100.0	100.0						100.0	100.0
				LIABILITIES						
Notes Payable-Short Term	12.1	11.2	13.2						11.6	10.8
Cur. Mat.-L.T.D.	2.5	3.1	2.8						3.0	2.4
Trade Payables	18.6	16.8	21.1						16.8	22.2
Income Taxes Payable	.4	.4	.4						.3	.6
All Other Current	9.8	10.7	9.4						9.0	7.6
Total Current	43.4	42.2	46.9						40.7	43.7
Long-Term Debt	12.3	13.7	10.4						10.3	10.8
Deferred Taxes	.2	.3	.4						.2	.6
All Other Non-Current	5.1	6.9	3.6						4.5	4.3
Net Worth	39.0	36.9	38.8						44.4	40.7
Total Liabilities & Net Worth	100.0	100.0	100.0						100.0	100.0
				INCOME DATA						
Net Sales	100.0	100.0	100.0						100.0	100.0
Gross Profit	41.3	39.2	37.4						38.7	34.0
Operating Expenses	34.3	32.5	31.5						31.1	27.5
Operating Profit	7.0	6.6	5.9						7.5	6.5
All Other Expenses (net)	1.8	1.9	1.3						1.8	1.0
Profit Before Taxes	5.2	4.8	4.6						5.7	5.5
				RATIOS						
Current	2.6	2.9	2.1						2.7	2.0
	1.6	1.6	1.5						1.7	1.6
	1.1	1.1	1.1						1.3	1.2
Quick	1.5	1.7	1.2						1.6	1.3
	.8	.7	.8						.9	.8
	.5	.5	.5						.6	.5
Sales/Receivables	33 11.0	33 11.0	31 11.9						32 11.6	33 11.2
	48 7.6	45 8.1	43 8.4						44 8.4	46 7.9
	65 5.6	57 6.4	60 6.0						60 6.1	65 5.6
Cost of Sales/Inventory	64 5.7	60 6.1	55 6.6						60 6.1	55 6.7
	89 4.1	91 4.0	92 4.0						100 3.6	86 4.2
	141 2.6	134 2.7	141 2.6						127 2.9	146 2.5
Cost of Sales/Payables	31 11.7	25 14.7	32 11.4						23 16.1	28 12.9
	52 7.0	48 7.5	50 7.3						44 8.3	49 7.5
	79 4.6	73 5.0	77 4.7						60 6.1	81 4.5
Sales/Working Capital	4.6	4.4	5.2						5.2	4.6
	7.9	8.3	10.1						7.7	10.2
	29.9	31.6	29.9						15.3	18.0
EBIT/Interest	15.4	15.6	17.5						29.2	17.7
	(83) 5.3	(84) 3.9	(87) 5.2						(23) 6.6	(44) 5.4
	1.6	1.4	1.5						4.9	1.7
Net Profit + Depr., Dep., Amort./Cur. Mat. L/T/D	8.1	21.4	13.3							12.3
	(28) 3.2	(26) 5.7	(21) 5.9							(15) 5.7
	.4	-.1	2.2							2.5
Fixed/Worth	.2	.3	.2						.1	.2
	.4	.6	.7						.6	.6
	1.4	2.4	1.5						1.1	2.1
Debt/Worth	.7	.7	1.1						.8	.9
	2.1	2.2	2.3						2.0	2.3
	7.4	14.0	4.8						3.9	16.4
% Profit Before Taxes/Tangible Net Worth	54.5	55.4	53.8						53.8	62.8
	(76) 24.2	(71) 17.8	(79) 28.2						(23) 41.4	(37) 29.7
	7.3	6.9	8.0						18.6	12.2
% Profit Before Taxes/Total Assets	19.9	15.4	14.6						26.0	15.1
	6.3	6.8	8.1						12.1	8.9
	1.2	1.2	1.1						3.9	2.7
Sales/Net Fixed Assets	45.8	23.5	36.3						64.3	33.4
	16.1	14.0	15.4						14.7	15.9
	7.8	7.8	7.6						7.4	8.3
Sales/Total Assets	2.8	2.6	2.6						3.3	2.6
	2.0	2.1	2.0						2.0	1.9
	1.3	1.3	1.4						1.5	1.4
% Depr., Dep., Amort./Sales	.5	1.1	.8						.7	.8
	(79) 1.4	(78) 1.7	(77) 1.8						(21) 1.7	(37) 1.8
	2.2	2.6	3.0						3.1	2.5
% Officers', Directors' Owners' Comp/Sales	1.6	1.6	1.3							
	(24) 3.5	(20) 2.5	(25) 3.2							
	7.3	5.1	5.3							
Net Sales ($)	4615734M	4733329M	4223748M		1084M	15304M	21327M	70940M	400414M	3714679M
Total Assets ($)	2856815M	3116788M	2642988M		679M	8474M	13718M	41003M	225170M	2353944M

Current Data Sorted by Assets | **Comparative Historical Data**

Type of Statement

0-500M	500M-2MM	2-10MM	10-50MM	50-100MM	100-250MM	Type of Statement	4/1/05-3/31/06 ALL	4/1/06-3/31/07 ALL
		1	6		1	Unqualified	7	8
	2	5	3			Reviewed	7	6
	2	1				Compiled	2	6
1	6	5				Tax Returns		1
1	1	7	6	1	1	Other	8	14
	10 (4/1-9/30/09)		40 (10/1/09-3/31/10)				8	14
2	11	19	15	1	2	NUMBER OF STATEMENTS	24	35

Data

0-500M	500M-2MM	2-10MM	10-50MM	50-100MM	100-250MM		4/1/05-3/31/06 ALL	4/1/06-3/31/07 ALL
%	%	%	%	%	%		%	%
						ASSETS		
	14.8	11.5	4.9			Cash & Equivalents	5.2	6.7
	26.2	32.7	26.2			Trade Receivables (net)	28.0	27.9
	23.5	25.7	30.3			Inventory	33.8	29.8
	.4	1.2	3.3			All Other Current	2.6	3.1
	65.0	71.2	64.6			Total Current	69.7	67.5
	17.4	21.8	22.0			Fixed Assets (net)	17.2	21.0
	2.2	2.6	8.8			Intangibles (net)	5.0	9.0
	15.3	4.5	4.6			All Other Non-Current	8.1	2.6
	100.0	100.0	100.0			Total	100.0	100.0
						LIABILITIES		
	5.0	10.0	12.9			Notes Payable-Short Term	15.1	10.2
	.9	1.7	1.8			Cur. Mat.-L.T.D.	2.3	2.7
	23.7	18.4	14.3			Trade Payables	23.1	16.9
	.0	.1	.2			Income Taxes Payable	.3	.5
	10.3	6.5	8.7			All Other Current	8.3	11.7
	40.0	36.7	37.9			Total Current	49.1	42.0
	15.2	16.5	4.9			Long-Term Debt	6.9	16.1
	.4	1.9	1.6			Deferred Taxes	.3	.7
	4.3	5.0	.7			All Other Non-Current	7.5	6.4
	40.1	39.9	54.9			Net Worth	36.1	34.7
	100.0	100.0	100.0			Total Liabilities & Net Worth	100.0	100.0
						INCOME DATA		
	100.0	100.0	100.0			Net Sales	100.0	100.0
	44.3	36.1	30.1			Gross Profit	31.0	35.8
	40.8	28.0	26.2			Operating Expenses	26.8	29.9
	3.5	8.1	4.0			Operating Profit	4.2	5.9
	.6	.8	-1.1			All Other Expenses (net)	.7	.8
	2.9	7.3	5.1			Profit Before Taxes	3.6	5.1
						RATIOS		
	5.2	4.4	2.4			Current	1.9	2.3
	1.2	2.2	1.7				1.5	1.7
	1.0	1.5	1.2				1.2	1.1
	2.7	2.1	1.2			Quick	.9	1.0
	.8	1.1	.8				.7	.8
	.4	.9	.5				.6	
13	28.2	35 10.5	43 8.5			Sales/Receivables	35 10.5	39 9.4
27	13.7	40 9.0	48 7.7				46 8.0	47 7.8
41	8.9	53 6.9	58 6.3				51 7.1	54 6.7
20	18.7	21 17.4	56 6.5			Cost of Sales/Inventory	56 6.5	49 7.5
37	10.0	48 7.6	81 4.5				82 4.5	81 4.5
47	7.8	106 3.4	104 3.5				114 3.2	114 3.2
23	15.6	19 19.2	19 19.1			Cost of Sales/Payables	24 15.1	27 13.4
43	8.5	31 11.7	34 10.9				33 11.1	36 10.2
56	6.5	52 7.1	52 7.1				70 5.2	51 7.2
	4.8	3.8	5.5			Sales/Working Capital	7.7	5.5
	38.0	6.2	7.1				10.4	8.4
	-304.1	15.0	17.0				55.9	35.0
		17.0	39.2			EBIT/Interest	16.1	13.8
	(18)	9.7	9.5				(21) 3.3	(31) 8.8
		3.9	3.8				1.0	1.4
						Net Profit + Depr., Dep.,		22.4
						Amort./Cur. Mat. L/T/D	(13)	5.9
								1.6
	.1	.3	.3			Fixed/Worth	.3	.4
	.8	.6	.5				.6	.7
	1.1	1.3	.9				1.1	5.7
	.3	.7	.5			Debt/Worth	1.0	1.0
	2.3	1.9	.8				1.9	1.7
	2.9	4.5	3.2				4.3	23.0
		81.1	27.5			% Profit Before Taxes/Tangible	45.4	49.9
	(17)	40.8	17.2			Net Worth	(22) 13.6	(27) 31.5
		13.7	8.1				.3	3.0
	15.4	24.0	14.3			% Profit Before Taxes/Total	15.4	20.2
	7.4	14.0	10.1			Assets	5.8	12.1
	-9.1	4.2	3.8				.4	.6
	30.4	42.9	26.2			Sales/Net Fixed Assets	26.9	24.7
	23.8	15.4	10.0				13.6	14.1
	17.6	6.2	6.4				8.1	7.9
	4.7	3.2	2.4			Sales/Total Assets	2.8	3.0
	3.7	2.4	2.0				2.2	2.2
	1.9	1.7	1.7				1.9	1.6
		.6	1.3			% Depr., Dep., Amort./Sales	1.2	1.0
	(17)	1.2	(13) 2.4				(21) 1.6	(32) 1.6
		3.5	4.0				2.1	2.2
						% Officers', Directors'		1.1
						Owners' Comp/Sales	(11)	3.0
								8.5
612M	50448M	261815M	693153M	47366M	624567M	Net Sales ($)	1133205M	1307642M
138M	14947M	96972M	335815M	76084M	342839M	Total Assets ($)	596891M	705280M

M = $ thousand   MM = $ million
See Pages 9 through 22 for Explanation of Ratios and Data

Comparative Historical Data

Current Data Sorted by Sales

			Type of Statement	0-1MM	1-3MM	3-5MM	5-10MM	10-25MM	25MM & OVER
8	12	8	Unqualified					3	5
10	14	10	Reviewed		1	1	2	4	2
5		3	Compiled		1	1	1	2	1
3	9	12	Tax Returns	2		3	4		
14	16	17	Other	1	1		2	4	9
	4/1/07-	4/1/08-	4/1/09-			10 (4/1-9/30/09)			40 (10/1/09-3/31/10)
	3/31/08	3/31/09	3/31/10						
	ALL	ALL	ALL						
40	**51**	**50**	**NUMBER OF STATEMENTS**	**3**	**3**	**5**	**9**	**13**	**17**
%	%	%	**ASSETS**	%	%	%	%	%	%
5.9	10.7	10.8	Cash & Equivalents					6.1	4.9
27.2	25.5	27.5	Trade Receivables (net)					35.1	27.4
33.2	30.2	27.5	Inventory					24.8	28.5
2.5	3.2	1.9	All Other Current					1.7	2.7
68.8	69.6	67.7	Total Current					67.7	63.5
20.3	19.3	19.8	Fixed Assets (net)					25.0	20.3
7.0	7.0	4.6	Intangibles (net)					3.1	8.0
3.9	4.2	7.9	All Other Non-Current					4.2	8.2
100.0	100.0	100.0	Total					100.0	100.0
			LIABILITIES						
10.8	11.1	9.1	Notes Payable-Short Term					12.8	10.1
2.8	3.1	1.9	Cur. Mat.-L.T.D.					2.4	1.6
16.4	16.8	18.2	Trade Payables					18.3	16.9
.4	.1	.2	Income Taxes Payable					.1	.4
13.8	11.3	8.8	All Other Current					10.0	8.8
44.2	42.4	38.1	Total Current					43.6	37.8
8.9	13.7	12.2	Long-Term Debt					18.3	5.2
.3	.3	1.4	Deferred Taxes					1.4	1.0
5.7	5.5	3.7	All Other Non-Current					2.8	2.0
40.9	38.1	44.7	Net Worth					33.9	54.0
100.0	100.0	100.0	Total Liabilities & Net Worth					100.0	100.0
			INCOME DATA						
100.0	100.0	100.0	Net Sales					100.0	100.0
31.6	31.9	36.7	Gross Profit					34.6	29.5
26.5	27.2	29.7	Operating Expenses					30.1	24.0
5.1	4.6	7.0	Operating Profit					4.4	5.5
.9	1.0	.4	All Other Expenses (net)					.0	.2
4.2	3.7	6.6	Profit Before Taxes					4.4	5.3
			RATIOS						
2.5	2.7	2.9	Current					2.8	2.3
1.7	1.7	1.7						1.9	1.6
1.1	1.2	1.2						1.1	1.4
1.2	1.7	1.5	Quick					1.4	1.2
.7	.9	.9						.9	.9
.6	.5	.7						.7	.6
37 9.9	34 10.9	32 11.4	Sales/Receivables					39 9.3	34 10.7
43 8.6	41 8.9	42 8.8						52 7.1	47 7.8
49 7.4	49 7.4	52 7.0						64 5.7	50 7.2
56 6.5	47 7.8	34 10.8	Cost of Sales/Inventory					19 18.9	53 6.9
76 4.8	65 5.6	59 6.1						48 7.6	65 5.6
113 3.2	88 4.1	107 3.4						110 3.3	86 4.2
23 16.0	17 21.5	20 18.5	Cost of Sales/Payables					26 13.8	18 20.1
35 10.4	32 11.3	33 11.0						35 10.4	33 11.0
50 7.3	53 6.9	55 6.6						67 5.4	52 7.1
5.4	5.4	4.9	Sales/Working Capital					4.5	6.0
8.5	8.3	7.4						6.3	8.0
39.8	22.4	22.3						79.4	16.0
21.9	13.4	21.5	EBIT/Interest					17.1	37.8
(35) 7.2	(46) 3.8	(47) 7.7						5.8	9.5
2.6	.9	3.0						3.1	4.2
9.8	21.6	15.4	Net Profit + Depr., Dep.,						
(13) 3.6	(16) 4.1	(15) 3.7	Amort./Cur. Mat. L/T/D						
1.6	1.8	1.6							
.3	.3	.2	Fixed/Worth					.3	.3
.5	.5	.5						.7	.4
1.2	1.3	1.0						5.7	.8
.7	.8	.5	Debt/Worth					.8	.5
1.7	2.4	1.2						1.9	.9
6.2	4.9	3.5						11.1	2.9
48.2	36.6	69.4	% Profit Before Taxes/Tangible					87.9	67.3
(36) 20.1	(46) 22.2	(46) 25.0	Net Worth					(11) 28.0	18.0
7.4	.1	5.9						3.1	11.0
15.3	16.4	19.8	% Profit Before Taxes/Total					18.1	18.7
8.1	4.4	10.5	Assets					9.2	10.1
3.4	-.2	3.7						3.0	4.1
23.4	35.1	33.1	Sales/Net Fixed Assets					24.6	26.9
14.5	14.6	16.9						10.4	10.9
7.5	7.0	7.2						5.7	6.9
2.8	2.9	3.4	Sales/Total Assets					3.1	2.6
2.3	2.4	2.2						2.2	2.1
1.7	1.7	1.8						1.7	1.9
1.0	1.1	.9	% Depr., Dep., Amort./Sales					1.0	.7
(37) 1.6	(42) 1.5	(38) 1.4						(12) 1.6	(13) 1.8
2.2	2.7	3.5						4.2	2.5
1.0		1.6	% Officers', Directors'						
(10) 2.3		(16) 4.9	Owners' Comp/Sales						
3.0		12.2							
1707998M	1984967M	1677961M	Net Sales ($)	1584M	6551M	17770M	61560M	220850M	1369646M
905877M	1184116M	866795M	Total Assets ($)	1453M	6443M	6623M	21949M	105619M	724708M

M = $ thousand   MM = $ million
See Pages 9 through 22 for Explanation of Ratios and Data

Current Data Sorted by Assets | **Comparative Historical Data**

0-500M	500M-2MM	2-10MM	10-50MM	50-100MM	100-250MM		4/1/05-3/31/06 ALL	4/1/06-3/31/07 ALL
						Type of Statement		
		2	3		2	Unqualified	5	5
		1	3			Reviewed	3	4
			2			Compiled	5	3
	1	3				Tax Returns		
	1	5	6	1		Other	16	12
	4 (4/1-9/30/09)		26 (10/1/09-3/31/10)					
	2	11	14	1	2	**NUMBER OF STATEMENTS**	29	24
%	%	%	%	%	%	**ASSETS**	%	%
DATA NOT AVAILABLE		10.8	1.8			Cash & Equivalents	4.1	3.4
		23.4	22.1			Trade Receivables (net)	26.8	24.6
		20.6	17.6			Inventory	25.9	25.9
		.7	3.5			All Other Current	1.9	2.7
		55.6	45.0			Total Current	58.6	56.6
		35.4	44.3			Fixed Assets (net)	31.8	35.1
		7.2	4.4			Intangibles (net)	4.4	4.0
		1.8	6.3			All Other Non-Current	5.2	4.3
		100.0	100.0			Total	100.0	100.0
						LIABILITIES		
		7.9	12.4			Notes Payable-Short Term	15.2	13.6
		6.0	7.3			Cur. Mat.-L.T.D.	2.7	2.6
		15.8	14.1			Trade Payables	15.7	17.0
		1.6	.0			Income Taxes Payable	.1	.0
		2.5	5.9			All Other Current	6.6	5.5
		33.9	39.8			Total Current	40.2	38.7
		23.8	16.6			Long-Term Debt	12.7	18.2
		.3	.5			Deferred Taxes	.4	.2
		5.4	2.1			All Other Non-Current	4.1	6.0
		36.7	41.0			Net Worth	42.7	36.9
		100.0	100.0			Total Liabilties & Net Worth	100.0	100.0
						INCOME DATA		
		100.0	100.0			Net Sales	100.0	100.0
		31.9	17.7			Gross Profit	25.3	27.0
		24.3	16.5			Operating Expenses	20.0	22.9
		7.6	1.2			Operating Profit	5.3	4.1
		1.9	1.0			All Other Expenses (net)	1.6	1.5
		5.7	.2			Profit Before Taxes	3.7	2.6
						RATIOS		
		3.1	2.1				2.1	2.2
		1.7	.9			Current	1.4	1.7
		.9	.7				1.1	1.2
		2.6	1.2				1.2	1.3
		.8	.5			Quick	.7	1.0
		.4	.4				.5	.5
		34 10.8	**37** 9.9				**33** 11.0	**36** 10.1
		53 6.8	**54** 6.8			Sales/Receivables	**42** 8.7	**42** 8.7
		63 5.8	**63** 5.8				**49** 7.5	**48** 7.6
		37 9.9	**21** 17.1				**42** 8.7	**37** 9.9
		49 7.5	**39** 9.4			Cost of Sales/Inventory	**55** 6.6	**52** 7.0
		87 4.2	**76** 4.8				**77** 4.8	**70** 5.2
		21 17.2	**26** 14.0				**22** 16.7	**24** 15.4
		29 12.7	**42** 8.7			Cost of Sales/Payables	**29** 12.5	**31** 11.7
		73 5.0	**59** 6.1				**45** 8.1	**52** 7.0
		4.4	9.5				6.5	6.7
		5.9	-39.4			Sales/Working Capital	14.4	10.3
		-38.0	-8.9				34.9	35.8
			5.5				11.9	11.5
			.9			EBIT/Interest	(26) 2.3	(23) 3.9
			-.4				1.4	1.2
						Net Profit + Depr., Dep., Amort./Cur. Mat. L/T/D		
		.4	.6				.5	.7
		1.1	1.0			Fixed/Worth	.9	1.4
		-4.9	2.3				1.5	2.8
		.6	.9				.8	1.1
		2.0	1.8			Debt/Worth	1.4	2.5
		-11.4	3.5				3.9	5.1
			21.5				41.4	43.3
			-.1			% Profit Before Taxes/Tangible Net Worth	(28) 19.9	27.5
			-11.5				6.1	3.2
		24.6	7.9				14.1	11.4
		2.9	-.5			% Profit Before Taxes/Total Assets	5.3	7.3
		-2.6	-3.9				1.7	.3
		29.5	7.8				16.6	12.5
		6.9	5.0			Sales/Net Fixed Assets	6.3	6.4
		1.9	1.8				4.8	3.7
		2.4	2.3				2.8	3.3
		2.0	1.3			Sales/Total Assets	2.2	2.1
		1.1	1.1				1.7	1.7
		1.6	1.7				1.2	1.9
		(10) 4.0	(13) 6.3			% Depr., Dep., Amort./Sales	(27) 2.5	(20) 2.8
		7.7	11.0				3.8	3.9
						% Officers', Directors' Owners' Comp/Sales		
	5164M	112335M	592255M	141212M	484350M	Net Sales ($)	1556984M	1844283M
	2539M	58850M	360086M	89042M	299332M	Total Assets ($)	785445M	908471M

M = $ thousand MM = $ million

See Pages 9 through 22 for Explanation of Ratios and Data

Comparative Historical Data   Current Data Sorted by Sales

	4/1/07-3/31/08 ALL	4/1/08-3/31/09 ALL	4/1/09-3/31/10 ALL	Type of Statement	0-1MM	1-3MM	3-5MM	5-10MM	10-25MM	25MM & OVE
	7	6	7	Unqualified				2	2	5
	2	3	4	Reviewed					4	
	3	4	2	Compiled					2	
	5	5	4	Tax Returns					1	
	10	11	13	Other	1	2	1	2	1	6
						4 (4/1-9/30/09)			26 (10/1/09-3/31/10)	
	22	29	30	NUMBER OF STATEMENTS	1	2	1	4	11	11
	%	%	%	ASSETS	%	%	%	%	%	%
	5.3	7.5	6.6	Cash & Equivalents					6.5	3.5
	29.7	24.4	24.2	Trade Receivables (net)					27.3	23.9
	17.1	22.2	18.1	Inventory					23.3	16.8
	4.0	6.2	2.0	All Other Current					.5	4.3
	56.1	60.3	50.9	Total Current					57.5	48.5
	34.0	30.6	39.7	Fixed Assets (net)					33.4	42.6
	2.4	5.4	5.5	Intangibles (net)					3.5	4.4
	7.5	3.8	3.9	All Other Non-Current					5.6	4.4
	100.0	100.0	100.0	Total					100.0	100.0
				LIABILITIES						
	13.0	10.1	9.1	Notes Payable-Short Term					12.6	6.9
	1.6	4.6	6.3	Cur. Mat.-L.T.D.					7.7	4.7
	14.9	23.8	15.3	Trade Payables					19.6	15.1
	.1	.1	.6	Income Taxes Payable					.0	.0
	8.8	7.5	4.8	All Other Current					2.9	7.1
	38.4	46.1	36.1	Total Current					42.7	33.8
	10.9	20.4	19.7	Long-Term Debt					10.9	22.1
	.1	.1	.3	Deferred Taxes					.1	.6
	6.7	8.2	3.5	All Other Non-Current					.8	2.7
	43.9	25.2	40.4	Net Worth					45.6	40.9
	100.0	100.0	100.0	Total Liabilties & Net Worth					100.0	100.0
				INCOME DATA						
	100.0	100.0	100.0	Net Sales					100.0	100.0
	24.8	30.3	25.5	Gross Profit					21.2	17.4
	18.7	25.9	21.4	Operating Expenses					20.6	13.8
	6.2	4.3	4.2	Operating Profit					.6	3.5
	1.5	1.4	1.3	All Other Expenses (net)					1.2	1.2
	4.7	3.0	2.9	Profit Before Taxes					-.6	2.4
				RATIOS						
	2.3	2.2	2.3						2.7	2.1
	1.7	1.9	1.4	Current					1.0	1.7
	1.4	1.2	.8						.7	.9
	1.6	1.6	1.4						1.7	1.3
	1.1	.7	.7	Quick					.7	.8
	.9	.4	.4						.4	.5
	31 11.8	26 14.3	37 9.9						45 8.1	35 10.3
	45 8.2	34 10.9	54 6.8	Sales/Receivables					54 6.7	50 7.3
	69 5.3	45 8.1	64 5.7						64 5.7	62 5.9
	10 36.2	33 11.1	33 11.2						36 10.3	15 23.8
	40 9.2	43 8.5	46 8.0	Cost of Sales/Inventory					49 7.5	33 11.0
	54 6.8	65 5.6	76 4.8						87 4.2	61 6.0
	17 22.0	19 18.9	26 14.2						29 12.7	26 14.1
	26 14.2	31 11.7	42 8.7	Cost of Sales/Payables					54 6.7	43 8.5
	41 8.9	43 8.5	61 5.9						67 5.4	55 6.6
	6.7	6.3	5.7						5.3	6.4
	9.0	10.5	15.6	Sales/Working Capital					-372.0	14.8
	26.1	32.2	-13.4						-9.2	-21.7
	15.1	5.4	8.0						4.9	10.8
	(18) 4.5	(23) 3.8	(28) 1.7	EBIT/Interest				(10)	.1	4.9
	1.2	1.4	-.2						-2.9	.1
				Net Profit + Depr., Dep., Amort./Cur. Mat. L/T/D						
	.6	.3	.6						.4	.6
	.7	1.1	1.0	Fixed/Worth					.7	.9
	2.1	2.4	2.8						2.7	2.2
	.3	1.0	.7						.4	.9
	1.3	1.6	1.7	Debt/Worth					1.7	1.4
	4.3	8.2	3.8						3.5	3.6
	32.8	31.5	20.9						14.2	23.0
	(20) 24.2	(26) 17.4	(27) 5.2	% Profit Before Taxes/Tangible Net Worth				(10)	-.4	19.2
	4.4	3.1	-10.7						-11.5	-10.7
	12.0	11.1	9.1						3.7	9.5
	9.4	7.4	3.1	% Profit Before Taxes/Total Assets					-2.4	7.5
	1.1	1.4	-3.1						-3.9	-3.2
	18.8	18.0	9.1						12.3	8.2
	7.5	11.4	4.7	Sales/Net Fixed Assets					6.7	5.1
	3.9	4.4	1.9						2.2	1.9
	3.2	3.3	2.3						2.4	2.4
	2.1	2.5	1.5	Sales/Total Assets					2.0	1.6
	1.5	1.8	1.1						1.2	1.2
	1.3	1.5	1.9						1.8	
	(19) 1.7	(26) 2.2	(25) 4.5	% Depr., Dep., Amort./Sales					4.5	
	3.5	3.4	8.1						7.3	
		2.6	1.4							
		(13) 5.9	(12) 3.8	% Officers', Directors' Owners' Comp/Sales						
		13.6	6.6							
	2091969M	1832262M	1335316M	Net Sales ($)	618M	4970M	4546M	29040M	195093M	1101049M
	998813M	831723M	809849M	Total Assets ($)	1245M	5023M	1294M	21781M	132425M	648081M

M = $ thousand   MM = $ million
See Pages 9 through 22 for Explanation of Ratios and Data

Current Data Sorted by Assets | Comparative Historical Data

Type of Statement

Type of Statement	0-500M	500M-2MM	2-10MM	10-50MM	50-100MM	100-250MM	4/1/05-3/31/06 ALL	4/1/06-3/31/07 ALL
Unqualified	1		10	24	4	9	42	50
Reviewed		7	27	9			24	38
Compiled	1	9	7	2			18	19
Tax Returns	6	10	4	1			17	22
Other	2	15	32	25	10	11	76	91
		43 (4/1-9/30/09)		183 (10/1/09-3/31/10)			4/1/05-3/31/06 ALL	4/1/06-3/31/07 ALL
NUMBER OF STATEMENTS	10	41	80	61	14	20	177	220

	0-500M	500M-2MM	2-10MM	10-50MM	50-100MM	100-250MM		4/1/05-3/31/06	4/1/06-3/31/07
	%	%	%	%	%	%	**ASSETS**	%	%
	16.3	10.0	9.7	9.4	6.9	5.7	Cash & Equivalents	8.3	8.0
	22.9	33.8	29.3	24.5	18.1	14.1	Trade Receivables (net)	31.3	28.7
	6.5	24.5	25.1	25.1	16.6	21.6	Inventory	22.6	24.0
	9.3	2.7	3.6	2.9	4.7	3.1	All Other Current	1.9	2.8
	54.9	70.9	67.8	62.0	46.3	44.6	Total Current	64.1	63.4
	32.0	21.2	23.0	24.2	38.7	38.8	Fixed Assets (net)	23.2	23.3
	.8	2.6	4.8	7.6	10.6	7.8	Intangibles (net)	6.1	7.5
	12.3	5.3	4.4	6.2	4.3	8.8	All Other Non-Current	6.6	5.7
	100.0	100.0	100.0	100.0	100.0	100.0	Total	100.0	100.0
							LIABILITIES		
	24.4	18.4	10.8	8.4	5.1	.8	Notes Payable-Short Term	9.8	11.9
	7.1	3.2	4.7	2.6	3.9	3.0	Cur. Mat.-L.T.D.	2.7	3.3
	13.0	19.7	18.6	14.0	8.7	8.0	Trade Payables	21.3	18.0
	.0	.1	.3	.1	.3	.3	Income Taxes Payable	.2	.3
	8.0	18.3	9.3	6.9	8.9	12.3	All Other Current	9.4	10.2
	52.5	59.8	43.7	32.1	26.7	24.3	Total Current	43.4	43.6
	50.1	13.2	11.1	13.0	19.6	20.3	Long-Term Debt	14.2	15.5
	.0	.0	.8	.5	.6	2.4	Deferred Taxes	.6	.7
	5.0	4.4	4.9	8.9	7.6	6.5	All Other Non-Current	7.1	6.8
	-7.6	22.7	39.4	45.5	45.4	46.5	Net Worth	34.7	33.5
	100.0	100.0	100.0	100.0	100.0	100.0	Total Liabilities & Net Worth	100.0	100.0
							INCOME DATA		
	100.0	100.0	100.0	100.0	100.0	100.0	Net Sales	100.0	100.0
	37.2	44.5	35.0	28.3	23.8	23.0	Gross Profit	32.8	33.0
	39.1	40.4	29.5	21.3	15.6	17.3	Operating Expenses	27.5	27.6
	-1.9	4.1	5.5	7.0	8.1	5.7	Operating Profit	5.3	5.4
	1.0	.9	.9	1.4	1.2	1.6	All Other Expenses (net)	1.2	1.2
	-2.9	3.2	4.6	5.6	6.9	4.1	Profit Before Taxes	4.0	4.2
							RATIOS		
	3.9	2.5	2.3	3.5	2.2	3.1	Current	2.3	2.4
	1.5	1.5	1.6	1.8	1.7	1.8		1.5	1.6
	.3	.9	1.3	1.3	1.5	1.3		1.1	1.1
	3.9	1.4	1.5	1.8	1.2	1.3	Quick	1.4	1.4
	1.2	.7	.9	.9	1.0	1.0		.9	.9
	.3	.4	.5	.6	.7	.7		.5	.6
	0 UND	30 12.2	29 12.8	32 11.5	32 11.5	16 22.9	Sales/Receivables	33 11.1	34 10.8
	11 32.3	40 9.0	44 8.3	42 8.6	48 7.6	41 9.0		46 7.9	46 8.0
	26 14.3	59 6.2	55 6.7	53 6.8	55 6.7	60 6.1		57 6.4	60 6.1
	0 UND	14 26.3	34 10.9	36 10.3	38 9.7	34 10.7	Cost of Sales/Inventory	26 14.2	32 11.4
	0 UND	52 7.0	62 5.9	64 5.7	47 7.7	49 7.5		50 7.3	55 6.6
	7 51.4	105 3.5	92 3.9	90 4.1	96 3.8	125 2.9		85 4.3	98 3.7
	0 UND	23 15.9	21 17.4	20 18.4	18 20.2	10 36.7	Cost of Sales/Payables	26 14.1	23 15.9
	19 19.6	41 8.8	32 11.3	28 13.0	29 12.4	25 14.7		39 9.3	39 9.3
	32 11.5	65 5.6	59 6.2	45 8.0	40 9.2	42 8.6		60 6.1	62 5.9
	4.6	7.0	5.3	4.2	5.4	4.5	Sales/Working Capital	6.4	5.5
	34.6	20.9	11.1	8.2	8.2	6.8		12.1	10.5
	-13.5	-17.3	22.4	15.8	13.7	15.5		62.4	64.1
		9.7	21.3	24.9	10.4	9.4	EBIT/Interest	13.5	10.0
		(34) 3.4	(72) 6.1	(54) 5.5	(13) 6.0	(18) 3.8		(157) 4.3	(194) 3.9
		.1	1.6	.9	3.8	1.3		1.6	1.6
			10.4	63.2			Net Profit + Depr., Dep., Amort./Cur. Mat. L/T/D	9.3	8.4
			(20) 3.2	(19) 13.9				(48) 2.5	(68) 3.5
			1.1	1.6				1.2	1.1
	.3	.2	.2	.2	.7	.4	Fixed/Worth	.3	.2
	NM	.7	.5	.6	1.1	.8		.6	.7
	-.3	-7.8	1.1	1.5	1.8	2.1		2.1	3.2
	.5	.5	.9	.5	.9	.6	Debt/Worth	.9	.9
	NM	2.7	1.5	1.5	1.3	1.6		2.4	2.0
	-2.8	-39.0	3.0	3.3	2.0	2.5		7.6	10.1
		61.5	53.2	71.9	40.4	27.9	% Profit Before Taxes/Tangible Net Worth	54.6	54.4
		(29) 29.3	(75) 25.2	(51) 31.3	(12) 20.3	(18) 13.9		(151) 27.7	(182) 26.9
		3.0	5.5	10.0	9.3	.6		10.0	6.4
	27.8	20.8	25.4	22.1	13.7	10.7	% Profit Before Taxes/Total Assets	17.0	15.6
	1.7	6.3	9.1	9.6	9.1	4.9		7.0	7.0
	-43.8	-.8	1.6	.8	4.2	.6		2.2	1.8
	UND	59.8	34.6	23.8	6.9	9.1	Sales/Net Fixed Assets	34.8	38.7
	19.0	22.1	14.1	9.3	3.9	3.6		11.7	11.4
	7.3	7.4	6.3	3.9	2.8	2.0		5.9	5.4
	5.3	3.7	3.3	2.4	1.6	1.6	Sales/Total Assets	3.3	3.1
	3.5	2.7	2.4	1.9	1.4	1.1		2.3	2.1
	2.7	1.9	1.6	1.3	1.1	1.0		1.4	1.4
		.4	.7	1.0	2.7	1.3	% Depr., Dep., Amort./Sales	.8	.8
		(34) 1.3	(67) 1.5	(54) 1.9	(13) 3.9	(12) 3.7		(143) 1.7	(176) 1.6
		3.2	2.7	4.1	5.1	4.1		3.5	4.1
		3.8	1.6				% Officers', Directors' Owners' Comp/Sales	2.3	2.0
		(25) 6.8	(20) 3.2					(46) 4.4	(55) 3.4
		13.0	5.5					8.4	6.4
	11239M	138092M	1784126M	3096803M	1552891M	4163606M	Net Sales ($)	7728618M	9519079M
	2868M	48608M	421559M	1486110M	1116132M	3102120M	Total Assets ($)	3991558M	5509255M

© RMA 2010

M = $ thousand   MM = $ million
See Pages 9 through 22 for Explanation of Ratios and Data

Comparative Historical Data / Current Data Sorted by Sales

			Type of Statement						
41	41	48	Unqualified	1	1		2	14	30
40	43	43	Reviewed		4	5	10	15	9
21	18	19	Compiled	1	3	4	6	3	2
17	23	21	Tax Returns	3	7	5	4	1	1
84	94	95	Other	3	12	6	9	22	43
4/1/07-3/31/08	4/1/08-3/31/09	4/1/09-3/31/10			43 (4/1-9/30/09)		183 (10/1/09-3/31/10)		
ALL	ALL	ALL		0-1MM	1-3MM	3-5MM	5-10MM	10-25MM	25MM & OVER
203	219	226	**NUMBER OF STATEMENTS**	8	27	20	31	55	85
%	%	%	**ASSETS**	%	%	%	%	%	%
7.7	7.6	9.4	Cash & Equivalents		12.6	9.6	8.4	7.4	10.2
28.4	25.9	26.5	Trade Receivables (net)		19.9	34.6	29.7	27.6	24.6
25.8	26.1	23.3	Inventory		21.5	20.5	25.1	28.4	21.5
3.4	2.7	3.5	All Other Current		1.8	3.8	3.3	3.3	3.5
65.2	62.2	62.8	Total Current		55.8	68.4	66.5	66.7	59.8
23.2	23.1	25.8	Fixed Assets (net)		34.2	21.8	24.7	21.4	28.3
6.7	7.5	5.6	Intangibles (net)		3.8	4.9	2.9	6.3	6.8
4.9	7.2	5.8	All Other Non-Current		6.2	4.8	5.9	5.7	5.1
100.0	100.0	100.0	Total		100.0	100.0	100.0	100.0	100.0
			LIABILITIES						
11.7	10.7	10.9	Notes Payable-Short Term		13.7	15.1	14.8	12.6	4.4
3.5	3.8	3.8	Cur. Mat.-L.T.D.		4.1	4.2	3.7	4.3	2.8
18.3	16.2	15.8	Trade Payables		14.5	24.1	18.6	16.9	13.2
.4	.2	.2	Income Taxes Payable		.0	.1	.1	.3	.2
11.4	10.3	10.5	All Other Current		24.0	3.5	7.4	7.5	10.0
45.3	41.3	41.1	Total Current		56.2	47.0	44.6	41.6	30.7
16.3	14.6	15.1	Long-Term Debt		29.9	11.9	8.1	10.3	14.0
.7	.5	.7	Deferred Taxes		.2	.0	1.2	.6	.9
5.9	5.4	6.2	All Other Non-Current		8.3	.0	6.0	5.9	7.8
31.8	38.1	36.9	Net Worth		5.4	41.1	40.1	41.6	46.7
100.0	100.0	100.0	Total Liabilities & Net Worth		100.0	100.0	100.0	100.0	100.0
			INCOME DATA						
100.0	100.0	100.0	Net Sales		100.0	100.0	100.0	100.0	100.0
33.0	32.7	33.3	Gross Profit		43.8	38.3	40.0	35.5	24.0
27.0	26.2	27.7	Operating Expenses		40.5	33.6	38.4	28.4	16.8
5.9	6.4	5.5	Operating Profit		3.4	4.7	1.6	7.1	7.1
1.8	1.1	1.1	All Other Expenses (net)		2.6	.9	.4	1.2	.9
4.1	5.3	4.4	Profit Before Taxes		.7	3.8	1.2	5.9	6.2
			RATIOS						
2.4	2.3	2.7	Current		3.0	2.7	2.5	2.3	3.0
1.5	1.5	1.7			1.3	1.8	1.4	1.6	1.8
1.0	1.1	1.2			.5	1.0	1.2	1.3	1.4
1.3	1.3	1.6	Quick		1.4	2.1	1.4	1.5	1.7
.8	.8	.9			.6	1.1	.9	.8	1.1
.5	.5	.6			.3	.5	.5	.6	.7
32 11.3	26 13.8	29 12.7	Sales/Receivables	18 19.8	37 9.9	31 11.7	34 10.8	28 12.8	
42 8.7	39 9.4	42 8.7		33 11.0	42 8.6	46 7.9	43 8.5	40 9.1	
52 7.1	49 7.5	54 6.7		61 6.0	60 6.1	54 6.8	58 6.3	51 7.2	
33 10.9	28 13.2	28 13.1	Cost of Sales/Inventory	11 33.1	8 48.1	38 9.6	45 8.1	28 13.3	
55 6.6	61 5.9	57 6.4		56 6.5	41 8.8	66 5.6	71 5.2	46 7.9	
101 3.6	100 3.7	93 3.9		107 3.4	99 3.7	103 3.5	105 3.5	76 4.8	
21 17.2	18 20.1	20 18.6	Cost of Sales/Payables	20 18.5	19 19.3	28 12.9	22 16.9	17 21.8	
37 10.0	31 11.7	31 11.6		39 9.4	31 11.6	41 8.8	31 11.9	25 14.6	
56 6.5	52 7.1	50 7.3		68 5.3	83 4.4	60 6.0	52 7.0	41 8.9	
6.1	6.3	4.9	Sales/Working Capital		4.0	5.2	6.3	5.1	4.9
12.3	12.5	10.0			21.7	9.8	11.6	10.8	8.2
92.1	63.4	26.8			-3.9	-73.6	33.8	22.1	16.5
9.6	11.8	18.0	EBIT/Interest	9.3	19.5	17.8	14.3	26.0	
(179) 3.4	(200) 4.2	(197) 5.3		(21) 3.2	(18) 6.3	(27) 3.2	(52) 5.7	(75) 7.4	
1.5	1.4	1.5		-1.5	.8	.4	1.6	2.0	
8.8	7.2	13.9	Net Profit + Depr., Dep., Amort./Cur. Mat. L/T/D				24.2	18.0	
(65) 3.1	(68) 2.4	(55) 3.0				(18) 4.3	(24) 4.5		
1.7	.9	1.1				1.5	1.7		
.2	.2	.3	Fixed/Worth		.5	.2	.3	.3	.3
.8	.7	.7			1.4	.6	.8	.5	.7
2.5	2.1	1.6			-1.3	5.0	1.2	1.1	1.3
1.0	1.0	.7	Debt/Worth		.5	.4	.9	.8	.7
2.2	2.0	1.6			7.0	1.5	1.5	1.7	1.4
12.3	5.4	4.6			-6.8	10.3	3.1	3.0	2.5
58.8	53.1	50.0	% Profit Before Taxes/Tangible Net Worth	78.0	39.5	40.2	53.3	56.7	
(171) 29.0	(191) 20.4	(190) 25.6		(17) 29.3	(16) 27.9	(30) 14.7	(49) 29.4	(75) 30.9	
9.5	2.7	5.8		.8	2.3	1.0	5.4	10.0	
16.8	20.6	20.8	% Profit Before Taxes/Total Assets		22.7	20.1	11.3	16.8	23.1
7.2	7.2	8.5			6.3	9.1	5.6	8.5	9.7
1.8	1.6	1.2			-6.1	-.9	-.2	1.6	3.4
43.6	43.8	30.8	Sales/Net Fixed Assets		24.7	45.0	32.1	28.8	22.0
12.7	14.2	10.4			7.0	20.1	12.5	12.8	7.9
5.9	5.4	4.3			3.3	7.2	4.9	6.0	3.4
3.3	3.4	3.0	Sales/Total Assets		3.1	3.6	3.7	2.8	2.9
2.3	2.3	2.1			2.0	2.4	2.1	2.1	1.9
1.7	1.5	1.4			1.3	1.6	1.6	1.4	1.3
.6	.6	.8	% Depr., Dep., Amort./Sales		.8	.4	.9	.9	1.0
(178) 1.6	(181) 1.7	(185) 1.8		(21) 3.1	(15) 1.8	(27) 1.7	(49) 1.6	(69) 1.7	
3.0	3.3	3.9		10.2	3.5	3.4	2.9	4.0	
1.6	1.5	2.0	% Officers', Directors' Owners' Comp/Sales		6.3	3.6	2.0	1.5	
(53) 3.3	(59) 3.2	(56) 4.7		(11) 9.4	(11) 7.6	(14) 4.2	(11) 3.0		
6.3	5.2	8.2		15.5	12.0	5.9	6.1		
9621034M	15154316M	10746757M	Net Sales ($)	4886M	53256M	78640M	223376M	934978M	9451621M
4880927M	6007778M	6177397M	Total Assets ($)	3568M	40147M	35268M	131796M	512194M	5454424M

M = $ thousand   MM = $ million
See Pages 9 through 22 for Explanation of Ratios and Data

Current Data Sorted by Assets   Comparative Historical Data

0-500M	500M-2MM	2-10MM	10-50MM	50-100MM	100-250MM	Type of Statement	4/1/05-3/31/06 ALL	4/1/06-3/31/07 ALL
		2	5	1	1	Unqualified	6	6
	1	2				Reviewed	5	6
	2	3				Compiled	1	5
3	1	2				Tax Returns		
2	4	6	7	2		Other	8	11
	8 (4/1-9/30/09)		36 (10/1/09-3/31/10)					
5	8	15	12	3	1	NUMBER OF STATEMENTS	20	28
%	%	%	%	%	%	ASSETS	%	%
		4.1	1.6			Cash & Equivalents	2.6	5.6
		28.9	22.2			Trade Receivables (net)	24.5	24.8
		25.3	22.8			Inventory	23.8	21.8
		3.8	2.5			All Other Current	3.5	1.4
		62.1	49.1			Total Current	54.5	53.6
		29.0	44.9			Fixed Assets (net)	36.7	35.7
		3.5	2.6			Intangibles (net)	3.2	5.1
		5.4	3.4			All Other Non-Current	5.6	5.7
		100.0	100.0			Total	100.0	100.0
						LIABILITIES		
		22.4	17.6			Notes Payable-Short Term	15.0	12.5
		4.7	4.2			Cur. Mat.-L.T.D.	3.8	5.9
		18.5	14.9			Trade Payables	21.4	15.8
		.1	-.1			Income Taxes Payable	.4	.8
		5.7	9.8			All Other Current	5.3	7.5
		51.4	46.7			Total Current	45.8	42.6
		11.9	20.4			Long-Term Debt	19.7	19.9
		.7	.8			Deferred Taxes	1.2	1.2
		.8	2.9			All Other Non-Current	3.8	2.6
		35.3	29.3			Net Worth	29.5	33.8
		100.0	100.0			Total Liabilities & Net Worth	100.0	100.0
						INCOME DATA		
		100.0	100.0			Net Sales	100.0	100.0
		25.6	23.9			Gross Profit	18.8	21.5
		22.1	17.8			Operating Expenses	13.7	16.4
		3.5	6.2			Operating Profit	5.1	5.1
		1.5	2.5			All Other Expenses (net)	1.5	1.6
		1.9	3.7			Profit Before Taxes	3.6	3.4
						RATIOS		
		1.3	2.1				1.3	2.1
		1.1	1.2			Current	1.0	1.2
		1.0	.7				.9	1.0
		.9	.8				.8	1.0
		.6	.6			Quick	.6	.6
		.4	.4				.4	.5
		36 10.2	33 11.0				35 10.5	33 10.9
		48 7.5	40 9.2			Sales/Receivables	43 8.6	39 9.4
		52 7.0	47 7.7				50 7.3	48 7.5
		42 8.8	44 8.3				39 9.3	27 13.4
		58 6.3	56 6.6			Cost of Sales/Inventory	54 6.8	46 7.9
		68 5.4	84 4.4				59 6.1	62 5.9
		34 10.8	18 19.8				26 13.9	18 20.0
		36 10.0	33 11.2			Cost of Sales/Payables	50 7.3	33 11.2
		48 7.6	47 7.8				62 5.9	51 7.2
		11.3	8.9				11.6	7.7
		40.2	36.6			Sales/Working Capital	103.4	37.5
		327.2	-11.3				-50.5	UND
		3.7	8.1				6.0	5.4
		2.4	3.9			EBIT/Interest	(19) 2.0	(27) 2.5
		2.0	1.3				1.6	.8
						Net Profit + Depr., Dep.,		2.4
						Amort./Cur. Mat. L/T/D	(11) 1.6
								.5
		.5	.8				.7	.8
		1.0	2.5			Fixed/Worth	1.9	1.2
		1.7	6.3				4.4	2.7
		1.1	1.0				1.3	1.1
		2.5	3.3			Debt/Worth	3.2	2.8
		5.5	10.4				7.6	6.8
		32.6	33.4				44.7	30.1
		21.6	(11) 14.8			% Profit Before Taxes/Tangible Net Worth	(18) 24.7	(23) 13.1
		7.5	5.7				12.1	3.4
		7.6	11.6				11.8	12.8
		3.5	6.5			% Profit Before Taxes/Total Assets	4.1	4.0
		1.0	1.2				1.6	-.5
		10.4	6.6				9.9	12.2
		6.9	4.6			Sales/Net Fixed Assets	6.2	6.0
		4.6	2.6				4.1	4.3
		2.5	2.3				2.5	2.6
		2.1	1.8			Sales/Total Assets	2.0	2.2
		1.8	1.2				1.7	1.7
		1.4	2.7				1.4	1.4
		(12) 3.1	3.4			% Depr., Dep., Amort./Sales	(18) 2.3	(25) 2.6
		4.5	6.2				4.2	3.9
								1.5
						% Officers', Directors' Owners' Comp/Sales		(10) 2.7
								3.9
5820M	32056M	171536M	557198M	422050M	302374M	Net Sales ($)	1122592M	1976986M
1778M	10602M	80722M	301923M	211238M	129378M	Total Assets ($)	654746M	1098782M

M = $ thousand   MM = $ million
See Pages 9 through 22 for Explanation of Ratios and Data

Comparative Historical Data   Current Data Sorted by Sales

Type of Statement

4/1/07-3/31/08 ALL	4/1/08-3/31/09 ALL	4/1/09-3/31/10 ALL	Type of Statement	0-1MM	1-3MM	3-5MM	5-10MM	10-25MM	25MM & OVER
6	10	9	Unqualified					3	6
5	3	3	Reviewed					1	
4	5	5	Compiled		3	1	3		
4	3	6	Tax Returns		3	2	2		
10	15	21	Other	1		2	3	8	6
					8 (4/1-9/30/09)			36 (10/1/09-3/31/10)	
29	36	44	NUMBER OF STATEMENTS	1	6	5	8	12	12

4/1/07-3/31/08 ALL	4/1/08-3/31/09 ALL	4/1/09-3/31/10 ALL		0-1MM	1-3MM	3-5MM	5-10MM	10-25MM	25MM & OVER
%	%	%	**ASSETS**	%	%	%	%	%	%
6.6	3.3	3.5	Cash & Equivalents					3.2	1.0
27.7	28.2	29.5	Trade Receivables (net)					25.4	25.1
23.1	26.7	24.0	Inventory					29.3	23.3
.9	2.7	2.7	All Other Current					2.1	4.0
58.4	60.9	59.7	Total Current					60.1	53.4
31.4	30.5	30.9	Fixed Assets (net)					31.9	38.1
3.5	3.6	4.3	Intangibles (net)					4.8	4.3
6.8	5.0	5.1	All Other Non-Current					3.1	4.2
100.0	100.0	100.0	Total					100.0	100.0
			LIABILITIES						
15.6	18.9	18.4	Notes Payable-Short Term					21.8	16.7
3.4	4.0	3.7	Cur. Mat.-L.T.D.					4.4	4.7
20.4	18.3	19.6	Trade Payables					16.0	17.5
.3	.4	.1	Income Taxes Payable					.0	.2
5.8	4.5	7.7	All Other Current					13.1	3.2
45.6	46.0	49.6	Total Current					55.3	42.3
18.8	16.7	16.2	Long-Term Debt					13.2	16.4
1.2	1.1	.6	Deferred Taxes					.0	1.1
4.7	5.3	3.3	All Other Non-Current					2.4	3.7
29.7	30.9	30.2	Net Worth					29.1	36.6
100.0	100.0	100.0	Total Liabilities & Net Worth					100.0	100.0
			INCOME DATA						
100.0	100.0	100.0	Net Sales					100.0	100.0
19.5	20.7	26.5	Gross Profit					24.5	20.7
16.5	17.9	22.0	Operating Expenses					19.9	14.0
3.0	2.8	4.5	Operating Profit					4.6	6.7
1.4	1.5	1.5	All Other Expenses (net)					2.1	1.4
1.5	1.2	3.0	Profit Before Taxes					2.5	5.4
			RATIOS						
1.6	1.6	1.9	Current					1.8	2.1
1.2	1.2	1.3						1.1	1.3
1.0	1.1	1.0						.9	1.1
1.3	.9	1.1	Quick					.9	.8
.6	.6	.6						.6	.6
.5	.5	.4						.4	.5
34 10.7	32 11.2	34 10.8	Sales/Receivables					39 9.4	32 11.4
40 9.2	38 9.5	42 8.7						44 8.2	38 9.5
51 7.1	45 8.2	52 7.0						51 7.1	58 6.3
26 13.9	37 9.8	32 11.5	Cost of Sales/Inventory					58 6.3	41 8.9
44 8.3	46 7.9	52 7.0						67 5.5	49 7.4
58 6.3	63 5.8	69 5.3						71 5.1	62 5.9
16 22.3	20 18.2	25 14.4	Cost of Sales/Payables					33 11.2	18 19.8
45 8.1	26 13.9	35 10.4						35 10.6	34 10.8
59 6.2	46 7.9	50 7.2						42 8.6	52 7.0
8.0	10.5	10.7	Sales/Working Capital					13.5	8.6
30.5	31.6	21.8						45.7	17.2
NM	49.5	269.2						NM	73.6
5.4	4.3	10.0	EBIT/Interest					4.7	11.2
1.8	2.1	(43) 2.4						2.0	5.9
1.2	.8	1.4						1.4	2.1
2.1	6.6	4.0	Net Profit + Depr., Dep., Amort./Cur. Mat. L/T/D						
(13) 1.8	(15) 2.9	(15) 2.5							
1.3	1.3	1.2							
.7	.8	.5	Fixed/Worth					.7	.6
1.2	1.0	1.1						1.5	1.2
7.4	2.9	3.3						6.2	8.7
1.2	1.2	.9	Debt/Worth					1.4	.8
3.2	2.2	2.9						3.6	1.5
19.4	13.5	9.0						10.4	21.2
28.2	31.9	35.6	% Profit Before Taxes/Tangible Net Worth					36.4	46.7
(25) 16.1	(31) 18.7	(38) 18.2						18.2	(10) 27.7
5.8	1.7	6.4						6.9	9.5
9.2	9.4	13.5	% Profit Before Taxes/Total Assets					8.9	16.2
3.9	3.5	4.6						3.5	11.3
.8	-.9	1.1						1.1	4.5
22.9	17.8	17.4	Sales/Net Fixed Assets					10.4	9.7
7.8	7.5	7.4						6.8	5.6
4.5	5.7	4.7						3.0	4.2
3.3	3.1	2.9	Sales/Total Assets					2.5	2.4
2.3	2.4	2.3						2.1	2.1
1.8	2.0	1.8						1.6	1.5
1.1	1.2	1.4	% Depr., Dep., Amort./Sales					1.4	2.6
(28) 1.6	(34) 2.2	(40) 2.8						2.5	(11) 3.5
3.5	3.4	3.6						4.2	4.0
1.7		1.7	% Officers', Directors' Owners' Comp/Sales						
(12) 3.1	(16) 4.5								
4.8	7.8								
1182272M	2330457M	1491034M	Net Sales ($)	707M	9086M	20360M	53109M	194510M	1213262M
558422M	1023726M	735641M	Total Assets ($)	92M	3000M	8517M	26891M	98550M	598591M

© RMA 2010   M = $ thousand   MM = $ million

See Pages 9 through 22 for Explanation of Ratios and Data

Current Data Sorted by Assets

Comparative Historical Data

0-500M	500M-2MM	2-10MM	10-50MM	50-100MM	100-250MM	Type of Statement	4/1/05-3/31/06 ALL	4/1/06-3/31/07 ALL
			2	3	3	Unqualified	3	8
		6	2			Reviewed	2	2
	1					Compiled		
		1	1			Tax Returns	3	2
1	2	1	6		1	Other	5	8
2(4/1-9/30/09)			28(10/1/09-3/31/10)				13	20
2	3	8	10	3	4	NUMBER OF STATEMENTS		
%	%	%	%	%	%	**ASSETS**	%	%
			5.4			Cash & Equivalents	13.2	5.2
			28.7			Trade Receivables (net)	30.2	36.4
			22.3			Inventory	22.7	20.0
			3.9			All Other Current	1.2	1.3
			60.3			Total Current	67.3	62.9
			27.7			Fixed Assets (net)	26.2	28.1
			.5			Intangibles (net)	2.9	4.9
			11.5			All Other Non-Current	3.6	4.2
			100.0			Total	100.0	100.0
						LIABILITIES		
			17.4			Notes Payable-Short Term	11.8	11.4
			3.1			Cur. Mat.-L.T.D.	1.4	3.4
			15.0			Trade Payables	19.0	20.7
			.4			Income Taxes Payable	.7	.2
			6.1			All Other Current	6.9	6.4
			42.0			Total Current	39.9	42.0
			17.1			Long-Term Debt	28.8	24.8
			.5			Deferred Taxes	.0	.6
			8.5			All Other Non-Current	2.0	2.0
			31.9			Net Worth	29.4	30.6
			100.0			Total Liabilties & Net Worth	100.0	100.0
						INCOME DATA		
			100.0			Net Sales	100.0	100.0
			24.7			Gross Profit	29.8	25.5
			24.5			Operating Expenses	21.5	21.6
			.2			Operating Profit	8.2	4.0
			1.2			All Other Expenses (net)	.4	1.2
			-.9			Profit Before Taxes	7.8	2.8
						RATIOS		
			2.6				3.2	2.0
			1.9			Current	1.3	1.6
			1.2				1.1	1.2
			1.4				2.1	1.3
			.9			Quick	.8	.9
			.6				.6	.7
		44	8.3				27 13.6	40 9.2
		48	7.5			Sales/Receivables	39 9.3	49 7.5
		57	6.4				52 7.0	64 5.7
		38	9.7				29 12.8	29 12.6
		61	5.9			Cost of Sales/Inventory	42 8.7	45 8.0
		87	4.2				76 4.8	58 6.3
		20	18.1				17 21.7	19 19.3
		36	10.2			Cost of Sales/Payables	41 8.8	33 11.1
		64	5.7				59 6.2	69 5.3
			4.7				4.6	7.1
			7.8			Sales/Working Capital	12.4	10.9
			23.5				48.9	44.4
			28.3				13.6	10.7
			3.1			EBIT/Interest	(11) 3.9	5.1
			-.9				2.4	.6
						Net Profit + Depr., Dep., Amort./Cur. Mat. L/T/D		
			.3				.3	.4
			.6			Fixed/Worth	1.1	1.1
			2.2				2.7	UND
			.5				.9	1.0
			1.5			Debt/Worth	2.9	1.8
			3.4				4.5	UND
						% Profit Before Taxes/Tangible Net Worth	52.8 (12) 27.7	58.0 (16) 29.5
							7.2	6.3
			8.8				31.3	15.6
			6.2			% Profit Before Taxes/Total Assets	6.6	7.0
			-3.2				2.2	-1.8
			18.4				71.3	25.5
			6.2			Sales/Net Fixed Assets	7.6	7.4
			3.7				4.3	5.4
			2.2				2.8	3.1
			1.7			Sales/Total Assets	2.2	2.4
			1.3				1.5	1.6
							.6	.8
						% Depr., Dep., Amort./Sales	(10) 1.9	(18) 2.8
							3.3	3.7
						% Officers', Directors' Owners' Comp/Sales		
2843M	6236M	82647M	501809M	450240M	1365797M	Net Sales ($)	855463M	1446480M
447M	3438M	34720M	259208M	277395M	784608M	Total Assets ($)	341348M	721593M

M = $ thousand   MM = $ million
See Pages 9 through 22 for Explanation of Ratios and Data

Comparative Historical Data | Current Data Sorted by Sales

4/1/07-3/31/08 ALL	4/1/08-3/31/09 ALL	4/1/09-3/31/10 ALL	Type of Statement	0-1MM	1-3MM	3-5MM	5-10MM	10-25MM	25MM & OVER
8	5	8	Unqualified						8
2	4	8	Reviewed					2	5
1	1	1	Compiled		1			1	
4	3	2	Tax Returns		1			1	
7	12	11	Other	1	1	1	1	2	5

Historical columns: 4/1/07-3/31/08 ALL; 4/1/08-3/31/09 ALL; 4/1/09-3/31/10 ALL. Current data groups: 2 (4/1-9/30/09); 28 (10/1/09-3/31/10).

22	25	30	NUMBER OF STATEMENTS	1	3	1	4	7	14
%	%	%	**ASSETS**	%	%	%	%	%	%
4.4	3.5	7.5	Cash & Equivalents						3.5
23.9	27.3	28.9	Trade Receivables (net)						26.0
23.7	28.6	21.7	Inventory						21.6
2.2	3.4	2.6	All Other Current						2.9
54.2	62.7	60.7	Total Current						54.0
38.8	31.7	27.2	Fixed Assets (net)						30.5
2.1	2.3	4.4	Intangibles (net)						7.2
5.0	3.4	7.7	All Other Non-Current						8.2
100.0	100.0	100.0	Total						100.0
			LIABILITIES						
6.7	12.4	11.5	Notes Payable-Short Term						5.7
6.1	3.8	4.7	Cur. Mat.-L.T.D.						4.4
17.6	17.4	16.0	Trade Payables						15.5
.1	.0	.4	Income Taxes Payable						.4
6.5	5.3	6.8	All Other Current						7.4
37.1	38.8	39.4	Total Current						33.4
28.3	20.1	16.4	Long-Term Debt						20.5
.7	.9	.7	Deferred Taxes						.7
3.0	2.8	8.8	All Other Non-Current						6.2
30.9	37.4	34.9	Net Worth						39.2
100.0	100.0	100.0	Total Liabilities & Net Worth						100.0
			INCOME DATA						
100.0	100.0	100.0	Net Sales						100.0
25.6	20.4	25.9	Gross Profit						21.6
22.7	16.8	21.5	Operating Expenses						15.9
2.9	3.6	4.4	Operating Profit						5.7
.8	1.2	1.7	All Other Expenses (net)						1.8
2.1	2.4	2.8	Profit Before Taxes						3.9
			RATIOS						
2.5	3.2	2.6	Current						2.4
1.8	1.6	1.8							1.5
1.2	1.2	1.1							1.2
1.3	1.5	1.5	Quick						1.3
.9	.7	.8							.8
.6	.5	.6							.6
30 12.0	30 12.3	33 11.2	Sales/Receivables						41 9.0
35 10.3	40 9.0	45 8.1							47 7.7
45 8.2	45 8.1	53 6.9							57 6.5
39 9.4	33 11.1	33 10.9	Cost of Sales/Inventory						39 9.5
52 7.0	43 8.5	49 7.5							56 6.6
68 5.4	62 5.9	68 5.4							70 5.2
17 21.5	18 20.2	22 16.8	Cost of Sales/Payables						21 17.1
37 9.8	30 12.1	36 10.2							39 9.3
59 6.2	44 8.3	52 7.0							53 6.9
5.6	5.8	7.2	Sales/Working Capital						7.6
9.3	10.2	9.3							9.2
42.9	44.1	55.5							16.9
10.7	6.7	24.5	EBIT/Interest						17.5
3.4	(24) 3.3	(28) 4.4							3.6
1.1	1.1	1.8							.6
	3.8	16.9	Net Profit + Depr., Dep., Amort./Cur. Mat. L/T/D						
	(11) 2.2	(12) 5.5							
	1.2	1.0							
.5	.5	.3	Fixed/Worth						.4
.9	.8	.8							.9
3.3	1.8	3.3							2.6
.8	.9	.7	Debt/Worth						.7
1.6	1.8	1.9							1.9
6.2	3.3	8.6							6.1
40.9	37.6	68.3	% Profit Before Taxes/Tangible Net Worth						35.5
(19) 24.1	(23) 19.4	(26) 25.3						(13)	20.6
6.7	4.2	8.0							2.8
11.4	10.1	17.6	% Profit Before Taxes/Total Assets						11.6
5.0	5.9	6.7							6.8
.8	.5	.7							-1.7
8.3	14.3	18.4	Sales/Net Fixed Assets						18.4
4.3	7.2	7.3							6.8
2.6	4.6	4.3							3.2
2.6	3.2	2.7	Sales/Total Assets						2.5
1.9	2.2	2.0							1.8
1.5	1.8	1.4							1.4
2.0	1.8	1.1	% Depr., Dep., Amort./Sales						1.1
(16) 3.2	(18) 2.7	(24) 1.8						(13)	1.3
4.5	3.9	4.4							4.4
			% Officers', Directors' Owners' Comp/Sales						
1531812M	1965843M	2409572M	Net Sales ($)	317M	5550M	3212M	26312M	109752M	2264429M
855200M	931092M	1359816M	Total Assets ($)	35M	2578M	1272M	16143M	60163M	1279625M

Current Data Sorted by Assets   Comparative Historical Data

Type of Statement

	0-500M	500M-2MM	2-10MM	10-50MM	50-100MM	100-250MM		4/1/05-3/31/06 ALL	4/1/06-3/31/07 ALL
Unqualified			2	12	3	4		29	31
Reviewed		2	11	9		1		17	25
Compiled		4	6					6	14
Tax Returns		11	8					6	4
Other	2	2	14	17	5	3		19	29
		17 (4/1-9/30/09)		99 (10/1/09-3/31/10)					
NUMBER OF STATEMENTS	2	19	41	38	8	8		77	103

Data

0-500M	500M-2MM	2-10MM	10-50MM	50-100MM	100-250MM		4/1/05-3/31/06 ALL	4/1/06-3/31/07 ALL
%	%	%	%	%	%	**ASSETS**	%	%
	9.4	9.2	8.2			Cash & Equivalents	4.6	4.7
	32.6	28.6	23.7			Trade Receivables (net)	31.4	29.1
	27.5	27.6	21.8			Inventory	26.7	28.0
	.3	2.5	3.0			All Other Current	1.2	1.8
	69.8	67.8	56.6			Total Current	64.0	63.6
	20.3	24.9	36.2			Fixed Assets (net)	30.3	28.3
	3.0	2.0	2.7			Intangibles (net)	1.5	3.2
	6.9	5.3	4.5			All Other Non-Current	4.3	4.9
	100.0	100.0	100.0			Total	100.0	100.0
						LIABILITIES		
	4.7	12.9	8.6			Notes Payable-Short Term	11.4	14.0
	1.9	4.8	5.3			Cur. Mat.-L.T.D.	5.2	3.6
	21.9	18.4	16.1			Trade Payables	18.8	19.2
	.0	.0	.4			Income Taxes Payable	.4	.3
	5.3	13.9	5.4			All Other Current	7.0	8.1
	33.8	50.1	35.9			Total Current	42.8	45.2
	10.7	14.0	15.5			Long-Term Debt	13.4	15.8
	.0	.2	.6			Deferred Taxes	.7	.6
	4.6	3.2	4.2			All Other Non-Current	7.3	8.7
	50.9	32.5	43.9			Net Worth	35.8	29.7
	100.0	100.0	100.0			Total Liabilties & Net Worth	100.0	100.0
						INCOME DATA		
	100.0	100.0	100.0			Net Sales	100.0	100.0
	35.4	27.5	23.5			Gross Profit	22.7	22.8
	30.1	23.1	17.7			Operating Expenses	17.9	18.4
	5.4	4.4	5.8			Operating Profit	4.8	4.4
	.0	.7	1.0			All Other Expenses (net)	1.0	1.2
	5.4	3.7	4.8			Profit Before Taxes	3.8	3.2
						RATIOS		
	2.8	1.9	2.6				2.3	2.3
	1.9	1.5	1.6			Current	1.6	1.6
	1.1	1.1	1.1				1.1	1.0
	1.8	1.4	1.6				1.2	1.2
	1.1	.8	.9			Quick	.9	.8
	.7	.5	.5				.5	.5
	20 18.4	34 10.8	33 11.2				38 9.7	34 10.7
	40 9.1	44 8.4	46 8.0			Sales/Receivables	49 7.5	42 8.6
	53 6.9	53 6.9	51 7.1				60 6.0	52 7.1
	21 17.0	33 10.9	38 9.6				39 9.3	37 9.7
	54 6.8	59 6.2	49 7.4			Cost of Sales/Inventory	55 6.7	51 7.1
	115 3.2	83 4.4	69 5.3				72 5.1	73 5.0
	17 21.1	24 15.2	26 13.9				22 16.7	21 17.7
	36 10.1	40 9.1	36 10.1			Cost of Sales/Payables	32 11.3	33 11.0
	63 5.8	55 6.6	48 7.6				52 7.0	51 7.1
	3.7	6.2	5.6				5.6	5.9
	8.4	11.2	11.2			Sales/Working Capital	9.8	11.5
	65.1	42.8	106.8				39.3	131.4
	57.3	8.9	12.9				10.7	10.1
	(17) 25.0	(36) 3.7	(36) 5.8			EBIT/Interest	(71) 4.1	(99) 3.6
	5.1	1.7	1.6				1.9	1.3
			5.1			Net Profit + Depr., Dep.,	4.2	5.0
			(18) 2.4			Amort./Cur. Mat. L/T/D	(23) 2.0	(31) 2.7
			.3				1.4	1.5
	.1	.3	.6				.4	.5
	.3	.6	1.0			Fixed/Worth	.8	.9
	1.5	1.1	1.3				1.7	2.3
	.4	.8	.8				.9	1.1
	.7	2.2	1.5			Debt/Worth	1.9	2.7
	6.1	4.5	2.9				4.1	5.6
	60.0	39.6	34.7			% Profit Before Taxes/Tangible	40.6	56.0
	(18) 28.7	(38) 19.0	(37) 18.6			Net Worth	(69) 17.7	(88) 23.1
	6.9	3.9	6.3				7.1	8.0
	21.4	12.4	16.0			% Profit Before Taxes/Total	12.5	14.3
	15.4	5.2	7.7			Assets	6.5	6.7
	3.1	1.1	1.8				1.8	1.1
	81.6	49.1	11.2				16.2	15.6
	27.3	10.9	4.9			Sales/Net Fixed Assets	7.9	9.1
	9.2	6.0	3.6				4.1	5.2
	4.1	3.0	2.6				3.0	3.0
	2.8	2.3	2.0			Sales/Total Assets	2.2	2.5
	2.1	1.7	1.6				1.7	1.8
	.8	.7	1.7				1.0	1.2
	(15) 1.0	(36) 2.2	(33) 2.4			% Depr., Dep., Amort./Sales	(67) 2.3	(89) 2.1
	3.1	3.6	7.2				3.3	3.5
	1.2	1.3				% Officers', Directors'	1.3	1.4
	(11) 2.6	(23) 2.7				Owners' Comp/Sales	(20) 2.2	(24) 2.6
	6.0	4.6					4.6	6.8
2321M	89469M	422423M	1724410M	903229M	2161279M	Net Sales ($)	3738625M	4463622M
420M	28506M	193040M	927950M	585189M	1309014M	Total Assets ($)	2024524M	2296095M

© RMA 2010

M = $ thousand   MM = $ million
See Pages 9 through 22 for Explanation of Ratios and Data

Comparative Historical Data | Current Data Sorted by Sales

Type of Statement

4/1/07-3/31/08 ALL	4/1/08-3/31/09 ALL	4/1/09-3/31/10 ALL	Type of Statement	0-1MM	1-3MM	3-5MM	5-10MM	10-25MM	25MM & OVER
21	21	21	Unqualified				1	2	18
19	22	23	Reviewed			1	7	7	8
9	10	10	Compiled		2	1	4	3	
5	14	21	Tax Returns		4	4	10	2	
35	32	41	Other	1		2	5	10	23
					17 (4/1-9/30/09)			99 (10/1/09-3/31/10)	
89	99	116	**NUMBER OF STATEMENTS**	1	7	8	27	24	49

%	%	%	ASSETS	%	%	%	%	%	%
5.7	7.7	8.3	Cash & Equivalents				8.6	13.1	5.7
26.1	25.7	27.3	Trade Receivables (net)				31.4	30.0	24.4
28.1	26.4	23.9	Inventory				26.8	24.4	20.9
1.7	1.6	2.4	All Other Current				.8	2.7	2.6
61.6	61.4	61.8	Total Current				67.6	70.2	53.7
29.2	29.3	30.0	Fixed Assets (net)				24.8	22.9	37.5
4.3	2.8	3.1	Intangibles (net)				2.4	1.1	4.4
4.9	6.4	5.1	All Other Non-Current				5.2	5.8	4.4
100.0	100.0	100.0	Total				100.0	100.0	100.0
			LIABILITIES						
11.2	10.5	9.0	Notes Payable-Short Term				9.8	14.4	7.6
4.1	4.3	4.4	Cur. Mat.-L.T.D.				4.2	2.1	5.4
18.0	16.4	17.4	Trade Payables				20.9	19.2	15.5
.3	.2	.3	Income Taxes Payable				.0	.1	.7
7.5	7.5	9.3	All Other Current				8.5	11.3	7.1
41.0	38.8	40.4	Total Current				43.5	47.2	36.3
16.2	16.7	14.1	Long-Term Debt				14.7	11.3	15.8
.6	.8	.5	Deferred Taxes				.2	.3	1.0
5.7	4.2	3.8	All Other Non-Current				3.9	5.3	3.9
36.4	39.5	41.1	Net Worth				37.7	36.0	43.1
100.0	100.0	100.0	Total Liabilities & Net Worth				100.0	100.0	100.0
			INCOME DATA						
100.0	100.0	100.0	Net Sales				100.0	100.0	100.0
23.8	22.9	27.0	Gross Profit				34.4	24.4	22.4
19.4	18.0	21.6	Operating Expenses				27.3	22.1	15.4
4.4	4.8	5.4	Operating Profit				7.1	2.3	7.0
1.5	1.1	.7	All Other Expenses (net)				1.3	.4	.9
2.9	3.7	4.7	Profit Before Taxes				5.8	1.9	6.0
			RATIOS						
2.5	2.4	2.3	Current				1.9	3.5	2.3
1.6	1.6	1.6					1.4	1.7	1.6
1.1	1.2	1.1					1.1	1.1	1.1
1.2	1.4	1.6	Quick				1.5	2.2	1.4
.8	.9	.9					.9	.9	.9
.5	.5	.6					.6	.6	.5
35 10.5	30 12.1	34 10.8	Sales/Receivables				32 11.4	34 10.6	34 10.7
44 8.3	38 9.7	45 8.2					43 8.4	46 8.0	47 7.7
53 6.9	49 7.5	54 6.8					51 7.2	57 6.4	55 6.6
42 8.7	31 11.8	36 10.2	Cost of Sales/Inventory				25 14.3	33 11.2	38 9.6
56 6.5	51 7.2	54 6.8					59 6.2	53 6.9	49 7.5
81 4.5	76 4.8	73 5.0					103 3.5	72 5.1	65 5.6
23 15.6	19 19.7	23 16.2	Cost of Sales/Payables				25 14.7	18 19.8	26 13.9
35 10.4	26 14.2	37 9.8					43 8.6	38 9.5	35 10.4
51 7.1	45 8.0	51 7.2					52 7.0	56 6.5	43 8.5
5.8	5.7	5.6	Sales/Working Capital				6.3	5.3	5.9
10.6	10.8	11.0					13.0	10.7	11.0
42.0	28.0	41.7					47.3	35.0	47.0
9.5	11.0	21.7	EBIT/Interest				32.4	20.4	12.3
(83) 3.3	(92) 3.0	(105) 4.9					(26) 5.0	(21) 3.7	(46) 5.3
1.8	1.1	2.1					2.3	2.1	1.7
3.5	4.0	5.4	Net Profit + Depr., Dep., Amort./Cur. Mat. L/T/D						5.2
(26) 2.3	(32) 2.1	(34) 2.4							(24) 2.0
1.2	.5	.4							.5
.4	.5	.3	Fixed/Worth				.3	.1	.6
.9	.8	.7					.6	.6	.9
2.0	2.3	1.3					1.5	1.1	1.6
.9	.6	.7	Debt/Worth				.7	.7	.9
2.1	1.8	1.6					2.4	1.4	1.5
4.6	5.7	3.7					6.3	4.4	2.9
39.2	43.3	38.7	% Profit Before Taxes/Tangible Net Worth				60.0	27.3	36.1
(79) 22.8	(90) 22.5	(110) 20.8					(26) 33.8	(22) 17.8	(47) 23.0
7.9	1.0	5.4					8.1	1.3	8.1
14.9	15.3	16.0	% Profit Before Taxes/Total Assets				21.2	11.2	16.7
6.6	6.4	7.0					9.4	4.2	8.7
2.0	.3	2.2					2.7	1.4	3.0
16.7	16.7	25.1	Sales/Net Fixed Assets				31.5	50.3	8.8
8.7	8.9	8.3					14.3	9.4	4.8
4.7	4.7	4.0					6.5	6.2	3.3
2.8	2.8	2.8	Sales/Total Assets				3.4	3.1	2.5
2.2	2.3	2.2					2.5	2.4	1.9
1.7	1.9	1.6					1.8	1.5	1.5
1.2	1.2	1.3	% Depr., Dep., Amort./Sales				.9	.7	1.7
(78) 2.3	(87) 2.6	(98) 2.4					(25) 1.9	(19) 2.5	(41) 2.6
3.8	4.4	4.1					3.3	3.7	4.8
1.9	1.5	1.2	% Officers', Directors' Owners' Comp/Sales				1.1	1.3	
(21) 4.0	(30) 3.0	(46) 2.6					(17) 2.6	(10) 2.9	
6.1	4.9	4.6					4.6	5.2	
3946948M	5829730M	5303131M	Net Sales ($)	867M	15140M	30198M	202762M	374093M	4680071M
2237107M	3047510M	3044119M	Total Assets ($)	195M	9476M	15443M	89752M	228250M	2701003M

M = $ thousand   MM = $ million
See Pages 9 through 22 for Explanation of Ratios and Data

Current Data Sorted by Assets							Comparative Historical Data	

0-500M	500M-2MM	2-10MM	10-50MM	50-100MM	100-250MM	Type of Statement	4/1/05-3/31/06 ALL	4/1/06-3/31/07 ALL
		5	5	1	5	Unqualified	21	14
	2	12	2			Reviewed	24	16
1	3	5	1			Compiled	13	17
3	1	1				Tax Returns	6	7
	6	13	6	2	1	Other	23	31
	14 (4/1-9/30/09)		61 (10/1/09-3/31/10)					
4	12	36	14	3	6	NUMBER OF STATEMENTS	87	85
%	%	%	%	%	%	ASSETS	%	%
	7.0	8.8	3.8			Cash & Equivalents	6.2	8.3
	27.6	20.7	23.5			Trade Receivables (net)	26.0	25.4
	21.9	21.5	31.6			Inventory	26.2	25.0
	2.2	1.4	.5			All Other Current	1.0	1.5
	58.7	52.4	59.5			Total Current	59.3	60.2
	31.8	34.5	30.2			Fixed Assets (net)	30.0	31.3
	4.7	2.6	1.4			Intangibles (net)	4.9	3.4
	4.9	10.4	8.8			All Other Non-Current	5.8	5.1
	100.0	100.0	100.0			Total	100.0	100.0
						LIABILITIES		
	20.2	8.9	13.0			Notes Payable-Short Term	10.8	9.3
	7.0	5.4	3.3			Cur. Mat.-L.T.D.	5.7	5.3
	13.6	13.1	16.5			Trade Payables	17.1	15.3
	.1	.4	.2			Income Taxes Payable	.2	.0
	13.6	6.2	5.1			All Other Current	8.8	9.3
	54.4	34.0	38.0			Total Current	42.5	39.3
	14.6	18.9	11.4			Long-Term Debt	17.1	19.3
	.0	.7	.6			Deferred Taxes	.4	.8
	16.8	2.3	3.5			All Other Non-Current	7.0	6.2
	14.2	44.0	46.4			Net Worth	33.0	34.5
	100.0	100.0	100.0			Total Liabilities & Net Worth	100.0	100.0
						INCOME DATA		
	100.0	100.0	100.0			Net Sales	100.0	100.0
	28.3	31.1	23.3			Gross Profit	27.6	28.4
	32.0	25.7	18.2			Operating Expenses	22.8	23.0
	-3.7	5.4	5.1			Operating Profit	4.8	5.4
	.4	1.3	.3			All Other Expenses (net)	1.7	1.4
	-4.1	4.1	4.8			Profit Before Taxes	3.0	4.0
						RATIOS		
	4.1	2.8	2.1				2.1	3.1
	1.2	1.7	1.6			Current	1.4	1.6
	.7	1.1	1.1				1.0	1.0
	2.5	1.7	1.1				1.1	1.7
	.6	.9	.6			Quick	.7	1.0
	.2	.6	.5				.5	.4
19 19.4	34 10.7	38 9.5					34 10.7	31 11.8
42 8.6	42 8.7	43 8.5				Sales/Receivables	42 8.8	38 9.5
49 7.4	58 6.3	50 7.3					55 6.7	53 7.0
22 16.5	52 7.1	53 6.9					34 10.7	35 10.5
58 6.3	68 5.4	76 4.8				Cost of Sales/Inventory	58 6.3	59 6.2
109 3.4	100 3.6	117 3.1					88 4.1	91 4.0
6 66.0	18 19.9	27 13.3					23 15.9	17 21.1
35 10.4	38 9.6	46 7.9				Cost of Sales/Payables	37 9.8	28 13.0
54 6.7	52 7.0	52 7.0					52 7.0	54 6.7
	4.8	4.4	4.7				6.9	5.0
	17.4	8.4	11.2			Sales/Working Capital	13.2	11.1
	-35.8	47.5	58.5				-492.4	-237.6
	5.1	11.2	9.9				9.8	10.5
	(11) 2.6	(33) 2.5	(13) 3.1			EBIT/Interest	(78) 3.1	(77) 2.9
	-3.1	.8	1.2				.9	1.1
		3.4					4.9	7.4
		(13) 1.3				Net Profit + Depr., Dep., Amort./Cur. Mat. L/T/D	(19) 1.5	(17) 3.8
		-.1					1.3	1.3
	.7	.4	.2				.4	.4
	2.2	.8	.8			Fixed/Worth	1.2	1.1
	-2.5	1.7	1.6				3.4	4.5
	.8	.5	.7				.8	.8
	11.3	.9	1.2			Debt/Worth	2.4	2.3
	-18.1	3.2	3.9				8.5	9.6
		37.2	25.7				33.3	43.1
		(34) 15.7	16.8			% Profit Before Taxes/Tangible Net Worth	(75) 16.4	(70) 20.6
		2.5	5.1				.0	4.5
	7.0	11.2	17.4				12.1	17.2
	3.0	4.3	6.7			% Profit Before Taxes/Total Assets	4.9	6.0
	-24.1	.3	1.0				-.3	.2
	12.9	11.0	17.0				21.1	18.0
	7.2	5.7	5.1			Sales/Net Fixed Assets	7.1	6.2
	4.2	3.8	4.1				4.3	3.5
	2.9	2.1	2.5				3.0	2.9
	2.0	1.7	1.9			Sales/Total Assets	2.2	2.1
	1.6	1.1	1.2				1.6	1.5
	2.1	2.1	1.0				1.5	1.7
	(10) 3.5	(35) 3.6	(13) 3.1			% Depr., Dep., Amort./Sales	(74) 2.9	(72) 2.9
	5.4	5.1	3.6				4.4	4.5
		1.7					2.1	2.1
		(17) 3.1				% Officers', Directors' Owners' Comp/Sales	(28) 3.4	(33) 3.7
		6.8					5.4	6.9
4104M	36891M	308607M	589759M	295817M	831318M	Net Sales ($)	2730376M	2217994M
1147M	14055M	183314M	308382M	225793M	841801M	Total Assets ($)	1503971M	1469436M

M = $ thousand   MM = $ million
See Pages 9 through 22 for Explanation of Ratios and Data

Comparative Historical Data | Current Data Sorted by Sales

			Type of Statement	0-1MM	1-3MM	3-5MM	5-10MM	10-25MM	25MM & OVER
15	16	16	Unqualified		2	2	3	2	11
20	17	16	Reviewed				6	5	1
20	14	10	Compiled		4	4	1		1
3	10	5	Tax Returns	3	1	1			1
22	21	28	Other	1	3	4	7	7	6
4/1/07-3/31/08 ALL	4/1/08-3/31/09 ALL	4/1/09-3/31/10 ALL			14 (4/1-9/30/09)		61 (10/1/09-3/31/10)		
80	78	75	**NUMBER OF STATEMENTS**	4	10	11	17	14	19
%	%	%	**ASSETS**	%	%	%	%	%	%
7.3	6.6	7.4	Cash & Equivalents		9.9	4.6	6.3	8.9	5.9
26.1	25.5	22.0	Trade Receivables (net)		20.2	21.7	23.8	23.3	19.9
24.8	24.2	22.8	Inventory		27.5	19.0	22.1	25.2	22.3
1.3	1.8	1.4	All Other Current		.8	1.8	2.0	1.1	1.4
59.5	58.2	53.6	Total Current		58.4	47.2	54.1	58.6	49.5
32.9	32.0	32.0	Fixed Assets (net)		34.7	31.3	34.8	28.6	32.2
1.8	3.0	6.2	Intangibles (net)		4.4	2.4	4.1	1.0	13.3
5.8	6.8	8.2	All Other Non-Current		2.4	19.1	7.0	11.8	4.9
100.0	100.0	100.0	Total		100.0	100.0	100.0	100.0	100.0
			LIABILITIES						
11.9	10.7	11.4	Notes Payable-Short Term		17.6	6.6	14.5	11.5	6.1
4.6	4.8	5.0	Cur. Mat.-L.T.D.		3.3	9.6	7.0	3.0	3.7
16.0	14.7	13.0	Trade Payables		8.6	16.4	12.3	14.0	13.8
.3	.3	.3	Income Taxes Payable		.4	.0	.0	1.0	.1
8.1	10.5	6.9	All Other Current		2.0	3.5	15.9	5.0	5.6
40.9	40.9	36.6	Total Current		31.8	36.1	49.6	34.6	29.4
18.2	17.1	17.1	Long-Term Debt		15.8	26.9	17.6	12.1	17.2
.4	.6	.8	Deferred Taxes		.0	.0	.9	1.1	1.6
6.0	5.5	5.2	All Other Non-Current		12.4	11.8	1.9	2.7	3.6
34.6	35.9	40.3	Net Worth		40.0	25.2	30.0	49.5	48.3
100.0	100.0	100.0	Total Liabilties & Net Worth		100.0	100.0	100.0	100.0	100.0
			INCOME DATA						
100.0	100.0	100.0	Net Sales		100.0	100.0	100.0	100.0	100.0
25.6	27.0	30.3	Gross Profit		35.6	29.5	29.7	29.3	23.4
22.1	23.4	26.8	Operating Expenses		40.6	23.7	25.6	24.7	17.6
3.5	3.6	3.5	Operating Profit		-5.0	5.8	4.1	4.7	5.9
1.0	.7	1.3	All Other Expenses (net)		1.3	1.9	1.5	-.1	2.4
2.5	2.9	2.2	Profit Before Taxes		-6.3	3.9	2.5	4.8	3.5

RATIOS

			Ratio	0-1MM	1-3MM	3-5MM	5-10MM	10-25MM	25MM & OVER
2.3	2.6	2.7	Current		5.2	2.1	2.7	2.9	2.0
1.6	1.5	1.6			2.1	1.8	1.2	1.8	1.7
1.0	1.0	1.1			1.1	1.0	.9	1.1	1.1
1.3	1.4	1.6	Quick		3.6	1.4	1.2	1.5	1.4
.8	.7	.9			1.3	.9	.7	.8	.9
.5	.5	.5			.4	.6	.5	.6	.5
33 11.1	25 14.8	35 10.6	Sales/Receivables		20 18.3	36 10.1	29 12.4	36 10.1	36 10.2
41 8.9	38 9.7	42 8.7			44 8.3	52 7.0	37 10.0	44 8.3	40 9.2
52 7.0	49 7.4	52 7.0			54 6.8	68 5.3	47 7.7	52 7.0	52 7.0
39 9.5	35 10.4	48 7.6	Cost of Sales/Inventory		48 7.6	35 10.5	60 6.1	41 9.0	47 7.7
52 7.1	50 7.3	68 5.4			84 4.4	61 6.0	84 4.3	76 4.8	55 6.6
75 4.9	75 4.8	110 3.3			113 3.2	92 4.0	115 3.2	120 3.0	82 4.4
18 20.5	17 21.7	20 18.1	Cost of Sales/Payables		7 54.1	21 17.6	17 21.8	19 19.2	21 17.6
33 11.0	27 13.8	37 9.9			32 11.3	48 7.5	26 14.2	42 8.6	37 9.8
48 7.5	48 7.6	51 7.1			41 9.0	60 6.1	52 7.1	48 7.6	49 7.4
6.1	7.0	4.8	Sales/Working Capital		3.2	5.5	4.2	4.3	5.5
10.7	13.4	9.5			8.3	8.2	33.6	6.9	9.0
-131.9	NM	54.9			28.7	-87.6	-72.7	NM	31.1
8.0	6.5	7.0	EBIT/Interest		5.3	4.2		16.6	10.2
(72) 2.1	(68) 2.3	(69) 2.5			(10) 2.8	2.0		(13) 2.8	(16) 3.7
.4	.8	.6			1.1	-.4		2.1	.9
4.2	4.1	4.1	Net Profit + Depr., Dep., Amort./Cur. Mat. L/T/D						
(22) 1.8	(20) 2.9	(22) 2.1							
.1	1.6	.9							
.3	.5	.4	Fixed/Worth		.4	.2	.5	.2	.6
.9	1.0	.9			.8	1.0	1.4	.8	1.1
2.4	2.3	2.1			NM	6.5	5.2	1.4	2.2
.7	.7	.6	Debt/Worth		.4	.5	.9	.6	.6
1.6	1.6	1.4			1.0	2.7	1.9	.8	2.2
5.1	5.6	4.8			NM	18.9	15.7	3.0	4.2
37.2	26.4	34.9	% Profit Before Taxes/Tangible Net Worth		78.7		45.6	35.0	54.3
(69) 10.4	(68) 10.5	(66) 14.5			(10) 15.6		(14) 13.2	19.9	(16) 15.0
.8	1.9	-3.2			2.6		1.1	6.5	-2.3
13.4	10.9	10.8	% Profit Before Taxes/Total Assets		8.8	9.8	8.8	25.5	17.0
3.9	3.5	4.2			-9.4	7.1	3.6	4.9	5.2
-.5	.1	-1.5			-39.8	1.5	-4.6	3.1	-.7
18.2	15.2	13.2	Sales/Net Fixed Assets		9.1	13.2	10.3	15.7	10.1
6.9	7.6	5.6			5.9	6.1	6.1	5.9	4.5
3.3	4.6	3.7			3.4	3.8	3.0	4.8	3.2
2.8	3.4	2.2	Sales/Total Assets		2.2	2.3	2.6	2.0	2.5
2.2	2.2	1.8			1.8	1.4	1.7	1.9	1.8
1.5	1.5	1.1			1.3	.8	1.1	1.7	1.0
1.8	1.6	1.8	% Depr., Dep., Amort./Sales			1.9	2.2	.6	1.3
(73) 2.9	(67) 2.5	(63) 3.3				3.1	(16) 3.0	(13) 3.6	(12) 2.5
4.6	4.1	5.1				6.9	4.9	4.1	5.0
2.1	2.4	1.9	% Officers', Directors' Owners' Comp/Sales						
(30) 3.5	(31) 5.4	(29) 3.7							
7.0	6.7	7.4							
2412150M	2274218M	2066496M	Net Sales ($)	2973M	21486M	45477M	117714M	229092M	1649754M
1479683M	1369138M	1574492M	Total Assets ($)	1796M	13732M	37283M	71249M	128106M	1322326M

M = $ thousand   MM = $ million
See Pages 9 through 22 for Explanation of Ratios and Data

Current Data Sorted by Assets   Comparative Historical Data

Type of Statement	0-500M	500M-2MM	2-10MM	10-50MM	50-100MM	100-250MM		4/1/05-3/31/06 ALL	4/1/06-3/31/07 ALL
Unqualified			8	12	3	7		36	28
Reviewed	1	1	14	2	1			31	22
Compiled	1	10	9	2				25	22
Tax Returns	1	5	1					4	5
Other	1	9	13	10	3	2		57	40
		19 (4/1-9/30/09)		96 (10/1/09-3/31/10)					
NUMBER OF STATEMENTS	3	25	45	26	7	9		153	117
	%	%	%	%	%	%	ASSETS	%	%
		14.8	5.5	5.9			Cash & Equivalents	4.7	7.6
		23.9	24.4	23.3			Trade Receivables (net)	28.9	25.1
		30.0	29.3	23.2			Inventory	23.0	24.7
		1.2	2.0	2.2			All Other Current	2.2	2.3
		69.8	61.1	54.5			Total Current	58.9	59.7
		21.5	29.5	34.8			Fixed Assets (net)	31.1	31.6
		2.2	2.8	3.4			Intangibles (net)	2.3	3.8
		6.4	6.6	7.3			All Other Non-Current	7.6	4.9
		100.0	100.0	100.0			Total	100.0	100.0
							LIABILITIES		
		15.5	12.6	8.4			Notes Payable-Short Term	12.6	10.7
		4.9	3.7	3.4			Cur. Mat.-L.T.D.	4.5	3.8
		11.9	14.8	11.3			Trade Payables	16.9	14.3
		.1	.1	.0			Income Taxes Payable	.4	.2
		8.2	8.3	7.1			All Other Current	7.4	8.1
		40.5	39.5	30.2			Total Current	41.7	37.1
		14.0	14.8	14.7			Long-Term Debt	14.3	14.5
		.1	1.0	.4			Deferred Taxes	1.0	1.0
		8.7	9.4	8.5			All Other Non-Current	6.7	6.0
		36.7	35.3	46.2			Net Worth	36.3	41.3
		100.0	100.0	100.0			Total Liabilties & Net Worth	100.0	100.0
							INCOME DATA		
		100.0	100.0	100.0			Net Sales	100.0	100.0
		24.2	22.0	26.5			Gross Profit	24.1	27.0
		25.4	22.7	23.1			Operating Expenses	19.5	21.1
		-1.2	-.8	3.3			Operating Profit	4.6	5.9
		-.4	2.4	1.7			All Other Expenses (net)	.9	.8
		-.8	-3.1	1.6			Profit Before Taxes	3.7	5.1
							RATIOS		
		4.9	2.2	3.5				2.3	2.9
		2.6	1.7	2.1			Current	1.4	1.7
		1.2	1.2	1.1				1.0	1.1
		3.1	1.2	1.7				1.2	1.5
		1.8	.7	1.0			Quick	(152) .8	.9
		.5	.5	.6				.5	.5
	23 15.9	35 10.4	43 8.4				Sales/Receivables	36 10.0	28 12.9
	46 7.9	46 7.9	51 7.1					49 7.5	38 9.7
	57 6.4	69 5.3	62 5.9					64 5.7	52 7.0
	29 12.4	48 7.6	41 8.9				Cost of Sales/Inventory	34 10.6	35 10.3
	61 6.0	69 5.3	66 5.6					49 7.5	50 7.3
	103 3.5	94 3.9	114 3.2					73 5.0	83 4.4
	9 42.9	20 18.7	19 19.7				Cost of Sales/Payables	21 17.7	14 26.5
	17 21.0	30 12.1	33 11.2					36 10.2	25 14.4
	36 10.2	50 7.3	47 7.8					54 6.7	44 8.2
		3.4	4.9	3.4			Sales/Working Capital	5.9	5.3
		6.8	8.2	6.4				12.0	9.3
		18.3	24.6	52.8				-143.6	46.1
		5.3	4.3	12.2			EBIT/Interest	13.1	14.0
	(20)	2.1	(44) .5	4.7				(145) 3.5	(108) 5.8
		-5.4	-7.9	-4.1				1.2	1.8
			1.7				Net Profit + Depr., Dep.,	9.8	7.0
		(11)	.7				Amort./Cur. Mat. L/T/D	(52) 3.3	(37) 4.1
			-1.6					1.4	1.5
		.2	.3	.3			Fixed/Worth	.5	.4
		.6	.9	.6				.9	.7
		1.5	1.8	1.8				2.0	1.5
		.5	.8	.3			Debt/Worth	.8	.7
		1.1	1.4	.7				1.7	1.3
		3.7	5.2	2.8				4.9	3.2
		27.7	18.7	27.0			% Profit Before Taxes/Tangible Net Worth	41.4	49.8
	(20)	1.8	(43) -2.2	(23) 10.1				(134) 22.6	(107) 23.4
		-13.3	-27.3	-6.2				5.2	5.7
		8.8	4.7	11.8			% Profit Before Taxes/Total Assets	17.6	20.1
		1.0	-1.1	3.6				5.6	9.5
		-10.2	-10.3	-6.3				.8	1.6
		31.5	15.4	6.8			Sales/Net Fixed Assets	12.2	12.9
		12.6	6.5	4.6				6.9	7.2
		6.3	3.1	2.9				4.2	4.4
		2.6	2.2	2.0			Sales/Total Assets	2.5	2.9
		2.2	1.7	1.5				1.9	2.1
		1.4	1.3	1.2				1.5	1.6
		1.1	1.7	2.3			% Depr., Dep., Amort./Sales	1.5	1.7
	(22)	2.8	(41) 2.8	(25) 4.0				(136) 2.8	(102) 2.8
		4.9	5.9	4.9				4.6	4.4
		2.0	2.0				% Officers', Directors' Owners' Comp/Sales	1.4	1.4
	(12)	5.1	(16) 4.2					(54) 3.1	(42) 3.3
		6.2	5.1					5.4	6.7
1325M	62400M	417541M	1083077M	642613M	1894793M		Net Sales ($)	6358139M	5901083M
511M	26673M	228914M	703329M	435132M	1586011M		Total Assets ($)	3281119M	3465145M

M = $ thousand   MM = $ million
See Pages 9 through 22 for Explanation of Ratios and Data

Comparative Historical Data

Current Data Sorted by Sales

4/1/07-3/31/08 ALL	4/1/08-3/31/09 ALL	4/1/09-3/31/10 ALL	Type of Statement	0-1MM	1-3MM	3-5MM	5-10MM	10-25MM	25MM & OVER
31	28	30	Unqualified	1	3	3	4	8	18
32	27	19	Reviewed				4	6	2
18	14	22	Compiled	1	11	1	4	3	2
5	4	6	Tax Returns			2		1	
45	40	38	Other	3	3	6	9	5	12
					19 (4/1-9/30/09)		96 (10/1/09-3/31/10)		
131	113	115	**NUMBER OF STATEMENTS**	5	20	12	21	23	34
%	%	%	**ASSETS**	%	%	%	%	%	%
5.7	5.9	7.6	Cash & Equivalents		11.1	12.6	10.2	4.8	4.8
26.6	21.4	23.0	Trade Receivables (net)		23.9	20.4	20.8	25.9	23.2
24.9	25.6	26.5	Inventory		27.1	27.0	25.6	33.6	20.7
1.8	1.8	2.8	All Other Current		.5	2.6	1.6	2.4	5.0
59.1	54.8	59.9	Total Current		62.6	62.5	58.2	66.8	53.7
30.5	31.9	29.2	Fixed Assets (net)		25.4	30.3	32.0	26.7	29.9
4.9	6.4	4.5	Intangibles (net)		2.1	2.6	5.0	.3	9.6
5.6	7.0	6.4	All Other Non-Current		9.8	4.6	4.8	6.1	6.9
100.0	100.0	100.0	Total		100.0	100.0	100.0	100.0	100.0
			LIABILITIES						
10.4	13.2	12.3	Notes Payable-Short Term		15.4	7.0	14.1	10.8	12.1
5.1	5.0	3.7	Cur. Mat.-L.T.D.		5.4	2.6	4.8	3.2	2.9
14.2	10.8	12.6	Trade Payables		6.5	14.4	13.5	16.0	11.6
.2	.0	.1	Income Taxes Payable		.0	.1	.1	.1	.2
8.1	9.2	8.5	All Other Current		8.4	8.1	6.1	8.6	8.4
38.0	38.3	37.2	Total Current		35.7	32.4	38.5	38.6	35.2
16.9	18.1	14.5	Long-Term Debt		15.1	19.1	12.3	14.5	14.6
.8	.7	.7	Deferred Taxes		.1	.7	1.2	.8	.7
6.5	7.5	8.5	All Other Non-Current		6.9	4.9	2.0	11.8	9.8
37.8	35.3	39.2	Net Worth		42.2	43.0	46.0	34.3	39.6
100.0	100.0	100.0	Total Liabilities & Net Worth		100.0	100.0	100.0	100.0	100.0
			INCOME DATA						
100.0	100.0	100.0	Net Sales		100.0	100.0	100.0	100.0	100.0
24.7	24.9	24.2	Gross Profit		27.5	25.0	22.9	21.7	25.8
20.2	21.0	22.9	Operating Expenses		29.2	23.6	23.2	20.8	19.8
4.5	3.9	1.3	Operating Profit		-1.8	1.4	-.3	.9	6.0
1.4	1.3	1.5	All Other Expenses (net)		.6	.2	3.5	1.1	1.9
3.1	2.5	-.3	Profit Before Taxes		-2.4	1.2	-3.8	-.1	4.2
			RATIOS						
2.7	2.8	3.3	Current		4.6	4.8	3.7	2.7	2.8
1.6	1.5	1.7			2.6	2.0	1.4	1.7	1.6
1.1	1.0	1.1			1.3	1.2	1.0	1.4	1.0
1.5	1.4	1.8	Quick		3.1	2.6	2.1	1.2	1.6
.9	.7	.8			1.7	1.0	.6	.7	.8
.5	.5	.5			.6	.6	.5	.5	.5
31 11.6	27 13.5	36 10.2	Sales/Receivables	36 10.2	18 20.4	32 11.2	36 10.3	42 8.8	
45 8.1	35 10.3	48 7.7		51 7.2	31 11.8	44 8.3	46 8.0	51 7.2	
57 6.4	47 7.7	63 5.8		66 5.5	69 5.3	67 5.5	59 6.2	62 5.9	
32 11.4	37 9.9	41 8.8	Cost of Sales/Inventory	36 10.1	45 8.1	45 8.1	48 7.6	39 9.4	
53 6.9	56 6.5	64 5.7		62 5.9	62 5.9	69 5.3	69 5.3	56 6.5	
76 4.8	95 3.8	98 3.7		121 3.0	95 3.8	108 3.4	96 3.8	108 3.4	
17 22.0	12 29.4	17 21.4	Cost of Sales/Payables	10 38.3	9 41.0	15 24.7	21 17.2	21 17.2	
32 11.6	22 16.8	30 12.1		17 20.9	29 12.5	30 12.3	30 12.1	34 10.6	
45 8.2	35 10.3	43 8.4		30 12.2	68 5.4	40 9.2	48 7.6	46 8.0	
5.3	5.1	4.2	Sales/Working Capital		2.6	4.3	4.5	4.4	4.5
9.0	11.7	7.6			4.3	8.4	11.0	6.4	8.1
60.9	230.8	25.5			17.7	22.2	92.1	14.0	77.7
11.8	7.1	6.4	EBIT/Interest		5.2	6.0	5.1	6.3	14.8
(122) 3.1	(106) 2.6	(107) 1.2		(17) 1.9	(11) 1.0	(19) .1	1.2	(32) 4.3	
.9	.3	-5.3			-8.3	-3.0	-8.6	-7.3	-3.2
8.0	4.0	3.1	Net Profit + Depr., Dep., Amort./Cur. Mat. L/T/D						9.0
(41) 2.5	(31) 1.9	(34) 1.3						(14)	1.7
1.5	.8	.0							-3.1
.4	.4	.3	Fixed/Worth		.2	.1	.3	.3	.4
.7	1.0	.7			.6	.9	.9	.7	.8
2.6	3.9	1.8			1.9	3.7	1.5	1.3	2.5
.7	.5	.4	Debt/Worth		.5	.4	.4	.4	.4
1.3	1.6	1.5			1.0	1.5	1.1	1.5	2.1
6.0	9.4	4.6			3.5	6.5	5.4	4.4	4.9
35.6	29.2	24.4	% Profit Before Taxes/Tangible Net Worth		14.5	24.6	22.1	15.3	54.3
(112) 17.9	(91) 12.1	(100) 1.8		(17) 1.2	(11) .2	(20) -1.3	(22) 2.7	(27) 21.6	
1.4	-1.7	-19.6			-20.4	-2.2	-26.4	-29.9	-5.1
15.1	13.0	9.6	% Profit Before Taxes/Total Assets		8.1	8.0	6.5	8.4	15.9
6.9	4.2	.9			.9	.7	-1.1	.0	6.3
.2	-1.6	-9.4			-11.7	-.9	-9.7	-10.2	-4.4
14.9	13.7	13.1	Sales/Net Fixed Assets		20.2	44.0	12.3	24.7	7.5
7.8	6.2	6.4			7.2	11.8	4.2	8.6	5.3
4.0	3.9	3.6			4.5	2.6	3.0	2.9	3.5
2.7	2.6	2.2	Sales/Total Assets		2.2	2.7	1.8	2.5	2.0
2.0	2.0	1.7			1.7	2.2	1.5	1.9	1.6
1.6	1.4	1.3			1.2	1.4	1.2	1.4	1.2
1.6	1.8	1.8	% Depr., Dep., Amort./Sales		1.1	.7	2.5	1.3	2.1
(116) 2.8	(101) 2.9	(103) 3.4		(19) 3.6	(11) 2.8	(19) 5.5	(21) 1.9	(29) 3.4	
4.2	4.4	5.4			6.4	5.2	6.2	4.1	4.4
1.4	1.7	1.9	% Officers', Directors' Owners' Comp/Sales		3.4				
(45) 3.8	(39) 3.8	(34) 4.2		(12) 5.1					
7.3	6.9	5.8			6.9				
5760168M	5166648M	4101749M	Net Sales ($)	3055M	42092M	44791M	153265M	389717M	3468829M
3190810M	3023015M	2980570M	Total Assets ($)	1785M	29077M	27467M	102679M	238443M	2581119M

Current Data Sorted by Assets — **Comparative Historical Data**

Type of Statement	05-06 ALL	06-07 ALL
Unqualified	8	15
Reviewed	9	6
Compiled	6	3
Tax Returns		2
Other	15	15

	0-500M	500M-2MM	2-10MM	10-50MM	50-100MM	100-250MM	4/1/05-3/31/06 ALL	4/1/06-3/31/07 ALL
			2	2	4	2		
			11	2				
		3	4	1				
	1	1	2	9	2	1		
	1							
date range	9 (4/1-9/30/09)			47 (10/1/09-3/31/10)				
NUMBER OF STATEMENTS	1	6	26	14	6	3	38	41
	%	%	%	%	%	%	%	%
ASSETS								
Cash & Equivalents			5.9	2.4			6.2	8.4
Trade Receivables (net)			25.5	20.1			26.0	23.2
Inventory			30.8	24.3			23.9	21.3
All Other Current			1.1	2.4			1.3	1.4
Total Current			63.3	49.3			57.4	54.2
Fixed Assets (net)			24.9	31.2			34.1	34.9
Intangibles (net)			6.6	13.8			4.8	4.0
All Other Non-Current			5.2	5.7			3.8	6.9
Total			100.0	100.0			100.0	100.0
LIABILITIES								
Notes Payable-Short Term			13.7	6.6			9.6	6.7
Cur. Mat.-L.T.D.			9.5	7.4			3.6	4.5
Trade Payables			16.2	12.8			16.4	18.3
Income Taxes Payable			.1	.0			.1	.3
All Other Current			7.1	5.3			7.4	9.9
Total Current			46.5	32.0			37.1	39.8
Long-Term Debt			17.6	18.5			17.5	17.0
Deferred Taxes			.8	.2			1.4	1.4
All Other Non-Current			5.4	9.4			10.6	6.8
Net Worth			29.7	39.8			33.5	35.1
Total Liabilities & Net Worth			100.0	100.0			100.0	100.0
INCOME DATA								
Net Sales			100.0	100.0			100.0	100.0
Gross Profit			26.4	28.2			27.3	22.4
Operating Expenses			22.4	22.1			23.4	19.0
Operating Profit			4.0	6.0			3.8	3.4
All Other Expenses (net)			1.0	2.1			1.7	1.5
Profit Before Taxes			3.1	3.9			2.1	1.9
RATIOS								
Current			2.9	5.5			2.6	2.2
			1.4	1.4			1.5	1.3
			1.0	.8			1.1	1.1
Quick			1.5	1.7			1.4	1.3
			.7	.6			.9	.9
			.4	.5			.5	.4
Sales/Receivables			28 13.0	33 11.2			36 10.0	27 13.3
			38 9.5	40 9.1			47 7.8	39 9.4
			48 7.7	53 6.9			53 6.8	50 7.3
Cost of Sales/Inventory			35 10.5	46 8.0			39 9.4	34 10.8
			50 7.3	66 5.5			58 6.3	41 8.9
			104 3.5	106 3.4			84 4.3	71 5.1
Cost of Sales/Payables			19 19.0	16 23.0			30 12.4	26 14.3
			33 11.2	35 10.3			38 9.6	37 9.9
			45 8.0	56 6.5			47 7.7	47 7.7
Sales/Working Capital			5.2	3.8			5.2	7.2
			15.6	13.0			10.4	16.9
			NM	-36.3			51.0	94.4
EBIT/Interest			4.5	4.4			5.5	9.1
		(24)	1.8	(13) 1.8			(37) 2.2	(38) 4.1
			.4	1.3			1.0	1.4
Net Profit + Depr., Dep., Amort./Cur. Mat. L/T/D							4.5	4.1
							(11) 2.2	(15) 2.4
							.7	1.8
Fixed/Worth			.5	.7			.4	.5
			.8	1.8			1.1	1.0
			NM	NM			2.5	3.3
Debt/Worth			.8	.6			.8	.8
			2.5	3.4			2.1	1.8
			NM	NM			4.3	5.5
% Profit Before Taxes/Tangible Net Worth			30.7	51.5			29.0	49.2
		(20)	11.6	(11) 22.2			(32) 13.3	(34) 19.3
			2.4	2.6			.6	5.2
% Profit Before Taxes/Total Assets			9.0	10.5			9.7	13.3
			2.7	4.2			4.5	5.5
			-.4	1.0			.1	.6
Sales/Net Fixed Assets			20.2	11.6			10.7	13.0
			8.9	5.7			5.1	6.7
			6.2	3.5			3.5	3.5
Sales/Total Assets			3.0	2.1			2.3	3.0
			2.3	1.8			1.8	2.0
			1.8	1.5			1.5	1.5
% Depr., Dep., Amort./Sales			.9	1.6			1.6	1.6
		(22)	1.7	(12) 2.6			(34) 3.4	(36) 2.8
			3.6	4.1			5.0	4.7
% Officers', Directors' Owners' Comp/Sales			1.4				3.6	.9
		(14)	4.3				(11) 3.8	(12) 3.4
			5.9				5.8	5.0
Net Sales ($)	677M	17543M	326485M	403177M	701026M	568782M	1605222M	2313399M
Total Assets ($)	310M	6267M	132545M	254728M	462690M	485743M	958817M	1297650M

M = $ thousand   MM = $ million
See Pages 9 through 22 for Explanation of Ratios and Data

Comparative Historical Data | Current Data Sorted by Sales

Type of Statement	4/1/07-3/31/08 ALL	4/1/08-3/31/09 ALL	4/1/09-3/31/10 ALL	0-1MM	1-3MM	3-5MM	5-10MM	10-25MM	25MM & OVER
Unqualified	11	11	10					3	7
Reviewed	12	9	13			1		9	1
Compiled	4	3	8			3	2	2	
Tax Returns	8	4	2	1		1	2		
Other	16	21	23	1	1	2	5	6	9
						9 (4/1-9/30/09)		47 (10/1/09-3/31/10)	
NUMBER OF STATEMENTS	51	48	56	2	1	7	9	20	17
ASSETS	%	%	%	%	%	%	%	%	%
Cash & Equivalents	7.6	4.5	4.4					4.3	3.6
Trade Receivables (net)	23.7	21.5	23.5					25.5	20.0
Inventory	25.9	31.7	26.6					25.8	23.5
All Other Current	2.2	2.3	1.4					1.4	2.6
Total Current	59.3	60.0	55.9					57.0	49.7
Fixed Assets (net)	27.7	28.2	26.5					31.3	25.4
Intangibles (net)	6.0	6.7	12.3					6.7	18.2
All Other Non-Current	6.9	5.1	5.3					5.0	6.8
Total	100.0	100.0	100.0					100.0	100.0
LIABILITIES									
Notes Payable-Short Term	12.3	10.8	9.4					11.7	5.5
Cur. Mat.-L.T.D.	4.9	5.6	8.3					11.7	4.9
Trade Payables	15.7	15.9	15.3					15.1	13.1
Income Taxes Payable	.2	.1	.2					.1	.6
All Other Current	8.2	7.0	7.1					4.6	9.0
Total Current	41.3	39.4	40.4					43.2	33.0
Long-Term Debt	18.7	24.7	22.2					14.4	28.2
Deferred Taxes	1.0	.9	.9					.5	1.5
All Other Non-Current	8.0	7.0	7.3					7.6	8.5
Net Worth	31.0	28.0	29.3					34.3	28.8
Total Liabilities & Net Worth	100.0	100.0	100.0					100.0	100.0
INCOME DATA									
Net Sales	100.0	100.0	100.0					100.0	100.0
Gross Profit	23.7	28.2	27.8					23.9	28.7
Operating Expenses	19.5	23.2	23.2					18.1	23.3
Operating Profit	4.3	5.0	4.6					5.8	5.4
All Other Expenses (net)	1.8	2.3	1.7					.8	2.5
Profit Before Taxes	2.5	2.7	2.9					5.1	2.8
RATIOS									
Current	2.4	2.9	2.4					3.9	3.2
Current	1.5	1.6	1.3					1.2	1.8
Current	1.2	1.1	1.0					.8	1.1
Quick	1.5	1.3	1.4					2.4	1.6
Quick	.9	.8	.7					.7	.9
Quick	.5	.4	.5					.4	.5
Sales/Receivables	29 12.6	23 16.2	32 11.5					27 13.7	31 11.8
Sales/Receivables	41 8.9	37 9.9	40 9.2					39 9.4	47 7.7
Sales/Receivables	50 7.3	51 7.2	51 7.1					50 7.2	60 6.1
Cost of Sales/Inventory	31 11.7	39 9.3	39 9.3					32 11.2	47 7.8
Cost of Sales/Inventory	52 7.0	71 5.2	57 6.5					46 7.9	66 5.5
Cost of Sales/Inventory	91 4.0	108 3.4	100 3.6					73 5.0	107 3.4
Cost of Sales/Payables	22 16.8	21 17.1	20 18.1					17 21.9	19 19.0
Cost of Sales/Payables	32 11.4	31 11.8	35 10.4					33 11.2	35 10.4
Cost of Sales/Payables	47 7.8	43 8.5	48 7.6					40 9.2	48 7.6
Sales/Working Capital	6.3	5.4	5.2					8.4	4.4
Sales/Working Capital	11.5	11.7	14.6					19.9	10.7
Sales/Working Capital	30.7	58.1	536.7					-28.0	27.9
EBIT/Interest	14.2	8.3	4.2					7.2	3.2
EBIT/Interest	(47) 3.7	(46) 1.8	(50) 1.7					(17) 2.2	(15) 1.5
EBIT/Interest	1.0	-.5	.9					1.4	1.1
Net Profit + Depr., Dep., Amort./Cur. Mat. L/T/D	3.7	3.5	2.8						
Net Profit + Depr., Dep., Amort./Cur. Mat. L/T/D	(18) 2.4	(14) 1.1	(18) 1.6						
Net Profit + Depr., Dep., Amort./Cur. Mat. L/T/D	.7	.0	.2						
Fixed/Worth	.4	.6	.6					.5	.8
Fixed/Worth	1.0	1.4	1.3					1.0	1.9
Fixed/Worth	3.3	-8.0	-5.2					2.3	-3.0
Debt/Worth	.9	1.0	1.2					.8	1.7
Debt/Worth	2.4	3.4	3.3					2.1	4.8
Debt/Worth	9.2	-20.6	-15.4					5.1	-10.5
% Profit Before Taxes/Tangible Net Worth	48.5	41.7	41.4					40.0	51.5
% Profit Before Taxes/Tangible Net Worth	(40) 17.6	(34) 17.7	(40) 15.0					(17) 21.0	(11) 8.6
% Profit Before Taxes/Tangible Net Worth	5.1	-14.1	2.7					2.6	-8.9
% Profit Before Taxes/Total Assets	14.6	16.4	8.7					18.8	8.4
% Profit Before Taxes/Total Assets	6.2	4.0	3.1					6.5	2.1
% Profit Before Taxes/Total Assets	.1	-4.1	.1					1.4	-1.2
Sales/Net Fixed Assets	17.9	16.1	17.1					14.5	9.9
Sales/Net Fixed Assets	8.2	7.5	7.8					7.3	6.2
Sales/Net Fixed Assets	4.9	4.6	4.8					4.7	4.6
Sales/Total Assets	2.5	2.7	2.5					2.6	2.3
Sales/Total Assets	2.1	2.2	2.0					2.2	1.6
Sales/Total Assets	1.5	1.6	1.5					1.9	1.1
% Depr., Dep., Amort./Sales	1.5	1.2	1.4					1.4	1.8
% Depr., Dep., Amort./Sales	(46) 2.6	(44) 2.3	(48) 2.3					(17) 2.0	(16) 2.8
% Depr., Dep., Amort./Sales	4.5	3.6	4.2					4.4	4.8
% Officers', Directors' Owners' Comp/Sales	1.2	1.7	1.8						
% Officers', Directors' Owners' Comp/Sales	(17) 1.9	(15) 2.7	(18) 4.3						
% Officers', Directors' Owners' Comp/Sales	6.3	7.5	6.0						
Net Sales ($)	1751145M	2624494M	2017690M	1455M	2748M	27487M	61636M	360229M	1564135M
Total Assets ($)	1053354M	1674757M	1342283M	863M	1162M	12483M	34776M	173967M	1119032M

M = $ thousand   MM = $ million
See Pages 9 through 22 for Explanation of Ratios and Data

MANUFACTURING—Polystyrene Foam Product Manufacturing NAICS 326140

| Current Data Sorted by Assets | | | | | | | Comparative Historical Data | |

Type of Statement

0-500M	500M-2MM	2-10MM	10-50MM	50-100MM	100-250MM	Type of Statement	4/1/05-3/31/06 ALL	4/1/06-3/31/07 ALL
		3	10	3	2	Unqualified	14	25
	2	6	5	1		Reviewed	17	19
2	3	1	1	1		Compiled	15	11
	1	2				Tax Returns	6	6
	6	9	6	1	1	Other	23	34
	12 (4/1-9/30/09)		54 (10/1/09-3/31/10)					
2	12	21	22	6	3	NUMBER OF STATEMENTS	75	95

Data Table

0-500M %	500M-2MM %	2-10MM %	10-50MM %	50-100MM %	100-250MM %		4/1/05-3/31/06 ALL %	4/1/06-3/31/07 ALL %
						ASSETS		
	5.4	9.0	6.1			Cash & Equivalents	7.6	8.1
	28.7	27.2	23.4			Trade Receivables (net)	29.0	28.2
	22.0	20.1	20.7			Inventory	20.4	21.3
	2.4	2.7	2.1			All Other Current	1.5	1.8
	58.5	59.0	52.2			Total Current	58.4	59.4
	33.3	32.4	37.7			Fixed Assets (net)	32.4	30.7
	5.9	4.5	6.3			Intangibles (net)	3.9	4.1
	2.2	4.2	3.8			All Other Non-Current	5.3	5.9
	100.0	100.0	100.0			Total	100.0	100.0
						LIABILITIES		
	15.4	8.8	6.5			Notes Payable-Short Term	9.7	9.8
	5.6	7.6	5.5			Cur. Mat.-L.T.D.	5.7	3.7
	22.7	12.1	11.2			Trade Payables	19.6	16.2
	.0	.0	.0			Income Taxes Payable	.2	.1
	13.8	5.7	6.7			All Other Current	6.6	7.6
	57.5	34.2	30.0			Total Current	41.8	37.4
	15.1	17.7	20.1			Long-Term Debt	17.9	21.0
	.3	.4	.5			Deferred Taxes	.3	.5
	13.1	3.1	2.1			All Other Non-Current	4.7	5.7
	13.9	44.7	47.4			Net Worth	35.2	35.4
	100.0	100.0	100.0			Total Liabilities & Net Worth	100.0	100.0
						INCOME DATA		
	100.0	100.0	100.0			Net Sales	100.0	100.0
	30.1	27.2	26.1			Gross Profit	27.9	25.3
	36.3	24.6	18.9			Operating Expenses	22.8	20.3
	-6.2	2.6	7.2			Operating Profit	5.2	5.0
	.8	.6	2.1			All Other Expenses (net)	.8	.8
	-7.0	2.1	5.1			Profit Before Taxes	4.4	4.2
						RATIOS		
	2.8	3.3	2.7				2.0	2.6
	1.0	2.2	1.5			Current	1.5	1.7
	.5	1.2	1.1				1.0	1.1
	1.4	1.9	1.7				1.3	1.6
	.6	1.1	.9			Quick	.9	.9
	.3	.6	.6				.6	.6
	22 16.5	41 8.9	29 12.5				35 10.4	31 11.8
	49 7.4	53 6.9	37 9.9			Sales/Receivables	44 8.4	39 9.3
	64 5.7	61 6.0	54 6.8				54 6.7	55 6.6
	11 31.7	32 11.5	33 10.9				32 11.5	27 13.5
	39 9.2	52 7.0	48 7.6			Cost of Sales/Inventory	45 8.0	43 8.4
	77 4.7	69 5.3	62 5.9				57 6.4	61 6.0
	27 13.3	16 23.0	14 26.9				20 18.1	17 20.9
	47 7.8	25 14.7	24 15.5			Cost of Sales/Payables	36 10.1	27 13.8
	66 5.5	42 8.8	36 10.2				54 6.8	43 8.5
	6.4	4.6	5.3				7.6	6.8
	556.0	6.9	12.4			Sales/Working Capital	13.2	12.5
	-4.5	29.9	NM				-291.9	47.0
		11.9	11.4				11.6	10.4
		(18) 4.4	(20) 4.1			EBIT/Interest	(67) 4.1	(88) 4.1
		.7	1.5				1.8	1.8
							5.0	6.2
						Net Profit + Depr., Dep., Amort./Cur. Mat. L/T/D	(21) 2.9	(27) 3.7
							1.5	1.7
	1.0	.4	.5				.4	.4
	5.7	.6	1.2			Fixed/Worth	.9	.8
	-2.3	2.8	2.4				3.3	2.5
	1.7	.4	.8				1.1	.8
	14.2	.9	1.5			Debt/Worth	2.1	1.8
	-6.9	4.0	3.7				5.7	6.8
		42.7	67.1				52.6	53.0
	(19)	20.6	24.9			% Profit Before Taxes/Tangible Net Worth	(65) 23.1	(84) 27.3
		-1.6	4.2				6.2	8.9
	2.3	15.2	19.1				15.1	17.5
	-10.2	7.1	6.1			% Profit Before Taxes/Total Assets	6.9	7.7
	-22.1	-2.7	1.3				2.2	2.7
	18.3	13.0	13.2				16.1	15.0
	10.6	8.0	5.0			Sales/Net Fixed Assets	7.3	8.2
	6.2	4.2	3.3				4.0	5.1
	3.4	2.6	2.3				3.3	3.2
	2.3	2.1	2.0			Sales/Total Assets	2.2	2.4
	1.7	1.5	1.6				1.6	1.7
	2.2	1.6	2.2				1.7	1.5
	(11) 2.9	2.4	(19) 3.8			% Depr., Dep., Amort./Sales	(67) 2.9	(80) 2.4
	4.5	6.4	4.6				4.8	3.8
							1.6	1.0
						% Officers', Directors' Owners' Comp/Sales	(26) 3.8	(30) 3.3
							6.9	6.6
3644M	38324M	240159M	1005623M	613823M	624610M	Net Sales ($)	2342109M	4848850M
862M	15178M	113878M	490581M	414301M	465531M	Total Assets ($)	1218339M	2394881M

M = $ thousand   MM = $ million
See Pages 9 through 22 for Explanation of Ratios and Data

Comparative Historical Data | Current Data Sorted by Sales

Hist 1	Hist 2	Hist 3	Type of Statement	0-1MM	1-3MM	3-5MM	5-10MM	10-25MM	25MM & OVER
20	20	18	Unqualified		2	2	1	3	14
18	13	14	Reviewed		6			5	4
8	13	8	Compiled						2
3	3	3	Tax Returns			1	1		
31	40	23	Other		2	4	4	7	6
4/1/07-3/31/08 ALL	4/1/08-3/31/09 ALL	4/1/09-3/31/10 ALL			12 (4/1-9/30/09)		54 (10/1/09-3/31/10)		
80	89	66	NUMBER OF STATEMENTS	10	10	7	7	16	26
%	%	%	**ASSETS**	%	%	%	%	%	%
8.5	4.8	7.5	Cash & Equivalents		7.6			8.8	7.3
25.7	25.9	25.1	Trade Receivables (net)		25.5			28.1	22.7
20.7	24.0	19.8	Inventory		23.1			17.5	19.3
3.1	4.1	2.6	All Other Current		2.4			1.5	3.1
58.1	58.8	55.0	Total Current		58.6			55.9	52.5
33.6	33.2	34.0	Fixed Assets (net)		38.6			38.6	30.9
2.3	3.2	5.5	Intangibles (net)		1.5			1.3	7.2
6.0	4.8	5.5	All Other Non-Current		1.3			4.1	9.4
100.0	100.0	100.0	Total		100.0			100.0	100.0
			LIABILITIES						
5.9	12.0	9.0	Notes Payable-Short Term		19.9			6.6	5.8
3.3	4.7	6.0	Cur. Mat.-L.T.D.		3.3			4.4	4.7
14.7	14.4	14.5	Trade Payables		17.0			12.6	12.0
.1	.1	.0	Income Taxes Payable		.0			.0	.0
7.7	7.5	7.0	All Other Current		3.6			5.8	6.1
31.6	38.7	36.6	Total Current		43.7			29.3	28.6
22.1	19.5	17.0	Long-Term Debt		20.7			20.8	13.6
.4	.6	.5	Deferred Taxes		.0			.8	.6
5.2	6.5	8.6	All Other Non-Current		27.2			.7	6.6
40.6	34.8	37.2	Net Worth		8.4			48.4	50.6
100.0	100.0	100.0	Total Liabilities & Net Worth		100.0			100.0	100.0
			INCOME DATA						
100.0	100.0	100.0	Net Sales		100.0			100.0	100.0
23.2	23.6	25.8	Gross Profit		29.2			27.1	22.9
18.3	21.3	23.4	Operating Expenses		37.1			21.0	16.6
4.9	2.2	2.4	Operating Profit		-7.9			6.1	6.3
1.1	1.1	1.6	All Other Expenses (net)		.1			1.6	2.4
3.8	1.1	.8	Profit Before Taxes		-7.9			4.5	3.9
			RATIOS						
2.7	2.6	2.8	Current		3.6			3.0	2.8
1.8	1.5	1.6			1.6			2.0	1.8
1.2	1.2	1.0			.6			1.2	1.3
1.6	1.4	1.7	Quick		1.7			1.9	1.8
1.1	.8	.9			1.1			1.1	.8
.6	.5	.5			.3			.9	.6
30 12.1	25 14.4	32 11.3	Sales/Receivables		35 10.6			42 8.8	29 12.6
42 8.8	37 9.9	47 7.8			52 7.1			52 7.0	37 9.8
52 7.1	50 7.3	57 6.4			63 5.8			66 5.5	54 6.8
24 15.3	30 12.2	30 12.0	Cost of Sales/Inventory		25 14.7			31 11.7	31 11.6
40 9.1	38 9.7	43 8.5			69 5.3			39 9.4	43 8.4
57 6.5	67 5.5	67 5.5			127 2.9			61 6.0	59 6.1
16 22.5	14 26.5	15 24.7	Cost of Sales/Payables		19 19.1			19 19.1	14 26.9
28 13.3	25 14.9	28 13.0			42 8.8			27 13.3	23 15.7
39 9.4	34 10.6	44 8.3			65 5.6			44 8.3	39 9.3
6.0	6.2	5.3	Sales/Working Capital		2.5			5.5	5.3
10.3	13.1	12.0			12.4			7.9	11.3
24.3	55.6	NM			-6.2			35.4	20.9
7.7	9.0	8.6	EBIT/Interest					11.3	12.2
(74) 3.9	(84) 3.3	(57) 2.7						(15) 4.4	(23) 3.9
.7	-.1	-1.2						1.1	1.2
5.5	4.5	7.8	Net Profit + Depr., Dep., Amort./Cur. Mat. L/T/D						8.2
(27) 2.5	(28) 2.8	(22) 3.7							(10) 3.7
1.3	1.7	1.1							1.8
.4	.5	.5	Fixed/Worth		1.1			.4	.4
.9	.9	1.1			NM			.6	.7
1.8	5.3	3.8			-.8			2.1	1.5
.5	.7	.8	Debt/Worth		.9			.5	.5
1.4	1.9	1.8			NM			.9	1.4
4.8	10.8	8.4			-4.2			2.5	2.8
36.1	32.3	42.8	% Profit Before Taxes/Tangible Net Worth					41.3	54.3
(73) 20.0	(76) 14.6	(57) 15.7						21.0	(25) 20.5
.3	3.3	-8.8						3.2	1.6
16.0	12.8	15.0	% Profit Before Taxes/Total Assets		3.3			16.7	24.1
7.9	4.4	3.9			-10.4			8.5	5.0
-.7	-1.8	-10.1			-19.3			1.4	-.4
13.7	15.5	13.2	Sales/Net Fixed Assets		20.4			9.7	13.2
7.4	8.3	7.1			7.9			6.2	5.1
3.5	4.1	3.4			1.0			2.9	3.6
3.0	3.3	2.6	Sales/Total Assets		3.6			2.5	2.7
2.3	2.4	2.0			1.8			2.0	1.9
1.5	1.7	1.5			.7			1.5	1.5
1.5	1.4	2.2	% Depr., Dep., Amort./Sales					1.8	2.1
(74) 2.7	(77) 2.1	(62) 3.1						2.7	(23) 3.8
4.4	3.9	5.3						6.0	4.9
1.0	1.7	.7	% Officers', Directors' Owners' Comp/Sales						
(22) 2.7	(22) 3.4	(16) 4.4							
4.7	4.8	9.0							
4432832M	4188094M	2526183M	Net Sales ($)		18234M	30261M	49770M	264819M	2163099M
2227113M	2095623M	1500331M	Total Assets ($)		15705M	13899M	22263M	144239M	1304225M

Note: For 0-1MM column (and certain small-size columns) in the Assets, Liabilities and Income Data sections, DATA NOT AVAILABLE.

M = $ thousand   MM = $ million
See Pages 9 through 22 for Explanation of Ratios and Data

Current Data Sorted by Assets   **Comparative Historical Data**

Periods: 9 (4/1-9/30/09)   25 (10/1/09-3/31/10)

0-500M	500M-2MM	2-10MM	10-50MM	50-100MM	100-250MM		4/1/05-3/31/06 ALL	4/1/06-3/31/07 ALL
		Type of Statement						
		4	3		5	Unqualified	12	13
		5	2			Reviewed	4	4
						Compiled	1	
		1	1			Tax Returns	2	2
		4	4		4	Other	15	14
1		14	10		9	**NUMBER OF STATEMENTS**	34	33
%	%	%	%	%	%	**ASSETS**	%	%
		6.1	10.1			Cash & Equivalents	3.9	8.8
		23.0	17.4			Trade Receivables (net)	21.6	22.4
		22.8	10.1			Inventory	16.0	15.4
		1.2	11.8			All Other Current	1.6	2.5
		53.1	49.3			Total Current	43.0	49.1
		40.5	41.8			Fixed Assets (net)	47.3	42.2
		3.2	2.3			Intangibles (net)	5.0	4.0
		3.3	6.5			All Other Non-Current	4.8	4.7
		100.0	100.0			Total	100.0	100.0
						LIABILITIES		
		7.2	6.2			Notes Payable-Short Term	6.6	6.7
		4.8	4.0			Cur. Mat.-L.T.D.	6.9	5.6
		12.1	12.2			Trade Payables	16.0	13.2
		.3	.0			Income Taxes Payable	.1	.2
		7.2	27.2			All Other Current	7.3	12.8
		31.5	49.5			Total Current	36.9	38.6
		13.5	17.4			Long-Term Debt	31.5	25.6
		1.0	.4			Deferred Taxes	.9	1.0
		1.0	.1			All Other Non-Current	5.9	6.4
		53.0	32.5			Net Worth	24.8	28.4
		100.0	100.0			Total Liabilities & Net Worth	100.0	100.0
						INCOME DATA		
		100.0	100.0			Net Sales	100.0	100.0
		24.0	18.5			Gross Profit	26.5	28.3
		16.6	18.0			Operating Expenses	20.3	20.8
		7.4	.5			Operating Profit	6.2	7.4
		.8	.7			All Other Expenses (net)	2.4	2.1
		6.6	-.1			Profit Before Taxes	3.8	5.4
						RATIOS		
		3.8	2.8			Current	1.7	2.1
		1.9	.9				1.3	1.3
		.9	.8				.8	.8
		2.1	2.3			Quick	1.1	1.4
		1.0	.6				.7	.8
		.5	.1				.5	.5
		29 12.6	14 26.7			Sales/Receivables	30 12.1	29 12.6
		36 10.3	44 8.3				44 8.3	43 8.6
		41 8.8	50 7.3				49 7.4	66 5.6
		26 14.0	0 UND			Cost of Sales/Inventory	31 11.6	26 13.8
		44 8.3	27 13.5				43 8.5	39 9.4
		68 5.4	65 5.6				61 6.0	55 6.6
		11 32.3	0 UND			Cost of Sales/Payables	20 18.3	20 18.0
		23 15.8	35 10.4				36 10.3	33 10.9
		32 11.3	46 7.9				56 6.5	46 7.9
		4.8	4.9			Sales/Working Capital	9.3	7.5
		11.6	NM				13.1	16.1
		NM	-13.6				-25.0	-27.5
		11.7				EBIT/Interest	8.3	10.6
		(12) 7.1					4.0	(31) 3.5
		2.8					.9	1.2
						Net Profit + Depr., Dep., Amort./Cur. Mat. L/T/D	4.5	6.0
							(13) 1.4	(16) 2.4
							.9	1.5
		.3	.5			Fixed/Worth	.9	.6
		.8	1.9				1.7	1.8
		1.7	4.7				5.4	11.4
		.4	.7			Debt/Worth	1.0	1.0
		1.2	4.4				1.6	2.5
		1.8	13.4				14.1	14.4
		36.2				% Profit Before Taxes/Tangible Net Worth	32.1	42.2
		19.4					(27) 25.9	(26) 31.5
		13.7					8.3	8.3
		22.0	10.4			% Profit Before Taxes/Total Assets	16.7	21.7
		10.5	4.4				4.5	8.7
		4.8	-1.3				-.6	.7
		20.3	60.4			Sales/Net Fixed Assets	6.1	11.1
		6.3	4.0				2.9	4.1
		2.1	2.0				1.7	1.9
		3.3	3.3			Sales/Total Assets	2.0	2.3
		2.5	1.5				1.5	1.8
		1.4	1.1				1.2	1.1
		.6				% Depr., Dep., Amort./Sales	2.7	2.5
		(13) 2.7					(30) 5.9	(26) 4.6
		4.9					7.9	5.4
						% Officers', Directors' Owners' Comp/Sales	2.2	
							(10) 4.8	
							7.4	
	2659M	232372M	438226M		1732864M	Net Sales ($)	2245018M	2138624M
	1512M	91590M	212327M		1443041M	Total Assets ($)	1482927M	1304711M

Note: Columns 0-500M, 500M-2MM, 50-100MM, and 100-250MM are marked "DATA NOT AVAILABLE" for the statement percentages and ratios.

M = $ thousand   MM = $ million
See Pages 9 through 22 for Explanation of Ratios and Data

Comparative Historical Data | | | Current Data Sorted by Sales

			Type of Statement							
10	11	12	Unqualified				1		1	10
7	6	7	Reviewed			1		4		2
1	1		Compiled				1		1	
	3	2	Tax Returns			2		1		
10	13	13	Other	1	1		1			8
4/1/07-	4/1/08-	4/1/09-			9 (4/1-9/30/09)		25 (10/1/09-3/31/10)			
3/31/08	3/31/09	3/31/10								
ALL	ALL	ALL		0-1MM	1-3MM	3-5MM	5-10MM	10-25MM		25MM & OVER
28	34	34	**NUMBER OF STATEMENTS**	1	2		4	7		20
%	%	%	**ASSETS**	%	%	%	%	%		%
7.3	7.0	7.0	Cash & Equivalents							6.5
22.8	21.6	18.3	Trade Receivables (net)							17.7
15.1	16.3	17.2	Inventory							15.0
1.9	2.0	4.4	All Other Current							7.0
47.1	46.9	46.9	Total Current							46.1
40.8	41.3	43.6	Fixed Assets (net)							42.3
5.1	5.3	5.5	Intangibles (net)							7.0
7.0	6.5	4.0	All Other Non-Current							4.6
100.0	100.0	100.0	Total							100.0
			LIABILITIES							
7.7	7.7	5.0	Notes Payable-Short Term							3.8
4.0	3.7	4.3	Cur. Mat.-L.T.D.							4.2
13.8	13.6	11.2	Trade Payables							13.4
.1	.1	.2	Income Taxes Payable							.4
6.1	7.6	14.2	All Other Current							14.5
31.7	32.8	34.9	Total Current							36.4
27.8	21.2	22.1	Long-Term Debt							25.8
1.0	.9	.7	Deferred Taxes							.7
3.9	3.6	1.8	All Other Non-Current							2.8
35.6	41.5	40.6	Net Worth							34.4
100.0	100.0	100.0	Total Liabilties & Net Worth							100.0
			INCOME DATA							
100.0	100.0	100.0	Net Sales							100.0
23.4	22.6	23.0	Gross Profit							21.8
16.9	17.7	17.2	Operating Expenses							13.8
6.6	4.9	5.8	Operating Profit							8.0
1.8	1.4	1.7	All Other Expenses (net)							2.1
4.7	3.5	4.1	Profit Before Taxes							5.8
			RATIOS							
1.7	2.4	2.6								2.1
1.3	1.4	1.3	Current							1.3
1.0	.9	.9								1.0
1.1	1.4	1.3								1.1
.7	.7	.8	Quick							.8
.6	.5	.4								.4
30 12.1	24 15.4	28 12.9							27	13.6
42 8.6	32 11.4	37 10.0	Sales/Receivables						33	11.1
54 6.7	45 8.1	47 7.8							46	7.9
28 13.2	23 16.1	27 13.6							26	14.3
35 10.4	30 12.1	39 9.3	Cost of Sales/Inventory						37	9.9
51 7.1	43 8.4	77 4.7							70	5.2
22 16.3	17 22.1	16 23.3							23	15.8
33 11.2	30 12.1	31 11.9	Cost of Sales/Payables						37	9.8
54 6.8	39 9.4	44 8.3							48	7.7
8.8	7.3	5.9								6.9
20.0	12.0	14.0	Sales/Working Capital							20.3
91.0	-36.8	-74.1								NM
8.0	10.4	15.9								20.1
(27) 2.8	(32) 1.9	(30) 4.4	EBIT/Interest						(18)	9.5
1.3	1.2	1.8								1.9
13.7	3.3		Net Profit + Depr., Dep.,							
(12) 3.4	(12) 2.1		Amort./Cur. Mat. L/T/D							
1.6	1.0									
.6	.4	.7								.8
1.6	1.2	1.4	Fixed/Worth							2.4
2.5	2.4	3.2								5.1
1.3	.8	.6								1.3
2.1	2.1	2.1	Debt/Worth							3.5
4.4	3.8	6.2								19.7
30.2	36.1	33.8	% Profit Before Taxes/Tangible							41.7
(25) 12.8	(31) 6.9	(30) 18.0	Net Worth						(17)	20.9
1.8	.2	11.5								14.6
10.9	18.0	16.9	% Profit Before Taxes/Total							17.1
4.3	2.8	7.0	Assets							7.0
1.0	.8	2.7								3.0
8.8	17.6	8.2								8.2
4.3	4.5	3.4	Sales/Net Fixed Assets							3.1
2.4	2.7	2.1								2.3
2.2	2.8	2.8								3.3
1.6	2.0	1.6	Sales/Total Assets							1.5
1.1	1.5	1.2								1.1
1.6	1.7	.8								.3
(24) 3.9	(29) 2.9	(22) 2.9	% Depr., Dep., Amort./Sales						(10)	2.9
5.4	5.2	5.7								4.6
			% Officers', Directors'							
			Owners' Comp/Sales							
2143560M	2587317M	2406121M	Net Sales ($)	2659M	9249M	31317M	121802M	2241094M		
1372486M	1466133M	1748470M	Total Assets ($)	1512M	7341M	26628M	61524M	1651465M		

Note on right-side columns: the center sales-range columns (0-1MM, 1-3MM, 3-5MM, 5-10MM, 10-25MM) display "DATA NOT AVAILABLE" for the upper asset/liabilities/income/ratio sections; only the 25MM & OVER column and the statement counts and dollar figures contain values.

M = $ thousand   MM = $ million
See Pages 9 through 22 for Explanation of Ratios and Data

MANUFACTURING—Plastics Plumbing Fixture Manufacturing NAICS 326191

		Current Data Sorted by Assets				Comparative Historical Data		
		2	3	2	1	Type of Statement		
		4	2			Unqualified	4	6
		1				Reviewed	4	3
1	1	3	4	1	1	Compiled	2	3
	3	5				Tax Returns	1	
	3 (4/1-9/30/09)		28 (10/1/09-3/31/10)			Other	5	6
							4/1/05-3/31/06	4/1/06-3/31/07
0-500M	500M-2MM	2-10MM	10-50MM	50-100MM	100-250MM		ALL	ALL
1	4	12	9	3	2	NUMBER OF STATEMENTS	16	18
%	%	%	%	%	%		%	%
						ASSETS		
		6.0				Cash & Equivalents	3.3	6.1
		22.7				Trade Receivables (net)	28.0	23.6
		33.9				Inventory	35.2	31.6
		4.8				All Other Current	1.7	1.9
		67.4				Total Current	68.2	63.2
		25.4				Fixed Assets (net)	24.0	21.9
		4.9				Intangibles (net)	4.8	9.6
		2.3				All Other Non-Current	3.0	5.3
		100.0				Total	100.0	100.0
						LIABILITIES		
		11.9				Notes Payable-Short Term	12.2	4.6
		2.9				Cur. Mat.-L.T.D.	3.9	6.0
		15.5				Trade Payables	24.1	16.6
		.0				Income Taxes Payable	.0	.0
		8.2				All Other Current	8.0	10.3
		38.4				Total Current	48.1	37.6
		7.8				Long-Term Debt	11.9	27.7
		.1				Deferred Taxes	.1	.5
		1.8				All Other Non-Current	3.2	19.1
		51.9				Net Worth	36.7	15.1
		100.0				Total Liabilities & Net Worth	100.0	100.0
						INCOME DATA		
		100.0				Net Sales	100.0	100.0
		26.3				Gross Profit	28.0	29.4
		22.1				Operating Expenses	26.4	23.3
		4.2				Operating Profit	1.6	6.1
		.4				All Other Expenses (net)	.8	1.9
		3.8				Profit Before Taxes	.8	4.2
						RATIOS		
		4.0					2.0	2.8
		1.6				Current	1.6	2.1
		1.1					1.1	1.2
		1.7					1.1	1.8
		.8				Quick	.9	.9
		.4					.3	.6
	15	25.1					21	17.4	17	22.0
	31	11.6				Sales/Receivables	32	11.3	34	10.7
	38	9.6					53	6.9	55	6.7
	35	10.3					41	8.9	48	7.5
	57	6.4				Cost of Sales/Inventory	54	6.7	60	6.1
	85	4.3					74	4.9	103	3.5
	20	18.7					19	19.1	13	28.5
	29	12.5				Cost of Sales/Payables	31	11.7	23	16.0
	32	11.6					51	7.1	49	7.4
		6.5					8.3	5.1
		15.3				Sales/Working Capital	10.9	8.3
		40.2					755.9	27.8
							8.8	10.1
						EBIT/Interest	(15) 4.2	(17) 2.9
							-2.4	1.2
						Net Profit + Depr., Dep., Amort./Cur. Mat. L/T/D		
		.1					.3	.2
		.7				Fixed/Worth	.7	.7
		1.0					1.7	-22.2
		.3					.7	.7
		.9				Debt/Worth	1.2	1.9
		1.9					6.5	-75.1
		50.9					47.0	31.6
	(11)	23.0				% Profit Before Taxes/Tangible Net Worth	(14) 19.9	(13) 23.7
		-9.8					-11.1	.0
		29.9					20.2	21.1
		12.8				% Profit Before Taxes/Total Assets	1.9	9.9
		-5.9					-9.3	1.0
		50.0					32.5	29.9
		12.1				Sales/Net Fixed Assets	13.4	10.1
		7.3					8.3	7.2
		3.4					3.9	3.2
		2.5				Sales/Total Assets	3.1	2.7
		2.3					2.8	1.9
		1.4					1.0	1.0
	(11)	1.9				% Depr., Dep., Amort./Sales	(13) 1.7	(16) 1.9
		4.5					3.0	4.1
						% Officers', Directors' Owners' Comp/Sales		
1406M	8752M	181634M	292286M	273676M	644561M	Net Sales ($)	356470M	872076M
418M	4371M	62029M	190550M	233549M	418924M	Total Assets ($)	115824M	513178M

M = $ thousand   MM = $ million
See Pages 9 through 22 for Explanation of Ratios and Data

Comparative Historical Data   Current Data Sorted by Sales

Type of Statement

	4/1/07-3/31/08 ALL	4/1/08-3/31/09 ALL	4/1/09-3/31/10 ALL	0-1MM	1-3MM	3-5MM	5-10MM	10-25MM	25MM & OVER
Unqualified	4	6	8					1	7
Reviewed	4	3	6			1	2	2	1
Compiled	1		1					1	
Tax Returns	2	2	2		2				
Other	9	10	14		2	1	3	3	5
	4/1/07-3/31/08	4/1/08-3/31/09	4/1/09-3/31/10			3 (4/1-9/30/09)		28 (10/1/09-3/31/10)	
NUMBER OF STATEMENTS	20	21	31		4	2	5	7	13
ASSETS	%	%	%	%	%	%	%	%	%
Cash & Equivalents	5.7	4.0	6.5						7.8
Trade Receivables (net)	17.7	23.5	23.7						24.5
Inventory	31.6	30.8	25.9						18.6
All Other Current	3.1	4.0	5.5						9.3
Total Current	58.1	62.4	61.6						60.2
Fixed Assets (net)	29.4	24.6	24.8						19.8
Intangibles (net)	8.3	6.4	8.8						16.9
All Other Non-Current	4.3	6.6	4.8						3.0
Total	100.0	100.0	100.0						100.0
LIABILITIES									
Notes Payable-Short Term	11.4	11.4	9.8						7.2
Cur. Mat.-L.T.D.	4.5	2.4	3.3						4.0
Trade Payables	15.0	12.6	15.4						16.5
Income Taxes Payable	.0	.8	.2						.4
All Other Current	11.6	8.6	9.7						12.0
Total Current	42.5	35.8	38.4						40.0
Long-Term Debt	13.4	16.9	15.8						20.7
Deferred Taxes	.9	.1	.3						.5
All Other Non-Current	5.5	7.2	7.8						13.2
Net Worth	37.6	39.9	37.8						25.6
Total Liabilties & Net Worth	100.0	100.0	100.0						100.0
INCOME DATA									
Net Sales	100.0	100.0	100.0						100.0
Gross Profit	24.8	24.5	29.9						30.9
Operating Expenses	24.4	22.6	25.2						25.4
Operating Profit	.5	1.9	4.6						5.5
All Other Expenses (net)	1.9	1.6	1.0						1.2
Profit Before Taxes	-1.4	.3	3.6						4.4

(Current columns 0-1MM through 10-25MM: DATA NOT AVAILABLE)

RATIOS

Ratio	4/1/07-3/31/08	4/1/08-3/31/09	4/1/09-3/31/10	25MM & OVER
Current	2.7 / 1.6 / 1.0	3.0 / 1.8 / 1.2	2.9 / 1.7 / 1.1	3.1 / 1.6 / .9
Quick	1.3 / .6 / .3	1.4 / .7 / .4	1.7 / 1.1 / .5	1.8 / 1.3 / .3
Sales/Receivables	14 25.8 / 25 14.5 / 39 9.4	23 15.9 / 35 10.6 / 49 7.5	30 12.2 / 40 9.1 / 59 6.2	32 11.3 / 46 8.0 / 66 5.6
Cost of Sales/Inventory	47 7.7 / 64 5.7 / 78 4.7	42 8.7 / 56 6.5 / 78 4.7	44 8.4 / 63 5.8 / 79 4.6	42 8.8 / 58 6.3 / 79 4.6
Cost of Sales/Payables	12 30.3 / 23 16.0 / 43 8.4	10 36.6 / 25 14.6 / 35 10.5	27 13.3 / 32 11.3 / 42 8.7	31 11.8 / 35 10.3 / 54 6.7
Sales/Working Capital	6.9 / 13.3 / -95.3	6.1 / 8.3 / 27.4	4.2 / 12.1 / 48.0	4.4 / 12.1 / -56.2
EBIT/Interest	11.1 / (17) .3 / -2.0	2.7 / (20) -.4 / -3.7	22.3 / (27) 4.9 / .3	5.0 / (11) 2.0 / .3
Net Profit + Depr., Dep., Amort./Cur. Mat. L/T/D			(10) 6.7 / 2.6 / .5	
Fixed/Worth	.4 / 1.4 / 3.7	.3 / .6 / 233.6	.3 / .9 / 7.3	.3 / 1.2 / -1.3
Debt/Worth	.9 / 1.4 / 6.7	.7 / 1.7 / 501.7	.7 / 1.6 / 33.7	.8 / 6.3 / -4.4
% Profit Before Taxes/Tangible Net Worth	42.9 / (17) 5.7 / -44.6	25.9 / (17) -1.7 / -18.0	50.1 / (24) 22.4 / 3.5	
% Profit Before Taxes/Total Assets	15.5 / -.2 / -11.8	5.9 / -3.4 / -12.9	19.8 / 5.3 / -3.4	22.7 / 5.3 / -2.8
Sales/Net Fixed Assets	28.0 / 8.3 / 5.6	23.5 / 13.3 / 5.4	16.5 / 8.3 / 6.1	15.2 / 8.3 / 6.3
Sales/Total Assets	3.5 / 2.8 / 1.7	3.1 / 2.3 / 1.9	2.9 / 2.1 / 1.5	2.8 / 1.5 / 1.2
% Depr., Dep., Amort./Sales	1.2 / (17) 2.5 / 4.3	1.1 / (19) 1.4 / 2.1	1.6 / (26) 2.3 / 4.6	2.0 / (10) 2.9 / 5.3
% Officers', Directors' Owners' Comp/Sales				

	4/1/07-3/31/08	4/1/08-3/31/09	4/1/09-3/31/10	1-3MM	3-5MM	5-10MM	10-25MM	25MM & OVER
Net Sales ($)	495672M	1031152M	1402315M	7101M	7774M	34895M	124811M	1227734M
Total Assets ($)	326018M	518675M	909841M	4007M	17525M	13807M	55129M	819373M

M = $ thousand   MM = $ million
See Pages 9 through 22 for Explanation of Ratios and Data

Current Data Sorted by Assets   Comparative Historical Data

Type of Statement	0-500M	500M-2MM	2-10MM	10-50MM	50-100MM	100-250MM	4/1/05-3/31/06 ALL	4/1/06-3/31/07 ALL
Unqualified	3	2	26	71	29	19	178	183
Reviewed		15	123	48	1		194	220
Compiled	5	20	41	10			114	105
Tax Returns	10	29	21	1			44	60
Other	12	35	116	108	21	19	340	300
		142 (4/1-9/30/09)		643 (10/1/09-3/31/10)				
NUMBER OF STATEMENTS	30	101	327	238	51	38	870	868
ASSETS	%	%	%	%	%	%	%	%
Cash & Equivalents	19.9	10.4	8.4	7.4	4.0	4.5	6.5	6.2
Trade Receivables (net)	22.5	28.1	26.0	22.4	23.0	17.4	27.6	26.9
Inventory	20.1	26.1	23.9	21.5	19.5	16.9	21.9	22.6
All Other Current	5.4	2.0	1.7	2.7	3.4	3.2	1.8	2.0
Total Current	67.9	66.6	60.0	53.9	49.8	42.0	57.8	57.6
Fixed Assets (net)	24.6	26.6	31.4	35.8	31.9	35.9	33.2	32.5
Intangibles (net)	2.2	3.4	3.9	5.1	10.9	18.4	3.5	4.5
All Other Non-Current	5.3	3.4	4.7	5.2	7.4	3.7	5.5	5.4
Total	100.0	100.0	100.0	100.0	100.0	100.0	100.0	100.0
LIABILITIES								
Notes Payable-Short Term	18.0	13.1	12.3	10.4	7.5	2.5	11.3	12.1
Cur. Mat.-L.T.D.	3.4	5.1	4.9	4.0	3.5	9.1	4.8	5.0
Trade Payables	19.5	16.8	15.1	12.8	13.6	10.6	17.6	16.4
Income Taxes Payable	.0	.2	.2	.2	.4	.2	.2	.2
All Other Current	10.0	6.9	7.6	8.5	10.0	8.0	8.6	9.3
Total Current	50.8	42.0	40.1	36.1	35.0	30.5	42.5	43.0
Long-Term Debt	22.0	21.9	15.9	17.5	20.4	25.9	19.6	20.1
Deferred Taxes	.1	.1	.4	1.0	.6	2.7	.7	.7
All Other Non-Current	14.8	6.9	5.3	6.7	7.7	9.6	7.6	6.8
Net Worth	12.1	29.1	38.3	38.8	36.4	31.4	29.5	29.4
Total Liabilities & Net Worth	100.0	100.0	100.0	100.0	100.0	100.0	100.0	100.0
INCOME DATA								
Net Sales	100.0	100.0	100.0	100.0	100.0	100.0	100.0	100.0
Gross Profit	43.2	33.3	27.7	24.3	24.9	24.6	25.4	26.3
Operating Expenses	42.6	31.2	23.7	19.2	20.6	17.9	20.9	21.3
Operating Profit	.6	2.1	4.0	5.1	4.3	6.7	4.5	5.1
All Other Expenses (net)	1.6	1.0	1.3	1.4	2.7	3.2	1.3	1.6
Profit Before Taxes	-1.0	1.1	2.7	3.6	1.6	3.5	3.2	3.5
RATIOS								
Current	3.8	2.9	2.6	2.4	2.1	2.3	2.1	2.2
	2.1	1.6	1.6	1.6	1.3	1.6	1.4	1.4
	.9	1.1	1.1	1.1	1.1	1.2	1.0	1.0
Quick	1.9	1.8	1.6	1.5	1.2	1.3	1.3	1.3
	.8	.9	.9	.8	.7	.8	.8 (867)	.8
	.5	.6	.5	.5	.5	.6	.5	.5
Sales/Receivables	6 58.1	28 13.1	34 10.8	37 9.9	42 8.8	39 9.4	36 10.1	34 10.7
	26 14.0	41 8.9	45 8.1	47 7.8	52 7.1	47 7.8	48 7.7	44 8.3
	51 7.1	54 6.8	59 6.2	60 6.1	65 5.6	55 6.6	61 6.0	57 6.4
Cost of Sales/Inventory	0 UND	34 10.7	37 9.8	36 10.3	43 8.4	39 9.5	32 11.3	32 11.3
	37 9.9	51 7.2	58 6.3	57 6.4	64 5.7	55 6.7	48 7.6	49 7.4
	88 4.2	86 4.3	89 4.1	83 4.4	78 4.7	78 4.7	71 5.2	70 5.2
Cost of Sales/Payables	6 63.9	18 20.6	19 19.2	21 17.8	26 13.9	21 17.0	21 17.0	20 18.2
	35 10.3	30 12.2	32 11.4	31 11.7	38 9.5	36 10.0	37 9.8	33 11.2
	70 5.2	51 7.1	49 7.5	48 7.5	48 7.6	49 7.4	54 6.8	50 7.3
Sales/Working Capital	4.3	5.6	5.1	5.0	4.9	4.8	6.4	6.2
	14.7	9.2	9.7	9.4	14.2	9.8	13.5	13.6
	-42.9	44.7	39.1	56.6	65.5	21.7	288.7	999.8
EBIT/Interest	2.3	7.5	10.0	11.5	6.6	7.9	9.3	8.1
	(18) .5	(87) 2.4	(297) 3.2	(228) 3.9	(50) 2.1	(36) 3.0	(811) 3.0	(804) 3.0
	-.7	-.4	.7	.9	.8	.5	1.0	1.1
Net Profit + Depr., Dep., Amort./Cur. Mat. L/T/D		8.5	4.6	9.6	4.1		4.6	4.6
	(19) 1.6	(95) 1.9	(92) 3.4	(31) 2.3			(258) 2.2	(241) 2.3
	.3	.8	1.0	1.0			1.0	1.4
Fixed/Worth	.3	.3	.4	.5	.7	.8	.5	.5
	1.5	.9	.9	1.0	1.2	2.4	1.2	1.1
	-1.1	4.8	2.2	2.3	5.1	-3.1	3.4	4.0
Debt/Worth	.6	.8	.6	.7	.8	1.3	1.0	.9
	7.3	1.8	1.7	1.7	2.4	2.9	2.3	2.3
	-8.4	13.0	4.7	4.0	12.0	-7.6	8.3	10.3
% Profit Before Taxes/Tangible Net Worth	46.9	50.9	33.8	36.8	26.4	36.8	39.7	43.6
	(17) 8.6	(80) 11.9	(288) 14.5	(213) 16.2	(42) 10.7	(24) 17.6	(732) 16.4	(710) 21.1
	-33.0	-2.7	.8	2.2	-1.9	4.1	3.1	5.2
% Profit Before Taxes/Total Assets	9.9	14.5	14.5	12.5	8.6	9.6	13.5	13.7
	-1.9	3.0	4.3	5.3	2.1	4.1	4.9	6.3
	-12.2	-5.4	-.7	-.3	-1.6	-1.2	-.1	.4
Sales/Net Fixed Assets	64.7	30.2	14.2	8.6	7.4	5.8	12.6	13.1
	13.9	12.9	6.9	4.8	4.9	3.8	6.2	6.6
	5.9	4.8	3.7	2.7	3.4	2.7	3.7	3.8
Sales/Total Assets	3.9	3.3	2.6	2.1	2.0	1.7	2.7	2.7
	2.6	2.3	1.9	1.6	1.5	1.5	2.0	2.1
	2.0	1.7	1.5	1.2	1.1	.9	1.5	1.6
% Depr., Dep., Amort./Sales	.7	1.2	1.8	2.3	2.4	2.5	1.7	1.7
	(22) 1.9	(86) 1.9	(294) 3.2	(209) 3.8	(46) 4.1	(13) 3.7	(774) 2.9	(766) 2.8
	3.3	4.7	5.2	5.5	6.3	5.4	4.6	4.4
% Officers', Directors' Owners' Comp/Sales	2.8	3.3	1.7	1.2			1.8	1.7
	(13) 10.5	(58) 4.7	(113) 3.7	(37) 2.6			(253) 3.1	(263) 3.3
	19.4	8.5	6.2	5.0			6.1	5.9
Net Sales ($)	24985M	326996M	3319250M	8469302M	5757850M	7653026M	32867327M	31059173M
Total Assets ($)	7991M	127279M	1634999M	5139725M	3583032M	5684106M	17027451M	17823292M

M = $ thousand   MM = $ million
See Pages 9 through 22 for Explanation of Ratios and Data

Comparative Historical Data   Current Data Sorted by Sales

			Type of Statement						
155	152	150	Unqualified	3	4	3	11	27	102
178	171	187	Reviewed		11	17	46	85	28
89	98	76	Compiled	4	14	16	22	15	5
50	72	61	Tax Returns	12	16	12	17	4	
300	335	311	Other	12	21	30	55	74	119
4/1/07- 3/31/08 ALL	4/1/08- 3/31/09 ALL	4/1/09- 3/31/10 ALL		142 (4/1-9/30/09)			643 (10/1/09-3/31/10)		
				0-1MM	1-3MM	3-5MM	5-10MM	10-25MM	25MM & OVER
772	828	785	**NUMBER OF STATEMENTS**	31	66	78	151	205	254
%	%	%	**ASSETS**	%	%	%	%	%	%
7.2	6.6	8.3	Cash & Equivalents	18.6	10.4	9.1	9.6	8.0	5.7
26.2	24.2	24.4	Trade Receivables (net)	20.9	21.9	24.6	26.2	25.0	23.9
22.9	24.5	22.7	Inventory	16.8	21.6	25.7	24.2	23.0	21.7
2.3	2.7	2.3	All Other Current	3.1	3.4	1.2	1.3	2.2	3.0
58.6	58.0	57.8	Total Current	59.4	57.4	60.5	61.3	58.3	54.3
31.8	31.6	32.1	Fixed Assets (net)	32.0	32.0	30.2	30.8	33.0	32.9
4.4	5.2	5.3	Intangibles (net)	4.5	4.9	5.2	3.1	4.1	7.8
5.1	5.3	4.9	All Other Non-Current	4.0	5.8	4.1	4.8	4.7	5.1
100.0	100.0	100.0	Total	100.0	100.0	100.0	100.0	100.0	100.0
			LIABILITIES						
10.9	12.2	11.3	Notes Payable-Short Term	16.5	10.5	14.2	12.2	11.2	9.4
5.0	4.8	4.7	Cur. Mat.-L.T.D.	4.6	6.0	4.4	4.2	5.0	4.5
16.2	15.1	14.5	Trade Payables	14.6	13.1	14.9	14.2	15.7	13.9
.2	.2	.2	Income Taxes Payable	.0	.3	.1	.1	.2	.3
8.0	9.3	8.1	All Other Current	4.8	8.8	7.6	6.9	7.8	9.4
40.4	41.6	38.7	Total Current	40.5	38.6	41.1	37.6	39.9	37.5
19.1	17.9	18.2	Long-Term Debt	25.6	22.8	21.1	16.2	15.6	18.4
.6	.6	.7	Deferred Taxes	.1	.1	.2	.4	.6	1.2
6.8	7.0	6.6	All Other Non-Current	10.3	8.3	8.1	4.8	4.9	7.8
33.1	32.9	35.8	Net Worth	23.4	30.2	29.5	41.0	39.0	35.0
100.0	100.0	100.0	Total Liabilties & Net Worth	100.0	100.0	100.0	100.0	100.0	100.0
			INCOME DATA						
100.0	100.0	100.0	Net Sales	100.0	100.0	100.0	100.0	100.0	100.0
26.7	25.3	27.6	Gross Profit	45.0	34.5	31.9	28.7	24.7	24.1
21.5	21.5	23.5	Operating Expenses	46.1	33.4	28.0	24.4	21.0	18.4
5.2	3.8	4.1	Operating Profit	-1.1	1.1	3.9	4.3	3.7	5.7
1.5	1.4	1.5	All Other Expenses (net)	1.6	1.7	1.1	.9	1.6	1.8
3.7	2.4	2.6	Profit Before Taxes	-2.7	-.6	2.8	3.4	2.1	3.9
			RATIOS						
2.4	2.4	2.5	Current	4.5	2.7	2.8	2.8	2.4	2.2
1.5	1.5	1.6		2.2	1.6	1.5	1.7	1.5	1.5
1.1	1.0	1.1		.9	1.1	1.1	1.2	1.1	1.1
1.4	1.3	1.5	Quick	2.4	1.5	1.7	1.9	1.5	1.2
.8	.8	.8		1.0	.9	.9	.9	.8	.8
.5	.5	.5		.6	.6	.5	.5	.5	.5
32 11.4	30 12.1	34 10.8	Sales/Receivables	15 25.1	27 13.6	34 10.7	34 10.8	34 10.8	36 10.0
43 8.5	40 9.1	46 8.0		35 10.4	44 8.3	46 8.0	44 8.4	46 7.9	47 7.8
53 6.9	51 7.2	59 6.2		54 6.8	65 5.6	61 6.0	57 6.4	58 6.3	59 6.2
32 11.2	34 10.7	36 10.0	Cost of Sales/Inventory	8 46.5	35 10.6	39 9.3	34 10.6	36 10.0	37 9.8
51 7.2	52 7.0	57 6.5		53 6.8	66 5.6	65 5.6	55 6.7	54 6.7	56 6.5
76 4.8	79 4.6	84 4.3		99 3.7	112 3.3	101 3.6	86 4.2	80 4.5	77 4.7
20 18.0	18 20.1	20 18.1	Cost of Sales/Payables	9 39.9	14 25.3	21 17.3	18 20.7	23 16.1	21 17.5
32 11.3	29 12.5	33 11.2		45 8.1	28 13.1	40 9.2	31 11.7	32 11.3	34 10.8
47 7.7	44 8.3	49 7.4		85 4.3	51 7.2	61 6.0	47 7.7	48 7.5	48 7.7
5.9	5.8	5.0	Sales/Working Capital	3.9	4.0	5.5	4.7	5.3	5.3
12.1	12.4	9.8		5.2	8.6	8.9	8.5	10.8	11.3
82.2	999.8	43.6		-47.0	28.1	125.7	27.6	70.9	46.5
8.5	7.7	8.9	EBIT/Interest	4.2	2.8	9.3	12.2	7.0	13.6
(709) 2.9	(769) 2.6	(716) 3.2		(21) 1.0	(57) .8	(69) 2.4	(139) 4.2	(185) 3.2	(245) 4.0
1.1	.7	.7		-.2	-2.3	.5	.7	.8	1.1
5.4	4.3	5.6	Net Profit + Depr., Dep., Amort./Cur. Mat. L/T/D		2.3	6.7	4.7	4.7	8.3
(228) 2.5	(267) 2.4	(244) 2.3			(16) 1.4	(14) 1.3	(40) 2.1	(75) 2.2	(99) 2.7
1.3	1.0	.9			.0	.2	1.0	.7	1.1
.5	.4	.4	Fixed/Worth	.3	.5	.4	.4	.4	.6
1.1	1.1	1.0		1.0	1.4	1.0	.7	1.0	1.1
3.7	3.5	2.8		-4.2	16.3	4.0	1.7	2.1	3.3
.8	.9	.7	Debt/Worth	.3	.9	.7	.5	.7	.8
2.1	2.0	1.9		4.7	2.5	2.3	1.4	1.8	2.0
8.7	7.7	6.0		-13.4	44.1	15.7	3.4	4.5	6.4
42.4	34.9	35.5	% Profit Before Taxes/Tangible Net Worth	42.4	20.3	34.5	43.6	29.0	40.9
(638) 22.4	(682) 15.6	(664) 14.2		(20) 10.9	(51) 3.8	(60) 13.3	(136) 18.4	(185) 11.1	(212) 20.1
5.2	.7	.7		-27.5	-21.4	1.6	.8	.0	5.0
15.5	12.0	12.8	% Profit Before Taxes/Total Assets	8.2	4.5	13.7	17.0	10.2	13.6
6.2	4.6	4.3		.0	.0	4.0	6.0	3.9	6.1
.5	-1.0	-1.0		-12.5	-7.9	-1.1	-1.0	-.3	5.0
13.9	14.5	13.0	Sales/Net Fixed Assets	28.8	19.9	21.4	13.6	13.3	10.2
6.9	6.9	5.9		6.2	5.9	8.4	7.1	5.8	5.2
4.2	4.0	3.4		2.9	2.6	2.8	3.8	3.6	3.4
2.8	2.8	2.5	Sales/Total Assets	2.5	2.6	2.8	2.6	2.6	2.3
2.1	2.1	1.8		1.9	1.7	1.7	2.0	1.8	1.7
1.6	1.5	1.3		1.1	1.1	1.2	1.5	1.3	1.3
1.7	1.7	1.8	% Depr., Dep., Amort./Sales	1.5	1.3	1.4	2.2	1.8	2.2
(684) 2.9	(724) 3.0	(670) 3.3		(25) 3.4	(61) 3.0	(60) 2.2	(136) 3.3	(190) 3.3	(198) 3.5
4.5	4.6	5.2		7.2	6.3	5.1	6.1	5.1	4.9
1.4	1.7	2.0	% Officers', Directors' Owners' Comp/Sales	3.1	3.7	2.7	2.4	1.1	1.1
(241) 3.2	(242) 3.8	(223) 3.9		(14) 5.8	(35) 6.2	(34) 3.9	(63) 4.5	(52) 2.4	(25) 3.1
6.1	6.2	7.0		15.5	11.2	7.4	6.9	3.8	5.2
28074274M	31305117M	25551409M	Net Sales ($)	17541M	135614M	309809M	1100382M	3296498M	20691565M
15758336M	18684007M	16177132M	Total Assets ($)	12759M	101592M	216610M	609435M	1978621M	13258115M

M = $ thousand   MM = $ million
See Pages 9 through 22 for Explanation of Ratios and Data

Current Data Sorted by Assets   Comparative Historical Data

0-500M	500M-2MM	2-10MM	10-50MM	50-100MM	100-250MM	Type of Statement	4/1/05-3/31/06 ALL	4/1/06-3/31/07 ALL
		1	2		1	Unqualified	2	2
	1	2	1			Reviewed	7	7
1	1	4	1	1		Compiled	11	7
3	5	5	1			Tax Returns	8	10
1	2	5	4	1		Other	18	14
		6 (4/1-9/30/09)	37 (10/1/09-3/31/10)					
5	9	17	9	2	1	NUMBER OF STATEMENTS	46	40
%	%	%	%	%	%	**ASSETS**	%	%
		4.3				Cash & Equivalents	4.7	8.4
		27.4				Trade Receivables (net)	28.6	27.2
		36.2				Inventory	35.0	31.6
		1.1				All Other Current	2.1	2.8
		69.1				Total Current	70.4	69.9
		20.4				Fixed Assets (net)	20.9	24.3
		2.6				Intangibles (net)	4.1	2.4
		8.0				All Other Non-Current	4.6	3.4
		100.0				Total	100.0	100.0
						LIABILITIES		
		11.0				Notes Payable-Short Term	9.7	8.2
		3.3				Cur. Mat.-L.T.D.	5.9	2.9
		23.9				Trade Payables	32.2	38.2
		.3				Income Taxes Payable	.3	.4
		9.5				All Other Current	8.4	7.8
		48.0				Total Current	56.5	57.5
		12.8				Long-Term Debt	19.0	11.8
		.1				Deferred Taxes	.4	.7
		3.1				All Other Non-Current	3.9	5.3
		35.9				Net Worth	20.2	24.6
		100.0				Total Liabilities & Net Worth	100.0	100.0
						INCOME DATA		
		100.0				Net Sales	100.0	100.0
		30.5				Gross Profit	32.7	32.3
		28.9				Operating Expenses	30.5	29.2
		1.6				Operating Profit	2.2	3.1
		.4				All Other Expenses (net)	-.3	-.1
		1.2				Profit Before Taxes	2.5	3.2
						RATIOS		
		2.2				Current	1.7	1.8
		1.6					1.2	1.4
		1.0					1.0	1.0
		1.3				Quick	.9	1.0
		.6					.5	.7
		.3					.4	.4
		27 13.6				Sales/Receivables	20 18.3	15 24.9
		41 8.9					36 10.1	35 10.3
		61 6.0					49 7.4	49 7.4
		40 9.2				Cost of Sales/Inventory	39 9.3	38 9.5
		89 4.1					69 5.3	61 6.0
		117 3.1					96 3.8	80 4.6
		33 11.1				Cost of Sales/Payables	41 9.0	30 12.3
		45 8.1					58 6.3	54 6.8
		78 4.7					77 4.7	72 5.1
		4.9				Sales/Working Capital	10.1	8.6
		10.6					18.8	16.7
		NM					230.2	107.8
		13.6				EBIT/Interest	7.4	14.3
		2.8					(42) 3.7	(37) 4.6
		.6					1.3	2.3
						Net Profit + Depr., Dep.,	4.6	4.2
						Amort./Cur. Mat. L/T/D	(12) 1.7	(12) 2.8
							1.2	1.2
		.2				Fixed/Worth	.4	.3
		.4					1.1	1.0
		9.8					8.4	1.6
		.6				Debt/Worth	1.6	1.1
		1.1					4.5	2.8
		33.2					81.3	4.9
		112.2				% Profit Before Taxes/Tangible	38.3	47.6
		(15) 4.6				Net Worth	(36) 26.2	(35) 25.7
		1.1					12.4	9.9
		6.7				% Profit Before Taxes/Total	9.7	12.5
		2.1				Assets	4.4	5.3
		-.1					.6	1.6
		38.9				Sales/Net Fixed Assets	30.0	31.0
		13.3					17.6	12.4
		6.6					7.6	6.3
		3.4				Sales/Total Assets	3.6	3.6
		2.5					2.6	2.9
		1.3					1.9	2.2
		1.2				% Depr., Dep., Amort./Sales	.9	1.1
		(16) 1.6					(42) 1.7	(37) 2.1
		2.7					2.7	2.7
						% Officers', Directors'	1.0	.6
						Owners' Comp/Sales	(19) 2.5	(17) 1.6
							3.9	3.4
6149M	28822M	237559M	498908M	416154M	223433M	Net Sales ($)	1172047M	890828M
1390M	9457M	91673M	200289M	132834M	116761M	Total Assets ($)	529791M	343679M

M = $ thousand   MM = $ million
See Pages 9 through 22 for Explanation of Ratios and Data

Comparative Historical Data   Current Data Sorted by Sales

			Type of Statement	0-1MM	1-3MM	3-5MM	5-10MM	10-25MM	25MM & OVER
3	5	4	Unqualified						3
5	4	4	Reviewed		1			1	2
9	6	8	Compiled		1	1	1	2	2
6	11	14	Tax Returns	1	7	2	2	2	1
16	12	13	Other		1	2	2	2	6
4/1/07-3/31/08	4/1/08-3/31/09	4/1/09-3/31/10			6 (4/1-9/30/09)			37 (10/1/09-3/31/10)	
ALL	ALL	ALL							
39	38	43	**NUMBER OF STATEMENTS**	1	10	5	5	8	14
%	%	%	**ASSETS**	%	%	%	%	%	%
8.3	5.3	9.5	Cash & Equivalents		21.4				6.5
26.3	25.4	22.4	Trade Receivables (net)		9.0				24.1
31.6	40.3	34.5	Inventory		35.7				32.1
2.4	1.7	1.4	All Other Current		1.6				2.6
68.7	72.7	67.9	Total Current		67.7				65.3
27.2	19.6	20.5	Fixed Assets (net)		18.4				26.6
1.4	4.2	4.1	Intangibles (net)		4.3				3.6
2.8	3.6	7.5	All Other Non-Current		9.6				4.5
100.0	100.0	100.0	Total		100.0				100.0
			LIABILITIES						
10.7	11.1	8.2	Notes Payable-Short Term		5.7				3.8
3.5	2.2	4.4	Cur. Mat.-L.T.D.		7.3				2.4
28.3	27.1	26.6	Trade Payables		23.5				29.3
.2	.0	.1	Income Taxes Payable		.0				.0
9.1	9.3	9.1	All Other Current		6.4				13.1
51.8	49.7	48.4	Total Current		42.8				48.6
15.5	13.0	20.2	Long-Term Debt		22.2				21.0
.5	.2	.1	Deferred Taxes		.0				.1
3.7	5.6	4.6	All Other Non-Current		12.7				2.7
28.4	31.5	26.7	Net Worth		22.3				27.6
100.0	100.0	100.0	Total Liabilities & Net Worth		100.0				100.0
			INCOME DATA						
100.0	100.0	100.0	Net Sales		100.0				100.0
34.5	31.0	31.2	Gross Profit		35.3				31.4
30.3	28.8	29.0	Operating Expenses		30.4				29.2
4.2	2.2	2.2	Operating Profit		4.9				2.1
.9	-.3	.5	All Other Expenses (net)		2.2				-.1
3.3	2.5	1.7	Profit Before Taxes		2.7				2.3
			RATIOS						
1.6	2.0	2.2			5.1				1.9
1.3	1.3	1.4	Current		2.6				1.4
1.0	1.2	1.0			.9				1.1
1.0	.8	1.3			3.8				.8
.7	.5	.6	Quick		1.0				.5
.4	.4	.3			.3				.4
21 17.5	21 17.5	12 29.6		0 UND					17 21.6
35 10.6	34 10.7	32 11.6	Sales/Receivables	4 81.7					27 13.4
50 7.3	46 7.9	46 7.9		29 12.8					47 7.7
54 6.7	59 6.2	33 11.2		32 11.6					51 7.1
67 5.5	79 4.6	64 5.7	Cost of Sales/Inventory	55 6.6					66 5.5
95 3.8	116 3.1	97 3.7		118 3.1					78 4.7
27 13.5	29 12.5	31 11.8		0 UND					35 10.5
66 5.6	52 7.0	54 6.7	Cost of Sales/Payables	52 7.0					53 6.9
83 4.4	73 5.0	76 4.8		82 4.4					62 5.9
10.7	7.6	6.8			4.5				12.3
19.6	15.4	16.4	Sales/Working Capital		17.1				21.0
-122.8	25.8	106.0			NM				47.2
8.6	6.7	8.6							8.3
(35) 3.1	(36) 2.7	(38) 2.7	EBIT/Interest					(13)	3.8
1.3	1.0	.8							1.4
3.7	6.5	4.1	Net Profit + Depr., Dep.,						
(13) 1.7	(11) 1.7	(10) 1.0	Amort./Cur. Mat. L/T/D						
1.0	1.2	.4							
.4	.3	.2			.1				.4
.9	.6	.5	Fixed/Worth		.3				1.1
3.4	1.6	6.8			NM				3.8
1.2	1.3	.8			.4				1.6
3.3	2.8	2.7	Debt/Worth		1.5				2.8
9.7	6.6	12.3			NM				10.7
69.3	40.0	42.7	% Profit Before Taxes/Tangible						53.1
(34) 22.4	(34) 18.3	(37) 10.2	Net Worth						12.9
10.8	2.4	1.2							3.7
9.7	9.7	9.0	% Profit Before Taxes/Total		32.6				7.1
4.9	3.2	3.1	Assets		6.3				3.0
1.4	.0	.3			-1.8				1.5
26.3	37.1	37.1			34.4				42.6
10.3	15.9	14.4	Sales/Net Fixed Assets		19.8				12.7
5.5	8.2	7.2			9.2				6.6
3.2	3.3	3.9			4.3				3.9
2.5	2.7	2.8	Sales/Total Assets		3.2				2.9
1.9	2.0	1.9			2.3				2.0
1.2	.8	.8							.6
(36) 2.0	(33) 1.5	(37) 1.6	% Depr., Dep., Amort./Sales					(13)	1.7
3.1	2.4	2.8							2.8
.6	.5	.7							
(17) .9	(17) 1.0	(16) 1.3	% Officers', Directors' Owners' Comp/Sales						
4.3	2.0	3.0							
989823M	1510190M	1411025M	Net Sales ($)	935M	16633M	17548M	37181M	123934M	1214794M
418367M	615928M	552404M	Total Assets ($)	266M	7562M	10069M	19915M	50159M	464433M

M = $ thousand   MM = $ million
See Pages 9 through 22 for Explanation of Ratios and Data

Current Data Sorted by Assets | **Comparative Historical Data**

0-500M	500M-2MM	2-10MM	10-50MM	50-100MM	100-250MM	Type of Statement	4/1/05-3/31/06 ALL	4/1/06-3/31/07 ALL
		3	4	2	2	Unqualified	10	11
		4	2			Reviewed	11	10
	1	3	1			Compiled	6	7
	1	1				Tax Returns		3
	2	4	7	3		Other	18	15
	13 (4/1-9/30/09)		27 (10/1/09-3/31/10)					
4	15	14	5	2		NUMBER OF STATEMENTS	45	46
%	%	%	%	%	%	**ASSETS**	%	%
D		6.5	8.8			Cash & Equivalents	4.7	6.9
A		25.6	24.3			Trade Receivables (net)	27.4	26.0
T		36.3	28.4			Inventory	31.8	31.0
A		.5	2.8			All Other Current	2.5	1.8
		68.9	64.3			Total Current	66.4	65.7
N		18.3	20.7			Fixed Assets (net)	21.2	22.5
O		6.9	3.2			Intangibles (net)	5.1	5.7
T		5.9	11.8			All Other Non-Current	7.3	6.0
		100.0	100.0			Total	100.0	100.0
A						**LIABILITIES**		
V		12.5	7.4			Notes Payable-Short Term	10.3	8.4
A		2.8	3.6			Cur. Mat.-L.T.D.	3.1	3.2
I		11.9	10.1			Trade Payables	14.9	14.1
L		.0	.2			Income Taxes Payable	.2	.5
A		10.6	7.1			All Other Current	8.7	9.1
B		37.9	28.4			Total Current	37.2	35.3
L		15.2	10.0			Long-Term Debt	10.9	14.2
E		.0	.4			Deferred Taxes	.4	.4
		4.4	8.2			All Other Non-Current	4.7	6.4
		42.4	53.0			Net Worth	46.8	43.7
		100.0	100.0			Total Liabilities & Net Worth	100.0	100.0
						INCOME DATA		
		100.0	100.0			Net Sales	100.0	100.0
		33.6	28.8			Gross Profit	27.7	31.5
		25.4	22.1			Operating Expenses	22.1	24.6
		8.1	6.8			Operating Profit	5.6	6.9
		1.8	-.4			All Other Expenses (net)	.8	.9
		6.4	7.2			Profit Before Taxes	4.8	6.1
						RATIOS		
		4.4	4.8				2.8	3.0
		1.6	2.5			Current	1.9	2.2
		1.2	1.5				1.4	1.3
		2.0	1.8				1.3	1.5
		.9	1.1			Quick	.9	1.0
		.6	.7				.5	.7
		36 10.2	47 7.8				35 10.5	35 10.5
		47 7.8	52 7.0			Sales/Receivables	49 7.4	45 8.0
		57 6.4	60 6.1				55 6.6	60 6.1
		54 6.8	65 5.6				40 9.1	46 8.0
		110 3.3	87 4.2			Cost of Sales/Inventory	70 5.2	66 5.5
		143 2.5	130 2.8				114 3.2	109 3.4
		17 21.2	17 21.0				22 16.5	22 16.7
		34 10.6	28 12.9			Cost of Sales/Payables	27 13.6	32 11.4
		45 8.2	31 11.9				43 8.5	48 7.7
		2.9	2.4				4.4	4.4
		6.3	6.1			Sales/Working Capital	6.4	6.1
		31.8	9.4				17.0	14.8
		14.0	22.3				13.6	23.8
		(12) 5.8	9.3			EBIT/Interest	(43) 7.3	(44) 7.9
		3.2	1.8				3.0	1.9
						Net Profit + Depr., Dep.,	5.7	11.9
						Amort./Cur. Mat. L/T/D	(12) 2.8	(17) 3.7
							1.8	1.0
		.1	.2				.2	.2
		.3	.4			Fixed/Worth	.5	.5
		2.1	.8				.7	1.2
		.6	.6				.6	.7
		1.2	1.1			Debt/Worth	1.1	1.0
		4.4	1.8				2.9	3.5
		37.2	39.9			% Profit Before Taxes/Tangible	39.3	55.8
		(12) 25.7	13.9			Net Worth	(43) 18.2	(41) 22.6
		16.1	3.9				8.9	3.0
		18.5	18.4			% Profit Before Taxes/Total	13.7	17.9
		12.5	6.7			Assets	8.7	10.9
		4.1	1.6				4.5	1.7
		79.6	15.1				19.3	22.7
		8.3	9.1			Sales/Net Fixed Assets	9.8	10.3
		5.1	5.3				6.5	5.9
		2.3	2.2				2.8	2.6
		1.6	1.7			Sales/Total Assets	2.1	2.0
		1.1	1.1				1.5	1.5
		.7	.8				1.1	.9
		(12) 1.2	(12) 1.9			% Depr., Dep., Amort./Sales	(40) 1.9	(43) 1.8
		2.3	2.9				3.5	2.9
							1.1	2.4
		(12)				% Officers', Directors' Owners' Comp/Sales	(12) 3.9	(18) 3.9
							7.4	7.0
	5615M	127816M	502963M	536772M	322327M	Net Sales ($)	1398964M	1660319M
	3587M	62286M	317099M	396777M	271072M	Total Assets ($)	729206M	810816M

M = $ thousand   MM = $ million
See Pages 9 through 22 for Explanation of Ratios and Data

Comparative Historical Data

Current Data Sorted by Sales

				Type of Statement						
	15	13	11	Unqualified		1		1		9
	10	8	6	Reviewed		1		3	2	
	2	7	5	Compiled			3	3		1
	2	4	2	Tax Returns	1				1	
	13	16	16	Other	3	2	2	2	2	7
	4/1/07-3/31/08	4/1/08-3/31/09	4/1/09-3/31/10		0-1MM	13 (4/1-9/30/09) 1-3MM	3-5MM	27 (10/1/09-3/31/10) 5-10MM	10-25MM	25MM & OVER
	ALL	ALL	ALL							
	42	48	40	**NUMBER OF STATEMENTS**	5	4	9	5	17	
	%	%	%	**ASSETS**	%	%	%	%	%	%
	9.6	8.4	8.1	Cash & Equivalents						10.2
	24.3	22.3	22.8	Trade Receivables (net)						24.2
	32.8	29.1	29.7	Inventory						28.7
	2.6	3.0	4.1	All Other Current						3.8
	69.3	62.8	64.6	Total Current						67.0
	18.4	21.0	20.7	Fixed Assets (net)						21.1
	5.8	7.7	6.4	Intangibles (net)						8.6
	6.4	8.5	8.3	All Other Non-Current						3.3
	100.0	100.0	100.0	Total						100.0
				LIABILITIES						
	7.2	10.2	9.0	Notes Payable-Short Term						8.5
	3.0	2.7	3.4	Cur. Mat.-L.T.D.						4.0
	12.7	12.0	11.2	Trade Payables						9.3
	.2	.2	.1	Income Taxes Payable						.2
	10.5	8.5	8.7	All Other Current						8.9
	33.7	33.6	32.4	Total Current						30.9
	15.5	12.8	11.4	Long-Term Debt						8.7
	.6	.5	.5	Deferred Taxes						1.2
	7.0	8.7	8.7	All Other Non-Current						7.8
	43.2	44.4	47.0	Net Worth						51.5
	100.0	100.0	100.0	Total Liabilities & Net Worth						100.0
				INCOME DATA						
	100.0	100.0	100.0	Net Sales						100.0
	30.6	29.6	31.7	Gross Profit						28.8
	24.1	22.1	24.7	Operating Expenses						22.1
	6.6	7.5	7.1	Operating Profit						6.7
	.9	.9	.8	All Other Expenses (net)						.6
	5.7	6.6	6.3	Profit Before Taxes						6.1
				RATIOS						
	3.2	3.8	3.9							3.4
	2.4	2.2	2.1	Current						2.6
	1.7	1.3	1.4							1.5
	1.9	1.9	1.9							1.9
	1.2	.9 (39)	1.1	Quick						1.1
	.7	.5	.7							.7
35	10.3	30 12.0	40 9.1						42	8.6
43	8.5	38 9.5	48 7.6	Sales/Receivables					48	7.7
52	7.0	51 7.2	56 6.5						53	6.8
55	6.6	51 7.1	63 5.8						56	6.5
67	5.4	68 6.4	99 3.7	Cost of Sales/Inventory					89	4.1
113	3.2	105 3.5	140 2.6						120	3.0
15	23.9	18 19.9	18 19.8						17	21.9
29	12.7	29 12.5	30 12.3	Cost of Sales/Payables					25	14.8
38	9.5	41 9.0	41 9.0						31	11.9
	3.0	4.2	2.8							2.6
	5.7	7.6	6.1	Sales/Working Capital						4.4
	10.1	21.9	10.5							9.6
	16.8	24.9	16.8							25.0
(38)	3.6	(44) 9.4	(37) 8.6	EBIT/Interest					(16)	13.0
	2.2	3.0	2.2							3.5
	10.0	8.7	6.6	Net Profit + Depr., Dep.,						
(18)	4.7	(17) 4.4	(15) 4.0	Amort./Cur. Mat. L/T/D						
	2.1	2.6	2.0							
	.2	.2	.2							.3
	.5	.4	.5	Fixed/Worth						.5
	1.0	1.8	.9							.8
	.5	.5	.7							.6
	1.4	1.4	1.2	Debt/Worth						1.2
	3.7	3.7	2.4							2.4
	36.9	41.8	39.5	% Profit Before Taxes/Tangible						57.5
(36)	24.0	(43) 24.1	(35) 21.4	Net Worth					(16)	25.8
	10.7	10.3	5.0							6.2
	18.7	16.8	18.4	% Profit Before Taxes/Total						19.8
	8.1	10.2	7.2	Assets						9.2
	3.4	4.4	2.1							2.5
	27.8	24.9	17.6							16.2
	10.7	10.1	7.8	Sales/Net Fixed Assets						9.1
	6.9	6.5	4.7							5.0
	2.8	2.6	2.1							2.3
	1.9	1.9	1.6	Sales/Total Assets						1.7
	1.4	1.4	1.1							1.1
	.5	.5	.7							1.2
(37)	1.6	(45) 1.1	(33) 1.5	% Depr., Dep., Amort./Sales					(15)	2.3
	2.8	2.5	2.6							3.5
	2.3	1.5	1.9							
(10)	3.9	(13) 3.5	(12) 3.1	% Officers', Directors'						
	9.8	4.8	5.6	Owners' Comp/Sales						
	1959491M	1867386M	1495493M	Net Sales ($)	8014M	16961M	63431M	86806M	1320281M	
	1152968M	1168204M	1050821M	Total Assets ($)	5820M	13253M	81604M	60678M	889466M	

M = $ thousand   MM = $ million
See Pages 9 through 22 for Explanation of Ratios and Data

Current Data Sorted by Assets   Comparative Historical Data

Type of Statement	0-500M	500M-2MM	2-10MM	10-50MM	50-100MM	100-250MM		4/1/05-3/31/06 ALL	4/1/06-3/31/07 ALL
Unqualified		1	7	4	1	1		6	12
Reviewed		3	3	1				3	12
Compiled		2	3					9	4
Tax Returns	2	2	1					3	5
Other	2	3	6	6	1			17	18
		4 (4/1-9/30/09)		42 (10/1/09-3/31/10)					
NUMBER OF STATEMENTS	4	8	20	11	2	1		38	51
	%	%	%	%	%	%		%	%
ASSETS									
Cash & Equivalents			8.0	2.1				5.3	6.4
Trade Receivables (net)			27.9	18.3				26.4	29.2
Inventory			22.6	22.2				22.3	22.6
All Other Current			2.4	3.8				4.3	3.3
Total Current			60.9	46.4				58.3	61.4
Fixed Assets (net)			31.0	36.6				31.7	31.0
Intangibles (net)			.7	6.1				3.9	3.2
All Other Non-Current			7.4	10.9				6.2	4.4
Total			100.0	100.0				100.0	100.0
LIABILITIES									
Notes Payable-Short Term			14.7	12.2				11.7	12.4
Cur. Mat.-L.T.D.			5.2	5.6				6.6	3.0
Trade Payables			15.0	9.8				18.9	15.3
Income Taxes Payable			.0	.3				1.1	.4
All Other Current			10.2	14.1				9.5	9.0
Total Current			45.1	42.0				47.8	40.1
Long-Term Debt			9.3	13.1				21.1	15.9
Deferred Taxes			1.1	1.3				.8	.9
All Other Non-Current			5.1	35.1				5.0	7.3
Net Worth			39.5	8.5				25.2	35.8
Total Liabilties & Net Worth			100.0	100.0				100.0	100.0
INCOME DATA									
Net Sales			100.0	100.0				100.0	100.0
Gross Profit			31.0	34.1				30.5	27.0
Operating Expenses			25.2	27.2				25.2	22.6
Operating Profit			5.8	7.0				5.3	4.4
All Other Expenses (net)			.3	1.6				1.2	1.2
Profit Before Taxes			5.5	5.3				4.1	3.2
RATIOS									
Current			3.1	3.5				2.2	3.0
			1.3	1.3				1.3	1.6
			.8	1.0				.9	1.1
Quick			1.6	1.0				1.4	2.0
			.7	.7				.8	.8
			.4	.5				.4	.6
Sales/Receivables			30 12.1	35 10.3				30 12.2	39 9.3
			51 7.1	45 8.0				40 9.1	46 7.9
			62 5.9	62 5.9				57 6.4	56 6.5
Cost of Sales/Inventory			35 10.4	43 8.5				23 16.2	24 15.0
			59 6.2	63 5.8				51 7.2	44 8.2
			69 5.3	133 2.7				87 4.2	82 4.5
Cost of Sales/Payables			17 21.3	16 23.1				24 15.4	18 20.8
			27 13.5	30 12.1				39 9.3	25 14.7
			51 7.2	42 8.6				53 6.9	48 7.6
Sales/Working Capital			5.2	7.5				6.8	5.6
			15.6	9.5				14.9	8.6
			-46.8	-66.0				-43.2	60.8
EBIT/Interest			9.7	14.6				10.3	12.8
			(19) 5.1	(10) 2.4				(36) 4.9	(47) 3.4
			1.5	1.4				1.2	.9
Net Profit + Depr., Dep., Amort./Cur. Mat. L/T/D								3.6	7.9
								(14) 2.1	(13) 3.0
								1.3	.9
Fixed/Worth			.2	.7				.4	.3
			.8	-6.8				1.0	.9
			2.4	-1.7				3.7	2.5
Debt/Worth			.8	.5				1.1	.7
			1.8	-15.7				2.4	2.2
			3.5	-8.2				6.7	5.0
% Profit Before Taxes/Tangible Net Worth			32.1					70.1	44.6
			(18) 16.0					(32) 32.9	(43) 19.7
			2.8					5.9	2.8
% Profit Before Taxes/Total Assets			15.8	15.9				16.6	13.9
			7.8	6.3				6.5	5.8
			2.6	.6				.8	-.7
Sales/Net Fixed Assets			20.9	7.9				12.5	15.2
			6.1	3.5				7.8	8.0
			3.2	2.8				3.9	4.1
Sales/Total Assets			2.4	1.7				3.2	2.9
			1.9	1.4				2.2	2.0
			1.4	1.0				1.7	1.6
% Depr., Dep., Amort./Sales			1.8	3.5				1.2	1.6
			(17) 2.4	(10) 4.2				(33) 2.7	(37) 2.9
			5.4	6.1				3.9	4.2
% Officers', Directors' Owners' Comp/Sales								3.5	3.5
								(17) 9.0	(16) 4.9
								13.1	10.0
Net Sales ($)	5849M	23669M	193908M	285447M	137192M	82711M		618186M	1240735M
Total Assets ($)	1034M	9707M	106832M	211965M	105212M	113082M		312293M	726265M

M = $ thousand   MM = $ million
See Pages 9 through 22 for Explanation of Ratios and Data

Comparative Historical Data

Current Data Sorted by Sales

				Type of Statement						
8	7	14		Unqualified		1	3	6	4
8	8	4		Reviewed			1	3	
2	7	5		Compiled		1	2		
2	2	5		Tax Returns	1	2	1	1	
22	13	18		Other	3	3	3	5	4
4/1/07-3/31/08 ALL	4/1/08-3/31/09 ALL	4/1/09-3/31/10 ALL				4 (4/1-9/30/09)		42 (10/1/09-3/31/10)	
					0-1MM	1-3MM	3-5MM	5-10MM	10-25MM	25MM & OVER
42	37	46		NUMBER OF STATEMENTS	1	6	7	9	15	8
%	%	%		ASSETS	%	%	%	%	%	%
8.4	7.0	8.0		Cash & Equivalents					4.4	
27.8	24.3	25.0		Trade Receivables (net)					24.5	
20.0	25.5	24.6		Inventory					22.1	
2.0	1.7	3.8		All Other Current					1.9	
58.1	58.5	61.5		Total Current					52.8	
34.1	34.7	27.9		Fixed Assets (net)					29.4	
2.0	2.3	3.4		Intangibles (net)					3.5	
5.8	4.5	7.2		All Other Non-Current					14.2	
100.0	100.0	100.0		Total					100.0	
				LIABILITIES						
18.4	16.1	12.8		Notes Payable-Short Term					11.1	
2.4	3.1	4.0		Cur. Mat.-L.T.D.					3.7	
14.3	16.9	13.2		Trade Payables					11.5	
.2	.3	.4		Income Taxes Payable					.2	
9.4	12.0	14.1		All Other Current					11.1	
44.8	48.4	44.6		Total Current					37.5	
16.9	15.1	9.3		Long-Term Debt					9.6	
.8	1.0	.8		Deferred Taxes					1.2	
6.6	8.1	13.9		All Other Non-Current					18.1	
30.9	27.4	31.4		Net Worth					33.6	
100.0	100.0	100.0		Total Liabilities & Net Worth					100.0	
				INCOME DATA						
100.0	100.0	100.0		Net Sales					100.0	
29.3	26.7	33.7		Gross Profit					35.8	
23.4	22.0	28.2		Operating Expenses					28.4	
6.0	4.7	5.5		Operating Profit					7.4	
1.5	1.8	.8		All Other Expenses (net)					.8	
4.4	2.9	4.7		Profit Before Taxes					6.6	
				RATIOS						
2.4	2.0	3.3							3.5	
1.3	1.2	1.4		Current					1.6	
1.0	.9	1.0							.9	
1.3	1.1	1.3							1.8	
.7	.6	.7		Quick					.8	
.5	.4	.5							.5	
35 10.3	31 11.9	30 12.3							30 12.1	
46 8.0	37 9.8	47 7.8		Sales/Receivables					49 7.5	
54 6.7	46 7.9	58 6.3							62 5.9	
28 12.8	31 11.8	35 10.3							40 9.2	
39 9.3	51 7.1	59 6.2		Cost of Sales/Inventory					63 5.8	
76 4.8	65 5.6	82 4.4							90 4.1	
17 21.1	20 18.4	17 21.9							16 23.0	
26 13.9	26 14.1	29 12.8		Cost of Sales/Payables					30 12.1	
44 8.2	43 8.5	46 7.9							50 7.3	
6.6	6.5	5.0							5.0	
20.5	24.9	13.2		Sales/Working Capital					9.5	
-141.8	-44.2	-296.1							-57.7	
11.6	9.6	10.1							35.0	
(39) 2.9	(33) 2.4	(41) 3.6		EBIT/Interest					(14) 5.8	
.5	.3	1.6							-.6	
5.5	3.2	8.7		Net Profit + Depr., Dep.,						
(10) 2.3	(13) 1.9	(15) 3.6		Amort./Cur. Mat. L/T/D						
1.1	.5	.9								
.5	.6	.2							.2	
1.2	1.2	1.0		Fixed/Worth					2.0	
2.9	2.3	2.5							-4.9	
.8	.8	.6							.4	
2.5	2.4	2.0		Debt/Worth					3.4	
5.9	4.6	6.1							-12.0	
44.9	49.4	44.9		% Profit Before Taxes/Tangible						
(35) 23.1	(32) 24.8	(37) 17.7		Net Worth						
-3.4	-2.3	4.0								
19.5	14.2	13.7		% Profit Before Taxes/Total					24.2	
7.2	5.2	6.7		Assets					10.9	
-1.9	-3.8	1.1							-3.1	
14.0	15.8	21.4							19.7	
5.8	7.2	8.2		Sales/Net Fixed Assets					5.6	
3.5	3.5	3.5							3.1	
2.6	2.9	2.6							2.1	
2.0	2.0	1.8		Sales/Total Assets					1.7	
1.6	1.6	1.3							1.2	
2.3	1.3	1.7							2.0	
(35) 3.1	(34) 2.8	(37) 3.4		% Depr., Dep., Amort./Sales					(12) 3.7	
4.7	4.9	5.3							6.0	
2.6	1.4			% Officers', Directors'						
(12) 8.4	(10) 3.5			Owners' Comp/Sales						
11.8	9.7									
1053442M	844131M	728776M		Net Sales ($)	807M	9700M	25763M	71104M	243076M	378326M
685534M	523617M	547832M		Total Assets ($)	574M	3012M	13333M	41010M	167112M	322791M

| Current Data Sorted by Assets | | | | | | | Comparative Historical Data | |

Type of Statement

0-500M	500M-2MM	2-10MM	10-50MM	50-100MM	100-250MM	Type of Statement	4/1/05-3/31/06 ALL	4/1/06-3/31/07 ALL
	1	5	10	7	2	Unqualified	26	21
	1	17	6			Reviewed	25	37
1	5	8				Compiled	16	18
4	6	4				Tax Returns	6	6
4	4	18	12	5	2	Other	36	34
	31 (4/1-9/30/09)		91 (10/1/09-3/31/10)					
9	17	52	28	12	4	NUMBER OF STATEMENTS	109	116
%	%	%	%	%	%		%	%

ASSETS

0-500M	500M-2MM	2-10MM	10-50MM	50-100MM	100-250MM		Hist 1	Hist 2
	12.1	11.0	5.4	6.4		Cash & Equivalents	7.4	7.1
	30.5	28.1	27.3	18.2		Trade Receivables (net)	27.9	27.9
	21.8	24.9	25.8	18.6		Inventory	23.8	22.2
	1.4	2.9	2.3	3.5		All Other Current	1.4	2.0
	65.9	66.9	60.8	46.6		Total Current	60.5	59.2
	23.6	26.5	27.4	41.6		Fixed Assets (net)	30.2	28.2
	2.3	.7	6.5	5.2		Intangibles (net)	2.9	4.4
	8.3	5.8	5.4	6.5		All Other Non-Current	6.4	8.2
	100.0	100.0	100.0	100.0		Total	100.0	100.0

LIABILITIES

500M-2MM	2-10MM	10-50MM	50-100MM		Hist 1	Hist 2
10.0	8.4	15.0	7.7	Notes Payable-Short Term	13.6	10.9
2.4	2.9	5.3	3.1	Cur. Mat.-L.T.D.	3.3	2.6
21.2	15.2	12.2	10.5	Trade Payables	15.1	16.2
.1	.1	.1	.6	Income Taxes Payable	.2	.1
6.7	8.4	6.8	10.4	All Other Current	10.0	9.9
40.4	35.0	39.4	32.3	Total Current	42.3	39.6
14.5	13.1	15.0	19.2	Long-Term Debt	15.9	12.2
.1	.5	.3	1.7	Deferred Taxes	.9	.7
9.4	6.3	13.3	14.4	All Other Non-Current	8.8	5.1
35.7	45.1	32.0	32.4	Net Worth	32.1	42.4
100.0	100.0	100.0	100.0	Total Liabilities & Net Worth	100.0	100.0

INCOME DATA

500M-2MM	2-10MM	10-50MM	50-100MM		Hist 1	Hist 2
100.0	100.0	100.0	100.0	Net Sales	100.0	100.0
32.1	28.8	24.0	28.0	Gross Profit	27.1	26.4
27.9	25.2	17.8	23.9	Operating Expenses	23.0	21.8
4.3	3.5	6.1	4.2	Operating Profit	4.1	4.6
.3	1.3	1.7	3.6	All Other Expenses (net)	.7	1.4
4.0	2.2	4.4	.6	Profit Before Taxes	3.4	3.1

RATIOS

500M-2MM	2-10MM	10-50MM	50-100MM		Hist 1	Hist 2
4.1	3.8	2.6	3.1	Current	2.5	2.7
1.7	2.2	1.6	1.8		1.6	1.7
1.1	1.2	1.2	1.5		1.0	1.1
2.7	2.4	1.6	1.7	Quick	1.7	1.6
1.1	1.1	.8	1.0		.9	1.0
.5	.6	.6	.7		.5	.6

Sales/Receivables

0-500M		2-10MM		10-50MM		50-100MM			Hist 1		Hist 2	
25	14.6	37	9.9	41	8.8	37	10.0	Sales/Receivables	36	10.0	35	10.5
43	8.5	45	8.1	55	6.7	46	7.9		44	8.2	43	8.4
52	7.0	53	6.9	68	5.4	58	6.2		55	6.6	53	6.9

Cost of Sales/Inventory

30	12.3	32	11.3	45	8.1	40	9.2	Cost of Sales/Inventory	28	13.3	28	13.1
43	8.4	48	7.6	71	5.1	54	6.7		44	8.3	44	8.2
57	6.4	102	3.6	101	3.6	69	5.3		83	4.4	84	4.4

Cost of Sales/Payables

12	30.4	19	18.9	20	18.1	18	20.3	Cost of Sales/Payables	19	19.6	17	21.2
34	10.7	29	12.5	28	13.2	23	15.5		28	12.9	29	12.6
52	7.0	38	9.7	39	9.4	49	7.4		45	8.2	41	8.9

500M-2MM	2-10MM	10-50MM	50-100MM		Hist 1	Hist 2
5.5	4.1	4.3	4.3	Sales/Working Capital	6.0	5.6
10.1	6.5	7.9	6.7		10.0	9.8
NM	29.6	20.9	10.7		269.3	59.2

EBIT/Interest

	31.0		10.8		16.2	7.9	EBIT/Interest		10.8		10.5
(14)	5.9	(42)	4.0	(25)	3.3	3.5		(95)	4.0	(104)	3.1
	1.2		.6		1.6	1.3			.7		1.2

Net Profit + Depr., Dep., Amort./Cur. Mat. L/T/D

		8.0		6.9	Net Profit + Depr., Dep., Amort./Cur. Mat. L/T/D		6.1		8.3
	(13)	2.0	(10)	4.9		(36)	3.3	(37)	2.5
		.6		.9			1.3		1.2

500M-2MM	2-10MM	10-50MM	50-100MM		Hist 1	Hist 2
.2	.2	.5	.8	Fixed/Worth	.4	.3
.4	.5	1.1	1.3		.9	.7
.8	2.0	6.0	3.0		2.3	1.6
.4	.4	1.5	1.0	Debt/Worth	.6	.4
1.0	1.0	3.1	1.7		1.9	1.6
NM	4.2	20.1	5.7		8.4	4.2

% Profit Before Taxes/Tangible Net Worth

	41.8		25.8		83.8	18.1	% Profit Before Taxes/Tangible Net Worth		34.2		47.3
(13)	20.3	(46)	11.5	(23)	20.4	(10) 14.7		(95)	13.4	(103)	15.0
	3.1		-3.4		4.6	6.3			.9		3.8

500M-2MM	2-10MM	10-50MM	50-100MM		Hist 1	Hist 2
25.0	16.0	11.9	8.3	% Profit Before Taxes/Total Assets	13.2	15.0
5.5	4.9	5.8	3.7		5.5	4.9
-.4	-4.0	.9	1.2		.3	.4
40.2	28.0	13.7	6.0	Sales/Net Fixed Assets	26.6	21.5
15.0	9.5	6.5	3.9		7.8	9.7
10.2	4.9	4.2	2.5		3.5	4.4
3.7	3.0	2.1	1.9	Sales/Total Assets	2.9	3.2
2.8	2.3	1.7	1.4		2.0	2.0
2.2	1.6	1.2	1.2		1.5	1.4

% Depr., Dep., Amort./Sales

	1.0		.9		1.5	3.6	% Depr., Dep., Amort./Sales		1.1		1.0
(11)	1.6	(45)	1.9	(27)	2.6	(11) 3.9		(98)	2.2	(106)	2.1
	5.1		3.7		3.9	6.0			3.6		3.5

% Officers', Directors' Owners' Comp/Sales

	1.2	% Officers', Directors' Owners' Comp/Sales		2.0		1.6
(17)	3.1		(39)	3.8	(37)	3.8
	4.4			6.9		5.5

0-500M	500M-2MM	2-10MM	10-50MM	50-100MM	100-250MM		Hist 1	Hist 2
10353M	60541M	588722M	914785M	1681916M	990001M	Net Sales ($)	2813936M	2902188M
2659M	21006M	245775M	531805M	833930M	882436M	Total Assets ($)	1498637M	1587742M

Comparative Historical Data | Current Data Sorted by Sales

Type of Statement

	ALL	ALL	ALL	0-1MM	1-3MM	3-5MM	5-10MM	10-25MM	25MM & OVER
Unqualified	24	15	25		1	1	2	5	16
Reviewed	34	36	24		1	2	10	6	5
Compiled	12	16	14		4	2	6	2	
Tax Returns	7	7	14	2	7	3	1	1	
Other	46	60	45	3	3	4	9	11	15
	4/1/07-3/31/08	4/1/08-3/31/09	4/1/09-3/31/10		31 (4/1-9/30/09)		91 (10/1/09-3/31/10)		
NUMBER OF STATEMENTS	123	134	122	5	16	12	28	25	36

ASSETS (%)

	ALL	ALL	ALL	0-1MM	1-3MM	3-5MM	5-10MM	10-25MM	25MM & OVER
Cash & Equivalents	6.9	8.1	9.2		7.1	10.8	11.1	13.3	4.0
Trade Receivables (net)	27.5	26.1	26.7		23.8	25.4	26.2	30.3	24.7
Inventory	25.2	24.7	24.2		29.6	23.6	25.3	22.5	23.5
All Other Current	2.2	2.3	2.7		.4	1.7	4.8	1.4	3.6
Total Current	61.9	61.2	62.9		60.9	61.5	67.3	67.5	55.7
Fixed Assets (net)	26.8	25.8	27.2		25.6	27.1	27.0	24.5	30.5
Intangibles (net)	4.5	5.4	4.1		2.9	1.5	.2	3.2	9.5
All Other Non-Current	6.9	7.5	5.9		10.6	9.9	5.4	4.7	4.3
Total	100.0	100.0	100.0		100.0	100.0	100.0	100.0	100.0

LIABILITIES

	ALL	ALL	ALL	0-1MM	1-3MM	3-5MM	5-10MM	10-25MM	25MM & OVER
Notes Payable-Short Term	11.5	12.1	12.5		26.7	8.4	10.2	9.5	9.9
Cur. Mat.-L.T.D.	3.0	3.5	3.2		1.9	3.6	2.6	4.6	3.6
Trade Payables	14.7	14.6	14.8		14.8	11.3	16.3	14.7	14.2
Income Taxes Payable	.2	.2	.1		.0	.1	.1	.2	.2
All Other Current	9.6	11.3	7.9		3.7	11.5	6.3	7.9	9.8
Total Current	39.1	41.7	38.6		47.2	34.9	35.6	36.9	37.8
Long-Term Debt	14.5	14.0	16.2		32.1	4.3	15.6	10.3	18.7
Deferred Taxes	.6	.6	.7		.6	.4	.4	.4	1.5
All Other Non-Current	8.0	8.2	10.2		13.0	5.8	4.7	10.2	13.4
Net Worth	37.8	35.6	34.3		7.2	54.5	43.8	42.3	28.6
Total Liabilities & Net Worth	100.0	100.0	100.0		100.0	100.0	100.0	100.0	100.0

INCOME DATA

	ALL	ALL	ALL	0-1MM	1-3MM	3-5MM	5-10MM	10-25MM	25MM & OVER
Net Sales	100.0	100.0	100.0		100.0	100.0	100.0	100.0	100.0
Gross Profit	26.6	27.2	29.6		38.4	35.9	27.9	24.0	25.5
Operating Expenses	22.7	22.7	25.1		35.2	29.0	25.7	19.8	18.9
Operating Profit	3.9	4.4	4.5		3.1	6.9	2.2	4.2	6.5
All Other Expenses (net)	1.4	1.2	1.6		.7	1.7	1.0	1.3	2.5
Profit Before Taxes	2.6	3.3	2.9		2.4	5.2	1.2	2.8	4.0

RATIOS

Values are given as upper quartile / median / lower quartile. For turnover ratios the first number is days and the second is times. Parenthetical figures are the number of statements used.

	ALL	ALL	ALL	0-1MM	1-3MM	3-5MM	5-10MM	10-25MM	25MM & OVER
Current	2.8 / 1.7 / 1.1	3.0 / 1.7 / 1.1	3.3 / 1.9 / 1.2		4.0 / 1.7 / 1.0	4.1 / 1.9 / 1.0	3.3 / 2.2 / 1.3	3.7 / 2.4 / 1.3	2.5 / 1.7 / 1.2
Quick	1.7 / (122) .9 / .5	1.8 / 1.0 / .5	2.0 / 1.0 / .6		1.8 / .9 / .3	2.8 / 1.2 / .4	2.0 / 1.0 / .6	2.8 / 1.6 / .6	1.4 / .7 / .5
Sales/Receivables (days / times)	37 10.0 / 45 8.1 / 56 6.6	31 11.9 / 40 9.0 / 50 7.3	35 10.3 / 45 8.0 / 56 6.5		13 28.9 / 38 9.5 / 57 6.4	38 9.7 / 48 7.6 / 54 6.8	28 13.2 / 44 8.3 / 50 7.4	39 9.5 / 51 7.2 / 65 5.6	33 11.0 / 43 8.6 / 55 6.6
Cost of Sales/Inventory (days / times)	32 11.2 / 53 6.9 / 97 3.8	31 11.7 / 51 7.2 / 88 4.1	34 10.6 / 54 6.8 / 92 4.0		32 11.5 / 58 6.3 / 134 2.7	36 10.0 / 56 6.5 / 133 2.7	34 10.8 / 42 8.7 / 87 4.2	28 12.8 / 64 5.7 / 93 3.9	40 9.2 / 60 6.1 / 85 4.3
Cost of Sales/Payables (days / times)	18 20.5 / 29 12.7 / 42 8.6	18 20.1 / 26 13.8 / 39 9.4	20 18.3 / 29 12.7 / 43 8.6		9 39.8 / 25 14.5 / 61 5.9	13 27.3 / 32 11.4 / 51 7.2	19 19.2 / 31 11.8 / 38 9.6	21 17.0 / 29 12.7 / 41 8.9	22 16.7 / 28 13.2 / 37 9.8
Sales/Working Capital	5.0 / 9.6 / 32.2	5.2 / 9.9 / 59.6	4.4 / 7.9 / 26.9		4.6 / 13.2 / NM	5.1 / 7.3 / 766.4	4.9 / 8.5 / 24.4	4.1 / 5.4 / 16.8	4.6 / 7.9 / 25.9
EBIT/Interest	9.5 / (108) 2.8 / 1.0	10.5 / (120) 3.3 / 1.2	11.4 / (105) 3.3 / 1.1		26.0 / (14) 4.0 / -.6		7.9 / (22) 1.8 / .6	15.2 / (20) 2.5 / -1.2	8.8 / (35) 3.6 / 1.8
Net Profit + Depr., Dep., Amort./Cur. Mat. L/T/D	5.1 / (31) 2.0 / .8	5.0 / (41) 2.8 / 1.6	7.0 / (32) 3.1 / .6						7.0 / (15) 4.8 / 1.7
Fixed/Worth	.2 / .6 / 2.0	.2 / .6 / 3.0	.3 / .8 / 2.6		.2 / .5 / NM	.4 / .5 / .9	.2 / .5 / 2.1	.2 / .7 / 2.1	.8 / 1.4 / -2.9
Debt/Worth	.6 / 1.8 / 5.9	.5 / 1.6 / 14.9	.5 / 1.7 / 10.1		.3 / 1.9 / -6.9	.3 / .8 / 1.2	.4 / 1.0 / 4.0	.4 / 1.6 / 7.8	1.4 / 2.9 / -17.7
% Profit Before Taxes/Tangible Net Worth	42.3 / (107) 15.1 / 2.1	37.9 / (106) 15.4 / 3.2	32.8 / (98) 15.6 / .4		20.3 / (11) 5.6 / -15.8	52.8 / (11) 23.6 / 2.1	25.9 / (25) 8.8 / -3.2	33.1 / (22) 16.8 / .9	60.2 / (26) 16.8 / 7.6
% Profit Before Taxes/Total Assets	14.0 / 5.6 / -.1	14.6 / 5.2 / .4	13.9 / 5.2 / .0		14.0 / 3.3 / -5.7	23.4 / 9.8 / .7	16.3 / 1.6 / -5.2	11.3 / 4.9 / -1.1	12.8 / 6.0 / 3.3
Sales/Net Fixed Assets	20.4 / 10.1 / 4.5	21.0 / 11.2 / 5.2	25.3 / 9.0 / 4.7		35.1 / 14.2 / 6.1	32.2 / 10.3 / 4.0	30.2 / 9.5 / 5.1	22.9 / 8.1 / 4.4	14.3 / 6.9 / 4.3
Sales/Total Assets	2.9 / 2.0 / 1.6	3.0 / 2.1 / 1.7	2.9 / 2.0 / 1.4		3.5 / 2.3 / 1.3	2.8 / 2.1 / 1.6	3.0 / 2.4 / 1.7	2.5 / 1.9 / 1.2	2.5 / 1.7 / 1.3
% Depr., Dep., Amort./Sales	1.1 / (105) 2.0 / 3.3	1.1 / (115) 1.9 / 3.9	1.3 / (101) 2.0 / 4.1		1.2 / (12) 1.8 / 4.2		.8 / (23) 1.9 / 5.1	.7 / (23) 1.8 / 2.9	1.7 / (31) 3.2 / 4.1
% Officers', Directors' Owners' Comp/Sales	2.8 / (36) 4.2 / 6.4	1.9 / (38) 3.9 / 7.6	1.9 / (33) 4.0 / 6.3		3.3 / (10) 5.3 / 8.9				
Net Sales ($)	3634434M	4548540M	4246318M	3442M	34871M	45909M	216780M	442129M	3503187M
Total Assets ($)	1967695M	2324881M	2517611M	1340M	19311M	24785M	103918M	258655M	2109602M

M = $ thousand   MM = $ million
See Pages 9 through 22 for Explanation of Ratios and Data

Current Data Sorted by Assets							Comparative Historical Data	

0-500M	500M-2MM	2-10MM	10-50MM	50-100MM	100-250MM	Type of Statement		
		3	3	3	3	Unqualified	16	19
	2	3	2		1	Reviewed	10	6
	2	2	1			Compiled	5	6
3	2	2				Tax Returns	2	1
2	1	5	9		5	Other	16	12

	8 (4/1-9/30/09)		46 (10/1/09-3/31/10)				4/1/05-3/31/06 ALL	4/1/06-3/31/07 ALL
0-500M	500M-2MM	2-10MM	10-50MM	50-100MM	100-250MM	NUMBER OF STATEMENTS	49	44
5	7	15	15	3	9			
%	%	%	%	%	%	ASSETS	%	%
		10.0	6.5			Cash & Equivalents	11.4	6.8
		17.2	8.4			Trade Receivables (net)	19.3	19.0
		38.5	24.2			Inventory	21.7	24.4
		1.0	1.2			All Other Current	1.0	2.9
		66.7	40.4			Total Current	53.4	53.1
		21.2	43.8			Fixed Assets (net)	38.1	35.1
		8.3	6.7			Intangibles (net)	2.3	5.4
		3.9	9.1			All Other Non-Current	6.2	6.4
		100.0	100.0			Total	100.0	100.0
						LIABILITIES		
		10.9	7.2			Notes Payable-Short Term	10.9	7.1
		2.6	5.8			Cur. Mat.-L.T.D.	2.7	2.6
		10.1	4.6			Trade Payables	11.6	10.7
		.0	.1			Income Taxes Payable	.1	.3
		11.3	11.1			All Other Current	6.3	6.4
		35.0	28.7			Total Current	31.6	27.1
		16.9	23.6			Long-Term Debt	21.2	23.4
		.4	1.0			Deferred Taxes	2.5	1.3
		11.1	.7			All Other Non-Current	7.3	5.3
		36.6	46.0			Net Worth	37.4	42.9
		100.0	100.0			Total Liabilities & Net Worth	100.0	100.0
						INCOME DATA		
		100.0	100.0			Net Sales	100.0	100.0
		30.8	28.7			Gross Profit	31.8	32.8
		29.5	26.1			Operating Expenses	22.5	23.9
		1.4	2.6			Operating Profit	9.3	8.9
		1.9	1.7			All Other Expenses (net)	1.5	1.6
		-.6	.9			Profit Before Taxes	7.8	7.3
						RATIOS		
		3.0	2.1				3.5	3.9
		2.3	1.3			Current	2.2	2.1
		1.6	1.1				1.3	1.7
		1.1	.7				2.1	1.8
		.9	.4			Quick	1.2	1.0
		.2	.3				.6	.5
		21 17.2	31 11.6				30 12.1	31 11.7
		32 11.5	34 10.6			Sales/Receivables	35 10.3	36 10.1
		45 8.1	41 8.8				47 7.8	45 8.1
		84 4.3	107 3.4				34 10.7	42 8.7
		92 4.0	179 2.0			Cost of Sales/Inventory	76 4.8	76 4.8
		230 1.6	258 1.4				126 2.9	102 3.6
		10 38.3	8 43.5				23 15.9	17 21.3
		29 12.5	24 15.0			Cost of Sales/Payables	32 11.6	25 14.3
		46 8.0	42 8.8				40 9.1	41 8.9
		2.6	2.4				3.5	4.0
		5.8	9.7			Sales/Working Capital	5.2	6.1
		11.2	43.8				15.2	11.8
		8.4	4.9				16.4	15.8
		(14) 1.0	1.3			EBIT/Interest	(47) 5.0	(40) 3.7
		-1.1	-1.0				1.8	2.1
						Net Profit + Depr., Dep., Amort./Cur. Mat. L/T/D	12.4	8.1
							(11) 5.9	(15) 2.8
							3.1	1.5
		.1	.6				.4	.3
		.4	1.0			Fixed/Worth	.9	.8
		4.0	2.4				2.0	2.4
		.5	.6				.8	.3
		3.7	1.6			Debt/Worth	1.6	1.4
		9.0	3.7				4.5	5.8
		26.5	26.6			% Profit Before Taxes/Tangible Net Worth	36.1	47.1
		(12) 2.1	(14) 1.7				(46) 19.5	(39) 24.7
		-36.3	-19.5				10.1	12.2
		5.0	5.4			% Profit Before Taxes/Total Assets	14.0	19.1
		.3	1.1				9.0	9.5
		-12.9	-5.0				3.4	4.3
		52.2	2.9				22.8	19.9
		13.5	1.4			Sales/Net Fixed Assets	3.1	4.5
		2.1	.8				1.6	2.0
		2.3	1.0				3.0	2.3
		1.5	.7			Sales/Total Assets	1.3	1.5
		.9	.5				.9	1.0
		.7	5.2				1.4	1.2
		(11) 2.6	(12) 10.9			% Depr., Dep., Amort./Sales	(36) 4.8	(37) 2.8
		6.2	18.3				6.7	5.5
						% Officers', Directors' Owners' Comp/Sales	3.0	
							(11) 4.7	
							13.6	
4326M	22493M	122676M	279695M	187605M	948418M	Net Sales ($)	2185623M	1332586M
1634M	8140M	78745M	369209M	238934M	1198170M	Total Assets ($)	1544387M	1190295M

M = $ thousand   MM = $ million
See Pages 9 through 22 for Explanation of Ratios and Data

Comparative Historical Data   Current Data Sorted by Sales

			Type of Statement						
18	16	12	Unqualified			1	1	3	7
10	9	8	Reviewed		1	2	2	2	1
4	6	5	Compiled		2	1	2		
3	2	7	Tax Returns		3	1		1	
18	20	22	Other	2	1	1	5	6	8
4/1/07-3/31/08	4/1/08-3/31/09	4/1/09-3/31/10		2					
ALL	ALL	ALL			8 (4/1-9/30/09)		46 (10/1/09-3/31/10)		
				0-1MM	1-3MM	3-5MM	5-10MM	10-25MM	25MM & OVER
53	53	54	NUMBER OF STATEMENTS	4	6	6	10	12	16
%	%	%	ASSETS	%	%	%	%	%	%
8.5	10.9	8.1	Cash & Equivalents				6.2	7.0	4.7
20.1	17.6	15.0	Trade Receivables (net)				10.5	14.4	8.9
23.5	25.4	29.7	Inventory				31.3	37.7	21.7
1.5	1.8	1.5	All Other Current				1.7	1.1	1.0
53.7	55.8	54.3	Total Current				49.8	60.2	36.3
36.2	35.2	34.2	Fixed Assets (net)				33.0	34.1	46.2
4.7	4.0	5.6	Intangibles (net)				12.1	2.6	7.5
5.5	5.0	5.9	All Other Non-Current				5.1	3.2	9.9
100.0	100.0	100.0	Total				100.0	100.0	100.0
			LIABILITIES						
6.5	6.7	6.9	Notes Payable-Short Term				9.9	8.9	4.9
2.4	5.2	5.4	Cur. Mat.-L.T.D.				5.7	4.8	9.4
11.9	10.0	9.1	Trade Payables				7.2	9.5	4.9
.2	.4	.1	Income Taxes Payable				.0	.1	.0
7.1	8.4	12.0	All Other Current				6.4	13.9	9.7
28.0	30.7	33.5	Total Current				29.1	37.2	28.9
24.2	19.8	19.1	Long-Term Debt				17.9	24.2	21.0
1.6	1.2	1.1	Deferred Taxes				.4	1.2	2.6
3.5	6.5	4.7	All Other Non-Current				10.9	5.3	3.1
42.6	41.8	41.6	Net Worth				41.6	32.1	44.5
100.0	100.0	100.0	Total Liabilites & Net Worth				100.0	100.0	100.0
			INCOME DATA						
100.0	100.0	100.0	Net Sales				100.0	100.0	100.0
33.1	29.3	30.5	Gross Profit				29.5	29.9	27.3
24.9	26.1	30.7	Operating Expenses				30.6	24.9	31.2
8.3	3.1	-.3	Operating Profit				-1.1	5.0	-3.9
2.0	1.6	1.9	All Other Expenses (net)				1.3	3.4	2.3
6.2	1.5	-2.2	Profit Before Taxes				-2.4	1.6	-6.2
			RATIOS						
3.7	3.9	3.0					5.6	2.5	2.8
2.3	2.0	1.9	Current				1.9	1.8	1.4
1.4	1.2	1.2					1.0	1.1	1.1
1.8	1.8	1.1					1.7	.9	1.0
.9	1.0	.7	Quick				.7	.7	.6
.4	.4	.3					.2	.3	.3
29 12.7	23 15.7	27 13.3					27 13.5	32 11.5	32 11.3
37 10.0	28 12.9	34 10.6	Sales/Receivables				31 11.8	42 8.6	35 10.5
48 7.7	39 9.3	43 8.4					35 10.5	45 8.1	39 9.3
58 6.3	39 9.3	80 4.6					88 4.1	96 3.8	81 4.5
82 4.5	90 4.1	115 3.2	Cost of Sales/Inventory				131 2.8	177 2.1	111 3.3
152 2.4	158 2.3	233 1.6					256 1.4	248 1.5	192 1.9
15 23.7	15 24.9	13 28.3					16 22.2	9 40.8	15 24.3
28 13.2	21 17.0	24 15.2	Cost of Sales/Payables				30 12.0	24 15.2	22 17.0
45 8.0	33 11.0	38 9.5					40 9.2	47 7.8	36 10.2
3.4	3.2	2.6					2.8	2.5	3.6
7.0	5.8	6.5	Sales/Working Capital				4.6	6.5	11.7
14.6	31.5	22.8					NM	40.9	38.2
5.0	7.7	4.7					4.3	25.1	1.1
(47) 2.3	(48) 2.2	(48) 1.1	EBIT/Interest				1.5	1.2	(14) -1.4
1.0	-.8	-1.4					-4.3	.0	-8.4
4.2			Net Profit + Depr., Dep.,						
(11) 2.1			Amort./Cur. Mat. L/T/D						
1.4									
.3	.4	.3					.2	.3	.6
1.0	.9	.8	Fixed/Worth				.8	1.2	1.1
2.3	2.4	2.6					NM	2.3	3.1
.5	.6	.5					.4	.9	.5
2.0	1.4	1.6	Debt/Worth				2.6	1.9	1.3
3.7	4.8	4.7					NM	7.2	4.2
39.4	30.9	21.2	% Profit Before Taxes/Tangible					27.9	3.2
(48) 14.9	(49) 6.3	(47) .6	Net Worth				(11) 5.2	(14) -13.2
.2	-8.4	-31.8						-2.1	-37.3
16.5	12.6	5.7	% Profit Before Taxes/Total				7.3	8.1	.2
5.2	4.0	.2	Assets				.7	.8	-5.0
.1	-2.5	-9.9					-13.9	-3.7	-10.0
19.1	20.9	17.5					40.5	42.5	2.9
3.4	5.1	2.9	Sales/Net Fixed Assets				5.6	3.6	1.7
1.4	1.4	1.0					.8	.9	.8
2.3	2.3	2.1					2.2	2.0	1.2
1.6	1.4	1.1	Sales/Total Assets				.9	1.1	.9
.8	.8	.6					.5	.6	.5
1.4	1.1	1.6							3.0
(44) 3.6	(41) 3.7	(38) 5.3	% Depr., Dep., Amort./Sales				(10) 7.2	(11) 6.1
7.2	8.8	10.6						18.7	10.3
1.2	2.9		% Officers', Directors'						
(12) 3.4	(13) 4.4		Owners' Comp/Sales						
5.2	9.3								
2268332M	1565121M	1565213M	Net Sales ($)	1794M	12992M	24193M	73366M	176780M	1276088M
2250966M	1580363M	1894832M	Total Assets ($)	1164M	8716M	16274M	92905M	207963M	1567810M

Current Data Sorted by Assets | Comparative Historical Data

1	6	2	10	2			Type of Statement		
	7	15	10				Unqualified	14	10
	4	5	1				Reviewed	30	35
9	4	5					Compiled	10	15
2	6	18	12	1	7		Tax Returns	15	17
							Other	43	40

	20 (4/1-9/30/09)		107 (10/1/09-3/31/10)					4/1/05-3/31/06	4/1/06-3/31/07
0-500M	500M-2MM	2-10MM	10-50MM	50-100MM	100-250MM			ALL	ALL
12	27	45	33	3	7		NUMBER OF STATEMENTS	112	117
%	%	%	%	%	%		ASSETS	%	%
10.9	4.4	8.0	10.9				Cash & Equivalents	6.7	9.3
34.7	29.7	23.7	21.8				Trade Receivables (net)	29.4	28.1
14.5	26.1	23.1	18.5				Inventory	24.2	23.5
3.7	1.1	2.2	2.9				All Other Current	2.9	3.8
63.8	61.3	57.0	54.2				Total Current	63.2	64.7
28.4	27.6	34.1	33.1				Fixed Assets (net)	26.8	26.8
.1	4.3	1.4	7.2				Intangibles (net)	4.0	3.4
7.8	6.8	7.5	5.4				All Other Non-Current	6.0	5.1
100.0	100.0	100.0	100.0				Total	100.0	100.0
							LIABILITIES		
17.3	14.5	11.2	8.3				Notes Payable-Short Term	11.3	11.8
5.7	5.7	5.5	5.1				Cur. Mat.-L.T.D.	4.6	3.9
17.7	20.2	13.2	11.6				Trade Payables	14.9	14.7
.0	.2	.0	.3				Income Taxes Payable	.6	.2
42.2	16.4	9.8	9.1				All Other Current	8.3	9.3
82.9	57.0	39.7	34.4				Total Current	39.7	40.0
40.2	16.1	19.6	22.3				Long-Term Debt	16.5	17.1
.0	.6	.0	1.0				Deferred Taxes	.6	.4
8.3	3.2	5.6	6.4				All Other Non-Current	7.9	6.3
-31.4	23.2	35.1	36.0				Net Worth	35.3	36.2
100.0	100.0	100.0	100.0				Total Liabilties & Net Worth	100.0	100.0
							INCOME DATA		
100.0	100.0	100.0	100.0				Net Sales	100.0	100.0
50.4	36.0	28.4	27.9				Gross Profit	30.7	31.8
49.8	34.1	29.2	23.8				Operating Expenses	27.5	27.0
.5	1.9	-.8	4.1				Operating Profit	3.2	4.9
1.6	.8	.7	.6				All Other Expenses (net)	1.0	1.0
-1.1	1.1	-1.5	3.5				Profit Before Taxes	2.2	3.8
							RATIOS		
2.2	1.8	3.1	2.7					2.7	3.1
1.0	1.2	1.5	1.7				Current	1.6	1.8
.6	.7	1.0	1.0					1.2	1.1
1.5	.9	1.4	2.0					1.5	1.8
.5	.7	.9	1.0				Quick	1.0	.9
.1	.4	.4	.5					.6	.6

0	UND	29	12.5	35	10.5	32	11.6			Sales/Receivables	32	11.3	34	10.6
34	10.7	40	9.1	43	8.5	44	8.4				45	8.1	43	8.5
73	5.0	61	6.0	55	6.7	55	6.6				59	6.2	57	6.4
0	UND	29	12.6	19	19.1	26	13.9			Cost of Sales/Inventory	24	15.4	18	19.9
9	39.5	47	7.8	62	5.9	45	8.2				43	8.5	47	7.7
74	4.9	73	5.0	114	3.2	73	5.0				85	4.3	89	4.1
0	UND	13	28.9	13	27.3	15	24.3			Cost of Sales/Payables	16	22.2	15	24.6
30	12.3	31	11.9	27	13.7	30	12.1				29	12.6	28	13.1
86	4.2	53	6.9	51	7.1	48	7.6				43	8.5	49	7.5

9.6	8.4	3.6	4.2					5.0	4.6
NM	24.0	17.2	8.0				Sales/Working Capital	9.5	8.8
-7.2	-15.3	NM	301.0					25.0	31.2

	3.3		8.8		8.8		12.0					6.5		15.0
(10)	1.2	(25)	1.8	(43)	1.7	(29)	4.1			EBIT/Interest	(103)	2.8	(105)	3.6
	-2.3		-4.8		-3.4		1.3					1.1		1.1

					1.9		4.4						4.6		10.0
				(10)	1.4	(15)	2.7			Net Profit + Depr., Dep., Amort./Cur. Mat. L/T/D	(34)	1.9	(27)	2.4
					.0		.6					1.0		1.7

.8	.6	.3	.4					.3	.3
-10.7	1.0	1.2	.8				Fixed/Worth	.8	.6
-.5	-2.9	2.6	4.4					2.5	2.9
2.6	.7	.7	.7					.7	.6
-25.8	1.8	2.2	1.7				Debt/Worth	1.8	1.6
-2.2	-7.2	4.5	5.8					8.1	6.2

			31.6		34.7		38.9					34.5		42.1
		(19)	23.2	(40)	6.5	(27)	21.6			% Profit Before Taxes/Tangible Net Worth	(93)	13.6	(101)	20.8
			-.6		-18.2		3.5					1.6		2.7

24.5	13.5	9.7	14.5					11.9	20.0
1.0	5.6	1.9	5.7				% Profit Before Taxes/Total Assets	4.8	6.5
-17.5	-14.5	-8.6	.8					.4	.3
40.6	41.2	16.7	11.7					19.7	23.9
15.0	9.8	7.4	5.7				Sales/Net Fixed Assets	9.6	10.2
4.9	5.3	2.3	2.8					4.7	5.3
3.8	3.2	2.6	2.1					3.0	3.1
2.8	2.4	1.8	1.5				Sales/Total Assets	2.1	2.2
1.7	2.1	1.2	1.2					1.7	1.7

	.7		.5		1.3		1.8					1.2		1.1
(11)	2.1	(22)	1.8	(41)	2.1	(31)	3.2			% Depr., Dep., Amort./Sales	(98)	2.3	(107)	2.1
	12.8		3.4		6.0		4.8					3.9		3.6

			2.6		2.5							1.6		2.3
		(10)	3.6	(15)	4.6					% Officers', Directors' Owners' Comp/Sales	(42)	2.8	(40)	3.9
			7.2		9.4							5.7		9.6

10407M	94122M	477578M	1221822M	357779M	1379991M		Net Sales ($)	2998917M	1981223M
3590M	35071M	243637M	713097M	249487M	1121470M		Total Assets ($)	1358873M	1002929M

M = $ thousand   MM = $ million
See Pages 9 through 22 for Explanation of Ratios and Data

Comparative Historical Data | Current Data Sorted by Sales

				Type of Statement	0-1MM	1-3MM	3-5MM	5-10MM	10-25MM	25MM & OVE
	20	21	21	Unqualified		2	4	2	3	10
	22	35	32	Reviewed		3	4	9	13	3
	10	11	10	Compiled		3	4	1	1	1
	12	15	18	Tax Returns	6	6	3	2	1	
	38	42	46	Other	3	4	1	8	10	20
	4/1/07-3/31/08 ALL	4/1/08-3/31/09 ALL	4/1/09-3/31/10 ALL			20 (4/1-9/30/09)		107 (10/1/09-3/31/10)		
	102	124	127	NUMBER OF STATEMENTS	9	18	16	22	28	34
	%	%	%	ASSETS	%	%	%	%	%	%
	7.9	8.5	8.2	Cash & Equivalents		7.8	4.3	9.0	10.0	8.3
	24.9	26.6	24.7	Trade Receivables (net)		31.1	30.6	24.4	22.4	22.7
	22.4	24.2	21.8	Inventory		15.6	28.3	22.8	23.4	20.5
	4.0	2.7	2.4	All Other Current		.9	1.6	1.6	2.1	3.6
	59.2	61.9	57.1	Total Current		55.4	64.7	57.8	57.9	55.1
	28.9	27.6	31.4	Fixed Assets (net)		31.8	27.7	31.8	32.8	29.0
	6.2	4.0	4.1	Intangibles (net)		5.3	.4	2.2	3.5	7.9
	5.7	6.5	7.4	All Other Non-Current		7.5	7.2	8.2	5.8	7.9
	100.0	100.0	100.0	Total		100.0	100.0	100.0	100.0	100.0
				LIABILITIES						
	8.2	9.2	11.1	Notes Payable-Short Term		10.1	5.7	6.9	14.1	7.6
	4.5	4.0	5.1	Cur. Mat.-L.T.D.		5.9	5.0	6.2	5.3	2.9
	13.0	12.9	14.2	Trade Payables		21.3	20.2	13.5	12.3	11.8
	.2	.2	.1	Income Taxes Payable		.3	.0	.1	.0	.3
	10.2	9.8	13.7	All Other Current		35.7	12.1	11.6	9.8	7.6
	36.1	36.1	44.3	Total Current		73.4	43.0	38.3	41.5	30.3
	19.9	18.2	23.4	Long-Term Debt		21.4	17.6	19.4	20.7	26.0
	.7	.4	.5	Deferred Taxes		.8	.0	.1	.3	1.3
	7.0	6.1	5.6	All Other Non-Current		1.7	3.6	1.6	9.6	6.7
	36.2	39.2	26.2	Net Worth		2.6	35.8	40.6	28.0	35.8
	100.0	100.0	100.0	Total Liabilties & Net Worth		100.0	100.0	100.0	100.0	100.0
				INCOME DATA						
	100.0	100.0	100.0	Net Sales		100.0	100.0	100.0	100.0	100.0
	34.8	32.3	31.6	Gross Profit		37.4	28.7	29.0	31.0	22.5
	29.9	27.8	30.2	Operating Expenses		41.9	29.7	27.2	28.3	19.8
	4.9	4.6	1.4	Operating Profit		-4.5	-1.0	1.9	2.7	2.7
	1.4	.7	1.0	All Other Expenses (net)		.2	1.1	.8	.0	1.5
	3.5	3.9	.5	Profit Before Taxes		-4.7	-2.1	1.0	2.7	1.1
				RATIOS						
	3.1	3.1	2.6	Current		1.8	2.9	3.2	3.0	3.2
	1.7	1.8	1.5			1.0	1.9	1.2	1.5	1.8
	1.2	1.2	.9			.5	.9	.9	1.0	1.2
	1.5	1.7	1.4	Quick		1.3	1.4	1.6	1.4	1.6
	1.0	1.0	.8			.7	.9	.8	.8	1.0
	.6	.6	.4			.3	.5	.4	.5	.6
	30 12.1	30 12.1	31 11.9	Sales/Receivables	26 13.9	32 11.6	35 10.4	35 10.3	29 12.5	
	42 8.7	42 8.7	42 8.8		41 9.0	55 6.7	43 8.6	41 9.0	43 8.4	
	52 7.0	60 6.1	55 6.7		52 7.1	70 5.2	50 7.4	54 6.7	55 6.7	
	24 15.5	23 16.2	23 16.1	Cost of Sales/Inventory	6 58.3	24 15.1	27 13.8	19 19.2	32 11.5	
	51 7.2	48 7.6	47 7.7		31 11.7	59 6.2	64 5.7	42 8.6	48 7.6	
	84 4.3	100 3.6	91 4.0		76 4.8	123 3.0	95 3.9	133 2.7	69 5.3	
	16 23.1	15 24.6	14 26.1	Cost of Sales/Payables	14 25.9	15 24.2	15 24.9	15 23.9	14 25.7	
	26 13.9	26 14.1	29 12.7		47 7.8	33 11.2	27 13.5	30 12.1	28 13.1	
	46 7.9	45 8.2	49 7.4		89 4.1	56 6.6	41 8.8	56 6.5	39 9.4	
	5.3	4.6	5.0	Sales/Working Capital		14.3	3.7	4.0	3.5	4.5
	9.7	9.5	14.4			NM	8.2	19.6	15.8	8.1
	22.5	33.0	-36.6			-5.3	NM	-25.7	61.2	35.5
	9.7	11.8	7.3	EBIT/Interest	4.9	7.2	8.7	10.4	6.9	
(92)	3.3	(112) 3.4	(116) 1.9		(16) .1	.3	(19) 2.6	(25) 2.6	(32) 3.8	
	1.1	.4	-1.8		-15.7	-3.7	-3.5	-1.3	1.1	
	5.6	6.5	3.3	Net Profit + Depr., Dep., Amort./Cur. Mat. L/T/D				2.2	5.4	
(27)	2.3	(36) 1.5	(32) 1.5					(10) 1.7	(15) 3.2	
	.9	.3	.4					.5	.6	
	.4	.3	.5	Fixed/Worth		.9	.2	.2	.4	.6
	1.1	.8	1.1			2.1	.9	.9	1.1	.9
	5.6	2.0	19.5			-2.3	NM	2.0	4.8	34.1
	.6	.6	.8	Debt/Worth		1.0	.5	.4	1.0	1.1
	1.8	1.8	2.2			16.0	1.3	1.8	2.2	1.8
	39.8	5.1	73.6			-5.2	NM	4.4	6.2	86.6
	46.0	38.3	36.2	% Profit Before Taxes/Tangible Net Worth	43.3	27.5	30.3	41.1	38.9	
(81)	20.7	(108) 19.6	(97) 11.9		(10) 7.7	(12) 5.0	(20) 9.9	(24) 23.2	(27) 21.6	
	4.1	-1.9	-6.1		-40.6	-15.2	.2	-18.8	3.5	
	19.3	16.1	10.8	% Profit Before Taxes/Total Assets		7.4	12.5	8.6	15.8	10.8
	6.3	6.4	3.1			-4.8	-2.0	3.4	5.1	4.3
	.0	-1.3	-8.0			-24.2	-7.1	-4.0	-6.0	-.8
	16.4	20.3	17.1	Sales/Net Fixed Assets		30.2	26.6	32.9	15.7	14.0
	9.6	9.4	7.2			8.7	8.9	8.9	5.5	8.2
	4.2	5.1	3.5			4.0	4.8	2.0	2.9	4.2
	2.9	2.8	2.8	Sales/Total Assets		3.3	2.7	3.2	2.3	2.6
	2.2	2.2	1.9			2.3	2.1	1.8	1.8	1.7
	1.5	1.6	1.3			1.9	1.6	1.1	1.3	1.3
	1.4	1.3	1.3	% Depr., Dep., Amort./Sales	1.2	.8	1.0	1.5	1.4	
(87)	2.5	(112) 2.3	(112) 2.7		(15) 2.2	(15) 1.9	(18) 2.5	(26) 2.9	(30) 2.8	
	4.2	3.5	5.6		7.2	6.8	6.1	5.2	4.4	
	2.4	2.0	2.1	% Officers', Directors' Owners' Comp/Sales					1.3	
(33)	4.5	(43) 3.0	(36) 3.6						(10) 2.5	
	9.4	6.0	7.7						5.4	
	3249674M	4104065M	3541699M	Net Sales ($)	4522M	31525M	63167M	146525M	445941M	2850019M
	1586902M	2234772M	2366352M	Total Assets ($)	3776M	18831M	31762M	94054M	273766M	1944163M

M = $ thousand   MM = $ million
See Pages 9 through 22 for Explanation of Ratios and Data

Current Data Sorted by Assets   **Comparative Historical Data**

0-500M	500M-2MM	2-10MM	10-50MM	50-100MM	100-250MM	Type of Statement	4/1/05-3/31/06 ALL	4/1/06-3/31/07 ALL
1	7	5	21	10	10	Unqualified	54	65
3	16	24	19	1	1	Reviewed	46	53
2	11	18	5		1	Compiled	33	37
2	9	11				Tax Returns	16	35
		26	19	6	7	Other	80	86
	33 (4/1-9/30/09)		202 (10/1/09-3/31/10)					
8	43	84	64	17	19	**NUMBER OF STATEMENTS**	229	276
%	%	%	%	%	%	**ASSETS**	%	%
	11.2	11.0	11.5	5.9	5.7	Cash & Equivalents	9.5	9.2
	22.6	24.5	17.9	13.9	12.8	Trade Receivables (net)	25.4	24.2
	8.0	7.0	9.4	8.2	8.0	Inventory	6.9	7.4
	1.9	3.8	1.7	2.5	2.9	All Other Current	2.8	2.8
	43.6	46.4	40.5	30.6	29.3	Total Current	44.6	43.6
	48.0	44.8	45.6	51.3	54.1	Fixed Assets (net)	44.4	45.7
	2.2	2.0	4.6	9.0	12.0	Intangibles (net)	3.3	4.0
	6.1	6.8	9.3	9.2	4.6	All Other Non-Current	7.7	6.7
	100.0	100.0	100.0	100.0	100.0	Total	100.0	100.0
						LIABILITIES		
	9.8	5.2	4.8	2.8	2.3	Notes Payable-Short Term	5.5	5.6
	6.8	5.5	6.7	4.7	4.1	Cur. Mat.-L.T.D.	5.9	5.3
	8.8	13.8	8.8	6.8	5.3	Trade Payables	13.7	14.2
	.1	.1	.2	.7	.0	Income Taxes Payable	.3	.2
	6.3	7.7	6.7	6.8	7.2	All Other Current	6.6	6.4
	31.8	32.2	27.3	21.7	19.0	Total Current	31.9	31.7
	33.8	25.6	17.6	29.4	25.5	Long-Term Debt	21.9	23.2
	.0	.3	1.4	1.8	1.2	Deferred Taxes	1.2	1.2
	7.6	4.3	2.6	5.5	2.7	All Other Non-Current	3.2	3.2
	26.8	37.6	51.1	41.6	51.6	Net Worth	41.7	40.7
	100.0	100.0	100.0	100.0	100.0	Total Liabilties & Net Worth	100.0	100.0
						INCOME DATA		
	100.0	100.0	100.0	100.0	100.0	Net Sales	100.0	100.0
	37.5	28.4	22.1	18.8	17.1	Gross Profit	28.4	30.0
	36.5	30.5	23.0	16.9	18.0	Operating Expenses	23.9	25.1
	1.1	-2.1	-.9	1.9	-.9	Operating Profit	4.5	4.9
	1.2	.8	.3	1.6	.7	All Other Expenses (net)	.5	.5
	-.2	-3.0	-1.2	.3	-1.6	Profit Before Taxes	3.9	4.4
						RATIOS		
	4.3	3.6	2.5	2.0	3.0		2.4	2.2
	1.5	1.5	1.6	1.3	1.4	Current	1.4	1.4
	.6	.9	.9	1.1	1.2		1.0	1.0
	2.6	2.9	2.0	1.5	1.6		1.8	1.7
	1.2	1.2	1.0	.9	1.0	Quick	1.1	1.1
	.4	.6	.6	.6	.6		.7	.7
	16 23.2	33 11.2	35 10.4	29 12.4	30 12.3		34 10.8	33 11.0
	31 11.9	44 8.4	45 8.0	42 8.7	42 8.6	Sales/Receivables	44 8.4	43 8.5
	54 6.8	60 6.1	57 6.5	60 6.1	55 6.7		56 6.5	54 6.7
	0 UND	7 50.7	8 43.6	25 14.7	20 18.7		5 72.6	6 63.8
	8 46.2	16 23.4	23 16.1	37 9.8	25 14.3	Cost of Sales/Inventory	12 29.6	14 25.7
	33 11.0	29 12.5	48 7.5	44 8.3	41 8.8		26 14.0	31 11.6
	5 75.4	17 21.8	16 22.1	13 27.1	13 28.8		18 20.1	20 18.3
	15 23.6	32 11.4	26 14.1	24 15.0	15 24.0	Cost of Sales/Payables	32 11.5	30 12.3
	38 9.7	49 7.4	42 8.6	35 10.5	27 13.8		44 8.2	44 8.2
	6.2	5.1	5.0	5.3	4.7		7.5	7.4
	18.1	12.7	10.8	9.8	14.4	Sales/Working Capital	15.1	15.8
	-14.4	-93.5	-38.2	79.6	48.7		UND	469.5
	3.0	4.3	3.9	3.7	6.4		12.0	10.5
	(37) .5	(74) 1.1	(61) 1.1	1.1	1.2	EBIT/Interest	(211) 4.5	(257) 3.9
	-1.7	-2.2	-2.7	-.3	-3.4		1.5	1.6
		3.1	3.2	3.7		Net Profit + Depr., Dep.,	4.1	5.5
		(17) 2.0	(25) 1.6	(11) 1.7		Amort./Cur. Mat. L/T/D	(78) 2.0	(82) 2.5
		.9	.3	.5			1.4	1.2
	.6	.5	.6	.8	.8		.6	.7
	2.0	1.1	1.0	1.2	1.3	Fixed/Worth	1.1	1.2
	-19.0	4.7	1.6	6.2	2.4		2.1	2.3
	.5	.5	.5	.7	.4		.7	.7
	3.2	1.4	1.0	1.9	1.2	Debt/Worth	1.4	1.6
	-75.0	6.1	2.1	7.8	3.2		3.3	3.9
	37.6	18.0	10.5	11.7	22.8	% Profit Before Taxes/Tangible	35.9	41.2
	(32) 2.1	(69) 3.9	(61) 1.7	(15) -.3	(18) 1.8	Net Worth	(213) 17.0	(252) 18.8
	-15.4	-13.0	-11.5	-11.6	-32.7		5.2	7.1
	5.0	6.3	4.8	6.1	7.7	% Profit Before Taxes/Total	14.1	14.9
	.0	.5	.5	.4	.7	Assets	7.2	6.6
	-7.6	-7.7	-4.6	-3.4	-10.3		1.1	1.7
	8.1	7.1	4.3	3.2	2.7		7.7	6.9
	3.7	4.6	2.8	1.9	2.0	Sales/Net Fixed Assets	4.6	4.4
	2.1	2.4	1.8	1.5	1.6		3.0	2.8
	3.1	2.2	1.6	1.4	1.3		2.5	2.5
	1.8	1.7	1.3	1.0	1.1	Sales/Total Assets	2.0	2.0
	1.3	1.2	1.0	.8	.9		1.5	1.4
	3.3	3.5	4.0	5.0	3.0		2.7	3.1
	(38) 5.1	(79) 5.5	(60) 6.0	7.2	(10) 6.5	% Depr., Dep., Amort./Sales	(203) 4.4	(245) 4.6
	9.4	9.1	9.0	8.0	7.4		5.8	6.2
	1.6	1.9	.5				1.2	1.5
	(18) 2.9	(32) 3.4	(15) 1.1			% Officers', Directors' Owners' Comp/Sales	(73) 2.8	(89) 3.2
	8.2	6.4	2.8				6.0	5.8
10228M	121504M	734387M	1973785M	1408795M	3260856M	Net Sales ($)	9368947M	11752949M
2638M	55236M	403258M	1482436M	1242193M	2858922M	Total Assets ($)	5871456M	7375872M

M = $ thousand   MM = $ million
See Pages 9 through 22 for Explanation of Ratios and Data

Comparative Historical Data | Current Data Sorted by Sales

4/1/07-3/31/08 ALL	4/1/08-3/31/09 ALL	4/1/09-3/31/10 ALL	Type of Statement	0-1MM	1-3MM	3-5MM	5-10MM	10-25MM	25MM & OVER
44	49	46	Unqualified			1	2	12	31
55	58	53	Reviewed	3	2	3	13	18	14
50	41	43	Compiled	3	17	7	4	7	5
34	26	24	Tax Returns	1	9	6	5	3	
78	101	69	Other	2	9	7	13	16	22
					33 (4/1-9/30/09)		202 (10/1/09-3/31/10)		
261	275	235	**NUMBER OF STATEMENTS**	9	37	24	37	56	72
%	%	%	**ASSETS**	%	%	%	%	%	%
8.6	8.3	10.7	Cash & Equivalents		14.5	9.4	13.6	10.7	8.8
22.9	23.1	20.2	Trade Receivables (net)		15.2	23.2	25.3	23.4	17.6
7.1	8.6	8.3	Inventory		8.5	5.0	5.6	7.7	10.3
2.8	2.9	2.6	All Other Current		3.7	3.7	2.3	2.5	2.2
41.4	43.0	41.8	Total Current		41.9	41.2	46.8	44.2	38.9
48.2	46.5	46.6	Fixed Assets (net)		46.6	48.3	45.4	43.1	48.3
2.8	3.2	4.1	Intangibles (net)		2.9	2.1	1.0	5.7	5.8
7.5	7.3	7.6	All Other Non-Current		8.6	8.3	6.8	6.9	7.0
100.0	100.0	100.0	Total		100.0	100.0	100.0	100.0	100.0
			LIABILITIES						
4.9	5.6	5.7	Notes Payable-Short Term		6.8	9.5	5.4	5.5	3.5
5.6	6.5	5.8	Cur. Mat.-L.T.D.		4.6	6.4	5.8	6.8	4.8
11.8	13.2	10.2	Trade Payables		6.7	10.8	14.0	13.3	7.9
.2	.1	.2	Income Taxes Payable		.1	.2	.1	.2	.3
6.5	7.4	7.3	All Other Current		11.8	3.6	4.3	7.6	6.7
29.0	32.8	29.2	Total Current		30.0	30.4	29.6	33.4	23.3
24.5	24.8	26.0	Long-Term Debt		33.1	41.4	24.8	20.8	20.7
1.0	1.1	.7	Deferred Taxes		.0	.4	.7	.5	1.5
3.5	4.8	4.3	All Other Non-Current		4.9	7.3	5.7	2.0	3.4
42.0	36.5	39.7	Net Worth		32.0	20.5	39.3	43.3	51.2
100.0	100.0	100.0	Total Liabilties & Net Worth		100.0	100.0	100.0	100.0	100.0
			INCOME DATA						
100.0	100.0	100.0	Net Sales		100.0	100.0	100.0	100.0	100.0
29.3	25.0	27.5	Gross Profit		37.9	29.0	29.4	25.1	20.6
25.1	24.8	28.3	Operating Expenses		39.0	28.5	31.4	26.6	20.1
4.1	.2	-.8	Operating Profit		-1.2	.4	-2.0	-1.5	.5
.8	.7	.8	All Other Expenses (net)		.7	1.4	.6	.6	.4
3.3	-.4	-1.5	Profit Before Taxes		-1.9	-1.0	-2.6	-2.1	.1
			RATIOS						
2.4	2.3	3.0	Current		7.6	3.7	3.2	2.2	2.7
1.5	1.4	1.5			1.9	1.3	1.5	1.3	1.6
1.0	.9	.9			.6	.7	.9	.9	1.1
1.7	1.5	2.1	Quick		7.4	3.0	2.6	2.0	1.6
(260) 1.1	.9	1.0			1.5	1.1	1.3	1.0	1.0
.7	.6	.6			.4	.5	.8	.6	.7
29 12.5	29 12.6	30 12.3	Sales/Receivables	9 41.0	26 13.8	30 12.3	35 10.5	32 11.4	
38 9.6	40 9.1	42 8.6		31 11.9	39 9.5	40 9.0	49 7.5	43 8.6	
51 7.1	51 7.1	57 6.4		57 6.4	50 7.3	54 6.7	62 5.9	55 6.7	
6 59.1	7 52.6	7 49.4	Cost of Sales/Inventory	1 665.7	0 UND	4 93.8	10 35.8	18 20.5	
12 30.0	15 23.7	20 18.7		11 34.0	7 54.8	13 28.3	21 17.5	28 12.9	
30 12.0	33 11.0	39 9.3		24 14.9	24 15.1	23 15.7	31 11.6	45 8.1	
16 22.3	14 25.5	14 26.6	Cost of Sales/Payables	4 81.8	7 52.0	15 24.7	22 16.5	14 26.6	
25 14.4	24 15.3	26 14.1		17 21.6	26 14.1	32 11.3	37 9.9	21 17.8	
41 9.0	41 8.9	43 8.5		46 7.9	51 7.2	40 9.0	58 6.3	32 11.4	
7.6	7.0	5.3	Sales/Working Capital		3.0	7.0	5.7	5.7	5.0
15.9	16.5	13.1			10.4	22.6	13.1	16.6	9.6
-616.1	-41.7	-43.9			-16.6	-19.7	-40.5	-25.9	47.8
9.3	4.9	3.9	EBIT/Interest		2.7	5.2	2.7	4.8	5.4
(237) 2.7	(253) 1.4	(213) 1.1		(29) .1	(23) 1.0	(32) 1.1	(52) .2	(70) 1.8	
1.1	-1.5	-1.9		-2.5	-1.5	-2.1	-2.8	-.9	
3.7	3.3	3.1	Net Profit + Depr., Dep., Amort./Cur. Mat. L/T/D					3.0	3.3
(67) 1.7	(72) 1.6	(60) 1.3					(17) 1.2	(30) 1.6	
1.2	.6	.4					.2	.6	
.6	.7	.6	Fixed/Worth		.5	.7	.5	.6	.7
1.3	1.3	1.2			1.2	2.7	1.2	1.1	1.0
2.5	2.8	3.3			-17.2	-4.8	4.8	2.7	1.6
.6	.7	.5	Debt/Worth		.4	.7	.4	.5	.6
1.4	1.5	1.4			1.6	3.2	1.4	1.3	1.0
3.5	4.8	5.5			-48.4	-15.9	6.1	4.3	2.1
36.2	18.1	16.1	% Profit Before Taxes/Tangible Net Worth		27.9	31.9	10.7	13.3	14.6
(237) 13.7	(232) 4.3	(199) 2.2		(27) -.3	(16) 16.2	(31) 2.1	(50) .5	(69) 4.7	
1.3	-13.6	-14.9		-13.0	-8.4	-14.9	-20.7	-9.8	
14.2	6.8	5.3	% Profit Before Taxes/Total Assets		5.7	7.1	2.7	5.4	6.6
4.3	.8	.4			.5	-1.0	.0	-1.6	.9
.1	-6.4	-7.0			-7.7	-11.9	-7.7	-7.0	-3.5
6.1	7.1	6.1	Sales/Net Fixed Assets		6.2	7.9	8.7	6.2	4.1
4.0	3.9	3.2			3.3	4.5	4.6	4.4	2.7
2.6	2.5	1.9			2.1	2.2	2.3	2.0	1.7
2.5	2.6	2.0	Sales/Total Assets		2.1	2.9	2.5	2.3	1.6
1.8	1.8	1.5			1.4	1.7	1.7	1.7	1.3
1.5	1.3	1.1			1.1	1.3	1.4	1.0	1.0
3.2	3.2	3.5	% Depr., Dep., Amort./Sales		2.6	3.5	3.3	3.6	3.6
(232) 4.8	(240) 5.0	(210) 5.8		(33) 5.6	(23) 5.3	(35) 5.0	(52) 5.6	(60) 6.1	
6.4	7.3	8.9		9.2	8.0	9.4	9.7	7.7	
1.3	1.0	1.3	% Officers', Directors' Owners' Comp/Sales		2.7	1.6	1.6	.6	
(91) 2.4	(84) 2.4	(72) 2.8			(17) 6.1	(13) 2.7	(16) 2.4	(16) 2.0	
4.7	4.1	6.6			8.2	6.7	4.4	4.7	
11205252M	11302451M	7509555M	Net Sales ($)	5010M	76422M	99885M	255705M	861734M	6210799M
7046906M	7403917M	6044683M	Total Assets ($)	7309M	58584M	60058M	172380M	745093M	5001259M

M = $ thousand   MM = $ million
See Pages 9 through 22 for Explanation of Ratios and Data

Current Data Sorted by Assets   **Comparative Historical Data**

0-500M	500M-2MM	2-10MM	10-50MM	50-100MM	100-250MM	Type of Statement	4/1/05-3/31/06 ALL	4/1/06-3/31/07 ALL
	1	1	3	5	6	Unqualified	25	35
	2	13	6	1	1	Reviewed	37	32
3	7	3	2			Compiled	20	13
1	6	4				Tax Returns	6	9
2	11	15	17	5	5	Other	35	47
	15 (4/1-9/30/09)		105 (10/1/09-3/31/10)					
6	27	36	28	11	12	**NUMBER OF STATEMENTS**	123	136
%	%	%	%	%	%	**ASSETS**	%	%
	8.4	10.7	8.5	4.0	7.6	Cash & Equivalents	9.3	6.9
	21.0	18.7	13.5	12.0	6.9	Trade Receivables (net)	22.3	18.5
	24.0	22.4	16.4	19.7	26.4	Inventory	18.2	19.3
	5.4	4.2	3.3	3.0	5.1	All Other Current	1.6	2.9
	58.9	55.9	41.6	38.6	45.9	Total Current	51.3	47.6
	32.8	34.0	49.6	46.9	45.8	Fixed Assets (net)	39.4	43.1
	3.9	.4	3.4	10.4	3.4	Intangibles (net)	2.6	2.9
	4.5	9.7	5.4	4.1	4.8	All Other Non-Current	6.6	6.5
	100.0	100.0	100.0	100.0	100.0	Total	100.0	100.0
						LIABILITIES		
	10.2	4.4	9.0	12.0	8.2	Notes Payable-Short Term	7.2	8.0
	6.0	3.9	9.7	16.0	4.6	Cur. Mat.-L.T.D.	4.9	4.4
	12.6	9.6	6.8	7.1	6.2	Trade Payables	11.1	10.3
	.0	.0	.0	.0	.1	Income Taxes Payable	.4	.2
	14.9	4.8	4.8	5.4	6.9	All Other Current	6.9	7.3
	43.8	22.6	30.4	40.5	26.0	Total Current	30.5	30.2
	28.5	19.0	25.3	15.4	21.9	Long-Term Debt	24.7	22.5
	.0	.7	.6	2.5	.1	Deferred Taxes	.6	.5
	12.0	9.3	.8	9.3	25.6	All Other Non-Current	3.8	5.3
	15.6	48.3	42.8	32.3	26.4	Net Worth	40.4	41.5
	100.0	100.0	100.0	100.0	100.0	Total Liabilities & Net Worth	100.0	100.0
						INCOME DATA		
	100.0	100.0	100.0	100.0	100.0	Net Sales	100.0	100.0
	37.2	34.8	31.2	36.1	18.8	Gross Profit	31.1	32.2
	39.0	31.1	29.6	31.1	18.9	Operating Expenses	23.7	24.1
	-1.8	3.6	1.6	5.0	-.1	Operating Profit	7.4	8.1
	.7	1.2	3.3	3.7	4.8	All Other Expenses (net)	1.4	1.5
	-2.5	2.4	-1.7	1.3	-4.8	Profit Before Taxes	6.0	6.6
						RATIOS		
	3.0	4.5	3.8	2.7	3.0	Current	2.8	2.5
	1.6	3.1	2.0	1.1	2.2		1.7	1.6
	1.0	1.4	.8	.6	1.2		1.2	1.1
	1.6	3.0	1.8	1.6	1.6	Quick	1.8	1.6
	.7	1.4	.8	.4	.6		1.1	.9
	.4	.6	.3	.2	.2		.5	.4
	12 29.6	26 14.0	30 12.1	33 11.1	17 21.8	Sales/Receivables	27 13.4	27 13.4
	30 12.0	38 9.7	38 9.6	45 8.0	33 11.2		39 9.4	37 9.9
	51 7.2	51 7.1	57 6.4	59 6.2	42 8.7		56 6.5	49 7.5
	23 16.1	39 9.2	46 8.0	92 4.0	87 4.2	Cost of Sales/Inventory	22 16.8	31 11.6
	57 6.4	67 5.5	69 5.3	121 3.0	104 3.5		55 6.7	59 6.2
	98 3.7	124 2.9	121 3.0	192 1.9	179 2.0		92 4.0	97 3.8
	11 33.1	14 26.5	15 24.4	23 15.6	14 25.6	Cost of Sales/Payables	18 20.8	20 18.6
	24 15.0	26 14.2	27 13.7	27 13.5	26 14.2		27 13.5	27 13.5
	44 8.3	39 9.5	39 9.3	57 6.4	56 6.5		45 8.2	43 8.5
	5.3	3.1	3.1	4.2	2.1	Sales/Working Capital	5.1	5.9
	10.5	4.8	6.1	41.2	4.4		7.8	10.4
	-522.2	9.6	-14.9	-8.4	12.1		28.8	40.0
	4.5	5.1	3.6	6.1	4.3	EBIT/Interest	13.2	17.5
	(24) 1.2	(30) 1.8	(25) 1.5	(10) 3.0	(11) .7		(111) 4.5	(128) 4.5
	-5.7	-1.5	-1.3	.6	-2.0		1.6	1.6
		2.8				Net Profit + Depr., Dep., Amort./Cur. Mat. L/T/D	7.5	7.8
		(11) 1.6					(42) 2.6	(37) 3.6
		.8					1.5	1.9
	.3	.4	.7	1.1	.7	Fixed/Worth	.5	.6
	1.6	.7	1.5	3.0	1.5		.9	1.0
	-10.0	1.6	2.3	5.5	3.1		2.2	2.3
	.6	.4	.4	1.4	.5	Debt/Worth	.6	.6
	2.7	.9	1.6	4.8	1.4		1.4	1.4
	-16.5	2.1	4.6	6.8	4.8		3.9	3.2
	20.5	28.6	7.4		7.3	% Profit Before Taxes/Tangible Net Worth	39.5	38.8
	(19) 7.9	(34) 9.9	(25) 5.0		(11) -9.7		(111) 20.1	(124) 24.8
	-26.4	-2.3	-7.8		-21.6		8.7	10.2
	7.5	10.2	5.4	8.2	4.4	% Profit Before Taxes/Total Assets	19.5	16.8
	1.8	4.2	.8	1.6	-1.9		7.3	8.1
	-16.2	-2.7	-6.4	-2.2	-9.5		2.0	3.0
	22.3	9.8	4.2	3.3	2.4	Sales/Net Fixed Assets	8.3	7.2
	8.6	4.2	1.9	1.9	1.8		4.6	3.6
	5.1	2.8	1.2	1.8	1.3		2.4	2.2
	3.2	2.1	1.2	1.0	1.0	Sales/Total Assets	2.3	2.2
	1.8	1.5	1.0	.9	.8		1.6	1.6
	1.3	1.2	.7	.7	.7		1.2	1.1
	1.6	3.4	2.7	5.9		% Depr., Dep., Amort./Sales	2.5	2.1
	(23) 3.0	(32) 4.8	(27) 6.8	7.5			(111) 3.4	(122) 3.7
	4.9	7.1	8.6	12.7			5.6	5.7
	2.5	1.9				% Officers', Directors' Owners' Comp/Sales	1.8	2.1
	(15) 4.8	(12) 3.1					(38) 3.0	(28) 2.9
	8.6	4.6					4.7	4.2
5236M	91752M	266342M	596655M	674915M	1532271M	Net Sales ($)	3744454M	4625493M
2130M	38514M	174519M	634599M	716737M	1738477M	Total Assets ($)	2436910M	3267613M

M = $ thousand   MM = $ million
See Pages 9 through 22 for Explanation of Ratios and Data

Comparative Historical Data | | Type of Statement | | Current Data Sorted by Sales | | | | |

33	23	16	Unqualified		1	1		1	13
19	23	23	Reviewed		2	1	11	8	1
14	15	15	Compiled	3	2	2	4	4	
9	10	11	Tax Returns	1	5	1	3	1	
55	52	55	Other	3	7	7	7	14	17
4/1/07-3/31/08 ALL	4/1/08-3/31/09 ALL	4/1/09-3/31/10 ALL			15 (4/1-9/30/09)			105 (10/1/09-3/31/10)	
				0-1MM	1-3MM	3-5MM	5-10MM	10-25MM	25MM & OVER
130	123	120	NUMBER OF STATEMENTS	7	17	12	25	28	31
%	%	%	ASSETS	%	%	%	%	%	%
9.2	7.6	8.5	Cash & Equivalents		6.6	12.7	8.6	8.2	8.7
16.3	16.5	16.3	Trade Receivables (net)		20.6	19.5	20.0	15.5	11.7
18.6	23.3	21.6	Inventory		19.5	24.7	25.0	19.0	20.2
3.7	3.4	4.1	All Other Current		5.3	4.8	4.7	2.9	3.5
47.8	50.8	50.6	Total Current		52.1	61.7	58.3	45.6	44.0
43.3	39.5	40.1	Fixed Assets (net)		38.8	27.6	34.3	47.2	44.3
2.9	2.7	3.2	Intangibles (net)		3.8	2.3	.2	.6	7.6
5.9	7.0	6.2	All Other Non-Current		5.2	8.4	7.2	6.7	4.2
100.0	100.0	100.0	Total		100.0	100.0	100.0	100.0	100.0
			LIABILITIES						
6.3	8.6	8.3	Notes Payable-Short Term		10.4	3.8	7.9	8.0	7.9
5.3	5.5	7.1	Cur. Mat.-L.T.D.		5.7	2.1	6.2	8.5	9.0
8.5	10.3	9.5	Trade Payables		11.0	6.1	14.1	9.3	6.5
.2	.1	.0	Income Taxes Payable		.0	.0	.0	.0	.0
9.8	6.5	8.1	All Other Current		13.1	7.5	11.1	3.9	6.1
30.0	31.0	33.0	Total Current		40.2	19.4	39.3	29.7	29.5
22.6	22.2	24.2	Long-Term Debt		40.5	13.7	26.5	22.0	19.1
.7	.9	.6	Deferred Taxes		.0	.7	.2	1.1	1.0
7.9	6.2	9.2	All Other Non-Current		7.9	8.0	10.5	6.4	13.2
38.7	39.7	32.9	Net Worth		11.4	58.2	23.5	40.8	37.1
100.0	100.0	100.0	Total Liabilties & Net Worth		100.0	100.0	100.0	100.0	100.0
			INCOME DATA						
100.0	100.0	100.0	Net Sales		100.0	100.0	100.0	100.0	100.0
31.9	31.6	33.4	Gross Profit		37.4	37.0	34.8	30.5	28.0
25.0	29.0	32.0	Operating Expenses		43.3	32.7	34.3	28.2	24.8
6.9	2.6	1.4	Operating Profit		-5.8	4.4	.5	2.3	3.2
2.2	1.8	2.2	All Other Expenses (net)		1.3	.2	1.3	2.8	3.1
4.7	.9	-.8	Profit Before Taxes		-7.1	4.2	-.8	-.5	.1
			RATIOS						
3.4	3.3	3.9			2.0	7.0	4.1	3.8	3.3
1.7	1.9	1.9	Current		1.6	4.4	1.9	2.7	1.3
1.0	1.1	1.1			1.1	1.7	1.3	.8	.9
1.6	1.7	1.9			1.1	4.5	2.3	1.8	2.2
.9	.9	.8	Quick		.7	1.6	.9	1.2	.6
.4	.4	.3			.4	.8	.4	.4	.3
25 14.9	23 15.9	26 14.0		14 25.5	28 13.1	25 14.4	27 13.6	32 11.3	
35 10.3	31 11.8	36 10.1	Sales/Receivables	38 9.6	40 9.1	37 9.7	35 10.5	41 8.8	
47 7.8	48 7.7	53 6.9		74 4.9	54 6.7	49 7.5	50 7.2	56 6.6	
36 10.1	44 8.3	40 9.2		22 17.0	42 8.7	38 9.5	36 10.2	51 7.2	
68 5.4	78 4.7	78 4.7	Cost of Sales/Inventory	48 7.6	81 4.5	75 4.9	65 5.6	94 3.9	
93 3.9	112 3.2	127 2.9		125 2.9	150 2.4	120 3.0	121 3.0	133 2.7	
15 24.9	13 27.3	14 26.3		11 32.7	11 32.9	15 25.0	15 23.9	16 23.4	
25 14.4	21 17.2	26 14.0	Cost of Sales/Payables	32 11.5	17 21.7	30 12.3	27 13.5	26 14.0	
37 9.9	42 8.7	43 8.4		50 7.4	30 12.0	47 7.8	41 9.0	42 8.7	
4.4	4.6	3.2			3.9	2.2	3.5	3.4	2.5
9.2	7.8	6.1	Sales/Working Capital		6.5	4.4	6.4	5.4	9.0
NM	44.5	62.8			NM	9.6	19.6	-39.2	-61.2
7.4	5.4	4.4			1.8	11.8	4.4	6.2	5.2
(112) 2.3	(114) 1.3	(105) 1.5	EBIT/Interest	(16) 1.0	(10) 2.9	(21) .3	(24) 1.6	(29) 1.5	
1.0	-1.0	-1.6			-5.8	-.1	-3.1	-1.1	.5
3.0	4.1	2.7	Net Profit + Depr., Dep., Amort./Cur. Mat. L/T/D						
(37) 1.9	(32) 1.8	(28) 1.4							
.7	.4	.2							
.6	.5	.5			1.1	.2	.3	.6	.7
1.2	1.0	1.2	Fixed/Worth		2.3	.5	.9	1.1	1.6
2.8	2.2	3.6			-1.9	1.3	2.0	5.5	3.0
.5	.5	.5			.7	.2	.5	.4	.6
1.5	1.4	1.6	Debt/Worth		5.0	.6	1.4	1.4	1.6
4.8	4.3	6.1			-13.5	1.6	NM	7.5	4.8
33.9	18.1	16.2			6.7	32.6	26.0	21.5	9.3
(113) 14.0	(108) 5.5	(101) 5.5	% Profit Before Taxes/Tangible Net Worth	(12) -13.6	17.3	(19) 13.9	(25) 5.5	(28) 5.3	
4.4	-7.9	-10.0			-116.6	-.3	-8.8	-7.0	-15.5
12.5	7.7	6.1			4.3	12.9	9.9	5.9	5.9
5.3	1.1	1.6	% Profit Before Taxes/Total Assets		-.1	4.1	4.2	.4	1.8
.0	-4.9	-6.5			-16.6	-.3	-11.1	-5.9	-2.2
7.5	8.8	8.1			12.3	22.1	17.7	5.8	4.4
3.9	4.1	3.6	Sales/Net Fixed Assets		6.1	7.5	5.0	3.6	1.9
2.4	2.1	1.8			1.9	3.6	2.8	1.2	1.5
2.1	2.1	1.9			2.2	2.4	3.2	1.9	1.1
1.5	1.4	1.2	Sales/Total Assets		1.4	1.8	1.6	1.2	1.0
1.1	1.0	.9			1.1	1.2	1.2	.8	.7
2.2	2.4	2.7			1.9	2.8	3.9	3.3	2.5
(117) 3.8	(112) 4.0	(105) 4.9	% Depr., Dep., Amort./Sales	(16) 3.1	(10) 3.7	(20) 5.2	(27) 5.3	(25) 6.2	
5.9	5.9	7.6			7.7	5.1	7.6	7.7	8.1
1.7	1.9	2.1			2.2				
(33) 3.4	(38) 3.1	(36) 3.4	% Officers', Directors' Owners' Comp/Sales	(10) 4.0					
5.2	5.3	5.5			7.3				
4093921M	3246691M	3167171M	Net Sales ($)	4810M	33850M	47855M	165427M	430240M	2484989M
3186357M	2849871M	3304976M	Total Assets ($)	8131M	25008M	35399M	113135M	453951M	2669352M

M = $ thousand   MM = $ million
See Pages 9 through 22 for Explanation of Ratios and Data

Current Data Sorted by Assets   **Comparative Historical Data**

0-500M	500M-2MM	2-10MM	10-50MM	50-100MM	100-250MM	Type of Statement	4/1/05-3/31/06 ALL	4/1/06-3/31/07 ALL
		2	3		1	Unqualified	6	8
		3				Reviewed	3	6
	2	2		1		Compiled	1	5
		1				Tax Returns	1	2
	2	4	1	1		Other	2	14
	4 (4/1-9/30/09)		19 (10/1/09-3/31/10)					
4	4	12	4	2	1	**NUMBER OF STATEMENTS**	13	35
%	%	%	%	%	%	**ASSETS**	%	%
		11.7				Cash & Equivalents	4.3	7.3
		23.3				Trade Receivables (net)	20.8	26.4
		18.1				Inventory	14.5	17.2
		1.3				All Other Current	2.8	2.2
		54.5				Total Current	42.3	53.1
		39.6				Fixed Assets (net)	47.6	38.9
		3.0				Intangibles (net)	3.5	4.8
		2.9				All Other Non-Current	6.6	3.2
		100.0				Total	100.0	100.0
						LIABILITIES		
		6.5				Notes Payable-Short Term	4.3	6.1
		3.0				Cur. Mat.-L.T.D.	6.0	4.5
		8.7				Trade Payables	8.0	11.4
		.2				Income Taxes Payable	.0	.3
		3.6				All Other Current	9.4	7.2
		22.0				Total Current	27.7	29.4
		18.3				Long-Term Debt	23.4	18.3
		.1				Deferred Taxes	1.8	.8
		3.0				All Other Non-Current	3.2	7.3
		56.6				Net Worth	43.8	44.2
		100.0				Total Liabilities & Net Worth	100.0	100.0
						INCOME DATA		
		100.0				Net Sales	100.0	100.0
		24.4				Gross Profit	25.8	25.2
		23.9				Operating Expenses	20.5	17.5
		.5				Operating Profit	5.3	7.7
		1.1				All Other Expenses (net)	1.7	1.2
		-.6				Profit Before Taxes	3.5	6.5
						RATIOS		
		5.9				Current	2.6	3.1
		3.8					2.1	1.8
		1.7					1.0	1.2
		3.8				Quick	1.4	2.0
		3.0					1.1	1.0
		.6					.6	.8
	37	9.8				Sales/Receivables	20 18.6	36 10.2
	56	6.5					40 9.1	43 8.4
	96	3.8					61 6.0	66 5.5
	43	8.5				Cost of Sales/Inventory	4 97.9	18 19.8
	64	5.7					41 8.9	36 10.0
	91	4.0					70 5.2	68 5.4
	15	23.6				Cost of Sales/Payables	11 34.2	17 21.5
	24	15.2					21 17.8	23 15.8
	46	7.9					32 11.3	34 10.7
		2.8				Sales/Working Capital	5.6	4.8
		3.4					9.6	9.1
		10.5					NM	19.3
		6.2				EBIT/Interest	6.1	15.9
		2.4					(11) 5.1	(33) 5.0
		-5.3					1.4	1.5
						Net Profit + Depr., Dep., Amort./Cur. Mat. L/T/D		6.4
							(15)	4.2
								1.4
		.4				Fixed/Worth	.5	.5
		.7					1.3	1.1
		1.3					4.2	2.2
		.2				Debt/Worth	.5	.6
		.9					1.3	1.7
		1.3					7.9	5.2
		18.5				% Profit Before Taxes/Tangible Net Worth	16.5	31.8
		3.1					(11) 7.0	(32) 24.4
		-15.9					-1.6	8.7
		9.1				% Profit Before Taxes/Total Assets	11.6	20.0
		2.1					3.3	9.4
		-12.4					-.3	2.0
		5.0				Sales/Net Fixed Assets	7.9	9.5
		2.7					4.5	5.1
		2.0					2.1	2.8
		1.8				Sales/Total Assets	2.5	2.3
		1.2					1.9	1.9
		1.0					1.1	1.4
		3.3				% Depr., Dep., Amort./Sales	2.9	1.3
		4.9					(12) 4.4	(32) 3.4
		7.9					6.9	4.8
						% Officers', Directors' Owners' Comp/Sales		.7
							(17)	2.6
								5.1
	12753M	77310M	183566M	99751M	326638M	Net Sales ($)	658416M	1387999M
	5526M	59335M	136734M	162782M	204442M	Total Assets ($)	365694M	871298M

M = $ thousand   MM = $ million
See Pages 9 through 22 for Explanation of Ratios and Data

Comparative Historical Data | Current Data Sorted by Sales

	4/1/07-3/31/08 ALL	4/1/08-3/31/09 ALL	4/1/09-3/31/10 ALL	Type of Statement	0-1MM	1-3MM	3-5MM	5-10MM	10-25MM	25MM & OVER
	5	5	6	Unqualified				1	1	4
	6	4	3	Reviewed			1	1	1	
	4	4	5	Compiled		1	1	2		1
			1	Tax Returns		1				
	16	13	8	Other		2	2	3		1
						4 (4/1-9/30/09)		19 (10/1/09-3/31/10)		
	31	26	23	NUMBER OF STATEMENTS		4	4	7	2	6
	%	%	%	**ASSETS**	%	%	%	%	%	%
	8.5	7.2	9.7	Cash & Equivalents	D					
	20.9	23.4	21.1	Trade Receivables (net)	A					
	17.2	16.7	17.4	Inventory	T					
	2.2	2.0	1.4	All Other Current	A					
	48.9	49.2	49.6	Total Current						
	44.6	43.9	41.3	Fixed Assets (net)	N					
	3.0	2.5	3.7	Intangibles (net)	O					
	3.5	4.3	5.4	All Other Non-Current	T					
	100.0	100.0	100.0	Total						
				LIABILITIES	A					
	6.5	7.1	4.8	Notes Payable-Short Term	V					
	5.6	5.8	3.3	Cur. Mat.-L.T.D.	A					
	7.9	9.0	9.1	Trade Payables	I					
	.0	.2	.2	Income Taxes Payable	L					
	6.5	5.1	3.7	All Other Current	A					
	26.6	27.1	21.1	Total Current	B					
	19.7	20.3	25.3	Long-Term Debt	L					
	1.1	2.0	.6	Deferred Taxes	E					
	6.4	5.1	4.6	All Other Non-Current						
	46.2	45.5	48.3	Net Worth						
	100.0	100.0	100.0	Total Liabilities & Net Worth						
				INCOME DATA						
	100.0	100.0	100.0	Net Sales						
	29.1	21.6	25.4	Gross Profit						
	22.2	21.8	23.9	Operating Expenses						
	6.9	-.2	1.5	Operating Profit						
	1.4	1.6	1.2	All Other Expenses (net)						
	5.5	-1.8	.3	Profit Before Taxes						
				RATIOS						
	3.4	3.7	4.6	Current						
	2.2	2.0	2.6							
	1.2	1.3	1.5							
	2.7	2.3	3.4	Quick						
	1.1	1.1	1.1							
	.6	.5	.7							
	33 11.1	24 15.0	39 9.5	Sales/Receivables						
	37 9.8	49 7.5	51 7.1							
	57 6.4	67 5.4	61 6.0							
	22 16.7	18 20.3	41 8.9	Cost of Sales/Inventory						
	64 5.7	65 5.6	74 4.9							
	93 3.9	89 4.1	92 4.0							
	18 20.7	13 27.7	13 28.7	Cost of Sales/Payables						
	24 15.2	19 19.3	23 15.9							
	35 10.6	30 12.1	42 8.8							
	4.7	4.4	3.2	Sales/Working Capital						
	7.2	7.5	4.5							
	20.0	28.9	10.4							
	11.1	4.5	5.2	EBIT/Interest						
	(30) 3.6	(24) 2.2	1.0							
	.7	-3.3	-.1							
	6.7	6.2		Net Profit + Depr., Dep., Amort./Cur. Mat. L/T/D						
	(14) 3.7	(13) 3.6								
	2.1	1.6								
	.6	.7	.5	Fixed/Worth						
	1.0	1.0	1.1							
	1.9	1.7	1.6							
	.6	.6	.4	Debt/Worth						
	1.3	1.3	1.0							
	3.0	2.7	3.5							
	33.8	14.3	21.2	% Profit Before Taxes/Tangible Net Worth						
	22.2	(23) 8.2	(22) 1.0							
	-1.1	.1	-9.7							
	19.9	6.4	5.7	% Profit Before Taxes/Total Assets						
	10.0	4.0	.1							
	-.5	-7.2	-2.9							
	4.9	4.6	4.7	Sales/Net Fixed Assets						
	3.7	3.8	3.3							
	2.3	1.9	2.0							
	1.9	2.3	1.8	Sales/Total Assets						
	1.6	1.2	1.4							
	1.2	1.0	1.0							
	2.6	3.8	3.4	% Depr., Dep., Amort./Sales						
	(30) 3.6	(24) 5.0	(22) 5.0							
	5.7	7.1	7.2							
	.8		1.2	% Officers', Directors' Owners' Comp/Sales						
	(13) 1.7		(12) 2.2							
	4.3		4.8							
	1089860M	747309M	700018M	Net Sales ($)		9778M	16796M	43798M	29522M	600124M
	897547M	618164M	568819M	Total Assets ($)		6796M	13556M	38030M	17916M	492521M

M = $ thousand   MM = $ million
See Pages 9 through 22 for Explanation of Ratios and Data

Current Data Sorted by Assets   Comparative Historical Data

0-500M	500M-2MM	2-10MM	10-50MM	50-100MM	100-250MM	Type of Statement	4/1/05-3/31/06 ALL	4/1/06-3/31/07 ALL
		6	12	5	6	Unqualified	34	35
	7	20	8			Reviewed	31	37
2	10	10	1			Compiled	27	29
2	10	4				Tax Returns	11	25
2	9	20	23	7	4	Other	68	44
		27 (4/1-9/30/09)		141 (10/1/09-3/31/10)				
6	36	60	44	12	10	**NUMBER OF STATEMENTS**	171	170
%	%	%	%	%	%		%	%
	7.6	10.3	13.3	6.4	7.2	Cash & Equivalents	8.7	8.6
	27.3	23.4	23.9	27.2	23.9	Trade Receivables (net)	30.3	27.3
	22.8	16.2	14.6	11.4	13.3	Inventory	15.8	16.3
	1.3	4.1	3.3	3.2	2.3	All Other Current	2.5	2.9
	59.0	54.0	55.1	48.2	46.7	Total Current	57.3	55.1
	33.9	38.5	34.0	37.0	45.7	Fixed Assets (net)	32.9	34.2
	1.1	3.5	1.7	6.7	3.0	Intangibles (net)	3.1	3.3
	6.0	4.0	9.2	8.1	4.6	All Other Non-Current	6.7	7.4
	100.0	100.0	100.0	100.0	100.0	Total	100.0	100.0
						LIABILITIES		
	15.1	7.5	6.5	5.3	5.2	Notes Payable-Short Term	6.5	5.9
	4.4	7.9	3.8	3.3	4.4	Cur. Mat.-L.T.D.	4.6	4.3
	15.2	13.8	8.5	13.3	8.8	Trade Payables	15.2	12.4
	.0	.2	1.3	.2	.2	Income Taxes Payable	.4	.3
	8.4	9.2	11.6	15.1	13.1	All Other Current	8.5	8.5
	43.2	38.7	31.6	37.2	31.8	Total Current	35.2	31.5
	21.8	21.1	14.2	6.5	14.5	Long-Term Debt	20.2	23.6
	.0	.3	1.1	1.1	.3	Deferred Taxes	.6	.7
	8.3	4.9	2.8	8.7	4.2	All Other Non-Current	5.5	4.8
	26.7	35.0	50.2	46.5	49.3	Net Worth	38.4	39.5
	100.0	100.0	100.0	100.0	100.0	Total Liabilties & Net Worth	100.0	100.0
						INCOME DATA		
	100.0	100.0	100.0	100.0	100.0	Net Sales	100.0	100.0
	35.6	32.5	28.1	25.0	16.7	Gross Profit	32.3	33.7
	36.2	28.8	22.9	20.7	16.0	Operating Expenses	25.7	26.4
	-.7	3.7	5.1	4.4	.7	Operating Profit	6.6	7.3
	.5	2.0	.5	.9	2.4	All Other Expenses (net)	.9	1.1
	-1.2	1.7	4.6	3.5	-1.7	Profit Before Taxes	5.7	6.2
						RATIOS		
	3.5	2.7	3.0	2.0	3.1		2.8	3.3
	1.5	1.8	1.8	1.4	1.9	Current	1.7	1.9
	1.0	1.1	1.3	1.1	1.4		1.2	1.2
	2.5	1.8	2.4	1.4	2.7		1.9	2.0
	1.0	1.0	1.1	.8	1.4	Quick	1.2	1.1
	.5	.5	.7	.6	.5		.8	.7
	31 11.7	31 11.7	40 9.2	38 9.6	37 9.9		35 10.5	34 10.8
	42 8.7	48 7.7	52 7.1	57 6.4	50 7.4	Sales/Receivables	49 7.5	46 7.9
	60 6.1	67 5.4	71 5.1	94 3.9	79 4.6		72 5.1	71 5.1
	19 19.5	19 18.7	22 16.3	7 54.6	8 43.5		12 29.8	11 32.2
	47 7.7	41 8.9	47 7.8	44 8.3	29 12.7	Cost of Sales/Inventory	32 11.4	38 9.7
	98 3.7	87 4.2	89 4.1	66 5.6	97 3.8		60 6.1	74 5.0
	22 16.7	16 23.2	16 22.5	16 23.2	14 26.6		17 20.9	17 21.9
	34 10.7	34 10.9	27 13.6	26 14.3	17 21.2	Cost of Sales/Payables	32 11.3	29 12.8
	49 7.5	62 5.9	38 9.6	36 10.1	32 11.4		50 7.3	46 7.9
	4.5	4.3	3.6	5.3	4.3		5.0	4.8
	15.1	8.7		14.5	6.3	Sales/Working Capital	9.6	9.0
	-176.8	39.1	11.2	59.1	NM		22.0	31.7
	2.3	12.0	12.3		10.1		14.8	10.6
	(32) .3	(56) 2.4	(40) 3.9		2.8	EBIT/Interest	(157) 5.9	(150) 4.9
	-4.4	.0	.3		1.3		2.4	1.7
		8.1	5.3			Net Profit + Depr., Dep.,	5.9	11.1
		(15) 2.2	(14) 1.7			Amort./Cur. Mat. L/T/D	(53) 3.5	(41) 3.9
		1.2	.9				1.6	1.6
	.4	.4	.4	.5	.6		.4	.4
	1.0	1.0	.7	1.0	.8	Fixed/Worth	.8	.9
	8.0	5.2	1.4	2.0	2.4		1.7	2.1
	.8	.5	.4	.9	.5		.8	.8
	2.1	1.2	1.1	1.5	.9	Debt/Worth	1.4	1.5
	18.5	6.6	2.2	3.5	4.0		3.7	4.0
	18.3	36.2	27.5	35.1	21.4	% Profit Before Taxes/Tangible	46.6	54.5
	(28) -1.1	(50) 12.8	(41) 9.4	(11) 15.2	6.9	Net Worth	(151) 25.6	(149) 28.3
	-14.5	.5	-4.5	3.0	2.3		9.8	9.8
	6.1	14.4	12.4	8.2	5.4	% Profit Before Taxes/Total	20.1	21.8
	-.9	3.3	3.9	6.2	3.3	Assets	10.1	11.4
	-10.1	-1.9	-1.5	-1.6	.4		3.2	2.7
	14.4	10.6	7.0	6.0	4.0		12.3	12.6
	7.7	4.6	4.2	3.7	3.0	Sales/Net Fixed Assets	6.9	6.1
	3.8	2.6	2.3	2.2	2.5		4.3	3.7
	2.7	2.2	1.8	2.0	1.6		2.7	2.6
	2.2	1.6	1.3	1.6	1.5	Sales/Total Assets	2.1	1.9
	1.6	1.3	.9	1.1	1.1		1.6	1.4
	1.9	2.2	2.6				1.6	1.9
	(32) 3.8	(55) 3.1	(37) 3.5			% Depr., Dep., Amort./Sales	(156) 2.7	(146) 3.1
	5.4	5.8	6.3				4.5	4.9
	4.1	1.6					1.6	1.6
	(17) 5.7	(19) 3.0				% Officers', Directors', Owners' Comp/Sales	(65) 3.4	(62) 2.9
	10.2	5.2					6.5	5.3
5313M	102802M	586303M	1367647M	1414371M	2298680M	Net Sales ($)	4978457M	5778113M
2123M	45360M	335734M	1002419M	852098M	1712520M	Total Assets ($)	2675627M	3342519M

M = $ thousand   MM = $ million
See Pages 9 through 22 for Explanation of Ratios and Data

Comparative Historical Data | Current Data Sorted by Sales

4/1/07-3/31/08 ALL	4/1/08-3/31/09 ALL	4/1/09-3/31/10 ALL	Type of Statement	0-1MM	1-3MM	3-5MM	5-10MM	10-25MM	25MM & OVER
33	29	29	Unqualified			1	1	10	17
41	41	35	Reviewed		4	4	9	16	2
23	23	23	Compiled	1	7	8	4	2	1
16	14	16	Tax Returns	3	5	4	1	3	
52	53	65	Other	3	8	6	11	13	24
					27 (4/1-9/30/09)		141 (10/1/09-3/31/10)		
165	160	168	NUMBER OF STATEMENTS	7	24	23	26	44	44
%	%	%	**ASSETS**	%	%	%	%	%	%
7.1	7.9	10.2	Cash & Equivalents		5.1	9.1	8.2	14.6	9.2
28.6	27.1	24.5	Trade Receivables (net)		23.8	23.9	23.8	26.4	25.3
15.4	17.0	17.0	Inventory		22.2	15.7	16.7	15.6	14.8
2.5	3.2	3.0	All Other Current		.7	3.4	3.1	4.3	3.0
53.6	55.1	54.6	Total Current		51.8	52.1	51.8	60.9	52.3
35.3	36.0	36.4	Fixed Assets (net)		36.8	42.6	34.7	33.1	37.4
3.2	2.7	2.6	Intangibles (net)		5.4	.7	2.9	1.1	3.8
7.9	6.2	6.4	All Other Non-Current		6.0	4.6	10.6	4.9	6.5
100.0	100.0	100.0	Total		100.0	100.0	100.0	100.0	100.0
			LIABILITIES						
7.6	8.8	9.1	Notes Payable-Short Term		12.4	14.6	10.0	7.2	5.3
4.7	4.1	5.4	Cur. Mat.-L.T.D.		6.2	12.3	4.6	4.2	3.5
11.7	12.6	12.4	Trade Payables		13.2	15.9	13.8	11.0	10.3
.3	.2	.4	Income Taxes Payable		.0	.0	.1	1.1	.6
9.7	8.5	11.0	All Other Current		12.8	13.2	8.2	7.7	14.6
34.0	34.2	38.3	Total Current		44.6	55.9	36.7	31.1	34.3
19.9	20.8	18.3	Long-Term Debt		29.3	19.1	22.0	13.1	11.6
.7	.6	.5	Deferred Taxes		.0	.0	.1	.7	1.1
4.0	6.0	5.2	All Other Non-Current		10.0	4.2	7.9	3.4	3.8
41.3	38.5	37.7	Net Worth		16.1	20.8	33.3	51.7	49.3
100.0	100.0	100.0	Total Liabilties & Net Worth		100.0	100.0	100.0	100.0	100.0
			INCOME DATA						
100.0	100.0	100.0	Net Sales		100.0	100.0	100.0	100.0	100.0
32.1	30.3	31.1	Gross Profit		43.7	24.2	30.2	31.6	25.0
26.1	25.9	28.1	Operating Expenses		46.7	25.7	29.3	24.6	19.4
6.0	4.4	3.1	Operating Profit		-3.0	-1.5	.9	7.1	5.6
1.3	1.3	1.2	All Other Expenses (net)		2.6	1.2	1.7	.2	1.3
4.7	3.1	1.9	Profit Before Taxes		-5.6	-2.7	-.7	6.9	4.3
			RATIOS						
3.0	2.8	2.7			3.3	2.2	2.5	3.1	2.5
1.7	1.7	1.7	Current		1.7	1.1	1.5	1.8	1.7
1.1	1.2	1.1			.9	.6	1.0	1.2	1.3
1.8	1.7	2.1			2.4	1.4	2.0	2.7	2.0
1.1	1.1	1.0	Quick		1.0	.7	1.0	1.2	1.1
.7	.6	.5			.4	.3	.5	.7	.7
34 10.6	38 9.7	33 11.0			28 12.8	31 11.6	31 11.7	34 10.7	39 9.5
50 7.3	47 7.7	46 8.0	Sales/Receivables		41 8.8	46 8.0	49 7.5	46 8.0	52 7.1
72 5.1	68 5.4	68 5.4			60 6.1	62 5.8	64 5.7	74 5.0	71 5.1
16 22.5	16 23.0	19 19.7			38 9.7	10 38.0	26 13.8	15 24.5	12 29.3
35 10.3	45 8.1	44 8.3	Cost of Sales/Inventory		66 5.5	41 8.9	40 9.2	42 8.8	45 8.1
76 4.8	88 4.1	89 4.1			136 2.7	58 6.3	96 3.8	77 4.8	86 4.2
16 22.8	16 22.5	16 22.6			16 22.3	24 15.0	16 22.6	15 24.1	15 24.9
25 14.6	27 13.7	29 12.6	Cost of Sales/Payables		33 11.2	40 9.0	34 10.7	24 15.5	25 14.4
39 9.3	51 7.1	46 8.0			57 6.4	47 7.7	51 7.2	42 8.6	37 9.9
5.1	5.1	4.3			4.2	6.2	3.6	3.7	4.4
8.4	7.7	8.1	Sales/Working Capital		10.4	30.0	9.7	7.3	6.9
39.3	21.3	47.9			-45.3	-6.9	NM	11.5	17.4
11.6	7.5	9.0			1.1	7.9	5.1	29.6	11.6
(156) 3.7	(147) 2.4	(150) 2.1	EBIT/Interest		-1.5	(18) 1.2	(25) 1.5	(40) 7.7	(39) 4.0
1.4	.1	-.2			-6.0	-2.2	-.1	1.2	1.3
9.5	10.3	7.7	Net Profit + Depr., Dep.,					8.1	21.1
(49) 3.4	(41) 2.7	(42) 1.8	Amort./Cur. Mat. L/T/D					(15) 1.9	(17) 5.2
2.0	1.5	.8						.5	1.5
.4	.4	.5			.7	.4	.2	.3	.5
.9	.9	.8	Fixed/Worth		1.3	4.2	1.0	.7	.7
2.3	2.2	3.0			-3.6	73.2	4.8	1.6	1.7
.7	.7	.6			.8	.9	.7	.3	.6
1.4	1.5	1.2	Debt/Worth		4.5	5.5	1.6	.8	1.2
3.3	4.8	5.5			-13.0	91.3	6.4	2.8	2.2
43.0	29.4	28.3	% Profit Before Taxes/Tangible		.5	18.9	23.1	35.7	31.7
(147) 22.0	(142) 11.3	(143) 8.9	Net Worth		(16) -10.1	(18) .6	(21) 3.1	(42) 13.2	(42) 9.6
6.7	-1.2	-3.6			-74.8	-57.9	-3.6	2.4	3.0
16.4	10.7	12.3	% Profit Before Taxes/Total		.4	4.5	7.8	20.4	12.4
7.1	4.7	2.4	Assets		-5.4	-.4	.9	10.0	4.3
1.3	-2.3	-2.5			-22.4	-14.2	-2.7	1.1	1.0
10.2	10.0	9.2			11.2	9.3	7.6	11.7	6.8
5.6	4.8	4.5	Sales/Net Fixed Assets		4.8	4.3	4.6	5.6	3.9
3.6	3.0	2.8			3.6	2.5	2.8	3.6	2.4
2.5	2.3	2.1			2.6	2.5	2.0	2.2	1.9
1.9	1.8	1.6	Sales/Total Assets		1.8	1.8	1.3	1.8	1.6
1.3	1.3	1.2			1.1	1.3	.8	1.4	1.1
1.8	1.9	2.1			2.5	1.9	2.5	1.5	2.4
(152) 3.0	(136) 3.2	(142) 3.5	% Depr., Dep., Amort./Sales		(22) 4.5	(20) 3.9	(23) 3.6	(41) 2.5	(31) 3.5
4.8	5.0	5.5			7.2	7.8	5.8	3.8	5.2
2.0	1.8	2.1			3.5			3.1	
(59) 3.2	(49) 3.4	(45) 4.5	% Officers', Directors'		(12) 7.1			(14) 4.9	
5.6	5.1	5.9	Owners' Comp/Sales		9.5			5.6	
6143799M	6644540M	5775116M	Net Sales ($)	5123M	44286M	89831M	189507M	711412M	4734957M
3940422M	4132100M	3950254M	Total Assets ($)	4053M	30722M	61234M	166111M	452406M	3235728M

© RMA 2010

M = $ thousand   MM = $ million
See Pages 9 through 22 for Explanation of Ratios and Data

Current Data Sorted by Assets   —   Comparative Historical Data

Type of Statement	0-500M	500M-2MM	2-10MM	10-50MM	50-100MM	100-250MM		4/1/05-3/31/06 ALL	4/1/06-3/31/07 ALL
Unqualified		1	3	2	1	1		10	10
Reviewed		2	9	1				16	16
Compiled		5	1					8	6
Tax Returns	1		4					2	
Other	1	4	10	11		1		14	22
	9 (4/1-9/30/09)			49 (10/1/09-3/31/10)					
NUMBER OF STATEMENTS	2	12	27	14	1	2		50	54
	%	%	%	%	%	%		%	%
ASSETS									
Cash & Equivalents		7.6	9.9	3.1				9.6	7.0
Trade Receivables (net)		25.9	23.9	23.0				25.8	24.9
Inventory		35.7	29.0	32.2				29.9	32.3
All Other Current		4.1	4.7	4.5				2.0	1.4
Total Current		73.3	67.5	62.8				67.3	65.6
Fixed Assets (net)		15.2	23.5	21.7				25.5	27.1
Intangibles (net)		3.4	1.8	2.7				1.6	1.2
All Other Non-Current		8.1	7.1	12.8				5.6	6.2
Total		100.0	100.0	100.0				100.0	100.0
LIABILITIES									
Notes Payable-Short Term		14.1	10.9	17.4				11.6	12.3
Cur. Mat.-L.T.D.		3.2	5.7	4.8				3.4	2.8
Trade Payables		13.7	10.4	17.1				15.0	17.1
Income Taxes Payable		.0	.0	2.9				1.0	.3
All Other Current		5.4	5.4	14.3				6.7	7.0
Total Current		36.4	32.5	56.5				37.6	39.6
Long-Term Debt		13.1	10.0	2.9				12.5	13.9
Deferred Taxes		.0	.4	.6				.3	.3
All Other Non-Current		3.9	9.5	6.8				6.3	4.6
Net Worth		46.6	47.6	33.1				43.2	41.6
Total Liabilties & Net Worth		100.0	100.0	100.0				100.0	100.0
INCOME DATA									
Net Sales		100.0	100.0	100.0				100.0	100.0
Gross Profit		31.4	28.6	22.1				31.1	28.1
Operating Expenses		31.2	25.8	20.7				24.5	21.9
Operating Profit		.2	2.8	1.4				6.6	6.2
All Other Expenses (net)		.8	1.5	1.5				1.4	.8
Profit Before Taxes		-.6	1.3	-.1				5.2	5.4
RATIOS									
Current		2.6	4.0	2.1				3.2	2.9
		1.9	2.3	1.1				1.7	1.8
		1.6	1.4	.8				1.2	1.2
Quick		1.3	2.0	1.0				1.6	1.6
		.9	1.2	.5				1.0	.9
		.6	.6	.2				.5	.5
Sales/Receivables		33 10.9	29 12.5	31 11.7				36 10.2	34 10.9
		36 10.0	57 6.4	51 7.2				45 8.1	41 9.0
		61 6.0	62 5.9	67 5.4				57 6.4	53 6.9
Cost of Sales/Inventory		32 11.3	44 8.4	56 6.5				47 7.7	55 6.6
		107 3.4	88 4.2	90 4.0				83 4.4	68 5.3
		163 2.2	119 3.1	165 2.2				126 2.9	91 4.0
Cost of Sales/Payables		20 17.9	11 31.8	16 22.8				13 28.0	18 19.7
		29 12.7	26 14.3	24 15.4				33 10.9	33 11.1
		43 8.5	46 7.9	44 8.4				49 7.5	50 7.2
Sales/Working Capital		2.8	3.0	6.3				3.8	5.0
		8.0	5.7	43.1				6.3	7.1
		12.8	10.2	-6.9				20.6	36.2
EBIT/Interest		12.8	9.7	33.1				25.0	20.3
	(11)	2.6	(24) 3.1	(13) 3.8				(48) 6.1	(51) 5.9
		-2.1	-1.7	-8.2				1.2	1.9
Net Profit + Depr., Dep., Amort./Cur. Mat. L/T/D								9.8	5.5
								(13) 6.2	(15) 3.1
								2.0	1.2
Fixed/Worth		.1	.2	.2				.2	.3
		.3	.3	1.1				.6	.6
		1.7	.8	-7.3				1.1	1.4
Debt/Worth		.5	.3	.7				.4	.5
		1.1	.9	1.7				1.6	1.4
		6.6	2.3	-51.6				2.8	3.2
% Profit Before Taxes/Tangible Net Worth		29.7	15.0	28.6				39.8	39.2
	(11)	14.7	(26) 2.6	(10) 16.0				(47) 22.0	(49) 24.1
		-14.3	-5.3	-9.9				5.8	10.7
% Profit Before Taxes/Total Assets		11.9	10.0	9.7				22.3	21.0
		3.5	.5	4.8				7.6	11.1
		-11.2	-4.1	-6.6				.9	2.8
Sales/Net Fixed Assets		68.2	17.2	12.5				15.1	17.7
		23.1	9.0	8.1				10.1	9.0
		7.1	4.6	4.8				4.0	4.7
Sales/Total Assets		3.4	2.4	1.9				2.6	2.8
		1.8	1.7	1.4				1.9	2.0
		1.4	1.2	1.0				1.5	1.7
% Depr., Dep., Amort./Sales			1.3	.9				1.1	1.0
		(25)	2.6	(11) 1.6				(45) 2.1	(50) 1.9
			5.1	2.6				3.8	3.2
% Officers', Directors' Owners' Comp/Sales			3.6					2.1	.9
		(11)	4.2					(19) 3.3	(14) 2.6
			8.1					7.4	9.1
Net Sales ($)	2045M	27211M	243859M	474015M	57791M	208753M		1358881M	1451193M
Total Assets ($)	934M	13140M	146704M	311190M	51413M	301407M		804461M	843084M

© RMA 2010

M = $ thousand   MM = $ million
See Pages 9 through 22 for Explanation of Ratios and Data

Comparative Historical Data | Current Data Sorted by Sales

			Type of Statement	0-1MM	1-3MM	3-5MM	5-10MM	10-25MM	25MM & OVE
15	13	8	Unqualified	1			2	1	4
11	12	12	Reviewed		2		1	6	
8	7	6	Compiled		4	1	1		
4	5	5	Tax Returns		1	1	2		
19	14	27	Other	1	3	3	6	7	7
4/1/07-3/31/08 ALL	4/1/08-3/31/09 ALL	4/1/09-3/31/10 ALL			9 (4/1-9/30/09)			49 (10/1/09-3/31/10)	
57	51	58	**NUMBER OF STATEMENTS**	2	10	8	12	15	11
%	%	%	**ASSETS**	%	%	%	%	%	%
8.6	7.7	7.8	Cash & Equivalents		11.8		9.5	8.6	5.9
24.0	19.1	23.5	Trade Receivables (net)		24.5		24.9	21.4	22.2
30.6	30.3	30.4	Inventory		30.7		26.3	32.1	32.9
3.6	3.3	4.3	All Other Current		3.4		4.5	1.7	4.5
66.9	60.4	65.9	Total Current		70.4		65.2	63.7	65.5
23.0	27.1	22.1	Fixed Assets (net)		15.3		25.4	22.1	20.7
4.4	3.9	3.6	Intangibles (net)		3.5		2.0	6.8	3.4
5.7	8.6	8.3	All Other Non-Current		10.8		7.4	7.4	10.4
100.0	100.0	100.0	Total		100.0		100.0	100.0	100.0
			LIABILITIES						
10.6	11.8	13.1	Notes Payable-Short Term		7.9		6.5	10.5	15.5
3.1	4.2	4.5	Cur. Mat.-L.T.D.		2.1		5.4	6.0	2.8
16.9	10.7	13.1	Trade Payables		16.6		10.7	16.3	11.4
.2	.5	.7	Income Taxes Payable		.0		.0	2.2	.7
7.2	7.9	7.5	All Other Current		3.4		6.1	10.8	9.6
38.0	35.1	38.8	Total Current		30.0		28.6	45.8	40.0
11.1	15.0	12.0	Long-Term Debt		26.5		14.7	6.5	3.5
.5	.4	.5	Deferred Taxes		.0		.7	.9	.7
4.6	5.3	7.5	All Other Non-Current		.7		18.7	7.5	3.1
45.8	44.2	41.2	Net Worth		42.9		37.3	39.4	52.6
100.0	100.0	100.0	Total Liabilities & Net Worth		100.0		100.0	100.0	100.0
			INCOME DATA						
100.0	100.0	100.0	Net Sales		100.0		100.0	100.0	100.0
28.4	28.2	28.5	Gross Profit		34.5		33.1	24.6	24.8
21.1	23.7	26.7	Operating Expenses		30.2		29.7	22.2	20.9
7.3	4.5	1.8	Operating Profit		4.2		3.3	2.4	4.0
1.3	.9	1.3	All Other Expenses (net)		.9		.8	1.7	.7
6.0	3.6	.5	Profit Before Taxes		3.3		2.5	.7	3.2
			RATIOS						
2.7	3.7	2.9	Current		5.4		2.8	2.9	5.0
1.7	1.8	1.9			2.0		2.3	1.4	1.8
1.3	1.2	1.2			1.7		1.8	.9	1.1
1.4	1.6	1.6	Quick		2.7		2.1	1.7	2.2
.9	.8	.9			.9		1.3	.6	.9
.5	.5	.5			.8		.8	.4	.4
31 11.8	29 12.8	32 11.4	Sales/Receivables	33 11.0		29 12.5	29 12.5	31 11.9
37 9.9	35 10.3	51 7.2		39 9.3		56 6.5	51 7.1	47 7.7
50 7.4	45 8.1	64 5.7		59 6.2		61 5.9	74 4.9	65 5.6
42 8.7	35 10.3	47 7.7	Cost of Sales/Inventory	38 9.7		35 10.5	59 6.1	67 5.4
75 4.9	81 4.5	91 4.0		87 4.2		67 5.4	97 3.8	92 4.0
101 3.6	115 3.2	143 2.6		148 2.5		119 3.1	126 2.9	162 2.3
19 19.4	14 25.2	16 22.8	Cost of Sales/Payables	16 22.3		8 46.5	17 21.6	16 22.7
31 11.8	22 16.5	27 13.6		32 11.4		34 10.6	31 11.6	21 17.2
47 7.8	38 9.7	46 8.0		46 8.0		48 7.6	50 7.4	34 10.7
4.4	4.6	3.0	Sales/Working Capital		2.4		3.4	3.2	2.8
7.9	9.3	6.9			5.5		6.1	16.1	6.8
21.3	36.2	16.2			10.5		9.5	-10.2	24.1
25.6	10.8	15.2	EBIT/Interest				17.6	10.8	57.2
(53) 7.0	(47) 3.7	(53) 2.9					(11) 5.3	(14) 1.0	(10) 14.6
2.2	.8	-2.0					-1.0	-5.8	3.2
6.9	5.6	3.6	Net Profit + Depr., Dep., Amort./Cur. Mat. L/T/D						
(15) 2.2	(14) 2.3	(13) .1							
1.1	.2	-1.1							
.2	.2	.2	Fixed/Worth		.1		.2	.3	.2
.5	.6	.4			.2		.5	.7	.4
1.1	1.6	2.1			.9		1.4	-8.4	1.5
.6	.5	.4	Debt/Worth		.2		.4	.6	.2
1.3	1.3	1.2			.5		1.3	1.4	.9
2.9	4.4	5.0			3.0		2.3	-59.4	2.0
46.0	39.0	22.5	% Profit Before Taxes/Tangible Net Worth				29.3	37.5	22.5
(50) 23.6	(46) 12.4	(50) 5.5					(11) 9.8	(11) 5.6	(10) 12.8
9.9	1.5	-5.9					-15.8	.5	4.3
23.2	14.5	9.2	% Profit Before Taxes/Total Assets		14.9		10.9	10.5	9.3
9.6	6.4	1.8			4.1		4.6	.1	7.8
4.2	-.8	-4.2			-3.0		-5.6	-4.6	2.3
21.4	16.4	18.9	Sales/Net Fixed Assets		63.3		28.6	12.5	17.8
11.4	10.8	9.1			15.1		9.1	6.7	10.2
5.3	4.1	4.5			7.2		5.3	4.4	4.2
2.8	2.5	2.2	Sales/Total Assets		2.7		2.7	2.2	1.9
2.0	1.9	1.5			1.6		2.1	1.4	1.5
1.6	1.4	1.1			1.4		1.4	.9	1.1
.9	1.0	1.2	% Depr., Dep., Amort./Sales				1.4	1.2	
(49) 1.7	(45) 1.7	(49) 2.2					(10) 2.8	2.2	
2.7	3.4	4.4					5.0	5.0	
1.1	1.9	2.3	% Officers', Directors' Owners' Comp/Sales						
(22) 2.6	(12) 3.7	(21) 5.0							
7.2	8.1	9.3							
1608811M	1605590M	1013674M	Net Sales ($)	1646M	19213M	32448M	90126M	216420M	653821M
1148738M	1088780M	824788M	Total Assets ($)	1124M	10885M	30193M	52836M	244101M	485649M

M = $ thousand   MM = $ million
See Pages 9 through 22 for Explanation of Ratios and Data

Current Data Sorted by Assets   Comparative Historical Data

		3	4	1		Type of Statement		11	11
1	3	10	3			Unqualified		15	18
5	8	4				Reviewed		29	26
9	6	5				Compiled		29	25
8	18	15	6	4	1	Tax Returns		49	47
	14 (4/1-9/30/09)		100 (10/1/09-3/31/10)			Other		4/1/05-3/31/06	4/1/06-3/31/07
0-500M	500M-2MM	2-10MM	10-50MM	50-100MM	100-250MM			ALL	ALL
23	35	37	13	5	1	NUMBER OF STATEMENTS		133	127
%	%	%	%	%	%	ASSETS		%	%
13.8	3.3	8.2	3.7			Cash & Equivalents		7.5	6.9
16.9	24.7	19.9	13.9			Trade Receivables (net)		25.3	26.3
18.8	25.4	28.0	18.7			Inventory		21.4	23.4
3.8	3.3	1.5	4.2			All Other Current		2.8	4.0
53.3	56.8	57.6	40.4			Total Current		57.0	60.6
31.6	32.3	34.0	41.6			Fixed Assets (net)		34.0	32.4
.6	5.4	1.5	14.4			Intangibles (net)		2.8	1.9
14.5	5.6	6.9	3.5			All Other Non-Current		6.2	5.1
100.0	100.0	100.0	100.0			Total		100.0	100.0
						LIABILITIES			
20.6	21.6	7.7	6.0			Notes Payable-Short Term		10.6	10.5
5.4	5.3	3.5	4.8			Cur. Mat.-L.T.D.		4.3	3.8
11.3	19.2	10.2	6.5			Trade Payables		15.7	15.8
.0	.5	.1	.0			Income Taxes Payable		.2	.3
21.0	8.3	10.3	3.8			All Other Current		8.3	9.5
58.3	54.9	31.8	21.1			Total Current		39.0	39.8
34.5	38.0	19.6	21.1			Long-Term Debt		25.2	26.8
.0	.0	.1	.2			Deferred Taxes		.3	.3
5.9	6.9	3.4	13.2			All Other Non-Current		5.5	8.6
1.2	.2	45.1	44.3			Net Worth		30.0	24.5
100.0	100.0	100.0	100.0			Total Liabilities & Net Worth		100.0	100.0
						INCOME DATA			
100.0	100.0	100.0	100.0			Net Sales		100.0	100.0
48.6	35.7	34.2	33.9			Gross Profit		37.2	36.9
46.1	35.2	34.9	27.2			Operating Expenses		32.3	31.0
2.5	.5	-.6	6.7			Operating Profit		4.9	5.8
1.1	1.9	1.2	3.4			All Other Expenses (net)		1.1	1.4
1.4	-1.4	-1.8	3.3			Profit Before Taxes		3.7	4.4
						RATIOS			
2.9	1.7	3.5	3.5					2.6	2.5
.9	1.0	2.2	1.9			Current		1.5	1.6
.5	.7	1.4	1.1					1.0	1.1
1.8	.9	2.6	1.2					1.4	1.7
.5	.5	.9	.9			Quick		.8	.8
.2	.3	.4	.5					.5	.4
0 UND	22 16.3	26 14.3	29 12.7					22 16.4	22 16.4
16 22.2	35 10.3	41 8.8	32 11.6			Sales/Receivables		37 10.0	38 9.5
34 10.8	51 7.2	59 6.2	52 7.1					46 7.9	55 6.6
0 UND	26 14.1	27 13.6	47 7.8					18 20.2	15 24.1
4 97.2	54 6.8	79 4.6	65 5.6			Cost of Sales/Inventory		32 11.5	54 6.8
78 4.7	127 2.9	205 1.8	176 2.1					88 4.2	114 3.2
0 UND	27 13.8	10 37.4	16 22.6					15 23.6	16 23.4
8 44.4	43 8.4	16 22.9	33 10.9			Cost of Sales/Payables		28 13.1	31 11.9
32 11.4	62 5.9	36 10.2	45 8.0					51 7.2	55 6.7
9.4	9.1	3.4	1.9					6.3	6.9
-79.4	444.7	6.9	8.5			Sales/Working Capital		14.5	12.0
-15.8	-9.0	16.6	36.3					-165.0	57.7
7.9	3.0	7.3	4.6					10.6	10.0
(20) 2.4	(34) .6	(34) 1.8	1.5			EBIT/Interest		(119) 3.5	(116) 3.7
-.9	-2.8	-5.0	.6					1.5	1.4
						Net Profit + Depr., Dep.,		2.4	5.8
						Amort./Cur. Mat. L/T/D		(27) 2.0 (30) 2.6	
								1.1	1.5
.3	1.3	.4	.7					.3	.5
4.2	6.5	.7	1.7			Fixed/Worth		1.1	1.2
-1.3	-.8	1.8	10.0					3.3	4.3
1.6	1.9	.4	.8					.9	1.0
18.4	8.4	1.2	1.8			Debt/Worth		2.2	2.3
-4.3	-3.7	4.7	16.9					5.9	11.8
157.3	45.2	22.0	19.4					58.2	54.7
(14) 31.7	(20) 11.1	(33) 4.7	(11) 6.0			% Profit Before Taxes/Tangible Net Worth		(112) 29.9	(104) 20.5
1.6	-32.5	-25.1	-33.7					9.0	7.3
12.0	9.2	10.4	7.4					20.9	20.5
4.6	-1.7	1.0	1.4			% Profit Before Taxes/Total Assets		9.7	8.4
-9.2	-13.5	-10.5	-1.6					1.1	1.9
29.7	14.2	9.1	5.8					21.8	18.6
17.3	8.3	4.7	1.8			Sales/Net Fixed Assets		8.5	8.0
11.7	4.7	2.9	.9					3.4	3.8
6.2	3.3	2.1	1.5					3.8	3.5
3.7	2.2	1.8	1.0			Sales/Total Assets		2.5	2.4
2.4	1.4	1.0	.5					1.6	1.4
1.7	1.4	1.7	2.1					1.4	1.3
(18) 3.2	(32) 3.0	(35) 3.2	4.5			% Depr., Dep., Amort./Sales		(109) 2.4	(106) 2.3
4.5	5.7	5.5	11.1					4.1	4.4
2.0	3.9	2.5						2.6	1.8
(11) 5.0	(14) 5.6	(19) 3.0				% Officers', Directors' Owners' Comp/Sales		(56) 4.1	(63) 3.2
18.4	8.3	5.0						5.8	5.8
28973M	94054M	279222M	221667M	366573M	240684M	Net Sales ($)		1372683M	2777545M
6534M	41116M	169900M	233974M	410472M	148829M	Total Assets ($)		874698M	1213093M

M = $ thousand   MM = $ million
See Pages 9 through 22 for Explanation of Ratios and Data

Comparative Historical Data   **Current Data Sorted by Sales**

Type of Statement	4/1/07-3/31/08 ALL	4/1/08-3/31/09 ALL	4/1/09-3/31/10 ALL	0-1MM	1-3MM	3-5MM	5-10MM	10-25MM	25MM & OV
Unqualified	10	10	8		1		2	3	2
Reviewed	20	25	17	1	1	2	8	5	
Compiled	22	15	17	2	7	5	3		
Tax Returns	25	26	20	8	7	1	3	1	
Other	46	41	52	8	14	7	10	7	6
				14 (4/1-9/30/09)			100 (10/1/09-3/31/10)		
NUMBER OF STATEMENTS	123	117	114	19	29	16	26	16	8
ASSETS	%	%	%	%	%	%	%	%	%
Cash & Equivalents	7.2	8.0	7.0	7.4	9.4	8.5	5.4	5.6	
Trade Receivables (net)	23.1	22.5	19.8	16.0	20.7	18.0	22.2	22.9	
Inventory	22.9	23.4	24.0	19.6	23.5	24.0	28.5	23.5	
All Other Current	2.5	1.5	2.8	4.0	3.8	3.5	1.9	1.2	
Total Current	55.7	55.4	53.7	47.0	57.4	54.0	58.1	53.2	
Fixed Assets (net)	35.3	34.7	34.1	37.8	30.3	35.4	33.8	35.1	
Intangibles (net)	3.0	3.7	4.5	4.9	3.6	6.4	1.4	4.7	
All Other Non-Current	6.0	6.3	7.7	10.3	8.7	4.2	6.7	7.1	
Total	100.0	100.0	100.0	100.0	100.0	100.0	100.0	100.0	
LIABILITIES									
Notes Payable-Short Term	10.0	16.7	14.4	27.7	19.5	3.1	10.2	10.7	
Cur. Mat.-L.T.D.	4.1	4.1	4.6	4.6	4.7	3.3	5.7	4.0	
Trade Payables	14.3	14.7	12.5	7.6	17.7	14.7	13.0	9.3	
Income Taxes Payable	.4	.3	.2	.0	.7	.1	.0	.1	
All Other Current	10.2	11.5	10.9	16.3	11.6	13.3	7.5	8.4	
Total Current	39.0	47.3	42.7	56.3	54.2	34.4	36.3	32.5	
Long-Term Debt	22.6	24.9	28.3	40.9	29.3	30.1	28.6	15.6	
Deferred Taxes	.6	.3	.2	.0	.0	.0	.0	.2	
All Other Non-Current	5.6	4.4	6.1	3.5	8.9	8.0	5.4	4.6	
Net Worth	32.2	23.1	22.7	-.7	7.6	27.4	29.6	47.1	
Total Liabilities & Net Worth	100.0	100.0	100.0	100.0	100.0	100.0	100.0	100.0	
INCOME DATA									
Net Sales	100.0	100.0	100.0	100.0	100.0	100.0	100.0	100.0	
Gross Profit	35.5	34.5	37.0	49.7	39.6	40.7	33.3	26.5	
Operating Expenses	30.0	32.9	35.7	47.4	41.2	38.1	31.9	22.8	
Operating Profit	5.4	1.6	1.3	2.3	-1.6	2.6	1.5	3.7	
All Other Expenses (net)	1.6	2.0	1.7	2.5	1.3	1.8	1.4	1.8	
Profit Before Taxes	3.8	-.4	-.4	-.3	-2.9	.8	.1	1.9	
RATIOS									
Current	2.7	2.7	2.5	2.9	2.2	6.9	2.5	2.4	
	1.5	1.5	1.5	.9	1.0	1.6	1.6	1.9	
	.9	.8	.9	.5	.6	.9	1.1	1.4	
Quick	1.4	1.3	1.5	1.3	.9	4.6	1.7	1.6	
	.7	.7	.7	.5	.5	.9	.6	1.0	
	.4	.4	.3	.2	.2	.2	.4	.7	
Sales/Receivables	20 17.8	22 16.2	22 16.3	0 UND	19 19.5	21 17.2	22 16.8	27 13.6	
	35 10.4	37 9.9	34 10.6	34 10.8	31 11.7	31 11.6	37 10.0	36 10.3	
	54 6.8	51 7.2	51 7.2	54 6.7	44 8.3	45 8.1	49 7.4	63 5.8	
Cost of Sales/Inventory	21 17.6	19 19.3	22 16.7	0 UND	29 12.5	21 17.0	22 16.6	10 37.3	
	49 7.5	52 7.1	60 6.1	46 8.0	57 6.5	112 3.2	61 6.0	54 6.8	
	118 3.1	126 2.9	144 2.5	144 2.5	128 2.8	153 2.4	193 1.9	118 3.1	
Cost of Sales/Payables	13 28.1	10 35.1	12 30.4	0 UND	15 24.3	5 67.7	12 31.7	11 31.9	
	30 12.2	19 19.0	25 14.5	24 15.3	42 8.7	24 15.4	18 20.4	20 18.5	
	47 7.8	40 9.2	47 7.8	45 8.2	72 5.0	51 7.1	38 9.6	35 10.3	
Sales/Working Capital	6.0	5.2	4.6	6.2	5.0	2.9	3.9	5.3	
	11.7	15.1	12.9	-65.0	444.7	25.0	8.2	8.3	
	-141.7	-27.6	-38.2	-6.3	-10.2	-38.8	45.8	19.0	
EBIT/Interest	11.1	4.4	6.6	7.0	2.7	8.6	6.9	9.8	
	(116) 3.0	(109) 1.3	(107) 1.6	(18) 1.5	(26) 1.0	(13) 3.0	2.2	1.4	
	1.1	-.9	-1.2	-3.3	-1.6	.8	-1.2	-3.9	
Net Profit + Depr., Dep., Amort./Cur. Mat. L/T/D	9.0	5.1	2.0						
	(29) 3.2	(23) 2.0	(20) 1.1						
	1.3	1.0	-.1						
Fixed/Worth	.4	.4	.6	.4	.6	.5	.6	.6	
	1.1	1.5	1.6	6.5	4.2	9.5	1.1	.7	
	3.4	10.7	-27.2	-.9	-1.6	-6.1	2.1	1.5	
Debt/Worth	.9	.9	1.0	1.7	1.2	1.0	1.0	.5	
	2.0	2.3	2.7	10.3	8.1	19.2	2.1	1.2	
	5.9	19.1	-26.6	-3.7	-5.3	-14.2	5.5	3.8	
% Profit Before Taxes/Tangible Net Worth	47.0	18.7	26.6	48.3	20.9	153.9	24.9	19.5	
	(104) 21.5	(92) 6.3	(84) 6.7	(11) 35.9	(18) 4.8	(10) 20.3	(22) 8.7	(15) 6.7	
	6.9	-10.3	-21.8	-35.5	-23.9	-16.8	-31.7	-29.7	
% Profit Before Taxes/Total Assets	16.0	7.2	10.1	10.2	5.7	25.3	14.5	13.8	
	5.0	1.2	2.0	.0	.2	2.9	3.7	1.9	
	.3	-5.9	-9.5	-17.2	-13.4	-3.6	-8.0	-6.6	
Sales/Net Fixed Assets	17.1	17.7	14.9	18.4	18.7	13.8	12.4	14.3	
	7.0	7.1	6.9	11.6	10.8	6.2	6.7	5.8	
	3.2	3.2	2.9	1.8	4.8	2.3	3.1	2.9	
Sales/Total Assets	3.3	3.2	3.2	3.5	3.5	4.9	2.9	2.7	
	2.1	2.0	1.8	1.5	2.2	1.7	1.9	1.9	
	1.4	1.3	1.1	.9	1.5	.9	1.1	1.4	
% Depr., Dep., Amort./Sales	1.4	1.5	1.8	3.6	1.4	1.3	1.8	1.6	
	(107) 2.5	(101) 3.4	(104) 3.2	(15) 4.1	(26) 3.1	(14) 2.3	(25) 2.8	2.3	
	4.9	5.0	6.1	10.8	5.0	11.1	5.4	4.8	
% Officers', Directors' Owners' Comp/Sales	1.5	1.8	2.6		2.8		2.5		
	(66) 2.9	(53) 3.0	(45) 4.7		(16) 5.5		(11) 3.0		
	6.2	5.6	7.1		8.4		4.9		
Net Sales ($)	1884309M	2231357M	1231173M	11598M	54075M	61265M	176219M	255297M	672719M
Total Assets ($)	1136900M	1306950M	1010825M	8719M	29958M	71755M	123703M	179338M	597352M

M = $ thousand   MM = $ million
See Pages 9 through 22 for Explanation of Ratios and Data

Current Data Sorted by Assets   Comparative Historical Data

	0-500M	500M-2MM	2-10MM	10-50MM	50-100MM	100-250MM	Type of Statement	4/1/05-3/31/06 ALL	4/1/06-3/31/07 ALL
	1		2	2	1		Unqualified	4	4
		2	4	6	1		Reviewed	9	8
	2	1					Compiled	2	5
	1	1	1				Tax Returns	3	3
	1	1	3	2	2		Other	11	18
		8 (4/1-9/30/09)		26 (10/1/09-3/31/10)					
NUMBER OF STATEMENTS	5	5	10	10	4			29	38
	%	%	%	%	%	%	ASSETS	%	%
			12.9	8.1			Cash & Equivalents	9.0	8.6
			26.7	16.3			Trade Receivables (net)	31.9	26.1
			28.6	24.9			Inventory	20.2	18.8
			3.3	3.5			All Other Current	2.3	1.7
			71.4	52.8			Total Current	63.4	55.1
			25.0	34.1			Fixed Assets (net)	31.1	33.0
			.9	3.2			Intangibles (net)	.7	3.0
			2.7	9.9			All Other Non-Current	4.8	8.8
			100.0	100.0			Total	100.0	100.0
							LIABILITIES		
			8.2	3.7			Notes Payable-Short Term	7.9	7.2
			4.0	6.1			Cur. Mat.-L.T.D.	2.9	5.8
			12.2	5.0			Trade Payables	16.7	15.2
			.0	.3			Income Taxes Payable	.2	.3
			4.1	8.8			All Other Current	9.6	7.1
			28.5	23.8			Total Current	37.2	35.6
			12.2	15.8			Long-Term Debt	13.6	19.3
			.4	.7			Deferred Taxes	1.0	.6
			6.4	11.1			All Other Non-Current	3.7	5.3
			52.5	48.6			Net Worth	44.5	39.2
			100.0	100.0			Total Liabilties & Net Worth	100.0	100.0
							INCOME DATA		
			100.0	100.0			Net Sales	100.0	100.0
			31.4	20.9			Gross Profit	33.1	33.8
			27.1	17.6			Operating Expenses	25.8	25.9
			4.3	3.3			Operating Profit	7.3	7.9
			.3	.7			All Other Expenses (net)	.5	.6
			4.1	2.7			Profit Before Taxes	6.8	7.3
							RATIOS		
			10.9	3.4			Current	2.9	4.2
			2.1	2.7				1.8	1.7
			1.6	1.9				1.1	1.0
			6.0	1.6			Quick	1.8	2.1
			1.0	1.2				1.1	1.1
			.7	.7				.7	.6
			37 9.9	40 9.1			Sales/Receivables	34 10.9	35 10.5
			49 7.4	44 8.3				45 8.2	43 8.5
			54 6.7	60 6.0				71 5.2	55 6.6
			32 11.3	68 5.4			Cost of Sales/Inventory	15 24.4	20 18.0
			78 4.7	96 3.8				47 7.7	42 8.6
			99 3.7	126 2.9				81 4.5	82 4.5
			14 26.4	13 27.4			Cost of Sales/Payables	21 17.1	15 24.0
			27 13.3	17 21.1				27 13.6	25 14.6
			44 8.3	21 17.7				50 7.2	45 8.1
			2.8	2.8			Sales/Working Capital	5.3	5.4
			6.6	4.0				9.5	10.0
			10.8	8.0				49.2	NM
				15.4			EBIT/Interest	21.7	17.1
				3.0				(26) 7.7	(32) 4.4
				-4.9				2.2	1.7
							Net Profit + Depr., Dep., Amort./Cur. Mat. L/T/D		
			.2	.5			Fixed/Worth	.3	.3
			.5	.9				.5	.9
			.9	1.2				1.6	2.1
			.3	.6			Debt/Worth	.5	.5
			1.2	1.1				1.0	1.0
			2.2	3.9				2.6	4.9
			44.0	67.5			% Profit Before Taxes/Tangible Net Worth	51.7	44.3
			12.2	14.7				(27) 33.4	(32) 27.9
			-1.0	-19.9				21.7	10.4
			18.3	13.6			% Profit Before Taxes/Total Assets	20.9	25.5
			6.4	5.9				15.3	11.2
			-.3	-11.1				4.6	3.0
			25.3	15.3			Sales/Net Fixed Assets	15.5	13.1
			10.9	3.6				10.0	6.1
			4.8	1.6				4.3	3.8
			2.5	1.9			Sales/Total Assets	2.8	2.7
			2.3	1.0				2.3	2.3
			1.6	.7				1.6	1.5
			1.4	2.9			% Depr., Dep., Amort./Sales	.5	1.4
			2.1	5.0				(26) 1.7	(28) 3.3
			3.4	9.3				3.7	4.8
							% Officers', Directors' Owners' Comp/Sales	3.5	.7
								(14) 4.8	(14) 5.5
								10.1	11.1
Net Sales ($)	6167M	15479M	106210M	293421M	258046M			574629M	708117M
Total Assets ($)	1523M	5551M	52783M	230378M	288510M			241934M	419192M

DATA NOT AVAILABLE

M = $ thousand   MM = $ million
See Pages 9 through 22 for Explanation of Ratios and Data

Comparative Historical Data | Current Data Sorted by Sales

4/1/07-3/31/08 ALL	4/1/08-3/31/09 ALL	4/1/09-3/31/10 ALL	Type of Statement	0-1MM	1-3MM	3-5MM	5-10MM	10-25MM	25MM & OVER
6	3	6	Unqualified		1		1	2	2
9	8	13	Reviewed	1	1		1	7	3
5	5	3	Compiled	1	1	1			
6	3	3	Tax Returns	1			1		
13	22	9	Other	1			1	3	3
					8 (4/1-9/30/09)			26 (10/1/09-3/31/10)	
39	41	34	NUMBER OF STATEMENTS	4	3	3	4	12	8
%	%	%	ASSETS	%	%	%	%	%	%
9.1	10.3	10.9	Cash & Equivalents					9.4	
22.9	23.1	20.6	Trade Receivables (net)					20.4	
22.6	22.3	22.5	Inventory					22.9	
2.4	1.8	3.5	All Other Current					.7	
56.9	57.6	57.4	Total Current					53.5	
34.6	26.6	31.1	Fixed Assets (net)					38.2	
2.4	5.2	4.2	Intangibles (net)					1.3	
6.1	10.6	7.3	All Other Non-Current					7.0	
100.0	100.0	100.0	Total					100.0	
			LIABILITIES						
9.2	11.0	8.6	Notes Payable-Short Term					5.9	
3.9	4.0	3.5	Cur. Mat.-L.T.D.					7.0	
14.9	12.9	12.0	Trade Payables					8.4	
.2	.3	.1	Income Taxes Payable					.1	
12.3	17.0	9.9	All Other Current					4.2	
40.4	45.1	34.1	Total Current					25.6	
19.2	13.5	15.6	Long-Term Debt					12.6	
.4	.7	.3	Deferred Taxes					.5	
5.3	5.1	6.6	All Other Non-Current					10.6	
34.7	35.6	43.4	Net Worth					50.7	
100.0	100.0	100.0	Total Liabilties & Net Worth					100.0	
			INCOME DATA						
100.0	100.0	100.0	Net Sales					100.0	
32.9	28.6	30.0	Gross Profit					28.2	
25.5	22.2	26.3	Operating Expenses					25.5	
7.4	6.4	3.7	Operating Profit					2.7	
.8	1.0	.5	All Other Expenses (net)					.5	
6.6	5.4	3.2	Profit Before Taxes					2.2	
			RATIOS						
3.1	2.7	3.2	Current					3.7	
1.9	1.4	2.1						2.2	
1.0	1.0	1.2						1.4	
2.1	1.4	2.2	Quick					2.0	
1.0	.8	1.0						1.1	
.5	.5	.6						.8	
33 11.0	29 12.4	30 12.3	Sales/Receivables					42 8.7	
41 9.0	38 9.5	44 8.3						52 7.0	
55 6.7	53 6.9	60 6.0						61 6.0	
37 9.9	27 13.3	27 13.5	Cost of Sales/Inventory					36 10.0	
57 6.4	62 5.9	65 5.6						89 4.1	
87 4.2	97 3.8	105 3.5						118 3.1	
20 18.5	15 23.6	14 25.7	Cost of Sales/Payables					14 26.3	
35 10.3	26 13.8	18 20.3						17 21.5	
53 6.9	59 6.2	43 8.5						42 8.7	
4.7	4.2	3.4	Sales/Working Capital					2.8	
6.8	10.2	7.4						5.1	
161.4	NM	29.2						15.4	
9.4	9.1	20.8	EBIT/Interest					12.6	
(34) 4.8	(36) 3.0	(30) 4.7						4.1	
1.4	-.8	.8						-10.3	
8.3	7.4	7.3	Net Profit + Depr., Dep., Amort./Cur. Mat. L/T/D						
(16) 3.4	(19) 1.9	(10) 3.8							
2.4	.1	.5							
.3	.3	.4	Fixed/Worth					.5	
1.1	.8	.7						.8	
2.5	1.6	1.4						1.0	
.6	.9	.6	Debt/Worth					.6	
1.4	1.7	1.3						1.0	
4.2	3.7	3.9						2.0	
43.5	33.1	32.7	% Profit Before Taxes/Tangible Net Worth					25.8	
(32) 22.3	(35) 15.5	(29) 14.5						11.6	
11.6	-2.7	-2.0						-23.9	
18.5	17.8	13.4	% Profit Before Taxes/Total Assets					13.3	
8.5	5.2	5.9						7.9	
2.6	-2.0	-.3						-12.2	
21.7	19.2	15.7	Sales/Net Fixed Assets					12.0	
7.7	8.6	6.6						3.3	
3.2	3.9	2.9						1.9	
2.5	2.3	2.5	Sales/Total Assets					2.4	
2.0	1.8	1.6						1.4	
1.2	1.3	.9						.8	
1.9	.9	1.5	% Depr., Dep., Amort./Sales					2.2	
(31) 3.5	(37) 2.5	(33) 3.3						4.5	
4.7	3.5	4.2						7.9	
1.7	3.0		% Officers', Directors' Owners' Comp/Sales						
(13) 8.2	(15) 3.8								
11.7	10.9								
893767M	1441500M	679323M	Net Sales ($)	2334M	6720M	11241M	28014M	166749M	464265M
627232M	800961M	578745M	Total Assets ($)	1592M	1073M	7960M	9929M	155064M	403127M

M = $ thousand   MM = $ million
See Pages 9 through 22 for Explanation of Ratios and Data

MANUFACTURING—Iron and Steel Mills NAICS 331111

Current Data Sorted by Assets   **Comparative Historical Data**

	0-500M	500M-2MM	2-10MM	10-50MM	50-100MM	100-250MM		ALL 4/1/05-3/31/06	ALL 4/1/06-3/31/07
Type of Statement									
Unqualified		2	10	13	5	6		30	24
Reviewed		1	14	8	1			15	22
Compiled	2	5	5	1				9	15
Tax Returns	1	1	3					11	14
Other	2	7	24	21	7	3		48	40
		27 (4/1-9/30/09)		115 (10/1/09-3/31/10)					
NUMBER OF STATEMENTS	5	16	56	43	13	9		113	115
	%	%	%	%	%	%		%	%
ASSETS									
Cash & Equivalents		10.7	8.4	9.6	4.1			8.3	6.7
Trade Receivables (net)		31.8	28.9	21.7	14.2			31.3	30.9
Inventory		17.4	23.4	23.5	25.2			21.8	25.1
All Other Current		3.7	2.4	3.2	5.7			3.0	3.3
Total Current		63.5	63.0	57.9	49.1			64.4	65.9
Fixed Assets (net)		29.1	30.0	29.1	36.0			28.9	25.6
Intangibles (net)		2.6	2.2	3.7	4.6			2.4	2.6
All Other Non-Current		4.8	4.8	9.3	10.3			4.2	5.8
Total		100.0	100.0	100.0	100.0			100.0	100.0
LIABILITIES									
Notes Payable-Short Term		8.5	10.5	12.3	9.6			15.5	12.2
Cur. Mat.-L.T.D.		3.6	5.1	4.0	6.3			3.1	3.1
Trade Payables		17.8	17.7	12.1	9.2			19.4	19.4
Income Taxes Payable		.1	.2	.2	.4			.3	.2
All Other Current		7.0	12.9	9.7	8.9			10.3	8.1
Total Current		36.9	46.5	38.4	34.5			48.6	43.0
Long-Term Debt		25.3	18.2	13.6	19.9			18.4	17.4
Deferred Taxes		.6	.6	.9	1.8			.6	.9
All Other Non-Current		19.2	4.6	7.9	9.0			7.5	6.3
Net Worth		18.0	30.1	39.2	34.8			24.9	32.4
Total Liabilities & Net Worth		100.0	100.0	100.0	100.0			100.0	100.0
INCOME DATA									
Net Sales		100.0	100.0	100.0	100.0			100.0	100.0
Gross Profit		33.6	22.6	18.3	14.7			23.6	23.5
Operating Expenses		35.9	22.9	15.2	11.4			17.7	17.5
Operating Profit		-2.2	-.3	3.1	3.3			5.9	6.0
All Other Expenses (net)		1.5	.8	2.9	2.9			1.0	1.3
Profit Before Taxes		-3.7	-1.1	.2	.4			4.8	4.7
RATIOS									
Current		3.8	3.2	2.6	2.4			2.4	2.3
		2.2	1.3	1.4	1.4			1.5	1.5
		1.1	.9	1.1	.9			1.1	1.1
Quick		2.5	1.5	1.6	1.3			1.4	1.4
		1.1	.7	.6	.4			.9	.9
		.6	.4	.4	.3			.6	.5
Sales/Receivables		28 13.1	33 11.0	35 10.5	23 15.8			31 11.7	30 12.3
		43 8.5	46 8.0	44 8.3	31 11.7			44 8.2	41 8.8
		53 6.8	63 5.8	63 5.8	48 7.6			60 6.1	57 6.5
Cost of Sales/Inventory		11 34.6	16 23.0	34 10.6	18 20.8			14 25.9	17 21.1
		30 12.2	48 7.6	65 5.6	51 7.2			41 8.8	45 8.0
		66 5.5	82 4.5	99 3.7	124 2.9			72 5.1	72 5.1
Cost of Sales/Payables		20 18.3	16 22.6	16 22.7	14 26.8			21 17.5	22 16.6
		32 11.5	32 11.3	30 12.2	28 13.2			32 11.4	33 11.1
		59 6.2	53 6.9	43 8.5	37 10.0			48 7.6	55 6.7
Sales/Working Capital		2.9	5.2	4.1	5.2			6.0	6.1
		7.7	16.6	9.8	9.2			11.7	10.9
		29.2	-44.6	27.7	-123.2			68.6	78.6
EBIT/Interest		7.3	4.8	12.9	1.3			14.8	13.5
		(11) 2.1	(47) 1.2	(42) 3.8	(12) .0			(104) 5.5	(102) 4.7
		-5.5	-1.3	-.5	-2.0			2.2	1.7
Net Profit + Depr., Dep., Amort./Cur. Mat. L/T/D			2.4	17.8				17.6	13.4
			(11) 1.3	(13) 2.6				(32) 4.4	(34) 4.8
			.3	.5				2.6	1.5
Fixed/Worth		.2	.3	.3	.8			.4	.3
		.9	.8	.7	1.1			.9	.7
		NM	3.2	1.4	2.6			4.0	3.5
Debt/Worth		.8	.6	.7	1.2			.9	.9
		1.7	2.3	1.4	3.0			2.2	2.0
		-12.6	8.1	5.0	4.7			12.6	8.0
% Profit Before Taxes/Tangible Net Worth		11.0	28.4	32.4	12.9			66.3	59.4
		(11) -3.7	(45) 7.1	(39) 9.2	(12) -.6			(95) 33.9	(98) 29.9
		-21.6	-6.1	-10.0	-27.8			13.8	13.2
% Profit Before Taxes/Total Assets		4.0	7.3	10.7	2.8			17.1	21.8
		-.4	1.0	4.1	-1.2			8.3	9.8
		-17.2	-4.6	-6.7	-7.8			2.6	2.6
Sales/Net Fixed Assets		34.3	18.8	12.2	12.7			21.6	24.9
		8.3	10.3	5.2	3.1			9.5	12.0
		2.2	4.5	2.8	2.8			5.1	5.7
Sales/Total Assets		4.0	2.9	2.3	2.1			3.2	3.1
		1.6	2.2	1.6	1.4			2.4	2.5
		1.0	1.5	1.0	.9			1.6	1.8
% Depr., Dep., Amort./Sales		1.0	.9	1.3	1.4			1.0	.9
		(12) 2.2	(48) 1.6	(37) 3.1	(12) 2.8			(103) 1.7	(97) 1.6
		4.3	3.7	5.1	5.2			2.7	2.3
% Officers', Directors' Owners' Comp/Sales			1.8					1.0	1.2
			(14) 4.4					(35) 3.5	(33) 2.9
			6.7					6.0	5.9
Net Sales ($)	4141M	43186M	669680M	1676577M	1400303M	2230147M		7058865M	6130458M
Total Assets ($)	1563M	16608M	309302M	1037708M	859287M	1478379M		3598872M	3160940M

M = $ thousand   MM = $ million
See Pages 9 through 22 for Explanation of Ratios and Data

Comparative Historical Data   Current Data Sorted by Sales

			Type of Statement						
27	29	36	Unqualified	1	1	1	3	7	23
15	27	24	Reviewed		1		4	10	7
8	12	13	Compiled	3	3	2	2	3	
13	15	5	Tax Returns	1	1		1	1	
47	60	64	Other	5	5	3	5	24	22
4/1/07-3/31/08 ALL	4/1/08-3/31/09 ALL	4/1/09-3/31/10 ALL		27 (4/1-9/30/09)			115 (10/1/09-3/31/10)		
				0-1MM	1-3MM	3-5MM	5-10MM	10-25MM	25MM & OV
110	143	142	NUMBER OF STATEMENTS	10	11	9	15	45	52
%	%	%	**ASSETS**	%	%	%	%	%	%
8.0	7.1	8.5	Cash & Equivalents	5.7	8.3		9.9	9.0	8.0
29.2	27.4	24.5	Trade Receivables (net)	19.8	22.0		22.7	28.7	20.6
22.8	25.4	22.8	Inventory	11.1	18.9		25.9	21.6	25.9
2.5	2.9	3.4	All Other Current	2.5	4.5		1.2	2.6	5.1
62.6	62.8	59.1	Total Current	39.1	53.7		59.6	61.9	59.6
28.9	27.7	30.9	Fixed Assets (net)	52.0	36.2		33.1	28.6	28.6
3.4	2.7	3.3	Intangibles (net)	6.7	3.4		2.0	3.2	2.9
5.1	6.8	6.7	All Other Non-Current	2.3	6.8		5.3	6.4	9.0
100.0	100.0	100.0	Total	100.0	100.0		100.0	100.0	100.0
			LIABILITIES						
12.2	12.9	10.7	Notes Payable-Short Term	5.4	14.1		6.2	11.1	11.4
3.4	3.6	4.6	Cur. Mat.-L.T.D.	4.2	4.9		5.1	4.7	3.7
19.6	15.5	14.3	Trade Payables	11.5	8.7		12.5	15.8	13.4
.2	.5	.2	Income Taxes Payable	.0	.2		.1	.3	.2
9.5	9.0	11.1	All Other Current	14.9	12.6		8.9	11.1	11.4
44.9	41.5	40.9	Total Current	36.0	40.4		32.7	43.0	40.1
15.6	14.6	18.2	Long-Term Debt	50.0	17.9		15.6	17.1	12.4
.6	.6	.9	Deferred Taxes	.8	1.4		.8	.5	1.4
6.3	6.4	7.6	All Other Non-Current	4.2	16.1		4.9	2.9	8.4
32.8	36.9	32.3	Net Worth	9.0	24.2		45.9	36.5	37.6
100.0	100.0	100.0	Total Liabilties & Net Worth	100.0	100.0		100.0	100.0	100.0
			INCOME DATA						
100.0	100.0	100.0	Net Sales	100.0	100.0		100.0	100.0	100.0
22.2	22.5	21.5	Gross Profit	37.7	25.2		22.0	22.7	15.8
15.8	16.7	20.3	Operating Expenses	44.0	26.2		20.9	20.7	12.5
6.4	5.8	1.2	Operating Profit	-6.3	-1.0		1.1	2.0	3.3
1.1	1.0	1.8	All Other Expenses (net)	2.4	1.4		4.9	.8	1.9
5.4	4.8	-.7	Profit Before Taxes	-8.7	-2.4		-3.7	1.2	1.4
			RATIOS						
2.5	2.6	3.1		5.1	2.7		4.0	3.1	2.5
1.4	1.7	1.4	Current	1.1	1.5		1.2	1.4	1.4
1.0	1.1	1.0		.2	.9		1.1	.9	1.1
1.6	1.4	1.6		1.7	2.0		1.9	2.0	1.2
.9	.9	.7	Quick	.8	1.0		.7	.8	.6
.5	.5	.4		.1	.3		.6	.6	.4
32 11.3	23 15.6	31 12.0		12 30.3	23 16.2		33 11.0	34 10.7	28 12.9
44 8.4	39 9.3	43 8.6	Sales/Receivables	38 9.6	42 8.7		45 8.0	45 8.2	37 10.0
56 6.5	57 6.4	60 6.1		72 5.1	79 4.6		57 6.4	63 5.7	50 7.3
10 36.5	18 20.4	20 18.2		0 UND	13 28.9		23 15.9	16 23.0	28 13.1
39 9.4	45 8.1	49 7.4	Cost of Sales/Inventory	22 16.9	48 7.7		56 6.5	45 8.0	57 6.4
72 5.1	76 4.8	84 4.4		53 6.8	67 5.4		181 2.0	82 4.4	96 3.8
19 18.7	12 29.8	16 23.1		5 78.9	14 26.2		18 20.0	15 23.6	16 22.5
31 11.8	25 14.8	30 12.0	Cost of Sales/Payables	35 10.5	32 11.3		28 13.2	30 12.2	29 12.6
46 7.9	43 8.6	46 8.0		79 4.6	53 6.9		45 8.2	44 8.3	41 9.0
5.8	5.3	4.5		3.6	5.3		2.8	4.5	4.9
13.4	11.2	10.5	Sales/Working Capital	21.9	9.5		13.4	11.4	9.6
246.9	67.4	-478.2		-2.0	-23.3		42.9	-63.7	29.1
18.5	17.3	6.5			8.1		1.6	11.6	7.6
(101) 4.5	(134) 5.6	(124) 1.5	EBIT/Interest	(10) 1.6		(13) -.4	(40) 1.9	(48) 2.7	
1.4	2.0	-1.4			-3.4		-3.1	-.2	-.8
7.9	11.8	6.5						9.9	14.3
(24) 1.9	(35) 3.7	(36) 2.3	Net Profit + Depr., Dep., Amort./Cur. Mat. L/T/D				(12) 2.3	(14) 5.2	
1.2	2.3	.2						1.4	.0
.3	.3	.3		.8	.6		.2	.3	.4
.8	.8	.8	Fixed/Worth	3.3	1.1		.8	.8	.6
2.6	1.8	2.1		-.6	-9.6		2.0	2.7	1.4
1.0	.8	.7		.7	1.6		.5	.7	.7
2.2	1.7	1.8	Debt/Worth	2.4	2.2		1.6	1.6	1.7
6.5	4.6	5.1		-1.9	-30.8		2.4	4.6	5.0
58.8	62.0	23.8					12.4	28.1	32.4
(96) 26.4	(127) 29.4	(118) 6.0	% Profit Before Taxes/Tangible Net Worth			(14) -7.4	(38) 11.1	(47) 10.0	
7.0	11.1	-8.5					-12.7	-.3	-10.0
22.2	19.3	8.6		.1	12.0		4.5	9.6	10.7
10.1	10.8	1.7	% Profit Before Taxes/Total Assets	-8.1	1.1		-2.5	3.6	3.0
2.1	2.6	-7.0		-14.3	-16.3		-6.6	-2.3	-6.5
23.3	23.7	17.6		8.3	35.6		19.4	16.4	13.5
11.5	10.8	7.0	Sales/Net Fixed Assets	2.5	3.0		9.0	9.3	5.6
4.3	5.5	3.1		1.0	1.9		1.8	4.3	3.6
2.9	3.3	2.6		1.7	2.2		2.9	2.8	2.4
2.3	2.4	1.8	Sales/Total Assets	1.2	.9		1.7	2.2	1.7
1.6	1.7	1.2		.7	.6		.8	1.5	1.3
.7	.7	1.0					1.0	.8	1.1
(98) 1.4	(127) 1.3	(119) 2.2	% Depr., Dep., Amort./Sales				1.6	(37) 2.6	(44) 2.2
2.7	2.7	4.2					4.2	3.9	3.6
1.2	1.1	1.9							
(28) 4.1	(41) 2.8	(25) 3.3	% Officers', Directors' Owners' Comp/Sales						
6.3	4.7	6.8							
6552594M	10441471M	6024034M	Net Sales ($)	7633M	21799M	35775M	124941M	703817M	5130069M
3141943M	4322972M	3702847M	Total Assets ($)	8156M	23825M	22820M	102568M	435523M	3109955M

M = $ thousand   MM = $ million
See Pages 9 through 22 for Explanation of Ratios and Data

Current Data Sorted by Assets   Comparative Historical Data

Type of Statement	0-500M	500M-2MM	2-10MM	10-50MM	50-100MM	100-250MM		4/1/05-3/31/06 ALL	4/1/06-3/31/07 ALL
Unqualified			3	16	9	5		30	24
Reviewed		4	21	16	1			16	17
Compiled	2	4	7	1				11	13
Tax Returns	7	8	3	1				6	12
Other	2	12	28	22	4	5		36	50
		20 (4/1-9/30/09)		161 (10/1/09-3/31/10)					
NUMBER OF STATEMENTS	11	28	62	56	14	10		99	116
ASSETS	%	%	%	%	%	%		%	%
Cash & Equivalents	6.2	11.6	10.2	7.1	7.6	4.1		6.8	7.3
Trade Receivables (net)	23.3	31.4	27.6	25.4	15.6	16.5		31.6	31.4
Inventory	33.1	28.4	20.8	26.5	36.4	32.4		30.6	33.3
All Other Current	12.6	3.7	4.4	3.3	3.0	2.9		2.5	2.3
Total Current	75.2	75.2	63.1	62.4	62.6	55.9		71.5	74.3
Fixed Assets (net)	21.5	16.7	27.5	27.4	29.9	31.2		21.6	20.4
Intangibles (net)	2.2	3.4	3.4	4.8	3.9	6.1		1.7	1.9
All Other Non-Current	1.1	4.7	6.0	5.4	3.6	6.7		5.2	3.4
Total	100.0	100.0	100.0	100.0	100.0	100.0		100.0	100.0
LIABILITIES									
Notes Payable-Short Term	16.8	16.1	9.5	9.1	6.8	4.5		9.1	10.9
Cur. Mat.-L.T.D.	.7	5.7	3.8	3.6	2.6	5.7		2.6	2.0
Trade Payables	19.5	17.3	16.0	11.1	10.7	9.1		18.6	19.8
Income Taxes Payable	.1	.0	.1	.3	.0	.1		.5	.4
All Other Current	63.4	8.6	13.0	10.0	8.7	7.0		12.0	9.3
Total Current	100.5	47.7	42.4	34.0	28.8	26.5		42.8	42.3
Long-Term Debt	10.4	15.8	15.3	13.6	16.3	19.5		12.4	13.1
Deferred Taxes	.0	.1	.4	.5	.4	2.2		.9	.8
All Other Non-Current	10.3	.9	4.3	3.1	11.3	8.8		5.0	4.1
Net Worth	-21.1	35.4	37.6	48.9	43.1	43.1		38.9	39.7
Total Liabilites & Net Worth	100.0	100.0	100.0	100.0	100.0	100.0		100.0	100.0
INCOME DATA									
Net Sales	100.0	100.0	100.0	100.0	100.0	100.0		100.0	100.0
Gross Profit	39.0	32.8	27.8	23.6	11.2	11.2		21.8	22.4
Operating Expenses	41.3	30.2	26.2	17.5	13.4	11.5		14.4	15.3
Operating Profit	-2.4	2.6	1.6	6.1	-2.2	-.3		7.4	7.1
All Other Expenses (net)	4.6	1.1	.8	1.0	.9	2.5		.5	.5
Profit Before Taxes	-7.0	1.5	.7	5.1	-3.1	-2.8		6.9	6.6
RATIOS									
Current	1.9	2.9	4.0	3.5	3.2	2.5		3.1	2.9
	1.0	1.8	1.2	1.7	2.4	2.0		1.8	1.7
	.4	1.2	.8	1.2	1.5	1.8		1.2	1.3
Quick	.7	2.5	2.1	1.7	1.2	.9		1.8	1.6
	.2	1.0	.8	.9	.8	.8		.9	.9
	.1	.4	.5	.5	.5	.5		.6	.6
Sales/Receivables	0 UND	24 14.9	28 13.0	36 10.1	29 12.5	28 13.0		37 9.9	32 11.3
	18 20.2	43 8.5	46 7.9	49 7.4	42 8.8	33 11.2		46 8.0	48 7.6
	25 14.8	63 5.8	64 5.7	61 5.9	50 7.3	50 7.3		57 6.4	56 6.5
Cost of Sales/Inventory	6 58.7	7 52.5	20 18.3	32 11.3	65 5.6	47 7.8		33 11.1	32 11.5
	60 6.1	58 6.3	39 9.3	72 5.0	98 3.7	82 4.5		59 6.2	66 5.6
	141 2.6	168 2.2	78 4.7	126 2.9	144 2.5	121 3.0		93 3.9	110 3.3
Cost of Sales/Payables	1 289.0	8 48.3	18 19.8	14 25.5	22 16.8	13 27.2		20 18.1	21 17.2
	14 26.2	28 13.2	34 10.8	30 12.0	26 13.8	24 15.0		32 11.4	35 10.4
	57 6.4	42 8.6	57 6.4	44 8.4	32 11.4	32 11.5		47 7.8	48 7.5
Sales/Working Capital	8.7	4.9	4.3	4.0	3.0	4.1		4.8	4.2
	-66.5	10.1	14.1	7.3	4.9	5.2		8.8	7.7
	-5.4	36.1	-34.7	20.5	8.3	12.6		20.1	15.8
EBIT/Interest		9.6	14.2	16.7	9.4	5.6		22.5	22.8
		(26) 2.5	(51) 2.6	(53) 5.3	(13) -.6	.6		(82) 8.2	(100) 7.7
		-5.3	-1.4	1.3	-9.0	-1.5		3.3	2.6
Net Profit + Depr., Dep., Amort./Cur. Mat. L/T/D			6.9	7.2				37.7	14.9
			(12) 1.5	(10) 2.6				(27) 6.0	(22) 7.0
			-.7	.2				1.3	2.4
Fixed/Worth	.0	.2	.2	.3	.2	.4		.2	.2
	1.4	.6	.8	.6	.9	.6		.5	.5
	-.1	3.5	4.9	2.1	NM	NM		1.4	1.1
Debt/Worth	3.2	.8	.5	.5	.4	.7		.8	.7
	4.9	2.3	2.3	.9	1.0	.9		1.5	1.6
	-2.0	13.1	9.2	2.6	NM	NM		5.0	3.9
% Profit Before Taxes/Tangible Net Worth		74.0	42.8	33.7	18.0			58.9	58.6
		(24) 11.7	(52) 11.2	(51) 12.4	(11) 5.1			(91) 38.0	(109) 33.4
		-28.6	-5.9	1.2	-36.8			21.4	14.5
% Profit Before Taxes/Total Assets	-.5	18.3	10.2	15.3	7.4	12.0		25.8	22.3
	-24.3	4.9	4.2	7.2	-1.5	-.7		13.6	12.4
	-40.5	-9.9	-4.7	.6	-14.8	-11.5		5.2	4.4
Sales/Net Fixed Assets	999.8	64.1	25.2	13.4	14.2	13.6		29.7	42.7
	44.6	19.1	9.1	6.4	4.6	6.0		11.5	15.3
	8.2	6.9	3.6	4.2	2.9	3.2		5.4	6.6
Sales/Total Assets	5.5	3.9	3.0	2.3	1.8	2.6		3.1	3.0
	4.1	2.6	1.8	1.6	1.4	1.6		2.2	2.3
	2.7	1.5	1.3	1.3	1.2	1.3		1.7	1.7
% Depr., Dep., Amort./Sales		.5	1.0	.9	1.3			.6	.5
		(19) 1.8	(51) 2.2	(51) 2.1	(13) 2.8			(86) 1.6	(104) 1.2
		3.2	4.6	4.2	4.6			2.9	2.4
% Officers', Directors' Owners' Comp/Sales		2.5	1.4					1.7	1.1
		(16) 4.0	(24) 2.8					(29) 3.6	(37) 2.4
		7.7	7.3					6.3	5.7
Net Sales ($)	9379M	97189M	744198M	1966254M	1515640M	3277248M		6444414M	6782453M
Total Assets ($)	2465M	33441M	303317M	1147235M	972648M	1839389M		2920536M	3221173M

Comparative Historical Data / Current Data Sorted by Sales

	4/1/07-3/31/08 ALL	4/1/08-3/31/09 ALL	4/1/09-3/31/10 ALL	0-1MM	1-3MM	3-5MM	5-10MM	10-25MM	25MM & OVER
					20 (4/1-9/30/09)		161 (10/1/09-3/31/10)		
Type of Statement									
Unqualified	31	37	33		1	4	14	15	26
Reviewed	23	26	42		2	1	2	3	8
Compiled	17	23	14	3	3		5	2	3
Tax Returns	13	15	19	7		2	1	6	
Other	50	70	73	4	11	6	13	15	24
NUMBER OF STATEMENTS	134	171	181	14	17	13	35	41	61
ASSETS	%	%	%	%	%	%	%	%	%
Cash & Equivalents	7.3	8.2	8.7	3.8	11.3	10.3	11.9	8.9	6.8
Trade Receivables (net)	27.2	26.1	25.7	23.2	29.4	30.7	26.6	27.5	22.5
Inventory	30.9	27.9	26.3	30.9	28.1	26.9	16.2	25.0	31.3
All Other Current	4.7	4.9	4.3	10.8	8.8	3.4	3.3	2.6	3.4
Total Current	70.0	67.1	65.0	68.7	77.6	71.2	58.0	64.0	64.0
Fixed Assets (net)	22.9	23.9	25.9	25.3	18.6	16.6	29.6	27.6	26.6
Intangibles (net)	4.0	3.9	3.9	4.2	.9	6.3	4.3	2.9	4.7
All Other Non-Current	3.1	5.2	5.2	1.8	2.9	5.9	8.0	5.4	4.7
Total	100.0	100.0	100.0	100.0	100.0	100.0	100.0	100.0	100.0
LIABILITIES									
Notes Payable-Short Term	12.8	12.3	10.4	21.5	14.6	11.3	7.3	11.5	7.4
Cur. Mat.-L.T.D.	2.9	2.7	3.9	2.5	1.4	6.4	5.6	3.5	3.5
Trade Payables	17.6	15.9	14.1	9.2	18.6	15.0	15.9	15.6	11.8
Income Taxes Payable	.4	.5	.1	.0	.1	.0	.1	.1	.2
All Other Current	8.5	10.3	13.8	50.1	15.2	11.6	11.6	8.4	10.4
Total Current	42.2	41.6	42.2	83.4	49.8	44.4	40.6	39.1	33.3
Long-Term Debt	12.8	11.6	14.8	11.8	18.5	19.5	17.2	10.7	15.0
Deferred Taxes	.3	.4	.4	.0	.6	.6	.2	.2	.7
All Other Non-Current	4.0	4.6	4.6	1.0	7.6	5.4	1.5	3.7	6.7
Net Worth	40.7	41.8	37.9	3.8	23.5	30.2	40.5	46.2	44.3
Total Liabilities & Net Worth	100.0	100.0	100.0	100.0	100.0	100.0	100.0	100.0	100.0
INCOME DATA									
Net Sales	100.0	100.0	100.0	100.0	100.0	100.0	100.0	100.0	100.0
Gross Profit	23.7	24.4	25.8	33.8	39.4	30.0	29.2	26.1	17.0
Operating Expenses	17.0	17.5	23.3	37.4	40.8	28.2	25.7	20.6	14.5
Operating Profit	6.7	6.9	2.5	-3.6	-1.4	1.9	3.5	5.5	2.5
All Other Expenses (net)	.9	1.2	1.3	4.7	1.1	1.2	.8	.6	1.2
Profit Before Taxes	5.8	5.7	1.2	-8.3	-2.4	.6	2.7	4.9	1.3
RATIOS									
Current	3.0	3.0	3.1	2.0	8.0	7.0	2.8	2.8	3.4
	1.6	1.6	1.7	1.0	1.8	2.5	1.3	1.4	2.0
	1.2	1.1	1.1	.5	1.0	1.2	.7	1.1	1.3
Quick	1.4	1.5	1.6	.6	2.8	3.2	2.1	1.5	1.4
	.8	.8	.8	.4	.8	2.2	1.0	.8	.8
	.5	.5	.5	.1	.5	.4	.4	.6	.5
Sales/Receivables	27 13.4	26 14.1	29 12.6	0 UND	26 14.2	35 10.3	28 13.3	32 11.3	30 12.2
	38 9.5	37 10.0	43 8.5	22 16.5	38 9.6	43 8.5	44 8.3	49 7.4	42 8.7
	48 7.7	48 7.6	58 6.3	106 3.4	87 4.2	50 7.3	56 6.5	63 5.8	54 6.8
Cost of Sales/Inventory	23 15.8	24 15.5	25 14.4	6 58.0	20 18.3	17 22.1	17 21.7	25 14.3	33 11.1
	57 6.4	45 8.0	60 6.1	88 4.1	80 4.6	57 6.4	40 9.0	60 6.0	71 5.1
	92 4.0	88 4.2	108 3.4	273 1.3	166 2.2	89 4.1	68 5.3	112 3.3	110 3.3
Cost of Sales/Payables	15 24.2	11 32.6	15 24.0	1 398.8	10 38.2	10 37.9	19 19.2	19 19.6	16 23.5
	28 13.1	26 14.0	27 13.4	9 38.6	35 10.5	26 13.8	30 12.2	38 9.5	25 14.8
	41 8.8	42 8.8	47 7.8	61 6.0	116 3.1	45 8.1	52 7.1	53 6.9	38 9.5
Sales/Working Capital	5.1	4.9	4.3	6.7	2.1	2.8	4.7	4.1	4.3
	9.6	10.4	8.7	-82.3	11.3	6.8	22.0	9.8	6.6
	32.2	50.2	60.0	-5.1	-152.8	34.2	-11.1	35.5	14.5
EBIT/Interest	13.7	24.0	10.5	3.9	15.1	7.4	11.7	13.9	12.8
	(116) 5.0	(142) 5.2	(162) 2.4	(12) -2.6	(15) 1.5	(12) 1.8	(29) 2.2	(35) 3.4	(59) 2.4
	2.0	1.6	-1.4	-8.9	-6.7	-3.1	-2.1	.9	-.4
Net Profit + Depr., Dep., Amort./Cur. Mat. L/T/D	12.4	8.0	6.0						6.1
	(32) 4.7	(39) 4.0	(35) 1.5						(22) 2.1
	1.5	1.6	-.1						.1
Fixed/Worth	.2	.2	.2	.2	.1	.2	.2	.2	.3
	.5	.6	.7	1.3	.6	.7	.8	.6	.6
	1.5	1.6	2.9	-2.9	-2.0	3.1	4.8	2.0	2.1
Debt/Worth	.6	.5	.5	.9	.5	1.3	.5	.6	.5
	1.6	1.4	1.7	3.9	2.3	3.3	2.3	1.3	1.0
	4.2	4.5	7.7	-5.3	-12.4	15.6	8.4	2.7	5.3
% Profit Before Taxes/Tangible Net Worth	59.2	65.9	34.7		8.4	200.0	50.5	30.8	27.9
	(113) 28.3	(151) 28.4	(152) 8.9		(11) -6.8	(11) 29.1	(32) 23.6	(37) 13.2	(52) 8.6
	11.8	7.7	-4.6		-31.6	-13.2	-5.9	1.1	-2.0
% Profit Before Taxes/Total Assets	21.5	24.3	11.8	1.6	6.9	13.2	16.6	13.3	12.2
	10.5	9.7	3.5	-14.2	-.9	5.8	4.2	7.7	3.1
	2.5	2.0	-3.7	-38.0	-15.1	-4.7	-7.3	.6	-2.2
Sales/Net Fixed Assets	34.8	32.1	26.1	60.3	65.6	63.8	33.8	17.1	25.2
	15.1	14.0	8.4	7.4	14.0	21.1	9.3	6.5	6.8
	7.4	6.2	4.1	4.1	4.9	6.7	3.6	3.8	4.0
Sales/Total Assets	3.4	3.4	2.7	3.7	3.6	3.5	3.0	2.2	2.6
	2.4	2.4	1.8	1.8	1.5	2.5	2.0	1.6	1.8
	1.8	1.8	1.3	.8	1.1	1.3	1.4	1.3	1.3
% Depr., Dep., Amort./Sales	.5	.6	.9			.8	1.0	1.2	.7
	(120) 1.1	(147) 1.4	(148) 2.1			(11) 2.0	(32) 2.0	(37) 2.3	(52) 1.9
	2.3	2.7	4.4			4.3	4.5	5.0	3.4
% Officers', Directors' Owners' Comp/Sales	1.4	1.9	1.7		1.9		.9		
	(47) 2.3	(50) 2.7	(54) 3.4		(12) 4.0		(13) 3.1		
	5.7	7.8	7.3		9.9		5.5		
Net Sales ($)	7484970M	11396480M	7609908M	9567M	33885M	52247M	242683M	680142M	6591384M
Total Assets ($)	3537587M	5027076M	4298495M	9500M	27172M	25596M	141884M	432224M	3662119M

M = $ thousand   MM = $ million
See Pages 9 through 22 for Explanation of Ratios and Data

Current Data Sorted by Assets **Comparative Historical Data**

0-500M	500M-2MM	2-10MM	10-50MM	50-100MM	100-250MM	Type of Statement	ALL	ALL
		3	8	1	1	Unqualified	19	25
1	1	10	9			Reviewed	19	18
	2	7	2			Compiled	8	13
2	4	6				Tax Returns	5	6
	2	7	15	8	3	Other	27	29
	21 (4/1-9/30/09)		71 (10/1/09-3/31/10)				4/1/05-3/31/06	4/1/06-3/31/07
0-500M	500M-2MM	2-10MM	10-50MM	50-100MM	100-250MM		ALL	ALL
3	9	33	34	9	4	NUMBER OF STATEMENTS	78	91
%	%	%	%	%	%	ASSETS	%	%
		9.3	11.1			Cash & Equivalents	8.6	7.4
		27.1	17.7			Trade Receivables (net)	29.0	27.7
		29.8	29.7			Inventory	28.4	30.6
		2.1	4.4			All Other Current	2.6	2.0
		68.3	62.9			Total Current	68.5	67.7
		24.5	28.1			Fixed Assets (net)	25.0	24.6
		4.0	3.9			Intangibles (net)	1.5	2.8
		3.2	5.1			All Other Non-Current	5.0	4.8
		100.0	100.0			Total	100.0	100.0
						LIABILITIES		
		12.9	10.7			Notes Payable-Short Term	18.6	13.8
		4.1	2.7			Cur. Mat.-L.T.D.	2.6	3.4
		17.4	11.2			Trade Payables	16.0	18.9
		.3	.2			Income Taxes Payable	.2	.2
		6.4	6.2			All Other Current	5.6	8.0
		41.1	31.1			Total Current	43.2	44.4
		10.5	12.4			Long-Term Debt	14.6	15.6
		.4	.7			Deferred Taxes	.8	.3
		4.1	7.2			All Other Non-Current	7.3	6.0
		43.9	48.6			Net Worth	34.2	33.7
		100.0	100.0			Total Liabilities & Net Worth	100.0	100.0
						INCOME DATA		
		100.0	100.0			Net Sales	100.0	100.0
		23.0	17.5			Gross Profit	22.8	21.5
		20.2	13.4			Operating Expenses	17.0	16.0
		2.7	4.2			Operating Profit	5.8	5.6
		1.3	1.2			All Other Expenses (net)	1.4	1.6
		1.4	3.0			Profit Before Taxes	4.4	3.9
						RATIOS		
		2.9	4.6			Current	2.7	2.3
		1.4	1.9				1.9	1.6
		1.0	1.2				1.3	1.1
		1.8	2.2			Quick	1.4	1.2
		.7	.7				.9	.8
		.5	.4				.6	.5
	33	11.0	25 14.9			Sales/Receivables	33 11.0	32 11.6
	49	7.4	40 9.1				42 8.6	42 8.6
	66	5.5	52 7.1				50 7.3	54 6.7
	33	11.1	39 9.4			Cost of Sales/Inventory	33 11.2	39 9.3
	57	6.4	71 5.1				51 7.2	60 6.1
	91	4.0	106 3.4				80 4.6	89 4.1
	15	25.0	13 27.1			Cost of Sales/Payables	16 23.5	21 17.6
	26	14.2	21 17.7				30 12.1	33 11.1
	43	8.5	46 7.9				42 8.7	49 7.4
		4.0	2.7			Sales/Working Capital	4.7	5.7
		8.1	6.4				9.0	10.8
		NM	20.6				17.0	33.5
		5.0	9.2			EBIT/Interest	17.2	9.0
		(29) 2.0	(31) 2.2				(68) 4.6	(81) 3.5
		-1.8	.7				1.5	1.0
		12.4				Net Profit + Depr., Dep.,	15.9	8.4
		(10) 1.8				Amort./Cur. Mat. L/T/D	(23) 5.2	(34) 4.0
		-.3					1.9	1.7
		.2	.3			Fixed/Worth	.2	.3
		.5	.5				.5	.6
		1.9	1.5				1.6	2.0
		.5	.6			Debt/Worth	.6	.9
		2.0	1.1				1.7	2.0
		4.4	2.5				3.4	5.9
		18.7	22.5			% Profit Before Taxes/Tangible	49.8	50.3
		(32) 10.1	(31) 8.0			Net Worth	(68) 22.4	(75) 22.8
		-9.7	-3.0				5.7	7.2
		7.2	9.5			% Profit Before Taxes/Total	19.4	14.1
		3.5	2.9			Assets	9.4	8.3
		-3.5	-1.5				1.4	.9
		54.1	16.2			Sales/Net Fixed Assets	32.7	24.1
		11.4	8.0				12.8	12.4
		3.9	4.0				5.9	5.6
		2.7	2.2			Sales/Total Assets	3.3	2.9
		2.1	1.7				2.4	2.3
		1.1	1.3				1.7	1.8
		.7	1.2			% Depr., Dep., Amort./Sales	.8	.9
		(31) 1.4	(30) 1.8				(63) 1.6	(85) 1.6
		4.3	3.5				3.1	2.9
		1.5				% Officers', Directors'	.7	.9
		(14) 2.2				Owners' Comp/Sales	(14) 2.9	(21) 2.1
		3.1					6.3	5.0
2351M	29767M	383172M	1212816M	1336510M	1158377M	Net Sales ($)	5092486M	5019590M
765M	9462M	174384M	691218M	703015M	554932M	Total Assets ($)	2204307M	2330996M

M = $ thousand   MM = $ million
See Pages 9 through 22 for Explanation of Ratios and Data

Comparative Historical Data | Current Data Sorted by Sales

Type of Statement periods (Comparative Historical Data): 4/1/07-3/31/08 ALL · 4/1/08-3/31/09 ALL · 4/1/09-3/31/10 ALL

Current Data: 21 (4/1-9/30/09) covers 0-1MM, 1-3MM, 3-5MM · 71 (10/1/09-3/31/10) covers 5-10MM, 10-25MM, 25MM & OVER

4/1/07-3/31/08 ALL	4/1/08-3/31/09 ALL	4/1/09-3/31/10 ALL	Type of Statement	0-1MM	1-3MM	3-5MM	5-10MM	10-25MM	25MM & OVER
18	17	13	Unqualified	1			1	3	9
11	19	21	Reviewed				2	9	6
10	10	11	Compiled		1	3	3	2	2
2	8	12	Tax Returns	1	2	3	3	2	1
34	36	35	Other		4	4	4	7	19
75	90	92	NUMBER OF STATEMENTS	2	7	10	13	23	37
%	%	%		%	%	%	%	%	%
			ASSETS						
5.3	7.3	9.4	Cash & Equivalents			9.6	18.4	8.2	7.3
25.6	25.0	23.4	Trade Receivables (net)			28.3	22.9	23.4	21.2
29.5	27.8	28.8	Inventory			29.1	28.5	32.4	29.0
2.0	2.1	2.9	All Other Current			.3	3.9	2.5	3.7
62.3	62.2	64.5	Total Current			67.3	73.7	66.6	61.1
29.4	29.4	27.1	Fixed Assets (net)			30.1	19.3	24.8	30.3
2.7	2.4	3.1	Intangibles (net)			.8	5.0	3.5	2.3
5.7	6.0	5.3	All Other Non-Current			1.7	2.0	5.2	6.3
100.0	100.0	100.0	Total			100.0	100.0	100.0	100.0
			LIABILITIES						
13.0	13.5	11.5	Notes Payable-Short Term			18.7	8.5	9.6	10.3
3.3	2.7	3.0	Cur. Mat.-L.T.D.			3.1	3.6	2.9	2.7
18.8	18.5	14.4	Trade Payables			22.4	8.0	17.2	13.5
.4	.2	.2	Income Taxes Payable			.0	.2	.3	.3
5.8	6.7	7.0	All Other Current			6.4	10.7	3.6	7.0
41.3	41.7	36.2	Total Current			50.6	31.0	33.7	33.8
14.0	17.6	12.8	Long-Term Debt			28.8	4.5	12.5	10.5
.8	.4	.7	Deferred Taxes			.0	.6	.4	1.2
7.5	6.2	7.0	All Other Non-Current			6.5	2.8	6.9	9.5
36.4	34.1	43.3	Net Worth			14.0	61.2	46.6	45.1
100.0	100.0	100.0	Total Liabilities & Net Worth			100.0	100.0	100.0	100.0
			INCOME DATA						
100.0	100.0	100.0	Net Sales			100.0	100.0	100.0	100.0
20.3	21.2	20.8	Gross Profit			29.2	23.5	16.3	16.8
13.1	15.9	18.3	Operating Expenses			29.2	22.1	14.6	12.6
7.2	5.4	2.4	Operating Profit			.1	1.4	1.7	4.2
1.4	1.3	1.0	All Other Expenses (net)			2.4	.5	1.1	1.2
5.8	4.0	1.4	Profit Before Taxes			-2.3	.9	.6	3.0
			RATIOS						
2.4	2.5	3.9	Current			2.8	7.5	4.6	3.3
1.6	1.5	1.8				1.1	2.7	1.9	2.0
1.1	1.1	1.1				.9	1.3	1.1	1.3
1.3	1.4	1.8	Quick			1.9	3.7	1.7	1.7
.7	.7	.8				.7	1.7	.7	1.0
.5	.5	.5				.5	.5	.5	.4
33 11.1	27 13.7	29 12.7	Sales/Receivables			29 12.6	30 12.1	31 11.9	24 15.1
39 9.3	34 10.8	43 8.6				55 6.7	49 7.4	47 7.8	34 10.8
48 7.6	45 8.1	55 6.7				68 5.3	71 5.2	51 7.1	48 7.6
35 10.4	23 16.2	33 11.0	Cost of Sales/Inventory			26 14.2	29 12.4	38 9.7	39 9.3
59 6.2	47 7.8	61 6.0				58 6.2	71 5.2	61 6.0	61 6.0
80 4.6	77 4.7	86 4.2				178 2.0	129 2.8	114 3.2	79 4.6
20 18.5	13 27.5	14 25.6	Cost of Sales/Payables			25 14.8	6 58.1	17 21.3	14 26.0
33 10.9	26 13.8	24 15.1				47 7.7	18 19.8	27 13.5	23 15.9
41 9.0	43 8.6	44 8.4				94 3.9	27 13.7	46 8.0	45 8.2
5.6	6.4	3.8	Sales/Working Capital			4.0	1.8	2.3	4.5
12.3	12.6	7.9				NM	5.2	8.1	8.6
41.6	72.4	52.4				-52.5	11.6	49.6	19.7
17.1	11.1	7.0	EBIT/Interest				6.6	3.9	19.0
(67) 4.4	(83) 3.7	(82) 2.2					(11) -.3	(20) 1.7	(35) 3.7
1.9	1.6	-1.1					-4.6	-.9	1.3
8.9	14.9	13.3	Net Profit + Depr., Dep., Amort./Cur. Mat. L/T/D						67.7
(31) 3.0	(22) 2.3	(22) 2.8							(12) 4.3
1.0	1.4	.3							1.1
.3	.3	.3	Fixed/Worth			.5	.1	.1	.3
.6	.7	.6				2.4	.3	.5	.6
1.6	1.8	1.8				-1.8	.8	1.5	1.5
.6	.8	.5	Debt/Worth			1.6	.2	.5	.6
1.5	2.0	1.6				3.8	.5	1.6	1.7
3.9	5.2	3.4				-4.5	1.5	2.6	2.6
47.1	45.1	24.0	% Profit Before Taxes/Tangible Net Worth				11.6	23.3	38.6
(66) 25.4	(81) 24.1	(82) 8.6					2.5	(22) 7.5	(34) 14.3
9.3	4.7	-7.8					-15.9	-6.8	.6
18.8	14.7	8.2	% Profit Before Taxes/Total Assets			3.9	7.1	8.2	14.6
8.6	6.8	3.0				-4.0	1.3	3.1	4.0
2.4	.8	-5.0				-13.7	-7.4	-3.5	-.5
19.4	28.4	20.4	Sales/Net Fixed Assets			36.2	42.9	42.2	14.9
8.1	10.8	8.2				11.0	14.3	10.0	8.2
4.7	5.0	4.0				3.6	3.5	3.9	4.6
2.9	3.1	2.7	Sales/Total Assets			3.3	2.2	2.7	2.8
2.2	2.5	1.9				1.8	1.6	1.9	2.0
1.8	1.6	1.4				1.4	1.0	1.2	1.6
.9	.7	1.0	% Depr., Dep., Amort./Sales				.8	.7	1.0
(67) 1.7	(81) 1.4	(76) 1.8					(12) 1.6	(21) 1.8	(28) 1.5
2.8	2.7	4.0					3.7	3.5	3.3
.7	1.0	1.5	% Officers', Directors' Owners' Comp/Sales						
(18) 1.5	(20) 1.6	(25) 2.3							
2.7	3.2	4.2							
4110201M	5016861M	4122993M	Net Sales ($)	312M	13623M	39342M	88872M	442211M	3538633M
1954521M	2363393M	2133776M	Total Assets ($)	283M	11934M	20922M	71153M	293452M	1736032M

M = $ thousand   MM = $ million
See Pages 9 through 22 for Explanation of Ratios and Data

Current Data Sorted by Assets

Comparative Historical Data

0-500M	500M-2MM	2-10MM	10-50MM	50-100MM	100-250MM	Type of Statement	4/1/05-3/31/06 ALL	4/1/06-3/31/07 ALL
			2	1	2	Unqualified	13	12
	1	4	3			Reviewed	8	9
1	3					Compiled	5	4
2	3	1				Tax Returns	3	2
1	2	4	8	1	2	Other	18	14
	13 (4/1-9/30/09)		28 (10/1/09-3/31/10)					
4	9	9	13	2	4	NUMBER OF STATEMENTS	47	41
%	%	%	%	%	%	**ASSETS**	%	%
			6.0			Cash & Equivalents	5.5	4.6
			22.4			Trade Receivables (net)	28.0	25.2
			31.5			Inventory	29.7	32.8
			.4			All Other Current	1.2	1.0
			60.3			Total Current	64.4	63.6
			31.4			Fixed Assets (net)	29.0	29.8
			.6			Intangibles (net)	3.2	1.6
			7.7			All Other Non-Current	3.5	5.0
			100.0			Total	100.0	100.0
						LIABILITIES		
			18.4			Notes Payable-Short Term	13.3	16.7
			3.3			Cur. Mat.-L.T.D.	3.3	4.0
			13.3			Trade Payables	15.8	15.4
			.2			Income Taxes Payable	.2	.2
			4.3			All Other Current	8.8	5.9
			39.6			Total Current	41.3	42.2
			10.4			Long-Term Debt	14.9	17.5
			.7			Deferred Taxes	.8	.7
			4.1			All Other Non-Current	4.8	2.8
			45.1			Net Worth	38.2	36.8
			100.0			Total Liabilities & Net Worth	100.0	100.0
						INCOME DATA		
			100.0			Net Sales	100.0	100.0
			19.6			Gross Profit	22.7	20.9
			15.2			Operating Expenses	18.3	16.4
			4.4			Operating Profit	4.4	4.6
			.1			All Other Expenses (net)	1.1	1.0
			4.3			Profit Before Taxes	3.2	3.6
						RATIOS		
			5.1			Current	2.9	3.0
			2.2				1.5	1.4
			1.1				1.1	1.0
			2.6			Quick	1.7	1.4
			.8				.8	.7
			.4				.5	.5
		30	12.3			Sales/Receivables	35 · 10.4	31 · 11.6
		45	8.1				45 · 8.1	42 · 8.7
		55	6.7				62 · 5.9	53 · 6.9
		41	8.8			Cost of Sales/Inventory	37 · 9.8	47 · 7.8
		61	6.0				77 · 4.7	72 · 5.1
		153	2.4				97 · 3.8	98 · 3.7
		12	30.3			Cost of Sales/Payables	15 · 24.9	20 · 18.6
		20	18.0				34 · 10.8	29 · 12.8
		37	9.9				48 · 7.6	44 · 8.4
			3.4			Sales/Working Capital	4.9	5.3
			4.5				10.7	10.3
			65.5				34.7	235.8
			17.8			EBIT/Interest	9.0	11.4
		(11)	6.4				(41) · 3.6	(38) · 2.2
			2.1				1.1	1.3
						Net Profit + Depr., Dep., Amort./Cur. Mat. L/T/D	10.6	5.8
							(14) · 3.8	(13) · 2.5
							.5	1.6
			.3			Fixed/Worth	.3	.3
			.7				.8	1.0
			1.5				1.9	1.6
			.6			Debt/Worth	.8	1.0
			1.2				1.8	1.9
			2.9				4.6	3.9
			16.6			% Profit Before Taxes/Tangible Net Worth	36.5	28.8
		(12)	11.5				(41) · 21.1	(38) · 14.5
			5.5				2.5	6.3
			7.5			% Profit Before Taxes/Total Assets	13.7	14.1
			3.0				6.4	3.3
			1.5				.7	1.1
			16.7			Sales/Net Fixed Assets	21.0	20.1
			7.5				7.8	8.5
			3.8				4.0	4.5
			2.1			Sales/Total Assets	2.8	2.9
			1.6				2.0	2.2
			1.4				1.3	1.6
						% Depr., Dep., Amort./Sales	.5	1.0
							(44) · 1.5	(38) · 1.7
							2.6	4.0
						% Officers', Directors' Owners' Comp/Sales	3.0	2.4
							(13) · 3.6	(10) · 4.3
							10.5	5.9
3414M	28323M	109049M	614888M	287279M	1072376M	Net Sales ($)	1747439M	2257938M
750M	10916M	46612M	315541M	146200M	775234M	Total Assets ($)	740286M	1158928M

M = $ thousand   MM = $ million
See Pages 9 through 22 for Explanation of Ratios and Data

Comparative Historical Data | Current Data Sorted by Sales

Type of Statement	07-08	08-09	09-10	0-1MM	1-3MM	3-5MM	5-10MM	10-25MM	25MM & OVER
Unqualified	14	17	5						5
Reviewed	8	10	8		2			3	3
Compiled	8	1	4	1	1	2			
Tax Returns	1	4	6	1	2	3			
Other	17	8	18		2	1	2	4	9
	4/1/07-3/31/08 ALL	4/1/08-3/31/09 ALL	4/1/09-3/31/10 ALL		13 (4/1-9/30/09)			28 (10/1/09-3/31/10)	
NUMBER OF STATEMENTS	48	40	41	2	7	6	2	7	17

	%	%	%	%	%	%	%	%	%
ASSETS									
Cash & Equivalents	8.0	7.8	9.3						7.5
Trade Receivables (net)	26.5	24.0	27.2						23.6
Inventory	31.7	35.1	27.3						33.6
All Other Current	2.3	3.9	4.4						1.8
Total Current	68.4	70.8	68.2						66.6
Fixed Assets (net)	22.8	21.6	21.7						26.5
Intangibles (net)	1.4	2.2	1.8						2.7
All Other Non-Current	7.4	5.4	8.4						4.2
Total	100.0	100.0	100.0						100.0
LIABILITIES									
Notes Payable-Short Term	12.3	16.7	14.8						18.5
Cur. Mat.-L.T.D.	2.5	4.1	3.1						3.7
Trade Payables	16.1	14.0	17.8						14.0
Income Taxes Payable	.3	.2	.1						.1
All Other Current	5.2	5.5	5.4						5.5
Total Current	36.3	40.5	41.1						41.7
Long-Term Debt	9.7	10.7	9.2						8.6
Deferred Taxes	.5	.4	.4						1.0
All Other Non-Current	3.2	6.7	13.7						5.3
Net Worth	50.3	41.7	35.5						43.3
Total Liabilties & Net Worth	100.0	100.0	100.0						100.0
INCOME DATA									
Net Sales	100.0	100.0	100.0						100.0
Gross Profit	20.0	19.2	21.8						16.8
Operating Expenses	14.5	15.7	21.4						15.4
Operating Profit	5.5	3.5	.3						1.4
All Other Expenses (net)	.4	.6	.2						.1
Profit Before Taxes	5.1	2.9	.1						1.3
RATIOS									
Current	4.3	4.9	3.8						3.7
	2.0	1.7	1.9						1.9
	1.3	1.1	1.1						1.1
Quick	1.8	2.1	2.3						2.1
	1.0	.8	.9						.7
	.5	.4	.6						.4
Sales/Receivables	37 10.0	26 14.2	34 10.8						34 10.8
	44 8.3	36 10.1	41 8.8						45 8.1
	53 6.9	50 7.3	54 6.8						57 6.4
Cost of Sales/Inventory	43 8.5	39 9.3	34 10.8						47 7.7
	69 5.3	69 5.3	55 6.6						79 4.6
	100 3.7	97 3.8	96 3.8						106 3.4
Cost of Sales/Payables	17 21.3	12 31.0	13 28.4						17 21.5
	30 12.0	25 14.4	26 14.2						26 14.2
	45 8.1	39 9.3	60 6.1						38 9.5
Sales/Working Capital	3.7	4.6	3.6						3.5
	6.0	8.6	8.2						4.5
	14.7	28.4	62.3						65.5
EBIT/Interest	15.7	8.0	11.4						15.7
	(37) 4.6	(33) 1.8	(33) 2.6					(16)	4.2
	1.8	-1.6	-4.2						-1.8
Net Profit + Depr., Dep., Amort./Cur. Mat. L/T/D	3.5	2.4							
	(12) 1.8	(12) 1.0							
	.9	.0							
Fixed/Worth	.2	.1	.1						.3
	.3	.4	.5						.6
	1.0	1.0	1.1						1.1
Debt/Worth	.4	.4	.5						.9
	1.0	1.6	1.4						1.3
	2.8	4.8	4.7						2.5
% Profit Before Taxes/Tangible Net Worth	32.6	37.1	29.4						18.4
	(46) 18.7	(35) 13.4	(36) 9.7					(16)	9.8
	7.5	-4.3	-17.2						-8.5
% Profit Before Taxes/Total Assets	20.1	17.7	7.5						7.3
	7.7	4.2	2.8						2.9
	2.7	-2.1	-10.2						-4.4
Sales/Net Fixed Assets	23.9	57.8	66.4						13.4
	11.7	14.2	11.6						7.6
	5.6	6.7	6.4						4.8
Sales/Total Assets	2.8	2.9	3.0						2.1
	2.0	2.2	2.0						1.8
	1.4	1.8	1.5						1.5
% Depr., Dep., Amort./Sales	.9	.4	.8						1.4
	(41) 1.6	(32) 1.5	(31) 1.5					(13)	1.7
	2.4	2.8	2.5						2.7
% Officers', Directors' Owners' Comp/Sales	1.7								
	(12) 3.7								
	5.2								
Net Sales ($)	2122318M	2521552M	2115329M	909M	12636M	24434M	16305M	102807M	1958238M
Total Assets ($)	1217935M	1253196M	1295253M	414M	9047M	10218M	25162M	38599M	1211813M

© RMA 2010   M = $ thousand   MM = $ million
See Pages 9 through 22 for Explanation of Ratios and Data

Current Data Sorted by Assets   Comparative Historical Data

Type of Statement	0-500M	500M-2MM	2-10MM	10-50MM	50-100MM	100-250MM		4/1/05-3/31/06 ALL	4/1/06-3/31/07 ALL
Unqualified			2	8	2			4	8
Reviewed			1	2	1			6	4
Compiled		1						1	1
Tax Returns									1
Other	1	1	3	6				7	16
	0 (4/1-9/30/09)			28 (10/1/09-3/31/10)					
NUMBER OF STATEMENTS	1	2	6	16	3			18	30

Current-data asset/liability/income percentages are reported only for the 10-50MM column; columns 50-100MM and 100-250MM are marked **DATA NOT AVAILABLE**.

	0-500M %	500M-2MM %	2-10MM %	10-50MM %	50-100MM %	100-250MM %		4/1/05-3/31/06 ALL %	4/1/06-3/31/07 ALL %
ASSETS									
Cash & Equivalents				4.6				7.5	7.1
Trade Receivables (net)				27.3				33.0	34.0
Inventory				21.9				28.4	25.2
All Other Current				2.9				.5	1.1
Total Current				56.6				69.4	67.3
Fixed Assets (net)				36.4				19.4	24.5
Intangibles (net)				1.4				3.0	1.7
All Other Non-Current				5.6				8.2	6.5
Total				100.0				100.0	100.0
LIABILITIES									
Notes Payable-Short Term				18.7				16.3	16.6
Cur. Mat.-L.T.D.				4.0				1.0	4.6
Trade Payables				18.5				23.3	19.6
Income Taxes Payable				.1				.2	.2
All Other Current				8.8				11.8	7.7
Total Current				50.1				52.5	48.7
Long-Term Debt				15.4				7.3	12.1
Deferred Taxes				.1				.4	.5
All Other Non-Current				6.4				4.4	3.9
Net Worth				28.0				35.4	34.7
Total Liabilities & Net Worth				100.0				100.0	100.0
INCOME DATA									
Net Sales				100.0				100.0	100.0
Gross Profit				14.9				19.9	21.4
Operating Expenses				13.2				16.8	15.0
Operating Profit				1.7				3.2	6.4
All Other Expenses (net)				1.0				.9	1.1
Profit Before Taxes				.7				2.3	5.3

RATIOS

Ratio	10-50MM (current)	4/1/05-3/31/06 ALL	4/1/06-3/31/07 ALL
Current	2.1 / 1.1 / .8	2.9 / 1.3 / 1.0	2.8 / 1.4 / 1.0
Quick	1.2 / .6 / .4	1.2 / .8 / .5	1.9 / .8 / .6
Sales/Receivables	36 10.2 / 43 8.4 / 59 6.2	31 11.6 / 44 8.3 / 52 7.0	28 13.1 / 37 9.8 / 54 6.8
Cost of Sales/Inventory	19 18.8 / 39 9.4 / 68 5.4	24 15.5 / 45 8.2 / 62 5.9	16 22.8 / 36 10.0 / 53 6.9
Cost of Sales/Payables	23 15.8 / 30 12.2 / 52 7.0	7 55.3 / 35 10.5 / 67 5.4	14 25.5 / 31 11.6 / 43 8.5
Sales/Working Capital	7.6 / NM / -21.1	8.5 / 16.2 / NM	7.1 / 16.4 / -339.8
EBIT/Interest	12.3 / 3.3 / -2.7	(17) 8.6 / 3.9 / 1.4	(27) 13.4 / 4.0 / 2.4
Net Profit + Depr., Dep., Amort./Cur. Mat. L/T/D			(11) 8.1 / 4.4 / 1.4
Fixed/Worth	.5 / 1.5 / 26.1	.2 / .7 / 2.5	.3 / .9 / 2.8
Debt/Worth	1.1 / 2.9 / 57.5	.8 / 3.1 / 10.3	.7 / 3.2 / 7.3
% Profit Before Taxes/Tangible Net Worth	41.9 / (13) 24.4 / -3.7	44.3 / (15) 13.6 / 2.9	57.1 / (29) 38.0 / 20.9
% Profit Before Taxes/Total Assets	11.4 / 5.4 / -9.6	9.4 / 3.2 / 1.4	19.8 / 9.6 / 5.5
Sales/Net Fixed Assets	9.8 / 6.3 / 4.7	58.6 / 12.6 / 6.5	29.3 / 15.4 / 8.8
Sales/Total Assets	2.6 / 2.2 / 1.9	3.5 / 2.7 / 2.0	4.3 / 3.0 / 1.8
% Depr., Dep., Amort./Sales	1.0 / (15) 2.2 / 4.3	.5 / (16) 1.3 / 2.9	.7 / (26) 1.0 / 2.2
% Officers', Directors' Owners' Comp/Sales			

	0-500M	500M-2MM	2-10MM	10-50MM	50-100MM	100-250MM		4/1/05-3/31/06 ALL	4/1/06-3/31/07 ALL
Net Sales ($)	157M	4184M	81097M	895535M	369613M			736105M	2537308M
Total Assets ($)	148M	1704M	29012M	408422M	154320M			232222M	807271M

M = $ thousand   MM = $ million
See Pages 9 through 22 for Explanation of Ratios and Data

Comparative Historical Data / Current Data Sorted by Sales

Type of Statement	4/1/07-3/31/08 ALL	4/1/08-3/31/09 ALL	4/1/09-3/31/10 ALL	0-1MM	1-3MM	3-5MM	5-10MM	10-25MM	25MM & OVER
Unqualified	5	7	10						10
Reviewed	4	2	5		1		1	1	3
Compiled	2	1	2			1		1	
Tax Returns	1								
Other	10	10	11	1				5	4
				1	1	0 (4/1-9/30/09)		28 (10/1/09-3/31/10)	5
NUMBER OF STATEMENTS	22	20	28	1	1	1	1	7	17

	%	%	%	%	%	%	%	%	%
ASSETS									
Cash & Equivalents	8.0	6.8	5.2						4.2
Trade Receivables (net)	39.6	37.2	32.0						28.0
Inventory	23.9	17.5	20.2						23.0
All Other Current	1.4	2.6	3.4						2.1
Total Current	72.9	64.1	60.9						57.4
Fixed Assets (net)	21.5	30.1	34.0						38.5
Intangibles (net)	1.9	2.2	.9						1.5
All Other Non-Current	3.7	3.6	4.2						2.7
Total	100.0	100.0	100.0						100.0
LIABILITIES									
Notes Payable-Short Term	16.7	18.8	19.0						20.8
Cur. Mat.-L.T.D.	1.9	7.4	2.9						3.5
Trade Payables	20.6	17.1	18.1						17.7
Income Taxes Payable	.1	.0	.1						.1
All Other Current	7.1	12.6	7.1						7.3
Total Current	46.4	55.9	47.2						49.3
Long-Term Debt	14.3	17.5	14.1						14.1
Deferred Taxes	.2	.1	.5						.7
All Other Non-Current	3.8	5.5	4.0						2.7
Net Worth	35.3	20.9	34.2						33.2
Total Liabilities & Net Worth	100.0	100.0	100.0						100.0
INCOME DATA									
Net Sales	100.0	100.0	100.0						100.0
Gross Profit	21.6	14.6	17.3						12.3
Operating Expenses	14.8	12.9	15.2						12.4
Operating Profit	6.8	1.7	2.1						-.1
All Other Expenses (net)	1.7	1.4	.8						.0
Profit Before Taxes	5.2	.2	1.3						.0
RATIOS									
Current	2.3	1.9	2.1						2.1
	1.5	1.1	1.4						1.3
	1.2	.8	.9						.8
Quick	1.7	1.6	1.4						1.2
	1.2	.6	.8						.6
	.6	.4	.4						.4
Sales/Receivables	31 11.7	18 20.4	39 9.4						37 9.9
	45 8.1	27 13.3	46 8.0						43 8.6
	55 6.6	41 8.9	60 6.1						52 7.0
Cost of Sales/Inventory	10 36.1	5 75.6	16 22.9						18 19.8
	35 10.5	13 27.1	34 10.6						37 9.8
	70 5.2	43 8.5	63 5.8						71 5.1
Cost of Sales/Payables	17 21.0	6 57.0	14 26.4						21 17.6
	30 12.2	14 26.1	30 12.2						30 12.3
	38 9.6	29 12.8	48 7.7						39 9.3
Sales/Working Capital	8.7	13.6	8.0						7.7
	13.4	43.2	14.3						13.2
	23.0	-22.8	-43.2						-24.0
EBIT/Interest	16.2	8.0	14.7						15.5
	(20) 5.5	(19) 2.6	(25) 3.4						4.5
	1.4	1.1	-1.9						-1.9
Net Profit + Depr., Dep., Amort./Cur. Mat. L/T/D			25.6						
			(10) 2.6						
			-1.1						
Fixed/Worth	.3	.5	.5						.5
	.4	1.9	1.0						1.1
	1.6	NM	8.8						2.4
Debt/Worth	.6	1.0	.8						.9
	2.2	4.7	2.0						2.1
	12.5	NM	10.6						4.2
% Profit Before Taxes/Tangible Net Worth	46.6	90.0	37.7						37.7
	(19) 40.1	(15) 12.3	(24) 21.0						(16) 21.9
	13.6	4.0	.5						-5.5
% Profit Before Taxes/Total Assets	23.3	15.5	11.5						12.9
	14.5	4.3	6.5						6.4
	3.4	.2	-3.2						-7.2
Sales/Net Fixed Assets	57.8	42.4	15.8						12.5
	18.9	18.9	7.2						6.7
	7.9	7.7	4.1						4.2
Sales/Total Assets	4.0	5.7	2.8						2.7
	2.8	4.0	2.3						2.2
	2.1	3.3	1.9						2.0
% Depr., Dep., Amort./Sales	.5	.4	.8						1.0
	(20) 1.0	(18) 1.1	(26) 1.9						(16) 2.1
	1.8	1.8	3.2						4.3
% Officers', Directors' Owners' Comp/Sales									
Net Sales ($)	1744102M	2878759M	1350586M	157M	1075M	3109M	8220M	120647M	1217378M
Total Assets ($)	579780M	776183M	593606M	148M	567M	1137M	2393M	53633M	535728M

M = $ thousand   MM = $ million
See Pages 9 through 22 for Explanation of Ratios and Data

Current Data Sorted by Assets

Comparative Historical Data

Type of Statement	0-500M	500M-2MM	2-10MM	10-50MM	50-100MM	100-250MM		ALL 4/1/05-3/31/06	ALL 4/1/06-3/31/07
Unqualified			7	12	5			23	37
Reviewed			4	6				12	18
Compiled	1	1	1					6	7
Tax Returns	1	1	1	1				3	7
Other	5	10	10	12	3	2		33	21
		8 (4/1-9/30/09)		64 (10/1/09-3/31/10)					
NUMBER OF STATEMENTS	1	7	23	31	8	2		77	90
	%	%	%	%	%	%		%	%
ASSETS									
Cash & Equivalents			7.2	4.1				5.4	5.6
Trade Receivables (net)			26.9	20.4				30.7	27.8
Inventory			25.4	23.9				25.4	26.2
All Other Current			4.0	3.2				2.9	2.7
Total Current			63.6	51.6				64.3	62.3
Fixed Assets (net)			27.2	37.9				30.1	29.2
Intangibles (net)			1.9	5.1				2.1	3.8
All Other Non-Current			7.4	5.4				3.4	4.7
Total			100.0	100.0				100.0	100.0
LIABILITIES									
Notes Payable-Short Term			14.8	15.0				12.5	10.5
Cur. Mat.-L.T.D.			5.2	4.3				4.1	3.0
Trade Payables			14.2	12.5				19.8	18.5
Income Taxes Payable			.0	.1				.3	.2
All Other Current			7.0	7.1				10.0	8.5
Total Current			41.2	38.9				46.7	40.8
Long-Term Debt			22.6	15.1				16.3	16.7
Deferred Taxes			.5	.5				.7	1.1
All Other Non-Current			3.7	5.6				4.1	9.7
Net Worth			32.0	39.9				32.2	31.9
Total Liabilities & Net Worth			100.0	100.0				100.0	100.0
INCOME DATA									
Net Sales			100.0	100.0				100.0	100.0
Gross Profit			20.7	19.1				20.6	19.8
Operating Expenses			17.2	18.0				15.1	14.5
Operating Profit			3.5	1.1				5.5	5.4
All Other Expenses (net)			.4	1.1				1.1	1.4
Profit Before Taxes			3.2	.0				4.4	3.9
RATIOS									
Current			2.8	2.1				2.1	2.1
			1.5	1.4				1.4	1.6
			1.2	.9				1.1	1.2
Quick			1.4	1.2				1.0	1.2
			.7	.6				.8	.8
			.4	.3				.5	.6
Sales/Receivables			34 10.8	27 13.3				35 10.4	29 12.7
			40 9.1	39 9.4				45 8.1	43 8.5
			51 7.2	51 7.1				57 6.4	53 6.9
Cost of Sales/Inventory			19 19.7	28 13.0				29 12.8	28 13.2
			37 9.9	45 8.2				50 7.3	49 7.5
			78 4.7	85 4.3				72 5.1	68 5.4
Cost of Sales/Payables			7 51.2	15 23.6				22 16.7	21 17.5
			27 13.4	24 15.4				33 11.2	30 12.1
			47 7.8	37 9.8				46 8.0	43 8.4
Sales/Working Capital			5.0	6.9				6.7	6.8
			11.1	11.0				17.1	12.4
			76.0	-23.1				72.5	26.8
EBIT/Interest			5.7	6.5				9.9	12.8
			(20) 1.9	(30) .6				(71) 4.6	(85) 5.3
			.2	-2.0				1.9	2.0
Net Profit + Depr., Dep., Amort./Cur. Mat. L/T/D								7.7	7.9
								(24) 2.6	(28) 3.3
								1.6	2.0
Fixed/Worth			.2	.6				.5	.5
			.7	1.3				1.0	1.0
			4.9	3.2				2.0	2.2
Debt/Worth			.6	.8				1.3	.9
			1.7	2.0				2.4	2.0
			9.6	4.2				6.1	7.8
% Profit Before Taxes/Tangible Net Worth			46.3	18.3				65.4	51.8
			(19) 15.9	(27) .9				(73) 29.0	(76) 30.7
			2.9	-15.2				7.6	12.1
% Profit Before Taxes/Total Assets			13.9	6.6				15.3	18.3
			2.8	-.8				8.0	8.1
			-1.0	-4.6				2.1	3.4
Sales/Net Fixed Assets			23.1	6.9				18.8	17.9
			10.3	5.6				7.2	8.3
			5.3	3.6				4.5	4.7
Sales/Total Assets			2.7	2.6				3.0	3.3
			2.4	1.8				2.3	2.3
			1.8	1.4				1.8	1.7
% Depr., Dep., Amort./Sales			1.2	1.6				1.2	1.0
			(18) 1.5	(25) 2.6				(66) 1.9	(78) 1.6
			3.7	4.3				3.3	2.6
% Officers', Directors' Owners' Comp/Sales								1.1	1.1
								(19) 2.7	(19) 2.1
								3.9	3.1
Net Sales ($)	537M	20101M	303792M	1371307M	1117655M	335601M		3994374M	5414080M
Total Assets ($)	252M	7237M	122871M	695377M	568542M	390849M		1852256M	2503556M

M = $ thousand   MM = $ million
See Pages 9 through 22 for Explanation of Ratios and Data

Comparative Historical Data   Current Data Sorted by Sales

Type of Statement				0-1MM	1-3MM	3-5MM	5-10MM	10-25MM	25MM & OVER
Unqualified	20	23	24				1	9	14
Reviewed	8	8	10			1	1	3	5
Compiled	4	6	3	1	1	1			
Tax Returns	2	3	3			1	1	1	
Other	44	46	32		3	3	3	9	14
	4/1/07-3/31/08 ALL	4/1/08-3/31/09 ALL	4/1/09-3/31/10 ALL		8 (4/1-9/30/09)			64 (10/1/09-3/31/10)	
NUMBER OF STATEMENTS	78	86	72	1	4	6	6	22	33
	%	%	%	%	%	%	%	%	%
ASSETS									
Cash & Equivalents	4.2	4.6	6.8					9.7	3.5
Trade Receivables (net)	29.9	25.8	24.2					24.6	23.3
Inventory	24.5	26.2	23.7					22.2	22.8
All Other Current	2.2	3.3	3.6					3.8	3.3
Total Current	60.9	59.8	58.3					60.2	53.0
Fixed Assets (net)	31.8	30.5	32.7					29.2	38.9
Intangibles (net)	3.5	2.6	3.2					2.5	4.4
All Other Non-Current	3.8	7.1	5.8					8.1	3.8
Total	100.0	100.0	100.0					100.0	100.0
LIABILITIES									
Notes Payable-Short Term	15.6	14.7	14.3					12.6	12.0
Cur. Mat.-L.T.D.	4.6	3.3	4.5					3.5	4.0
Trade Payables	17.5	14.6	14.7					13.1	13.5
Income Taxes Payable	.2	.2	.1					.0	.1
All Other Current	5.8	7.5	10.6					8.8	6.6
Total Current	43.7	40.5	44.2					37.9	36.1
Long-Term Debt	21.6	21.3	20.7					24.3	19.1
Deferred Taxes	.4	.8	.7					.2	1.1
All Other Non-Current	5.2	5.3	5.8					3.7	6.7
Net Worth	29.1	32.2	28.6					33.9	36.9
Total Liabilties & Net Worth	100.0	100.0	100.0					100.0	100.0
INCOME DATA									
Net Sales	100.0	100.0	100.0					100.0	100.0
Gross Profit	20.1	18.7	20.9					21.1	15.6
Operating Expenses	15.3	15.7	18.3					18.1	13.9
Operating Profit	4.8	3.0	2.6					3.0	1.8
All Other Expenses (net)	1.6	1.2	.9					.8	1.3
Profit Before Taxes	3.2	1.8	1.7					2.2	.5
RATIOS									
Current	2.1	2.5	2.4					3.2	2.4
	1.5	1.7	1.6					1.7	1.7
	1.1	1.1	.9					1.1	.9
Quick	1.2	1.3	1.4					2.0	1.4
	.9	.8	.8					.9	1.0
	.6	.5	.4					.6	.4
Sales/Receivables	34 10.6	29 12.6	31 11.9					34 10.8	28 13.0
	42 8.7	36 10.1	41 8.9					43 8.4	39 9.3
	50 7.3	46 8.0	51 7.1					61 6.0	52 7.0
Cost of Sales/Inventory	20 18.6	22 16.4	25 14.6					21 17.3	25 14.3
	41 8.9	33 11.0	42 8.7					44 8.2	40 9.2
	62 5.9	83 4.4	82 4.4					79 4.6	82 4.5
Cost of Sales/Payables	21 17.3	14 26.2	15 23.7					11 34.2	17 21.6
	27 13.3	23 16.0	25 14.8					23 15.9	24 15.4
	36 10.2	31 11.9	45 8.1					52 7.0	37 9.9
Sales/Working Capital	8.2	6.4	5.8					4.5	6.4
	15.5	9.9	10.3					8.8	10.3
	59.4	57.6	-66.1					NM	-74.4
EBIT/Interest	6.9	8.5	7.2					6.3	8.4
	(77) 2.9	(81) 2.8	(68) 2.1					(19) .7	(32) 3.4
	1.0	.0	-.6					-1.2	-.6
Net Profit + Depr., Dep., Amort./Cur. Mat. L/T/D	4.1	6.6	4.2						6.4
	(25) 2.4	(27) 2.4	(19) 1.8						(11) 1.8
	.8	.0	.1						-.1
Fixed/Worth	.6	.3	.4					.2	.6
	1.3	.8	1.2					.8	1.3
	2.3	2.2	3.7					4.0	3.2
Debt/Worth	1.4	.8	.7					.4	.5
	3.0	1.9	2.0					2.1	1.9
	7.5	4.7	7.9					6.0	7.2
% Profit Before Taxes/Tangible Net Worth	52.4	38.8	33.8					41.9	27.5
	(67) 24.6	(75) 14.9	(59) 9.1					(18) 9.3	(27) 9.0
	2.8	1.2	-9.7					-13.2	-16.1
% Profit Before Taxes/Total Assets	12.4	12.5	10.6					17.7	9.0
	6.9	4.5	2.1					1.1	2.5
	.2	-2.1	-4.2					-5.4	-4.4
Sales/Net Fixed Assets	19.0	21.7	16.7					22.4	8.4
	7.4	7.8	6.4					7.4	5.7
	4.9	4.5	4.1					3.5	3.8
Sales/Total Assets	3.2	3.1	2.6					2.6	2.7
	2.5	2.4	2.1					1.8	2.1
	1.9	1.6	1.4					1.4	1.4
% Depr., Dep., Amort./Sales	.9	.9	1.3					1.2	1.6
	(73) 1.7	(76) 1.5	(58) 2.4					(18) 1.7	(26) 2.5
	2.8	3.2	4.2					4.3	4.4
% Officers', Directors' Owners' Comp/Sales	.7	.9	1.0						
	(19) 1.5	(21) 2.0	(15) 1.6						
	3.5	5.1	2.7						
Net Sales ($)	4455405M	5506351M	3148993M	537M	7031M	24409M	41241M	382361M	2693414M
Total Assets ($)	1912080M	2738973M	1785128M	252M	4822M	10756M	19949M	221187M	1528162M

M = $ thousand   MM = $ million
See Pages 9 through 22 for Explanation of Ratios and Data

MANUFACTURING—Copper Wire (except Mechanical) Drawing   NAICS 331422

Current Data Sorted by Assets   **Comparative Historical Data**

Type of Statement	0-500M	500M-2MM	2-10MM	10-50MM	50-100MM	100-250MM		4/1/05-3/31/06 ALL	4/1/06-3/31/07 ALL
Unqualified			2	3	4	2		10	11
Reviewed		1	4	4				5	8
Compiled		1	1	2				2	4
Tax Returns		1	3					1	3
Other			4	6	5			15	17
	0-500M	9 (4/1-9/30/09) 500M-2MM	2-10MM	33 (10/1/09-3/31/10) 10-50MM	50-100MM	100-250MM			
NUMBER OF STATEMENTS	2		14	15	9	2		33	43
	%		%	%	%	%		%	%

	0-500M	500M-2MM	2-10MM	10-50MM	50-100MM	100-250MM	4/1/05-3/31/06 ALL	4/1/06-3/31/07 ALL
ASSETS								
Cash & Equivalents			17.8	4.6			6.1	4.4
Trade Receivables (net)			22.8	31.7			28.5	33.9
Inventory			24.3	31.5			28.5	30.5
All Other Current			6.9	1.9			2.3	1.5
Total Current			71.8	69.7			65.4	70.3
Fixed Assets (net)			21.7	19.3			26.1	23.4
Intangibles (net)			2.7	2.2			3.2	2.4
All Other Non-Current			3.8	8.8			5.3	3.8
Total			100.0	100.0			100.0	100.0
LIABILITIES								
Notes Payable-Short Term			5.9	13.3			11.7	13.9
Cur. Mat.-L.T.D.			2.8	1.6			5.2	4.8
Trade Payables			14.4	23.9			16.8	21.9
Income Taxes Payable			.0	.2			.3	.3
All Other Current			16.3	10.7			6.3	8.0
Total Current			39.4	49.6			40.2	48.9
Long-Term Debt			16.1	13.4			10.2	13.9
Deferred Taxes			.6	.1			.8	.5
All Other Non-Current			5.9	8.3			7.0	5.6
Net Worth			38.1	28.5			41.7	31.1
Total Liabilities & Net Worth			100.0	100.0			100.0	100.0
INCOME DATA								
Net Sales			100.0	100.0			100.0	100.0
Gross Profit			32.9	13.2			21.7	20.0
Operating Expenses			26.7	14.2			16.8	14.5
Operating Profit			6.2	-1.1			4.9	5.5
All Other Expenses (net)			1.3	1.3			1.1	1.3
Profit Before Taxes			5.0	-2.3			3.8	4.2
RATIOS								
Current			2.9	2.2			2.9	2.1
			2.1	1.4			1.7	1.4
			1.3	1.1			1.2	1.1
Quick			1.9	1.1			1.6	1.0
			1.2	.8			.8	.8
			.7	.4			.6	.5
Sales/Receivables			25 14.7	29 12.4			41 8.9	34 10.7
			36 10.2	57 6.4			46 7.9	41 8.9
			55 6.6	73 5.0			52 7.0	50 7.4
Cost of Sales/Inventory			32 11.2	20 18.3			33 11.2	28 13.0
			58 6.3	91 4.0			75 4.8	53 6.9
			93 3.9	114 3.2			106 3.5	74 5.0
Cost of Sales/Payables			22 16.7	28 13.0			21 17.5	21 17.3
			34 10.9	46 7.9			38 9.7	34 10.7
			45 8.1	74 5.0			43 8.4	41 8.9
Sales/Working Capital			4.1	4.0			4.2	6.3
			6.0	8.0			7.8	12.3
			16.0	20.1			23.3	57.5
EBIT/Interest			23.7	5.3			20.1	15.5
			(12) 2.1	(13) 2.6			(32) 5.1	(41) 3.2
			.4	-2.4			1.6	1.7
Net Profit + Depr., Dep., Amort./Cur. Mat. L/T/D								6.0
							(14) 3.1	
								1.8
Fixed/Worth			.1	.3			.3	.2
			.5	.6			.6	.8
			5.1	1.5			1.0	1.9
Debt/Worth			.6	1.7			.7	1.1
			2.2	2.3			1.3	3.5
			10.6	4.2			4.0	9.2
% Profit Before Taxes/Tangible Net Worth			53.9	22.8			31.3	73.3
			(13) 29.6	(14) 11.6			(30) 18.8	(38) 30.9
			.1	-3.1			2.0	10.9
% Profit Before Taxes/Total Assets			18.8	5.6			14.1	17.0
			3.1	3.2			5.9	9.6
			-1.8	-5.3			.1	2.0
Sales/Net Fixed Assets			45.5	41.5			15.7	29.6
			19.5	20.7			9.4	15.6
			7.6	4.7			4.7	8.1
Sales/Total Assets			2.9	2.9			2.8	3.7
			2.2	2.0			1.9	2.8
			1.5	1.4			1.5	2.0
% Depr., Dep., Amort./Sales			.3	1.1			1.1	.7
			(10) 1.2	(12) 2.0			(27) 2.4	(39) 1.3
			4.2	5.0			3.2	2.6
% Officers', Directors' Owners' Comp/Sales								
Net Sales ($)	3384M		146667M	662879M	1274107M	692667M	3492996M	5357995M
Total Assets ($)	1599M		75144M	318454M	681425M	323665M	1731594M	1988903M

M = $ thousand   MM = $ million
See Pages 9 through 22 for Explanation of Ratios and Data

Comparative Historical Data | Current Data Sorted by Sales

			Type of Statement						
7	7	11	Unqualified				1	1	9
10	12	9	Reviewed		1		1	4	3
1	2	3	Compiled						2
2	2	4	Tax Returns		1		3	1	
13	19	15	Other		1		2	3	9
4/1/07-3/31/08 ALL	4/1/08-3/31/09 ALL	4/1/09-3/31/10 ALL		0-1MM	9 (4/1-9/30/09) 1-3MM	3-5MM	33 (10/1/09-3/31/10) 5-10MM	10-25MM	25MM & OVE
33	42	42	**NUMBER OF STATEMENTS**	3			7	9	23
%	%	%	**ASSETS**	%	%	%	%	%	%
5.4	8.6	10.2	Cash & Equivalents						7.0
31.6	27.1	28.2	Trade Receivables (net)	D	D				32.6
31.8	30.8	26.6	Inventory	A	A				26.7
1.2	2.2	3.9	All Other Current	T	T				2.5
69.9	68.7	68.9	Total Current	A	A				68.7
17.8	19.6	21.5	Fixed Assets (net)						18.1
2.7	3.2	2.6	Intangibles (net)	N	N				3.1
9.5	8.5	7.0	All Other Non-Current	O	O				10.1
100.0	100.0	100.0	Total	T	T				100.0
			LIABILITIES	A	A				
16.3	11.8	10.0	Notes Payable-Short Term	V	V				12.9
4.0	2.6	1.8	Cur. Mat.-L.T.D.	A	A				1.1
19.4	18.1	18.2	Trade Payables	I	I				21.0
1.6	.4	.1	Income Taxes Payable	L	L				.2
8.4	7.1	10.6	All Other Current	A	A				9.0
49.7	39.9	40.8	Total Current	B	B				44.2
11.0	12.0	14.1	Long-Term Debt	L	L				8.4
.4	.4	.4	Deferred Taxes	E	E				.4
7.1	7.1	6.2	All Other Non-Current						5.8
31.8	40.6	38.4	Net Worth						41.1
100.0	100.0	100.0	Total Liabilities & Net Worth						100.0
			INCOME DATA						
100.0	100.0	100.0	Net Sales						100.0
22.8	19.2	21.8	Gross Profit						15.3
19.2	16.6	19.0	Operating Expenses						13.2
3.6	2.6	2.8	Operating Profit						2.1
1.1	.2	1.4	All Other Expenses (net)						1.5
2.5	2.4	1.4	Profit Before Taxes						.6
			RATIOS						
2.2	2.8	3.1							3.6
1.6	1.8	1.6	Current						1.4
1.1	1.2	1.2							1.1
1.2	1.6	1.8							1.9
.8	.9	1.0	Quick						.9
.6	.6	.7							.7
35 10.3	24 14.9	33 10.9						39	9.4
39 9.3	33 11.0	50 7.3	Sales/Receivables					54	6.8
48 7.6	41 8.9	60 6.1						61	6.0
43 8.5	21 17.7	32 11.2						22	16.4
54 6.8	47 7.7	70 5.2	Cost of Sales/Inventory					67	5.5
61 5.9	67 5.5	94 3.9						94	3.9
19 19.4	15 24.2	22 16.9						21	17.5
30 12.2	20 17.9	37 9.8	Cost of Sales/Payables					37	9.8
42 8.6	35 10.5	49 7.4						52	7.1
6.6	5.5	3.6							3.6
9.8	9.6	7.4	Sales/Working Capital						10.9
46.9	28.8	20.8							35.0
10.8	12.7	11.6							24.7
(31) 4.4	3.8	(38) 2.6	EBIT/Interest					(21)	2.6
1.7	1.6	-.4							-1.0
9.4	11.0	7.7	Net Profit + Depr., Dep.,						
(14) 4.4	(14) 3.6	(12) 2.6	Amort./Cur. Mat. L/T/D						
1.9	1.4	.5							
.2	.1	.2							.2
.4	.3	.4	Fixed/Worth						.4
1.4	1.0	1.5							.7
1.2	.6	.6							.4
1.8	1.4	2.0	Debt/Worth						1.7
7.2	3.7	4.4							3.9
67.0	43.5	29.6	% Profit Before Taxes/Tangible						19.8
(30) 32.5	(39) 22.5	(39) 12.4	Net Worth					(22)	11.7
7.4	5.5	-2.8							-3.2
15.2	15.4	8.1	% Profit Before Taxes/Total						5.6
8.0	7.3	3.6	Assets						3.2
1.9	1.6	-1.8							-3.6
42.6	48.0	36.6							39.8
22.0	26.6	16.3	Sales/Net Fixed Assets						16.9
8.2	10.3	4.7							4.7
3.6	4.3	2.8							2.9
3.1	3.0	2.0	Sales/Total Assets						2.0
2.1	1.8	1.3							1.4
.8	.6	1.0							1.0
(30) 1.3	(36) .9	(33) 1.6	% Depr., Dep., Amort./Sales					(19)	1.6
2.1	2.3	4.1							4.3
	2.1	2.5							
	(11) 4.6	(13) 3.6	% Officers', Directors'						
	8.3	7.0	Owners' Comp/Sales						
2513937M	5822310M	2779704M	Net Sales ($)	5936M			49498M	147933M	2576337M
1129457M	1828683M	1400287M	Total Assets ($)	6202M			51902M	77959M	1264224M

© RMA 2010

M = $ thousand   MM = $ million
See Pages 9 through 22 for Explanation of Ratios and Data

Current Data Sorted by Assets   **Comparative Historical Data**

0-500M	500M-2MM	2-10MM	10-50MM	50-100MM	100-250MM		4/1/05-3/31/06 ALL	4/1/06-3/31/07 ALL
						Type of Statement		
		1	3			Unqualified	6	9
	3	6	5			Reviewed	14	10
		3	1			Compiled	1	3
2	3		1			Tax Returns	3	4
	3	7	5	3	4	Other	10	12
	8 (4/1-9/30/09)		41 (10/1/09-3/31/10)					
2	8	17	15	3	4	**NUMBER OF STATEMENTS**	34	38
%	%	%	%	%	%		%	%
						ASSETS		
		10.5	13.0			Cash & Equivalents	5.9	5.2
		23.9	24.9			Trade Receivables (net)	26.6	27.0
		30.4	25.1			Inventory	32.6	32.3
		2.3	4.7			All Other Current	4.1	3.4
		67.2	67.7			Total Current	69.2	67.9
		23.1	25.6			Fixed Assets (net)	24.0	26.1
		8.2	1.1			Intangibles (net)	2.0	3.1
		1.6	5.6			All Other Non-Current	4.9	2.9
		100.0	100.0			Total	100.0	100.0
						LIABILITIES		
		13.8	10.8			Notes Payable-Short Term	15.8	16.1
		1.3	4.2			Cur. Mat.-L.T.D.	2.9	2.9
		12.5	13.7			Trade Payables	17.9	16.5
		.0	.6			Income Taxes Payable	.7	1.2
		5.8	9.7			All Other Current	10.1	7.9
		33.5	38.9			Total Current	47.4	44.7
		10.5	12.2			Long-Term Debt	10.4	13.9
		1.1	.8			Deferred Taxes	.3	.4
		12.7	12.6			All Other Non-Current	7.5	5.5
		42.3	35.5			Net Worth	34.5	35.5
		100.0	100.0			Total Liabilties & Net Worth	100.0	100.0
						INCOME DATA		
		100.0	100.0			Net Sales	100.0	100.0
		29.9	14.6			Gross Profit	22.1	23.6
		23.8	12.9			Operating Expenses	15.9	16.0
		6.1	1.7			Operating Profit	6.2	7.5
		1.7	.2			All Other Expenses (net)	1.0	.8
		4.4	1.5			Profit Before Taxes	5.3	6.8
						RATIOS		
		2.7	3.1			Current	2.3	2.4
		1.8	1.7				1.3	1.5
		1.4	1.2				1.1	1.1
		1.6	1.8			Quick	.9	1.2
		.9	1.2				.6	.7
		.6	.5				.4	.4
		31 11.8	35 10.6			Sales/Receivables	32 11.4	35 10.5
		44 8.3	48 7.7				46 8.0	44 8.2
		52 7.0	63 5.8				59 6.2	60 6.1
		28 12.9	39 9.3			Cost of Sales/Inventory	37 9.8	29 12.7
		79 4.6	54 6.8				76 4.8	80 4.6
		127 2.9	92 4.0				114 3.2	106 3.4
		13 28.0	9 39.4			Cost of Sales/Payables	21 17.6	18 19.9
		23 16.1	32 11.4				36 10.2	36 10.1
		43 8.4	46 7.9				50 7.3	51 7.1
		3.3	3.3			Sales/Working Capital	5.6	4.3
		7.8	8.2				13.4	9.3
		19.8	12.5				31.4	28.8
		14.0	81.4			EBIT/Interest	15.3	11.0
		(15) 3.3	(14) 4.9				(32) 5.9	(36) 4.4
		.1	-.1				.5	1.2
						Net Profit + Depr., Dep., Amort./Cur. Mat. L/T/D	23.7	13.7
							(12) 2.7	(11) 3.3
							-1.5	1.6
		.2	.4			Fixed/Worth	.4	.2
		.5	.5				.6	.6
		2.7	3.1				1.1	2.2
		.7	.5			Debt/Worth	.8	.9
		1.4	1.1				2.2	1.8
		5.8	9.7				7.2	6.9
		60.5	17.6			% Profit Before Taxes/Tangible Net Worth	52.8	50.6
		(14) 12.3	(13) 9.7				(32) 30.0	(32) 27.4
		-3.6	-7.5				.4	9.9
		15.6	10.8			% Profit Before Taxes/Total Assets	22.5	22.8
		5.3	3.0				8.3	7.9
		-2.2	-4.5				-.6	1.4
		26.1	18.8			Sales/Net Fixed Assets	18.5	33.7
		11.6	6.7				9.9	8.7
		4.7	3.6				5.0	4.5
		2.7	2.4			Sales/Total Assets	2.6	2.8
		1.6	2.0				2.0	1.9
		1.3	1.0				1.5	1.4
		.5	1.0			% Depr., Dep., Amort./Sales	.7	.4
		(15) 1.7	(14) 2.6				(32) 1.5	(37) 1.9
		3.0	3.7				3.0	3.4
						% Officers', Directors' Owners' Comp/Sales		.8
								(12) 3.8
								6.0
1431M	27546M	179529M	609034M	436047M	900735M	Net Sales ($)	1746862M	1459571M
367M	9103M	85853M	321500M	214078M	700658M	Total Assets ($)	918000M	775521M

M = $ thousand   MM = $ million
See Pages 9 through 22 for Explanation of Ratios and Data

Comparative Historical Data   **Current Data Sorted by Sales**

			Type of Statement						
7	8	4	Unqualified		2	3	1	4	4
7	13	14	Reviewed		1		1	1	4
	4	4	Compiled	3	2				1
2	2	6	Tax Returns						1
12	20	21	Other	1		1	4	5	10
4/1/07-3/31/08 ALL	4/1/08-3/31/09 ALL	4/1/09-3/31/10 ALL			8 (4/1-9/30/09)			41 (10/1/09-3/31/10)	
				0-1MM	1-3MM	3-5MM	5-10MM	10-25MM	25MM & OVER
28	**47**	**49**	**NUMBER OF STATEMENTS**	**4**	**5**	**4**	**6**	**10**	**20**
%	%	%	**ASSETS**	%	%	%	%	%	%
9.8	7.1	10.9	Cash & Equivalents					8.9	10.5
25.0	22.8	23.8	Trade Receivables (net)					27.2	24.9
32.0	30.6	26.9	Inventory					21.9	26.1
3.5	3.1	2.8	All Other Current					2.2	4.8
70.3	63.5	64.4	Total Current					60.2	66.2
21.9	28.7	26.7	Fixed Assets (net)					35.0	26.7
5.0	3.2	3.7	Intangibles (net)					2.8	1.4
2.8	4.6	5.1	All Other Non-Current					2.1	5.7
100.0	100.0	100.0	Total					100.0	100.0
			LIABILITIES						
14.0	12.5	14.2	Notes Payable-Short Term					20.1	8.7
3.0	2.4	2.9	Cur. Mat.-L.T.D.					1.1	3.3
14.0	14.1	15.4	Trade Payables					16.9	15.3
.3	.2	.2	Income Taxes Payable					.1	.4
8.3	10.3	7.6	All Other Current					5.5	10.2
39.6	39.6	40.4	Total Current					43.7	38.0
9.6	15.8	14.6	Long-Term Debt					16.0	8.0
.3	.7	1.0	Deferred Taxes					.9	1.1
7.7	5.4	19.8	All Other Non-Current					24.7	2.4
42.8	38.5	24.2	Net Worth					14.7	50.4
100.0	100.0	100.0	Total Liabilties & Net Worth					100.0	100.0
			INCOME DATA						
100.0	100.0	100.0	Net Sales					100.0	100.0
24.9	23.4	23.4	Gross Profit					12.9	15.7
17.0	17.0	20.0	Operating Expenses					12.6	10.9
7.9	6.4	3.4	Operating Profit					.3	4.8
1.0	1.5	.6	All Other Expenses (net)					.3	.5
6.9	4.9	2.8	Profit Before Taxes					.0	4.2
			RATIOS						
3.4	2.8	2.7						2.3	3.2
2.0	1.7	1.6	Current					1.4	1.7
1.2	1.1	1.2						1.2	1.3
1.7	1.2	1.5						1.3	1.7
.8	.7	.9	Quick					.9	1.0
.5	.5	.5							.8
30 12.1	22 16.3	29 12.5						29 12.5	26 13.9
36 10.2	33 10.9	45 8.1	Sales/Receivables					50 7.4	40 9.0
47 7.7	44 8.4	53 6.8						64 5.7	52 7.0
27 13.5	20 18.6	33 11.1						21 17.8	36 10.1
54 6.8	48 7.6	55 6.6	Cost of Sales/Inventory					48 7.6	42 8.6
112 3.2	111 3.3	109 3.4						84 4.3	93 3.9
13 28.0	11 33.6	14 26.9						16 22.8	10 36.4
22 16.9	22 16.6	27 13.7	Cost of Sales/Payables					32 11.3	23 15.8
42 8.8	42 8.6	44 8.3						45 8.0	41 8.9
3.6	4.7	3.5						4.9	3.3
7.2	10.4	9.6	Sales/Working Capital					12.1	8.9
21.8	60.0	21.8						20.9	17.4
15.1	13.8	14.1							70.5
(25) 7.3	(42) 7.2	(46) 2.0	EBIT/Interest						(19) 10.1
1.0	.1	.1							2.4
4.2	7.7	3.9	Net Profit + Depr., Dep.,						
(11) 2.0	(13) 4.3	(12) .6	Amort./Cur. Mat. L/T/D						
.7	-.2	.1							
.3	.4	.3						.4	.3
.5	.9	.7	Fixed/Worth					2.2	.4
2.9	2.7	2.7						-17.8	1.2
.6	.7	.7						1.2	.5
1.2	1.9	1.8	Debt/Worth					3.8	1.1
13.1	5.3	6.0						-30.3	2.0
63.0	50.3	34.7	% Profit Before Taxes/Tangible						39.1
(23) 26.0	(41) 27.5	(40) 10.2	Net Worth						(19) 11.4
16.7	7.5	-4.4							5.0
25.6	19.3	12.8	% Profit Before Taxes/Total					7.0	15.4
10.7	8.8	3.0	Assets					-2.3	7.6
.3	-.2	-2.7						-6.1	2.1
34.4	21.9	32.0						19.1	22.4
12.7	7.5	9.3	Sales/Net Fixed Assets					5.9	8.0
5.9	4.9	4.4						2.4	4.1
3.6	3.3	2.9						3.5	3.1
2.1	2.3	1.9	Sales/Total Assets					2.1	2.1
1.5	1.2	1.2						1.1	1.3
.9	.8	.5						.9	.5
(27) 1.6	(40) 2.3	(39) 1.7	% Depr., Dep., Amort./Sales					3.3	(14) 1.1
2.4	3.4	3.6						5.4	2.5
.8	1.1	2.4	% Officers', Directors'						
(10) 1.4	(15) 2.5	(11) 4.0	Owners' Comp/Sales						
9.0	5.4	6.5							
1494817M	2615226M	2154322M	Net Sales ($)	3117M	12924M	14784M	44463M	161042M	1917992M
912634M	1510743M	1331559M	Total Assets ($)	1703M	6969M	12508M	30859M	103897M	1175623M

M = $ thousand   MM = $ million
See Pages 9 through 22 for Explanation of Ratios and Data

Current Data Sorted by Assets							Comparative Historical Data	

Type of Statement

0-500M	500M-2MM	2-10MM	10-50MM	50-100MM	100-250MM	Type of Statement		
			9	5	2	Unqualified	23	15
		1	6			Reviewed	12	9
	2					Compiled	1	9
1	1					Tax Returns	1	3
	9 (4/1-9/30/09)	4	10	5	2	Other	26	22
			40 (10/1/09-3/31/10)				4/1/05-3/31/06 ALL	4/1/06-3/31/07 ALL
1	4	5	25	10	4	NUMBER OF STATEMENTS	63	58
%	%	%	%	%	%	ASSETS	%	%
			8.4	8.8		Cash & Equivalents	5.7	5.9
			24.5	20.1		Trade Receivables (net)	26.7	30.7
			33.5	39.9		Inventory	34.9	34.4
			3.9	6.4		All Other Current	3.2	2.5
			70.4	75.2		Total Current	70.5	73.5
			21.8	15.1		Fixed Assets (net)	22.0	18.9
			1.2	5.3		Intangibles (net)	2.1	2.7
			6.6	4.4		All Other Non-Current	5.4	4.8
			100.0	100.0		Total	100.0	100.0
						LIABILITIES		
			19.0	14.1		Notes Payable-Short Term	18.4	17.3
			3.6	.6		Cur. Mat.-L.T.D.	2.8	3.5
			18.2	13.0		Trade Payables	22.4	23.2
			.0	.8		Income Taxes Payable	.3	.8
			8.4	13.4		All Other Current	13.1	10.2
			49.3	41.9		Total Current	57.0	54.9
			8.7	8.1		Long-Term Debt	11.3	13.6
			.4	1.1		Deferred Taxes	1.0	.5
			3.9	5.1		All Other Non-Current	4.2	1.5
			37.7	43.9		Net Worth	26.4	29.4
			100.0	100.0		Total Liabilities & Net Worth	100.0	100.0
						INCOME DATA		
			100.0	100.0		Net Sales	100.0	100.0
			9.8	16.8		Gross Profit	16.4	16.6
			7.7	10.8		Operating Expenses	12.3	11.4
			2.1	6.0		Operating Profit	4.1	5.2
			.3	-.8		All Other Expenses (net)	.8	1.1
			1.8	6.8		Profit Before Taxes	3.3	4.1
						RATIOS		
			2.9	5.2			2.2	2.1
			1.5	1.6		Current	1.3	1.5
			1.0	1.2			1.0	1.0
			1.2	1.8			1.0	1.2
			.6	1.0		Quick	.7	.8
			.5	.2			.4	.3
		17 21.1	4 85.1			Sales/Receivables	24 15.2	18 20.7
		36 10.2	23 16.0				35 10.4	37 9.9
		47 7.7	64 5.7				49 7.4	48 7.5
		25 14.8	29 12.6			Cost of Sales/Inventory	24 15.2	23 15.7
		43 8.4	40 9.2				48 7.7	45 8.0
		63 5.8	78 4.7				87 4.2	74 4.9
		6 59.9	1 308.4			Cost of Sales/Payables	15 24.4	15 24.1
		21 17.8	23 16.0				33 10.9	25 14.7
		42 8.7	60 6.1				49 7.4	48 7.6
			6.1	4.4		Sales/Working Capital	7.7	8.1
			13.5	7.6			16.2	19.1
			521.1	26.5			-237.1	-814.3
			20.0	126.7		EBIT/Interest	15.5	11.1
			(24) 2.5	12.0			(59) 3.7	(53) 6.3
			-.6	6.0			1.4	1.9
			4.3			Net Profit + Depr., Dep.,	13.0	12.7
			(10) .8			Amort./Cur. Mat. L/T/D	(27) 2.7	(19) 3.8
			-.3				1.3	1.4
			.1	.1		Fixed/Worth	.4	.2
			.6	.3			.8	.5
			1.4	.7			2.4	1.9
			.6	.7		Debt/Worth	1.3	1.0
			1.7	1.8			3.0	2.1
			3.9	4.6			6.9	8.8
			51.7	43.4		% Profit Before Taxes/Tangible	49.8	68.2
			(23) 16.7	22.0		Net Worth	(57) 29.3	(49) 36.7
			-6.5	18.0			6.1	15.0
			15.2	17.7		% Profit Before Taxes/Total	17.2	23.1
			4.7	12.1		Assets	6.4	9.0
			-5.5	4.1			1.1	3.4
			71.8	129.2		Sales/Net Fixed Assets	37.0	71.7
			15.2	32.5			14.9	24.0
			7.7	7.3			6.9	9.9
			4.0	5.2		Sales/Total Assets	3.7	4.5
			3.0	2.6			2.5	3.4
			2.1	1.3			1.7	2.3
			.4			% Depr., Dep., Amort./Sales	.4	.3
			(22) .8				(59) .9	(51) 1.1
			2.5				2.3	1.9
						% Officers', Directors'	.5	.4
						Owners' Comp/Sales	(17) 1.4	(17) 1.3
							4.1	4.4
2041M	11478M	64704M	2053895M	2857952M	1011277M	Net Sales ($)	4951848M	5135752M
305M	5520M	23799M	564528M	802949M	547176M	Total Assets ($)	1922003M	1796972M

M = $ thousand   MM = $ million
See Pages 9 through 22 for Explanation of Ratios and Data

Comparative Historical Data				Current Data Sorted by Sales					
			Type of Statement						
17	16	17	Unqualified		1		1	1	14
7	8	7	Reviewed						7
6	1	2	Compiled		1	1			
7	2	2	Tax Returns		1	1			
25	17	21	Other			2	1	4	14
4/1/07-3/31/08 ALL	4/1/08-3/31/09 ALL	4/1/09-3/31/10 ALL			9 (4/1-9/30/09)		40 (10/1/09-3/31/10)		
				0-1MM	1-3MM	3-5MM	5-10MM	10-25MM	25MM & OVER
62	44	49	**NUMBER OF STATEMENTS**		3	4	2	5	35
%	%	%	**ASSETS**	%	%	%	%	%	%
8.0	11.4	9.2	Cash & Equivalents	DATA NOT AVAILABLE					8.8
25.6	25.7	24.3	Trade Receivables (net)						25.3
32.2	35.6	31.5	Inventory						37.6
4.2	1.7	4.0	All Other Current						5.2
70.0	74.4	68.9	Total Current						76.8
19.8	17.6	21.3	Fixed Assets (net)						16.3
2.3	2.2	2.7	Intangibles (net)						1.9
7.9	5.8	7.1	All Other Non-Current						5.0
100.0	100.0	100.0	Total						100.0
			LIABILITIES						
16.0	20.6	17.8	Notes Payable-Short Term						18.5
2.3	1.5	2.9	Cur. Mat.-L.T.D.						1.7
17.9	15.8	17.3	Trade Payables						17.3
.4	.4	.2	Income Taxes Payable						.3
13.1	9.0	11.2	All Other Current						10.4
49.8	47.1	49.6	Total Current						48.2
12.4	8.2	9.8	Long-Term Debt						6.8
.4	.6	.5	Deferred Taxes						.6
2.8	3.8	4.6	All Other Non-Current						5.1
34.6	40.2	35.5	Net Worth						39.3
100.0	100.0	100.0	Total Liabilties & Net Worth						100.0
			INCOME DATA						
100.0	100.0	100.0	Net Sales						100.0
18.9	13.8	16.7	Gross Profit						11.4
12.6	9.3	13.3	Operating Expenses						8.4
6.2	4.5	3.4	Operating Profit						3.0
.7	.6	.0	All Other Expenses (net)						-.2
5.6	4.0	3.4	Profit Before Taxes						3.2
			RATIOS						
2.5	2.1	2.6							3.5
1.4	1.5	1.5	Current						1.7
1.1	1.2	1.1							1.3
1.2	1.1	1.3							1.3
.7	.8	.7	Quick						.8
.4	.5	.5							.5
14 26.2	**15** 24.3	**20** 18.6							**14** 26.2
35 10.5	**24** 15.4	**36** 10.2	Sales/Receivables						**28** 13.1
44 8.4	**39** 9.5	**53** 6.9							**47** 7.7
16 22.4	**16** 22.6	**26** 14.0							**27** 13.7
36 10.1	**38** 9.5	**43** 8.4	Cost of Sales/Inventory						**43** 8.4
66 5.5	**63** 5.8	**69** 5.3							**66** 5.5
8 46.0	**9** 40.0	**10** 35.1							**5** 70.2
24 15.1	**15** 24.1	**24** 15.4	Cost of Sales/Payables						**23** 16.2
43 8.5	**33** 11.0	**43** 8.5							**39** 9.3
6.9	8.7	5.0							5.1
16.4	15.9	13.1	Sales/Working Capital						12.8
50.7	51.5	86.1							26.7
19.5	15.2	18.4							25.7
(57) 6.6	(43) 6.3	(47) 4.0	EBIT/Interest						(34) 6.2
3.1	1.9	-.4							.5
12.5	11.0	10.9							11.9
(14) 6.2	(20) 5.7	(16) 1.6	Net Profit + Depr., Dep., Amort./Cur. Mat. L/T/D						(14) 2.6
2.7	2.5	.2							.1
.2	.2	.2							.1
.4	.4	.5	Fixed/Worth						.4
1.2	1.1	1.3							.8
1.0	.9	.7							.6
2.2	1.7	2.0	Debt/Worth						1.6
4.1	4.3	5.7							3.8
69.3	66.7	46.7							49.2
(58) 35.0	(43) 33.6	(43) 20.5	% Profit Before Taxes/Tangible Net Worth						(33) 21.3
20.5	6.2	-.2							9.0
21.7	20.1	16.8							17.6
12.1	10.9	6.5	% Profit Before Taxes/Total Assets						7.9
5.8	2.9	-2.6							-.1
85.3	77.4	55.0							74.1
34.4	31.8	14.7	Sales/Net Fixed Assets						25.0
7.5	11.5	6.8							8.4
4.6	5.9	3.9							4.1
3.3	3.4	2.7	Sales/Total Assets						3.0
1.7	2.2	1.5							2.1
.2	.3	.4							.3
(55) .6	(41) .5	(44) 1.2	% Depr., Dep., Amort./Sales						(31) .6
2.4	1.4	3.0							1.9
1.1	.4								
(17) 2.0	(13) 1.6		% Officers', Directors' Owners' Comp/Sales						
5.4	3.0								
5777088M	6628877M	6001347M	Net Sales ($)		6112M	15625M	16186M	72760M	5890664M
1827655M	1748066M	1944277M	Total Assets ($)		3148M	10336M	99975M	50344M	1780474M

M = $ thousand MM = $ million

See Pages 9 through 22 for Explanation of Ratios and Data

Current Data Sorted by Assets　　　　　　　　　　　**Comparative Historical Data**

0-500M	500M-2MM	2-10MM	10-50MM	50-100MM	100-250MM	Type of Statement	4/1/05-3/31/06 ALL	4/1/06-3/31/07 ALL
		2	8	1	2	Unqualified	20	20
	2	7	2			Reviewed	14	15
	2	3	1			Compiled	10	10
	1					Tax Returns	3	2
1	2	4	13	4	3	Other	22	23
	16 (4/1-9/30/09)		42 (10/1/09-3/31/10)					
1	7	16	24	5	5	**NUMBER OF STATEMENTS**	69	70
%	%	%	%	%	%	**ASSETS**	%	%
		7.5	6.0			Cash & Equivalents	6.9	8.2
		21.9	19.0			Trade Receivables (net)	29.1	26.4
		25.4	18.0			Inventory	18.3	18.2
		1.2	6.8			All Other Current	1.4	2.3
		56.0	49.8			Total Current	55.8	55.1
		35.5	40.7			Fixed Assets (net)	34.4	35.7
		3.7	2.5			Intangibles (net)	3.3	3.5
		4.7	7.0			All Other Non-Current	6.5	5.7
		100.0	100.0			Total	100.0	100.0
						LIABILITIES		
		14.3	7.5			Notes Payable-Short Term	9.0	7.7
		5.4	3.0			Cur. Mat.-L.T.D.	3.2	3.5
		11.7	8.9			Trade Payables	15.0	15.9
		.0	.1			Income Taxes Payable	.2	.4
		6.4	7.3			All Other Current	9.0	6.0
		37.9	26.8			Total Current	36.5	33.5
		15.1	12.3			Long-Term Debt	16.2	17.3
		.3	2.0			Deferred Taxes	1.3	1.4
		3.3	9.1			All Other Non-Current	5.4	3.4
		43.5	49.9			Net Worth	40.6	44.3
		100.0	100.0			Total Liabilities & Net Worth	100.0	100.0
						INCOME DATA		
		100.0	100.0			Net Sales	100.0	100.0
		21.0	19.8			Gross Profit	21.6	22.2
		20.7	16.6			Operating Expenses	15.1	15.7
		.3	3.2			Operating Profit	6.5	6.5
		1.1	.4			All Other Expenses (net)	1.0	1.0
		-.7	2.8			Profit Before Taxes	5.4	5.5
						RATIOS		
		3.0	3.9				2.5	2.5
		1.4	2.2			Current	1.5	1.7
		.9	1.1				1.2	1.1
		1.8	2.0				1.5	1.7
		.8	.8			Quick	.9	1.1
		.4	.5				.7	.7
		36　10.0	41　8.9				39　9.4	39　9.4
		44　8.4	45　8.1			Sales/Receivables	47　7.8	45　8.1
		48　7.6	51　7.2				54　6.7	54　6.7
		26　14.1	24　15.5				22　16.6	20　18.2
		57　6.4	37　9.8			Cost of Sales/Inventory	30　12.0	33　11.0
		86　4.3	80　4.6				51　7.2	62　5.9
		13　27.4	16　23.5				20　18.2	19　18.7
		26　13.9	21　17.2			Cost of Sales/Payables	28　13.1	31　11.9
		41　8.9	29　12.4				38　9.7	39　9.2
		5.3	3.1				7.4	5.4
		12.8	5.8			Sales/Working Capital	13.2	10.8
		NM	186.2				38.4	40.7
		4.6	14.1				11.9	12.6
		(15) .5	(21) 2.5			EBIT/Interest	(62) 5.5	(66) 4.0
		-1.3	-.3				2.4	2.7
							7.3	6.8
						Net Profit + Depr., Dep., Amort./Cur. Mat. L/T/D	(25) 3.0	(33) 3.8
							2.0	1.7
		.4	.4				.5	.5
		1.1	.8			Fixed/Worth	1.1	.9
		8.0	1.9				2.4	1.6
		.4	.4				.6	.6
		1.3	.8			Debt/Worth	1.7	1.2
		13.2	2.8				5.0	3.2
		8.5	20.8				41.7	47.2
		(15) .7	(23) 12.4			% Profit Before Taxes/Tangible Net Worth	(63) 21.0	(63) 23.1
		-105.4	-1.6				7.9	10.0
		4.3	10.5				17.1	17.4
		-.3	3.6			% Profit Before Taxes/Total Assets	8.2	8.9
		-4.6	-2.3				4.0	3.8
		8.8	6.1				10.2	9.4
		6.0	4.6			Sales/Net Fixed Assets	6.6	6.1
		2.6	3.2				4.3	3.6
		2.2	1.8				3.0	2.7
		1.7	1.5			Sales/Total Assets	2.2	2.1
		1.5	1.1				1.6	1.5
		1.6	2.6				1.6	1.5
		(15) 3.0	4.0			% Depr., Dep., Amort./Sales	(64) 2.4	(64) 2.4
		5.2	5.1				3.5	4.1
							.7	1.2
						% Officers', Directors' Owners' Comp/Sales	(16) 1.8	(19) 2.0
							7.5	5.4
1189M	23098M	136201M	703043M	355366M	817726M	Net Sales ($)	2376650M	2812039M
459M	8702M	75670M	471064M	456684M	808010M	Total Assets ($)	1257663M	1887142M

© RMA 2010　　　　　　　　M = $ thousand　　MM = $ million
See Pages 9 through 22 for Explanation of Ratios and Data

Comparative Historical Data | Current Data Sorted by Sales

			Type of Statement	0-1MM	1-3MM	3-5MM	5-10MM	10-25MM	25MM & OVER
19	20	13	Unqualified					3	10
13	15	11	Reviewed		1	4	3	3	
8	4	6	Compiled		1	1	3	1	
2	2	1	Tax Returns				1		
31	20	27	Other	1	2	1	2	9	12
4/1/07-3/31/08 ALL	4/1/08-3/31/09 ALL	4/1/09-3/31/10 ALL			16 (4/1-9/30/09)			42 (10/1/09-3/31/10)	
73	61	58	**NUMBER OF STATEMENTS**	1	4	6	9	16	22
%	%	%	**ASSETS**	%	%	%	%	%	%
8.2	8.7	7.6	Cash & Equivalents					8.2	7.2
26.0	24.9	21.2	Trade Receivables (net)					19.0	18.0
16.9	18.8	18.2	Inventory					25.6	13.5
2.0	1.9	3.5	All Other Current					6.9	3.7
53.1	54.3	50.5	Total Current					59.7	42.4
36.2	36.1	36.9	Fixed Assets (net)					35.3	35.8
5.0	3.9	4.3	Intangibles (net)					.2	8.6
5.6	5.8	8.2	All Other Non-Current					4.8	13.2
100.0	100.0	100.0	Total					100.0	100.0
			LIABILITIES						
7.8	10.3	10.6	Notes Payable-Short Term					9.3	7.1
3.6	3.5	4.4	Cur. Mat.-L.T.D.					2.7	3.7
13.9	14.2	11.0	Trade Payables					7.8	10.0
.3	.2	.1	Income Taxes Payable					.1	.2
7.4	6.1	7.9	All Other Current					7.8	5.8
32.9	34.3	34.1	Total Current					27.7	26.9
16.2	14.2	13.9	Long-Term Debt					9.7	14.9
1.2	1.2	1.0	Deferred Taxes					1.5	1.5
6.8	4.7	6.2	All Other Non-Current					9.2	8.3
42.9	45.6	44.8	Net Worth					52.0	48.4
100.0	100.0	100.0	Total Liabilities & Net Worth					100.0	100.0
			INCOME DATA						
100.0	100.0	100.0	Net Sales					100.0	100.0
21.9	17.7	20.6	Gross Profit					21.0	19.6
15.9	12.6	19.6	Operating Expenses					17.6	17.7
6.0	5.0	1.0	Operating Profit					3.3	1.9
1.3	1.1	1.5	All Other Expenses (net)					.5	2.6
4.7	3.9	-.5	Profit Before Taxes					2.8	-.7
			RATIOS						
2.5	2.9	3.5	Current					4.0	3.8
1.6	1.6	1.8						2.5	1.9
1.1	1.1	1.0						1.4	1.0
1.8	1.7	1.8	Quick					2.0	2.2
1.1	1.0	.8						1.1	.8
.7	.7	.5						.5	.7
38 9.6	32 11.4	38 9.5	Sales/Receivables					38 9.6	38 9.6
46 7.9	42 8.7	44 8.3						43 8.4	44 8.2
55 6.6	57 6.5	53 6.9						46 7.9	55 6.7
19 19.3	21 17.7	25 14.4	Cost of Sales/Inventory					27 13.8	28 12.8
32 11.6	33 11.2	45 8.2						65 5.6	47 7.7
59 6.2	62 5.9	70 5.2						125 2.9	68 5.4
18 20.4	14 25.9	15 24.9	Cost of Sales/Payables					13 28.5	18 20.8
29 12.7	27 13.8	21 17.2						17 21.2	24 15.3
40 9.1	34 10.8	36 10.1						27 13.3	37 9.9
5.9	5.4	3.3	Sales/Working Capital					2.6	3.2
11.1	11.4	10.5						4.8	9.5
67.2	50.5	-193.3						14.3	NM
13.9	13.1	4.9	EBIT/Interest					9.4	9.4
(65) 4.2	(57) 4.3	(50) 1.4						(14) 1.5	(17) 2.5
1.3	1.5	-1.3						-1.3	-1.0
10.2	9.7	4.7	Net Profit + Depr., Dep., Amort./Cur. Mat. L/T/D						
(31) 3.3	(24) 3.0	(16) 2.9							
1.5	.8	.9							
.5	.4	.4	Fixed/Worth					.3	.4
.9	1.0	.9						.7	.7
2.7	1.8	3.3						1.4	4.3
.7	.4	.4	Debt/Worth					.4	.2
1.3	1.2	1.1						.9	.8
3.9	3.7	8.4						1.4	6.5
36.7	34.4	19.5	% Profit Before Taxes/Tangible Net Worth					21.2	19.2
(66) 17.5	(57) 16.9	(52) 3.0						10.3	(18) 5.0
5.0	3.3	-10.5						-11.5	-3.4
16.6	15.3	8.9	% Profit Before Taxes/Total Assets					12.0	8.8
7.4	5.1	.7						5.0	1.1
1.9	1.4	-6.3						-5.2	-3.7
10.5	10.2	7.7	Sales/Net Fixed Assets					7.8	5.7
5.3	6.2	4.8						4.6	4.7
3.2	3.8	2.6						3.2	2.1
2.5	2.5	2.0	Sales/Total Assets					1.8	2.0
2.0	2.0	1.6						1.5	1.6
1.3	1.4	1.0						1.2	.8
1.7	1.5	1.7	% Depr., Dep., Amort./Sales					1.2	2.9
(63) 2.6	(57) 2.7	(52) 3.7						3.3	(18) 4.2
4.2	4.0	5.2						4.9	5.2
1.3	.8	1.4	% Officers', Directors' Owners' Comp/Sales						
(18) 2.5	(14) 1.9	(15) 3.3							
5.3	5.9	5.3							
4116715M	2743167M	2036623M	Net Sales ($)	838M	7375M	23098M	63467M	272235M	1669610M
2470641M	1810612M	1820589M	Total Assets ($)	682M	5793M	12125M	50327M	195891M	1555771M

M = $ thousand   MM = $ million
See Pages 9 through 22 for Explanation of Ratios and Data

Current Data Sorted by Assets

Comparative Historical Data

0-500M	500M-2MM	2-10MM	10-50MM	50-100MM	100-250MM	Type of Statement	4/1/05-3/31/06 ALL	4/1/06-3/31/07 ALL
		2	4	1	2	Unqualified	14	13
	2	10	2			Reviewed	20	17
1	2	4	1			Compiled	10	9
		1				Tax Returns	1	5
	1 8 (4/1-9/30/09)	6	3 38 (10/1/09-3/31/10)	1	3	Other	22	26
1	5	23	10	2	5	**NUMBER OF STATEMENTS**	67	70
%	%	%	%	%	%	**ASSETS**	%	%
		6.7	14.9			Cash & Equivalents	5.2	7.3
		30.5	18.0			Trade Receivables (net)	32.3	34.1
		25.2	38.0			Inventory	24.5	21.3
		1.9	2.5			All Other Current	3.6	3.4
		64.3	73.5			Total Current	65.6	66.2
		29.5	23.0			Fixed Assets (net)	28.2	27.3
		2.5	.4			Intangibles (net)	1.6	3.0
		3.7	3.2			All Other Non-Current	4.6	3.6
		100.0	100.0			Total	100.0	100.0
						LIABILITIES		
		12.8	8.7			Notes Payable-Short Term	14.2	12.0
		4.0	1.8			Cur. Mat.-L.T.D.	2.3	3.0
		18.4	10.9			Trade Payables	18.2	22.4
		.1	.0			Income Taxes Payable	.2	.2
		6.3	12.8			All Other Current	9.7	11.1
		41.6	34.3			Total Current	44.7	48.7
		9.5	5.2			Long-Term Debt	12.0	14.6
		.1	.1			Deferred Taxes	.4	.4
		12.4	11.3			All Other Non-Current	6.6	5.5
		36.4	49.1			Net Worth	36.4	30.8
		100.0	100.0			Total Liabilities & Net Worth	100.0	100.0
						INCOME DATA		
		100.0	100.0			Net Sales	100.0	100.0
		21.0	19.7			Gross Profit	22.6	23.7
		22.0	19.8			Operating Expenses	16.7	16.7
		-1.0	-.1			Operating Profit	6.0	7.1
		1.0	1.2			All Other Expenses (net)	1.0	1.0
		-2.0	-1.3			Profit Before Taxes	5.0	6.1
						RATIOS		
		2.6	5.1				2.1	1.9
		1.7	2.4			Current	1.5	1.5
		1.1	1.4				1.1	1.1
		1.8	2.9				1.1	1.3
		.9	1.0			Quick	.9	.9
		.6	.5				.6	.6
		47 7.7	26 14.3				37 9.8	41 9.0
		52 7.1	50 7.3			Sales/Receivables	47 7.7	48 7.6
		61 6.0	60 6.1				61 6.0	61 6.0
		27 13.4	56 6.5				21 17.1	13 27.7
		45 8.1	100 3.6			Cost of Sales/Inventory	47 7.7	36 10.3
		95 3.8	129 2.8				62 5.9	56 6.5
		22 16.9	10 35.8				25 14.7	24 15.2
		32 11.6	21 17.4			Cost of Sales/Payables	34 10.8	36 10.2
		53 6.8	46 7.9				43 8.4	49 7.5
		4.4	1.8				6.1	6.6
		7.7	3.3			Sales/Working Capital	11.0	12.7
		34.4	10.5				45.8	50.5
		7.8	14.0				13.9	13.6
		(21) 3.0	1.1			EBIT/Interest	(65) 5.2	(66) 6.0
		-1.5	-16.8				2.0	2.3
							5.7	18.1
						Net Profit + Depr., Dep., Amort./Cur. Mat. L/T/D	(16) 3.6	(21) 5.7
							2.0	2.7
		.4	.2				.3	.4
		.6	.4			Fixed/Worth	.7	.8
		3.3	.8				1.2	1.7
		.6	.6				1.1	1.0
		1.7	1.1			Debt/Worth	1.8	1.8
		4.4	1.7				3.5	6.3
		17.6	22.8				60.4	61.1
		(21) 7.2	.8			% Profit Before Taxes/Tangible Net Worth	(64) 24.6	(64) 39.1
		-11.6	-22.3				7.0	11.9
		5.6	8.8				19.7	20.7
		2.1	.3			% Profit Before Taxes/Total Assets	8.6	10.5
		-6.0	-7.9				2.3	4.7
		21.2	12.5				26.0	20.4
		7.6	6.5			Sales/Net Fixed Assets	9.0	10.4
		3.6	5.1				5.0	5.1
		2.8	1.9				2.9	2.9
		1.9	1.7			Sales/Total Assets	2.4	2.4
		1.5	.9				1.7	1.8
		.9					.9	.9
		2.6				% Depr., Dep., Amort./Sales	(55) 1.8	(63) 1.7
		4.0					3.5	3.0
							1.7	1.4
						% Officers', Directors' Owners' Comp/Sales	(18) 2.8	(18) 3.3
							5.6	4.0
581M	21578M	255122M	325502M	484439M	1033651M	Net Sales ($)	3794054M	4018832M
198M	7599M	127902M	243986M	126664M	623989M	Total Assets ($)	1878827M	1998727M

© RMA 2010

M = $ thousand   MM = $ million
See Pages 9 through 22 for Explanation of Ratios and Data

Comparative Historical Data | Current Data Sorted by Sales

			Type of Statement						
8	10	9	Unqualified				1	2	6
13	14	14	Reviewed				5	4	3
5	7	8	Compiled			2	5		1
2	2	1	Tax Returns					1	
12	18	14	Other	1	1		4	2	7
4/1/07-3/31/08 ALL	4/1/08-3/31/09 ALL	4/1/09-3/31/10 ALL		0-1MM	1-3MM	3-5MM	5-10MM	10-25MM	25MM & OVER
	8 (4/1-9/30/09)						38 (10/1/09-3/31/10)		
40	51	46	NUMBER OF STATEMENTS	1	2	2	15	9	17
%	%	%	**ASSETS**	%	%	%	%	%	%
7.3	7.2	9.2	Cash & Equivalents				10.1		11.5
27.6	30.1	27.8	Trade Receivables (net)				29.1		25.4
23.7	27.2	25.5	Inventory				22.0		26.8
2.8	2.8	2.4	All Other Current				.7		3.6
61.3	67.2	64.9	Total Current				61.8		67.4
32.6	25.0	28.7	Fixed Assets (net)				32.0		25.0
1.7	3.2	2.9	Intangibles (net)				3.9		4.3
4.4	4.5	3.5	All Other Non-Current				2.3		3.3
100.0	100.0	100.0	Total				100.0		100.0
			LIABILITIES						
9.3	11.3	9.4	Notes Payable-Short Term				9.1		7.5
2.7	2.5	3.8	Cur. Mat.-L.T.D.				5.0		3.5
15.4	16.9	16.5	Trade Payables				16.2		16.6
.1	.2	.1	Income Taxes Payable				.2		.0
13.1	10.9	8.7	All Other Current				6.0		13.9
40.6	41.8	38.4	Total Current				36.6		41.6
16.6	11.6	12.7	Long-Term Debt				10.7		11.8
.5	.4	.1	Deferred Taxes				.0		.2
5.2	9.1	13.6	All Other Non-Current				14.4		14.0
37.2	37.1	35.2	Net Worth				38.4		32.4
100.0	100.0	100.0	Total Liabilties & Net Worth				100.0		100.0
			INCOME DATA						
100.0	100.0	100.0	Net Sales				100.0		100.0
24.1	21.0	20.8	Gross Profit				23.3		14.2
17.6	17.0	20.6	Operating Expenses				25.5		11.6
6.5	4.0	.1	Operating Profit				-2.1		2.7
1.1	.7	1.2	All Other Expenses (net)				.8		1.2
5.4	3.3	-1.1	Profit Before Taxes				-3.0		1.5
			RATIOS						
2.3	2.6	2.9	Current				2.9		3.3
1.6	1.6	1.8					1.8		1.6
1.1	1.2	1.1					1.1		1.1
1.4	1.4	1.9	Quick				2.1		1.8
.9	.9	1.0					1.1		.8
.6	.6	.6					.6		.6
34 10.6	33 11.0	35 10.3	Sales/Receivables				47 7.7	30 12.4	
43 8.5	44 8.4	51 7.2					52 7.1	47 7.7	
52 7.0	58 6.3	58 6.3					61 6.0	57 6.4	
17 21.0	22 16.7	27 13.7	Cost of Sales/Inventory				29 12.6	26 14.0	
40 9.0	46 7.9	48 7.6					43 8.5	52 7.1	
82 4.4	72 5.1	96 3.8					57 6.4	98 3.7	
16 22.1	13 28.4	17 21.8	Cost of Sales/Payables				14 26.3	15 25.0	
30 12.3	27 13.4	27 13.3					32 11.6	25 14.6	
38 9.5	44 8.3	48 7.6					53 6.8	42 8.7	
6.1	5.8	4.2	Sales/Working Capital				4.2		4.5
9.4	8.5	7.9					6.9		10.0
28.1	31.5	27.9					79.9		69.2
16.7	14.0	7.0	EBIT/Interest				10.3		6.6
(38) 4.2	(46) 4.4	(43) 2.6					(13) 3.0	(16) 2.7	
2.1	1.8	-2.8					-2.4		-4.4
7.3	11.5	5.0	Net Profit + Depr., Dep., Amort./Cur. Mat. L/T/D						
(12) 4.4	(13) 2.4	(13) 1.0							
2.6	1.6	-.3							
.4	.4	.3	Fixed/Worth				.4		.2
.8	.7	.6					.6		.7
1.9	1.4	2.1					6.1		1.7
.8	.8	.6	Debt/Worth				.4		.8
1.7	1.8	1.5					1.6		1.5
3.7	4.2	4.9					20.8		10.1
52.8	53.4	19.3	% Profit Before Taxes/Tangible Net Worth				13.9		32.1
(37) 25.8	(45) 28.0	(40) 5.9					(13) 2.9	(14) 8.2	
9.0	2.3	-11.6					-15.6		-12.7
18.0	16.7	6.6	% Profit Before Taxes/Total Assets				5.6		8.9
8.5	8.3	2.0					1.8		3.8
3.0	1.7	-5.5					-6.0		-5.8
12.5	21.7	16.1	Sales/Net Fixed Assets				16.4		75.1
7.7	11.2	7.2					10.2		6.8
5.6	6.1	4.7					3.1		5.4
3.0	3.2	2.8	Sales/Total Assets				2.7		2.6
2.6	2.4	1.8					1.9		1.8
1.8	1.8	1.5					1.4		1.5
1.0	.7	.9	% Depr., Dep., Amort./Sales				.9		.4
(38) 1.9	(47) 1.3	(43) 2.4					2.4	(14) 1.4	
3.2	2.7	3.6					4.2		3.4
3.2	.6	2.2	% Officers', Directors' Owners' Comp/Sales						
(11) 4.0	(12) 2.0	(10) 3.8							
6.1	4.3	4.9							
2269488M	2662556M	2120873M	Net Sales ($)	581M	4229M	9644M	113023M	136304M	1857092M
1128733M	1275243M	1130338M	Total Assets ($)	198M	2711M	3420M	63756M	106255M	953998M

M = $ thousand   MM = $ million
See Pages 9 through 22 for Explanation of Ratios and Data

Current Data Sorted by Assets | Comparative Historical Data

Type of Statement	0-500M	500M-2MM	2-10MM	10-50MM	50-100MM	100-250MM	4/1/05-3/31/06 ALL	4/1/06-3/31/07 ALL
Unqualified			1	3	3	3	13	10
Reviewed		1	6	4	1		9	18
Compiled		4	5	3			14	10
Tax Returns	1	2	1				6	5
Other		1	7			1	20	16
	10 (4/1-9/30/09)			44 (10/1/09-3/31/10)				
NUMBER OF STATEMENTS	1	8	20	17	4	4	62	59
ASSETS	%	%	%	%	%	%	%	%
Cash & Equivalents			11.4	7.9			6.2	5.4
Trade Receivables (net)			22.3	22.6			29.1	31.5
Inventory			22.0	15.0			17.3	19.7
All Other Current			3.3	3.5			1.9	1.2
Total Current			58.9	49.0			54.5	57.7
Fixed Assets (net)			32.9	39.7			34.4	33.9
Intangibles (net)			3.0	2.6			5.8	2.8
All Other Non-Current			5.1	8.7			5.3	5.6
Total			100.0	100.0			100.0	100.0
LIABILITIES								
Notes Payable-Short Term			12.6	6.7			9.7	7.9
Cur. Mat.-L.T.D.			4.3	4.1			3.5	3.9
Trade Payables			12.8	14.6			17.7	16.3
Income Taxes Payable			.0	.1			.1	.2
All Other Current			13.0	10.0			9.4	9.7
Total Current			42.7	35.4			40.4	37.9
Long-Term Debt			20.9	19.4			23.0	18.1
Deferred Taxes			.4	1.5			.6	.5
All Other Non-Current			5.0	4.5			8.3	5.3
Net Worth			31.0	39.3			27.7	38.2
Total Liabilities & Net Worth			100.0	100.0			100.0	100.0
INCOME DATA								
Net Sales			100.0	100.0			100.0	100.0
Gross Profit			21.6	13.8			21.7	19.5
Operating Expenses			18.6	12.9			16.4	15.7
Operating Profit			3.0	.9			5.3	3.8
All Other Expenses (net)			2.4	.9			1.4	1.0
Profit Before Taxes			.6	.0			4.0	2.8
RATIOS								
Current			3.3	2.1			1.9	2.4
			1.6	1.3			1.4	1.5
			1.0	.9			1.0	1.2
Quick			1.8	1.5			1.3	1.7
			.8	.8			.8	.9
			.6	.4			.6	.6
Sales/Receivables			34 10.6	41 9.0			41 8.9	45 8.1
			51 7.2	57 6.4			53 6.9	57 6.4
			70 5.2	74 4.9			63 5.8	66 5.6
Cost of Sales/Inventory			33 11.0	28 13.0			20 18.4	24 15.5
			56 6.5	36 10.1			33 11.1	37 9.9
			105 3.5	59 6.1			56 6.5	61 6.0
Cost of Sales/Payables			13 28.3	20 18.2			21 17.0	18 20.4
			23 15.8	39 9.2			38 9.7	33 11.2
			42 8.7	60 6.1			59 6.1	51 7.2
Sales/Working Capital			4.3	5.4			6.7	5.5
			7.6	14.3			15.1	10.4
			NM	NM			-115.7	30.4
EBIT/Interest			4.9	9.5			9.1	8.2
			.8	1.6			(58) 3.2	(53) 3.0
			-1.6	-.2			1.4	.9
Net Profit + Depr., Dep., Amort./Cur. Mat. L/T/D							6.2	9.9
							(25) 1.7	(20) 3.6
							.5	.5
Fixed/Worth			.4	.4			.5	.4
			1.1	1.2			1.7	.9
			3.2	10.9			28.4	2.0
Debt/Worth			.5	.5			.9	.8
			1.9	1.6			3.4	1.4
			10.9	23.3			51.7	3.8
% Profit Before Taxes/Tangible Net Worth			29.1	7.7			56.0	35.2
			(16) 5.7	(14) 3.0			(48) 24.8	(53) 15.7
			-6.5	-3.6			3.8	1.8
% Profit Before Taxes/Total Assets			5.3	3.6			14.6	12.5
			-.2	.9			6.0	5.2
			-4.5	-3.0			1.0	.0
Sales/Net Fixed Assets			16.7	5.6			9.6	13.1
			3.4	3.0			5.8	7.3
			2.3	2.6			3.5	3.4
Sales/Total Assets			2.2	1.7			2.6	2.4
			1.5	1.5			1.8	2.0
			1.0	1.2			1.4	1.7
% Depr., Dep., Amort./Sales			2.4	2.9			1.5	1.4
			(17) 4.4	(14) 3.9			(53) 2.7	(54) 2.4
			6.7	5.7			4.2	4.3
% Officers', Directors' Owners' Comp/Sales							1.6	1.4
							(31) 2.8	(27) 1.9
							5.0	3.7
Net Sales ($)	731M	22776M	168164M	570812M	246693M	954440M	2090379M	2392127M
Total Assets ($)	326M	10802M	111045M	403779M	255788M	677151M	1175249M	1340437M

© RMA 2010

M = $ thousand   MM = $ million
See Pages 9 through 22 for Explanation of Ratios and Data

Comparative Historical Data | Current Data Sorted by Sales

4/1/07-3/31/08 ALL	4/1/08-3/31/09 ALL	4/1/09-3/31/10 ALL	Type of Statement	0-1MM	1-3MM	3-5MM	5-10MM	10-25MM	25MM & OVER
							10 (4/1-9/30/09)	44 (10/1/09-3/31/10)	
11	12	10	Unqualified				3	1	8
16	11	12	Reviewed		1		5	3	3
9	10	12	Compiled		2	2	1	3	
2	4	4	Tax Returns	1	1	2			
22	16	16	Other			4	2	4	8
60	53	54	**NUMBER OF STATEMENTS**	1	4	8	11	11	19
%	%	%	**ASSETS**	%	%	%	%	%	%
7.1	8.0	10.3	Cash & Equivalents				9.7	18.9	8.0
29.8	25.7	22.4	Trade Receivables (net)				22.3	24.2	20.2
21.1	21.9	18.3	Inventory				18.1	20.3	15.1
1.6	2.1	3.4	All Other Current				6.0	1.3	2.8
59.7	57.8	54.4	Total Current				56.1	64.8	46.2
33.5	31.6	35.9	Fixed Assets (net)				32.5	23.6	45.9
.8	3.7	2.7	Intangibles (net)				5.2	2.3	1.5
5.9	6.9	7.1	All Other Non-Current				6.2	9.3	6.4
100.0	100.0	100.0	Total				100.0	100.0	100.0
			LIABILITIES						
9.6	11.7	8.5	Notes Payable-Short Term				11.5	7.5	6.0
3.1	3.7	3.9	Cur. Mat.-L.T.D.				3.9	1.7	4.6
16.2	15.1	12.5	Trade Payables				15.6	10.8	14.3
.2	.0	.1	Income Taxes Payable				.0	.0	.1
9.5	8.4	10.4	All Other Current				13.2	14.2	10.6
38.6	38.9	35.4	Total Current				44.2	34.2	35.6
16.4	17.0	21.1	Long-Term Debt				17.0	11.7	19.9
.6	.3	.8	Deferred Taxes				.7	.8	1.4
5.2	5.6	8.5	All Other Non-Current				4.3	4.1	8.5
39.2	38.2	34.1	Net Worth				33.8	49.3	34.7
100.0	100.0	100.0	Total Liabilities & Net Worth				100.0	100.0	100.0
			INCOME DATA						
100.0	100.0	100.0	Net Sales				100.0	100.0	100.0
21.1	17.6	19.9	Gross Profit				17.7	24.7	13.6
15.9	15.3	18.0	Operating Expenses				17.5	19.4	12.5
5.2	2.2	1.9	Operating Profit				.2	5.3	1.1
1.1	.9	1.6	All Other Expenses (net)				1.6	1.0	1.6
4.0	1.3	.3	Profit Before Taxes				-1.4	4.3	-.5
			RATIOS						
2.6	2.7	3.4	Current				2.5	4.3	2.0
1.6	1.7	1.6					1.3	2.3	1.3
1.0	1.1	1.1					1.0	1.5	.9
1.8	1.7	1.9	Quick				1.9	2.2	1.2
.9	.8	.9					.7	1.6	.8
.6	.6	.6					.5	.8	.4
40 9.2	31 11.7	38 9.6	Sales/Receivables				34 10.8	38 9.6	38 9.6
51 7.2	49 7.5	50 7.2					49 7.4	52 7.0	53 6.8
58 6.2	59 6.2	67 5.4					95 3.8	60 6.0	69 5.3
25 14.6	27 13.6	29 12.4	Cost of Sales/Inventory				30 12.3	31 11.7	27 13.7
43 8.5	36 10.0	48 7.6					41 8.9	50 7.2	36 10.1
68 5.4	57 6.4	81 4.5					80 4.6	98 3.7	70 5.2
15 24.2	15 24.3	15 23.8	Cost of Sales/Payables				14 25.3	12 29.3	19 19.6
31 11.8	23 15.8	29 12.8					30 12.3	21 17.7	39 9.3
46 7.9	42 8.6	48 7.7					51 7.2	49 7.4	58 6.3
5.7	5.2	4.9	Sales/Working Capital				5.2	3.4	6.2
9.5	11.3	7.8					7.5	5.5	19.5
103.1	40.6	31.2					74.0	10.9	-17.9
4.7	4.3	6.6	EBIT/Interest				4.3	41.0	11.6
(53) 2.4	(48) 2.0	(36) 1.9					1.8	6.4	1.0
1.2	-2.8	-.9					-2.0	-.7	-1.5
5.2	5.3	6.6	Net Profit + Depr., Dep., Amort./Cur. Mat. L/T/D						
(21) 3.0	(23) 1.3	(17) 2.7							
1.8	.2	.0							
.4	.3	.5	Fixed/Worth				.4	.1	.7
.9	.8	1.1					1.0	.6	1.3
2.1	2.4	2.6					2.5	1.1	2.4
.6	.5	.5	Debt/Worth				.3	.4	.9
1.6	1.3	1.8					2.2	.5	2.5
4.6	6.6	9.0					11.6	4.0	5.8
37.3	24.8	13.7	% Profit Before Taxes/Tangible Net Worth					29.1	8.8
(56) 13.6	(44) 9.8	(45) 3.9						(10) 3.0	(16) 2.0
5.4	-.6	-5.7						-5.0	-25.8
13.4	7.5	4.9	% Profit Before Taxes/Total Assets				3.5	15.3	5.8
5.4	3.3	1.5					1.5	2.2	-.1
1.2	-3.2	-4.9					-6.5	-2.2	-8.9
13.5	14.3	10.7	Sales/Net Fixed Assets				15.2	24.9	4.8
7.3	6.6	3.7					3.5	14.9	2.9
4.1	4.1	2.4					2.3	3.3	2.2
2.7	2.6	2.0	Sales/Total Assets				2.1	2.6	1.7
2.1	1.9	1.6					1.6	1.8	1.3
1.5	1.4	1.1					.8	1.3	.9
1.1	1.3	2.2	% Depr., Dep., Amort./Sales				3.3		2.9
(54) 2.4	(49) 2.4	(46) 3.7					4.4	(15)	5.4
4.3	4.0	5.9					6.3		6.3
1.9	1.4	1.9	% Officers', Directors' Owners' Comp/Sales						
(21) 2.6	(26) 3.8	(22) 3.7							
4.3	5.5	5.2							
2776002M	2180097M	1963616M	Net Sales ($)	731M	7455M	32426M	76577M	191272M	1655155M
1480244M	1297251M	1458891M	Total Assets ($)	326M	4499M	25526M	63556M	109807M	1255177M

© RMA 2010   M = $ thousand   MM = $ million
See Pages 9 through 22 for Explanation of Ratios and Data

Current Data Sorted by Assets   Comparative Historical Data

						Type of Statement	2	4
			1			Unqualified		
		5	3			Reviewed	10	7
	3	2	2			Compiled	7	9
1	1	7	6		1	Tax Returns	1	3
	12 (4/1-9/30/09)		19 (10/1/09-3/31/10)			Other	6	5
							4/1/05-3/31/06	4/1/06-3/31/07
0-500M	500M-2MM	2-10MM	10-50MM	50-100MM	100-250MM		ALL	ALL
1	4	14	11		1	NUMBER OF STATEMENTS	26	28
%	%	%	%	%	%	**ASSETS**	%	%
		8.3	9.4			Cash & Equivalents	7.2	7.1
		25.4	24.6			Trade Receivables (net)	28.5	29.6
		18.9	22.8			Inventory	22.1	23.7
		1.4	2.9			All Other Current	1.3	1.8
		54.0	59.7			Total Current	59.1	62.2
		32.9	25.0			Fixed Assets (net)	30.6	28.7
		1.5	6.4			Intangibles (net)	2.6	4.6
		11.6	8.8			All Other Non-Current	7.7	4.5
		100.0	100.0			Total	100.0	100.0
						LIABILITIES		
		10.5	13.3			Notes Payable-Short Term	17.6	8.9
		7.0	2.2			Cur. Mat.-L.T.D.	2.7	2.3
		12.3	10.7			Trade Payables	12.4	16.6
		.0	.4			Income Taxes Payable	.2	.1
		6.3	11.4			All Other Current	7.2	9.3
		36.2	37.9			Total Current	40.1	37.2
		29.2	10.1			Long-Term Debt	11.8	17.9
		.9	1.7			Deferred Taxes	.8	.7
		2.0	7.7			All Other Non-Current	6.5	3.4
		31.7	42.6			Net Worth	40.8	40.8
		100.0	100.0			Total Liabilities & Net Worth	100.0	100.0
						INCOME DATA		
		100.0	100.0			Net Sales	100.0	100.0
		22.9	19.7			Gross Profit	21.3	24.9
		21.1	23.8			Operating Expenses	18.1	20.6
		1.8	-4.1			Operating Profit	3.2	4.2
		1.2	1.5			All Other Expenses (net)	.6	.2
		.6	-5.6			Profit Before Taxes	2.6	4.0
						RATIOS		
		2.2	2.2				2.2	2.1
		1.5	1.8			Current	1.6	1.7
		1.1	.9				1.2	1.2
		1.6	1.5				1.5	1.4
		.9	.8			Quick	1.0	.9
		.5	.6				.6	.6
		43 8.5	44 8.2				41 8.8	38 9.6
		57 6.4	53 6.8			Sales/Receivables	48 7.6	48 7.7
		73 5.0	62 5.9				59 6.2	55 6.6
		24 15.5	27 13.4				27 13.6	24 15.2
		37 9.9	36 10.1			Cost of Sales/Inventory	34 10.7	40 9.1
		62 5.9	91 4.0				86 4.2	69 5.3
		20 18.1	19 18.9				10 36.5	16 22.6
		45 8.2	35 10.5			Cost of Sales/Payables	25 14.5	29 12.5
		59 6.2	39 9.3				43 8.6	46 7.9
		4.3	4.1				5.2	7.1
		10.3	6.7			Sales/Working Capital	11.1	11.4
		NM	-27.6				32.9	27.8
		1.7					10.1	16.0
		(13) 1.1				EBIT/Interest	(22) 2.9	(25) 5.2
		-2.8					.6	2.0
						Net Profit + Depr., Dep.,	4.3	
						Amort./Cur. Mat. L/T/D	(10) 2.5	
							-.3	
		.4	.2				.3	.3
		1.4	.7			Fixed/Worth	.8	.8
		2.1	2.0				3.4	3.3
		1.0	.6				.5	.7
		2.3	1.5			Debt/Worth	1.0	1.5
		5.6	3.9				4.6	3.9
		12.0	18.8			% Profit Before Taxes/Tangible	22.9	46.6
		(12) 2.6	(10) -.2			Net Worth	(22) 10.4	(24) 19.4
		-4.8	-27.7				-6.7	4.2
		1.9	8.1			% Profit Before Taxes/Total	11.4	14.3
		.8	-1.5			Assets	3.9	6.6
		-4.2	-16.7				-2.2	2.3
		12.8	16.9				12.0	19.3
		4.5	8.3			Sales/Net Fixed Assets	6.5	7.3
		2.2	3.2				3.6	4.1
		1.8	2.1				2.2	3.3
		1.5	1.4			Sales/Total Assets	1.8	2.1
		1.1	1.2				1.4	1.6
		.6					1.9	2.3
		(12) 2.6				% Depr., Dep., Amort./Sales	(24) 3.4	(24) 3.7
		5.3					5.5	5.2
						% Officers', Directors'	2.1	1.3
						Owners' Comp/Sales	(11) 2.9	(14) 3.1
							4.5	6.9
354M	11143M	95601M	367130M		231385M	Net Sales ($)	594204M	807298M
241M	4516M	66457M	243056M		121282M	Total Assets ($)	359565M	494930M

(Columns 50-100MM and 100-250MM on the current-data side: DATA NOT AVAILABLE)

M = $ thousand   MM = $ million
See Pages 9 through 22 for Explanation of Ratios and Data

Comparative Historical Data   **Current Data Sorted by Sales**

							Type of Statement						
	3		6		4		Unqualified				1	1	3
	11		7		7		Reviewed						1
	6		3		5		Compiled		3	1 2	5		
	1		1				Tax Returns						
	7		7		15		Other	1	1	3	2	3	5
	4/1/07-3/31/08 ALL		4/1/08-3/31/09 ALL		4/1/09-3/31/10 ALL				12 (4/1-9/30/09)		19 (10/1/09-3/31/10)		
								0-1MM	1-3MM	3-5MM	5-10MM	10-25MM	25MM & OVE
	28		24		31		NUMBER OF STATEMENTS	1	4	6	7	4	9
	%		%		%		ASSETS	%	%	%	%	%	%
	5.0		4.5		7.7		Cash & Equivalents						
	32.8		25.5		25.2		Trade Receivables (net)						
	24.1		25.0		20.6		Inventory						
	2.7		3.2		2.4		All Other Current						
	64.7		58.1		56.0		Total Current						
	27.1		28.8		31.6		Fixed Assets (net)						
	3.1		4.9		3.2		Intangibles (net)						
	5.1		8.1		9.2		All Other Non-Current						
	100.0		100.0		100.0		Total						
							LIABILITIES						
	8.8		14.5		12.5		Notes Payable-Short Term						
	2.8		3.6		5.1		Cur. Mat.-L.T.D.						
	14.0		15.4		12.4		Trade Payables						
	.4		.5		.2		Income Taxes Payable						
	11.3		10.0		9.5		All Other Current						
	37.3		44.1		39.6		Total Current						
	12.2		19.6		23.4		Long-Term Debt						
	.7		.6		1.0		Deferred Taxes						
	5.9		4.8		5.7		All Other Non-Current						
	43.8		31.0		30.3		Net Worth						
	100.0		100.0		100.0		Total Liabilties & Net Worth						
							INCOME DATA						
	100.0		100.0		100.0		Net Sales						
	23.2		22.5		22.8		Gross Profit						
	17.4		19.8		24.7		Operating Expenses						
	5.9		2.7		-1.9		Operating Profit						
	.9		.9		1.4		All Other Expenses (net)						
	4.9		1.8		-3.2		Profit Before Taxes						
							RATIOS						
	2.2		1.9		2.2								
	1.9		1.3		1.5		Current						
	1.5		1.0		1.0								
	1.4		1.0		1.1								
	1.0		.7		.8		Quick						
	.7		.5		.5								
40	9.1	32	11.5	44	8.2								
50	7.4	42	8.7	53	6.9		Sales/Receivables						
61	6.0	52	7.1	67	5.4								
27	13.6	26	14.1	22	16.3								
45	8.0	40	9.2	36	10.1		Cost of Sales/Inventory						
81	4.5	83	4.4	76	4.8								
19	19.2	21	17.1	20	18.1								
33	11.2	31	11.8	35	10.5		Cost of Sales/Payables						
44	8.3	38	9.6	54	6.8								
	4.8		8.8		4.3								
	8.1		17.5		10.3		Sales/Working Capital						
	13.5		NM		-127.9								
	15.1		7.4		7.0								
(27)	3.4	(22)	1.8	(27)	1.1		EBIT/Interest						
	.8		.4		-3.2								
					11.3								
		(10)			1.7		Net Profit + Depr., Dep., Amort./Cur. Mat. L/T/D						
					1.1								
	.3		.4		.5								
	.6		.8		1.3		Fixed/Worth						
	2.1		5.1		2.1								
	.6		1.4		.8								
	1.2		2.8		2.3		Debt/Worth						
	3.2		17.0		4.2								
	55.2		31.3		17.3		% Profit Before Taxes/Tangible Net Worth						
(24)	16.2	(19)	17.0	(26)	2.2								
	-.1		2.0		-5.7								
	21.6		9.6		4.4		% Profit Before Taxes/Total Assets						
	4.9		4.2		-.2								
	-.4		-2.2		-6.4								
	24.8		30.6		11.6									
	8.3		9.3		5.9		Sales/Net Fixed Assets						
	4.6		3.4		3.2								
	2.7		2.9		1.9								
	1.9		2.0		1.6		Sales/Total Assets						
	1.5		1.3		1.2								
	.7		.9		1.1								
(25)	2.4	(20)	2.1	(27)	2.6		% Depr., Dep., Amort./Sales						
	3.4		2.8		5.9								
			1.8		1.1								
		(10)	2.7	(11)	3.1		% Officers', Directors' Owners' Comp/Sales						
			5.4		4.6								
	765663M		1271467M		705613M		Net Sales ($)	354M	8015M	24455M	58648M	64789M	549352M
	401748M		488382M		435552M		Total Assets ($)	241M	6027M	16057M	46550M	65461M	301216M

M = $ thousand   MM = $ million
See Pages 9 through 22 for Explanation of Ratios and Data

Current Data Sorted by Assets   Comparative Historical Data

						Type of Statement		
	1	3				Unqualified	5	4
	1	6	4			Reviewed	10	8
2	1	1				Compiled	6	6
1	1	1				Tax Returns	2	1
	2	4	3			Other	12	13
	9 (4/1-9/30/09)		24 (10/1/09-3/31/10)				4/1/05-3/31/06	4/1/06-3/31/07
0-500M	500M-2MM	2-10MM	10-50MM	50-100MM	100-250MM		ALL	ALL
3	8	15	7			NUMBER OF STATEMENTS	35	32
%	%	%	%	%	%	ASSETS	%	%
		11.0				Cash & Equivalents	3.8	6.0
		24.6		D	D	Trade Receivables (net)	31.0	30.5
		16.4		A	A	Inventory	23.1	18.5
		1.3		T	T	All Other Current	2.1	.9
		53.3		A	A	Total Current	60.1	55.9
		42.4				Fixed Assets (net)	32.0	38.7
		1.2		N	N	Intangibles (net)	2.8	1.7
		3.1		O	O	All Other Non-Current	5.0	3.7
		100.0		T	T	Total	100.0	100.0
						LIABILITIES		
		8.7		A	A	Notes Payable-Short Term	11.4	10.7
		4.8		V	V	Cur. Mat.-L.T.D.	4.6	4.5
		11.0		A	A	Trade Payables	15.6	14.5
		.0		I	I	Income Taxes Payable	.0	.0
		6.4		L	L	All Other Current	8.9	7.7
		31.0		A	A	Total Current	40.6	37.3
		22.6		B	B	Long-Term Debt	17.7	21.9
		.5		L	L	Deferred Taxes	.6	.3
		2.0		E	E	All Other Non-Current	21.0	4.4
		44.0				Net Worth	20.0	36.0
		100.0				Total Liabilities & Net Worth	100.0	100.0
						INCOME DATA		
		100.0				Net Sales	100.0	100.0
		23.9				Gross Profit	20.1	26.1
		19.8				Operating Expenses	17.3	20.4
		4.2				Operating Profit	2.8	5.7
		1.4				All Other Expenses (net)	1.2	1.3
		2.8				Profit Before Taxes	1.6	4.4
						RATIOS		
		4.7					2.2	2.6
		2.2				Current	1.4	1.5
		.8					1.0	1.0
		3.3					1.6	1.8
		1.8				Quick	.8	.9
		.4					.5	.6
	37	9.7					41 8.8	41 8.9
	46	8.0				Sales/Receivables	48 7.6	49 7.5
	68	5.4					59 6.2	60 6.1
	25	14.4					26 14.2	24 15.3
	36	10.2				Cost of Sales/Inventory	41 8.8	40 9.2
	76	4.8					63 5.8	56 6.5
	13	27.1					16 23.3	15 24.7
	27	13.5				Cost of Sales/Payables	29 12.5	28 13.0
	44	8.3					49 7.5	51 7.1
		3.7					6.8	6.1
		6.2				Sales/Working Capital	14.5	12.0
		-15.2					122.1	108.4
		36.9					5.4	8.6
	(14)	1.7				EBIT/Interest	(31) 1.3	(29) 2.9
		.3					-.7	1.2
						Net Profit + Depr., Dep.,	1.6	
						Amort./Cur. Mat. L/T/D	(11) 1.1	
							.0	
		.4					.6	.6
		1.3				Fixed/Worth	1.1	1.3
		2.0					3.1	2.0
		.4					.9	.9
		1.6				Debt/Worth	2.4	2.5
		3.3					8.6	4.8
		25.6				% Profit Before Taxes/Tangible	24.6	47.9
	(13)	4.1				Net Worth	(30) 3.6	(30) 20.9
		.2					-14.7	4.5
		18.7				% Profit Before Taxes/Total	10.2	17.3
		1.5				Assets	1.0	5.4
		.1					-3.2	1.1
		5.7					11.0	11.0
		3.9				Sales/Net Fixed Assets	6.6	5.7
		2.4					4.6	3.3
		2.1					2.8	2.9
		1.7				Sales/Total Assets	2.1	2.0
		1.4					1.7	1.5
		2.8					2.1	1.8
	(14)	4.8				% Depr., Dep., Amort./Sales	2.8	(29) 2.8
		6.3					3.9	5.8
						% Officers', Directors'	1.9	1.5
	(12)					Owners' Comp/Sales	3.9	(10) 2.8
							10.2	8.7
2891M	21557M	138714M	242873M			Net Sales ($)	692785M	598277M
1067M	9778M	74285M	151444M			Total Assets ($)	336178M	270705M

M = $ thousand   MM = $ million
See Pages 9 through 22 for Explanation of Ratios and Data

Comparative Historical Data

Current Data Sorted by Sales

4/1/07-3/31/08 ALL	4/1/08-3/31/09 ALL	4/1/09-3/31/10 ALL	Type of Statement	0-1MM	1-3MM	3-5MM	5-10MM	10-25MM	25MM & OVER
4	3	4	Unqualified		1		1	2	
5	9	11	Reviewed		1	2	2	3	3
5	4	6	Compiled	2	1	2	1		
2	4	3	Tax Returns	1	1	1	2		
13	12	9	Other		1		2	3	1
				9 (4/1-9/30/09)			24 (10/1/09-3/31/10)		
29	32	33	**NUMBER OF STATEMENTS**	3	5	7	6	8	4
%	%	%	**ASSETS**	%	%	%	%	%	%
5.2	11.6	12.1	Cash & Equivalents						
33.8	28.7	25.5	Trade Receivables (net)						
20.2	20.2	17.0	Inventory						
1.9	2.3	1.3	All Other Current						
61.1	62.8	55.9	Total Current						
31.1	31.1	38.2	Fixed Assets (net)						
2.7	1.7	2.8	Intangibles (net)						
5.1	4.4	3.1	All Other Non-Current						
100.0	100.0	100.0	Total						
			LIABILITIES						
24.1	10.8	8.7	Notes Payable-Short Term						
4.9	4.8	5.1	Cur. Mat.-L.T.D.						
20.9	15.8	13.3	Trade Payables						
.1	.0	.0	Income Taxes Payable						
8.6	12.1	6.9	All Other Current						
58.6	43.6	34.0	Total Current						
16.5	17.0	20.9	Long-Term Debt						
.4	.8	.7	Deferred Taxes						
5.8	2.1	1.8	All Other Non-Current						
18.6	36.6	42.7	Net Worth						
100.0	100.0	100.0	Total Liabilities & Net Worth						
			INCOME DATA						
100.0	100.0	100.0	Net Sales						
23.8	24.3	24.6	Gross Profit						
18.6	16.3	21.9	Operating Expenses						
5.2	8.0	2.7	Operating Profit						
1.3	.6	1.2	All Other Expenses (net)						
4.0	7.4	1.5	Profit Before Taxes						
			RATIOS						
2.2	2.9	3.4	Current						
1.2	1.5	2.1							
.9	1.0	1.2							
1.5	1.6	2.5	Quick						
.7	1.0	1.4							
.5	.5	.6							
40 9.2	35 10.3	38 9.6	Sales/Receivables						
53 6.9	45 8.1	45 8.2							
59 6.1	62 5.9	65 5.6							
20 18.5	19 19.2	29 12.5	Cost of Sales/Inventory						
35 10.3	40 9.1	40 9.2							
62 5.9	56 6.5	57 6.4							
18 20.1	17 21.1	13 28.1	Cost of Sales/Payables						
39 9.4	27 13.5	24 15.1							
59 6.2	54 6.8	39 9.4							
7.2	5.2	4.3	Sales/Working Capital						
15.4	11.6	8.2							
-28.7	NM	386.1							
14.7	32.1	13.1	EBIT/Interest						
(28) 2.1	(31) 5.3	(31) 2.6							
.6	2.1	1.1							
			Net Profit + Depr., Dep., Amort./Cur. Mat. L/T/D						
.5	.4	.4	Fixed/Worth						
1.6	.7	.8							
NM	2.6	2.3							
.6	.5	.4	Debt/Worth						
3.1	2.3	1.6							
NM	6.2	3.8							
48.6	62.2	23.7	% Profit Before Taxes/Tangible Net Worth						
(22) 19.3	(30) 29.3	(28) 7.4							
5.5	19.5	.2							
12.4	23.5	10.7	% Profit Before Taxes/Total Assets						
2.2	11.8	1.9							
-1.8	2.7	-1.0							
23.3	20.1	12.1	Sales/Net Fixed Assets						
7.8	7.9	5.1							
3.8	4.4	2.7							
3.4	3.0	2.5	Sales/Total Assets						
2.0	2.2	1.8							
1.6	1.6	1.2							
.7	.9	2.4	% Depr., Dep., Amort./Sales						
(26) 2.0	(26) 2.5	(32) 3.5							
4.0	4.8	5.9							
1.6		2.3	% Officers', Directors' Owners' Comp/Sales						
(11) 7.3		(11) 5.8							
13.2		10.5							
562757M	778545M	406035M	Net Sales ($)	2471M	8354M	28072M	38805M	135120M	193213M
256681M	308547M	236574M	Total Assets ($)	1440M	5736M	16382M	26027M	83488M	103501M

© RMA 2010

M = $ thousand   MM = $ million

See Pages 9 through 22 for Explanation of Ratios and Data

Current Data Sorted by Assets							Comparative Historical Data	
						Type of Statement		
		1	3		1	Unqualified	7	7
	1	6	4			Reviewed	10	8
		3				Compiled	5	7
	1					Tax Returns	3	4
	1	4	3	1	1	Other	14	11
	3 (4/1-9/30/09)		27 (10/1/09-3/31/10)				4/1/05-3/31/06	4/1/06-3/31/07
0-500M	500M-2MM	2-10MM	10-50MM	50-100MM	100-250MM		ALL	ALL
	3	14	10	1	2	**NUMBER OF STATEMENTS**	39	37
%	%	%	%	%	%	**ASSETS**	%	%
DATA NOT AVAILABLE		9.2	10.1			Cash & Equivalents	6.4	8.1
		33.6	22.9			Trade Receivables (net)	29.8	29.6
		18.2	32.3			Inventory	23.3	23.7
		1.1	3.3			All Other Current	2.3	1.4
		62.0	68.6			Total Current	61.7	62.7
		30.1	25.3			Fixed Assets (net)	29.5	30.5
		2.0	.3			Intangibles (net)	4.5	3.5
		5.9	5.9			All Other Non-Current	4.3	3.3
		100.0	100.0			Total	100.0	100.0
						LIABILITIES		
		8.8	15.2			Notes Payable-Short Term	10.1	10.6
		7.1	4.6			Cur. Mat.-L.T.D.	4.8	3.2
		18.0	15.6			Trade Payables	16.8	18.4
		.0	.4			Income Taxes Payable	.5	.1
		7.3	6.2			All Other Current	10.7	9.0
		41.1	42.0			Total Current	42.8	41.3
		7.6	2.9			Long-Term Debt	13.8	14.6
		.0	.5			Deferred Taxes	1.0	.7
		3.2	4.5			All Other Non-Current	5.5	4.4
		48.1	50.0			Net Worth	36.9	39.0
		100.0	100.0			Total Liabilties & Net Worth	100.0	100.0
						INCOME DATA		
		100.0	100.0			Net Sales	100.0	100.0
		23.5	15.9			Gross Profit	26.0	23.7
		21.6	13.8			Operating Expenses	18.9	15.7
		1.9	2.1			Operating Profit	7.1	8.0
		.7	.5			All Other Expenses (net)	.8	.9
		1.2	1.6			Profit Before Taxes	6.3	7.1
						RATIOS		
		2.8	4.8				2.2	2.0
		1.6	2.2			Current	1.5	1.5
		1.0	.8				1.1	1.1
		1.8	2.5				1.2	1.4
		1.1	1.3			Quick	.8	.8
		.7	.4				.6	.6
		36 10.1	25 14.5				41 8.8	40 9.2
		55 6.6	38 9.5			Sales/Receivables	53 6.9	53 6.9
		74 4.9	63 5.8				70 5.2	64 5.7
		20 17.9	38 9.7				30 12.3	25 14.6
		40 9.1	90 4.1			Cost of Sales/Inventory	53 6.9	47 7.8
		75 4.9	108 3.4				89 4.1	67 5.4
		17 22.1	18 20.1				27 13.3	25 14.6
		26 14.2	25 14.5			Cost of Sales/Payables	33 11.1	35 10.3
		56 6.5	44 8.3				59 6.1	57 6.4
		5.7	2.9				5.4	4.9
		9.5	6.8			Sales/Working Capital	14.4	11.8
		-199.0	-13.9				71.1	36.6
		36.0	121.9				23.8	9.9
		(13) 2.9	4.3			EBIT/Interest	(35) 5.0	(33) 5.3
		-6.4	-1.6				1.8	2.1
							8.2	6.9
						Net Profit + Depr., Dep., Amort./Cur. Mat. L/T/D	(14) 3.7	(10) 2.3
							2.1	1.9
		.3	.2				.5	.4
		.5	.5			Fixed/Worth	1.0	1.0
		1.4	1.7				2.0	1.9
		.4	.3				1.0	1.0
		1.0	.8			Debt/Worth	1.8	2.3
		3.3	2.7				7.1	5.2
		22.6					68.8	57.8
		3.1				% Profit Before Taxes/Tangible Net Worth	(34) 20.7	(34) 36.5
		-32.4					2.7	13.5
		10.9	10.8				19.3	20.7
		.7	2.8			% Profit Before Taxes/Total Assets	7.6	9.4
		-11.8	-6.1				1.2	3.4
		11.9	21.2				13.7	14.2
		8.9	7.1			Sales/Net Fixed Assets	7.7	7.2
		4.2	4.5				4.9	3.9
		2.4	2.3				2.7	2.6
		1.8	1.7			Sales/Total Assets	2.0	2.0
		1.4	1.4				1.5	1.5
		1.4					1.4	1.6
		(12) 2.7				% Depr., Dep., Amort./Sales	(36) 2.4	(34) 2.8
		5.1					3.6	4.5
							1.6	2.8
						% Officers', Directors' Owners' Comp/Sales	(13) 4.3	(10) 5.0
							6.5	6.6
	11820M	143491M	495757M	90456M	1175846M	Net Sales ($)	815610M	759233M
	5118M	70044M	250010M	74104M	472327M	Total Assets ($)	436412M	514812M

M = $ thousand MM = $ million

See Pages 9 through 22 for Explanation of Ratios and Data

Comparative Historical Data
Current Data Sorted by Sales

	Comparative Historical Data			Type of Statement	0-1MM	1-3MM	3-5MM	5-10MM	10-25MM	25MM & OVE
	9	5	5	Unqualified		1	3	3	2
	11	14	11	Reviewed		1	1	2	5
	6	3	3	Compiled			1	1	
		6	1	Tax Returns			1		
	12	12	10	Other	1	3	3	1	5
	4/1/07- 3/31/08 ALL	4/1/08- 3/31/09 ALL	4/1/09- 3/31/10 ALL			3 (4/1-9/30/09)		27 (10/1/09-3/31/10)		
	38	40	30	**NUMBER OF STATEMENTS**	1	2	8	7	12
	%	%	%		%	%	%	%	%	%
				ASSETS						
	6.3	8.9	9.4	Cash & Equivalents						12.1
	29.6	31.2	28.2	Trade Receivables (net)						25.7
	22.7	25.2	24.0	Inventory	DATA					30.2
	1.8	3.6	2.2	All Other Current	NOT					3.6
	60.5	68.8	63.8	Total Current						71.5
	31.3	26.6	29.7	Fixed Assets (net)	AVAILABLE					21.2
	2.2	.9	1.4	Intangibles (net)						1.1
	6.1	3.6	5.1	All Other Non-Current						6.1
	100.0	100.0	100.0	Total						100.0
				LIABILITIES						
	15.2	10.2	9.5	Notes Payable-Short Term						9.6
	4.6	3.2	6.1	Cur. Mat.-L.T.D.						3.1
	17.2	13.6	18.0	Trade Payables						20.1
	.2	1.1	.1	Income Taxes Payable						.0
	8.8	11.2	7.4	All Other Current						7.1
	45.9	39.4	41.1	Total Current						39.9
	14.0	11.9	10.1	Long-Term Debt						10.1
	.4	.6	.3	Deferred Taxes						.7
	2.6	4.1	3.8	All Other Non-Current						4.2
	37.1	44.0	44.7	Net Worth						45.1
	100.0	100.0	100.0	Total Liabilties & Net Worth						100.0
				INCOME DATA						
	100.0	100.0	100.0	Net Sales						100.0
	21.8	21.5	18.8	Gross Profit						16.0
	15.9	15.9	17.5	Operating Expenses						13.4
	6.0	5.6	1.3	Operating Profit						2.6
	1.1	.2	1.2	All Other Expenses (net)						1.6
	4.9	5.4	.1	Profit Before Taxes						1.0
				RATIOS						
	2.0	2.7	3.1							4.0
	1.4	1.9	1.7	Current						1.8
	1.0	1.3	1.0							1.5
	1.3	1.5	1.8							2.3
	.8	1.0	1.1	Quick						1.1
	.5	.7	.5							.9
30	12.0	32 11.3	36 10.1	Sales/Receivables					29	12.6
50	7.4	45 8.1	49 7.5						40	9.0
63	5.8	55 6.7	62 5.9						56	6.5
24	15.3	22 16.9	32 11.4	Cost of Sales/Inventory					36	10.1
48	7.6	45 8.1	55 6.6						50	7.3
69	5.3	77 4.8	80 4.6						103	3.5
20	17.9	13 27.5	18 20.1	Cost of Sales/Payables					23	15.8
29	12.5	20 18.1	27 13.6						28	13.2
39	9.4	32 11.5	63 5.8						61	6.0
	8.2	4.6	4.3	Sales/Working Capital						2.9
	18.4	8.3	9.1							5.9
	-135.6	25.1	-199.9							19.1
	11.0	20.9	36.0	EBIT/Interest						82.9
(37)	4.0	(39) 6.2	(29) 2.9							1.1
	2.0	.9	-2.3							-1.4
	10.2	13.8		Net Profit + Depr., Dep., Amort./Cur. Mat. L/T/D						
(11)	3.8	(10) 3.3								
	2.7	.7								
	.4	.3	.3	Fixed/Worth						.2
	1.1	.5	.6							.5
	1.8	1.3	1.6							1.6
	1.0	.6	.5	Debt/Worth						.3
	1.9	1.1	1.0							1.1
	4.0	2.5	4.9							5.9
	49.8	51.0	20.8	% Profit Before Taxes/Tangible Net Worth						15.3
(35)	26.1	(38) 20.8	(28) 6.0						(11)	5.4
	10.4	-.1	-12.8							-8.9
	16.0	25.4	10.8	% Profit Before Taxes/Total Assets						8.8
	8.9	11.6	1.0							-.1
	2.8	-.2	-6.1							-6.5
	21.1	20.9	14.8	Sales/Net Fixed Assets						43.5
	6.9	8.7	7.1							13.0
	4.6	5.3	4.1							4.3
	3.0	3.2	2.3	Sales/Total Assets						3.5
	2.3	2.5	1.7							1.9
	1.5	1.8	1.4							1.3
	.9	.5	.9	% Depr., Dep., Amort./Sales						
(34)	2.2	(34) 1.5	(24) 2.2							
	4.3	3.8	5.1							
	1.4	2.8		% Officers', Directors' Owners' Comp/Sales						
(12)	3.1	(15) 4.8								
	5.2	8.0								
	1120342M	904472M	1917370M	Net Sales ($)		2225M	8561M	49902M	102736M	1753946M
	531872M	415072M	871603M	Total Assets ($)		1611M	4783M	31481M	61691M	772037M

M = $ thousand   MM = $ million
See Pages 9 through 22 for Explanation of Ratios and Data

Current Data Sorted by Assets   Comparative Historical Data

	0-500M	500M-2MM	2-10MM	10-50MM	50-100MM	100-250MM		4/1/05-3/31/06 ALL	4/1/06-3/31/07 ALL
Type of Statement									
Unqualified		3	5	7	3	5		20	26
Reviewed		3	9	7				19	25
Compiled		3	6	3				7	10
Tax Returns	2	4	3	2				4	8
Other	2	6	13	28	6	5		38	26
		28 (4/1-9/30/09)		94 (10/1/09-3/31/10)					
NUMBER OF STATEMENTS	4	16	36	47	9	10		88	95
	%	%	%	%	%	%		%	%
ASSETS									
Cash & Equivalents		9.2	6.7	9.9		8.0		6.9	7.3
Trade Receivables (net)		32.1	23.4	19.0		16.7		25.8	24.7
Inventory		15.4	28.7	27.2		23.9		29.7	27.3
All Other Current		1.2	.9	4.9		2.1		2.1	2.4
Total Current		57.9	59.7	61.0		50.7		64.4	61.7
Fixed Assets (net)		26.6	31.3	30.9		39.5		27.6	30.9
Intangibles (net)		8.1	4.7	3.8		6.7		2.8	3.3
All Other Non-Current		7.4	4.3	4.3		3.1		5.2	4.1
Total		100.0	100.0	100.0		100.0		100.0	100.0
LIABILITIES									
Notes Payable-Short Term		8.9	11.6	9.8		2.3		8.2	8.7
Cur. Mat.-L.T.D.		2.1	4.9	3.7		2.8		3.0	3.5
Trade Payables		10.9	10.7	10.5		15.0		15.8	15.5
Income Taxes Payable		.0	.0	.2		.0		.2	.2
All Other Current		6.8	8.3	12.0		6.0		7.5	10.3
Total Current		28.6	35.4	36.3		26.2		34.6	38.3
Long-Term Debt		25.6	15.6	14.8		22.4		16.9	20.8
Deferred Taxes		.0	.9	.8		2.3		.9	.4
All Other Non-Current		8.7	10.9	6.8		5.3		7.5	4.8
Net Worth		37.1	37.3	41.4		43.8		40.1	35.8
Total Liabilities & Net Worth		100.0	100.0	100.0		100.0		100.0	100.0
INCOME DATA									
Net Sales		100.0	100.0	100.0		100.0		100.0	100.0
Gross Profit		30.9	27.8	23.5		17.8		23.7	25.6
Operating Expenses		29.0	25.0	16.1		12.5		17.0	18.7
Operating Profit		1.8	2.8	7.4		5.3		6.7	6.9
All Other Expenses (net)		1.0	1.0	1.9		1.7		.7	.8
Profit Before Taxes		.8	1.8	5.6		3.6		6.0	6.1
RATIOS									
Current		4.6	3.3	3.0		3.2		3.2	2.5
		2.7	1.7	1.9		1.9		1.8	1.7
		1.5	1.0	1.2		1.2		1.3	1.2
Quick		2.9	1.7	1.4		1.4		1.6	1.4
		1.9	.7	.8		.8		1.0	.9
		.9	.5	.5		.7		.6	.6
Sales/Receivables	33 11.2	33 11.0	31 11.8	32 11.3				38 9.5	33 10.9
	49 7.5	42 8.6	45 8.1	40 9.1				49 7.4	45 8.1
	73 5.0	59 6.2	62 5.9	45 8.1				61 6.0	57 6.4
Cost of Sales/Inventory	12 31.0	42 8.8	39 9.4	32 11.3				41 8.9	29 12.4
	32 11.3	60 6.1	88 4.1	75 4.9				69 5.3	60 6.1
	56 6.5	151 2.4	128 2.8	135 2.7				102 3.6	107 3.4
Cost of Sales/Payables	13 28.0	14 26.9	17 21.0	26 14.1				22 16.7	22 16.3
	19 19.5	26 13.9	31 11.9	38 9.7				33 11.1	32 11.5
	31 11.6	37 9.8	46 7.9	56 6.6				48 7.5	51 7.2
Sales/Working Capital		4.9	3.9	3.3		2.9		3.8	5.1
		7.0	9.6	6.0		8.2		7.1	8.7
		10.3	-102.4	14.0		28.1		13.7	24.2
EBIT/Interest		19.5	8.4	22.9		3.8		9.3	11.7
	(13) 1.3		1.7	(44) 5.0		2.5		(76) 4.9	(86) 4.1
		-.2	-.7	-.5		.4		2.3	1.9
Net Profit + Depr., Dep., Amort./Cur. Mat. L/T/D				13.2				6.5	11.1
			(12) 2.8					(27) 2.6	(33) 3.1
				.5				1.8	2.0
Fixed/Worth		.3	.3	.4		.5		.3	.4
		.6	.9	.7		1.3		.7	.8
		UND	5.9	2.3		NM		1.3	2.2
Debt/Worth		.3	.9	.8		.7		.7	.8
		1.1	1.8	1.5		1.2		1.6	1.8
		UND	34.4	4.7		NM		2.8	4.0
% Profit Before Taxes/Tangible Net Worth		66.9	32.6	49.5				37.4	46.9
	(12) 13.0	(30) 11.4	(42) 19.8					(80) 23.9	(84) 25.1
		-5.1	-11.2	-2.0				8.9	9.9
% Profit Before Taxes/Total Assets		13.6	12.3	18.6		7.6		19.2	19.0
		.2	1.5	6.1		5.2		8.4	9.2
		-3.7	-5.5	-3.8		-.4		3.1	2.5
Sales/Net Fixed Assets		24.4	11.7	9.8		4.9		17.5	14.6
		7.6	7.9	5.0		4.0		7.0	6.2
		4.7	3.2	3.2		2.4		4.1	3.8
Sales/Total Assets		3.0	2.2	1.9		2.1		2.5	2.5
		2.2	1.8	1.4		1.5		2.0	2.0
		1.8	1.2	1.2		1.1		1.4	1.5
% Depr., Dep., Amort./Sales		2.1	1.6	1.4				1.0	1.4
	(11) 2.9	(33) 3.0	(43) 3.0					(77) 2.4	(85) 2.7
		5.2	5.0	5.4				3.9	4.1
% Officers', Directors' Owners' Comp/Sales			1.8	1.4				1.7	1.3
		(11) 5.2	(12) 3.3					(22) 3.3	(26) 3.0
			11.8	5.0				6.4	7.3
Net Sales ($)	3358M	39045M	370219M	1437867M	747476M	2551729M		3593946M	3606235M
Total Assets ($)	586M	19219M	204221M	934359M	622586M	1607885M		2097549M	2222800M

M = $ thousand   MM = $ million
See Pages 9 through 22 for Explanation of Ratios and Data

Comparative Historical Data   Current Data Sorted by Sales

H1	H2	H3	Type of Statement	0-1MM	1-3MM	3-5MM	5-10MM	10-25MM	25MM & OVER
22	23	20	Unqualified			1	1	7	11
18	13	19	Reviewed		3	2	2	7	5
11	15	12	Compiled		4	1	3	3	1
10	10	11	Tax Returns	2	1	4	2	2	
46	44	60	Other	1	6	4	5	18	26
4/1/07-3/31/08 ALL	4/1/08-3/31/09 ALL	4/1/09-3/31/10 ALL			28 (4/1-9/30/09)		94 (10/1/09-3/31/10)		
107	105	122	NUMBER OF STATEMENTS	3	14	12	13	37	43
%	%	%	ASSETS	%	%	%	%	%	%
5.5	7.8	9.8	Cash & Equivalents		10.3	8.6	9.6	9.4	10.0
26.1	23.1	21.7	Trade Receivables (net)		29.4	27.4	19.5	20.1	20.6
27.2	29.5	24.2	Inventory		12.1	18.4	35.3	27.6	25.0
3.5	2.3	3.0	All Other Current		1.0	.3	1.6	4.9	2.6
62.3	62.8	58.7	Total Current		52.8	54.8	66.1	62.0	58.2
29.9	28.3	32.0	Fixed Assets (net)		32.2	35.2	27.7	28.4	33.8
2.9	4.3	4.5	Intangibles (net)		8.0	5.0	2.6	4.7	4.0
4.9	4.6	4.8	All Other Non-Current		7.0	5.0	3.7	4.9	3.9
100.0	100.0	100.0	Total		100.0	100.0	100.0	100.0	100.0
			LIABILITIES						
9.7	10.4	10.3	Notes Payable-Short Term		7.3	8.6	11.2	9.6	8.2
3.2	3.6	3.5	Cur. Mat.-L.T.D.		3.4	3.2	4.9	3.4	3.6
15.5	12.4	10.8	Trade Payables		11.2	8.9	10.7	10.7	12.2
.2	.1	.1	Income Taxes Payable		.0	.0	.0	.1	.1
10.7	7.9	10.0	All Other Current		7.6	9.9	7.0	10.7	9.3
39.2	34.4	34.8	Total Current		29.5	30.7	33.9	34.5	33.5
20.6	14.3	18.8	Long-Term Debt		30.4	27.9	14.1	13.1	15.3
.4	.8	.8	Deferred Taxes		.0	.3	2.5	.4	1.1
8.6	9.2	10.7	All Other Non-Current		5.0	10.3	3.3	8.3	8.5
31.2	41.4	35.0	Net Worth		35.1	30.9	46.2	43.7	41.6
100.0	100.0	100.0	Total Liabilities & Net Worth		100.0	100.0	100.0	100.0	100.0
			INCOME DATA						
100.0	100.0	100.0	Net Sales		100.0	100.0	100.0	100.0	100.0
25.1	25.6	26.1	Gross Profit		40.0	27.3	25.1	26.5	19.1
18.1	18.8	21.4	Operating Expenses		38.2	23.6	26.2	19.2	13.0
7.0	6.9	4.7	Operating Profit		1.8	3.7	-1.0	7.3	6.1
1.3	1.1	1.3	All Other Expenses (net)		1.4	1.8	.3	1.2	1.7
5.7	5.8	3.3	Profit Before Taxes		.4	1.9	-1.4	6.2	4.3
			RATIOS						
2.6	3.1	3.4	Current		6.8	3.7	5.3	3.3	3.3
1.9	2.0	1.9			1.9	2.1	1.8	1.9	1.9
1.2	1.3	1.2			1.3	.9	1.0	1.2	1.3
1.4	1.7	2.1	Quick		3.0	2.7	2.9	1.5	1.7
.9	.8	.9			1.7	1.5	.6	.8	.9
.5	.5	.6			.6	.4	.4	.5	.7
36 10.1	30 12.0	33 11.1	Sales/Receivables		29 12.4	28 13.0	28 12.9	33 11.0	33 11.0
47 7.8	41 8.8	44 8.4			51 7.2	45 8.1	37 9.9	49 7.4	43 8.5
54 6.7	49 7.4	60 6.1			69 5.3	87 4.2	58 6.3	61 6.0	52 7.0
29 12.4	37 9.9	35 10.4	Cost of Sales/Inventory		5 67.5	31 11.8	47 7.8	40 9.2	37 9.9
58 6.3	68 5.3	59 6.2			13 29.0	43 8.4	87 4.2	87 4.2	60 6.1
93 3.9	108 3.4	111 3.3			87 4.2	98 3.7	196 1.9	128 2.8	104 3.5
21 17.3	16 22.9	15 24.6	Cost of Sales/Payables		13 29.0	15 24.8	11 33.0	18 20.5	18 20.0
33 11.2	24 14.9	26 13.8			23 15.7	22 16.9	28 12.9	29 12.7	31 11.9
47 7.8	41 8.8	42 8.6			38 9.6	36 10.2	44 8.2	45 8.1	45 8.1
5.0	4.5	3.7	Sales/Working Capital		5.0	4.7	3.3	3.3	3.1
8.6	7.3	7.2			9.6	6.3	7.2	5.9	7.6
21.7	16.8	27.9			NM	-35.4	NM	13.6	16.5
19.7	24.5	14.6	EBIT/Interest		2.1	22.5	4.6	26.0	11.9
(100) 4.5	(95) 5.5	(113) 2.6			(11) .6	5.7	.3	(34) 6.4	2.6
1.8	1.3	-.5			-2.3	-.4	-4.4	.7	-.5
9.5	12.3	4.1	Net Profit + Depr., Dep., Amort./Cur. Mat. L/T/D						11.1
(36) 4.2	(31) 4.2	(28) 1.6							(16) 2.2
2.4	1.7	.5							.5
.4	.3	.4	Fixed/Worth		.2	.4	.2	.3	.4
.8	.7	.7			1.1	4.4	.5	.6	.7
2.9	2.3	3.2			-2.7	50.0	2.9	1.5	2.5
.9	.6	.7	Debt/Worth		.4	.5	.5	.5	.7
1.8	1.3	1.5			1.3	8.6	1.2	1.5	1.4
7.5	5.7	7.1			-8.2	85.9	5.7	3.4	5.2
65.8	55.4	39.9	% Profit Before Taxes/Tangible Net Worth		97.8	17.9		50.4	27.7
(92) 35.2	(90) 30.6	(102) 14.5			(10) 45.4	(11) -2.0		(35) 22.0	(36) 10.7
10.6	3.0	-6.0			-3.0	-13.8		4.8	-6.3
23.9	24.7	14.5	% Profit Before Taxes/Total Assets		11.2	15.5	7.0	18.4	11.7
9.5	11.2	3.3			-1.0	6.3	-1.2	9.2	3.8
3.0	.4	-4.6			-5.1	-7.6	-6.0	.7	-4.5
15.7	16.9	11.1	Sales/Net Fixed Assets		27.1	13.4	16.7	11.1	8.8
7.7	7.4	5.3			6.4	7.6	10.2	6.1	4.9
4.4	4.3	3.4			3.8	2.7	2.9	3.4	3.4
2.6	2.7	2.2	Sales/Total Assets		3.3	2.5	2.2	2.0	2.1
2.0	2.1	1.6			1.9	1.7	1.4	1.7	1.5
1.5	1.4	1.2			1.2	1.2	1.0	1.2	1.3
1.3	1.2	1.7	% Depr., Dep., Amort./Sales			2.0	1.8	1.7	1.5
(91) 2.3	(94) 2.1	(103) 3.0			(10) 4.3	3.7	(33) 2.5	(35) 3.0	
4.3	4.3	5.2			6.5	5.7	3.9	4.4	
1.9	1.8	1.8	% Officers', Directors' Owners' Comp/Sales					2.1	
(27) 3.2	(30) 2.9	(34) 3.8					(12) 4.4		
6.4	7.4	8.2					7.3		
5127544M	5005417M	5149694M	Net Sales ($)	1315M	27558M	45011M	93462M	641805M	4340543M
2909387M	2671541M	3388856M	Total Assets ($)	1948M	16738M	34004M	66914M	484721M	2784531M

M = $ thousand   MM = $ million
See Pages 9 through 22 for Explanation of Ratios and Data

Current Data Sorted by Assets　　　　　　　　　　　　　　　　**Comparative Historical Data**

Type of Statement								
		3	20	7	4	Unqualified	55	47
1	6	40	25			Reviewed	97	91
3	5	19	4			Compiled	54	54
4	7	8				Tax Returns	19	26
6	12	58	36	2	2	Other	92	103
	43 (4/1-9/30/09)		229 (10/1/09-3/31/10)				4/1/05-3/31/06	4/1/06-3/31/07
0-500M	500M-2MM	2-10MM	10-50MM	50-100MM	100-250MM		ALL	ALL
14	30	128	85	9	6	**NUMBER OF STATEMENTS**	317	321
%	%	%	%	%	%	**ASSETS**	%	%
7.0	9.1	7.9	5.4			Cash & Equivalents	6.1	6.9
26.2	24.8	25.0	21.4			Trade Receivables (net)	29.1	27.1
22.4	24.2	23.8	21.1			Inventory	21.5	23.1
11.6	1.3	2.2	2.1			All Other Current	1.7	1.8
67.2	59.4	58.9	50.1			Total Current	58.4	58.9
18.6	33.7	32.2	38.1			Fixed Assets (net)	32.4	31.1
6.4	4.3	3.4	6.0			Intangibles (net)	3.8	4.1
7.7	2.5	5.5	5.8			All Other Non-Current	5.3	5.9
100.0	100.0	100.0	100.0			Total	100.0	100.0
						LIABILITIES		
19.6	13.3	10.0	12.4			Notes Payable-Short Term	10.0	9.4
.8	5.6	4.9	5.1			Cur. Mat.-L.T.D.	4.6	4.7
23.0	17.7	13.4	12.1			Trade Payables	16.3	14.7
.6	.0	.1	.2			Income Taxes Payable	.1	.3
11.3	6.1	8.1	6.7			All Other Current	7.7	8.3
55.3	42.8	36.5	36.5			Total Current	38.7	37.3
42.3	15.9	16.9	18.1			Long-Term Debt	17.1	17.5
.0	.3	.3	.6			Deferred Taxes	.7	.5
53.1	3.2	5.2	5.6			All Other Non-Current	7.5	7.1
-50.7	37.8	41.0	39.3			Net Worth	35.9	37.6
100.0	100.0	100.0	100.0			Total Liabilities & Net Worth	100.0	100.0
						INCOME DATA		
100.0	100.0	100.0	100.0			Net Sales	100.0	100.0
32.0	29.3	25.2	17.8			Gross Profit	24.1	25.0
36.1	29.0	22.6	15.9			Operating Expenses	19.2	20.0
-4.1	.3	2.6	2.0			Operating Profit	4.8	4.9
1.6	.7	.5	1.7			All Other Expenses (net)	1.0	.9
-5.6	-.5	2.1	.3			Profit Before Taxes	3.8	4.0
						RATIOS		
6.5	2.8	3.1	2.1			Current	2.5	2.6
1.7	1.7	1.5	1.5				1.5	1.6
.8	.8	1.1	1.0				1.1	1.1
2.6	1.7	1.7	1.2			Quick	1.5	1.5
1.0	.9	.9	.7				.9	.9
.4	.5	.5	.5				.6	.6
13　27.8	31　11.9	34　10.6	43　8.5			Sales/Receivables	37　9.8	35　10.3
27　13.6	41　9.0	51　7.1	53　6.9				48　7.6	45　8.2
60　6.1	57　6.4	67　5.5	67　5.5				58　6.3	56　6.5
0　UND	31　11.8	34　10.6	45　8.1			Cost of Sales/Inventory	27　13.3	30　12.3
43　8.5	51　7.2	58　6.3	64　5.7				43　8.4	48　7.7
116　3.1	83　4.4	86　4.3	86　4.3				65　5.6	71　5.2
8　45.6	22　16.9	18　20.5	20　18.0			Cost of Sales/Payables	19　18.8	19　19.6
33　11.1	29　12.7	29　12.7	31　11.9				32　11.4	30　12.3
82　4.4	49　7.5	50　7.3	51　7.2				48　7.6	42　8.7
3.1	5.4	4.3	5.2			Sales/Working Capital	6.1	5.8
26.7	10.6	9.3	10.4				12.4	10.7
-18.4	-31.8	58.9	-124.0				77.1	44.7
	4.8	7.6	5.6			EBIT/Interest	9.3	9.0
	(26)　1.0	(122)　1.8	(84)　1.8				(292)　3.1	(298)　3.3
	-5.7	-.7	-1.3				1.3	1.4
		3.0	3.6			Net Profit + Depr., Dep., Amort./Cur. Mat. L/T/D	4.5	4.4
	(26)　1.5	(22)　2.0					(111)　2.2	(88)　2.2
	.8	.4					1.3	1.2
.1	.5	.3	.7			Fixed/Worth	.5	.5
NM	1.0	.8	1.2				1.0	.9
-.3	2.3	2.3	2.7				2.7	2.7
.4	.6	.6	.8			Debt/Worth	.8	.7
-10.5	1.5	1.4	2.0				1.9	1.8
-1.5	4.3	4.4	4.9				6.6	6.3
	24.1	28.8	18.0			% Profit Before Taxes/Tangible Net Worth	47.4	49.0
	(28)　.4	(115)　8.2	(75)　6.2				(272)　17.4	(280)　21.7
	-29.5	-9.6	-8.2				3.7	5.5
10.3	6.8	10.3	6.5			% Profit Before Taxes/Total Assets	15.0	15.9
.4	.0	1.7	1.1				5.3	6.1
-39.1	-9.6	-4.9	-4.3				.7	1.2
UND	25.9	12.9	6.6			Sales/Net Fixed Assets	12.7	14.1
41.6	7.3	6.6	3.9				7.1	7.0
8.5	3.5	3.6	2.6				4.3	4.7
3.9	2.8	2.2	1.8			Sales/Total Assets	2.7	2.7
2.8	2.2	1.7	1.5				2.2	2.1
1.8	1.4	1.3	1.1				1.7	1.7
	1.3	1.9	3.0			% Depr., Dep., Amort./Sales	1.9	1.7
	(28)　3.7	(116)　3.5	(74)　4.3				(295)　2.8	(295)　2.6
	6.2	5.7	6.3				3.9	3.8
	2.7	1.6	1.2			% Officers', Directors' Owners' Comp/Sales	1.5	1.8
	(13)　5.2	(48)　3.6	(18)　2.6				(119)　3.2	(122)　3.9
	14.1	5.9	4.6				6.8	7.4
10700M	83775M	1117942M	2533258M	636598M	1364977M	Net Sales ($)	8069916M	7631524M
3570M	39291M	613869M	1785530M	579352M	988604M	Total Assets ($)	4320740M	4258545M

M = $ thousand　　　MM = $ million
See Pages 9 through 22 for Explanation of Ratios and Data

Comparative Historical Data   Current Data Sorted by Sales

			Type of Statement						
42	36	34	Unqualified	3	5	12	13	13	21
83	80	72	Reviewed	2	6	6	12	27	12
47	37	31	Compiled	2	8	3	4	4	1
17	20	19	Tax Returns					2	
96	126	116	Other	6	11	10	34	29	26
4/1/07-3/31/08 ALL	4/1/08-3/31/09 ALL	4/1/09-3/31/10 ALL		43 (4/1-9/30/09)			229 (10/1/09-3/31/10)		
				0-1MM	1-3MM	3-5MM	5-10MM	10-25MM	25MM & OVER
285	299	272	NUMBER OF STATEMENTS	13	30	31	63	75	60
%	%	%	**ASSETS**	%	%	%	%	%	%
7.3	7.4	7.2	Cash & Equivalents	4.5	10.5	12.7	7.8	5.6	4.7
25.9	23.0	23.5	Trade Receivables (net)	19.7	23.8	22.7	24.1	24.6	22.4
22.5	25.0	22.5	Inventory	17.8	23.5	21.0	24.1	23.0	21.4
1.5	1.9	2.9	All Other Current	11.8	1.7	1.9	1.4	2.4	4.3
57.2	57.3	56.0	Total Current	53.8	59.5	58.3	57.3	55.7	52.7
32.2	32.5	33.7	Fixed Assets (net)	32.4	30.4	33.8	32.6	32.6	38.1
5.0	4.0	5.0	Intangibles (net)	7.0	3.9	3.1	4.7	6.5	4.4
5.6	6.1	5.3	All Other Non-Current	6.6	6.1	4.8	5.4	5.3	4.8
100.0	100.0	100.0	Total	100.0	100.0	100.0	100.0	100.0	100.0
			LIABILITIES						
9.6	10.7	11.2	Notes Payable-Short Term	16.9	12.6	7.2	14.7	9.8	9.5
4.9	4.2	4.7	Cur. Mat.-L.T.D.	1.6	4.6	6.4	4.6	4.8	4.5
14.5	12.6	13.7	Trade Payables	19.4	15.7	11.5	13.9	13.1	13.4
.1	.2	.1	Income Taxes Payable	.6	.0	.0	.1	.0	.2
7.7	7.0	7.8	All Other Current	11.7	7.1	6.4	8.4	6.4	9.1
36.8	34.7	37.6	Total Current	50.2	39.9	31.5	41.7	34.2	36.7
16.6	18.0	18.5	Long-Term Debt	41.9	18.9	16.8	17.2	18.2	16.0
.4	.5	.4	Deferred Taxes	.0	.2	.5	.3	.2	1.1
6.4	6.6	7.9	All Other Non-Current	35.0	12.7	2.4	5.5	6.3	7.1
39.8	40.3	35.5	Net Worth	-27.0	28.3	48.9	35.4	41.0	39.1
100.0	100.0	100.0	Total Liabilities & Net Worth	100.0	100.0	100.0	100.0	100.0	100.0
			INCOME DATA						
100.0	100.0	100.0	Net Sales	100.0	100.0	100.0	100.0	100.0	100.0
23.8	24.2	23.4	Gross Profit	35.4	29.3	25.2	25.7	20.2	18.5
18.8	19.6	21.5	Operating Expenses	35.1	30.8	24.9	23.7	16.8	15.7
5.0	4.6	1.9	Operating Profit	.3	-1.5	.3	1.9	3.4	2.8
1.1	1.1	1.0	All Other Expenses (net)	4.3	.4	.4	.4	1.6	.9
4.0	3.4	.9	Profit Before Taxes	-4.0	-1.9	-.1	1.5	1.8	1.9
			RATIOS						
2.7	2.7	2.7	Current	5.9	3.2	4.0	3.1	2.6	2.2
1.6	1.7	1.5		1.0	1.7	1.7	1.4	1.6	1.4
1.1	1.1	1.0		.7	1.0	1.2	1.0	1.1	1.0
1.5	1.4	1.6	Quick	2.1	1.6	2.1	1.9	1.5	1.0
.9	.8	.8		.8	1.0	.9	.8	.9	.7
.6	.5	.5		.4	.5	.6	.5	.5	.5
36 10.3	30 12.2	35 10.3	Sales/Receivables	13 28.2	26 14.2	38 9.6	32 11.4	38 9.6	40 9.2
45 8.2	40 9.2	50 7.3		27 13.3	45 8.1	52 7.1	50 7.3	50 7.3	52 7.1
55 6.7	51 7.1	64 5.7		60 6.1	60 6.1	67 5.4	68 5.4	66 5.6	65 5.6
30 12.3	35 10.5	36 10.1	Cost of Sales/Inventory	0 UND	28 13.1	31 11.8	38 9.6	36 10.1	38 9.5
48 7.6	55 6.7	58 6.3		41 8.9	52 7.1	52 7.1	63 5.8	62 5.9	59 6.2
72 5.1	80 4.6	86 4.3		100 3.7	108 3.4	79 4.6	86 4.3	86 4.3	84 4.3
19 19.7	16 23.3	19 19.1	Cost of Sales/Payables	2 230.1	20 18.1	17 20.9	18 20.4	18 20.0	24 15.1
29 12.7	24 14.9	30 12.1		28 13.0	29 12.6	27 13.5	29 12.5	30 12.1	33 11.2
42 8.8	39 9.5	50 7.3		86 4.2	48 7.6	47 7.8	52 7.0	49 7.4	52 7.0
5.5	5.5	4.6	Sales/Working Capital	4.1	4.5	3.4	4.4	4.4	5.0
10.5	9.7	9.9		-627.0	7.9	7.1	13.3	8.9	11.9
71.8	46.6	306.2		-9.4	NM	19.8	-96.2	41.6	299.1
8.7	10.0	6.5	EBIT/Interest		2.3	6.9	6.1	7.8	8.5
(269) 3.1	(273) 3.5	(254) 1.6		(26) .8	(28) 1.5	(61) 1.4	(74) 2.5	(58) 1.8	
1.2	1.1	-1.0			-6.3	-1.1	-2.0	-.2	-1.0
6.0	5.3	3.5	Net Profit + Depr., Dep., Amort./Cur. Mat. L/T/D				3.4	4.1	3.4
(79) 2.7	(85) 2.4	(59) 1.6				(16) 1.9	(11) 1.5	(18) 2.2	
.8	1.2	.6				1.0	-.1	1.0	
.4	.4	.5	Fixed/Worth	.1	.4	.2	.6	.4	.7
.9	.9	1.0		2.4	.8	.7	1.0	1.0	1.4
2.3	2.0	2.6		-.4	4.6	2.0	2.4	2.7	2.8
.7	.6	.6	Debt/Worth	.9	.4	.3	.8	.6	.7
1.7	1.6	1.7		6.1	1.3	1.3	2.0	1.6	2.0
5.2	3.7	5.8		-1.7	13.9	2.0	8.3	6.0	5.0
41.5	36.5	24.8	% Profit Before Taxes/Tangible Net Worth		14.3	16.5	25.8	30.2	22.7
(252) 19.0	(266) 15.0	(236) 6.5		(26) -.6	(28) 2.9	(54) 7.7	(67) 11.3	(54) 7.0	
3.4	2.2	-10.8		-16.0	-13.4	-13.5	-2.7	-10.1	
14.1	13.7	8.3	% Profit Before Taxes/Total Assets	15.2	4.4	8.4	9.0	9.1	8.2
6.0	5.9	1.4		.6	-.3	1.4	1.5	2.9	1.7
.5	.2	-5.1		-27.8	-10.0	-7.6	-7.5	-2.8	-4.6
12.4	13.1	10.7	Sales/Net Fixed Assets	UND	20.3	11.7	11.7	10.7	6.4
6.5	6.5	5.2		19.9	8.4	6.0	5.5	5.2	4.3
4.4	4.3	3.2		2.2	2.7	3.5	3.6	3.2	2.8
2.6	2.5	2.2	Sales/Total Assets	3.3	2.7	2.1	2.2	2.1	2.0
2.0	2.0	1.7		1.9	1.7	1.5	1.7	1.7	1.6
1.7	1.6	1.2		.6	1.2	1.2	1.4	1.2	1.2
1.8	1.7	2.2	% Depr., Dep., Amort./Sales		1.3	1.4	2.3	1.9	2.9
(260) 2.7	(273) 2.7	(237) 3.8			(28) 4.0	3.4	(57) 4.2	(65) 3.8	(49) 3.7
4.2	4.5	5.9			6.7	4.4	5.9	5.5	5.9
1.4	1.6	2.1	% Officers', Directors' Owners' Comp/Sales		2.8	1.8	2.1	1.4	
(99) 3.2	(99) 3.6	(87) 3.7			(15) 5.9	(14) 4.2	(26) 3.4	(19) 3.1	
5.3	7.1	7.1			14.1	5.1	6.6	7.9	
8015387M	7614453M	5747250M	Net Sales ($)	6379M	61643M	127872M	465981M	1218575M	3866800M
4412735M	4141483M	4010216M	Total Assets ($)	8660M	38499M	92422M	287090M	849731M	2733814M

© RMA 2010

M = $ thousand   MM = $ million
See Pages 9 through 22 for Explanation of Ratios and Data

Current Data Sorted by Assets   Comparative Historical Data

0-500M	500M-2MM	2-10MM	10-50MM	50-100MM	100-250MM	Type of Statement	4/1/05-3/31/06 ALL	4/1/06-3/31/07 ALL
		1	2		1	Unqualified		
		2	3			Reviewed	9	11
1	4	5	4			Compiled	3	4
2	4	2				Tax Returns	4	2
2	3			1		Other	7	10
		10 (4/1-9/30/09)	27 (10/1/09-3/31/10)					
5	11	10	9	1	1	**NUMBER OF STATEMENTS**	23	29
%	%	%	%	%	%		%	%
						ASSETS		
	18.7	8.7				Cash & Equivalents	8.3	8.8
	23.9	19.6				Trade Receivables (net)	31.1	25.8
	16.3	17.6				Inventory	29.4	29.8
	.4	.3				All Other Current	.7	3.2
	59.3	46.2				Total Current	69.4	67.6
	33.9	45.6				Fixed Assets (net)	20.1	22.9
	3.6	5.1				Intangibles (net)	4.2	2.2
	3.2	3.1				All Other Non-Current	6.3	7.3
	100.0	100.0				Total	100.0	100.0
						LIABILITIES		
	8.4	1.0				Notes Payable-Short Term	11.7	11.9
	2.0	4.0				Cur. Mat.-L.T.D.	2.4	3.2
	20.4	7.1				Trade Payables	18.4	13.1
	.0	.0				Income Taxes Payable	.0	.0
	5.9	3.1				All Other Current	7.1	13.9
	36.7	15.1				Total Current	39.6	42.1
	34.2	38.3				Long-Term Debt	19.2	11.4
	.0	.0				Deferred Taxes	.0	.0
	8.5	1.1				All Other Non-Current	8.6	5.0
	20.6	45.5				Net Worth	32.6	41.5
	100.0	100.0				Total Liabilities & Net Worth	100.0	100.0
						INCOME DATA		
	100.0	100.0				Net Sales	100.0	100.0
	29.6	27.1				Gross Profit	30.8	28.0
	33.6	20.5				Operating Expenses	23.7	21.5
	-4.0	6.5				Operating Profit	7.2	6.5
	1.6	2.5				All Other Expenses (net)	1.4	.7
	-5.6	4.1				Profit Before Taxes	5.8	5.8
						RATIOS		
	4.1	5.1				Current	2.8	3.2
	2.3	2.5					2.0	1.9
	1.2	1.6					1.2	1.4
	3.7	3.5				Quick	1.9	1.9
	1.2	1.7					1.0	.9
	.8	1.1					.5	.6
	[22] 16.7	[39] 9.3				Sales/Receivables	[23] 16.1	[34] 10.7
	[29] 12.5	[46] 7.9					[50] 7.3	[37] 9.8
	[54] 6.8	[52] 7.0					[56] 6.5	[55] 6.7
	[2] 183.6	[21] 17.0				Cost of Sales/Inventory	[29] 12.7	[32] 11.5
	[50] 7.2	[40] 9.2					[65] 5.6	[68] 5.4
	[77] 4.8	[63] 5.8					[78] 4.7	[85] 4.3
	[3] 144.1	[13] 28.0				Cost of Sales/Payables	[19] 19.3	[14] 27.0
	[14] 27.0	[24] 15.4					[34] 10.9	[29] 12.7
	[58] 6.3	[33] 10.9					[51] 7.2	[44] 8.2
	5.4	3.9				Sales/Working Capital	5.6	4.2
	6.6	6.2					7.6	7.3
	34.2	10.6					82.4	17.6
	4.9					EBIT/Interest	16.9	15.0
	(10) -.5						(22) 6.0	(26) 5.4
	-5.3						1.5	1.4
						Net Profit + Depr., Dep., Amort./Cur. Mat. L/T/D		
	.3	.5				Fixed/Worth	.3	.2
	1.2	1.1					.4	.5
	-1.3	3.9					1.7	1.3
	.6	.5				Debt/Worth	1.0	.5
	179.3	1.5					1.6	1.2
	-5.5	4.7					5.1	3.3
						% Profit Before Taxes/Tangible Net Worth	57.1	41.3
							(19) 37.4	(26) 22.3
							10.6	1.8
	9.1	19.2				% Profit Before Taxes/Total Assets	26.6	20.6
	-2.3	2.0					8.7	11.3
	-11.2	-3.2					2.6	.8
	14.9	11.8				Sales/Net Fixed Assets	36.7	21.5
	6.6	3.4					12.9	13.4
	2.8	1.3					7.0	6.0
	2.7	2.1				Sales/Total Assets	3.5	2.7
	2.2	1.7					2.6	2.1
	1.5	.9					1.7	1.7
	1.2					% Depr., Dep., Amort./Sales	.6	1.2
	(10) 4.0						(18) 1.8	(25) 2.1
	7.6						4.7	2.8
						% Officers', Directors' Owners' Comp/Sales	2.1	
							(14) 3.8	
							4.9	
5287M	27991M	77516M	271543M	32517M	164898M	Net Sales ($)	241613M	491673M
1350M	11797M	52542M	185838M	56463M	225176M	Total Assets ($)	126403M	258346M

Comparative Historical Data | Current Data Sorted by Sales

				Type of Statement						
	7	6	4	Unqualified				1	1	2
	6	8	2	Reviewed					1	
	5	13	13	Compiled	2	2	2	2	5	
	3	6	6	Tax Returns	1	4	1			
	10	10	12	Other	2	2	1	2	1	4
	4/1/07-3/31/08	4/1/08-3/31/09	4/1/09-3/31/10			10 (4/1-9/30/09)			27 (10/1/09-3/31/10)	
	ALL	ALL	ALL		0-1MM	1-3MM	3-5MM	5-10MM	10-25MM	25MM & OVER
	31	43	37	NUMBER OF STATEMENTS	5	8	5	5	8	6
	%	%	%	ASSETS	%	%	%	%	%	%
	8.8	8.4	12.8	Cash & Equivalents						
	27.1	24.1	23.2	Trade Receivables (net)						
	24.6	23.2	17.8	Inventory						
	1.6	2.2	.5	All Other Current						
	62.1	57.9	54.4	Total Current						
	25.9	32.0	31.7	Fixed Assets (net)						
	6.3	4.7	9.1	Intangibles (net)						
	5.8	5.4	4.8	All Other Non-Current						
	100.0	100.0	100.0	Total						
				LIABILITIES						
	7.6	7.6	4.8	Notes Payable-Short Term						
	5.1	3.8	4.9	Cur. Mat.-L.T.D.						
	13.7	15.3	14.7	Trade Payables						
	.0	.0	.0	Income Taxes Payable						
	7.9	5.0	4.9	All Other Current						
	34.3	31.7	29.2	Total Current						
	20.7	25.2	30.3	Long-Term Debt						
	.7	.2	.8	Deferred Taxes						
	4.8	9.3	15.3	All Other Non-Current						
	39.6	33.5	24.5	Net Worth						
	100.0	100.0	100.0	Total Liabilities & Net Worth						
				INCOME DATA						
	100.0	100.0	100.0	Net Sales						
	27.5	28.9	28.8	Gross Profit						
	18.5	22.6	27.2	Operating Expenses						
	9.0	6.3	1.6	Operating Profit						
	.9	.7	2.2	All Other Expenses (net)						
	8.1	5.6	-.6	Profit Before Taxes						
				RATIOS						
	2.7	3.2	4.2							
	2.0	2.2	2.5	Current						
	1.2	1.4	1.4							
	1.8	2.1	3.4							
	1.1	1.1	1.5	Quick						
	.7	.7	.9							
33	11.0	29 12.6	31 11.9	Sales/Receivables						
47	7.7	39 9.4	45 8.0							
67	5.4	55 6.7	56 6.5							
35	10.4	33 11.2	17 21.0	Cost of Sales/Inventory						
67	5.5	65 5.7	52 7.0							
91	4.0	88 4.1	89 4.1							
17	20.9	13 28.2	10 35.3	Cost of Sales/Payables						
29	12.7	31 11.9	26 14.1							
49	7.5	49 7.4	42 8.7							
	3.6	4.3	3.5	Sales/Working Capital						
	6.6	7.8	6.1							
	17.8	18.1	17.2							
	18.0	11.5	5.3	EBIT/Interest						
(28)	4.5	(38) 4.1	(33) .5							
	2.6	1.7	-1.7							
	10.2			Net Profit + Depr., Dep.,						
(10)	3.9			Amort./Cur. Mat. L/T/D						
	1.9									
	.3	.4	.3	Fixed/Worth						
	.7	.7	1.0							
	1.5	2.3	-10.2							
	.6	.5	.4	Debt/Worth						
	1.4	1.4	2.2							
	5.4	6.9	-15.7							
	45.8	66.6	33.3	% Profit Before Taxes/Tangible						
(26)	23.6	(37) 28.5	(26) 12.7	Net Worth						
	15.0	5.8	-7.8							
	16.8	16.8	10.8	% Profit Before Taxes/Total						
	13.1	7.8	-.6	Assets						
	4.0	2.1	-7.3							
	16.3	15.7	13.7	Sales/Net Fixed Assets						
	7.6	6.0	6.2							
	4.8	3.9	3.2							
	2.4	2.6	2.6	Sales/Total Assets						
	2.0	1.9	1.9							
	1.4	1.4	1.0							
	1.5	1.1	2.1	% Depr., Dep., Amort./Sales						
(27)	2.7	(39) 2.4	(29) 4.1							
	3.9	3.3	7.0							
		1.7	3.0	% Officers', Directors'						
	(17)	2.5	(12) 3.9	Owners' Comp/Sales						
		4.4	9.1							
	913778M	845918M	579752M	Net Sales ($)	4024M	13458M	20448M	36547M	113018M	392257M
	641629M	512627M	533166M	Total Assets ($)	3005M	7049M	17014M	18337M	101836M	385925M

M = $ thousand   MM = $ million
See Pages 9 through 22 for Explanation of Ratios and Data

MANUFACTURING—Hand and Edge Tool Manufacturing NAICS 332212

Current Data Sorted by Assets							Comparative Historical Data	

0-500M	500M-2MM	2-10MM	10-50MM	50-100MM	100-250MM	Type of Statement		
		3	8	3	4	Unqualified	20	17
	6	9	5	1		Reviewed	18	24
	3	5				Compiled	17	16
2	2	4				Tax Returns	6	8
3	6	11	7	1		Other	19	32
	15 (4/1-9/30/09)		68 (10/1/09-3/31/10)				4/1/05-3/31/06 ALL	4/1/06-3/31/07 ALL
5	17	32	20	5	4	NUMBER OF STATEMENTS	80	97
%	%	%	%	%	%	ASSETS	%	%
	9.4	6.2	4.6			Cash & Equivalents	5.8	6.7
	24.3	19.4	19.3			Trade Receivables (net)	23.9	24.5
	32.5	44.9	32.2			Inventory	33.7	30.6
	1.4	.9	5.0			All Other Current	2.0	1.7
	67.7	71.4	61.1			Total Current	65.4	63.5
	23.9	20.7	22.0			Fixed Assets (net)	23.1	22.2
	6.6	2.5	10.6			Intangibles (net)	6.1	7.6
	1.9	5.4	6.2			All Other Non-Current	5.4	6.7
	100.0	100.0	100.0			Total	100.0	100.0
						LIABILITIES		
	2.2	11.0	7.5			Notes Payable-Short Term	12.9	12.4
	3.9	2.3	2.5			Cur. Mat.-L.T.D.	2.9	3.3
	10.0	6.8	10.7			Trade Payables	11.1	13.2
	.0	.3	.7			Income Taxes Payable	.3	.2
	9.5	10.0	7.8			All Other Current	7.8	9.1
	25.7	30.4	29.1			Total Current	35.0	38.1
	24.3	12.9	16.7			Long-Term Debt	13.0	22.2
	.4	.9	.8			Deferred Taxes	.3	.5
	6.7	4.8	8.4			All Other Non-Current	7.2	4.8
	42.9	51.0	45.0			Net Worth	44.5	34.4
	100.0	100.0	100.0			Total Liabilities & Net Worth	100.0	100.0
						INCOME DATA		
	100.0	100.0	100.0			Net Sales	100.0	100.0
	42.0	34.3	31.9			Gross Profit	35.6	36.1
	38.3	33.6	26.1			Operating Expenses	30.2	29.4
	3.7	.7	5.7			Operating Profit	5.4	6.6
	1.3	.4	2.6			All Other Expenses (net)	1.0	1.6
	2.4	.2	3.1			Profit Before Taxes	4.4	5.0
						RATIOS		
	14.2	4.2	3.7				3.4	2.9
	2.3	2.4	2.1			Current	1.9	1.8
	1.8	1.5	1.5				1.4	1.2
	4.8	1.6	1.2				1.4	1.5
	1.1	.7	.8			Quick	.8	.9
	.9	.4	.5				.6	.6
31	11.8	29 / 12.4	39 / 9.5				37 / 9.8	32 / 11.3
40	9.1	39 / 9.3	50 / 7.4			Sales/Receivables	45 / 8.1	43 / 8.5
51	7.2	56 / 6.5	60 / 6.1				56 / 6.5	58 / 6.2
52	7.0	104 / 3.5	99 / 3.7				68 / 5.4	53 / 6.9
99	3.7	175 / 2.1	130 / 2.8			Cost of Sales/Inventory	103 / 3.6	92 / 4.0
155	2.4	262 / 1.4	181 / 2.0				139 / 2.6	138 / 2.6
7	54.4	14 / 26.8	20 / 18.1				16 / 22.4	16 / 22.7
31	11.6	19 / 18.8	30 / 12.2			Cost of Sales/Payables	26 / 14.0	30 / 12.4
44	8.4	30 / 12.2	47 / 7.7				47 / 7.8	53 / 6.8
	3.0	2.6	2.7				3.9	4.0
	5.0	4.0	5.1			Sales/Working Capital	6.3	7.1
	10.5	6.4	8.7				10.8	16.9
	16.6	7.0	8.2				17.8	8.9
	3.2	(28) 3.3	(19) 2.4			EBIT/Interest	(77) 3.2	(90) 2.9
	.1	-.4	.3				1.5	1.3
							7.5	4.5
						Net Profit + Depr., Dep., Amort./Cur. Mat. L/T/D	(23) 3.3	(27) 1.8
							2.1	1.1
	.1	.1	.4				.2	.2
	.5	.3	.8			Fixed/Worth	.6	.7
	11.3	1.0	4.8				1.4	2.5
	.6	.4	.6				.6	.7
	1.0	1.3	1.4			Debt/Worth	1.4	1.8
	54.3	1.9	13.4				3.4	10.3
	27.3	21.6	13.9				29.1	37.6
(14)	9.2	(30) 10.1	(16) 8.2			% Profit Before Taxes/Tangible Net Worth	(70) 15.0	(79) 15.6
	-.1	-9.0	-1.8				3.1	4.0
	10.5	10.4	11.3				11.9	15.7
	2.4	2.6	4.5			% Profit Before Taxes/Total Assets	5.7	5.8
	-1.7	-4.8	-.6				1.4	1.7
	40.4	39.9	28.8				21.4	28.1
	10.2	9.2	7.5			Sales/Net Fixed Assets	8.5	11.7
	5.2	4.9	3.7				5.0	4.8
	2.7	1.9	1.8				2.2	2.5
	2.1	1.5	1.2			Sales/Total Assets	1.8	1.8
	1.4	1.2	1.0				1.4	1.4
	1.3	1.4	1.3				1.4	1.2
(14)	3.0	(27) 3.0	(16) 2.6			% Depr., Dep., Amort./Sales	(71) 2.6	(81) 2.2
	5.0	5.0	4.0				4.1	4.1
		3.1					2.7	2.4
		(10) 4.4				% Officers', Directors' Owners' Comp/Sales	(28) 5.8	(31) 4.6
		6.6					7.0	7.7
4002M	46819M	223150M	703581M	443448M	579748M	Net Sales ($)	3053680M	2488513M
1259M	21281M	132849M	463290M	338405M	696459M	Total Assets ($)	1819600M	1537664M

M = $ thousand   MM = $ million
See Pages 9 through 22 for Explanation of Ratios and Data

Comparative Historical Data | Current Data Sorted by Sales

					Type of Statement						
	13		13	18	Unqualified		4	2	2	6	10
	18		21	21	Reviewed				7	4	4
	17		16	8	Compiled		3		5		
	9		6	8	Tax Returns	1	2	2	3		
	30		34	28	Other	5	5	7	2	6	3
	4/1/07-		4/1/08-	4/1/09-			15 (4/1-9/30/09)		68 (10/1/09-3/31/10)		
	3/31/08		3/31/09	3/31/10							
	ALL		**ALL**	**ALL**		**0-1MM**	**1-3MM**	**3-5MM**	**5-10MM**	**10-25MM**	**25MM & OVER**
	87		90	83	**NUMBER OF STATEMENTS**	6	14	11	19	16	17
	%		%	%	**ASSETS**	%	%	%	%	%	%
	8.5		6.2	7.0	Cash & Equivalents		10.8	6.2	6.1	7.1	5.1
	23.9		23.1	20.5	Trade Receivables (net)		18.0	15.3	24.8	21.3	19.7
	34.6		33.7	36.5	Inventory		42.1	55.3	32.5	34.2	27.8
	1.4		2.3	2.1	All Other Current		.8	.6	1.6	1.9	5.5
	68.3		65.2	66.1	Total Current		71.8	77.4	65.0	64.5	58.0
	21.7		22.9	21.4	Fixed Assets (net)		17.6	17.2	25.1	22.8	19.7
	4.8		6.1	7.3	Intangibles (net)		3.8	2.7	7.7	6.5	13.1
	5.2		5.8	5.2	All Other Non-Current		6.8	2.7	2.2	6.2	9.1
	100.0		100.0	100.0	Total		100.0	100.0	100.0	100.0	100.0
					LIABILITIES						
	12.1		12.1	8.6	Notes Payable-Short Term		3.6	11.4	6.5	8.9	10.5
	3.0		3.2	3.0	Cur. Mat.-L.T.D.		2.6	2.3	4.1	2.1	1.8
	10.7		12.0	9.5	Trade Payables		6.6	4.8	11.2	6.1	12.4
	.2		.0	.3	Income Taxes Payable		.0	.3	.3	.9	.2
	9.3		8.5	9.0	All Other Current		9.4	7.8	11.3	8.4	10.0
	35.3		35.9	30.4	Total Current		22.3	26.6	33.4	26.3	35.0
	13.8		17.5	15.9	Long-Term Debt		19.6	13.2	15.4	12.5	14.0
	.7		.7	.7	Deferred Taxes		.4	.7	1.4	.6	.7
	6.6		7.6	9.1	All Other Non-Current		10.4	2.8	3.1	7.2	9.7
	43.7		38.4	43.9	Net Worth		47.3	56.8	46.6	53.4	40.7
	100.0		100.0	100.0	Total Liabilities & Net Worth		100.0	100.0	100.0	100.0	100.0
					INCOME DATA						
	100.0		100.0	100.0	Net Sales		100.0	100.0	100.0	100.0	100.0
	35.8		34.7	35.0	Gross Profit		43.9	29.1	37.2	34.9	27.4
	30.3		30.6	32.3	Operating Expenses		42.0	31.1	34.4	29.7	23.6
	5.5		4.0	2.7	Operating Profit		1.9	-2.0	2.8	5.2	3.8
	1.5		1.8	1.3	All Other Expenses (net)		.8	-.6	2.1	1.5	1.4
	4.0		2.2	1.5	Profit Before Taxes		1.1	-1.3	.7	3.7	2.4
					RATIOS						
	4.4		3.8	4.0			15.7	5.1	3.6	4.4	3.3
	2.1		1.9	2.3	Current		3.6	2.5	1.9	2.4	1.6
	1.3		1.3	1.5			2.1	2.2	1.3	1.7	1.2
	2.1		1.5	1.6			6.2	1.2	2.0	1.9	1.2
	1.0		.8	.9	Quick		1.1	1.1	.7	1.1	.7
	.6		.4	.5			.6	.3	.4	.5	.5
29	12.4	27	13.5	33	11.2		29	12.6	24	15.4	33	11.2	35	10.5	41	8.9
40	9.2	41	8.9	42	8.6	Sales/Receivables	38	9.5	34	10.6	39	9.4	50	7.4	49	7.5
57	6.4	51	7.1	55	6.7		50	7.3	58	6.3	49	7.5	63	5.8	54	6.7
60	6.1	50	7.3	79	4.6		123	3.0	176	2.1	47	7.7	104	3.5	79	4.6
98	3.7	99	3.7	133	2.8	Cost of Sales/Inventory	160	2.3	235	1.6	105	3.5	137	2.7	103	3.5
154	2.4	164	2.2	193	1.9		291	1.3	280	1.3	174	2.1	176	2.1	127	2.9
15	23.6	14	26.5	16	23.2		6	63.1	4	99.7	19	19.4	13	28.7	20	18.6
24	15.2	26	14.1	24	15.3	Cost of Sales/Payables	23	15.7	14	25.9	28	13.0	20	18.1	32	11.5
45	8.1	48	7.5	41	8.8		50	7.3	24	15.3	39	9.3	34	10.9	47	7.8
	3.7		3.6	2.8			2.3	2.3	3.7	2.7	3.8
	5.3		6.4	5.1	Sales/Working Capital		3.0	2.6	6.8	4.1	8.2
	14.8		13.2	9.1			4.6	6.2	16.0	5.8	12.8
	9.8		6.0	8.6			19.0	13.7	8.9	9.7	10.0
(77)	2.9	(83)	1.7	(76)	2.8	EBIT/Interest	(13)	1.9	(10)	1.1	(17)	4.0	(15)	3.8	2.6
	1.0		.0	-.3			-1.0	-4.4	.2	1.5	.6
	5.3		5.8	5.1	Net Profit + Depr., Dep.,						
(26)	2.5	(31)	1.2	(26)	1.7	Amort./Cur. Mat. L/T/D						
	1.4		.1	.4							
	.2		.3	.2			.1	.1	.2	.1	.5
	.5		.6	.6	Fixed/Worth		.4	.2	.5	.4	.8
	1.2		1.6	1.7			1.3	.7	2.7	1.0	-3.4
	.6		.7	.6			.6	.3	.4	.6	.7
	1.3		1.6	1.3	Debt/Worth		1.0	.5	1.3	1.2	2.6
	4.2		5.4	4.8			2.4	2.5	4.8	1.5	-25.3
	34.2		37.6	21.8			22.0	20.9	25.5	13.8	48.1
(79)	15.0	(78)	11.2	(68)	8.2	% Profit Before Taxes/Tangible Net Worth	(12)	8.6	-4.1	(17)	12.8	(15)	6.7	(12)	8.7
	3.4		-6.6	-3.7			1.3	-18.4	-3.6	.5	-3.6
	13.7		10.8	10.1			11.6	12.6	8.4	12.0	10.5
	6.5		2.7	3.6	% Profit Before Taxes/Total Assets		2.3	-1.0	6.2	4.5	4.3
	.5		-2.9	-3.4			-3.2	-9.5	-4.4	.3	-1.0
	24.9		21.0	31.2			53.9	15.2	31.1	52.1	23.6
	11.2		9.8	8.8	Sales/Net Fixed Assets		17.0	8.4	9.7	5.4	7.4
	5.3		4.7	4.7			5.8	6.6	4.7	3.5	4.2
	2.6		2.4	2.2			2.2	1.8	2.8	1.8	2.1
	1.9		1.7	1.6	Sales/Total Assets		1.8	1.5	1.9	1.4	1.4
	1.5		1.3	1.1			1.0	1.2	1.4	1.1	.7
	1.5		1.2	1.4			.6		1.7	1.6	1.4
(74)	2.4	(80)	2.7	(68)	2.8	% Depr., Dep., Amort./Sales	(11)	2.2	(18)	3.0	(10)	3.6	(15)	2.1
	4.1		3.9	4.8			3.9		7.0	4.8	3.9
	2.2		1.9	3.1							
(31)	4.4	(35)	5.6	(22)	5.5	% Officers', Directors' Owners' Comp/Sales						
	7.4		8.0	9.0							
	1814444M		1975566M	2000748M	Net Sales ($)	3271M	27349M	47214M	131163M	264245M	1527506M
	1188162M		1428892M	1653543M	Total Assets ($)	2593M	19234M	34896M	86069M	194952M	1315799M

M = $ thousand   MM = $ million
See Pages 9 through 22 for Explanation of Ratios and Data

Current Data Sorted by Assets   Comparative Historical Data

0-500M	500M-2MM	2-10MM	10-50MM	50-100MM	100-250MM	Type of Statement	4/1/05-3/31/06 ALL	4/1/06-3/31/07 ALL
		3	5	4	4	Unqualified	15	23
	2	8	1			Reviewed	20	17
1	5	4	2			Compiled	10	14
2	5	4				Tax Returns	4	11
1	8	12	12	4	2	Other	24	27
	23 (4/1-9/30/09)		66 (10/1/09-3/31/10)					
4	20	31	20	8	6	NUMBER OF STATEMENTS	73	92
%	%	%	%	%	%	**ASSETS**	%	%
	18.7	14.6	15.1			Cash & Equivalents	10.1	7.3
	26.1	27.6	16.0			Trade Receivables (net)	32.5	30.9
	22.6	26.2	22.6			Inventory	23.4	25.7
	2.3	2.7	5.2			All Other Current	4.0	4.5
	69.6	71.1	58.9			Total Current	70.0	68.4
	22.0	19.1	34.7			Fixed Assets (net)	23.0	23.7
	3.6	1.4	1.0			Intangibles (net)	2.1	3.0
	4.9	8.4	5.4			All Other Non-Current	4.9	4.8
	100.0	100.0	100.0			Total	100.0	100.0
						LIABILITIES		
	8.5	5.9	12.1			Notes Payable-Short Term	9.5	8.5
	5.8	3.5	5.4			Cur. Mat.-L.T.D.	4.6	2.6
	14.1	16.0	9.6			Trade Payables	20.9	17.8
	.6	.3	.0			Income Taxes Payable	.4	.4
	14.6	11.2	13.4			All Other Current	16.1	18.6
	43.6	36.9	40.4			Total Current	51.5	48.0
	24.3	18.1	16.0			Long-Term Debt	12.7	13.3
	.8	.6	.7			Deferred Taxes	.2	.4
	19.0	8.1	11.8			All Other Non-Current	7.4	5.5
	12.4	36.3	31.1			Net Worth	28.2	32.9
	100.0	100.0	100.0			Total Liabilities & Net Worth	100.0	100.0
						INCOME DATA		
	100.0	100.0	100.0			Net Sales	100.0	100.0
	40.8	31.6	29.0			Gross Profit	26.6	27.0
	35.2	29.1	30.3			Operating Expenses	22.3	20.4
	5.6	2.6	-1.3			Operating Profit	4.3	6.6
	1.5	1.8	2.7			All Other Expenses (net)	.8	.9
	4.1	.8	-3.9			Profit Before Taxes	3.5	5.6
						RATIOS		
	5.3	3.8	4.2				2.0	2.1
	2.5	1.7	1.4			Current	1.4	1.5
	1.3	1.2	1.0				1.1	1.2
	4.8	2.3	2.4				1.2	1.2
	1.4	1.2	.7			Quick	.9	.9
	.4	.7	.3				.6	.5
	16 23.3	27 13.6	19 19.3				33 11.2	27 13.6
	26 13.9	45 8.1	33 10.9			Sales/Receivables	44 8.4	43 8.5
	60 6.1	65 5.6	54 6.7				64 5.7	66 5.5
	4 84.6	30 12.1	32 11.4				19 18.8	24 15.3
	25 14.8	56 6.5	54 6.8			Cost of Sales/Inventory	40 9.2	46 8.0
	77 4.7	119 3.1	138 2.6				64 5.7	76 4.8
	9 40.3	18 20.5	15 23.7				21 17.1	20 18.6
	14 26.2	34 10.6	24 15.0			Cost of Sales/Payables	35 10.3	30 12.2
	36 10.1	53 6.8	38 9.7				49 7.4	44 8.3
	4.1	3.8	3.5				7.2	6.8
	6.7	6.9	9.6			Sales/Working Capital	12.2	10.8
	30.0	25.5	NM				45.9	29.4
	9.3	5.1	18.8				13.3	16.1
	(19) 1.9	(28) 1.8	(19) .3			EBIT/Interest	(68) 5.3	(85) 6.5
	.7	-4.3	-10.4				2.3	3.1
							7.5	17.6
						Net Profit + Depr., Dep., Amort./Cur. Mat. L/T/D	(27) 3.1	(32) 5.6
							1.7	2.6
	.2	.1	.3				.3	.3
	.5	.5	1.1			Fixed/Worth	.7	.7
	1.3	1.3	3.2				1.8	1.5
	.6	.8	.5				1.2	1.0
	1.1	1.8	1.7			Debt/Worth	2.4	1.7
	3.7	5.0	5.6				5.4	3.1
	43.9	21.7	18.0				59.2	54.6
	(16) 12.7	(26) 10.6	(18) -7.8			% Profit Before Taxes/Tangible Net Worth	(64) 27.8	(83) 27.1
	-2.1	-11.5	-28.2				12.4	14.9
	24.9	8.9	8.8				15.6	17.7
	6.9	3.3	-4.2			% Profit Before Taxes/Total Assets	9.6	11.4
	-.8	-8.4	-16.7				3.1	5.4
	45.0	39.2	13.3				27.0	25.9
	14.4	15.3	6.0			Sales/Net Fixed Assets	12.7	10.7
	7.1	8.2	2.3				8.0	6.6
	3.8	2.9	2.7				3.2	3.5
	3.0	2.1	1.6			Sales/Total Assets	2.5	2.4
	2.0	1.6	.9				2.0	1.8
	.4	.7	.9				.7	.8
	(13) 1.1	(28) 1.2	(19) 2.5			% Depr., Dep., Amort./Sales	(65) 1.4	(86) 1.5
	1.9	2.6	3.7				2.2	2.1
	5.3	2.1					1.1	2.3
	(11) 6.9	(13) 4.1				% Officers', Directors' Owners' Comp/Sales	(21) 3.0	(24) 4.9
	11.4	7.0					7.3	6.4
3020M	70175M	342558M	642137M	977092M	1721251M	Net Sales ($)	4091816M	5852125M
888M	21915M	162504M	409000M	506328M	856594M	Total Assets ($)	1735141M	2522908M

M = $ thousand   MM = $ million
See Pages 9 through 22 for Explanation of Ratios and Data

Comparative Historical Data

Current Data Sorted by Sales

Type of Statement	4/1/07-3/31/08 ALL	4/1/08-3/31/09 ALL	4/1/09-3/31/10 ALL	0-1MM	1-3MM	3-5MM	5-10MM	10-25MM	25MM & OVE
Unqualified	21	17	16				2	1	13
Reviewed	20	14	11		2	1	1	6	1
Compiled	11	10	12	2		3	5	2	
Tax Returns	11	10	11		1	3	5	2	
Other	32	40	39	1	6	2	10	6	14
				23 (4/1-9/30/09)			66 (10/1/09-3/31/10)		
NUMBER OF STATEMENTS	95	91	89	3	9	9	23	17	28
	%	%	%	%	%	%	%	%	%
ASSETS									
Cash & Equivalents	11.0	12.8	14.9				19.7	14.1	15.2
Trade Receivables (net)	27.8	28.1	22.8				25.3	26.0	20.0
Inventory	24.1	25.9	25.2				24.3	21.8	27.8
All Other Current	4.1	3.8	3.2				1.2	4.6	4.8
Total Current	67.0	70.6	66.1				70.5	66.4	67.9
Fixed Assets (net)	25.1	21.4	25.1				24.6	24.3	25.9
Intangibles (net)	2.7	1.8	2.3				1.2	1.3	1.0
All Other Non-Current	5.2	6.1	6.5				3.7	8.1	5.2
Total	100.0	100.0	100.0				100.0	100.0	100.0
LIABILITIES									
Notes Payable-Short Term	12.7	15.8	10.2				9.3	4.9	11.1
Cur. Mat.-L.T.D.	3.8	3.0	4.0				2.0	3.3	3.8
Trade Payables	14.0	16.6	15.0				11.6	15.6	14.9
Income Taxes Payable	.3	.3	.2				.1	.3	.1
All Other Current	19.3	19.6	13.2				9.8	8.7	16.2
Total Current	50.2	55.4	42.7				32.9	32.9	46.1
Long-Term Debt	13.9	15.3	17.3				19.8	10.9	8.7
Deferred Taxes	.2	.4	.7				.5	.4	1.0
All Other Non-Current	3.1	3.2	11.2				13.0	3.2	12.8
Net Worth	32.6	25.7	28.0				33.9	52.6	31.5
Total Liabilities & Net Worth	100.0	100.0	100.0				100.0	100.0	100.0
INCOME DATA									
Net Sales	100.0	100.0	100.0				100.0	100.0	100.0
Gross Profit	29.1	27.5	32.2				34.0	30.6	25.6
Operating Expenses	23.3	24.1	30.1				32.2	30.4	22.8
Operating Profit	5.8	3.4	2.1				1.8	.2	2.7
All Other Expenses (net)	1.3	.5	1.7				3.5	.3	1.1
Profit Before Taxes	4.5	2.9	.5				-1.6	-.1	1.6
RATIOS									
Current	2.2	2.9	3.5				5.1	4.7	3.0
	1.5	1.5	1.7				1.7	2.5	1.5
	1.1	1.1	1.2				1.5	1.2	1.1
Quick	1.4	1.5	2.3				2.8	2.8	1.3
	.8	.7	1.0				1.2	1.7	.7
	.6	.5	.4				.8	.7	.4
Sales/Receivables	24 15.2	21 17.5	19 19.7				27 13.6	29 12.7	15 24.9
	38 9.7	36 10.3	36 10.3				42 8.7	38 9.6	31 11.6
	62 5.8	51 7.1	58 6.3				88 4.1	56 6.6	49 7.4
Cost of Sales/Inventory	17 21.7	24 14.9	21 17.4				30 12.1	8 43.4	32 11.4
	41 9.0	50 7.3	48 7.6				56 6.5	48 7.7	55 6.7
	81 4.5	86 4.3	107 3.4				119 3.1	122 3.0	107 3.4
Cost of Sales/Payables	16 23.2	12 29.3	14 26.1				13 27.7	15 24.1	17 21.0
	26 14.2	26 14.3	29 12.7				28 13.3	27 13.6	33 11.0
	39 9.3	40 9.2	50 7.3				53 6.8	42 8.8	53 6.8
Sales/Working Capital	6.2	5.0	3.8				3.2	3.4	4.9
	12.0	12.1	7.5				5.6	5.2	11.1
	104.6	73.2	31.1				14.5	26.4	25.4
EBIT/Interest	19.7	13.1	9.1				3.2	8.9	19.2
	(85) 5.2	(79) 4.1	(81) 1.4				(22) -.1	(15) -.1	(25) 2.8
	1.4	1.3	-2.5				-5.0	-12.3	.6
Net Profit + Depr., Dep., Amort./Cur. Mat. L/T/D	14.9	10.7	16.7						35.9
	(30) 4.2	(23) 4.6	(26) 2.8						(15) 7.7
	1.5	1.6	.8						.9
Fixed/Worth	.2	.2	.3				.1	.2	.4
	.6	.7	.7				.7	.4	.7
	1.6	2.1	1.5				4.1	.9	1.4
Debt/Worth	.9	.7	.7				.8	.4	.7
	1.7	2.3	1.8				2.3	.9	2.0
	4.7	4.5	5.3				5.6	1.5	5.4
% Profit Before Taxes/Tangible Net Worth	54.5	47.8	27.5				15.4	22.0	30.2
	(85) 30.3	(79) 27.8	(75) 6.1				(20) .3	(16) 7.8	(25) 7.4
	8.2	5.9	-13.3				-22.2	-18.7	-1.6
% Profit Before Taxes/Total Assets	19.9	19.9	11.5				7.0	13.9	12.7
	9.9	6.4	1.6				-1.9	.6	3.1
	.8	.9	-7.4				-11.6	-9.4	-1.4
Sales/Net Fixed Assets	33.4	38.4	25.2				43.8	20.0	13.3
	12.5	14.3	11.3				14.7	12.4	8.3
	6.4	7.5	6.0				5.0	4.7	5.9
Sales/Total Assets	3.3	3.3	3.0				2.9	2.8	2.7
	2.4	2.6	2.1				2.1	2.1	2.0
	1.7	1.9	1.6				1.3	1.7	1.4
% Depr., Dep., Amort./Sales	.8	.7	.7				.7	.8	1.1
	(84) 1.4	(75) 1.3	(76) 1.8				(20) 1.5	(16) 1.3	(26) 2.2
	2.2	1.9	2.9				2.8	3.1	3.1
% Officers', Directors', Owners' Comp/Sales	1.4	2.1	2.4				1.9		
	(22) 3.5	(24) 3.6	(32) 6.0				(11) 4.7		
	6.2	6.0	9.5				9.2		
Net Sales ($)	4315287M	5042422M	3756233M	1176M	13402M	35721M	174678M	240045M	3291211M
Total Assets ($)	1820120M	2279140M	1957229M	439M	5946M	16090M	129230M	127795M	1677729M

M = $ thousand   MM = $ million
See Pages 9 through 22 for Explanation of Ratios and Data

Current Data Sorted by Assets   Comparative Historical Data

						Type of Statement		
1	19	12	33	4	12	Unqualified	93	83
4	20	76	30			Reviewed	158	157
6	25	26				Compiled	57	73
8	19	19				Tax Returns	47	49
		55	48	9	7	Other	150	131
	93 (4/1-9/30/09)		340 (10/1/09-3/31/10)				4/1/05-3/31/06	4/1/06-3/31/07
0-500M	500M-2MM	2-10MM	10-50MM	50-100MM	100-250MM		ALL	ALL
19	83	188	111	13	19	NUMBER OF STATEMENTS	505	493
%	%	%	%	%	%	ASSETS	%	%
21.0	11.3	13.7	16.6	14.4	10.8	Cash & Equivalents	8.0	8.1
26.8	31.3	31.6	27.2	27.8	22.4	Trade Receivables (net)	37.3	37.1
16.9	20.6	17.1	18.1	24.1	14.4	Inventory	18.3	18.7
3.8	4.6	4.0	5.8	6.0	11.6	All Other Current	5.2	5.0
68.5	67.7	66.4	67.6	72.2	59.1	Total Current	68.8	68.9
23.8	23.8	27.4	24.9	21.1	25.6	Fixed Assets (net)	24.0	23.7
1.2	2.9	2.1	2.6	4.3	9.6	Intangibles (net)	1.3	1.8
6.5	5.6	4.1	4.8	2.3	5.7	All Other Non-Current	6.0	5.6
100.0	100.0	100.0	100.0	100.0	100.0	Total	100.0	100.0
						LIABILITIES		
19.7	14.4	9.6	6.4	7.5	5.7	Notes Payable-Short Term	11.5	11.1
9.4	3.2	3.7	2.5	1.0	2.2	Cur. Mat.-L.T.D.	3.6	3.4
17.7	14.3	14.0	12.0	12.8	10.9	Trade Payables	18.5	18.6
.0	.4	.3	.4	.2	.3	Income Taxes Payable	.4	.5
12.9	11.0	10.0	10.8	17.1	13.0	All Other Current	11.2	11.8
59.8	43.3	37.5	32.1	38.5	32.1	Total Current	45.1	45.4
20.8	15.5	12.2	11.5	8.0	11.9	Long-Term Debt	15.4	15.0
.0	.4	.3	.7	.6	1.6	Deferred Taxes	.4	.4
9.5	4.1	3.8	4.3	3.6	4.2	All Other Non-Current	4.2	3.1
9.8	36.6	46.2	51.3	49.3	50.3	Net Worth	34.9	36.1
100.0	100.0	100.0	100.0	100.0	100.0	Total Liabilities & Net Worth	100.0	100.0
						INCOME DATA		
100.0	100.0	100.0	100.0	100.0	100.0	Net Sales	100.0	100.0
37.0	28.9	24.5	22.6	23.1	20.2	Gross Profit	25.5	25.9
42.3	32.4	21.9	16.2	12.7	15.1	Operating Expenses	20.4	20.1
-5.3	-3.5	2.6	6.4	10.4	5.1	Operating Profit	5.0	5.8
.7	.5	.7	.9	1.1	.6	All Other Expenses (net)	.7	.6
-5.9	-4.0	1.9	5.5	9.3	4.5	Profit Before Taxes	4.4	5.2
						RATIOS		
2.7	3.4	3.5	3.7	2.7	2.2	Current	2.2	2.3
1.1	1.7	1.8	2.0	1.9	2.0		1.5	1.5
.8	1.1	1.2	1.4	1.5	1.5		1.2	1.1
1.8	2.0	2.1	2.7	1.6	1.3	Quick	1.6	1.5
.8	1.0	1.3	1.2	1.2	1.1		1.0	1.0
.5	.5	.7	.7	.8	.9		.7	.7
11 33.7	28 12.8	35 10.4	35 10.5	46 7.9	40 9.1	Sales/Receivables	38 9.7	37 9.9
27 13.4	41 8.9	50 7.3	52 7.1	57 6.4	55 6.7		53 6.8	55 6.7
45 8.1	62 5.9	73 5.0	68 5.3	66 5.5	62 5.9		75 4.8	74 5.0
1 352.7	6 58.2	10 38.0	16 22.5	38 9.6	8 47.8	Cost of Sales/Inventory	9 39.0	10 38.1
18 20.7	33 11.0	28 13.0	41 8.8	70 5.2	38 9.6		31 11.7	32 11.4
50 7.3	87 4.2	63 5.8	71 5.1	104 3.5	73 5.0		60 6.0	62 5.9
8 47.5	11 31.8	16 23.4	16 22.8	16 22.4	25 14.5	Cost of Sales/Payables	19 19.0	19 18.9
22 16.7	22 16.6	28 13.1	27 13.4	30 12.2	31 11.7		33 11.2	33 11.2
68 5.4	43 8.5	41 8.9	41 8.9	44 8.3	41 9.0		50 7.2	49 7.5
8.5	4.8	4.0	3.2	3.8	3.9	Sales/Working Capital	6.0	5.8
34.1	8.5	7.7	5.8	4.7	7.5		10.5	10.2
-16.8	41.0	25.5	10.9	9.5	9.4		29.5	31.1
7.0	5.4	12.6	29.8	72.8	10.1	EBIT/Interest	14.8	17.1
(16) .2	(73) .8	(171) 3.3	(101) 6.4	(10) 16.5	(18) 7.6		(464) 5.5	(458) 5.7
-9.9	-9.1	.5	1.3	5.5	1.1		2.0	2.1
	2.6	7.8	12.5			Net Profit + Depr., Dep.,	8.1	8.8
	(13) 1.0	(53) 2.1	(35) 1.7			Amort./Cur. Mat. L/T/D	(140) 3.4	(128) 4.2
	-1.2	.8	.5				1.7	2.0
.3	.2	.2	.2	.2	.5	Fixed/Worth	.3	.3
1.4	.5	.5	.4	.5	.6		.6	.6
-2.3	2.4	1.6	1.0	.9	.9		1.4	1.6
1.7	.5	.5	.4	.7	.8	Debt/Worth	.8	.9
6.6	1.2	1.1	1.3	1.1	1.1		1.8	1.8
-5.2	7.8	3.4	2.2	2.1	1.8		4.5	4.4
20.1	20.0	30.4	31.7	56.0	38.0	% Profit Before Taxes/Tangible	49.6	49.6
(12) -6.6	(69) 1.9	(173) 10.2	(108) 16.9	(12) 46.3	(18) 17.5	Net Worth	(466) 25.9	(455) 30.2
-152.0	-24.2	.4	1.3	19.2	7.0		8.6	14.5
7.5	6.5	11.3	17.7	27.6	12.6	% Profit Before Taxes/Total	16.9	18.9
-14.4	.0	4.3	6.1	21.8	7.0	Assets	8.6	10.2
-30.6	-18.5	-1.2	.7	7.8	3.9		2.6	3.6
52.4	40.4	21.0	15.0	17.9	11.5	Sales/Net Fixed Assets	25.4	27.2
22.4	12.1	9.9	8.7	8.7	6.2		13.2	14.0
7.8	5.9	4.4	4.4	6.6	4.5		6.5	6.9
3.9	3.0	2.7	2.2	2.2	1.8	Sales/Total Assets	3.0	3.1
3.2	2.2	2.1	1.7	1.9	1.6		2.3	2.4
2.3	1.7	1.5	1.3	1.5	1.3		1.8	1.9
1.4	.7	.9	.9	.7	1.3	% Depr., Dep., Amort./Sales	.7	.8
(12) 1.7	(68) 1.8	(175) 2.0	(108) 1.6	(11) 1.5	(12) 1.9		(449) 1.4	(440) 1.4
3.8	3.8	4.1	3.5	2.8	2.5		2.6	2.5
3.6	3.7	1.6	.8			% Officers', Directors'	1.7	1.7
(11) 9.8	(55) 5.5	(83) 3.2	(25) 1.9			Owners' Comp/Sales	(199) 3.3	(179) 3.1
18.2	8.8	6.0	3.9				6.1	6.0
18337M	248022M	1865256M	4001839M	1754986M	5061207M	Net Sales ($)	14434389M	16043368M
5896M	101379M	897562M	2291083M	964295M	3291906M	Total Assets ($)	6774892M	7296738M

M = $ thousand   MM = $ million
See Pages 9 through 22 for Explanation of Ratios and Data

Comparative Historical Data | | | Type of Statement | ## Current Data Sorted by Sales

			Type of Statement						
81	81	61	Unqualified	1	7	17	6	16	39
139	148	126	Reviewed				28	53	20
64	66	50	Compiled	2	16	11	15	6	
44	47	50	Tax Returns	6	14	13	11	6	
174	180	146	Other	8	16	18	22	28	54
4/1/07- 3/31/08 ALL	4/1/08- 3/31/09 ALL	4/1/09- 3/31/10 ALL		93 (4/1-9/30/09)			340 (10/1/09-3/31/10)		
				0-1MM	1-3MM	3-5MM	5-10MM	10-25MM	25MM & OVER
502	522	433	NUMBER OF STATEMENTS	17	53	59	82	109	113
%	%	%	**ASSETS**	%	%	%	%	%	%
10.6	10.3	14.2	Cash & Equivalents	12.0	14.3	13.8	12.9	14.0	15.8
34.4	34.2	29.7	Trade Receivables (net)	25.3	23.0	31.7	32.1	32.7	27.6
18.5	19.2	18.1	Inventory	18.4	21.6	16.1	16.9	18.2	18.2
5.3	5.3	5.0	All Other Current	3.4	5.2	3.1	4.5	4.4	7.0
68.8	69.0	66.9	Total Current	59.0	64.2	64.6	66.4	69.3	68.6
23.4	23.7	25.6	Fixed Assets (net)	32.1	26.9	26.0	28.8	24.3	22.9
2.4	2.4	2.7	Intangibles (net)	1.9	3.2	3.1	1.7	2.3	3.7
5.5	5.0	4.7	All Other Non-Current	7.0	5.8	6.3	3.1	4.1	4.8
100.0	100.0	100.0	Total	100.0	100.0	100.0	100.0	100.0	100.0
			LIABILITIES						
9.7	10.2	9.9	Notes Payable-Short Term	24.9	13.5	10.9	10.2	8.7	6.3
4.3	3.2	3.4	Cur. Mat.-L.T.D.	7.4	4.2	4.1	3.6	3.1	2.2
17.3	15.9	13.5	Trade Payables	15.1	12.5	14.4	12.9	14.8	12.5
.4	.4	.3	Income Taxes Payable	.0	.4	.4	.3	.5	.3
13.9	13.1	10.9	All Other Current	7.3	12.5	10.0	9.6	10.4	12.5
45.6	42.8	38.0	Total Current	54.7	43.2	39.8	36.5	37.6	33.7
14.2	14.0	12.9	Long-Term Debt	27.2	20.6	14.3	12.4	9.8	9.7
.3	.4	.5	Deferred Taxes	.0	.2	.1	.4	.7	.7
3.0	2.7	4.2	All Other Non-Current	6.0	5.8	2.6	4.8	3.9	4.0
36.9	40.1	44.4	Net Worth	12.1	30.2	43.2	45.9	48.0	51.9
100.0	100.0	100.0	Total Liabilities & Net Worth	100.0	100.0	100.0	100.0	100.0	100.0
			INCOME DATA						
100.0	100.0	100.0	Net Sales	100.0	100.0	100.0	100.0	100.0	100.0
27.1	26.1	25.1	Gross Profit	36.9	30.0	28.5	24.1	23.2	22.0
20.4	20.1	22.8	Operating Expenses	44.3	36.6	27.8	21.6	19.2	14.7
6.7	6.0	2.4	Operating Profit	-7.4	-6.7	.7	2.5	4.0	7.3
.7	.7	.7	All Other Expenses (net)	.8	.8	.6	.8	.5	.9
6.0	5.3	1.7	Profit Before Taxes	-8.2	-7.4	.1	1.7	3.4	6.4
			RATIOS						
2.4	2.6	3.3	Current	3.7	3.4	3.2	3.8	3.1	3.3
1.6	1.7	1.8		1.0	1.7	1.6	1.9	1.8	2.1
1.2	1.2	1.3		.6	1.0	1.0	1.2	1.3	1.4
1.6	1.7	2.1	Quick	1.6	1.9	2.0	2.1	2.3	2.0
(501) 1.0	1.0	1.1		.5	.9	1.0	1.2	1.3	1.2
.7	.7	.7		.3	.5	.6	.7	.7	.8
35 10.4	32 11.3	34 10.8	Sales/Receivables	21 17.0	22 16.9	32 11.5	34 10.7	36 10.3	36 10.2
49 7.5	49 7.4	49 7.4		36 10.1	40 9.1	59 6.2	46 8.0	51 7.1	51 7.2
66 5.5	67 5.4	70 5.2		54 6.7	65 6.7	77 4.7	72 5.1	73 5.0	63 5.8
9 42.7	10 36.6	11 32.8	Cost of Sales/Inventory	0 UND	13 27.1	7 53.4	9 41.7	12 29.7	13 29.2
31 11.7	32 11.5	35 10.3		24 14.9	45 8.1	24 15.0	32 11.5	36 10.0	38 9.6
65 5.6	63 5.8	70 5.2		71 5.1	101 3.6	69 5.3	60 6.1	65 5.6	72 5.1
18 20.4	16 22.6	15 24.4	Cost of Sales/Payables	11 34.2	12 30.9	15 24.8	15 24.4	16 22.4	16 22.5
29 12.6	27 13.6	26 14.0		27 13.7	22 17.0	25 14.7	25 14.9	29 12.4	29 12.8
45 8.2	42 8.7	41 8.8		65 5.6	51 7.1	45 8.2	40 9.2	43 8.5	40 9.1
5.8	5.3	4.0	Sales/Working Capital	4.2	4.1	4.9	4.0	4.1	3.5
9.7	8.7	7.4		-70.0	9.2	8.4	7.0	7.5	5.8
23.9	21.9	19.6		-14.0	NM	85.0	25.3	18.5	10.5
19.0	20.2	13.0	EBIT/Interest	5.9	2.0	13.3	9.6	20.2	28.1
(458) 5.8	(476) 6.5	(389) 3.3		(14) 1.1	(47) -.2	(53) 1.6	(76) 4.2	(97) 3.5	(102) 7.3
2.4	2.4	-.1		-8.1	-18.1	-1.6	.9	.8	2.1
9.1	10.4	8.6	Net Profit + Depr., Dep., Amort./Cur. Mat. L/T/D			5.3	8.8	6.6	13.3
(132) 3.4	(134) 3.9	(114) 2.0				(11) 1.8	(19) 1.0	(35) 2.1	(42) 3.3
1.5	1.7	.7				.7	.4	.9	.8
.2	.2	.2	Fixed/Worth	.2	.2	.2	.2	.2	.3
.5	.5	.5		2.3	.8	.6	.5	.4	.5
1.3	1.3	1.4		-1.7	NM	2.3	1.4	1.3	.8
.8	.6	.5	Debt/Worth	.5	.5	.5	.6	.5	.5
1.6	1.5	1.2		19.3	1.9	1.3	1.1	1.1	1.2
4.0	3.6	3.1		-5.2	NM	6.0	3.0	3.2	2.0
58.3	52.2	30.1	% Profit Before Taxes/Tangible Net Worth	29.0	7.1	29.3	27.6	30.8	38.4
(448) 32.6	(469) 26.2	(392) 10.7		(11) .7	(40) -3.7	(52) 2.8	(75) 9.0	(104) 11.6	(110) 18.1
14.2	9.8	-.9		-42.6	-55.0	-13.8	.6	1.3	8.0
24.3	19.5	12.5	% Profit Before Taxes/Total Assets	3.1	2.4	11.0	11.2	13.1	21.9
11.4	9.4	4.4		-11.9	-3.2	.9	5.0	5.1	7.6
4.1	3.1	-2.6		-28.5	-25.7	-10.1	-.1	.4	3.6
26.5	26.7	21.3	Sales/Net Fixed Assets	26.8	40.2	25.7	21.4	23.1	14.8
13.4	12.4	9.7		8.8	7.8	10.5	7.7	10.9	9.0
6.9	6.7	4.7		3.4	3.6	3.8	4.4	6.1	4.8
3.1	3.1	2.6	Sales/Total Assets	2.9	3.0	2.7	2.8	2.7	2.3
2.5	2.3	2.0		2.2	2.0	2.0	2.0	2.1	1.9
1.9	1.8	1.5		1.0	1.2	1.3	1.6	1.6	1.5
.7	.8	.9	% Depr., Dep., Amort./Sales	1.4	.9	.9	1.0	.9	.8
(441) 1.3	(457) 1.4	(386) 1.8		(11) 2.1	(43) 2.1	(51) 1.9	(77) 2.2	(103) 1.5	(101) 1.5
2.4	2.5	3.6		9.1	6.9	4.4	4.2	3.3	2.7
1.7	1.7	1.8	% Officers', Directors' Owners' Comp/Sales		4.0	2.8	1.6	1.1	.7
(201) 3.1	(202) 3.2	(175) 3.9			(28) 6.1	(36) 4.6	(43) 3.6	(39) 2.4	(21) 1.8
6.7	6.1	7.3			10.1	7.3	6.6	4.9	3.3
16970525M	18167322M	12949647M	Net Sales ($)	11346M	98690M	228843M	596824M	1737970M	10275974M
7847073M	8290672M	7552121M	Total Assets ($)	7355M	61705M	132328M	328393M	933643M	6088697M

M = $ thousand   MM = $ million
See Pages 9 through 22 for Explanation of Ratios and Data

MANUFACTURING—Plate Work Manufacturing NAICS 332313

| Current Data Sorted by Assets | | | | | | Comparative Historical Data | | |

Type of Statement

0-500M	500M-2MM	2-10MM	10-50MM	50-100MM	100-250MM		4/1/05-3/31/06 ALL	4/1/06-3/31/07 ALL
		8	9	1	1	Unqualified	28	29
	4	16	7			Reviewed	31	30
	12	11	1			Compiled	19	18
2	9	3	1			Tax Returns	7	10
2	6	20	15	3	3	Other	39	42
	27 (4/1-9/30/09)		107 (10/1/09-3/31/10)					
4	31	58	33	4	4	NUMBER OF STATEMENTS	124	129
%	%	%	%	%	%	ASSETS	%	%
	15.6	13.6	13.4			Cash & Equivalents	8.4	9.5
	19.3	22.5	20.9			Trade Receivables (net)	30.5	29.4
	15.4	20.9	19.1			Inventory	23.4	22.1
	2.3	3.4	8.2			All Other Current	4.5	4.5
	52.6	60.5	61.6			Total Current	66.9	65.5
	38.5	29.1	26.6			Fixed Assets (net)	24.0	25.4
	1.9	2.1	4.8			Intangibles (net)	2.9	3.3
	7.0	8.4	7.0			All Other Non-Current	6.3	5.8
	100.0	100.0	100.0			Total	100.0	100.0
						LIABILITIES		
	7.7	7.9	5.6			Notes Payable-Short Term	8.5	9.1
	4.3	3.5	5.0			Cur. Mat.-L.T.D.	3.9	2.4
	11.2	10.5	10.4			Trade Payables	15.9	14.9
	.0	.4	.1			Income Taxes Payable	.3	.4
	6.8	10.8	15.2			All Other Current	13.9	17.4
	29.9	33.1	36.3			Total Current	42.5	44.1
	24.2	13.7	13.2			Long-Term Debt	13.7	14.4
	.0	.3	.4			Deferred Taxes	.4	.5
	10.0	6.3	12.4			All Other Non-Current	7.1	7.1
	35.9	46.7	37.7			Net Worth	36.3	33.9
	100.0	100.0	100.0			Total Liabilities & Net Worth	100.0	100.0
						INCOME DATA		
	100.0	100.0	100.0			Net Sales	100.0	100.0
	38.8	26.9	24.8			Gross Profit	23.9	25.7
	42.0	22.8	20.5			Operating Expenses	18.8	19.3
	-3.2	4.1	4.3			Operating Profit	5.1	6.4
	.3	1.8	.5			All Other Expenses (net)	.7	.7
	-3.5	2.4	3.8			Profit Before Taxes	4.4	5.7
						RATIOS		
	4.0	3.4	3.0			Current	2.7	2.4
	2.3	2.0	2.1				1.7	1.6
	.8	1.1	1.3				1.2	1.2
	2.9	2.0	1.9			Quick	1.6	1.5
	.8	1.2	1.3				.9	.8
	.6	.5	.5				.6	.6
	20 18.0	24 14.9	39 9.3			Sales/Receivables	34 10.7	33 11.1
	31 11.7	43 8.4	52 7.1				46 8.0	46 8.0
	49 7.5	61 6.0	59 6.2				60 6.0	63 5.8
	17 21.3	26 14.3	24 15.1			Cost of Sales/Inventory	20 17.8	21 17.6
	31 11.8	49 7.4	58 6.3				47 7.8	47 7.7
	85 4.3	101 3.6	98 3.7				77 4.7	81 4.5
	13 27.6	14 25.4	12 31.7			Cost of Sales/Payables	18 20.4	17 21.5
	22 16.6	25 14.9	30 12.3				29 12.4	32 11.3
	46 8.0	39 9.4	44 8.4				43 8.5	46 8.0
	3.5	3.6	2.5			Sales/Working Capital	4.5	5.3
	7.4	5.9	4.3				8.0	9.9
	-45.2	157.5	16.8				24.2	24.5
	5.9	18.9	16.4			EBIT/Interest	15.3	17.1
	(26) -.5	(49) 2.4	(31) 3.3				(114) 6.5	(115) 5.2
	-5.2	-.6	.5				1.8	1.7
		13.7	2.4			Net Profit + Depr., Dep., Amort./Cur. Mat. L/T/D	10.5	8.0
		(12) 6.2	(12) 1.6				(35) 4.0	(32) 3.2
		.7	.5				1.6	1.3
	.5	.2	.3			Fixed/Worth	.3	.3
	1.2	.4	.5				.7	.6
	10.6	1.3	1.7				1.5	1.9
	.5	.4	.6			Debt/Worth	.8	.7
	2.2	.8	1.4				1.8	1.8
	11.8	2.2	3.7				5.2	5.3
	34.7	32.9	46.0			% Profit Before Taxes/Tangible Net Worth	51.7	55.7
	(24) 6.9	(52) 12.2	(30) 8.6				(114) 25.5	(112) 25.8
	-19.8	-.7	-1.0				6.6	11.7
	11.8	12.6	13.7			% Profit Before Taxes/Total Assets	17.9	19.9
	-1.6	3.7	3.9				6.9	9.0
	-15.3	-3.9	-.6				2.5	2.4
	12.2	20.8	10.7			Sales/Net Fixed Assets	19.0	20.2
	6.7	7.1	5.7				10.5	9.9
	2.5	3.4	3.6				5.6	5.3
	2.7	2.3	2.0			Sales/Total Assets	2.7	2.7
	2.1	1.7	1.2				2.2	2.2
	1.4	1.2	1.0				1.8	1.6
	1.3	1.1	1.3			% Depr., Dep., Amort./Sales	.9	.9
	(24) 3.1	(51) 2.6	(30) 3.0				(115) 1.5	(115) 1.6
	6.4	4.2	4.3				2.5	2.5
	3.6	2.1				% Officers', Directors' Owners' Comp/Sales	1.5	1.8
	(20) 6.9	(17) 3.8					(43) 3.8	(58) 4.3
	8.3	5.9					7.3	7.3
2559M	76471M	513215M	1049855M	309774M	957575M	Net Sales ($)	4048991M	5459858M
1694M	36001M	296687M	704843M	227683M	703682M	Total Assets ($)	2014759M	2525986M

M = $ thousand   MM = $ million
See Pages 9 through 22 for Explanation of Ratios and Data

Comparative Historical Data   Current Data Sorted by Sales

Hist 1	Hist 2	Hist 3	Type of Statement	0-1MM	1-3MM	3-5MM	5-10MM	10-25MM	25MM & OVE
22	26	19	Unqualified				6	3	10
35	35	27	Reviewed		3	4	9	8	3
20	23	24	Compiled	1	5	7	10	1	
8	12	15	Tax Returns	1	11		1	2	
42	45	49	Other	4	4	1	13	13	14
4/1/07-3/31/08 ALL	4/1/08-3/31/09 ALL	4/1/09-3/31/10 ALL			27 (4/1-9/30/09)		107 (10/1/09-3/31/10)		
127	141	134	**NUMBER OF STATEMENTS**	6	23	12	39	27	27
%	%	%	**ASSETS**	%	%	%	%	%	%
9.2	11.8	14.1	Cash & Equivalents		18.5	10.5	12.3	15.3	15.9
26.7	26.0	21.1	Trade Receivables (net)		17.3	26.5	23.6	19.4	21.6
22.0	22.1	18.9	Inventory		14.7	25.7	19.4	22.2	18.8
5.2	4.1	4.1	All Other Current		2.9	.5	3.4	5.6	7.1
63.1	63.9	58.2	Total Current		53.3	63.2	58.7	62.5	63.4
27.2	26.9	30.7	Fixed Assets (net)		40.1	27.9	26.6	29.5	24.5
2.4	3.8	3.4	Intangibles (net)		.8	2.7	2.2	3.2	7.1
7.2	5.4	7.7	All Other Non-Current		5.7	6.2	12.5	4.8	5.0
100.0	100.0	100.0	Total		100.0	100.0	100.0	100.0	100.0
			LIABILITIES						
7.9	8.7	7.3	Notes Payable-Short Term		8.0	12.2	6.6	4.9	6.4
2.9	4.4	4.2	Cur. Mat.-L.T.D.		4.0	2.4	2.9	4.3	4.7
13.6	13.3	10.8	Trade Payables		10.3	13.0	12.0	8.1	10.7
.2	.2	.2	Income Taxes Payable		.0	.0	.6	.1	.1
14.3	13.1	11.2	All Other Current		6.7	5.5	11.9	11.3	17.1
39.0	39.7	33.7	Total Current		29.1	33.1	33.9	28.8	39.0
16.6	16.4	17.1	Long-Term Debt		24.0	14.4	10.4	15.1	14.9
.3	.4	.3	Deferred Taxes		.0	.0	.2	.3	.9
6.0	6.0	8.9	All Other Non-Current		12.3	13.2	6.1	5.7	10.7
38.1	37.5	39.9	Net Worth		34.6	39.3	49.4	50.1	34.5
100.0	100.0	100.0	Total Liabilties & Net Worth		100.0	100.0	100.0	100.0	100.0
			INCOME DATA						
100.0	100.0	100.0	Net Sales		100.0	100.0	100.0	100.0	100.0
26.3	28.4	29.5	Gross Profit		33.5	30.6	28.8	26.5	24.9
19.7	21.5	26.9	Operating Expenses		38.3	29.8	25.8	19.3	17.2
6.7	6.9	2.6	Operating Profit		-4.8	.8	3.0	7.2	7.7
1.0	.8	1.2	All Other Expenses (net)		.3	.2	2.0	.4	1.5
5.7	6.1	1.4	Profit Before Taxes		-5.1	.6	1.0	6.7	6.2
			RATIOS						
2.8	2.7	3.4	Current		4.3	3.9	3.0	3.5	3.2
1.7	1.9	2.0			3.1	2.6	2.0	2.1	1.9
1.2	1.3	1.1			.7	1.1	1.1	1.5	1.2
1.5	1.7	2.0	Quick		2.9	2.8	1.8	2.0	2.0
.9	1.0	1.1			1.3	.9	1.2	1.5	1.1
.6	.6	.5			.5	.6	.6	.5	.6
28 13.1	29 12.7	26 13.8	Sales/Receivables	19 19.4	28 12.9	26 13.9	22 16.5	38 9.5	
43 8.6	40 9.2	44 8.4		34 10.6	49 7.5	45 8.1	39 9.3	51 7.1	
62 5.9	51 7.2	58 6.2		49 7.5	76 4.8	61 6.0	53 6.9	58 6.3	
23 15.8	18 20.2	22 16.7	Cost of Sales/Inventory	19 19.5	22 16.5	26 13.8	23 15.7	19 19.3	
47 7.8	48 7.6	49 7.5		36 10.2	49 7.5	50 7.2	50 7.2	52 7.0	
85 4.3	84 4.3	92 3.9		86 4.3	99 3.7	91 4.0	123 3.0	79 4.6	
16 22.2	15 24.0	15 25.0	Cost of Sales/Payables	12 31.3	14 26.4	16 23.2	11 34.3	16 22.2	
27 13.3	23 16.0	25 14.5		21 17.6	30 12.0	26 13.9	17 21.3	27 13.4	
46 8.0	39 9.4	43 8.4		46 8.0	48 7.5	43 8.4	36 10.2	36 10.2	
4.4	4.6	3.4	Sales/Working Capital		2.6	4.1	4.0	3.2	2.9
7.6	7.8	6.0			7.0	6.7	6.0	4.7	5.8
20.9	16.2	146.6			-19.7	466.5	117.2	16.8	20.8
(112) 16.0	(126) 16.6	(116) 10.9	EBIT/Interest	(19) 3.1	(11) 16.7	(32) 8.8	(22) 22.1	(26) 25.6	
4.8	5.2	2.2		.2	3.3	1.9	2.4	5.5	
1.4	1.9	-1.5		-9.1	-5.0	-2.0	.8	1.3	
(29) 28.1	(37) 10.4	(30) 9.1	Net Profit + Depr., Dep., Amort./Cur. Mat. L/T/D					(13) 3.2	
5.7	5.2	2.0						1.8	
1.8	1.8	.6						1.0	
.3	.3	.2	Fixed/Worth		.5	.1	.2	.2	.2
.7	.6	.7			1.2	.6	.4	.5	.7
1.3	2.1	1.8			-4.2	1.4	1.6	1.0	3.7
.7	.7	.5	Debt/Worth		.3	.5	.4	.5	.6
1.3	1.4	1.3			1.5	2.0	1.0	.9	2.3
3.2	4.4	3.9			-12.0	4.8	2.3	2.3	6.4
(111) 52.5	(119) 57.9	(113) 36.3	% Profit Before Taxes/Tangible Net Worth	(17) 32.0	(11) 33.3	(36) 20.6	(25) 39.6	(23) 64.5	
27.2	32.0	11.3		4.7	15.0	3.2	14.4	19.1	
10.4	8.4	-2.5		-11.7	-39.3	-5.4	1.8	6.1	
21.1	22.0	12.1	% Profit Before Taxes/Total Assets		8.6	17.7	9.9	20.9	21.9
9.3	9.3	3.3			-1.6	6.0	1.6	8.6	7.1
1.3	1.9	-4.3			-17.0	-15.6	-3.9	.1	1.2
16.7	22.4	16.1	Sales/Net Fixed Assets		11.6	85.3	20.8	16.1	12.9
8.5	9.2	6.4			3.9	8.3	7.1	5.7	6.4
4.9	5.3	3.1			2.2	4.9	4.4	3.5	3.9
2.5	3.0	2.3	Sales/Total Assets		2.3	2.8	2.3	2.1	2.1
2.0	2.1	1.6			1.8	2.4	1.7	1.6	1.6
1.6	1.6	1.1			1.1	1.6	1.2	1.2	1.1
(114) .9	(118) 1.1	(115) 1.3	% Depr., Dep., Amort./Sales	(20) 1.7		(36) 1.2	(23) 1.2	(25) 1.2	
1.6	2.0	2.9		4.0		2.6	2.2	2.9	
3.0	3.8	4.5		6.4		4.2	4.5	3.8	
(50) 2.0	(49) 2.1	(43) 2.8	% Officers', Directors' Owners' Comp/Sales	(18) 3.8		(10) 2.3			
4.2	3.2	5.6		6.9		4.2			
6.2	7.2	8.3		9.5		11.0			
3472589M	5158448M	2909449M	Net Sales ($)	3130M	43800M	48024M	286613M	411620M	2116262M
1805743M	2632063M	1970590M	Total Assets ($)	2993M	29617M	26652M	197834M	277601M	1435893M

M = $ thousand   MM = $ million
See Pages 9 through 22 for Explanation of Ratios and Data

Current Data Sorted by Assets   Comparative Historical Data

0-500M	500M-2MM	2-10MM	10-50MM	50-100MM	100-250MM	Type of Statement	4/1/05-3/31/06 ALL	4/1/06-3/31/07 ALL
		3	14	2	4	Unqualified	29	24
1	6	18	9			Reviewed	37	43
	7	9				Compiled	15	10
3	4	4				Tax Returns	20	17
4	9	17	21	1	1	Other	67	59
	19 (4/1-9/30/09)		118 (10/1/09-3/31/10)					
8	26	51	44	3	5	NUMBER OF STATEMENTS	168	153
%	%	%	%	%	%	**ASSETS**	%	%
	16.5	11.4	10.2			Cash & Equivalents	8.0	8.3
	28.3	28.0	24.4			Trade Receivables (net)	33.6	32.2
	29.7	25.0	16.6			Inventory	25.0	23.4
	1.7	4.2	5.1			All Other Current	2.0	3.3
	76.2	68.5	56.2			Total Current	68.6	67.3
	17.3	23.9	32.4			Fixed Assets (net)	22.7	24.3
	1.5	2.1	6.7			Intangibles (net)	3.0	3.7
	5.1	5.5	4.7			All Other Non-Current	5.7	4.7
	100.0	100.0	100.0			Total	100.0	100.0
						LIABILITIES		
	13.9	11.1	7.3			Notes Payable-Short Term	11.0	14.2
	1.8	3.2	3.6			Cur. Mat.-L.T.D.	3.1	2.6
	16.2	15.0	8.8			Trade Payables	17.9	15.9
	.0	.0	.3			Income Taxes Payable	.2	.2
	6.8	9.7	9.4			All Other Current	11.8	10.7
	38.7	38.9	29.4			Total Current	44.1	43.6
	8.4	17.9	22.6			Long-Term Debt	14.5	15.5
	.0	.4	.8			Deferred Taxes	.5	.4
	9.5	9.5	9.1			All Other Non-Current	5.6	4.7
	43.3	33.3	38.2			Net Worth	35.3	35.7
	100.0	100.0	100.0			Total Liabilities & Net Worth	100.0	100.0
						INCOME DATA		
	100.0	100.0	100.0			Net Sales	100.0	100.0
	34.4	29.3	27.8			Gross Profit	28.7	29.1
	33.5	27.4	22.6			Operating Expenses	24.4	25.1
	.9	1.9	5.2			Operating Profit	4.4	4.0
	.4	.7	2.0			All Other Expenses (net)	.6	.7
	.5	1.2	3.2			Profit Before Taxes	3.8	3.3
						RATIOS		
	5.3	4.2	3.2			Current	2.6	2.6
	2.1	2.1	2.1				1.6	1.6
	1.1	1.2	1.5				1.2	1.2
	2.3	2.8	2.1			Quick	1.7	1.5
	1.4	1.2	1.1				1.0	.9
	.6	.6	.7				.6	.6
19 18.9		32 11.4	35 10.4			Sales/Receivables	31 11.7	27 13.4
35 10.3		46 7.9	42 8.7				44 8.2	42 8.7
40 9.2		65 5.6	61 6.0				69 5.3	63 5.8
23 15.9		20 18.1	27 13.3			Cost of Sales/Inventory	32 11.3	29 12.4
57 6.4		53 6.8	48 7.6				46 7.9	47 7.7
88 4.2		81 4.5	74 5.0				72 5.1	68 5.4
11 33.9		18 20.5	11 33.8			Cost of Sales/Payables	17 21.9	16 23.5
20 18.0		28 12.8	22 16.9				29 12.6	25 14.9
38 9.7		41 9.0	31 11.6				45 8.0	44 8.3
	4.9	3.4	3.9			Sales/Working Capital	5.9	5.7
	8.9	7.3	6.9				11.1	10.8
	NM	29.1	13.4				23.4	34.9
	27.6	13.3	9.2			EBIT/Interest	13.3	9.3
	(20) 2.2	(47) 4.2	(42) 3.7				(147) 4.2	(140) 3.5
	1.0	.5	.5				1.4	1.4
		1.6	5.3			Net Profit + Depr., Dep.,	8.9	4.6
		(12) .8	(16) 2.6			Amort./Cur. Mat. L/T/D	(42) 3.7	(44) 2.5
		-.2	.7				1.7	.9
	.2	.2	.4			Fixed/Worth	.3	.2
	.4	.5	.9				.7	.7
	6.6	1.9	4.0				2.2	1.6
	.2	.6	.8			Debt/Worth	.8	.8
	.8	1.7	1.7				2.2	1.9
	53.6	4.7	6.1				6.7	5.4
	42.4	28.6	32.0			% Profit Before Taxes/Tangible	51.8	46.3
	(21) 8.7	(43) 12.9	(37) 14.3			Net Worth	(146) 21.6	(136) 22.0
	-10.3	1.8	-4.8				7.0	7.0
	22.2	12.4	15.6			% Profit Before Taxes/Total	14.8	15.8
	5.4	7.2	6.6			Assets	7.8	7.6
	-1.2	-1.1	-1.2				1.3	1.2
	48.9	27.8	16.0			Sales/Net Fixed Assets	35.0	32.9
	22.2	13.0	6.1				12.9	13.2
	12.9	5.9	3.5				6.1	5.9
	4.0	3.1	2.3			Sales/Total Assets	3.2	3.2
	3.3	2.3	1.8				2.5	2.6
	2.5	1.7	1.2				1.9	1.9
	.7	.7	1.2			% Depr., Dep., Amort./Sales	.9	.8
	(21) .9	(48) 1.4	(39) 2.3				(139) 1.7	(134) 1.5
	2.2	2.9	3.3				2.5	2.4
	3.8	1.1				% Officers', Directors'	1.4	1.9
	(11) 4.8	(19) 2.2				Owners' Comp/Sales	(65) 2.6	(51) 2.7
	8.1	4.5					5.0	5.4
8997M	90989M	553005M	1723756M	272792M	1196146M	Net Sales ($)	5416703M	6021998M
2125M	29488M	249534M	1021998M	221440M	864001M	Total Assets ($)	2495416M	2727447M

M = $ thousand   MM = $ million
See Pages 9 through 22 for Explanation of Ratios and Data

Comparative Historical Data | Current Data Sorted by Sales

Type of Statement

Type	4/1/07-3/31/08 ALL	4/1/08-3/31/09 ALL	4/1/09-3/31/10 ALL	0-1MM	1-3MM	3-5MM	5-10MM	10-25MM	25MM & OVER
Unqualified	20	27	23				2	2	19
Reviewed	38	30	34		2	4	10	14	4
Compiled	11	13	16		4	2	4	6	
Tax Returns	15	16	11	2	2	4	3		
Other	58	65	53	1	10	5	8	14	15

Historical periods: 4/1/07-3/31/08 ALL; 4/1/08-3/31/09 ALL; 4/1/09-3/31/10 ALL. Current period splits: 19 (4/1-9/30/09); 118 (10/1/09-3/31/10).

	4/1/07-3/31/08 ALL	4/1/08-3/31/09 ALL	4/1/09-3/31/10 ALL	0-1MM	1-3MM	3-5MM	5-10MM	10-25MM	25MM & OVER
NUMBER OF STATEMENTS	142	151	137	3	18	15	27	36	38
	%	%	%	%	%	%	%	%	%
ASSETS									
Cash & Equivalents	7.4	7.6	11.7		15.6	15.6	12.3	8.4	11.6
Trade Receivables (net)	31.7	28.9	25.9		22.9	27.8	27.6	28.3	23.4
Inventory	22.5	24.8	22.0		23.9	30.9	22.4	21.9	16.9
All Other Current	3.5	3.7	3.9		1.9	.8	2.9	6.1	5.1
Total Current	65.1	65.0	63.5		64.3	75.2	65.2	64.7	57.1
Fixed Assets (net)	25.5	23.9	26.4		28.3	16.3	24.0	27.6	28.8
Intangibles (net)	4.8	5.7	4.6		.5	.7	6.3	3.2	8.2
All Other Non-Current	4.6	5.3	5.5		6.9	7.7	4.6	4.6	5.9
Total	100.0	100.0	100.0		100.0	100.0	100.0	100.0	100.0
LIABILITIES									
Notes Payable-Short Term	12.4	13.1	11.6		11.1	15.1	9.9	10.8	11.5
Cur. Mat.-L.T.D.	3.0	3.8	3.3		4.5	3.1	2.8	3.5	3.2
Trade Payables	14.9	14.2	12.5		9.9	19.1	12.0	14.7	9.2
Income Taxes Payable	.1	.1	.1		.0	.0	.0	.1	.3
All Other Current	10.5	12.4	9.5		8.6	9.5	10.2	9.1	10.3
Total Current	40.9	43.6	37.1		34.1	46.9	34.8	38.2	34.6
Long-Term Debt	18.8	15.5	20.0		32.1	7.3	20.5	19.2	18.7
Deferred Taxes	.6	.4	.6		.0	.0	.1	.8	1.2
All Other Non-Current	4.6	5.8	9.6		13.1	6.8	10.4	8.3	10.5
Net Worth	35.2	34.6	32.7		20.7	39.1	34.1	33.5	34.9
Total Liabilties & Net Worth	100.0	100.0	100.0		100.0	100.0	100.0	100.0	100.0
INCOME DATA									
Net Sales	100.0	100.0	100.0		100.0	100.0	100.0	100.0	100.0
Gross Profit	29.2	30.9	31.2		40.2	33.8	33.4	27.8	27.8
Operating Expenses	24.8	27.1	28.3		41.8	29.2	30.6	25.1	22.5
Operating Profit	4.4	3.8	3.0		-1.6	4.6	2.8	2.7	5.4
All Other Expenses (net)	1.7	1.6	1.5		2.1	-.1	1.0	1.8	2.1
Profit Before Taxes	2.8	2.1	1.4		-3.6	4.7	1.8	.8	3.3
RATIOS									
Current	2.7	2.8	3.8		5.1	4.8	4.4	2.7	2.9
	1.6	1.5	1.9		1.9	1.9	2.5	1.7	2.2
	1.1	1.1	1.2		.9	1.0	1.4	1.2	1.5
Quick	1.7	1.7	2.2		3.2	2.3	2.8	1.9	2.1
	.9	.8	1.1		.8	1.3	1.7	.9	1.3
	.6	.5	.6		.4	.5	.7	.6	.7
Sales/Receivables	30 12.3	29 12.8	31 11.7		6 60.8	21 17.7	31 11.6	27 13.5	35 10.5
	44 8.3	42 8.8	40 9.2		36 10.1	39 9.4	52 7.0	40 9.0	41 9.0
	65 5.6	59 6.2	57 6.4		51 7.2	66 5.5	66 5.5	66 5.5	52 7.0
Cost of Sales/Inventory	24 15.5	29 12.8	26 14.1		16 22.1	32 11.6	20 18.3	26 13.8	27 13.4
	45 8.2	48 7.7	50 7.3		35 10.3	62 5.9	53 6.9	50 7.3	48 7.6
	69 5.3	83 4.4	78 4.7		98 3.7	86 4.2	92 4.0	74 5.0	61 6.0
Cost of Sales/Payables	16 22.7	14 27.0	11 33.1		5 71.1	23 16.2	10 36.6	14 25.4	10 34.8
	28 13.1	22 16.2	23 15.8		14 26.2	31 11.8	30 12.2	26 13.8	17 20.9
	44 8.2	40 9.2	37 9.8		38 9.7	62 5.9	40 9.2	35 10.4	31 11.9
Sales/Working Capital	5.5	5.9	4.1		4.6	2.6	3.6	4.2	4.6
	9.7	9.7	8.3		9.4	12.0	5.2	9.7	7.0
	34.1	76.1	24.1		-114.8	-256.6	13.7	21.5	13.4
EBIT/Interest	7.1	9.3	12.3		9.3	50.4	16.9	12.4	8.1
	(126) 2.9	(137) 2.3	(123) 2.6		(14) 1.2	(11) 9.7	(26) 3.4	(33) 3.4	(37) 3.8
	1.0	-.1	.5		-6.6	2.0	.4	.3	.8
Net Profit + Depr., Dep., Amort./Cur. Mat. L/T/D	6.3	3.7	4.8					4.0	9.6
	(45) 2.3	(44) 2.2	(37) 1.7					(13) 1.2	(15) 2.7
	1.4	.5	-.1					-.1	1.3
Fixed/Worth	.3	.3	.3		.2	.1	.2	.3	.4
	.8	.8	.7		.9	.4	.6	.8	.9
	2.0	3.1	5.7		-5.1	6.9	3.9	2.0	6.3
Debt/Worth	1.0	.9	.6		.3	.2	.4	.7	.8
	1.9	1.9	1.7		1.7	1.2	1.7	1.8	1.7
	6.4	7.7	13.4		-15.5	76.5	15.0	4.9	12.0
% Profit Before Taxes/Tangible Net Worth	44.9	36.1	36.0		45.8	35.3	38.0	36.2	33.9
	(119) 19.5	(123) 11.5	(109) 13.9		(12) .3	(12) 10.6	(21) 14.8	(31) 15.0	(31) 16.6
	4.5	-5.8	-2.5		-54.8	4.8	-2.1	-5.7	-2.1
% Profit Before Taxes/Total Assets	11.8	12.8	13.0		23.1	16.5	15.7	12.6	14.0
	6.0	3.1	5.6		.2	6.3	6.5	8.3	6.6
	.6	-3.1	-1.7		-16.2	1.8	-1.9	-2.0	-.1
Sales/Net Fixed Assets	25.1	28.7	24.5		33.0	48.5	37.0	26.8	15.6
	12.1	12.0	12.3		18.3	21.1	12.3	12.3	6.4
	6.0	6.3	4.8		6.4	8.7	5.5	4.4	4.4
Sales/Total Assets	2.9	3.1	3.1		4.0	4.3	2.7	3.3	2.3
	2.4	2.3	2.2		3.2	3.3	1.9	2.5	1.8
	1.8	1.7	1.5		1.4	1.3	1.5	1.8	1.5
% Depr., Dep., Amort./Sales	.8	.9	.8		.7	.7	.9	.7	1.2
	(128) 1.8	(133) 1.5	(120) 1.7		(14) 1.2	(13) .9	2.2	(31) 1.3	(32) 2.3
	2.7	2.6	3.0		4.2	2.4	3.4	2.7	3.4
% Officers', Directors' Owners' Comp/Sales	1.9	1.5	1.7				2.1		
	(45) 2.9	(47) 3.2	(38) 3.7				(13) 3.9		
	5.9	6.1	6.0				5.4		
Net Sales ($)	4570846M	5411060M	3845685M	1774M	36082M	61388M	197830M	603019M	2945592M
Total Assets ($)	2417488M	2571153M	2388586M	694M	16994M	38720M	120555M	398595M	1813028M

M = $ thousand   MM = $ million
See Pages 9 through 22 for Explanation of Ratios and Data

Current Data Sorted by Assets   Comparative Historical Data

Type of Statement	0-500M	500M-2MM	2-10MM	10-50MM	50-100MM	100-250MM	4/1/05-3/31/06 ALL	4/1/06-3/31/07 ALL
Unqualified			8	12	7	1	46	49
Reviewed	5	16	46	12			91	96
Compiled	4	24	22	3	1		54	69
Tax Returns	16	22	14				36	29
Other	9	17	37	20	2	2	105	92
		57 (4/1-9/30/09)		243 (10/1/09-3/31/10)				
NUMBER OF STATEMENTS	34	79	127	47	10	3	332	335
ASSETS	%	%	%	%	%	%	%	%
Cash & Equivalents	12.7	9.4	10.4	11.7	13.5		8.2	8.0
Trade Receivables (net)	29.7	30.4	27.9	24.0	15.1		31.1	31.7
Inventory	23.1	19.3	19.5	21.5	19.6		20.8	20.6
All Other Current	3.3	3.2	2.7	4.3	5.1		2.7	2.4
Total Current	68.8	62.3	60.5	61.4	53.4		62.9	62.7
Fixed Assets (net)	26.3	28.2	30.1	27.3	25.5		29.5	28.7
Intangibles (net)	.4	2.9	2.6	6.2	14.5		2.3	3.2
All Other Non-Current	4.6	6.7	6.8	5.1	6.6		5.3	5.4
Total	100.0	100.0	100.0	100.0	100.0		100.0	100.0
LIABILITIES								
Notes Payable-Short Term	20.2	11.5	9.5	11.2	4.8		11.0	10.6
Cur. Mat.-L.T.D.	5.8	4.9	4.7	4.3	5.4		5.2	4.1
Trade Payables	20.2	13.2	12.3	10.7	3.8		15.5	14.6
Income Taxes Payable	.0	.2	.1	.1	.4		.4	.3
All Other Current	12.3	7.2	6.4	10.6	6.8		10.1	11.3
Total Current	58.5	37.1	33.1	36.9	21.1		42.2	40.8
Long-Term Debt	25.5	19.8	18.1	16.6	11.6		17.2	17.8
Deferred Taxes	.1	.2	.4	.7	.7		.5	.5
All Other Non-Current	22.4	8.9	6.6	3.5	6.9		5.9	4.9
Net Worth	-6.5	34.0	41.8	42.3	59.6		34.3	36.0
Total Liabilities & Net Worth	100.0	100.0	100.0	100.0	100.0		100.0	100.0
INCOME DATA								
Net Sales	100.0	100.0	100.0	100.0	100.0		100.0	100.0
Gross Profit	39.6	33.1	27.4	24.4	25.3		28.5	28.0
Operating Expenses	37.5	31.8	24.6	18.7	25.7		23.5	21.9
Operating Profit	2.1	1.3	2.8	5.7	-.3		5.0	6.1
All Other Expenses (net)	.8	.9	1.0	1.5	.8		.9	.9
Profit Before Taxes	1.3	.5	1.8	4.2	-1.1		4.1	5.2
RATIOS								
Current	5.3	3.6	3.5	3.1	10.1		2.6	2.6
	1.5	1.8	1.8	1.6	2.8		1.6	1.6
	.8	1.1	1.3	1.2	1.3		1.2	1.2
Quick	2.3	2.2	2.3	1.9	6.7		1.6	1.7
	1.0	1.1	1.1	1.0	1.4		1.0	1.0
	.5	.5	.7	.5	.5		.6	.7
Sales/Receivables	6 60.2	29 12.8	32 11.4	31 11.8	30 12.0		31 11.7	31 11.7
	28 13.0	42 8.6	45 8.2	42 8.6	46 7.9		44 8.2	43 8.4
	42 8.7	61 6.0	60 6.1	51 7.2	63 5.8		59 6.2	57 6.4
Cost of Sales/Inventory	5 71.1	10 37.0	19 19.0	28 13.0	37 9.9		17 20.9	14 26.3
	28 13.0	32 11.6	47 7.7	53 7.0	71 5.1		40 9.1	37 9.8
	50 7.3	55 6.6	77 4.7	99 3.7	134 2.7		68 5.4	68 5.4
Cost of Sales/Payables	3 134.2	9 42.5	17 21.7	16 22.4	5 77.2		18 19.9	16 22.4
	16 23.1	23 15.6	27 13.5	21 17.2	10 35.6		29 12.7	26 13.8
	42 8.7	43 8.5	39 9.4	40 9.2	19 19.7		42 8.7	37 9.9
Sales/Working Capital	5.8	5.9	4.9	4.1	2.1		6.1	6.3
	23.1	10.9	7.6	9.1	4.1		10.5	11.1
	-46.9	31.0	16.0	21.5	38.1		30.5	29.2
EBIT/Interest	11.1	8.6	8.1	15.2	4.8		12.1	12.8
	(28) 2.2	(72) 1.8	(120) 2.7	(41) 5.1	-.6		(304) 4.0	(308) 4.6
	-1.1	-1.3	.4	1.8	-19.2		1.7	1.8
Net Profit + Depr., Dep., Amort./Cur. Mat. L/T/D		2.5	14.1	7.1			8.4	6.5
		(16) 1.5	(30) 3.9	(18) 2.3			(83) 3.3	(94) 3.0
		.4	1.9	.6			1.5	1.6
Fixed/Worth	.2	.3	.3	.4	.2		.3	.3
	1.6	.7	.7	.7	.7		.8	.7
	-2.0	12.1	2.3	1.8	NM		2.3	2.0
Debt/Worth	.6	.7	.5	.8	.1		.8	.7
	11.9	2.0	1.6	1.7	.9		1.8	1.8
	-3.3	21.2	4.7	3.5	NM		5.2	4.4
% Profit Before Taxes/Tangible Net Worth	117.8	40.3	31.9	42.4			55.0	50.4
	(21) 29.3	(60) 13.8	(113) 11.8	(45) 23.3			(296) 25.9	(299) 27.0
	1.1	-2.6	-1.4	6.5			8.0	10.0
% Profit Before Taxes/Total Assets	21.6	13.3	11.8	15.5	11.4		16.4	21.4
	6.2	3.3	4.2	7.5	-2.3		8.3	9.1
	-7.5	-6.4	-1.2	1.8	-7.4		2.1	2.6
Sales/Net Fixed Assets	95.4	26.8	16.4	16.9	10.1		21.6	18.6
	25.1	11.2	7.8	8.7	5.0		9.4	10.0
	10.8	5.5	3.7	4.1	2.8		5.2	5.8
Sales/Total Assets	7.5	3.3	2.7	2.6	1.6		3.1	3.1
	3.9	2.4	1.8	1.9	1.2		2.4	2.5
	2.6	1.9	1.5	1.3	.9		1.8	1.9
% Depr., Dep., Amort./Sales	.6	.9	1.4	1.0			1.3	1.2
	(24) 1.2	(71) 2.0	(118) 2.8	(42) 2.8			(298) 2.4	(313) 2.2
	3.3	4.4	5.2	3.9			3.8	3.8
% Officers', Directors' Owners' Comp/Sales	4.6	3.6	2.1				2.3	2.2
	(22) 8.3	(48) 6.2	(66) 3.4				(139) 4.2	(152) 3.7
	11.3	9.6	5.5				7.6	7.4
Net Sales ($)	52894M	234323M	1160015M	2143293M	887670M	779868M	6484462M	7056412M
Total Assets ($)	10477M	91859M	587975M	1011177M	701188M	372822M	2908281M	3226870M

M = $ thousand   MM = $ million
See Pages 9 through 22 for Explanation of Ratios and Data

Comparative Historical Data

Current Data Sorted by Sales

© RMA 2010   M = $ thousand   MM = $ million
See Pages 9 through 22 for Explanation of Ratios and Data

4/1/07-3/31/08 ALL	4/1/08-3/31/09 ALL	4/1/09-3/31/10 ALL	Type of Statement	0-1MM	1-3MM	3-5MM	5-10MM	10-25MM	25MM & OVER
39	34	28	Unqualified			1		8	19
93	78	79	Reviewed	3	11	11	25	21	8
59	61	54	Compiled	1	16	17	16	2	2
41	52	52	Tax Returns	7	23	11	8	3	
87	101	87	Other	6	15	9	25	13	19
				57 (4/1-9/30/09)			243 (10/1/09-3/31/10)		
319	326	300	**NUMBER OF STATEMENTS**	17	65	49	74	47	48
%	%	%	**ASSETS**	%	%	%	%	%	%
8.9	9.4	10.8	Cash & Equivalents	6.8	11.2	8.8	11.9	10.3	12.3
32.1	29.4	27.7	Trade Receivables (net)	24.0	30.4	24.7	29.0	29.0	25.0
21.3	22.1	20.3	Inventory	21.6	19.2	20.1	17.7	23.5	22.1
2.5	2.7	3.3	All Other Current	5.7	2.7	3.4	2.5	3.0	4.5
64.8	63.7	62.0	Total Current	58.1	63.5	57.0	61.2	65.8	63.9
26.5	27.4	28.5	Fixed Assets (net)	34.9	27.2	34.0	26.3	29.2	25.0
3.0	3.4	3.4	Intangibles (net)	.4	2.6	.7	5.8	1.7	6.0
5.8	5.5	6.2	All Other Non-Current	6.7	6.7	8.4	6.7	3.3	5.1
100.0	100.0	100.0	Total	100.0	100.0	100.0	100.0	100.0	100.0
			LIABILITIES						
10.8	11.2	11.3	Notes Payable-Short Term	14.6	13.9	11.8	9.5	9.9	10.4
4.1	4.1	4.8	Cur. Mat.-L.T.D.	6.2	4.0	8.5	3.8	2.9	5.0
14.7	15.3	12.9	Trade Payables	8.0	16.8	12.3	12.7	12.1	10.9
.2	.3	.1	Income Taxes Payable	.0	.2	.2	.1	.1	.2
9.3	8.5	8.1	All Other Current	5.3	8.4	8.3	6.5	8.2	10.6
39.1	39.3	37.2	Total Current	34.0	43.3	41.1	32.7	33.2	37.1
16.3	17.2	18.8	Long-Term Debt	33.9	22.0	21.4	17.3	12.7	15.0
.4	.5	.4	Deferred Taxes	.0	.2	.3	.4	.6	.8
5.2	7.1	8.5	All Other Non-Current	32.5	12.4	3.3	6.8	6.2	4.9
38.9	35.9	35.0	Net Worth	-.5	22.1	33.9	42.8	47.4	42.2
100.0	100.0	100.0	Total Liabilities & Net Worth	100.0	100.0	100.0	100.0	100.0	100.0
			INCOME DATA						
100.0	100.0	100.0	Net Sales	100.0	100.0	100.0	100.0	100.0	100.0
27.9	27.8	29.7	Gross Profit	43.9	35.4	31.5	27.3	24.5	24.0
22.5	23.2	27.0	Operating Expenses	43.8	34.3	30.1	23.8	21.0	18.7
5.4	4.5	2.7	Operating Profit	.2	1.1	1.4	3.5	3.5	5.3
.9	.8	1.0	All Other Expenses (net)	2.4	1.0	.8	.9	.9	.9
4.5	3.7	1.7	Profit Before Taxes	-2.2	.1	.6	2.5	2.5	4.4
			RATIOS						
2.7	2.9	3.7	Current	7.9	4.1	3.7	3.5	3.7	3.1
1.7	1.7	1.8		1.8	1.6	1.6	1.8	1.8	1.7
1.2	1.1	1.2		.7	1.0	1.0	1.3	1.3	1.2
1.8	1.8	2.2	Quick	2.1	2.3	2.0	2.8	2.3	1.9
1.0	1.0	1.1		1.0	1.1	.9	1.2	1.1	1.1
.6	.6	.6		.4	.7	.5	.7	.6	.6
33 11.2	29 12.5	29 12.6	Sales/Receivables	28 12.8	23 16.2	25 14.4	32 11.3	31 11.7	31 11.7
44 8.3	41 8.9	42 8.6		39 9.3	36 10.0	39 9.3	47 7.8	43 8.4	41 8.9
60 6.1	54 6.8	57 6.4		53 6.9	60 6.1	52 7.0	61 5.9	59 6.2	53 6.6
17 21.4	19 19.5	17 21.4	Cost of Sales/Inventory	14 26.6	8 44.0	17 21.8	14 25.9	27 13.4	28 12.9
42 8.8	40 9.0	42 8.6		45 8.0	32 11.6	44 8.3	47 7.7	53 6.9	44 8.4
71 5.2	72 5.1	73 5.0		62 5.9	58 6.3	71 5.1	79 4.6	78 4.7	81 4.5
16 22.7	14 25.2	13 27.9	Cost of Sales/Payables	6 66.1	8 44.3	11 33.3	14 25.9	16 22.8	12 31.5
28 13.0	25 14.3	22 16.4		21 17.0	28 13.2	21 17.4	24 14.9	23 15.8	21 17.8
42 8.7	41 8.8	40 9.2		51 7.2	50 7.3	34 10.9	40 9.0	36 10.0	33 11.0
5.5	5.8	5.0	Sales/Working Capital	5.7	5.6	5.3	4.9	4.5	4.1
9.6	10.0	9.0		9.3	9.6	11.7	8.0	7.7	8.4
26.9	33.2	26.2		-10.2	UND	-230.6	16.0	14.6	21.4
12.3	13.7	9.1	EBIT/Interest	5.5	7.3	14.3	9.2	13.3	15.6
(292) 4.7	(306) 4.0	(274) 2.7		(14) 1.7	(56) 1.5	(48) 1.5	(66) 3.9	(46) 4.0	(44) 3.6
1.6	1.3	-.4		-7.0	-1.2	-2.0	1.2	1.2	.4
7.1	7.7	7.5	Net Profit + Depr., Dep., Amort./Cur. Mat. L/T/D		2.6	25.6	7.7	18.8	6.8
(79) 2.8	(103) 3.8	(72) 2.4			(11) 1.6	(11) 1.8	(16) 3.5	(15) 3.6	(19) 2.3
1.7	1.7	.9			.6	.2	1.2	1.0	.8
.3	.3	.3	Fixed/Worth	.1	.3	.4	.3	.3	.3
.6	.8	.7		1.1	1.3	.9	.7	.6	.6
1.7	1.9	2.6		20.2	-2.2	3.0	2.0	1.6	1.9
.7	.7	.7	Debt/Worth	.8	1.0	.5	.5	.4	.7
1.6	1.9	1.7		16.5	3.4	1.6	1.7	1.0	1.8
4.8	4.8	6.7		-17.9	-10.0	5.9	5.0	2.5	4.4
48.5	44.9	38.1	% Profit Before Taxes/Tangible Net Worth	66.5	49.4	27.7	40.9	23.6	52.7
(284) 21.4	(290) 21.5	(250) 13.6		(12) 18.0	(43) 9.9	(43) 4.4	(63) 17.0	(45) 10.4	(44) 34.0
7.4	6.8	-.3		-42.9	.4	-26.1	3.2	2.0	3.2
19.4	15.9	13.7	% Profit Before Taxes/Total Assets	14.0	13.0	12.6	13.7	10.7	20.2
7.9	7.8	4.0		1.5	2.0	1.7	5.6	4.4	8.2
2.4	1.2	-2.0		-24.7	-6.9	-6.7	-.6	.4	-.1
21.5	19.5	23.8	Sales/Net Fixed Assets	55.6	46.4	19.1	21.9	18.8	17.5
11.1	10.1	9.6		6.3	16.5	7.1	9.4	7.9	8.7
5.8	5.5	4.4		2.7	5.6	3.9	4.5	3.7	4.8
3.1	3.1	3.0	Sales/Total Assets	3.6	3.6	3.3	3.0	2.9	2.6
2.3	2.4	2.2		1.8	2.6	2.2	2.1	1.9	2.2
1.8	1.8	1.6		1.0	1.7	1.7	1.4	1.5	1.5
1.1	1.3	1.1	% Depr., Dep., Amort./Sales	1.1	.7	1.6	1.3	1.5	.8
(290) 2.0	(290) 2.1	(266) 2.5		(11) 2.9	(57) 1.8	(45) 3.0	(67) 2.6	(43) 2.7	(43) 2.2
3.5	3.7	4.4		6.6	4.1	6.1	4.3	4.3	3.5
2.1	2.4	2.6	% Officers', Directors' Owners' Comp/Sales	7.2	5.3	2.8	2.6	1.4	
(159) 3.8	(146) 4.0	(147) 4.4		(10) 10.9	(38) 6.9	(31) 3.8	(39) 3.4	(23) 2.3	
6.6	6.4	8.5		16.9	9.9	6.2	5.9	3.4	
6278311M	11372069M	5258063M	Net Sales ($)	10687M	134131M	193331M	549233M	747930M	3622751M
2906512M	3832592M	2775498M	Total Assets ($)	6450M	64867M	89349M	336071M	392965M	1885796M

Current Data Sorted by Assets   Comparative Historical Data

	0-500M	500M-2MM	2-10MM	10-50MM	50-100MM	100-250MM	Type of Statement	4/1/05-3/31/06 ALL	4/1/06-3/31/07 ALL
		7	2	2		1	Unqualified	13	10
	1	1	17	4			Reviewed	20	25
	1	1	4	1			Compiled	9	12
		4	1				Tax Returns	12	15
	6	13	11	7	3	2	Other	22	26
	8	25	35	14	3	3	**NUMBER OF STATEMENTS**	76	88
	%	%	%	%	%	%	**ASSETS**	%	%
		5.2	11.6	4.4			Cash & Equivalents	7.7	8.1
		36.0	33.0	22.9			Trade Receivables (net)	34.6	40.6
		20.9	14.8	21.9			Inventory	21.4	19.0
		5.8	6.1	6.6			All Other Current	3.2	4.9
		67.9	65.5	55.7			Total Current	66.8	72.6
		18.3	25.2	28.9			Fixed Assets (net)	23.3	17.1
		4.2	3.0	6.3			Intangibles (net)	3.3	4.6
		9.6	6.4	9.1			All Other Non-Current	6.6	5.6
		100.0	100.0	100.0			Total	100.0	100.0
							LIABILITIES		
		11.6	8.6	9.2			Notes Payable-Short Term	10.7	10.6
		2.3	3.5	4.2			Cur. Mat.-L.T.D.	3.6	2.7
		16.5	12.5	13.1			Trade Payables	17.7	15.1
		.5	.8	.1			Income Taxes Payable	.9	.8
		15.7	12.0	6.7			All Other Current	12.2	16.4
		46.6	37.3	33.3			Total Current	45.1	45.6
		18.5	14.6	20.4			Long-Term Debt	16.7	12.2
		1.1	1.0	1.2			Deferred Taxes	.5	.3
		8.9	6.7	9.3			All Other Non-Current	7.8	8.7
		24.9	40.4	35.8			Net Worth	29.8	33.2
		100.0	100.0	100.0			Total Liabilities & Net Worth	100.0	100.0
							INCOME DATA		
		100.0	100.0	100.0			Net Sales	100.0	100.0
		35.0	30.3	31.9			Gross Profit	32.6	33.3
		34.5	26.3	29.7			Operating Expenses	28.7	27.1
		.6	4.0	2.1			Operating Profit	3.9	6.2
		.9	1.3	1.4			All Other Expenses (net)	.7	.6
		-.4	2.7	.7			Profit Before Taxes	3.2	5.6

RATIOS

	500M-2MM	2-10MM	10-50MM	Ratio	4/1/05-3/31/06	4/1/06-3/31/07
	2.5	2.7	2.2	Current	2.2	2.4
	1.4	1.7	1.6		1.5	1.6
	1.1	1.4	1.2		1.2	1.2
	1.6	1.9	1.1	Quick	1.6	1.6
	1.0	1.2	.6		1.0	1.1
	.5	.6	.6		.6	.8
	26 14.1	36 10.3	32 11.6	Sales/Receivables	31 11.7	37 9.8
	48 7.6	56 6.5	42 8.7		52 7.0	58 6.3
	77 4.8	72 5.1	53 6.9		74 5.0	81 4.5
	11 33.5	2 207.5	39 9.4	Cost of Sales/Inventory	9 39.2	5 76.8
	30 12.2	38 9.7	70 5.2		47 7.8	37 9.9
	63 5.8	75 4.8	97 3.7		83 4.4	76 4.8
	20 18.2	14 25.7	18 20.6	Cost of Sales/Payables	21 17.0	19 19.4
	30 12.1	25 14.8	27 13.5		31 11.9	31 11.6
	37 9.8	49 7.5	50 7.3		47 7.7	48 7.6
	5.2	3.9	5.2	Sales/Working Capital	5.8	5.1
	11.1	7.0	7.9		10.7	8.3
	99.5	14.7	18.0		38.7	21.6
	8.3	10.3	3.8	EBIT/Interest	13.2	11.8
	(22) 3.4	(32) 3.2	2.7		(72) 5.9	(77) 5.3
	-1.1	.6	.4		1.4	1.6
				Net Profit + Depr., Dep., Amort./Cur. Mat. L/T/D	22.1	7.8
					(22) 3.0	(20) 3.0
					1.2	1.6
	.3	.2	.8	Fixed/Worth	.3	.2
	.6	.5	1.0		.7	.5
	17.1	1.2	NM		1.5	1.4
	.9	.7	1.3	Debt/Worth	.9	.9
	7.2	1.2	2.0		2.2	2.4
	NM	5.8	NM		6.0	5.4
	66.8	39.8	11.9	% Profit Before Taxes/Tangible Net Worth	51.4	78.0
	(19) 11.0	(32) 15.2	(11) 5.9		(64) 22.8	(78) 36.1
	-5.3	1.6	-1.6		7.0	13.9
	11.5	13.1	5.7	% Profit Before Taxes/Total Assets	18.3	23.7
	5.2	5.0	2.6		8.5	11.4
	-6.8	-.9	-1.2		1.7	2.7
	33.7	25.8	7.6	Sales/Net Fixed Assets	30.3	37.3
	16.6	12.7	5.9		12.8	19.3
	8.0	4.4	4.4		7.2	8.9
	3.3	2.5	2.1	Sales/Total Assets	3.2	3.0
	2.5	1.8	1.7		2.6	2.4
	1.9	1.3	1.4		1.9	2.0
	.8	.9	1.4	% Depr., Dep., Amort./Sales	.9	.7
	(18) 1.5	(32) 1.7	(12) 2.4		(67) 1.7	(72) 1.1
	3.2	3.5	4.5		2.5	1.8
	2.7	1.6		% Officers', Directors' Owners' Comp/Sales	2.6	2.3
	(10) 6.1	(18) 2.8			(33) 5.1	(38) 4.4
	10.3	4.8			9.4	7.2

	0-500M	500M-2MM	2-10MM	10-50MM	50-100MM	100-250MM		4/1/05-3/31/06	4/1/06-3/31/07
	7607M	88980M	364778M	599271M	348996M	802772M	Net Sales ($)	1729355M	1681839M
	3090M	33546M	184787M	343191M	220415M	477961M	Total Assets ($)	833633M	838829M

Comparative Historical Data | Current Data Sorted by Sales

Type of Statement	8	9	5						
Unqualified	8	9	5		2		2		3
Reviewed	29	22	29			7	8	10	2
Compiled	12	10	7	1		2	2	1	1
Tax Returns	11	11	5	1		4			
Other	21	36	42	4	9	7	6	5	11
	4/1/07-3/31/08 ALL	4/1/08-3/31/09 ALL	4/1/09-3/31/10 ALL	0-1MM	1-3MM	3-5MM	5-10MM	10-25MM	25MM & OVER
					13 (4/1-9/30/09)		75 (10/1/09-3/31/10)		
NUMBER OF STATEMENTS	81	88	88	6	11	20	18	16	17

	%	%	%	%	%	%	%	%	%
ASSETS									
Cash & Equivalents	9.5	8.5	8.0		9.3	2.8	15.9	9.5	5.1
Trade Receivables (net)	34.4	37.1	32.1		31.4	36.8	32.7	29.0	27.0
Inventory	23.0	19.0	18.7		13.2	17.9	13.9	19.6	25.6
All Other Current	4.9	4.7	5.8		8.5	4.6	5.3	5.9	6.5
Total Current	71.7	69.3	64.6		62.3	62.2	67.8	64.0	64.2
Fixed Assets (net)	20.5	20.0	23.6		23.3	24.1	24.1	18.8	28.3
Intangibles (net)	2.1	5.2	3.9		9.5	4.3	.5	5.2	1.1
All Other Non-Current	5.6	5.5	8.0		4.9	9.5	7.6	12.1	6.5
Total	100.0	100.0	100.0		100.0	100.0	100.0	100.0	100.0
LIABILITIES									
Notes Payable-Short Term	9.7	13.1	10.0		4.8	13.4	9.5	5.6	10.2
Cur. Mat.-L.T.D.	3.8	4.8	3.1		2.9	3.3	4.2	2.4	3.0
Trade Payables	15.0	15.2	14.1		16.0	18.3	7.6	15.4	14.5
Income Taxes Payable	.5	.5	.5		.1	.5	.2	1.4	.1
All Other Current	17.7	14.0	13.9		16.8	9.5	14.5	14.9	9.6
Total Current	46.7	47.6	41.6		40.8	45.1	35.9	39.8	37.5
Long-Term Debt	12.0	15.0	16.2		22.9	23.8	14.4	8.1	13.4
Deferred Taxes	.6	.5	.9		.0	1.4	1.9	.9	.2
All Other Non-Current	5.6	6.3	7.5		17.3	6.2	6.7	7.4	5.6
Net Worth	35.1	30.7	33.9		19.1	23.6	41.1	43.7	43.3
Total Liabilities & Net Worth	100.0	100.0	100.0		100.0	100.0	100.0	100.0	100.0
INCOME DATA									
Net Sales	100.0	100.0	100.0		100.0	100.0	100.0	100.0	100.0
Gross Profit	33.8	32.5	33.7		44.7	27.7	30.2	35.0	26.9
Operating Expenses	26.9	27.7	31.1		45.2	27.6	24.3	31.6	22.4
Operating Profit	6.9	4.8	2.6		-.5	.1	5.9	3.4	4.5
All Other Expenses (net)	.7	.9	1.2		2.0	1.5	.8	.5	1.0
Profit Before Taxes	6.2	3.9	1.4		-2.6	-1.5	5.1	2.9	3.5
RATIOS									
Current	2.6	2.3	2.5		7.9	2.2	3.1	2.6	2.2
	1.6	1.7	1.6		1.5	1.4	1.9	1.7	1.6
	1.2	1.2	1.2		.7	1.1	1.3	1.1	1.4
Quick	1.6	1.6	1.7		6.6	1.2	2.9	1.5	1.3
	.9	1.0	.9		1.1	.9	1.7	.9	.6
	.6	.6	.6		.4	.6	.6	.5	.6
Sales/Receivables	35 10.3	33 11.2	34 10.8		23 15.8	27 13.3	35 10.3	29 12.7	31 11.7
	50 7.4	47 7.8	50 7.2		39 9.3	55 6.7	64 5.7	44 8.3	42 8.6
	71 5.2	68 5.4	69 5.3		83 4.4	80 4.6	80 4.6	63 5.8	60 6.1
Cost of Sales/Inventory	15 24.3	10 38.4	13 28.7		7 54.3	10 35.0	0 UND	27 13.6	34 10.6
	46 7.9	36 10.2	46 7.9		45 8.2	31 11.6	25 14.7	49 7.4	61 6.0
	80 4.6	65 5.6	86 4.2		54 6.8	70 5.2	68 5.3	95 3.8	86 4.2
Cost of Sales/Payables	15 24.3	16 22.1	17 21.7		17 21.4	25 14.8	6 63.6	17 21.7	22 16.6
	27 13.5	27 13.3	28 13.1		25 14.4	32 11.4	17 21.5	29 12.8	32 11.3
	44 8.3	39 9.3	48 7.5		96 3.8	44 8.4	29 12.7	55 6.6	45 8.2
Sales/Working Capital	5.5	6.2	4.7		2.9	5.7	3.1	4.8	5.1
	9.2	9.5	8.4		10.4	12.5	5.0	8.5	7.7
	23.1	32.0	47.8		-12.2	68.0	18.5	109.6	15.0
EBIT/Interest	20.4	10.5	8.4			5.2	6.8	40.5	12.8
	(71) 5.6	(79) 3.6	(80) 3.1			1.8	(15) 3.1	5.2	3.9
	2.1	1.5	.4			-5.3	1.8	.7	2.9
Net Profit + Depr., Dep., Amort./Cur. Mat. L/T/D	14.2	10.9	7.2						
	(23) 4.0	(16) 2.2	(18) 1.5						
	1.7	1.5	.4						
Fixed/Worth	.2	.2	.3		.1	.5	.2	.2	.4
	.7	.6	.7		.3	.9	.5	.5	.8
	1.9	6.7	3.3		-.6	8.2	1.3	1.1	1.0
Debt/Worth	.7	.9	.7		.1	1.2	.6	.7	.7
	2.2	2.3	1.8		7.8	6.6	1.3	1.1	1.5
	6.3	28.9	11.9		-2.4	13.9	3.1	10.3	2.3
% Profit Before Taxes/Tangible Net Worth	77.8	65.8	34.6			62.6	27.2	58.9	25.3
	(69) 38.5	(70) 25.3	(73) 11.6		(17) 11.6	(15) 15.0		(14) 17.5	(16) 13.0
	22.0	9.8	.3			-56.5	3.9	1.7	3.7
% Profit Before Taxes/Total Assets	23.4	18.5	11.1		11.8	10.1	13.9	13.8	8.7
	13.0	8.1	4.4		.8	3.4	5.6	5.8	5.8
	4.3	1.2	-3.0		-28.8	-10.3	1.2	-.4	2.6
Sales/Net Fixed Assets	37.2	41.3	25.3		35.1	22.7	27.3	47.6	9.1
	13.3	19.4	10.1		14.2	12.1	13.0	13.9	7.1
	8.2	7.1	5.7		5.8	5.7	2.5	7.3	5.6
Sales/Total Assets	3.2	3.6	2.7		3.0	2.8	2.5	3.0	2.3
	2.5	2.6	2.0		2.0	2.2	1.6	1.9	1.9
	1.8	1.9	1.4		1.2	1.8	1.0	1.6	1.7
% Depr., Dep., Amort./Sales	.6	.7	1.1			1.2	.8	.7	1.2
	(72) 1.2	(69) 1.4	(71) 1.7		(15)	1.7	(17) 1.8	(14) 1.7	(13) 1.6
	2.2	2.9	3.4			4.9	3.4	3.8	2.6
% Officers', Directors' Owners' Comp/Sales	1.9	1.8	2.5						
	(43) 3.5	(30) 4.0	(32) 4.0						
	6.9	7.0	7.3						
Net Sales ($)	2186388M	2430094M	2212404M	4285M	20138M	77703M	127952M	252935M	1729391M
Total Assets ($)	1054245M	1180874M	1262990M	2581M	13477M	40663M	88614M	165465M	952190M

Current Data Sorted by Assets   Comparative Historical Data

Type of Statement

Type of Statement	0-500M	500M-2MM	2-10MM	10-50MM	50-100MM	100-250MM		ALL 4/1/05-3/31/06	ALL 4/1/06-3/31/07
Unqualified			4	6	1			9	13
Reviewed		1	4	2				8	10
Compiled		1	4	1				9	4
Tax Returns		4	3					4	9
Other		2	12	6	4	3		8	18
		7 (4/1-9/30/09)	51 (10/1/09-3/31/10)						
NUMBER OF STATEMENTS		8	27	15	5	3		38	54

Columns 0-500M and 500M-2MM marked "DATA NOT AVAILABLE" for the ratio body below.

	0-500M %	500M-2MM %	2-10MM %	10-50MM %	50-100MM %	100-250MM %		ALL %	ALL %
ASSETS									
Cash & Equivalents			7.6	10.2				5.2	6.3
Trade Receivables (net)			30.4	20.7				35.6	28.5
Inventory			21.8	24.7				22.6	25.8
All Other Current			4.4	1.6				6.0	2.9
Total Current			64.1	57.2				69.3	63.6
Fixed Assets (net)			22.5	30.0				23.2	25.9
Intangibles (net)			9.0	10.4				4.3	6.6
All Other Non-Current			4.4	2.4				3.2	3.8
Total			100.0	100.0				100.0	100.0
LIABILITIES									
Notes Payable-Short Term			9.6	8.9				9.4	8.1
Cur. Mat.-L.T.D.			4.5	2.3				5.7	3.7
Trade Payables			15.6	11.1				16.8	16.5
Income Taxes Payable			.2	.1				.3	.7
All Other Current			6.9	6.5				13.3	12.1
Total Current			36.8	29.1				45.5	41.1
Long-Term Debt			16.4	13.7				12.1	21.3
Deferred Taxes			.0	1.1				.8	.6
All Other Non-Current			8.5	7.4				8.0	4.1
Net Worth			38.3	48.7				33.7	32.9
Total Liabilities & Net Worth			100.0	100.0				100.0	100.0
INCOME DATA									
Net Sales			100.0	100.0				100.0	100.0
Gross Profit			32.6	22.3				26.9	28.1
Operating Expenses			29.0	18.5				21.0	22.4
Operating Profit			3.6	3.8				5.9	5.8
All Other Expenses (net)			1.7	1.4				1.2	1.3
Profit Before Taxes			1.9	2.4				4.6	4.5
RATIOS									
Current			3.2	3.3				2.5	2.5
			1.6	1.9				1.6	1.6
			1.2	1.3				1.0	1.1
Quick			2.1	1.7				1.5	1.4
			.9	1.1				.8	.8
			.7	.6				.6	.5
Sales/Receivables			38 9.6	35 10.4				38 9.5	34 10.7
			48 7.6	48 7.6				48 7.6	45 8.1
			58 6.3	58 6.3				58 6.3	56 6.5
Cost of Sales/Inventory			28 12.8	41 9.0				18 20.3	31 11.9
			40 9.0	62 5.9				35 10.4	55 6.7
			76 4.8	124 3.0				59 6.2	83 4.4
Cost of Sales/Payables			20 18.6	9 39.0				20 17.9	18 19.8
			37 9.9	27 13.3				31 12.0	30 12.1
			55 6.6	43 8.5				43 8.6	47 7.8
Sales/Working Capital			3.7	3.5				6.7	5.8
			7.9	6.5				13.8	10.1
			23.9	14.6				177.7	68.1
EBIT/Interest			12.4	5.8				21.8	10.7
			(25) 1.9	(14) 3.1				(37) 5.8	(50) 4.5
			.2	-2.4				2.4	2.4
Net Profit + Depr., Dep., Amort./Cur. Mat. L/T/D								10.2	7.9
								(12) 4.1	(20) 2.0
								1.2	1.1
Fixed/Worth			.2	.4				.3	.3
			.6	.8				.7	.6
			1.8	1.7				2.4	4.2
Debt/Worth			.8	.4				.9	.8
			2.1	1.4				2.3	1.7
			6.9	4.5				7.8	9.0
% Profit Before Taxes/Tangible Net Worth			38.6	36.0				45.9	48.1
			(23) 14.2	(13) 6.1				(33) 27.7	(43) 25.5
			1.7	-2.8				19.7	12.0
% Profit Before Taxes/Total Assets			17.5	6.9				18.8	17.7
			2.4	2.8				10.8	8.1
			-2.0	-.8				3.1	3.0
Sales/Net Fixed Assets			29.0	10.0				23.7	22.8
			12.3	4.8				11.7	11.4
			5.2	3.1				7.4	4.8
Sales/Total Assets			2.7	2.6				3.7	3.1
			2.3	1.4				2.9	2.4
			1.5	1.0				1.8	1.8
% Depr., Dep., Amort./Sales			1.0	1.5				.9	1.1
			(22) 2.2	(14) 3.0				(33) 1.8	(47) 1.7
			3.5	4.3				3.2	3.3
% Officers', Directors' Owners' Comp/Sales								1.0	2.5
								(14) 3.5	(17) 4.9
								5.8	7.9
Net Sales ($)		25726M	269871M	729154M	500797M	525032M		1581649M	1923417M
Total Assets ($)		11452M	125552M	440868M	343810M	615684M		577753M	1142326M

M = $ thousand   MM = $ million
See Pages 9 through 22 for Explanation of Ratios and Data

Comparative Historical Data   Current Data Sorted by Sales

			Type of Statement						
10	12	11	Uniqualified			3	1	5	6
7	12	7	Reviewed		1	1	2	2	1
6	7	6	Compiled			1	3	1	1
5	6	7	Tax Returns	1		2	3		
17	29	27	Other	1	2	1	7	4	12
4/1/07-3/31/08 ALL	4/1/08-3/31/09 ALL	4/1/09-3/31/10 ALL				7 (4/1-9/30/09)		51 (10/1/09-3/31/10)	
				0-1MM	1-3MM	3-5MM	5-10MM	10-25MM	25MM & OVE
45	66	58	NUMBER OF STATEMENTS	2	3	7	13	13	20
%	%	%	ASSETS	%	%	%	%	%	%
9.1	7.3	7.5	Cash & Equivalents				11.0	1.2	10.2
26.9	25.2	25.6	Trade Receivables (net)				30.6	31.1	21.0
22.6	25.2	22.3	Inventory				19.4	21.8	21.2
1.9	3.1	4.0	All Other Current				7.0	3.7	3.6
60.5	60.9	59.4	Total Current				68.1	57.8	56.0
29.1	26.8	28.1	Fixed Assets (net)				25.5	28.5	29.6
6.6	6.5	8.7	Intangibles (net)				4.1	7.6	11.6
3.8	5.9	3.7	All Other Non-Current				2.4	6.2	2.8
100.0	100.0	100.0	Total				100.0	100.0	100.0
			LIABILITIES						
15.4	10.6	8.1	Notes Payable-Short Term				7.7	16.7	4.3
4.2	2.9	3.6	Cur. Mat.-L.T.D.				3.7	3.0	2.2
15.0	12.2	13.5	Trade Payables				15.8	16.0	10.4
1.0	.3	.2	Income Taxes Payable				.0	.4	.1
8.5	11.3	8.9	All Other Current				9.1	7.7	9.6
44.2	37.2	34.2	Total Current				36.3	43.8	26.6
20.7	16.9	18.2	Long-Term Debt				19.4	15.6	14.5
.5	.9	1.0	Deferred Taxes				.0	.6	2.4
6.7	6.0	6.3	All Other Non-Current				2.3	6.4	3.9
27.9	39.0	40.3	Net Worth				42.0	33.5	52.5
100.0	100.0	100.0	Total Liabilities & Net Worth				100.0	100.0	100.0
			INCOME DATA						
100.0	100.0	100.0	Net Sales				100.0	100.0	100.0
32.7	28.2	29.0	Gross Profit				36.9	27.4	22.0
23.8	21.7	25.2	Operating Expenses				33.4	22.0	16.8
8.8	6.5	3.8	Operating Profit				3.6	5.5	5.2
1.8	1.2	1.8	All Other Expenses (net)				1.2	2.1	1.5
7.0	5.3	2.1	Profit Before Taxes				2.4	3.3	3.7
			RATIOS						
2.1	2.5	3.2					4.6	2.1	3.3
1.6	1.6	1.6	Current				1.7	1.2	1.8
1.2	1.2	1.2					1.3	1.0	1.4
1.4	1.3	1.8					3.1	1.1	2.0
.9	.9	.9	Quick				1.1	.8	1.1
.5	.6	.6					.8	.4	.6
32 11.5	30 12.0	37 9.7					34 10.8	42 8.6	31 11.6
44 8.3	40 9.2	50 7.4	Sales/Receivables				49 7.4	57 6.4	45 8.2
55 6.6	51 7.2	60 6.1					60 6.1	66 5.5	55 6.6
26 14.0	31 11.8	29 12.6					23 15.8	12 30.6	35 10.4
54 6.8	55 6.6	51 7.1	Cost of Sales/Inventory				40 9.0	36 10.2	53 6.9
83 4.4	87 4.2	100 3.7					75 4.9	104 3.5	88 4.2
22 16.4	12 31.7	19 18.8					15 23.9	19 19.0	13 29.1
28 12.9	21 17.1	32 11.6	Cost of Sales/Payables				38 9.7	37 9.9	24 15.5
41 9.0	36 10.1	49 7.5					57 6.4	54 6.7	32 11.3
6.6	5.2	4.1					3.6	7.1	4.2
11.6	9.9	9.3	Sales/Working Capital				11.5	23.9	7.9
22.4	21.4	20.0					17.3	-563.0	14.2
14.5	18.9	5.5					15.4	6.7	11.3
(44) 7.1	(61) 4.5	(55) 2.4	EBIT/Interest			(12) 2.6		2.4	(19) 4.3
2.6	2.2	-1.3					.7	-5.5	-.9
7.9	18.5	6.1	Net Profit + Depr., Dep.,						7.2
(15) 3.1	(19) 6.0	(14) 2.1	Amort./Cur. Mat. L/T/D						(10) 3.4
1.6	3.1	-.1							1.0
.4	.3	.4					.2	.4	.4
.8	.8	.9	Fixed/Worth				.7	1.0	.8
3.5	2.3	1.8					1.5	2.5	1.5
.8	.8	.9					.7	1.2	.5
1.6	1.7	1.7	Debt/Worth				1.4	1.7	1.3
6.3	6.3	6.7					2.3	4.8	2.5
55.2	45.7	36.8	% Profit Before Taxes/Tangible				35.7	38.6	41.5
(37) 22.6	(54) 24.6	(49) 14.2	Net Worth			(12) 12.5		(11) 15.5	(18) 23.2
12.5	11.2	-2.0					1.8	-8.7	-1.4
24.1	19.1	11.6	% Profit Before Taxes/Total				17.9	15.0	11.1
9.1	8.0	2.7	Assets				3.3	2.8	6.2
4.5	3.8	-2.2					-.8	-3.9	-.6
20.6	24.4	16.8					21.9	22.7	13.2
9.7	9.7	7.4	Sales/Net Fixed Assets				11.8	8.5	6.4
4.9	5.6	3.7					5.5	4.2	3.2
3.4	3.0	2.5					3.1	2.7	2.6
2.3	2.2	1.8	Sales/Total Assets				2.5	2.3	1.5
1.4	1.6	1.2					1.7	1.3	1.0
1.0	.9	1.4					1.5	1.7	1.0
(41) 2.4	(53) 1.5	(48) 2.6	% Depr., Dep., Amort./Sales			(11) 2.6		(11) 2.7	(15) 2.9
3.8	3.4	4.2					5.1	3.5	5.4
1.5	1.9	1.3	% Officers', Directors'						
(17) 3.7	(20) 4.0	(15) 7.4	Owners' Comp/Sales						
4.5	8.6	11.6							
1506243M	3333095M	2050580M	Net Sales ($)	1782M	7034M	27170M	86240M	239636M	1688718M
959894M	1515239M	1537366M	Total Assets ($)	1417M	7823M	17729M	42735M	218236M	1249426M

M = $ thousand   MM = $ million
See Pages 9 through 22 for Explanation of Ratios and Data

Current Data Sorted by Assets   **Comparative Historical Data**

	0-500M	500M-2MM	2-10MM	10-50MM	50-100MM	100-250MM	Type of Statement	4/1/05-3/31/06 ALL	4/1/06-3/31/07 ALL
			8	6	2	2	Unqualified	22	20
		2	10	1		1	Reviewed	19	27
	3	7	9	1			Compiled	15	17
	3	5	8				Tax Returns	18	12
	2	6	18	7	1	3	Other	42	25
		18 (4/1-9/30/09)		87 (10/1/09-3/31/10)					
NUMBER OF STATEMENTS	8	20	53	15	3	6		116	101

0-500M	500M-2MM	2-10MM	10-50MM	50-100MM	100-250MM		4/1/05-3/31/06 ALL	4/1/06-3/31/07 ALL
%	%	%	%	%	%	**ASSETS**	%	%
		12.6	6.2	7.8		Cash & Equivalents	6.5	7.7
		20.0	24.6	20.2		Trade Receivables (net)	22.6	23.3
		35.7	42.4	25.7		Inventory	32.4	33.4
		4.1	1.1	2.9		All Other Current	2.1	1.4
		72.3	74.3	56.5		Total Current	63.7	65.8
		16.9	19.2	25.0		Fixed Assets (net)	25.3	22.8
		2.2	2.1	7.5		Intangibles (net)	4.6	4.4
		8.5	4.4	11.0		All Other Non-Current	6.4	7.0
		100.0	100.0	100.0		Total	100.0	100.0
						LIABILITIES		
		10.5	15.1	6.1		Notes Payable-Short Term	11.5	10.3
		3.8	3.5	1.7		Cur. Mat.-L.T.D.	2.5	3.0
		13.8	13.8	8.7		Trade Payables	14.6	13.4
		.0	.4	.3		Income Taxes Payable	.3	.2
		9.7	5.5	7.7		All Other Current	8.3	10.4
		37.8	38.3	24.4		Total Current	37.1	37.3
		12.5	13.5	12.9		Long-Term Debt	18.3	15.9
		.0	.4	1.1		Deferred Taxes	.7	.6
		18.5	6.0	6.3		All Other Non-Current	8.8	8.0
		31.1	41.8	55.4		Net Worth	35.1	38.2
		100.0	100.0	100.0		Total Liabilities & Net Worth	100.0	100.0
						INCOME DATA		
		100.0	100.0	100.0		Net Sales	100.0	100.0
		30.3	32.0	33.0		Gross Profit	30.3	34.5
		30.2	29.2	25.8		Operating Expenses	24.6	28.5
		.0	2.8	7.2		Operating Profit	5.7	6.1
		1.1	1.8	1.1		All Other Expenses (net)	1.4	1.1
		-1.0	1.0	6.1		Profit Before Taxes	4.3	5.0
						RATIOS		
		3.0	4.5	5.2		Current	3.2	3.2
		2.1	2.1	2.4			2.0	2.1
		1.1	1.3	1.9			1.3	1.3
		1.4	1.8	1.7		Quick	1.6	1.5
		.8	.7	1.3			.9	.9
		.4	.5	.8			.5	.5
	19 18.9	33 11.1	33 11.1			Sales/Receivables	32 11.4	28 13.0
	33 11.0	40 9.1	46 7.9				40 9.1	39 9.3
	46 7.9	51 7.2	55 6.7				50 7.2	48 7.5
	30 12.2	67 5.5	61 6.0			Cost of Sales/Inventory	49 7.4	47 7.7
	93 3.9	142 2.6	91 4.0				80 4.6	86 4.3
	149 2.4	259 1.4	149 2.5				125 2.9	147 2.5
	8 47.2	12 30.4	15 24.8			Cost of Sales/Payables	18 20.5	15 24.3
	32 11.5	25 14.8	24 15.5				29 12.5	28 13.2
	61 6.0	50 7.3	51 7.2				45 8.1	46 7.9
		2.9	2.8	3.1		Sales/Working Capital	4.6	3.9
		6.3	5.1	4.8			7.0	6.4
		25.2	15.0	7.5			19.6	18.6
		19.1	5.2	11.2		EBIT/Interest	11.0	13.6
	(17) 2.6	(48) 1.8	(13) 5.2				(108) 3.7	(90) 4.7
	-2.1	-.2	2.1				1.8	2.0
		8.0				Net Profit + Depr., Dep., Amort./Cur. Mat. L/T/D	6.0	7.7
	(10) .6						(31) 3.0	(30) 3.9
	-5.4						1.4	1.6
		.0	.2	.3		Fixed/Worth	.3	.3
		.2	.4	.5			.6	.6
		.9	1.2	.9			2.8	1.7
		.8	.4	.4		Debt/Worth	.7	.6
		1.4	1.3	1.0			1.7	1.6
		7.0	3.9	1.9			8.5	5.6
		61.6	22.7	37.7		% Profit Before Taxes/Tangible Net Worth	45.1	47.4
	(18) 10.5	(49) 7.6	9.0				(93) 24.0	(87) 23.1
	-14.7	-.6	3.7				9.0	9.8
		22.2	8.5	13.6		% Profit Before Taxes/Total Assets	14.4	17.2
		5.4	2.5	6.9			8.6	7.9
		-9.2	-.6	1.7			2.1	2.3
		203.5	34.6	10.9		Sales/Net Fixed Assets	20.4	25.7
		19.2	11.6	7.0			9.0	10.5
		7.4	6.2	5.2			5.0	5.3
		3.0	2.7	2.3		Sales/Total Assets	2.6	2.9
		2.3	1.7	1.5			2.0	1.9
		1.2	1.3	1.2			1.5	1.5
		.8	.7	1.4		% Depr., Dep., Amort./Sales	1.1	.8
	(15) 1.6	(46) 2.1	(14) 2.1				(99) 2.0	(91) 2.0
	5.0	4.0	3.3				3.4	2.7
		2.0	1.3			% Officers', Directors' Owners' Comp/Sales	2.4	2.7
	(14) 3.6	(26) 3.5					(43) 4.3	(30) 3.7
	6.1	7.2					6.4	6.1
7625M	70028M	496477M	610559M	280789M	1155982M	Net Sales ($)	3883638M	3109317M
1821M	26646M	260050M	375653M	199092M	904386M	Total Assets ($)	2404817M	1869020M

M = $ thousand   MM = $ million
See Pages 9 through 22 for Explanation of Ratios and Data

Comparative Historical Data | Current Data Sorted by Sales

			Type of Statement	0-1MM	1-3MM	3-5MM	5-10MM	10-25MM	25MM & OVER
14	18	18	Unqualified		1		2	7	8
22	20	14	Reviewed			2	7	3	2
12	14	20	Compiled	1	7	4	3	5	
21	16	16	Tax Returns	1	3	4	7	1	
36	39	37	Other	3	4	5	9	6	10
4/1/07-3/31/08 ALL	4/1/08-3/31/09 ALL	4/1/09-3/31/10 ALL			18 (4/1-9/30/09)		87 (10/1/09-3/31/10)		
105	107	105	**NUMBER OF STATEMENTS**	5	15	15	28	22	20

ASSETS

Yr1 %	Yr2 %	Yr3 %		0-1MM %	1-3MM %	3-5MM %	5-10MM %	10-25MM %	25MM&OVER %
7.5	8.5	9.3	Cash & Equivalents		13.8	10.5	6.5	7.6	9.6
24.7	25.3	22.4	Trade Receivables (net)		19.0	21.0	25.4	22.3	23.5
31.8	33.9	34.5	Inventory		39.2	36.4	39.8	39.1	22.2
1.1	2.0	2.3	All Other Current		1.4	3.4	1.1	2.1	2.3
65.2	69.7	68.6	Total Current		73.4	71.4	72.8	71.1	57.6
22.9	20.9	20.3	Fixed Assets (net)		17.7	20.8	19.6	18.8	24.5
5.7	4.0	4.0	Intangibles (net)		3.1	2.1	3.7	.7	9.0
6.3	5.4	7.2	All Other Non-Current		5.8	5.7	3.8	9.4	9.0
100.0	100.0	100.0	Total		100.0	100.0	100.0	100.0	100.0

LIABILITIES

Yr1	Yr2	Yr3		0-1MM	1-3MM	3-5MM	5-10MM	10-25MM	25MM&OVER
10.1	13.5	13.0	Notes Payable-Short Term		19.2	10.1	13.2	15.9	5.7
3.3	3.4	3.2	Cur. Mat.-L.T.D.		4.6	5.0	3.6	2.5	1.5
15.6	13.6	11.8	Trade Payables		9.5	12.7	13.7	14.9	8.3
.2	.2	.3	Income Taxes Payable		.0	.0	.7	.2	.3
7.7	9.1	10.9	All Other Current		34.5	5.7	7.1	5.8	8.2
36.9	39.8	39.2	Total Current		67.8	33.5	38.3	39.2	24.1
17.4	15.6	12.6	Long-Term Debt		11.6	22.5	8.3	11.0	12.3
.5	.4	.5	Deferred Taxes		.2	.0	1.0	.4	.7
9.5	5.2	8.9	All Other Non-Current		19.4	6.6	5.4	5.8	7.2
35.7	39.0	38.9	Net Worth		1.0	37.3	47.0	43.6	55.7
100.0	100.0	100.0	Total Liabilities & Net Worth		100.0	100.0	100.0	100.0	100.0

INCOME DATA

Yr1	Yr2	Yr3		0-1MM	1-3MM	3-5MM	5-10MM	10-25MM	25MM&OVER
100.0	100.0	100.0	Net Sales		100.0	100.0	100.0	100.0	100.0
31.5	30.7	32.4	Gross Profit		34.9	36.3	33.3	27.7	32.5
25.4	25.1	29.4	Operating Expenses		41.9	29.6	30.2	23.7	25.7
6.2	5.6	3.0	Operating Profit		-7.1	6.7	3.1	4.0	6.8
1.5	1.4	1.5	All Other Expenses (net)		2.9	1.2	.9	1.5	1.2
4.7	4.2	1.5	Profit Before Taxes		-10.0	5.5	2.2	2.5	5.6

RATIOS

Yr1	Yr2	Yr3		0-1MM	1-3MM	3-5MM	5-10MM	10-25MM	25MM&OVER
3.4	3.8	3.8	Current		5.3	3.1	4.7	3.4	3.8
2.1	2.1	2.4			2.3	1.7	2.5	2.3	2.4
1.2	1.3	1.3			1.1	1.3	1.4	1.2	1.9
1.7	1.9	1.8	Quick		1.7	2.2	1.8	1.9	1.9
.9	.8	.9			.7	.9	.7	.8	1.5
.6	.5	.5			.4	.4	.5	.4	1.0
30 12.0	25 14.9	27 13.7	Sales/Receivables	10 37.0	24 15.0	34 10.9	25 14.4	34 10.8	
38 9.6	36 10.2	39 9.5		31 11.8	32 11.3	41 8.9	37 9.9	48 7.6	
48 7.5	57 6.4	50 7.2		47 7.8	56 6.6	50 7.3	50 7.2	57 6.5	
51 7.1	44 8.3	50 7.3	Cost of Sales/Inventory	50 7.2	48 7.6	61 5.9	51 7.1	49 7.4	
82 4.5	75 4.9	87 4.2		85 4.3	114 3.2	114 3.2	94 3.9	67 5.5	
133 2.7	154 2.4	167 2.2		385 .9	187 2.0	252 1.4	172 2.1	122 3.0	
15 24.0	10 34.9	12 30.4	Cost of Sales/Payables	3 114.3	16 23.2	13 28.6	12 30.6	15 24.6	
29 12.4	24 15.3	24 15.4		28 12.9	28 13.2	23 16.2	29 12.5	24 15.5	
51 7.1	42 8.7	50 7.3		77 4.7	53 6.9	49 7.5	51 7.1	44 8.2	
4.0	4.1	3.3	Sales/Working Capital		2.2	4.0	2.5	3.7	3.5
7.1	6.4	5.3			8.1	5.7	5.3	5.4	5.0
19.5	16.4	12.9			35.0	18.3	13.3	13.9	6.6
11.1	12.5	9.6	EBIT/Interest		2.5	21.4	7.3	21.7	11.7
(93) 3.7	(91) 3.2	(91) 2.6		(14) -1.5	(12) 4.2	(25) 1.6	(20) 3.8	(16) 5.9	
1.5	.9	.1			-24.8	1.3	-1.9	1.4	2.6
11.2	12.9	45.8	Net Profit + Depr., Dep., Amort./Cur. Mat. L/T/D						
(24) 2.8	(21) 1.1	(20) 3.6							
1.7	.1	.6							
.3	.2	.2	Fixed/Worth		.1	.1	.1	.2	.3
.5	.5	.4			.3	.5	.4	.4	.4
2.1	1.5	1.0			1.0	1.2	1.2	.6	.9
.6	.5	.5	Debt/Worth		.8	.5	.3	.4	.4
2.2	1.8	1.3			2.5	1.3	1.3	1.1	1.0
6.4	5.5	4.1			5.3	3.8	4.4	5.3	1.7
43.9	50.8	31.0	% Profit Before Taxes/Tangible Net Worth		6.8	58.0	31.8	32.9	31.1
(86) 19.6	(91) 17.7	(96) 9.1		(13) -18.6	(14) 15.1	(27) 7.6	(20) 8.9	(19) 14.0	
6.5	1.0	.8			-41.7	5.4	-14.7	4.0	5.6
15.3	16.2	11.1	% Profit Before Taxes/Total Assets		2.6	28.2	11.5	11.2	13.4
5.7	6.7	3.9			-7.8	7.0	2.0	4.4	6.7
1.2	-.7	-.6			-23.8	1.2	-4.1	.9	1.9
28.4	40.1	26.8	Sales/Net Fixed Assets		25.9	30.6	49.8	39.6	15.1
12.4	12.2	10.7			18.4	9.2	11.3	11.7	5.9
5.7	5.5	5.5			4.3	6.2	5.7	7.2	4.2
2.6	2.8	2.7	Sales/Total Assets		4.2	3.0	3.0	2.7	2.2
2.0	2.0	1.8			1.6	1.8	1.8	1.9	1.5
1.5	1.5	1.3			.9	1.3	1.3	1.6	1.2
.8	.9	1.0	% Depr., Dep., Amort./Sales		1.2	1.3	.8	.6	1.4
(84) 2.2	(91) 1.7	(88) 2.3		(13) 2.2	(12) 3.5	(23) 1.9	(18) 1.7	(19) 2.6	
3.1	3.1	4.0			4.2	6.4	4.0	2.9	3.7
1.8	2.3	1.9	% Officers', Directors', Owners' Comp/Sales		5.4		1.3		
(40) 2.8	(43) 3.2	(48) 3.8		(11) 7.8		(16) 2.8			
5.5	4.9	7.4			11.6		4.2		
2440692M	2885470M	2621460M	Net Sales ($)	3135M	24992M	59491M	206813M	333058M	1993971M
1534982M	1712372M	1767648M	Total Assets ($)	2432M	21260M	33419M	126939M	179411M	1404187M

© RMA 2010

M = $ thousand   MM = $ million
See Pages 9 through 22 for Explanation of Ratios and Data

MANUFACTURING—Spring (Light Gauge) Manufacturing NAICS 332612

Current Data Sorted by Assets   **Comparative Historical Data**

Note: For the 100-250MM current-data column the data is marked **DATA NOT AVAILABLE**.

0-500M	500M-2MM	2-10MM	10-50MM	50-100MM	100-250MM		4/1/05-3/31/06 ALL	4/1/06-3/31/07 ALL
						Type of Statement		
		2	5			Unqualified	12	9
	2	7	3			Reviewed	18	11
	1	8				Compiled	9	6
1	4	1				Tax Returns	4	5
	3	5	3		1	Other	9	9
	5 (4/1-9/30/09)		41 (10/1/09-3/31/10)					
1	10	23	11		1	**NUMBER OF STATEMENTS**	52	40
%	%	%	%	%	%	**ASSETS**	%	%
	7.7	11.9	9.1			Cash & Equivalents	6.1	6.5
	25.7	21.0	22.0			Trade Receivables (net)	27.4	25.3
	18.3	23.5	28.9			Inventory	22.7	25.1
	9.7	.7	2.1			All Other Current	1.2	1.9
	61.5	57.1	62.0			Total Current	57.4	58.8
	28.0	31.5	27.5			Fixed Assets (net)	29.4	30.0
	8.7	5.6	5.1			Intangibles (net)	4.1	4.1
	1.8	5.8	5.4			All Other Non-Current	9.2	7.1
	100.0	100.0	100.0			Total	100.0	100.0
						LIABILITIES		
	12.7	8.1	14.4			Notes Payable-Short Term	11.1	9.3
	3.6	7.4	1.0			Cur. Mat.-L.T.D.	4.3	5.9
	8.9	9.4	5.8			Trade Payables	13.5	12.9
	.0	.0	.3			Income Taxes Payable	.1	.1
	2.7	5.8	5.7			All Other Current	11.0	10.3
	27.9	30.6	27.2			Total Current	40.0	38.5
	20.7	18.9	6.7			Long-Term Debt	15.3	15.1
	.0	.2	.6			Deferred Taxes	1.0	.8
	.2	9.0	5.7			All Other Non-Current	5.6	5.2
	51.1	41.3	59.8			Net Worth	38.1	40.5
	100.0	100.0	100.0			Total Liabilities & Net Worth	100.0	100.0
						INCOME DATA		
	100.0	100.0	100.0			Net Sales	100.0	100.0
	35.4	27.1	27.9			Gross Profit	24.8	28.0
	25.3	25.2	20.7			Operating Expenses	19.7	23.4
	10.1	1.8	7.2			Operating Profit	5.1	4.6
	3.6	1.4	.1			All Other Expenses (net)	1.3	1.3
	6.5	.4	7.2			Profit Before Taxes	3.9	3.3
						RATIOS		
	6.8	3.6	4.7			Current	2.8	2.5
	2.6	2.1	2.7				1.6	1.9
	1.4	1.1	1.3				1.1	1.4
	3.0	2.6	3.3			Quick	1.5	1.6
	1.6	1.0	1.3				.9	.9
	.9	.5	.6				.6	.6
	21 17.2	40 9.1	40 9.2			Sales/Receivables	43 8.5	36 10.1
	37 9.9	46 7.9	55 6.6				53 6.9	47 7.7
	61 5.9	55 6.6	73 5.0				58 6.2	56 6.6
	12 30.8	51 7.1	54 6.7			Cost of Sales/Inventory	41 9.0	38 9.6
	41 9.0	72 5.1	87 4.2				52 7.1	63 5.8
	89 4.1	98 3.7	119 3.1				75 4.9	88 4.1
	8 44.5	13 27.1	12 31.2			Cost of Sales/Payables	19 19.5	15 24.2
	21 17.7	26 14.2	22 16.9				28 12.9	24 15.4
	36 10.3	35 10.3	28 12.8				43 8.5	38 9.6
	3.2	3.4	2.8			Sales/Working Capital	4.7	5.3
	5.9	7.2	3.8				8.9	7.5
	16.8	16.9	9.7				35.1	14.2
		7.9	87.1			EBIT/Interest	12.3	16.1
		(20) 1.3	(10) 9.7				(49) 2.7	(39) 6.2
		-.3	1.8				1.4	1.3
						Net Profit + Depr., Dep.,	8.9	8.5
						Amort./Cur. Mat. L/T/D	(20) 1.7	(14) 5.8
							.9	1.4
	.2	.4	.3			Fixed/Worth	.4	.4
	1.1	1.0	.5				.7	.7
	2.6	3.3	1.1				2.1	2.6
	.2	.3	.2			Debt/Worth	.6	.6
	1.8	2.3	.9				1.4	.9
	6.8	5.9	2.1				5.0	6.4
		15.3	40.9			% Profit Before Taxes/Tangible	32.2	36.2
		(19) 3.2	19.8			Net Worth	(45) 14.7	(33) 18.4
		-14.2	5.5				2.1	4.3
	13.1	6.5	23.1			% Profit Before Taxes/Total	13.0	16.2
	3.4	1.1	6.2			Assets	6.0	5.8
	-3.8	-3.3	1.6				1.6	1.1
	26.3	9.6	7.9			Sales/Net Fixed Assets	12.4	17.5
	11.4	4.9	4.7				6.9	7.1
	5.7	3.4	3.2				4.1	4.3
	3.0	1.9	2.0			Sales/Total Assets	2.2	2.7
	2.2	1.5	1.6				1.8	1.9
	1.2	1.0	1.2				1.4	1.5
		2.2	1.7			% Depr., Dep., Amort./Sales	2.2	2.3
		(22) 4.1	3.6				(48) 2.9	(34) 3.4
		5.9	5.3				4.2	5.3
						% Officers', Directors'	2.8	2.3
						Owners' Comp/Sales	(17) 4.7	(15) 6.2
							9.1	10.7
1269M	21583M	180057M	399291M	69257M		Net Sales ($)	907014M	721788M
480M	10005M	120281M	262492M	50180M		Total Assets ($)	525672M	411140M

M = $ thousand   MM = $ million
See Pages 9 through 22 for Explanation of Ratios and Data

Comparative Historical Data / Current Data Sorted by Sales

4/1/07-3/31/08 ALL	4/1/08-3/31/09 ALL	4/1/09-3/31/10 ALL	Type of Statement	0-1MM	1-3MM	3-5MM	5-10MM	10-25MM	25MM & OVER
8	8	7	Unqualified			1	6	2	5
10	10	12	Reviewed	1			5	3	1
11	9	9	Compiled		1	2	1	1	
2	6	6	Tax Returns		3	2	1		
14	12	12	Other	1	2	1	4		4
					5 (4/1-9/30/09)		41 (10/1/09-3/31/10)		
45	45	46	NUMBER OF STATEMENTS	2	6	6	16	6	10
%	%	%	**ASSETS**	%	%	%	%	%	%
8.3	6.8	10.1	Cash & Equivalents				11.6		9.6
23.0	21.7	22.4	Trade Receivables (net)				23.0		24.4
24.0	32.3	24.4	Inventory				21.1		30.8
.9	1.1	3.1	All Other Current				.6		2.8
56.1	62.0	60.0	Total Current				56.3		67.7
29.1	28.2	29.5	Fixed Assets (net)				28.3		28.3
6.7	2.6	5.9	Intangibles (net)				9.1		1.4
8.1	7.3	4.6	All Other Non-Current				6.3		2.7
100.0	100.0	100.0	Total				100.0		100.0
			LIABILITIES						
9.1	12.5	10.6	Notes Payable-Short Term				10.6		14.7
3.4	4.2	4.7	Cur. Mat.-L.T.D.				6.1		.7
8.2	11.1	8.5	Trade Payables				10.1		6.5
.1	.0	.1	Income Taxes Payable				.0		.6
7.0	7.9	5.1	All Other Current				5.4		6.5
27.7	35.8	29.1	Total Current				32.2		29.0
17.2	20.2	15.5	Long-Term Debt				20.4		3.4
.7	.4	.3	Deferred Taxes				.2		.6
5.0	7.1	8.0	All Other Non-Current				6.9		6.9
49.5	36.5	47.1	Net Worth				40.3		60.0
100.0	100.0	100.0	Total Liabilities & Net Worth				100.0		100.0
			INCOME DATA						
100.0	100.0	100.0	Net Sales				100.0		100.0
26.4	25.1	29.4	Gross Profit				32.8		23.5
20.5	21.8	24.6	Operating Expenses				29.5		18.0
5.8	3.2	4.8	Operating Profit				3.3		5.5
1.0	.8	1.5	All Other Expenses (net)				1.4		-.3
4.8	2.4	3.3	Profit Before Taxes				1.9		5.8
			RATIOS						
3.0	2.9	4.7	Current				3.5		6.1
2.3	2.2	2.3					2.0		2.4
1.4	1.3	1.4					1.2		1.4
2.1	1.7	2.9	Quick				2.5		4.0
1.1	.9	1.2					1.2		1.2
.7	.6	.7					.6		.7
37 9.9	31 11.8	38 9.6	Sales/Receivables				42 8.8		32 11.3
46 7.9	40 9.1	48 7.6					53 6.8		55 6.6
54 6.7	48 7.6	61 5.9					69 5.3		75 4.9
35 10.3	44 8.3	50 7.3	Cost of Sales/Inventory				49 7.4		53 6.9
56 6.5	70 5.2	71 5.2					74 4.9		71 5.1
83 4.4	102 3.6	98 3.7					100 3.6		104 3.5
11 34.1	12 29.3	13 28.0	Cost of Sales/Payables				14 26.7		11 31.9
20 18.5	17 21.1	23 15.9					27 13.5		17 21.0
29 12.7	31 11.8	35 10.5					45 8.1		27 13.5
4.9	4.5	3.5	Sales/Working Capital				3.0		3.4
7.1	7.1	6.0					8.1		4.9
15.2	15.6	14.0					19.4		8.7
9.9	6.4	10.0	EBIT/Interest				7.2		
(42) 3.9	(42) 2.7	(39) 2.0					(14) 1.3		
1.4	.3	-.3					-.4		
4.0	4.5	31.8	Net Profit + Depr., Dep., Amort./Cur. Mat. L/T/D						
(11) 3.2	(14) 2.6	(12) 3.3							
2.7	1.2	1.2							
.4	.3	.4	Fixed/Worth				.5		.3
.7	.8	1.0					1.3		.5
1.2	1.7	1.7					3.2		1.1
.5	.5	.3	Debt/Worth				.5		.1
1.1	2.0	1.8					2.8		.7
2.6	4.3	4.5					5.7		2.2
31.6	29.2	26.6	% Profit Before Taxes/Tangible Net Worth				27.4		31.1
(41) 15.2	(40) 8.6	(41) 5.8					(13) 8.3		6.5
4.3	-2.6	-7.8					-7.4		4.3
12.8	12.1	7.7	% Profit Before Taxes/Total Assets				7.8		23.2
8.3	3.6	2.2					1.3		5.2
1.3	-.9	-2.7					-3.0		1.5
11.5	16.2	11.3	Sales/Net Fixed Assets				11.0		15.5
7.0	7.5	6.0					5.3		4.9
4.4	5.1	3.4					2.6		3.5
2.3	2.6	2.2	Sales/Total Assets				2.4		2.0
1.9	1.9	1.6					1.4		1.7
1.6	1.7	1.2					1.0		1.4
2.3	1.5	2.2	% Depr., Dep., Amort./Sales				2.2		1.9
(43) 3.0	(43) 2.8	(43) 3.3					3.8		3.7
4.4	4.4	5.4					6.0		5.4
1.9	1.8	3.6	% Officers', Directors' Owners' Comp/Sales						
(14) 5.3	(14) 3.7	(17) 6.9							
8.5	10.6	10.0							
846020M	923729M	671457M	Net Sales ($)	602M	10310M	24838M	104311M	88875M	442521M
480793M	483366M	443438M	Total Assets ($)	1713M	5163M	17916M	82033M	57066M	279547M

M = $ thousand   MM = $ million
See Pages 9 through 22 for Explanation of Ratios and Data

Current Data Sorted by Assets / Comparative Historical Data

0-500M	500M-2MM	2-10MM	10-50MM	50-100MM	100-250MM	Type of Statement	4/1/05-3/31/06 ALL	4/1/06-3/31/07 ALL
		7	10	4	3	Unqualified	35	51
	7	20	6			Reviewed	34	36
	4	8	2			Compiled	29	24
1	5	3				Tax Returns	23	13
	5	20	22	3	2	Other	68	58
	24 (4/1-9/30/09)		108 (10/1/09-3/31/10)					
1	21	58	40	7	5	NUMBER OF STATEMENTS	189	182
%	%	%	%	%	%	ASSETS	%	%
	10.7	10.3	3.5			Cash & Equivalents	7.5	7.5
	32.1	23.7	24.0			Trade Receivables (net)	27.6	29.1
	29.1	31.9	34.6			Inventory	29.6	29.2
	3.5	2.7	4.0			All Other Current	1.2	1.6
	75.5	68.7	66.1			Total Current	65.9	67.4
	16.4	25.2	27.2			Fixed Assets (net)	25.8	24.0
	3.1	2.4	2.9			Intangibles (net)	3.3	3.5
	5.0	3.7	3.8			All Other Non-Current	5.0	5.0
	100.0	100.0	100.0			Total	100.0	100.0
						LIABILITIES		
	20.2	13.4	13.1			Notes Payable-Short Term	12.8	11.8
	2.6	4.8	4.5			Cur. Mat.-L.T.D.	3.5	3.2
	25.6	15.0	11.0			Trade Payables	16.6	17.2
	.1	.1	.6			Income Taxes Payable	.2	.4
	8.3	6.4	6.7			All Other Current	8.7	10.1
	56.8	39.7	36.1			Total Current	41.8	42.6
	21.8	12.5	10.7			Long-Term Debt	18.7	14.4
	.2	.2	.6			Deferred Taxes	.6	.6
	13.4	3.8	8.7			All Other Non-Current	6.5	4.6
	7.8	43.9	43.9			Net Worth	32.4	37.8
	100.0	100.0	100.0			Total Liabilties & Net Worth	100.0	100.0
						INCOME DATA		
	100.0	100.0	100.0			Net Sales	100.0	100.0
	25.6	27.3	20.4			Gross Profit	27.2	26.7
	29.8	25.4	16.5			Operating Expenses	22.1	20.3
	-4.3	1.9	3.9			Operating Profit	5.1	6.4
	.3	.9	1.5			All Other Expenses (net)	1.2	.9
	-4.6	1.0	2.4			Profit Before Taxes	3.9	5.5
						RATIOS		
	2.7	3.3	2.7			Current	2.7	2.4
	1.4	1.8	1.9				1.6	1.7
	1.0	1.1	1.2				1.2	1.2
	1.5	1.6	1.2			Quick	1.4	1.4
	.6	.8	.9				.9	.9
	.5	.5	.5				.5	.6
	30 12.3	30 12.1	38 9.7			Sales/Receivables	32 11.4	34 10.8
	47 7.8	38 9.6	54 6.7				45 8.2	44 8.2
	57 6.4	51 7.2	62 5.9				57 6.4	58 6.3
	25 14.5	42 8.8	67 5.4			Cost of Sales/Inventory	32 11.5	35 10.6
	66 5.5	70 5.2	90 4.1				62 5.9	62 5.8
	102 3.6	111 3.3	134 2.7				95 3.9	89 4.1
	22 16.5	19 19.6	14 26.9			Cost of Sales/Payables	16 22.9	18 20.2
	43 8.5	31 11.7	26 13.9				29 12.4	30 12.1
	61 6.0	54 6.7	44 8.4				49 7.4	46 8.0
	4.6	3.9	3.6			Sales/Working Capital	5.3	5.1
	18.0	5.4	6.4				9.3	7.9
	-93.6	35.0	15.6				28.7	22.9
	3.1	7.3	17.9			EBIT/Interest	9.1	11.0
	(18) .7	(52) 1.9	1.9				(178) 3.9	(167) 3.7
	-4.1	-.2	-2.4				1.4	1.8
		4.8	3.1			Net Profit + Depr., Dep., Amort./Cur. Mat. L/T/D	6.3	6.6
		(14) 2.5	(17) 1.4				(45) 2.1	(60) 2.1
		.5	-.8				1.2	1.3
	.3	.2	.3			Fixed/Worth	.2	.3
	.7	.5	.7				.6	.5
	UND	1.4	1.4				1.9	1.5
	.9	.6	.5			Debt/Worth	.7	.6
	5.7	1.6	1.3				1.7	1.3
	-5.3	3.0	3.8				5.2	5.7
	28.7	16.1	28.0			% Profit Before Taxes/Tangible Net Worth	45.6	46.6
	(14) 4.3	(53) 6.1	(38) 13.7				(162) 17.5	(162) 20.6
	-76.9	-4.5	-10.9				6.5	8.2
	5.0	7.5	15.4			% Profit Before Taxes/Total Assets	15.5	16.6
	-2.4	2.2	3.8				6.4	8.0
	-26.4	-1.8	-4.1				1.1	2.0
	100.9	20.1	13.1			Sales/Net Fixed Assets	30.7	30.8
	18.1	9.6	7.3				9.4	10.6
	7.9	4.9	4.0				5.8	4.7
	3.2	2.5	2.2			Sales/Total Assets	3.0	2.8
	2.2	2.1	1.7				2.3	2.1
	1.6	1.5	1.1				1.7	1.6
	.9	1.4	1.5			% Depr., Dep., Amort./Sales	.7	.9
	(16) 2.1	(50) 2.2	(37) 2.4				(167) 1.9	(162) 1.7
	2.8	4.5	3.8				2.9	3.2
	1.3	2.6				% Officers', Directors' Owners' Comp/Sales	1.7	2.1
	(10) 2.1	(23) 3.6					(72) 3.6	(55) 4.9
	11.1	8.1					6.5	7.5
975M	58083M	644195M	1459870M	885224M	1147937M	Net Sales ($)	5647095M	8325512M
464M	23198M	307152M	866989M	509712M	873705M	Total Assets ($)	2668040M	3286362M

M = $ thousand MM = $ million
See Pages 9 through 22 for Explanation of Ratios and Data

Comparative Historical Data / Current Data Sorted by Sales

4/1/07-3/31/08 ALL	4/1/08-3/31/09 ALL	4/1/09-3/31/10 ALL	Type of Statement	0-1MM	1-3MM 24 (4/1-9/30/09)	3-5MM	5-10MM 108 (10/1/09-3/31/10)	10-25MM	25MM & OVER
36	25	24	Unqualified		3	5	3	5	16
33	21	33	Reviewed				7	16	2
26	19	14	Compiled		3	4	4	3	
18	8	9	Tax Returns	1	2	4	2		
77	44	52	Other	2	3	2	7	17	21
190	117	132	**NUMBER OF STATEMENTS**	3	11	15	23	41	39
%	%	%	**ASSETS**	%	%	%	%	%	%
7.2	7.4	8.0	Cash & Equivalents		6.5	12.3	8.7	9.8	4.3
27.7	25.5	24.5	Trade Receivables (net)		27.2	25.2	26.2	23.6	23.6
32.8	32.9	31.3	Inventory		32.8	26.1	34.5	32.7	29.0
2.2	2.0	3.3	All Other Current		4.4	1.3	3.3	3.2	4.0
69.8	67.7	67.0	Total Current		70.8	65.0	72.7	69.3	60.9
21.5	24.4	25.4	Fixed Assets (net)		18.6	27.6	23.1	25.4	28.3
3.2	3.7	3.4	Intangibles (net)		1.3	4.6	.9	1.9	5.8
5.5	4.2	4.2	All Other Non-Current		9.4	2.8	3.3	3.4	5.0
100.0	100.0	100.0	Total		100.0	100.0	100.0	100.0	100.0
			LIABILITIES						
13.5	15.1	13.8	Notes Payable-Short Term		27.3	12.0	16.5	11.5	11.7
3.8	2.5	4.1	Cur. Mat.-L.T.D.		3.0	2.8	4.7	4.7	4.0
18.5	15.6	15.4	Trade Payables		24.0	19.0	16.3	14.1	11.5
.2	.5	.3	Income Taxes Payable		.0	.1	.0	.2	.6
10.5	10.1	6.7	All Other Current		4.3	11.2	5.3	7.1	6.3
46.5	43.8	40.3	Total Current		58.7	45.2	42.9	37.6	34.1
13.0	13.1	13.6	Long-Term Debt		19.4	10.4	18.9	9.5	12.6
.4	.7	.4	Deferred Taxes		.2	.3	.1	.3	.9
5.0	4.1	8.0	All Other Non-Current		2.3	20.5	2.8	4.4	10.2
35.1	38.3	37.7	Net Worth		19.3	23.7	35.3	48.2	42.2
100.0	100.0	100.0	Total Liabilties & Net Worth		100.0	100.0	100.0	100.0	100.0
			INCOME DATA						
100.0	100.0	100.0	Net Sales		100.0	100.0	100.0	100.0	100.0
25.6	24.5	23.8	Gross Profit		25.2	33.4	27.7	22.6	17.9
21.0	20.0	22.5	Operating Expenses		29.7	32.9	26.5	20.4	15.5
4.6	4.6	1.3	Operating Profit		-4.5	.4	1.2	2.2	2.4
1.0	.9	1.1	All Other Expenses (net)		.4	.5	1.1	.5	2.0
3.6	3.6	.2	Profit Before Taxes		-4.9	-.1	.1	1.7	.4
			RATIOS						
2.5	2.8	2.6	Current		2.1	3.4	2.6	3.5	2.6
1.6	1.7	1.8			1.2	1.4	1.8	1.9	1.9
1.1	1.1	1.2			.9	1.0	1.2	1.1	1.5
1.3	1.4	1.3	Quick		.9	2.0	1.5	1.7	1.3
.8	.7	.8			.6	.7	.8	.8	.9
.5	.4	.5			.3	.5	.6	.4	.6
33 11.1	28 12.9	32 11.3	Sales/Receivables		28 12.8	24 15.5	32 11.4	31 11.8	34 10.8
42 8.8	39 9.3	43 8.6			39 9.3	41 8.8	47 7.8	40 9.2	44 8.4
52 7.0	48 7.5	57 6.4			56 6.6	64 5.7	72 5.1	53 6.9	60 6.1
38 9.5	43 8.4	43 8.4	Cost of Sales/Inventory		26 14.2	25 14.9	42 8.7	45 8.1	57 6.4
65 5.6	64 5.7	75 4.9			73 5.0	71 5.2	69 5.3	70 5.2	77 4.7
99 3.4	108 3.4	113 3.2			148 2.5	99 3.7	144 2.5	115 3.2	101 3.6
18 20.8	17 22.0	17 21.1	Cost of Sales/Payables		28 13.3	16 22.3	13 27.3	18 19.8	16 23.2
31 11.7	28 13.2	30 12.3			51 7.2	29 12.6	44 8.3	30 12.2	26 13.8
49 7.4	43 8.5	47 7.8			67 5.5	42 8.7	68 5.3	48 7.5	35 10.4
5.0	4.5	4.0	Sales/Working Capital		5.5	4.1	3.8	3.5	4.1
9.1	10.0	6.7			18.0	7.1	5.4	6.1	6.6
37.7	34.3	27.5			-87.2	-74.2	34.2	35.8	10.6
9.1	10.6	8.6	EBIT/Interest		3.0	5.1	7.3	22.0	15.3
(172) 2.4	(110) 3.3	(123) 1.6			.8	(12) 2.4	(20) 1.4	(38) 2.1	1.6
.9	1.0	-1.3			-6.1	-.1	-1.1	.0	-3.5
3.2	5.4	3.6	Net Profit + Depr., Dep., Amort./Cur. Mat. L/T/D						3.2	4.3
(47) 2.1	(41) 2.6	(38) 1.5						(10) 1.6	(17) 1.5
.8	.9	.2						.5	-2.6
.2	.3	.3	Fixed/Worth		.4	.3	.2	.2	.4
.6	.8	.6			.7	.8	.6	.4	.7
1.9	1.7	1.4			UND	1.3	1.7	1.4	1.4
.7	.6	.6	Debt/Worth		2.0	.7	.6	.4	.5
1.8	1.8	1.7			3.5	1.5	2.3	1.5	1.5
7.3	6.0	3.9			-30.1	2.8	5.9	2.8	3.7
42.2	32.6	21.9	% Profit Before Taxes/Tangible Net Worth			18.9	11.1	23.8	36.7
(162) 19.6	(103) 15.4	(115) 6.1				(13) 6.7	(20) 3.8	(38) 6.0	(35) 12.0
2.8	3.0	-10.9				-3.9	-25.5	-4.8	-22.2
15.2	13.3	8.5	% Profit Before Taxes/Total Assets		4.2	11.4	5.2	12.2	13.5
4.5	5.2	1.5			-.3	2.3	.9	2.1	3.1
-.1	.6	-7.2			-22.4	-3.1	-11.9	-4.3	-10.0
37.7	20.2	17.9	Sales/Net Fixed Assets		103.2	30.1	22.6	22.5	10.7
13.0	11.2	8.4			12.2	8.8	10.0	11.6	6.8
6.2	5.3	4.4			6.4	3.9	6.9	5.2	3.6
3.0	3.1	2.4	Sales/Total Assets		2.8	2.9	2.4	2.6	2.2
2.2	2.3	1.8			1.8	1.7	2.1	2.0	1.7
1.7	1.6	1.4			1.3	1.4	1.4	1.5	1.3
.8	1.0	1.5	% Depr., Dep., Amort./Sales			1.2	1.5	1.3	1.8
(160) 1.5	(107) 1.8	(113) 2.4				(14) 3.1	(20) 3.3	(36) 1.7	(33) 2.5
2.8	2.6	4.0				7.4	4.9	3.1	3.0
2.1	2.4	2.0	% Officers', Directors', Owners' Comp/Sales					2.4	1.8
(61) 3.9	(39) 4.6	(42) 3.0						(10) 2.9	(14) 3.5
8.0	7.8	7.9						5.9	8.9
7328735M	4628051M	4196284M	Net Sales ($)	2747M	21429M	57132M	173778M	671495M	3269703M
3467814M	2157112M	2581220M	Total Assets ($)	1656M	11218M	32737M	105399M	366402M	2063808M

M = $ thousand   MM = $ million
See Pages 9 through 22 for Explanation of Ratios and Data

Current Data Sorted by Assets   **Comparative Historical Data**

Type of Statement	0-500M	500M-2MM	2-10MM	10-50MM	50-100MM	100-250MM		4/1/05-3/31/06 ALL	4/1/06-3/31/07 ALL
Unqualified	1	1	10	19	3	4		51	58
Reviewed	1	22	94	22	2			141	157
Compiled	9	66	72	7	1			167	201
Tax Returns	48	67	54	1				160	197
Other	25	74	103	39	4			278	244
	155 (4/1-9/30/09)			594 (10/1/09-3/31/10)					
NUMBER OF STATEMENTS	84	230	333	88	10	4		797	857
ASSETS	%	%	%	%	%	%		%	%
Cash & Equivalents	14.2	10.7	10.0	7.3	4.6			8.7	8.8
Trade Receivables (net)	25.8	22.3	21.2	19.6	21.3			26.9	25.3
Inventory	12.2	15.8	19.9	24.1	21.6			18.4	18.1
All Other Current	.9	2.5	2.0	2.5	4.2			1.7	2.0
Total Current	53.1	51.3	53.1	53.6	51.6			55.7	54.3
Fixed Assets (net)	35.8	39.9	38.4	35.9	26.4			35.6	36.6
Intangibles (net)	2.8	3.1	2.9	6.0	15.8			2.8	3.5
All Other Non-Current	8.3	5.7	5.7	4.6	6.3			5.9	5.5
Total	100.0	100.0	100.0	100.0	100.0			100.0	100.0
LIABILITIES									
Notes Payable-Short Term	20.0	9.6	8.6	7.0	9.2			10.4	9.5
Cur. Mat.-L.T.D.	7.4	6.7	6.1	5.8	2.5			6.6	6.5
Trade Payables	12.8	10.1	9.2	10.5	10.7			13.1	12.2
Income Taxes Payable	.1	.1	.3	.1	.1			.3	.2
All Other Current	12.9	7.2	6.5	7.9	8.8			8.8	7.5
Total Current	53.0	33.6	30.6	31.2	31.3			39.2	35.9
Long-Term Debt	39.6	30.4	21.5	20.3	13.9			24.8	25.6
Deferred Taxes	.1	.4	.7	1.0	1.1			.6	.4
All Other Non-Current	12.5	7.2	5.5	6.4	7.3			6.8	5.9
Net Worth	-5.3	28.4	41.7	41.1	46.4			28.7	32.2
Total Liabilities & Net Worth	100.0	100.0	100.0	100.0	100.0			100.0	100.0
INCOME DATA									
Net Sales	100.0	100.0	100.0	100.0	100.0			100.0	100.0
Gross Profit	52.1	40.0	30.8	20.6	23.4			34.4	35.4
Operating Expenses	50.1	38.7	26.8	16.3	16.7			28.3	28.2
Operating Profit	1.9	1.3	4.0	4.3	6.7			6.1	7.2
All Other Expenses (net)	1.3	1.6	1.5	1.8	1.4			1.4	1.6
Profit Before Taxes	.6	-.3	2.6	2.4	5.3			4.7	5.6
RATIOS									
Current	3.4	3.3	3.3	2.8	3.8			2.5	2.6
	1.2	1.7	1.8	1.6	1.3			1.5	1.6
	.6	1.0	1.1	1.2	1.2			1.0	1.1
Quick	2.0	2.4	2.2	1.3	1.7			1.7	1.7
	.9	1.1	1.0	.8	.7			.9	1.0
	.3	.6	.5	.5	.6			.6	.6
Sales/Receivables	6 65.3	27 13.7	31 11.8	39 9.4	46 8.0			31 11.8	29 12.6
	29 12.7	41 8.8	43 8.5	50 7.3	54 6.8			45 8.0	44 8.4
	48 7.7	57 6.4	60 6.1	61 6.0	60 6.1			58 6.2	56 6.5
Cost of Sales/Inventory	0 UND	5 73.5	27 13.3	45 8.1	37 9.8			10 37.3	11 34.1
	11 33.6	28 12.9	56 6.5	65 5.6	50 7.3			34 10.6	36 10.1
	61 6.0	73 5.0	104 3.5	108 3.4	85 4.3			75 4.9	70 5.2
Cost of Sales/Payables	0 UND	13 28.2	13 28.9	17 21.9	28 12.9			14 25.2	13 27.5
	18 20.3	23 15.7	23 16.1	26 13.8	32 11.3			27 13.5	25 14.7
	46 7.9	41 8.9	40 9.2	47 7.8	36 10.2			43 8.5	43 8.6
Sales/Working Capital	8.5	5.3	4.0	3.9	3.6			5.9	5.8
	48.5	9.9	8.3	7.5	18.3			12.2	11.8
	-15.2	-230.1	72.5	17.6	27.0			114.7	68.6
EBIT/Interest	5.7	4.2	7.9	8.4	38.1			9.0	9.9
	(66) 1.4	(209) 1.0	(314) 2.8	(83) 2.8	7.3			(745) 3.8	(793) 3.9
	-4.0	-1.6	.1	.0	-1.0			1.5	1.7
Net Profit + Depr., Dep., Amort./Cur. Mat. L/T/D		1.5	4.5	5.3				4.3	4.5
	(24) .8	(88) 2.2	(30) 2.0					(154) 2.1	(181) 2.3
	-1.0	.5	.6					1.2	1.2
Fixed/Worth	.5	.4	.5	.5	.3			.5	.5
	2.8	1.3	1.0	1.0	1.1			1.2	1.1
	-.9	6.7	2.3	2.4	NM			4.4	3.1
Debt/Worth	1.2	.8	.6	.8	.6			1.0	.9
	9.0	2.0	1.7	1.5	1.6			2.2	1.9
	-2.9	33.3	3.6	3.7	NM			10.0	6.3
% Profit Before Taxes/Tangible Net Worth	86.0	31.0	35.3	24.4				60.7	60.5
	(48) 23.5	(179) 1.9	(304) 10.3	(76) 12.0				(661) 25.5	(731) 27.6
	-7.1	-16.5	-2.1	-5.8				7.1	7.8
% Profit Before Taxes/Total Assets	23.9	10.5	12.6	11.4	17.0			16.8	18.7
	4.9	.3	4.9	4.0	1.9			7.4	8.1
	-9.0	-8.6	-2.0	-3.5	-6.4			1.5	2.5
Sales/Net Fixed Assets	27.8	11.5	9.0	7.0	9.4			14.5	12.8
	10.6	5.0	4.6	3.7	5.3			6.3	6.1
	4.8	2.9	2.5	2.4	4.1			3.6	3.6
Sales/Total Assets	4.5	2.5	2.1	1.8	2.1			2.9	2.8
	3.1	1.8	1.5	1.4	1.3			2.0	2.0
	2.0	1.4	1.2	1.0	.9			1.5	1.5
% Depr., Dep., Amort./Sales	1.0	2.4	2.7	1.8	1.2			1.8	2.1
	(66) 3.1	(206) 4.5	(313) 4.8	(84) 4.1	5.1			(688) 3.6	(758) 3.8
	6.2	8.1	7.8	7.1	5.6			6.0	5.9
% Officers', Directors' Owners' Comp/Sales	5.6	3.7	2.1	.9				2.9	2.7
	(63) 9.2	(149) 6.7	(173) 3.8	(18) 2.4				(405) 5.3	(452) 4.9
	15.4	10.1	6.5	3.8				8.4	8.7
Net Sales ($)	77392M	532259M	2599683M	3065354M	1060507M	1163236M		11155381M	11007224M
Total Assets ($)	23441M	269866M	1591509M	1777596M	751998M	672653M		5093686M	5603292M

M = $ thousand   MM = $ million
See Pages 9 through 22 for Explanation of Ratios and Data

Comparative Historical Data

Current Data Sorted by Sales

			Type of Statement						
41	30	38	Unqualified	1	1	1	6	10	19
131	117	141	Reviewed		21	21	53	37	9
180	149	155	Compiled	15	50	31	31	26	2
169	160	170	Tax Returns	36	68	32	25	8	1
259	200	245	Other	29	65	45	40	39	27
4/1/07-3/31/08 ALL	4/1/08-3/31/09 ALL	4/1/09-3/31/10 ALL		155 (4/1-9/30/09) 0-1MM	1-3MM	3-5MM	594 (10/1/09-3/31/10) 5-10MM	10-25MM	25MM & OVER
780	656	749	NUMBER OF STATEMENTS	81	205	130	155	120	58
%	%	%	ASSETS	%	%	%	%	%	%
9.8	9.8	10.3	Cash & Equivalents	12.1	11.7	6.9	11.8	9.8	6.7
24.6	23.2	21.9	Trade Receivables (net)	20.1	21.7	22.1	21.4	23.5	22.9
18.1	17.4	18.3	Inventory	14.1	15.0	18.6	19.3	22.0	24.7
1.8	1.9	2.1	All Other Current	1.2	1.7	2.1	2.6	2.7	2.8
54.4	52.3	52.6	Total Current	47.6	50.1	49.7	55.1	58.0	57.1
37.2	39.2	38.0	Fixed Assets (net)	41.1	39.3	40.7	37.9	34.7	29.7
3.0	3.2	3.5	Intangibles (net)	3.2	4.1	3.0	2.5	3.1	6.8
5.4	5.3	5.9	All Other Non-Current	8.0	6.5	6.7	4.4	4.2	6.4
100.0	100.0	100.0	Total	100.0	100.0	100.0	100.0	100.0	100.0
			LIABILITIES						
8.1	9.8	10.0	Notes Payable-Short Term	19.1	10.4	9.2	8.2	7.1	8.5
6.3	6.4	6.3	Cur. Mat.-L.T.D.	6.2	6.8	7.1	6.1	5.9	4.4
11.2	10.3	10.1	Trade Payables	11.1	9.2	9.8	9.1	11.2	12.6
.3	.2	.2	Income Taxes Payable	.1	.1	.2	.5	.2	.1
7.6	6.6	7.7	All Other Current	11.8	7.6	5.6	6.2	7.9	9.8
33.4	33.3	34.2	Total Current	48.3	34.1	31.9	30.0	32.3	35.4
26.2	26.8	26.0	Long-Term Debt	42.0	31.6	26.6	19.0	18.0	17.8
.4	.5	.6	Deferred Taxes	.0	.5	.3	.9	.7	1.0
5.5	5.5	7.0	All Other Non-Current	14.5	5.9	7.8	4.6	5.1	8.2
34.4	33.9	32.3	Net Worth	-4.8	27.9	33.3	45.6	44.0	37.5
100.0	100.0	100.0	Total Liabilties & Net Worth	100.0	100.0	100.0	100.0	100.0	100.0
			INCOME DATA						
100.0	100.0	100.0	Net Sales	100.0	100.0	100.0	100.0	100.0	100.0
35.7	35.1	34.7	Gross Profit	52.5	41.4	31.4	31.2	26.2	20.0
28.2	28.9	31.6	Operating Expenses	54.3	39.1	29.4	25.8	21.2	15.7
7.6	6.2	3.0	Operating Profit	-1.8	2.4	2.0	5.4	5.0	4.3
1.5	1.2	1.5	All Other Expenses (net)	1.9	1.5	1.8	1.3	1.3	1.6
6.0	5.0	1.5	Profit Before Taxes	-3.7	.8	.2	4.0	3.8	2.7
			RATIOS						
2.9	3.2	3.2	Current	3.8	3.3	3.1	3.8	3.3	2.7
1.7	1.7	1.6		1.2	1.6	1.6	1.8	1.8	1.6
1.1	1.1	1.0		.6	1.0	1.0	1.1	1.2	1.2
2.0	2.2	2.1	Quick	1.9	2.6	2.0	2.4	1.9	1.4
1.0	1.0	1.0		.8	1.0	1.0	1.1	.9	.8
.6	.5	.5		.3	.5	.5	.6	.5	.6
30 12.0	27 13.5	29 12.6	Sales/Receivables	16 22.9	24 15.4	30 12.2	32 11.5	33 11.2	39 9.4
43 8.4	40 9.1	43 8.5		36 10.0	40 9.0	45 8.1	41 8.8	45 8.1	46 7.9
56 6.5	53 6.8	58 6.2		53 6.9	57 6.4	65 5.6	53 6.8	60 6.1	57 6.4
14 26.3	10 38.1	14 25.5	Cost of Sales/Inventory	0 UND	4 95.3	22 16.3	21 17.2	30 12.3	42 8.6
40 9.1	36 10.0	45 8.0		26 13.8	30 12.3	49 7.5	45 8.1	52 7.1	57 6.5
77 4.7	70 5.2	91 4.0		82 4.5	83 4.4	91 4.0	105 3.5	89 4.1	94 3.9
14 25.9	11 32.1	13 28.7	Cost of Sales/Payables	9 41.0	9 39.8	13 28.2	12 29.8	15 24.4	17 21.7
26 14.2	23 16.1	23 15.9		30 12.2	20 17.9	25 14.4	19 19.2	28 13.2	28 12.9
41 8.9	39 9.3	42 8.8		70 5.2	45 8.1	39 9.5	37 9.8	40 9.2	45 8.1
5.4	5.5	4.5	Sales/Working Capital	5.1	5.0	4.7	3.8	4.1	4.2
10.0	11.4	9.6		48.8	10.1	10.1	8.8	7.4	10.6
45.6	87.1	160.3		-6.7	-93.6	-792.2	27.3	19.4	24.9
9.6	9.8	6.6	EBIT/Interest	2.6	4.8	5.3	8.2	14.7	12.8
(710) 4.2	(595) 4.1	(686) 2.0		(66) .3	(182) 1.4	(123) 1.0	(145) 3.3	(114) 4.4	(56) 2.9
1.6	1.3	-.7		-3.5	-1.4	-1.1	1.0	.0	.8
5.1	4.1	3.3	Net Profit + Depr., Dep., Amort./Cur. Mat. L/T/D		1.7	2.6	3.5	4.3	6.2
(174) 2.5	(114) 2.1	(151) 1.6			(20) 1.0	(21) 1.2	(49) 2.0	(36) 1.9	(21) 2.1
1.4	1.1	.4			-.6	.5	.5	.5	1.5
.5	.5	.5	Fixed/Worth	.5	.5	.6	.4	.4	.4
1.1	1.1	1.1		5.4	1.4	1.1	1.0	.8	.9
2.8	2.8	3.5		-1.0	9.6	3.7	2.0	1.7	2.8
.8	.7	.7	Debt/Worth	.8	.9	.7	.5	.6	.7
2.0	1.7	1.9		27.5	2.3	1.9	1.4	1.4	1.8
5.0	5.8	7.4		-3.5	33.9	6.1	3.4	2.9	7.5
57.3	55.8	35.5	% Profit Before Taxes/Tangible Net Worth	50.0	38.2	27.2	36.4	43.7	29.2
(676) 28.6	(558) 26.7	(618) 8.9		(43) 2.3	(157) 5.5	(111) 2.1	(145) 12.8	(114) 14.5	(48) 12.2
8.6	6.0	-7.0		-16.5	-15.8	-13.3	.3	-2.3	-3.2
21.0	19.8	12.4	% Profit Before Taxes/Total Assets	12.3	11.6	8.8	14.4	15.3	11.8
9.7	9.2	3.0		-2.2	1.3	.2	6.0	6.5	4.0
2.1	1.1	-4.6		-14.1	-6.0	-5.1	.0	-1.1	-4.0
11.4	12.0	10.4	Sales/Net Fixed Assets	13.8	12.8	7.7	10.5	10.0	9.7
5.8	5.6	4.9		5.0	4.9	4.5	4.6	6.2	5.2
3.5	3.2	2.8		1.8	2.7	2.3	2.7	3.2	3.4
2.7	2.8	2.4	Sales/Total Assets	2.7	2.7	2.2	2.2	2.3	2.2
2.0	2.0	1.7		1.8	1.8	1.6	1.7	1.7	1.6
1.5	1.5	1.2		1.1	1.3	1.2	1.3	1.2	1.2
2.1	2.0	2.3	% Depr., Dep., Amort./Sales	2.2	2.4	2.9	2.9	2.0	1.5
(695) 3.8	(562) 3.7	(682) 4.5		(64) 5.3	(182) 4.6	(121) 5.2	(146) 4.6	(114) 3.7	(55) 3.5
6.3	6.2	7.6		10.2	8.4	8.3	7.0	6.5	5.3
2.8	2.5	2.7	% Officers', Directors' Owners' Comp/Sales	6.3	4.3	2.7	2.2	1.2	
(434) 4.8	(359) 4.8	(405) 5.4		(55) 10.8	(131) 6.8	(73) 4.8	(82) 3.9	(57) 2.9	
8.8	7.8	9.2		17.3	10.2	6.8	6.6	5.2	
9680374M	7702159M	8498431M	Net Sales ($)	47257M	401667M	503526M	1106155M	1888404M	4551422M
4901691M	4387194M	5087063M	Total Assets ($)	32995M	273407M	358699M	720412M	1170556M	2530994M

© RMA 2010

M = $ thousand   MM = $ million
See Pages 9 through 22 for Explanation of Ratios and Data

Current Data Sorted by Assets

Comparative Historical Data

						Type of Statement		
1		3	9	1		Unqualified	21	18
1	8	41	6			Reviewed	83	67
3	18	13	1			Compiled	33	40
8	5	8				Tax Returns	16	14
4	10	18	14		2	Other	45	61
	38 (4/1-9/30/09)		**136 (10/1/09-3/31/10)**				4/1/05-3/31/06	4/1/06-3/31/07
0-500M	500M-2MM	2-10MM	10-50MM	50-100MM	100-250MM		ALL	ALL
17	41	83	30	1	2	**NUMBER OF STATEMENTS**	198	200
%	%	%	%	%	%	**ASSETS**	%	%
18.5	7.5	8.1	1.3			Cash & Equivalents	6.1	6.7
22.6	20.7	21.2	17.4			Trade Receivables (net)	24.8	25.0
8.9	25.7	25.4	27.8			Inventory	22.3	22.5
.7	2.4	1.5	1.9			All Other Current	1.3	1.2
50.7	56.2	56.2	48.3			Total Current	54.5	55.4
41.0	36.6	35.2	40.9			Fixed Assets (net)	37.0	36.8
.1	2.0	3.3	6.2			Intangibles (net)	3.3	2.7
8.3	5.2	5.3	4.5			All Other Non-Current	5.3	5.1
100.0	100.0	100.0	100.0			Total	100.0	100.0
						LIABILITIES		
15.4	9.5	8.1	14.7			Notes Payable-Short Term	10.4	9.9
8.9	8.7	6.6	7.7			Cur. Mat.-L.T.D.	6.2	7.5
9.8	11.0	10.8	11.1			Trade Payables	13.1	13.0
.0	.4	.2	.2			Income Taxes Payable	.1	.2
8.6	4.5	6.2	5.8			All Other Current	6.8	6.3
42.8	34.1	32.0	39.5			Total Current	36.5	37.0
27.4	28.1	19.5	19.3			Long-Term Debt	22.9	21.9
.0	.4	.8	1.4			Deferred Taxes	.7	.7
19.2	8.9	6.8	6.6			All Other Non-Current	6.8	4.5
10.6	28.5	40.9	33.2			Net Worth	33.1	35.8
100.0	100.0	100.0	100.0			Total Liabilties & Net Worth	100.0	100.0
						INCOME DATA		
100.0	100.0	100.0	100.0			Net Sales	100.0	100.0
55.4	31.6	23.8	19.7			Gross Profit	25.9	27.2
45.0	33.6	21.8	17.4			Operating Expenses	21.3	22.0
10.3	-1.9	2.0	2.3			Operating Profit	4.6	5.2
1.2	2.2	1.1	2.4			All Other Expenses (net)	1.3	1.6
9.2	-4.2	.9	-.1			Profit Before Taxes	3.2	3.6
						RATIOS		
2.9	2.9	3.0	1.6				2.4	2.2
1.5	1.4	1.8	1.2			Current	1.5	1.5
.6	1.1	1.2	1.0				1.1	1.0
2.5	1.7	1.7	.8				1.4	1.3
(16) 1.3	.8	.9	.6			Quick	.9	.8
.6	.4	.5	.3				.5	.5
0 UND	32 11.4	28 13.0	37 9.9				38 9.5	35 10.4
22 16.8	40 9.0	43 8.5	48 7.6			Sales/Receivables	47 7.7	43 8.4
61 6.0	60 6.1	57 6.4	63 5.8				59 6.2	56 6.5
0 UND	48 7.6	40 9.0	62 5.9				32 11.5	31 11.6
13 27.3	71 5.1	59 6.2	89 4.1			Cost of Sales/Inventory	54 6.8	55 6.7
70 5.2	126 2.9	91 4.0	134 2.7				83 4.4	80 4.5
0 UND	12 29.6	11 32.7	25 14.7				20 18.4	15 23.9
7 50.3	31 11.8	20 17.8	39 9.2			Cost of Sales/Payables	30 12.2	27 13.7
44 8.3	64 5.7	41 8.9	53 6.9				46 8.0	42 8.8
4.2	4.8	4.3	6.1				5.8	5.9
42.8	7.7	7.5	17.0			Sales/Working Capital	10.1	11.7
-22.4	103.3	22.6	64.9				66.3	557.2
2.5	1.1	7.6	2.7				6.5	6.1
(11) .6	(38) -.4	(81) 1.7	(29) 1.1			EBIT/Interest	(180) 2.4	(178) 2.7
-6.0	-3.2	-1.2	-1.3				1.1	1.5
		4.0	2.0				3.9	4.4
	(28) 1.9	(15) 1.1				Net Profit + Depr., Dep., Amort./Cur. Mat. L/T/D	(63) 1.8	(65) 1.9
		1.0	.3				.8	1.2
.4	.6	.4	.9				.5	.5
1.3	1.5	.9	1.6			Fixed/Worth	1.2	1.1
NM	33.5	2.1	2.0				4.0	2.6
1.1	.9	.6	1.5				.8	.8
3.0	1.9	1.3	2.4			Debt/Worth	1.9	1.8
-13.3	69.3	5.4	4.0				7.8	4.9
112.6	8.7	27.3	13.2				30.1	33.2
(12) 9.2	(32) -12.0	(70) 5.3	(28) .4			% Profit Before Taxes/Tangible Net Worth	(165) 13.5	(169) 16.4
-9.2	-23.4	-9.4	-12.9				1.7	5.6
45.0	1.1	10.8	3.3				10.2	12.5
3.8	-4.8	1.6	.8			% Profit Before Taxes/Total Assets	4.4	5.4
-3.5	-11.7	-6.0	-4.5				.2	1.3
19.1	8.3	9.9	4.9				9.5	12.7
10.0	4.0	5.0	3.2			Sales/Net Fixed Assets	4.9	5.3
4.7	2.4	3.1	2.3				3.1	3.1
4.2	1.9	2.3	1.5				2.4	2.7
2.3	1.6	1.7	1.2			Sales/Total Assets	1.8	1.8
1.3	1.1	1.3	1.0				1.3	1.4
3.2	3.7	2.6	4.7				2.4	2.0
(11) 3.4	(35) 6.0	(79) 4.6	(29) 6.4			% Depr., Dep., Amort./Sales	(191) 4.3	(183) 4.4
7.0	10.9	6.6	7.8				6.2	6.2
3.5	3.0	1.8					1.7	2.0
(10) 5.4	(25) 7.6	(48) 3.3				% Officers', Directors' Owners' Comp/Sales	(85) 3.3	(87) 3.5
10.9	13.0	6.4					6.4	6.4
14414M	88909M	695172M	795920M	71937M	428278M	Net Sales ($)	2284671M	2710579M
4532M	52602M	401607M	646221M	91575M	375839M	Total Assets ($)	1440701M	1609167M

M = $ thousand   MM = $ million
See Pages 9 through 22 for Explanation of Ratios and Data

Comparative Historical Data   Current Data Sorted by Sales

Type of Statement	4/1/07-3/31/08 ALL	4/1/08-3/31/09 ALL	4/1/09-3/31/10 ALL	0-1MM	1-3MM	3-5MM	5-10MM	10-25MM	25MM & OVER
Unqualified	16	13	14	1			1	6	6
Reviewed	60	56	56	1	6	8	20	17	4
Compiled	36	37	35	6	16	5	3	5	
Tax Returns	18	16	21	3	8	6	3	1	
Other	55	55	48	4	8	3	11	16	6
				38 (4/1-9/30/09)			136 (10/1/09-3/31/10)		
NUMBER OF STATEMENTS	185	177	174	15	38	22	38	45	16
ASSETS	%	%	%	%	%	%	%	%	%
Cash & Equivalents	7.5	6.4	7.7	12.4	10.4	8.0	7.9	5.6	2.3
Trade Receivables (net)	22.8	21.5	20.5	19.8	18.7	23.5	21.6	20.6	18.7
Inventory	23.1	24.6	24.1	15.3	21.0	25.5	24.9	27.8	25.7
All Other Current	1.4	1.3	1.8	4.5	1.0	.8	1.5	2.3	1.6
Total Current	54.8	53.9	54.2	52.0	51.0	57.8	55.9	56.3	48.3
Fixed Assets (net)	36.9	36.6	37.1	33.5	42.8	35.3	33.1	36.1	41.2
Intangibles (net)	2.8	4.6	3.2	2.5	2.2	1.9	5.8	2.4	4.5
All Other Non-Current	5.6	4.9	5.5	12.0	3.9	4.9	5.2	5.1	6.0
Total	100.0	100.0	100.0	100.0	100.0	100.0	100.0	100.0	100.0
LIABILITIES									
Notes Payable-Short Term	9.0	12.8	10.2	11.2	12.3	8.8	7.9	11.5	8.0
Cur. Mat.-L.T.D.	6.2	6.7	7.4	11.9	7.8	7.1	5.9	7.3	6.6
Trade Payables	12.3	11.6	10.8	9.1	9.9	10.9	11.5	11.3	11.6
Income Taxes Payable	.1	.2	.2	.0	.3	.2	.3	.2	.2
All Other Current	6.3	5.5	6.1	8.1	4.3	5.3	4.9	7.6	8.0
Total Current	33.9	36.7	34.8	40.4	34.6	32.3	30.5	37.9	34.4
Long-Term Debt	23.3	25.0	22.3	22.7	29.9	23.5	19.7	19.1	17.8
Deferred Taxes	1.0	.7	.8	.0	.4	.4	.9	1.1	1.9
All Other Non-Current	4.7	5.0	8.4	24.3	8.3	11.0	5.3	4.3	9.4
Net Worth	37.1	32.6	33.7	12.6	26.8	32.8	43.6	37.6	36.6
Total Liabilities & Net Worth	100.0	100.0	100.0	100.0	100.0	100.0	100.0	100.0	100.0
INCOME DATA									
Net Sales	100.0	100.0	100.0	100.0	100.0	100.0	100.0	100.0	100.0
Gross Profit	28.3	26.4	28.0	45.9	34.5	30.2	23.5	23.0	17.9
Operating Expenses	23.3	22.8	26.3	38.1	36.4	26.2	21.8	20.3	18.7
Operating Profit	5.0	3.6	1.8	7.8	-1.8	4.0	1.8	2.7	-.8
All Other Expenses (net)	1.4	1.4	1.6	2.6	1.9	1.0	1.5	1.3	2.0
Profit Before Taxes	3.6	2.2	.2	5.2	-3.7	3.0	.3	1.4	-2.8
RATIOS									
Current	2.5	2.5	2.6	2.2	3.0	3.1	2.9	2.2	1.7
	1.6	1.6	1.6	1.4	1.3	1.9	2.0	1.4	1.5
	1.1	1.1	1.1	.8	1.0	1.4	1.2	1.1	1.2
Quick	1.6	1.5	1.5	1.5	2.6	1.8	1.6	1.1	.9
	.9	.8	(173) .8	.5	(37) .8	1.0	.9	.6	.8
	.5	.5	.4	.4	.4	.5	.6	.4	.5
Sales/Receivables	33 11.0	29 12.4	30 12.1	0 UND	28 13.1	32 11.5	30 12.1	29 12.6	35 10.6
	44 8.4	40 9.1	44 8.3	44 8.3	38 9.5	44 8.2	44 8.3	44 8.3	54 6.8
	53 6.9	52 7.1	59 6.2	102 3.6	55 6.6	67 5.4	54 6.7	56 6.5	68 5.4
Cost of Sales/Inventory	31 11.9	33 11.2	42 8.7	4 95.0	26 14.1	36 10.1	48 7.6	44 8.3	46 7.9
	54 6.7	59 6.2	66 5.5	49 7.5	66 5.5	71 5.1	65 5.6	66 5.5	76 4.8
	93 3.9	90 4.0	106 3.4	261 1.4	115 3.2	131 2.8	86 4.3	109 3.4	126 2.9
Cost of Sales/Payables	16 23.0	14 26.5	13 27.6	0 UND	8 43.2	10 35.0	14 27.0	18 19.8	25 14.4
	27 13.6	25 14.5	27 13.6	18 19.8	22 16.4	20 17.8	27 13.7	24 15.0	39 9.2
	40 9.2	39 9.3	48 7.6	59 6.2	63 5.8	45 8.1	41 8.8	44 8.2	58 6.3
Sales/Working Capital	5.5	5.7	4.6	3.4	4.5	3.2	4.8	5.6	4.1
	10.0	9.5	8.4	6.7	13.5	6.0	6.9	11.6	9.0
	36.3	52.2	46.4	-12.5	-94.4	14.4	26.2	35.8	20.3
EBIT/Interest	6.1	5.6	3.6	.6	1.2	8.8	4.4	8.0	1.8
	(171) 2.6	(167) 2.2	(162) .7	(11) -.8	(33) -1.3	(21) 1.1	(37) 1.5	(44) 2.0	-.4
	1.0	.4	-2.1	-15.4	-4.8	-.4	-1.1	-1.1	-3.1
Net Profit + Depr., Dep., Amort./Cur. Mat. L/T/D	4.0	4.2	3.1					3.7	
	(63) 2.3	(51) 1.9	(51) 1.3					(20) 1.6	
	1.4	1.3	.5					.4	
Fixed/Worth	.6	.6	.6	.6	.7	.5	.4	.5	.8
	1.0	1.2	1.2	1.5	1.7	.8	1.0	1.2	1.2
	2.2	2.9	2.6	-1.5	-13.5	3.4	2.7	1.8	2.0
Debt/Worth	.8	.8	.8	1.1	.6	.7	.6	.8	1.0
	1.7	1.8	1.8	3.0	2.0	1.8	1.3	2.0	1.9
	4.5	6.0	6.2	-7.5	-21.3	7.6	6.1	3.2	3.7
% Profit Before Taxes/Tangible Net Worth	35.5	32.7	21.2	43.3	11.8	43.3	15.0	34.6	4.5
	(161) 14.6	(147) 11.1	(145) 1.3	(10) -12.5	(28) -9.1	(19) 5.0	(31) 1.3	(42) 11.9	(15) -11.8
	.9	-2.6	-17.0	-38.9	-19.5	-7.9	-15.0	-5.8	-23.4
% Profit Before Taxes/Total Assets	14.6	11.8	7.7	5.2	3.9	16.0	7.8	10.6	2.2
	6.1	3.4	.3	-2.7	-4.8	1.0	.7	2.3	-3.3
	.0	-2.5	-7.0	-14.7	-11.4	-4.2	-5.6	-3.6	-7.8
Sales/Net Fixed Assets	10.7	10.3	9.3	12.5	9.1	10.0	9.6	9.6	6.2
	5.6	5.3	4.6	3.9	4.4	5.6	5.0	4.8	3.1
	3.2	3.2	2.8	2.3	2.1	2.7	3.7	3.0	2.1
Sales/Total Assets	2.6	2.7	2.1	1.6	2.4	2.3	2.1	2.3	1.6
	1.9	1.9	1.6	1.2	1.6	1.6	1.8	1.7	1.2
	1.3	1.4	1.2	.9	1.1	1.3	1.2	1.3	1.1
% Depr., Dep., Amort./Sales	1.7	2.1	3.2	3.0	4.0	3.2	2.5	3.0	4.2
	(174) 3.8	(165) 4.0	(155) 5.1	(10) 4.0	(32) 6.4	4.6	(36) 4.5	(41) 4.8	(14) 6.4
	6.4	6.4	7.2	15.0	11.2	7.7	6.1	6.8	9.7
% Officers', Directors', Owners' Comp/Sales	2.1	2.3	1.9		2.6	3.0	1.3	1.7	
	(91) 3.9	(83) 3.7	(90) 4.2		(25) 5.6	(14) 5.4	(22) 2.7	(24) 3.2	
	7.0	6.3	8.1		9.1	10.0	7.1	5.4	
Net Sales ($)	2565289M	2435181M	2094630M	7955M	69837M	89787M	272486M	668385M	986180M
Total Assets ($)	1510989M	1536238M	1572376M	7400M	47869M	60235M	175904M	424854M	856114M

Current Data Sorted by Assets / Comparative Historical Data

Type of Statement	0-500M	500M-2MM	2-10MM	10-50MM	50-100MM	100-250MM		ALL 4/1/05-3/31/06	ALL 4/1/06-3/31/07
Unqualified	1	6	5	7	2	1		27	26
Reviewed		3	12	6				33	37
Compiled			4	1				15	19
Tax Returns	3	4	4					9	8
Other	4	3	21	17	2	2		54	43
		27 (4/1-9/30/09)		81 (10/1/09-3/31/10)					
NUMBER OF STATEMENTS	8	16	46	31	4	3		138	133

ASSETS	0-500M %	500M-2MM %	2-10MM %	10-50MM %	50-100MM %	100-250MM %		ALL %	ALL %
Cash & Equivalents		8.1	9.0	9.0				5.2	5.5
Trade Receivables (net)		27.6	22.0	19.4				26.9	25.3
Inventory		40.3	34.9	28.8				34.3	33.4
All Other Current		1.1	2.1	2.5				1.7	1.7
Total Current		77.1	68.1	59.8				68.2	65.8
Fixed Assets (net)		16.5	22.4	29.1				24.2	26.0
Intangibles (net)		.3	3.0	5.5				1.7	3.0
All Other Non-Current		6.1	6.5	5.6				6.0	5.1
Total		100.0	100.0	100.0				100.0	100.0

LIABILITIES									
Notes Payable-Short Term		8.5	11.2	11.5				13.5	11.3
Cur. Mat.-L.T.D.		3.5	2.5	3.8				4.3	5.0
Trade Payables		18.6	10.8	11.6				16.4	15.1
Income Taxes Payable		.1	.4	.4				.2	.3
All Other Current		12.5	6.1	7.2				8.0	8.5
Total Current		43.2	31.0	34.6				42.5	40.2
Long-Term Debt		13.4	11.6	11.5				13.0	15.9
Deferred Taxes		1.0	.4	.7				.6	.6
All Other Non-Current		5.2	3.1	6.4				4.4	6.3
Net Worth		37.2	54.0	46.8				39.6	36.9
Total Liabilties & Net Worth		100.0	100.0	100.0				100.0	100.0

INCOME DATA									
Net Sales		100.0	100.0	100.0				100.0	100.0
Gross Profit		30.8	27.4	24.5				26.5	28.2
Operating Expenses		28.6	24.9	22.5				21.4	22.8
Operating Profit		2.2	2.5	2.0				5.1	5.5
All Other Expenses (net)		2.0	.9	.5				1.1	1.3
Profit Before Taxes		.2	1.6	1.5				4.0	4.2

RATIOS									
Current		4.1	4.8	3.1				2.4	3.0
		1.5	2.5	1.9				1.6	1.7
		1.1	1.4	1.3				1.1	1.2
Quick		2.7	2.5	2.0				1.3	1.2
		.7	1.1	.7				.8	.8
		.6	.4	.4				.5	.5
Sales/Receivables		37 9.8	37 9.8	36 10.1				39 9.4	37 9.9
		51 7.1	48 7.7	48 7.7				46 7.9	44 8.2
		73 5.0	61 6.0	61 6.0				54 6.7	53 6.9
Cost of Sales/Inventory		55 6.6	72 5.1	58 6.3				50 7.3	56 6.6
		127 2.9	104 3.5	99 3.7				73 5.0	86 4.2
		198 1.8	137 2.7	142 2.6				120 3.0	119 3.1
Cost of Sales/Payables		11 32.3	13 27.8	18 20.5				23 16.2	18 20.1
		41 9.0	28 13.0	35 10.6				36 10.2	33 10.9
		82 4.5	40 9.1	46 7.9				48 7.6	48 7.6
Sales/Working Capital		3.8	3.3	3.7				4.6	4.3
		6.9	4.2	5.9				8.3	6.8
		20.0	11.7	18.3				28.5	26.6
EBIT/Interest		18.5	10.5	8.0				10.1	8.0
		(13) 1.6	(36) 1.9	(30) 1.1				(123) 3.7	(124) 3.0
		-1.6	-.1	-2.3				1.3	1.6
Net Profit + Depr., Dep., Amort./Cur. Mat. L/T/D			9.6	7.4				7.8	5.1
			(11) 2.1	(12) 3.2				(46) 3.3	(44) 3.0
			.5	1.7				1.1	1.2
Fixed/Worth		.1	.2	.3				.3	.3
		.5	.4	.8				.6	.7
		1.3	1.1	1.3				1.2	1.9
Debt/Worth		.3	.3	.5				.6	.6
		2.2	.7	1.3				1.8	1.7
		12.7	2.7	3.5				3.3	5.4
% Profit Before Taxes/Tangible Net Worth		9.9	20.2	27.6				38.0	45.5
		(14) 1.0	(43) 3.7	(29) .8				(126) 18.5	(118) 18.8
		-33.2	-5.2	-14.0				4.8	6.6
% Profit Before Taxes/Total Assets		5.5	11.6	11.1				16.2	15.0
		.5	1.9	.3				6.3	5.7
		-7.4	-2.3	-4.9				1.2	2.1
Sales/Net Fixed Assets		56.5	27.3	8.4				22.4	16.1
		17.8	9.4	5.6				10.0	8.4
		7.3	4.4	3.5				5.6	4.7
Sales/Total Assets		2.3	2.1	2.0				2.7	2.5
		1.7	1.7	1.4				2.1	2.0
		1.3	1.3	1.1				1.6	1.6
% Depr., Dep., Amort./Sales		.9	1.0	2.3				1.1	1.3
		(13) 1.3	(39) 1.9	(28) 3.2				(127) 2.1	(121) 2.4
		2.8	3.1	5.6				3.6	3.8
% Officers', Directors' Owners' Comp/Sales			3.6					2.1	2.3
			(15) 6.0					(47) 4.1	(49) 3.6
			8.9					8.7	8.4
Net Sales ($)	7512M	38017M	373270M	1112408M	347886M	996939M		3555313M	3009329M
Total Assets ($)	1860M	20490M	221025M	730562M	254840M	549247M		2028308M	1764976M

M = $ thousand   MM = $ million
See Pages 9 through 22 for Explanation of Ratios and Data

Comparative Historical Data / Current Data Sorted by Sales

Hist 4/1/07-3/31/08 ALL	Hist 4/1/08-3/31/09 ALL	Hist 4/1/09-3/31/10 ALL	Type of Statement	0-1MM	1-3MM	3-5MM	5-10MM	10-25MM	25MM & OVE
22	27	15	Unqualified		1		2	5	7
36	37	25	Reviewed	6	3		6	6	4
16	15	8	Compiled	2	2		1	2	1
12	12	11	Tax Returns	6	2		1		
36	41	49	Other	2 3	5 1		15	9	16
					27 (4/1-9/30/09)		81 (10/1/09-3/31/10)		
122	132	108	**NUMBER OF STATEMENTS**	5	19	9	25	22	28
%	%	%	**ASSETS**	%	%	%	%	%	%
6.6	6.3	9.1	Cash & Equivalents		12.2		9.7	8.3	8.6
24.8	23.2	21.6	Trade Receivables (net)		22.8		24.1	21.4	20.3
33.5	32.5	31.9	Inventory		34.9		36.5	32.3	27.4
2.1	1.7	2.4	All Other Current		1.7		1.9	2.5	1.9
67.0	63.7	64.9	Total Current		71.5		72.2	64.6	58.1
24.4	26.8	24.7	Fixed Assets (net)		22.2		21.2	23.9	29.4
2.4	3.8	4.4	Intangibles (net)		2.3		1.2	4.8	7.2
6.2	5.7	6.0	All Other Non-Current		4.0		5.3	6.7	5.2
100.0	100.0	100.0	Total		100.0		100.0	100.0	100.0
			LIABILITIES						
13.5	11.7	13.3	Notes Payable-Short Term		13.4		10.5	12.7	9.7
3.5	3.3	3.2	Cur. Mat.-L.T.D.		4.1		2.5	3.6	3.3
14.5	11.7	12.5	Trade Payables		15.4		14.1	11.0	11.7
.3	.4	.3	Income Taxes Payable		.1		.2	1.1	.1
5.9	5.1	7.4	All Other Current		12.3		6.2	4.9	8.0
37.8	32.1	36.6	Total Current		45.3		33.4	33.2	32.8
14.2	14.7	13.3	Long-Term Debt		15.7		9.6	17.6	9.4
.7	.6	.8	Deferred Taxes		.5		.4	.6	1.0
4.8	5.8	4.4	All Other Non-Current		7.2		2.3	4.3	5.9
42.5	46.8	44.9	Net Worth		31.3		54.3	44.3	50.8
100.0	100.0	100.0	Total Liabilities & Net Worth		100.0		100.0	100.0	100.0
			INCOME DATA						
100.0	100.0	100.0	Net Sales		100.0		100.0	100.0	100.0
28.3	25.7	29.4	Gross Profit		36.3		26.4	24.2	27.3
22.6	20.7	27.3	Operating Expenses		35.3		22.2	21.5	24.1
5.7	5.0	2.1	Operating Profit		1.1		4.3	2.7	3.2
1.3	1.0	1.3	All Other Expenses (net)		2.1		1.0	1.5	.9
4.4	4.0	.9	Profit Before Taxes		-1.1		3.3	1.3	2.3
			RATIOS						
2.8	3.6	4.1	Current		3.9		5.6	2.9	4.6
1.9	2.0	1.9			1.3		2.3	2.1	1.9
1.2	1.3	1.2			1.1		1.2	1.6	1.3
1.5	1.8	1.9	Quick		1.8		4.2	1.5	1.9
.8	.9	.8			.7		1.0	1.0	.9
.5	.5	.4			.5		.4	.5	.5
35 10.5	31 11.6	36 10.2	Sales/Receivables		26 14.1		37 10.0	39 9.3	35 10.4
44 8.3	40 9.1	48 7.7			50 7.4		53 6.8	49 7.5	46 7.9
54 6.8	49 7.5	60 6.0			63 5.8		61 5.9	61 5.9	61 7.9
54 6.8	48 7.6	58 6.2	Cost of Sales/Inventory		47 7.7		62 5.9	72 5.1	53 6.9
83 4.4	80 4.5	102 3.6			138 2.7		105 3.5	102 3.6	78 4.7
124 3.0	123 3.0	138 2.6			215 1.7		128 2.8	142 2.6	129 2.8
19 19.0	12 29.3	15 23.9	Cost of Sales/Payables		9 38.6		16 22.5	26 14.0	17 21.4
31 11.9	23 16.0	31 11.7			32 11.6		29 12.4	33 11.2	33 11.1
46 7.9	41 8.8	46 7.9			76 4.8		44 8.2	47 7.8	45 8.1
4.9	4.0	3.5	Sales/Working Capital		3.8		3.0	3.7	3.5
7.3	6.0	6.0			8.8		4.1	5.2	6.3
16.7	14.3	18.0			26.0		14.7	8.4	14.7
9.4	13.3	8.1	EBIT/Interest		5.9		18.8	6.3	16.4
(113) 3.5	(121) 3.6	(92) 1.4		(14) 1.2		(17) 3.6	(21) 1.7	(27) 1.1	
1.3	.8	-2.1			-3.6		.8	.2	-4.3
4.1	8.5	6.0	Net Profit + Depr., Dep.,						17.5
(37) 2.7	(51) 3.2	(32) 2.6	Amort./Cur. Mat. L/T/D					(13) 3.4	
1.6	1.6	1.0							2.4
.3	.3	.2	Fixed/Worth		.1		.1	.2	.3
.6	.6	.6			.9		.3	.6	.8
1.2	1.2	1.3			2.6		.9	1.0	1.2
.6	.5	.3	Debt/Worth		.3		.3	.6	.5
1.3	1.2	1.3			2.6		.7	1.4	1.1
4.3	3.6	4.8			14.5		2.8	2.3	3.4
46.5	37.2	23.2	% Profit Before Taxes/Tangible		4.2		28.6	26.5	30.1
(113) 19.7	(125) 11.5	(96) 1.5	Net Worth	(15) .8		(24) 10.0	(20) 3.0	(26) -13.8	
4.5	1.4	-8.1			-43.4		-2.4	.4	-13.8
16.0	14.9	9.3	% Profit Before Taxes/Total		4.2		12.9	8.9	12.7
6.3	4.7	.4	Assets		.3		3.0	.8	-.3
1.0	-.4	-4.9			-8.2		-.8	-4.4	-6.0
20.1	16.5	14.9	Sales/Net Fixed Assets		39.6		32.1	12.2	9.5
9.5	7.5	7.8			14.6		9.5	7.3	5.7
5.2	4.2	4.1			3.5		3.9	4.1	3.6
2.6	2.5	2.2	Sales/Total Assets		2.3		2.3	2.0	2.1
2.0	2.0	1.6			1.5		1.8	1.5	1.5
1.5	1.5	1.3			1.1		1.3	1.2	1.2
1.3	1.0	1.2	% Depr., Dep., Amort./Sales		.9		.6	1.4	2.3
(114) 2.1	(123) 2.2	(94) 2.5		(17) 1.3		(20) 1.6	(20) 2.3	(26) 3.3	
3.2	3.7	4.9			3.5		3.8	3.2	5.5
1.8	1.5	2.5	% Officers', Directors'						
(51) 3.3	(48) 4.3	(34) 6.4	Owners' Comp/Sales						
7.9	8.0	11.1							
2905891M	3561606M	2876032M	Net Sales ($)	2375M	37968M	35375M	184396M	349526M	2266392M
1602136M	2102480M	1778024M	Total Assets ($)	947M	24792M	22948M	112371M	244988M	1371978M

© RMA 2010

M = $ thousand   MM = $ million
See Pages 9 through 22 for Explanation of Ratios and Data

Current Data Sorted by Assets   **Comparative Historical Data**

0-500M	500M-2MM	2-10MM	10-50MM	50-100MM	100-250MM	Type of Statement	4/1/05-3/31/06 ALL	4/1/06-3/31/07 ALL
		1	1	2		Unqualified	10	7
	5	8	7			Reviewed	22	23
	11	4	2			Compiled	11	17
2	5					Tax Returns	6	6
6	9	15	7	1	2	Other	22	31
	15 (4/1-9/30/09)		73 (10/1/09-3/31/10)					
8	30	28	17	3	2	**NUMBER OF STATEMENTS**	71	84
%	%	%	%	%	%	**ASSETS**	%	%
	9.6	9.2	10.2			Cash & Equivalents	7.7	6.7
	28.1	19.4	14.6			Trade Receivables (net)	25.7	28.7
	8.4	10.6	7.0			Inventory	6.3	7.9
	2.6	3.6	4.4			All Other Current	1.0	1.7
	48.8	42.8	36.2			Total Current	40.7	45.1
	41.5	47.9	50.0			Fixed Assets (net)	47.8	43.0
	5.1	2.2	7.2			Intangibles (net)	4.2	5.0
	4.6	7.0	6.5			All Other Non-Current	7.4	7.0
	100.0	100.0	100.0			Total	100.0	100.0
						LIABILITIES		
	13.3	11.0	2.8			Notes Payable-Short Term	4.9	7.4
	8.0	6.9	4.2			Cur. Mat.-L.T.D.	5.9	6.3
	11.8	7.3	4.2			Trade Payables	10.2	11.0
	.1	.1	.1			Income Taxes Payable	.3	.5
	6.3	6.4	4.3			All Other Current	11.7	14.4
	39.5	31.7	15.6			Total Current	33.0	39.6
	30.5	21.3	20.3			Long-Term Debt	30.2	23.5
	.1	1.2	2.0			Deferred Taxes	.9	.6
	12.6	8.9	7.2			All Other Non-Current	6.6	7.9
	17.3	36.9	54.9			Net Worth	29.3	28.3
	100.0	100.0	100.0			Total Liabilities & Net Worth	100.0	100.0
						INCOME DATA		
	100.0	100.0	100.0			Net Sales	100.0	100.0
	32.2	33.7	35.6			Gross Profit	36.6	36.2
	37.9	33.0	32.1			Operating Expenses	28.8	29.6
	-5.7	.6	3.5			Operating Profit	7.8	6.7
	1.4	1.5	3.8			All Other Expenses (net)	2.3	1.8
	-7.2	-.9	-.2			Profit Before Taxes	5.5	4.8
						RATIOS		
	2.6	2.3	3.4			Current	2.3	2.4
	1.3	1.3	2.3				1.4	1.4
	.6	.9	1.1				.8	.8
	2.4	2.0	2.2			Quick	2.2	2.1
	.8	.9	1.7				1.1	1.0
	.5	.5	.7				.7	.6
	26 13.9	42 8.7	41 8.9			Sales/Receivables	43 8.4	43 8.6
	44 8.2	47 7.7	48 7.6				54 6.8	51 7.1
	55 6.6	60 6.1	67 5.5				62 5.9	60 6.1
	0 UND	0 UND	0 UND			Cost of Sales/Inventory	0 UND	0 UND
	3 120.6	2 185.3	16 23.0				5 76.8	6 60.7
	23 15.9	24 15.3	54 6.7				19 19.0	35 10.5
	12 30.3	13 27.1	15 24.8			Cost of Sales/Payables	14 25.2	16 23.5
	24 15.2	24 15.5	21 17.3				30 12.1	25 14.5
	40 9.1	51 7.2	28 13.1				47 7.8	35 10.3
	7.6	6.5	3.4			Sales/Working Capital	7.1	7.7
	57.0	25.4	5.6				14.2	16.4
	-12.1	-18.0	NM				-31.0	-29.5
	1.5	9.6	6.6			EBIT/Interest	8.6	9.1
	(25) -4.1	1.5	(15) 1.9				(68) 3.3	(78) 2.6
	-21.0	-2.3	-2.8				1.3	1.1
						Net Profit + Depr., Dep., Amort./Cur. Mat. L/T/D	6.5	4.1
							(23) 2.5	(24) 2.6
							1.6	1.5
	.5	.7	.6			Fixed/Worth	.8	.8
	3.4	1.2	1.1				1.4	1.6
	-1.5	4.8	1.6				4.2	5.7
	.6	.5	.5			Debt/Worth	.7	.7
	5.6	1.3	.8				1.7	1.8
	-3.6	10.2	1.2				13.7	20.6
	13.5	14.9	16.9			% Profit Before Taxes/Tangible Net Worth	40.7	53.3
	(21) -2.8	(23) 5.5	(15) 3.0				(58) 24.0	(66) 25.2
	-41.1	-13.1	-4.0				2.7	10.3
	1.9	7.3	9.3			% Profit Before Taxes/Total Assets	16.7	14.8
	-12.5	1.6	1.4				6.0	7.2
	-27.2	-6.8	-2.6				1.3	.8
	12.1	5.2	4.1			Sales/Net Fixed Assets	8.4	11.3
	7.0	2.7	1.8				3.1	4.3
	3.3	1.6	1.0				1.7	2.6
	3.3	2.0	1.4			Sales/Total Assets	2.3	2.8
	2.6	1.3	1.0				1.7	1.9
	1.6	.8	.6				1.1	1.2
	1.5	3.4	4.3			% Depr., Dep., Amort./Sales	2.7	2.3
	(29) 3.2	(24) 6.0	(14) 8.3				(69) 4.8	(82) 4.3
	4.5	11.0	18.2				7.8	6.8
	3.9					% Officers', Directors' Owners' Comp/Sales	3.0	3.9
	(13) 10.8						(29) 5.1	(36) 6.1
	13.5						8.7	8.4
5791M	88451M	209995M	324255M	214559M	454176M	Net Sales ($)	744253M	1000243M
1813M	36174M	137702M	333937M	193533M	419073M	Total Assets ($)	560689M	652105M

© RMA 2010

M = $ thousand   MM = $ million
See Pages 9 through 22 for Explanation of Ratios and Data

Comparative Historical Data   Current Data Sorted by Sales

9	10	4	Type of Statement					1	3
14	20	20	Unqualified		6	1	4	7	2
17	13	17	Reviewed		7	5	3		1
5	6	7	Compiled	1	2	2	2		
27	26	40	Tax Returns / Other	4	11	6	7	8	4

4/1/07-3/31/08 ALL	4/1/08-3/31/09 ALL	4/1/09-3/31/10 ALL		0-1MM	1-3MM 15 (4/1-9/30/09)	3-5MM	5-10MM 73 (10/1/09-3/31/10)	10-25MM	25MM & OVER
72	75	88	NUMBER OF STATEMENTS	7	26	13	16	16	10
%	%	%	ASSETS	%	%	%	%	%	%
8.4	8.2	9.4	Cash & Equivalents		9.7	7.2	9.9	12.4	13.0
26.9	25.1	22.4	Trade Receivables (net)		25.6	24.4	19.7	19.2	16.0
10.8	6.4	9.4	Inventory		8.7	9.7	7.8	12.5	11.8
1.6	1.2	3.3	All Other Current		1.0	7.3	5.3	2.3	4.4
47.8	41.0	44.6	Total Current		45.1	48.6	42.7	46.4	45.2
41.5	45.3	43.5	Fixed Assets (net)		43.4	44.2	51.7	45.2	28.5
5.2	5.7	6.4	Intangibles (net)		4.7	1.3	1.1	4.3	19.1
5.5	8.1	5.5	All Other Non-Current		6.8	5.9	4.5	4.1	7.2
100.0	100.0	100.0	Total		100.0	100.0	100.0	100.0	100.0
			LIABILITIES						
6.3	6.6	9.4	Notes Payable-Short Term		9.1	14.2	12.4	6.9	2.1
7.7	7.0	6.4	Cur. Mat.-L.T.D.		6.0	8.0	6.0	3.6	3.1
10.7	8.8	9.5	Trade Payables		13.0	11.2	7.3	5.8	5.1
.2	.1	.1	Income Taxes Payable		.1	.0	.0	.3	.1
10.7	5.8	8.1	All Other Current		9.4	6.4	4.9	7.0	6.4
35.5	28.4	33.5	Total Current		37.5	39.7	30.6	23.6	16.8
25.1	22.9	24.9	Long-Term Debt		33.3	21.2	20.7	18.4	17.1
1.4	1.0	1.0	Deferred Taxes		.5	1.1	.9	1.0	3.1
6.6	7.3	11.6	All Other Non-Current		8.6	18.3	8.3	4.6	7.3
31.4	40.5	29.0	Net Worth		20.1	19.7	39.4	52.3	55.7
100.0	100.0	100.0	Total Liabilities & Net Worth		100.0	100.0	100.0	100.0	100.0
			INCOME DATA						
100.0	100.0	100.0	Net Sales		100.0	100.0	100.0	100.0	100.0
36.5	36.0	35.2	Gross Profit		37.3	33.4	34.7	34.5	34.7
28.3	30.2	35.5	Operating Expenses		42.3	37.9	31.7	30.6	25.2
8.3	5.8	-.3	Operating Profit		-5.0	-4.5	3.0	3.9	9.5
2.3	1.3	1.9	All Other Expenses (net)		2.1	1.1	2.4	2.7	.7
6.0	4.5	-2.1	Profit Before Taxes		-7.1	-5.6	.7	1.2	8.8
			RATIOS						
3.2	2.5	2.6	Current		2.4	2.5	3.6	3.5	8.2
1.7	1.5	1.4			1.0	1.4	1.1	2.1	2.4
.8	.8	.8			.6	.9	.8	1.3	1.1
2.2	2.1	2.0	Quick		2.0	2.0	1.5	2.2	3.7
1.1	1.0	.9			.8	.8	.8	1.8	1.6
.7	.7	.6			.5	.4	.7	1.1	.9
43 8.5 / 38 9.6 / 34 10.6			Sales/Receivables		34 10.7	28 12.8	34 10.6	41 8.9	36 10.2
50 7.3 / 48 7.6 / 46 7.9					51 7.1	48 7.7	44 8.3	45 8.1	53 6.9
62 5.9 / 58 6.3 / 57 6.4					63 5.8	57 6.4	53 6.9	51 7.1	63 5.8
0 UND / 0 UND / 0 UND			Cost of Sales/Inventory		0 UND	0 UND	0 UND	2 218.3	0 UND
9 41.1 / 7 50.1 / 6 59.7					2 221.6	7 50.2	0 UND	17 20.9	39 9.3
53 6.8 / 28 12.8 / 35 10.5					21 17.2	25 14.8	15 25.0	73 5.0	92 4.0
16 23.0 / 15 24.6 / 14 26.8			Cost of Sales/Payables		14 25.3	18 20.8	13 27.1	13 28.5	12 30.9
27 13.3 / 24 15.2 / 24 15.5					34 10.7	25 14.8	20 18.7	18 20.6	26 14.1
42 8.7 / 40 9.1 / 41 8.9					55 6.7	46 7.9	28 13.2	24 15.0	33 11.1
4.7	6.7	5.5	Sales/Working Capital		8.0	7.0	4.0	4.3	3.1
12.4	13.8	30.1			NM	23.8	97.5	9.0	4.0
-25.4	-22.9	-18.5			-6.8	-81.4	-22.8	25.1	NM
6.7	9.9	4.8	EBIT/Interest		1.6	-.3	2.5	13.8	
(66) 2.3	(68) 2.6	(79) .6			(23) -2.7	(11) -2.0	(15) 1.4	(15) 3.2	
.4	.2	-4.7			-18.2	-15.3	-2.8	.4	
1.9	3.6	3.3	Net Profit + Depr., Dep., Amort./Cur. Mat. L/T/D						
(17) 1.3	(30) 1.9	(22) 1.9							
.6	1.2	.7							
.6	.6	.6	Fixed/Worth		.4	.7	1.0	.7	.4
1.5	1.3	1.3			1.9	3.5	1.3	.8	.8
12.6	3.2	21.3			-1.4	NM	2.4	1.4	-1.2
.7	.5	.5	Debt/Worth		.4	.7	.8	.4	.4
1.9	1.3	1.3			4.0	5.8	1.1	.7	1.0
28.5	7.0	NM			-4.7	NM	3.7	1.7	-4.0
55.3	39.5	17.1	% Profit Before Taxes/Tangible Net Worth		8.3	12.7	16.7	22.8	
(55) 25.0	(65) 16.3	(66) 3.2			(16) -6.7	(10) -16.7	(15) 5.5	(15) 11.7	
-.1	-1.5	-13.6			-29.6	-159.2	-10.6	.8	
15.5	16.4	7.7	% Profit Before Taxes/Total Assets		4.1	3.3	7.7	9.0	18.3
6.7	6.8	.7			-10.2	-7.0	2.1	5.5	10.4
-.9	-1.2	-10.6			-23.1	-14.0	-4.2	-.4	4.0
11.3	7.3	7.9	Sales/Net Fixed Assets		9.2	11.7	7.0	5.8	6.1
4.2	4.0	4.1			4.1	5.8	2.7	3.9	4.6
2.0	1.9	1.8			1.6	2.2	1.3	1.7	2.7
2.7	3.0	2.7	Sales/Total Assets		2.8	3.3	2.8	2.1	1.6
1.8	1.8	1.5			1.7	2.6	1.4	1.6	1.1
1.1	1.0	1.0			1.1	1.1	.7	1.1	.8
2.5	2.9	2.8	% Depr., Dep., Amort./Sales		2.9	2.0	3.2	2.9	
(64) 4.6	(68) 4.8	(73) 4.7			(22) 4.2	(11) 3.7	(14) 8.3	(14) 3.8	
6.9	7.8	9.9			6.7	10.0	18.7	8.4	
2.6	2.4	4.6	% Officers', Directors' Owners' Comp/Sales		3.9				
(27) 4.6	(28) 4.5	(27) 6.1			(13) 7.0				
9.7	8.3	11.6			12.4				
1613019M	1110014M	1297227M	Net Sales ($)	4071M	50215M	49380M	116041M	227267M	850253M
1239084M	864420M	1122232M	Total Assets ($)	3291M	36651M	31068M	114244M	173679M	763299M

M = $ thousand   MM = $ million
See Pages 9 through 22 for Explanation of Ratios and Data

Current Data Sorted by Assets							Comparative Historical Data	

Type of Statement

0-500M	500M-2MM	2-10MM	10-50MM	50-100MM	100-250MM		4/1/05-3/31/06 ALL	4/1/06-3/31/07 ALL
	2	6	7		2	Unqualified	16	19
	9	13	1			Reviewed	38	40
3	11	7	1			Compiled	15	20
6	6	5	1			Tax Returns	14	13
5	13	20	9	4	2	Other	63	54
	27 (4/1-9/30/09)		105 (10/1/09-3/31/10)					
14	41	51	18	4	4	NUMBER OF STATEMENTS	146	146
%	%	%	%	%	%	ASSETS	%	%
10.1	12.7	7.6	12.6			Cash & Equivalents	6.1	7.0
31.9	33.7	22.3	22.3			Trade Receivables (net)	30.1	28.8
9.3	8.8	13.1	18.0			Inventory	12.3	13.7
6.7	2.2	2.7	2.0			All Other Current	1.9	2.8
58.0	57.5	45.7	55.0			Total Current	50.3	52.3
32.9	30.5	38.3	35.7			Fixed Assets (net)	38.6	36.5
2.6	2.5	8.2	2.7			Intangibles (net)	4.2	4.6
6.5	9.6	7.7	6.6			All Other Non-Current	7.0	6.7
100.0	100.0	100.0	100.0			Total	100.0	100.0
						LIABILITIES		
34.2	12.7	9.4	8.5			Notes Payable-Short Term	10.5	10.6
7.9	4.4	4.6	1.4			Cur. Mat.-L.T.D.	5.4	4.7
11.0	12.2	8.2	10.0			Trade Payables	13.9	13.5
.0	.2	.1	.3			Income Taxes Payable	.4	.2
20.4	7.8	7.2	8.6			All Other Current	10.1	11.6
73.6	37.3	29.5	28.8			Total Current	40.3	40.7
34.3	21.4	24.1	20.1			Long-Term Debt	19.8	18.4
.0	.3	.5	.8			Deferred Taxes	.4	.5
5.5	5.2	6.1	2.8			All Other Non-Current	8.3	7.9
-13.4	35.8	39.8	47.5			Net Worth	31.2	32.4
100.0	100.0	100.0	100.0			Total Liabilities & Net Worth	100.0	100.0
						INCOME DATA		
100.0	100.0	100.0	100.0			Net Sales	100.0	100.0
56.1	38.5	29.4	27.4			Gross Profit	29.9	30.5
55.0	37.2	26.9	20.3			Operating Expenses	23.8	24.2
1.1	1.3	2.5	7.1			Operating Profit	6.1	6.2
.7	1.0	1.6	2.3			All Other Expenses (net)	1.3	1.4
.4	.3	.9	4.8			Profit Before Taxes	4.8	4.8
						RATIOS		
2.1	4.7	3.4	5.1				2.2	2.3
.9	2.0	1.8	1.8			Current	1.3	1.4
.4	.9	1.0	1.2				.9	.9
1.1	3.5	2.2	3.1				1.5	1.5
.6	1.5	1.3	1.1			Quick	1.0	1.0
.4	.7	.5	.6				.6	.6
0 UND	36 10.0	35 10.5	36 10.1				40 9.1	37 9.9
31 11.9	43 8.4	43 8.5	45 8.2			Sales/Receivables	51 7.2	48 7.6
58 6.3	57 6.4	56 6.5	55 6.6				63 5.8	61 6.0
0 UND	0 UND	9 40.2	13 27.5				6 57.9	10 35.9
0 UND	13 29.1	23 15.9	50 7.3			Cost of Sales/Inventory	23 15.9	22 16.8
31 11.9	31 11.6	57 6.4	64 5.7				53 6.9	48 7.6
0 UND	14 26.7	12 31.1	11 33.2				19 19.4	15 23.8
17 21.9	27 13.7	22 16.7	21 17.5			Cost of Sales/Payables	28 13.1	26 13.9
56 6.5	46 8.0	29 12.5	49 7.5				42 8.7	40 9.1
9.0	4.6	5.1	3.1				6.7	6.6
-46.4	11.0	8.1	7.2			Sales/Working Capital	17.4	15.1
-8.5	-62.8	-213.3	95.3				-48.9	-103.2
9.9	8.4	18.1	9.3				9.6	9.7
(12) 1.6	(36) 3.0	(50) 2.3	(16) 4.0			EBIT/Interest	(137) 4.6	(133) 3.8
-1.7	-.2	-1.1	-1.0				1.4	1.2
		7.1				Net Profit + Depr., Dep.,	3.6	3.9
	(14) 1.4					Amort./Cur. Mat. L/T/D	(34) 1.6	(36) 2.1
		.0					.9	.8
.6	.3	.6	.4				.6	.5
NM	.7	.9	.8			Fixed/Worth	1.2	1.1
-.7	6.6	4.6	2.2				3.2	3.3
.7	.3	.7	.3				.8	.6
NM	1.5	1.3	1.3			Debt/Worth	1.9	1.9
-3.8	9.0	5.9	4.0				7.6	8.8
	32.5	30.8	46.9			% Profit Before Taxes/Tangible	50.1	62.5
	(33) 13.6	(42) 12.5	(16) 16.9			Net Worth	(121) 24.0	(123) 25.6
	.1	-6.3	-28.0				8.4	7.2
21.2	11.9	15.2	20.4			% Profit Before Taxes/Total	16.0	17.1
2.3	4.5	3.4	7.5			Assets	8.5	9.5
-14.6	-4.1	-7.3	-6.0				2.0	.9
24.7	19.9	10.2	11.2				10.6	13.7
15.1	9.6	4.3	6.0			Sales/Net Fixed Assets	5.9	6.3
7.9	4.8	2.2	2.5				2.8	3.5
5.7	3.3	2.1	2.1				2.7	2.9
4.0	2.4	1.4	1.7			Sales/Total Assets	2.0	2.2
2.9	1.8	1.1	1.1				1.4	1.5
1.5	2.4	1.6	.8				1.9	1.8
(10) 2.0	(30) 3.3	(48) 3.8	(17) 2.3			% Depr., Dep., Amort./Sales	(125) 3.1	(124) 3.1
3.3	6.0	6.6	4.3				5.7	4.5
	4.2	2.9				% Officers', Directors'	2.2	3.1
	(21) 6.8	(22) 4.9				Owners' Comp/Sales	(44) 5.2	(47) 4.9
	13.5	6.4					7.1	8.5
13541M	133591M	368080M	698788M	265798M	691197M	Net Sales ($)	4034958M	3781106M
3494M	49525M	224654M	383998M	286518M	598406M	Total Assets ($)	2272383M	2163090M

Comparative Historical Data | | | | Current Data Sorted by Sales

Hist 1	Hist 2	Hist 3	Type of Statement	0-1MM	1-3MM	3-5MM	5-10MM	10-25MM	25MM & OVER
11	11	17	Unqualified			4	3	1	9
33	27	23	Reviewed		2	7	10	4	
23	21	22	Compiled	4	8	6	1	2	1
16	20	17	Tax Returns	4	6	4	3		
52	48	53	Other	5	13	4	13	9	9
4/1/07-3/31/08 ALL	4/1/08-3/31/09 ALL	4/1/09-3/31/10 ALL		27 (4/1-9/30/09)			105 (10/1/09-3/31/10)		
135	127	132	NUMBER OF STATEMENTS	13	29	25	30	16	19
%	%	%	**ASSETS**	%	%	%	%	%	%
8.1	7.9	10.7	Cash & Equivalents	10.6	13.8	5.9	10.2	9.4	13.9
28.8	26.2	26.6	Trade Receivables (net)	26.5	28.7	26.2	28.3	25.0	22.5
13.3	11.1	11.6	Inventory	10.4	3.9	15.9	11.9	16.6	14.0
2.7	3.5	2.9	All Other Current	3.4	4.8	4.1	1.0	1.1	2.5
52.9	48.7	51.7	Total Current	50.9	51.2	52.2	51.4	52.2	52.8
33.4	40.5	35.4	Fixed Assets (net)	40.1	34.0	32.2	34.8	37.8	37.1
4.9	3.8	5.2	Intangibles (net)	2.9	3.5	4.0	9.8	4.0	4.6
8.7	7.0	7.7	All Other Non-Current	6.1	11.3	11.6	4.0	6.1	5.5
100.0	100.0	100.0	Total	100.0	100.0	100.0	100.0	100.0	100.0
			LIABILITIES						
10.6	12.2	12.4	Notes Payable-Short Term	25.6	10.1	20.5	8.8	8.1	5.7
3.9	5.4	4.3	Cur. Mat.-L.T.D.	8.8	3.1	4.3	6.0	2.6	1.5
12.3	10.5	10.2	Trade Payables	6.6	9.7	10.1	11.3	10.3	11.9
.5	.2	.2	Income Taxes Payable	.0	.0	.2	.3	.3	.1
10.7	11.3	9.0	All Other Current	21.9	7.5	8.9	6.6	5.4	9.2
38.1	39.6	36.1	Total Current	62.9	30.5	44.1	33.0	26.7	28.4
23.6	21.8	24.1	Long-Term Debt	50.0	26.7	21.9	19.9	16.3	18.6
.4	.4	.5	Deferred Taxes	.0	.2	.5	.5	1.0	.8
5.2	4.5	5.1	All Other Non-Current	5.9	8.1	4.2	5.2	3.2	2.9
32.8	33.7	34.2	Net Worth	-18.8	34.4	29.2	41.4	52.8	49.3
100.0	100.0	100.0	Total Liabilities & Net Worth	100.0	100.0	100.0	100.0	100.0	100.0
			INCOME DATA						
100.0	100.0	100.0	Net Sales	100.0	100.0	100.0	100.0	100.0	100.0
31.4	34.5	34.6	Gross Profit	53.9	42.0	30.9	31.0	28.3	25.6
25.4	30.3	31.5	Operating Expenses	52.2	41.3	32.7	27.6	20.4	16.6
5.9	4.2	3.0	Operating Profit	1.8	.6	-1.8	3.4	8.0	9.0
1.5	1.4	1.6	All Other Expenses (net)	1.7	1.3	1.7	1.8	.6	2.3
4.4	2.8	1.5	Profit Before Taxes	.1	-.6	-3.5	1.7	7.4	6.7
			RATIOS						
2.5	2.6	3.4	Current	2.1	5.7	2.3	2.8	3.8	4.8
1.6	1.3	1.7		1.2	2.7	1.3	1.9	2.0	1.6
1.0	.8	.9		.4	.9	.8	1.0	1.3	1.2
1.9	1.7	2.4	Quick	1.4	4.6	1.9	2.3	2.3	2.5
1.0	.9	1.2		.6	2.1	.8	1.4	1.3	1.2
.6	.5	.6		.4	.7	.4	.6	.7	.7
37 9.8	32 11.4	35 10.4	Sales/Receivables	0 UND	38 9.6	36 10.1	34 10.9	34 10.8	37 9.9
46 8.0	43 8.4	43 8.4		36 10.3	53 6.8	41 8.8	44 8.3	42 8.7	45 8.1
56 6.5	54 6.8	56 6.5		60 6.1	58 6.3	50 7.3	58 6.3	63 5.8	52 7.1
7 49.5	8 44.6	3 109.8	Cost of Sales/Inventory	0 UND	0 UND	13 29.2	5 72.4	6 61.2	22 16.4
25 14.7	21 17.1	22 16.5		5 69.0	3 122.4	26 13.9	17 22.1	26 14.3	45 8.2
55 6.6	49 7.5	46 7.9		37 9.9	28 13.1	61 6.0	43 8.5	96 3.8	56 6.5
16 22.7	14 25.2	12 31.0	Cost of Sales/Payables	0 UND	11 32.4	12 31.2	14 26.3	10 36.9	12 30.7
25 14.4	25 14.8	24 15.5		12 30.2	26 13.9	26 14.1	22 16.2	22 16.6	26 14.2
40 9.0	41 8.8	42 8.8		41 8.9	52 7.1	34 10.7	29 12.8	44 8.3	51 7.2
6.5	6.5	5.0	Sales/Working Capital	7.5	3.8	5.5	5.6	4.1	3.6
13.8	21.1	10.8		36.1	7.6	19.0	9.4	8.1	8.0
-229.0	-15.7	-53.6		-8.2	-41.6	-17.9	NM	30.0	23.2
13.5	9.8	9.2	EBIT/Interest	9.9	6.2	5.1	8.7	70.6	29.7
(122) 4.5	(111) 3.7	(121) 2.4		(12) 1.6	(24) 2.2	(24) 1.4	2.5	(14) 19.4	(17) 7.0
1.4	1.1	-.7		-.2	-1.2	-3.1	-.9	1.6	-1.2
2.5	2.5	2.9	Net Profit + Depr., Dep., Amort./Cur. Mat. L/T/D						
(28) 1.8	(22) 1.6	(26) 1.6							
.8	.9	.2							
.4	.5	.4	Fixed/Worth	.5	.4	.6	.4	.4	.4
1.0	1.1	.9		-7.3	1.0	.8	.9	.7	.7
3.5	3.2	7.1		-1.2	NM	NM	4.9	1.8	1.9
.7	.7	.5	Debt/Worth		.3	.9	.6	.2	.3
1.8	1.9	1.4		-21.8	2.2	2.6	1.3	1.2	1.2
6.8	5.9	9.9		-3.1	NM	NM	6.3	3.9	2.1
56.7	45.3	32.6	% Profit Before Taxes/Tangible Net Worth		27.4	13.1	51.5	41.7	68.1
(115) 25.7	(106) 18.1	(104) 13.6			(22) 13.9	(19) 2.6	(25) 14.7	(15) 23.3	(17) 21.1
4.0	.7	-3.7			-1.0	-53.0	-7.4	.4	-19.9
20.9	15.8	15.6	% Profit Before Taxes/Total Assets	21.5	8.5	6.7	15.5	22.7	19.9
8.1	5.5	4.4		3.7	3.5		5.1	14.9	9.4
.8	-.2	-6.1		-7.2	-4.1	-16.5	-5.2	.3	-6.3
18.0	11.6	14.3	Sales/Net Fixed Assets	20.8	15.8	14.3	17.2	9.9	12.4
6.8	5.4	6.9		9.9	7.3	7.7	6.8	7.3	4.2
3.8	3.1	2.8		3.7	3.1	2.9	2.5	2.8	2.7
2.9	3.0	2.9	Sales/Total Assets	4.3	2.6	2.6	3.2	2.5	2.3
1.9	2.0	2.0		3.5	2.0	1.6	2.0	1.9	1.8
1.4	1.3	1.2		1.9	1.4	1.2	1.1	1.2	1.0
1.3	1.6	1.8	% Depr., Dep., Amort./Sales	1.5	2.3	1.6	2.1	1.3	.4
(114) 2.8	(102) 3.0	(110) 3.3		(10) 3.1	(21) 5.2	(23) 2.8	(26) 3.8	(15) 2.7	(15) 2.1
4.4	5.5	6.1		5.8	6.5	8.2	7.2	4.0	4.8
3.4	2.7	3.6	% Officers', Directors' Owners' Comp/Sales		3.5	4.0	4.6		
(39) 5.2	(46) 5.7	(48) 5.7			(13) 6.7	(10) 5.4	(14) 5.7		
8.3	7.4	10.1			10.6	13.7	15.3		
3540245M	2990099M	2170995M	Net Sales ($)	9371M	62946M	99224M	204420M	234471M	1560563M
2207264M	1944148M	1546595M	Total Assets ($)	4055M	35950M	66631M	130566M	149990M	1159403M

M = $ thousand   MM = $ million
See Pages 9 through 22 for Explanation of Ratios and Data

Current Data Sorted by Assets							Type of Statement	Comparative Historical Data	
			6	4	1		Unqualified	17	15
	2		23	3			Reviewed	36	40
2	8		11	2			Compiled	39	33
7	6		2				Tax Returns	14	23
7	18		20	8			Other	60	60
	25 (4/1-9/30/09)			105 (10/1/09-3/31/10)				4/1/05-3/31/06	4/1/06-3/31/07
0-500M	500M-2MM	2-10MM	10-50MM	50-100MM	100-250MM			ALL	ALL
16	34	62	17	1			NUMBER OF STATEMENTS	166	171
%	%	%	%	%	%		ASSETS	%	%
7.1	3.8	9.2	6.1			D	Cash & Equivalents	8.8	8.2
39.9	27.2	26.1	21.2			A	Trade Receivables (net)	27.9	29.6
13.0	9.4	12.5	19.2			T	Inventory	11.4	10.5
3.3	4.8	3.0	1.4			A	All Other Current	2.0	1.5
63.4	45.2	50.8	48.0				Total Current	50.1	49.8
29.2	41.0	38.8	39.2			N	Fixed Assets (net)	38.8	40.9
.7	5.6	2.3	5.9			O	Intangibles (net)	3.2	3.1
6.7	8.3	8.2	6.9			T	All Other Non-Current	7.9	6.2
100.0	100.0	100.0	100.0				Total	100.0	100.0
						A	LIABILITIES		
16.9	13.0	10.5	12.7			V	Notes Payable-Short Term	10.5	10.2
6.6	3.5	4.5	8.1			A	Cur. Mat.-L.T.D.	5.2	5.2
22.0	14.7	12.4	14.3			I	Trade Payables	13.3	14.2
.0		.1	.0			L	Income Taxes Payable	.1	.4
26.1	7.1	6.0	5.4			A	All Other Current	9.2	9.3
71.7	38.4	33.4	40.4			B	Total Current	38.4	39.3
20.3	29.8	17.5	16.2			L	Long-Term Debt	18.9	23.3
.0	.9	.7	1.3			E	Deferred Taxes	.6	.5
34.3	8.2	5.4	6.8				All Other Non-Current	11.1	9.1
-26.3	22.6	43.1	35.3				Net Worth	31.0	27.8
100.0	100.0	100.0	100.0				Total Liabilties & Net Worth	100.0	100.0
							INCOME DATA		
100.0	100.0	100.0	100.0				Net Sales	100.0	100.0
50.5	42.3	28.4	17.6				Gross Profit	32.5	33.0
51.8	35.5	26.5	16.5				Operating Expenses	28.3	27.4
-1.3	6.9	1.9	1.1				Operating Profit	4.2	5.6
2.1	1.9	.6	2.3				All Other Expenses (net)	1.1	1.8
-3.4	5.0	1.3	-1.2				Profit Before Taxes	3.1	3.8
							RATIOS		
2.6	2.5	3.1	1.8					2.1	2.6
1.3	1.2	1.6	1.0				Current	1.3	1.3
.7	.9	.9	.9					.9	.9
1.7	1.9	2.0	1.4					1.7	2.0
1.1	1.0	1.1	.6				Quick	1.0	1.0
.5	.6	.6	.4					.6	.6
27 13.7	37 9.9	38 9.6	40 9.1					40 9.2	37 9.8
39 9.3	43 8.6	48 7.6	53 6.8				Sales/Receivables	48 7.5	47 7.8
54 6.8	64 5.7	58 6.3	61 6.0					57 6.4	55 6.7
0 UND	6 65.0	9 42.6	20 18.5					7 49.6	4 81.9
7 49.3	16 23.0	19 19.6	54 6.7				Cost of Sales/Inventory	17 21.7	14 25.5
78 4.7	34 10.7	43 8.6	66 5.6					41 8.9	39 9.3
16 23.1	16 22.7	16 23.3	23 16.2					16 22.2	13 27.1
39 9.4	32 11.4	30 12.0	32 11.4				Cost of Sales/Payables	26 14.0	28 13.1
58 6.3	69 5.3	45 8.1	42 8.7					43 8.4	42 8.6
6.7	6.8	5.7	10.0					7.2	8.0
36.6	25.2	11.8	127.1				Sales/Working Capital	17.7	18.3
-23.6	-200.1	-30.9	-27.2					-50.1	-37.7
5.4	9.5	8.4	3.0					8.0	9.6
(14) -.7	(33) 3.6	(56) 2.4	(16) 1.9				EBIT/Interest	(154) 3.3	(156) 3.7
-12.4	.5	.2	.0					.8	1.0
		4.0					Net Profit + Depr., Dep.,	4.8	8.7
	(16) 2.1						Amort./Cur. Mat. L/T/D	(39) 2.1	(48) 2.9
		.4						1.2	1.1
.2	.9	.5	.7					.6	.6
1.2	2.1	.9	2.4				Fixed/Worth	1.1	1.3
-.4	-3.0	2.1	9.7					3.4	9.6
.8	1.0	.5	.8					.8	.8
6.9	3.0	1.5	2.4				Debt/Worth	1.8	2.0
-1.7	-16.1	3.1	20.0					7.2	29.3
	43.4	28.6	32.3				% Profit Before Taxes/Tangible	45.1	49.6
	(24) 27.4	(56) 8.2	(14) 6.1				Net Worth	(141) 17.7	(133) 22.4
	.2	-.5	.2					2.1	3.3
6.6	16.8	8.8	5.5				% Profit Before Taxes/Total	16.4	16.1
-2.7	7.9	3.0	2.6				Assets	5.4	7.1
-29.3	-.7	-1.0	-.9					-.3	.2
58.6	19.5	8.5	7.0					11.1	12.0
10.4	4.8	5.1	4.3				Sales/Net Fixed Assets	5.9	5.6
5.6	2.0	2.6	2.4					3.3	3.3
4.7	3.1	2.6	2.2					2.9	3.3
3.4	2.1	1.9	1.4				Sales/Total Assets	2.1	2.2
2.1	1.2	1.5	1.1					1.5	1.5
.5	1.2	1.5	1.5					1.6	1.5
(12) 1.2	(27) 3.7	(59) 3.3	(14) 3.8				% Depr., Dep., Amort./Sales	(152) 3.0	(163) 3.0
3.0	5.5	5.2	7.1					5.0	4.8
2.8	4.4	1.6						3.7	3.3
(12) 7.0	(19) 6.6	(28) 3.3					% Officers', Directors' Owners' Comp/Sales	(78) 5.7	(79) 5.3
11.7	8.5	6.7						9.5	8.4
17815M	89678M	547075M	472156M	48960M			Net Sales ($)	2478407M	2260219M
4860M	40226M	271210M	346456M	66009M			Total Assets ($)	1254450M	1144396M

© RMA 2010

M = $ thousand   MM = $ million
See Pages 9 through 22 for Explanation of Ratios and Data

Comparative Historical Data

Current Data Sorted by Sales

4/1/07-3/31/08 ALL	4/1/08-3/31/09 ALL	4/1/09-3/31/10 ALL	Type of Statement	0-1MM	1-3MM	3-5MM	5-10MM	10-25MM	25MM & OVE
8	13	11	Unqualified				2	4	5
30	36	28	Reviewed		1	6	11	7	3
35	32	23	Compiled		9	4	6	4	
14	15	15	Tax Returns	5	6	2	1	1	
59	64	53	Other	9	12	6	14	7	5
					25 (4/1-9/30/09)		**105 (10/1/09-3/31/10)**		
146	160	130	**NUMBER OF STATEMENTS**	14	28	18	34	23	13
%	%	%	**ASSETS**	%	%	%	%	%	%
9.2	8.1	7.0	Cash & Equivalents	6.9	4.6	7.3	7.1	11.9	3.4
29.3	26.5	27.3	Trade Receivables (net)	23.9	30.9	23.6	27.4	28.5	26.1
9.4	14.2	12.5	Inventory	11.9	8.2	7.3	11.8	18.3	21.3
2.5	3.3	3.3	All Other Current	1.7	5.9	1.6	3.6	2.2	2.9
50.3	52.0	50.2	Total Current	44.4	49.7	39.8	49.8	60.9	53.7
39.4	37.6	38.1	Fixed Assets (net)	39.2	37.8	49.9	39.5	28.6	34.7
4.0	4.4	3.9	Intangibles (net)	6.4	4.7	2.1	1.6	4.4	7.0
6.3	5.9	7.8	All Other Non-Current	9.9	7.8	8.2	9.1	6.0	4.6
100.0	100.0	100.0	Total	100.0	100.0	100.0	100.0	100.0	100.0
			LIABILITIES						
12.4	11.4	12.1	Notes Payable-Short Term	13.6	14.9	10.7	10.7	9.7	14.7
5.2	5.7	5.0	Cur. Mat.-L.T.D.	6.9	3.6	4.3	5.5	3.2	8.7
14.0	14.1	14.4	Trade Payables	12.1	16.7	13.7	12.9	13.9	17.2
.1	.1	.0	Income Taxes Payable	.0	.0	.0	.1	.1	.0
10.0	7.5	8.6	All Other Current	24.3	9.5	4.8	6.1	5.2	7.9
41.7	38.8	40.2	Total Current	56.9	44.7	33.6	35.3	32.0	48.5
17.9	20.3	21.0	Long-Term Debt	24.8	30.4	25.3	18.2	11.4	14.8
.6	.6	.7	Deferred Taxes	.0	.4	1.4	.9	.9	.7
10.7	8.0	10.0	All Other Non-Current	28.6	12.2	7.5	7.5	2.6	8.3
29.1	32.2	28.1	Net Worth	-10.4	12.2	32.2	38.2	53.1	27.7
100.0	100.0	100.0	Total Liabilities & Net Worth	100.0	100.0	100.0	100.0	100.0	100.0
			INCOME DATA						
100.0	100.0	100.0	Net Sales	100.0	100.0	100.0	100.0	100.0	100.0
31.0	30.1	33.5	Gross Profit	50.8	46.2	31.7	26.5	27.1	20.1
25.8	25.0	30.8	Operating Expenses	46.2	43.1	30.0	24.6	24.3	16.5
5.3	5.1	2.7	Operating Profit	4.6	3.1	1.7	1.9	2.7	3.7
1.4	1.5	1.4	All Other Expenses (net)	3.6	1.5	1.3	.6	.9	2.0
3.8	3.6	1.3	Profit Before Taxes	1.0	1.7	.5	1.3	1.8	1.7
			RATIOS						
2.2	2.4	2.7	Current	2.4	2.6	2.7	2.7	3.8	1.9
1.3	1.3	1.2		1.0	1.2	1.1	1.5	1.9	1.0
.9	.9	.9		.5	1.0	.7	.9	1.1	.8
1.6	1.7	1.8	Quick	2.2	1.7	2.1	1.9	3.3	.8
1.0	.9	.9		.7	1.0	1.0	1.1	1.3	.6
.6	.6	.6		.2	.8	.6	.6	.6	.5
38 9.7	31 11.7	38 9.7	Sales/Receivables	32 11.2	27 13.6	37 9.8	40 9.1	43 8.4	35 10.4
46 7.9	42 8.7	47 7.8		56 6.5	40 9.2	42 8.8	50 7.4	53 6.8	50 7.3
55 6.6	53 6.9	58 6.3		78 4.7	54 6.7	50 7.3	57 6.4	61 6.0	62 5.9
4 100.9	8 44.1	8 45.5	Cost of Sales/Inventory	0 UND	2 194.6	6 63.8	11 33.9	10 36.4	22 16.9
12 30.7	21 17.5	18 20.7		33 11.0	6 59.8	15 24.8	20 18.3	33 11.1	51 7.2
29 12.4	46 -7.9	45 8.1		124 2.9	17 22.0	26 14.2	38 9.6	85 4.3	60 6.1
15 24.0	13 27.3	17 20.9	Cost of Sales/Payables	15 23.7	14 26.8	11 33.3	20 18.4	22 16.7	22 16.6
25 14.5	25 14.5	32 11.4		41 8.8	36 10.1	22 16.4	32 11.3	35 10.4	32 11.4
38 9.6	41 8.9	46 8.0		138 2.6	53 6.9	40 9.1	41 8.9	45 8.1	45 8.1
8.4	7.1	6.4	Sales/Working Capital	5.4	8.5	6.7	6.4	5.1	9.3
22.4	21.3	22.1		NM	36.1	UND	12.1	8.8	-176.6
-61.0	-138.9	-33.5		-4.8	NM	-16.5	-42.0	29.2	-16.6
10.4	7.6	6.9	EBIT/Interest	8.2	10.0	2.6	7.7	14.7	4.4
(134) 3.4	(144) 2.7	(120) 2.4		(12) .5	(27) 3.6	(16) 1.4	(32) 2.4	(20) 1.9	2.4
1.0	1.0	-.4		-10.2	-1.4	-.4	.3	-1.7	1.3
5.5	4.9	3.7	Net Profit + Depr., Dep., Amort./Cur. Mat. L/T/D				3.9		
(42) 2.4	(41) 1.9	(29) 1.6					(11) 2.0		
.9	1.1	.6					.3		
.6	.5	.6	Fixed/Worth	1.1	.6	.9	.5	.3	.7
1.0	1.0	1.2		2.3	2.0	1.3	.9	.5	2.9
3.8	3.7	7.4		-.3	-3.9	NM	2.6	1.2	NM
.7	.7	.8	Debt/Worth	1.2	1.1	.9	.5	.3	1.1
1.9	1.9	2.0		5.0	3.0	1.4	1.6	1.0	4.9
10.0	9.0	15.9		-2.2	-9.5	NM	3.4	2.6	NM
40.6	40.1	31.5	% Profit Before Taxes/Tangible Net Worth		43.4	25.4	22.8	29.4	46.8
(118) 19.5	(126) 18.0	(103) 8.5			(20) 21.7	(14) 5.2	(29) 8.1	(22) 8.1	(10) 17.9
4.1	2.9	-.5			-1.1	-1.7	-1.1	.3	-3.8
14.9	13.3	8.8	% Profit Before Taxes/Total Assets	14.2	16.7	5.2	8.5	11.8	8.4
6.2	5.0	3.2		-.3	7.2	1.0	2.6	3.5	3.4
.2	-.8	-2.9		-16.3	-6.0	-2.5	-1.5	-.4	1.3
12.0	13.2	10.8	Sales/Net Fixed Assets	14.5	35.5	6.7	7.8	18.7	9.5
6.1	6.2	5.3		5.7	5.3	3.4	5.2	7.5	5.2
3.4	3.4	2.9		1.4	3.6	2.2	2.4	3.8	3.3
3.0	3.1	2.8	Sales/Total Assets	2.2	3.5	2.4	2.6	2.9	2.5
2.2	2.1	1.9		1.4	2.5	1.9	1.9	1.9	2.2
1.6	1.5	1.4		.8	1.7	1.4	1.4	1.3	1.4
1.6	1.4	1.3	% Depr., Dep., Amort./Sales	1.2	.8	2.4	1.5	1.3	1.1
(134) 2.9	(147) 2.5	(113) 3.3		(10) 2.9	(21) 4.0	3.5	3.5	(19) 3.2	(11) 3.4
4.8	4.4	5.2		10.4	5.0	5.6	4.9	6.5	6.3
2.1	2.6	2.6	% Officers', Directors' Owners' Comp/Sales		3.1	2.8	1.4		
(71) 4.9	(62) 4.8	(62) 5.5			(17) 7.8	(13) 5.3	(15) 3.5		
7.7	8.1	7.8			10.9	7.5	7.4		
2076297M	2702961M	1175684M	Net Sales ($)	9083M	52284M	74358M	239547M	336180M	464232M
1045949M	1342564M	728761M	Total Assets ($)	8140M	25403M	42132M	132979M	240186M	279921M

M = $ thousand   MM = $ million
See Pages 9 through 22 for Explanation of Ratios and Data

Current Data Sorted by Assets

Comparative Historical Data

	0-500M	500M-2MM	2-10MM	10-50MM	50-100MM	100-250MM	Type of Statement	4/1/05-3/31/06 ALL	4/1/06-3/31/07 ALL
		1	1	5	4	2	Unqualified	12	17
		3	16	4			Reviewed	16	10
	3	13	16				Compiled	22	9
	13	22	5	2			Tax Returns	25	13
	3	18	22	11	6	3	Other	35	36
		28 (4/1-9/30/09)		145 (10/1/09-3/31/10)					
NUMBER OF STATEMENTS	19	57	60	22	10	5		110	85
	%	%	%	%	%	%	**ASSETS**	%	%
Cash & Equivalents	14.6	10.1	10.6	7.4	9.0			9.8	7.8
Trade Receivables (net)	17.9	23.7	20.7	27.8	31.9			27.3	28.0
Inventory	13.3	23.9	27.3	30.7	35.3			26.2	30.1
All Other Current	1.1	2.1	1.3	4.5	3.6			2.5	2.0
Total Current	46.8	59.9	59.9	70.5	79.8			65.9	67.9
Fixed Assets (net)	32.9	28.8	32.8	21.3	14.2			25.6	22.8
Intangibles (net)	9.6	4.4	1.6	2.0	4.4			2.3	3.6
All Other Non-Current	10.8	6.9	5.6	6.2	1.7			6.2	5.7
Total	100.0	100.0	100.0	100.0	100.0			100.0	100.0
							LIABILITIES		
Notes Payable-Short Term	9.8	12.6	11.2	9.8	7.4			10.9	11.2
Cur. Mat.-L.T.D.	6.1	4.5	5.8	4.2	8.3			3.6	4.1
Trade Payables	14.5	13.4	11.6	15.6	10.9			14.9	14.2
Income Taxes Payable	.3	.1	.4	.2	2.3			.2	.2
All Other Current	22.5	11.4	6.7	10.8	16.4			10.5	9.7
Total Current	53.2	42.0	35.7	40.4	45.2			40.2	39.5
Long-Term Debt	39.3	31.2	17.5	18.1	13.0			16.2	15.3
Deferred Taxes	.0	.3	.1	.1	.0			.2	.4
All Other Non-Current	15.4	7.2	8.0	18.5	10.0			6.5	4.3
Net Worth	-7.9	19.4	38.8	22.9	31.8			37.0	40.5
Total Liabilties & Net Worth	100.0	100.0	100.0	100.0	100.0			100.0	100.0
							INCOME DATA		
Net Sales	100.0	100.0	100.0	100.0	100.0			100.0	100.0
Gross Profit	52.5	40.5	31.9	33.8	39.1			36.7	33.7
Operating Expenses	58.3	36.5	26.8	26.3	21.2			29.3	24.9
Operating Profit	-5.8	4.1	5.1	7.5	17.9			7.4	8.8
All Other Expenses (net)	1.5	1.8	1.2	.2	2.6			.8	1.1
Profit Before Taxes	-7.3	2.2	3.9	7.3	15.3			6.6	7.6
							RATIOS		
Current	1.8	2.8	3.6	3.5	2.8			3.0	2.8
	1.1	1.7	1.9	1.9	1.9			1.8	1.9
	.4	1.0	1.1	1.1	1.3	1.4		1.3	1.2
Quick	1.5	2.1	1.8	1.7	1.4			1.6	1.6
	.7	.8	.8	.9	1.1			.9	.9
	.2	.6	.6	.5	.6			.6	.5
Sales/Receivables	0 UND	24 15.3	34 10.9	41 8.8	56 6.5			35 10.5	41 8.9
	12 30.5	41 9.0	43 8.4	51 7.2	64 5.7			46 7.9	49 7.5
	53 6.9	53 6.8	52 7.0	64 5.7	71 5.1			59 6.2	61 6.0
Cost of Sales/Inventory	0 UND	23 15.9	31 11.6	49 7.5	92 4.0			36 10.3	42 8.8
	12 30.6	58 6.3	78 4.7	102 3.6	107 3.4			70 5.2	84 4.3
	23 15.8	119 3.1	130 2.8	165 2.2	146 2.5			124 3.0	139 2.6
Cost of Sales/Payables	1 292.5	14 25.3	14 26.5	20 18.0	23 15.9			21 17.2	14 25.5
	24 15.3	31 11.8	27 13.5	38 9.6	29 12.5			36 10.1	31 11.7
	98 3.7	50 7.3	42 8.7	55 6.6	50 7.3			53 6.9	49 7.4
Sales/Working Capital	12.2	4.0	4.1	2.5	2.4			4.1	3.9
	98.7	10.1	7.1	5.1	4.9			7.9	8.0
	-6.2	139.4	62.9	16.2	12.6			25.7	24.7
EBIT/Interest	1.3	6.9	8.2	27.2	255.8			27.1	10.0
	(15) -.8	(54) 2.0	(57) 2.7	(21) 7.8	20.3			(97) 5.1	(77) 6.2
	-13.0	-.6	.6	2.4	5.7			1.7	2.9
Net Profit + Depr., Dep., Amort./Cur. Mat. L/T/D			4.3					5.6	5.9
		(13) 1.9						(21) 2.0	(26) 2.8
			.7					1.7	1.4
Fixed/Worth	.4	.3	.4	.3	.2			.3	.2
	2.0	1.7	.8	.6	.6			.5	.5
	-.4	-3.0	2.4	1.8	2.7			2.1	1.3
Debt/Worth	1.0	1.2	.6	.7	.8			.5	.8
	3.9	3.4	2.1	1.5	2.1			1.4	1.8
	-1.8	-8.7	5.2	6.4	10.9			5.9	4.1
% Profit Before Taxes/Tangible Net Worth	82.0	52.3	44.1	83.2				57.6	59.7
	(10) 11.4	(38) 19.5	(55) 16.3	(19) 35.6				(94) 28.2	(76) 27.6
	-49.2	-11.6	-3.3	17.7				8.8	17.5
% Profit Before Taxes/Total Assets	21.7	15.6	15.3	19.8	37.5			24.2	20.1
	-9.0	3.7	3.6	11.1	21.9			8.9	11.6
	-27.3	-6.7	-1.0	2.3	16.0			2.5	4.9
Sales/Net Fixed Assets	142.5	20.9	10.4	20.8	20.0			22.5	33.6
	11.0	11.9	5.7	10.2	13.6			9.6	11.3
	5.4	4.1	3.4	6.4	8.1			4.5	5.5
Sales/Total Assets	6.5	2.8	2.4	2.2	2.0			2.7	2.8
	3.4	2.1	1.8	1.8	1.8			2.0	1.9
	1.4	1.5	1.3	1.4	1.4			1.4	1.4
% Depr., Dep., Amort./Sales	1.2	1.5	1.7	.8	.7			1.1	1.1
	(11) 2.2	(44) 2.4	(54) 3.5	(18) 1.8	1.0			(97) 2.3	(73) 2.3
	22.0	4.7	7.2	3.0	2.0			4.0	3.4
% Officers', Directors' Owners' Comp/Sales	3.3	3.0	1.8					1.7	1.7
	(13) 10.1	(37) 5.2	(32) 4.1					(42) 3.5	(32) 3.2
	18.1	7.2	5.7					7.2	5.6
Net Sales ($)	15389M	140393M	520266M	1349590M	1205644M	893183M		2003113M	2478571M
Total Assets ($)	4428M	63398M	293550M	497432M	713702M	768182M		1227879M	1526789M

Comparative Historical Data

Current Data Sorted by Sales

4/1/07-3/31/08 ALL	4/1/08-3/31/09 ALL	4/1/09-3/31/10 ALL	Type of Statement	0-1MM	1-3MM	3-5MM	5-10MM	10-25MM	25MM & OVER
16	8	13	Unqualified			1	1	2	9
10	11	23	Reviewed		3	2	7	9	2
10	18	32	Compiled	4	10	7	10	1	
8	25	42	Tax Returns	12	18	6	3	1	2
25	39	63	Other	5	9	8	15	8	18
				28 (4/1-9/30/09)		145 (10/1/09-3/31/10)			
69	101	173	**NUMBER OF STATEMENTS**	21	40	24	36	21	31
%	%	%	**ASSETS**	%	%	%	%	%	%
6.2	8.8	10.2	Cash & Equivalents	11.1	11.2	10.5	8.8	13.6	7.1
28.2	26.0	23.0	Trade Receivables (net)	12.2	22.5	26.7	23.2	21.5	28.8
32.3	30.5	25.9	Inventory	22.5	20.1	18.4	28.5	30.5	35.1
2.7	1.5	2.2	All Other Current	2.1	.5	2.3	2.5	3.3	3.2
69.5	66.9	61.2	Total Current	48.0	54.4	57.9	63.0	68.8	74.2
21.0	24.2	28.7	Fixed Assets (net)	38.5	31.0	29.3	32.2	23.3	18.1
4.1	3.1	3.8	Intangibles (net)	5.5	6.7	3.6	.5	2.2	4.0
5.5	5.8	6.3	All Other Non-Current	8.1	7.9	9.1	4.3	5.6	3.7
100.0	100.0	100.0	Total	100.0	100.0	100.0	100.0	100.0	100.0
			LIABILITIES						
10.0	12.1	11.1	Notes Payable-Short Term	8.3	11.1	13.1	10.9	14.4	9.7
3.7	3.4	5.3	Cur. Mat.-L.T.D.	7.1	4.7	5.3	6.0	2.7	5.8
12.9	16.4	13.1	Trade Payables	10.9	13.6	12.1	14.1	10.8	15.2
1.2	.3	.3	Income Taxes Payable	.0	.2	.1	.5	.1	.9
9.8	14.2	11.1	All Other Current	16.2	13.3	10.8	6.3	8.5	12.1
37.6	46.4	40.9	Total Current	42.5	43.0	41.3	37.7	36.5	43.8
16.9	15.4	24.0	Long-Term Debt	46.8	37.2	14.1	14.6	18.5	14.0
.8	.7	.2	Deferred Taxes	.0	.4	.0	.1	.1	.2
3.5	5.1	9.8	All Other Non-Current	15.3	6.9	6.1	9.4	5.8	15.6
41.2	32.5	25.1	Net Worth	-4.7	12.6	38.5	38.2	39.1	26.4
100.0	100.0	100.0	Total Liabilities & Net Worth	100.0	100.0	100.0	100.0	100.0	100.0
			INCOME DATA						
100.0	100.0	100.0	Net Sales	100.0	100.0	100.0	100.0	100.0	100.0
34.4	35.5	37.7	Gross Profit	51.0	40.9	39.8	30.6	29.6	36.6
24.3	28.7	33.0	Operating Expenses	55.4	38.2	34.3	26.4	22.4	25.2
10.1	6.9	4.6	Operating Profit	-4.4	2.7	5.6	4.2	7.2	11.3
.7	1.0	1.4	All Other Expenses (net)	2.4	2.3	1.8	.2	.8	1.0
9.4	5.8	3.3	Profit Before Taxes	-6.8	.4	3.7	4.0	6.4	10.3
			RATIOS						
3.1	3.1	2.9	Current	4.8	2.6	3.1	2.7	5.2	2.8
2.0	1.9	1.7		1.6	1.4	1.9	1.7	1.9	2.0
1.3	1.1	1.1		.5	.9	.8	1.2	1.1	1.3
1.7	1.8	1.7	Quick	1.9	2.1	2.1	1.4	2.7	1.4
1.0	.8	.8		.7	.8	1.2	.8	.9	.8
.6	.5	.5		.2	.5	.6	.5	.6	.5
40 9.1	30 12.2	28 13.0	Sales/Receivables	2 151.4	24 15.4	30 12.1	33 11.1	35 10.4	45 8.1
51 7.2	40 9.0	44 8.2		15 23.8	39 9.4	45 8.1	45 8.1	41 9.0	57 6.4
63 5.8	51 7.2	58 6.3		51 7.2	56 6.6	60 6.1	59 6.2	46 7.9	64 5.7
47 7.8	26 14.0	24 15.2	Cost of Sales/Inventory	0 UND	17 20.9	20 17.9	36 10.0	33 11.1	86 4.2
96 3.8	85 4.3	72 5.1		23 15.8	60 6.1	28 12.9	72 5.0	88 4.1	108 3.4
150 2.4	147 2.5	129 2.8		277 1.3	114 3.2	61 6.0	137 2.7	126 2.9	193 1.9
19 19.7	16 22.2	15 24.2	Cost of Sales/Payables	6 63.0	10 37.7	19 19.6	15 24.4	8 47.4	25 14.6
33 11.2	30 12.3	29 12.6		33 11.1	33 11.0	29 12.6	28 13.3	27 13.7	36 10.2
50 7.2	45 8.2	50 7.3		119 3.1	57 6.4	40 9.2	46 7.9	42 8.7	55 6.6
3.2	4.3	4.1	Sales/Working Capital	4.1	4.7	5.1	4.3	3.4	2.6
5.7	7.8	8.3		18.0	23.4	11.3	7.2	5.1	4.8
14.1	40.5	80.1		-8.4	-30.7	-22.5	42.5	51.1	13.2
15.8	16.5	8.7	EBIT/Interest	2.4	4.4	11.7	7.9	25.0	52.2
(63) 5.7	(91) 5.1	(162) 2.8		(18) -.6	(37) .7	(23) 3.2	(34) 2.6	(19) 4.5	7.7
2.6	2.2	.1		-5.9	-1.2	.8	-.6	1.1	5.7
3.6	4.1	5.7	Net Profit + Depr., Dep., Amort./Cur. Mat. L/T/D				5.0		21.0
(22) 2.5	(23) 2.5	(35) 1.8					(12) 2.4		(12) 3.5
1.3	.8	.9					.6		1.1
.2	.2	.3	Fixed/Worth	.4	.4	.3	.4	.2	.2
.6	.7	.8		5.6	NM	.6	.8	.6	.6
1.3	4.0	5.6		-.5	-1.1	1.6	1.8	2.6	1.1
.7	.6	.8	Debt/Worth	.7	1.7	.8	.6	.7	.8
1.5	1.8	2.3		5.7	NM	2.0	2.1	1.1	1.6
4.6	24.7	9.5		-2.7	-6.0	4.8	5.8	5.4	5.6
48.8	62.1	51.7	% Profit Before Taxes/Tangible Net Worth	29.3	83.3	49.0	37.4	63.5	89.4
(59) 36.9	(80) 30.8	(136) 21.3		(13) -31.2	(20) 20.3	(23) 5.1	(34) 9.4	(18) 24.1	(28) 43.0
20.2	11.9	-.1		-72.3	-6.6	-3.9	-4.1	11.6	20.2
22.8	22.0	19.4	% Profit Before Taxes/Total Assets	3.9	14.9	22.2	14.2	22.9	22.7
13.6	9.1	5.1		-9.0	.0	4.7	3.6	10.1	14.9
4.9	2.8	-2.7		-23.4	-8.1	-.8	-1.6	1.8	5.7
28.5	26.2	18.2	Sales/Net Fixed Assets	18.5	18.5	22.1	11.8	24.2	23.8
12.6	12.0	9.4		6.6	10.6	10.3	5.7	7.2	12.0
5.5	5.6	4.4		2.1	3.6	3.6	3.6	6.0	7.4
2.5	3.0	2.5	Sales/Total Assets	5.0	2.8	2.9	2.4	2.4	2.1
1.8	2.1	1.9		1.4	1.8	2.4	1.9	2.1	1.8
1.5	1.5	1.3		.9	1.4	1.5	1.3	1.5	1.3
1.0	1.0	1.3	% Depr., Dep., Amort./Sales	.7	1.8	1.5	1.9	1.4	.8
(59) 1.8	(85) 2.0	(142) 2.6		(15) 2.7	(29) 3.6	(21) 2.6	(32) 3.4	(17) 1.7	(28) 1.2
2.9	3.0	4.8		22.0	6.6	7.6	6.6	3.5	3.2
1.6	2.4	2.7	% Officers', Directors' Owners' Comp/Sales	4.0	3.1	2.3	1.8		
(23) 4.0	(43) 5.3	(89) 4.5		(13) 6.5	(26) 5.9	(16) 4.1	(23) 4.3		
7.2	7.9	7.9		17.6	9.6	6.0	5.3		
2051014M	1984905M	4124465M	Net Sales ($)	11975M	76077M	90961M	264625M	341117M	3339710M
1391976M	1202179M	2340692M	Total Assets ($)	8162M	44921M	50224M	153425M	182951M	1901009M

M = $ thousand   MM = $ million
See Pages 9 through 22 for Explanation of Ratios and Data

Current Data Sorted by Assets							Comparative Historical Data	

0-500M	500M-2MM	2-10MM	10-50MM	50-100MM	100-250MM	**Type of Statement**	4/1/05-3/31/06 ALL	4/1/06-3/31/07 ALL
			5	1	2	Unqualified	11	9
	3	6	4	1		Reviewed	13	16
1		5		1		Compiled	8	5
1	5	3	1			Tax Returns	4	6
1	1	6	5	1	1	Other	10	25
	8 (4/1-9/30/09)		46 (10/1/09-3/31/10)					
3	9	20	15	4	3	**NUMBER OF STATEMENTS**	46	61
%	%	%	%	%	%	**ASSETS**	%	%
		8.9	8.1			Cash & Equivalents	8.3	6.5
		26.3	25.9			Trade Receivables (net)	25.0	24.3
		36.4	27.2			Inventory	33.2	32.1
		7.2	3.2			All Other Current	2.7	4.8
		78.8	64.4			Total Current	69.2	67.7
		15.6	20.9			Fixed Assets (net)	21.0	23.7
		2.7	4.0			Intangibles (net)	3.3	3.8
		2.8	10.7			All Other Non-Current	6.5	4.8
		100.0	100.0			Total	100.0	100.0
						LIABILITIES		
		7.3	6.9			Notes Payable-Short Term	10.3	12.5
		1.9	2.8			Cur. Mat.-L.T.D.	4.2	3.6
		8.8	8.2			Trade Payables	11.9	12.6
		.0	1.7			Income Taxes Payable	.5	.5
		10.4	10.3			All Other Current	9.8	10.1
		28.5	29.9			Total Current	36.7	39.2
		9.4	6.5			Long-Term Debt	18.6	15.1
		.1	1.1			Deferred Taxes	.3	.4
		7.2	7.2			All Other Non-Current	5.7	9.0
		54.8	55.2			Net Worth	38.7	36.3
		100.0	100.0			Total Liabilities & Net Worth	100.0	100.0
						INCOME DATA		
		100.0	100.0			Net Sales	100.0	100.0
		36.7	33.4			Gross Profit	31.3	32.0
		30.4	23.3			Operating Expenses	24.9	25.7
		6.3	10.1			Operating Profit	6.4	6.3
		2.0	-.4			All Other Expenses (net)	1.1	1.2
		4.3	10.5			Profit Before Taxes	5.3	5.1
						RATIOS		
		8.4	3.0				3.1	3.2
		3.9	1.9			Current	1.9	1.9
		1.4	1.6				1.4	1.3
		4.0	1.6				1.4	1.2
		1.0	1.0			Quick	.8	.8
		.7	.7				.6	.6
		40 9.0	37 9.8				34 10.8	38 9.5
		52 7.0	49 7.4			Sales/Receivables	46 8.0	48 7.6
		63 5.8	67 5.5				59 6.2	59 6.2
		57 6.4	34 10.7				50 7.3	40 9.2
		116 3.1	99 3.7			Cost of Sales/Inventory	82 4.4	93 3.9
		224 1.6	146 2.5				145 2.5	142 2.6
		14 25.9	12 29.7				19 18.8	19 19.6
		23 16.1	22 16.6			Cost of Sales/Payables	29 12.6	33 11.2
		36 10.1	32 11.5				39 9.4	51 7.2
		2.1	3.0				3.2	3.7
		3.9	5.2			Sales/Working Capital	6.2	5.5
		9.0	9.1				13.7	14.0
		17.3	252.7				12.3	9.7
		(19) 3.6	(13) 9.4			EBIT/Interest	(39) 5.1	(55) 4.5
		-.3	.8				2.3	1.4
						Net Profit + Depr., Dep.,	10.5	6.9
						Amort./Cur. Mat. L/T/D	(10) 5.1	(23) 3.8
							3.2	2.0
		.1	.1				.2	.2
		.3	.5			Fixed/Worth	.5	.6
		.5	.9				1.1	1.1
		.3	.4				.6	.8
		1.2	.9			Debt/Worth	1.3	1.4
		2.1	1.7				4.3	3.1
		26.1	58.4			% Profit Before Taxes/Tangible	57.8	38.2
		16.0	22.6			Net Worth	(40) 22.9	(56) 21.3
		-1.9	17.6				10.3	10.1
		15.1	33.4			% Profit Before Taxes/Total	14.7	14.4
		7.4	11.5			Assets	8.1	8.1
		-1.3	2.8				2.4	2.6
		35.3	30.0				33.1	20.1
		14.9	8.9			Sales/Net Fixed Assets	11.1	9.7
		8.5	3.9				4.9	4.2
		2.3	2.2				2.6	2.3
		1.8	1.6			Sales/Total Assets	1.9	1.9
		1.3	1.3				1.4	1.3
		.8	.6				.7	1.3
		(16) 1.5	(14) 2.3			% Depr., Dep., Amort./Sales	(41) 2.1	(59) 2.1
		2.6	4.7				3.3	3.3
						% Officers', Directors'	3.2	1.7
						Owners' Comp/Sales	(10) 5.2	(23) 5.0
							15.4	8.2
2192M	32572M	186225M	559347M	379162M	411432M	Net Sales ($)	1319142M	2232236M
1140M	11066M	104224M	328258M	275027M	441133M	Total Assets ($)	914500M	1683603M

M = $ thousand   MM = $ million
See Pages 9 through 22 for Explanation of Ratios and Data

Comparative Historical Data | **Current Data Sorted by Sales**

4/1/07-3/31/08 ALL	4/1/08-3/31/09 ALL	4/1/09-3/31/10 ALL	Type of Statement	0-1MM	1-3MM	3-5MM	5-10MM	10-25MM	25MM & OVER
6	7	8	Unqualified		2	2	3	2	6
13	15	14	Reviewed		2	2	3	3	4
7	13	7	Compiled			1	2	2	1
3	9	10	Tax Returns	1	3	1	4	2	1
29	22	15	Other	1	3	1			5
				8 (4/1-9/30/09)			46 (10/1/09-3/31/10)		
58	66	54	NUMBER OF STATEMENTS	2	8	5	9	13	17
%	%	%	ASSETS	%	%	%	%	%	%
7.3	11.0	13.1	Cash & Equivalents					9.6	12.9
26.6	23.1	25.5	Trade Receivables (net)					25.3	21.1
32.6	30.7	31.3	Inventory					26.3	31.8
4.1	3.3	3.9	All Other Current					11.9	2.1
70.7	68.1	73.8	Total Current					73.0	67.9
20.9	21.9	17.0	Fixed Assets (net)					18.6	20.4
2.5	3.5	3.0	Intangibles (net)					.1	5.7
5.9	6.5	6.2	All Other Non-Current					8.3	5.9
100.0	100.0	100.0	Total					100.0	100.0
			LIABILITIES						
10.8	8.4	6.9	Notes Payable-Short Term					8.5	7.5
3.3	3.2	3.2	Cur. Mat.-L.T.D.					3.3	3.8
12.5	10.7	10.7	Trade Payables					9.5	6.2
.7	.6	.5	Income Taxes Payable					.2	1.3
8.2	8.5	10.7	All Other Current					10.0	8.4
35.6	31.4	31.9	Total Current					31.5	27.3
12.6	10.4	7.9	Long-Term Debt					10.3	4.4
.5	.4	.4	Deferred Taxes					.1	1.2
8.2	5.2	5.8	All Other Non-Current					9.6	6.6
43.0	52.6	54.0	Net Worth					48.5	60.5
100.0	100.0	100.0	Total Liabilities & Net Worth					100.0	100.0
			INCOME DATA						
100.0	100.0	100.0	Net Sales					100.0	100.0
30.1	33.5	34.8	Gross Profit					33.5	32.1
21.7	24.9	27.9	Operating Expenses					26.8	23.7
8.5	8.7	6.9	Operating Profit					6.8	8.4
1.4	1.0	.9	All Other Expenses (net)					.5	.1
7.1	7.7	6.1	Profit Before Taxes					6.3	8.4
			RATIOS						
3.3	4.1	6.3	Current					4.2	7.5
2.1	2.3	2.8						2.0	2.6
1.4	1.6	1.6						1.5	1.6
1.9	2.1	3.6	Quick					2.9	3.7
.9	.9	1.1						.9	1.2
.6	.6	.7						.6	.6
36 10.1	33 11.0	36 10.1	Sales/Receivables					38 9.5	37 9.9
47 7.7	42 8.7	46 7.9						52 7.0	46 7.9
61 6.0	52 7.1	60 6.1						61 6.0	60 6.1
51 7.1	43 8.5	53 6.9	Cost of Sales/Inventory					19 19.5	81 4.5
94 3.9	89 4.1	95 3.8						57 6.4	105 3.5
135 2.7	136 2.7	150 2.4						125 2.9	158 2.3
20 18.1	16 23.2	13 28.0	Cost of Sales/Payables					17 21.0	11 31.8
29 12.6	23 15.6	22 16.3						22 16.6	21 17.7
39 9.3	39 9.4	37 10.0						38 9.5	27 13.3
3.1	3.3	2.5	Sales/Working Capital					3.4	2.4
5.0	5.1	4.0						5.2	3.3
11.9	10.2	9.2						8.8	7.1
16.8	23.9	17.4	EBIT/Interest					20.6	237.7
(52) 5.7	(59) 8.8	(46) 3.8						(12) 7.9	(13) 4.6
2.1	3.0	-.4						2.3	-.1
11.0	14.6	3.5	Net Profit + Depr., Dep.,						
(23) 3.4	(26) 4.2	(15) 2.1	Amort./Cur. Mat. L/T/D						
1.7	2.2	.4							
.2	.1	.1	Fixed/Worth					.1	.1
.5	.4	.3						.4	.3
1.0	.7	.6						.9	.6
.6	.5	.3	Debt/Worth					.6	.1
1.2	1.0	1.1						1.1	.9
2.6	1.6	2.0						2.5	1.6
42.9	48.6	37.1	% Profit Before Taxes/Tangible					44.9	35.3
(52) 25.6	(63) 29.6	(53) 17.6	Net Worth					23.2	15.4
10.3	9.7	-1.7						16.5	5.0
20.2	25.2	21.1	% Profit Before Taxes/Total					21.2	24.8
12.1	14.3	8.0	Assets					11.5	9.4
3.9	2.9	-1.4						3.8	2.9
28.7	26.3	40.3	Sales/Net Fixed Assets					33.0	46.0
10.2	12.7	13.7						12.5	6.5
5.7	5.7	6.5						8.4	4.5
2.4	2.7	2.4	Sales/Total Assets					2.3	1.8
1.9	2.0	1.6						2.0	1.4
1.4	1.5	1.3						1.5	1.2
.7	.7	.6	% Depr., Dep., Amort./Sales					.7	.7
(55) 1.9	(56) 2.0	(44) 1.5						(11) 2.3	(15) 1.9
3.9	3.5	3.0						3.0	4.0
1.6	1.8	1.7	% Officers', Directors'						
(21) 2.9	(15) 3.1	(12) 3.5	Owners' Comp/Sales						
6.8	16.6	9.9							
2511986M	3114674M	1570930M	Net Sales ($)	1098M	17042M	20068M	65627M	221762M	1245333M
1563332M	2067730M	1160848M	Total Assets ($)	805M	10177M	10946M	39604M	115136M	984180M

Current Data Sorted by Assets							Comparative Historical Data	
		1	6	3	1	**Type of Statement** Unqualified	10	12
		4	4			Reviewed	3	7
						Compiled	5	3
		1	1			Tax Returns		1
		3	4	2	2	Other	13	10
	4 (4/1-9/30/09)		28 (10/1/09-3/31/10)				4/1/05-3/31/06 ALL	4/1/06-3/31/07 ALL
0-500M	500M-2MM	2-10MM	10-50MM	50-100MM	100-250MM			
		9	15	5	3	NUMBER OF STATEMENTS	31	33
%	%	%	%	%	%	**ASSETS**	%	%
DATA NOT AVAILABLE	DATA NOT AVAILABLE		7.3			Cash & Equivalents	8.6	11.1
			23.3			Trade Receivables (net)	27.1	26.2
			32.6			Inventory	35.8	34.5
			4.7			All Other Current	1.9	1.8
			67.9			Total Current	73.4	73.6
			19.6			Fixed Assets (net)	16.2	15.3
			6.0			Intangibles (net)	5.3	3.8
			6.5			All Other Non-Current	5.1	7.4
			100.0			Total	100.0	100.0
						LIABILITIES		
			12.5			Notes Payable-Short Term	14.1	11.0
			2.9			Cur. Mat.-L.T.D.	2.6	3.5
			10.0			Trade Payables	15.6	10.8
			.8			Income Taxes Payable	.1	.8
			10.0			All Other Current	13.7	13.0
			36.3			Total Current	46.1	39.1
			16.7			Long-Term Debt	11.2	16.1
			.2			Deferred Taxes	.4	.4
			9.6			All Other Non-Current	3.8	3.5
			37.2			Net Worth	38.4	40.9
			100.0			Total Liabilties & Net Worth	100.0	100.0
						INCOME DATA		
			100.0			Net Sales	100.0	100.0
			28.9			Gross Profit	31.2	37.8
			26.6			Operating Expenses	26.8	29.5
			2.4			Operating Profit	4.4	8.3
			1.6			All Other Expenses (net)	.3	1.0
			.8			Profit Before Taxes	4.0	7.3
						RATIOS		
			3.8				2.0	3.9
			1.9			Current	1.6	1.9
			1.2				1.4	1.4
			2.0				1.3	2.1
			.6			Quick	.8	1.0
			.4				.4	.5
			41 8.9				**38** 9.6	**38** 9.5
			45 8.1			Sales/Receivables	**44** 8.2	**45** 8.1
			60 6.1				**54** 6.8	**58** 6.3
			85 4.3				**56** 6.5	**74** 4.9
			110 3.3			Cost of Sales/Inventory	**78** 4.7	**100** 3.7
			133 2.7				**122** 3.0	**145** 2.5
			21 17.6				**21** 17.7	**14** 25.4
			26 13.9			Cost of Sales/Payables	**30** 12.0	**31** 11.7
			30 12.1				**53** 6.9	**42** 8.7
			3.0				4.1	4.0
			4.8			Sales/Working Capital	7.2	6.2
			13.3				11.6	14.8
			14.8				13.5	22.4
			5.8			EBIT/Interest	(27) 3.7	(29) 3.9
			-1.6				1.6	1.7
							10.5	11.9
						Net Profit + Depr., Dep., Amort./Cur. Mat. L/T/D	(14) 3.1	(11) 2.5
							1.3	2.3
			.3				.2	.2
			.6			Fixed/Worth	.4	.3
			2.2				1.8	1.1
			.6				.6	.6
			2.4			Debt/Worth	1.8	1.5
			14.4				5.4	3.7
			86.5				49.3	62.8
			(12) 12.4			% Profit Before Taxes/Tangible Net Worth	(26) 26.4	(30) 35.6
			1.3				7.7	16.7
			15.0				14.5	18.4
			3.9			% Profit Before Taxes/Total Assets	6.7	12.0
			-6.3				2.8	3.3
			13.1				41.7	32.2
			10.0			Sales/Net Fixed Assets	15.1	14.7
			6.2				7.6	8.8
			2.1				2.3	2.4
			1.9			Sales/Total Assets	2.1	2.1
			1.3				1.8	1.6
			1.2				.5	.6
			(14) 2.5			% Depr., Dep., Amort./Sales	(26) 1.3	(30) 1.0
			5.3				2.2	1.6
						% Officers', Directors' Owners' Comp/Sales		
		110152M	731324M	764405M	478343M	Net Sales ($)	1997549M	2008389M
		48720M	404037M	415496M	508864M	Total Assets ($)	971712M	1231551M

M = $ thousand MM = $ million

See Pages 9 through 22 for Explanation of Ratios and Data

Comparative Historical Data | Current Data Sorted by Sales

4/1/07-3/31/08 ALL	4/1/08-3/31/09 ALL	4/1/09-3/31/10 ALL	Type of Statement	0-1MM	1-3MM	3-5MM	5-10MM	10-25MM	25MM & OVER
14	10	11	Unqualified					1	10
3	10	8	Reviewed				3	3	2
1	1		Compiled						
1	6	2	Tax Returns				1	1	
10	9	11	Other		1			5	5
					1 (4/1-9/30/09)		28 (10/1/09-3/31/10)		
29	36	32	**NUMBER OF STATEMENTS**		1		4	10	17
%	%	%	**ASSETS**	%	%	%	%	%	%
8.4	6.2	11.1	Cash & Equivalents					12.9	10.3
23.6	23.0	21.8	Trade Receivables (net)	*DATA*		*DATA*		21.9	23.9
35.7	38.3	31.2	Inventory	*NOT*		*NOT*		27.6	29.4
3.3	3.2	4.3	All Other Current	*AVAILABLE*		*AVAILABLE*		8.1	3.0
70.9	70.7	68.3	Total Current					70.5	66.5
16.8	18.4	19.5	Fixed Assets (net)					20.8	20.8
7.1	6.4	7.2	Intangibles (net)					3.7	8.4
5.2	4.5	4.9	All Other Non-Current					4.9	4.4
100.0	100.0	100.0	Total					100.0	100.0
			LIABILITIES						
12.5	9.9	9.8	Notes Payable-Short Term					12.0	9.4
2.7	3.1	2.4	Cur. Mat.-L.T.D.					3.8	2.0
11.7	11.9	10.6	Trade Payables					14.0	8.9
.7	.4	.5	Income Taxes Payable					.0	.8
11.7	10.8	9.8	All Other Current					10.8	10.4
39.2	36.0	33.2	Total Current					40.6	31.5
23.4	15.0	16.2	Long-Term Debt					13.4	14.2
.1	.4	.2	Deferred Taxes					.3	.2
6.2	7.4	6.7	All Other Non-Current					3.6	10.2
31.1	41.2	43.7	Net Worth					42.0	43.8
100.0	100.0	100.0	Total Liabilities & Net Worth					100.0	100.0
			INCOME DATA						
100.0	100.0	100.0	Net Sales					100.0	100.0
36.3	29.9	34.7	Gross Profit					34.2	30.9
29.0	27.5	30.7	Operating Expenses					33.6	24.5
7.2	2.4	4.0	Operating Profit					.6	6.4
1.8	.6	1.3	All Other Expenses (net)					1.0	.9
5.4	1.8	2.7	Profit Before Taxes					-.4	5.5
			RATIOS						
3.2	3.7	4.4	Current					5.9	3.7
2.5	2.1	2.2						1.4	2.2
1.5	1.6	1.4						1.0	1.5
1.7	1.5	2.2	Quick					2.6	2.4
.9	.7	.7						.6	1.2
.6	.5	.6						.4	.6
31 11.7	26 13.8	36 10.0	Sales/Receivables					33 11.2	41 8.8
46 7.9	35 10.5	44 8.3						43 8.4	45 8.1
56 6.5	53 6.9	54 6.8						56 6.5	57 6.4
79 4.6	73 5.0	68 5.4	Cost of Sales/Inventory					26 14.2	58 6.3
98 3.7	97 3.8	102 3.6						104 3.5	96 3.8
124 3.0	147 2.5	134 2.7						155 2.3	118 3.1
17 21.6	12 29.6	21 17.4	Cost of Sales/Payables					23 16.2	18 19.7
34 10.7	24 14.9	25 14.3						29 12.5	25 14.8
49 7.4	39 9.4	37 9.8						61 5.9	29 12.8
4.2	3.4	3.1	Sales/Working Capital					2.9	3.4
5.2	5.5	4.9						9.0	6.2
9.0	8.6	10.8						NM	8.8
8.5	13.7	16.5	EBIT/Interest						17.7
(25) 3.1	(32) 2.1	(29) 2.6						(15) 7.8	
1.3	-1.3	1.1							1.6
	4.6	9.0	Net Profit + Depr., Dep., Amort./Cur. Mat. L/T/D						7.4
	(11) 2.1	(16) 4.0						(10) 4.9	
	.6	.8							2.3
.2	.2	.2	Fixed/Worth					.2	.3
.7	.5	.6						.5	.6
8.5	1.1	2.0						NM	2.2
.9	.6	.5	Debt/Worth					.4	.6
2.9	1.5	1.7						1.6	2.2
33.5	5.1	7.8						NM	7.6
61.1	23.5	33.3	% Profit Before Taxes/Tangible Net Worth						55.5
(23) 37.8	(31) 17.1	(27) 13.6						(15) 18.4	
15.8	-.7	3.0							9.6
19.0	13.9	14.1	% Profit Before Taxes/Total Assets					10.8	14.8
11.9	4.6	4.4						2.0	12.1
3.1	-3.3	.7						-10.0	1.7
22.7	20.7	16.8	Sales/Net Fixed Assets					43.1	12.5
14.8	11.9	9.9						10.1	9.2
7.7	8.4	6.2						5.5	6.4
2.3	2.7	2.2	Sales/Total Assets					2.5	2.2
1.9	2.0	1.9						1.9	1.9
1.6	1.5	1.3						1.3	1.5
1.1	.7	1.2	% Depr., Dep., Amort./Sales						1.2
(23) 1.8	(33) 1.4	(28) 2.0						(16) 2.0	
2.7	2.4	3.3							3.0
			% Officers', Directors' Owners' Comp/Sales						
1978979M	2332914M	2084224M	Net Sales ($)		2951M		35740M	182126M	1863407M
1127025M	1333520M	1377117M	Total Assets ($)		2057M		29545M	108399M	1237116M

© RMA 2010

M = $ thousand   MM = $ million

See Pages 9 through 22 for Explanation of Ratios and Data

Current Data Sorted by Assets
Comparative Historical Data

0-500M	500M-2MM	2-10MM	10-50MM	50-100MM	100-250MM	Type of Statement	4/1/05-3/31/06 ALL	4/1/06-3/31/07 ALL
		6	11	2	1	Unqualified	23	33
	1	10	5			Reviewed	25	13
1	2	7	1			Compiled	11	10
3	7	3				Tax Returns	5	5
	8	10	15	2	3	Other	31	34
	25 (4/1-9/30/09)		73 (10/1/09-3/31/10)					
4	18	36	32	4	4	NUMBER OF STATEMENTS	95	95
%	%	%	%	%	%	ASSETS	%	%
	10.5	9.7	9.1			Cash & Equivalents	7.4	7.8
	22.5	24.0	21.2			Trade Receivables (net)	28.4	26.9
	17.4	31.5	32.6			Inventory	29.4	31.7
	4.5	.9	3.1			All Other Current	2.6	2.3
	54.9	66.3	66.1			Total Current	67.7	68.6
	27.6	25.3	19.6			Fixed Assets (net)	20.1	19.1
	14.1	1.7	7.0			Intangibles (net)	5.7	5.3
	3.4	6.7	7.4			All Other Non-Current	6.5	7.0
	100.0	100.0	100.0			Total	100.0	100.0
						LIABILITIES		
	8.9	8.9	7.3			Notes Payable-Short Term	13.6	12.3
	2.9	4.4	4.9			Cur. Mat.-L.T.D.	3.5	3.1
	11.5	13.9	9.0			Trade Payables	16.2	16.3
	.1	.2	.1			Income Taxes Payable	.5	.5
	6.4	6.0	8.3			All Other Current	9.1	9.5
	29.9	33.4	29.6			Total Current	42.8	41.7
	19.1	19.1	15.8			Long-Term Debt	14.8	13.7
	.0	.3	.5			Deferred Taxes	.4	.4
	10.3	4.9	10.9			All Other Non-Current	5.8	3.2
	40.8	42.3	43.2			Net Worth	36.1	40.9
	100.0	100.0	100.0			Total Liabilities & Net Worth	100.0	100.0
						INCOME DATA		
	100.0	100.0	100.0			Net Sales	100.0	100.0
	36.3	30.5	27.3			Gross Profit	29.9	32.1
	31.7	26.4	23.1			Operating Expenses	24.9	25.6
	4.6	4.1	4.2			Operating Profit	5.0	6.4
	1.2	1.1	1.3			All Other Expenses (net)	.8	1.0
	3.4	3.0	2.9			Profit Before Taxes	4.2	5.5
						RATIOS		
	3.7	4.4	3.5				2.9	3.1
	2.1	1.9	2.3			Current	1.7	1.7
	.8	1.3	1.7				1.2	1.2
	2.4	2.8	1.7				1.6	1.8
	1.3	1.2	1.0			Quick	.9	.9
	.4	.6	.6				.5	.5
23	15.9	39 9.3	37 9.8				38 9.6	34 10.9
37	10.0	45 8.1	47 7.8			Sales/Receivables	51 7.2	45 8.1
53	6.9	61 6.0	63 5.8				68 5.4	58 6.3
0	UND	51 7.2	72 5.0				44 8.3	45 8.0
47	7.8	91 4.0	100 3.7			Cost of Sales/Inventory	81 4.5	81 4.5
73	5.0	161 2.3	140 2.6				125 2.9	121 3.0
16	23.0	18 20.4	16 22.5				20 18.4	16 23.1
31	11.9	30 12.2	25 14.4			Cost of Sales/Payables	35 10.5	31 11.8
41	9.0	53 6.8	36 10.0				54 6.8	54 6.8
	4.0	3.6	3.8				4.3	4.5
	7.9	6.2	4.9			Sales/Working Capital	7.4	6.4
	-63.6	15.7	6.4				25.2	21.0
	6.3	18.5	14.6				10.0	18.9
(13)	3.7	(33) 3.9	(31) 3.7			EBIT/Interest	(88) 4.2	(84) 5.2
	.2	.7	.7				1.8	2.0
		8.0	6.5			Net Profit + Depr., Dep.,	7.4	11.9
		(16) 1.8	(22) 3.4			Amort./Cur. Mat. L/T/D	(39) 3.7	(35) 4.3
		1.6	.4				1.8	1.8
	.2	.3	.3				.3	.2
	.9	.6	.6			Fixed/Worth	.5	.4
	-3.3	2.3	1.5				1.5	1.4
	.7	.7	.7				.9	.5
	2.3	1.3	1.5			Debt/Worth	2.0	1.9
	-7.7	4.9	5.3				5.6	5.5
	51.5	34.3	40.5			% Profit Before Taxes/Tangible	47.4	46.8
(13)	22.7	(31) 17.7	(29) 12.5			Net Worth	(81) 21.2	(82) 27.6
	4.1	-2.8	-7.6				8.6	7.6
	11.8	17.6	12.4			% Profit Before Taxes/Total	16.4	17.4
	7.4	4.3	6.3			Assets	5.7	7.9
	.1	-1.2	-2.3				3.2	3.6
	40.7	21.3	13.6				28.5	26.7
	7.8	8.0	9.4			Sales/Net Fixed Assets	10.8	11.3
	3.9	4.4	6.2				7.2	7.5
	3.3	2.1	2.2				2.4	2.6
	1.9	1.9	1.5			Sales/Total Assets	1.9	2.1
	1.1	1.5	1.2				1.4	1.5
	.7	1.0	1.1				.8	1.0
(15)	1.8	(35) 1.8	(28) 2.5			% Depr., Dep., Amort./Sales	(90) 2.0	(80) 1.9
	5.4	6.6	4.5				3.1	3.1
	3.5	1.6					1.1	.9
(11)	5.1	(13) 4.4				% Officers', Directors'	(24) 3.3	(23) 2.8
	8.2	8.2				Owners' Comp/Sales	8.2	9.4
1624M	47448M	303491M	1132199M	349516M	840386M	Net Sales ($)	3164711M	3654539M
930M	22195M	176346M	693976M	286382M	570125M	Total Assets ($)	1882383M	2133352M

M = $ thousand   MM = $ million
See Pages 9 through 22 for Explanation of Ratios and Data

Comparative Historical Data | Current Data Sorted by Sales

Type of Statement	4/1/07-3/31/08	4/1/08-3/31/09	4/1/09-3/31/10		0-1MM	1-3MM	3-5MM	5-10MM	10-25MM	25MM & OVER
Unqualified	25	28	20			1	3	4	4	12
Reviewed	10	15	16			2		3	6	3
Compiled	9	9	11		1	2	1	4	3	
Tax Returns	3	9	13		3	5	2	2	1	
Other	34	35	38		2	5	2	6	10	13
	ALL	ALL	ALL		25 (4/1-9/30/09)			73 (10/1/09-3/31/10)		
NUMBER OF STATEMENTS	81	96	98		6	13	8	19	24	28

	%	%	%	ASSETS	%	%	%	%	%	%
	8.4	9.2	9.7	Cash & Equivalents		8.9		8.4	11.2	8.3
	23.0	22.2	23.1	Trade Receivables (net)		15.8		29.0	24.8	21.9
	32.0	31.7	28.1	Inventory		21.4		29.4	27.1	32.4
	3.0	3.2	2.7	All Other Current		1.8		4.3	3.3	1.6
	66.5	66.4	63.5	Total Current		48.0		71.1	66.5	64.1
	20.5	20.2	23.8	Fixed Assets (net)		36.8		23.1	19.6	21.4
	6.9	7.5	6.3	Intangibles (net)		13.7		.2	5.1	7.2
	6.1	5.9	6.3	All Other Non-Current		1.5		5.7	8.8	7.3
	100.0	100.0	100.0	Total		100.0		100.0	100.0	100.0

				LIABILITIES						
	9.3	9.1	7.5	Notes Payable-Short Term		7.5		8.6	4.4	7.3
	3.5	3.2	5.4	Cur. Mat.-L.T.D.		3.9		4.6	2.4	5.9
	11.8	13.1	11.3	Trade Payables		7.3		16.7	10.8	10.3
	.4	.5	.1	Income Taxes Payable		.1		.0	.4	.1
	7.7	8.8	7.1	All Other Current		3.3		7.6	6.7	8.3
	32.7	34.7	31.4	Total Current		22.1		37.5	24.7	31.9
	15.2	13.6	22.8	Long-Term Debt		21.6		17.1	15.5	14.1
	.4	.5	.4	Deferred Taxes		.0		.3	.6	.8
	7.7	7.3	7.5	All Other Non-Current		9.9		8.6	5.0	9.3
	44.0	43.9	37.8	Net Worth		46.4		36.5	54.2	43.8
	100.0	100.0	100.0	Total Liabilties & Net Worth		100.0		100.0	100.0	100.0

				INCOME DATA						
	100.0	100.0	100.0	Net Sales		100.0		100.0	100.0	100.0
	33.2	34.1	31.4	Gross Profit		31.9		29.6	31.2	25.9
	25.3	25.1	27.1	Operating Expenses		28.3		26.6	23.1	20.7
	7.9	8.9	4.4	Operating Profit		3.5		2.9	8.1	5.2
	1.3	1.0	1.4	All Other Expenses (net)		1.5		.8	.8	1.6
	6.6	7.9	3.0	Profit Before Taxes		2.0		2.1	7.3	3.6

				RATIOS						
	4.3	3.2	3.6	Current		4.8		4.9	3.7	3.3
	2.1	2.0	2.1			2.5		1.8	2.8	2.0
	1.3	1.3	1.4			.8		1.3	1.9	1.6
	1.8	1.9	2.0	Quick		2.4		2.9	2.5	1.6
	1.0	.9	1.1			1.2		.8	1.3	1.0
	.6	.5	.6			.3		.6	.9	.5
35	10.6	30 12.1	35 10.5	Sales/Receivables	25 14.5		38 9.6	40 9.2	30 12.1	
45	8.2	39 9.5	45 8.1		37 9.8		44 8.2	50 7.3	45 8.1	
56	6.5	51 7.2	60 6.1		56 6.6		53 6.9	66 5.5	59 6.2	
65	5.6	62 5.9	47 7.7	Cost of Sales/Inventory	47 7.8		17 21.5	52 7.0	68 5.4	
91	4.0	99 3.7	85 4.3		68 5.4		59 6.2	86 4.2	101 3.6	
124	2.9	133 2.7	142 2.6		113 3.2		117 3.1	135 2.7	140 2.6	
16	22.1	14 25.3	17 21.2	Cost of Sales/Payables	19 19.0		19 19.4	12 31.0	20 18.5	
29	12.6	27 13.6	28 13.2		24 15.1		40 9.1	29 12.7	26 13.8	
41	8.9	42 8.8	43 8.4		39 9.3		53 6.9	47 7.8	37 9.9	
	3.5	4.3	3.7	Sales/Working Capital		4.0		4.6	2.8	3.9
	6.0	7.1	5.3			7.5		8.9	4.3	5.0
	12.4	14.1	14.2			-39.9		16.3	6.2	8.0
	19.5	21.7	10.5	EBIT/Interest		7.2		5.7	34.9	10.5
(74)	6.3	(81) 7.0	(87) 3.7		(12) 2.7		(17) 3.7	(22) 14.2	(27) 4.8	
	2.0	3.0	.7			-3.3		.8	1.4	.4
	11.6	9.8	6.7	Net Profit + Depr., Dep., Amort./Cur. Mat. L/T/D					9.7	8.1
(28)	3.5	(42) 3.5	(42) 2.0					(13) 4.4	(18) 1.1	
	1.3	1.7	.7						2.5	.0
	.2	.2	.2	Fixed/Worth		.5		.3	.2	.3
	.5	.5	.6			1.4		.6	.4	.6
	1.4	1.7	2.2			NM		1.3	.8	1.8
	.4	.6	.7	Debt/Worth		.6		.8	.4	.7
	1.4	1.5	1.6			2.4		1.8	.7	1.5
	5.6	3.8	6.8			NM		4.0	2.2	6.2
	55.0	58.4	40.2	% Profit Before Taxes/Tangible Net Worth		50.9		25.9	47.8	44.5
(70)	28.8	(80) 27.4	(82) 17.8		(10) 4.1		(17) 17.1	(22) 25.1	(26) 15.3	
	10.1	10.6	-1.6			-26.8		-2.5	4.2	-8.7
	20.5	23.3	12.8	% Profit Before Taxes/Total Assets		10.7		9.7	26.3	12.6
	12.1	10.1	6.0			6.7		5.4	9.1	6.3
	3.2	4.0	-1.4			-8.4		.1	.8	-2.3
	24.1	31.9	17.4	Sales/Net Fixed Assets		8.6		24.5	16.3	15.0
	10.2	10.8	8.4			5.6		11.2	8.9	9.6
	5.9	6.4	4.7			2.0		4.7	5.4	5.1
	2.3	2.4	2.3	Sales/Total Assets		2.1		2.7	2.0	2.3
	1.9	1.9	1.8			1.4		2.0	1.7	1.5
	1.5	1.3	1.2			1.0		1.8	1.3	1.2
	1.1	.6	1.1	% Depr., Dep., Amort./Sales		1.3		.9	1.0	1.3
(73)	2.0	(84) 1.5	(88) 2.0		(12) 2.8		1.4	(21) 1.8	(25) 2.7	
	3.4	3.2	5.3			6.8		6.6	4.9	4.2
	1.2	1.2	2.7	% Officers', Directors' Owners' Comp/Sales				1.9		
(18)	2.5	(18) 3.8	(30) 4.7			(10)	3.1			
	7.0	6.6	8.2					5.6		
2725889M		4034028M	2674664M	Net Sales ($)	2557M	27488M	33997M	133395M	387897M	2089330M
1589412M		2447944M	1749954M	Total Assets ($)	2800M	20840M	31404M	64288M	259869M	1370753M

M = $ thousand   MM = $ million
See Pages 9 through 22 for Explanation of Ratios and Data

MANUFACTURING—Ball and Roller Bearing Manufacturing NAICS 332991

	Current Data Sorted by Assets						Comparative Historical Data	
Type of Statement	**0-500M**	**500M-2MM**	**2-10MM**	**10-50MM**	**50-100MM**	**100-250MM**	**4/1/05-3/31/06 ALL**	**4/1/06-3/31/07 ALL**
Unqualified				6	6		4	10
Reviewed			5	1			5	9
Compiled			1				10	6
Tax Returns	2	1					1	
Other	1	1	2	3	4	3	7	9
(period)		5 (4/1-9/30/09)		31 (10/1/09-3/31/10)				
NUMBER OF STATEMENTS	3	2	8	10	10	3	27	34
	%	%	%	%	%	%	%	%
ASSETS								
Cash & Equivalents				4.3	2.7		8.9	7.0
Trade Receivables (net)				18.0	19.1		29.1	23.9
Inventory				32.4	28.3		30.7	31.0
All Other Current				4.4	3.4		2.2	3.2
Total Current				59.0	53.5		70.9	65.2
Fixed Assets (net)				27.7	24.7		18.9	22.7
Intangibles (net)				8.9	5.2		2.0	2.9
All Other Non-Current				4.4	16.7		8.3	9.2
Total				100.0	100.0		100.0	100.0
LIABILITIES								
Notes Payable-Short Term				14.4	10.4		10.6	12.3
Cur. Mat.-L.T.D.				4.6	4.7		2.7	2.8
Trade Payables				9.3	11.7		16.4	11.4
Income Taxes Payable				.0	.0		.5	.2
All Other Current				9.1	8.1		9.6	10.7
Total Current				37.4	34.9		39.7	37.4
Long-Term Debt				17.4	14.6		10.9	9.7
Deferred Taxes				.4	1.7		.4	.4
All Other Non-Current				4.6	5.5		10.0	6.9
Net Worth				40.4	43.4		38.9	45.6
Total Liabilities & Net Worth				100.0	100.0		100.0	100.0
INCOME DATA								
Net Sales				100.0	100.0		100.0	100.0
Gross Profit				23.2	17.7		30.7	27.5
Operating Expenses				19.6	15.8		22.5	19.8
Operating Profit				3.6	1.9		8.1	7.7
All Other Expenses (net)				2.4	.3		.7	2.0
Profit Before Taxes				1.2	1.6		7.4	5.7
RATIOS								
Current				2.5	3.0		3.6	3.5
				1.4	2.2		2.4	1.8
				1.1	1.0		1.2	1.2
Quick				1.0	1.1		1.9	1.7
				.4	1.0		.9	.8
				.3	.4		.5	.5
Sales/Receivables				28 13.1	33 11.1		34 10.6	41 8.8
				43 8.6	53 6.8		48 7.6	53 6.9
				57 6.4	66 5.5		56 6.5	62 5.9
Cost of Sales/Inventory				44 8.4	67 5.5		43 8.5	54 6.8
				118 3.1	89 4.1		72 5.1	96 3.8
				175 2.1	146 2.5		127 2.9	139 2.6
Cost of Sales/Payables				19 19.6	10 35.8		14 25.8	15 24.6
				26 14.1	36 10.1		35 10.5	33 11.0
				39 9.5	46 7.9		52 7.0	51 7.2
Sales/Working Capital				4.5	2.9		3.0	3.1
				9.9	5.0		5.2	5.5
				NM	NM		29.8	18.6
EBIT/Interest				8.7	8.6		22.5	18.7
				2.4	1.9		(22) 5.9	(31) 4.4
				1.0	-.7		2.2	2.1
Net Profit + Depr., Dep., Amort./Cur. Mat. L/T/D								8.9
							(11)	4.9
								1.1
Fixed/Worth				.4	.2		.1	.1
				1.1	1.0		.4	.5
				1.9	1.8		1.5	.9
Debt/Worth				1.0	.4		.6	.5
				2.0	2.3		.9	1.4
				3.0	4.2		5.4	2.9
% Profit Before Taxes/Tangible Net Worth					14.2		54.3	38.9
					-.9		(22) 21.6	(31) 21.1
					-44.3		13.1	2.5
% Profit Before Taxes/Total Assets				6.9	6.5		21.0	15.3
				2.8	.3		9.4	7.2
				.3	-6.9		3.6	2.1
Sales/Net Fixed Assets				13.1	7.6		40.6	20.9
				5.1	4.9		11.2	7.0
				3.6	4.7		5.9	4.3
Sales/Total Assets				2.0	1.7		2.8	2.1
				1.4	1.5		1.9	1.7
				1.3	1.0		1.5	1.3
% Depr., Dep., Amort./Sales				1.4			1.1	1.4
				2.7			(22) 2.0	(29) 2.3
				4.7			3.9	3.8
% Officers', Directors' Owners' Comp/Sales								
Net Sales ($)	3493M	8803M	75351M	335625M	1028178M	392122M	407133M	1497887M
Total Assets ($)	1126M	3331M	46315M	219599M	715359M	498269M	274204M	918297M

© RMA 2010

M = $ thousand   MM = $ million
See Pages 9 through 22 for Explanation of Ratios and Data

Comparative Historical Data

Current Data Sorted by Sales

						Type of Statement	0-1MM	1-3MM	3-5MM	5-10MM	10-25MM	25MM & OVER
	8		7		12	Unqualified					3	9
	6		7		6	Reviewed			1	2	2	1
	2		4		1	Compiled				1		
	5		2		3	Tax Returns						
	9		14		14	Other	1	3		2	2	9
	4/1/07-3/31/08 ALL		4/1/08-3/31/09 ALL		4/1/09-3/31/10 ALL			5 (4/1-9/30/09)			31 (10/1/09-3/31/10)	
	30		34		36	NUMBER OF STATEMENTS	1	3	1	5	7	19
	%		%		%	ASSETS	%	%	%	%	%	%
	12.2		8.9		10.9	Cash & Equivalents						5.5
	25.1		22.4		21.5	Trade Receivables (net)						18.6
	32.1		31.7		28.2	Inventory						28.0
	3.4		1.8		2.8	All Other Current						3.9
	72.7		64.8		63.3	Total Current						56.0
	18.9		20.9		24.2	Fixed Assets (net)						25.3
	3.3		4.8		4.2	Intangibles (net)						4.8
	5.0		9.6		8.3	All Other Non-Current						13.9
	100.0		100.0		100.0	Total						100.0
						LIABILITIES						
	10.7		10.1		9.3	Notes Payable-Short Term						9.6
	2.0		1.9		3.0	Cur. Mat.-L.T.D.						3.8
	13.3		9.9		9.3	Trade Payables						10.3
	.4		.2		.0	Income Taxes Payable						.1
	12.1		9.7		9.4	All Other Current						8.7
	38.5		31.7		31.0	Total Current						32.5
	9.7		9.9		14.6	Long-Term Debt						15.2
	.4		.4		.6	Deferred Taxes						1.2
	8.7		7.3		4.4	All Other Non-Current						6.6
	42.8		50.9		49.4	Net Worth						44.4
	100.0		100.0		100.0	Total Liabilities & Net Worth						100.0
						INCOME DATA						
	100.0		100.0		100.0	Net Sales						100.0
	29.6		28.7		26.4	Gross Profit						18.6
	20.3		19.4		22.0	Operating Expenses						16.1
	9.3		9.3		4.4	Operating Profit						2.6
	1.8		.9		1.7	All Other Expenses (net)						1.7
	7.5		8.4		2.7	Profit Before Taxes						.8
						RATIOS						
	4.4		4.5		4.2	Current						3.6
	2.2		2.1		2.1							2.0
	1.4		1.5		1.2							1.2
	1.8		2.3		2.5	Quick						1.1
	.9		1.0		.9							.9
	.6		.4		.4							.4
36	10.2	40	9.1	30	12.0	Sales/Receivables					33	11.0
45	8.0	45	8.1	47	7.8						48	7.7
53	6.8	58	6.3	66	5.5						66	5.5
43	8.6	42	8.7	46	7.9	Cost of Sales/Inventory					59	6.2
93	3.9	115	3.2	81	4.5						97	3.8
131	2.8	159	2.3	147	2.5						148	2.5
17	21.3	17	21.2	12	29.6	Cost of Sales/Payables					12	30.5
30	12.1	29	12.6	26	14.1						31	12.0
47	7.8	42	8.7	46	8.0						45	8.1
	3.1		3.0		2.8	Sales/Working Capital						2.9
	4.3		4.2		5.2							5.0
	10.5		13.6		13.8							15.4
	18.1		28.5		12.5	EBIT/Interest						8.6
(27)	7.2	(29)	6.1	(33)	2.9						(18)	3.1
	2.6		2.7		.4							.0
	51.2		13.6		2.9	Net Profit + Depr., Dep., Amort./Cur. Mat. L/T/D						
(12)	8.1	(11)	2.6	(10)	1.1							
	2.7		1.4		.4							
	.1		.1		.2	Fixed/Worth						.3
	.4		.5		.6							.9
	1.4		1.2		1.5							1.7
	.4		.3		.3	Debt/Worth						.4
	1.5		1.6		1.9							2.0
	3.8		2.5		2.6							3.8
	42.4		49.8		16.7	% Profit Before Taxes/Tangible Net Worth						16.7
(26)	24.5	(32)	20.2	(34)	4.5						(18)	3.0
	12.2		14.4		-5.6							-13.6
	16.5		15.9		9.0	% Profit Before Taxes/Total Assets						6.2
	11.5		7.8		1.8							1.8
	3.1		4.2		-1.2							-1.3
	42.3		17.4		14.1	Sales/Net Fixed Assets						11.0
	9.4		8.0		5.5							4.9
	5.4		4.6		4.2							4.0
	2.3		1.9		1.9	Sales/Total Assets						2.0
	1.6		1.7		1.4							1.5
	1.3		1.1		1.1							.9
	.9		1.0		1.8	% Depr., Dep., Amort./Sales						1.5
(24)	1.9	(29)	1.9	(31)	2.6						(17)	2.6
	3.0		3.4		3.3							3.1
						% Officers', Directors' Owners' Comp/Sales						
	1087561M		1257695M		1843572M	Net Sales ($)	275M	5658M	3709M	33453M	118022M	1682455M
	772286M		1046857M		1483999M	Total Assets ($)	283M	2751M	3878M	19239M	80537M	1377311M

M = $ thousand   MM = $ million
See Pages 9 through 22 for Explanation of Ratios and Data

Current Data Sorted by Assets | **Comparative Historical Data**

Type of Statement	0-500M	500M-2MM	2-10MM	10-50MM	50-100MM	100-250MM		4/1/05-3/31/06 ALL	4/1/06-3/31/07 ALL
Unqualified			6	10	5	1		19	22
Reviewed		1	12	5				20	23
Compiled		2	5					18	21
Tax Returns		4						12	5
Other	2	5	12	15	5	3		23	25
NUMBER OF STATEMENTS	2	12	35	30	10	4		92	96
ASSETS	%	%	%	%	%	%		%	%
Cash & Equivalents		9.9	8.9	9.2	17.9			8.3	9.6
Trade Receivables (net)		34.8	27.1	27.7	16.9			33.7	35.4
Inventory		19.3	25.0	25.3	22.4			25.5	25.1
All Other Current		3.6	5.4	2.5	10.6			2.8	3.2
Total Current		67.8	66.4	64.6	67.8			70.3	73.3
Fixed Assets (net)		22.1	25.9	25.4	21.1			22.8	20.8
Intangibles (net)		.5	3.6	6.4	6.9			1.7	1.9
All Other Non-Current		9.7	4.1	3.6	4.2			5.2	4.0
Total		100.0	100.0	100.0	100.0			100.0	100.0
LIABILITIES									
Notes Payable-Short Term		22.0	11.6	8.7	5.8			11.7	12.0
Cur. Mat.-L.T.D.		1.6	3.7	2.4	4.9			3.5	3.4
Trade Payables		20.0	14.4	11.1	5.1			16.4	16.4
Income Taxes Payable		.0	.5	.4	2.7			.6	.3
All Other Current		4.2	9.9	10.2	17.3			8.9	8.5
Total Current		47.8	40.1	32.9	35.7			41.1	40.6
Long-Term Debt		14.0	13.2	11.7	9.8			17.2	14.8
Deferred Taxes		.0	.6	.8	.8			.6	.5
All Other Non-Current		4.1	2.5	6.5	5.3			5.1	4.4
Net Worth		34.1	43.7	48.1	48.5			35.9	39.7
Total Liabilities & Net Worth		100.0	100.0	100.0	100.0			100.0	100.0
INCOME DATA									
Net Sales		100.0	100.0	100.0	100.0			100.0	100.0
Gross Profit		34.3	29.7	24.2	19.5			29.0	28.0
Operating Expenses		31.9	25.0	16.1	8.0			23.4	19.9
Operating Profit		2.4	4.7	8.1	11.5			5.6	8.1
All Other Expenses (net)		.7	.6	.9	2.7			.9	.9
Profit Before Taxes		1.7	4.1	7.2	8.7			4.7	7.3
RATIOS									
Current		2.9	3.2	2.7	4.7			2.6	3.1
		1.4	1.5	2.1	2.1			1.8	1.9
		1.2	1.0	1.5	1.2			1.3	1.3
Quick		1.8	2.0	1.5	2.2			1.6	1.9
		.9	.8	1.1	.9			1.0	1.1
		.7	.4	.7	.6			.7	.7
Sales/Receivables	31 11.9	32 11.3	43 8.4	30 12.1				39 9.4	40 9.1
	52 7.0	41 8.8	52 7.0	41 8.9				52 7.0	51 7.2
	64 5.7	63 5.8	62 5.9	66 5.6				66 5.5	65 5.6
Cost of Sales/Inventory	8 47.9	26 14.2	45 8.1	17 21.4				27 13.6	21 17.7
	45 8.0	56 6.5	55 6.6	93 3.9				50 7.3	58 6.3
	79 4.6	116 3.2	86 4.2	146 2.5				92 4.0	87 4.2
Cost of Sales/Payables	23 16.0	19 19.3	12 31.5	1 273.9				21 17.5	15 24.0
	32 11.3	30 12.1	22 16.4	14 26.6				31 11.7	29 12.6
	85 4.3	54 6.7	34 10.7	27 13.4				52 7.0	53 6.9
Sales/Working Capital		6.6	5.2	4.7	2.3			5.1	4.4
		10.7	8.5	6.7	3.2			7.4	7.1
		49.9	-999.8	10.6	65.2			15.2	13.8
EBIT/Interest		14.5	18.4	15.1				14.4	18.5
	(11) 4.2	(32) 3.0	(28) 4.5					(86) 5.8	(87) 6.8
	-8.0	.9	1.8					2.1	2.9
Net Profit + Depr., Dep., Amort./Cur. Mat. L/T/D			3.4	22.0				7.4	17.7
		(10) 2.5	(11) 2.5					(27) 3.9	(31) 5.2
		1.5	2.1					1.9	2.2
Fixed/Worth		.3	.2	.3	.2			.3	.2
		.6	.5	.6	.4			.5	.4
		1.2	2.2	1.3	2.1			1.3	.9
Debt/Worth		.8	.4	.7	.5			.7	.5
		1.5	2.1	1.4	1.9			1.7	1.3
		7.5	3.9	2.3	4.0			3.3	3.2
% Profit Before Taxes/Tangible Net Worth		66.8	58.3	48.9	67.3			51.2	60.3
	(10) 45.2	(32) 10.0	(28) 22.5	31.9				(84) 23.4	(86) 32.0
	-4.1	1.7	4.5	8.9				5.9	14.6
% Profit Before Taxes/Total Assets		26.2	30.6	20.4	12.8			20.2	23.1
		9.7	3.4	9.5	9.2			8.0	13.7
		-3.5	-1.2	2.1	5.1			1.7	5.0
Sales/Net Fixed Assets		32.9	28.4	15.3	17.7			26.3	32.3
		14.2	8.3	8.0	6.1			12.1	14.1
		7.6	4.3	4.3	5.0			6.0	7.9
Sales/Total Assets		3.0	3.0	2.7	2.4			3.0	3.3
		2.7	2.1	1.8	1.2			2.2	2.2
		2.1	1.3	1.5	.7			1.7	1.7
% Depr., Dep., Amort./Sales		1.2	.8	1.4				1.0	.8
	(10) 2.4	(33) 1.6	(29) 2.7					(85) 1.7	(85) 1.6
	3.0	3.2	4.5					2.9	2.8
% Officers', Directors' Owners' Comp/Sales			2.2					1.9	1.6
	(13) 3.2							(41) 2.5	(32) 2.9
		5.5						7.2	6.3
Net Sales ($)	3100M	34136M	371748M	1207667M	2796560M	1120247M		3580176M	3364256M
Total Assets ($)	707M	13205M	176722M	618432M	762059M	680686M		1892572M	1756949M

17 (4/1-9/30/09) 76 (10/1/09-3/31/10)

© RMA 2010

M = $ thousand   MM = $ million
See Pages 9 through 22 for Explanation of Ratios and Data

Comparative Historical Data

Current Data Sorted by Sales

			Type of Statement						
16	28	22	Unqualified		1	1	1	7	12
18	18	18	Reviewed		3	6		4	4
18	16	7	Compiled		1	2	2	2	
9	10	4	Tax Returns		2				
31	37	42	Other		6	3		16	17
4/1/07-3/31/08	4/1/08-3/31/09	4/1/09-3/31/10			17 (4/1-9/30/09)			76 (10/1/09-3/31/10)	
ALL	ALL	ALL		0-1MM	1-3MM	3-5MM	5-10MM	10-25MM	25MM & OVER
92	109	93	NUMBER OF STATEMENTS		13	9	9	29	33
%	%	%	ASSETS	%	%	%	%	%	%
11.3	11.5	11.1	Cash & Equivalents	D	22.5			6.6	13.6
32.5	28.5	26.6	Trade Receivables (net)	A	22.3			29.6	25.8
21.3	26.3	24.0	Inventory	T	16.5			23.8	25.8
5.3	4.0	4.6	All Other Current	A	6.4			4.1	4.7
70.3	70.4	66.4	Total Current		67.8			64.1	69.9
22.4	23.2	24.6	Fixed Assets (net)	N	22.6			23.5	23.5
3.3	2.5	4.5	Intangibles (net)	O	3.4			8.0	2.9
4.0	3.9	4.5	All Other Non-Current	T	6.2			4.4	3.7
100.0	100.0	100.0	Total		100.0			100.0	100.0
			LIABILITIES	A					
9.2	10.3	11.3	Notes Payable-Short Term	V	18.7			12.3	6.2
4.0	4.1	3.1	Cur. Mat.-L.T.D.	A	1.2			3.3	3.0
14.9	14.0	12.6	Trade Payables	I	15.1			14.4	9.4
.5	.5	.6	Income Taxes Payable	L	.4			.5	1.1
13.0	10.6	9.7	All Other Current	A	4.7			7.6	12.4
41.5	39.5	37.3	Total Current	B	40.2			38.1	32.2
15.5	13.6	12.0	Long-Term Debt	L	15.1			10.0	11.2
.6	.5	.6	Deferred Taxes	E	.4			.8	.8
4.7	4.5	4.3	All Other Non-Current		2.6			5.1	5.0
37.6	41.8	45.7	Net Worth		41.6			46.0	50.8
100.0	100.0	100.0	Total Liabilities & Net Worth		100.0			100.0	100.0
			INCOME DATA						
100.0	100.0	100.0	Net Sales		100.0			100.0	100.0
29.6	28.7	27.2	Gross Profit		32.5			26.7	23.3
21.0	20.1	21.0	Operating Expenses		32.2			21.0	13.4
8.6	8.6	6.2	Operating Profit		.3			5.6	9.9
1.3	1.0	.9	All Other Expenses (net)		.9			.3	1.3
7.3	7.7	5.3	Profit Before Taxes		-.6			5.3	8.5
			RATIOS						
2.9	3.0	3.0			4.3			2.5	3.4
1.7	1.9	1.9	Current		1.4			1.9	2.3
1.2	1.2	1.2			1.1			1.2	1.6
1.8	2.1	1.9			3.6			1.5	2.0
1.0	.9	1.0	Quick		1.0			.9	1.2
.7	.6	.6			.6			.7	.8
35 10.5	31 11.7	34 10.9		26 13.9			34 10.9	37 9.8
47 7.7	40 9.1	49 7.5	Sales/Receivables	37 9.8			49 7.5	51 7.2
66 5.6	54 6.8	62 5.9		67 5.4			63 5.8	61 6.0
19 19.5	28 13.3	31 11.8		12 29.5			31 11.8	35 10.4
41 8.9	50 7.4	56 6.5	Cost of Sales/Inventory	65 5.7			48 7.6	57 6.4
69 5.3	93 3.9	96 3.8		101 3.6			82 4.4	96 3.8
16 22.8	15 24.9	14 25.2		12 30.3			19 19.4	11 34.1
26 14.1	24 15.2	24 15.1	Cost of Sales/Payables	28 13.2			30 12.1	19 18.8
46 7.9	43 8.5	40 9.1		77 4.8			47 7.8	31 11.8
4.7	5.0	4.3			5.7			5.6	3.1
8.2	8.4	7.2	Sales/Working Capital		9.9			7.4	5.2
22.5	23.6	25.7			42.9			31.8	9.0
19.3	22.2	14.1			10.8			18.5	18.9
(84) 6.2	(97) 5.8	(85) 4.5	EBIT/Interest	(10) 3.3			(27) 3.3	(30) 7.3
2.2	2.1	1.5			-2.0			1.1	3.1
10.8	17.2	8.0	Net Profit + Depr., Dep.,					3.2	12.9
(28) 4.2	(33) 4.2	(28) 2.5	Amort./Cur. Mat. L/T/D				(10) 2.2	(15) 3.0
1.8	2.1	1.6						1.5	1.8
.2	.2	.2			.1			.3	.2
.5	.4	.5	Fixed/Worth		.8			.5	.4
1.6	1.3	1.6			2.6			1.6	1.0
.7	.5	.6			.5			.5	.5
1.6	1.4	1.4	Debt/Worth		1.4			1.5	1.2
5.4	3.0	3.3			7.0			3.3	2.3
59.8	64.1	54.3			57.3			54.3	53.9
(81) 42.9	(100) 37.5	(86) 20.5	% Profit Before Taxes/Tangible Net Worth	(11) 35.5			(26) 19.3	31.7
12.6	14.2	4.1			-2.9			2.2	11.2
25.0	26.3	21.2			22.6			32.1	20.1
13.2	12.8	7.6	% Profit Before Taxes/Total Assets		7.3			5.0	11.7
4.5	4.9	.9			-4.5			.3	5.1
33.0	26.3	23.8			78.0			27.6	17.2
13.3	11.8	9.1	Sales/Net Fixed Assets		8.8			11.1	9.2
7.1	6.3	4.5			4.7			4.6	5.0
3.1	3.2	2.9			3.2			3.1	2.8
2.3	2.3	2.0	Sales/Total Assets		2.0			2.0	2.1
1.6	1.7	1.4			1.1			1.5	1.3
.7	.6	1.0						1.2	.9
(83) 1.4	(94) 1.7	(84) 2.2	% Depr., Dep., Amort./Sales				(28) 1.8	(30) 2.3
2.5	2.9	3.2						3.7	2.8
2.0	1.5	2.1							
(35) 3.0	(39) 3.4	(28) 3.1	% Officers', Directors' Owners' Comp/Sales					
8.3	5.2	5.7							
4012676M	5355596M	5533458M	Net Sales ($)		28705M	34400M	61325M	489367M	4919661M
1954561M	2467769M	2251811M	Total Assets ($)		19927M	24044M	40992M	261150M	1905698M

M = $ thousand   MM = $ million
See Pages 9 through 22 for Explanation of Ratios and Data

Current Data Sorted by Assets | Comparative Historical Data

Type of Statement dates: 103 (4/1–9/30/09); 433 (10/1/09–3/31/10). Comparative periods: 4/1/05–3/31/06 ALL; 4/1/06–3/31/07 ALL.

Type of Statement	0-500M	500M-2MM	2-10MM	10-50MM	50-100MM	100-250MM	4/1/05-3/31/06 ALL	4/1/06-3/31/07 ALL
Unqualified		3	11	24	8	11	70	69
Reviewed		8	78	23			134	118
Compiled	6	36	42	6			97	86
Tax Returns	34	43	28	2			69	98
Other	7	38	67	42	10	9	195	192
NUMBER OF STATEMENTS	47	128	226	97	18	20	565	563

ASSETS	%	%	%	%	%	%	%	%
Cash & Equivalents	8.1	12.2	10.2	10.1	11.9	7.8	8.9	8.2
Trade Receivables (net)	23.9	25.0	22.3	19.0	16.1	18.0	28.9	27.4
Inventory	12.6	22.5	25.6	26.2	20.8	19.1	23.8	24.7
All Other Current	3.3	2.3	2.9	2.8	2.4	4.8	2.5	3.0
Total Current	47.9	62.1	61.0	58.1	51.3	49.7	64.1	63.3
Fixed Assets (net)	39.2	26.0	29.2	28.1	25.8	25.5	27.1	28.3
Intangibles (net)	6.1	5.2	3.5	8.1	18.9	17.7	2.7	3.1
All Other Non-Current	6.6	6.8	6.3	5.8	4.0	7.0	6.1	5.3
Total	100.0	100.0	100.0	100.0	100.0	100.0	100.0	100.0

LIABILITIES								
Notes Payable-Short Term	24.4	15.2	10.1	7.0	11.3	6.0	12.0	11.1
Cur. Mat.-L.T.D.	6.3	6.1	4.3	3.1	1.9	3.8	3.9	5.3
Trade Payables	21.1	12.2	11.3	9.9	11.4	8.4	15.4	15.3
Income Taxes Payable	.0	.1	.2	.2	.2	.4	.3	.3
All Other Current	15.6	8.2	8.1	8.3	8.0	9.4	10.2	9.6
Total Current	67.4	41.7	33.9	28.6	32.8	28.0	41.8	41.7
Long-Term Debt	32.1	21.3	17.3	15.5	16.9	25.0	18.8	17.8
Deferred Taxes	.0	.2	.6	.8	.5	2.9	.5	.4
All Other Non-Current	25.3	7.5	5.2	6.3	12.2	4.6	5.6	6.9
Net Worth	-24.7	29.4	43.0	48.8	37.5	39.5	33.3	33.2
Total Liabilities & Net Worth	100.0	100.0	100.0	100.0	100.0	100.0	100.0	100.0

INCOME DATA								
Net Sales	100.0	100.0	100.0	100.0	100.0	100.0	100.0	100.0
Gross Profit	45.0	37.5	29.0	23.4	24.1	22.7	30.4	30.2
Operating Expenses	42.4	35.0	25.4	18.4	20.1	16.8	24.8	24.3
Operating Profit	2.6	2.5	3.6	5.0	4.0	5.9	5.6	5.9
All Other Expenses (net)	2.8	1.5	1.5	1.5	3.4	3.1	.9	1.2
Profit Before Taxes	-.2	1.0	2.2	3.5	.6	2.8	4.7	4.6

RATIOS

Ratio	0-500M	500M-2MM	2-10MM	10-50MM	50-100MM	100-250MM	4/1/05-3/31/06 ALL	4/1/06-3/31/07 ALL
Current	1.7	3.3	3.5	3.3	3.6	2.4	2.6	2.9
	1.1	1.8	1.9	2.1	1.4	2.0	1.6	1.7
	.5	1.0	1.2	1.4	1.0	1.3	1.2	1.1
Quick	1.3	2.4	2.1	1.8	2.0	1.4	1.6	1.6
	.6	1.1	.9	1.0	.8	.9	.9 (562)	.9
	.5	.5	.5	.6	.5	.6	.6	.5
Sales/Receivables	0 UND	25 14.4	29 12.6	30 12.2	36 10.3	39 9.4	31 11.8	28 13.0
	18 19.8	38 9.7	39 9.3	41 9.0	46 8.0	54 6.8	44 8.2	42 8.6
	43 8.5	50 7.2	54 6.8	54 6.7	51 7.2	65 5.6	59 6.2	58 6.3
Cost of Sales/Inventory	0 UND	21 17.8	29 12.6	44 8.2	45 8.1	46 8.0	20 18.3	22 16.4
	11 34.2	46 8.0	62 5.9	66 5.5	81 4.5	73 5.0	50 7.3	51 7.2
	51 7.2	85 4.3	115 3.2	108 3.4	95 3.9	99 3.7	82 4.4	83 4.4
Cost of Sales/Payables	0 UND	12 31.3	14 26.6	15 23.7	15 24.0	21 17.1	17 21.8	16 23.3
	16 23.3	23 16.0	25 14.5	22 16.6	26 13.9	30 12.3	30 12.2	29 12.8
	54 6.8	39 9.4	41 9.0	36 10.1	48 7.7	38 9.5	44 8.4	46 7.9
Sales/Working Capital	14.2	4.5	3.5	3.8	3.1	3.6	5.4	5.4
	204.0	9.0	8.0	5.5	5.6	6.4	9.8	9.2
	-13.1	NM	27.3	10.7	NM	11.9	33.2	39.6
EBIT/Interest	8.8	5.8	8.6	17.6	5.5	7.0	12.3	12.8
	(38) .6	(109) 1.7	(205) 2.1	(89) 4.1	(16) 1.1	3.3	(505) 4.4	(513) 4.2
	-2.9	-2.6	-.3	-.6	-4.8	.8	1.6	1.6
Net Profit + Depr., Dep., Amort./Cur. Mat. L/T/D		4.7	4.7	12.5	8.7	2.8	6.4	7.2
	(16) 2.1	(67) 2.1	(31) 2.5	(11) 2.2	(10) 1.8		(141) 2.6	(144) 3.1
		-.5	.8	.3	-.1	-.2	1.3	1.5
Fixed/Worth	.3	.3	.3	.3	.5	.5	.3	.3
	-18.3	.9	.7	.7	1.7	.9	.7	.7
	-.8	-3.2	2.0	1.4	-1.2	NM	1.9	2.3
Debt/Worth	3.9	.6	.6	.5	.7	1.1	.7	.7
	-14.9	1.9	1.5	1.1	3.7	2.0	1.8	1.8
	-2.7	-11.7	4.1	2.8	-4.1	NM	5.0	6.0
% Profit Before Taxes/Tangible Net Worth	27.3	47.6	36.2	30.0	24.8	27.2	50.3	49.0
	(18) 3.9	(93) 11.9	(201) 11.1	(84) 13.9	(11) 8.3	(15) 9.0	(497) 23.2	(492) 24.7
	-17.4	-13.0	-4.4	-4.1	-24.2	4.7	6.2	8.2
% Profit Before Taxes/Total Assets	10.6	12.4	13.5	14.4	9.2	8.5	18.9	18.9
	-1.1	3.0	2.9	6.3	1.8	3.8	7.8	8.5
	-13.5	-8.9	-3.5	-2.6	-5.9	-.5	2.0	2.0
Sales/Net Fixed Assets	34.0	26.9	17.6	11.6	18.1	7.3	24.0	21.9
	13.1	13.8	7.6	6.3	5.1	5.5	10.2	9.2
	5.7	5.5	3.6	3.7	2.9	3.7	5.5	5.1
Sales/Total Assets	5.6	3.0	2.5	2.0	1.5	1.7	3.0	3.1
	3.6	2.3	1.7	1.5	1.3	1.4	2.2	2.2
	2.0	1.7	1.3	1.1	.9	.7	1.7	1.6
% Depr., Dep., Amort./Sales	1.5	1.3	1.1	1.7	1.5	1.9	1.0	1.0
	(36) 2.9	(100) 3.2	(208) 2.8	(84) 2.7	3.0	(14) 2.8	(498) 2.1	(479) 2.2
	5.8	5.5	5.8	5.1	6.8	5.6	3.6	4.0
% Officers', Directors' Owners' Comp/Sales	3.2	4.0	2.1	.8			2.2	2.2
	(31) 7.5	(70) 5.9	(101) 4.4	(20) 2.5			(247) 4.4	(240) 4.0
	11.2	9.7	7.0	3.6			7.9	6.9
Net Sales ($)	52816M	345740M	2147448M	3249951M	1497915M	4712069M	13591316M	15580360M
Total Assets ($)	13445M	142799M	1100770M	2006866M	1209392M	3524122M	6137112M	7417099M

Comparative Historical Data

Current Data Sorted by Sales

66	55	57	Type of Statement: Unqualified	1	1	2	3	17	33
114	121	109	Reviewed		9	16	30	42	12
92	79	90	Compiled	5	29	19	24	10	3
84	83	107	Tax Returns	19	39	27	15	6	1
186	199	173	Other	7	32	20	27	41	46
4/1/07-3/31/08 ALL	4/1/08-3/31/09 ALL	4/1/09-3/31/10 ALL		0-1MM	103 (4/1-9/30/09) 1-3MM	3-5MM	5-10MM	433 (10/1/09-3/31/10) 10-25MM	25MM & OVER
542	537	536	NUMBER OF STATEMENTS	32	110	84	99	116	95
%	%	%	ASSETS	%	%	%	%	%	%
9.0	9.1	10.4	Cash & Equivalents	7.9	10.5	12.0	9.4	12.4	8.4
26.6	25.5	22.2	Trade Receivables (net)	19.9	22.5	21.6	23.5	22.8	20.9
24.5	25.6	23.4	Inventory	13.8	19.6	22.2	25.7	26.4	26.0
2.5	2.9	2.9	All Other Current	3.4	2.6	2.3	2.8	3.1	3.4
62.6	63.1	58.8	Total Current	45.0	55.2	58.0	61.4	64.7	58.7
27.6	27.3	28.9	Fixed Assets (net)	46.3	31.2	26.7	29.2	24.9	26.9
3.9	3.9	6.0	Intangibles (net)	5.3	6.8	4.7	3.3	4.9	10.5
5.9	5.8	6.3	All Other Non-Current	3.4	6.8	10.6	6.1	5.6	3.9
100.0	100.0	100.0	Total	100.0	100.0	100.0	100.0	100.0	100.0
			LIABILITIES						
11.4	12.3	11.9	Notes Payable-Short Term	28.5	15.1	11.8	9.1	9.7	8.4
3.7	4.0	4.6	Cur. Mat.-L.T.D.	8.0	6.2	5.0	4.2	3.3	3.1
13.6	13.3	12.0	Trade Payables	21.1	11.5	10.5	10.1	12.9	11.9
.3	.2	.2	Income Taxes Payable	.0	.1	.1	.2	.3	.2
10.0	10.0	8.8	All Other Current	18.2	8.6	5.2	7.7	10.0	9.1
39.1	39.9	37.5	Total Current	75.9	41.5	32.5	31.2	36.1	32.6
17.8	16.5	19.5	Long-Term Debt	45.5	24.0	20.6	15.0	12.2	18.0
.4	.5	.6	Deferred Taxes	.1	.2	.6	.5	.7	.9
6.2	5.4	7.9	All Other Non-Current	19.9	11.9	5.9	6.9	4.5	6.3
36.5	37.7	34.6	Net Worth	-41.4	22.4	40.3	46.4	46.5	42.2
100.0	100.0	100.0	Total Liabilities & Net Worth	100.0	100.0	100.0	100.0	100.0	100.0
			INCOME DATA						
100.0	100.0	100.0	Net Sales	100.0	100.0	100.0	100.0	100.0	100.0
32.0	29.2	31.0	Gross Profit	49.3	36.5	32.9	31.3	26.1	22.6
25.3	23.7	27.4	Operating Expenses	46.0	35.3	29.4	28.4	21.1	17.0
6.7	5.5	3.6	Operating Profit	3.3	1.2	3.5	2.9	4.9	5.7
1.2	1.0	1.7	All Other Expenses (net)	5.0	1.7	1.4	1.3	1.0	2.1
5.4	4.5	1.9	Profit Before Taxes	-1.7	-.6	2.1	1.5	4.0	3.5
			RATIOS						
2.9	3.0	3.3	Current	1.7	3.3	3.7	3.7	3.2	2.7
1.7	1.7	1.8		.9	1.5	2.1	1.9	1.9	2.1
1.2	1.1	1.1		.4	.9	1.2	1.2	1.2	1.3
1.7	1.8	2.0	Quick	1.0	2.0	2.6	2.4	2.0	1.5
.9	.8	.9		.5	.9	1.1	1.0	1.1	.9
.6	.5	.5		.2	.5	.5	.5	.6	.6
29 12.6	26 14.1	27 13.5	Sales/Receivables	1 348.7	23 15.7	22 16.6	29 12.7	29 12.5	32 11.3
42 8.8	38 9.6	39 9.3		26 14.3	39 9.4	38 9.6	38 9.6	40 9.1	42 8.7
56 6.5	52 7.0	52 7.0		52 7.0	51 7.2	54 6.8	54 6.7	55 6.6	
23 15.7	22 16.8	26 14.1	Cost of Sales/Inventory	2 151.9	11 32.7	19 19.1	26 14.2	39 9.4	43 8.5
53 6.9	50 7.3	57 6.4		45 8.1	45 8.1	46 8.0	65 5.6	62 5.8	67 5.4
91 4.0	94 3.9	100 3.6		96 3.8	90 4.0	86 4.2	116 3.1	104 3.5	98 3.7
15 23.6	13 28.4	13 27.3	Cost of Sales/Payables	1 293.3	11 33.4	12 29.7	10 35.3	15 23.6	16 22.2
27 13.5	23 15.6	24 15.5		30 12.2	23 16.0	23 16.0	21 17.1	28 12.9	25 14.5
43 8.5	38 9.6	40 9.1		64 5.7	42 8.8	38 9.5	36 10.2	40 9.1	42 8.7
5.3	5.3	4.1	Sales/Working Capital	8.3	4.3	3.7	3.9	3.8	4.0
9.0	9.6	8.1		-97.8	14.3	7.3	8.1	6.5	6.5
29.8	31.7	42.1		-5.6	-51.0	37.1	18.0	21.8	13.6
12.8	12.4	8.5	EBIT/Interest	4.6	5.5	6.5	5.3	15.6	15.4
(491) 4.0	(493) 3.9	(477) 2.2		(26) .3	(97) 1.5	(74) 1.3	(85) 1.2	(104) 4.0	(91) 3.8
1.7	1.2	-1.0		-2.4	-2.7	-1.5	-1.1	.5	.1
8.5	6.6	5.1	Net Profit + Depr., Dep., Amort./Cur. Mat. L/T/D		5.5	2.1	4.8	5.1	14.5
(139) 3.1	(145) 2.8	(135) 2.1			(10) 2.5	(18) .8	(27) 2.3	(42) 2.2	(37) 2.5
1.4	1.1	.5			-.3	-.4	.4	.9	.0
.3	.3	.3	Fixed/Worth	2.1	.3	.2	.2	.2	.4
.7	.7	.8		-3.9	1.3	.7	.7	.6	.8
2.0	1.7	3.6		-.5	-2.8	2.8	1.6	1.4	2.2
.7	.7	.6	Debt/Worth	NM	.6	.5	.5	.5	.8
1.7	1.6	1.7		-7.6	4.0	1.6	1.3	1.3	1.5
5.3	4.3	14.4		-2.1	-8.4	7.6	3.3	3.8	5.1
53.7	49.3	35.4	% Profit Before Taxes/Tangible Net Worth		35.6	52.0	28.7	35.6	35.2
(470) 25.4	(471) 21.9	(422) 11.2		(71) 7.0	(69) 5.3	(90) 5.4	(108) 16.0	(76) 14.8	
8.5	6.0	-5.2			-13.9	-10.6	-6.3	2.1	-.9
19.6	17.9	12.7	% Profit Before Taxes/Total Assets	11.3	11.7	11.7	12.2	15.7	14.2
7.9	7.7	3.0		-3.5	1.4	1.8	2.4	5.5	6.1
2.6	1.0	-4.7		-21.1	-8.2	-7.1	-3.6	-.5	-1.5
23.5	23.1	18.6	Sales/Net Fixed Assets	18.3	23.7	20.3	18.0	22.9	14.2
10.0	9.4	8.2		4.3	8.7	8.9	7.9	8.4	6.6
5.0	5.1	3.9		1.4	3.7	4.7	3.6	4.5	4.0
2.9	3.0	2.6	Sales/Total Assets	3.1	3.0	2.9	2.5	2.5	2.3
2.2	2.2	1.8		1.7	2.0	1.9	1.9	1.7	1.7
1.6	1.6	1.3		.9	1.4	1.3	1.3	1.3	1.3
1.1	1.2	1.3	% Depr., Dep., Amort./Sales	2.3	1.7	1.1	1.3	1.1	1.4
(466) 2.2	(446) 2.3	(460) 2.8		(28) 4.9	(82) 4.1	(73) 2.9	(91) 3.0	(107) 2.2	(79) 2.4
4.1	4.1	5.5		17.1	7.1	5.0	6.6	4.5	4.9
2.3	1.9	2.5	% Officers', Directors' Owners' Comp/Sales	4.9	4.1	2.6	2.0	1.4	.5
(225) 4.2	(209) 3.7	(224) 4.9		(17) 8.8	(65) 6.7	(48) 4.6	(43) 4.5	(39) 2.5	(12) 3.3
7.5	7.6	8.2		12.5	10.7	7.1	6.3	4.8	7.2
14233757M	14298619M	12005939M	Net Sales ($)	18162M	207839M	330299M	711949M	1893990M	8843700M
7243192M	7686824M	7997394M	Total Assets ($)	12887M	122655M	201561M	428273M	1207277M	6024741M

M = $ thousand   MM = $ million
See Pages 9 through 22 for Explanation of Ratios and Data

Current Data Sorted by Assets

Comparative Historical Data

Type of Statement (counts by size)

	0-500M	500M-2MM	2-10MM	10-50MM	50-100MM	100-250MM	Type of Statement		
			7	15	4	5	Unqualified	32	34
	1		13	15		1	Reviewed	21	32
	1	9	16	3			Compiled	20	24
	1	4	4				Tax Returns	8	11
		5	20	13	3	1	Other	51	46
		34 (4/1-9/30/09)		107 (10/1/09-3/31/10)				4/1/05-3/31/06 ALL	4/1/06-3/31/07 ALL

Main Data

0-500M	500M-2MM	2-10MM	10-50MM	50-100MM	100-250MM		4/1/05-3/31/06 ALL	4/1/06-3/31/07 ALL
2	19	60	46	8	6	NUMBER OF STATEMENTS	132	147
%	%	%	%	%	%	ASSETS	%	%
	9.3	7.1	7.5			Cash & Equivalents	5.7	6.0
	16.8	18.9	20.6			Trade Receivables (net)	20.2	18.0
	43.9	46.7	40.2			Inventory	43.3	47.2
	.6	2.4	2.3			All Other Current	2.7	2.5
	70.7	75.1	70.6			Total Current	72.0	73.7
	21.7	17.4	21.8			Fixed Assets (net)	20.2	18.1
	.5	3.0	3.1			Intangibles (net)	4.0	3.8
	7.1	4.5	4.5			All Other Non-Current	3.9	4.4
	100.0	100.0	100.0			Total	100.0	100.0
						LIABILITIES		
	9.5	15.7	17.7			Notes Payable-Short Term	16.3	16.9
	6.3	2.6	2.9			Cur. Mat.-L.T.D.	2.6	2.9
	15.0	9.9	7.2			Trade Payables	12.1	10.8
	.0	.2	.5			Income Taxes Payable	.3	.2
	8.6	13.0	11.6			All Other Current	11.7	10.2
	39.4	41.4	39.8			Total Current	42.9	41.0
	26.3	15.0	8.9			Long-Term Debt	13.4	14.4
	.1	.4	.5			Deferred Taxes	.3	.3
	2.1	9.8	3.3			All Other Non-Current	5.7	6.2
	32.0	33.4	47.6			Net Worth	37.7	38.0
	100.0	100.0	100.0			Total Liabilities & Net Worth	100.0	100.0
						INCOME DATA		
	100.0	100.0	100.0			Net Sales	100.0	100.0
	36.9	29.3	27.1			Gross Profit	25.3	26.6
	38.6	25.7	22.1			Operating Expenses	20.2	21.8
	-1.6	3.6	4.9			Operating Profit	5.1	4.9
	.9	1.3	.6			All Other Expenses (net)	1.0	1.4
	-2.6	2.3	4.3			Profit Before Taxes	4.1	3.4
						RATIOS		
	3.1	3.2	3.0			Current	2.9	2.8
	2.3	2.0	1.8				1.8	1.8
	1.4	1.3	1.4				1.3	1.3
	1.2	1.5	.9			Quick	1.2	1.1
	.5	.7	.7				.6	.6
	.4	.2	.5				.3	.3
	13 28.8	18 19.9	25 14.4			Sales/Receivables	19 18.8	17 21.2
	28 13.2	30 12.0	38 9.6				38 9.6	34 10.6
	41 8.9	48 7.5	68 5.4				58 6.3	56 6.5
	67 5.4	67 5.4	82 4.5			Cost of Sales/Inventory	74 4.9	82 4.5
	164 2.2	136 2.7	129 2.8				120 3.0	120 3.0
	228 1.6	234 1.6	198 1.8				167 2.2	197 1.9
	17 20.9	10 37.1	10 38.4			Cost of Sales/Payables	15 24.3	13 28.5
	39 9.3	19 19.5	18 19.9				25 14.4	25 14.8
	60 6.1	34 10.7	29 12.6				41 9.0	40 9.1
	3.3	3.4	2.8			Sales/Working Capital	3.4	3.6
	3.8	5.8	5.1				6.2	5.8
	14.8	10.8	10.5				14.4	12.1
	2.1	9.1	12.1			EBIT/Interest	8.9	5.9
	(16) -.1	(55) 3.3	(42) 4.4				(120) 3.0	(138) 2.8
	-4.1	.9	1.5				1.2	1.3
		13.3	20.0			Net Profit + Depr., Dep.,	6.5	4.3
		(13) 5.1	(12) 4.6			Amort./Cur. Mat. L/T/D	(34) 2.7	(34) 2.6
		1.9	1.7				1.6	1.4
	.2	.2	.2			Fixed/Worth	.2	.2
	.5	.4	.5				.6	.5
	2.0	1.0	.9				1.5	1.0
	.6	.6	.5			Debt/Worth	.7	.9
	2.1	1.5	1.1				1.9	1.7
	6.9	7.3	2.7				5.9	5.1
	7.6	30.2	25.1			% Profit Before Taxes/Tangible	35.8	31.5
	(17) .1	(52) 16.0	(45) 15.3			Net Worth	(119) 17.3	(137) 15.2
	-61.4	4.2	2.4				6.2	3.8
	4.0	10.8	13.3			% Profit Before Taxes/Total	11.8	10.9
	-.9	5.6	6.9			Assets	5.0	4.3
	-15.7	-.3	1.3				.9	.9
	34.4	48.6	17.5			Sales/Net Fixed Assets	24.6	32.8
	7.2	16.8	9.0				11.4	11.4
	4.8	5.5	4.1				6.4	6.6
	2.1	2.5	1.9			Sales/Total Assets	2.3	2.3
	1.8	1.7	1.5				1.8	1.8
	1.4	1.2	1.2				1.3	1.3
	.6	.9	1.1			% Depr., Dep., Amort./Sales	1.0	.9
	(16) 2.7	(53) 1.4	(44) 2.0				(119) 1.5	(124) 1.5
	4.8	3.0	3.1				2.4	2.4
	2.9	1.3				% Officers', Directors'	1.0	1.0
	(10) 5.5	(20) 1.8				Owners' Comp/Sales	(31) 2.8	(43) 2.5
	7.9	5.2					6.8	4.6
2170M	45625M	526468M	1743534M	889199M	1200939M	Net Sales ($)	4682180M	4738641M
425M	22504M	286375M	1092252M	511273M	977094M	Total Assets ($)	2990433M	3078298M

M = $ thousand   MM = $ million
See Pages 9 through 22 for Explanation of Ratios and Data

Comparative Historical Data | | | Current Data Sorted by Sales

4/1/07-3/31/08 ALL	4/1/08-3/31/09 ALL	4/1/09-3/31/10 ALL	Type of Statement	0-1MM	1-3MM	3-5MM	5-10MM	10-25MM	25MM & OVER
33	37	31	Unqualified		1		4	5	21
32	30	30	Reviewed	1	1	3	4	9	12
23	25	29	Compiled	1	8	5	7	8	
12	14	9	Tax Returns	1	4		3	1	
41	44	42	Other	2	3	3	13	7	14
					34 (4/1-9/30/09)		107 (10/1/09-3/31/10)		
141	150	141	**NUMBER OF STATEMENTS**	5	17	11	31	30	47
%	%	%	**ASSETS**	%	%	%	%	%	%
5.4	5.4	7.5	Cash & Equivalents		3.1	6.5	6.8	6.7	8.7
20.0	20.9	19.4	Trade Receivables (net)		13.6	14.3	21.8	22.5	20.7
43.6	45.8	42.3	Inventory		51.3	38.3	45.6	47.8	35.8
3.2	2.2	2.1	All Other Current		.6	1.3	3.2	2.8	1.9
72.2	74.3	71.3	Total Current		68.6	60.4	77.5	79.8	67.1
18.8	18.3	19.6	Fixed Assets (net)		24.1	28.6	16.2	11.8	23.0
4.6	2.5	3.8	Intangibles (net)		1.2	.4	3.2	5.1	5.6
4.5	4.8	5.3	All Other Non-Current		6.1	10.6	3.1	3.4	4.3
100.0	100.0	100.0	Total		100.0	100.0	100.0	100.0	100.0
			LIABILITIES						
16.5	15.6	14.7	Notes Payable-Short Term		16.9	18.8	11.3	16.8	13.9
2.5	3.3	3.1	Cur. Mat.-L.T.D.		4.7	3.2	3.0	2.3	2.8
11.5	11.6	9.5	Trade Payables		11.0	8.1	12.4	8.9	8.5
.2	.3	.3	Income Taxes Payable		.0	.0	.2	.3	.5
10.2	11.5	11.6	All Other Current		8.9	6.5	13.5	15.8	10.7
40.9	42.3	39.2	Total Current		41.4	36.6	40.3	44.1	36.4
13.8	11.4	13.9	Long-Term Debt		34.9	12.1	9.1	15.5	9.7
.3	.5	.6	Deferred Taxes		.0	.9	.1	.5	1.0
3.8	3.6	6.0	All Other Non-Current		2.2	.7	16.7	3.8	3.5
41.1	42.3	40.4	Net Worth		21.3	49.6	33.8	36.1	49.4
100.0	100.0	100.0	Total Liabilities & Net Worth		100.0	100.0	100.0	100.0	100.0
			INCOME DATA						
100.0	100.0	100.0	Net Sales		100.0	100.0	100.0	100.0	100.0
26.6	27.5	29.4	Gross Profit		26.4	36.2	30.8	27.5	26.5
21.0	21.6	25.8	Operating Expenses		30.7	33.1	26.4	23.7	20.1
5.6	5.9	3.7	Operating Profit		-4.3	3.1	4.4	3.8	6.4
1.2	.8	1.0	All Other Expenses (net)		2.5	.4	1.2	.8	.8
4.4	5.1	2.6	Profit Before Taxes		-6.9	2.7	3.2	3.0	5.6
			RATIOS						
2.8	2.6	3.1	Current		3.1	3.2	3.4	2.8	3.1
1.9	1.8	2.0			2.2	1.9	2.1	1.7	2.2
1.2	1.4	1.3			1.1	.9	1.6	1.4	1.3
1.2	1.2	1.3	Quick		.6	1.3	1.7	1.0	1.4
(140) .7	.7	.7			.4	.4	.7	.7	.9
.3	.4	.4			.2	.2	.5	.3	.5
20 17.9	19 18.8	19 19.2	Sales/Receivables	11 33.5	13 28.8	21 17.8	23 16.1	25 14.4	
33 11.2	34 10.8	34 10.6		22 16.9	29 12.6	37 9.9	38 9.6	36 10.1	
54 6.8	55 6.6	56 6.5		36 10.3	45 8.0	56 6.5	66 5.5	63 5.8	
70 5.2	68 5.4	70 5.2	Cost of Sales/Inventory	82 4.4	46 7.9	60 6.1	87 4.2	52 7.1	
106 3.4	111 3.3	126 2.9		173 2.1	147 2.5	142 2.6	110 3.3	108 3.4	
164 2.2	164 2.2	209 1.7		268 1.4	243 1.5	210 1.7	239 1.5	157 2.3	
14 25.7	11 31.8	11 31.8	Cost of Sales/Payables	7 55.4	15 24.6	10 37.3	14 25.9	11 32.4	
25 14.4	23 15.7	20 18.0		25 14.7	22 16.4	20 18.6	19 19.5	22 16.7	
39 9.3	37 9.9	35 10.3		45 8.0	52 7.0	34 10.6	28 13.1	32 11.4	
3.7	3.9	3.2	Sales/Working Capital		3.2	3.3	2.5	3.5	3.0
6.3	6.7	5.5			6.1	6.8	5.3	5.6	5.6
14.0	13.1	11.1			27.6	-70.6	10.3	7.7	14.9
8.8	16.3	10.8	EBIT/Interest		.3	6.9	7.2	11.5	14.8
(135) 3.7	(144) 5.6	(129) 3.7		(16) -1.1	4.0	(27) 2.8	(27) 5.5	(44) 5.2	
1.6	2.1	.9			-3.7	1.2	1.0	1.0	3.1
5.7	7.7	16.7	Net Profit + Depr., Dep., Amort./Cur. Mat. L/T/D						23.2
(42) 2.6	(38) 3.2	(34) 4.2						(14)	4.9
1.9	.8	1.6							1.8
.2	.2	.2	Fixed/Worth		.2	.4	.2	.1	.3
.5	.4	.4			.8	.6	.3	.2	.5
1.1	.9	1.0			NM	1.0	1.0	.6	1.0
.7	.7	.6	Debt/Worth		.7	.4	.6	.6	.5
1.5	1.4	1.1			5.4	1.1	1.9	1.2	.9
3.9	3.2	3.5			NM	2.7	3.5	3.0	2.7
42.5	43.7	29.8	% Profit Before Taxes/Tangible Net Worth		10.4	23.3	30.1	30.3	33.2
(129) 19.4	(142) 24.0	(127) 12.1		(13) -5.6	9.2	(27) 11.3	(27) 17.0	(44) 17.3	
6.2	6.6	1.2			-84.8	1.2	2.1	5.1	5.6
13.6	16.8	11.4	% Profit Before Taxes/Total Assets		.4	9.9	9.7	14.5	15.4
7.4	8.7	5.2			-7.6	2.2	4.2	7.9	8.3
2.1	2.6	-.3			-16.0	.3	.0	1.6	3.3
30.7	36.6	33.8	Sales/Net Fixed Assets		34.8	18.9	48.8	59.9	13.2
10.7	13.4	11.1			8.0	4.9	26.4	17.1	8.3
6.4	6.8	5.1			4.3	4.2	5.4	10.3	4.4
2.4	2.5	2.2	Sales/Total Assets		1.9	2.0	2.8	2.6	2.0
1.8	1.9	1.6			1.4	1.4	1.9	1.6	1.6
1.4	1.5	1.2			1.0	1.2	1.3	1.4	1.2
.8	.9	1.1	% Depr., Dep., Amort./Sales		1.0	2.5	.7	.6	1.4
(123) 1.4	(127) 1.4	(126) 1.9		(16) 1.8	(10) 3.2	(28) 1.2	(27) 1.4	(43) 2.3	
2.3	2.3	3.2			4.4	4.2	2.9	2.6	3.2
1.2	1.0	1.5	% Officers', Directors' Owners' Comp/Sales					1.3	
(36) 2.4	(51) 2.1	(39) 2.8					(13)	2.8	
4.4	4.5	5.9						6.0	
5004293M	5953923M	4407935M	Net Sales ($)	3480M	33126M	41924M	228278M	498313M	3602814M
3307552M	3266627M	2889923M	Total Assets ($)	3870M	27447M	29342M	140097M	322354M	2366813M

© RMA 2010

M = $ thousand   MM = $ million
See Pages 9 through 22 for Explanation of Ratios and Data

Current Data Sorted by Assets   Comparative Historical Data

0-500M	500M-2MM	2-10MM	10-50MM	50-100MM	100-250MM		4/1/05-3/31/06 ALL	4/1/06-3/31/07 ALL
						Type of Statement		
						Unqualified	8	8
						Reviewed	4	9
						Compiled	2	4
						Tax Returns	4	7
						Other	22	16
3	7	13	13		3	**NUMBER OF STATEMENTS**	40	44
%	%	%	%	%	%	**ASSETS**	%	%
		7.8	9.9			Cash & Equivalents	8.8	8.2
		18.8	14.2			Trade Receivables (net)	19.7	18.9
		41.4	41.0			Inventory	43.3	40.8
		.7	3.5			All Other Current	3.1	3.2
		68.6	68.6			Total Current	74.9	71.1
		20.5	21.6			Fixed Assets (net)	16.9	19.3
		1.1	5.0			Intangibles (net)	4.3	5.0
		9.7	4.8			All Other Non-Current	3.9	4.7
		100.0	100.0			Total	100.0	100.0
						LIABILITIES		
		19.2	13.1			Notes Payable-Short Term	21.5	22.1
		3.6	2.5			Cur. Mat.-L.T.D.	1.1	1.8
		14.8	11.7			Trade Payables	16.4	17.5
		1.0	.1			Income Taxes Payable	.5	.5
		4.7	11.5			All Other Current	10.0	9.6
		43.3	38.9			Total Current	49.4	51.5
		13.3	10.2			Long-Term Debt	10.9	11.4
		.0	.3			Deferred Taxes	.6	.4
		3.2	6.0			All Other Non-Current	5.4	5.3
		40.1	44.6			Net Worth	33.8	31.4
		100.0	100.0			Total Liabilities & Net Worth	100.0	100.0
						INCOME DATA		
		100.0	100.0			Net Sales	100.0	100.0
		32.0	22.2			Gross Profit	28.7	28.3
		31.8	21.6			Operating Expenses	25.5	25.0
		.3	.6			Operating Profit	3.2	3.2
		1.8	2.2			All Other Expenses (net)	2.1	1.6
		-1.5	-1.6			Profit Before Taxes	1.2	1.7
						RATIOS		
		2.2	4.3				2.3	2.5
		1.4	1.6			Current	1.5	1.6
		1.2	1.4				1.1	1.2
		1.1	1.8				1.0	1.1
		.6	.6			Quick	.6	.6
		.4	.2				.3	.3
		5 67.5	14 25.2				13 28.5	17 21.3
		43 8.4	27 13.6			Sales/Receivables	35 10.5	36 10.1
		54 6.8	46 7.9				61 6.0	53 6.8
		63 5.8	81 4.5				63 5.8	72 5.1
		135 2.7	120 3.0			Cost of Sales/Inventory	105 3.5	100 3.7
		230 1.6	151 2.4				158 2.3	134 2.7
		7 54.0	14 25.4				13 28.9	16 23.3
		41 8.9	20 18.6			Cost of Sales/Payables	33 11.2	32 11.4
		75 4.9	35 10.3				60 6.1	60 6.1
		4.3	2.9				4.2	4.4
		7.2	6.1			Sales/Working Capital	8.9	8.2
		16.3	15.3				21.7	18.4
		12.8	9.8				5.4	4.7
		.7	3.0			EBIT/Interest	(38) 2.9	(42) 1.4
		-.2	-4.8				1.1	.6
						Net Profit + Depr., Dep.,		22.0
						Amort./Cur. Mat. L/T/D	(10) 1.7	1.7
								.9
		.1	.2				.1	.3
		.6	.4			Fixed/Worth	.4	.5
		1.1	1.1				1.0	1.1
		1.0	.6				.9	.7
		1.6	1.2			Debt/Worth	1.7	1.9
		2.5	2.6				3.8	5.4
		5.9	20.4			% Profit Before Taxes/Tangible	30.5	27.3
	(12) -.9	(12) 10.2				Net Worth	(34) 13.6	(35) 11.3
		-11.8	-19.5				6.5	-3.0
		3.9	9.5			% Profit Before Taxes/Total	8.2	11.9
		-.9	4.3			Assets	4.1	3.2
		-3.8	-17.4				-1.1	-1.0
		74.0	47.5				41.9	25.2
		10.6	10.1			Sales/Net Fixed Assets	17.1	12.6
		4.3	4.7				8.7	6.7
		2.4	2.3				2.7	2.6
		1.5	1.7			Sales/Total Assets	2.0	2.0
		1.3	1.1				1.4	1.4
		.5	1.2				.6	1.3
		1.1	(12) 1.8			% Depr., Dep., Amort./Sales	(33) 1.3	(39) 1.7
		2.3	3.0				2.3	2.7
							1.2	1.5
						% Officers', Directors'	(10) 1.8	(10) 2.3
						Owners' Comp/Sales	9.3	5.3
2074M	15163M	109009M	572078M		936214M	Net Sales ($)	1724468M	2190445M
637M	6680M	56024M	335103M		410520M	Total Assets ($)	921061M	1206273M

(Current data columns 50-100MM and 100-250MM: DATA NOT AVAILABLE)

12 (4/1-9/30/09)   27 (10/1/09-3/31/10)

M = $ thousand   MM = $ million
See Pages 9 through 22 for Explanation of Ratios and Data

Comparative Historical Data | Current Data Sorted by Sales

	8 9 5 4 24 4/1/07- 3/31/08 ALL	10 3 5 6 20 4/1/08- 3/31/09 ALL	8 6 5 4 16 4/1/09- 3/31/10 ALL	Type of Statement Unqualified Reviewed Compiled Tax Returns Other	0-1MM	1-3MM	3-5MM	5-10MM	10-25MM	25MM & OVE
				Type of Statement		2	2		1	7
				Unqualified		2	2		1	2
				Reviewed	1	2	1		1	
				Compiled	2	1	3	3	4	5
				Tax Returns						
				Other	12 (4/1-9/30/09)			27 (10/1/09-3/31/10)		
					0-1MM	1-3MM	3-5MM	5-10MM	10-25MM	25MM & OVE
	50	44	39	NUMBER OF STATEMENTS	3	7	6	3	6	14
	%	%	%	ASSETS	%	%	%	%	%	%
	5.7	7.6	10.4	Cash & Equivalents						13.0
	22.5	15.3	14.8	Trade Receivables (net)						12.6
	44.3	48.8	42.7	Inventory						42.2
	1.5	2.4	1.9	All Other Current						3.3
	74.0	74.1	69.8	Total Current						71.2
	15.8	15.7	17.6	Fixed Assets (net)						16.4
	5.9	6.3	5.0	Intangibles (net)						5.4
	4.4	3.9	7.7	All Other Non-Current						7.0
	100.0	100.0	100.0	Total						100.0
				LIABILITIES						
	19.6	17.8	17.5	Notes Payable-Short Term						11.9
	3.2	3.0	3.3	Cur. Mat.-L.T.D.						1.3
	17.6	16.8	17.4	Trade Payables						13.5
	.4	.1	.4	Income Taxes Payable						.2
	9.4	8.5	10.6	All Other Current						9.4
	50.2	46.3	49.2	Total Current						36.2
	13.6	11.9	8.1	Long-Term Debt						5.4
	.3	.1	.3	Deferred Taxes						.9
	9.6	5.9	10.7	All Other Non-Current						5.7
	26.4	35.8	31.7	Net Worth						51.8
	100.0	100.0	100.0	Total Liabilties & Net Worth						100.0
				INCOME DATA						
	100.0	100.0	100.0	Net Sales						100.0
	28.1	29.7	30.9	Gross Profit						22.6
	24.6	27.7	28.9	Operating Expenses						23.1
	3.6	2.0	2.0	Operating Profit						-.5
	2.0	1.3	1.4	All Other Expenses (net)						.9
	1.6	.7	.6	Profit Before Taxes						-1.4
				RATIOS						
	3.1	2.8	5.5	Current						5.8
	1.6	1.5	1.5							1.8
	1.1	1.1	1.2							1.4
	1.5	.9	1.6	Quick						2.8
	.5	.5	.6							.7
	.3	.3	.2							.2
24	15.0	17 21.7	8 48.4	Sales/Receivables						14 26.4
37	9.9	34 10.9	27 13.6							25 14.9
58	6.3	45 8.2	47 7.8							39 9.4
69	5.3	100 3.7	69 5.3	Cost of Sales/Inventory						92 3.9
101	3.6	134 2.7	120 3.0							110 3.3
156	2.3	195 1.9	178 2.0							140 2.6
16	22.3	18 19.8	11 33.5	Cost of Sales/Payables						16 23.3
34	10.7	31 11.7	20 18.6							26 14.1
54	6.7	71 5.1	48 7.6							40 9.2
	4.0	3.4	3.5	Sales/Working Capital						2.1
	8.6	7.8	7.2							4.4
	30.4	31.5	20.2							19.1
	5.3	5.5	10.3	EBIT/Interest						19.2
(46)	1.7	(41) 2.3	(37) 1.6							3.3
	.2	.4	-1.9							-4.8
		4.0		Net Profit + Depr., Dep., Amort./Cur. Mat. L/T/D						
		(15) 2.9								
		2.3								
	.2	.2	.1	Fixed/Worth						.2
	.5	.4	.4							.2
	NM	1.3	1.1							.7
	.7	.6	.7	Debt/Worth						.3
	2.0	1.9	1.2							.9
	-11.3	12.9	2.7							1.9
	32.3	27.7	19.2	% Profit Before Taxes/Tangible Net Worth						18.3
(37)	17.3	(35) 14.4	(34) 3.9						(13)	5.1
	4.0	2.6	-19.1							-19.3
	10.4	9.3	9.6	% Profit Before Taxes/Total Assets						9.6
	5.0	4.0	1.1							3.3
	-2.5	-1.2	-6.8							-14.0
	43.7	34.3	51.8	Sales/Net Fixed Assets						45.4
	18.0	13.7	15.6							12.7
	8.3	8.4	6.1							7.3
	2.7	2.3	2.6	Sales/Total Assets						2.7
	2.0	1.7	1.7							1.8
	1.5	1.3	1.3							1.1
	.6	.8	.6	% Depr., Dep., Amort./Sales						.9
(38)	1.5	(37) 1.7	(38) 1.5						(13)	1.7
	2.5	2.3	2.4							2.9
	1.7	1.6	1.7	% Officers', Directors' Owners' Comp/Sales						
(10)	2.6	(10) 2.9	(16) 3.0							
	4.4	7.4	6.8							
	1921653M	1927255M	1634538M	Net Sales ($)	1959M	14431M	23661M	21419M	100147M	1472921M
	1011123M	1040757M	808964M	Total Assets ($)	846M	6635M	19454M	14109M	55406M	712514M

© RMA 2010

M = $ thousand   MM = $ million
See Pages 9 through 22 for Explanation of Ratios and Data

MANUFACTURING—Construction Machinery Manufacturing   NAICS 333120

Current Data Sorted by Assets							Comparative Historical Data	

0-500M	500M-2MM	2-10MM	10-50MM	50-100MM	100-250MM	Type of Statement	4/1/05-3/31/06 ALL	4/1/06-3/31/07 ALL
1		8	19	6	2	Unqualified	41	38
	2	10	7	1		Reviewed	35	27
1		5	3			Compiled	12	13
1	7	1				Tax Returns	15	9
3	8	15	20	6	7	Other	43	38
	29 (4/1-9/30/09)		104 (10/1/09-3/31/10)					
6	17	39	49	13	9	NUMBER OF STATEMENTS	146	125
%	%	%	%	%	%	**ASSETS**	%	%
9.7	8.2	7.2	21.5			Cash & Equivalents	8.8	8.1
25.3	19.9	15.9	15.9			Trade Receivables (net)	23.9	23.9
33.4	39.8	35.6	22.4			Inventory	31.5	32.3
2.9	2.5	7.7	5.1			All Other Current	3.0	4.0
71.2	70.4	66.4	65.0			Total Current	67.2	68.4
17.1	24.1	26.5	23.5			Fixed Assets (net)	23.1	23.3
2.6	2.7	2.1	6.1			Intangibles (net)	4.3	3.5
9.0	2.7	5.0	5.4			All Other Non-Current	5.4	4.8
100.0	100.0	100.0	100.0			Total	100.0	100.0
						LIABILITIES		
6.0	13.6	14.0	5.9			Notes Payable-Short Term	13.6	12.7
1.3	2.7	3.9	1.9			Cur. Mat.-L.T.D.	3.5	2.8
16.4	11.4	8.4	10.6			Trade Payables	14.4	14.9
.0	.1	.3	.5			Income Taxes Payable	1.3	.4
18.1	11.1	13.2	14.3			All Other Current	11.1	12.4
41.8	38.8	39.9	33.2			Total Current	43.9	43.2
12.4	15.5	9.8	10.5			Long-Term Debt	11.1	15.7
.3	.2	.7	.1			Deferred Taxes	.5	.4
19.7	2.8	3.8	9.2			All Other Non-Current	5.5	5.5
25.9	42.7	45.8	47.0			Net Worth	38.6	35.1
100.0	100.0	100.0	100.0			Total Liabilities & Net Worth	100.0	100.0
						INCOME DATA		
100.0	100.0	100.0	100.0			Net Sales	100.0	100.0
31.5	26.2	24.4	24.2			Gross Profit	28.0	27.0
32.4	25.4	23.4	24.0			Operating Expenses	21.1	20.2
-.8	.8	1.0	.2			Operating Profit	6.9	6.8
.3	.9	.7	-.1			All Other Expenses (net)	.9	1.0
-1.2	-.1	.3	.4			Profit Before Taxes	6.0	5.7
						RATIOS		
3.0	2.7	3.7	6.2			Current	2.2	2.2
2.2	1.7	1.6	2.2				1.5	1.6
1.2	1.4	1.1	1.3				1.1	1.2
1.6	1.5	1.3	3.7			Quick	1.2	1.2
.9	.6	.6	1.4				.7	.7
.4	.4	.4	.6				.5	.5
15 24.3	22 16.4	33 11.0	31 11.9			Sales/Receivables	29 12.7	29 12.7
42 8.7	38 9.6	48 7.7	40 9.2				42 8.8	42 8.6
61 6.0	55 6.7	66 5.5	65 5.6				54 6.7	61 6.0
4 87.6	64 5.7	96 3.8	46 7.9			Cost of Sales/Inventory	37 9.9	42 8.6
92 4.0	105 3.5	137 2.7	126 2.9				83 4.4	91 4.0
152 2.4	176 2.1	227 1.6	207 1.8				128 2.9	126 2.9
16 22.9	15 24.6	16 22.8	18 20.2			Cost of Sales/Payables	16 22.8	19 19.7
40 9.0	23 15.7	22 16.7	24 15.5				31 11.9	28 13.1
57 6.4	51 7.1	42 8.8	40 9.2				46 8.0	48 7.5
3.5	3.9	3.0	1.5			Sales/Working Capital	5.0	4.9
5.6	7.5	4.2	2.5				9.0	8.6
NM	13.2	11.3	NM				31.4	18.7
9.5	4.9	6.8	591.4			EBIT/Interest	12.0	12.2
(15) 1.9	(38) 2.9	(42) 1.6	(12) 5.2				(135) 5.1	(116) 4.9
-5.8	-6.4	-1.9	-2.0				2.1	2.1
	12.3	4.9				Net Profit + Depr., Dep., Amort./Cur. Mat. L/T/D	12.2	5.7
	(10) .9	(18) 1.5					(45) 2.6	(34) 2.4
	-2.0	.0					1.9	1.5
.1	.2	.3	.2			Fixed/Worth	.3	.3
.2	.6	.6	.6				.5	.6
1.3	1.9	1.4	3.9				1.5	1.6
.7	.7	.3	.2			Debt/Worth	1.0	1.0
1.3	1.3	1.4	1.4				1.9	2.1
21.2	3.3	2.8	9.6				4.8	5.2
22.3	29.2	18.6	145.0			% Profit Before Taxes/Tangible Net Worth	58.8	66.3
(14) 5.9	(37) 6.0	(45) 2.9	(12) 11.3				(134) 21.4	(113) 25.4
-12.5	-11.4	-5.2	-7.9				10.2	12.9
7.6	7.3	5.5	14.2			% Profit Before Taxes/Total Assets	15.5	17.0
2.3	2.7	1.1	5.6				8.4	8.7
-9.8	-10.2	-3.9	-2.7				2.8	3.1
80.1	28.9	12.7	10.4			Sales/Net Fixed Assets	27.9	22.2
15.5	9.4	5.4	7.3				11.1	9.5
6.2	4.5	2.4	2.8				5.9	6.0
2.6	2.5	1.7	1.5			Sales/Total Assets	2.7	2.6
1.9	1.8	1.1	1.1				2.0	1.9
1.5	1.2	.8	.7				1.4	1.5
.9	1.1	1.5	1.7			% Depr., Dep., Amort./Sales	.7	.8
(13) 1.5	(33) 1.7	(43) 2.6	2.3				(122) 1.5	(108) 1.7
4.4	3.6	4.4	4.6				3.1	2.9
	.2					% Officers', Directors' Owners' Comp/Sales	1.6	2.4
	(12) 1.8						(35) 3.5	(27) 3.6
	3.1						6.6	5.0
3424M	52821M	375666M	1410712M	1145953M	1122988M	Net Sales ($)	6409252M	5486966M
1676M	23900M	204462M	1165669M	996531M	1427928M	Total Assets ($)	3497604M	3296535M

M = $ thousand   MM = $ million
See Pages 9 through 22 for Explanation of Ratios and Data

Comparative Historical Data | Current Data Sorted by Sales

37	44	36	Type of Statement / Unqualified	1	3		3	12	20
24	22	20	Reviewed			1	7	6	3
16	14	9	Compiled	1		1	4	1	2
7	7	9	Tax Returns	2	2	3	2		
44	56	59	Other	4	5	4	11	13	22
4/1/07-3/31/08 ALL	4/1/08-3/31/09 ALL	4/1/09-3/31/10 ALL			29 (4/1-9/30/09)			104 (10/1/09-3/31/10)	
				0-1MM	1-3MM	3-5MM	5-10MM	10-25MM	25MM & OVER
128	143	133	NUMBER OF STATEMENTS	8	10	9	27	32	47
%	%	%	ASSETS	%	%	%	%	%	%
7.2	6.3	10.9	Cash & Equivalents		13.6		9.7	6.7	15.0
22.8	18.7	18.5	Trade Receivables (net)		23.4		19.8	16.7	17.6
31.9	38.3	34.1	Inventory		22.1		40.2	37.6	29.2
4.5	4.1	4.8	All Other Current		1.5		1.8	7.3	6.4
66.4	67.3	68.3	Total Current		60.6		71.6	68.3	68.2
24.4	23.2	23.5	Fixed Assets (net)		23.8		21.1	25.9	22.1
4.3	5.4	3.0	Intangibles (net)		4.0		3.3	2.1	3.6
5.0	4.1	5.3	All Other Non-Current		11.5		3.9	3.8	6.0
100.0	100.0	100.0	Total		100.0		100.0	100.0	100.0
			LIABILITIES						
14.9	14.9	12.5	Notes Payable-Short Term		5.3		15.2	14.0	9.7
4.5	2.7	2.8	Cur. Mat.-L.T.D.		3.2		2.6	2.8	3.2
12.2	11.3	10.6	Trade Payables		10.2		14.4	7.8	9.5
.3	.3	.2	Income Taxes Payable		.0		.1	.4	.3
12.3	12.6	14.2	All Other Current		17.6		13.6	12.4	13.8
44.2	41.7	40.3	Total Current		36.3		45.8	37.6	36.6
15.8	15.1	13.1	Long-Term Debt		20.1		15.9	9.9	8.0
.3	.6	.4	Deferred Taxes		.3		.3	.7	.4
4.1	5.1	6.3	All Other Non-Current		9.3		4.2	1.6	6.5
35.6	37.4	39.8	Net Worth		34.0		33.8	50.2	48.5
100.0	100.0	100.0	Total Liabilities & Net Worth		100.0		100.0	100.0	100.0
			INCOME DATA						
100.0	100.0	100.0	Net Sales		100.0		100.0	100.0	100.0
29.7	27.2	26.5	Gross Profit		32.6		26.0	24.8	23.8
22.9	23.1	26.6	Operating Expenses		31.7		25.2	26.8	22.0
6.7	4.1	-.1	Operating Profit		.9		.8	-2.0	1.9
1.3	1.1	.6	All Other Expenses (net)		1.7		.9	1.0	.1
5.4	3.0	-.7	Profit Before Taxes		-.9		-.2	-3.0	1.8
			RATIOS						
2.4 / 1.6 / 1.1	2.9 / 1.6 / 1.1	3.5 / 1.8 / 1.2	Current		6.0 / 2.1 / .7		3.0 / 1.5 / 1.0	3.4 / 1.7 / 1.4	5.7 / 2.1 / 1.2
1.2 / .6 / .3	1.0 / .6 / .3	1.5 / .7 / .3	Quick		2.9 / 1.0 / .5		1.7 / .6 / .3	1.0 / .6 / .3	2.0 / 1.0 / .5
26 14.1 / 41 8.9 / 57 6.3	23 16.0 / 37 10.0 / 56 6.6	29 12.6 / 45 8.2 / 62 5.9	Sales/Receivables		36 10.3 / 57 6.4 / 61 5.5		20 17.9 / 39 9.3 / 66 5.5	30 12.3 / 42 8.7 / 61 5.9	33 11.1 / 48 7.7 / 59 6.2
35 10.3 / 91 4.0 / 149 2.4	65 5.6 / 107 3.4 / 170 2.1	68 5.3 / 118 3.1 / 199 1.8	Cost of Sales/Inventory		2 202.3 / 64 5.7 / 148 2.5		75 4.8 / 111 3.3 / 210 1.7	88 4.2 / 130 2.8 / 208 1.8	77 4.7 / 121 3.0 / 171 2.1
16 22.5 / 29 12.8 / 44 8.4	15 24.8 / 27 13.6 / 41 9.0	16 23.5 / 23 15.6 / 46 8.0	Cost of Sales/Payables		13 28.3 / 27 13.5 / 47 7.8		19 18.8 / 37 9.8 / 63 5.8	15 23.8 / 20 18.4 / 36 10.1	16 22.8 / 23 16.0 / 40 9.2
4.7 / 9.3 / 24.4	4.1 / 6.7 / 21.9	2.6 / 5.3 / 13.2	Sales/Working Capital		2.9 / 4.4 / -9.7		2.6 / 9.3 / 74.7	3.0 / 4.8 / 8.8	1.6 / 4.0 / 13.0
10.0 / (121) 4.1 / 1.3	10.2 / (132) 3.2 / .4	6.7 / (120) 2.3 / -2.9	EBIT/Interest				5.1 / (26) 2.9 / -2.1	7.2 / (30) 2.0 / -7.9	13.8 / (41) 1.7 / -3.5
7.4 / (45) 2.6 / 1.0	6.5 / (44) 3.0 / .7	6.2 / (37) 1.4 / .0	Net Profit + Depr., Dep., Amort./Cur. Mat. L/T/D					9.6 / (11) 1.2 / .0	8.4 / (17) 2.0 / .0
.2 / .5 / 1.7	.2 / .5 / 1.9	.2 / .6 / 1.8	Fixed/Worth		.1 / .2 / 1.3		.2 / 1.0 / 6.3	.2 / .5 / .8	.2 / .4 / 1.4
.8 / 2.2 / 5.2	.6 / 1.8 / 7.7	.6 / 1.4 / 4.1	Debt/Worth		.6 / 1.3 / 5.8		.7 / 2.5 / 15.4	.4 / 1.1 / 2.4	.3 / 1.4 / 3.8
44.3 / (116) 22.0 / 5.3	36.4 / (122) 16.4 / 1.8	21.1 / (119) 5.2 / -8.4	% Profit Before Taxes/Tangible Net Worth				35.0 / (23) 9.4 / .2	8.6 / (31) 1.0 / -17.0	30.9 / (44) 5.5 / -4.9
15.7 / 7.5 / 1.5	13.2 / 5.3 / -.8	7.3 / 2.1 / -5.0	% Profit Before Taxes/Total Assets		9.3 / .6 / -11.3		7.3 / 3.3 / -4.5	4.8 / -.3 / -7.5	10.5 / 3.1 / -4.0
25.3 / 10.1 / 5.1	18.7 / 9.9 / 5.1	18.2 / 7.5 / 3.7	Sales/Net Fixed Assets		UND / 12.4 / 2.2		34.6 / 10.7 / 4.2	14.5 / 6.2 / 2.9	13.4 / 7.3 / 3.8
2.5 / 1.7 / 1.2	2.4 / 1.6 / 1.2	2.1 / 1.3 / .9	Sales/Total Assets		2.0 / 1.5 / 1.1		2.6 / 1.6 / 1.1	2.0 / 1.3 / .8	1.9 / 1.1 / .8
.9 / (108) 1.9 / 3.4	1.0 / (121) 1.8 / 3.4	1.3 / (112) 2.3 / 4.0	% Depr., Dep., Amort./Sales				1.1 / (24) 2.0 / 3.8	1.3 / (27) 2.3 / 3.2	1.6 / (40) 2.3 / 4.3
2.2 / (25) 3.8 / 5.4	1.1 / (23) 3.1 / 5.7	1.2 / (26) 2.9 / 7.1	% Officers', Directors' Owners' Comp/Sales				.6 / (10) 1.8 / 2.7		
5064454M	6771288M	4111564M	Net Sales ($)	4730M	22623M	36190M	195823M	555894M	3296304M
3197587M	4623437M	3820166M	Total Assets ($)	3490M	16281M	29349M	146084M	534260M	3090702M

M = $ thousand   MM = $ million
See Pages 9 through 22 for Explanation of Ratios and Data

Current Data Sorted by Assets   Comparative Historical Data

0-500M	500M-2MM	2-10MM	10-50MM	50-100MM	100-250MM		4/1/05-3/31/06 ALL	4/1/06-3/31/07 ALL
1		1	6	2	2	Type of Statement		
3		5	4	1		Unqualified	12	9
		2				Reviewed	6	18
		3				Compiled	4	9
						Tax Returns	1	
1	4	7	10	1	1	Other	20	19
	11 (4/1-9/30/09)		43 (10/1/09-3/31/10)					
1	8	18	20	4	3	NUMBER OF STATEMENTS	43	55
%	%	%	%	%	%	ASSETS	%	%
		7.6	5.8			Cash & Equivalents	8.4	6.7
		18.4	18.9			Trade Receivables (net)	25.8	25.0
		37.7	42.3			Inventory	30.5	35.4
		3.6	3.4			All Other Current	2.3	3.6
		67.3	70.3			Total Current	67.0	70.7
		27.1	22.4			Fixed Assets (net)	23.1	19.8
		2.3	4.1			Intangibles (net)	3.3	3.4
		3.3	3.3			All Other Non-Current	6.7	6.1
		100.0	100.0			Total	100.0	100.0
						LIABILITIES		
		7.7	18.2			Notes Payable-Short Term	7.2	10.7
		7.5	3.2			Cur. Mat.-L.T.D.	4.7	2.8
		11.5	11.1			Trade Payables	19.2	17.0
		.0	1.8			Income Taxes Payable	.7	.3
		6.8	12.6			All Other Current	13.1	13.4
		33.4	46.9			Total Current	45.0	44.2
		22.6	11.4			Long-Term Debt	17.8	13.7
		.3	1.0			Deferred Taxes	.4	.4
		4.8	2.9			All Other Non-Current	4.2	7.4
		38.9	37.8			Net Worth	32.6	34.4
		100.0	100.0			Total Liabilites & Net Worth	100.0	100.0
						INCOME DATA		
		100.0	100.0			Net Sales	100.0	100.0
		29.6	26.7			Gross Profit	30.2	30.7
		24.6	22.0			Operating Expenses	22.9	23.9
		4.9	4.7			Operating Profit	7.3	6.9
		1.5	1.0			All Other Expenses (net)	1.1	.8
		3.5	3.8			Profit Before Taxes	6.1	6.0
						RATIOS		
		3.1	2.0				2.2	2.6
		1.8	1.3			Current	1.6	1.7
		1.4	1.1				1.0	1.2
		1.7	.8				1.1	1.2
		1.0	.4			Quick	.7	.8
		.2	.3				.6	.5
		25 14.5	35 10.5				30 12.3	29 12.7
		35 10.5	52 7.1			Sales/Receivables	43 8.5	42 8.6
		49 7.4	67 5.4				58 6.3	61 6.0
		55 6.7	78 4.7				30 12.4	46 7.9
		127 2.9	148 2.5			Cost of Sales/Inventory	66 5.6	90 4.0
		206 1.8	222 1.6				127 2.9	155 2.4
		19 19.2	23 15.9				21 17.4	20 18.3
		25 14.7	40 9.1			Cost of Sales/Payables	39 9.3	36 10.2
		49 7.5	55 6.7				62 5.9	55 6.6
		2.6	3.1				5.2	3.9
		5.0	7.1			Sales/Working Capital	7.7	6.4
		13.1	37.6				-295.2	19.0
		24.8	8.1				21.8	30.4
		(16) 2.2	3.4			EBIT/Interest	(40) 6.8	(53) 6.9
		-1.9	1.7				2.4	2.1
			23.0			Net Profit + Depr., Dep.,	8.9	25.0
		(12)	3.6			Amort./Cur. Mat. L/T/D	(15) 4.0	(13) 5.7
			1.6				1.3	3.8
		.3	.3				.3	.2
		.8	.5			Fixed/Worth	.5	.4
		1.8	1.4				1.1	2.1
		.6	1.3				1.0	.8
		2.0	2.2			Debt/Worth	1.8	1.5
		3.9	3.4				5.5	6.0
		61.8	31.3			% Profit Before Taxes/Tangible	69.6	49.8
		(16) 31.1	(19) 17.1			Net Worth	(36) 27.2	(46) 28.3
		-12.1	3.6				14.0	13.6
		30.9	10.3			% Profit Before Taxes/Total	20.8	22.5
		7.1	3.9			Assets	9.1	10.3
		-6.1	1.1				3.7	2.3
		10.2	18.1				25.8	37.7
		7.0	9.0			Sales/Net Fixed Assets	10.5	10.8
		3.8	3.3				6.7	7.0
		2.5	1.8				2.8	2.4
		1.9	1.2			Sales/Total Assets	2.2	1.9
		.9	1.0				1.5	1.6
		1.5	1.7				.9	.7
		(17) 2.5	(18) 2.8			% Depr., Dep., Amort./Sales	(37) 1.2	(49) 1.3
		5.0	4.5				2.1	2.6
								2.1
						% Officers', Directors'		(15) 3.9
						Owners' Comp/Sales		7.6
2092M	17784M	154064M	612351M	439542M	806412M	Net Sales ($)	2826589M	2445335M
484M	9143M	90817M	432115M	284914M	442756M	Total Assets ($)	1465884M	1300492M

MANUFACTURING—Mining Machinery and Equipment Manufacturing NAICS 333131

Comparative Historical Data | Current Data Sorted by Sales

12	9	12	Type of Statement				1			1	1	9
12	14	13	Unqualified				3			3	5	2
9	8	2	Reviewed							2		
3	3	3	Compiled							1		
15	22	24	Tax Returns	2			3			5	11	3
4/1/07-3/31/08	4/1/08-3/31/09	4/1/09-3/31/10	Other			11 (4/1-9/30/09)				43 (10/1/09-3/31/10)		
ALL	ALL	ALL		0-1MM	1-3MM	3-5MM				5-10MM	10-25MM	25MM & OVER
51	56	54	NUMBER OF STATEMENTS	2	9					12	17	14
%	%	%	ASSETS	%	%	%				%	%	%
6.3	7.1	7.4	Cash & Equivalents							8.1	6.5	7.7
24.1	23.9	20.2	Trade Receivables (net)			D				18.9	16.8	24.1
33.0	33.2	36.2	Inventory			A				31.5	38.8	35.2
3.6	2.4	4.3	All Other Current			T				5.2	2.8	6.8
67.0	66.7	68.2	Total Current			A				63.7	64.9	73.8
23.2	22.8	24.1	Fixed Assets (net)							30.9	26.6	20.8
3.2	5.1	4.0	Intangibles (net)			N				3.4	4.8	3.0
6.5	5.5	3.7	All Other Non-Current			O				2.0	3.7	2.4
100.0	100.0	100.0	Total			T				100.0	100.0	100.0
			LIABILITIES			A						
10.4	12.7	12.0	Notes Payable-Short Term			V				5.5	19.4	9.0
3.3	4.3	4.5	Cur. Mat.-L.T.D.			A				7.6	3.6	2.5
15.3	15.0	11.6	Trade Payables			I				12.5	10.5	10.4
.1	.5	.9	Income Taxes Payable			L				.0	1.4	1.7
14.8	10.2	10.3	All Other Current			A				5.9	10.9	13.8
43.9	42.7	39.3	Total Current			B				31.4	45.8	37.4
18.3	16.6	14.6	Long-Term Debt			L				16.2	13.9	7.5
.3	.2	.6	Deferred Taxes			E				.2	.9	.9
4.0	4.2	7.0	All Other Non-Current							3.4	2.7	3.2
33.4	36.4	38.6	Net Worth							48.8	36.7	51.1
100.0	100.0	100.0	Total Liabilities & Net Worth							100.0	100.0	100.0
			INCOME DATA									
100.0	100.0	100.0	Net Sales							100.0	100.0	100.0
29.0	29.5	28.9	Gross Profit							26.4	28.6	26.8
22.0	24.2	25.1	Operating Expenses							18.8	23.7	19.1
7.0	5.2	3.8	Operating Profit							7.7	4.9	7.7
.8	1.5	.7	All Other Expenses (net)							1.1	.8	.5
6.2	3.7	3.0	Profit Before Taxes							6.6	4.1	7.2
			RATIOS									
2.7	2.1	2.6								3.2	1.9	2.9
1.9	1.6	1.7	Current							1.8	1.4	1.9
1.3	1.2	1.3								1.4	1.1	1.5
1.2	1.1	1.5								1.5	.8	1.5
.8	.7	.7	Quick							1.2	.4	1.1
.5	.5	.3								.3	.2	.4
31 11.8	28 12.8	29 12.5								19 19.0	34 10.9	34 10.6
49 7.5	39 9.4	41 8.9	Sales/Receivables							29 12.4	47 7.8	54 6.8
61 5.9	53 6.9	62 5.9								37 9.9	67 5.4	65 5.7
45 8.1	35 10.5	56 6.5								36 10.2	39 9.3	64 5.7
69 5.3	76 4.8	110 3.3	Cost of Sales/Inventory							80 4.6	130 2.8	78 4.7
155 2.4	136 2.7	202 1.8								139 2.6	256 1.4	145 2.5
18 20.2	14 25.7	19 19.2								18 19.7	23 16.1	14 26.0
32 11.5	29 12.5	30 12.0	Cost of Sales/Payables							21 17.5	44 8.4	26 13.8
63 5.8	51 7.2	51 7.2								42 8.7	53 6.9	38 9.6
3.4	4.7	3.0								3.1	3.1	3.8
6.2	9.5	5.8	Sales/Working Capital							9.9	7.0	5.5
14.4	21.6	15.6								16.9	51.6	9.0
15.0	18.7	16.0								16.0	8.1	52.5
(50) 5.9	(52) 5.3	(50) 3.6	EBIT/Interest						(11)	2.9	(16) 3.4	8.6
1.5	1.7	-.7								-2.0	1.4	4.3
5.0	7.5	13.9										
(15) 2.9	(20) 2.6	(18) 3.6	Net Profit + Depr., Dep., Amort./Cur. Mat. L/T/D									
.3	.7	1.3										
.3	.3	.3								.3	.3	.3
.6	.7	.7	Fixed/Worth							.9	.7	.4
1.8	1.4	1.5								1.5	1.7	.6
.9	1.0	.7								.6	1.5	.5
2.0	1.7	1.9	Debt/Worth							1.0	2.1	1.0
5.2	3.8	3.2								2.8	2.9	2.2
49.6	59.8	37.9								54.9	37.7	38.4
(44) 25.9	(46) 31.5	(48) 18.4	% Profit Before Taxes/Tangible Net Worth							29.9	(16) 16.3	18.4
13.2	5.5	2.8								-10.4	3.2	10.4
21.3	20.5	16.1								26.6	11.3	24.2
10.1	7.3	5.3	% Profit Before Taxes/Total Assets							7.1	4.1	7.7
1.0	-.8	-3.7								-6.4	.9	3.4
28.4	27.9	13.4								9.2	9.8	21.5
12.4	10.9	7.0	Sales/Net Fixed Assets							7.0	6.8	7.1
4.5	5.4	4.2								4.3	3.1	5.8
2.5	2.9	2.1								2.7	1.9	2.0
2.0	2.1	1.6	Sales/Total Assets							2.3	1.1	1.7
1.4	1.5	1.0								1.3	1.0	1.6
.9	1.1	1.5								2.1	2.1	.8
(47) 1.6	(50) 1.7	(50) 2.8	% Depr., Dep., Amort./Sales							3.1	(15) 3.0	(13) 1.7
3.2	2.7	4.4								5.1	5.5	2.8
1.5	1.4											
(13) 2.2	(14) 1.7		% Officers', Directors' Owners' Comp/Sales									
4.1	6.3											
2025816M	2177751M	2032245M	Net Sales ($)	1168M	17538M					92795M	317837M	1602907M
1112012M	1224053M	1260229M	Total Assets ($)	1668M	13526M					54413M	268877M	921745M

© RMA 2010

M = $ thousand   MM = $ million
See Pages 9 through 22 for Explanation of Ratios and Data

Current Data Sorted by Assets   Comparative Historical Data

0-500M	500M-2MM	2-10MM	10-50MM	50-100MM	100-250MM		4/1/05-3/31/06 ALL	4/1/06-3/31/07 ALL
						Type of Statement		
		4	5	4	5	Unqualified	15	13
		4	2	1		Reviewed	3	6
1	1	6	1	1		Compiled	8	14
1	1	6				Tax Returns	7	4
	2	24	17	4	4	Other	32	41
		14 (4/1-9/30/09)	80 (10/1/09-3/31/10)					
2	4	44	25	10	9	**NUMBER OF STATEMENTS**	65	78
%	%	%	%	%	%	**ASSETS**	%	%
		14.8	8.5	20.2		Cash & Equivalents	9.3	7.3
		19.3	16.3	17.4		Trade Receivables (net)	30.2	28.5
		24.7	25.1	13.3		Inventory	25.0	25.3
		6.3	3.9	3.9		All Other Current	3.5	5.1
		65.1	53.8	54.8		Total Current	68.0	66.3
		20.4	31.3	19.8		Fixed Assets (net)	21.8	26.0
		4.5	11.9	15.6		Intangibles (net)	5.1	4.5
		10.0	3.0	9.8		All Other Non-Current	5.1	3.2
		100.0	100.0	100.0		Total	100.0	100.0
						LIABILITIES		
		8.6	6.4	.1		Notes Payable-Short Term	7.4	8.0
		2.2	2.8	1.9		Cur. Mat.-L.T.D.	3.0	3.0
		10.2	6.4	9.4		Trade Payables	16.8	15.6
		.5	.3	.4		Income Taxes Payable	.6	.3
		9.5	8.9	15.0		All Other Current	12.6	13.4
		30.9	24.8	26.9		Total Current	40.4	40.3
		8.2	16.8	12.0		Long-Term Debt	15.5	15.8
		1.1	1.7	2.5		Deferred Taxes	.5	.6
		5.5	3.1	12.7		All Other Non-Current	6.3	5.4
		54.4	53.6	46.0		Net Worth	37.3	37.9
		100.0	100.0	100.0		Total Liabilities & Net Worth	100.0	100.0
						INCOME DATA		
		100.0	100.0	100.0		Net Sales	100.0	100.0
		35.5	33.0	38.4		Gross Profit	35.6	35.1
		31.6	26.2	26.4		Operating Expenses	26.7	24.9
		3.9	6.8	12.0		Operating Profit	8.9	10.3
		.7	3.0	2.2		All Other Expenses (net)	1.1	1.3
		3.1	3.8	9.8		Profit Before Taxes	7.8	9.0
						RATIOS		
		3.9	3.2	3.7		Current	2.6	2.3
		2.4	2.5	1.7			1.8	1.6
		1.3	1.6	1.1			1.3	1.3
		2.9	1.7	2.4		Quick	1.4	1.6
		1.0	1.0	1.1			1.0	.8
		.5	.5	.9			.7	.5
		25 14.8	37 10.0	62 5.9		Sales/Receivables	44 8.3	38 9.5
		40 9.2	52 7.0	70 5.2			61 5.9	56 6.5
		55 6.6	64 5.7	105 3.5			81 4.5	71 5.2
		24 15.2	56 6.5	3 130.8		Cost of Sales/Inventory	32 11.2	30 12.1
		81 4.5	116 3.1	96 3.8			80 4.6	70 5.2
		183 2.0	164 2.2	174 2.1			126 2.9	148 2.5
		11 32.3	13 28.4	37 9.7		Cost of Sales/Payables	28 12.8	21 17.1
		20 18.5	21 17.1	67 5.4			47 7.8	47 7.8
		37 9.9	47 7.8	75 4.8			70 5.2	68 5.3
		3.1	2.7	2.2		Sales/Working Capital	4.4	4.5
		4.7	4.1	4.7			6.6	8.0
		15.9	9.8	12.0			11.9	14.6
		24.8	22.1			EBIT/Interest	14.7	13.5
		(35) 4.3	(24) 5.2				(60) 6.7	(72) 6.3
		-1.4	.5				2.8	3.2
						Net Profit + Depr., Dep.,	7.6	16.2
						Amort./Cur. Mat. L/T/D	(25) 3.5	(22) 5.1
							2.1	2.0
		.1	.3	.1		Fixed/Worth	.3	.3
		.3	.6	.4			.6	.9
		.7	2.0	NM			1.2	1.6
		.4	.4	.5		Debt/Worth	.9	1.0
		.8	1.1	1.3			2.2	1.9
		2.1	1.9	NM			3.3	4.9
		30.5	19.6			% Profit Before Taxes/Tangible	60.9	60.7
		(43) 14.7	(22) 10.3			Net Worth	(61) 29.3	(72) 38.9
		2.6	1.4				14.7	18.6
		15.7	11.2	16.2		% Profit Before Taxes/Total	17.3	21.5
		6.2	4.9	8.3		Assets	10.5	11.1
		.0	-2.0	3.5			5.4	6.8
		27.4	8.4	53.7		Sales/Net Fixed Assets	26.4	19.8
		11.0	4.7	6.7			9.7	7.7
		3.8	2.9	2.5			5.0	4.5
		2.2	1.6	1.1		Sales/Total Assets	2.6	2.5
		1.5	1.2	.8			1.8	1.7
		1.0	.7	.5			1.3	1.3
		.8	2.7			% Depr., Dep., Amort./Sales	1.0	1.1
		(38) 1.6	(22) 4.7				(57) 1.7	(66) 2.1
		4.4	12.3				3.6	3.0
		2.6				% Officers', Directors'	2.1	1.7
		(19) 4.8				Owners' Comp/Sales	(17) 4.3	(18) 2.4
		8.4					8.0	5.6
1304M	10239M	359339M	708136M	581724M	1287789M	Net Sales ($)	1935731M	2791109M
720M	3994M	214283M	623777M	704748M	1509216M	Total Assets ($)	1599644M	1931830M

M = $ thousand   MM = $ million
See Pages 9 through 22 for Explanation of Ratios and Data

Comparative Historical Data | Current Data Sorted by Sales

			Type of Statement	0-1MM	1-3MM	3-5MM	5-10MM	10-25MM	25MM & OVER
11	19	18	Unqualified				2	5	11
17	11	8	Reviewed	1		1	2	1	3
17	9	10	Compiled	1		3	4	1	1
5	6	7	Tax Returns		2	2	1		1
47	60	51	Other	2	7	3	7	17	15
4/1/07-3/31/08 ALL	4/1/08-3/31/09 ALL	4/1/09-3/31/10 ALL			14 (4/1-9/30/09)		80 (10/1/09-3/31/10)		
97	105	94	**NUMBER OF STATEMENTS**	4	9	9	16	25	31
%	%	%	**ASSETS**	%	%	%	%	%	%
8.2	9.9	12.1	Cash & Equivalents				14.1	13.4	12.5
28.8	23.2	18.2	Trade Receivables (net)				22.1	16.0	18.7
24.4	24.7	21.8	Inventory				29.1	19.8	21.3
8.0	6.3	5.8	All Other Current				4.1	7.4	3.6
69.3	64.1	58.0	Total Current				69.4	56.6	56.1
22.1	23.2	24.8	Fixed Assets (net)				19.3	24.8	27.4
3.7	6.7	9.2	Intangibles (net)				2.3	14.2	12.1
4.9	5.9	8.0	All Other Non-Current				9.0	4.4	4.4
100.0	100.0	100.0	Total				100.0	100.0	100.0
			LIABILITIES						
9.3	9.0	6.3	Notes Payable-Short Term				11.4	6.9	1.5
2.9	2.9	2.6	Cur. Mat.-L.T.D.				1.8	3.0	2.5
15.5	11.9	9.0	Trade Payables				12.9	6.2	8.1
.8	.8	.4	Income Taxes Payable				.6	.3	.6
11.7	12.2	9.6	All Other Current				5.9	13.9	10.0
40.2	36.9	28.0	Total Current				32.7	30.2	22.8
13.1	12.6	16.8	Long-Term Debt				7.0	14.5	15.1
.7	1.4	1.3	Deferred Taxes				1.3	1.9	1.2
1.9	3.8	6.2	All Other Non-Current				1.1	1.5	7.5
44.1	45.4	47.7	Net Worth				57.9	51.8	53.4
100.0	100.0	100.0	Total Liabilities & Net Worth				100.0	100.0	100.0
			INCOME DATA						
100.0	100.0	100.0	Net Sales				100.0	100.0	100.0
37.1	37.5	35.1	Gross Profit				34.1	29.5	32.3
25.1	25.2	29.3	Operating Expenses				30.6	25.5	23.5
12.0	12.3	5.8	Operating Profit				3.5	4.0	8.8
1.5	1.5	1.9	All Other Expenses (net)				-.1	1.8	2.5
10.5	10.7	4.0	Profit Before Taxes				3.6	2.2	6.3
			RATIOS						
2.7	2.6	3.6	Current				3.9	3.5	3.8
1.8	1.8	2.2					2.9	2.2	2.3
1.3	1.2	1.3					1.5	1.1	1.5
1.6	1.6	2.0	Quick				3.1	1.9	1.8
1.0	.9	1.0					1.2	.9	1.1
.6	.5	.5					.5		.8
38 9.7	39 9.4	28 13.3	Sales/Receivables	27 13.7		26 14.2			49 7.4
57 6.4	54 6.8	50 7.3		40 9.2		38 9.5			55 6.6
69 5.3	72 5.1	66 5.5		56 6.5		54 6.7			69 5.3
18 19.8	16 23.5	16 22.8	Cost of Sales/Inventory	18 20.8		13 28.0			24 15.4
66 5.5	83 4.4	88 4.1		80 4.6		77 4.8			109 3.4
145 2.5	154 2.4	165 2.2		188 1.9		138 2.6			155 2.4
22 16.7	20 18.4	14 26.7	Cost of Sales/Payables	13 28.9		11 31.9			21 17.4
40 9.2	34 10.7	26 14.0		29 12.4		18 22.0			28 13.0
60 6.1	62 5.9	50 7.3		50 7.3		34 10.9			65 5.6
4.5	3.6	2.8	Sales/Working Capital				2.9	3.3	2.7
7.3	6.2	4.7					4.5	5.3	4.4
18.2	14.3	11.7					10.2	26.2	8.0
23.4	44.7	23.1	EBIT/Interest				24.1	25.9	30.2
(85) 8.2	(94) 12.3	(81) 4.7					(13) 4.3	(23) 8.9	(28) 6.5
3.2	4.4	1.2					-12.3	-1.4	2.2
29.2	20.1	6.4	Net Profit + Depr., Dep., Amort./Cur. Mat. L/T/D						
(26) 5.2	(33) 3.3	(20) 1.8							
2.7	1.5	.2							
.2	.2	.2	Fixed/Worth				.0	.2	.3
.5	.4	.5					.2	.5	.4
1.2	1.4	1.3					.7	1.9	2.0
.7	.7	.4	Debt/Worth				.3	.4	.4
1.4	1.4	1.1					.5	1.0	1.2
3.7	3.2	3.7					1.7	4.8	2.6
75.7	64.6	30.1	% Profit Before Taxes/Tangible Net Worth				24.3	38.7	36.2
(94) 42.7	(93) 35.0	(82) 14.9					10.2	(22) 18.3	(27) 18.1
22.5	19.3	2.4					-13.4	-14.1	8.0
28.5	27.6	14.3	% Profit Before Taxes/Total Assets				14.9	18.3	13.8
15.7	13.4	6.2					4.7	6.1	7.5
5.7	7.1	.4					-7.8	-7.3	2.9
32.6	28.1	15.6	Sales/Net Fixed Assets				82.1	15.2	12.8
9.6	9.2	7.0					14.6	7.4	5.5
5.5	4.3	3.0					5.1	3.5	2.3
2.7	2.2	1.8	Sales/Total Assets				2.4	2.0	1.4
1.8	1.7	1.3					1.7	1.6	1.1
1.3	1.0	.7					1.5	.9	.7
.5	.7	1.2	% Depr., Dep., Amort./Sales				.8	.9	2.5
(77) 1.8	(82) 2.6	(77) 3.0					(13) 1.3	(23) 2.6	(23) 3.8
4.1	5.1	6.3					5.4	6.3	6.2
1.4	1.6	2.6	% Officers', Directors' Owners' Comp/Sales						
(24) 3.4	(27) 3.4	(25) 4.3							
7.7	8.0	7.6							
3450700M	4239960M	2948531M	Net Sales ($)	2828M	19035M	33293M	117970M	413022M	2362383M
2435625M	3618243M	3056738M	Total Assets ($)	9566M	30638M	29534M	77075M	399966M	2509959M

M = $ thousand   MM = $ million
See Pages 9 through 22 for Explanation of Ratios and Data

Current Data Sorted by Assets   Comparative Historical Data

	0-500M	500M-2MM	2-10MM	10-50MM	50-100MM	100-250MM		4/1/05-3/31/06 ALL	4/1/06-3/31/07 ALL
Type of Statement									
Unqualified	1	3	5	6				5	13
Reviewed		3	9	4				9	12
Compiled		2		2				3	5
Tax Returns	2	5	2					2	3
Other		5	11	8	4			10	12
		8 (4/1-9/30/09)		61 (10/1/09-3/31/10)					
NUMBER OF STATEMENTS	3	15	27	20	4			29	45
	%	%	%	%	%	%		%	%
ASSETS									
Cash & Equivalents		17.5	3.8	11.9				5.8	7.9
Trade Receivables (net)		18.3	24.4	23.7		D		27.0	22.2
Inventory		31.8	27.7	22.9		A		24.3	24.7
All Other Current		1.8	3.8	3.3		T		1.4	3.1
Total Current		69.5	59.7	61.8		A		58.4	57.9
Fixed Assets (net)		23.7	27.6	24.3				26.0	30.3
Intangibles (net)		4.2	4.8	2.7		N		5.0	6.2
All Other Non-Current		2.6	7.9	11.2		O		10.6	5.6
Total		100.0	100.0	100.0		T		100.0	100.0
LIABILITIES						A			
Notes Payable-Short Term		18.1	12.0	11.8		V		11.1	11.7
Cur. Mat.-L.T.D.		2.4	2.9	4.4		A		6.0	4.3
Trade Payables		10.6	13.4	13.7		I		19.8	15.9
Income Taxes Payable		.1	.1	.1		L		.3	.1
All Other Current		20.8	17.9	15.3		A		10.8	10.1
Total Current		51.9	46.3	45.1		B		48.0	42.1
Long-Term Debt		7.2	21.2	8.5		L		14.7	13.6
Deferred Taxes		.4	.9	.8		E		.8	.5
All Other Non-Current		2.1	4.7	8.9				4.0	6.0
Net Worth		38.3	26.9	36.6				32.4	37.9
Total Liabilities & Net Worth		100.0	100.0	100.0				100.0	100.0
INCOME DATA									
Net Sales		100.0	100.0	100.0				100.0	100.0
Gross Profit		38.7	28.8	24.2				24.1	25.6
Operating Expenses		33.9	24.5	20.7				20.1	19.1
Operating Profit		4.7	4.3	3.6				4.0	6.5
All Other Expenses (net)		2.0	1.2	.9				1.2	1.3
Profit Before Taxes		2.8	3.1	2.7				2.8	5.2
RATIOS									
Current		3.2	1.6	2.0				1.5	2.1
		1.6	1.3	1.6				1.3	1.2
		.7	1.0	1.0				1.0	1.0
Quick		2.6	.9	1.4				1.1	.9
		.9	.6	.7				.7	.6
		.3	.3	.5				.5	.4
Sales/Receivables	9	40.3	38 9.5	45 8.1				36 10.1	30 12.2
	40	9.1	57 6.4	51 7.2				57 6.4	46 8.0
	55	6.6	65 5.6	71 5.1				73 5.0	59 6.1
Cost of Sales/Inventory	18	20.2	45 8.1	38 9.5				33 11.1	40 9.2
	70	5.2	75 4.9	66 5.5				63 5.8	61 6.0
	168	2.2	158 2.3	144 2.5				97 3.7	89 4.1
Cost of Sales/Payables	12	31.7	16 23.3	18 20.3				31 11.7	22 16.4
	42	8.7	46 7.9	33 11.0				46 7.9	34 10.7
	58	6.3	73 5.0	59 6.2				63 5.8	46 7.9
Sales/Working Capital		2.5	5.1	4.6				8.4	5.5
		9.9	12.9	6.4				17.7	20.6
		-5.2	-864.3	NM				NM	-150.6
EBIT/Interest		36.2	13.3	11.3				5.5	10.0
	(10)	1.0	1.8	(18) 1.5				(26) 2.7	(39) 3.4
		-2.9	1.2	-.4				1.6	1.5
Net Profit + Depr., Dep., Amort./Cur. Mat. L/T/D			3.0					2.1	2.7
			(11) 1.7					(11) 1.5	(11) 1.3
			-1.3					1.4	.4
Fixed/Worth		.2	.3	.3				.4	.4
		.3	.9	.8				1.0	1.2
		4.4	12.4	2.0				3.0	2.4
Debt/Worth		.5	1.0	.7				1.4	.9
		1.4	3.8	2.4				3.5	2.3
		7.2	41.6	38.4				7.2	6.4
% Profit Before Taxes/Tangible Net Worth		53.2	31.3	30.8				41.0	52.2
	(12)	7.2	(21) 9.1	(16) 5.1				(26) 12.7	(42) 23.7
		-6.5	-8.8	-1.7				5.2	4.0
% Profit Before Taxes/Total Assets		12.4	10.4	11.1				7.4	14.2
		.5	2.2	1.5				3.6	6.9
		-6.1	.6	-3.9				.6	2.3
Sales/Net Fixed Assets		25.9	11.1	16.0				16.7	16.3
		13.3	6.3	5.3				6.3	5.8
		6.4	3.8	3.6				4.1	3.2
Sales/Total Assets		2.7	1.9	1.6				2.5	2.5
		1.7	1.4	1.3				1.6	1.8
		1.1	1.2	.9				1.3	1.3
% Depr., Dep., Amort./Sales		1.0	1.3	1.6				1.6	1.9
	(13)	1.8	(24) 2.3	(19) 2.1				(28) 3.4	(38) 2.9
		4.7	5.2	5.1				4.3	4.7
% Officers', Directors' Owners' Comp/Sales								1.9	1.4
								(11) 3.1	(13) 3.1
								6.6	8.7
Net Sales ($)	4298M	36562M	244010M	635748M	210840M			878715M	1440879M
Total Assets ($)	1077M	18407M	155239M	432716M	224175M			559239M	1044502M

M = $ thousand   MM = $ million
See Pages 9 through 22 for Explanation of Ratios and Data

Comparative Historical Data

Current Data Sorted by Sales

					Type of Statement						
	8		15	11	Unqualified		1		1	9	1
	16		17	17	Reviewed		3	1	5	7	1
	6		3	4	Compiled		1			2	
	2		7	9	Tax Returns	1	3	2	2		
	16		21	28	Other	2	3	3	5	6	9
	4/1/07-		4/1/08-	4/1/09-		2	3				
	3/31/08		3/31/09	3/31/10			8 (4/1-9/30/09)		61 (10/1/09-3/31/10)		
	ALL		ALL	ALL		0-1MM	1-3MM	3-5MM	5-10MM	10-25MM	25MM & OVER
	48		63	69	NUMBER OF STATEMENTS	5	10	6	13	24	11
	%		%	%	ASSETS	%	%	%	%	%	%
	6.6		7.4	9.7	Cash & Equivalents		12.3		10.1	9.3	8.9
	25.6		24.7	21.9	Trade Receivables (net)		17.3		24.5	25.9	20.7
	24.7		23.7	25.9	Inventory		27.7		30.8	23.2	22.0
	2.1		2.6	2.9	All Other Current		2.6		3.2	3.6	4.5
	59.1		58.4	60.4	Total Current		59.9		68.6	61.9	56.2
	29.1		26.2	25.2	Fixed Assets (net)		29.8		20.0	28.5	18.4
	5.0		6.4	5.3	Intangibles (net)		.6		4.6	2.2	14.1
	6.9		9.0	9.0	All Other Non-Current		9.8		6.8	7.3	11.3
	100.0		100.0	100.0	Total		100.0		100.0	100.0	100.0
					LIABILITIES						
	9.8		10.4	12.9	Notes Payable-Short Term		18.6		6.6	13.7	9.1
	3.8		3.7	3.4	Cur. Mat.-L.T.D.		5.4		3.7	3.9	2.9
	15.5		14.1	12.4	Trade Payables		14.0		11.0	12.3	13.5
	.1		.1	.1	Income Taxes Payable		.2		.1	.0	.2
	10.7		13.2	16.8	All Other Current		11.7		19.3	15.5	17.0
	39.8		41.4	45.7	Total Current		49.9		40.7	45.4	42.7
	16.4		17.5	15.9	Long-Term Debt		25.6		8.7	11.4	18.2
	.2		.8	.8	Deferred Taxes		.0		1.5	.7	1.1
	4.0		4.9	5.8	All Other Non-Current		2.0		3.8	6.8	14.1
	39.5		35.4	31.9	Net Worth		22.5		45.3	35.8	23.9
	100.0		100.0	100.0	Total Liabilties & Net Worth		100.0		100.0	100.0	100.0
					INCOME DATA						
	100.0		100.0	100.0	Net Sales		100.0		100.0	100.0	100.0
	28.8		29.0	30.4	Gross Profit		39.1		31.4	25.9	23.1
	22.2		23.7	26.5	Operating Expenses		36.6		30.0	20.4	23.5
	6.7		5.3	3.9	Operating Profit		2.4		1.4	5.5	-.5
	1.3		1.8	1.4	All Other Expenses (net)		2.5		.7	.6	2.0
	5.3		3.5	2.5	Profit Before Taxes		-.1		.7	4.9	-2.5
					RATIOS						
	2.0		2.0	1.9			2.8		2.1	1.8	2.4
	1.5		1.4	1.4	Current		1.0		1.6	1.4	1.4
	1.1		1.1	.9			.7		1.3	1.1	.9
	1.1		1.2	1.1			1.7		1.3	1.1	.9
	.8		.8	.6	Quick		.7		.8	.7	.6
	.6		.6	.4			.2		.4	.5	.5
34	10.6	31	11.7	37	10.0		12	30.2	34	10.9	43	8.5	43	8.4
46	7.9	44	8.3	49	7.5	Sales/Receivables	32	11.5	52	7.0	56	6.5	50	7.3
58	6.3	55	6.6	64	5.7		51	7.1	78	4.7	66	5.5	62	5.9
35	10.3	30	12.0	39	9.4		18	20.0	27	13.6	41	8.9	42	8.6
59	6.2	54	6.8	70	5.2	Cost of Sales/Inventory	66	5.5	140	2.6	62	5.9	88	4.2
81	4.5	91	4.0	147	2.5		144	2.5	192	1.9	118	3.1	138	2.7
22	16.7	17	21.1	16	22.2		16	23.4	15	23.8	17	21.1	18	20.7
32	11.3	35	10.6	37	9.9	Cost of Sales/Payables	43	8.4	26	14.0	37	10.0	36	10.0
53	6.9	43	8.4	61	6.0		70	5.2	72	5.1	58	6.3	50	7.3

				Sales/Working Capital					
6.7		6.9	4.9		3.3		3.6	4.9	4.9
12.0		11.6	9.9		NM		8.1	8.2	11.0
33.4		44.1	-49.9		-3.7		14.8	28.5	-21.2

						EBIT/Interest						
	10.8		9.5		6.6					4.8	15.9	
(44)	3.3	(58)	4.0	(61)	1.5			(12)	1.7	(23)	3.9	
	1.4		1.6		-.7				-7.3	1.4	

						Net Profit + Depr., Dep., Amort./Cur. Mat. L/T/D				
	3.0		8.8		2.9					
(11)	2.1	(19)	3.3	(22)	1.2					
	1.8		2.5		-.4					

				Fixed/Worth					
.4		.4	.3		.1		.2	.3	1.1
.9		1.0	.9		2.7		.4	.6	1.9
1.7		2.3	UND		-2.1		2.6	2.0	-2.0

				Debt/Worth					
.9		.9	.7		.5		.6	.7	2.0
2.0		2.8	2.8		3.5		1.4	1.7	46.3
3.7		6.9	UND		-4.9		9.6	3.8	-6.1

						% Profit Before Taxes/Tangible Net Worth					
	35.3		59.8		32.8				60.9	33.2	
(42)	21.1	(57)	23.3	(53)	7.0				8.8	(20)	17.9
	9.1		6.4		-4.5				-11.4	2.3	

				% Profit Before Taxes/Total Assets					
14.9		14.6	10.6		6.3		11.4	14.3	1.7
6.7		5.5	1.6		-5.7		1.4	3.2	-2.4
1.7		1.5	-4.7		-7.9		-5.4	.8	-5.5

				Sales/Net Fixed Assets					
15.2		18.5	14.8		32.8		17.0	10.6	17.2
6.8		8.7	7.1		13.3		8.6	5.0	9.1
3.4		4.5	3.7		5.1		5.3	3.6	4.3

				Sales/Total Assets					
2.5		2.3	1.9		3.0		2.3	1.8	1.6
1.9		1.9	1.4		1.7		1.4	1.5	1.2
1.4		1.5	1.0		1.0		1.2	1.1	.9

						% Depr., Dep., Amort./Sales				
	1.1		1.1		1.4				.9	1.8
(44)	2.5	(58)	2.6	(61)	2.3			(12)	2.2	3.0
	4.4		4.3		5.2				5.2	4.7

						% Officers', Directors' Owners' Comp/Sales		
	2.1		1.2		2.1			
(11)	3.7	(15)	2.6	(18)	4.8			
	17.1		10.3		10.8			

				Net Sales ($)					
1166512M		1649618M	1131458M	Net Sales ($)	2850M	19180M	21231M	92263M	371860M	624074M
768371M		1052100M	831614M	Total Assets ($)	4050M	12784M	18905M	61482M	284169M	450224M

M = $ thousand   MM = $ million
See Pages 9 through 22 for Explanation of Ratios and Data

Current Data Sorted by Assets

Comparative Historical Data

0-500M	500M-2MM	2-10MM	10-50MM	50-100MM	100-250MM		4/1/05-3/31/06 ALL	4/1/06-3/31/07 ALL
1	2 / 1 / 2	5 / 2	1	1	3	Type of Statement		
						Unqualified	4	8
						Reviewed	8	12
						Compiled	4	6
						Tax Returns	2	4
	2 (4/1-9/30/09)	6	7 30 (10/1/09-3/31/10)		1	Other	11	9
1	5	13	8	2	3	NUMBER OF STATEMENTS	29	39
%	%	%	%	%	%		%	%
						ASSETS		
		13.0				Cash & Equivalents	12.6	13.0
		23.4				Trade Receivables (net)	23.9	29.7
		37.0				Inventory	32.5	29.3
		2.6				All Other Current	2.7	2.6
		76.0				Total Current	71.6	74.5
		17.6				Fixed Assets (net)	18.2	17.7
		2.4				Intangibles (net)	4.0	3.6
		4.0				All Other Non-Current	6.1	4.1
		100.0				Total	100.0	100.0
						LIABILITIES		
		15.1				Notes Payable-Short Term	13.4	7.7
		1.7				Cur. Mat.-L.T.D.	1.5	2.8
		17.1				Trade Payables	15.7	17.2
		.0				Income Taxes Payable	.1	.3
		19.0				All Other Current	20.9	21.9
		52.9				Total Current	51.7	50.0
		8.4				Long-Term Debt	5.9	7.4
		1.4				Deferred Taxes	.4	.1
		6.8				All Other Non-Current	5.7	4.5
		30.4				Net Worth	36.3	38.0
		100.0				Total Liabilties & Net Worth	100.0	100.0
						INCOME DATA		
		100.0				Net Sales	100.0	100.0
		26.9				Gross Profit	29.3	28.8
		27.3				Operating Expenses	25.5	23.8
		-.4				Operating Profit	3.8	5.0
		1.3				All Other Expenses (net)	.5	1.6
		-1.7				Profit Before Taxes	3.4	3.4
						RATIOS		
		2.9					2.1	2.3
		1.6				Current	1.4	1.6
		1.0					1.1	1.1
		1.5					.8	1.5
		.6				Quick	.7	.8
		.4					.5	.6
		38 9.5					30 12.3 / 36 10.3	
		46 8.0				Sales/Receivables	47 7.8 / 48 7.6	
		57 6.4					58 6.3 / 58 6.2	
		39 9.4					47 7.8 / 32 11.3	
		93 3.9				Cost of Sales/Inventory	95 3.8 / 64 5.7	
		162 2.3					174 2.1 / 110 3.3	
		22 16.5					15 23.9 / 13 27.2	
		33 11.0				Cost of Sales/Payables	35 10.5 / 33 11.1	
		93 3.9					60 6.1 / 49 7.4	
		3.5					4.1	4.2
		6.1				Sales/Working Capital	8.7	10.5
		NM					52.1	27.5
		8.5					6.7	23.3
		-.5				EBIT/Interest	(24) 4.5	(33) 5.7
		-2.1					2.0	2.2
						Net Profit + Depr., Dep., Amort./Cur. Mat. L/T/D		
		.2					.2	.2
		.4				Fixed/Worth	.3	.4
		68.6					1.4	1.2
		.7					.7	.6
		4.1				Debt/Worth	1.7	1.6
		255.5					3.6	4.1
		16.3					39.3	55.1
	(11) -3.9					% Profit Before Taxes/Tangible Net Worth	(26) 12.8	(35) 20.9
		-19.6					1.5	7.6
		3.5					10.7	17.4
		-2.6				% Profit Before Taxes/Total Assets	6.1	8.3
		-7.0					.5	3.9
		30.4					42.5	44.6
		15.7				Sales/Net Fixed Assets	15.3	12.6
		6.7					5.9	7.8
		2.1					2.5	3.0
		1.7				Sales/Total Assets	1.8	2.1
		1.4					1.2	1.6
		.9					.8	.6
	(12) 1.1					% Depr., Dep., Amort./Sales	(27) 1.6	(38) 1.0
		1.7					2.8	2.4
							1.9	1.7
						% Officers', Directors' Owners' Comp/Sales	(14) 2.6	(12) 2.4
							3.9	3.8
5M	13039M	119625M	272431M	88696M	440437M	Net Sales ($)	613482M	1205785M
3M	6590M	68106M	212783M	114479M	455103M	Total Assets ($)	585056M	798657M

M = $ thousand   MM = $ million
See Pages 9 through 22 for Explanation of Ratios and Data

Comparative Historical Data | Current Data Sorted by Sales

			Type of Statement	0-1MM	1-3MM	3-5MM	5-10MM	10-25MM	25MM & OVER
5		5	Unqualified						5
6	7	6	Reviewed	1			3	2	
4	7	4	Compiled		2	1	3	2	1
2	2	2	Tax Returns			1	1		
12	15	16	Other		3	1	4	4	4
4/1/07-3/31/08	4/1/08-3/31/09	4/1/09-3/31/10			2 (4/1-9/30/09)		30 (10/1/09-3/31/10)		
ALL	ALL	ALL							
29	31	32	NUMBER OF STATEMENTS	1	5	3	7	7	9
%	%	%	**ASSETS**	%	%	%	%	%	%
10.1	10.4	15.2	Cash & Equivalents						
23.7	25.2	20.6	Trade Receivables (net)						
32.5	32.6	30.7	Inventory						
3.9	3.5	2.5	All Other Current						
70.2	71.8	68.9	Total Current						
19.8	20.6	22.2	Fixed Assets (net)						
6.8	4.2	3.5	Intangibles (net)						
3.2	3.5	5.4	All Other Non-Current						
100.0	100.0	100.0	Total						
			LIABILITIES						
5.0	10.6	9.9	Notes Payable-Short Term						
3.9	3.3	1.9	Cur. Mat.-L.T.D.						
17.2	17.2	12.2	Trade Payables						
.5	.1	.0	Income Taxes Payable						
22.4	18.8	17.3	All Other Current						
49.1	50.0	41.3	Total Current						
9.7	12.3	11.2	Long-Term Debt						
.5	.6	.8	Deferred Taxes						
4.2	6.3	6.1	All Other Non-Current						
36.6	30.9	40.6	Net Worth						
100.0	100.0	100.0	Total Liabilities & Net Worth						
			INCOME DATA						
100.0	100.0	100.0	Net Sales						
28.6	30.4	29.9	Gross Profit						
23.1	26.0	28.1	Operating Expenses						
5.5	4.4	1.8	Operating Profit						
.9	.7	.5	All Other Expenses (net)						
4.6	3.7	1.3	Profit Before Taxes						
			RATIOS						
2.3	2.4	3.8	Current						
1.8	1.3	1.7							
1.0	.9	1.1							
1.3	1.3	2.0	Quick						
.7	.6	.7							
.3	.4	.4							
38 9.5	30 12.2	38 9.7	Sales/Receivables						
49 7.4	39 9.5	44 8.4							
59 6.2	49 7.5	57 6.4							
52 7.1	43 8.6	42 8.7	Cost of Sales/Inventory						
81 4.5	71 5.1	92 4.0							
181 2.0	111 3.3	164 2.2							
20 18.4	20 18.6	17 21.6	Cost of Sales/Payables						
41 8.9	31 11.7	32 11.3							
63 5.8	52 7.0	54 6.8							
3.4	5.0	2.6	Sales/Working Capital						
9.4	11.1	6.0							
NM	-75.7	28.8							
34.4	20.5	8.7	EBIT/Interest						
(23) 7.4	(27) 3.5	(28) 1.6							
.4	.1	-1.1							
			Net Profit + Depr., Dep., Amort./Cur. Mat. L/T/D						
.2	.2	.2	Fixed/Worth						
.6	.6	.4							
4.7	-4.9	3.3							
.6	.9	.5	Debt/Worth						
2.6	2.9	1.0							
10.7	-38.8	32.9							
60.8	55.5	17.4	% Profit Before Taxes/Tangible Net Worth						
(23) 18.8	(23) 19.3	(26) 3.6							
-5.3	8.4	-4.9							
14.6	13.5	5.2	% Profit Before Taxes/Total Assets						
8.0	7.5	1.6							
-1.4	.2	-3.9							
35.4	26.9	18.5	Sales/Net Fixed Assets						
10.9	13.0	8.0							
3.7	7.7	5.2							
2.3	3.5	1.9	Sales/Total Assets						
1.7	2.1	1.5							
1.1	1.7	1.1							
.5	.5	.9	% Depr., Dep., Amort./Sales						
1.4	(24) 1.0	(29) 1.6							
3.5	2.1	2.3							
			% Officers', Directors' Owners' Comp/Sales						
923136M	817392M	934233M	Net Sales ($)	5M	12217M	12381M	51542M	114916M	743172M
934191M	497241M	857064M	Total Assets ($)	3M	8046M	6723M	53525M	103316M	685451M

M = $ thousand   MM = $ million
See Pages 9 through 22 for Explanation of Ratios and Data

Current Data Sorted by Assets   Comparative Historical Data

0-500M	500M-2MM	2-10MM	10-50MM	50-100MM	100-250MM	Type of Statement	6	6
		1				Unqualified	6	6
		4				Reviewed	9	14
2	2	3	2	1		Compiled	9	9
1	1					Tax Returns	1	4
		3	4			Other	18	18
							4/1/05-3/31/06	4/1/06-3/31/07
0-500M	0 (4/1-9/30/09) 500M-2MM	2-10MM	21 (10/1/09-3/31/10) 10-50MM	50-100MM	100-250MM		ALL	ALL
	3	11	6	1		NUMBER OF STATEMENTS	43	51
%	%	%	%	%	%	**ASSETS**	%	%
D		11.5			D	Cash & Equivalents	9.9	11.5
A		24.6			A	Trade Receivables (net)	28.5	24.4
T		34.2			T	Inventory	32.7	28.8
A		5.9			A	All Other Current	2.8	1.8
		76.3				Total Current	73.9	66.6
N		16.6			N	Fixed Assets (net)	13.8	17.2
O		2.7			O	Intangibles (net)	4.7	7.6
T		4.4			T	All Other Non-Current	7.5	8.6
		100.0				Total	100.0	100.0
A					A	**LIABILITIES**		
V		18.2			V	Notes Payable-Short Term	13.2	10.1
A		1.1			A	Cur. Mat.-L.T.D.	4.0	4.9
I		12.8			I	Trade Payables	16.7	13.7
L		.0			L	Income Taxes Payable	.2	.1
A		8.5			A	All Other Current	14.3	16.4
B		40.7			B	Total Current	48.4	45.1
L		11.3			L	Long-Term Debt	11.0	14.1
E		.2			E	Deferred Taxes	.3	.2
		2.1				All Other Non-Current	3.4	2.8
		45.7				Net Worth	36.9	37.8
		100.0				Total Liabilties & Net Worth	100.0	100.0
						INCOME DATA		
		100.0				Net Sales	100.0	100.0
		29.1				Gross Profit	29.0	31.0
		25.1				Operating Expenses	24.4	27.0
		4.0				Operating Profit	4.7	3.9
		2.9				All Other Expenses (net)	.4	1.5
		1.1				Profit Before Taxes	4.3	2.4
						RATIOS		
		2.5					2.5	2.7
		2.0				Current	1.7	1.7
		1.3					1.4	1.2
		1.1					1.4	1.4
		.8				Quick	.8	.8
		.6					.5	.5
	32	11.5					37 10.0	36 10.1
	44	8.2				Sales/Receivables	47 7.7	50 7.3
	68	5.4					74 4.9	64 5.7
	24	15.0					40 9.2	29 12.6
	105	3.5				Cost of Sales/Inventory	109 3.4	82 4.4
	180	2.0					132 2.8	138 2.6
	9	40.7					19 19.0	15 23.7
	20	18.3				Cost of Sales/Payables	30 12.2	26 14.1
	46	7.9					60 6.1	53 6.9
		3.5					3.8	3.7
		4.1				Sales/Working Capital	5.8	6.1
		10.4					25.3	25.2
		9.7					(39) 12.1	5.2
		(10) 1.8				EBIT/Interest	4.2	(41) 2.9
		-1.5					1.6	-.4
						Net Profit + Depr., Dep.,	40.6	
						Amort./Cur. Mat. L/T/D	(12) 5.6	
							.5	
		.2					.1	.1
		.4				Fixed/Worth	.3	.3
		.9					1.1	2.1
		.5					.6	.6
		1.4				Debt/Worth	2.3	1.7
		3.2					8.1	6.1
		27.6				% Profit Before Taxes/Tangible	62.3	22.6
		(10) 12.9				Net Worth	(38) 8.6	(42) 6.9
		-.8					3.3	-.4
		8.5				% Profit Before Taxes/Total	14.2	13.9
		3.9				Assets	4.3	3.0
		-6.5					1.3	-.8
		17.2					47.8	42.7
		15.1				Sales/Net Fixed Assets	19.0	14.5
		6.1					7.8	5.2
		2.3					2.4	2.1
		1.8				Sales/Total Assets	1.7	1.7
		1.1					1.1	1.1
		.5					.6	.6
		1.5				% Depr., Dep., Amort./Sales	1.2	1.3
		2.6					2.0	3.7
						% Officers', Directors'	2.4	3.2
						Owners' Comp/Sales	(13) 3.3	(19) 4.1
							6.1	6.8
	7142M	92729M	151212M	97090M		Net Sales ($)	937279M	762933M
	3213M	49770M	130006M	98040M		Total Assets ($)	651606M	609480M

Comparative Historical Data				Current Data Sorted by Sales					
			Type of Statement						
10	4	1	Unqualified					1	
10	6	7	Reviewed				1	4	2
5	4	5	Compiled		3	1	1		
	1	1	Tax Returns		1				
12	9	7	Other				3	2	2
4/1/07-3/31/08	**4/1/08-3/31/09**	**4/1/09-3/31/10**			**0 (4/1-9/30/09)**		**21 (10/1/09-3/31/10)**		
ALL	**ALL**	**ALL**		**0-1MM**	**1-3MM**	**3-5MM**	**5-10MM**	**10-25MM**	**25MM & OVER**
37	24	21	**NUMBER OF STATEMENTS**		4	1	5	7	4
%	%	%	**ASSETS**	%	%	%	%	%	%
11.9	11.5	15.8	Cash & Equivalents	**DATA NOT AVAILABLE**					
24.2	19.7	20.6	Trade Receivables (net)						
29.6	35.2	29.5	Inventory						
3.7	3.8	9.3	All Other Current						
69.4	70.2	75.2	Total Current						
17.6	17.2	16.6	Fixed Assets (net)						
5.8	6.0	1.6	Intangibles (net)						
7.2	6.6	6.6	All Other Non-Current						
100.0	100.0	100.0	Total						
			LIABILITIES						
11.0	9.6	11.0	Notes Payable-Short Term						
3.2	1.6	2.2	Cur. Mat.-L.T.D.						
15.4	12.6	10.2	Trade Payables						
.2	.2	.0	Income Taxes Payable						
13.1	14.5	11.5	All Other Current						
42.9	38.5	34.9	Total Current						
14.2	11.8	6.5	Long-Term Debt						
.1	.2	.2	Deferred Taxes						
4.2	3.5	3.4	All Other Non-Current						
38.5	46.0	55.0	Net Worth						
100.0	100.0	100.0	Total Liabilties & Net Worth						
			INCOME DATA						
100.0	100.0	100.0	Net Sales						
31.7	32.8	31.3	Gross Profit						
24.6	25.9	27.2	Operating Expenses						
7.1	6.9	4.0	Operating Profit						
.8	1.6	1.3	All Other Expenses (net)						
6.3	5.3	2.7	Profit Before Taxes						
			RATIOS						
3.3	3.6	5.2							
2.1	2.2	2.4	Current						
1.2	1.2	1.5							
1.7	2.0	2.4							
.8	.9	.9	Quick						
.6	.4	.6							
38 9.7	**22** 16.9	**29** 12.5							
52 7.0	**35** 10.3	**44** 8.2	Sales/Receivables						
72 5.1	**57** 6.4	**59** 6.2							
45 8.1	**33** 11.2	**29** 12.5							
103 3.6	**117** 3.1	**105** 3.5	Cost of Sales/Inventory						
174 2.1	**159** 2.3	**176** 2.1							
20 18.2	**10** 34.9	**9** 42.4							
32 11.5	**23** 16.0	**20** 18.3	Cost of Sales/Payables						
76 4.8	**54** 6.7	**46** 7.9							
2.7	3.9	2.3							
5.7	5.5	4.1	Sales/Working Capital						
13.0	18.3	9.7							
10.3	5.1	8.2							
(32) 3.7	(19) 2.3	(15) 2.3	EBIT/Interest						
1.0	.0	-2.6							
			Net Profit + Depr., Dep., Amort./Cur. Mat. L/T/D						
.1	.2	.2							
.4	.4	.3	Fixed/Worth						
1.6	1.5	.4							
.7	.5	.2							
2.0	1.2	.6	Debt/Worth						
3.9	3.9	2.9							
34.0	45.2	26.2							
(30) 14.2	(21) 20.5	(20) 8.6	% Profit Before Taxes/Tangible Net Worth						
.3	-3.5	1.5							
17.4	20.2	10.1							
5.6	6.1	5.5	% Profit Before Taxes/Total Assets						
.0	-1.4	-.2							
32.2	30.4	26.3							
11.3	9.6	9.1	Sales/Net Fixed Assets						
4.6	5.9	5.3							
2.0	2.2	2.2							
1.5	1.7	1.5	Sales/Total Assets						
1.0	1.1	1.1							
.4	.4	.6							
(34) 1.4	(21) 2.1	(20) 1.8	% Depr., Dep., Amort./Sales						
4.0	3.9	3.1							
2.4									
(11) 4.7			% Officers', Directors' Owners' Comp/Sales						
6.3									
647522M	**520324M**	**348173M**	Net Sales ($)		**7142M**	**3952M**	**37927M**	**97925M**	**201227M**
572405M	**393524M**	**281029M**	Total Assets ($)		**6207M**	**1336M**	**24974M**	**80836M**	**167676M**

M = $ thousand MM = $ million

See Pages 9 through 22 for Explanation of Ratios and Data

Current Data Sorted by Assets

Comparative Historical Data

0-500M	500M-2MM	2-10MM	10-50MM	50-100MM	100-250MM	Type of Statement	4/1/05-3/31/06 ALL	4/1/06-3/31/07 ALL
	1	3	2	1	1	Unqualified	10	12
	2	8	1			Reviewed	15	14
	1	1				Compiled	4	7
3	3	2				Tax Returns	2	7
2	3	8	5		5	Other	20	18
	10 (4/1-9/30/09)	42 (10/1/09-3/31/10)						
5	10	22	8	1	6	NUMBER OF STATEMENTS	51	58
%	%	%	%	%	%	ASSETS	%	%
	7.1	11.3				Cash & Equivalents	8.0	7.7
	24.2	22.8				Trade Receivables (net)	25.5	25.4
	41.8	26.6				Inventory	29.7	29.1
	1.6	1.1				All Other Current	2.8	2.0
	74.7	61.8				Total Current	66.0	64.2
	17.8	24.3				Fixed Assets (net)	22.6	23.8
	.3	10.0				Intangibles (net)	5.7	5.9
	7.3	4.0				All Other Non-Current	5.7	6.0
	100.0	100.0				Total	100.0	100.0
						LIABILITIES		
	8.9	9.2				Notes Payable-Short Term	9.2	10.3
	6.3	4.5				Cur. Mat.-L.T.D.	5.5	4.4
	42.3	14.5				Trade Payables	13.5	16.2
	.0	.3				Income Taxes Payable	.3	.2
	16.1	11.2				All Other Current	17.1	21.2
	73.6	39.7				Total Current	45.5	52.3
	9.7	13.6				Long-Term Debt	17.6	22.6
	.0	.5				Deferred Taxes	.2	.3
	7.2	4.8				All Other Non-Current	6.8	7.1
	9.6	41.5				Net Worth	29.9	17.8
	100.0	100.0				Total Liabilities & Net Worth	100.0	100.0
						INCOME DATA		
	100.0	100.0				Net Sales	100.0	100.0
	35.1	36.1				Gross Profit	35.2	34.7
	36.7	33.4				Operating Expenses	30.9	29.1
	-1.6	2.6				Operating Profit	4.3	5.6
	2.2	1.0				All Other Expenses (net)	1.3	2.1
	-3.8	1.7				Profit Before Taxes	3.1	3.5
						RATIOS		
	3.3	2.3					2.3	1.9
	1.2	1.6				Current	1.5	1.4
	.6	1.3					1.1	.9
	1.2	1.6					1.3	1.1
	.4	.9				Quick	.7	.7
	.1	.5					.5	.4
	13 28.8	40 9.1					30 12.1	30 12.0
	30 12.1	49 7.4				Sales/Receivables	47 7.8	46 7.9
	52 7.0	60 6.1					59 6.2	61 6.0
	22 16.3	34 10.6					32 11.5	36 10.0
	71 5.1	86 4.2				Cost of Sales/Inventory	72 5.1	74 4.9
	214 1.7	152 2.4					117 3.1	127 2.9
	22 16.2	33 11.0					21 17.8	19 18.9
	37 9.7	44 8.3				Cost of Sales/Payables	30 12.2	36 10.2
	85 4.3	54 6.8					46 8.0	55 6.7
	4.2	5.2					4.7	5.5
	21.4	8.1				Sales/Working Capital	8.1	11.3
	-6.5	23.7					35.1	-66.2
	12.2	11.9					7.7	9.4
	3.0	4.6				EBIT/Interest	(42) 3.7	(57) 3.1
	-2.9	.7					1.2	1.1
		7.4				Net Profit + Depr., Dep.,	7.5	14.8
		(10) 3.5				Amort./Cur. Mat. L/T/D	(12) 2.9	(12) 3.7
		.7					.5	.4
	.5	.3					.3	.3
	1.6	.6				Fixed/Worth	.7	1.1
	-.6	2.5					2.2	-8.9
	2.3	.8					1.1	1.7
	3.7	1.6				Debt/Worth	2.7	5.5
	-8.3	8.4					55.1	-75.3
		35.4				% Profit Before Taxes/Tangible	45.3	61.4
		(19) 21.9				Net Worth	(41) 19.3	(42) 23.6
		2.4					6.0	3.7
	7.8	14.7				% Profit Before Taxes/Total	10.2	14.5
	2.6	7.4				Assets	6.1	4.7
	-9.0	-1.2					1.2	.8
	63.5	21.7					35.5	33.9
	13.2	8.3				Sales/Net Fixed Assets	9.3	10.6
	6.6	4.9					6.5	6.2
	3.3	2.0					2.5	2.6
	1.9	1.8				Sales/Total Assets	1.9	1.9
	1.7	1.2					1.4	1.4
		1.4					.7	.7
		(20) 3.3				% Depr., Dep., Amort./Sales	(47) 1.5	(51) 1.6
		4.9					3.2	3.6
							1.3	2.4
						% Officers', Directors'	(13) 2.8	(18) 5.2
						Owners' Comp/Sales	7.6	7.4
4247M	34672M	221739M	263521M	92034M	1031424M	Net Sales ($)	2071534M	2201639M
1257M	13535M	127677M	172711M	80531M	845430M	Total Assets ($)	1271105M	1496359M

M = $ thousand   MM = $ million
See Pages 9 through 22 for Explanation of Ratios and Data

Comparative Historical Data | Current Data Sorted by Sales

			Type of Statement	0-1MM	1-3MM	3-5MM	5-10MM	10-25MM	25MM & OVER
8	6	8	Unqualified				3	2	3
18	11	11	Reviewed	1	2	3	2	3	
7	3	2	Compiled		1		1		
5	9	8	Tax Returns	2			2	1	
26	27	23	Other	2	1	3	4	5	8
4/1/07-3/31/08 ALL	4/1/08-3/31/09 ALL	4/1/09-3/31/10 ALL			10 (4/1-9/30/09)		42 (10/1/09-3/31/10)		
64	56	52	NUMBER OF STATEMENTS	5	4	9	12	11	11
%	%	%	**ASSETS**	%	%	%	%	%	%
7.9	8.1	9.9	Cash & Equivalents				9.4	11.6	8.8
27.2	21.9	21.9	Trade Receivables (net)				24.1	25.9	22.2
29.0	30.1	30.2	Inventory				26.5	33.4	23.6
2.7	2.3	2.9	All Other Current				1.3	.9	7.1
66.8	62.5	64.9	Total Current				61.2	71.9	61.7
23.3	23.1	20.6	Fixed Assets (net)				17.6	19.9	14.3
2.5	6.9	7.9	Intangibles (net)				11.0	5.7	14.4
7.4	7.5	6.6	All Other Non-Current				10.3	2.6	9.6
100.0	100.0	100.0	Total				100.0	100.0	100.0
			LIABILITIES						
8.3	11.2	8.4	Notes Payable-Short Term				6.9	10.2	5.3
4.1	4.1	7.0	Cur. Mat.-L.T.D.				6.5	2.5	6.6
18.3	12.7	18.6	Trade Payables				29.1	16.6	15.0
.2	.3	.2	Income Taxes Payable				.3	.3	.2
18.5	20.9	13.3	All Other Current				12.6	5.9	17.7
49.5	49.2	47.5	Total Current				55.4	35.5	44.9
16.2	18.8	23.3	Long-Term Debt				7.3	16.7	8.7
.0	.1	.3	Deferred Taxes				.3	.7	.4
4.6	8.3	6.4	All Other Non-Current				5.3	9.1	6.8
29.7	23.7	22.5	Net Worth				31.8	38.1	39.3
100.0	100.0	100.0	Total Liabilities & Net Worth				100.0	100.0	100.0
			INCOME DATA						
100.0	100.0	100.0	Net Sales				100.0	100.0	100.0
35.0	34.1	34.2	Gross Profit				30.8	33.6	29.9
30.4	29.5	34.1	Operating Expenses				33.8	27.2	33.8
4.6	4.6	.1	Operating Profit				-2.9	6.4	-3.9
1.2	1.5	1.9	All Other Expenses (net)				2.0	.9	3.9
3.4	3.1	-1.8	Profit Before Taxes				-5.0	5.6	-7.8
			RATIOS						
2.4	2.9	2.2	Current				1.9	4.3	1.7
1.6	1.6	1.5					1.4	1.9	1.4
1.0	1.0	1.1					1.0	1.5	1.1
1.1	1.4	1.4	Quick				1.5	2.4	1.3
.8	.7	.7					.7	1.0	.7
.4	.3	.4					.4	.6	.6
32 11.4	19 19.7	32 11.5	Sales/Receivables				30 12.1	43 8.5	46 8.0
47 7.8	44 8.3	49 7.5					49 7.5	50 7.4	61 6.0
59 6.2	55 6.7	61 6.0					58 6.2	72 5.1	67 5.4
28 13.1	31 11.8	43 8.5	Cost of Sales/Inventory				34 10.7	36 10.0	65 5.6
64 5.7	75 4.9	77 4.7					68 5.3	133 2.8	75 4.8
116 3.2	97 3.8	159 2.3					131 2.8	161 2.3	116 3.1
22 16.3	13 27.7	21 17.5	Cost of Sales/Payables				30 12.0	21 17.6	25 14.4
37 10.0	26 13.9	39 9.3					43 8.4	41 9.0	39 9.3
55 6.6	39 9.4	54 6.8					51 7.1	58 6.2	68 5.3
5.6	5.1	4.6	Sales/Working Capital				6.8	4.2	5.0
8.7	7.7	8.6					9.5	5.1	8.6
107.0	288.3	43.2					NM	9.9	22.7
9.9	6.5	11.1	EBIT/Interest				14.5	15.0	15.3
(61) 3.1	(51) 2.9	(50) 2.1					2.3	7.0	(10) -1.1
1.0	.6	-.7					-5.6	2.4	-10.5
12.7	13.9	5.7	Net Profit + Depr., Dep., Amort./Cur. Mat. L/T/D						
(17) 7.2	(18) 3.5	(16) 1.2							
1.1	1.2	-1.9							
.2	.3	.3	Fixed/Worth				.2	.1	.3
.6	.7	.6					.6	.5	.5
2.4	NM	5.1					3.3	1.9	13.1
.8	1.0	1.0	Debt/Worth				1.0	.9	.9
2.4	3.6	2.5					2.0	1.5	3.1
11.8	NM	54.5					12.4	7.1	61.1
47.4	38.8	38.9	% Profit Before Taxes/Tangible Net Worth				24.7		
(54) 15.5	(42) 9.7	(40) 14.6				(10) 7.5			
2.1	-3.8	-26.0					-8.5		
12.9	11.1	11.8	% Profit Before Taxes/Total Assets				8.6	21.9	1.7
3.8	3.4	1.8					3.4	11.6	-9.5
.2	-1.5	-9.4					-13.2	.1	-29.1
51.8	48.1	33.8	Sales/Net Fixed Assets				48.3	104.2	21.3
13.7	12.2	10.4					14.0	9.4	10.3
5.9	6.9	5.6					3.8	6.7	5.9
2.8	2.7	2.1	Sales/Total Assets				2.5	2.1	1.7
2.2	2.1	1.7					1.9	1.8	1.3
1.5	1.5	1.2					1.1	1.4	1.1
.7	.7	1.2	% Depr., Dep., Amort./Sales					.4	
(59) 1.2	(50) 1.7	(43) 3.0						2.0	
3.7	3.4	4.7						4.2	
1.7	2.0	1.9	% Officers', Directors' Owners' Comp/Sales						
(16) 6.0	(16) 4.6	(16) 5.7							
8.4	6.7	7.1							
2113365M	2050886M	1647637M	Net Sales ($)	2214M	8614M	33810M	84101M	181651M	1337247M
1228451M	1277343M	1241141M	Total Assets ($)	1361M	5761M	22442M	57751M	107542M	1046284M

M = $ thousand   MM = $ million
See Pages 9 through 22 for Explanation of Ratios and Data

Current Data Sorted by Assets   Comparative Historical Data

	0-500M	500M-2MM	2-10MM	10-50MM	50-100MM	100-250MM	Type of Statement	4/1/05-3/31/06 ALL	4/1/06-3/31/07 ALL
			4	4		3	Unqualified	17	15
	2		13	5			Reviewed	21	26
		2	5	1			Compiled	9	12
		3	6				Tax Returns	11	5
	1	3	5	13	5	1	Other	26	33
			12 (4/1-9/30/09)	64 (10/1/09-3/31/10)					
NUMBER OF STATEMENTS	3	8	33	23	5	4		84	91
	%	%	%	%	%	%		%	%
							ASSETS		
			10.9	18.1			Cash & Equivalents	11.1	10.4
			20.1	15.6			Trade Receivables (net)	26.3	24.5
			34.0	23.6			Inventory	29.8	31.1
			2.9	4.5			All Other Current	2.8	2.8
			68.0	61.8			Total Current	70.0	68.8
			18.6	23.1			Fixed Assets (net)	19.2	18.9
			7.1	8.8			Intangibles (net)	4.4	5.8
			6.4	6.3			All Other Non-Current	6.4	6.5
			100.0	100.0			Total	100.0	100.0
							LIABILITIES		
			9.4	3.0			Notes Payable-Short Term	8.1	6.0
			3.4	2.4			Cur. Mat.-L.T.D.	2.3	2.9
			10.6	10.0			Trade Payables	16.7	12.6
			.2	.5			Income Taxes Payable	.4	.3
			17.1	14.8			All Other Current	14.8	18.9
			40.8	30.6			Total Current	42.3	40.8
			14.9	8.9			Long-Term Debt	15.1	13.4
			.3	.0			Deferred Taxes	.3	.3
			19.2	3.0			All Other Non-Current	6.9	3.3
			24.8	57.4			Net Worth	35.4	42.2
			100.0	100.0			Total Liabilties & Net Worth	100.0	100.0
							INCOME DATA		
			100.0	100.0			Net Sales	100.0	100.0
			35.6	34.8			Gross Profit	35.4	36.1
			33.1	28.9			Operating Expenses	30.5	29.7
			2.5	5.9			Operating Profit	4.9	6.5
			1.8	.4			All Other Expenses (net)	1.3	.9
			.8	5.5			Profit Before Taxes	3.5	5.6
							RATIOS		
			2.2	4.0			Current	2.6	2.9
			1.7	2.0				1.6	1.8
			1.4	1.4				1.3	1.2
			1.5	1.9			Quick	1.4	1.5
			.7	1.3				.9	.9
			.5	.5				.6	.5
			29 12.5	27 13.4			Sales/Receivables	30 12.3	32 11.5
			38 9.7	36 10.0				37 9.8	41 8.9
			51 7.2	49 7.4				54 6.8	52 7.0
			48 7.7	52 7.0			Cost of Sales/Inventory	40 9.2	52 7.0
			107 3.4	84 4.4				71 5.1	88 4.1
			192 1.9	155 2.4				129 2.8	145 2.5
			17 21.5	16 23.4			Cost of Sales/Payables	19 19.7	21 17.2
			26 14.0	28 13.1				35 10.5	31 11.6
			50 7.3	40 9.1				57 6.4	43 8.4
			4.4	3.2			Sales/Working Capital	4.5	4.3
			6.5	5.1				8.3	6.4
			10.6	10.1				21.3	17.7
			17.2	60.1			EBIT/Interest	17.3	20.8
			(28) 4.5	(21) 13.8				(75) 5.9	(77) 5.1
			1.1	4.9				1.1	2.4
							Net Profit + Depr., Dep., Amort./Cur. Mat. L/T/D	15.3	10.8
								(31) 5.1	(27) 7.3
								1.7	2.3
			.3	.2			Fixed/Worth	.2	.2
			.6	.4				.5	.4
			3.1	.9				1.1	1.1
			.7	.3			Debt/Worth	.8	.7
			1.7	.9				1.7	1.7
			9.8	2.1				5.2	4.0
			28.8	29.6			% Profit Before Taxes/Tangible Net Worth	50.8	49.2
			(27) 19.7	(22) 14.9				(73) 21.4	(82) 21.9
			5.1	7.3				3.9	8.7
			11.8	14.5			% Profit Before Taxes/Total Assets	20.5	18.3
			5.3	9.4				6.9	8.4
			-1.3	3.2				.5	3.1
			32.2	14.7			Sales/Net Fixed Assets	34.0	30.4
			10.1	9.1				15.9	13.7
			5.2	3.2				7.8	6.3
			2.2	1.9			Sales/Total Assets	3.1	2.6
			1.7	1.4				2.2	1.9
			1.3	1.1				1.6	1.6
			.8	1.4			% Depr., Dep., Amort./Sales	.8	.7
			(30) 2.0	(20) 2.1				(75) 1.5	(75) 1.3
			3.2	2.9				2.5	2.0
							% Officers', Directors' Owners' Comp/Sales	2.9	2.7
								(21) 4.5	(24) 5.0
								9.2	9.4
	950M	31720M	321970M	738449M	431028M	985972M	Net Sales ($)	1861635M	2850213M
	463M	11105M	173478M	502225M	329313M	689950M	Total Assets ($)	1038829M	1727455M

© RMA 2010

M = $ thousand   MM = $ million
See Pages 9 through 22 for Explanation of Ratios and Data

Comparative Historical Data   Current Data Sorted by Sales

			Type of Statement						
10	14	11	Unqualified		2		2	1	8
18	19	20	Reviewed				5	9	2
13	7	8	Compiled	2	1	2	1	2	
6	6	9	Tax Returns		3	1	4	1	
35	37	28	Other	1	1	2	4	6	14
4/1/07-3/31/08 ALL	4/1/08-3/31/09 ALL	4/1/09-3/31/10 ALL		0-1MM	1-3MM 12 (4/1-9/30/09)	3-5MM	5-10MM	10-25MM 64 (10/1/09-3/31/10)	25MM & OVER
82	83	76	NUMBER OF STATEMENTS	3	7	7	16	19	24
%	%	%	ASSETS	%	%	%	%	%	%
9.5	9.9	14.0	Cash & Equivalents				18.6	14.7	14.3
24.9	23.1	18.1	Trade Receivables (net)				16.8	19.9	17.2
29.6	31.7	29.4	Inventory				40.5	27.3	22.1
4.7	4.7	3.3	All Other Current				1.5	5.2	4.7
68.6	69.4	64.8	Total Current				77.4	67.1	58.3
19.5	19.1	20.1	Fixed Assets (net)				13.6	23.3	22.1
5.4	4.6	8.9	Intangibles (net)				4.7	4.0	13.3
6.5	6.8	6.2	All Other Non-Current				4.4	5.6	6.2
100.0	100.0	100.0	Total				100.0	100.0	100.0
			LIABILITIES						
6.8	7.7	6.3	Notes Payable-Short Term				6.5	4.9	3.1
3.3	2.1	2.6	Cur. Mat.-L.T.D.				.9	2.8	1.7
15.7	12.9	11.3	Trade Payables				10.8	11.5	11.0
.2	.5	.3	Income Taxes Payable				.0	.3	.4
17.3	20.6	16.1	All Other Current				20.3	19.0	16.0
43.3	43.8	36.7	Total Current				38.5	38.6	32.2
14.7	11.4	13.6	Long-Term Debt				11.2	11.3	10.4
.1	.4	.4	Deferred Taxes				.1	.5	.6
3.0	4.4	10.6	All Other Non-Current				31.7	2.2	3.0
38.9	40.0	38.8	Net Worth				18.6	47.4	53.7
100.0	100.0	100.0	Total Liabilties & Net Worth				100.0	100.0	100.0
			INCOME DATA						
100.0	100.0	100.0	Net Sales				100.0	100.0	100.0
35.0	32.6	35.5	Gross Profit				35.8	33.6	35.0
28.7	28.0	32.2	Operating Expenses				33.4	28.2	29.7
6.2	4.6	3.3	Operating Profit				2.5	5.4	5.3
.2	.7	1.2	All Other Expenses (net)				.7	-.2	1.2
6.0	3.8	2.1	Profit Before Taxes				1.8	5.6	4.1
			RATIOS						
2.7	2.6	2.9	Current				3.7	3.6	3.1
1.5	1.5	1.9					1.8	2.0	2.0
1.2	1.2	1.4					1.4	1.3	1.4
1.5	1.4	1.8	Quick				1.7	1.8	1.7
.7	.7	.9					.7	1.1	1.2
.5	.4	.5					.5	.6	.6
31 11.9	26 14.0	27 13.3	Sales/Receivables				18 20.5	30 12.0	30 12.1
39 9.3	38 9.7	38 9.7					31 11.6	37 9.8	38 9.6
50 7.4	48 7.6	48 7.7					52 7.1	44 8.3	47 7.8
43 8.5	40 9.1	50 7.3	Cost of Sales/Inventory				91 4.0	44 8.4	40 9.2
76 4.8	80 4.5	92 4.0					119 3.1	76 4.8	70 5.2
117 3.1	129 2.8	146 2.5					190 1.9	107 3.4	140 2.6
22 16.8	18 20.0	16 23.0	Cost of Sales/Payables				15 24.0	14 25.4	23 15.9
36 10.1	28 13.2	29 12.8					24 15.5	25 14.7	32 11.5
55 6.7	43 8.5	48 7.6					59 6.2	37 9.8	44 8.4
4.8	5.1	4.1	Sales/Working Capital				2.4	4.4	4.1
8.8	8.0	6.2					6.7	5.7	5.9
27.2	25.9	10.7					10.1	9.7	10.4
15.9	20.8	23.5	EBIT/Interest				29.2	94.9	30.9
(74) 7.1	(73) 6.1	(67) 6.7					(11) 8.4	(17) 14.4	(22) 8.4
2.9	2.0	1.3					2.4	3.2	2.0
10.5	18.7	13.4	Net Profit + Depr., Dep., Amort./Cur. Mat. L/T/D						
(25) 5.4	(24) 4.7	(20) 4.1							
1.0	2.7	2.5							
.1	.2	.2	Fixed/Worth				.1	.3	.2
.5	.5	.5					.3	.5	.5
1.3	1.3	1.3					2.6	1.0	1.0
.7	.6	.6	Debt/Worth				.5	.7	.4
1.7	1.6	1.3					1.2	.9	1.0
5.0	4.1	4.7					7.0	2.8	2.2
55.5	42.3	29.4	% Profit Before Taxes/Tangible Net Worth				29.4	29.2	32.1
(75) 32.5	(76) 23.2	(65) 15.5					(13) 19.7	(18) 17.4	(23) 13.6
12.7	5.3	4.9					11.8	5.0	6.1
16.4	18.2	13.2	% Profit Before Taxes/Total Assets				15.3	18.4	12.9
9.8	7.8	6.2					6.5	7.5	7.3
3.6	2.3	.1					-1.5	3.0	2.9
44.5	34.9	22.8	Sales/Net Fixed Assets				55.5	17.6	17.1
14.3	14.6	9.4					11.8	9.4	6.6
6.9	6.5	4.8					4.8	4.6	3.6
2.9	2.7	2.2	Sales/Total Assets				3.1	2.2	2.0
2.0	2.0	1.6					1.7	1.9	1.4
1.5	1.5	1.2					1.1	1.4	1.2
.7	.7	1.0	% Depr., Dep., Amort./Sales				.9	.9	1.1
(69) 1.5	(69) 1.3	(64) 2.0					(12) 1.9	(17) 1.8	(21) 2.1
2.5	2.3	3.1					2.9	3.1	3.6
2.6	1.8	3.3	% Officers', Directors' Owners' Comp/Sales						
(22) 4.6	(24) 3.7	(22) 4.5							
8.6	6.3	9.6							
2818427M	3724888M	2510089M	Net Sales ($)	950M	17133M	27833M	111166M	323655M	2029352M
1528821M	1984808M	1706534M	Total Assets ($)	463M	14160M	21684M	82315M	197339M	1390573M

© RMA 2010

M = $ thousand   MM = $ million
See Pages 9 through 22 for Explanation of Ratios and Data

Current Data Sorted by Assets   **Comparative Historical Data**

Type of Statement	0-500M	500M-2MM	2-10MM	10-50MM	50-100MM	100-250MM	4/1/05-3/31/06 ALL	4/1/06-3/31/07 ALL
Unqualified		1	10	23	11	3	38	38
Reviewed		8	28	11	1		39	40
Compiled	2	11	13			1	34	41
Tax Returns	8	11	4				24	20
Other	5	8	27	35	7	7	85	62
		44 (4/1-9/30/09)		191 (10/1/09-3/31/10)				

	0-500M	500M-2MM	2-10MM	10-50MM	50-100MM	100-250MM		4/1/05-3/31/06 ALL	4/1/06-3/31/07 ALL
NUMBER OF STATEMENTS	15	39	82	69	19	11		220	201
	%	%	%	%	%	%	**ASSETS**	%	%
	17.8	10.7	12.8	13.5	16.8	13.7	Cash & Equivalents	9.6	12.4
	31.5	26.0	22.8	23.4	16.8	16.2	Trade Receivables (net)	27.5	27.0
	23.5	31.2	30.4	22.5	13.6	20.1	Inventory	28.4	26.7
	4.0	3.0	3.4	8.2	7.8	8.2	All Other Current	3.7	3.7
	76.9	70.9	69.4	67.5	55.1	58.1	Total Current	69.2	69.8
	16.7	20.7	21.3	17.3	24.2	18.3	Fixed Assets (net)	20.5	19.6
	1.4	.9	4.2	5.7	12.0	17.4	Intangibles (net)	3.9	4.4
	5.0	7.5	5.2	9.5	8.7	6.2	All Other Non-Current	6.4	6.2
	100.0	100.0	100.0	100.0	100.0	100.0	Total	100.0	100.0
							LIABILITIES		
	19.8	16.1	9.9	6.2	1.7	5.6	Notes Payable-Short Term	11.8	9.2
	1.8	5.6	3.3	2.4	3.9	.9	Cur. Mat.-L.T.D.	3.7	2.9
	21.6	14.6	13.9	11.4	7.8	7.8	Trade Payables	16.3	13.9
	.0	.9	.5	.5	.5	.5	Income Taxes Payable	.3	.2
	18.7	11.9	14.6	18.8	20.4	20.3	All Other Current	15.1	16.9
	61.9	49.0	42.1	38.9	34.4	35.1	Total Current	47.3	43.2
	34.6	15.2	12.0	7.4	15.7	14.0	Long-Term Debt	15.9	14.0
	.0	.1	.5	.4	.3	2.2	Deferred Taxes	.5	.4
	12.0	5.8	8.1	9.0	5.5	8.4	All Other Non-Current	5.3	5.7
	-8.6	29.9	37.3	44.2	44.1	40.3	Net Worth	31.0	36.8
	100.0	100.0	100.0	100.0	100.0	100.0	Total Liabilities & Net Worth	100.0	100.0
							INCOME DATA		
	100.0	100.0	100.0	100.0	100.0	100.0	Net Sales	100.0	100.0
	34.7	34.6	31.7	29.4	28.5	24.9	Gross Profit	32.6	34.2
	32.8	33.7	29.5	23.9	23.6	23.9	Operating Expenses	27.2	26.9
	1.9	.8	2.3	5.5	4.9	1.0	Operating Profit	5.4	7.3
	2.0	.6	1.2	2.0	1.5	.3	All Other Expenses (net)	1.2	1.1
	-.1	.2	1.1	3.5	3.4	.7	Profit Before Taxes	4.2	6.2
							RATIOS		
	2.6	3.7	3.0	2.9	2.6	2.6	Current	2.4	2.8
	1.4	1.5	1.6	1.9	1.9	1.7		1.6	1.7
	1.1	.8	1.1	1.3	1.0	.9		1.1	1.2
	2.0	1.5	1.7	1.6	1.5	1.5	Quick	1.4	1.5
	1.2	.7	.8	.9	1.0	.7		(219) .8	.9
	.3	.5	.4	.5	.6	.6		.5	.6
	20 18.0	21 17.2	28 13.0	37 9.9	39 9.4	28 13.2	Sales/Receivables	32 11.4	34 10.7
	25 14.5	35 10.4	45 8.1	50 7.2	48 7.5	50 7.3		46 7.9	47 7.8
	31 11.8	64 5.7	60 6.0	64 5.7	66 5.6	77 4.7		66 5.5	61 5.9
	3 141.8	14 25.9	42 8.8	35 10.4	37 9.8	42 8.7	Cost of Sales/Inventory	30 12.3	34 10.7
	32 11.5	70 5.2	86 4.2	81 4.5	65 5.6	90 4.1		73 5.0	75 4.9
	61 6.0	178 2.1	156 2.3	141 2.6	101 3.6	128 2.8		134 2.7	124 2.9
	3 121.6	11 32.9	17 21.2	17 21.3	16 22.4	17 21.3	Cost of Sales/Payables	20 18.1	16 22.4
	25 14.3	25 14.5	33 11.2	29 12.6	25 14.9	27 13.8		38 9.7	34 10.8
	47 7.8	38 9.6	56 6.5	48 7.6	41 9.0	54 6.8		59 6.1	53 6.9
	9.2	4.2	3.1	3.5	2.7	3.1	Sales/Working Capital	4.3	4.3
	23.1	13.6	6.7	5.7	6.0	6.0		8.1	7.6
	58.4	-19.4	24.7	12.6	115.9	-38.0		28.8	23.6
		6.6	16.3	15.8	28.7	13.9	EBIT/Interest	14.2	20.1
	(35) 2.5	(72) 2.1	(58) 3.3	3.1	(10) 2.6		(195) 3.6	(169) 5.0
		-.2	-2.0	.0	.0	-.8		1.1	1.7
		7.6	4.3	44.2			Net Profit + Depr., Dep., Amort./Cur. Mat. L/T/D	5.6	8.2
	(24) 1.1	(27) 2.3	(14) 2.4				(49) 2.7	(51) 3.4
		-.2	-.1	.7				1.4	1.5
	.1	.1	.2	.2	.3	.2	Fixed/Worth	.2	.2
	2.2	.6	.5	.4	.5	.5		.5	.5
	-.5	8.3	1.5	1.1	8.5	-1.2		1.9	1.5
	.5	.7	.6	.5	.6	.7	Debt/Worth	.8	.7
	79.5	1.6	1.5	1.2	1.7	1.4		2.0	1.8
	-9.3	59.6	5.6	4.2	10.9	-10.9		6.0	5.8
		36.4	29.3	31.7	34.1		% Profit Before Taxes/Tangible Net Worth	55.4	57.4
	(30) 5.6	(73) 8.0	(58) 11.5	(15) 10.3			(187) 22.0	(175) 27.4
		-10.6	-13.9	.3	.4			5.8	9.6
	37.1	12.1	10.8	15.3	7.1	6.6	% Profit Before Taxes/Total Assets	16.6	19.8
	.6	2.3	1.8	5.3	3.3	2.9		6.3	10.7
	-14.5	-7.5	-5.3	-.8	-1.9	-5.3		.4	2.0
	121.8	45.4	28.3	20.2	11.9	14.3	Sales/Net Fixed Assets	40.9	30.3
	34.4	15.1	11.2	12.0	7.0	9.1		13.0	13.1
	17.3	6.7	5.2	5.2	3.7	4.6		5.8	6.2
	5.9	3.3	2.3	2.1	1.3	1.6	Sales/Total Assets	2.7	2.7
	4.2	2.0	1.7	1.5	1.2	1.3		1.9	1.8
	2.6	1.2	1.3	1.1	1.0	.8		1.4	1.4
		.7	.9	1.0	1.3		% Depr., Dep., Amort./Sales	.9	.6
	(31) 1.5	(70) 1.8	(56) 1.8	(18) 3.3			(185) 1.6	(173) 1.5
		4.5	3.4	4.6	6.4			3.1	2.9
	4.7	3.6	2.0				% Officers', Directors' Owners' Comp/Sales	2.1	2.6
(11) 9.1	(23) 6.2	(27) 3.5					(78) 4.8	(68) 4.5
	11.0	10.9	6.9					7.5	8.4
	16296M	111309M	706312M	2226916M	1497338M	1959654M	Net Sales ($)	5592229M	5724554M
	4058M	46552M	394123M	1462752M	1221544M	1518421M	Total Assets ($)	3273377M	3623483M

© RMA 2010

M = $ thousand   MM = $ million
See Pages 9 through 22 for Explanation of Ratios and Data

Comparative Historical Data | Current Data Sorted by Sales

				Type of Statement	0-1MM	1-3MM	3-5MM	5-10MM	10-25MM	25MM & OVER
36		47	48	Unqualified			1	5	14	28
38		45	48	Reviewed	2	7	5	15	14	5
29		27	27	Compiled	2	7	6	9	2	1
14		27	23	Tax Returns	5	10	6	1	1	
75		90	89	Other	2	9	12	11	19	36
4/1/07-3/31/08 ALL		4/1/08-3/31/09 ALL	4/1/09-3/31/10 ALL		44 (4/1-9/30/09)			191 (10/1/09-3/31/10)		
192		236	235	**NUMBER OF STATEMENTS**	11	33	30	41	50	70
%		%	%	**ASSETS**	%	%	%	%	%	%
11.7		9.9	13.3	Cash & Equivalents	12.1	12.4	8.5	14.9	15.1	13.8
26.4		25.6	23.3	Trade Receivables (net)	19.4	23.3	23.0	26.7	20.7	23.7
25.8		25.9	25.9	Inventory	31.2	32.9	29.2	29.5	27.5	17.1
4.6		5.4	5.4	All Other Current	2.5	2.6	4.1	3.4	4.8	9.3
68.4		66.7	67.9	Total Current	65.2	71.3	64.7	74.6	68.1	63.9
19.9		20.3	19.8	Fixed Assets (net)	19.9	22.4	21.1	19.0	19.4	18.8
5.9		6.0	5.1	Intangibles (net)	2.3	.3	8.5	3.5	3.8	8.4
5.7		6.9	7.2	All Other Non-Current	12.6	6.0	5.7	2.9	8.7	8.9
100.0		100.0	100.0	Total	100.0	100.0	100.0	100.0	100.0	100.0
				LIABILITIES						
9.4		11.0	9.6	Notes Payable-Short Term	4.4	22.7	13.5	8.7	7.8	4.4
3.1		3.8	3.2	Cur. Mat.-L.T.D.	2.9	4.9	3.0	3.7	3.2	2.3
16.1		13.4	13.0	Trade Payables	10.6	14.7	15.4	13.2	13.2	11.2
.2		.3	.4	Income Taxes Payable	.0	.0	1.1	.1	.7	.4
17.2		16.5	16.4	All Other Current	10.4	14.6	11.6	17.0	15.2	20.7
46.1		44.9	42.6	Total Current	28.3	56.9	44.7	42.7	40.2	38.9
13.6		13.4	13.0	Long-Term Debt	39.4	18.5	14.1	10.8	7.4	11.1
.3		.3	.4	Deferred Taxes	.0	.2	.4	.2	.8	.5
6.6		6.6	8.0	All Other Non-Current	3.7	7.7	9.1	7.5	8.7	8.3
33.5		34.7	35.9	Net Worth	28.7	16.8	31.7	38.7	42.8	41.1
100.0		100.0	100.0	Total Liabilities & Net Worth	100.0	100.0	100.0	100.0	100.0	100.0
				INCOME DATA						
100.0		100.0	100.0	Net Sales	100.0	100.0	100.0	100.0	100.0	100.0
31.7		30.8	31.1	Gross Profit	36.7	33.0	37.7	30.9	29.7	27.7
25.9		25.7	28.0	Operating Expenses	35.3	34.2	33.4	30.6	25.4	22.0
5.7		5.0	3.1	Operating Profit	1.5	-1.2	4.2	.3	4.2	5.8
1.3		1.1	1.4	All Other Expenses (net)	1.5	1.0	1.6	1.2	1.9	1.1
4.4		4.0	1.7	Profit Before Taxes	.0	-2.2	2.6	-.9	2.4	4.6
				RATIOS						
2.3		2.3	2.7		5.2	3.0	2.9	3.3	2.5	2.6
1.4		1.6	1.6	Current	1.9	1.4	1.3	2.0	1.7	1.7
1.1		1.1	1.1		1.4	.9	.8	1.2	1.4	1.1
1.4		1.3	1.5		1.8	1.2	1.6	1.9	1.6	1.5
(191) .8		.8	.8	Quick	1.3	.7	.6	1.1	.9	.9
.5		.5	.5		.3	.4	.4	.5	.4	.6
35 10.6	31	11.9	28 13.0		10 38.3	22 16.4	23 16.2	38 9.7	30 12.0	40 9.1
47 7.7	45	8.0	45 8.1	Sales/Receivables	26 14.2	34 10.7	34 10.6	53 6.9	41 8.9	51 7.1
63 5.8	59	6.2	61 6.0		31 11.8	64 5.7	61 6.0	63 5.8	56 6.6	67 5.4
33 10.9	30	12.1	33 11.0		1 346.0	31 12.0	35 10.6	44 8.2	32 11.4	29 12.5
76 4.8	66	5.5	75 4.9	Cost of Sales/Inventory	97 3.8	76 4.8	80 4.6	83 4.4	95 3.8	59 6.2
116 3.1	111	3.3	143 2.6		192 1.9	190 1.9	147 2.5	171 2.1	150 2.4	102 3.6
21 17.1	17	22.0	16 22.4		4 102.7	8 44.4	20 18.3	14 26.1	18 20.7	17 21.6
35 10.4	29	12.5	27 13.6	Cost of Sales/Payables	21 17.2	27 13.6	34 10.8	25 14.9	28 13.3	29 12.6
54 6.7	44	8.2	52 7.0		35 10.4	61 6.0	60 6.1	45 8.0	48 7.6	52 7.0
4.5		4.4	3.6		5.0	4.2	4.0	2.9	3.7	3.6
9.8		8.8	7.2	Sales/Working Capital	13.2	14.2	9.4	6.8	6.2	6.3
47.0		40.7	23.8		27.9	-25.9	-21.8	19.7	11.1	22.6
11.3		16.8	12.0			6.0	6.4	12.9	33.8	21.0
(164) 4.2	(202)	3.7	(203) 2.6	EBIT/Interest	(27) 1.4	(26) 2.8	(36) 1.0	(45) 4.2	(62) 4.2	
1.1		1.1	-.2			-2.1	1.0	-5.9	-.2	.8
11.7		10.1	7.0	Net Profit + Depr., Dep.,				6.5	5.9	15.2
(55) 3.7	(59)	3.3	(75) 2.1	Amort./Cur. Mat. L/T/D			(12) 2.6	(17) 2.0	(36) 2.4	
1.4		1.0	-.1					-.6	-.6	.2
.2		.2	.2		.1	.2	.1	.1	.2	.2
.6		.6	.5	Fixed/Worth	.5	.8	.9	.4	.4	.4
2.4		2.1	2.3		35.5	5.3	-1.8	1.4	1.3	3.3
1.0		.7	.6		.3	1.0	.6	.5	.6	.6
2.4		2.1	1.4	Debt/Worth	.6	2.8	3.3	1.1	1.4	1.4
6.4		8.3	10.2		106.5	NM	-7.0	3.9	4.9	10.8
55.0		42.2	31.5	% Profit Before Taxes/Tangible		34.1	32.1	25.3	35.9	34.1
(164) 26.7	(191)	21.2	(193) 10.1	Net Worth	(25) 6.8	(21) 8.0	(35) .4	(47) 10.3	(56) 16.5	
6.6		5.0	-3.7			-12.6	1.9	-20.1	-7.5	-2.8
19.1		16.7	11.4	% Profit Before Taxes/Total	37.1	7.0	9.9	9.7	12.2	13.9
7.4		7.2	2.8	Assets	.4	.2	3.3	-.2	3.8	5.6
.8		.4	-3.1		-7.5	-13.1	.2	-10.3	-1.5	.3
34.1		31.7	28.0		121.8	35.6	32.8	33.3	25.4	19.7
12.3		13.2	11.7	Sales/Net Fixed Assets	17.3	10.1	15.7	13.1	11.5	11.1
5.3		5.8	5.6		6.9	3.8	5.5	5.9	4.7	5.8
2.6		2.6	2.4		4.4	3.2	3.1	2.7	2.1	2.1
1.8		1.9	1.6	Sales/Total Assets	2.3	1.7	1.7	1.8	1.6	1.5
1.3		1.4	1.2		1.2	1.2	1.1	1.2	1.1	1.2
.7		.8	.9			.9	.7	.8	.8	1.3
(161) 1.5	(192)	1.6	(190) 1.8	% Depr., Dep., Amort./Sales	(23) 1.6	(25) 1.7	(35) 1.8	(42) 1.9	(58) 2.0	
3.1		3.0	4.4			6.2	5.3	3.3	4.4	4.5
2.6		2.5	2.2			4.5	3.0	2.1	1.1	
(51) 4.4	(75)	3.4	(72) 4.7	% Officers', Directors' Owners' Comp/Sales	(21) 7.1	(15) 3.3	(12) 4.1	(12) 2.4		
7.6		6.0	9.0			11.8	5.3	8.3	10.7	
5849345M		7804340M	6517825M	Net Sales ($)	7762M	61182M	121082M	293518M	863130M	5171151M
4289625M		4824063M	4647450M	Total Assets ($)	4482M	38931M	77456M	193874M	605807M	3726900M

M = $ thousand   MM = $ million
See Pages 9 through 22 for Explanation of Ratios and Data

Current Data Sorted by Assets   Comparative Historical Data

Type of Statement

	0-500M	500M-2MM	2-10MM	10-50MM	50-100MM	100-250MM		4/1/05-3/31/06 ALL	4/1/06-3/31/07 ALL
Unqualified			1	7	4	1		11	13
Reviewed		1	11	4				6	13
Compiled	1	1	3					6	11
Tax Returns	1	2	2					2	5
Other		2	9	6	4	2		16	15
		11 (4/1-9/30/09)		51 (10/1/09-3/31/10)					
NUMBER OF STATEMENTS	2	6	26	17	8	3		41	57
	%	%	%	%	%	%		%	%
ASSETS									
Cash & Equivalents			11.5	6.4				12.1	11.3
Trade Receivables (net)			23.1	18.8				23.1	23.0
Inventory			31.2	24.2				27.0	27.2
All Other Current			2.5	3.8				1.7	3.2
Total Current			68.3	53.2				63.9	64.7
Fixed Assets (net)			25.5	24.8				25.6	26.8
Intangibles (net)			.4	19.6				6.2	3.9
All Other Non-Current			5.8	2.4				4.2	4.6
Total			100.0	100.0				100.0	100.0
LIABILITIES									
Notes Payable-Short Term			10.1	6.0				5.1	14.6
Cur. Mat.-L.T.D.			3.7	2.9				5.9	4.4
Trade Payables			15.1	6.9				15.2	15.2
Income Taxes Payable			.2	.2				.3	.1
All Other Current			11.2	10.1				10.1	9.9
Total Current			40.4	26.1				36.4	44.3
Long-Term Debt			11.9	11.1				17.1	15.2
Deferred Taxes			.5	1.4				.8	.6
All Other Non-Current			2.2	14.1				6.2	6.3
Net Worth			44.9	47.2				39.4	33.5
Total Liabilities & Net Worth			100.0	100.0				100.0	100.0
INCOME DATA									
Net Sales			100.0	100.0				100.0	100.0
Gross Profit			32.0	37.0				36.6	39.0
Operating Expenses			29.3	27.6				32.1	33.0
Operating Profit			2.7	9.5				4.5	6.1
All Other Expenses (net)			.3	4.5				2.9	1.4
Profit Before Taxes			2.4	5.0				1.7	4.6
RATIOS									
Current			3.4	3.8				2.8	2.7
			1.7	2.5				1.8	1.6
			1.4	1.4				1.4	1.2
Quick			1.4	2.0				1.4	1.3
			1.0	1.2				1.1	.9
			.6	.6				.6	.5
Sales/Receivables			28 13.0	35 10.3				33 11.0	33 10.9
			40 9.0	42 8.6				43 8.6	41 9.0
			48 7.6	55 6.6				57 6.4	55 6.7
Cost of Sales/Inventory			29 12.5	71 5.2				38 9.6	33 11.0
			76 4.8	94 3.9				94 3.9	89 4.1
			128 2.8	132 2.8				141 2.6	131 2.8
Cost of Sales/Payables			13 28.4	11 33.6				21 17.6	20 18.5
			26 14.2	18 20.7				32 11.6	35 10.5
			44 8.2	39 9.4				51 7.1	50 7.4
Sales/Working Capital			3.8	3.4				3.7	4.1
			7.8	5.8				5.8	7.8
			16.8	9.9				14.2	30.4
EBIT/Interest			6.8	6.1				10.4	8.2
			(20) 3.4	(13) 3.9				(35) 3.0	(48) 3.5
			2.2	3.1				.9	1.7
Net Profit + Depr., Dep., Amort./Cur. Mat. L/T/D								3.0	2.6
								(13) 2.2	(17) 1.8
								.8	1.3
Fixed/Worth			.2	.3				.2	.2
			.5	.7				.6	.7
			1.5	3.1				2.1	1.5
Debt/Worth			.4	.5				.7	1.0
			1.1	1.3				1.2	1.5
			3.8	8.1				4.9	3.8
% Profit Before Taxes/Tangible Net Worth			35.8	83.4				31.1	53.6
			(25) 10.4	(16) 19.6				(35) 14.2	(51) 26.9
			1.4	5.4				6.5	8.9
% Profit Before Taxes/Total Assets			10.6	9.9				13.6	16.1
			4.6	6.1				5.8	6.3
			.4	1.2				-.6	2.7
Sales/Net Fixed Assets			28.7	21.6				26.1	27.3
			14.4	6.7				8.7	9.4
			4.1	3.3				3.6	4.2
Sales/Total Assets			2.6	1.9				2.6	2.5
			2.1	1.4				1.8	2.0
			1.5	1.0				1.0	1.3
% Depr., Dep., Amort./Sales			1.5	.9				1.1	1.6
			(22) 3.2	(14) 3.4				(38) 1.9	(48) 3.4
			5.3	5.6				4.0	5.2
% Officers', Directors' Owners' Comp/Sales			.6						2.8
			(10) 2.3						(15) 5.8
			6.4						6.4
Net Sales ($)	843M	17441M	251884M	446606M	843059M	821282M		983745M	1203352M
Total Assets ($)	617M	8454M	124665M	336974M	542403M	412665M		783431M	831219M

© RMA 2010

M = $ thousand   MM = $ million
See Pages 9 through 22 for Explanation of Ratios and Data

Comparative Historical Data | Current Data Sorted by Sales

			Type of Statement						
10	11	13	Unqualified		1		1	3	9
7	10	16	Reviewed				3	8	1
7	5	5	Compiled	1		2		2	
4	4	5	Tax Returns	2		1	2		
30	26	23	Other		1	3	2	9	8
4/1/07- 3/31/08 ALL	4/1/08- 3/31/09 ALL	4/1/09- 3/31/10 ALL		11 (4/1-9/30/09)			51 (10/1/09-3/31/10)		
				0-1MM	1-3MM	3-5MM	5-10MM	10-25MM	25MM & OVER
58	56	62	NUMBER OF STATEMENTS	3	2	9	8	22	18
%	%	%	**ASSETS**	%	%	%	%	%	%
13.0	8.2	11.2	Cash & Equivalents					10.2	11.4
20.9	22.2	21.6	Trade Receivables (net)					21.9	19.7
25.4	29.4	28.6	Inventory					29.8	25.3
3.6	2.6	2.7	All Other Current					3.3	2.6
62.8	62.3	64.1	Total Current					65.2	59.0
26.6	23.1	22.9	Fixed Assets (net)					23.5	19.2
3.8	9.1	8.5	Intangibles (net)					7.2	17.7
6.7	5.4	4.4	All Other Non-Current					4.0	4.1
100.0	100.0	100.0	Total					100.0	100.0
			LIABILITIES						
5.1	7.5	7.8	Notes Payable-Short Term					5.1	5.8
4.5	3.1	2.9	Cur. Mat.-L.T.D.					3.6	2.6
14.4	14.6	12.4	Trade Payables					15.0	10.0
.2	.2	.2	Income Taxes Payable					.4	.1
9.3	11.7	10.9	All Other Current					13.5	9.1
33.6	37.0	34.2	Total Current					37.7	27.7
14.8	13.2	11.3	Long-Term Debt					10.3	11.5
.6	.5	.9	Deferred Taxes					.8	1.5
4.8	6.1	6.0	All Other Non-Current					3.7	14.0
46.3	43.2	47.6	Net Worth					47.6	45.3
100.0	100.0	100.0	Total Liabilities & Net Worth					100.0	100.0
			INCOME DATA						
100.0	100.0	100.0	Net Sales					100.0	100.0
41.8	38.2	36.8	Gross Profit					33.7	41.4
35.2	31.1	31.8	Operating Expenses					27.1	35.5
6.5	7.1	5.0	Operating Profit					6.7	5.9
1.4	1.3	1.5	All Other Expenses (net)					.9	4.0
5.1	5.7	3.4	Profit Before Taxes					5.8	1.9
			RATIOS						
3.4	2.5	3.4	Current					3.4	3.3
1.9	1.6	2.0						1.6	2.1
1.4	1.3	1.4						1.4	1.5
1.6	1.2	1.6	Quick					1.4	2.0
1.0	.8	1.0						.9	1.0
.6	.6	.6						.5	.7
28 12.8	35 10.5	34 10.7	Sales/Receivables					34 10.7	35 10.5
42 8.7	47 7.8	42 8.6						39 9.3	44 8.4
56 6.5	56 6.5	53 6.9						52 7.0	54 6.7
45 8.1	59 6.2	53 6.9	Cost of Sales/Inventory					47 7.7	69 5.3
91 4.0	93 3.9	92 4.0						94 3.9	101 3.6
130 2.8	140 2.6	140 2.6						130 2.8	145 2.5
23 15.9	19 18.8	14 26.5	Cost of Sales/Payables					14 26.3	13 29.0
37 9.8	36 10.0	29 12.7						29 12.8	29 12.7
59 6.1	63 5.8	49 7.4						52 7.1	53 6.9
3.6	3.9	3.6	Sales/Working Capital					3.8	3.5
7.2	8.3	6.2						9.6	5.3
15.5	19.6	10.9						14.0	9.8
8.6	11.4	8.9	EBIT/Interest					6.5	14.1
(45) 3.6	(48) 4.2	(49) 3.8						(17) 3.4	(15) 4.9
1.1	1.5	2.5						2.6	2.8
2.6	4.0	3.4	Net Profit + Depr., Dep.,						
(20) 2.2	(19) 2.3	(16) 2.7	Amort./Cur. Mat. L/T/D						
1.1	1.6	1.6							
.2	.2	.2	Fixed/Worth					.1	.3
.6	.7	.5						.5	.7
1.5	1.6	1.2						1.2	1.6
.5	.9	.5	Debt/Worth					.4	1.1
1.1	1.6	1.2						1.3	1.8
3.3	3.8	3.0						3.0	7.9
45.6	46.3	38.3	% Profit Before Taxes/Tangible					76.9	42.6
(52) 13.3	(48) 19.9	(59) 15.5	Net Worth					11.9	(17) 18.6
.9	3.3	3.3						3.7	10.9
18.1	16.3	9.5	% Profit Before Taxes/Total					9.6	8.7
5.3	6.7	6.0	Assets					4.6	6.4
.5	1.9	.9						1.8	2.0
39.0	28.2	29.5	Sales/Net Fixed Assets					33.1	18.6
8.5	9.7	10.1						14.0	8.1
3.9	5.2	4.2						3.4	5.7
2.7	2.3	2.3	Sales/Total Assets					2.5	2.1
1.8	1.8	1.8						1.8	1.6
1.2	1.3	1.2						1.2	1.2
.8	.7	1.5	% Depr., Dep., Amort./Sales					1.3	1.0
(53) 3.0	(45) 2.2	(50) 3.3						(17) 3.1	(15) 3.3
5.0	4.1	4.8						4.8	4.1
2.2	1.3	1.5	% Officers', Directors'						
(18) 3.1	(14) 3.5	(20) 5.0	Owners' Comp/Sales						
5.7	11.6	8.8							
1946228M	2396070M	2381115M	Net Sales ($)	1756M	3403M	37067M	64985M	354579M	1919325M
1332204M	1516911M	1425778M	Total Assets ($)	1509M	3185M	22328M	36544M	244167M	1118045M

M = $ thousand   MM = $ million
See Pages 9 through 22 for Explanation of Ratios and Data

Current Data Sorted by Assets   **Comparative Historical Data**

						Type of Statement		
			1	1		Unqualified	11	5
			1	1		Reviewed	7	5
	3	4				Compiled		1
	2	1				Tax Returns	1	3
	1	2	6	2	3	Other	11	11
	5 (4/1-9/30/09)			23 (10/1/09-3/31/10)			4/1/05-3/31/06 ALL	4/1/06-3/31/07 ALL
0-500M	500M-2MM	2-10MM	10-50MM	50-100MM	100-250MM	NUMBER OF STATEMENTS	30	25
	6	7	8	4	3			
%	%	%	%	%	%	ASSETS	%	%
						Cash & Equivalents	9.0	11.1
						Trade Receivables (net)	21.7	22.7
						Inventory	28.9	24.8
						All Other Current	3.9	4.0
						Total Current	63.5	62.5
						Fixed Assets (net)	24.4	21.7
						Intangibles (net)	5.6	8.4
						All Other Non-Current	6.6	7.3
						Total	100.0	100.0
						LIABILITIES		
						Notes Payable-Short Term	9.7	12.5
						Cur. Mat.-L.T.D.	5.9	6.3
						Trade Payables	11.9	17.5
						Income Taxes Payable	.5	.5
						All Other Current	9.1	6.5
						Total Current	37.1	43.3
						Long-Term Debt	23.2	27.1
						Deferred Taxes	.5	.5
						All Other Non-Current	3.3	7.3
						Net Worth	35.9	21.8
						Total Liabilities & Net Worth	100.0	100.0
						INCOME DATA		
						Net Sales	100.0	100.0
						Gross Profit	37.6	36.1
						Operating Expenses	30.4	32.1
						Operating Profit	7.1	4.0
						All Other Expenses (net)	2.4	1.7
						Profit Before Taxes	4.7	2.3
						RATIOS		
						Current	2.9	3.7
							2.1	2.1
							1.2	1.0
						Quick	1.8	2.1
							.9	.8
							.5	.5
						Sales/Receivables	31 11.8	30 12.2
							42 8.6	42 8.7
							59 6.1	65 5.7
						Cost of Sales/Inventory	46 8.0	43 8.5
							94 3.9	78 4.7
							143 2.5	121 3.0
						Cost of Sales/Payables	20 18.6	18 19.9
							36 10.2	37 9.9
							45 8.0	57 6.4
						Sales/Working Capital	3.1	3.2
							6.6	8.0
							28.6	NM
						EBIT/Interest	8.2	7.9
							(28) 5.2	(24) 3.1
							1.7	1.4
						Net Profit + Depr., Dep., Amort./Cur. Mat. L/T/D	7.9	
							(11) 1.9	
							1.1	
						Fixed/Worth	.3	.2
							.6	.7
							NM	NM
						Debt/Worth	.5	.7
							1.9	2.4
							NM	-27.7
						% Profit Before Taxes/Tangible Net Worth	30.9	39.9
							(23) 18.1	(18) 15.3
							4.5	3.5
						% Profit Before Taxes/Total Assets	15.7	13.4
							9.3	6.8
							2.2	.9
						Sales/Net Fixed Assets	20.2	40.7
							8.8	8.9
							3.9	4.1
						Sales/Total Assets	2.5	2.6
							1.8	1.9
							1.3	1.2
						% Depr., Dep., Amort./Sales	1.3	.7
							(27) 3.2	(21) 1.6
							4.7	5.0
						% Officers', Directors' Owners' Comp/Sales		
27550M	64466M	360676M	391806M	712707M		Net Sales ($)	1639850M	930266M
7688M	36586M	242396M	276383M	554699M		Total Assets ($)	1186831M	665341M

DATA NOT AVAILABLE

© RMA 2010

M = $ thousand   MM = $ million
See Pages 9 through 22 for Explanation of Ratios and Data

Comparative Historical Data   Current Data Sorted by Sales

Type of Statement									
	4	9	2					1	1
	3	4	2						2
		4	7		1		4	2	
		2	3			2	1	1	
	14	11	14			1	1	2	10

	4/1/07-3/31/08 ALL	4/1/08-3/31/09 ALL	4/1/09-3/31/10 ALL		5 (4/1-9/30/09)		23 (10/1/09-3/31/10)		
				0-1MM	1-3MM	3-5MM	5-10MM	10-25MM	25MM & OVER
NUMBER OF STATEMENTS	21	30	28		1	3	6	5	13
ASSETS	%	%	%	%	%	%	%	%	%
Cash & Equivalents	8.5	9.6	13.2	D					9.8
Trade Receivables (net)	22.5	23.2	23.2	A					23.5
Inventory	23.0	26.9	26.1	T					25.8
All Other Current	2.7	2.2	4.1	A					4.4
Total Current	56.7	62.0	66.6						63.5
Fixed Assets (net)	27.4	23.4	23.2	N					21.5
Intangibles (net)	9.4	6.9	6.5	O					10.2
All Other Non-Current	6.5	7.8	3.8	T					4.9
Total	100.0	100.0	100.0						100.0
LIABILITIES				A					
Notes Payable-Short Term	12.3	8.6	8.4	V					8.0
Cur. Mat.-L.T.D.	3.8	2.9	1.4	A					1.1
Trade Payables	16.3	15.0	13.6	I					11.9
Income Taxes Payable	.5	.7	.3	L					.4
All Other Current	9.4	15.2	18.2	A					16.5
Total Current	42.2	42.4	41.8	B					38.0
Long-Term Debt	18.0	16.3	12.4	L					20.0
Deferred Taxes	.2	.3	.2	E					.3
All Other Non-Current	8.2	6.0	5.4						3.9
Net Worth	31.4	35.0	40.1						37.8
Total Liabilities & Net Worth	100.0	100.0	100.0						100.0
INCOME DATA									
Net Sales	100.0	100.0	100.0						100.0
Gross Profit	34.8	34.4	35.7						30.5
Operating Expenses	31.4	29.3	29.7						23.3
Operating Profit	3.3	5.1	6.0						7.2
All Other Expenses (net)	2.3	1.6	.8						2.2
Profit Before Taxes	1.0	3.6	5.2						5.0
RATIOS									
Current	2.0	2.9	3.1						3.1
	1.3	1.6	1.8						1.6
	.9	1.1	1.2						1.2
Quick	1.2	1.7	1.8						1.9
	.6	.8	.8						.7
	.5	.5	.6						.6
Sales/Receivables	34 10.6	33 10.9	32 11.3						38 9.6
	46 7.9	49 7.4	43 8.5						49 7.4
	64 5.7	62 5.9	65 5.6						72 5.1
Cost of Sales/Inventory	38 9.6	34 10.6	42 8.8						46 8.0
	75 4.8	87 4.2	57 6.4						63 5.8
	133 2.8	124 2.9	111 3.3						118 3.1
Cost of Sales/Payables	31 11.9	24 15.3	16 22.7						17 21.7
	44 8.3	44 8.3	31 11.8						25 14.5
	60 6.1	55 6.7	61 5.9						65 5.6
Sales/Working Capital	4.5	2.8	2.7						2.5
	12.0	9.5	6.7						5.4
	-50.1	56.9	38.3						28.8
EBIT/Interest	6.2	23.5	111.3						67.0
	(19) 1.6	(27) 2.8	(27) 7.7						3.5
	-.8	-.9	1.5						1.5
Net Profit + Depr., Dep., Amort./Cur. Mat. L/T/D		7.4							
		(10) 3.3							
		.8							
Fixed/Worth	.4	.2	.1						.2
	1.1	.5	.4						.5
	-239.1	4.8	2.1						9.0
Debt/Worth	1.3	.5	.4						.4
	3.4	1.6	1.5						1.7
	-539.2	14.4	10.1						NM
% Profit Before Taxes/Tangible Net Worth	68.1	65.5	54.8						39.5
	(15) 28.9	(25) 17.0	(23) 24.4						(10) 16.1
	2.0	.7	2.9						2.5
% Profit Before Taxes/Total Assets	9.6	16.5	20.7						18.2
	6.1	3.9	7.0						8.1
	-.3	-2.0	1.2						1.3
Sales/Net Fixed Assets	20.8	37.3	43.0						22.4
	6.8	17.5	20.9						8.1
	4.1	5.3	6.7						4.7
Sales/Total Assets	2.3	2.6	2.7						2.2
	1.8	1.7	1.8						1.7
	1.3	1.1	1.3						1.0
% Depr., Dep., Amort./Sales	.9	.6	1.0						
	(17) 1.7	(25) 1.5	(21) 1.8						
	7.0	3.4	3.5						
% Officers', Directors' Owners' Comp/Sales			1.7						
		(10)	3.8						
			5.8						
Net Sales ($)	959023M	1464188M	1557205M		1826M	12900M	41915M	77249M	1423315M
Total Assets ($)	676562M	1028635M	1117752M		1427M	3659M	17106M	75210M	1020350M

M = $ thousand   MM = $ million
See Pages 9 through 22 for Explanation of Ratios and Data

Current Data Sorted by Assets   **Comparative Historical Data**

Type of Statement									
							Unqualified	32	33
	1	12	9 34	20 12	4	2	Reviewed	42	46
	4	21	25	1			Compiled	24	45
	6	33	26	2			Tax Returns	9	22
	7	26	41	23	5	5	Other	59	62
		64 (4/1-9/30/09)		255 (10/1/09-3/31/10)				4/1/05-3/31/06	4/1/06-3/31/07
	0-500M	500M-2MM	2-10MM	10-50MM	50-100MM	100-250MM		ALL	ALL
NUMBER OF STATEMENTS	18	92	135	58	9	7		166	208
ASSETS	%	%	%	%	%	%		%	%
Cash & Equivalents	11.5	10.3	12.5	8.0				6.6	7.9
Trade Receivables (net)	35.5	32.6	24.7	23.5				31.7	29.2
Inventory	27.0	27.1	26.1	25.7				27.4	28.2
All Other Current	.2	1.1	4.2	4.5				4.0	3.1
Total Current	74.3	71.1	67.6	61.6				69.7	68.4
Fixed Assets (net)	15.6	17.4	22.3	22.5				18.5	18.1
Intangibles (net)	3.0	2.4	4.0	8.7				4.0	5.8
All Other Non-Current	7.1	9.1	6.1	7.2				7.7	7.7
Total	100.0	100.0	100.0	100.0				100.0	100.0
LIABILITIES									
Notes Payable-Short Term	13.9	15.2	9.0	7.6				12.5	11.9
Cur. Mat.-L.T.D.	4.0	2.5	4.3	3.7				2.7	3.9
Trade Payables	23.1	18.3	14.0	11.8				16.0	14.4
Income Taxes Payable	.0	.1	.1	.7				.5	.3
All Other Current	8.6	7.0	12.7	14.2				13.2	15.0
Total Current	49.5	43.1	40.1	37.9				44.7	45.4
Long-Term Debt	22.6	17.4	13.5	12.8				13.3	13.7
Deferred Taxes	.0	.3	.3	.6				.3	.5
All Other Non-Current	12.8	5.1	4.9	5.6				5.3	5.4
Net Worth	15.1	34.1	41.2	43.1				36.3	34.9
Total Liabilities & Net Worth	100.0	100.0	100.0	100.0				100.0	100.0
INCOME DATA									
Net Sales	100.0	100.0	100.0	100.0				100.0	100.0
Gross Profit	36.5	33.2	34.5	34.0				33.6	32.4
Operating Expenses	34.6	33.0	31.4	30.0				29.1	26.2
Operating Profit	1.9	.2	3.1	4.0				4.5	6.2
All Other Expenses (net)	.7	.5	.4	1.1				.9	1.2
Profit Before Taxes	1.2	-.4	2.7	2.9				3.6	5.0
RATIOS									
Current	2.8	3.2	3.0	2.7				2.3	2.4
	1.7	1.7	1.7	1.7				1.5	1.7
	1.0	1.1	1.1	1.1				1.2	1.1
Quick	1.6	2.2	1.8	1.5				1.3	1.4
	1.1	.9	.9	.9				(165) .8	(207) .8
	.7	.6	.5	.5				.6	.5
Sales/Receivables	15 24.8	29 12.6	29 12.7	34 10.8				34 10.7	29 12.5
	40 9.1	40 9.2	43 8.5	47 7.8				47 7.7	44 8.3
	49 7.5	54 6.8	54 6.7	67 5.4				62 5.9	61 6.0
Cost of Sales/Inventory	0 UND	15 24.2	31 11.7	53 6.9				31 11.8	30 12.3
	28 13.0	45 8.2	68 5.4	81 4.5				59 6.2	62 5.9
	101 3.6	109 3.3	122 3.0	115 3.2				102 3.6	101 3.6
Cost of Sales/Payables	10 37.9	14 25.9	16 22.5	19 19.4				20 18.2	17 20.9
	27 13.7	31 11.9	30 12.2	31 11.7				33 10.9	29 12.8
	46 7.9	50 7.2	53 6.9	66 5.6				50 7.3	45 8.1
Sales/Working Capital	9.1	5.0	4.1	4.5				5.5	5.2
	18.6	10.4	7.2	6.5				10.1	8.3
	NM	34.1	21.6	38.1				21.5	30.2
EBIT/Interest	6.6	8.9	9.1	21.3				10.6	13.6
	(13) .9	(82) 2.5	(110) 3.6	(52) 2.9				(144) 3.8	(178) 4.7
	-7.1	-3.7	.8	.6				1.5	2.0
Net Profit + Depr., Dep., Amort./Cur. Mat. L/T/D		3.7	18.3	7.8				5.9	10.5
		(11) 1.4	(26) 2.5	(19) 2.3				(42) 2.6	(57) 3.5
		-.5	.8	.5				1.1	1.2
Fixed/Worth	.1	.1	.1	.2				.2	.2
	.4	.4	.5	.4				.4	.5
	-1.0	1.3	1.7	1.9				1.3	1.5
Debt/Worth	1.1	.8	.5	.6				.7	.8
	2.7	2.0	1.6	1.6				1.8	1.8
	-5.3	6.1	4.1	3.0				4.2	5.3
% Profit Before Taxes/Tangible Net Worth	61.7	31.6	36.8	38.3				44.3	58.1
	(12) 6.9	(80) 10.1	(119) 15.1	(50) 20.7				(146) 21.1	(177) 25.5
	-39.8	-10.1	.6	4.9				6.3	8.0
% Profit Before Taxes/Total Assets	17.9	10.8	12.4	17.2				14.5	20.4
	.9	2.6	4.1	4.5				6.8	7.9
	-16.0	-8.1	-.4	.3				1.4	3.2
Sales/Net Fixed Assets	307.8	83.2	33.8	17.5				43.1	36.5
	34.5	21.2	15.2	9.6				17.2	16.2
	11.9	11.0	4.6	5.7				7.3	6.9
Sales/Total Assets	5.4	3.5	2.7	2.2				3.0	3.0
	3.6	2.5	1.9	1.6				2.2	2.2
	2.6	1.7	1.4	1.1				1.7	1.7
% Depr., Dep., Amort./Sales		.6	.8	1.1				.7	.7
		(70) 1.7	(117) 1.9	(44) 2.1				(146) 1.4	(176) 1.4
		3.3	3.7	4.1				3.0	2.7
% Officers', Directors' Owners' Comp/Sales		2.7	2.4	.7				2.0	2.6
		(53) 5.4	(57) 4.2	(10) 2.0				(48) 4.1	(77) 4.4
		8.2	6.3	4.9				10.5	7.6
Net Sales ($)	25820M	309375M	1337270M	2161638M	830765M	1670569M		6734458M	6396161M
Total Assets ($)	5494M	111276M	632370M	1216869M	576759M	1209446M		2621788M	3501112M

M = $ thousand   MM = $ million
See Pages 9 through 22 for Explanation of Ratios and Data

Comparative Historical Data | Current Data Sorted by Sales

					Type of Statement						
	31		39	35	Unqualified		1	2	2	10	20
	44		50	59	Reviewed		8	10	17	18	6
	34		43	51	Compiled	3	15	9	13	11	
	15		49	67	Tax Returns	7	13	23	16	6	2
	63		88	107	Other	6	18	17	22	21	23
	4/1/07-3/31/08		4/1/08-3/31/09	4/1/09-3/31/10			64 (4/1-9/30/09)		255 (10/1/09-3/31/10)		
	ALL		ALL	ALL		0-1MM	1-3MM	3-5MM	5-10MM	10-25MM	25MM & OVER
	187		269	319	NUMBER OF STATEMENTS	16	55	61	70	66	51
	%		%	%	ASSETS	%	%	%	%	%	%
	9.5		9.8	10.6	Cash & Equivalents	7.2	8.0	8.1	15.2	12.2	8.9
	27.0		26.5	27.2	Trade Receivables (net)	28.9	24.7	29.1	28.9	25.6	26.9
	28.2		28.2	25.9	Inventory	22.3	27.8	31.0	21.4	27.9	22.2
	3.8		3.0	3.3	All Other Current	.2	4.1	3.0	1.8	3.3	5.6
	68.5		67.6	66.9	Total Current	58.5	64.6	71.2	67.3	69.0	63.5
	18.5		20.2	20.6	Fixed Assets (net)	26.5	19.1	19.3	22.7	20.7	18.7
	6.1		5.8	4.8	Intangibles (net)	8.3	2.8	3.4	4.9	4.1	8.4
	6.9		6.4	7.7	All Other Non-Current	6.6	13.4	6.1	5.1	6.2	9.4
	100.0		100.0	100.0	Total	100.0	100.0	100.0	100.0	100.0	100.0
					LIABILITIES						
	11.7		10.4	10.4	Notes Payable-Short Term	14.2	15.6	14.4	6.5	8.8	6.6
	5.4		5.4	3.6	Cur. Mat.-L.T.D.	7.5	2.7	2.9	4.6	3.3	3.3
	16.4		16.1	15.1	Trade Payables	21.7	12.8	19.3	13.3	15.8	12.2
	.3		.4	.2	Income Taxes Payable	.0	.0	.0	.2	.1	.8
	16.7		13.7	11.4	All Other Current	3.8	11.2	10.2	7.9	13.0	17.9
	50.5		46.0	40.8	Total Current	47.2	42.3	46.8	32.6	41.0	40.8
	17.9		15.4	15.2	Long-Term Debt	40.4	17.3	16.9	12.7	11.9	10.8
	.4		.4	.3	Deferred Taxes	.0	.1	.4	.3	.5	.6
	5.4		5.2	5.8	All Other Non-Current	7.9	7.4	6.3	5.0	3.0	7.2
	25.8		33.0	37.9	Net Worth	4.5	32.8	29.6	49.5	43.6	40.6
	100.0		100.0	100.0	Total Liabilties & Net Worth	100.0	100.0	100.0	100.0	100.0	100.0
					INCOME DATA						
	100.0		100.0	100.0	Net Sales	100.0	100.0	100.0	100.0	100.0	100.0
	31.8		32.3	33.9	Gross Profit	37.6	34.5	33.9	34.2	33.2	32.8
	27.9		28.7	31.3	Operating Expenses	36.6	36.0	33.3	30.5	29.1	26.0
	4.0		3.7	2.6	Operating Profit	1.1	-1.6	.5	3.7	4.1	6.8
	1.2		1.2	.8	All Other Expenses (net)	1.7	.4	-.2	.9	.7	1.8
	2.8		2.5	1.9	Profit Before Taxes	-.7	-2.0	.7	2.8	3.4	5.0
					RATIOS						
	2.2		2.6	2.8		1.9	3.1	2.4	4.5	2.9	2.5
	1.5		1.6	1.7	Current	1.2	1.7	1.5	1.9	1.7	1.7
	1.1		1.1	1.1		.8	1.0	1.1	1.3	1.2	1.3
	1.3		1.5	1.7		1.2	1.5	1.4	3.0	1.8	1.3
(186)	.8		.8	.9	Quick	.8	.8	.8	1.2	.9	.9
	.5		.5	.6		.5	.4	.5	.7	.5	.7
29	12.6	28	12.8	30	12.1	28	13.1	26	14.3	31	11.8	30	12.0	31	11.7	33	11.2
43	8.5	41	9.0	42	8.7	Sales/Receivables	49	7.5	40	9.2	41	9.0	45	8.1	38	9.5	45	8.2
58	6.3	55	6.6	56	6.5		96	3.8	57	6.4	54	6.7	57	6.6	55	6.6	57	6.4
29	12.5	29	12.5	28	13.2		19	19.4	17	21.1	31	11.6	14	25.9	32	11.2	42	8.7
64	5.7	61	6.0	62	5.9	Cost of Sales/Inventory	56	6.6	63	5.8	68	5.3	49	7.4	64	5.7	61	6.0
102	3.6	103	3.5	114	3.2		152	2.4	137	2.7	118	3.1	110	3.3	108	3.4	86	4.2
18	20.5	16	23.0	17	21.7		21	17.7	13	29.0	22	16.2	11	32.0	21	17.7	17	21.7
33	11.1	30	12.2	30	12.2	Cost of Sales/Payables	46	7.9	24	14.9	35	10.3	28	13.1	34	10.8	27	13.7
53	6.9	48	7.7	52	7.0		165	2.2	49	7.5	71	5.1	45	8.1	54	6.7	44	8.3
	5.7		5.2	4.7		3.8	3.5	4.8	4.1	4.6	5.4
	9.7		9.6	8.3	Sales/Working Capital	40.7	9.6	8.5	6.9	7.9	7.7
	42.7		79.2	27.9		-13.3	165.0	30.3	19.7	19.8	15.8
	11.7		13.9	9.6		3.5	4.0	7.6	12.2	10.3	25.9
(168)	3.3	(234)	3.8	(273)	2.9	EBIT/Interest	(12)	1.8	(50)	1.1	(52)	2.6	(57)	5.4	(55)	4.0	(47)	6.6
	.8		.8	.2		-.4	-5.9	-.7	1.1	1.5	1.4
	6.8		7.1	7.5				4.5	3.0	27.4	13.2
(58)	2.9	(71)	1.6	(61)	2.3	Net Profit + Depr., Dep., Amort./Cur. Mat. L/T/D		(10)	2.2	(12)	1.1	(21)	2.8	(15)	3.4
	.8		.4	.5				.2	.0	.6	1.6
	.2		.2	.2		.3	.1	.1	.1	.1	.3
	.6		.5	.5	Fixed/Worth	1.0	.4	.6	.4	.4	.5
	2.2		2.0	1.5		-.7	1.5	1.5	1.7	1.3	1.6
	1.0		.8	.7		1.5	.9	.9	.3	.6	.7
	2.5		2.1	1.8	Debt/Worth	5.1	2.6	2.8	1.1	1.3	1.7
	11.1		6.9	4.7		-2.8	9.4	6.0	2.8	3.2	5.1
	54.7		45.2	36.6		48.1	23.2	42.0	29.9	39.3	65.2
(148)	21.2	(222)	22.3	(276)	15.2	% Profit Before Taxes/Tangible Net Worth	(10)	5.7	(45)	5.1	(52)	8.1	(64)	14.9	(61)	19.1	(44)	28.7
	2.6		8.3	.5		-8.0	-11.6	-11.6	.6	5.4	13.3
	16.7		14.4	12.1		9.2	5.1	12.2	13.5	16.0	20.5
	6.4		6.4	4.1	% Profit Before Taxes/Total Assets	.8	.5	2.6	5.4	5.8	7.3
	-.4		-.4	-1.6		-5.0	-14.6	-5.1	.4	1.0	1.9
	36.4		36.6	35.7		37.1	48.0	57.4	41.4	34.2	22.0
	15.9		16.0	15.8	Sales/Net Fixed Assets	12.5	16.9	18.0	15.4	15.7	12.8
	7.2		7.5	6.1		1.1	5.6	7.4	5.1	6.1	6.2
	2.9		3.0	2.9		3.4	2.8	3.1	3.7	2.9	2.7
	2.2		2.3	2.0	Sales/Total Assets	1.6	1.7	2.2	1.9	2.1	2.0
	1.5		1.6	1.4		.6	1.1	1.6	1.4	1.3	1.3
	.8		.8	.8			.9	.8	.8	.5	1.1
(157)	1.5	(224)	1.4	(250)	1.9	% Depr., Dep., Amort./Sales		(41)	2.4	(47)	1.8	(60)	2.0	(57)	1.1	(36)	2.0
	2.8		2.8	3.6			3.9	3.5	4.2	2.7	3.6
	1.9		2.5	2.5			3.0	3.2	2.4	2.1	
(56)	4.5	(100)	4.9	(130)	4.6	% Officers', Directors' Owners' Comp/Sales		(29)	5.4	(31)	5.5	(39)	4.2	(18)	3.5	
	10.2		8.5	7.8			10.2	8.2	6.7	6.2	
	4785446M		7543137M	6335437M	Net Sales ($)	10564M	105175M	236234M	521639M	1094234M	4367591M
	2715591M		4072850M	3752214M	Total Assets ($)	17207M	75792M	121483M	297154M	638173M	2602405M

© RMA 2010

M = $ thousand   MM = $ million
See Pages 9 through 22 for Explanation of Ratios and Data

Current Data Sorted by Assets

Comparative Historical Data

0-500M	500M-2MM	2-10MM	10-50MM	50-100MM	100-250MM	Type of Statement	4/1/05-3/31/06 ALL	4/1/06-3/31/07 ALL
		2	4	1	3	Unqualified	13	16
	2	5		1		Reviewed	13	6
	1	2				Compiled	9	9
	3	4	1			Tax Returns	4	3
1	1	9	5	3	1	Other	11	21
	6 (4/1-9/30/09)		43 (10/1/09-3/31/10)					
1	7	22	10	5	4	NUMBER OF STATEMENTS	50	55
%	%	%	%	%	%	**ASSETS**	%	%
		11.5	14.2			Cash & Equivalents	8.8	10.1
		27.3	22.2			Trade Receivables (net)	34.6	30.4
		23.8	16.3			Inventory	20.5	21.1
		3.5	4.3			All Other Current	4.2	5.9
		66.0	57.0			Total Current	68.2	67.6
		21.6	26.4			Fixed Assets (net)	22.2	20.8
		4.4	11.2			Intangibles (net)	5.0	6.7
		8.1	5.3			All Other Non-Current	4.6	4.9
		100.0	100.0			Total	100.0	100.0
						LIABILITIES		
		7.9	3.6			Notes Payable-Short Term	11.5	7.5
		2.2	1.6			Cur. Mat.-L.T.D.	2.5	2.0
		11.5	5.7			Trade Payables	16.0	14.7
		.1	.4			Income Taxes Payable	.6	.5
		8.5	13.0			All Other Current	15.3	15.6
		30.2	24.3			Total Current	46.0	40.4
		12.0	7.1			Long-Term Debt	15.2	12.4
		.0	1.7			Deferred Taxes	.5	.4
		8.5	7.1			All Other Non-Current	7.1	8.2
		49.3	59.8			Net Worth	31.2	38.5
		100.0	100.0			Total Liabilities & Net Worth	100.0	100.0
						INCOME DATA		
		100.0	100.0			Net Sales	100.0	100.0
		38.9	35.0			Gross Profit	31.3	30.8
		35.1	27.1			Operating Expenses	26.1	22.1
		3.9	7.9			Operating Profit	5.2	8.7
		.2	1.8			All Other Expenses (net)	.5	.8
		3.6	6.1			Profit Before Taxes	4.7	7.9
						RATIOS		
		4.1	5.0				2.7	2.5
		2.2	2.3			Current	1.5	1.8
		1.7	1.5				1.3	1.3
		1.9	2.9				2.0	1.6
		1.2	1.4			Quick	.9	1.0
		.9	1.1				.7	.8
		34 10.8	39 9.4				49 7.5	40 9.2
		38 9.7	48 7.6			Sales/Receivables	60 6.1	54 6.8
		58 6.3	57 6.4				75 4.9	73 5.0
		36 10.2	36 10.1				26 14.1	34 10.6
		71 5.2	47 7.7			Cost of Sales/Inventory	50 7.3	52 7.0
		102 3.6	87 4.2				71 5.1	81 4.5
		20 17.9	3 131.3				24 15.4	21 17.8
		30 12.4	18 20.0			Cost of Sales/Payables	35 10.4	33 10.9
		40 9.1	32 11.3				50 7.3	49 7.4
		3.5	3.6				4.4	5.0
		5.2	6.1			Sales/Working Capital	7.9	7.5
		11.9	7.7				15.5	15.4
		14.1					38.4	31.0
		(21) 5.8				EBIT/Interest	(47) 9.2	(45) 8.8
		2.3					2.2	2.8
						Net Profit + Depr., Dep.,	9.2	9.8
		(15) 4.8				Amort./Cur. Mat. L/T/D	(21) 3.7	
		2.0					2.0	1.6
		.2	.4				.3	.3
		.4	.5			Fixed/Worth	.5	.5
		.7	2.2				2.5	1.2
		.5	.2				.7	1.0
		1.0	.8			Debt/Worth	1.5	1.5
		2.4	4.3				6.3	3.5
		24.1				% Profit Before Taxes/Tangible	47.0	58.0
		(20) 16.5				Net Worth	(41) 17.5	(47) 34.4
		3.5					9.5	19.4
		14.0	20.1			% Profit Before Taxes/Total	16.1	21.6
		6.1	8.7			Assets	7.2	11.3
		1.6	-3.9				3.4	5.2
		39.9	10.8				38.0	26.5
		13.8	6.7			Sales/Net Fixed Assets	12.5	10.4
		5.1	4.8				4.9	6.1
		2.7	2.5				2.6	2.5
		1.8	1.8			Sales/Total Assets	1.9	2.0
		1.6	1.2				1.6	1.6
		.9	1.8				.7	.9
		(17) 1.7	2.3			% Depr., Dep., Amort./Sales	(45) 1.4	(49) 1.5
		2.7	3.8				2.0	2.3
						% Officers', Directors'	1.8	
						Owners' Comp/Sales	(12) 5.5	
							11.5	
1025M	26117M	195106M	413949M	680410M	711243M	Net Sales ($)	1642751M	2535000M
365M	11853M	106637M	248285M	424119M	532312M	Total Assets ($)	978011M	1376943M

M = $ thousand   MM = $ million
See Pages 9 through 22 for Explanation of Ratios and Data

Comparative Historical Data | | Current Data Sorted by Sales

4/1/07-3/31/08 ALL	4/1/08-3/31/09 ALL	4/1/09-3/31/10 ALL	Type of Statement	0-1MM	1-3MM	3-5MM	5-10MM	10-25MM	25MM & OVER
14	8	10	Unqualified				1	2	7
7	10	8	Reviewed		1		2	4	1
8	9	3	Compiled			1	3	2	
4	8	8	Tax Returns			2			1
13	21	20	Other	1	1	2	7	3	7
				6 (4/1-9/30/09)			43 (10/1/09-3/31/10)		
46	56	49	**NUMBER OF STATEMENTS**	1	2	6	13	11	16
%	%	%	**ASSETS**	%	%	%	%	%	%
9.8	12.2	13.8	Cash & Equivalents				15.1	13.4	13.8
27.8	27.6	24.2	Trade Receivables (net)				29.2	23.5	24.5
21.3	23.6	22.6	Inventory				22.3	24.1	17.2
3.2	2.1	3.8	All Other Current				5.4	.3	6.2
62.1	65.5	64.5	Total Current				72.0	61.3	61.6
24.4	24.1	22.5	Fixed Assets (net)				16.0	21.6	25.0
7.3	6.0	6.7	Intangibles (net)				2.4	15.2	6.6
6.3	4.3	6.3	All Other Non-Current				9.5	2.0	6.7
100.0	100.0	100.0	Total				100.0	100.0	100.0
			LIABILITIES						
7.5	9.0	5.8	Notes Payable-Short Term				6.7	3.5	4.4
2.2	1.6	1.7	Cur. Mat.-L.T.D.				1.7	2.6	1.4
14.7	14.4	9.8	Trade Payables				12.5	10.3	8.6
.5	.4	.2	Income Taxes Payable				.1	.2	.5
15.1	13.7	13.3	All Other Current				7.5	9.0	15.9
40.0	39.1	30.8	Total Current				28.5	25.4	30.8
13.7	14.9	10.0	Long-Term Debt				12.7	8.8	7.3
.8	.5	.6	Deferred Taxes				.0	.7	1.2
7.1	8.9	5.8	All Other Non-Current				9.4	10.7	2.5
38.4	36.6	52.8	Net Worth				49.4	54.4	58.1
100.0	100.0	100.0	Total Liabilities & Net Worth				100.0	100.0	100.0
			INCOME DATA						
100.0	100.0	100.0	Net Sales				100.0	100.0	100.0
29.0	30.6	36.4	Gross Profit				36.6	39.8	28.5
22.5	25.1	29.9	Operating Expenses				34.3	30.7	21.8
6.5	5.5	6.5	Operating Profit				2.4	9.1	6.8
1.2	.4	.4	All Other Expenses (net)				.1	1.1	.4
5.3	5.1	6.1	Profit Before Taxes				2.3	8.0	6.3
			RATIOS						
2.3	2.7	4.2	Current				4.7	4.3	3.9
1.6	1.6	2.1					2.8	2.2	1.9
1.2	1.2	1.4					2.0	1.7	1.3
1.4	1.7	2.0	Quick				2.3	1.8	1.9
.9	1.0	1.2					1.5	1.5	1.0
.6	.7	.9					1.1	.9	.8
37 10.0	29 12.8	34 10.8	Sales/Receivables				36 10.3	22 16.3	42 8.8
53 6.9	44 8.4	46 7.9					46 7.9	37 9.9	58 6.3
72 5.1	59 6.2	61 6.0					73 5.0	53 6.9	62 5.9
31 11.9	28 12.9	35 10.5	Cost of Sales/Inventory				24 15.2	46 8.0	30 12.3
48 7.6	55 6.7	72 5.1					94 3.9	68 5.4	54 6.7
86 4.3	79 4.6	94 3.9					109 3.3	86 4.3	72 5.1
17 21.8	13 28.2	13 27.4	Cost of Sales/Payables				21 17.1	11 34.6	14 26.7
35 10.5	23 16.1	29 12.7					31 11.7	22 16.8	28 12.9
52 7.0	39 9.4	40 9.1					39 9.4	36 10.2	40 9.1
5.6	5.5	3.6	Sales/Working Capital				3.2	3.4	3.9
9.2	9.6	5.9					4.1	5.7	6.9
19.8	19.4	11.3					5.8	11.7	10.5
20.8	24.1	27.6	EBIT/Interest				11.1	14.7	117.6
(41) 5.5	(49) 7.2	(45) 9.4					(11) 4.0	(10) 10.0	32.2
1.7	2.4	2.3					2.7	1.5	4.2
8.6	12.7	13.7	Net Profit + Depr., Dep.,						
(17) 3.1	(19) 6.1	(13) 8.4	Amort./Cur. Mat. L/T/D						
1.6	2.3	1.9							
.2	.3	.2	Fixed/Worth				.1	.4	.4
.6	.6	.5					.3	.5	.5
1.4	2.6	.8					.6	-.9	.8
1.0	.7	.4	Debt/Worth				.5	.4	.3
1.6	1.9	1.1					1.3	.9	1.0
2.9	19.4	2.3					2.4	-10.6	1.4
49.6	48.8	34.7	% Profit Before Taxes/Tangible				27.8		47.4
(40) 29.8	(44) 24.0	(46) 19.4	Net Worth				13.8		23.8
9.1	12.3	7.0					5.7		9.7
19.5	17.9	16.4	% Profit Before Taxes/Total				8.2	16.4	17.3
10.5	10.4	7.9	Assets				5.0	14.0	9.3
1.6	4.0	2.5					2.5	1.4	5.3
28.5	27.3	23.0	Sales/Net Fixed Assets				57.6	17.6	9.6
9.6	10.9	9.9					17.3	10.4	6.8
4.5	5.5	5.0					5.4	4.9	4.6
2.3	2.8	2.5	Sales/Total Assets				2.6	3.3	2.1
1.8	2.4	1.8					1.8	1.8	1.6
1.3	1.7	1.4					1.5	1.4	1.4
.9	.9	1.4	% Depr., Dep., Amort./Sales				.3		1.8
(41) 1.6	(49) 1.4	(41) 1.8					(10) 1.6	(15) 2.2	
2.1	2.2	2.7					5.9		2.8
		3.6	% Officers', Directors'						
	(14) 5.1		Owners' Comp/Sales						
		6.5							
1962418M	2503145M	2027850M	Net Sales ($)	705M	2990M	23882M	92495M	141123M	1766655M
1189963M	1263358M	1323571M	Total Assets ($)	796M	4671M	11316M	61753M	93903M	1151132M

M = $ thousand   MM = $ million
See Pages 9 through 22 for Explanation of Ratios and Data

Current Data Sorted by Assets | Comparative Historical Data

0-500M	500M-2MM	2-10MM	10-50MM	50-100MM	100-250MM	Type of Statement	4/1/05-3/31/06 ALL	4/1/06-3/31/07 ALL
		4	9	3	3	Unqualified	25	30
		13	9	1		Reviewed	17	16
	1	4	1			Compiled	7	12
1	2	1				Tax Returns	6	6
3	4	9	10	3	1	Other	28	25
13 (4/1-9/30/09)			69 (10/1/09-3/31/10)					
4	7	31	29	7	4	**NUMBER OF STATEMENTS**	83	89
%	%	%	%	%	%	**ASSETS**	%	%
		9.4	10.0			Cash & Equivalents	9.1	11.9
		27.3	26.9			Trade Receivables (net)	29.0	26.9
		34.5	29.1			Inventory	32.2	31.1
		3.1	3.3			All Other Current	1.9	3.6
		74.2	69.3			Total Current	72.2	73.5
		17.0	18.9			Fixed Assets (net)	19.2	16.2
		2.7	4.2			Intangibles (net)	3.1	4.4
		6.1	7.5			All Other Non-Current	5.5	5.8
		100.0	100.0			Total	100.0	100.0
						LIABILITIES		
		16.5	7.7			Notes Payable-Short Term	8.8	9.7
		2.7	2.4			Cur. Mat.-L.T.D.	2.6	2.6
		13.4	14.1			Trade Payables	16.6	15.7
		.2	.1			Income Taxes Payable	.3	.4
		14.0	13.7			All Other Current	13.6	12.3
		46.9	38.1			Total Current	41.9	40.7
		11.2	9.2			Long-Term Debt	14.0	11.0
		.2	1.0			Deferred Taxes	.2	.4
		3.4	7.7			All Other Non-Current	6.9	8.0
		38.3	44.0			Net Worth	37.0	39.9
		100.0	100.0			Total Liabilities & Net Worth	100.0	100.0
						INCOME DATA		
		100.0	100.0			Net Sales	100.0	100.0
		31.8	30.2			Gross Profit	31.4	30.6
		26.7	23.4			Operating Expenses	25.3	25.3
		5.1	6.9			Operating Profit	6.1	5.3
		.7	.8			All Other Expenses (net)	1.6	1.2
		4.3	6.1			Profit Before Taxes	4.5	4.2
						RATIOS		
		3.0	2.9				3.1	3.2
		1.7	2.0			Current	1.8	1.9
		1.2	1.3				1.2	1.3
		1.5	1.5				1.7	1.8
		.7	1.1			Quick	.9	.9
		.4	.6				.6	.5
		34 10.8	35 10.5				35 10.5	36 10.1
		41 9.0	43 8.4			Sales/Receivables	48 7.5	44 8.4
		54 6.8	65 5.6				68 5.3	60 6.1
		48 7.6	41 9.0				53 6.9	39 9.4
		110 3.3	79 4.6			Cost of Sales/Inventory	79 4.6	77 4.7
		140 2.6	126 2.9				116 3.2	130 2.8
		15 24.0	21 17.4				21 17.2	18 20.3
		27 13.5	29 12.4			Cost of Sales/Payables	34 10.7	33 10.9
		44 8.4	39 9.4				59 6.2	49 7.4
		3.7	3.6				4.0	4.1
		8.0	5.2			Sales/Working Capital	7.0	6.4
		17.3	12.1				20.9	15.2
		20.8	19.1				10.9	13.0
		(27) 4.0	6.8			EBIT/Interest	(71) 3.1	(73) 4.5
		1.2	3.1				1.1	.8
			10.3				4.2	6.7
			(11) 3.8			Net Profit + Depr., Dep., Amort./Cur. Mat. L/T/D	(27) 2.6	(27) 2.3
			2.3				1.2	.7
		.1	.2				.2	.1
		.4	.5			Fixed/Worth	.6	.3
		1.1	.8				1.3	1.4
		.6	.7				.6	.7
		1.9	1.3			Debt/Worth	1.6	1.5
		5.8	4.0				4.8	5.1
		47.8	45.3				53.4	54.6
		(27) 5.2	(27) 21.7			% Profit Before Taxes/Tangible Net Worth	(72) 20.3	(78) 29.3
		3.1	5.4				4.8	5.6
		17.4	16.0				18.5	21.3
		3.9	9.7			% Profit Before Taxes/Total Assets	6.7	7.6
		.7	2.4				.5	1.0
		46.9	29.1				28.6	46.7
		16.4	10.9			Sales/Net Fixed Assets	13.3	17.2
		4.1	5.5				6.0	6.2
		3.0	2.3				2.8	2.8
		1.8	1.8			Sales/Total Assets	2.1	2.1
		1.4	1.3				1.5	1.5
		.8	.8				.7	.6
		(25) 1.2	(26) 1.4			% Depr., Dep., Amort./Sales	(71) 1.4	(73) 1.2
		2.6	2.4				2.3	1.9
							1.3	1.8
						% Officers', Directors' Owners' Comp/Sales	(16) 2.8	(22) 6.7
							6.0	13.5
5346M	20288M	352142M	1216824M	636385M	1296029M	Net Sales ($)	3314532M	3616266M
994M	7969M	164957M	663606M	432468M	728074M	Total Assets ($)	1912582M	2182365M

M = $ thousand   MM = $ million
See Pages 9 through 22 for Explanation of Ratios and Data

Comparative Historical Data | | | Current Data Sorted by Sales

Type of Statement

4/1/07-3/31/08 ALL	4/1/08-3/31/09 ALL	4/1/09-3/31/10 ALL	Type of Statement	0-1MM	1-3MM	3-5MM	5-10MM	10-25MM	25MM & OVER
22	19	19	Unqualified		1		5	5	13
20	17	23	Reviewed		1	1		9	7
8	13	6	Compiled		1		4	1	
6	7	4	Tax Returns		2		1	1	
20	37	30	Other	3	4	1	4	5	13
				3	9	2	14	21	33
				13 (4/1-9/30/09)			69 (10/1/09-3/31/10)		
76	93	82	**NUMBER OF STATEMENTS**	3	9	2	14	21	33
%	%	%		%	%	%	%	%	%

ASSETS

4/1/07-3/31/08	4/1/08-3/31/09	4/1/09-3/31/10		0-1MM	1-3MM	3-5MM	5-10MM	10-25MM	25MM & OVER
8.7	9.9	10.5	Cash & Equivalents				13.3	9.2	10.7
26.4	27.2	26.6	Trade Receivables (net)				24.1	28.4	27.8
32.6	29.5	31.8	Inventory				31.5	31.3	26.6
4.9	4.1	3.7	All Other Current				2.8	3.9	4.4
72.6	70.8	72.6	Total Current				71.7	72.8	69.6
15.9	19.2	17.4	Fixed Assets (net)				19.0	14.9	19.6
4.9	3.3	3.6	Intangibles (net)				2.5	5.9	3.2
6.6	6.7	6.4	All Other Non-Current				6.8	6.4	7.6
100.0	100.0	100.0	Total				100.0	100.0	100.0

LIABILITIES

4/1/07-3/31/08	4/1/08-3/31/09	4/1/09-3/31/10		0-1MM	1-3MM	3-5MM	5-10MM	10-25MM	25MM & OVER
9.9	13.6	12.1	Notes Payable-Short Term				16.1	9.9	7.0
3.5	2.6	2.5	Cur. Mat.-L.T.D.				1.4	3.6	2.1
15.2	12.8	13.2	Trade Payables				10.9	13.4	14.7
.3	.4	.2	Income Taxes Payable				.0	.1	.3
16.1	14.4	12.8	All Other Current				10.1	16.5	13.7
45.1	43.9	40.8	Total Current				38.6	43.5	37.8
12.3	11.2	10.8	Long-Term Debt				9.0	12.6	9.5
.5	.4	.5	Deferred Taxes				.2	.4	.9
5.5	6.9	8.1	All Other Non-Current				.8	2.8	10.4
36.6	37.6	39.7	Net Worth				51.5	40.8	41.4
100.0	100.0	100.0	Total Liabilties & Net Worth				100.0	100.0	100.0

INCOME DATA

4/1/07-3/31/08	4/1/08-3/31/09	4/1/09-3/31/10		0-1MM	1-3MM	3-5MM	5-10MM	10-25MM	25MM & OVER
100.0	100.0	100.0	Net Sales				100.0	100.0	100.0
30.4	30.6	32.2	Gross Profit				33.6	32.0	28.0
25.2	25.4	26.9	Operating Expenses				30.7	24.2	21.7
5.2	5.2	5.3	Operating Profit				2.9	7.8	6.3
1.5	1.0	1.1	All Other Expenses (net)				.2	1.2	1.1
3.7	4.2	4.2	Profit Before Taxes				2.7	6.6	5.2

RATIOS

4/1/07-3/31/08	4/1/08-3/31/09	4/1/09-3/31/10		0-1MM	1-3MM	3-5MM	5-10MM	10-25MM	25MM & OVER
2.6	2.6	3.0	Current				5.2	3.0	2.8
1.7	1.7	2.0					1.6	1.8	2.0
1.2	1.3	1.3					1.2	1.2	1.4
1.2	1.3	1.7	Quick				3.0	1.5	1.7
.8	.9	.9					.8	1.0	.9
.5	.5	.5					.5	.4	.6
36 10.3	31 11.8	34 10.8	Sales/Receivables				32 11.3	37 9.9	33 10.9
49 7.5	44 8.4	44 8.4					38 9.7	46 7.9	47 7.8
63 5.8	60 6.1	57 6.4					49 7.5	60 6.1	57 6.4
51 7.2	45 8.1	46 8.0	Cost of Sales/Inventory				57 6.4	53 6.8	34 10.8
88 4.1	73 5.0	94 3.9					116 3.1	107 3.4	77 4.7
131 2.8	111 3.3	129 2.8					138 2.6	133 2.8	104 3.5
20 18.5	12 29.4	18 20.1	Cost of Sales/Payables				12 30.4	12 30.7	20 18.2
37 9.9	27 13.4	28 13.1					26 14.0	26 14.2	27 13.5
53 6.9	41 9.0	44 8.3					39 9.3	44 8.3	42 8.6
4.1	4.6	3.7	Sales/Working Capital				4.0	4.1	4.1
7.8	7.3	6.3					8.4	7.4	6.0
19.2	17.6	12.4					11.6	16.3	10.0
13.1	12.3	20.8	EBIT/Interest				49.4	28.6	27.2
(69) 5.0	(83) 3.6	(75) 5.4					(12) 4.0	(20) 5.2	(31) 6.2
1.0	1.5	1.6					2.1	2.4	1.7
19.8	5.5	9.6	Net Profit + Depr., Dep., Amort./Cur. Mat. L/T/D						14.1
(30) 3.8	(22) 2.7	(20) 2.4						(13)	3.8
.9	1.3	.5							1.3
.2	.2	.2	Fixed/Worth				.1	.2	.2
.4	.5	.5					.2	.5	.5
1.4	1.2	1.1					.6	2.0	.8
.9	.8	.6	Debt/Worth				.2	.6	.8
2.2	1.6	1.6					1.0	1.5	1.4
4.5	4.2	5.6					2.8	18.7	4.4
48.3	48.8	44.0	% Profit Before Taxes/Tangible Net Worth				20.3	111.7	61.5
(67) 18.1	(85) 16.6	(72) 10.6					(12) 5.0	(18) 23.9	(32) 21.7
.3	4.1	3.1					3.6	3.9	3.7
15.9	14.0	17.0	% Profit Before Taxes/Total Assets				8.0	23.3	17.7
5.6	6.2	4.4					3.7	6.3	8.9
.0	1.1	.9					1.1	1.6	1.0
41.1	35.1	31.8	Sales/Net Fixed Assets				32.7	41.9	28.1
16.6	18.4	16.3					15.5	16.6	16.2
6.3	5.8	5.0					4.0	5.6	5.4
2.7	2.8	2.7	Sales/Total Assets				2.7	3.2	2.4
1.9	2.0	1.8					1.7	2.0	1.8
1.4	1.5	1.3					1.4	1.2	1.4
.7	.6	.8	% Depr., Dep., Amort./Sales				1.1	.8	.8
(67) 1.3	(82) 1.2	(68) 1.4					(13) 1.5	(16) 1.3	(30) 1.4
2.4	2.6	2.6					2.6	1.6	2.6
1.7	2.7	1.1	% Officers', Directors' Owners' Comp/Sales						
(15) 2.8	(20) 4.1	(17) 3.2							
6.1	7.5	5.0							
3529520M	3643920M	3527014M	Net Sales ($)	864M	18408M	8686M	95883M	365867M	3037306M
2123172M	1880668M	1998068M	Total Assets ($)	2180M	17980M	3698M	54287M	238408M	1681515M

M = $ thousand   MM = $ million
See Pages 9 through 22 for Explanation of Ratios and Data

Current Data Sorted by Assets | Comparative Historical Data

Type of Statement	0-500M	500M-2MM	2-10MM	10-50MM	50-100MM	100-250MM		4/1/05-3/31/06 ALL	4/1/06-3/31/07 ALL
Unqualified		1	4	14	3	4		31	43
Reviewed		2	15	5				22	21
Compiled		11	8					11	16
Tax Returns	5	2	2					12	9
Other		6	18	17	1	2		33	32
		19 (4/1-9/30/09)		101 (10/1/09-3/31/10)					
NUMBER OF STATEMENTS	5	22	47	36	4	6		109	121
	%	%	%	%	%	%	ASSETS	%	%
		10.5	12.5	16.9			Cash & Equivalents	9.5	9.6
		31.5	31.2	25.5			Trade Receivables (net)	35.9	31.3
		20.0	31.0	25.1			Inventory	22.6	25.6
		2.7	4.4	2.6			All Other Current	4.1	2.9
		64.6	79.1	70.1			Total Current	72.1	69.3
		20.8	14.9	18.3			Fixed Assets (net)	17.8	19.0
		8.3	3.0	7.0			Intangibles (net)	3.6	6.2
		6.3	3.0	4.6			All Other Non-Current	6.4	5.5
		100.0	100.0	100.0			Total	100.0	100.0
							LIABILITIES		
		8.8	10.2	4.4			Notes Payable-Short Term	11.9	10.7
		5.0	3.0	2.6			Cur. Mat.-L.T.D.	3.6	2.2
		16.0	14.4	10.7			Trade Payables	20.5	17.2
		2.7	.4	.1			Income Taxes Payable	.5	.6
		10.2	13.6	12.0			All Other Current	14.6	13.4
		42.6	41.5	29.9			Total Current	51.0	44.2
		17.1	9.0	8.3			Long-Term Debt	10.6	14.7
		.4	.9	1.0			Deferred Taxes	.6	.7
		3.9	6.3	7.8			All Other Non-Current	5.0	6.0
		36.0	42.1	53.0			Net Worth	32.9	34.4
		100.0	100.0	100.0			Total Liabilties & Net Worth	100.0	100.0
							INCOME DATA		
		100.0	100.0	100.0			Net Sales	100.0	100.0
		33.4	29.7	29.5			Gross Profit	29.2	28.4
		31.4	25.1	21.0			Operating Expenses	24.0	22.8
		1.9	4.5	8.5			Operating Profit	5.2	5.6
		.7	.5	.7			All Other Expenses (net)	1.0	1.1
		1.2	4.1	7.8			Profit Before Taxes	4.2	4.4
							RATIOS		
		2.3	3.3	4.9				2.3	2.4
		1.7	1.8	2.6			Current	1.5	1.6
		1.1	1.5	1.4				1.1	1.2
		1.4	1.9	3.1				1.5	1.5
		1.0	1.1	1.5			Quick	1.0	1.0
		.6	.5	.9				.6	.6
	20	17.9	29 12.6	34 10.7				36 10.0	34 10.9
	36	10.2	42 8.7	44 8.3			Sales/Receivables	49 7.4	45 8.1
	51	7.2	56 6.5	54 6.8				64 5.7	58 6.3
	9	40.2	30 12.3	35 10.5				18 20.0	23 15.7
	32	11.4	80 4.6	60 6.0			Cost of Sales/Inventory	52 7.1	54 6.7
	48	7.6	107 3.4	126 2.9				73 5.0	91 4.0
	13	28.2	14 25.3	15 24.0				21 17.5	17 21.1
	34	10.9	31 11.7	23 16.1			Cost of Sales/Payables	35 10.5	31 11.9
	44	8.3	45 8.2	32 11.4				53 6.8	46 7.9
		7.4	3.2	3.0				6.2	5.4
		12.0	7.1	4.4			Sales/Working Capital	10.9	9.5
		111.7	16.0	12.4				30.8	26.9
		7.5	15.5	97.3				11.2	13.9
	(20)	2.1	(42) 3.7	(30) 20.1			EBIT/Interest	(94) 4.6	(107) 5.4
		-1.5	1.5	3.8				1.8	1.8
			43.5	14.4				12.0	11.7
			(11) 2.3	(12) 8.7			Net Profit + Depr., Dep., Amort./Cur. Mat. L/T/D	(26) 3.7	(45) 4.6
			.3	4.0				.8	1.4
		.3	.2	.1				.2	.2
		1.0	.4	.3			Fixed/Worth	.5	.5
		1.6	.7	1.2				1.5	1.8
		.9	.6	.3				.8	.8
		2.3	1.4	.9			Debt/Worth	1.8	1.8
		6.1	4.7	3.0				5.7	6.8
		58.8	34.8	65.2				47.7	60.5
	(18)	13.6	(45) 18.7	(33) 32.3			% Profit Before Taxes/Tangible Net Worth	(94) 20.9	(99) 31.5
		-5.0	4.0	11.0				8.4	16.0
		12.4	15.4	25.2				15.7	19.5
		5.2	4.5	9.8			% Profit Before Taxes/Total Assets	7.2	9.1
		-4.8	.9	3.4				2.8	2.9
		54.1	45.3	29.4				46.6	41.6
		21.0	20.7	11.8			Sales/Net Fixed Assets	17.5	15.2
		8.2	10.3	7.0				8.9	7.1
		4.7	2.9	2.5				3.3	3.4
		3.2	2.3	1.9			Sales/Total Assets	2.5	2.4
		2.0	1.7	1.4				1.8	1.6
		.7	.6	.7				.6	.5
	(19)	1.4	(41) 1.1	(28) 1.3			% Depr., Dep., Amort./Sales	(90) 1.3	(112) 1.3
		2.7	2.4	2.4				1.8	2.2
		2.6	1.5					1.5	.8
	(10)	4.4	(13) 2.8				% Officers', Directors' Owners' Comp/Sales	(31) 3.3	(31) 2.1
		9.4	4.2					6.2	4.5
Net Sales ($)	11163M	79150M	557990M	1448422M	359747M	1970909M		4202040M	5283228M
Total Assets ($)	1186M	25111M	226460M	751551M	236671M	1142934M		1946728M	3234142M

© RMA 2010

M = $ thousand   MM = $ million
See Pages 9 through 22 for Explanation of Ratios and Data

Comparative Historical Data   Current Data Sorted by Sales

4/1/07-3/31/08 ALL	4/1/08-3/31/09 ALL	4/1/09-3/31/10 ALL		0-1MM	1-3MM	3-5MM	5-10MM	10-25MM	25MM & OVER
					19 (4/1-9/30/09)		101 (10/1/09-3/31/10)		
			Type of Statement						
33	26	26	Unqualified		1			8	17
16	34	22	Reviewed		1	1	9	9	2
9	12	19	Compiled		3	5	9	2	
7	12	9	Tax Returns	2	4	1	2		
46	50	44	Other		4	2	10	10	18
111	134	120	**NUMBER OF STATEMENTS**	2	13	9	30	29	37
%	%	%	**ASSETS**	%	%	%	%	%	%
7.9	8.3	13.7	Cash & Equivalents		15.1		11.4	14.6	12.2
31.3	28.4	29.5	Trade Receivables (net)		20.9		33.4	29.3	27.5
27.8	30.1	25.7	Inventory		25.5		28.3	28.4	24.0
3.4	4.0	3.3	All Other Current		3.1		3.8	3.3	3.3
70.4	70.8	72.2	Total Current		64.6		76.9	75.6	66.9
17.7	19.5	17.7	Fixed Assets (net)		20.6		16.4	13.7	22.3
5.4	6.0	5.6	Intangibles (net)		14.3		2.3	7.2	5.4
6.5	3.8	4.4	All Other Non-Current		.6		4.4	3.5	5.4
100.0	100.0	100.0	Total		100.0		100.0	100.0	100.0
			LIABILITIES						
8.9	9.7	7.1	Notes Payable-Short Term		4.6		10.6	8.3	3.8
2.4	4.0	3.2	Cur. Mat.-L.T.D.		4.0		2.3	2.9	2.5
15.9	14.0	13.3	Trade Payables		15.8		15.5	12.8	10.5
.2	.4	.7	Income Taxes Payable		4.0		.3	.4	.1
12.2	11.9	12.1	All Other Current		15.2		8.7	15.6	13.3
39.6	40.0	36.5	Total Current		43.6		37.3	40.1	30.2
14.2	12.5	11.4	Long-Term Debt		27.0		6.3	9.0	10.6
.9	.7	.9	Deferred Taxes		.5		1.4	1.2	.7
4.7	4.8	7.5	All Other Non-Current		8.9		7.1	5.1	10.7
40.7	42.1	43.7	Net Worth		20.0		47.8	44.6	47.8
100.0	100.0	100.0	Total Liabilties & Net Worth		100.0		100.0	100.0	100.0
			INCOME DATA						
100.0	100.0	100.0	Net Sales		100.0		100.0	100.0	100.0
29.0	30.7	30.1	Gross Profit		34.7		29.3	31.9	27.0
22.9	24.3	24.7	Operating Expenses		33.4		24.1	26.2	19.3
6.1	6.5	5.4	Operating Profit		1.3		5.2	5.7	7.6
1.1	1.0	.7	All Other Expenses (net)		1.0		.3	1.1	.7
5.0	5.5	4.7	Profit Before Taxes		.3		4.9	4.6	7.0
			RATIOS						
2.9	2.6	3.6			2.2		3.6	3.5	4.4
1.9	1.8	2.0	Current		1.5		2.2	1.8	2.2
1.3	1.4	1.4			1.2		1.5	1.2	1.4
1.5	1.4	2.3			1.3		2.5	2.0	2.4
1.0	.9	1.2	Quick		.8		1.2	1.1	1.2
.6	.5	.8			.4		.7	.6	.8
33 11.1	28 12.9	31 11.7			20 18.1		29 12.8	32 11.2	32 11.3
47 7.8	39 9.5	42 8.6	Sales/Receivables		29 12.4		42 8.7	44 8.4	44 8.2
62 5.9	57 6.4	54 6.7			50 7.4		55 6.6	60 6.1	54 6.7
31 11.6	30 12.1	26 14.1			15 23.9		23 16.0	52 7.0	29 12.8
63 5.8	64 5.7	57 6.3	Cost of Sales/Inventory		50 7.3		68 5.4	85 4.3	55 6.6
102 3.6	109 3.3	100 3.6			125 2.9		101 3.6	134 2.7	80 4.6
19 19.5	16 22.9	14 26.5			29 12.6		10 38.0	18 20.8	13 27.5
27 13.3	28 13.1	28 13.1	Cost of Sales/Payables		37 10.0		29 12.6	29 12.6	22 16.8
44 8.4	41 9.0	37 10.0			52 7.0		45 8.0	36 10.2	32 11.5
4.5	4.7	3.7			7.4		3.2	3.1	3.8
7.5	7.9	7.2	Sales/Working Capital		10.2		6.7	5.6	5.6
13.4	16.9	15.9			37.1		17.6	15.8	14.4
21.0	23.4	22.6			3.8		17.8	19.9	99.7
(101) 4.9	(120) 7.0	(104) 7.2	EBIT/Interest	(10) .1		(24) 8.1	(26) 3.7	(33) 15.0	
1.5	2.6	1.3			-7.2		2.4	1.2	6.0
11.4	14.3	12.8							13.7
(41) 3.2	(41) 5.6	(32) 3.5	Net Profit + Depr., Dep., Amort./Cur. Mat. L/T/D					(17) 8.5	
1.1	1.8	1.0							2.1
.2	.2	.2			.7		.2	.1	.2
.4	.5	.4	Fixed/Worth		1.5		.4	.4	.4
1.2	1.2	1.1			-.1		.8	1.3	1.1
.6	.7	.5			2.0		.4	.5	.4
1.8	1.6	1.4	Debt/Worth		3.3		1.1	1.6	1.0
4.1	3.2	3.7			-3.0		3.2	9.6	2.9
57.9	57.6	46.5					34.9	57.7	63.2
(95) 24.4	(120) 27.8	(107) 19.2	% Profit Before Taxes/Tangible Net Worth			(29) 19.4	(26) 15.4	(33) 33.9	
8.4	11.5	5.1					6.1	1.2	13.3
18.0	18.9	18.4			8.9		19.0	15.0	25.1
9.5	10.2	7.9	% Profit Before Taxes/Total Assets		2.9		6.8	4.1	11.3
1.9	3.4	.9			-8.2		2.9	.8	4.2
43.5	36.5	40.2			77.9		34.1	55.6	26.7
14.7	15.1	17.1	Sales/Net Fixed Assets		12.1		20.4	20.7	10.4
6.7	7.0	8.1			6.0		10.6	10.0	6.0
3.2	3.1	3.1			3.3		3.3	2.8	2.8
2.2	2.2	2.2	Sales/Total Assets		2.0		2.4	1.9	2.1
1.5	1.6	1.6			1.3		1.7	1.3	1.5
.5	.6	.6			.3		.6	.7	.6
(97) 1.3	(116) 1.2	(99) 1.3	% Depr., Dep., Amort./Sales	(11) 2.7		(25) 1.1	(22) 1.2	(33) 1.4	
2.0	2.1	2.5			5.5		2.8	2.1	2.5
.8	1.1	1.7					2.0		
(26) 1.8	(19) 2.3	(30) 2.9	% Officers', Directors' Owners' Comp/Sales				(10) 2.8		
5.2	7.3	5.1					5.1		
5492622M	5512865M	4427381M	Net Sales ($)	1512M	28428M	35383M	220523M	456690M	3684845M
3049924M	2921438M	2383913M	Total Assets ($)	249M	16199M	13937M	98610M	265557M	1989361M

M = $ thousand   MM = $ million
See Pages 9 through 22 for Explanation of Ratios and Data

Current Data Sorted by Assets   Comparative Historical Data

0-500M	500M-2MM	2-10MM	10-50MM	50-100MM	100-250MM	Type of Statement	4/1/05-3/31/06 ALL	4/1/06-3/31/07 ALL
		1	5	1		Unqualified	21	16
	9	17	12			Reviewed	44	51
3	8	9	1			Compiled	25	26
5	4	3				Tax Returns	11	18
2	8	18	1	3	1	Other	24	55
24 (4/1-9/30/09)			87 (10/1/09-3/31/10)					
10	29	48	19	4	1	NUMBER OF STATEMENTS	125	166
%	%	%	%	%	%	**ASSETS**	%	%
6.8	8.7	9.9	7.6			Cash & Equivalents	7.4	8.0
24.3	27.5	24.7	24.3			Trade Receivables (net)	26.6	28.6
22.0	18.3	19.6	18.5			Inventory	17.8	17.0
1.1	1.1	1.7	2.7			All Other Current	3.7	3.7
54.1	55.6	55.8	53.1			Total Current	55.5	57.2
37.6	34.0	35.5	37.4			Fixed Assets (net)	34.3	35.2
.1	2.9	4.3	6.8			Intangibles (net)	3.4	2.9
8.0	7.5	4.3	2.7			All Other Non-Current	6.8	4.7
100.0	100.0	100.0	100.0			Total	100.0	100.0
						LIABILITIES		
24.6	13.5	9.6	10.6			Notes Payable-Short Term	11.0	9.2
14.0	5.2	7.3	5.6			Cur. Mat.-L.T.D.	5.3	4.9
21.0	12.2	11.5	10.3			Trade Payables	11.3	12.7
.0	.1	.1	.0			Income Taxes Payable	.1	.2
8.6	10.0	9.6	8.9			All Other Current	10.5	11.8
68.2	41.1	38.1	35.4			Total Current	38.2	38.7
52.6	19.9	20.4	19.8			Long-Term Debt	18.2	19.6
.0	.1	.8	1.8			Deferred Taxes	.8	.8
6.4	11.6	5.3	2.5			All Other Non-Current	7.1	5.9
-27.1	27.2	35.5	40.5			Net Worth	35.6	35.0
100.0	100.0	100.0	100.0			Total Liabilities & Net Worth	100.0	100.0
						INCOME DATA		
100.0	100.0	100.0	100.0			Net Sales	100.0	100.0
37.0	27.5	28.2	20.4			Gross Profit	29.6	28.8
39.9	27.9	27.8	15.3			Operating Expenses	24.5	23.7
-2.8	-.3	.4	5.1			Operating Profit	5.1	5.1
2.0	1.4	1.3	1.5			All Other Expenses (net)	1.4	1.3
-4.8	-1.8	-.9	3.6			Profit Before Taxes	3.7	3.9
						RATIOS		
2.2	1.9	2.3	2.9				2.4	2.2
.8	1.3	1.4	1.5			Current	1.4	1.5
.4	.9	1.1	1.0				1.1	1.1
1.6	1.3	1.4	1.4				1.5	1.5
.5	.9	.9	.9			Quick	.9	.9
.2	.6	.7	.5				.6	.6
0 UND	30 12.2	36 10.2	37 9.9				38 9.5	35 10.5
25 14.3	40 9.0	47 7.7	55 6.6			Sales/Receivables	49 7.4	49 7.4
46 7.9	65 5.6	70 5.2	84 4.3				65 5.6	63 5.8
3 117.7	15 25.0	27 13.3	31 11.8				20 18.3	17 21.7
28 13.1	33 10.9	45 8.1	40 9.2			Cost of Sales/Inventory	39 9.5	39 9.3
61 6.0	56 6.5	106 3.4	63 5.8				67 5.4	66 5.6
8 45.9	17 21.3	10 34.9	21 17.5				14 25.8	15 24.6
25 14.7	26 13.8	28 13.0	28 12.8			Cost of Sales/Payables	27 13.7	25 14.3
105 3.5	49 7.5	45 8.1	49 7.5				45 8.1	40 9.2
9.2	6.8	5.1	3.5				5.6	6.3
-97.7	17.7	9.3	12.7			Sales/Working Capital	10.9	11.9
-4.7	-49.9	87.8	-171.9				48.6	72.9
	5.4	3.5	7.3				5.8	8.4
	(27) 2.3	(44) .7	(18) 3.2			EBIT/Interest	(114) 2.7	(154) 2.8
	-2.2	-2.6	.0				1.1	1.3
		1.7	2.6			Net Profit + Depr., Dep.,	3.0	4.2
		(15) 1.2	(11) 1.4			Amort./Cur. Mat. L/T/D	(35) 2.1	(43) 2.0
		.4	.5				1.2	1.4
.2	.6	.6	.7				.6	.6
1.8	1.7	1.2	1.4			Fixed/Worth	1.1	1.2
-.5	14.1	2.8	5.5				3.4	2.4
1.9	1.2	.9	.7				.9	1.0
17.3	2.8	1.9	1.6			Debt/Worth	2.0	2.1
-2.6	125.3	4.3	14.6				6.4	5.8
	32.4	32.0	12.2			% Profit Before Taxes/Tangible	32.0	42.1
	(23) 7.2	(42) 3.2	(16) 6.1			Net Worth	(106) 13.1	(151) 18.7
	-106.3	-14.0	-5.6				4.5	3.6
13.7	7.5	6.7	8.1			% Profit Before Taxes/Total	13.7	14.1
-2.8	2.5	-.5	3.0			Assets	5.4	4.7
-35.7	-11.0	-6.7	-1.8				.4	.7
UND	14.4	6.2	5.0				9.4	12.7
15.5	9.1	4.7	3.8			Sales/Net Fixed Assets	5.4	5.6
4.8	3.8	2.8	2.5				3.5	3.4
5.2	2.6	2.3	1.8				2.3	2.6
2.9	2.2	1.6	1.3			Sales/Total Assets	1.8	1.9
2.3	1.5	1.3	1.0				1.3	1.4
	1.9	2.5	2.5				2.7	2.2
	(27) 2.6	(47) 4.3	4.6			% Depr., Dep., Amort./Sales	(113) 4.0	(149) 3.7
	6.5	7.4	6.1				5.5	5.4
	2.7	2.0				% Officers', Directors'	2.3	2.4
	(16) 4.3	(25) 4.6				Owners' Comp/Sales	(55) 4.5	(85) 4.5
	7.9	6.2					8.0	7.4
10735M	70995M	313199M	479292M	333252M	300638M	Net Sales ($)	1415558M	2173992M
2626M	33834M	178133M	340809M	276318M	242861M	Total Assets ($)	925070M	1260816M

M = $ thousand   MM = $ million
See Pages 9 through 22 for Explanation of Ratios and Data

Comparative Historical Data   ## Current Data Sorted by Sales

4/1/07-3/31/08 ALL	4/1/08-3/31/09 ALL	4/1/09-3/31/10 ALL	Type of Statement	0-1MM	1-3MM	3-5MM	5-10MM	10-25MM	25MM & OVER
10	9	7	Unqualified	1	9	7	7	4	3
41	35	38	Reviewed	4	6	1	9	11	3
28	23	21	Compiled		6			1	
17	10	12	Tax Returns	3	6	3			
35	54	33	Other	3	6	11	6	2	5
					24 (4/1-9/30/09)		87 (10/1/09-3/31/10)		
131	131	111	NUMBER OF STATEMENTS	11	27	22	22	18	11
%	%	%	**ASSETS**	%	%	%	%	%	%
7.1	9.3	8.5	Cash & Equivalents	4.8	9.2	10.3	11.4	8.2	1.9
26.8	26.2	24.9	Trade Receivables (net)	25.0	21.7	25.9	27.8	27.3	20.4
16.9	18.0	19.1	Inventory	22.0	17.1	19.3	23.8	15.4	17.2
2.7	2.2	1.7	All Other Current	.5	1.0	2.2	.8	4.3	1.8
53.5	55.7	54.2	Total Current	52.3	49.0	57.7	63.8	55.2	41.4
37.3	34.7	36.5	Fixed Assets (net)	39.6	36.8	34.3	30.3	38.9	44.9
3.4	3.7	3.9	Intangibles (net)	.4	7.3	3.2	.5	3.4	8.0
5.8	5.9	5.4	All Other Non-Current	7.7	6.8	4.7	5.4	2.5	5.6
100.0	100.0	100.0	Total	100.0	100.0	100.0	100.0	100.0	100.0
			LIABILITIES						
9.1	9.4	11.9	Notes Payable-Short Term	14.7	10.4	17.5	10.7	10.4	6.7
5.9	5.5	6.9	Cur. Mat.-L.T.D.	8.4	6.5	7.8	4.4	8.9	6.3
12.5	11.4	12.0	Trade Payables	19.5	9.3	8.8	16.0	11.4	10.5
.2	.2	.1	Income Taxes Payable	.3	.0	.2	.0	.0	.1
10.5	13.1	9.6	All Other Current	3.8	9.2	10.3	10.8	10.8	10.6
38.2	39.6	40.5	Total Current	46.6	35.5	44.5	41.9	41.5	34.0
22.1	23.7	23.5	Long-Term Debt	36.6	28.9	21.7	14.9	19.9	24.0
1.0	.7	.7	Deferred Taxes	.0	.1	.9	.9	.6	2.0
6.8	7.4	6.4	All Other Non-Current	15.1	9.8	5.8	2.8	2.5	4.7
32.0	28.6	28.9	Net Worth	1.6	25.6	27.1	39.5	35.6	35.3
100.0	100.0	100.0	Total Liabilities & Net Worth	100.0	100.0	100.0	100.0	100.0	100.0
			INCOME DATA						
100.0	100.0	100.0	Net Sales	100.0	100.0	100.0	100.0	100.0	100.0
28.0	28.1	27.2	Gross Profit	38.8	28.5	30.9	26.4	18.1	21.6
24.4	25.0	26.2	Operating Expenses	40.3	30.1	32.3	24.3	13.9	14.6
3.6	3.1	1.0	Operating Profit	-1.5	-1.6	-1.4	2.0	4.3	7.0
1.5	1.3	1.5	All Other Expenses (net)	2.7	2.2	.9	.8	1.1	2.0
2.1	1.8	-.5	Profit Before Taxes	-4.1	-3.8	-2.3	1.2	3.2	5.0
			RATIOS						
1.9	2.6	2.3	Current	1.9	2.7	3.4	2.1	2.6	1.7
1.5	1.5	1.4		1.0	1.3	1.5	1.5	1.3	1.2
1.0	1.0	1.0		.4	.9	1.2	1.2	1.0	1.0
1.2	1.6	1.3	Quick	1.2	1.6	1.7	1.3	1.6	1.0
.9	.9	.8		.6	.7	1.0	1.0	.8	.7
.6	.6	.6		.3	.4	.7	.7	.6	.5
33 10.9	31 11.6	33 11.1	Sales/Receivables	23 15.5	28 12.9	31 11.6	25 14.4	43 8.5	40 9.1
47 7.7	47 7.7	44 8.3		38 9.6	48 7.7	51 7.1	42 8.7	55 6.7	42 8.6
63 5.8	61 6.0	69 5.3		44 8.4	69 5.3	80 4.5	54 6.7	80 4.6	47 7.8
16 22.3	19 18.8	22 16.8	Cost of Sales/Inventory	4 93.7	7 50.5	29 12.4	25 14.8	23 16.1	35 10.4
38 9.5	39 9.4	40 9.2		39 9.3	36 10.2	51 7.1	43 8.6	35 10.3	43 8.6
59 6.2	69 5.3	79 4.6		80 4.5	86 4.2	113 3.2	78 4.7	56 6.5	63 5.8
15 24.3	13 28.9	13 28.4	Cost of Sales/Payables	17 20.9	9 39.0	8 47.6	22 16.5	16 22.9	11 32.7
26 13.8	22 16.5	27 13.4		49 7.4	23 15.6	23 15.7	29 12.7	27 13.4	25 14.5
43 8.5	36 10.1	46 7.9		97 3.8	44 8.3	42 8.6	49 7.4	46 8.0	31 11.7
6.7	5.8	5.2	Sales/Working Capital	9.8	5.7	3.8	6.5	4.5	10.0
13.8	13.4	13.8		-174.2	15.6	5.9	10.5	16.6	22.1
343.4	151.7	-135.8		-4.6	-45.1	29.1	26.0	-118.5	-171.9
5.9	5.9	5.4	EBIT/Interest		4.1	2.6	7.4	6.0	7.8
(126) 2.3	(119) 3.2	(103) 1.9		(26) .9	-1.3	(19) 2.8	(16) 3.2		5.0
.1	-.1	-2.2		-3.2	-3.9	.1	.9		1.4
3.2	6.8	2.1	Net Profit + Depr., Dep., Amort./Cur. Mat. L/T/D						
(37) 2.0	(33) 2.7	(34) 1.4							
1.3	1.7	.6							
.6	.6	.6	Fixed/Worth	.3	.9	.4	.4	.7	1.1
1.4	1.4	1.4		1.9	1.7	.8	.8	1.5	1.6
3.6	3.7	3.2		-3.2	-1.6	1.8	1.9	2.9	541.0
1.0	.9	.9	Debt/Worth	2.1	1.1	.8	.8	.9	.9
2.1	2.5	2.1		4.7	3.1	1.4	1.3	2.1	2.0
7.5	11.1	8.3		-4.5	-8.3	4.1	3.8	6.4	999.8
37.6	42.2	31.8	% Profit Before Taxes/Tangible Net Worth		31.2	10.8	41.0	30.1	
(108) 11.8	(106) 17.7	(92) 5.8		(19) 5.0	(20) -12.5	(20) 8.5	(16) 8.1		
-1.2	-.5	-13.2		-42.2	-23.1	-3.2	1.2		
11.9	13.5	7.4	% Profit Before Taxes/Total Assets	10.3	7.2	5.0	8.0	9.3	17.7
3.7	5.0	1.7		-5.2	-.5	-5.7	3.4	2.7	7.0
-1.6	-2.1	-6.4		-19.6	-12.9	-10.2	-3.7	-.2	1.3
11.4	11.1	10.3	Sales/Net Fixed Assets	284.3	10.3	12.4	18.5	5.3	4.3
5.7	5.6	4.8		6.2	5.6	4.9	6.0	4.7	2.7
3.1	3.6	2.8		1.3	2.4	3.7	4.3	3.2	2.3
2.5	2.5	2.4	Sales/Total Assets	2.4	2.3	2.3	3.0	2.0	2.1
1.8	1.9	1.7		2.0	1.6	1.7	2.2	1.6	1.4
1.4	1.3	1.3		1.1	1.1	1.3	1.3	1.2	1.2
2.1	1.8	2.3	% Depr., Dep., Amort./Sales		1.8	2.9	1.5	3.5	3.2
(125) 3.8	(120) 3.6	(105) 4.3		(26) 3.8	(20) 4.7	2.7	4.7		(10) 5.7
6.3	5.9	7.3		8.8	7.4	4.1	6.2		7.2
2.7	2.5	2.0	% Officers', Directors' Owners' Comp/Sales		1.0	2.9	2.0	1.7	
(64) 5.1	(58) 4.5	(57) 4.2		(14) 5.0	(13) 5.5	(12) 4.0	(11) 2.3		
7.8	7.5	6.3		7.3	6.8	5.4	4.4		
1275390M	1737766M	1508111M	Net Sales ($)	6970M	54948M	84036M	158422M	305218M	898517M
747340M	1128144M	1074581M	Total Assets ($)	4908M	39396M	54492M	95220M	207810M	672755M

M = $ thousand   MM = $ million
See Pages 9 through 22 for Explanation of Ratios and Data

Current Data Sorted by Assets | Comparative Historical Data

Type of Statement

Type of Statement	0-500M	500M-2MM	2-10MM	10-50MM	50-100MM	100-250MM	4/1/05-3/31/06 ALL	4/1/06-3/31/07 ALL
Unqualified			6	12	3	3	20	24
Reviewed	1	8	43	11			64	61
Compiled	3	17	12	4			45	51
Tax Returns	7	10	7				27	28
Other	3	18	13	16	7	3	73	66
		36 (4/1-9/30/09)			171 (10/1/09-3/31/10)			
NUMBER OF STATEMENTS	14	53	81	43	10	6	229	230

Assets / Liabilities / Income Data (%)

	0-500M %	500M-2MM %	2-10MM %	10-50MM %	50-100MM %	100-250MM %	4/1/05-3/31/06 ALL %	4/1/06-3/31/07 ALL %
ASSETS								
Cash & Equivalents	15.3	8.1	7.7	10.0	5.7		8.1	10.1
Trade Receivables (net)	26.5	27.5	21.8	19.9	19.7		28.5	25.6
Inventory	15.7	22.9	26.5	23.8	17.1		21.9	20.1
All Other Current	8.3	4.4	3.4	4.7	11.4		2.2	2.3
Total Current	65.8	63.0	59.5	58.4	53.8		60.7	58.2
Fixed Assets (net)	30.2	29.5	33.2	27.7	31.2		30.7	34.2
Intangibles (net)	.2	2.7	2.1	8.6	9.2		3.1	2.1
All Other Non-Current	3.7	4.8	5.2	5.2	5.8		5.5	5.5
Total	100.0	100.0	100.0	100.0	100.0		100.0	100.0
LIABILITIES								
Notes Payable-Short Term	11.3	15.0	12.5	5.4	9.8		10.1	8.1
Cur. Mat.-L.T.D.	2.1	5.6	4.0	3.1	2.7		5.1	5.3
Trade Payables	19.8	13.4	10.8	9.3	6.8		13.2	11.8
Income Taxes Payable	.2	.1	.2	.1	.0		.3	.1
All Other Current	17.1	7.6	8.6	13.2	10.0		11.0	10.5
Total Current	50.5	41.7	36.1	31.1	29.3		39.7	35.8
Long-Term Debt	17.4	24.5	16.3	12.6	7.9		18.8	20.2
Deferred Taxes	.3	.8	.5	.2	2.5		.5	.5
All Other Non-Current	7.4	5.6	2.6	11.5	6.2		5.1	4.7
Net Worth	24.5	27.4	44.4	44.6	54.1		35.9	38.8
Total Liabilties & Net Worth	100.0	100.0	100.0	100.0	100.0		100.0	100.0
INCOME DATA								
Net Sales	100.0	100.0	100.0	100.0	100.0		100.0	100.0
Gross Profit	48.5	35.3	27.1	25.8	23.6		33.0	33.2
Operating Expenses	46.6	37.4	26.4	20.1	26.5		27.8	27.1
Operating Profit	1.8	-2.1	.8	5.7	-2.8		5.2	6.1
All Other Expenses (net)	1.1	1.0	.9	.7	1.1		.9	1.1
Profit Before Taxes	.8	-3.1	-.1	5.0	-3.9		4.4	5.0

Ratios

	0-500M	500M-2MM	2-10MM	10-50MM	50-100MM	100-250MM	4/1/05-3/31/06 ALL	4/1/06-3/31/07 ALL
Current	4.3	2.4	2.3	4.7	2.8		2.6	2.8
	1.2	1.5	1.7	2.1	2.1		1.6	1.6
	.9	1.1	1.2	1.1	1.3		1.1	1.1
Quick	3.7	1.4	1.4	1.6	1.3		1.7	1.7
	.8	.9	.8	.9	.8		1.0	1.0
	.6	.6	.5	.6	.6		.6	.6
Sales/Receivables	0 UND	25 14.3	35 10.5	39 9.3	45 8.1		39 9.4	37 9.8
	22 16.4	43 8.6	45 8.1	50 7.2	56 6.5		50 7.2	47 7.8
	50 7.2	64 5.7	59 6.2	65 5.6	64 5.7		66 5.6	61 6.0
Cost of Sales/Inventory	0 UND	6 65.9	39 9.3	50 7.3	0 UND		18 19.9	15 25.1
	6 64.1	40 9.2	78 4.7	63 5.8	80 4.6		44 8.3	42 8.7
	30 12.0	94 3.9	122 3.0	112 3.3	187 2.0		107 3.4	97 3.8
Cost of Sales/Payables	0 UND	13 27.8	18 20.6	16 22.7	12 31.4		21 17.6	16 22.3
	18 20.2	29 12.8	26 14.0	28 13.3	29 12.7		30 12.0	29 12.6
	49 7.4	51 7.1	44 8.3	45 8.1	36 10.0		49 7.5	42 8.6
Sales/Working Capital	12.9	5.2	4.3	2.7	2.6		4.8	4.9
	65.2	10.1	5.1	5.1	4.1		8.9	9.2
	-244.2	105.6	17.9	37.0	260.0		35.1	37.8
EBIT/Interest	11.1	4.3	6.2	11.7	3.1		10.8	10.2
	(10) 1.9	(50) 1.3	(76) 1.8	(42) 4.0	-1.8		(209) 4.3	(213) 3.6
	-9.1	-3.0	-3.0	-.1	-9.2		1.3	1.3
Net Profit + Depr., Dep., Amort./Cur. Mat. L/T/D		3.3	3.9	4.2			4.0	4.6
		(13) .6	(29) 1.0	(10) 1.5			(57) 2.3	(51) 2.2
		-.1	.4	.1			1.0	1.3
Fixed/Worth	.4	.2	.3	.3	.2		.3	.4
	.8	1.0	.8	.7	.9		.8	.7
	NM	4.2	1.5	2.8	2.2		2.4	2.0
Debt/Worth	1.1	1.3	.7	.5	.5		.8	.8
	3.7	3.0	1.5	1.5	.8		1.9	1.7
	NM	9.8	2.9	4.1	4.5		5.5	3.4
% Profit Before Taxes/Tangible Net Worth	95.5	24.5	19.4	28.7	8.7		40.9	43.3
	(11) -3.9	(47) 3.8	(79) 1.3	(37) 11.2	-3.3		(209) 19.7	(215) 21.3
	-36.3	-54.4	-18.5	-2.3	-11.0		4.9	5.2
% Profit Before Taxes/Total Assets	25.7	8.0	7.5	15.2	3.2		14.9	15.0
	.8	.8	.1	4.4	-2.0		6.7	7.3
	-18.4	-15.0	-6.6	-.9	-6.8		1.2	1.2
Sales/Net Fixed Assets	140.6	29.9	9.2	8.4	5.6		17.1	14.8
	14.8	11.2	5.5	5.9	4.1		6.9	6.7
	7.6	4.8	2.8	3.6	2.9		3.9	3.4
Sales/Total Assets	4.5	2.7	2.0	1.7	1.5		2.5	2.5
	3.7	2.0	1.6	1.2	1.0		1.8	1.9
	3.1	1.6	1.3	.9	.8		1.4	1.3
% Depr., Dep., Amort./Sales	.3	1.2	1.3	1.8	2.7		1.3	1.3
	(10) 3.4	(46) 3.1	(76) 3.6	(41) 3.0	4.1		(210) 2.8	(217) 2.8
	6.1	6.3	6.3	5.2	6.7		5.2	5.8
% Officers', Directors' Owners' Comp/Sales		3.9	2.9				2.7	2.6
		(39) 6.9	(31) 3.9				(91) 4.5	(92) 4.8
		9.1	6.2				9.1	8.3
Net Sales ($)	19445M	136801M	586654M	1392109M	735725M	1090522M	3565639M	5315508M
Total Assets ($)	4171M	64793M	364698M	993666M	676409M	969143M	2314661M	3006020M

© RMA 2010

M = $ thousand   MM = $ million
See Pages 9 through 22 for Explanation of Ratios and Data

Comparative Historical Data

Current Data Sorted by Sales

						Type of Statement						
	27		29		24	Unqualified				4	8	12
	54		50		63	Reviewed	2	6	9	29	13	4
	32		35		36	Compiled	2	16	9	5	4	
	19		22		24	Tax Returns	6	9	4	4	1	
	73		65		60	Other	1	18	3	9	8	21
	4/1/07-3/31/08 ALL		4/1/08-3/31/09 ALL		4/1/09-3/31/10 ALL			36 (4/1-9/30/09)		171 (10/1/09-3/31/10)		
							0-1MM	1-3MM	3-5MM	5-10MM	10-25MM	25MM & OVER
	205		201		207	NUMBER OF STATEMENTS	11	49	25	51	34	37
	%		%		%	ASSETS	%	%	%	%	%	%
	8.3		7.9		8.7	Cash & Equivalents	9.3	8.0	13.4	7.8	9.9	6.7
	25.7		23.7		23.2	Trade Receivables (net)	13.7	27.6	20.8	23.1	22.0	22.9
	22.1		24.4		24.1	Inventory	14.8	20.9	26.0	28.4	25.4	22.4
	3.0		2.9		4.7	All Other Current	7.4	4.7	2.7	3.9	5.0	6.4
	59.0		58.9		60.7	Total Current	45.1	61.2	62.8	63.2	62.3	58.4
	32.4		33.0		30.3	Fixed Assets (net)	46.5	32.2	28.1	30.8	26.3	27.6
	3.6		2.8		3.9	Intangibles (net)	3.4	3.7	1.8	.8	4.5	9.2
	5.0		5.3		5.1	All Other Non-Current	5.0	3.0	7.3	5.2	6.9	4.7
	100.0		100.0		100.0	Total	100.0	100.0	100.0	100.0	100.0	100.0
						LIABILITIES						
	10.3		11.9		11.2	Notes Payable-Short Term	6.8	18.4	7.2	12.3	7.4	7.4
	4.8		5.3		3.9	Cur. Mat.-L.T.D.	2.4	5.2	5.6	3.9	2.5	3.9
	11.6		11.1		11.5	Trade Payables	9.3	11.6	10.8	13.8	11.8	8.9
	.1		.0		.2	Income Taxes Payable	.0	.3	.1	.2	.2	.1
	13.3		11.4		10.4	All Other Current	17.1	5.7	9.3	10.4	11.9	14.0
	40.1		39.7		37.2	Total Current	35.6	41.2	33.0	40.7	33.8	33.4
	22.2		19.4		16.9	Long-Term Debt	22.9	25.3	17.8	14.7	11.9	10.8
	.6		.6		.7	Deferred Taxes	.4	.9	.7	.4	.3	1.1
	5.7		6.1		5.9	All Other Non-Current	11.3	4.2	4.5	2.5	7.6	10.5
	31.5		34.1		39.5	Net Worth	29.8	28.4	44.0	41.7	46.5	44.3
	100.0		100.0		100.0	Total Liabilties & Net Worth	100.0	100.0	100.0	100.0	100.0	100.0
						INCOME DATA						
	100.0		100.0		100.0	Net Sales	100.0	100.0	100.0	100.0	100.0	100.0
	33.8		32.7		30.3	Gross Profit	48.8	34.0	38.0	28.1	23.6	24.0
	27.5		28.4		29.4	Operating Expenses	51.0	36.2	36.2	26.6	20.0	22.1
	6.3		4.2		.9	Operating Profit	-2.3	-2.1	1.8	1.5	3.6	1.9
	1.3		1.0		.9	All Other Expenses (net)	1.8	1.1	.8	.8	.6	1.1
	4.9		3.2		.0	Profit Before Taxes	-4.1	-3.2	1.1	.7	2.9	.8
						RATIOS						
	2.5		2.6		2.6		4.3	2.6	2.6	2.2	3.8	3.4
	1.6		1.7		1.7	Current	1.2	1.5	2.0	1.5	1.8	2.1
	1.1		1.1		1.1		.7	1.1	1.4	1.1	1.2	1.0
	1.7		1.4		1.5		3.5	1.4	1.8	1.0	1.6	1.5
	.9		.8		.8	Quick	.7	.9	1.0	.7	.9	.8
	.6		.5		.6		.5	.6	.7	.4	.6	.6
34	10.6	31	11.6	35	10.5		0 UND	36 10.2	28 13.2	33 11.2	34 10.8	45 8.1
47	7.7	41	8.8	47	7.8	Sales/Receivables	36 10.1	53 6.9	40 9.0	42 8.6	45 8.0	57 6.4
59	6.2	56	6.5	61	6.0		48 7.5	67 5.5	53 6.9	57 6.4	61 6.0	69 5.3
16	23.3	20	18.7	29	12.4		0 UND	4 99.5	36 10.0	38 9.5	39 9.4	51 7.2
47	7.7	62	5.9	63	5.8	Cost of Sales/Inventory	8 45.9	34 10.6	74 4.9	72 5.1	68 5.4	63 5.8
103	3.5	108	3.4	110	3.3		104 3.5	99 3.7	121 3.0	110 3.3	128 2.9	101 3.6
15	24.7	14	26.6	16	23.3		0 UND	11 32.6	14 26.9	20 18.0	20 18.2	15 24.4
27	13.4	26	14.3	28	13.3	Cost of Sales/Payables	19 19.2	21 17.4	35 10.4	27 13.6	28 13.0	28 13.1
42	8.7	41	8.9	44	8.3		70 5.2	42 8.8	51 7.1	45 8.2	45 8.1	39 9.3
	5.1		4.8		4.1		5.0	4.7	4.6	4.6	2.7	2.9
	9.3		8.9		7.4	Sales/Working Capital	99.4	9.2	6.5	8.3	6.6	4.4
	28.2		47.7		45.1		-8.5	43.5	14.4	66.8	-15.7	69.3
	9.0		7.2		6.3			3.4	6.9	8.3	13.3	8.3
(187)	3.8	(187)	3.1	(194)	1.6	EBIT/Interest	(48) .8	(23) 2.4	(46) .5	(33) 2.5	(36) 1.3
	1.7		1.0		-2.9			-3.3	.5	-2.9	-1.1	-4.7
	5.4		5.9		3.5	Net Profit + Depr., Dep.,				2.6	15.3	4.9
(48)	2.1	(53)	2.1	(59)	1.0	Amort./Cur. Mat. L/T/D		(20) .9	(10) 2.0	(12) 2.0
	1.4		.9		.4					.2	.2	.9
	.4		.4		.3		.4	.5	.2	.3	.3	.3
	.9		.9		.8	Fixed/Worth	1.8	1.2	.7	.7	.4	.8
	2.3		2.0		2.2		12.5	4.2	1.9	1.5	1.0	2.8
	.8		.8		.7		1.0	1.3	.6	.8	.6	.5
	2.0		1.9		1.7	Debt/Worth	2.9	3.0	1.3	1.6	1.1	1.5
	5.4		5.0		4.6		17.1	10.1	6.6	3.0	2.9	5.2
	47.0		40.3		23.9	% Profit Before Taxes/Tangible		24.5	15.3	25.8	24.8	30.0
(175)	24.4	(172)	17.2	(190)	3.8	Net Worth	(43) -5.4	(24) 7.4	(50) 3.7	(32) 9.7	(32) 3.2
	6.6		1.9		-18.3			-54.4	-7.5	-18.3	-2.8	-13.1
	15.9		14.9		8.9	% Profit Before Taxes/Total	2.6	9.3	6.7	9.0	12.9	11.7
	7.6		5.2		1.1	Assets	-3.4	-1.9	2.9	.1	3.0	.9
	1.7		.3		-6.7		-21.9	-13.7	-2.7	-6.4	-2.4	-5.4
	16.1		13.8		13.8		21.8	24.1	14.7	12.3	16.7	8.5
	6.7		7.1		6.3	Sales/Net Fixed Assets	6.1	7.7	8.7	5.5	6.7	5.4
	3.7		3.4		3.7		1.0	2.8	4.5	3.2	3.8	3.7
	2.4		2.5		2.2		4.2	2.6	2.2	2.0	2.1	1.8
	1.8		1.9		1.6	Sales/Total Assets	2.8	1.9	1.8	1.7	1.5	1.4
	1.3		1.3		1.1		.9	1.2	1.4	1.4	1.0	.9
	1.4		1.3		1.3			1.4	1.7	.8	1.1	1.8
(185)	3.0	(175)	2.7	(188)	3.2	% Depr., Dep., Amort./Sales	(43) 3.8	(23) 2.7	(46) 2.8	(32) 3.3	(35) 3.1
	5.1		4.8		5.9			6.5	5.1	5.3	6.0	4.4
	3.0		2.4		3.0			3.4	4.3	2.7	1.0	
(83)	5.6	(74)	4.2	(86)	5.0	% Officers', Directors' Owners' Comp/Sales	(32) 7.2	(14) 6.4	(20) 3.8	(11) 2.3
	10.8		6.8		8.2			12.3	8.3	5.9	3.9	
3798528M		3941084M		3961256M		Net Sales ($)	8232M	96892M	92884M	363914M	568816M	2830518M
2318095M		2416030M		3072880M		Total Assets ($)	8140M	61599M	56218M	243558M	431046M	2272319M

M = $ thousand   MM = $ million
See Pages 9 through 22 for Explanation of Ratios and Data

Current Data Sorted by Assets   **Comparative Historical Data**

						Type of Statement		
						Unqualified	17	16
		3	5	2		Reviewed	21	25
3	3	8	4			Compiled	23	22
	8	5	2			Tax Returns	9	10
4	5					Other	40	44
2	5	11	12				4/1/05-	4/1/06-
	14 (4/1-9/30/09)		68 (10/1/09-3/31/10)				3/31/06	3/31/07
0-500M	500M-2MM	2-10MM	10-50MM	50-100MM	100-250MM		ALL	ALL
9	21	27	23	2		NUMBER OF STATEMENTS	110	117
%	%	%	%	%	%	ASSETS	%	%
	9.4	7.4	11.2		D	Cash & Equivalents	9.5	8.9
	22.1	24.6	22.9		A	Trade Receivables (net)	26.4	28.3
	30.1	30.8	24.6		T	Inventory	22.6	24.0
	4.8	3.8	7.4		A	All Other Current	4.5	4.0
	66.3	66.6	66.1			Total Current	63.0	65.2
	26.8	26.4	24.1		N	Fixed Assets (net)	26.5	25.5
	2.6	1.5	3.6		O	Intangibles (net)	4.5	2.9
	4.3	5.5	6.2		T	All Other Non-Current	6.0	6.4
	100.0	100.0	100.0			Total	100.0	100.0
					A	LIABILITIES		
	9.2	16.7	7.1		V	Notes Payable-Short Term	9.4	11.6
	5.6	3.2	3.3		A	Cur. Mat.-L.T.D.	4.9	3.5
	9.8	9.3	14.7		I	Trade Payables	13.1	15.5
	.7	.1	.3		L	Income Taxes Payable	.2	.3
	14.5	8.6	16.5		A	All Other Current	13.3	13.9
	39.8	38.0	41.9		B	Total Current	40.9	44.7
	14.0	11.9	9.4		L	Long-Term Debt	17.6	14.7
	.2	.2	.3		E	Deferred Taxes	.4	.2
	6.8	4.8	4.7			All Other Non-Current	7.2	7.6
	39.2	45.1	43.8			Net Worth	33.9	32.7
	100.0	100.0	100.0			Total Liabilities & Net Worth	100.0	100.0
						INCOME DATA		
	100.0	100.0	100.0			Net Sales	100.0	100.0
	37.3	27.1	28.1			Gross Profit	30.1	28.3
	37.3	24.9	21.3			Operating Expenses	24.6	21.7
	.0	2.2	6.7			Operating Profit	5.6	6.6
	2.1	2.0	1.9			All Other Expenses (net)	1.1	1.3
	-2.0	.1	4.9			Profit Before Taxes	4.5	5.3
						RATIOS		
	4.2	3.0	2.2				2.7	2.5
	1.6	2.2	1.7			Current	1.6	1.5
	1.0	1.1	1.1				1.0	1.1
	2.5	1.4	1.6				1.6	1.5
	.8	.8	.6			Quick	.8	.9
	.3	.5	.4				.5	.5
28	13.1	35 10.5	39 9.3				35 10.4	36 10.3
38	9.7	48 7.6	55 6.7			Sales/Receivables	49 7.4	48 7.6
48	7.5	73 5.0	74 5.0				62 5.9	63 5.8
29	12.7	44 8.4	56 6.5				33 11.2	25 14.8
67	5.4	83 4.4	82 4.5			Cost of Sales/Inventory	55 6.6	55 6.6
126	2.9	136 2.7	156 2.3				94 3.9	96 3.8
14	26.0	12 31.2	26 13.8				18 20.7	17 21.3
25	14.6	19 19.1	41 8.9			Cost of Sales/Payables	31 11.8	29 12.7
36	10.2	33 11.1	94 3.9				47 7.7	47 7.8
	4.5	3.5	2.8				4.7	4.8
	8.8	7.5	8.4			Sales/Working Capital	9.5	11.0
	-94.5	94.2	17.3				55.3	46.8
	9.0	13.7	9.3				11.2	12.2
(20)	1.8	(25) 5.8	(18) 3.0			EBIT/Interest	(95) 3.3	(103) 4.6
	-6.4	-3.4	.8				1.5	1.4
						Net Profit + Depr., Dep.,	3.9	8.9
						Amort./Cur. Mat. L/T/D	(30) 2.5	(27) 1.9
							1.4	.8
	.2	.2	.2				.3	.3
	.5	.5	.6			Fixed/Worth	.7	.6
	2.4	1.8	.8				3.0	3.0
	.3	.6	.3				.7	.7
	1.4	1.5	1.3			Debt/Worth	1.7	1.9
	4.2	2.8	3.7				10.9	11.2
	24.6	38.9	33.1			% Profit Before Taxes/Tangible	59.9	65.7
(19)	6.1	15.8	8.6			Net Worth	(90) 30.8	(98) 36.2
	-31.1	-16.0	.0				7.5	11.3
	12.5	14.0	13.5			% Profit Before Taxes/Total	18.1	19.3
	2.3	4.5	3.9			Assets	6.2	8.1
	-14.7	-7.4	.0				1.5	1.9
	26.0	15.3	18.8				19.2	26.0
	11.6	10.1	5.4			Sales/Net Fixed Assets	7.7	10.4
	4.9	4.7	3.2				4.7	4.7
	2.9	2.4	1.6				2.4	2.6
	2.1	1.8	1.3			Sales/Total Assets	1.8	1.9
	1.5	1.4	1.0				1.3	1.4
	1.3	1.2	.8				1.5	1.2
(18)	2.2	(24) 2.4	(21) 2.1			% Depr., Dep., Amort./Sales	(92) 2.7	(102) 1.9
	3.5	4.3	3.8				5.0	3.7
	2.7	1.6					3.2	1.4
(15)	5.7	(12) 2.9				% Officers', Directors'	(43) 5.4	(41) 3.3
	11.7	9.6				Owners' Comp/Sales	9.7	10.5
7733M	52417M	273582M	711951M	90187M		Net Sales ($)	1801825M	2407134M
2516M	25647M	152358M	519128M	122760M		Total Assets ($)	1217792M	1514840M

M = $ thousand   MM = $ million
See Pages 9 through 22 for Explanation of Ratios and Data

Comparative Historical Data   Current Data Sorted by Sales

4/1/07-3/31/08 ALL	4/1/08-3/31/09 ALL	4/1/09-3/31/10 ALL	Type of Statement	0-1MM	1-3MM	3-5MM	5-10MM	10-25MM	25MM & OVER
17	16	10	Unqualified				2	2	6
22	14	18	Reviewed	3	3	4	5	5	2
20	15	15	Compiled		5		3	2	1
6	9	9	Tax Returns	3	4	1			
37	42	30	Other	1	5	3	7	10	5
				14 (4/1-9/30/09)			68 (10/1/09-3/31/10)		
102	96	82	**NUMBER OF STATEMENTS**	7	17	8	17	19	14
%	%	%	**ASSETS**	%	%	%	%	%	%
10.0	9.6	9.4	Cash & Equivalents		11.5		6.6	10.2	10.4
26.5	25.3	23.8	Trade Receivables (net)		21.3		25.0	21.9	25.0
25.1	26.2	27.0	Inventory		23.4		28.9	29.0	22.7
4.0	3.3	5.6	All Other Current		4.2		5.4	5.0	10.1
65.6	64.4	65.8	Total Current		60.5		65.9	66.1	68.3
25.2	26.3	26.2	Fixed Assets (net)		32.2		24.5	25.0	22.4
3.4	4.0	3.0	Intangibles (net)		3.0		2.4	3.4	4.4
5.8	5.4	5.0	All Other Non-Current		4.4		7.2	5.5	5.0
100.0	100.0	100.0	Total		100.0		100.0	100.0	100.0
			LIABILITIES						
9.6	9.9	13.1	Notes Payable-Short Term		10.1		20.1	11.1	4.4
4.0	4.3	4.9	Cur. Mat.-L.T.D.		5.4		2.9	3.4	3.7
12.3	14.2	11.4	Trade Payables		9.9		8.1	12.5	15.8
.1	.4	.3	Income Taxes Payable		.0		.2	.0	.5
12.5	13.9	14.0	All Other Current		9.8		8.2	11.3	19.2
38.5	42.6	43.7	Total Current		35.3		39.5	38.2	43.7
17.4	15.4	12.1	Long-Term Debt		14.0		12.3	9.1	8.6
.4	.4	.2	Deferred Taxes		.0		.0	.3	.6
5.2	12.7	6.5	All Other Non-Current		9.2		6.4	3.8	6.8
38.6	28.9	37.4	Net Worth		41.6		41.7	48.6	40.4
100.0	100.0	100.0	Total Liabilities & Net Worth		100.0		100.0	100.0	100.0
			INCOME DATA						
100.0	100.0	100.0	Net Sales		100.0		100.0	100.0	100.0
30.0	31.2	31.1	Gross Profit		40.1		27.9	25.3	26.6
23.0	25.7	28.8	Operating Expenses		40.6		26.0	19.2	21.3
7.0	5.6	2.3	Operating Profit		-.5		1.9	6.1	5.3
.9	1.5	2.0	All Other Expenses (net)		1.2		1.6	1.2	2.3
6.1	4.1	.2	Profit Before Taxes		-1.7		.3	4.9	3.0
			RATIOS						
3.1	2.7	2.9	Current		4.6		3.3	2.6	2.4
1.8	1.7	1.9			2.7		2.0	2.0	1.5
1.3	1.1	1.1			.8		.9	1.1	1.1
1.9	1.6	1.6	Quick		2.6		1.3	1.9	1.4
1.0	.8	.8			1.1		.8	.9	.7
.6	.5	.5			.5		.5	.5	.5
35 10.4	31 11.6	32 11.4	Sales/Receivables	31 11.6		35 10.5	38 9.7	37 9.8
43 8.4	43 8.4	46 8.0		38 9.7		61 6.0	47 7.8	51 7.1
60 6.1	55 6.6	64 5.7		47 7.8		75 4.9	57 6.4	79 4.6
23 15.9	25 14.8	42 8.7	Cost of Sales/Inventory	25 14.7		49 7.5	38 9.6	50 7.3
68 5.4	65 5.6	70 5.2		60 6.0		99 3.7	76 4.8	78 4.7
109 3.4	119 3.1	126 2.9		134 2.7		149 2.5	123 3.0	121 3.0
17 21.8	16 22.6	14 26.9	Cost of Sales/Payables	15 23.8		9 39.2	16 23.1	25 14.8
28 13.3	29 12.7	26 14.3		23 16.1		16 22.8	33 11.1	43 8.4
45 8.2	48 7.6	45 8.1		37 9.8		42 8.7	49 7.4	96 3.8
3.6	3.9	3.5	Sales/Working Capital		3.0		3.2	2.8	2.4
8.1	7.9	8.4			8.8		6.2	5.6	10.3
14.6	90.6	54.0			-19.6		-48.3	19.7	16.7
12.3	13.8	10.2	EBIT/Interest		10.5		10.0	14.7	17.4
(88) 5.0	(88) 4.8	(73) 2.5		(15) 1.4		(16) 2.6	(15) 5.8	(13) 7.5
2.1	1.0	-2.7			-7.0		-4.5	1.0	.3
6.1	10.4	3.7	Net Profit + Depr., Dep., Amort./Cur. Mat. L/T/D						
(27) 3.5	(22) 2.8	(15) 2.1							
1.3	1.2	.5							
.2	.3	.2	Fixed/Worth		.1		.3	.1	.2
.7	.9	.6			.9		.5	.6	.5
1.6	3.1	1.8			3.1		1.7	.9	1.5
.6	.8	.6	Debt/Worth		.3		.7	.6	1.1
1.7	1.5	1.4			.9		1.8	1.0	1.8
4.5	8.8	3.9			4.6		3.3	1.8	4.0
52.3	51.0	29.1	% Profit Before Taxes/Tangible Net Worth		12.9		32.3	38.9	50.6
(92) 27.0	(79) 22.8	(74) 9.5		(15) 3.9		8.6	11.9	(13) 16.8
10.6	3.8	-13.7			-31.1		-19.4	.0	2.1
17.6	17.9	13.9	% Profit Before Taxes/Total Assets		10.1		12.6	15.5	13.7
9.1	7.6	2.8			2.0		3.9	3.4	5.7
3.6	.0	-6.7			-14.7		-7.9	.0	-.9
18.7	22.2	17.9	Sales/Net Fixed Assets		13.6		15.3	17.7	40.4
8.8	7.6	9.6			10.0		11.8	5.7	6.1
5.3	4.6	4.5			4.5		4.1	3.7	3.8
2.4	2.7	2.4	Sales/Total Assets		2.9		2.2	2.3	1.7
1.9	1.8	1.7			1.8		1.8	1.4	1.5
1.5	1.4	1.3			1.2		1.4	1.2	.7
1.1	1.2	1.2	% Depr., Dep., Amort./Sales		1.3		1.8	1.1	.5
(92) 2.0	(82) 2.5	(69) 2.5		(16) 2.3		(14) 2.8	(17) 2.1	(12) 1.9
4.2	3.7	4.5			4.7		4.9	3.4	3.4
2.6	1.9	2.6	% Officers', Directors' Owners' Comp/Sales		2.3				
(38) 3.4	(36) 3.4	(34) 5.1		(12) 5.9					
9.9	9.9	11.4			11.4				
1985266M	1733339M	1135870M	Net Sales ($)	4340M	31571M	30241M	124169M	322249M	623300M
1270384M	1185835M	822409M	Total Assets ($)	1709M	19343M	13659M	88268M	218030M	481400M

M = $ thousand   MM = $ million
See Pages 9 through 22 for Explanation of Ratios and Data

Current Data Sorted by Assets   Comparative Historical Data

Type of Statement

Type of Statement	0-500M	500M-2MM	2-10MM	10-50MM	50-100MM	100-250MM		4/1/05-3/31/06 ALL	4/1/06-3/31/07 ALL
Unqualified			4	14	5	3		35	34
Reviewed	2	14	53	16		1		148	126
Compiled	14	15	27	8				104	116
Tax Returns	8	14	8	21	6	1		48	33
Other	8	17	36					155	100
		60 (4/1-9/30/09)		227 (10/1/09-3/31/10)					
NUMBER OF STATEMENTS	32	60	128	52	11	4		490	409

ASSETS

	0-500M %	500M-2MM %	2-10MM %	10-50MM %	50-100MM %	100-250MM %		ALL %	ALL %
Cash & Equivalents	13.6	12.9	9.5	7.4	5.8			7.4	7.7
Trade Receivables (net)	30.3	31.1	27.5	23.5	17.3			31.3	30.1
Inventory	17.2	18.2	18.1	15.6	11.5			16.6	16.9
All Other Current	3.5	1.6	5.2	5.6	10.2			4.0	2.8
Total Current	64.6	63.8	60.3	52.0	44.9			59.3	57.6
Fixed Assets (net)	32.3	30.3	33.0	35.0	40.2			33.4	33.2
Intangibles (net)	1.4	1.6	1.9	5.1	6.0			2.1	3.6
All Other Non-Current	1.7	4.4	4.8	7.8	8.9			5.2	5.6
Total	100.0	100.0	100.0	100.0	100.0			100.0	100.0

LIABILITIES

	0-500M	500M-2MM	2-10MM	10-50MM	50-100MM	100-250MM		ALL	ALL
Notes Payable-Short Term	16.8	9.1	11.8	8.0	6.1			12.8	12.7
Cur. Mat.-L.T.D.	12.4	6.0	5.2	5.2	3.1			5.9	6.2
Trade Payables	12.2	11.7	10.9	8.9	10.8			12.8	11.5
Income Taxes Payable	.0	.1	.2	.1	.2			.2	.2
All Other Current	13.9	6.0	10.6	9.0	8.8			10.8	10.1
Total Current	55.3	33.0	38.7	31.2	29.0			42.4	40.7
Long-Term Debt	35.0	18.2	17.6	17.0	21.8			17.8	18.5
Deferred Taxes	.1	.4	.7	.9	1.6			.5	.6
All Other Non-Current	8.9	7.9	5.7	3.3	11.7			8.6	7.5
Net Worth	.7	40.4	37.4	47.7	35.9			30.7	32.7
Total Liabilties & Net Worth	100.0	100.0	100.0	100.0	100.0			100.0	100.0

INCOME DATA

	0-500M	500M-2MM	2-10MM	10-50MM	50-100MM	100-250MM		ALL	ALL
Net Sales	100.0	100.0	100.0	100.0	100.0			100.0	100.0
Gross Profit	42.8	31.9	22.0	18.5	16.8			27.5	28.8
Operating Expenses	43.2	33.0	21.4	19.0	19.6			22.9	23.8
Operating Profit	-.4	-1.0	.6	-.5	-2.8			4.6	5.0
All Other Expenses (net)	.9	.4	1.1	1.6	.7			1.3	1.3
Profit Before Taxes	-1.3	-1.5	-.4	-2.2	-3.5			3.3	3.7

RATIOS

	0-500M	500M-2MM	2-10MM	10-50MM	50-100MM	100-250MM		ALL	ALL
Current	4.3	4.0	2.9	3.5	2.0			2.3	2.6
	1.0	2.6	1.7	1.8	1.5			1.5	1.5
	.7	1.3	1.1	1.0	1.0			1.1	1.0
Quick	2.3	2.9	2.2	2.0	1.1			1.6	1.7
	.6	1.4	1.0	1.1	.7			1.0	.9
	.4	.8	.6	.6	.6			.6	.6
Sales/Receivables	32 11.3	39 9.3	42 8.7	47 7.8	52 7.0			42 8.7	37 9.9
	39 9.3	54 6.8	56 6.5	61 6.0	53 6.9			55 6.7	51 7.1
	54 6.7	72 5.0	80 4.5	85 4.3	64 5.7			76 4.8	65 5.6
Cost of Sales/Inventory	6 62.9	13 27.7	26 14.3	26 14.1	31 11.7			15 23.9	14 27.0
	23 16.1	35 10.3	48 7.6	49 7.5	45 8.2			38 9.5	35 10.4
	67 5.5	97 3.7	78 4.7	71 5.1	48 7.6			67 5.4	62 5.9
Cost of Sales/Payables	7 54.5	11 33.0	15 23.6	20 18.2	23 15.6			15 23.7	13 28.7
	22 16.4	21 17.3	27 13.4	28 13.2	36 10.1			29 12.7	24 15.3
	36 10.2	42 8.8	42 8.7	43 8.5	44 8.3			47 7.7	38 9.6
Sales/Working Capital	7.1	3.5	3.5	2.9	5.8			5.3	5.4
	NM	6.1	7.1	5.0	8.6			10.9	11.1
	-11.5	15.4	48.7	NM	-167.3			56.4	104.5
EBIT/Interest	3.2	3.3	8.6	4.7	.8			7.4	7.4
	(28) .8	(52) 1.4	(121) 2.5	(51) 1.9	(10) -.3			(459) 3.2	(373) 2.9
	-3.2	-2.0	-.8	-1.7	-1.7			1.3	1.3
Net Profit + Depr., Dep., Amort./Cur. Mat. L/T/D		2.0	2.6	2.9				3.9	3.7
		(12) .7	(35) 1.5	(22) 1.9				(129) 2.2	(107) 2.0
		-.1	.8	1.1				1.0	1.0
Fixed/Worth	.9	.3	.3	.4	.6			.5	.4
	2.5	.7	.9	.8	1.5			1.0	1.0
	-1.6	2.5	2.3	2.0	3.6			2.8	2.9
Debt/Worth	1.7	.4	.6	.5	1.1			.8	.7
	14.7	1.4	1.6	1.2	2.8			2.0	1.8
	-5.6	4.3	4.6	3.8	5.2			6.4	7.2
% Profit Before Taxes/Tangible Net Worth	82.6	14.7	20.1	12.4				41.3	39.2
	(19) .0	(51) 2.4	(118) 6.9	(49) 3.4				(425) 16.7	(340) 17.4
	-96.2	-8.2	-7.0	-13.6				3.8	3.0
% Profit Before Taxes/Total Assets	15.8	5.5	7.6	4.5	-.3			12.2	14.7
	-.6	.9	2.7	2.0	-5.8			5.2	5.4
	-21.3	-5.0	-5.2	-3.8	-7.3			.9	.6
Sales/Net Fixed Assets	25.9	13.4	10.8	6.5	3.0			12.0	13.3
	8.2	9.2	5.1	4.1	2.6			6.2	6.7
	4.7	5.0	3.0	2.3	2.2			3.7	3.8
Sales/Total Assets	3.2	2.6	1.9	1.6	1.5			2.5	2.7
	2.4	2.0	1.5	1.2	1.1			1.9	1.9
	1.7	1.4	1.1	.9	.7			1.3	1.4
% Depr., Dep., Amort./Sales	1.2	2.0	2.2	3.3	5.2			2.0	2.0
	(27) 3.6	(55) 3.4	(118) 4.8	(46) 4.9	(10) 6.9			(460) 3.5	(370) 3.5
	7.0	5.2	6.5	7.0	7.2			5.3	5.7
% Officers', Directors' Owners' Comp/Sales	9.7	2.9	2.1	1.9				2.4	2.5
	(18) 16.3	(43) 4.6	(64) 3.9	(13) 2.4				(262) 4.5	(206) 4.3
	24.7	8.2	6.8	2.9				8.9	7.4
Net Sales ($)	26675M	147712M	997825M	1255304M	858470M	597360M		6283093M	5560509M
Total Assets ($)	10348M	73802M	628141M	1072738M	785241M	522768M		3998042M	3543094M

M = $ thousand   MM = $ million
See Pages 9 through 22 for Explanation of Ratios and Data

Comparative Historical Data

Current Data Sorted by Sales

				Type of Statement						
36		37	26	Unqualified			1	2	11	12
87		90	85	Reviewed		12	18	25	24	6
93		65	57	Compiled	12	21	12	9	2	1
24		34	30	Tax Returns	4	11	6	8	1	
96		118	89	Other	9	14	16	11	23	16
4/1/07-		4/1/08-	4/1/09-			60 (4/1-9/30/09)		227 (10/1/09-3/31/10)		
3/31/08		3/31/09	3/31/10							
ALL		ALL	ALL		0-1MM	1-3MM	3-5MM	5-10MM	10-25MM	25MM & OVER
336		344	287	NUMBER OF STATEMENTS	25	58	53	55	61	35
%		%	%	ASSETS	%	%	%	%	%	%
7.6		8.2	10.1	Cash & Equivalents	9.1	15.5	10.7	9.6	7.7	5.9
30.0		28.7	27.3	Trade Receivables (net)	25.7	29.7	30.1	25.3	26.4	25.1
17.7		18.2	17.3	Inventory	23.3	15.6	18.7	16.3	16.3	16.7
3.4		2.8	4.4	All Other Current	4.1	2.2	2.5	4.1	8.5	4.7
58.6		58.0	59.1	Total Current	62.2	63.0	62.0	55.3	59.0	52.4
33.4		32.3	33.2	Fixed Assets (net)	33.0	31.6	31.8	37.0	30.6	36.7
2.6		3.7	2.7	Intangibles (net)	2.3	1.5	1.8	2.0	3.5	5.5
5.3		6.0	5.0	All Other Non-Current	2.4	3.9	4.4	5.7	6.9	5.5
100.0		100.0	100.0	Total	100.0	100.0	100.0	100.0	100.0	100.0
				LIABILITIES						
13.1		12.2	10.7	Notes Payable-Short Term	16.2	10.9	10.7	8.8	11.1	9.2
5.7		5.9	6.0	Cur. Mat.-L.T.D.	10.6	6.6	5.3	6.2	5.0	4.5
13.0		12.6	10.9	Trade Payables	8.0	12.5	10.6	10.2	10.5	12.3
.2		.2	.1	Income Taxes Payable	.0	.1	.2	.1	.1	.2
10.1		8.8	9.6	All Other Current	12.1	6.0	8.2	13.7	9.9	9.1
42.0		39.7	37.4	Total Current	47.0	36.0	34.9	39.1	36.6	35.2
18.3		19.6	19.7	Long-Term Debt	30.3	22.1	17.8	19.4	17.6	15.2
.6		.7	.7	Deferred Taxes	.1	.5	.5	1.0	.5	1.6
7.0		6.5	6.3	All Other Non-Current	11.9	7.3	5.2	6.2	4.1	6.1
32.1		33.6	36.0	Net Worth	10.7	34.2	41.6	34.3	41.1	41.9
100.0		100.0	100.0	Total Liabilities & Net Worth	100.0	100.0	100.0	100.0	100.0	100.0
				INCOME DATA						
100.0		100.0	100.0	Net Sales	100.0	100.0	100.0	100.0	100.0	100.0
27.0		26.5	25.6	Gross Profit	42.1	33.3	23.4	23.9	18.9	18.6
22.4		22.7	25.7	Operating Expenses	44.4	34.5	23.4	24.3	17.5	17.7
4.7		3.7	-.1	Operating Profit	-2.3	-1.3	-.1	-.4	1.4	.9
1.1		.9	1.1	All Other Expenses (net)	.7	.5	.9	1.7	1.3	1.3
3.6		2.8	-1.2	Profit Before Taxes	-2.9	-1.7	-1.0	-2.1	.2	-.4
				RATIOS						
2.5		2.7	3.3		5.0	5.0	3.8	2.6	3.3	2.1
1.4		1.6	1.7	Current	1.3	2.1	2.0	1.7	1.7	1.7
1.0		1.1	1.1		.7	1.1	1.1	1.1	1.0	1.0
1.5		1.7	2.2		2.5	3.4	2.4	1.8	1.8	1.2
.9	(343)	.9	1.0	Quick	.6	1.3	1.1	1.1	1.0	.9
.6		.6	.6		.4	.7	.7	.6	.5	.6
39	9.4	36 10.2	41 9.0	Sales/Receivables	34 10.8	40 9.1	36 10.1	37 9.7	46 7.9	50 7.3
52	7.0	49 7.4	54 6.7		52 7.0	51 7.1	57 6.4	51 7.1	56 6.5	54 6.8
68	5.4	67 5.5	75 4.8		91 4.0	72 5.1	106 3.5	69 5.3	74 4.9	72 5.1
16	22.2	17 21.2	21 17.5	Cost of Sales/Inventory	22 16.6	6 61.4	23 15.7	26 14.3	24 15.3	28 13.0
40	9.2	39 9.4	45 8.2		49 7.5	24 15.4	47 7.8	44 8.3	48 7.6	45 8.2
69	5.3	71 5.1	72 5.1		171 2.1	93 3.9	100 3.7	69 5.3	69 5.3	68 5.4
14	25.4	15 25.0	15 23.6	Cost of Sales/Payables	5 67.6	12 30.0	14 25.4	14 25.9	19 19.6	23 15.8
27	13.6	26 14.2	26 14.2		24 15.3	23 15.8	23 15.6	25 14.9	26 13.9	36 10.2
43	8.4	39 9.4	42 8.7		52 7.0	51 7.2	39 9.4	43 8.4	42 8.7	43 8.5
	4.7	4.8	3.4	Sales/Working Capital	2.7	2.7	2.9	4.0	3.3	4.3
	11.3	10.2	7.4		13.2	6.1	5.3	8.4	6.8	8.0
	UND	62.5	75.2		-11.8	35.1	32.1	87.1	98.0	71.9
	6.7	7.2	5.5	EBIT/Interest	3.2	3.3	6.3	6.6	8.6	6.4
(314)	2.9	(325) 2.9	(266) 1.8		(20) 1.5	(49) 1.1	(50) 1.9	(54) 1.8	(59) 2.9	(34) 1.2
	1.0	.5	-1.2		-1.3	-5.8	-1.2	-2.1	.7	1.4
	3.1	3.4	2.6	Net Profit + Depr., Dep.,			1.8	2.7	4.0	2.6
(84)	1.9	(95) 1.7	(81) 1.6	Amort./Cur. Mat. L/T/D		(14) 1.1	(18) 1.5	(20) 2.4	(19) 1.3
	.8	.9	.5				.5	.7	1.7	.5
	.4	.4	.3	Fixed/Worth	.4	.2	.3	.4	.3	.5
	1.0	.9	.9		2.3	.9	.9	.8	.7	1.2
	2.8	2.9	2.6		-1.6	2.5	1.7	2.6	2.2	3.1
	.7	.8	.6	Debt/Worth	1.0	.5	.5	.7	.6	.8
	2.1	2.1	1.7		8.6	1.6	1.3	1.5	1.8	2.0
	6.5	7.2	5.9		-5.7	6.9	3.9	4.3	5.6	4.8
	34.7	33.8	17.7	% Profit Before Taxes/Tangible Net Worth	73.6	15.7	16.0	19.7	20.0	10.9
(288)	14.7	(291) 14.2	(249) 4.7		(15) 1.2	(49) .7	(47) 3.8	(51) 6.2	(55) 8.8	(32) 1.5
	2.5	-.3	-12.3		-29.6	-28.6	-15.6	-10.7	-1.4	-9.8
	12.7	11.9	6.6	% Profit Before Taxes/Total Assets	10.9	6.6	6.0	7.7	6.9	4.7
	5.1	4.3	1.4		.7	-.2	1.2	2.7	3.1	.1
	.3	-1.0	-6.7		-17.4	-13.8	-5.9	-7.9	-1.0	-3.9
	12.3	12.8	10.8	Sales/Net Fixed Assets	13.3	14.2	12.8	8.8	10.5	6.7
	5.9	6.1	5.4		7.7	7.4	6.4	4.7	4.9	3.6
	3.5	3.6	2.9		2.6	4.1	3.2	2.9	2.7	2.6
	2.6	2.6	2.1	Sales/Total Assets	2.4	2.6	2.1	1.9	2.0	1.9
	1.9	1.8	1.5		1.6	1.8	1.4	1.5	1.5	1.3
	1.3	1.3	1.1		1.1	1.2	1.1	1.2	1.0	1.1
	2.0	1.9	2.5	% Depr., Dep., Amort./Sales	2.4	1.9	2.6	3.0	2.2	3.0
(308)	3.5	(307) 3.5	(259) 4.5		(21) 4.4	(54) 3.6	(45) 4.7	(54) 5.0	(54) 3.9	(31) 5.5
	5.5	5.1	6.7		7.0	6.7	6.8	6.4	5.7	6.9
	2.5	2.4	2.5	% Officers', Directors' Owners' Comp/Sales	5.2	4.2	2.8	2.2	2.1	
(180)	4.8	(177) 4.6	(138) 4.5		(10) 18.1	(40) 6.6	(29) 6.2	(30) 3.4	(22) 2.5	
	7.6	8.3	8.1		26.9	11.6	8.5	6.4	3.7	
4844617M		4808539M	3883346M	Net Sales ($)	15748M	108940M	208077M	390665M	984624M	2175292M
3107992M		3407732M	3093038M	Total Assets ($)	12066M	77584M	152173M	275547M	837543M	1738125M

    M = $ thousand   MM = $ million
See Pages 9 through 22 for Explanation of Ratios and Data

Current Data Sorted by Assets   Comparative Historical Data

Type of Statement	0-500M	500M-2MM	2-10MM	10-50MM	50-100MM	100-250MM		4/1/05-3/31/06 ALL	4/1/06-3/31/07 ALL
Unqualified		1	4	6	1	1		21	22
Reviewed		7	16	8				53	52
Compiled	5	12	12					32	21
Tax Returns	5	8	2					16	17
Other		7	20	15	2	3		51	43
		35 (4/1-9/30/09)		100 (10/1/09-3/31/10)					
NUMBER OF STATEMENTS	10	35	54	29	3	4		173	155
	%	%	%	%	%	%		%	%
ASSETS									
Cash & Equivalents	10.7	8.3	9.7	7.5				7.5	6.8
Trade Receivables (net)	26.3	24.2	20.1	19.2				28.8	26.3
Inventory	16.7	22.8	32.4	25.6				24.6	28.8
All Other Current	1.1	1.5	3.1	5.4				1.9	1.6
Total Current	54.8	56.8	65.4	57.7				62.8	63.5
Fixed Assets (net)	28.5	29.2	25.5	24.7				29.0	27.2
Intangibles (net)	6.2	4.9	3.3	9.0				2.2	2.8
All Other Non-Current	10.5	9.1	5.8	8.7				6.0	6.5
Total	100.0	100.0	100.0	100.0				100.0	100.0
LIABILITIES									
Notes Payable-Short Term	11.0	14.3	11.6	7.8				10.8	12.0
Cur. Mat.-L.T.D.	6.7	8.6	4.3	3.8				5.5	5.0
Trade Payables	11.9	10.4	10.5	6.8				12.9	12.7
Income Taxes Payable	.1	.3	.0	.1				.5	.2
All Other Current	8.6	10.8	6.2	10.2				8.1	8.8
Total Current	38.2	44.4	32.7	28.7				37.8	38.7
Long-Term Debt	31.2	16.0	12.8	18.5				18.8	16.1
Deferred Taxes	.5	.4	.9	1.0				.7	.4
All Other Non-Current	60.2	13.6	5.8	9.0				6.7	9.2
Net Worth	-30.1	25.7	47.8	42.8				36.1	35.7
Total Liabilities & Net Worth	100.0	100.0	100.0	100.0				100.0	100.0
INCOME DATA									
Net Sales	100.0	100.0	100.0	100.0				100.0	100.0
Gross Profit	35.1	35.2	33.3	30.4				33.9	33.3
Operating Expenses	43.6	38.4	31.2	28.3				28.7	27.7
Operating Profit	-8.5	-3.3	2.1	2.0				5.3	5.6
All Other Expenses (net)	2.9	.8	1.5	2.3				1.3	1.5
Profit Before Taxes	-11.4	-4.0	.6	-.3				4.0	4.0
RATIOS									
Current	3.3	2.3	3.6	4.1				2.6	2.7
	1.9	1.3	2.1	1.8				1.7	1.8
	1.1	.7	1.4	1.3				1.2	1.2
Quick	2.1	1.4	1.8	1.9				1.7	1.5
	1.2	.7	.8	.8				.9	.9
	.8	.4	.5	.6				.6	.5
Sales/Receivables	26 13.8	37 10.0	36 10.3	38 9.5				41 8.8	37 9.8
	45 8.2	50 7.4	44 8.2	51 7.1				50 7.3	46 8.0
	67 5.4	57 6.4	56 6.5	67 5.5				63 5.8	58 6.3
Cost of Sales/Inventory	5 66.9	18 20.3	50 7.3	58 6.2				29 12.5	37 9.9
	29 12.7	51 7.1	121 3.0	111 3.3				72 5.1	77 4.8
	56 6.5	147 2.5	174 2.1	200 1.8				119 3.1	129 2.8
Cost of Sales/Payables	12 29.5	15 24.6	15 23.6	11 32.1				19 19.6	17 21.9
	17 21.6	26 13.9	33 11.0	23 15.7				30 12.3	28 13.3
	33 11.1	49 7.5	43 8.5	40 9.1				44 8.3	44 8.3
Sales/Working Capital	5.0	4.6	2.6	2.5				4.9	4.7
	12.2	20.2	5.0	4.1				8.6	7.5
	NM	-10.0	12.4	8.7				19.9	17.0
EBIT/Interest		4.3	6.5	8.1				8.7	7.4
		(34) .7	(46) 1.6	(27) 2.0				(162) 3.7	(142) 2.8
		-4.5	-.9	-.1				1.5	1.0
Net Profit + Depr., Dep., Amort./Cur. Mat. L/T/D			2.4	1.7				4.1	3.9
			(20) 1.1	(13) .6				(60) 2.2	(53) 2.1
			-.4	-.1				1.0	1.1
Fixed/Worth	.3	.3	.2	.3				.4	.4
	NM	1.1	.6	.7				.7	.7
	-.7	UND	1.1	2.7				1.9	1.7
Debt/Worth	1.5	.8	.5	.7				.8	.7
	NM	3.5	1.4	1.1				1.9	1.7
	-2.6	UND	2.5	6.6				4.0	5.1
% Profit Before Taxes/Tangible Net Worth		32.1	14.3	16.0				41.0	29.8
		(27) 4.7	(51) 4.9	(25) 4.4				(158) 18.6	(140) 16.1
		-37.8	-7.7	-10.1				4.7	1.3
% Profit Before Taxes/Total Assets	4.1	8.5	5.4	6.4				13.9	14.7
	-12.8	-1.1	2.0	2.9				5.8	4.7
	-28.0	-14.9	-4.1	-2.5				1.3	.2
Sales/Net Fixed Assets	22.2	18.1	11.7	13.9				16.5	15.9
	8.1	7.5	7.6	4.6				6.9	7.1
	3.3	3.0	3.9	3.2				4.2	4.6
Sales/Total Assets	2.9	2.5	2.0	1.6				2.4	2.5
	1.7	1.6	1.5	1.2				1.8	1.9
	1.4	1.1	1.1	.9				1.4	1.5
% Depr., Dep., Amort./Sales	1.6	2.1	1.5	2.6				1.6	1.4
	3.3	(30) 4.4	(51) 2.6	(24) 4.2				(161) 3.3	(141) 2.8
	6.6	7.4	5.0	5.7				5.2	4.2
% Officers', Directors' Owners' Comp/Sales		3.1	2.2					2.9	3.2
		(23) 7.1	(25) 5.4					(77) 5.1	(64) 4.6
		12.6	8.1					7.8	8.1
Net Sales ($)	6551M	94689M	424464M	704799M	302129M	614356M		2505235M	3489318M
Total Assets ($)	3437M	43993M	273032M	588194M	220936M	647946M		1616227M	2202379M

Comparative Historical Data | | | | Current Data Sorted by Sales

4/1/07-3/31/08 ALL	4/1/08-3/31/09 ALL	4/1/09-3/31/10 ALL	Type of Statement	0-1MM	1-3MM	3-5MM	5-10MM	10-25MM	25MM & OVER
11	15	13	Unqualified		3		2	3	5
48	41	31	Reviewed	1	3	6	10	7	4
15	22	29	Compiled	5	12	7	5		
15	13	15	Tax Returns	5	4	2	2	2	
43	36	47	Other	1	8	1	12	16	9
				35 (4/1-9/30/09)			100 (10/1/09-3/31/10)		
132	127	135	NUMBER OF STATEMENTS	12	30	16	31	28	18
%	%	%	ASSETS	%	%	%	%	%	%
6.6	7.4	8.7	Cash & Equivalents	8.7	9.1	11.8	9.3	7.0	7.1
26.4	23.5	21.2	Trade Receivables (net)	22.2	20.4	24.9	20.3	21.9	19.2
27.2	31.0	27.1	Inventory	18.3	22.0	27.3	33.7	30.3	24.6
2.4	1.7	3.0	All Other Current	3.5	.7	4.2	1.8	6.5	1.8
62.6	63.6	60.0	Total Current	52.7	52.2	68.3	65.2	65.7	52.6
27.5	28.0	26.3	Fixed Assets (net)	28.1	33.0	24.0	22.4	23.5	27.3
3.2	2.4	6.0	Intangibles (net)	5.2	8.3	.5	4.7	5.5	10.5
6.7	5.9	7.7	All Other Non-Current	14.0	6.4	7.1	7.8	5.3	9.6
100.0	100.0	100.0	Total	100.0	100.0	100.0	100.0	100.0	100.0
			LIABILITIES						
11.7	13.0	11.0	Notes Payable-Short Term	10.7	14.1	10.9	12.3	10.3	5.3
4.9	5.1	5.4	Cur. Mat.-L.T.D.	5.9	8.5	5.3	5.0	3.7	3.0
13.5	11.1	9.7	Trade Payables	12.6	8.6	7.0	10.4	10.8	8.9
.4	.2	.1	Income Taxes Payable	.0	.2	.3	.0	.1	.1
9.1	8.1	8.5	All Other Current	12.4	8.1	3.8	7.3	11.0	9.0
39.6	37.5	34.7	Total Current	41.7	39.5	27.4	35.0	35.8	26.4
17.9	15.8	16.3	Long-Term Debt	27.8	17.5	13.8	14.7	14.7	14.2
.7	.8	.8	Deferred Taxes	.5	.3	.3	1.3	.9	1.5
5.0	8.1	12.6	All Other Non-Current	34.9	13.6	19.7	9.8	5.2	6.5
36.9	37.8	35.5	Net Worth	-4.8	29.1	38.9	39.2	43.4	51.4
100.0	100.0	100.0	Total Liabilties & Net Worth	100.0	100.0	100.0	100.0	100.0	100.0
			INCOME DATA						
100.0	100.0	100.0	Net Sales	100.0	100.0	100.0	100.0	100.0	100.0
34.6	33.6	33.5	Gross Profit	32.5	33.9	32.3	38.4	32.0	28.5
29.4	28.9	33.6	Operating Expenses	43.6	36.3	29.0	37.6	28.8	27.1
5.2	4.7	-.1	Operating Profit	-11.1	-2.4	3.3	.8	3.2	1.4
1.7	1.1	1.7	All Other Expenses (net)	2.4	1.0	1.4	2.0	1.9	1.7
3.5	3.6	-1.8	Profit Before Taxes	-13.5	-3.4	1.9	-1.2	1.4	-.3
			RATIOS						
2.4	2.8	3.4	Current	3.0	3.5	8.4	2.5	3.3	3.7
1.5	1.7	1.8		1.2	1.7	2.8	1.7	2.0	2.0
1.1	1.2	1.2		.8	.9	1.5	1.3	1.3	1.2
1.4	1.4	1.8	Quick	1.8	2.1	3.2	1.2	1.8	1.9
.8	.8	.8		.9	.8	1.3	.8	.7	1.0
.5	.5	.5		.4	.4	.7	.4	.6	.7
35 10.3	32 11.4	36 10.0	Sales/Receivables	33 11.1	38 9.5	44 8.3	33 11.1	35 10.5	36 10.0
47 7.8	41 9.0	48 7.6		45 8.2	50 7.3	53 6.9	41 8.8	48 7.6	47 7.8
62 5.9	50 7.3	62 5.9		63 5.8	64 5.7	67 5.5	55 6.6	57 6.4	66 5.6
36 10.2	37 9.9	39 9.3	Cost of Sales/Inventory	12 30.4	32 11.5	28 12.9	92 4.0	47 7.7	56 6.5
76 4.8	84 4.4	99 3.7		38 9.6	64 5.7	77 4.7	139 2.6	115 3.2	81 4.5
128 2.9	145 2.5	162 2.2		117 3.1	139 2.6	146 2.5	227 1.6	165 2.2	140 2.6
20 17.9	15 25.1	15 25.1	Cost of Sales/Payables	13 28.1	14 25.2	9 41.0	14 25.7	14 25.7	16 22.7
32 11.4	27 13.4	27 13.6		23 16.1	27 13.3	21 17.7	33 11.1	30 12.4	27 13.5
47 7.8	44 8.3	43 8.5		59 6.2	49 7.4	33 11.1	49 7.4	42 8.7	39 9.5
5.2	4.4	2.9	Sales/Working Capital	4.3	3.1	1.8	2.6	2.9	2.5
10.2	7.6	5.8		19.3	8.2	5.3	4.9	5.2	7.2
24.2	17.7	30.2		-38.8	-126.7	9.9	18.6	12.2	20.9
6.9	9.5	5.7	EBIT/Interest		4.0	7.1	2.5	8.5	7.6
(117) 2.2	(118) 3.4	(121) 1.4		(29) .1	(13) 2.3	(28) 1.0	(25) 2.6	(17) .7	
.9	1.0	-2.8		-5.5	1.1	-1.3	.6	-4.9	
2.2	4.1	1.9	Net Profit + Depr., Dep., Amort./Cur. Mat. L/T/D				1.7	3.8	
(42) 1.3	(50) 1.3	(41) 1.1				(11) .6	(12) 1.2		
.7	.4	-.4				.5	-.4		
.3	.4	.3	Fixed/Worth	.1	.4	.2	.2	.3	.4
.7	.7	.7		1.3	1.2	.8	.7	.6	.6
1.6	1.6	2.2		-1.6	-8.1	1.3	1.7	1.1	2.0
.9	.8	.6	Debt/Worth	1.0	.5	.4	.7	.6	.3
1.8	1.6	1.6		3.3	5.4	1.8	1.5	1.5	1.1
4.6	4.2	9.0		-5.7	-28.4	3.8	7.6	3.9	11.0
35.4	39.2	16.0	% Profit Before Taxes/Tangible Net Worth		39.5	14.6	17.2	15.8	11.8
(115) 14.4	(116) 15.4	(113) 3.6		(22) 9.7	(14) 2.7	(28) 3.9	(26) 6.5	(15) -2.5	
.1	1.8	-13.0		-25.3	-12.9	-8.4	-3.3	-18.4	
13.9	14.6	6.1	% Profit Before Taxes/Total Assets	2.4	8.7	9.2	4.6	6.0	7.5
4.9	6.2	.8		-12.8	-3.3	1.9	.0	3.0	.2
-.2	.2	-5.9		-22.1	-14.9	-2.2	-4.6	-1.0	-3.9
17.2	15.9	14.7	Sales/Net Fixed Assets	45.3	12.6	14.1	17.7	12.7	11.3
8.1	7.3	6.9		11.1	4.2	7.1	10.0	7.8	4.6
4.3	4.2	3.3		2.9	2.5	4.2	3.4	4.3	3.2
2.5	2.4	1.9	Sales/Total Assets	1.9	1.8	2.1	2.0	1.9	2.2
2.0	1.9	1.4		1.6	1.2	1.6	1.5	1.5	1.2
1.4	1.4	1.0		.8	1.0	1.1	1.0	1.2	1.0
1.2	1.3	1.7	% Depr., Dep., Amort./Sales	1.6	2.5	1.5	1.4	2.0	1.8
(117) 2.6	(118) 2.9	(121) 3.6		(11) 2.7	(27) 4.8	(15) 3.1	(27) 3.6	(25) 3.2	(16) 4.2
4.9	4.9	5.8		11.4	7.6	4.5	5.7	4.3	6.9
2.5	2.3	2.8	% Officers', Directors' Owners' Comp/Sales		6.1	2.5	3.4		
(52) 5.4	(57) 4.7	(57) 5.9			(17) 8.9	(10) 3.5	(14) 5.9		
8.1	9.2	9.6			13.0	11.2	7.1		
2657695M	1993863M	2146988M	Net Sales ($)	7552M	54822M	64149M	228380M	449503M	1342582M
1623446M	1371120M	1777538M	Total Assets ($)	6179M	49534M	43126M	194984M	311855M	1171860M

M = $ thousand   MM = $ million
See Pages 9 through 22 for Explanation of Ratios and Data

Current Data Sorted by Assets   **Comparative Historical Data**

Type of Statement	0-500M	500M-2MM	2-10MM	10-50MM	50-100MM	100-250MM		4/1/05-3/31/06 ALL	4/1/06-3/31/07 ALL
Unqualified			2	3	1	1		9	5
Reviewed		1	5	5	.1			20	24
Compiled		5	5	1				9	10
Tax Returns	2	5	4					8	12
Other	4	10	7	7	2			21	26
		18 (4/1-9/30/09)		53 (10/1/09-3/31/10)					
NUMBER OF STATEMENTS	6	21	23	16	4	1		67	77

	0-500M %	500M-2MM %	2-10MM %	10-50MM %	50-100MM %	100-250MM %		ALL %	ALL %
ASSETS									
Cash & Equivalents		11.1	10.6	10.4				8.3	10.3
Trade Receivables (net)		27.0	22.2	13.5				32.6	28.5
Inventory		18.4	29.2	21.9				23.1	24.8
All Other Current		3.3	4.8	7.6				5.2	3.4
Total Current		59.8	66.8	53.5				69.2	66.9
Fixed Assets (net)		31.9	24.3	38.5				23.6	23.0
Intangibles (net)		4.1	4.4	5.1				3.3	5.7
All Other Non-Current		4.2	4.5	3.0				4.0	4.4
Total		100.0	100.0	100.0				100.0	100.0
LIABILITIES									
Notes Payable-Short Term		12.6	6.6	1.2				12.4	10.6
Cur. Mat.-L.T.D.		3.3	5.1	5.1				4.1	5.1
Trade Payables		21.5	9.2	5.2				15.3	14.0
Income Taxes Payable		.1	.1	.1				.1	.4
All Other Current		14.2	10.4	12.4				14.3	12.5
Total Current		51.7	31.4	24.0				46.2	42.5
Long-Term Debt		29.2	21.4	18.8				17.1	15.8
Deferred Taxes		.1	.0	.1				.4	.5
All Other Non-Current		18.6	8.1	4.0				9.2	6.9
Net Worth		.5	39.1	53.2				27.1	34.3
Total Liabilities & Net Worth		100.0	100.0	100.0				100.0	100.0
INCOME DATA									
Net Sales		100.0	100.0	100.0				100.0	100.0
Gross Profit		32.1	34.0	22.3				32.7	30.9
Operating Expenses		35.1	29.1	22.0				27.3	24.9
Operating Profit		-3.0	5.0	.3				5.4	6.0
All Other Expenses (net)		1.7	1.6	1.5				1.1	1.4
Profit Before Taxes		-4.6	3.3	-1.2				4.3	4.6
RATIOS									
Current		2.0	5.0	4.9				2.5	2.7
		1.3	2.7	2.1				1.5	1.6
		1.0	1.3	1.6				1.1	1.1
Quick		1.4	2.5	2.6				1.6	1.6
		.9	1.4	1.4				.9	.9
		.4	.6	.7				.5	.6
Sales/Receivables	21 17.0	28 13.0	18 20.7					33 11.0	33 11.2
	39 9.3	39 9.3	40 9.1					54 6.7	46 7.9
	56 6.5	52 7.0	58 6.3					74 4.9	62 5.8
Cost of Sales/Inventory	11 32.1	26 14.3	11 33.7					23 16.0	18 20.1
	26 13.9	96 3.8	65 5.7					53 6.9	64 5.7
	83 4.4	168 2.2	118 3.1					95 3.8	109 3.3
Cost of Sales/Payables	12 31.6	9 38.7	9 38.6					20 18.7	18 20.5
	26 14.1	23 15.9	19 19.0					29 12.5	30 12.0
	73 5.0	38 9.7	34 10.6					57 6.4	49 7.5
Sales/Working Capital		5.9	2.5	2.2				4.8	4.5
		22.9	5.1	3.4				10.2	8.4
		NM	9.4	13.7				25.1	28.9
EBIT/Interest		5.0	17.1	14.4				15.9	13.8
	(18) .8	(19) 3.7	1.6					(59) 3.3	(70) 3.3
		-.8	1.0	-25.5				1.5	.7
Net Profit + Depr., Dep., Amort./Cur. Mat. L/T/D								4.6	3.2
								(16) 2.2	(19) 2.0
								1.0	.6
Fixed/Worth		.3	.2	.3				.2	.2
		1.2	.5	.9				.7	.6
		-3.6	5.2	2.2				3.5	-8.2
Debt/Worth		1.1	.4	.5				1.1	.7
		13.6	1.4	1.0				2.6	1.6
		-4.3	7.7	2.0				10.4	-25.7
% Profit Before Taxes/Tangible Net Worth		62.4	29.8	12.7				59.4	50.3
	(14) 1.5	(20) 14.6	(15) 3.7					(53) 21.8	(56) 21.7
		-3.1	.0	-12.7				8.0	4.5
% Profit Before Taxes/Total Assets		9.3	17.0	5.8				16.0	19.2
		-.5	4.3	1.3				5.8	8.2
		-10.5	-1.1	-6.0				1.3	.1
Sales/Net Fixed Assets		21.4	23.7	10.2				32.8	34.2
		6.4	8.1	3.8				12.3	12.9
		3.3	5.2	1.2				4.5	4.4
Sales/Total Assets		3.2	2.6	1.3				2.7	2.7
		1.9	1.7	1.1				1.9	1.9
		1.4	1.1	.7				1.4	1.4
% Depr., Dep., Amort./Sales		1.1	.7	2.1				1.0	1.0
	(16) 3.4	(22) 1.6	3.2					(54) 2.2	(62) 2.0
		8.7	5.1	6.9				3.8	5.0
% Officers', Directors' Owners' Comp/Sales			2.0					2.8	2.8
		(12)	4.9					(26) 5.6	(33) 5.2
			8.6					8.1	8.5
Net Sales ($)	9495M	64489M	171602M	324110M	215972M	164898M		1147601M	1598746M
Total Assets ($)	1474M	26887M	95558M	279644M	293321M	225176M		687612M	1070429M

M = $ thousand   MM = $ million
See Pages 9 through 22 for Explanation of Ratios and Data

Comparative Historical Data | | | Current Data Sorted by Sales

Comparative Historical Data			Type of Statement		Current Data Sorted by Sales				
5	10	7	Unqualified			1	3	1	3
19	21	12	Reviewed			1	5	1	3
12	16	13	Compiled		1	3	4		1
7	8	13	Tax Returns		2	3	4	4	
18	27	26	Other		3	6	1	5	7	4
4/1/07-3/31/08 ALL	4/1/08-3/31/09 ALL	4/1/09-3/31/10 ALL				18 (4/1-9/30/09)		53 (10/1/09-3/31/10)	
				0-1MM	1-3MM	3-5MM	5-10MM	10-25MM	25MM & OV
61	82	71	**NUMBER OF STATEMENTS**	6	13	11	21	9	11
%	%	%	**ASSETS**	%	%	%	%	%	%
6.7	7.1	13.0	Cash & Equivalents		13.7	19.5	9.7		11.7
27.8	24.5	21.8	Trade Receivables (net)		23.2	20.5	25.0		16.1
25.4	28.2	21.2	Inventory		15.0	28.2	21.9		16.9
4.3	4.4	4.7	All Other Current		3.5	4.1	4.0		8.6
64.2	64.3	60.7	Total Current		55.4	72.3	60.7		53.3
25.9	22.8	28.9	Fixed Assets (net)		32.3	22.6	30.3		24.9
6.7	6.4	5.8	Intangibles (net)		5.8	2.4	4.9		14.2
3.2	6.5	4.6	All Other Non-Current		6.6	2.8	4.1		7.6
100.0	100.0	100.0	Total		100.0	100.0	100.0		100.0
			LIABILITIES						
9.9	7.5	8.1	Notes Payable-Short Term		12.3	15.6	8.6		1.7
6.3	5.0	4.0	Cur. Mat.-L.T.D.		3.5	2.3	7.4		1.5
10.7	11.1	12.4	Trade Payables		18.8	17.4	13.3		4.8
.1	.2	.1	Income Taxes Payable		.0	.1	.1		.2
12.6	13.8	13.9	All Other Current		9.9	17.2	11.6		16.2
39.6	37.7	38.4	Total Current		44.5	52.6	41.0		24.5
19.2	17.6	24.7	Long-Term Debt		30.6	16.4	26.6		16.0
.2	.3	.2	Deferred Taxes		.0	.0	.1		1.0
8.2	8.6	9.3	All Other Non-Current		11.5	19.8	5.9		2.0
32.8	35.9	27.3	Net Worth		13.4	11.1	26.4		56.6
100.0	100.0	100.0	Total Liabilities & Net Worth		100.0	100.0	100.0		100.0
			INCOME DATA						
100.0	100.0	100.0	Net Sales		100.0	100.0	100.0		100.0
29.5	30.9	32.4	Gross Profit		28.5	41.1	31.1		23.4
25.9	24.6	30.3	Operating Expenses		33.4	35.0	27.6		17.8
3.6	6.3	2.1	Operating Profit		-4.9	6.1	3.5		5.6
1.8	1.2	1.5	All Other Expenses (net)		1.3	1.6	1.6		.5
1.8	5.1	.5	Profit Before Taxes		-6.2	4.5	1.8		5.1
			RATIOS						
2.8	3.0	4.3			7.8	5.4	2.4		4.3
1.9	1.8	1.9	Current		1.4	2.8	1.4		1.9
1.1	1.2	1.1			.9	.9	1.0		1.8
1.5	1.4	1.9			3.6	2.5	1.6		1.9
.9	.9	1.0	Quick		.7	1.5	.8		1.1
.6	.6	.6			.4	.6	.5		.7
40 9.1	31 11.6	24 15.4		5 74.3	16 23.4	20 18.1		27 13.5
52 7.1	43 8.5	39 9.3	Sales/Receivables	35 10.4	39 9.3	38 9.7		57 6.4
65 5.6	57 6.4	57 6.4		60 6.1	50 7.3	47 7.7		70 5.2
23 15.8	20 18.1	13 27.4		6 63.1	5 67.8	11 32.1		30 12.3
71 5.1	78 4.7	50 7.3	Cost of Sales/Inventory	26 13.9	79 4.6	26 13.8		67 5.5
129 2.8	128 2.9	110 3.3		77 4.8	146 2.5	109 3.3		98 3.7
14 25.8	14 26.9	10 38.2		9 40.9	11 31.9	13 28.2		9 42.4
27 13.6	25 14.4	21 17.4	Cost of Sales/Payables	23 15.8	23 15.9	26 14.1		20 17.9
46 8.0	38 9.6	40 9.1		62 5.9	58 6.3	38 9.7		28 13.2
4.5	4.5	3.3			4.4	2.5	5.3		3.3
6.6	7.4	7.0	Sales/Working Capital		14.3	5.1	14.2		4.3
27.4	18.7	88.4			-39.2	-37.9	312.9		12.1
11.2	11.9	6.8			1.9	10.3	6.2		18.8
(55) 2.9	(71) 4.8	(62) 2.0	EBIT/Interest	(10) -.4	(10) 2.8	(19) 2.6	(10) 5.4
.8	1.5	-.8			-7.4	-.8	1.1		2.2
11.3	10.4	6.1							
(14) 2.5	(20) 2.2	(14) 2.2	Net Profit + Depr., Dep., Amort./Cur. Mat. L/T/D					
.7	1.1	.8							
.3	.3	.3			.2	.2	.3		.2
.9	.6	1.1	Fixed/Worth		1.2	1.2	1.2		.5
17.8	2.8	26.4			-.8	-.9	5.5		1.4
.8	.7	.8			.4	.4	.9		.6
2.0	1.8	1.6	Debt/Worth		60.2	1.5	2.0		1.0
99.4	6.2	236.0			-2.7	-6.5	20.7		2.9
35.7	37.9	25.8					77.3		17.3
(47) 14.3	(66) 21.5	(54) 9.2	% Profit Before Taxes/Tangible Net Worth			(18) 8.5	(10) 12.8
3.1	7.7	-2.0					1.2		6.6
13.0	15.7	9.2			1.9	18.2	9.8		6.8
4.4	8.7	1.8	% Profit Before Taxes/Total Assets		-2.0	8.1	4.3		5.7
-.5	1.5	-2.9			-49.0	-1.6	.5		4.9
31.6	26.9	23.7			60.1	36.3	33.9		7.7
7.3	11.8	7.7	Sales/Net Fixed Assets		5.7	13.1	10.9		7.1
4.2	5.9	3.4			2.7	6.3	2.6		3.4
2.5	2.7	2.6			3.5	2.9	3.5		1.6
1.7	1.8	1.5	Sales/Total Assets		1.5	1.7	2.0		1.1
1.4	1.3	.9			1.1	1.5	1.0		.7
1.0	1.1	1.0			1.1		.7		
(56) 2.4	(71) 2.0	(60) 2.8	% Depr., Dep., Amort./Sales	(11) 3.9	(18) 1.4	
4.7	3.9	5.7			9.4		8.4		
2.0	2.7	2.2					2.3		
(21) 4.6	(34) 4.9	(30) 4.6	% Officers', Directors' Owners' Comp/Sales			(11) 4.0	
8.1	6.7	7.7					9.6		
939716M	2005985M	950566M	Net Sales ($)	3965M	23324M	39525M	149190M	146317M	588245M
705096M	1413567M	922060M	Total Assets ($)	4917M	14552M	23141M	115519M	106463M	657468M

M = $ thousand   MM = $ million
See Pages 9 through 22 for Explanation of Ratios and Data

Current Data Sorted by Assets   Comparative Historical Data

0-500M	500M-2MM	2-10MM	10-50MM	50-100MM	100-250MM	Type of Statement	4/1/05-3/31/06 ALL	4/1/06-3/31/07 ALL
		2	3		2	Unqualified	6	7
	1	3	2			Reviewed	7	9
	1	4				Compiled	3	6
1	1					Tax Returns	1	1
1	4	3	3	2		Other	11	7
	5 (4/1-9/30/09)		28 (10/1/09-3/31/10)					
2	7	12	8	2	2	NUMBER OF STATEMENTS	28	30
%	%	%	%	%	%	ASSETS	%	%
		10.1				Cash & Equivalents	3.9	5.3
		18.1				Trade Receivables (net)	28.4	22.0
		25.8				Inventory	30.5	30.0
		.9				All Other Current	2.7	1.0
		55.0				Total Current	65.4	58.4
		30.8				Fixed Assets (net)	26.1	29.2
		5.7				Intangibles (net)	2.9	4.8
		8.6				All Other Non-Current	5.6	7.7
		100.0				Total	100.0	100.0
						LIABILITIES		
		5.8				Notes Payable-Short Term	12.0	9.6
		5.2				Cur. Mat.-L.T.D.	3.6	4.3
		7.5				Trade Payables	13.0	10.4
		.1				Income Taxes Payable	.2	.2
		6.1				All Other Current	10.6	10.3
		24.7				Total Current	39.4	34.9
		22.9				Long-Term Debt	11.3	17.8
		.3				Deferred Taxes	.1	.4
		6.5				All Other Non-Current	9.3	5.9
		45.7				Net Worth	39.8	41.1
		100.0				Total Liabilities & Net Worth	100.0	100.0
						INCOME DATA		
		100.0				Net Sales	100.0	100.0
		28.5				Gross Profit	26.2	27.6
		24.9				Operating Expenses	21.6	20.2
		3.5				Operating Profit	4.6	7.4
		1.0				All Other Expenses (net)	.3	1.2
		2.5				Profit Before Taxes	4.3	6.2
						RATIOS		
		4.4					2.3	2.1
		2.4				Current	1.6	1.6
		1.2					1.3	1.3
		2.6					1.1	1.2
		1.1				Quick	.8	.8
		.7					.6	.6
	34	10.8					42 8.7	42 8.6
	44	8.3				Sales/Receivables	51 7.1	52 7.1
	51	7.2					67 5.4	59 6.2
	44	8.3					59 6.1	68 5.4
	107	3.4				Cost of Sales/Inventory	81 4.5	99 3.7
	127	2.9					108 3.4	115 3.2
	11	33.7					19 19.6	12 29.5
	27	13.4				Cost of Sales/Payables	29 12.8	30 12.1
	34	10.8					37 9.7	42 8.6
		3.0					5.2	5.0
		4.8				Sales/Working Capital	7.4	7.8
		40.6					18.5	14.9
		4.8					8.9	8.8
		1.5				EBIT/Interest	(26) 6.1	5.9
		-1.5					1.5	3.1
								4.9
						Net Profit + Depr., Dep., Amort./Cur. Mat. L/T/D	(10) 2.4	
								.9
		.2					.2	.4
		.5				Fixed/Worth	.8	.9
		1.7					1.3	2.0
		.8					.7	1.0
		1.5				Debt/Worth	1.7	2.0
		2.5					3.2	3.6
		31.0					37.9	50.8
	(11)	4.5				% Profit Before Taxes/Tangible Net Worth	(26) 21.0	(26) 20.1
		-6.2					2.0	3.7
		12.7					13.9	15.6
		1.7				% Profit Before Taxes/Total Assets	6.7	9.7
		-3.3					.8	4.2
		23.5					16.0	11.3
		7.7				Sales/Net Fixed Assets	7.3	5.3
		1.7					4.7	3.5
		1.8					2.2	2.0
		1.4				Sales/Total Assets	1.9	1.6
		1.0					1.4	1.2
		1.6					1.8	2.2
	(11)	4.2				% Depr., Dep., Amort./Sales	(27) 3.0	3.7
		5.5					4.6	5.1
								1.9
						% Officers', Directors' Owners' Comp/Sales	(13) 5.7	
								8.0
133M	23131M	77081M	275766M	116162M	528753M	Net Sales ($)	719804M	672328M
157M	10419M	54370M	172653M	127608M	387234M	Total Assets ($)	474591M	507976M

RMA 2010

M = $ thousand   MM = $ million
See Pages 9 through 22 for Explanation of Ratios and Data

Comparative Historical Data   Current Data Sorted by Sales

4/1/07-3/31/08 ALL	4/1/08-3/31/09 ALL	4/1/09-3/31/10 ALL	Type of Statement	0-1MM	1-3MM	3-5MM	5-10MM	10-25MM	25MM & OVER
7	12	7	Unqualified		1		1	3	3
4	6	6	Reviewed		2	2	2	2	1
2	4	5	Compiled			1	1		
1	3	2	Tax Returns	1		1			
11	14	13	Other	1	2	3	2	1	4
				5 (4/1-9/30/09)			28 (10/1/09-3/31/10)		
25	39	33	NUMBER OF STATEMENTS	2	5	6	6	6	8
%	%	%	ASSETS	%	%	%	%	%	%
5.8	4.9	8.9	Cash & Equivalents						
23.9	23.9	20.5	Trade Receivables (net)						
32.7	32.8	29.9	Inventory						
1.4	1.9	2.2	All Other Current						
63.7	63.5	61.4	Total Current						
29.0	23.7	29.1	Fixed Assets (net)						
3.5	6.3	3.9	Intangibles (net)						
3.8	6.5	5.6	All Other Non-Current						
100.0	100.0	100.0	Total						
			LIABILITIES						
9.1	13.1	11.6	Notes Payable-Short Term						
3.5	3.9	3.4	Cur. Mat.-L.T.D.						
16.1	16.7	12.0	Trade Payables						
2.2	.4	.1	Income Taxes Payable						
9.4	9.1	10.7	All Other Current						
40.3	43.3	37.9	Total Current						
14.5	14.8	18.3	Long-Term Debt						
.5	.7	.7	Deferred Taxes						
4.0	12.7	9.6	All Other Non-Current						
40.8	28.6	33.4	Net Worth						
100.0	100.0	100.0	Total Liabilties & Net Worth						
			INCOME DATA						
100.0	100.0	100.0	Net Sales						
33.7	29.5	26.9	Gross Profit						
24.4	23.0	27.6	Operating Expenses						
9.3	6.5	-.7	Operating Profit						
1.0	1.3	1.2	All Other Expenses (net)						
8.3	5.2	-2.0	Profit Before Taxes						
			RATIOS						
3.2	2.7	4.1	Current						
1.8	1.5	2.0	Current						
1.0	1.1	1.2	Current						
1.5	1.0	1.8	Quick						
1.0	.7	1.0	Quick						
.5	.4	.5	Quick						
37 9.9	35 10.6	35 10.3	Sales/Receivables						
52 7.0	43 8.5	47 7.8	Sales/Receivables						
62 5.9	55 6.7	53 6.9	Sales/Receivables						
73 5.0	70 5.2	57 6.4	Cost of Sales/Inventory						
99 3.7	85 4.3	98 3.7	Cost of Sales/Inventory						
116 3.1	106 3.4	124 2.9	Cost of Sales/Inventory						
17 21.0	19 18.9	11 31.8	Cost of Sales/Payables						
36 10.3	31 11.7	25 14.7	Cost of Sales/Payables						
70 5.2	69 5.3	54 6.8	Cost of Sales/Payables						
3.8	4.9	2.9	Sales/Working Capital						
6.0	7.8	4.9	Sales/Working Capital						
NM	53.0	32.0	Sales/Working Capital						
11.3	16.6	5.4	EBIT/Interest						
(23) 7.1	(37) 5.0	(29) 1.2	EBIT/Interest						
4.5	1.6	-1.7	EBIT/Interest						
	5.6	3.5	Net Profit + Depr., Dep., Amort./Cur. Mat. L/T/D						
	(10) 2.9	(11) 1.0	Net Profit + Depr., Dep., Amort./Cur. Mat. L/T/D						
	1.8	-1.4	Net Profit + Depr., Dep., Amort./Cur. Mat. L/T/D						
.4	.5	.4	Fixed/Worth						
.9	.8	.9	Fixed/Worth						
6.2	3.9	2.6	Fixed/Worth						
.5	.9	.9	Debt/Worth						
1.5	2.2	2.3	Debt/Worth						
33.6	7.1	4.1	Debt/Worth						
46.7	53.3	15.9	% Profit Before Taxes/Tangible Net Worth						
(20) 27.7	(31) 22.9	(27) .0	% Profit Before Taxes/Tangible Net Worth						
16.2	3.8	-35.7	% Profit Before Taxes/Tangible Net Worth						
20.3	21.7	9.5	% Profit Before Taxes/Total Assets						
13.6	9.3	.1	% Profit Before Taxes/Total Assets						
7.4	2.8	-9.1	% Profit Before Taxes/Total Assets						
11.9	20.9	22.6	Sales/Net Fixed Assets						
5.5	11.5	6.8	Sales/Net Fixed Assets						
3.5	4.3	2.1	Sales/Net Fixed Assets						
2.1	2.5	2.1	Sales/Total Assets						
1.7	2.0	1.5	Sales/Total Assets						
1.2	1.3	1.0	Sales/Total Assets						
2.1	1.0	1.6	% Depr., Dep., Amort./Sales						
(23) 3.0	(31) 2.2	(29) 3.2	% Depr., Dep., Amort./Sales						
4.7	5.3	5.3	% Depr., Dep., Amort./Sales						
	1.6		% Officers', Directors' Owners' Comp/Sales						
	(10) 4.5		% Officers', Directors' Owners' Comp/Sales						
	7.8		% Officers', Directors' Owners' Comp/Sales						
909489M	1689273M	1021026M	Net Sales ($)	133M	11092M	24476M	42635M	96676M	846014M
579729M	1159657M	752441M	Total Assets ($)	157M	8415M	13999M	29570M	109065M	591235M

M = $ thousand   MM = $ million
See Pages 9 through 22 for Explanation of Ratios and Data

Current Data Sorted by Assets | Comparative Historical Data

0-500M	500M-2MM	2-10MM	10-50MM	50-100MM	100-250MM	Type of Statement	ALL 4/1/05-3/31/06	ALL 4/1/06-3/31/07
		2	7	1	2	Unqualified	6	12
	1	4	2			Reviewed	8	10
		2				Compiled	4	4
	1	1				Tax Returns	3	5
1		10	4	3	1	Other	11	15
	13 (4/1-9/30/09)		29 (10/1/09-3/31/10)					
1	2	19	13	4	3	**NUMBER OF STATEMENTS**	32	46
%	%	%	%	%	%	**ASSETS**	%	%
		8.0	7.5			Cash & Equivalents	5.2	5.8
		17.6	25.1			Trade Receivables (net)	30.8	25.8
		40.5	32.8			Inventory	32.6	30.9
		4.7	1.6			All Other Current	1.7	3.5
		70.8	67.1			Total Current	70.2	66.0
		20.6	20.1			Fixed Assets (net)	22.7	25.4
		2.7	6.5			Intangibles (net)	3.8	2.8
		5.9	6.3			All Other Non-Current	3.3	5.8
		100.0	100.0			Total	100.0	100.0
						LIABILITIES		
		18.9	6.0			Notes Payable-Short Term	8.8	24.6
		4.2	4.8			Cur. Mat.-L.T.D.	4.3	4.2
		11.6	8.4			Trade Payables	14.8	14.2
		.1	.0			Income Taxes Payable	.5	.3
		10.6	19.1			All Other Current	11.3	9.5
		45.4	38.3			Total Current	39.7	52.9
		16.1	7.5			Long-Term Debt	9.9	19.8
		1.1	.2			Deferred Taxes	1.0	.5
		14.2	2.7			All Other Non-Current	3.1	6.5
		23.3	51.3			Net Worth	46.3	20.3
		100.0	100.0			Total Liabilites & Net Worth	100.0	100.0
						INCOME DATA		
		100.0	100.0			Net Sales	100.0	100.0
		33.3	33.8			Gross Profit	32.4	33.6
		27.3	26.2			Operating Expenses	25.5	25.7
		6.0	7.6			Operating Profit	6.9	7.9
		1.6	1.8			All Other Expenses (net)	.8	2.2
		4.4	5.9			Profit Before Taxes	6.1	5.7
						RATIOS		
		3.4	2.5			Current	3.1	2.9
		1.9	1.8				1.9	1.7
		1.4	1.5				1.2	1.2
		1.4	1.3			Quick	1.6	1.3
		.7	1.0				1.0	.9
		.3	.6				.5	.5
	29	12.4	47 7.7			Sales/Receivables	37 9.9	40 9.2
	34	10.7	66 5.5				50 7.3	50 7.3
	46	7.9	71 5.1				63 5.8	61 6.0
	69	5.3	50 7.3			Cost of Sales/Inventory	45 8.1	37 9.9
	146	2.5	125 2.9				78 4.7	79 4.6
	252	1.4	265 1.4				151 2.4	143 2.6
	18	20.2	13 28.1			Cost of Sales/Payables	18 20.6	20 18.6
	30	12.2	23 15.9				27 13.3	31 11.8
	40	9.1	42 8.6				47 7.7	55 6.7
		3.0	3.4			Sales/Working Capital	4.2	3.7
		5.0	5.9				7.0	8.2
		8.5	13.2				14.5	20.6
		11.7	17.9			EBIT/Interest	22.7	16.6
	(17)	4.8	(10) 5.3				(30) 8.4	(43) 6.0
		-.7	.1				2.8	2.6
						Net Profit + Depr., Dep., Amort./Cur. Mat. L/T/D	4.3	7.4
							(12) 2.1 (19) 3.0	
							1.2	1.9
		.1	.2			Fixed/Worth	.3	.3
		.5	.5				.5	.6
		1.2	1.0				1.2	1.5
		.4	.5			Debt/Worth	.5	.6
		1.5	1.1				1.3	1.7
		3.8	3.1				2.8	3.9
		43.2	70.6			% Profit Before Taxes/Tangible Net Worth	38.8	36.9
	(16)	20.0	(12) 10.7				(31) 24.7 (38) 20.8	
		4.7	-.5				15.2	10.8
		19.7	22.1			% Profit Before Taxes/Total Assets	20.3	18.2
		7.3	5.7				9.7	10.3
		-4.5	-.2				4.0	4.9
		62.1	20.9			Sales/Net Fixed Assets	26.2	21.5
		8.1	7.8				8.4	8.2
		4.7	5.2				5.1	4.4
		2.1	2.1			Sales/Total Assets	3.2	2.4
		1.7	1.4				2.1	1.9
		1.1	.9				1.6	1.5
		1.2	1.6			% Depr., Dep., Amort./Sales	1.3	1.1
	(15)	2.7	(12) 2.6				(26) 2.2 (39) 2.4	
		6.7	4.7				2.7	4.1
						% Officers', Directors' Owners' Comp/Sales	2.0	
							(10) 2.8	
							7.0	
552M	2078M	168988M	478495M	289116M	214035M	Net Sales ($)	898779M	1184947M
278M	1877M	101298M	281066M	280392M	441996M	Total Assets ($)	434747M	733707M

M = $ thousand   MM = $ million
See Pages 9 through 22 for Explanation of Ratios and Data

Comparative Historical Data   Current Data Sorted by Sales

4/1/07-3/31/08 ALL	4/1/08-3/31/09 ALL	4/1/09-3/31/10 ALL	Type of Statement	0-1MM	1-3MM	3-5MM	5-10MM	10-25MM	25MM & OVER
					13 (4/1-9/30/09)			29 (10/1/09-3/31/10)	
11	13	12	Unqualified		1		1	4	6
7	7	7	Reviewed			1	3	3	
4	1	2	Compiled				1	1	
1	2	2	Tax Returns	1				1	
22	20	19	Other	1	1	2	4	4	7
45	43	42	**NUMBER OF STATEMENTS**	2	2	3	9	13	13
%	%	%	**ASSETS**	%	%	%	%	%	%
4.0	4.6	7.5	Cash & Equivalents					7.5	7.8
27.1	25.3	21.3	Trade Receivables (net)					22.2	22.1
30.6	31.8	33.9	Inventory					37.1	21.6
4.7	3.2	4.2	All Other Current					6.3	5.2
66.4	65.0	66.9	Total Current					73.1	56.7
24.4	29.8	21.1	Fixed Assets (net)					18.9	21.2
4.0	1.7	5.7	Intangibles (net)					2.8	12.8
5.2	3.6	6.3	All Other Non-Current					5.2	9.3
100.0	100.0	100.0	Total					100.0	100.0
			LIABILITIES						
19.1	21.0	13.0	Notes Payable-Short Term					7.2	6.8
3.6	3.8	4.1	Cur. Mat.-L.T.D.					5.0	2.1
13.3	10.0	9.6	Trade Payables					11.5	9.4
.5	.1	.2	Income Taxes Payable					.0	.3
12.8	14.7	13.0	All Other Current					19.3	13.3
49.3	49.5	39.8	Total Current					43.0	31.9
15.6	16.9	12.1	Long-Term Debt					9.6	5.7
.7	1.0	1.1	Deferred Taxes					.2	1.8
5.7	1.7	10.3	All Other Non-Current					.2	7.9
28.6	30.9	36.6	Net Worth					47.0	52.7
100.0	100.0	100.0	Total Liabilities & Net Worth					100.0	100.0
			INCOME DATA						
100.0	100.0	100.0	Net Sales					100.0	100.0
33.5	30.4	33.7	Gross Profit					36.0	27.4
25.7	22.8	29.1	Operating Expenses					27.4	27.4
7.8	7.5	4.6	Operating Profit					8.6	.0
.9	.8	1.5	All Other Expenses (net)					.5	1.9
7.0	6.7	3.1	Profit Before Taxes					8.1	-1.9
			RATIOS						
2.8	2.6	3.2	Current					2.5	4.0
1.9	1.7	1.9						1.8	1.9
1.2	1.2	1.3						1.3	1.2
1.2	1.3	1.5	Quick					1.3	2.3
.7	.8	.8						1.0	.7
.6	.4	.4						.3	.6
40 9.2	33 11.2	34 10.8	Sales/Receivables					29 12.7	42 8.6
47 7.8	44 8.3	47 7.8						40 9.1	60 6.0
60 6.1	61 6.0	69 5.3						68 5.3	76 4.8
42 8.8	46 7.9	52 7.0	Cost of Sales/Inventory					55 6.6	45 8.0
89 4.1	70 5.2	119 3.1						125 2.9	95 3.8
144 2.5	148 2.5	247 1.5						219 1.7	133 2.8
17 22.0	16 23.1	21 17.4	Cost of Sales/Payables					16 23.4	23 15.8
29 12.8	27 13.5	29 12.7						26 14.3	28 13.2
44 8.3	38 9.6	41 8.9						43 8.5	41 8.9
3.9	4.3	2.6	Sales/Working Capital					4.0	1.8
6.0	7.5	5.0						6.5	5.9
14.9	18.7	13.5						17.4	16.6
15.2	13.3	14.3	EBIT/Interest					29.4	14.9
(38) 6.7	(41) 5.3	(35) 3.0						(11) 3.2	(10) 5.1
3.3	1.3	-.6						-.7	-1.0
8.1	11.0	6.3	Net Profit + Depr., Dep., Amort./Cur. Mat. L/T/D						
(18) 4.2	(20) 4.4	(12) 3.1							
1.8	1.7	.8							
.3	.4	.2	Fixed/Worth					.2	.2
.7	.8	.5						.5	.4
1.1	1.1	1.0						1.0	1.8
.6	.9	.6	Debt/Worth					.5	.4
1.6	1.5	1.3						1.0	1.3
8.5	2.8	3.3						3.4	2.6
62.0	65.5	38.3	% Profit Before Taxes/Tangible Net Worth					59.0	42.8
(39) 23.8	(41) 20.8	(37) 14.0						(12) 28.4	(11) 7.5
14.2	1.6	-.4						-.5	-7.8
16.7	19.3	16.9	% Profit Before Taxes/Total Assets					28.3	14.3
10.4	10.8	5.6						14.2	3.1
5.4	.8	-4.5						-2.4	-6.9
19.4	11.5	24.0	Sales/Net Fixed Assets					93.4	20.9
9.1	8.1	6.9						7.8	6.3
4.0	3.4	3.6						5.3	2.2
2.3	2.2	2.0	Sales/Total Assets					2.1	2.0
1.9	2.0	1.3						1.7	.8
1.5	1.4	.9						1.3	.6
1.2	1.4	1.6	% Depr., Dep., Amort./Sales					1.3	1.6
(39) 1.9	(41) 2.0	(34) 2.9						(11) 2.3	(10) 3.0
2.9	3.9	5.7						3.0	6.6
			% Officers', Directors' Owners' Comp/Sales						
1206163M	1425466M	1153264M	Net Sales ($)	1047M	3569M	11523M	66722M	210847M	859556M
811377M	844326M	1106907M	Total Assets ($)	1156M	3162M	10361M	52357M	124379M	915492M

© RMA 2010

M = $ thousand   MM = $ million

See Pages 9 through 22 for Explanation of Ratios and Data

Current Data Sorted by Assets · Comparative Historical Data

0-500M	500M-2MM	2-10MM	10-50MM	50-100MM	100-250MM	Type of Statement	4/1/05-3/31/06 ALL	4/1/06-3/31/07 ALL
	1	2	15	6	2	Unqualified	28	21
	1	14	9	1		Reviewed	15	21
1	6	6	1			Compiled	12	10
2	7	4	1			Tax Returns	5	8
1	7	13	12	3	2	Other	33	23
	34 (4/1-9/30/09)		83 (10/1/09-3/31/10)					
4	22	39	38	10	4	NUMBER OF STATEMENTS	93	83
%	%	%	%	%	%	**ASSETS**	%	%
	9.8	11.4	7.6	21.1		Cash & Equivalents	8.3	6.9
	28.8	25.4	26.7	22.1		Trade Receivables (net)	28.7	27.3
	33.6	35.1	29.3	19.3		Inventory	33.4	33.8
	1.5	3.7	3.6	5.6		All Other Current	2.4	2.4
	73.7	75.7	67.3	68.1		Total Current	72.8	70.5
	16.8	16.3	25.3	16.3		Fixed Assets (net)	19.0	19.4
	3.6	2.0	2.9	9.0		Intangibles (net)	3.3	4.2
	5.9	5.9	4.5	6.5		All Other Non-Current	4.9	5.9
	100.0	100.0	100.0	100.0		Total	100.0	100.0
						LIABILITIES		
	10.6	7.7	4.8	2.1		Notes Payable-Short Term	13.7	7.5
	4.0	3.4	3.0	.5		Cur. Mat.-L.T.D.	2.3	2.4
	15.9	16.2	9.7	6.3		Trade Payables	15.3	14.3
	.2	.4	.5	.3		Income Taxes Payable	.3	.5
	9.1	16.7	15.2	16.6		All Other Current	11.8	12.0
	39.9	44.4	33.3	25.7		Total Current	43.5	36.8
	10.1	10.6	11.2	8.9		Long-Term Debt	13.8	11.3
	.3	.8	1.3	.6		Deferred Taxes	.6	.5
	5.8	1.8	2.1	3.9		All Other Non-Current	7.2	6.3
	43.8	42.4	52.0	60.9		Net Worth	34.9	45.1
	100.0	100.0	100.0	100.0		Total Liabilties & Net Worth	100.0	100.0
						INCOME DATA		
	100.0	100.0	100.0	100.0		Net Sales	100.0	100.0
	44.1	33.9	30.3	34.4		Gross Profit	32.9	32.3
	39.6	27.7	25.4	24.0		Operating Expenses	27.9	24.6
	4.5	6.2	4.9	10.5		Operating Profit	5.0	7.6
	1.6	.7	.7	-.2		All Other Expenses (net)	1.1	.6
	2.9	5.6	4.2	10.6		Profit Before Taxes	3.9	7.0
						RATIOS		
	4.2	5.3	3.4	8.8		Current	2.6	3.0
	1.9	1.9	2.1	2.8			1.8	2.1
	1.2	1.4	1.5	1.5			1.2	1.5
	2.0	2.5	2.1	5.5		Quick	1.4	1.6
	.8	.8	1.1	1.5			.8	.9
	.5	.6	.6	1.0			.6	.7
22 16.9	33 11.2	42 8.7	40 9.1			Sales/Receivables	42 8.7	38 9.6
41 9.0	40 9.0	52 7.0	57 6.4				53 6.9	47 7.7
63 5.8	59 6.2	71 5.2	87 4.2				65 5.6	61 6.0
22 16.3	53 6.9	46 7.9	49 7.5			Cost of Sales/Inventory	61 6.0	58 6.3
93 3.9	92 4.0	75 4.9	86 4.2				102 3.6	87 4.2
156 2.3	139 2.6	155 2.4	150 2.4				129 2.8	123 3.0
17 21.9	16 22.3	19 18.9	8 47.1			Cost of Sales/Payables	22 16.6	20 18.6
34 10.7	30 12.0	28 13.0	22 16.9				35 10.5	29 12.6
50 7.3	53 6.9	36 10.2	41 8.9				58 6.3	47 7.7
	3.2	2.9	2.9	1.4		Sales/Working Capital	4.3	3.8
	7.6	6.0	4.9	3.4			5.9	6.5
	18.7	12.4	11.9	6.9			16.8	10.6
	7.9	30.3	25.8			EBIT/Interest	11.5	36.3
	(18) 2.9	6.0	(36) 8.6				(82) 4.9	(79) 7.1
	-1.3	.8	1.6				1.3	2.7
		14.4	8.0			Net Profit + Depr., Dep., Amort./Cur. Mat. L/T/D	8.3	9.1
		(12) 3.2	(23) 3.1				(28) 4.7	(27) 5.1
		.7	1.2				1.3	1.6
	.1	.2	.2	.1		Fixed/Worth	.2	.2
	.5	.3	.5	.4			.5	.3
	15.9	.6	.9	.9			1.3	1.0
	.4	.4	.5	.1		Debt/Worth	.7	.6
	1.3	1.5	1.0	.7			1.6	1.2
	78.5	2.5	1.8	2.3			5.5	2.9
	42.6	38.7	24.5			% Profit Before Taxes/Tangible Net Worth	36.3	49.3
	(18) 6.0	(36) 14.1	15.9				(85) 19.4	(80) 27.8
	-2.7	4.2	4.4				9.2	15.6
	12.3	22.0	12.6	20.3		% Profit Before Taxes/Total Assets	16.2	21.6
	3.3	7.4	7.2	16.6			7.3	10.7
	-6.1	-1.1	2.3	9.6			1.4	6.2
	49.9	36.0	16.3	21.2		Sales/Net Fixed Assets	32.8	39.0
	22.5	17.7	7.6	11.5			11.3	12.3
	10.5	9.0	5.3	5.8			6.1	6.3
	3.0	2.7	2.1	1.7		Sales/Total Assets	2.3	2.5
	2.5	1.9	1.8	1.4			1.9	2.0
	1.8	1.6	1.2	.9			1.5	1.5
	.7	.6	.9			% Depr., Dep., Amort./Sales	.8	.7
	(17) 2.0	(34) 1.2	(35) 1.8				(82) 1.6	(72) 1.4
	3.4	2.0	3.2				2.7	2.2
	3.5	.8				% Officers', Directors' Owners' Comp/Sales	2.7	1.7
	(14) 8.3	(14) 2.8					(32) 3.9	(27) 3.5
	11.8	4.7					7.0	6.5
3288M	63213M	394583M	1380679M	989801M	801064M	Net Sales ($)	2759021M	2991531M
1106M	26055M	198073M	807257M	729212M	713438M	Total Assets ($)	1562015M	1595522M

Comparative Historical Data

Current Data Sorted by Sales

4/1/07-3/31/08 ALL	4/1/08-3/31/09 ALL	4/1/09-3/31/10 ALL	Type of Statement	0-1MM	34 (4/1-9/30/09) 1-3MM	3-5MM	83 (10/1/09-3/31/10) 5-10MM	10-25MM	25MM & OVER
25	26	26	Unqualified	1		1		5	19
23	24	25	Reviewed			1	5	11	8
17	13	14	Compiled	1	2	4	4	3	
13	10	14	Tax Returns	1	5	4		4	
31	35	38	Other	2	3	4	6	13	10
109	108	117	**NUMBER OF STATEMENTS**	5	10	14	15	36	37
%	%	%	**ASSETS**	%	%	%	%	%	%
9.2	8.9	10.2	Cash & Equivalents		5.0	12.7	10.5	11.9	9.9
28.2	25.1	25.5	Trade Receivables (net)		32.1	27.5	25.2	26.7	24.6
33.2	33.6	31.8	Inventory		39.5	29.0	33.1	30.0	30.0
2.7	3.5	3.4	All Other Current		.1	1.9	5.6	3.1	4.5
73.3	71.1	70.9	Total Current		76.8	71.2	74.4	71.6	68.9
18.8	20.0	20.1	Fixed Assets (net)		14.1	21.4	15.2	20.4	22.0
3.8	4.2	3.5	Intangibles (net)		4.2	.2	3.8	2.5	4.9
4.2	4.7	5.5	All Other Non-Current		4.9	7.2	6.6	5.4	4.2
100.0	100.0	100.0	Total		100.0	100.0	100.0	100.0	100.0
			LIABILITIES						
8.9	9.8	8.1	Notes Payable-Short Term		13.7	11.6	12.4	3.3	5.9
2.9	2.7	3.9	Cur. Mat.-L.T.D.		6.1	2.6	2.7	3.3	2.2
14.1	12.9	13.3	Trade Payables		19.6	16.8	11.6	14.7	9.4
.3	.3	.4	Income Taxes Payable		.3	.1	.3	.6	.4
9.6	11.0	14.7	All Other Current		16.8	3.2	5.6	21.5	16.0
35.7	36.8	40.4	Total Current		56.5	34.2	32.6	43.5	33.9
12.8	11.6	11.6	Long-Term Debt		13.7	9.1	11.4	9.7	10.4
.5	.5	.9	Deferred Taxes		.1	.9	.3	1.2	.9
3.8	5.5	3.0	All Other Non-Current		1.1	5.0	1.3	1.7	2.9
47.1	45.5	44.2	Net Worth		28.7	50.9	54.4	43.8	51.8
100.0	100.0	100.0	Total Liabilties & Net Worth		100.0	100.0	100.0	100.0	100.0
			INCOME DATA						
100.0	100.0	100.0	Net Sales		100.0	100.0	100.0	100.0	100.0
34.1	32.8	34.2	Gross Profit		43.0	44.6	39.7	30.8	28.1
25.5	26.2	29.2	Operating Expenses		39.4	40.6	34.9	24.4	22.9
8.6	6.6	5.1	Operating Profit		3.6	4.1	4.8	6.5	5.2
.6	.7	1.0	All Other Expenses (net)		.4	.7	1.1	.7	.4
7.9	6.0	4.1	Profit Before Taxes		3.2	3.4	3.8	5.8	4.7
			RATIOS						
3.1	3.2	4.0			3.6	4.2	5.3	4.2	3.6
2.0	2.0	2.0	Current		1.3	1.8	2.5	2.3	2.1
1.4	1.4	1.3			.8	1.3	1.4	1.3	1.4
1.7	1.6	2.0			1.1	3.3	3.0	2.5	1.9
.9	1.0	1.0	Quick		.8	1.1	1.4	1.2	1.1
.7	.6	.6			.4	.5	.6	.7	.6
38 9.6	32 11.4	33 11.2			26 14.1	22 16.9	36 10.0	33 11.1	38 9.6
49 7.4	46 7.9	47 7.7	Sales/Receivables		44 8.3	40 9.2	42 8.6	48 7.6	51 7.1
60 6.0	57 6.4	65 5.6			76 4.8	60 6.1	59 6.2	70 5.2	68 5.3
52 7.1	57 6.4	47 7.7			27 13.5	19 19.3	73 5.0	44 8.4	51 7.1
87 4.2	90 4.1	87 4.2	Cost of Sales/Inventory		108 3.4	78 4.7	133 2.7	68 5.4	80 4.5
140 2.6	139 2.6	146 2.5			286 1.3	107 3.4	144 2.5	132 2.8	158 2.3
20 18.5	18 20.0	17 21.7			21 17.1	16 23.1	16 22.3	17 22.0	18 20.5
32 11.2	29 12.7	28 12.9	Cost of Sales/Payables		45 8.1	26 14.0	36 10.1	29 12.8	23 15.6
48 7.6	43 8.4	47 7.8			58 6.3	45 8.1	47 7.7	49 7.5	40 9.2
3.5	3.7	3.0			2.8	5.7	2.9	2.5	3.0
6.0	6.9	5.9	Sales/Working Capital		13.7	7.7	5.0	5.6	4.9
11.2	13.5	13.5			-18.7	15.5	8.8	13.6	11.3
23.2	16.4	26.6			18.6	7.3	12.4	46.4	28.9
(101) 6.4	(94) 5.3	(108) 5.8	EBIT/Interest		1.2	(12) 2.1	(14) 1.8	(34) 10.3	(34) 8.6
2.7	1.7	1.0			-3.5	.6	-.6	1.9	1.7
10.0	10.3	9.4	Net Profit + Depr., Dep., Amort./Cur. Mat. L/T/D						10.4	8.2
(38) 3.2	(36) 3.1	(44) 2.8						(17) 5.2	(17) 2.7
1.5	1.2	.9						1.6	1.1
.1	.2	.2			.0	.2	.1	.2	.2
.3	.4	.4	Fixed/Worth		10.7	.3	.2	.3	.5
.9	1.1	1.0			-329.6	.8	.5	.7	.9
.6	.6	.4			.5	.3	.3	.4	.5
1.4	1.2	1.4	Debt/Worth		66.5	1.3	1.0	.9	1.3
2.9	3.3	2.5			-753.5	3.0	1.7	2.1	1.8
58.7	43.4	34.3	% Profit Before Taxes/Tangible Net Worth			21.3	13.9	38.7	24.7
(105) 34.8	(97) 21.8	(106) 15.7				5.0	(14) 7.8	(34) 22.0	(35) 16.1
14.4	7.2	3.6				-5.6	-4.0	6.7	6.7
24.1	17.4	15.3	% Profit Before Taxes/Total Assets		23.1	12.3	7.7	20.7	16.4
12.2	8.3	7.0			-1.6	2.1	1.7	9.7	7.8
5.2	2.5	.0			-16.6	-1.3	-4.1	1.6	3.2
48.9	34.5	25.2			346.6	35.8	32.9	35.4	15.4
12.9	13.8	13.0	Sales/Net Fixed Assets		33.2	21.1	14.5	15.9	9.1
5.8	6.5	5.6			8.8	8.9	7.7	6.8	5.1
2.7	2.6	2.5			3.0	3.0	2.6	2.7	2.1
2.1	2.0	1.8	Sales/Total Assets		2.0	2.7	1.6	1.9	1.6
1.5	1.4	1.3			1.7	1.9	1.2	1.3	1.1
.7	.8	.8				.6	.7	.8	1.2
(90) 1.3	(90) 1.6	(98) 1.6	% Depr., Dep., Amort./Sales			1.7	(12) 1.2	(33) 1.2	(30) 1.9
2.2	2.6	2.9				2.1	2.8	2.4	3.3
1.8	2.0	1.9	% Officers', Directors' Owners' Comp/Sales						.8
(39) 3.5	(30) 3.9	(36) 4.1						(10) 2.0	
8.2	8.7	8.4						4.0	
2843777M	3850714M	3632628M	Net Sales ($)	2431M	19963M	56672M	111844M	559178M	2882540M
1680249M	2306591M	2475141M	Total Assets ($)	3160M	9417M	25105M	72765M	329182M	2035512M

M = $ thousand   MM = $ million
See Pages 9 through 22 for Explanation of Ratios and Data

Current Data Sorted by Assets   Comparative Historical Data

0-500M	500M-2MM	2-10MM	10-50MM	50-100MM	100-250MM	Type of Statement	4/1/05-3/31/06 ALL	4/1/06-3/31/07 ALL
						Unqualified	8	6
						Reviewed	9	8
						Compiled	2	2
						Tax Returns	2	
						Other	9	11
1	1		1	1	1			
	2		3					
	2							
1	4	4	8	2				
4	8 (4/1-9/30/09)		23 (10/1/09-3/31/10)					
1	7	7	12	3	1	NUMBER OF STATEMENTS	30	27
%	%	%	%	%	%		%	%
						ASSETS		
			9.7			Cash & Equivalents	4.2	3.1
			22.8			Trade Receivables (net)	26.6	22.7
			29.8			Inventory	36.1	34.0
			6.9			All Other Current	1.2	4.1
			69.1			Total Current	68.1	63.9
			22.0			Fixed Assets (net)	23.7	22.9
			3.9			Intangibles (net)	2.4	9.1
			5.0			All Other Non-Current	5.8	4.2
			100.0			Total	100.0	100.0
						LIABILITIES		
			4.0			Notes Payable-Short Term	13.2	14.5
			4.9			Cur. Mat.-L.T.D.	5.1	4.6
			8.4			Trade Payables	14.9	12.7
			.0			Income Taxes Payable	.1	.2
			18.6			All Other Current	7.3	11.8
			35.8			Total Current	40.6	43.7
			10.9			Long-Term Debt	15.6	15.5
			1.8			Deferred Taxes	.8	1.4
			6.5			All Other Non-Current	10.8	13.0
			45.0			Net Worth	32.1	26.5
			100.0			Total Liabilities & Net Worth	100.0	100.0
						INCOME DATA		
			100.0			Net Sales	100.0	100.0
			25.5			Gross Profit	30.9	33.7
			19.6			Operating Expenses	26.1	23.7
			6.0			Operating Profit	4.8	10.0
			.9			All Other Expenses (net)	2.0	3.4
			5.0			Profit Before Taxes	2.8	6.6
						RATIOS		
			3.3				2.6	1.8
			2.2			Current	1.6	1.5
			1.3				1.2	1.3
			2.0				1.2	.9
			1.0			Quick	.8	.6
			.6				.5	.5
			29 12.4				44 8.3	37 9.9
			45 8.2			Sales/Receivables	52 7.0	46 7.9
			66 5.5				74 5.0	63 5.8
			45 8.1				80 4.6	72 5.0
			100 3.6			Cost of Sales/Inventory	108 3.4	93 3.9
			161 2.3				138 2.6	115 3.2
			13 28.5				33 11.0	23 16.0
			21 17.5			Cost of Sales/Payables	42 8.7	33 11.1
			33 11.2				67 5.4	49 7.5
			3.1				3.6	4.7
			4.7			Sales/Working Capital	6.9	8.2
			15.7				17.6	14.4
			17.6				6.6	8.4
			(10) 14.9			EBIT/Interest	(27) 2.8	(24) 3.7
			3.9				.3	1.7
						Net Profit + Depr., Dep.,	7.1	7.7
						Amort./Cur. Mat. L/T/D	(11) 2.7	(13) 4.6
							1.4	2.9
			.2				.3	.3
			.3			Fixed/Worth	1.0	1.4
			1.7				3.0	7.5
			.4				1.0	1.4
			1.9			Debt/Worth	2.5	3.6
			3.0				7.3	-44.9
			51.5				33.3	92.8
			17.1			% Profit Before Taxes/Tangible Net Worth	(27) 12.1	(20) 44.2
			5.3				-4.8	15.9
			14.4				11.1	18.3
			7.0			% Profit Before Taxes/Total Assets	3.5	9.5
			2.3				-.9	2.7
			12.9				21.7	21.9
			7.4			Sales/Net Fixed Assets	10.1	9.5
			3.8				3.9	5.8
			2.1				2.2	2.3
			1.5			Sales/Total Assets	1.7	1.9
			1.1				1.0	1.0
			.9				.8	.8
			(10) 1.7			% Depr., Dep., Amort./Sales	(27) 1.8	(24) 2.1
			2.8				3.1	3.1
						% Officers', Directors' Owners' Comp/Sales		
905M	16175M	77123M	446785M	239715M	67794M	Net Sales ($)	427514M	552890M
351M	6489M	39458M	266753M	207914M	186871M	Total Assets ($)	365883M	437737M

M = $ thousand   MM = $ million
See Pages 9 through 22 for Explanation of Ratios and Data

Comparative Historical Data   Current Data Sorted by Sales

					Type of Statement						
	9		7		4	Unqualified				1	3
	5		4		5	Reviewed			1	3	1
	4		3		2	Compiled	1	1				
	1		1		2	Tax Returns		1	1			
	12		15		18	Other	4	2	2	1	2	9
	4/1/07-		4/1/08-		4/1/09-			8 (4/1-9/30/09)			23 (10/1/09-3/31/10)	
	3/31/08		3/31/09		3/31/10		0-1MM	1-3MM	3-5MM	5-10MM	10-25MM	25MM & OVER
	ALL		ALL		ALL							
	31		30		31	**NUMBER OF STATEMENTS**	1	6	3	2	6	13
	%		%		%	**ASSETS**	%	%	%	%	%	%
	7.3		4.8		9.7	Cash & Equivalents						8.6
	22.5		23.6		22.9	Trade Receivables (net)						23.7
	30.0		33.7		29.7	Inventory						27.6
	1.6		3.4		4.8	All Other Current						7.6
	61.4		65.5		67.2	Total Current						67.5
	25.1		24.8		22.3	Fixed Assets (net)						21.0
	10.5		4.1		4.3	Intangibles (net)						2.7
	3.0		5.6		6.2	All Other Non-Current						8.8
	100.0		100.0		100.0	Total						100.0
						LIABILITIES						
	10.4		14.6		11.4	Notes Payable-Short Term						7.4
	4.0		3.4		3.8	Cur. Mat.-L.T.D.						4.8
	14.4		14.7		11.1	Trade Payables						7.8
	.2		.2		.1	Income Taxes Payable						.1
	11.9		9.1		12.0	All Other Current						17.2
	40.9		42.0		38.4	Total Current						37.4
	15.7		14.0		12.7	Long-Term Debt						5.7
	1.4		1.8		1.5	Deferred Taxes						3.1
	4.2		5.4		7.6	All Other Non-Current						5.4
	37.8		36.8		39.8	Net Worth						48.4
	100.0		100.0		100.0	Total Liabilties & Net Worth						100.0
						INCOME DATA						
	100.0		100.0		100.0	Net Sales						100.0
	33.5		31.6		35.0	Gross Profit						27.7
	25.2		23.9		28.6	Operating Expenses						21.6
	8.3		7.6		6.4	Operating Profit						6.1
	2.3		1.7		.6	All Other Expenses (net)						.7
	6.0		5.9		5.8	Profit Before Taxes						5.4
						RATIOS						
	2.4		2.5		3.4							3.8
	1.4		1.7		2.2	Current						1.6
	1.0		1.0		1.2							1.2
	1.3		1.2		1.7							2.2
	.7		.6		1.0	Quick						1.0
	.4		.4		.5							.5
34	10.7	37	9.8	35	10.6						37	9.9
50	7.3	49	7.5	46	8.0	Sales/Receivables					45	8.1
65	5.6	62	5.9	59	6.2						71	5.1
63	5.8	67	5.4	62	5.9						58	6.3
98	3.7	97	3.8	92	4.0	Cost of Sales/Inventory					110	3.3
144	2.5	128	2.8	141	2.6						154	2.4
31	11.7	21	17.0	20	18.5						14	26.5
47	7.7	37	9.8	25	14.4	Cost of Sales/Payables					21	17.4
59	6.1	60	6.1	49	7.5						42	8.6
	4.5		4.5		3.1							2.9
	8.1		8.1		5.3	Sales/Working Capital						4.1
	62.7		64.0		26.0							20.9
	9.3		14.0		19.1							29.4
(27)	3.7	(27)	4.6	(27)	5.4	EBIT/Interest					(11)	14.5
	1.1		1.5		3.1							4.0
	5.3		10.0									
(10)	3.1	(12)	2.3			Net Profit + Depr., Dep., Amort./Cur. Mat. L/T/D						
	-.4		1.7									
	.4		.3		.2							.2
	.7		.7		.4	Fixed/Worth						.3
	2.9		2.2		2.5							1.0
	.9		1.0		.5							.3
	2.6		2.2		1.7	Debt/Worth						1.7
	6.6		3.5		3.2							2.3
	77.7		44.7		34.3							21.1
(29)	21.4	(27)	20.3	(27)	14.1	% Profit Before Taxes/Tangible Net Worth						14.1
	3.9		9.2		4.9							5.0
	16.3		15.0		16.0							9.9
	8.8		10.7		6.3	% Profit Before Taxes/Total Assets						5.7
	1.1		2.1		2.9							2.3
	17.0		18.9		31.3							11.9
	8.0		8.9		8.9	Sales/Net Fixed Assets						8.5
	5.1		4.0		4.0							3.2
	2.1		2.1		2.2							1.8
	1.5		1.7		1.7	Sales/Total Assets						1.4
	1.1		1.3		1.1							1.0
	1.2		.9		1.1							.9
(28)	1.9	(26)	1.8	(24)	1.9	% Depr., Dep., Amort./Sales					(10)	2.0
	2.9		2.9		3.4							3.5
	1.5				.8							
(10)	4.5			(14)	2.1	% Officers', Directors' Owners' Comp/Sales						
	12.4				9.7							
	700916M		1022799M		848497M	Net Sales ($)	905M	12356M	11310M	16487M	110645M	696794M
	539778M		853880M		707836M	Total Assets ($)	351M	10061M	4531M	9566M	68283M	615044M

M = $ thousand   MM = $ million
See Pages 9 through 22 for Explanation of Ratios and Data

Current Data Sorted by Assets

Comparative Historical Data

	0-500M	500M-2MM	2-10MM	10-50MM	50-100MM	100-250MM	Type of Statement		4/1/05-3/31/06 ALL	4/1/06-3/31/07 ALL
		2	4	10	3	2	Unqualified		19	21
		4	24	14	1		Reviewed		38	41
	1	8	3	1			Compiled		16	20
		1	2				Tax Returns		9	6
		3	18	8	2	4	Other		34	37
		27 (4/1-9/30/09)		88 (10/1/09-3/31/10)						
NUMBER OF STATEMENTS	1	18	51	33	6	6	NUMBER OF STATEMENTS		116	125
	%	%	%	%	%	%	ASSETS		%	%
		10.3	8.7	16.9			Cash & Equivalents		10.6	9.5
		27.3	29.1	24.4			Trade Receivables (net)		34.7	32.3
		32.7	26.1	21.9			Inventory		24.4	26.8
		5.9	4.4	3.2			All Other Current		3.3	3.7
		76.1	68.3	66.4			Total Current		73.0	72.3
		15.6	21.1	21.2			Fixed Assets (net)		17.5	17.7
		4.8	3.8	4.5			Intangibles (net)		3.2	2.8
		3.4	6.7	7.9			All Other Non-Current		6.2	7.3
		100.0	100.0	100.0			Total		100.0	100.0
							LIABILITIES			
		23.1	11.1	7.0			Notes Payable-Short Term		11.1	9.9
		2.0	2.4	3.3			Cur. Mat.-L.T.D.		1.8	2.1
		14.0	15.0	9.8			Trade Payables		17.9	19.6
		.2	.4	.2			Income Taxes Payable		.5	.3
		14.3	17.1	13.4			All Other Current		14.4	19.4
		53.7	46.1	33.6			Total Current		45.7	51.4
		10.6	10.2	11.2			Long-Term Debt		9.6	12.3
		.6	.1	.3			Deferred Taxes		.3	.3
		3.9	3.2	7.2			All Other Non-Current		5.2	5.6
		31.3	40.4	47.7			Net Worth		39.2	30.3
		100.0	100.0	100.0			Total Liabilties & Net Worth		100.0	100.0
							INCOME DATA			
		100.0	100.0	100.0			Net Sales		100.0	100.0
		35.4	30.2	30.4			Gross Profit		30.9	29.9
		36.2	27.5	28.0			Operating Expenses		26.2	25.2
		-.7	2.7	2.5			Operating Profit		4.6	4.7
		.8	1.0	2.1			All Other Expenses (net)		.6	1.0
		-1.5	1.7	.4			Profit Before Taxes		4.1	3.7
							RATIOS			
		4.1	2.1	3.4			Current		2.5	2.1
		1.9	1.5	2.1					1.6	1.5
		1.0	1.2	1.4					1.3	1.1
		2.5	1.3	2.0			Quick		1.4	1.2
		.9	.8	1.1					1.0	.8
		.4	.6	.8					.7	.6
	25 14.6		35 10.4	41 8.8			Sales/Receivables		43 8.6	40 9.1
	38 9.5		51 7.1	48 7.6					56 6.5	51 7.2
	67 5.4		72 5.0	75 4.9					77 4.7	67 5.5
	20 18.0		33 11.2	41 8.8			Cost of Sales/Inventory		34 10.9	34 10.9
	59 6.2		62 5.9	62 5.9					60 6.1	58 6.3
	132 2.8		118 3.1	101 3.6					96 3.8	112 3.3
	12 30.6		14 25.3	16 23.3			Cost of Sales/Payables		24 15.2	26 13.8
	21 17.7		31 11.8	25 14.7					37 9.8	40 9.1
	35 10.4		61 5.9	44 8.4					59 6.1	56 6.5
		4.0	4.8	3.2			Sales/Working Capital		4.3	5.2
		6.6	9.8	5.2					7.8	9.5
		NM	22.9	9.8					18.0	48.8
		7.6	7.3	7.3			EBIT/Interest		15.6	17.2
	(16) 3.3		(48) 2.8	(27) 1.3				(103)	6.3 (113)	4.0
		-2.2	.9	-6.0					2.0	1.6
			3.0	4.5			Net Profit + Depr., Dep., Amort./Cur. Mat. L/T/D		13.8	9.3
		(14) 1.7		(11) .3				(39)	4.0 (37)	2.8
		1.1		-.6					1.8	1.7
		.1	.2	.2			Fixed/Worth		.2	.2
		.4	.4	.4					.5	.5
		1.9	1.4	1.1					.8	1.4
		.4	.7	.5			Debt/Worth		.7	1.0
		2.4	2.0	1.2					1.6	2.4
		20.4	3.6	2.4					3.8	7.3
		61.5	28.2	22.3			% Profit Before Taxes/Tangible Net Worth		41.0	47.2
	(15) 9.1		(47) 6.8	(31) 2.1				(107)	19.6 (108)	22.1
		-6.6	-1.5	-14.4					5.9	3.8
		8.3	8.3	13.0			% Profit Before Taxes/Total Assets		14.8	14.8
		4.7	2.2	1.4					6.8	6.8
		-7.6	-.6	-6.1					2.0	.9
		42.3	30.0	16.7			Sales/Net Fixed Assets		37.7	37.3
		22.1	11.2	9.5					16.7	15.1
		10.5	5.0	4.8					6.6	6.9
		3.5	2.6	2.1			Sales/Total Assets		2.8	2.7
		2.6	2.1	1.5					2.1	2.1
		1.9	1.3	1.1					1.6	1.7
		.5	.8	1.2			% Depr., Dep., Amort./Sales		.7	.7
	(15) 1.4		(42) 1.6	(30) 1.5				(98)	1.4 (114)	1.4
		3.5	3.2	2.1					2.5	2.1
			1.9				% Officers', Directors' Owners' Comp/Sales		2.2	2.2
		(12) 3.7						(38)	3.2 (32)	4.5
		9.7							4.8	9.6
	925M	73720M	488768M	1046877M	672579M	1368812M	Net Sales ($)		3225550M	3615137M
	342M	23613M	241350M	659759M	391024M	967818M	Total Assets ($)		2170228M	2155352M

M = $ thousand   MM = $ million
See Pages 9 through 22 for Explanation of Ratios and Data

Comparative Historical Data | Current Data Sorted by Sales

4/1/07-3/31/08 ALL	4/1/08-3/31/09 ALL	4/1/09-3/31/10 ALL	Type of Statement	0-1MM	1-3MM	3-5MM	5-10MM	10-25MM	25MM & OVER
26	23	21	Unqualified			1	4	4	12
27	39	43	Reviewed		2	5	11	20	5
15	17	13	Compiled	2	2	4	3	1	1
4	6	3	Tax Returns			2		1	
35	32	35	Other	1	5	3	7	8	11
				27 (4/1-9/30/09)		88 (10/1/09-3/31/10)			
107	117	115	NUMBER OF STATEMENTS	3	9	15	25	34	29
%	%	%	**ASSETS**	%	%	%	%	%	%
14.7	10.3	11.3	Cash & Equivalents			10.8	10.8	12.9	12.9
33.7	32.2	26.9	Trade Receivables (net)			29.1	27.3	26.9	26.1
22.7	26.5	24.9	Inventory			33.1	21.1	24.7	19.0
3.2	5.4	5.0	All Other Current			4.9	4.1	4.8	6.5
74.4	74.5	68.1	Total Current			77.8	63.3	69.2	64.5
16.7	15.9	20.0	Fixed Assets (net)			12.9	24.0	21.0	20.0
3.8	3.6	5.3	Intangibles (net)			4.8	4.0	1.8	9.8
5.1	6.0	6.6	All Other Non-Current			4.6	8.7	8.0	5.7
100.0	100.0	100.0	Total			100.0	100.0	100.0	100.0
			LIABILITIES						
8.8	11.0	11.1	Notes Payable-Short Term			24.0	9.4	9.2	4.8
2.1	2.6	2.6	Cur. Mat.-L.T.D.			1.4	2.6	2.9	3.2
17.1	16.7	13.2	Trade Payables			18.2	13.8	11.9	12.1
.7	.4	.3	Income Taxes Payable			.1	.4	.5	.2
17.7	18.9	15.6	All Other Current			8.8	14.6	17.6	15.6
46.5	49.6	42.8	Total Current			52.5	40.7	42.0	35.9
9.9	10.3	10.0	Long-Term Debt			10.2	11.5	10.4	6.8
.4	.4	.3	Deferred Taxes			.0	.3	.3	.3
5.5	5.2	6.0	All Other Non-Current			1.3	3.8	2.2	14.8
37.8	34.5	41.0	Net Worth			36.0	43.6	45.0	42.2
100.0	100.0	100.0	Total Liabilties & Net Worth			100.0	100.0	100.0	100.0
			INCOME DATA						
100.0	100.0	100.0	Net Sales			100.0	100.0	100.0	100.0
29.9	29.5	30.1	Gross Profit			36.7	30.0	28.4	25.9
23.9	24.5	27.8	Operating Expenses			35.7	25.8	26.6	21.8
6.0	5.0	2.3	Operating Profit			1.1	4.3	1.8	4.1
.8	.7	1.3	All Other Expenses (net)			1.9	1.0	1.0	1.8
5.2	4.3	1.0	Profit Before Taxes			-.8	3.3	.8	2.2
			RATIOS						
2.5	2.5	2.7				3.3	2.5	2.8	2.6
1.6	1.6	1.7	Current			1.9	1.6	1.6	1.9
1.2	1.1	1.2				1.2	1.3	1.2	1.4
1.8	1.4	1.6				2.1	1.8	1.7	1.8
1.0	.8	.9	Quick			.9	1.1	.8	1.0
.7	.5	.6				.5	.6	.6	.7
39 9.5	**37** 9.8	**35** 10.4				**38** 9.7	**29** 12.5	**32** 11.5	**42** 8.7
52 7.0	**52** 7.1	**49** 7.4	Sales/Receivables			**60** 6.1	**43** 8.4	**49** 7.5	**47** 7.8
68 5.4	**71** 5.1	**71** 5.1				**77** 4.8	**64** 5.7	**70** 5.2	**63** 5.8
23 15.8	**31** 11.9	**35** 10.4				**60** 6.1	**14** 26.3	**40** 9.1	**32** 11.4
56 6.5	**59** 6.2	**60** 6.1	Cost of Sales/Inventory			**115** 3.2	**52** 7.1	**56** 6.5	**52** 7.0
83 4.4	**109** 3.4	**105** 3.5				**133** 2.7	**87** 4.2	**74** 4.9	**78** 4.7
22 16.8	**20** 17.9	**17** 22.0				**21** 17.7	**9** 42.1	**14** 25.3	**20** 18.2
35 10.3	**35** 10.5	**30** 12.2	Cost of Sales/Payables			**31** 11.8	**28** 13.0	**22** 16.7	**33** 11.2
60 6.1	**58** 6.2	**52** 7.1				**78** 4.7	**52** 7.1	**50** 7.3	**44** 8.3
4.4	4.3	4.1				3.9	5.5	3.2	4.2
7.6	7.4	6.9	Sales/Working Capital			5.0	8.7	11.2	5.8
20.9	29.4	20.9				27.1	14.5	21.8	14.9
24.8	22.8	8.0				7.5	7.4	6.6	31.0
(86) 7.3	(97) 5.1	(103) 2.6	EBIT/Interest			(13) 4.5	(23) 2.9	(29) 1.6	(26) 4.1
1.8	1.3	-.7				1.3	.8	-3.9	-6.0
18.0	9.9	3.8						2.4	7.4
(26) 6.7	(36) 4.2	(34) 1.4	Net Profit + Depr., Dep., Amort./Cur. Mat. L/T/D					(12) 1.0	(11) 2.5
2.1	1.9	.2						-.5	.3
.2	.1	.2				.1	.2	.2	.2
.4	.4	.5	Fixed/Worth			.2	.5	.4	.7
1.4	1.0	1.3				2.3	1.8	1.1	2.3
.6	.8	.6				.3	.6	.5	.5
1.9	2.2	1.9	Debt/Worth			1.1	1.2	1.7	1.9
5.5	6.5	4.1				24.7	4.0	2.7	6.6
63.3	49.5	29.9				27.8	43.6	21.1	33.8
(93) 23.0	(100) 21.2	(104) 8.9	% Profit Before Taxes/Tangible Net Worth			(12) 7.5	(23) 9.3	5.1	(25) 13.9
5.3	5.0	-3.4				3.2	-1.8	-13.2	-11.4
20.2	16.5	10.6				7.1	10.1	12.7	15.5
9.0	7.7	2.2	% Profit Before Taxes/Total Assets			2.0	2.7	1.9	1.8
1.2	.9	-1.7				.6	-.8	-4.2	-1.8
32.3	36.6	26.3				54.4	32.4	25.9	21.2
15.7	17.8	12.0	Sales/Net Fixed Assets			26.5	11.2	9.3	12.1
9.1	9.0	5.7				13.3	3.9	5.3	6.0
2.7	2.7	2.5				2.7	3.0	2.6	2.2
2.1	2.1	1.9	Sales/Total Assets			2.3	2.2	1.9	1.7
1.6	1.5	1.3				1.2	1.4	1.3	1.5
.6	.8	.9				.5	1.0	.8	1.1
(96) 1.4	(106) 1.2	(98) 1.6	% Depr., Dep., Amort./Sales			(10) .7	(22) 1.8	(31) 1.2	(25) 1.8
2.1	2.3	2.8				2.9	3.5	2.0	2.7
2.1	2.2	2.0							
(33) 4.2	(25) 3.4	(23) 4.1	% Officers', Directors' Owners' Comp/Sales						
6.9	6.3	6.1							
4585537M	4516392M	3651681M	Net Sales ($)	2549M	20697M	61543M	170105M	573504M	2823283M
2567486M	2479482M	2283906M	Total Assets ($)	2090M	17035M	38118M	98235M	338494M	1789934M

M = $ thousand MM = $ million

See Pages 9 through 22 for Explanation of Ratios and Data

Current Data Sorted by Assets **Comparative Historical Data**

Type of Statement

	0-500M	500M-2MM	2-10MM	10-50MM	50-100MM	100-250MM		4/1/05-3/31/06 ALL	4/1/06-3/31/07 ALL
Unqualified			1	1		3		7	7
Reviewed		1	4	3				7	14
Compiled		3	5					6	9
Tax Returns	1	2						2	7
Other	3	5	8			1		8	11
		7 (4/1-9/30/09)		34 (10/1/09-3/31/10)					
NUMBER OF STATEMENTS	1	9	15	12		4		30	48

0-500M %	500M-2MM %	2-10MM %	10-50MM %	50-100MM %	100-250MM %		4/1/05-3/31/06 ALL %	4/1/06-3/31/07 ALL %
						ASSETS		
		15.1	13.8			Cash & Equivalents	9.2	8.3
		21.3	25.6			Trade Receivables (net)	35.0	32.8
		30.9	32.6			Inventory	27.2	28.1
		3.5	6.6	D A T A		All Other Current	6.7	6.6
		70.7	78.7			Total Current	78.0	75.8
		17.1	16.1	N O T		Fixed Assets (net)	13.7	18.1
		2.0	1.2			Intangibles (net)	3.5	2.2
		10.2	4.0	A V A I L A B L E		All Other Non-Current	4.8	3.9
		100.0	100.0			Total	100.0	100.0
						LIABILITIES		
		11.0	10.3			Notes Payable-Short Term	8.5	8.9
		2.1	1.6			Cur. Mat.-L.T.D.	3.5	2.4
		7.9	11.0			Trade Payables	17.7	18.2
		.0	.0			Income Taxes Payable	.8	.6
		15.6	16.6			All Other Current	15.1	16.0
		36.6	39.4			Total Current	45.7	46.1
		7.8	7.7			Long-Term Debt	9.5	11.8
		.7	.9			Deferred Taxes	.2	.1
		2.4	3.9			All Other Non-Current	6.0	5.0
		52.5	48.1			Net Worth	38.6	37.0
		100.0	100.0			Total Liabilties & Net Worth	100.0	100.0
						INCOME DATA		
		100.0	100.0			Net Sales	100.0	100.0
		32.9	23.0			Gross Profit	27.1	31.0
		29.5	16.5			Operating Expenses	22.6	22.6
		3.4	6.5			Operating Profit	4.5	8.4
		.4	.7			All Other Expenses (net)	.6	1.2
		3.0	5.8			Profit Before Taxes	3.8	7.3
						RATIOS		
		4.8	5.1			Current	2.8	2.4
		2.5	1.8				1.8	1.7
		1.2	1.3				1.3	1.2
		2.9	2.7			Quick	1.8	1.3
		.9	1.0				1.0	.9
		.4	.5				.7	.6
	28 12.9	35 10.3				Sales/Receivables	46 7.9	38 9.7
	35 10.4	48 7.5					59 6.1	56 6.5
	49 7.4	61 6.0					71 5.2	69 5.3
	25 14.6	43 8.6				Cost of Sales/Inventory	29 12.7	27 13.5
	97 3.7	76 4.8					68 5.4	61 6.0
	185 2.0	133 2.7					97 3.8	87 4.2
	11 34.7	15 23.8				Cost of Sales/Payables	22 16.3	24 15.3
	21 17.0	25 14.5					34 10.8	34 10.9
	33 10.9	43 8.4					53 6.8	50 7.4
		2.4	3.1			Sales/Working Capital	4.3	4.1
		6.1	5.9				7.2	6.8
		21.2	9.7				18.2	19.7
		23.5				EBIT/Interest	(27) 23.6	(42) 22.0
	(14) 4.3						6.9	5.7
		1.3					1.8	3.2
						Net Profit + Depr., Dep., Amort./Cur. Mat. L/T/D	(11) 24.8	37.4
								3.8
		.1	.1			Fixed/Worth	.2	.1
		.4	.5				.3	.3
		1.0	.8				1.0	1.3
		.2	.3			Debt/Worth	.6	.8
		.7	1.9				1.9	2.0
		3.5	2.8				4.7	4.1
		39.4	40.9			% Profit Before Taxes/Tangible Net Worth	(29) 38.9	(43) 58.2
	(14) 10.8	22.1					15.2	30.1
		1.7	2.9				4.7	11.6
		10.6	20.0			% Profit Before Taxes/Total Assets	12.5	20.0
		4.2	8.4				5.1	11.1
		1.2	1.0				1.0	4.6
		24.1	77.8			Sales/Net Fixed Assets	48.6	50.7
		15.8	14.4				18.7	22.6
		5.2	6.8				9.0	10.7
		2.5	2.3			Sales/Total Assets	2.9	3.0
		1.9	2.1				2.3	2.4
		1.4	1.4				1.6	1.7
		1.1	.6			% Depr., Dep., Amort./Sales	.6	(42) .7
	(13) 1.6	(10) 1.3					1.1	.9
		3.3	2.3				2.0	1.7
						% Officers', Directors' Owners' Comp/Sales	(14) 1.8	(22) 2.2
							4.1	4.4
							7.5	6.0
2341M	41688M	150557M	513321M		694456M	Net Sales ($)	545370M	1480020M
169M	11363M	76006M	255565M		673102M	Total Assets ($)	297320M	823648M

M = $ thousand   MM = $ million
See Pages 9 through 22 for Explanation of Ratios and Data

Comparative Historical Data | Current Data Sorted by Sales

8	7	5	Type of Statement						
				0-1MM	1-3MM	3-5MM	5-10MM	10-25MM	25MM & OVER
8	7	5	Unqualified					1	4
9	11	8	Reviewed		1	2	2	5	2
11	8	8	Compiled		1	2	1	3	
2	3	3	Tax Returns			1	3		
16	15	17	Other	1		2	1	1	8
4/1/07-3/31/08 ALL	4/1/08-3/31/09 ALL	4/1/09-3/31/10 ALL				7 (4/1-9/30/09)		34 (10/1/09-3/31/10)	
46	44	41	NUMBER OF STATEMENTS	1	2	7	7	10	14
%	%	%		%	%	%	%	%	%
			ASSETS						
10.9	9.4	16.0	Cash & Equivalents					18.2	13.0
31.8	30.7	23.4	Trade Receivables (net)					28.1	22.4
27.8	28.6	27.9	Inventory					26.9	27.8
5.2	6.2	4.9	All Other Current					5.5	7.0
75.7	74.9	72.2	Total Current					78.7	70.3
16.2	17.4	17.5	Fixed Assets (net)					16.8	18.4
2.9	3.4	3.8	Intangibles (net)					2.3	8.4
5.2	4.3	6.6	All Other Non-Current					2.3	3.0
100.0	100.0	100.0	Total					100.0	100.0
			LIABILITIES						
7.3	10.3	14.3	Notes Payable-Short Term					9.8	8.2
1.7	1.9	2.1	Cur. Mat.-L.T.D.					3.1	1.5
17.5	16.4	10.0	Trade Payables					9.0	9.6
.3	.0	.0	Income Taxes Payable					.0	.0
17.1	17.1	14.5	All Other Current					15.4	13.8
43.8	45.7	40.9	Total Current					37.3	33.2
9.2	10.2	9.1	Long-Term Debt					9.8	11.0
.1	.2	.7	Deferred Taxes					1.0	1.2
4.1	2.6	2.3	All Other Non-Current					.9	3.6
42.8	41.3	47.0	Net Worth					50.9	51.0
100.0	100.0	100.0	Total Liabilities & Net Worth					100.0	100.0
			INCOME DATA						
100.0	100.0	100.0	Net Sales					100.0	100.0
30.0	29.5	29.1	Gross Profit					32.2	24.0
22.5	23.0	24.9	Operating Expenses					25.8	16.7
7.5	6.5	4.2	Operating Profit					6.3	7.3
.5	.7	2.1	All Other Expenses (net)					.9	4.9
7.0	5.8	2.1	Profit Before Taxes					5.4	2.5
			RATIOS						
2.6 / 1.6 / 1.3	3.0 / 1.6 / 1.2	4.7 / 2.1 / 1.3	Current					5.8 / 2.1 / 1.2	4.8 / 2.0 / 1.3
1.7 / 1.0 / .7	1.4 / .8 / .4	2.5 / 1.1 / .6	Quick					3.3 / 1.4 / .7	2.7 / 1.1 / .5
36 10.2 / 46 7.9 / 62 5.8	33 11.2 / 52 7.0 / 61 6.0	28 12.8 / 41 8.9 / 56 6.6	Sales/Receivables					26 14.0 / 41 8.8 / 53 6.8	35 10.5 / 48 7.6 / 62 5.9
34 10.7 / 61 6.0 / 106 3.4	17 21.7 / 68 5.4 / 118 3.1	26 14.3 / 60 6.1 / 129 2.8	Cost of Sales/Inventory					23 16.0 / 40 9.2 / 105 3.5	41 8.9 / 64 5.7 / 110 3.3
21 17.6 / 30 12.2 / 45 8.2	19 19.0 / 33 11.2 / 55 6.6	11 32.1 / 22 16.8 / 38 9.6	Cost of Sales/Payables					9 39.2 / 15 23.9 / 27 13.3	16 23.3 / 29 12.7 / 43 8.5
4.4 / 7.7 / 16.3	4.3 / 9.0 / 22.0	3.0 / 6.1 / 18.8	Sales/Working Capital					3.1 / 6.2 / 22.8	3.1 / 5.9 / 12.2
31.3 / (42) 7.0 / 3.5	34.9 / (40) 9.6 / 3.9	13.9 / (34) 4.2 / 1.0	EBIT/Interest						43.3 / (10) 6.3 / .7
96.3 / (13) 9.8 / 3.1		44.8 / (12) 10.4 / 1.6	Net Profit + Depr., Dep., Amort./Cur. Mat. L/T/D						
.1 / .2 / .5	.2 / .3 / .8	.1 / .4 / 1.0	Fixed/Worth					.1 / .5 / 1.0	.1 / .4 / 2.1
.7 / 1.7 / 2.9	.6 / 1.5 / 4.1	.3 / 1.2 / 3.2	Debt/Worth					.2 / 1.6 / 4.4	.3 / 1.9 / 3.1
56.0 / (44) 40.9 / 19.6	58.8 / (41) 35.6 / 11.8	34.1 / (38) 10.8 / .9	% Profit Before Taxes/Tangible Net Worth					52.5 / 20.6 / 9.5	38.5 / (13) 24.7 / 7.0
20.0 / 12.9 / 6.5	21.0 / 11.6 / 4.1	12.7 / 5.8 / .0	% Profit Before Taxes/Total Assets					20.4 / 7.0 / 2.6	15.2 / 8.4 / 1.4
40.6 / 22.4 / 12.8	34.1 / 21.6 / 8.1	38.2 / 16.7 / 7.2	Sales/Net Fixed Assets					28.4 / 16.1 / 9.4	76.6 / 13.1 / 7.0
2.8 / 2.4 / 1.9	3.0 / 2.5 / 1.7	3.2 / 2.1 / 1.4	Sales/Total Assets					3.0 / 2.4 / 2.0	2.2 / 1.5 / 1.4
.5 / (38) 1.0 / 1.5	.5 / (40) 1.0 / 1.5	.9 / (34) 1.5 / 2.5	% Depr., Dep., Amort./Sales						.7 / (11) 1.5 / 1.9
1.7 / (15) 3.8 / 5.6	1.5 / (14) 2.6 / 5.7	1.9 / (14) 3.1 / 8.0	% Officers', Directors' Owners' Comp/Sales						
1255829M	1535551M	1402363M	Net Sales ($)	652M	4262M	29014M	44099M	143961M	1180375M
744796M	805443M	1016205M	Total Assets ($)	537M	3165M	22984M	21166M	61396M	906957M

M = $ thousand   MM = $ million
See Pages 9 through 22 for Explanation of Ratios and Data

MANUFACTURING—Industrial Truck, Tractor, Trailer, and Stacker Machinery Manufacturing   NAICS 333924

Current Data Sorted by Assets — **Comparative Historical Data**

Type of Statement

Type of Statement	0-500M	500M-2MM	2-10MM	10-50MM	50-100MM	100-250MM	4/1/05-3/31/06 ALL	4/1/06-3/31/07 ALL
Unqualified			1	4	3	1	11	17
Reviewed		1	5	3	1		8	10
Compiled		3	2	1			8	10
Tax Returns		3	2	1			8	8
Other		3	14	9		2	22	19
		14 (4/1-9/30/09)		45 (10/1/09-3/31/10)				
NUMBER OF STATEMENTS		10	24	18	4	3	57	64

(0-500M column: DATA NOT AVAILABLE)

Assets / Liabilities / Income Data / Ratios

500M-2MM %	2-10MM %	10-50MM %	Item	4/1/05-3/31/06 ALL %	4/1/06-3/31/07 ALL %
			ASSETS		
10.0	4.8	9.1	Cash & Equivalents	6.3	5.6
19.7	20.2	15.8	Trade Receivables (net)	25.0	22.8
40.0	37.1	29.6	Inventory	32.8	34.8
2.0	4.3	5.2	All Other Current	1.6	4.3
71.7	66.4	59.8	Total Current	65.8	67.5
21.7	23.3	30.1	Fixed Assets (net)	23.0	22.8
1.0	8.4	3.0	Intangibles (net)	3.8	3.1
5.6	1.8	7.1	All Other Non-Current	7.4	6.7
100.0	100.0	100.0	Total	100.0	100.0
			LIABILITIES		
6.9	13.1	9.1	Notes Payable-Short Term	16.1	14.4
6.7	5.1	3.3	Cur. Mat.-L.T.D.	3.8	4.5
8.2	11.0	9.1	Trade Payables	17.2	14.3
.5	.0	.2	Income Taxes Payable	.3	.4
10.5	9.7	18.5	All Other Current	10.4	16.7
32.9	38.9	40.3	Total Current	47.7	50.3
27.8	15.1	13.3	Long-Term Debt	15.2	17.3
.0	.2	.7	Deferred Taxes	.6	.4
6.7	3.4	8.9	All Other Non-Current	5.2	4.4
32.7	42.4	36.8	Net Worth	31.4	27.6
100.0	100.0	100.0	Total Liabilities & Net Worth	100.0	100.0
			INCOME DATA		
100.0	100.0	100.0	Net Sales	100.0	100.0
26.1	24.1	25.4	Gross Profit	23.6	24.0
24.5	25.6	24.0	Operating Expenses	18.9	18.8
1.7	-1.6	1.4	Operating Profit	4.7	5.2
.5	1.2	2.9	All Other Expenses (net)	1.6	1.2
1.1	-2.8	-1.4	Profit Before Taxes	3.1	4.0
			RATIOS		
4.7	3.0	2.3	Current	1.7	2.3
1.8	1.8	1.7		1.3	1.3
1.3	1.2	1.0		1.0	.9
2.5	1.1	1.2	Quick	.8	1.2
.7	.6	.6		.6	.5
.3	.4	.3		.4	.4
8 45.6	24 15.3	15 23.9	Sales/Receivables	25 14.8	24 15.5
29 12.5	38 9.6	35 10.6		35 10.5	37 9.9
34 10.6	60 6.1	57 6.4		47 7.7	49 7.4
38 9.5	65 5.6	46 8.0	Cost of Sales/Inventory	31 11.8	43 8.5
104 3.5	95 3.8	68 5.4		61 6.0	70 5.2
158 2.3	134 2.7	174 2.1		81 4.5	127 2.9
8 43.7	14 25.8	11 32.9	Cost of Sales/Payables	17 21.7	15 23.8
14 26.9	25 14.8	31 11.7		27 13.4	27 13.6
23 16.1	46 8.0	36 10.1		39 9.3	40 9.0
2.8	4.1	3.0	Sales/Working Capital	8.3	6.5
9.5	7.9	8.6		16.8	15.3
NM	20.3	NM		787.2	-79.9
	3.6	9.8	EBIT/Interest	9.4	7.0
	(23) 1.4	(17) 2.0		(54) 3.1	(59) 2.9
	-3.1	-2.2		1.3	1.4
			Net Profit + Depr., Dep., Amort./Cur. Mat. L/T/D	7.8	3.5
				(15) 2.1	(26) 2.2
				1.7	1.2
.0	.3	.3	Fixed/Worth	.3	.3
.2	.8	.9		.7	.9
-2.0	2.5	1.6		3.5	4.2
.3	.6	.8	Debt/Worth	1.2	1.1
1.5	1.5	1.8		2.5	2.7
-6.0	8.2	5.1		9.4	13.4
	15.6	16.3	% Profit Before Taxes/Tangible Net Worth	50.7	46.7
	(21) 6.4	(17) 8.9		(51) 23.5	(54) 27.5
	-21.7	-30.5		11.3	14.8
15.5	5.8	6.2	% Profit Before Taxes/Total Assets	15.3	14.9
.6	1.3	1.7		7.9	6.6
-8.0	-10.0	-8.0		1.4	1.7
116.4	22.9	10.4	Sales/Net Fixed Assets	45.3	29.2
35.5	9.9	7.1		14.1	13.7
5.3	5.0	3.6		6.4	6.1
3.4	2.5	2.3	Sales/Total Assets	3.7	2.9
2.8	1.9	1.4		2.5	2.1
1.4	1.6	.9		1.6	1.5
	1.2	2.1	% Depr., Dep., Amort./Sales	.6	.6
	(22) 2.3	(15) 3.9		(50) 1.1	(60) 1.4
	3.1	5.4		2.4	3.1
			% Officers', Directors' Owners' Comp/Sales	2.1	1.5
				(18) 3.7	(21) 3.6
				5.1	5.3

Net Sales / Total Assets ($)

0-500M	500M-2MM	2-10MM	10-50MM	50-100MM	Item	4/1/05-3/31/06 ALL	4/1/06-3/31/07 ALL
31316M	259935M	717118M	461769M	470172M	Net Sales ($)	1834468M	2511599M
13124M	135759M	401260M	306614M	423364M	Total Assets ($)	895250M	1127744M

M = $ thousand   MM = $ million
See Pages 9 through 22 for Explanation of Ratios and Data

Comparative Historical Data | Current Data Sorted by Sales

				Type of Statement						
17		9	9	Unqualified				4	1	8
11		10	10	Reviewed			1	2	3	2
10		9	6	Compiled	1		2	1	1	
6		6	6	Tax Returns			2	1	2	
29		39	28	Other	1		1	6	6	9
4/1/07-3/31/08 ALL		4/1/08-3/31/09 ALL	4/1/09-3/31/10 ALL		14 (4/1-9/30/09)			45 (10/1/09-3/31/10)		
					0-1MM	1-3MM	3-5MM	5-10MM	10-25MM	25MM & OVER
73		73	59	NUMBER OF STATEMENTS	1	4	6	13	16	19
%		%	%	ASSETS	%	%	%	%	%	%
7.1		5.9	7.8	Cash & Equivalents				3.2	4.0	10.7
24.3		20.4	18.5	Trade Receivables (net)				21.0	16.8	18.7
35.2		38.4	33.9	Inventory				41.6	36.4	24.7
3.5		2.5	3.8	All Other Current				.7	4.0	6.6
70.1		67.1	64.0	Total Current				66.5	61.1	60.8
23.2		20.6	25.1	Fixed Assets (net)				18.4	34.0	24.7
3.7		7.7	6.2	Intangibles (net)				13.7	3.3	6.0
3.0		4.5	4.7	All Other Non-Current				1.5	1.5	8.5
100.0		100.0	100.0	Total				100.0	100.0	100.0
				LIABILITIES						
14.2		13.8	9.7	Notes Payable-Short Term				10.6	15.6	6.0
3.9		4.8	4.4	Cur. Mat.-L.T.D.				5.2	5.4	1.8
15.5		12.2	9.7	Trade Payables				11.5	5.4	1.8
.4		.3	.3	Income Taxes Payable				.1	.2	11.1
9.8		15.6	12.2	All Other Current				18.1	8.4	.4
43.9		46.8	36.3	Total Current				45.5	8.7	13.5
17.3		15.8	16.7	Long-Term Debt				17.5	38.2	32.7
.3		.6	.4	Deferred Taxes				.4	15.5	11.6
4.3		4.1	5.8	All Other Non-Current				7.6	.6	.5
34.2		32.6	40.7	Net Worth				29.0	2.1	6.0
100.0		100.0	100.0	Total Liabilties & Net Worth				100.0	43.6	49.3
				INCOME DATA					100.0	100.0
100.0		100.0	100.0	Net Sales				100.0	100.0	100.0
24.9		23.6	23.8	Gross Profit				22.0	29.9	19.9
18.9		21.9	23.7	Operating Expenses				26.8	28.7	17.4
6.0		1.6	.2	Operating Profit				-4.8	1.3	2.5
1.0		1.2	1.5	All Other Expenses (net)				1.5	1.5	1.9
5.0		.4	-1.3	Profit Before Taxes				-6.2	-.2	.6
				RATIOS						
2.4		2.1	3.1					3.1	2.1	3.7
1.5		1.4	1.8	Current				1.4	1.8	2.0
1.1		1.1	1.2					.9	1.2	1.2
1.1		.9	1.5					1.0	.7	2.4
.6		.5	.7	Quick				.5	.6	.8
.4		.3	.4					.2	.3	.5
24	15.2	18	20.1	21	17.0		Sales/Receivables	25	14.5	16	22.8	25	14.7
37	9.8	33	11.2	36	10.2			35	10.4	38	9.6	41	8.8
51	7.2	51	7.2	57	6.4			67	5.5	56	6.5	58	6.3
42	8.8	52	7.0	51	7.1		Cost of Sales/Inventory	82	4.5	61	6.0	36	10.0
66	5.5	82	4.5	90	4.1			95	3.8	101	3.6	66	5.5
97	3.8	141	2.6	144	2.5			133	2.7	177	2.1	100	3.6
13	28.4	10	35.9	13	28.5		Cost of Sales/Payables	14	27.0	14	25.8	17	22.0
27	13.4	26	13.8	23	16.2			26	14.2	27	13.6	23	16.2
42	8.6	41	9.0	36	10.1			49	7.5	36	10.1	33	11.1
	5.8		5.4		3.1		Sales/Working Capital		4.6		3.6		2.8
	10.3		10.9		7.4				12.9		8.9		6.5
	59.0		28.1		23.0				-103.1		22.8		25.9
	8.3		7.6		6.2		EBIT/Interest		2.6		5.6		27.0
(63)	3.2	(65)	1.7	(54)	1.7				-.8		1.9	(16)	3.2
	1.2		-2.7		-3.2				-3.8		-2.2		.1
	9.7		7.9		10.6		Net Profit + Depr., Dep., Amort./Cur. Mat. L/T/D						
(17)	3.2	(15)	5.6	(20)	3.4								
	.9		2.2		.3								
	.2		.2		.2		Fixed/Worth		.1		.4		.3
	.6		.7		.7				1.0		.9		.5
	3.7		5.8		1.8				-4.4		2.5		1.7
	.7		1.1		.6		Debt/Worth		1.1		.6		.3
	2.4		2.8		1.6				3.8		1.4		1.2
	11.2		143.8		9.3				-13.0		7.1		3.5
	52.1		44.7		17.2		% Profit Before Taxes/Tangible Net Worth				13.9		18.4
(60)	23.3	(56)	10.4	(51)	6.2						6.1	(18)	7.5
	9.4		-9.3		-11.0						-9.7		-6.1
	16.7		11.6		5.8		% Profit Before Taxes/Total Assets		3.8		6.8		7.6
	7.0		2.3		1.3				-7.4		2.3		2.0
	.8		-7.0		-8.0				-15.9		-6.3		-1.7
	50.2		39.0		19.9		Sales/Net Fixed Assets		43.6		11.3		11.1
	13.2		12.6		8.4				10.5		6.5		8.0
	6.8		6.6		4.4				4.2		2.2		4.4
	3.1		3.0		2.6		Sales/Total Assets		2.5		2.2		2.8
	2.4		2.2		1.8				1.7		1.7		2.0
	1.6		1.4		1.2				1.1		1.0		1.2
	.6		.8		1.2		% Depr., Dep., Amort./Sales		.5		2.1		1.2
(63)	1.1	(60)	1.3	(52)	2.7			(12)	2.4	(13)	2.9	(18)	2.8
	2.0		2.8		4.3				3.3		6.2		4.5
	.9		1.1		1.8		% Officers', Directors' Owners' Comp/Sales						
(20)	2.7	(14)	2.9	(14)	2.9								
	4.2		5.0		4.0								
2793468M		3165029M	1940310M	Net Sales ($)	749M	7989M	24028M	100575M	233835M	1573134M
1312721M		1566961M	1280121M	Total Assets ($)	592M	4760M	14181M	65459M	182647M	1012482M

© RMA 2010

M = $ thousand   MM = $ million
See Pages 9 through 22 for Explanation of Ratios and Data

MANUFACTURING—Welding and Soldering Equipment Manufacturing   NAICS 333992

							Comparative Historical Data	
Current Data Sorted by Assets								
						Type of Statement		
						Unqualified	2	5
						Reviewed	11	13
	2	3	4			Compiled	6	8
	2	5	4			Tax Returns	5	5
1	3	2 / 2 / 9	1 / 8		2	Other	26	14
	8 (4/1-9/30/09)		40 (10/1/09-3/31/10)				4/1/05-3/31/06	4/1/06-3/31/07
0-500M	500M-2MM	2-10MM	10-50MM	50-100MM	100-250MM		ALL	ALL
1	7	21	17		2	NUMBER OF STATEMENTS	50	45
%	%	%	%	%	%	**ASSETS**	%	%
		11.1	9.3			Cash & Equivalents	10.9	11.8
		23.0	24.8			Trade Receivables (net)	28.9	26.6
		30.9	23.5			Inventory	25.7	26.7
		4.3	5.7			All Other Current	3.4	2.7
		69.3	63.3			Total Current	68.9	67.8
		21.2	20.3			Fixed Assets (net)	23.1	21.3
		2.7	7.4			Intangibles (net)	1.0	2.2
		6.8	9.0			All Other Non-Current	7.0	8.6
		100.0	100.0			Total	100.0	100.0
						LIABILITIES		
		14.4	15.5			Notes Payable-Short Term	12.2	10.1
		5.7	3.8			Cur. Mat.-L.T.D.	2.3	2.6
		9.5	14.9			Trade Payables	13.3	13.0
		.1	.2			Income Taxes Payable	.3	.1
		8.6	9.3			All Other Current	14.2	13.2
		38.3	43.8			Total Current	42.3	39.0
		10.7	4.4			Long-Term Debt	11.8	10.5
		.4	1.1			Deferred Taxes	.4	.3
		7.3	14.2			All Other Non-Current	6.2	5.1
		43.3	36.5			Net Worth	39.3	45.1
		100.0	100.0			Total Liabilties & Net Worth	100.0	100.0
						INCOME DATA		
		100.0	100.0			Net Sales	100.0	100.0
		34.6	20.8			Gross Profit	31.5	35.6
		32.6	17.7			Operating Expenses	27.8	28.7
		2.0	3.1			Operating Profit	3.7	6.9
		1.8	1.7			All Other Expenses (net)	1.4	.6
		.2	1.5			Profit Before Taxes	2.3	6.3
						RATIOS		
		5.0	2.4			Current	3.0	2.7
		1.9	1.4				1.8	1.9
		1.1	.9				1.2	1.2
		2.9	1.3			Quick	2.0	1.6
		.8	.7				.8	1.1
		.4	.4				.6	.7
		39 9.4	52 7.0			Sales/Receivables	37 10.0	35 10.5
		52 7.1	64 5.7				49 7.4	47 7.8
		64 5.7	74 4.9				69 5.3	62 5.9
		62 5.9	34 10.8			Cost of Sales/Inventory	14 26.7	30 12.2
		118 3.1	62 5.8				78 4.7	66 5.5
		154 2.4	152 2.4				135 2.7	117 3.1
		13 28.8	15 24.7			Cost of Sales/Payables	17 21.0	21 17.3
		21 17.4	28 13.2				31 11.8	26 14.2
		44 8.3	46 7.9				46 7.9	46 8.0
		2.5	3.1			Sales/Working Capital	3.7	3.3
		5.9	8.6				9.3	6.5
		NM	NM				18.8	12.3
		7.2	6.2			EBIT/Interest	7.6	15.8
		(19) .0	(15) 1.6				(45) 3.1	(34) 4.8
		-4.6	.4				.4	2.1
						Net Profit + Depr., Dep., Amort./Cur. Mat. L/T/D	10.1	6.1
							(13) 2.4	(10) 3.2
							1.4	2.0
		.2	.3			Fixed/Worth	.2	.1
		.5	.6				.6	.4
		5.2	NM				1.1	.9
		.4	.7			Debt/Worth	.5	.6
		1.2	4.3				1.6	1.3
		11.3	NM				4.9	2.6
		19.3	30.8			% Profit Before Taxes/Tangible Net Worth	38.5	53.8
		(17) -4.8	(13) 17.2				(45) 17.5	(42) 30.2
		-32.9	-2.3				1.8	10.1
		13.3	9.3			% Profit Before Taxes/Total Assets	13.7	20.8
		-2.9	2.6				4.3	9.2
		-11.6	-.9				.4	3.6
		18.6	13.4			Sales/Net Fixed Assets	37.1	39.8
		10.6	7.5				12.0	11.6
		6.0	4.1				4.4	6.4
		2.2	1.5			Sales/Total Assets	2.7	2.8
		1.6	1.3				1.8	2.0
		1.2	1.0				1.2	1.4
		1.3	1.0			% Depr., Dep., Amort./Sales	.9	.7
		(19) 2.3	(15) 2.7				(40) 1.5	(35) 1.4
		4.0	4.0				2.9	2.6
						% Officers', Directors' Owners' Comp/Sales	1.3	1.7
							(17) 3.4	(14) 3.5
							4.9	13.1
1009M	21302M	150073M	546511M		768375M	Net Sales ($)	1234773M	910158M
485M	7200M	91034M	408239M		326348M	Total Assets ($)	681244M	609185M

(The 50-100MM column is marked vertically: "DATA NOT AVAILABLE")

M = $ thousand   MM = $ million
See Pages 9 through 22 for Explanation of Ratios and Data

Comparative Historical Data | Current Data Sorted by Sales

4/1/07-3/31/08 ALL	4/1/08-3/31/09 ALL	4/1/09-3/31/10 ALL	Type of Statement	0-1MM	1-3MM	3-5MM	5-10MM	10-25MM	25MM & OVER
2	5	7	Unqualified				2	3	2
17	14	9	Reviewed		1		4	3	2
7	4	5	Compiled			1	2		1
2	5	4	Tax Returns			1	3		
21	26	23	Other	1	4	3	3	5	7
					8 (4/1-9/30/09)			40 (10/1/09-3/31/10)	
49	54	48	NUMBER OF STATEMENTS	1	5	5	14	11	12
%	%	%	ASSETS	%	%	%	%	%	%
8.1	9.2	11.6	Cash & Equivalents				15.0	9.5	9.4
27.6	26.0	26.0	Trade Receivables (net)				21.7	22.1	33.4
28.6	28.7	24.2	Inventory				32.4	27.2	18.8
3.8	3.1	4.9	All Other Current				4.0	3.6	7.7
68.1	67.1	66.7	Total Current				73.2	62.4	69.2
23.9	18.6	21.5	Fixed Assets (net)				18.0	23.2	17.2
1.9	4.8	4.6	Intangibles (net)				1.1	8.2	4.4
6.0	9.5	7.3	All Other Non-Current				7.7	6.2	9.1
100.0	100.0	100.0	Total				100.0	100.0	100.0
			LIABILITIES						
13.5	13.4	13.0	Notes Payable-Short Term				13.9	17.2	12.6
2.8	2.2	4.7	Cur. Mat.-L.T.D.				6.9	5.4	1.8
14.5	13.5	14.1	Trade Payables				9.5	8.1	19.9
.1	.1	.4	Income Taxes Payable				.1	.1	.4
13.1	8.8	9.4	All Other Current				7.2	11.7	11.7
44.0	38.0	41.6	Total Current				37.5	42.5	46.4
11.9	7.6	11.4	Long-Term Debt				10.3	6.3	7.1
.5	.7	.7	Deferred Taxes				.6	1.3	.5
5.8	6.7	9.1	All Other Non-Current				8.9	11.8	10.8
37.8	47.0	37.3	Net Worth				42.7	38.0	35.2
100.0	100.0	100.0	Total Liabilities & Net Worth				100.0	100.0	100.0
			INCOME DATA						
100.0	100.0	100.0	Net Sales				100.0	100.0	100.0
31.3	28.7	28.8	Gross Profit				33.1	23.1	24.6
26.8	23.0	27.2	Operating Expenses				30.4	22.6	18.4
4.5	5.7	1.5	Operating Profit				2.8	.5	6.2
1.1	.7	1.5	All Other Expenses (net)				1.8	1.2	1.5
3.4	5.0	.0	Profit Before Taxes				.9	-.6	4.7
			RATIOS						
2.4	2.9	2.9	Current				7.3	2.6	2.4
1.7	1.9	1.7					1.9	1.4	1.5
1.1	1.3	1.1					1.4	.8	1.1
1.4	1.5	2.0	Quick				3.6	1.3	1.4
1.0	1.0	.8					.8	.6	.8
.4	.6	.4					.4	.3	.5
37 9.8	25 14.5	41 8.8	Sales/Receivables				30 12.3	44 8.2	59 6.2
49 7.5	41 8.8	62 5.9					45 8.2	64 5.7	68 5.4
73 5.0	56 6.5	67 5.4					61 6.0	66 5.5	75 4.8
41 8.8	31 11.9	28 12.9	Cost of Sales/Inventory				55 6.6	47 7.7	3 131.9
78 4.7	69 5.3	80 4.6					112 3.3	118 3.1	61 6.0
138 2.6	117 3.1	146 2.5					144 2.5	156 2.3	101 3.6
16 22.9	17 21.4	15 25.0	Cost of Sales/Payables				11 34.7	11 32.6	15 23.6
29 12.5	24 15.3	27 13.6					22 16.8	20 18.4	33 10.9
51 7.2	38 9.7	45 8.1					43 8.5	28 13.2	71 5.2
3.9	3.5	2.8	Sales/Working Capital				3.1	2.5	3.5
9.4	6.2	6.3					6.1	8.6	8.5
36.9	18.4	34.7					NM	-30.3	33.8
10.2	11.7	5.5	EBIT/Interest				12.6	3.6	11.7
(40) 5.1	(45) 5.3	(44) .5				(13)	.5	(10) .8	(10) 2.7
1.8	1.6	-6.9					-2.1	-18.9	.3
7.4	6.3	2.1	Net Profit + Depr., Dep., Amort./Cur. Mat. L/T/D						
(10) 3.5	(11) 4.1	(10) .2							
1.9	1.4	-2.3							
.2	.1	.2	Fixed/Worth				.2	.2	.3
.6	.4	.6					.4	3.0	.6
1.3	1.3	5.0					NM	5.4	NM
.8	.5	.6	Debt/Worth				.4	.7	.8
1.7	1.3	1.5					1.1	4.3	2.0
4.6	3.4	19.0					NM	23.4	NM
57.1	51.8	23.0	% Profit Before Taxes/Tangible Net Worth				25.4		
(45) 31.6	(49) 25.1	(39) .5				(11)	18.5		
6.8	6.5	-23.7					-43.2		
18.0	17.0	9.5	% Profit Before Taxes/Total Assets				14.5	7.5	18.0
7.8	8.1	-.9					-2.3	.1	6.4
1.9	2.1	-11.0					-11.3	-7.3	-.3
28.1	35.7	20.5	Sales/Net Fixed Assets				23.7	14.5	36.4
9.8	12.8	8.9					11.5	6.3	8.8
4.8	7.9	5.6					8.2	3.9	5.2
2.5	2.7	2.2	Sales/Total Assets				2.4	1.6	2.3
2.0	2.1	1.5					2.0	1.3	1.5
1.4	1.5	1.2					1.4	1.0	1.2
.5	.5	1.2	% Depr., Dep., Amort./Sales				1.6	.9	
(42) .9	(44) 1.1	(40) 2.4				(12)	2.4	(10) 1.2	
2.5	2.1	3.9					3.1	3.0	
1.0	1.1	1.8	% Officers', Directors' Owners' Comp/Sales						
(15) 2.9	(15) 2.0	(16) 2.9							
6.2	4.8	5.4							
873289M	1320905M	1487270M	Net Sales ($)	343M	8470M	19348M	96717M	171564M	1190828M
455562M	724545M	833306M	Total Assets ($)	924M	7703M	10119M	51715M	141311M	621534M

M = $ thousand   MM = $ million
See Pages 9 through 22 for Explanation of Ratios and Data

Current Data Sorted by Assets

Comparative Historical Data

0-500M	500M-2MM	2-10MM	10-50MM	50-100MM	100-250MM	Type of Statement	4/1/05-3/31/06 ALL	4/1/06-3/31/07 ALL
		6	7	1	1	Unqualified	20	24
	2	11	7			Reviewed	25	25
1	2	2	1			Compiled	12	11
1	3	1				Tax Returns	6	6
1	2	13	4	1	1	Other	25	22
	16 (4/1-9/30/09)		52 (10/1/09-3/31/10)					
3	9	33	19	2	2	NUMBER OF STATEMENTS	88	88
%	%	%	%	%	%	ASSETS	%	%
		12.0	14.7			Cash & Equivalents	8.7	10.9
		20.4	20.3			Trade Receivables (net)	27.9	27.7
		36.5	33.4			Inventory	32.6	32.7
		3.7	4.4			All Other Current	3.6	3.6
		72.6	72.8			Total Current	72.8	75.0
		14.2	13.8			Fixed Assets (net)	13.7	15.0
		4.0	5.6			Intangibles (net)	6.9	4.4
		9.2	7.8			All Other Non-Current	6.5	5.6
		100.0	100.0			Total	100.0	100.0
						LIABILITIES		
		10.2	2.7			Notes Payable-Short Term	8.7	6.6
		2.9	1.3			Cur. Mat.-L.T.D.	2.2	2.1
		11.5	6.5			Trade Payables	18.7	16.2
		.1	.2			Income Taxes Payable	.3	.3
		23.1	25.5			All Other Current	25.5	28.2
		47.8	36.1			Total Current	55.4	53.4
		7.0	1.9			Long-Term Debt	9.8	9.1
		.1	.6			Deferred Taxes	.6	.3
		3.2	14.1			All Other Non-Current	8.2	10.8
		41.9	47.2			Net Worth	26.0	26.3
		100.0	100.0			Total Liabilities & Net Worth	100.0	100.0
						INCOME DATA		
		100.0	100.0			Net Sales	100.0	100.0
		34.2	31.8			Gross Profit	32.1	31.4
		33.0	26.3			Operating Expenses	28.4	27.7
		1.2	5.5			Operating Profit	3.7	3.7
		1.3	.1			All Other Expenses (net)	.8	.5
		-.1	5.4			Profit Before Taxes	2.9	3.2
						RATIOS		
		2.6	3.7				2.1	2.2
		1.5	2.1			Current	1.4	1.6
		1.0	1.4				1.0	1.2
		1.4	1.4				1.0	1.0
		.7	.9			Quick	.7	.7
		.4	.7				.4	.5
	30	12.1	30 12.0				33 10.9	33 11.2
	37	9.9	40 9.1			Sales/Receivables	45 8.0	42 8.6
	51	7.2	77 4.8				60 6.1	54 6.7
		68 5.3	54 6.7				49 7.5	43 8.5
		125 2.9	104 3.5			Cost of Sales/Inventory	77 4.7	84 4.4
		182 2.0	189 1.9				126 2.9	127 2.9
		11 33.1	11 33.1				19 19.4	17 21.8
		22 16.2	22 16.7			Cost of Sales/Payables	33 11.0	28 12.9
		52 7.0	28 13.2				59 6.2	51 7.2
		4.3	2.8				5.6	4.7
		7.0	5.2			Sales/Working Capital	10.0	8.0
		254.9	7.8				246.4	22.0
		16.8	139.8				15.3	16.0
		(29) 5.8	(15) 23.2			EBIT/Interest	(74) 3.5	(72) 4.1
		.1	2.9				1.6	1.4
						Net Profit + Depr., Dep.,	5.9	11.0
						Amort./Cur. Mat. L/T/D	(29) 3.2	(30) 3.6
							.9	1.7
		.1	.1				.2	.2
		.3	.4			Fixed/Worth	.5	.4
		1.4	.8				1.9	1.3
		.7	.5				.9	.9
		1.9	1.0			Debt/Worth	3.0	2.5
		4.2	6.6				35.5	7.7
		31.3	28.3			% Profit Before Taxes/Tangible	49.1	36.0
		(30) 11.4	(18) 19.8			Net Worth	(72) 14.0	(72) 19.6
		-5.0	8.7				2.9	3.7
		10.1	14.1			% Profit Before Taxes/Total	11.1	13.3
		4.4	7.0			Assets	4.4	5.1
		-4.3	3.0				.4	.7
		43.2	27.1				49.0	39.6
		22.3	11.5			Sales/Net Fixed Assets	23.0	20.6
		7.5	7.7				9.2	10.3
		2.3	1.9				2.7	2.7
		1.7	1.7			Sales/Total Assets	2.1	2.1
		1.2	1.2				1.6	1.6
		.7	.9				.7	.6
		(28) 1.3	1.4			% Depr., Dep., Amort./Sales	(76) 1.1	(79) 1.0
		1.6	2.3				2.1	2.5
		1.9				% Officers', Directors'	1.2	2.1
		(10) 3.7				Owners' Comp/Sales	(19) 3.3	(21) 3.1
		8.0					6.6	4.3
4736M	21422M	304333M	611996M	167670M	424308M	Net Sales ($)	2424256M	2157239M
925M	10708M	165505M	390957M	151042M	312828M	Total Assets ($)	1424434M	1127056M

M = $ thousand   MM = $ million
See Pages 9 through 22 for Explanation of Ratios and Data

Comparative Historical Data

Current Data Sorted by Sales

			Type of Statement						
14	17	15	Unqualified		2	1	2	4	8
20	17	20	Reviewed		2	3	4	7	4
9	13	6	Compiled		2	1	2		1
6	5	5	Tax Returns	1	2	1	1		
25	18	22	Other	1	3	2	7	5	4
4/1/07-3/31/08 ALL	4/1/08-3/31/09 ALL	4/1/09-3/31/10 ALL		0-1MM	16 (4/1-9/30/09) 1-3MM	3-5MM	52 (10/1/09-3/31/10) 5-10MM	10-25MM	25MM & OVER
74	70	68	NUMBER OF STATEMENTS	2	9	8	16	16	17
%	%	%	ASSETS	%	%	%	%	%	%
11.9	12.0	11.6	Cash & Equivalents				7.1	15.3	9.3
26.9	24.9	19.7	Trade Receivables (net)				22.3	19.3	21.8
32.7	31.9	35.6	Inventory				39.4	32.1	37.2
4.6	4.3	4.4	All Other Current				3.5	3.8	5.7
76.0	73.2	71.3	Total Current				72.3	70.5	74.1
13.3	14.5	15.4	Fixed Assets (net)				15.7	15.0	14.1
6.5	6.5	5.0	Intangibles (net)				6.4	6.2	6.3
4.2	5.8	8.3	All Other Non-Current				5.6	8.3	5.5
100.0	100.0	100.0	Total				100.0	100.0	100.0
			LIABILITIES						
9.9	10.7	8.1	Notes Payable-Short Term				12.3	6.7	5.7
3.3	2.8	2.2	Cur. Mat.-L.T.D.				3.8	2.3	.9
19.5	16.5	11.0	Trade Payables				13.2	9.8	6.9
.3	.4	.3	Income Taxes Payable				.1	.1	.7
24.2	24.2	24.2	All Other Current				19.3	26.8	27.2
57.3	54.6	45.8	Total Current				48.7	45.6	41.4
8.7	6.9	6.2	Long-Term Debt				7.2	4.8	5.1
.4	.5	.4	Deferred Taxes				.0	1.0	.5
6.3	4.6	8.6	All Other Non-Current				5.3	9.6	10.6
27.3	33.5	39.0	Net Worth				38.9	39.0	42.4
100.0	100.0	100.0	Total Liabilties & Net Worth				100.0	100.0	100.0
			INCOME DATA						
100.0	100.0	100.0	Net Sales				100.0	100.0	100.0
30.6	29.6	34.7	Gross Profit				32.8	35.4	25.1
26.7	26.1	32.7	Operating Expenses				29.5	29.8	23.2
3.8	3.5	2.0	Operating Profit				3.3	5.6	1.9
.7	.5	.9	All Other Expenses (net)				.8	.5	.4
3.2	3.0	1.1	Profit Before Taxes				2.5	5.1	1.5
			RATIOS						
2.1	2.1	2.7					2.4	2.2	2.6
1.4	1.5	1.6	Current				1.2	1.5	1.7
1.1	1.1	1.1					1.0	1.2	1.3
1.0	1.0	1.3					1.2	1.4	1.2
.7	.7	.7	Quick				.5	.8	.8
.5	.4	.4					.3	.5	.5
29 12.8	26 13.8	28 12.8	Sales/Receivables		34 10.9	29 12.8	30 12.3		
41 9.0	38 9.7	39 9.5	Sales/Receivables		40 9.1	37 9.8	41 8.9		
56 6.5	54 6.8	58 6.3	Sales/Receivables		50 7.3	68 5.3	59 6.1		
42 8.6	39 9.5	55 6.6	Cost of Sales/Inventory		73 5.0	50 7.3	56 6.5		
86 4.3	78 4.7	126 2.9	Cost of Sales/Inventory		124 2.9	129 2.8	101 3.6		
137 2.7	128 2.8	189 1.9	Cost of Sales/Inventory		187 2.0	177 2.1	156 2.3		
15 23.9	15 24.3	11 32.6	Cost of Sales/Payables		10 36.5	13 27.7	8 44.7		
32 11.3	26 13.9	24 15.1	Cost of Sales/Payables		25 14.5	26 14.2	17 21.7		
49 7.4	46 8.0	50 7.4	Cost of Sales/Payables		37 9.9	48 7.6	25 14.6		
4.6	4.5	3.7	Sales/Working Capital				5.1	4.4	3.5
9.5	10.3	6.5	Sales/Working Capital				19.1	7.4	6.2
50.3	25.9	44.2	Sales/Working Capital				NM	22.2	9.4
16.0	20.2	22.8	EBIT/Interest				34.0	32.5	55.0
(66) 2.6	(60) 5.2	(58) 5.1	EBIT/Interest				(15) 6.2	(13) 2.9	(14) 14.3
1.5	1.3	.1	EBIT/Interest				-1.0	2.0	-3.0
8.3	17.2	14.3	Net Profit + Depr., Dep., Amort./Cur. Mat. L/T/D						
(31) 3.2	(15) 5.0	(13) 1.3	Net Profit + Depr., Dep., Amort./Cur. Mat. L/T/D						
.6	.0	-.8	Net Profit + Depr., Dep., Amort./Cur. Mat. L/T/D						
.2	.2	.1	Fixed/Worth				.1	.1	.3
.5	.4	.4	Fixed/Worth				.7	.6	.4
2.1	1.6	1.4	Fixed/Worth				1.6	1.5	.8
.8	.8	.6	Debt/Worth				1.6	.9	.5
2.2	2.2	1.8	Debt/Worth				2.4	2.3	1.4
8.7	11.5	5.2	Debt/Worth				5.4	6.6	4.8
37.2	49.3	27.9	% Profit Before Taxes/Tangible Net Worth				25.3	38.2	31.6
(59) 20.6	(57) 19.1	(59) 15.6	% Profit Before Taxes/Tangible Net Worth				(14) 8.7	(15) 20.0	(15) 17.7
5.1	3.4	.9	% Profit Before Taxes/Tangible Net Worth				-9.9	9.4	7.2
15.1	14.6	11.2	% Profit Before Taxes/Total Assets				9.2	13.9	12.3
5.7	7.0	4.6	% Profit Before Taxes/Total Assets				3.7	8.0	4.8
.7	.6	-.4	% Profit Before Taxes/Total Assets				-.7	2.3	-.1
45.6	41.9	39.1	Sales/Net Fixed Assets				43.1	32.4	19.5
21.1	19.9	15.3	Sales/Net Fixed Assets				18.9	13.1	11.8
11.3	9.0	7.7	Sales/Net Fixed Assets				8.7	6.8	10.2
2.8	3.0	2.1	Sales/Total Assets				2.4	2.2	2.2
2.1	2.0	1.7	Sales/Total Assets				1.8	1.6	1.8
1.6	1.5	1.2	Sales/Total Assets				1.4	1.4	1.3
.5	.6	.8	% Depr., Dep., Amort./Sales				.5	.9	.8
(66) 1.1	(61) 1.0	(60) 1.3	% Depr., Dep., Amort./Sales				(15) 1.1	1.6	1.4
1.7	1.7	1.8	% Depr., Dep., Amort./Sales				1.6	2.2	2.3
2.5	1.9	2.2	% Officers', Directors' Owners' Comp/Sales						
(20) 3.5	(16) 4.1	(20) 4.2	% Officers', Directors' Owners' Comp/Sales						
6.0	6.7	6.8	% Officers', Directors' Owners' Comp/Sales						
1816315M	2081778M	1534465M	Net Sales ($)	1077M	15737M	30250M	120999M	258531M	1107871M
951276M	1176255M	1031965M	Total Assets ($)	792M	15354M	24172M	70273M	172553M	748821M

Current Data Sorted by Assets | Comparative Historical Data

Columns for 0-500M and 500M-2MM (left) and 10-50MM, 50-100MM, 100-250MM (right) are marked **DATA NOT AVAILABLE** for the balance-sheet / income percentages; values shown below appear in the 2-10MM column and the two comparative-historical columns.

0-500M	500M-2MM	2-10MM	10-50MM	50-100MM	100-250MM	Type of Statement	4/1/05-3/31/06 ALL	4/1/06-3/31/07 ALL
		4	3		1	Unqualified	13	7
	2	7	4			Reviewed	10	15
	3	2				Compiled	5	8
	2					Tax Returns	2	4
	1	8	2		1	Other	13	11
	10 (4/1-9/30/09)		30 (10/1/09-3/31/10)					
	8	21	9		2	**NUMBER OF STATEMENTS** 43 / 45	43	45

0-500M	500M-2MM	2-10MM	10-50MM	50-100MM	100-250MM		4/1/05-3/31/06 ALL	4/1/06-3/31/07 ALL
%	%	%	%	%	%	**ASSETS**	%	%
		13.4				Cash & Equivalents	8.3	13.2
		27.9				Trade Receivables (net)	32.0	35.7
		20.6				Inventory	18.1	20.8
		6.3				All Other Current	5.6	6.4
		68.3				Total Current	64.1	76.1
		20.9				Fixed Assets (net)	20.5	16.4
		2.2				Intangibles (net)	7.4	3.8
		8.6				All Other Non-Current	8.1	3.7
		100.0				Total	100.0	100.0
						LIABILITIES		
		12.8				Notes Payable-Short Term	10.7	8.8
		2.0				Cur. Mat.-L.T.D.	3.5	3.0
		12.8				Trade Payables	17.8	20.1
		.2				Income Taxes Payable	.1	.4
		20.6				All Other Current	16.0	27.4
		48.3				Total Current	48.1	59.7
		11.2				Long-Term Debt	12.3	7.8
		.3				Deferred Taxes	.4	.2
		5.4				All Other Non-Current	5.9	7.3
		34.8				Net Worth	33.3	25.0
		100.0				Total Liabilities & Net Worth	100.0	100.0
						INCOME DATA		
		100.0				Net Sales	100.0	100.0
		29.0				Gross Profit	30.7	29.5
		25.7				Operating Expenses	24.7	24.1
		3.2				Operating Profit	6.0	5.4
		1.1				All Other Expenses (net)	.8	1.0
		2.2				Profit Before Taxes	5.2	4.5
						RATIOS		
		1.9				Current	2.3	2.1
		1.6					1.5	1.3
		1.0					1.0	1.0
		1.3				Quick	1.6	1.3
		1.0					1.0	.9
		.5					.6	.6
		38 9.6				Sales/Receivables	48 7.6	31 11.8
		48 7.5					62 5.9	49 7.4
		60 6.1					85 4.3	60 6.0
		15 24.9				Cost of Sales/Inventory	17 21.3	10 37.3
		37 9.8					47 7.8	34 10.6
		98 3.7					82 4.5	81 4.5
		19 19.7				Cost of Sales/Payables	24 15.1	19 19.0
		31 11.8					37 9.9	32 11.5
		39 9.3					65 5.6	52 7.0
		4.1				Sales/Working Capital	5.7	6.2
		8.0					8.7	17.0
		579.0					-69.0	-48.8
		14.7				EBIT/Interest	14.1	13.9
	(20)	1.6					(38) 4.3	(39) 6.0
		-1.2					1.1	1.2
						Net Profit + Depr., Dep., Amort./Cur. Mat. L/T/D	5.9	9.1
							(15) 1.9	(11) 2.1
							.6	1.0
		.2				Fixed/Worth	.3	.3
		.6					.7	.6
		1.0					20.7	1.6
		.9				Debt/Worth	.8	1.0
		2.6					1.9	2.5
		5.5					81.4	12.6
		62.5				% Profit Before Taxes/Tangible Net Worth	74.8	53.9
		10.0					(34) 24.9	(38) 30.0
		-24.5					8.3	8.2
		12.6				% Profit Before Taxes/Total Assets	13.6	18.4
		2.7					7.3	3.9
		-4.0					.8	.5
		64.8				Sales/Net Fixed Assets	22.4	74.9
		13.2					11.8	27.4
		4.4					4.2	10.5
		2.8				Sales/Total Assets	2.5	3.5
		2.0					1.6	2.5
		1.1					1.4	1.8
		.3				% Depr., Dep., Amort./Sales	.8	.4
	(18)	1.2					(38) 1.7	(40) 1.0
		3.1					2.8	2.0
						% Officers', Directors', Owners' Comp/Sales	1.6	3.2
							(14) 3.5	(11) 3.7
							6.5	8.8
	24382M	213254M	236458M		391991M	Net Sales ($)	763145M	1082283M
	9842M	109320M	142796M		283445M	Total Assets ($)	521483M	645298M

M = $ thousand   MM = $ million
See Pages 9 through 22 for Explanation of Ratios and Data

Comparative Historical Data   ## Current Data Sorted by Sales

				Type of Statement						
9		8	8	Unqualified			2		2	3	3
18		11	13	Reviewed			5		5	3	3
5		9	5	Compiled			1	2	1		
2		2	2	Tax Returns			1		1		
13		13	12	Other			1		6	4	1
4/1/07-3/31/08 ALL		4/1/08-3/31/09 ALL	4/1/09-3/31/10 ALL		0-1MM	1-3MM	10 (4/1-9/30/09)	3-5MM	30 (10/1/09-3/31/10) 5-10MM	10-25MM	25MM & OVE
47		43	40	NUMBER OF STATEMENTS	6	2		15		10	7

%		%	%	ASSETS	%	%	%	%	%	%
13.9		11.9	15.1	Cash & Equivalents				11.8	17.9	
35.3		32.9	29.3	Trade Receivables (net)	D			28.9	26.9	
15.3		20.5	20.3	Inventory	A			15.9	23.0	
8.2		6.0	4.9	All Other Current	T			6.3	4.3	
72.7		71.3	69.5	Total Current	A			62.9	72.1	
16.3		15.4	17.9	Fixed Assets (net)				24.2	15.5	
5.8		4.9	4.9	Intangibles (net)	N			2.7	8.6	
5.2		8.5	7.7	All Other Non-Current	O			10.3	3.7	
100.0		100.0	100.0	Total	T			100.0	100.0	

				LIABILITIES						
10.6		13.0	12.2	Notes Payable-Short Term	A			11.9	16.0	
2.3		2.3	4.0	Cur. Mat.-L.T.D.	V			2.2	1.3	
17.2		19.0	12.3	Trade Payables	A			13.3	13.5	
.7		.2	.9	Income Taxes Payable	I			.2	.1	
21.3		22.8	20.3	All Other Current	L			14.8	29.8	
52.2		57.3	49.7	Total Current	A			42.4	60.8	
8.0		8.7	11.3	Long-Term Debt	B			11.1	14.7	
.3		.1	.2	Deferred Taxes	L			.4	.2	
5.9		6.0	7.0	All Other Non-Current	E			6.4	.1	
33.7		28.0	31.8	Net Worth				39.7	24.3	
100.0		100.0	100.0	Total Liabilities & Net Worth				100.0	100.0	

				INCOME DATA						
100.0		100.0	100.0	Net Sales				100.0	100.0	
31.8		30.4	30.1	Gross Profit				29.5	27.0	
26.0		25.9	26.1	Operating Expenses				26.6	22.7	
5.8		4.5	4.0	Operating Profit				3.0	4.4	
.6		.7	1.4	All Other Expenses (net)				.9	2.4	
5.3		3.8	2.7	Profit Before Taxes				2.0	1.9	

				RATIOS						
2.1		2.2	2.0					2.5	1.7	
1.5		1.6	1.5	Current				1.6	1.1	
1.0		1.1	1.1					1.0	1.0	
1.4		1.3	1.4					1.4	1.3	
1.0		.9	.9	Quick				1.1	.7	
.7		.5	.6					.6	.5	
35 10.4		36 10.1	38 9.6					44 8.3	32 11.5	
53 6.9		53 6.9	50 7.2	Sales/Receivables				56 6.5	44 8.2	
66 5.5		68 5.4	71 5.1					73 5.0	60 6.1	
7 49.9		7 50.9	10 35.9					11 33.8	9 39.3	
24 15.3		37 9.8	37 9.8	Cost of Sales/Inventory				33 11.1	41 8.9	
63 5.8		84 4.3	101 3.6					94 3.9	123 3.0	
21 17.2		23 15.8	18 19.9					18 20.0	24 15.5	
33 11.0		37 10.0	30 12.0	Cost of Sales/Payables				35 10.3	29 12.4	
45 8.2		60 6.1	43 8.5					54 6.8	42 8.7	
6.2		5.3	4.4					4.0	11.8	
9.4		9.6	10.9	Sales/Working Capital				7.1	35.9	
146.4		44.2	56.1					158.3	NM	
27.0		29.6	15.7					17.1		
(43) 10.3		(37) 3.6	(37) 3.2	EBIT/Interest				1.8		
1.9		.7	.8					-1.8		
18.6		116.3	5.3	Net Profit + Depr., Dep.,						
(10) 6.4		(10) 3.7	(11) 2.3	Amort./Cur. Mat. L/T/D						
2.5		-3.1	-10.5							
.2		.2	.2					.2	.4	
.5		.5	.7	Fixed/Worth				.6	.9	
2.2		1.4	1.4					.9	NM	
1.1		1.0	.9					.8	1.6	
2.1		2.9	2.7	Debt/Worth				1.6	4.0	
8.1		11.9	8.7					4.3	NM	
81.6		49.9	62.5	% Profit Before Taxes/Tangible				25.7		
(40) 27.3		(35) 28.3	(37) 10.0	Net Worth				8.6		
5.8		5.4	.2					-37.8		
16.9		15.8	10.7	% Profit Before Taxes/Total				13.0	10.5	
9.2		5.7	2.3	Assets				2.7	5.1	
1.9		.8	.0					-6.3	-4.0	
48.6		61.3	43.3					49.9	71.4	
21.2		21.4	13.7	Sales/Net Fixed Assets				8.2	22.9	
9.8		9.0	5.7					3.6	3.9	
3.2		3.2	2.8					2.5	3.4	
2.4		2.0	1.9	Sales/Total Assets				1.6	2.2	
1.6		1.4	1.1					1.1	1.1	
.4		.6	.7					.4	.3	
(40) 1.0		(35) 1.3	(36) 1.0	% Depr., Dep., Amort./Sales			(12)	2.1	.8	
2.2		2.2	2.7					5.2	3.2	
2.3		1.9	1.6							
(12) 3.5		(12) 4.9	(13) 4.9	% Officers', Directors'						
6.8		7.8	6.1	Owners' Comp/Sales						
1120977M		1184984M	866085M	Net Sales ($)	14074M	8458M		108115M	160991M	574447M
565281M		641046M	545403M	Total Assets ($)	7406M	5647M		72664M	96808M	362878M

© RMA 2010

M = $ thousand   MM = $ million
See Pages 9 through 22 for Explanation of Ratios and Data

Current Data Sorted by Assets   **Comparative Historical Data**

	0-500M	500M-2MM	2-10MM	10-50MM	50-100MM	100-250MM		4/1/05-3/31/06 ALL	4/1/06-3/31/07 ALL
Type of Statement									
Unqualified	1	2	14	11	3	6		41	57
Reviewed	1	9	36	12				58	60
Compiled	4	6	27	2				37	36
Tax Returns	8	14	11	1				19	29
Other	1	18	37	19	8	3		63	66
	49 (4/1-9/30/09)			205 (10/1/09-3/31/10)					
NUMBER OF STATEMENTS	15	49	125	45	11	9		218	248
	%	%	%	%	%	%		%	%
ASSETS									
Cash & Equivalents	8.4	11.1	11.9	7.4	6.0			8.7	8.9
Trade Receivables (net)	23.3	27.7	24.0	21.1	16.4			30.3	28.9
Inventory	19.2	22.1	26.7	24.4	15.0			25.2	25.1
All Other Current	1.3	4.8	4.1	6.6	4.4			4.4	3.6
Total Current	52.2	65.7	66.8	59.6	41.8			68.6	66.5
Fixed Assets (net)	23.7	26.7	23.5	24.3	30.0			21.8	23.3
Intangibles (net)	11.2	1.0	3.3	10.7	24.5			4.2	4.6
All Other Non-Current	12.8	6.6	6.3	5.5	3.7			5.3	5.6
Total	100.0	100.0	100.0	100.0	100.0			100.0	100.0
LIABILITIES									
Notes Payable-Short Term	18.2	16.1	11.5	8.8	7.0			12.8	9.9
Cur. Mat.-L.T.D.	2.5	2.5	3.5	3.8	5.7			3.1	3.4
Trade Payables	26.1	15.9	11.4	10.9	9.0			15.8	15.3
Income Taxes Payable	.3	.2	.2	.4	.1			.3	.4
All Other Current	21.1	14.9	13.8	13.7	11.4			13.9	15.1
Total Current	68.3	49.7	40.4	37.6	33.2			45.8	44.2
Long-Term Debt	33.2	18.2	12.5	11.5	19.5			13.0	14.6
Deferred Taxes	.0	.1	.5	1.0	1.1			.5	.4
All Other Non-Current	13.4	12.3	5.1	12.3	12.6			9.7	5.8
Net Worth	-15.0	19.8	41.5	37.6	33.6			31.0	34.9
Total Liabilities & Net Worth	100.0	100.0	100.0	100.0	100.0			100.0	100.0
INCOME DATA									
Net Sales	100.0	100.0	100.0	100.0	100.0			100.0	100.0
Gross Profit	36.9	37.4	30.6	25.0	31.4			32.2	32.8
Operating Expenses	38.4	36.9	27.4	22.0	23.1			26.9	26.0
Operating Profit	-1.5	.5	3.1	3.0	8.4			5.3	6.8
All Other Expenses (net)	1.1	1.1	1.1	1.4	5.6			.9	1.3
Profit Before Taxes	-2.6	-.6	2.1	1.5	2.7			4.5	5.5
RATIOS									
Current	3.2	3.1	3.2	3.0	3.8			2.5	2.5
	1.0	1.4	1.7	1.6	1.0			1.5	1.5
	.5	.9	1.1	1.1	.7			1.1	1.1
Quick	1.4	2.4	2.0	1.5	1.6			1.5	1.4
	.6	.8	.8	.9	.6			.8	.9
	.3	.3	.5		.4			.5	.5
Sales/Receivables	0 UND	23 15.9	30 12.1	33 11.2	48 7.6			38 9.7	35 10.5
	21 17.1	38 9.5	42 8.6	48 7.7	50 7.3			50 7.3	48 7.6
	41 9.0	56 6.6	58 6.2	64 5.7	52 7.0			64 5.7	62 5.9
Cost of Sales/Inventory	7 48.9	8 43.7	29 12.8	35 10.4	34 10.7			29 12.7	29 12.7
	25 14.8	59 6.2	65 5.6	69 5.3	89 4.1			66 5.5	61 6.0
	73 5.0	119 3.1	128 2.8	124 3.0	111 3.3			100 3.7	100 3.6
Cost of Sales/Payables	0 UND	15 24.5	15 23.8	17 21.8	24 15.3			20 18.6	21 17.0
	26 14.2	24 15.2	24 15.1	28 13.3	40 9.2			32 11.6	32 11.3
	72 5.1	48 7.6	40 9.1	44 8.4	60 6.1			52 7.0	47 7.8
Sales/Working Capital	26.8	4.9	4.0	3.7	3.6			4.7	4.8
	97.3	18.9	7.6	8.5	-154.4			9.6	9.5
	-9.6	-34.4	28.3	43.0	-10.3			44.8	29.1
EBIT/Interest	3.5	7.1	7.7	8.6	18.7			12.6	16.9
	(11) 1.2	(43) 1.4	(110) 2.7	(44) 2.0	(10) 2.2			(196) 5.2	(218) 6.1
	-15.7	-4.2	-.4	.3	.3			2.0	1.8
Net Profit + Depr., Dep., Amort./Cur. Mat. L/T/D			9.0		2.9			6.9	9.0
		(24)	2.5	(16) 1.3				(57) 3.0	(68) 3.5
			1.0		.5			1.2	1.3
Fixed/Worth	.6	.2	.2	.3	.8			.3	.3
	18.4	1.1	.5	.7	-14.1			.6	.7
	-.2	NM	1.5	1.7	-.8			1.9	2.0
Debt/Worth	1.8	1.1	.5	.6	1.2			.8	.8
	35.8	3.9	1.3	2.1	-24.1			2.2	1.8
	-2.3	NM	5.5	9.3	-3.0			7.7	6.0
% Profit Before Taxes/Tangible Net Worth		38.5	32.7	22.9				52.0	55.3
	(37)	19.4	(108) 11.1	(38) 9.8				(178) 25.0	(210) 27.0
		-22.2	-.9	-3.7				6.5	11.4
% Profit Before Taxes/Total Assets	6.8	15.3	11.7	9.4	7.6			17.5	19.5
	3.1	1.5	4.2	3.8	6.8			7.7	8.8
	-26.8	-12.9	-1.1	-2.1	-3.7			1.7	2.9
Sales/Net Fixed Assets	49.3	47.7	25.8	16.8	7.8			27.8	25.5
	27.8	12.4	9.5	9.1	3.8			12.0	10.4
	20.9	4.5	4.3	4.8	3.6			6.1	5.9
Sales/Total Assets	4.7	3.4	2.5	2.0	1.6			2.8	2.8
	3.2	2.2	1.9	1.5	1.3			2.1	2.0
	2.5	1.5	1.3	1.1	.6			1.5	1.5
% Depr., Dep., Amort./Sales		.6	.8	1.3	2.2			.9	1.0
	(36)	1.8	(113) 2.1	(40) 2.4	(10) 3.8			(192) 1.7	(225) 1.9
		5.6	4.3	4.1	5.3			3.3	3.4
% Officers', Directors' Owners' Comp/Sales	2.9	3.2	2.5					2.3	2.4
	(12) 6.9	(21) 7.4	(46) 4.9					(76) 4.0	(85) 4.7
	10.4	10.0	5.9					6.9	8.3
Net Sales ($)	16975M	136073M	1129623M	1528290M	823800M	1679229M		4883498M	5498834M
Total Assets ($)	4257M	56141M	594626M	960458M	699129M	1194696M		2714332M	3040546M

© RMA 2010   M = $ thousand   MM = $ million
See Pages 9 through 22 for Explanation of Ratios and Data

Comparative Historical Data | Current Data Sorted by Sales

Type of Statement									
	51	62	37	Unqualified	1		2	4	11	19
	54	76	58	Reviewed	1	6	7	20	16	8
	31	63	39	Compiled	3	7	8	16	4	1
	21	46	34	Tax Returns	6	14	8	4	2	
	75	122	86	Other	4	12	7	23	15	25
	4/1/07-3/31/08 ALL	4/1/08-3/31/09 ALL	4/1/09-3/31/10 ALL		49 (4/1-9/30/09)			205 (10/1/09-3/31/10)		
					0-1MM	1-3MM	3-5MM	5-10MM	10-25MM	25MM & OVE

	08 ALL	09 ALL	10 ALL		0-1MM	1-3MM	3-5MM	5-10MM	10-25MM	25MM & OVE
NUMBER OF STATEMENTS	232	369	254		15	39	32	67	48	53
	%	%	%	**ASSETS**	%	%	%	%	%	%
	8.6	9.9	10.5	Cash & Equivalents	7.1	6.4	16.7	12.4	10.9	8.0
	29.6	25.7	23.8	Trade Receivables (net)	8.8	26.2	23.9	24.0	27.6	22.7
	24.4	22.7	24.2	Inventory	20.8	22.4	23.9	28.1	23.8	22.3
	4.0	3.9	4.8	All Other Current	.9	4.1	3.5	3.3	5.3	8.4
	66.5	62.2	63.4	Total Current	37.6	59.1	67.9	67.9	67.7	61.4
	24.5	27.0	24.5	Fixed Assets (net)	36.2	30.4	22.9	22.7	19.3	24.6
	4.0	4.9	5.8	Intangibles (net)	9.3	2.5	2.9	2.9	8.5	10.2
	5.0	5.9	6.4	All Other Non-Current	16.9	8.1	6.3	6.4	4.5	3.8
	100.0	100.0	100.0	Total	100.0	100.0	100.0	100.0	100.0	100.0
				LIABILITIES						
	11.6	10.6	11.7	Notes Payable-Short Term	5.0	22.0	11.8	12.5	9.5	7.0
	3.5	4.4	3.4	Cur. Mat.-L.T.D.	2.5	3.9	3.5	3.3	2.8	3.8
	15.3	12.1	12.9	Trade Payables	6.4	18.4	14.5	10.0	13.1	13.1
	.4	.3	.3	Income Taxes Payable	.3	.3	.2	.3	.2	.3
	12.9	11.9	14.2	All Other Current	8.6	14.4	19.0	13.3	15.8	12.6
	43.7	39.4	42.4	Total Current	22.8	59.0	49.0	39.3	41.4	36.8
	16.4	17.0	15.2	Long-Term Debt	27.0	27.2	17.9	9.6	8.6	14.4
	.4	.6	.5	Deferred Taxes	.0	.3	.3	.7	.3	1.0
	6.1	5.6	8.8	All Other Non-Current	19.4	13.6	1.6	6.1	11.3	8.0
	33.5	37.3	33.0	Net Worth	30.7	-.1	31.2	44.3	38.4	39.8
	100.0	100.0	100.0	Total Liabilities & Net Worth	100.0	100.0	100.0	100.0	100.0	100.0
				INCOME DATA						
	100.0	100.0	100.0	Net Sales	100.0	100.0	100.0	100.0	100.0	100.0
	32.8	32.3	31.4	Gross Profit	46.7	35.9	34.3	29.6	27.9	27.5
	26.6	25.8	28.6	Operating Expenses	43.6	39.0	31.6	25.4	26.1	21.1
	6.2	6.4	2.8	Operating Profit	3.2	-3.2	2.7	4.2	1.9	6.4
	1.2	1.2	1.4	All Other Expenses (net)	1.2	1.4	1.8	.6	1.6	1.9
	5.0	5.2	1.5	Profit Before Taxes	1.9	-4.6	.9	3.6	.3	4.5
				RATIOS						
	2.2	2.8	3.2		6.9	2.3	3.1	4.1	2.7	3.1
	1.6	1.6	1.6	Current	3.0	1.1	1.5	1.7	1.9	1.6
	1.1	1.1	1.0		.9	.6	1.0	1.1	1.2	1.1
	1.4	1.6	1.9		2.5	1.0	2.1	2.3	1.8	1.8
	.8	.9	.8	Quick	.6	.6	1.0	.8	.9	.9
	.6	.5	.5		.2	.3	.4	.5	.6	.5
	36 10.1	31 11.7	29 12.4		6 65.3	21 17.1	26 14.3	30 12.2	37 10.0	35 10.6
	48 7.6	44 8.3	43 8.4	Sales/Receivables	16 23.1	41 8.9	41 8.9	38 9.5	47 7.7	49 7.4
	63 5.8	58 6.3	58 6.3		45 8.0	59 6.1	55 6.6	54 6.8	60 6.1	60 6.1
	22 16.8	20 18.3	26 13.9		9 42.3	19 19.6	13 27.9	26 13.8	31 11.8	31 11.8
	58 6.3	55 6.7	62 5.9	Cost of Sales/Inventory	98 3.7	61 5.9	66 5.5	65 5.6	53 6.8	57 6.4
	92 4.0	99 3.7	121 3.0		280 1.3	120 3.0	139 2.6	128 2.9	100 3.6	112 3.3
	21 17.7	14 26.7	16 23.5		5 74.2	9 39.6	11 33.0	13 28.2	18 20.3	19 19.3
	30 12.2	24 15.2	27 13.7	Cost of Sales/Payables	20 18.7	26 14.2	30 12.0	23 16.2	30 12.3	30 12.0
	53 6.9	44 8.3	44 8.3		75 4.8	55 6.6	54 6.8	34 10.7	44 8.3	48 7.7
	4.9	4.6	4.0		2.8	7.0	3.3	3.9	4.7	3.6
	10.0	8.8	9.0	Sales/Working Capital	28.5	66.3	12.3	8.3	6.8	8.6
	26.5	45.1	264.5		-57.6	-11.4	479.3	25.6	20.3	66.2
	10.7	15.3	8.2		7.7	2.9	5.0	12.3	8.8	12.0
	(209) 4.0	(337) 4.8	(227) 2.5	EBIT/Interest	(12) 4.0	(35) .2	(27) 2.5	(59) 3.4	(45) 1.2	(49) 5.8
	1.6	1.6	-.4		-1.2	-5.8	-1.3	.7	-3.8	1.2
	11.9	7.5	5.3	Net Profit + Depr., Dep.,				7.0		5.0
	(60) 3.5	(103) 2.5	(53) 1.8	Amort./Cur. Mat. L/T/D				(13) 2.1		(23) 2.1
	1.2	1.4	.9					.9		1.0
	.3	.3	.2		.6	.4	.3	.2	.2	.4
	.7	.7	.7	Fixed/Worth	1.3	1.8	.7	.4	.5	.7
	3.0	2.4	4.0		-19.1	-2.2	11.8	1.2	1.3	23.1
	.9	.7	.6		1.0	.8	.6	.4	.6	.6
	2.1	1.7	2.1	Debt/Worth	2.9	11.4	2.7	1.3	1.2	2.1
	8.5	6.0	18.4		-32.2	-6.2	36.1	4.1	6.2	51.4
	59.1	54.3	37.1	% Profit Before Taxes/Tangible	53.7	22.8	32.6	37.7	32.4	42.3
	(201) 26.1	(311) 25.5	(203) 14.5	Net Worth	(11) 32.5	(26) 4.9	(26) 13.9	(59) 11.7	(40) 14.2	(41) 20.9
	9.9	10.1	-.5		9.3	-74.9	-3.9	.2	-14.7	9.6
	17.0	17.6	11.7	% Profit Before Taxes/Total	16.8	3.1	10.3	17.3	12.3	12.8
	8.7	8.3	3.9	Assets	6.1	-1.3	4.8	4.8	2.6	6.7
	2.9	2.5	-2.6		.3	-17.8	-4.9	-.4	-3.8	1.1
	25.0	21.5	25.0		22.5	29.6	23.7	32.6	34.9	15.9
	10.4	8.8	9.9	Sales/Net Fixed Assets	5.0	9.5	11.5	9.6	12.0	7.8
	5.2	4.6	4.4		1.5	3.4	4.6	4.8	7.4	4.2
	2.8	2.7	2.5		1.8	3.6	2.9	2.5	2.6	2.2
	2.1	2.0	1.8	Sales/Total Assets	1.5	1.9	1.7	2.0	2.0	1.6
	1.6	1.5	1.2		.8	1.3	1.1	1.3	1.2	1.2
	.9	1.2	1.0		1.7	1.2	.7	.8	.8	1.3
	(206) 1.8	(322) 2.3	(216) 2.3	% Depr., Dep., Amort./Sales	(12) 4.2	(30) 2.9	(28) 1.5	(56) 2.2	(42) 1.8	(48) 2.4
	3.5	4.2	4.3		8.7	6.0	4.0	4.2	3.6	4.0
	3.1	2.2	2.5	% Officers', Directors'		2.6	4.1	2.5	2.0	
	(80) 4.5	(139) 4.4	(86) 4.9	Owners' Comp/Sales		(23) 7.4	(18) 5.5	(19) 3.4	(16) 3.6	
	6.8	7.4	7.6			9.4	7.0	6.2	5.0	
	6968061M	9479556M	5313990M	Net Sales ($)	10824M	76817M	127744M	487171M	726907M	3884527M
	4012450M	5853905M	3509307M	Total Assets ($)	11881M	48386M	86169M	292878M	448266M	2621727M

© RMA 2010

M = $ thousand   MM = $ million
See Pages 9 through 22 for Explanation of Ratios and Data

Current Data Sorted by Assets   Comparative Historical Data

	0-500M	500M-2MM	2-10MM	10-50MM	50-100MM	100-250MM		4/1/05-3/31/06 ALL	4/1/06-3/31/07 ALL
Type of Statement									
Unqualified			1	5	3	5		15	13
Reviewed		2	9	4				5	6
Compiled		1	2					6	4
Tax Returns	4	6	6	1				5	3
Other	3	8	13	8	2	1		24	20
		21 (4/1-9/30/09)		63 (10/1/09-3/31/10)					
NUMBER OF STATEMENTS	7	17	31	18	5	6		55	46
	%	%	%	%	%	%		%	%
ASSETS									
Cash & Equivalents		13.2	12.0	9.1				14.0	15.3
Trade Receivables (net)		32.2	30.2	29.3				31.3	31.7
Inventory		29.9	25.7	24.2				28.1	27.6
All Other Current		2.4	3.5	4.2				3.0	3.1
Total Current		77.6	71.4	66.7				76.3	77.7
Fixed Assets (net)		11.3	15.4	20.1				14.5	11.2
Intangibles (net)		1.8	3.3	9.9				5.0	5.7
All Other Non-Current		9.3	9.9	3.2				4.1	5.4
Total		100.0	100.0	100.0				100.0	100.0
LIABILITIES									
Notes Payable-Short Term		11.2	16.3	10.1				14.6	12.2
Cur. Mat.-L.T.D.		3.1	1.2	4.2				1.2	2.4
Trade Payables		12.2	15.6	17.3				18.8	16.8
Income Taxes Payable		.9	1.1	.0				1.3	.6
All Other Current		20.9	10.1	6.5				10.0	11.1
Total Current		48.4	44.3	38.1				45.9	43.2
Long-Term Debt		11.4	8.6	8.1				9.4	11.3
Deferred Taxes		-.0	.1	1.0				.2	.1
All Other Non-Current		2.6	8.3	6.1				15.6	9.8
Net Worth		37.6	38.7	46.7				28.9	35.6
Total Liabilities & Net Worth		100.0	100.0	100.0				100.0	100.0
INCOME DATA									
Net Sales		100.0	100.0	100.0				100.0	100.0
Gross Profit		44.5	39.8	29.5				36.2	31.9
Operating Expenses		40.6	37.4	25.7				32.4	27.2
Operating Profit		3.9	2.4	3.8				3.8	4.7
All Other Expenses (net)		1.0	.8	.4				1.0	1.0
Profit Before Taxes		2.9	1.5	3.4				2.8	3.7
RATIOS									
Current		2.5	3.0	2.3				2.9	2.8
		1.3	1.4	1.7				1.6	1.7
		1.1	1.2	1.2				1.2	1.3
Quick		2.0	2.0	1.3				1.5	1.9
		.9	.9	1.0				.9	1.0
		.4	.5	.5				.6	.6
Sales/Receivables	18 19.9		35 10.4	43 8.6				30 12.2	32 11.5
	34 10.8		47 7.8	49 7.4				42 8.6	49 7.4
	66 5.5		62 5.9	61 6.0				60 6.0	63 5.8
Cost of Sales/Inventory	19 19.4		29 12.8	34 10.7				17 21.0	22 16.5
	33 11.1		62 5.9	68 5.4				64 5.7	53 6.9
	341 1.1		144 2.5	99 3.7				112 3.3	100 3.7
Cost of Sales/Payables	8 48.3		21 17.0	19 18.9				22 16.7	16 22.3
	19 19.2		39 9.4	30 12.2				40 9.2	36 10.2
	63 5.8		58 6.3	49 7.4				54 6.8	61 6.0
Sales/Working Capital		2.9	5.0	5.0				4.0	3.6
		11.6	9.0	8.4				8.2	7.7
		51.7	16.1	15.3				21.6	19.0
EBIT/Interest		19.0	22.0	28.7				19.8	11.5
	(11) 4.4		(26) 3.0	(15) 5.3				(49) 4.7	(39) 4.4
		1.9	1.2	.4				1.3	1.4
Net Profit + Depr., Dep., Amort./Cur. Mat. L/T/D									9.3
								(11) 1.8	
								.9	
Fixed/Worth		.1	.1	.0				.1	.1
		.2	.3	.6				.3	.2
		.9	1.9	1.7				1.2	.9
Debt/Worth		.6	.9	.7				.6	.6
		1.8	1.9	1.6				1.8	2.0
		4.3	4.4	4.5				5.3	5.1
% Profit Before Taxes/Tangible Net Worth		41.7	38.8	54.8				71.4	51.0
	(16) 16.9		(28) 10.9	(16) 23.4				(49) 22.5	(41) 21.6
		6.1	-4.9	-4.1				5.1	7.3
% Profit Before Taxes/Total Assets		17.8	15.6	14.6				14.5	19.5
		6.6	3.5	7.2				7.3	7.4
		2.7	.2	-2.3				1.4	2.2
Sales/Net Fixed Assets		455.0	68.8	59.6				65.9	114.8
		32.1	31.8	16.4				32.4	42.8
		14.1	9.9	4.2				9.7	9.9
Sales/Total Assets		4.4	3.1	3.1				3.4	3.1
		2.7	2.5	1.9				2.4	2.4
		1.1	1.4	1.2				1.6	1.6
% Depr., Dep., Amort./Sales			.7	.4				.5	.3
		(22) 1.5	(14) 1.9					(44) 1.1	(31) .9
			3.4	3.3				2.6	2.2
% Officers', Directors' Owners' Comp/Sales			2.2						1.7
		(13) 5.8						(15) 4.0	
			8.5					6.9	
Net Sales ($)	9423M	60127M	324588M	632440M	535874M	1014437M		2644447M	3522331M
Total Assets ($)	1926M	18943M	149910M	300144M	300333M	989080M		1278641M	2003733M

© RMA 2010

M = $ thousand   MM = $ million
See Pages 9 through 22 for Explanation of Ratios and Data

Comparative Historical Data | Current Data Sorted by Sales

	4/1/07-3/31/08 ALL	4/1/08-3/31/09 ALL	4/1/09-3/31/10 ALL	Type of Statement	0-1MM	1-3MM	3-5MM	5-10MM	10-25MM	25MM & OVER
	19	15	14	Unqualified		1		4	1	13
	4	12	15	Reviewed		6	2	6	8	1
	5	3	3	Compiled			1		1	
	10	12	17	Tax Returns	2		2		2	
	27	27	35	Other	5	4		9	6	9
						21 (4/1-9/30/09)			63 (10/1/09-3/31/10)	
	65	69	84	NUMBER OF STATEMENTS	7	11	6	19	18	23
	%	%	%	**ASSETS**	%	%	%	%	%	%
	14.4	14.7	13.3	Cash & Equivalents		9.8		16.2	13.3	14.8
	30.9	26.5	29.3	Trade Receivables (net)		35.6		35.2	28.5	30.3
	23.2	26.8	23.9	Inventory		22.6		22.7	27.1	18.7
	3.2	5.3	3.3	All Other Current		1.0		5.2	1.9	4.9
	71.7	73.3	69.7	Total Current		68.9		79.3	70.8	68.7
	12.8	14.7	15.3	Fixed Assets (net)		16.8		13.0	20.2	10.1
	9.0	5.0	7.2	Intangibles (net)		3.3		1.2	5.4	16.5
	6.5	7.1	7.8	All Other Non-Current		11.1		6.6	3.7	4.8
	100.0	100.0	100.0	Total		100.0		100.0	100.0	100.0
				LIABILITIES						
	11.2	14.7	14.2	Notes Payable-Short Term		25.2		14.8	10.7	8.5
	2.2	2.9	2.9	Cur. Mat.-L.T.D.		9.5		.8	2.0	3.3
	19.1	16.5	14.1	Trade Payables		9.6		17.8	14.1	17.0
	.2	.2	.6	Income Taxes Payable		.0		.8	2.0	.1
	12.1	9.1	12.4	All Other Current		13.4		11.8	13.4	11.5
	44.8	43.5	44.3	Total Current		57.7		46.0	42.1	40.4
	9.2	9.2	10.9	Long-Term Debt		22.8		3.2	8.2	7.7
	.1	.2	.3	Deferred Taxes		.1		.3	.5	.4
	8.7	6.1	6.7	All Other Non-Current		4.0		4.6	9.4	7.9
	37.1	41.0	37.8	Net Worth		15.4		45.9	39.8	43.6
	100.0	100.0	100.0	Total Liabilities & Net Worth		100.0		100.0	100.0	100.0
				INCOME DATA						
	100.0	100.0	100.0	Net Sales		100.0		100.0	100.0	100.0
	34.8	34.1	40.2	Gross Profit		49.3		44.4	30.0	34.1
	29.7	31.3	38.0	Operating Expenses		46.5		45.1	23.7	32.8
	5.1	2.8	2.1	Operating Profit		2.8		-.7	6.2	1.4
	.1	1.2	.9	All Other Expenses (net)		1.8		.1	.0	1.3
	5.0	1.6	1.3	Profit Before Taxes		1.0		-.8	6.3	.0
				RATIOS						
	3.0	3.3	2.4	Current		5.6		3.0	2.7	2.3
	1.8	1.8	1.5			1.2		1.9	1.4	1.8
	1.2	1.2	1.1			.8		1.0	1.2	1.2
	1.8	1.9	1.8	Quick		2.3		2.0	1.6	1.8
	1.1	.9	.9			.9		1.3	1.0	1.1
	.6	.5	.6			.6		.6	.6	.8
30	12.3	25 — 14.6	33 — 11.1	Sales/Receivables		23 — 16.1		25 — 14.3	42 — 8.8	45 — 8.1
44	8.3	38 — 9.5	47 — 7.8			37 — 9.9		47 — 7.8	52 — 7.0	55 — 6.7
66	5.5	52 — 7.0	62 — 5.9			67 — 5.5		58 — 6.3	62 — 5.9	72 — 5.1
27	13.6	29 — 12.4	26 — 14.2	Cost of Sales/Inventory		16 — 22.3		19 — 19.2	33 — 11.2	26 — 14.3
44	8.3	52 — 7.0	59 — 6.2			33 — 11.1		58 — 6.3	75 — 4.8	60 — 6.1
83	4.4	128 — 2.9	106 — 3.5			188 — 1.9		106 — 3.4	100 — 3.7	73 — 5.0
21	17.6	17 — 21.6	17 — 20.9	Cost of Sales/Payables		1 — 401.8		22 — 16.4	13 — 28.3	28 — 12.9
42	8.6	31 — 11.9	34 — 10.7			10 — 37.9		37 — 9.9	20 — 18.2	44 — 8.2
72	5.1	54 — 6.8	54 — 6.8			37 — 9.9		53 — 6.9	49 — 7.4	62 — 5.9
	4.3	4.4	4.1	Sales/Working Capital		3.4		5.5	5.3	3.1
	7.9	9.7	9.0			26.9		9.0	9.2	8.0
	27.7	29.3	33.7			-25.5		609.3	15.0	16.2
	26.7	10.3	15.1	EBIT/Interest				19.1	36.9	20.6
(59)	6.3	(55) — 2.2	(66) — 3.7					(14) — 6.1	(14) — 12.6	(21) — 2.9
	1.5	-1.4	.4					.1	1.5	-1.9
	42.3	6.0	12.3	Net Profit + Depr., Dep., Amort./Cur. Mat. L/T/D						
(16)	6.5	(13) — 2.0	(16) — 1.7							
	1.8	.3	-.9							
	.1	.0	.1	Fixed/Worth		.0		.1	.0	.1
	.4	.3	.3			.9		.2	.5	.2
	1.5	1.3	1.6			-7.8		.5	2.1	2.4
	.8	.6	.8	Debt/Worth		1.8		.5	.6	.9
	1.8	1.5	2.0			4.3		1.5	2.3	1.8
	9.0	5.5	4.6			-17.3		2.7	4.5	6.0
	71.6	54.3	43.2	% Profit Before Taxes/Tangible Net Worth				40.0	54.8	60.0
(53)	26.9	(59) — 14.7	(74) — 13.2					8.2	(16) — 30.2	(19) — 9.5
	8.6	-5.2	-.6					-12.6	17.3	-3.2
	21.0	18.8	15.1	% Profit Before Taxes/Total Assets				18.7	20.9	9.4
	11.8	5.1	3.6			17.4		3.3	9.5	3.2
	1.3	-4.0	-2.0			3.9		-9.3	4.0	-3.3
						-1.5				
	71.6	136.7	68.2	Sales/Net Fixed Assets		999.8		68.8	81.7	63.8
	27.4	34.3	28.6			27.6		30.4	39.0	25.8
	12.5	10.6	10.1			15.1		13.8	3.7	10.2
	3.2	3.7	3.5	Sales/Total Assets		5.3		4.3	3.0	3.1
	2.2	2.2	2.2			2.5		3.0	2.0	1.6
	1.4	1.3	1.2			1.5		2.2	1.2	1.1
	.5	.3	.8	% Depr., Dep., Amort./Sales				.7	.4	.6
(44)	1.3	(45) — 1.5	(52) — 1.6					(12) — 1.3	(13) — 2.1	(16) — 1.7
	2.6	3.2	3.2					2.8	3.5	3.1
	1.5	1.9	1.9	% Officers', Directors' Owners' Comp/Sales						
(17)	3.6	(14) — 5.0	(27) — 3.5							
	7.1	12.6	8.0							
	3214682M	2506877M	2576889M	Net Sales ($)	2487M	21211M	26686M	137525M	296414M	2092566M
	2078851M	1434081M	1760336M	Total Assets ($)	4413M	15431M	19812M	62319M	156569M	1501792M

M = $ thousand   MM = $ million
See Pages 9 through 22 for Explanation of Ratios and Data

Current Data Sorted by Assets | Comparative Historical Data

Type of Statement	0-500M	500M-2MM	2-10MM	10-50MM	50-100MM	100-250MM		4/1/05-3/31/06 ALL	4/1/06-3/31/07 ALL
Unqualified			5	12	4	5		26	33
Reviewed		2	7	2				13	7
Compiled		1	2	1	1			2	4
Tax Returns	1	2						6	11
Other	1	3	21	22	3	2		36	38
		15 (4/1-9/30/09)		82 (10/1/09-3/31/10)					
NUMBER OF STATEMENTS	2	8	35	37	8	7		83	93
ASSETS	%	%	%	%	%	%		%	%
Cash & Equivalents			9.2	15.6				14.8	15.5
Trade Receivables (net)			30.8	24.4				28.5	29.3
Inventory			27.5	22.4				22.5	23.0
All Other Current			3.0	5.7				4.6	2.9
Total Current			70.5	68.1				70.4	70.7
Fixed Assets (net)			12.8	12.9				14.5	12.2
Intangibles (net)			7.7	10.9				8.5	9.6
All Other Non-Current			9.0	8.1				6.6	7.5
Total			100.0	100.0				100.0	100.0
LIABILITIES									
Notes Payable-Short Term			14.0	7.5				8.9	8.5
Cur. Mat.-L.T.D.			3.5	1.1				1.6	2.5
Trade Payables			13.2	14.6				15.1	16.0
Income Taxes Payable			.3	.4				.7	.4
All Other Current			12.2	16.8				11.6	13.0
Total Current			43.2	40.4				37.9	40.4
Long-Term Debt			11.1	8.3				13.7	15.7
Deferred Taxes			.5	.5				.3	.4
All Other Non-Current			4.5	17.5				7.7	9.3
Net Worth			40.6	33.2				40.4	34.2
Total Liabilities & Net Worth			100.0	100.0				100.0	100.0
INCOME DATA									
Net Sales			100.0	100.0				100.0	100.0
Gross Profit			37.3	36.8				38.6	39.5
Operating Expenses			34.0	36.9				33.5	36.6
Operating Profit			3.4	-.1				5.2	3.0
All Other Expenses (net)			.7	1.1				.2	.9
Profit Before Taxes			2.7	-1.2				5.0	2.1
RATIOS									
Current			2.6	5.3				4.2	3.2
			1.5	2.2				1.7	1.7
			1.3	1.3				1.3	1.2
Quick			1.4	3.2				2.7	2.3
			.8	1.2				1.1	1.1
			.6	.6				.7	.6
Sales/Receivables			30 12.0	42 8.7				38 9.7	34 10.6
			45 8.1	49 7.5				53 6.8	51 7.1
			60 6.1	58 6.3				67 5.4	68 5.4
Cost of Sales/Inventory			28 12.9	41 8.8				31 11.9	32 11.5
			75 4.9	81 4.5				70 5.2	73 5.0
			134 2.7	118 3.1				106 3.5	105 3.5
Cost of Sales/Payables			20 17.9	23 15.6				27 13.8	26 14.1
			30 12.2	38 9.6				38 9.7	41 8.8
			53 6.9	53 6.9				55 6.6	65 5.6
Sales/Working Capital			4.6	2.4				3.1	3.7
			8.0	3.9				6.4	6.9
			14.9	18.6				21.6	36.0
EBIT/Interest			5.1	22.5				26.6	13.6
			(32) 1.9	(30) 3.5				(68) 6.7	(73) 3.9
			.3	.9				1.7	.9
Net Profit + Depr., Dep., Amort./Cur. Mat. L/T/D				6.0				14.7	16.5
				(15) 2.1				(18) 4.8	(21) 3.1
				.5				1.8	2.3
Fixed/Worth			.1	.2				.1	.1
			.3	.4				.3	.3
			.9	5.8				1.4	1.7
Debt/Worth			.9	.3				.5	.6
			1.8	2.6				1.5	1.8
			3.3	18.1				6.0	8.8
% Profit Before Taxes/Tangible Net Worth			60.8	28.2				47.3	51.3
			(30) 4.2	(29) 15.8				(70) 19.6	(78) 21.6
			-2.6	5.5				6.2	4.5
% Profit Before Taxes/Total Assets			11.9	9.2				16.2	13.9
			1.4	2.6				6.3	6.3
			-1.0	-6.4				1.1	-.8
Sales/Net Fixed Assets			71.5	41.2				51.3	54.9
			28.7	21.1				20.0	24.4
			11.9	10.6				8.8	10.3
Sales/Total Assets			3.0	2.2				2.8	2.8
			2.1	1.8				1.9	2.0
			1.6	.7				1.2	1.3
% Depr., Dep., Amort./Sales			.8	.8				.8	1.0
			(26) 1.5	(28) 1.5				(65) 1.7	(62) 1.6
			2.7	3.1				3.0	2.4
% Officers', Directors' Owners' Comp/Sales								1.9	.6
								(13) 6.9	(12) 3.7
								14.7	8.5
Net Sales ($)	1472M	41764M	425797M	1272087M	867998M	1663297M		4007153M	5719779M
Total Assets ($)	459M	11092M	193104M	795769M	507882M	1061749M		2680978M	3395226M

Comparative Historical Data | Current Data Sorted by Sales

	4/1/07-3/31/08 ALL	4/1/08-3/31/09 ALL	4/1/09-3/31/10 ALL	Type of Statement	0-1MM	1-3MM	3-5MM	5-10MM	10-25MM	25MM & OVER
	24	35	26	Unqualified				2	7	17
	10	13	11	Reviewed				6	4	1
	6	4	5	Compiled				1	2	2
	4	6	3	Tax Returns						
	38	53	52	Other	1	3 / 4		9	21	17
						15 (4/1-9/30/09)		82 (10/1/09-3/31/10)		
NUMBER OF STATEMENTS	82	111	97		1	7		18	34	37
	%	%	%	**ASSETS**	%	%	%	%	%	%
	10.5	11.6	14.2	Cash & Equivalents			D	9.9	15.4	13.1
	28.5	29.4	26.6	Trade Receivables (net)			A	30.3	23.8	30.8
	26.2	25.0	22.9	Inventory			T	25.0	24.8	21.6
	5.2	6.3	4.7	All Other Current			A	1.4	7.0	4.4
	70.4	72.2	68.3	Total Current				66.6	71.0	70.0
	13.8	11.7	13.6	Fixed Assets (net)			N	12.0	13.2	13.3
	9.7	9.1	10.1	Intangibles (net)			O	12.5	6.3	10.9
	6.2	7.0	7.9	All Other Non-Current			T	8.9	9.6	5.8
	100.0	100.0	100.0	Total				100.0	100.0	100.0
				LIABILITIES			A			
	9.8	9.9	9.7	Notes Payable-Short Term			V	14.5	7.8	9.7
	2.1	2.7	2.2	Cur. Mat.-L.T.D.			A	3.6	2.4	1.7
	16.0	16.2	14.1	Trade Payables			I	9.1	12.4	19.6
	.5	.9	.3	Income Taxes Payable			L	.6	.2	.2
	11.9	16.2	13.8	All Other Current			A	6.1	11.6	19.1
	40.3	46.0	40.1	Total Current			B	33.8	34.4	50.4
	14.8	9.1	10.4	Long-Term Debt			L	10.6	9.4	7.4
	.4	.4	.5	Deferred Taxes			E	.6	.6	.6
	7.0	6.7	9.0	All Other Non-Current				4.0	7.8	13.9
	37.4	37.7	40.0	Net Worth				51.1	47.8	27.7
	100.0	100.0	100.0	Total Liabilities & Net Worth				100.0	100.0	100.0
				INCOME DATA						
	100.0	100.0	100.0	Net Sales				100.0	100.0	100.0
	38.5	38.0	36.6	Gross Profit				45.5	37.2	29.8
	35.8	35.1	35.0	Operating Expenses				43.3	33.3	31.5
	2.7	2.9	1.6	Operating Profit				2.2	3.8	-1.7
	1.0	.7	.8	All Other Expenses (net)				.4	.4	1.3
	1.8	2.2	.7	Profit Before Taxes				1.8	3.4	-3.0
				RATIOS						
	2.5 / 1.8 / 1.2	2.9 / 1.8 / 1.2	3.5 / 1.8 / 1.3	Current				3.7 / 1.7 / 1.4	4.3 / 2.4 / 1.3	2.7 / 1.4 / 1.1
	1.4 / .9 / .6	1.6 / 1.0 / .6	2.1 / 1.0 / .6	Quick				1.9 / 1.2 / .6	3.3 / 1.1 / .7	1.9 / .9 / .5
	(35) 10.5 / (50) 7.3 / (65) 5.6	(38) 9.6 / (51) 7.2 / (64) 5.7	(36) 10.1 / (49) 7.5 / (60) 6.0	Sales/Receivables				(33) 11.1 / (47) 7.8 / (62) 5.9	(33) 11.1 / (46) 8.0 / (57) 6.4	(43) 8.5 / (53) 6.9 / (70) 5.2
	(42) 8.6 / (75) 4.8 / (122) 3.0	(33) 11.0 / (65) 5.6 / (102) 3.6	(31) 11.8 / (65) 5.6 / (114) 3.2	Cost of Sales/Inventory				(32) 11.2 / (97) 3.7 / (202) 1.8	(34) 10.8 / (69) 5.3 / (135) 2.7	(33) 11.2 / (58) 6.3 / (87) 4.2
	(26) 13.9 / (40) 9.2 / (61) 6.0	(23) 15.8 / (37) 9.9 / (54) 6.8	(21) 17.0 / (34) 10.7 / (54) 6.7	Cost of Sales/Payables				(19) 19.0 / (27) 13.7 / (59) 6.2	(21) 17.8 / (30) 12.0 / (50) 7.3	(27) 13.3 / (43) 8.5 / (66) 5.5
	3.7 / 7.1 / 22.4	4.2 / 6.6 / 25.3	3.2 / 6.9 / 18.6	Sales/Working Capital				2.8 / 5.5 / 11.7	2.8 / 4.7 / 12.6	3.6 / 9.7 / 103.5
	(70) 12.6 / 2.5 / -.3	(91) 10.6 / 3.8 / .3	(81) 12.0 / 2.7 / .3	EBIT/Interest				(16) 9.5 / 2.2 / .3	(30) 15.7 / 3.7 / -.1	(31) 16.1 / 2.9 / 1.1
	(27) 18.7 / 3.3 / 1.0	(36) 9.5 / 2.3 / 1.2	(25) 4.8 / 2.1 / .8	Net Profit + Depr., Dep., Amort./Cur. Mat. L/T/D						(12) 5.9 / 2.2 / .6
	.1 / .3 / 1.1	.1 / .3 / .9	.1 / .4 / 1.2	Fixed/Worth				.1 / .3 / 1.0	.1 / .2 / .6	.2 / .5 / 5.8
	.6 / 2.0 / 5.7	.6 / 1.9 / 5.7	.5 / 1.8 / 4.8	Debt/Worth				.3 / 1.3 / 1.9	.5 / 1.0 / 2.8	.5 / 2.9 / 18.1
	(72) 38.8 / 15.8 / -8.2	(95) 44.2 / 13.9 / .1	(82) 31.6 / 11.2 / .7	% Profit Before Taxes/Tangible Net Worth				(16) 63.9 / 6.4 / -3.4	(31) 36.6 / 10.9 / -3.8	(29) 17.2 / 13.3 / 5.3
	16.0 / 3.9 / -3.8	12.9 / 4.7 / -.8	9.1 / 2.7 / -2.6	% Profit Before Taxes/Total Assets				19.6 / 2.7 / -.4	10.2 / 2.2 / -4.1	5.4 / 2.9 / -2.6
	67.8 / 24.5 / 8.1	63.4 / 27.7 / 13.0	45.7 / 23.2 / 8.9	Sales/Net Fixed Assets				62.5 / 26.4 / 9.1	51.6 / 27.6 / 11.1	45.5 / 19.6 / 7.9
	2.9 / 2.0 / 1.2	3.0 / 2.2 / 1.3	2.5 / 1.9 / 1.2	Sales/Total Assets				2.2 / 1.8 / 1.2	3.0 / 2.1 / 1.2	2.5 / 1.9 / 1.4
	(60) .7 / 1.6 / 2.9	(83) .8 / 1.3 / 2.5	(69) .9 / 1.7 / 3.1	% Depr., Dep., Amort./Sales				(15) .9 / 2.0 / 3.0	(26) .9 / 1.6 / 2.4	(23) .5 / 1.4 / 3.0
	(14) .9 / 3.5 / 7.7	(18) 3.2 / 4.6 / 10.4	(15) 3.7 / 5.6 / 8.4	% Officers', Directors' Owners' Comp/Sales						
	4491862M	7129412M	4272415M	Net Sales ($)	10M	11661M		122298M	569366M	3569080M
	2915406M	4070890M	2570055M	Total Assets ($)	4M	9971M		87211M	373816M	2099053M

M = $ thousand   MM = $ million
See Pages 9 through 22 for Explanation of Ratios and Data

Current Data Sorted by Assets   Comparative Historical Data

	0-500M	500M-2MM	2-10MM	10-50MM	50-100MM	100-250MM	Type of Statement	4/1/05-3/31/06 ALL	4/1/06-3/31/07 ALL
			2	5		2	Unqualified	8	9
	1		2	1			Reviewed	5	4
			2				Compiled	2	2
			2				Tax Returns	3	6
	2	1	5	7	2	5	Other	17	18
		9 (4/1-9/30/09)		32 (10/1/09-3/31/10)					
NUMBER OF STATEMENTS	2	4	13	13	2	7		35	39
	%	%	%	%	%	%	**ASSETS**	%	%
			12.6	25.0			Cash & Equivalents	14.1	17.2
			33.4	21.7			Trade Receivables (net)	27.3	26.8
			28.1	22.5			Inventory	23.4	25.6
			4.7	7.9			All Other Current	3.0	3.8
			78.8	77.2			Total Current	67.9	73.4
			11.0	9.2			Fixed Assets (net)	10.3	11.9
			1.2	6.1			Intangibles (net)	11.3	7.2
			9.0	7.5			All Other Non-Current	10.6	7.5
			100.0	100.0			Total	100.0	100.0
							LIABILITIES		
			8.7	8.0			Notes Payable-Short Term	13.1	9.8
			5.1	8.8			Cur. Mat.-L.T.D.	4.5	5.1
			17.8	11.3			Trade Payables	14.7	16.5
			.0	.1			Income Taxes Payable	.3	.8
			14.9	24.6			All Other Current	10.3	14.2
			46.6	52.7			Total Current	42.9	46.3
			4.4	6.1			Long-Term Debt	16.7	7.4
			.0	.2			Deferred Taxes	.1	.2
			21.7	7.3			All Other Non-Current	7.0	3.9
			27.3	33.7			Net Worth	33.3	42.2
			100.0	100.0			Total Liabilties & Net Worth	100.0	100.0
							INCOME DATA		
			100.0	100.0			Net Sales	100.0	100.0
			47.6	39.6			Gross Profit	40.2	39.3
			45.6	35.0			Operating Expenses	33.2	34.4
			2.0	4.6			Operating Profit	7.0	4.9
			1.2	2.9			All Other Expenses (net)	1.1	.4
			.7	1.7			Profit Before Taxes	5.9	4.5
							RATIOS		
			5.2	3.6			Current	3.3	3.6
			1.6	1.6				1.7	1.8
			1.3	1.0				.9	1.1
			1.6	2.1			Quick	2.0	1.8
			1.0	1.3				1.2	1.0
			.8	.6				.5	.6
			45 8.1	30 12.1			Sales/Receivables	35 10.3	31 11.9
			55 6.7	48 7.6				47 7.8	61 6.0
			60 6.1	67 5.5				66 5.5	80 4.6
			15 24.3	52 7.1			Cost of Sales/Inventory	26 13.8	34 10.7
			122 3.0	76 4.8				82 4.5	83 4.4
			173 2.1	104 3.5				117 3.1	112 3.3
			20 18.2	20 18.1			Cost of Sales/Payables	29 12.7	21 17.4
			32 11.5	27 13.5				41 9.0	33 11.2
			83 4.4	55 6.7				62 5.9	64 5.7
			3.5	2.9			Sales/Working Capital	2.5	3.0
			4.3	4.4				10.1	6.2
			14.7	NM				-91.3	33.7
			28.2	63.0			EBIT/Interest	25.5	27.2
		(12)	8.8	(10) 3.2				(27) 6.8	(32) 5.1
			-2.0	.3				.7	.7
							Net Profit + Depr., Dep., Amort./Cur. Mat. L/T/D		16.5
								(10)	1.8
									.3
			.1	.1			Fixed/Worth	.1	.1
			.2	.2				.3	.3
			5.2	3.5				3.7	1.1
			.6	.4			Debt/Worth	.4	.4
			2.5	1.5				1.5	1.5
			71.0	14.3				41.3	7.2
			112.5	24.6			% Profit Before Taxes/Tangible Net Worth	43.8	64.2
		(11)	19.0	(11) 20.0				(29) 27.9	(32) 18.4
			-43.1	2.5				5.7	5.6
			24.1	14.3			% Profit Before Taxes/Total Assets	19.3	16.4
			10.9	3.1				7.1	5.8
			-16.8	-.6				-1.5	-.2
			55.0	77.9			Sales/Net Fixed Assets	64.7	65.1
			29.3	26.6				27.2	24.1
			15.4	7.3				9.3	9.2
			3.4	2.0			Sales/Total Assets	3.0	3.4
			2.2	1.7				2.2	1.7
			1.3	1.0				1.0	1.1
			.8	.6			% Depr., Dep., Amort./Sales	.6	.5
		(10)	1.2	(11) 1.4				(26) 1.6	(33) 1.6
			1.6	4.0				2.6	2.6
							% Officers', Directors' Owners' Comp/Sales		
Net Sales ($)	5888M	15299M	140108M	518131M	280581M	1271519M		1796310M	1729221M
Total Assets ($)	967M	4830M	68051M	354756M	149396M	1146293M		1352792M	1283139M

M = $ thousand   MM = $ million
See Pages 9 through 22 for Explanation of Ratios and Data

Comparative Historical Data / Current Data Sorted by Sales

			Type of Statement						
8	12	9	Unqualified					4	5
3	1	4	Reviewed					1	
5	1	2	Compiled				3		
3	7	4	Tax Returns				2 1		
18	16	22	Other		2 3	1 1	1 2 2		14
4/1/07-3/31/08 ALL	4/1/08-3/31/09 ALL	4/1/09-3/31/10 ALL		0-1MM	9 (4/1-9/30/09) 1-3MM	3-5MM	32 (10/1/09-3/31/10) 5-10MM	10-25MM	25MM & OVER
37	37	41	NUMBER OF STATEMENTS		5	2	8	7	19
%	%	%	ASSETS	%	%	%	%	%	%
16.2	17.7	19.3	Cash & Equivalents						25.6
26.1	26.0	29.0	Trade Receivables (net)	D					23.6
21.9	22.6	21.4	Inventory	A					20.3
5.3	2.7	6.0	All Other Current	T					5.5
69.5	69.1	75.6	Total Current	A					75.0
10.5	13.8	12.0	Fixed Assets (net)						8.8
11.6	9.5	6.1	Intangibles (net)	N					10.5
8.4	7.7	6.3	All Other Non-Current	O					5.7
100.0	100.0	100.0	Total	T					100.0
			LIABILITIES						
7.2	9.7	7.5	Notes Payable-Short Term	A					6.5
3.4	3.9	5.8	Cur. Mat.-L.T.D.	V					8.1
17.1	24.6	17.3	Trade Payables	A					14.7
.3	.1	.1	Income Taxes Payable	I					.1
15.9	15.7	16.6	All Other Current	L					21.1
44.0	54.0	47.4	Total Current	A					50.6
7.4	9.4	6.2	Long-Term Debt	B					7.4
.2	.4	.3	Deferred Taxes	L					.4
7.0	11.4	13.1	All Other Non-Current	E					10.6
41.3	24.8	33.1	Net Worth						31.0
100.0	100.0	100.0	Total Liabilities & Net Worth						100.0
			INCOME DATA						
100.0	100.0	100.0	Net Sales						100.0
38.8	40.7	42.2	Gross Profit						40.7
36.0	41.4	41.3	Operating Expenses						41.6
2.8	-.8	.9	Operating Profit						-.9
1.4	.9	1.7	All Other Expenses (net)						2.6
1.4	-1.7	-.8	Profit Before Taxes						-3.5
			RATIOS						
3.0	4.0	3.2	Current						2.9
1.5	1.6	1.6							1.6
1.1	1.0	1.2							1.1
1.7	2.5	2.0	Quick						1.6
1.0	.9	1.0							1.0
.6	.6	.7							.6
37 9.9	33 11.0	38 9.7	Sales/Receivables						38 9.7
58 6.3	52 7.1	54 6.7							58 6.3
79 4.6	65 5.6	63 5.8							79 4.6
30 12.1	23 16.0	34 10.7	Cost of Sales/Inventory						50 7.3
80 4.6	74 4.9	79 4.6							76 4.8
128 2.9	123 3.0	131 2.8							91 4.0
27 13.8	21 17.1	24 15.0	Cost of Sales/Payables						28 12.9
56 6.5	38 9.6	43 8.4							58 6.3
88 4.2	70 5.2	71 5.2							78 4.7
3.0	3.4	3.2	Sales/Working Capital						2.5
8.3	7.3	7.0							4.5
96.5	255.2	31.8							69.2
11.1	6.2	17.4	EBIT/Interest						8.4
(29) 1.0	(31) 1.2	(33) 1.8						(14)	1.3
-4.0	-7.5	-4.6							-4.8
		7.5	Net Profit + Depr., Dep.,						
	(13) 3.4		Amort./Cur. Mat. L/T/D						
	-4.4								
.1	.1	.1	Fixed/Worth						.1
.2	.2	.2							.2
1.1	1.0	3.5							-1.5
.5	.4	.5	Debt/Worth						.6
1.3	2.3	1.5							1.5
9.8	11.1	18.8							-12.6
24.4	50.5	25.4	% Profit Before Taxes/Tangible						20.3
(31) 5.5	(30) 5.8	(33) 10.3	Net Worth					(14)	6.4
-9.3	-22.1	-22.0							-17.3
10.7	10.2	13.4	% Profit Before Taxes/Total						7.8
.7	1.3	.9	Assets						.8
-3.7	-13.8	-16.2							-14.8
85.8	67.5	52.2	Sales/Net Fixed Assets						49.3
33.4	20.4	26.6							21.9
9.8	6.6	12.0							18.0
2.3	2.8	3.0	Sales/Total Assets						1.9
1.7	1.9	1.8							1.4
.9	1.0	1.0							1.0
.4	.9	.8	% Depr., Dep., Amort./Sales						.7
(24) 1.4	(24) 2.0	(31) 1.4						(13)	1.4
4.0	4.4	2.0							1.7
	4.4		% Officers', Directors'						
	(12) 7.3		Owners' Comp/Sales						
	14.4								
2142730M	2045527M	2231526M	Net Sales ($)		11922M	7128M	64592M	145258M	2002626M
1785362M	1497386M	1724293M	Total Assets ($)		10615M	6336M	26883M	112627M	1567832M

M = $ thousand   MM = $ million
See Pages 9 through 22 for Explanation of Ratios and Data

Current Data Sorted by Assets   **Comparative Historical Data**

0-500M	500M-2MM	2-10MM	10-50MM	50-100MM	100-250MM	Type of Statement	4/1/05-3/31/06 ALL	4/1/06-3/31/07 ALL
		3	17	4	6	Unqualified	32	35
1	1	10	3			Reviewed	16	21
	2	2	1			Compiled	6	11
1	2	2				Tax Returns	5	6
1	9	17	10	5	3	Other	30	43
26 (4/1-9/30/09)			74 (10/1/09-3/31/10)					
3	14	34	31	9	9	**NUMBER OF STATEMENTS**	89	116
%	%	%	%	%	%	**ASSETS**	%	%
	9.3	11.7	17.5			Cash & Equivalents	12.5	11.2
	29.1	20.0	24.5			Trade Receivables (net)	26.5	27.9
	26.5	33.1	26.8			Inventory	27.6	26.4
	4.0	5.3	5.2			All Other Current	3.4	3.4
	68.9	70.2	73.9			Total Current	70.0	68.9
	24.2	17.2	11.5			Fixed Assets (net)	19.2	19.8
	.0	7.0	8.5			Intangibles (net)	4.5	6.0
	6.9	5.6	6.1			All Other Non-Current	6.2	5.3
	100.0	100.0	100.0			Total	100.0	100.0
						LIABILITIES		
	15.3	13.2	7.4			Notes Payable-Short Term	10.8	8.0
	2.1	5.0	1.6			Cur. Mat.-L.T.D.	2.7	3.5
	11.2	13.1	10.4			Trade Payables	15.1	14.1
	.0	.3	.1			Income Taxes Payable	.4	.8
	6.3	12.9	9.3			All Other Current	11.3	11.2
	34.9	44.5	28.8			Total Current	40.2	37.6
	19.7	9.0	5.4			Long-Term Debt	13.9	11.7
	.0	.4	.5			Deferred Taxes	.9	.6
	2.7	3.6	5.9			All Other Non-Current	6.4	5.6
	42.7	42.5	59.4			Net Worth	38.6	44.4
	100.0	100.0	100.0			Total Liabilities & Net Worth	100.0	100.0
						INCOME DATA		
	100.0	100.0	100.0			Net Sales	100.0	100.0
	48.9	39.6	35.9			Gross Profit	38.4	37.5
	46.1	34.7	30.9			Operating Expenses	32.5	30.8
	2.8	4.9	4.9			Operating Profit	5.9	6.7
	1.5	1.7	1.3			All Other Expenses (net)	1.1	1.1
	1.3	3.2	3.6			Profit Before Taxes	4.9	5.5
						RATIOS		
	3.0	3.1	4.5			Current	3.9	3.7
	2.2	1.6	2.7				2.1	1.9
	1.4	1.2	1.8				1.2	1.3
	1.9	1.5	3.3			Quick	2.0	2.3
	1.3	.7	1.4				1.0	1.0
	.6	.4	.8				.5	.6
21	17.1	25 14.8	39 9.3			Sales/Receivables	33 11.0	35 10.4
33	10.9	38 9.6	54 6.7				48 7.6	45 8.0
61	6.0	54 6.7	66 5.6				63 5.8	62 5.9
25	14.7	64 5.7	60 6.1			Cost of Sales/Inventory	47 7.8	34 10.6
61	6.0	111 3.3	100 3.7				86 4.3	80 4.6
100	3.7	168 2.2	161 2.3				129 2.8	122 3.0
10	38.3	21 17.0	18 19.9			Cost of Sales/Payables	23 16.2	21 17.0
33	11.1	36 10.1	33 11.2				38 9.7	35 10.3
48	7.6	54 6.7	46 8.0				59 6.1	53 6.9
	5.4	3.4	2.0			Sales/Working Capital	3.4	3.4
	8.0	6.1	3.7				5.8	6.4
	15.7	31.9	5.8				17.3	15.1
	25.8	12.6	38.3			EBIT/Interest	15.3	20.6
(13)	-.3	(29) 3.7	(22) 5.7				(65) 4.5	(100) 5.3
	-3.6	-2.1	.0				2.1	1.6
			6.3			Net Profit + Depr., Dep., Amort./Cur. Mat. L/T/D	9.9	9.2
			(10) 1.6				(30) 3.4	(32) 3.0
			-.2				1.4	.9
	.2	.2	.1			Fixed/Worth	.1	.1
	.6	.4	.2				.4	.4
	2.4	1.2	.4				1.7	1.2
	.4	.8	.3			Debt/Worth	.5	.5
	1.0	1.5	.7				1.5	1.2
	6.1	4.7	1.8				5.9	3.4
	46.1	47.1	24.2			% Profit Before Taxes/Tangible Net Worth	49.5	47.0
(12)	-2.8	(31) 11.6	(30) 11.8				(81) 22.2	(104) 18.4
	-20.8	-14.0	.8				5.9	2.8
	21.6	14.3	9.8			% Profit Before Taxes/Total Assets	17.0	20.3
	-2.4	2.4	6.5				7.2	6.8
	-11.0	-7.9	.4				.5	1.1
	25.7	45.5	46.9			Sales/Net Fixed Assets	32.4	35.5
	12.9	22.5	20.1				17.5	16.6
	4.9	5.9	7.3				7.1	6.9
	3.4	2.6	1.9			Sales/Total Assets	2.8	2.9
	2.4	1.8	1.5				1.9	2.1
	1.7	.9	1.2				1.3	1.3
		.8	.6			% Depr., Dep., Amort./Sales	.8	.7
	(27)	(27) 1.8	(27) 1.4				(73) 1.9	(104) 1.6
		2.9	2.4				3.2	2.5
		2.2				% Officers', Directors' Owners' Comp/Sales	1.9	2.5
	(13)	(13) 8.6					(20) 4.2	(26) 4.0
		15.4					7.5	9.0
5273M	43182M	310072M	1154343M	1152053M	1924344M	Net Sales ($)	3253213M	4112645M
520M	16081M	175865M	762409M	644868M	1414022M	Total Assets ($)	2610967M	3179740M

Comparative Historical Data

Current Data Sorted by Sales

	4/1/07-3/31/08 ALL	4/1/08-3/31/09 ALL	4/1/09-3/31/10 ALL	Type of Statement	0-1MM	1-3MM (26 / 4/1-9/30/09)	3-5MM	5-10MM (74 / 10/1/09-3/31/10)	10-25MM	25MM & OVER
	26	38	30	Unqualified	1	2		1	4	24
	18	11	15	Reviewed			1	6	3	2
	7	7	5	Compiled	1		2	1	1	1
	9	7	5	Tax Returns		3		2		1
	47	47	45	Other	1	7	3	10	14	10
	107	110	100	**NUMBER OF STATEMENTS**	2	12	7	20	22	37
	%	%	%	**ASSETS**	%	%	%	%	%	%
	13.2	13.2	13.8	Cash & Equivalents		13.0		17.1	14.9	12.3
	23.8	25.0	22.8	Trade Receivables (net)		20.3		24.1	18.4	26.3
	26.5	27.9	26.7	Inventory		23.2		33.4	30.1	22.5
	3.0	3.4	6.0	All Other Current		4.7		4.0	10.7	5.4
	66.5	69.4	69.3	Total Current		61.2		78.5	74.1	66.5
	19.1	15.8	16.9	Fixed Assets (net)		21.5		11.9	16.4	15.5
	8.9	7.8	7.5	Intangibles (net)		7.6		4.1	6.2	10.1
	5.4	6.9	6.4	All Other Non-Current		9.7		5.4	3.3	7.9
	100.0	100.0	100.0	Total		100.0		100.0	100.0	100.0
				LIABILITIES						
	13.6	10.5	11.1	Notes Payable-Short Term		12.2		11.4	13.2	7.8
	3.1	2.4	3.0	Cur. Mat.-L.T.D.		2.1		2.2	2.1	2.0
	12.1	13.1	13.5	Trade Payables		16.7		11.3	12.3	12.5
	.6	.3	.2	Income Taxes Payable		.2		.2	.1	.2
	10.5	12.7	10.7	All Other Current		3.9		14.8	13.4	10.0
	39.9	39.1	38.5	Total Current		35.1		40.0	41.2	32.6
	10.3	13.2	13.0	Long-Term Debt		14.8		11.1	6.6	17.4
	.4	.2	.4	Deferred Taxes		.0		.6	.3	.6
	5.4	10.7	3.8	All Other Non-Current		.6		1.2	4.5	3.8
	44.1	36.7	44.3	Net Worth		49.5		47.1	47.5	45.6
	100.0	100.0	100.0	Total Liabilities & Net Worth		100.0		100.0	100.0	100.0
				INCOME DATA						
	100.0	100.0	100.0	Net Sales		100.0		100.0	100.0	100.0
	39.8	38.9	39.4	Gross Profit		56.6		41.1	39.8	34.1
	32.1	32.7	34.1	Operating Expenses		47.1		40.6	36.5	26.2
	7.7	6.2	5.4	Operating Profit		9.5		.5	3.3	7.9
	2.0	1.8	2.0	All Other Expenses (net)		2.7		.8	.8	2.9
	5.7	4.4	3.4	Profit Before Taxes		6.8		-.3	2.5	5.0
				RATIOS						
	4.0	3.4	3.5	Current		2.9		4.3	3.7	4.3
	2.0	2.2	2.0			2.1		2.2	1.7	2.4
	1.2	1.3	1.3			1.3		1.2	1.2	1.7
	2.5	1.9	2.0	Quick		1.4		2.4	2.7	2.1
	1.0	1.2	1.1			1.3		1.3	.6	1.2
	.5	.6	.5			.7		.5	.3	.8
	31 11.8	31 11.8	29 12.6	Sales/Receivables	20 18.4		34 10.7	24 15.2	38 9.7	
	44 8.3	43 8.5	44 8.4		30 12.3		44 8.2	31 11.9	52 7.1	
	59 6.1	65 5.6	62 5.9		96 3.8		60 6.1	47 7.8	66 5.5	
	28 13.0	46 7.9	38 9.5	Cost of Sales/Inventory	17 21.6		68 5.4	51 7.1	31 11.9	
	71 5.1	86 4.2	87 4.2		89 4.1		137 2.7	84 4.3	79 4.6	
	117 3.1	137 2.7	148 2.5		236 1.5		187 2.0	160 2.3	111 3.3	
	16 22.1	22 16.4	20 18.4	Cost of Sales/Payables	11 32.3		21 17.7	19 19.7	22 16.3	
	31 11.6	36 10.3	34 10.7		51 7.1		36 10.2	28 13.1	34 10.6	
	54 6.7	57 6.4	49 7.5		171 2.1		49 7.5	39 9.4	45 8.1	
	3.5	3.0	2.7	Sales/Working Capital		2.4		2.6	2.6	2.5
	6.4	5.3	5.1			7.0		4.7	5.9	4.3
	23.1	13.9	13.8			15.3		13.9	16.2	8.5
	16.1	17.9	17.8	EBIT/Interest	9.6		14.2	29.6	25.8	
	(93) 6.3	(94) 3.8	(80) 2.6		(11) -.3		(16) 1.7	(17) 6.3	(28) 5.9	
	1.3	.6	-1.3		-3.4		-5.2	-5.7	1.5	
	15.9	16.3	5.2	Net Profit + Depr., Dep., Amort./Cur. Mat. L/T/D						7.7
	(26) 3.8	(20) 2.5	(26) 2.6						(13) 2.9	
	-.1	-.1	.4							1.4
	.1	.1	.1	Fixed/Worth		.2		.1	.2	.1
	.4	.3	.3			.7		.2	.3	.3
	1.0	1.1	1.0			3.8		.9	1.2	.7
	.4	.4	.4	Debt/Worth		.5		.4	.3	.4
	1.4	1.3	1.3			1.1		1.2	1.4	1.1
	3.4	4.7	4.5			8.7		4.5	4.4	3.6
	69.7	44.7	35.6	% Profit Before Taxes/Tangible Net Worth	25.4		44.0	52.1	29.7	
	(93) 24.5	(96) 18.0	(87) 11.6		(10) -7.6		(19) -2.1	(21) 13.3	(31) 15.2	
	3.1	2.4	-6.3		-21.4		-23.9	-6.4	6.2	
	23.7	21.2	13.1	% Profit Before Taxes/Total Assets		9.2		16.2	14.3	14.2
	9.8	7.9	4.0			-2.4		.0	6.5	4.8
	.8	-.4	-3.7			-10.5		-11.5	-3.2	1.6
	44.9	47.9	38.9	Sales/Net Fixed Assets		25.6		46.6	38.7	40.9
	18.3	18.2	14.6			7.7		27.6	21.8	11.7
	6.3	8.0	6.4			3.8		8.3	7.6	6.9
	2.8	2.6	2.3	Sales/Total Assets		2.5		2.6	2.5	2.1
	1.9	1.8	1.7			1.6		2.1	1.8	1.6
	1.2	1.3	1.2			.7		1.0	1.2	1.2
	.6	.8	.8	% Depr., Dep., Amort./Sales				.7	1.3	.8
	(82) 1.5	(84) 1.5	(76) 1.8					(15) 1.4	(17) 2.1	(30) 2.1
	2.8	2.6	3.1					1.9	2.7	3.4
	2.3	2.0	2.2	% Officers', Directors', Owners' Comp/Sales				2.3		
	(24) 5.5	(18) 4.4	(21) 6.0					(10) 6.5		
	8.1	8.0	13.7					14.6		
	3951466M	5071150M	4589267M	Net Sales ($)	702M	21831M	28902M	145203M	393294M	3999335M
	2820366M	3317319M	3013765M	Total Assets ($)	2853M	20516M	13806M	96041M	276043M	2604506M

© RMA 2010

M = $ thousand   MM = $ million
See Pages 9 through 22 for Explanation of Ratios and Data

Current Data Sorted by Assets   Comparative Historical Data

Type of Statement

	0-500M	500M-2MM	2-10MM	10-50MM	50-100MM	100-250MM		4/1/05-3/31/06 ALL	4/1/06-3/31/07 ALL
Unqualified			8	8		5		17	17
Reviewed		4	7	3	2			14	18
Compiled		3	2					5	10
Tax Returns		2	2					6	6
Other	2	3	11	15	3	6		31	35
		11 (4/1-9/30/09)	75 (10/1/09-3/31/10)						
NUMBER OF STATEMENTS	2	12	30	26	5	11		73	86

0-500M	500M-2MM	2-10MM	10-50MM	50-100MM	100-250MM		4/1/05-3/31/06	4/1/06-3/31/07
%	%	%	%	%	%	**ASSETS**	%	%
	16.1	13.0	11.6		21.3	Cash & Equivalents	10.0	11.6
	31.0	29.1	35.7		21.0	Trade Receivables (net)	33.8	32.2
	32.8	26.5	24.2		14.4	Inventory	23.5	25.7
	1.2	5.2	5.3		5.1	All Other Current	3.6	3.0
	81.1	73.7	76.8		61.7	Total Current	71.0	72.5
	10.2	16.3	14.2		15.0	Fixed Assets (net)	15.5	16.1
	2.6	4.2	4.5		16.7	Intangibles (net)	7.5	6.5
	6.1	5.8	4.5		6.6	All Other Non-Current	6.1	4.8
	100.0	100.0	100.0		100.0	Total	100.0	100.0
						LIABILITIES		
	26.8	14.4	9.8		1.6	Notes Payable-Short Term	11.7	8.9
	2.5	2.7	1.8		2.4	Cur. Mat.-L.T.D.	2.8	3.1
	14.5	18.4	16.1		11.9	Trade Payables	16.3	15.9
	.2	.2	.3		.0	Income Taxes Payable	.2	.2
	5.4	9.5	14.3		12.7	All Other Current	11.6	12.2
	49.4	45.2	42.3		28.5	Total Current	42.6	40.3
	4.9	10.9	7.1		13.2	Long-Term Debt	10.1	11.7
	.1	.2	.5		.9	Deferred Taxes	.4	.4
	12.9	4.1	5.8		17.1	All Other Non-Current	5.2	5.3
	32.7	39.6	44.3		40.2	Net Worth	41.7	42.3
	100.0	100.0	100.0		100.0	Total Liabilities & Net Worth	100.0	100.0
						INCOME DATA		
	100.0	100.0	100.0		100.0	Net Sales	100.0	100.0
	46.2	38.9	35.8		42.2	Gross Profit	37.1	39.7
	39.8	33.8	29.3		43.9	Operating Expenses	31.7	33.4
	6.4	5.1	6.5		-1.7	Operating Profit	5.4	6.3
	1.4	1.0	.2		7.4	All Other Expenses (net)	.8	1.5
	5.0	4.0	6.3		-9.2	Profit Before Taxes	4.7	4.8
						RATIOS		
	6.2	3.1	3.0		3.1		2.7	3.1
	2.2	1.6	1.8		2.4	Current	1.8	1.8
	1.0	1.1	1.3		1.4		1.2	1.3
	4.4	1.9	1.7		2.5		1.6	1.7
	.9	.9	1.2		1.6	Quick	1.1	1.1
	.6	.7	.6		.6		.7	.7
25 14.6	36 10.2	54 6.8		54 6.8		Sales/Receivables	35 10.5	36 10.2
35 10.4	50 7.2	62 5.9		70 5.2			49 7.4	51 7.1
57 6.4	57 6.4	74 4.9		97 3.7			69 5.3	64 5.7
58 6.3	41 8.9	28 13.1		55 6.7		Cost of Sales/Inventory	24 15.4	32 11.2
82 4.4	90 4.1	77 4.7		69 5.3			60 6.1	61 5.9
113 3.2	135 2.7	103 3.5		99 3.7			99 3.7	119 3.1
9 41.9	21 17.0	23 15.6		41 8.9		Cost of Sales/Payables	22 16.7	23 15.6
28 13.2	36 10.0	34 10.8		57 6.3			33 11.2	33 11.0
56 6.5	56 6.5	61 6.0		72 5.1			50 7.3	53 6.9
	3.7	2.6	3.5		1.7	Sales/Working Capital	4.7	4.4
	8.5	7.9	6.2		2.9		8.4	7.7
	NM	34.2	11.0		11.4		22.6	15.1
	24.0	15.2	17.6				13.8	19.0
	(11) 2.0	(25) 3.6	(19) 4.8			EBIT/Interest	(61) 5.6	(76) 6.0
	1.0	1.3	2.8				1.6	1.6
			10.4			Net Profit + Depr., Dep.,	17.8	10.2
			(11) 5.7			Amort./Cur. Mat. L/T/D	(19) 7.0	(28) 3.5
			2.0				1.3	.9
	.0	.1	.1		.2		.2	.1
	.3	.3	.4		.4	Fixed/Worth	.4	.4
	1.1	1.2	.8		-.9		1.0	1.0
	.2	.4	.4		.7		.7	.6
	4.7	1.6	1.2		1.9	Debt/Worth	1.8	1.6
	NM	4.8	4.6		-6.2		4.5	3.3
		61.9	51.5			% Profit Before Taxes/Tangible	56.3	56.7
	(26)	23.5 (23)	15.8			Net Worth	(64) 18.6	(77) 29.0
		3.3	4.9				3.9	3.1
	27.9	22.0	24.8		7.2	% Profit Before Taxes/Total	18.1	22.6
	11.3	5.1	7.7		-5.5	Assets	8.5	11.8
	.1	-.4	1.8		-13.4		2.3	1.7
	225.9	81.5	33.4		16.9	Sales/Net Fixed Assets	54.5	45.8
	98.0	16.4	19.1		7.1		20.3	18.8
	23.2	6.0	11.7		5.1		9.1	8.8
	3.6	3.1	2.2		1.0	Sales/Total Assets	3.2	3.1
	2.5	1.8	1.9		.9		2.6	2.4
	2.0	1.1	1.3		.6		1.6	1.5
		1.0	.7			% Depr., Dep., Amort./Sales	.5	.7
	(24)	1.9 (21)	1.2				(62) 1.2	(70) 1.5
		4.2	1.8				3.1	2.7
						% Officers', Directors'	2.4	2.5
						Owners' Comp/Sales	(16) 5.4	(27) 4.6
							8.6	8.4
4194M	43433M	259076M	1156726M	417150M	1975073M	Net Sales ($)	2604869M	3145340M
916M	16001M	138861M	608843M	331255M	1664996M	Total Assets ($)	1781542M	2214175M

M = $ thousand   MM = $ million
See Pages 9 through 22 for Explanation of Ratios and Data

Comparative Historical Data   ## Current Data Sorted by Sales

					Type of Statement							
	16		21		21	Unqualified				2	7	12
	14		15		16	Reviewed			2	3	5	1	5
	5		8		5	Compiled			2	1	2		
	9		5		6	Tax Returns			3	1	1	1	
	47		40		38	Other			1	6	6	3	22
	4/1/07-		4/1/08-		4/1/09-				11 (4/1-9/30/09)		75 (10/1/09-3/31/10)		
	3/31/08		3/31/09		3/31/10								
	ALL		ALL		ALL		0-1MM	1-3MM	3-5MM	5-10MM	10-25MM	25MM & OVER
	91		89		86	NUMBER OF STATEMENTS		8	11	16	12	39
	%		%		%	ASSETS	%	%	%	%	%	%
	14.8		11.7		13.5	Cash & Equivalents			8.5	20.1	9.3	14.5
	28.6		29.4		30.4	Trade Receivables (net)	D		24.4	27.8	40.2	29.2
	22.7		24.7		24.0	Inventory	A		37.0	28.0	16.5	20.1
	4.7		5.0		4.5	All Other Current	T		1.2	2.8	10.3	5.0
	70.8		70.9		72.4	Total Current	A		71.1	78.7	76.3	68.9
	16.8		15.3		14.6	Fixed Assets (net)			13.0	13.7	18.1	14.3
	6.2		6.5		7.6	Intangibles (net)	N		5.9	3.1	1.5	11.7
	6.2		7.3		5.4	All Other Non-Current	O		10.0	4.4	4.1	5.1
	100.0		100.0		100.0	Total	T		100.0	100.0	100.0	100.0
					LIABILITIES	A					
	10.0		8.2		12.0	Notes Payable-Short Term	V		14.0	9.0	18.7	5.9
	2.0		3.0		2.6	Cur. Mat.-L.T.D.	A		2.0	1.5	3.6	2.7
	17.7		14.5		15.9	Trade Payables	I		13.6	13.3	26.4	14.3
	.6		.4		.2	Income Taxes Payable	L		.2	.2	.4	.2
	13.6		10.7		11.0	All Other Current	A		6.3	10.3	8.7	13.3
	43.9		36.8		41.8	Total Current	B		36.0	34.3	57.9	36.4
	12.6		9.0		9.5	Long-Term Debt	L		9.2	6.6	12.6	8.7
	.5		.5		.4	Deferred Taxes	E		.3	.2	.0	.7
	10.0		8.7		7.5	All Other Non-Current			8.8	7.6	1.0	8.5
	33.0		45.1		40.8	Net Worth			45.6	51.3	28.5	45.7
	100.0		100.0		100.0	Total Liabilties & Net Worth			100.0	100.0	100.0	100.0
					INCOME DATA						
	100.0		100.0		100.0	Net Sales			100.0	100.0	100.0	100.0
	38.5		38.3		39.5	Gross Profit			42.5	42.8	36.0	37.5
	34.4		33.4		34.8	Operating Expenses			37.9	38.4	30.1	33.2
	4.1		4.9		4.7	Operating Profit			4.7	4.4	5.9	4.3
	.9		2.1		1.8	All Other Expenses (net)			1.0	.7	.8	2.7
	3.2		2.8		2.9	Profit Before Taxes			3.6	3.7	5.1	1.5
					RATIOS						
	3.8		3.8		3.1				5.2	6.3	1.9	3.0
	2.2		1.8		1.9	Current			3.0	2.7	1.5	2.0
	1.3		1.3		1.2				1.1	1.5	1.0	1.3
	2.6		2.1		1.9				2.1	4.3	1.2	1.9
	1.2		1.0		1.1	Quick			.9	1.5	.8	1.3
	.8		.6		.6				.5	.8	.7	.6
30	12.0	35	10.4	46	8.0		27	13.3	28	13.0	52	7.0	53	6.9
52	7.0	51	7.1	56	6.6	Sales/Receivables	38	9.7	49	7.5	56	6.5	64	5.7
70	5.2	66	5.5	71	5.1		61	6.0	54	6.8	75	4.9	74	4.9
26	14.1	45	8.0	50	7.3		81	4.5	58	6.3	2	169.1	51	7.2
59	6.2	79	4.6	78	4.7	Cost of Sales/Inventory	120	3.0	93	3.9	28	12.8	78	4.7
101	3.6	109	3.4	109	3.3		201	1.8	121	3.0	78	4.7	102	3.6
20	18.2	19	18.9	24	15.0		19	19.5	15	24.8	36	10.2	30	12.3
31	11.8	35	10.5	39	9.4	Cost of Sales/Payables	26	14.1	31	11.8	49	7.4	41	9.0
57	6.4	49	7.5	62	5.9		54	6.8	47	7.8	78	4.7	63	5.8
	3.5		3.3		3.0			2.7	2.7	4.5	2.8
	6.2		6.9		6.2	Sales/Working Capital		3.6	5.7	13.1	5.6
	16.3		16.2		17.0			30.2	10.9	NM	11.2
	15.4		36.8		12.7			24.0	27.6	17.6	13.0
(70)	5.0	(75)	6.6	(71)	3.6	EBIT/Interest	3.6	(12) 4.0	(10) 2.9	(30) 4.5
	-1.1		2.0		1.0			-.9	1.8	-1.8	.0
	6.5		8.9		9.0	Net Profit + Depr., Dep.,					8.7
(19)	2.8	(21)	3.7	(22)	4.3	Amort./Cur. Mat. L/T/D				(13) 5.7
	1.8		.7		1.8						1.6
	.1		.1		.1			.2	.1	.1	.2
	.3		.3		.4	Fixed/Worth		.4	.2	.5	.4
	1.8		1.0		1.2			1.0	.8	16.8	1.5
	.5		.4		.5			.3	.3	1.3	.5
	1.5		1.3		1.5	Debt/Worth		1.2	1.0	2.3	1.2
	7.3		3.3		8.1			25.7	2.6	32.8	7.8
	63.7		45.6		51.4	% Profit Before Taxes/Tangible		50.2	209.4	38.8
(77)	25.1	(75)	20.6	(71)	15.0	Net Worth	(15) 22.8	(11) 31.0	(32) 13.0
	-1.6		3.6		2.7			2.7	1.0	-2.6
	22.8		22.1		20.3	% Profit Before Taxes/Total		25.9	30.4	42.7	15.8
	9.1		8.4		6.3	Assets		1.8	6.3	6.9	6.1
	-1.9		-.3		-3.0			-4.7	1.4	-3.9	-4.1
	54.8		46.1		53.7			79.4	118.9	133.4	28.2
	21.6		21.3		17.5	Sales/Net Fixed Assets		17.3	31.1	20.1	14.9
	9.2		9.0		7.2			6.1	5.9	7.6	7.1
	3.1		2.8		2.7			2.5	3.3	3.2	2.1
	2.2		2.1		1.8	Sales/Total Assets		1.8	2.2	2.3	1.5
	1.4		1.4		1.2			1.1	1.4	1.9	.9
	.7		.5		.7			.4	.4	.6	.7
(67)	1.5	(70)	1.0	(67)	1.5	% Depr., Dep., Amort./Sales	(10) 2.1	(11) 1.6	(11) 1.4	(30) 1.5
	3.2		2.4		3.6			4.3	2.5	3.6	3.7
	3.4		2.6		2.9	% Officers', Directors'				
(21)	5.7	(25)	4.9	(18)	5.1	Owners' Comp/Sales				
	9.7		7.4		8.5					
	2854767M		4029757M		3855652M	Net Sales ($)		17902M	44603M	112493M	193628M	3487026M
	2053880M		2604621M		2760872M	Total Assets ($)		8636M	32447M	66246M	84001M	2569542M

Current Data Sorted by Assets   Comparative Historical Data

	0-500M	500M-2MM	2-10MM	10-50MM	50-100MM	100-250MM	Type of Statement	4/1/05-3/31/06 ALL	4/1/06-3/31/07 ALL
			2	7	4	3	Unqualified	19	18
		5	5	4			Reviewed	9	12
			4	1			Compiled	4	6
		2	3	1			Tax Returns	3	6
	1	5	18	9	6	3	Other	30	46
	18 (4/1-9/30/09)			65 (10/1/09-3/31/10)					
	1	12	32	22	10	6	NUMBER OF STATEMENTS	65	88
	%	%	%	%	%	%	ASSETS	%	%
		14.2	9.8	13.3	9.3		Cash & Equivalents	8.6	10.5
		23.0	34.0	26.3	31.5		Trade Receivables (net)	30.7	32.2
		41.5	30.2	32.0	28.0		Inventory	36.6	33.0
		1.2	3.4	2.8	6.6		All Other Current	3.3	4.0
		79.9	77.3	74.4	75.5		Total Current	79.2	79.8
		13.9	14.6	11.3	10.4		Fixed Assets (net)	13.2	12.9
		4.1	2.7	10.2	7.2		Intangibles (net)	3.5	2.9
		2.1	5.4	4.1	6.8		All Other Non-Current	4.1	4.4
		100.0	100.0	100.0	100.0		Total	100.0	100.0
							LIABILITIES		
		15.2	13.2	6.9	8.5		Notes Payable-Short Term	15.7	13.7
		.6	2.0	2.1	6.5		Cur. Mat.-L.T.D.	2.9	2.6
		20.3	16.8	8.2	20.6		Trade Payables	16.8	17.0
		.0	.1	.2	.9		Income Taxes Payable	.5	.5
		9.7	11.3	9.7	13.1		All Other Current	9.7	13.5
		45.8	43.4	27.1	49.7		Total Current	45.5	47.2
		11.8	9.6	5.1	8.7		Long-Term Debt	10.8	8.3
		.0	.0	.3	.3		Deferred Taxes	.4	.2
		7.6	3.6	2.8	25.1		All Other Non-Current	5.2	4.1
		34.8	43.3	64.7	16.1		Net Worth	38.1	40.2
		100.0	100.0	100.0	100.0		Total Liabilities & Net Worth	100.0	100.0
							INCOME DATA		
		100.0	100.0	100.0	100.0		Net Sales	100.0	100.0
		59.8	34.8	39.2	34.4		Gross Profit	39.2	37.9
		53.0	34.1	34.7	29.2		Operating Expenses	33.9	32.3
		6.7	.7	4.5	5.2		Operating Profit	5.4	5.6
		.8	.7	1.2	2.2		All Other Expenses (net)	.9	1.1
		5.9	.0	3.3	3.0		Profit Before Taxes	4.5	4.5
							RATIOS		
		5.0	2.9	6.3	1.7		Current	2.9	3.4
		1.5	1.6	3.0	1.6			1.9	1.7
		1.1	1.3	1.9	1.2			1.3	1.3
		1.3	1.7	3.0	1.2		Quick	1.3	1.6
		.6	1.0	1.6	.7			.9	1.0
		.4	.7	.9	.5			.7	.6
		14 26.5	33 11.1	40 9.1	38 9.6		Sales/Receivables	38 9.7	34 10.7
		29 12.7	48 7.5	54 6.7	45 8.1			47 7.7	47 7.8
		43 8.4	71 5.2	70 5.2	78 4.7			66 5.5	66 5.5
		40 9.2	32 11.3	82 4.5	31 11.6		Cost of Sales/Inventory	72 5.1	45 8.1
		101 3.6	74 5.0	109 3.3	66 5.6			105 3.5	92 4.0
		221 1.7	148 2.5	149 2.5	127 2.9			152 2.4	151 2.4
		17 21.3	19 19.0	13 28.7	34 10.8		Cost of Sales/Payables	27 13.8	20 18.0
		37 9.8	33 11.0	23 15.8	56 6.6			42 8.7	33 11.2
		102 3.6	53 6.9	44 8.3	68 5.4			58 6.2	58 6.3
		3.0	3.4	1.7	5.8		Sales/Working Capital	4.0	3.8
		13.2	7.6	4.5	9.8			5.7	7.9
		40.3	21.6	6.2	14.8			12.7	15.9
		29.0	20.5	15.5	8.9		EBIT/Interest	12.3	15.5
		(10) 8.2	(29) 2.7	(18) 5.5	2.4			(55) 3.7	(75) 4.0
		1.8	-.4	2.5	-1.4			1.3	1.6
							Net Profit + Depr., Dep.,	17.3	6.0
							Amort./Cur. Mat. L/T/D	(28) 4.1	(21) 2.6
								1.6	1.8
		.0	.1	.1	.1		Fixed/Worth	.1	.1
		.2	.3	.2	.9			.4	.2
		.4	1.4	.5	NM			.9	.6
		.6	.5	.2	1.3		Debt/Worth	.6	.6
		2.3	1.3	.5	4.9			2.0	1.6
		5.2	5.3	1.9	NM			5.3	3.8
		104.5	16.3	17.6			% Profit Before Taxes/Tangible	28.5	48.7
		(11) 43.9	(27) 3.6	(20) 9.0			Net Worth	(55) 16.0	(80) 26.9
		20.9	.7	-2.5				4.0	9.3
		31.4	8.1	10.3	24.6		% Profit Before Taxes/Total	14.2	18.4
		18.1	1.9	6.2	5.7		Assets	5.3	8.1
		5.6	-.9	.2	-6.0			.8	2.4
		122.9	76.3	39.5	87.3		Sales/Net Fixed Assets	65.9	77.8
		49.4	27.6	25.3	39.0			25.5	31.5
		16.3	10.8	9.3	13.7			13.3	13.7
		3.6	2.8	2.5	2.7		Sales/Total Assets	2.9	3.2
		2.9	2.4	1.4	2.2			2.1	2.2
		2.5	1.8	1.0	1.3			1.5	1.7
			.4	.9			% Depr., Dep., Amort./Sales	.6	.5
		(25)	1.2	(16) 1.5				(55) 1.3	(64) 1.1
			2.5	2.3				2.4	2.1
			2.2				% Officers', Directors'	1.3	2.0
		(12)	3.1				Owners' Comp/Sales	(16) 3.5	(24) 4.6
			5.1					5.1	6.1
	129M	44898M	353326M	782000M	1511202M	1466867M	Net Sales ($)	3596638M	5716675M
	2M	14939M	155697M	455869M	705924M	1071050M	Total Assets ($)	1864546M	2856616M

M = $ thousand   MM = $ million
See Pages 9 through 22 for Explanation of Ratios and Data

Comparative Historical Data | | | Current Data Sorted by Sales

			Type of Statement	0-1MM	1-3MM	3-5MM	5-10MM	10-25MM	25MM & OVER
13	19	16	Unqualified				2	3	11
15	14	9	Reviewed			1	2	4	2
9	11	7	Compiled			3	1	3	
7	10	10*	Tax Returns		1	3	1		
33	37	41	Other	1	2	5	6	11	17
4/1/07-3/31/08 ALL	4/1/08-3/31/09 ALL	4/1/09-3/31/10 ALL			18 (4/1-9/30/09)		65 (10/1/09-3/31/10)		
77	91	83	**NUMBER OF STATEMENTS**	1	3	12	14	22	31
%	%	%	**ASSETS**	%	%	%	%	%	%
9.9	9.2	13.3	Cash & Equivalents			13.3	15.4	13.4	10.5
29.6	29.1	29.1	Trade Receivables (net)			22.5	30.9	31.4	31.6
34.2	33.2	31.1	Inventory			33.0	33.1	25.4	30.1
3.1	4.2	3.4	All Other Current			1.4	1.4	4.5	4.6
76.8	75.7	76.9	Total Current			70.1	80.9	74.8	76.8
13.6	13.3	13.0	Fixed Assets (net)			20.7	8.3	14.3	12.6
4.7	5.5	5.5	Intangibles (net)			5.3	5.8	5.8	5.5
4.9	5.4	4.6	All Other Non-Current			3.9	5.0	5.1	5.0
100.0	100.0	100.0	Total			100.0	100.0	100.0	100.0
			LIABILITIES						
15.4	15.7	10.4	Notes Payable-Short Term			18.2	6.3	13.8	6.7
1.5	3.1	2.6	Cur. Mat.-L.T.D.			1.4	1.3	2.6	3.9
16.3	14.1	15.8	Trade Payables			13.6	21.8	13.6	15.6
.4	.3	.2	Income Taxes Payable			.0	.1	.1	.4
9.4	10.3	14.2	All Other Current			8.2	8.5	12.5	13.7
43.1	43.5	43.2	Total Current			41.4	38.0	42.6	40.3
12.2	11.5	7.9	Long-Term Debt			16.6	8.2	5.6	7.1
.1	.2	.1	Deferred Taxes			.0	.1	.2	.1
7.0	4.2	6.4	All Other Non-Current			4.3	1.1	4.0	9.4
37.6	40.5	42.3	Net Worth			37.6	52.6	47.6	43.1
100.0	100.0	100.0	Total Liabilities & Net Worth			100.0	100.0	100.0	100.0
			INCOME DATA						
100.0	100.0	100.0	Net Sales			100.0	100.0	100.0	100.0
38.4	39.9	41.1	Gross Profit			55.2	39.9	32.0	39.9
33.9	35.6	37.8	Operating Expenses			53.6	38.0	29.1	34.7
4.5	4.3	3.3	Operating Profit			1.6	2.0	2.9	5.2
1.4	1.4	1.0	All Other Expenses (net)			1.2	.8	.9	1.1
3.2	2.9	2.3	Profit Before Taxes			.5	1.1	2.0	4.1
			RATIOS						
3.1	3.6	3.9				3.1	6.7	3.5	3.9
1.9	1.7	1.8	Current			1.5	1.7	1.8	2.2
1.3	1.3	1.3				.9	1.5	1.2	1.4
1.5	1.8	2.0				1.4	2.8	1.9	2.2
1.0	.8	1.0	Quick			.8	1.1	1.0	1.3
.6	.5	.6				.3	.8	.7	.7
32 · 11.4	32 · 11.5	34 · 10.7				11 · 32.1	25 · 14.4	39 · 9.3	43 · 8.5
45 · 8.2	44 · 8.3	45 · 8.1	Sales/Receivables			37 · 10.0	37 · 10.0	50 · 7.3	57 · 6.4
62 · 5.9	61 · 6.0	69 · 5.3				48 · 7.6	62 · 5.9	72 · 5.1	77 · 4.8
53 · 6.9	48 · 7.7	53 · 6.9				82 · 4.4	54 · 6.8	20 · 18.0	58 · 6.3
94 · 3.9	100 · 3.7	85 · 4.3	Cost of Sales/Inventory			101 · 3.6	78 · 4.7	68 · 5.4	93 · 3.9
159 · 2.3	136 · 2.7	148 · 2.5				209 · 1.7	153 · 2.4	134 · 2.7	143 · 2.6
21 · 17.0	18 · 20.5	18 · 20.0				20 · 18.7	19 · 19.6	12 · 30.4	20 · 17.9
38 · 9.7	33 · 11.2	35 · 10.5	Cost of Sales/Payables			43 · 8.4	32 · 11.4	31 · 11.8	37 · 9.8
61 · 6.0	58 · 6.3	57 · 6.5				80 · 4.5	60 · 6.1	51 · 7.1	62 · 5.9
3.9	3.8	3.2				3.9	2.6	3.0	3.3
6.8	6.5	7.2	Sales/Working Capital			5.0	8.2	7.4	5.1
14.9	17.2	15.9				NM	14.3	23.1	10.3
16.9	14.4	16.0				21.4	24.2	24.0	14.2
(70) 2.9	(81) 3.6	(69) 3.7	EBIT/Interest			(10) 2.4	(12) 5.2	(21) 3.3	(24) 3.8
.8	1.1	.3				-.8	1.2	.0	.4
11.2	8.5	13.8							37.5
(16) 5.3	(24) 2.9	(19) 3.5	Net Profit + Depr., Dep., Amort./Cur. Mat. L/T/D					(10) 6.6	
1.6	.6	1.0							-.1
.1	.1	.1				.1	.0	.1	.1
.3	.2	.2	Fixed/Worth			.4	.1	.4	.3
1.4	.7	.9				1.8	.5	1.5	.8
.6	.5	.4				.4	.4	.4	.4
1.6	1.5	1.2	Debt/Worth			1.6	.9	1.1	.8
9.3	5.0	5.2				4.7	3.4	14.8	5.7
38.8	45.1	29.8				75.7	18.0	18.0	33.8
(66) 18.1	(78) 17.5	(71) 9.7	% Profit Before Taxes/Tangible Net Worth			(10) 16.1	(12) 7.1	(18) 3.1	(28) 12.5
3.6	4.7	.7				-.1	1.0	-4.3	.3
17.9	16.9	11.1				28.9	8.0	11.0	11.8
5.4	6.1	4.6	% Profit Before Taxes/Total Assets			1.2	2.8	3.3	7.3
-.2	.3	-.2				-4.7	.4	-1.2	-.2
62.9	66.4	66.4				46.5	110.7	78.0	35.7
25.0	31.8	27.6	Sales/Net Fixed Assets			17.8	50.7	27.8	26.6
14.1	11.5	10.3				7.2	24.0	10.0	8.0
2.9	2.9	2.8				2.9	2.9	2.8	2.7
2.2	2.1	2.2	Sales/Total Assets			2.6	2.4	2.1	1.9
1.5	1.6	1.3				1.5	1.6	1.3	1.3
.8	.6	.6				.7		.9	.9
(56) 1.2	(66) 1.3	(57) 1.4	% Depr., Dep., Amort./Sales			(10) 1.6	(16) 1.5	(22) 1.7	
2.0	2.1	2.5				3.3		2.5	2.7
2.2	3.6	2.7							
(20) 3.7	(27) 4.7	(23) 4.7	% Officers', Directors' Owners' Comp/Sales						
6.3	7.2	6.1							
5550368M	4593992M	4158422M	Net Sales ($)	129M	4749M	49364M	96517M	343269M	3664394M
2929230M	2531105M	2403481M	Total Assets ($)	2M	2935M	28155M	48686M	197442M	2126261M

	Current Data Sorted by Assets							Comparative Historical Data	

			6	4	2	2	Type of Statement	14	26
	2		12	8			Unqualified	17	20
	9		2				Reviewed	19	20
1	3		2				Compiled	8	11
1	6		19	15	3	5	Tax Returns	47	40
							Other	4/1/05-	4/1/06-
	18 (4/1-9/30/09)			84 (10/1/09-3/31/10)				3/31/06	3/31/07
0-500M	500M-2MM		2-10MM	10-50MM	50-100MM	100-250MM		ALL	ALL
2	20		41	27	5	7	NUMBER OF STATEMENTS	105	117
%	%		%	%	%	%	**ASSETS**	%	%
	13.2		6.0	7.8			Cash & Equivalents	7.0	7.5
	26.1		30.6	25.2			Trade Receivables (net)	31.8	31.2
	25.0		28.4	29.7			Inventory	24.2	26.0
	.9		1.4	2.6			All Other Current	1.5	1.3
	65.2		66.4	65.2			Total Current	64.5	65.9
	26.0		24.2	23.2			Fixed Assets (net)	25.3	22.2
	2.7		4.5	7.0			Intangibles (net)	4.6	5.3
	6.1		4.9	4.6			All Other Non-Current	5.6	6.6
	100.0		100.0	100.0			Total	100.0	100.0
							LIABILITIES		
	11.0		12.6	10.8			Notes Payable-Short Term	11.9	11.1
	3.7		5.5	3.2			Cur. Mat.-L.T.D.	4.4	4.9
	15.5		18.2	14.1			Trade Payables	19.6	20.8
	.0		.1	.5			Income Taxes Payable	.2	.2
	7.7		8.0	9.5			All Other Current	8.5	9.2
	37.9		44.4	38.1			Total Current	44.5	46.2
	21.6		10.4	9.2			Long-Term Debt	14.1	15.3
	.0		.6	.5			Deferred Taxes	.4	.2
	6.7		4.0	5.9			All Other Non-Current	5.8	6.8
	33.8		40.5	46.3			Net Worth	35.2	31.5
	100.0		100.0	100.0			Total Liabilties & Net Worth	100.0	100.0
							INCOME DATA		
	100.0		100.0	100.0			Net Sales	100.0	100.0
	38.8		25.0	23.7			Gross Profit	26.5	27.0
	37.3		21.9	21.8			Operating Expenses	23.1	21.5
	1.5		3.1	1.9			Operating Profit	3.3	5.5
	2.6		.6	1.3			All Other Expenses (net)	1.4	1.4
	-1.1		2.6	.5			Profit Before Taxes	2.0	4.2
							RATIOS		
	3.0		2.4	3.0				2.0	2.2
	1.7		1.6	1.5			Current	1.5	1.5
	1.4		1.1	1.1				1.1	1.1
	1.5		1.6	2.0				1.4	1.5
	.9		1.0	.8			Quick	.8	.9
	.7		.6	.6				.6	.6
37 / 9.8	37 / 9.8		37 / 9.9	42 / 8.6				41 / 8.9	39 / 9.3
45 / 8.0	45 / 8.0		46 / 7.9	49 / 7.4			Sales/Receivables	51 / 7.1	47 / 7.7
62 / 5.9	62 / 5.9		55 / 6.6	68 / 5.4				60 / 6.1	57 / 6.4
8 / 46.5	8 / 46.5		28 / 12.9	44 / 8.2				28 / 13.2	25 / 14.6
41 / 8.9	41 / 8.9		59 / 6.2	67 / 5.4			Cost of Sales/Inventory	52 / 7.0	50 / 7.2
96 / 3.8	96 / 3.8		85 / 4.3	108 / 3.4				79 / 4.6	79 / 4.6
13 / 28.3	13 / 28.3		22 / 16.3	18 / 19.8				24 / 15.1	24 / 15.3
22 / 16.5	22 / 16.5		33 / 11.1	32 / 11.2			Cost of Sales/Payables	36 / 10.1	38 / 9.7
73 / 5.0	73 / 5.0		50 / 7.2	54 / 6.8				51 / 7.1	54 / 6.7
	4.3		6.0	3.4				6.6	5.9
	10.6		8.9	7.5			Sales/Working Capital	10.7	12.6
	16.1		40.8	64.4				30.6	35.8
	5.6		7.1	8.0				6.7	11.9
	1.1	(38)	3.8	(24) 1.8			EBIT/Interest	(97) 3.1	(107) 3.4
	-7.4		1.2	-.4				1.0	1.1
			5.3	4.9			Net Profit + Depr., Dep.,	6.4	8.0
		(14)	2.7	(12) 2.1			Amort./Cur. Mat. L/T/D	(26) 2.7	(32) 4.0
			1.9	.5				.7	1.6
	.1		.3	.2				.4	.3
	.4		.6	.7			Fixed/Worth	.7	.6
	3.1		1.6	1.4				1.6	1.6
	.6		.7	.6				.9	.9
	1.4		1.8	1.7			Debt/Worth	1.9	2.2
	13.2		3.3	5.5				5.4	6.4
	89.9		28.9	18.5			% Profit Before Taxes/Tangible	32.9	47.9
	(17) 1.1	(36)	16.0	(25) 4.8			Net Worth	(90) 11.3	(100) 21.6
	-10.2		1.3	-6.3				3.1	1.4
	8.0		12.2	8.1			% Profit Before Taxes/Total	10.9	16.2
	.4		6.1	2.4			Assets	5.0	8.1
	-14.7		.8	-4.2				.4	.2
	38.7		22.2	22.0				21.0	25.1
	17.1		10.0	13.4			Sales/Net Fixed Assets	12.1	13.3
	3.7		5.1	4.2				5.6	6.7
	2.9		3.1	2.1				2.8	2.9
	2.0		2.2	1.8			Sales/Total Assets	2.3	2.3
	1.4		1.7	1.3				1.8	1.8
	1.8		1.1	1.6				1.5	1.3
	(15) 2.4	(38)	2.2	2.3			% Depr., Dep., Amort./Sales	(92) 2.6	(106) 2.3
	5.7		3.5	3.9				4.9	4.1
	3.1		1.8				% Officers', Directors'	1.3	3.1
	(12) 5.6	(13)	4.3				Owners' Comp/Sales	(30) 2.9	(32) 4.6
	18.5		6.3					5.4	8.5
2486M	58628M		490674M	833451M	661540M	1460441M	Net Sales ($)	3048053M	3893947M
637M	25758M		206732M	493628M	404781M	1104362M	Total Assets ($)	1451011M	1866964M

M = $ thousand   MM = $ million
See Pages 9 through 22 for Explanation of Ratios and Data

Comparative Historical Data   Current Data Sorted by Sales

4/1/07-3/31/08 ALL	4/1/08-3/31/09 ALL	4/1/09-3/31/10 ALL	Type of Statement	0-1MM	1-3MM	3-5MM	5-10MM	10-25MM	25MM & OVER
14	12	14	Unqualified			1	1	7	6
18	22	22	Reviewed	1	6	1	8	9	1
21	18	11	Compiled		1	1	3	2	1
6	19	6	Tax Returns		1	3	2	1	
57	47	49	Other	1	3	6	8	15	16
					18 (4/1-9/30/09)		**84 (10/1/09-3/31/10)**		
116	118	102	**NUMBER OF STATEMENTS**	2	10	11	21	32	26
%	%	%	**ASSETS**	%	%	%	%	%	%
7.9	10.7	8.0	Cash & Equivalents		5.3	19.0	8.9	6.2	6.4
28.9	28.3	28.9	Trade Receivables (net)		28.2	25.4	30.3	30.6	27.7
26.9	23.8	26.7	Inventory		29.7	17.2	25.4	26.9	29.4
1.8	2.4	1.6	All Other Current		.6	1.1	1.1	2.1	2.1
65.6	65.1	65.1	Total Current		63.8	62.8	65.6	65.8	65.6
23.7	25.4	23.8	Fixed Assets (net)		23.3	26.1	27.3	26.1	16.5
5.9	4.8	5.9	Intangibles (net)		3.6	8.6	1.5	2.7	13.4
4.9	4.8	5.2	All Other Non-Current		9.3	2.6	5.5	5.4	4.5
100.0	100.0	100.0	Total		100.0	100.0	100.0	100.0	100.0
			LIABILITIES						
10.4	10.2	11.8	Notes Payable-Short Term		13.0	10.2	9.5	15.7	7.4
4.7	4.1	4.3	Cur. Mat.-L.T.D.		3.2	1.9	7.8	3.7	3.5
18.0	17.1	18.2	Trade Payables		12.6	16.9	19.9	13.5	21.1
.1	.1	.2	Income Taxes Payable		.0	.0	.0	.2	.6
9.2	7.9	8.3	All Other Current		11.1	6.7	9.2	7.1	9.0
42.5	39.5	42.9	Total Current		39.9	35.8	46.4	40.3	41.7
15.4	14.1	12.4	Long-Term Debt		10.8	29.8	11.5	9.0	10.3
.3	.4	.5	Deferred Taxes		.0	.0	.9	.4	.7
4.5	10.6	7.9	All Other Non-Current		2.9	6.2	7.3	3.9	7.7
37.4	35.3	36.3	Net Worth		46.4	28.2	33.9	46.4	39.6
100.0	100.0	100.0	Total Liabilities & Net Worth		100.0	100.0	100.0	100.0	100.0
			INCOME DATA						
100.0	100.0	100.0	Net Sales		100.0	100.0	100.0	100.0	100.0
28.5	27.3	26.8	Gross Profit		46.8	34.5	24.2	25.3	17.9
22.1	22.8	24.4	Operating Expenses		48.0	30.5	23.0	22.1	15.2
6.4	4.5	2.4	Operating Profit		-1.2	4.0	1.2	3.2	2.7
1.2	.8	1.5	All Other Expenses (net)		.8	3.6	.3	.7	2.3
5.2	3.7	.9	Profit Before Taxes		-2.0	.4	.9	2.5	.4
			RATIOS						
2.9	2.9	2.4	Current		2.9	3.5	2.4	3.0	1.8
1.6	1.9	1.6			1.8	1.4	1.6	1.7	1.5
1.2	1.2	1.2			.8	1.2	1.1	1.1	1.4
1.7	1.9	1.4	Quick		1.1	2.6	1.7	1.9	1.0
.8	1.0	.9			.8	1.3	1.3	.8	.8
.6	.6	.6			.7	.6	.5	.7	.6
35 10.3	34 10.9	39 9.4	Sales/Receivables		39 9.4	40 9.1	35 10.3	38 9.6	42 8.6
48 7.6	41 8.9	48 7.6			48 7.5	48 7.6	46 7.9	51 7.2	49 7.5
58 6.3	51 7.1	62 5.9			64 5.7	63 5.8	55 6.7	66 5.5	66 5.5
35 10.5	20 18.5	28 12.9	Cost of Sales/Inventory		12 31.3	6 63.5	27 13.7	38 9.6	44 8.2
53 6.9	45 8.1	59 6.2			49 7.4	41 8.9	51 7.2	59 6.2	62 5.9
87 4.2	75 4.8	93 3.9			177 2.1	79 4.6	92 4.0	97 3.8	85 4.3
18 20.1	18 20.3	21 17.6	Cost of Sales/Payables		8 46.0	20 18.1	23 15.9	21 17.6	21 17.3
35 10.6	31 11.8	33 11.2			23 15.6	29 12.4	40 9.1	27 13.4	46 8.0
56 6.5	44 8.3	54 6.7			83 4.4	79 4.6	65 5.6	42 8.7	71 5.2
5.4	5.2	5.3	Sales/Working Capital		4.4	3.9	6.7	4.6	5.7
8.5	9.1	8.9			6.8	13.9	8.7	6.1	9.5
34.4	25.7	20.1			-30.8	24.9	NM	58.6	13.4
11.9	14.2	6.8	EBIT/Interest		2.9	7.5	5.0	11.4	6.2
(107) 4.3	(104) 4.3	(95) 1.9			.5	(10) 3.3	(20) 2.7	(27) 4.8	1.8
.8	1.0	-.4			-16.9	-14.8	-.7	1.0	-.7
11.9	7.2	4.8	Net Profit + Depr., Dep.,						5.1
(28) 2.5	(28) 3.0	(31) 2.3	Amort./Cur. Mat. L/T/D						(15) 2.0
.8	1.6	1.3							.7
.3	.2	.2	Fixed/Worth		.1	.1	.3	.2	.2
.5	.8	.6			.2	2.5	.6	.7	.5
1.5	1.8	1.9			1.8	-9.9	2.8	1.2	2.0
.8	.7	.8	Debt/Worth		.5	.5	.7	.5	1.2
1.9	1.7	1.8			1.3	16.0	1.9	1.3	2.3
4.2	4.5	4.8			4.0	-16.3	6.0	2.9	5.6
55.9	43.8	22.4	% Profit Before Taxes/Tangible				26.8	29.3	18.8
(102) 28.4	(103) 18.4	(88) 7.6	Net Worth				(18) 12.3	(31) 10.7	(22) 5.3
2.7	5.8	-3.3					-2.6	.5	-16.3
20.9	18.0	8.7	% Profit Before Taxes/Total		2.8	12.7	10.1	13.8	6.1
8.2	7.3	2.8	Assets		-.6	6.4	3.8	4.3	1.6
.5	.1	-2.1			-9.6	-17.1	-3.0	.1	-4.3
23.2	26.4	24.0	Sales/Net Fixed Assets		70.6	57.8	17.3	22.1	26.9
12.5	13.3	13.1			24.4	7.3	9.5	10.6	16.7
7.3	5.5	4.2			4.2	3.5	4.6	4.3	10.3
2.8	3.3	2.5	Sales/Total Assets		2.5	2.8	2.7	2.8	2.1
2.2	2.5	2.0			1.8	2.1	2.2	1.9	1.9
1.8	1.9	1.5			1.3	1.6	1.7	1.5	1.5
1.2	1.3	1.4	% Depr., Dep., Amort./Sales				1.9	1.4	1.0
(105) 2.1	(100) 2.2	(89) 2.3					2.7	(28) 2.5	(23) 1.6
3.8	3.7	3.8					5.5	4.7	3.0
2.2	2.0	2.9	% Officers', Directors'						
(38) 5.5	(43) 4.0	(30) 4.8	Owners' Comp/Sales						
8.3	6.4	12.6							
3483286M	3519141M	3507220M	Net Sales ($)	1759M	18609M	40048M	162810M	532689M	2751305M
1640985M	1662355M	2235898M	Total Assets ($)	1058M	10585M	21905M	82760M	371240M	1748350M

© RMA 2010

M = $ thousand   MM = $ million
See Pages 9 through 22 for Explanation of Ratios and Data

MANUFACTURING—Semiconductor and Related Device Manufacturing   NAICS 334413

| Current Data Sorted by Assets | | | | | | | Comparative Historical Data | |

Type of Statement

0-500M	500M-2MM	2-10MM	10-50MM	50-100MM	100-250MM		4/1/05-3/31/06 ALL	4/1/06-3/31/07 ALL
	1	4	14	2	9	Unqualified	14	25
	1	4	2			Reviewed	8	6
	3	1				Compiled	5	2
1	3	5				Tax Returns	2	2
3	3	11	16	3	6	Other	43	32
	12 (4/1-9/30/09)		80 (10/1/09-3/31/10)					
4	11	25	32	5	15	**NUMBER OF STATEMENTS**	72	67

0-500M	500M-2MM	2-10MM	10-50MM	50-100MM	100-250MM		4/1/05-3/31/06 ALL	4/1/06-3/31/07 ALL
%	%	%	%	%	%	**ASSETS**	%	%
	16.8	14.7	17.7		27.3	Cash & Equivalents	14.7	18.2
	24.3	25.3	20.9		15.3	Trade Receivables (net)	25.1	23.0
	13.1	22.6	20.6		15.4	Inventory	27.1	23.7
	1.4	2.9	2.7		6.3	All Other Current	3.5	2.5
	55.6	65.5	61.9		64.4	Total Current	70.4	67.3
	29.2	22.7	24.6		18.3	Fixed Assets (net)	17.2	23.1
	.0	6.2	6.8		11.4	Intangibles (net)	6.2	3.6
	15.2	5.6	6.7		5.9	All Other Non-Current	6.2	5.9
	100.0	100.0	100.0		100.0	Total	100.0	100.0
						LIABILITIES		
	12.5	6.8	4.8		.9	Notes Payable-Short Term	11.1	7.9
	2.6	2.8	3.0		1.0	Cur. Mat.-L.T.D.	3.3	2.1
	22.7	13.7	12.5		10.6	Trade Payables	16.2	11.1
	.0	.5	.2		.1	Income Taxes Payable	.6	.3
	10.4	11.0	13.3		14.3	All Other Current	15.0	11.5
	48.2	34.9	33.7		26.9	Total Current	46.2	32.9
	13.3	8.8	10.3		6.9	Long-Term Debt	9.7	10.1
	.4	.0	.6		.9	Deferred Taxes	.4	.4
	10.4	8.0	7.0		1.7	All Other Non-Current	10.6	10.3
	27.8	48.3	48.3		63.6	Net Worth	33.1	46.3
	100.0	100.0	100.0		100.0	Total Liabilties & Net Worth	100.0	100.0
						INCOME DATA		
	100.0	100.0	100.0		100.0	Net Sales	100.0	100.0
	46.8	42.7	30.8		31.2	Gross Profit	33.4	33.8
	43.8	39.6	29.5		30.6	Operating Expenses	31.0	28.9
	3.0	3.1	1.3		.6	Operating Profit	2.4	4.8
	-2.0	1.4	1.3		1.2	All Other Expenses (net)	1.1	1.1
	5.0	1.7	.0		-.6	Profit Before Taxes	1.3	3.7
						RATIOS		
	5.0	3.3	3.8		6.2	Current	2.9	4.1
	1.8	1.7	2.4		2.9		1.8	2.3
	.4	1.2	1.6		1.7		1.2	1.4
	3.2	2.0	2.1		5.0	Quick	1.9	2.8
	1.5	.9	1.4		1.8		1.0	1.2
	.2	.6	.8		.9		.6	.7
	10 36.1	32 11.5	40 9.1		14 26.7	Sales/Receivables	41 8.9	36 10.1
	30 12.1	55 6.6	50 7.3		44 8.3		51 7.2	49 7.5
	50 7.3	64 5.7	70 5.2		65 5.6		61 6.0	68 5.4
	7 55.7	34 10.8	61 6.0		42 8.6	Cost of Sales/Inventory	51 7.1	34 10.9
	10 35.9	72 5.0	82 4.4		67 5.4		85 4.3	76 4.8
	58 6.3	160 2.3	134 2.7		117 3.1		143 2.5	137 2.7
	17 21.0	26 13.8	16 23.5		22 16.3	Cost of Sales/Payables	27 13.4	20 18.3
	34 10.8	51 7.1	38 9.5		42 8.6		38 9.5	32 11.2
	158 2.3	66 5.6	73 5.0		54 6.8		56 6.5	47 7.8
	6.4	2.8	2.6		1.4	Sales/Working Capital	3.1	2.6
	8.8	7.7	3.8		3.5		7.2	3.9
	-4.4	24.3	7.3		7.5		22.6	9.9
		15.9	15.6		9.2	EBIT/Interest	8.8	17.7
		(24) 5.7	(27) 1.9		(10) .2		(61) 4.0	(53) 5.5
		2.1	-4.0		-37.3		.7	.9
			25.3			Net Profit + Depr., Dep., Amort./Cur. Mat. L/T/D	11.2	12.1
			(10) 5.6				(19) 4.9	(14) 7.0
			1.1				2.8	1.7
	.2	.1	.2		.1	Fixed/Worth	.2	.2
	.6	.7	.5		.3		.5	.4
	1.2	1.1	1.2		.7		7.2	.9
	.7	.7	.3		.1	Debt/Worth	.6	.3
	.8	1.3	1.0		.4		1.5	.8
	14.8	2.7	3.6		3.8		51.9	1.9
		35.4	29.1		15.1	% Profit Before Taxes/Tangible Net Worth	30.4	32.7
		(24) 17.8	(28) 16.0		(13) -.1		(55) 11.9	(62) 14.8
		2.2	-14.7		-30.4		1.0	-5.8
	11.8	15.1	13.6		6.7	% Profit Before Taxes/Total Assets	11.5	15.9
	2.2	6.5	3.0		-.4		4.1	5.2
	1.2	-.3	-11.2		-12.2		-1.1	-3.6
	29.4	18.3	13.7		28.4	Sales/Net Fixed Assets	26.0	18.3
	15.4	11.7	6.0		9.2		13.8	8.3
	2.4	4.5	2.9		3.2		6.1	3.0
	3.7	2.2	1.5		1.6	Sales/Total Assets	2.4	2.1
	1.8	1.5	1.2		.9		1.5	1.3
	1.3	1.3	1.0		.6		1.1	.9
		1.1	2.4			% Depr., Dep., Amort./Sales	1.3	1.8
		(23) 3.2	(24) 4.8				(60) 2.2	(53) 2.8
		5.5	11.8				3.9	4.7
		.9				% Officers', Directors' Owners' Comp/Sales	2.6	2.2
	(11) 4.5						(15) 3.1	(12) 4.4
		4.8					9.0	7.4
2737M	36783M	209161M	1033768M	413333M	3673650M	Net Sales ($)	4046445M	3833387M
1039M	14637M	127388M	823594M	344101M	2472037M	Total Assets ($)	2775103M	2804336M

M = $ thousand   MM = $ million
See Pages 9 through 22 for Explanation of Ratios and Data

Comparative Historical Data

Current Data Sorted by Sales

4/1/07-3/31/08 ALL	4/1/08-3/31/09 ALL	4/1/09-3/31/10 ALL	Type of Statement	0-1MM	1-3MM	3-5MM	5-10MM	10-25MM	25MM & OVER
24	22	30	Unqualified			1	2	6	21
7	6	7	Reviewed	1	2		1	3	
6	4	4	Compiled		2	1	1		
5	6	9	Tax Returns	1	3	3	1	1	
36	40	42	Other	3	2		10	12	15
				12 (4/1-9/30/09)			80 (10/1/09-3/31/10)		
78	78	92	NUMBER OF STATEMENTS	5	9	5	15	22	36
%	%	%	ASSETS	%	%	%	%	%	%
16.1	19.1	19.1	Cash & Equivalents				24.3	12.5	24.5
24.6	20.0	21.4	Trade Receivables (net)				21.2	23.1	19.7
25.5	25.8	20.3	Inventory				19.5	23.6	19.2
4.1	2.8	3.3	All Other Current				3.2	2.8	4.8
70.2	67.6	64.1	Total Current				68.2	62.1	68.2
21.2	21.6	22.1	Fixed Assets (net)				22.5	25.4	17.5
4.0	5.2	6.4	Intangibles (net)				1.5	4.6	8.8
4.6	5.6	7.5	All Other Non-Current				7.8	7.9	5.6
100.0	100.0	100.0	Total				100.0	100.0	100.0
			LIABILITIES						
7.1	5.7	6.1	Notes Payable-Short Term				4.6	7.0	3.0
3.0	2.3	2.4	Cur. Mat.-L.T.D.				2.9	4.0	1.6
13.6	11.5	13.5	Trade Payables				11.6	10.4	14.0
.2	.2	.3	Income Taxes Payable				.0	.4	.2
12.2	12.9	13.9	All Other Current				9.7	13.5	16.3
36.2	32.6	36.2	Total Current				28.7	35.3	35.1
9.9	9.8	9.6	Long-Term Debt				8.1	13.0	5.8
.4	.4	.4	Deferred Taxes				.1	.4	.6
8.8	5.9	6.7	All Other Non-Current				7.3	9.2	3.7
44.7	51.2	47.2	Net Worth				55.8	42.1	54.8
100.0	100.0	100.0	Total Liabilties & Net Worth				100.0	100.0	100.0
			INCOME DATA						
100.0	100.0	100.0	Net Sales				100.0	100.0	100.0
35.3	36.2	38.0	Gross Profit				36.8	36.8	30.0
29.9	30.9	36.6	Operating Expenses				37.8	31.9	30.3
5.4	5.3	1.5	Operating Profit				-1.1	5.0	-.3
.8	.5	.8	All Other Expenses (net)				1.5	1.2	.9
4.6	4.8	.7	Profit Before Taxes				-2.6	3.7	-1.2
			RATIOS						
3.5	4.4	3.8	Current				3.8	5.3	3.8
2.3	2.3	2.1					2.6	2.4	2.1
1.6	1.5	1.3					1.7	1.2	1.5
2.2	2.9	2.2	Quick				2.4	2.1	2.3
1.3	1.3	1.3					1.7	1.2	1.5
.9	.7	.8					.8	.5	.8
(35) 10.3	(28) 12.9	(30) 12.1	Sales/Receivables				(25) 14.6	(37) 9.8	(38) 9.6
(49) 7.5	(39) 9.3	(46) 7.9					(28) 12.9	(48) 7.5	(51) 7.2
(63) 5.8	(56) 6.6	(65) 5.6					(67) 5.5	(69) 5.3	(70) 5.2
(46) 8.0	(52) 7.0	(42) 8.7	Cost of Sales/Inventory				(46) 7.9	(61) 6.0	(42) 8.7
(82) 4.5	(80) 4.5	(74) 4.9					(61) 5.9	(82) 4.4	(74) 4.9
(122) 3.0	(142) 2.6	(129) 2.8					(134) 2.7	(156) 2.3	(119) 3.1
(24) 15.4	(20) 18.2	(22) 16.8	Cost of Sales/Payables				(21) 17.3	(14) 27.0	(22) 16.3
(38) 9.7	(32) 11.4	(43) 8.4					(34) 10.6	(32) 11.3	(48) 7.7
(51) 7.1	(50) 7.2	(73) 5.0					(51) 7.1	(57) 6.4	(74) 4.9
2.8	2.6	2.6	Sales/Working Capital				2.3	2.6	2.2
4.1	4.1	5.2					3.3	3.9	3.9
9.0	9.2	14.9					9.2	31.0	10.4
27.7	31.6	14.0	EBIT/Interest				9.2	16.6	28.6
(63) 4.5	(64) 6.1	(76) 3.3					(13) 3.2	(21) 3.6	(25) 1.8
1.2	.7	-3.1					-5.3	-.8	-10.5
12.5	21.3	20.9	Net Profit + Depr., Dep., Amort./Cur. Mat. L/T/D						
(25) 7.5	(18) 9.3	(18) 5.5							
2.3	2.4	.9							
.2	.2	.2	Fixed/Worth				.1	.4	.2
.4	.4	.5					.5	.7	.3
1.0	.9	1.0					.8	1.6	.9
.5	.3	.4	Debt/Worth				.5	.2	.3
1.1	.8	1.1					1.0	1.6	.9
3.7	2.3	3.3					1.4	6.3	3.3
43.9	42.7	28.6	% Profit Before Taxes/Tangible Net Worth				20.6	57.8	23.5
(70) 14.4	(71) 15.1	(81) 13.3					14.2	(19) 22.0	(32) 5.4
6.6	.8	-5.4					-8.2	2.2	-24.6
14.7	21.6	10.3	% Profit Before Taxes/Total Assets				8.6	19.2	8.1
7.6	6.6	3.0					5.8	5.8	.9
.7	-1.3	-4.9					-6.9	-2.1	-12.9
24.4	17.6	20.2	Sales/Net Fixed Assets				34.6	13.8	29.5
8.7	9.5	10.9					8.6	6.1	11.7
3.8	4.6	3.8					3.2	3.0	4.4
2.3	2.1	1.9	Sales/Total Assets				2.5	1.9	1.7
1.5	1.5	1.4					1.4	1.4	1.2
1.0	.9	.9					1.2	1.0	.9
1.4	1.2	1.3	% Depr., Dep., Amort./Sales				.5	2.3	1.3
(65) 3.2	(61) 2.6	(64) 3.1					(13) 3.6	(19) 3.2	(19) 2.8
4.8	4.2	7.8					5.6	8.0	7.0
1.7	2.2	1.8	% Officers', Directors' Owners' Comp/Sales						
(16) 2.7	(15) 3.1	(22) 4.4							
5.6	6.3	10.7							
5523053M	6481287M	5369432M	Net Sales ($)	3259M	19082M	22629M	112649M	345894M	4865919M
3407538M	4250286M	3782796M	Total Assets ($)	2050M	20176M	10884M	111862M	285379M	3352445M

© RMA 2010

M = $ thousand   MM = $ million
See Pages 9 through 22 for Explanation of Ratios and Data

Current Data Sorted by Assets / Comparative Historical Data

0-500M	500M-2MM	2-10MM	10-50MM	50-100MM	100-250MM	Type of Statement	4/1/05-3/31/06 ALL	4/1/06-3/31/07 ALL
		3	2	3		Unqualified	7	8
	1	5				Reviewed	10	9
	1	1				Compiled	2	1
						Tax Returns		
	2	3	9		2	Other	12	12
	6 (4/1-9/30/09)		26 (10/1/09-3/31/10)					
	4	12	11	3	2	NUMBER OF STATEMENTS	31	30
%	%	%	%	%	%	**ASSETS**	%	%
DATA NOT AVAILABLE		9.3	4.1			Cash & Equivalents	5.5	8.7
		31.5	31.3			Trade Receivables (net)	32.4	32.5
		24.6	26.7			Inventory	25.6	26.3
		1.4	3.4			All Other Current	3.6	2.6
		66.9	65.4			Total Current	67.1	70.2
		27.2	20.6			Fixed Assets (net)	19.0	20.6
		.1	8.0			Intangibles (net)	5.9	4.4
		5.7	6.0			All Other Non-Current	7.9	4.9
		100.0	100.0			Total	100.0	100.0
						LIABILITIES		
		6.6	9.5			Notes Payable-Short Term	11.7	13.5
		3.2	1.4			Cur. Mat.-L.T.D.	3.1	2.4
		26.1	15.5			Trade Payables	19.6	18.9
		.0	.2			Income Taxes Payable	.5	.2
		7.3	15.8			All Other Current	8.9	12.6
		43.2	42.4			Total Current	43.8	47.5
		14.9	6.7			Long-Term Debt	9.9	11.8
		.3	.5			Deferred Taxes	.3	.5
		7.2	8.1			All Other Non-Current	5.7	9.9
		34.5	42.3			Net Worth	40.2	30.2
		100.0	100.0			Total Liabilities & Net Worth	100.0	100.0
						INCOME DATA		
		100.0	100.0			Net Sales	100.0	100.0
		29.6	19.3			Gross Profit	28.8	30.0
		25.6	15.4			Operating Expenses	22.4	22.5
		4.0	3.9			Operating Profit	6.3	7.6
		1.0	.3			All Other Expenses (net)	.4	1.1
		3.0	3.6			Profit Before Taxes	5.9	6.4
						RATIOS		
		3.1	3.1				2.6	2.4
		1.8	1.6			Current	1.4	1.5
		1.3	1.0				1.1	1.1
		1.5	1.3				1.5	1.7
		1.3	.8			Quick	.9	.9
		.7	.7				.5	.6
		39 9.4	**47** 7.7				**41** 9.0	**46** 7.9
		49 7.5	**67** 5.4			Sales/Receivables	**53** 6.9	**53** 6.8
		62 5.9	**74** 4.9				**66** 5.5	**61** 6.0
		21 17.2	**45** 8.1				**33** 10.9	**31** 11.6
		71 5.1	**66** 5.5			Cost of Sales/Inventory	**67** 5.5	**57** 6.4
		97 3.7	**95** 3.8				**93** 3.9	**102** 3.6
		23 15.6	**29** 12.4				**30** 12.4	**23** 15.8
		38 9.6	**34** 10.8			Cost of Sales/Payables	**43** 8.5	**43** 8.5
		60 6.1	**54** 6.8				**58** 6.3	**59** 6.2
		4.4	4.4				4.8	5.0
		11.0	8.1			Sales/Working Capital	8.0	10.1
		13.9	-125.3				56.3	28.7
		23.4	24.8				16.8	21.4
		(10) 2.2	6.3			EBIT/Interest	(28) 5.7	(27) 5.0
		.6	.6				1.6	1.3
						Net Profit + Depr., Dep., Amort./Cur. Mat. L/T/D		
		.3	.4				.2	.3
		.5	1.1			Fixed/Worth	.4	.7
		1.2	1.5				1.1	NM
		.5	.4				.7	.8
		1.8	3.5			Debt/Worth	1.5	1.5
		2.5	8.2				4.2	NM
		38.4	37.0				57.5	61.1
		(11) 3.7	16.1			% Profit Before Taxes/Tangible Net Worth	(28) 19.9	(23) 39.7
		-.8	-1.6				5.2	7.9
		20.2	12.0				19.8	22.2
		1.9	5.2			% Profit Before Taxes/Total Assets	9.6	14.3
		-.7	-.5				2.6	1.1
		26.8	14.3				18.6	29.3
		10.3	11.0			Sales/Net Fixed Assets	11.1	11.5
		6.6	5.6				8.0	5.0
		3.3	2.4				2.7	2.9
		2.0	1.9			Sales/Total Assets	1.9	2.0
		1.7	1.3				1.6	1.6
		1.4					1.2	.9
		(11) 2.0				% Depr., Dep., Amort./Sales	(26) 1.9	(26) 1.7
		2.9					3.2	3.2
						% Officers', Directors' Owners' Comp/Sales		
	13933M	133995M	504446M	234834M	516413M	Net Sales ($)	892136M	1088557M
	5156M	51401M	273467M	223558M	395988M	Total Assets ($)	630519M	573809M

M = $ thousand MM = $ million

See Pages 9 through 22 for Explanation of Ratios and Data

Comparative Historical Data   **Current Data Sorted by Sales**

			Type of Statement						
8	6	8	Unqualified						
14	5	6	Reviewed		1	1	1		5
3	4	2	Compiled		1	3	1		1
2		2	Tax Returns		1		1		
14	10	16	Other						
4/1/07-3/31/08 ALL	4/1/08-3/31/09 ALL	4/1/09-3/31/10 ALL		0-1MM	6 (4/1-9/30/09) 1-3MM	3-5MM	26 (10/1/09-3/31/10) 5-10MM	10-25MM	25MM & OVER
41	27	32	NUMBER OF STATEMENTS		2	4	5	7	14
%	%	%	ASSETS	%	%	%	%	%	%
10.3	9.8	8.0	Cash & Equivalents	D					8.4
30.9	29.0	31.6	Trade Receivables (net)	A					28.0
28.0	28.9	25.9	Inventory	T					27.9
2.2	1.3	3.1	All Other Current	A					5.1
71.3	68.9	68.6	Total Current						69.4
19.3	21.4	22.6	Fixed Assets (net)	N					22.4
4.1	5.6	3.0	Intangibles (net)	O					4.6
5.3	4.1	5.8	All Other Non-Current	T					3.5
100.0	100.0	100.0	Total						100.0
			LIABILITIES	A					
6.8	8.0	8.7	Notes Payable-Short Term	V					12.8
2.7	2.2	2.6	Cur. Mat.-L.T.D.	A					1.3
16.5	14.6	18.1	Trade Payables	I					15.0
.3	.2	.7	Income Taxes Payable	L					1.0
9.0	8.6	15.1	All Other Current	A					15.3
35.3	33.7	45.2	Total Current	B					45.4
14.9	11.3	11.5	Long-Term Debt	L					8.9
.2	.1	.3	Deferred Taxes	E					.4
7.1	9.9	6.1	All Other Non-Current						5.6
42.5	45.0	36.9	Net Worth						39.8
100.0	100.0	100.0	Total Liabilities & Net Worth						100.0
			INCOME DATA						
100.0	100.0	100.0	Net Sales						100.0
31.9	32.2	30.6	Gross Profit						29.2
24.5	24.5	24.9	Operating Expenses						23.1
7.4	7.8	5.7	Operating Profit						6.1
.7	.8	.8	All Other Expenses (net)						1.2
6.6	7.0	4.8	Profit Before Taxes						5.0
			RATIOS						
3.2	3.6	3.0							3.1
2.2	2.2	1.7	Current						1.6
1.5	1.6	1.1							1.1
2.0	1.8	1.4							1.4
1.1	1.1	.9	Quick						.9
.8	.7	.6							.5
38 9.7	37 10.0	45 8.2							46 7.9
47 7.7	49 7.4	58 6.3	Sales/Receivables						68 5.4
58 6.3	61 5.9	70 5.2							75 4.9
36 10.1	48 7.7	40 9.0							48 7.6
66 5.5	68 5.4	75 4.9	Cost of Sales/Inventory						92 4.0
103 3.6	87 4.2	110 3.3							148 2.5
20 18.6	19 19.1	23 15.6							31 11.8
32 11.4	26 14.3	37 9.9	Cost of Sales/Payables						41 8.8
53 6.9	37 10.0	55 6.6							66 5.5
4.1	3.3	4.6							4.3
8.2	6.0	10.5	Sales/Working Capital						10.5
11.5	10.0	24.1							27.4
23.6	22.0	22.0							29.8
(39) 10.9	(24) 7.8	(28) 5.4	EBIT/Interest					(13)	6.0
2.1	3.4	1.3							1.2
15.6		23.3	Net Profit + Depr., Dep.,						
(11) 5.4		(10) 2.6	Amort./Cur. Mat. L/T/D						
2.5		1.3							
.3	.3	.3							.3
.5	.5	.6	Fixed/Worth						.7
.9	1.4	1.3							1.6
.5	.5	.9							.8
1.3	1.4	2.0	Debt/Worth						2.4
2.8	4.6	3.9							5.3
54.4	66.4	42.1							63.6
(36) 27.0	(23) 29.3	(30) 20.6	% Profit Before Taxes/Tangible Net Worth						24.0
12.0	8.3	.4							-2.4
22.1	24.0	19.0							19.5
11.4	12.9	6.4	% Profit Before Taxes/Total Assets						7.3
3.8	3.3	-.2							-.7
27.9	20.2	21.2							15.3
11.8	13.2	10.9	Sales/Net Fixed Assets						6.7
7.3	8.5	4.5							4.0
3.0	3.0	2.5							2.3
2.3	2.1	2.0	Sales/Total Assets						1.5
1.7	1.8	1.3							1.1
.9	.6	.9							.8
(36) 1.6	(25) 1.4	(25) 1.8	% Depr., Dep., Amort./Sales					(11)	2.0
2.5	2.1	3.0							3.7
1.6									
(11) 3.5			% Officers', Directors' Owners' Comp/Sales						
8.6									
1156786M	1248846M	1403621M	Net Sales ($)		4262M	16566M	31659M	121145M	1229989M
608528M	648508M	949570M	Total Assets ($)		2594M	9838M	14456M	53786M	868896M

© RMA 2010

M = $ thousand   MM = $ million
See Pages 9 through 22 for Explanation of Ratios and Data

Current Data Sorted by Assets

Comparative Historical Data

Type of Statement

0-500M	500M-2MM	2-10MM	10-50MM	50-100MM	100-250MM	Type of Statement	4/1/05-3/31/06 ALL	4/1/06-3/31/07 ALL
		1	4	1		Unqualified	10	7
		4				Reviewed	10	7
	2	7				Compiled	2	6
	2	1	1			Tax Returns	6	5
1	6	7	4	4	2	Other	16	16
1	9 (4/1-9/30/09)	20	38 (10/1/09-3/31/10)	5	2			
0-500M	500M-2MM	2-10MM	10-50MM	50-100MM	100-250MM			
1	10	20	9	5	2	NUMBER OF STATEMENTS	44	41

0-500M %	500M-2MM %	2-10MM %	10-50MM %	50-100MM %	100-250MM %		4/1/05-3/31/06 ALL %	4/1/06-3/31/07 ALL %
						ASSETS		
	1.7	14.3				Cash & Equivalents	13.2	13.3
	32.9	28.9				Trade Receivables (net)	25.4	25.1
	34.8	29.8				Inventory	31.6	26.0
	.8	3.3				All Other Current	1.5	3.9
	70.2	76.2				Total Current	71.7	68.3
	15.5	20.8				Fixed Assets (net)	20.5	19.4
	5.5	.9				Intangibles (net)	3.3	5.6
	8.7	2.1				All Other Non-Current	4.5	6.6
	100.0	100.0				Total	100.0	100.0
						LIABILITIES		
	13.7	11.8				Notes Payable-Short Term	7.6	7.7
	2.4	3.0				Cur. Mat.-L.T.D.	2.9	4.0
	17.8	16.7				Trade Payables	15.4	14.0
	.0	.0				Income Taxes Payable	.3	.1
	3.6	10.0				All Other Current	9.9	9.5
	37.5	41.7				Total Current	36.1	35.3
	6.3	9.8				Long-Term Debt	15.2	15.6
	.0	1.1				Deferred Taxes	.6	.8
	7.8	5.9				All Other Non-Current	9.3	12.0
	48.4	41.5				Net Worth	38.8	36.3
	100.0	100.0				Total Liabilities & Net Worth	100.0	100.0
						INCOME DATA		
	100.0	100.0				Net Sales	100.0	100.0
	34.5	31.8				Gross Profit	34.7	37.5
	32.6	26.7				Operating Expenses	28.8	29.3
	1.9	5.1				Operating Profit	5.9	8.3
	.8	.8				All Other Expenses (net)	.5	.6
	1.2	4.3				Profit Before Taxes	5.4	7.7
						RATIOS		
	2.6	3.1				Current	2.9	4.1
	2.0	2.0					2.0	2.6
	1.5	1.2					1.4	1.2
	1.3	2.0				Quick	1.8	2.6
	.9	.9					1.0	1.1
	.6	.6					.6	.6
29	12.6	35 10.3				Sales/Receivables	36 10.2	33 11.0
46	8.0	47 7.7					44 8.3	41 8.9
52	7.0	60 6.1					58 6.3	51 7.1
39	9.5	42 8.7				Cost of Sales/Inventory	55 6.6	52 7.0
55	6.7	63 5.8					79 4.6	73 5.0
118	3.1	101 3.6					110 3.3	96 3.8
10	36.1	22 16.8				Cost of Sales/Payables	19 19.1	22 16.8
36	10.2	28 12.8					39 9.5	29 12.6
53	6.9	53 6.9					55 6.6	46 7.9
	6.3	4.0				Sales/Working Capital	4.2	3.3
	8.3	6.0					6.4	6.1
	14.8	32.5					11.2	22.0
		48.5				EBIT/Interest	30.3	73.5
	(18)	9.2					(37) 7.4	(37) 7.0
		1.6					3.4	1.9
						Net Profit + Depr., Dep., Amort./Cur. Mat. L/T/D		
	.1	.1				Fixed/Worth	.2	.2
	.1	.2					.5	.4
	1.3	1.9					1.8	1.8
	.6	.5				Debt/Worth	.6	.4
	1.1	1.0					1.4	1.2
	3.5	5.1					8.0	5.1
	27.3	46.9				% Profit Before Taxes/Tangible Net Worth	76.0	65.3
	(17) 15.1	29.2					(38) 31.1	(33) 43.2
	-5.5	11.0					13.8	21.3
	13.4	23.0				% Profit Before Taxes/Total Assets	18.1	30.5
	2.7	14.4					10.8	16.2
	-3.3	2.7					5.2	2.2
	155.2	41.7				Sales/Net Fixed Assets	26.3	22.9
	48.9	16.8					13.1	13.2
	6.0	7.1					5.0	7.4
	4.0	2.8				Sales/Total Assets	2.7	2.9
	2.6	2.3					2.1	2.1
	2.0	1.9					1.5	1.6
		.4				% Depr., Dep., Amort./Sales	1.5	1.2
	(16)	1.5					(38) 2.1	(31) 1.8
		2.9					3.4	3.2
						% Officers', Directors' Owners' Comp/Sales	2.1	3.1
	(15)						(15) 4.2	(14) 5.0
							10.2	9.0
3291M	39552M	213058M	299249M	534664M	264171M	Net Sales ($)	940879M	1183403M
398M	12972M	92316M	214554M	331723M	256043M	Total Assets ($)	567765M	698111M

M = $ thousand   MM = $ million
See Pages 9 through 22 for Explanation of Ratios and Data

Comparative Historical Data   **Current Data Sorted by Sales**

			Type of Statement						
7	12	6	Unqualified				2	2	2
6	6	4	Reviewed				2	2	
5	6	11	Compiled		2		1	6	
8	4	3	Tax Returns		2		1		
15	22	23	Other		2	3	5	3	10
4/1/07- 3/31/08	4/1/08- 3/31/09	4/1/09- 3/31/10			9 (4/1-9/30/09)		38 (10/1/09-3/31/10)		
ALL	ALL	ALL		0-1MM	1-3MM	3-5MM	5-10MM	10-25MM	25MM & OVER
41	50	47	NUMBER OF STATEMENTS		6	5	11	13	12
%	%	%	ASSETS	%	%	%	%	%	%
15.5	10.7	12.9	Cash & Equivalents				15.5	16.0	15.2
28.6	27.3	26.8	Trade Receivables (net)				32.8	24.6	19.7
23.3	26.1	29.1	Inventory				25.0	28.0	29.6
3.4	2.6	2.5	All Other Current				3.4	3.0	2.6
70.8	66.8	71.3	Total Current				76.7	71.7	67.1
18.8	20.5	18.3	Fixed Assets (net)				14.0	23.9	18.0
5.6	8.9	6.4	Intangibles (net)				7.8	.3	12.1
4.9	3.8	4.0	All Other Non-Current				1.6	4.1	2.9
100.0	100.0	100.0	Total				100.0	100.0	100.0
			LIABILITIES						
10.4	20.3	9.9	Notes Payable-Short Term				14.1	6.4	4.8
2.3	4.3	3.1	Cur. Mat.-L.T.D.				2.5	2.5	1.4
14.7	13.7	14.3	Trade Payables				13.9	17.7	9.3
.2	.2	.1	Income Taxes Payable				.1	.0	.3
6.7	7.4	7.5	All Other Current				10.6	8.8	5.9
34.3	46.0	34.9	Total Current				41.1	35.5	21.8
10.5	16.8	10.6	Long-Term Debt				6.8	4.7	9.2
.8	1.3	.8	Deferred Taxes				.0	1.7	1.3
5.9	11.5	5.7	All Other Non-Current				6.6	3.4	5.9
48.4	24.4	48.0	Net Worth				45.5	54.8	61.9
100.0	100.0	100.0	Total Liabilties & Net Worth				100.0	100.0	100.0
			INCOME DATA						
100.0	100.0	100.0	Net Sales				100.0	100.0	100.0
32.0	34.2	35.3	Gross Profit				34.6	33.9	35.2
24.8	26.2	29.5	Operating Expenses				27.4	27.8	25.9
7.2	8.0	5.8	Operating Profit				7.2	6.1	9.3
.1	1.4	.2	All Other Expenses (net)				1.1	-.3	-1.0
7.1	6.6	5.6	Profit Before Taxes				6.2	6.4	10.3
			RATIOS						
4.2	3.9	3.6					3.3	3.6	4.3
2.0	2.2	2.5	Current				2.3	2.1	3.6
1.4	1.3	1.6					1.1	1.5	2.7
3.3	1.9	2.1					2.1	2.5	2.4
1.1	1.0	1.2	Quick				1.2	.9	1.5
.8	.7	.6					.5	.6	1.0
35 10.5	30 12.2	34 10.8					43 8.5	26 14.1	37 10.0
44 8.3	42 8.8	43 8.4	Sales/Receivables				57 6.4	43 8.4	42 8.7
58 6.3	51 7.2	55 6.6					68 5.4	51 7.2	52 7.0
30 12.0	39 9.3	46 7.9					41 8.9	40 9.2	91 4.0
59 6.2	70 5.2	89 4.1	Cost of Sales/Inventory				61 6.0	61 6.0	99 3.7
93 3.9	96 3.8	112 3.3					105 3.5	89 4.1	125 2.9
20 18.7	16 22.5	22 16.3					26 14.0	23 16.0	17 22.0
29 12.6	28 12.9	33 11.1	Cost of Sales/Payables				30 12.0	31 11.9	32 11.5
47 7.8	37 9.9	52 7.0					47 7.8	55 6.6	49 7.5
3.9	4.3	3.5					3.5	3.0	2.8
6.3	6.4	5.4	Sales/Working Capital				6.0	6.1	3.8
15.6	21.6	11.5					36.8	16.5	4.6
36.7	40.6	18.9					72.0	26.4	
(34) 6.2	(45) 7.5	(39) 3.8	EBIT/Interest			(10) 6.8	(11) 13.0	
1.4	1.7	1.6					1.4	2.7	
	18.6	11.3	Net Profit + Depr., Dep.,						
(11) 4.3	(14) 5.2		Amort./Cur. Mat. L/T/D						
2.1	1.9								
.2	.2	.1					.1	.1	.1
.3	.4	.2	Fixed/Worth				.1	.4	.2
1.3	NM	1.1					2.1	1.1	.6
.3	.5	.4					.5	.4	.4
.9	1.6	.8	Debt/Worth				1.1	.7	.6
2.7	-28.3	3.7					-62.5	2.1	1.5
57.5	57.5	38.7	% Profit Before Taxes/Tangible				44.5		37.2
(34) 24.4	(37) 34.1	(41) 26.1	Net Worth					26.1 (11)	31.1
6.5	16.8	7.2						9.7	10.2
29.8	24.4	20.3	% Profit Before Taxes/Total				31.9	21.8	27.9
10.8	12.7	11.9	Assets				12.9	13.7	17.6
2.8	2.9	2.1					1.0	3.4	4.6
37.1	43.6	61.2					43.8	38.5	38.4
18.1	16.3	18.3	Sales/Net Fixed Assets				15.3	18.3	11.7
6.8	5.7	6.2					9.4	5.9	4.1
3.0	3.3	2.7					2.8	3.7	1.9
2.3	2.2	2.0	Sales/Total Assets				2.3	2.3	1.6
1.5	1.6	1.6					1.5	1.7	1.4
.5	1.0	.6						.3	1.2
(32) 1.4	(40) 2.5	(36) 2.1	% Depr., Dep., Amort./Sales					(11) .6	(11) 2.6
3.0	4.0	3.7						2.2	5.3
2.3	2.3	2.7	% Officers', Directors'						
(18) 3.8	(15) 4.0	(13) 4.6	Owners' Comp/Sales						
6.0	10.0	7.7							
1306965M	1701745M	1353985M	Net Sales ($)		14717M	18283M	86393M	203493M	1031099M
765320M	1124499M	908006M	Total Assets ($)		6379M	7732M	81000M	98453M	714442M

M = $ thousand   MM = $ million
See Pages 9 through 22 for Explanation of Ratios and Data

Current Data Sorted by Assets — Comparative Historical Data

0-500M	500M-2MM	2-10MM	10-50MM	50-100MM	100-250MM		4/1/05-3/31/06 ALL	4/1/06-3/31/07 ALL
						Type of Statement		
1	9	5	15	5	5	Unqualified	33	45
	8	32	11			Reviewed	32	31
	11	9	1			Compiled	29	21
		6				Tax Returns	12	14
2	13	46	30	4	2	Other	78	71
	41 (4/1-9/30/09)		174 (10/1/09-3/31/10)					
3	41	98	57	9	7	**NUMBER OF STATEMENTS**	184	182
%	%	%	%	%	%	**ASSETS**	%	%
	10.1	11.8	10.5			Cash & Equivalents	10.8	8.1
	32.8	26.0	24.7			Trade Receivables (net)	30.5	30.3
	29.0	31.3	26.8			Inventory	28.7	29.9
	2.5	2.8	2.6			All Other Current	2.4	3.3
	74.5	71.9	64.7			Total Current	72.4	71.6
	17.4	17.9	22.7			Fixed Assets (net)	18.1	18.6
	2.6	3.7	7.6			Intangibles (net)	4.0	4.5
	5.5	6.5	5.1			All Other Non-Current	5.6	5.2
	100.0	100.0	100.0			Total	100.0	100.0
						LIABILITIES		
	14.2	10.6	8.1			Notes Payable-Short Term	11.9	11.6
	2.9	2.2	3.4			Cur. Mat.-L.T.D.	3.1	3.3
	21.2	15.6	13.2			Trade Payables	14.7	17.0
	.2	.1	.1			Income Taxes Payable	.4	.3
	9.3	9.1	14.7			All Other Current	9.5	10.3
	47.9	37.5	39.5			Total Current	39.6	42.5
	10.8	11.3	12.8			Long-Term Debt	10.5	11.7
	.1	.3	.7			Deferred Taxes	.5	.3
	6.0	4.9	15.5			All Other Non-Current	6.8	4.6
	35.2	46.0	31.6			Net Worth	42.5	40.9
	100.0	100.0	100.0			Total Liabilities & Net Worth	100.0	100.0
						INCOME DATA		
	100.0	100.0	100.0			Net Sales	100.0	100.0
	35.3	32.8	30.4			Gross Profit	32.5	32.7
	30.3	27.2	26.5			Operating Expenses	27.0	26.9
	5.1	5.6	4.0			Operating Profit	5.5	5.8
	.5	1.0	1.4			All Other Expenses (net)	.9	.8
	4.6	4.6	2.6			Profit Before Taxes	4.6	5.0
						RATIOS		
	3.2	3.4	3.1				3.1	2.8
	1.6	2.0	1.8			Current	1.8	1.8
	1.1	1.4	1.3				1.3	1.2
	1.9	1.9	1.5				1.9	1.6
	.9	1.0	1.1			Quick	1.0	.9
	.5	.5	.6				.7	.6
	32 11.4	35 10.4	44 8.2				42 8.6	39 9.4
	40 9.1	46 7.9	56 6.5			Sales/Receivables	52 7.1	50 7.3
	53 6.9	58 6.3	65 5.6				63 5.8	62 5.9
	29 12.7	44 8.3	61 6.0				42 8.7	45 8.1
	64 5.7	87 4.2	88 4.2			Cost of Sales/Inventory	78 4.7	79 4.6
	86 4.3	144 2.5	140 2.6				111 3.3	114 3.2
	19 19.0	19 19.4	23 15.5				22 16.6	21 17.4
	29 12.7	33 11.1	33 11.0			Cost of Sales/Payables	32 11.5	36 10.1
	60 6.1	57 6.4	50 7.4				45 8.1	55 6.6
	5.1	3.9	3.5				3.8	4.3
	10.7	5.5	5.7			Sales/Working Capital	7.1	6.8
	34.9	10.4	13.2				13.3	18.4
	15.0	16.2	14.5				18.5	16.9
	(36) 5.6	(82) 4.0	(51) 2.3			EBIT/Interest	(163) 6.2	(161) 4.9
	1.7	1.2	-.4				1.7	2.0
		6.2	4.3			Net Profit + Depr., Dep.,	7.2	7.9
		(25) 3.2	(23) 1.4			Amort./Cur. Mat. L/T/D	(53) 2.9	(46) 3.3
		1.4	.3				1.7	1.6
	.1	.1	.3				.2	.2
	.5	.3	.6			Fixed/Worth	.4	.4
	1.4	1.0	1.7				.8	1.2
	.7	.5	.6				.6	.7
	1.8	1.2	1.4			Debt/Worth	1.5	1.6
	9.9	3.4	4.0				3.3	4.8
	67.0	47.1	38.1			% Profit Before Taxes/Tangible	42.9	49.5
	(32) 25.5	(92) 17.1	(49) 7.9			Net Worth	(170) 19.0	(162) 26.1
	3.8	2.6	.2				4.9	6.5
	24.2	19.8	9.8			% Profit Before Taxes/Total	15.6	16.7
	11.4	5.0	2.4			Assets	7.7	8.2
	1.3	.6	-1.7				1.9	1.5
	154.7	49.9	20.2				29.4	28.3
	16.9	14.6	7.8			Sales/Net Fixed Assets	13.3	14.8
	10.1	7.1	4.5				8.3	6.9
	3.5	2.6	2.0				2.6	2.6
	2.6	1.9	1.5			Sales/Total Assets	2.1	2.0
	2.1	1.4	1.0				1.6	1.6
	.5	.6	1.7				.9	.9
	(30) 1.2	(82) 1.6	(46) 2.9			% Depr., Dep., Amort./Sales	(146) 1.8	(148) 1.6
	3.7	3.0	5.0				2.9	2.6
	3.3	2.6	1.1			% Officers', Directors'	2.1	2.3
	(25) 5.1	(30) 5.0	(12) 1.3			Owners' Comp/Sales	(52) 5.1	(51) 6.1
	9.3	7.8	3.2				9.0	11.0
1478M	151331M	1065305M	1643761M	688941M	1473524M	Net Sales ($)	5769763M	4320432M
346M	50162M	528590M	1077338M	645225M	997902M	Total Assets ($)	3621770M	2950940M

M = $ thousand MM = $ million
See Pages 9 through 22 for Explanation of Ratios and Data

Comparative Historical Data · **Current Data Sorted by Sales**

Type of Statement										
Unqualified	34	27	31		1			3	7	20
Reviewed	34	38	52			6	6	11	22	7
Compiled	18	23	18			2	5	6	4	1
Tax Returns	19	15	17			8	3	4	2	
Other	71	90	97		2	7	16	18	28	26
	4/1/07-3/31/08	4/1/08-3/31/09	4/1/09-3/31/10			41 (4/1-9/30/09)		174 (10/1/09-3/31/10)		
	ALL	ALL	ALL		0-1MM	1-3MM	3-5MM	5-10MM	10-25MM	25MM & OVER
NUMBER OF STATEMENTS	176	193	215		3	23	30	42	63	54
	%	%	%	**ASSETS**	%	%	%	%	%	%
Cash & Equivalents	11.2	10.0	11.2			10.3	8.3	12.9	11.2	12.4
Trade Receivables (net)	29.6	26.5	26.6			28.3	23.0	27.2	26.9	26.5
Inventory	28.1	30.8	28.4			28.0	27.5	29.8	32.1	24.3
All Other Current	2.7	2.2	3.2			3.0	1.9	1.2	3.8	3.7
Total Current	71.6	69.6	69.3			69.6	60.7	71.1	74.0	67.0
Fixed Assets (net)	18.4	19.8	18.8			18.7	28.6	16.0	17.2	17.1
Intangibles (net)	5.2	5.5	6.2			3.5	3.7	6.9	3.9	11.1
All Other Non-Current	4.8	5.2	5.7			8.2	7.0	5.9	5.0	4.8
Total	100.0	100.0	100.0			100.0	100.0	100.0	100.0	100.0
				LIABILITIES						
Notes Payable-Short Term	10.0	13.3	9.8			13.2	15.8	9.3	10.0	5.4
Cur. Mat.-L.T.D.	2.8	2.8	2.6			3.0	4.2	1.2	2.7	2.9
Trade Payables	15.5	14.0	15.6			16.0	13.4	15.4	16.4	16.3
Income Taxes Payable	.3	.3	.1			.1	.1	.2	.1	.2
All Other Current	9.4	9.2	10.9			7.1	8.5	9.5	10.1	14.3
Total Current	38.0	39.5	39.1			39.4	42.1	35.5	39.2	39.1
Long-Term Debt	12.0	12.8	13.6			13.7	17.9	11.1	9.2	13.9
Deferred Taxes	.2	.5	.4			.0	.2	.1	.8	.4
All Other Non-Current	5.9	6.8	8.7			3.6	4.1	7.7	4.8	19.1
Net Worth	43.9	40.4	38.2			43.2	35.8	45.6	46.0	27.5
Total Liabilties & Net Worth	100.0	100.0	100.0			100.0	100.0	100.0	100.0	100.0
				INCOME DATA						
Net Sales	100.0	100.0	100.0			100.0	100.0	100.0	100.0	100.0
Gross Profit	33.7	32.6	33.0			36.5	39.1	37.2	27.7	29.3
Operating Expenses	27.0	27.5	27.6			31.5	33.4	31.8	23.0	22.9
Operating Profit	6.7	5.2	5.4			5.0	5.7	5.4	4.7	6.4
All Other Expenses (net)	1.3	1.2	1.2			.8	1.9	.9	.8	1.6
Profit Before Taxes	5.4	3.9	4.3			4.2	3.8	4.6	4.0	4.8
				RATIOS						
Current	3.2 / 1.8 / 1.4	3.0 / 1.9 / 1.3	3.2 / 1.9 / 1.3			3.3 / 2.1 / 1.2	2.7 / 1.5 / 1.0	3.7 / 2.1 / 1.4	3.1 / 2.0 / 1.4	2.8 / 2.0 / 1.3
Quick	1.9 / 1.0 / .7	1.8 / .9 / .6	1.7 / 1.0 / .6			2.1 / 1.0 / .5	1.5 / .6 / .4	1.9 / 1.0 / .7	1.8 / 1.1 / .6	1.6 / 1.2 / .7
Sales/Receivables	38 9.7 / 49 7.4 / 61 6.0	34 10.6 / 44 8.2 / 57 6.4	37 9.9 / 49 7.5 / 61 6.0			34 10.9 / 47 7.8 / 59 6.2	31 11.7 / 37 9.8 / 50 7.3	35 10.5 / 47 7.8 / 63 5.8	40 9.0 / 49 7.4 / 60 6.1	44 8.4 / 55 6.6 / 63 5.8
Cost of Sales/Inventory	35 10.4 / 68 5.3 / 114 3.2	46 7.9 / 78 4.7 / 122 3.0	43 8.4 / 79 4.6 / 122 3.0			22 16.4 / 74 5.0 / 132 2.8	38 9.6 / 81 4.5 / 140 2.6	47 7.8 / 87 4.2 / 152 2.4	54 6.7 / 82 4.4 / 119 3.1	41 8.9 / 76 4.8 / 100 3.7
Cost of Sales/Payables	21 17.5 / 33 11.2 / 51 7.2	17 21.9 / 29 12.4 / 49 7.4	21 17.3 / 33 11.0 / 55 6.7			21 17.6 / 34 10.7 / 64 5.7	16 22.2 / 28 13.2 / 59 6.2	17 21.8 / 29 12.5 / 59 6.2	21 17.4 / 31 11.8 / 53 6.9	28 12.9 / 37 10.0 / 53 6.8
Sales/Working Capital	3.9 / 6.9 / 14.3	4.1 / 6.5 / 16.2	3.9 / 6.1 / 13.1			3.9 / 6.1 / 19.1	4.2 / 11.7 / -144.3	3.7 / 5.6 / 9.9	3.9 / 5.2 / 9.7	3.6 / 6.0 / 14.9
EBIT/Interest	(142) 13.4 / 4.6 / 2.0	(173) 15.8 / 4.4 / 1.4	(185) 14.4 / 3.6 / 1.1			(20) 8.6 / 2.8 / -1.2	(27) 12.7 / 4.6 / 1.0	(33) 8.4 / 2.6 / .5	(56) 22.7 / 4.0 / 1.2	(48) 20.1 / 3.7 / .8
Net Profit + Depr., Dep., Amort./Cur. Mat. L/T/D	(40) 6.0 / 2.8 / 1.1	(44) 6.4 / 2.1 / 1.3	(62) 5.4 / 2.8 / .8					(11) 5.4 / 3.7 / 2.6	(17) 6.2 / 2.6 / .3	(29) 8.1 / 3.1 / 1.1
Fixed/Worth	.2 / .4 / 1.0	.2 / .4 / 1.4	.1 / .5 / 1.4			.1 / .4 / 1.4	.4 / .8 / 3.0	.1 / .3 / 1.3	.1 / .3 / .8	.2 / .5 / 1.4
Debt/Worth	.5 / 1.3 / 3.0	.7 / 1.4 / 5.0	.6 / 1.4 / 4.3			.4 / 1.8 / 4.5	.7 / 1.8 / 8.8	.6 / 1.2 / 4.6	.5 / 1.1 / 2.7	.9 / 1.7 / 4.7
% Profit Before Taxes/Tangible Net Worth	(156) 52.6 / 25.5 / 10.6	(164) 46.8 / 21.6 / 4.1	(186) 47.1 / 15.7 / 2.1			(18) 32.4 / 6.8 / -.1	(25) 77.8 / 25.0 / 5.3	(38) 42.7 / 13.5 / .0	(58) 49.2 / 13.4 / 1.7	(45) 41.3 / 16.8 / 2.7
% Profit Before Taxes/Total Assets	18.8 / 9.8 / 3.8	16.2 / 7.0 / .8	18.9 / 4.5 / .4			16.9 / 4.3 / 1.1	21.9 / 9.4 / -.3	17.8 / 3.7 / -.5	18.5 / 4.5 / .5	15.0 / 4.4 / .3
Sales/Net Fixed Assets	36.5 / 14.8 / 7.1	33.6 / 14.9 / 6.3	42.0 / 13.5 / 6.0			34.4 / 12.9 / 7.4	20.4 / 8.9 / 3.0	54.6 / 17.0 / 9.5	48.8 / 13.6 / 5.8	28.4 / 10.7 / 6.8
Sales/Total Assets	2.9 / 2.1 / 1.6	2.8 / 2.0 / 1.5	2.6 / 1.9 / 1.4			2.7 / 2.3 / 1.6	2.7 / 1.9 / 1.4	2.7 / 1.8 / 1.2	2.5 / 1.9 / 1.5	2.4 / 1.7 / 1.3
% Depr., Dep., Amort./Sales	(142) .7 / 1.8 / 3.3	(155) 1.0 / 2.1 / 3.2	(176) .8 / 2.1 / 3.6			(17) .6 / 2.4 / 3.9	(25) .9 / 2.6 / 4.7	(34) .5 / 1.4 / 3.3	(52) .8 / 1.8 / 3.3	(46) 1.3 / 2.6 / 3.6
% Officers', Directors' Owners' Comp/Sales	(45) 2.0 / 3.6 / 5.8	(55) 2.7 / 4.6 / 8.6	(69) 2.3 / 4.5 / 7.4			(13) 3.7 / 5.1 / 10.3	(13) 2.4 / 4.7 / 5.6	(20) 2.8 / 6.1 / 10.0	(16) 1.4 / 2.9 / 5.2	
Net Sales ($)	4590926M	5475372M	5024340M		1478M	52266M	123687M	304307M	977008M	3565594M
Total Assets ($)	2853621M	3180933M	3299563M		346M	30204M	77552M	209573M	568623M	2413265M

© RMA 2010

M = $ thousand   MM = $ million
See Pages 9 through 22 for Explanation of Ratios and Data

Current Data Sorted by Assets   **Comparative Historical Data**

0-500M	500M-2MM	2-10MM	10-50MM	50-100MM	100-250MM	Type of Statement	4/1/05-3/31/06 ALL	4/1/06-3/31/07 ALL
		7	7	2	3	Unqualified	13	22
1	1	4	5			Reviewed	2	4
1		2				Compiled	5	3
1	2	2				Tax Returns	5	1
2	3	8	6	4	4	Other	25	23
	8 (4/1-9/30/09)		55 (10/1/09-3/31/10)					
5	6	21	18	6	7	**NUMBER OF STATEMENTS**	50	53
%	%	%	%	%	%	**ASSETS**	%	%
		14.0	10.3			Cash & Equivalents	19.0	15.4
		28.5	17.3			Trade Receivables (net)	25.3	20.9
		25.2	19.2			Inventory	21.0	22.8
		4.3	2.6			All Other Current	2.5	3.6
		72.0	49.5			Total Current	67.9	62.7
		10.5	32.3			Fixed Assets (net)	20.5	19.4
		9.0	12.5			Intangibles (net)	7.9	13.2
		8.5	5.7			All Other Non-Current	3.6	4.7
		100.0	100.0			Total	100.0	100.0
						LIABILITIES		
		8.0	4.5			Notes Payable-Short Term	8.8	6.3
		1.7	4.3			Cur. Mat.-L.T.D.	1.7	2.5
		10.8	7.8			Trade Payables	12.2	10.2
		.0	.6			Income Taxes Payable	1.9	.5
		19.9	12.9			All Other Current	12.9	10.1
		40.5	30.0			Total Current	37.4	29.6
		7.2	9.5			Long-Term Debt	12.7	10.6
		1.1	.8			Deferred Taxes	.7	.5
		6.4	7.1			All Other Non-Current	8.3	3.7
		44.9	52.6			Net Worth	40.8	55.6
		100.0	100.0			Total Liabilties & Net Worth	100.0	100.0
						INCOME DATA		
		100.0	100.0			Net Sales	100.0	100.0
		45.2	38.6			Gross Profit	50.9	49.1
		41.2	32.1			Operating Expenses	45.0	42.4
		4.0	6.5			Operating Profit	5.8	6.7
		1.0	2.2			All Other Expenses (net)	.5	1.6
		3.0	4.3			Profit Before Taxes	5.4	5.1
						RATIOS		
		3.1	3.1				3.8	4.2
		2.2	1.6			Current	2.0	2.7
		1.1	1.2				1.2	1.7
		2.1	1.8				2.7	2.3
		1.0	.7			Quick	1.2	1.5
		.6	.5				.8	.8
		40 9.1	26 14.2				38 9.6	35 10.5
		48 7.7	50 7.3			Sales/Receivables	54 6.8	50 7.3
		57 6.4	67 5.5				69 5.3	73 5.0
		54 6.7	58 6.3				36 10.1	77 4.8
		90 4.1	73 5.0			Cost of Sales/Inventory	96 3.8	114 3.2
		126 2.9	123 3.0				144 2.5	158 2.3
		12 29.3	19 19.2				30 12.1	27 13.4
		33 10.9	32 11.3			Cost of Sales/Payables	49 7.4	43 8.5
		60 6.0	56 6.5				65 5.6	72 5.1
		4.0	3.9				2.5	2.2
		6.1	6.8			Sales/Working Capital	6.5	3.3
		17.4	18.6				23.7	8.9
		9.6	15.6				17.9	23.5
		(15) 3.0	7.1			EBIT/Interest	(44) 9.7	(43) 4.0
		1.4	1.6				1.5	.5
						Net Profit + Depr., Dep.,	20.3	22.8
						Amort./Cur. Mat. L/T/D	(11) 5.0	(14) 4.1
							2.3	-.4
		.1	.4				.1	.2
		.2	.6			Fixed/Worth	.4	.4
		1.1	1.0				.9	.6
		.4	.4				.6	.4
		1.0	.9			Debt/Worth	1.0	.8
		6.8	2.3				4.6	2.8
		49.4	28.1			% Profit Before Taxes/Tangible	42.1	34.4
		(18) 27.0	(16) 13.5			Net Worth	(42) 18.0	(50) 17.2
		4.5	4.5				3.9	2.3
		22.9	13.3			% Profit Before Taxes/Total	22.6	12.6
		8.4	4.5			Assets	7.8	7.1
		.7	1.8				.4	.3
		89.0	13.5				21.5	19.5
		34.1	4.2			Sales/Net Fixed Assets	12.3	9.3
		12.2	2.3				6.2	4.5
		2.5	1.6				2.5	2.1
		1.6	1.1			Sales/Total Assets	1.7	1.3
		1.3	1.0				1.1	.8
		.5	1.6				1.4	1.6
		(15) 1.9	(17) 3.3			% Depr., Dep., Amort./Sales	(41) 2.3	(45) 2.9
		4.5	6.9				4.8	4.9
							1.9	
						% Officers', Directors'	(18) 5.3	
						Owners' Comp/Sales	8.7	
4192M	30199M	246823M	526968M	358596M	1082461M	Net Sales ($)	2419942M	3096348M
1428M	6623M	128402M	402610M	337378M	1006463M	Total Assets ($)	2052873M	2928948M

Comparative Historical Data   **Current Data Sorted by Sales**

17	17	19	Type of Statement						
17	17	19	Unqualified				1	3	7	8
4	7	11	Reviewed	1		1	2	5	2
1	4	1	Compiled		1				
2	4	5	Tax Returns	1		1	3		
31	22	27	Other	1	2	2	3	7	14
4/1/07-3/31/08 ALL	4/1/08-3/31/09 ALL	4/1/09-3/31/10 ALL		\[8 (4/1-9/30/09)\] 0-1MM	1-3MM	3-5MM	\[55 (10/1/09-3/31/10)\] 5-10MM	10-25MM	25MM & OVER
55	54	63	**NUMBER OF STATEMENTS**	3	3	5	9	19	24
%	%	%	**ASSETS**	%	%	%	%	%	%
15.4	14.7	15.6	Cash & Equivalents					13.2	20.4
21.9	22.4	23.9	Trade Receivables (net)					27.3	15.5
18.4	21.5	20.2	Inventory					22.9	18.3
4.1	2.8	3.4	All Other Current					4.5	3.1
59.8	61.4	63.1	Total Current					68.0	57.3
20.4	21.5	20.0	Fixed Assets (net)					17.9	23.2
16.4	11.3	10.4	Intangibles (net)					8.9	13.5
3.4	5.8	6.4	All Other Non-Current					5.2	6.1
100.0	100.0	100.0	Total					100.0	100.0
			LIABILITIES						
8.3	9.6	7.7	Notes Payable-Short Term					6.9	3.0
2.3	4.5	2.9	Cur. Mat.-L.T.D.					2.1	4.1
10.0	8.4	10.5	Trade Payables					11.3	7.3
.3	.4	.2	Income Taxes Payable					.0	.5
13.2	11.7	16.1	All Other Current					16.4	13.2
34.2	34.5	37.4	Total Current					36.7	28.0
10.3	13.9	8.6	Long-Term Debt					8.5	8.1
.5	.5	.8	Deferred Taxes					.5	1.0
7.0	7.7	8.0	All Other Non-Current					8.4	9.1
47.9	43.3	45.3	Net Worth					46.0	53.8
100.0	100.0	100.0	Total Liabilties & Net Worth					100.0	100.0
			INCOME DATA						
100.0	100.0	100.0	Net Sales					100.0	100.0
49.0	50.0	44.0	Gross Profit					39.4	46.5
40.8	47.3	40.5	Operating Expenses					32.8	41.3
8.1	2.7	3.5	Operating Profit					6.6	5.2
1.3	1.1	1.3	All Other Expenses (net)					1.9	1.7
6.9	1.6	2.2	Profit Before Taxes					4.6	3.5
			RATIOS						
3.2	2.9	3.3	Current					3.4	4.0
2.2	2.0	1.8	Current					2.4	1.6
1.1	1.3	1.2	Current					1.3	1.2
2.2	2.0	2.5	Quick					2.8	2.5
1.1	1.4	1.0	Quick					1.2	.9
.6	.6	.5	Quick					.5	.5
34 10.6	29 12.4	35 10.4	Sales/Receivables					39 9.5	33 11.2
48 7.7	44 8.2	46 7.9	Sales/Receivables					49 7.4	45 8.0
75 4.9	59 6.2	57 6.5	Sales/Receivables					66 5.5	54 6.8
37 9.9	51 7.2	49 7.4	Cost of Sales/Inventory					38 9.6	68 5.4
90 4.1	87 4.2	77 4.7	Cost of Sales/Inventory					68 5.4	95 3.8
144 2.5	146 2.5	123 3.0	Cost of Sales/Inventory					108 3.4	162 2.3
25 14.8	14 26.8	16 23.2	Cost of Sales/Payables					16 22.9	21 17.6
37 9.8	31 11.8	32 11.4	Cost of Sales/Payables					32 11.4	38 9.6
67 5.4	53 6.9	54 6.8	Cost of Sales/Payables					54 6.8	59 6.2
2.8	3.2	4.0	Sales/Working Capital					3.5	2.6
5.3	6.1	6.9	Sales/Working Capital					6.2	6.3
25.6	14.1	18.1	Sales/Working Capital					14.7	13.7
24.5	9.9	14.0	EBIT/Interest					14.7	14.3
(46) 5.3	(42) 2.2	(50) 3.6	EBIT/Interest				(16) 3.2	(19) 6.1	
1.4	-1.1	.9	EBIT/Interest					1.6	1.7
45.2	4.4	3.2	Net Profit + Depr., Dep., Amort./Cur. Mat. L/T/D						
(18) 7.0	(15) 2.4	(15) 2.1	Net Profit + Depr., Dep., Amort./Cur. Mat. L/T/D						
1.0	.9	1.3	Net Profit + Depr., Dep., Amort./Cur. Mat. L/T/D						
.2	.2	.1	Fixed/Worth					.1	.2
.4	.7	.5	Fixed/Worth					.4	.5
1.5	2.2	1.3	Fixed/Worth					1.0	1.1
.5	.6	.4	Debt/Worth					.4	.3
1.4	1.4	1.0	Debt/Worth					1.0	1.0
4.8	9.7	4.8	Debt/Worth					6.3	2.3
68.5	37.8	41.3	% Profit Before Taxes/Tangible Net Worth					56.1	31.5
(48) 20.8	(45) 10.1	(52) 14.9	% Profit Before Taxes/Tangible Net Worth				(17) 18.4	(20) 12.3	
8.4	-16.9	1.5	% Profit Before Taxes/Tangible Net Worth					6.8	-.7
17.4	15.2	16.0	% Profit Before Taxes/Total Assets					27.2	14.1
8.2	2.9	3.8	% Profit Before Taxes/Total Assets					3.8	5.1
1.0	-7.6	-3.7	% Profit Before Taxes/Total Assets					.8	-.6
21.9	29.2	39.6	Sales/Net Fixed Assets					108.5	16.2
12.0	11.3	13.4	Sales/Net Fixed Assets					26.8	6.9
5.1	5.3	4.2	Sales/Net Fixed Assets					4.2	3.6
2.4	2.2	2.4	Sales/Total Assets					2.6	1.6
1.3	1.6	1.5	Sales/Total Assets					1.6	1.2
.8	1.1	1.1	Sales/Total Assets					1.1	.9
1.4	1.1	1.3	% Depr., Dep., Amort./Sales					1.5	1.6
(49) 2.9	(41) 2.0	(50) 2.4	% Depr., Dep., Amort./Sales				(13) 1.9	(22) 2.9	
5.5	3.8	5.4	% Depr., Dep., Amort./Sales					6.9	5.5
		2.8	% Officers', Directors' Owners' Comp/Sales						
	(15) 7.7	(16) 3.1	% Officers', Directors' Owners' Comp/Sales						
	11.8	10.6	% Officers', Directors' Owners' Comp/Sales						
3006329M	1897427M	2249239M	Net Sales ($)	1405M	4192M	21158M	58033M	313975M	1850476M
2603989M	1512811M	1882904M	Total Assets ($)	622M	1319M	13706M	35600M	200374M	1631283M

© RMA 2010   M = $ thousand   MM = $ million
See Pages 9 through 22 for Explanation of Ratios and Data

Current Data Sorted by Assets							Comparative Historical Data	

							Type of Statement		
		4	16	3	6		Unqualified	20	22
	2	9	5				Reviewed	14	8
	1	1					Compiled	9	7
	1						Tax Returns	1	
	1	7	8	2	3		Other	19	16
	20 (4/1-9/30/09)		49 (10/1/09-3/31/10)					4/1/05-3/31/06	4/1/06-3/31/07
0-500M	500M-2MM	2-10MM	10-50MM	50-100MM	100-250MM			ALL	ALL
5	5	21	29	5	9		**NUMBER OF STATEMENTS**	63	53
%	%	%	%	%	%		**ASSETS**	%	%
		12.4	13.5				Cash & Equivalents	12.4	13.7
D		22.3	23.5				Trade Receivables (net)	23.8	26.3
A		30.2	30.7				Inventory	25.9	25.4
T		9.3	4.1				All Other Current	5.8	6.3
A		74.3	71.8				Total Current	68.0	71.7
		13.6	18.1				Fixed Assets (net)	18.7	15.2
N		9.2	5.2				Intangibles (net)	7.2	7.6
O		2.9	4.9				All Other Non-Current	6.2	5.4
T		100.0	100.0				Total	100.0	100.0
							LIABILITIES		
A		4.4	6.0				Notes Payable-Short Term	6.4	6.8
V		2.3	2.8				Cur. Mat.-L.T.D.	1.9	2.5
A		7.6	12.1				Trade Payables	12.1	10.7
I		.4	1.9				Income Taxes Payable	.7	.8
L		16.1	9.2				All Other Current	10.5	10.4
A		30.7	32.0				Total Current	31.7	31.1
B		6.8	7.9				Long-Term Debt	8.1	11.3
L		.5	.5				Deferred Taxes	.7	.7
E		3.2	7.8				All Other Non-Current	9.9	9.6
		58.6	51.8				Net Worth	49.6	47.2
		100.0	100.0				Total Liabilties & Net Worth	100.0	100.0
							INCOME DATA		
		100.0	100.0				Net Sales	100.0	100.0
		43.2	36.5				Gross Profit	36.8	36.3
		33.4	29.3				Operating Expenses	28.9	27.8
		9.8	7.2				Operating Profit	7.8	8.5
		.7	2.1				All Other Expenses (net)	.5	1.1
		9.1	5.1				Profit Before Taxes	7.4	7.4
							RATIOS		
		5.1	4.3					4.0	4.0
		2.7	2.5				Current	2.5	2.6
		1.4	1.4					1.4	1.5
		3.1	2.2					2.1	2.4
		1.0	1.4				Quick	1.2	1.2
		.6	.5					.7	.8
	26	13.8	36	10.0				32	11.5	43	8.4
	38	9.7	49	7.4			Sales/Receivables	50	7.4	57	6.4
	52	7.0	79	4.6				66	5.5	78	4.7
	52	7.0	91	4.0				34	10.6	39	9.3
	93	3.9	136	2.7			Cost of Sales/Inventory	101	3.6	95	3.8
	180	2.0	183	2.0				150	2.4	150	2.4
	11	32.7	16	22.4				19	19.7	19	18.9
	24	15.0	42	8.7			Cost of Sales/Payables	31	11.7	34	10.7
	35	10.3	85	4.3				52	7.1	51	7.2
		3.0	2.4					2.8	2.4
		4.4	3.2				Sales/Working Capital	4.8	3.8
		12.8	8.4					11.4	8.2
		75.5	76.6					26.0	31.8
	(17)	21.1	(25)	7.8			EBIT/Interest	(51)	12.3	(47)	7.4
		2.6	2.4					1.4	1.3
							Net Profit + Depr., Dep.,	15.5	21.3
							Amort./Cur. Mat. L/T/D	(18)	5.0	(23)	6.4
								1.8	1.3
		.1	.1					.1	.1
		.3	.3				Fixed/Worth	.3	.3
		.6	.7					.7	.9
		.3	.4					.4	.4
		1.2	.6				Debt/Worth	.8	1.2
		2.8	2.1					2.9	2.8
		73.8	33.2					57.9	51.3
	(20)	24.5	(26)	13.4			% Profit Before Taxes/Tangible Net Worth	(58)	27.3	(47)	19.7
		7.5	3.5					11.8	4.1
		33.7	14.3					27.2	20.4
		17.4	9.0				% Profit Before Taxes/Total Assets	9.5	8.6
		3.9	1.0					2.8	.5
		38.5	23.2					20.3	24.8
		13.3	13.2				Sales/Net Fixed Assets	9.2	11.4
		8.3	5.5					5.6	6.4
		2.6	1.6					2.2	2.0
		1.8	1.3				Sales/Total Assets	1.5	1.5
		1.3	1.0					1.0	1.2
		.8	1.3					1.3	1.1
	(20)	1.5	(22)	2.5			% Depr., Dep., Amort./Sales	(57)	2.0	(49)	2.0
		3.0	4.4					3.2	3.1
							% Officers', Directors' Owners' Comp/Sales	2.0	
								(13)	4.6	
								9.0	
21278M	234324M	989251M	468110M	1670972M			Net Sales ($)	2697050M	2777228M
7993M	120169M	691555M	402830M	1583440M			Total Assets ($)	2332820M	2177754M

M = $ thousand   MM = $ million
See Pages 9 through 22 for Explanation of Ratios and Data

Comparative Historical Data

Current Data Sorted by Sales

						Type of Statement							
	20		19		29	Unqualified			1	2	7	19	
	5		8		16	Reviewed	1	2	4		7	2	
	4		5		2	Compiled			1	1	1		
	3		6		1	Tax Returns	1						
	24		24		21	Other		2	2	6	11		
	4/1/07-3/31/08 ALL		4/1/08-3/31/09 ALL		4/1/09-3/31/10 ALL		0-1MM	20 (4/1-9/30/09) 1-3MM	3-5MM	49 (10/1/09-3/31/10) 5-10MM	10-25MM	25MM & OVER	
	56		62		69	NUMBER OF STATEMENTS	2	5	9	21	32		
	%		%		%	ASSETS	%	%	%	%	%	%	
	11.6		10.9		14.0	Cash & Equivalents					11.3	16.6	
	25.5		24.8		22.1	Trade Receivables (net)					20.7	22.9	
	23.3		26.2		27.8	Inventory					29.9	27.8	
	6.6		5.2		6.1	All Other Current					8.1	5.1	
	67.0		67.1		70.1	Total Current					70.0	72.4	
	16.5		15.6		16.2	Fixed Assets (net)					16.9	14.3	
	10.9		10.3		9.6	Intangibles (net)					8.1	9.1	
	5.7		7.0		4.1	All Other Non-Current					5.0	4.2	
	100.0		100.0		100.0	Total					100.0	100.0	
						LIABILITIES							
	6.5		7.7		4.9	Notes Payable-Short Term					6.1	4.8	
	4.1		2.6		2.7	Cur. Mat.-L.T.D.					2.4	2.2	
	10.9		13.3		9.8	Trade Payables					8.8	12.0	
	.3		.3		.9	Income Taxes Payable					.5	1.4	
	14.7		13.5		12.8	All Other Current					17.0	9.9	
	36.6		37.3		31.2	Total Current					34.9	30.3	
	15.2		13.6		10.0	Long-Term Debt					9.5	7.2	
	.9		1.1		.8	Deferred Taxes					.6	1.2	
	7.4		4.5		4.8	All Other Non-Current					4.6	2.5	
	40.0		43.6		53.2	Net Worth					50.4	58.9	
	100.0		100.0		100.0	Total Liabilties & Net Worth					100.0	100.0	
						INCOME DATA							
	100.0		100.0		100.0	Net Sales					100.0	100.0	
	37.6		37.8		37.7	Gross Profit					37.8	33.0	
	28.2		31.2		30.9	Operating Expenses					28.1	27.4	
	9.4		6.6		6.8	Operating Profit					9.7	5.6	
	1.5		1.0		2.0	All Other Expenses (net)					1.4	2.5	
	7.9		5.6		4.8	Profit Before Taxes					8.3	3.1	
						RATIOS							
	3.5		3.8		4.4						4.0	4.3	
	2.0		2.2		2.6	Current					2.1	2.6	
	1.3		1.3		1.5						1.3	1.7	
	1.9		2.0		2.5						2.1	2.4	
	1.0		.9		1.1	Quick					.8	1.4	
	.6		.6		.6						.5	.8	
38	9.6	31	11.7	34	10.6					27	13.4	39 9.5	
48	7.7	50	7.4	48	7.6	Sales/Receivables				43	8.5	56 6.5	
67	5.4	65	5.6	65	5.6					55	6.6	81 4.5	
28	13.2	38	9.5	65	5.7					52	7.0	84 4.3	
85	4.3	103	3.5	123	3.0	Cost of Sales/Inventory				111	3.3	123 3.0	
146	2.5	149	2.4	163	2.2					191	1.9	148 2.5	
19	18.9	19	19.3	18	20.3					18	20.8	22 16.9	
30	12.2	31	11.6	28	12.9	Cost of Sales/Payables				26	14.1	39 9.3	
52	7.1	54	6.8	51	7.2					37	9.8	66 5.5	
	2.6		3.2		2.4						2.9	2.0	
	6.1		5.6		4.0	Sales/Working Capital					3.4	3.4	
	17.6		13.5		9.4						14.2	5.9	
	41.4		23.5		66.8						84.3	58.6	
(50)	11.3	(56)	4.4	(61)	6.5	EBIT/Interest			(19)	21.1	(29) 7.8	
	1.9		1.2		.8						3.3	-2.4	
	28.1		18.4		10.1	Net Profit + Depr., Dep.,							
(19)	2.2	(20)	2.8	(19)	2.4	Amort./Cur. Mat. L/T/D							
	.4		1.0		1.3								
	.1		.2		.1						.1	.1	
	.3		.4		.3	Fixed/Worth					.4	.3	
	1.5		1.5		.7						.8	.5	
	.5		.5		.4						.4	.3	
	1.6		1.4		1.0	Debt/Worth					1.5	.7	
	7.8		5.1		2.5						2.8	1.7	
	80.4		57.1		36.6	% Profit Before Taxes/Tangible				63.8	32.3		
(47)	31.6	(51)	20.4	(61)	13.6	Net Worth			(19)	22.0	(30) 12.5	
	7.6		4.7		2.1						7.0	-4.2	
	25.3		19.4		18.2	% Profit Before Taxes/Total				23.9	13.2		
	11.0		6.4		7.0	Assets					10.1	6.9	
	3.8		1.6		-.6						4.4	-1.9	
	24.1		29.5		23.2						31.9	21.0	
	11.6		12.6		11.9	Sales/Net Fixed Assets					13.3	11.1	
	7.0		7.9		6.3						5.5	5.8	
	2.3		2.7		2.0						2.3	1.6	
	1.5		1.6		1.4	Sales/Total Assets					1.5	1.3	
	1.0		1.2		1.1						1.0	1.0	
	1.2		.8		1.2						1.0	1.3	
(45)	1.9	(52)	1.7	(58)	2.1	% Depr., Dep., Amort./Sales			(19)	1.5	(24) 2.2	
	2.9		2.6		3.0						2.9	3.0	
			2.8		2.4								
		(18)	5.7	(12)	5.1	% Officers', Directors' Owners' Comp/Sales							
			10.5		7.8								
	3072344M		2549041M		3383935M	Net Sales ($)		4612M	20528M	67842M	350014M	2940939M	
	2246521M		2096510M		2805987M	Total Assets ($)		2269M	14502M	43992M	250052M	2495172M	

M = $ thousand   MM = $ million
See Pages 9 through 22 for Explanation of Ratios and Data

Current Data Sorted by Assets   Comparative Historical Data

0-500M	500M-2MM	2-10MM	10-50MM	50-100MM	100-250MM	Type of Statement	4/1/05-3/31/06 ALL	4/1/06-3/31/07 ALL
			4		2	Unqualified	11	11
	2	5	2			Reviewed	13	9
1	1	3				Compiled	4	4
	2	1				Tax Returns	1	6
	2	7	1	1		Other	7	9
						5 (4/1-9/30/09) 29 (10/1/09-3/31/10)		
1	7	16	7	1	2	**NUMBER OF STATEMENTS**	36	39
%	%	%	%	%	%		%	%
						ASSETS		
		6.7				Cash & Equivalents	9.4	14.7
		42.0				Trade Receivables (net)	35.5	35.2
		23.5				Inventory	23.2	24.6
		3.6				All Other Current	4.9	2.8
		75.9				Total Current	73.0	77.2
		14.7				Fixed Assets (net)	16.9	15.0
		4.0				Intangibles (net)	4.5	3.6
		5.4				All Other Non-Current	5.7	4.2
		100.0				Total	100.0	100.0
						LIABILITIES		
		12.4				Notes Payable-Short Term	13.8	10.6
		1.8				Cur. Mat.-L.T.D.	4.1	2.8
		16.4				Trade Payables	14.0	16.0
		.0				Income Taxes Payable	.1	.2
		11.6				All Other Current	13.7	13.7
		42.3				Total Current	45.7	43.2
		9.6				Long-Term Debt	13.3	11.2
		.3				Deferred Taxes	.8	.4
		3.2				All Other Non-Current	4.7	5.0
		44.7				Net Worth	35.5	40.1
		100.0				Total Liabilties & Net Worth	100.0	100.0
						INCOME DATA		
		100.0				Net Sales	100.0	100.0
		38.4				Gross Profit	31.9	36.1
		30.8				Operating Expenses	27.4	29.5
		7.6				Operating Profit	4.6	6.6
		.2				All Other Expenses (net)	.3	.7
		7.4				Profit Before Taxes	4.2	5.8
						RATIOS		
		2.9					2.2	3.4
		1.9				Current	1.4	1.7
		1.3					1.2	1.3
		1.7					1.3	1.8
		1.2				Quick	.9	1.0
		.7					.6	.8
	41	9.0					43 8.6	49 7.4
	54	6.7				Sales/Receivables	55 6.6	56 6.6
	77	4.8					69 5.3	65 5.6
	8	45.7					27 13.4	34 10.8
	54	6.8				Cost of Sales/Inventory	55 6.6	64 5.7
	102	3.6					112 3.3	114 3.2
	21	17.1					21 17.1	19 19.6
	35	10.4				Cost of Sales/Payables	33 11.1	29 12.4
	50	7.3					52 7.1	54 6.8
		5.2					4.7	3.9
		7.4				Sales/Working Capital	8.6	7.5
		15.1					18.1	16.9
		17.4					8.4	20.0
		(15) 11.3				EBIT/Interest	(32) 2.9	(34) 8.0
		3.4					1.7	1.5
						Net Profit + Depr., Dep.,	2.9	5.9
						Amort./Cur. Mat. L/T/D	(11) 1.9	(12) 2.9
							1.0	1.4
		.1					.2	.2
		.3				Fixed/Worth	.5	.3
		.8					1.4	.7
		.8					.9	.6
		1.1				Debt/Worth	2.8	1.7
		2.9					5.1	3.7
		63.7				% Profit Before Taxes/Tangible	64.7	79.8
		(15) 31.7				Net Worth	(33) 21.2	(37) 31.4
		12.3					3.4	8.3
		33.0				% Profit Before Taxes/Total	15.8	20.2
		14.2				Assets	6.5	11.7
		2.9					1.6	1.6
		48.2					44.7	59.9
		23.7				Sales/Net Fixed Assets	19.4	21.6
		12.5					6.9	7.9
		3.7					2.4	3.5
		2.5				Sales/Total Assets	1.9	2.1
		2.3					1.3	1.6
		.4					.6	.5
		(15) 1.1				% Depr., Dep., Amort./Sales	(34) 1.4	(34) 1.2
		1.7					2.5	3.0
							2.1	2.2
						% Officers', Directors'	(13) 3.1	(13) 4.9
						Owners' Comp/Sales	8.3	7.3
1427M	32546M	170786M	323635M	158131M	635673M	Net Sales ($)	1046496M	1386681M
296M	9117M	70769M	139013M	93841M	279007M	Total Assets ($)	734548M	844175M

M = $ thousand   MM = $ million
See Pages 9 through 22 for Explanation of Ratios and Data

Comparative Historical Data | Current Data Sorted by Sales

4/1/07-3/31/08 ALL	4/1/08-3/31/09 ALL	4/1/09-3/31/10 ALL	Type of Statement	0-1MM	1-3MM	3-5MM	5-10MM	10-25MM	25MM & OVER
					5 (4/1-9/30/09)		29 (10/1/09-3/31/10)		
10	8	6	Unqualified					1	5
12	11	9	Reviewed		1		4	4	
5	5	5	Compiled		2	1	2		
5	4	3	Tax Returns			2	1		
20	16	11	Other				4	5	2
52	44	34	**NUMBER OF STATEMENTS**		3	3	11	10	7
%	%	%	**ASSETS**	%	%	%	%	%	%
13.9	14.4	13.7	Cash & Equivalents				8.3	11.1	
35.6	38.3	38.3	Trade Receivables (net)				41.3	39.4	
21.0	19.4	22.0	Inventory				25.0	21.2	
4.7	3.5	4.6	All Other Current				2.8	6.7	
75.2	75.6	78.6	Total Current				77.4	78.3	
13.1	14.5	12.4	Fixed Assets (net)				14.8	14.0	
3.4	4.1	4.1	Intangibles (net)				3.8	2.2	
8.4	5.8	5.0	All Other Non-Current				4.0	5.4	
100.0	100.0	100.0	Total				100.0	100.0	
			LIABILITIES						
11.7	9.0	9.6	Notes Payable-Short Term				14.2	10.2	
3.1	3.9	3.1	Cur. Mat.-L.T.D.				1.0	3.5	
16.4	14.0	13.2	Trade Payables				18.3	13.4	
.3	.2	.0	Income Taxes Payable				.0	.0	
19.6	16.0	16.6	All Other Current				11.3	11.9	
51.0	43.1	42.6	Total Current				44.8	39.1	
10.0	8.0	6.5	Long-Term Debt				7.5	11.1	
.2	.3	.7	Deferred Taxes				.4	.1	
7.2	4.6	9.0	All Other Non-Current				3.8	2.0	
31.5	44.0	41.1	Net Worth				43.4	47.7	
100.0	100.0	100.0	Total Liabilities & Net Worth				100.0	100.0	
			INCOME DATA						
100.0	100.0	100.0	Net Sales				100.0	100.0	
36.7	36.0	37.5	Gross Profit				39.0	38.5	
30.6	28.5	29.5	Operating Expenses				31.6	30.4	
6.1	7.6	7.9	Operating Profit				7.4	8.1	
.6	.5	.4	All Other Expenses (net)				.0	.6	
5.5	7.1	7.5	Profit Before Taxes				7.4	7.5	
			RATIOS						
3.6	3.4	3.6	Current				3.0	5.0	
1.8	1.8	2.0					1.9	2.1	
1.3	1.2	1.2					1.3	1.2	
2.0	2.1	2.2	Quick				1.5	3.7	
1.1	1.4	1.3					1.3	1.1	
.8	.8	.8					.8	.7	
37 9.9	41 8.8	36 10.2	Sales/Receivables				41 9.0	32 11.4	
52 7.0	51 7.1	48 7.6					55 6.7	44 8.3	
71 5.1	68 5.4	62 5.9					82 4.5	70 5.2	
18 20.2	11 31.9	7 51.0	Cost of Sales/Inventory				40 9.1	0 UND	
54 6.8	48 7.6	50 7.3					52 7.0	17 21.3	
94 3.9	86 4.3	96 3.8					104 3.5	103 3.5	
18 20.4	13 27.0	11 32.7	Cost of Sales/Payables				22 16.6	11 33.6	
31 11.7	31 11.8	24 15.0					39 9.3	27 13.5	
52 7.1	49 7.5	39 9.3					53 6.8	37 9.9	
4.2	4.1	4.4	Sales/Working Capital				4.7	4.6	
6.6	7.3	6.7					7.6	7.8	
15.7	21.9	21.2					15.4	21.5	
39.0	44.3	210.9	EBIT/Interest				27.2		
(44) 8.1	(39) 16.8	(29) 12.0					(10) 9.5		
.8	3.5	1.9					2.1		
			Net Profit + Depr., Dep., Amort./Cur. Mat. L/T/D						
.1	.1	.1	Fixed/Worth				.2	.1	
.3	.2	.3					.3	.3	
1.0	.9	.5					.9	.8	
.6	.5	.6	Debt/Worth				.8	.2	
1.6	1.3	1.0					1.0	1.4	
7.0	4.8	3.1					3.1	4.3	
67.7	69.8	57.3	% Profit Before Taxes/Tangible Net Worth				67.0		
(45) 31.3	(39) 37.5	(32) 30.4					29.0		
6.0	14.0	9.1					12.3		
24.2	27.2	32.7	% Profit Before Taxes/Total Assets				34.7	30.8	
11.3	16.4	15.0					9.8	16.7	
1.1	5.1	1.5					1.5	.3	
35.8	43.6	63.6	Sales/Net Fixed Assets				48.3	45.6	
22.5	25.7	25.0					22.3	19.6	
11.8	11.4	12.0					12.1	9.6	
3.0	3.3	3.5	Sales/Total Assets				3.5	3.8	
2.3	2.3	2.6					2.5	2.5	
1.8	1.7	1.7					1.7	1.6	
.5	.4	.4	% Depr., Dep., Amort./Sales				.3		
(44) 1.3	(36) 1.1	(27) 1.1					(10) .9		
2.2	2.1	1.8					1.7		
2.7	3.0	2.8	% Officers', Directors' Owners' Comp/Sales						
(13) 4.1	(12) 4.1	(11) 4.8							
7.4	7.3	9.9							
1988884M	1202524M	1322198M	Net Sales ($)		5228M	12306M	88643M	154181M	1061840M
1102314M	664087M	592043M	Total Assets ($)		2112M	3611M	42137M	71890M	472293M

M = $ thousand   MM = $ million
See Pages 9 through 22 for Explanation of Ratios and Data

Current Data Sorted by Assets   **Comparative Historical Data**

0-500M	500M-2MM	2-10MM	10-50MM	50-100MM	100-250MM	Type of Statement	4/1/05-3/31/06 ALL	4/1/06-3/31/07 ALL
	1	7	7	8	6	Unqualified	22	26
	2	24	6			Reviewed	33	41
	4	5				Compiled	17	20
	2					Tax Returns	6	8
1	10	16	13	5	6	Other	52	56
	24 (4/1-9/30/09)		99 (10/1/09-3/31/10)					
1	19	52	26	13	12	NUMBER OF STATEMENTS	130	151
%	%	%	%	%	%	**ASSETS**	%	%
	13.0	12.2	18.4	14.0	15.3	Cash & Equivalents	9.5	9.1
	34.2	24.2	25.6	15.7	15.8	Trade Receivables (net)	31.0	30.1
	30.2	28.4	21.2	16.5	17.3	Inventory	26.9	28.0
	1.3	7.9	5.2	8.1	3.2	All Other Current	3.4	4.3
	78.8	72.8	70.5	54.3	51.7	Total Current	70.9	71.5
	16.9	15.2	15.0	12.7	17.9	Fixed Assets (net)	17.3	16.0
	1.3	6.7	5.2	25.0	21.9	Intangibles (net)	4.5	6.0
	3.1	5.3	9.3	8.0	8.5	All Other Non-Current	7.3	6.6
	100.0	100.0	100.0	100.0	100.0	Total	100.0	100.0
						LIABILITIES		
	19.5	11.3	4.4	1.2	.4	Notes Payable-Short Term	11.8	10.5
	2.4	2.3	3.7	1.4	2.8	Cur. Mat.-L.T.D.	2.6	2.8
	11.0	10.4	10.6	5.0	9.3	Trade Payables	13.7	12.5
	.0	.2	3.4	.1	.6	Income Taxes Payable	.8	.6
	10.3	11.7	15.8	7.7	9.4	All Other Current	14.0	14.6
	43.2	35.9	37.8	15.4	22.5	Total Current	42.9	41.0
	9.7	9.7	7.9	17.9	12.6	Long-Term Debt	10.1	11.6
	.1	.2	.4	.7	1.9	Deferred Taxes	.4	.5
	10.2	9.0	9.1	9.6	5.6	All Other Non-Current	7.5	6.3
	36.8	45.2	44.8	56.4	57.4	Net Worth	39.1	40.7
	100.0	100.0	100.0	100.0	100.0	Total Liabilities & Net Worth	100.0	100.0
						INCOME DATA		
	100.0	100.0	100.0	100.0	100.0	Net Sales	100.0	100.0
	44.9	41.8	40.2	41.9	35.5	Gross Profit	41.8	41.3
	39.7	35.6	31.7	35.4	31.8	Operating Expenses	34.9	34.3
	5.2	6.2	8.5	6.5	3.7	Operating Profit	6.8	7.0
	.5	.9	2.0	4.1	.3	All Other Expenses (net)	.9	1.4
	4.7	5.4	6.5	2.4	3.4	Profit Before Taxes	5.9	5.6
						RATIOS		
	3.8	3.4	3.5	5.3	3.3	Current	2.9	3.0
	2.0	2.1	2.2	3.4	2.8		1.8	2.0
	1.4	1.4	1.5	2.2	1.2		1.3	1.4
	2.1	1.8	2.0	2.5	2.2	Quick	1.8	1.7
	.9	1.1	1.5	1.5	1.9		1.1 (150)	1.1
	.7	.6	.9	1.2	.7		.7	.7
33 11.1	34 10.7	42 8.8	50 7.3	46 7.8		Sales/Receivables	42 8.7	43 8.5
50 7.4	48 7.6	49 7.4	57 6.4	54 6.7			55 6.6	51 7.2
63 5.8	65 5.6	64 5.7	73 5.0	76 4.8			67 5.5	63 5.8
54 6.7	54 6.8	44 8.4	80 4.6	59 6.2		Cost of Sales/Inventory	54 6.7	57 6.4
81 4.5	92 4.0	81 4.5	89 4.1	85 4.3			88 4.2	91 4.0
145 2.5	137 2.7	108 3.4	130 2.8	125 2.9			140 2.6	134 2.7
12 29.4	18 20.0	20 18.5	20 18.5	27 13.7		Cost of Sales/Payables	21 17.4	22 16.3
29 12.5	29 12.7	28 13.1	35 10.5	45 8.1			32 11.2	35 10.4
39 9.3	42 8.6	59 6.2	45 8.1	61 6.0			57 6.4	51 7.1
	3.3	3.2	3.0	2.0	2.5	Sales/Working Capital	3.6	3.8
	5.9	5.3	4.1	3.5	3.2		6.7	6.1
	14.7	10.7	10.4	5.3	15.0		14.4	10.5
	19.8	25.0	30.9	12.7	34.6	EBIT/Interest	17.2	18.0
	(18) 5.8	(46) 3.3	(21) 5.1	(11) 1.5	(11) 1.4		(106) 3.9	(135) 5.4
	1.9	1.7	-1.1	.0	-1.0		1.9	1.5
		5.6	32.2			Net Profit + Depr., Dep., Amort./Cur. Mat. L/T/D	12.0	18.0
	(16)	1.9	(10) 9.2				(45) 4.1	(45) 6.0
		1.1	1.7				1.7	1.9
	.1	.1	.1	.2	.2	Fixed/Worth	.1	.2
	.3	.3	.3	.4	.4		.4	.4
	1.4	2.0	.9	-.5	1.5		1.0	1.3
	.3	.4	.4	.2	.4	Debt/Worth	.6	.6
	1.5	1.3	.9	.9	1.2		1.3	1.5
	7.4	5.3	2.8	-7.5	2.1		5.6	5.0
	71.4	33.9	34.4		36.9	% Profit Before Taxes/Tangible Net Worth	49.6	48.8
	(16) 15.0	(44) 16.8	(23) 21.0	(10)			(116) 22.1	(133) 24.6
	5.5	6.5	5.3		-10.5		10.9	8.8
	13.3	15.5	17.5	12.8	15.8	% Profit Before Taxes/Total Assets	16.7	18.3
	7.5	5.6	9.0	2.9	1.2		7.9	9.0
	2.6	1.4	-3.0	-2.7	-4.2		2.8	2.0
	46.5	46.2	27.4	13.2	12.4	Sales/Net Fixed Assets	39.4	38.9
	18.5	16.6	11.6	6.9	8.2		13.2	14.9
	6.0	7.9	6.6	6.2	4.7		6.8	7.8
	3.0	2.2	2.0	1.4	1.2	Sales/Total Assets	2.6	2.7
	2.2	1.7	1.7	.8	1.0		1.8	1.8
	1.8	1.3	1.1	.6	.7		1.4	1.4
	.8	.9	1.3		1.4	% Depr., Dep., Amort./Sales	1.0	.8
	(16) 1.4	(47) 1.3	(20) 1.7	(10) 2.9			(105) 1.7	(129) 1.7
	2.4	2.3	2.4	4.0			2.8	3.0
		2.5				% Officers', Directors' Owners' Comp/Sales	3.0	2.4
		(11) 3.7					(39) 5.7	(36) 5.6
		7.7					12.6	9.6
480M	47056M	462354M	843242M	936738M	1848795M	Net Sales ($)	2774067M	4502077M
449M	19533M	253004M	529676M	1000655M	1881005M	Total Assets ($)	1881769M	3352550M

M = $ thousand   MM = $ million
See Pages 9 through 22 for Explanation of Ratios and Data

Comparative Historical Data

Current Data Sorted by Sales

			Type of Statement						
29	30	29	Unqualified			1	2	7	19
36	27	32	Reviewed	1	2	5	12	9	3
12	8	9	Compiled		3	1	5		
11	5	3	Tax Returns	1	2				
39	49	50	Other		8	6	7	12	17
4/1/07-3/31/08	4/1/08-3/31/09	4/1/09-3/31/10			24 (4/1-9/30/09)		99 (10/1/09-3/31/10)		
ALL	ALL	ALL		0-1MM	1-3MM	3-5MM	5-10MM	10-25MM	25MM & OVER
127	119	123	NUMBER OF STATEMENTS	2	15	13	26	28	39
%	%	%	ASSETS	%	%	%	%	%	%
12.4	11.9	14.0	Cash & Equivalents		12.9	5.8	13.8	20.5	13.1
29.6	26.9	24.2	Trade Receivables (net)		32.1	23.6	25.8	22.4	22.6
24.1	24.9	25.2	Inventory		23.1	29.9	29.3	27.3	18.6
5.0	5.0	5.8	All Other Current		8.9	8.0	3.0	5.2	6.4
71.2	68.6	69.2	Total Current		77.0	67.3	71.9	75.5	60.7
15.6	14.7	15.4	Fixed Assets (net)		17.7	13.3	15.7	16.0	14.5
6.7	8.6	9.0	Intangibles (net)		3.3	11.0	5.8	4.1	16.4
6.5	8.1	6.4	All Other Non-Current		2.1	8.5	6.6	4.5	8.4
100.0	100.0	100.0	Total		100.0	100.0	100.0	100.0	100.0
			LIABILITIES						
12.2	9.0	8.9	Notes Payable-Short Term		18.4	18.0	8.7	8.4	3.1
3.4	2.5	2.6	Cur. Mat.-L.T.D.		3.0	2.5	2.7	2.6	2.3
13.4	11.0	9.9	Trade Payables		7.8	11.9	8.9	11.6	9.5
.3	1.0	.9	Income Taxes Payable		.0	.0	.1	3.1	.4
15.0	13.7	11.6	All Other Current		9.3	7.9	9.6	14.6	13.1
44.2	37.2	33.9	Total Current		38.6	40.4	30.1	40.4	28.3
14.0	11.4	10.8	Long-Term Debt		11.6	5.4	12.2	9.3	11.7
.4	.8	.5	Deferred Taxes		.1	.0	.4	.1	1.0
5.6	7.7	9.6	All Other Non-Current		9.7	12.5	12.1	2.5	10.2
35.8	42.9	45.2	Net Worth		40.0	41.8	45.2	47.8	48.8
100.0	100.0	100.0	Total Liabilities & Net Worth		100.0	100.0	100.0	100.0	100.0
			INCOME DATA						
100.0	100.0	100.0	Net Sales		100.0	100.0	100.0	100.0	100.0
42.3	42.2	41.2	Gross Profit		47.7	47.8	42.5	40.6	36.6
34.0	34.6	35.1	Operating Expenses		41.1	41.7	33.7	35.2	31.2
8.3	7.6	6.2	Operating Profit		6.6	6.1	8.7	5.4	5.4
1.5	1.6	1.4	All Other Expenses (net)		-.1	1.7	1.0	1.0	2.3
6.7	6.0	4.8	Profit Before Taxes		6.7	4.5	7.7	4.4	3.1
			RATIOS						
3.3	3.5	3.5			8.6	2.3	4.3	3.5	3.5
2.0	2.0	2.3	Current		2.1	1.6	2.6	2.2	2.7
1.3	1.3	1.4			1.5	1.2	1.5	1.1	1.6
1.8	1.8	2.1			4.7	1.2	2.1	2.0	2.2
1.1	1.1	1.3	Quick		1.2	.8	1.3	1.4	1.5
.7	.7	.7			.6	.5	.9	.6	.9

							Sales/Receivables						
39	9.5	38	9.6	40	9.1		25	14.9	33	11.1	40	9.0	34 10.9	48 7.6
48	7.6	48	7.6	51	7.2		60	6.1	50	7.4	48	7.6	42 8.7	56 6.5
65	5.6	65	5.6	64	5.7		65	5.6	79	4.6	67	5.4	58 6.3	74 5.0

							Cost of Sales/Inventory						
43	8.6	52	7.0	56	6.5		40	9.1	44	8.3	61	6.0	72 5.1	56 6.5
79	4.6	83	4.4	88	4.1		81	4.5	71	5.2	85	4.3	96 3.8	82 4.4
112	3.3	138	2.7	126	2.9		140	2.6	161	2.3	177	2.1	126 2.9	106 3.5

							Cost of Sales/Payables						
23	16.0	20	18.6	19	19.0		12	29.4	18	20.5	24	15.5	16 22.4	23 16.1
35	10.3	32	11.4	30	12.0		30	12.2	32	11.6	31	11.7	23 15.6	35 10.5
57	6.4	48	7.6	46	8.0		40	9.1	94	3.9	36	10.3	44 8.2	54 6.8

			Sales/Working Capital						
3.6	3.2	2.9			3.3	3.8	3.0	2.9	2.6
6.2	5.4	4.4			4.2	7.6	4.9	5.0	3.7
15.3	13.4	9.9			14.7	74.5	9.5	25.1	7.7

					EBIT/Interest						
	14.3		27.1		26.4		20.9	7.3	40.6	34.9	27.9
(111)	3.8	(106)	5.4	(108)	3.1	(14)	8.7	(11) 2.0	(23) 5.1	(24) 3.9	(34) 1.5
	1.8		1.6		.9		1.9	1.4	2.2		-1.0

					Net Profit + Depr., Dep., Amort./Cur. Mat. L/T/D						
	13.1		15.3		11.1					19.1	9.8
(36)	4.7	(41)	3.3	(41)	3.9				(10) 5.8	(18) 3.5	
	1.9		1.7		1.0					3.3	.1

			Fixed/Worth						
.2	.1	.1			.1	.1	.1	.1	.1
.5	.4	.3			.4	.1	.4	.3	.3
2.4	1.9	1.6			1.4	NM	3.1	1.3	14.8

			Debt/Worth						
.5	.5	.4			.3	.7	.3	.4	.4
1.8	1.5	1.2			1.2	2.0	.9	1.0	1.1
13.0	8.9	5.9			7.4	NM	10.3	2.7	111.2

					% Profit Before Taxes/Tangible Net Worth						
	51.3		50.0		35.2		125.4	21.3	39.0	34.8	36.8
(105)	29.7	(98)	22.6	(101)	17.8	(13)	14.9	(10) 7.3	(22) 17.7	(25) 20.3	(30) 19.1
	9.9		7.3		5.2		7.2	-1.1	8.8	6.7	-6.7

			% Profit Before Taxes/Total Assets						
19.5	19.7	14.5			13.3	7.5	19.9	16.0	15.1
8.3	7.7	5.4			8.6	2.5	8.0	7.3	2.8
2.8	1.4	.7			2.6	-1.2	2.1	.8	-4.5

			Sales/Net Fixed Assets						
49.2	28.2	30.6			34.9	52.8	51.7	29.7	15.7
15.5	14.1	13.0			15.1	27.8	16.6	14.0	8.8
7.5	8.1	6.8			6.0	6.6	7.3	7.4	6.6

			Sales/Total Assets						
2.7	2.3	2.1			2.9	2.2	2.2	2.4	1.8
1.9	1.7	1.6			1.8	1.2	1.7	1.9	1.2
1.4	1.4	1.1			1.7	1.0	1.4	1.3	.7

					% Depr., Dep., Amort./Sales						
	.8		1.2		1.1		1.1	.9	.4	1.2	1.4
(105)	1.5	(92)	1.7	(103)	1.6	(13)	1.5	(12) 1.2	(23) 1.1	(23) 1.6	(30) 2.6
	2.3		2.5		2.8		2.4	2.3	2.2	2.3	3.7

					% Officers', Directors' Owners' Comp/Sales						
	2.4		1.3		2.5						
(31)	5.9	(23)	4.1	(22)	6.7						
	8.6		6.1		9.6						

			Net Sales ($)						
4004238M	4739494M	4138665M	Net Sales ($)	1264M	30716M	51885M	183919M	467565M	3403316M
2924124M	3553653M	3684322M	Total Assets ($)	1056M	17954M	46321M	105853M	301882M	3211256M

M = $ thousand   MM = $ million
See Pages 9 through 22 for Explanation of Ratios and Data

Current Data Sorted by Assets

Comparative Historical Data

0-500M	500M-2MM	2-10MM	10-50MM	50-100MM	100-250MM	Type of Statement		4/1/05-3/31/06		4/1/06-3/31/07
		5	1			Unqualified		7		10
	3	5	1		1	Reviewed		9		8
	1	1				Compiled		5		6
	1	3				Tax Returns		1		4
1	1	4	6		1	Other		17		18
	4 (4/1-9/30/09)		31 (10/1/09-3/31/10)					ALL		ALL
1	6	18	8	1	1	NUMBER OF STATEMENTS		39		46
%	%	%	%	%	%	ASSETS		%		%
		8.9				Cash & Equivalents		10.3		9.4
		20.7				Trade Receivables (net)		27.2		29.6
		32.7				Inventory		31.9		30.0
		8.1				All Other Current		3.0		6.4
		70.5				Total Current		72.4		75.4
		18.5				Fixed Assets (net)		14.7		18.1
		3.2				Intangibles (net)		6.0		2.5
		7.8				All Other Non-Current		6.9		4.0
		100.0				Total		100.0		100.0
						LIABILITIES				
		9.4				Notes Payable-Short Term		8.4		10.4
		2.8				Cur. Mat.-L.T.D.		1.9		3.2
		12.9				Trade Payables		12.2		15.3
		.2				Income Taxes Payable		1.7		.6
		8.9				All Other Current		12.8		8.9
		34.2				Total Current		36.9		38.5
		6.6				Long-Term Debt		12.5		13.1
		.2				Deferred Taxes		.4		.3
		6.3				All Other Non-Current		8.3		6.4
		52.7				Net Worth		41.8		41.6
		100.0				Total Liabilities & Net Worth		100.0		100.0
						INCOME DATA				
		100.0				Net Sales		100.0		100.0
		39.3				Gross Profit		38.4		37.9
		36.9				Operating Expenses		31.5		28.9
		2.4				Operating Profit		6.8		9.0
		.1				All Other Expenses (net)		.8		.8
		2.3				Profit Before Taxes		6.0		8.2
						RATIOS				
		3.8						3.4		3.3
		2.0				Current		2.2		1.9
		1.5						1.5		1.4
		1.4						1.8		1.6
		1.0				Quick		1.1		.9
		.5						.6		.6
	35	10.4					38	9.5	39	9.3
	42	8.6				Sales/Receivables	45	8.0	49	7.4
	58	6.3					60	6.0	65	5.6
	37	9.8					54	6.8	43	8.4
	114	3.2				Cost of Sales/Inventory	92	4.0	93	3.9
	162	2.2					152	2.4	130	2.8
	24	15.4					17	21.6	19	18.9
	38	9.6				Cost of Sales/Payables	33	11.1	37	9.9
	68	5.4					51	7.2	59	6.2
		2.7						4.0		3.9
		4.4				Sales/Working Capital		5.6		6.1
		8.5						8.6		9.9
		11.3						23.3		19.9
	(17)	3.4				EBIT/Interest	(33)	9.7	(42)	6.6
		.5						2.3		1.9
						Net Profit + Depr., Dep.,		27.0		10.5
						Amort./Cur. Mat. L/T/D	(10)	2.6	(13)	5.6
								1.4		2.9
		.1						.1		.1
		.2				Fixed/Worth		.3		.3
		.8						.7		.9
		.4						.5		.5
		.9				Debt/Worth		1.0		1.4
		1.9						2.6		2.6
		26.1				% Profit Before Taxes/Tangible		44.9		63.1
	(17)	10.1				Net Worth	(34)	19.7	(41)	25.2
		-1.7						7.2		6.7
		11.2				% Profit Before Taxes/Total		15.6		27.4
		5.4				Assets		9.4		9.0
		-.1						2.4		2.5
		23.1						32.2		25.9
		14.8				Sales/Net Fixed Assets		14.2		13.9
		6.4						7.4		7.9
		2.5						2.7		2.5
		1.6				Sales/Total Assets		2.1		2.1
		1.3						1.4		1.6
		.9						.7		1.0
	(17)	1.7				% Depr., Dep., Amort./Sales	(30)	1.4	(36)	1.9
		3.1						2.2		2.9
						% Officers', Directors'		2.3		
						Owners' Comp/Sales	(10)	5.8		
								20.0		
1476M	14327M	155422M	259818M	42925M	250337M	Net Sales ($)		1124998M		2153188M
436M	8667M	89078M	163615M	50943M	191016M	Total Assets ($)		761772M		1052739M

M = $ thousand   MM = $ million
See Pages 9 through 22 for Explanation of Ratios and Data

Comparative Historical Data | **Current Data Sorted by Sales**

4/1/07-3/31/08 ALL	4/1/08-3/31/09 ALL	4/1/09-3/31/10 ALL	Type of Statement	0-1MM	1-3MM	3-5MM	5-10MM	10-25MM	25MM & OVER
7	6	6	Unqualified				4	1	1
9	11	10	Reviewed		2	2	3	1	2
3	5	2	Compiled		1		1		
5	3	4	Tax Returns		1	1	2		
17	14	13	Other		2	2		4	5
					4 (4/1-9/30/09)		31 (10/1/09-3/31/10)		
41	39	35	**NUMBER OF STATEMENTS**		6	5	10	6	8
%	%	%	**ASSETS**	%	%	%	%	%	%
11.8	12.8	9.0	Cash & Equivalents	DATA NOT AVAILABLE			4.6		
26.8	24.6	20.7	Trade Receivables (net)				21.7		
29.7	33.7	34.6	Inventory				29.1		
3.1	4.3	6.7	All Other Current				4.5		
71.5	75.4	70.9	Total Current				59.9		
15.9	16.4	16.9	Fixed Assets (net)				23.6		
6.8	4.1	4.1	Intangibles (net)				5.4		
5.9	4.1	8.1	All Other Non-Current				11.1		
100.0	100.0	100.0	Total				100.0		
			LIABILITIES						
7.3	9.6	10.3	Notes Payable-Short Term				12.3		
3.0	3.3	2.4	Cur. Mat.-L.T.D.				4.2		
13.2	14.0	11.1	Trade Payables				12.5		
.2	.2	.1	Income Taxes Payable				.2		
10.6	14.6	12.6	All Other Current				10.0		
34.3	41.8	36.5	Total Current				39.2		
12.5	16.1	6.2	Long-Term Debt				10.9		
.4	.5	.4	Deferred Taxes				.1		
3.7	6.8	9.5	All Other Non-Current				3.1		
49.1	34.8	47.4	Net Worth				46.6		
100.0	100.0	100.0	Total Liabilties & Net Worth				100.0		
			INCOME DATA						
100.0	100.0	100.0	Net Sales				100.0		
40.6	37.3	38.8	Gross Profit				37.6		
34.5	33.8	36.5	Operating Expenses				37.5		
6.0	3.5	2.3	Operating Profit				.1		
.0	.7	.4	All Other Expenses (net)				.1		
6.1	2.8	1.9	Profit Before Taxes				.0		
			RATIOS						
4.1	3.9	3.5					2.3		
2.2	2.0	1.9	Current				1.7		
1.4	1.4	1.5					1.1		
2.3	2.1	1.4					1.2		
1.1	1.0	1.0	Quick				.6		
.6	.5	.5					.4		
35 10.5	**30** 12.2	**37** 10.0					**33** 10.9		
48 7.7	**41** 9.0	**49** 7.5	Sales/Receivables				**50** 7.3		
59 6.2	**49** 7.5	**63** 5.8					**64** 5.7		
67 5.5	**86** 4.3	**75** 4.9					**6** 59.3		
109 3.4	**111** 3.3	**111** 3.3	Cost of Sales/Inventory				**109** 3.3		
141 2.6	**164** 2.2	**173** 2.1					**162** 2.2		
19 18.8	**20** 17.8	**21** 17.5					**21** 17.5		
34 10.9	**35** 10.5	**35** 10.4	Cost of Sales/Payables				**33** 11.0		
51 7.1	**48** 7.6	**51** 7.1					**55** 6.7		
3.5	2.6	2.5					4.1		
5.7	5.9	4.5	Sales/Working Capital				7.7		
9.9	11.3	8.2					NM		
30.1	8.4	8.9					8.3		
(36) 3.9	(31) 2.7	(26) 3.3	EBIT/Interest				3.7		
1.6	1.6	.3					1.7		
10.8	6.6								
(15) 3.9	(10) 1.4		Net Profit + Depr., Dep., Amort./Cur. Mat. L/T/D						
1.3	-253.1								
.2	.1	.1					.2		
.3	.2	.3	Fixed/Worth				.3		
.8	1.0	.6					1.0		
.3	.5	.5					.7		
.9	1.2	.8	Debt/Worth				1.2		
3.2	3.7	1.4					3.6		
53.0	41.4	25.0					25.7		
(35) 20.2	(35) 13.6	(32) 12.4	% Profit Before Taxes/Tangible Net Worth				13.8		
6.9	4.0	1.0					2.7		
22.6	13.6	11.9					8.4		
7.8	5.0	5.0	% Profit Before Taxes/Total Assets				4.7		
1.7	2.0	-1.3					1.5		
27.1	43.4	22.3					29.6		
14.9	14.8	14.0	Sales/Net Fixed Assets				12.5		
7.9	7.3	6.9					4.3		
2.4	2.7	2.3					2.7		
1.9	2.1	1.5	Sales/Total Assets				1.9		
1.5	1.5	1.2					1.2		
1.0	1.1	1.1							
(36) 1.8	(32) 1.7	(30) 1.8	% Depr., Dep., Amort./Sales						
2.8	2.8	2.9							
			% Officers', Directors' Owners' Comp/Sales						
1149490M	1602890M	724305M	Net Sales ($)		11752M	20676M	75645M	103700M	512532M
748056M	841765M	503755M	Total Assets ($)		7249M	13977M	45033M	66855M	370641M

M = $ thousand MM = $ million

See Pages 9 through 22 for Explanation of Ratios and Data

Current Data Sorted by Assets | Comparative Historical Data

						Type of Statement		
		3	5	4	3	Unqualified	15	19
	2	6	2			Reviewed	7	10
	3	3				Compiled	7	8
2	4					Tax Returns		3
	2	10	4		1	Other	21	17
	14 (4/1-9/30/09)		40 (10/1/09-3/31/10)				21 4/1/05- 3/31/06	17 4/1/06- 3/31/07
0-500M	500M-2MM	2-10MM	10-50MM	50-100MM	100-250MM		ALL	ALL
2	11	22	11	5	3	NUMBER OF STATEMENTS	50	57
%	%	%	%	%	%	ASSETS	%	%
	16.4	9.1	15.2			Cash & Equivalents	13.2	11.5
	28.8	27.6	23.1			Trade Receivables (net)	27.7	26.9
	32.1	31.3	23.5			Inventory	30.3	26.5
	.6	3.8	1.8			All Other Current	1.8	2.3
	77.8	71.8	63.6			Total Current	73.1	67.2
	11.6	14.7	20.7			Fixed Assets (net)	15.3	15.7
	3.6	3.8	7.1			Intangibles (net)	4.3	8.7
	7.0	9.7	8.6			All Other Non-Current	7.4	8.4
	100.0	100.0	100.0			Total	100.0	100.0
						LIABILITIES		
	10.0	9.3	4.3			Notes Payable-Short Term	10.9	7.9
	2.0	3.3	1.5			Cur. Mat.-L.T.D.	2.9	2.2
	16.2	11.3	9.2			Trade Payables	10.5	10.6
	.0	.0	.9			Income Taxes Payable	.5	.6
	10.3	15.8	9.6			All Other Current	9.5	9.6
	38.7	39.7	25.6			Total Current	34.3	30.8
	8.2	7.3	12.3			Long-Term Debt	8.4	10.2
	.3	.4	.8			Deferred Taxes	.3	.5
	4.0	7.2	5.2			All Other Non-Current	10.6	4.7
	48.9	45.4	56.1			Net Worth	46.4	53.8
	100.0	100.0	100.0			Total Liabilties & Net Worth	100.0	100.0
						INCOME DATA		
	100.0	100.0	100.0			Net Sales	100.0	100.0
	41.5	41.2	39.6			Gross Profit	43.8	45.5
	37.4	34.1	34.5			Operating Expenses	38.1	38.4
	4.1	7.1	5.0			Operating Profit	5.7	7.1
	-.2	.8	.8			All Other Expenses (net)	1.0	.6
	4.3	6.4	4.3			Profit Before Taxes	4.7	6.5
						RATIOS		
	2.8	2.9	11.9				3.8	4.2
	1.9	1.8	2.3			Current	2.3	2.1
	1.4	1.4	1.4				1.6	1.6
	2.1	1.4	5.4				2.3	2.7
	1.3	.8	1.7			Quick	1.2	1.1
	.8	.5	.8				.8	.7
20 17.8	30 12.2	50 7.3					43 8.6	43 8.5
38 9.5	44 8.2	60 6.1				Sales/Receivables	52 7.0	58 6.3
48 7.6	63 5.8	66 5.5					66 5.5	71 5.1
66 5.6	71 5.2	61 5.9					73 5.0	63 5.8
87 4.2	98 3.7	107 3.4				Cost of Sales/Inventory	103 3.5	95 3.8
160 2.3	119 3.1	144 2.5					147 2.5	137 2.7
23 15.7	16 22.3	12 30.5					17 21.0	21 17.5
33 11.0	26 14.3	31 11.7				Cost of Sales/Payables	36 10.2	31 11.8
43 8.5	47 7.8	59 6.2					49 7.5	51 7.1
	3.7	3.8	1.9				2.9	3.1
	5.4	5.5	4.9			Sales/Working Capital	5.5	5.2
	12.1	12.9	9.2				7.9	8.7
		33.5					36.1	46.1
		(20) 8.6				EBIT/Interest	(43) 3.7	(46) 4.9
		2.3					1.5	1.4
							9.0	20.6
						Net Profit + Depr., Dep., Amort./Cur. Mat. L/T/D	(15) 2.7	(16) 3.9
							.8	1.0
	.1	.1	.1				.1	.1
	.3	.4	.7			Fixed/Worth	.3	.3
	.4	.6	1.1				1.1	.9
	.5	.7	.1				.3	.3
	1.0	1.1	.4			Debt/Worth	.9	1.2
	3.0	2.2	2.9				3.3	2.3
	59.9	45.0	41.2				37.4	44.0
(10) 18.5	(20) 17.1	(10) 13.9				% Profit Before Taxes/Tangible Net Worth	(44) 16.0	(53) 21.3
	3.0	4.3	.4				5.1	4.3
	28.9	17.4	16.9				18.8	21.0
	5.4	8.5	8.3			% Profit Before Taxes/Total Assets	8.7	7.4
	1.2	2.3	-.8				1.1	1.9
	78.1	26.5	24.0				30.7	33.0
	24.3	16.1	10.0			Sales/Net Fixed Assets	16.8	13.1
	9.5	9.0	7.1				8.1	7.4
	2.9	2.8	1.9				2.5	2.3
	2.3	1.8	1.5			Sales/Total Assets	1.9	1.7
	1.5	1.5	1.0				1.3	1.0
		.9					.9	1.0
		(19) 1.7				% Depr., Dep., Amort./Sales	(46) 1.7	(49) 2.0
		2.3					3.0	2.9
							2.9	3.7
						% Officers', Directors' Owners' Comp/Sales	(11) 5.1	(13) 7.4
							11.2	11.0
2694M	31045M	220622M	345268M	353814M	437424M	Net Sales ($)	1112437M	1654460M
572M	14258M	113108M	224301M	361113M	452577M	Total Assets ($)	999828M	1382760M

M = $ thousand   MM = $ million
See Pages 9 through 22 for Explanation of Ratios and Data

Comparative Historical Data

Current Data Sorted by Sales

					Type of Statement						
	16		13		15	Unqualified				1	4	10
	12		15		10	Reviewed			1	7	2	
	6		7		6	Compiled		2	1	1	2	
	3		2		6	Tax Returns		4	1			
	17		20		17	Other	1	2	2	4	6	3
	4/1/07-3/31/08		4/1/08-3/31/09		4/1/09-3/31/10			14 (4/1-9/30/09)		40 (10/1/09-3/31/10)		
	ALL		ALL		ALL		0-1MM	1-3MM	3-5MM	5-10MM	10-25MM	25MM & OVER
	54		57		54	NUMBER OF STATEMENTS	1	8	5	13	14	13
	%		%		%	ASSETS	%	%	%	%	%	%
	14.9		16.0		14.4	Cash & Equivalents				6.4	8.8	21.3
	23.3		28.4		24.6	Trade Receivables (net)				21.2	28.0	20.2
	26.8		27.1		27.6	Inventory				35.0	29.2	20.0
	2.7		4.8		2.5	All Other Current				2.2	3.6	2.8
	67.7		76.3		69.2	Total Current				64.7	69.5	64.3
	15.9		12.7		15.5	Fixed Assets (net)				16.0	18.2	17.8
	9.4		4.9		6.2	Intangibles (net)				10.2	1.6	11.0
	7.0		6.1		9.1	All Other Non-Current				9.0	10.7	6.9
	100.0		100.0		100.0	Total				100.0	100.0	100.0
						LIABILITIES						
	5.9		7.4		7.7	Notes Payable-Short Term				6.8	10.9	1.5
	2.9		1.3		3.6	Cur. Mat.-L.T.D.				4.7	1.3	1.7
	10.0		11.7		10.7	Trade Payables				9.7	13.3	7.6
	.3		.3		.2	Income Taxes Payable				.1	.2	.7
	11.0		13.0		11.9	All Other Current				14.4	14.4	10.2
	30.0		33.7		34.3	Total Current				35.8	40.0	21.8
	10.0		6.2		11.4	Long-Term Debt				12.5	7.8	13.5
	.1		.3		.4	Deferred Taxes				.6	.1	.9
	4.0		4.1		6.4	All Other Non-Current				5.9	8.3	8.6
	55.9		55.6		47.5	Net Worth				45.2	43.8	55.3
	100.0		100.0		100.0	Total Liabilties & Net Worth				100.0	100.0	100.0
						INCOME DATA						
	100.0		100.0		100.0	Net Sales				100.0	100.0	100.0
	46.1		43.2		42.6	Gross Profit				47.4	34.1	41.4
	39.2		36.4		37.8	Operating Expenses				43.0	26.3	40.9
	6.9		6.8		4.8	Operating Profit				4.4	7.8	.5
	1.0		1.3		1.1	All Other Expenses (net)				1.3	.5	1.3
	5.9		5.6		3.7	Profit Before Taxes				3.1	7.3	-.8
						RATIOS						
	4.3		4.4		3.3					2.8	7.1	4.2
	2.2		2.3		2.1	Current				1.8	1.7	2.7
	1.6		1.8		1.4					1.4	1.3	2.2
	2.4		2.5		2.1					1.4	3.7	2.8
	1.3		1.5		1.2	Quick				.8	.8	1.7
	.8		.9		.7					.5	.7	1.1
33	11.2	39	9.4	34	10.8		28	13.2	34	10.8	44	8.3
49	7.4	48	7.6	49	7.4	Sales/Receivables	42	8.6	59	6.2	55	6.6
64	5.7	63	5.8	67	5.4		61	6.0	68	5.4	71	5.1
68	5.4	61	6.0	72	5.1		96	3.8	47	7.8	67	5.5
120	3.0	101	3.6	107	3.4	Cost of Sales/Inventory	109	3.3	93	3.9	108	3.4
162	2.3	159	2.3	146	2.5		138	2.7	128	2.8	147	2.5
19	19.0	18	20.4	16	22.3		15	24.4	16	22.3	29	12.4
30	12.3	24	15.3	32	11.3	Cost of Sales/Payables	31	11.9	20	17.9	38	9.6
48	7.7	39	9.3	44	8.3		68	5.4	41	9.0	45	8.1
	2.9		2.9		2.9					4.1	2.5	2.5
	4.4		4.3		4.6	Sales/Working Capital				6.2	9.3	3.2
	7.4		8.5		10.4					12.3	13.8	5.3
	15.0		28.1		29.3					16.8	66.8	27.5
(44)	5.0	(45)	8.5	(45)	4.4	EBIT/Interest	(12)	4.2	(13)	13.0	(10)	.5
	1.1		1.5		1.1					2.3	2.6	-2.7
	8.5		21.2		7.5	Net Profit + Depr., Dep.,						
(13)	2.5	(17)	7.8	(17)	3.0	Amort./Cur. Mat. L/T/D						
	-18.7		2.1		.8							
	.1		.1		.1					.2	.1	.2
	.3		.2		.4	Fixed/Worth				.5	.5	.6
	.7		.5		.8					.7	.9	1.4
	.3		.3		.5					.7	.5	.3
	1.0		.8		1.1	Debt/Worth				1.2	1.1	1.2
	1.8		1.5		2.9					3.0	2.5	5.2
	35.8		44.7		44.0	% Profit Before Taxes/Tangible				28.4	51.9	20.1
(50)	13.9	(54)	20.1	(47)	14.1	Net Worth	(12)	13.5	(12)	24.4	(11)	4.2
	1.2		4.4		1.4					4.1	4.9	-8.3
	17.8		26.5		16.1	% Profit Before Taxes/Total				8.3	22.6	9.8
	6.5		11.5		6.3	Assets				6.1	12.1	-.8
	1.0		1.4		.0					.7	5.3	-6.4
	28.9		67.8		26.5					24.7	29.9	9.6
	13.2		16.7		12.9	Sales/Net Fixed Assets				15.2	14.3	6.1
	7.9		10.6		6.5					7.2	6.7	5.0
	2.4		2.5		2.3					2.8	2.5	1.8
	1.6		1.8		1.6	Sales/Total Assets				1.8	1.8	1.3
	1.0		1.4		1.2					1.1	1.3	.7
	.7		.9		1.1					1.0	1.3	2.2
(43)	1.5	(46)	1.8	(44)	2.1	% Depr., Dep., Amort./Sales			(12)	1.7	(11)	2.0	3.8
	2.7		2.4		3.4					2.5	2.4	4.5
	1.8		2.3		3.1	% Officers', Directors'						
(13)	3.5	(18)	5.3	(14)	5.9	Owners' Comp/Sales						
	9.4		9.1		9.6							
	1573317M		1762725M		1390867M	Net Sales ($)	446M	16389M	18747M	89920M	214154M	1051211M
	1481991M		1316941M		1165929M	Total Assets ($)	471M	9345M	8583M	62997M	133151M	951382M

M = $ thousand   MM = $ million
See Pages 9 through 22 for Explanation of Ratios and Data

Current Data Sorted by Assets   Comparative Historical Data

0-500M	500M-2MM	2-10MM	10-50MM	50-100MM	100-250MM	Type of Statement	4/1/05-3/31/06 ALL	4/1/06-3/31/07 ALL
		4	9	5	3	Unqualified	17	20
		5	1			Reviewed	10	10
		1				Compiled	4	3
2	1					Tax Returns	2	5
1	1	14	6	1	3	Other	23	20
	9 (4/1-9/30/09)		47 (10/1/09-3/31/10)					
2	2	24	16	6	6	NUMBER OF STATEMENTS	56	58
%	%	%	%	%	%	ASSETS	%	%
		10.1	25.3			Cash & Equivalents	9.3	11.8
		27.4	20.2			Trade Receivables (net)	26.6	26.6
		30.2	19.4			Inventory	26.4	24.9
		1.4	2.1			All Other Current	2.9	1.7
		69.1	67.0			Total Current	65.1	65.0
		18.3	15.6			Fixed Assets (net)	16.4	13.8
		6.0	11.5			Intangibles (net)	10.2	11.8
		6.7	5.9			All Other Non-Current	8.2	9.4
		100.0	100.0			Total	100.0	100.0
						LIABILITIES		
		10.6	1.2			Notes Payable-Short Term	10.7	8.1
		2.2	1.0			Cur. Mat.-L.T.D.	1.9	1.4
		12.9	7.1			Trade Payables	12.0	11.8
		.0	.2			Income Taxes Payable	.8	.6
		8.0	11.5			All Other Current	12.7	14.3
		33.7	21.0			Total Current	38.1	36.1
		16.3	6.7			Long-Term Debt	10.4	9.4
		.5	.3			Deferred Taxes	.3	.8
		7.6	3.2			All Other Non-Current	7.0	6.5
		41.9	68.7			Net Worth	44.1	47.2
		100.0	100.0			Total Liabilities & Net Worth	100.0	100.0
						INCOME DATA		
		100.0	100.0			Net Sales	100.0	100.0
		46.5	50.9			Gross Profit	46.0	45.6
		41.4	43.3			Operating Expenses	39.7	39.5
		5.1	7.5			Operating Profit	6.3	6.1
		1.5	.2			All Other Expenses (net)	1.0	1.1
		3.6	7.3			Profit Before Taxes	5.3	5.0
						RATIOS		
		3.9	5.7			Current	3.5	3.7
		2.2	3.4				2.0	2.2
		1.6	2.5				1.5	1.4
		2.2	3.5			Quick	1.8	2.1
		1.1	2.0				1.0	1.2
		.6	1.3				.7	.7
		38 9.7	52 7.1			Sales/Receivables	45 8.1	46 8.0
		49 7.4	61 6.0				57 6.4	58 6.2
		65 5.6	67 5.4				67 5.4	70 5.2
		57 6.4	71 5.2			Cost of Sales/Inventory	68 5.3	62 5.8
		103 3.5	128 2.9				105 3.5	102 3.6
		148 2.5	181 2.0				145 2.5	146 2.5
		28 12.9	23 15.8			Cost of Sales/Payables	27 13.7	22 16.2
		38 9.6	33 11.1				43 8.6	44 8.4
		60 6.1	63 5.8				58 6.3	62 5.9
		3.5	1.9			Sales/Working Capital	2.9	3.0
		4.9	2.5				5.8	4.8
		11.8	3.5				9.6	10.4
		8.6	74.4			EBIT/Interest	20.0	33.4
		(22) 4.1	(12) 4.5				(47) 6.6	(50) 6.4
		-1.2	-12.8				2.4	2.1
						Net Profit + Depr., Dep., Amort./Cur. Mat. L/T/D	25.7	40.0
							(22) 9.6	(18) 5.1
							3.4	1.2
		.2	.1			Fixed/Worth	.2	.1
		.4	.3				.4	.3
		1.3	.7				1.1	1.5
		.6	.2			Debt/Worth	.4	.4
		1.0	.5				1.3	1.1
		3.0	1.3				4.8	5.0
		25.3	45.7			% Profit Before Taxes/Tangible Net Worth	42.1	36.2
		(20) 7.3	(15) 19.0				(47) 29.5	(48) 22.5
		-10.0	-2.6				8.4	4.3
		15.3	29.6			% Profit Before Taxes/Total Assets	16.2	17.0
		5.8	7.9				8.6	8.9
		-4.3	-2.3				2.6	2.4
		39.5	22.6			Sales/Net Fixed Assets	28.4	28.3
		13.4	11.1				12.2	16.6
		5.1	4.7				5.8	7.5
		2.3	1.6			Sales/Total Assets	2.2	2.2
		1.8	1.3				1.6	1.6
		1.5	.9				1.1	1.1
		1.1	1.6			% Depr., Dep., Amort./Sales	1.0	1.0
		(18) 2.2	2.2				(47) 1.9	(44) 1.7
		3.1	3.2				4.0	2.7
						% Officers', Directors' Owners' Comp/Sales		2.1
								(12) 5.0
								12.4
1784M	10481M	237699M	579320M	485299M	813622M	Net Sales ($)	2343863M	2233156M
664M	2566M	123490M	451751M	430676M	892519M	Total Assets ($)	2043841M	2001228M

M = $ thousand   MM = $ million
See Pages 9 through 22 for Explanation of Ratios and Data

Comparative Historical Data / Current Data Sorted by Sales

4/1/07-3/31/08 ALL	4/1/08-3/31/09 ALL	4/1/09-3/31/10 ALL	Type of Statement	0-1MM	1-3MM	3-5MM	5-10MM	10-25MM	25MM & OVER
15	14	21	Unqualified				3	3	15
11	3	6	Reviewed		1	1	1	3	
4	4	1	Compiled					1	
2	7	3	Tax Returns	1	2				
20	25	25	Other		1		9	8	7
				1			9 (4/1-9/30/09)	47 (10/1/09-3/31/10)	
52	53	56	NUMBER OF STATEMENTS	1	4	1	13	15	22
%	%	%	ASSETS	%	%	%	%	%	%
11.3	13.8	17.5	Cash & Equivalents				12.3	11.8	26.1
23.8	25.2	23.6	Trade Receivables (net)				25.3	27.0	18.7
25.7	26.1	24.7	Inventory				28.8	29.9	17.1
3.1	3.0	1.6	All Other Current				.6	2.7	1.9
63.9	68.2	67.5	Total Current				67.0	71.4	63.8
15.5	17.1	15.3	Fixed Assets (net)				13.9	18.6	13.8
14.6	9.9	11.6	Intangibles (net)				11.4	4.8	17.2
6.0	4.8	5.6	All Other Non-Current				7.7	5.2	5.2
100.0	100.0	100.0	Total				100.0	100.0	100.0
			LIABILITIES						
5.0	5.3	5.6	Notes Payable-Short Term				10.0	6.1	1.7
3.0	3.1	1.6	Cur. Mat.-L.T.D.				1.4	2.0	.9
9.6	8.4	10.3	Trade Payables				13.1	12.7	8.0
.5	.6	.1	Income Taxes Payable				.1	.0	.2
12.6	12.7	10.7	All Other Current				6.3	11.3	11.5
30.8	30.0	28.3	Total Current				30.9	32.1	22.3
10.8	7.7	12.7	Long-Term Debt				20.0	7.3	9.8
.6	.3	.6	Deferred Taxes				.2	.7	1.0
5.1	5.2	6.5	All Other Non-Current				6.3	12.7	3.6
52.7	56.8	52.0	Net Worth				42.6	47.2	63.3
100.0	100.0	100.0	Total Liabilities & Net Worth				100.0	100.0	100.0
			INCOME DATA						
100.0	100.0	100.0	Net Sales				100.0	100.0	100.0
47.0	47.1	47.0	Gross Profit				44.8	44.7	51.7
41.0	43.4	41.5	Operating Expenses				37.3	39.9	45.7
6.0	3.7	5.5	Operating Profit				7.5	4.9	6.0
1.3	.9	1.2	All Other Expenses (net)				1.2	1.1	1.0
4.7	2.8	4.3	Profit Before Taxes				6.3	3.8	5.0
			RATIOS						
3.2	4.3	4.5	Current				4.1	4.7	5.3
2.3	2.4	2.7					2.7	2.2	2.9
1.6	1.6	1.8					1.8	1.6	1.9
1.8	2.4	2.7	Quick				2.7	2.4	3.7
1.2	1.2	1.6					1.4	1.1	2.0
.9	.8	1.0					.7	.9	1.3
46 8.0	40 9.2	47 7.8	Sales/Receivables				33 11.1	39 9.5	53 6.9
53 6.9	50 7.3	54 6.8					47 7.7	49 7.4	59 6.2
65 5.6	62 5.9	64 5.7					68 5.4	59 6.2	63 5.8
72 5.1	69 5.3	66 5.6	Cost of Sales/Inventory				59 6.1	42 8.7	77 4.7
110 3.3	99 3.7	104 3.5					97 3.8	106 3.5	112 3.2
151 2.4	152 2.4	149 2.4					147 2.5	181 2.0	151 2.4
22 16.7	23 15.5	25 14.8	Cost of Sales/Payables				31 11.7	21 17.2	26 14.1
38 9.5	33 11.1	35 10.4					35 10.4	31 11.9	42 8.6
57 6.4	50 7.2	60 6.1					53 6.9	61 6.0	80 4.6
3.1	3.0	2.4	Sales/Working Capital				2.7	3.1	2.0
4.4	4.3	3.8					4.3	4.6	2.9
9.6	8.0	6.3					12.5	7.7	4.3
20.5	46.9	12.6	EBIT/Interest				17.0	7.8	22.8
(49) 6.6	(47) 5.9	(49) 3.2					(12) 3.7	(12) 4.6	(19) 1.5
1.8	.6	-2.2					-1.3	2.5	-22.4
20.2	4.9	5.5	Net Profit + Depr., Dep., Amort./Cur. Mat. L/T/D						
(23) 7.6	(17) 2.4	(15) 2.4							
.9	-.3	-1.5							
.1	.1	.2	Fixed/Worth				.1	.2	.2
.3	.3	.3					.4	.4	.3
1.2	.6	.8					NM	.8	.4
.5	.3	.3	Debt/Worth				.8	.3	.3
.8	.8	.9					1.2	.8	.8
4.9	1.7	2.7					-110.1	2.7	1.7
44.4	32.8	36.8	% Profit Before Taxes/Tangible Net Worth					29.8	36.8
(43) 18.9	(49) 10.0	(48) 8.8						(14) 13.1	(20) 10.7
2.3	-7.5	-8.0						.8	-12.7
18.1	16.2	13.6	% Profit Before Taxes/Total Assets				21.6	14.3	13.0
8.0	4.4	5.8					9.2	6.8	5.2
1.8	-2.3	-3.0					-3.9	1.4	-3.8
33.7	35.0	27.1	Sales/Net Fixed Assets				83.5	31.7	14.8
16.1	11.0	13.0					16.5	12.7	10.8
7.4	5.9	5.1					5.6	5.9	4.8
2.3	2.4	1.9	Sales/Total Assets				2.2	2.4	1.5
1.4	1.7	1.5					1.6	1.9	1.0
1.1	1.1	1.0					1.3	1.5	.9
.8	1.2	1.4	% Depr., Dep., Amort./Sales					.9	1.9
(45) 1.9	(40) 2.1	(44) 2.3						(13) 2.3	(19) 2.8
3.0	3.8	3.6						3.3	3.8
3.1	2.6	3.2	% Officers', Directors' Owners' Comp/Sales						
(12) 6.9	(10) 5.2	(12) 6.9							
11.5	8.1	20.7							
1977478M	2085476M	2128205M	Net Sales ($)	493M	7328M	3922M	100069M	232525M	1783868M
1868804M	1847969M	1901666M	Total Assets ($)	258M	6111M	2824M	68420M	131218M	1692835M

M = $ thousand   MM = $ million
See Pages 9 through 22 for Explanation of Ratios and Data

Current Data Sorted by Assets   Comparative Historical Data

Type of Statement

0-500M	500M-2MM	2-10MM	10-50MM	50-100MM	100-250MM		4/1/05-3/31/06 ALL	4/1/06-3/31/07 ALL
	1	5	7	4	6	Unqualified	26	27
	1	23	3			Reviewed	18	26
	6	5				Compiled	9	11
1	5	1	1			Tax Returns	7	1
4	5	8	13	2	2	Other	40	40
	19 (4/1-9/30/09)		84 (10/1/09-3/31/10)					
5	18	42	24	6	8	NUMBER OF STATEMENTS	100	105

Data Table

0-500M	500M-2MM	2-10MM	10-50MM	50-100MM	100-250MM		4/1/05-3/31/06	4/1/06-3/31/07
%	%	%	%	%	%	**ASSETS**	%	%
	17.4	9.6	9.5			Cash & Equivalents	8.5	12.5
	28.4	28.3	23.5			Trade Receivables (net)	29.7	29.5
	20.7	28.7	22.8			Inventory	27.3	26.1
	2.4	6.0	3.3			All Other Current	2.6	3.7
	68.8	72.6	59.1			Total Current	68.2	71.7
	20.5	18.2	23.9			Fixed Assets (net)	17.7	17.3
	5.3	3.2	14.1			Intangibles (net)	7.4	5.9
	5.4	6.0	2.9			All Other Non-Current	6.6	5.1
	100.0	100.0	100.0			Total	100.0	100.0
						LIABILITIES		
	11.7	9.6	8.4			Notes Payable-Short Term	8.6	11.5
	1.4	2.4	3.3			Cur. Mat.-L.T.D.	2.8	3.1
	11.7	11.7	9.3			Trade Payables	12.9	12.7
	.2	.7	3.2			Income Taxes Payable	.7	.7
	16.9	13.5	10.6			All Other Current	14.1	14.2
	42.0	38.0	34.7			Total Current	39.0	42.3
	11.4	7.7	10.7			Long-Term Debt	13.9	9.3
	1.2	.2	.7			Deferred Taxes	.4	.4
	8.3	7.9	6.0			All Other Non-Current	8.2	4.0
	37.1	46.2	48.0			Net Worth	38.4	44.0
	100.0	100.0	100.0			Total Liabilities & Net Worth	100.0	100.0
						INCOME DATA		
	100.0	100.0	100.0			Net Sales	100.0	100.0
	54.7	40.6	34.2			Gross Profit	41.4	41.4
	51.8	36.1	28.5			Operating Expenses	33.7	33.8
	2.9	4.4	5.7			Operating Profit	7.7	7.6
	.5	.8	.7			All Other Expenses (net)	1.5	1.0
	2.4	3.7	4.9			Profit Before Taxes	6.1	6.6
						RATIOS		
	4.5	3.0	3.3				3.2	3.1
	2.8	1.9	1.9			Current	2.0	1.9
	1.3	1.4	1.1				1.3	1.2
	3.9	1.7	2.5				2.0	2.1
	1.8	.9	.8			Quick	(99) 1.1	1.0
	.6	.7	.6				.6	.6
	20 17.9	37 9.9	41 8.9				43 8.5	41 9.0
	36 10.0	53 6.9	51 7.2			Sales/Receivables	53 6.8	59 6.2
	53 6.9	73 5.0	63 5.8				69 5.3	81 4.5
	21 17.7	48 7.7	40 9.2				45 8.0	48 7.6
	40 9.1	98 3.7	85 4.3			Cost of Sales/Inventory	96 3.8	104 3.5
	108 3.4	152 2.4	139 2.6				136 2.7	148 2.5
	15 24.1	13 27.2	19 19.5				19 19.0	19 18.8
	25 14.5	34 10.7	28 13.0			Cost of Sales/Payables	32 11.4	38 9.7
	45 8.0	54 6.8	49 7.4				51 7.1	59 6.2
	4.1	3.4	4.6				3.5	3.1
	6.6	4.5	6.1			Sales/Working Capital	5.9	5.6
	25.2	9.3	31.8				13.5	24.1
	7.1	14.3	33.7				23.3	14.9
	(14) 1.6	(34) 3.7	(20) 8.1			EBIT/Interest	(86) 6.4	(91) 5.1
	-.2	1.0	1.5				1.6	1.7
		4.6					14.1	12.3
		(10) 1.9				Net Profit + Depr., Dep., Amort./Cur. Mat. L/T/D	(29) 3.8	(30) 3.5
		1.4					1.0	1.7
	.1	.1	.3				.2	.2
	.5	.4	.6			Fixed/Worth	.5	.4
	2.4	.7	1.6				1.0	.9
	.4	.6	.5				.6	.5
	.8	1.0	1.4			Debt/Worth	1.5	1.5
	5.3	2.2	4.6				5.4	3.9
	64.0	33.1	39.0				48.8	42.9
	(15) 11.3	(40) 13.3	(20) 23.1			% Profit Before Taxes/Tangible Net Worth	(89) 30.1	(95) 30.4
	-9.3	3.6	6.6				11.3	9.1
	25.9	15.0	16.7				19.0	17.8
	2.2	4.9	11.0			% Profit Before Taxes/Total Assets	10.0	9.6
	-6.0	-.8	1.4				2.9	2.2
	87.9	33.9	20.6				31.5	28.4
	21.5	14.6	8.8			Sales/Net Fixed Assets	12.3	12.7
	9.6	6.1	4.5				6.6	6.8
	3.6	2.4	2.0				2.4	2.4
	2.6	1.7	1.6			Sales/Total Assets	1.8	1.6
	1.9	1.2	1.0				1.3	1.3
	.4	.9	1.3				.9	.9
	(15) 1.4	(39) 1.9	(17) 2.0			% Depr., Dep., Amort./Sales	(85) 2.0	(85) 1.7
	2.1	2.7	4.0				2.8	2.8
		2.9					2.5	4.2
		(16) 4.1				% Officers', Directors' Owners' Comp/Sales	(22) 5.8	(16) 6.2
		5.4					9.0	9.4
4682M	52071M	382796M	874797M	437649M	1124381M	Net Sales ($)	2645779M	2669268M
1719M	19679M	213725M	537097M	376581M	1284999M	Total Assets ($)	1778784M	1962524M

M = $ thousand   MM = $ million
See Pages 9 through 22 for Explanation of Ratios and Data

Comparative Historical Data / Current Data Sorted by Sales

'07-'08 ALL	'08-'09 ALL	'09-'10 ALL	Type of Statement	0-1MM	1-3MM	3-5MM	5-10MM	10-25MM	25MM & OVER
23	18	23	Unqualified			1	3	5	14
24	27	27	Reviewed			8	10	8	1
5	12	11	Compiled		3	4	1	1	
4	4	8	Tax Returns		5	1	1	1	
42	51	34	Other	2	8	1	3	7	13
4/1/07-3/31/08 ALL	4/1/08-3/31/09 ALL	4/1/09-3/31/10 ALL			19 (4/1-9/30/09)		84 (10/1/09-3/31/10)		
98	112	103	NUMBER OF STATEMENTS	2	17	14	18	24	28
%	%	%	**ASSETS**	%	%	%	%	%	%
10.1	11.0	11.4	Cash & Equivalents		15.8	5.5	13.7	9.6	12.4
28.4	24.4	25.1	Trade Receivables (net)		18.6	33.4	23.2	29.7	21.1
27.0	27.9	25.4	Inventory		30.5	24.6	30.9	20.4	23.6
3.6	4.8	4.7	All Other Current		6.2	4.6	4.4	4.7	4.3
69.2	68.1	66.5	Total Current		71.1	68.0	72.2	64.2	61.4
14.1	16.9	19.1	Fixed Assets (net)		17.0	23.5	16.1	25.0	15.2
8.5	7.3	9.2	Intangibles (net)		5.6	4.0	6.0	5.2	19.6
8.2	7.7	5.1	All Other Non-Current		6.3	4.5	5.6	5.6	3.8
100.0	100.0	100.0	Total		100.0	100.0	100.0	100.0	100.0
			LIABILITIES						
8.2	8.9	9.1	Notes Payable-Short Term		13.6	13.7	9.4	9.3	4.0
2.8	1.7	2.7	Cur. Mat.-L.T.D.		3.8	1.9	2.3	2.8	2.9
10.7	10.5	10.3	Trade Payables		10.3	10.5	11.7	12.2	7.7
.3	.4	1.2	Income Taxes Payable		.4	.0	.4	3.7	.8
13.6	13.6	13.4	All Other Current		21.0	4.9	14.2	14.3	12.6
35.5	35.0	36.7	Total Current		49.1	31.0	38.2	42.2	28.0
9.0	9.3	11.3	Long-Term Debt		7.9	18.6	5.0	6.7	17.7
.4	.6	.5	Deferred Taxes		1.1	.4	.6	.4	.4
4.9	4.6	9.3	All Other Non-Current		10.9	4.0	7.4	13.4	4.2
50.2	50.5	42.2	Net Worth		31.1	45.9	48.8	37.3	49.7
100.0	100.0	100.0	Total Liabilities & Net Worth		100.0	100.0	100.0	100.0	100.0
			INCOME DATA						
100.0	100.0	100.0	Net Sales		100.0	100.0	100.0	100.0	100.0
41.6	44.2	42.9	Gross Profit		51.3	49.8	44.1	34.4	38.6
31.8	36.7	37.8	Operating Expenses		49.6	46.7	36.7	32.3	30.8
9.9	7.5	5.1	Operating Profit		1.6	3.1	7.4	2.1	7.7
1.2	1.0	.8	All Other Expenses (net)		-.4	2.0	.2	1.5	.6
8.7	6.5	4.3	Profit Before Taxes		2.0	1.1	7.1	.6	7.1
			RATIOS						
3.8	3.7	3.5	Current		4.3	4.1	3.4	2.3	3.9
2.3	2.2	1.9			1.4	2.5	2.0	1.6	2.1
1.4	1.3	1.4			1.1	1.5	1.3	1.1	1.6
2.4	2.3	2.1	Quick		3.7	2.6	2.0	1.8	2.1
1.2	1.1	(102) 1.0		(16)	.7	1.0	1.1	.8	1.1
.7	.6	.6			.4	.5	.7	.6	.7
39 9.5	31 11.7	35 10.3	Sales/Receivables		19 19.0	37 9.9	27 13.7	41 9.0	45 8.0
53 6.9	47 7.8	50 7.3			28 13.0	54 6.8	49 7.5	55 6.6	51 7.2
77 4.7	61 6.0	67 5.5			47 7.8	90 4.0	59 6.2	78 4.7	62 5.9
44 8.2	56 6.5	40 9.1	Cost of Sales/Inventory		58 6.2	13 28.0	63 5.8	33 11.2	54 6.7
102 3.6	117 3.1	94 3.9			115 3.2	53 6.9	98 3.7	68 5.3	98 3.7
148 2.5	160 2.3	148 2.5			149 2.5	314 1.2	164 2.2	110 3.3	150 2.4
14 25.3	16 22.8	15 25.0	Cost of Sales/Payables		16 22.8	13 28.2	11 32.1	13 28.2	19 19.7
28 13.2	29 12.5	32 11.3			27 13.4	37 9.8	29 12.6	39 9.5	28 13.1
46 7.9	57 6.4	52 7.0			42 8.6	90 4.0	53 6.9	54 6.8	46 8.0
3.0	3.1	3.5	Sales/Working Capital		4.0	2.6	3.5	3.9	3.1
5.3	5.3	5.2			5.5	4.1	5.1	8.4	5.0
12.9	17.3	11.1			31.8	8.5	12.0	128.3	8.6
20.7	27.7	13.7	EBIT/Interest		23.0	2.9	17.3	11.3	37.6
(76) 6.1	(86) 6.1	(83) 4.0		(12) 2.3		(13) 1.9	(13) 7.7	(19) 1.8	(25) 7.6
2.2	2.4	.8			-22.0	.7	1.4	-2.0	3.3
14.7	13.7	5.9	Net Profit + Depr., Dep., Amort./Cur. Mat. L/T/D						11.2
(26) 5.4	(26) 4.0	(22) 2.1						(10)	4.2
2.0	2.0	1.6							1.7
.1	.1	.1	Fixed/Worth		.1	.2	.1	.2	.3
.3	.4	.5			.5	.6	.5	.6	.4
.8	.7	1.5			NM	1.1	.5	1.6	.9
.4	.3	.5	Debt/Worth		.4	.7	.5	.6	.5
1.0	1.1	1.2			1.2	1.5	.9	1.1	1.4
3.3	3.1	3.8			NM	3.8	1.9	3.4	5.9
55.1	47.9	33.8	% Profit Before Taxes/Tangible Net Worth		70.0	15.5	43.0	19.4	39.8
(86) 26.6	(103) 20.9	(87) 14.4		(13)	22.0	(16) 7.6	(20) 27.8	(23) 5.7	21.9
12.4	10.8	1.9			-31.4	-.9	7.5	-3.1	7.6
26.2	18.9	15.2	% Profit Before Taxes/Total Assets		27.9	4.8	20.8	9.7	15.6
10.9	10.5	5.3			2.8	2.3	11.6	2.3	12.5
4.1	3.9	.3			-17.2	-.5	2.3	-4.5	4.1
45.7	34.4	26.4	Sales/Net Fixed Assets		62.7	20.9	73.9	25.2	21.2
17.9	14.3	11.9			20.0	10.7	17.1	11.3	10.8
7.9	6.4	6.5			9.0	5.2	6.1	4.3	7.1
2.5	2.3	2.4	Sales/Total Assets		3.0	3.6	2.6	2.4	1.8
1.7	1.7	1.6			2.1	1.4	1.8	1.7	1.5
1.3	1.2	1.2			1.3	.9	1.3	1.3	.8
.8	.7	1.0	% Depr., Dep., Amort./Sales		.5	.6	.6	1.1	1.3
(78) 1.6	(85) 1.6	(83) 1.8		(13)	1.4	(16) 2.1	(21) 1.7	(19) 1.9	2.0
2.3	3.0	2.9			2.2	4.0	2.7	3.2	2.9
2.7	3.4	2.7	% Officers', Directors' Owners' Comp/Sales						
(17) 4.8	(23) 4.2	(27) 4.7							
6.3	8.8	7.8							
3079775M	3340485M	2876376M	Net Sales ($)	639M	34113M	57808M	132233M	385817M	2265766M
2232572M	2627305M	2433800M	Total Assets ($)	352M	18765M	44675M	80677M	251081M	2038250M

M = $ thousand   MM = $ million
See Pages 9 through 22 for Explanation of Ratios and Data

Current Data Sorted by Assets   **Comparative Historical Data**

0-500M	500M-2MM	2-10MM	10-50MM	50-100MM	100-250MM	Type of Statement	4/1/05-3/31/06 ALL	4/1/06-3/31/07 ALL
			4	1	1	Unqualified	11	12
		2	4			Reviewed	7	3
		1				Compiled	4	3
1	3	4				Tax Returns	8	5
1	4	4	8	1	1	Other	18	11
	3 (4/1-9/30/09)		37 (10/1/09-3/31/10)					
2	7	11	16	2	2	NUMBER OF STATEMENTS	48	34
%	%	%	%	%	%		%	%
						ASSETS		
		4.0	7.7			Cash & Equivalents	7.5	8.2
		25.2	20.5			Trade Receivables (net)	24.9	27.3
		46.5	30.2			Inventory	36.6	38.7
		5.7	6.4			All Other Current	1.4	1.9
		81.3	64.8			Total Current	70.4	76.0
		10.0	19.9			Fixed Assets (net)	16.8	17.4
		3.8	8.9			Intangibles (net)	7.7	2.3
		4.9	6.4			All Other Non-Current	5.0	4.2
		100.0	100.0			Total	100.0	100.0
						LIABILITIES		
		14.4	12.7			Notes Payable-Short Term	13.1	10.3
		6.8	4.6			Cur. Mat.-L.T.D.	1.7	2.9
		12.6	8.7			Trade Payables	14.8	18.1
		.1	.0			Income Taxes Payable	.4	.7
		9.5	8.8			All Other Current	8.9	9.3
		43.4	34.8			Total Current	38.9	41.2
		13.0	9.8			Long-Term Debt	14.3	14.8
		1.2	.0			Deferred Taxes	.3	.3
		5.1	3.1			All Other Non-Current	12.6	9.3
		37.4	52.3			Net Worth	33.8	34.5
		100.0	100.0			Total Liabilities & Net Worth	100.0	100.0
						INCOME DATA		
		100.0	100.0			Net Sales	100.0	100.0
		41.7	41.5			Gross Profit	41.3	42.1
		39.8	37.5			Operating Expenses	34.6	35.3
		1.9	4.0			Operating Profit	6.6	6.8
		1.6	1.5			All Other Expenses (net)	1.3	1.1
		.4	2.5			Profit Before Taxes	5.3	5.6
						RATIOS		
		3.0	4.4				2.8	2.9
		1.6	2.0			Current	2.2	2.0
		1.3	1.2				1.3	1.3
		1.0	2.2				1.4	1.5
		.6	.6			Quick	.9	.8
		.3	.4				.6	.5
	27	13.5	31 11.7				33 10.9	32 11.3
	43	8.5	47 7.7			Sales/Receivables	45 8.1	49 7.5
	53	6.8	57 6.4				61 6.0	66 5.6
	74	5.0	56 6.5				79 4.6	60 6.1
	125	2.9	145 2.5			Cost of Sales/Inventory	114 3.2	137 2.7
	195	1.9	188 1.9				143 2.6	168 2.2
	15	23.9	21 17.1				22 16.9	26 14.2
	29	12.8	29 12.5			Cost of Sales/Payables	40 9.2	48 7.6
	74	4.9	45 8.2				67 5.5	82 4.5
		3.7	2.7				4.4	4.0
		6.6	6.8			Sales/Working Capital	6.3	5.8
		14.4	21.1				12.2	19.2
		9.7	9.1				12.7	19.1
		2.9	(15) 2.5			EBIT/Interest	(43) 3.8	(30) 4.5
		-1.7	-1.0				1.8	1.5
							34.5	
						Net Profit + Depr., Dep., Amort./Cur. Mat. L/T/D	(12) 4.7	
							1.1	
		.1	.2				.3	.1
		.2	.5			Fixed/Worth	.5	.4
		.9	.8				2.5	1.6
		1.1	.5				.9	.7
		2.2	1.3			Debt/Worth	2.3	1.5
		6.5	1.9				9.0	4.7
		37.2	7.4				48.8	52.3
	(10)	12.2	(15) 3.5			% Profit Before Taxes/Tangible Net Worth	(40) 22.2	(30) 25.7
		-15.3	-14.7				6.5	10.5
		12.2	4.4				19.1	23.7
		3.2	2.9			% Profit Before Taxes/Total Assets	7.1	10.6
		-3.4	-3.2				2.0	1.1
		55.1	21.6				47.5	42.7
		27.0	9.9			Sales/Net Fixed Assets	19.4	18.9
		12.1	5.4				9.3	9.0
		3.0	2.1				2.7	2.4
		2.6	1.6			Sales/Total Assets	2.2	2.1
		1.4	1.2				1.5	1.7
			.9				.7	.6
		(15)	2.5			% Depr., Dep., Amort./Sales	(44) 1.0	(27) 1.1
			4.4				1.8	2.8
							1.3	1.4
						% Officers', Directors' Owners' Comp/Sales	(19) 3.7	(12) 2.3
							6.4	4.5
1179M	18242M	121869M	462663M	297201M	328707M	Net Sales ($)	1488753M	1752679M
311M	9096M	52921M	316214M	168693M	205370M	Total Assets ($)	895759M	970361M

M = $ thousand   MM = $ million
See Pages 9 through 22 for Explanation of Ratios and Data

Comparative Historical Data / Current Data Sorted by Sales

Type of Statement

4/1/07-3/31/08	4/1/08-3/31/09	4/1/09-3/31/10	Type of Statement	0-1MM	1-3MM	3-5MM	5-10MM	10-25MM	25MM & OVER
11	10	6	Unqualified					1	5
4	5	6	Reviewed				1	2	3
3	5	1	Compiled			1			
7	8	8	Tax Returns	1	1	2	2	2	
10	15	19	Other	2	2	3	1	2	9
ALL	ALL	ALL		3 (4/1-9/30/09)			37 (10/1/09-3/31/10)		
35	43	40	NUMBER OF STATEMENTS	3	3	6	4	7	17

Data

4/1/07-3/31/08 ALL	4/1/08-3/31/09 ALL	4/1/09-3/31/10 ALL		0-1MM	1-3MM	3-5MM	5-10MM	10-25MM	25MM & OVER
%	%	%	**ASSETS**	%	%	%	%	%	%
11.0	7.3	9.7	Cash & Equivalents						8.5
24.2	23.4	21.8	Trade Receivables (net)						26.6
40.3	41.0	36.2	Inventory						30.5
1.4	4.0	4.4	All Other Current						4.7
77.0	75.7	72.1	Total Current						70.4
13.9	16.1	17.6	Fixed Assets (net)						18.1
5.1	4.2	6.1	Intangibles (net)						7.3
4.0	4.0	4.2	All Other Non-Current						4.2
100.0	100.0	100.0	Total						100.0
			LIABILITIES						
9.5	12.1	11.9	Notes Payable-Short Term						11.3
3.1	3.8	4.8	Cur. Mat.-L.T.D.						2.8
14.2	15.2	10.6	Trade Payables						9.0
.8	.5	.0	Income Taxes Payable						.0
11.4	8.5	8.4	All Other Current						8.9
39.0	40.2	35.7	Total Current						32.1
11.3	10.8	15.0	Long-Term Debt						8.7
.3	.4	.3	Deferred Taxes						.0
7.1	6.8	5.4	All Other Non-Current						4.2
42.2	41.9	43.6	Net Worth						55.0
100.0	100.0	100.0	Total Liabilities & Net Worth						100.0
			INCOME DATA						
100.0	100.0	100.0	Net Sales						100.0
42.1	43.6	41.6	Gross Profit						39.6
35.3	38.0	38.4	Operating Expenses						34.4
6.7	5.5	3.2	Operating Profit						5.2
1.4	1.5	1.6	All Other Expenses (net)						1.4
5.3	4.0	1.6	Profit Before Taxes						3.8
			RATIOS						
3.3 / 2.0 / 1.4	3.0 / 1.9 / 1.4	4.4 / 1.9 / 1.2	Current						4.4 / 2.3 / 1.2
1.3 / .9 / .7	1.4 / .6 / .4	2.3 / .8 / .4	Quick						2.6 / 1.0 / .5
21 17.8 / 43 8.4 / 65 5.6	23 16.1 / 39 9.5 / 60 6.1	27 13.5 / 44 8.4 / 59 6.2	Sales/Receivables						43 8.5 / 56 6.5 / 73 5.0
96 3.8 / 130 2.8 / 183 2.0	65 5.6 / 132 2.8 / 182 2.0	63 5.8 / 112 3.3 / 187 1.9	Cost of Sales/Inventory						58 6.3 / 114 3.2 / 165 2.2
21 17.2 / 31 11.9 / 54 6.8	23 15.8 / 38 9.6 / 70 5.2	21 17.1 / 29 12.6 / 45 8.2	Cost of Sales/Payables						23 16.1 / 28 12.9 / 39 9.4
3.5 / 6.0 / 8.8	3.4 / 7.0 / 14.0	2.9 / 5.8 / 15.9	Sales/Working Capital						2.3 / 3.6 / 17.4
20.6 / (31) 4.1 / 1.3	9.1 / (39) 2.6 / 1.3	12.6 / (38) 2.4 / -1.7	EBIT/Interest					(16)	36.1 / 3.8 / 1.2
	(13)	5.8 / 1.2 / .3	Net Profit + Depr., Dep., Amort./Cur. Mat. L/T/D						
.1 / .4 / .8	.1 / .4 / 1.0	.2 / .4 / .9	Fixed/Worth						.2 / .3 / .9
.8 / 1.6 / 3.5	.7 / 1.6 / 3.2	.5 / 1.7 / 4.5	Debt/Worth						.3 / 1.3 / 1.8
50.8 / (32) 27.6 / 7.3	48.1 / (40) 14.5 / 1.6	15.4 / (35) 4.9 / -14.7	% Profit Before Taxes/Tangible Net Worth					(15)	8.6 / 4.9 / .1
21.5 / 11.9 / 1.1	16.8 / 5.8 / .9	6.2 / 3.2 / -4.0	% Profit Before Taxes/Total Assets						5.7 / 3.9 / .5
49.6 / 22.5 / 7.6	35.8 / 22.5 / 7.6	47.1 / 12.2 / 6.2	Sales/Net Fixed Assets						31.0 / 9.6 / 6.2
2.6 / 2.1 / 1.5	2.8 / 1.9 / 1.6	2.4 / 1.7 / 1.4	Sales/Total Assets						2.0 / 1.6 / 1.3
(27) .8 / 1.2 / 2.4	(34) .6 / 1.4 / 2.7	(34) .7 / 1.5 / 2.7	% Depr., Dep., Amort./Sales					(15)	1.0 / 2.1 / 3.3
(13) 1.7 / 2.6 / 5.0	(16) 1.4 / 2.6 / 6.0	(11) 2.0 / 3.6 / 8.9	% Officers', Directors' Owners' Comp/Sales						
1342859M	1413151M	1229861M	Net Sales ($)	1470M	5454M	21632M	26010M	132820M	1042475M
701190M	733318M	752605M	Total Assets ($)	1506M	4924M	21287M	11580M	60371M	652937M

M = $ thousand   MM = $ million
See Pages 9 through 22 for Explanation of Ratios and Data

Current Data Sorted by Assets / Comparative Historical Data

						Type of Statement		
		4	6	3	1	Unqualified	10	19
	2	12	7			Reviewed	13	12
	2	3				Compiled	2	6
2	9	3				Tax Returns	8	8
1	6	10	7	2	5	Other	18	26
	15 (4/1-9/30/09)		70 (10/1/09-3/31/10)				4/1/05-3/31/06	4/1/06-3/31/07
0-500M	500M-2MM	2-10MM	10-50MM	50-100MM	100-250MM		ALL	ALL
3	19	32	20	5	6	NUMBER OF STATEMENTS	51	71
%	%	%	%	%	%	ASSETS	%	%
	13.6	6.7	13.3			Cash & Equivalents	7.6	5.8
	24.5	27.0	21.4			Trade Receivables (net)	33.3	32.8
	22.8	35.5	29.0			Inventory	28.3	28.2
	1.0	3.8	4.1			All Other Current	4.9	3.8
	62.0	73.0	67.9			Total Current	74.2	70.6
	24.5	17.6	18.0			Fixed Assets (net)	16.2	17.2
	5.6	4.8	11.1			Intangibles (net)	4.4	6.7
	8.0	4.6	3.0			All Other Non-Current	5.3	5.4
	100.0	100.0	100.0			Total	100.0	100.0
						LIABILITIES		
	15.0	15.2	8.1			Notes Payable-Short Term	10.5	11.3
	3.9	1.9	4.8			Cur. Mat.-L.T.D.	3.3	3.6
	16.0	20.8	10.5			Trade Payables	16.5	18.0
	.1	.1	.1			Income Taxes Payable	.6	.4
	10.7	13.1	8.9			All Other Current	11.5	12.4
	45.6	51.2	32.3			Total Current	42.3	45.8
	18.0	12.4	12.1			Long-Term Debt	11.7	16.1
	.0	.2	1.1			Deferred Taxes	.4	.4
	7.2	7.0	6.0			All Other Non-Current	3.4	4.7
	29.2	29.1	48.5			Net Worth	42.1	33.0
	100.0	100.0	100.0			Total Liabilities & Net Worth	100.0	100.0
						INCOME DATA		
	100.0	100.0	100.0			Net Sales	100.0	100.0
	47.1	36.4	35.5			Gross Profit	38.4	34.6
	40.0	32.1	33.4			Operating Expenses	32.8	27.6
	7.2	4.3	2.1			Operating Profit	5.6	7.0
	.1	1.5	1.5			All Other Expenses (net)	.7	1.1
	7.1	2.8	.6			Profit Before Taxes	4.8	5.9
						RATIOS		
	3.1	2.2	3.8				2.6	2.6
	1.5	1.6	2.0			Current	1.7	1.6
	.8	1.3	1.4				1.2	1.2
	1.4	1.1	2.2				1.7	1.5
	.8	.7	1.0			Quick	1.0	1.0
	.6	.4	.7				.6	.5
	28 / 13.2	33 / 10.9	41 / 9.0				41 / 9.0	40 / 9.0
	33 / 11.1	42 / 8.6	49 / 7.5			Sales/Receivables	50 / 7.3	52 / 7.0
	53 / 7.0	52 / 7.0	62 / 5.9				61 / 6.0	60 / 6.1
	17 / 21.7	50 / 7.2	62 / 5.9				40 / 9.1	39 / 9.2
	82 / 4.5	99 / 3.7	113 / 3.2			Cost of Sales/Inventory	84 / 4.3	74 / 4.9
	130 / 2.8	140 / 2.6	151 / 2.4				105 / 3.5	107 / 3.4
	12 / 31.0	23 / 16.1	13 / 28.9				20 / 18.4	25 / 14.7
	27 / 13.5	46 / 8.0	33 / 11.0			Cost of Sales/Payables	39 / 9.3	38 / 9.7
	88 / 4.2	71 / 5.1	51 / 7.2				60 / 6.1	56 / 6.5
	4.5	5.4	3.2				4.7	5.3
	10.5	8.4	6.3			Sales/Working Capital	6.8	8.4
	-26.1	17.1	8.4				9.9	21.8
	7.9	4.7	11.1				24.6	19.2
	(17) 4.9	(28) 3.0	(18) 2.0			EBIT/Interest	(48) 5.6	(69) 4.6
	.9	.8	.3				1.8	2.1
		2.5				Net Profit + Depr., Dep.,		7.8	6.8
		(14) 2.0				Amort./Cur. Mat. L/T/D	(15) 2.7	(24) 2.6
		1.2					.1	.6
	.2	.2	.2				.2	.2
	.8	.5	.7			Fixed/Worth	.3	.6
	2.7	1.3	1.1				.9	1.5
	1.0	1.0	.4				.7	1.0
	2.2	1.9	1.3			Debt/Worth	1.5	2.4
	6.5	4.2	3.9				2.9	5.1
	119.9	43.2	28.0			% Profit Before Taxes/Tangible	43.2	56.0
	(16) 72.4	(28) 6.5	(17) 8.7			Net Worth	(45) 22.7	(57) 30.3
	10.5	-1.5	-1.7				7.5	13.5
	24.3	15.3	11.5			% Profit Before Taxes/Total	17.8	18.8
	7.0	3.0	2.1			Assets	8.9	9.8
	1.0	-.5	-1.6				1.1	3.4
	36.1	45.9	22.0				37.7	39.0
	16.1	17.8	11.6			Sales/Net Fixed Assets	20.5	19.5
	5.7	6.1	5.6				10.4	8.9
	2.5	2.7	2.2				2.9	2.9
	2.1	2.1	1.6			Sales/Total Assets	2.2	2.2
	1.5	1.6	1.1				1.6	1.7
	1.2	.7	1.0				.7	.8
	(14) 1.4	(28) 1.5	(16) 2.2			% Depr., Dep., Amort./Sales	(42) 1.5	(59) 1.7
	2.6	2.5	2.7				2.7	2.3
		2.8				% Officers', Directors'		2.0	1.2
		(11) 3.8				Owners' Comp/Sales	(17) 3.9	(25) 3.3
		5.8					5.7	5.0
3922M	51212M	344488M	628166M	580199M	1125640M	Net Sales ($)	2498479M	2878658M
531M	24679M	158512M	401424M	304822M	1025541M	Total Assets ($)	1364811M	1658916M

M = $ thousand   MM = $ million
See Pages 9 through 22 for Explanation of Ratios and Data

Comparative Historical Data   Current Data Sorted by Sales

			Type of Statement						
15	14	14	Unqualified		1	2	3	7	7
12	13	21	Reviewed		3		1	12	3
5	6	5	Compiled			1	1	1	
7	12	14	Tax Returns	1	5	5	3	1	
23	28	31	Other	2	3	4	3	8	11
4/1/07-3/31/08	4/1/08-3/31/09	4/1/09-3/31/10			15 (4/1-9/30/09)		70 (10/1/09-3/31/10)		
ALL	ALL	ALL		0-1MM	1-3MM	3-5MM	5-10MM	10-25MM	25MM & OVER
62	73	85	**NUMBER OF STATEMENTS**	3	12	11	10	28	21
%	%	%	**ASSETS**	%	%	%	%	%	%
7.2	10.5	11.0	Cash & Equivalents		9.5	21.5	12.2	9.5	8.0
29.1	29.4	24.1	Trade Receivables (net)		23.5	25.0	24.5	25.4	23.8
29.0	28.6	29.4	Inventory		26.6	31.9	31.8	29.3	27.9
6.0	5.2	2.9	All Other Current		1.7	.3	5.6	2.7	4.5
71.3	73.7	67.5	Total Current		61.4	78.7	74.1	67.0	64.2
15.8	15.4	19.6	Fixed Assets (net)		31.0	14.6	17.2	19.2	20.1
7.4	4.4	8.0	Intangibles (net)		5.6	2.9	4.6	9.4	11.2
5.4	6.6	4.9	All Other Non-Current		2.1	3.8	4.0	4.5	4.6
100.0	100.0	100.0	Total		100.0	100.0	100.0	100.0	100.0
			LIABILITIES						
15.4	13.6	14.0	Notes Payable-Short Term		13.4	13.6	5.0	15.2	11.7
3.3	2.7	2.8	Cur. Mat.-L.T.D.		4.0	2.6	1.6	3.3	2.7
16.2	16.4	16.3	Trade Payables		17.9	14.4	21.2	16.6	13.6
.1	.3	.1	Income Taxes Payable		.1	.0	.2	.0	.3
11.7	11.7	11.6	All Other Current		6.5	8.8	13.7	11.7	12.3
46.8	44.6	44.9	Total Current		41.9	39.4	41.7	46.8	40.6
14.1	12.5	14.3	Long-Term Debt		24.3	14.1	16.2	10.5	14.8
.5	.1	.4	Deferred Taxes		.0	.0	.1	.9	.4
6.4	5.4	6.7	All Other Non-Current		4.5	8.3	6.6	8.0	6.4
32.3	37.3	33.7	Net Worth		29.3	38.2	35.4	33.8	37.8
100.0	100.0	100.0	Total Liabilities & Net Worth		100.0	100.0	100.0	100.0	100.0
			INCOME DATA						
100.0	100.0	100.0	Net Sales		100.0	100.0	100.0	100.0	100.0
40.9	38.5	37.5	Gross Profit		49.1	40.0	34.2	37.1	33.2
33.7	32.3	32.9	Operating Expenses		44.5	34.6	32.1	32.8	26.4
7.2	6.2	4.6	Operating Profit		4.5	5.4	2.1	4.2	6.8
2.2	1.1	1.4	All Other Expenses (net)		.0	.8	1.2	1.9	2.1
5.1	5.1	3.2	Profit Before Taxes		4.5	4.6	.9	2.3	4.7
			RATIOS						
2.8	2.6	2.6	Current		2.7	5.4	6.3	2.3	3.1
1.4	1.7	1.6			1.8	1.7	1.5	1.6	2.1
1.1	1.2	1.1			.8	1.5	1.3	1.2	1.0
1.2	1.5	1.3	Quick		1.1	3.3	4.5	1.2	1.4
.7	.9	.8			.8	.8	.8	.9	1.0
.5	.5	.5			.7	.7	.4	.5	.5
37 10.0	33 11.1	32 11.3	Sales/Receivables	22 16.2	27 13.6	36 10.1	34 10.8	42 8.7	
46 8.0	44 8.3	44 8.3		35 10.6	33 11.1	47 7.8	43 8.5	53 6.8	
58 6.3	57 6.4	59 6.2		72 5.1	53 7.0	62 5.9	53 6.9	66 5.5	
43 8.5	38 9.6	55 6.7	Cost of Sales/Inventory	8 47.6	27 13.8	57 6.4	55 6.7	60 6.1	
85 4.3	71 5.1	90 4.1		86 4.3	100 3.6	88 4.1	109 3.4	84 4.3	
112 3.3	109 3.3	140 2.6		180 2.0	130 2.8	107 3.4	140 2.6	141 2.6	
25 14.8	20 17.8	15 23.8	Cost of Sales/Payables	12 30.3	11 33.6	24 15.3	19 19.6	20 18.5	
35 10.5	33 11.1	36 10.0		49 7.4	13 27.7	50 7.3	36 10.1	30 12.0	
52 7.0	54 6.8	61 6.0		97 3.8	59 6.2	80 4.6	49 7.5	53 6.9	
4.8	5.0	3.9	Sales/Working Capital		4.0	3.3	5.0	4.9	3.3
12.1	8.7	7.9			21.4	6.3	7.3	8.6	6.3
32.7	20.5	35.5			NM	10.8	12.0	20.0	NM
14.6	16.5	6.7	EBIT/Interest		6.4	16.5		4.5	19.1
(58) 5.9	(67) 4.2	(75) 3.0		(11) 3.0	(10) 3.2		(23) 2.9	4.4	
2.1	1.9	.7			1.5	-2.0		.9	.1
25.1	6.8	4.5	Net Profit + Depr., Dep.,					4.7	
(18) 4.4	(21) 2.4	(25) 2.1	Amort./Cur. Mat. L/T/D				(12) 1.9		
2.2	1.3	.9						.6	
.2	.1	.2	Fixed/Worth		.2	.1	.1	.2	.3
.7	.5	.8			1.1	.4	.4	.8	1.1
2.2	1.4	2.3			NM	.8	1.4	1.3	-2.6
1.3	.7	.9	Debt/Worth		1.1	.8	1.2	.8	.5
2.9	2.1	1.9			1.5	2.2	2.0	1.8	2.9
12.5	8.3	9.9			NM	6.4	16.4	3.3	-10.7
75.7	76.3	55.6	% Profit Before Taxes/Tangible		124.5		15.7	49.8	
(53) 41.7	(64) 26.2	(67) 11.3	Net Worth		74.2		(23) 6.2	(14) 26.0	
21.7	9.3	-.4			-5.4		-.4	-.3	
15.8	17.0	15.0	% Profit Before Taxes/Total		29.0	24.7	9.6	7.7	14.4
11.0	8.1	3.0	Assets		4.7	9.9	2.4	2.5	5.5
3.0	2.5	-.5			-3.0	-3.7	-.5	-1.2	
43.0	54.0	36.3	Sales/Net Fixed Assets		22.4	36.2	45.4	58.9	19.3
22.9	23.7	13.6			6.5	24.4	24.1	12.7	9.2
8.3	9.9	5.6			2.8	8.0	6.1	5.9	5.5
2.9	3.3	2.4	Sales/Total Assets		3.0	2.9	2.9	2.4	2.2
2.2	2.4	2.0			1.8	2.4	2.0	2.1	1.6
1.7	1.6	1.4			1.4	2.0	1.5	1.5	1.3
.6	.5	.9	% Depr., Dep., Amort./Sales		1.2			.8	1.0
(49) 1.4	(53) 1.3	(67) 1.8		(10) 1.6			(23) 2.1	(16) 2.1	
2.2	2.0	2.7			3.1			2.9	2.7
2.8	2.3	3.0	% Officers', Directors'						
(18) 3.9	(20) 2.8	(29) 3.8	Owners' Comp/Sales						
5.5	4.5	5.6							
2641097M	2659525M	2733627M	Net Sales ($)	2059M	25703M	40466M	71206M	426171M	2168022M
1582876M	1442081M	1915509M	Total Assets ($)	2706M	17918M	18958M	41472M	256560M	1577895M

MANUFACTURING—Other Lighting Equipment Manufacturing NAICS 335129

| Current Data Sorted by Assets | | | | | | | Comparative Historical Data | |

Type of Statement

0-500M	500M-2MM	2-10MM	10-50MM	50-100MM	100-250MM		4/1/05-3/31/06 ALL	4/1/06-3/31/07 ALL
		6	2	2		Unqualified	7	6
		5	5			Reviewed	12	9
		2	1			Compiled	6	8
1	4	2	1			Tax Returns	6	3
2		6	5	3	2	Other	19	19
	4 (4/1-9/30/09)		47 (10/1/09-3/31/10)					
3	8	19	14	5	2	NUMBER OF STATEMENTS	50	45

Data

0-500M	500M-2MM	2-10MM	10-50MM	50-100MM	100-250MM		4/1/05-3/31/06 ALL	4/1/06-3/31/07 ALL
%	%	%	%	%	%	**ASSETS**	%	%
		9.7	16.1			Cash & Equivalents	11.6	9.6
		29.0	18.6			Trade Receivables (net)	27.3	26.6
		30.4	31.5			Inventory	27.3	29.9
		2.3	1.9			All Other Current	2.0	2.5
		71.4	68.0			Total Current	68.2	68.5
		18.3	23.5			Fixed Assets (net)	20.7	17.0
		2.4	.1			Intangibles (net)	4.5	6.3
		8.0	8.3			All Other Non-Current	6.7	8.2
		100.0	100.0			Total	100.0	100.0
						LIABILITIES		
		15.6	13.1			Notes Payable-Short Term	10.7	13.6
		2.8	4.6			Cur. Mat.-L.T.D.	2.0	2.4
		16.6	7.1			Trade Payables	13.5	15.8
		.3	.2			Income Taxes Payable	.3	.2
		6.7	6.0			All Other Current	8.3	9.9
		42.0	31.0			Total Current	34.9	41.9
		9.5	7.4			Long-Term Debt	12.8	13.0
		.1	.2			Deferred Taxes	.3	.1
		2.8	5.7			All Other Non-Current	6.1	6.8
		45.6	55.7			Net Worth	45.9	38.1
		100.0	100.0			Total Liabilties & Net Worth	100.0	100.0
						INCOME DATA		
		100.0	100.0			Net Sales	100.0	100.0
		36.1	35.3			Gross Profit	37.7	35.3
		31.5	27.7			Operating Expenses	31.9	28.0
		4.6	7.7			Operating Profit	5.8	7.3
		.7	1.3			All Other Expenses (net)	.8	1.2
		3.9	6.4			Profit Before Taxes	5.0	6.1
						RATIOS		
		2.4	5.8				3.4	3.3
		1.7	4.0			Current	2.3	2.1
		1.3	1.2				1.3	1.1
		1.7	4.2				2.1	1.6
		1.0	1.4			Quick	1.3	1.0
		.5	.4				.6	.5
	37	9.9	31 11.6				37 9.9	30 12.1
	47	7.8	44 8.4			Sales/Receivables	47 7.7	45 8.0
	58	6.3	49 7.5				60 6.0	58 6.3
	33	11.2	67 5.5				54 6.7	51 7.1
	112	3.3	97 3.7			Cost of Sales/Inventory	77 4.7	81 4.5
	131	2.8	163 2.2				105 3.5	109 3.3
	25	14.7	12 31.0				24 15.3	18 20.2
	36	10.1	17 21.7			Cost of Sales/Payables	37 9.8	36 10.2
	54	6.7	38 9.6				54 6.8	56 6.5
		5.1	2.0				4.2	3.5
		7.3	4.1			Sales/Working Capital	5.9	5.7
		18.6	NM				9.2	46.3
		17.3	33.4				19.7	10.6
	(18)	8.3	(10) 3.5			EBIT/Interest	(44) 9.2	(39) 5.4
		1.8	1.9				1.9	2.8
						Net Profit + Depr., Dep., Amort./Cur. Mat. L/T/D		
		.0	.2				.2	.2
		.3	.4			Fixed/Worth	.4	.4
		1.0	.9				1.2	2.4
		.5	.2				.5	.6
		1.1	.8			Debt/Worth	1.3	1.6
		2.3	1.4				3.9	17.9
		43.0	49.3				55.4	52.7
	(18)	13.7	20.7			% Profit Before Taxes/Tangible Net Worth	(45) 22.0	(38) 24.3
		2.3	5.2				6.9	7.4
		19.7	17.7				20.2	20.0
		5.8	7.3			% Profit Before Taxes/Total Assets	9.4	10.3
		2.0	3.2				2.5	4.0
		61.9	27.5				28.5	42.5
		19.8	5.0			Sales/Net Fixed Assets	12.1	19.1
		7.5	2.7				5.3	6.0
		2.5	2.3				2.5	2.5
		2.3	1.2			Sales/Total Assets	1.9	2.0
		1.9	.9				1.5	1.5
		.6	1.0				.8	.8
	(17)	1.4	(13) 1.8			% Depr., Dep., Amort./Sales	(44) 1.7	(39) 1.9
		3.1	3.5				2.7	2.4
							4.0	3.7
						% Officers', Directors' Owners' Comp/Sales	(17) 5.3	(13) 6.0
							7.9	8.3
2061M	27579M	200752M	458738M	525853M	368361M	Net Sales ($)	1401303M	1784301M
438M	9933M	91307M	268813M	337428M	280640M	Total Assets ($)	825738M	1046430M

M = $ thousand   MM = $ million
See Pages 9 through 22 for Explanation of Ratios and Data

Comparative Historical Data   **Current Data Sorted by Sales**

Comparative Historical Data			Type of Statement	Current Data Sorted by Sales					
			Unqualified				1	6	3
8	7	10	Reviewed		1		5	3	3
8	13	12	Compiled			2			1
7	5	3	Tax Returns			2	3		
5	6	8	Other	2	1	2	2	5	8
21	32	18							
4/1/07-3/31/08	4/1/08-3/31/09	4/1/09-3/31/10		4 (4/1-9/30/09)			47 (10/1/09-3/31/10)		
ALL	ALL	ALL		0-1MM	1-3MM	3-5MM	5-10MM	10-25MM	25MM & OVER
49	63	51	NUMBER OF STATEMENTS	4	3	4	11	14	15
%	%	%	**ASSETS**	%	%	%	%	%	%
9.9	9.4	12.9	Cash & Equivalents				9.1	13.1	15.9
25.5	24.4	24.4	Trade Receivables (net)				24.0	27.9	21.1
32.8	32.4	30.3	Inventory				31.7	26.2	35.1
2.7	3.8	2.0	All Other Current				1.4	2.5	3.0
70.9	70.0	69.5	Total Current				66.2	69.6	75.1
18.0	22.0	21.2	Fixed Assets (net)				25.3	21.4	16.9
6.2	2.3	2.6	Intangibles (net)				.8	2.9	5.1
4.9	5.7	6.6	All Other Non-Current				7.8	6.0	3.0
100.0	100.0	100.0	Total				100.0	100.0	100.0
			LIABILITIES						
14.1	12.0	14.7	Notes Payable-Short Term				17.5	12.9	10.7
2.2	2.4	2.8	Cur. Mat.-L.T.D.				5.1	3.2	2.3
16.8	15.5	12.7	Trade Payables				19.4	11.6	9.2
.1	.3	.4	Income Taxes Payable				.3	.4	.1
8.2	9.2	6.9	All Other Current				5.9	6.8	8.0
41.5	39.4	37.5	Total Current				48.3	34.8	30.3
13.3	10.4	10.0	Long-Term Debt				14.7	4.9	10.2
.2	.2	.2	Deferred Taxes				.2	.2	.2
12.9	10.0	4.3	All Other Non-Current				2.9	2.2	7.4
32.0	40.1	48.0	Net Worth				34.0	57.8	52.0
100.0	100.0	100.0	Total Liabilties & Net Worth				100.0	100.0	100.0
			INCOME DATA						
100.0	100.0	100.0	Net Sales				100.0	100.0	100.0
35.0	37.2	36.9	Gross Profit				36.8	35.2	35.2
30.4	31.7	32.9	Operating Expenses				32.5	28.3	26.9
4.6	5.4	4.0	Operating Profit				4.3	6.9	8.3
1.8	.6	.8	All Other Expenses (net)				.6	.6	1.5
2.8	4.9	3.2	Profit Before Taxes				3.7	6.3	6.8
			RATIOS						
2.9	2.9	3.2	Current				1.9	3.6	5.6
1.9	1.8	2.2					1.5	2.4	3.1
1.3	1.2	1.3					1.2	1.3	1.7
1.7	1.5	1.9	Quick				1.0	2.2	3.8
.9	.8	1.0					.7	1.4	1.5
.5	.5	.5					.4	.5	.9
28 13.1	30 12.2	29 12.5	Sales/Receivables				29 12.5	34 10.8	25 14.6
41 9.0	41 8.9	44 8.3					49 7.4	44 8.4	44 8.2
56 6.6	51 7.1	57 6.4					62 5.9	56 6.6	57 6.4
46 8.0	55 6.6	54 6.8	Cost of Sales/Inventory				29 12.8	35 10.5	76 4.8
91 4.0	93 3.9	84 4.4					116 3.1	67 5.4	99 3.7
129 2.8	126 2.9	128 2.8					128 2.8	138 2.6	147 2.5
24 15.3	22 17.0	15 24.3	Cost of Sales/Payables				27 13.7	14 26.7	15 24.3
36 10.2	32 11.5	30 12.2					47 7.7	27 13.5	27 13.7
50 7.3	55 6.7	43 8.5					69 5.3	37 10.0	38 9.6
4.0	3.9	3.0	Sales/Working Capital				5.5	2.9	2.4
7.1	7.2	6.9					7.3	6.9	2.9
17.6	19.8	13.7					26.9	13.3	6.8
13.2	28.1	17.3	EBIT/Interest				9.7	56.5	416.5
(43) 5.3	(51) 9.6	(42) 3.9				(10) 3.9	(12) 9.9	(12) 8.0
1.4	2.4	1.2					1.4	2.1	2.1
38.3	19.6		Net Profit + Depr., Dep.,						
(15) 7.8	(12) 5.2		Amort./Cur. Mat. L/T/D						
3.3	1.9								
.2	.2	.2	Fixed/Worth				.2	.1	.2
.4	.5	.5					.6	.3	.4
1.0	2.0	1.0					1.2	.9	.8
.8	.5	.4	Debt/Worth				1.1	.4	.3
1.7	1.1	1.1					1.8	.5	1.2
3.5	3.2	2.3					3.1	1.4	1.9
51.1	53.5	34.0	% Profit Before Taxes/Tangible				35.7	36.6	63.7
(44) 26.2	(58) 27.1	(47) 11.9	Net Worth				(10) 17.1	(13) 6.2	23.6
4.9	4.4	1.1					7.6	.0	11.9
19.4	21.3	13.7	% Profit Before Taxes/Total				12.2	21.3	18.8
8.5	9.4	5.2	Assets				5.8	4.4	9.5
1.8	2.1	.7					2.6	.3	5.2
46.9	41.4	38.0	Sales/Net Fixed Assets				19.8	38.7	28.2
18.2	15.6	15.3					7.5	15.4	10.0
5.6	5.5	4.6					5.6	4.1	4.4
2.8	2.7	2.6	Sales/Total Assets				2.6	2.4	2.5
2.2	2.0	2.0					2.4	2.0	1.6
1.5	1.5	1.2					1.1	1.2	1.2
.6	.7	.8	% Depr., Dep., Amort./Sales				1.1	1.1	.8
(37) 1.4	(49) 1.6	(45) 1.5				(10) 2.8	(13) 1.4	(13) 1.2
2.4	2.8	3.1					5.1	3.5	2.8
2.9	1.6	2.1	% Officers', Directors'						
(15) 4.7	(22) 3.8	(13) 5.1	Owners' Comp/Sales						
9.0	8.9	9.3							
1350904M	2220200M	1583344M	Net Sales ($)	2597M	5919M	16460M	82416M	210553M	1265399M
743831M	1374478M	988559M	Total Assets ($)	4515M	2263M	5365M	53082M	124988M	798346M

© RMA 2010

M = $ thousand   MM = $ million
See Pages 9 through 22 for Explanation of Ratios and Data

Current Data Sorted by Assets

Comparative Historical Data

						Type of Statement		
	1	5	7	3	2	Unqualified	15	18
	1	10	4			Reviewed	10	12
		1	1			Compiled	6	4
3	1	4				Tax Returns	3	3
1	3	13	14	5	2	Other	26	30
	14 (4/1-9/30/09)		67 (10/1/09-3/31/10)				4/1/05-3/31/06	4/1/06-3/31/07
0-500M	500M-2MM	2-10MM	10-50MM	50-100MM	100-250MM		ALL	ALL
4	6	33	26	8	4	NUMBER OF STATEMENTS	60	67
%	%	%	%	%	%	ASSETS	%	%
		11.9	13.3			Cash & Equivalents	6.6	6.9
		26.2	22.5			Trade Receivables (net)	27.2	31.3
		29.2	28.5			Inventory	27.2	27.6
		2.8	3.8			All Other Current	1.9	1.3
		70.1	68.1			Total Current	62.9	67.2
		19.2	21.0			Fixed Assets (net)	21.9	18.9
		4.3	6.4			Intangibles (net)	6.4	8.8
		6.4	4.5			All Other Non-Current	8.8	5.2
		100.0	100.0			Total	100.0	100.0
						LIABILITIES		
		13.0	8.3			Notes Payable-Short Term	10.9	9.9
		3.0	1.6			Cur. Mat.-L.T.D.	2.0	2.4
		18.6	13.1			Trade Payables	13.3	18.5
		.3	.6			Income Taxes Payable	.2	.3
		9.4	14.5			All Other Current	11.9	10.6
		44.4	38.1			Total Current	38.4	41.7
		13.4	7.0			Long-Term Debt	14.2	14.6
		.3	.8			Deferred Taxes	.4	.9
		1.8	.9			All Other Non-Current	6.8	5.0
		40.1	53.3			Net Worth	40.1	37.8
		100.0	100.0			Total Liabilties & Net Worth	100.0	100.0
						INCOME DATA		
		100.0	100.0			Net Sales	100.0	100.0
		27.0	30.0			Gross Profit	31.6	29.0
		24.6	23.7			Operating Expenses	24.9	22.5
		2.4	6.4			Operating Profit	6.7	6.5
		1.4	.8			All Other Expenses (net)	1.0	1.9
		1.1	5.5			Profit Before Taxes	5.7	4.6
						RATIOS		
		3.9	2.2				2.2	2.4
		1.6	1.8			Current	1.7	1.7
		1.0	1.4				1.3	1.1
		2.6	1.5				1.3	1.5
		.7	.9			Quick	.9	.9
		.6	.6				.6	.6
		27 13.4	37 9.7				41 8.9	38 9.7
		38 9.6	47 7.8			Sales/Receivables	50 7.3	52 7.1
		44 8.3	61 6.0				62 5.9	68 5.4
		36 10.2	56 6.5				37 9.8	38 9.6
		53 6.9	69 5.3			Cost of Sales/Inventory	67 5.4	69 5.3
		83 4.4	115 3.2				113 3.2	113 3.2
		13 27.9	19 19.0				22 16.4	27 13.5
		30 12.4	31 11.9			Cost of Sales/Payables	33 11.2	40 9.2
		48 7.6	49 7.5				48 7.6	52 7.0
		5.6	4.6				4.5	4.7
		12.6	7.7			Sales/Working Capital	8.1	8.4
		107.5	10.8				16.5	29.8
		23.2	41.5				15.4	9.7
		(30) 6.7	(22) 10.9			EBIT/Interest	(57) 6.0	(66) 3.7
		.9	1.3				2.0	1.9
		11.7	13.1			Net Profit + Depr., Dep.,	11.6	31.3
		(10) 7.3	(10) 3.2			Amort./Cur. Mat. L/T/D	(23) 4.1	(24) 10.1
		3.0	.8				1.1	3.3
		.1	.2				.2	.2
		.5	.4			Fixed/Worth	.5	.7
		1.1	.7				1.3	1.6
		.6	.6				.7	.9
		1.4	1.0			Debt/Worth	1.5	2.6
		5.8	2.3				5.0	6.3
		60.7	47.0			% Profit Before Taxes/Tangible	51.7	57.6
		(31) 23.2	13.2			Net Worth	(51) 27.7	(59) 31.4
		.3	1.2				10.8	7.8
		18.0	14.5			% Profit Before Taxes/Total	19.1	15.5
		7.5	6.7			Assets	8.7	8.6
		.1	.5				2.3	2.2
		46.1	27.3				31.2	29.8
		19.4	12.2			Sales/Net Fixed Assets	9.2	11.4
		9.7	5.4				6.2	8.0
		3.3	2.3				2.7	2.9
		2.7	1.6			Sales/Total Assets	1.9	2.0
		2.0	1.2				1.4	1.4
		.5	1.0				.8	.7
		(30) 1.3	(23) 2.1			% Depr., Dep., Amort./Sales	(54) 1.2	(59) 1.4
		2.1	3.8				2.3	2.6
							3.1	1.7
						% Officers', Directors' Owners' Comp/Sales	(10) 6.1	(13) 4.0
							8.3	6.3
3508M	26098M	463649M	1218682M	811187M	598235M	Net Sales ($)	2806132M	2974458M
1122M	8162M	168339M	670535M	530437M	492358M	Total Assets ($)	1720294M	1863904M

M = $ thousand   MM = $ million
See Pages 9 through 22 for Explanation of Ratios and Data

Comparative Historical Data

Current Data Sorted by Sales

			Type of Statement	0-1MM	1-3MM	3-5MM	5-10MM	10-25MM	25MM & OVER
19	20	18	Unqualified		2		2	2	12
15	20	15	Reviewed		3		3	7	5
2	2	2	Compiled				1		1
5	3	8	Tax Returns	1	3	1		3	
24	25	38	Other	1		2	7	10	18
4/1/07-3/31/08 ALL	4/1/08-3/31/09 ALL	4/1/09-3/31/10 ALL			14 (4/1-9/30/09)			67 (10/1/09-3/31/10)	
65	70	81	**NUMBER OF STATEMENTS**	2	5	3	13	22	36
%	%	%	**ASSETS**	%	%	%	%	%	%
8.8	8.8	12.3	Cash & Equivalents				14.2	10.8	13.6
30.3	29.9	24.1	Trade Receivables (net)				25.1	29.6	22.4
28.4	30.0	30.5	Inventory				33.4	27.8	28.7
1.6	2.8	3.0	All Other Current				2.0	2.1	4.5
69.0	71.6	69.8	Total Current				74.7	70.3	69.2
15.7	16.9	19.4	Fixed Assets (net)				13.3	21.0	18.9
9.0	6.5	5.6	Intangibles (net)				7.0	3.1	6.3
6.3	5.0	5.2	All Other Non-Current				5.0	5.5	5.6
100.0	100.0	100.0	Total				100.0	100.0	100.0
			LIABILITIES						
8.7	9.8	10.9	Notes Payable-Short Term				11.2	13.8	6.9
2.2	2.8	2.0	Cur. Mat.-L.T.D.				3.1	2.0	1.4
16.5	17.1	15.4	Trade Payables				14.3	19.0	13.3
.2	.5	.3	Income Taxes Payable				.1	.1	.6
10.6	11.4	12.6	All Other Current				5.7	10.4	15.1
38.2	41.5	41.3	Total Current				34.4	45.4	37.3
13.5	9.9	9.4	Long-Term Debt				10.0	14.4	5.6
.4	.5	.5	Deferred Taxes				.1	.4	.9
5.9	4.4	4.7	All Other Non-Current				16.0	1.2	4.1
42.1	43.7	44.1	Net Worth				39.5	38.6	52.0
100.0	100.0	100.0	Total Liabilities & Net Worth				100.0	100.0	100.0
			INCOME DATA						
100.0	100.0	100.0	Net Sales				100.0	100.0	100.0
30.3	27.3	28.0	Gross Profit				31.3	27.7	26.2
21.7	19.3	24.0	Operating Expenses				27.8	20.6	20.9
8.5	7.9	4.0	Operating Profit				3.5	7.1	5.3
1.1	1.0	1.0	All Other Expenses (net)				.3	1.0	.7
7.4	6.9	2.9	Profit Before Taxes				3.2	6.1	4.6
			RATIOS						
2.5	2.7	3.3	Current				6.4	3.0	2.7
1.9	1.7	1.8					1.8	1.8	1.8
1.3	1.3	1.2					1.4	1.0	1.5
1.5	1.5	1.9	Quick				4.4	2.2	1.7
1.0	1.0	.9					.8	1.1	1.0
.7	.6	.6					.6	.6	.6
36 10.2	31 11.7	30 12.0	Sales/Receivables				27 13.4	35 10.4	34 10.7
49 7.5	44 8.2	42 8.7					34 10.6	44 8.3	44 8.2
62 5.9	59 6.1	53 6.9					44 8.4	54 6.8	58 6.3
41 8.9	43 8.5	44 8.2	Cost of Sales/Inventory				34 10.7	41 9.0	56 6.5
64 5.7	66 5.5	66 5.6					70 5.2	49 7.4	74 4.9
106 3.5	85 4.3	105 3.5					119 3.1	73 5.0	108 3.4
20 18.1	17 21.3	15 24.3	Cost of Sales/Payables				9 40.5	19 19.3	14 26.7
39 9.4	28 12.9	28 13.0					23 15.6	28 13.0	29 12.5
52 7.0	49 7.4	47 7.8					50 7.3	48 7.6	43 8.4
5.1	5.0	4.3	Sales/Working Capital				4.1	5.3	3.5
7.8	8.0	7.4					7.3	10.3	6.7
14.7	20.2	17.3					12.2	164.8	11.9
20.4	30.1	20.6	EBIT/Interest				71.7	17.2	44.5
(61) 6.5	(65) 9.4	(71) 6.8					(12) 10.4	(19) 8.6	(32) 7.3
2.0	3.0	1.0					-.9	1.6	1.5
34.0	20.3	10.1	Net Profit + Depr., Dep., Amort./Cur. Mat. L/T/D						8.9
(22) 15.6	(26) 8.8	(25) 5.2							(14) 3.6
2.9	2.8	1.3							1.1
.2	.2	.2	Fixed/Worth				.1	.2	.2
.4	.4	.4					.2	.5	.4
1.0	.9	.8					.9	1.3	.7
.6	.7	.5	Debt/Worth				.5	.5	.5
1.3	1.6	1.2					1.2	1.6	1.0
4.3	3.2	3.1					2.9	9.8	2.2
60.0	62.4	50.4	% Profit Before Taxes/Tangible Net Worth				39.5	84.3	45.9
(54) 34.5	(62) 31.0	(75) 16.6					(12) 16.7	(21) 28.0	(35) 13.1
14.7	10.6	.8					-1.5	11.5	3.5
26.4	23.2	16.0	% Profit Before Taxes/Total Assets				20.4	18.2	15.4
12.7	11.3	5.6					4.0	9.1	5.4
4.4	4.4	-.5					-3.1	3.5	.6
31.9	41.1	38.2	Sales/Net Fixed Assets				54.5	30.3	26.8
13.9	17.9	13.4					20.8	18.1	11.3
9.2	9.1	7.5					10.4	9.5	5.7
3.0	3.2	3.2	Sales/Total Assets				3.1	3.3	2.5
2.2	2.4	2.1					2.3	2.8	1.7
1.7	1.8	1.4					1.8	1.6	1.4
.7	.7	.6	% Depr., Dep., Amort./Sales				.5	.5	.9
(56) 1.4	(58) 1.1	(70) 1.4					(10) 1.2	(20) 1.4	(32) 1.4
2.1	2.1	2.6					1.9	2.1	2.9
1.6	1.3	2.1	% Officers', Directors' Owners' Comp/Sales						
(15) 3.8	(14) 2.6	(15) 3.6							
7.6	4.0	5.6							
3680109M	3967326M	3121359M	Net Sales ($)	1212M	8935M	12600M	98591M	347640M	2652381M
1970508M	2166204M	1870953M	Total Assets ($)	532M	9415M	11742M	50255M	167665M	1631344M

M = $ thousand   MM = $ million
See Pages 9 through 22 for Explanation of Ratios and Data

Current Data Sorted by Assets   Comparative Historical Data

Period subtotals: 14 (4/1-9/30/09)   41 (10/1/09-3/31/10)

0-500M		500M-2MM		2-10MM		10-50MM	50-100MM	100-250MM			4/1/05-3/31/06 ALL		4/1/06-3/31/07 ALL
				Type of Statement									
						3	1	1	Unqualified		15		15
		5		6		5			Reviewed		14		15
		1		2					Compiled		9		5
		4		1					Tax Returns		3		5
1				4		7	1	3	Other		26		30
1		10		16		22	2	4	**NUMBER OF STATEMENTS**		67		70
%		%		%		%	%	%	**ASSETS**		%		%
		4.6		6.4		6.5			Cash & Equivalents		5.9		9.1
		40.4		32.9		21.6			Trade Receivables (net)		29.6		28.4
		28.1		28.2		25.3			Inventory		31.1		29.8
		.8		2.8		1.9			All Other Current		1.8		2.6
		74.0		70.2		55.2			Total Current		68.4		69.8
		11.9		20.0		32.1			Fixed Assets (net)		22.1		21.3
		9.5		4.1		6.0			Intangibles (net)		4.8		4.4
		4.6		5.7		6.6			All Other Non-Current		4.7		4.4
		100.0		100.0		100.0			Total		100.0		100.0
									LIABILITIES				
		8.4		20.6		8.5			Notes Payable-Short Term		14.3		11.0
		2.3		2.0		3.7			Cur. Mat.-L.T.D.		3.8		3.6
		21.1		19.2		9.3			Trade Payables		13.7		13.9
		.1		.5		.7			Income Taxes Payable		.4		.3
		6.9		9.8		9.2			All Other Current		12.0		13.3
		38.8		52.2		31.3			Total Current		44.2		42.1
		24.2		11.4		13.2			Long-Term Debt		14.5		14.5
		.0		.8		.8			Deferred Taxes		.5		.5
		9.1		1.6		4.4			All Other Non-Current		9.1		4.9
		28.0		34.0		50.2			Net Worth		31.7		37.9
		100.0		100.0		100.0			Total Liabilities & Net Worth		100.0		100.0
									INCOME DATA				
		100.0		100.0		100.0			Net Sales		100.0		100.0
		44.1		26.0		22.7			Gross Profit		27.6		30.3
		36.5		23.2		18.3			Operating Expenses		22.7		23.4
		7.6		2.8		4.4			Operating Profit		4.9		6.9
		4.6		1.1		2.4			All Other Expenses (net)		1.2		.7
		3.0		1.7		2.0			Profit Before Taxes		3.7		6.1
									RATIOS				
		3.2		2.2		2.3					2.4		2.7
		2.0		1.3		1.8			Current		1.4		1.7
		1.3		1.0		1.4					1.1		1.2
		2.0		1.0		1.3					1.2		1.5
		1.2		.8		.9			Quick		.8		.9
		.8		.5		.5					.5		.6
37		9.8	40	9.0	42	8.8			Sales/Receivables	43	8.5	42	8.6
52		7.1	48	7.6	47	7.7				51	7.2	52	7.0
59		6.2	52	7.0	61	6.0				62	5.9	61	6.0
37		10.0	40	9.2	61	6.0			Cost of Sales/Inventory	53	6.9	54	6.8
64		5.7	54	6.8	78	4.7				68	5.4	72	5.1
226		1.6	84	4.4	87	4.2				110	3.3	101	3.6
23		15.5	25	14.8	17	22.1			Cost of Sales/Payables	22	16.3	22	16.7
39		9.2	34	10.7	23	15.9				26	13.9	33	10.9
56		6.5	45	8.1	39	9.3				44	8.3	50	7.4
		4.1		6.0		4.2			Sales/Working Capital		4.8		4.9
		6.2		14.9		6.4					8.8		8.1
		19.0		101.4		11.6					26.3		26.2
				4.8		14.0			EBIT/Interest		7.5		16.8
			(14)	1.0	(20)	5.0				(62)	3.3	(62)	3.7
				-1.7		-1.9					1.1		1.6
									Net Profit + Depr., Dep.,		4.8		5.9
									Amort./Cur. Mat. L/T/D	(30)	2.0	(25)	3.2
											1.1		.7
		.1		.3		.5			Fixed/Worth		.3		.3
		.3		.6		.7					.8		.5
		NM		1.8		1.4					2.2		1.6
		.7		1.3		.6			Debt/Worth		.7		.8
		2.6		1.7		.9					2.2		2.1
		NM		18.0		2.5					7.7		5.1
				28.1		22.8			% Profit Before Taxes/Tangible		33.6		60.1
			(14)	1.1	(20)	6.9			Net Worth	(57)	20.4	(63)	25.8
				-13.4		-18.7					3.7		13.1
		9.7		10.0		11.9			% Profit Before Taxes/Total		13.7		17.9
		4.6		1.1		4.6			Assets		5.0		8.7
		-.3		-4.6		-5.6					.4		1.6
		67.0		22.4		7.2			Sales/Net Fixed Assets		21.3		29.4
		23.7		13.5		6.2					9.8		12.4
		12.6		7.2		2.7					5.0		5.8
		3.9		2.8		2.0			Sales/Total Assets		2.5		2.6
		2.4		2.2		1.5					2.0		2.0
		2.0		1.6		1.2					1.5		1.5
				.9		1.9			% Depr., Dep., Amort./Sales		.9		1.0
			(15)	1.7	(21)	2.5				(62)	2.0	(62)	1.7
				2.3		3.8					3.4		2.7
									% Officers', Directors'		2.0		1.7
									Owners' Comp/Sales	(23)	5.1	(25)	3.3
											6.6		5.6
1642M		40671M		206026M		746122M	402567M	677751M	Net Sales ($)		3342629M		2922011M
417M		13857M		93487M		511905M	151487M	517289M	Total Assets ($)		1871084M		1352204M

M = $ thousand   MM = $ million
See Pages 9 through 22 for Explanation of Ratios and Data

Comparative Historical Data | | | | Current Data Sorted by Sales

4/1/07-3/31/08 ALL	4/1/08-3/31/09 ALL	4/1/09-3/31/10 ALL	Type of Statement	0-1MM	1-3MM	3-5MM	5-10MM	10-25MM	25MM & OVER
15	12	15	Unqualified					4	11
13	12	11	Reviewed					9	2
9	7	7	Compiled	1	1	2	2	1	
6	2	2	Tax Returns			1	3		
22	23	20	Other		1	3		5	7
				14 (4/1-9/30/09)			41 (10/1/09-3/31/10)		
65	56	55	NUMBER OF STATEMENTS	1	2	6	7	19	20
%	%	%		%	%	%	%	%	%
			ASSETS						
8.6	8.0	6.4	Cash & Equivalents					8.0	6.0
28.8	25.7	28.5	Trade Receivables (net)					28.7	24.7
28.9	32.7	26.8	Inventory					24.2	27.7
2.4	2.4	2.1	All Other Current					3.2	2.2
68.6	68.7	63.8	Total Current					64.2	60.7
19.9	20.1	23.5	Fixed Assets (net)					25.6	26.3
7.1	5.9	7.2	Intangibles (net)					4.2	9.8
4.4	5.2	5.5	All Other Non-Current					6.0	3.2
100.0	100.0	100.0	Total					100.0	100.0
			LIABILITIES						
10.1	12.0	11.4	Notes Payable-Short Term					14.7	8.0
2.6	2.6	2.6	Cur. Mat.-L.T.D.					3.7	1.8
14.8	13.4	14.5	Trade Payables					17.1	10.2
.1	.1	.5	Income Taxes Payable					.3	.5
15.8	19.5	9.2	All Other Current					8.7	11.4
43.4	47.7	38.3	Total Current					44.5	31.9
14.6	13.1	14.0	Long-Term Debt					13.9	9.8
.3	.6	.6	Deferred Taxes					.8	.4
7.4	5.6	4.5	All Other Non-Current					1.4	6.6
34.2	33.0	42.6	Net Worth					39.4	51.4
100.0	100.0	100.0	Total Liabilties & Net Worth					100.0	100.0
			INCOME DATA						
100.0	100.0	100.0	Net Sales					100.0	100.0
30.2	27.8	29.3	Gross Profit					24.4	23.9
25.5	23.0	24.0	Operating Expenses					21.9	18.1
4.8	4.7	5.3	Operating Profit					2.5	5.8
1.1	1.1	2.3	All Other Expenses (net)					1.2	2.5
3.7	3.7	3.0	Profit Before Taxes					1.3	3.3
			RATIOS						
2.8	2.5	2.4	Current					2.4	2.6
1.9	1.8	1.8						1.6	2.0
1.2	1.3	1.3						1.1	1.4
1.5	1.3	1.4	Quick					1.2	1.4
.9	.8	.9						.9	.9
.6	.6	.6						.6	.5
40 9.1	32 11.4	40 9.1	Sales/Receivables					45 8.2	42 8.7
48 7.5	45 8.2	49 7.4						49 7.4	48 7.6
62 5.9	56 6.5	57 6.4						55 6.6	57 6.4
44 8.3	52 7.0	51 7.2	Cost of Sales/Inventory					43 8.4	62 5.9
70 5.2	85 4.3	66 5.5						58 6.3	78 4.7
117 3.1	107 3.4	87 4.2						82 4.4	84 4.3
22 16.8	17 21.4	22 17.0	Cost of Sales/Payables					23 16.0	15 24.9
33 11.1	26 14.1	31 11.8						31 11.8	25 14.6
46 7.9	42 8.7	44 8.4						46 8.0	36 10.1
3.4	4.3	4.6	Sales/Working Capital					4.6	4.3
7.5	7.2	7.4						10.5	6.4
20.3	16.3	15.9						98.8	11.1
		13.3	EBIT/Interest					6.0	17.6
(57) 3.7	(53) 3.6	(49) 3.9					(17) 1.0	(18) 5.7
1.4	1.3	-1.3						-1.4	1.3
8.3	17.7	6.2	Net Profit + Depr., Dep.,					6.0	
(22) 4.3	(18) 4.3	(20) 3.0	Amort./Cur. Mat. L/T/D					(10) 2.8	
2.1	.7	.5						.1	
.3	.4	.3	Fixed/Worth					.5	.4
.5	.6	.6						.6	.7
1.2	1.2	1.4						1.4	1.4
.6	.7	.7	Debt/Worth					.7	.7
1.5	1.7	1.3						1.3	.9
5.6	5.0	3.9						5.3	2.6
42.0	35.3	27.3	% Profit Before Taxes/Tangible					22.7	30.1
(56) 25.8	(51) 20.1	(48) 10.0	Net Worth					(18) 1.1	(17) 15.3
7.2	3.8	-8.0						-15.5	.4
14.0	13.4	11.8	% Profit Before Taxes/Total					11.5	14.6
8.2	5.7	4.7	Assets					.2	6.2
1.6	1.1	-1.2						-5.9	2.6
27.0	38.9	16.0	Sales/Net Fixed Assets					22.4	9.6
11.8	9.7	8.6						7.0	7.3
6.2	6.0	6.0						3.6	6.2
2.6	2.9	2.5	Sales/Total Assets					2.7	2.2
1.9	2.0	1.9						1.8	1.8
1.3	1.5	1.5						1.3	1.5
1.2	.9	.9	% Depr., Dep., Amort./Sales					1.0	1.6
(58) 2.0	(53) 1.6	(50) 1.9					(18) 2.4	(19) 1.9
3.1	2.6	2.8						2.9	2.2
1.8	1.6	1.2	% Officers', Directors'						
(22) 4.1	(15) 5.4	(13) 2.1	Owners' Comp/Sales						
6.2	7.2	6.1							
1974319M	2657124M	2074779M	Net Sales ($)	145M	3353M	21720M	47533M	300560M	1701468M
1107867M	1494710M	1288442M	Total Assets ($)	1016M	1313M	52947M	16348M	182730M	1034088M

M = $ thousand   MM = $ million
See Pages 9 through 22 for Explanation of Ratios and Data

Current Data Sorted by Assets   Comparative Historical Data

0-500M	500M-2MM	2-10MM	10-50MM	50-100MM	100-250MM	Type of Statement	4/1/05-3/31/06 ALL	4/1/06-3/31/07 ALL
		1	6	2	1	Unqualified	10	6
	3	11	2			Reviewed	7	14
1	5	3				Compiled	5	1
2	3	1				Tax Returns	3	1
	3	2	4		1	Other	19	12
	9 (4/1-9/30/09)		39 (10/1/09-3/31/10)					
3	11	18	12	2	2	NUMBER OF STATEMENTS	44	34
%	%	%	%	%	%	**ASSETS**	%	%
	11.6	15.3	21.9			Cash & Equivalents	6.9	10.3
	32.3	33.9	24.4			Trade Receivables (net)	37.5	32.4
	31.0	24.2	21.6			Inventory	27.3	27.4
	1.7	3.5	7.1			All Other Current	3.6	3.8
	76.6	76.9	75.0			Total Current	75.3	73.9
	18.9	15.0	20.1			Fixed Assets (net)	14.5	16.9
	.9	3.1	1.0			Intangibles (net)	3.4	4.7
	3.5	5.1	4.0			All Other Non-Current	6.8	4.4
	100.0	100.0	100.0			Total	100.0	100.0
						LIABILITIES		
	23.8	11.4	1.8			Notes Payable-Short Term	11.8	11.3
	2.1	3.1	2.3			Cur. Mat.-L.T.D.	1.7	3.1
	19.2	17.2	10.0			Trade Payables	17.7	17.8
	.0	.2	1.0			Income Taxes Payable	.2	.4
	6.9	9.0	12.2			All Other Current	11.2	9.5
	52.0	40.7	27.3			Total Current	42.7	42.0
	8.3	7.9	7.5			Long-Term Debt	7.0	4.7
	.0	.3	.8			Deferred Taxes	.1	.1
	23.7	5.0	2.9			All Other Non-Current	6.6	4.4
	16.0	46.1	61.4			Net Worth	43.6	48.8
	100.0	100.0	100.0			Total Liabilties & Net Worth	100.0	100.0
						INCOME DATA		
	100.0	100.0	100.0			Net Sales	100.0	100.0
	23.8	24.8	36.0			Gross Profit	27.8	29.0
	26.9	21.7	27.7			Operating Expenses	22.4	23.3
	-3.0	3.1	8.3			Operating Profit	5.4	5.7
	2.0	.6	.2			All Other Expenses (net)	.3	1.3
	-5.0	2.4	8.1			Profit Before Taxes	5.1	4.4
						RATIOS		
	3.8	3.4	4.7				3.8	3.6
	1.7	2.0	3.0			Current	1.8	1.8
	.9	1.4	1.9				1.3	1.3
	2.6	2.1	2.9				1.9	1.9
	.8	1.3	2.1			Quick	1.2	1.1
	.4	.8	1.2				.7	.7
20 17.9	36 10.1	44 8.3					42 8.7	41 9.0
38 9.5	48 7.6	49 7.5				Sales/Receivables	53 6.9	48 7.6
52 7.0	77 4.7	56 6.5					68 5.4	56 6.5
32 11.5	17 20.9	36 10.0					37 9.9	35 10.5
51 7.2	43 8.4	62 5.9				Cost of Sales/Inventory	60 6.1	66 5.5
70 5.2	81 4.5	136 2.7					87 4.2	91 4.0
15 24.9	22 16.9	19 18.9					22 16.4	23 15.9
34 10.8	33 10.9	29 12.6				Cost of Sales/Payables	32 11.4	36 10.3
46 7.9	53 6.9	47 7.8					54 6.7	48 7.6
	6.4	4.0	2.1				3.5	4.1
	7.9	6.3	4.1			Sales/Working Capital	7.3	7.8
	-18.6	10.4	4.8				13.0	20.6
	51.5	12.4					36.6	39.5
	(10) -.4	(17) 3.5				EBIT/Interest	(38) 10.7	(29) 7.0
	-10.3	1.8					2.0	1.5
								26.2
						Net Profit + Depr., Dep., Amort./Cur. Mat. L/T/D		(10) 4.3
								.2
	.0	.1	.2				.1	.1
	.5	.3	.3			Fixed/Worth	.3	.3
	-6.2	.6	.5				.7	.8
	.3	.6	.2				.4	.4
	1.7	1.6	.7			Debt/Worth	1.1	1.2
	-34.8	2.4	1.0				2.8	2.3
		28.4	43.2				52.3	42.3
	(17) 12.2	27.0				% Profit Before Taxes/Tangible Net Worth	(38) 26.2	(31) 29.0
		3.2	-10.3				6.6	11.3
	3.7	9.1	26.3				21.0	16.4
	-16.3	4.6	15.3			% Profit Before Taxes/Total Assets	10.2	11.9
	-29.0	1.2	-5.7				2.0	.9
	311.9	74.4	18.6				48.8	58.6
	22.3	31.3	10.9			Sales/Net Fixed Assets	19.1	20.8
	10.3	7.9	4.6				9.5	7.0
	3.2	2.6	2.4				2.9	3.0
	3.0	2.1	1.5			Sales/Total Assets	2.3	2.3
	2.3	1.6	1.1				1.5	1.6
		.3	1.1				.3	.6
		.8	(10) 1.7			% Depr., Dep., Amort./Sales	(36) 1.1	(28) 1.7
		2.0	3.7				2.2	2.4
								1.8
						% Officers', Directors' Owners' Comp/Sales	(17) 5.8	
								9.1
1791M	41841M	170177M	537014M	122520M	305524M	Net Sales ($)	1385973M	1369742M
720M	14856M	77670M	298309M	127289M	365791M	Total Assets ($)	1069397M	851223M

M = $ thousand   MM = $ million
See Pages 9 through 22 for Explanation of Ratios and Data

Comparative Historical Data   Current Data Sorted by Sales

					Type of Statement						
	3		5	10	Unqualified				1	2	7
	9		11	16	Reviewed		1		8	5	
	7		8	9	Compiled		3	2	4		
	1		4	6	Tax Returns	1	1	1		1	
	19		14	7	Other	2		2		3	4
	4/1/07-		4/1/08-	4/1/09-							
	3/31/08		3/31/09	3/31/10			9 (4/1-9/30/09)			39 (10/1/09-3/31/10)	
	ALL		ALL	ALL		0-1MM	1-3MM	3-5MM	5-10MM	10-25MM	25MM & OVER
	39		42	48	NUMBER OF STATEMENTS	3	5	5	13	11	11
	%		%	%	ASSETS	%	%	%	%	%	%
	8.0		13.3	16.2	Cash & Equivalents				7.1	23.0	22.2
	35.5		31.5	30.2	Trade Receivables (net)				38.1	22.3	23.1
	28.1		28.9	23.6	Inventory				21.2	26.5	18.1
	3.6		3.2	3.7	All Other Current				4.1	3.7	6.2
	75.3		77.0	73.7	Total Current				70.5	75.5	69.6
	16.1		13.9	17.5	Fixed Assets (net)				18.6	20.3	14.1
	6.2		6.0	4.9	Intangibles (net)				4.3	1.2	12.9
	2.5		3.1	4.0	All Other Non-Current				6.5	3.0	3.4
	100.0		100.0	100.0	Total				100.0	100.0	100.0
					LIABILITIES						
	14.2		11.5	14.6	Notes Payable-Short Term				15.2	5.8	1.0
	2.2		2.1	2.7	Cur. Mat.-L.T.D.				2.5	1.4	3.0
	18.3		14.1	15.7	Trade Payables				17.8	12.4	10.1
	.2		.5	.3	Income Taxes Payable				.2	1.0	.1
	8.5		8.9	9.3	All Other Current				7.6	10.4	14.6
	43.5		37.0	42.6	Total Current				43.3	31.1	28.7
	8.6		8.0	8.2	Long-Term Debt				8.0	9.5	7.8
	.1		.2	.5	Deferred Taxes				.4	.6	.7
	5.9		8.7	8.4	All Other Non-Current				4.7	5.9	2.2
	41.9		46.1	40.3	Net Worth				43.6	52.9	60.5
	100.0		100.0	100.0	Total Liabilties & Net Worth				100.0	100.0	100.0
					INCOME DATA						
	100.0		100.0	100.0	Net Sales				100.0	100.0	100.0
	32.6		31.0	30.0	Gross Profit				22.5	31.3	37.7
	24.0		22.3	26.9	Operating Expenses				21.1	25.4	27.6
	8.6		8.7	3.1	Operating Profit				1.4	5.9	10.1
	1.0		.9	1.1	All Other Expenses (net)				.7	.0	1.4
	7.7		7.8	2.1	Profit Before Taxes				.7	5.9	8.7
					RATIOS						
	2.8		3.9	3.6					3.6	3.7	7.6
	2.0		2.2	2.2	Current				1.6	3.4	2.4
	1.4		1.6	1.4					1.2	2.0	1.8
	1.9		2.2	2.5					2.4	3.2	3.1
	1.2		1.5	1.3	Quick				1.0	2.0	1.5
	.6		.7	.8					.7	.8	1.1
38	9.6	37	10.0	38 9.6		45 8.2	33 11.0	46 7.9			
55	6.6	45	8.2	46 7.9	Sales/Receivables	51 7.1	42 8.7	49 7.5			
64	5.7	54	6.8	57 6.5		78 4.7	47 7.8	54 6.7			
31	11.8	30	12.0	32 11.3		21 17.0	27 13.5	33 11.0			
58	6.3	63	5.8	53 6.9	Cost of Sales/Inventory	37 9.7	60 6.1	63 5.8			
81	4.5	91	4.0	87 4.2		69 5.3	104 3.5	92 4.0			
20	18.0	15	23.6	20 18.1		23 16.0	12 29.4	26 14.0			
30	12.2	22	16.3	32 11.2	Cost of Sales/Payables	35 10.5	29 12.5	36 10.2			
50	7.2	41	9.0	47 7.7		48 7.6	34 10.7	49 7.5			
	4.7		4.4	4.1					5.2	2.7	1.7
	7.4		5.6	6.4	Sales/Working Capital				8.7	4.2	4.9
	12.7		9.4	12.0					26.6	6.2	7.8
	39.4		23.4	22.1					14.1		
(38)	6.4	(35)	9.6	(41) 2.9	EBIT/Interest		(12) 3.1				
	2.0		3.5	-2.5			1.5				
	29.3		7.6	10.5							
(13)	4.4	(11)	5.1	(15) 3.7	Net Profit + Depr., Dep., Amort./Cur. Mat. L/T/D						
	2.4		1.5	1.8							
	.1		.2	.1					.3	.1	.2
	.3		.3	.3	Fixed/Worth				.4	.3	.2
	.9		.6	.8					1.1	.6	.5
	.7		.3	.5					.4	.5	.3
	1.3		1.1	1.1	Debt/Worth				2.0	1.0	.8
	4.8		3.0	2.6					4.1	1.8	2.6
	59.4		59.3	32.3					31.2	43.6	
(36)	39.3	(37)	32.9	(40) 11.5	% Profit Before Taxes/Tangible Net Worth		(11) 10.8			17.9	
	20.5		16.0	-2.9			1.9			-3.6	
	30.5		29.5	14.2					5.5	27.1	24.1
	14.7		13.1	3.8	% Profit Before Taxes/Total Assets				3.6	10.0	12.8
	4.0		4.4	-5.7					-.1	-2.2	1.2
	64.6		61.6	44.6					61.3	71.4	21.8
	16.9		21.5	16.9	Sales/Net Fixed Assets				22.3	12.7	16.8
	11.9		10.0	7.1					7.5	4.5	9.1
	3.2		3.0	2.9					3.0	2.9	2.5
	2.5		2.3	2.1	Sales/Total Assets				2.4	1.7	1.3
	1.7		1.7	1.4					1.9	1.2	.8
	.4		.3	.6					.3	.4	
(33)	.9	(32)	1.0	(41) 1.2	% Depr., Dep., Amort./Sales				1.6	(10) 1.5	
	1.9		2.0	2.7					3.0	2.3	
	2.4		2.8	1.6							
(13)	3.6	(10)	6.3	(18) 4.1	% Officers', Directors' Owners' Comp/Sales						
	14.5		11.9	12.9							
	1433960M		1580284M	1178867M	Net Sales ($)	1791M	8547M	22217M	90846M	186537M	868929M
	805272M		1018234M	884635M	Total Assets ($)	720M	5117M	9092M	39004M	118151M	712551M

© RMA 2010

M = $ thousand   MM = $ million
See Pages 9 through 22 for Explanation of Ratios and Data

Current Data Sorted by Assets   Comparative Historical Data

						Type of Statement		
	1	3	7	2		Unqualified	15	22
1	2	8	5			Reviewed	16	16
3	6	7				Compiled	15	12
	2	1	1			Tax Returns	8	7
	2	11	5	4	1	Other	32	41
	15 (4/1-9/30/09)		57 (10/1/09-3/31/10)				4/1/05-3/31/06	4/1/06-3/31/07
0-500M	500M-2MM	2-10MM	10-50MM	50-100MM	100-250MM		ALL	ALL
4	13	30	18	6	1	NUMBER OF STATEMENTS	86	98
%	%	%	%	%	%	ASSETS	%	%
	11.6	11.5	12.7			Cash & Equivalents	9.7	8.9
	35.1	23.4	28.4			Trade Receivables (net)	32.2	30.9
	27.0	31.8	27.3			Inventory	27.6	30.8
	5.2	3.6	2.2			All Other Current	2.6	2.8
	78.9	70.3	70.7			Total Current	72.1	73.4
	13.5	16.3	18.8			Fixed Assets (net)	18.3	16.8
	2.2	5.5	8.2			Intangibles (net)	3.2	4.2
	5.3	7.9	2.3			All Other Non-Current	6.3	5.7
	100.0	100.0	100.0			Total	100.0	100.0
						LIABILITIES		
	14.5	9.4	7.5			Notes Payable-Short Term	10.8	7.8
	1.6	2.1	4.0			Cur. Mat.-L.T.D.	2.0	2.5
	8.2	8.8	13.2			Trade Payables	15.2	15.3
	.0	.1	.1			Income Taxes Payable	.3	.3
	14.5	12.3	9.4			All Other Current	10.8	13.0
	38.8	32.7	34.1			Total Current	39.2	39.0
	13.8	8.0	7.6			Long-Term Debt	9.7	12.2
	.0	.3	.3			Deferred Taxes	.2	.2
	4.6	5.5	8.3			All Other Non-Current	7.4	6.7
	42.8	53.5	49.7			Net Worth	43.4	42.0
	100.0	100.0	100.0			Total Liabilities & Net Worth	100.0	100.0
						INCOME DATA		
	100.0	100.0	100.0			Net Sales	100.0	100.0
	36.6	37.2	35.4			Gross Profit	37.5	34.5
	34.8	33.5	26.2			Operating Expenses	31.3	27.7
	1.9	3.6	9.2			Operating Profit	6.2	6.8
	.4	.8	1.5			All Other Expenses (net)	.6	.5
	1.5	2.9	7.6			Profit Before Taxes	5.6	6.3
						RATIOS		
	4.5	5.4	4.0			Current	3.5	2.9
	2.0	2.1	2.3				1.9	1.9
	1.4	1.4	1.4				1.3	1.4
	1.9	3.1	2.3			Quick	1.9	1.6
	1.3	1.1	1.3				1.0	1.0
	.8	.6	.8				.7	.6
	32 11.3	29 12.5	43 8.4			Sales/Receivables	42 8.7	39 9.3
	46 8.0	43 8.5	59 6.2				52 7.0	49 7.4
	59 6.2	52 7.0	62 5.9				65 5.6	65 5.6
	1 270.0	57 6.4	58 6.3			Cost of Sales/Inventory	40 9.1	39 9.4
	73 5.0	95 3.8	99 3.7				88 4.1	88 4.2
	146 2.5	184 2.0	113 3.2				133 2.7	145 2.5
	7 51.5	9 38.6	16 23.0			Cost of Sales/Payables	17 21.5	20 18.6
	15 23.9	18 20.0	26 13.9				35 10.3	33 11.1
	31 11.9	36 10.1	43 8.4				56 6.5	54 6.8
	4.5	3.4	3.7			Sales/Working Capital	3.7	3.6
	7.0	4.5	5.0				6.8	6.7
	14.8	10.5	9.8				15.4	13.1
	9.0	20.0	22.2			EBIT/Interest	17.1	16.6
	(12) 2.5	(25) 2.1	(17) 8.3				(76) 6.6	(85) 4.9
	-4.5	-2.0	2.4				1.4	1.9
						Net Profit + Depr., Dep., Amort./Cur. Mat. L/T/D	9.6	15.3
							(25) 3.2	(32) 3.4
							1.5	1.3
	.0	.2	.2			Fixed/Worth	.2	.2
	.1	.3	.5				.4	.4
	.5	.9	.8				1.0	1.0
	.6	.3	.4			Debt/Worth	.5	.6
	1.0	1.0	.8				1.4	1.4
	3.2	1.9	3.9				3.2	3.6
	25.7	42.5	47.2			% Profit Before Taxes/Tangible Net Worth	49.0	56.4
	(12) 16.8	(27) 9.3	(17) 25.3				(77) 21.8	(86) 21.2
	-8.9	-4.6	13.5				3.0	7.5
	14.4	13.1	26.8			% Profit Before Taxes/Total Assets	19.9	18.1
	3.7	3.0	9.6				8.4	7.9
	-1.8	-4.1	3.5				.8	2.6
	131.8	42.3	27.0			Sales/Net Fixed Assets	33.6	34.1
	36.4	14.0	9.8				13.0	15.1
	13.4	7.2	6.2				6.9	7.8
	4.3	3.0	2.2			Sales/Total Assets	2.7	2.7
	2.5	2.0	1.8				2.0	2.0
	2.0	1.3	1.4				1.6	1.5
	.4	.5	.9			% Depr., Dep., Amort./Sales	.8	.8
	(11) .8	(28) 1.4	(17) 1.7				(69) 1.6	(82) 1.6
	1.6	2.7	2.8				2.6	2.6
						% Officers', Directors' Owners' Comp/Sales	3.0	2.8
							(27) 5.4	(24) 5.8
							10.3	10.0
5071M	49062M	302653M	620553M	490937M	141641M	Net Sales ($)	3043225M	3421537M
1072M	15972M	146504M	361651M	428725M	102433M	Total Assets ($)	1687821M	2010419M

M = $ thousand   MM = $ million
See Pages 9 through 22 for Explanation of Ratios and Data

Comparative Historical Data   Current Data Sorted by Sales

Type of Statement	4/1/07-3/31/08 ALL	4/1/08-3/31/09 ALL	4/1/09-3/31/10 ALL	0-1MM	1-3MM	3-5MM	5-10MM	10-25MM	25MM & OVER
					15 (4/1-9/30/09)			57 (10/1/09-3/31/10)	
Unqualified	19	15	13				3	1	9
Reviewed	14	18	16	1	1		5	6	3
Compiled	11	11	13	1	1	5	6		
Tax Returns	2	8	7	1	3	1	1	1	
Other	27	25	23		3	3	2	6	9
NUMBER OF STATEMENTS	73	77	72	3	8	9	17	14	21
ASSETS	%	%	%	%	%	%	%	%	%
Cash & Equivalents	10.6	9.8	13.4				13.5	8.5	13.9
Trade Receivables (net)	30.9	29.1	26.6				24.4	29.0	23.5
Inventory	27.4	29.4	28.6				26.1	33.1	27.1
All Other Current	3.9	4.5	3.5				8.4	.6	3.3
Total Current	72.9	72.9	72.1				72.4	71.1	67.9
Fixed Assets (net)	16.6	14.5	16.1				13.5	23.7	16.5
Intangibles (net)	4.7	6.4	6.4				6.9	3.4	12.0
All Other Non-Current	5.8	6.3	5.4				7.2	1.8	3.7
Total	100.0	100.0	100.0				100.0	100.0	100.0
LIABILITIES									
Notes Payable-Short Term	7.9	10.1	9.5				8.4	9.3	7.3
Cur. Mat.-L.T.D.	2.2	3.6	2.6				1.5	1.5	3.4
Trade Payables	11.5	12.5	10.5				5.0	12.0	13.9
Income Taxes Payable	.2	.3	.1				.1	.1	.0
All Other Current	13.9	12.5	11.8				14.3	8.7	10.1
Total Current	35.7	39.0	34.4				29.3	31.6	34.8
Long-Term Debt	11.1	8.9	9.9				5.2	8.3	9.0
Deferred Taxes	.3	.2	.3				.2	.2	.7
All Other Non-Current	3.4	6.5	7.2				4.5	4.5	13.0
Net Worth	49.5	45.3	48.2				60.8	55.5	42.5
Total Liabilties & Net Worth	100.0	100.0	100.0				100.0	100.0	100.0
INCOME DATA									
Net Sales	100.0	100.0	100.0				100.0	100.0	100.0
Gross Profit	32.4	32.5	35.9				37.5	32.5	32.2
Operating Expenses	25.0	26.9	30.9				34.5	24.2	25.1
Operating Profit	7.4	5.5	5.0				3.0	8.3	7.1
All Other Expenses (net)	.8	1.0	1.0				1.2	.5	1.7
Profit Before Taxes	6.6	4.5	4.0				1.7	7.8	5.3
RATIOS									
Current	3.2	3.4	4.2				5.1	4.5	3.7
Current	1.8	2.1	2.1				2.6	2.3	1.9
Current	1.5	1.4	1.4				1.4	1.8	1.4
Quick	1.7	2.1	2.4				2.8	3.5	2.3
Quick	1.1	.9	1.3				1.4	1.2	.8
Quick	.7	.6	.7				.8	.8	.7
Sales/Receivables	42 8.6	37 9.8	37 10.0				29 12.6	36 10.2	41 9.0
Sales/Receivables	53 6.9	46 7.9	47 7.7				41 8.9	49 7.4	50 7.2
Sales/Receivables	66 5.5	61 6.0	59 6.1				48 7.5	63 5.8	59 6.2
Cost of Sales/Inventory	38 9.6	43 8.5	50 7.3				1 418.7	58 6.3	57 6.4
Cost of Sales/Inventory	79 4.6	82 4.4	95 3.8				94 3.9	92 4.0	103 3.5
Cost of Sales/Inventory	118 3.1	117 3.1	132 2.8				208 1.8	112 3.3	121 3.0
Cost of Sales/Payables	16 22.8	15 23.7	13 29.1				6 62.2	12 30.9	20 18.4
Cost of Sales/Payables	30 12.0	28 13.1	23 15.9				14 26.8	24 15.2	29 12.5
Cost of Sales/Payables	40 9.2	40 9.0	40 9.0				22 16.5	36 10.0	43 8.5
Sales/Working Capital	3.9	4.2	3.7				3.6	3.1	3.7
Sales/Working Capital	5.7	5.9	5.1				4.7	5.0	5.2
Sales/Working Capital	9.1	13.3	10.8				9.1	11.2	11.4
EBIT/Interest	14.1	24.4	18.4				89.5	11.5	19.9
EBIT/Interest	(62) 5.3	(67) 5.9	(61) 2.7				(16) 6.8	(10) 4.6	(19) 4.3
EBIT/Interest	1.3	1.7	.5				-.2	-.2	.5
Net Profit + Depr., Dep., Amort./Cur. Mat. L/T/D	9.4	9.4	11.8						
Net Profit + Depr., Dep., Amort./Cur. Mat. L/T/D	(14) 4.6	(21) 3.2	(17) 4.5						
Net Profit + Depr., Dep., Amort./Cur. Mat. L/T/D	1.7	.6	.2						
Fixed/Worth	.1	.1	.1				.1	.3	.2
Fixed/Worth	.4	.4	.4				.2	.5	.4
Fixed/Worth	.7	1.1	.9				.5	.8	1.8
Debt/Worth	.5	.4	.4				.3	.3	.4
Debt/Worth	1.2	1.2	1.0				.9	.8	2.5
Debt/Worth	2.1	3.3	3.5				1.5	1.8	6.4
% Profit Before Taxes/Tangible Net Worth	48.0	45.0	38.6				13.4	56.4	56.6
% Profit Before Taxes/Tangible Net Worth	(69) 25.2	(67) 22.8	(64) 13.7				(16) 8.8	(13) 16.8	(18) 24.1
% Profit Before Taxes/Tangible Net Worth	9.8	5.3	-.3				-7.4	-.2	.8
% Profit Before Taxes/Total Assets	19.7	18.4	16.1				9.7	29.7	15.2
% Profit Before Taxes/Total Assets	11.3	6.3	4.6				3.5	9.2	7.5
% Profit Before Taxes/Total Assets	2.4	1.0	-.2				-5.8	.0	-.3
Sales/Net Fixed Assets	44.3	54.3	40.7				38.9	27.0	26.7
Sales/Net Fixed Assets	15.9	19.2	16.2				18.1	9.5	10.2
Sales/Net Fixed Assets	7.0	9.2	7.2				10.7	5.4	6.6
Sales/Total Assets	2.7	2.8	2.8				3.0	3.1	2.2
Sales/Total Assets	2.1	2.2	1.9				2.2	2.2	1.6
Sales/Total Assets	1.4	1.5	1.4				1.3	1.5	1.2
% Depr., Dep., Amort./Sales	.8	.6	.6				.4	.6	.8
% Depr., Dep., Amort./Sales	(62) 1.3	(62) 1.4	(64) 1.4				1.2	(12) 1.8	(19) 1.7
% Depr., Dep., Amort./Sales	2.4	2.2	2.4				2.1	2.1	3.0
% Officers', Directors' Owners' Comp/Sales	2.8	3.1	2.5						
% Officers', Directors' Owners' Comp/Sales	(20) 4.8	(27) 6.7	(24) 5.1						
% Officers', Directors' Owners' Comp/Sales	9.6	10.3	11.2						
Net Sales ($)	2115855M	2395640M	1609917M	1616M	13767M	36623M	128040M	234251M	1195620M
Total Assets ($)	1332757M	1383535M	1056357M	2376M	13925M	14286M	70373M	117388M	838009M

M = $ thousand   MM = $ million
See Pages 9 through 22 for Explanation of Ratios and Data

Current Data Sorted by Assets | **Comparative Historical Data**

0-500M	500M-2MM	2-10MM	10-50MM	50-100MM	100-250MM	Type of Statement	4/1/05-3/31/06 ALL	4/1/06-3/31/07 ALL
		3	5	3	4	Unqualified	22	19
	2	6	3			Reviewed	15	14
	5	4	2			Compiled	7	8
		3	1			Tax Returns	4	7
	4	6		2	5	Other	30	33
	7 (4/1-9/30/09)		56 (10/1/09-3/31/10)					
	11	22	16	5	9	NUMBER OF STATEMENTS	78	81
%	%	%	%	%	%	**ASSETS**	%	%
	13.6	6.9	14.4			Cash & Equivalents	6.7	6.9
	30.1	20.9	23.7			Trade Receivables (net)	31.8	34.0
	35.5	36.4	21.2			Inventory	29.5	29.5
	.4	3.3	1.2			All Other Current	1.6	1.9
	79.5	67.4	60.5			Total Current	69.5	72.3
	10.7	19.6	22.4			Fixed Assets (net)	18.3	16.9
	5.5	5.3	6.9			Intangibles (net)	5.7	6.0
	4.3	7.7	10.2			All Other Non-Current	6.5	4.8
	100.0	100.0	100.0			Total	100.0	100.0
						LIABILITIES		
	11.7	8.9	5.5			Notes Payable-Short Term	10.9	8.9
	1.7	5.1	2.0			Cur. Mat.-L.T.D.	3.7	3.3
	14.8	13.0	9.7			Trade Payables	16.7	19.1
	.0	.1	.1			Income Taxes Payable	.4	.4
	11.2	8.1	9.2			All Other Current	7.6	10.7
	39.5	35.3	26.5			Total Current	39.3	42.4
	4.4	14.6	12.7			Long-Term Debt	11.6	11.1
	.2	.7	3.0			Deferred Taxes	.5	.4
	3.9	4.0	6.2			All Other Non-Current	5.9	4.2
	52.1	45.5	51.6			Net Worth	42.8	42.0
	100.0	100.0	100.0			Total Liabilities & Net Worth	100.0	100.0
						INCOME DATA		
	100.0	100.0	100.0			Net Sales	100.0	100.0
	31.4	29.4	31.6			Gross Profit	27.7	27.0
	27.0	24.6	22.5			Operating Expenses	22.3	20.3
	4.4	4.9	9.1			Operating Profit	5.4	6.7
	.2	1.0	1.7			All Other Expenses (net)	.7	1.0
	4.3	3.8	7.4			Profit Before Taxes	4.6	5.7
						RATIOS		
	3.7	4.3	3.8				2.8	2.5
	2.4	1.8	2.6			Current	1.9	1.9
	1.1	1.1	1.5				1.3	1.3
	1.8	2.2	2.3				1.5	1.4
	1.2	.7	1.6			Quick	1.0	1.0
	.7	.2	.7				.7	.7

Data not available for 0-500M column (ASSETS through RATIOS/Quick).

RATIOS (with count columns)

	500M-2MM		2-10MM		10-50MM	Ratio		Hist 4/1/05-3/31/06		Hist 4/1/06-3/31/07
22	16.4	22	16.6	41	9.0		41	8.9	37	9.9
31	11.9	37	9.9	46	8.0	Sales/Receivables	53	7.0	51	7.2
57	6.4	51	7.1	59	6.2		67	5.4	68	5.4
32	11.3	70	5.2	40	9.1		43	8.5	45	8.2
91	4.0	100	3.6	61	6.0	Cost of Sales/Inventory	65	5.6	67	5.5
118	3.1	159	2.3	82	4.4		100	3.6	92	4.0
12	29.5	19	19.0	9	41.6		24	14.9	22	16.4
26	13.9	27	13.4	23	15.8	Cost of Sales/Payables	31	11.8	35	10.5
42	8.7	45	8.2	34	10.8		48	7.6	46	8.0
	3.9		3.5		3.5			5.0		4.4
	6.3		7.0		4.5	Sales/Working Capital		7.8		7.5
	47.0		41.5		12.2			18.9		24.1
			15.0		25.4			12.4		15.5
		(19)	4.7	(12)	3.9	EBIT/Interest	(68)	5.3	(71)	5.9
			1.5		1.3			1.9		2.0
						Net Profit + Depr., Dep.,		11.1		11.0
						Amort./Cur. Mat. L/T/D	(24)	2.8	(21)	6.5
								1.7		2.0
	.1		.1		.2			.2		.2
	.2		.3		.7	Fixed/Worth		.5		.5
	.5		1.4		1.3			.8		1.0
	.5		.5		.4			.6		.6
	1.0		1.5		1.0	Debt/Worth		1.4		1.3
	2.3		4.8		4.0			3.9		6.1
	69.7		39.5		41.2			41.4		49.1
(10)	10.3	(20)	15.3	(14)	26.0	% Profit Before Taxes/Tangible Net Worth	(68)	25.3	(69)	29.9
	-8.6		1.3		7.8			5.1		12.4
	24.9		18.2		18.4			17.4		19.5
	7.4		5.0		7.6	% Profit Before Taxes/Total Assets		7.7		11.4
	-.2		1.0		3.5			1.3		3.4
	72.3		37.5		24.3			28.9		38.9
	35.1		13.6		7.7	Sales/Net Fixed Assets		14.7		14.3
	25.2		5.2		4.3			8.1		7.9
	3.9		2.6		2.1			2.9		3.0
	2.7		2.1		1.6	Sales/Total Assets		2.2		2.4
	2.3		1.3		1.4			1.6		1.7
			.6		.7			.9		.7
		(20)	2.0	(13)	2.5	% Depr., Dep., Amort./Sales	(69)	1.5	(60)	1.4
			3.5		4.1			2.3		2.0
						% Officers', Directors'		2.0		1.6
						Owners' Comp/Sales	(24)	5.1	(20)	3.8
								7.8		6.4

0-500M	500M-2MM	2-10MM	10-50MM	50-100MM	100-250MM		Hist	Hist
47956M	277323M	635945M	443013M	2865308M		Net Sales ($)	3827053M	5021621M
15718M	118807M	356580M	329474M	1659312M		Total Assets ($)	2054512M	2669163M

© RMA 2010

M = $ thousand   MM = $ million
See Pages 9 through 22 for Explanation of Ratios and Data

Comparative Historical Data   ## Current Data Sorted by Sales

Type of Statement

4/1/07-3/31/08	4/1/08-3/31/09	4/1/09-3/31/10	Type of Statement	0-1MM	1-3MM	3-5MM	5-10MM	10-25MM	25MM & OVER
14	15	15	Unqualified			2		3	10
10	10	11	Reviewed		2	1	4	2	4
7	8	11	Compiled	2	1	2	2	2	3
2	1	4	Tax Returns	1	2	1	2	2	
21	21	22	Other		3	4	1	2	12
4/1/07-3/31/08 ALL	4/1/08-3/31/09 ALL	4/1/09-3/31/10 ALL			7 (4/1-9/30/09)		56 (10/1/09-3/31/10)		
54	55	63	NUMBER OF STATEMENTS		5	8	11	10	29

(Columns 0-1MM, 1-3MM and 3-5MM are marked **DATA NOT AVAILABLE** for the common-size statements and ratios below.)

4/1/07-3/31/08 ALL	4/1/08-3/31/09 ALL	4/1/09-3/31/10 ALL		5-10MM	10-25MM	25MM & OVER
%	%	%	**ASSETS**	%	%	%
7.8	10.7	10.6	Cash & Equivalents	11.0	5.2	13.8
30.9	27.6	23.9	Trade Receivables (net)	26.3	24.5	25.0
33.0	31.3	29.3	Inventory	32.6	34.9	23.4
2.2	2.5	2.1	All Other Current	3.2	2.1	2.1
74.0	72.1	65.9	Total Current	73.1	66.6	64.3
16.8	16.1	20.2	Fixed Assets (net)	19.1	20.7	21.9
4.7	5.3	6.5	Intangibles (net)	.5	3.6	7.9
4.4	6.5	7.4	All Other Non-Current	7.2	9.1	5.8
100.0	100.0	100.0	Total	100.0	100.0	100.0
			LIABILITIES			
11.8	9.1	7.4	Notes Payable-Short Term	8.3	14.3	4.7
2.1	1.9	3.6	Cur. Mat.-L.T.D.	3.8	2.5	2.8
17.7	15.0	12.1	Trade Payables	10.7	14.3	11.6
.3	.1	.1	Income Taxes Payable	.1	.0	.3
7.6	9.3	8.9	All Other Current	7.3	7.9	8.7
39.6	35.4	32.2	Total Current	30.3	38.9	28.1
10.5	11.3	10.3	Long-Term Debt	17.6	14.4	5.8
.4	.2	1.0	Deferred Taxes	.4	.4	1.7
4.8	3.2	6.2	All Other Non-Current	2.1	4.4	9.0
44.8	49.9	50.2	Net Worth	49.7	41.9	55.4
100.0	100.0	100.0	Total Liabilities & Net Worth	100.0	100.0	100.0
			INCOME DATA			
100.0	100.0	100.0	Net Sales	100.0	100.0	100.0
27.6	29.8	30.4	Gross Profit	31.2	32.3	27.2
21.9	23.8	25.1	Operating Expenses	28.4	28.7	21.2
5.7	6.0	5.4	Operating Profit	2.8	3.6	6.1
.9	.4	1.0	All Other Expenses (net)	1.9	.9	.6
4.8	5.5	4.4	Profit Before Taxes	.9	2.7	5.4
			RATIOS			
2.7 / 2.0 / 1.4	3.3 / 2.2 / 1.5	3.7 / 2.2 / 1.3	Current	6.3 / 4.1 / 1.3	2.7 / 1.7 / 1.1	3.5 / 2.4 / 1.7
1.6 / 1.1 / .6	1.7 / 1.1 / .7	2.2 / 1.2 / .6	Quick	2.3 / 2.2 / .7	1.4 / .7 / .4	2.2 / 1.3 / .9
40 9.1 / 48 7.6 / 58 6.3	28 13.1 / 40 9.1 / 49 7.5	33 11.1 / 46 7.9 / 52 7.0	Sales/Receivables	29 12.7 / 39 9.5 / 51 7.1	27 13.3 / 41 8.9 / 52 7.0	41 9.0 / 49 7.4 / 60 6.1
51 7.1 / 71 5.1 / 106 3.5	43 8.5 / 66 5.5 / 105 3.5	53 6.9 / 84 4.3 / 118 3.1	Cost of Sales/Inventory	32 11.3 / 84 4.3 / 104 3.5	56 6.5 / 94 3.9 / 125 2.9	53 6.8 / 65 5.6 / 101 3.6
24 15.4 / 32 11.6 / 44 8.4	17 22.0 / 29 12.7 / 42 8.6	17 21.0 / 28 13.2 / 43 8.4	Cost of Sales/Payables	12 29.5 / 18 20.3 / 43 8.4	25 14.6 / 34 10.7 / 43 8.4	13 27.6 / 29 12.6 / 43 8.4
4.6 / 7.4 / 12.5	4.5 / 7.2 / 14.8	3.6 / 6.2 / 13.0	Sales/Working Capital	3.2 / 6.3 / 10.7	4.0 / 8.9 / 41.5	3.0 / 4.9 / 9.9
21.3 / (49) 4.5 / 1.8	36.6 / (47) 7.2 / 1.8	16.9 / (54) 4.4 / .4	EBIT/Interest		(25) 4.6	35.2 / 4.6 / -.4
8.3 / (20) 3.6 / 2.2	8.5 / (19) 3.4 / 1.3	8.0 / (19) 2.9 / .2	Net Profit + Depr., Dep., Amort./Cur. Mat. L/T/D		(10) 4.0	7.5 / 4.0 / 1.8
.2 / .3 / .9	.1 / .3 / .8	.2 / .5 / .9	Fixed/Worth	.1 / .3 / .9	.1 / .7 / 1.5	.2 / .5 / .9
.6 / 1.5 / 3.9	.5 / 1.2 / 2.4	.5 / 1.1 / 3.3	Debt/Worth	.3 / 1.1 / 2.3	.7 / 1.6 / 4.8	.4 / 1.0 / 2.0
47.1 / (49) 22.3 / 7.1	54.4 / (52) 21.6 / 6.4	39.9 / (57) 14.8 / -1.4	% Profit Before Taxes/Tangible Net Worth	18.0 / (10) 5.0 / -38.2	40.9 / 13.4 / -17.4	42.7 / (27) 25.7 / -2.4
22.6 / 9.3 / 2.8	27.6 / 11.9 / 2.8	18.7 / 5.9 / -.2	% Profit Before Taxes/Total Assets	14.5 / 1.1 / -10.0	11.8 / 6.2 / -2.5	19.8 / 7.4 / -.6
40.3 / 13.4 / 9.0	57.8 / 16.0 / 8.7	34.6 / 12.0 / 5.1	Sales/Net Fixed Assets	41.5 / 24.2 / 5.1	45.0 / 11.8 / 5.4	17.8 / 8.1 / 4.5
3.0 / 2.3 / 1.7	3.5 / 2.5 / 1.9	2.4 / 2.0 / 1.4	Sales/Total Assets	3.9 / 2.5 / 1.4	2.4 / 2.1 / 1.8	2.1 / 1.7 / 1.4
.7 / (45) 1.6 / 2.1	.7 / (47) 1.0 / 2.3	.9 / (52) 2.1 / 3.4	% Depr., Dep., Amort./Sales		(23) 2.0	.8 / 2.0 / 3.4
1.8 / (20) 3.4 / 5.5	2.8 / (15) 4.2 / 8.0	2.7 / (19) 4.4 / 7.0	% Officers', Directors' Owners' Comp/Sales			
3826778M	4308514M	4269545M	Net Sales ($)	11905M (1-3MM) · 31124M (3-5MM) · 77372M	154836M	3994308M
2011654M	1940061M	2479891M	Total Assets ($)	10683M (1-3MM) · 20685M (3-5MM) · 44552M	78038M	2325933M

© RMA 2010

M = $ thousand   MM = $ million
See Pages 9 through 22 for Explanation of Ratios and Data

Current Data Sorted by Assets | **Comparative Historical Data**

						Type of Statement		
1	1	11	20	7	6	Unqualified	50	45
	5	27	5		1	Reviewed	30	30
1	12	14	1			Compiled	18	19
9	15	7	2			Tax Returns	14	28
5	14	42	25	6	9	Other	86	78
	36 (4/1-9/30/09)		210 (10/1/09-3/31/10)				4/1/05-3/31/06	4/1/06-3/31/07
0-500M	500M-2MM	2-10MM	10-50MM	50-100MM	100-250MM		ALL	ALL
16	47	101	53	14	15	NUMBER OF STATEMENTS	198	200
%	%	%	%	%	%	ASSETS	%	%
15.2	9.6	10.8	9.2	12.0	8.9	Cash & Equivalents	9.9	8.9
36.2	26.8	26.1	26.6	21.2	22.6	Trade Receivables (net)	30.7	31.7
22.1	36.7	30.8	27.6	21.3	18.0	Inventory	29.9	28.6
3.5	2.8	3.1	3.8	7.5	6.0	All Other Current	2.0	3.4
77.0	75.9	70.8	67.2	62.1	55.6	Total Current	72.5	72.6
11.4	12.7	17.8	19.4	20.1	24.1	Fixed Assets (net)	15.4	16.1
5.2	5.1	6.5	9.0	13.0	15.0	Intangibles (net)	6.3	5.0
6.5	6.3	4.9	4.3	4.9	5.3	All Other Non-Current	5.8	6.3
100.0	100.0	100.0	100.0	100.0	100.0	Total	100.0	100.0
						LIABILITIES		
22.7	14.8	11.6	7.0	3.2	2.5	Notes Payable-Short Term	11.9	9.6
9.3	2.6	2.8	2.3	5.7	1.5	Cur. Mat.-L.T.D.	2.2	2.3
17.0	16.8	14.2	11.4	13.2	11.9	Trade Payables	17.1	16.3
.0	.3	.1	.6	1.1	.1	Income Taxes Payable	.4	.4
15.2	9.6	11.1	13.6	15.7	15.1	All Other Current	11.4	11.1
64.2	44.1	40.0	34.8	38.8	31.0	Total Current	43.0	39.7
15.4	7.3	13.3	12.5	11.1	18.2	Long-Term Debt	10.9	10.8
.0	.1	.2	.7	.8	.3	Deferred Taxes	.4	.3
6.1	10.0	3.7	4.5	4.1	5.6	All Other Non-Current	5.6	5.6
14.3	38.5	42.9	47.5	45.3	44.8	Net Worth	40.1	43.7
100.0	100.0	100.0	100.0	100.0	100.0	Total Liabilities & Net Worth	100.0	100.0
						INCOME DATA		
100.0	100.0	100.0	100.0	100.0	100.0	Net Sales	100.0	100.0
47.5	38.7	33.9	31.2	32.5	26.3	Gross Profit	34.1	34.1
41.3	34.0	30.4	25.5	29.0	22.0	Operating Expenses	28.6	26.4
6.2	4.7	3.5	5.7	3.6	4.3	Operating Profit	5.5	7.7
1.0	.6	1.0	.9	3.7	4.8	All Other Expenses (net)	1.3	.7
5.2	4.1	2.5	4.8	-.1	-.6	Profit Before Taxes	4.2	6.9
						RATIOS		
2.0	3.2	3.1	3.5	2.5	3.6	Current	2.8	3.0
1.3	1.6	1.9	2.0	1.7	2.1		1.7	1.9
.8	1.2	1.2	1.4	1.3	1.1		1.3	1.3
1.3	1.4	1.6	1.8	1.5	1.9	Quick	1.5	1.7
.8	.8	.9	1.1	1.0	1.3		.9	1.1
.4	.5	.5	.6	.6	.6		.6	.7
7 53.7	23 16.1	30 12.3	41 8.9	38 9.7	49 7.4	Sales/Receivables	38 9.5	35 10.4
39 9.4	35 10.5	43 8.5	52 7.0	54 6.7	54 6.8		51 7.2	47 7.8
48 7.6	46 7.9	55 6.6	64 5.7	69 5.3	70 5.2		66 5.6	64 5.7
0 UND	39 9.4	44 8.2	50 7.4	50 7.3	44 8.4	Cost of Sales/Inventory	46 7.9	33 11.2
21 17.8	75 4.9	82 4.5	82 4.4	95 3.8	72 5.1		83 4.4	74 5.0
75 4.9	136 2.7	118 3.1	116 3.2	118 3.1	98 3.7		121 3.0	115 3.2
6 64.3	18 20.7	18 20.4	19 18.8	31 11.9	22 16.8	Cost of Sales/Payables	21 17.2	19 19.0
25 14.4	31 11.7	29 12.8	31 11.9	44 8.3	40 9.1		37 9.9	34 10.7
56 6.5	55 6.7	44 8.2	47 7.8	61 6.0	52 7.0		55 6.6	50 7.3
9.3	4.4	3.9	3.3	3.3	2.9	Sales/Working Capital	4.3	4.1
28.7	8.3	7.8	5.9	5.0	5.5		7.0	6.9
-29.6	17.8	18.0	9.6	18.8	32.5		17.0	13.8
17.5	17.5	15.8	21.9	6.4	3.7	EBIT/Interest	16.4	19.4
(13) 3.6	(44) 4.7	(90) 5.2	(48) 5.2	(13) .4	(13) 1.9		(169) 4.1	(177) 6.8
1.5	1.0	1.1	1.3	-6.0	-.6		1.6	2.8
		4.7	9.6			Net Profit + Depr., Dep., Amort./Cur. Mat. L/T/D	14.0	14.7
	(19) 2.4	(18) 2.3					(51) 3.5	(53) 3.9
		1.1	.6				1.8	2.0
.1	.1	.1	.2	.3	.3	Fixed/Worth	.1	.1
1.0	.3	.4	.4	.5	.8		.4	.3
-3.7	.9	1.4	1.2	.7	-5.7		1.0	.7
1.9	.5	.7	.5	1.0	.8	Debt/Worth	.6	.6
6.5	1.9	1.5	1.1	1.5	2.3		1.7	1.3
-30.3	4.4	4.5	3.1	NM	-11.2		5.4	3.3
262.6	39.9	45.6	46.0	25.7	32.2	% Profit Before Taxes/Tangible Net Worth	42.3	57.6
(10) 50.7	(41) 16.6	(92) 22.7	(47) 18.3	(11) -7.2	(11) 5.9		(167) 19.5	(183) 30.5
19.9	1.5	4.8	2.3	-12.4	.1		5.8	11.0
46.3	15.8	16.0	17.6	6.7	7.4	% Profit Before Taxes/Total Assets	14.7	23.7
11.3	7.3	6.4	6.3	-.6	1.1		7.9	11.1
4.0	.2	.8	1.0	-4.8	-4.4		1.7	3.6
444.8	85.8	48.0	25.7	14.1	17.5	Sales/Net Fixed Assets	43.1	51.4
98.5	39.7	17.1	10.4	6.8	6.1		18.1	18.8
19.1	13.2	8.0	5.3	3.9	3.5		8.2	8.5
6.7	3.7	2.8	2.2	1.7	1.8	Sales/Total Assets	2.8	3.1
4.5	2.8	2.1	1.6	1.2	1.5		2.0	2.3
2.9	1.9	1.7	1.2	1.0	.8		1.3	1.6
	.4	.7	.7	2.8	1.3	% Depr., Dep., Amort./Sales	.7	.8
	(32) 1.1	(80) 1.4	(47) 2.1	(12) 3.7	2.2		(162) 1.4	(167) 1.4
	2.7	3.0	3.3	4.9	5.2		2.5	2.5
4.3	3.2	1.6				% Officers', Directors' Owners' Comp/Sales	2.3	2.2
(12) 7.3	(26) 5.9	(31) 3.4					(61) 4.6	(68) 4.5
13.3	11.3	5.0					7.6	7.9
27707M	165295M	1122829M	2327440M	1418826M	3338884M	Net Sales ($)	6343230M	7012109M
5003M	58473M	513615M	1245576M	1000421M	2155209M	Total Assets ($)	4319960M	3844307M

© RMA 2010

M = $ thousand   MM = $ million

See Pages 9 through 22 for Explanation of Ratios and Data

Comparative Historical Data | Current Data Sorted by Sales

			Type of Statement		36 (4/1-9/30/09)		210 (10/1/09-3/31/10)		
				0-1MM	1-3MM	3-5MM	5-10MM	10-25MM	25MM & OVER
35	35	46	Unqualified	1		1	4	14	26
43	31	38	Reviewed		3	2	14	15	4
28	21	28	Compiled	1	4	10	7	5	1
26	33	33	Tax Returns	1	14	5	9	2	2
94	108	101	Other	4	7	12	26	19	33
4/1/07-3/31/08 ALL	4/1/08-3/31/09 ALL	4/1/09-3/31/10 ALL							
226	228	246	**NUMBER OF STATEMENTS**	7	28	30	60	55	66
%	%	%	**ASSETS**	%	%	%	%	%	%
9.4	8.7	10.5	Cash & Equivalents		13.3	10.6	7.3	13.7	10.3
30.7	30.2	26.5	Trade Receivables (net)		27.5	23.2	27.2	26.3	27.2
28.5	31.5	29.4	Inventory		33.0	37.5	26.2	31.8	25.3
3.3	3.0	3.6	All Other Current		4.4	3.2	3.0	2.0	5.0
71.9	73.4	70.0	Total Current		78.1	74.5	63.8	73.8	67.8
15.7	15.5	17.3	Fixed Assets (net)		13.0	11.3	22.0	15.4	19.1
7.1	6.1	7.6	Intangibles (net)		4.0	8.9	8.3	5.8	9.2
5.3	5.0	5.2	All Other Non-Current		4.8	5.2	5.9	5.0	3.9
100.0	100.0	100.0	Total		100.0	100.0	100.0	100.0	100.0
			LIABILITIES						
11.2	12.7	10.9	Notes Payable-Short Term		13.9	14.2	14.7	8.0	5.1
2.6	2.4	3.2	Cur. Mat.-L.T.D.		3.8	5.8	3.2	2.4	2.6
15.1	15.8	14.1	Trade Payables		14.6	16.8	12.3	14.3	13.8
.5	.3	.3	Income Taxes Payable		.1	.4	.1	.4	.6
11.4	11.1	12.1	All Other Current		9.8	9.5	9.8	14.8	13.8
40.8	42.2	40.6	Total Current		42.3	46.6	40.1	39.9	35.9
12.3	11.9	12.3	Long-Term Debt		12.7	10.0	17.4	6.8	13.7
.4	.4	.3	Deferred Taxes		.0	.1	.1	.6	.5
6.9	7.0	5.3	All Other Non-Current		16.4	2.3	4.3	3.3	4.8
39.5	38.5	41.4	Net Worth		28.7	41.0	38.1	49.5	45.1
100.0	100.0	100.0	Total Liabilities & Net Worth		100.0	100.0	100.0	100.0	100.0
			INCOME DATA						
100.0	100.0	100.0	Net Sales		100.0	100.0	100.0	100.0	100.0
36.0	33.7	34.6	Gross Profit		40.6	39.0	36.3	32.8	27.8
28.7	28.1	30.1	Operating Expenses		39.8	35.4	32.2	26.4	23.2
7.3	5.6	4.4	Operating Profit		.8	3.6	4.1	6.4	4.6
1.6	1.3	1.3	All Other Expenses (net)		.6	1.0	1.3	.5	2.3
5.7	4.3	3.2	Profit Before Taxes		.3	2.6	2.8	5.9	2.3
			RATIOS						
3.2	3.0	3.1	Current		4.2	2.9	3.1	3.2	3.2
2.0	1.8	1.8			2.1	1.6	1.6	1.9	2.0
1.3	1.2	1.2			1.2	1.3	1.1	1.3	1.5
1.9	1.7	1.7	Quick		2.0	1.4	1.6	1.7	1.7
1.1	.9	.9			.9	.8	.9	1.0	1.1
.6	.6	.5			.5	.4	.5	.6	.7
34 10.6	33 11.1	32 11.6	Sales/Receivables	24 15.1	22 16.6	29 12.5	35 10.4	39 9.3	
48 7.6	44 8.4	44 8.3		38 9.5	35 10.4	43 8.5	44 8.3	54 6.8	
62 5.9	56 6.5	59 6.2		60 6.1	48 7.6	55 6.6	56 6.5	64 5.7	
43 8.5	48 7.6	44 8.4	Cost of Sales/Inventory	29 12.5	62 5.9	41 8.9	38 9.6	45 8.2	
75 4.9	76 4.8	75 4.9		103 3.5	89 4.1	67 5.5	89 4.1	72 5.1	
123 3.0	113 3.2	115 3.2		202 1.8	116 3.2	114 3.2	138 2.6	101 3.6	
18 20.1	18 19.7	19 19.3	Cost of Sales/Payables	18 20.7	20 18.2	20 18.3	16 22.2	23 16.2	
32 11.3	32 11.4	31 11.8		36 10.1	30 12.3	26 13.8	26 13.9	35 10.6	
51 7.2	52 7.1	50 7.4		60 6.1	56 6.5	41 9.0	50 7.4	49 7.5	
3.9	4.8	3.8	Sales/Working Capital		3.1	4.2	4.0	3.7	3.7
6.5	7.3	7.6			6.9	8.8	9.6	6.1	6.0
15.0	18.3	18.4			18.4	20.5	131.2	15.5	9.1
14.7	22.5	15.8	EBIT/Interest		10.7	21.0	10.2	22.6	17.0
(205) 5.1	(203) 5.6	(221) 4.0			(24) 3.0	(29) 6.0	(54) 3.0	(48) 7.8	(61) 3.2
1.7	1.3	1.0			-.7	1.0	.8	2.2	.0
9.1	17.5	4.6	Net Profit + Depr., Dep., Amort./Cur. Mat. L/T/D				3.6	4.4	6.2
(51) 3.7	(55) 3.5	(56) 2.2					(11) 2.4	(13) 1.6	(26) 2.6
1.3	1.2	.4					1.6	.9	-.1
.1	.1	.2	Fixed/Worth		.1	.1	.2	.1	.2
.4	.4	.4			.4	.2	.6	.3	.5
1.2	1.2	1.4			3.3	1.2	4.1	.8	1.1
.6	.8	.7	Debt/Worth		.6	.5	.8	.6	.7
1.7	1.6	1.6			2.1	1.6	2.5	1.0	1.5
5.5	5.3	5.3			23.1	4.8	7.7	3.3	3.2
58.9	59.1	45.0	% Profit Before Taxes/Tangible Net Worth		39.4	44.5	50.3	38.8	46.0
(196) 29.2	(200) 25.6	(212) 18.5		(22) 10.0	(24) 28.5	(53) 14.5	(53) 26.1	(55) 14.3	
10.4	7.5	1.9			-17.6	2.9	.9	10.7	-.2
19.7	19.1	14.9	% Profit Before Taxes/Total Assets		10.1	20.5	13.1	17.1	13.8
9.8	8.9	6.2			5.1	10.3	3.6	9.6	4.5
2.8	.9	.1			-3.5	.1	-.4	3.8	-1.7
54.8	59.2	51.4	Sales/Net Fixed Assets		125.1	88.4	45.6	45.6	25.2
18.3	19.9	16.0			40.2	38.6	13.0	18.5	10.5
8.1	8.8	6.7			8.3	15.2	5.6	7.4	5.6
3.0	3.1	3.0	Sales/Total Assets		3.8	3.6	2.8	2.7	2.8
2.2	2.3	2.0			2.1	2.7	2.2	2.0	1.7
1.4	1.6	1.5			1.5	1.8	1.5	1.6	1.2
.7	.6	.7	% Depr., Dep., Amort./Sales		.3	.4	1.1	.5	.8
(175) 1.5	(185) 1.6	(195) 1.6		(22) .9	(15) 1.4	(47) 1.6	(47) 1.4	(60) 2.2	
2.3	2.6	3.4			3.7	4.4	3.5	2.6	3.7
2.0	2.0	2.5	% Officers', Directors' Owners' Comp/Sales		3.4	3.9	2.8	1.2	
(74) 4.6	(69)* 3.9	(73) 4.6		(19) 5.8	(12) 6.5	(24) 4.4	(12) 1.5		
8.3	9.0				11.4	10.3	7.3	3.5	
6995107M	7779040M	8400981M	Net Sales ($)	4540M	54803M	121401M	452608M	897318M	6870311M
4344424M	4224101M	4978297M	Total Assets ($)	1569M	34475M	60578M	273839M	522126M	4085710M

© RMA 2010

M = $ thousand   MM = $ million
See Pages 9 through 22 for Explanation of Ratios and Data

Current Data Sorted by Assets   Comparative Historical Data

Type of Statement

0-500M	500M-2MM	2-10MM	10-50MM	50-100MM	100-250MM		4/1/05-3/31/06 ALL	4/1/06-3/31/07 ALL
		1	3		2	Unqualified	6	14
	1	4	4			Reviewed	6	6
	3	3				Compiled	6	7
1	3	1				Tax Returns	4	3
		3	9	3	1	Other	20	20
		3 (4/1-9/30/09)	40 (10/1/09-3/31/10)					
1	8	12	16	3	3	**NUMBER OF STATEMENTS**	42	50
%	%	%	%	%	%	**ASSETS**	%	%
		6.3	11.2			Cash & Equivalents	7.5	7.0
		18.4	19.4			Trade Receivables (net)	21.0	23.3
		31.7	27.3			Inventory	36.4	29.2
		5.6	4.6			All Other Current	4.0	2.7
		62.0	62.4			Total Current	68.9	62.2
		28.4	25.0			Fixed Assets (net)	22.2	26.2
		1.4	3.2			Intangibles (net)	4.1	4.7
		8.3	9.4			All Other Non-Current	4.8	6.9
		100.0	100.0			Total	100.0	100.0
						LIABILITIES		
		19.3	16.4			Notes Payable-Short Term	12.1	11.7
		3.4	6.5			Cur. Mat.-L.T.D.	2.0	1.9
		17.7	12.0			Trade Payables	19.0	14.9
		.0	.3			Income Taxes Payable	.9	.1
		12.0	8.9			All Other Current	16.9	16.3
		52.5	44.1			Total Current	50.9	44.8
		8.0	6.8			Long-Term Debt	15.7	14.7
		.3	.9			Deferred Taxes	.6	.8
		5.0	8.3			All Other Non-Current	10.1	8.8
		34.3	39.9			Net Worth	22.7	30.9
		100.0	100.0			Total Liabilities & Net Worth	100.0	100.0
						INCOME DATA		
		100.0	100.0			Net Sales	100.0	100.0
		20.5	20.6			Gross Profit	23.2	22.5
		18.9	18.7			Operating Expenses	19.8	18.1
		1.7	1.9			Operating Profit	3.5	4.3
		.6	.6			All Other Expenses (net)	1.2	1.4
		1.0	1.3			Profit Before Taxes	2.3	2.9
						RATIOS		
		2.0	2.3			Current	2.4	2.2
		1.2	1.4				1.5	1.6
		.9	1.1				1.0	1.0
		1.2	1.5			Quick	.9	1.2
		.5	.7				.5	.7
		.3	.3				.3	.4
		19 / 19.4	15 / 23.8			Sales/Receivables	11 / 34.1	30 / 12.1
		35 / 10.4	51 / 7.1				36 / 10.2	44 / 8.2
		54 / 6.8	61 / 5.9				48 / 7.7	57 / 6.3
		43 / 8.5	28 / 13.0			Cost of Sales/Inventory	29 / 12.5	24 / 15.0
		56 / 6.5	49 / 7.5				62 / 5.9	63 / 5.8
		105 / 3.5	111 / 3.3				109 / 3.3	111 / 3.3
		11 / 33.0	19 / 19.3			Cost of Sales/Payables	14 / 26.1	26 / 14.1
		33 / 11.2	31 / 11.9				37 / 9.9	35 / 10.4
		73 / 5.0	50 / 7.4				52 / 7.0	57 / 6.4
		6.6	3.2			Sales/Working Capital	5.6	4.5
		29.5	11.6				11.3	9.9
		-28.6	67.9				-70.9	-41.6
		6.7	7.8			EBIT/Interest	16.8	12.7
		2.7	(14) 3.7				(37) 4.9	(40) 3.4
		-.8	-1.2				.8	.8
						Net Profit + Depr., Dep., Amort./Cur. Mat. L/T/D	8.5	
							(10) 5.0	
							2.1	
		.3	.2			Fixed/Worth	.2	.3
		.9	.5				1.5	1.5
		NM	2.0				-473.5	16.4
		.8	.6			Debt/Worth	.8	.7
		1.9	1.9				5.5	3.3
		NM	2.8				-758.6	63.5
			34.3			% Profit Before Taxes/Tangible Net Worth	89.7	54.6
			(15) 14.2				(31) 23.7	(39) 19.3
			-6.1				13.7	6.9
		7.8	10.0			% Profit Before Taxes/Total Assets	14.6	17.0
		2.8	5.1				8.1	7.7
		-3.9	-3.6				-1.0	.7
		59.7	32.8			Sales/Net Fixed Assets	31.7	21.8
		13.0	8.3				14.3	10.8
		2.6	3.4				6.1	4.1
		2.9	2.2			Sales/Total Assets	3.2	2.4
		1.9	1.4				2.2	1.8
		1.3	1.1				1.7	1.2
		.6	1.0			% Depr., Dep., Amort./Sales	.7	1.2
		(10) 1.8	(13) 1.6				(35) 1.4	(42) 2.2
		4.3	6.5				2.2	3.7
						% Officers', Directors' Owners' Comp/Sales	1.2	
							(13) 2.6	
							4.6	
1927M	19704M	131149M	640990M	409954M	379231M	Net Sales ($)	2568969M	3168636M
245M	9312M	63987M	379329M	165762M	465491M	Total Assets ($)	1277916M	1861075M

M = $ thousand   MM = $ million
See Pages 9 through 22 for Explanation of Ratios and Data

Comparative Historical Data / Current Data Sorted by Sales

	4/1/07-3/31/08 ALL	4/1/08-3/31/09 ALL	4/1/09-3/31/10 ALL	0-1MM	1-3MM 3 (4/1-9/30/09)	3-5MM	5-10MM	10-25MM 40 (10/1/09-3/31/10)	25MM & OVER
Type of Statement									
Unqualified	12	10	6	1					5
Reviewed	7	4	9			2		3	3
Compiled	7	7	3		3	2	2		
Tax Returns	1	4	5		2		1		
Other	19	21	20			2	2	6	9
NUMBER OF STATEMENTS	46	46	43	1	5	6	5	9	17
	%	%	%	%	%	%	%	%	%
ASSETS									
Cash & Equivalents	10.4	10.7	9.9						11.3
Trade Receivables (net)	17.8	19.8	20.1						20.6
Inventory	33.6	30.9	30.7						26.9
All Other Current	4.4	2.4	5.2						9.2
Total Current	66.2	63.9	65.7						68.1
Fixed Assets (net)	21.7	25.2	23.2						16.5
Intangibles (net)	4.8	3.4	3.3						3.4
All Other Non-Current	7.3	7.6	7.8						12.0
Total	100.0	100.0	100.0						100.0
LIABILITIES									
Notes Payable-Short Term	12.8	13.1	18.0						11.6
Cur. Mat.-L.T.D.	5.6	8.0	4.6						5.3
Trade Payables	13.0	13.9	13.7						13.5
Income Taxes Payable	1.1	.3	.2						.2
All Other Current	14.7	13.5	14.2						14.4
Total Current	47.2	48.8	50.7						45.0
Long-Term Debt	15.3	10.0	9.3						10.1
Deferred Taxes	.5	.3	.4						.2
All Other Non-Current	11.5	16.5	7.9						9.8
Net Worth	25.6	24.4	31.6						34.9
Total Liabilities & Net Worth	100.0	100.0	100.0						100.0
INCOME DATA									
Net Sales	100.0	100.0	100.0						100.0
Gross Profit	24.2	23.2	21.9						22.1
Operating Expenses	19.7	21.3	21.5						21.8
Operating Profit	4.6	1.9	.4						.3
All Other Expenses (net)	1.0	1.6	.9						.8
Profit Before Taxes	3.5	.2	-.5						-.5
RATIOS									
Current	2.1	2.2	1.9						2.0
	1.4	1.4	1.4						1.5
	1.1	.9	1.1						1.1
Quick	1.2	1.1	1.0						1.1
	.5	.5	.5						.8
	.3	.3	.2						.3
Sales/Receivables	13 28.4	20 18.7	15 24.7						16 22.2
	27 13.4	33 11.1	37 9.8						40 9.1
	47 7.7	50 7.3	61 6.0						60 6.1
Cost of Sales/Inventory	31 11.7	15 23.9	27 13.6						10 35.2
	55 6.6	48 7.6	57 6.4						72 5.1
	112 3.3	105 3.5	118 3.1						108 3.4
Cost of Sales/Payables	14 26.0	13 28.3	15 24.9						17 21.3
	26 14.0	36 10.2	31 11.7						35 10.3
	43 8.5	59 6.2	53 6.8						54 6.8
Sales/Working Capital	5.0	5.1	5.6						4.3
	9.9	11.0	11.3						11.3
	NM	-17.2	63.2						37.6
EBIT/Interest	13.0	12.3	6.6						10.6
	(42) 3.7	(41) 2.7	(40) 2.6					(14) 3.6	
	.6	.5	-1.6						-1.1
Net Profit + Depr., Dep., Amort./Cur. Mat. L/T/D	3.2	2.5	4.3						
	(16) 1.3	(10) .7	(13) 1.9						
	.7	-1.3	-.1						
Fixed/Worth	.2	.2	.2						.2
	1.2	.5	.9						.4
	-2.5	-5.5	2.2						1.4
Debt/Worth	1.2	.8	1.0						.9
	3.6	2.3	2.3						2.0
	-14.9	-8.2	5.8						3.4
% Profit Before Taxes/Tangible Net Worth	36.8	36.9	27.2						34.3
	(34) 23.0	(34) 19.1	(35) 7.0					(15) 14.2	
	10.0	6.0	-14.2						5.0
% Profit Before Taxes/Total Assets	14.4	16.8	8.3						9.9
	6.3	3.1	3.1						4.6
	-1.8	-1.2	-4.6						-.4
Sales/Net Fixed Assets	43.5	39.9	34.6						36.4
	13.7	14.5	13.1						16.3
	7.9	4.8	4.0						5.1
Sales/Total Assets	3.0	2.6	2.6						2.7
	2.1	1.9	1.6						2.1
	1.5	1.2	1.1						1.1
% Depr., Dep., Amort./Sales	.6	.6	.9						1.1
	(38) 1.6	(36) 1.4	(33) 2.0					(12) 2.1	
	4.4	3.7	4.7						4.7
% Officers', Directors' Owners' Comp/Sales	.9	1.0	1.9						
	(11) 1.9	(10) 3.7	(10) 3.4						
	7.1	10.9	7.1						
Net Sales ($)	3185472M	2853685M	1582955M	753M	9119M	23765M	40474M	154851M	1353993M
Total Assets ($)	1750852M	1685617M	1084126M	745M	5474M	13732M	35582M	105911M	922682M

M = $ thousand   MM = $ million
See Pages 9 through 22 for Explanation of Ratios and Data

Current Data Sorted by Assets   Comparative Historical Data

0-500M	500M-2MM	2-10MM	10-50MM	50-100MM	100-250MM	Type of Statement	4/1/05-3/31/06 ALL	4/1/06-3/31/07 ALL
		4	14	4	3	Unqualified	46	33
1	7	14	9	1		Reviewed	31	27
	3	6				Compiled	22	26
5	4	4				Tax Returns	9	9
6	5	18	8	10	7	Other	61	69
	22 (4/1-9/30/09)		111 (10/1/09-3/31/10)					
12	19	46	31	15	10	**NUMBER OF STATEMENTS**	169	164
%	%	%	%	%	%	**ASSETS**	%	%
10.8	11.5	6.9	8.3	6.4	10.2	Cash & Equivalents	5.4	5.9
26.4	19.3	21.0	21.0	16.6	18.1	Trade Receivables (net)	23.6	21.9
27.6	43.2	43.3	31.2	30.2	22.6	Inventory	31.0	34.9
1.5	1.8	4.6	1.6	3.4	5.8	All Other Current	2.5	3.3
66.3	75.9	75.8	62.0	56.7	56.7	Total Current	62.5	66.0
22.3	18.5	18.5	20.5	23.5	27.7	Fixed Assets (net)	25.4	23.2
2.8	3.0	.7	8.2	14.0	11.7	Intangibles (net)	4.5	5.4
8.5	2.6	5.0	9.4	5.9	3.9	All Other Non-Current	7.6	5.4
100.0	100.0	100.0	100.0	100.0	100.0	Total	100.0	100.0
						LIABILITIES		
19.5	14.5	19.2	15.2	12.4	3.3	Notes Payable-Short Term	13.4	15.9
6.8	5.4	2.3	4.4	7.6	3.7	Cur. Mat.-L.T.D.	4.2	3.4
20.0	20.4	16.0	13.8	12.0	11.4	Trade Payables	18.7	19.2
.0	.0	.0	.0	1.8	2.5	Income Taxes Payable	.4	.3
30.9	12.4	17.3	16.2	11.3	13.6	All Other Current	11.7	12.7
77.1	52.8	54.8	49.7	45.1	34.5	Total Current	48.4	51.5
44.3	18.4	6.1	7.8	14.0	22.1	Long-Term Debt	15.1	13.8
.0	.0	.3	.7	.8	1.0	Deferred Taxes	.7	.5
12.2	2.7	8.5	8.6	5.2	10.4	All Other Non-Current	7.5	7.1
-33.6	26.1	30.3	33.2	34.9	32.0	Net Worth	28.4	27.1
100.0	100.0	100.0	100.0	100.0	100.0	Total Liabilities & Net Worth	100.0	100.0
						INCOME DATA		
100.0	100.0	100.0	100.0	100.0	100.0	Net Sales	100.0	100.0
26.8	28.7	21.4	16.5	15.7	15.4	Gross Profit	22.2	23.3
27.8	29.9	20.2	14.9	15.9	14.0	Operating Expenses	17.3	19.9
-1.0	-1.1	1.1	1.6	-.2	1.4	Operating Profit	4.8	3.5
-.2	.6	2.2	.8	2.3	3.4	All Other Expenses (net)	1.1	1.1
-.8	-1.8	-1.1	.8	.8	-2.1	Profit Before Taxes	3.8	2.4
						RATIOS		
3.4	2.7	2.1	2.3	1.9	2.8	Current	2.2	2.2
1.0	1.7	1.3	1.3	1.4	1.6		1.4	1.4
.5	.9	1.2	1.0	.9	1.3		1.0	1.0
1.1	1.2	.9	1.4	1.1	1.7	Quick	1.1	1.0
.4	.5	.5	.5	.6	.6		.6	.6
.2	.3	.3	.3	.2	.4		.4	.4
2 150.0	4 87.7	13 27.7	23 15.7	29 12.5	35 10.4	Sales/Receivables	23 15.7	18 19.8
11 33.2	26 14.2	32 11.3	38 9.5	33 11.1	42 8.7		38 9.6	35 10.4
36 10.2	41 8.9	55 6.6	63 5.8	46 7.9	46 7.9		51 7.1	52 7.1
0 UND	51 7.2	54 6.7	34 10.8	39 9.3	43 8.4	Cost of Sales/Inventory	30 12.2	34 10.8
27 13.4	67 5.4	88 4.1	56 6.6	78 4.7	65 5.6		56 6.5	60 6.1
68 5.3	125 2.9	127 2.9	112 3.3	112 3.3	77 4.8		92 4.0	105 3.5
0 773.9	9 40.5	12 29.3	13 28.3	20 18.5	20 18.7	Cost of Sales/Payables	16 23.4	17 22.0
14 25.6	14 26.3	24 15.2	19 18.8	28 13.2	32 11.5		28 12.9	31 11.6
37 9.9	69 5.3	47 7.7	47 7.8	47 7.7	43 8.5		48 7.6	48 7.6
11.6	5.7	4.4	6.0	5.8	3.0	Sales/Working Capital	7.0	6.0
NM	7.3	10.4	18.4	11.7	8.8		12.4	12.9
-6.3	-55.0	26.7	-76.6	-44.6	24.4		294.3	207.1
	8.7	4.5	14.3	8.0		EBIT/Interest	9.6	6.1
	(15) .9	(42) 1.4	(28) 2.4	.0			(154) 3.6	(151) 2.7
	-1.5	-.6	.4	-3.7			1.2	1.2
			12.7			Net Profit + Depr., Dep., Amort./Cur. Mat. L/T/D	6.3	9.3
			(11) 2.0				(47) 3.3	(47) 3.8
			.1				1.4	1.8
.2	.1	.1	.3	.5	.5	Fixed/Worth	.4	.3
-.7	.8	.4	.5	1.0	1.0		.9	.8
-.3	-1.3	1.0	1.6	-54.3	-.4		2.7	2.5
6.6	.5	.8	.8	.8	.5	Debt/Worth	1.1	1.2
-6.0	1.2	1.9	2.4	2.6	1.3		2.6	2.9
-2.2	-4.7	5.2	8.7	-169.2	-3.2		6.9	11.8
	34.0	31.3	36.8	60.6		% Profit Before Taxes/Tangible Net Worth	45.7	42.2
	(14) -3.6	(41) 3.8	(26) 8.1	(11) -9.6			(139) 23.1	(135) 19.4
	-52.3	-6.8	-1.4	-16.5			8.2	4.6
9.1	8.4	9.9	9.6	13.1	5.4	% Profit Before Taxes/Total Assets	15.5	13.2
.0	-1.7	1.3	2.2	-5.3	2.1		5.7	5.0
-19.3	-21.5	-4.1	-5.6	-9.4	-16.3		1.1	.7
190.2	93.5	44.8	20.4	15.1	10.7	Sales/Net Fixed Assets	36.8	35.3
19.9	34.2	23.6	11.1	7.2	7.7		10.9	13.4
7.3	6.8	7.3	6.2	3.8	3.8		6.1	5.6
6.9	3.7	2.9	2.6	2.2	2.0	Sales/Total Assets	3.1	3.1
3.7	2.9	2.1	2.0	1.3	1.7		2.3	2.2
3.3	2.2	1.6	1.2	1.1	1.1		1.7	1.6
	.7	.7	.9	.8		% Depr., Dep., Amort./Sales	.8	.7
	(14) 1.4	(39) 1.3	(29) 1.6	(14) 3.7			(138) 1.6	(141) 1.4
	2.5	3.1	3.4	5.8			2.7	3.2
	2.2	1.3				% Officers', Directors' Owners' Comp/Sales	1.5	1.4
	(12) 3.4	(18) 2.0					(51) 3.1	(48) 2.9
	4.9	3.9					4.8	5.1
13509M	67231M	530841M	1412720M	1991708M	2315361M	Net Sales ($)	9834514M	8967945M
3140M	23209M	243689M	697511M	1097441M	1557423M	Total Assets ($)	4839850M	4760275M

M = $ thousand   MM = $ million
See Pages 9 through 22 for Explanation of Ratios and Data

Comparative Historical Data   **Current Data Sorted by Sales**

4/1/07-3/31/08 ALL	4/1/08-3/31/09 ALL	4/1/09-3/31/10 ALL	Type of Statement	0-1MM	1-3MM	3-5MM	5-10MM	10-25MM	25MM & OVER
40	32	25	Unqualified				1	3	21
30	37	32	Reviewed		6	3	8	9	6
15	13	9	Compiled		3		4	2	
20	10	13	Tax Returns	2	7	1	2	1	
67	59	54	Other	4	2	4	4	18	22
					22 (4/1-9/30/09)		111 (10/1/09-3/31/10)		
172	151	133	**NUMBER OF STATEMENTS**	6	18	8	19	33	49
%	%	%	**ASSETS**	%	%	%	%	%	%
5.9	5.7	8.4	Cash & Equivalents		10.1		6.7	7.2	7.6
22.7	20.8	20.5	Trade Receivables (net)		16.4		17.8	24.0	19.9
34.1	37.7	36.0	Inventory		35.4		45.3	38.6	30.0
2.5	2.4	3.2	All Other Current		2.1		3.8	4.6	3.1
65.2	66.6	68.1	Total Current		63.9		73.6	74.4	60.7
24.0	22.4	20.6	Fixed Assets (net)		25.9		18.9	16.1	23.4
5.2	5.1	5.3	Intangibles (net)		5.0		.4	5.6	8.6
5.6	5.9	6.0	All Other Non-Current		5.1		7.2	3.9	7.3
100.0	100.0	100.0	Total		100.0		100.0	100.0	100.0
			LIABILITIES						
15.0	18.1	15.7	Notes Payable-Short Term		15.1		21.3	19.8	11.7
3.6	4.2	4.3	Cur. Mat.-L.T.D.		6.9		.6	4.4	4.3
17.6	15.2	15.7	Trade Payables		14.9		19.6	19.5	12.7
.1	.4	.4	Income Taxes Payable		.0		.0	.0	1.1
14.0	13.6	16.6	All Other Current		26.5		10.9	12.5	16.2
50.3	51.5	52.7	Total Current		63.4		52.5	56.3	45.9
14.9	14.0	13.8	Long-Term Debt		36.0		7.9	3.7	13.0
.5	.6	.5	Deferred Taxes		.0		.0	1.3	.3
6.8	4.9	7.8	All Other Non-Current		5.1		7.9	7.3	8.4
27.5	28.9	25.3	Net Worth		-4.5		31.7	31.4	32.4
100.0	100.0	100.0	Total Liabilities & Net Worth		100.0		100.0	100.0	100.0
			INCOME DATA						
100.0	100.0	100.0	Net Sales		100.0		100.0	100.0	100.0
22.8	20.2	20.7	Gross Profit		24.6		20.3	21.7	14.7
19.6	18.6	20.1	Operating Expenses		26.4		20.5	20.1	14.0
3.2	1.6	.6	Operating Profit		-1.8		-.2	1.6	.6
1.4	1.7	1.6	All Other Expenses (net)		1.5		2.4	.8	1.8
1.8	-.1	-1.0	Profit Before Taxes		-3.3		-2.6	.8	-1.2
			RATIOS						
2.3	2.3	2.1	Current		2.8		2.0	2.0	2.1
1.4	1.5	1.4			1.1		1.5	1.3	1.4
1.1	1.1	1.0			.8		1.0	1.0	1.0
1.1	1.0	1.1	Quick		1.2		.9	1.0	1.1
.6	.6	.5			.5		.4	.5	.6
.4	.3	.3			.2		.3	.4	.3
23 16.1	21 17.7	15 24.6	Sales/Receivables		3 135.2		9 39.6	18 19.8	24 15.2
36 10.0	33 11.1	37 9.9			18 20.7		29 12.4	44 8.3	37 9.8
50 7.3	43 8.4	49 7.5			40 9.1		55 6.6	53 6.8	47 7.8
36 10.1	42 8.6	43 8.4	Cost of Sales/Inventory		25 14.8		55 6.6	40 9.1	36 10.1
61 6.0	70 5.2	67 5.4			64 5.7		88 4.1	69 5.3	62 5.9
108 3.4	106 3.5	112 3.3			136 2.7		128 2.8	113 3.2	84 4.4
16 22.8	12 29.9	12 29.4	Cost of Sales/Payables		5 66.7		14 26.3	15 23.6	13 27.4
31 11.8	25 14.4	21 17.1			14 25.9		29 12.5	33 11.1	21 17.1
44 8.3	41 8.9	47 7.8			42 8.7		48 7.6	58 6.3	36 10.0
5.6	5.6	5.6	Sales/Working Capital		5.6		6.1	5.9	5.9
12.7	10.8	10.7			NM		12.8	14.0	9.3
64.0	56.3	-186.1			-13.7		-999.8	NM	409.0
5.5	5.8	6.3	EBIT/Interest		4.6		4.3	7.8	8.5
(156) 2.3	(136) 1.5	(117) 1.4			(15) .9		(16) 1.2	(30) 1.7	(46) 1.8
.8	-1.1	-1.3			-5.8		-.8	.5	-2.7
5.1	5.4	4.2	Net Profit + Depr., Dep., Amort./Cur. Mat. L/T/D					4.1	10.9
(54) 3.0	(42) 2.1	(33) 1.4						(10) 2.1	(17) 1.8
.9	-.1	-.2						.2	.0
.3	.3	.2	Fixed/Worth		.3		.1	.1	.4
.9	.7	.6			NM		.7	.4	.7
3.1	7.7	4.1			-.4		1.7	.9	2.7
1.0	.9	.8	Debt/Worth		.8		.8	.9	.7
2.8	2.4	2.4			NM		1.8	2.7	2.2
13.1	16.0	22.0			-3.1		17.9	6.4	12.8
37.3	29.1	30.6	% Profit Before Taxes/Tangible Net Worth				34.6	55.3	31.8
(137) 17.4	(118) 8.6	(102) 5.2					(17) 5.0	(28) 5.6	(38) 7.6
2.5	-8.0	-9.7					-18.2	-.5	-10.3
11.2	9.3	8.3	% Profit Before Taxes/Total Assets		7.2		6.8	11.6	8.9
3.6	1.7	1.1			-.3		-.3	1.5	2.2
-.4	-4.9	-6.8			-19.8		-6.1	-2.0	-9.5
31.5	31.0	34.7	Sales/Net Fixed Assets		130.2		55.2	47.5	17.1
12.2	13.5	15.1			11.2		27.7	21.4	9.3
5.8	5.4	5.5			4.2		12.5	8.3	4.4
3.0	3.1	3.1	Sales/Total Assets		3.6		4.0	2.9	2.6
2.2	2.2	2.1			2.7		2.1	2.2	1.9
1.7	1.6	1.3			1.2		1.5	1.7	1.3
.7	.7	.7	% Depr., Dep., Amort./Sales		.7		.7	.7	.9
(145) 1.5	(127) 1.3	(109) 1.5			(13) 1.9		(16) 1.1	(29) 1.4	(44) 1.8
3.0	3.0	3.3			6.5		1.7	2.7	3.5
1.2	1.1	1.4	% Officers', Directors' Owners' Comp/Sales		3.0		1.5	1.2	
(50) 2.6	(35) 3.3	(44) 2.6			(10) 4.2		(10) 2.3	(14) 2.0	
5.3	4.9	4.4			5.1		3.6	3.9	
10323874M	8280571M	6331370M	Net Sales ($)	3798M	33164M	31579M	138866M	509304M	5614659M
5690788M	4876854M	3622413M	Total Assets ($)	1261M	22150M	32611M	71939M	306071M	3188381M

M = $ thousand   MM = $ million
See Pages 9 through 22 for Explanation of Ratios and Data

MANUFACTURING—Truck Trailer Manufacturing NAICS 336212

Current Data Sorted by Assets							Comparative Historical Data	

						Type of Statement		
		1	3	1	3	Unqualified	13	14
		3	5			Reviewed	10	15
1	6	6	2	1		Compiled	22	22
1	5					Tax Returns	10	10
1	3	15	8	3	3	Other	20	31
	11 (4/1-9/30/09)		60 (10/1/09-3/31/10)				4/1/05-3/31/06	4/1/06-3/31/07
0-500M	500M-2MM	2-10MM	10-50MM	50-100MM	100-250MM		ALL	ALL
3	14	25	18	5	6	**NUMBER OF STATEMENTS**	75	92
%	%	%	%	%	%	**ASSETS**	%	%
	10.5	9.5	6.6			Cash & Equivalents	7.9	5.8
	13.0	15.3	15.4			Trade Receivables (net)	20.7	19.0
	53.0	40.8	37.1			Inventory	38.2	43.2
	.8	7.4	1.4			All Other Current	1.2	2.5
	77.3	73.0	60.4			Total Current	68.1	70.5
	15.0	22.3	27.5			Fixed Assets (net)	24.0	22.5
	1.0	1.0	8.0			Intangibles (net)	3.8	3.6
	6.8	3.8	4.0			All Other Non-Current	4.1	3.4
	100.0	100.0	100.0			Total	100.0	100.0
						LIABILITIES		
	23.0	13.2	15.7			Notes Payable-Short Term	13.7	15.0
	1.3	2.5	3.3			Cur. Mat.-L.T.D.	3.5	3.2
	16.1	12.9	9.3			Trade Payables	20.0	15.9
	.0	.0	.2			Income Taxes Payable	.2	.2
	21.8	9.8	13.5			All Other Current	10.5	14.7
	62.1	38.4	41.9			Total Current	47.9	49.0
	12.8	15.2	13.8			Long-Term Debt	14.8	12.5
	.0	.1	1.4			Deferred Taxes	.5	.3
	7.1	15.3	3.1			All Other Non-Current	4.8	4.3
	18.0	31.1	39.9			Net Worth	31.9	33.8
	100.0	100.0	100.0			Total Liabilities & Net Worth	100.0	100.0
						INCOME DATA		
	100.0	100.0	100.0			Net Sales	100.0	100.0
	20.9	18.7	15.5			Gross Profit	19.0	19.1
	23.9	14.4	14.3			Operating Expenses	14.8	15.5
	-3.0	4.3	1.2			Operating Profit	4.2	3.5
	-.1	.9	1.6			All Other Expenses (net)	.4	.5
	-2.9	3.4	-.4			Profit Before Taxes	3.8	3.0
						RATIOS		
	3.3	3.6	3.5				2.1	2.2
	1.9	1.9	1.9			Current	1.4	1.4
	1.0	1.3	.9				1.0	1.1
	.9	1.0	1.5				1.0	.8
	.5	.5	.5			Quick	.6	.5
	.2	.2	.3				.3	.3
4	92.9	8	48.4	11	34.1		12	31.4	9	41.4
7	52.3	17	21.6	23	16.0	Sales/Receivables	24	15.4	20	18.5
22	16.3	30	12.1	33	11.2		38	9.6	32	11.5
42	8.7	44	8.4	51	7.2		34	10.6	37	9.8
81	4.5	68	5.4	78	4.7	Cost of Sales/Inventory	55	6.6	62	5.9
109	3.3	122	3.0	140	2.6		84	4.3	95	3.8
5	72.5	10	35.7	8	43.5		11	32.5	9	40.8
18	19.8	17	21.5	13	28.4	Cost of Sales/Payables	22	16.5	18	20.1
31	11.9	38	9.7	26	14.0		39	9.3	35	10.4
	5.1	3.5	3.2				7.8	6.9
	13.5	7.6	10.6			Sales/Working Capital	18.1	14.6
	NM	21.6	-65.1				-999.8	62.3
	3.9	18.4	16.0				15.7	14.1
(13)	1.5	(21)	6.9		.8	EBIT/Interest	(71)	7.8	(82)	4.8
	-6.3	1.4	-2.2				2.5	1.3
						Net Profit + Depr., Dep.,		14.4		18.8
						Amort./Cur. Mat. L/T/D	(14)	3.9	(18)	9.9
							1.6	3.3
	.1	.1	.3				.2	.3
	.5	.6	.7			Fixed/Worth	.7	.7
	1.2	1.5	NM				1.9	2.3
	.9	.5	.8				.9	.7
	2.8	1.9	2.0			Debt/Worth	2.0	2.1
	NM	5.6	NM				9.9	6.0
	8.4	50.8	29.5				53.9	61.4
(11)	.7	(23)	17.1	(14)	-2.3	% Profit Before Taxes/Tangible Net Worth	(64)	33.4	(81)	29.9
	-87.8	-3.5	-17.4				12.3	6.6
	4.3	19.3	18.9				22.8	19.0
	.4	9.3	-1.0			% Profit Before Taxes/Total Assets	9.8	10.2
	-19.9	-.1	-9.2				3.3	.7
	57.3	66.9	32.3				53.5	51.4
	30.2	23.3	6.5			Sales/Net Fixed Assets	24.6	20.2
	15.5	4.7	3.4				6.5	8.2
	5.1	3.6	3.8				4.1	4.8
	3.5	2.7	1.9			Sales/Total Assets	3.3	3.2
	2.5	1.7	1.0				2.3	2.2
	1.0	.4	.9				.5	.5
(12)	1.2	(20)	1.0	(17)	1.9	% Depr., Dep., Amort./Sales	(63)	.9	(82)	.8
	1.6	2.1	2.8				2.0	1.6
						% Officers', Directors'		.8		1.2
						Owners' Comp/Sales	(19)	3.2	(26)	2.2
							4.3	5.8
1002M	58357M	350587M	839684M	530397M	1892444M	Net Sales ($)	3239164M	3404664M
522M	13646M	131167M	371013M	315460M	1138794M	Total Assets ($)	1201371M	1289162M

M = $ thousand   MM = $ million
See Pages 9 through 22 for Explanation of Ratios and Data

Comparative Historical Data   ## Current Data Sorted by Sales

					Type of Statement							
	15		12		8	Unqualified					1	7
	14		11		8	Reviewed					5	3
	23		19		16	Compiled	1	4	3	3	2	3
	11		8		6	Tax Returns	1	3	1	1		
	36		28		33	Other	1	1	2	6	8	15
	4/1/07- 3/31/08 ALL		4/1/08- 3/31/09 ALL		4/1/09- 3/31/10 ALL			11 (4/1-9/30/09)			60 (10/1/09-3/31/10)	
							0-1MM	1-3MM	3-5MM	5-10MM	10-25MM	25MM & OVER
	99		78		71	NUMBER OF STATEMENTS	3	8	6	10	16	28
	%		%		%	ASSETS	%	%	%	%	%	%
	5.7		5.8		7.9	Cash & Equivalents				8.5	14.0	5.2
	15.7		12.8		14.4	Trade Receivables (net)				7.5	19.7	15.7
	44.7		45.6		38.6	Inventory				47.9	36.9	32.9
	2.9		2.3		3.6	All Other Current				1.0	.7	7.8
	69.0		66.5		64.5	Total Current				64.9	71.3	61.5
	20.9		20.9		23.0	Fixed Assets (net)				26.7	17.4	24.2
	4.9		7.5		6.0	Intangibles (net)				.1	6.6	10.7
	5.2		5.1		6.6	All Other Non-Current				8.3	4.8	3.6
	100.0		100.0		100.0	Total				100.0	100.0	100.0
					LIABILITIES						
	14.7		21.2		15.8	Notes Payable-Short Term				10.6	17.1	11.5
	3.2		3.5		3.8	Cur. Mat.-L.T.D.				2.3	2.0	2.6
	15.0		15.6		15.6	Trade Payables				9.9	13.2	12.1
	.2		.0		.1	Income Taxes Payable				.1	.0	.2
	10.6		11.4		13.7	All Other Current				10.0	22.9	13.3
	43.7		51.7		48.9	Total Current				32.8	55.3	39.6
	15.3		18.4		15.5	Long-Term Debt				22.8	13.9	11.2
	.3		.5		.8	Deferred Taxes				.8	.9	1.3
	7.9		9.1		9.5	All Other Non-Current				4.1	3.3	3.6
	32.8		20.4		25.2	Net Worth				39.5	26.6	44.3
	100.0		100.0		100.0	Total Liabilities & Net Worth				100.0	100.0	100.0
					INCOME DATA						
	100.0		100.0		100.0	Net Sales				100.0	100.0	100.0
	21.0		19.7		18.7	Gross Profit				24.2	16.1	16.0
	17.4		17.6		18.2	Operating Expenses				23.4	15.3	13.7
	3.6		2.1		.4	Operating Profit				.8	.8	2.3
	1.0		1.3		1.2	All Other Expenses (net)				.6	1.9	1.4
	2.5		.8		-.8	Profit Before Taxes				.2	-1.1	.9
					RATIOS						
	3.0		3.0		2.8					4.3	2.7	2.8
	1.6		1.5		1.8	Current				2.2	1.6	1.6
	1.1		1.1		1.1					1.4	1.1	1.1
	.9		.7		1.0					1.5	1.0	1.0
	.4		.4		.6	Quick				.7	.6	.6
	.2		.3		.2					.1	.3	.2
8	44.0	7	51.2	7	51.4		5 70.8	7 49.9				13 27.7
18	20.5	15	24.0	20	18.3	Sales/Receivables	10 35.6	16 22.7				23 16.0
29	12.7	27	13.6	31	11.7		21 17.2	41 8.9				37 9.8
40	9.1	45	8.1	46	8.0		66 5.6	42 8.8				43 8.5
64	5.7	69	5.3	68	5.4	Cost of Sales/Inventory	95 3.8	63 5.8				56 6.5
99	3.7	115	3.2	108	3.4		199 1.8	141 2.6				78 4.7
9	38.9	7	51.3	9	41.2		10 35.2	5 75.3				9 41.4
15	23.8	15	24.4	17	21.3	Cost of Sales/Payables	16 23.0	15 25.0				19 18.9
32	11.4	33	10.9	34	10.8		27 13.6	39 9.4				30 12.1
	7.2		5.5		4.6					3.5	3.7	6.0
	11.0		11.0		9.4	Sales/Working Capital				6.3	10.6	11.8
	50.5		46.8		40.8					23.5	146.7	59.6
	11.2		8.3		10.6						10.9	19.0
(92)	3.1	(72)	1.8	(66)	1.9	EBIT/Interest			(15)		6.9 (26)	1.7
	1.3		-.2		-2.8						-1.2	-2.2
	11.6		8.5		7.1	Net Profit + Depr., Dep.,						
(19)	5.8	(18)	2.3	(12)	2.8	Amort./Cur. Mat. L/T/D						
	1.3		1.0		-.2							
	.2		.2		.3					.1	.1	.3
	.7		.7		.7	Fixed/Worth				1.0	.5	.7
	2.4		3.0		5.2					2.4	1.2	6.8
	.8		.9		.7					.4	.7	.7
	2.4		2.0		2.6	Debt/Worth				1.8	2.6	2.5
	11.6		26.1		16.8					6.1	11.5	18.6
	54.4		29.9		27.0	% Profit Before Taxes/Tangible					53.3	24.4
(83)	19.7	(60)	8.2	(55)	5.1	Net Worth				(13)	25.6 (22)	4.9
	3.4		-6.1		-18.9						-24.6	-21.0
	16.2		9.5		9.9	% Profit Before Taxes/Total				5.7	21.4	13.7
	6.9		2.1		2.2	Assets				2.0	2.4	3.6
	.2		-3.3		-9.0					-5.2	-9.0	-6.2
	46.2		39.5		39.5					31.8	146.8	35.9
	17.4		15.1		12.3	Sales/Net Fixed Assets				16.9	25.8	10.1
	8.8		7.2		5.5					3.9	6.8	6.0
	4.1		4.1		3.6					3.7	3.6	3.8
	3.0		2.7		2.3	Sales/Total Assets				2.3	2.6	2.2
	2.1		1.8		1.4					1.3	1.3	1.4
	.5		.7		.8						.3	.8
(88)	1.0	(60)	1.2	(57)	1.3	% Depr., Dep., Amort./Sales				(12)	.9 (23)	1.2
	1.5		2.1		2.5						2.6	2.4
	.8		.9		1.2	% Officers', Directors'						
(30)	1.9	(21)	2.0	(19)	3.0	Owners' Comp/Sales						
	3.8		4.1		4.5							
	4410820M		5057652M		3672471M	Net Sales ($)	1002M	18886M	21761M	67774M	244383M	3318665M
	1826745M		2389823M		1970602M	Total Assets ($)	522M	10594M	11283M	88974M	127481M	1731748M

M = $ thousand   MM = $ million
See Pages 9 through 22 for Explanation of Ratios and Data

Current Data Sorted by Assets   Comparative Historical Data

0-500M	500M-2MM	2-10MM	10-50MM	50-100MM	100-250MM	Type of Statement	4/1/05-3/31/06 ALL	4/1/06-3/31/07 ALL
		1	5	2	2	Unqualified	14	14
	1	6	2			Reviewed	9	7
1	7	2				Compiled	10	11
		2				Tax Returns	2	5
	3	3	3	1	1	Other	11	13
	8 (4/1-9/30/09)		34 (10/1/09-3/31/10)					
1	11	14	10	3	3	**NUMBER OF STATEMENTS**	46	50
%	%	%	%	%	%	**ASSETS**	%	%
	20.5	2.8	5.9			Cash & Equivalents	7.3	9.6
	12.4	13.3	21.4			Trade Receivables (net)	21.8	16.9
	55.3	58.9	36.6			Inventory	42.5	44.1
	1.1	1.9	7.9			All Other Current	1.4	1.9
	89.3	76.8	71.7			Total Current	73.0	72.4
	5.9	14.4	16.0			Fixed Assets (net)	17.6	17.5
	1.5	3.2	9.5			Intangibles (net)	5.1	3.5
	3.3	5.6	2.8			All Other Non-Current	4.3	6.6
	100.0	100.0	100.0			Total	100.0	100.0
						LIABILITIES		
	23.9	25.1	4.9			Notes Payable-Short Term	16.8	16.4
	4.2	1.8	6.8			Cur. Mat.-L.T.D.	1.3	2.7
	8.9	13.1	14.6			Trade Payables	17.4	18.3
	.1	.1	.0			Income Taxes Payable	.1	.0
	17.5	12.8	17.7			All Other Current	12.1	10.9
	54.6	52.8	44.0			Total Current	47.7	48.3
	19.9	9.1	19.6			Long-Term Debt	12.2	11.2
	.0	.0	.0			Deferred Taxes	.1	.2
	.7	19.7	11.0			All Other Non-Current	8.1	7.5
	24.8	18.5	25.4			Net Worth	31.9	32.8
	100.0	100.0	100.0			Total Liabilities & Net Worth	100.0	100.0
						INCOME DATA		
	100.0	100.0	100.0			Net Sales	100.0	100.0
	21.2	17.3	12.2			Gross Profit	18.7	17.9
	24.3	18.1	17.9			Operating Expenses	15.4	15.9
	-3.1	-.7	-5.7			Operating Profit	3.3	2.0
	.8	1.6	1.5			All Other Expenses (net)	.9	.8
	-4.0	-2.3	-7.2			Profit Before Taxes	2.4	1.2
						RATIOS		
	3.0	3.0	3.0				2.1	2.2
	2.5	1.3	1.9			Current	1.5	1.6
	1.0	1.0	.9				1.2	1.1
	1.4	.5	1.1				.9	.9
	.9	.4	.7			Quick	.6	.5
	.3	.1	.4				.4	.3
	(5) 69.3	(5) 68.3	(14) 26.7				(13) 28.0	(4) 87.5
	(14) 25.6	(8) 43.1	(36) 10.3			Sales/Receivables	(20) 18.6	(15) 24.2
	(29) 12.4	(28) 12.8	(41) 8.8				(29) 12.6	(21) 17.5
	(63) 5.8	(43) 8.5	(45) 8.1				(35) 10.4	(31) 11.7
	(104) 3.5	(72) 5.1	(65) 5.6			Cost of Sales/Inventory	(45) 8.1	(48) 7.6
	(157) 2.3	(215) 1.7	(84) 4.4				(67) 5.5	(65) 5.6
	(3) 142.1	(9) 41.4	(8) 47.2				(11) 33.0	(9) 41.5
	(8) 43.3	(16) 23.3	(22) 16.6			Cost of Sales/Payables	(17) 21.1	(14) 26.1
	(27) 13.4	(27) 13.7	(37) 9.9				(28) 12.9	(33) 11.1
	2.3	9.9	3.2				8.6	9.0
	7.9	26.5	8.2			Sales/Working Capital	16.9	19.3
	-793.9	NM	-93.6				37.8	69.9
	12.9	13.1	-.4				17.9	6.6
	1.3	(12) 5.4	-7.4			EBIT/Interest	(41) 4.3	(46) 2.6
	-13.8	-4.5	-18.0				1.7	.2
						Net Profit + Depr., Dep.,		13.3
						Amort./Cur. Mat. L/T/D		(10) 1.0
								-3.3
	.1	.6	.1				.2	.2
	.4	.7	4.1			Fixed/Worth	.7	.4
	1.7	1.4	NM				1.7	2.9
	.4	2.2	.6				1.2	.8
	4.3	6.3	16.4			Debt/Worth	2.7	1.6
	91.9	14.9	NM				6.6	10.9
		203.9				% Profit Before Taxes/Tangible	58.0	46.5
		(12) 38.7				Net Worth	(40) 40.0	(42) 29.1
		-72.9					14.3	1.0
	8.4	27.0	-3.8			% Profit Before Taxes/Total	18.3	16.0
	1.4	4.2	-7.8			Assets	9.7	7.6
	-24.9	-15.1	-16.2				1.9	-1.1
	288.7	62.1	45.5				72.7	63.8
	87.5	34.2	27.8			Sales/Net Fixed Assets	24.8	27.4
	28.5	8.8	10.8				13.6	13.7
	4.6	4.3	3.7				4.9	5.2
	2.2	3.1	2.6			Sales/Total Assets	3.8	3.9
	1.6	1.2	1.8				2.6	2.4
		.4					.3	.3
		(11) .6				% Depr., Dep., Amort./Sales	(39) .6	(42) .6
		1.7					1.1	1.0
							1.0	.8
						% Officers', Directors' Owners' Comp/Sales	(12) 2.1	(17) 1.6
							3.0	2.4
2134M	30329M	230907M	569441M	417397M	1059300M	Net Sales ($)	3089575M	4031693M
96M	10531M	70846M	229333M	201148M	452260M	Total Assets ($)	825323M	1135313M

© RMA 2010

M = $ thousand   MM = $ million

See Pages 9 through 22 for Explanation of Ratios and Data

Comparative Historical Data   Current Data Sorted by Sales

4/1/07-3/31/08 ALL	4/1/08-3/31/09 ALL	4/1/09-3/31/10 ALL	Type of Statement	0-1MM	1-3MM	3-5MM	5-10MM	10-25MM	25MM & OVER
8	8	10	Unqualified	1			3	1	8
8	5	9	Reviewed	1			2	2	3
15	8	10	Compiled		7		2		1
2	3	2	Tax Returns				1	1	1
23	22	11	Other		3		1		5
					8 (4/1-9/30/09)		34 (10/1/09-3/31/10)		
56	46	42	NUMBER OF STATEMENTS	2	10		8	4	18
%	%	%	**ASSETS**	%	%	%	%	%	%
9.0	12.1	11.2	Cash & Equivalents		27.7				5.8
16.9	12.4	13.8	Trade Receivables (net)		10.5				19.2
43.3	43.5	48.1	Inventory		54.1				40.8
1.0	2.7	3.2	All Other Current		.7				5.3
70.2	70.7	76.3	Total Current		93.0				71.2
16.8	16.6	13.0	Fixed Assets (net)		4.4				17.2
7.6	6.3	6.0	Intangibles (net)		.6				7.4
5.4	6.4	4.7	All Other Non-Current		2.0				4.2
100.0	100.0	100.0	Total		100.0				100.0
			LIABILITIES						
18.5	16.8	17.7	Notes Payable-Short Term		23.7				13.4
1.2	2.5	3.6	Cur. Mat.-L.T.D.		6.7				4.2
17.7	12.0	11.4	Trade Payables		5.2				13.4
.2	.1	.2	Income Taxes Payable		.1				.2
13.6	15.0	16.5	All Other Current		10.3				18.7
51.3	46.3	49.4	Total Current		45.9				50.0
12.5	15.4	15.8	Long-Term Debt		19.1				12.2
.1	.1	.0	Deferred Taxes		.0				.0
10.3	6.7	11.1	All Other Non-Current		5.4				9.7
25.9	31.5	23.6	Net Worth		29.6				28.1
100.0	100.0	100.0	Total Liabilities & Net Worth		100.0				100.0
			INCOME DATA						
100.0	100.0	100.0	Net Sales		100.0				100.0
16.0	15.6	15.4	Gross Profit		26.0				9.8
14.3	16.0	18.5	Operating Expenses		25.6				12.3
1.6	-.4	-3.1	Operating Profit		.4				-2.5
.9	1.4	1.5	All Other Expenses (net)		.5				1.1
.8	-1.9	-4.6	Profit Before Taxes		-.1				-3.7
			RATIOS						
2.2 / 1.4 / 1.0	2.5 / 1.3 / 1.1	2.8 / 1.4 / 1.0	Current		4.1 / 2.7 / 1.1				2.3 / 1.3 / 1.0
1.0 / .5 / .2	1.1 / .4 / .2	1.1 / .5 / .3	Quick		2.1 / 1.0 / .3				.8 / .5 / .3
8 45.0 / 15 25.0 / 26 14.0	4 85.1 / 10 37.0 / 17 21.1	6 64.0 / 14 25.6 / 31 11.9	Sales/Receivables		0 UND / 8 45.2 / 30 12.0				11 34.3 / 23 15.9 / 38 9.7
33 10.9 / 49 7.4 / 78 4.7	30 12.2 / 46 7.9 / 90 4.1	48 7.7 / 70 5.2 / 139 2.6	Cost of Sales/Inventory		66 5.5 / 136 2.7 / 188 1.9				41 8.8 / 59 6.2 / 73 5.0
8 43.6 / 22 16.5 / 40 9.1	6 65.4 / 13 29.2 / 35 10.4	7 54.8 / 14 26.1 / 28 13.2	Cost of Sales/Payables		0 UND / 4 103.5 / 15 24.9				11 32.8 / 15 23.6 / 31 12.0
10.3 / 20.0 / NM	7.5 / 16.3 / 99.5	4.7 / 21.6 / -687.4	Sales/Working Capital		2.3 / 5.2 / 36.8				7.1 / 21.6 / -186.4
(51) 11.9 / 2.0 / .3	(43) 9.6 / 1.2 / -3.2	(39) 11.6 / -.5 / -7.7	EBIT/Interest		12.1 / 2.9 / -5.5				(17) 9.4 / -1.2 / -8.0
(10) 11.5 / 7.2 / 3.0			Net Profit + Depr., Dep., Amort./Cur. Mat. L/T/D						
.2 / .5 / UND	.2 / .6 / 184.3	.2 / .8 / 3.9	Fixed/Worth		.0 / .3 / .9				.3 / .8 / 9.8
.8 / 2.4 / UND	.8 / 1.6 / 999.8	1.4 / 6.3 / 86.9	Debt/Worth		.5 / 3.1 / 28.5				1.4 / 6.1 / 88.0
(43) 45.9 / 13.2 / -3.7	(36) 25.5 / 2.5 / -19.3	(34) 80.9 / .7 / -66.2	% Profit Before Taxes/Tangible Net Worth						(15) 19.3 / -16.6 / -92.1
16.7 / 3.7 / -2.7	14.0 / .4 / -9.5	9.9 / -4.3 / -16.5	% Profit Before Taxes/Total Assets		9.9 / 3.8 / -18.3				8.9 / -5.8 / -14.2
58.2 / 25.8 / 13.5	68.4 / 25.5 / 12.0	62.1 / 35.5 / 12.1	Sales/Net Fixed Assets		999.8 / 108.7 / 25.3				45.5 / 20.9 / 10.7
5.4 / 3.4 / 2.2	4.7 / 3.2 / 1.8	3.9 / 2.8 / 1.6	Sales/Total Assets		4.0 / 2.1 / 1.4				3.9 / 3.3 / 1.8
(48) .4 / .6 / 1.2	(36) .3 / .7 / 1.3	(33) .4 / 1.0 / 1.4	% Depr., Dep., Amort./Sales						(16) .6 / 1.0 / 1.4
(17) 1.4 / 2.2 / 4.5	(13) 1.5 / 1.9 / 2.7	(11) 2.2 / 2.8 / 3.7	% Officers', Directors' Owners' Comp/Sales						
5062746M	3906028M	2309508M	Net Sales ($)	1575M	19834M		56067M	84592M	2147440M
1633932M	1212954M	964214M	Total Assets ($)	3124M	10023M		30392M	37204M	883471M

Note: Columns 0-1MM, 3-5MM, 5-10MM, and 10-25MM are marked **DATA NOT AVAILABLE** for the Assets/Liabilities/Income/Ratios sections.

M = $ thousand   MM = $ million
See Pages 9 through 22 for Explanation of Ratios and Data

Current Data Sorted by Assets   **Comparative Historical Data**

0-500M	500M-2MM	2-10MM	10-50MM	50-100MM	100-250MM	Type of Statement	4/1/05-3/31/06 ALL	4/1/06-3/31/07 ALL
		3	6	2	3	Unqualified	7	12
		4	2			Reviewed	9	7
		3	1			Compiled	7	7
		1				Tax Returns	1	3
2	1	9	6	1	2	Other	23	20
	7 (4/1-9/30/09)		39 (10/1/09-3/31/10)					
2	1	20	15	3	5	**NUMBER OF STATEMENTS**	47	49
%	%	%	%	%	%	**ASSETS**	%	%
		11.8	3.6			Cash & Equivalents	7.2	5.9
		29.8	23.4			Trade Receivables (net)	28.4	28.6
		31.3	24.7			Inventory	28.9	30.0
		2.3	2.8			All Other Current	3.2	1.7
		75.1	54.6			Total Current	67.7	66.1
		16.2	26.3			Fixed Assets (net)	24.7	22.2
		3.3	11.5			Intangibles (net)	3.0	8.0
		5.3	7.6			All Other Non-Current	4.5	3.8
		100.0	100.0			Total	100.0	100.0
						LIABILITIES		
		11.0	13.1			Notes Payable-Short Term	10.8	11.0
		5.1	2.5			Cur. Mat.-L.T.D.	2.0	2.9
		12.4	15.6			Trade Payables	16.4	17.9
		.1	.0			Income Taxes Payable	.3	.3
		12.1	16.3			All Other Current	8.4	9.4
		40.7	47.6			Total Current	38.0	41.4
		10.8	20.1			Long-Term Debt	13.7	17.8
		1.2	.3			Deferred Taxes	.4	.8
		12.0	5.6			All Other Non-Current	5.0	5.8
		35.4	26.4			Net Worth	42.9	34.1
		100.0	100.0			Total Liabilities & Net Worth	100.0	100.0
						INCOME DATA		
		100.0	100.0			Net Sales	100.0	100.0
		24.1	21.4			Gross Profit	27.0	27.6
		22.5	22.4			Operating Expenses	21.6	22.4
		1.6	-1.0			Operating Profit	5.5	5.2
		.7	3.0			All Other Expenses (net)	.9	1.2
		.9	-4.1			Profit Before Taxes	4.6	3.9
						RATIOS		
		3.8	1.5			Current	3.8	2.7
		1.9	1.2				1.9	1.6
		1.2	.9				1.3	1.2
		1.9	.8			Quick	1.9	1.5
		1.1	.5				1.0	.9
		.6	.4				.5	.5
		21 17.4	58 6.3			Sales/Receivables	30 12.0	27 13.7
		45 8.1	69 5.3				41 8.9	41 8.9
		65 5.6	81 4.5				56 6.6	54 6.7
		32 11.6	33 11.1			Cost of Sales/Inventory	33 11.1	27 13.4
		43 8.5	76 4.8				49 7.5	41 8.9
		88 4.2	165 2.2				81 4.5	102 3.6
		11 33.6	20 18.0			Cost of Sales/Payables	14 27.0	15 24.8
		20 18.3	44 8.4				30 12.0	30 12.3
		36 10.0	78 4.7				51 7.1	44 8.4
		4.0	4.1			Sales/Working Capital	4.4	6.1
		7.9	19.9				8.3	13.1
		20.6	-23.5				19.4	26.2
		12.5	2.5			EBIT/Interest	18.4	14.0
		(18) 2.7	.5				(44) 8.2	(48) 5.1
		-4.3	-3.1				2.5	1.1
						Net Profit + Depr., Dep., Amort./Cur. Mat. L/T/D	12.6	8.6
							(14) 3.7	(11) 4.5
							1.8	1.9
		.1	.4			Fixed/Worth	.2	.3
		.3	.9				.5	.7
		1.0	92.1				1.4	3.1
		.4	1.6			Debt/Worth	.5	.6
		1.3	3.1				1.4	1.9
		3.4	178.1				3.1	9.3
		56.7	6.8			% Profit Before Taxes/Tangible Net Worth	41.9	55.7
		(16) 11.6	(12) -5.2				(43) 21.3	(40) 29.0
		1.7	-61.3				5.8	7.1
		23.2	2.7			% Profit Before Taxes/Total Assets	18.2	22.4
		3.5	-2.1				10.1	9.7
		-16.2	-9.1				3.6	1.0
		55.4	14.6			Sales/Net Fixed Assets	29.6	29.4
		18.9	7.8				11.3	14.7
		8.7	3.5				5.0	8.4
		2.9	2.4			Sales/Total Assets	3.1	3.8
		2.4	1.2				2.4	2.5
		2.0	.9				1.7	1.7
		.7	1.5			% Depr., Dep., Amort./Sales	.7	.8
		(14) 1.1	(14) 3.3				(39) 1.6	(42) 1.6
		2.6	6.7				2.9	2.7
						% Officers', Directors' Owners' Comp/Sales	3.5	2.4
							(13) 6.3	(15) 3.9
							11.5	5.9
2146M	5119M	262950M	632013M	305757M	958416M	Net Sales ($)	2083668M	2566329M
554M	961M	108370M	356051M	195074M	643010M	Total Assets ($)	1057560M	1077554M

M = $ thousand   MM = $ million
See Pages 9 through 22 for Explanation of Ratios and Data

Comparative Historical Data

Current Data Sorted by Sales

Comparative Historical Data columns: 4/1/07-3/31/08 ALL | 4/1/08-3/31/09 ALL | 4/1/09-3/31/10 ALL

Current Data columns date note: 7 (4/1-9/30/09) · 39 (10/1/09-3/31/10)

4/1/07-3/31/08 ALL	4/1/08-3/31/09 ALL	4/1/09-3/31/10 ALL		0-1MM	1-3MM	3-5MM	5-10MM	10-25MM	25MM & OVER
			Type of Statement						
7	7	14	Unqualified				1	5	8
8	7	6	Reviewed					5	1
7	7	4	Compiled					1	3
2	4	3	Tax Returns					1	
20	14	19	Other	1	1	1	1	6	7
44	39	46	**NUMBER OF STATEMENTS**	1	1	1	8	19	16
%	%	%	**ASSETS**	%	%	%	%	%	%
9.8	8.1	9.0	Cash & Equivalents					8.0	9.8
28.4	26.8	27.2	Trade Receivables (net)					27.6	23.6
29.7	29.8	24.5	Inventory					30.4	15.4
2.5	2.8	2.8	All Other Current					2.2	5.0
70.4	67.6	63.5	Total Current					68.2	53.8
23.3	20.4	23.8	Fixed Assets (net)					17.7	32.2
2.9	4.7	6.1	Intangibles (net)					6.6	7.0
3.2	7.3	6.7	All Other Non-Current					7.5	7.0
100.0	100.0	100.0	Total					100.0	100.0
			LIABILITIES						
10.1	8.1	9.3	Notes Payable-Short Term					11.8	5.9
1.0	2.4	3.8	Cur. Mat.-L.T.D.					1.5	1.6
17.5	16.0	14.1	Trade Payables					12.4	15.8
.0	.1	.1	Income Taxes Payable					.1	.2
17.0	15.4	13.8	All Other Current					10.3	18.3
45.6	42.1	41.1	Total Current					36.1	41.8
14.9	18.3	25.1	Long-Term Debt					15.2	14.5
.1	.1	.7	Deferred Taxes					.3	.4
8.3	4.3	14.3	All Other Non-Current					14.2	4.8
31.1	35.2	18.7	Net Worth					34.3	38.6
100.0	100.0	100.0	Total Liabilities & Net Worth					100.0	100.0
			INCOME DATA						
100.0	100.0	100.0	Net Sales					100.0	100.0
25.5	23.7	22.2	Gross Profit					22.7	15.9
21.4	23.1	21.8	Operating Expenses					20.5	16.0
4.2	.5	.3	Operating Profit					2.2	-.1
.7	1.7	1.5	All Other Expenses (net)					1.4	1.4
3.4	-1.2	-1.2	Profit Before Taxes					.8	-1.5
			RATIOS						
3.6	2.9	2.9	Current					3.1	2.0
1.7	1.8	1.5						1.7	1.2
1.1	1.1	1.1						1.3	1.0
1.8	1.4	1.3	Quick					1.4	.9
.9	.9	.9						1.0	.7
.5	.5	.5						.5	.6
22 16.8	21 17.5	32 11.2	Sales/Receivables					33 11.1	32 11.3
40 9.2	33 11.1	55 6.6						69 5.3	51 7.1
56 6.5	46 7.9	73 5.0						81 4.5	63 5.8
24 15.2	27 13.7	20 18.3	Cost of Sales/Inventory					33 11.0	17 21.8
43 8.4	46 7.9	41 8.9						59 6.2	25 14.6
114 3.2	86 4.2	98 3.7						165 2.2	64 5.7
13 27.2	15 24.5	15 24.9	Cost of Sales/Payables					15 24.0	15 24.4
30 12.3	23 15.6	32 11.5						32 11.5	33 11.0
38 9.7	38 9.5	58 6.3						57 6.4	61 6.0
4.6	5.1	4.9	Sales/Working Capital					3.5	5.7
10.2	9.8	11.9						7.0	41.5
63.4	34.5	54.1						12.4	NM
20.8	15.4	4.0	EBIT/Interest					3.7	3.5
(39) 7.3	(37) 1.9	(42) 1.4						(17) 1.2	(14) 2.1
1.3	-3.4	-3.3						-3.4	-7.5
		2.5	Net Profit + Depr., Dep., Amort./Cur. Mat. L/T/D						
	(11) .9	.9							
		-1.6							
.3	.3	.2	Fixed/Worth					.2	.6
.5	.5	.3						.4	1.0
2.4	2.8	2.5						.9	2.5
.3	.6	.8	Debt/Worth					.4	.7
1.7	2.2	2.0						1.9	2.4
10.5	8.4	7.7						3.1	4.3
50.4	34.0	28.1	% Profit Before Taxes/Tangible Net Worth					56.7	20.2
(37) 21.4	(34) 5.2	(37) 5.8						(16) 6.7	(14) 2.0
9.6	-16.0	-10.2						-10.6	-33.1
19.0	12.7	5.3	% Profit Before Taxes/Total Assets					18.1	4.8
8.2	1.8	1.7						1.8	1.1
2.0	-10.9	-8.9						-5.9	-7.9
36.5	37.7	22.5	Sales/Net Fixed Assets					34.9	11.6
17.3	13.6	11.1						15.6	6.7
6.2	7.7	4.8						7.4	3.2
3.8	3.6	2.5	Sales/Total Assets					2.4	2.4
2.6	2.9	1.9						2.2	1.8
1.6	2.0	1.2						.9	1.2
.6	.9	1.0	% Depr., Dep., Amort./Sales					.6	2.3
(40) 1.5	(29) 1.4	(36) 2.4						(15) 1.1	(14) 3.2
2.9	3.9	4.6						3.9	4.5
1.0			% Officers', Directors' Owners' Comp/Sales						
(13) 3.6									
7.3									
1900503M	2375292M	2166401M	Net Sales ($)	408M	1738M	4930M	52847M	312660M	1793818M
918341M	1127128M	1304020M	Total Assets ($)	260M	294M	3639M	32902M	201895M	1065030M

M = $ thousand   MM = $ million
See Pages 9 through 22 for Explanation of Ratios and Data

Current Data Sorted by Assets | **Comparative Historical Data**

Type of Statement	0-500M	500M-2MM	2-10MM	10-50MM	50-100MM	100-250MM		
Unqualified			2	6	3	1	24	23
Reviewed		1	7	7			27	21
Compiled			3				12	15
Tax Returns		1	1				5	4
Other	1	1	16	6	8	3	47	35
	11 (4/1-9/30/09)			56 (10/1/09-3/31/10)			4/1/05-3/31/06 ALL	4/1/06-3/31/07 ALL
NUMBER OF STATEMENTS	1	3	29	19	11	4	115	98
ASSETS	%	%	%	%	%	%	%	%
Cash & Equivalents			6.9	8.0	2.5		5.2	4.6
Trade Receivables (net)			26.7	21.7	24.9		29.0	29.6
Inventory			20.5	14.0	11.0		18.3	16.9
All Other Current			1.4	1.8	2.8		2.4	1.9
Total Current			55.5	45.5	41.2		54.8	53.0
Fixed Assets (net)			34.4	42.9	48.6		35.5	37.9
Intangibles (net)			4.9	3.0	3.0		4.4	3.8
All Other Non-Current			5.3	8.5	7.2		5.3	5.2
Total			100.0	100.0	100.0		100.0	100.0
LIABILITIES								
Notes Payable-Short Term			12.3	9.4	9.6		11.6	13.5
Cur. Mat.-L.T.D.			4.2	5.1	4.3		5.6	3.9
Trade Payables			14.7	12.3	15.3		19.6	17.9
Income Taxes Payable			.0	.0	.0		.1	.1
All Other Current			6.4	7.1	8.1		8.3	7.5
Total Current			37.5	33.9	37.3		45.1	42.9
Long-Term Debt			15.1	17.7	13.9		17.8	17.4
Deferred Taxes			.4	.4	1.8		.9	1.7
All Other Non-Current			4.8	8.9	8.6		5.5	6.7
Net Worth			42.2	39.0	38.4		30.7	31.3
Total Liabilities & Net Worth			100.0	100.0	100.0		100.0	100.0
INCOME DATA								
Net Sales			100.0	100.0	100.0		100.0	100.0
Gross Profit			19.4	14.2	13.1		18.1	18.8
Operating Expenses			19.9	12.4	14.6		14.7	15.6
Operating Profit			-.5	1.8	-1.5		3.4	3.2
All Other Expenses (net)			.7	.2	1.2		1.0	1.3
Profit Before Taxes			-1.2	1.6	-2.7		2.4	2.0
RATIOS								
Current			3.1	2.2	1.3		1.8	2.0
			1.5	1.2	1.2		1.3	1.3
			.9	.9	1.0		.9	.8
Quick			2.0	1.2	1.0		1.2	1.3
			.8	.8	.8		(114) .8	.8
			.5	.6	.6		.5	.6
Sales/Receivables			46 7.9	52 7.1	53 6.9		40 9.2	36 10.2
			55 6.7	58 6.3	68 5.3		53 6.9	50 7.2
			65 5.6	69 5.3	82 4.5		69 5.3	63 5.8
Cost of Sales/Inventory			30 12.1	32 11.5	30 12.2		25 14.8	22 16.7
			51 7.2	37 9.8	33 11.1		36 10.0	32 11.5
			83 4.4	57 6.4	47 7.7		54 6.8	51 7.1
Cost of Sales/Payables			22 16.4	23 16.1	31 11.7		27 13.4	20 18.5
			41 9.0	36 10.1	52 7.0		38 9.5	32 11.3
			58 6.3	43 8.5	65 5.6		54 6.8	43 8.4
Sales/Working Capital			4.4	5.2	17.0		6.1	8.2
			10.3	22.9	27.3		17.3	17.1
			-43.5	-37.6	-88.6		-23.4	-27.7
EBIT/Interest			11.8	5.0	4.1		6.5	5.7
			.3	(18) .8	2.6		(104) 2.2	(94) 2.3
			-3.3	-.3	-7.1		.6	.2
Net Profit + Depr., Dep., Amort./Cur. Mat. L/T/D							5.4	4.8
							(35) 2.0	(33) 2.0
							.8	1.4
Fixed/Worth			.4	.6	.9		.6	.7
			.9	1.3	1.5		1.3	1.2
			2.0	2.0	2.1		2.9	3.3
Debt/Worth			.7	.5	1.7		1.0	.9
			1.7	1.7	1.9		2.9	2.2
			4.6	3.1	3.1		5.8	5.5
% Profit Before Taxes/Tangible Net Worth			14.8	35.0	13.4		27.5	32.3
		(27)	-8.3	(16) 1.0	10.6		(98) 14.5	(84) 11.6
			-27.3	-2.7	-38.8		.6	-2.9
% Profit Before Taxes/Total Assets			7.4	10.8	4.7		11.4	9.0
			-2.2	-.4	3.0		3.9	3.2
			-7.6	-5.4	-12.2		-.7	-1.7
Sales/Net Fixed Assets			8.0	4.9	4.4		10.0	10.2
			5.5	3.6	3.1		6.0	5.8
			3.4	2.5	1.5		3.4	3.2
Sales/Total Assets			2.2	1.8	1.6		2.4	2.7
			1.7	1.2	1.5		1.9	2.0
			1.3	1.0	1.0		1.5	1.5
% Depr., Dep., Amort./Sales			2.2	4.4	2.7		2.1	2.1
		(27)	3.4	(16) 6.0	(10) 4.4		(97) 3.3	(90) 3.4
			5.4	7.4	5.7		4.8	4.5
% Officers', Directors' Owners' Comp/Sales			2.2					.9
		(12)	4.8				(27) 4.2	(27) 4.0
			6.2				7.3	7.4
Net Sales ($)	172M	9885M	293061M	606521M	1130139M	1019660M	6544754M	5398039M
Total Assets ($)	84M	3788M	169748M	466747M	820693M	575712M	3756930M	2918904M

M = $ thousand   MM = $ million
See Pages 9 through 22 for Explanation of Ratios and Data

Comparative Historical Data

Current Data Sorted by Sales

			Type of Statement						
13	14	12	Unqualified				5	3	9
17	12	15	Reviewed		1	1		4	4
6	11	3	Compiled				3		
2	1	2	Tax Returns		1			1	
39	38	35	Other	1	2	2	7	9	14
4/1/07-3/31/08 ALL	4/1/08-3/31/09 ALL	4/1/09-3/31/10 ALL		0-1MM	11 (4/1-9/30/09) 1-3MM	3-5MM	56 (10/1/09-3/31/10) 5-10MM	10-25MM	25MM & OVER
77	76	67	**NUMBER OF STATEMENTS**	1	4	3	15	17	27
%	%	%	**ASSETS**	%	%	%	%	%	%
5.3	6.4	6.2	Cash & Equivalents				10.1	7.5	3.9
26.2	23.7	25.1	Trade Receivables (net)				23.5	27.6	25.0
17.8	19.0	16.3	Inventory				20.2	17.3	13.6
2.2	2.2	2.2	All Other Current				.9	2.3	3.0
51.5	51.3	49.7	Total Current				54.8	54.7	45.6
37.8	38.6	40.3	Fixed Assets (net)				36.9	28.7	47.3
2.9	2.8	3.7	Intangibles (net)				4.2	6.2	2.1
7.8	7.4	6.3	All Other Non-Current				4.1	10.4	5.1
100.0	100.0	100.0	Total				100.0	100.0	100.0
			LIABILITIES						
12.9	12.2	10.8	Notes Payable-Short Term				12.3	11.4	8.1
4.5	5.4	4.6	Cur. Mat.-L.T.D.				6.0	2.4	5.4
16.1	15.4	15.3	Trade Payables				13.7	15.8	16.2
.1	.2	.0	Income Taxes Payable				.0	.0	.0
7.3	6.7	8.7	All Other Current				6.7	7.6	7.3
41.0	39.8	39.4	Total Current				38.8	37.1	37.1
17.1	16.5	19.1	Long-Term Debt				16.9	11.3	18.4
.8	.6	.7	Deferred Taxes				.7	.1	1.3
6.9	5.8	7.0	All Other Non-Current				3.5	.8	11.6
34.3	37.2	33.8	Net Worth				40.2	50.6	31.6
100.0	100.0	100.0	Total Liabilties & Net Worth				100.0	100.0	100.0
			INCOME DATA						
100.0	100.0	100.0	Net Sales				100.0	100.0	100.0
18.8	19.6	16.2	Gross Profit				23.2	16.1	13.2
14.8	17.4	16.9	Operating Expenses				24.1	12.4	13.3
4.0	2.2	-.6	Operating Profit				-.9	3.7	-.1
1.2	1.0	1.0	All Other Expenses (net)				1.1	.1	1.4
2.8	1.3	-1.6	Profit Before Taxes				-1.9	3.6	-1.6
			RATIOS						
2.2	2.0	2.2					4.2	2.6	1.5
1.3	1.3	1.2	Current				1.6	1.3	1.2
.9	1.0	.9					.8	.9	1.0
1.5	1.3	1.2					2.6	1.8	1.0
.8	.8	.8	Quick				.8	.9	.8
.5	.5	.6					.4	.6	.6
41 9.0	32 11.3	46 7.9					45 8.0	47 7.8	52 7.1
49 7.4	45 8.2	60 6.1	Sales/Receivables				49 7.5	58 6.3	64 5.7
58 6.3	54 6.7	69 5.3					62 5.9	72 5.1	75 4.8
24 15.3	24 15.0	29 12.7					25 14.3	30 12.1	30 12.2
40 9.2	42 8.8	38 9.6	Cost of Sales/Inventory				54 6.8	45 8.2	36 10.1
58 6.3	66 5.6	64 5.7					76 4.8	61 5.9	53 6.9
23 16.0	18 20.8	24 15.3					18 20.4	25 14.7	27 13.3
35 10.5	28 12.9	41 9.0	Cost of Sales/Payables				31 11.6	41 8.9	41 8.8
45 8.1	47 7.8	59 6.2					51 7.2	56 6.5	61 6.0
6.8	7.0	5.6					4.2	5.4	7.1
15.7	19.3	20.3	Sales/Working Capital				5.6	20.3	23.3
-36.4	NM	-42.3					-18.5	-42.9	-88.6
6.6	4.7	4.1					3.4	16.6	2.9
(73) 2.2	(70) 1.8	(66) .5	EBIT/Interest				-2.2	(16) 7.8	.8
.1	-1.7	-2.9					-10.1	.0	-.6
3.7	3.0	1.9							
(26) 1.7	(26) 1.9	(15) .9	Net Profit + Depr., Dep., Amort./Cur. Mat. L/T/D						
1.2	.8	.1							
.5	.6	.7					.5	.4	.9
1.3	1.3	1.3	Fixed/Worth				1.2	.8	1.6
3.5	2.6	2.3					3.5	1.3	2.3
.8	.8	.8					1.0	.5	.9
2.0	2.2	1.9	Debt/Worth				1.7	1.2	2.6
7.3	5.5	4.7					6.4	2.9	4.4
41.6	30.2	14.7					3.5	39.6	13.4
(65) 15.6	(68) 7.0	(60) -.3	% Profit Before Taxes/Tangible Net Worth			(14) -9.8	1.9	(23) 3.7
-.7	-11.2	-19.2					-82.2	-12.7	-3.8
12.3	9.4	6.4					2.9	16.1	4.4
5.3	1.7	-.6	% Profit Before Taxes/Total Assets				-4.2	1.3	-.5
-1.3	-4.8	-7.6					-18.6	-2.0	-7.1
8.9	9.8	7.1					8.2	9.1	5.1
5.1	5.7	4.3	Sales/Net Fixed Assets				5.5	6.1	3.1
3.2	3.2	2.6					3.1	4.0	1.7
2.3	2.5	2.0					2.2	2.3	1.8
1.9	2.0	1.5	Sales/Total Assets				1.5	1.7	1.5
1.5	1.3	1.0					1.3	1.1	1.0
2.2	2.4	2.6					3.2	1.9	3.5
(64) 3.5	(65) 3.3	(57) 4.3	% Depr., Dep., Amort./Sales				4.0	(16) 3.6	(21) 5.6
5.1	4.8	5.9					6.0	4.9	6.4
1.6	2.0	2.2							
(21) 3.1	(23) 3.3	(16) 4.8	% Officers', Directors' Owners' Comp/Sales						
4.7	5.4	6.4							
4540296M	4777342M	3059438M	Net Sales ($)	172M	8330M	13212M	111375M	303205M	2623144M
2412961M	2510707M	2036772M	Total Assets ($)	84M	12562M	14254M	78572M	206801M	1724499M

© RMA 2010

M = $ thousand   MM = $ million
See Pages 9 through 22 for Explanation of Ratios and Data

Current Data Sorted by Assets   **Comparative Historical Data**

0-500M	500M-2MM	2-10MM	10-50MM	50-100MM	100-250MM	Type of Statement	4/1/05-3/31/06 ALL	4/1/06-3/31/07 ALL
1	1	15	27	12	17	Unqualified	99	102
2	4	41	14			Reviewed	76	64
1	13	19	2			Compiled	61	57
6	6	8				Tax Returns	26	27
4	22	41	58	22	14	Other	181	151
	55 (4/1-9/30/09)		295 (10/1/09-3/31/10)					
14	46	124	101	34	31	**NUMBER OF STATEMENTS**	443	401
%	%	%	%	%	%	**ASSETS**	%	%
18.5	12.2	8.3	6.2	6.7	6.0	Cash & Equivalents	6.6	5.5
30.8	23.5	22.9	25.7	23.8	21.0	Trade Receivables (net)	27.6	26.1
14.2	31.0	33.8	28.0	18.3	16.4	Inventory	26.0	26.7
.4	2.0	2.3	4.0	3.0	5.7	All Other Current	2.7	2.7
63.9	68.6	67.2	64.0	51.8	49.2	Total Current	62.9	61.0
22.8	24.0	24.1	27.5	38.3	31.3	Fixed Assets (net)	28.3	29.5
3.6	2.8	4.2	3.7	4.7	13.6	Intangibles (net)	3.2	4.2
9.3	4.6	4.5	4.8	5.2	6.0	All Other Non-Current	5.5	5.3
100.0	100.0	100.0	100.0	100.0	100.0	Total	100.0	100.0
						LIABILITIES		
17.1	17.3	13.2	13.3	7.2	3.3	Notes Payable-Short Term	13.2	12.9
6.2	4.8	4.3	3.6	3.1	3.6	Cur. Mat.-L.T.D.	3.9	4.1
23.2	17.8	13.7	17.3	19.1	19.7	Trade Payables	19.1	18.0
.0	.0	.2	.1	.0	.1	Income Taxes Payable	.4	.3
10.6	11.5	8.3	10.2	9.4	14.8	All Other Current	10.4	11.2
57.0	51.4	39.7	44.4	38.9	41.5	Total Current	47.0	46.5
9.8	16.4	15.0	16.1	19.4	15.4	Long-Term Debt	15.7	16.3
.6	.6	.5	.3	.9	1.7	Deferred Taxes	.7	.7
7.2	8.3	7.8	5.6	5.9	12.0	All Other Non-Current	6.1	5.6
25.2	23.2	37.0	33.5	35.0	29.5	Net Worth	30.5	30.9
100.0	100.0	100.0	100.0	100.0	100.0	Total Liabilities & Net Worth	100.0	100.0
						INCOME DATA		
100.0	100.0	100.0	100.0	100.0	100.0	Net Sales	100.0	100.0
40.9	37.1	27.4	20.6	15.6	14.1	Gross Profit	25.9	25.4
36.0	35.7	25.6	17.8	14.9	12.7	Operating Expenses	21.9	20.8
4.9	1.4	1.7	2.8	.7	1.3	Operating Profit	3.9	4.6
1.0	1.0	1.2	1.3	1.6	3.4	All Other Expenses (net)	1.1	1.2
3.9	.4	.6	1.5	-.9	-2.1	Profit Before Taxes	2.8	3.3
						RATIOS		
2.1	2.5	3.2	2.6	2.6	2.2		2.1	2.1
1.1	1.5	1.8	1.5	1.4	1.2	Current	1.4	1.3
.7	1.0	1.2	1.1	.9	.9		1.0	1.0
1.8	1.5	1.5	1.2	1.3	1.1		1.1	1.1
.9	.8	.7	.8	1.0	.8	Quick	(442) .8	(400) .7
.3	.4	.5	.5	.5	.5		.5	.5
20 18.7	25 14.8	24 15.2	37 9.9	37 9.8	31 11.6		33 10.9	32 11.5
37 9.7	39 9.4	39 9.4	51 7.2	50 7.3	50 7.3	Sales/Receivables	47 7.8	46 8.0
75 4.9	50 7.3	56 6.5	66 5.5	69 5.3	65 5.6		61 6.0	59 6.2
0 UND	31 11.9	45 8.1	41 9.0	23 16.1	17 21.2		25 14.3	28 13.2
23 15.6	77 4.8	76 4.8	68 5.4	45 8.1	46 8.0	Cost of Sales/Inventory	49 7.4	55 6.6
47 7.8	110 3.3	140 2.6	106 3.4	83 4.4	66 5.5		90 4.0	93 3.9
28 13.0	14 26.1	13 27.6	24 15.1	29 12.6	31 11.7		22 16.6	22 16.3
38 9.5	31 11.9	30 12.3	37 9.9	38 9.6	40 9.1	Cost of Sales/Payables	36 10.0	36 10.0
55 6.6	62 5.9	45 8.1	52 7.0	58 6.3	62 5.9		56 6.6	55 6.6
10.3	5.6	4.0	4.2	4.2	5.1		6.4	6.3
41.8	11.4	7.3	7.9	10.5	18.9	Sales/Working Capital	13.0	15.4
-6.9	NM	17.8	45.5	-36.0	-37.0		999.8	-136.2
	6.3	5.9	7.4	7.6	3.5		9.6	8.5
	(43) 2.3	(114) 1.7	(95) 3.9	(33) .1	(29) 1.0	EBIT/Interest	(397) 3.1	(360) 3.1
	-3.7	-1.6	.8	-2.5	-2.5		1.1	1.0
5.6	3.1	6.1	6.6	4.2		Net Profit + Depr., Dep., Amort./Cur. Mat. L/T/D	6.2	5.2
(10) 1.3	(31) 1.4	(34) 2.1	(14) 2.6	(11) 2.6			(132) 2.7	(126) 2.6
-.4	.9	.6	1.0	.1			1.1	
.1	.1	.2	.4	.6	.8		.3	.4
.5	1.0	.5	.7	1.0	1.4	Fixed/Worth	1.0	1.0
NM	3.1	1.5	1.8	1.9	-5.1		2.7	3.0
.5	.8	.5	.9	.7	.9		.9	.9
1.7	2.6	1.7	2.1	1.4	3.1	Debt/Worth	2.4	2.4
-13.5	74.0	4.3	4.7	3.8	-12.1		8.0	7.6
70.5	38.1	33.0	35.8	12.6	15.0		40.9	43.7
(10) 12.5	(36) 18.0	(106) 6.7	(90) 11.1	(29) .1	(22) .9	% Profit Before Taxes/Tangible Net Worth	(376) 17.7	(335) 20.5
-1.3	-12.8	-2.4	-4.1	-8.7	-16.8		2.4	5.0
24.6	15.7	11.1	10.8	6.5	2.3		11.8	12.9
2.5	3.8	2.2	4.9	-.7	-1.8	% Profit Before Taxes/Total Assets	4.8	6.0
-3.7	-11.7	-5.2	-1.5	-4.9	-8.2		.3	.4
UND	57.6	30.1	19.8	6.8	9.9		21.3	18.4
22.5	17.0	9.5	6.0	3.6	6.0	Sales/Net Fixed Assets	8.8	8.2
4.2	4.7	4.7	3.2	2.8	3.2		4.5	4.4
5.8	3.1	2.5	2.3	2.1	2.0		2.8	2.7
2.5	2.3	1.9	1.6	1.6	1.6	Sales/Total Assets	2.1	2.1
1.7	1.6	1.4	1.2	1.1	1.0		1.5	1.5
.6	.7	1.1	1.6	2.0	1.8		1.1	1.2
(10) 1.3	(36) 1.6	(110) 2.5	(81) 3.2	(22) 3.7	(19) 3.5	% Depr., Dep., Amort./Sales	(370) 2.3	(342) 2.4
2.9	4.9	4.8	5.1	6.9	5.1		4.1	4.2
	3.6	2.8	.5				2.0	1.9
	(19) 6.5	(48) 4.6	(13) 1.6			% Officers', Directors' Owners' Comp/Sales	(125) 3.8	(106) 4.0
	8.6	7.9	2.8				7.2	6.8
7601M	146261M	1308306M	4704868M	4611760M	7934644M	Net Sales ($)	25583082M	25627169M
2449M	61527M	636910M	2351542M	2651997M	4812693M	Total Assets ($)	13239514M	12943175M

M = $ thousand   MM = $ million
See Pages 9 through 22 for Explanation of Ratios and Data

Comparative Historical Data   ## Current Data Sorted by Sales

				Type of Statement						
69		77	73	Unqualified	1	1	1	3	14	53
66		62	61	Reviewed	2	4	3	25	19	8
34		41	35	Compiled	1	9	10	10	3	2
24		32	20	Tax Returns	4	6	5	4	1	
165		148	161	Other	5	15	10	19	34	78
4/1/07-3/31/08 ALL		4/1/08-3/31/09 ALL	4/1/09-3/31/10 ALL		55 (4/1-9/30/09)			295 (10/1/09-3/31/10)		
					0-1MM	1-3MM	3-5MM	5-10MM	10-25MM	25MM & OVER
358		360	350	NUMBER OF STATEMENTS	13	35	29	61	71	141
%		%	%	ASSETS	%	%	%	%	%	%
6.8		7.9	8.3	Cash & Equivalents	13.5	10.5	10.4	8.6	7.7	6.9
25.3		23.4	24.0	Trade Receivables (net)	26.1	23.8	19.8	19.8	25.6	25.7
29.3		29.3	27.9	Inventory	22.5	24.3	30.7	37.3	29.9	23.7
2.6		2.5	3.0	All Other Current	1.0	1.7	3.2	1.3	2.7	4.5
64.0		63.1	63.2	Total Current	63.1	60.3	64.1	67.1	66.0	60.7
26.3		26.5	27.0	Fixed Assets (net)	24.9	28.2	25.0	23.7	27.6	28.5
4.8		4.7	4.7	Intangibles (net)	3.5	5.1	6.1	4.5	1.4	6.2
4.9		5.7	5.0	All Other Non-Current	8.0	6.4	4.8	4.8	5.0	4.5
100.0		100.0	100.0	Total	100.0	100.0	100.0	100.0	100.0	100.0
				LIABILITIES						
12.2		14.1	12.5	Notes Payable-Short Term	21.2	14.4	19.6	12.2	11.7	10.2
4.6		4.5	4.1	Cur. Mat.-L.T.D.	8.5	4.2	6.1	4.2	3.8	3.3
17.0		16.2	16.7	Trade Payables	14.6	18.0	10.4	14.0	16.4	19.2
.2		.2	.1	Income Taxes Payable	.0	.1	.5	.1	.1	.1
10.0		9.3	10.1	All Other Current	16.8	8.6	12.0	6.3	7.3	12.4
44.1		44.4	43.4	Total Current	61.0	45.3	48.6	36.9	39.3	45.1
16.3		15.3	15.8	Long-Term Debt	16.0	16.6	13.3	18.0	13.0	16.4
.7		.6	.6	Deferred Taxes	.6	.8	.6	.4	.5	.8
5.9		6.6	7.4	All Other Non-Current	7.7	11.2	11.2	5.4	9.6	5.4
33.0		33.1	32.8	Net Worth	14.3	26.2	26.3	39.3	37.6	32.3
100.0		100.0	100.0	Total Liabilties & Net Worth	100.0	100.0	100.0	100.0	100.0	100.0
				INCOME DATA						
100.0		100.0	100.0	Net Sales	100.0	100.0	100.0	100.0	100.0	100.0
25.3		25.8	24.9	Gross Profit	39.1	41.2	30.6	30.6	22.8	17.0
20.9		22.7	22.9	Operating Expenses	37.3	40.8	31.0	28.3	20.6	14.3
4.4		3.1	2.0	Operating Profit	1.8	.3	-.3	2.2	2.2	2.7
1.5		1.1	1.4	All Other Expenses (net)	1.9	.8	2.2	.9	.8	1.9
2.9		2.0	.6	Profit Before Taxes	-.1	-.4	-2.5	1.3	1.4	.7
				RATIOS						
2.3		2.5	2.6		1.6	2.9	2.6	3.4	3.4	2.3
1.5		1.5	1.5	Current	.9	1.6	1.4	1.9	1.9	1.5
1.1		1.0	1.1		.7	.9	1.1	1.3	1.2	1.0
1.2		1.2	1.3		1.3	1.6	1.1	1.3	1.5	1.1
.7		.7	.8	Quick	.5	.8	.8	.7	.8	.8
.4		.4	.5		.3	.4	.3	.5	.5	.5
30	12.2	25	14.4	30	12.1	Sales/Receivables	22	16.9	26	14.0	24	14.9	20	18.3	35	10.6	33	11.2

Sales/Receivables:

30	12.2	25	14.4	30	12.1	22	16.9	26	14.0	24	14.9	20	18.3	35	10.6	33	11.2
44	8.3	38	9.6	46	8.0	70	5.2	41	8.8	41	8.8	36	10.1	48	7.6	48	7.6
57	6.4	53	6.9	63	5.8	82	4.4	59	6.2	70	5.2	55	6.7	66	5.5	64	5.7

Cost of Sales/Inventory:

34	10.6	31	11.7	36	10.0	0	UND	17	21.1	58	6.3	60	6.1	42	8.8	28	13.2
58	6.3	61	6.0	66	5.5	37	10.0	68	5.4	83	4.4	92	4.0	73	5.0	53	6.9
115	3.2	108	3.4	109	3.3	143	2.6	127	2.9	145	2.5	142	2.6	118	3.1	87	4.2

Cost of Sales/Payables:

22	16.8	18	20.1	19	19.1	26	14.1	13	27.6	10	35.3	13	27.7	23	16.2	22	16.9
35	10.4	32	11.4	35	10.3	42	8.7	37	9.8	29	12.6	28	13.1	36	10.2	37	9.9
52	7.0	49	7.5	54	6.8	61	6.0	62	5.9	45	8.2	54	6.7	58	6.3	52	7.0

Sales/Working Capital:

5.2		5.4		4.5	19.1	4.4	3.8	4.0	3.7	5.8
10.9		11.1		9.4	-23.3	9.4	7.8	6.4	8.9	10.2
57.6		206.9		49.7	-5.6	-24.3	57.8	13.7	25.7	290.1

EBIT/Interest:

	8.9		7.1		6.4			6.2	3.2	6.1	8.8	6.9
(315)	2.6	(316)	2.4	(322)	2.2	(32)	.5	1.3	(56)	2.5	(64)	3.4	(133)	2.6
	1.0		-.4		-1.0		-4.2	-3.5	-.9	.6	-.5

Net Profit + Depr., Dep., Amort./Cur. Mat. L/T/D:

	4.6		5.1		4.3					3.3	4.7	5.4
(92)	2.1	(96)	2.2	(100)	2.0			(17)	1.4	(21)	1.4	(48)	2.4
	1.2		.8		.6				1.0	-.4	.7

Fixed/Worth:

.3		.3	.3	.3	.1	.3	.2	.3	.4
.9		.8	.8	1.8	1.0	.8	.5	.7	.9
2.5		2.2	2.0	-4.2	2.8	-4.1	1.6	1.6	1.8

Debt/Worth:

.8		.8	.7	.6	.6	1.1	.4	.6	.9
2.3		2.2	2.0	4.4	2.7	2.5	1.5	1.9	1.9
7.4		6.9	5.6	-9.6	-61.6	-14.0	4.0	4.4	4.9

% Profit Before Taxes/Tangible Net Worth:

	44.0		36.3		33.6			39.1	12.2	28.2	35.4	35.3
(305)	18.3	(307)	13.5	(293)	7.9	(26)	8.0	(21)	3.9	(54)	7.4	(63)	8.6	(120)	9.4
	2.2		-4.5		-5.7		-16.4	-21.7	-5.6	-4.1	-5.0

% Profit Before Taxes/Total Assets:

14.0		11.2	9.8	24.7	12.7	5.4	11.8	9.9	8.9
5.7		3.5	2.3	1.2	-.4	.5	3.4	3.2	2.2
-.1		-3.2	-4.7	-5.2	-15.1	-10.7	-2.1	-2.1	-4.1

Sales/Net Fixed Assets:

20.9		24.2	23.3	134.0	30.5	33.6	39.0	19.6	19.5
8.8		8.1	7.2	15.5	7.2	8.2	10.4	6.6	6.2
4.7		4.5	3.6	3.4	3.5	3.7	4.1	4.0	3.4

Sales/Total Assets:

2.7		2.8	2.5	2.8	2.5	2.3	2.6	2.4	2.5
2.0		2.0	1.8	1.9	1.7	1.6	2.0	1.8	1.8
1.5		1.5	1.3	1.3	1.2	1.0	1.3	1.3	1.3

% Depr., Dep., Amort./Sales:

	1.2		1.1		1.2				.9	1.3	1.1	.9	1.5
(287)	2.4	(288)	2.5	(278)	2.6	(29)	2.2	(26)	2.8	(53)	2.4	(58)	3.0	(103)	2.9
	4.0		4.2		4.9				6.1	4.8	4.0	5.3	4.8

% Officers', Directors' Owners' Comp/Sales:

	1.5		2.1		2.6			3.9	3.5	-2.6	2.0	
(92)	3.5	(94)	3.8	(88)	4.2	(20)	7.2	(17)	4.2	(21)	3.7	(18)	2.7	
	7.5		6.8		7.7			9.7	8.6	7.8	5.6	

21943075M		20680657M	18713440M	Net Sales ($)	5454M	75836M	118516M	417181M	1192200M	16904253M
10925804M		10336026M	10517118M	Total Assets ($)	3500M	50156M	92194M	273241M	722967M	9375060M

M = $ thousand   MM = $ million
See Pages 9 through 22 for Explanation of Ratios and Data

Current Data Sorted by Assets   Comparative Historical Data

0-500M	500M-2MM	2-10MM	10-50MM	50-100MM	100-250MM	Type of Statement	4/1/05-3/31/06 ALL	4/1/06-3/31/07 ALL
		3	10	7	4	Unqualified	22	17
	1	15	5			Reviewed	16	21
	1	2	1			Compiled	10	5
	5	4				Tax Returns	4	7
1	1	19	16	5	5	Other	35	39
	21 (4/1-9/30/09)		84 (10/1/09-3/31/10)					
1	8	43	32	12	9	NUMBER OF STATEMENTS	87	89
%	%	%	%	%	%	ASSETS	%	%
		7.0	7.2	6.8		Cash & Equivalents	6.5	5.3
		23.4	17.7	13.1		Trade Receivables (net)	20.3	20.7
		40.3	35.0	35.2		Inventory	37.5	38.5
		2.0	1.8	4.5		All Other Current	1.6	2.5
		72.7	61.7	59.6		Total Current	66.0	67.0
		20.1	28.8	27.5		Fixed Assets (net)	26.1	25.3
		2.7	4.5	9.8		Intangibles (net)	2.3	3.6
		4.6	4.9	3.1		All Other Non-Current	5.6	4.1
		100.0	100.0	100.0		Total	100.0	100.0
						LIABILITIES		
		16.1	9.6	18.4		Notes Payable-Short Term	11.6	11.4
		2.5	5.0	2.7		Cur. Mat.-L.T.D.	4.7	3.6
		13.0	7.9	7.6		Trade Payables	15.1	14.8
		1.2	.1	.0		Income Taxes Payable	.3	.0
		7.9	9.6	10.5		All Other Current	12.8	12.4
		40.6	32.2	39.2		Total Current	44.4	42.3
		12.4	18.1	16.7		Long-Term Debt	16.5	16.8
		1.1	.9	.3		Deferred Taxes	.3	.3
		1.9	3.6	8.1		All Other Non-Current	10.2	8.6
		43.9	45.2	35.7		Net Worth	28.5	32.0
		100.0	100.0	100.0		Total Liabilities & Net Worth	100.0	100.0
						INCOME DATA		
		100.0	100.0	100.0		Net Sales	100.0	100.0
		29.1	22.9	21.3		Gross Profit	27.3	29.6
		23.0	14.5	13.8		Operating Expenses	21.5	21.9
		6.1	8.4	7.5		Operating Profit	5.7	7.7
		1.2	1.7	3.4		All Other Expenses (net)	1.4	1.2
		4.9	6.8	4.1		Profit Before Taxes	4.3	6.5
						RATIOS		
		3.1	3.4	2.4		Current	2.6	2.3
		1.9	1.7	1.5			1.5	1.6
		1.3	1.3	1.2			1.1	1.2
		1.5	1.4	.9		Quick	1.2	1.0
		.6	.7	.6			.6	.6
		.4	.4	.2			.3	.3
		27 13.4	32 11.4	39 9.4		Sales/Receivables	29 12.6	28 13.2
		40 9.1	41 8.9	44 8.3			41 8.9	46 8.0
		56 6.5	61 5.9	50 7.2			61 5.9	59 6.2
		56 6.6	76 4.8	64 5.7		Cost of Sales/Inventory	60 6.1	68 5.4
		113 3.2	116 3.2	123 3.0			109 3.4	109 3.3
		166 2.2	172 2.1	140 2.6			162 2.3	172 2.1
		14 25.7	12 29.3	12 29.4		Cost of Sales/Payables	22 16.9	22 16.5
		28 12.9	24 15.1	26 14.2			33 11.2	37 9.9
		41 9.0	37 9.8	43 8.5			51 7.2	54 6.8
		3.7	2.6	2.8		Sales/Working Capital	4.0	3.8
		5.1	5.4	6.7			8.0	6.1
		13.4	12.6	10.0			22.9	18.3
		17.7	6.1	5.6		EBIT/Interest	9.5	9.4
		(41) 5.3	(31) 4.0	(11) 2.0			(80) 3.8	(83) 3.6
		2.5	1.7	1.2			1.5	1.8
			3.5			Net Profit + Depr., Dep., Amort./Cur. Mat. L/T/D	3.9	8.4
		(13) 1.8					(26) 2.6	(31) 2.5
		1.2					1.1	1.3
		.1	.4	.2		Fixed/Worth	.2	.3
		.4	.8	.9			.7	.8
		1.0	1.4	5.3			2.1	2.1
		.7	.4	1.0		Debt/Worth	.9	1.1
		1.4	2.2	3.4			1.9	2.1
		3.6	3.2	23.9			6.5	5.4
		49.9	39.4	34.0		% Profit Before Taxes/Tangible Net Worth	44.4	65.9
		(41) 24.6	(31) 20.3	(10) 7.7			(74) 23.3	(78) 24.7
		13.3	5.2	4.4			12.2	7.7
		18.0	13.2	6.2		% Profit Before Taxes/Total Assets	15.5	17.4
		11.4	5.6	2.6			7.9	7.1
		3.8	2.3	.9			2.3	2.9
		42.1	9.3	12.2		Sales/Net Fixed Assets	17.6	18.2
		14.8	4.4	5.8			7.9	8.8
		7.0	3.1	2.3			3.7	3.9
		2.5	1.7	1.6		Sales/Total Assets	2.6	2.5
		2.0	1.4	1.0			1.5	1.7
		1.3	1.0	.6			1.2	1.3
		.5	2.1	2.1		% Depr., Dep., Amort./Sales	1.6	1.8
		(38) 1.4	(31) 3.5	2.6			(69) 3.1	(76) 2.9
		3.6	4.3	6.4			5.1	4.0
		2.9				% Officers', Directors' Owners' Comp/Sales	1.4	1.7
		(11) 6.1					(20) 3.8	(23) 5.0
		10.9					9.8	7.1
595M	25220M	454161M	885208M	857345M	2359609M	Net Sales ($)	2743771M	2928496M
376M	8913M	231063M	669580M	776380M	1440620M	Total Assets ($)	2026868M	1922681M

Comparative Historical Data

Current Data Sorted by Sales

			Type of Statement						
23	30	24	Unqualified			1		1	7	16
21	21	21	Reviewed		1	3	7	8	2
7	5	4	Compiled		1			3	
7	9	10	Tax Returns	1	3		2	1	
48	52	46	Other		3	4	10	14	18
4/1/07-3/31/08 ALL	4/1/08-3/31/09 ALL	4/1/09-3/31/10 ALL			21 (4/1-9/30/09)		84 (10/1/09-3/31/10)		
				0-1MM	1-3MM	3-5MM	5-10MM	10-25MM	25MM & OVER
106	117	105	NUMBER OF STATEMENTS	1	5	10	20	33	36
%	%	%	**ASSETS**	%	%	%	%	%	%
6.6	7.0	7.4	Cash & Equivalents			3.0	5.8	6.9	9.1
20.8	21.2	20.3	Trade Receivables (net)			15.8	22.4	22.2	17.8
38.5	38.7	36.3	Inventory			41.7	44.0	38.5	32.2
4.2	2.2	2.4	All Other Current			2.0	2.1	1.7	3.3
70.1	69.1	66.4	Total Current			62.5	74.3	69.3	62.3
21.2	22.3	24.7	Fixed Assets (net)			24.4	22.1	22.2	26.9
4.3	4.9	4.2	Intangibles (net)			9.4	1.0	2.3	7.0
4.4	3.7	4.6	All Other Non-Current			3.7	2.7	6.2	3.9
100.0	100.0	100.0	Total			100.0	100.0	100.0	100.0
			LIABILITIES						
12.1	11.6	12.5	Notes Payable-Short Term			18.3	15.4	14.5	9.0
3.9	4.7	3.7	Cur. Mat.-L.T.D.			5.0	2.8	3.6	3.2
13.9	12.3	10.4	Trade Payables			18.7	8.6	11.7	8.4
.6	.6	.6	Income Taxes Payable			.0	.6	1.4	.1
12.7	10.2	8.9	All Other Current			4.1	7.3	9.0	11.0
43.2	39.3	36.0	Total Current			46.2	34.6	40.2	31.7
15.4	18.2	15.8	Long-Term Debt			22.4	11.5	12.5	18.5
.3	.6	.9	Deferred Taxes			.0	.7	1.3	.9
6.9	7.2	4.2	All Other Non-Current			1.7	1.5	3.1	7.4
34.2	34.7	43.1	Net Worth			29.7	51.7	42.8	41.5
100.0	100.0	100.0	Total Liabilities & Net Worth			100.0	100.0	100.0	100.0
			INCOME DATA						
100.0	100.0	100.0	Net Sales			100.0	100.0	100.0	100.0
31.6	30.2	26.1	Gross Profit			35.2	29.8	23.4	23.0
22.4	22.0	18.9	Operating Expenses			30.2	20.4	18.8	14.1
9.3	8.2	7.1	Operating Profit			5.1	9.4	4.6	8.9
2.2	1.4	1.6	All Other Expenses (net)			1.4	1.2	1.7	2.1
7.1	6.8	5.5	Profit Before Taxes			3.7	8.2	2.8	6.8
			RATIOS						
2.6	2.7	3.1	Current			1.9	4.4	2.6	3.3
1.6	1.9	1.9				1.4	2.6	1.9	1.8
1.3	1.3	1.3				1.1	1.3	1.3	1.3
1.1	1.4	1.3	Quick			.6	2.4	1.2	1.2
.6	.7	.7				.5	.7	.7	.7
.4	.4	.5				.3	.4	.4	.5
25 14.5	29 12.6	32 11.6	Sales/Receivables			27 13.7	26 13.9	26 14.1	34 10.6
42 8.7	42 8.6	42 8.7				42 8.7	36 10.1	41 8.9	45 8.1
55 6.6	56 6.5	55 6.7				64 5.7	56 6.6	53 6.8	54 6.8
70 5.2	61 6.0	62 5.9	Cost of Sales/Inventory			71 5.1	61 6.0	60 6.1	65 5.6
109 3.4	113 3.2	107 3.4				135 2.7	126 2.9	104 3.5	98 3.7
156 2.3	195 1.9	169 2.2				344 1.1	224 1.6	158 2.3	138 2.6
20 18.7	19 19.6	14 26.1	Cost of Sales/Payables			14 26.8	11 34.1	16 23.4	16 23.0
34 10.7	30 12.2	25 14.5				29 12.5	19 18.8	28 13.2	25 14.5
54 6.7	44 8.2	38 9.6				121 3.0	39 9.3	39 9.3	36 10.2
3.3	3.2	2.9	Sales/Working Capital			4.1	2.8	3.1	2.6
7.0	5.2	5.4				9.9	3.9	7.2	5.3
15.1	15.3	12.7				29.6	6.9	12.1	12.6
9.7	11.1	11.8	EBIT/Interest			5.4	17.9	11.3	10.1
(95) 3.9	(100) 4.7	(96) 4.1				3.8	(18) 10.6	(32) 4.5	(32) 3.2
2.0	1.8	1.8				2.1	3.1	1.5	1.6
5.9	8.0	6.1	Net Profit + Depr., Dep., Amort./Cur. Mat. L/T/D					5.2	5.4
(31) 2.5	(34) 2.7	(25) 3.0					(12) 3.5	(10) 1.6
.7	1.2	1.4						2.4	1.2
.2	.2	.1	Fixed/Worth			.5	.1	.1	.3
.6	.6	.6				.9	.4	.5	.9
1.7	1.8	1.5				NM	.8	1.0	1.9
.8	.8	.6	Debt/Worth			1.4	.3	.7	.6
1.7	2.0	1.6				3.8	1.1	1.6	2.4
4.6	5.7	3.7				NM	2.2	3.6	4.0
70.1	59.8	44.8	% Profit Before Taxes/Tangible Net Worth				38.7	41.4	41.1
(93) 28.1	(100) 25.3	(98) 23.3					24.1	18.6	(31) 20.2
11.4	8.7	8.5					12.9	6.4	7.3
17.6	20.0	16.1	% Profit Before Taxes/Total Assets			12.6	21.8	12.3	14.0
9.6	9.4	7.6				8.3	15.3	8.0	5.7
3.6	2.8	2.4				.5	5.2	1.3	2.2
29.3	20.6	24.7	Sales/Net Fixed Assets			36.2	41.8	32.7	9.0
9.6	9.4	8.2				11.4	10.5	12.1	5.4
4.9	4.8	3.4				2.6	3.5	3.6	3.2
2.6	2.3	2.1	Sales/Total Assets			2.0	2.5	2.3	1.6
1.8	1.6	1.5				1.0	1.7	1.8	1.4
1.2	1.2	1.1				.9	1.1	1.2	1.0
1.3	1.1	1.2	% Depr., Dep., Amort./Sales				.5	1.1	1.8
(88) 2.2	(103) 1.9	(94) 2.4				(18) 1.5	(29) 3.0	(32) 2.5
3.6	3.3	4.0					4.1	3.7	4.5
1.6	2.1	2.7	% Officers', Directors' Owners' Comp/Sales						
(31) 4.4	(22) 4.9	(22) 4.5							
9.1	8.0	9.6							
4435095M	5414105M	4582138M	Net Sales ($)	595M	10120M	39707M	150399M	575225M	3806092M
2811581M	3676039M	3126932M	Total Assets ($)	376M	4837M	34367M	100400M	391147M	2595805M

© RMA 2010

M = $ thousand   MM = $ million
See Pages 9 through 22 for Explanation of Ratios and Data

Current Data Sorted by Assets							Comparative Historical Data	
Type of Statement								
Unqualified	1		8	17	4	5	30	24
Reviewed		2	18	14			30	34
Compiled		4	13	2	1		16	15
Tax Returns	2	10	5	1			18	12
Other	1	10	33	33	5	10	68	65
	37 (4/1-9/30/09)			162 (10/1/09-3/31/10)			4/1/05-3/31/06 ALL	4/1/06-3/31/07 ALL
	0-500M	500M-2MM	2-10MM	10-50MM	50-100MM	100-250MM		
NUMBER OF STATEMENTS	4	26	77	67	10	15	162	150
ASSETS	%	%	%	%	%	%	%	%
Cash & Equivalents		14.1	11.7	6.6	11.2	6.0	7.4	8.9
Trade Receivables (net)		29.8	18.6	17.3	14.2	12.1	21.2	23.6
Inventory		22.9	35.7	39.0	23.3	25.2	33.7	34.9
All Other Current		3.2	2.6	3.3	17.3	6.1	3.7	3.6
Total Current		69.9	68.6	66.2	66.0	49.5	66.0	71.0
Fixed Assets (net)		24.1	24.1	25.6	17.3	19.3	25.9	21.8
Intangibles (net)		1.5	3.6	5.4	6.6	29.3	3.8	2.9
All Other Non-Current		4.5	3.7	2.7	10.1	2.0	4.4	4.3
Total		100.0	100.0	100.0	100.0	100.0	100.0	100.0
LIABILITIES								
Notes Payable-Short Term		11.9	10.6	9.5	1.5	.6	10.4	9.3
Cur. Mat.-L.T.D.		5.0	5.0	4.0	1.5	2.5	3.8	3.1
Trade Payables		14.6	10.0	7.8	5.2	6.6	11.9	13.1
Income Taxes Payable		.2	.2	.6	.6	.2	.2	.4
All Other Current		7.3	9.2	7.3	12.5	7.2	8.0	9.9
Total Current		39.0	35.0	29.2	21.3	17.0	34.3	35.7
Long-Term Debt		16.2	15.3	15.2	14.6	25.2	15.8	14.0
Deferred Taxes		.0	.7	.7	1.3	3.5	.5	.5
All Other Non-Current		6.3	9.3	4.6	7.5	4.4	7.5	4.9
Net Worth		38.5	39.7	50.4	55.3	50.0	41.7	44.9
Total Liabilties & Net Worth		100.0	100.0	100.0	100.0	100.0	100.0	100.0
INCOME DATA								
Net Sales		100.0	100.0	100.0	100.0	100.0	100.0	100.0
Gross Profit		34.0	31.6	29.8	31.5	26.9	31.1	31.9
Operating Expenses		29.3	25.5	19.9	21.7	19.9	24.5	22.6
Operating Profit		4.7	6.1	9.9	9.8	7.0	6.5	9.4
All Other Expenses (net)		.4	1.7	1.8	.4	3.6	1.4	1.6
Profit Before Taxes		4.3	4.4	8.1	9.4	3.4	5.1	7.8
RATIOS								
Current		4.8	4.0	4.1	4.3	4.4	3.8	3.6
		2.1	2.1	2.3	3.1	2.7	2.0	2.1
		1.0	1.4	1.7	2.2	2.3	1.4	1.4
Quick		3.3	2.1	1.7	2.1	1.6	1.6	1.6
		1.4	.8	.7	.9	1.1	.8	.9
		.4	.4	.4	.6	.9	.4	.5
Sales/Receivables		**23** 15.8	**25** 14.6	**36** 10.2	**26** 14.3	**37** 9.9	**31** 11.6	**35** 10.5
		32 11.5	**38** 9.5	**43** 8.5	**43** 8.5	**48** 7.6	**43** 8.6	**48** 7.6
		50 7.3	**55** 6.7	**56** 6.5	**69** 5.3	**54** 6.7	**57** 6.4	**63** 5.8
Cost of Sales/Inventory		**10** 36.7	**58** 6.3	**88** 4.2	**61** 6.0	**89** 4.1	**60** 6.1	**56** 6.5
		49 7.4	**108** 3.4	**148** 2.5	**101** 3.6	**108** 3.4	**106** 3.4	**111** 3.3
		80 4.6	**189** 1.9	**198** 1.8	**160** 2.3	**181** 2.0	**169** 2.2	**160** 2.3
Cost of Sales/Payables		**11** 32.0	**15** 24.1	**16** 22.2	**13** 28.8	**24** 15.3	**18** 20.0	**21** 17.8
		20 18.2	**25** 14.3	**22** 16.6	**30** 12.3	**28** 13.3	**31** 11.7	**32** 11.3
		33 11.1	**47** 7.7	**39** 9.4	**49** 7.4	**36** 10.2	**46** 7.9	**56** 6.5
Sales/Working Capital		4.9	2.9	2.4	1.6	2.4	3.2	3.1
		11.3	4.8	3.8	2.8	3.4	5.2	5.0
		-218.6	8.6	6.2	4.3	5.2	10.0	10.3
EBIT/Interest		14.5	12.0	20.5		10.4	12.9	11.9
		(22) 2.5	(72) 4.0	(64) 5.6		(14) 2.3	(146) 4.0	(130) 5.0
		-1.8	1.4	3.6		-.3	1.4	2.4
Net Profit + Depr., Dep., Amort./Cur. Mat. L/T/D			4.2	6.5			5.2	7.9
			(21) 2.6	(30) 2.8			(46) 2.5	(38) 3.4
			1.3	1.7			1.1	1.6
Fixed/Worth		.1	.3	.3	.0	.3	.3	.2
		.4	.5	.6	.4	1.6	.6	.5
		2.0	1.7	.9	.7	10.4	1.2	1.1
Debt/Worth		.5	.6	.5	.3	.7	.6	.6
		1.8	1.5	1.0	1.0	2.3	1.4	1.2
		3.9	4.8	2.3	2.2	20.2	3.2	3.2
% Profit Before Taxes/Tangible Net Worth		41.7	33.8	34.4		26.1	44.9	47.7
		(22) 14.2	(71) 18.7	(60) 19.9		(12) 20.9	(148) 19.5	(136) 27.7
		.6	5.3	12.1		-11.6	7.7	10.3
% Profit Before Taxes/Total Assets		19.4	16.0	16.6	15.8	8.9	18.6	22.4
		8.1	6.4	10.9	10.1	4.1	7.6	9.9
		-.8	1.2	5.5	4.6	-3.0	1.3	4.7
Sales/Net Fixed Assets		106.1	22.2	11.7	40.4	10.9	15.7	22.4
		10.2	7.6	5.3	6.9	4.5	7.0	9.1
		4.9	4.0	3.3	3.6	3.6	4.2	4.6
Sales/Total Assets		3.8	2.1	1.6	1.3	1.3	2.1	2.3
		2.6	1.6	1.3	.9	1.0	1.7	1.7
		2.3	1.2	1.0	.8	.7	1.2	1.2
% Depr., Dep., Amort./Sales		.4	1.6	1.5			1.2	1.0
		(22) 3.2	(61) 2.6	(63) 2.9			(140) 2.6	(126) 2.1
		6.3	4.5	5.3			4.4	3.9
% Officers', Directors' Owners' Comp/Sales		4.3	1.6	1.1			1.7	1.2
		(17) 6.5	(26) 4.7	(17) 1.8			(49) 3.6	(49) 3.0
		11.9	8.0	5.5			6.0	5.4
Net Sales ($)	**4938M**	**95197M**	**651453M**	**2062534M**	**905507M**	**2415019M**	**4269588M**	**3665802M**
Total Assets ($)	**1278M**	**33123M**	**401190M**	**1479071M**	**703320M**	**2496078M**	**3171748M**	**2498599M**

M = $ thousand MM = $ million

See Pages 9 through 22 for Explanation of Ratios and Data

Comparative Historical Data | Current Data Sorted by Sales

4/1/07-3/31/08 ALL	4/1/08-3/31/09 ALL	4/1/09-3/31/10 ALL		0-1MM	1-3MM	3-5MM	5-10MM	10-25MM	25MM & OVER
			Type of Statement		37 (4/1-9/30/09)		162 (10/1/09-3/31/10)		
24	30	35	Unqualified	1		1	3	13	17
39	35	34	Reviewed		1	6	8	13	6
18	20	20	Compiled		3	2	9	5	1
23	16	18	Tax Returns	1	5	8	3	1	
69	85	92	Other	2	6	11	17	19	37
173	186	199	**NUMBER OF STATEMENTS**	4	15	28	40	51	61
%	%	%	**ASSETS**	%	%	%	%	%	%
10.0	8.4	9.9	Cash & Equivalents		12.0	12.2	14.4	6.5	7.9
22.0	19.0	18.9	Trade Receivables (net)		24.0	17.4	21.9	17.2	18.4
33.4	32.7	33.2	Inventory		27.5	32.2	32.2	36.5	34.3
3.7	4.1	3.9	All Other Current		5.5	1.4	2.2	3.8	6.1
69.2	64.3	65.9	Total Current		69.1	63.3	70.7	63.9	66.8
21.2	24.4	23.9	Fixed Assets (net)		20.8	28.5	21.6	26.6	20.7
5.6	7.3	6.3	Intangibles (net)		2.5	4.8	4.3	5.4	9.2
4.0	4.1	3.9	All Other Non-Current		7.6	3.4	3.5	4.0	3.3
100.0	100.0	100.0	Total		100.0	100.0	100.0	100.0	100.0
			LIABILITIES						
8.9	9.6	9.0	Notes Payable-Short Term		14.3	8.8	9.2	8.9	7.7
4.8	3.5	4.3	Cur. Mat.-L.T.D.		2.7	5.9	2.5	7.2	2.6
11.4	9.5	9.4	Trade Payables		8.0	8.6	14.4	8.1	8.2
.5	.4	.3	Income Taxes Payable		.0	.1	.0	.5	.6
9.2	8.9	8.3	All Other Current		7.0	7.4	9.5	6.2	10.0
34.7	31.9	31.4	Total Current		31.9	30.8	35.6	30.9	29.0
17.6	16.7	16.3	Long-Term Debt		20.3	21.2	11.8	16.7	15.2
.4	.7	.8	Deferred Taxes		.3	.2	.7	.7	1.4
8.0	8.7	7.3	All Other Non-Current		14.3	6.3	7.3	9.8	4.1
39.2	42.1	44.3	Net Worth		33.2	41.5	44.5	42.0	50.3
100.0	100.0	100.0	Total Liabilties & Net Worth		100.0	100.0	100.0	100.0	100.0
			INCOME DATA						
100.0	100.0	100.0	Net Sales		100.0	100.0	100.0	100.0	100.0
32.2	33.2	31.4	Gross Profit		39.1	34.8	27.9	30.6	29.8
21.9	23.6	23.9	Operating Expenses		34.0	31.7	22.0	21.8	20.2
10.2	9.6	7.5	Operating Profit		5.0	3.2	5.9	8.8	9.6
1.8	1.6	1.7	All Other Expenses (net)		.8	1.8	1.6	1.6	1.8
8.5	8.0	5.8	Profit Before Taxes		4.2	1.3	4.3	7.1	7.9
			RATIOS						
3.6	3.3	4.1	Current		6.3	4.3	4.6	3.1	4.2
2.1	2.1	2.3			2.2	2.6	2.1	1.9	2.5
1.4	1.5	1.6			1.2	1.2	1.4	1.7	1.8
1.7	1.4	1.9	Quick		3.7	2.9	2.6	1.5	1.8
.9	.8	.9			1.4	1.0	1.0	.6	1.0
.5	.4	.4			.2	.2	.5	.4	.5
28 12.9	25 14.7	29 12.8	Sales/Receivables		15 24.2	19 19.1	29 12.4	26 14.3	38 9.6
44 8.2	40 9.0	41 8.8			28 13.1	34 10.7	39 9.2	40 9.1	46 7.9
61 6.0	51 7.1	54 6.7			45 8.1	57 6.4	56 6.5	51 7.1	56 6.5
54 6.8	67 5.5	63 5.8	Cost of Sales/Inventory		16 22.4	45 8.1	22 16.5	81 4.5	87 4.2
107 3.4	111 3.3	105 3.5			50 7.3	99 3.7	84 4.3	109 3.3	136 2.7
168 2.2	172 2.1	178 2.1			94 3.9	203 1.8	156 2.3	198 1.8	181 2.0
18 19.8	18 20.7	15 24.0	Cost of Sales/Payables		8 48.3	18 19.9	17 21.2	16 22.4	17 21.7
28 12.8	27 13.3	25 14.6			13 29.0	24 15.1	27 13.6	20 15.8	31 11.9
47 7.8	44 8.2	41 8.9			25 14.8	53 7.0	46 7.9	33 11.1	45 8.1
3.1	3.4	2.8	Sales/Working Capital		4.1	3.4	2.7	3.2	2.4
5.0	5.0	4.3			7.1	4.7	5.2	4.8	3.4
10.1	10.0	8.2			14.1	14.2	9.9	7.1	6.3
12.6	18.1	12.0	EBIT/Interest		7.8	10.0	15.2	8.9	23.6
(158) 5.3	(172) 5.2	(185) 4.6			(13) 2.3	(25) 2.4	(37) 5.0	(50) 4.8	(57) 6.4
2.4	1.9	1.9			.7	-1.8	1.3	2.9	2.7
14.2	9.1	6.2	Net Profit + Depr., Dep., Amort./Cur. Mat. L/T/D				14.0	2.7	7.1
(48) 3.1	(66) 3.9	(63) 2.6				(11) 3.0	(18) 1.9	(28) 3.2
1.7	1.9	1.5					1.0	1.7	1.7
.2	.2	.2	Fixed/Worth		.1	.4	.2	.3	.2
.5	.6	.6			.4	1.0	.4	.7	.5
1.5	1.5	1.6			8.8	2.0	1.7	1.0	1.1
.8	.7	.6	Debt/Worth		1.0	.6	.4	.6	.6
1.7	1.4	1.3			2.3	1.5	1.5	1.2	1.0
4.6	3.8	3.7			12.0	4.6	5.9	3.1	3.4
58.6	51.2	33.3	% Profit Before Taxes/Tangible Net Worth		68.5	30.8	33.7	32.0	37.8
(151) 33.1	(165) 27.7	(176) 19.7			(12) 21.6	(24) 15.5	(36) 16.4	(47) 18.3	(54) 22.0
13.7	8.4	7.2			.7	-5.3	3.3	10.5	13.2
22.1	20.0	15.8	% Profit Before Taxes/Total Assets		31.9	14.4	16.9	13.6	17.6
11.3	10.7	8.9			4.9	3.7	9.7	8.0	9.4
5.2	2.5	2.1			-.4	-7.9	1.2	3.8	4.2
31.3	18.0	17.0	Sales/Net Fixed Assets		102.9	16.2	26.3	15.0	12.4
10.0	7.7	6.6			11.5	5.1	10.2	5.2	7.3
4.6	3.8	3.7			4.4	3.4	5.7	3.4	3.7
2.2	2.2	2.1	Sales/Total Assets		3.7	2.1	2.8	1.8	1.6
1.7	1.6	1.4			2.6	1.4	1.7	1.5	1.3
1.2	1.1	1.0			.8	.9	1.3	1.1	.9
1.0	1.1	1.2	% Depr., Dep., Amort./Sales		.7	1.0	.6	1.8	1.2
(151) 2.4	(160) 2.4	(164) 2.9			(13) 2.8	(23) 3.8	(31) 2.1	(45) 3.2	(49) 2.4
4.0	4.5	5.2			6.6	6.1	4.2	5.1	4.1
2.4	1.7	1.7	% Officers', Directors' Owners' Comp/Sales			5.0	2.2	1.2	.5
(48) 4.2	(55) 3.6	(65) 5.0				(12) 6.2	(17) 4.6	(14) 2.2	(12) 1.8
8.0	6.6	8.9				10.6		6.1	
4790994M	6254351M	6134648M	Net Sales ($)	2483M	34275M	110759M	295770M	854102M	4837259M
3757282M	5017101M	5114060M	Total Assets ($)	3628M	22570M	84694M	202125M	651329M	4149714M

M = $ thousand   MM = $ million
See Pages 9 through 22 for Explanation of Ratios and Data

Current Data Sorted by Assets | Comparative Historical Data

Type of Statement	0-500M	500M-2MM	2-10MM	10-50MM	50-100MM	100-250MM		4/1/05-3/31/06 ALL	4/1/06-3/31/07 ALL
	5 (4/1-9/30/09)		40 (10/1/09-3/31/10)						
Unqualified			2	5	5	3		9	7
Reviewed		1	2	2				4	7
Compiled		1	2	2				7	4
Tax Returns		1	2					2	2
Other		1	7	3	4	2		16	18
NUMBER OF STATEMENTS		4	15	12	9	5		38	38
	%	%	%	%	%	%		%	%
ASSETS									
Cash & Equivalents			7.1	11.3				8.6	8.4
Trade Receivables (net)			22.0	20.6				26.1	24.5
Inventory			21.2	18.5				26.4	27.0
All Other Current			4.7	4.8				2.0	2.6
Total Current			55.0	55.2				63.1	62.6
Fixed Assets (net)			25.7	27.1				25.0	22.7
Intangibles (net)			11.6	10.5				6.2	9.5
All Other Non-Current			7.8	7.2				5.7	5.1
Total			100.0	100.0				100.0	100.0
LIABILITIES									
Notes Payable-Short Term			8.2	2.4				10.5	8.7
Cur. Mat.-L.T.D.			3.2	4.8				3.4	2.6
Trade Payables			14.2	6.8				14.8	14.4
Income Taxes Payable			.0	.6				.5	.2
All Other Current			6.5	14.1				13.7	9.2
Total Current			32.2	28.7				42.9	35.1
Long-Term Debt			14.4	14.0				15.2	21.3
Deferred Taxes			.3	.6				.2	.4
All Other Non-Current			8.5	5.4				3.9	3.1
Net Worth			44.6	51.3				37.7	40.0
Total Liabilities & Net Worth			100.0	100.0				100.0	100.0
INCOME DATA									
Net Sales			100.0	100.0				100.0	100.0
Gross Profit			42.0	32.9				31.0	30.1
Operating Expenses			33.8	21.7				23.0	20.5
Operating Profit			8.2	11.1				8.1	9.6
All Other Expenses (net)			1.7	.9				1.4	.8
Profit Before Taxes			6.5	10.2				6.6	8.8
RATIOS									
Current			3.3 / 1.7 / 1.2	3.1 / 1.9 / 1.3				2.4 / 1.5 / 1.0	2.9 / 1.7 / 1.3
Quick			1.6 / .7 / .5	1.6 / 1.2 / .5				1.1 / .8 / .5	1.4 / .7 / .5
Sales/Receivables			(26) 14.2 / (36) 10.1 / (48) 7.6	(29) 12.6 / (48) 7.7 / (81) 4.5				(29) 12.8 / (42) 8.7 / (54) 6.7	(30) 12.1 / (42) 8.7 / (65) 5.6
Cost of Sales/Inventory			(29) 12.6 / (50) 7.3 / (83) 4.4	(25) 14.9 / (65) 5.6 / (78) 4.7				(37) 10.0 / (65) 5.6 / (116) 3.1	(27) 13.3 / (73) 5.0 / (104) 3.5
Cost of Sales/Payables			(20) 18.7 / (47) 7.8 / (66) 5.5	(14) 25.5 / (19) 19.3 / (37) 9.8				(22) 16.3 / (36) 10.0 / (51) 7.1	(20) 18.0 / (32) 11.4 / (50) 7.4
Sales/Working Capital			6.0 / 10.5 / 23.5	3.9 / 7.0 / 13.8				5.0 / 9.6 / NM	3.8 / 6.9 / 24.7
EBIT/Interest			28.1 / (13) 9.6 / 1.9	96.2 / 13.9 / 3.3				36.4 / (36) 4.5 / 1.9	17.2 / (33) 6.1 / 2.4
Net Profit + Depr., Dep., Amort./Cur. Mat. L/T/D									10.3 / (12) 5.0 / 2.2
Fixed/Worth			.3 / .8 / 1.9	.3 / .6 / 2.1				.3 / .7 / 4.0	.3 / .9 / 2.1
Debt/Worth			.8 / 1.9 / 2.9	.4 / 1.8 / 6.5				.6 / 1.8 / 7.3	.9 / 1.7 / 10.9
% Profit Before Taxes/Tangible Net Worth			51.1 / (14) 20.2 / 6.7	63.8 / 41.3 / 16.7				71.9 / (32) 33.6 / 9.5	62.1 / (33) 36.5 / 15.7
% Profit Before Taxes/Total Assets			19.4 / 8.3 / 3.9	20.4 / 10.1 / 5.2				29.3 / 10.5 / 2.6	21.6 / 13.8 / 3.6
Sales/Net Fixed Assets			18.9 / 8.2 / 4.7	14.3 / 6.6 / 5.3				29.1 / 8.4 / 5.2	17.8 / 9.6 / 6.3
Sales/Total Assets			2.4 / 1.7 / .9	2.1 / 1.5 / .9				3.0 / 2.0 / 1.3	2.5 / 2.0 / 1.1
% Depr., Dep., Amort./Sales			1.4 / (13) 2.5 / 4.7	1.2 / 2.3 / 3.7				.8 / (33) 1.7 / 2.9	1.3 / (32) 2.1 / 3.2
% Officers', Directors' Owners' Comp/Sales									
Net Sales ($)		15763M	130194M	371820M	749991M	883936M		2563966M	1843496M
Total Assets ($)		5423M	80901M	272581M	621290M	877005M		1066868M	1056928M

(For the 0-500M and 500M-2MM columns: DATA NOT AVAILABLE)

M = $ thousand   MM = $ million
See Pages 9 through 22 for Explanation of Ratios and Data

Comparative Historical Data

Current Data Sorted by Sales

			Type of Statement						
10	14	15	Unqualified			3			12
3	1	5	Reviewed		1		1	2	1
2	2	5	Compiled		1		1	3	
4	4	3	Tax Returns			1	1		
23	18	17	Other	1	1	1	2	7	7
4/1/07- 3/31/08 ALL	4/1/08- 3/31/09 ALL	4/1/09- 3/31/10 ALL		0-1MM	5 (4/1-9/30/09) 1-3MM	3-5MM	40 (10/1/09-3/31/10) 5-10MM	10-25MM	25MM & OVER
42	39	45	NUMBER OF STATEMENTS	1	2	3	7	12	20
%	%	%	ASSETS	%	%	%	%	%	%
12.2	9.2	9.6	Cash & Equivalents					6.5	14.0
22.4	19.5	19.9	Trade Receivables (net)					25.1	17.0
23.7	32.3	25.4	Inventory					25.3	32.8
3.0	4.4	4.1	All Other Current					8.5	2.7
61.3	65.5	59.0	Total Current					65.3	66.6
21.4	23.4	25.0	Fixed Assets (net)					20.6	23.7
10.9	7.1	8.7	Intangibles (net)					9.9	4.9
6.4	4.0	7.3	All Other Non-Current					4.1	4.8
100.0	100.0	100.0	Total					100.0	100.0
			LIABILITIES						
8.0	9.8	6.9	Notes Payable-Short Term					6.0	9.0
5.1	3.4	3.3	Cur. Mat.-L.T.D.					2.4	2.2
12.6	13.8	9.3	Trade Payables					16.2	8.0
.1	.2	.4	Income Taxes Payable					.1	.4
11.8	14.5	10.9	All Other Current					8.4	16.0
37.6	41.8	30.8	Total Current					33.1	35.6
19.2	11.6	12.4	Long-Term Debt					10.3	10.4
.7	.8	1.1	Deferred Taxes					.4	2.0
2.8	12.2	7.2	All Other Non-Current					5.6	9.2
39.7	33.6	48.5	Net Worth					50.6	42.7
100.0	100.0	100.0	Total Liabilities & Net Worth					100.0	100.0
			INCOME DATA						
100.0	100.0	100.0	Net Sales					100.0	100.0
34.7	27.0	32.3	Gross Profit					26.3	25.1
25.3	20.7	24.0	Operating Expenses					20.6	16.6
9.4	6.3	8.3	Operating Profit					5.7	8.4
2.3	1.5	1.3	All Other Expenses (net)					.6	1.0
7.1	4.8	7.0	Profit Before Taxes					5.1	7.4
			RATIOS						
3.4	2.4	3.8	Current					3.1	3.4
2.1	1.6	2.1						1.7	2.4
1.2	1.1	1.2						1.4	1.3
2.1	1.2	1.6	Quick					1.6	1.5
1.0	.8	1.0						.9	1.1
.6	.3	.5						.5	.4
31 11.9	33 11.1	29 12.4	Sales/Receivables					27 13.7	32 11.6
43 8.5	38 9.5	38 9.5						38 9.6	44 8.3
56 6.5	53 6.9	63 5.8						64 5.7	55 6.7
34 10.9	49 7.4	30 12.1	Cost of Sales/Inventory					26 14.3	73 5.0
65 5.6	88 4.1	77 4.7						50 7.3	86 4.2
103 3.6	171 2.1	138 2.6						102 3.6	176 2.1
18 20.6	23 15.7	16 23.4	Cost of Sales/Payables					19 19.7	15 24.2
29 12.8	33 11.0	27 13.3						27 13.5	27 13.7
47 7.7	43 8.5	54 6.8						48 7.7	50 7.3
3.9	3.7	3.2	Sales/Working Capital					3.8	2.6
7.7	6.1	6.0						9.7	3.7
16.1	33.7	12.5						12.8	6.4
19.9	21.5	38.7	EBIT/Interest					38.6	38.9
(37) 8.2	(38) 5.6	(42) 9.8						(11) 9.6	(19) 10.3
1.7	2.7	2.0						2.7	1.8
13.9	6.1		Net Profit + Depr., Dep., Amort./Cur. Mat. L/T/D						
(11) 5.0	(14) 2.6								
2.8	1.4								
.2	.3	.3	Fixed/Worth					.2	.3
.7	.7	.6						.7	.6
2.1	2.3	1.4						2.0	1.1
.6	1.0	.3	Debt/Worth					.7	.6
1.5	2.6	1.7						1.6	2.0
5.1	7.2	3.3						4.7	3.8
73.4	38.2	51.0	% Profit Before Taxes/Tangible Net Worth					72.0	52.0
(34) 29.0	(33) 26.8	(42) 19.4						20.2	(18) 16.2
11.6	13.8	8.6						10.2	7.7
30.7	16.5	17.8	% Profit Before Taxes/Total Assets					18.4	17.9
14.6	9.3	6.9						9.1	6.0
2.6	1.4	2.9						3.9	1.9
21.0	19.1	14.6	Sales/Net Fixed Assets					23.1	14.2
10.6	8.7	6.3						8.9	5.4
6.6	5.2	3.9						5.5	3.6
3.0	2.2	2.2	Sales/Total Assets					2.9	1.7
1.8	1.5	1.3						1.8	1.2
1.2	1.1	.9						1.2	.9
.7	.9	1.2	% Depr., Dep., Amort./Sales					1.1	1.3
(34) 1.6	(36) 2.0	(38) 2.4						(10) 2.1	(15) 2.5
2.5	3.2	3.9						3.0	3.0
			% Officers', Directors' Owners' Comp/Sales						
2388783M	2530898M	2151704M	Net Sales ($)	676M	4896M	11790M	48543M	173082M	1912717M
1457006M	2026028M	1857200M	Total Assets ($)	804M	9710M	9720M	77770M	109246M	1649950M

M = $ thousand   MM = $ million
See Pages 9 through 22 for Explanation of Ratios and Data

Current Data Sorted by Assets   Comparative Historical Data

0-500M	500M-2MM	2-10MM	10-50MM	50-100MM	100-250MM	Type of Statement	4/1/05-3/31/06 ALL	4/1/06-3/31/07 ALL
		4	6	5	5	Unqualified	18	25
		6	6			Reviewed	11	15
1	4	5	1			Compiled	11	16
1	2	2	1			Tax Returns	1	4
	2	7	16	3	13	Other	24	19
	18 (4/1-9/30/09)		72 (10/1/09-3/31/10)					
2	8	24	30	8	18	NUMBER OF STATEMENTS	65	79
%	%	%	%	%	%	**ASSETS**	%	%
		18.0	10.5		10.1	Cash & Equivalents	11.8	13.9
		21.4	19.7		15.1	Trade Receivables (net)	17.7	19.6
		6.1	11.8		9.8	Inventory	14.9	13.2
		6.7	16.1		13.8	All Other Current	10.9	12.0
		52.2	58.1		48.7	Total Current	55.2	58.7
		39.4	35.0		41.6	Fixed Assets (net)	34.4	31.4
		.9	2.7		5.6	Intangibles (net)	1.8	2.7
		7.6	4.2		4.1	All Other Non-Current	8.6	7.2
		100.0	100.0		100.0	Total	100.0	100.0
						LIABILITIES		
		7.5	8.0		7.9	Notes Payable-Short Term	13.7	10.1
		2.7	2.5		2.8	Cur. Mat.-L.T.D.	3.3	3.7
		10.3	12.8		7.4	Trade Payables	10.9	12.4
		.2	.1		1.0	Income Taxes Payable	.4	1.1
		10.0	17.8		12.8	All Other Current	14.8	17.6
		30.7	41.2		31.9	Total Current	43.1	45.0
		16.7	23.2		24.2	Long-Term Debt	18.3	14.0
		.8	.9		1.3	Deferred Taxes	.7	.7
		1.0	1.8		2.6	All Other Non-Current	3.2	4.5
		50.8	32.8		40.0	Net Worth	34.8	35.8
		100.0	100.0		100.0	Total Liabilties & Net Worth	100.0	100.0
						INCOME DATA		
		100.0	100.0		100.0	Net Sales	100.0	100.0
		32.4	21.3		17.5	Gross Profit	26.9	28.6
		27.2	16.7		12.7	Operating Expenses	24.1	22.3
		5.2	4.5		4.7	Operating Profit	2.8	6.3
		.1	1.4		1.4	All Other Expenses (net)	.6	.7
		5.1	3.1		3.3	Profit Before Taxes	2.2	5.6
						RATIOS		
		3.0	1.9		2.9		2.0	2.2
		1.8	1.4		1.7	Current	1.3	1.5
		1.0	1.1		1.0		1.1	1.0
		2.5	1.2		1.5		1.3	1.3
		1.3	.7		1.1	Quick	.6	.8
		.6	.3		.4		.3	.4
		15 24.6	14 26.1		17 21.0		11 34.6	19 19.2
		37 9.9	30 12.4		39 9.4	Sales/Receivables	27 13.6	37 9.7
		52 7.0	42 8.8		46 7.9		50 7.3	57 6.4
		0 UND	1 386.4		1 251.4		1 249.3	1 433.8
		2 234.8	5 75.1		9 40.7	Cost of Sales/Inventory	7 55.8	5 66.7
		26 14.1	53 6.9		79 4.6		64 5.7	56 6.5
		11 32.4	16 23.3		14 25.2		14 26.1	17 21.8
		23 16.2	31 11.9		17 21.5	Cost of Sales/Payables	24 15.2	25 14.5
		39 9.5	41 8.8		33 11.2		50 7.3	41 8.9
		5.3	7.1		4.0		6.5	6.0
		9.7	10.4		6.1	Sales/Working Capital	10.5	9.0
		NM	53.0		NM		51.3	159.8
		18.3	24.4		10.3		9.6	13.4
		(23) 6.9	(29) 9.3		(15) 1.8	EBIT/Interest	(57) 3.0	(68) 3.7
		2.7	1.4		.2		.9	2.2
			8.2			Net Profit + Depr., Dep.,	5.6	9.3
			(12) 1.5			Amort./Cur. Mat. L/T/D	(25) 2.6	(32) 4.0
			.4				1.3	2.4
		.3	.4		.7		.4	.4
		.7	1.2		.8	Fixed/Worth	.8	.8
		1.4	1.9		3.0		1.9	1.8
		.5	1.1		.7		.8	.8
		1.0	2.2		1.6	Debt/Worth	2.0	1.7
		2.0	3.8		4.2		3.9	4.5
		30.0	61.5		27.8	% Profit Before Taxes/Tangible	38.8	39.6
		(23) 14.5	(28) 34.1		(16) 7.0	Net Worth	(62) 13.3	(72) 24.8
		5.3	6.1		-6.8		.4	10.0
		11.8	22.8		13.7	% Profit Before Taxes/Total	9.8	15.1
		6.1	9.4		1.2	Assets	4.8	6.7
		3.5	.1		-2.2		-.3	2.5
		16.6	17.2		7.0		11.9	12.1
		5.6	5.9		3.2	Sales/Net Fixed Assets	5.9	5.7
		2.3	2.6		1.6		3.1	3.1
		3.1	2.6		1.7		2.5	2.6
		1.9	1.7		1.2	Sales/Total Assets	1.7	1.6
		1.3	1.3		.9		1.2	1.2
		1.6	1.0		2.2		1.1	1.0
		(21) 2.7	(29) 1.9		(14) 2.5	% Depr., Dep., Amort./Sales	(60) 2.0	(77) 2.0
		3.7	3.4		4.0		3.3	3.1
							2.6	1.7
						% Officers', Directors' Owners' Comp/Sales	(18) 3.9	(20) 6.1
							7.1	10.9
2742M	32489M	279720M	1277991M	958291M	3103564M	Net Sales ($)	2358295M	4063802M
707M	11331M	128691M	655013M	542018M	2458517M	Total Assets ($)	1513053M	2750587M

M = $ thousand   MM = $ million
See Pages 9 through 22 for Explanation of Ratios and Data

Comparative Historical Data

Current Data Sorted by Sales

29	23	20	Type of Statement — Unqualified				4	6	14
14	10	12	Reviewed		1		3	3	4
6	9	11	Compiled		4		2	4	
6	6	6	Tax Returns			2	2	1	
34	28	41	Other	1	3		3	7	28
4/1/07-3/31/08 ALL	4/1/08-3/31/09 ALL	4/1/09-3/31/10 ALL		0-1MM	1-3MM	3-5MM	5-10MM	10-25MM	25MM & OVER

18 (4/1-9/30/09)   72 (10/1/09-3/31/10)

89	76	90	NUMBER OF STATEMENTS	1	8	2	12	21	46
%	%	%	**ASSETS**	%	%	%	%	%	%
13.5	11.8	11.8	Cash & Equivalents				25.9	10.8	9.9
20.5	18.3	20.0	Trade Receivables (net)				17.8	24.9	19.6
11.9	11.4	11.6	Inventory				5.2	7.1	9.2
11.9	12.6	11.4	All Other Current				3.7	10.2	16.4
57.8	54.1	54.7	Total Current				52.5	53.0	55.1
33.7	36.2	36.7	Fixed Assets (net)				37.1	37.9	37.1
3.0	3.4	2.5	Intangibles (net)				.6	3.0	3.2
5.4	6.2	6.0	All Other Non-Current				9.8	6.1	4.6
100.0	100.0	100.0	Total				100.0	100.0	100.0
			LIABILITIES						
7.7	9.4	8.5	Notes Payable-Short Term				4.7	8.2	7.7
3.4	2.8	2.9	Cur. Mat.-L.T.D.				3.5	2.4	2.7
11.4	10.1	11.1	Trade Payables				9.0	15.2	11.2
.8	.6	.4	Income Taxes Payable				.2	.1	.6
19.7	15.2	13.3	All Other Current				8.1	17.4	14.2
42.9	38.2	36.1	Total Current				25.6	43.3	36.3
15.5	20.8	21.1	Long-Term Debt				19.1	21.8	19.9
.9	1.1	1.0	Deferred Taxes				1.2	.5	1.2
7.2	2.9	3.0	All Other Non-Current				.8	1.4	2.6
33.6	37.0	38.8	Net Worth				53.3	32.9	40.0
100.0	100.0	100.0	Total Liabilities & Net Worth				100.0	100.0	100.0
			INCOME DATA						
100.0	100.0	100.0	Net Sales				100.0	100.0	100.0
25.0	24.6	25.2	Gross Profit				33.6	26.6	21.3
18.5	18.5	20.7	Operating Expenses				30.5	23.5	14.5
6.5	6.1	4.5	Operating Profit				3.1	3.0	6.8
.4	1.1	.9	All Other Expenses (net)				-.3	2.0	.7
6.1	5.0	3.6	Profit Before Taxes				3.4	1.1	6.1
			RATIOS						
2.0	2.1	2.4	Current				4.2	1.7	2.4
1.5	1.4	1.5					2.2	1.2	1.5
1.1	1.0	1.1					1.4	.9	1.1
1.4	1.4	1.5	Quick				3.0	1.3	1.3
.9	.7	.9					1.5	.9	.9
.4	.4	.4					1.1	.2	.4
15 25.1	14 26.8	16 23.5	Sales/Receivables				20 18.2	11 32.3	21 17.4
31 11.7	31 11.7	34 10.7					35 10.3	41 8.9	35 10.3
56 6.5	46 7.9	47 7.7					53 6.9	54 6.7	45 8.1
0 999.8	0 999.8	1 476.5	Cost of Sales/Inventory				1 405.6	0 UND	1 292.7
5 71.1	8 43.8	5 75.7					6 56.2	2 182.4	4 84.8
53 6.9	32 11.4	45 8.2					35 10.4	28 12.8	32 11.4
16 22.4	11 34.4	12 30.9	Cost of Sales/Payables				6 58.4	18 20.5	14 25.2
24 14.9	20 18.6	24 15.2					21 17.2	32 11.3	24 15.3
35 10.5	40 9.2	39 9.5					38 9.7	44 8.3	36 10.0
6.5	5.5	5.8	Sales/Working Capital				4.6	8.8	5.6
11.9	13.4	10.4					5.9	18.6	9.6
59.6	NM	53.0					18.9	-117.6	51.1
17.3	12.4	12.9	EBIT/Interest				6.9	11.3	31.1
(78) 5.3	(69) 6.1	(83) 5.2					(11) 3.8	(19) 4.4	(43) 10.9
2.1	1.6	.8					.2	2.7	1.8
7.8	6.5	9.2	Net Profit + Depr., Dep., Amort./Cur. Mat. L/T/D						9.6
(30) 2.6	(27) 4.5	(30) 2.7							(19) 2.5
1.4	2.1	.9							.9
.5	.6	.5	Fixed/Worth				.2	.6	.6
1.0	1.1	.8					.6	1.4	.8
2.4	2.5	1.9					1.7	1.9	1.7
.9	.9	.7	Debt/Worth				.5	1.1	.8
1.8	1.9	1.6					.7	2.1	1.8
6.0	4.5	3.1					1.8	3.6	3.1
66.0	51.8	43.8	% Profit Before Taxes/Tangible Net Worth				20.2	49.3	59.5
(82) 31.1	(66) 29.6	(82) 16.3					(11) 5.3	(19) 14.9	(43) 27.2
11.0	8.3	1.3					-3.6	5.9	3.8
18.8	21.5	15.4	% Profit Before Taxes/Total Assets				10.2	12.0	24.1
8.6	10.5	5.7					3.8	4.6	9.8
3.7	.9	-.3					-1.7	1.1	1.0
16.2	10.1	13.7	Sales/Net Fixed Assets				14.4	18.1	10.3
5.8	5.0	5.6					6.5	3.8	5.5
3.5	3.0	2.6					2.4	2.5	2.6
2.8	2.4	2.5	Sales/Total Assets				2.7	3.3	2.4
1.9	1.9	1.7					1.8	1.6	1.8
1.3	1.3	1.2					1.3	1.2	1.1
1.0	1.4	1.2	% Depr., Dep., Amort./Sales				1.3	1.1	1.1
(83) 1.8	(66) 2.3	(81) 2.4					2.4	(19) 2.5	(41) 2.3
3.3	3.7	3.6					3.4	4.2	3.8
1.0	1.6	1.1	% Officers', Directors' Owners' Comp/Sales						
(14) 1.9	(21) 2.3	(18) 2.7							
6.9	5.6	4.1							
6163786M	5384796M	5654797M	Net Sales ($)	941M	16717M	9260M	91260M	376007M	5160612M
3875066M	3313183M	3796277M	Total Assets ($)	235M	13098M	3275M	52904M	249027M	3477738M

© RMA 2010

M = $ thousand   MM = $ million
See Pages 9 through 22 for Explanation of Ratios and Data

Current Data Sorted by Assets   Comparative Historical Data

Type of Statement

						Type of Statement		
	1	3	11	3	2	Unqualified	25	33
		6	1			Reviewed	16	16
	4	3				Compiled	11	9
	3	8	14	4	1	Tax Returns	10	7
	18 (4/1-9/30/09)		46 (10/1/09-3/31/10)			Other	33	34
0-500M	500M-2MM	2-10MM	10-50MM	50-100MM	100-250MM		4/1/05-3/31/06 ALL	4/1/06-3/31/07 ALL
8	8	20	26	7	3	NUMBER OF STATEMENTS	95	99

0-500M %	500M-2MM %	2-10MM %	10-50MM %	50-100MM %	100-250MM %		ALL %	ALL %
						ASSETS		
		10.1	9.0			Cash & Equivalents	10.0	10.4
		12.5	8.5			Trade Receivables (net)	12.2	14.0
		35.2	31.2			Inventory	33.0	32.1
		4.7	6.7			All Other Current	4.5	3.6
		62.5	55.5			Total Current	59.7	60.2
		31.7	33.6			Fixed Assets (net)	29.0	28.7
D A T A N O T A V A I L A B L E		2.7	4.5			Intangibles (net)	6.4	6.0
		3.1	6.4			All Other Non-Current	5.0	5.1
		100.0	100.0			Total	100.0	100.0
						LIABILITIES		
		13.4	13.6			Notes Payable-Short Term	10.7	10.2
		2.1	2.7			Cur. Mat.-L.T.D.	2.5	2.2
		8.6	9.4			Trade Payables	15.1	15.7
		1.4	.0			Income Taxes Payable	.2	.3
		8.8	14.9			All Other Current	12.2	15.3
		34.3	40.6			Total Current	40.6	43.7
		22.3	13.6			Long-Term Debt	19.7	17.5
		.3	.0			Deferred Taxes	.4	.3
		8.5	6.7			All Other Non-Current	11.2	7.6
		34.7	39.0			Net Worth	28.0	30.8
		100.0	100.0			Total Liabilities & Net Worth	100.0	100.0
						INCOME DATA		
		100.0	100.0			Net Sales	100.0	100.0
		22.1	13.8			Gross Profit	24.3	24.0
		24.2	20.9			Operating Expenses	19.2	19.1
		-2.0	-7.1			Operating Profit	5.1	4.9
		.4	1.8			All Other Expenses (net)	1.3	1.1
		-2.5	-8.9			Profit Before Taxes	3.8	3.8

RATIOS

2-10MM	10-50MM	Ratio	ALL (4/1/05-3/31/06)	ALL (4/1/06-3/31/07)
4.7	3.0	Current	3.0	2.1
2.0	1.5		1.6	1.5
1.2	.9		1.2	1.1
2.7	1.0	Quick	1.0	1.0
.7	.3		.6	.6
.2	.1		.3	.3
8 46.1	7 49.5	Sales/Receivables	6 63.8	9 40.9
14 25.6	13 28.3		16 22.2	17 20.9
34 10.8	39 9.3		26 14.2	34 10.7
46 8.0	28 13.1	Cost of Sales/Inventory	31 11.7	31 11.6
84 4.4	93 3.9		49 7.4	54 6.8
211 1.7	151 2.4		97 3.8	94 3.9
14 26.5	15 23.8	Cost of Sales/Payables	11 31.8	14 25.8
23 15.8	19 19.3		23 15.7	23 16.1
36 10.0	33 11.2		35 10.4	37 9.8
2.6	4.1	Sales/Working Capital	6.3	6.9
6.3	9.5		11.3	12.0
25.2	-18.5		35.3	45.9
4.0	.1	EBIT/Interest	11.6	10.9
(18) -.2	(22) -4.3		(85) 2.8	(94) 4.4
-3.2	-19.5		1.6	1.8
		Net Profit + Depr., Dep., Amort./Cur. Mat. L/T/D	8.1	19.7
			(24) 3.4	(20) 5.8
			1.9	2.3
.5	.3	Fixed/Worth	.4	.4
.9	1.0		1.2	.9
NM	3.4		260.0	1.9
.5	.7	Debt/Worth	1.0	1.0
1.4	1.3		3.0	2.1
NM	8.2		291.0	6.8
24.2	4.1	% Profit Before Taxes/Tangible Net Worth	49.4	59.9
(15) -4.7	(23) -26.1		(72) 27.8	(86) 21.1
-31.6	-66.8		7.1	10.4
7.7	-.7	% Profit Before Taxes/Total Assets	16.4	18.3
-2.2	-8.1		4.6	7.3
-16.0	-22.0		1.7	2.8
13.1	10.5	Sales/Net Fixed Assets	23.5	17.2
4.4	4.5		10.5	9.0
2.5	2.4		5.3	5.0
2.3	2.2	Sales/Total Assets	3.1	3.0
1.5	1.3		2.2	2.3
1.2	.9		1.6	1.6
.9	1.9	% Depr., Dep., Amort./Sales	.6	.8
(19) 2.1	(24) 2.6		(89) 1.3	(95) 1.5
4.5	4.8		2.5	2.6
1.7		% Officers', Directors' Owners' Comp/Sales	1.1	.9
(10) 3.4			(30) 2.0	(22) 1.8
4.8			4.1	3.8

500M-2MM	2-10MM	10-50MM	50-100MM	100-250MM		ALL	ALL
31750M	160974M	930613M	433180M	425334M	Net Sales ($)	4023962M	4504086M
10141M	100463M	630059M	476456M	471825M	Total Assets ($)	1910455M	2289436M

M = $ thousand   MM = $ million
See Pages 9 through 22 for Explanation of Ratios and Data

Comparative Historical Data				Current Data Sorted by Sales					
			Type of Statement						
23	20	16	Unqualified				1	4	11
17	8	5	Reviewed			1	2	2	
7	10	6	Compiled		1	1	3	1	
5	9	7	Tax Returns		3		3	1	
40	41	30	Other		2	3	5	5	15
4/1/07-3/31/08 ALL	**4/1/08-3/31/09 ALL**	**4/1/09-3/31/10 ALL**		**18 (4/1-9/30/09)**			**46 (10/1/09-3/31/10)**		
				0-1MM	**1-3MM**	**3-5MM**	**5-10MM**	**10-25MM**	**25MM & OVER**
92	88	64	**NUMBER OF STATEMENTS**		6	5	14	13	26
%	%	%	**ASSETS**	%	%	%	%	%	%
10.5	7.1	9.5	Cash & Equivalents	**DATA NOT AVAILABLE**			8.7	14.2	6.9
12.5	11.0	10.8	Trade Receivables (net)				15.7	8.4	10.6
32.0	37.5	32.3	Inventory				35.5	30.3	28.4
3.9	2.5	5.0	All Other Current				5.5	7.6	5.1
59.0	58.2	57.6	Total Current				65.4	60.5	51.0
29.8	31.4	33.0	Fixed Assets (net)				29.8	27.0	36.8
5.9	5.3	4.4	Intangibles (net)				2.7	5.8	5.7
5.4	5.2	5.0	All Other Non-Current				2.1	6.8	6.5
100.0	100.0	100.0	Total				100.0	100.0	100.0
			LIABILITIES						
10.3	13.1	12.3	Notes Payable-Short Term				15.7	15.0	10.0
4.3	3.1	2.3	Cur. Mat.-L.T.D.				1.9	1.6	3.1
14.2	13.0	10.9	Trade Payables				12.0	7.4	9.9
.2	.1	.4	Income Taxes Payable				.8	.7	.3
16.3	11.3	12.4	All Other Current				11.9	13.1	15.5
45.2	40.6	38.2	Total Current				42.2	37.9	38.7
17.1	21.4	18.5	Long-Term Debt				21.9	11.3	18.7
.5	.3	.1	Deferred Taxes				.0	.3	.1
3.8	5.6	7.0	All Other Non-Current				13.2	3.0	6.8
33.4	32.1	36.2	Net Worth				22.7	47.5	35.6
100.0	100.0	100.0	Total Liabilties & Net Worth				100.0	100.0	100.0
			INCOME DATA						
100.0	100.0	100.0	Net Sales				100.0	100.0	100.0
21.6	22.2	19.9	Gross Profit				22.1	15.5	15.5
18.5	20.9	23.4	Operating Expenses				24.5	18.2	20.6
3.1	1.4	-3.5	Operating Profit				-2.4	-2.7	-5.0
1.2	1.0	1.2	All Other Expenses (net)				1.3	2.0	1.5
1.9	.3	-4.7	Profit Before Taxes				-3.7	-4.8	-6.6
			RATIOS						
2.2	2.5	3.1					2.6	3.4	2.0
1.4	1.3	1.5	Current				1.7	2.2	1.3
1.1	1.0	1.1					1.0	1.1	.9
.9	.8	1.2					2.1	1.5	.9
.5	.4	.6	Quick				.5	.8	.4
.2	.2	.2					.2	.4	.2
6 63.4	**6** 58.6	**8** 46.6					**9** 41.7	**5** 73.9	**10** 37.9
16 22.9	**14** 25.8	**16** 22.9	Sales/Receivables				**23** 15.7	**10** 36.8	**18** 20.5
26 14.2	**26** 13.8	**38** 9.5					**37** 9.8	**45** 8.2	**40** 9.1
31 11.8	**40** 9.0	**34** 10.9					**29** 12.5	**3** 139.0	**20** 18.0
53 6.8	**68** 5.4	**86** 4.2	Cost of Sales/Inventory				**84** 4.4	**86** 4.2	**68** 5.3
84 4.4	**123** 3.0	**185** 2.0					**278** 1.3	**154** 2.4	**152** 2.4
13 28.4	**12** 30.8	**15** 23.6					**14** 25.4	**10** 37.9	**17** 21.5
21 17.3	**22** 16.8	**23** 15.6	Cost of Sales/Payables				**24** 14.9	**18** 20.8	**24** 15.0
32 11.4	**37** 9.9	**37** 9.9					**42** 8.8	**25** 14.4	**36** 10.1
6.6	6.0	3.0					2.9	2.4	5.3
13.2	13.7	9.5	Sales/Working Capital				8.7	4.9	14.3
265.2	NM	57.9					NM	NM	-19.2
8.7	5.7	2.5					4.8	.0	2.2
(83) 2.7	(82) 1.3	(55) -.9	EBIT/Interest				(12) .4	(11) -1.9	(21) -2.4
.7	-1.1	-6.0					-5.3	-3.5	-13.0
9.1	9.7	4.8							
(21) 1.8	(17) 2.3	(13) 1.7	Net Profit + Depr., Dep., Amort./Cur. Mat. L/T/D						
-.1	.4	-4.9							
.4	.5	.4					.5	.2	.5
.9	1.4	1.0	Fixed/Worth				2.1	.9	1.0
2.9	4.1	6.7					-22.8	10.1	2.7
.6	1.0	.7					1.0	.5	.8
1.9	2.6	1.7	Debt/Worth				6.0	1.0	1.7
7.4	16.0	13.3					-86.8	20.9	8.2
46.4	28.7	19.1					18.3	20.0	14.5
(75) 13.0	(71) 6.7	(52) -3.8	% Profit Before Taxes/Tangible Net Worth				(10) -22.6	(11) -4.2	(21) -1.5
.0	-15.5	-39.2					-130.7	-47.1	-47.1
13.6	10.2	5.5					8.2	4.8	1.7
5.5	1.2	-2.7	% Profit Before Taxes/Total Assets				-4.4	-4.5	-4.6
-1.0	-5.7	-19.7					-13.3	-16.7	-23.9
21.8	14.9	11.4					16.6	10.6	10.5
9.4	7.4	4.2	Sales/Net Fixed Assets				5.0	5.4	3.1
5.2	4.2	2.4					2.8	3.4	2.1
3.2	2.9	2.3					2.3	1.6	2.3
2.5	2.1	1.3	Sales/Total Assets				1.7	1.2	1.2
1.6	1.4	1.0					.7	1.1	.9
.8	.9	1.4					1.1	1.4	1.9
(83) 1.3	(79) 1.6	(58) 2.5	% Depr., Dep., Amort./Sales				(13) 2.7	2.4	(23) 3.9
2.4	3.1	4.9					4.7	3.8	5.2
1.0	1.2	1.3							
(21) 2.0	(21) 1.6	(18) 2.7	% Officers', Directors' Owners' Comp/Sales						
5.8	2.5	4.0							
4471746M	**4080234M**	**1981851M**	Net Sales ($)		**12822M**	**20867M**	**98000M**	**206764M**	**1643398M**
2424477M	**2369519M**	**1688944M**	Total Assets ($)		**9358M**	**15627M**	**80506M**	**170476M**	**1412977M**

M = $ thousand MM = $ million

See Pages 9 through 22 for Explanation of Ratios and Data

Current Data Sorted by Assets | Comparative Historical Data

0-500M	500M-2MM	2-10MM	10-50MM	50-100MM	100-250MM	Type of Statement	4/1/05-3/31/06 ALL	4/1/06-3/31/07 ALL
			1		1	Unqualified	4	4
		3				Reviewed	5	5
	2	3				Compiled	1	6
	7	5	4			Tax Returns		4
1	3	6	1		2	Other	10	16
	2 (4/1-9/30/09)	37 (10/1/09-3/31/10)						
1	12	17	6		3	NUMBER OF STATEMENTS	20	35
%	%	%	%	%	%	ASSETS	%	%
	11.7	9.1				Cash & Equivalents	7.1	9.7
	15.6	12.4				Trade Receivables (net)	20.9	16.5
	44.4	46.7				Inventory	42.3	45.9
	.2	3.2				All Other Current	1.6	1.8
	71.9	71.4				Total Current	71.9	74.0
	14.9	17.9				Fixed Assets (net)	17.5	15.4
	6.4	8.0				Intangibles (net)	7.9	5.9
	6.9	2.6				All Other Non-Current	2.6	4.7
	100.0	100.0				Total	100.0	100.0
						LIABILITIES		
	10.8	19.8				Notes Payable-Short Term	22.9	18.8
	1.7	5.8				Cur. Mat.-L.T.D.	2.6	6.2
	13.3	9.8				Trade Payables	13.6	16.5
	.0	.1				Income Taxes Payable	.1	.1
	12.0	10.9				All Other Current	9.0	13.1
	37.8	46.4				Total Current	48.2	54.6
	30.6	15.6				Long-Term Debt	14.1	13.5
	.0	.1				Deferred Taxes	.1	.6
	1.1	7.0				All Other Non-Current	9.5	12.5
	30.4	31.0				Net Worth	28.2	18.9
	100.0	100.0				Total Liabilities & Net Worth	100.0	100.0
						INCOME DATA		
	100.0	100.0				Net Sales	100.0	100.0
	39.7	34.4				Gross Profit	33.8	33.5
	33.8	32.7				Operating Expenses	26.1	28.0
	5.9	1.7				Operating Profit	7.7	5.5
	2.7	3.2				All Other Expenses (net)	1.3	2.0
	3.2	-1.5				Profit Before Taxes	6.4	3.5
						RATIOS		
	6.4	3.9					2.2	2.6
	1.8	1.4				Current	1.6	1.6
	1.1	1.1					1.2	1.1
	3.5	1.0					1.3	1.0
	.7	.3				Quick	.6	.5
	.2	.2					.3	.2
	3 111.5	8 43.0					9 41.0	8 45.7
	20 18.3	21 17.1				Sales/Receivables	29 12.7	23 15.8
	29 12.5	38 9.6					50 7.3	42 8.7
	61 5.9	105 3.5					46 8.0	61 6.0
	77 4.7	172 2.1				Cost of Sales/Inventory	112 3.3	98 3.7
	277 1.3	224 1.6					167 2.2	148 2.5
	10 35.4	14 25.3					10 36.1	15 24.0
	36 10.2	23 16.2				Cost of Sales/Payables	24 15.5	30 12.2
	53 6.8	40 9.1					41 8.8	51 7.1
	5.3	3.5					5.9	5.4
	7.8	6.5				Sales/Working Capital	10.3	8.3
	NM	21.5					16.1	39.7
	12.4	7.0					9.3	9.7
	(11) 3.7	(16) .4				EBIT/Interest	(18) 3.0	(33) 2.4
	1.8	-2.1					2.0	1.4
						Net Profit + Depr., Dep., Amort./Cur. Mat. L/T/D		8.1
							(10)	1.8
								.6
	.1	.1					.3	.2
	.5	.5				Fixed/Worth	.4	.5
	10.5	NM					NM	-13.8
	1.0	.5					1.1	.9
	3.2	2.5				Debt/Worth	3.4	4.0
	59.6	NM					NM	-185.6
	96.4	28.2				% Profit Before Taxes/Tangible	89.9	74.0
	(10) 32.5	(13) 8.1				Net Worth	(15) 22.3	(25) 30.6
	12.2	-21.1					11.4	16.8
	23.6	8.7				% Profit Before Taxes/Total	19.5	17.0
	4.9	-1.6				Assets	8.7	7.7
	3.6	-10.7					2.9	1.9
	174.1	40.4					36.1	57.6
	19.1	18.8				Sales/Net Fixed Assets	17.3	27.2
	6.5	7.8					9.5	10.8
	3.4	2.1					3.7	3.6
	2.2	1.7				Sales/Total Assets	2.1	2.6
	1.1	1.3					1.4	1.7
		1.0					.6	.5
	(14)	1.5				% Depr., Dep., Amort./Sales	(18) 1.2	(31) .9
		6.1					2.4	3.0
						% Officers', Directors'		1.7
						Owners' Comp/Sales	(15) 3.6	
								6.5
149M	36420M	131111M	171175M		993354M	Net Sales ($)	611284M	1107353M
330M	15691M	74470M	77047M		559402M	Total Assets ($)	386920M	701787M

(Note: columns 0-500M, 10-50MM, 50-100MM, and 100-250MM display "DATA NOT AVAILABLE" for the asset, liability, income, and ratio sections.)

M = $ thousand   MM = $ million
See Pages 9 through 22 for Explanation of Ratios and Data

Comparative Historical Data / Current Data Sorted by Sales

				Type of Statement	0-1MM	1-3MM	3-5MM	5-10MM	10-25MM	25MM & OVER
4		3	2	Unqualified				2	1	2
4		6	3	Reviewed		5	3	1	1	
5		4	5	Compiled		5		3	1	1
6		11	13	Tax Returns	1		3			
13		14	16	Other				1		4
4/1/07-3/31/08 ALL		4/1/08-3/31/09 ALL	4/1/09-3/31/10 ALL			2 (4/1-9/30/09)		37 (10/1/09-3/31/10)		
32		38	39	**NUMBER OF STATEMENTS**	1	10	6	8	7	7
%		%	%	**ASSETS**	%	%	%	%	%	%
6.4		6.0	9.6	Cash & Equivalents		6.2				
17.3		17.9	14.9	Trade Receivables (net)		6.8				
42.1		41.3	44.7	Inventory		44.4				
1.5		1.7	1.9	All Other Current		1.1				
67.3		66.8	71.1	Total Current		58.6				
14.4		17.1	15.2	Fixed Assets (net)		24.5				
11.4		9.6	10.1	Intangibles (net)		8.9				
6.9		6.5	3.6	All Other Non-Current		8.1				
100.0		100.0	100.0	Total		100.0				
				LIABILITIES						
19.4		22.0	16.7	Notes Payable-Short Term		24.2				
1.4		3.3	3.7	Cur. Mat.-L.T.D.		1.4				
12.6		14.1	12.6	Trade Payables		9.9				
.3		.2	.1	Income Taxes Payable		.0				
13.8		9.5	13.3	All Other Current		12.8				
47.6		49.1	46.4	Total Current		48.2				
13.7		17.6	23.1	Long-Term Debt		24.9				
.4		.0	.0	Deferred Taxes		.0				
11.7		14.0	6.2	All Other Non-Current		9.3				
26.6		19.3	24.2	Net Worth		17.5				
100.0		100.0	100.0	Total Liabilities & Net Worth		100.0				
				INCOME DATA						
100.0		100.0	100.0	Net Sales		100.0				
32.6		31.6	32.9	Gross Profit		46.4				
26.8		27.6	30.2	Operating Expenses		44.0				
5.8		4.0	2.7	Operating Profit		2.3				
2.0		3.3	3.1	All Other Expenses (net)		3.6				
3.8		.7	-.4	Profit Before Taxes		-1.3				
				RATIOS						
2.7		2.3	3.1	Current		9.9				
1.4		1.5	1.4			1.3				
.9		1.1	1.0			.6				
1.0		1.0	1.1	Quick		3.4				
.6		.5	.3			.3				
.2		.2	.2			.1				
9	42.5 / 10	36.2 / 11	32.2	Sales/Receivables		1 277.7				
23	16.0 / 26	14.0 / 22	16.9			14 25.2				
60	6.1 / 51	7.1 / 38	9.6			35 10.3				
68	5.4 / 63	5.8 / 62	5.9	Cost of Sales/Inventory		96 3.8				
102	3.6 / 115	3.2 / 116	3.1			303 1.2				
141	2.6 / 157	2.3 / 220	1.7			336 1.1				
13	27.1 / 15	24.2 / 18	20.8	Cost of Sales/Payables		14 26.9				
24	15.0 / 27	13.3 / 28	12.9			41 9.0				
50	7.3 / 47	7.7 / 59	6.2			80 4.6				
6.3		7.0	4.0	Sales/Working Capital		4.7				
11.1		10.6	8.5			8.7				
-39.8		170.0	58.0			-9.5				
12.3		7.7	8.2	EBIT/Interest						
(29) 3.3		(37) 1.8	(36) 2.4							
1.6		.6	-1.1							
				Net Profit + Depr., Dep., Amort./Cur. Mat. L/T/D						
.2		.1	.2	Fixed/Worth		.5				
.9		.6	.5			1.0				
-1.1		-1.7	-1.3			-1.2				
1.8		1.0	.9	Debt/Worth		1.0				
4.4		3.9	3.4			1.8				
-8.4		-6.2	-9.4			-7.7				
91.7		56.8	56.2	% Profit Before Taxes/Tangible Net Worth						
(22) 37.1		(26) 24.5	(28) 16.7							
8.4		7.3	-1.4							
19.9		15.2	10.2	% Profit Before Taxes/Total Assets		13.5				
7.7		2.9	4.0			4.9				
.0		.0	-8.1			-14.5				
43.1		98.7	51.9	Sales/Net Fixed Assets		27.3				
28.5		26.6	18.8			7.0				
10.4		9.7	9.5			3.0				
3.4		3.1	2.9	Sales/Total Assets		1.9				
1.8		2.0	1.8			1.2				
1.2		1.3	1.3			1.0				
.8		.5	1.0	% Depr., Dep., Amort./Sales						
(26) 1.3		(28) 1.0	(25) 1.6							
2.6		2.9	4.9							
2.4		3.1	1.8	% Officers', Directors' Owners' Comp/Sales						
(12) 5.6		(14) 4.8	(17) 3.9							
11.0		10.6	8.9							
1378295M		1045256M	1332209M	Net Sales ($)	149M	20796M	27437M	53199M	100448M	1130180M
909511M		730927M	726940M	Total Assets ($)	330M	16006M	12314M	30958M	55686M	611646M

M = $ thousand   MM = $ million
See Pages 9 through 22 for Explanation of Ratios and Data

Current Data Sorted by Assets   Comparative Historical Data

							Type of Statement			
		2	1	5	1		Unqualified		9	10
	1	2	4				Reviewed		7	8
	3	2	1				Compiled		7	9
4	4	1	1				Tax Returns		10	11
	6	9	10	3	4		Other		23	23
	10 (4/1-9/30/09)		54 (10/1/09-3/31/10)						4/1/05-	4/1/06-
									3/31/06	3/31/07
0-500M	500M-2MM	2-10MM	10-50MM	50-100MM	100-250MM				ALL	ALL
4	14	16	17	8	5		NUMBER OF STATEMENTS		56	61
%	%	%	%	%	%		ASSETS		%	%
	4.4	10.9	4.7				Cash & Equivalents		7.8	6.8
	17.2	17.3	22.9				Trade Receivables (net)		20.4	23.2
	43.1	37.7	32.0				Inventory		42.1	41.2
	6.4	3.1	5.5				All Other Current		2.2	2.7
	71.2	69.0	65.2				Total Current		72.6	73.9
	16.9	20.7	22.6				Fixed Assets (net)		18.5	17.9
	8.4	3.7	1.7				Intangibles (net)		4.4	3.9
	3.5	6.6	10.5				All Other Non-Current		4.4	4.3
	100.0	100.0	100.0				Total		100.0	100.0
							LIABILITIES			
	24.4	11.0	14.7				Notes Payable-Short Term		15.1	19.3
	10.0	1.6	4.8				Cur. Mat.-L.T.D.		4.9	4.0
	17.7	7.1	16.3				Trade Payables		14.8	15.9
	.0	.1	.3				Income Taxes Payable		.3	.0
	5.8	12.4	12.7				All Other Current		15.1	9.7
	58.0	32.1	48.8				Total Current		50.2	48.8
	18.0	12.6	14.8				Long-Term Debt		14.6	12.4
	.0	.0	.1				Deferred Taxes		.1	.1
	26.1	6.8	4.2				All Other Non-Current		13.9	13.8
	-2.0	48.4	32.0				Net Worth		21.2	24.9
	100.0	100.0	100.0				Total Liabilties & Net Worth		100.0	100.0
							INCOME DATA			
	100.0	100.0	100.0				Net Sales		100.0	100.0
	41.3	32.2	19.9				Gross Profit		27.6	29.0
	48.4	29.5	18.7				Operating Expenses		24.9	23.4
	-7.1	2.7	1.2				Operating Profit		2.7	5.6
	.8	.7	2.0				All Other Expenses (net)		.8	1.4
	-8.0	2.0	-.8				Profit Before Taxes		1.8	4.2
							RATIOS			
	3.1	4.5	1.7						2.2	2.4
	1.4	2.1	1.2				Current		1.5	1.5
	.9	1.2	.9						1.1	1.1
	1.0	1.9	1.0						1.0	1.3
	.5	.7	.7				Quick	(55)	.6	.6
	.2	.4	.3						.4	.3

16	22.8	1	656.9	27	13.3			12	30.2	12	31.3
28	12.9	24	15.5	43	8.5	Sales/Receivables	33	11.2	30	12.2
46	7.9	52	7.0	53	6.8		42	8.6	48	7.6
41	9.0	6	66.0	25	14.5		40	9.1	41	9.0
91	4.0	102	3.6	66	5.5	Cost of Sales/Inventory	90	4.1	72	5.0
346	1.1	205	1.8	89	4.1		160	2.3	123	3.0
11	34.2	11	33.6	19	19.3		11	34.3	12	31.2
34	10.7	17	22.0	36	10.3	Cost of Sales/Payables	22	16.8	30	12.2
59	6.2	36	10.2	43	8.5		38	9.6	45	8.1

	2.3	2.2	6.3		5.5	6.7
	12.1	5.3	19.2	Sales/Working Capital	9.9	11.2
	-110.2	23.0	-52.8		26.7	38.6

	3.0		17.9	8.5			12.0		9.9
(10)	-.3	(14)	1.5	2.7	EBIT/Interest	(49)	3.0	(56)	3.4
	-10.1		-.1	-2.6			1.4		1.7

					Net Profit + Depr., Dep.,		
					Amort./Cur. Mat. L/T/D		

	.1	.2	.3		.2	.2
	.2	.4	.9	Fixed/Worth	.6	.7
	-13.7	.9	2.7		3.7	3.5
	1.4	.4	1.2		.8	1.2
	2.3	1.0	3.1	Debt/Worth	1.9	3.1
	-45.6	2.5	7.9		28.7	16.7

	41.3	51.3	61.6		% Profit Before Taxes/Tangible		48.2		70.0
(10)	-3.3	7.0	7.5	Net Worth	(46)	22.8	(51)	30.6
	-59.7	-19.6	-27.1			10.4		15.7
	4.5	19.6	7.0	% Profit Before Taxes/Total		14.9		20.7
	-9.6	1.5	2.1	Assets		5.5		8.2
	-20.5	-5.8	-8.3			2.0		1.6

	90.5	20.7	23.4		47.0	58.9
	35.8	12.8	11.9	Sales/Net Fixed Assets	18.2	21.0
	7.0	5.3	5.2		7.6	9.6
	3.8	2.6	3.2		3.6	3.5
	1.7	2.1	2.1	Sales/Total Assets	2.5	2.4
	1.0	1.2	1.1		1.5	1.8

			.8	1.0			.6		.5
		(15)	1.3	(15) 1.6	% Depr., Dep., Amort./Sales	(52)	1.1	(50)	.9
			4.0	2.1			1.8		1.8

					% Officers', Directors'		1.9		2.1
					Owners' Comp/Sales	(12)	2.1	(20)	4.7
							10.2		7.9

7325M	30517M	151812M	692123M	1328829M	1444105M	Net Sales ($)		1790733M	2110568M
967M	14500M	74763M	334894M	582446M	1036486M	Total Assets ($)		705293M	896320M

       M = $ thousand   MM = $ million
See Pages 9 through 22 for Explanation of Ratios and Data

Comparative Historical Data

Current Data Sorted by Sales

4/1/07-3/31/08 ALL	4/1/08-3/31/09 ALL	4/1/09-3/31/10 ALL	Type of Statement	0-1MM	1-3MM	3-5MM	5-10MM	10-25MM	25MM & OVER
10	10	9	Unqualified					2	7
5	15	7	Reviewed		1	1		3	2
7	9	6	Compiled	1	1	2		1	1
11	11	10	Tax Returns	5	1		3	1	1
29	25	32	Other	2	3	5	2	3	16
				10 (4/1-9/30/09)			54 (10/1/09-3/31/10)		
62	70	64	**NUMBER OF STATEMENTS**	8	6	8	5	10	27
%	%	%	**ASSETS**	%	%	%	%	%	%
9.8	10.6	8.1	Cash & Equivalents					4.8	6.7
22.9	20.1	17.7	Trade Receivables (net)					18.7	21.0
34.6	36.7	35.0	Inventory					27.4	31.9
2.8	3.5	4.6	All Other Current					3.0	5.5
70.0	71.0	65.4	Total Current					54.0	65.0
16.7	19.5	20.7	Fixed Assets (net)					31.7	17.9
9.0	4.9	7.6	Intangibles (net)					2.5	11.0
4.3	4.6	6.3	All Other Non-Current					11.8	6.1
100.0	100.0	100.0	Total					100.0	100.0
			LIABILITIES						
13.8	16.4	15.5	Notes Payable-Short Term					7.1	12.4
3.2	3.7	5.4	Cur. Mat.-L.T.D.					5.1	4.8
16.0	11.4	13.9	Trade Payables					7.5	14.9
.2	.1	.5	Income Taxes Payable					.2	1.0
11.1	10.7	10.4	All Other Current					13.8	12.7
44.3	42.4	45.7	Total Current					33.6	45.8
13.3	17.8	19.5	Long-Term Debt					18.9	18.0
.1	.2	.1	Deferred Taxes					.0	.3
7.4	8.7	10.8	All Other Non-Current					4.0	7.7
34.9	31.0	23.7	Net Worth					43.5	28.2
100.0	100.0	100.0	Total Liabilities & Net Worth					100.0	100.0
			INCOME DATA						
100.0	100.0	100.0	Net Sales					100.0	100.0
31.2	25.8	31.0	Gross Profit					25.8	21.4
24.6	21.6	30.2	Operating Expenses					23.0	18.6
6.6	4.3	.8	Operating Profit					2.8	2.8
1.7	.7	1.4	All Other Expenses (net)					.2	1.6
5.0	3.5	-.6	Profit Before Taxes					2.6	1.2
			RATIOS						
2.7	3.1	2.7	Current					3.4	2.5
1.5	1.6	1.5						1.3	1.4
1.0	1.2	1.0						1.0	1.1
1.4	1.5	1.1	Quick					1.4	1.0
.7	.7	.7						.6	.7
.4	.3	.4						.3	.4
15 24.4	7 48.7	16 23.4	Sales/Receivables					12 29.3	23 15.6
28 13.1	31 11.8	30 12.3						24 14.9	31 11.7
51 7.2	52 7.0	50 7.3						58 6.3	47 7.8
25 14.5	26 14.2	27 13.6	Cost of Sales/Inventory					0 UND	31 11.8
62 5.9	69 5.3	80 4.6						50 7.3	68 5.3
99 3.7	127 2.9	128 2.9						137 2.7	86 4.2
11 32.6	7 54.4	12 29.5	Cost of Sales/Payables					12 31.5	15 23.6
29 12.6	19 19.2	26 14.0						15 25.0	26 14.2
42 8.6	34 10.7	43 8.4						37 10.0	39 9.2
6.2	5.5	3.8	Sales/Working Capital					8.8	5.8
12.9	10.4	11.1						13.1	11.3
119.7	37.8	85.6						-415.1	79.5
21.6	13.6	6.1	EBIT/Interest						5.6
(48) 4.3	(64) 2.0	(56) 1.8							(26) 3.0
2.1	.5	-1.3							.2
5.9	6.5	4.3	Net Profit + Depr., Dep., Amort./Cur. Mat. L/T/D						4.8
(12) 3.6	(20) 1.6	(15) 2.1							(10) 1.6
1.8	-.2	.4							.3
.2	.2	.2	Fixed/Worth					.3	.3
.6	.6	.7						.4	1.3
5.0	1.9	3.6						2.1	4.2
.7	.7	1.0	Debt/Worth					.8	1.3
2.7	2.6	2.5						1.3	4.2
19.8	7.7	12.9						3.1	25.9
64.3	48.0	56.6	% Profit Before Taxes/Tangible Net Worth					42.1	68.4
(49) 27.5	(61) 15.4	(52) 8.6						(22) 5.5	25.0
13.9	-1.8	-21.4						-2.3	-15.0
18.0	15.8	9.3	% Profit Before Taxes/Total Assets					9.8	9.9
9.0	3.8	1.7						1.8	3.0
3.1	-.7	-9.5						-.1	-1.7
39.4	38.6	35.2	Sales/Net Fixed Assets					20.4	25.7
20.1	17.5	12.8						12.1	11.9
10.3	7.4	5.9						4.3	6.4
3.9	3.5	3.2	Sales/Total Assets					2.7	3.1
2.4	2.6	2.0						2.2	2.1
1.5	1.4	1.1						1.0	1.6
.7	.7	1.0	% Depr., Dep., Amort./Sales					.7	.9
(46) 1.0	(60) 1.2	(51) 1.5						1.4	(21) 1.5
2.4	2.4	3.6						7.7	2.4
2.1	1.8	2.1	% Officers', Directors' Owners' Comp/Sales						
(16) 3.9	(25) 2.8	(12) 6.7							
6.3	4.9	15.1							
2809477M	3280429M	3654711M	Net Sales ($)	5079M	13996M	28856M	29774M	126035M	3450971M
1237189M	1620358M	2044056M	Total Assets ($)	4942M	8824M	24184M	20982M	88897M	1896227M

© RMA 2010

M = $ thousand   MM = $ million
See Pages 9 through 22 for Explanation of Ratios and Data

Current Data Sorted by Assets   Comparative Historical Data

							Type of Statement		
			8	8	2	2	Unqualified	22	21
1	5	19	7				Reviewed	32	42
3	17	17	1				Compiled	45	37
18	19	9					Tax Returns	46	54
15	21	18	9	1	2		Other	55	80
	36 (4/1-9/30/09)		166 (10/1/09-3/31/10)					4/1/05-3/31/06	4/1/06-3/31/07
0-500M	500M-2MM	2-10MM	10-50MM	50-100MM	100-250MM			ALL	ALL
37	62	71	25	3	4	**NUMBER OF STATEMENTS**	200	234
%	%	%	%	%	%	**ASSETS**	%	%
12.5	7.3	9.6	8.9			Cash & Equivalents	9.2	9.2
20.9	23.1	22.5	18.8			Trade Receivables (net)	27.1	28.5
17.3	26.7	26.8	17.7			Inventory	21.0	20.3
1.7	2.0	1.5	3.0			All Other Current	2.4	2.1
52.3	58.9	60.4	48.4			Total Current	59.6	60.1
35.5	32.4	29.0	34.4			Fixed Assets (net)	31.3	31.9
1.6	1.9	4.1	6.6			Intangibles (net)	3.2	3.2
10.6	6.8	6.5	10.6			All Other Non-Current	5.8	4.8
100.0	100.0	100.0	100.0			Total	100.0	100.0
						LIABILITIES		
36.7	16.7	13.2	7.3			Notes Payable-Short Term	12.2	10.3
5.9	2.9	5.6	5.3			Cur. Mat.-L.T.D.	4.2	4.2
14.1	19.1	12.1	9.0			Trade Payables	15.3	13.5
.0	.0	.2	.4			Income Taxes Payable	.2	.2
20.7	14.1	14.5	10.7			All Other Current	13.7	15.0
77.5	52.9	45.6	32.7			Total Current	45.6	43.3
32.2	23.1	14.1	15.3			Long-Term Debt	19.1	21.0
.0	.4	1.0	.8			Deferred Taxes	.4	.4
20.0	12.9	8.8	4.1			All Other Non-Current	7.4	6.6
-29.6	10.7	30.6	47.1			Net Worth	27.5	28.7
100.0	100.0	100.0	100.0			Total Liabilities & Net Worth	100.0	100.0
						INCOME DATA		
100.0	100.0	100.0	100.0			Net Sales	100.0	100.0
43.9	32.1	25.4	28.0			Gross Profit	34.4	33.1
46.7	33.7	27.3	27.5			Operating Expenses	30.4	28.9
-2.8	-1.6	-1.9	.5			Operating Profit	4.0	4.2
.9	.4	.9	2.3			All Other Expenses (net)	.8	1.1
-3.7	-1.9	-2.8	-1.8			Profit Before Taxes	3.2	3.1
						RATIOS		
1.3	2.4	2.7	5.2				2.2	2.9
.8	1.1	1.4	1.6			Current	1.3	1.6
.5	.7	.9	1.1				1.0	1.0
.8	1.1	1.4	3.0				1.3	1.8
.5	.6	.7	1.0			Quick	.8	1.0
.2	.3	.4	.6				.5	.5
0 UND	14 26.7	24 14.9	29 12.4				16 23.1	19 18.9
15 23.6	26 13.9	35 10.4	36 10.1			Sales/Receivables	31 11.9	33 11.2
34 10.8	40 9.1	52 7.0	48 7.5				47 7.8	51 7.1
0 UND	24 15.0	31 11.8	28 13.2				12 29.2	14 26.8
18 20.3	40 9.1	49 7.5	39 9.2			Cost of Sales/Inventory	32 11.3	32 11.3
38 9.7	73 5.0	99 3.7	77 4.7				56 6.5	54 6.8
0 UND	13 27.4	10 36.8	8 43.2				9 39.2	9 41.7
16 23.5	24 15.2	23 15.9	12 31.6			Cost of Sales/Payables	21 17.4	18 20.0
37 10.0	51 7.1	41 8.9	28 13.2				38 9.5	37 10.0
24.5	9.1	5.6	4.1				8.6	7.0
-64.0	47.0	12.8	11.4			Sales/Working Capital	19.8	14.5
-7.9	-17.5	-21.7	114.5				-140.5	623.3
3.8	3.5	2.3	7.3				12.5	16.7
(33) 1.0	(53) 1.0	(68) .1	(22) 2.3			EBIT/Interest	(180) 3.9	(207) 4.9
-4.2	-4.3	-3.4	-1.8				1.2	1.6
		2.4				Net Profit + Depr., Dep.,	8.1	11.9
		(17) .6				Amort./Cur. Mat. L/T/D	(30) 3.1	(44) 3.1
		-1.6					1.1	1.2
.4	.5	.3	.3				.4	.4
56.7	1.8	1.2	.6			Fixed/Worth	1.1	1.0
-.4	-4.9	441.4	1.8				6.9	4.1
1.5	.8	.7	.3				.8	.6
-19.3	3.9	2.9	1.3			Debt/Worth	2.3	1.9
-2.6	-9.6	664.4	2.3				15.7	12.6
116.8	23.5	7.5	17.8			% Profit Before Taxes/Tangible	58.6	60.8
(18) 19.6	(43) 1.4	(54) -4.7	(21) 5.1			Net Worth	(155) 30.3	(187) 28.3
-21.8	-31.3	-35.5	-5.3				6.6	8.1
16.2	5.3	2.7	7.5			% Profit Before Taxes/Total	21.0	23.4
-.8	-1.1	-2.0	2.2			Assets	7.2	8.2
-36.6	-18.1	-9.4	-2.9				.8	1.6
50.2	29.8	17.8	12.7				24.6	23.1
14.8	12.4	7.9	4.3			Sales/Net Fixed Assets	11.4	10.7
7.1	4.7	4.8	2.9				6.7	6.0
6.8	3.7	2.8	2.1				4.1	3.8
4.2	2.7	2.2	1.6			Sales/Total Assets	3.1	3.0
2.9	2.1	1.4	1.3				2.3	2.2
1.2	1.0	1.2	1.2				1.0	1.1
(28) 2.1	(47) 1.7	(64) 2.4	(24) 3.4			% Depr., Dep., Amort./Sales	(167) 1.8	(196) 1.8
3.3	3.5	3.5	4.5				2.5	2.9
3.3	2.0	1.6				% Officers', Directors'	2.1	2.1
(26) 8.7	(42) 3.3	(26) 2.6				Owners' Comp/Sales	(96) 3.5	(105) 3.7
13.8	5.1	5.7					7.6	7.6
35388M	207165M	798406M	924224M	372141M	1970304M	Net Sales ($)	6653993M	7783377M
9081M	68395M	369206M	522889M	263325M	527690M	Total Assets ($)	2091848M	2863380M

© RMA 2010

M = $ thousand   MM = $ million
See Pages 9 through 22 for Explanation of Ratios and Data

Comparative Historical Data | Current Data Sorted by Sales

			Type of Statement						
25	18	20	Unqualified		4	1	2	9	9
30	39	32	Reviewed				8	13	6
34	36	38	Compiled	1	13	6	11	6	1
53	63	46	Tax Returns	13	16	8	6	3	
78	85	66	Other	11	17	7	12	8	11
4/1/07-3/31/08	4/1/08-3/31/09	4/1/09-3/31/10			36 (4/1-9/30/09)		166 (10/1/09-3/31/10)		
ALL	ALL	ALL		0-1MM	1-3MM	3-5MM	5-10MM	10-25MM	25MM & OVER
220	241	202	NUMBER OF STATEMENTS	25	50	22	39	39	27
%	%	%	**ASSETS**	%	%	%	%	%	%
9.2	7.8	9.4	Cash & Equivalents	16.5	7.8	4.8	11.1	8.7	8.0
26.9	24.0	22.0	Trade Receivables (net)	17.9	21.7	20.4	24.2	24.2	21.3
21.1	21.1	23.3	Inventory	15.9	23.3	33.5	23.6	26.2	17.3
2.7	2.3	1.9	All Other Current	2.0	1.7	.9	2.2	1.3	3.5
59.9	55.2	56.6	Total Current	52.3	54.4	59.7	61.1	60.5	50.1
29.6	33.6	32.1	Fixed Assets (net)	35.8	34.3	31.4	28.8	29.1	34.5
4.5	3.6	3.5	Intangibles (net)	2.9	1.6	1.1	4.2	4.9	6.1
6.0	7.5	7.8	All Other Non-Current	8.9	9.7	7.9	5.9	5.5	9.3
100.0	100.0	100.0	Total	100.0	100.0	100.0	100.0	100.0	100.0
			LIABILITIES						
10.5	14.9	17.5	Notes Payable-Short Term	45.1	17.5	12.2	15.9	12.5	6.2
4.4	4.4	4.6	Cur. Mat.-L.T.D.	5.3	3.7	3.2	5.2	6.3	3.9
13.9	14.3	14.0	Trade Payables	6.6	20.6	12.2	15.0	13.4	9.4
.2	.4	.1	Income Taxes Payable	.0	.0	.0	.2	.4	.0
13.9	16.4	14.8	All Other Current	27.2	14.5	9.4	14.0	13.2	11.9
43.0	50.3	51.1	Total Current	84.1	56.2	37.1	50.2	45.8	31.3
20.4	20.6	20.2	Long-Term Debt	33.0	25.0	22.0	14.9	13.3	16.0
.4	.3	.6	Deferred Taxes	.0	1.1	.3	.4	.3	.8
6.9	6.9	11.7	All Other Non-Current	26.4	12.0	6.2	12.9	7.2	7.1
29.3	21.9	16.4	Net Worth	-43.4	5.7	34.4	21.6	33.3	44.8
100.0	100.0	100.0	Total Liabilties & Net Worth	100.0	100.0	100.0	100.0	100.0	100.0
			INCOME DATA						
100.0	100.0	100.0	Net Sales	100.0	100.0	100.0	100.0	100.0	100.0
32.9	32.2	31.2	Gross Profit	49.2	35.5	25.1	26.3	24.5	28.3
29.3	31.4	32.7	Operating Expenses	51.0	38.8	28.1	27.8	24.4	27.2
3.6	.9	-1.5	Operating Profit	-1.9	-3.3	-3.0	-1.5	.1	1.0
1.1	1.2	1.0	All Other Expenses (net)	1.9	.0	.5	.6	1.0	2.7
2.5	-.3	-2.5	Profit Before Taxes	-3.8	-3.3	-3.5	-2.0	-.9	-1.7
			RATIOS						
2.7	2.4	2.5	Current	1.9	1.8	3.2	2.7	2.5	3.5
1.5	1.2	1.2		.8	1.0	1.4	1.2	1.4	1.8
1.0	.7	.7		.3	.7	1.0	.8	1.0	1.2
1.6	1.4	1.3	Quick	1.3	1.0	1.2	1.4	1.1	2.2
.9	(240) .7	.7		.4	.5	.8	.7	.7	1.0
.4	.4	.3		.1	.3	.2	.4	.4	.7
17 20.9	14 25.4	17 21.0	Sales/Receivables	0 UND	18 20.6	9 41.3	24 15.3	22 16.7	29 12.7
30 12.2	28 13.1	31 12.0		7 48.7	28 12.9	23 15.9	35 10.3	34 10.9	36 10.1
44 8.3	44 8.2	46 8.0		31 11.9	39 9.3	46 7.9	53 6.9	50 7.3	51 7.2
16 22.6	16 22.7	24 15.5	Cost of Sales/Inventory	0 UND	14 25.4	29 12.4	30 12.2	26 13.9	27 13.4
31 11.9	32 11.4	39 9.4		24 15.3	39 9.4	39 9.3	41 8.8	45 8.1	33 11.0
56 6.5	60 6.1	76 4.8		84 4.3	72 5.1	105 3.5	65 5.6	89 4.1	48 7.7
9 40.0	9 42.6	9 42.2	Cost of Sales/Payables	0 UND	12 30.1	7 53.8	11 34.7	9 42.7	8 43.8
20 18.0	19 19.0	21 17.4		5 67.5	30 12.2	20 18.3	25 14.8	18 19.9	13 28.6
39 9.3	34 10.7	41 9.0		29 12.7	57 6.5	28 13.3	43 8.5	37 9.9	27 13.3
7.8	8.4	7.3	Sales/Working Capital	18.1	11.1	5.1	5.8	6.8	4.9
16.2	30.3	28.3		-20.0	205.6	12.7	39.2	12.2	11.4
-527.6	-17.9	-17.5		-4.5	-11.3	-743.4	-12.0	-104.1	31.3
7.3	4.9	3.5	EBIT/Interest	3.6	3.2	2.7	2.2	3.7	6.6
(195) 3.0	(215) 1.5	(183) .8		(20) 1.6	(43) .6	(20) .2	.4	(36) 1.5	(25) .4
.6	-2.1	-3.1		-4.4	-5.6	-5.6	-3.5	-1.4	-2.3
8.7	6.7	5.3	Net Profit + Depr., Dep., Amort./Cur. Mat. L/T/D					3.7	
(38) 1.9	(37) 2.1	(36) .7						(10) .5	
.9	.2	-.1						-.5	
.4	.5	.4	Fixed/Worth	.3	.5	.5	.3	.4	.5
1.0	1.5	1.3		-5.5	2.0	1.2	1.3	1.0	.6
6.8	-7.4	-3.9		-.3	-2.1	2.3	-1.9	5.8	1.8
.8	.9	.8	Debt/Worth	1.6	1.0	1.0	.7	.8	.5
2.3	3.5	2.7		-10.0	4.5	3.3	2.9	2.1	1.2
17.5	-20.9	-10.3		-1.9	-5.0	6.5	-5.9	14.1	2.3
55.9	42.6	16.0	% Profit Before Taxes/Tangible Net Worth	88.6	50.4	7.2	6.5	29.5	16.4
(173) 28.4	(173) 10.4	(142) 1.8		(10) 19.6	(32) 1.1	(21) -11.4	(26) -5.9	(30) 4.7	(23) 2.3
6.9	-5.1	-26.9		-6.4	-28.8	-45.8	-33.1	-21.9	-7.3
18.6	10.3	5.6	% Profit Before Taxes/Total Assets	13.7	5.8	2.4	2.5	6.7	6.6
7.2	2.1	-1.1		1.9	-1.7	-3.0	-2.0	1.2	-.9
-2.2	-9.2	-10.0		-47.0	-20.5	-10.3	-9.2	-7.9	-3.0
31.5	22.3	24.1	Sales/Net Fixed Assets	73.1	28.2	19.4	21.6	40.9	11.2
11.5	9.5	9.8		15.8	9.9	10.7	9.0	12.5	5.8
6.1	4.7	4.7		5.1	5.1	5.0	4.8	4.7	3.6
4.0	3.7	3.5	Sales/Total Assets	7.7	3.8	3.2	3.6	2.8	2.3
2.8	2.7	2.4		3.4	2.8	2.4	2.3	2.5	1.9
2.1	2.0	1.6		1.5	1.8	2.3	1.4	1.5	1.5
1.0	1.2	1.2	% Depr., Dep., Amort./Sales	1.5	1.4	.9	1.3	.5	1.2
(187) 2.0	(208) 2.1	(170) 2.3		(16) 2.0	(39) 2.8	(18) 1.8	(35) 2.4	(36) 2.0	(26) 3.0
3.2	3.8	4.0		3.3	5.2	2.9	3.2	4.1	5.1
1.9	2.1	1.9	% Officers', Directors', Owners' Comp/Sales	3.9	3.1	2.0	1.6	1.4	
(94) 4.2	(106) 3.1	(100) 3.5		(18) 12.7	(34) 4.3	(14) 2.4	(17) 2.6	(15) 2.0	
7.6	6.7	7.6		17.0	8.3	3.6	4.5	3.0	
6531850M	5689639M	4307628M	Net Sales ($)	13976M	95337M	84298M	286689M	641493M	3185835M
2940134M	2484522M	1760586M	Total Assets ($)	5448M	45142M	32860M	147719M	305480M	1223937M

M = $ thousand   MM = $ million
See Pages 9 through 22 for Explanation of Ratios and Data

Current Data Sorted by Assets **Comparative Historical Data**

0-500M	500M-2MM	2-10MM	10-50MM	50-100MM	100-250MM	Type of Statement	4/1/05-3/31/06 ALL	4/1/06-3/31/07 ALL
	1	5	9	4		Unqualified	21	15
1		8	3			Reviewed	18	21
	3	6				Compiled	15	14
1	4	2				Tax Returns	7	17
4	3	8	9	5	4	Other	28	29
	14 (4/1-9/30/09)		66 (10/1/09-3/31/10)					
6	11	29	21	9	4	NUMBER OF STATEMENTS	89	96
%	%	%	%	%	%	**ASSETS**	%	%
	9.1	7.9	7.3			Cash & Equivalents	6.0	7.8
	17.0	26.0	28.2			Trade Receivables (net)	26.8	23.7
	34.8	35.6	29.2			Inventory	35.2	36.4
	.6	2.9	3.6			All Other Current	2.9	2.8
	61.5	72.4	68.3			Total Current	70.9	70.6
	31.0	17.3	21.9			Fixed Assets (net)	17.6	18.6
	.2	1.1	1.3			Intangibles (net)	4.1	2.3
	7.2	9.1	8.5			All Other Non-Current	7.4	8.4
	100.0	100.0	100.0			Total	100.0	100.0
						LIABILITIES		
	6.6	21.7	3.8			Notes Payable-Short Term	11.5	11.6
	1.1	2.8	5.2			Cur. Mat.-L.T.D.	2.5	2.1
	10.0	18.4	13.4			Trade Payables	17.5	16.5
	.0	.0	.7			Income Taxes Payable	.2	.2
	5.0	7.8	8.9			All Other Current	10.4	10.5
	22.8	50.7	32.0			Total Current	41.9	41.0
	20.9	12.9	19.1			Long-Term Debt	12.8	13.0
	.0	.3	.8			Deferred Taxes	.3	.5
	12.6	3.6	5.8			All Other Non-Current	5.5	5.9
	43.7	32.6	42.3			Net Worth	39.4	39.6
	100.0	100.0	100.0			Total Liabilities & Net Worth	100.0	100.0
						INCOME DATA		
	100.0	100.0	100.0			Net Sales	100.0	100.0
	34.6	24.9	24.7			Gross Profit	24.6	29.0
	34.2	23.8	21.2			Operating Expenses	21.4	25.1
	.4	1.1	3.5			Operating Profit	3.2	3.8
	-.1	.7	.7			All Other Expenses (net)	.7	.5
	.5	.4	2.8			Profit Before Taxes	2.5	3.4
						RATIOS		
	6.1	3.2	4.7				2.9	3.4
	1.9	1.7	2.3			Current	1.7	2.1
	1.2	1.1	1.7				1.2	1.2
	1.7	1.4	2.6				1.3	1.5
	.6	.8	1.3			Quick	.8	.9
	.5	.5	.7				.5	.4
	4 101.1	16 22.9	28 13.1				19 19.4	12 29.8
	31 11.9	28 12.9	41 8.9			Sales/Receivables	31 11.6	29 12.4
	41 8.9	40 9.0	46 8.0				44 8.3	42 8.6
	23 16.0	35 10.5	36 10.2				32 11.3	36 10.3
	72 5.1	73 5.0	47 7.7			Cost of Sales/Inventory	48 7.6	54 6.7
	108 3.4	95 3.8	65 5.7				75 4.9	91 4.0
	6 62.6	16 23.2	7 49.9				14 26.4	12 30.9
	30 12.0	24 15.0	19 18.8			Cost of Sales/Payables	21 17.5	20 17.9
	48 7.6	35 10.6	30 12.1				38 9.7	35 10.4
	2.3	5.7	4.6				6.2	5.3
	8.3	10.6	8.7			Sales/Working Capital	11.9	9.8
	33.6	52.5	11.3				28.7	27.5
		5.1	17.0				11.4	13.1
	(28)	2.4	(19) 10.1			EBIT/Interest	(81) 4.2	(84) 3.2
		-.5	.1				.9	1.3
							4.0	4.4
						Net Profit + Depr., Dep., Amort./Cur. Mat. L/T/D	(20) 1.4	(20) 2.4
							.7	.5
	.2	.1	.2				.2	.2
	.3	.4	.3			Fixed/Worth	.5	.4
	2.8	1.1	1.6				1.7	1.0
	.3	.8	.3				.5	.5
	2.1	1.4	.8			Debt/Worth	1.7	1.3
	7.5	3.8	4.1				6.3	4.2
	17.5	20.3	43.0				42.8	37.4
(10) 5.0		(26) 3.2	(18) 15.4			% Profit Before Taxes/Tangible Net Worth	(77) 18.1	(86) 19.8
	-31.9	-13.0	-1.9				.5	4.2
	14.7	8.4	14.0				17.1	16.2
	1.3	.5	9.1			% Profit Before Taxes/Total Assets	8.2	6.2
	-7.4	-3.9	-1.3				.0	1.3
	28.2	67.9	24.4				52.7	43.9
	15.8	19.9	11.4			Sales/Net Fixed Assets	20.2	19.2
	4.3	11.0	8.2				11.1	10.1
	3.0	4.2	3.6				4.2	4.4
	2.8	3.0	2.8			Sales/Total Assets	2.9	2.9
	1.3	1.9	2.2				2.3	2.2
		.4	.8				.5	.4
	(26)	1.0	(20) 1.1			% Depr., Dep., Amort./Sales	(74) .8	(81) 1.0
		2.0	1.5				1.5	1.4
		1.4					1.0	2.3
	(13)	2.8				% Officers', Directors' Owners' Comp/Sales	(29) 2.3	(39) 3.9
		4.0					3.0	6.8
12047M	35859M	448587M	1180518M	1595552M	893737M	Net Sales ($)	4365919M	4932490M
1738M	13931M	143296M	411862M	699474M	595663M	Total Assets ($)	1821630M	2048606M

Comparative Historical Data

Current Data Sorted by Sales

				Type of Statement						
	14		18		19	Unqualified			2	3	14
	19		15		12	Reviewed			5	4	3
	13		10		9	Compiled		2	3	2	
	7		10		7	Tax Returns	2	2		1	1	1
	35		35		33	Other	2	3	1	3	7	17
	4/1/07-		4/1/08-		4/1/09-			14 (4/1-9/30/09)		66 (10/1/09-3/31/10)		
	3/31/08		3/31/09		3/31/10						
	ALL		ALL		ALL		0-1MM	1-3MM	3-5MM	5-10MM	10-25MM	25MM & OVER
	88		88		80	NUMBER OF STATEMENTS	4	7	3	14	17	35
	%		%		%	ASSETS	%	%	%	%	%	%
	6.9		7.7		9.5	Cash & Equivalents				7.7	10.5	9.0
	24.0		22.9		24.2	Trade Receivables (net)				16.0	26.4	29.2
	35.2		37.0		32.3	Inventory				39.4	33.9	27.7
	4.6		2.6		2.5	All Other Current				.5	4.1	3.4
	70.7		70.3		68.5	Total Current				63.6	74.9	69.2
	18.4		20.6		19.6	Fixed Assets (net)				20.9	17.2	18.8
	2.7		2.1		3.4	Intangibles (net)				.8	.7	5.2
	8.2		7.0		8.5	All Other Non-Current				14.7	7.2	6.7
	100.0		100.0		100.0	Total				100.0	100.0	100.0
						LIABILITIES						
	12.9		17.6		10.8	Notes Payable-Short Term				28.0	15.2	3.3
	2.6		2.7		3.3	Cur. Mat.-L.T.D.				2.9	1.9	3.7
	17.1		13.6		14.0	Trade Payables				13.0	15.7	16.4
	.2		.1		.3	Income Taxes Payable				.1	.0	.6
	14.1		13.2		8.0	All Other Current				6.8	6.6	10.0
	47.0		47.2		36.5	Total Current				50.8	39.4	34.0
	16.2		19.0		19.7	Long-Term Debt				14.8	12.7	22.6
	.5		.3		.3	Deferred Taxes				1.0	.0	.3
	5.6		7.8		5.4	All Other Non-Current				1.9	3.8	6.0
	30.7		25.7		38.1	Net Worth				31.5	44.1	37.1
	100.0		100.0		100.0	Total Liabilties & Net Worth				100.0	100.0	100.0
						INCOME DATA						
	100.0		100.0		100.0	Net Sales				100.0	100.0	100.0
	27.5		25.8		26.4	Gross Profit				25.9	24.9	21.6
	25.0		25.7		23.9	Operating Expenses				25.8	23.2	18.3
	2.6		.1		2.5	Operating Profit				.1	1.7	3.3
	.5		1.2		.7	All Other Expenses (net)				1.3	.7	.9
	2.1		-1.1		1.8	Profit Before Taxes				-1.2	1.0	2.5
						RATIOS						
	2.8		4.0		4.1					3.1	4.0	4.1
	1.7		1.8		2.2	Current				1.7	2.2	2.3
	1.1		1.0		1.2					1.3	1.3	1.6
	1.4		1.9		2.1					1.4	2.3	2.5
	.6		.8		1.1	Quick				.5	1.0	1.3
	.4		.4		.5					.4	.5	.8

12	29.8	19	19.3	23	16.1		5	73.2	24	15.5	30	12.2			
28	12.8	31	11.8	36	10.2	Sales/Receivables	20	18.5	28	13.2	41	9.0			
40	9.1	40	9.1	46	7.9		41	8.9	40	9.0	46	7.9			
37	9.9	36	10.1	34	10.6		65	5.6	35	10.5	30	12.3			
53	6.9	60	6.0	51	7.2	Cost of Sales/Inventory	92	4.0	47	7.8	44	8.3			
81	4.5	102	3.6	91	4.0		114	3.2	90	4.1	62	5.9			
11	33.6	10	38.0	10	35.3		6	61.0	12	30.0	13	28.3			
20	18.5	17	21.5	22	16.7	Cost of Sales/Payables	19	19.6	21	17.1	23	15.9			
34	10.6	31	11.6	35	10.6		36	10.1	33	10.9	31	11.7			
	5.7		5.0		4.8					4.8	5.3	4.2			
	12.7		11.3		8.4	Sales/Working Capital				9.7	8.1	8.7			
	79.5		202.1		31.6					33.4	29.3	17.7			
	10.1		6.1		11.5					3.0	10.3	16.3			
(79)	2.1	(79)	1.1	(71)	2.5	EBIT/Interest	(13)	.4	(16)	3.5	(32)	7.1			
	-.1		-2.4		-.2			-2.7		.0		-.2			
	5.3		7.4		4.2	Net Profit + Depr., Dep.,									
(23)	.8	(21)	2.3	(14)	1.1	Amort./Cur. Mat. L/T/D									
	.2		-5.6		-.2										
	.2		.2		.2					.1	.1	.2			
	.6		.5		.4	Fixed/Worth				.5	.4	.4			
	1.3		2.2		1.4					1.4	.8	2.3			
	.5		.5		.4					.6	.8	.3			
	1.9		1.5		1.1	Debt/Worth				1.2	1.2	.7			
	6.6		13.9		4.1					3.7	2.5	13.1			
	38.5		16.0		40.1					11.1	22.4	46.0			
(75)	12.7	(71)	5.0	(68)	8.7	% Profit Before Taxes/Tangible Net Worth	(13)	-2.0		6.2	(27)	16.4			
	-2.0		-10.2		-10.0			-26.5		-7.2		3.4			
	17.0		7.9		14.1					5.7	11.3	25.7			
	5.0		.7		3.7	% Profit Before Taxes/Total Assets				-1.9	1.5	8.5			
	-2.2		-11.8		-4.0					-7.6	-3.2	-3.0			
	63.4		31.8		32.3					21.9	71.3	27.7			
	19.7		18.3		16.4	Sales/Net Fixed Assets				17.9	16.6	14.4			
	10.0		10.0		9.4					10.2	11.0	9.2			
	4.0		4.1		3.7					3.0	4.2	3.7			
	3.0		2.9		2.8	Sales/Total Assets				2.7	3.2	2.6			
	2.3		2.2		1.7					1.3	2.2	2.1			
	.4		.6		.7					1.0	.2	.7			
(75)	.8	(80)	.9	(65)	1.1	% Depr., Dep., Amort./Sales			(13)	1.5	(15)	.7	(29)	1.0	
	1.4		1.5		2.0					2.0	2.0	1.6			
	2.3		1.6		1.4	% Officers', Directors'									
(29)	3.4	(33)	2.8	(18)	3.0	Owners' Comp/Sales									
	5.9		5.3		3.8										

5511356M	4058096M	4166300M	Net Sales ($)	1621M	12658M	11231M	100159M	276930M	3763701M
2167492M	1601647M	1865964M	Total Assets ($)	1388M	6357M	4974M	53103M	98983M	1701159M

M = $ thousand   MM = $ million
See Pages 9 through 22 for Explanation of Ratios and Data

Current Data Sorted by Assets | Comparative Historical Data

	0-500M	500M-2MM	2-10MM	10-50MM	50-100MM	100-250MM	Type of Statement	4/1/05-3/31/06 ALL	4/1/06-3/31/07 ALL
			2	2	2	3	Unqualified	20	20
		1	6	4			Reviewed	20	19
	2	5					Compiled	32	28
	4	8	3	2			Tax Returns	16	14
	3	8	9	5	4	2	Other	46	41
		11 (4/1-9/30/09)		64 (10/1/09-3/31/10)					
NUMBER OF STATEMENTS	9	22	20	13	6	5		134	122
	%	%	%	%	%	%	ASSETS	%	%
		6.8	5.7	5.5			Cash & Equivalents	7.1	6.9
		15.7	17.9	18.8			Trade Receivables (net)	19.9	22.1
		42.5	39.9	33.6			Inventory	38.3	35.5
		.9	4.6	5.1			All Other Current	2.4	3.7
		65.9	68.1	62.9			Total Current	67.6	68.2
		29.1	25.4	28.2			Fixed Assets (net)	25.0	23.7
		.9	.6	2.7			Intangibles (net)	2.0	2.9
		4.0	5.9	6.2			All Other Non-Current	5.4	5.3
		100.0	100.0	100.0			Total	100.0	100.0
							LIABILITIES		
		10.5	17.7	13.2			Notes Payable-Short Term	16.3	14.9
		2.4	2.8	3.5			Cur. Mat.-L.T.D.	2.9	2.5
		16.8	17.3	11.2			Trade Payables	15.3	14.0
		.0	.0	.0			Income Taxes Payable	.3	.2
		12.4	8.3	9.2			All Other Current	14.1	17.2
		42.1	46.0	37.1			Total Current	48.9	49.0
		18.7	17.1	22.3			Long-Term Debt	19.3	16.8
		.0	.1	.0			Deferred Taxes	.3	.4
		10.4	10.3	6.4			All Other Non-Current	4.6	5.3
		28.7	26.4	34.2			Net Worth	26.9	28.5
		100.0	100.0	100.0			Total Liabilities & Net Worth	100.0	100.0
							INCOME DATA		
		100.0	100.0	100.0			Net Sales	100.0	100.0
		40.0	29.7	25.0			Gross Profit	29.7	28.3
		39.0	32.1	27.5			Operating Expenses	27.9	25.3
		1.0	-2.4	-2.5			Operating Profit	1.8	3.0
		1.3	-.7	.2			All Other Expenses (net)	1.1	1.1
		-.3	-1.7	-2.7			Profit Before Taxes	.7	1.9
							RATIOS		
		4.7	2.6	3.3			Current	2.5	3.0
		1.8	1.6	1.6				1.5	1.6
		1.0	1.1	1.3				1.1	1.1
		2.4	1.1	1.4			Quick	1.1	1.2
		.6	.5	.7				.6	.7
		.1	.2	.4				.3	.4
	0 UND	12 30.2	29 12.4				Sales/Receivables	10 38.1	16 22.9
	14 26.2	30 12.1	39 9.2					28 13.1	27 13.3
	33 11.0	44 8.4	44 8.3					42 8.8	43 8.5
	47 7.7	41 8.9	49 7.5				Cost of Sales/Inventory	39 9.3	32 11.6
	95 3.8	82 4.4	90 4.0					69 5.3	62 5.9
	151 2.4	179 2.0	119 3.1					117 3.1	98 3.7
	15 24.8	15 25.0	13 27.6				Cost of Sales/Payables	12 29.6	10 35.6
	22 16.3	29 12.5	26 14.0					21 17.6	20 18.2
	40 9.1	60 6.0	46 8.0					39 9.5	36 10.2
		4.2	5.2	2.8			Sales/Working Capital	5.5	6.0
		8.6	8.0	9.0				12.3	10.8
		-417.8	18.0	13.3				62.8	233.2
		4.6	8.9	1.3			EBIT/Interest	7.0	7.7
	(20) .6	(18) 1.1	(12) .6				(126) 2.8	(116) 3.4
		-1.1	-3.0	-2.7				.2	1.0
							Net Profit + Depr., Dep., Amort./Cur. Mat. L/T/D	5.0	7.2
								(36) 2.2 (32) 4.1	
								.5	1.6
		.2	.2	.3			Fixed/Worth	.3	.3
		1.2	.9	.4				.7	.6
		-7.6	-18.8	-4.3				2.4	2.6
		.6	1.0	.4			Debt/Worth	1.1	.9
		2.6	2.3	1.8				2.2	1.8
		-18.1	-29.6	-9.2				8.1	7.2
		33.6	17.7				% Profit Before Taxes/Tangible Net Worth	39.2	45.3
	(16) 2.3	(14) 6.1					(115) 14.3	(104) 17.7
		-35.5	-21.4					-.2	2.8
		5.7	7.8	1.6			% Profit Before Taxes/Total Assets	12.3	15.6
		-.5	.5	-.1				5.1	6.9
		-8.6	-11.2	-9.0				-3.4	.0
		42.5	24.4	34.9			Sales/Net Fixed Assets	26.8	31.6
		13.6	9.3	7.6				13.3	15.6
		3.7	4.7	4.0				6.2	6.8
		3.7	2.7	2.5			Sales/Total Assets	3.6	3.6
		2.3	2.1	1.7				2.5	2.5
		1.4	1.4	1.2				1.8	2.0
		.4	.9	1.1			% Depr., Dep., Amort./Sales	.8	.8
	(20) 1.6	(19) 2.6	(12) 1.9				(116) 1.4	(103) 1.4
		4.9	3.6	2.8				2.3	2.5
		2.8					% Officers', Directors' Owners' Comp/Sales	1.7	1.7
	(13) 4.4						(62) 3.0	(49) 3.1
		9.2						6.3	5.9
	10028M	62477M	219589M	476355M	956491M	1094174M	Net Sales ($)	5113923M	6772905M
	2754M	21379M	103110M	266938M	365260M	752167M	Total Assets ($)	2355843M	2928046M

M = $ thousand   MM = $ million
See Pages 9 through 22 for Explanation of Ratios and Data

Comparative Historical Data | Current Data Sorted by Sales

Type of Statement

4/1/07-3/31/08 ALL	4/1/08-3/31/09 ALL	4/1/09-3/31/10 ALL	Type of Statement	0-1MM	1-3MM	3-5MM	5-10MM	10-25MM	25MM & OVER
10	9	9	Unqualified					1	7
19	15	11	Reviewed		1		2	3	2
15	13	7	Compiled	2	3	1	1	5	
14	21	17	Tax Returns	3	8	2	2	1	
39	44	31	Other	1	7	4	4	3	12
					11 (4/1-9/30/09)		64 (10/1/09-3/31/10)		
97	102	75	**NUMBER OF STATEMENTS**	6	19	7	9	13	21

ASSETS (%)

07-08 ALL	08-09 ALL	09-10 ALL		0-1MM	1-3MM	3-5MM	5-10MM	10-25MM	25MM & OVER
8.1	6.8	6.5	Cash & Equivalents		6.6			6.7	6.5
21.5	19.8	17.9	Trade Receivables (net)		16.4			21.7	20.0
35.9	41.0	39.5	Inventory		43.8			32.8	37.8
3.9	2.6	3.4	All Other Current		2.1			4.8	4.9
69.4	70.2	67.3	Total Current		68.9			66.0	69.1
23.0	21.8	26.6	Fixed Assets (net)		26.7			27.6	23.2
2.3	1.8	1.0	Intangibles (net)		.6			1.3	1.7
5.3	6.2	5.1	All Other Non-Current		3.9			5.1	5.9
100.0	100.0	100.0	Total		100.0			100.0	100.0

LIABILITIES

07-08 ALL	08-09 ALL	09-10 ALL		0-1MM	1-3MM	3-5MM	5-10MM	10-25MM	25MM & OVER
15.9	15.4	14.7	Notes Payable-Short Term		23.1			18.3	9.8
3.4	2.5	4.3	Cur. Mat.-L.T.D.		1.1			1.5	3.8
14.7	13.5	15.0	Trade Payables		17.3			23.0	10.6
.2	.1	.0	Income Taxes Payable		.0			.0	.0
13.1	14.2	13.8	All Other Current		13.9			9.1	9.4
47.3	45.7	47.8	Total Current		55.5			51.9	33.6
19.5	15.0	17.3	Long-Term Debt		18.0			13.3	17.0
.1	.1	.1	Deferred Taxes		.0			.0	.1
6.5	6.3	8.9	All Other Non-Current		7.9			7.5	8.1
26.7	32.9	25.9	Net Worth		18.6			27.4	41.2
100.0	100.0	100.0	Total Liabilties & Net Worth		100.0			100.0	100.0

INCOME DATA

07-08 ALL	08-09 ALL	09-10 ALL		0-1MM	1-3MM	3-5MM	5-10MM	10-25MM	25MM & OVER
100.0	100.0	100.0	Net Sales		100.0			100.0	100.0
31.4	29.7	31.7	Gross Profit		37.7			31.0	22.6
28.7	29.2	33.1	Operating Expenses		38.2			35.1	23.4
2.7	.6	-1.4	Operating Profit		-.6			-4.2	-.9
.4	.9	.3	All Other Expenses (net)		.8			-.8	1.0
2.3	-.3	-1.7	Profit Before Taxes		-1.3			-3.3	-1.9

RATIOS (values shown upper / median / lower; counts in parentheses)

07-08 ALL	08-09 ALL	09-10 ALL		0-1MM	1-3MM	3-5MM	5-10MM	10-25MM	25MM & OVER
3.2 / 1.7 / 1.0	3.3 / 1.6 / 1.1	3.2 / 1.7 / 1.2	Current		4.5 / 1.4 / .7			2.1 / 1.5 / .7	3.1 / 2.0 / 1.5
1.5 / .6 / .3	1.5 / (100) .6 / .3	1.4 / .6 / .2	Quick		2.2 / .4 / .2			1.1 / .6 / .3	1.4 / .8 / .4
(13) 27.2 / (27) 13.3 / (41) 8.8	(10) 35.7 / (29) 12.8 / (40) 9.2	(9) 38.6 / (30) 12.0 / (43) 8.5	Sales/Receivables		(8) 44.5 / (13) 27.8 / (37) 10.0			(19) 18.8 / (37) 9.8 / (48) 7.6	(27) 13.7 / (37) 9.8 / (45) 8.1
(31) 11.8 / (65) 5.6 / (99) 3.7	(46) 8.0 / (81) 4.5 / (136) 2.7	(47) 7.8 / (82) 4.5 / (133) 2.8	Cost of Sales/Inventory		(50) 7.3 / (79) 4.6 / (148) 2.5			(34) 10.8 / (42) 8.7 / (166) 2.2	(64) 5.7 / (90) 4.0 / (102) 3.6
(14) 26.8 / (22) 16.9 / (39) 9.4	(10) 34.8 / (21) 17.3 / (38) 9.6	(14) 27.0 / (26) 14.1 / (39) 9.4	Cost of Sales/Payables		(15) 23.8 / (28) 12.8 / (49) 7.4			(28) 12.9 / (36) 10.0 / (71) 5.1	(13) 27.4 / (21) 17.6 / (29) 12.5
4.7 / 9.7 / 303.0	4.4 / 9.2 / 33.9	4.4 / 8.4 / 18.3	Sales/Working Capital		4.4 / 10.8 / -17.5			4.7 / 8.6 / -10.3	4.0 / 7.1 / 10.2
(86) 7.6 / 2.4 / .0	(91) 7.3 / 1.9 / -1.9	(70) 3.5 / .4 / -4.1	EBIT/Interest		(18) 1.7 / -.5 / -8.2			(20) 3.0 / .9 / -12.0	9.3 / .3 / -3.7
(21) 7.2 / 1.7 / -.3	(19) 6.0 / .7 / -8.0	(12) 1.9 / .8 / -3.3	Net Profit + Depr., Dep., Amort./Cur. Mat. L/T/D						
.2 / .5 / 2.2	.2 / .5 / 3.0	.2 / .7 / -43.6	Fixed/Worth		.2 / 1.3 / -.8			.1 / .5 / NM	.2 / .4 / 1.4
.8 / 2.1 / 8.8	.6 / 1.8 / 9.0	.7 / 1.8 / -18.3	Debt/Worth		.7 / 1.9 / -6.0			1.0 / 1.8 / NM	.5 / 1.0 / 6.5
(81) 63.0 / 18.2 / -.1	(83) 22.6 / 7.0 / -11.7	(55) 20.7 / .1 / -19.8	% Profit Before Taxes/Tangible Net Worth		(13) 8.6 / -8.7 / -49.0			(10) 36.8 / 2.3 / -21.4	(17) 14.1 / -4.3 / -19.7
14.4 / 4.5 / -4.4	10.8 / 1.9 / -6.9	5.0 / -1.7 / -11.1	% Profit Before Taxes/Total Assets		2.6 / -5.0 / -12.3			7.6 / -.1 / -15.1	4.2 / -1.7 / -9.4
38.1 / 12.7 / 7.0	38.7 / 15.5 / 6.8	30.6 / 11.0 / 4.7	Sales/Net Fixed Assets		39.6 / 13.7 / 4.6			45.4 / 7.0 / 3.3	23.3 / 8.9 / 4.9
3.8 / 2.7 / 1.9	3.5 / 2.6 / 1.9	3.1 / 2.2 / 1.5	Sales/Total Assets		3.5 / 2.7 / 1.9			3.0 / 2.0 / 1.1	2.8 / 2.0 / 1.7
(80) .6 / 1.4 / 2.5	(84) .9 / 1.6 / 2.7	(65) .8 / 2.1 / 3.2	% Depr., Dep., Amort./Sales		(15) .5 / .7 / 5.6			(17) .8 / 1.3 / 3.7	1.4 / 2.1 / 2.8
(43) 2.2 / 3.7 / 6.7	(43) 2.1 / 3.6 / 5.4	(32) 2.2 / 4.6 / 8.3	% Officers', Directors' Owners' Comp/Sales		(14) 2.1 / 4.0 / 6.9				
3846608M	3604471M	2819114M	Net Sales ($)	4136M	32139M	28197M	65831M	189588M	2499223M
1903848M	1821421M	1511608M	Total Assets ($)	2683M	15006M	11609M	39454M	115382M	1327474M

M = $ thousand   MM = $ million
See Pages 9 through 22 for Explanation of Ratios and Data

MANUFACTURING—Institutional Furniture Manufacturing NAICS 337127

Current Data Sorted by Assets							Comparative Historical Data	
		3	6	5	2	Type of Statement		
	2	13	7			Unqualified	35	31
2	2	6				Reviewed	27	31
1	5	2				Compiled	19	20
1	3	22	13	5	5	Tax Returns	15	19
1	10					Other	48	56
	14 (4/1-9/30/09)		100 (10/1/09-3/31/10)				4/1/05-3/31/06	4/1/06-3/31/07
0-500M	500M-2MM	2-10MM	10-50MM	50-100MM	100-250MM		ALL	ALL
5	20	46	26	10	7	NUMBER OF STATEMENTS	144	157
%	%	%	%	%	%	ASSETS	%	%
	4.7	10.2	11.4	9.5		Cash & Equivalents	6.2	7.1
	25.8	25.2	24.1	24.9		Trade Receivables (net)	30.4	29.1
	34.7	29.4	25.0	15.4		Inventory	26.2	27.4
	2.5	2.1	4.2	2.0		All Other Current	3.3	2.7
	67.7	66.8	64.7	51.8		Total Current	66.0	66.2
	25.1	23.5	24.0	14.5		Fixed Assets (net)	24.1	22.5
	2.6	2.9	7.3	24.7		Intangibles (net)	5.1	4.2
	4.6	6.8	4.0	9.0		All Other Non-Current	4.7	7.1
	100.0	100.0	100.0	100.0		Total	100.0	100.0
						LIABILITIES		
	23.0	10.7	9.7	5.5		Notes Payable-Short Term	16.6	14.8
	4.4	3.1	2.9	2.5		Cur. Mat.-L.T.D.	2.9	2.3
	13.4	14.5	13.1	8.6		Trade Payables	16.7	15.4
	.0	.2	.5	.2		Income Taxes Payable	.2	.2
	9.8	13.1	10.8	10.6		All Other Current	12.0	12.2
	50.5	41.6	37.0	27.3		Total Current	48.4	44.8
	21.3	13.9	15.6	25.1		Long-Term Debt	14.6	15.8
	.0	.4	.3	2.3		Deferred Taxes	.4	.4
	10.9	5.7	8.7	4.7		All Other Non-Current	8.1	5.4
	17.3	38.4	38.4	40.5		Net Worth	28.5	33.6
	100.0	100.0	100.0	100.0		Total Liabilties & Net Worth	100.0	100.0
						INCOME DATA		
	100.0	100.0	100.0	100.0		Net Sales	100.0	100.0
	36.8	30.5	26.2	25.3		Gross Profit	29.2	28.9
	37.3	27.5	21.8	17.5		Operating Expenses	26.3	24.5
	-.5	3.0	4.4	7.7		Operating Profit	2.9	4.4
	1.2	.8	1.6	1.9		All Other Expenses (net)	1.5	1.3
	-1.7	2.2	2.8	5.8		Profit Before Taxes	1.4	3.2
						RATIOS		
	3.8	3.1	2.6	2.6			2.3	2.4
	1.3	1.5	1.7	2.1		Current	1.5	1.6
	.8	1.1	1.2	1.7			1.1	1.1
	1.0	1.6	1.7	1.8			1.6	1.5
	.5	.7	.7	1.3		Quick	.8	.8
	.3	.4	.5	1.1			.5	.5
24 15.2	20 18.4	33 10.9	36 10.1				27 13.3	29 12.4
31 11.7	34 10.6	42 8.8	56 6.5			Sales/Receivables	40 9.0	40 9.1
51 7.2	45 8.1	50 7.2	77 4.7				58 6.3	59 6.2
32 11.3	30 12.1	31 11.8	31 11.7				29 12.5	30 12.0
73 5.0	53 6.9	44 8.3	46 8.0			Cost of Sales/Inventory	47 7.8	51 7.2
135 2.7	98 3.7	107 3.4	88 4.1				77 4.8	87 4.2
11 32.5	14 26.9	15 24.8	13 27.7				15 23.8	16 22.7
23 16.1	25 14.6	26 14.3	21 17.2			Cost of Sales/Payables	28 13.2	27 13.7
58 6.3	37 9.8	46 7.9	41 8.8				43 8.5	41 9.0
	5.5	5.0	4.6	4.2			6.2	6.0
	13.6	12.4	9.6	5.1		Sales/Working Capital	13.1	11.1
	-23.4	70.7	22.0	9.3			49.7	41.5
	3.0	12.3	25.5	23.0			9.6	8.3
	(19) .2	(40) 2.2	(25) 5.4	7.1		EBIT/Interest	(134) 3.5	(148) 3.1
	-2.4	-.2	1.1	3.6			.9	1.1
		3.7	12.5			Net Profit + Depr., Dep.,	6.0	6.5
		(12) 1.5	(11) 3.4			Amort./Cur. Mat. L/T/D	(31) 2.1	(40) 2.7
		.6	1.5				1.0	1.0
	.2	.3	.2	.5			.3	.3
	.8	.5	.6	.6		Fixed/Worth	.7	.6
	NM	1.8	1.8	-.9			2.8	1.7
	1.2	.7	.7	2.5			.8	.9
	3.1	1.5	1.6	7.9		Debt/Worth	1.9	1.8
	NM	4.5	4.3	-6.0			9.6	6.1
	44.4	46.5	40.9			% Profit Before Taxes/Tangible	42.0	41.3
	(15) -3.9	(38) 18.3	(24) 23.5			Net Worth	(115) 18.1	(135) 20.9
	-69.7	-3.2	4.3				6.3	2.9
	9.0	14.0	16.7	11.8		% Profit Before Taxes/Total	12.3	15.4
	-2.6	6.5	8.4	8.7		Assets	5.4	6.8
	-18.3	-2.2	.6	3.4			-.3	.4
	28.2	29.1	18.5	30.4			34.4	41.6
	15.3	12.3	10.9	9.5		Sales/Net Fixed Assets	12.1	11.0
	6.4	6.9	7.0	5.9			6.0	6.3
	3.3	3.5	2.8	2.0			3.5	3.3
	2.3	2.4	2.2	1.3		Sales/Total Assets	2.5	2.4
	1.6	1.8	1.8	.9			1.7	1.8
	.8	.6	1.1				.8	.6
	(15) 1.9	(40) 1.7	(23) 1.9			% Depr., Dep., Amort./Sales	(121) 1.7	(138) 1.4
	3.0	2.7	2.4				2.8	2.4
	2.4	2.6					1.8	1.8
	(11) 5.6	(15) 3.4				% Officers', Directors' Owners' Comp/Sales	(51) 4.3	(56) 3.2
	8.0	5.6					7.7	5.1
2388M	57927M	685200M	1063300M	968589M	1996460M	Net Sales ($)	4723403M	4242755M
964M	23833M	245263M	503569M	690676M	1057065M	Total Assets ($)	1787974M	2242635M

M = $ thousand   MM = $ million
See Pages 9 through 22 for Explanation of Ratios and Data

Comparative Historical Data / Current Data Sorted by Sales

4/1/07-3/31/08 ALL	4/1/08-3/31/09 ALL	4/1/09-3/31/10 ALL	Type of Statement	0-1MM	1-3MM	3-5MM	5-10MM	10-25MM	25MM & OVER
23	22	16	Unqualified			5	3	3	13
29	28	24	Reviewed	2		5	3	9	5
18	20	12	Compiled	2	4	2	2	1	1
14	11	6	Tax Returns		2		3	1	
61	35	56	Other	1	7	4	6	18	20
				14 (4/1-9/30/09)		100 (10/1/09-3/31/10)			
145	116	114	NUMBER OF STATEMENTS	5	13	11	14	32	39
%	%	%	ASSETS	%	%	%	%	%	%
6.3	7.5	9.0	Cash & Equivalents		3.0	11.0	8.3	9.7	10.3
30.4	28.3	24.6	Trade Receivables (net)		21.7	20.4	26.6	24.1	26.7
25.7	25.4	27.1	Inventory		36.6	25.9	28.1	30.4	21.3
3.3	2.8	2.5	All Other Current		2.8	2.4	1.5	2.0	3.6
65.7	64.1	63.2	Total Current		64.0	59.7	64.6	66.3	61.9
22.6	25.7	24.1	Fixed Assets (net)		30.0	30.8	24.0	22.1	21.1
5.6	5.2	6.2	Intangibles (net)		2.0	.5	2.1	6.5	11.3
6.1	5.1	6.5	All Other Non-Current		4.0	9.0	9.3	5.1	5.7
100.0	100.0	100.0	Total		100.0	100.0	100.0	100.0	100.0
			LIABILITIES						
13.6	11.1	12.1	Notes Payable-Short Term		23.3	11.0	10.6	12.9	6.6
2.5	3.0	3.1	Cur. Mat.-L.T.D.		4.2	4.6	2.3	3.2	2.6
15.4	14.3	13.4	Trade Payables		12.2	9.9	11.4	16.1	12.2
.1	.1	.2	Income Taxes Payable		.0	.0	.1	.2	.4
14.9	15.4	11.6	All Other Current		8.0	11.7	14.2	10.3	12.7
46.5	43.9	40.5	Total Current		47.7	37.2	38.6	42.6	34.5
15.4	17.4	18.1	Long-Term Debt		28.6	18.9	11.6	13.3	19.3
.3	.5	.5	Deferred Taxes		.0	.5	.0	.4	1.1
5.4	4.9	7.0	All Other Non-Current		16.7	1.0	4.0	6.5	8.0
32.4	33.4	33.9	Net Worth		7.0	42.3	45.9	37.2	37.1
100.0	100.0	100.0	Total Liabilties & Net Worth		100.0	100.0	100.0	100.0	100.0
			INCOME DATA						
100.0	100.0	100.0	Net Sales		100.0	100.0	100.0	100.0	100.0
31.2	30.2	30.4	Gross Profit		40.5	32.3	32.5	28.2	25.7
25.9	25.1	27.8	Operating Expenses		42.9	33.9	29.5	25.0	19.5
5.3	5.1	2.6	Operating Profit		-2.4	-1.6	3.0	3.2	6.3
1.3	1.2	1.4	All Other Expenses (net)		1.7	.4	.4	1.5	2.0
3.9	3.9	1.1	Profit Before Taxes		-4.1	-2.0	2.5	1.7	4.2
			RATIOS						
2.1	2.6	2.7	Current		5.6	4.3	3.2	2.4	2.6
1.5	1.6	1.7			1.2	2.1	1.7	1.4	1.9
1.1	1.2	1.1			.8	.8	1.1	1.0	1.3
1.3	1.6	1.6	Quick		.8	2.8	1.6	1.6	1.7
.8	.8	.8			.5	.7	.8	.7	1.0
.5	.5	.5			.2	.4	.3	.4	.7
27 13.3	27 13.6	25 14.4	Sales/Receivables	18 19.8	17 21.9	29 12.4	23 16.0	35 10.3	
41 8.8	38 9.6	37 9.8		30 12.0	31 11.8	41 9.0	34 10.9	42 8.6	
57 6.4	53 6.9	49 7.4		50 7.2	47 7.7	58 6.3	44 8.3	50 7.4	
33 11.2	29 12.5	31 11.7	Cost of Sales/Inventory	27 13.6	38 9.5	40 9.2	31 11.8	24 15.4	
49 7.5	50 7.3	49 7.4		108 3.4	68 5.4	53 6.9	53 6.9	38 9.6	
86 4.3	92 4.0	102 3.6		152 2.4	97 3.8	107 3.4	110 3.3	66 5.6	
16 23.4	14 25.2	14 26.9	Cost of Sales/Payables	6 60.1	11 33.5	17 22.0	14 26.0	14 25.8	
26 13.9	25 14.8	24 15.0		27 13.3	15 24.7	30 12.4	31 11.7	22 16.9	
43 8.5	39 9.4	40 9.1		67 5.4	47 7.7	33 11.1	42 8.8	33 11.0	
6.4	6.2	4.6	Sales/Working Capital		3.6	3.8	4.5	6.6	4.8
12.4	11.2	10.0			15.2	4.3	10.4	12.4	8.4
81.5	40.0	59.2			-14.8	-26.7	46.8	149.3	20.1
8.7	17.1	12.6	EBIT/Interest		2.0	10.5	15.3	16.6	18.4
(133) 3.8	(109) 4.7	(104) 2.7			(12) -1.1	-.1	(13) 1.6	(28) 2.8	(37) 5.8
1.6	1.4	-.2			-6.6	-9.3	-1.4	1.0	1.2
8.4	12.9	11.1	Net Profit + Depr., Dep., Amort./Cur. Mat. L/T/D					6.6	17.4
(32) 3.3	(33) 3.4	(36) 1.6						(10) 1.5	(20) 3.1
1.4	1.0	.8						1.0	1.3
.3	.3	.3	Fixed/Worth		.4	.4	.2	.2	.4
.6	.8	.6			1.3	.5	.4	.6	.7
4.1	5.0	4.9			-2.1	2.2	1.1	4.7	2.1
.9	.8	.8	Debt/Worth		1.8	.6	.5	.8	.8
2.5	2.2	2.1			4.0	1.3	1.0	1.8	2.7
10.4	13.0	12.0			-7.4	2.3	2.6	15.3	10.6
53.3	51.6	48.4	% Profit Before Taxes/Tangible Net Worth		21.0		62.9	53.4	64.6
(121) 27.9	(94) 22.5	(93) 15.5			(10) -10.7		(13) 6.5	(26) 22.2	(32) 25.2
10.2	6.5	-2.5			-52.3		-5.1	2.2	6.6
16.4	17.9	12.7	% Profit Before Taxes/Total Assets		8.3	8.9	17.0	13.3	17.2
9.3	7.0	4.1			-3.2	-3.4	3.1	6.5	9.2
2.0	1.1	-2.7			-29.3	-17.3	-3.3	.0	1.1
35.8	29.2	25.8	Sales/Net Fixed Assets		24.8	13.1	42.2	30.0	18.4
13.0	9.9	11.3			8.9	7.6	16.8	12.8	9.9
6.5	6.4	6.1			3.6	4.6	3.9	8.1	6.1
3.3	3.2	2.9	Sales/Total Assets		2.7	2.4	3.1	3.5	2.8
2.5	2.4	2.2			2.0	1.8	2.5	2.3	2.2
1.8	1.8	1.7			1.3	1.2	1.7	1.8	1.6
.7	.8	.8	% Depr., Dep., Amort./Sales			1.8	.8	.6	.8
(125) 1.6	(102) 1.9	(94) 1.9				3.3	(13) 1.5	(25) 1.7	(34) 1.5
2.5	2.7	3.0				4.3	3.0	2.2	2.6
1.9	1.7	1.7	% Officers', Directors' Owners' Comp/Sales						
(45) 4.0	(35) 2.9	(34) 3.8							
6.3	5.4	8.2							
4861713M	3786059M	4773864M	Net Sales ($)	2312M	23583M	43564M	100544M	567404M	4036457M
2401610M	1792355M	2521370M	Total Assets ($)	1056M	12920M	30058M	76596M	260153M	2140587M

M = $ thousand   MM = $ million
See Pages 9 through 22 for Explanation of Ratios and Data

Current Data Sorted by Assets

Comparative Historical Data

0-500M	500M-2MM	2-10MM	10-50MM	50-100MM	100-250MM		4/1/05-3/31/06 ALL	4/1/06-3/31/07 ALL
		1	3	1		Type of Statement		
	1	11	3			Unqualified	6	8
	6	1	1			Reviewed	16	26
2	3					Compiled	5	11
2	4	5	2		1	Tax Returns	5	5
	15 (4/1-9/30/09)		32 (10/1/09-3/31/10)			Other	18	14
4	14	18	9	1	1	**NUMBER OF STATEMENTS**	50	64
%	%	%	%	%	%	**ASSETS**	%	%
	7.3	2.9				Cash & Equivalents	9.8	5.9
	35.5	40.1				Trade Receivables (net)	28.5	33.0
	28.7	15.3				Inventory	26.1	21.5
	2.8	5.0				All Other Current	2.9	5.6
	74.3	63.3				Total Current	67.2	66.0
	19.5	29.0				Fixed Assets (net)	23.2	27.0
	1.3	1.6				Intangibles (net)	3.2	1.5
	4.9	6.1				All Other Non-Current	6.4	5.5
	100.0	100.0				Total	100.0	100.0
						LIABILITIES		
	14.7	13.1				Notes Payable-Short Term	13.3	12.5
	4.9	4.0				Cur. Mat.-L.T.D.	3.5	3.6
	18.2	16.4				Trade Payables	17.2	15.8
	.0	.0				Income Taxes Payable	.7	.2
	13.9	8.7				All Other Current	12.8	11.2
	51.7	42.2				Total Current	47.4	43.3
	20.9	20.1				Long-Term Debt	15.1	17.1
	.1	.8				Deferred Taxes	1.0	.9
	1.8	3.3				All Other Non-Current	4.8	6.1
	25.5	33.6				Net Worth	31.6	32.6
	100.0	100.0				Total Liabilities & Net Worth	100.0	100.0
						INCOME DATA		
	100.0	100.0				Net Sales	100.0	100.0
	29.8	21.0				Gross Profit	27.3	27.4
	30.9	18.5				Operating Expenses	25.1	24.2
	-1.1	2.5				Operating Profit	2.2	3.2
	.5	1.0				All Other Expenses (net)	1.0	1.1
	-1.6	1.5				Profit Before Taxes	1.2	2.1
						RATIOS		
	2.3	1.9					1.9	2.3
	1.6	1.5				Current	1.5	1.6
	1.0	1.3					1.1	1.1
	1.9	1.3					1.0	1.3
	.8	.9				Quick	.7	.9
	.6	.8					.5	.6
	26 13.9	42 8.7					27 13.8	30 12.0
	41 9.0	56 6.5				Sales/Receivables	35 10.3	42 8.8
	55 6.6	72 5.0					53 6.9	61 6.0
	7 54.5	9 41.6					21 17.4	15 23.8
	34 10.6	19 18.8				Cost of Sales/Inventory	48 7.7	38 9.6
	112 3.3	46 7.9					79 4.6	62 5.9
	13 28.2	14 26.1					15 23.9	16 22.3
	22 16.6	27 13.5				Cost of Sales/Payables	24 15.0	22 16.5
	39 9.4	40 9.2					36 10.2	37 9.8
	6.4	8.3					8.4	6.1
	10.6	11.7				Sales/Working Capital	18.9	12.0
	NM	16.8					110.6	45.4
	9.4	3.7					6.3	9.7
	(13) -.3	1.9				EBIT/Interest	(45) 2.7	(59) 4.2
	-11.3	1.1					-.4	1.4
						Net Profit + Depr., Dep.,	4.1	7.6
						Amort./Cur. Mat. L/T/D	(15) 2.5	(27) 5.4
							.0	2.2
	.4	.4					.3	.4
	.6	.8				Fixed/Worth	.6	.6
	27.2	1.4					1.5	1.8
	1.0	1.2					1.2	.8
	5.0	1.9				Debt/Worth	2.1	1.8
	68.0	5.1					3.8	5.4
	18.3	23.0				% Profit Before Taxes/Tangible	34.8	37.9
	(12) -4.0	(17) 6.0				Net Worth	(45) 16.5	(53) 21.5
	-44.1	.0					-.3	4.9
	10.3	6.6				% Profit Before Taxes/Total	9.2	15.1
	-1.3	1.6				Assets	4.6	8.1
	-25.7	.2					-2.1	1.3
	75.2	27.7					39.6	22.1
	17.9	12.2				Sales/Net Fixed Assets	12.4	13.3
	10.8	5.4					6.2	5.5
	4.0	3.3					3.8	3.5
	2.9	2.7				Sales/Total Assets	2.4	2.6
	2.5	1.8					1.7	2.0
	.5	.8					.8	.9
	(12) 1.0	(17) 1.9				% Depr., Dep., Amort./Sales	(41) 2.0	(58) 1.7
	3.3	3.4					3.3	2.7
						% Officers', Directors'	1.6	2.0
						Owners' Comp/Sales	(16) 3.3	(25) 4.0
							6.5	7.0
6304M	56987M	182850M	354133M	151352M	185297M	Net Sales ($)	1069946M	1407239M
1364M	17622M	69896M	181892M	63681M	114260M	Total Assets ($)	475695M	646161M

M = $ thousand   MM = $ million
See Pages 9 through 22 for Explanation of Ratios and Data

Comparative Historical Data — Current Data Sorted by Sales

			Type of Statement	0-1MM	1-3MM	3-5MM	5-10MM	10-25MM	25MM & OVER
			Unqualified						
6	5	5	Reviewed		1	2	5	6	4
14	14	15	Compiled		2	2	3	1	1
8	8	8	Tax Returns	1	1	2	1		1
10	5	5	Other	1	3	2	3	1	4
15	16	14							
4/1/07-3/31/08 ALL	4/1/08-3/31/09 ALL	4/1/09-3/31/10 ALL			15 (4/1-9/30/09)		32 (10/1/09-3/31/10)		
53	48	47	**NUMBER OF STATEMENTS**	2	7	8	12	8	10
%	%	%	**ASSETS**	%	%	%	%	%	%
7.5	6.6	5.7	Cash & Equivalents				7.2		5.3
36.9	35.0	32.9	Trade Receivables (net)				40.6		26.0
19.0	19.4	21.3	Inventory				14.6		27.4
3.9	6.6	5.1	All Other Current				5.1		3.2
67.3	67.6	65.0	Total Current				67.6		61.9
25.1	27.3	28.0	Fixed Assets (net)				24.9		30.3
1.8	1.0	1.7	Intangibles (net)				.1		3.3
5.9	4.1	5.2	All Other Non-Current				7.4		4.5
100.0	100.0	100.0	Total				100.0		100.0
			LIABILITIES						
9.5	8.5	11.2	Notes Payable-Short Term				16.5		9.0
2.8	3.6	3.6	Cur. Mat.-L.T.D.				4.4		2.5
15.1	15.5	16.3	Trade Payables				18.6		19.0
.3	.1	.1	Income Taxes Payable				.0		.3
15.6	13.0	12.0	All Other Current				13.1		8.9
43.3	40.8	43.1	Total Current				52.6		39.8
16.9	19.0	20.4	Long-Term Debt				18.2		29.8
.7	.6	.6	Deferred Taxes				.4		1.3
6.6	4.2	3.7	All Other Non-Current				3.2		5.3
32.5	35.5	32.2	Net Worth				25.6		23.7
100.0	100.0	100.0	Total Liabilties & Net Worth				100.0		100.0
			INCOME DATA						
100.0	100.0	100.0	Net Sales				100.0		100.0
31.6	28.4	25.2	Gross Profit				24.0		25.8
27.5	25.0	23.0	Operating Expenses				22.0		21.5
4.0	3.5	2.2	Operating Profit				2.0		4.2
.7	1.0	.8	All Other Expenses (net)				.6		1.3
3.3	2.5	1.4	Profit Before Taxes				1.4		3.0
			RATIOS						
2.6	2.9	2.3	Current				2.1		2.6
1.5	1.7	1.6					1.4		1.7
1.1	1.4	1.2					.9		1.1
1.5	1.8	1.3	Quick				1.5		1.0
1.0	1.1	.9					.9		.8
.6	.7	.6					.6		.6
29 12.4	35 10.5	33 11.0	Sales/Receivables				33 11.2		31 11.7
44 8.3	48 7.6	42 8.6					46 8.0		38 9.6
63 5.8	71 5.2	61 6.0					67 5.5		47 7.7
5 67.1	9 39.0	7 51.8	Cost of Sales/Inventory				4 89.3		36 10.0
33 10.9	23 15.6	35 10.5					11 33.9		55 6.6
68 5.4	66 5.6	77 4.7					29 12.5		80 4.6
14 26.6	16 23.4	14 25.9	Cost of Sales/Payables				11 32.7		14 26.0
23 15.9	23 15.8	22 16.8					19 19.6		23 16.1
37 9.9	37 9.9	38 9.6					35 10.4		50 7.3
5.7	5.2	6.1	Sales/Working Capital				8.1		5.3
12.8	9.5	11.4					13.1		10.1
30.4	16.2	34.9					NM		35.3
12.9	10.4	8.5	EBIT/Interest				5.1		
(48) 4.4	(47) 3.5	(43) 1.9					(11) 1.9		
2.3	1.1	.1					-.3		
11.2	6.6	5.3	Net Profit + Depr., Dep., Amort./Cur. Mat. L/T/D						
(16) 6.6	(19) 1.4	(13) 3.6							
2.0	.3	1.3							
.3	.4	.5	Fixed/Worth				.5		.6
.6	.7	.8					.8		1.4
2.8	1.3	2.0					1.4		NM
.8	.9	.8	Debt/Worth				1.6		.5
2.3	1.5	2.2					2.9		3.1
6.3	3.7	6.5					9.0		NM
40.8	28.9	21.1	% Profit Before Taxes/Tangible Net Worth				67.3		
(43) 22.4	(43) 15.2	(42) 7.1					6.7		
9.8	3.2	-6.4					-6.3		
18.2	11.1	10.1	% Profit Before Taxes/Total Assets				11.7		12.0
8.2	6.3	2.6					2.0		4.1
2.8	.3	-1.2					-2.9		-1.3
23.7	18.3	25.7	Sales/Net Fixed Assets				38.9		20.5
13.7	10.7	12.2					13.3		8.5
6.7	4.5	6.2					7.3		3.9
3.7	3.3	3.3	Sales/Total Assets				4.1		2.8
2.7	2.4	2.6					2.9		2.2
2.2	1.9	1.9					2.5		1.7
.8	1.2	.7	% Depr., Dep., Amort./Sales				.6		
(50) 1.5	(46) 1.8	(42) 1.5					1.8		
2.9	3.1	3.2					3.2		
2.3	2.0	2.1	% Officers', Directors' Owners' Comp/Sales						
(29) 4.7	(23) 5.3	(18) 2.4							
8.2	7.1	6.4							
897453M	845706M	936923M	Net Sales ($)	1514M	13571M	30929M	80952M	119821M	690136M
396110M	400058M	448715M	Total Assets ($)	390M	7363M	19120M	26393M	51990M	343459M

M = $ thousand   MM = $ million
See Pages 9 through 22 for Explanation of Ratios and Data

Current Data Sorted by Assets   **Comparative Historical Data**

Type of Statement	0-500M	500M-2MM	2-10MM	10-50MM	50-100MM	100-250MM		4/1/05-3/31/06 ALL	4/1/06-3/31/07 ALL
Unqualified		2	6	8	4	2		18	16
Reviewed		3	12	2	1			19	18
Compiled		2	1					3	3
Tax Returns		2						8	5
Other		3	9	8	2	2		26	27
		13 (4/1-9/30/09)		54 (10/1/09-3/31/10)					
NUMBER OF STATEMENTS		10	28	18	7	4		74	69

(0-500M column: DATA NOT AVAILABLE)

	500M-2MM %	2-10MM %	10-50MM %		4/1/05-3/31/06 ALL %	4/1/06-3/31/07 ALL %
ASSETS						
Cash & Equivalents	7.1	11.0	7.0		7.5	6.4
Trade Receivables (net)	33.4	30.8	28.3		31.5	30.3
Inventory	32.1	29.2	20.9		21.7	24.6
All Other Current	2.8	4.8	2.5		3.3	3.4
Total Current	75.5	75.8	58.7		64.0	64.7
Fixed Assets (net)	20.5	15.7	27.8		22.4	19.3
Intangibles (net)	.0	2.0	8.2		8.3	10.5
All Other Non-Current	4.0	6.5	5.3		5.3	5.5
Total	100.0	100.0	100.0		100.0	100.0
LIABILITIES						
Notes Payable-Short Term	15.2	8.5	9.6		11.8	12.4
Cur. Mat.-L.T.D.	5.9	3.5	5.7		4.2	4.5
Trade Payables	16.5	17.2	14.9		18.1	17.5
Income Taxes Payable	1.6	.1	.1		.3	.2
All Other Current	22.0	12.1	11.5		12.6	11.4
Total Current	61.1	41.5	41.8		47.0	45.9
Long-Term Debt	12.3	11.4	29.0		20.3	18.3
Deferred Taxes	.2	.4	.3		.5	.6
All Other Non-Current	3.8	5.5	15.3		5.1	7.0
Net Worth	22.6	41.2	13.6		27.1	28.1
Total Liabilties & Net Worth	100.0	100.0	100.0		100.0	100.0
INCOME DATA						
Net Sales	100.0	100.0	100.0		100.0	100.0
Gross Profit	36.1	30.6	31.4		33.0	32.1
Operating Expenses	33.5	28.0	26.1		28.8	27.3
Operating Profit	2.6	2.6	5.3		4.2	4.8
All Other Expenses (net)	.0	.5	3.7		1.2	1.2
Profit Before Taxes	2.5	2.1	1.6		2.9	3.6
RATIOS						
Current	1.6	3.4	2.2		2.2	2.2
	1.3	2.1	1.6		1.4	1.4
	1.1	1.3	1.4		1.1	1.1
Quick	1.3	2.1	1.3		1.3	1.3
	.9	1.1	1.0		.9	.8
	.2	.5	.7		.5	.5
Sales/Receivables	15 24.6	29 12.8	35 10.5		31 11.8	29 12.5
	45 8.1	37 9.8	48 7.6		43 8.5	42 8.7
	60 6.1	44 8.3	62 5.9		55 6.7	55 6.7
Cost of Sales/Inventory	15 24.6	25 14.8	27 13.6		24 14.9	23 16.0
	33 11.2	50 7.3	53 6.8		35 10.3	42 8.7
	121 3.0	92 4.0	78 4.7		68 5.4	83 4.4
Cost of Sales/Payables	6 57.5	13 27.3	21 17.7		19 19.1	14 25.3
	39 9.2	27 13.6	36 10.1		33 10.9	31 11.9
	65 5.6	36 10.1	48 7.6		49 7.5	47 7.8
Sales/Working Capital	15.8	4.6	6.5		7.9	7.5
	24.1	9.4	9.5		15.3	13.2
	NM	18.5	16.0		93.1	95.7
EBIT/Interest		(26) 20.5	(16) 6.9		(65) 10.5	(64) 8.6
		3.9	1.5		3.6	3.5
		1.1	.7		1.4	1.4
Net Profit + Depr., Dep., Amort./Cur. Mat. L/T/D		(10) 5.1			(23) 4.6	(28) 7.0
		2.6			2.9	2.6
		.4			1.1	1.0
Fixed/Worth	.4	.1	.8		.4	.3
	.8	.4	1.2		1.2	.9
	-1.0	.7	NM		-4.3	-9.7
Debt/Worth	.9	.6	1.2		1.0	1.0
	2.5	1.3	2.6		3.6	2.5
	-6.8	3.1	NM		-23.2	-32.8
% Profit Before Taxes/Tangible Net Worth		(24) 39.4	(14) 43.6		(55) 49.3	(50) 51.7
		16.6	11.1		29.0	23.9
		-.9	.0		9.3	2.8
% Profit Before Taxes/Total Assets	20.5	14.4	5.7		15.9	15.3
	4.3	5.6	1.6		5.3	6.6
	-4.5	-.9	-1.4		1.9	1.1
Sales/Net Fixed Assets	106.6	61.9	16.9		44.7	39.4
	18.0	22.3	6.2		14.2	18.2
	12.7	9.8	5.2		5.8	7.6
Sales/Total Assets	5.7	3.8	2.5		3.8	3.7
	3.1	2.8	2.1		2.4	2.6
	2.3	2.1	1.6		1.9	1.7
% Depr., Dep., Amort./Sales		(24) .5	(16) 2.1		(66) .8	(63) .5
		1.2	2.9		1.6	1.4
		2.0	4.1		2.8	2.4
% Officers', Directors' Owners' Comp/Sales		(21) 2.2	(17) 2.0			
		4.9	2.7			
		6.8	7.3			

	0-500M	500M-2MM	2-10MM	10-50MM	50-100MM	100-250MM		'05-'06 ALL	'06-'07 ALL
Net Sales ($)		44406M	462007M	1077542M	784937M	1589820M		3476244M	2988289M
Total Assets ($)		11319M	154175M	485069M	468283M	791269M		1425370M	1561824M

M = $ thousand   MM = $ million
See Pages 9 through 22 for Explanation of Ratios and Data

Comparative Historical Data				Current Data Sorted by Sales					
			Type of Statement						
12	15	20	Unqualified					4	16
16	12	17	Reviewed		1	2	2	9	3
6	2	4	Compiled		2	1	1		
3	2	2	Tax Returns			1		1	
24	29	24	Other		1	2	3	7	11
4/1/07-3/31/08 ALL	**4/1/08-3/31/09 ALL**	**4/1/09-3/31/10 ALL**			**13 (4/1-9/30/09)**			**54 (10/1/09-3/31/10)**	
				0-1MM	**1-3MM**	**3-5MM**	**5-10MM**	**10-25MM**	**25MM & OVER**
61	60	67	**NUMBER OF STATEMENTS**		4	6	6	21	30
%	%	%	**ASSETS**	%	%	%	%	%	%
7.5	5.9	8.0	Cash & Equivalents	D A T A N O T A V A I L A B L E				7.1	6.9
36.2	32.4	29.9	Trade Receivables (net)					26.2	32.7
21.2	24.2	25.9	Inventory					30.9	20.2
3.2	3.1	3.9	All Other Current					5.5	3.3
68.1	65.5	67.6	Total Current					69.7	63.0
19.6	21.3	20.4	Fixed Assets (net)					21.4	20.8
7.6	7.3	6.5	Intangibles (net)					5.7	9.9
4.7	5.9	5.5	All Other Non-Current					3.1	6.3
100.0	100.0	100.0	Total					100.0	100.0
			LIABILITIES						
14.9	11.6	9.0	Notes Payable-Short Term					8.5	7.4
3.0	2.6	4.1	Cur. Mat.-L.T.D.					5.1	3.3
18.3	15.3	15.5	Trade Payables					12.9	17.2
.3	.4	.4	Income Taxes Payable					.0	.4
12.8	12.4	13.2	All Other Current					14.3	11.9
49.3	42.3	42.2	Total Current					40.9	40.1
18.0	17.2	17.1	Long-Term Debt					18.0	20.1
.5	.6	.6	Deferred Taxes					.2	.8
5.2	5.3	8.4	All Other Non-Current					5.5	9.8
27.0	34.5	31.7	Net Worth					35.5	29.1
100.0	100.0	100.0	Total Liabilties & Net Worth					100.0	100.0
			INCOME DATA						
100.0	100.0	100.0	Net Sales					100.0	100.0
30.4	30.3	31.3	Gross Profit					32.9	27.6
26.6	26.0	27.5	Operating Expenses					27.9	23.5
3.8	4.3	3.8	Operating Profit					4.9	4.1
1.4	1.2	1.5	All Other Expenses (net)					1.4	2.3
2.4	3.1	2.3	Profit Before Taxes					3.5	1.8
			RATIOS						
2.2	2.7	2.4						2.7	2.3
1.6	1.6	1.7	Current					1.8	1.7
1.1	1.2	1.3						1.4	1.4
1.4	1.4	1.5						1.8	1.4
.9	.9	.9	Quick					.7	1.0
.6	.6	.7						.5	.8
36 10.0	**34** 10.8	**33** 11.0						**26** 13.9	**36** 10.0
48 7.6	**42** 8.6	**41** 8.8	Sales/Receivables					**35** 10.4	**48** 7.6
64 5.7	**53** 7.0	**53** 6.8						**39** 9.3	**57** 6.4
20 18.0	**22** 16.6	**25** 14.3						**30** 12.1	**24** 15.1
36 10.2	**40** 9.2	**49** 7.5	Cost of Sales/Inventory					**63** 5.8	**39** 9.3
67 5.4	**73** 5.0	**84** 4.4						**96** 3.8	**68** 5.4
20 18.6	**14** 26.9	**17** 21.8						**13** 27.3	**21** 17.5
31 11.6	**23** 15.8	**30** 12.0	Cost of Sales/Payables					**23** 15.9	**32** 11.3
44 8.3	**42** 8.7	**45** 8.1						**34** 10.8	**52** 7.1
7.4	6.6	5.7						5.4	6.0
12.3	11.3	10.0	Sales/Working Capital					8.3	11.3
50.6	32.3	21.9						19.0	19.1
9.1	8.0	11.8						17.3	10.6
(57) 2.9	(54) 4.1	(62) 3.3	EBIT/Interest					6.6	(27) 2.6
1.2	1.5	1.2						1.8	.9
11.3	8.3	5.5							6.4
(27) 2.5	(30) 2.8	(27) 2.3	Net Profit + Depr., Dep., Amort./Cur. Mat. L/T/D						(14) 2.6
1.8	.1	.3							1.0
.5	.4	.3						.4	.3
1.0	.7	.7	Fixed/Worth					.5	.8
-30.2	2.3	2.0						1.3	5.2
1.3	.9	.8						.8	1.1
3.7	2.4	1.8	Debt/Worth					1.7	3.1
-147.3	9.2	11.6						2.9	14.5
39.1	45.7	43.3						43.9	46.9
(45) 17.7	(48) 21.2	(54) 18.8	% Profit Before Taxes/Tangible Net Worth					(17) 21.7	(25) 20.8
4.9	11.0	1.2						8.0	1.3
12.5	18.8	13.3						14.2	10.1
5.1	7.4	4.1	% Profit Before Taxes/Total Assets					8.8	2.7
.8	3.0	-.3						2.5	-.6
44.3	43.5	32.6						31.8	32.7
14.9	14.2	14.0	Sales/Net Fixed Assets					17.9	10.9
8.6	8.5	6.4						6.1	5.8
3.6	3.9	3.3						3.5	3.4
2.6	2.6	2.4	Sales/Total Assets					2.8	2.2
1.9	1.9	1.7						1.8	1.7
.8	.8	.7						.5	.7
(51) 1.3	(54) 1.4	(58) 1.9	% Depr., Dep., Amort./Sales					(18) 1.4	(25) 2.2
2.5	2.2	2.6						2.5	3.6
2.8		1.1							
(14) 3.4		(15) 2.8	% Officers', Directors' Owners' Comp/Sales						
6.1		4.4							
3209410M	**3030620M**	**3958712M**	Net Sales ($)		**8694M**	**22844M**	**45539M**	**353137M**	**3528498M**
1598090M	**1323590M**	**1910115M**	Total Assets ($)		**3757M**	**10361M**	**22939M**	**154120M**	**1718938M**

M = $ thousand MM = $ million

See Pages 9 through 22 for Explanation of Ratios and Data

Current Data Sorted by Assets | Comparative Historical Data

0-500M	500M-2MM	2-10MM	10-50MM	50-100MM	100-250MM	Type of Statement	4/1/05-3/31/06 ALL	4/1/06-3/31/07 ALL
		4	10		1	Unqualified	31	22
	3	12	3	1		Reviewed	35	38
2	6	4	4			Compiled	23	16
2	4	3				Tax Returns	19	12
1	5	21	14	4	1	Other	48	34
	15 (4/1-9/30/09)		86 (10/1/09-3/31/10)					
5	18	44	27	5	2	NUMBER OF STATEMENTS	156	122
%	%	%	%	%	%	ASSETS	%	%
	9.4	8.1	5.5			Cash & Equivalents	6.9	7.6
	35.3	28.1	23.2			Trade Receivables (net)	31.4	33.5
	18.3	23.7	31.6			Inventory	23.7	23.1
	2.6	1.7	1.9			All Other Current	3.1	2.3
	65.5	61.6	62.2			Total Current	65.0	66.6
	24.0	30.0	24.1			Fixed Assets (net)	25.1	25.4
	4.6	4.5	8.4			Intangibles (net)	5.6	4.5
	5.9	4.0	5.3			All Other Non-Current	4.3	3.5
	100.0	100.0	100.0			Total	100.0	100.0
						LIABILITIES		
	10.0	12.3	14.5			Notes Payable-Short Term	13.2	13.8
	4.1	4.9	4.0			Cur. Mat.-L.T.D.	2.9	3.7
	19.1	13.3	13.2			Trade Payables	17.1	15.1
	.1	.0	.1			Income Taxes Payable	.2	.3
	6.7	13.6	11.7			All Other Current	12.7	11.6
	40.0	44.1	43.6			Total Current	46.1	44.5
	18.9	16.0	24.3			Long-Term Debt	15.2	18.8
	.5	.3	.2			Deferred Taxes	.4	.4
	7.3	4.1	9.6			All Other Non-Current	8.1	3.2
	33.3	35.5	22.4			Net Worth	30.2	33.0
	100.0	100.0	100.0			Total Liabilities & Net Worth	100.0	100.0
						INCOME DATA		
	100.0	100.0	100.0			Net Sales	100.0	100.0
	29.7	27.2	22.8			Gross Profit	29.5	29.4
	31.7	27.1	21.1			Operating Expenses	25.2	24.3
	-2.1	.2	1.7			Operating Profit	4.3	5.1
	.8	1.0	2.2			All Other Expenses (net)	1.0	1.1
	-2.9	-.8	-.5			Profit Before Taxes	3.3	4.0
						RATIOS		
	3.2	2.7	2.1				2.2	2.1
	1.8	1.6	1.5			Current	1.5	1.4
	1.1	1.0	1.1				1.1	1.1
	2.2	1.6	1.1				1.3	1.3
	1.2	.8	.6			Quick	.8	.8
	.7	.5	.4				.5	.6
33	11.2 · 28	12.9 · 31	11.6				32 · 11.5	33 · 11.1
47	7.7 · 39	9.3 · 40	9.0			Sales/Receivables	44 · 8.2	45 · 8.1
63	5.8 · 67	5.4 · 51	7.1				63 · 5.8	62 · 5.9
8	46.2 · 25	14.8 · 48	7.6				22 · 16.7	21 · 17.1
16	22.8 · 48	7.6 · 83	4.4			Cost of Sales/Inventory	45 · 8.2	44 · 8.4
73	5.0 · 65	5.6 · 118	3.1				72 · 5.1	71 · 5.1
13	27.9 · 16	22.9 · 14	25.5				17 · 21.6	17 · 21.7
25	14.9 · 23	15.7 · 27	13.5			Cost of Sales/Payables	26 · 13.9	27 · 13.7
50	7.4 · 38	9.5 · 39	9.3				41 · 8.8	41 · 8.8
	5.3	5.7	5.3				6.2	6.6
	10.4	10.3	8.5			Sales/Working Capital	11.9	13.8
	NM	772.1	27.3				64.4	43.1
	9.4	6.6	8.6				8.7	9.9
(16)	1.5	(42) 1.5	1.0			EBIT/Interest	(149) 3.2	(114) 3.5
	-9.0	-2.8	-1.6				1.3	1.7
		5.3	7.1			Net Profit + Depr., Dep.,	6.8	6.9
	(12)	1.4	(10) 1.9			Amort./Cur. Mat. L/T/D	(32) 3.3	(43) 3.3
		-.9	1.3				1.6	1.1
	.2	.3	.4				.3	.3
	.9	.9	2.2			Fixed/Worth	.9	.7
	-13.8	3.2	-1.4				2.7	1.8
	.6	.8	1.1				.9	1.0
	.8	1.8	8.1			Debt/Worth	2.0	2.1
	-166.4	4.7	-11.5				7.1	4.5
	41.3	17.8	58.2			% Profit Before Taxes/Tangible	47.2	50.0
(13)	3.7	(38) 3.8	(20) 5.9			Net Worth	(131) 22.9	(110) 18.1
	-42.9	-35.9	-50.2				9.4	6.5
	4.9	6.4	11.8			% Profit Before Taxes/Total	14.2	17.9
	2.2	1.5	-.1			Assets	5.2	6.3
	-26.5	-10.0	-10.3				.9	1.8
	36.4	24.9	20.0				26.7	28.5
	19.9	9.0	10.9			Sales/Net Fixed Assets	12.6	11.7
	5.4	4.3	5.0				6.7	6.8
	3.5	3.2	2.5				3.3	3.3
	2.6	2.3	1.9			Sales/Total Assets	2.4	2.7
	2.1	1.6	1.5				1.7	1.9
	1.2	1.3	1.8				1.0	1.0
(15)	1.8	(43) 2.4	(21) 2.0			% Depr., Dep., Amort./Sales	(134) 1.7	(106) 1.6
	2.6	4.3	3.3				2.8	2.8
	4.5	1.3				% Officers', Directors'	2.2	1.9
(13)	5.4	(14) 3.4				Owners' Comp/Sales	(53) 4.9	(48) 3.9
	8.0	6.4					8.1	6.4
9873M	62885M	541894M	1126406M	504667M	581080M	Net Sales ($)	3435135M	3199665M
1524M	21755M	236583M	578675M	309725M	334916M	Total Assets ($)	1844600M	1513065M

M = $ thousand   MM = $ million
See Pages 9 through 22 for Explanation of Ratios and Data

Comparative Historical Data | Current Data Sorted by Sales

	4/1/07-3/31/08 ALL	4/1/08-3/31/09 ALL	4/1/09-3/31/10 ALL	0-1MM	1-3MM	3-5MM	5-10MM	10-25MM	25MM & OVER
Type of Statement									
Unqualified	22	21	15					8	7
Reviewed	42	39	19			4	6	6	3
Compiled	27	20	12	2	4	1	4	1	
Tax Returns	13	12	9	1	3	3	1	1	
Other	47	40	46	1	2	3	11	10	19
				15 (4/1-9/30/09)			86 (10/1/09-3/31/10)		
NUMBER OF STATEMENTS	151	132	101	4	9	11	22	26	29
	%	%	%	%	%	%	%	%	%
ASSETS									
Cash & Equivalents	8.3	9.6	7.7			4.1	7.9	10.6	7.0
Trade Receivables (net)	32.6	26.9	27.3			23.8	26.0	31.2	24.5
Inventory	23.2	23.6	23.7			8.9	20.9	26.3	29.6
All Other Current	3.2	2.4	2.2			4.3	.6	2.4	2.4
Total Current	67.3	62.5	61.0			41.1	55.5	70.5	63.5
Fixed Assets (net)	24.0	27.0	26.8			33.2	36.4	19.8	23.3
Intangibles (net)	4.5	5.0	6.8			11.9	5.7	6.5	7.5
All Other Non-Current	4.2	5.5	5.4			13.8	2.4	3.2	5.6
Total	100.0	100.0	100.0			100.0	100.0	100.0	100.0
LIABILITIES									
Notes Payable-Short Term	16.4	11.1	14.8			10.1	12.7	13.4	11.1
Cur. Mat.-L.T.D.	3.8	3.6	4.1			7.3	3.5	5.1	2.8
Trade Payables	17.5	14.1	14.1			13.8	15.4	13.8	12.9
Income Taxes Payable	.5	.3	.1			.2	.1	.0	.2
All Other Current	12.7	11.5	11.4			2.7	9.3	16.7	12.5
Total Current	51.0	40.6	44.6			34.2	41.0	49.0	39.5
Long-Term Debt	18.7	21.7	19.4			20.2	20.8	14.8	20.9
Deferred Taxes	.2	.2	.3			1.4	.1	.1	.2
All Other Non-Current	6.3	5.8	7.8			4.3	4.4	5.6	7.1
Net Worth	23.7	31.7	27.9			39.9	33.7	30.5	32.3
Total Liabilities & Net Worth	100.0	100.0	100.0			100.0	100.0	100.0	100.0
INCOME DATA									
Net Sales	100.0	100.0	100.0			100.0	100.0	100.0	100.0
Gross Profit	29.6	28.6	26.9			29.2	24.3	27.4	25.1
Operating Expenses	24.6	25.2	26.4			27.4	26.9	25.1	22.5
Operating Profit	4.9	3.4	.5			1.8	-2.6	2.4	2.5
All Other Expenses (net)	1.4	1.4	1.7			1.2	1.2	1.0	1.7
Profit Before Taxes	3.6	2.0	-1.3			.7	-3.8	1.3	.8
RATIOS									
Current	2.2	2.4	2.6			2.8	2.3	2.2	2.8
	1.5	1.6	1.6			1.7	1.3	1.5	1.7
	1.1	1.1	1.0			.7	.9	1.2	1.1
Quick	1.3	1.6	1.5			2.2	1.7	1.2	1.4
	.8	.9	.8			1.1	.6	.8	.8
	.6	.5	.5			.4	.5	.6	.5
Sales/Receivables	28 12.9	27 13.6	30 12.2			9 40.5	27 13.6	34 10.7	29 12.4
	44 8.4	38 9.7	40 9.0			43 8.5	36 10.3	41 8.8	40 9.0
	60 6.1	51 7.1	60 6.1			55 6.7	69 5.3	57 6.4	51 7.1
Cost of Sales/Inventory	20 18.4	17 21.4	22 16.6			2 152.8	24 15.1	26 14.1	37 9.7
	44 8.4	49 7.4	50 7.4			11 33.8	49 7.4	52 7.0	74 4.9
	71 5.1	77 4.7	85 4.3			20 18.1	93 3.9	105 3.5	85 4.3
Cost of Sales/Payables	15 23.9	14 25.3	14 25.5			13 27.5	19 19.2	16 23.1	11 34.4
	26 14.1	27 13.4	25 14.7			17 21.6	32 11.5	22 16.4	26 14.1
	39 9.4	37 9.9	39 9.4			19 19.0	47 7.7	39 9.4	38 9.6
Sales/Working Capital	6.9	6.0	5.4			8.1	7.3	5.1	4.5
	12.4	10.6	10.2			12.3	18.9	9.7	9.2
	66.3	56.3	550.2			-42.3	-165.2	31.9	25.5
EBIT/Interest	9.1	8.8	7.4			(10) 9.3	(20) 2.7	12.6	(27) 13.0
	(137) 3.5	(118) 2.2	(95) 1.3			2.0	-.7	3.0	1.3
	1.5	.0	-2.2			.7	-3.8	-2.8	-1.4
Net Profit + Depr., Dep., Amort./Cur. Mat. L/T/D	6.8	4.4	5.8						7.2
	(42) 3.5	(39) 2.1	(29) 1.7						(13) 2.1
	1.5	.7	-.6						1.3
Fixed/Worth	.3	.4	.3			.3	.4	.3	.3
	.8	1.0	1.0			.9	1.7	.8	.9
	3.0	4.2	18.4			3.9	6.5	9.9	NM
Debt/Worth	1.0	.9	.8			.7	.8	1.1	.8
	2.5	2.5	2.9			.9	2.7	3.0	2.8
	10.5	10.3	54.9			7.3	15.0	33.4	NM
% Profit Before Taxes/Tangible Net Worth	64.7	47.2	28.4				13.6	26.1	52.6
	(124) 24.2	(107) 19.1	(78) 5.6				(20) -5.3	(21) 6.5	(22) 16.3
	9.1	2.0	-31.0				-47.5	-44.6	2.2
% Profit Before Taxes/Total Assets	16.7	13.8	8.2			6.7	3.4	16.6	11.0
	8.7	4.5	1.6			3.0	-2.3	2.4	1.6
	1.5	-3.0	-10.2			.0	-18.4	-8.3	-3.7
Sales/Net Fixed Assets	29.6	24.8	25.4			59.8	17.5	32.2	19.6
	15.0	10.8	10.4			11.2	5.8	15.2	10.5
	7.1	6.4	4.6			4.6	2.3	6.9	5.5
Sales/Total Assets	3.6	3.1	2.9			6.1	2.4	3.3	2.7
	2.6	2.4	2.1			2.7	1.9	2.4	2.0
	1.9	1.9	1.6			1.6	1.2	1.6	1.7
% Depr., Dep., Amort./Sales	.9	1.1	1.4			1.3	1.6	1.1	1.3
	(129) 1.5	(113) 1.6	(90) 2.2			(10) 2.1	(21) 3.6	(24) 2.1	(24) 1.9
	2.9	3.1	3.8			3.4	5.7	3.3	3.0
% Officers', Directors' Owners' Comp/Sales	2.2	1.9	2.8						
	(61) 3.9	(52) 3.2	(34) 4.6						
	5.9	6.0	7.2						
Net Sales ($)	4027661M	4005616M	2826805M	1887M	21295M	46077M	155658M	474586M	2127302M
Total Assets ($)	1930541M	1976262M	1483178M	1441M	9352M	22349M	94073M	221925M	1134038M

M = $ thousand   MM = $ million
See Pages 9 through 22 for Explanation of Ratios and Data

Current Data Sorted by Assets   Comparative Historical Data

	0-500M	500M-2MM	2-10MM	10-50MM	50-100MM	100-250MM		ALL 4/1/05- 3/31/06	ALL 4/1/06- 3/31/07
Type of Statement									
Unqualified				1	1	1		8	13
Reviewed		2	6	3				6	8
Compiled	3	1	2	1				14	9
Tax Returns		2						3	1
Other		2	11	6	1			15	13
		4 (4/1-9/30/09)		39 (10/1/09-3/31/10)					
NUMBER OF STATEMENTS	3	7	19	11	2	1		46	44
	%	%	%	%	%	%		%	%
ASSETS									
Cash & Equivalents			9.8	16.1				13.0	10.7
Trade Receivables (net)			25.7	21.1				27.7	25.8
Inventory			28.7	20.1				26.0	22.3
All Other Current			1.3	8.0				1.9	2.7
Total Current			65.5	65.4				68.5	61.5
Fixed Assets (net)			23.9	31.7				21.3	25.9
Intangibles (net)			5.1	.6				2.5	5.1
All Other Non-Current			5.5	2.4				7.7	7.5
Total			100.0	100.0				100.0	100.0
LIABILITIES									
Notes Payable-Short Term			9.5	1.1				7.5	7.4
Cur. Mat.-L.T.D.			2.1	3.9				3.3	3.6
Trade Payables			25.2	10.5				22.4	18.9
Income Taxes Payable			.1	.1				.2	.2
All Other Current			7.3	10.2				9.6	11.0
Total Current			44.3	25.9				43.0	41.0
Long-Term Debt			11.0	18.5				10.6	12.6
Deferred Taxes			.0	1.3				.5	.8
All Other Non-Current			10.3	4.0				4.8	7.6
Net Worth			34.4	50.4				41.2	38.0
Total Liabilities & Net Worth			100.0	100.0				100.0	100.0
INCOME DATA									
Net Sales			100.0	100.0				100.0	100.0
Gross Profit			32.1	29.9				34.2	34.1
Operating Expenses			32.2	27.2				29.8	30.3
Operating Profit			-.1	2.7				4.4	3.8
All Other Expenses (net)			.2	-.5				.3	.2
Profit Before Taxes			-.3	3.2				4.1	3.6
RATIOS									
Current			2.3	4.9				2.8	2.7
			1.1	2.7				1.7	1.7
			1.0	2.3				1.2	1.1
Quick			1.1	3.8				1.5	1.7
			.6	1.9				.9	.9
			.5	.5				.6	.6
Sales/Receivables			17 21.7	16 22.9				19 19.2	18 19.8
			34 10.9	28 13.2				34 10.6	32 11.4
			44 8.3	48 7.7				42 8.7	43 8.5
Cost of Sales/Inventory			32 11.3	22 16.8				23 15.7	23 15.9
			42 8.6	30 12.2				35 10.6	33 10.9
			79 4.6	93 3.9				57 6.4	44 8.4
Cost of Sales/Payables			22 16.8	9 39.8				16 22.3	16 23.0
			28 13.0	19 19.1				31 12.0	25 14.9
			52 7.0	27 13.5				42 8.7	38 9.6
Sales/Working Capital			6.8	3.1				6.7	6.7
			45.0	7.1				11.5	13.3
			-999.8	11.3				58.1	131.3
EBIT/Interest			8.7	156.8				68.8	19.2
			(15) 2.3	(10) 7.2				(41) 7.5	(42) 6.1
			-.2	-1.9				1.9	1.1
Net Profit + Depr., Dep., Amort./Cur. Mat. L/T/D								14.1	10.6
								(12) 3.7	(14) 3.8
								.8	-.3
Fixed/Worth			.1	.3				.3	.4
			1.0	.5				.5	.6
			42.1	1.7				1.1	1.2
Debt/Worth			.5	.4				.7	.7
			2.2	.9				1.4	1.3
			135.6	2.6				7.5	5.2
% Profit Before Taxes/Tangible Net Worth			42.7	28.4				61.8	41.9
			(16) 4.4	17.0				(43) 31.3	(36) 16.7
			-8.2	-4.8				6.2	2.2
% Profit Before Taxes/Total Assets			11.5	20.6				28.1	21.4
			2.9	6.2				11.6	9.9
			-3.1	-3.4				2.6	1.0
Sales/Net Fixed Assets			41.0	15.9				37.6	31.2
			16.1	7.4				18.3	17.0
			9.6	3.8				10.4	7.5
Sales/Total Assets			4.2	3.6				4.4	4.4
			3.5	2.3				3.7	3.5
			1.8	1.4				2.5	2.3
% Depr., Dep., Amort./Sales			.7	1.2				.7	1.1
			(16) 1.4	1.3				(39) 1.2	(40) 1.4
			2.7	2.7				1.5	1.8
% Officers', Directors' Owners' Comp/Sales								1.1	1.5
								(18) 2.1	(14) 3.6
								4.7	4.4
Net Sales ($)	3384M	32446M	236517M	538482M	291906M	544202M		1771276M	2011355M
Total Assets ($)	829M	10012M	78076M	231900M	135294M	118240M		707936M	788643M

Comparative Historical Data | Current Data Sorted by Sales

6	5	3	Type of Statement						3
11	11	11	Unqualified			1	4	4	2
7	13	7	Reviewed	1	2		1	1	2
2	4	2	Compiled			2			
11	13	20	Tax Returns	1			1		6
4/1/07-3/31/08	4/1/08-3/31/09	4/1/09-3/31/10	Other	1	4 (4/1-9/30/09)		3	39 (10/1/09-3/31/10) 9	6
ALL	ALL	ALL		0-1MM	1-3MM	3-5MM	5-10MM	10-25MM	25MM & OVER
37	46	43	NUMBER OF STATEMENTS	2	3	3	8	14	13
%	%	%	**ASSETS**	%	%	%	%	%	%
12.2	8.8	12.3	Cash & Equivalents					10.3	14.3
26.8	24.8	22.2	Trade Receivables (net)					23.1	23.9
22.1	22.3	25.7	Inventory					26.1	20.1
3.1	3.8	3.3	All Other Current					4.4	3.4
64.1	59.7	63.5	Total Current					63.9	61.8
24.4	27.8	26.3	Fixed Assets (net)					24.7	31.0
4.8	3.8	4.9	Intangibles (net)					6.4	.6
6.6	8.7	5.4	All Other Non-Current					5.0	6.6
100.0	100.0	100.0	Total					100.0	100.0
			LIABILITIES						
8.1	12.7	7.1	Notes Payable-Short Term					7.4	.3
3.5	2.0	3.4	Cur. Mat.-L.T.D.					2.5	2.3
17.5	17.6	18.9	Trade Payables					27.5	12.7
.2	.7	.1	Income Taxes Payable					.1	.1
11.2	8.5	8.3	All Other Current					7.9	13.1
40.5	41.5	37.9	Total Current					45.3	28.4
14.3	17.0	15.0	Long-Term Debt					11.9	15.5
.6	.4	.3	Deferred Taxes					.8	.3
3.8	5.7	6.3	All Other Non-Current					13.3	5.5
40.8	35.4	40.4	Net Worth					28.7	50.3
100.0	100.0	100.0	Total Liabilities & Net Worth					100.0	100.0
			INCOME DATA						
100.0	100.0	100.0	Net Sales					100.0	100.0
33.4	30.3	33.5	Gross Profit					33.0	33.7
30.5	31.3	31.4	Operating Expenses					32.0	30.4
2.9	-1.0	2.1	Operating Profit					1.0	3.4
.5	.9	.1	All Other Expenses (net)					-.3	.2
2.5	-1.8	2.0	Profit Before Taxes					1.3	3.2
			RATIOS						
3.4	3.1	3.2	Current					3.2	4.7
1.5	1.4	1.7						1.1	2.6
1.1	1.0	1.0						.9	1.5
2.1	1.8	2.1	Quick					1.4	2.8
.9	.7	.8						.6	1.9
.6	.5	.4						.4	.7
17 21.6	18 20.1	16 22.9	Sales/Receivables					14 25.7	13 27.3
30 12.0	33 11.2	28 13.2						25 14.7	29 12.6
44 8.4	47 7.8	43 8.6						35 10.4	48 7.5
20 17.9	27 13.7	27 13.3	Cost of Sales/Inventory					29 12.8	22 16.3
33 11.1	38 9.7	42 8.7						40 9.2	30 12.2
47 7.8	52 7.0	79 4.6						81 4.5	53 6.8
16 22.2	14 26.2	16 23.0	Cost of Sales/Payables					19 19.3	12 31.1
24 15.1	24 15.2	27 13.6						26 14.1	18 20.2
41 8.8	46 7.9	49 7.5						53 6.9	33 11.1
5.9	5.9	5.2	Sales/Working Capital					7.0	5.2
15.8	18.7	12.7						77.6	7.7
79.3	-174.5	247.8						-46.0	129.5
14.0	4.0	13.7	EBIT/Interest					4.7	35.9
(32) 2.4	(40) .1	(36) 3.5					(11) -.1	(12) 6.8	
-.8	-6.3	-.4						-.8	-.3
	2.9	5.4	Net Profit + Depr., Dep.,						
	(15) 1.3	(15) 2.2	Amort./Cur. Mat. L/T/D						
	-10.4	1.5							
.3	.3	.2	Fixed/Worth					.2	.2
.5	.7	.6						2.2	.6
2.6	2.1	3.7						NM	1.7
.4	.6	.5	Debt/Worth					.8	.4
1.4	1.6	1.4						9.1	.9
4.3	7.0	11.6						NM	2.6
38.7	16.8	57.7	% Profit Before Taxes/Tangible					43.8	43.3
(32) 18.8	(39) 1.5	(37) 17.5	Net Worth					(11) -.7	13.6
-4.5	-42.9	-2.8						-29.0	-2.8
18.9	6.8	16.0	% Profit Before Taxes/Total					14.0	15.1
7.1	-5.7	6.2	Assets					1.2	6.2
-1.8	-18.4	-3.1						-3.4	-1.8
34.4	29.9	29.5	Sales/Net Fixed Assets					28.9	20.4
16.2	12.1	14.3						13.0	13.1
7.9	5.3	6.6						7.2	5.0
4.9	4.0	4.0	Sales/Total Assets					4.5	3.8
3.1	3.1	2.8						3.8	2.6
2.1	2.1	2.0						2.4	2.1
1.1	1.1	1.0	% Depr., Dep., Amort./Sales					.7	1.2
(32) 1.5	(38) 1.4	(37) 1.5					(13) 1.5	(12) 1.3	
2.6	2.6	2.7						3.8	1.8
1.2	1.0	.8	% Officers', Directors'						
(15) 2.2	(13) 3.0	(14) 1.7	Owners' Comp/Sales						
4.1	5.9	5.8							
1808364M	2355476M	1646937M	Net Sales ($)	1192M	4223M	11352M	61244M	192209M	1376717M
578486M	774157M	574351M	Total Assets ($)	2327M	1531M	4351M	28516M	68058M	469568M

© RMA 2010

M = $ thousand   MM = $ million
See Pages 9 through 22 for Explanation of Ratios and Data

Current Data Sorted by Assets   **Comparative Historical Data**

Type of Statement

0-500M	500M-2MM	2-10MM	10-50MM	50-100MM	100-250MM		4/1/05-3/31/06 ALL	4/1/06-3/31/07 ALL
					1	Unqualified	5	8
		6	1			Reviewed	8	5
		2				Compiled	4	8
1						Tax Returns	3	2
2	1	6	5			Other	11	7
	4 (4/1-9/30/09)		21 (10/1/09-3/31/10)					
3	1	14	6		1	**NUMBER OF STATEMENTS**	31	30
%	%	%	%	%	%	**ASSETS**	%	%
		6.9				Cash & Equivalents	8.6	9.4
		27.6				Trade Receivables (net)	34.6	28.1
		46.1		D		Inventory	27.9	34.7
		3.2		A		All Other Current	1.8	2.7
		83.8		T		Total Current	72.8	75.0
		13.6		A		Fixed Assets (net)	16.9	15.0
		.5				Intangibles (net)	5.3	6.1
		2.0		N		All Other Non-Current	5.0	3.8
		100.0		O		Total	100.0	100.0
				T		**LIABILITIES**		
		25.2				Notes Payable-Short Term	16.9	15.3
		1.7		A		Cur. Mat.-L.T.D.	2.4	2.8
		20.3		V		Trade Payables	24.4	16.0
		.0		A		Income Taxes Payable	.2	.3
		14.5		I		All Other Current	16.0	12.3
		61.8		L		Total Current	59.9	46.7
		3.2		A		Long-Term Debt	14.3	12.9
		.2		B		Deferred Taxes	.2	.3
		5.3		L		All Other Non-Current	5.6	14.3
		29.5		E		Net Worth	20.0	25.9
		100.0				Total Liabilities & Net Worth	100.0	100.0
						INCOME DATA		
		100.0				Net Sales	100.0	100.0
		33.3				Gross Profit	32.0	33.1
		31.5				Operating Expenses	28.5	26.7
		1.8				Operating Profit	3.6	6.4
		.9				All Other Expenses (net)	.7	1.2
		.9				Profit Before Taxes	2.8	5.2
						RATIOS		
		2.0				Current	1.7	4.1
		1.3					1.3	1.8
		1.0					.9	1.1
		.9				Quick	1.0	1.9
		.6					.8	.9
		.2					.4	.6
		17 21.3				Sales/Receivables	27 13.4	27 13.7
		33 11.2					33 10.9	35 10.5
		42 8.6					41 8.9	42 8.7
		58 6.3				Cost of Sales/Inventory	21 17.1	37 9.9
		72 5.1					45 8.1	55 6.6
		104 3.5					62 5.9	80 4.6
		18 20.6				Cost of Sales/Payables	18 20.0	14 25.2
		35 10.4					29 12.6	27 13.4
		46 8.0					50 7.3	39 9.3
		6.6				Sales/Working Capital	10.5	4.9
		17.5					20.4	9.8
		NM					-34.0	66.0
		9.7				EBIT/Interest	7.4	15.2
	(12)	3.5					(27) 2.4	(25) 5.5
		-3.4					.9	2.6
						Net Profit + Depr., Dep., Amort./Cur. Mat. L/T/D		
		.2				Fixed/Worth	.2	.1
		.3					1.6	.4
		8.7					-5.7	NM
		1.3				Debt/Worth	1.3	.3
		3.1					5.4	2.0
		18.5					-48.6	NM
		74.2				% Profit Before Taxes/Tangible Net Worth	98.8	36.3
	(12)	11.5					(23) 22.0	(23) 17.7
		-18.4					7.1	9.9
		11.3				% Profit Before Taxes/Total Assets	18.8	18.0
		2.7					3.4	11.0
		-10.1					.1	5.4
		50.6				Sales/Net Fixed Assets	50.7	57.2
		39.6					27.3	31.4
		19.2					12.5	15.2
		4.3				Sales/Total Assets	5.2	4.1
		3.3					3.1	2.8
		2.2					2.3	2.3
		.8				% Depr., Dep., Amort./Sales	.5	.4
	(11)	1.3					(28) .8	(22) .8
		2.1					1.7	2.4
						% Officers', Directors' Owners' Comp/Sales	1.3	1.4
							(16) 3.4	(11) 4.1
							5.4	7.2
5167M	3521M	236550M	228678M		509903M	Net Sales ($)	704287M	1181808M
1082M	1935M	65499M	120558M		248122M	Total Assets ($)	285115M	493991M

Comparative Historical Data   Current Data Sorted by Sales

				Type of Statement						
5	4	1	Unqualified						1
6	4	7	Reviewed				1	4	2
3	4	2	Compiled				2		
1	1	1	Tax Returns				1	2	
15	13	14	Other	1	1	1	5	2	2
4/1/07-3/31/08 ALL	4/1/08-3/31/09 ALL	4/1/09-3/31/10 ALL		0-1MM	1-3MM	3-5MM	5-10MM	10-25MM	25MM & OVER
					4 (4/1-9/30/09)		21 (10/1/09-3/31/10)		
30	26	25	NUMBER OF STATEMENTS	1	1	3	7	6	7
%	%	%	**ASSETS**	%	%	%	%	%	%
7.4	5.0	7.1	Cash & Equivalents						
32.1	29.3	25.5	Trade Receivables (net)						
34.3	34.9	35.4	Inventory						
4.0	3.3	3.0	All Other Current						
77.9	72.5	71.0	Total Current						
16.2	17.9	17.1	Fixed Assets (net)						
3.3	4.1	7.0	Intangibles (net)						
2.7	5.5	4.9	All Other Non-Current						
100.0	100.0	100.0	Total						
			LIABILITIES						
17.7	15.8	20.8	Notes Payable-Short Term						
3.0	1.8	2.0	Cur. Mat.-L.T.D.						
22.1	21.0	19.2	Trade Payables						
.6	.2	.1	Income Taxes Payable						
13.8	13.2	12.2	All Other Current						
57.2	51.9	54.4	Total Current						
9.1	16.2	12.5	Long-Term Debt						
.2	.3	.8	Deferred Taxes						
4.8	4.1	5.9	All Other Non-Current						
28.7	27.5	26.5	Net Worth						
100.0	100.0	100.0	Total Liabilties & Net Worth						
			INCOME DATA						
100.0	100.0	100.0	Net Sales						
31.8	31.5	34.0	Gross Profit						
28.2	29.5	32.3	Operating Expenses						
3.6	2.0	1.7	Operating Profit						
1.6	1.5	2.0	All Other Expenses (net)						
1.9	.5	-.4	Profit Before Taxes						
			RATIOS						
2.2	2.2	2.1							
1.4	1.5	1.5	Current						
1.1	1.1	1.1							
1.1	1.0	1.1							
.8	.8	.8	Quick						
.4	.4	.3							
26 13.9	26 14.2	25 14.6							
38 9.5	36 10.1	34 10.6	Sales/Receivables						
49 7.4	49 7.4	46 7.9							
36 10.2	47 7.7	55 6.7							
61 6.0	62 5.9	70 5.2	Cost of Sales/Inventory						
81 4.5	89 4.1	87 4.2							
20 18.2	19 18.9	20 18.5							
31 11.8	32 11.3	35 10.5	Cost of Sales/Payables						
56 6.5	43 8.4	42 8.6							
7.2	6.6	6.5							
15.8	10.8	12.2	Sales/Working Capital						
62.4	34.4	45.0							
7.6	4.5	9.5							
(27) 3.6	(24) 2.2	(23) 2.3	EBIT/Interest						
1.2	-3.0	-3.5							
			Net Profit + Depr., Dep., Amort./Cur. Mat. L/T/D						
.3	.3	.3							
.4	.5	.4	Fixed/Worth						
16.0	NM	-25.5							
.8	.9	.9							
2.8	2.4	2.9	Debt/Worth						
95.2	NM	-59.0							
43.9	28.4	34.8							
(24) 18.1	(20) 10.2	(18) 3.6	% Profit Before Taxes/Tangible Net Worth						
1.9	-12.2	-19.5							
13.3	8.2	11.3							
5.2	4.2	1.3	% Profit Before Taxes/Total Assets						
.6	-6.6	-10.6							
43.0	40.2	48.3							
33.0	23.1	20.8	Sales/Net Fixed Assets						
12.1	11.8	12.0							
4.6	4.0	3.7							
3.3	2.9	2.8	Sales/Total Assets						
2.3	2.2	1.9							
.7	.6	.8							
(23) 1.1	(19) 1.2	(19) 1.3	% Depr., Dep., Amort./Sales						
2.0	2.1	2.5							
1.5	1.5	1.9							
(15) 2.8	(10) 3.4	(11) 4.2	% Officers', Directors' Owners' Comp/Sales						
5.7	4.8	5.6							
736946M	1782762M	983819M	Net Sales ($)	573M	1234M	11630M	49060M	91312M	830010M
296718M	735327M	437196M	Total Assets ($)	234M	398M	5029M	37569M	44895M	349071M

M = $ thousand   MM = $ million
See Pages 9 through 22 for Explanation of Ratios and Data

Current Data Sorted by Assets   Comparative Historical Data

Type of Statement	0-500M	500M-2MM	2-10MM	10-50MM	50-100MM	100-250MM		4/1/05-3/31/06 ALL	4/1/06-3/31/07 ALL
Unqualified		2	9	19	13	11		34	51
Reviewed	5	1	21	4				14	17
Compiled	2	7	10	1				7	12
Tax Returns	5	9	2	1	5	7		8	6
Other		6	28	29				71	80
		29 (4/1-9/30/09)		168 (10/1/09-3/31/10)					
NUMBER OF STATEMENTS	12	25	70	54	18	18		134	166

ASSETS	%	%	%	%	%	%		%	%
Cash & Equivalents	21.1	11.9	9.2	13.2	15.1	11.9		11.3	11.1
Trade Receivables (net)	29.1	23.8	26.2	23.2	20.8	14.0		23.7	22.6
Inventory	22.0	29.9	26.9	19.8	16.5	12.8		23.6	23.2
All Other Current	.1	3.7	2.1	4.0	3.5	2.8		2.5	2.2
Total Current	72.2	69.5	64.5	60.1	56.0	41.5		61.2	59.0
Fixed Assets (net)	19.6	17.4	20.8	22.1	13.4	25.3		22.5	21.2
Intangibles (net)	1.5	2.3	9.4	11.7	24.1	28.3		9.0	14.2
All Other Non-Current	6.8	10.8	5.3	6.1	6.4	4.9		7.4	5.5
Total	100.0	100.0	100.0	100.0	100.0	100.0		100.0	100.0

LIABILITIES									
Notes Payable-Short Term	5.0	11.6	12.8	5.1	6.2	.5		6.1	5.7
Cur. Mat.-L.T.D.	4.1	2.8	4.9	2.1	2.6	4.1		3.1	4.2
Trade Payables	19.3	12.4	13.0	8.3	7.5	4.3		11.7	10.6
Income Taxes Payable	.0	.5	.2	.6	.3	.3		.4	.5
All Other Current	7.9	13.5	11.4	10.1	8.6	6.2		10.5	9.6
Total Current	36.3	40.9	42.2	26.2	25.1	15.5		31.8	30.5
Long-Term Debt	22.0	9.2	12.4	16.1	9.3	15.6		14.1	14.1
Deferred Taxes	.0	.0	.6	1.3	1.1	3.0		.5	.6
All Other Non-Current	52.6	6.7	2.8	5.9	9.3	5.9		5.6	5.6
Net Worth	-10.9	43.1	42.0	50.5	55.2	60.1		47.9	49.3
Total Liabilities & Net Worth	100.0	100.0	100.0	100.0	100.0	100.0		100.0	100.0

INCOME DATA									
Net Sales	100.0	100.0	100.0	100.0	100.0	100.0		100.0	100.0
Gross Profit	57.2	49.1	43.5	43.9	51.7	44.9		47.4	45.9
Operating Expenses	40.3	45.2	36.4	33.9	43.6	33.0		37.9	37.8
Operating Profit	17.0	3.9	7.1	9.9	8.1	11.9		9.5	8.1
All Other Expenses (net)	11.5	.6	.7	2.3	2.2	2.4		1.2	1.9
Profit Before Taxes	5.4	3.2	6.3	7.6	5.9	9.5		8.3	6.2

RATIOS									
Current	8.3	3.9	3.2	4.1	5.8	4.0		3.7	3.9
	2.2	2.3	1.6	2.7	1.9	2.1		2.1	2.1
	.9	1.4	1.1	1.5	1.1	1.5		1.3	1.3
Quick	4.3	1.9	1.6	2.5	4.0	2.7		2.2	2.3
	1.4	1.1	.8	1.3	1.1	1.4		1.2 (165)	1.1
	.6	.6	.5	.9	.6	.8		.7	.7
Sales/Receivables	15 23.6	34 10.9	33 11.1	41 8.9	40 9.0	34 10.6		41 9.0	38 9.7
	37 9.8	43 8.6	41 9.0	48 7.6	60 6.0	44 8.3		49 7.4	49 7.4
	42 8.6	61 6.0	51 7.1	57 6.4	70 5.2	60 6.1		58 6.3	62 5.9
Cost of Sales/Inventory	1 337.3	50 7.3	48 7.6	55 6.6	83 4.4	42 8.8		58 6.3	59 6.2
	58 6.3	122 3.0	77 4.7	96 3.8	114 3.2	65 5.6		100 3.7	95 3.8
	147 2.5	193 1.9	128 2.8	126 2.9	173 2.1	127 2.9		123 3.0	141 2.6
Cost of Sales/Payables	7 51.2	19 19.1	19 19.3	18 20.6	30 12.2	18 20.7		22 16.6	20 17.9
	36 10.3	36 10.1	32 11.4	28 13.0	39 9.4	24 15.3		36 10.0	35 10.3
	52 7.0	65 5.6	49 7.5	45 8.2	52 7.0	35 10.4		57 6.4	64 5.7
Sales/Working Capital	4.0	3.4	4.8	2.8	1.6	2.6		3.6	3.4
	15.5	4.9	10.6	4.6	5.6	5.7		7.1	5.7
	NM	14.0	92.2	7.7	21.1	12.5		12.2	16.4
EBIT/Interest		26.6	16.0	18.1	59.0	17.1		24.1	16.2
		(20) 3.0	(62) 6.5	(48) 5.8	(17) 3.7	(14) 5.5		(118) 7.0	(139) 4.9
		.7	2.5	2.2	.5	1.3		2.0	1.8
Net Profit + Depr., Dep., Amort./Cur. Mat. L/T/D			4.7	9.9				22.8	15.1
			(22) 3.1	(28) 3.3				(49) 3.8	(57) 3.2
			1.3	1.4				1.8	.8
Fixed/Worth	.1	.2	.2	.2	.1	.5		.2	.2
	5.0	.4	.6	.4	.5	.9		.6	.6
	-.3	.8	1.9	1.3	NM	-8.7		1.4	2.6
Debt/Worth	3.1	.4	.5	.3	.3	.5		.4	.4
	-195.1	1.5	1.9	.8	1.4	1.4		1.3	1.3
	-3.2	3.1	7.9	4.2	NM	-42.6		3.5	6.0
% Profit Before Taxes/Tangible Net Worth		52.5	62.3	34.2	46.2	38.6		52.8	48.8
		(22) 13.3	(61) 30.8	(44) 18.3	(14) 15.1	(12) 25.0		(121) 25.3	(134) 26.4
		.8	15.8	3.4	.9	13.2		6.6	6.7
% Profit Before Taxes/Total Assets	39.7	25.0	23.4	18.8	13.5	15.5		21.1	19.3
	11.9	7.6	12.3	6.8	3.2	7.6		12.1	10.5
	2.3	-1.3	4.2	1.7	.0	2.5		2.1	2.3
Sales/Net Fixed Assets	268.5	34.8	33.4	16.0	24.0	6.9		18.8	21.9
	48.2	16.9	15.1	7.4	14.1	4.0		8.8	9.2
	10.8	9.2	5.3	4.4	6.0	2.3		4.9	4.6
Sales/Total Assets	6.7	2.7	2.8	1.9	1.6	1.3		2.4	2.2
	2.7	1.9	1.9	1.5	1.0	.9		1.7	1.6
	1.9	1.5	1.5	1.0	.6	.6		1.1	1.0
% Depr., Dep., Amort./Sales		.8	1.0	1.6	2.0			1.1	1.5
		(18) 1.4	(62) 2.1	(45) 3.2	(14) 3.0			(113) 2.5	(138) 2.6
		3.1	4.6	5.4	4.6			4.0	4.8
% Officers', Directors' Owners' Comp/Sales		3.1	2.5					2.4	2.9
		(13) 6.0	(16) 5.6					(37) 6.2	(34) 5.5
		10.6	9.1					11.1	9.2
Net Sales ($)	17245M	68290M	798298M	1962110M	1581964M	3376861M		6708537M	6560031M
Total Assets ($)	4540M	31783M	366821M	1408718M	1356607M	2825211M		5216848M	5465559M

M = $ thousand   MM = $ million
See Pages 9 through 22 for Explanation of Ratios and Data

Comparative Historical Data

Current Data Sorted by Sales

			Type of Statement						
47	50	54	Unqualified		1	2	2	11	39
18	22	26	Reviewed		6	4	10	12	3
12	15	23	Compiled	2	6	4	5	6	
6	9	14	Tax Returns	2			1	1	
68	82	80	Other	5	4	4	13	21	33
4/1/07-3/31/08	4/1/08-3/31/09	4/1/09-3/31/10			29 (4/1-9/30/09)		168 (10/1/09-3/31/10)		
ALL	ALL	ALL		0-1MM	1-3MM	3-5MM	5-10MM	10-25MM	25MM & OVER
151	178	197	**NUMBER OF STATEMENTS**	9	17	14	31	51	75
%	%	%	**ASSETS**	%	%	%	%	%	%
12.9	11.3	12.2	Cash & Equivalents		13.6	13.4	13.8	9.5	12.4
22.2	23.4	23.7	Trade Receivables (net)		23.1	24.3	20.6	26.7	22.7
23.4	23.8	22.8	Inventory		22.7	29.8	24.6	25.6	18.5
2.6	2.3	2.9	All Other Current		1.4	6.6	1.6	2.3	3.9
61.0	60.7	61.5	Total Current		60.8	74.1	60.7	64.1	57.5
22.2	20.1	20.4	Fixed Assets (net)		20.4	15.6	19.4	23.0	19.9
11.9	14.1	11.7	Intangibles (net)		8.9	4.1	12.4	8.8	16.8
4.9	5.0	6.4	All Other Non-Current		9.9	6.3	7.5	4.1	5.8
100.0	100.0	100.0	Total		100.0	100.0	100.0	100.0	100.0
			LIABILITIES						
7.6	8.2	8.3	Notes Payable-Short Term		12.2	9.3	5.2	15.6	4.3
3.2	3.6	3.5	Cur. Mat.-L.T.D.		3.8	6.1	4.4	3.6	2.7
11.2	12.2	10.7	Trade Payables		12.5	13.6	9.9	11.3	9.0
.3	.3	.3	Income Taxes Payable		.8	.2	.3	.2	.4
10.2	10.8	10.4	All Other Current		7.7	16.7	6.7	12.7	10.0
32.5	35.1	33.3	Total Current		37.0	45.9	26.5	43.5	26.4
14.8	17.0	13.6	Long-Term Debt		20.2	9.4	14.5	10.8	14.6
.7	.7	.9	Deferred Taxes		.1	.4	1.1	.6	1.5
6.9	7.5	8.1	All Other Non-Current		17.1	15.4	.7	4.9	6.6
45.1	39.6	44.1	Net Worth		25.7	28.9	57.3	40.2	50.9
100.0	100.0	100.0	Total Liabilities & Net Worth		100.0	100.0	100.0	100.0	100.0
			INCOME DATA						
100.0	100.0	100.0	Net Sales		100.0	100.0	100.0	100.0	100.0
45.2	44.8	46.0	Gross Profit		51.3	45.4	48.6	42.9	44.2
37.5	36.6	37.4	Operating Expenses		45.5	40.7	39.4	35.9	34.7
7.6	8.2	8.6	Operating Profit		5.7	4.7	9.2	7.0	9.5
1.6	2.1	2.1	All Other Expenses (net)		1.7	.2	.5	1.4	2.2
6.0	6.2	6.5	Profit Before Taxes		4.0	4.5	8.7	5.6	7.3
			RATIOS						
3.5	3.4	3.9			4.4	3.1	4.9	3.0	3.9
2.2	1.9	2.1	Current		1.9	2.2	2.6	1.7	2.4
1.3	1.2	1.2			.8	.9	1.4	1.0	1.4
2.1	2.2	2.2			2.4	1.7	2.3	1.8	2.4
1.2	1.1	1.1	Quick		1.0	1.2	1.4	.8	1.2
.6	.6	.6			.6	.3	.6	.5	.8
37 9.9	38 9.7	34 10.7			27 13.7	22 17.0	34 10.7	34 10.8	38 9.5
47 7.8	46 7.9	44 8.2	Sales/Receivables		43 8.6	36 10.1	41 8.9	42 8.6	49 7.5
60 6.1	58 6.3	58 6.3			55 6.6	51 7.2	58 6.3	52 7.0	62 5.9
60 6.1	60 6.1	50 7.3			3 133.1	37 9.8	50 7.3	45 8.1	57 6.4
91 4.0	84 4.4	90 4.1	Cost of Sales/Inventory		117 3.1	74 5.0	97 3.8	81 4.5	92 4.0
148 2.5	131 2.8	134 2.7			196 1.9	141 2.6	154 2.4	129 2.8	121 3.0
20 18.4	22 16.8	19 19.4			13 29.0	13 29.0	18 20.3	19 19.3	19 19.4
33 11.2	35 10.5	32 11.5	Cost of Sales/Payables		47 7.8	30 12.1	32 11.3	32 11.3	28 13.2
57 6.4	56 6.5	49 7.5			77 4.8	50 7.3	63 5.8	47 7.7	43 8.5
3.4	3.5	3.2			3.7	4.7	3.3	3.7	2.7
5.4	5.8	6.4	Sales/Working Capital		7.6	6.8	4.8	9.3	5.8
13.6	16.2	19.7			-38.0	-50.9	13.5	-86.6	12.1
15.8	14.2	17.6			32.4	25.2	15.6	14.0	23.9
(124) 4.0	(153) 4.3	(169) 5.7	EBIT/Interest		(13) 2.4	(13) 5.5	(24) 7.0	(48) 6.2	(66) 4.7
1.4	1.8	1.7			.8	-.1	2.3	2.7	1.3
6.8	14.9	6.3						6.3	7.6
(42) 2.5	(52) 3.7	(67) 3.3	Net Profit + Depr., Dep., Amort./Cur. Mat. L/T/D					(20) 3.5	(34) 3.3
1.4	1.9	1.6						1.3	1.7
.2	.2	.2			.3	.1	.1	.2	.2
.5	.6	.5	Fixed/Worth		.6	.4	.3	.8	.5
1.9	6.6	2.3			-.5	-1.8	1.7	2.6	1.7
.4	.5	.4			.4	.6	.2	.5	.4
1.2	1.6	1.5	Debt/Worth		2.8	2.0	.8	2.0	1.0
3.9	18.3	8.9			-5.8	-5.6	2.9	10.5	6.3
40.9	46.2	45.1			62.2	52.5	44.5	67.6	43.6
(125) 19.0	(138) 26.7	(158) 22.2	% Profit Before Taxes/Tangible Net Worth		(12) 14.0	(10) 25.4	(27) 25.4	(43) 25.8	(60) 20.8
6.9	12.5	6.5			.3	1.1	12.0	11.0	4.7
20.1	19.4	21.6			23.7	29.6	24.4	15.5	19.6
9.2	8.2	8.6	% Profit Before Taxes/Total Assets		8.6	14.1	13.1	9.1	5.9
1.6	2.5	1.6			-1.3	-.1	4.0	1.8	1.1
21.7	23.1	26.4			45.3	45.4	27.4	21.8	18.5
8.8	10.1	10.8	Sales/Net Fixed Assets		10.8	30.4	14.7	12.9	7.7
4.0	4.6	4.6			5.1	12.0	4.7	4.5	4.1
2.3	2.5	2.3			3.3	2.9	2.4	2.8	1.9
1.6	1.6	1.7	Sales/Total Assets		1.7	2.2	1.5	1.8	1.5
1.0	1.0	1.1			1.3	1.9	1.2	1.3	.8
1.2	.9	1.1			.8	.8	.6	1.2	1.4
(127) 2.9	(142) 2.3	(155) 2.3	% Depr., Dep., Amort./Sales		(12) 2.2	(11) 1.3	(27) 2.1	(43) 2.2	(58) 2.7
4.6	4.2	4.7			6.7	3.0	5.2	4.5	4.7
3.2	2.9	2.6			3.7				
(26) 5.4	(34) 5.6	(39) 5.9	% Officers', Directors' Owners' Comp/Sales		(10) 8.8				
11.5	9.2	9.4			13.7				
5493474M	8755231M	7804768M	Net Sales ($)	5764M	32206M	52377M	225790M	785462M	6703169M
5010160M	6984919M	5993680M	Total Assets ($)	4018M	17871M	22168M	170499M	573708M	5205416M

M = $ thousand   MM = $ million
See Pages 9 through 22 for Explanation of Ratios and Data

Current Data Sorted by Assets

Comparative Historical Data

0-500M	500M-2MM	2-10MM	10-50MM	50-100MM	100-250MM	Type of Statement	4/1/05-3/31/06 ALL	4/1/06-3/31/07 ALL
1	8	8	9	5	2	Unqualified	22	32
1	5	14	8			Reviewed	22	21
1	9	9	1			Compiled	13	22
6	6	6	1			Tax Returns	14	10
3	8	12	22	10	11	Other	40	50
	18 (4/1-9/30/09)		141 (10/1/09-3/31/10)					
11	30	49	41	15	13	NUMBER OF STATEMENTS	111	135
%	%	%	%	%	%	**ASSETS**	%	%
12.8	11.0	8.2	15.3	10.5	6.9	Cash & Equivalents	9.0	8.2
38.2	27.9	34.1	26.3	18.4	13.2	Trade Receivables (net)	28.9	29.5
14.7	31.9	26.2	21.5	23.8	15.0	Inventory	26.2	24.1
.2	5.4	2.0	2.3	3.5	5.0	All Other Current	2.5	3.1
66.1	76.2	70.5	65.5	56.3	40.1	Total Current	66.5	65.0
24.6	13.5	20.6	21.7	19.7	29.7	Fixed Assets (net)	22.8	20.5
5.6	6.9	2.4	7.1	20.2	22.9	Intangibles (net)	4.6	8.5
3.8	3.4	6.5	5.6	3.8	7.3	All Other Non-Current	6.1	6.0
100.0	100.0	100.0	100.0	100.0	100.0	Total	100.0	100.0
						LIABILITIES		
24.4	10.2	9.1	4.6	7.8	.6	Notes Payable-Short Term	10.3	9.5
3.5	2.6	3.0	3.3	1.8	4.3	Cur. Mat.-L.T.D.	3.3	3.5
23.0	16.6	15.1	13.7	7.0	4.9	Trade Payables	13.6	12.9
.0	.0	.2	.2	.5	.7	Income Taxes Payable	.2	.1
11.1	16.4	11.7	9.9	7.4	9.9	All Other Current	9.9	11.0
62.0	45.8	39.1	31.7	24.5	20.3	Total Current	37.2	37.0
28.9	14.7	9.8	7.3	14.7	13.1	Long-Term Debt	18.0	15.0
.0	.0	.3	.6	.7	2.0	Deferred Taxes	.3	.5
12.1	11.1	3.4	7.0	4.5	3.8	All Other Non-Current	4.4	3.9
-3.0	28.4	47.5	53.4	55.5	60.8	Net Worth	40.2	43.5
100.0	100.0	100.0	100.0	100.0	100.0	Total Liabilties & Net Worth	100.0	100.0
						INCOME DATA		
100.0	100.0	100.0	100.0	100.0	100.0	Net Sales	100.0	100.0
44.8	42.0	41.2	44.3	47.4	45.5	Gross Profit	43.4	40.6
41.1	37.8	33.9	33.6	41.9	35.7	Operating Expenses	37.3	34.6
3.7	4.2	7.3	10.7	5.5	9.9	Operating Profit	6.2	5.9
.4	1.4	.7	.6	2.7	3.7	All Other Expenses (net)	.9	1.3
3.3	2.8	6.6	10.1	2.8	6.2	Profit Before Taxes	5.3	4.6
						RATIOS		
4.0	2.7	3.8	3.2	2.8	4.4	Current	3.1	3.2
1.8	1.9	1.8	2.4	2.4	1.8		2.0	1.8
.5	1.1	1.2	1.5	1.8	1.4		1.3	1.2
3.5	1.8	2.3	2.2	1.6	1.8	Quick	2.0	1.9
1.5	.9	1.0	1.4	1.0	.9		1.2	1.0
.4	.5	.7	.8	.7	.6		.6	.6
33 10.9	22 16.9	34 10.8	40 9.2	43 8.5	33 11.0	Sales/Receivables	32 11.4	38 9.6
43 8.5	39 9.4	45 8.1	46 7.9	61 6.0	44 8.2		46 8.0	49 7.4
57 6.4	53 6.9	71 5.2	60 6.1	65 5.6	66 5.6		59 6.2	64 5.7
0 UND	21 17.0	44 8.4	38 9.7	76 4.8	50 7.4	Cost of Sales/Inventory	36 10.1	39 9.4
14 27.0	63 5.8	65 5.6	62 5.8	123 3.0	75 4.9		65 5.6	71 5.1
59 6.1	114 3.2	118 3.1	96 3.8	223 1.6	159 2.3		111 3.3	118 3.1
6 61.2	17 21.9	14 26.0	22 17.0	27 13.5	17 22.1	Cost of Sales/Payables	16 23.1	17 20.9
23 15.9	33 10.9	29 12.7	31 11.7	36 10.1	23 16.2		31 11.8	34 10.8
113 3.2	52 7.0	59 6.1	53 6.9	49 7.4	42 8.7		53 6.9	50 7.3
5.7	5.1	4.3	3.3	2.8	2.6	Sales/Working Capital	4.7	4.3
9.9	8.7	9.2	6.1	5.1	5.2		7.9	8.1
-7.9	26.2	23.1	9.4	7.0	15.2		15.5	18.2
	7.3	32.0	68.2	15.3	14.5	EBIT/Interest	19.5	12.5
	(24) 2.7	(42) 11.5	(37) 12.2	(12) 3.5	(11) 5.0		(99) 5.2	(122) 3.6
	1.0	1.9	5.5	1.6	-.8		1.7	1.3
			35.5	16.9		Net Profit + Depr., Dep., Amort./Cur. Mat. L/T/D	11.3	7.2
			(12) 14.5	(11) 4.5			(44) 2.7	(45) 2.2
			2.1	1.7			1.0	1.1
.0	.1	.1	.2	.2	.5	Fixed/Worth	.3	.2
.4	.5	.3	.5	.6	.8		.6	.6
-.8	-2.6	.7	.8	1.4	3.7		1.2	1.6
.7	.7	.4	.3	.7	-.4	Debt/Worth	.6	.6
3.5	2.8	.8	.8	.9	1.2		1.3	1.6
-2.2	-10.4	3.2	2.6	3.0	5.2		3.5	4.3
	64.6	51.9	48.3	39.3	36.1	% Profit Before Taxes/Tangible Net Worth	54.8	41.3
	(22) 13.3	(45) 27.3	(40) 33.5	(12) 18.2	(11) 17.7		(97) 23.7	(119) 19.2
	2.4	6.1	16.1	1.0	-5.1		6.5	4.1
35.0	20.3	26.8	25.5	16.1	12.3	% Profit Before Taxes/Total Assets	21.3	14.7
3.9	5.1	11.2	17.3	4.9	8.5		9.0	8.0
-3.9	-.1	.8	6.5	.4	.2		1.7	1.2
320.7	75.3	46.9	17.6	12.3	6.8	Sales/Net Fixed Assets	27.0	26.1
17.0	27.5	16.3	9.4	6.5	4.1		10.6	11.9
9.3	13.2	5.9	5.7	4.6	2.7		5.7	5.6
4.3	3.9	3.0	2.5	1.8	1.3	Sales/Total Assets	3.3	3.0
2.7	2.7	2.3	1.9	1.3	1.0		2.1	2.0
2.1	1.9	1.8	1.5	.9	.8		1.6	1.4
	.9	.8	1.0	2.1		% Depr., Dep., Amort./Sales	.9	.9
	(21) 1.4	(43) 1.7	(39) 1.6	(14) 3.4			(97) 1.9	(112) 1.8
	2.3	2.7	3.1	6.5			3.2	3.1
	4.3	1.5				% Officers', Directors' Owners' Comp/Sales	2.8	3.9
	(18) 7.9	(21) 3.6					(44) 6.0	(43) 5.4
	12.7	4.8					11.0	10.1
10245M	110306M	559056M	1846019M	1547067M	2185880M	Net Sales ($)	3448390M	5409810M
3174M	38102M	240130M	931033M	1179555M	1982972M	Total Assets ($)	2259295M	4048330M

© RMA 2010

M = $ thousand   MM = $ million
See Pages 9 through 22 for Explanation of Ratios and Data

Comparative Historical Data   Current Data Sorted by Sales

4/1/07-3/31/08 ALL	4/1/08-3/31/09 ALL	4/1/09-3/31/10 ALL	Type of Statement	0-1MM	1-3MM	3-5MM	5-10MM	10-25MM	25MM & OVER
40	34	24	Unqualified			1	5	4	14
22	32	31	Reviewed	1	3	3	8	9	7
21	26	16	Compiled	1	3	3	5	4	
12	27	22	Tax Returns	1	10	4	3	4	
49	72	66	Other	2	3	3	7	10	41
					18 (4/1-9/30/09)		141 (10/1/09-3/31/10)		
144	191	159	NUMBER OF STATEMENTS	5	19	14	28	31	62
%	%	%	ASSETS	%	%	%	%	%	%
11.5	9.3	11.0	Cash & Equivalents		8.5	11.6	7.5	10.6	12.9
26.6	26.2	28.0	Trade Receivables (net)		25.6	30.9	33.7	33.6	22.1
22.7	25.5	24.1	Inventory		26.5	34.3	25.1	26.1	20.1
3.4	3.0	3.0	All Other Current		5.4	2.9	2.3	2.0	3.3
64.3	64.0	66.1	Total Current		66.0	79.6	68.6	72.3	58.4
19.7	21.1	20.5	Fixed Assets (net)		18.3	12.9	23.8	20.3	21.5
10.4	8.9	8.0	Intangibles (net)		11.7	1.8	1.6	2.8	14.3
5.7	5.9	5.3	All Other Non-Current		4.0	5.6	5.9	4.6	5.8
100.0	100.0	100.0	Total		100.0	100.0	100.0	100.0	100.0
			LIABILITIES						
8.2	9.6	8.4	Notes Payable-Short Term		17.7	8.1	9.7	9.2	4.5
2.2	2.6	3.0	Cur. Mat.-L.T.D.		4.0	2.1	2.6	3.3	3.2
13.8	12.7	14.0	Trade Payables		10.1	18.3	14.3	17.0	10.8
.3	.2	.2	Income Taxes Payable		.0	.3	.1	.1	.4
8.6	11.6	11.5	All Other Current		13.4	12.4	13.2	11.3	9.9
33.1	36.6	37.1	Total Current		45.2	41.2	39.9	41.0	28.7
14.1	14.7	12.1	Long-Term Debt		21.4	14.6	11.1	7.3	9.8
.5	.2	.5	Deferred Taxes		.0	.0	.4	.3	.9
4.7	7.5	6.5	All Other Non-Current		4.9	10.6	5.9	3.8	6.1
47.6	41.0	43.7	Net Worth		28.5	33.6	42.6	47.7	54.5
100.0	100.0	100.0	Total Liabilties & Net Worth		100.0	100.0	100.0	100.0	100.0
			INCOME DATA						
100.0	100.0	100.0	Net Sales		100.0	100.0	100.0	100.0	100.0
42.1	41.3	43.3	Gross Profit		44.8	42.5	43.3	39.7	45.3
35.7	34.6	35.9	Operating Expenses		41.0	40.3	35.7	31.1	36.0
6.4	6.7	7.4	Operating Profit		3.8	2.1	7.7	8.6	9.3
1.4	1.3	1.2	All Other Expenses (net)		1.2	1.5	1.0	.6	1.8
5.0	5.4	6.2	Profit Before Taxes		2.6	.6	6.7	8.0	7.5
			RATIOS						
3.5	3.3	3.4	Current		6.0	4.4	3.3	4.1	3.0
2.2	1.9	2.1			1.9	2.4	1.7	2.4	2.1
1.4	1.1	1.3			1.1	1.5	1.3	1.2	1.6
2.0	2.0	2.2	Quick		3.1	2.2	1.7	2.4	2.0
1.1	1.0	1.1			.9	1.5	1.0	1.2	1.1
.7	.5	.7			.4	.5	.8	.7	.7
34 10.7	30 12.2	34 10.6	Sales/Receivables		28 12.8	36 10.2	29 12.5	39 9.4	40 9.2
45 8.1	41 8.9	45 8.1			39 9.3	44 8.3	37 10.0	49 7.4	46 7.9
59 6.1	55 6.7	63 5.8			57 6.4	51 7.2	67 5.5	68 5.4	62 5.8
31 11.8	30 12.1	35 10.4	Cost of Sales/Inventory		14 27.0	21 17.0	32 11.3	35 10.4	43 8.5
65 5.6	64 5.7	70 5.2			86 4.3	93 3.9	59 6.2	72 5.1	73 5.0
121 3.0	121 3.0	117 3.1			123 3.0	152 2.4	113 3.2	94 3.9	123 3.0
18 20.4	17 21.4	18 20.8	Cost of Sales/Payables		0 UND	29 12.7	13 28.0	19 19.6	20 18.2
32 11.5	29 12.6	31 11.9			23 15.9	38 9.6	23 15.6	31 11.7	31 11.8
52 7.0	48 7.6	52 7.0			46 8.0	58 6.3	44 8.2	64 5.7	50 7.3
4.0	4.4	4.0	Sales/Working Capital		4.0	4.5	4.8	4.2	3.3
6.5	7.3	6.7			9.3	6.2	10.6	6.5	5.8
19.5	43.7	18.3			26.1	14.3	30.6	15.4	9.9
15.8	13.3	24.6	EBIT/Interest		5.3	3.9	31.0	36.1	22.6
(126) 4.9	(167) 4.0	(134) 6.3			(16) 2.1	(10) 2.6	(24) 14.1	(28) 7.9	(53) 8.2
2.1	1.4	2.0			-.8	1.7	1.7	2.7	3.2
9.7	10.5	13.7	Net Profit + Depr., Dep., Amort./Cur. Mat. L/T/D						24.5
(51) 4.0	(45) 4.1	(41) 4.5						(27) 4.5	
1.7	1.6	1.5							1.7
.2	.2	.2	Fixed/Worth		.3	.1	.2	.1	.3
.5	.6	.5			1.0	.2	.3	.4	.5
1.5	2.1	1.4			-1.9	-2.6	1.2	.7	1.0
.5	.6	.4	Debt/Worth		.2	.6	.4	.4	.4
1.3	1.7	1.2			4.9	1.4	1.0	.8	.9
4.0	11.4	4.7			-6.2	-10.2	4.2	3.1	2.7
50.6	51.3	50.1	% Profit Before Taxes/Tangible Net Worth		48.8	43.6	89.2	45.3	48.3
(123) 23.5	(157) 22.5	(136) 25.0			(13) 8.0	(10) 4.3	(25) 39.0	(29) 20.1	(56) 24.4
8.0	6.6	7.3			-15.7	2.5	19.7	11.3	11.1
19.0	17.2	23.9	% Profit Before Taxes/Total Assets		16.4	7.5	39.2	26.2	22.9
9.3	8.8	9.8			1.9	2.2	16.1	8.4	10.8
2.4	1.1	1.5			-3.9	.7	2.7	2.0	3.9
32.4	32.6	28.5	Sales/Net Fixed Assets		29.3	75.3	62.0	33.1	13.7
12.6	12.5	12.3			16.1	44.0	17.7	13.1	7.5
6.4	6.0	5.5			7.8	14.2	4.9	4.8	4.9
2.9	3.3	2.9	Sales/Total Assets		3.6	3.4	3.5	2.9	2.1
2.0	2.1	2.1			2.3	2.6	2.8	2.2	1.6
1.3	1.5	1.5			1.6	2.1	2.0	1.8	1.0
.9	.9	1.0	% Depr., Dep., Amort./Sales		1.4	.7	.9	.7	1.1
(115) 1.8	(159) 1.7	(132) 1.9			(15) 2.2	(10) 1.1	(23) 1.9	(27) 1.7	(55) 2.2
3.5	3.4	3.6			4.0	2.3	2.7	3.0	3.7
2.5	1.9	2.6	% Officers', Directors' Owners' Comp/Sales			4.4	3.3	1.0	
(50) 4.3	(53) 4.8	(51) 4.4			(10) 10.9	(12) 4.3	(13) 1.9		
8.2	9.8	9.9			14.7	8.7	4.7		
5123530M	6469088M	6258573M	Net Sales ($)	2638M	35628M	56591M	210726M	510534M	5442456M
3872816M	4742981M	4374966M	Total Assets ($)	994M	17249M	25563M	85170M	242806M	4003184M

© RMA 2010

M = $ thousand   MM = $ million
See Pages 9 through 22 for Explanation of Ratios and Data

Current Data Sorted by Assets   Comparative Historical Data

0-500M	500M-2MM	2-10MM	10-50MM	50-100MM	100-250MM	Type of Statement	4/1/05-3/31/06 ALL	4/1/06-3/31/07 ALL
		1	4	1	3	Unqualified	12	6
	1	3	1	1		Reviewed	9	11
	1					Compiled	2	1
3		2				Tax Returns	1	7
	5	5	3		7	Other	18	11
	4 (4/1-9/30/09)		37 (10/1/09-3/31/10)					
3	7	11	8	2	10	**NUMBER OF STATEMENTS**	42	36
%	%	%	%	%	%	**ASSETS**	%	%
		5.1			4.8	Cash & Equivalents	9.4	10.6
		18.8			16.1	Trade Receivables (net)	24.8	25.1
		32.5			17.9	Inventory	25.4	18.1
		4.2			2.5	All Other Current	3.9	2.6
		60.5			41.3	Total Current	63.5	56.5
		24.6			23.8	Fixed Assets (net)	23.3	28.5
		10.3			33.0	Intangibles (net)	6.9	8.7
		4.5			1.9	All Other Non-Current	6.3	6.3
		100.0			100.0	Total	100.0	100.0
						LIABILITIES		
		6.1			8.3	Notes Payable-Short Term	13.8	10.5
		4.5			2.2	Cur. Mat.-L.T.D.	2.4	5.0
		10.7			6.9	Trade Payables	13.7	11.7
		.8			.0	Income Taxes Payable	.1	.1
		15.3			9.0	All Other Current	10.0	10.5
		37.4			26.5	Total Current	40.1	37.7
		22.1			18.5	Long-Term Debt	11.8	19.4
		.1			1.7	Deferred Taxes	.7	.6
		2.3			2.9	All Other Non-Current	6.8	6.2
		38.0			50.4	Net Worth	40.7	36.1
		100.0			100.0	Total Liabilties & Net Worth	100.0	100.0
						INCOME DATA		
		100.0			100.0	Net Sales	100.0	100.0
		43.4			46.6	Gross Profit	46.0	47.8
		38.7			38.0	Operating Expenses	37.5	42.2
		4.7			8.6	Operating Profit	8.5	5.7
		2.0			2.1	All Other Expenses (net)	1.2	1.2
		2.7			6.5	Profit Before Taxes	7.3	4.4
						RATIOS		
		2.0			2.2		4.0	2.8
		1.5			1.6	Current	1.9	1.6
		1.4			1.3		1.2	1.1
		.8			1.2		1.7	1.5
		.6			.9	Quick	1.1	1.0
		.5			.7		.7	.7
		18 20.1			43 8.4		29 12.5	33 11.2
		29 12.6			47 7.7	Sales/Receivables	40 9.1	43 8.6
		53 6.9			52 7.0		47 7.8	54 6.8
		66 5.5			62 5.9		18 19.9	20 18.1
		106 3.4			104 3.5	Cost of Sales/Inventory	77 4.7	59 6.2
		155 2.3			135 2.7		124 2.9	112 3.3
		19 19.2			24 15.2		20 18.3	24 15.2
		30 12.2			53 6.8	Cost of Sales/Payables	29 12.7	36 10.1
		42 8.6			72 5.1		50 7.2	54 6.7
		6.7			6.1		4.3	5.0
		9.6			7.4	Sales/Working Capital	8.8	11.5
		18.6			13.3		23.9	80.9
		19.5			6.3		16.1	26.6
		(10) 5.9			4.8	EBIT/Interest	(37) 7.6	(34) 3.6
		.3			2.5		2.0	1.6
						Net Profit + Depr., Dep.,	8.7	3.6
						Amort./Cur. Mat. L/T/D	(18) 3.6	(15) 2.0
							2.0	.9
		.5			.9		.3	.4
		1.0			1.2	Fixed/Worth	.5	1.0
		-4.1			2.4		1.1	2.2
		.8			1.2		.4	.7
		1.3			2.4	Debt/Worth	1.3	1.8
		-14.3			9.8		3.9	4.9
						% Profit Before Taxes/Tangible	57.1	68.3
						Net Worth	(39) 29.0	(33) 25.5
							12.0	10.6
		15.9			13.2	% Profit Before Taxes/Total	20.6	17.0
		3.3			7.0	Assets	11.3	8.1
		.4			2.3		4.2	1.9
		19.1			15.7		23.1	17.9
		7.1			5.1	Sales/Net Fixed Assets	11.6	8.2
		6.7			2.8		6.3	3.6
		2.3			1.8		3.4	2.7
		1.9			1.1	Sales/Total Assets	2.3	1.9
		1.6			.8		1.5	1.3
							1.3	1.3
						% Depr., Dep., Amort./Sales	(38) 1.8	(34) 1.8
							2.9	4.2
							3.7	3.0
						% Officers', Directors'	(12) 5.2	(17) 5.3
						Owners' Comp/Sales	9.3	9.9
3144M	26695M	126553M	525842M	141345M	1728077M	Net Sales ($)	1965791M	1044834M
823M	9665M	65705M	233502M	108939M	1387934M	Total Assets ($)	961018M	697398M

M = $ thousand   MM = $ million
See Pages 9 through 22 for Explanation of Ratios and Data

Comparative Historical Data / Current Data Sorted by Sales

			Type of Statement	0-1MM	1-3MM	3-5MM	5-10MM	10-25MM	25MM & OVER
8	9	9	Unqualified					1	8
4	4	6	Reviewed		1				1
2	2	1	Compiled					1	
2	5	5	Tax Returns				1	1	
22	22	20	Other	2	1		1	5	8
4/1/07-3/31/08 ALL	4/1/08-3/31/09 ALL	4/1/09-3/31/10 ALL		0-1MM	4 (4/1-9/30/09) 1-3MM	3-5MM	5-10MM	37 (10/1/09-3/31/10) 10-25MM	25MM & OVER
38	42	41	**NUMBER OF STATEMENTS**	2	4	3	5	10	17
%	%	%	**ASSETS**	%	%	%	%	%	%
12.6	10.6	6.8	Cash & Equivalents					3.9	6.8
24.8	24.2	22.0	Trade Receivables (net)					18.6	21.9
22.5	22.9	27.0	Inventory					29.3	21.6
3.2	2.4	2.7	All Other Current					4.0	2.0
63.1	60.1	58.4	Total Current					55.7	52.4
22.3	22.3	20.1	Fixed Assets (net)					19.2	21.0
12.1	13.0	16.3	Intangibles (net)					18.6	22.2
2.5	4.7	5.3	All Other Non-Current					6.4	4.4
100.0	100.0	100.0	Total					100.0	100.0
			LIABILITIES						
13.2	9.2	10.4	Notes Payable-Short Term					10.2	10.4
3.0	9.4	2.6	Cur. Mat.-L.T.D.					4.2	2.1
8.4	10.8	9.1	Trade Payables					10.5	6.8
.2	.2	.3	Income Taxes Payable					.1	.3
8.9	12.1	10.7	All Other Current					8.5	10.6
33.8	41.8	33.2	Total Current					33.6	30.2
13.7	22.0	13.7	Long-Term Debt					14.8	13.4
.7	.8	.5	Deferred Taxes					.2	1.1
5.2	3.9	2.8	All Other Non-Current					2.9	3.9
46.6	31.4	49.7	Net Worth					48.5	51.4
100.0	100.0	100.0	Total Liabilities & Net Worth					100.0	100.0
			INCOME DATA						
100.0	100.0	100.0	Net Sales					100.0	100.0
44.3	46.0	45.5	Gross Profit					42.8	43.1
36.4	39.2	40.9	Operating Expenses					45.7	34.5
7.9	6.8	4.6	Operating Profit					-2.9	8.5
1.5	2.1	1.4	All Other Expenses (net)					2.1	1.6
6.5	4.7	3.2	Profit Before Taxes					-5.0	7.0
			RATIOS						
2.7	3.2	2.7	Current					2.0	2.7
1.8	1.9	1.7						1.5	1.7
1.3	1.2	1.4						1.3	1.4
1.5	1.4	1.4	Quick					1.0	1.4
1.1	1.1	.8						.6	.9
.7	.7	.6						.5	.7
34 10.9	30 12.2	30 12.3	Sales/Receivables					19 19.4	42 8.7
47 7.8	39 9.4	41 8.9						36 10.1	44 8.3
53 6.9	45 8.1	50 7.2						53 6.9	51 7.2
31 11.9	45 8.1	59 6.2	Cost of Sales/Inventory					52 7.1	60 6.1
76 4.8	81 4.5	98 3.7						102 3.6	74 5.0
121 3.0	151 2.4	142 2.6						155 2.3	136 2.7
14 26.4	16 23.0	16 23.0	Cost of Sales/Payables					20 18.2	16 23.0
27 13.5	31 11.9	30 12.2						38 9.6	25 14.6
48 7.6	48 7.7	58 6.3						64 5.7	68 5.4
3.8	4.5	6.2	Sales/Working Capital					5.4	5.6
8.3	8.4	8.1						8.1	7.9
21.3	24.5	14.3						16.1	13.3
12.2	11.1	11.9	EBIT/Interest						12.3
(37) 3.9	(41) 3.1	(38) 4.8							(16) 5.1
2.0	.8	1.2							3.1
10.9	10.7	4.1	Net Profit + Depr., Dep., Amort./Cur. Mat. L/T/D						
(14) 3.8	(12) 3.8	(14) 2.2							
1.5	.9	1.5							
.2	.2	.2	Fixed/Worth					.4	.2
.7	.7	.6						.5	1.2
1.8	2.5	1.2						NM	1.5
.9	.8	.8	Debt/Worth					.9	1.0
1.4	1.5	1.2						1.3	1.4
4.0	NM	3.3						NM	3.4
55.1	66.7	55.5	% Profit Before Taxes/Tangible Net Worth						64.0
(34) 24.3	(32) 12.2	(37) 24.5						(16)	32.9
10.3	.1	5.9							18.7
16.6	13.3	17.6	% Profit Before Taxes/Total Assets					16.9	19.4
9.9	4.8	7.5						3.6	8.6
3.7	-.9	.8						-7.3	3.7
21.0	19.8	26.0	Sales/Net Fixed Assets					14.6	26.0
10.2	11.7	11.4						8.0	11.4
5.2	5.3	5.2						6.3	3.7
2.8	2.9	2.8	Sales/Total Assets					2.3	2.3
1.9	2.0	1.9						1.6	1.7
1.2	1.2	1.1						1.1	.8
1.2	1.6	.9	% Depr., Dep., Amort./Sales						.8
(34) 1.9	(34) 2.1	(33) 2.5						(15)	2.7
4.3	3.3	3.9							4.1
2.4	1.5		% Officers', Directors' Owners' Comp/Sales						
(12) 5.4	(10) 5.1								
9.0	7.1								
2824284M	3171281M	2551656M	Net Sales ($)	1589M	5798M	13402M	42346M	145567M	2342954M
1789806M	1609088M	1806568M	Total Assets ($)	382M	4068M	4278M	19752M	153586M	1624502M

M = $ thousand   MM = $ million
See Pages 9 through 22 for Explanation of Ratios and Data

Current Data Sorted by Assets							Comparative Historical Data	
						Type of Statement		
		2	5	3	4	Unqualified	8	9
	2	1				Reviewed	7	7
	2	2				Compiled	5	6
	3					Tax Returns	1	2
	2	4	2	3	1	Other	11	10
	7 (4/1-9/30/09)		29 (10/1/09-3/31/10)				**4/1/05-3/31/06 ALL**	**4/1/06-3/31/07 ALL**
0-500M	**500M-2MM**	**2-10MM**	**10-50MM**	**50-100MM**	**100-250MM**			
	9	9	7	6	5	**NUMBER OF STATEMENTS**	32	34
%	%	%	%	%	%	**ASSETS**	%	%
D A T A N O T A V A I L A B L E						Cash & Equivalents	9.0	10.8
						Trade Receivables (net)	22.7	22.7
						Inventory	23.2	21.3
						All Other Current	3.4	3.3
						Total Current	58.3	58.1
						Fixed Assets (net)	27.0	20.1
						Intangibles (net)	8.5	10.5
						All Other Non-Current	6.2	11.3
						Total	100.0	100.0
						LIABILITIES		
						Notes Payable-Short Term	10.7	8.7
						Cur. Mat.-L.T.D.	7.0	3.6
						Trade Payables	17.2	15.7
						Income Taxes Payable	.2	.2
						All Other Current	10.3	8.8
						Total Current	45.6	37.0
						Long-Term Debt	11.5	17.7
						Deferred Taxes	.8	.3
						All Other Non-Current	10.4	11.5
						Net Worth	31.7	33.5
						Total Liabilities & Net Worth	100.0	100.0
						INCOME DATA		
						Net Sales	100.0	100.0
						Gross Profit	42.2	44.7
						Operating Expenses	35.6	37.9
						Operating Profit	6.6	6.8
						All Other Expenses (net)	1.2	1.7
						Profit Before Taxes	5.4	5.2
						RATIOS		
						Current	2.7	2.2
							1.4	1.6
							1.0	1.0
						Quick	1.4	1.4
							.7	.8
							.4	.5
						Sales/Receivables	**24** 15.1	**24** 15.1
							38 9.6	**43** 8.5
							46 7.9	**57** 6.4
						Cost of Sales/Inventory	**26** 13.8	**27** 13.6
							68 5.4	**75** 4.8
							136 2.7	**115** 3.2
						Cost of Sales/Payables	**29** 12.7	**25** 14.8
							41 9.0	**43** 8.4
							71 5.1	**80** 4.5
						Sales/Working Capital	6.6	7.2
							15.0	14.4
							NM	NM
						EBIT/Interest	11.3	10.1
							(29) 3.8	(32) 4.0
							1.5	1.5
						Net Profit + Depr., Dep., Amort./Cur. Mat. L/T/D	14.5	
							(15) 6.3	
							1.8	
						Fixed/Worth	.4	.2
							1.1	.5
							3.8	2.0
						Debt/Worth	.8	.7
							2.6	1.9
							15.6	5.8
						% Profit Before Taxes/Tangible Net Worth	79.5	54.1
							(27) 32.0	(29) 17.6
							11.1	5.2
						% Profit Before Taxes/Total Assets	12.6	12.4
							8.6	6.2
							.5	1.3
						Sales/Net Fixed Assets	25.1	61.2
							11.0	13.8
							4.5	6.1
						Sales/Total Assets	3.4	3.6
							2.3	2.1
							1.4	1.4
						% Depr., Dep., Amort./Sales	1.3	.7
							(29) 2.6	(29) 2.1
							3.9	2.9
						% Officers', Directors' Owners' Comp/Sales	3.5	
							(10) 5.0	
							11.1	
	29339M	**106890M**	**267725M**	**461330M**	**903819M**	Net Sales ($)	**1228250M**	**1503789M**
	8800M	**44085M**	**161482M**	**421137M**	**703699M**	Total Assets ($)	**782312M**	**1122330M**

M = $ thousand MM = $ million

See Pages 9 through 22 for Explanation of Ratios and Data

Comparative Historical Data   **Current Data Sorted by Sales**

Type of Statement	4/1/07-3/31/08 ALL	4/1/08-3/31/09 ALL	4/1/09-3/31/10 ALL		0-1MM	1-3MM	3-5MM	5-10MM	10-25MM	25MM & OVER
Unqualified	9	11	14					1	2	11
Reviewed	5	4	3				1		1	1
Compiled	6	3	4			2	1			1
Tax Returns	2	2	3			3				
Other	15	11	12		1		1	5	2	4
					7 (4/1-9/30/09)			29 (10/1/09-3/31/10)		
NUMBER OF STATEMENTS	37	31	36		1	5	3	6	6	15

	%	%	%	ASSETS	%	%	%	%	%	%
	7.9	7.6	7.8	Cash & Equivalents						11.4
	24.3	20.7	23.2	Trade Receivables (net)						15.5
	25.5	26.6	21.5	Inventory						20.7
	3.1	2.9	3.8	All Other Current						5.0
	60.7	57.8	56.3	Total Current						52.6
	20.4	22.6	21.6	Fixed Assets (net)						22.9
	9.7	9.3	14.0	Intangibles (net)						18.3
	9.3	10.3	8.1	All Other Non-Current						6.2
	100.0	100.0	100.0	Total						100.0

				LIABILITIES						
	7.6	10.7	8.0	Notes Payable-Short Term						2.3
	3.8	4.0	3.7	Cur. Mat.-L.T.D.						3.8
	16.6	15.8	16.3	Trade Payables						10.1
	.1	.3	.4	Income Taxes Payable						.9
	11.3	6.3	9.6	All Other Current						9.0
	39.5	37.0	38.0	Total Current						26.1
	20.5	15.7	14.7	Long-Term Debt						16.0
	.8	.8	.5	Deferred Taxes						1.0
	2.6	3.0	7.9	All Other Non-Current						8.4
	36.6	43.4	38.8	Net Worth						48.5
	100.0	100.0	100.0	Total Liabilities & Net Worth						100.0

				INCOME DATA						
	100.0	100.0	100.0	Net Sales						100.0
	43.8	47.0	44.9	Gross Profit						45.4
	36.5	38.6	38.4	Operating Expenses						36.6
	7.3	8.3	6.5	Operating Profit						8.8
	1.3	1.1	1.3	All Other Expenses (net)						2.7
	6.0	7.2	5.1	Profit Before Taxes						6.1

RATIOS

	4/1/07-3/31/08 ALL	4/1/08-3/31/09 ALL	4/1/09-3/31/10 ALL		25MM & OVER
Current	2.4 / 1.6 / 1.0	3.0 / 1.4 / 1.1	2.7 / 1.4 / 1.1		2.9 / 1.8 / 1.3
Quick	1.1 / .7 / .5	1.3 / .7 / .4	1.3 / .8 / .5		1.3 / .9 / .7
Sales/Receivables	31 11.7 / 44 8.4 / 51 7.1	26 13.8 / 40 9.0 / 49 7.5	30 12.1 / 39 9.5 / 45 8.1		34 10.6 / 39 9.5 / 42 8.7
Cost of Sales/Inventory	32 11.5 / 86 4.2 / 136 2.7	27 13.6 / 97 3.7 / 156 2.3	34 10.8 / 81 4.5 / 126 2.9		60 6.1 / 98 3.7 / 133 2.7
Cost of Sales/Payables	26 14.1 / 46 8.0 / 85 4.3	28 13.2 / 46 7.9 / 84 4.4	25 14.9 / 41 8.9 / 67 5.5		25 14.7 / 48 7.6 / 82 4.4
Sales/Working Capital	4.9 / 9.5 / NM	5.9 / 9.7 / 56.9	4.6 / 12.1 / 67.5		3.1 / 6.6 / 12.1
EBIT/Interest	(35) 9.7 / 3.6 / 1.2	(27) 13.5 / 2.2 / 1.1	(35) 15.9 / 2.5 / 1.0		39.8 / 3.5 / 1.5
Net Profit + Depr., Dep., Amort./Cur. Mat. L/T/D	(13) 38.0 / 3.6 / 1.5	(13) 3.8 / 2.2 / .9	(13) 8.8 / 3.1 / .6		
Fixed/Worth	.2 / .8 / 2.9	.2 / .7 / 1.0	.3 / .7 / 4.0		.5 / .7 / 6.2
Debt/Worth	1.0 / 2.0 / 9.7	.8 / 1.4 / 4.9	.7 / 1.8 / 16.3		.6 / 1.3 / 103.8
% Profit Before Taxes/Tangible Net Worth	(31) 53.0 / 20.1 / 3.5	(27) 50.4 / 17.6 / 3.9	(29) 38.1 / 10.4 / -1.0		(12) 37.8 / 10.8 / .9
% Profit Before Taxes/Total Assets	16.2 / 6.0 / 1.0	17.4 / 7.3 / 1.5	12.9 / 4.0 / .1		14.0 / 4.8 / .4
Sales/Net Fixed Assets	54.7 / 11.3 / 6.2	24.3 / 9.0 / 4.7	34.9 / 12.7 / 5.1		13.8 / 7.9 / 3.7
Sales/Total Assets	3.4 / 2.0 / 1.2	2.4 / 1.9 / 1.4	3.1 / 1.6 / .9		2.0 / 1.4 / .8
% Depr., Dep., Amort./Sales	(30) .8 / 2.1 / 3.6	(25) 1.3 / 2.1 / 3.9	(28) 1.2 / 2.0 / 3.0		(11) 1.7 / 2.0 / 3.0
% Officers', Directors' Owners' Comp/Sales					

	4/1/07-3/31/08 ALL	4/1/08-3/31/09 ALL	4/1/09-3/31/10 ALL		0-1MM	1-3MM	3-5MM	5-10MM	10-25MM	25MM & OVER
Net Sales ($)	2063753M	1795085M	1769103M		881M	11476M	13825M	44897M	94143M	1603881M
Total Assets ($)	1561789M	1246214M	1339203M		613M	9670M	5756M	47002M	38147M	1238015M

© RMA 2010
M = $ thousand MM = $ million
See Pages 9 through 22 for Explanation of Ratios and Data

Current Data Sorted by Assets   Comparative Historical Data

	0-500M	500M-2MM	2-10MM	10-50MM	50-100MM	100-250MM		4/1/05-3/31/06 ALL	4/1/06-3/31/07 ALL
		10 (4/1-9/30/09)		35 (10/1/09-3/31/10)			**Type of Statement**		
			1			1	Unqualified	2	3
		1	1				Reviewed	3	9
	2	2	1				Compiled	7	9
	12	4	1		1		Tax Returns	21	16
	8	7	3	1			Other	15	17
	22	14	7	1	1	1	**NUMBER OF STATEMENTS**	48	54
	%	%	%	%	%	%	**ASSETS**	%	%
	15.8	15.4					Cash & Equivalents	13.1	13.1
	21.3	39.3					Trade Receivables (net)	26.7	24.5
	5.1	12.0		D			Inventory	4.8	7.8
	4.7	4.3		A			All Other Current	4.9	4.8
	47.0	71.0		T			Total Current	49.5	50.2
	35.2	18.8		A			Fixed Assets (net)	32.6	28.1
	6.5	3.2					Intangibles (net)	9.9	13.4
	11.3	7.0		N			All Other Non-Current	8.0	8.3
	100.0	100.0		O			Total	100.0	100.0
				T			**LIABILITIES**		
	15.8	13.7					Notes Payable-Short Term	12.2	7.5
	5.3	2.5		A			Cur. Mat.-L.T.D.	3.9	6.5
	6.1	13.1		V			Trade Payables	8.2	10.8
	.0	.9		A			Income Taxes Payable	.3	.2
	12.5	6.8		I			All Other Current	10.2	7.8
	39.7	37.0		L			Total Current	34.7	32.8
	35.5	15.2		A			Long-Term Debt	25.6	24.2
	.1	.6		B			Deferred Taxes	.7	.8
	2.9	3.0		L			All Other Non-Current	5.2	5.5
	21.8	44.2		E			Net Worth	33.8	36.8
	100.0	100.0					Total Liabilties & Net Worth	100.0	100.0
							INCOME DATA		
	100.0	100.0					Net Sales	100.0	100.0
							Gross Profit		
	92.7	94.7					Operating Expenses	94.3	92.9
	7.3	5.3					Operating Profit	5.7	7.1
	1.2	.5					All Other Expenses (net)	.7	1.4
	6.1	4.8					Profit Before Taxes	5.0	5.7
							RATIOS		
	3.4	7.6						2.7	3.0
	1.6	2.8					Current	1.7	1.6
	.6	1.0						.9	1.3
	2.6	5.4						2.4	2.5
	.9	2.3					Quick	1.1	1.4
	.2	.7						.6	.8
	0 UND	29 12.7						5 70.0	25 14.4
	4 82.9	35 10.5					Sales/Receivables	33 11.2	36 10.2
	39 9.5	43 8.4						40 9.1	42 8.8
							Cost of Sales/Inventory		
							Cost of Sales/Payables		
	8.5	6.5						10.5	7.8
	63.8	10.6					Sales/Working Capital	23.5	16.4
	-37.8	-532.4						-98.7	28.0
	22.8	91.4						12.1	12.6
	(15) 4.8	(13) 7.4					EBIT/Interest	(40) 4.0	(49) 3.5
	2.7	1.4						.5	1.4
									2.7
							Net Profit + Depr., Dep., Amort./Cur. Mat. L/T/D	(11)	1.8
									1.6
	.5	.2						.5	.4
	.9	.4					Fixed/Worth	1.1	1.0
	UND	3.7						NM	5.0
	.5	.3						.7	.8
	3.8	2.3					Debt/Worth	1.7	2.5
	UND	17.5						NM	18.9
	645.0	74.7					% Profit Before Taxes/Tangible	62.3	82.5
	(17) 106.3	(12) 34.4					Net Worth	(36) 23.1	(43) 27.5
	23.6	13.5						1.8	14.3
	55.7	24.9					% Profit Before Taxes/Total	31.8	28.7
	20.6	13.1					Assets	7.2	7.8
	5.6	2.2						-.7	2.1
	69.7	48.3						25.8	31.8
	33.8	17.4					Sales/Net Fixed Assets	14.4	12.3
	5.1	14.0						9.7	6.3
	8.6	5.7						5.0	4.0
	4.4	3.7					Sales/Total Assets	3.9	2.7
	2.2	3.0						2.8	1.3
	.5	1.2						1.2	1.4
	(11) 1.7	(11) 1.7					% Depr., Dep., Amort./Sales	(42) 2.1	(41) 2.5
	2.7	3.4						2.9	3.9
	5.3	5.0					% Officers', Directors'	4.5	5.3
	(16) 12.0	(11) 8.3					Owners' Comp/Sales	(27) 11.6	(30) 7.1
	16.9	9.9						16.7	12.5
	27910M	68028M	77847M		86459M	161195M	Net Sales ($)	1372777M	2107905M
	4983M	15598M	32438M		61894M	155295M	Total Assets ($)	451518M	564854M

© RMA 2010

M = $ thousand   MM = $ million
See Pages 9 through 22 for Explanation of Ratios and Data

Comparative Historical Data

Current Data Sorted by Sales

© RMA 2010

				Type of Statement									
1		2	2	Unqualified		1			1	1	1		
3		3	2	Reviewed						1	1		
6		10	5	Compiled		2	1		1	1	1		
9		15	17	Tax Returns	5	7	3		1	1	1		
14		10	19	Other	6	5			7	1	1	1	
4/1/07- 3/31/08 ALL		4/1/08- 3/31/09 ALL	4/1/09- 3/31/10 ALL		0-1MM	10 (4/1-9/30/09) 1-3MM	3-5MM		35 (10/1/09-3/31/10) 5-10MM	10-25MM		25MM & OVER	
33		40	45	NUMBER OF STATEMENTS	11	15	4		9	4		2	
%		%	%	ASSETS	%	%	%		%	%		%	
11.1		18.2	13.7	Cash & Equivalents	16.6	15.6							
25.9		21.2	27.0	Trade Receivables (net)	10.9	32.7							
9.2		6.3	7.1	Inventory	7.4	7.0							
2.0		2.5	3.9	All Other Current	9.7	2.8							
48.2		48.2	51.6	Total Current	44.6	58.2							
34.1		31.3	29.2	Fixed Assets (net)	43.8	23.5							
3.2		8.5	7.5	Intangibles (net)	9.5	4.4							
14.4		12.1	11.7	All Other Non-Current	2.1	13.9							
100.0		100.0	100.0	Total	100.0	100.0							
				LIABILITIES									
16.3		22.6	12.9	Notes Payable-Short Term	22.0	17.2							
4.6		3.0	4.8	Cur. Mat.-L.T.D.	6.6	4.0							
9.8		8.8	8.7	Trade Payables	2.9	10.6							
.5		.4	.4	Income Taxes Payable	.0	.1							
9.1		9.0	10.4	All Other Current	6.4	10.4							
40.3		43.9	37.3	Total Current	37.9	42.3							
17.5		22.6	27.4	Long-Term Debt	29.2	33.4							
1.3		.8	.4	Deferred Taxes	.0	.4							
1.6		1.9	3.2	All Other Non-Current	.0	4.7							
39.2		30.9	31.7	Net Worth	32.9	19.3							
100.0		100.0	100.0	Total Liabilities & Net Worth	100.0	100.0							
				INCOME DATA									
100.0		100.0	100.0	Net Sales	100.0	100.0							
				Gross Profit									
92.6		94.9	93.7	Operating Expenses	87.9	96.0							
7.4		5.1	6.3	Operating Profit	12.1	4.0							
1.5		1.2	.9	All Other Expenses (net)	2.7	.3							
5.9		3.9	5.5	Profit Before Taxes	9.4	3.8							
				RATIOS									
2.5		2.3	3.4		2.9	8.5							
1.6		1.4	1.5	Current	1.6	1.0							
.7		1.1	.8		.7	.8							
2.0		1.9	2.6		1.7	7.6							
1.3		1.1	1.1	Quick	.9	.9							
.4		.8	.6		.2	.5							
24 15.1	0	UND	1 309.9		0 UND	23 16.1							
35 10.3	32	11.3	35 10.5	Sales/Receivables	2 152.8	35 10.5							
41 9.0	42	8.8	40 9.0		31 11.7	45 8.1							
				Cost of Sales/Inventory									
				Cost of Sales/Payables									
10.7		14.1	8.2		9.0	7.0							
19.8		27.7	31.2	Sales/Working Capital	24.6	999.8							
-14.1		479.2	-56.3		-23.9	-27.4							
		21.9	24.2			45.0							
(31) 11.8 6.1	(36)	3.6	(37) 5.0	EBIT/Interest		(14) 9.4							
1.1		.1	1.7			2.6							
4.8		2.0		Net Profit + Depr., Dep.,									
(10) 2.3	(10)	1.1		Amort./Cur. Mat. L/T/D									
1.8		.5											
.5		.3	.3		.7	.2							
.9		.7	1.0	Fixed/Worth	7.4	1.0							
1.9		4.0	UND		UND	-1.0							
.7		.6	.4		.4	.4							
1.7		1.4	3.7	Debt/Worth	12.3	3.7							
5.0		6.5	UND		UND	-5.1							
74.6		58.8	109.6	% Profit Before Taxes/Tangible		106.3							
(30) 30.1	(35)	24.8	(35) 52.2	Net Worth		(11) 44.9							
7.5		2.7	19.7			19.7							
27.6		28.8	36.1	% Profit Before Taxes/Total	53.9	38.0							
10.5		8.0	12.9	Assets	18.4	17.3							
1.0		-1.1	3.0		1.6	3.4							
23.9		42.0	51.7		56.8	57.8							
12.4		16.1	18.2	Sales/Net Fixed Assets	16.5	27.1							
5.9		7.6	6.5		2.4	14.4							
4.0		6.1	5.5		6.2	5.5							
3.2		3.9	3.6	Sales/Total Assets	1.9	4.1							
1.9		2.2	2.2		1.5	3.4							
1.2		1.3	1.2			.9							
(29) 1.8	(30)	2.0	(31) 1.8	% Depr., Dep., Amort./Sales		(12) 1.6							
3.4		3.3	3.6			2.8							
6.6		6.1	5.0	% Officers', Directors'		3.4							
(22) 12.6	(23)	8.2	(30) 8.6	Owners' Comp/Sales		(11) 6.1							
17.2		14.3	13.5			12.9							
591272M		1452494M	421439M	Net Sales ($)	5254M	27140M	15559M		70738M	55094M		247654M	
377354M		509397M	270208M	Total Assets ($)	2404M	6558M	2367M		20444M	21246M		217189M	

M = $ thousand   MM = $ million
See Pages 9 through 22 for Explanation of Ratios and Data

Current Data Sorted by Assets

Comparative Historical Data

				7	1	Type of Statement		
	7	6 22	19 7			Unqualified	47	32
	6	12	2			Reviewed	50	53
11	16	12	4			Compiled	14	12
4	14	26	16	2		Tax Returns	14	16
	34 (4/1-9/30/09)		160 (10/1/09-3/31/10)			Other	50	36
0-500M	500M-2MM	2-10MM	10-50MM	50-100MM	100-250MM		4/1/05- 3/31/06 ALL	4/1/06- 3/31/07 ALL
15	43	78	48	9	1	NUMBER OF STATEMENTS	175	149
%	%	%	%	%	%	ASSETS	%	%
13.1	8.5	6.9	11.5			Cash & Equivalents	5.3	6.0
27.5	29.3	24.3	25.7			Trade Receivables (net)	28.4	28.0
23.7	31.5	41.0	40.7			Inventory	48.5	48.7
1.1	1.3	1.1	.6			All Other Current	1.9	1.2
65.5	70.6	73.3	78.4			Total Current	84.2	83.9
21.8	20.1	19.7	12.5			Fixed Assets (net)	10.2	9.4
.1	1.8	1.5	2.2			Intangibles (net)	1.3	2.8
12.6	7.5	5.5	6.8			All Other Non-Current	4.3	3.9
100.0	100.0	100.0	100.0			Total	100.0	100.0
						LIABILITIES		
40.5	10.6	16.2	19.1			Notes Payable-Short Term	28.8	27.5
6.5	3.2	2.7	4.4			Cur. Mat.-L.T.D.	2.0	1.9
30.4	18.5	15.8	13.2			Trade Payables	17.2	17.9
.0	.1	.0	.1			Income Taxes Payable	.3	.3
17.8	14.1	8.3	9.9			All Other Current	8.1	6.3
95.2	46.6	43.0	46.8			Total Current	56.4	53.8
18.0	10.4	14.1	6.7			Long-Term Debt	6.2	7.0
.0	.1	.1	.5			Deferred Taxes	.1	.4
8.7	6.4	5.5	2.5			All Other Non-Current	4.5	3.6
-21.9	36.6	37.2	43.6			Net Worth	32.7	35.2
100.0	100.0	100.0	100.0			Total Liabilities & Net Worth	100.0	100.0
						INCOME DATA		
100.0	100.0	100.0	100.0			Net Sales	100.0	100.0
50.7	38.2	31.2	27.5			Gross Profit	26.3	27.0
52.3	38.3	29.3	20.7			Operating Expenses	22.5	22.2
-1.5	-.1	1.8	6.9			Operating Profit	3.8	4.9
.6	.4	1.4	1.3			All Other Expenses (net)	1.6	1.6
-2.2	-.5	.5	5.5			Profit Before Taxes	2.2	3.3
						RATIOS		
4.2	3.2	3.0	2.7				2.1	2.1
.7	1.6	1.8	1.6			Current	1.4	1.4
.4	1.0	1.2	1.3				1.2	1.2
2.6	2.2	1.5	1.4				1.0	1.0
.5	.9	.7	.8			Quick	.6 (148)	.6
.1	.4	.4	.4				.3	.4
0 UND	31 11.9	31 11.9	33 11.0				33 11.0	29 12.6
28 13.1	46 8.0	50 7.3	53 6.8			Sales/Receivables	56 6.5	55 6.6
51 7.2	61 5.9	70 5.2	83 4.4				79 4.6	78 4.7
0 UND	22 16.9	51 7.1	50 7.3				74 4.9	74 4.9
30 12.2	65 5.6	89 4.1	111 3.3			Cost of Sales/Inventory	157 2.3	137 2.7
162 2.3	178 2.1	225 1.6	241 1.5				242 1.5	227 1.6
0 UND	16 23.2	14 25.3	13 28.9				13 28.4	12 29.6
27 13.5	27 13.4	38 9.6	29 12.6			Cost of Sales/Payables	33 11.1	39 9.3
63 5.8	53 6.9	69 5.3	48 7.5				78 4.7	81 4.5
6.5	4.0	3.0	2.4				3.6	3.8
-35.6	8.2	5.5	7.1			Sales/Working Capital	6.6	7.2
-10.4	853.3	15.9	14.2				13.2	13.8
6.2	4.4	7.4	12.5				4.5	4.5
(10) .6	(32) 1.4	(75) 1.8	(43) 2.1			EBIT/Interest	(162) 2.3	(138) 2.0
-8.6	-4.7	-.2	1.4				1.1	1.3
		4.4					7.0	10.4
		(13) 1.2				Net Profit + Depr., Dep., Amort./Cur. Mat. L/T/D	(31) 2.4	(28) 3.4
		.0					.2	1.5
.0	.1	.1	.1				.1	.1
.4	.5	.3	.2			Fixed/Worth	.2	.2
-.5	1.5	1.2	.6				.6	.5
1.0	.6	.7	.5				1.1	1.2
31.9	1.3	1.7	1.5			Debt/Worth	2.4	2.3
-2.1	6.6	7.5	4.7				4.8	4.7
	27.4	28.0	34.3				23.5	31.3
	(38) 4.5	(71) 9.1	(44) 11.7			% Profit Before Taxes/Tangible Net Worth	(163) 9.9	(137) 11.4
	-25.4	-.4	3.3				2.3	3.1
29.6	6.6	9.4	12.4				6.8	7.9
3.6	2.0	1.6	3.4			% Profit Before Taxes/Total Assets	3.0	3.2
-28.5	-9.2	-3.7	1.2				.4	.7
UND	49.7	61.3	76.3				84.0	122.7
105.2	17.4	18.5	22.0			Sales/Net Fixed Assets	33.3	34.4
8.7	7.0	6.8	9.4				12.8	12.3
11.5	3.0	2.4	2.5				2.6	2.4
4.7	2.4	1.7	1.7			Sales/Total Assets	1.5	1.6
2.0	1.7	1.1	.8				1.2	1.2
	.5	.4	.4				.3	.3
	(38) 1.6	(70) 1.2	(40) 1.0			% Depr., Dep., Amort./Sales	(154) .7	(130) .8
	2.9	3.4	1.7				1.4	1.3
	3.3	1.2	.7				1.0	1.3
	(28) 4.4	(43) 3.1	(15) 1.2			% Officers', Directors' Owners' Comp/Sales	(90) 2.9	(79) 2.3
	5.8	4.3	2.9				5.7	5.5
14257M	117255M	751276M	1793259M	843493M	202296M	Net Sales ($)	6134520M	5486358M
3146M	51713M	375398M	1012489M	593459M	138293M	Total Assets ($)	4329697M	3659601M

M = $ thousand   MM = $ million
See Pages 9 through 22 for Explanation of Ratios and Data

Comparative Historical Data

Current Data Sorted by Sales

			Type of Statement						
25	28	33	Unqualified		7	1	2	6	24
46	36	36	Reviewed		6	9	9	9	5
14	15	20	Compiled		5	7	3	5	
17	25	43	Tax Returns	7	18	7	7	2	2
32	68	62	Other	6	7	8	17	15	9
4/1/07-3/31/08	4/1/08-3/31/09	4/1/09-3/31/10			34 (4/1-9/30/09)		160 (10/1/09-3/31/10)		
ALL	ALL	ALL		0-1MM	1-3MM	3-5MM	5-10MM	10-25MM	25MM & OVE
134	172	194	NUMBER OF STATEMENTS	13	37	29	38	37	40
%	%	%	ASSETS	%	%	%	%	%	%
5.8	7.2	8.8	Cash & Equivalents	12.4	9.2	6.2	6.2	12.5	8.3
27.7	23.9	25.6	Trade Receivables (net)	21.7	25.1	24.2	27.6	22.8	28.9
47.1	43.0	37.9	Inventory	28.1	39.4	31.2	36.1	44.5	40.3
1.8	1.5	1.0	All Other Current	.8	1.4	.2	1.3	1.0	.8
82.4	75.6	73.3	Total Current	62.9	75.1	61.7	71.2	80.8	78.5
10.2	14.2	18.0	Fixed Assets (net)	24.3	17.7	29.8	18.6	11.6	13.1
1.9	2.5	1.9	Intangibles (net)	.5	1.6	1.0	1.7	1.0	4.1
5.6	7.7	6.8	All Other Non-Current	12.3	5.6	7.5	8.4	6.6	4.3
100.0	100.0	100.0	Total	100.0	100.0	100.0	100.0	100.0	100.0
			LIABILITIES						
25.7	23.9	18.1	Notes Payable-Short Term	31.9	20.0	10.0	14.8	17.4	21.5
2.4	3.1	3.4	Cur. Mat.-L.T.D.	7.4	2.3	4.5	3.8	2.3	3.1
18.7	14.2	16.6	Trade Payables	14.7	19.7	19.8	17.6	12.2	14.9
.5	.5	.1	Income Taxes Payable	.0	.0	.0	.2	.1	.4
7.8	14.0	11.0	All Other Current	21.3	10.1	10.2	7.0	13.5	10.7
55.1	55.6	49.2	Total Current	75.2	52.2	44.5	43.3	45.5	50.6
5.8	10.4	11.4	Long-Term Debt	20.6	10.1	19.6	13.3	6.1	6.9
.3	.3	.2	Deferred Taxes	.0	.0	.1	.5	.1	.5
5.2	3.7	5.0	All Other Non-Current	4.6	7.6	5.9	8.0	1.3	2.8
33.6	30.0	34.1	Net Worth	-.4	30.1	29.9	34.9	47.0	39.3
100.0	100.0	100.0	Total Liabilities & Net Worth	100.0	100.0	100.0	100.0	100.0	100.0
			INCOME DATA						
100.0	100.0	100.0	Net Sales	100.0	100.0	100.0	100.0	100.0	100.0
27.4	33.2	33.2	Gross Profit	50.3	41.8	35.8	30.0	29.1	24.7
23.6	29.2	30.5	Operating Expenses	55.2	40.6	36.3	28.3	22.2	18.8
3.8	3.9	2.7	Operating Profit	-4.8	1.2	-.5	1.7	6.8	5.9
1.2	1.6	1.2	All Other Expenses (net)	.5	.9	1.6	.9	1.3	1.7
2.6	2.4	1.5	Profit Before Taxes	-5.3	.3	-2.0	.9	5.5	4.2
			RATIOS						
2.0	2.3	2.9		3.7	3.7	2.8	2.4	5.5	2.0
1.4	1.5	1.6	Current	.8	1.8	1.3	1.7	1.8	1.5
1.2	1.1	1.1		.5	1.2	.8	1.2	1.2	1.3
1.0	1.0	1.5		2.0	2.3	1.0	1.2	3.2	1.0
.6	.5	.7	Quick	.5	.9	.7	.7	.8	.7
.3	.4	.4		.2	.3	.4	.6	.3	.4

							Sales/Receivables											
24	15.0	18	20.5	30	12.2			0	UND	31	11.8	32	11.5	33	11.1	26	14.2	26	13.8

						Sales/Receivables										
24	15.0	18	20.5	30	12.2	0 UND	31	11.8	32	11.5	33	11.1	26	14.2	26	13.8
48	7.6	40	9.1	48	7.5	37 10.0	50	7.3	45	8.1	51	7.2	53	6.9	41	9.0
82	4.5	62	5.9	70	5.2	72 5.1	61	6.0	71	5.2	78	4.7	83	4.4	72	5.1
58	6.3	51	7.1	35	10.3	0 UND	22	16.5	28	13.0	53	6.9	70	5.2	35	10.4
116	3.1	114	3.2	92	4.0	36 10.0	109	3.4	68	5.4	89	4.1	116	3.1	75	4.9
225	1.6	236	1.5	212	1.7	201 1.8	488	.7	206	1.8	200	1.8	320	1.1	145	2.5

						Cost of Sales/Inventory			

Hist						Cost of Sales/Payables										
11	34.2	9	40.8	14	25.6	0 UND	11	31.9	21	17.3	22	16.7	8	44.9	20	18.5
40	9.2	25	14.5	31	11.8	33 11.2	27	13.5	45	8.1	41	8.9	24	15.0	30	12.3
81	4.5	58	6.3	61	6.0	68 5.4	60	6.0	111	3.3	67	5.4	49	7.5	45	8.2
3.8	3.9	3.5				Sales/Working Capital	3.0	2.4	4.0	4.0	1.9	5.2
7.9	8.1	6.8					-35.6	4.8	12.0	6.2	4.3	8.9
17.2	37.1	27.9					-4.2	34.0	-15.4	19.2	14.2	14.3

					EBIT/Interest							
	4.9		5.4		7.7		4.4		3.3		6.5	15.3	13.6
(123)	1.9	(157)	2.2	(170)	2.0	(30)	1.5	(25)	.6	(35)	2.3	(34) 3.2	(38) 2.9
	1.1		.9		-.2		-3.5		-1.2		-.4	1.2	1.5

	14.1		7.7		5.9	Net Profit + Depr., Dep.,							
(20)	3.6	(31)	2.3	(30)	1.3	Amort./Cur. Mat. L/T/D							
	.8		.6		.1								

	.1		.1		.1	Fixed/Worth	.0	.0	.3	.1	.0	.1
	.2		.2		.3		.4	.2	1.2	.6	.2	.2
	.5		.8		1.1		16.4	1.4	4.0	1.1	.5	.7
	1.2		.8		.7	Debt/Worth	1.2	.5	.8	.8	.3	1.0
	2.3		1.9		1.7		2.5	1.1	2.5	1.7	1.2	2.0
	4.6		3.8		6.8		-3.4	4.8	9.9	7.5	3.8	3.8

	28.7		31.5		32.7	% Profit Before Taxes/Tangible		22.3		12.7		32.7	38.4	36.1
(128)	8.7	(158)	8.4	(171)	8.8	Net Worth	(31)	5.3	(24) 1.8	(35) 10.1	(35) 10.9	(37) 16.7
	1.1		.4		-.4			-5.6		-19.3		-.4	3.0	4.3

	8.1		10.7		11.5	% Profit Before Taxes/Total	21.5	9.3	3.7	8.4	18.9	13.3
	2.5		3.0		2.5	Assets	-4.9	1.1	-.6	2.9	3.6	4.5
	.3		-.1		-3.1		-20.5	-8.5	-6.3	-3.7	3.0	1.3

	133.7		98.5		74.0	Sales/Net Fixed Assets	UND	120.7	25.6	63.7	71.9	108.8
	40.8		31.3		21.0		17.1	26.8	9.5	20.9	22.5	39.6
	14.6		10.7		7.4		3.5	7.4	3.8	5.6	10.6	9.8

	2.6		3.0		2.8	Sales/Total Assets	4.8	2.9	2.9	2.6	2.3	3.1
	1.8		1.9		1.8		2.0	1.8	1.7	1.8	1.7	2.2
	1.2		1.2		1.2		1.1	.8	1.2	1.3	.9	1.5

	.2		.3		.5	% Depr., Dep., Amort./Sales		.5		.8		.5	.4	.3
(111)	.7	(141)	1.0	(165)	1.2		(29)	1.5	(28) 1.5	(35) 1.2	(30) 1.2	(36) .7
	1.2		1.8		2.8			2.8		4.5		2.9	2.2	1.7

	1.1		1.7		1.4	% Officers', Directors'		3.8		3.1		1.4	1.2	.3
(69)	2.7	(82)	3.4	(97)	3.5	Owners' Comp/Sales	(24)	5.8	(17) 3.7	(22) 3.5	(13) 2.1	(15) .9
	6.4		6.3		5.6			8.2		4.5		5.0	3.0	1.2

5586316M	4749716M	3721836M	Net Sales ($)	6497M	71017M	113480M	270806M	637536M	2622500M
2894524M	2658158M	2174498M	Total Assets ($)	5292M	54117M	84669M	175472M	512297M	1342651M

M = $ thousand   MM = $ million
See Pages 9 through 22 for Explanation of Ratios and Data

Current Data Sorted by Assets   **Comparative Historical Data**

	0-500M	500M-2MM	2-10MM	10-50MM	50-100MM	100-250MM	Type of Statement	4/1/05-3/31/06 ALL	4/1/06-3/31/07 ALL
	1	2	6	3			Unqualified	5	3
			1				Reviewed	6	9
			1				Compiled	5	2
		2	4	1			Tax Returns		2
		5 (4/1-9/30/09)		16 (10/1/09-3/31/10)			Other	6	7
	0-500M	500M-2MM	2-10MM	10-50MM	50-100MM	100-250MM	NUMBER OF STATEMENTS	22	23
	1	4	12	4					
	%	%	%	%	%	%	**ASSETS**	%	%
			12.9				Cash & Equivalents	9.4	11.1
			32.3				Trade Receivables (net)	39.6	34.3
			32.0		DATA	DATA	Inventory	27.4	24.7
			3.7		NOT	NOT	All Other Current	.2	1.7
			80.9		AVAILABLE	AVAILABLE	Total Current	76.6	71.7
			10.8				Fixed Assets (net)	15.7	16.1
			.5				Intangibles (net)	3.0	7.3
			7.9				All Other Non-Current	4.7	4.9
			100.0				Total	100.0	100.0
							LIABILITIES		
			16.8				Notes Payable-Short Term	18.7	12.7
			3.4				Cur. Mat.-L.T.D.	2.5	2.5
			18.2				Trade Payables	19.2	18.4
			.2				Income Taxes Payable	.1	.2
			11.3				All Other Current	9.3	7.0
			50.0				Total Current	49.6	40.9
			6.8				Long-Term Debt	8.7	10.4
			.0				Deferred Taxes	.0	.0
			3.5				All Other Non-Current	3.8	3.0
			39.7				Net Worth	37.9	45.7
			100.0				Total Liabilties & Net Worth	100.0	100.0
							INCOME DATA		
			100.0				Net Sales	100.0	100.0
			34.1				Gross Profit	32.1	41.6
			29.2				Operating Expenses	25.9	32.9
			4.9				Operating Profit	6.2	8.7
			-.4				All Other Expenses (net)	1.0	.7
			5.3				Profit Before Taxes	5.2	7.9
							RATIOS		
			2.8					2.7	3.5
			1.9				Current	1.6	2.2
			1.2					1.1	1.2
			1.6					1.5	2.0
			1.0				Quick	1.0	1.0
			.4					.6	.8
		35	10.4					32 11.3	24 15.2
		56	6.5				Sales/Receivables	53 6.9	47 7.8
		71	5.1					70 5.2	72 5.1
		23	15.9					19 19.6	18 20.2
		82	4.5				Cost of Sales/Inventory	39 9.5	57 6.4
		137	2.7					64 5.7	86 4.3
		27	13.7					19 19.3	12 30.7
		33	11.2				Cost of Sales/Payables	23 15.6	48 7.6
		66	5.5					48 7.7	56 6.6
			3.4					5.2	5.1
			6.4				Sales/Working Capital	11.2	7.7
			17.5					NM	32.0
			15.0					26.0	19.6
		(11)	3.6				EBIT/Interest	(19) 5.8	(22) 8.4
			1.2					2.1	3.8
							Net Profit + Depr., Dep., Amort./Cur. Mat. L/T/D		
			.1					.1	.1
			.1				Fixed/Worth	.2	.4
			.6					1.1	.9
			.8					.8	.4
			1.3				Debt/Worth	1.4	1.6
			4.5					6.2	6.4
			50.8					96.6	87.1
			15.0				% Profit Before Taxes/Tangible Net Worth	(19) 23.9	(19) 33.9
			3.1					9.9	14.8
			19.6					20.7	32.7
			6.5				% Profit Before Taxes/Total Assets	9.4	17.8
			.5					5.6	7.6
			108.1					58.4	45.3
			30.3				Sales/Net Fixed Assets	28.3	23.0
			9.4					14.8	17.7
			2.7					3.8	3.4
			2.2				Sales/Total Assets	2.8	2.3
			1.6					2.2	1.9
			.2					.4	.5
		(11)	.9				% Depr., Dep., Amort./Sales	(21) .8	(21) .6
			1.4					2.0	2.4
			.9					2.2	2.4
		(10)	3.2				% Officers', Directors' Owners' Comp/Sales	(11) 5.7	(11) 4.1
			5.4					9.4	7.1
	384M	7855M	117953M	207018M			Net Sales ($)	349246M	376280M
	76M	3667M	55794M	88318M			Total Assets ($)	121618M	161476M

Comparative Historical Data

Current Data Sorted by Sales

				Type of Statement						
3		3	3	Unqualified			1	3	1 2	2
11		11	6	Reviewed						
4		5	4	Compiled				1		
1		2	1	Tax Returns	1	2			1	
3		5	7	Other				3	1	1
4/1/07-3/31/08		4/1/08-3/31/09	4/1/09-3/31/10			2 5 (4/1-9/30/09)		16 (10/1/09-3/31/10)		
ALL		ALL	ALL		0-1MM	1-3MM	3-5MM	5-10MM	10-25MM	25MM & OVER
22		26	21	NUMBER OF STATEMENTS	1	4		7	5	3
%		%	%	ASSETS	%	%	%	%	%	%
14.8		9.3	14.5	Cash & Equivalents						
33.8		30.3	33.1	Trade Receivables (net)						
30.0		32.3	29.9	Inventory						
1.0		2.4	4.2	All Other Current						
79.6		74.2	81.8	Total Current						
11.7		14.2	9.9	Fixed Assets (net)						
4.0		3.4	1.7	Intangibles (net)						
4.6		8.1	6.6	All Other Non-Current						
100.0		100.0	100.0	Total						
				LIABILITIES						
19.0		17.0	16.8	Notes Payable-Short Term						
1.4		4.8	3.0	Cur. Mat.-L.T.D.						
16.6		18.2	16.9	Trade Payables						
.0		.0	.1	Income Taxes Payable						
9.2		9.7	9.6	All Other Current						
46.2		49.8	46.3	Total Current						
4.9		12.8	6.6	Long-Term Debt						
.3		.3	.0	Deferred Taxes						
30.3		6.5	8.8	All Other Non-Current						
18.2		30.6	38.3	Net Worth						
100.0		100.0	100.0	Total Liabilties & Net Worth						
				INCOME DATA						
100.0		100.0	100.0	Net Sales						
35.6		38.0	37.7	Gross Profit						
31.9		34.8	31.8	Operating Expenses						
3.6		3.2	5.8	Operating Profit						
.5		1.2	.2	All Other Expenses (net)						
3.1		2.0	5.7	Profit Before Taxes						
				RATIOS						
3.1		2.7	3.4							
2.0		1.7	1.9	Current						
1.1		1.1	1.2							
1.9		1.3	2.1							
.9		.7	1.0	Quick						
.8		.4	.5							
26 14.0	28	12.9	33 11.0							
50 7.2	38	9.6	57 6.4	Sales/Receivables						
71 5.1	57	6.4	70 5.2							
28 13.0	27	13.5	25 14.8							
57 6.4	57	6.4	66 5.5	Cost of Sales/Inventory						
124 2.9	123	3.0	133 2.7							
16 22.3	27	13.7	21 17.7							
30 12.1	37	9.7	31 11.7	Cost of Sales/Payables						
44 8.3	55	6.7	68 5.4							
5.4		5.0	3.1							
8.4		8.5	6.0	Sales/Working Capital						
23.7		34.0	19.4							
9.5		12.5	18.2							
(21) 2.7		2.2	(18) 4.5	EBIT/Interest						
.3		.7	1.3							
				Net Profit + Depr., Dep., Amort./Cur. Mat. L/T/D						
.1		.1	.1							
.2		.3	.2	Fixed/Worth						
.5		.8	.6							
.5		.9	.8							
1.6		2.6	1.7	Debt/Worth						
3.8		6.6	4.1							
94.2		77.0	53.6	% Profit Before Taxes/Tangible Net Worth						
(20) 17.6	(22)	16.9	(19) 13.2							
-3.3		3.2	5.8							
34.0		20.9	24.4	% Profit Before Taxes/Total Assets						
8.6		4.3	7.3							
-2.2		.1	2.1							
76.2		102.3	120.9	Sales/Net Fixed Assets						
34.2		23.8	35.6							
14.6		13.7	15.2							
3.8		3.7	3.3	Sales/Total Assets						
2.7		2.8	2.3							
1.9		1.9	1.6							
.4		.4	.2	% Depr., Dep., Amort./Sales						
(19) .6	(24)	.8	(17) .9							
1.2		2.2	1.5							
2.3		2.3	1.1	% Officers', Directors' Owners' Comp/Sales						
(12) 4.7	(14)	3.3	(12) 4.2							
8.1		5.4	6.9							
450803M		604524M	333210M	Net Sales ($)	384M	7855M	4955M	53020M	79311M	187685M
208636M		302129M	147855M	Total Assets ($)	76M	3667M	3454M	27615M	42392M	70651M

M = $ thousand   MM = $ million
See Pages 9 through 22 for Explanation of Ratios and Data

Current Data Sorted by Assets   **Comparative Historical Data**

0-500M	500M-2MM	2-10MM	10-50MM	50-100MM	100-250MM		4/1/05-3/31/06 ALL	4/1/06-3/31/07 ALL
						Type of Statement		
	1	6	18	4	5	Unqualified	39	45
1	2	15	11	1	1	Reviewed	17	31
1	6	6	1			Compiled	15	24
11	7	5				Tax Returns	15	20
·6	14	23	30	12	9	Other	60	63
	33 (4/1-9/30/09)		163 (10/1/09-3/31/10)					
19	30	55	60	17	15	**NUMBER OF STATEMENTS**	146	183
%	%	%	%	%	%	**ASSETS**	%	%
12.8	9.5	5.8	7.8	9.2	6.8	Cash & Equivalents	6.6	5.6
8.9	23.4	23.9	24.1	25.3	14.9	Trade Receivables (net)	26.5	25.1
38.3	36.5	37.3	32.5	25.2	19.1	Inventory	36.9	39.6
1.6	1.4	1.6	4.2	6.4	7.7	All Other Current	2.6	2.9
61.5	70.8	68.6	68.6	66.2	48.5	Total Current	72.6	73.1
19.9	18.3	16.2	15.3	15.5	14.3	Fixed Assets (net)	16.8	14.9
5.0	5.0	8.4	10.4	13.0	33.8	Intangibles (net)	5.7	5.7
14.0	6.0	6.7	5.7	5.3	3.4	All Other Non-Current	4.9	6.3
100.0	100.0	100.0	100.0	100.0	100.0	Total	100.0	100.0
						LIABILITIES		
27.6	25.9	14.5	13.5	5.0	4.1	Notes Payable-Short Term	14.4	17.6
4.7	1.1	3.5	2.7	1.8	1.8	Cur. Mat.-L.T.D.	2.2	2.4
4.9	11.4	14.5	13.5	9.5	9.4	Trade Payables	12.4	13.4
.1	.0	.3	.2	.1	.3	Income Taxes Payable	.3	.3
8.7	13.3	9.7	8.6	17.3	8.1	All Other Current	11.1	9.4
46.1	51.7	42.5	38.5	33.8	23.7	Total Current	40.4	43.1
33.7	16.3	13.8	17.2	14.5	26.9	Long-Term Debt	12.4	10.3
.0	.1	.4	.3	.3	1.8	Deferred Taxes	.4	.3
9.8	20.5	4.2	6.9	10.9	7.6	All Other Non-Current	4.9	7.2
10.4	11.5	39.1	37.1	40.5	40.0	Net Worth	41.8	39.1
100.0	100.0	100.0	100.0	100.0	100.0	Total Liabilities & Net Worth	100.0	100.0
						INCOME DATA		
100.0	100.0	100.0	100.0	100.0	100.0	Net Sales	100.0	100.0
52.1	42.8	34.8	35.9	35.3	33.3	Gross Profit	36.5	35.1
43.4	42.4	30.4	31.5	32.4	29.1	Operating Expenses	31.0	30.1
8.7	.5	4.4	4.4	2.9	4.2	Operating Profit	5.4	5.0
1.7	2.1	1.7	2.2	3.9	8.6	All Other Expenses (net)	1.2	1.4
7.0	-1.7	2.7	2.2	-1.1	-4.4	Profit Before Taxes	4.2	3.7
						RATIOS		
5.2	2.4	3.2	3.8	3.2	3.5	Current	3.8	2.9
1.3	1.5	1.6	1.8	2.2	1.9		2.0	1.9
.7	1.3	1.0	1.2	1.4	1.5		1.3	1.3
3.0	1.2	1.4	1.5	1.7	1.2	Quick	1.7	1.4
.3	.6	.7	.8	1.1	.9		.8	.8
.1	.2	.4	.6	.8	.6		.5	.4
0 UND	18 20.0	22 16.7	31 12.0	41 8.9	36 10.2	Sales/Receivables	30 12.1	26 14.0
2 202.3	36 10.2	40 9.0	51 7.2	51 7.2	54 6.8		45 8.1	41 8.9
18 20.5	49 7.5	53 6.9	76 4.8	76 4.8	59 6.2		67 5.5	62 5.9
20 18.1	50 7.3	64 5.7	83 4.4	65 5.6	53 6.8	Cost of Sales/Inventory	62 5.9	71 5.2
70 5.2	123 3.0	90 4.1	109 3.3	91 4.0	103 3.5		91 4.0	97 3.7
169 2.2	263 1.4	138 2.6	144 2.5	104 3.5	115 3.2		157 2.3	148 2.5
0 UND	13 27.4	12 30.9	23 15.9	15 24.4	21 17.5	Cost of Sales/Payables	16 22.3	18 20.8
1 323.0	35 10.5	26 14.0	35 10.4	22 16.8	30 12.1		26 14.3	29 12.5
16 23.5	52 7.1	39 9.3	51 7.1	46 8.0	46 8.0		49 7.5	45 8.1
6.8	4.6	4.5	3.0	3.2	2.4	Sales/Working Capital	3.5	4.0
31.5	6.9	8.6	5.7	4.0	6.7		6.2	6.9
-14.3	26.2	119.3	16.0	9.8	10.6		15.7	14.6
28.4	13.7	10.6	7.8	7.1	3.1	EBIT/Interest	11.7	8.5
(16) 6.3	(26) 1.5	(52) 3.7	(54) 2.3	(15) .6	(13) 1.5		(135) 4.4	(168) 3.1
.7	-1.5	-.7	.5	-1.2	-1.3		1.3	1.0
			2.9			Net Profit + Depr., Dep., Amort./Cur. Mat. L/T/D	10.8	7.3
			(18) 1.2				(42) 3.6	(46) 2.4
			.0				1.5	1.0
.1	.1	.1	.1	.2	.3	Fixed/Worth	.2	.1
.3	.4	.4	.4	.4	1.0		.4	.4
-2.6	-1.3	2.7	3.5	NM	-.1		1.1	1.1
.9	.6	.5	.5	.7	1.0	Debt/Worth	.6	.7
2.8	3.8	1.6	2.3	1.3	1.9		1.4	1.8
-3.8	-6.8	6.6	10.9	NM	-1.9		3.7	4.9
537.5	45.9	38.0	22.2	19.0		% Profit Before Taxes/Tangible Net Worth	40.4	40.2
(13) 94.8	(19) 26.5	(45) 17.1	(47) 9.8	(13) -1.3			(130) 18.2	(161) 14.2
12.5	.8	.5	-1.5	-14.7			3.6	2.4
59.6	10.9	14.5	9.0	9.0	5.6	% Profit Before Taxes/Total Assets	16.2	16.8
15.9	6.3	7.6	3.3	-2.2	1.6		6.2	6.6
-1.0	-12.4	-5.4	-1.7	-7.8	-13.7		1.2	.3
133.1	78.5	50.9	46.6	25.5	17.0	Sales/Net Fixed Assets	34.5	52.3
36.7	21.3	19.8	12.1	11.2	10.9		17.5	21.0
13.1	7.1	9.2	7.0	6.8	6.5		8.3	8.8
5.1	2.6	2.9	2.0	1.8	1.6	Sales/Total Assets	2.9	2.9
4.4	1.7	2.0	1.4	1.5	1.1		2.0	2.1
2.5	1.1	1.5	1.2	1.3	.7		1.5	1.5
.8	.6	.7	1.1	2.4		% Depr., Dep., Amort./Sales	.8	.7
(11) 1.8	(19) 1.6	(42) 1.5	(49) 2.5	(10) 2.6			(121) 1.5	(150) 1.4
3.7	3.5	2.8	3.4	4.3			2.7	2.2
	2.6	1.9				% Officers', Directors' Owners' Comp/Sales	1.4	2.6
	(10) 4.7	(17) 4.4					(40) 3.6	(43) 4.2
	8.5	6.2					6.7	7.1
18642M	69887M	572800M	2266038M	1727351M	3101257M	Net Sales ($)	5818616M	5878327M
4686M	34268M	264512M	1412380M	1153398M	2589205M	Total Assets ($)	3347662M	3512663M

Comparative Historical Data | Current Data Sorted by Sales

	4/1/07-3/31/08 ALL	4/1/08-3/31/09 ALL	4/1/09-3/31/10 ALL	Type of Statement	0-1MM	1-3MM	3-5MM	5-10MM	10-25MM	25MM & OVER
	41	39	34	Unqualified			1	2	8	23
	34	29	31	Reviewed	1	2	2	7	13	6
	17	16	14	Compiled		5	3	4		2
	14	22	23	Tax Returns	9	8	2	4	4	
	61	90	94	Other	8	12	2	12	17	43
					33 (4/1-9/30/09)			163 (10/1/09-3/31/10)		
	167	196	196	**NUMBER OF STATEMENTS**	18	27	10	29	38	74
	%	%	%	**ASSETS**	%	%	%	%	%	%
	6.8	7.6	8.0	Cash & Equivalents	11.5	10.1	10.2	6.3	6.3	7.7
	24.1	21.7	21.9	Trade Receivables (net)	9.0	18.0	21.6	23.9	26.5	23.3
	39.2	40.0	33.4	Inventory	38.3	36.3	38.6	32.9	35.0	29.7
	3.0	3.1	3.2	All Other Current	2.0	.9	1.3	1.4	2.8	5.6
	73.1	72.5	66.5	Total Current	60.9	65.2	71.7	64.6	70.6	66.4
	13.3	13.9	16.4	Fixed Assets (net)	22.5	17.5	13.7	20.9	13.2	14.7
	6.7	7.8	10.5	Intangibles (net)	4.5	7.5	8.3	9.0	10.8	13.8
	6.9	5.8	6.6	All Other Non-Current	12.5	9.8	6.4	5.6	5.4	5.1
	100.0	100.0	100.0	Total	100.0	100.0	100.0	100.0	100.0	100.0
				LIABILITIES						
	19.3	17.7	15.6	Notes Payable-Short Term	38.5	19.3	27.0	11.0	13.3	10.1
	2.9	2.9	2.7	Cur. Mat.-L.T.D.	2.6	2.6	1.6	5.4	2.5	2.0
	13.5	13.8	12.0	Trade Payables	4.4	10.4	8.0	9.3	19.1	12.3
	.6	.5	.2	Income Taxes Payable	.1	.1	.1	.6	.2	.2
	10.9	10.4	10.3	All Other Current	9.9	10.3	8.8	12.3	8.2	11.0
	47.1	45.4	40.8	Total Current	55.5	42.7	45.4	38.7	43.3	35.5
	13.1	13.0	18.2	Long-Term Debt	40.7	16.0	15.8	17.7	15.1	15.6
	.3	.3	.4	Deferred Taxes	.0	.0	.1	.6	.4	.6
	7.5	9.4	8.9	All Other Non-Current	8.5	23.4	3.8	4.2	5.7	7.9
	32.0	32.0	31.7	Net Worth	-4.6	17.8	34.8	38.7	35.4	40.4
	100.0	100.0	100.0	Total Liabilities & Net Worth	100.0	100.0	100.0	100.0	100.0	100.0
				INCOME DATA						
	100.0	100.0	100.0	Net Sales	100.0	100.0	100.0	100.0	100.0	100.0
	36.5	35.5	38.0	Gross Profit	50.4	47.0	36.4	36.0	35.1	34.1
	30.5	32.6	33.9	Operating Expenses	47.9	42.0	34.7	28.6	31.6	30.6
	6.0	2.9	4.1	Operating Profit	2.4	5.0	1.6	7.4	3.4	3.5
	1.8	1.9	2.6	All Other Expenses (net)	3.7	1.0	3.1	1.6	1.8	3.8
	4.2	1.0	1.4	Profit Before Taxes	-1.2	4.0	-1.4	5.8	1.6	-.3
				RATIOS						
	3.0	3.3	3.3	Current	3.6	4.0	3.5	3.1	3.5	3.2
	1.7	1.7	1.7		1.4	1.7	1.4	1.6	1.6	2.0
	1.1	1.2	1.2		.6	1.2	1.2	1.0	1.1	1.3
	1.4	1.4	1.5	Quick	3.0	2.0	2.3	1.8	1.5	1.4
	.6	.7	.8		.2	.7	.5	.7	.8	1.0
	.4	.4	.4		.1	.3	.3	.4	.4	.6
24	15.0	22 16.4	24 15.4	Sales/Receivables	0 UND	6 60.9	23 15.6	27 13.7	24 15.5	38 9.7
41	8.9	37 9.9	41 9.0		3 116.1	26 14.0	33 11.1	45 8.1	40 9.1	50 7.3
62	5.9	56 6.5	58 6.3		26 13.9	45 8.0	55 6.6	55 6.7	75 4.8	65 5.7
73	5.0	75 4.8	65 5.6	Cost of Sales/Inventory	28 12.9	49 7.4	63 5.8	42 8.7	69 5.3	71 5.1
110	3.3	112 3.3	98 3.7		181 2.0	92 4.0	154 2.4	99 3.7	93 3.9	95 3.8
167	2.2	161 2.3	146 2.5		309 1.2	169 2.2	243 1.5	154 2.4	140 2.6	125 2.9
13	27.3	16 23.0	14 26.4	Cost of Sales/Payables	0 UND	4 95.0	9 38.8	11 33.8	23 16.1	20 18.0
28	13.2	30 12.1	29 12.5		10 37.2	31 11.8	19 19.4	17 21.4	33 11.0	32 11.4
52	7.1	50 7.2	45 8.1		32 11.6	52 7.1	35 10.6	35 10.5	63 5.8	48 7.6
	4.0	3.8	3.7	Sales/Working Capital	4.5	4.5	4.7	4.2	3.7	3.3
	8.1	7.0	6.4		21.8	6.4	9.1	7.3	7.3	5.9
	23.3	17.7	21.6		-8.2	68.0	20.3	NM	24.2	12.0
	8.9	6.5	9.6	EBIT/Interest	13.5	16.3		13.4	11.4	6.4
(149)	3.0	(179) 1.9	(176) 2.3		(15) .4	(24) 2.8	(26) 6.4	(36) 2.8	(66) 1.6	
	1.1	.0	-.2		-3.0	.6		1.2	-.5	-.1
	11.8	5.9	3.9	Net Profit + Depr., Dep., Amort./Cur. Mat. L/T/D						4.4
(46)	2.1	(38) 1.7	(38) 1.7						(25) 1.2	
	.4	.4	.0							.2
	.1	.1	.1	Fixed/Worth	.1	.1	.2	.2	.1	.2
	.3	.4	.4		1.0	.5	.5	.5	.2	.4
	1.6	1.7	NM		-1.7	-1.4	NM	NM	2.9	NM
	.7	.7	.6	Debt/Worth	.9	.5	.3	.5	.5	.7
	2.3	1.9	1.9		8.1	2.8	4.0	1.5	2.2	1.8
	10.6	11.8	-63.2		-3.1	-10.1	NM	NM	7.1	NM
	46.6	36.7	33.3	% Profit Before Taxes/Tangible Net Worth	113.8	89.7		43.4	32.1	19.8
(134)	18.9	(157) 13.0	(146) 12.7		(10) 71.2	(18) 30.5		(22) 23.4	(32) 12.7	(56) 6.5
	4.3	-3.7	-2.9		-30.3	8.1		10.0	-1.0	-5.4
	15.7	10.8	11.4	% Profit Before Taxes/Total Assets	40.1	15.9	7.6	20.7	11.3	6.9
	6.6	3.2	3.6		-.3	9.8	1.0	9.6	3.9	2.0
	.7	-2.4	-3.0		-22.2	-.6	-7.9	.8	-2.7	-3.7
	55.7	48.5	49.3	Sales/Net Fixed Assets	93.9	67.9	36.2	22.6	74.2	26.8
	22.3	21.8	15.8		18.5	31.4	17.3	12.9	26.9	11.1
	10.0	8.9	7.4		7.3	9.3	8.8	5.9	12.4	7.1
	2.8	2.6	2.5	Sales/Total Assets	4.4	3.5	2.3	2.6	2.7	1.9
	2.0	1.8	1.7		1.9	2.2	1.6	1.8	1.9	1.5
	1.4	1.4	1.3		1.0	1.5	1.2	1.2	1.3	1.2
	.7	.8	1.0	% Depr., Dep., Amort./Sales	1.2	.7		.7	.7	1.5
(132)	1.5	(150) 1.5	(138) 2.1		(10) 1.6	(17) 1.9		(24) 1.8	(26) 1.9	(53) 2.5
	2.6	2.7	3.4		4.5	3.5		3.4	2.7	3.6
	3.1	1.9	2.3	% Officers', Directors', Owners' Comp/Sales		3.2				
(41)	5.6	(48) 4.5	(42) 4.5			(12) 4.6				
	10.8	8.0	7.7			6.5				
	5142252M	6999057M	7755975M	Net Sales ($)	11023M	55304M	40558M	210564M	640554M	6797972M
	3262106M	4317975M	5458449M	Total Assets ($)	6915M	28646M	26120M	138647M	365221M	4892900M

Current Data Sorted by Assets · **Comparative Historical Data**

Type of Statement

	0-500M	500M-2MM	2-10MM	10-50MM	50-100MM	100-250MM	Type of Statement	4/1/05-3/31/06 ALL	4/1/06-3/31/07 ALL
			2	7	3	2	Unqualified	12	19
			9	2			Reviewed	5	9
		1	2				Compiled	4	3
		4	1				Tax Returns	2	2
	2	2	7	5	2	2	Other	24	15
0-500M	500M-2MM	7 (4/1-9/30/09)		46 (10/1/09-3/31/10)					
2	7	21	14	5	4	NUMBER OF STATEMENTS	47	48

Main Data

0-500M	500M-2MM	2-10MM	10-50MM	50-100MM	100-250MM		4/1/05-3/31/06 ALL	4/1/06-3/31/07 ALL
%	%	%	%	%	%	**ASSETS**	%	%
		13.4	9.1			Cash & Equivalents	6.0	5.2
		27.5	30.0			Trade Receivables (net)	31.1	32.4
		29.0	28.8			Inventory	33.6	34.8
		5.7	3.0			All Other Current	3.1	1.9
		75.6	71.0			Total Current	73.8	74.4
		13.0	10.9			Fixed Assets (net)	13.5	12.0
		4.8	7.6			Intangibles (net)	4.8	8.8
		6.5	10.5			All Other Non-Current	8.0	4.9
		100.0	100.0			Total	100.0	100.0
						LIABILITIES		
		9.6	16.5			Notes Payable-Short Term	19.5	26.5
		1.8	2.5			Cur. Mat.-L.T.D.	2.5	5.0
		18.5	11.5			Trade Payables	14.8	17.4
		.0	1.0			Income Taxes Payable	.2	.1
		11.0	9.6			All Other Current	9.8	9.4
		40.9	41.1			Total Current	46.8	58.5
		6.7	3.1			Long-Term Debt	8.9	11.3
		.0	1.0			Deferred Taxes	.3	.4
		5.7	6.3			All Other Non-Current	5.4	5.8
		46.8	48.6			Net Worth	38.5	24.1
		100.0	100.0			Total Liabilities & Net Worth	100.0	100.0
						INCOME DATA		
		100.0	100.0			Net Sales	100.0	100.0
		39.4	36.6			Gross Profit	37.9	36.5
		34.7	28.6			Operating Expenses	34.1	34.1
		4.7	8.0			Operating Profit	3.8	2.3
		.0	2.1			All Other Expenses (net)	1.7	2.2
		4.7	6.0			Profit Before Taxes	2.1	.1
						RATIOS		
		5.4	2.3			Current	2.5	2.1
		2.2	1.8				1.7	1.5
		1.5	1.2				1.2	1.0
		2.4	1.8			Quick	1.3	1.2
		1.1	.9				.8	.7
		.5	.6				.6	.4
		25 14.8	46 7.9			Sales/Receivables	41 8.9	39 9.3
		49 7.4	65 5.6				63 5.8	65 5.6
		56 6.5	78 4.7				88 4.1	86 4.2
		39 9.3	65 5.6			Cost of Sales/Inventory	73 5.0	59 6.2
		77 4.8	106 3.4				114 3.2	120 3.0
		150 2.4	126 2.9				161 2.3	151 2.4
		20 17.8	15 23.6			Cost of Sales/Payables	19 18.9	23 16.0
		38 9.5	28 13.0				36 10.1	46 8.0
		61 6.0	54 6.8				81 4.5	82 4.4
		3.1	5.2			Sales/Working Capital	3.8	4.7
		6.0	7.9				7.0	9.2
		9.1	16.3				15.8	-159.1
		22.4	96.4			EBIT/Interest	9.4	7.4
		(18) 8.9	(13) 10.6				(45) 2.2	(45) 2.3
		1.0	2.4				.7	.0
						Net Profit + Depr., Dep., Amort./Cur. Mat. L/T/D	14.3	10.1
							(14) 5.8	(11) 1.6
							.4	.9
		.0	.0			Fixed/Worth	.1	.2
		.2	.2				.2	.5
		.9	.6				1.4	-5.9
		.2	.6			Debt/Worth	.6	1.0
		.8	.9				1.6	3.5
		17.6	3.3				5.1	-22.9
		59.3	75.6			% Profit Before Taxes/Tangible Net Worth	30.1	48.4
		(19) 37.5	(13) 52.5				(41) 11.8	(33) 21.3
		-6.5	8.1				-8.5	7.4
		28.5	25.1			% Profit Before Taxes/Total Assets	10.8	10.8
		12.1	10.5				4.0	4.1
		-4.9	4.7				-5.0	-6.8
		133.5	111.8			Sales/Net Fixed Assets	61.6	44.8
		26.8	27.9				22.8	17.7
		10.9	7.3				7.0	9.4
		2.8	2.4			Sales/Total Assets	2.3	2.2
		2.1	1.6				1.8	1.8
		1.6	1.2				1.4	1.3
		.7	.3			% Depr., Dep., Amort./Sales	.6	.8
		(14) 1.8	(13) 1.1				(41) 1.9	(44) 1.7
		3.4	2.1				3.1	3.2
						% Officers', Directors' Owners' Comp/Sales	.7	.7
							(12) 2.1	(14) 1.6
							4.0	4.5
860M	27514M	317216M	601591M	517299M	1072736M	Net Sales ($)	2039038M	2228183M
365M	7873M	132049M	326331M	413823M	718817M	Total Assets ($)	1173102M	1220601M

M = $ thousand   MM = $ million
See Pages 9 through 22 for Explanation of Ratios and Data

Comparative Historical Data | Current Data Sorted by Sales

4/1/07-3/31/08 ALL	4/1/08-3/31/09 ALL	4/1/09-3/31/10 ALL	Type of Statement	0-1MM	1-3MM	3-5MM	5-10MM	10-25MM	25MM & OVER
15	15	14	Unqualified					3	11
8	10	11	Reviewed				4	7	
2	3	3	Compiled			2	2		
4	1	5	Tax Returns		1	2	1		
18	27	20	Other	3				7	9
				7 (4/1-9/30/09)			46 (10/1/09-3/31/10)		
47	56	53	NUMBER OF STATEMENTS	3	1	5	6	17	21
%	%	%	**ASSETS**	%	%	%	%	%	%
12.2	10.1	10.1	Cash & Equivalents					10.8	8.7
27.0	27.0	26.1	Trade Receivables (net)					28.6	29.4
33.5	32.8	28.5	Inventory					28.0	25.6
2.9	2.9	3.7	All Other Current					7.1	2.7
75.6	72.8	68.4	Total Current					74.5	66.4
13.3	12.8	15.1	Fixed Assets (net)					14.0	12.0
7.6	7.5	8.0	Intangibles (net)					5.2	15.1
3.5	6.9	8.6	All Other Non-Current					6.3	6.5
100.0	100.0	100.0	Total					100.0	100.0
			LIABILITIES						
16.0	15.5	12.5	Notes Payable-Short Term					15.1	8.5
6.2	1.5	1.9	Cur. Mat.-L.T.D.					2.1	1.7
14.4	16.1	14.7	Trade Payables					17.7	12.1
.1	.1	.3	Income Taxes Payable					.0	.8
11.0	19.5	10.5	All Other Current					12.6	8.3
47.8	52.7	39.9	Total Current					47.6	31.4
10.1	9.8	9.7	Long-Term Debt					4.8	13.0
.8	.5	.4	Deferred Taxes					.1	.9
6.7	8.0	6.3	All Other Non-Current					6.6	7.8
34.7	29.0	43.9	Net Worth					40.9	46.9
100.0	100.0	100.0	Total Liabilties & Net Worth					100.0	100.0
			INCOME DATA						
100.0	100.0	100.0	Net Sales					100.0	100.0
36.4	34.7	38.7	Gross Profit					38.7	34.5
32.1	35.0	33.3	Operating Expenses					33.6	29.1
4.3	-.3	5.3	Operating Profit					5.1	5.5
1.5	1.2	2.0	All Other Expenses (net)					.9	3.9
2.8	-1.5	3.4	Profit Before Taxes					4.2	1.6
			RATIOS						
3.1	2.7	3.2	Current					2.2	3.5
2.0	1.5	1.9						1.9	2.2
1.2	1.2	1.2						1.2	1.3
1.7	1.2	1.9	Quick					1.5	2.1
.9	.7	.9						.8	1.1
.5	.5	.6						.6	.6
28 12.8	31 11.9	28 13.2	Sales/Receivables					37 9.8	33 11.0
49 7.4	51 7.2	51 7.1						51 7.1	64 5.7
79 4.6	73 5.0	66 5.5						63 5.8	90 4.1
58 6.3	61 6.0	51 7.2	Cost of Sales/Inventory					46 8.0	59 6.2
102 3.6	100 3.7	92 4.0						91 4.0	94 3.9
122 3.0	133 2.7	124 2.9						126 2.9	116 3.2
13 27.7	17 21.1	15 24.1	Cost of Sales/Payables					23 15.8	17 21.2
38 9.7	38 9.7	33 10.9						41 9.0	33 10.9
66 5.5	63 5.8	58 6.3						63 5.8	58 6.3
3.8	4.2	4.1	Sales/Working Capital					5.4	4.1
6.0	9.2	6.8						6.2	7.2
18.1	23.0	16.5						12.8	10.6
9.3	8.7	18.3	EBIT/Interest					22.3	21.4
(40) 3.9	(51) 2.4	(48) 6.8						(16) 6.8	(20) 8.9
.3	1.0	1.3						.6	1.8
9.3	7.7	13.9	Net Profit + Depr., Dep.,						
(11) 2.4	(15) 3.3	(15) 4.5	Amort./Cur. Mat. L/T/D						
1.8	1.8	2.4							
.1	.1	.1	Fixed/Worth					.1	.1
.4	.4	.3						.3	.3
UND	1.3	1.1						5.3	1.2
.5	.8	.6	Debt/Worth					.5	.7
2.7	2.4	1.5						1.4	2.1
UND	19.3	8.7						28.4	7.2
56.0	46.1	75.0	% Profit Before Taxes/Tangible					54.0	81.3
(37) 17.5	(44) 11.0	(47) 37.5	Net Worth					(15) 28.7	(19) 52.5
-2.9	.1	2.8						-3.7	5.9
16.9	11.5	24.2	% Profit Before Taxes/Total					24.2	24.2
7.3	2.8	11.2	Assets					9.3	13.2
-2.9	-4.7	.5						-3.0	3.6
57.9	85.3	69.5	Sales/Net Fixed Assets					100.7	77.9
18.6	25.2	25.8						15.5	34.4
9.4	6.8	7.8						9.1	9.4
2.7	2.6	2.7	Sales/Total Assets					2.8	2.7
2.0	2.0	1.9						2.1	1.8
1.5	1.4	1.3						1.6	1.2
.9	.6	.7	% Depr., Dep., Amort./Sales					.8	.4
(35) 1.8	(46) 1.4	(38) 1.6						(12) 2.1	(16) 1.1
3.3	2.8	3.3						3.6	3.1
2.4	2.1	1.5	% Officers', Directors'						
(10) 4.1	(11) 2.8	(19) 3.3	Owners' Comp/Sales						
7.8	5.2	4.9							
1923559M	2248261M	2537216M	Net Sales ($)	1602M	1576M	19818M	46409M	280468M	2187343M
1116828M	1358878M	1599258M	Total Assets ($)	937M	938M	8114M	31858M	139829M	1417582M

M = $ thousand   MM = $ million
See Pages 9 through 22 for Explanation of Ratios and Data

MANUFACTURING—Sign Manufacturing NAICS 339950

	Current Data Sorted by Assets						Comparative Historical Data	
Type of Statement								
Unqualified			4	12	3	1	22	29
Reviewed		5	23	14			53	55
Compiled	5	8	17	1			43	39
Tax Returns	17	12	1	1		2	34	27
Other	13	19	31	21		1	84	75
		30 (4/1-9/30/09)		181 (10/1/09-3/31/10)			4/1/05-3/31/06 ALL	4/1/06-3/31/07 ALL
	0-500M	500M-2MM	2-10MM	10-50MM	50-100MM	100-250MM		
NUMBER OF STATEMENTS	35	44	76	49	3	4	236	225
	%	%	%	%	%	%	%	%
ASSETS								
Cash & Equivalents	9.3	9.4	11.7	7.9			6.7	7.9
Trade Receivables (net)	30.9	32.8	32.5	26.2			34.3	35.6
Inventory	14.2	14.4	18.7	19.6			18.7	19.9
All Other Current	3.0	3.0	3.5	4.7			3.3	3.0
Total Current	57.4	59.7	66.4	58.4			63.0	66.3
Fixed Assets (net)	28.8	26.4	24.3	24.4			25.7	22.9
Intangibles (net)	7.0	2.8	3.3	9.6			5.2	4.6
All Other Non-Current	6.8	11.1	6.0	7.6			6.2	6.2
Total	100.0	100.0	100.0	100.0			100.0	100.0
LIABILITIES								
Notes Payable-Short Term	31.8	10.2	8.4	7.4			13.9	13.2
Cur. Mat.-L.T.D.	8.7	4.3	3.0	4.3			5.1	5.8
Trade Payables	17.6	12.7	12.2	13.9			16.1	18.1
Income Taxes Payable	.0	.0	.5	.1			.3	.3
All Other Current	12.5	15.2	11.0	10.6			14.6	14.2
Total Current	70.7	42.5	35.1	36.3			50.1	51.6
Long-Term Debt	34.8	20.4	12.8	18.1			18.9	18.5
Deferred Taxes	.0	.0	1.0	.3			.4	.4
All Other Non-Current	13.2	4.4	6.6	7.6			7.3	4.4
Net Worth	-18.7	32.7	44.4	37.7			23.3	25.2
Total Liabilties & Net Worth	100.0	100.0	100.0	100.0			100.0	100.0
INCOME DATA								
Net Sales	100.0	100.0	100.0	100.0			100.0	100.0
Gross Profit	58.4	46.3	34.1	31.1			37.5	36.9
Operating Expenses	55.5	46.0	32.0	26.5			33.9	33.1
Operating Profit	3.0	.4	2.1	4.5			3.6	3.7
All Other Expenses (net)	1.4	.5	.6	2.3			1.1	1.0
Profit Before Taxes	1.5	-.2	1.6	2.3			2.5	2.7
RATIOS								
Current	1.5	2.7	3.1	2.4			2.0	2.1
	1.1	1.4	1.9	1.7			1.4	1.5
	.6	.9	1.4	1.2			1.0	1.1
Quick	1.3	2.1	2.1	1.6			1.3	1.5
	.8	.9	1.3	1.0			.9	.9
	.4	.6	.8	.7			.6	.6
Sales/Receivables	9 39.1	27 13.3	30 12.2	35 10.5			35 10.3	35 10.3
	29 12.7	39 9.3	47 7.7	55 6.7			50 7.3	49 7.4
	60 6.1	51 7.1	63 5.8	72 5.1			65 5.6	63 5.8
Cost of Sales/Inventory	5 75.2	13 28.0	21 17.2	30 12.3			19 19.6	17 21.0
	31 11.6	36 10.2	37 9.9	53 6.9			41 8.9	39 9.3
	63 5.8	54 6.8	60 6.0	92 4.0			68 5.4	65 5.6
Cost of Sales/Payables	0 UND	14 26.2	18 20.0	25 14.7			20 17.9	20 18.1
	34 10.6	26 14.1	25 14.8	38 9.6			34 10.9	33 11.1
	58 6.3	41 9.0	40 9.1	59 6.2			50 7.3	54 6.8
Sales/Working Capital	14.4	7.5	4.4	4.8			6.9	7.1
	56.1	14.6	8.1	8.0			16.2	13.7
	-13.5	-46.5	15.4	21.3			365.9	66.8
EBIT/Interest	5.3	6.1	12.7	6.7			8.0	11.3
	(32) 1.4	(38) 1.9	(66) 3.6	(44) 4.2			(213) 2.9	(213) 3.6
	-2.2	-2.1	-2.8	.9			1.0	1.3
Net Profit + Depr., Dep., Amort./Cur. Mat. L/T/D			4.3	2.9			4.8	4.4
		(19) 2.0	(12) 1.4				(60) 1.7	(52) 2.8
		-1.5	-.9				.5	1.3
Fixed/Worth	1.6	.3	.2	.4			.4	.3
	-1.9	.9	.5	.8			1.1	.8
	-.4	2.7	1.3	2.5			3.9	2.5
Debt/Worth	2.7	.8	.5	.7			1.4	1.1
	-8.4	2.0	1.1	1.9			3.2	2.6
	-3.1	9.2	3.2	9.1			11.2	9.8
% Profit Before Taxes/Tangible Net Worth	160.0	51.1	28.5	32.1			47.7	54.4
	(15) 50.0	(35) 11.8	(70) 12.1	(42) 15.1			(187) 23.5	(183) 24.8
	-1.0	-4.9	-5.4	7.6			5.7	10.1
% Profit Before Taxes/Total Assets	29.5	16.0	15.4	9.7			14.9	15.7
	4.4	2.5	5.4	5.6			5.6	6.8
	-17.3	-6.6	-2.4	.1			.2	1.0
Sales/Net Fixed Assets	30.9	37.9	30.3	22.2			22.7	30.2
	21.2	13.7	11.0	7.8			12.0	14.8
	9.1	6.4	5.8	4.3			6.5	8.0
Sales/Total Assets	5.0	3.6	3.0	2.0			3.3	3.3
	3.3	2.7	2.3	1.6			2.5	2.6
	2.6	2.1	1.7	1.3			1.9	2.0
% Depr., Dep., Amort./Sales	1.6	.9	1.0	1.0			1.1	1.0
	(23) 2.7	(36) 2.9	(66) 1.9	(38) 2.0			(205) 1.9	(200) 1.8
	3.3	3.5	3.3	2.9			3.1	2.8
% Officers', Directors' Owners' Comp/Sales	4.6	2.4	2.1				2.1	2.4
	(20) 6.9	(24) 3.7	(27) 4.2				(92) 5.0	(89) 4.5
	10.8	7.7	7.1				7.5	7.2
Net Sales ($)	36009M	136965M	784393M	1790397M	376016M	1278702M	4215784M	4008176M
Total Assets ($)	9857M	48702M	350390M	1065326M	225240M	796171M	2146975M	1881883M

M = $ thousand   MM = $ million
See Pages 9 through 22 for Explanation of Ratios and Data

Comparative Historical Data / Current Data Sorted by Sales

			Type of Statement	0-1MM	1-3MM	3-5MM	5-10MM	10-25MM	25MM & OVER
23	23	20	Unqualified				1	6	13
42	51	42	Reviewed		3	3	9	21	6
36	36	31	Compiled	3	6	7	9	5	1
28	40	33	Tax Returns	9	18	2	1		3
75	92	85	Other	9	14	10	16	21	15
4/1/07-3/31/08 ALL	4/1/08-3/31/09 ALL	4/1/09-3/31/10 ALL		30 (4/1-9/30/09)			181 (10/1/09-3/31/10)		
204	242	211	NUMBER OF STATEMENTS	21	41	22	36	53	38
%	%	%	ASSETS	%	%	%	%	%	%
8.8	9.5	9.7	Cash & Equivalents	8.0	8.7	11.9	11.6	10.6	7.3
34.8	30.7	30.4	Trade Receivables (net)	27.2	27.3	32.9	35.3	32.4	26.7
17.2	18.9	17.2	Inventory	17.6	9.0	21.8	13.9	21.9	19.4
3.6	4.0	3.6	All Other Current	1.0	3.4	1.5	6.4	2.2	5.6
64.3	63.1	60.8	Total Current	53.8	48.4	68.1	67.4	67.2	58.9
25.1	25.7	25.8	Fixed Assets (net)	28.8	35.1	22.4	23.1	21.3	24.7
4.8	4.7	5.6	Intangibles (net)	9.2	5.4	2.8	3.6	5.6	7.5
5.7	6.5	7.8	All Other Non-Current	8.3	11.1	6.8	6.0	5.8	8.9
100.0	100.0	100.0	Total	100.0	100.0	100.0	100.0	100.0	100.0
			LIABILITIES						
13.5	13.1	12.4	Notes Payable-Short Term	29.5	19.3	9.6	7.9	9.2	5.9
6.6	5.7	4.5	Cur. Mat.-L.T.D.	8.9	5.9	3.9	3.0	3.1	4.4
15.8	15.1	13.5	Trade Payables	16.0	12.5	14.1	11.7	13.3	14.7
.6	.2	.2	Income Taxes Payable	.0	.0	.9	.6	.0	.2
14.8	13.5	12.0	All Other Current	8.7	13.8	15.9	12.6	10.3	11.2
51.4	47.6	42.6	Total Current	63.0	51.5	44.4	35.9	36.0	36.3
21.1	20.5	19.8	Long-Term Debt	40.0	29.2	13.9	11.3	15.4	16.1
.3	.3	.5	Deferred Taxes	.0	.1	.6	1.3	.5	.4
7.8	5.3	7.3	All Other Non-Current	14.3	8.5	1.4	7.0	5.6	8.5
19.4	26.3	29.7	Net Worth	-17.3	10.7	39.6	44.5	42.6	38.7
100.0	100.0	100.0	Total Liabilities & Net Worth	100.0	100.0	100.0	100.0	100.0	100.0
			INCOME DATA						
100.0	100.0	100.0	Net Sales	100.0	100.0	100.0	100.0	100.0	100.0
39.6	38.2	40.2	Gross Profit	60.0	52.4	38.9	34.2	33.0	32.7
35.0	34.8	37.7	Operating Expenses	56.4	51.5	40.2	31.6	29.3	28.4
4.6	3.4	2.5	Operating Profit	3.6	.9	-1.4	2.5	3.7	4.3
1.4	1.0	1.2	All Other Expenses (net)	1.7	1.1	.3	1.5	.8	1.6
3.2	2.4	1.4	Profit Before Taxes	1.9	-.2	-1.7	1.0	2.9	2.7
			RATIOS						
2.1 / 1.4 / 1.0	2.2 / 1.5 / 1.1	2.5 / 1.6 / 1.1	Current	1.5 / 1.0 / .4	1.6 / 1.2 / .7	2.4 / 1.7 / 1.2	3.6 / 1.9 / 1.2	2.7 / 2.0 / 1.4	2.5 / 1.6 / 1.2
1.4 / .9 / .6	1.5 / .9 / .6	1.7 / 1.0 / .6	Quick	1.0 / .8 / .4	1.4 / .7 / .4	2.1 / 1.2 / .6	2.2 / 1.4 / .8	1.8 / 1.3 / .8	1.3 / 1.0 / .8
31 11.8 / 47 7.8 / 61 6.0	26 14.3 / 40 9.2 / 56 6.5	27 13.3 / 42 8.6 / 63 5.8	Sales/Receivables	8 47.1 / 21 17.6 / 62 5.9	21 17.6 / 33 11.0 / 50 7.3	28 13.2 / 38 9.7 / 70 5.2	32 11.4 / 48 7.6 / 86 4.2	36 10.2 / 48 7.6 / 58 6.3	30 12.2 / 53 6.9 / 71 5.1
16 23.5 / 35 10.5 / 58 6.3	15 23.8 / 36 10.2 / 63 5.8	16 22.6 / 39 9.5 / 68 5.4	Cost of Sales/Inventory	0 UND / 63 5.8 / 85 4.3	10 37.6 / 27 13.7 / 46 8.0	21 17.7 / 47 7.8 / 56 6.6	10 34.8 / 32 11.6 / 51 7.2	29 12.7 / 43 8.5 / 71 5.1	30 12.0 / 55 6.6 / 85 4.3
17 21.6 / 31 11.7 / 49 7.5	17 21.3 / 28 13.2 / 45 8.2	18 20.1 / 29 12.6 / 48 7.5	Cost of Sales/Payables	0 UND / 21 17.1 / 65 5.7	11 32.6 / 35 10.4 / 59 6.2	16 22.9 / 24 15.2 / 48 7.6	14 26.0 / 27 13.4 / 40 9.2	20 18.0 / 28 13.2 / 38 9.5	19 19.4 / 47 7.7 / 63 5.8
7.8 / 15.1 / NM	6.9 / 13.9 / 106.6	5.6 / 11.1 / 70.6	Sales/Working Capital	15.9 / -49.1 / -10.6	11.8 / 31.7 / -20.3	4.4 / 9.8 / 43.9	4.5 / 6.6 / 20.4	5.4 / 8.2 / 15.0	4.8 / 7.7 / 20.0
(191) 11.6 / 3.3 / 1.0	(222) 9.6 / 3.1 / .9	(187) 8.5 / 2.9 / -.9	EBIT/Interest	(17) 9.1 / 2.0 / -1.3	(40) 5.4 / 1.2 / -6.6	(17) 3.5 / .0 / -6.7	(29) 11.8 / 1.9 / -2.8	(50) 16.0 / 4.7 / .9	(34) 7.0 / 4.4 / 1.1
(45) 9.4 / 2.1 / 1.4	(52) 6.4 / 2.0 / 1.0	(41) 4.6 / 2.0 / -.6	Net Profit + Depr., Dep., Amort./Cur. Mat. L/T/D					(14) 4.0 / 2.0 / .7	(14) 8.2 / 2.9 / -.1
.3 / 1.0 / 88.5	.3 / .8 / 3.1	.3 / .8 / 5.4	Fixed/Worth	1.9 / -1.2 / -.3	1.0 / 2.4 / -1.8	.3 / .6 / 1.0	.1 / .6 / 1.5	.2 / .5 / 1.3	.4 / .8 / 2.2
1.2 / 3.2 / NM	.9 / 2.4 / 9.5	.8 / 1.9 / 9.8	Debt/Worth	4.2 / -8.4 / -2.4	1.5 / 3.6 / -5.3	.7 / 1.8 / 3.4	.5 / 1.2 / 3.3	.6 / 1.2 / 4.1	.7 / 1.7 / 6.4
(153) 57.6 / 26.0 / 7.1	(197) 50.3 / 21.9 / 5.7	(167) 35.9 / 12.3 / -1.0	% Profit Before Taxes/Tangible Net Worth		(27) 51.1 / 15.7 / -23.3	(19) 22.1 / 10.6 / -14.7	(33) 26.9 / 5.0 / -11.4	(48) 48.3 / 17.6 / 2.8	(32) 27.1 / 11.9 / 5.0
17.1 / 6.4 / .3	15.4 / 6.3 / -.5	13.7 / 4.0 / -4.9	% Profit Before Taxes/Total Assets	27.6 / 5.5 / -16.2	16.0 / 1.9 / -16.8	8.6 / -2.1 / -13.4	10.7 / 2.2 / -6.1	16.7 / 7.2 / .1	9.3 / 5.4 / 1.1
31.6 / 14.6 / 7.2	30.7 / 13.7 / 6.7	27.8 / 11.1 / 5.6	Sales/Net Fixed Assets	36.4 / 18.4 / 7.4	22.9 / 9.4 / 3.9	25.7 / 14.1 / 7.5	47.6 / 11.7 / 6.4	32.7 / 13.0 / 6.6	19.5 / 8.3 / 4.3
3.4 / 2.6 / 1.9	3.5 / 2.6 / 2.0	3.1 / 2.3 / 1.6	Sales/Total Assets	3.7 / 2.8 / 2.2	4.0 / 2.8 / 1.8	3.3 / 2.4 / 1.7	3.1 / 2.3 / 1.7	3.1 / 2.3 / 1.8	2.0 / 1.6 / 1.3
(173) .9 / 1.6 / 3.1	(209) .9 / 2.0 / 3.0	(168) 1.1 / 2.2 / 3.5	% Depr., Dep., Amort./Sales	(13) 1.6 / 2.4 / 3.3	(33) 2.4 / 3.4 / 6.6	(18) .8 / 2.3 / 3.4	(30) .9 / 1.6 / 3.8	(42) 1.0 / 1.7 / 2.5	(32) .9 / 2.0 / 3.4
(84) 3.2 / 4.8 / 8.3	(103) 2.7 / 5.2 / 9.3	(78) 2.6 / 4.4 / 7.9	% Officers', Directors' Owners' Comp/Sales	(12) 5.4 / 8.0 / 11.4	(24) 3.2 / 5.1 / 10.1	(15) 1.8 / 3.0 /	(14) 2.1 / 4.6 /		
4204965M	4548104M	4402482M	Net Sales ($)	12231M	77646M	78028M	255479M	905584M	3073514M
2026325M	2154924M	2495686M	Total Assets ($)	4800M	38803M	40335M	154547M	444969M	1812232M

© RMA 2010

M = $ thousand   MM = $ million
See Pages 9 through 22 for Explanation of Ratios and Data

Current Data Sorted by Assets | Comparative Historical Data

Type of Statement

0-500M	500M-2MM	2-10MM	10-50MM	50-100MM	100-250MM	Type of Statement	4/1/05-3/31/06 ALL	4/1/06-3/31/07 ALL
			6	3	2	Unqualified	15	11
	1	15	3			Reviewed	23	17
	5	8	1			Compiled	16	11
	5					Tax Returns	8	10
1	3	11	10	6	3	Other	24	20
24 (4/1-9/30/09)			59 (10/1/09-3/31/10)					
1	14	34	20	9	5	NUMBER OF STATEMENTS	86	69

Financial Data

0-500M %	500M-2MM %	2-10MM %	10-50MM %	50-100MM %	100-250MM %	Item	4/1/05-3/31/06 ALL %	4/1/06-3/31/07 ALL %
						ASSETS		
	10.5	9.1	11.7			Cash & Equivalents	7.1	9.5
	30.9	24.0	22.8			Trade Receivables (net)	31.6	28.4
	26.0	27.2	18.8			Inventory	28.8	25.4
	4.0	1.9	3.3			All Other Current	1.1	1.4
	71.3	62.2	56.6			Total Current	68.6	64.6
	16.6	27.2	27.1			Fixed Assets (net)	22.2	24.1
	5.8	3.3	12.4			Intangibles (net)	4.1	4.8
	6.3	7.2	3.9			All Other Non-Current	5.1	6.4
	100.0	100.0	100.0			Total	100.0	100.0
						LIABILITIES		
	9.6	10.8	4.6			Notes Payable-Short Term	11.4	8.5
	4.7	4.1	3.7			Cur. Mat.-L.T.D.	4.8	1.8
	14.3	14.1	8.9			Trade Payables	16.5	14.5
	.6	.1	.2			Income Taxes Payable	.4	.3
	4.9	5.2	6.1			All Other Current	8.4	11.9
	34.1	34.3	23.6			Total Current	41.4	36.9
	10.1	15.3	14.6			Long-Term Debt	16.8	15.1
	.3	.7	1.3			Deferred Taxes	.5	.7
	2.1	3.3	6.6			All Other Non-Current	4.2	6.0
	53.3	46.3	53.9			Net Worth	37.2	41.4
	100.0	100.0	100.0			Total Liabilities & Net Worth	100.0	100.0
						INCOME DATA		
	100.0	100.0	100.0			Net Sales	100.0	100.0
	31.6	28.6	29.3			Gross Profit	31.3	34.4
	29.4	25.4	22.5			Operating Expenses	26.0	28.2
	2.2	3.2	6.8			Operating Profit	5.3	6.1
	.5	.3	.9			All Other Expenses (net)	1.5	.9
	1.6	2.9	5.9			Profit Before Taxes	3.8	5.3
						RATIOS		
	4.3	3.3	5.2			Current	2.6	3.4
	2.3	1.6	2.4				1.8	1.9
	1.5	1.3	1.4				1.3	1.3
	2.7	1.9	3.2			Quick	1.7	2.2
	1.3	.8	1.5				1.0	1.0
	.8	.6	.8				.6	.7
	34 10.8	37 9.8	39 9.5			Sales/Receivables	40 9.1	36 10.1
	40 9.1	41 9.0	49 7.5				46 7.9	42 8.7
	43 8.5	52 7.0	58 6.3				57 6.4	53 6.8
	31 11.8	36 10.2	42 8.7			Cost of Sales/Inventory	35 10.5	34 10.9
	48 7.6	70 5.2	69 5.3				59 6.2	60 6.0
	73 5.0	108 3.4	88 4.2				93 3.9	101 3.6
	7 52.3	20 17.8	18 19.7			Cost of Sales/Payables	20 18.5	19 19.7
	23 15.6	34 10.7	28 13.2				32 11.5	28 12.9
	41 9.0	44 8.2	38 9.5				48 7.6	45 8.1
	4.5	3.8	3.4			Sales/Working Capital	5.2	4.4
	7.6	7.3	5.0				7.9	9.0
	17.4	19.8	10.6				18.0	14.2
	8.9	4.3	31.5			EBIT/Interest	11.5	14.5
	(11) 3.9	(27) 2.3	4.6				(80) 5.7	(60) 4.7
	-2.9	-.1	2.0				2.5	1.9
						Net Profit + Depr., Dep., Amort./Cur. Mat. L/T/D	12.2	14.9
							(30) 2.3	(17) 3.5
							.8	1.5
	.1	.4	.4			Fixed/Worth	.2	.2
	.2	.6	.6				.5	.6
	.6	1.0	1.4				1.7	1.6
	.4	.8	.5			Debt/Worth	.7	.5
	1.3	1.3	1.2				2.0	1.5
	2.4	2.7	2.2				11.1	6.5
	46.5	37.9	35.5			% Profit Before Taxes/Tangible Net Worth	55.4	41.6
	(13) 5.3	(33) 7.6	(19) 14.7				(74) 26.2	(61) 20.1
	2.3	.4	4.2				9.7	8.7
	19.1	9.9	13.4			% Profit Before Taxes/Total Assets	14.9	15.2
	4.2	4.1	6.1				8.4	8.9
	-.2	-.4	2.0				3.0	3.1
	79.9	17.5	12.9			Sales/Net Fixed Assets	34.9	32.8
	28.6	7.6	7.2				13.0	9.7
	8.9	4.0	2.8				6.4	4.6
	3.5	2.2	1.9			Sales/Total Assets	3.0	3.0
	2.9	1.8	1.5				2.4	2.3
	2.3	1.5	1.0				1.7	1.5
		.6	.9			% Depr., Dep., Amort./Sales	.7	.8
		(30) 2.1	(17) 2.1				(78) 1.6	(59) 1.5
		3.7	4.4				2.9	3.4
	3.2	1.6				% Officers', Directors' Owners' Comp/Sales	2.8	2.8
	(10) 4.8	(12) 4.5					(33) 5.3	(25) 5.1
	7.8	9.3					7.8	9.7
1679M	48648M	315763M	756698M	796965M	850138M	Net Sales ($)	1723555M	1875748M
378M	17172M	164058M	551214M	591721M	727095M	Total Assets ($)	1119011M	1419161M

M = $ thousand   MM = $ million
See Pages 9 through 22 for Explanation of Ratios and Data

Comparative Historical Data				Current Data Sorted by Sales					
			Type of Statement						
9	14	11	Unqualified					1	10
21	18	19	Reviewed		1	4	4	8	2
14	12	14	Compiled		3	4	4	2	1
7	9	6	Tax Returns		4	1	1		
19	27	33	Other		1	3	6	5	18
					24 (4/1-9/30/09)		59 (10/1/09-3/31/10)		
4/1/07-3/31/08 ALL	4/1/08-3/31/09 ALL	4/1/09-3/31/10 ALL		0-1MM	1-3MM	3-5MM	5-10MM	10-25MM	25MM & OVER
70	80	83	**NUMBER OF STATEMENTS**		9	12	15	16	31
%	%	%	**ASSETS**	%	%	%	%	%	%
10.5	9.6	10.4	Cash & Equivalents	D A T A		11.2	8.0	9.6	11.6
24.4	25.8	24.4	Trade Receivables (net)			23.0	28.6	25.2	22.4
25.1	23.6	22.8	Inventory			33.0	28.4	20.6	17.8
2.4	2.9	2.9	All Other Current			3.0	1.2	.9	3.8
62.5	61.9	60.5	Total Current			70.3	66.3	56.3	55.6
24.8	21.7	25.2	Fixed Assets (net)	N O T		20.6	19.5	32.2	27.3
6.2	10.1	7.8	Intangibles (net)			1.1	7.4	6.7	10.8
6.5	6.3	6.4	All Other Non-Current			8.0	6.9	4.8	6.3
100.0	100.0	100.0	Total			100.0	100.0	100.0	100.0
			LIABILITIES	A V A I L A B L E					
11.8	7.2	7.5	Notes Payable-Short Term			13.7	12.7	4.8	4.3
3.2	3.5	4.3	Cur. Mat.-L.T.D.			2.3	4.7	5.9	3.4
16.0	12.7	12.4	Trade Payables			14.5	12.7	13.7	10.7
.2	.2	.2	Income Taxes Payable			.0	.1	.1	.3
7.5	6.8	7.3	All Other Current			5.0	6.8	4.2	11.1
38.6	30.4	31.7	Total Current			35.5	36.9	28.6	29.8
14.9	15.2	13.2	Long-Term Debt			11.0	9.9	22.6	11.3
.6	.7	.9	Deferred Taxes			.9	.7	.9	1.1
7.2	10.4	6.9	All Other Non-Current			5.5	2.5	2.8	13.4
38.7	43.3	47.4	Net Worth			47.1	50.0	45.2	44.3
100.0	100.0	100.0	Total Liabilties & Net Worth			100.0	100.0	100.0	100.0
			INCOME DATA						
100.0	100.0	100.0	Net Sales			100.0	100.0	100.0	100.0
30.1	33.4	30.7	Gross Profit			29.9	29.4	32.1	31.2
25.8	27.8	26.8	Operating Expenses			25.1	26.6	26.6	26.7
4.3	5.6	3.9	Operating Profit			4.9	2.8	5.5	4.5
1.1	1.0	.7	All Other Expenses (net)			.7	.0	.7	1.3
3.3	4.6	3.2	Profit Before Taxes			4.2	2.8	4.8	3.3
			RATIOS						
3.4 1.8 1.2	3.8 2.0 1.3	3.5 2.0 1.3	Current			3.2 2.1 1.3	2.2 1.6 1.4	3.6 2.2 1.3	3.6 2.1 1.3
2.4 .9 .6	2.1 1.1 .7	2.1 1.2 .7	Quick			2.0 1.0 .5	1.3 .9 .7	2.1 1.2 .7	2.3 1.3 .7
33 11.0 **42** 8.7 **49** 7.4	**33** 11.1 **41** 8.9 **48** 7.7	**38** 9.7 **43** 8.5 **54** 6.8	Sales/Receivables			**39** 9.4 **40** 9.1 **46** 7.9	**39** 9.2 **45** 8.0 **52** 7.1	**36** 10.1 **39** 9.4 **54** 6.8	**39** 9.5 **51** 7.2 **60** 6.0
33 11.1 **54** 6.7 **89** 4.1	**27** 13.3 **52** 7.0 **87** 4.2	**39** 9.3 **61** 6.0 **90** 4.0	Cost of Sales/Inventory			**46** 8.0 **86** 4.2 **102** 3.6	**42** 8.8 **70** 5.2 **118** 3.1	**29** 12.6 **50** 7.3 **77** 4.8	**42** 8.6 **62** 5.8 **84** 4.4
20 18.4 **28** 12.9 **41** 8.8	**18** 19.8 **26** 13.9 **39** 9.4	**19** 18.8 **28** 13.0 **44** 8.4	Cost of Sales/Payables			**21** 17.4 **37** 9.7 **58** 6.3	**19** 18.8 **27** 13.4 **38** 9.7	**21** 17.3 **29** 12.7 **45** 8.1	**17** 21.6 **28** 13.0 **42** 8.8
4.7 8.9 21.5	5.0 8.8 16.7	3.7 6.3 16.9	Sales/Working Capital			3.9 5.7 10.6	4.3 7.8 17.4	4.0 6.5 19.9	3.3 5.6 13.4
8.2 (63) 4.3 1.2	10.9 (70) 2.9 1.6	8.3 (70) 3.6 .9	EBIT/Interest			13.7 (10) 2.7 1.3	6.3 (14) 4.0 -.3	4.5 (12) 3.7 1.8	14.1 (28) 3.8 1.1
5.8 (21) 2.2 .7	2.0 (16) 1.2 .6	2.8 (20) 1.4 .3	Net Profit + Depr., Dep., Amort./Cur. Mat. L/T/D						3.1 (10) 2.7 .2
.3 .6 2.6	.2 .7 2.1	.3 .6 1.3	Fixed/Worth			.2 .4 .8	.1 .4 .9	.4 .8 1.5	.4 .7 2.4
.6 1.7 5.0	.6 1.8 6.2	.5 1.4 3.0	Debt/Worth			.6 1.2 1.8	.9 1.4 2.3	.9 1.3 3.3	.5 1.4 7.6
37.9 (60) 16.0 6.5	33.0 (67) 15.9 6.0	34.6 (74) 8.5 .1	% Profit Before Taxes/Tangible Net Worth			35.5 (11) 13.7 2.0	40.2 6.5 -5.7	70.4 (15) 15.9 4.3	33.9 (25) 12.0 -3.6
14.6 6.2 .8	11.9 6.4 2.0	11.1 3.6 .2	% Profit Before Taxes/Total Assets			19.1 4.8 1.0	7.9 4.9 -2.5	12.9 6.7 2.6	11.9 3.4 -.6
28.8 10.3 4.4	51.0 11.4 5.3	18.3 7.9 3.9	Sales/Net Fixed Assets			29.0 10.5 4.1	19.6 12.1 7.5	18.1 7.2 3.1	9.0 7.4 2.9
2.8 2.1 1.5	3.0 2.2 1.6	2.4 1.7 1.3	Sales/Total Assets			3.0 1.7 1.5	2.7 1.8 1.5	3.2 1.8 1.6	2.0 1.5 1.0
.8 (62) 1.7 3.0	.8 (65) 1.7 2.9	1.0 (69) 2.6 4.0	% Depr., Dep., Amort./Sales				.6 (14) 2.6 4.6	.8 (13) 2.1 3.2	1.3 (27) 2.9 4.7
3.0 (25) 6.2 9.8	2.9 (29) 4.6 7.8	2.6 (28) 4.8 8.2	% Officers', Directors' Owners' Comp/Sales						
1641741M	2279084M	2769891M	Net Sales ($)		20840M	47446M	103358M	222115M	2376132M
1168963M	1505367M	2051638M	Total Assets ($)		11292M	31293M	78033M	138118M	1792902M

M = $ thousand MM = $ million
See Pages 9 through 22 for Explanation of Ratios and Data

Current Data Sorted by Assets

Comparative Historical Data

Type of Statement	0-500M	500M-2MM	2-10MM	10-50MM	50-100MM	100-250MM		4/1/05-3/31/06 ALL	4/1/06-3/31/07 ALL
Unqualified			2	4	3			8	11
Reviewed			1	1	1			7	5
Compiled		2	2					5	6
Tax Returns		2	1					3	3
Other		1	1	7	2	2		5	10
		6 (4/1-9/30/09)		26 (10/1/09-3/31/10)					
NUMBER OF STATEMENTS		5	7	12	6	2		28	35

Data Not Available for columns 0-500M, 500M-2MM, 2-10MM, 50-100MM, 100-250MM.

	10-50MM		ASSETS	4/1/05-3/31/06 ALL %	4/1/06-3/31/07 ALL %
	16.1		Cash & Equivalents	8.8	5.6
	15.9		Trade Receivables (net)	22.2	22.6
	37.4		Inventory	36.5	36.4
	5.8		All Other Current	2.2	1.5
	75.2		Total Current	69.7	66.1
	18.2		Fixed Assets (net)	20.4	21.6
	4.3		Intangibles (net)	2.3	2.9
	2.3		All Other Non-Current	7.6	9.4
	100.0		Total	100.0	100.0
			LIABILITIES		
	4.9		Notes Payable-Short Term	8.5	11.7
	.6		Cur. Mat.-L.T.D.	2.0	2.0
	10.5		Trade Payables	10.0	12.5
	.2		Income Taxes Payable	.6	.3
	5.2		All Other Current	11.2	12.6
	21.4		Total Current	32.3	39.1
	8.1		Long-Term Debt	11.5	22.0
	.8		Deferred Taxes	.6	.2
	4.8		All Other Non-Current	7.8	7.9
	64.9		Net Worth	47.8	30.8
	100.0		Total Liabilities & Net Worth	100.0	100.0
			INCOME DATA		
	100.0		Net Sales	100.0	100.0
	32.2		Gross Profit	37.5	35.8
	26.9		Operating Expenses	31.4	31.2
	5.3		Operating Profit	6.1	4.7
	.7		All Other Expenses (net)	1.2	2.2
	4.6		Profit Before Taxes	4.9	2.5

RATIOS

	10-50MM (current)	RATIO	4/1/05-3/31/06 ALL	4/1/06-3/31/07 ALL
	8.8	Current	4.6	3.4
	6.3		2.3	1.9
	2.0		1.2	1.1
	5.1	Quick	1.7	1.1
	1.7		1.0	.8
	.6		.6	.6
	28 12.9	Sales/Receivables	27 13.7	25 14.5
	42 8.7		42 8.7	37 9.8
	65 5.6		51 7.2	58 6.3
	98 3.7	Cost of Sales/Inventory	77 4.7	83 4.4
	174 2.1		109 3.3	132 2.8
	200 1.8		185 2.0	185 2.0
	8 47.6	Cost of Sales/Payables	16 22.9	14 26.2
	13 27.0		21 17.3	32 11.3
	53 6.9		43 8.4	52 7.1
	1.7	Sales/Working Capital	2.7	3.0
	2.4		5.1	5.1
	3.3		12.5	20.9
		EBIT/Interest	37.3	12.0
			(25) 7.3	(32) 4.0
			1.1	.7
		Net Profit + Depr., Dep., Amort./Cur. Mat. L/T/D	12.3	15.4
			(12) 7.5	(13) 5.7
			2.1	2.0
	.1	Fixed/Worth	.2	.1
	.2		.3	.4
	.5		1.0	-16.0
	.1	Debt/Worth	.4	.4
	.3		.9	2.2
	2.2		3.0	-14.2
	19.1	% Profit Before Taxes/Tangible Net Worth	35.7	34.8
	11.7		(25) 12.0	(25) 20.2
	-3.1		4.3	2.3
	13.6	% Profit Before Taxes/Total Assets	21.7	13.9
	7.6		8.0	7.4
	-.9		1.0	-.5
	15.5	Sales/Net Fixed Assets	19.9	26.0
	9.9		10.8	11.3
	5.7		6.6	6.7
	1.8	Sales/Total Assets	2.1	2.1
	1.4		1.8	1.6
	.9		1.3	1.3
	.8	% Depr., Dep., Amort./Sales	.9	1.0
	(10) 1.6		(27) 1.7	(32) 1.7
	3.0		3.1	2.6
		% Officers', Directors' Owners' Comp/Sales		2.8
				(10) 6.4
				12.6

0-500M	500M-2MM	2-10MM	10-50MM	50-100MM	100-250MM		4/1/05-3/31/06 ALL	4/1/06-3/31/07 ALL
	13658M	49166M	398235M	644640M	478383M	Net Sales ($)	879657M	1839767M
	5385M	37893M	283120M	457288M	291149M	Total Assets ($)	579049M	1180316M

M = $ thousand MM = $ million
See Pages 9 through 22 for Explanation of Ratios and Data

Comparative Historical Data

Current Data Sorted by Sales

			Type of Statement	0-1MM	1-3MM	3-5MM	5-10MM	10-25MM	25MM & OVER
6	5	9	Unqualified	1			1	3	4
7	9	2	Reviewed				1		1
7	4	5	Compiled		1	2	1	1	
1	1	3	Tax Returns		1	1	1		
10	19	13	Other			1	1	2	9
4/1/07-3/31/08 ALL	4/1/08-3/31/09 ALL	4/1/09-3/31/10 ALL			6 (4/1-9/30/09)			26 (10/1/09-3/31/10)	
31	38	32	NUMBER OF STATEMENTS	1	2	4	5	6	14
%	%	%	ASSETS	%	%	%	%	%	%
5.5	8.1	13.9	Cash & Equivalents						12.2
23.6	22.1	16.3	Trade Receivables (net)						18.1
39.2	38.0	34.9	Inventory						29.7
2.5	2.5	3.5	All Other Current						3.5
70.8	70.7	68.6	Total Current						63.6
18.5	19.2	20.6	Fixed Assets (net)						23.0
2.9	1.7	4.1	Intangibles (net)						4.9
7.8	8.3	6.7	All Other Non-Current						8.5
100.0	100.0	100.0	Total						100.0
			LIABILITIES						
25.1	10.9	9.7	Notes Payable-Short Term						6.1
3.4	2.7	1.4	Cur. Mat.-L.T.D.						1.4
9.6	9.1	10.4	Trade Payables						8.5
.2	.4	.2	Income Taxes Payable						.0
10.7	11.7	6.3	All Other Current						8.5
48.9	34.8	28.1	Total Current						24.5
16.3	14.2	16.4	Long-Term Debt						23.0
.3	.4	.3	Deferred Taxes						.0
7.8	7.3	7.3	All Other Non-Current						5.7
26.7	43.3	48.0	Net Worth						46.8
100.0	100.0	100.0	Total Liabilities & Net Worth						100.0
			INCOME DATA						
100.0	100.0	100.0	Net Sales						100.0
38.5	36.6	38.2	Gross Profit						38.2
32.3	30.8	33.2	Operating Expenses						28.8
6.2	5.8	5.0	Operating Profit						9.4
1.7	1.2	1.4	All Other Expenses (net)						1.2
4.5	4.6	3.6	Profit Before Taxes						8.2
			RATIOS						
3.2	3.8	6.3	Current						6.3
2.2	2.1	2.6							2.9
1.5	1.4	1.5							1.9
1.3	1.5	1.8	Quick						2.2
.9	.8	1.1							1.1
.6	.5	.6							.7
31 11.6	31 11.7	27 13.8	Sales/Receivables						31 11.6
45 8.1	41 9.0	38 9.7							39 9.3
61 6.0	63 5.8	53 6.8							53 6.9
96 3.8	97 3.8	92 4.0	Cost of Sales/Inventory						91 4.0
136 2.7	134 2.7	123 3.0							113 3.2
186 2.0	186 2.0	184 2.0							128 2.8
10 35.5	10 35.1	12 30.2	Cost of Sales/Payables						15 24.8
26 14.0	22 16.3	21 17.7							23 15.6
61 6.0	49 7.4	58 6.3							50 7.3
3.0	3.2	2.4	Sales/Working Capital						2.7
5.2	4.8	3.6							3.6
9.0	9.9	7.3							5.7
11.9	8.3	15.2	EBIT/Interest						32.4
(28) 2.6	(33) 3.2	(26) 3.4						(12)	7.5
1.4	1.6	.5							3.1
10.7	12.1		Net Profit + Depr., Dep., Amort./Cur. Mat. L/T/D						
(11) 4.2	(16) 9.0								
1.2	2.5								
.2	.2	.1	Fixed/Worth						.2
.3	.3	.4							.4
5.8	1.1	1.5							6.0
.4	.4	.2	Debt/Worth						.2
1.1	.8	.8							.9
-43.0	5.3	3.6							15.1
25.6	26.7	19.2	% Profit Before Taxes/Tangible Net Worth						39.6
(23) 9.2	(32) 12.4	(27) 10.8						(12)	20.8
1.5	2.1	.9							17.2
14.3	16.3	13.4	% Profit Before Taxes/Total Assets						14.9
4.6	6.2	7.3							13.1
1.0	.8	.1							8.0
25.8	25.9	26.1	Sales/Net Fixed Assets						11.5
10.9	9.6	8.1							7.1
6.6	5.6	5.3							4.2
1.9	2.1	1.9	Sales/Total Assets						1.8
1.6	1.6	1.6							1.7
1.3	1.2	1.0							1.0
.9	.7	.7	% Depr., Dep., Amort./Sales						1.4
(28) 1.9	(35) 1.7	(28) 2.0						(12)	2.4
3.1	2.8	3.0							3.1
			% Officers', Directors' Owners' Comp/Sales						
1386547M	2308964M	1584082M	Net Sales ($)	608M	4934M	16576M	40706M	107967M	1413291M
918876M	1365003M	1074835M	Total Assets ($)	641M	1950M	12239M	28448M	108160M	923397M

M = $ thousand   MM = $ million
See Pages 9 through 22 for Explanation of Ratios and Data

Current Data Sorted by Assets   **Comparative Historical Data**

© RMA 2010

							Type of Statement		
		1	1	1			Unqualified	6	9
		5	1				Reviewed	4	7
	2	2					Compiled	4	5
		1					Tax Returns	1	3
	1	2	1	3			Other	12	8
	7 (4/1-9/30/09)		14 (10/1/09-3/31/10)					4/1/05-3/31/06	4/1/06-3/31/07
0-500M	500M-2MM	2-10MM	10-50MM	50-100MM	100-250MM			ALL	ALL
	3	11	3	4			**NUMBER OF STATEMENTS**	27	32
%	%	%	%	%	%		**ASSETS**	%	%
		7.9					Cash & Equivalents	7.1	4.9
D		24.8			D		Trade Receivables (net)	27.4	22.9
A		34.8			A		Inventory	32.8	34.6
T		1.3			T		All Other Current	1.5	1.5
A		68.8			A		Total Current	68.8	63.9
		19.5					Fixed Assets (net)	20.5	23.8
N		6.8			N		Intangibles (net)	5.4	5.8
O		4.9			O		All Other Non-Current	5.3	6.5
T		100.0			T		Total	100.0	100.0
							LIABILITIES		
A		4.0			A		Notes Payable-Short Term	12.3	11.3
V		6.1			V		Cur. Mat.-L.T.D.	2.6	5.2
A		13.0			A		Trade Payables	11.8	16.0
I		.0			I		Income Taxes Payable	.2	.5
L		6.3			L		All Other Current	9.8	8.7
A		29.4			A		Total Current	36.7	41.6
B		19.9			B		Long-Term Debt	13.4	16.5
L		.5			L		Deferred Taxes	.5	.5
E		3.4			E		All Other Non-Current	3.4	3.8
		46.7					Net Worth	46.0	37.5
		100.0					Total Liabilities & Net Worth	100.0	100.0
							INCOME DATA		
		100.0					Net Sales	100.0	100.0
		33.9					Gross Profit	32.5	32.4
		25.6					Operating Expenses	27.7	27.3
		8.4					Operating Profit	4.8	5.0
		1.5					All Other Expenses (net)	1.2	.8
		6.9					Profit Before Taxes	3.5	4.2
							RATIOS		
		3.7						3.0	3.1
		2.7					Current	2.1	2.2
		1.6						1.4	1.2
		2.0						1.6	1.4
		1.0					Quick	.9	.9
		.5						.6	.5
	34	10.7				33		11.1	33	10.9
	39	9.4				44	Sales/Receivables	8.3	40	9.0
	45	8.1				55		6.6	50	7.3
	57	6.4				55		6.6	57	6.4
	104	3.5				78	Cost of Sales/Inventory	4.7	86	4.2
	134	2.7				115		3.2	122	3.0
	14	26.9				15		24.2	17	21.2
	20	18.3				29	Cost of Sales/Payables	12.7	27	13.3
	48	7.6				48		7.6	43	8.6
		4.4						4.4	3.9
		5.6					Sales/Working Capital	7.0	6.6
		10.3						13.7	27.6
		88.7						13.5	9.3
	(10)	1.7				(25)	EBIT/Interest	4.1	(30)	2.7
		.2						.6	.8
							Net Profit + Depr., Dep., Amort./Cur. Mat. L/T/D		
		.2						.2	.2
		.5					Fixed/Worth	.3	.5
		1.2						1.4	2.1
		.5						.5	.5
		1.7					Debt/Worth	1.6	1.8
		2.7						3.4	4.9
		51.6						27.1	30.2
	(10)	19.6				(24)	% Profit Before Taxes/Tangible Net Worth	14.5	(26)	16.6
		-4.6						-8.6	2.5
		41.4						15.2	19.7
		4.5					% Profit Before Taxes/Total Assets	5.3	5.4
		-.8						-1.2	-.9
		38.8						25.0	24.4
		15.1					Sales/Net Fixed Assets	10.1	9.7
		5.1						6.7	5.1
		2.7						2.6	2.6
		1.9					Sales/Total Assets	2.0	1.9
		1.5						1.7	1.5
								1.0	.9
							% Depr., Dep., Amort./Sales	(25)	1.6	(26)	1.9
								3.3	3.2
							% Officers', Directors' Owners' Comp/Sales		
	12788M	100560M	121589M	455419M			Net Sales ($)	983547M	998928M
	4179M	43219M	75007M	308688M			Total Assets ($)	622941M	699693M

Comparative Historical Data

Current Data Sorted by Sales

4/1/07-3/31/08 ALL	4/1/08-3/31/09 ALL	4/1/09-3/31/10 ALL	Type of Statement	0-1MM	1-3MM	3-5MM	5-10MM	10-25MM	25MM & OVER
4	2	3	Unqualified						
5	6	6	Reviewed		1	1	1	2	2
4	1	4	Compiled			2	1	2	1
1	1	1	Tax Returns			1	1		
7	13	7	Other			1			4
					7 (4/1-9/30/09)		14 (10/1/09-3/31/10)		
21	23	21	NUMBER OF STATEMENTS		1	4	7	2	7
%	%	%	**ASSETS**	%	%	%	%	%	%
7.0	6.4	8.9	Cash & Equivalents						
22.6	21.5	24.9	Trade Receivables (net)						
35.7	36.1	31.3	Inventory						
1.1	2.0	1.2	All Other Current						
66.5	66.1	66.4	Total Current						
23.0	21.5	20.3	Fixed Assets (net)						
3.0	6.0	8.1	Intangibles (net)						
7.6	6.4	5.2	All Other Non-Current						
100.0	100.0	100.0	Total						
			LIABILITIES						
8.5	9.9	8.6	Notes Payable-Short Term						
4.6	3.3	5.2	Cur. Mat.-L.T.D.						
14.0	13.1	13.8	Trade Payables						
.0	.1	.0	Income Taxes Payable						
9.0	4.5	7.0	All Other Current						
36.0	30.9	34.7	Total Current						
18.6	16.5	15.4	Long-Term Debt						
.3	.2	.3	Deferred Taxes						
1.6	3.2	4.3	All Other Non-Current						
43.5	49.1	45.3	Net Worth						
100.0	100.0	100.0	Total Liabilities & Net Worth						
			INCOME DATA						
100.0	100.0	100.0	Net Sales						
31.1	27.7	30.4	Gross Profit						
24.8	25.6	24.8	Operating Expenses						
6.4	2.2	5.6	Operating Profit						
1.3	.7	1.4	All Other Expenses (net)						
5.0	1.4	4.2	Profit Before Taxes						
			RATIOS						
4.0	4.5	3.7	Current						
2.1	2.5	1.9							
1.4	1.3	1.4							
2.0	2.0	1.8	Quick						
.9	.8	.9							
.4	.4	.6							
26 14.1	30 12.1	34 10.7	Sales/Receivables						
33 11.2	37 9.9	42 8.7							
41 8.8	46 7.9	49 7.5							
64 5.7	68 5.4	58 6.3	Cost of Sales/Inventory						
82 4.5	100 3.7	79 4.6							
97 3.7	113 3.2	132 2.8							
15 24.3	13 27.9	17 21.7	Cost of Sales/Payables						
20 17.9	30 12.3	26 14.0							
39 9.4	39 9.3	46 7.9							
3.8	4.3	4.1	Sales/Working Capital						
6.4	6.4	5.7							
14.9	13.3	11.5							
18.7	8.8	15.5	EBIT/Interest						
(19) 3.6	(19) 1.0	(19) 1.5							
1.2	-.6	.4							
			Net Profit + Depr., Dep., Amort./Cur. Mat. L/T/D						
.2	.3	.2	Fixed/Worth						
.4	.5	.5							
1.7	1.4	4.6							
.3	.3	.4	Debt/Worth						
2.1	1.2	1.7							
3.0	2.4	12.0							
33.0	16.0	31.9	% Profit Before Taxes/Tangible Net Worth						
(19) 17.9	(20) 4.5	(17) 7.8							
2.0	-11.5	-1.9							
21.2	11.3	12.0	% Profit Before Taxes/Total Assets						
4.4	.3	4.5							
1.2	-3.6	-.6							
35.9	25.1	31.4	Sales/Net Fixed Assets						
11.8	9.2	12.2							
6.2	5.5	4.7							
2.8	2.3	2.7	Sales/Total Assets						
2.0	2.1	1.9							
1.8	1.8	1.4							
.8	1.2	.9	% Depr., Dep., Amort./Sales						
(17) 2.3	(16) 2.8	(17) 2.5							
3.1	3.7	3.9							
			% Officers', Directors' Owners' Comp/Sales						
368382M	580915M	690356M	Net Sales ($)		2404M	15011M	56075M	31455M	585411M
241868M	343149M	431093M	Total Assets ($)		2077M	8462M	24663M	15481M	380410M

Data for right-hand sales categories (0-1MM): DATA NOT AVAILABLE

Current Data Sorted by Assets / Comparative Historical Data

Type of Statement

	4/1/05-3/31/06 ALL	4/1/06-3/31/07 ALL
Unqualified	109	104
Reviewed	82	96
Compiled	61	68
Tax Returns	70	83
Other	237	179

			1	17	45	22	12
			14	61	15		
	1		14	22	6		
	26		39	31	3	1	
	20		47	96	70	13	11
		88 (4/1-9/30/09)			499 (10/1/09-3/31/10)		

0-500M	500M-2MM	2-10MM	10-50MM	50-100MM	100-250MM		4/1/05-3/31/06 ALL	4/1/06-3/31/07 ALL
47	115	227	139	36	23	NUMBER OF STATEMENTS	559	530
%	%	%	%	%	%	ASSETS	%	%
19.1	10.3	9.1	9.1	5.5	6.3	Cash & Equivalents	7.9	8.2
26.3	25.2	24.0	21.5	20.9	18.2	Trade Receivables (net)	27.8	27.1
25.1	23.9	29.8	26.0	24.8	20.7	Inventory	26.4	27.2
.9	3.9	3.2	4.1	3.7	4.6	All Other Current	3.3	2.6
71.4	63.2	66.1	60.8	55.0	49.9	Total Current	65.3	65.0
21.1	25.0	23.5	25.2	24.1	17.7	Fixed Assets (net)	22.8	23.4
1.9	6.1	4.0	7.3	15.5	25.6	Intangibles (net)	5.2	5.9
5.5	5.6	6.3	6.8	5.4	6.8	All Other Non-Current	6.6	5.7
100.0	100.0	100.0	100.0	100.0	100.0	Total	100.0	100.0
						LIABILITIES		
26.8	11.3	13.1	10.1	8.0	3.9	Notes Payable-Short Term	12.8	13.5
5.3	4.7	3.9	3.8	2.5	4.6	Cur. Mat.-L.T.D.	3.2	3.2
29.5	16.6	14.4	11.2	10.4	7.3	Trade Payables	15.0	15.9
.0	.3	.2	.3	.3	.5	Income Taxes Payable	.2	.3
19.8	16.9	10.3	10.5	12.1	10.5	All Other Current	9.2	10.5
81.4	49.8	41.8	35.9	33.3	26.8	Total Current	40.3	43.3
21.4	22.1	16.3	13.7	21.6	18.1	Long-Term Debt	17.0	16.0
.0	.1	.2	.8	.8	1.2	Deferred Taxes	.6	.5
22.1	5.3	6.2	8.9	6.7	6.1	All Other Non-Current	7.0	7.4
-24.9	22.8	35.5	40.6	37.6	47.9	Net Worth	35.1	32.8
100.0	100.0	100.0	100.0	100.0	100.0	Total Liabilities & Net Worth	100.0	100.0
						INCOME DATA		
100.0	100.0	100.0	100.0	100.0	100.0	Net Sales	100.0	100.0
43.8	40.4	33.4	29.4	28.3	30.7	Gross Profit	34.0	33.7
43.9	37.2	30.3	23.9	20.4	25.2	Operating Expenses	28.2	28.5
-.1	3.2	3.0	5.5	7.9	5.5	Operating Profit	5.8	5.2
1.4	2.1	1.6	1.6	3.1	2.7	All Other Expenses (net)	1.1	1.5
-1.6	1.1	1.5	3.9	4.8	2.8	Profit Before Taxes	4.7	3.7
						RATIOS		
3.5	3.2	2.9	3.6	2.5	2.3	Current	2.8	2.6
1.1	1.5	1.7	1.7	1.7	2.1		1.7	1.6
.7	.8	1.1	1.2	1.2	1.7		1.2	1.1
1.9	2.0	1.5	1.9	1.4	1.2	Quick	1.5	1.4
.6	.8	.8	.9	.8	1.0		(558) .9	.9
.3	.4	.5	.5	.5	.7		.5	.5
3 136.7	24 15.2	29 12.6	32 11.3	34 10.8	46 8.0	Sales/Receivables	30 12.3	29 12.8
23 15.7	38 9.5	42 8.7	47 7.8	47 7.8	54 6.8		45 8.2	44 8.3
41 8.8	56 6.5	57 6.4	62 5.9	59 6.2	65 5.6		61 5.9	59 6.2
0 999.8	19 19.7	47 7.8	49 7.5	44 8.4	65 5.6	Cost of Sales/Inventory	31 11.8	37 9.9
27 13.4	52 7.0	81 4.5	87 4.2	69 5.3	80 4.6		62 5.9	65 5.6
104 3.5	112 3.3	132 2.8	133 2.7	110 3.3	111 3.3		104 3.5	109 3.3
11 34.5	15 23.8	17 21.3	16 22.2	23 15.8	25 14.7	Cost of Sales/Payables	17 21.5	18 20.0
27 13.4	34 10.8	29 12.5	27 13.7	33 10.9	30 12.3		31 11.9	33 11.2
67 5.5	67 5.5	52 7.0	47 7.8	42 8.6	49 7.5		53 6.9	53 6.9
7.1	4.8	4.1	3.5	4.1	3.7	Sales/Working Capital	4.6	5.0
42.2	10.2	8.5	7.1	7.9	5.0		9.0	9.3
-21.4	-24.5	33.3	23.4	27.3	8.4		30.2	42.9
4.4	5.2	9.9	12.1	14.5	10.7	EBIT/Interest	11.4	10.6
(29) .0	(100) 1.8	(211) 2.7	(123) 3.6	(33) 5.0	2.6		(507) 4.4	(480) 3.6
-6.6	-1.7	.2	.8	1.5	1.6		1.8	1.1
	6.5	5.2	4.7	14.5		Net Profit + Depr., Dep., Amort./Cur. Mat. L/T/D	5.0	8.3
(12) 3.0	(45) 1.2	(47) 2.4	(16) 4.1				(120) 2.5	(121) 3.0
.9	-.1	.6	2.4				1.4	1.4
.1	.2	.2	.2	.3	.4	Fixed/Worth	.2	.3
.7	.9	.6	.7	.7	.6		.7	.7
-1.2	-8.5	2.0	1.8	NM	-3.3		2.3	2.4
.8	.7	.7	.5	1.0	.8	Debt/Worth	.8	.8
8.7	2.6	2.0	1.5	1.9	2.2		1.9	2.1
-3.4	-16.9	7.1	5.1	NM	-50.3		6.1	9.3
60.9	46.5	34.2	35.3	41.5	44.9	% Profit Before Taxes/Tangible Net Worth	49.5	57.0
(25) 25.3	(83) 12.5	(195) 14.8	(120) 16.3	(27) 24.4	(17) 11.2		(475) 22.7	(437) 24.1
-2.4	-9.5	1.8	.8	11.3	5.3		7.1	5.5
23.9	12.1	11.2	12.1	13.8	7.1	% Profit Before Taxes/Total Assets	16.3	17.5
.0	3.6	4.6	5.5	8.1	3.4		7.6	7.2
-21.5	-10.6	-1.2	-1.2	1.8	1.4		2.2	.4
350.4	27.4	29.0	19.7	15.7	12.9	Sales/Net Fixed Assets	28.7	30.8
32.5	13.5	11.3	6.5	7.9	7.5		12.3	11.8
9.9	5.6	4.7	3.4	4.5	4.0		6.0	5.5
6.1	2.8	2.6	2.1	2.1	1.4	Sales/Total Assets	3.0	2.9
3.3	2.3	1.9	1.5	1.6	1.2		2.1	2.1
2.0	1.5	1.3	1.1	1.1	.9		1.5	1.5
.7	1.1	.9	1.2	1.3	1.6	% Depr., Dep., Amort./Sales	.9	.9
(26) 1.5	(88) 2.5	(194) 2.1	(113) 2.7	(28) 2.3	(16) 2.9		(457) 1.7	(447) 1.8
6.0	4.6	3.9	5.4	4.6	3.8		3.1	3.2
4.1	2.5	1.5	.9			% Officers', Directors' Owners' Comp/Sales	2.3	2.2
(18) 7.6	(44) 6.8	(85) 3.1	(22) 1.6				(174) 4.1	(171) 3.8
13.5	10.0	4.9	3.1				7.3	7.2
52355M	314247M	2428217M	4943691M	4042503M	4325913M	Net Sales ($)	15605233M	15845763M
11927M	130753M	1176962M	2836932M	2525555M	3615505M	Total Assets ($)	9383765M	9279684M

© RMA 2010

M = $ thousand   MM = $ million
See Pages 9 through 22 for Explanation of Ratios and Data

Comparative Historical Data   Current Data Sorted by Sales

	83	92	97	Type of Statement	0-1MM	1-3MM	3-5MM	5-10MM	10-25MM	25MM & OVER
	83	92	97	Unqualified	1	2	2	6	26	61
	76	79	90	Reviewed		7	10	24	36	12
	62	50	43	Compiled		8	8	18	8	1
	71	85	100	Tax Returns	27	26	19	17	9	2
	179	213	257	Other	20	39	28	35	67	68
	4/1/07-3/31/08 ALL	4/1/08-3/31/09 ALL	4/1/09-3/31/10 ALL		88 (4/1-9/30/09)			499 (10/1/09-3/31/10)		
	471	519	587	NUMBER OF STATEMENTS	48	82	67	100	146	144
	%	%	%	ASSETS	%	%	%	%	%	%
	9.5	9.3	9.8	Cash & Equivalents	14.1	10.1	11.1	8.8	10.4	7.6
	24.8	23.9	23.4	Trade Receivables (net)	19.5	24.4	23.8	21.0	24.3	24.7
	27.5	28.9	26.7	Inventory	22.5	25.0	26.0	28.0	28.6	26.6
	3.1	3.0	3.4	All Other Current	3.4	3.4	2.7	3.2	3.7	3.7
	64.9	65.1	63.4	Total Current	59.5	63.0	63.6	61.0	67.1	62.6
	23.2	21.6	23.8	Fixed Assets (net)	29.3	23.9	26.0	27.0	21.7	20.9
	5.3	6.8	6.6	Intangibles (net)	6.3	4.4	4.6	5.6	5.7	10.5
	6.6	6.5	6.2	All Other Non-Current	5.0	8.7	5.9	6.4	5.5	6.0
	100.0	100.0	100.0	Total	100.0	100.0	100.0	100.0	100.0	100.0
				LIABILITIES						
	12.9	13.2	12.4	Notes Payable-Short Term	12.9	18.9	13.9	12.5	10.6	9.9
	4.3	3.4	4.1	Cur. Mat.-L.T.D.	8.9	4.0	2.5	6.4	3.0	2.8
	13.2	14.3	14.8	Trade Payables	22.0	17.2	14.9	13.8	13.9	12.4
	.2	.3	.2	Income Taxes Payable	.0	.0	.4	.0	.4	.4
	11.8	11.1	12.5	All Other Current	16.3	19.2	11.2	10.8	10.3	11.5
	42.4	42.3	44.1	Total Current	60.1	59.3	42.9	43.5	38.1	36.9
	16.0	18.0	17.6	Long-Term Debt	26.2	24.0	17.7	19.1	13.4	14.4
	.4	.3	.4	Deferred Taxes	.0	.0	.0	.5	.7	.5
	4.8	7.1	8.0	All Other Non-Current	23.6	6.2	2.0	7.6	5.6	9.1
	36.4	32.3	30.0	Net Worth	-10.0	10.4	37.3	29.2	42.2	39.2
	100.0	100.0	100.0	Total Liabilties & Net Worth	100.0	100.0	100.0	100.0	100.0	100.0
				INCOME DATA						
	100.0	100.0	100.0	Net Sales	100.0	100.0	100.0	100.0	100.0	100.0
	35.1	32.9	34.2	Gross Profit	46.4	42.4	36.5	32.4	31.9	28.0
	28.7	27.9	30.4	Operating Expenses	44.2	40.7	33.8	30.7	26.3	22.3
	6.4	4.9	3.8	Operating Profit	2.2	1.7	2.7	1.7	5.6	5.7
	1.3	1.4	1.8	All Other Expenses (net)	4.2	2.0	1.4	1.5	1.2	1.9
	5.1	3.5	2.0	Profit Before Taxes	-2.0	-.3	1.3	.2	4.4	3.8
				RATIOS						
	2.6 / 1.7 / 1.1	2.9 / 1.7 / 1.1	3.1 / 1.7 / 1.1	Current	3.7 / 1.3 / .7	2.7 / 1.4 / .7	3.3 / 1.7 / 1.0	2.8 / 1.6 / 1.0	3.7 / 1.9 / 1.2	2.8 / 1.8 / 1.3
	1.5 / .8 / .5	1.7 / .8 / .5	1.7 / .8 / .5	Quick	1.8 / .6 / .3	1.5 / .6 / .3	2.1 / .9 / .5	1.3 / .7 / .4	1.9 / 1.0 / .5	1.5 / .9 / .6
	26 14.0 / 40 9.1 / 58 6.2	25 14.5 / 37 9.7 / 54 6.8	27 13.3 / 43 8.6 / 58 6.3	Sales/Receivables	9 41.2 / 31 11.7 / 56 6.5	21 17.6 / 38 9.7 / 52 7.0	26 14.0 / 41 8.8 / 66 5.6	28 13.0 / 41 8.9 / 50 7.3	28 12.9 / 44 8.3 / 58 6.3	33 11.1 / 47 7.8 / 62 5.9
	36 10.2 / 64 5.7 / 113 3.2	37 9.9 / 73 5.0 / 109 3.4	38 9.7 / 76 4.8 / 123 3.0	Cost of Sales/Inventory	0 UND / 61 6.0 / 207 1.8	18 19.8 / 63 5.8 / 145 2.5	35 10.5 / 62 5.9 / 120 3.0	44 8.3 / 88 4.1 / 147 2.5	47 7.7 / 79 4.6 / 125 2.9	42 8.6 / 74 4.9 / 106 3.5
	16 22.4 / 29 12.7 / 47 7.8	15 24.5 / 27 13.4 / 48 7.6	17 21.2 / 30 12.4 / 52 7.0	Cost of Sales/Payables	15 25.1 / 38 9.5 / 109 3.4	19 19.4 / 34 10.8 / 67 5.4	13 28.2 / 29 12.7 / 50 7.4	17 20.9 / 33 11.1 / 54 6.8	16 23.4 / 27 13.6 / 49 7.4	19 19.1 / 30 12.3 / 41 8.9
	4.7 / 8.6 / 32.5	4.6 / 9.0 / 34.3	4.1 / 8.3 / 61.9	Sales/Working Capital	3.5 / 17.6 / -5.9	5.2 / 11.9 / -15.4	4.1 / 8.3 / 118.8	4.1 / 9.6 / -355.0	4.0 / 8.1 / 20.6	7.3 / 17.2
	10.8 / (414) 3.7 / 1.3	10.7 / (455) 3.2 / .8	9.9 / (519) 2.7 / .0	EBIT/Interest	1.8 / (33) .0 / -6.6	5.2 / (73) 1.6 / -3.4	4.8 / (57) 1.8 / -.1	4.8 / (96) 2.1 / -2.0	13.7 / (124) 3.7 / 1.1	15.2 / (136) 5.2 / 1.6
	6.5 / (121) 2.7 / .9	6.2 / (119) 3.0 / 1.1	5.7 / (129) 2.4 / .6	Net Profit + Depr., Dep., Amort./Cur. Mat. L/T/D				2.1 / (20) 1.2 / -.1	5.0 / (44) 1.4 / .5	12.3 / (52) 4.1 / 2.2
	.2 / .6 / 1.5	.2 / .6 / 2.2	.2 / .7 / 3.3	Fixed/Worth	.2 / 4.0 / -1.8	.2 / .7 / -4.1	.1 / .6 / 2.1	.3 / 1.0 / NM	.2 / .5 / 1.6	.3 / .6 / 1.9
	.6 / 1.7 / 5.5	.7 / 1.8 / 8.0	.7 / 2.0 / 14.8	Debt/Worth	1.9 / NM / -3.9	.9 / 2.6 / -6.1	.5 / 1.5 / 7.7	.8 / 2.1 / NM	.5 / 1.7 / 7.2	.7 / 1.7 / 8.0
	58.6 / (410) 25.5 / 5.3	43.6 / (429) 19.4 / 1.7	38.6 / (467) 15.9 / 1.7	% Profit Before Taxes/Tangible Net Worth	34.7 / (24) 14.5 / -13.4	40.7 / (58) 9.0 / -13.2	19.8 / (59) 6.2 / -4.5	28.2 / (75) 11.2 / -1.6	47.4 / (130) 19.4 / 5.7	46.1 / (121) 21.8 / 7.1
	19.0 / 7.7 / 1.3	16.3 / 5.9 / -.1	12.1 / 4.4 / -2.5	% Profit Before Taxes/Total Assets	8.6 / -1.6 / -16.1	12.6 / 1.6 / -14.5	8.7 / 2.4 / -2.3	9.9 / 3.9 / -6.3	14.4 / 6.5 / .9	12.8 / 6.6 / 2.2
	32.5 / 12.2 / 5.5	34.5 / 13.0 / 6.0	29.7 / 10.2 / 4.5	Sales/Net Fixed Assets	47.5 / 10.6 / 2.7	29.3 / 11.0 / 5.7	31.2 / 10.3 / 4.2	19.9 / 8.7 / 3.6	33.4 / 11.5 / 4.7	31.4 / 10.0 / 4.9
	3.0 / 2.1 / 1.4	2.9 / 2.1 / 1.4	2.6 / 1.9 / 1.2	Sales/Total Assets	3.2 / 1.5 / .7	2.8 / 2.2 / 1.5	2.7 / 1.9 / 1.2	2.3 / 1.8 / 1.2	2.7 / 1.9 / 1.4	2.6 / 1.9 / 1.2
	.9 / (394) 1.9 / 3.3	.8 / (425) 1.8 / 3.1	1.0 / (465) 2.3 / 4.4	% Depr., Dep., Amort./Sales	.7 / (36) 2.3 / 7.3	1.7 / (55) 3.1 / 5.1	.9 / (53) 2.4 / 4.4	1.5 / (82) 2.9 / 5.9	.9 / (127) 2.0 / 3.8	1.0 / (112) 2.1 / 3.7
	2.2 / (157) 3.9 / 6.8	1.9 / (156) 3.8 / 7.3	1.6 / (171) 3.5 / 6.8	% Officers', Directors' Owners' Comp/Sales	5.7 / (18) 9.7 / 15.1	3.2 / (27) 5.8 / 8.8	2.4 / (28) 4.7 / 6.7	1.8 / (40) 3.3 / 5.9	1.3 / (43) 1.8 / 3.5	.5 / (15) 1.5 / 6.3
	12453260M	18464887M	16106926M	Net Sales ($)	26782M	164716M	266366M	740979M	2368170M	12539913M
	7296445M	11019501M	10297634M	Total Assets ($)	27789M	89949M	176830M	563101M	1441541M	7998424M

© RMA 2010

M = $ thousand   MM = $ million
See Pages 9 through 22 for Explanation of Ratios and Data

WHOLESALE TRADE

WHOLESALE—Automobile and Other Motor Vehicle Merchant Wholesalers NAICS 423110

Current Data Sorted by Assets   **Comparative Historical Data**

Type of Statement

Type of Statement	0-500M	500M-2MM	2-10MM	10-50MM	50-100MM	100-250MM	4/1/05-3/31/06 ALL	4/1/06-3/31/07 ALL
Unqualified			10	17	10	11	40	37
Reviewed	1	3	23	25	5		54	58
Compiled	6	14	27	4			50	60
Tax Returns	20	32	15	5	1	1	42	46
Other	6	23	59	48	6	6	116	137
NUMBER OF STATEMENTS	33	72	134	99	22	18	302	338

Date ranges: 42 (4/1-9/30/09); 336 (10/1/09-3/31/10)

Data

	0-500M %	500M-2MM %	2-10MM %	10-50MM %	50-100MM %	100-250MM %	4/1/05-3/31/06 ALL %	4/1/06-3/31/07 ALL %
ASSETS								
Cash & Equivalents	25.2	11.2	9.4	12.2	7.6	18.0	8.6	7.0
Trade Receivables (net)	17.8	16.5	19.2	16.3	13.2	6.6	18.9	19.8
Inventory	37.4	51.6	42.4	36.2	44.1	27.8	45.8	47.5
All Other Current	2.0	1.1	3.0	3.5	3.2	9.5	2.4	2.9
Total Current	82.4	80.3	74.0	68.3	68.2	61.9	75.8	77.2
Fixed Assets (net)	8.4	12.5	15.5	19.6	23.8	22.4	17.1	15.5
Intangibles (net)	1.8	2.4	3.3	5.2	1.5	5.1	1.9	2.5
All Other Non-Current	7.4	4.7	7.2	7.0	6.5	10.7	5.2	4.8
Total	100.0	100.0	100.0	100.0	100.0	100.0	100.0	100.0
LIABILITIES								
Notes Payable-Short Term	29.0	28.5	23.3	28.2	34.8	15.8	31.0	33.5
Cur. Mat.-L.T.D.	4.6	3.6	2.9	2.8	4.0	6.5	3.3	2.8
Trade Payables	13.5	16.1	12.9	10.6	9.2	5.7	12.2	10.9
Income Taxes Payable	.0	.0	.2	.2	.1	.2	.1	.1
All Other Current	11.4	6.9	12.2	11.8	8.3	9.3	10.5	10.7
Total Current	58.5	55.0	51.4	53.6	56.4	37.3	57.1	58.1
Long-Term Debt	12.3	12.4	10.5	12.0	16.8	21.2	12.4	12.0
Deferred Taxes	.0	.1	.5	.4	1.6	.9	.4	.3
All Other Non-Current	4.7	6.7	4.9	4.0	2.0	3.5	5.7	4.3
Net Worth	24.5	25.8	32.7	30.1	23.1	37.1	24.5	25.4
Total Liabilities & Net Worth	100.0	100.0	100.0	100.0	100.0	100.0	100.0	100.0
INCOME DATA								
Net Sales	100.0	100.0	100.0	100.0	100.0	100.0	100.0	100.0
Gross Profit	26.9	23.1	26.4	25.6	19.8	26.9	23.2	23.2
Operating Expenses	25.0	20.6	24.1	23.1	18.8	19.7	20.0	19.6
Operating Profit	1.9	2.5	2.3	2.5	1.0	7.2	3.3	3.6
All Other Expenses (net)	.7	.7	.5	.9	.4	3.7	.8	.8
Profit Before Taxes	1.2	1.8	1.8	1.7	.7	3.5	2.5	2.9
RATIOS								
Current	3.8	3.0	2.1	1.6	1.3	2.2	1.8	1.7
	1.8	1.5	1.5	1.3	1.2	1.3	1.3	1.2
	1.0	1.0	1.1	1.1	1.0	1.0	1.1	1.0
Quick	2.0	1.1	1.1	.8	.5	1.1	.9	.9
	.8	(71) .4	.5	.5	.3	.4	(301) .4	.4
	.3	.2	.3	.2	.2	.2	.2	.2
Sales/Receivables	0 UND	0 UND	8 45.6	12 31.7	9 40.8	8 43.5	6 64.3	6 60.6
	1 322.5	5 66.7	20 18.3	18 20.5	15 24.2	23 16.0	16 22.9	15 23.6
	21 17.2	20 17.9	37 10.0	36 10.2	23 16.1	37 9.9	34 10.7	33 11.0
Cost of Sales/Inventory	3 126.6	20 18.6	38 9.5	40 9.2	61 6.0	23 16.1	30 12.3	33 11.0
	21 17.8	57 6.4	66 5.6	67 5.4	81 4.5	58 6.3	61 6.0	63 5.8
	69 5.3	114 3.2	110 3.3	104 3.5	112 3.3	154 2.4	94 3.9	95 3.8
Cost of Sales/Payables	0 UND	0 UND	4 100.0	9 40.4	7 55.1	5 73.2	3 107.5	3 128.0
	2 194.0	6 62.7	14 26.1	16 23.5	15 24.3	14 27.0	10 38.2	8 44.0
	18 20.6	29 12.5	35 10.5	38 9.6	34 10.6	22 16.4	30 12.3	24 15.4
Sales/Working Capital	8.1	6.4	6.5	7.8	11.0	5.3	9.0	8.8
	22.4	24.5	13.7	16.5	27.2	8.6	24.8	23.2
	-196.2	UND	54.9	67.9	NM	NM	77.7	99.4
EBIT/Interest	14.8	5.3	6.4	5.3	3.8	9.3	6.4	4.7
	(22) 3.3	(58) 2.0	(121) 2.5	(88) 2.4	(21) 2.1	(15) 2.4	(275) 2.9	(290) 2.2
	-2.2	.9	1.1	1.1	1.0	1.2	1.4	1.2
Net Profit + Depr., Dep., Amort./Cur. Mat. L/T/D			7.2	5.9	2.6		5.8	4.6
		(19) 2.2	(21) 1.4	(14) 1.1			(54) 2.4	(53) 1.5
		.8	.9	.8			.8	.9
Fixed/Worth	.0	.0	.1	.2	.2	.1	.1	.1
	.1	.4	.3	.5	1.2	1.2	.5	.4
	.9	3.0	1.3	2.2	2.6	2.1	1.8	1.6
Debt/Worth	.6	1.3	1.0	1.4	2.5	1.0	1.7	1.5
	1.2	3.6	2.2	3.3	3.2	2.4	3.7	3.9
	NM	UND	5.5	10.8	8.4	8.4	8.4	12.0
% Profit Before Taxes/Tangible Net Worth	123.7	52.3	33.1	32.6	32.6	32.0	50.4	44.3
	(25) 19.7	(56) 14.8	(122) 10.0	(89) 14.6	(21) 13.4	(16) 11.0	(267) 26.2	(292) 22.3
	1.2	5.1	1.5	3.9	-.1	5.8	9.3	6.7
% Profit Before Taxes/Total Assets	43.4	10.3	8.4	8.0	4.3	11.8	10.9	11.4
	8.4	3.8	2.6	3.5	2.2	2.4	5.1	4.4
	-8.7	.8	.1	.5	.2	1.0	1.3	.9
Sales/Net Fixed Assets	UND	721.5	101.6	51.1	42.8	137.3	119.8	154.6
	283.7	46.4	37.2	17.6	8.7	6.8	41.4	46.2
	48.7	18.9	11.3	5.5	5.9	3.1	11.5	12.8
Sales/Total Assets	11.7	8.2	3.9	3.1	2.8	2.8	4.5	4.4
	6.0	4.2	2.9	2.3	2.1	1.4	3.0	3.1
	3.4	2.1	1.8	1.5	1.6	.8	2.1	1.9
% Depr., Dep., Amort./Sales	.1	.1	.3	.4	.4	.1	.2	.2
	(16) .7	(43) .7	(107) .6	(90) 1.0	(18) 1.4	(11) .9	(240) .5	(268) .5
	2.2	1.6	1.5	3.3	3.3	3.3	1.4	1.6
% Officers', Directors' Owners' Comp/Sales	1.0	1.1	.9	.5			.6	.6
	(16) 4.2	(37) 1.7	(48) 1.7	(26) 1.0			(115) 1.3	(135) 1.2
	6.6	3.6	4.5	2.4			3.5	2.7
Net Sales ($)	78935M	556457M	2118272M	4937186M	3765162M	7496461M	14794418M	19082781M
Total Assets ($)	8778M	82281M	666547M	2164122M	1584715M	3062859M	5691224M	5850871M

M = $ thousand   MM = $ million
See Pages 9 through 22 for Explanation of Ratios and Data

Comparative Historical Data

Current Data Sorted by Sales

			Type of Statement						
39	41	48	Unqualified				2	9	37
62	62	57	Reviewed	4	3	2	7	15	30
50	54	51	Compiled	9	7	8	15	12	5
57	70	74	Tax Returns	9	14	9	20	11	11
137	168	148	Other	5	13	14	15	41	60
4/1/07-3/31/08 ALL	4/1/08-3/31/09 ALL	4/1/09-3/31/10 ALL			42 (4/1-9/30/09)		336 (10/1/09-3/31/10)		
				0-1MM	1-3MM	3-5MM	5-10MM	10-25MM	25MM & OVER
345	395	378	NUMBER OF STATEMENTS	18	37	33	59	88	143
%	%	%	ASSETS	%	%	%	%	%	%
8.1	8.3	12.2	Cash & Equivalents	15.8	13.6	12.4	13.8	8.9	12.6
18.0	17.0	16.8	Trade Receivables (net)	11.6	17.7	19.8	17.5	20.1	14.3
44.9	45.4	41.5	Inventory	51.4	43.9	42.3	36.3	41.0	41.9
3.2	3.1	3.0	All Other Current	1.1	.3	2.0	2.4	2.8	4.5
74.2	73.8	73.5	Total Current	79.9	75.6	76.4	70.1	72.8	73.4
17.7	17.1	16.2	Fixed Assets (net)	11.5	16.5	15.8	17.5	14.2	17.5
2.9	2.6	3.5	Intangibles (net)	1.5	.9	3.3	5.0	5.3	2.7
5.3	6.4	6.8	All Other Non-Current	7.2	7.0	4.5	7.5	7.6	6.5
100.0	100.0	100.0	Total	100.0	100.0	100.0	100.0	100.0	100.0
			LIABILITIES						
30.6	26.4	26.4	Notes Payable-Short Term	26.2	20.6	34.5	18.8	25.9	29.4
3.3	4.1	3.4	Cur. Mat.-L.T.D.	6.5	1.7	1.3	2.1	3.4	4.4
10.4	11.3	12.4	Trade Payables	17.4	12.8	12.8	13.0	12.9	10.9
.1	.1	.1	Income Taxes Payable	.0	.0	.0	.1	.1	.2
9.3	12.4	10.6	All Other Current	11.7	7.3	12.8	11.0	11.9	10.0
53.7	54.4	52.9	Total Current	61.8	42.5	61.5	45.0	54.2	55.0
13.2	15.9	12.3	Long-Term Debt	18.5	22.8	7.2	13.2	10.9	10.4
.5	.3	.4	Deferred Taxes	.0	.0	.7	.2	.4	.6
4.8	5.9	4.7	All Other Non-Current	1.2	4.6	8.9	4.0	6.4	3.6
27.9	23.5	29.6	Net Worth	18.5	30.1	21.7	37.6	28.1	30.4
100.0	100.0	100.0	Total Liabilities & Net Worth	100.0	100.0	100.0	100.0	100.0	100.0
			INCOME DATA						
100.0	100.0	100.0	Net Sales	100.0	100.0	100.0	100.0	100.0	100.0
24.3	23.8	25.3	Gross Profit	38.1	34.5	25.0	31.2	25.0	19.1
20.2	21.4	22.8	Operating Expenses	36.7	30.7	22.6	28.0	23.0	16.7
4.1	2.4	2.5	Operating Profit	1.4	3.8	2.4	3.2	2.0	2.4
.9	1.1	.8	All Other Expenses (net)	2.3	1.1	.2	.9	.8	.6
3.2	1.4	1.7	Profit Before Taxes	-.9	2.7	2.2	2.3	1.2	1.8
			RATIOS						
2.0	1.9	2.1		3.3	5.0	2.4	2.9	2.0	1.6
1.3	1.4	1.4	Current	1.4	1.8	1.4	1.6	1.4	1.3
1.1	1.1	1.1		.8	1.0	.9	1.2	1.0	1.1
1.0	.8	1.0		1.2	2.2	1.2	1.7	.9	.7
(344) .4	.4 (377) .5		Quick	.3	.7 (32) .5	.7	.5	.4	
.2	.2			.1	.3	.3	.3	.3	.2
5 70.4	7 52.7	5 66.6		0 UND	1 335.9	1 559.0	6 62.3	7 52.1	8 48.5
16 23.3	15 23.7	16 23.0	Sales/Receivables	0 UND	18 20.6	19 19.5	21 17.7	19 18.8	14 26.0
31 11.8	29 12.5	32 11.3		27 13.7	38 9.6	55 6.6	39 9.4	35 10.5	24 14.9
35 10.4	34 10.6	31 11.9		30 12.1	37 9.9	26 13.9	31 11.7	25 14.7	34 10.9
64 5.7	65 5.6	62 5.9	Cost of Sales/Inventory	180 2.0	71 5.1	66 5.5	73 5.0	53 6.9	61 6.0
105 3.5	102 3.6	107 3.4		412 .9	199 1.8	101 3.6	144 2.5	99 3.7	92 4.0
3 125.5	4 86.5	3 113.5		0 UND	1 320.4	1 626.3	4 95.5	2 164.0	5 73.3
9 40.1	11 33.1	13 27.7	Cost of Sales/Payables	13 27.4	21 17.6	10 36.9	19 19.4	12 29.5	12 29.8
23 15.7	28 13.2	30 12.3		24 15.3	46 7.9	40 9.1	43 8.4	34 10.9	20 17.9
7.1	7.9	7.4		3.4	3.8	5.6	6.0	8.7	9.4
18.3	18.2	15.9	Sales/Working Capital	16.4	8.0	15.9	13.3	16.4	19.7
60.8	128.5	89.1		-10.0	-114.4	-64.9	56.7	403.5	55.0
5.2	5.5	5.5		5.5	13.7	5.3	4.1	5.7	6.0
(308) 2.4	(363) 2.2	(325) 2.2	EBIT/Interest	(14) 1.0	(30) 1.8	(31) 2.5	(50) 2.1	(77) 2.1	(123) 2.6
1.3	.9	1.1		-2.4	-.7	1.3	1.0	.8	1.3
4.1	4.8	4.9						5.5	4.3
(58) 1.5	(66) 1.5	(62) 1.6	Net Profit + Depr., Dep., Amort./Cur. Mat. L/T/D				(13) 1.7	(41) 1.7	1.4
.9	.8	.8						.5	.8
.1	.1	.1		.0	.1	.1	.1	.1	.2
.5	.5	.4	Fixed/Worth	.1	.6	.5	.4	.4	.4
1.5	2.0	1.7		5.4	-56.5	12.7	1.6	1.7	1.4
1.4	1.5	1.1		.9	.4	.9	.7	1.5	1.5
3.3	3.3	2.8	Debt/Worth	21.6	1.9	2.3	1.5	3.0	3.1
8.3	9.6	11.7		-56.3	-98.2	NM	5.7	14.9	7.9
45.9	40.3	34.9		716.6	74.4	31.4	40.9	37.6	33.2
(308) 19.7	(341) 15.4	(329) 13.8	% Profit Before Taxes/Tangible Net Worth	(13) 13.9	(27) 15.5	(25) 16.8	(52) 9.9	(77) 11.0	(135) 15.2
6.7	3.7	3.5		-17.1	3.7	5.7	.4	1.0	4.8
13.0	10.2	8.5		19.6	17.0	8.6	9.5	8.1	8.0
4.4	3.7	3.0	% Profit Before Taxes/Total Assets	1.8	6.0	3.7	2.7	2.8	3.4
1.3	-.3	.4		-8.8	-1.8	1.4	.1	-.3	1.0
106.9	109.0	121.6		UND	96.2	196.1	159.8	148.8	83.3
32.7	31.1	32.7	Sales/Net Fixed Assets	65.5	22.3	42.9	25.5	44.1	28.6
9.9	10.0	9.4		6.5	8.4	18.2	7.8	12.5	8.4
4.2	4.0	4.3		4.5	4.2	5.6	4.7	4.9	3.9
2.9	2.9	2.8	Sales/Total Assets	2.0	2.2	3.0	2.9	3.1	2.7
1.9	2.0	1.7		.9	1.2	1.5	1.4	2.1	2.0
.3	.3	.3			.6	.3	.5	.2	.3
(264) .6	(310) .7	(285) .9	% Depr., Dep., Amort./Sales	(27) 1.0	(23) 1.1	(43) 1.2	(70) .5	(115) .8	
1.7	2.1	2.1			2.3	1.7	2.2	2.0	1.9
.6	.8	.8			2.7	1.4	1.0	.8	.3
(115) 1.4	(152) 1.7	(134) 1.6	% Officers', Directors' Owners' Comp/Sales	(17) 3.5	(12) 2.0	(37) 1.7	(28) 1.5	(35) .6	
3.1	3.3	4.0			4.3	4.3	4.4	3.6	1.7
19387565M	15443253M	18952473M	Net Sales ($)	10241M	71650M	131532M	430506M	1433090M	16875454M
6360001M	6447458M	7569302M	Total Assets ($)	6510M	41155M	64763M	269606M	671596M	6515672M

M = $ thousand   MM = $ million
See Pages 9 through 22 for Explanation of Ratios and Data

Current Data Sorted by Assets — Comparative Historical Data

0-500M	500M-2MM	2-10MM	10-50MM	50-100MM	100-250MM	Type of Statement	4/1/05-3/31/06 ALL	4/1/06-3/31/07 ALL
1	1	13	36	11	4	Unqualified	73	78
1	7	61	41			Reviewed	107	117
6	30	40	9			Compiled	100	101
11	33	19				Tax Returns	70	67
9	32	77	62	10	7	Other	183	146
	79 (4/1-9/30/09)			442 (10/1/09-3/31/10)				
28	103	210	148	21	11	NUMBER OF STATEMENTS	533	509

0-500M %	500M-2MM %	2-10MM %	10-50MM %	50-100MM %	100-250MM %		ALL %	ALL %
						ASSETS		
12.9	8.9	7.6	4.3	1.6	8.5	Cash & Equivalents	6.1	5.1
25.5	20.4	24.5	22.2	23.5	18.4	Trade Receivables (net)	24.8	24.6
42.6	48.7	48.5	48.6	44.7	34.4	Inventory	47.6	49.6
1.1	2.6	2.6	2.6	1.6	1.6	All Other Current	1.5	1.8
82.2	80.7	83.2	77.8	71.5	62.9	Total Current	79.9	81.1
12.5	12.6	11.0	11.2	12.0	13.2	Fixed Assets (net)	12.2	11.2
4.2	2.0	2.2	6.0	13.8	18.3	Intangibles (net)	2.7	2.8
1.1	4.8	3.6	5.0	2.7	5.6	All Other Non-Current	5.2	4.8
100.0	100.0	100.0	100.0	100.0	100.0	Total	100.0	100.0
						LIABILITIES		
42.2	16.0	18.1	19.3	27.9	5.4	Notes Payable-Short Term	16.0	17.9
3.8	3.8	1.6	2.4	1.5	.7	Cur. Mat.-L.T.D.	2.2	2.2
19.3	17.9	20.2	20.4	17.3	18.7	Trade Payables	20.8	21.8
.3	.2	.1	.2	.4	.0	Income Taxes Payable	.3	.2
18.8	7.9	5.8	5.7	5.9	8.3	All Other Current	8.3	9.1
84.5	45.7	45.8	47.9	53.0	33.3	Total Current	47.5	51.1
15.5	13.3	8.0	7.5	8.0	14.5	Long-Term Debt	12.7	11.8
.1	.0	.1	.4	.1	1.5	Deferred Taxes	.2	.3
10.5	11.5	6.2	4.7	7.9	6.5	All Other Non-Current	6.0	5.8
-10.7	29.5	39.8	39.6	31.0	44.2	Net Worth	33.6	31.0
100.0	100.0	100.0	100.0	100.0	100.0	Total Liabilities & Net Worth	100.0	100.0
						INCOME DATA		
100.0	100.0	100.0	100.0	100.0	100.0	Net Sales	100.0	100.0
38.7	33.9	29.5	30.8	28.6	29.6	Gross Profit	31.5	31.2
36.4	33.1	26.4	27.3	24.5	26.6	Operating Expenses	27.9	27.7
2.3	.8	3.1	3.5	4.1	3.0	Operating Profit	3.6	3.5
3.2	.7	.7	1.0	2.4	1.9	All Other Expenses (net)	.6	.9
-.9	.1	2.4	2.5	1.7	1.1	Profit Before Taxes	3.0	2.6
						RATIOS		
5.0	3.8	2.9	2.5	1.9	2.9	Current	2.7	2.6
1.6	1.8	1.8	1.6	1.4	2.5		1.7	1.7
.9	1.2	1.3	1.2	1.1	1.0		1.3	1.3
1.5	1.4	1.2	1.0	.8	1.0	Quick	1.0	1.0
.7	.6	.6	.5	.4	.8		.6	.6
.4	.3	.4	.3	.3	.5		.4	.4
17 21.9	13 28.3	23 15.9	27 13.7	30 12.3	28 12.9	Sales/Receivables	23 15.6	24 15.0
25 14.4	25 14.3	36 10.2	36 10.2	36 10.0	41 8.9		34 10.8	34 10.8
38 9.5	39 9.4	46 8.0	54 6.8	48 7.7	63 5.8		47 7.7	47 7.8
41 8.9	64 5.7	68 5.4	87 4.2	76 4.8	59 6.2	Cost of Sales/Inventory	66 5.6	67 5.4
83 4.4	100 3.7	98 3.7	131 2.8	122 3.0	163 2.2		103 3.6	111 3.3
135 2.7	181 2.0	155 2.4	212 1.7	145 2.5	190 1.9		157 2.3	167 2.2
9 39.2	15 23.6	21 17.6	23 15.6	29 12.7	53 6.9	Cost of Sales/Payables	21 17.0	23 16.2
24 15.0	32 11.2	35 10.5	48 7.7	36 10.1	57 6.4		39 9.4	40 9.1
43 8.4	53 7.0	55 6.6	74 4.9	61 6.0	77 4.7		63 5.8	66 5.5
4.5	3.7	4.0	3.9	6.3	2.8	Sales/Working Capital	4.6	4.3
7.7	7.4	6.2	7.3	8.0	4.7		8.1	7.6
-85.0	38.2	14.0	12.1	26.1	-508.8		15.8	18.1
6.2	6.7	8.3	10.7	9.6	9.6	EBIT/Interest	8.4	6.6
(23) 2.5	(88) 2.3	(191) 3.2	(139) 3.8	(20) 3.4	(10) 3.4		(481) 3.5	(465) 2.8
-2.4	-.7	1.2	1.4	1.1	-.1		1.6	1.3
		5.0	7.5	21.4		Net Profit + Depr., Dep., Amort./Cur. Mat. L/T/D	8.0	6.6
		(48) 2.1	(56) 3.5	(10) 4.9			(130) 3.1	(133) 2.0
		.6	1.4	.8			1.3	.9
.0	.1	.1	.1	.2	.1	Fixed/Worth	.1	.1
.5	.2	.2	.3	.6	.4		.3	.2
-.5	.9	.6	.8	NM	1.3		.8	.8
1.1	.7	.8	.8	1.7	1.1	Debt/Worth	.9	.9
10.2	2.4	1.6	1.9	5.9	2.0		2.0	2.1
-5.6	6.4	3.9	5.0	NM	8.1		5.5	5.9
104.0	32.1	24.1	29.3	40.3		% Profit Before Taxes/Tangible Net Worth	39.5	36.7
(17) 16.7	(84) 8.7	(192) 10.4	(134) 14.1	(16) 17.1			(474) 18.3	(454) 16.1
4.2	-1.2	2.2	2.9	5.8			5.4	4.4
12.6	9.2	9.7	9.5	10.5	9.4	% Profit Before Taxes/Total Assets	12.8	12.0
4.0	2.5	3.5	3.7	3.9	5.7		5.7	4.4
-6.2	-2.4	.7	.8	.4	-7.0		1.5	.8
UND	121.9	87.7	68.0	69.8	44.1	Sales/Net Fixed Assets	71.3	86.5
293.8	40.6	40.1	36.2	31.4	14.3		34.4	37.0
19.5	17.2	19.0	13.2	14.4	10.0		17.1	17.8
4.7	3.7	3.0	2.6	2.4	1.8	Sales/Total Assets	3.2	3.1
3.0	2.5	2.4	1.9	2.1	1.5		2.5	2.4
2.0	1.6	1.8	1.4	1.6	1.2		1.8	1.8
.1	.4	.4	.5	.5		% Depr., Dep., Amort./Sales	.4	.4
(18) .5	(69) .8	(176) .7	(137) .8	(19) 1.0			(456) .8	(437) .8
1.4	1.3	1.3	1.3	1.5			1.4	1.3
3.3	1.8	1.5	1.0			% Officers', Directors' Owners' Comp/Sales	1.5	1.7
(17) 4.3	(53) 4.2	(93) 2.6	(35) 2.1				(220) 2.8	(192) 2.9
8.9	8.9	4.2	3.1				6.1	5.7
26013M	349272M	2713225M	6611810M	2966033M	2622519M	Net Sales ($)	14222047M	14133794M
7782M	119855M	1097767M	3310195M	1491366M	1669145M	Total Assets ($)	7320577M	6768111M

M = $ thousand   MM = $ million
See Pages 9 through 22 for Explanation of Ratios and Data

Comparative Historical Data — Current Data Sorted by Sales

4/1/07-3/31/08 ALL	4/1/08-3/31/09 ALL	4/1/09-3/31/10 ALL	Type of Statement	0-1MM	1-3MM	3-5MM	5-10MM	10-25MM	25MM & OVER
65	69	66	Unqualified	1	1	2	3	13	46
104	108	110	Reviewed	2	1	6	16	48	37
101	101	85	Compiled	2	20	8	28	24	3
58	64	63	Tax Returns	6	25	11	11	10	
164	197	197	Other	13	20	11	30	51	72
				79 (4/1-9/30/09)			442 (10/1/09-3/31/10)		
492	539	521	NUMBER OF STATEMENTS	24	67	38	88	146	158
%	%	%	**ASSETS**	%	%	%	%	%	%
6.0	5.6	7.0	Cash & Equivalents	9.0	8.1	6.6	10.6	6.2	5.0
23.9	22.7	22.9	Trade Receivables (net)	16.3	20.5	18.3	24.3	23.9	24.4
49.3	50.8	47.8	Inventory	42.2	51.3	50.6	43.9	48.3	48.1
2.1	2.6	2.5	All Other Current	.6	2.9	2.9	3.3	2.3	2.3
81.2	81.7	80.2	Total Current	68.2	82.9	78.4	82.0	80.7	79.8
11.3	10.6	11.6	Fixed Assets (net)	22.1	11.5	15.1	11.4	11.0	9.8
3.7	3.7	4.1	Intangibles (net)	4.5	2.3	2.4	1.9	4.2	6.5
3.8	4.0	4.1	All Other Non-Current	5.2	3.3	4.1	4.7	4.1	3.9
100.0	100.0	100.0	Total	100.0	100.0	100.0	100.0	100.0	100.0
			LIABILITIES						
17.9	19.0	19.4	Notes Payable-Short Term	49.6	15.7	20.0	15.9	18.1	19.5
2.2	2.4	2.3	Cur. Mat.-L.T.D.	2.2	4.5	3.2	1.7	1.7	2.2
21.7	19.7	19.6	Trade Payables	12.8	16.7	14.8	22.2	18.7	22.5
.2	.2	.2	Income Taxes Payable	.3	.2	.2	.0	.2	.2
6.7	7.9	6.9	All Other Current	18.2	8.4	8.5	5.2	5.6	6.5
48.7	49.2	48.5	Total Current	83.2	45.6	46.7	45.1	44.1	50.8
11.0	10.0	9.4	Long-Term Debt	22.8	14.4	13.5	7.9	7.5	7.0
.2	.1	.2	Deferred Taxes	.1	.0	.3	.1	.3	.3
6.7	5.1	7.1	All Other Non-Current	14.7	15.6	2.9	4.7	6.5	5.4
33.5	35.5	34.7	Net Worth	-20.9	24.4	36.6	42.3	41.7	36.5
100.0	100.0	100.0	Total Liabilities & Net Worth	100.0	100.0	100.0	100.0	100.0	100.0
			INCOME DATA						
100.0	100.0	100.0	Net Sales	100.0	100.0	100.0	100.0	100.0	100.0
30.4	31.0	31.2	Gross Profit	42.8	35.8	32.0	29.3	30.4	29.1
26.5	27.9	28.5	Operating Expenses	41.2	34.7	30.8	26.6	27.4	25.4
3.9	3.0	2.8	Operating Profit	1.6	1.0	1.1	2.7	3.0	3.8
1.0	.8	1.0	All Other Expenses (net)	6.1	1.0	.4	.4	.9	.9
2.9	2.2	1.7	Profit Before Taxes	-4.5	.1	.7	2.4	2.1	2.9
			RATIOS						
2.6	2.6	2.9	Current	5.8	3.8	3.1	3.1	2.8	2.4
1.6	1.7	1.7		1.6	2.0	1.7	1.8	1.8	1.5
1.3	1.2	1.2		.4	1.4	1.1	1.2	1.3	1.2
1.0	.9	1.1	Quick	1.4	1.5	1.0	1.3	1.1	1.0
.6	.5	.6		.4	.6	.4	.8	.6	.5
.4	.3	.4		.2	.3	.3	.5	.4	.3
23 15.6	21 17.0	23 16.0	Sales/Receivables	21 17.7	16 22.7	19 19.7	23 15.8	26 14.1	25 14.5
33 11.2	31 11.8	34 10.8		33 11.2	25 14.3	26 14.2	37 10.0	37 9.9	35 10.3
45 8.1	44 8.4	46 8.0		51 7.2	38 9.6	36 10.0	48 7.6	46 7.9	51 7.1
67 5.4	70 5.2	69 5.3	Cost of Sales/Inventory	90 4.1	77 4.7	60 6.1	63 5.8	75 4.9	71 5.1
109 3.4	114 3.2	109 3.4		161 2.3	115 3.2	126 2.9	87 4.2	107 3.4	116 3.1
157 2.3	179 2.0	178 2.0		228 1.6	203 1.8	190 1.9	148 2.5	168 2.2	174 2.1
24 15.3	20 18.6	21 17.6	Cost of Sales/Payables	14 26.1	14 26.3	14 25.3	23 15.7	20 17.9	24 15.2
41 8.9	34 10.9	36 10.1		34 10.8	34 10.8	23 15.8	35 10.6	35 10.6	48 7.7
62 5.8	56 6.6	61 6.0		73 5.0	51 7.1	52 7.1	60 6.1	53 6.8	68 5.4
4.6	4.3	4.0	Sales/Working Capital	2.1	3.6	4.0	3.8	4.1	4.7
7.7	7.6	6.8		5.0	5.4	7.1	6.4	6.3	8.4
15.1	18.6	15.8		-2.7	20.9	40.1	17.0	12.7	18.0
(444) 6.6	(495) 7.5	(471) 8.7	EBIT/Interest	(20) 2.2	(57) 6.0	(33) 5.1	(78) 9.8	(132) 8.9	(151) 10.8
2.6	2.9	3.3		.5	2.8	2.2	2.6	3.5	4.5
1.4	1.1	1.1		-6.2	-.8	-.4	.9	1.4	1.6
(136) 5.5	(144) 6.8	(128) 7.3	Net Profit + Depr., Dep., Amort./Cur. Mat. L/T/D				6.9	6.6	13.1
2.5	3.0	2.7				(12) 2.1	(43) 3.0	(61) 3.8	
.8	.9	1.0				-.2	1.0	1.3	
.1	.1	.1	Fixed/Worth	.0	.0	.1	.1	.1	.1
.3	.2	.2		2.3	.3	.3	.2	.2	.3
.8	.7	.7		-.8	1.5	.6	.6	.7	.7
1.0	.9	.9	Debt/Worth	1.7	1.1	.9	.6	.8	1.0
2.1	2.0	2.0		9.3	3.1	1.8	1.7	1.6	2.3
5.5	5.6	5.5		-3.0	-94.3	4.7	3.3	3.9	6.1
(442) 39.3	(480) 33.3	(452) 28.0	% Profit Before Taxes/Tangible Net Worth	(13) 20.0	(49) 37.6	(35) 28.0	(83) 20.8	(133) 23.9	(139) 34.0
17.4	14.5	11.9		3.1	8.5	10.6	8.2	9.8	17.1
5.7	2.9	2.1		-9.7	-1.1	-6.5	.6	2.2	6.4
13.0	10.7	9.7	% Profit Before Taxes/Total Assets	5.7	9.2	7.2	9.8	9.3	11.0
5.1	4.6	3.7		.3	2.5	2.8	2.8	3.8	4.9
1.4	.2	.3		-19.5	-5.3	-2.4	.1	.9	1.3
86.5	92.1	89.3	Sales/Net Fixed Assets	150.8	443.3	108.3	76.1	71.9	80.4
36.9	37.1	39.3		23.4	55.2	39.0	35.1	37.8	42.5
17.5	17.3	16.3		2.8	17.2	10.0	17.3	16.8	16.4
3.2	3.2	2.9	Sales/Total Assets	2.2	3.5	2.9	3.1	2.9	2.9
2.4	2.4	2.3		1.3	2.3	2.2	2.4	2.3	2.3
1.8	1.7	1.6		.9	1.6	1.6	1.6	1.7	1.6
(422) .4	(445) .4	(427) .4	% Depr., Dep., Amort./Sales	(16) .4	(40) .3	(30) .5	(71) .4	(124) .5	(146) .4
.8	.7	.8		1.0	.7	.9	.7	.8	.8
1.3	1.2	1.4		5.9	1.5	1.4	1.2	1.4	1.3
(191) 1.5	(206) 1.4	(201) 1.6	% Officers', Directors' Owners' Comp/Sales	(11) 3.3	(38) 3.2	(23) 1.6	(40) 1.8	(59) 1.3	(30) .7
2.8	2.6	2.8		4.0	6.0	2.9	3.1	2.1	1.3
5.1	4.7	5.4		12.5	9.4	6.9	5.5	3.2	3.1
16845240M	21023396M	15288872M	Net Sales ($)	13841M	129022M	147168M	643100M	2326670M	12029071M
7905636M	9561307M	7696110M	Total Assets ($)	17444M	61604M	67158M	325356M	1190942M	6033606M

M = $ thousand   MM = $ million
See Pages 9 through 22 for Explanation of Ratios and Data

Current Data Sorted by Assets   Comparative Historical Data

Type of Statement

0-500M	500M-2MM	2-10MM	10-50MM	50-100MM	100-250MM	Type of Statement	4/1/05-3/31/06 ALL	4/1/06-3/31/07 ALL
		1	9	5	8	Unqualified	16	17
		10	14	2		Reviewed	41	38
1	9	13	7			Compiled	40	36
1	2	7				Tax Returns	18	25
2	5	12	23	2	5	Other	69	57
	28 (4/1-9/30/09)		110 (10/1/09-3/31/10)					
4	16	43	53	9	13	NUMBER OF STATEMENTS	184	173

0-500M	500M-2MM	2-10MM	10-50MM	50-100MM	100-250MM		4/1/05-3/31/06 ALL	4/1/06-3/31/07 ALL
%	%	%	%	%	%	ASSETS	%	%
	8.0	5.0	6.0		3.7	Cash & Equivalents	6.4	6.0
	23.7	27.2	27.7		21.5	Trade Receivables (net)	27.9	26.2
	46.0	44.7	38.9		41.6	Inventory	41.3	39.8
	1.2	2.5	3.1		2.9	All Other Current	3.0	3.1
	78.9	79.5	75.7		69.6	Total Current	78.6	75.1
	12.4	15.2	17.3		17.8	Fixed Assets (net)	15.7	19.2
	6.5	1.3	1.4		10.9	Intangibles (net)	1.8	1.8
	2.1	4.1	5.5		1.7	All Other Non-Current	3.8	3.8
	100.0	100.0	100.0		100.0	Total	100.0	100.0
						LIABILITIES		
	6.3	15.7	13.2		5.0	Notes Payable-Short Term	12.3	12.9
	2.7	3.0	2.2		1.8	Cur. Mat.-L.T.D.	2.4	3.0
	35.0	34.8	29.9		28.7	Trade Payables	34.3	32.7
	.5	.1	.4		.6	Income Taxes Payable	.2	.2
	16.5	9.7	5.5		4.7	All Other Current	6.9	6.3
	61.0	63.2	51.1		40.7	Total Current	56.1	55.0
	26.4	7.4	6.8		21.8	Long-Term Debt	9.0	10.9
	.0	.1	.4		.5	Deferred Taxes	.2	.3
	7.8	3.6	2.6		6.0	All Other Non-Current	2.5	4.9
	4.8	25.7	39.1		30.9	Net Worth	32.2	28.9
	100.0	100.0	100.0		100.0	Total Liabilities & Net Worth	100.0	100.0
						INCOME DATA		
	100.0	100.0	100.0		100.0	Net Sales	100.0	100.0
	30.3	25.7	20.7		22.8	Gross Profit	26.8	26.0
	28.7	25.1	18.9		21.2	Operating Expenses	23.8	24.1
	1.6	.6	1.8		1.6	Operating Profit	3.0	1.9
	.2	-.1	-.1		.8	All Other Expenses (net)	.1	.3
	1.4	.7	1.9		.7	Profit Before Taxes	2.9	1.6
						RATIOS		
	2.2	1.6	2.0		2.0		1.9	1.8
	1.4	1.2	1.5		1.6	Current	1.3	1.3
	.9	1.0	1.2		1.3		1.2	1.1
	.9	.7	.9		.8		.9	.8
	.4	.4	.6		.6	Quick	(183) .6	.5
	.2	.3	.4		.5		.4	.4
	5 72.0	21 17.5	28 12.9		22 16.9		24 15.0	20 18.6
	19 18.8	35 10.4	38 9.7		34 10.7	Sales/Receivables	34 10.9	31 11.8
	33 11.1	44 8.3	47 7.8		48 7.6		45 8.1	42 8.6
	39 9.4	52 7.0	53 6.9		65 5.7		54 6.8	46 7.9
	67 5.4	83 4.4	65 5.6		77 4.8	Cost of Sales/Inventory	70 5.2	68 5.4
	106 3.5	106 3.5	81 4.5		103 3.5		93 3.9	87 4.2
	22 16.5	39 9.4	32 11.4		46 8.0		33 11.2	33 11.0
	40 9.1	54 6.8	53 6.9		58 6.3	Cost of Sales/Payables	57 6.4	50 7.3
	68 5.3	79 4.6	71 5.1		73 5.0		78 4.7	71 5.2
	9.0	8.3	7.1		5.9		7.9	8.6
	15.1	23.4	10.6		8.0	Sales/Working Capital	13.7	16.8
	-64.1	132.3	45.5		19.1		28.1	50.5
	10.0	6.0	15.1		18.9		16.4	8.0
	(15) 1.8	(40) 2.7	(52) 5.3		(12) 9.1	EBIT/Interest	(172) 5.6	(160) 3.4
	.7	1.1	2.2		1.6		2.4	1.6
		6.5	5.4				8.6	4.8
		(10) 2.9	(15) 1.2			Net Profit + Depr., Dep., Amort./Cur. Mat. L/T/D	(51) 3.1	(49) 2.3
		1.4	.4				1.9	1.3
	.1	.2	.2		.4		.2	.2
	.6	.5	.4		1.4	Fixed/Worth	.4	.5
	-.2	1.4	.9		8.3		.9	1.4
	1.1	1.9	.9		1.4		1.1	1.3
	8.0	3.5	1.7		2.8	Debt/Worth	2.3	2.6
	-2.5	6.5	3.3		27.3		4.8	5.1
	212.7	31.1	20.4		41.1		39.6	38.0
	(10) 12.3	(41) 12.9	11.4		(11) 24.8	% Profit Before Taxes/Tangible Net Worth	(176) 21.0	(158) 19.0
	.6	1.1	6.4		14.6		10.4	4.4
	13.1	5.9	7.8		12.4		12.1	9.1
	2.9	3.6	4.0		5.5	% Profit Before Taxes/Total Assets	6.0	4.5
	-1.8	.7	1.9		1.8		2.8	.8
	143.4	86.3	42.0		33.4		58.0	54.8
	67.1	36.3	19.9		19.4	Sales/Net Fixed Assets	26.0	24.8
	21.1	15.5	7.3		7.7		12.8	10.8
	4.8	3.6	3.3		2.9		3.7	3.8
	3.6	2.9	2.6		2.3	Sales/Total Assets	3.0	3.1
	2.5	2.0	2.1		1.9		2.3	2.4
	.3	.5	.5		1.0		.5	.5
	(11) .6	(37) .9	(51) .9		(12) 1.4	% Depr., Dep., Amort./Sales	(157) 1.0	(156) 1.0
	1.7	1.5	1.5		2.0		1.6	1.6
		.8	.8				.8	.9
		(22) 1.3	(16) 1.1			% Officers', Directors' Owners' Comp/Sales	(60) 1.8	(62) 2.0
		2.5	1.9				3.0	4.5
5524M	74671M	630892M	3150708M	1701529M	5091319M	Net Sales ($)	7747927M	9605214M
949M	18701M	221741M	1248860M	652508M	2048640M	Total Assets ($)	3186374M	3475371M

M = $ thousand   MM = $ million
See Pages 9 through 22 for Explanation of Ratios and Data

Comparative Historical Data

Current Data Sorted by Sales

					Type of Statement							
	18		21		23	Unqualified				1	1	22
	34		35		26	Reviewed				10	10	15
	41		35		30	Compiled	1	2	3	9	7	8
	16		11		10	Tax Returns		2		5	3	
	55		57		49	Other	2	1	1	6	7	32
	4/1/07-3/31/08		4/1/08-3/31/09		4/1/09-3/31/10			28 (4/1-9/30/09)		110 (10/1/09-3/31/10)		
	ALL		ALL		ALL		0-1MM	1-3MM	3-5MM	5-10MM	10-25MM	25MM & OVER
	164		159		138	NUMBER OF STATEMENTS	3	5	4	21	28	77
	%		%		%	ASSETS	%	%	%	%	%	%
	5.3		5.1		5.9	Cash & Equivalents				8.4	3.4	6.0
	27.5		24.7		26.0	Trade Receivables (net)				27.5	26.6	26.5
	41.4		44.7		41.4	Inventory				43.6	44.9	39.5
	3.3		3.0		2.7	All Other Current				4.0	2.0	2.9
	77.5		77.6		76.0	Total Current				83.5	76.9	74.9
	15.5		15.7		16.9	Fixed Assets (net)				14.2	15.6	17.7
	2.5		1.9		2.9	Intangibles (net)				.8	2.2	2.8
	4.5		4.9		4.2	All Other Non-Current				1.5	5.3	4.5
	100.0		100.0		100.0	Total				100.0	100.0	100.0
					LIABILITIES						
	13.0		14.8		12.6	Notes Payable-Short Term				12.9	16.5	11.9
	3.1		2.6		2.5	Cur. Mat.-L.T.D.				4.1	1.8	2.2
	32.5		30.9		32.1	Trade Payables				34.8	38.6	29.6
	.1		.1		.3	Income Taxes Payable				.1	.1	.3
	6.9		7.1		8.1	All Other Current				8.8	9.5	5.7
	55.5		55.5		55.5	Total Current				60.7	66.5	49.8
	10.3		10.0		11.3	Long-Term Debt				19.0	6.3	9.3
	.3		.2		.2	Deferred Taxes				.0	.1	.4
	4.4		4.7		3.8	All Other Non-Current				1.1	2.6	3.9
	29.5		29.6		29.1	Net Worth				19.2	24.6	36.7
	100.0		100.0		100.0	Total Liabilities & Net Worth				100.0	100.0	100.0
					INCOME DATA						
	100.0		100.0		100.0	Net Sales				100.0	100.0	100.0
	24.7		25.2		24.1	Gross Profit				25.6	26.8	20.9
	22.4		23.3		22.6	Operating Expenses				25.7	25.3	18.9
	2.3		2.0		1.5	Operating Profit				-.1	1.5	1.9
	.3		.4		.0	All Other Expenses (net)				-.4	.0	.1
	2.0		1.6		1.5	Profit Before Taxes				.3	1.5	1.8
					RATIOS						
	1.7		1.9		1.8					1.8	1.4	1.9
	1.4		1.4		1.4	Current				1.4	1.1	1.5
	1.1		1.1		1.1					1.1	1.0	1.2
	.7		.7		.8					.9	.6	.9
	.5		.5		.6	Quick				.7	.4	.6
	.4		.3		.4					.3	.3	.4
23	15.9	18	20.7	20	18.0	Sales/Receivables	21	17.7	18 20.2	25 14.3		
33	11.2	30	12.1	34	10.7		35	10.4	28 13.0	36 10.0		
43	8.4	41	8.8	44	8.3		48	7.6	42 8.8	45 8.0		
49	7.5	53	6.8	53	6.9	Cost of Sales/Inventory	49	7.4	52 7.0	54 6.8		
69	5.3	73	5.0	71	5.1		68	5.4	82 4.4	67 5.4		
93	3.9	97	3.7	96	3.8		112	3.3	106 3.4	81 4.5		
32	11.3	29	12.6	32	11.5	Cost of Sales/Payables	34	10.8	40 9.1	32 11.5		
53	6.9	51	7.2	52	7.0		48	7.6	54 6.7	54 6.7		
73	5.0	69	5.3	71	5.1		74	4.9	80 4.6	67 5.4		
	8.2		7.7		7.2	Sales/Working Capital				6.1	13.9	6.9
	15.5		14.6		14.1					15.0	63.6	10.7
	42.0		34.3		77.1					84.8	-187.0	22.1
	7.9		7.6		10.9	EBIT/Interest				5.2	7.1	15.0
(154)	3.3	(150)	3.4	(132)	4.1		(19)	2.5	(27) 2.8	(74) 5.5		
	1.7		1.4		1.8					.5	1.5	2.1
	6.3		4.4		9.8	Net Profit + Depr., Dep., Amort./Cur. Mat. L/T/D						10.3
(43)	3.1	(48)	2.2	(40)	2.6						(31) 2.4	
	1.5		1.3		.8							1.0
	.2		.2		.2	Fixed/Worth				.2	.2	.2
	.4		.5		.5					.3	.5	.4
	1.1		1.1		1.4					2.3	1.4	1.0
	1.3		1.3		1.4	Debt/Worth				1.6	2.2	1.2
	2.5		2.6		2.5					3.7	3.7	2.0
	4.9		5.9		5.8					10.1	8.2	3.7
	34.3		31.7		30.4	% Profit Before Taxes/Tangible Net Worth				24.6	42.6	25.8
(151)	16.1	(147)	13.2	(127)	13.5		(18)	8.0	(26) 15.9	(75) 14.6		
	6.9		3.8		6.4					-13.7	4.3	7.8
	9.4		8.3		8.8	% Profit Before Taxes/Total Assets				9.1	8.2	8.9
	5.2		4.3		4.1					3.6	3.2	5.1
	1.7		.9		1.7					-1.6	.9	2.0
	55.2		61.8		62.1	Sales/Net Fixed Assets				87.5	110.0	43.4
	29.4		28.1		25.8					36.3	37.6	21.5
	13.1		13.2		9.9					16.1	13.4	8.2
	3.8		3.6		3.5	Sales/Total Assets				4.2	3.7	3.3
	3.0		2.9		2.8					2.8	3.0	2.6
	2.3		2.2		2.1					1.9	2.5	2.1
	.5		.5		.5	% Depr., Dep., Amort./Sales				.3	.6	.5
(147)	.9	(142)	.8	(123)	.9		(17)	.7	(24) 1.1	(73) 1.0		
	1.4		1.3		1.6					1.4	1.8	1.6
	.6		1.0		.8	% Officers', Directors' Owners' Comp/Sales				.9	.6	.7
(68)	1.2	(57)	1.6	(52)	1.4		(13)	2.2	(12) 1.2	(21) .9		
	3.0		3.5		3.2					5.1	1.7	1.8
9808360M		13499898M		10654643M		Net Sales ($)	1879M	8556M	17614M	154501M	433044M	10039049M
4004875M		4678550M		4191399M		Total Assets ($)	947M	2470M	5266M	66252M	158359M	3958105M

M = $ thousand   MM = $ million
See Pages 9 through 22 for Explanation of Ratios and Data

Current Data Sorted by Assets   Comparative Historical Data

Type of Statement

0-500M	500M-2MM	2-10MM	10-50MM	50-100MM	100-250MM	Type of Statement	4/1/05-3/31/06 ALL	4/1/06-3/31/07 ALL
		1	2	3	1	Unqualified	7	5
	3	5	7			Reviewed	12	17
1	2	8	1			Compiled	12	13
6	3	3				Tax Returns	18	18
	2	9	3			Other	17	17
	16 (4/1-9/30/09)		44 (10/1/09-3/31/10)				4/1/05-3/31/06	4/1/06-3/31/07
7	10	26	13	3	1	NUMBER OF STATEMENTS	66	70

0-500M %	500M-2MM %	2-10MM %	10-50MM %	50-100MM %	100-250MM %		ALL %	ALL %
						ASSETS		
	7.3	8.0	3.5			Cash & Equivalents	6.8	6.7
	29.9	19.6	24.7			Trade Receivables (net)	18.2	18.2
	39.8	44.4	46.1			Inventory	43.9	43.9
	1.8	5.6	1.6			All Other Current	2.6	2.8
	78.8	77.6	76.0			Total Current	71.6	71.6
	6.5	17.4	12.6			Fixed Assets (net)	21.9	18.2
	1.0	2.8	5.3			Intangibles (net)	2.1	2.0
	13.8	2.3	6.1			All Other Non-Current	4.5	8.2
	100.0	100.0	100.0			Total	100.0	100.0
						LIABILITIES		
	13.7	17.0	21.9			Notes Payable-Short Term	12.8	11.6
	4.7	2.3	3.3			Cur. Mat.-L.T.D.	3.7	2.2
	20.2	13.4	13.0			Trade Payables	11.6	13.8
	.0	.2	.1			Income Taxes Payable	.2	.2
	7.6	9.2	7.9			All Other Current	9.6	11.9
	46.1	42.2	46.1			Total Current	38.0	39.6
	4.0	3.4	8.3			Long-Term Debt	19.7	16.0
	.1	.2	.3			Deferred Taxes	.3	.1
	6.7	5.5	12.8			All Other Non-Current	5.7	5.1
	43.1	48.7	32.5			Net Worth	36.4	39.2
	100.0	100.0	100.0			Total Liabilities & Net Worth	100.0	100.0
						INCOME DATA		
	100.0	100.0	100.0			Net Sales	100.0	100.0
	33.9	34.8	30.9			Gross Profit	40.5	36.9
	31.4	30.9	29.1			Operating Expenses	36.8	33.1
	2.5	3.9	1.8			Operating Profit	3.7	3.8
	.6	.5	.8			All Other Expenses (net)	1.0	.4
	1.9	3.4	1.0			Profit Before Taxes	2.7	3.4
						RATIOS		
	2.5	4.5	2.4			Current	3.7	3.6
	1.8	1.6	1.6				1.9	2.2
	1.2	1.2	1.3				1.4	1.5
	1.4	2.2	1.2			Quick	1.2	1.3
	.8	.6	.6				(65) .5	.7
	.5	.2	.4				.3	.3
28 12.8	11 32.2	29 12.7				Sales/Receivables	10 34.9	8 47.4
37 9.8	26 13.9	35 10.3					26 14.3	23 16.1
50 7.3	39 9.4	66 5.5					41 8.9	35 10.4
37 9.8	59 6.2	80 4.5				Cost of Sales/Inventory	58 6.3	46 7.9
63 5.8	89 4.1	138 2.7					95 3.8	88 4.1
122 3.0	158 2.3	179 2.0					195 1.9	140 2.6
14 25.3	5 77.7	7 50.9				Cost of Sales/Payables	7 51.5	5 75.7
27 13.6	22 16.9	32 11.5					17 20.9	17 20.9
65 5.6	38 9.6	62 5.9					49 7.4	52 7.0
	4.5	3.2	3.6			Sales/Working Capital	3.7	4.1
	11.5	8.4	6.8				7.4	7.7
	39.1	16.1	17.0				18.3	17.4
		13.8	6.3			EBIT/Interest	7.5	8.9
		(21) 4.1	3.0				(59) 3.0	(60) 3.8
		1.9	2.3				1.2	1.5
						Net Profit + Depr., Dep., Amort./Cur. Mat. L/T/D	6.3	3.2
							(13) 2.8	(12) 1.7
							1.3	1.0
	.0	.1	.1			Fixed/Worth	.1	.1
	.1	.2	.3				.3	.3
	.7	.6	NM				1.5	.9
	.5	.5	.9			Debt/Worth	.7	.5
	1.6	1.6	2.0				1.9	1.5
	3.3	2.3	NM				3.5	3.0
		20.5	17.3			% Profit Before Taxes/Tangible Net Worth	37.3	34.3
		(10) 12.1	12.1				(59) 10.4	(63) 13.6
		2.2	8.7				1.7	4.5
	19.1	10.5	10.4			% Profit Before Taxes/Total Assets	11.7	19.2
	10.4	4.3	4.5				4.4	7.0
	3.3	1.1	2.5				.3	1.1
	999.8	113.6	64.6			Sales/Net Fixed Assets	48.5	55.9
	48.6	28.8	17.7				17.4	24.3
	24.2	8.1	11.7				9.2	11.0
	4.5	3.4	2.3			Sales/Total Assets	3.3	3.8
	2.8	2.5	2.0				2.4	2.7
	2.3	1.4	1.7				1.5	1.7
		.5	.4			% Depr., Dep., Amort./Sales	.7	.6
		(24) 1.0	(12) 1.1				(53) 1.4	(59) 1.0
		2.6	2.7				2.3	2.0
		5.0				% Officers', Directors' Owners' Comp/Sales	2.7	2.3
		(11) 7.7					(30) 5.2	(37) 4.3
		9.1					8.0	9.9
8131M	42874M	270344M	503371M	564679M	295133M	Net Sales ($)	1318431M	1182649M
2721M	13606M	122071M	258304M	212357M	119802M	Total Assets ($)	522663M	411615M

M = $ thousand   MM = $ million
See Pages 9 through 22 for Explanation of Ratios and Data

Comparative Historical Data | Current Data Sorted by Sales

			Type of Statement	0-1MM	1-3MM	3-5MM	5-10MM	10-25MM	25MM & OVER
4	5	7	Unqualified					1	6
14	13	15	Reviewed		2	2	2	7	4
14	21	12	Compiled		4	3	4	1	2
10	11	12	Tax Returns	4	1	1	3		
11	7	14	Other			3	4	3	3
4/1/07-3/31/08 ALL	4/1/08-3/31/09 ALL	4/1/09-3/31/10 ALL					16 (4/1-9/30/09)		44 (10/1/09-3/31/10)
53	57	60	NUMBER OF STATEMENTS	4	7	9	13	12	15
%	%	%	ASSETS	%	%	%	%	%	%
4.8	6.9	7.2	Cash & Equivalents				10.3	5.0	2.8
17.5	20.5	21.9	Trade Receivables (net)				18.5	32.3	22.1
45.4	45.2	46.6	Inventory				33.0	53.6	48.3
3.3	2.6	3.2	All Other Current				5.8	.9	1.9
71.0	75.1	78.9	Total Current				67.5	91.8	75.0
19.0	16.5	13.4	Fixed Assets (net)				21.0	5.0	13.2
2.8	1.8	2.9	Intangibles (net)				4.4	.3	6.2
7.1	6.5	4.8	All Other Non-Current				7.0	2.9	5.5
100.0	100.0	100.0	Total				100.0	100.0	100.0
			LIABILITIES						
15.7	14.6	15.5	Notes Payable-Short Term				6.3	28.2	14.2
3.7	3.7	3.6	Cur. Mat.-L.T.D.				3.2	.7	2.8
10.6	14.9	16.0	Trade Payables				9.8	22.2	17.4
.0	.3	.1	Income Taxes Payable				.5	.0	.1
13.4	13.1	9.2	All Other Current				7.0	8.5	11.9
43.5	46.5	44.5	Total Current				26.8	59.6	46.4
12.1	11.2	7.9	Long-Term Debt				6.8	2.1	8.1
.2	.3	.2	Deferred Taxes				.5	.1	.2
3.8	4.1	8.7	All Other Non-Current				4.0	4.2	12.6
40.4	38.0	38.6	Net Worth				61.9	34.0	32.7
100.0	100.0	100.0	Total Liabilities & Net Worth				100.0	100.0	100.0
			INCOME DATA						
100.0	100.0	100.0	Net Sales				100.0	100.0	100.0
34.3	31.3	35.3	Gross Profit				33.8	25.8	30.7
29.3	27.7	32.7	Operating Expenses				30.7	23.4	28.8
5.0	3.6	2.6	Operating Profit				3.1	2.4	1.8
1.0	.7	.7	All Other Expenses (net)				-.2	.7	.3
4.0	2.9	1.9	Profit Before Taxes				3.4	1.7	1.5
			RATIOS						
2.7	2.7	2.7					6.1	1.6	2.3
1.7	1.7	1.6	Current				2.5	1.4	1.6
1.3	1.2	1.3					1.3	1.2	1.3
.8	1.4	1.2					3.1	.7	.9
.5	.6	.6	Quick				1.1	.6	.6
.3	.3	.3					.3	.4	.3
9 41.6	10 38.0	14 25.7					3 117.0	32 11.5	28 13.2
23 16.0	25 14.5	30 12.1	Sales/Receivables				15 23.8	41 8.9	34 10.9
36 10.1	38 9.6	40 9.0					30 12.1	77 4.7	39 9.5
54 6.8	51 7.1	56 6.5					36 10.1	63 5.8	87 4.2
97 3.8	81 4.5	102 3.6	Cost of Sales/Inventory				50 7.3	106 3.4	110 3.3
200 1.8	131 2.8	164 2.2					100 3.7	154 2.4	155 2.4
7 54.1	7 51.2	7 50.2					3 108.3	13 27.9	22 16.7
17 21.0	18 20.2	25 14.5	Cost of Sales/Payables				7 49.3	28 13.3	32 11.5
42 8.8	47 7.8	61 6.0					25 14.9	72 5.0	61 6.0
3.9	5.0	3.9					3.2	4.8	4.8
8.1	10.1	7.2	Sales/Working Capital				6.7	10.2	6.8
20.3	24.9	15.3					26.5	14.3	24.1
8.0	9.1	13.8						3.4	17.7
(45) 3.6	(50) 3.9	(53) 3.7	EBIT/Interest					(10) 3.0	5.9
1.5	1.7	2.3						2.6	2.4
2.6	4.1	7.1	Net Profit + Depr., Dep.,						
(12) 1.6	(13) 1.3	(18) 2.3	Amort./Cur. Mat. L/T/D						
.6	.1	1.1							
.1	.1	.1					.1	.0	.1
.3	.3	.2	Fixed/Worth				.3	.1	.3
.8	.9	.8					.8	.3	1.2
.6	.6	.8					.3	1.6	1.5
1.7	1.8	2.0	Debt/Worth				.7	2.1	2.0
2.6	3.7	3.2					1.5	3.1	3.9
38.2	35.7	24.9					23.2	16.7	42.7
(52) 14.1	(52) 16.3	(53) 13.4	% Profit Before Taxes/Tangible Net Worth				15.0	9.9	(12) 15.3
4.4	5.8	5.3					3.5	3.1	8.5
13.2	14.1	11.2					19.2	4.8	11.3
6.2	5.1	4.7	% Profit Before Taxes/Total Assets				7.3	3.4	4.8
1.4	1.4	1.9					1.9	1.5	2.9
55.5	86.5	93.2					40.4	312.2	59.2
29.1	30.3	34.7	Sales/Net Fixed Assets				11.4	73.2	18.0
6.6	10.0	11.1					7.5	50.4	14.8
3.5	3.9	3.4					3.5	3.6	3.3
2.3	2.8	2.5	Sales/Total Assets				3.1	2.2	2.2
1.5	1.6	1.8					2.0	1.8	1.8
.7	.3	.4					.7	.1	.3
(45) 1.1	(49) 1.0	(51) .9	% Depr., Dep., Amort./Sales				(11) 1.5	(11) .4	1.1
2.2	2.1	2.1					2.6	.8	3.1
2.7	2.4	1.7							
(19) 4.9	(27) 4.2	(28) 5.4	% Officers', Directors' Owners' Comp/Sales						
11.0	7.9	9.0							
1087990M	1655383M	1684532M	Net Sales ($)	1863M	13666M	37199M	102250M	194597M	1334957M
487047M	638739M	728861M	Total Assets ($)	1748M	8744M	21425M	43619M	93658M	559667M

© RMA 2010

M = $ thousand   MM = $ million
See Pages 9 through 22 for Explanation of Ratios and Data

Current Data Sorted by Assets

Comparative Historical Data

1	2	14	12	2	2	Type of Statement		
1	16	51	9			Unqualified	34	45
5	16	6	2			Reviewed	68	79
9	19	11	2			Compiled	31	40
3	22	42	27	3		Tax Returns	27	26
						Other	100	89
	48 (4/1-9/30/09)		229 (10/1/09-3/31/10)				4/1/05-3/31/06 ALL	4/1/06-3/31/07 ALL
0-500M	500M-2MM	2-10MM	10-50MM	50-100MM	100-250MM			
19	75	124	52	5	2	NUMBER OF STATEMENTS	260	279
%	%	%	%	%	%	ASSETS	%	%
9.1	11.9	10.4	8.4			Cash & Equivalents	7.1	7.7
24.9	32.3	36.0	33.6			Trade Receivables (net)	40.3	38.5
32.3	35.2	28.2	27.6			Inventory	30.8	30.1
1.9	2.7	3.8	4.7			All Other Current	2.3	3.9
68.1	82.1	78.3	74.3			Total Current	80.5	80.2
14.5	10.4	12.2	13.7			Fixed Assets (net)	11.5	11.9
8.4	1.6	4.0	5.7			Intangibles (net)	2.2	2.5
9.0	5.8	5.5	6.2			All Other Non-Current	5.8	5.5
100.0	100.0	100.0	100.0			Total	100.0	100.0
						LIABILITIES		
50.5	14.6	14.9	12.3			Notes Payable-Short Term	17.4	18.5
1.7	2.5	2.0	2.0			Cur. Mat.-L.T.D.	2.0	1.7
16.2	21.2	17.9	16.5			Trade Payables	19.7	20.6
.0	.3	.2	.0			Income Taxes Payable	.2	.2
12.4	12.8	13.4	13.1			All Other Current	16.4	17.1
80.8	51.5	48.3	43.9			Total Current	55.7	58.0
15.7	6.1	7.8	8.3			Long-Term Debt	7.6	7.2
.0	.2	.2	.2			Deferred Taxes	.1	.1
3.8	11.9	5.0	5.5			All Other Non-Current	5.8	5.7
-.2	30.3	38.6	42.2			Net Worth	30.7	29.0
100.0	100.0	100.0	100.0			Total Liabilities & Net Worth	100.0	100.0
						INCOME DATA		
100.0	100.0	100.0	100.0			Net Sales	100.0	100.0
37.4	29.2	28.0	28.2			Gross Profit	29.6	28.9
38.7	27.8	26.3	27.6			Operating Expenses	26.6	25.8
-1.3	1.4	1.7	.7			Operating Profit	3.0	3.1
2.7	.6	.3	.8			All Other Expenses (net)	.3	.6
-4.0	.8	1.4	-.2			Profit Before Taxes	2.6	2.5
						RATIOS		
2.8	2.9	2.5	2.9				2.2	2.1
1.1	1.6	1.6	1.8			Current	1.4	1.4
.5	1.1	1.1	1.2				1.2	1.1
1.2	1.6	1.5	1.7				1.3	1.2
.4	(74) .9	.9	1.1			Quick	.9	.8
.2	.5	.6	.5				.5	.5
0 UND	12 31.6	23 15.6	31 11.7				27 13.4	24 15.2
30 12.1	26 14.1	37 9.9	41 8.8			Sales/Receivables	41 9.0	42 8.7
49 7.4	54 6.8	51 7.1	55 6.7				59 6.2	55 6.6
1 343.8	9 42.8	12 29.5	19 19.4				13 28.8	12 30.4
38 9.5	44 8.2	27 13.4	38 9.7			Cost of Sales/Inventory	38 9.5	38 9.5
193 1.9	109 3.3	107 3.4	100 3.6				93 3.9	94 3.9
0 UND	8 47.1	13 28.2	12 30.6				14 26.2	15 23.8
11 34.4	22 16.3	23 15.8	21 17.5			Cost of Sales/Payables	25 14.5	26 14.3
63 5.8	49 7.4	37 9.9	35 10.5				40 9.2	42 8.8
10.7	5.3	5.9	4.1				6.8	7.9
78.0	11.7	11.9	9.7			Sales/Working Capital	15.0	15.4
-11.1	37.5	33.2	30.4				31.6	75.8
2.8	13.5	8.8	12.1				11.9	9.6
(16) .2	(65) 2.5	(110) 2.7	(49) 1.6			EBIT/Interest	(234) 4.0	(256) 3.4
-10.4	-1.1	.9	-.7				1.4	1.3
		5.5	39.3			Net Profit + Depr., Dep.,	8.8	13.4
		(22) 3.0	(12) 3.7			Amort./Cur. Mat. L/T/D	(41) 3.2	(43) 3.5
		.6	-4.3				.9	1.1
.0	.1	.1	.1				.1	.1
.4	.3	.2	.3			Fixed/Worth	.3	.3
-.1	1.0	.8	1.2				1.1	1.2
.4	1.1	.8	.6				1.0	1.1
13.5	2.4	1.8	1.4			Debt/Worth	2.2	2.5
-2.4	9.2	4.9	7.2				7.7	11.1
97.3	46.8	32.6	22.0			% Profit Before Taxes/Tangible	53.0	53.2
(10) 36.0	(63) 16.0	(111) 10.7	(48) 5.5			Net Worth	(226) 25.2	(234) 26.5
-16.5	-4.5	-.3	-6.8				4.0	8.3
7.5	12.7	10.5	6.0			% Profit Before Taxes/Total	16.4	16.4
-1.2	4.0	3.6	1.7			Assets	6.3	6.2
-23.4	-2.2	.4	-3.2				.9	1.0
848.5	164.9	93.6	86.8				95.4	112.3
170.5	55.5	48.9	40.0			Sales/Net Fixed Assets	48.8	52.7
19.4	24.9	22.7	14.2				21.2	21.5
8.7	4.7	4.4	4.0				4.5	4.4
3.6	3.6	3.1	2.7			Sales/Total Assets	3.4	3.3
1.3	2.4	2.3	1.9				2.4	2.4
	.3	.2	.4				.3	.3
	(60) .5	(105) .5	(51) .8			% Depr., Dep., Amort./Sales	(215) .6	(228) .5
	.9	1.0	1.5				.9	.9
	2.0	1.1	.9				1.5	1.6
	(33) 3.0	(46) 1.9	(12) 1.4			% Officers', Directors' Owners' Comp/Sales	(100) 2.9	(101) 2.8
	6.3	3.6	4.5				5.4	5.2
16015M	346060M	2004177M	3224292M	836823M	556151M	Net Sales ($)	6741256M	7906078M
4880M	91829M	569953M	1136638M	324191M	323382M	Total Assets ($)	2124201M	2617757M

M = $ thousand   MM = $ million
See Pages 9 through 22 for Explanation of Ratios and Data

Comparative Historical Data | Current Data Sorted by Sales

4/1/07-3/31/08 ALL	4/1/08-3/31/09 ALL	4/1/09-3/31/10 ALL	Type of Statement	0-1MM	1-3MM	3-5MM	5-10MM	10-25MM	25MM & OVER
38	33	33	Unqualified	1			4	8	20
59	71	77	Reviewed	1	6	4	25	24	17
37	43	29	Compiled	6	7	3	8	5	
28	32	41	Tax Returns	5	17	7	7	3	2
82	106	97	Other	4	6	12	19	21	35
				48 (4/1-9/30/09)			229 (10/1/09-3/31/10)		
244	285	277	NUMBER OF STATEMENTS	17	36	26	63	61	74
%	%	%	**ASSETS**	%	%	%	%	%	%
8.1	7.6	10.4	Cash & Equivalents	10.6	7.1	17.4	11.2	9.5	9.5
40.4	36.7	33.5	Trade Receivables (net)	15.0	31.7	23.2	33.4	37.0	39.6
29.3	31.1	30.2	Inventory	39.0	41.3	36.9	32.6	22.9	24.4
3.7	4.6	3.6	All Other Current	1.2	2.0	3.8	2.9	4.1	5.2
81.5	80.0	77.8	Total Current	65.8	82.1	81.3	80.1	73.5	78.7
10.2	11.1	12.2	Fixed Assets (net)	14.4	9.9	9.4	11.7	16.2	10.9
2.8	3.6	3.9	Intangibles (net)	9.3	1.8	3.4	2.1	6.4	3.4
5.4	5.3	6.1	All Other Non-Current	10.4	6.2	5.9	6.1	3.9	7.1
100.0	100.0	100.0	Total	100.0	100.0	100.0	100.0	100.0	100.0
			LIABILITIES						
19.1	17.0	16.5	Notes Payable-Short Term	49.1	23.1	14.6	12.4	14.4	11.6
2.1	1.6	2.1	Cur. Mat.-L.T.D.	1.8	1.5	2.8	2.3	3.2	1.0
19.2	19.8	18.6	Trade Payables	10.8	23.1	16.3	17.1	17.8	21.0
.2	.2	.2	Income Taxes Payable	.0	.0	.4	.4	.1	.1
14.8	15.4	13.0	All Other Current	10.4	9.4	10.3	11.7	15.1	15.7
55.4	54.1	50.4	Total Current	72.2	57.1	44.5	44.0	50.6	49.5
5.6	6.0	8.3	Long-Term Debt	17.1	4.3	10.0	7.3	7.7	9.0
.1	.1	.2	Deferred Taxes	.0	.0	.3	.2	.4	.1
5.2	5.4	6.9	All Other Non-Current	9.0	15.2	1.6	9.1	3.4	5.4
33.7	34.5	34.2	Net Worth	1.9	23.4	43.6	39.4	37.8	36.0
100.0	100.0	100.0	Total Liabilities & Net Worth	100.0	100.0	100.0	100.0	100.0	100.0
			INCOME DATA						
100.0	100.0	100.0	Net Sales	100.0	100.0	100.0	100.0	100.0	100.0
28.4	28.6	29.0	Gross Profit	37.9	33.0	34.3	28.1	27.0	25.6
25.2	26.3	27.9	Operating Expenses	44.9	32.5	30.8	26.3	24.9	24.5
3.2	2.3	1.1	Operating Profit	-7.0	.5	3.4	1.8	2.1	1.1
.6	.3	.7	All Other Expenses (net)	2.4	1.1	.3	.3	.7	.6
2.5	2.0	.4	Profit Before Taxes	-9.4	-.6	3.1	1.5	1.4	.5
			RATIOS						
2.2	2.2	2.8	Current	3.8	2.8	2.9	3.2	2.0	2.4
1.5	1.5	1.6		1.1	1.5	1.6	2.0	1.4	1.7
1.1	1.2	1.1		.6	1.1	1.3	1.3	1.1	1.2
1.3	1.3	1.6	Quick	2.2	1.1	1.6	1.9	1.4	1.7
.9	.8 (276)	.9		.4 (35)	.7	.8	1.0	.9	1.2
.6	.5	.5		.1	.4	.4	.6	.6	.7
23 15.5	23 15.8	22 16.6	Sales/Receivables	0 UND	13 27.7	20 18.1	22 16.7	24 15.0	28 13.0
40 9.1	35 10.6	36 10.0		22 16.5	41 9.0	35 10.3	31 11.7	35 10.5	42 8.8
57 6.4	51 7.2	53 6.9		42 8.7	70 5.2	53 6.9	46 7.9	47 7.7	60 6.1
11 34.7	11 32.6	13 28.9	Cost of Sales/Inventory	0 UND	18 20.2	31 11.7	10 35.6	6 57.8	14 26.1
33 11.1	35 10.5	36 10.2		138 2.6	105 3.5	80 4.6	44 8.3	15 24.0	28 13.2
90 4.1	92 4.0	103 3.5		290 1.3	197 1.9	146 2.5	82 4.5	78 4.7	63 5.8
12 29.4	12 31.3	12 30.7	Cost of Sales/Payables	0 UND	6 64.3	17 21.1	12 30.1	11 32.8	14 26.3
24 15.2	21 17.3	22 16.3		17 21.2	45 8.1	25 14.7	20 18.1	21 17.0	23 15.6
37 10.0	37 9.8	41 8.9		30 12.4	88 4.1	49 7.4	31 11.6	38 9.5	36 10.3
7.4	7.9	5.5	Sales/Working Capital	1.9	4.4	3.7	5.6	6.5	7.5
14.4	14.2	11.5		31.4	10.3	7.8	8.4	18.6	12.3
32.3	34.7	43.8		-13.5	47.0	20.6	30.5	106.5	33.3
8.1	11.5	9.1	EBIT/Interest	1.3	2.6	18.4	8.4	8.1	14.9
(220) 3.7	(261) 3.9	(245) 2.4		(14) -1.3	(30) .9	(22) 3.8	(57) 3.0	(55) 2.4	(67) 4.0
1.4	1.1	-.1		-11.9	-4.0	-.4	-.9	.9	.0
13.4	8.4	6.8	Net Profit + Depr., Dep., Amort./Cur. Mat. L/T/D					5.1	19.0
(42) 4.0	(38) 4.1	(42) 2.5						(13) 2.7	(19) 3.4
1.1	2.2	.3						.3	1.0
.1	.1	.1	Fixed/Worth	.0	.1	.0	.1	.1	.1
.2	.3	.3		.3	.3	.3	.2	.4	.3
.7	.7	1.1		-.6	-1.9	.7	.7	1.8	1.0
.9	.9	.8	Debt/Worth	.3	1.0	.4	.8	1.0	.7
2.3	2.2	2.1		13.5	3.0	1.9	1.6	1.8	2.2
5.9	5.1	7.1		-2.2	-19.6	4.0	3.8	5.6	8.5
49.2	42.3	35.3	% Profit Before Taxes/Tangible Net Worth		40.2	37.5	36.9	29.9	36.5
(217) 23.5	(263) 19.1	(238) 10.5			(26) 3.1	(24) 11.2	(60) 11.0	(52) 8.1	(67) 17.7
5.4	2.9	-2.7			-18.2	-11.1	.4	-.7	.2
14.3	13.8	10.0	% Profit Before Taxes/Total Assets	5.3	5.7	11.6	10.5	8.9	13.4
6.6	5.9	3.2		-5.9	1.3	6.0	3.6	2.8	3.7
1.3	.5	-1.8		-15.0	-10.5	.4	.2	.0	-.3
118.9	105.9	114.3	Sales/Net Fixed Assets	UND	169.1	89.6	121.2	86.4	94.0
56.1	52.5	48.3		204.0	37.0	44.3	56.3	44.9	49.3
26.4	24.9	20.2		17.4	13.8	16.3	26.8	16.1	24.7
4.5	4.8	4.4	Sales/Total Assets	4.9	4.0	3.7	4.7	4.9	4.5
3.4	3.4	3.1		2.0	2.4	2.6	3.6	3.3	3.7
2.5	2.4	2.2		.7	1.6	1.5	2.6	2.4	2.5
.3	.3	.3	% Depr., Dep., Amort./Sales		.3	.3	.2	.3	.3
(211) .5	(231) .5	(231) .5			(28) .7	(20) .6	(52) .4	(55) .6	(70) .6
.9	1.0	1.1			1.5	.9	.8	1.1	1.2
1.4	1.1	1.4	% Officers', Directors' Owners' Comp/Sales		3.0	2.3	1.1	1.4	.5
(92) 3.1	(98) 2.6	(100) 2.6			(18) 4.7	(12) 3.8	(27) 1.9	(23) 1.8	(14) 1.0
5.4	5.5				7.9	5.0	5.1	2.7	3.3
8736602M	8791888M	6983518M	Net Sales ($)	8902M	79777M	102738M	483421M	1019778M	5288902M
2501692M	2709360M	2450873M	Total Assets ($)	7201M	42137M	47040M	168701M	347354M	1838440M

© RMA 2010

M = $ thousand   MM = $ million
See Pages 9 through 22 for Explanation of Ratios and Data

Current Data Sorted by Assets | | | | | | **Comparative Historical Data**

0-500M	500M-2MM	2-10MM	10-50MM	50-100MM	100-250MM	Type of Statement	4/1/05-3/31/06 ALL	4/1/06-3/31/07 ALL
	1	8	16	6	5	Unqualified	55	60
1	6	48	23	1		Reviewed	60	70
1	20	17	3			Compiled	37	44
5	17	18	1			Tax Returns	34	50
1	17	39	39	7	3	Other	103	124
	40 (4/1-9/30/09)		263 (10/1/09-3/31/10)					
8	61	130	82	14	8	**NUMBER OF STATEMENTS**	289	348
%	%	%	%	%	%	**ASSETS**	%	%
	12.9	7.5	6.5	7.3		Cash & Equivalents	6.7	8.1
	24.5	30.6	28.4	19.6		Trade Receivables (net)	32.0	31.6
	41.5	41.9	38.7	31.8		Inventory	39.4	39.8
	5.5	2.6	3.8	5.9		All Other Current	3.0	2.3
	84.3	82.5	77.5	64.6		Total Current	81.1	81.8
	6.6	10.6	10.8	9.2		Fixed Assets (net)	10.2	9.7
	1.9	2.1	5.1	9.1		Intangibles (net)	2.7	2.6
	7.2	4.8	6.6	17.1		All Other Non-Current	6.1	5.9
	100.0	100.0	100.0	100.0		Total	100.0	100.0
						LIABILITIES		
	19.9	18.5	17.7	4.7		Notes Payable-Short Term	17.1	16.8
	2.0	2.0	2.7	1.7		Cur. Mat.-L.T.D.	2.0	1.9
	20.9	19.4	14.6	14.4		Trade Payables	20.9	19.7
	.0	.6	.1	.1		Income Taxes Payable	.2	.2
	13.7	7.6	11.6	8.3		All Other Current	11.2	11.5
	56.6	48.0	46.7	29.2		Total Current	51.4	50.2
	6.2	8.7	8.6	18.4		Long-Term Debt	10.7	7.3
	.0	.0	.4	.9		Deferred Taxes	.2	.1
	6.1	5.1	8.7	2.6		All Other Non-Current	6.9	6.7
	31.1	38.1	35.6	48.9		Net Worth	30.8	35.7
	100.0	100.0	100.0	100.0		Total Liabilities & Net Worth	100.0	100.0
						INCOME DATA		
	100.0	100.0	100.0	100.0		Net Sales	100.0	100.0
	32.4	31.3	29.9	32.7		Gross Profit	31.2	31.0
	31.8	29.3	26.1	30.0		Operating Expenses	27.4	26.6
	.6	2.0	3.8	2.7		Operating Profit	3.8	4.4
	1.1	.6	1.3	3.2		All Other Expenses (net)	.8	1.3
	-.5	1.4	2.5	-.4		Profit Before Taxes	3.0	3.1
						RATIOS		
	3.0	2.7	2.3	4.4		Current	2.4	2.6
	1.9	1.7	1.7	2.5			1.6	1.7
	1.0	1.2	1.3	1.4			1.2	1.2
	1.4	1.3	1.1	1.7		Quick	1.2	1.3
	.6	.7	.8	.9			.7	.7
	.3	.5	.5	.5			.5	.5
13	29.1	29 · 12.8	30 · 12.2	32 · 11.2		Sales/Receivables	29 · 12.7	28 · 12.9
26	14.1	40 · 9.0	45 · 8.2	37 · 9.9			40 · 9.2	40 · 9.1
44	8.3	59 · 6.2	70 · 5.2	49 · 7.4			53 · 6.8	56 · 6.5
28	13.0	45 · 8.1	59 · 6.2	64 · 5.7		Cost of Sales/Inventory	41 · 8.8	38 · 9.5
77	4.7	82 · 4.5	82 · 4.5	106 · 3.5			72 · 5.1	79 · 4.6
161	2.3	160 · 2.3	132 · 2.8	178 · 2.0			124 · 3.0	128 · 2.8
9	41.3	18 · 20.2	15 · 25.1	13 · 27.4		Cost of Sales/Payables	18 · 20.4	15 · 24.6
26	14.2	29 · 12.4	27 · 13.4	32 · 11.4			32 · 11.4	29 · 12.5
60	6.1	56 · 6.6	54 · 6.8	73 · 5.0			53 · 6.9	53 · 6.9
	4.3	4.7	4.1	2.7		Sales/Working Capital	5.5	5.0
	8.5	7.4	6.6	4.3			9.8	9.1
	154.0	17.6	12.4	11.0			22.1	19.9
	4.6	6.8	14.5	45.8		EBIT/Interest	10.5	10.1
(44)	1.8	(121) · 2.8	(78) · 3.8	(13) · 5.2			(262) · 3.7	(314) · 3.4
	-5.8	.8	1.1	1.1			1.4	1.5
		6.5	15.6			Net Profit + Depr., Dep., Amort./Cur. Mat. L/T/D	11.6	17.9
	(20)	1.8	(14) · 1.3				(61) · 3.8	(70) · 3.8
		-.2	-.6				1.2	1.1
	.0	.1	.1	.1		Fixed/Worth	.1	.1
	.1	.2	.2	.2			.2	.2
	.5	.6	1.2	NM			.5	.5
	.8	.7	.9	.5		Debt/Worth	.9	.8
	2.3	1.8	1.9	1.0			2.3	1.9
	9.9	4.0	4.2	NM			5.1	4.7
	28.2	31.9	28.9	14.5		% Profit Before Taxes/Tangible Net Worth	46.8	43.9
(50)	8.5	(121) · 8.1	(68) · 14.2	(11) · 10.1			(262) · 21.8	(311) · 18.7
	-6.9	.8	1.9	5.4			5.5	5.9
	10.1	9.5	12.2	7.3		% Profit Before Taxes/Total Assets	15.5	16.2
	2.0	2.2	3.8	4.8			5.3	5.8
	-3.2	-.2	.2	-1.9			1.1	1.2
	158.6	104.9	91.7	77.3		Sales/Net Fixed Assets	106.2	112.8
	79.4	46.7	33.3	42.5			48.4	48.6
	30.6	22.1	15.8	9.6			21.9	23.1
	4.5	3.4	2.9	3.0		Sales/Total Assets	3.8	3.8
	2.8	2.6	2.0	1.6			2.8	2.8
	2.1	1.8	1.5	1.1			2.0	1.9
	.2	.3	.3	.5		% Depr., Dep., Amort./Sales	.3	.3
(43)	.4	(102) · .6	(66) · .7	(10) · .9			(246) · .6	(291) · .6
	.7	1.1	1.1	1.7			1.0	1.0
	1.9	1.2	.9			% Officers', Directors' Owners' Comp/Sales	1.3	1.4
(36)	3.3	(71) · 2.3	(27) · 1.7				(122) · 2.6	(156) · 2.4
	7.4	3.5					5.3	4.6
6931M	240574M	1839070M	3968920M	1597507M	1632706M	Net Sales ($)	10649498M	14491988M
1470M	72112M	679862M	1806645M	934893M	1215467M	Total Assets ($)	3990779M	5396338M

M = $ thousand   MM = $ million
See Pages 9 through 22 for Explanation of Ratios and Data

Comparative Historical Data

Current Data Sorted by Sales

Comparative Historical Data			Type of Statement	0-1MM	1-3MM	3-5MM	5-10MM	10-25MM	25MM & OVER
56	47	36	Unqualified	1	1	1	1	7	26
69	84	79	Reviewed	1	2	6	9	40	21
38	39	41	Compiled		13	9	8	7	4
35	46	41	Tax Returns	5	9	6	14	5	2
129	121	106	Other	2	10	6	15	33	40
4/1/07-3/31/08	4/1/08-3/31/09	4/1/09-3/31/10			40 (4/1-9/30/09)		263 (10/1/09-3/31/10)		
ALL	ALL	ALL							
327	337	303	NUMBER OF STATEMENTS	8	35	28	47	92	93
%	%	%	ASSETS	%	%	%	%	%	%
8.0	8.4	8.5	Cash & Equivalents		8.7	6.4	12.6	7.8	7.0
28.8	28.3	28.0	Trade Receivables (net)		20.8	21.6	28.6	30.3	30.4
40.3	40.9	39.7	Inventory		45.8	47.0	38.4	40.9	35.6
3.0	3.9	3.6	All Other Current		2.7	6.0	2.5	2.8	4.4
80.1	81.5	79.7	Total Current		77.9	81.0	82.0	81.8	77.4
10.3	9.8	9.7	Fixed Assets (net)		8.3	6.5	11.9	10.3	9.6
4.1	2.5	3.8	Intangibles (net)		3.1	2.6	1.2	3.2	6.7
5.5	6.3	6.8	All Other Non-Current		10.8	9.8	4.8	4.8	6.3
100.0	100.0	100.0	Total		100.0	100.0	100.0	100.0	100.0
			LIABILITIES						
17.7	18.1	18.7	Notes Payable-Short Term		24.8	22.9	12.5	19.7	13.9
2.5	2.8	2.6	Cur. Mat.-L.T.D.		2.1	1.3	3.5	2.0	2.5
18.5	17.8	18.3	Trade Payables		18.4	19.6	18.8	19.9	15.9
.1	.2	.3	Income Taxes Payable		1.4	.0	.2	.0	.3
10.0	10.2	11.2	All Other Current		12.9	12.6	10.8	8.4	11.9
48.7	49.1	51.1	Total Current		59.7	56.4	45.7	50.0	44.5
9.3	6.3	8.6	Long-Term Debt		11.0	5.0	8.8	8.2	9.3
.3	.1	.2	Deferred Taxes		.1	.0	.0	.0	.5
6.3	6.3	6.2	All Other Non-Current		6.3	7.7	6.0	5.9	6.3
35.6	38.2	34.0	Net Worth		22.9	30.9	39.5	35.8	39.4
100.0	100.0	100.0	Total Liabilities & Net Worth		100.0	100.0	100.0	100.0	100.0
			INCOME DATA						
100.0	100.0	100.0	Net Sales		100.0	100.0	100.0	100.0	100.0
32.8	31.4	31.6	Gross Profit		35.7	32.2	30.9	31.4	30.2
28.8	28.5	29.2	Operating Expenses		38.0	31.8	27.9	28.9	25.8
4.1	2.8	2.4	Operating Profit		-2.3	.3	3.0	2.6	4.4
1.3	.9	1.1	All Other Expenses (net)		1.2	1.1	.8	.6	1.5
2.8	2.0	1.3	Profit Before Taxes		-3.5	-.8	2.2	1.9	3.0
			RATIOS						
2.8 / 1.6 / 1.2	2.7 / 1.7 / 1.3	2.5 / 1.7 / 1.2	Current		2.4 / 1.9 / .9	2.4 / 1.7 / .8	2.7 / 2.0 / 1.4	2.8 / 1.7 / 1.3	2.5 / 1.8 / 1.4
1.2 / .7 / .5	1.3 / .7 / .5	1.3 / .7 / .4	Quick		.9 / .6 / .2	.9 / .5 / .3	1.3 / .9 / .5	1.3 / .7 / .5	1.3 / .9 / .5
27 13.8 / 40 9.2 / 60 6.1	26 14.1 / 37 9.9 / 55 6.7	25 14.4 / 39 9.4 / 58 6.3	Sales/Receivables	10 35.7 / 34 10.7 / 63 5.8	21 17.5 / 28 12.8 / 63 5.8	21 17.5 / 30 12.1 / 54 6.7	29 12.4 / 40 9.2 / 58 6.3	30 12.2 / 43 8.5 / 58 6.3	
51 7.1 / 85 4.3 / 142 2.6	44 8.3 / 87 4.2 / 142 2.6	49 7.4 / 81 4.5 / 147 2.5	Cost of Sales/Inventory	65 5.6 / 120 3.0 / 222 1.6	66 5.6 / 138 2.7 / 182 2.0	28 13.1 / 66 5.6 / 173 2.1	48 7.6 / 92 4.0 / 145 2.5	53 6.9 / 72 5.1 / 110 3.3	
16 22.7 / 28 12.9 / 52 7.0	13 28.2 / 26 14.2 / 47 7.8	15 24.2 / 29 12.8 / 58 6.3	Cost of Sales/Payables	6 58.2 / 31 11.7 / 85 4.3	8 48.0 / 31 11.6 / 85 4.3	15 24.3 / 26 14.1 / 56 6.5	19 19.2 / 33 11.1 / 55 6.7	14 25.2 / 25 14.7 / 47 7.7	
4.6 / 8.5 / 20.3	4.6 / 8.1 / 18.3	4.4 / 7.4 / 18.8	Sales/Working Capital		3.5 / 8.3 / -23.0	3.0 / 6.6 / -9.7	4.6 / 6.8 / 14.8	4.6 / 7.5 / 17.0	4.7 / 7.0 / 15.0
(286) 6.0 / 2.9 / 1.3	(293) 6.2 / 2.3 / .3	(270) 7.4 / 2.8 / .8	EBIT/Interest	(29) 2.8 / -1.4 / -7.2	(24) 6.4 / 2.2 / .7	(37) 6.3 / 2.7 / .9	(83) 6.6 / 2.8 / .8	(91) 21.9 / 4.5 / 1.3	
(64) 8.7 / 3.1 / 1.4	(58) 6.3 / 1.6 / -.1	(44) 6.1 / 1.8 / .1	Net Profit + Depr., Dep., Amort./Cur. Mat. L/T/D					(13) 17.6 / 5.1 / -.7	(19) 6.3 / 2.2 / .6
.1 / .2 / .7	.1 / .2 / .5	.1 / .2 / .7	Fixed/Worth		.0 / .2 / 4.3	.0 / .3 / 3.9	.1 / .1 / .4	.1 / .2 / .6	.1 / .2 / .8
.8 / 2.0 / 4.2	.8 / 1.8 / 4.6	.8 / 1.9 / 4.6	Debt/Worth		.7 / 2.5 / -29.3	.9 / 2.2 / 60.2	.5 / 2.6 / 4.2	1.0 / 2.2 / 4.1	.8 / 1.5 / 3.6
(289) 37.0 / 16.2 / 4.2	(307) 31.6 / 11.1 / .0	(258) 30.9 / 8.3 / 1.0	% Profit Before Taxes/Tangible Net Worth	(26) 19.1 / 1.3 / -24.5	(22) 28.8 / 8.3 / -3.4	(43) 42.4 / 8.3 / 1.8	(84) 31.5 / 10.2 / -.2	(79) 25.2 / 13.1 / 4.4	
12.7 / 4.9 / .9	11.1 / 2.8 / -1.9	10.5 / 2.8 / -.2	% Profit Before Taxes/Total Assets		7.2 / -1.3 / -18.1	6.2 / .8 / -1.6	11.1 / 4.0 / .3	11.9 / 2.7 / -.3	11.1 / 3.9 / .8
111.4 / 44.3 / 20.0	121.8 / 47.4 / 20.0	104.9 / 46.4 / 22.1	Sales/Net Fixed Assets		135.3 / 65.0 / 16.0	144.8 / 50.3 / 25.8	149.0 / 54.7 / 23.3	97.1 / 44.9 / 20.1	109.0 / 44.1 / 18.9
3.5 / 2.5 / 1.8	3.5 / 2.5 / 1.8	3.4 / 2.3 / 1.7	Sales/Total Assets		2.7 / 2.1 / 1.3	3.2 / 2.1 / 1.5	4.4 / 2.7 / 2.0	3.3 / 2.5 / 1.7	3.3 / 2.3 / 1.6
(271) .3 / .6 / 1.1	(263) .3 / .6 / 1.2	(229) .3 / .6 / 1.1	% Depr., Dep., Amort./Sales	(26) .2 / .5 / 1.3	(18) .4 / .7 / 1.4	(35) .2 / .6 / 1.2	(75) .3 / .6 / 1.0	(73) .3 / .7 / 1.2	
(121) 1.6 / 2.9 / 6.8	(138) 1.1 / 2.4 / 5.5	(141) 1.3 / 2.3 / 4.2	% Officers', Directors' Owners' Comp/Sales	(22) 2.3 / 3.8 / 6.2	(13) 1.9 / 4.2 / 9.0	(29) 1.4 / 2.3 /	(49) .9 / 1.7 / 3.3	(24) 1.1 / 1.8 / 2.7	
12231275M	13416415M	9285708M	Net Sales ($)	3662M	69106M	108222M	351254M	1536578M	7216886M
5411266M	5697910M	4710449M	Total Assets ($)	4595M	43950M	147493M	143622M	739928M	3630861M

M = $ thousand   MM = $ million
See Pages 9 through 22 for Explanation of Ratios and Data

WHOLESALE—Lumber, Plywood, Millwork, and Wood Panel Merchant Wholesalers   NAICS 423310

	Current Data Sorted by Assets							Comparative Historical Data	
Type of Statement									
Unqualified		1	26	63	14	6		178	168
Reviewed	1	31	132	45	7			262	273
Compiled	7	40	58	10				147	160
Tax Returns	24	45	25	4				62	93
Other	15	63	107	95	17	8		241	291
		135 (4/1-9/30/09)		709 (10/1/09-3/31/10)				4/1/05-3/31/06	4/1/06-3/31/07
	0-500M	500M-2MM	2-10MM	10-50MM	50-100MM	100-250MM		ALL	ALL
NUMBER OF STATEMENTS	47	180	348	217	38	14		890	985
	%	%	%	%	%	%	**ASSETS**	%	%
	12.8	8.4	7.6	6.3	7.1	4.8	Cash & Equivalents	5.8	6.1
	30.1	34.0	29.6	25.4	23.9	24.6	Trade Receivables (net)	35.7	33.4
	29.6	33.9	34.1	33.8	28.0	25.2	Inventory	34.3	34.3
	3.5	3.4	2.8	4.5	3.7	4.2	All Other Current	2.1	2.5
	76.0	79.8	74.0	70.0	62.8	58.8	Total Current	78.0	76.3
	16.7	12.8	17.5	20.6	21.7	25.9	Fixed Assets (net)	14.7	15.8
	1.3	1.4	1.8	2.7	4.9	7.5	Intangibles (net)	1.7	2.2
	6.0	6.1	6.7	6.7	10.6	7.8	All Other Non-Current	5.7	5.7
	100.0	100.0	100.0	100.0	100.0	100.0	Total	100.0	100.0
							LIABILITIES		
	16.9	21.5	20.4	18.6	16.5	10.7	Notes Payable-Short Term	21.1	20.1
	5.5	1.7	2.5	2.6	3.0	2.1	Cur. Mat.-L.T.D.	2.1	2.4
	14.5	16.7	11.5	11.1	11.0	17.1	Trade Payables	15.4	13.9
	.0	.1	.3	.1	.1	.2	Income Taxes Payable	.3	.2
	20.8	9.7	7.6	5.9	6.0	7.9	All Other Current	9.8	9.1
	57.6	49.7	42.2	38.3	36.6	38.0	Total Current	48.7	45.7
	18.5	8.1	9.7	11.0	9.5	21.7	Long-Term Debt	9.8	9.3
	.0	.2	.2	.6	.2	.0	Deferred Taxes	.2	.2
	8.1	7.8	6.5	5.0	4.9	10.5	All Other Non-Current	4.3	4.3
	15.7	34.2	41.4	45.2	48.8	29.9	Net Worth	37.0	40.3
	100.0	100.0	100.0	100.0	100.0	100.0	Total Liabilities & Net Worth	100.0	100.0
							INCOME DATA		
	100.0	100.0	100.0	100.0	100.0	100.0	Net Sales	100.0	100.0
	28.7	22.7	22.4	19.3	20.6	22.4	Gross Profit	21.0	21.5
	29.2	22.2	23.1	20.4	20.3	23.1	Operating Expenses	17.8	18.6
	-.5	.4	-.7	-1.1	.3	-.8	Operating Profit	3.2	2.9
	1.3	.6	.6	.5	1.2	1.3	All Other Expenses (net)	.4	.5
	-1.8	-.2	-1.3	-1.6	-.9	-2.1	Profit Before Taxes	2.8	2.4
							RATIOS		
	2.7	3.3	3.1	3.5	3.9	2.7	Current	2.5	2.7
	1.5	1.8	1.8	1.7	1.8	1.5		1.6	1.6
	.9	1.2	1.2	1.3	1.2	1.2		1.2	1.2
	2.1	1.6	1.6	1.5	1.8	1.2	Quick	1.4	1.5
	.8	.9	.8	.8	.9	.8		.9	.8
	.3	.4	.5	.5	.5	.5		.5	.5
	8 45.7	19 19.3	23 15.9	26 13.8	28 13.1	27 13.5	Sales/Receivables	23 15.8	23 16.2
	19 19.3	31 11.7	34 10.6	35 10.4	34 10.6	29 12.4		34 10.9	32 11.5
	37 9.9	51 7.2	48 7.5	46 8.0	43 8.5	42 8.6		45 8.1	42 8.6
	0 UND	15 24.8	33 11.2	39 9.4	37 9.9	26 13.9	Cost of Sales/Inventory	28 13.2	27 13.6
	21 17.1	49 7.5	54 6.3	58 6.3	57 6.4	49 7.4		43 8.4	45 8.1
	115 3.2	79 4.6	89 4.1	81 4.5	86 4.2	75 4.9		66 5.6	68 5.4
	0 UND	8 45.1	8 44.7	10 35.3	11 31.8	16 23.2	Cost of Sales/Payables	9 40.3	9 42.1
	11 33.4	17 21.6	15 24.3	17 21.9	19 18.8	24 15.2		16 22.4	15 24.5
	24 15.0	31 11.8	26 13.9	23 15.9	27 13.7	35 10.5		27 13.8	24 15.4
	6.7	5.6	5.0	4.9	3.8	6.1	Sales/Working Capital	7.4	6.8
	24.7	10.2	9.7	8.9	8.7	9.6		13.0	11.8
	-110.7	26.0	25.0	18.9	24.6	NM		26.5	28.9
	4.3	4.2	4.1	3.7	2.6	.7	EBIT/Interest	10.0	8.6
	(35) .4	(160) 1.1	(318) 1.1	(206) .8	(37) .1	(13) -.4		(829) 4.1	(929) 3.2
	-3.9	-3.4	-2.6	-2.9	-1.1	-1.6		1.9	1.3
		3.3	7.0	2.6			Net Profit + Depr., Dep., Amort./Cur. Mat. L/T/D	9.3	9.0
		(16) .5	(71) 1.1	(75) 1.1				(234) 3.7	(272) 3.3
		-1.4	-.9	-1.1				1.7	1.4
	.0	.0	.1	.2	.3	.5	Fixed/Worth	.1	.1
	.3	.2	.3	.4	.4	1.2		.3	.3
	-.6	.7	.8	1.0	.9	-5.6		.7	.8
	.6	.7	.6	.5	.4	.9	Debt/Worth	.9	.7
	2.5	1.6	1.3	1.3	1.5	4.1		1.7	1.6
	-6.0	5.3	3.5	3.4	3.9	-12.9		3.7	3.5
	21.9	22.0	11.7	10.1	4.8		% Profit Before Taxes/Tangible Net Worth	43.4	37.7
	(31) .5	(153) 1.7	(324) 1.6	(209) .0	-2.4			(831) 22.3	(928) 17.0
	-28.0	-10.9	-15.2	-16.4	-20.7			8.2	4.3
	10.9	7.8	4.6	4.3	1.6	-.6	% Profit Before Taxes/Total Assets	16.3	14.1
	.0	.6	.4	-.2	-.8	-6.4		7.5	6.0
	-13.1	-7.2	-6.9	-6.4	-5.3	-9.8		2.4	1.3
	291.0	284.3	76.6	39.8	23.0	43.4	Sales/Net Fixed Assets	85.4	83.7
	65.2	48.9	23.6	16.8	9.5	8.6		32.4	30.0
	17.6	21.0	8.8	6.8	5.1	4.2		15.0	12.9
	7.1	4.5	3.6	3.3	2.9	4.8	Sales/Total Assets	4.6	4.6
	3.4	3.4	2.7	2.4	2.0	1.9		3.5	3.4
	2.1	2.3	1.9	1.7	1.2	1.6		2.6	2.5
	.3	.2	.4	.5	.7	.6	% Depr., Dep., Amort./Sales	.3	.4
	(34) .8	(133) .6	(304) .9	(203) 1.1	(36) 1.4	(13) 2.2		(785) .7	(871) .7
	2.1	1.2	1.8	2.0	2.6	2.9		1.1	1.3
	2.8	2.0	1.3	.5			% Officers', Directors' Owners' Comp/Sales	1.1	1.2
	(22) 7.1	(90) 3.3	(143) 2.5	(47) 1.0				(320) 2.1	(352) 2.4
	12.4	5.3	4.1	2.6				4.3	4.2
	67029M	819685M	4941205M	12482237M	6200095M	5892321M	Net Sales ($)	47580276M	55023383M
	14311M	220778M	1712533M	4709802M	2595675M	1930700M	Total Assets ($)	13435804M	15945681M

M = $ thousand   MM = $ million
See Pages 9 through 22 for Explanation of Ratios and Data

Comparative Historical Data / Current Data Sorted by Sales

			Type of Statement						
139	127	110	Unqualified		2		5	20	83
260	233	216	Reviewed		4	16	53	84	59
132	127	115	Compiled	5	12	27	31	28	12
90	85	98	Tax Returns	11	32	20	16	17	2
353	365	305	Other	13	30	33	45	78	106
4/1/07-3/31/08	4/1/08-3/31/09	4/1/09-3/31/10			135 (4/1-9/30/09)		709 (10/1/09-3/31/10)		
ALL	ALL	ALL		0-1MM	1-3MM	3-5MM	5-10MM	10-25MM	25MM & OVER
974	937	844	**NUMBER OF STATEMENTS**	29	80	96	150	227	262
%	%	%	**ASSETS**	%	%	%	%	%	%
6.6	6.5	7.7	Cash & Equivalents	13.1	9.0	10.4	10.3	6.0	5.6
32.1	29.4	29.1	Trade Receivables (net)	15.2	28.6	31.2	29.9	29.2	29.6
34.7	35.7	33.3	Inventory	28.4	33.0	31.9	33.1	35.1	33.1
2.7	2.9	3.5	All Other Current	2.6	4.9	2.9	2.8	3.0	4.1
76.2	74.5	73.6	Total Current	59.2	75.5	76.4	76.0	73.3	72.4
16.1	16.8	17.6	Fixed Assets (net)	30.7	15.9	15.1	14.8	19.0	17.8
2.1	2.0	2.2	Intangibles (net)	1.9	1.8	1.5	2.7	1.2	3.1
5.7	6.6	6.7	All Other Non-Current	8.2	6.8	7.0	6.5	6.5	6.7
100.0	100.0	100.0	Total	100.0	100.0	100.0	100.0	100.0	100.0
			LIABILITIES						
20.4	21.9	19.6	Notes Payable-Short Term	15.1	21.4	19.5	18.6	20.2	19.8
2.4	2.8	2.5	Cur. Mat.-L.T.D.	2.3	4.4	2.2	2.2	2.3	2.4
13.0	11.8	12.7	Trade Payables	4.9	18.4	14.3	13.0	11.0	12.6
.1	.2	.2	Income Taxes Payable	.0	.0	.2	.3	.2	.1
9.0	8.1	8.3	All Other Current	18.7	14.9	7.9	6.7	7.6	6.7
45.0	44.8	43.3	Total Current	41.1	59.1	44.1	40.8	41.3	41.6
9.6	9.6	10.4	Long-Term Debt	33.7	10.1	9.6	7.4	10.3	9.9
.2	.2	.3	Deferred Taxes	.0	.4	.1	.2	.2	.4
5.6	5.4	6.5	All Other Non-Current	12.0	7.6	7.2	8.9	5.0	5.2
39.6	40.0	39.5	Net Worth	13.2	22.8	38.9	42.7	43.2	42.9
100.0	100.0	100.0	Total Liabilities & Net Worth	100.0	100.0	100.0	100.0	100.0	100.0
			INCOME DATA						
100.0	100.0	100.0	Net Sales	100.0	100.0	100.0	100.0	100.0	100.0
21.5	21.2	21.9	Gross Profit	38.2	26.3	24.2	23.2	20.2	18.7
19.7	21.0	22.4	Operating Expenses	34.7	28.1	24.2	24.6	21.2	18.6
1.7	.2	-.5	Operating Profit	3.5	-1.8	.0	-1.5	-.9	.1
.6	.6	.6	All Other Expenses (net)	4.2	.7	.5	.3	.6	.5
1.2	-.4	-1.1	Profit Before Taxes	-.7	-2.5	-.4	-1.8	-1.5	-.3
			RATIOS						
2.9	3.1	3.2	Current	5.0	2.5	3.7	4.2	2.9	2.8
1.7	1.7	1.8		1.5	1.5	2.0	2.1	1.7	1.7
1.2	1.2	1.2		.7	1.0	1.2	1.3	1.2	1.3
1.5	1.6	1.6	Quick	2.0	1.2	2.0	2.4	1.4	1.5
.8	.8	.8		.5	.7	1.0	1.0	.8	.8
.5	.4	.5		.2	.3	.4	.5	.5	.5
22 16.4	20 17.9	23 16.1	Sales/Receivables	0 UND	19 19.6	20 18.5	23 15.9	26 14.0	26 14.0
32 11.5	29 12.5	34 10.8		16 23.3	34 10.8	34 10.7	32 11.2	35 10.5	34 10.9
44 8.3	41 8.8	47 7.7		46 8.0	53 6.9	53 6.9	51 7.2	48 7.6	43 8.4
28 12.8	30 12.2	30 12.3	Cost of Sales/Inventory	0 UND	14 25.3	24 15.4	25 14.6	33 10.9	35 10.3
48 7.6	51 7.2	54 6.8		72 5.0	53 6.9	58 6.3	52 7.1	56 6.5	53 6.9
75 4.8	78 4.7	84 4.3		160 2.3	115 3.2	90 4.1	87 4.2	93 3.9	69 5.3
8 47.1	6 60.2	9 41.7	Cost of Sales/Payables	0 UND	10 37.1	10 38.3	9 40.3	8 47.4	10 36.6
15 25.0	13 27.6	16 22.7		7 51.5	19 18.9	20 18.7	16 22.6	14 26.3	16 22.7
25 14.7	23 15.9	26 14.0		23 16.1	44 8.2	36 10.1	25 13.0	25 14.4	23 16.2
6.3	6.0	5.1	Sales/Working Capital	3.4	5.1	4.9	4.3	5.6	6.1
11.3	10.6	9.9		8.1	11.3	7.8	7.4	10.3	10.3
25.6	27.7	25.6		-30.3	-203.6	25.0	20.2	21.9	23.0
5.8	4.4	3.8	EBIT/Interest	6.4	1.5	4.3	3.0	3.9	4.8
(920) 2.1	(871) 1.4	(769) 1.0		(16) .7	(70) -.3	(86) 1.3	(135) -.2	(209) .7	(253) 1.3
.8	-.9	-2.7		-3.4	-9.5	-1.3	-3.6	-2.8	-1.4
7.2	4.7	3.3	Net Profit + Depr., Dep., Amort./Cur. Mat. L/T/D			4.7	1.1	3.4	4.0
(245) 2.7	(224) 1.4	(179) .8				(15) .8	(31) -.7	(45) 1.0	(87) 1.3
.8	-.3	-.9				.1	-4.7	-1.0	-.2
.1	.1	.1	Fixed/Worth	.1	.1	.0	.1	.1	.1
.4	.3	.3		1.6	.4	.2	.2	.3	.4
.9	.9	.9		-.6	2.0	.8	.7	.9	.8
.7	.6	.6	Debt/Worth	.5	.8	.6	.5	.6	.7
1.6	1.5	1.4		7.0	2.5	1.3	1.2	1.3	1.5
3.8	3.6	4.0		-5.3	-28.3	4.3	3.4	3.2	3.7
25.9	17.6	12.6	% Profit Before Taxes/Tangible Net Worth	19.4	10.6	16.1	10.9	11.7	13.8
(894) 10.5	(858) 3.5	(764) .8		(17) 3.8	(58) -.6	(90) 1.4	(135) -1.3	(215) 1.2	(249) 1.6
.0	-9.6	-15.1		-2.6	-42.7	-9.4	-19.8	-20.0	-11.8
10.5	7.0	4.7	% Profit Before Taxes/Total Assets	3.9	5.6	6.0	3.7	4.9	5.0
3.7	1.0	.1		.0	-1.4	.6	-1.1	-.1	.5
-.7	-5.0	-7.2		-11.8	-15.8	-4.9	-10.3	-7.5	-5.1
83.2	79.9	76.4	Sales/Net Fixed Assets	183.6	107.2	184.4	86.8	66.1	60.5
29.0	28.6	24.8		7.3	33.2	49.6	32.8	19.3	22.5
11.8	10.5	8.2		2.5	11.7	10.7	10.4	7.2	8.7
4.2	4.1	3.7	Sales/Total Assets	2.3	3.8	3.9	3.8	3.7	3.8
3.2	3.0	2.7		1.8	2.4	2.6	2.7	2.7	2.9
2.4	2.2	1.9		1.4	1.6	1.8	1.9	1.9	2.2
.3	.4	.4	% Depr., Dep., Amort./Sales	.6	.5	.3	.4	.5	.4
(857) .8	(824) .9	(723) .9		(20) 2.0	(52) 1.0	(77) .7	(128) .9	(207) 1.0	(239) .9
1.4	1.7	1.9		4.5	2.2	1.7	1.9	2.0	1.6
1.2	1.1	1.4	% Officers', Directors' Owners' Comp/Sales	5.0	2.5	2.0	1.8	.9	.5
(354) 2.3	(352) 2.2	(308) 2.6		(11) 12.2	(40) 3.9	(50) 3.3	(68) 2.9	(87) 1.9	(52) 1.1
4.7	4.0	4.8		19.1	6.5	5.3	4.5	3.7	2.3
46893140M	40857294M	30402572M	Net Sales ($)	16163M	153145M	389704M	1073593M	3598028M	25171939M
15218062M	13386766M	11183799M	Total Assets ($)	17462M	73510M	176581M	509994M	1653351M	8752901M

M = $ thousand   MM = $ million
See Pages 9 through 22 for Explanation of Ratios and Data

WHOLESALE—Brick, Stone, and Related Construction Material Merchant Wholesalers NAICS 423320

Current Data Sorted by Assets							Comparative Historical Data	

Type of Statement

0-500M	500M-2MM	2-10MM	10-50MM	50-100MM	100-250MM	Type of Statement	4/1/05-3/31/06 ALL	4/1/06-3/31/07 ALL
	4	6	9	3	1	Unqualified	47	45
	11	46	9			Reviewed	79	78
4	11	16	8			Compiled	54	64
7	37	17	1			Tax Returns	35	44
7	13	47	32	3	2	Other	112	110
	43 (4/1-9/30/09)		251 (10/1/09-3/31/10)					
18	76	132	59	6	3	**NUMBER OF STATEMENTS**	327	341
%	%	%	%	%	%	**ASSETS**	%	%
9.7	7.2	6.5	5.7			Cash & Equivalents	6.8	6.0
22.4	24.2	23.7	21.4			Trade Receivables (net)	28.6	30.6
33.2	36.7	35.9	32.6			Inventory	31.8	33.7
2.0	3.5	2.8	2.9			All Other Current	2.3	2.0
67.3	71.6	68.9	62.6			Total Current	69.5	72.4
26.9	17.4	23.0	28.8			Fixed Assets (net)	21.8	20.0
.0	3.2	3.2	2.6			Intangibles (net)	2.6	2.3
5.8	7.8	4.8	6.0			All Other Non-Current	6.1	5.3
100.0	100.0	100.0	100.0			Total	100.0	100.0
						LIABILITIES		
17.7	14.5	12.0	11.0			Notes Payable-Short Term	12.9	13.4
2.4	4.0	2.8	3.5			Cur. Mat.-L.T.D.	2.9	3.0
23.2	27.1	22.4	15.6			Trade Payables	23.6	21.4
.0	.0	.1	.2			Income Taxes Payable	.3	.4
16.3	9.8	7.8	6.1			All Other Current	9.9	8.9
59.6	55.4	45.0	36.5			Total Current	49.6	47.1
20.8	19.7	18.3	14.6			Long-Term Debt	13.1	12.7
.0	.0	.5	.5			Deferred Taxes	.5	.3
25.4	7.4	5.5	6.0			All Other Non-Current	4.3	4.7
-5.8	17.5	30.7	42.3			Net Worth	32.5	35.2
100.0	100.0	100.0	100.0			Total Liabilities & Net Worth	100.0	100.0
						INCOME DATA		
100.0	100.0	100.0	100.0			Net Sales	100.0	100.0
31.3	33.8	29.5	31.0			Gross Profit	29.2	29.8
32.8	35.1	30.8	31.1			Operating Expenses	24.6	25.0
-1.6	-1.3	-1.3	-.1			Operating Profit	4.6	4.8
1.8	1.0	.5	.7			All Other Expenses (net)	.5	.6
-3.3	-2.4	-1.8	-.8			Profit Before Taxes	4.1	4.2
						RATIOS		
2.7	2.6	2.5	3.0			Current	2.1	2.3
1.7	1.5	1.6	1.6				1.5	1.6
.7	.9	1.2	1.1				1.1	1.2
1.1	1.4	1.2	1.3			Quick	1.2	1.2
.5	.6	.7	.6				.7	.8
.3	.3	.4	.4				.5	.5
0 UND	18 20.0	26 13.9	28 13.2			Sales/Receivables	28 13.1	27 13.3
13 27.0	38 9.6	37 9.7	38 9.6				39 9.4	38 9.5
39 9.4	49 7.4	57 6.4	57 6.4				53 6.8	52 7.0
0 UND	33 11.1	41 8.9	60 6.1			Cost of Sales/Inventory	28 12.9	31 11.8
36 10.1	69 5.3	89 4.1	106 3.4				58 6.3	55 6.7
132 2.8	146 2.5	167 2.2	148 2.5				101 3.6	100 3.7
0 UND	16 22.8	22 16.5	18 20.3			Cost of Sales/Payables	21 17.2	20 18.0
15 24.4	39 9.3	35 10.5	41 9.0				35 10.3	33 11.0
42 8.8	76 4.8	70 5.2	64 5.7				64 5.7	60 6.1
8.2	4.2	4.7	3.3			Sales/Working Capital	6.5	6.5
44.7	10.5	8.6	7.2				11.4	10.3
-17.8	-39.9	21.3	19.6				33.0	31.7
2.3	6.9	2.0	3.4			EBIT/Interest	11.1	13.1
(14) .6	(68) .1	(119) .5	(55) 1.7				(301) 4.7	(309) 4.7
-6.3	-3.9	-3.8	-.4				2.1	1.8
		2.0	3.0			Net Profit + Depr., Dep., Amort./Cur. Mat. L/T/D	9.7	8.9
		(25) .6	(19) 1.5				(90) 4.3	(82) 4.1
		-.8	.3				2.0	2.0
.3	.1	.2	.1			Fixed/Worth	.2	.2
UND	.6	.6	.7				.6	.5
-.5	-2.6	1.6	1.5				1.4	1.1
1.1	1.2	.8	.6			Debt/Worth	1.0	.9
UND	3.1	2.1	1.7				2.0	2.1
-2.8	-21.5	6.4	3.1				5.1	4.7
	25.8	10.9	13.9			% Profit Before Taxes/Tangible Net Worth	56.1	59.5
	(53) 1.2	(113) -.1	(56) 5.0				(289) 26.9	(319) 29.5
	-23.4	-20.5	-4.1				8.2	8.5
12.1	5.7	2.6	4.4			% Profit Before Taxes/Total Assets	16.9	17.7
-2.6	-2.1	-.5	1.6				8.2	9.3
-25.0	-13.7	-8.2	-3.1				2.4	2.2
87.2	68.8	36.6	22.3			Sales/Net Fixed Assets	43.5	53.3
17.2	24.1	14.0	7.2				17.4	19.8
6.4	9.7	5.2	2.6				6.9	8.4
6.1	3.2	2.7	1.9			Sales/Total Assets	3.5	3.5
3.9	2.2	1.9	1.5				2.6	2.7
2.3	1.6	1.3	1.1				1.8	1.9
.6	.6	.7	.8			% Depr., Dep., Amort./Sales	.7	.6
(13) 1.8	(57) 1.4	(109) 1.7	(51) 2.0				(270) 1.3	(284) 1.2
3.9	2.7	3.8	5.2				2.6	2.5
		2.7	1.7			% Officers', Directors' Owners' Comp/Sales	1.6	1.7
	(41) 4.3	(61) 2.5	(18) 2.4				(104) 3.1	(121) 2.9
		6.5	3.8	4.8			5.4	5.7
19672M	270776M	1287503M	1975341M	680307M	704647M	Net Sales ($)	9807374M	10674602M
5182M	99984M	658859M	1236807M	405711M	335512M	Total Assets ($)	4602807M	4540653M

M = $ thousand   MM = $ million
See Pages 9 through 22 for Explanation of Ratios and Data

Comparative Historical Data

Current Data Sorted by Sales

	4/1/07-3/31/08 ALL	4/1/08-3/31/09 ALL	4/1/09-3/31/10 ALL	Type of Statement	0-1MM	1-3MM	3-5MM	5-10MM	10-25MM	25MM & OVER
	37	28	23	Unqualified		1	1	2	9	10
	71	68	66	Reviewed		3	11	27	19	6
	47	41	39	Compiled	4	9	6	4	10	6
	48	41	62	Tax Returns	5	27	18	6	6	6
	101	102	104	Other	4	10	13	25	24	28
						43 (4/1-9/30/09)		251 (10/1/09-3/31/10)		
NUMBER OF STATEMENTS	304	280	294		13	50	49	64	68	50
	%	%	%	**ASSETS**	%	%	%	%	%	%
	6.4	7.4	6.6	Cash & Equivalents	6.4	6.9	7.4	7.4	6.6	4.6
	26.9	25.7	23.4	Trade Receivables (net)	15.6	22.0	21.3	25.7	25.0	23.6
	33.5	33.8	35.2	Inventory	35.8	32.4	45.9	32.2	34.9	31.7
	2.9	3.2	3.0	All Other Current	3.4	3.6	1.3	2.8	2.9	4.2
	69.8	70.2	68.2	Total Current	61.2	64.8	75.9	68.2	69.4	64.1
	21.8	22.1	23.0	Fixed Assets (net)	35.3	22.7	17.2	23.6	22.4	25.6
	2.8	2.0	2.9	Intangibles (net)	.1	2.2	2.5	2.8	4.0	3.3
	5.6	5.7	6.0	All Other Non-Current	3.4	10.2	4.4	5.4	4.2	6.9
	100.0	100.0	100.0	Total	100.0	100.0	100.0	100.0	100.0	100.0
				LIABILITIES						
	12.5	13.5	12.6	Notes Payable-Short Term	12.7	12.6	12.8	13.4	12.8	11.4
	3.7	3.1	3.3	Cur. Mat.-L.T.D.	3.3	4.1	2.8	3.8	2.0	3.9
	20.4	20.2	21.9	Trade Payables	13.9	31.0	22.5	20.4	18.9	20.6
	.1	.3	.1	Income Taxes Payable	.0	.0	.0	.1	.1	.3
	9.2	9.7	8.5	All Other Current	17.8	9.1	9.8	6.9	8.7	6.3
	45.9	46.8	46.5	Total Current	47.6	56.8	48.0	44.6	42.4	42.4
	15.4	12.5	18.1	Long-Term Debt	30.9	23.4	20.1	15.4	15.2	14.6
	.4	.4	.4	Deferred Taxes	.0	.0	.0	.6	.6	.7
	5.1	6.0	7.4	All Other Non-Current	30.7	8.8	4.6	9.7	1.7	7.6
	33.2	34.3	27.7	Net Worth	-9.2	11.0	27.3	29.7	40.0	34.7
	100.0	100.0	100.0	Total Liabilities & Net Worth	100.0	100.0	100.0	100.0	100.0	100.0
				INCOME DATA						
	100.0	100.0	100.0	Net Sales	100.0	100.0	100.0	100.0	100.0	100.0
	30.4	30.8	30.9	Gross Profit	32.3	37.3	33.6	29.4	27.4	28.4
	27.3	29.4	31.9	Operating Expenses	33.0	39.5	33.8	32.1	27.3	28.2
	3.2	1.4	-1.0	Operating Profit	-.8	-2.2	-.2	-2.7	.1	.3
	.8	.5	.8	All Other Expenses (net)	2.0	1.6	.6	.6	.4	.4
	2.3	.9	-1.7	Profit Before Taxes	-2.8	-3.8	-.8	-3.3	-.4	-.1
				RATIOS						
	2.4	2.6	2.7		3.0	2.5	3.4	2.4	2.6	2.8
	1.6	1.7	1.6	Current	2.1	1.3	1.9	1.5	1.7	1.5
	1.1	1.2	1.1		.8	.7	1.2	1.2	1.2	1.1
	1.2	1.2	1.3		1.1	1.0	1.4	1.3	1.3	1.2
	.7	.7	.6	Quick	.5	.5	.8	.7	.7	.6
	.4	.4	.4		.3	.2	.4	.3	.4	.4
	25 14.4	23 16.0	24 15.1		0 UND	23 15.8	20 18.6	26 13.9	27 13.3	26 14.3
	37 10.0	35 10.3	37 9.8	Sales/Receivables	11 33.9	43 8.5	36 10.2	38 9.5	37 9.7	33 10.9
	52 7.1	53 6.9	54 6.8		46 8.0	62 5.9	48 7.7	54 6.8	55 6.7	56 6.5
	33 11.2	33 10.9	40 9.1		0 UND	30 12.2	67 5.5	39 9.4	39 9.4	44 8.2
	65 5.6	69 5.3	83 4.4	Cost of Sales/Inventory	45 8.0	90 4.1	106 3.5	77 4.7	76 4.8	85 4.3
	122 3.0	118 3.1	148 2.5		147 2.5	222 1.6	195 1.9	128 2.9	139 2.6	138 2.6
	18 19.7	19 19.4	19 19.0		6 61.0	25 14.4	22 16.8	20 18.5	20 18.6	20 18.7
	32 11.3	31 11.6	35 10.4	Cost of Sales/Payables	11 32.5	57 6.4	40 9.2	37 10.0	33 11.2	31 11.9
	60 6.1	56 6.5	67 5.4		25 14.9	162 2.3	70 5.3	67 5.4	57 6.4	57 6.4
	5.9	4.9	4.2		3.8	3.5	3.8	5.0	4.5	4.6
	10.3	8.8	8.8	Sales/Working Capital	20.7	13.7	6.8	9.3	7.9	10.4
	39.5	28.9	36.6		-38.0	-16.3	20.1	24.6	19.3	27.0
	7.2	5.6	3.4			3.3	4.2	1.6	3.0	5.8
	(284) 2.5	(252) 2.0	(264) .8	EBIT/Interest	(45) -.3	(43) 1.1	(58) -.4	(62) 1.0	(47) 2.0	
	.6	-.1	-3.3		-3.6	-2.7	-4.9	-2.1	-.7	
	6.8	6.0	2.6					1.8	1.9	11.3
	(76) 2.5	(64) 2.8	(58) .6	Net Profit + Depr., Dep., Amort./Cur. Mat. L/T/D		(13) .2	(18) 1.2	(19) 2.2		
	.8	.7	-.4			-.8	.2	.4		
	.2	.2	.2		.7	.2	.1	.2	.1	.3
	.6	.5	.6	Fixed/Worth	3.3	.9	.6	.6	.4	.6
	1.9	1.3	2.5		-1.6	-1.5	3.2	1.8	1.3	1.5
	.8	.8	.9		1.3	1.3	1.1	.9	.6	.7
	2.3	1.8	2.2	Debt/Worth	UND	5.0	2.4	2.2	1.6	2.1
	6.7	4.5	8.1		-2.4	-5.5	35.3	6.6	3.7	4.2
	38.8	23.4	14.6			17.2	22.8	8.0	12.0	14.1
	(263) 16.7	(248) 8.2	(240) 1.2	% Profit Before Taxes/Tangible Net Worth	(31) -4.3	(40) 5.3	(55) -2.1	(62) 1.1	(45) 6.3	
	1.8	-2.8	-13.8		-34.2	-9.1	-33.2	-9.0	-6.3	
	13.5	8.2	4.3		16.0	3.1	5.5	3.0	4.3	4.7
	4.7	2.4	-.3	% Profit Before Taxes/Total Assets	-3.9	-2.7	1.0	-1.3	.1	1.6
	-.8	-2.7	-8.5		-29.7	-15.0	-10.5	-10.9	-4.9	-3.8
	45.0	50.7	44.6		92.2	51.3	57.6	40.1	46.6	33.5
	16.1	16.6	15.4	Sales/Net Fixed Assets	13.2	14.4	20.1	11.8	16.1	12.1
	6.9	6.5	4.8		2.4	4.4	9.7	4.5	4.5	4.7
	3.4	3.1	2.8		6.3	2.4	3.1	2.9	3.1	2.6
	2.4	2.4	1.9	Sales/Total Assets	2.4	1.6	2.1	2.0	2.0	1.8
	1.6	1.6	1.3		1.0	1.0	1.4	1.2	1.5	1.4
	.7	.7	.7			.9	.6	.6	.7	.7
	(250) 1.4	(231) 1.6	(239) 1.7	% Depr., Dep., Amort./Sales	(36) 2.1	(35) 1.3	(59) 1.8	(57) 1.6	(44) 1.7	
	2.6	3.5	3.6		4.6	2.1	4.6	3.0	5.1	
	1.5	1.5	2.0			2.8	2.4	2.0	1.3	1.3
	(121) 2.8	(117) 2.9	(129) 3.3	% Officers', Directors' Owners' Comp/Sales	(28) 4.5	(25) 3.0	(31) 3.4	(31) 1.9	(11) 3.1	
	6.3	4.6	6.3		7.3	5.1	4.7	3.4	9.8	
	9310961M	6962194M	4938246M	Net Sales ($)	8171M	92001M	188562M	456647M	1045123M	3147742M
	4242952M	3475496M	2742055M	Total Assets ($)	4540M	68119M	117029M	283036M	569526M	1699805M

M = $ thousand   MM = $ million
See Pages 9 through 22 for Explanation of Ratios and Data

Current Data Sorted by Assets   Comparative Historical Data

	0-500M	500M-2MM	2-10MM	10-50MM	50-100MM	100-250MM		Type of Statement		4/1/05-3/31/06 ALL	4/1/06-3/31/07 ALL
			6	8	2	2		Unqualified		23	29
	4		18	10	1			Reviewed		35	38
2	9		7	5				Compiled		26	33
2	13		4	3	1			Tax Returns		12	12
2	5		19	15	3	2		Other		47	41
	15 (4/1-9/30/09)			128 (10/1/09-3/31/10)							
6	31		54	41	7	4		**NUMBER OF STATEMENTS**		143	153
%	%		%	%	%	%		**ASSETS**		%	%
	13.5		7.8	7.6				Cash & Equivalents		4.8	7.0
	28.0		32.3	30.7				Trade Receivables (net)		41.3	38.6
	34.4		37.5	36.4				Inventory		33.0	32.7
	3.8		5.3	3.3				All Other Current		1.9	2.5
	79.6		83.0	78.0				Total Current		81.0	80.7
	13.8		13.3	13.4				Fixed Assets (net)		12.5	14.0
	.5		.9	1.9				Intangibles (net)		1.4	1.5
	6.1		2.9	6.7				All Other Non-Current		5.1	3.8
	100.0		100.0	100.0				Total		100.0	100.0
								LIABILITIES			
	17.5		13.5	9.8				Notes Payable-Short Term		16.4	13.5
	2.6		2.9	2.5				Cur. Mat.-L.T.D.		3.0	2.5
	18.0		18.4	22.6				Trade Payables		27.5	23.2
	.0		.2	.1				Income Taxes Payable		.1	.2
	5.1		9.1	8.5				All Other Current		8.3	9.4
	43.2		44.2	43.5				Total Current		55.3	48.7
	11.7		8.4	9.5				Long-Term Debt		8.5	10.2
	1.0		.1	.2				Deferred Taxes		.3	.1
	3.4		5.9	4.6				All Other Non-Current		3.5	3.6
	40.7		41.4	42.2				Net Worth		32.3	37.3
	100.0		100.0	100.0				Total Liabilties & Net Worth		100.0	100.0
								INCOME DATA			
	100.0		100.0	100.0				Net Sales		100.0	100.0
	30.8		24.1	24.8				Gross Profit		24.7	25.2
	29.8		21.7	23.2				Operating Expenses		21.2	20.8
	1.1		2.4	1.6				Operating Profit		3.5	4.4
	-.2		.3	-.4				All Other Expenses (net)		.4	.2
	1.3		2.1	2.0				Profit Before Taxes		3.2	4.2
								RATIOS			
	4.1		3.3	2.8						2.1	2.3
	1.7		1.8	1.6				Current		1.5	1.7
	1.3		1.4	1.3						1.1	1.3
	2.3		2.1	1.5						1.2	1.4
	.8		.8	.8				Quick		.8	.9
	.4		.6	.5						.6	.6
	25 14.8	28 12.9		27 13.5					34 10.8	30 12.3
	33 11.0	36 10.2		40 9.0				Sales/Receivables	50 7.3	43 8.6
	49 7.5	53 6.9		58 6.3					61 6.0	56 6.5
	33 11.2	36 10.1		47 7.8					34 10.8	30 12.0
	53 6.9	63 5.8		67 5.5				Cost of Sales/Inventory	52 7.0	48 7.5
	86 4.3	79 4.6		88 4.2					72 5.1	71 5.1
	16 23.4	13 27.7		25 14.6					24 15.4	19 19.6
	26 14.2	27 13.3		44 8.4				Cost of Sales/Payables	37 9.8	31 11.6
	45 8.0	41 8.9		55 6.7					62 5.9	50 7.3
	5.3		5.1	4.7						7.8	6.5
	9.5		8.3	9.2				Sales/Working Capital		11.9	9.9
	22.2		18.9	16.7						42.5	20.7
	6.9		9.1	19.2						15.5	16.0
	(28) 2.6	(49) 4.2		(40) 6.0				EBIT/Interest	(136) 6.8	(146) 5.3
	-2.2		1.5	1.1						2.6	2.2
				6.5				Net Profit + Depr., Dep.,		8.8	10.8
			(11)	4.3				Amort./Cur. Mat. L/T/D	(30) 4.3	(41) 4.4
				1.8						1.7	1.9
	.1		.1	.1						.2	.1
	.3		.2	.3				Fixed/Worth		.3	.3
	.7		.5	.8						.9	.7
	.7		.6	.6						1.0	.9
	2.4		1.7	1.3				Debt/Worth		2.3	1.8
	4.2		3.6	2.8						7.4	3.8
	47.9		37.4	31.3				% Profit Before Taxes/Tangible		55.8	56.2
	(30) 13.1	(52) 13.2		(39) 11.4				Net Worth	(131) 28.8	(145) 31.4
	-9.7		2.1	.6						11.1	11.4
	12.5		11.8	11.3				% Profit Before Taxes/Total		17.5	21.9
	3.4		4.9	3.7				Assets		9.6	10.4
	-2.3		1.1	.0						2.3	3.0
	100.6		78.2	54.5						72.5	75.7
	28.3		41.4	25.5				Sales/Net Fixed Assets		33.4	31.8
	15.3		16.1	17.2						17.7	17.6
	4.2		3.9	3.0						3.7	3.9
	2.7		3.2	2.6				Sales/Total Assets		3.1	3.2
	2.2		2.2	2.2						2.3	2.6
	.2		.4	.6						.4	.4
	(22) 1.1	(47) .7		(38) .9				% Depr., Dep., Amort./Sales	(126) .7	(136) .7
	1.9		1.3	1.4						1.3	1.1
	2.0		1.6	1.2				% Officers', Directors'		1.8	1.8
	(19) 2.9	(21) 3.1		(14) 1.7				Owners' Comp/Sales	(47) 2.8	(51) 3.0
	4.9		3.4	4.6						5.0	4.6
4759M	131636M		852121M	2047201M	1606368M	1001392M		Net Sales ($)		5040804M	7319960M
1358M	40660M		256020M	787345M	446792M	552837M		Total Assets ($)		1687810M	2234246M

M = $ thousand   MM = $ million
See Pages 9 through 22 for Explanation of Ratios and Data

Comparative Historical Data · Current Data Sorted by Sales

Sub-period headers for Current Data: **15 (4/1-9/30/09)** spans the 0-1MM and 1-3MM columns; **128 (10/1/09-3/31/10)** spans the 3-5MM, 5-10MM, 10-25MM and 25MM & OVER columns.

4/1/07-3/31/08 ALL	4/1/08-3/31/09 ALL	4/1/09-3/31/10 ALL	Type of Statement	0-1MM	1-3MM	3-5MM	5-10MM	10-25MM	25MM & OVER
19	23	18	Unqualified			1	1	3	13
32	33	33	Reviewed			3	7	7	16
30	23	23	Compiled	1	5	2	8	2	5
13	16	23	Tax Returns	1	6	8	3	1	4
56	60	46	Other	3		4	6	12	21
150	155	143	**NUMBER OF STATEMENTS**	5	11	18	25	25	59
%	%	%	**ASSETS**	%	%	%	%	%	%
7.9	7.4	9.2	Cash & Equivalents		14.2	15.0	6.0	6.9	9.4
33.5	31.3	30.0	Trade Receivables (net)		25.4	28.3	29.2	31.9	32.5
33.1	34.9	34.1	Inventory		28.0	35.1	38.1	35.6	33.1
3.6	2.4	4.3	All Other Current		7.7	1.3	7.6	5.4	2.9
78.1	76.0	77.6	Total Current		75.4	79.7	81.0	79.9	77.8
14.2	14.9	13.2	Fixed Assets (net)		17.4	13.6	17.6	11.6	11.8
2.6	3.8	3.1	Intangibles (net)		.4	.5	.3	1.5	5.4
5.0	5.4	6.1	All Other Non-Current		6.8	6.2	1.1	7.1	5.0
100.0	100.0	100.0	Total		100.0	100.0	100.0	100.0	100.0
			LIABILITIES						
13.7	13.9	13.9	Notes Payable-Short Term		22.3	15.0	16.5	12.6	10.4
1.7	2.4	2.7	Cur. Mat.-L.T.D.		3.1	2.1	4.1	3.0	2.2
19.9	18.8	19.5	Trade Payables		24.6	15.7	17.7	18.9	21.8
.2	.2	.1	Income Taxes Payable		.0	.0	.1	.4	.1
10.0	8.9	7.7	All Other Current		4.9	4.7	7.3	11.7	8.2
45.4	44.2	43.9	Total Current		54.9	37.4	45.7	46.5	42.7
9.6	12.5	12.0	Long-Term Debt		27.2	12.9	10.4	9.7	9.5
.2	.8	.4	Deferred Taxes		2.9	.1	.2	.1	.2
4.0	3.7	5.0	All Other Non-Current		4.0	1.7	9.6	2.3	5.4
40.7	38.8	38.7	Net Worth		11.1	47.9	34.1	41.3	42.2
100.0	100.0	100.0	Total Liabilities & Net Worth		100.0	100.0	100.0	100.0	100.0
			INCOME DATA						
100.0	100.0	100.0	Net Sales		100.0	100.0	100.0	100.0	100.0
24.9	25.1	26.7	Gross Profit		35.9	27.2	24.0	23.8	25.6
21.7	22.1	25.0	Operating Expenses		34.3	27.1	21.7	21.7	23.2
3.2	3.0	1.6	Operating Profit		1.7	.1	2.3	2.1	2.4
.1	.5	.2	All Other Expenses (net)		-.7	.3	1.0	-.4	.0
3.1	2.5	1.5	Profit Before Taxes		2.3	-.2	1.3	2.5	2.4
			RATIOS						
2.6	2.9	3.2	Current		4.3	4.5	3.4	3.1	2.9
1.8	1.8	1.7			1.7	1.9	1.7	1.8	1.6
1.3	1.3	1.3			1.1	1.4	1.1	1.2	1.4
1.5	1.4	1.8	Quick		2.0	2.9	1.3	2.1	1.6
.9	.8	.8			.8	1.2	.7	.7	.8
.6	.5	.5			.3	.6	.5	.5	.6
26 14.0	24 15.1	27 13.4	Sales/Receivables		22 16.6	28 12.8	28 13.0	20 18.4	28 12.8
39 9.3	38 9.5	36 10.0			29 12.7	37 9.8	33 10.9	40 9.1	40 9.0
53 6.8	55 6.7	54 6.7			44 8.3	55 6.7	45 8.0	56 6.5	59 6.2
33 11.1	36 10.1	37 9.9	Cost of Sales/Inventory		10 36.1	41 8.9	33 11.0	36 10.2	39 9.3
50 7.4	54 6.8	58 6.3			53 6.9	61 5.9	68 5.4	62 5.9	53 6.9
75 4.8	79 4.6	84 4.4			126 2.9	78 4.7	99 3.7	75 4.9	75 4.9
16 23.3	14 25.5	16 22.4	Cost of Sales/Payables		10 36.2	16 22.5	15 24.8	12 29.4	20 18.1
29 12.5	27 13.4	32 11.5			40 9.0	22 16.2	27 13.5	31 11.9	37 9.8
44 8.3	45 8.1	50 7.4			68 5.4	35 10.4	40 9.2	45 8.1	52 7.0
6.0	5.9	5.1	Sales/Working Capital		4.3	3.7	5.1	6.0	4.8
8.9	8.8	9.2			9.5	6.4	9.4	10.8	9.3
18.8	18.1	21.0			37.7	14.8	40.6	29.7	18.7
11.0	11.3	10.7	EBIT/Interest		15.1	3.9	5.6	12.8	13.5
(138) 3.9	(144) 3.7	(133) 3.4			(10) 1.5	(15) 2.2	(24) 2.5	(23) 4.6	(56) 5.2
1.4	1.3	.6			-4.7	-3.8	.3	2.0	1.3
12.9	4.1	6.5	Net Profit + Depr., Dep., Amort./Cur. Mat. L/T/D						6.5
(38) 3.3	(31) 2.4	(23) 2.5							(15) 4.3
1.5	1.1	.9							1.8
.1	.1	.1	Fixed/Worth		.2	.1	.1	.1	.1
.3	.3	.3			.3	.2	.3	.2	.3
.8	.8	.8			12.4	.6	1.9	.6	.7
.6	.7	.7	Debt/Worth		1.4	.2	.9	.5	.8
1.5	1.7	1.8			4.0	1.0	2.4	2.1	1.5
3.8	4.1	4.6			18.0	3.6	10.9	4.6	2.8
48.6	40.1	38.9	% Profit Before Taxes/Tangible Net Worth			14.1	39.4	51.7	35.0
(140) 18.3	(141) 18.0	(133) 13.0				5.1	(23) 11.5	(24) 22.6	(55) 13.6
4.1	5.3	1.4				-17.4	-.5	8.4	2.3
15.5	14.9	11.6	% Profit Before Taxes/Total Assets		27.8	5.3	12.4	17.0	11.6
8.3	5.9	3.7			3.4	1.7	3.7	7.1	3.7
1.0	.9	-.3			-10.3	-14.1	-1.2	2.2	.3
68.5	71.4	61.8	Sales/Net Fixed Assets		40.1	106.1	113.1	83.3	61.0
28.4	30.8	33.9			24.6	31.5	36.6	42.6	34.6
15.7	12.2	16.4			11.5	13.8	10.4	20.1	18.1
3.7	3.6	3.6	Sales/Total Assets		2.6	3.9	3.9	3.9	3.5
3.0	2.9	2.7			2.3	2.9	3.0	3.4	2.8
2.3	2.2	2.1			1.7	2.0	2.1	2.3	2.2
.4	.5	.5	% Depr., Dep., Amort./Sales				.1	.1	.1	.1
(134) .9	(132) .9	(117) .8				(11) 1.3	(21) .8	(23) .8	(51) .7
1.4	1.4	1.4				2.2	1.5	1.0	1.4
1.4	1.1	1.3	% Officers', Directors' Owners' Comp/Sales			2.1	2.0	.9	
(60) 2.4	(53) 2.5	(57) 2.9				(11) 3.0	(11) 3.0	(11) 1.8	(17) 1.9
4.1	4.3	4.8				4.9	3.5	3.2	9.8
6781047M	6709454M	5643477M	Net Sales ($)	2571M	21218M	71786M	182043M	386514M	4979345M
2437540M	2604509M	2085012M	Total Assets ($)	3530M	10194M	26886M	70484M	149248M	1824670M

M = $ thousand   MM = $ million
See Pages 9 through 22 for Explanation of Ratios and Data

Current Data Sorted by Assets   Comparative Historical Data

	0-500M	500M-2MM	2-10MM	10-50MM	50-100MM	100-250MM	Type of Statement	4/1/05-3/31/06 ALL	4/1/06-3/31/07 ALL
		3	9	17	3	2	Unqualified	38	41
		14	45	15	1		Reviewed	81	82
	2	17	19				Compiled	53	49
	9	20	13				Tax Returns	32	35
	6	23	49	26	6	4	Other	89	94
		51 (4/1-9/30/09)		252 (10/1/09-3/31/10)					
	17	77	135	58	10	6	NUMBER OF STATEMENTS	293	301
	%	%	%	%	%	%	**ASSETS**	%	%
	20.4	9.0	9.1	6.3	3.2		Cash & Equivalents	8.0	7.3
	28.7	27.2	31.3	27.8	27.4		Trade Receivables (net)	36.3	36.3
	28.5	34.2	31.7	29.7	36.7		Inventory	30.6	30.0
	.1	1.6	2.8	3.4	4.3		All Other Current	1.9	3.1
	77.7	72.1	74.9	67.2	71.7		Total Current	76.8	76.7
	19.3	20.2	17.4	21.6	16.7		Fixed Assets (net)	16.9	16.5
	.1	1.4	2.9	4.7	7.5		Intangibles (net)	2.1	1.7
	2.9	6.3	4.8	6.5	4.1		All Other Non-Current	4.2	5.1
	100.0	100.0	100.0	100.0	100.0		Total	100.0	100.0
							LIABILITIES		
	21.0	12.9	16.5	11.1	12.7		Notes Payable-Short Term	15.6	15.5
	2.2	2.3	3.1	3.4	1.4		Cur. Mat.-L.T.D.	2.4	2.7
	23.3	14.1	18.2	11.3	11.6		Trade Payables	19.5	19.3
	.0	.0	.1	.2	.0		Income Taxes Payable	.3	.2
	15.6	6.5	6.1	8.5	10.6		All Other Current	10.4	10.5
	62.1	35.8	44.1	34.4	36.3		Total Current	48.1	48.2
	8.5	15.4	10.5	12.2	12.8		Long-Term Debt	11.4	12.7
	.0	.1	.2	.3	.5		Deferred Taxes	.2	.2
	10.7	4.1	8.0	2.4	2.9		All Other Non-Current	4.6	4.8
	18.7	44.5	37.2	50.7	47.5		Net Worth	35.6	34.1
	100.0	100.0	100.0	100.0	100.0		Total Liabilities & Net Worth	100.0	100.0
							INCOME DATA		
	100.0	100.0	100.0	100.0	100.0		Net Sales	100.0	100.0
	37.7	31.9	26.3	25.5	23.4		Gross Profit	27.1	27.8
	40.4	29.3	24.7	23.3	21.4		Operating Expenses	23.0	23.6
	-2.7	2.6	1.6	2.2	2.0		Operating Profit	4.1	4.3
	-.8	.4	.7	.0	1.0		All Other Expenses (net)	.4	.6
	-1.9	2.2	.9	2.2	1.1		Profit Before Taxes	3.7	3.6
							RATIOS		
	2.4	4.0	3.1	3.3	3.2		Current	2.7	2.6
	1.5	2.1	1.6	2.0	2.1			1.6	1.6
	.8	1.3	1.3	1.3	1.4			1.2	1.2
	1.8	1.9	1.5	1.8	1.8		Quick	1.5	1.6
	.8	1.1	.9	1.0	.9			.9	.9
	.3	.5	.6	.6	.5			.6	.6
	4 88.6	17 21.7	29 12.7	32 11.6	25 14.7		Sales/Receivables	32 11.6	28 12.8
	19 19.0	32 11.2	41 9.0	41 8.9	36 10.0			43 8.4	42 8.8
	31 11.9	50 7.3	57 6.4	53 6.9	63 5.8			55 6.6	56 6.5
	0 UND	21 17.6	36 10.2	35 10.3	36 10.1		Cost of Sales/Inventory	28 13.2	26 14.0
	30 12.1	59 6.2	58 6.3	58 6.3	69 5.3			46 7.8	45 8.2
	62 5.9	100 3.7	94 3.9	85 4.3	106 3.4			71 5.1	74 4.9
	7 49.3	11 32.9	13 27.2	12 30.3	13 29.1		Cost of Sales/Payables	16 23.1	16 23.1
	24 15.0	22 16.7	28 13.1	19 18.8	20 18.7			27 13.3	27 13.5
	39 9.4	35 10.5	50 7.3	33 10.9	39 9.4			43 8.5	43 8.5
	8.3	4.7	5.3	4.0	4.7		Sales/Working Capital	6.8	6.4
	15.9	8.5	8.3	7.5	6.4			10.5	10.7
	-26.3	19.5	16.3	14.3	8.6			26.1	29.8
	13.5	11.8	6.7	7.7	6.0		EBIT/Interest	11.3	11.0
	(12) 2.1	(66) 1.7	(122) 2.1	(55) 1.4	2.5			(266) 4.7	(279) 4.6
	-8.2	-.7	-.4	-.3	.2			2.0	1.9
		5.5	3.4	4.2			Net Profit + Depr., Dep., Amort./Cur. Mat. L/T/D	8.5	10.8
		(10) .9	(30) 1.7	(14) 1.6				(64) 3.7	(77) 3.8
		-.1	-.2	.1				2.1	1.5
	.2	.1	.1	.2	.2		Fixed/Worth	.1	.1
	1.0	.3	.4	.4	.4			.3	.3
	NM	1.4	1.0	1.1	.7			.9	1.0
	1.7	.5	.8	.4	.8		Debt/Worth	.8	.8
	5.5	1.4	1.8	.9	1.5			1.9	2.0
	NM	3.0	4.3	2.5	2.1			4.6	4.3
	143.0	31.5	24.0	16.7	14.8		% Profit Before Taxes/Tangible Net Worth	44.8	53.3
	(13) 44.4	(72) 7.8	(120) 9.6	(54) 4.6	3.6			(268) 23.3	(273) 28.4
	-105.6	-6.2	-3.9	-4.5	-12.3			8.6	12.2
	37.0	14.8	8.9	7.8	8.4		% Profit Before Taxes/Total Assets	16.1	17.2
	5.1	3.0	2.7	1.5	2.4			8.2	8.7
	-28.1	-3.3	-3.0	-2.4	-3.1			2.6	3.2
	71.2	96.4	64.4	29.1	40.7		Sales/Net Fixed Assets	73.0	65.8
	38.2	28.2	23.4	16.4	12.4			29.4	28.4
	10.8	8.3	8.3	6.3	7.9			12.9	12.5
	5.8	3.7	3.4	2.7	2.8		Sales/Total Assets	3.8	3.9
	4.4	2.8	2.4	2.1	2.2			3.1	3.1
	3.6	2.1	1.7	1.5	1.8			2.4	2.4
	.9	.5	.5	.8			% Depr., Dep., Amort./Sales	.5	.5
	(12) 1.4	(53) 1.3	(125) 1.0	(50) 1.3				(241) .8	(252) .9
	3.4	2.5	1.9	3.3				1.5	1.6
	5.0	3.0	1.8				% Officers', Directors' Owners' Comp/Sales	1.7	1.4
	(10) 8.2	(45) 4.3	(63) 2.9					(95) 2.9	(97) 2.6
	18.0	5.9	5.8					5.1	5.0
	19579M	274301M	1710862M	3158086M	1814146M	1179147M	Net Sales ($)	10008795M	10166947M
	4593M	90783M	614469M	1361539M	639324M	930256M	Total Assets ($)	3375430M	3519887M

M = $ thousand   MM = $ million
See Pages 9 through 22 for Explanation of Ratios and Data

Comparative Historical Data | Current Data Sorted by Sales

Type of Statement	4/1/07-3/31/08 ALL	4/1/08-3/31/09 ALL	4/1/09-3/31/10 ALL	0-1MM	1-3MM	3-5MM	5-10MM	10-25MM	25MM & OVER
Unqualified	41	42	34		2	1		12	19
Reviewed	68	73	75		5	12	23	22	13
Compiled	46	55	38		10	6	12	9	1
Tax Returns	45	62	42	9	16	5	7	4	1
Other	99	108	114	4	15	15	22	20	38
				51 (4/1-9/30/09)		252 (10/1/09-3/31/10)			
NUMBER OF STATEMENTS	299	340	303	13	48	39	64	67	72
ASSETS	%	%	%	%	%	%	%	%	%
Cash & Equivalents	7.2	8.4	8.9	21.9	9.0	11.6	8.5	7.8	6.3
Trade Receivables (net)	34.7	31.0	29.4	23.5	21.7	26.0	32.8	32.4	31.6
Inventory	31.1	32.5	31.6	25.0	35.7	32.4	29.5	34.0	29.4
All Other Current	2.8	3.1	2.5	.3	1.7	1.2	2.7	3.0	3.6
Total Current	75.7	75.0	72.4	70.7	68.1	71.2	73.4	77.2	70.9
Fixed Assets (net)	15.5	17.2	19.2	20.9	26.1	17.9	18.0	17.0	18.2
Intangibles (net)	3.2	3.3	3.0	.0	1.2	4.1	2.9	2.0	5.3
All Other Non-Current	5.6	4.5	5.3	8.4	4.6	6.9	5.7	3.8	5.6
Total	100.0	100.0	100.0	100.0	100.0	100.0	100.0	100.0	100.0
LIABILITIES									
Notes Payable-Short Term	16.8	16.6	14.4	10.7	15.6	13.4	18.5	12.7	12.6
Cur. Mat.-L.T.D.	3.6	3.4	2.8	.6	3.1	2.6	3.1	2.9	2.9
Trade Payables	18.2	15.4	15.7	19.2	13.4	14.8	17.6	16.0	15.2
Income Taxes Payable	.2	.2	.1	.2	.0	.3	.0	.1	.2
All Other Current	9.1	7.9	7.3	10.6	7.0	8.1	4.8	7.1	8.9
Total Current	47.9	43.6	40.3	41.3	39.1	39.1	44.0	38.7	39.8
Long-Term Debt	11.2	12.2	12.5	18.7	18.2	13.1	10.9	8.1	12.8
Deferred Taxes	.3	.4	.2	.2	.1	.4	.1	.2	.4
All Other Non-Current	4.1	4.1	5.9	17.1	7.7	8.2	6.0	3.8	3.3
Net Worth	36.5	39.8	41.0	22.8	34.9	39.2	38.9	49.2	43.7
Total Liabilities & Net Worth	100.0	100.0	100.0	100.0	100.0	100.0	100.0	100.0	100.0
INCOME DATA									
Net Sales	100.0	100.0	100.0	100.0	100.0	100.0	100.0	100.0	100.0
Gross Profit	27.5	27.8	28.2	43.6	37.0	28.7	24.4	27.1	23.9
Operating Expenses	24.1	25.3	26.5	44.7	33.4	26.8	23.4	24.6	23.1
Operating Profit	3.4	2.6	1.7	-1.1	3.6	1.9	1.0	2.5	.7
All Other Expenses (net)	.4	.6	.5	-.6	.9	.7	.4	.5	.2
Profit Before Taxes	3.0	2.0	1.2	-.5	2.7	1.2	.6	2.0	.5
RATIOS									
Current	2.8	3.2	3.2	5.7	3.1	3.5	3.0	4.1	3.2
	1.7	1.8	1.9	2.3	1.9	1.9	1.6	2.0	1.9
	1.2	1.3	1.3	1.0	1.2	1.3	1.3	1.3	1.3
Quick	1.5	1.6	1.7	5.4	1.5	2.2	1.5	2.1	1.5
	.9	.9	1.0	1.2	.8	.8	1.0	1.2	.9
	.6	.5	.6	.5	.4	.4	.6	.6	.7
Sales/Receivables	30 12.3	24 15.1	26 14.2	10 34.9	16 23.3	18 20.0	29 12.6	29 12.6	29 12.5
	39 9.4	37 10.0	37 9.9	23 16.1	31 11.8	37 10.0	40 9.2	43 8.5	39 9.4
	53 6.9	51 7.1	54 6.7	49 7.5	42 8.7	67 5.5	57 6.4	57 6.5	54 6.7
Cost of Sales/Inventory	29 12.7	28 13.3	31 11.9	0 UND	23 15.7	29 12.6	29 12.4	39 9.3	29 12.5
	51 7.2	54 6.8	57 6.4	20 18.7	66 5.5	60 6.1	49 7.4	59 6.2	53 6.9
	75 4.9	82 4.4	91 4.0	148 2.5	121 3.0	120 3.0	76 4.8	94 3.9	78 4.7
Cost of Sales/Payables	16 22.9	11 32.8	13 29.2	7 49.3	14 26.3	13 28.4	11 34.7	14 26.8	12 31.2
	24 15.5	20 18.3	24 15.5	25 14.4	26 13.9	23 15.7	25 14.9	25 14.3	21 17.1
	40 9.1	38 9.7	38 9.5	115 3.2	41 8.9	53 6.9	46 7.9	36 10.1	34 10.8
Sales/Working Capital	6.0	5.3	5.0	3.6	4.6	4.0	5.4	4.9	4.5
	10.4	9.1	8.3	8.1	7.9	8.0	11.6	7.3	8.0
	22.5	20.1	16.5	NM	60.8	20.7	18.6	13.0	16.3
EBIT/Interest	10.6	10.7	7.1		11.1	11.0	9.8	7.8	4.7
	(278) 3.5	(306) 3.3	(271) 1.8	(41) 1.7	(34) 1.7	(59) 2.0	(60) 2.3	(69) 2.0	
	1.5	.9	-.6		-.1	-.8	-1.2	.0	-.5
Net Profit + Depr., Dep., Amort./Cur. Mat. L/T/D	7.1	5.9	4.5					3.5	5.4
	(69) 3.0	(70) 2.1	(62) 1.7				(17) 1.6	(21) 1.8	
	1.1	.4	.0					.0	.2
Fixed/Worth	.1	.1	.1	.2	.2	.1	.1	.1	.2
	.3	.3	.4	.9	.8	.4	.4	.3	.4
	.9	.9	1.2	NM	2.3	1.9	1.0	.7	.9
Debt/Worth	.8	.7	.6	1.0	.7	.9	.9	.4	.5
	1.7	1.7	1.6	7.7	2.0	1.8	1.8	1.1	1.7
	4.3	4.7	3.6	NM	5.6	4.3	3.3	2.2	3.4
% Profit Before Taxes/Tangible Net Worth	45.5	34.3	23.4	54.4	53.2	24.4	25.1	20.3	17.1
	(275) 21.3	(311) 15.6	(274) 7.4	(10) -8.6	(43) 14.5	(33) 8.4	(59) 7.5	(62) 6.3	(67) 6.6
	7.0	1.4	-5.9	-127.4	-4.7	-7.4	-11.8	-1.1	-5.1
% Profit Before Taxes/Total Assets	16.8	14.7	9.4	16.6	25.2	12.9	9.1	9.0	7.0
	6.9	5.1	2.6	.9	2.8	3.2	2.2	2.7	2.2
	1.7	-.1	-3.0	-22.3	-2.1	-3.4	-4.8	-.9	-2.5
Sales/Net Fixed Assets	74.1	72.0	55.1	75.1	45.0	79.8	61.4	70.8	39.2
	30.5	28.8	21.7	15.4	18.0	19.6	23.0	27.0	20.1
	13.5	11.3	7.9	4.0	5.5	7.2	9.0	8.3	8.9
Sales/Total Assets	3.8	3.7	3.5	4.9	3.9	3.2	3.7	3.4	3.4
	2.9	2.9	2.5	2.9	2.5	2.0	2.7	2.5	2.3
	2.2	2.1	1.7	1.0	1.8	1.5	1.8	1.7	1.8
% Depr., Dep., Amort./Sales	.5	.5	.5		.5	.7	.5	.5	.5
	(258) .9	(282) .9	(252) 1.1	(33) 1.4	(31) 1.6	(55) .9	(63) 1.0	(61) .9	
	1.8	2.0	2.3		2.9	3.6	2.1	2.0	1.8
% Officers', Directors' Owners' Comp/Sales	1.2	1.8	2.1		3.1	2.8	1.9	1.8	.8
	(105) 2.6	(141) 2.8	(126) 3.6	(29) 4.5	(23) 3.5	(33) 3.7	(23) 2.7	(11) 1.8	
	5.4	4.9	6.5		7.9	5.0	6.2	7.0	6.8
Net Sales ($)	10948669M	13065514M	8156121M	9442M	100286M	148257M	462035M	1090789M	6345312M
Total Assets ($)	4219611M	4337331M	3640964M	6396M	47988M	74553M	194185M	496953M	2820889M

M = $ thousand   MM = $ million
See Pages 9 through 22 for Explanation of Ratios and Data

Current Data Sorted by Assets   **Comparative Historical Data**

0-500M	500M-2MM	2-10MM	10-50MM	50-100MM	100-250MM	Type of Statement	4/1/05-3/31/06 ALL	4/1/06-3/31/07 ALL
		1	6		1	Unqualified	5	5
	1	14	2		1	Reviewed	8	13
	3	2				Compiled	3	3
1	9	4				Tax Returns	2	7
	1	7	2	1		Other	11	9
	13 (4/1-9/30/09)		43 (10/1/09-3/31/10)					
1	14	28	10	1	2	NUMBER OF STATEMENTS	29	37
%	%	%	%	%	%	**ASSETS**	%	%
	20.5	12.1	9.4			Cash & Equivalents	13.8	10.6
	26.6	24.9	30.0			Trade Receivables (net)	38.4	35.5
	30.5	34.8	40.8			Inventory	24.3	34.1
	.5	1.5	2.6			All Other Current	3.4	3.4
	78.1	73.4	82.8			Total Current	80.0	83.6
	13.1	12.6	15.3			Fixed Assets (net)	11.7	10.2
	6.4	4.9	.4			Intangibles (net)	4.4	3.1
	2.5	9.2	1.6			All Other Non-Current	3.9	3.2
	100.0	100.0	100.0			Total	100.0	100.0
						LIABILITIES		
	8.8	7.8	13.5			Notes Payable-Short Term	15.5	16.5
	2.0	3.2	1.1			Cur. Mat.-L.T.D.	2.2	1.6
	20.0	28.1	30.2			Trade Payables	20.1	23.6
	.0	.2	1.2			Income Taxes Payable	.1	.2
	16.0	9.2	12.6			All Other Current	13.6	15.9
	46.7	48.5	58.7			Total Current	51.5	57.8
	12.6	4.5	6.1			Long-Term Debt	6.0	6.5
	.1	.1	.1			Deferred Taxes	.0	.0
	4.4	5.6	4.8			All Other Non-Current	13.1	6.7
	36.2	41.3	30.2			Net Worth	29.4	29.0
	100.0	100.0	100.0			Total Liabilities & Net Worth	100.0	100.0
						INCOME DATA		
	100.0	100.0	100.0			Net Sales	100.0	100.0
	36.2	26.0	26.8			Gross Profit	29.8	30.7
	34.1	23.1	20.2			Operating Expenses	24.6	25.9
	2.1	2.9	6.6			Operating Profit	5.2	4.7
	.7	.3	.5			All Other Expenses (net)	.7	.8
	1.4	2.6	6.2			Profit Before Taxes	4.4	3.9
						RATIOS		
	3.9	2.6	2.0				2.4	2.3
	1.8	1.7	1.4			Current	1.5	1.5
	1.0	1.0	1.1				1.1	1.2
	2.2	1.2	.8				1.8	1.1
	1.0	.8	.6			Quick	1.0	.8
	.4	.5	.5				.5	.6
	16 22.9	15 25.1	25 14.3				32 11.5	30 12.3
	33 11.1	25 14.9	38 9.7			Sales/Receivables	45 8.0	42 8.6
	37 9.8	44 8.3	65 5.7				66 5.6	49 7.5
	22 16.9	25 14.8	40 9.2				0 UND	37 10.0
	34 10.7	43 8.6	66 5.5			Cost of Sales/Inventory	38 9.5	58 6.3
	107 3.4	72 5.1	123 3.0				93 3.9	110 3.3
	6 56.8	18 20.2	23 15.6				16 23.3	23 15.6
	40 9.1	31 11.9	62 5.9			Cost of Sales/Payables	32 11.3	37 10.0
	59 6.2	53 6.9	78 4.7				50 7.4	54 6.8
	3.7	8.2	4.5				6.5	6.7
	13.1	14.0	12.4			Sales/Working Capital	11.9	10.5
	-329.0	NM	51.4				47.0	34.9
	13.6	34.3					20.2	10.8
	(12) 5.6	(27) 10.1				EBIT/Interest	(22) 4.4	(35) 4.1
	1.6	2.7					1.5	1.2
		22.4						
		(10) 2.3				Net Profit + Depr., Dep., Amort./Cur. Mat. L/T/D		
		.8						
	.0	.1	.1				.1	.1
	.2	.2	.4			Fixed/Worth	.2	.3
	1.1	.7	2.1				1.7	1.0
	.7	.5	1.2				.8	.8
	3.2	2.5	2.6			Debt/Worth	2.2	2.5
	14.6	4.5	7.3				8.9	5.8
	48.3	43.8					61.7	71.5
	(12) 27.7	(26) 19.9				% Profit Before Taxes/Tangible Net Worth	(26) 25.6	(31) 30.3
	14.3	10.0					5.3	3.6
	14.9	13.1	20.9				17.0	17.3
	8.7	5.6	5.2			% Profit Before Taxes/Total Assets	7.4	7.1
	2.1	2.8	2.0				1.8	.8
	UND	166.6	455.7				194.8	247.2
	137.1	64.5	27.0			Sales/Net Fixed Assets	42.5	60.9
	21.8	21.9	8.2				21.7	26.6
	5.5	4.0	3.8				4.2	4.0
	2.8	3.6	2.5			Sales/Total Assets	3.2	3.2
	2.3	2.2	1.8				2.2	2.0
		.2	.1				.2	.3
		(25) .7				% Depr., Dep., Amort./Sales	(21) .8	(27) .9
		1.4					2.6	1.5
	2.3	.4						1.2
	(12) 3.6	(12) .9				% Officers', Directors' Owners' Comp/Sales		(15) 2.7
	5.5	2.7						6.2
396M	60249M	532069M	455569M	42795M	349468M	Net Sales ($)	1444252M	1430825M
172M	14342M	150811M	187210M	57733M	244779M	Total Assets ($)	507564M	582407M

M = $ thousand   MM = $ million
See Pages 9 through 22 for Explanation of Ratios and Data

Comparative Historical Data | Current Data Sorted by Sales

			Type of Statement						
5	7	8	Unqualified					1	7
11	15	18	Reviewed		2		4	5	7
5	2	5	Compiled				2		1
5	4	14	Tax Returns	2	4	1	3	3	1
13	13	11	Other	2	4	1	1	5	4
4/1/07-3/31/08 ALL	4/1/08-3/31/09 ALL	4/1/09-3/31/10 ALL		0-1MM	13 (4/1-9/30/09) 1-3MM	3-5MM	43 (10/1/09-3/31/10) 5-10MM	10-25MM	25MM & OVER
39	41	56	NUMBER OF STATEMENTS	2	7	3	10	14	20
%	%	%	ASSETS	%	%	%	%	%	%
7.6	8.2	13.5	Cash & Equivalents				5.6	14.0	11.4
35.5	31.9	26.6	Trade Receivables (net)				33.7	20.7	31.3
30.4	33.6	33.3	Inventory				31.7	37.0	35.0
3.4	1.6	1.4	All Other Current				.9	1.4	2.1
76.8	75.2	74.9	Total Current				71.9	73.0	79.8
13.6	12.2	13.6	Fixed Assets (net)				20.7	10.8	9.5
3.7	7.4	6.0	Intangibles (net)				1.1	5.2	6.8
5.9	5.3	5.6	All Other Non-Current				6.3	10.9	3.9
100.0	100.0	100.0	Total				100.0	100.0	100.0
			LIABILITIES						
16.9	13.2	9.5	Notes Payable-Short Term				4.9	12.0	13.1
1.8	3.2	3.1	Cur. Mat.-L.T.D.				3.2	3.0	3.6
22.2	17.1	25.2	Trade Payables				23.0	31.4	30.2
.3	.1	.4	Income Taxes Payable				.2	.1	.9
15.4	13.3	11.2	All Other Current				10.0	9.6	10.5
56.5	46.8	49.4	Total Current				41.3	56.2	58.3
7.4	9.6	7.3	Long-Term Debt				4.5	6.3	6.1
.1	.0	.1	Deferred Taxes				.3	.0	.1
6.0	4.1	4.8	All Other Non-Current				3.7	6.0	4.3
30.1	39.5	38.5	Net Worth				50.3	31.5	31.3
100.0	100.0	100.0	Total Liabilities & Net Worth				100.0	100.0	100.0
			INCOME DATA						
100.0	100.0	100.0	Net Sales				100.0	100.0	100.0
27.8	29.3	29.1	Gross Profit				35.8	22.4	21.7
24.2	26.6	25.8	Operating Expenses				32.0	20.4	17.4
3.6	2.7	3.3	Operating Profit				3.8	2.0	4.3
1.4	.6	.2	All Other Expenses (net)				.3	.3	-.4
2.2	2.1	3.1	Profit Before Taxes				3.5	1.7	4.7
			RATIOS						
1.9	2.3	2.4	Current				2.5	2.4	1.9
1.4	1.6	1.6					1.9	1.4	1.4
1.1	1.2	1.1					1.2	.9	1.1
1.0	1.1	1.4	Quick				1.9	.9	1.1
.8	.8	.8					1.0	.6	.6
.6	.5	.5					.7	.4	.5
28 12.9	27 13.8	16 22.5	Sales/Receivables				22 16.9	9 41.1	23 16.0
41 8.8	36 10.2	32 11.6					35 10.3	19 19.5	38 9.5
54 6.8	56 6.5	46 7.9					44 8.2	28 12.9	73 5.0
30 12.3	30 12.3	25 14.8	Cost of Sales/Inventory				22 16.9	24 15.5	37 9.9
45 8.1	48 7.7	46 7.9					33 10.9	37 9.8	50 7.3
88 4.2	87 4.2	93 3.9					78 4.7	72 5.1	78 4.7
18 20.3	13 27.8	17 21.2	Cost of Sales/Payables				17 21.6	20 18.2	23 16.1
29 12.4	24 15.2	37 9.8					22 16.9	32 11.4	43 8.4
47 7.8	52 7.0	66 5.6					49 7.4	79 4.6	66 5.5
8.7	5.8	6.1	Sales/Working Capital				7.6	8.7	7.2
11.4	12.3	14.0					13.7	31.2	17.5
51.6	25.8	106.9					35.9	-38.7	101.7
11.1	11.0	22.8	EBIT/Interest				36.7	60.1	33.0
(37) 4.7	(37) 2.3	(51) 7.0					10.8	7.5	(17) 5.5
1.7	.0	2.7					3.7	.6	2.9
5.9		13.4	Net Profit + Depr., Dep., Amort./Cur. Mat. L/T/D						
(13) 3.2		(17) 3.3							
1.3		.7							
.1	.1	.1	Fixed/Worth				.0	.2	.1
.4	.4	.3					.5	.3	.3
1.5	.9	.9					.8	NM	1.0
1.0	1.0	.7	Debt/Worth				.4	.7	1.8
2.7	2.8	2.6					1.1	4.1	3.3
9.1	6.6	6.3					2.6	NM	7.0
51.2	41.2	50.4	% Profit Before Taxes/Tangible Net Worth				37.0	90.9	68.0
(33) 23.9	(35) 17.2	(49) 22.1					18.5	(11) 27.2	(17) 29.3
5.6	-4.1	11.4					13.8	11.9	12.4
13.0	14.8	14.2	% Profit Before Taxes/Total Assets				18.5	12.6	15.6
5.6	4.8	6.1					7.7	5.8	5.0
1.6	-2.3	2.8					3.8	-1.1	2.3
183.5	157.7	184.0	Sales/Net Fixed Assets				255.4	144.7	252.1
43.0	44.9	57.5					65.3	52.1	66.4
14.2	19.3	18.0					6.3	24.1	37.9
3.9	4.2	4.0	Sales/Total Assets				5.5	4.7	3.9
3.0	2.8	2.9					3.8	3.8	3.1
2.3	2.1	2.1					2.0	2.3	1.9
.3	.5	.2	% Depr., Dep., Amort./Sales					.2	.2
(31) .7	(30) 1.0	(45) .8						(13) .5	(16) .7
1.5	1.6	2.0						1.2	1.4
.8	1.3	.9	% Officers', Directors' Owners' Comp/Sales						
(14) 2.7	(15) 2.4	(25) 2.7							
6.0	6.4	4.5							
1934990M	1597524M	1440546M	Net Sales ($)	1263M	14014M	11572M	70165M	230682M	1112850M
782547M	729891M	655047M	Total Assets ($)	1025M	6779M	6532M	22915M	70348M	547448M

M = $ thousand   MM = $ million
See Pages 9 through 22 for Explanation of Ratios and Data

Current Data Sorted by Assets   **Comparative Historical Data**

						Type of Statement		
	1	6	8	2	2	Unqualified	22	36
	4	21	14	1		Reviewed	41	49
2	10	11				Compiled	46	39
3	16	7	2		1	Tax Returns	19	23
6	15	27	20	1	1	Other	98	76
	41 (4/1-9/30/09)		139 (10/1/09-3/31/10)				4/1/05-3/31/06	4/1/06-3/31/07
0-500M	500M-2MM	2-10MM	10-50MM	50-100MM	100-250MM		ALL	ALL
11	46	72	44	4	3	**NUMBER OF STATEMENTS**	226	223
%	%	%	%	%	%	**ASSETS**	%	%
8.2	15.0	7.8	9.1			Cash & Equivalents	8.0	8.2
32.5	32.8	32.8	25.6			Trade Receivables (net)	33.8	32.2
33.6	27.0	27.4	25.2			Inventory	30.7	31.4
4.5	2.7	6.5	5.6			All Other Current	3.9	3.6
78.8	77.5	74.5	65.6			Total Current	76.5	75.5
12.3	12.2	11.7	15.3			Fixed Assets (net)	13.1	14.3
3.7	3.1	5.7	8.9			Intangibles (net)	4.7	3.7
5.2	7.2	8.2	10.2			All Other Non-Current	5.8	6.5
100.0	100.0	100.0	100.0			Total	100.0	100.0
						LIABILITIES		
23.4	11.7	11.5	11.0			Notes Payable-Short Term	14.4	13.6
1.2	4.5	5.2	2.5			Cur. Mat.-L.T.D.	3.1	3.1
23.6	23.6	20.0	15.3			Trade Payables	22.8	19.0
.1	.0	.2	.2			Income Taxes Payable	.2	.4
16.2	12.7	18.5	15.0			All Other Current	14.5	16.2
64.5	52.5	55.4	44.0			Total Current	55.0	52.2
9.9	14.1	8.5	10.7			Long-Term Debt	11.2	11.6
.0	.1	.3	.2			Deferred Taxes	.2	.3
8.9	5.4	6.3	4.5			All Other Non-Current	9.3	6.3
16.6	27.9	29.5	40.6			Net Worth	24.3	29.6
100.0	100.0	100.0	100.0			Total Liabilities & Net Worth	100.0	100.0
						INCOME DATA		
100.0	100.0	100.0	100.0			Net Sales	100.0	100.0
45.7	42.4	37.4	39.2			Gross Profit	36.4	37.8
45.9	38.7	34.1	31.9			Operating Expenses	33.6	34.6
-.2	3.6	3.3	7.3			Operating Profit	2.8	3.2
.3	.3	.2	1.5			All Other Expenses (net)	.4	.3
-.5	3.3	3.1	5.8			Profit Before Taxes	2.4	2.9
						RATIOS		
3.7	2.4	2.5	2.1				2.1	2.1
1.4	1.4	1.4	1.4			Current	1.4	1.5
1.0	1.0	1.0	1.2				1.1	1.1
1.8	1.5	1.4	1.2				1.2	1.1
(10) .9	.8	.8	.7			Quick	.8	.7
.5	.5	.5	.5				.5	.5
13 27.3	22 16.9	25 14.8	32 11.4				27 13.7	25 14.7
21 17.2	32 11.4	34 10.6	41 8.8			Sales/Receivables	36 10.2	35 10.4
32 11.3	40 9.0	44 8.4	51 7.2				48 7.6	44 8.3
0 UND	20 17.9	27 13.6	42 8.8				30 12.0	37 10.0
59 6.2	46 8.0	53 6.8	68 5.4			Cost of Sales/Inventory	60 6.1	65 5.6
158 2.3	101 3.6	78 4.7	119 3.1				87 4.2	92 4.0
4 84.4	23 15.9	17 22.1	20 17.9				17 21.2	14 26.6
29 12.7	34 10.9	32 11.3	33 11.1			Cost of Sales/Payables	35 10.6	30 12.3
57 6.4	69 5.3	54 6.7	47 7.8				55 6.7	49 7.4
4.1	7.5	7.4	5.8				8.0	7.7
19.1	14.6	15.3	8.8			Sales/Working Capital	14.6	14.7
UND	NM	141.6	30.9				39.0	46.8
	17.3	17.7	18.6				11.4	10.9
(40) 5.3	(64) 5.3	(40) 8.1				EBIT/Interest	(204) 3.4	(188) 3.9
1.0	1.6	3.3					1.2	1.6
	59.3	19.5	10.8				4.8	6.1
(13) 3.8	(11) 4.6	(11) 2.3				Net Profit + Depr., Dep., Amort./Cur. Mat. L/T/D	(51) 2.0	(50) 2.1
1.3	2.2	1.6					.6	.9
.0	.1	.1	.1				.1	.1
.2	.3	.4	.3			Fixed/Worth	.4	.3
2.6	8.6	3.9	1.3				1.2	1.5
.6	.9	1.0	1.0				1.3	1.1
3.0	2.6	3.0	1.9			Debt/Worth	2.8	2.3
48.8	19.1	15.6	3.5				10.7	8.0
	47.0	54.3	66.5				51.7	51.5
(36) 23.9	(60) 23.6	(40) 35.4				% Profit Before Taxes/Tangible Net Worth	(191) 22.8	(189) 23.8
.5	6.1	13.3					4.9	7.3
6.9	20.4	16.2	13.4				13.8	14.3
3.6	9.0	6.8	8.0			% Profit Before Taxes/Total Assets	5.4	7.1
-4.5	.1	.6	3.2				.5	1.8
999.8	84.5	92.9	89.7				89.5	82.6
42.1	44.7	42.9	19.8			Sales/Net Fixed Assets	36.8	33.0
28.6	24.9	20.6	6.8				17.0	15.2
7.2	4.4	4.0	3.2				4.4	4.3
4.0	3.4	3.3	1.8			Sales/Total Assets	3.0	3.1
2.7	2.6	2.5	1.3				2.3	2.3
	.5	.6	.4				.6	.4
(34) 1.2	(58) 1.0	(38) 1.2				% Depr., Dep., Amort./Sales	(189) 1.0	(194) 1.0
2.0	1.9	3.9					1.9	2.2
	2.1	1.2					2.5	2.7
(29) 3.4	(33) 2.4					% Officers', Directors' Owners' Comp/Sales	(77) 3.9	(73) 4.3
7.3	5.8						6.4	6.1
16115M	202440M	1143061M	1840931M	543577M	832440M	Net Sales ($)	5058114M	5283938M
3398M	55814M	339594M	860944M	291768M	521800M	Total Assets ($)	1724000M	2050876M

M = $ thousand   MM = $ million
See Pages 9 through 22 for Explanation of Ratios and Data

Comparative Historical Data   Current Data Sorted by Sales

Current Data period groupings: **41 (4/1-9/30/09)** and **139 (10/1/09-3/31/10)**

4/1/07-3/31/08 ALL	4/1/08-3/31/09 ALL	4/1/09-3/31/10 ALL		0-1MM	1-3MM	3-5MM	5-10MM	10-25MM	25MM & OVER
			Type of Statement						
36	27	19	Unqualified		1			8	10
46	40	40	Reviewed		1		12	16	11
25	32	23	Compiled	1	2	7	6	7	
18	24	28	Tax Returns	2	9	5	7	4	1
65	81	70	Other	3	6	7	8	19	27
190	204	180	**NUMBER OF STATEMENTS**	6	19	19	33	54	49
%	%	%	**ASSETS**	%	%	%	%	%	%
8.3	7.9	10.0	Cash & Equivalents		7.2	19.1	8.5	9.1	9.0
31.8	30.8	31.0	Trade Receivables (net)		26.5	34.4	30.9	31.7	31.6
29.8	28.5	26.9	Inventory		35.4	22.0	27.7	25.5	27.1
5.4	4.2	5.4	All Other Current		2.3	5.9	4.1	7.9	4.9
75.3	71.3	73.3	Total Current		71.5	81.3	71.2	74.2	72.7
14.5	14.8	12.4	Fixed Assets (net)		12.8	12.0	13.8	12.2	11.2
3.9	5.9	5.7	Intangibles (net)		3.6	.3	7.5	6.0	7.0
6.3	7.9	8.6	All Other Non-Current		12.1	6.4	7.4	7.7	9.1
100.0	100.0	100.0	Total		100.0	100.0	100.0	100.0	100.0
			LIABILITIES						
13.6	15.7	12.0	Notes Payable-Short Term		13.6	21.7	7.7	11.9	11.9
3.7	3.1	4.0	Cur. Mat.-L.T.D.		7.4	1.0	5.5	2.9	1.7
20.2	16.9	19.9	Trade Payables		23.1	22.9	21.1	19.2	17.7
.4	.2	.2	Income Taxes Payable		.0	.0	.3	.1	.3
17.0	15.4	16.0	All Other Current		13.4	15.5	11.5	16.6	19.7
54.9	51.3	52.1	Total Current		57.6	61.1	46.0	50.7	51.3
11.4	11.7	10.7	Long-Term Debt		22.1	11.5	9.1	9.6	8.5
.3	.2	.3	Deferred Taxes		.0	.4	.4	.2	.3
5.8	5.4	5.7	All Other Non-Current		12.8	.6	5.1	4.0	7.5
27.6	31.4	31.3	Net Worth		7.5	26.4	39.4	35.5	32.3
100.0	100.0	100.0	Total Liabilities & Net Worth		100.0	100.0	100.0	100.0	100.0
			INCOME DATA						
100.0	100.0	100.0	Net Sales		100.0	100.0	100.0	100.0	100.0
37.9	37.6	39.5	Gross Profit		51.2	35.7	42.3	37.7	34.9
34.1	34.5	35.2	Operating Expenses		47.5	33.8	39.2	32.3	29.9
3.7	3.1	4.3	Operating Profit		3.7	1.9	3.1	5.4	5.1
.5	.5	.6	All Other Expenses (net)		1.3	.2	.1	.0	1.5
3.2	2.6	3.7	Profit Before Taxes		2.4	1.7	3.0	5.4	3.6
			RATIOS						
2.0	2.1	2.2	Current		1.8	3.9	2.3	2.7	2.1
1.4	1.4	1.4			1.4	1.4	1.5	1.5	1.4
1.1	1.1	1.1			1.0	1.0	1.2	1.1	1.1
1.1	1.2	1.3	Quick		.8	3.7	1.5	1.5	1.2
.7	.8	(179) .8			(18) .7	.8	.8	.8	.8
.5	.5	.5			.5	.5	.5	.5	.5
26 13.8	26 14.0	25 14.7	Sales/Receivables		22 16.8	16 23.4	24 14.9	27 13.6	31 11.9
35 10.3	35 10.5	35 10.5			34 10.9	28 13.2	32 11.3	36 10.2	38 9.6
47 7.8	46 7.9	46 8.0			51 7.2	40 9.0	42 8.6	46 8.0	51 7.2
34 10.8	28 13.1	29 12.7	Cost of Sales/Inventory		46 8.0	7 53.3	23 15.8	26 14.2	40 9.1
59 6.1	58 6.2	57 6.4			100 3.6	33 11.1	61 6.0	50 7.3	63 5.8
83 4.4	89 4.1	90 4.1			165 2.2	64 5.7	86 4.3	75 4.9	79 4.6
17 21.6	14 25.5	18 20.3	Cost of Sales/Payables		33 10.9	23 15.7	19 19.6	13 27.2	19 18.8
30 12.0	24 15.1	33 11.1			57 6.4	31 11.8	39 9.4	27 13.7	33 11.1
50 7.3	48 7.7	58 6.3			93 3.9	56 6.5	63 5.8	47 7.8	48 7.7
7.5	8.2	6.3	Sales/Working Capital		7.6	6.2	7.5	6.2	6.1
13.9	16.2	12.8			19.2	12.3	13.1	11.0	10.3
59.4	85.4	82.7			-73.1	-102.1	35.1	43.1	53.3
9.6	8.2	17.4	EBIT/Interest		6.8	15.8	22.4	18.0	17.4
(160) 3.5	(178) 3.0	(158) 5.6			1.5	(16) 5.3	(30) 3.5	(44) 6.5	(46) 9.2
1.7	1.2	1.8			.8	1.0	.9	2.6	3.8
5.9	10.2	11.9	Net Profit + Depr., Dep., Amort./Cur. Mat. L/T/D				51.9	13.8	11.9
(46) 1.7	(44) 2.9	(38) 3.8					(10) 4.3	(12) 5.6	(10) 3.0
.6	.9	1.8					2.7	2.2	.3
.1	.1	.1	Fixed/Worth		.1	.1	.1	.1	.1
.4	.4	.3			.4	.3	.5	.3	.2
1.6	1.5	2.4			-.6	1.5	2.1	2.4	1.0
1.0	1.1	1.0	Debt/Worth		1.5	.3	1.0	.9	1.1
2.2	2.3	2.5			4.4	2.8	2.1	1.8	2.5
9.0	10.2	8.1			-5.8	8.0	7.4	7.4	5.9
45.8	40.4	47.2	% Profit Before Taxes/Tangible Net Worth		26.9	46.8	38.5	52.8	71.2
(156) 19.3	(166) 19.5	(152) 24.0			(13) 12.8	(16) 23.0	(28) 25.3	(45) 20.4	(45) 36.2
6.8	5.1	9.3			-4.3	1.7	1.4	8.8	16.7
14.3	12.4	15.0	% Profit Before Taxes/Total Assets		9.3	15.0	20.4	15.6	14.9
6.7	5.4	7.2			3.3	8.1	5.0	8.0	9.0
1.6	.7	1.0			-.5	.0	.1	2.4	4.7
82.3	83.4	90.6	Sales/Net Fixed Assets		72.7	304.8	54.8	87.0	138.7
35.2	35.5	41.7			35.9	65.5	29.7	44.5	43.7
12.6	11.9	16.1			28.6	16.7	16.6	12.8	13.4
4.0	4.1		Sales/Total Assets		3.7	5.1	3.6	4.3	3.8
3.1	3.0	2.9			2.6	3.7	3.1	3.1	2.6
2.2	2.1	2.2			1.9	2.8	2.6	2.0	1.7
.5	.5	.5	% Depr., Dep., Amort./Sales		.9	.3	.7	.5	.3
(163) .9	(169) 1.0	(139) 1.0			(12) 1.4	(12) 1.2	(27) 1.5	(46) .8	(39) .8
2.0	2.4	2.3			2.2	2.7	2.2	2.0	2.9
2.4	1.9	1.4	% Officers', Directors' Owners' Comp/Sales		3.2	2.1	1.5	1.0	
(56) 4.2	(71) 3.6	(77) 2.9			(14) 6.9	(12) 4.3	(15) 2.7	(25) 1.6	
6.6	6.8	7.7			12.6	8.4	6.7	3.6	
5913624M	5176938M	4578564M	Net Sales ($)	4846M	36702M	71571M	235986M	898791M	3330668M
2237934M	2158204M	2073318M	Total Assets ($)	3843M	14953M	22297M	80394M	386727M	1565104M

M = $ thousand   MM = $ million
See Pages 9 through 22 for Explanation of Ratios and Data

WHOLESALE—Computer and Computer Peripheral Equipment and Software Merchant Wholesalers NAICS 423430

Current Data Sorted by Assets | Comparative Historical Data

0-500M	500M-2MM	2-10MM	10-50MM	50-100MM	100-250MM	Type of Statement	ALL 4/1/05-3/31/06	ALL 4/1/06-3/31/07
	1	17	22	11	3	Unqualified	47	51
1	6	26	8	1		Reviewed	33	44
3	4	10	2			Compiled	18	27
7	10	11	1	1		Tax Returns	22	21
8	18	47	20	8	7	Other	104	101
	43 (4/1-9/30/09)		210 (10/1/09-3/31/10)					
19	39	111	53	21	10	NUMBER OF STATEMENTS	224	244
%	%	%	%	%	%	**ASSETS**	%	%
29.9	17.5	14.3	12.7	11.7	17.5	Cash & Equivalents	13.0	12.1
30.1	34.2	47.5	38.3	37.8	37.1	Trade Receivables (net)	43.7	44.4
21.8	19.9	19.5	22.3	13.8	13.4	Inventory	21.9	20.3
1.5	3.5	3.3	4.3	3.4	12.5	All Other Current	3.3	3.6
83.2	75.1	84.5	77.6	66.7	80.5	Total Current	82.0	80.4
11.1	11.0	7.9	5.8	10.4	3.1	Fixed Assets (net)	9.8	9.0
.7	6.4	1.6	11.4	15.2	6.8	Intangibles (net)	3.3	5.1
5.0	7.5	5.9	5.2	7.7	9.6	All Other Non-Current	5.0	5.5
100.0	100.0	100.0	100.0	100.0	100.0	Total	100.0	100.0
						LIABILITIES		
27.5	17.4	12.4	11.5	13.6	12.5	Notes Payable-Short Term	16.7	15.0
4.9	2.0	1.8	2.6	1.9	.1	Cur. Mat.-L.T.D.	1.7	1.8
17.1	26.5	29.6	29.8	21.9	19.0	Trade Payables	29.1	27.1
.0	.0	.3	.3	.4	.0	Income Taxes Payable	.7	.4
11.1	8.9	13.9	12.3	11.8	24.0	All Other Current	13.4	12.8
60.6	54.8	58.0	56.4	49.6	55.6	Total Current	61.7	57.0
17.3	4.5	5.3	5.5	10.5	2.9	Long-Term Debt	6.8	8.4
.0	.0	.2	.2	1.0	.2	Deferred Taxes	.3	.2
17.8	11.6	5.8	6.7	4.7	3.4	All Other Non-Current	6.0	6.6
4.3	29.1	30.7	31.1	34.3	37.9	Net Worth	25.3	27.7
100.0	100.0	100.0	100.0	100.0	100.0	Total Liabilities & Net Worth	100.0	100.0
						INCOME DATA		
100.0	100.0	100.0	100.0	100.0	100.0	Net Sales	100.0	100.0
45.7	33.1	27.7	22.8	24.2	34.3	Gross Profit	29.5	32.6
43.1	30.8	24.3	19.8	20.2	29.8	Operating Expenses	25.7	28.0
2.6	2.4	3.4	3.0	4.0	4.4	Operating Profit	3.8	4.6
.6	.0	.3	.9	.4	.7	All Other Expenses (net)	.5	.7
2.0	2.4	3.1	2.1	3.5	3.7	Profit Before Taxes	3.3	4.0
						RATIOS		
3.5	2.0	2.1	1.9	2.0	1.7		1.9	2.1
1.3	1.4	1.4	1.3	1.3	1.5	Current	1.4	1.4
.9	1.1	1.2	1.1	1.1	1.1		1.1	1.0
2.9	1.4	1.5	1.3	1.4	1.6		1.3	1.5
1.0	1.0	1.1	.9	1.1	1.2	Quick	1.0	.9
.4	.6	.8	.6	.7	.5		.7	.6
0 UND	19 18.8	25 14.5	34 10.8	38 9.5	44 8.3		29 12.6	28 12.9
23 15.9	31 11.7	43 8.5	47 7.8	50 7.3	60 6.1	Sales/Receivables	45 8.2	42 8.6
40 9.2	48 7.6	69 5.3	63 5.8	69 5.3	80 4.5		63 5.8	64 5.7
1 425.0	4 88.1	2 218.2	2 202.2	3 112.0	0 UND		6 56.6	3 144.9
6 64.0	20 18.7	16 22.9	27 13.6	18 20.2	18 20.1	Cost of Sales/Inventory	27 13.6	24 15.3
59 6.2	63 5.8	49 7.5	46 7.9	35 10.4	35 10.6		49 7.5	44 8.3
0 UND	11 33.1	20 17.9	23 15.9	15 24.7	23 15.7		23 16.1	20 17.9
16 23.2	26 14.1	33 11.0	39 9.3	34 10.8	27 13.4	Cost of Sales/Payables	36 10.2	35 10.5
36 10.1	57 6.4	54 6.7	69 5.3	54 6.8	39 9.5		58 6.3	54 6.7
7.5	6.9	7.1	7.9	7.6	3.1		8.0	8.5
19.9	22.6	16.9	16.7	16.1	9.9	Sales/Working Capital	18.2	17.0
-42.2	117.1	38.8	49.2	40.9	28.3		72.0	138.0
7.2	26.9	24.4	33.0	17.0			15.9	18.6
(14) 4.2	(32) 6.1	(94) 5.0	(46) 7.8	(19) 5.4		EBIT/Interest	(190) 4.9	(206) 4.6
-2.1	-3.0	1.5	1.7	2.3			1.7	1.7
		13.2	48.8			Net Profit + Depr., Dep.,	14.9	13.0
	(18) 2.5	(18) 3.3				Amort./Cur. Mat. L/T/D	(42) 4.9	(47) 4.5
		1.2	.9				1.5	1.4
.2	.0	.0	.1	.1	.0		.1	.1
.7	.2	.1	.1	.2	.1	Fixed/Worth	.2	.2
-.2	.7	.6	.5	1.5	.3		.9	1.1
.5	1.2	1.0	1.1	1.0	1.2		1.2	1.2
4.5	2.4	2.3	2.8	3.8	2.7	Debt/Worth	3.1	2.6
-3.9	6.5	5.5	11.8	7.8	4.0		9.3	13.8
24.2	80.2	46.9	74.3	40.6	65.8	% Profit Before Taxes/Tangible	64.1	63.4
(11) 7.9	(35) 20.3	(99) 22.7	(46) 26.6	(17) 21.2	16.2	Net Worth	(189) 28.9	(198) 29.2
.0	-30.6	4.4	5.5	7.4	1.4		8.8	10.4
19.5	17.9	15.6	12.3	11.1	15.3	% Profit Before Taxes/Total	15.7	19.4
13.1	5.5	5.6	7.0	5.1	5.7	Assets	6.9	8.2
-6.8	-7.0	1.4	.8	2.5	.5		1.5	1.9
394.0	999.8	439.6	249.8	235.7	156.3		239.8	228.2
55.0	148.5	92.1	114.0	80.6	81.1	Sales/Net Fixed Assets	82.5	81.1
36.4	37.7	30.1	36.8	21.1	37.4		27.3	31.7
7.9	6.3	4.8	4.0	4.4	4.3		4.9	5.0
5.2	3.5	3.6	3.1	2.4	1.9	Sales/Total Assets	3.6	3.7
3.6	2.4	2.5	1.8	.9	.9		2.5	2.6
.2	.1	.1	.1	.1			.2	.2
(11) .4	(23) .6	(83) .5	(41) .4	(15) .5		% Depr., Dep., Amort./Sales	(163) .4	(174) .4
1.3	1.7	1.0	1.1	1.5			1.1	1.2
3.4	2.0	1.0				% Officers', Directors'	1.5	1.2
(12) 7.5	(20) 3.8	(29) 1.4				Owners' Comp/Sales	(74) 2.7	(71) 3.4
12.2	6.1	2.5					5.4	6.8
28419M	226966M	2345386M	3701488M	3681464M	3965163M	Net Sales ($)	12728158M	13770370M
4813M	49114M	557006M	1170639M	1436020M	1768197M	Total Assets ($)	4201914M	4833975M

M = $ thousand   MM = $ million
See Pages 9 through 22 for Explanation of Ratios and Data

Comparative Historical Data   Current Data Sorted by Sales

	4/1/07-3/31/08 ALL	4/1/08-3/31/09 ALL	4/1/09-3/31/10 ALL	Type of Statement	0-1MM	1-3MM	3-5MM	5-10MM	10-25MM	25MM & OVER
	49	58	54	Unqualified			3	3	12	39
	33	38	42	Reviewed	2	2	2	5	14	17
	16	21	19	Compiled	2	2	2	3	6	4
	20	31	30	Tax Returns	1	8	4	4	8	5
	111	110	108	Other	4	8	10	18	27	41
						43 (4/1-9/30/09)		210 (10/1/09-3/31/10)		
	229	258	253	NUMBER OF STATEMENTS	9	20	18	33	67	106
	%	%	%	**ASSETS**	%	%	%	%	%	%
	12.3	13.4	15.5	Cash & Equivalents		27.0	15.0	13.6	15.8	13.2
	43.7	41.7	41.0	Trade Receivables (net)		36.7	35.6	39.8	44.1	44.0
	18.4	20.3	19.6	Inventory		15.1	22.9	17.8	17.9	20.4
	4.3	3.6	3.8	All Other Current		1.8	4.8	4.2	3.5	4.0
	78.8	79.0	79.9	Total Current		80.6	78.2	75.4	81.3	81.6
	8.6	8.3	8.2	Fixed Assets (net)		8.5	13.1	8.4	8.9	5.9
	7.1	6.2	5.7	Intangibles (net)		6.7	4.9	4.6	3.4	7.8
	5.5	6.5	6.2	All Other Non-Current		4.3	3.9	11.6	6.3	4.7
	100.0	100.0	100.0	Total		100.0	100.0	100.0	100.0	100.0
				LIABILITIES						
	14.0	12.1	14.2	Notes Payable-Short Term		18.2	26.8	13.4	10.8	12.0
	2.0	2.3	2.2	Cur. Mat.-L.T.D.		3.7	2.4	1.7	2.4	1.9
	25.0	26.4	27.2	Trade Payables		20.3	20.7	21.9	29.6	31.6
	.4	.3	.2	Income Taxes Payable		.0	.0	.5	.3	.2
	12.8	12.2	12.8	All Other Current		7.4	5.5	13.8	16.5	12.9
	54.2	53.3	56.6	Total Current		49.5	55.4	51.3	59.5	58.7
	7.6	9.4	6.5	Long-Term Debt		15.2	3.3	6.6	5.0	6.4
	.2	.2	.2	Deferred Taxes		.1	.0	.1	.2	.4
	6.8	6.4	7.6	All Other Non-Current		17.4	18.7	4.9	3.8	6.3
	31.2	30.8	29.1	Net Worth		17.8	22.6	37.1	31.5	28.2
	100.0	100.0	100.0	Total Liabilities & Net Worth		100.0	100.0	100.0	100.0	100.0
				INCOME DATA						
	100.0	100.0	100.0	Net Sales		100.0	100.0	100.0	100.0	100.0
	32.4	29.2	28.8	Gross Profit		37.7	42.5	39.4	27.9	20.4
	27.5	25.2	25.7	Operating Expenses		35.0	38.8	35.5	25.3	16.9
	4.9	4.0	3.2	Operating Profit		2.7	3.7	3.9	2.7	3.5
	.6	.8	.4	All Other Expenses (net)		.8	.1	.5	.3	.5
	4.2	3.2	2.7	Profit Before Taxes		1.9	3.7	3.4	2.3	3.0
				RATIOS						
	2.1	2.2	2.1	Current		5.6	2.3	2.7	2.0	1.8
	1.4	1.4	1.4			1.7	1.5	1.3	1.3	1.4
	1.1	1.1	1.1			1.0	1.1	1.0	1.2	1.1
	1.6	1.6	1.5	Quick		4.8	2.0	1.6	1.5	1.3
	1.1	1.0	1.0			1.2	1.1	1.0	1.0	1.0
	.7	.7	.7			.5	.5	.8	.7	.7
	32 / 11.5	27 / 13.6	25 / 14.5	Sales/Receivables	20 / 18.4	26 / 13.9	25 / 14.4	24 / 15.3	29 / 12.8	
	44 / 8.3	41 / 8.9	42 / 8.7		30 / 12.4	38 / 9.5	46 / 7.9	42 / 8.8	45 / 8.1	
	63 / 5.8	58 / 6.2	63 / 5.8		52 / 7.0	68 / 5.4	70 / 5.2	66 / 5.5	63 / 5.8	
	2 / 163.8	2 / 173.1	2 / 215.9	Cost of Sales/Inventory	1 / 372.1	9 / 39.3	2 / 223.6	1 / 376.7	3 / 120.0	
	21 / 17.3	21 / 17.7	18 / 20.0		9 / 39.0	29 / 12.6	29 / 12.5	14 / 27.0	18 / 20.2	
	50 / 7.2	47 / 7.8	48 / 7.5		54 / 6.8	67 / 5.4	70 / 5.2	49 / 7.4	37 / 10.0	
	19 / 19.2	17 / 21.3	17 / 21.2	Cost of Sales/Payables	5 / 69.9	7 / 49.4	20 / 18.1	17 / 21.0	22 / 16.7	
	33 / 11.1	30 / 12.2	33 / 11.0		19 / 19.3	27 / 13.6	35 / 10.3	35 / 10.4	33 / 10.9	
	54 / 6.8	51 / 7.1	54 / 6.8		55 / 6.6	62 / 5.9	91 / 4.0	61 / 6.0	47 / 7.8	
	8.2	8.1	7.5	Sales/Working Capital		4.6	6.0	4.8	7.6	9.0
	13.8	16.0	16.9			16.1	13.8	14.3	18.8	17.9
	44.7	51.3	50.3			NM	NM	124.7	41.0	42.1
	17.2	21.7	22.1	EBIT/Interest		9.6	12.2	50.2	29.5	22.1
	(193) 5.4	(216) 4.7	(213) 5.5		(16) 3.4	(13) 3.1	(32) 5.0	(57) 5.9	(90) 7.7	
	1.6	1.7	1.5			-15.6	-2.4	.5	1.2	2.4
	27.2	28.5	20.0	Net Profit + Depr., Dep., Amort./Cur. Mat. L/T/D					11.6	25.4
	(46) 5.3	(46) 4.1	(44) 3.2					(11) 2.3	(29) 7.6	
	1.4	1.3	1.2						1.2	1.2
	.1	.1	.1	Fixed/Worth		.1	.0	.0	.1	.1
	.2	.2	.2			.3	.2	.2	.2	.1
	.8	.7	.7			NM	2.2	.5	.6	.4
	.9	.9	1.0	Debt/Worth		.5	1.4	.9	1.0	1.3
	2.4	2.2	2.7			3.5	3.0	1.9	2.8	2.8
	7.2	6.1	7.7			-19.7	96.0	5.7	5.5	7.6
	74.7	65.1	54.4	% Profit Before Taxes/Tangible Net Worth		83.3	37.2	81.4	46.4	63.0
	(193) 34.1	(219) 23.0	(218) 21.4		(14) 3.6	(15) 6.7	(29) 22.7	(60) 26.9	(93) 23.0	
	8.7	6.3	4.2			-13.5	-47.7	2.7	4.0	8.3
	20.7	16.2	14.8	% Profit Before Taxes/Total Assets		18.1	15.8	24.6	15.3	12.2
	8.8	6.4	5.8			3.4	3.0	5.8	5.3	6.9
	1.9	1.8	.8			-5.8	-7.7	.0	.9	2.0
	193.6	290.7	314.1	Sales/Net Fixed Assets		902.5	265.6	406.0	224.6	316.6
	71.7	84.1	103.3			53.1	130.6	59.0	78.2	136.8
	30.6	33.3	36.6			31.4	12.9	22.6	28.5	50.7
	4.8	5.2	4.9	Sales/Total Assets		5.5	4.0	4.3	4.6	5.2
	3.5	3.6	3.3			3.7	3.1	2.8	3.6	3.5
	2.4	2.3	2.3			1.8	2.7	1.9	2.5	2.4
	.2	.1	.1	% Depr., Dep., Amort./Sales		.4	.1	.2	.1	.1
	(171) .5	(191) .4	(182) .5		(12) .8	(12) .7	(22) .8	(53) .5	(79) .3	
	1.0	1.0	1.1			1.2	2.8	1.3	1.1	.7
	1.1	1.0	1.0	% Officers', Directors' Owners' Comp/Sales		2.5		1.0	.7	.8
	(59) 2.5	(68) 2.3	(68) 2.4		(13) 5.2		(12) 2.4	(15) 1.3	(15) 1.0	
	6.8	4.7	5.4			7.7		2.7	1.3	
	17426211M	19252775M	13948886M	Net Sales ($)	5771M	39030M	71647M	241448M	1137106M	12453884M
	5657814M	5930116M	4985789M	Total Assets ($)	3352M	15500M	28699M	123118M	396758M	4418362M

M = $ thousand   MM = $ million
See Pages 9 through 22 for Explanation of Ratios and Data

Current Data Sorted by Assets   Comparative Historical Data

0-500M	500M-2MM	2-10MM	10-50MM	50-100MM	100-250MM	Type of Statement	4/1/05-3/31/06 ALL	4/1/06-3/31/07 ALL
	2	8	11	3	3	Unqualified	16	29
	4	33	18			Reviewed	40	47
1	17	15	4			Compiled	36	36
8	16	9				Tax Returns	25	35
5	16	33	19	2	5	Other	84	74
	39 (4/1-9/30/09)		193 (10/1/09-3/31/10)					
14	55	98	52	5	8	NUMBER OF STATEMENTS	201	221
%	%	%	%	%	%	ASSETS	%	%
12.4	11.5	9.4	9.4			Cash & Equivalents	8.5	8.5
27.9	31.3	32.8	25.7			Trade Receivables (net)	33.1	34.9
37.2	35.1	34.1	28.7			Inventory	35.2	32.5
.0	3.5	2.8	6.0			All Other Current	3.0	3.3
77.5	81.4	79.2	69.8			Total Current	79.9	79.1
14.5	11.6	12.1	19.9			Fixed Assets (net)	12.5	12.0
1.0	2.4	4.5	5.1			Intangibles (net)	2.8	4.1
7.0	4.6	4.2	5.2			All Other Non-Current	4.8	4.7
100.0	100.0	100.0	100.0			Total	100.0	100.0
						LIABILITIES		
21.7	11.0	14.8	11.4			Notes Payable-Short Term	16.3	15.1
1.0	5.2	1.6	2.7			Cur. Mat.-L.T.D.	3.0	2.8
13.5	20.0	17.9	15.4			Trade Payables	21.5	21.6
.0	.1	.2	.0			Income Taxes Payable	.2	.2
13.6	10.9	12.0	12.4			All Other Current	10.9	12.2
49.8	47.1	46.6	41.9			Total Current	51.9	51.9
18.4	10.8	10.3	12.3			Long-Term Debt	11.6	9.6
.0	.0	.3	.3			Deferred Taxes	.2	.3
7.1	7.0	5.0	3.4			All Other Non-Current	4.8	4.4
24.7	35.1	37.8	42.2			Net Worth	31.5	33.8
100.0	100.0	100.0	100.0			Total Liabilities & Net Worth	100.0	100.0
						INCOME DATA		
100.0	100.0	100.0	100.0			Net Sales	100.0	100.0
43.5	31.8	29.2	30.0			Gross Profit	30.4	29.3
40.9	29.5	26.2	25.3			Operating Expenses	26.6	24.8
2.6	2.3	3.0	4.7			Operating Profit	3.8	4.5
.5	1.0	.6	.2			All Other Expenses (net)	.6	.0
2.1	1.2	2.4	4.5			Profit Before Taxes	3.2	4.5
						RATIOS		
8.1	4.0	3.1	2.7			Current	2.3	2.2
1.9	1.9	1.5	1.8				1.6	1.5
.9	1.2	1.2	1.1				1.2	1.2
4.6	2.3	1.5	1.6			Quick	1.2	1.2
1.0	1.0	.9	.8			(200)	.8	.8
.3	.5	.5	.5				.5	.6
0 UND	19 19.1	26 13.9	34 10.7			Sales/Receivables	25 14.7	26 14.0
19 19.7	31 11.8	41 9.0	40 9.1				41 9.0	41 8.9
30 12.3	53 6.9	56 6.5	54 6.8				58 6.2	56 6.5
0 UND	26 13.8	35 10.4	39 9.4			Cost of Sales/Inventory	31 11.9	25 14.6
47 7.8	61 6.0	63 5.8	57 6.4				65 5.6	53 6.9
188 1.9	102 3.6	97 3.8	94 3.9				103 3.5	86 4.2
0 UND	10 37.0	15 24.4	16 22.3			Cost of Sales/Payables	15 24.9	15 24.2
16 23.4	29 12.6	28 13.1	27 13.5				33 10.9	31 11.8
69 5.3	47 7.8	45 8.1	46 8.0				60 6.1	52 7.0
4.2	4.9	5.1	5.4			Sales/Working Capital	5.6	6.9
13.5	8.5	10.1	7.6				11.1	12.2
NM	19.7	28.5	15.8				23.6	29.5
14.4	3.9	7.3	12.5			EBIT/Interest	10.3	12.2
(10) .8	(43) 1.5	(86) 2.6	(47) 5.8				(175) 3.9	(196) 5.0
-2.8	-2.4	.7	1.8				1.4	2.3
		20.3	9.2			Net Profit + Depr., Dep., Amort./Cur. Mat. L/T/D	7.0	11.3
	(14) 2.6		(13) 3.5				(31) 3.4	(42) 4.5
		1.2	1.5				1.2	1.7
.0	.1	.1	.1			Fixed/Worth	.1	.1
.3	.1	.2	.5				.3	.3
-.6	.5	1.0	1.1				1.1	.8
.1	.4	.7	.6			Debt/Worth	.9	1.0
1.7	1.2	1.8	1.5				2.4	2.3
-9.8	4.8	4.8	3.9				6.6	5.9
	36.6	42.1	41.9			% Profit Before Taxes/Tangible Net Worth	52.1	60.7
	(48) 8.0	(88) 9.0	(48) 20.5				(179) 25.1	(197) 29.2
	-1.3	.1	6.1				6.9	11.8
35.2	16.4	11.5	16.9			% Profit Before Taxes/Total Assets	14.5	17.5
.8	2.7	3.2	8.0				5.9	7.9
-5.7	-3.8	-.8	1.5				1.7	2.5
421.7	156.6	107.1	52.1			Sales/Net Fixed Assets	116.3	117.1
100.3	39.7	44.8	16.6				43.2	47.9
19.6	20.8	15.7	7.4				18.5	19.0
6.2	4.1	3.7	2.9			Sales/Total Assets	3.8	4.0
3.6	3.1	2.9	2.2				2.8	3.1
2.8	2.4	2.0	1.4				2.1	2.1
	.2	.4	.6			% Depr., Dep., Amort./Sales	.3	.3
	(42) .6	(82) .7	(47) .9				(165) .6	(182) .6
	1.2	1.5	1.8				1.4	1.1
	3.0	1.1	.5			% Officers', Directors' Owners' Comp/Sales	2.0	2.0
	(32) 4.6	(37) 2.9	(14) .8				(75) 3.0	(77) 3.6
	8.4	4.4	2.9				6.1	5.3
14082M	215910M	1396601M	2478002M	573771M	2489665M	Net Sales ($)	4492834M	6840362M
3433M	66128M	472796M	1125018M	352523M	1310719M	Total Assets ($)	1842469M	2745547M

M = $ thousand   MM = $ million
See Pages 9 through 22 for Explanation of Ratios and Data

Comparative Historical Data

Current Data Sorted by Sales

			Type of Statement						
19	23	27	Unqualified			2	1	9	15
41	55	55	Reviewed			6	13	14	22
26	35	37	Compiled	5	2	10	10	7	3
29	29	33	Tax Returns	8	10	5	5	5	
89	80	80	Other	3	9	6	19	17	26
4/1/07-3/31/08 ALL	4/1/08-3/31/09 ALL	4/1/09-3/31/10 ALL		0-1MM	1-3MM	3-5MM	5-10MM	10-25MM	25MM & OVER
				39 (4/1-9/30/09)			193 (10/1/09-3/31/10)		
204	222	232	NUMBER OF STATEMENTS	16	21	29	48	52	66
%	%	%	ASSETS	%	%	%	%	%	%
7.6	8.9	9.8	Cash & Equivalents	10.6	12.8	11.2	10.9	8.6	8.1
31.9	28.3	30.0	Trade Receivables (net)	27.1	24.7	25.8	30.6	33.7	30.9
33.6	34.0	32.6	Inventory	36.4	31.2	35.2	35.3	31.8	29.5
3.4	3.2	3.6	All Other Current	7.1	.7	1.3	2.3	6.4	3.4
76.4	74.5	75.9	Total Current	81.1	69.4	73.5	79.1	80.5	71.8
15.6	15.5	14.2	Fixed Assets (net)	8.7	19.7	21.0	11.4	11.8	14.9
3.1	4.0	5.1	Intangibles (net)	3.6	7.4	.4	5.0	2.6	8.7
4.9	6.1	4.8	All Other Non-Current	6.5	3.5	5.2	4.5	5.1	4.6
100.0	100.0	100.0	Total	100.0	100.0	100.0	100.0	100.0	100.0
			LIABILITIES						
13.8	14.7	13.7	Notes Payable-Short Term	20.7	7.0	12.7	13.8	14.7	13.6
2.9	2.8	2.7	Cur. Mat.-L.T.D.	2.9	6.2	5.0	1.6	1.7	2.1
20.9	17.3	17.3	Trade Payables	8.3	15.9	15.0	22.0	18.8	16.4
.2	.2	.1	Income Taxes Payable	.0	.1	.0	.2		.1
13.3	12.6	11.6	All Other Current	10.5	19.2	11.1	9.4	11.8	11.1
51.0	47.6	45.4	Total Current	42.4	48.3	43.8	46.9	47.3	43.3
10.2	12.5	12.1	Long-Term Debt	15.2	16.3	14.4	9.6	9.4	13.1
.3	.2	.4	Deferred Taxes	.0	.0	.1	.3	.2	1.0
4.0	5.5	5.1	All Other Non-Current	13.5	8.5	5.7	4.1	4.4	3.0
34.5	34.2	37.0	Net Worth	29.0	26.9	36.1	39.1	38.7	39.6
100.0	100.0	100.0	Total Liabilities & Net Worth	100.0	100.0	100.0	100.0	100.0	100.0
			INCOME DATA						
100.0	100.0	100.0	Net Sales	100.0	100.0	100.0	100.0	100.0	100.0
31.3	31.3	30.4	Gross Profit	46.0	34.7	36.4	30.6	27.5	24.7
26.4	26.7	27.2	Operating Expenses	43.7	29.4	34.2	27.4	24.0	21.8
5.0	4.6	3.2	Operating Profit	2.3	5.2	2.2	3.2	3.5	2.9
.7	.6	.7	All Other Expenses (net)	3.0	1.8	.2	.4	.7	.4
4.2	4.1	2.4	Profit Before Taxes	-.7	3.5	2.0	2.8	2.8	2.5
			RATIOS						
2.2	2.4	3.1	Current	8.3	3.8	2.9	3.5	3.6	2.6
1.6	1.6	1.8		2.8	1.7	1.5	1.7	1.5	1.9
1.1	1.1	1.2		1.6	1.0	1.1	1.2	1.1	1.3
1.2	1.3	1.6	Quick	6.9	2.7	1.2	1.6	1.7	1.4
.9	.8	.9		1.3	.8	.7	.9	.9	.9
.5	.4	.5		.3	.3	.5	.5	.5	.5
24 15.5	24 15.2	24 14.9	Sales/Receivables	14 26.2	20 18.1	17 21.2	27 13.6	26 13.9	32 11.3
37 9.9	34 10.6	37 9.8		27 13.6	35 10.6	34 10.8	34 10.8	45 8.2	39 9.3
52 7.1	46 7.9	54 6.8		126 2.9	50 7.3	64 5.7	49 7.5	56 6.5	52 7.0
28 13.0	30 12.1	30 12.1	Cost of Sales/Inventory	0 UND	16 23.0	47 7.8	38 9.5	30 12.3	32 11.3
59 6.2	63 5.8	60 6.1		168 2.2	57 6.4	78 4.7	69 5.3	58 6.3	51 7.1
93 3.9	96 3.8	99 3.7		469 .8	101 3.6	140 2.6	92 4.0	96 3.8	76 4.8
15 23.6	12 29.2	14 26.2	Cost of Sales/Payables	0 UND	15 24.8	10 36.9	14 25.6	14 25.5	16 23.4
28 12.8	25 14.6	28 13.3		14 26.7	26 14.1	35 10.3	30 12.0	24 15.1	27 13.7
48 7.6	46 8.0	46 8.0		110 3.3	45 8.0	55 6.6	48 7.6	39 9.3	37 9.8
6.3	6.5	5.1	Sales/Working Capital	2.4	4.4	5.1	5.0	5.1	5.8
10.4	10.9	8.7		4.1	13.3	9.7	9.8	8.6	8.6
37.4	35.2	23.8		22.3	694.8	33.3	31.2	22.5	20.2
10.5	9.8	9.3	EBIT/Interest	13.7	9.2	5.6	4.3	18.7	12.2
(181) 4.4	(198) 3.3	(198) 2.5		(11) .6	(15) 1.8	(23) 2.1	(43) 2.1	(47) 3.0	(59) 5.1
1.8	1.6	.6		-6.7	-3.2	-.1	-.4	.7	1.1
18.3	9.6	6.6	Net Profit + Depr., Dep., Amort./Cur. Mat. L/T/D						8.9
(40) 4.3	(44) 2.6	(40) 1.9						(17)	4.3
1.2	.7	1.1							1.6
.1	.1	.1	Fixed/Worth	.0	.1	.1	.1	.1	.1
.3	.3	.2		.1	.3	.5	.2	.2	.4
1.1	1.2	1.1		NM	NM	1.3	.7	1.1	1.0
.8	.8	.6	Debt/Worth	.2	.5	.8	.6	.4	.8
2.0	2.1	1.8		.9	1.8	2.0	1.7	1.7	1.9
5.6	5.3	5.4		-5.5	NM	4.8	6.1	5.5	4.1
51.7	55.2	40.9	% Profit Before Taxes/Tangible Net Worth	99.3	52.4	21.3	30.1	45.0	41.6
(177) 25.8	(191) 21.2	(201) 12.7		(11) 3.9	(16) 36.4	(26) 8.3	(42) 5.0	(49) 9.9	(57) 20.9
9.1	5.7	1.1		-7.1	2.3	.2	-6.3	1.2	7.2
15.7	16.4	12.6	% Profit Before Taxes/Total Assets	18.7	27.6	6.7	12.0	15.5	14.6
7.7	5.8	3.6		.2	8.4	2.5	2.7	2.9	6.4
2.4	1.4	-.8		-12.7	-3.7	-1.4	-1.2	-.2	.8
123.4	102.4	105.9	Sales/Net Fixed Assets	705.3	140.6	45.1	119.4	163.8	64.4
44.2	34.2	34.5		60.9	20.8	23.1	41.1	61.0	32.5
14.7	13.7	13.2		21.1	6.7	5.9	16.8	14.8	12.2
4.1	3.8	3.7	Sales/Total Assets	3.7	4.1	3.3	3.8	3.7	3.5
2.9	2.9	2.8		2.6	2.8	2.5	2.8	3.0	2.6
2.0	2.0	1.9		1.1	1.2	1.4	2.1	2.1	1.9
.3	.3	.4	% Depr., Dep., Amort./Sales		.2	.6	.4	.4	.4
(167) .7	(187) .7	(187) .8			(16) .6	(25) 1.2	(40) .6	(42) .7	(56) .7
1.4	1.6	1.5			2.5	1.7	1.6	1.4	1.3
1.8	1.8	1.6	% Officers', Directors' Owners' Comp/Sales		5.1	2.8	1.9	1.3	.5
(69) 3.2	(80) 3.4	(91) 3.5			(10) 7.7	(14) 4.7	(23) 3.2	(17) 2.8	(18) 1.0
6.1	6.4	6.7			13.5	7.2	4.7	4.1	2.7
6216107M	7768600M	7168031M	Net Sales ($)	10908M	45745M	111971M	354928M	817899M	5826580M
2397226M	3011899M	3330617M	Total Assets ($)	8061M	33770M	94740M	152175M	388545M	2653326M

M = $ thousand   MM = $ million
See Pages 9 through 22 for Explanation of Ratios and Data

Current Data Sorted by Assets   **Comparative Historical Data**

0-500M	500M-2MM	2-10MM	10-50MM	50-100MM	100-250MM	Type of Statement	4/1/05-3/31/06 ALL	4/1/06-3/31/07 ALL
1		14	26	6	7	Unqualified	52	56
	10	33	18	2		Reviewed	51	53
5	24	22	2			Compiled	55	50
18	28	16	2			Tax Returns	44	45
11	34	58	45	7	10	Other	127	139
	64 (4/1-9/30/09)		335 (10/1/09-3/31/10)					
35	96	143	93	15	17	**NUMBER OF STATEMENTS**	329	343
%	%	%	%	%	%	**ASSETS**	%	%
18.9	10.9	8.4	11.6	6.0	5.4	Cash & Equivalents	8.3	8.0
25.1	30.6	37.3	32.5	22.8	32.7	Trade Receivables (net)	35.0	35.6
18.7	33.2	27.6	26.4	23.8	23.7	Inventory	29.6	27.5
2.7	2.5	2.8	2.8	4.1	3.7	All Other Current	2.3	2.0
65.4	77.2	76.1	73.3	56.6	65.5	Total Current	75.1	73.1
21.4	10.7	15.7	14.7	20.5	11.4	Fixed Assets (net)	13.7	14.8
5.2	6.2	4.2	8.2	18.4	21.0	Intangibles (net)	5.3	6.6
8.0	5.8	4.0	3.8	4.6	2.1	All Other Non-Current	5.8	5.4
100.0	100.0	100.0	100.0	100.0	100.0	Total	100.0	100.0
						LIABILITIES		
20.7	17.0	13.9	11.4	15.0	6.3	Notes Payable-Short Term	17.1	15.4
6.4	2.7	2.8	3.6	2.8	2.0	Cur. Mat.-L.T.D.	2.5	3.9
19.1	22.3	23.4	19.4	11.2	17.8	Trade Payables	23.9	21.8
.1	.2	.2	.3	.2	.2	Income Taxes Payable	.3	.3
17.7	10.1	7.9	8.2	13.5	10.9	All Other Current	10.5	10.1
64.0	52.3	48.2	42.9	42.7	37.3	Total Current	54.4	51.6
31.2	9.8	9.9	9.5	11.5	20.0	Long-Term Debt	10.1	11.8
.0	.0	.1	.3	.9	1.4	Deferred Taxes	.2	.2
12.1	5.1	5.9	3.0	5.9	3.3	All Other Non-Current	5.2	4.3
-7.3	32.9	35.9	44.3	38.9	38.1	Net Worth	30.0	32.2
100.0	100.0	100.0	100.0	100.0	100.0	Total Liabilities & Net Worth	100.0	100.0
						INCOME DATA		
100.0	100.0	100.0	100.0	100.0	100.0	Net Sales	100.0	100.0
53.4	40.5	36.6	41.3	41.8	27.6	Gross Profit	38.3	41.8
48.8	36.4	30.4	34.0	35.9	20.5	Operating Expenses	33.6	36.3
4.6	4.2	6.2	7.3	5.9	7.1	Operating Profit	4.6	5.5
1.5	.4	.4	1.0	1.5	1.9	All Other Expenses (net)	.9	1.2
3.1	3.8	5.8	6.3	4.3	5.2	Profit Before Taxes	3.7	4.3
						RATIOS		
1.7	2.5	2.5	2.6	1.9	2.3	Current	2.1	2.3
1.2	1.5	1.5	1.5	1.4	1.7		1.4	1.4
.6	1.1	1.1	1.3	1.0	1.2		1.1	1.1
1.3	1.6	1.5	1.6	1.0	2.1	Quick	1.3	1.4
.6	.8	.8	1.0	.6	.8		.8	.8
.3	.5	.6	.7	.5	.7		.6	.6
0 UND	21 17.5	32 11.4	34 10.9	38 9.7	32 11.5	Sales/Receivables	31 11.7 / 33 11.0	
30 12.2	35 10.6	43 8.4	47 7.7	50 7.4	49 7.5		41 8.9 / 46 8.0	
52 7.0	51 7.2	59 6.2	63 5.8	52 7.0	57 6.3		55 6.7 / 60 6.1	
0 UND	28 13.2	25 14.9	36 10.2	48 7.6	9 42.5	Cost of Sales/Inventory	31 11.8 / 31 11.9	
22 16.9	55 6.6	49 7.4	62 5.9	99 3.7	51 7.1		53 6.9 / 54 6.7	
70 5.2	113 3.2	84 4.3	103 3.5	130 2.8	59 6.2		90 4.1 / 105 3.5	
0 UND	17 22.1	21 17.6	22 16.4	22 16.9	13 27.4	Cost of Sales/Payables	23 15.9 / 22 16.6	
41 9.0	40 9.2	40 9.2	43 8.6	36 10.3	37 9.8		42 8.8 / 38 9.5	
75 4.8	67 5.5	61 5.9	88 4.1	60 6.1	45 8.1		65 5.6 / 63 5.8	
17.9	6.2	5.2	4.9	7.0	5.2	Sales/Working Capital	7.3	6.4
143.2	10.4	11.7	8.9	8.0	8.2		13.3	14.3
-18.5	140.8	32.6	17.1	-104.0	18.2		43.0	49.1
(24) 14.0	(82) 16.0	(129) 21.3	(81) 46.3	22.2	39.4	EBIT/Interest	(294) 13.6	(311) 12.6
1.8	3.4	6.8	11.7	2.5	4.1		4.3	3.8
-1.6	1.2	2.0	4.8	1.6	3.2		1.8	1.4
		(17) 6.0	(35) 32.0			Net Profit + Depr., Dep., Amort./Cur. Mat. L/T/D	(73) 9.3	(62) 8.4
		3.5	5.6				3.4	2.9
		1.1	3.0				1.6	1.3
.1	.0	.1	.1	.5	.1	Fixed/Worth	.1	.1
1.5	.2	.3	.4	1.1	1.3		.4	.4
-.4	.9	1.4	.8	-2.2	-1.0		1.2	2.0
1.9	.9	.8	.7	1.7	2.2	Debt/Worth	1.0	1.0
20.7	2.0	2.1	1.6	2.5	4.8		2.6	2.6
-2.6	10.9	5.3	2.9	-19.1	-5.0		7.5	8.8
130.6	63.5	69.3	60.7	29.6	40.2	% Profit Before Taxes/Tangible Net Worth	61.8	65.3
(20) 29.2	(78) 26.6	(126) 34.4	(85) 32.4	(11) 13.7	(12) 24.2		(283) 28.6	(284) 23.8
-4.0	6.1	10.0	20.8	1.5	22.1		10.1	6.7
32.9	19.1	23.8	20.9	11.3	15.0	% Profit Before Taxes/Total Assets	18.2	21.2
1.9	7.3	9.7	11.4	3.7	6.7		7.5	6.7
-13.4	.5	2.8	5.7	1.0	3.7		2.1	1.0
250.3	232.1	141.0	70.7	22.6	42.3	Sales/Net Fixed Assets	112.1	108.2
65.6	74.7	55.7	22.1	9.7	20.6		37.9	32.6
20.4	24.1	9.3	9.7	5.2	11.9		14.6	12.2
8.0	4.2	3.9	3.4	2.0	3.5	Sales/Total Assets	4.2	3.8
3.6	2.9	2.7	2.2	1.5	2.5		3.2	2.9
2.5	2.2	1.9	1.6	1.2	.9		2.0	1.8
.4	.3	.3	.4	1.6	.5	% Depr., Dep., Amort./Sales	.3	.3
(21) .8	(58) .8	(117) .6	(78) 1.0	(11) 2.8	(13) .8		(268) .8	(268) .8
1.7	1.4	1.9	2.0	4.5	1.6		1.8	2.3
3.9	2.7	1.6	1.0			% Officers', Directors' Owners' Comp/Sales	2.3	2.0
(18) 9.8	(51) 4.4	(53) 2.7	(22) 2.2				(120) 4.4	(129) 4.1
16.7	9.5	4.8	4.7				8.8	8.0
45718M	410288M	2111674M	5112573M	1857557M	5978690M	Net Sales ($)	10010653M	10515648M
9250M	122021M	705386M	2072047M	1110227M	2593708M	Total Assets ($)	3765305M	4089966M

M = $ thousand   MM = $ million
See Pages 9 through 22 for Explanation of Ratios and Data

Comparative Historical Data | Current Data Sorted by Sales

53	52	54	Type of Statement						
53	52	54	Unqualified		1		4	9	40
49	63	63	Reviewed		5		11	25	18
45	55	53	Compiled	4	10	11	12	12	4
53	65	64	Tax Returns	9	20	8	15	10	2
122	168	165	Other	7	20	20	25	33	60
4/1/07-3/31/08 ALL	4/1/08-3/31/09 ALL	4/1/09-3/31/10 ALL		0-1MM	1-3MM	3-5MM	5-10MM	10-25MM	25MM & OVER
				64 (4/1-9/30/09)			335 (10/1/09-3/31/10)		
322	403	399	**NUMBER OF STATEMENTS**	20	56	43	67	89	124
%	%	%	**ASSETS**	%	%	%	%	%	%
9.2	8.7	10.4	Cash & Equivalents	11.7	16.1	8.9	10.9	8.6	9.3
33.1	33.7	32.8	Trade Receivables (net)	26.3	26.2	30.0	33.1	37.4	34.2
29.2	28.7	27.6	Inventory	24.7	27.1	29.3	28.2	27.6	27.3
2.0	3.2	2.8	All Other Current	2.7	2.0	4.5	1.7	2.3	3.5
73.6	74.3	73.6	Total Current	65.4	71.3	72.6	73.8	76.0	74.4
13.7	14.0	14.8	Fixed Assets (net)	21.1	14.2	18.7	14.2	14.2	13.4
7.1	6.1	7.0	Intangibles (net)	4.2	9.1	2.8	6.4	6.3	8.6
5.6	5.6	4.7	All Other Non-Current	9.4	5.4	6.0	5.6	3.5	3.5
100.0	100.0	100.0	Total	100.0	100.0	100.0	100.0	100.0	100.0
			LIABILITIES						
13.8	15.2	14.4	Notes Payable-Short Term	21.8	17.4	17.2	12.9	14.0	11.9
3.2	4.1	3.2	Cur. Mat.-L.T.D.	6.7	1.5	7.1	3.3	2.8	2.4
21.7	21.4	21.2	Trade Payables	22.3	19.7	20.4	20.7	21.6	21.8
.2	.2	.2	Income Taxes Payable	.2	.0	.3	.3	.2	.2
10.3	9.6	9.7	All Other Current	14.2	15.4	8.6	5.3	9.5	9.3
49.1	50.5	48.6	Total Current	65.3	54.1	53.5	42.5	48.1	45.6
12.0	12.0	12.1	Long-Term Debt	38.8	11.8	15.8	9.2	10.6	9.4
.2	.2	.2	Deferred Taxes	.0	.0	.0	.1	.1	.5
5.8	4.8	5.5	All Other Non-Current	10.9	6.4	7.2	5.8	5.9	3.1
32.9	32.5	33.5	Net Worth	-14.9	27.7	23.4	42.4	35.3	41.4
100.0	100.0	100.0	Total Liabilities & Net Worth	100.0	100.0	100.0	100.0	100.0	100.0
			INCOME DATA						
100.0	100.0	100.0	Net Sales	100.0	100.0	100.0	100.0	100.0	100.0
40.1	40.2	39.9	Gross Profit	56.9	46.3	48.7	38.5	35.5	35.2
34.2	34.5	34.1	Operating Expenses	49.8	42.8	43.2	31.6	30.2	28.5
5.9	5.7	5.9	Operating Profit	7.1	3.5	5.6	6.9	5.3	6.6
1.5	.9	.7	All Other Expenses (net)	2.3	.5	.8	.4	.7	.8
4.4	4.7	5.1	Profit Before Taxes	4.8	3.0	4.8	6.5	4.5	5.9
			RATIOS						
2.4	2.4	2.4	Current	1.5	2.9	2.2	3.1	2.3	2.4
1.5	1.5	1.5		1.1	1.5	1.3	1.7	1.5	1.5
1.1	1.1	1.2		.7	.9	.9	1.1	1.2	1.3
1.4	1.5	1.5	Quick	1.1	1.7	1.1	2.0	1.5	1.5
.9	.8	.9		.6	.8	.7	1.2	.9	1.0
.6	.5	.6		.3	.5	.5	.6	.6	.6
32 11.5	30 12.1	30 12.4	Sales/Receivables	30 12.1	12 31.7	25 14.8	30 12.2	32 11.3	32 11.3
42 8.7	42 8.6	42 8.7		42 8.7	35 10.5	40 9.2	38 9.5	44 8.2	44 8.4
58 6.2	59 6.2	57 6.4		60 6.1	58 6.3	64 5.7	52 7.0	60 6.1	53 6.9
32 11.3	29 12.4	28 13.1	Cost of Sales/Inventory	0 UND	21 17.1	25 14.4	31 11.8	25 14.7	31 11.7
60 6.1	54 6.7	52 7.0		54 6.8	67 5.4	54 6.8	57 6.4	46 8.0	54 6.7
105 3.5	101 3.6	96 3.8		142 2.6	141 2.6	141 2.6	96 3.8	70 5.2	99 3.7
24 15.4	21 17.1	20 18.5	Cost of Sales/Payables	43 8.5	2 147.8	23 15.9	20 18.2	20 18.0	20 18.0
39 9.3	38 9.6	40 9.2		72 5.1	47 7.8	44 8.4	39 9.4	36 10.1	37 9.8
66 5.5	67 5.5	67 5.5		91 4.0	83 4.4	67 5.5	63 5.8	61 6.0	55 6.6
6.0	6.0	6.0	Sales/Working Capital	6.1	6.2	6.7	5.0	6.4	6.1
11.9	12.3	11.3		NM	12.4	16.3	10.2	13.5	9.9
37.2	48.1	33.9		-14.3	-45.9	-94.2	47.1	29.2	18.5
12.3	14.9	21.6	EBIT/Interest	16.9	12.6	10.8	23.1	18.6	44.7
(286) 4.1	(346) 4.5	(348) 6.1		(13) 1.1	(43) 2.5	(40) 5.1	(59) 7.8	(82) 5.8	(111) 11.2
1.7	1.6	2.0		-1.8	-1.7	1.5	1.7	2.0	3.7
8.5	10.4	12.2	Net Profit + Depr., Dep., Amort./Cur. Mat. L/T/D					17.7	19.3
(55) 3.4	(70) 3.0	(72) 4.2						(16) 4.9	(42) 5.7
1.5	1.0	1.8						1.5	3.1
.1	.1	.1	Fixed/Worth	.0	.0	.1	.1	.1	.1
.4	.4	.3		1.2	.3	.5	.3	.3	.4
1.6	1.7	1.5		-.4	3.7	2.9	.9	1.0	1.1
.9	.9	.9	Debt/Worth	2.0	.9	1.3	.7	.9	.8
2.3	2.6	2.1		15.3	2.3	3.4	1.7	2.0	2.0
9.3	10.3	8.2		-2.9	-46.0	12.0	5.4	7.2	4.1
61.7	61.1	65.1	% Profit Before Taxes/Tangible Net Worth	79.8	46.9	62.8	79.8	69.8	59.3
(265) 27.9	(333) 27.4	(332) 30.7		(11) 20.6	(40) 20.2	(35) 30.9	(60) 30.5	(77) 31.8	(109) 31.3
8.9	9.2	11.2		.0	2.0	7.0	10.5	9.2	19.5
19.2	18.2	20.6	% Profit Before Taxes/Total Assets	15.9	18.1	19.3	27.2	21.1	20.1
7.8	6.9	9.6		.9	7.1	8.0	9.7	9.0	11.4
1.9	1.8	2.6		-12.6	-3.0	.8	1.3	2.9	4.8
133.1	130.4	134.2	Sales/Net Fixed Assets	179.4	199.4	102.7	140.6	213.4	103.2
34.9	36.9	33.0		66.3	44.1	31.9	32.3	37.0	27.1
12.1	14.0	11.0		8.6	12.2	5.8	12.9	12.2	10.6
3.8	3.9	3.8	Sales/Total Assets	3.3	3.5	3.8	3.9	4.1	3.9
2.8	2.7	2.7		2.1	2.5	2.6	2.6	2.8	2.8
1.7	1.8	1.8		1.3	1.8	1.9	1.9	2.1	1.7
.3	.3	.3	% Depr., Dep., Amort./Sales	.7	.4	.6	.2	.3	.3
(240) .8	(299) .7	(298) .8		(13) 1.6	(29) .8	(31) 1.4	(54) .6	(71) .7	(100) .8
2.0	1.9	1.8		5.2	1.9	5.7	1.8	1.8	1.8
2.5	2.0	1.9	% Officers', Directors' Owners' Comp/Sales		3.9	2.0	1.7	1.9	.8
(109) 4.2	(146) 3.6	(144) 3.6			(26) 6.1	(22) 4.5	(31) 2.9	(35) 3.5	(22) 2.2
7.6	7.4	6.9			14.7	9.7	4.1	4.7	4.8
10781124M	21124280M	15516500M	Net Sales ($)	10336M	115049M	175311M	510231M	1449976M	13255597M
4431483M	6455148M	6612639M	Total Assets ($)	6243M	52041M	75507M	249989M	614882M	5613977M

M = $ thousand   MM = $ million
See Pages 9 through 22 for Explanation of Ratios and Data

Current Data Sorted by Assets   Comparative Historical Data

0-500M	500M-2MM	2-10MM	10-50MM	50-100MM	100-250MM	Type of Statement	4/1/05-3/31/06 ALL	4/1/06-3/31/07 ALL
			2			Unqualified	8	9
	1	3	1			Reviewed	5	7
	1	4				Compiled	4	6
	2	1				Tax Returns		1
		5	5		2	Other	6	6
	6 (4/1-9/30/09)		21 (10/1/09-3/31/10)					
	4	13	8		2	NUMBER OF STATEMENTS	23	29
%	%	%	%	%	%	**ASSETS**	%	%
		4.4				Cash & Equivalents	8.7	7.2
D	D	32.7	D			Trade Receivables (net)	29.4	27.9
A	A	37.1	A			Inventory	40.3	39.7
T	T	3.5	T			All Other Current	2.7	2.3
A	A	77.6	A			Total Current	81.1	77.2
		6.4				Fixed Assets (net)	10.5	11.0
N	N	7.4	N			Intangibles (net)	1.9	5.6
O	O	8.6	O			All Other Non-Current	6.4	6.3
T	T	100.0	T			Total	100.0	100.0
						LIABILITIES		
A	A	16.3	A			Notes Payable-Short Term	14.7	11.2
V	V	1.3	V			Cur. Mat.-L.T.D.	2.1	2.5
A	A	32.0	A			Trade Payables	21.1	26.0
I	I	.2	I			Income Taxes Payable	.5	.1
L	L	6.7	L			All Other Current	14.2	12.6
A	A	56.4	A			Total Current	52.5	52.4
B	B	6.9	B			Long-Term Debt	14.6	8.0
L	L	.0	L			Deferred Taxes	.2	.0
E	E	3.7	E			All Other Non-Current	5.2	2.0
		33.0				Net Worth	27.5	37.6
		100.0				Total Liabilities & Net Worth	100.0	100.0
						INCOME DATA		
		100.0				Net Sales	100.0	100.0
		36.9				Gross Profit	40.4	37.4
		35.5				Operating Expenses	35.4	33.9
		1.4				Operating Profit	5.0	3.5
		.5				All Other Expenses (net)	.9	.9
		.9				Profit Before Taxes	4.2	2.6
						RATIOS		
		2.0					2.0	2.1
		1.5				Current	1.5	1.6
		1.0					1.3	1.1
		.9					1.2	1.1
		.7				Quick	.7 (28)	.8
		.5					.5	.5
		25 14.7					31 11.8	28 13.0
		35 10.3				Sales/Receivables	37 9.9	35 10.5
		63 5.8					52 7.0	44 8.4
		51 7.2					63 5.8	44 8.3
		75 4.9				Cost of Sales/Inventory	99 3.7	99 3.7
		165 2.2					176 2.1	150 2.4
		39 9.5					21 17.0	32 11.5
		56 6.5				Cost of Sales/Payables	45 8.2	38 9.7
		77 4.7					70 5.2	83 4.4
		7.1					5.8	5.5
		10.3				Sales/Working Capital	11.6	14.3
		NM					26.2	51.1
		14.6					9.3	18.3
		7.7				EBIT/Interest	(22) 3.7	(28) 4.0
		1.3					1.7	1.6
						Net Profit + Depr., Dep., Amort./Cur. Mat. L/T/D		
		.0					.1	.1
		.2				Fixed/Worth	.2	.2
		.5					.7	.6
		1.8					1.1	.9
		2.2				Debt/Worth	1.9	1.7
		7.6					4.2	4.0
		67.5					64.4	57.6
		(11) 22.7				% Profit Before Taxes/Tangible Net Worth	(21) 23.7	(26) 31.5
		2.7					3.5	9.3
		13.0					20.0	15.6
		5.8				% Profit Before Taxes/Total Assets	7.5	10.8
		.7					1.1	1.3
		425.6					95.0	163.7
		63.8				Sales/Net Fixed Assets	42.8	37.4
		25.6					13.0	13.0
		3.9					3.4	4.0
		3.1				Sales/Total Assets	2.7	2.9
		1.6					2.0	1.8
		.2					.3	.3
		(10) .4				% Depr., Dep., Amort./Sales	(20) .8	(20) .7
		1.0					1.7	1.9
							1.4	2.1
						% Officers', Directors' Owners' Comp/Sales	(10) 4.0	(10) 4.1
							5.8	10.8
	9355M	199296M	323064M		632137M	Net Sales ($)	366283M	1094723M
	3217M	72535M	138859M		386430M	Total Assets ($)	154130M	541407M

M = $ thousand   MM = $ million
See Pages 9 through 22 for Explanation of Ratios and Data

Comparative Historical Data

Current Data Sorted by Sales

				Type of Statement						
4		5	2	Unqualified					3	2
3		6	5	Reviewed	1				3	1
4		4	5	Compiled	1					1
2		3	3	Tax Returns		1	1	1		
9		10	12	Other					6	6
4/1/07-3/31/08 ALL		4/1/08-3/31/09 ALL	4/1/09-3/31/10 ALL		0-1MM	6 (4/1-9/30/09) 1-3MM	3-5MM	5-10MM	21 (10/1/09-3/31/10) 10-25MM	25MM & OVER
22		28	27	NUMBER OF STATEMENTS	2	1	1	1	12	10
%		%	%	ASSETS	%	%	%	%	%	%
8.2		6.6	3.4	Cash & Equivalents					2.7	6.1
31.6		28.9	30.9	Trade Receivables (net)					29.8	29.0
35.7		37.6	37.5	Inventory					41.5	27.3
3.2		3.2	3.8	All Other Current					2.9	6.4
78.7		76.3	75.7	Total Current					76.9	68.8
10.1		7.5	6.3	Fixed Assets (net)					5.4	6.3
7.6		5.2	11.8	Intangibles (net)					8.4	21.1
3.5		11.0	6.2	All Other Non-Current					9.3	3.8
100.0		100.0	100.0	Total					100.0	100.0
				LIABILITIES						
13.3		19.0	17.6	Notes Payable-Short Term					16.8	12.7
.7		.9	1.5	Cur. Mat.-L.T.D.					1.4	2.4
25.8		31.1	28.0	Trade Payables					29.5	23.1
.2		.3	.1	Income Taxes Payable					.2	.0
21.5		11.2	7.8	All Other Current					8.6	10.1
61.5		62.5	55.0	Total Current					56.4	48.3
6.1		7.3	6.7	Long-Term Debt					6.9	9.1
.2		.0	.5	Deferred Taxes					.0	1.3
3.4		1.7	4.1	All Other Non-Current					4.0	6.4
28.8		28.5	33.7	Net Worth					32.7	35.0
100.0		100.0	100.0	Total Liabilties & Net Worth					100.0	100.0
				INCOME DATA						
100.0		100.0	100.0	Net Sales					100.0	100.0
37.3		40.4	40.2	Gross Profit					39.4	40.7
33.7		35.4	37.4	Operating Expenses					36.2	35.4
3.6		5.0	2.8	Operating Profit					3.2	5.3
1.0		.6	1.1	All Other Expenses (net)					.4	1.9
2.6		4.4	1.7	Profit Before Taxes					2.8	3.4
				RATIOS						
1.8		1.9	1.9						2.1	1.6
1.3		1.2	1.3	Current					1.4	1.4
1.1		.9	1.1						.9	1.1
1.0		.9	.9						.8	1.1
.7		.6	.6	Quick					.7	.6
.4		.4	.4						.4	.4
28 13.0		33 11.0	32 11.3						23 15.7	35 10.6
40 9.2		41 8.8	41 8.9	Sales/Receivables					36 10.1	37 9.8
60 6.1		59 6.2	49 7.4						49 7.5	44 8.2
48 7.5		54 6.8	50 7.3						52 7.1	32 11.4
68 5.3		107 3.4	90 4.1	Cost of Sales/Inventory					81 4.5	99 3.7
136 2.7		193 1.9	175 2.1						170 2.1	158 2.3
23 16.0		31 11.9	40 9.1						38 9.6	38 9.5
44 8.3		59 6.2	56 6.5	Cost of Sales/Payables					61 6.0	53 6.9
87 4.2		107 3.4	80 4.5						79 4.6	74 4.9
7.4		6.4	8.1						6.9	10.4
14.7		16.2	12.8	Sales/Working Capital					10.5	17.9
55.2		-82.2	50.3						NM	22.1
12.1		10.5	15.3						14.9	23.0
(20) 3.9		(25) 4.9	7.6	EBIT/Interest					8.1	9.9
1.3		1.2	1.0						1.9	.7
				Net Profit + Depr., Dep., Amort./Cur. Mat. L/T/D						
.1		.1	.1						.0	.1
.2		.2	.2	Fixed/Worth					.1	.6
1.8		.6	.7						.4	-3.5
1.5		1.8	1.8						1.8	1.7
2.8		2.7	2.7	Debt/Worth					2.4	7.1
7.8		5.5	12.6						10.3	-56.9
118.5		61.9	73.9	% Profit Before Taxes/Tangible Net Worth					73.2	
(19) 21.8		(26) 29.4	(22) 25.9					(10) 25.9	
8.1		6.2	2.5						5.5	
15.1		15.1	14.5	% Profit Before Taxes/Total Assets					13.0	19.8
4.5		5.8	5.8						7.2	12.4
1.7		.9	.1						1.6	-1.6
211.6		162.5	148.1	Sales/Net Fixed Assets					280.7	80.0
47.9		42.6	63.8						64.0	48.6
23.3		20.2	22.5						31.0	16.5
3.8		3.3	3.8	Sales/Total Assets					3.7	4.6
2.8		2.3	2.5						2.9	2.1
2.0		1.6	1.4						1.9	-1.4
.1		.2	.3	% Depr., Dep., Amort./Sales						
(16) .3		(24) .5	(19) .6							
.7			1.2	1.2						
		2.7	1.6	% Officers', Directors' Owners' Comp/Sales						
		(13) 3.9	(11) 4.0							
		6.4	5.4							
541467M		472084M	1163852M	Net Sales ($)	1468M	2814M	4428M	5073M	188977M	961092M
311171M		202685M	601041M	Total Assets ($)	1113M	666M	3988M	1438M	75570M	518266M

M = $ thousand   MM = $ million
See Pages 9 through 22 for Explanation of Ratios and Data

Current Data Sorted by Assets   Comparative Historical Data

Type of Statement

	0-500M	500M-2MM	2-10MM	10-50MM	50-100MM	100-250MM		4/1/05-3/31/06 ALL	4/1/06-3/31/07 ALL
Unqualified			3	8	1			13	11
Reviewed		5	10	4				25	26
Compiled	1	7	8	1				11	17
Tax Returns	7	7	7					9	10
Other	1	9	17	11	6	1		29	23
		12 (4/1-9/30/09)		102 (10/1/09-3/31/10)				29	23
NUMBER OF STATEMENTS	9	28	45	24	7	1		87	87

0-500M	500M-2MM	2-10MM	10-50MM	50-100MM	100-250MM		4/1/05-3/31/06 ALL	4/1/06-3/31/07 ALL
%	%	%	%	%	%	**ASSETS**	%	%
	9.0	5.4	5.1			Cash & Equivalents	6.6	7.1
	41.0	33.0	33.0			Trade Receivables (net)	34.1	34.9
	24.7	38.5	25.8			Inventory	33.6	31.2
	3.6	3.6	4.5			All Other Current	2.0	3.2
	78.3	80.4	68.3			Total Current	76.4	76.4
	12.7	10.5	15.2			Fixed Assets (net)	13.2	13.3
	1.1	3.9	12.7			Intangibles (net)	5.0	4.9
	7.9	5.2	3.8			All Other Non-Current	5.5	5.4
	100.0	100.0	100.0			Total	100.0	100.0
						LIABILITIES		
	15.0	14.4	17.4			Notes Payable-Short Term	12.2	11.6
	2.0	1.9	3.8			Cur. Mat.-L.T.D.	2.8	3.2
	20.9	24.2	16.7			Trade Payables	22.2	21.7
	.2	.1	.3			Income Taxes Payable	.3	.1
	10.2	7.9	13.7			All Other Current	9.8	12.1
	48.2	48.5	52.1			Total Current	47.3	48.8
	11.0	8.7	9.5			Long-Term Debt	7.6	11.8
	.0	.0	.3			Deferred Taxes	.1	.0
	7.3	2.7	9.5			All Other Non-Current	4.8	4.2
	33.5	40.1	28.6			Net Worth	40.2	35.2
	100.0	100.0	100.0			Total Liabilities & Net Worth	100.0	100.0
						INCOME DATA		
	100.0	100.0	100.0			Net Sales	100.0	100.0
	36.1	34.0	31.2			Gross Profit	33.7	35.3
	32.0	30.8	26.6			Operating Expenses	29.5	30.3
	4.2	3.2	4.6			Operating Profit	4.2	5.1
	.2	-.1	2.1			All Other Expenses (net)	.8	1.5
	4.0	3.3	2.4			Profit Before Taxes	3.4	3.6
						RATIOS		
	3.4	2.8	2.0				2.5	2.6
	1.4	1.6	1.4			Current	1.6	1.6
	1.0	1.3	1.0				1.2	1.2
	1.7	1.2	1.3				1.3	1.2
	.9	.9	.7			Quick	.8 (86)	.9
	.6	.5	.4				.6	.6
	28 13.1	32 11.4	42 8.7				33 11.2	28 13.1
	38 9.5	44 8.3	48 7.5			Sales/Receivables	42 8.8	41 8.9
	57 6.4	61 6.0	69 5.3				52 7.1	53 6.9
	3 124.0	45 8.1	32 11.3				39 9.3	31 11.7
	23 15.7	69 5.3	65 5.6			Cost of Sales/Inventory	65 5.7	64 5.7
	83 4.4	137 2.7	103 3.5				120 3.0	103 3.5
	12 29.9	19 18.9	24 15.4				24 15.4	21 17.1
	24 15.0	36 10.2	37 9.9			Cost of Sales/Payables	32 11.3	33 10.9
	51 7.1	76 4.8	62 5.9				54 6.7	58 6.3
	4.8	5.7	5.5				5.4	5.6
	15.0	8.7	11.2			Sales/Working Capital	9.4	9.6
	NM	15.5	NM				24.9	35.3
	11.7	14.3	12.5				10.1	11.1
	(25) 4.5	(39) 3.7	(23) 8.1			EBIT/Interest	(78) 4.0	(82) 4.5
	.9	1.7	1.2				2.1	1.6
		11.7				Net Profit + Depr., Dep.,	6.4	27.5
		(10) 3.7				Amort./Cur. Mat. L/T/D	(21) 3.1	(19) 7.8
		1.1					1.8	2.0
	.1	.1	.1				.1	.1
	.3	.2	.7			Fixed/Worth	.3	.3
	1.1	.7	-3.3				.8	.9
	1.1	.9	1.5				.7	.9
	2.7	1.6	4.1			Debt/Worth	1.9	2.1
	11.5	4.6	-26.3				5.2	7.3
	126.5	39.8	34.8			% Profit Before Taxes/Tangible	38.4	60.3
	(25) 41.8	(42) 19.8	(17) 23.0			Net Worth	(76) 18.3	(77) 26.5
	8.5	4.2	12.1				6.9	7.7
	21.1	14.7	12.0			% Profit Before Taxes/Total	11.9	16.6
	7.6	6.4	6.8			Assets	6.3	6.1
	.3	1.6	1.3				1.6	1.6
	181.9	134.0	51.2				91.3	137.2
	41.7	45.2	31.8			Sales/Net Fixed Assets	37.2	45.4
	21.0	15.0	10.1				10.6	12.3
	5.0	3.3	2.8				3.6	3.9
	3.4	2.6	2.1			Sales/Total Assets	2.8	2.8
	2.2	1.9	1.5				2.0	2.0
	.2	.2	.4				.4	.3
	(16) .7	(41) .5	(22) .8			% Depr., Dep., Amort./Sales	(71) .9	(74) .8
	1.9	1.2	2.1				2.2	2.1
	1.7	1.0					1.5	2.1
	(15) 3.1	(24) 2.7				% Officers', Directors' Owners' Comp/Sales	(37) 2.9	(36) 3.1
	8.2	4.0					5.9	4.8
16610M	128466M	579925M	1289361M	910408M	125210M	Net Sales ($)	2109094M	1642442M
1991M	33091M	221551M	604357M	467722M	105797M	Total Assets ($)	948474M	830656M

Comparative Historical Data | Current Data Sorted by Sales

Type of Statement

07-08	08-09	09-10	Type of Statement	0-1MM	1-3MM	3-5MM	5-10MM	10-25MM	25MM & OVER
13	12	12	Unqualified					3	9
26	23	19	Reviewed		2	3	4	8	2
17	11	17	Compiled	1	1	2	9	2	2
12	15	21	Tax Returns	2	8	2	6	3	
29	34	45	Other		4	4	8	10	19
4/1/07-3/31/08	4/1/08-3/31/09	4/1/09-3/31/10			12 (4/1-9/30/09)			102 (10/1/09-3/31/10)	
ALL	ALL	ALL		0-1MM	1-3MM	3-5MM	5-10MM	10-25MM	25MM & OVER
97	95	114	NUMBER OF STATEMENTS	3	15	11	27	26	32

ASSETS

07-08	08-09	09-10		0-1MM	1-3MM	3-5MM	5-10MM	10-25MM	25MM & OVER
%	%	%	ASSETS	%	%	%	%	%	%
9.3	7.4	7.1	Cash & Equivalents		10.2	10.9	8.9	4.6	5.4
29.2	28.5	32.9	Trade Receivables (net)		30.4	42.0	32.9	33.0	32.0
31.8	35.9	31.1	Inventory		27.9	31.5	28.5	38.4	24.7
2.4	3.8	3.5	All Other Current		1.6	1.3	4.6	2.8	5.2
72.8	75.7	74.7	Total Current		70.1	85.6	74.9	78.8	67.3
13.9	12.5	13.0	Fixed Assets (net)		13.3	12.3	15.2	8.3	16.2
8.6	7.4	6.0	Intangibles (net)		.0	.7	3.4	7.6	12.2
4.6	4.4	6.3	All Other Non-Current		16.6	1.3	6.5	5.4	4.3
100.0	100.0	100.0	Total		100.0	100.0	100.0	100.0	100.0

LIABILITIES

07-08	08-09	09-10		0-1MM	1-3MM	3-5MM	5-10MM	10-25MM	25MM & OVER
14.3	21.1	17.2	Notes Payable-Short Term		22.4	9.6	18.6	14.5	15.6
2.7	2.0	2.4	Cur. Mat.-L.T.D.		3.1	.9	4.7	1.7	1.6
22.8	19.5	20.2	Trade Payables		15.6	21.6	27.8	17.4	17.2
.3	.2	.1	Income Taxes Payable		.0	.3	.1	.3	.1
11.3	10.1	9.3	All Other Current		10.8	7.4	6.1	9.1	12.7
51.4	52.9	49.2	Total Current		51.9	39.8	57.4	42.9	47.2
10.6	11.4	10.9	Long-Term Debt		13.7	9.1	7.9	11.6	13.1
.1	.2	.1	Deferred Taxes		.0	.1	.0	.1	.2
7.1	6.4	6.3	All Other Non-Current		11.8	4.3	3.9	3.1	9.6
30.7	29.2	33.4	Net Worth		22.6	46.7	30.8	42.3	29.9
100.0	100.0	100.0	Total Liabilities & Net Worth		100.0	100.0	100.0	100.0	100.0

INCOME DATA

07-08	08-09	09-10		0-1MM	1-3MM	3-5MM	5-10MM	10-25MM	25MM & OVER
100.0	100.0	100.0	Net Sales		100.0	100.0	100.0	100.0	100.0
36.0	33.5	33.7	Gross Profit		41.2	39.6	31.2	34.2	29.4
32.3	30.5	29.9	Operating Expenses		36.9	36.0	28.0	29.7	25.9
3.7	2.9	3.8	Operating Profit		4.4	3.6	3.2	4.5	3.4
1.3	1.5	.6	All Other Expenses (net)		.7	-.4	.0	.5	1.6
2.4	1.5	3.2	Profit Before Taxes		3.6	4.0	3.2	4.0	1.8

RATIOS

07-08	08-09	09-10		0-1MM	1-3MM	3-5MM	5-10MM	10-25MM	25MM & OVER
2.2	2.0	2.6	Current		2.7	8.9	2.2	3.0	2.1
1.6	1.5	1.5			1.3	1.7	1.4	1.9	1.5
1.1	1.1	1.2			.7	1.3	1.0	1.4	1.2
1.1	1.1	1.3	Quick		1.5	3.2	1.1	1.3	1.3
.8	.7	.8			.8	1.3	.8	.9	.8
.5	.5	.5			.5	.9	.4	.6	.5
28 13.1	25 14.4	30 12.3	Sales/Receivables		17 21.3	31 11.7	30 12.2	31 11.6	34 10.9
40 9.2	37 9.8	42 8.8			34 10.8	38 9.6	39 9.3	45 8.1	45 8.1
52 7.0	50 7.3	58 6.2			59 6.2	66 5.5	56 6.5	64 5.7	61 6.0
35 10.4	34 10.7	21 17.2	Cost of Sales/Inventory		0 UND	6 62.2	5 69.5	56 6.5	23 16.1
70 5.2	66 5.5	61 6.0			45 8.1	66 5.6	39 9.3	80 4.6	55 6.6
111 3.3	122 3.0	118 3.1			111 3.3	175 2.1	99 3.7	136 2.7	82 4.4
24 15.2	18 20.3	18 20.5	Cost of Sales/Payables		2 170.8	12 30.5	19 18.9	15 23.8	24 15.0
36 10.2	32 11.5	32 11.2			29 12.7	30 12.1	44 8.4	27 13.5	33 11.1
70 5.2	56 6.6	57 6.4			54 6.8	60 6.0	93 3.9	55 6.7	43 8.5
6.5	6.1	5.6	Sales/Working Capital		4.8	3.5	6.8	4.8	5.8
11.6	12.6	11.6			55.4	11.0	15.8	7.8	9.6
59.2	34.5	25.3			-37.8	12.6	309.3	14.3	24.1
(88) 9.9	(83) 7.9	(100) 12.3	EBIT/Interest		8.6		(24) 9.8	(23) 31.7	(30) 11.9
3.7	4.3	4.4			(12) 1.9		3.6	8.8	6.3
1.3	1.8	1.2			-2.8		1.2	2.4	.5
(18) 11.5	(20) 8.0	(25) 7.2	Net Profit + Depr., Dep., Amort./Cur. Mat. L/T/D						9.8
3.4	3.2	3.5						(12)	3.7
1.8	1.2	.4							-.5
.1	.1	.1	Fixed/Worth		.1	.1	.1	.1	.2
.4	.3	.3			.3	.3	.3	.1	.6
3.9	1.1	1.3			-7.8	.5	1.2	.7	NM
1.1	1.4	1.2	Debt/Worth		1.5	.1	1.3	.8	1.4
2.7	2.6	2.3			2.8	1.7	2.4	1.6	3.6
95.3	11.0	12.5			-18.3	4.0	16.8	6.6	NM
(78) 43.9	(82) 42.6	(95) 49.9	% Profit Before Taxes/Tangible Net Worth		(11) 124.4	119.2	(24) 83.1	(22) 41.6	(24) 33.1
18.3	21.9	23.0			38.8	26.1	21.7	30.7	19.9
5.4	7.7	5.6			4.4	3.5	3.8	11.1	-.5
13.9	10.9	14.9	% Profit Before Taxes/Total Assets		26.3	18.0	14.5	19.0	12.5
6.6	5.8	6.8			7.6	7.6	4.7	7.2	5.8
.7	1.7	1.0			-.3	3.1	.6	2.3	-2.5
82.6	93.2	120.6	Sales/Net Fixed Assets		591.3	112.7	121.1	185.2	63.2
33.9	38.6	38.3			40.9	39.1	42.6	49.0	24.4
11.3	15.4	15.3			23.2	12.6	14.4	27.3	10.7
3.5	3.8	3.6	Sales/Total Assets		5.9	4.5	4.7	3.5	3.1
2.6	2.7	2.6			2.8	2.4	2.9	2.6	2.2
1.9	1.9	1.9			2.0	2.1	1.9	2.0	1.6
(74) .5	(78) .3	(91) .3	% Depr., Dep., Amort./Sales			(10) .3	(21) .2	(23) .2	(29) .3
1.1	.6	.6				.6	.6	.5	.6
2.8	1.3	1.7				2.7	1.6	.9	1.8
(37) 2.4	(31) 2.5	(52) 1.3	% Officers', Directors' Owners' Comp/Sales		(10) .7		(19) 1.7	(12) 1.0	
3.9	4.0	3.1			6.6		2.8	2.4	
5.2	6.5	5.0			12.5		3.5	4.6	
1860265M	2914159M	3049980M	Net Sales ($)	1229M	28305M	46608M	193333M	403928M	2376577M
930534M	1397772M	1434509M	Total Assets ($)	585M	9588M	18504M	83054M	190467M	1132311M

M = $ thousand   MM = $ million
See Pages 9 through 22 for Explanation of Ratios and Data

Current Data Sorted by Assets							Comparative Historical Data	

						Type of Statement		
2	2	21	57	22	15	Unqualified	110	140
1	16	73	56	2		Reviewed	163	177
5	29	50	16			Compiled	103	104
7	21	27	4			Tax Returns	41	49
12	25	83	101	22	23	Other	201	207
	125 (4/1-9/30/09)		567 (10/1/09-3/31/10)				4/1/05-3/31/06	4/1/06-3/31/07
0-500M	500M-2MM	2-10MM	10-50MM	50-100MM	100-250MM		ALL	ALL
27	93	254	234	46	38	NUMBER OF STATEMENTS	618	677
%	%	%	%	%	%	ASSETS	%	%
23.9	12.1	7.9	8.0	4.4	7.0	Cash & Equivalents	6.5	6.0
23.5	33.6	30.7	26.5	23.7	21.3	Trade Receivables (net)	35.9	34.1
17.7	36.0	37.3	40.4	46.8	37.9	Inventory	36.6	40.4
3.4	2.3	1.8	2.9	2.0	5.0	All Other Current	1.8	2.0
68.5	84.0	77.7	77.9	76.9	71.1	Total Current	80.8	82.5
18.4	10.9	15.5	16.0	13.0	17.8	Fixed Assets (net)	13.0	11.9
6.3	1.3	2.1	2.3	5.1	4.6	Intangibles (net)	2.0	1.8
6.8	3.7	4.7	3.8	5.0	6.4	All Other Non-Current	4.2	3.8
100.0	100.0	100.0	100.0	100.0	100.0	Total	100.0	100.0
						LIABILITIES		
29.8	19.1	18.7	17.9	15.4	9.3	Notes Payable-Short Term	19.1	20.1
7.9	2.0	2.9	2.9	3.3	4.5	Cur. Mat.-L.T.D.	2.1	1.5
23.4	20.9	20.6	15.9	16.2	13.1	Trade Payables	22.5	22.4
.6	.4	.1	.2	.2	.4	Income Taxes Payable	.4	.4
24.6	4.4	5.7	5.4	7.0	7.6	All Other Current	6.9	7.7
86.3	46.8	48.0	42.4	42.0	34.9	Total Current	51.0	52.2
11.8	5.9	9.8	9.5	13.0	15.6	Long-Term Debt	8.8	8.8
.0	.1	.3	.5	.2	1.4	Deferred Taxes	.3	.3
16.5	9.2	4.4	4.3	4.1	4.6	All Other Non-Current	5.4	3.9
-14.6	38.0	37.4	43.4	40.7	43.4	Net Worth	34.4	34.8
100.0	100.0	100.0	100.0	100.0	100.0	Total Liabilties & Net Worth	100.0	100.0
						INCOME DATA		
100.0	100.0	100.0	100.0	100.0	100.0	Net Sales	100.0	100.0
32.6	23.7	21.1	17.4	12.0	14.2	Gross Profit	20.6	19.9
34.0	21.9	19.8	15.5	10.5	11.9	Operating Expenses	15.2	14.6
-1.4	1.8	1.2	1.9	1.5	2.2	Operating Profit	5.3	5.3
1.1	.5	.7	.9	1.2	2.1	All Other Expenses (net)	.7	.7
-2.5	1.3	.6	1.0	.3	.1	Profit Before Taxes	4.7	4.5
						RATIOS		
3.2	3.3	2.7	3.1	3.6	3.4		2.5	2.5
1.1	1.8	1.5	1.8	1.9	2.5	Current	1.5	1.6
.3	1.3	1.2	1.3	1.4	1.6		1.2	1.2
1.5	2.0	1.3	1.5	1.1	1.3		1.3	1.2
.6	.8	.8	.7	.8	1.0	Quick	.8	.8
.2	.5	.5	.5	.4	.7		.5	.5
0 UND	25 14.9	31 11.7	34 10.9	26 13.8	29 12.6		33 11.2	30 12.0
13 29.0	38 9.5	39 9.2	41 9.0	42 8.7	36 10.1	Sales/Receivables	41 9.0	40 9.2
39 9.3	52 7.1	55 6.6	52 7.1	53 6.9	47 7.7		52 7.0	50 7.3
0 UND	18 20.3	40 9.1	53 6.9	55 6.6	42 8.7		29 12.8	33 11.1
5 79.0	53 6.9	61 5.9	85 4.3	83 4.4	65 5.6	Cost of Sales/Inventory	56 6.5	65 5.6
35 10.3	100 3.7	108 3.4	121 3.0	162 2.2	110 3.3		86 4.2	99 3.7
0 UND	12 30.9	18 19.8	15 25.0	17 21.1	10 37.3		17 21.3	17 21.9
20 18.5	26 14.2	31 11.9	25 14.3	30 12.1	22 16.5	Cost of Sales/Payables	29 12.8	29 12.4
83 4.4	41 8.8	48 7.5	43 8.6	41 8.9	31 11.8		46 8.0	47 7.8
8.4	5.4	4.6	3.6	3.4	3.9		6.3	5.8
43.6	8.6	10.1	6.5	5.0	5.9	Sales/Working Capital	11.1	11.0
-8.5	20.2	25.4	18.0	12.2	8.6		26.7	24.7
32.2	10.4	8.0	8.8	7.2	6.0		14.6	13.0
(20) 8.9	(80) 2.2	(234) 2.1	(215) 2.5	(45) 1.5	(35) 2.2	EBIT/Interest	(574) 6.3	(622) 5.1
-5.5	-1.1	-.1	-.7	-1.1	-.4		2.3	1.9
		3.6	6.6	6.3	12.8	Net Profit + Depr., Dep.,	16.5	16.0
	(56) 1.7	(64) 2.0	(15) 2.0	(17) 1.7		Amort./Cur. Mat. L/T/D	(137) 5.4	(157) 6.0
	.8	.2	-.1	-.3			2.7	2.5
.0	.0	.1	.1	.1	.1		.1	.1
.5	.1	.3	.3	.3	.3	Fixed/Worth	.3	.2
-1.0	.4	.8	.9	.9	.9		.7	.7
.7	.7	.8	.6	.7	.6		1.0	1.0
UND	1.8	2.0	1.5	1.4	1.2	Debt/Worth	2.2	2.3
-2.3	5.3	4.3	4.0	4.4	4.6		4.9	5.2
219.9	38.9	28.1	25.8	17.8	23.2	% Profit Before Taxes/Tangible	64.0	60.2
(14) 84.5	(86) 4.7	(237) 8.8	(218) 9.6	(38) 1.4	(34) 6.2	Net Worth	(575) 34.5	(632) 30.6
-1.9	-16.7	-1.6	-6.3	-5.8	-5.8		15.4	12.9
40.7	11.9	8.5	10.2	7.4	7.9	% Profit Before Taxes/Total	21.0	18.9
15.1	3.2	2.3	3.2	.7	1.4	Assets	10.6	9.6
-6.1	-4.3	-1.6	-3.8	-3.7	-3.9		3.4	2.7
UND	506.6	118.2	81.0	152.5	62.1		155.5	184.8
143.0	76.9	35.7	16.4	26.8	15.0	Sales/Net Fixed Assets	39.2	42.4
6.4	24.4	10.3	7.7	7.1	7.8		14.7	15.8
7.9	4.3	3.2	2.7	3.1	3.0		4.0	3.8
2.9	2.9	2.5	2.1	1.8	2.2	Sales/Total Assets	2.9	2.9
1.9	2.0	1.8	1.6	1.3	1.6		2.2	2.2
.2	.2	.3	.4	.3	.2		.3	.3
(12) 1.3	(67) .7	(215) .8	(208) 1.1	(39) .7	(34) 1.0	% Depr., Dep., Amort./Sales	(506) .7	(549) .6
9.6	1.7	1.6	1.9	1.9	1.4		1.3	1.1
6.2	1.9	1.5	1.0				1.1	1.2
(10) 11.2	(51) 3.0	(115) 2.3	(65) 1.7			% Officers', Directors' Owners' Comp/Sales	(243) 2.3	(236) 2.2
17.6	5.2	5.7	3.2				4.1	4.2
39891M	407192M	3479273M	11897895M	6895197M	15994355M	Net Sales ($)	35344094M	46285245M
7282M	120949M	1304456M	5359270M	3044541M	6435675M	Total Assets ($)	12118703M	16122295M

© RMA 2010

M = $ thousand   MM = $ million
See Pages 9 through 22 for Explanation of Ratios and Data

Comparative Historical Data   Current Data Sorted by Sales

Hist 1	Hist 2	Hist 3	Type of Statement	0-1MM	1-3MM	3-5MM	5-10MM	10-25MM	25MM & OVER
130	116	119	Unqualified	1	3	1	2	19	93
168	172	148	Reviewed	2	8	11	24	53	50
108	101	100	Compiled	9	13	15	24	25	14
56	55	59	Tax Returns	5	8	12	15	12	7
211	269	266	Other	7	11	19	41	59	129
4/1/07-3/31/08 ALL	4/1/08-3/31/09 ALL	4/1/09-3/31/10 ALL		125 (4/1-9/30/09)			567 (10/1/09-3/31/10)		
673	713	692	**NUMBER OF STATEMENTS**	24	43	58	106	168	293
%	%	%	**ASSETS**	%	%	%	%	%	%
6.2	8.0	8.9	Cash & Equivalents	21.4	15.7	11.5	9.8	6.9	7.1
33.4	29.8	28.4	Trade Receivables (net)	12.8	23.9	32.5	30.6	29.3	28.3
39.8	40.7	38.1	Inventory	21.9	35.9	36.6	37.3	38.3	40.2
2.0	2.7	2.5	All Other Current	4.8	4.5	.6	1.4	2.2	2.9
81.4	81.2	77.9	Total Current	60.9	80.0	81.2	79.1	76.7	78.5
12.0	12.7	15.1	Fixed Assets (net)	25.0	9.9	15.2	14.9	15.7	14.8
2.3	2.2	2.6	Intangibles (net)	5.8	3.1	1.3	1.2	3.2	2.6
4.3	3.9	4.5	All Other Non-Current	8.3	7.0	2.3	4.7	4.4	4.1
100.0	100.0	100.0	Total	100.0	100.0	100.0	100.0	100.0	100.0
			LIABILITIES						
20.1	20.6	18.2	Notes Payable-Short Term	33.0	16.1	17.5	18.9	18.0	17.3
2.0	2.1	3.1	Cur. Mat.-L.T.D.	.7	2.0	3.5	4.3	3.7	2.6
21.5	18.9	18.4	Trade Payables	22.4	15.5	15.7	20.4	20.4	17.2
.2	.2	.2	Income Taxes Payable	.4	.4	.0	.2	.2	.2
7.6	8.0	6.4	All Other Current	19.5	7.6	4.9	5.1	5.7	6.3
51.4	49.8	46.3	Total Current	76.0	41.6	41.5	48.9	48.0	43.7
8.4	8.8	9.8	Long-Term Debt	13.5	7.9	10.0	10.8	9.2	9.7
.3	.2	.4	Deferred Taxes	.0	.0	.3	.2	.3	.6
3.8	5.2	5.5	All Other Non-Current	10.2	14.2	9.2	4.4	4.3	4.1
36.0	36.1	38.0	Net Worth	.3	36.4	39.0	35.7	38.2	41.9
100.0	100.0	100.0	Total Liabilities & Net Worth	100.0	100.0	100.0	100.0	100.0	100.0
			INCOME DATA						
100.0	100.0	100.0	Net Sales	100.0	100.0	100.0	100.0	100.0	100.0
19.3	19.5	19.6	Gross Profit	39.1	25.6	24.9	23.0	19.0	15.3
14.5	14.7	18.1	Operating Expenses	40.9	26.1	24.0	21.8	17.5	13.0
4.9	4.9	1.5	Operating Profit	-1.8	-.4	.9	1.3	1.5	2.2
.9	.9	.8	All Other Expenses (net)	1.2	1.0	.8	.7	.8	.9
3.9	3.9	.7	Profit Before Taxes	-3.0	-1.4	.1	.6	.8	1.3
			RATIOS						
2.4	2.8	3.1	Current	3.7	3.8	3.4	3.1	2.6	3.0
1.5	1.7	1.7		1.0	1.8	2.0	1.7	1.5	1.8
1.2	1.2	1.2		.3	1.2	1.4	1.1	1.2	1.3
1.3	1.4	1.4	Quick	1.2	2.4	2.0	1.6	1.2	1.3
.7	(712) .7	.8		.4	.9	.9	.8	.7	.8
.5	.5	.5		.2	.5	.6	.5	.5	.5
30 12.0	22 16.5	31 11.9	Sales/Receivables	0 UND	19 19.0	32 11.5	30 12.0	32 11.4	32 11.6
39 9.4	32 11.6	39 9.3		16 22.3	48 7.6	38 9.5	41 8.9	40 9.2	39 9.3
49 7.4	43 8.4	52 7.0		71 5.1	61 6.0	55 6.7	56 6.5	54 6.8	49 7.5
35 10.5	30 12.3	39 9.5	Cost of Sales/Inventory	0 UND	20 18.2	22 16.6	40 9.1	42 8.8	44 8.2
62 5.9	58 6.3	70 5.2		9 38.6	72 5.1	71 5.1	61 6.0	73 5.0	71 5.2
102 3.6	99 3.7	113 3.2		276 1.3	177 2.1	120 3.0	117 3.1	119 3.1	106 3.5
17 21.7	10 37.6	15 24.2	Cost of Sales/Payables	15 24.6	9 41.5	13 28.1	17 21.4	18 19.9	14 26.5
30 12.3	21 17.1	27 13.4		38 9.6	26 14.2	26 13.8	30 12.3	30 12.1	25 14.3
44 8.4	39 9.4	44 8.3		177 2.1	41 8.9	42 8.8	48 7.6	49 7.4	40 9.1
5.7	5.3	4.0	Sales/Working Capital	1.0	2.5	4.0	4.1	4.7	3.9
10.5	10.9	8.3		NM	5.3	7.8	8.3	10.9	7.2
25.7	29.2	21.0		-7.2	25.6	10.8	30.3	22.7	17.1
10.7	13.2	8.8	EBIT/Interest	11.8	6.5	6.0	7.3	9.3	9.3
(617) 4.0	(656) 5.1	(629) 2.3		(17) 1.8	(33) -.3	(53) 2.2	(94) 1.5	(153) 2.5	(279) 2.7
1.7	1.6	-.7		-6.2	-4.5	-1.9	-1.4	-.5	.0
10.2	13.2	6.3	Net Profit + Depr., Dep., Amort./Cur. Mat. L/T/D				4.2	3.1	8.2
(174) 4.0	(153) 4.3	(161) 1.9					(22) 1.7	(39) 1.4	(89) 2.3
1.7	1.6	.3					1.2	.0	.3
.1	.1	.1	Fixed/Worth	.0	.0	.0	.1	.1	.1
.2	.2	.3		.8	.1	.2	.2	.3	.3
.6	.7	.8		-1.1	.5	.7	.9	.9	.7
.9	.8	.7	Debt/Worth	.3	.4	.6	.6	1.0	.7
2.2	1.9	1.7		11.8	1.8	1.6	1.7	2.2	1.5
5.1	5.0	4.6		-2.8	11.6	4.7	5.1	4.4	4.0
51.0	57.5	28.1	% Profit Before Taxes/Tangible Net Worth	24.5	25.9	38.1	17.1	37.2	26.2
(634) 27.7	(649) 27.1	(627) 8.7		(14) 2.8	(36) -4.0	(55) 4.7	(95) 7.1	(157) 11.5	(270) 11.1
11.2	8.0	-5.3		-8.2	-24.3	-8.3	-5.1	-4.3	-3.6
17.4	19.9	10.0	% Profit Before Taxes/Total Assets	19.9	7.5	9.9	8.4	9.9	10.4
8.8	8.5	2.8		3.7	-1.3	2.0	1.8	3.1	3.3
2.3	1.9	-3.3		-8.8	-7.4	-2.7	-3.5	-3.2	-2.2
200.7	228.3	142.7	Sales/Net Fixed Assets	UND	202.4	374.2	120.0	112.3	127.7
38.1	42.6	28.4		20.2	61.9	41.0	46.2	27.7	19.9
14.7	16.6	9.0		2.4	17.7	9.2	10.6	8.0	8.6
3.9	4.4	3.2	Sales/Total Assets	2.8	2.8	3.5	3.2	3.1	3.2
2.8	3.1	2.4		1.3	2.0	2.4	2.5	2.3	2.4
2.1	2.2	1.7		.5	1.2	1.8	1.7	1.7	1.8
.2	.2	.3	% Depr., Dep., Amort./Sales	.7	.3	.4	.3	.4	.3
(568) .6	(577) .6	(575) .9		(15) 2.4	(30) .9	(43) 1.0	(86) .9	(140) .8	(261) .9
1.2	1.1	1.8		8.3	1.5	1.8	1.9	1.7	1.6
1.1	1.0	1.3	% Officers', Directors' Owners' Comp/Sales		2.9	2.1	1.9	1.1	.8
(256) 2.3	(269) 2.2	(249) 2.3		(19) 5.9	(32) 3.8	(54) 3.2	(73) 2.0	(67) 1.3	
3.9	4.7	4.7			10.3	6.2	5.5	3.9	2.4
41914843M	53073352M	38713803M	Net Sales ($)	13289M	91539M	234510M	820490M	2813942M	34740033M
15379804M	17351241M	16272173M	Total Assets ($)	23679M	61566M	108117M	408209M	1472047M	14198555M

Current Data Sorted by Assets | Comparative Historical Data

Type of Statement

		2-10MM	10-50MM	50-100MM	100-250MM	Type of Statement		
			3	6	1	Unqualified	10	10
	2	7	5			Reviewed	4	12
1	2	1	1			Compiled	11	11
1	2	3	1			Tax Returns		3
1	1	4	8	5	1	Other	17	14
	9 (4/1-9/30/09)		47 (10/1/09-3/31/10)				4/1/05-3/31/06 ALL	4/1/06-3/31/07 ALL
0-500M	500M-2MM	2-10MM	10-50MM	50-100MM	100-250MM			
3	7	15	18	11	2	NUMBER OF STATEMENTS	42	50
%	%	%	%	%	%		%	%

ASSETS

0-500M	500M-2MM	2-10MM	10-50MM	50-100MM	100-250MM		4/1/05-3/31/06	4/1/06-3/31/07
		14.6	11.9	8.5		Cash & Equivalents	9.9	8.3
		41.1	25.5	22.6		Trade Receivables (net)	33.3	40.7
		17.0	31.5	28.8		Inventory	19.9	22.1
		2.3	3.9	4.3		All Other Current	1.9	1.9
		74.9	72.9	64.2		Total Current	64.9	73.0
		16.4	14.9	27.5		Fixed Assets (net)	20.4	16.2
		.2	3.3	1.4		Intangibles (net)	2.8	2.2
		8.5	9.0	6.9		All Other Non-Current	11.8	8.5
		100.0	100.0	100.0		Total	100.0	100.0

LIABILITIES

0-500M	500M-2MM	2-10MM	10-50MM	50-100MM	100-250MM		4/1/05-3/31/06	4/1/06-3/31/07
		19.7	10.9	3.8		Notes Payable-Short Term	16.4	12.1
		1.1	3.2	1.6		Cur. Mat.-L.T.D.	3.6	5.1
		20.4	11.3	14.3		Trade Payables	20.0	24.8
		.6	.4	.0		Income Taxes Payable	.2	.2
		5.2	9.9	6.4		All Other Current	9.9	10.9
		47.0	35.6	26.1		Total Current	50.1	53.1
		12.4	17.3	7.7		Long-Term Debt	11.1	11.1
		.0	.0	.2		Deferred Taxes	.1	.1
		3.5	5.4	2.7		All Other Non-Current	4.1	5.3
		37.1	41.7	63.4		Net Worth	34.5	30.3
		100.0	100.0	100.0		Total Liabilities & Net Worth	100.0	100.0

INCOME DATA

0-500M	500M-2MM	2-10MM	10-50MM	50-100MM	100-250MM		4/1/05-3/31/06	4/1/06-3/31/07
		100.0	100.0	100.0		Net Sales	100.0	100.0
		11.1	16.9	19.2		Gross Profit	12.1	18.0
		9.2	12.4	9.2		Operating Expenses	10.8	13.7
		1.8	4.4	10.0		Operating Profit	1.3	4.3
		.8	2.1	1.8		All Other Expenses (net)	-.3	.4
		1.0	2.3	8.2		Profit Before Taxes	1.7	3.9

RATIOS

0-500M	500M-2MM	2-10MM	10-50MM	50-100MM	100-250MM		4/1/05-3/31/06	4/1/06-3/31/07
		2.8	4.3	3.3		Current	1.7	2.1
		1.7	2.2	2.5			1.3	1.2
		1.3	1.3	1.4			1.0	1.0
		2.1	3.4	1.9		Quick	1.3	1.3
		1.2	.9	1.4			.9	.9
		.8	.5	.7			.4	.5
		19 19.4	26 13.8	21 17.1		Sales/Receivables	19 18.8	22 16.3
		21 17.7	38 9.6	33 11.2			35 10.3	32 11.5
		44 8.3	47 7.7	51 7.2			48 7.6	45 8.1
		0 UND	18 20.5	14 26.1		Cost of Sales/Inventory	0 UND	0 UND
		9 39.8	50 7.3	45 8.1			20 18.6	29 12.8
		43 8.5	94 3.9	77 4.7			57 6.4	61 6.0
		8 47.9	8 44.7	18 19.9		Cost of Sales/Payables	14 25.9	10 37.5
		24 15.4	16 23.0	29 12.6			22 16.7	22 16.5
		34 10.7	31 11.9	57 6.4			29 12.6	40 9.1
		5.7	4.1	3.7		Sales/Working Capital	9.6	8.0
		16.7	7.1	6.6			18.4	45.8
		49.4	16.7	14.5			-755.9	-536.0
		51.8	21.4	21.2		EBIT/Interest	16.5	13.4
		2.4	(16) 4.4	7.5			(39) 5.3	(47) 4.3
		1.1	1.1	2.1			.8	1.7
						Net Profit + Depr., Dep., Amort./Cur. Mat. L/T/D		5.4
								(12) 3.0
								.9
		.0	.0	.1		Fixed/Worth	.1	.1
		.3	.2	.1			.5	.3
		3.2	1.2	1.1			1.7	1.7
		.7	.9	.3		Debt/Worth	1.0	1.0
		2.0	1.7	.5			2.4	2.9
		12.1	3.3	1.3			5.0	11.0
		31.5	55.5	35.4		% Profit Before Taxes/Tangible Net Worth	56.3	55.7
	(14)	16.6	(16) 21.5	13.6			(39) 26.2	(45) 29.8
		5.1	1.8	3.3			12.2	14.6
		13.7	17.2	18.5		% Profit Before Taxes/Total Assets	17.5	17.3
		3.2	7.0	7.4			9.5	7.2
		.3	.0	1.6			-.1	2.5
		999.8	312.6	112.4		Sales/Net Fixed Assets	231.7	336.9
		49.6	28.3	22.3			22.4	67.4
		9.3	9.4	2.1			5.6	11.8
		6.6	3.7	3.5		Sales/Total Assets	5.2	7.0
		4.2	2.5	2.3			3.1	3.7
		1.9	1.3	1.2			1.9	2.1
		.0	.1			% Depr., Dep., Amort./Sales	.1	.1
	(13)	.1	(10) 2.7				(35) .7	(40) .4
		3.7	5.2				3.2	1.7
						% Officers', Directors' Owners' Comp/Sales	1.0	.6
							(14) 1.7	(10) 1.4
							2.4	3.0
18471M	92501M	420595M	1174285M	1598321M	631946M	Net Sales ($)	2693111M	3272445M
925M	8830M	81563M	458916M	673011M	310353M	Total Assets ($)	1117648M	947670M

© RMA 2010

M = $ thousand   MM = $ million
See Pages 9 through 22 for Explanation of Ratios and Data

Comparative Historical Data

Current Data Sorted by Sales

4/1/07-3/31/08 ALL	4/1/08-3/31/09 ALL	4/1/09-3/31/10 ALL	Type of Statement	0-1MM	1-3MM	3-5MM	5-10MM	10-25MM	25MM & OVER
12	9	10	Unqualified					1	9
9	13	14	Reviewed				3	5	6
10	5	5	Compiled		1			2	2
4	3	7	Tax Returns		1	1	2	2	1
15	20	20	Other	2	1		2		15
					9 (4/1-9/30/09)			47 (10/1/09-3/31/10)	
50	50	56	NUMBER OF STATEMENTS	2	3	1	7	10	33
%	%	%	**ASSETS**	%	%	%	%	%	%
12.4	9.2	14.5	Cash & Equivalents					16.8	13.2
31.6	33.1	29.2	Trade Receivables (net)					30.9	29.5
23.8	23.6	24.0	Inventory					20.2	26.8
2.6	7.4	5.7	All Other Current					1.2	5.8
70.4	73.3	73.4	Total Current					69.1	75.4
22.6	17.4	16.5	Fixed Assets (net)					20.7	15.9
1.8	2.5	2.5	Intangibles (net)					.3	2.2
5.3	6.8	7.6	All Other Non-Current					9.9	6.5
100.0	100.0	100.0	Total					100.0	100.0
			LIABILITIES						
12.9	13.7	14.5	Notes Payable-Short Term					11.2	11.8
2.2	1.5	3.5	Cur. Mat.-L.T.D.					1.8	2.8
20.1	25.2	16.0	Trade Payables					16.9	16.5
.1	.3	.5	Income Taxes Payable					1.6	.2
10.6	14.1	11.3	All Other Current					14.3	8.4
45.9	54.9	45.8	Total Current					45.9	39.7
13.2	7.3	14.9	Long-Term Debt					16.4	12.2
.0	.1	.0	Deferred Taxes					.0	.1
4.9	4.3	3.5	All Other Non-Current					.8	4.6
35.9	33.3	35.7	Net Worth					36.9	43.4
100.0	100.0	100.0	Total Liabilities & Net Worth					100.0	100.0
			INCOME DATA						
100.0	100.0	100.0	Net Sales					100.0	100.0
21.8	12.4	18.6	Gross Profit					24.9	11.5
16.9	8.2	13.0	Operating Expenses					15.5	8.5
4.9	4.2	5.6	Operating Profit					9.4	3.0
.9	.6	1.7	All Other Expenses (net)					.1	.6
4.1	3.6	3.9	Profit Before Taxes					9.3	2.4
			RATIOS						
2.5	2.4	3.0	Current					4.1	3.0
1.5	1.3	1.7						1.8	2.1
1.0	1.0	1.1						1.1	1.3
1.7	1.3	1.7	Quick					2.3	1.9
.9	1.0	1.0						1.3	1.0
.5	.4	.6						.8	.6
21 17.7	18 20.4	19 18.8	Sales/Receivables					20 17.9	21 17.4
33 11.1	26 14.1	33 11.1						40 9.1	33 11.2
44 8.3	43 8.5	46 8.0						59 6.2	44 8.4
0 UND	0 UND	0 UND	Cost of Sales/Inventory					0 UND	13 27.5
28 12.8	15 24.4	35 10.5						31 11.8	37 9.9
52 7.0	56 6.6	72 5.0						87 4.2	72 5.1
11 32.6	10 36.3	8 44.1	Cost of Sales/Payables					15 24.2	9 40.3
22 16.6	23 16.1	22 16.8						35 10.5	22 16.9
39 9.3	39 9.2	35 10.3						37 10.0	32 11.6
7.4	7.6	4.9	Sales/Working Capital					3.1	4.9
18.2	23.6	10.8						10.9	9.7
NM	926.7	43.0						NM	29.4
35.9	28.5	20.8	EBIT/Interest						22.7
(49) 6.5	(47) 6.8	(52) 6.4						(32) 5.7	
1.9	1.4	1.6						1.4	
		10.0	Net Profit + Depr., Dep., Amort./Cur. Mat. L/T/D						
		(13) 2.3							
		-.7							
.0	.0	.0	Fixed/Worth					.0	.0
.3	.3	.3						1.1	.2
.8	1.5	1.4						-1.6	1.0
.7	.9	.7	Debt/Worth					.2	.7
2.0	2.9	1.9						1.7	1.3
4.5	6.4	8.3						-68.1	3.3
50.3	61.2	37.9	% Profit Before Taxes/Tangible Net Worth						42.9
(47) 25.7	(47) 28.5	(48) 19.2						(31) 13.6	
15.1	4.0	4.3							3.3
16.8	21.3	15.6	% Profit Before Taxes/Total Assets					15.9	17.4
9.1	6.8	7.0						14.0	6.6
3.3	.7	1.4						2.7	1.5
765.3	986.7	543.9	Sales/Net Fixed Assets					664.5	758.5
50.8	45.8	45.0						159.5	40.4
5.7	9.8	9.4						5.5	12.0
5.0	6.4	4.7	Sales/Total Assets					5.3	4.5
3.4	3.6	2.9						3.2	3.3
1.7	2.4	1.6						1.4	1.8
.1	.1	.1	% Depr., Dep., Amort./Sales						.1
(39) .8	(39) .7	(40) .9						(23) .9	
5.1	1.7	4.3							4.4
1.0	.3	.8	% Officers', Directors' Owners' Comp/Sales						
(11) 1.6	(12) 1.1	(17) 1.5							
4.1	2.4	3.1							
4610038M	5939018M	3936119M	Net Sales ($)	987M	5965M	4918M	47799M	161795M	3714655M
1153000M	1312159M	1533598M	Total Assets ($)	13897M	2210M	2630M	24358M	142674M	1347829M

M = $ thousand   MM = $ million
See Pages 9 through 22 for Explanation of Ratios and Data

Current Data Sorted by Assets   **Comparative Historical Data**

Type of Statement

0-500M	500M-2MM	2-10MM	10-50MM	50-100MM	100-250MM	Type of Statement	4/1/05-3/31/06 ALL	4/1/06-3/31/07 ALL
		12	24	17	8	Unqualified	89	88
2	20	80	41	2	2	Reviewed	136	154
2	34	43	6	4	1	Compiled	93	109
11	44	26	5			Tax Returns	46	52
5	38	82	64	16	14	Other	164	184
	94 (4/1-9/30/09)		509 (10/1/09-3/31/10)					
20	136	243	140	39	25	**NUMBER OF STATEMENTS**	528	587
%	%	%	%	%	%	**ASSETS**	%	%
16.8	11.8	8.1	7.9	6.6	9.6	Cash & Equivalents	6.1	7.0
16.5	33.7	37.4	35.5	30.5	35.9	Trade Receivables (net)	40.0	39.6
31.6	35.5	33.4	34.7	27.4	31.9	Inventory	33.4	33.1
6.5	1.8	2.4	2.2	3.7	3.0	All Other Current	2.1	2.1
71.3	82.8	81.3	80.4	68.2	80.5	Total Current	81.6	81.7
10.3	8.7	11.5	11.1	19.9	8.3	Fixed Assets (net)	10.5	10.5
7.2	2.4	2.1	4.0	6.5	8.7	Intangibles (net)	3.0	3.0
11.2	6.1	5.0	4.6	5.4	2.6	All Other Non-Current	4.9	4.8
100.0	100.0	100.0	100.0	100.0	100.0	Total	100.0	100.0
						LIABILITIES		
30.0	15.2	15.2	14.2	6.0	.9	Notes Payable-Short Term	15.1	15.8
4.8	3.2	2.3	1.4	2.6	1.0	Cur. Mat.-L.T.D.	2.2	2.4
17.9	21.7	22.5	20.1	16.3	19.4	Trade Payables	24.1	24.1
.1	.0	.2	.1	.2	.2	Income Taxes Payable	.3	.3
15.5	8.3	7.2	8.8	9.5	11.5	All Other Current	9.8	9.8
68.4	48.5	47.3	44.6	34.5	33.0	Total Current	51.5	52.4
5.2	8.0	6.0	7.7	21.0	8.0	Long-Term Debt	9.1	8.4
.0	.0	.3	.2	.0	.0	Deferred Taxes	.1	.1
15.2	6.0	4.5	4.4	2.9	5.8	All Other Non-Current	4.9	4.4
11.3	37.5	42.0	43.2	41.6	53.1	Net Worth	34.3	34.7
100.0	100.0	100.0	100.0	100.0	100.0	Total Liabilities & Net Worth	100.0	100.0
						INCOME DATA		
100.0	100.0	100.0	100.0	100.0	100.0	Net Sales	100.0	100.0
43.1	33.6	29.7	25.3	26.0	24.3	Gross Profit	27.7	28.2
42.6	31.6	26.6	22.0	21.2	21.9	Operating Expenses	23.8	23.5
.5	2.1	3.1	3.3	4.9	2.4	Operating Profit	3.9	4.7
.5	.5	.3	.5	.8	.0	All Other Expenses (net)	.5	.5
.0	1.5	2.8	2.8	4.0	2.3	Profit Before Taxes	3.4	4.3
						RATIOS		
3.2	2.9	2.8	2.5	3.1	4.0	Current	2.3	2.3
1.4	1.8	1.7	1.9	1.7	2.7		1.6	1.6
.7	1.3	1.3	1.4	1.4	1.7		1.2	1.2
1.3	1.8	1.5	1.4	2.1	2.1	Quick	1.3	1.3
.7	.9	.9	1.0	1.0	1.6		.9	.9
.2	.6	.6	.6	.7	.9		.7	.6
0 UND	29 12.7	37 9.7	44 8.3	39 9.5	42 8.7	Sales/Receivables	39 9.3	37 9.8
15 24.2	40 9.2	48 7.6	50 7.3	47 7.8	54 6.7		49 7.4	48 7.6
30 12.3	53 6.9	61 6.0	61 6.0	60 6.1	66 5.5		62 5.9	58 6.2
2 230.6	26 14.0	36 10.1	42 8.6	33 11.0	38 9.5	Cost of Sales/Inventory	34 10.6	32 11.3
51 7.1	70 5.2	58 6.3	61 5.9	55 6.6	56 6.5		56 6.6	52 7.0
74 4.9	120 3.1	102 3.6	114 3.2	87 4.2	109 3.4		85 4.3	85 4.3
2 154.9	18 20.0	27 13.6	24 15.1	22 16.3	28 13.3	Cost of Sales/Payables	27 13.6	24 14.9
32 11.5	32 11.3	38 9.7	37 9.9	27 13.3	34 10.6		40 9.2	36 10.1
54 6.8	53 6.8	53 6.9	49 7.4	36 10.2	54 6.8		52 7.0	49 7.4
8.7	4.8	5.0	5.1	4.1	3.7	Sales/Working Capital	6.0	6.2
27.4	8.5	7.9	7.4	8.5	5.5		10.5	9.7
-159.6	20.4	20.9	11.2	12.5	8.3		21.4	22.6
3.9	8.2	11.1	14.2	25.3	26.5	EBIT/Interest	11.8	15.1
(15) .2	(115) 1.8	(219) 3.6	(129) 5.0	(35) 6.5	(23) 11.9		(473) 4.7	(523) 5.2
-6.8	-1.1	1.2	1.4	2.3	1.8		2.0	2.2
	3.9	6.3	7.7	19.3		Net Profit + Depr., Dep., Amort./Cur. Mat. L/T/D	12.6	14.5
	(15) 1.9	(57) 2.8	(40) 2.0	(11) 11.4			(152) 4.7	(155) 5.4
	.1	1.3	.1	1.9			1.7	1.9
.0	.0	.1	.1	.1	.0	Fixed/Worth	.1	.1
.3	.1	.2	.2	.4	.1		.2	.2
3.0	.5	.5	.5	1.5	.4		.6	.6
.6	.6	.6	.8	.6	.5	Debt/Worth	1.0	.9
3.8	1.8	1.7	1.5	1.9	.9		2.2	1.9
-45.6	5.3	3.5	2.7	2.9	2.9		4.6	5.1
57.4	39.3	33.1	24.6	22.9	29.0	% Profit Before Taxes/Tangible Net Worth	45.1	54.1
(14) -5.3	(120) 5.9	(231) 11.1	(132) 9.9	(35) 16.3	(24) 17.1		(484) 23.8	(527) 30.9
-41.4	-6.9	1.4	2.5	3.7	1.9		7.8	13.7
15.8	12.4	10.1	9.1	14.3	11.9	% Profit Before Taxes/Total Assets	13.5	18.9
-.5	2.3	3.7	4.1	6.3	5.7		7.3	9.5
-7.9	-2.3	.4	1.1	2.2	.8		2.2	3.4
UND	243.9	104.2	72.6	55.2	118.6	Sales/Net Fixed Assets	93.4	117.0
191.3	59.7	43.6	37.4	17.4	63.8		42.3	46.8
32.0	26.1	20.1	14.2	7.8	17.8		21.7	21.1
6.6	4.0	3.4	3.2	3.4	3.1	Sales/Total Assets	3.6	3.7
3.5	3.0	2.7	2.4	2.5	2.3		2.9	3.0
2.6	2.2	2.1	1.8	1.8	2.1		2.2	2.3
.2	.2	.4	.4	.4	.3	% Depr., Dep., Amort./Sales	.3	.3
(10) .6	(93) .7	(204) .6	(124) .6	(33) 1.0	(21) .5		(452) .6	(493) .5
1.4	1.3	1.2	1.0	1.8	1.6		.9	1.0
	3.4	1.6	1.0			% Officers', Directors' Owners' Comp/Sales	1.7	1.7
	(76) 6.3	(110) 3.2	(37) 1.6				(208) 3.3	(213) 3.2
	10.9	5.7	2.8				6.4	6.2
29994M	495606M	3583470M	7175316M	7605753M	8671297M	Net Sales ($)	19739434M	25229382M
5891M	155727M	1291668M	2954181M	2952691M	3495052M	Total Assets ($)	7230374M	8711042M

M = $ thousand   MM = $ million
See Pages 9 through 22 for Explanation of Ratios and Data

Comparative Historical Data

Current Data Sorted by Sales

	69 75 61			Type of Statement						

	4/1/07-3/31/08 ALL	4/1/08-3/31/09 ALL	4/1/09-3/31/10 ALL		0-1MM	1-3MM	3-5MM	5-10MM	10-25MM	25MM & OVER
Unqualified	69	75	61					3	9	49
Reviewed	129	135	147		1	9	8	23	61	45
Compiled	104	100	90		3	16	16	18	21	16
Tax Returns	62	83	86		6	26	14	21	15	4
Other	170	203	219		3	26	12	29	53	96
					94 (4/1-9/30/09)			509 (10/1/09-3/31/10)		
NUMBER OF STATEMENTS	**534**	**596**	**603**		**13**	**77**	**50**	**94**	**159**	**210**
ASSETS	%	%	%		%	%	%	%	%	%
Cash & Equivalents	7.4	8.3	9.1		11.0	11.5	9.9	11.1	9.0	7.2
Trade Receivables (net)	37.4	35.2	34.9		16.4	26.0	34.3	36.1	36.7	37.6
Inventory	33.5	34.7	33.7		22.3	40.7	33.5	29.6	34.6	33.0
All Other Current	2.2	2.3	2.5		9.6	1.6	1.7	2.0	2.6	2.7
Total Current	80.6	80.5	80.2		59.2	79.8	79.4	78.8	83.0	80.5
Fixed Assets (net)	11.8	11.0	11.2		12.4	10.1	8.9	13.4	11.1	11.0
Intangibles (net)	3.2	2.9	3.3		7.9	4.2	3.4	2.4	1.8	4.3
All Other Non-Current	4.5	5.6	5.3		20.4	6.0	8.3	5.4	4.1	4.2
Total	100.0	100.0	100.0		100.0	100.0	100.0	100.0	100.0	100.0
LIABILITIES										
Notes Payable-Short Term	14.2	14.9	14.3		5.2	22.9	16.3	13.7	14.8	11.0
Cur. Mat.-L.T.D.	2.4	2.1	2.4		5.7	4.6	2.1	3.4	1.4	1.6
Trade Payables	23.6	21.6	21.1		14.6	17.6	20.9	21.7	22.3	21.6
Income Taxes Payable	.4	.1	.1		.0	.0	.1	.0	.3	.1
All Other Current	9.1	8.9	8.4		5.3	9.6	7.8	8.4	6.8	9.5
Total Current	49.6	47.7	46.2		30.7	54.7	47.2	47.2	45.7	43.8
Long-Term Debt	10.0	9.7	7.9		6.2	8.9	7.1	7.5	7.1	8.5
Deferred Taxes	.1	.2	.2		.0	.0	.0	.3	.2	.1
All Other Non-Current	5.5	4.2	5.1		12.3	10.3	2.8	4.4	3.9	4.5
Net Worth	34.9	38.2	40.7		50.7	26.1	42.9	40.6	43.0	43.1
Total Liabilities & Net Worth	100.0	100.0	100.0		100.0	100.0	100.0	100.0	100.0	100.0
INCOME DATA										
Net Sales	100.0	100.0	100.0		100.0	100.0	100.0	100.0	100.0	100.0
Gross Profit	28.9	28.9	29.5		43.0	35.7	32.4	34.3	29.3	23.8
Operating Expenses	24.2	25.1	26.6		42.3	33.9	32.3	30.4	25.8	20.6
Operating Profit	4.7	3.8	2.9		.7	1.8	.1	3.9	3.5	3.2
All Other Expenses (net)	.5	.4	.4		.9	.8	-.1	.3	.5	.3
Profit Before Taxes	4.2	3.3	2.5		-.2	1.0	.2	3.6	3.0	2.9
RATIOS										
Current	2.5	2.6	2.8		6.1	3.5	2.5	2.7	3.0	2.6
	1.7	1.7	1.8		1.6	1.9	1.7	1.6	1.8	1.9
	1.3	1.3	1.3		1.1	1.1	1.2	1.2	1.3	1.4
Quick	1.4	1.4	1.6		2.3	1.8	1.5	1.7	1.7	1.6
	.9	.9	.9		1.2	.8	.9	.9	1.0	1.0
	.6	.6	.6		.2	.4	.6	.6	.7	.7
Sales/Receivables	34 10.7	32 11.3	35 10.3		12 29.3	27 13.7	29 12.4	33 11.2	38 9.7	42 8.6
	46 7.9	40 9.0	47 7.8		28 13.2	37 9.9	42 8.6	46 8.0	48 7.6	48 7.6
	59 6.2	53 6.8	59 6.1		59 6.2	51 7.1	53 6.9	62 5.9	60 6.1	61 6.0
Cost of Sales/Inventory	34 10.9	32 11.3	36 10.2		0 UND	62 5.9	24 15.1	24 15.2	38 9.7	37 9.8
	55 6.6	57 6.5	60 6.1		49 7.4	101 3.6	57 6.4	57 6.4	64 5.7	53 6.9
	92 4.0	90 4.0	105 3.5		161 2.3	145 2.5	96 3.8	105 3.5	105 3.5	84 4.3
Cost of Sales/Payables	24 14.9	20 18.3	23 15.7		28 13.0	14 27.0	20 18.6	27 13.8	28 12.9	24 15.0
	36 10.0	31 11.7	36 10.2		45 8.1	28 13.1	34 10.6	36 10.1	38 9.5	34 10.6
	53 6.9	47 7.7	50 7.3		73 5.0	57 6.4	55 6.6	49 7.4	53 6.9	47 7.8
Sales/Working Capital	6.0	5.5	4.9		2.4	3.6	6.1	5.8	4.3	5.2
	9.7	9.1	7.8		5.7	6.8	9.1	9.1	7.5	7.8
	18.7	18.4	16.0		NM	81.6	21.7	21.9	18.6	11.7
EBIT/Interest	13.9	16.3	12.9			6.2	5.5	12.2	13.1	18.1
	(481) 5.1	(531) 5.4	(536) 3.7			(69) 1.7	(41) 1.4	(81) 3.9	(146) 3.4	(192) 5.9
	1.8	1.7	1.0			-2.2	-2.8	1.1	1.5	1.5
Net Profit + Depr., Dep., Amort./Cur. Mat. L/T/D	14.3	12.6	6.4					8.1	6.7	11.5
	(156) 4.7	(154) 4.2	(128) 2.5					(19) 3.6	(38) 2.3	(57) 3.3
	1.8	1.9	.9					.2	1.0	1.1
Fixed/Worth	.1	.1	.1		.0	.0	.0	.1	.1	.1
	.2	.2	.2		.2	.1	.2	.3	.2	.2
	.6	.6	.5		.5	1.3	.7	.7	.5	.5
Debt/Worth	.9	.7	.6		.2	.6	.6	.6	.7	.7
	1.8	1.6	1.6		.9	2.1	1.9	1.8	1.6	1.5
	4.3	4.1	3.6		3.4	NM	4.3	3.8	3.1	2.9
% Profit Before Taxes/Tangible Net Worth	48.2	43.8	30.8		8.3	34.7	38.0	40.9	29.3	28.6
	(486) 26.1	(544) 23.0	(556) 10.5		(12) -9.7	(58) 4.2	(46) 2.8	(88) 15.0	(153) 10.7	(199) 12.6
	8.9	6.9	.7		-26.4	-16.8	-6.7	1.0	2.4	3.1
% Profit Before Taxes/Total Assets	17.1	16.0	11.2		8.5	10.7	6.2	13.1	10.9	11.1
	9.0	7.5	3.7		-5.4	1.9	1.0	4.8	3.7	4.9
	2.3	1.6	.1		-14.3	-5.1	-3.4	.4	1.1	1.3
Sales/Net Fixed Assets	95.1	115.3	114.0		UND	183.5	211.0	116.7	99.0	91.2
	41.1	47.0	43.4		211.7	48.0	54.7	38.5	42.7	41.6
	19.0	20.2	17.7		7.5	18.6	25.2	12.9	19.2	16.9
Sales/Total Assets	3.6	3.8	3.5		2.4	3.2	4.1	3.8	3.3	3.4
	2.9	3.0	2.7		1.8	2.5	3.1	2.6	2.7	2.7
	2.2	2.3	2.0		.7	1.8	2.1	1.9	2.1	2.0
% Depr., Dep., Amort./Sales	.3	.3	.4			.5	.1	.3	.4	.4
	(437) .6	(476) .6	(485) .6			(49) .7	(39) .7	(76) .8	(134) .6	(182) .5
	1.1	1.0	1.2			1.3	1.3	1.6	1.1	1.1
% Officers', Directors' Owners' Comp/Sales	1.7	1.7	1.8			4.2	2.9	2.6	1.3	1.0
	(216) 3.5	(224) 3.4	(239) 3.5			(40) 7.6	(32) 5.1	(48) 3.6	(66) 2.5	(48) 1.9
	6.0	6.9	7.4			12.3	9.3	6.2	4.9	3.0
Net Sales ($)	26241237M	29206552M	27561436M		8051M	161272M	207223M	692739M	2569180M	23922971M
Total Assets ($)	9225007M	10307329M	10855210M		6257M	76378M	76063M	304007M	1104728M	9287777M

M = $ thousand   MM = $ million
See Pages 9 through 22 for Explanation of Ratios and Data

Current Data Sorted by Assets   Comparative Historical Data

	0-500M	500M-2MM	2-10MM	10-50MM	50-100MM	100-250MM	Type of Statement	ALL 4/1/05-3/31/06	ALL 4/1/06-3/31/07
			3	9	4	3	Unqualified	22	27
	1	1	17	6			Reviewed	28	27
	1	7	10				Compiled	21	20
	2	10	9	1			Tax Returns	11	11
	1	8	24	23	3	2	Other	47	50
		23 (4/1-9/30/09)		122 (10/1/09-3/31/10)					
	5	26	63	39	7	5	**NUMBER OF STATEMENTS**	129	135
	%	%	%	%	%	%	**ASSETS**	%	%
		9.5	10.9	11.1			Cash & Equivalents	9.1	8.2
		32.6	34.3	23.5			Trade Receivables (net)	33.2	34.7
		41.9	41.1	40.5			Inventory	41.5	40.5
		2.4	1.9	2.6			All Other Current	1.8	1.9
		86.4	88.1	77.6			Total Current	85.5	85.4
		8.3	8.1	11.8			Fixed Assets (net)	8.5	7.7
		2.1	.8	5.0			Intangibles (net)	1.9	2.6
		3.3	2.9	5.5			All Other Non-Current	4.1	4.3
		100.0	100.0	100.0			Total	100.0	100.0
							LIABILITIES		
		14.5	16.1	15.8			Notes Payable-Short Term	16.4	17.9
		1.7	1.2	1.4			Cur. Mat.-L.T.D.	1.7	1.7
		28.3	23.6	18.9			Trade Payables	24.3	24.4
		.1	.2	.1			Income Taxes Payable	.3	.2
		7.7	8.4	7.9			All Other Current	9.8	10.9
		52.3	49.4	44.1			Total Current	52.5	55.0
		5.4	5.1	8.0			Long-Term Debt	5.8	5.6
		.0	.0	.0			Deferred Taxes	.1	.1
		7.3	5.6	8.8			All Other Non-Current	3.1	2.9
		35.0	39.9	39.0			Net Worth	38.5	36.3
		100.0	100.0	100.0			Total Liabilities & Net Worth	100.0	100.0
							INCOME DATA		
		100.0	100.0	100.0			Net Sales	100.0	100.0
		30.7	21.7	22.5			Gross Profit	23.6	23.6
		28.4	19.5	20.6			Operating Expenses	20.0	20.6
		2.3	2.2	1.9			Operating Profit	3.7	3.0
		.2	.7	.0			All Other Expenses (net)	.5	.4
		2.2	1.4	1.9			Profit Before Taxes	3.1	2.6
							RATIOS		
		2.8	3.1	2.6			Current	2.4	2.2
		1.6	1.6	1.7				1.6	1.5
		1.4	1.3	1.4				1.2	1.2
		1.2	1.6	1.3			Quick	1.2	1.2
		.9	.9	.8				.8	.7
		.5	.6	.6				.5	.5
		19 19.4	24 15.2	22 16.4			Sales/Receivables	26 13.9	28 12.8
		28 13.2	32 11.3	30 12.1				36 10.3	37 9.9
		35 10.4	52 7.1	42 8.7				52 7.1	47 7.8
		24 15.5	32 11.3	53 6.8			Cost of Sales/Inventory	43 8.5	40 9.1
		59 6.2	57 6.4	72 5.1				63 5.8	62 5.9
		100 3.7	86 4.2	99 3.7				103 3.5	91 4.0
		12 29.3	17 20.9	16 22.2			Cost of Sales/Payables	18 20.6	19 18.8
		50 7.2	28 13.1	25 14.5				32 11.2	32 11.5
		64 5.7	38 9.5	39 9.3				52 7.1	48 7.6
		6.3	5.4	4.8			Sales/Working Capital	5.9	6.5
		9.5	8.7	8.9				10.3	10.6
		22.8	18.9	16.0				21.6	22.1
		7.5	15.4	43.1			EBIT/Interest	15.8	10.7
		(22) 3.4	(57) 4.2	3.6				(109) 5.8	(121) 3.4
		-.2	1.4	-.3				1.9	1.6
				59.8			Net Profit + Depr., Dep., Amort./Cur. Mat. L/T/D	14.8	9.7
			(13) 3.0					(26) 4.2	(29) 4.3
			-.2					1.8	1.1
		.0	.0	.1			Fixed/Worth	.0	.1
		.1	.1	.2				.2	.2
		.3	.3	.5				.5	.4
		.6	.8	.6			Debt/Worth	.8	.9
		1.7	1.7	1.4				1.9	2.0
		6.9	4.2	7.0				4.5	4.7
		21.3	28.2	41.4			% Profit Before Taxes/Tangible Net Worth	52.9	53.6
		(22) 9.4	(60) 11.7	(35) 11.9				(124) 22.2	(128) 18.3
		3.9	2.1	.1				7.5	7.9
		6.6	13.3	10.0			% Profit Before Taxes/Total Assets	16.1	15.0
		3.1	3.8	4.3				7.5	5.8
		-3.2	.3	-.7				2.4	2.0
		409.0	302.0	102.5			Sales/Net Fixed Assets	168.5	171.8
		108.6	86.9	46.9				59.3	60.3
		56.1	25.4	17.3				26.2	29.7
		4.8	4.5	3.4			Sales/Total Assets	4.0	4.0
		3.6	2.9	2.5				3.0	3.1
		2.9	2.4	1.8				2.3	2.5
		.2	.1	.3			% Depr., Dep., Amort./Sales	.2	.2
		(13) .4	(40) .3	(37) .7				(102) .4	(115) .4
		.7	.8	1.4				.7	.8
		1.7	.9				% Officers', Directors' Owners' Comp/Sales	1.4	1.4
		(15) 3.0	(20) 1.9					(44) 2.2	(45) 2.2
		5.4	2.7					4.2	4.4
	5629M	143288M	1114558M	2658589M	1344878M	3069048M	Net Sales ($)	5983439M	7616253M
	1978M	37033M	328895M	883442M	492320M	865159M	Total Assets ($)	2004744M	2493762M

© RMA 2010

M = $ thousand   MM = $ million
See Pages 9 through 22 for Explanation of Ratios and Data

Comparative Historical Data   **Current Data Sorted by Sales**

			Type of Statement	0-1MM	1-3MM	3-5MM	5-10MM	10-25MM	25MM & OVER
22	26	19	Unqualified		1		3	1	18
26	31	25	Reviewed				7	15	6
16	20	18	Compiled	1	1	3	3	6	
12	20	22	Tax Returns			3	3	9	1
51	44	61	Other	3	3	3	11	9	36
4/1/07-3/31/08 ALL	4/1/08-3/31/09 ALL	4/1/09-3/31/10 ALL		|— 23 (4/1-9/30/09) —|			|— 122 (10/1/09-3/31/10) —|		
127	141	145	NUMBER OF STATEMENTS	4	7	9	24	40	61
%	%	%	ASSETS	%	%	%	%	%	%
6.5	7.4	9.9	Cash & Equivalents				8.1	11.5	9.0
32.0	29.4	31.4	Trade Receivables (net)				35.0	32.6	31.0
44.1	42.4	40.6	Inventory				43.1	41.9	40.1
1.9	3.0	2.4	All Other Current				1.5	2.1	2.8
84.4	82.1	84.2	Total Current				87.8	88.0	82.9
8.1	10.0	8.9	Fixed Assets (net)				9.3	8.5	7.7
4.7	3.8	3.0	Intangibles (net)				1.4	.9	5.3
2.8	4.1	3.9	All Other Non-Current				1.6	2.6	4.1
100.0	100.0	100.0	Total				100.0	100.0	100.0
			LIABILITIES						
17.0	18.2	16.5	Notes Payable-Short Term				14.3	18.5	13.1
1.4	2.4	2.0	Cur. Mat.-L.T.D.				.9	1.5	2.1
24.9	23.1	23.4	Trade Payables				28.5	19.9	23.8
.3	.2	.2	Income Taxes Payable				.1	.2	.4
10.4	10.1	9.4	All Other Current				8.1	9.5	9.9
53.9	54.0	51.6	Total Current				51.8	49.7	49.3
6.3	7.8	6.1	Long-Term Debt				6.4	6.3	5.6
.1	.2	.0	Deferred Taxes				.0	.0	.1
3.6	3.1	6.7	All Other Non-Current				2.6	8.3	6.5
36.0	34.9	35.6	Net Worth				39.1	35.7	38.5
100.0	100.0	100.0	Total Liabilities & Net Worth				100.0	100.0	100.0
			INCOME DATA						
100.0	100.0	100.0	Net Sales				100.0	100.0	100.0
25.4	23.8	23.5	Gross Profit				26.3	21.8	21.4
22.0	22.1	21.6	Operating Expenses				25.1	21.4	18.7
3.4	1.7	1.9	Operating Profit				1.2	.4	2.7
1.0	.9	.4	All Other Expenses (net)				-.1	.1	.3
2.4	.8	1.5	Profit Before Taxes				1.3	.3	2.5
			RATIOS						
2.2	2.6	2.6	Current				2.5	3.5	2.5
1.6	1.6	1.6					1.6	1.6	1.6
1.2	1.2	1.2					1.4	1.2	1.3
1.1	1.1	1.5	Quick				1.2	1.9	1.4
.7	.7	.8					.7	.8	.8
.5	.4	.6					.6	.5	.6
26 14.3	21 17.2	23 15.9	Sales/Receivables				25 14.9	23 15.8	23 15.8
34 10.6	32 11.6	31 11.9					29 12.4	32 11.3	31 11.9
47 7.8	47 7.8	49 7.5					56 6.5	50 7.3	50 7.3
46 7.9	41 8.9	39 9.3	Cost of Sales/Inventory				22 16.3	38 9.5	40 9.1
69 5.3	60 6.1	62 5.9					63 5.8	64 5.7	61 6.0
102 3.6	106 3.4	96 3.8					108 3.4	90 4.1	89 4.1
19 19.7	18 20.8	17 21.9	Cost of Sales/Payables				16 22.8	15 23.6	21 17.4
32 11.3	30 12.0	31 11.7					46 7.9	25 14.9	28 13.1
50 7.3	46 8.0	46 7.9					70 5.2	38 9.7	39 9.5
6.6	5.7	5.5	Sales/Working Capital				5.4	5.1	5.6
10.5	11.4	9.7					8.9	9.9	10.5
22.4	27.8	20.7					15.9	24.6	19.2
8.0	13.8	14.1	EBIT/Interest				7.8	8.5	42.2
(111) 3.7	(129) 3.6	(133) 4.0					(20) 2.7	(37) 2.7	5.8
1.3	1.0	.5					.0	-.2	.9
14.1	19.9	54.2	Net Profit + Depr., Dep., Amort./Cur. Mat. L/T/D						228.5
(23) 7.0	(24) 6.0	(22) 2.8						(12) 12.1	
1.1	.8	.0							.1
.1	.1	.0	Fixed/Worth				.0	.1	.1
.2	.2	.2					.1	.1	.2
.5	.5	.4					.2	.5	.5
.9	.8	.8	Debt/Worth				.6	1.0	.7
2.3	2.1	1.9					1.7	2.0	1.7
5.0	5.6	5.0					3.1	4.7	4.9
49.7	31.6	31.1	% Profit Before Taxes/Tangible Net Worth				22.1	18.1	55.8
(115) 23.0	(124) 13.4	(129) 11.6					(21) 11.0	(37) 8.8	(56) 18.1
6.9	1.9	2.2					3.9	-8.3	2.9
13.7	8.5	10.0	% Profit Before Taxes/Total Assets				7.6	6.9	14.1
7.2	4.3	3.7					3.7	2.2	6.0
1.2	.0	-.8					-1.6	-3.1	-.1
178.3	168.0	223.7	Sales/Net Fixed Assets				259.4	189.5	165.7
63.8	62.0	68.7					140.4	71.2	58.8
25.7	22.9	29.9					49.9	21.9	30.4
4.0	4.3	4.3	Sales/Total Assets				4.5	4.5	4.5
3.0	3.1	2.9					3.4	2.9	3.0
2.3	2.0	2.2					2.3	2.4	2.1
.2	.2	.2	% Depr., Dep., Amort./Sales				.1	.2	.2
(105) .4	(116) .4	(103) .4					(13) .4	(29) .4	(52) .4
.9	.8	.8					1.2	.8	.9
1.3	1.2	1.0	% Officers', Directors' Owners' Comp/Sales				1.0	1.0	.5
(41) 2.6	(49) 1.8	(47) 2.0					(14) 2.1	(14) 1.9	(12) 1.2
4.1	4.0						4.2	3.8	1.8
6973602M	7797522M	8335990M	Net Sales ($)	2222M	16089M	37278M	170101M	663810M	7446490M
2711124M	2817052M	2608827M	Total Assets ($)	4636M	5607M	19002M	61506M	231279M	2286797M

M = $ thousand   MM = $ million
See Pages 9 through 22 for Explanation of Ratios and Data

Current Data Sorted by Assets | Comparative Historical Data

	0-500M	500M-2MM	2-10MM	10-50MM	50-100MM	100-250MM	Type of Statement	4/1/05-3/31/06 ALL	4/1/06-3/31/07 ALL
	1		16	27	9	6	Unqualified	67	72
	1	7	54	29	1		Reviewed	102	90
	3	11	28	5			Compiled	63	55
	7	25	7	1			Tax Returns	42	28
	10	27	70	44	12	12	Other	126	117
		75 (4/1-9/30/09)		338 (10/1/09-3/31/10)					
	22	70	175	106	22	18	NUMBER OF STATEMENTS	400	362
	%	%	%	%	%	%	ASSETS	%	%
	26.6	11.4	10.3	8.3	8.5	4.0	Cash & Equivalents	7.6	7.8
	19.0	33.9	33.4	33.7	38.7	36.3	Trade Receivables (net)	37.4	36.5
	30.9	32.8	35.7	34.2	34.2	25.1	Inventory	34.9	34.7
	3.8	3.0	3.2	3.7	4.3	1.6	All Other Current	2.5	2.7
	80.3	81.0	82.7	79.9	85.7	67.0	Total Current	82.4	81.8
	6.2	9.5	7.8	8.4	8.8	8.5	Fixed Assets (net)	9.7	8.8
	5.5	5.5	2.8	6.5	2.4	20.9	Intangibles (net)	3.0	4.0
	8.1	3.9	6.8	5.2	3.1	3.6	All Other Non-Current	4.8	5.4
	100.0	100.0	100.0	100.0	100.0	100.0	Total	100.0	100.0
							LIABILITIES		
	14.2	14.2	16.4	14.6	8.1	6.9	Notes Payable-Short Term	16.3	14.6
	4.0	2.2	1.8	1.6	2.2	1.2	Cur. Mat.-L.T.D.	1.8	1.8
	14.4	28.3	24.8	22.5	22.7	23.0	Trade Payables	24.4	23.8
	.0	.1	.1	.3	.3	.3	Income Taxes Payable	.3	.3
	20.6	9.1	7.9	7.9	11.7	7.2	All Other Current	10.1	10.4
	53.1	53.9	51.1	46.9	45.1	38.6	Total Current	52.8	51.0
	11.0	10.1	5.7	7.5	6.4	19.7	Long-Term Debt	8.0	8.1
	.0	.1	.2	.3	.1	.5	Deferred Taxes	.2	.2
	2.7	7.7	6.6	6.8	2.3	1.5	All Other Non-Current	4.3	3.8
	33.2	28.3	36.5	38.5	46.1	39.7	Net Worth	34.6	37.0
	100.0	100.0	100.0	100.0	100.0	100.0	Total Liabilities & Net Worth	100.0	100.0
							INCOME DATA		
	100.0	100.0	100.0	100.0	100.0	100.0	Net Sales	100.0	100.0
	33.2	34.7	28.3	25.2	22.5	21.6	Gross Profit	30.4	28.9
	29.3	33.4	26.5	21.7	19.7	18.3	Operating Expenses	26.4	25.1
	3.9	1.3	1.9	3.5	2.8	3.3	Operating Profit	4.0	3.8
	1.5	.6	.2	.5	.3	1.0	All Other Expenses (net)	.5	.5
	2.4	.7	1.6	3.0	2.5	2.3	Profit Before Taxes	3.5	3.3
							RATIOS		
	4.5	2.3	2.5	2.4	2.8	3.2	Current	2.2	2.3
	1.6	1.5	1.6	1.6	2.2	1.6		1.5	1.6
	1.1	1.1	1.2	1.3	1.4	1.1		1.2	1.2
	3.6	1.4	1.5	1.5	1.7	1.9	Quick	1.3	1.3
	.9	.8	.8	.8	1.1	.9		.8	.9
	.4	.4	.5	.5	.7	.6		.6	.6
	0 UND	18 20.0	32 11.4	35 10.4	42 8.6	42 8.8	Sales/Receivables	34 10.8	33 11.0
	11 33.4	35 10.3	42 8.6	47 7.7	57 6.4	49 7.4		45 8.1	45 8.1
	36 10.0	47 7.8	60 6.1	64 5.7	67 5.4	69 5.3		58 6.3	57 6.4
	0 UND	19 19.6	36 10.2	30 12.2	28 12.8	30 12.1	Cost of Sales/Inventory	34 10.8	35 10.4
	26 14.0	40 9.1	64 5.7	52 7.1	71 5.2	51 7.2		59 6.2	63 5.8
	70 5.2	101 3.6	109 3.4	110 3.3	133 2.8	78 4.7		97 3.8	98 3.7
	0 UND	16 22.4	26 14.2	25 14.6	22 16.5	28 13.1	Cost of Sales/Payables	24 15.0	21 17.2
	2 154.8	32 11.4	40 9.2	39 9.3	33 11.2	47 7.8		38 9.5	38 9.7
	41 8.8	64 5.7	63 5.8	59 6.2	51 7.2	57 6.5		56 6.5	59 6.2
	7.9	6.4	5.2	4.5	4.0	5.5	Sales/Working Capital	6.1	5.6
	20.4	15.6	9.5	8.7	5.4	9.9		11.1	10.1
	374.3	87.9	22.3	17.2	18.6	34.7		24.9	22.1
	19.5	11.9	12.9	25.5	55.8	10.0	EBIT/Interest	13.9	13.1
	(14) 3.9	(57) 3.7	(153) 3.2	(98) 6.5	(21) 7.9	(17) 3.6		(356) 4.7	(326) 4.2
	1.2	-.2	1.2	1.3	-2.5	2.1		1.8	1.7
			8.5	31.4	27.9		Net Profit + Depr., Dep., Amort./Cur. Mat. L/T/D	12.7	10.6
		(32) 1.9	1.9	(24) 4.3	(10) 10.5			(94) 3.8	(83) 3.5
		.7	.7	1.8	2.0			1.5	1.1
	.0	.0	.0	.1	.1	.2	Fixed/Worth	.1	.1
	.0	.3	.2	.1	.1	.4		.2	.2
	.3	1.2	.5	.7	.4	-.7		.6	.6
	.4	1.1	.8	.9	.7	1.5	Debt/Worth	1.0	.8
	1.8	2.3	2.2	2.0	1.3	3.4		2.1	2.0
	11.9	13.4	5.3	5.4	2.9	-5.6		4.7	4.8
	112.5	36.4	32.3	31.0	39.7	25.2	% Profit Before Taxes/Tangible Net Worth	47.5	46.5
	(18) 76.0	(57) 17.0	(158) 9.3	(93) 15.7	(21) 21.2	(12) 17.7		(371) 20.8	(327) 20.8
	13.9	-4.5	1.8	2.5	3.8	10.3		6.2	6.9
	46.1	13.1	9.9	14.5	17.5	8.9	% Profit Before Taxes/Total Assets	14.5	17.1
	15.8	4.1	2.7	4.6	9.7	4.9		6.9	6.9
	2.2	-2.8	.2	.6	-1.1	1.7		1.8	1.5
	UND	259.7	158.5	116.6	112.3	62.4	Sales/Net Fixed Assets	134.2	133.1
	413.9	66.0	63.9	63.0	32.7	25.4		54.5	51.4
	49.1	21.4	25.2	22.9	13.6	18.5		22.3	22.0
	9.3	4.9	3.6	3.2	3.4	3.2	Sales/Total Assets	3.8	3.8
	5.2	3.6	2.8	2.5	2.5	2.7		2.9	2.8
	2.8	2.2	2.0	1.7	1.9	1.4		2.2	2.2
		.2	.2	.2	.2	.3	% Depr., Dep., Amort./Sales	.3	.3
		(39) .9	(135) .5	(90) .5	(19) .5	(15) .7		(331) .6	(308) .5
		1.8	1.1	.9	1.3	1.0		1.2	1.1
		3.4	1.9	.9			% Officers', Directors' Owners' Comp/Sales	1.8	1.7
		(38) 5.5	(56) 2.5	(17) 1.3				(143) 4.0	(127) 3.0
		7.1	4.7	2.8				7.3	6.2
	64677M	373319M	2529274M	6347783M	3980836M	6193961M	Net Sales ($)	19388059M	15244374M
	5149M	86633M	917099M	2316518M	1536963M	2646011M	Total Assets ($)	6723973M	6056800M

M = $ thousand   MM = $ million
See Pages 9 through 22 for Explanation of Ratios and Data

Comparative Historical Data · Current Data Sorted by Sales

	4/1/07-3/31/08 ALL	4/1/08-3/31/09 ALL	4/1/09-3/31/10 ALL	Type of Statement	0-1MM	1-3MM	3-5MM	5-10MM	10-25MM	25MM & OVER
	63	80	59	Unqualified	1	1		6	10	41
	78	84	92	Reviewed	2	2	3	18	36	31
	46	42	47	Compiled	1	8	4	9	21	4
	34	44	40	Tax Returns	5	10	8	7	9	1
	105	142	175	Other	6	9	17	29	48	66
					75 (4/1-9/30/09)			338 (10/1/09-3/31/10)		
NUMBER OF STATEMENTS	326	392	413		15	30	32	69	124	143
	%	%	%	ASSETS	%	%	%	%	%	%
Cash & Equivalents	8.9	9.9	10.5		11.6	20.9	10.3	11.9	10.0	8.0
Trade Receivables (net)	37.9	35.0	33.2		18.6	19.3	36.1	31.8	33.3	37.6
Inventory	33.7	33.6	34.1		38.4	37.1	30.2	32.5	35.1	33.7
All Other Current	2.8	2.5	3.3		.7	5.5	4.0	3.9	2.8	3.1
Total Current	83.2	81.1	81.0		69.3	82.9	80.5	80.1	81.2	82.3
Fixed Assets (net)	8.8	8.9	8.2		12.1	5.6	9.7	8.8	8.6	7.4
Intangibles (net)	3.3	3.9	5.1		7.0	4.6	3.0	3.6	5.2	6.1
All Other Non-Current	4.7	6.1	5.6		11.6	6.9	6.8	7.5	5.0	4.2
Total	100.0	100.0	100.0		100.0	100.0	100.0	100.0	100.0	100.0
				LIABILITIES						
Notes Payable-Short Term	15.2	14.4	14.6		15.4	17.7	15.3	14.0	15.6	13.2
Cur. Mat.-L.T.D.	1.5	1.8	1.9		1.9	2.8	5.2	2.0	1.0	1.8
Trade Payables	23.9	22.8	24.1		11.4	19.6	31.8	23.7	23.1	25.6
Income Taxes Payable	.3	.2	.2		.0	.0	.1	.1	.2	.3
All Other Current	10.3	9.3	9.0		16.0	10.9	6.3	8.7	8.0	9.4
Total Current	51.3	48.6	49.7		44.6	50.9	58.7	48.4	47.9	50.2
Long-Term Debt	7.6	7.7	7.8		15.1	7.4	9.9	5.8	7.0	8.4
Deferred Taxes	.2	.1	.2		.0	.0	.0	.4	.2	.2
All Other Non-Current	4.2	4.3	6.2		3.3	11.3	5.7	9.1	5.7	4.5
Net Worth	36.8	39.3	36.1		37.0	30.3	25.7	36.3	39.2	36.7
Total Liabilities & Net Worth	100.0	100.0	100.0		100.0	100.0	100.0	100.0	100.0	100.0
				INCOME DATA						
Net Sales	100.0	100.0	100.0		100.0	100.0	100.0	100.0	100.0	100.0
Gross Profit	28.6	28.6	28.3		44.9	37.7	35.7	28.7	28.8	22.2
Operating Expenses	24.9	25.3	25.9		39.3	38.2	36.0	26.8	25.5	19.4
Operating Profit	3.7	3.4	2.4		5.6	-.5	-.3	1.8	3.2	2.8
All Other Expenses (net)	.5	.4	.5		2.6	.7	.2	.3	.2	.6
Profit Before Taxes	3.1	3.0	1.9		3.0	-1.2	-.5	1.5	3.1	2.3
				RATIOS						
Current	2.4	2.6	2.6		4.2	4.1	2.1	2.6	2.9	2.4
	1.6	1.7	1.6		1.6	1.8	1.3	1.6	1.6	1.6
	1.2	1.2	1.2		.9	1.1	1.0	1.3	1.3	1.2
Quick	1.4	1.5	1.5		2.2	2.8	1.2	1.7	1.5	1.4
	.9	.9	.8		.8	.7	.8	.9	.8	.9
	.6	.6	.5		.2	.3	.5	.5	.6	.6
Sales/Receivables	34 10.8	31 11.9	31 12.0		0 UND	10 35.0	30 12.3	29 12.8	30 12.2	37 10.0
	44 8.3	42 8.7	43 8.6		37 9.8	30 12.1	45 8.1	42 8.7	42 8.7	47 7.8
	58 6.3	54 6.7	60 6.1		56 6.6	44 8.3	68 5.3	54 6.7	61 6.0	61 6.0
Cost of Sales/Inventory	31 11.9	30 12.2	28 12.8		23 15.7	28 13.2	29 12.6	22 16.2	36 10.2	28 12.8
	56 6.6	54 6.7	55 6.7		123 3.0	72 5.1	55 6.7	49 7.4	63 5.8	49 7.4
	90 4.1	96 3.8	104 3.5		428 .9	167 2.2	135 2.7	114 3.2	106 3.4	81 4.5
Cost of Sales/Payables	20 18.5	20 18.7	22 16.6		0 UND	1 644.1	31 11.9	20 18.4	23 15.6	24 15.1
	36 10.1	32 11.5	38 9.6		7 51.4	34 10.8	55 6.6	37 9.9	40 9.2	36 10.2
	53 6.9	52 7.0	59 6.2		46 8.0	80 4.6	94 3.9	56 6.6	58 6.3	54 6.7
Sales/Working Capital	5.5	5.3	5.0		2.6	4.4	5.6	5.1	4.9	5.6
	10.1	9.5	10.4		18.8	10.2	17.0	10.4	8.9	11.0
	20.7	23.2	24.5		-14.6	87.9	55.5	19.3	20.5	23.2
EBIT/Interest	17.0	14.0	16.5		27.8	4.0	6.4	11.6	24.8	25.5
	(289) 4.2	(322) 4.2	(360) 3.7		(13) 2.0	(22) 1.7	(25) 1.7	(55) 3.0	(111) 5.8	(134) 5.9
	1.4	1.5	1.2		1.2	-1.1	.2	.0	1.5	1.3
Net Profit + Depr., Dep., Amort./Cur. Mat. L/T/D	18.6	13.7	14.5					3.9	37.4	31.8
	(64) 4.9	(83) 4.4	(79) 2.3				(11) 1.3	(18) 2.8	(42) 5.4	
	1.9	1.2	.8					.7	1.4	1.5
Fixed/Worth	.1	.1	.0		.0	.0	.0	.0	.0	.1
	.2	.2	.2		.3	.1	.5	.1	.2	.2
	.5	.5	.6		.5	1.1	6.0	.6	.6	.5
Debt/Worth	.8	.7	.9		.4	.5	1.4	.8	.7	1.0
	1.9	1.8	2.2		1.3	2.3	3.2	2.2	1.9	2.1
	4.7	4.3	5.4		-25.4	9.4	29.1	4.2	4.9	5.4
% Profit Before Taxes/Tangible Net Worth	45.1	38.7	35.1		100.0	55.9	34.0	25.0	33.1	43.5
	(296) 22.1	(347) 17.6	(359) 15.3		(11) 23.5	(26) 5.1	(25) 3.8	(60) 7.3	(111) 16.4	(126) 17.9
	7.2	3.8	1.9		4.0	-5.5	-12.1	-1.0	3.9	3.3
% Profit Before Taxes/Total Assets	15.7	15.4	12.8		36.8	10.5	9.1	11.7	13.8	13.9
	6.8	5.4	4.2		3.4	1.2	1.6	3.5	5.5	5.6
	1.3	.9	.3		.5	-6.1	-3.1	-.6	.8	.6
Sales/Net Fixed Assets	156.8	149.7	176.8		UND	449.9	139.6	207.2	209.1	123.0
	55.5	51.9	62.6		51.0	78.4	43.7	57.4	65.2	63.5
	21.7	24.9	24.2		10.4	23.0	16.8	27.0	22.1	25.0
Sales/Total Assets	3.8	4.0	3.7		3.0	5.1	3.8	4.2	3.6	3.7
	3.0	3.0	2.8		1.8	2.3	2.8	2.9	2.8	2.9
	2.2	2.1	1.9		.7	1.4	1.7	1.8	2.0	2.1
% Depr., Dep., Amort./Sales	.2	.2	.2			.5	.2	.2	.3	.2
	(267) .4	(319) .5	(306) .5			(15) 1.3	(18) .8	(47) .5	(91) .5	(126) .5
	1.0	1.1	1.1			2.7	1.8	1.1	1.3	.8
% Officers', Directors' Owners' Comp/Sales	1.2	1.4	1.8			2.5	3.3	2.2	1.8	.9
	(111) 2.6	(130) 3.2	(120) 3.0			(15) 5.9	(15) 4.9	(24) 4.2	(41) 2.5	(20) 1.7
	5.7	6.0	6.0			7.1	7.4	7.7	3.5	2.7
Net Sales ($)	14538678M	21097761M	19489850M		6843M	63775M	125447M	520890M	1981948M	16790947M
Total Assets ($)	5306933M	7304452M	7508373M		6781M	35880M	56554M	257113M	838966M	6313079M

M = $ thousand   MM = $ million
See Pages 9 through 22 for Explanation of Ratios and Data

Current Data Sorted by Assets

Comparative Historical Data

Type of Statement	0-500M	500M-2MM	2-10MM	10-50MM	50-100MM	100-250MM		
Unqualified	1	1	8	26	4	3		35	30
Reviewed		8	56	14	2		83	75
Compiled	1	15	25	3			42	47
Tax Returns	10	29	17	5			18	37
Other	6	28	37	41	2	3	67	72
		68 (4/1-9/30/09)			277 (10/1/09-3/31/10)		4/1/05-3/31/06 ALL	4/1/06-3/31/07 ALL
NUMBER OF STATEMENTS	18	81	143	89	8	6	245	261

	0-500M %	500M-2MM %	2-10MM %	10-50MM %	50-100MM %	100-250MM %	ALL %	ALL %
ASSETS								
Cash & Equivalents	9.7	10.0	8.0	5.8			6.1	7.6
Trade Receivables (net)	16.4	28.0	28.6	26.7			30.8	30.5
Inventory	49.0	40.7	44.2	41.4			44.2	42.6
All Other Current	1.7	2.2	3.2	3.5			1.1	1.2
Total Current	76.8	81.0	84.0	77.4			82.2	81.9
Fixed Assets (net)	16.2	11.1	10.2	12.6			12.3	11.9
Intangibles (net)	.6	2.9	1.7	4.4			1.4	1.8
All Other Non-Current	6.4	5.0	4.1	5.6			4.1	4.4
Total	100.0	100.0	100.0	100.0			100.0	100.0
LIABILITIES								
Notes Payable-Short Term	25.0	15.5	18.6	15.4			16.6	15.1
Cur. Mat.-L.T.D.	12.7	3.3	1.8	2.2			2.5	1.9
Trade Payables	15.9	19.5	16.0	17.3			19.6	19.9
Income Taxes Payable	.0	.1	.2	.1			.2	.3
All Other Current	25.6	8.1	5.9	6.1			8.6	7.7
Total Current	79.1	46.5	42.6	41.2			47.6	44.9
Long-Term Debt	31.2	8.4	6.4	9.9			10.5	10.9
Deferred Taxes	.0	.1	.2	.2			.2	.2
All Other Non-Current	12.5	3.6	5.1	4.2			5.2	3.4
Net Worth	-22.9	41.4	45.7	44.5			36.5	40.7
Total Liabilities & Net Worth	100.0	100.0	100.0	100.0			100.0	100.0
INCOME DATA								
Net Sales	100.0	100.0	100.0	100.0			100.0	100.0
Gross Profit	40.7	32.6	31.1	28.9			30.4	31.2
Operating Expenses	45.1	30.7	28.8	25.8			25.5	26.5
Operating Profit	-4.5	1.9	2.3	3.1			4.9	4.7
All Other Expenses (net)	.7	.4	.3	.4			.6	.6
Profit Before Taxes	-5.1	1.5	2.0	2.7			4.3	4.1
RATIOS								
Current	2.8	3.8	3.2	3.9			3.0	3.2
	1.1	2.1	2.0	2.0			1.8	1.9
	.9	1.2	1.4	1.3			1.3	1.4
Quick	.7	1.6	1.5	1.6			1.2	1.4
	(17) .3	.8	.8	.7			.8	.8
	.1	.5	.5	.5			.5	.5
Sales/Receivables	0 UND	26 14.1	30 12.3	33 11.2			31 11.9	30 12.4
	15 24.0	34 10.7	40 9.2	41 9.0			41 9.0	38 9.7
	28 12.9	46 7.9	50 7.3	60 6.1			51 7.1	48 7.7
Cost of Sales/Inventory	28 12.9	33 11.2	64 5.7	73 5.0			58 6.3	48 7.6
	97 3.8	83 4.4	93 3.9	99 3.7			91 4.0	86 4.3
	154 2.4	123 3.0	144 2.5	153 2.4			134 2.7	121 3.0
Cost of Sales/Payables	5 80.0	15 23.9	16 23.1	24 15.5			18 19.9	20 18.5
	24 14.9	35 10.3	28 13.1	35 10.3			32 11.4	31 11.6
	76 4.8	52 7.0	43 8.5	47 7.7			50 7.3	47 7.8
Sales/Working Capital	5.6	4.9	4.1	3.8			4.7	5.0
	28.9	7.9	5.9	6.1			7.3	7.8
	-39.3	25.4	9.5	12.2			13.3	13.8
EBIT/Interest	16.9	10.6	8.7	13.2			12.6	11.4
	(13) 1.7	(68) 3.3	(128) 2.4	(81) 4.3			(222) 4.7	(231) 4.2
	-4.5	.3	1.1	.9			2.1	1.8
Net Profit + Depr., Dep., Amort./Cur. Mat. L/T/D		5.4	6.4	10.3			7.4	10.2
		(11) 1.3	(39) 2.2	(25) 4.0			(64) 3.7	(65) 4.3
		.6	.5	1.6			2.0	2.0
Fixed/Worth	.1	.0	.1	.1			.1	.1
	.4	.2	.2	.2			.3	.2
	-.3	.6	.4	.8			.7	.6
Debt/Worth	1.6	.4	.5	.5			.9	.7
	9.2	1.5	1.2	1.6			1.7	1.5
	-2.2	3.8	3.0	3.9			3.6	3.4
% Profit Before Taxes/Tangible Net Worth	58.3	50.9	23.3	22.8			46.9	40.3
	(12) -6.4	(71) 10.3	(138) 7.1	(83) 10.8			(229) 20.1	(242) 20.3
	-41.4	1.5	.4	-1.5			7.7	7.1
% Profit Before Taxes/Total Assets	18.0	11.3	11.3	11.2			16.2	17.5
	-3.0	4.2	2.3	4.1			8.2	7.8
	-36.1	-1.2	.1	-.4			2.3	2.7
Sales/Net Fixed Assets	348.7	131.7	84.6	56.1			78.7	86.7
	21.4	49.0	40.0	29.1			37.4	38.9
	14.4	25.1	17.9	12.8			16.4	18.7
Sales/Total Assets	4.9	3.9	3.1	2.6			3.3	3.6
	3.3	2.9	2.5	2.0			2.6	2.8
	2.4	2.2	1.9	1.6			2.0	2.1
% Depr., Dep., Amort./Sales	.4	.3	.3	.5			.4	.4
	(11) .9	(63) .7	(130) .6	(78) .8			(216) .6	(219) .7
	6.7	1.1	1.1	1.3			1.1	1.1
% Officers', Directors' Owners' Comp/Sales	2.7	1.9	1.9	2.0			2.1	2.2
	(10) 7.7	(53) 4.5	(72) 3.7	(17) 3.4			(95) 3.6	(124) 3.5
	18.7	7.3	6.4	5.0			6.1	7.5
Net Sales ($)	18034M	316791M	1709498M	4009613M	1162837M	1954190M	6817850M	6777157M
Total Assets ($)	5395M	102177M	694418M	1884256M	500411M	1044178M	2609698M	2633625M

© RMA 2010

M = $ thousand   MM = $ million
See Pages 9 through 22 for Explanation of Ratios and Data

Comparative Historical Data

Current Data Sorted by Sales

Type of Statement	4/1/07-3/31/08	4/1/08-3/31/09	4/1/09-3/31/10	0-1MM	1-3MM	3-5MM	5-10MM	10-25MM	25MM & OVER
Unqualified	33	41	43	1	1	1	2	11	27
Reviewed	61	81	80		2	6	18	39	15
Compiled	39	38	44		7	11	12	11	3
Tax Returns	37	47	61	5	21	11	13	8	3
Other	86	107	117	4	14	15	20	26	38
	ALL	ALL	ALL	68 (4/1-9/30/09)			277 (10/1/09-3/31/10)		
NUMBER OF STATEMENTS	256	314	345	10	45	44	65	95	86
ASSETS	%	%	%	%	%	%	%	%	%
Cash & Equivalents	7.0	6.8	7.9	8.1	12.6	7.4	8.9	6.6	6.2
Trade Receivables (net)	28.9	28.5	27.1	13.8	21.6	27.7	29.6	27.2	29.1
Inventory	43.9	44.9	42.9	52.5	41.0	42.5	43.9	45.2	39.7
All Other Current	1.9	2.2	3.0	2.4	2.8	4.4	2.6	2.2	3.5
Total Current	81.6	82.4	80.8	76.8	78.0	82.0	85.1	81.2	78.5
Fixed Assets (net)	11.2	10.7	11.4	11.7	13.6	10.1	9.0	12.5	11.4
Intangibles (net)	2.4	3.0	2.9	.0	3.3	2.8	2.1	1.3	5.5
All Other Non-Current	4.8	3.9	4.9	11.4	5.1	5.0	3.8	4.9	4.6
Total	100.0	100.0	100.0	100.0	100.0	100.0	100.0	100.0	100.0
LIABILITIES									
Notes Payable-Short Term	17.9	19.2	17.2	36.4	12.7	18.3	19.5	18.0	14.1
Cur. Mat.-L.T.D.	5.2	2.2	2.8	2.9	8.1	2.1	1.5	2.3	2.0
Trade Payables	19.4	16.7	17.4	13.2	18.1	18.9	15.7	16.1	19.3
Income Taxes Payable	.2	.3	.2	.0	.1	.0	.1	.3	.1
All Other Current	7.2	7.8	7.6	11.2	11.8	10.0	7.1	4.6	7.3
Total Current	49.9	46.3	45.1	63.6	50.7	49.3	44.0	41.4	42.8
Long-Term Debt	10.3	9.0	9.2	33.5	11.2	9.9	6.5	7.4	8.9
Deferred Taxes	.2	.2	.2	.0	.0	.2	.1	.3	.3
All Other Non-Current	5.2	4.2	5.0	10.4	5.0	3.8	6.0	4.5	4.7
Net Worth	34.4	40.4	40.6	-7.7	33.0	36.8	43.5	46.4	43.4
Total Liabilities & Net Worth	100.0	100.0	100.0	100.0	100.0	100.0	100.0	100.0	100.0
INCOME DATA									
Net Sales	100.0	100.0	100.0	100.0	100.0	100.0	100.0	100.0	100.0
Gross Profit	31.7	31.4	31.2	36.0	32.2	37.1	31.7	30.2	28.0
Operating Expenses	27.4	28.0	29.2	42.7	32.7	34.0	29.6	27.3	25.0
Operating Profit	4.2	3.5	2.1	-6.7	-.4	3.1	2.0	2.9	2.9
All Other Expenses (net)	.7	.6	.4	1.5	.3	.6	.2	.4	.4
Profit Before Taxes	3.6	2.9	1.7	-8.2	-.7	2.5	1.9	2.5	2.5
RATIOS									
Current	2.9	3.1	3.3	2.1	5.0	3.1	3.4	3.2	3.0
	1.8	1.8	2.0	1.1	2.2	1.8	2.0	2.0	2.0
	1.3	1.3	1.3	1.0	1.1	1.2	1.3	1.5	1.3
Quick	1.3	1.3	1.5		2.6	1.2	1.7	1.4	1.6
	.7	.8 (344)	.7		.7	.8	.7	.8	.8
	.5	.4	.5		.3	.5	.5	.5	.5
Sales/Receivables	30 12.2	28 13.2	29 12.8	0 UND	21 17.1	26 13.8	31 11.9	29 12.5	33 11.2
	38 9.6	37 9.9	38 9.5	14 27.0	30 12.1	35 10.5	40 9.2	39 9.5	40 9.2
	51 7.2	48 7.6	50 7.2	62 5.9	45 8.1	47 7.8	53 6.9	50 7.3	60 6.1
Cost of Sales/Inventory	61 6.0	55 6.7	55 6.7	43 8.6	46 7.9	42 8.6	52 7.0	64 5.7	57 6.5
	97 3.8	95 3.9	95 3.8	107 3.4	108 3.4	98 3.7	83 4.4	101 3.6	90 4.1
	128 2.8	144 2.5	142 2.6	276 1.3	144 2.6	143 2.6	140 2.6	148 2.5	126 2.9
Cost of Sales/Payables	20 18.2	16 23.0	18 20.0	5 80.0	10 34.9	23 15.8	14 25.2	17 21.6	26 14.2
	34 10.7	30 12.2	32 11.3	26 14.0	31 11.7	38 9.6	29 12.5	28 13.1	37 9.9
	50 7.3	45 8.1	48 7.6	58 6.3	60 6.1	55 6.7	45 8.2	43 8.5	48 7.6
Sales/Working Capital	5.0	4.8	4.3	3.0	4.0	4.6	3.8	4.3	4.3
	7.8	7.6	6.4	26.1	6.0	7.1	5.7	5.9	6.7
	14.7	15.0	14.3	NM	28.9	20.2	16.0	10.1	16.2
EBIT/Interest	10.7	9.4	9.6		22.5	8.5	6.5	10.6	12.7
	(227) 3.3	(271) 3.0	(303) 2.8		(35) 3.3	(40) 2.7	(56) 2.0	(88) 2.5	(78) 4.4
	1.5	1.5	.9		.3	1.1	.1	1.1	1.0
Net Profit + Depr., Dep., Amort./Cur. Mat. L/T/D	6.7	7.5	6.7				6.4	7.9	8.9
	(63) 3.2	(76) 4.0	(82) 2.6				(15) 3.4	(30) 2.8	(26) 2.7
	.9	.8	.7				-.5	.7	1.2
Fixed/Worth	.1	.1	.1	.1	.0	.1	.1	.1	.1
	.2	.2	.2	.3	.1	.2	.2	.2	.2
	.6	.5	.6	NM	2.9	.5	.5	.5	.8
Debt/Worth	.7	.6	.6	1.6	.3	.5	.5	.5	.6
	1.7	1.8	1.4	5.7	1.0	2.4	1.5	1.2	1.6
	3.8	4.1	4.0	NM	35.7	3.6	4.8	2.4	3.9
% Profit Before Taxes/Tangible Net Worth	37.5	35.2	25.5		24.4	51.6	22.5	26.1	22.9
	(235) 16.0	(289) 14.6	(316) 8.2	(36) 4.9	(41) 17.2	(61) 7.1	(92) 6.7	(78) 11.7	
	4.4	3.2	-.2		-6.6	3.7	-.1	.2	-.1
% Profit Before Taxes/Total Assets	14.5	12.9	11.2	-1.1	8.4	11.8	9.5	11.8	11.2
	6.3	4.3	3.3	-7.4	3.1	4.5	2.3	3.3	4.8
	1.2	.9	-.4	-18.8	-4.1	1.4	-.6	.1	.0
Sales/Net Fixed Assets	92.8	96.0	84.2	UND	163.0	82.2	91.0	84.3	55.3
	41.3	38.6	36.4	36.5	41.1	37.0	51.5	35.2	31.5
	18.7	16.6	16.7	9.6	16.9	17.9	24.0	14.0	15.4
Sales/Total Assets	3.3	3.3	3.2	3.8	3.3	3.5	3.3	3.1	2.9
	2.6	2.6	2.4	2.3	2.5	2.8	2.6	2.4	2.3
	2.1	2.0	1.8	1.0	1.4	1.7	2.0	1.7	1.9
% Depr., Dep., Amort./Sales	.3	.4	.4		.2	.4	.4	.3	.5
	(216) .6	(264) .6	(292) .7	(35) .8	(36) .7	(54) .8	(87) .6	(74) .7	
	1.1	1.1	1.3		1.6	1.3	.9	1.2	1.3
% Officers', Directors' Owners' Comp/Sales	2.1	2.1	2.0		1.8	2.6	2.4	1.3	.7
	(116) 3.5	(122) 3.8	(152) 3.9	(31) 4.1	(28) 5.2	(38) 4.0	(39) 3.1	(13) 3.0	
	7.3	7.0	6.8		6.0	8.2	6.6	5.3	4.6
Net Sales ($)	7640239M	10309827M	9170963M	4961M	92339M	177168M	506894M	1567830M	6821771M
Total Assets ($)	3232255M	4578978M	4230835M	2647M	47137M	77391M	212224M	770492M	3120944M

© RMA 2010

M = $ thousand   MM = $ million
See Pages 9 through 22 for Explanation of Ratios and Data

Current Data Sorted by Assets   Comparative Historical Data

Type of Statement	0-500M	500M-2MM	2-10MM	10-50MM	50-100MM	100-250MM		4/1/05-3/31/06 ALL	4/1/06-3/31/07 ALL
Unqualified			6	28	7	1		47	47
Reviewed	3	9	65	24	1			118	116
Compiled	3	21	33	1		1		75	89
Tax Returns	13	27	20					32	41
Other	6	15	68	36	12			113	95
		65 (4/1-9/30/09)	335 (10/1/09-3/31/10)					4/1/05-3/31/06	4/1/06-3/31/07
NUMBER OF STATEMENTS	25	72	192	89	20	2		385	388
ASSETS	%	%	%	%	%	%		%	%
Cash & Equivalents	13.0	10.8	6.8	6.0	5.2			5.9	6.1
Trade Receivables (net)	32.3	28.8	31.0	29.8	28.1			34.7	34.1
Inventory	36.2	41.7	41.3	40.3	35.8			39.5	40.5
All Other Current	1.7	2.6	2.7	3.1	3.0			2.6	2.2
Total Current	83.1	83.9	81.8	79.2	72.1			82.7	82.9
Fixed Assets (net)	9.5	9.2	11.3	12.7	17.3			10.3	9.8
Intangibles (net)	1.0	1.6	1.1	3.7	1.1			1.5	2.0
All Other Non-Current	6.4	5.2	5.8	4.4	9.4			5.5	5.3
Total	100.0	100.0	100.0	100.0	100.0			100.0	100.0
LIABILITIES									
Notes Payable-Short Term	23.8	15.0	15.8	22.1	13.0			15.3	16.6
Cur. Mat.-L.T.D.	2.5	2.6	2.0	2.0	1.3			2.6	2.5
Trade Payables	19.4	21.5	19.9	16.8	13.0			21.6	19.9
Income Taxes Payable	.1	.2	.1	.2	.1			.4	.3
All Other Current	11.0	10.6	7.8	6.9	13.4			9.5	8.4
Total Current	56.7	49.9	45.6	48.1	40.9			49.5	47.8
Long-Term Debt	17.2	11.5	6.8	6.7	8.7			8.2	8.1
Deferred Taxes	.0	.3	.2	.4	.1			.1	.2
All Other-Non-Current	7.0	6.3	4.0	5.4	5.6			4.2	3.5
Net Worth	19.1	32.1	43.4	39.3	44.7			38.0	40.5
Total Liabilities & Net Worth	100.0	100.0	100.0	100.0	100.0			100.0	100.0
INCOME DATA									
Net Sales	100.0	100.0	100.0	100.0	100.0			100.0	100.0
Gross Profit	40.7	34.0	28.9	26.6	32.1			29.0	28.4
Operating Expenses	39.4	34.3	27.5	25.6	29.8			25.5	24.6
Operating Profit	1.3	-.3	1.4	1.0	2.3			3.5	3.8
All Other Expenses (net)	1.0	-.1	.3	.6	.4			.2	.2
Profit Before Taxes	.3	-.2	1.1	.4	1.9			3.3	3.7
RATIOS									
Current	3.9	2.7	2.6	2.4	3.0			2.4	2.7
	1.5	1.8	1.9	1.6	1.9			1.7	1.7
	1.0	1.4	1.4	1.2	1.3			1.3	1.4
Quick	2.6	1.4	1.3	1.1	1.3			1.3	1.3
	.8	.8	.8	.7	.8			.8	.8
	.4	.5	.5	.5	.6			.6	.6
Sales/Receivables	17 21.1	21 17.6	32 11.3	36 10.1	37 10.0			35 10.6	33 11.1
	35 10.4	34 10.8	42 8.8	44 8.2	44 8.3			43 8.4	42 8.7
	45 8.2	47 7.8	54 6.8	53 6.9	54 6.8			53 6.9	51 7.1
Cost of Sales/Inventory	19 19.1	46 8.0	54 6.7	61 5.9	69 5.3			48 7.6	46 8.0
	51 7.2	75 4.9	81 4.5	88 4.2	83 4.4			72 5.1	74 4.9
	107 3.4	111 3.3	131 2.8	120 3.0	99 3.7			100 3.7	102 3.6
Cost of Sales/Payables	7 55.5	18 20.4	23 15.6	23 16.0	17 21.2			24 15.2	21 17.5
	30 12.3	30 12.1	33 11.1	32 11.6	31 11.6			35 10.3	31 11.9
	55 6.6	50 7.3	48 7.6	42 8.8	45 8.0			50 7.3	44 8.3
Sales/Working Capital	6.1	5.7	4.3	5.0	4.3			5.6	5.3
	13.1	9.4	7.5	7.4	5.9			9.2	8.8
	NM	22.1	14.0	15.7	17.0			15.6	15.2
EBIT/Interest	14.6	14.8	10.6	5.7	8.5			11.7	12.4
	(20) 2.1	(61) 2.8	(176) 2.3	(84) 2.1	(18) 2.8			(336) 4.4	(355) 4.8
	-5.0	.1	.2	-.9	-.3			2.2	2.1
Net Profit + Depr., Dep., Amort./Cur. Mat. L/T/D		4.6	7.1	12.4				14.3	7.8
		(10) 2.0	(48) 2.3	(29) 3.0				(104) 4.6	(101) 3.2
		.4	.4	.6				2.1	1.7
Fixed/Worth	.0	.1	.1	.2	.2			.1	.1
	.2	.2	.2	.3	.4			.2	.2
	NM	1.2	.5	.7	.6			.5	.4
Debt/Worth	.3	.8	.6	.9	.7			.8	.8
	2.9	1.6	1.2	1.8	1.3			1.7	1.6
	-9.0	12.1	2.6	3.4	2.2			3.7	3.4
% Profit Before Taxes/Tangible Net Worth	77.6	26.6	17.9	17.2	15.7			37.1	42.8
	(18) 26.8	(61) 6.4	(180) 5.9	(80) 5.9	(19) 4.6			(362) 20.6	(368) 22.6
	1.5	-8.6	-3.0	-6.7	-3.0			7.2	8.8
% Profit Before Taxes/Total Assets	27.1	11.8	7.1	7.9	7.6			14.1	16.8
	6.0	2.2	2.5	1.9	2.8			6.3	8.0
	-10.9	-4.1	-.9	-3.5	-1.2			2.4	2.9
Sales/Net Fixed Assets	410.2	107.0	79.4	45.8	26.0			82.1	83.6
	59.2	54.3	39.0	24.5	15.7			39.2	40.6
	17.0	29.4	18.1	12.8	10.5			21.7	22.1
Sales/Total Assets	5.1	4.0	3.3	2.8	2.7			3.4	3.7
	3.7	3.3	2.6	2.5	2.3			2.8	2.9
	2.2	2.2	1.9	2.0	1.8			2.3	2.3
% Depr., Dep., Amort./Sales	.4	.4	.4	.6	.9			.4	.3
	(16) .7	(58) .6	(167) .6	(77) .8	(19) 1.0			(323) .6	(330) .6
	2.1	1.2	1.0	1.2	1.8			.9	.9
% Officers', Directors' Owners' Comp/Sales	2.2	2.5	1.4	.5				1.5	1.3
	(15) 5.9	(44) 4.5	(82) 3.0	(21) 1.4				(168) 2.7	(165) 2.8
	8.1	9.9	4.8	2.0				5.7	6.1
Net Sales ($)	24145M	283743M	2630727M	4964361M	3036828M	557370M		10861235M	13587240M
Total Assets ($)	6558M	87427M	988270M	2111136M	1354122M	292812M		4052104M	4677584M

Comparative Historical Data | | | Current Data Sorted by Sales

			Type of Statement						
38	36	42	Unqualified	1	3	3	1	6	35
101	123	102	Reviewed				24	44	27
85	74	59	Compiled	2	10	11	18	14	4
37	50	60	Tax Returns	8	20	10	13	9	
100	104	137	Other	4	13	9	18	46	47
4/1/07-3/31/08 ALL	4/1/08-3/31/09 ALL	4/1/09-3/31/10 ALL		0-1MM	65 (4/1-9/30/09) 1-3MM	3-5MM	335 (10/1/09-3/31/10) 5-10MM	10-25MM	25MM & OVER
361	387	400	**NUMBER OF STATEMENTS**	15	46	33	74	119	113
%	%	%	**ASSETS**	%	%	%	%	%	%
7.0	7.2	7.6	Cash & Equivalents	9.7	9.9	11.2	10.0	5.1	6.6
33.2	31.3	30.3	Trade Receivables (net)	28.1	26.9	22.4	31.3	31.8	32.0
39.7	40.4	40.5	Inventory	44.8	42.7	42.9	38.4	41.4	38.9
2.7	2.5	2.7	All Other Current	1.6	3.2	4.0	2.1	2.5	2.9
82.7	81.3	81.1	Total Current	84.2	82.8	80.4	81.7	80.7	80.4
11.2	11.1	11.5	Fixed Assets (net)	10.4	9.9	10.3	10.6	12.1	12.5
1.8	2.1	1.8	Intangibles (net)	.4	1.6	2.3	.8	2.3	2.2
4.4	5.5	5.6	All Other Non-Current	5.0	5.8	6.9	6.9	5.0	5.0
100.0	100.0	100.0	Total	100.0	100.0	100.0	100.0	100.0	100.0
			LIABILITIES						
16.9	17.0	17.4	Notes Payable-Short Term	25.5	16.3	16.9	12.8	18.4	18.9
2.2	2.6	2.1	Cur. Mat.-L.T.D.	3.3	1.8	2.5	2.5	2.4	1.4
20.3	18.9	19.1	Trade Payables	19.2	19.9	17.6	19.4	20.6	17.4
.3	.2	.2	Income Taxes Payable	.1	.1	.1	.1	.2	.2
7.8	8.8	8.6	All Other Current	9.7	13.7	4.7	7.4	8.4	8.5
47.3	47.5	47.3	Total Current	57.8	51.8	41.9	42.3	49.8	46.5
8.1	9.0	8.4	Long-Term Debt	14.4	18.2	9.1	7.2	6.4	6.4
.2	.4	.3	Deferred Taxes	.0	.0	.6	.3	.3	.3
4.3	4.2	5.0	All Other Non-Current	9.7	5.9	4.7	4.2	5.6	3.9
40.1	38.8	39.0	Net Worth	18.1	24.2	43.8	46.0	37.9	42.9
100.0	100.0	100.0	Total Liabilties & Net Worth	100.0	100.0	100.0	100.0	100.0	100.0
			INCOME DATA						
100.0	100.0	100.0	Net Sales	100.0	100.0	100.0	100.0	100.0	100.0
29.2	28.8	30.2	Gross Profit	40.6	37.7	34.2	28.9	28.8	26.8
25.6	26.4	29.1	Operating Expenses	41.4	37.6	33.6	27.7	27.6	25.2
3.6	2.5	1.1	Operating Profit	-.8	.1	.7	1.1	1.2	1.7
.2	.3	.4	All Other Expenses (net)	1.1	1.1	-.5	-.2	.4	.5
3.4	2.1	.7	Profit Before Taxes	-1.9	-1.0	1.1	1.3	.8	1.1
			RATIOS						
2.7	2.6	2.6	Current	2.8	3.5	3.2	2.9	2.3	2.5
1.8	1.7	1.8		1.7	1.9	2.1	2.0	1.6	1.7
1.4	1.3	1.3		1.0	1.2	1.5	1.4	1.3	1.3
1.4	1.3	1.4	Quick	2.6	1.8	1.4	1.6	1.1	1.3
.8	.8	.8		.6	.7	.7	.9	.7	.8
.5	.5	.5		.3	.4	.5	.6	.5	.6
32 11.4	29 12.4	31 11.6	Sales/Receivables	23 15.6	23 16.1	15 23.7	26 14.0	32 11.4	36 10.1
40 9.0	38 9.7	41 8.9		35 10.3	38 9.5	33 11.1	40 9.1	41 9.0	44 8.3
51 7.2	48 7.6	52 7.0		58 6.3	49 7.4	50 7.4	57 6.5	51 7.1	52 7.0
51 7.2	46 8.0	52 7.0	Cost of Sales/Inventory	46 7.9	51 7.2	59 6.2	45 8.1	55 6.6	56 6.5
73 5.0	76 4.8	81 4.5		129 2.8	89 4.1	107 3.4	71 5.1	82 4.4	79 4.6
102 3.6	103 3.6	121 3.0		212 1.7	207 1.8	172 2.1	101 3.6	119 3.1	105 3.5
21 17.1	19 19.5	22 16.6	Cost of Sales/Payables	4 90.0	18 20.5	18 20.5	21 17.1	23 15.8	23 16.0
33 11.1	27 13.3	32 11.4		31 11.7	38 9.5	34 10.8	31 11.7	33 11.2	31 11.6
46 7.9	44 8.2	46 7.9		81 4.5	74 5.0	57 6.4	46 8.0	47 7.8	40 9.2
5.0	5.1	4.8	Sales/Working Capital	4.5	3.3	3.8	4.3	5.5	5.1
8.2	9.6	7.9		8.0	7.1	6.1	7.2	9.6	7.4
15.3	15.8	16.7		-284.0	49.9	18.9	14.6	16.7	14.9
10.9	9.8	9.8	EBIT/Interest	11.4	5.6	27.6	11.9	10.2	8.2
(328) 4.0	(350) 3.4	(361) 2.4		(12) -1.5	(35) 1.3	(30) 2.2	(66) 2.8	(111) 2.2	(107) 2.7
1.6	1.2	-.3		-5.7	-1.3	-.4	1.0	.1	-.7
7.4	6.0	7.0	Net Profit + Depr., Dep., Amort./Cur. Mat. L/T/D				4.5	7.3	8.8
(114) 3.5	(104) 2.5	(98) 2.2				(17) 1.2	(32) 2.7	(39) 3.0	
1.6	1.2	.4					.3	.6	.9
.1	.1	.1	Fixed/Worth	.1	.0	.1	.1	.1	.2
.2	.2	.2		.7	.2	.1	.2	.2	.3
.5	.5	.6		-.6	1.1	.9	.4	.7	.5
.7	.8	.7	Debt/Worth	.5	.9	.5	.6	.7	.8
1.4	1.5	1.5		8.0	1.8	.9	1.1	1.6	1.4
3.3	3.2	3.4		-5.4	31.7	3.9	2.5	3.6	2.7
34.2	27.4	19.3	% Profit Before Taxes/Tangible Net Worth	84.3	21.0	18.7	21.4	22.1	16.5
(336) 20.8	(353) 15.1	(360) 6.4		(10) 32.5	(37) 1.8	(28) 4.2	(71) 7.7	(108) 7.5	(106) 6.7
6.6	2.4	-4.1		-50.0	-13.0	-3.6	.5	-2.8	-5.8
14.8	11.8	8.4	% Profit Before Taxes/Total Assets	32.7	7.7	12.9	10.7	7.4	8.6
7.4	5.2	2.4		-3.4	.2	2.1	2.9	2.5	2.4
2.1	.5	-3.2		-38.1	-5.5	-3.3	.0	-.9	-3.3
65.6	74.4	70.9	Sales/Net Fixed Assets	284.0	343.4	88.9	90.6	65.3	46.8
36.3	38.8	37.0		34.3	60.7	51.2	45.1	33.3	25.5
19.8	19.2	16.1		8.1	18.9	23.8	23.1	17.6	15.1
3.5	3.6	3.3	Sales/Total Assets	3.6	4.0	3.6	3.7	3.4	3.0
2.8	2.9	2.6		2.1	2.6	2.5	2.6	2.6	2.5
2.2	2.2	2.0		1.5	1.4	1.4	2.0	2.1	2.1
.4	.4	.4	% Depr., Dep., Amort./Sales	.5	.4	.4	.4	.4	.5
(315) .7	(330) .6	(339) .7		(10) 1.2	(31) .6	(25) .7	(63) .6	(107) .7	(103) .8
1.0	1.0	1.2		1.9	1.3	1.3	1.3	1.0	1.1
1.5	1.5	1.5	% Officers', Directors' Owners' Comp/Sales		3.4	2.5	2.3	1.3	.5
(152) 2.6	(164) 2.8	(162) 3.1		(24) 7.5	(22) 4.6	(44) 3.2	(45) 2.4	(20) .8	
5.5	5.6	6.3		11.0	5.7	5.8	3.8	2.8	
11999810M	14160590M	11497174M	Net Sales ($)	8581M	86570M	133058M	537008M	1958555M	8773402M
4461018M	5326975M	4840325M	Total Assets ($)	5267M	46593M	78518M	222487M	821893M	3665567M

RMA 2010

M = $ thousand   MM = $ million
See Pages 9 through 22 for Explanation of Ratios and Data

Current Data Sorted by Assets   **Comparative Historical Data**

						Type of Statement		
		6	22	9	1	Unqualified	32	38
	6	52	19			Reviewed	60	72
1	14	19	5	2	3	Compiled	36	39
7	13	9	2			Tax Returns	35	33
5	7	31	29			Other	84	61
	38 (4/1-9/30/09)		224 (10/1/09-3/31/10)				4/1/05-3/31/06 ALL	4/1/06-3/31/07 ALL
0-500M	500M-2MM	2-10MM	10-50MM	50-100MM	100-250MM			
13	40	117	77	11	4	NUMBER OF STATEMENTS	247	243
%	%	%	%	%	%	ASSETS	%	%
6.8	10.2	7.3	5.4	12.3		Cash & Equivalents	7.3	6.6
39.7	42.2	37.7	32.5	24.8		Trade Receivables (net)	41.3	39.7
26.8	30.1	35.4	44.5	35.8		Inventory	34.6	37.2
2.0	3.2	2.8	2.3	2.0		All Other Current	2.1	1.9
75.3	85.7	83.1	84.7	74.9		Total Current	85.3	85.3
16.7	5.8	10.0	9.1	16.7		Fixed Assets (net)	9.2	9.1
5.5	3.8	1.6	1.9	3.6		Intangibles (net)	1.3	1.2
2.6	4.6	5.3	4.4	4.9		All Other Non-Current	4.2	4.4
100.0	100.0	100.0	100.0	100.0		Total	100.0	100.0
						LIABILITIES		
16.9	12.2	13.8	20.1	13.4		Notes Payable-Short Term	19.3	19.0
13.6	1.3	1.2	1.4	2.4		Cur. Mat.-L.T.D.	1.5	2.0
26.9	31.1	23.3	16.8	13.0		Trade Payables	23.9	23.3
.1	.1	.2	.1	.4		Income Taxes Payable	.2	.3
13.0	11.3	12.3	10.7	5.6		All Other Current	11.5	10.4
70.5	56.0	50.9	49.2	34.9		Total Current	56.5	55.0
14.2	4.9	5.4	4.6	12.5		Long-Term Debt	7.1	6.8
.0	.0	.2	.2	.4		Deferred Taxes	.2	.1
47.0	2.9	3.0	3.2	2.6		All Other Non-Current	5.0	5.3
-31.7	36.2	40.6	42.7	49.6		Net Worth	31.3	32.7
100.0	100.0	100.0	100.0	100.0		Total Liabilties & Net Worth	100.0	100.0
						INCOME DATA		
100.0	100.0	100.0	100.0	100.0		Net Sales	100.0	100.0
30.8	31.2	27.5	25.3	26.3		Gross Profit	26.9	27.2
29.9	27.9	26.0	23.1	23.2		Operating Expenses	23.6	23.4
.9	3.4	1.5	2.2	3.1		Operating Profit	3.3	3.8
.9	.0	-.3	.2	.3		All Other Expenses (net)	.3	.3
.0	3.4	1.9	2.0	2.8		Profit Before Taxes	3.0	3.5
						RATIOS		
2.0	3.0	2.2	2.4	3.7			2.1	2.1
1.1	1.7	1.6	1.6	2.9		Current	1.4	1.5
.6	1.1	1.2	1.3	1.1			1.2	1.2
1.7	2.0	1.3	1.1	2.0			1.2	1.2
.8	1.1	.8	.7	1.1		Quick	.8	.8
.3	.6	.6	.5	.6			.6	.5
3 111.7	32 11.6	35 10.5	33 11.0	25 14.7			38 9.6	34 10.9
26 14.3	40 9.1	46 8.0	43 8.6	43 8.5		Sales/Receivables	49 7.5	44 8.4
50 7.3	56 6.6	61 6.0	55 6.6	60 6.0			62 5.9	58 6.3
0 UND	9 42.8	25 14.9	68 5.4	74 4.9			25 14.7	27 13.5
15 24.3	49 7.5	71 5.1	89 4.1	90 4.0		Cost of Sales/Inventory	64 5.7	70 5.2
75 4.9	98 3.7	110 3.3	116 3.1	108 3.4			96 3.8	99 3.7
5 73.5	21 17.6	23 15.7	17 21.0	19 19.6			22 16.8	17 21.6
37 10.0	39 9.4	39 9.4	25 14.5	25 14.6		Cost of Sales/Payables	37 9.8	32 11.3
54 6.8	64 5.7	56 6.5	48 7.6	33 11.0			51 7.1	54 6.7
10.0	6.3	5.6	4.7	2.3			6.6	6.2
67.1	10.8	8.5	8.0	4.6		Sales/Working Capital	10.6	10.0
-11.3	49.9	16.8	12.8	40.0			20.0	20.4
13.2	29.4	10.0	10.6				11.5	10.0
(11) 2.1	(35) 11.7	(110) 4.6	(72) 3.7			EBIT/Interest	(227) 5.0	(221) 3.8
-.4	-1.9	1.2	1.6				2.4	2.0
		8.0	8.2				8.6	10.6
	(30) 3.5	3.5	(22) 1.3			Net Profit + Depr., Dep., Amort./Cur. Mat. L/T/D	(61) 3.3	(60) 3.3
		1.0	.0				1.7	1.7
.5	.1	.1	.1	.1			.1	.1
-14.0	.1	.2	.2	.4		Fixed/Worth	.2	.2
-.5	.6	.5	.3	.7			.6	.5
6.5	.6	.8	.8	.3			1.2	1.0
-38.5	2.2	1.4	1.5	1.6		Debt/Worth	2.4	2.2
-3.2	9.1	3.3	2.9	3.0			4.8	4.3
	87.7	25.8	25.1	16.6			45.7	41.2
	(34) 23.8	(114) 8.6	(74) 11.3	13.6		% Profit Before Taxes/Tangible Net Worth	(226) 26.0	(226) 25.0
	1.8	2.0	5.3	-1.1			12.5	10.0
29.6	24.5	9.7	8.0	9.8			12.9	15.4
2.3	8.3	3.6	4.0	3.4		% Profit Before Taxes/Total Assets	7.7	7.4
-12.1	.3	.4	1.3	-.4			3.1	2.6
656.7	229.6	122.3	93.0	45.3			111.1	124.6
45.4	78.4	47.2	49.1	18.6		Sales/Net Fixed Assets	55.5	56.1
25.7	33.0	20.9	21.1	8.3			25.7	24.8
7.8	4.6	3.4	2.9	2.8			3.8	3.6
4.8	3.4	2.6	2.5	1.9		Sales/Total Assets	2.9	3.0
3.0	2.7	2.1	2.2	1.4			2.5	2.5
.1		.4	.3	.6			.3	.3
	(34) .3	(100) .5	(75) .6	.8		% Depr., Dep., Amort./Sales	(216) .5	(213) .5
	1.0	1.1	.8	1.6			.8	.9
	2.7	1.3	1.3				2.0	1.6
	(17) 4.9	(43) 2.6	(15) 2.5			% Officers', Directors' Owners' Comp/Sales	(107) 3.5	(96) 3.3
	6.8	5.3	3.3				5.9	6.2
27077M	191044M	1552115M	4079056M	1530414M	2188871M	Net Sales ($)	11923856M	9472276M
4751M	52152M	560448M	1580028M	748599M	696799M	Total Assets ($)	3223269M	3206660M

M = $ thousand   MM = $ million
See Pages 9 through 22 for Explanation of Ratios and Data

Comparative Historical Data & Current Data Sorted by Sales

	4/1/07-3/31/08 ALL	4/1/08-3/31/09 ALL	4/1/09-3/31/10 ALL	Type of Statement	0-1MM	1-3MM	3-5MM	5-10MM	10-25MM	25MM & OVER
	36	37	38	Unqualified				3	4	31
	64	80	77	Reviewed		3	3	17	34	20
	39	36	39	Compiled	1	4	8	11	9	6
	25	41	31	Tax Returns	1	7	9	8	4	2
	70	82	77	Other	1	4	4	4	22	31
					38 (4/1-9/30/09)			224 (10/1/09-3/31/10)		
	234	276	262	**NUMBER OF STATEMENTS**	3	18	24	54	73	90
	%	%	%	**ASSETS**	%	%	%	%	%	%
	5.9	6.6	7.3	Cash & Equivalents		5.3	9.7	8.5	6.9	6.8
	37.7	37.1	36.5	Trade Receivables (net)		31.9	38.8	37.3	38.1	35.4
	38.1	37.1	36.9	Inventory		34.4	31.8	34.4	36.5	39.9
	2.9	2.7	2.6	All Other Current		1.5	3.9	3.6	2.3	2.3
	84.6	83.4	83.4	Total Current		73.2	84.2	83.7	83.7	84.4
	9.7	9.3	9.6	Fixed Assets (net)		18.5	6.7	8.8	10.2	9.0
	1.6	2.0	2.3	Intangibles (net)		2.5	4.6	2.4	1.4	2.3
	4.1	5.4	4.7	All Other Non-Current		5.8	4.6	5.2	4.7	4.3
	100.0	100.0	100.0	Total		100.0	100.0	100.0	100.0	100.0
				LIABILITIES						
	17.9	20.1	15.5	Notes Payable-Short Term		15.5	11.3	11.3	16.9	17.3
	1.6	2.0	1.9	Cur. Mat.-L.T.D.		8.8	1.5	1.8	1.0	1.5
	22.2	21.4	22.6	Trade Payables		27.5	28.0	25.2	23.7	17.9
	.2	.3	.2	Income Taxes Payable		.4	.0	.2	.2	.1
	9.9	11.8	11.4	All Other Current		17.2	10.6	9.1	14.0	10.1
	51.8	55.6	51.6	Total Current		69.3	51.4	47.6	55.8	46.9
	7.6	7.2	5.7	Long-Term Debt		8.1	6.7	5.8	4.5	5.1
	.2	.2	.2	Deferred Taxes		.0	.0	.3	.1	.2
	4.0	3.9	5.2	All Other Non-Current		14.4	2.4	4.2	4.5	2.3
	36.4	33.0	37.3	Net Worth		8.3	39.5	42.2	35.1	45.4
	100.0	100.0	100.0	Total Liabilities & Net Worth		100.0	100.0	100.0	100.0	100.0
				INCOME DATA						
	100.0	100.0	100.0	Net Sales		100.0	100.0	100.0	100.0	100.0
	27.9	27.0	27.4	Gross Profit		30.8	30.8	29.9	26.0	25.1
	24.2	24.3	25.3	Operating Expenses		31.2	27.4	27.5	24.6	22.5
	3.6	2.6	2.0	Operating Profit		-.4	3.4	2.3	1.5	2.6
	.3	.1	.0	All Other Expenses (net)		.8	-.3	-.5	-.2	.2
	3.3	2.5	2.0	Profit Before Taxes		-1.2	3.7	2.9	1.7	2.4
				RATIOS						
	2.2	2.2	2.4	Current		3.4	2.6	2.7	1.9	2.8
	1.6	1.5	1.6			1.1	1.6	2.0	1.4	1.7
	1.3	1.2	1.2			.7	1.2	1.3	1.2	1.3
	1.2	1.2	1.3	Quick		1.6	1.5	1.6	1.2	1.3
	.8	.7	.8			.6	1.0	.8	.7	.8
	.6	.5	.5			.3	.6	.6	.5	.6
	33 11.1	31 11.8	33 11.0	Sales/Receivables		27 13.5	29 12.4	32 11.5	35 10.3	33 11.0
	42 8.7	41 8.9	43 8.5			40 9.1	40 9.1	43 8.4	43 8.4	43 8.5
	55 6.6	55 6.7	57 6.5			51 7.2	68 5.4	58 6.3	57 6.4	56 6.6
	33 11.0	27 13.4	30 12.2	Cost of Sales/Inventory		14 26.6	10 36.8	16 22.6	25 14.9	52 7.0
	70 5.2	67 5.4	77 4.8			79 4.6	70 5.2	70 5.2	68 5.4	82 4.5
	100 3.6	100 3.7	109 3.3			117 3.1	120 3.0	107 3.4	113 3.2	103 3.5
	19 19.1	18 20.7	20 18.2	Cost of Sales/Payables		23 15.5	26 13.8	22 16.3	21 17.5	17 21.5
	31 11.9	29 12.4	33 11.0			45 8.2	42 8.6	39 9.3	37 9.8	25 14.7
	48 7.7	49 7.4	55 6.6			69 5.3	65 5.6	58 6.3	56 6.6	43 8.5
	6.2	6.1	5.4	Sales/Working Capital		5.2	4.8	5.6	7.0	4.6
	8.7	10.1	8.8			87.6	7.9	7.1	10.4	7.6
	17.6	24.3	18.5			-11.6	22.7	15.6	21.8	14.5
	13.3	11.1	13.3	EBIT/Interest		8.7	41.4	11.8	10.3	16.3
	(221) 4.6	(257) 4.2	(241) 4.3		(16) 1.2	(22) 11.8	(50) 5.6	(68) 3.8	(83) 4.6
	2.1	1.5	1.1			-5.2	2.3	.1	1.1	2.3
	14.8	12.5	9.0	Net Profit + Depr., Dep., Amort./Cur. Mat. L/T/D				3.4	12.6	10.1
	(66) 4.1	(62) 4.8	(60) 2.9					(10) 2.1	(21) 3.0	(26) 3.0
	2.0	2.1	.4					.0	.8	.3
	.1	.1	.1	Fixed/Worth		.1	.0	.1	.1	.1
	.2	.2	.2			1.7	.1	.2	.2	.2
	.5	.5	.6			-.6	.6	.5	.7	.3
	.9	1.0	.8	Debt/Worth		.5	.7	.8	1.1	.7
	1.8	2.1	1.7			6.5	2.0	1.0	2.2	1.5
	3.9	5.1	4.3			-5.5	5.0	4.9	5.0	2.7
	46.3	38.5	28.4	% Profit Before Taxes/Tangible Net Worth		178.8	53.5	35.3	29.8	25.2
	(217) 22.8	(249) 16.4	(242) 12.1		(12) 2.7	(22) 23.8	(49) 11.2	(71) 9.4	(88) 13.0
	10.6	4.8	2.9			-14.4	5.5	-.3	.5	5.9
	16.1	12.6	9.8	% Profit Before Taxes/Total Assets		5.0	24.0	9.8	9.2	9.5
	7.7	5.5	4.0			.4	6.4	4.5	3.3	4.6
	3.6	.9	.3			-10.3	1.2	-.4	.2	2.3
	128.3	118.8	121.8	Sales/Net Fixed Assets		45.6	302.2	153.8	120.6	110.4
	51.7	49.3	49.1			26.6	73.7	45.7	49.5	50.0
	23.8	25.2	22.6			14.6	33.0	24.8	20.9	20.9
	3.6	3.7	3.5	Sales/Total Assets		4.9	4.0	3.6	3.6	3.2
	2.9	3.0	2.7			2.9	3.0	2.8	2.6	2.7
	2.5	2.4	2.2			2.2	2.5	2.3	2.1	2.3
	.3	.3	.3	% Depr., Dep., Amort./Sales		.6	.1	.3	.3	.3
	(194) .5	(237) .5	(232) .6		(17) 1.2	(17) .2	(44) .5	(65) .5	(88) .5
	.9	.8	.9			1.6	.8	1.2	.9	.8
	1.3	1.4	1.5	% Officers', Directors' Owners' Comp/Sales		3.2		1.9	1.2	1.3
	(91) 2.8	(99) 2.9	(83) 2.9		(11) 4.9		(22) 3.7	(25) 2.1	(15) 2.9
	5.1	5.1	5.9			7.4		6.2	3.6	4.5
	10222574M	10890428M	9568577M	Net Sales ($)	2232M	34298M	95457M	418206M	1211063M	7807321M
	3687623M	3948396M	3642777M	Total Assets ($)	848M	16210M	39439M	154029M	485900M	2946351M

© RMA 2010

M = $ thousand   MM = $ million
See Pages 9 through 22 for Explanation of Ratios and Data

Current Data Sorted by Assets   **Comparative Historical Data**

Type of Statement						12	13
Unqualified						12	13
Reviewed						18	13
Compiled						15	13
Tax Returns						7	11
Other						22	18

	0-500M	500M-2MM	2-10MM	10-50MM	50-100MM	100-250MM	4/1/05-3/31/06 ALL	4/1/06-3/31/07 ALL
	2/1	10/2/5 8 (4/1-9/30/09)	2/12/1/2/1/10	7/5/10 64 (10/1/09-3/31/10)	2/1/1			
NUMBER OF STATEMENTS	3	17	26	22	4		74	68
	%	%	%	%	%	%	%	%
ASSETS								
Cash & Equivalents		11.1	14.7	5.0		D	6.4	7.0
Trade Receivables (net)		27.6	25.6	27.4		A	29.7	28.6
Inventory		39.6	35.6	43.7		T	36.4	41.0
All Other Current		2.0	3.9	2.8		A	3.7	1.9
Total Current		80.3	79.9	79.0			76.3	78.5
Fixed Assets (net)		12.4	9.7	10.8		N	15.5	13.5
Intangibles (net)		3.0	6.3	5.6		O	3.9	4.5
All Other Non-Current		4.3	4.2	4.7		T	4.3	3.5
Total		100.0	100.0	100.0			100.0	100.0
LIABILITIES						A		
Notes Payable-Short Term		10.1	10.9	17.1		V	15.1	18.2
Cur. Mat.-L.T.D.		2.0	2.9	.8		A	3.8	2.2
Trade Payables		22.3	17.4	18.0		I	19.8	20.3
Income Taxes Payable		.3	.1	.0		L	.3	.3
All Other Current		6.7	8.1	5.7		A	8.0	8.3
Total Current		41.5	39.5	41.7		B	46.9	49.4
Long-Term Debt		12.0	8.4	5.6		L	12.6	10.1
Deferred Taxes		.0	.4	.1		E	.2	.3
All Other Non-Current		2.0	3.9	14.1			6.0	5.8
Net Worth		44.5	47.8	38.5			34.3	34.4
Total Liabilities & Net Worth		100.0	100.0	100.0			100.0	100.0
INCOME DATA								
Net Sales		100.0	100.0	100.0			100.0	100.0
Gross Profit		31.7	28.2	22.6			26.9	29.0
Operating Expenses		29.5	25.0	18.3			21.8	23.6
Operating Profit		2.2	3.2	4.4			5.0	5.4
All Other Expenses (net)		.0	.3	.7			.6	1.4
Profit Before Taxes		2.2	2.9	3.7			4.5	4.0
RATIOS								
Current		3.2 / 2.0 / 1.3	3.0 / 1.8 / 1.4	2.5 / 2.0 / 1.4			2.4 / 1.7 / 1.2	2.6 / 1.7 / 1.2
Quick		1.4 / .9 / .8	1.4 / 1.0 / .6	1.1 / .7 / .6			1.3 / .7 / .5	1.3 / .6 / .4
Sales/Receivables		17 21.1 / 32 11.4 / 39 9.3	25 14.8 / 34 10.7 / 64 5.7	27 13.6 / 34 10.6 / 42 8.8			30 12.2 / 37 9.8 / 47 7.7	25 14.8 / 34 10.7 / 47 7.7
Cost of Sales/Inventory		15 24.5 / 71 5.1 / 141 2.6	50 7.2 / 71 5.1 / 115 3.2	42 8.8 / 90 4.1 / 127 2.9			34 10.8 / 77 4.8 / 115 3.2	40 9.2 / 73 5.0 / 125 2.9
Cost of Sales/Payables		15 23.9 / 29 12.6 / 49 7.5	15 24.3 / 33 11.0 / 49 7.5	18 20.1 / 29 12.6 / 38 9.7			20 18.7 / 34 10.6 / 49 7.5	20 18.0 / 32 11.3 / 51 7.1
Sales/Working Capital		4.2 / 5.8 / 33.8	4.2 / 7.0 / 9.9	4.6 / 7.2 / 12.8			5.0 / 8.2 / 20.4	5.8 / 9.8 / 23.0
EBIT/Interest		16.5 / (14) 6.2 / 1.3	12.7 / (23) 4.9 / 2.3	10.7 / (21) 5.2 / 3.2			11.4 / (66) 4.8 / 2.5	9.2 / (62) 3.1 / 1.8
Net Profit + Depr., Dep., Amort./Cur. Mat. L/T/D							10.9 / (17) 2.9 / 1.7	40.7 / (13) 8.3 / 1.8
Fixed/Worth		.1 / .2 / .8	.0 / .1 / .4	.2 / .3 / .6			.1 / .3 / 1.2	.2 / .3 / .7
Debt/Worth		.5 / 1.0 / 3.0	.6 / 1.2 / 2.8	.7 / 1.3 / 3.9			.7 / 2.6 / 5.4	1.0 / 2.2 / 5.9
% Profit Before Taxes/Tangible Net Worth		29.5 / (16) 11.2 / 3.7	19.5 / (24) 11.9 / 4.6	37.7 / (19) 14.2 / 5.8			56.8 / (66) 19.4 / 10.2	42.2 / (62) 24.6 / 9.3
% Profit Before Taxes/Total Assets		11.0 / 4.0 / 1.3	10.9 / 4.5 / 2.1	11.4 / 6.8 / 2.3			15.2 / 6.8 / 3.4	14.5 / 7.6 / 2.6
Sales/Net Fixed Assets		76.1 / 35.9 / 24.6	184.7 / 49.9 / 24.3	58.7 / 36.8 / 18.1			76.0 / 33.3 / 12.7	75.5 / 38.9 / 12.3
Sales/Total Assets		3.5 / 3.2 / 2.4	3.0 / 2.6 / 1.8	3.4 / 2.7 / 2.0			3.4 / 2.6 / 2.0	3.4 / 2.7 / 2.2
% Depr., Dep., Amort./Sales		.5 / (12) .8 / 2.2	.5 / (19) .9 / 1.8	.4 / (21) .6 / .9			.4 / (62) .8 / 1.3	.3 / (57) .8 / 1.1
% Officers', Directors' Owners' Comp/Sales							2.3 / (28) 3.8 / 6.1	2.6 / (27) 3.7 / 7.8
Net Sales ($)	3674M	71633M	330990M	1261590M	532127M		1858647M	1859369M
Total Assets ($)	1123M	21038M	136341M	470204M	310907M		831021M	778296M

© RMA 2010

M = $ thousand   MM = $ million
See Pages 9 through 22 for Explanation of Ratios and Data

Comparative Historical Data   Current Data Sorted by Sales

Type of Statement

H1	H2	H3					0-1MM	1-3MM	3-5MM	5-10MM	10-25MM	25MM & OVER
7	8	11	Unqualified					1	1	4	5	10
15	20	18	Reviewed					4	2	3	2	7
14	12	12	Compiled				1	1	1	1	1	1
2	17	5	Tax Returns									
18	23	26	Other				1	2	2	7	6	8

H1 4/1/07-3/31/08 ALL	H2 4/1/08-3/31/09 ALL	H3 4/1/09-3/31/10 ALL		8 (4/1-9/30/09)			0-1MM	1-3MM	3-5MM	64 (10/1/09-3/31/10)		
56	80	72	**NUMBER OF STATEMENTS**				2	8	6	15	15	26

H1 %	H2 %	H3 %	Item				0-1MM %	1-3MM %	3-5MM %	5-10MM %	10-25MM %	25MM & OVER %
			ASSETS									
10.1	10.6	11.7	Cash & Equivalents							14.9	15.9	7.7
27.2	24.6	26.4	Trade Receivables (net)							26.0	24.7	28.0
37.0	38.0	38.5	Inventory							35.2	36.1	40.4
3.5	3.0	3.4	All Other Current							3.8	2.9	2.9
77.9	76.2	80.0	Total Current							79.8	79.6	79.0
13.3	12.9	11.2	Fixed Assets (net)							9.0	10.3	12.1
4.4	6.0	4.7	Intangibles (net)							5.9	6.4	4.3
4.5	5.0	4.1	All Other Non-Current							5.3	3.7	4.6
100.0	100.0	100.0	Total							100.0	100.0	100.0
			LIABILITIES									
17.3	20.0	13.3	Notes Payable-Short Term							8.9	11.1	14.5
2.0	2.4	2.2	Cur. Mat.-L.T.D.							3.9	1.9	1.8
16.7	17.2	18.5	Trade Payables							18.2	21.7	17.7
.4	.2	.1	Income Taxes Payable							.0	.1	.1
8.7	9.0	8.4	All Other Current							7.4	9.8	5.8
45.0	48.8	42.5	Total Current							38.5	44.6	39.9
8.9	11.8	7.8	Long-Term Debt							12.1	7.2	4.6
.1	.2	.2	Deferred Taxes							.6	.0	.2
6.1	5.5	6.7	All Other Non-Current							6.3	2.4	11.8
39.8	33.7	42.7	Net Worth							42.5	45.8	43.6
100.0	100.0	100.0	Total Liabilities & Net Worth							100.0	100.0	100.0
			INCOME DATA									
100.0	100.0	100.0	Net Sales							100.0	100.0	100.0
32.0	28.6	28.7	Gross Profit							28.7	27.6	23.7
25.1	25.1	25.0	Operating Expenses							24.3	24.5	19.0
6.9	3.5	3.7	Operating Profit							4.4	3.1	4.7
.9	.3	.3	All Other Expenses (net)							.2	.3	.6
6.0	3.2	3.4	Profit Before Taxes							4.2	2.8	4.2

RATIOS

H1	H2	H3	Item				0-1MM	1-3MM	3-5MM	5-10MM	10-25MM	25MM & OVER
2.6	2.8	3.1	Current							5.2	2.6	4.1
1.8	1.7	2.0								1.8	1.8	2.0
1.4	1.2	1.4								1.2	1.4	1.4
1.3	1.1	1.4	Quick							2.5	1.2	1.4
.8	.7	.9								.9	.9	.8
.4	.4	.6								.6	.7	.6
24 15.4	21 17.8	24 15.1	Sales/Receivables							24 15.4	24 15.1	27 13.6
35 10.6	27 13.5	34 10.8								33 11.1	34 10.8	35 10.5
45 8.2	39 9.4	40 9.0								66 5.5	39 9.4	46 7.9
31 11.8	34 10.8	44 8.2	Cost of Sales/Inventory							42 8.7	52 7.0	42 8.8
76 4.8	59 6.1	75 4.8								64 5.7	70 5.2	90 4.1
127 2.9	123 3.0	124 2.9								87 4.2	97 3.8	122 3.0
14 26.4	11 34.5	17 21.8	Cost of Sales/Payables							15 24.5	18 20.6	18 20.3
28 13.1	26 13.8	31 11.8								24 15.3	44 8.2	28 13.2
46 7.9	36 10.1	48 7.6								49 7.5	53 6.9	38 9.7
4.8	4.6	4.3	Sales/Working Capital							3.2	4.8	3.9
8.7	10.8	6.7								7.7	7.3	7.4
12.5	36.4	11.8								11.7	9.8	15.2
9.7	9.8	12.6	EBIT/Interest							23.7	21.4	12.3
(53) 4.0	(73) 3.5	(64) 5.5					(12)	(14)	(24)	4.6	9.4	4.8
2.4	1.6	2.7								1.4	2.7	3.0
31.4	42.1	6.6	Net Profit + Depr., Dep., Amort./Cur. Mat. L/T/D									
(18) 10.7	(19) 5.6	(16) 5.2										
1.4	2.0	2.8										
.2	.1	.1	Fixed/Worth							.0	.1	.2
.3	.3	.2								.2	.1	.2
.8	1.4	.5								.5	.6	.5
.9	.7	.5	Debt/Worth							.4	.8	.6
1.7	1.6	1.2								2.1	1.2	1.3
3.4	7.0	3.2								6.0	2.4	3.3
56.7	38.3	26.9	% Profit Before Taxes/Tangible Net Worth							29.0	26.8	29.9
(50) 24.8	(66) 16.5	(64) 13.9					(12)		(23)	9.2	18.7	14.2
8.8	7.1	4.7								3.8	6.6	7.5
16.4	12.9	11.4	% Profit Before Taxes/Total Assets							11.4	10.8	13.2
8.4	5.8	5.8								4.5	6.5	6.2
3.1	2.1	2.1								1.2	2.9	3.0
63.4	93.3	73.0	Sales/Net Fixed Assets							204.0	136.2	56.2
32.2	43.7	38.2								65.6	50.2	32.3
12.8	18.4	16.6								15.8	27.2	13.2
3.4	3.9	3.3	Sales/Total Assets							3.2	3.1	3.4
2.7	2.9	2.6								2.7	2.6	2.6
2.0	2.1	1.9								1.6	2.1	2.0
.4	.4	.5	% Depr., Dep., Amort./Sales							.5	.4	.4
(49) .8	(66) .7	(58) .8					(11)	(12)	(24)	1.3	.7	.7
1.2	1.0	1.3								1.8	1.3	.9
1.8	2.1	1.6	% Officers', Directors' Owners' Comp/Sales									
(24) 3.8	(35) 4.5	(14) 2.5										
5.9	6.8	4.4										
1537966M	2273007M	2200014M	Net Sales ($)				1798M	16147M	25206M	102267M	236634M	1817962M
622284M	993486M	939613M	Total Assets ($)				680M	8448M	7761M	49416M	95754M	777554M

© RMA 2010

M = $ thousand   MM = $ million
See Pages 9 through 22 for Explanation of Ratios and Data

Current Data Sorted by Assets | **Comparative Historical Data**

	0-500M	500M-2MM	2-10MM	10-50MM	50-100MM	100-250MM	Type of Statement	4/1/05-3/31/06 ALL	4/1/06-3/31/07 ALL
		2	23	45	20	34	Unqualified	100	115
		13	69	40	5		Reviewed	72	108
	1	22	44	5	2	1	Compiled	46	48
	16	32	11		16		Tax Returns	29	44
	8	30	79	66	16	28	Other	109	115

79 (4/1-9/30/09) 533 (10/1/09-3/31/10)

	0-500M	500M-2MM	2-10MM	10-50MM	50-100MM	100-250MM		ALL	ALL
	25	99	226	156	43	63	**NUMBER OF STATEMENTS**	356	430
	%	%	%	%	%	%	**ASSETS**	%	%
	13.5	12.8	8.1	4.5	3.6	2.9	Cash & Equivalents	6.1	5.3
	24.3	21.3	17.8	14.1	11.3	15.9	Trade Receivables (net)	20.1	20.0
	33.7	40.5	48.2	50.3	53.9	44.3	Inventory	46.4	46.0
	1.4	1.6	1.5	2.2	3.5	2.6	All Other Current	1.6	1.8
	72.9	76.2	75.6	71.1	72.2	65.7	Total Current	74.2	73.1
	19.8	15.0	17.7	23.3	21.0	27.6	Fixed Assets (net)	21.2	22.2
	.1	2.8	2.1	1.5	2.9	.7	Intangibles (net)	1.4	1.4
	7.2	6.0	4.6	4.0	3.8	6.0	All Other Non-Current	3.2	3.3
	100.0	100.0	100.0	100.0	100.0	100.0	Total	100.0	100.0
							LIABILITIES		
	15.6	18.3	24.7	27.1	28.1	21.8	Notes Payable-Short Term	27.2	25.6
	5.5	3.1	4.6	5.7	6.1	1.6	Cur. Mat.-L.T.D.	3.7	4.0
	18.3	18.4	10.8	8.1	6.5	7.3	Trade Payables	15.9	14.0
	.2	.1	.1	.4	1.3	.4	Income Taxes Payable	.4	.3
	38.5	14.6	6.3	5.7	6.6	8.1	All Other Current	8.0	8.3
	78.1	54.5	46.5	47.0	48.6	39.3	Total Current	55.1	52.1
	24.0	12.1	10.7	12.8	13.4	19.0	Long-Term Debt	12.6	12.5
	.1	.1	.5	.9	2.3	1.1	Deferred Taxes	.6	.5
	.4	4.9	4.7	2.3	2.4	2.9	All Other Non-Current	3.7	5.1
	-2.7	28.3	37.6	37.0	33.3	37.7	Net Worth	28.0	29.9
	100.0	100.0	100.0	100.0	100.0	100.0	Total Liabilities & Net Worth	100.0	100.0
							INCOME DATA		
	100.0	100.0	100.0	100.0	100.0	100.0	Net Sales	100.0	100.0
	38.0	33.6	28.6	25.7	21.6	26.3	Gross Profit	25.1	26.5
	37.0	31.5	27.5	23.2	19.3	23.7	Operating Expenses	20.4	20.6
	1.0	2.0	1.1	2.5	2.2	2.6	Operating Profit	4.7	5.9
	.9	.9	1.1	1.1	1.1	1.5	All Other Expenses (net)	.7	1.2
	.1	1.1	.0	1.4	1.2	1.1	Profit Before Taxes	4.0	4.7
							RATIOS		
	2.1	2.8	2.3	2.1	1.9	3.0	Current	1.8	1.9
	1.2	1.6	1.6	1.4	1.3	1.6		1.3	1.4
	.6	1.0	1.2	1.2	1.1	1.2		1.1	1.1
	1.1	1.4	1.0	.7	.6	.8	Quick	.8	.9
	.4	.6	.5	.4	.3	.5		.4 (429)	.4
	.2	.3	.3	.2	.2	.3		.3	.2
0 UND		12 30.9	20 18.1	22 16.9	26 14.0	37 9.8	Sales/Receivables	20 18.0	20 18.0
15 24.5		28 13.2	30 12.0	32 11.5	32 11.3	44 8.2		35 10.6	33 11.0
30 12.0		47 7.8	48 7.6	47 7.7	48 7.5	56 6.5		47 7.8	47 7.8
0 UND		35 10.5	65 5.6	94 3.9	131 2.8	118 3.1	Cost of Sales/Inventory	52 7.1	50 7.2
16 22.3		97 3.8	158 2.3	169 2.2	197 1.9	186 2.0		108 3.4	112 3.2
89 4.1		224 1.6	265 1.4	266 1.4	297 1.2	240 1.5		178 2.1	187 2.0
0 UND		5 78.9	10 38.0	11 34.6	12 30.9	16 22.7	Cost of Sales/Payables	12 31.3	10 38.2
17 22.0		29 12.6	20 18.1	19 19.1	19 19.4	25 14.4		25 14.5	23 15.9
41 8.9		64 5.7	43 8.4	33 11.1	34 10.7	34 10.8		58 6.3	48 7.7
	10.2	4.1	3.6	3.5	3.1	2.7	Sales/Working Capital	6.3	5.7
	47.6	8.5	6.2	6.9	6.7	4.6		10.7	10.2
	-13.6	-83.4	13.8	14.4	23.5	10.5		29.3	28.9
	13.8	5.8	4.3	3.9	4.4	2.9	EBIT/Interest	7.2	6.0
	(21) 2.8	(83) 1.8	(211) 1.6	(151) 1.7	(42) 1.8	(59) 1.8		(347) 3.5	(407) 2.8
	-.5	-1.3	-.4	.7	.9	.8		1.9	1.6
			5.1	5.2			Net Profit + Depr., Dep.,	9.7	8.6
		(47) 1.9	(49) 1.5				Amort./Cur. Mat. L/T/D	(95) 3.4	(114) 3.5
			.5	.6				1.9	1.0
	.2	.1	.1	.2	.1	.3	Fixed/Worth	.2	.2
	.7	.3	.3	.5	.3	.9		.5	.5
	-.6	2.0	.9	1.1	1.9	1.2		1.5	1.4
	1.0	.9	1.0	1.1	1.7	1.0	Debt/Worth	1.5	1.4
	7.2	2.5	1.9	2.0	2.6	1.7		3.0	3.0
	-5.0	28.9	3.8	4.0	4.6	3.4		5.2	5.0
	139.6	31.8	19.7	15.9	12.0	9.7	% Profit Before Taxes/Tangible	40.8	41.0
	(16) 16.0	(83) 11.1	(213) 4.7	(152) 5.4	(41) 7.0	4.3	Net Worth	(335) 22.9	(412) 23.2
	-15.5	-9.4	-8.5	-1.9	.3	-1.9		10.4	10.5
	23.4	10.2	5.9	5.1	3.8	4.3	% Profit Before Taxes/Total	10.9	11.5
	4.8	2.3	1.4	1.5	1.6	1.3	Assets	5.8	5.6
	-4.8	-3.5	-2.9	-.7	-.2	-.7		2.3	2.4
	851.8	125.8	38.5	30.6	46.1	8.9	Sales/Net Fixed Assets	49.6	46.5
	68.0	37.9	18.5	11.0	17.6	5.0		18.3	18.1
	13.0	14.2	6.7	3.8	3.3	2.9		5.5	5.5
	8.7	3.4	2.2	1.8	1.6	1.4	Sales/Total Assets	2.6	2.6
	4.4	2.1	1.5	1.4	1.1	1.2		1.9	1.9
	2.9	1.4	1.1	1.0	.8	1.0		1.4	1.4
	.4	.4	.6	1.1	.6	1.1	% Depr., Dep., Amort./Sales	.6	.6
	(12) 1.1	(68) 1.2	(182) 1.3	(112) 1.9	(26) 2.1	(21) 2.7		(281) 1.1	(341) 1.1
	2.1	2.4	3.1	6.8	8.3	4.8		4.5	3.9
	4.5	2.2	1.3	.7			% Officers', Directors'	1.1	1.3
	(13) 8.3	(59) 4.3	(83) 2.4	(23) 1.0			Owners' Comp/Sales	(116) 2.6	(120) 2.2
	11.2	7.6	4.1	2.8				4.5	5.1
	33079M	315477M	1998906M	5782920M	3770634M	12029300M	Net Sales ($)	18492330M	22652797M
	6339M	123054M	1163194M	3980498M	3008093M	9872458M	Total Assets ($)	11124845M	13652684M

M = $ thousand   MM = $ million
See Pages 9 through 22 for Explanation of Ratios and Data

Comparative Historical Data   Current Data Sorted by Sales

			Type of Statement						
120	145	124	Unqualified		2	2	12	15	93
118	128	127	Reviewed	2	7	13	37	44	24
70	63	75	Compiled	4	11	15	23	18	4
45	49	59	Tax Returns	11	23	10	10	4	1
177	222	227	Other	10	34	24	30	49	80
4/1/07-3/31/08 ALL	4/1/08-3/31/09 ALL	4/1/09-3/31/10 ALL		79 (4/1-9/30/09)			533 (10/1/09-3/31/10)		
				0-1MM	1-3MM	3-5MM	5-10MM	10-25MM	25MM & OVER
530	607	612	NUMBER OF STATEMENTS	27	77	64	112	130	202
%	%	%	ASSETS	%	%	%	%	%	%
5.6	5.4	7.3	Cash & Equivalents	16.4	9.3	7.7	7.3	10.3	3.4
16.9	16.0	17.0	Trade Receivables (net)	9.1	19.2	17.5	18.2	18.6	15.4
49.5	49.9	46.9	Inventory	32.6	45.6	50.6	49.5	41.4	50.2
2.0	2.1	1.9	All Other Current	.8	1.9	1.1	1.3	2.4	2.4
74.0	73.5	73.2	Total Current	58.9	76.0	77.0	76.3	72.7	71.4
21.3	20.9	20.0	Fixed Assets (net)	32.9	16.9	14.0	16.4	21.3	22.7
1.4	1.5	1.9	Intangibles (net)	3.6	1.8	3.6	2.2	1.2	1.4
3.3	4.2	4.9	All Other Non-Current	4.7	5.3	5.4	5.1	4.8	4.5
100.0	100.0	100.0	Total	100.0	100.0	100.0	100.0	100.0	100.0
			LIABILITIES						
27.8	29.5	23.8	Notes Payable-Short Term	9.3	19.6	29.3	24.0	23.1	26.0
5.2	4.4	4.5	Cur. Mat.-L.T.D.	6.2	4.1	2.7	5.8	4.7	4.1
12.7	11.2	11.0	Trade Payables	6.0	15.7	13.9	12.1	11.2	8.2
.3	.3	.3	Income Taxes Payable	.0	.2	.1	.1	.1	.7
7.5	7.8	9.0	All Other Current	25.1	14.6	10.2	6.8	7.3	6.7
53.6	53.1	48.6	Total Current	46.6	54.1	56.0	48.6	46.5	45.8
14.0	13.1	13.1	Long-Term Debt	37.2	14.2	9.0	8.9	11.9	13.7
.5	.6	.7	Deferred Taxes	.0	.3	.6	.4	.6	1.2
3.8	3.0	3.6	All Other Non-Current	1.8	5.6	4.0	5.8	2.5	2.4
28.2	30.2	34.0	Net Worth	14.4	25.7	30.3	36.2	38.5	36.9
100.0	100.0	100.0	Total Liabilities & Net Worth	100.0	100.0	100.0	100.0	100.0	100.0
			INCOME DATA						
100.0	100.0	100.0	Net Sales	100.0	100.0	100.0	100.0	100.0	100.0
26.0	26.0	28.3	Gross Profit	46.5	36.9	33.7	25.0	27.2	23.6
20.7	21.9	26.5	Operating Expenses	38.7	36.6	32.3	25.0	25.1	20.9
5.3	4.1	1.9	Operating Profit	7.7	.2	1.4	.0	2.1	2.7
1.3	1.1	1.1	All Other Expenses (net)	4.9	.7	1.6	.9	.6	1.1
3.9	3.0	.7	Profit Before Taxes	2.8	-.5	-.2	-.9	1.5	1.6
			RATIOS						
1.8	2.0	2.3	Current	3.0	3.1	2.0	2.3	2.3	2.2
1.3	1.3	1.5		1.5	1.7	1.3	1.6	1.5	1.5
1.1	1.1	1.2		.7	1.0	1.1	1.2	1.2	1.2
.7	.7	.9	Quick	2.4	1.1	.6	1.0	1.3	.6
.4 (606)	.3	.4		.7	.5	.4	.4	.5	.4
.2	.2	.2		.1	.2	.2	.2	.3	.2
17 21.1	17 21.2	20 18.3	Sales/Receivables	0 UND	15 23.8	17 21.2	17 21.7	21 17.1	27 13.6
30 12.4	28 13.0	33 11.0		16 22.5	30 12.0	30 12.1	30 12.3	32 11.5	38 9.7
45 8.1	43 8.5	48 7.6		58 6.3	49 7.5	51 7.2	45 8.2	51 7.1	48 7.7
59 6.2	69 5.3	67 5.5	Cost of Sales/Inventory	0 UND	56 6.5	73 5.0	52 7.0	44 8.3	100 3.7
124 2.9	136 2.7	156 2.3		90 4.1	159 2.3	186 2.0	132 2.8	117 3.1	171 2.1
207 1.8	219 1.7	253 1.4		266 1.4	276 1.3	299 1.2	265 1.4	202 1.8	243 1.5
11 34.2	9 42.1	10 35.9	Cost of Sales/Payables	0 UND	10 36.4	10 37.6	8 45.6	11 32.9	12 29.9
22 16.8	19 19.4	20 18.0		10 37.7	33 11.1	19 19.6	25 14.7	20 18.3	20 18.4
47 7.8	42 8.7	41 8.9		42 8.8	71 5.1	48 7.5	47 7.7	32 11.3	34 10.9
5.2	4.9	3.5	Sales/Working Capital	3.0	3.3	4.0	3.3	4.4	3.3
9.8	9.3	6.8		6.5	6.0	7.0	6.4	7.2	7.0
27.8	24.9	17.8		-13.9	238.2	19.3	15.2	14.4	15.2
4.9	5.2	4.1	EBIT/Interest	4.0	3.7	3.1	4.0	5.8	4.1
(509) 2.4	(578) 2.3	(567) 1.7		(25) 1.9	(64) 1.3	(56) 1.2	(107) 1.2	(121) 1.9	(194) 2.0
1.3	1.2	.3		-.5	-1.3	-.9	-1.2	.6	1.0
7.0	6.5	5.1	Net Profit + Depr., Dep., Amort./Cur. Mat. L/T/D				3.3	7.4	5.4
(137) 2.0	(144) 1.9	(119) 1.7				(26) 1.1	(25) 2.0	(53) 1.9	
.7	.5	.5				.0	.9	.5	
.1	.2	.1	Fixed/Worth	.2	.1	.1	.1	.1	.2
.4	.5	.4		.9	.3	.3	.3	.4	.5
1.5	1.4	1.2		43.8	1.8	1.2	1.0	1.0	1.2
1.6	1.4	1.0	Debt/Worth	1.0	.9	1.1	1.0	1.0	1.1
3.0	2.8	2.1		4.5	2.8	2.5	1.9	1.8	2.0
5.9	5.6	4.4		-4.1	8.6	7.9	5.5	3.7	3.7
39.1	28.8	17.8	% Profit Before Taxes/Tangible Net Worth	29.9	22.9	19.7	16.2	19.8	15.3
(498) 18.8	(572) 13.7	(568) 5.6		(20) 10.6	(66) 2.8	(56) 3.9	(102) 2.2	(127) 7.6	(197) 7.0
6.5	3.6	-3.6		-9.6	-14.5	-8.5	-14.1	-1.5	.7
9.6	8.8	5.6	% Profit Before Taxes/Total Assets	14.1	6.1	5.0	5.9	6.3	5.2
4.5	3.3	1.6		2.3	.9	1.2	.4	1.9	2.1
1.1	.4	-1.7		-3.0	-5.0	-2.6	-4.9	-.8	.1
51.9	41.0	39.8	Sales/Net Fixed Assets	90.1	73.8	76.2	53.1	34.3	31.7
19.4	16.8	16.5		8.6	29.1	19.3	21.7	15.9	10.6
5.4	5.1	5.2		2.9	8.0	9.6	7.3	4.8	3.8
2.5	2.4	2.2	Sales/Total Assets	3.0	2.7	2.2	2.8	2.5	1.8
1.8	1.7	1.4		1.1	1.6	1.6	1.5	1.6	1.3
1.3	1.2	1.0		.3	1.0	1.0	1.0	1.1	1.0
.6	.7	.7	% Depr., Dep., Amort./Sales	1.6	.6	.6	.5	.7	.9
(405) 1.1	(443) 1.3	(421) 1.5		(15) 7.6	(51) 1.2	(43) 1.4	(93) 1.3	(104) 1.8	(115) 1.5
4.8	4.4	4.7		18.1	2.8	2.5	2.7	5.6	4.9
1.0	1.3	1.5	% Officers', Directors' Owners' Comp/Sales		3.5	2.3	1.4	.9	.5
(121) 2.2	(155) 2.1	(183) 2.9			(47) 5.8	(27) 4.1	(44) 2.3	(42) 1.8	(16) .9
4.2	4.2	5.8			8.5	6.4	3.7	3.5	1.4
26164916M	32829823M	23930316M	Net Sales ($)	16885M	159374M	247962M	813342M	2076650M	20616103M
15861361M	20495425M	18153636M	Total Assets ($)	20958M	120006M	197211M	553529M	1504081M	15757851M

© RMA 2010

M = $ thousand   MM = $ million
See Pages 9 through 22 for Explanation of Ratios and Data

WHOLESALE—Farm and Garden Machinery and Equipment Merchant Wholesalers   NAICS 423820

Current Data Sorted by Assets							Comparative Historical Data	

			6	23	7	7	Type of Statement		
		3	37	31	1		Unqualified	37	42
4	10	30	7				Reviewed	64	81
5	12	18	7	1			Compiled	76	84
4	11	36	33	7	2		Tax Returns	34	55
							Other	95	94
	47 (4/1-9/30/09)			255 (10/1/09-3/31/10)				4/1/05-3/31/06	4/1/06-3/31/07
0-500M	500M-2MM	2-10MM	10-50MM	50-100MM	100-250MM			ALL	ALL
13	36	127	101	16	9		NUMBER OF STATEMENTS	306	356

%	%	%	%	%	%			%	%
							ASSETS		
11.2	7.3	7.3	5.8	1.4		Cash & Equivalents	5.9	5.7
22.3	12.6	15.4	12.3	15.3		Trade Receivables (net)	16.4	15.5
56.7	59.5	57.0	60.2	55.7		Inventory	59.7	59.3
.6	1.6	1.9	2.3	2.8		All Other Current	2.1	1.9
90.8	81.1	81.5	80.5	75.2		Total Current	84.0	82.3
8.9	11.6	12.0	13.9	14.5		Fixed Assets (net)	10.5	11.3
.0	.1	2.0	1.6	3.2		Intangibles (net)	1.4	1.7
.3	7.2	4.4	3.9	7.1		All Other Non-Current	4.1	4.7
100.0	100.0	100.0	100.0	100.0		Total	100.0	100.0
						LIABILITIES		
50.3	27.3	25.9	26.3	21.3		Notes Payable-Short Term	23.2	25.3
2.9	1.2	2.1	2.1	4.3		Cur. Mat.-L.T.D.	2.0	2.3
13.5	15.1	16.6	18.9	14.0		Trade Payables	20.2	19.1
.0	.0	.2	.1	.5		Income Taxes Payable	.2	.2
19.5	5.0	6.0	6.3	12.3		All Other Current	8.8	9.0
86.2	48.6	50.8	53.8	52.3		Total Current	54.5	55.9
11.4	11.0	7.6	7.9	8.7		Long-Term Debt	9.9	8.6
.0	.0	.4	.3	.2		Deferred Taxes	.2	.1
8.9	4.0	3.8	4.1	4.2		All Other Non-Current	2.8	3.4
-6.6	36.3	37.4	33.9	34.6		Net Worth	32.7	31.9
100.0	100.0	100.0	100.0	100.0		Total Liabilities & Net Worth	100.0	100.0
						INCOME DATA		
100.0	100.0	100.0	100.0	100.0		Net Sales	100.0	100.0
31.9	23.8	23.8	20.3	19.6		Gross Profit	22.5	21.7
30.2	21.9	21.5	17.8	14.6		Operating Expenses	19.5	19.1
1.8	1.9	2.3	2.5	5.0		Operating Profit	3.0	2.7
1.5	.6	.3	.2	.9		All Other Expenses (net)	.3	.6
.2	1.3	2.0	2.2	4.1		Profit Before Taxes	2.7	2.1
						RATIOS		
4.3	3.3	2.3	2.0	2.0		Current	1.9	2.0
1.5	1.8	1.5	1.4	1.4			1.5	1.4
.6	1.2	1.3	1.2	1.2			1.2	1.2
1.7	.9	.9	.6	.7		Quick	.7	.7
.4	.3	.4	.2	.2			.4	.3
.1	.1	.2	.1	.1			.1	.1
0 UND	5 71.4	9 42.5	7 52.0	6 61.5		Sales/Receivables	7 51.3	7 53.9
13 27.2	16 22.2	17 22.1	15 24.6	27 13.4			18 20.7	17 21.5
29 12.6	32 11.3	40 9.1	33 11.0	42 8.8			40 9.2	34 10.8
24 14.9	66 5.5	76 4.8	86 4.3	73 5.0		Cost of Sales/Inventory	79 4.6	73 5.0
85 4.3	131 2.8	115 3.2	127 2.9	105 3.5			122 3.0	114 3.2
197 1.9	214 1.7	181 2.0	190 1.9	227 1.6			177 2.1	177 2.1
0 UND	2 195.2	10 37.9	13 27.7	5 69.7		Cost of Sales/Payables	11 33.8	9 41.6
15 24.0	20 18.2	24 15.2	28 13.1	17 21.0			32 11.3	25 14.3
40 9.0	43 8.5	48 7.6	62 5.9	39 9.3			59 6.2	52 7.0
4.9	4.2	4.9	5.6	3.8		Sales/Working Capital	5.3	5.7
15.1	7.1	8.0	9.0	10.3			8.4	9.8
-12.0	11.0	14.1	16.2	19.6			15.1	20.0
28.8	6.3	7.8	7.9	9.1		EBIT/Interest	7.0	5.4
(12) 1.8	(32) 2.1	(122) 2.8	(96) 2.9	5.8			(290) 3.2	(345) 2.5
-1.8	.4	1.0	1.4	3.3			1.6	1.3
		4.9	7.0			Net Profit + Depr., Dep.,	5.4	4.1
	(38) 3.0	(34) 2.4			Amort./Cur. Mat. L/T/D	(87) 3.2	(89) 2.6
		.7	1.4				1.1	1.0
.0	.0	.1	.2	.1		Fixed/Worth	.1	.1
.0	.2	.2	.3	.4			.3	.3
-5.4	.7	.5	.6	.8			.6	.7
.3	.5	.9	1.1	1.3		Debt/Worth	1.3	1.1
2.6	1.6	1.9	2.6	2.3			2.2	2.4
-3.0	6.1	4.1	4.8	4.7			4.5	5.9
	34.5	26.2	25.1	42.6		% Profit Before Taxes/Tangible	30.4	28.4
(32) 13.1	(122) 10.4	(100) 14.7	(15) 20.0		Net Worth	(291) 15.5	(323) 14.5
	.6	.3	4.8	8.2			5.3	4.4
25.3	8.3	8.3	8.5	12.9		% Profit Before Taxes/Total	10.1	8.9
.6	2.0	3.4	3.9	7.4		Assets	4.0	4.0
-16.1	-1.4	.1	1.0	3.7			1.5	1.0
UND	225.8	66.3	51.5	64.1		Sales/Net Fixed Assets	70.8	70.6
102.0	47.3	31.7	22.7	30.6			30.5	33.1
28.4	15.1	13.3	12.4	11.0			16.1	16.3
5.4	3.2	2.8	2.6	3.1		Sales/Total Assets	3.0	3.1
3.5	2.7	2.2	2.0	2.2			2.3	2.3
2.6	1.4	1.6	1.6	1.3			1.7	1.8
	.2	.5	.5	.5		% Depr., Dep., Amort./Sales	.4	.4
(26) .5	(114) .9	(88) .8	(12) .6			(265) .7	(308) .7
	1.1	1.8	1.5	1.3			1.1	1.2
	1.7	1.0	.7			% Officers', Directors',	1.0	1.0
(16) 2.3	(60) 2.3	(28) 1.1			Owners' Comp/Sales	(138) 1.9	(166) 2.0
	3.8	4.1	1.6				3.5	3.9
15172M	110091M	1423486M	4941484M	2418141M	2865745M	Net Sales ($)	6898449M	8726333M
3814M	43688M	640274M	2331513M	1098061M	1471035M	Total Assets ($)	3139655M	3608731M

M = $ thousand   MM = $ million
See Pages 9 through 22 for Explanation of Ratios and Data

Comparative Historical Data | Current Data Sorted by Sales

	4/1/07-3/31/08 ALL	4/1/08-3/31/09 ALL	4/1/09-3/31/10 ALL		0-1MM	1-3MM	3-5MM	5-10MM	10-25MM	25MM & OVER
Type of Statement										
Unqualified	36	39	43			4	3	18	9	34
Reviewed	69	75	72			6	6	15	19	28
Compiled	94	74	51		6	12	8	5	14	4
Tax Returns	43	49	43		1				11	6
Other	105	91	93		2	9	3	16	24	39
						47 (4/1-9/30/09)		255 (10/1/09-3/31/10)		
NUMBER OF STATEMENTS	347	328	302		9	31	20	54	77	111
	%	%	%		%	%	%	%	%	%
ASSETS										
Cash & Equivalents	5.7	6.7	6.5			9.0	9.7	8.4	7.4	4.1
Trade Receivables (net)	15.0	14.0	14.3			18.8	12.3	15.0	16.0	12.6
Inventory	58.3	60.2	57.9			54.0	62.1	54.4	56.3	60.5
All Other Current	2.4	2.4	2.0			1.2	1.2	2.5	1.7	2.4
Total Current	81.5	83.3	80.7			82.9	85.4	80.4	81.4	79.6
Fixed Assets (net)	12.3	11.3	12.9			10.3	10.4	13.7	11.4	13.6
Intangibles (net)	1.6	1.1	1.7			.1	.4	.2	3.6	1.9
All Other Non-Current	4.6	4.2	4.7			6.7	3.9	5.8	3.6	4.9
Total	100.0	100.0	100.0			100.0	100.0	100.0	100.0	100.0
LIABILITIES										
Notes Payable-Short Term	24.2	25.2	26.8			25.4	27.0	28.1	24.4	25.0
Cur. Mat.-L.T.D.	2.5	2.7	2.1			.9	1.7	2.4	2.2	2.2
Trade Payables	18.5	18.5	17.0			17.4	15.8	13.3	16.0	20.2
Income Taxes Payable	.1	.3	.2			.2	.0	.0	.2	.3
All Other Current	9.9	9.2	7.1			9.2	5.1	6.0	7.1	7.5
Total Current	55.2	55.9	53.3			53.0	49.7	49.8	49.9	55.1
Long-Term Debt	8.7	7.2	8.2			10.5	15.6	6.6	8.7	6.3
Deferred Taxes	.2	.1	.4			.0	.1	.1	.5	.6
All Other Non-Current	4.0	4.0	4.2			5.2	5.0	3.9	2.3	4.4
Net Worth	31.8	32.8	34.0			31.3	29.6	39.5	38.6	33.6
Total Liabilties & Net Worth	100.0	100.0	100.0			100.0	100.0	100.0	100.0	100.0
INCOME DATA										
Net Sales	100.0	100.0	100.0			100.0	100.0	100.0	100.0	100.0
Gross Profit	22.9	22.3	22.7			29.7	21.4	24.4	22.9	19.6
Operating Expenses	20.0	19.0	20.2			26.4	18.9	21.2	20.8	16.8
Operating Profit	2.9	3.3	2.5			3.3	2.6	3.2	2.1	2.8
All Other Expenses (net)	.6	.3	.4			1.2	.9	.6	.0	.2
Profit Before Taxes	2.3	3.0	2.1			2.0	1.7	2.6	2.1	2.5
RATIOS										
Current	1.9	2.0	2.2			3.5	3.6	2.6	2.3	1.9
	1.5	1.5	1.5			1.6	1.5	1.5	1.6	1.4
	1.2	1.2	1.2			1.2	1.2	1.3	1.3	1.2
Quick	.7	.6	.8			1.0	1.0	1.2	.9	.6
	.3	.3	.3			.4	.2	.4	.4	.2
	.1	.1	.1			.2	.1	.2	.2	.1
Sales/Receivables	7 52.8	6 64.1	7 50.9		11 34.6	5 79.2	9 38.9	10 38.3	6 60.5	
	17 20.9	15 24.6	16 22.9		19 19.2	18 20.4	20 18.3	15 23.6	14 27.0	
	35 10.4	31 11.9	35 10.4		42 8.7	56 6.5	39 9.3	39 9.4	34 10.9	
Cost of Sales/Inventory	80 4.6	76 4.8	78 4.7		58 6.3	92 3.9	71 5.1	75 4.8	84 4.3	
	116 3.1	117 3.1	119 3.1		133 2.7	178 2.1	121 3.0	115 3.2	116 3.2	
	168 2.2	168 2.2	184 2.0		286 1.3	291 1.3	173 2.1	177 2.1	169 2.2	
Cost of Sales/Payables	9 40.0	7 48.9	9 39.1		5 76.4	8 48.0	11 32.3	9 39.2	11 31.8	
	26 14.1	22 16.3	24 14.9		21 17.4	32 11.5	18 19.7	28 13.2	28 12.9	
	54 6.8	53 6.8	53 6.9		67 5.4	64 5.7	36 10.1	48 7.7	60 6.0	
Sales/Working Capital	5.5	5.8	5.0		4.2	2.9	4.9	5.3	6.2	
	9.6	10.1	8.5		7.3	5.8	7.1	8.8	9.6	
	17.3	19.3	15.3		14.1	18.4	13.7	14.2	18.2	
EBIT/Interest	5.7	8.6	8.1		12.6	7.0	6.4	8.2	9.4	
	(337) 2.6	(317) 4.0	(287) 3.0		(29) 2.5	1.6	(49) 2.4	(74) 2.8	(107) 4.6	
	1.4	1.7	1.1		.5	-.2	1.0	1.0	1.9	
Net Profit + Depr., Dep., Amort./Cur. Mat. L/T/D	5.1	5.1	6.1						5.9	7.9
	(100) 2.6	(84) 2.9	(86) 3.4						(31) 3.0	(38) 4.5
	1.2	1.5	1.1						1.0	1.7
Fixed/Worth	.1	.1	.1			.0	.1	.1	.1	.2
	.3	.3	.2			.1	.3	.2	.2	.4
	.7	.6	.6			.4	.5	.5	.5	.6
Debt/Worth	1.1	1.1	1.0			.6	1.5	.7	.8	1.2
	2.6	2.1	2.1			1.9	2.6	1.6	2.0	2.6
	4.5	4.4	4.6			5.7	8.8	3.9	4.3	4.4
% Profit Before Taxes/Tangible Net Worth	28.7	35.4	28.5			34.5	53.3	32.3	22.3	30.1
	(323) 13.9	(309) 18.2	(285) 13.5		(28) 12.4	4.1	(51) 9.2	(74) 11.4	(109) 17.3	
	4.9	6.4	1.7		-2.6	-14.2	1.0	2.2	8.0	
% Profit Before Taxes/Total Assets	9.6	12.0	9.2			10.0	6.6	12.1	7.4	10.2
	3.8	5.1	3.7			3.6	1.0	3.1	3.7	5.3
	1.2	1.9	.3			-1.0	-2.7	.1	.4	1.9
Sales/Net Fixed Assets	72.3	74.8	66.6			415.8	90.8	53.1	66.5	55.3
	31.9	38.0	31.2			89.4	14.8	30.0	33.8	26.1
	14.4	16.5	13.4			18.9	10.3	12.3	14.1	14.6
Sales/Total Assets	2.9	3.2	2.9			3.5	2.2	2.7	3.1	2.8
	2.3	2.5	2.2			2.2	1.6	2.3	2.1	2.2
	1.8	1.8	1.6			1.3	1.1	1.7	1.8	1.7
% Depr., Dep., Amort./Sales	.4	.4	.4			.1	.5	.4	.5	.4
	(293) .8	(273) .7	(253) .8		(20) .5	(17) .9	(46) 1.0	(70) .9	(93) .7	
	1.4	1.3	1.6		1.6	2.2	1.8	1.6	1.2	
% Officers', Directors' Owners' Comp/Sales	1.0	.9	.9			2.5		1.6	.6	.7
	(148) 1.8	(129) 1.8	(115) 1.9		(16) 3.9		(29) 2.4	(34) 1.1	(25) 1.1	
	3.5	3.4	4.0		6.7		1.8	1.6	1.1	
Net Sales ($)	11011927M	12846978M	11774119M		5119M	61778M	82260M	381201M	1253369M	9990392M
Total Assets ($)	4713147M	5195260M	5588385M		3916M	33288M	77168M	191275M	618831M	4663907M

M = $ thousand   MM = $ million
See Pages 9 through 22 for Explanation of Ratios and Data

Current Data Sorted by Assets

Comparative Historical Data

						Type of Statement		
1	4	58	67	27	18	Unqualified	188	208
3	34	164	77	5	1	Reviewed	302	342
17	76	96	15			Compiled	216	238
36	64	42	3			Tax Returns	95	104
18	78	167	129	24	20	Other	348	349
	254 (4/1-9/30/09)		990 (10/1/09-3/31/10)				4/1/05-3/31/06	4/1/06-3/31/07
0-500M	500M-2MM	2-10MM	10-50MM	50-100MM	100-250MM		ALL	ALL
75	256	527	291	56	39	NUMBER OF STATEMENTS	1149	1241
%	%	%	%	%	%	ASSETS	%	%
12.9	9.2	8.5	7.6	3.8	6.3	Cash & Equivalents	7.0	6.9
28.0	32.3	28.4	25.5	20.7	18.5	Trade Receivables (net)	32.9	32.0
27.8	35.2	36.7	32.4	37.3	35.4	Inventory	34.6	35.8
5.7	3.0	2.6	3.5	5.1	5.4	All Other Current	2.5	2.5
74.5	79.8	76.2	69.0	66.8	65.6	Total Current	77.0	77.3
15.6	12.4	15.8	21.2	21.5	23.5	Fixed Assets (net)	15.0	14.7
2.4	2.3	2.6	4.2	7.7	5.9	Intangibles (net)	2.5	2.5
7.5	5.6	5.5	5.5	3.9	5.0	All Other Non-Current	5.6	5.5
100.0	100.0	100.0	100.0	100.0	100.0	Total	100.0	100.0
						LIABILITIES		
23.5	14.8	16.3	14.1	17.1	13.7	Notes Payable-Short Term	16.4	16.4
5.1	2.6	3.2	3.4	4.1	4.1	Cur. Mat.-L.T.D.	3.2	3.0
23.7	21.8	16.2	13.9	11.2	8.8	Trade Payables	21.0	19.9
.4	.1	.2	.2	.7	.3	Income Taxes Payable	.3	.3
11.4	8.7	8.7	10.8	9.7	10.6	All Other Current	10.6	11.0
64.1	48.0	44.6	42.4	42.8	37.5	Total Current	51.5	50.7
9.7	9.4	10.0	11.8	14.8	16.6	Long-Term Debt	9.8	10.7
.0	.1	.4	.5	1.2	1.5	Deferred Taxes	.3	.4
8.4	5.6	3.9	4.3	4.4	3.9	All Other Non-Current	3.9	3.6
17.8	36.9	41.1	41.0	36.8	40.6	Net Worth	34.4	34.7
100.0	100.0	100.0	100.0	100.0	100.0	Total Liabilities & Net Worth	100.0	100.0
						INCOME DATA		
100.0	100.0	100.0	100.0	100.0	100.0	Net Sales	100.0	100.0
37.1	32.3	31.2	29.1	28.0	27.5	Gross Profit	30.2	30.0
37.6	31.5	28.7	26.2	23.0	24.3	Operating Expenses	26.2	25.4
-.5	.7	2.5	2.9	5.0	3.2	Operating Profit	4.1	4.5
.6	.4	.6	.9	1.1	1.5	All Other Expenses (net)	.5	.7
-1.1	.3	1.8	2.0	3.9	1.7	Profit Before Taxes	3.6	3.9
						RATIOS		
3.0	2.9	2.8	2.4	2.4	3.2		2.1	2.3
1.3	1.8	1.7	1.6	1.6	1.8	Current	1.5	1.6
.8	1.2	1.3	1.2	1.2	1.3		1.2	1.2
1.6	1.6	1.5	1.3	1.0	1.1		1.1	1.2
.8	.9	.8	.8	.6	.5	Quick	.8 (1240)	.8
.3	.6	.5	.5	.4	.3		.5	.5
7 55.5	24 15.3	30 12.1	32 11.4	33 10.9	37 9.9	Sales/Receivables	33 11.1	32 11.5
26 14.2	38 9.7	40 9.1	42 8.7	41 8.9	49 7.4		43 8.4	42 8.6
45 8.1	52 7.0	52 7.0	54 6.7	62 5.9	63 5.8		55 6.6	53 6.9
7 50.5	25 14.7	41 8.9	48 7.7	61 6.0	86 4.2	Cost of Sales/Inventory	36 10.1	37 10.0
24 15.1	51 7.2	73 5.0	78 4.7	90 4.0	145 2.5		62 5.8	62 5.8
99 3.7	120 3.1	134 2.7	138 2.6	187 1.9	213 1.7		104 3.5	108 3.4
0 999.8	18 20.8	16 22.7	17 21.0	16 22.1	18 20.3	Cost of Sales/Payables	21 17.4	19 19.3
29 12.7	33 11.1	30 12.3	28 13.0	30 12.1	28 12.9		34 10.7	32 11.4
62 5.9	50 7.3	47 7.8	42 8.7	41 8.9	50 7.4		54 6.7	50 7.4
6.5	5.3	4.4	4.4	4.0	2.6	Sales/Working Capital	6.1	6.0
36.2	8.7	7.6	8.8	6.5	4.9		10.7	10.2
-89.9	28.2	17.3	20.3	22.1	10.4		27.8	25.3
5.8	10.7	8.9	11.7	8.3	6.2	EBIT/Interest	12.1	11.0
(55) 1.1	(229) 2.6	(478) 2.1	(271) 2.9	(54) 3.0	(38) 2.3		(1051) 4.4	(1125) 4.3
-4.9	-.4	.1	.8	1.0	.8		2.0	1.9
	3.2	8.8	14.7	11.8		Net Profit + Depr., Dep.,	6.5	7.6
(29)	1.8 (148)	2.2 (88)	3.4 (24)	3.8		Amort./Cur. Mat. L/T/D	(302) 2.8	(357) 3.2
	.1	.7	1.0	1.0			1.3	1.5
.0	.1	.1	.1	.2	.3	Fixed/Worth	.1	.1
.3	.2	.3	.5	.7	.6		.3	.3
1.5	.8	.8	1.2	1.7	1.5		1.0	1.0
.8	.7	.6	.8	1.2	.9	Debt/Worth	1.0	.9
3.0	1.8	1.6	1.8	2.9	1.8		2.1	2.0
-72.0	5.0	3.9	3.6	6.7	4.1		4.9	4.9
37.9	24.8	23.7	27.8	30.8	16.6	% Profit Before Taxes/Tangible Net Worth	44.9	45.3
(56) 4.1	(225) 7.0	(491) 8.1	(278) 8.6	(53) 11.3	(36) 6.2		(1044) 20.3	(1144) 23.7
-19.0	-3.0	-1.3	-1.3	.5	-.2		7.3	9.0
12.2	8.7	9.2	9.8	11.6	5.8	% Profit Before Taxes/Total Assets	13.1	15.0
.9	2.7	2.3	3.3	2.8	2.9		6.4	6.8
-15.4	-3.4	-1.3	-.1	.1	-.2		2.2	2.3
406.5	124.3	63.7	50.6	25.9	14.5	Sales/Net Fixed Assets	78.6	80.5
52.2	47.3	29.7	13.4	11.1	6.1		32.2	33.5
18.5	20.9	9.9	5.6	4.8	3.6		11.2	11.7
7.1	4.1	3.2	2.7	2.1	1.8	Sales/Total Assets	3.5	3.6
3.5	3.2	2.3	2.0	1.4	1.2		2.7	2.7
2.0	2.0	1.7	1.3	1.1	.9		1.9	1.9
.4	.3	.5	.6	.7	1.2	% Depr., Dep., Amort./Sales	.4	.4
(44) .7	(180) .7	(448) 1.0	(255) 1.5	(47) 1.7	(23) 2.0		(991) .8	(1054) .8
1.7	1.5	2.5	3.7	4.3	2.6		1.8	1.8
4.8	2.7	1.5	.9			% Officers', Directors' Owners' Comp/Sales	2.1	1.9
(40) 7.0	(153) 4.6	(193) 2.9	(37) 1.6				(434) 3.9	(438) 3.8
12.8	7.0	5.5	3.1				6.9	6.4
99502M	986887M	6454127M	12792803M	6656804M	7669886M	Net Sales ($)	33202777M	39004288M
21690M	314628M	2648193M	6227418M	4097823M	6057614M	Total Assets ($)	14956344M	17786929M

M = $ thousand MM = $ million
See Pages 9 through 22 for Explanation of Ratios and Data

Comparative Historical Data | Current Data Sorted by Sales

205	206	175	Type of Statement	1	3	3	18	40	110
284	317	284	Reviewed	3	14	18	73	107	69
208	224	204	Compiled	13	38	47	55	36	15
118	159	145	Tax Returns	21	37	32	41	14	15
416	533	436	Other	16	45	49	77	98	151
4/1/07-3/31/08 ALL	4/1/08-3/31/09 ALL	4/1/09-3/31/10 ALL		254 (4/1-9/30/09)			990 (10/1/09-3/31/10)		
				0-1MM	1-3MM	3-5MM	5-10MM	10-25MM	25MM & OVER
1231	1439	1244	NUMBER OF STATEMENTS	54	137	149	264	295	345
%	%	%	ASSETS	%	%	%	%	%	%
7.6	8.0	8.4	Cash & Equivalents	9.7	8.7	10.3	9.0	8.8	6.6
31.1	29.6	27.8	Trade Receivables (net)	19.1	23.6	28.8	29.8	28.9	28.1
35.7	35.7	34.9	Inventory	31.7	37.1	35.6	36.3	34.5	33.4
2.7	3.0	3.2	All Other Current	5.9	4.4	2.1	2.5	2.5	4.1
77.2	76.3	74.4	Total Current	66.4	73.8	76.7	77.7	74.6	72.2
15.2	15.4	16.8	Fixed Assets (net)	21.2	16.4	14.5	15.0	17.4	18.2
2.6	3.0	3.2	Intangibles (net)	2.0	3.9	2.8	2.3	2.7	4.6
5.1	5.3	5.5	All Other Non-Current	10.4	5.9	6.1	5.0	5.2	5.0
100.0	100.0	100.0	Total	100.0	100.0	100.0	100.0	100.0	100.0
			LIABILITIES						
17.1	17.5	15.9	Notes Payable-Short Term	26.7	18.3	15.6	15.7	13.7	15.3
3.3	3.2	3.3	Cur. Mat.-L.T.D.	5.6	3.1	3.3	2.8	3.6	3.2
19.0	18.7	16.8	Trade Payables	15.1	18.1	19.9	18.0	16.2	14.9
.3	.2	.2	Income Taxes Payable	.2	.1	.2	.1	.3	.2
10.8	10.4	9.4	All Other Current	7.7	9.9	6.9	9.1	9.8	10.6
50.4	50.0	45.6	Total Current	55.4	49.4	45.8	45.7	43.5	44.3
9.9	10.1	10.7	Long-Term Debt	16.9	11.9	10.4	9.9	8.9	11.6
.3	.3	.4	Deferred Taxes	.0	.1	.1	.4	.5	.7
4.0	4.5	4.6	All Other Non-Current	8.6	6.9	4.0	4.2	4.2	4.1
35.4	35.1	38.6	Net Worth	19.0	31.8	39.6	39.9	42.8	39.3
100.0	100.0	100.0	Total Liabilities & Net Worth	100.0	100.0	100.0	100.0	100.0	100.0
			INCOME DATA						
100.0	100.0	100.0	Net Sales	100.0	100.0	100.0	100.0	100.0	100.0
29.7	29.7	31.0	Gross Profit	43.9	37.4	32.3	29.5	30.5	27.4
25.1	26.0	28.8	Operating Expenses	43.5	37.0	30.9	27.5	28.1	24.0
4.6	3.6	2.2	Operating Profit	.4	.5	1.4	2.0	2.4	3.4
.7	.6	.7	All Other Expenses (net)	1.9	1.0	.7	.5	.4	.8
3.9	3.0	1.5	Profit Before Taxes	-1.5	-.6	.7	1.5	2.0	2.6
			RATIOS						
2.2	2.3	2.7		3.5	2.9	3.1	3.0	2.7	2.4
1.6	1.5	1.7	Current	1.6	1.6	1.8	1.8	1.7	1.6
1.2	1.2	1.2		.7	1.1	1.2	1.3	1.2	1.2
1.2	1.2	1.4		1.6	1.3	1.6	1.6	1.4	1.2
.8 (1438)	.8	.8	Quick	.7	.7	.9	.9	.8	.8
.5	.5	.5		.2	.3	.5	.5	.5	.5
30 12.2	27 13.7	29 12.6		8 47.4	22 16.9	28 12.9	28 13.2	31 11.7	33 11.0
40 9.2	38 9.7	40 9.1	Sales/Receivables	27 13.8	37 10.0	39 9.3	39 9.4	40 9.1	42 8.7
51 7.1	51 7.2	53 6.9		54 6.7	56 6.5	51 7.1	52 7.0	51 7.1	55 6.6
35 10.4	33 11.1	37 9.8		8 43.2	21 17.4	28 13.2	35 10.5	42 8.8	44 8.4
63 5.8	64 5.7	72 5.1	Cost of Sales/Inventory	92 4.0	100 3.6	69 5.3	69 5.3	70 5.2	71 5.1
107 3.4	114 3.2	135 2.7		194 1.9	215 1.7	158 2.3	126 2.9	113 3.2	117 3.1
18 20.7	16 23.0	16 22.5		7 50.5	14 25.9	15 24.9	17 21.0	17 21.5	17 21.5
31 11.9	28 13.2	30 12.3	Cost of Sales/Payables	28 13.1	36 10.2	36 10.2	30 12.3	28 12.9	28 12.8
47 7.8	47 7.8	47 7.7		69 5.3	66 5.5	56 6.5	48 7.7	39 9.3	41 8.8
5.9	5.7	4.5		3.7	4.0	4.1	4.8	4.4	4.9
10.2	10.6	8.2	Sales/Working Capital	8.3	8.4	8.0	7.5	9.3	9.1
25.9	25.8	22.7		-13.5	72.5	34.9	19.4	19.1	19.5
10.1	12.0	9.2		2.8	4.7	7.8	9.5	10.3	11.8
(1109) 3.8	(1296) 3.5	(1125) 2.3	EBIT/Interest	(40) .9	(119) 1.3	(133) 1.8	(237) 2.1	(269) 2.6	(327) 3.4
1.7	1.4	.3		-4.8	-3.0	-1.0	-.2	1.1	1.1
6.8	8.7	8.7			1.9	4.1	9.8	7.5	18.9
(329) 2.8	(342) 3.1	(304) 2.3	Net Profit + Depr., Dep., Amort./Cur. Mat. L/T/D		(16) .7	(20) .6	(58) 2.3	(98) 2.3	(109) 3.7
1.3	1.1	.7			-.4	-4.4	.5	1.0	1.1
.1	.1	.1		.0	.1	.1	.1	.1	.2
.3	.3	.3	Fixed/Worth	.3	.5	.2	.2	.3	.4
1.0	1.0	1.0		6.6	1.6	.7	.8	.9	1.1
.9	.9	.7		.7	.7	.6	.7	.6	.9
1.9	2.1	1.7	Debt/Worth	3.3	2.4	1.5	1.6	1.4	1.9
4.8	4.8	4.3		NM	13.6	4.8	3.8	3.3	4.1
44.2	40.2	25.0		24.3	20.1	22.7	20.3	25.2	30.5
(1130) 21.1	(1317) 16.6	(1139) 7.9	% Profit Before Taxes/Tangible Net Worth	(41) 3.3	(113) 2.7	(131) 3.5	(243) 7.2	(283) 9.4	(328) 11.3
7.4	4.1	-1.7		-18.8	-24.5	-5.8	-2.7	.6	.7
14.7	13.3	9.3		6.5	7.8	6.5	8.7	9.5	11.0
6.7	5.2	2.6	% Profit Before Taxes/Total Assets	.6	1.0	1.3	2.4	2.9	3.7
2.0	1.1	-1.2		-15.9	-7.1	-3.7	-2.0	.2	.2
75.1	81.4	67.9		UND	71.1	98.3	87.1	56.9	52.1
32.8	32.1	26.0	Sales/Net Fixed Assets	24.4	25.2	43.4	34.1	24.1	17.2
11.7	11.9	8.6		8.8	7.9	-14.6	12.4	7.7	7.2
3.6	3.6	3.3		2.5	3.1	4.0	3.5	3.2	3.1
2.7	2.7	2.3	Sales/Total Assets	1.8	2.2	2.5	2.5	2.4	2.2
1.9	1.9	1.5		1.0	1.3	1.5	1.7	1.7	1.5
.4	.4	.5		.7	.5	.3	.4	.5	.6
(1023) .7	(1151) .8	(997) 1.0	% Depr., Dep., Amort./Sales	(30) 2.4	(92) 1.1	(112) .7	(218) 1.0	(259) 1.0	(286) 1.2
1.8	1.9	2.6		11.4	2.9	1.5	2.1	3.0	2.7
1.8	1.8	1.8		3.5	4.0	2.5	1.9	1.4	.6
(438) 3.9	(475) 3.4	(429) 3.7	% Officers', Directors' Owners' Comp/Sales	(21) 8.9	(74) 6.0	(82) 4.6	(136) 3.2	(85) 2.3	(31) 1.4
6.7	6.1	6.5		15.8	9.1	6.7	5.5		3.0
41247601M	50340857M	34660009M	Net Sales ($)	30141M	283094M	586339M	1938826M	4769385M	27052224M
19071611M	23402505M	19367366M	Total Assets ($)	27093M	174097M	315505M	985251M	2469563M	15395857M

M = $ thousand   MM = $ million
See Pages 9 through 22 for Explanation of Ratios and Data

WHOLESALE—Industrial Supplies Merchant Wholesalers NAICS 423840

	Current Data Sorted by Assets						Comparative Historical Data	
Type of Statement								
Unqualified		5	26	33	4	4	63	72
Reviewed	1	16	80	35		1	148	164
Compiled	4	34	54	6			104	115
Tax Returns	8	33	15				41	47
Other	6	37	83	55	7	6	177	161
		106 (4/1-9/30/09)		447 (10/1/09-3/31/10)			4/1/05-3/31/06	4/1/06-3/31/07
	0-500M	500M-2MM	2-10MM	10-50MM	50-100MM	100-250MM	ALL	ALL
NUMBER OF STATEMENTS	19	125	258	129	11	11	533	559
	%	%	%	%	%	%	%	%
ASSETS								
Cash & Equivalents	11.6	8.8	8.5	6.8	9.9	4.2	5.6	5.5
Trade Receivables (net)	37.5	33.3	29.2	29.3	28.8	29.3	36.0	34.4
Inventory	28.0	37.3	39.2	35.2	29.5	28.2	36.7	37.9
All Other Current	2.8	1.8	2.3	3.0	6.2	4.1	2.1	2.0
Total Current	79.9	81.2	79.2	74.4	74.5	65.8	80.4	79.8
Fixed Assets (net)	14.3	9.9	12.4	14.6	16.9	5.4	11.9	12.1
Intangibles (net)	2.2	2.7	2.9	5.7	4.2	26.0	3.0	3.4
All Other Non-Current	3.6	6.3	5.5	5.3	4.5	2.8	4.8	4.7
Total	100.0	100.0	100.0	100.0	100.0	100.0	100.0	100.0
LIABILITIES								
Notes Payable-Short Term	10.2	18.2	15.4	16.9	11.0	8.3	16.7	16.7
Cur. Mat.-L.T.D.	8.3	3.0	2.6	2.7	.6	.7	2.0	2.1
Trade Payables	22.3	23.5	17.3	15.6	12.4	13.3	22.1	21.8
Income Taxes Payable	.0	.1	.1	.3	.1	.6	.4	.3
All Other Current	4.9	8.5	6.5	7.3	8.6	5.5	7.1	7.9
Total Current	45.6	53.4	41.9	42.8	32.6	28.4	48.3	48.8
Long-Term Debt	15.3	9.3	8.5	8.4	9.0	21.5	8.6	9.8
Deferred Taxes	.0	.0	.3	.2	1.0	2.3	.3	.3
All Other Non-Current	17.9	4.4	4.3	4.3	.4	3.7	5.0	4.1
Net Worth	21.1	32.9	45.0	44.3	57.1	44.2	37.8	37.0
Total Liabilities & Net Worth	100.0	100.0	100.0	100.0	100.0	100.0	100.0	100.0
INCOME DATA								
Net Sales	100.0	100.0	100.0	100.0	100.0	100.0	100.0	100.0
Gross Profit	35.5	32.1	31.0	30.6	25.8	28.6	30.1	29.9
Operating Expenses	31.0	29.9	27.8	26.4	20.5	24.5	26.2	24.9
Operating Profit	4.5	2.1	3.2	4.2	5.3	4.2	3.9	5.0
All Other Expenses (net)	.9	.4	.5	.8	.4	1.6	.6	.7
Profit Before Taxes	3.5	1.7	2.7	3.5	4.9	2.6	3.3	4.3
RATIOS								
Current	4.8	2.8	3.6	2.6	4.3	3.2	2.4	2.6
	3.0	1.6	1.9	1.7	2.1	2.2	1.7	1.7
	1.2	1.1	1.3	1.3	1.6	1.8	1.3	1.2
Quick	3.4	1.5	1.6	1.4	2.7	1.5	1.4	1.3
	1.1	.8	.9	.9	.8	1.2	.9	.8
	.7	.5	.5	.5	.6	1.0	.6	.5
Sales/Receivables	25 14.8	29 12.4	31 11.9	35 10.4	35 10.4	47 7.7	36 10.2	35 10.4
	30 12.1	37 9.8	39 9.3	44 8.4	44 8.3	50 7.3	44 8.3	42 8.7
	44 8.3	47 7.7	49 7.5	53 6.8	52 7.0	57 6.4	55 6.7	50 7.3
Cost of Sales/Inventory	7 49.9	31 11.8	42 8.6	36 10.0	54 6.7	38 9.6	39 9.3	39 9.3
	25 14.5	61 6.0	76 4.8	67 5.4	66 5.5	67 5.5	62 5.9	64 5.7
	56 6.5	106 3.4	127 2.9	134 2.7	96 3.8	88 4.1	100 3.6	101 3.6
Cost of Sales/Payables	3 145.7	20 18.0	19 19.3	19 19.3	18 19.9	22 16.5	23 15.7	23 16.2
	29 12.6	30 12.0	29 12.4	31 12.0	29 12.7	38 9.7	36 10.1	35 10.4
	41 8.9	52 7.0	47 7.8	46 7.9	35 10.4	44 8.3	51 7.2	49 7.4
Sales/Working Capital	4.3	6.0	4.1	4.5	3.3	4.3	5.7	5.9
	8.9	11.8	7.5	8.1	5.3	6.0	9.4	9.5
	27.9	54.5	17.3	14.3	8.7	7.4	18.9	22.1
EBIT/Interest	14.0	10.8	13.4	13.5	25.8	3.3	11.0	11.9
	(15) 3.7	(112) 3.3	(237) 3.5	(120) 4.9	(10) 13.0	(10) 2.0	(480) 4.7	(521) 4.6
	1.6	-.2	1.0	2.1	3.9	1.0	1.8	1.9
Net Profit + Depr., Dep., Amort./Cur. Mat. L/T/D		4.3	5.5	16.9			9.7	10.7
		(22) 1.4	(61) 2.3	(45) 3.4			(138) 4.2	(153) 4.1
		.2	1.0	1.4			2.1	1.3
Fixed/Worth	.0	.1	.1	.1	.1	.1	.1	.1
	.4	.3	.2	.3	.3	.3	.2	.3
	1.0	1.2	.6	.8	.4	-.4	.7	.8
Debt/Worth	.4	.8	.5	.7	.4	.8	.8	.8
	3.6	2.2	1.3	1.7	.9	4.1	1.7	1.8
	-13.6	18.6	3.3	3.0	1.1	-3.6	4.5	4.8
% Profit Before Taxes/Tangible Net Worth	56.3	47.0	26.6	31.1	33.6		41.0	48.1
	(14) 18.4	(101) 14.4	(239) 11.7	(118) 16.5	19.9		(480) 18.8	(499) 26.1
	5.9	.7	1.8	5.5	2.1		5.6	9.1
% Profit Before Taxes/Total Assets	22.6	13.7	11.0	11.5	16.6	4.7	14.0	16.3
	10.1	4.9	4.4	6.3	11.5	2.5	6.8	8.3
	.2	-1.3	.2	2.7	1.2	.2	2.1	2.4
Sales/Net Fixed Assets	999.8	186.4	88.7	54.3	88.3	150.4	97.4	102.8
	77.6	50.3	33.8	23.3	16.5	72.7	39.2	40.4
	27.1	22.2	14.7	9.8	7.4	18.6	17.9	17.3
Sales/Total Assets	5.5	4.0	3.3	2.9	2.4	2.4	3.7	3.7
	4.2	3.1	2.6	2.2	2.2	2.1	2.8	2.9
	3.0	2.3	1.9	1.6	1.6	1.3	2.2	2.1
% Depr., Dep., Amort./Sales	.5	.3	.4	.4	.2		.4	.4
	(12) .8	(87) .7	(218) .8	(110) .8	(10) .7		(451) .7	(478) .7
	1.2	1.3	1.4	1.8	2.5		1.2	1.2
% Officers', Directors' Owners' Comp/Sales	3.8	3.0	1.8	.7			2.0	1.8
	(11) 7.2	(69) 4.2	(99) 2.9	(18) 1.8			(211) 3.6	(198) 3.2
	10.4	7.1	5.0	6.3			6.3	5.6
Net Sales ($)	22956M	513332M	3259631M	5836512M	1745662M	3785920M	14975858M	16934650M
Total Assets ($)	5662M	155479M	1254223M	2525353M	827712M	1502017M	5726917M	6523371M

© RMA 2010

M = $ thousand   MM = $ million
See Pages 9 through 22 for Explanation of Ratios and Data

Comparative Historical Data | Current Data Sorted by Sales

			Type of Statement						
70	73	72	Unqualified		1	2	11	17	41
141	157	132	Reviewed		4	8	37	50	33
91	102	99	Compiled	2	17	8	40	24	8
51	70	56	Tax Returns	3	18	17	11	7	
151	183	194	Other	8	19	15	43	57	52
4/1/07-3/31/08 ALL	4/1/08-3/31/09 ALL	4/1/09-3/31/10 ALL		106 (4/1-9/30/09)			447 (10/1/09-3/31/10)		
				0-1MM	1-3MM	3-5MM	5-10MM	10-25MM	25MM & OVER
504	585	553	NUMBER OF STATEMENTS	13	59	50	142	155	134
%	%	%	ASSETS	%	%	%	%	%	%
6.4	6.8	8.2	Cash & Equivalents	13.4	11.4	9.8	7.9	7.5	6.9
32.9	32.2	30.4	Trade Receivables (net)	27.5	28.7	26.3	29.8	30.8	33.3
37.9	38.4	37.1	Inventory	26.6	37.8	36.5	40.1	38.2	33.3
2.2	2.1	2.5	All Other Current	.0	3.4	2.2	1.6	2.5	3.5
79.5	79.4	78.2	Total Current	67.6	81.2	74.8	79.4	79.0	76.9
12.6	11.7	12.4	Fixed Assets (net)	18.5	12.2	13.5	11.2	13.3	11.6
2.8	3.6	4.0	Intangibles (net)	2.5	1.9	3.2	3.1	3.6	6.6
5.2	5.3	5.5	All Other Non-Current	11.5	4.7	8.5	6.3	4.1	4.9
100.0	100.0	100.0	Total	100.0	100.0	100.0	100.0	100.0	100.0
			LIABILITIES						
16.1	17.5	16.0	Notes Payable-Short Term	13.2	17.3	15.9	15.5	16.8	15.1
2.4	2.2	2.8	Cur. Mat.-L.T.D.	9.4	3.2	4.8	2.7	2.1	2.4
21.1	19.7	18.3	Trade Payables	18.4	20.1	18.4	19.5	17.5	17.2
.2	.2	.2	Income Taxes Payable	.0	.1	.0	.1	.1	.3
7.2	7.7	7.1	All Other Current	5.3	10.2	4.4	6.3	7.4	7.4
46.9	47.3	44.4	Total Current	46.3	51.0	43.5	44.1	43.9	42.4
9.7	8.2	9.2	Long-Term Debt	18.0	10.3	12.8	8.0	8.0	9.1
.3	.2	.2	Deferred Taxes	.1	.0	.1	.3	.2	.4
4.3	5.2	4.7	All Other Non-Current	18.2	6.8	3.2	5.3	3.6	3.7
38.8	39.2	41.5	Net Worth	17.4	31.8	40.4	42.4	44.2	44.4
100.0	100.0	100.0	Total Liabilities & Net Worth	100.0	100.0	100.0	100.0	100.0	100.0
			INCOME DATA						
100.0	100.0	100.0	Net Sales	100.0	100.0	100.0	100.0	100.0	100.0
29.8	29.6	31.1	Gross Profit	46.3	33.5	34.7	30.7	31.0	27.8
25.0	25.0	27.8	Operating Expenses	39.9	32.0	31.0	28.6	26.7	24.1
4.8	4.6	3.3	Operating Profit	6.4	1.5	3.7	2.1	4.3	3.7
.6	.6	.6	All Other Expenses (net)	1.7	.6	.5	.5	.4	.7
4.2	4.0	2.7	Profit Before Taxes	4.7	.8	3.2	1.6	3.9	3.0
			RATIOS						
2.8	2.7	3.2	Current	4.8	3.7	3.3	3.3	2.6	2.9
1.7	1.7	1.8	Current	3.8	1.8	1.8	1.8	1.7	1.8
1.3	1.2	1.3	Current	.9	1.1	1.1	1.2	1.3	1.4
1.4	1.3	1.6	Quick	3.6	1.8	1.5	1.7	1.4	1.5
.9	.9	.9	Quick	.7	.8	.7	.9	.8	1.0
.6	.5	.5	Quick	.4	.4	.4	.5	.5	.6
33 10.9	30 12.2	31 11.7	Sales/Receivables	11 34.7	28 13.0	27 13.7	31 12.0	33 11.1	35 10.4
41 9.0	38 9.5	40 9.2	Sales/Receivables	48 7.5	37 10.0	34 10.8	37 9.8	41 8.9	44 8.3
50 7.4	48 7.6	50 7.3	Sales/Receivables	81 4.5	47 7.8	47 7.7	48 7.6	52 7.0	52 7.0
42 8.8	37 9.8	37 10.0	Cost of Sales/Inventory	6 61.2	31 11.6	37 9.9	39 9.3	39 9.4	35 10.4
68 5.4	63 5.8	67 5.4	Cost of Sales/Inventory	142 2.6	74 4.9	73 5.0	71 5.2	72 5.1	61 6.0
101 3.6	110 3.3	121 3.0	Cost of Sales/Inventory	588 .6	138 2.6	123 3.0	125 2.9	126 2.9	92 4.0
21 17.2	19 19.6	19 19.2	Cost of Sales/Payables	6 57.2	14 26.7	17 21.9	20 18.6	19 19.5	19 19.1
33 11.0	30 12.3	30 12.1	Cost of Sales/Payables	41 8.9	29 12.4	32 11.4	30 12.3	29 12.7	30 12.1
47 7.7	45 8.1	46 7.9	Cost of Sales/Payables	127 2.9	56 6.5	54 6.7	48 7.6	46 7.9	41 9.0
5.3	5.5	4.4	Sales/Working Capital	1.8	3.3	4.0	4.7	4.3	5.1
8.8	9.6	8.1	Sales/Working Capital	3.8	7.8	7.6	8.1	8.2	8.3
19.7	21.8	18.2	Sales/Working Capital	-15.0	35.8	35.4	18.2	18.3	14.8
11.5	14.5	13.0	EBIT/Interest		6.8	6.3	12.9	14.4	17.0
(458) 4.4	(535) 4.8	(504) 3.7	EBIT/Interest		(51) 2.1	(46) 3.6	(132) 2.9	(141) 4.0	(125) 5.7
1.9	1.7	1.2	EBIT/Interest		-1.0	1.1	.0	1.6	1.8
10.8	11.4	8.2	Net Profit + Depr., Dep., Amort./Cur. Mat. L/T/D			3.1	8.5	4.8	18.0
(128) 3.4	(142) 3.3	(138) 2.9	Net Profit + Depr., Dep., Amort./Cur. Mat. L/T/D			(10) .9	(32) 2.1	(38) 2.4	(50) 4.7
1.6	1.4	1.0	Net Profit + Depr., Dep., Amort./Cur. Mat. L/T/D			.2	.9	1.2	1.8
.1	.1	.1	Fixed/Worth	.0	.1	.1	.1	.1	.1
.2	.3	.3	Fixed/Worth	.2	.5	.3	.2	.2	.3
.7	.7	.7	Fixed/Worth	1.4	1.8	1.0	.6	.7	.7
.7	.7	.6	Debt/Worth	.5	.5	.5	.4	.7	.7
1.7	1.7	1.6	Debt/Worth	1.8	2.4	1.7	1.6	1.5	1.5
4.0	4.5	4.0	Debt/Worth	-28.2	40.8	7.4	4.9	3.1	3.6
42.0	46.0	30.2	% Profit Before Taxes/Tangible Net Worth		33.8	51.7	26.8	28.0	33.6
(458) 22.8	(517) 24.7	(491) 13.9	% Profit Before Taxes/Tangible Net Worth		(46) 12.3	(45) 13.9	(126) 9.7	(143) 14.0	(122) 16.7
9.8	6.9	2.8	% Profit Before Taxes/Tangible Net Worth		-2.6	2.4	-2.6	4.6	5.5
15.7	17.1	11.8	% Profit Before Taxes/Total Assets	22.6	12.2	13.0	10.9	11.1	13.0
7.9	7.6	5.2	% Profit Before Taxes/Total Assets	3.5	3.6	5.6	4.3	5.4	6.8
2.8	1.6	.5	% Profit Before Taxes/Total Assets	-4.6	-1.8	.9	-1.7	1.6	1.7
90.8	108.7	93.6	Sales/Net Fixed Assets	UND	219.2	142.3	101.8	90.7	74.3
40.3	43.5	36.1	Sales/Net Fixed Assets	15.8	40.1	33.1	43.9	28.0	38.3
17.0	18.2	15.3	Sales/Net Fixed Assets	5.8	15.7	15.0	19.0	12.1	16.4
3.7	3.8	3.4	Sales/Total Assets	4.5	3.7	3.4	3.7	3.3	3.3
2.8	2.9	2.6	Sales/Total Assets	1.7	2.7	2.7	2.7	2.5	2.6
2.1	2.1	1.8	Sales/Total Assets	.5	1.7	1.8	1.9	1.8	1.9
.4	.3	.4	% Depr., Dep., Amort./Sales		.6	.5	.3	.4	.4
(430) .6	(493) .6	(445) .8	% Depr., Dep., Amort./Sales		(42) .9	(36) 1.0	(114) .6	(127) .8	(120) .7
1.1	1.2	1.5	% Depr., Dep., Amort./Sales		1.7	1.8	1.2	1.5	1.3
1.9	1.6	1.9	% Officers', Directors', Owners' Comp/Sales		3.7	3.4	2.0	1.3	1.5
(194) 3.4	(233) 3.0	(198) 3.4	% Officers', Directors', Owners' Comp/Sales		(31) 5.7	(25) 4.5	(71) 3.2	(47) 2.1	(22) 2.2
6.0	6.2	6.6	% Officers', Directors', Owners' Comp/Sales		8.4	7.5	5.0	4.1	3.4
15481090M	22410395M	15164013M	Net Sales ($)	7766M	117247M	196341M	1025528M	2467481M	11349650M
5892633M	7872875M	6270446M	Total Assets ($)	6762M	65557M	94572M	433759M	1138368M	4531428M

M = $ thousand   MM = $ million
See Pages 9 through 22 for Explanation of Ratios and Data

Current Data Sorted by Assets   Comparative Historical Data

Type of Statement	0-500M	500M-2MM	2-10MM	10-50MM	50-100MM	100-250MM		4/1/05-3/31/06 ALL	4/1/06-3/31/07 ALL
Unqualified			7	6	1	3		14	10
Reviewed		8	28	8	1			40	43
Compiled	4	18	16	3	1			24	39
Tax Returns	4	15	6	1				16	28
Other	4	19	22	14	2	1		50	36
		32 (4/1-9/30/09)		159 (10/1/09-3/31/10)					
NUMBER OF STATEMENTS	12	60	79	32	4	4		144	156
ASSETS	%	%	%	%	%	%		%	%
Cash & Equivalents	9.3	8.2	7.5	3.5				8.2	7.0
Trade Receivables (net)	23.2	35.2	29.5	29.7				31.6	32.9
Inventory	35.8	29.9	38.7	29.6				34.8	34.6
All Other Current	2.2	4.0	3.0	4.6				2.2	3.5
Total Current	70.6	77.3	78.6	67.5				76.7	78.0
Fixed Assets (net)	10.2	14.5	10.7	18.3				13.3	13.0
Intangibles (net)	5.9	4.1	4.0	6.7				4.5	3.9
All Other Non-Current	13.3	4.1	6.6	7.5				5.5	5.1
Total	100.0	100.0	100.0	100.0				100.0	100.0
LIABILITIES									
Notes Payable-Short Term	20.6	12.1	16.5	17.4				13.7	11.6
Cur. Mat.-L.T.D.	4.1	2.6	2.6	2.0				2.7	2.9
Trade Payables	20.2	25.4	17.5	17.8				22.9	21.4
Income Taxes Payable	.0	.2	.1	.2				.2	.3
All Other Current	12.4	17.2	12.4	7.7				11.2	11.4
Total Current	57.3	57.6	49.1	45.1				50.7	47.6
Long-Term Debt	19.0	17.2	10.3	12.6				9.8	10.9
Deferred Taxes	.0	.0	.2	.2				.3	.2
All Other Non-Current	14.6	6.4	4.5	6.8				6.7	7.3
Net Worth	9.1	18.8	35.9	35.3				32.6	34.0
Total Liabilities & Net Worth	100.0	100.0	100.0	100.0				100.0	100.0
INCOME DATA									
Net Sales	100.0	100.0	100.0	100.0				100.0	100.0
Gross Profit	39.5	33.0	31.6	29.1				30.9	32.0
Operating Expenses	37.1	32.0	29.9	25.7				28.6	28.7
Operating Profit	2.4	1.1	1.7	3.4				2.3	3.3
All Other Expenses (net)	.9	.0	.5	.5				.1	.2
Profit Before Taxes	1.5	1.0	1.3	2.8				2.2	3.1
RATIOS									
Current	3.0	2.6	2.8	2.0				2.4	2.5
	1.7	1.4	1.6	1.5				1.5	1.7
	.7	1.0	1.2	1.3				1.2	1.2
Quick	1.5	1.4	1.2	1.0				1.2	1.3
	.6	.8	.8	.8				.8	.8
	.2	.5	.5	.5				.5	.5
Sales/Receivables	2 157.7	21 17.5	26 13.8	25 14.4				25 14.8	26 14.2
	21 17.4	34 10.8	34 10.7	36 10.0				36 10.1	36 10.2
	32 11.3	48 7.6	46 8.0	46 8.0				51 7.1	47 7.8
Cost of Sales/Inventory	21 17.7	25 14.9	46 7.9	34 10.8				36 10.2	33 11.2
	41 9.0	41 8.9	61 6.0	47 7.8				57 6.4	54 6.8
	102 3.6	64 5.7	99 3.7	78 4.7				87 4.2	84 4.3
Cost of Sales/Payables	0 UND	10 37.8	17 21.2	21 17.4				20 18.3	21 17.1
	21 17.3	31 11.7	27 13.3	28 13.2				34 10.7	33 11.2
	39 9.4	50 7.3	43 8.4	39 9.4				57 6.5	44 8.3
Sales/Working Capital	6.6	7.5	6.0	6.6				6.9	6.7
	15.1	23.8	11.0	14.1				11.0	11.2
	-22.4	-124.9	31.6	31.4				27.6	23.5
EBIT/Interest		13.0	9.1	8.2				8.2	8.0
		(51) 3.6	(75) 3.4	(29) 2.6				(129) 3.4	(138) 3.8
		.8	.5	1.4				1.8	1.8
Net Profit + Depr., Dep., Amort./Cur. Mat. L/T/D			10.8					5.7	6.4
			(20) 4.2					(36) 3.4	(54) 2.4
			1.4					1.4	1.1
Fixed/Worth	.1	.1	.1	.2				.2	.1
	NM	.4	.3	.4				.4	.4
	-.2	NM	1.0	1.7				1.3	1.7
Debt/Worth	1.1	1.1	.7	1.3				.9	.9
	NM	3.4	2.0	2.6				2.4	2.5
	-3.1	-20.6	6.4	6.4				7.0	6.0
% Profit Before Taxes/Tangible Net Worth		56.8	24.6	48.1				41.7	38.5
	(44) 23.3		(66) 14.5	(29) 22.6				(124) 18.5	(139) 19.9
		9.2	1.8	5.0				5.3	6.9
% Profit Before Taxes/Total Assets	8.9	11.3	8.9	11.0				11.3	12.5
	5.4	4.7	4.1	5.7				4.8	5.8
	-2.2	-1.1	-.6	1.3				1.5	2.3
Sales/Net Fixed Assets	149.7	143.6	106.0	71.9				69.5	73.1
	53.4	60.7	44.9	22.1				34.9	35.8
	21.0	23.4	23.7	10.0				16.4	19.9
Sales/Total Assets	7.3	5.0	3.8	3.6				4.1	4.2
	4.6	3.9	3.1	2.8				3.1	3.2
	2.8	2.6	2.4	2.1				2.2	2.4
% Depr., Dep., Amort./Sales	.1	.4	.3	.5				.4	.4
	(10) .3	(46) .6	(69) .7	(28) 1.0				(118) .8	(131) .7
	.4	1.5	1.4	1.8				1.2	1.1
% Officers', Directors' Owners' Comp/Sales		2.9	1.5					2.7	1.8
		(40) 4.8	(36) 3.8					(62) 4.6	(79) 3.2
		7.4	5.1					7.0	5.7
Net Sales ($)	13676M	334629M	1177360M	2115832M	961185M	2004561M		4036913M	6104866M
Total Assets ($)	3226M	73312M	393479M	713193M	284925M	571166M		1741903M	1701982M

M = $ thousand   MM = $ million
See Pages 9 through 22 for Explanation of Ratios and Data

Comparative Historical Data | Current Data Sorted by Sales

Type of Statement

	4/1/07-3/31/08 ALL	4/1/08-3/31/09 ALL	4/1/09-3/31/10 ALL		0-1MM	1-3MM	3-5MM	5-10MM	10-25MM	25MM & OVER
						32 (4/1-9/30/09)		159 (10/1/09-3/31/10)		
Unqualified	14	15	17					1	6	10
Reviewed	44	43	45				2	13	15	15
Compiled	25	30	41		4	5	6	9	14	3
Tax Returns	15	33	26		2	11	2	4	6	1
Other	54	56	62		2	11	3	16	13	17
NUMBER OF STATEMENTS	152	177	191		8	27	13	43	54	46
	%	%	%	**ASSETS**	%	%	%	%	%	%
	7.2	7.4	6.9	Cash & Equivalents		9.1	9.5	5.7	8.4	4.3
	33.1	31.7	30.9	Trade Receivables (net)		31.6	31.2	35.4	28.3	32.4
	34.2	32.5	33.3	Inventory		28.0	33.7	35.9	36.8	28.2
	3.9	3.7	3.7	All Other Current		6.5	2.1	2.1	3.4	4.6
	78.5	75.2	74.9	Total Current		75.3	76.6	79.1	77.0	69.4
	11.4	12.1	13.3	Fixed Assets (net)		13.4	16.1	10.4	11.9	15.3
	5.7	5.5	5.0	Intangibles (net)		3.7	2.4	3.3	4.9	7.5
	4.4	7.1	6.8	All Other Non-Current		7.7	5.0	7.2	6.1	7.8
	100.0	100.0	100.0	Total		100.0	100.0	100.0	100.0	100.0
				LIABILITIES						
	14.8	16.0	15.3	Notes Payable-Short Term		13.5	20.1	15.4	13.2	17.2
	2.6	2.6	2.7	Cur. Mat.-L.T.D.		3.1	3.7	2.4	2.5	2.6
	22.7	18.2	20.2	Trade Payables		22.1	31.1	23.2	16.8	18.4
	.2	.2	.2	Income Taxes Payable		.0	.7	.1	.1	.2
	12.6	12.0	13.1	All Other Current		15.1	25.6	12.2	14.2	8.8
	52.8	49.0	51.5	Total Current		53.8	81.3	53.4	46.8	47.2
	9.5	9.2	13.5	Long-Term Debt		21.5	9.2	11.1	14.4	10.3
	.2	.2	.2	Deferred Taxes		.0	.0	.1	.3	.3
	5.4	5.1	6.1	All Other Non-Current		10.9	3.1	5.9	3.6	6.4
	32.0	36.6	28.7	Net Worth		13.9	6.4	29.6	34.8	35.9
	100.0	100.0	100.0	Total Liabilities & Net Worth		100.0	100.0	100.0	100.0	100.0
				INCOME DATA						
	100.0	100.0	100.0	Net Sales		100.0	100.0	100.0	100.0	100.0
	30.2	32.7	31.6	Gross Profit		37.3	32.0	32.1	31.0	25.8
	27.3	29.5	29.7	Operating Expenses		37.2	30.4	31.0	28.7	22.9
	2.8	3.2	1.9	Operating Profit		.1	1.6	1.2	2.3	2.9
	.4	.5	.4	All Other Expenses (net)		.2	.8	.0	.6	.3
	2.4	2.7	1.5	Profit Before Taxes		.0	.8	1.1	1.7	2.6
				RATIOS						
	2.0	2.3	2.6	Current		3.0	1.6	2.3	3.1	2.0
	1.5	1.5	1.5			1.4	1.1	1.5	2.0	1.5
	1.1	1.1	1.1			.9	.8	1.1	1.2	1.2
	1.1	1.3	1.2	Quick		1.7	1.0	1.1	1.5	1.0
	.7	.8	.8			.8	.6	.7	.9	.8
	.5	.5	.5			.4	.4	.5	.5	.6
	25 14.4	22 16.4	23 15.9	Sales/Receivables		20 17.9	17 21.0	23 16.1	26 14.2	24 14.9
	38 9.7	35 10.4	34 10.9			41 8.9	28 13.0	34 10.8	33 10.9	33 10.9
	49 7.5	45 8.1	46 8.0			57 6.4	54 6.8	46 8.0	43 8.4	43 8.4
	33 11.0	27 13.6	31 11.6	Cost of Sales/Inventory		23 16.0	20 18.0	31 11.6	38 9.5	27 13.6
	49 7.4	50 7.3	52 7.0			51 7.2	52 7.0	50 7.3	59 6.2	40 9.1
	80 4.6	85 4.3	79 4.6			75 4.9	85 4.3	76 4.8	92 4.0	56 6.5
	18 19.8	14 26.8	16 23.1	Cost of Sales/Payables		11 33.7	8 44.1	15 24.7	17 21.1	17 21.1
	29 12.7	23 15.9	28 13.3			35 10.5	34 10.7	31 11.8	26 14.0	25 14.7
	48 7.6	39 9.4	43 8.4			59 6.2	51 7.2	46 7.9	39 9.4	35 10.4
	7.3	7.4	6.6	Sales/Working Capital		6.2	8.0	7.2	5.2	8.8
	12.9	13.7	14.3			16.3	95.9	11.8	8.5	15.1
	44.7	53.5	73.3			-39.7	-31.6	77.4	22.4	45.7
	7.4	12.8	9.1	EBIT/Interest		7.6	12.6	10.9	5.6	10.2
	(136) 3.0	(156) 4.1	(170) 2.9			(20) 1.5	4.0	(38) 3.8	(50) 2.5	(43) 5.4
	1.3	1.4	.9			-2.0	1.0	.3	.5	1.7
	5.0	10.1	7.3	Net Profit + Depr., Dep., Amort./Cur. Mat. L/T/D						12.1
	(47) 2.4	(48) 3.5	(41) 2.1							(20) 3.3
	.9	1.0	1.2							1.5
	.1	.1	.1	Fixed/Worth		.0	.1	.1	.1	.2
	.3	.3	.4			.3	1.2	.3	.3	.4
	1.2	.9	2.4			-2.8	-.3	1.1	.8	1.6
	1.2	.8	.9	Debt/Worth		.6	1.3	.8	.5	1.3
	2.6	2.1	2.6			9.9	2.8	3.2	2.2	2.3
	8.1	6.7	23.6			-5.8	-14.2	10.9	5.1	10.7
	44.2	36.8	32.3	% Profit Before Taxes/Tangible Net Worth		34.6		51.5	24.8	44.1
	(129) 18.3	(151) 17.9	(151) 17.8			(17) 13.5		(36) 16.3	(46) 14.6	(40) 21.8
	5.8	6.3	3.3			-19.9		3.7	2.6	7.4
	12.0	13.2	10.7	% Profit Before Taxes/Total Assets		10.9	12.7	11.1	8.3	12.8
	5.0	6.4	4.8			2.5	4.0	3.0	3.2	7.0
	1.3	1.1	-.4			-7.8	.0	-2.3	-.9	2.8
	86.6	107.6	106.0	Sales/Net Fixed Assets		154.2	646.3	106.8	109.0	73.5
	43.8	47.0	46.1			47.5	64.2	51.3	46.4	38.8
	20.9	20.7	19.5			13.2	20.0	31.1	20.3	13.9
	4.2	4.2	4.2	Sales/Total Assets		4.1	4.7	4.9	3.8	4.2
	3.2	3.2	3.2			3.2	3.7	3.7	3.1	3.4
	2.4	2.5	2.4			1.8	2.1	2.8	2.3	2.5
	.4	.4	.3	% Depr., Dep., Amort./Sales		.3	.3	.4	.3	.5
	(125) .7	(139) .7	(160) .7			(21) .9	(10) .7	(36) .6	(46) .6	(40) .7
	1.1	1.2	1.4			2.1	1.3	1.6	1.2	1.3
	1.6	1.8	1.8	% Officers', Directors' Owners' Comp/Sales		.9	1.7	3.8	1.1	
	(60) 3.4	(84) 3.3	(86) 4.1			(18) 5.0	(10) 4.0	(24) 5.3	(23) 3.7	
	6.0	6.1	7.1			6.0	16.7	11.9	5.0	
	5524602M	6960256M	6607243M	Net Sales ($)	5837M	50650M	54264M	312819M	855993M	5327680M
	1734646M	2090554M	2039301M	Total Assets ($)	3924M	21193M	17172M	95743M	330355M	1570914M

© RMA 2010

M = $ thousand   MM = $ million
See Pages 9 through 22 for Explanation of Ratios and Data

WHOLESALE—Transportation Equipment and Supplies (except Motor Vehicle) Merchant Wholesalers NAICS 423860

Current Data Sorted by Assets

Comparative Historical Data

Type of Statement	0-500M	500M-2MM	2-10MM	10-50MM	50-100MM	100-250MM	4/1/05-3/31/06 ALL	4/1/06-3/31/07 ALL
Unqualified		1	7	15	5	3	35	32
Reviewed	2	3	13	8	1		43	41
Compiled	3	5	11	2			33	32
Tax Returns	4	7	9				16	24
Other	5	13	41	23	8	2	61	68
	28 (4/1-9/30/09)		163 (10/1/09-3/31/10)					
NUMBER OF STATEMENTS	14	29	81	48	14	5	188	197
ASSETS	%	%	%	%	%	%	%	%
Cash & Equivalents	12.3	6.9	9.0	7.3	1.1		8.4	9.8
Trade Receivables (net)	28.2	24.8	22.2	19.8	22.0		26.0	24.6
Inventory	26.5	50.3	41.0	43.8	48.6		42.7	42.0
All Other Current	9.0	1.0	2.4	3.2	4.7		3.1	3.8
Total Current	76.0	83.1	74.6	74.1	76.4		80.1	80.3
Fixed Assets (net)	18.9	12.0	15.4	16.1	14.4		12.0	12.6
Intangibles (net)	.1	2.4	2.7	2.6	4.4		1.5	1.7
All Other Non-Current	4.9	2.5	7.3	7.1	4.8		6.4	5.5
Total	100.0	100.0	100.0	100.0	100.0		100.0	100.0
LIABILITIES								
Notes Payable-Short Term	21.8	18.6	18.9	17.7	31.5		20.6	20.7
Cur. Mat.-L.T.D.	8.7	3.1	2.1	2.7	3.9		3.5	2.8
Trade Payables	29.7	17.0	15.6	12.8	13.1		19.0	18.7
Income Taxes Payable	.0	.0	.0	.3	.0		.2	.3
All Other Current	34.6	11.8	9.2	8.1	5.8		10.2	9.0
Total Current	94.7	50.6	45.8	41.7	54.3		53.5	51.5
Long-Term Debt	5.2	7.5	9.0	12.0	8.2		8.4	9.2
Deferred Taxes	.2	.0	.1	.2	.2		.3	.2
All Other Non-Current	13.1	7.3	5.5	4.6	5.1		4.1	4.5
Net Worth	-13.2	34.7	39.5	41.6	32.1		33.7	34.5
Total Liabilities & Net Worth	100.0	100.0	100.0	100.0	100.0		100.0	100.0
INCOME DATA								
Net Sales	100.0	100.0	100.0	100.0	100.0		100.0	100.0
Gross Profit	35.7	33.1	25.4	30.3	30.3		28.3	28.0
Operating Expenses	34.8	31.2	22.5	24.0	22.6		23.4	22.7
Operating Profit	.8	1.9	2.9	6.4	7.7		4.9	5.4
All Other Expenses (net)	.0	.0	.4	1.6	4.0		.9	.9
Profit Before Taxes	.8	1.9	2.4	4.8	3.7		4.0	4.4
RATIOS								
Current	1.9	3.2	2.7	3.4	2.0		2.3	2.4
	1.1	1.6	1.7	1.7	1.3		1.4	1.5
	.4	1.2	1.2	1.2	1.2		1.1	1.2
Quick	.8	1.4	1.1	1.1	.7		1.0	1.2
	.5	.6	.6	.6	.5		.6 (196)	.6
	.2	.2	.3	.3	.2		.3	.3
Sales/Receivables	0 UND	13 27.2	16 22.2	27 13.4	32 11.3		15 23.8	12 29.4
	18 20.3	31 11.9	28 12.8	42 8.8	49 7.4		38 9.7	31 11.8
	37 9.9	50 7.3	51 7.1	60 6.1	66 5.6		54 6.7	54 6.8
Cost of Sales/Inventory	0 UND	54 6.7	36 10.1	75 4.9	89 4.1		38 9.7	24 15.5
	11 33.4	107 3.4	66 5.5	147 2.5	163 2.2		84 4.4	73 5.0
	56 6.6	239 1.5	136 2.7	248 1.5	502 .7		173 2.1	151 2.4
Cost of Sales/Payables	0 UND	13 27.8	15 24.0	21 17.0	20 17.9		17 21.5	13 28.7
	20 18.5	28 13.1	27 13.4	32 11.4	32 11.4		31 11.6	25 14.3
	60 6.1	52 7.0	43 8.6	50 7.3	51 7.1		55 6.6	50 7.4
Sales/Working Capital	9.4	4.4	4.5	3.1	2.3		5.1	4.4
	NM	8.0	7.3	6.0	6.7		11.8	11.2
	-9.1	16.8	30.8	22.7	28.1		37.1	32.5
EBIT/Interest		5.2	10.9	18.1	7.0		8.8	10.8
		(22) 2.1	(76) 3.9	(45) 3.3	3.0		(169) 4.0	(169) 3.7
		.1	1.7	1.2	1.2		2.0	1.6
Net Profit + Depr., Dep., Amort./Cur. Mat. L/T/D			6.1	18.3			8.8	9.8
			(13) 2.0	(10) 7.6			(40) 2.3	(44) 2.0
			1.2	1.8			1.3	1.3
Fixed/Worth	.0	.0	.1	.1	.1		.1	.1
	.7	.2	.3	.3	.4		.2	.2
	-1.0	1.2	.8	1.0	1.6		.6	.7
Debt/Worth	1.0	.5	.7	.9	1.7		1.1	.8
	NM	1.9	1.7	2.1	3.3		2.3	2.2
	-2.6	4.9	2.9	3.5	4.8		4.9	5.5
% Profit Before Taxes/Tangible Net Worth		21.2	37.5	31.9	37.0		51.3	54.4
	(25) 14.4	(70) 12.8	17.5	(12) 9.0		(179) 23.7	(183) 24.9
		1.5	2.7	3.1	4.0		9.4	9.1
% Profit Before Taxes/Total Assets	42.8	7.9	13.1	15.9	10.8		13.7	17.1
	11.2	3.5	3.4	4.1	3.6		7.0	6.9
	-14.0	-1.0	.1	.8	.8		2.4	2.7
Sales/Net Fixed Assets	UND	441.6	118.8	58.8	115.9		136.2	143.3
	182.4	60.7	30.1	22.1	13.5		53.3	48.3
	23.3	13.2	10.0	8.7	6.6		16.0	15.7
Sales/Total Assets	9.8	3.4	3.5	2.3	2.4		3.7	3.7
	6.5	2.4	2.6	1.9	1.2		2.4	2.5
	4.8	1.8	1.4	.9	.7		1.6	1.6
% Depr., Dep., Amort./Sales		.2	.3	.3	.3		.3	.3
	(21) .9	(71) .7	(40) .7	(13) 1.1		(139) .6	(154) .6
		2.0	1.3	1.1	3.4		1.3	1.2
% Officers', Directors' Owners' Comp/Sales		.2	.3	.3	.3			
		2.3	1.4	1.3			1.2	1.7
	(16) 6.3	(23) 2.6	(10) 2.5			(70) 3.3	(73) 4.1
		12.9	6.2	3.6			5.9	6.8
Net Sales ($)	22103M	97146M	1053727M	1925720M	1621662M	674086M	5443696M	5348387M
Total Assets ($)	2771M	37887M	417909M	1105784M	994196M	676475M	2452113M	2450687M

M = $ thousand   MM = $ million
See Pages 9 through 22 for Explanation of Ratios and Data

Comparative Historical Data | Current Data Sorted by Sales

			Type of Statement			28 (4/1-9/30/09)	163 (10/1/09-3/31/10)		
32	37	31	Unqualified			1	1	8	21
48	53	27	Reviewed	1		2	10	5	8
29	28	21	Compiled		6	2	7	4	2
14	24	20	Tax Returns	2	7	3	4	4	
89	89	92	Other	4	10	9	14	31	24
4/1/07-3/31/08 ALL	4/1/08-3/31/09 ALL	4/1/09-3/31/10 ALL		0-1MM	1-3MM	3-5MM	5-10MM	10-25MM	25MM & OVER
212	231	191	**NUMBER OF STATEMENTS**	7	24	17	36	52	55
%	%	%	**ASSETS**	%	%	%	%	%	%
6.3	8.2	7.8	Cash & Equivalents		13.1	8.3	5.4	7.0	7.5
22.0	22.6	22.2	Trade Receivables (net)		22.2	17.2	20.9	22.3	24.1
44.2	43.9	42.6	Inventory		34.4	48.0	44.7	41.0	44.6
2.8	2.4	3.0	All Other Current		3.0	1.5	2.1	3.7	2.6
75.3	77.1	75.6	Total Current		72.6	75.0	73.1	74.0	78.8
16.1	15.0	15.4	Fixed Assets (net)		20.0	13.7	17.0	15.5	13.0
2.3	1.9	2.6	Intangibles (net)		1.4	5.1	1.6	3.2	2.8
6.3	6.0	6.4	All Other Non-Current		6.0	6.2	8.3	7.3	5.4
100.0	100.0	100.0	Total		100.0	100.0	100.0	100.0	100.0
			LIABILITIES						
22.3	19.5	19.7	Notes Payable-Short Term		18.9	20.7	22.3	17.3	20.6
3.5	3.3	3.2	Cur. Mat.-L.T.D.		7.7	4.4	1.5	2.3	3.3
15.3	15.6	15.8	Trade Payables		20.9	11.9	16.0	12.5	18.4
.2	.2	.1	Income Taxes Payable		.0	.0	.0	.2	.1
9.3	11.5	11.0	All Other Current		21.7	4.1	6.8	8.6	8.5
50.6	50.1	49.9	Total Current		69.3	41.1	46.7	40.9	51.0
11.0	10.9	9.2	Long-Term Debt		4.0	10.1	10.7	12.6	7.2
.2	.3	.1	Deferred Taxes		.0	.1	.1	.2	.1
5.1	4.6	5.9	All Other Non-Current		7.2	10.1	6.1	6.1	3.5
33.1	34.2	34.9	Net Worth		19.5	38.5	36.5	40.2	38.2
100.0	100.0	100.0	Total Liabilties & Net Worth		100.0	100.0	100.0	100.0	100.0
			INCOME DATA						
100.0	100.0	100.0	Net Sales		100.0	100.0	100.0	100.0	100.0
29.0	28.4	29.2	Gross Profit		29.3	35.3	28.1	30.6	24.8
22.6	23.4	25.3	Operating Expenses		30.2	32.9	25.6	23.8	20.7
6.4	5.0	3.9	Operating Profit		-.9	2.4	2.4	6.8	4.1
1.3	1.1	.9	All Other Expenses (net)		-.1	.5	.9	1.6	1.0
5.1	3.9	3.0	Profit Before Taxes		-.8	1.9	1.6	5.2	3.1
			RATIOS						
2.4	2.4	2.7			2.6	2.7	2.7	2.9	2.0
1.5	1.5	1.5	Current		1.2	1.9	1.5	1.7	1.5
1.1	1.2	1.2			.6	1.3	1.1	1.2	1.2
.9	1.1	1.0			1.6	1.0	1.2	1.2	.9
(211) .6	.6	.6	Quick		.6	.4	.5	.6	.6
.3	.3	.3			.2	.3	.1	.4	.3
14 26.1	14 26.5	20 18.6			12 29.7	19 19.6	20 18.3	20 18.2	24 15.4
32 11.3	32 11.3	34 10.8	Sales/Receivables		24 15.2	25 14.7	32 11.4	34 10.7	39 9.5
47 7.8	48 7.6	55 6.6			45 8.1	49 7.4	51 7.2	61 5.9	56 6.5
41 8.9	37 9.8	43 8.5			3 118.4	71 5.1	37 9.9	44 8.4	44 8.2
80 4.6	95 3.8	99 3.7	Cost of Sales/Inventory		51 7.2	104 3.5	108 3.4	103 3.5	80 4.6
158 2.3	175 2.1	199 1.8			201 1.8	313 1.2	262 1.4	176 2.1	169 2.2
10 34.8	11 32.6	16 23.5			9 39.5	20 18.1	17 21.0	13 29.0	21 17.2
23 15.8	27 13.6	30 12.0	Cost of Sales/Payables		24 15.2	38 9.6	32 11.5	26 14.3	33 10.9
42 8.6	49 7.4	50 7.3			58 6.2	49 7.4	62 5.8	40 9.2	50 7.3
5.0	4.5	4.2			4.8	3.4	4.1	4.0	4.4
11.1	9.4	7.5	Sales/Working Capital		17.3	6.7	7.1	6.9	8.4
42.8	30.7	40.3			-6.9	13.9	45.2	21.1	24.7
9.4	10.5	10.2			4.5	7.9	8.6	10.4	19.6
(194) 3.3	(209) 3.0	(171) 3.2	EBIT/Interest		(18) 1.1	(16) 4.0	(32) 2.3	(49) 4.2	(52) 3.7
1.8	1.3	1.1			-4.9	.7	.2	1.9	1.2
8.0	13.2	7.4							15.0
(41) 2.3	(50) 2.8	(33) 2.8	Net Profit + Depr., Dep., Amort./Cur. Mat. L/T/D						(12) 4.4
1.2	.9	1.3							1.3
.1	.1	.1			.1	.0	.1	.1	.1
.3	.3	.3	Fixed/Worth		.7	.4	.3	.3	.3
1.0	.8	1.0			14.2	.6	1.2	.9	.9
.9	1.0	.8			.6	.9	.6	.8	.9
2.1	2.2	2.0	Debt/Worth		2.2	1.6	2.0	1.7	2.2
5.1	4.9	4.1			-14.0	2.8	4.0	3.5	4.5
46.4	45.9	33.1			16.8	19.8	25.9	37.5	33.1
(196) 25.4	(213) 22.8	(167) 14.7	% Profit Before Taxes/Tangible Net Worth		(17) 5.2	(16) 8.6	(30) 10.8	(48) 19.3	(51) 19.0
9.2	3.4	3.4			-9.5	-3.4	2.0	4.6	3.9
15.7	13.9	12.7			5.1	11.4	9.3	15.4	12.8
6.7	5.3	3.7	% Profit Before Taxes/Total Assets		.5	4.0	3.2	7.5	4.9
2.2	.9	.3			-9.1	-.7	-1.3	2.1	-.5
113.3	123.0	113.9			321.4	115.5	87.6	128.2	88.2
33.4	39.9	30.1	Sales/Net Fixed Assets		41.2	24.3	32.6	24.6	34.4
10.5	11.0	9.9			4.9	10.0	11.5	7.6	13.3
3.6	3.4	3.2			4.0	2.4	3.2	3.1	3.2
2.3	2.3	2.1	Sales/Total Assets		2.5	1.8	2.0	2.0	2.1
1.6	1.5	1.3			1.2	1.5	1.2	1.2	1.2
.3	.3	.3			.6	.5	.3	.3	.2
(169) .7	(175) .7	(154) .7	% Depr., Dep., Amort./Sales		(16) 2.0	(13) 1.2	(30) .7	(43) .7	(51) .6
1.6	1.7	1.4			7.3	1.4	1.5	2.0	1.1
1.0	1.3	1.9			3.6	1.3	1.3	1.5	1.0
(68) 2.3	(89) 4.0	(56) 3.3	% Officers', Directors' Owners' Comp/Sales		(11) 7.2	(10) 6.9	(13) 3.1	(10) 2.2	(10) 2.5
4.8	7.9	7.5			13.5	1.4	6.5	2.0	3.1
6892841M	7049465M	5394444M	Net Sales ($)	3658M	47704M	62793M	254652M	837858M	4187779M
3239597M	3563493M	3235022M	Total Assets ($)	1532M	37858M	35672M	172593M	675047M	2312320M

M = $ thousand   MM = $ million
See Pages 9 through 22 for Explanation of Ratios and Data

Current Data Sorted by Assets   Comparative Historical Data

Type of Statement

	0-500M	500M-2MM	2-10MM	10-50MM	50-100MM	100-250MM		4/1/05-3/31/06 ALL	4/1/06-3/31/07 ALL
Unqualified		14	18	24	11	9		48	44
Reviewed		15	58	17	2	1		68	71
Compiled		34	22	3	1			42	47
Tax Returns	1	33	18	2		1		38	51
Other	14/.16		56	26	17	9		126	126

Date ranges for current data columns: 69 (4/1-9/30/09); 353 (10/1/09-3/31/10)

	0-500M	500M-2MM	2-10MM	10-50MM	50-100MM	100-250MM		ALL	ALL
NUMBER OF STATEMENTS	31	96	172	72	31	20		322	339

ASSETS

	%	%	%	%	%	%		%	%
Cash & Equivalents	11.2	9.2	10.7	9.0	3.0	8.8		6.8	7.3
Trade Receivables (net)	18.7	25.9	27.4	28.5	32.3	26.0		27.6	27.0
Inventory	45.2	42.5	42.3	38.9	34.6	29.8		42.6	44.8
All Other Current	2.2	1.8	1.9	3.7	2.4	3.4		2.8	2.4
Total Current	77.4	79.3	82.2	80.2	72.3	68.0		79.8	81.5
Fixed Assets (net)	12.2	10.9	9.2	9.8	8.7	11.5		10.2	9.5
Intangibles (net)	6.3	6.5	3.7	2.3	12.2	14.4		4.7	4.2
All Other Non-Current	4.1	3.4	4.8	7.7	6.8	6.1		5.2	4.8
Total	100.0	100.0	100.0	100.0	100.0	100.0		100.0	100.0

LIABILITIES

Notes Payable-Short Term	38.7	19.4	15.3	20.0	11.7	19.4		18.2	17.8
Cur. Mat.-L.T.D.	2.3	2.2	2.4	1.7	1.7	2.4		1.7	2.1
Trade Payables	34.0	19.4	19.0	18.4	21.1	19.9		21.5	19.7
Income Taxes Payable	.0	.0	.1	.3	.3	.5		.3	.2
All Other Current	7.2	8.0	10.4	10.3	11.3	12.2		10.1	10.5
Total Current	82.2	49.1	47.3	50.7	46.0	54.4		51.8	50.2
Long-Term Debt	25.3	13.7	8.6	3.6	12.7	5.6		11.1	9.1
Deferred Taxes	.0	.1	.1	.3	.1	1.3		.2	.2
All Other Non-Current	21.6	9.0	5.4	4.3	3.7	5.6		10.3	8.4
Net Worth	-29.2	28.1	38.6	41.1	37.4	33.1		26.7	32.0
Total Liabilities & Net Worth	100.0	100.0	100.0	100.0	100.0	100.0		100.0	100.0

INCOME DATA

Net Sales	100.0	100.0	100.0	100.0	100.0	100.0		100.0	100.0
Gross Profit	36.5	36.2	31.1	29.1	27.4	28.9		32.5	32.3
Operating Expenses	35.5	32.1	27.7	25.0	22.2	25.0		28.9	28.2
Operating Profit	1.0	4.1	3.4	4.1	5.2	3.9		3.6	4.1
All Other Expenses (net)	1.4	1.5	.6	.5	1.4	2.2		1.1	1.0
Profit Before Taxes	-.4	2.6	2.9	3.6	3.8	1.7		2.4	3.1

RATIOS

Current	2.0	3.0	3.1	2.6	2.4	1.7		2.5	2.9
	1.2	1.6	1.9	1.6	1.5	1.2		1.5	1.5
	.7	1.2	1.2	1.2	1.1	1.0		1.2	1.2
Quick	.7	1.4	1.5	1.2	1.2	1.0		1.1	1.2
	.3	.7	.8	.8	.8	.6		.6	.6
	.1	.4	.4	.4	.4	.5		.4	.4
Sales/Receivables	2 223.8	13 28.6	20 18.4	25 14.3	35 10.5	34 10.8		21 17.7	16 23.0
	11 34.4	30 12.0	38 9.7	43 8.4	43 8.6	57 6.4		36 10.0	37 9.9
	39 9.5	56 6.5	53 6.8	67 5.5	66 5.6	76 4.8		62 5.9	60 6.1
Cost of Sales/Inventory	17 21.4	41 8.9	54 6.8	55 6.6	53 6.9	58 6.3		62 5.9	63 5.8
	109 3.4	92 4.0	88 4.2	84 4.3	75 4.9	89 4.1		97 3.8	101 3.6
	134 2.7	171 2.1	149 2.5	137 2.7	118 3.1	106 3.4		139 2.6	150 2.4
Cost of Sales/Payables	9 40.4	8 45.5	15 24.5	14 25.9	25 14.8	24 15.4		17 21.0	14 26.5
	26 13.8	27 13.5	28 12.9	27 13.6	34 10.8	40 9.2		33 11.0	32 11.5
	80 4.5	58 6.3	52 7.0	52 7.0	54 6.7	67 5.4		69 5.3	55 6.6
Sales/Working Capital	8.5	4.2	4.1	4.1	4.2	5.2		4.9	4.3
	15.9	9.7	7.3	8.4	10.3	13.8		8.7	8.4
	-17.4	38.3	21.3	21.4	50.3	NM		21.1	20.8
EBIT/Interest	5.3	7.7	13.2	21.4	10.2	52.6		9.4	7.9
	(24) 1.9	(87) 2.5	(160) 4.0	(65) 4.5	(30) 3.7	2.5		(300) 3.2	(307) 2.9
	-2.1	-.5	1.3	1.3	2.0	1.9		1.2	1.1
Net Profit + Depr., Dep., Amort./Cur. Mat. L/T/D			8.9	16.1				11.5	11.4
		(34) 2.3		(18) 3.0				(62) 5.2	(69) 3.2
			.5	1.3				1.3	.7
Fixed/Worth	.0	.0	.0	.1	.1	.1		.1	.1
	.4	.2	.2	.2	.3	.5		.3	.2
	-.7	3.3	.6	.5	1.2	-.4		.9	.9
Debt/Worth	3.3	.8	.6	.6	1.1	1.2		1.1	.8
	-47.2	2.9	1.8	1.9	2.8	2.2		2.6	2.2
	-2.1	18.6	6.3	5.1	6.9	-10.8		9.0	9.4
% Profit Before Taxes/Tangible Net Worth	77.4	63.6	43.8	43.0	40.3	56.0		40.6	38.2
	(15) 51.2	(76) 22.0	(157) 19.0	(70) 17.0	(27) 17.2	(14) 19.2		(270) 16.4	(284) 15.3
	2.4	3.1	4.2	3.0	5.5	1.7		3.0	3.6
% Profit Before Taxes/Total Assets	21.0	16.0	13.7	17.4	11.2	18.2		11.6	12.5
	9.2	4.8	5.5	5.3	6.3	4.5		4.2	4.6
	-6.4	-1.5	.5	.8	2.0	1.5		.6	.5
Sales/Net Fixed Assets	UND	213.8	168.3	125.5	259.5	72.3		136.3	130.1
	50.8	64.2	67.0	40.2	69.4	31.7		43.4	47.7
	22.8	19.8	20.8	15.4	9.8	8.1		18.4	21.3
Sales/Total Assets	4.7	3.3	3.2	2.9	3.3	2.5		3.2	3.3
	3.7	2.4	2.4	2.1	1.9	1.6		2.4	2.4
	2.3	1.7	1.8	1.5	1.4	1.0		1.6	1.7
% Depr., Dep., Amort./Sales	.4	.3	.2	.3	.2	.3		.3	.3
	(14) 1.4	(57) .8	(135) .6	(62) .6	(23) .7	(14) .6		(253) .6	(255) .7
	2.1	1.3	1.2	1.2	2.3	1.9		1.0	1.1
% Officers', Directors' Owners' Comp/Sales	3.6	2.1	1.6	.4				1.6	1.7
	(19) 5.6	(51) 3.7	(65) 3.3	(19) 2.0				(118) 3.0	(140) 3.8
	8.6	6.5	5.4	3.9				5.7	5.7
Net Sales ($)	36188M	341939M	2301300M	4444964M	5135393M	6978515M		8825629M	10252247M
Total Assets ($)	9114M	115440M	798542M	1656116M	2064482M	3003379M		3948651M	4469077M

© RMA 2010

M = $ thousand   MM = $ million
See Pages 9 through 22 for Explanation of Ratios and Data

Comparative Historical Data · Current Data Sorted by Sales

4/1/07-3/31/08 ALL	4/1/08-3/31/09 ALL	4/1/09-3/31/10 ALL	Type of Statement	0-1MM	1-3MM	3-5MM	5-10MM	10-25MM	25MM & OVER
43	60	62	Unqualified		1	2	4	13	42
80	82	92	Reviewed		7	7	25	30	23
40	54	42	Compiled		9	7	12	9	5
40	60	71	Tax Returns	10	28	13	10	7	3
133	138	155	Other	6	26	20	23	34	46
					69 (4/1-9/30/09)		353 (10/1/09-3/31/10)		
336	394	422	**NUMBER OF STATEMENTS**	16	71	49	74	93	119
%	%	%	**ASSETS**	%	%	%	%	%	%
8.3	8.1	9.4	Cash & Equivalents	10.7	8.9	10.8	11.1	10.6	7.0
26.6	24.0	26.9	Trade Receivables (net)	18.8	20.7	22.9	25.8	30.2	31.3
42.9	45.3	40.8	Inventory	47.0	43.2	41.1	45.5	40.7	35.6
3.0	2.7	2.3	All Other Current	1.1	2.2	1.2	2.2	2.2	3.2
80.8	80.0	79.4	Total Current	77.5	75.1	76.0	84.6	83.7	77.2
8.6	9.6	10.0	Fixed Assets (net)	12.2	12.1	12.4	8.4	9.0	9.2
5.3	5.8	5.4	Intangibles (net)	5.9	9.7	6.7	1.9	2.8	6.6
5.3	4.6	5.1	All Other Non-Current	4.5	3.1	4.9	5.1	4.5	7.0
100.0	100.0	100.0	Total	100.0	100.0	100.0	100.0	100.0	100.0
			LIABILITIES						
18.0	18.4	18.7	Notes Payable-Short Term	54.5	19.9	18.6	14.6	17.1	17.0
2.0	2.3	2.2	Cur. Mat.-L.T.D.	4.2	3.3	1.9	1.9	1.6	2.0
20.7	19.2	20.3	Trade Payables	26.4	19.5	18.8	18.5	21.7	20.5
.2	.1	.2	Income Taxes Payable	.0	.0	.1	.1	.2	.4
8.4	9.1	9.7	All Other Current	2.7	8.5	9.2	9.2	10.2	11.5
49.2	49.1	51.1	Total Current	87.8	51.2	48.7	44.3	50.9	51.4
7.6	8.4	10.3	Long-Term Debt	28.1	18.6	15.0	7.3	6.7	5.7
.2	.2	.2	Deferred Taxes	.0	.0	.1	.1	.2	.3
6.3	6.0	7.1	All Other Non-Current	40.3	6.1	12.1	5.2	3.9	4.9
36.7	36.3	31.3	Net Worth	-56.2	24.1	24.1	43.0	38.4	37.6
100.0	100.0	100.0	Total Liabilities & Net Worth	100.0	100.0	100.0	100.0	100.0	100.0
			INCOME DATA						
100.0	100.0	100.0	Net Sales	100.0	100.0	100.0	100.0	100.0	100.0
31.7	31.6	31.9	Gross Profit	43.4	36.8	37.1	31.8	29.9	27.1
27.2	28.0	28.3	Operating Expenses	46.6	32.7	33.0	29.1	25.4	23.0
4.5	3.6	3.7	Operating Profit	-3.2	4.1	4.1	2.7	4.6	4.1
1.2	.8	1.0	All Other Expenses (net)	2.3	1.7	1.3	.0	.7	1.0
3.4	2.8	2.7	Profit Before Taxes	-5.5	2.4	2.7	2.7	3.9	3.1
			RATIOS						
2.6	2.7	2.8	Current	2.3	3.0	3.1	3.3	2.7	2.4
1.7	1.7	1.6		1.3	1.5	2.1	2.0	1.7	1.5
1.2	1.2	1.2		.5	1.0	1.1	1.4	1.2	1.1
1.2	1.2	1.3	Quick	.9	1.2	1.5	1.9	1.4	1.1
(335) .7	.6	.7		.4	.6	.7	.8	.9	.8
.4	.4	.4		.2	.2	.3	.4	.5	.4
19 19.4	19 19.1	19 19.1	Sales/Receivables	12 31.5	6 56.2	18 20.1	18 20.8	21 17.1	25 14.6
36 10.2	36 10.2	37 9.8		29 12.7	27 13.4	32 11.3	33 11.1	39 9.2	42 8.7
54 6.7	53 6.9	59 6.2		53 6.9	59 6.2	52 7.0	59 6.2	53 6.9	64 5.7
53 6.9	58 6.3	52 7.0	Cost of Sales/Inventory	71 5.1	58 6.3	65 5.6	54 6.7	48 7.7	49 7.4
101 3.6	100 3.6	89 4.1		160 2.3	112 3.3	110 3.3	89 4.1	82 4.5	75 4.9
147 2.5	159 2.3	142 2.6		235 1.6	188 1.9	154 2.4	154 2.4	146 2.5	118 3.1
15 24.8	14 27.0	14 26.2	Cost of Sales/Payables	20 18.1	5 76.0	13 27.2	15 23.9	16 23.0	16 22.8
32 11.3	31 11.9	31 11.8		33 11.0	26 14.0	43 8.6	25 14.7	34 10.7	32 11.4
56 6.5	55 6.6	55 6.7		95 3.8	66 5.6	65 5.6	51 7.1	49 7.4	52 7.0
4.5	4.7	4.3	Sales/Working Capital	6.6	3.6	3.1	4.1	4.4	5.1
8.5	7.9	8.7		11.3	7.4	9.1	6.7	8.6	10.6
20.0	19.9	33.1		-82.8	91.3	70.2	13.7	23.9	49.5
9.7	9.4	12.6	EBIT/Interest	3.0	6.6	9.0	13.1	16.0	17.2
(303) 2.9	(357) 3.0	(386) 3.3		(13) .7	(63) 2.1	(45) 3.0	(65) 4.0	(88) 4.4	(112) 4.3
1.3	1.1	1.2		-4.6	-.4	.7	1.1	1.9	1.7
9.3	8.9	9.4	Net Profit + Depr., Dep., Amort./Cur. Mat. L/T/D				14.6	14.4	16.0
(59) 2.8	(76) 3.6	(72) 2.9					(13) .7	(20) 3.8	(29) 4.5
.9	1.1	.7					-.7	1.9	1.7
.1	.1	.0	Fixed/Worth	.0	.0	.1	.0	.1	.1
.2	.2	.2		.6	.2	.3	.2	.2	.2
.7	.9	.9		-.5	24.8	-4.8	.4	.7	.8
.8	.8	.7	Debt/Worth	3.5	.8	.6	.6	.6	1.0
1.8	1.9	2.2		-9.5	4.2	1.8	1.6	1.9	2.2
6.2	7.4	8.9		-1.7	-10.3	-23.9	3.6	6.6	6.7
43.5	41.4	48.1	% Profit Before Taxes/Tangible Net Worth		73.8	40.1	34.7	48.8	49.8
(292) 20.7	(340) 14.1	(359) 19.7			(53) 24.3	(35) 15.0	(72) 10.5	(84) 25.4	(109) 19.3
5.1	3.3	4.1			1.0	3.5	2.2	8.2	4.7
15.6	13.1	15.5	% Profit Before Taxes/Total Assets	10.5	15.6	13.5	11.8	17.0	17.5
6.6	4.5	5.5		-.8	4.8	5.4	4.2	7.4	5.8
1.0	.3	.6		-30.2	-1.2	-.3	.4	1.4	1.3
157.3	134.3	173.5	Sales/Net Fixed Assets	UND	243.6	123.2	164.0	183.5	182.0
52.7	53.2	56.9		31.5	52.1	67.7	52.8	56.2	64.4
22.6	19.9	18.4		11.7	20.0	12.8	17.0	23.1	17.5
3.4	3.4	3.5	Sales/Total Assets	3.1	3.2	3.0	3.2	3.6	3.5
2.5	2.3	2.3		2.3	2.1	2.2	2.3	2.7	2.2
1.7	1.7	1.7		1.7	1.4	1.4	1.8	2.0	1.6
.3	.3	.3	% Depr., Dep., Amort./Sales		.4	.2	.2	.2	.2
(254) .6	(294) .6	(305) .6			(43) .9	(32) .7	(54) .6	(74) .6	(97) .5
1.1	1.1	1.3			1.5	1.5	1.1	1.2	1.3
1.4	1.4	1.6	% Officers', Directors' Owners' Comp/Sales		3.2	3.2	1.4	1.5	.4
(143) 3.0	(154) 3.1	(158) 3.4			(37) 4.9	(28) 4.3	(32) 2.9	(28) 2.0	(24) 1.3
5.7	6.0	5.9			8.4	6.7	5.3	4.2	3.3
12932831M	14160930M	19238299M	Net Sales ($)	10031M	126989M	193418M	544590M	1515412M	16847859M
5776951M	6490458M	7647073M	Total Assets ($)	4318M	74491M	106847M	251355M	657821M	6552241M

© RMA 2010

M = $ thousand   MM = $ million
See Pages 9 through 22 for Explanation of Ratios and Data

Current Data Sorted by Assets   Comparative Historical Data

0-500M	500M-2MM	2-10MM	10-50MM	50-100MM	100-250MM	Type of Statement	4/1/05-3/31/06 ALL	4/1/06-3/31/07 ALL
	1	1	9	3	1	Unqualified	28	20
	1	14	7			Reviewed	22	24
	5	8	2			Compiled	18	17
4	16	6				Tax Returns	20	23
	11	25	12	5	7	Other	41	42
	25 (4/1-9/30/09)		113 (10/1/09-3/31/10)					
5	33	54	30	8	8	NUMBER OF STATEMENTS	129	126
%	%	%	%	%	%	ASSETS	%	%
	14.1	8.7	9.1			Cash & Equivalents	8.5	8.3
	23.8	26.0	32.1			Trade Receivables (net)	27.5	27.2
	45.5	41.6	29.5			Inventory	40.3	40.3
	1.3	3.4	5.0			All Other Current	2.7	2.9
	84.7	79.7	75.7			Total Current	79.1	78.7
	10.5	10.3	14.3			Fixed Assets (net)	11.1	12.3
	1.5	1.5	4.2			Intangibles (net)	3.3	3.8
	3.4	8.6	5.8			All Other Non-Current	6.4	5.2
	100.0	100.0	100.0			Total	100.0	100.0
						LIABILITIES		
	16.8	17.4	16.7			Notes Payable-Short Term	20.0	21.8
	2.3	1.1	2.9			Cur. Mat.-L.T.D.	2.2	2.0
	18.5	17.0	17.0			Trade Payables	18.8	19.0
	.4	.1	.7			Income Taxes Payable	.3	.2
	4.6	7.1	9.2			All Other Current	7.5	7.4
	42.6	42.7	46.5			Total Current	48.9	50.4
	10.0	4.3	7.5			Long-Term Debt	9.2	12.7
	.0	.1	.1			Deferred Taxes	.5	.1
	10.4	6.9	3.7			All Other Non-Current	6.4	8.1
	37.0	46.0	42.3			Net Worth	35.0	28.6
	100.0	100.0	100.0			Total Liabilities & Net Worth	100.0	100.0
						INCOME DATA		
	100.0	100.0	100.0			Net Sales	100.0	100.0
	38.2	33.7	31.0			Gross Profit	34.3	34.4
	36.6	30.1	25.0			Operating Expenses	31.2	30.3
	1.6	3.6	6.0			Operating Profit	3.0	4.2
	.4	.4	.6			All Other Expenses (net)	.9	1.4
	1.2	3.2	5.4			Profit Before Taxes	2.1	2.8
						RATIOS		
	3.3	2.9	2.2			Current	2.5	2.7
	2.3	1.9	1.8				1.7	1.7
	1.4	1.3	1.3				1.2	1.2
	1.4	1.4	1.5			Quick	1.4	1.4
	.8	.9	.9				(128) .7	.7
	.6	.4	.4				.4	.3
	13 27.6	20 17.9	29 12.4			Sales/Receivables	22 16.9	18 20.5
	22 16.3	41 9.0	49 7.4				38 9.6	33 11.2
	47 7.8	57 6.4	81 4.5				57 6.4	61 6.0
	39 9.3	45 8.2	31 11.7			Cost of Sales/Inventory	48 7.6	46 7.9
	109 3.3	104 3.5	80 4.6				98 3.7	96 3.8
	206 1.8	163 2.2	137 2.7				158 2.3	136 2.7
	11 33.4	14 26.2	21 17.7			Cost of Sales/Payables	17 21.9	14 25.4
	33 11.0	32 11.6	27 13.7				32 11.4	32 11.5
	57 6.4	49 7.5	36 10.3				56 6.5	54 6.7
	3.4	4.0	4.7			Sales/Working Capital	4.9	4.6
	7.6	6.8	6.5				8.5	8.5
	12.2	14.9	16.6				20.9	23.2
	16.3	21.7	31.2			EBIT/Interest	7.1	9.1
	(30) 2.6	(47) 4.5	9.8				(122) 3.3	(112) 2.8
	.3	1.6	3.0				1.0	1.5
						Net Profit + Depr., Dep., Amort./Cur. Mat. L/T/D	21.7	14.0
							(29) 4.7	(21) 3.8
							.2	-.4
	.0	.0	.0			Fixed/Worth	.1	.0
	.1	.1	.2				.2	.3
	.7	.4	.9				.8	1.2
	.5	.6	.8			Debt/Worth	.8	.8
	1.2	1.2	1.1				1.7	2.0
	4.7	2.2	3.4				5.1	8.5
	31.8	35.4	56.0			% Profit Before Taxes/Tangible Net Worth	47.2	52.9
	(29) 11.3	(52) 17.0	(27) 33.3				(116) 11.7	(108) 14.8
	.1	2.3	20.7				1.0	4.9
	11.2	16.7	24.6			% Profit Before Taxes/Total Assets	12.6	12.5
	3.4	6.2	13.6				4.3	5.5
	-1.7	1.1	4.3				.2	1.3
	529.0	170.6	164.0			Sales/Net Fixed Assets	115.7	114.4
	60.8	57.2	30.8				40.5	39.9
	23.5	17.3	9.4				14.5	13.4
	4.4	3.3	2.8			Sales/Total Assets	3.5	3.6
	2.4	2.3	2.0				2.4	2.6
	1.6	1.4	1.4				1.7	1.6
	.4	.3	.4			% Depr., Dep., Amort./Sales	.4	.3
	(18) .8	(38) .7	(20) 1.0				(104) .9	(102) .7
	1.7	1.1	1.6				1.5	1.5
	3.0	2.0				% Officers', Directors' Owners' Comp/Sales	2.0	1.4
	(22) 4.5	(22) 3.9					(59) 3.7	(49) 3.2
	8.7	11.6					6.9	5.9
3757M	117621M	751360M	1527589M	1368562M	1550197M	Net Sales ($)	4336015M	3875225M
1252M	36691M	277993M	663893M	572454M	1054811M	Total Assets ($)	2109888M	1716334M

M = $ thousand   MM = $ million
See Pages 9 through 22 for Explanation of Ratios and Data

Comparative Historical Data | **Current Data Sorted by Sales**

						Type of Statement												
	21		23		14	Unqualified										1		13
	22		26		23	Reviewed		1				2		4		11		5
	7		15		15	Compiled				4		2		4		3		2
	19		24		26	Tax Returns		4		10		4		6		1		1
	60		61		60	Other		1		6		4		8		17		24
	4/1/07-3/31/08 ALL		**4/1/08-3/31/09 ALL**		**4/1/09-3/31/10 ALL**					**25 (4/1-9/30/09)**						**113 (10/1/09-3/31/10)**		
								0-1MM		**1-3MM**		**3-5MM**		**5-10MM**		**10-25MM**		**25MM & OVER**
	129		149		138	**NUMBER OF STATEMENTS**		6		20		12		22		33		45
	%		%		%	**ASSETS**		%		%		%		%		%		%
	8.8		9.3		9.5	Cash & Equivalents				10.0		6.4		9.8		9.1		8.3
	25.7		25.4		26.2	Trade Receivables (net)				19.9		16.8		26.5		29.7		30.4
	40.3		40.4		39.7	Inventory				47.9		53.7		44.1		37.3		31.2
	5.0		4.3		3.0	All Other Current				1.1		3.0		2.0		3.1		4.2
	79.7		79.5		78.4	Total Current				79.0		79.9		82.4		79.3		74.1
	12.0		12.5		12.0	Fixed Assets (net)				12.7		14.8		9.0		10.9		13.3
	3.0		3.5		3.2	Intangibles (net)				2.5		.8		.9		4.2		4.9
	5.2		4.5		6.5	All Other Non-Current				5.8		4.5		7.7		5.6		7.8
	100.0		100.0		100.0	Total				100.0		100.0		100.0		100.0		100.0
						LIABILITIES												
	20.4		18.2		16.1	Notes Payable-Short Term				22.0		14.6		17.7		16.6		14.1
	2.2		3.1		2.6	Cur. Mat.-L.T.D.				6.8		.8		.5		1.7		3.1
	17.8		20.0		16.8	Trade Payables				11.2		15.4		18.1		18.2		17.3
	.7		.1		.3	Income Taxes Payable				.2		.6		.1		.2		.4
	8.2		6.9		6.9	All Other Current				3.4		7.7		3.5		8.6		9.6
	49.2		48.2		42.7	Total Current				43.6		39.1		40.0		45.4		44.6
	10.3		9.2		7.9	Long-Term Debt				9.0		9.2		7.9		5.0		9.5
	.1		.1		.1	Deferred Taxes				.0		.1		.0		.2		.1
	7.5		9.0		7.6	All Other Non-Current				13.8		9.5		4.2		6.5		5.7
	32.9		33.6		41.7	Net Worth				33.6		42.1		47.9		43.0		40.1
	100.0		100.0		100.0	Total Liabilties & Net Worth				100.0		100.0		100.0		100.0		100.0
						INCOME DATA												
	100.0		100.0		100.0	Net Sales				100.0		100.0		100.0		100.0		100.0
	35.6		33.1		34.7	Gross Profit				42.0		45.3		30.5		30.8		33.4
	31.7		30.9		30.7	Operating Expenses				42.5		43.5		27.8		25.2		27.1
	3.9		2.2		4.0	Operating Profit				-.5		1.8		2.7		5.5		6.2
	1.4		1.2		.6	All Other Expenses (net)				.9		1.3		.3		.4		.5
	2.5		1.0		3.5	Profit Before Taxes				-1.4		.5		2.4		5.2		5.7
						RATIOS												
	2.8		2.9		3.0					3.1		3.6		3.6		2.6		2.8
	1.7		1.8		1.9	Current				1.8		2.2		2.5		1.8		1.8
	1.2		1.2		1.3					1.3		1.4		1.4		1.3		1.2
	1.1		1.3		1.5					1.0		1.4		1.5		1.2		1.6
	.6		.7		.9	Quick				.7		.6		1.0		.8		.9
	.4		.4		.4					.3		.2		.6		.5		.4
21	17.2	**20**	18.7	**18**	20.5				**3**	108.0	**19**	18.9	**17**	22.0	**21**	17.7	**20**	18.1
34	10.6	**36**	10.2	**36**	10.0	Sales/Receivables			**34**	10.9	**26**	14.1	**41**	8.8	**40**	9.0	**38**	9.6
55	6.7	**56**	6.5	**57**	6.4				**57**	6.4	**40**	9.1	**57**	6.4	**57**	6.4	**70**	5.2
48	7.7	**43**	8.5	**44**	8.3				**101**	3.6	**101**	3.6	**37**	10.0	**38**	9.6	**30**	12.1
109	3.4	**108**	3.4	**101**	3.6	Cost of Sales/Inventory			**157**	2.3	**179**	2.0	**103**	3.6	**93**	3.9	**86**	4.2
163	2.2	**168**	2.2	**168**	2.2				**254**	1.4	**375**	1.0	**205**	1.8	**140**	2.6	**125**	2.9
19	19.3	**16**	22.2	**16**	23.0				**6**	56.6	**18**	20.5	**10**	38.3	**25**	14.5	**20**	18.3
32	11.5	**32**	11.2	**31**	11.8	Cost of Sales/Payables			**44**	8.4	**36**	10.2	**25**	14.6	**35**	10.5	**29**	12.5
67	5.5	**60**	6.1	**51**	7.2				**57**	6.3	**67**	5.5	**47**	7.7	**45**	8.2	**53**	6.8
	4.5		4.6		4.0					3.0		3.1		3.6		4.9		5.0
	7.6		8.2		6.9	Sales/Working Capital				5.1		4.7		7.8		7.4		9.0
	21.9		22.8		14.7					11.3		14.9		12.2		15.3		16.8
	6.4		6.9		18.7					2.5		18.5		16.3		24.2		25.3
(115)	2.1	(127)	2.1	(122)	5.3	EBIT/Interest			(18)	1.2	(11)	1.9	(17)	2.9	(32)	6.0	(42)	10.2
	1.0		.8		1.7					-1.9		-.8		1.2		3.2		3.1
	18.3		6.2		3.7													
(22)	3.0	(20)	2.2	(16)	1.8	Net Profit + Depr., Dep., Amort./Cur. Mat. L/T/D												
	.6		1.0		1.4													
	.0		.0		.0					.0		.1		.0		.0		.1
	.2		.2		.1	Fixed/Worth				.2		.2		.1		.1		.2
	1.2		.8		.6					.7		1.0		.4		.6		.9
	.8		.7		.7					.6		.6		.5		.9		.7
	1.9		1.9		1.3	Debt/Worth				1.6		1.2		1.1		1.3		1.4
	6.7		4.3		3.4					4.3		5.1		2.1		3.1		3.9
	41.6		32.1		43.8					26.1		27.2		19.4		50.7		59.9
(110)	14.2	(135)	9.0	(127)	22.7	% Profit Before Taxes/Tangible Net Worth			(17)	3.0	(11)	6.1	(21)	5.8	(32)	28.0	(41)	35.3
	1.7		.2		3.7					-.2		-9.4		.4		9.0		20.1
	13.4		10.8		16.7					4.4		8.5		11.1		18.3		26.5
	3.6		2.6		7.6	% Profit Before Taxes/Total Assets				.4		1.9		3.2		11.2		14.3
	.2		-1.2		1.1					-7.5		-6.9		.2		2.9		7.1
	126.7		287.1		229.2					610.2		37.0		213.9		246.9		103.5
	40.1		49.6		47.1	Sales/Net Fixed Assets				35.9		26.1		82.4		75.4		37.3
	14.2		11.7		14.6					7.3		7.5		17.4		16.4		12.1
	3.1		3.6		3.2					2.4		2.8		5.2		3.5		3.2
	2.2		2.2		2.2	Sales/Total Assets				1.8		2.0		2.1		2.6		2.2
	1.6		1.5		1.4					1.3		1.2		1.3		1.9		1.4
	.3		.3		.4					.8				.4		.3		.6
(99)	.8	(109)	.7	(88)	.9	% Depr., Dep., Amort./Sales			(12)	1.7			(15)	.6	(22)	.6	(29)	1.3
	1.9		2.0		1.6					2.0				.8		1.0		1.8
	1.7		1.8		1.9					4.0				1.7		1.5		
(50)	4.0	(60)	3.7	(56)	3.9	% Officers', Directors' Owners' Comp/Sales			(14)	6.8			(11)	3.1	(10)	2.4		
	7.4		6.1		7.5					9.4				11.6		4.7		
	4843369M		**5719380M**		**5319086M**	Net Sales ($)		**2499M**		**39192M**		**49298M**		**145399M**		**526030M**		**4556668M**
	2383819M		**2740491M**		**2607094M**	Total Assets ($)		**2170M**		**22990M**		**34866M**		**74142M**		**225329M**		**2247597M**

M = $ thousand MM = $ million

See Pages 9 through 22 for Explanation of Ratios and Data

Current Data Sorted by Assets   Comparative Historical Data

Type of Statement	0-500M	500M-2MM	2-10MM	10-50MM	50-100MM	100-250MM		4/1/05-3/31/06 ALL	4/1/06-3/31/07 ALL
Unqualified		1	5	22	6	5		36	33
Reviewed	3	6	37	31	3	1		84	83
Compiled	3	16	24	8				70	56
Tax Returns	11	35	26	3				28	54
Other	5	28	57	68	7	8		100	121
		60 (4/1-9/30/09)		359 (10/1/09-3/31/10)					
NUMBER OF STATEMENTS	22	86	149	132	16	14		318	347
ASSETS	%	%	%	%	%	%		%	%
Cash & Equivalents	11.8	13.8	12.8	7.1	9.4	8.3		9.2	10.3
Trade Receivables (net)	25.5	24.8	21.8	26.5	20.3	19.6		29.9	30.3
Inventory	7.7	16.8	17.0	20.6	23.9	11.4		18.4	19.3
All Other Current	.2	2.0	4.4	5.1	2.9	2.7		3.1	3.0
Total Current	45.3	57.3	56.0	59.3	56.5	42.1		60.6	62.8
Fixed Assets (net)	38.8	33.6	37.2	29.9	30.1	29.8		30.7	29.4
Intangibles (net)	1.4	2.4	1.9	3.3	7.8	23.0		1.7	2.2
All Other Non-Current	14.5	6.7	4.9	7.5	5.6	5.1		7.0	5.5
Total	100.0	100.0	100.0	100.0	100.0	100.0		100.0	100.0
LIABILITIES									
Notes Payable-Short Term	14.5	9.8	12.1	12.5	4.0	4.0		10.3	11.0
Cur. Mat.-L.T.D.	5.0	4.5	3.7	4.0	7.7	4.5		4.2	4.0
Trade Payables	14.0	16.8	13.7	15.6	12.0	12.4		19.0	18.2
Income Taxes Payable	.0	.0	.2	.6	.0	.1		.4	.4
All Other Current	10.5	10.3	6.7	6.6	6.1	3.1		8.0	8.4
Total Current	44.0	41.3	36.5	39.3	30.0	24.1		41.9	42.0
Long-Term Debt	25.4	19.3	16.5	13.2	11.5	18.5		16.2	17.4
Deferred Taxes	.0	.2	.4	.5	.7	1.5		.4	.3
All Other Non-Current	14.7	6.7	4.4	6.0	12.5	4.7		4.8	3.8
Net Worth	15.9	32.5	42.3	41.1	45.3	51.2		36.7	36.4
Total Liabilities & Net Worth	100.0	100.0	100.0	100.0	100.0	100.0		100.0	100.0
INCOME DATA									
Net Sales	100.0	100.0	100.0	100.0	100.0	100.0		100.0	100.0
Gross Profit	36.0	31.0	24.6	21.1	20.2	10.3		28.0	25.7
Operating Expenses	37.0	29.5	22.6	17.5	17.3	12.8		21.6	19.2
Operating Profit	-1.0	1.4	1.9	3.6	2.9	-2.5		6.4	6.5
All Other Expenses (net)	-.4	.3	.5	.7	.0	3.2		.7	.5
Profit Before Taxes	-.6	1.2	1.4	2.8	2.9	-5.7		5.7	6.0
RATIOS									
Current	4.2	4.4	3.3	2.2	4.2	2.7		2.3	2.7
	1.6	1.6	1.7	1.5	1.5	1.8		1.5	1.6
	.6	.9	1.0	1.1	1.2	1.3		1.0	1.1
Quick	3.6	2.5	2.1	1.3	2.2	2.1		1.5	1.7
	1.0	(85) 1.1	.9	.8	.8	1.0		.9	(346) 1.0
	.3	.6	.5	.5	.7	.8		.6	.6
Sales/Receivables	0 UND	7 51.3	13 27.7	28 13.0	27 13.3	31 11.8		17 21.4	16 22.2
	19 19.4	23 16.0	28 13.0	40 9.1	42 8.7	44 8.4		32 11.5	31 11.9
	41 9.0	39 9.3	45 8.0	53 6.9	48 7.6	54 6.8		43 8.6	43 8.5
Cost of Sales/Inventory	0 UND	5 68.6	5 69.1	14 25.8	25 14.6	11 32.3		6 64.5	6 60.8
	0 UND	16 22.5	24 15.2	33 11.1	47 7.7	24 15.5		18 20.1	17 20.9
	10 35.6	45 8.1	51 7.2	55 6.6	99 3.7	44 8.4		40 9.2	40 9.1
Cost of Sales/Payables	0 UND	2 195.9	10 38.1	13 27.1	15 25.0	16 22.7		11 32.9	8 44.2
	10 35.6	15 24.8	21 17.6	27 13.3	27 13.7	27 13.4		22 16.4	21 17.2
	34 10.9	41 8.8	36 10.1	44 8.2	39 9.4	36 10.3		37 9.9	35 10.4
Sales/Working Capital	12.6	7.0	6.3	6.7	3.9	6.4		9.6	8.9
	37.3	20.3	13.4	13.1	12.5	9.2		19.7	17.5
	-19.8	-62.5	-166.2	65.7	33.5	29.7		450.0	70.8
EBIT/Interest	11.6	12.5	10.5	13.8	13.7	1.5		21.9	25.3
	(15) 1.9	(75) 3.3	(133) 3.0	(126) 4.4	(14) 3.6	(13) -1.4		(283) 8.5	(319) 8.2
	-4.8	-2.3	-1.0	.7	1.1	-62.8		2.7	2.9
Net Profit + Depr., Dep., Amort./Cur. Mat. L/T/D			2.1	4.7				7.9	11.1
		(23) 1.5	(26) .8					(68) 3.0	(68) 3.8
		.4	-1.9					1.4	1.7
Fixed/Worth	.2	.3	.4	.2	.4	.3		.3	.3
	4.6	.8	.9	.7	.9	1.1		.8	.7
	-5.0	2.3	2.6	1.7	2.5	NM		1.8	1.7
Debt/Worth	.4	.5	.4	.7	.4	.3		.7	.7
	13.9	1.7	1.3	1.7	1.3	1.3		1.9	1.7
	-8.8	7.6	3.8	3.6	3.1	NM		4.4	4.9
% Profit Before Taxes/Tangible Net Worth	128.4	53.6	27.8	33.0	18.9	19.6		69.5	80.1
	(13) 30.4	(76) 10.6	(133) 9.5	(120) 15.2	(14) 7.8	(11) -7.2		(291) 37.7	(317) 47.8
	3.5	-11.0	-3.7	3.7	2.0	-15.0		18.1	22.0
% Profit Before Taxes/Total Assets	23.9	18.6	10.6	12.2	6.8	.4		28.4	33.5
	8.3	4.7	3.7	5.7	4.0	-3.9		12.6	15.6
	-16.7	-5.0	-3.2	-.4	-.1	-6.0		3.8	5.0
Sales/Net Fixed Assets	35.5	52.8	19.4	23.0	13.1	7.2		35.4	44.6
	18.5	10.7	6.8	9.9	5.7	3.2		13.4	14.9
	6.0	4.3	3.5	4.1	3.7	2.7		6.6	7.1
Sales/Total Assets	6.0	5.5	3.3	3.1	2.8	2.0		4.8	5.3
	4.4	2.9	2.3	2.2	1.9	1.2		3.5	3.5
	2.0	1.8	1.7	1.6	1.5	.7		2.4	2.5
% Depr., Dep., Amort./Sales	1.6	.7	1.5	.7	1.8	1.5		.7	.7
	(16) 2.6	(63) 2.2	(136) 3.5	(120) 1.9	(12) 3.6	(10) 3.3		(279) 1.8	(302) 1.5
	9.0	5.2	5.5	4.7	4.8	6.1		3.1	3.0
% Officers', Directors' Owners' Comp/Sales	2.1	2.4	1.1	.9				1.3	.8
	(10) 3.5	(48) 4.2	(73) 2.5	(30) 1.4				(137) 3.0	(148) 2.6
	9.1	5.5	3.8	3.3				6.2	5.5
Net Sales ($)	31827M	398287M	1934956M	7180923M	2263984M	3538280M		14255796M	18292630M
Total Assets ($)	6319M	102715M	741749M	2847003M	1136337M	2107918M		4188645M	5086591M

M = $ thousand   MM = $ million
See Pages 9 through 22 for Explanation of Ratios and Data

Comparative Historical Data | Current Data Sorted by Sales

			Type of Statement						
39	41	39	Unqualified		1	1	2	6	29
85	86	81	Reviewed	2	2	5	12	29	31
61	56	51	Compiled	3	6	5	16	17	4
65	60	75	Tax Returns	7	14	16	18	16	4
156	184	173	Other	4	23	8	22	41	75
4/1/07-3/31/08 ALL	4/1/08-3/31/09 ALL	4/1/09-3/31/10 ALL		60 (4/1-9/30/09)			359 (10/1/09-3/31/10)		
				0-1MM	1-3MM	3-5MM	5-10MM	10-25MM	25MM & OVER
406	427	419	NUMBER OF STATEMENTS	16	46	35	70	109	143
%	%	%	ASSETS	%	%	%	%	%	%
11.1	13.2	10.9	Cash & Equivalents	10.6	12.3	17.2	10.6	14.3	6.5
29.6	22.8	24.0	Trade Receivables (net)	23.5	17.6	23.3	20.6	23.6	28.2
18.5	15.8	17.7	Inventory	7.3	11.9	16.0	15.7	18.7	21.3
2.5	3.6	3.8	All Other Current	.3	2.6	1.4	6.0	2.7	4.9
61.7	55.4	56.3	Total Current	41.8	44.4	57.8	52.8	59.2	60.9
28.4	31.8	33.7	Fixed Assets (net)	47.6	41.5	34.2	37.2	33.5	28.0
3.1	4.0	3.4	Intangibles (net)	.8	4.0	1.9	2.6	3.0	4.5
6.7	8.8	6.6	All Other Non-Current	9.8	10.2	6.2	7.4	4.3	6.6
100.0	100.0	100.0	Total	100.0	100.0	100.0	100.0	100.0	100.0
			LIABILITIES						
11.0	12.3	11.3	Notes Payable-Short Term	13.4	14.3	6.4	8.9	12.9	11.3
4.0	3.8	4.2	Cur. Mat.-L.T.D.	5.8	3.7	5.7	4.9	3.2	4.3
17.9	15.6	14.8	Trade Payables	23.0	7.5	14.9	14.1	14.6	16.7
.3	.3	.3	Income Taxes Payable	.0	.1	.0	.3	.2	.5
8.5	7.3	7.5	All Other Current	8.4	13.8	7.1	8.4	5.2	6.6
41.6	39.3	38.1	Total Current	50.6	39.4	34.0	36.7	36.1	39.4
15.1	17.4	16.4	Long-Term Debt	26.0	21.5	18.1	20.8	14.7	12.4
.3	.3	.4	Deferred Taxes	.1	.2	.3	.6	.2	.6
4.7	5.3	6.2	All Other Non-Current	32.5	3.8	6.9	2.1	7.6	4.9
38.2	37.6	38.9	Net Worth	-9.1	35.1	40.7	39.9	41.4	42.8
100.0	100.0	100.0	Total Liabilities & Net Worth	100.0	100.0	100.0	100.0	100.0	100.0
			INCOME DATA						
100.0	100.0	100.0	Net Sales	100.0	100.0	100.0	100.0	100.0	100.0
24.4	20.7	24.7	Gross Profit	40.1	43.1	26.7	27.9	22.8	16.6
18.0	16.6	22.7	Operating Expenses	44.3	38.5	26.4	27.5	18.9	14.7
6.4	4.1	2.1	Operating Profit	-4.3	4.6	.3	.4	3.9	1.9
.5	.4	.6	All Other Expenses (net)	.2	1.0	.0	.5	•.4	.8
5.8	3.7	1.5	Profit Before Taxes	-4.4	3.6	.2	-.1	3.5	1.1
			RATIOS						
2.6	2.6	3.0	Current	4.4	3.5	5.4	3.4	3.4	2.2
1.5	1.5	1.6		1.5	1.3	1.7	1.4	1.9	1.5
1.1	.9	1.0		.4	.6	1.0	.7	1.0	1.2
1.8	1.8	2.0	Quick	3.9	2.8	4.6	1.8	2.4	1.4
(405) 1.1	.9	(418) .9		1.0	(45) .8	1.1	.8	1.0	.8
.6	.5	.5		.3	.3	.6	.4	.6	.5
15 24.3	6 62.0	16 23.1	Sales/Receivables	1 597.8	1 278.2	8 46.3	14 26.9	13 27.7	26 14.1
29 12.5	16 23.4	32 11.3		15 24.6	25 14.9	31 11.6	28 13.2	30 12.2	39 9.4
41 8.8	28 13.2	48 7.6		56 6.5	43 8.5	54 6.7	38 9.6	45 8.0	52 7.1
5 79.0	3 114.6	8 43.5	Cost of Sales/Inventory	0 UND	0 UND	6 61.4	8 43.6	6 59.1	14 25.8
14 26.1	10 35.6	26 14.1		2 161.3	21 17.6	20 18.7	23 15.5	23 15.8	29 12.5
34 10.7	22 16.4	53 6.9		46 7.9	58 6.3	49 7.4	46 8.0	58 6.3	54 6.8
7 50.3	4 90.2	10 36.8	Cost of Sales/Payables	3 108.5	1 395.1	10 35.6	14 27.0	8 46.8	12 29.9
19 19.1	11 33.3	22 16.9		44 8.3	18 20.4	15 24.1	22 16.6	19 19.0	25 14.9
35 10.3	24 15.1	41 9.0		92 4.0	48 7.6	46 8.0	41 9.0	37 10.0	36 10.0
9.1	12.1	6.7	Sales/Working Capital	8.4	5.8	4.9	7.3	6.2	7.5
21.4	33.0	14.4		40.1	14.6	12.3	24.7	14.2	13.3
86.8	-131.0	999.8		-4.1	-18.2	-118.6	-16.0	317.6	43.3
24.3	19.8	11.9	EBIT/Interest	2.8	12.5	11.8	7.0	15.6	13.3
(379) 8.3	(393) 6.0	(376) 3.4		(10) -1.4	(37) 2.5	(33) 3.6	(61) 1.7	(98) 4.0	(137) 4.4
2.8	1.8	-.3		-11.3	-.8	-6.6	-3.1	.8	.4
10.9	12.0	2.9	Net Profit + Depr., Dep., Amort./Cur. Mat. L/T/D				2.3	2.7	3.9
(87) 4.0	(87) 4.2	(62) 1.2					(12) 1.3	(16) 1.7	(29) .9
1.4	1.7	-.1					-.3	.7	-.8
.2	.3	.3	Fixed/Worth	.2	.5	.2	.3	.3	.2
.6	.9	.8		UND	1.6	.7	1.3	.8	.6
1.7	2.6	2.5		-3.9	6.6	3.5	3.0	2.0	1.5
.7	.7	.5	Debt/Worth	.4	.5	.3	.4	.5	.7
1.7	1.8	1.6		UND	2.1	1.3	1.8	1.3	1.6
4.4	4.9	4.7		-7.7	11.7	5.3	4.9	3.5	3.2
78.8	71.6	32.5	% Profit Before Taxes/Tangible Net Worth		36.1	31.7	23.1	40.5	32.5
(377) 43.8	(372) 36.8	(367) 12.1		(38) 10.3	(31) 10.1	(62) 5.2	(96) 16.7	(131) 15.7	
21.6	9.9	-3.8			-8.5	-28.9	-15.9	-1.1	.9
31.2	27.0	12.3	% Profit Before Taxes/Total Assets	12.0	16.6	12.3	10.0	19.2	11.0
15.4	12.7	4.2		-.9	3.7	2.4	1.8	5.4	5.1
5.4	1.9	-2.8		-21.5	-4.4	-12.6	-8.9	-.5	-2.0
41.1	46.1	24.6	Sales/Net Fixed Assets	28.8	10.0	37.7	20.9	29.5	25.6
16.9	17.9	9.0		4.4	5.2	10.9	6.5	10.4	10.1
7.0	7.9	3.8		1.4	2.2	3.1	3.5	4.0	4.7
5.3	6.8	3.6	Sales/Total Assets	2.9	2.9	4.3	3.8	3.7	3.6
3.7	4.5	2.4		1.4	1.9	2.4	2.2	2.4	2.5
2.4	2.6	1.6		1.1	1.1	1.4	1.6	1.8	1.8
.6	.6	1.1	% Depr., Dep., Amort./Sales	2.3	1.6	1.1	.9	1.1	.7
(362) 1.6	(357) 1.5	(357) 2.8		(12) 8.2	(33) 3.2	(28) 2.7	(63) 4.0	(97) 3.0	(124) 1.8
2.9	3.0	5.1		16.4	8.0	4.4	5.8	5.0	3.7
.9	1.0	1.2	% Officers', Directors' Owners' Comp/Sales		3.1	3.1	1.3	1.0	.8
(169) 2.0	(162) 2.3	(163) 2.7		(24) 5.4	(18) 5.0	(33) 2.7	(51) 2.4	(32) 1.2	
4.8	4.1	4.6		12.7	5.7	4.2	3.7	2.6	
26482551M	33145394M	15348257M	Net Sales ($)	8667M	84472M	138947M	525269M	1749210M	12841692M
7369954M	7846744M	6942041M	Total Assets ($)	8409M	55409M	72231M	288244M	854150M	5663598M

© RMA 2010

M = $ thousand   MM = $ million
See Pages 9 through 22 for Explanation of Ratios and Data

Current Data Sorted by Assets **Comparative Historical Data**

0-500M	500M-2MM	2-10MM	10-50MM	50-100MM	100-250MM	Type of Statement	ALL 4/1/05-3/31/06	ALL 4/1/06-3/31/07
		2	7	4	3	Unqualified	30	23
	2	28	25		2	Reviewed	73	64
1	7	20	2			Compiled	27	37
7	22	16	3			Tax Returns	33	36
3	4	26	18	7	4	Other	72	64
	46 (4/1-9/30/09)		167 (10/1/09-3/31/10)					
11	35	92	55	13	7	**NUMBER OF STATEMENTS**	235	224
%	%	%	%	%	%	**ASSETS**	%	%
22.7	16.1	7.7	6.9	10.9		Cash & Equivalents	6.6	7.5
6.0	23.3	33.3	29.7	28.6		Trade Receivables (net)	30.5	27.3
50.6	43.7	49.3	46.3	43.5		Inventory	51.6	50.3
.0	.5	1.1	2.7	1.8		All Other Current	1.2	2.0
79.4	83.7	91.4	85.6	84.9		Total Current	89.9	87.1
14.3	5.8	3.4	6.9	5.8		Fixed Assets (net)	4.7	6.7
.0	.9	1.3	1.6	5.1		Intangibles (net)	1.3	2.0
6.3	9.7	3.9	5.9	4.3		All Other Non-Current	4.2	4.1
100.0	100.0	100.0	100.0	100.0		Total	100.0	100.0
						LIABILITIES		
27.8	16.6	14.8	19.5	18.4		Notes Payable-Short Term	19.7	19.3
2.7	2.1	1.0	1.8	.0		Cur. Mat.-L.T.D.	1.5	2.3
17.3	22.2	27.9	29.0	17.4		Trade Payables	25.0	21.7
.0	.0	.1	.3	.2		Income Taxes Payable	.1	.3
9.0	10.2	6.8	6.8	17.8		All Other Current	9.8	10.3
56.8	51.1	50.6	57.4	53.8		Total Current	56.1	53.8
11.0	6.5	4.2	6.9	1.0		Long-Term Debt	5.6	6.0
.0	.0	.0	.2	.6		Deferred Taxes	.0	.1
7.7	13.6	7.2	6.4	1.5		All Other Non-Current	4.6	4.9
24.5	28.8	38.0	29.1	43.1		Net Worth	33.6	35.2
100.0	100.0	100.0	100.0	100.0		Total Liabilities & Net Worth	100.0	100.0
						INCOME DATA		
100.0	100.0	100.0	100.0	100.0		Net Sales	100.0	100.0
50.4	34.1	21.3	20.9	29.3		Gross Profit	26.8	28.9
47.2	31.2	17.9	18.0	28.4		Operating Expenses	22.7	25.1
3.2	2.9	3.3	2.9	.9		Operating Profit	4.1	3.8
.1	.4	.8	1.2	1.4		All Other Expenses (net)	1.3	1.1
3.1	2.5	2.6	1.6	-.5		Profit Before Taxes	2.8	2.7
						RATIOS		
3.9	3.7	2.6	2.0	2.4			2.3	2.4
2.1	1.6	1.6	1.5	1.4		Current	1.6	1.5
.6	1.2	1.4	1.2	1.2			1.3	1.2
1.6	1.8	1.2	.9	1.1			1.0	1.1
.7	.7	.7	.7	.8		Quick	(234) .6	(223) .6
.2	.3	.5	.4	.4			.4	.3
0 UND	2 224.8	33 10.9	33 11.1	12 29.8			24 15.1	15 24.1
5 67.6	15 23.8	55 6.6	59 6.2	67 5.4		Sales/Receivables	59 6.2	48 7.6
10 35.6	52 7.0	79 4.6	107 3.4	130 2.8			99 3.7	83 4.4
38 9.7	14 26.1	58 6.2	48 7.6	64 5.7			83 4.4	60 6.1
78 4.7	57 6.4	137 2.7	106 3.4	236 1.5		Cost of Sales/Inventory	154 2.4	129 2.8
268 1.4	170 2.1	222 1.6	192 1.9	400 .9			240 1.5	278 1.3
0 UND	4 88.3	20 18.3	17 21.2	20 18.0			21 17.8	12 29.6
22 17.0	36 10.2	52 7.0	60 6.1	44 8.4		Cost of Sales/Payables	56 6.6	47 7.8
52 7.0	61 6.0	86 4.2	130 2.8	145 2.5			106 3.5	99 3.7
4.7	4.2	2.7	3.6	2.4			3.3	3.3
15.6	10.1	5.0	6.1	5.1		Sales/Working Capital	5.1	6.2
-16.8	60.6	9.2	16.7	37.9			11.2	12.7
	10.6	8.4	15.3	4.1			7.8	6.3
	(26) 5.2	(77) 2.9	(49) 2.9	(11) 2.2		EBIT/Interest	(214) 2.4	(194) 2.2
	2.0	1.4	1.3	-2.5			1.3	1.3
							9.8	9.8
						Net Profit + Depr., Dep., Amort./Cur. Mat. L/T/D	(28) 2.4	(25) 2.2
							1.0	.5
.0	.0	.0	.0	.1			.0	.0
.0	.1	.0	.1	.1		Fixed/Worth	.1	.1
-2.8	1.2	.2	.2	.6			.2	.4
.3	1.1	.9	1.3	.7			1.1	.9
.8	2.8	1.9	2.3	1.9		Debt/Worth	2.2	2.2
-13.5	10.0	5.5	3.9	7.9			4.3	4.3
	78.9	36.7	26.4	12.9			27.8	31.9
	(29) 17.0	(90) 10.6	(51) 9.0	(12) 3.9		% Profit Before Taxes/Tangible Net Worth	(219) 10.5	(205) 10.3
	2.9	1.8	2.2	-1.3			3.2	2.6
65.9	18.7	10.2	11.5	2.7			8.7	10.1
15.2	5.4	3.0	1.7	.7		% Profit Before Taxes/Total Assets	2.8	3.3
-17.6	1.0	.7	.3	-1.4			.6	.7
UND	691.7	999.8	318.6	162.1			346.3	382.5
95.0	195.0	197.1	96.9	43.5		Sales/Net Fixed Assets	94.0	65.4
17.4	21.9	67.9	37.8	11.9			30.5	22.2
8.5	6.9	2.6	2.5	1.9			2.5	2.8
3.1	3.2	1.8	1.6	1.3		Sales/Total Assets	1.7	1.8
2.0	2.1	1.1	1.1	.9			1.1	1.2
	.1	.0	.1	.1			.1	.1
	(29) .3	(61) .2	(51) .2	(12) .6		% Depr., Dep., Amort./Sales	(180) .3	(180) .4
	.9	.4	.8	.7			.8	.9
	4.0	1.5	.5				1.2	1.1
	(29) 4.5	(58) 2.5	(28) 1.6			% Officers', Directors' Owners' Comp/Sales	(119) 2.7	(121) 2.8
	9.1	4.5	3.8				5.6	5.5
24794M	360616M	1322206M	7188448M	2312918M	10316998M	Net Sales ($)	6384255M	10549097M
2827M	42297M	451422M	1223560M	903316M	1169972M	Total Assets ($)	3840004M	3569170M

M = $ thousand   MM = $ million
See Pages 9 through 22 for Explanation of Ratios and Data

Comparative Historical Data / Current Data Sorted by Sales

4/1/07-3/31/08 ALL	4/1/08-3/31/09 ALL	4/1/09-3/31/10 ALL	Type of Statement	46 (4/1-9/30/09)		167 (10/1/09-3/31/10)			
				0-1MM	1-3MM	3-5MM	5-10MM	10-25MM	25MM & OVER
24	22	16	Unqualified			1		3	12
62	68	57	Reviewed	1	1	3	13	22	17
33	25	30	Compiled		6	6	9	4	5
31	32	48	Tax Returns	5	9	10	9	12	3
45	76	62	Other	3	5	8	8	10	28
195	**223**	**213**	**NUMBER OF STATEMENTS**	**9**	**21**	**28**	**39**	**51**	**65**
%	%	%	**ASSETS**	%	%	%	%	%	%
7.1	5.8	9.7	Cash & Equivalents		7.5	11.9	7.4	10.3	9.8
28.6	25.3	28.4	Trade Receivables (net)		19.7	27.2	29.8	36.6	27.9
49.7	53.8	47.5	Inventory		53.6	46.1	53.3	42.6	43.8
2.7	2.7	1.6	All Other Current		.2	.1	.8	1.4	3.5
88.1	87.7	87.2	Total Current		81.0	85.3	91.2	90.9	85.0
6.2	6.1	5.5	Fixed Assets (net)		10.6	3.4	3.6	4.8	6.3
1.8	1.4	1.5	Intangibles (net)		.5	2.6	.6	1.2	2.2
3.8	4.8	5.8	All Other Non-Current		7.9	8.7	4.5	3.1	6.5
100.0	100.0	100.0	Total		100.0	100.0	100.0	100.0	100.0
			LIABILITIES						
20.2	20.1	17.2	Notes Payable-Short Term		16.9	15.0	16.5	20.1	15.1
1.9	1.9	1.5	Cur. Mat.-L.T.D.		2.7	1.7	.9	.7	1.7
22.6	22.1	25.7	Trade Payables		19.0	21.1	31.2	28.1	26.0
.2	.1	.2	Income Taxes Payable		.0	.0	.0	.1	.4
9.1	11.3	8.4	All Other Current		10.9	7.0	8.1	4.9	11.6
54.0	55.4	52.9	Total Current		49.4	44.7	56.8	53.9	54.9
7.1	6.5	5.7	Long-Term Debt		9.8	7.5	2.2	5.4	6.0
.1	.1	.1	Deferred Taxes		.0	.0	.0	.0	.3
4.9	5.4	7.7	All Other Non-Current		11.5	7.7	5.6	5.8	6.8
33.8	32.6	33.7	Net Worth		29.2	40.0	35.4	34.9	32.0
100.0	100.0	100.0	Total Liabilities & Net Worth		100.0	100.0	100.0	100.0	100.0
			INCOME DATA						
100.0	100.0	100.0	Net Sales		100.0	100.0	100.0	100.0	100.0
25.0	26.4	25.3	Gross Profit		40.1	29.8	23.5	20.3	19.0
20.8	24.0	22.3	Operating Expenses		35.4	26.1	20.4	16.9	17.1
4.3	2.4	3.0	Operating Profit		4.7	3.7	3.1	3.4	1.9
1.2	1.2	.9	All Other Expenses (net)		1.6	.3	.7	1.1	1.0
3.1	1.2	2.1	Profit Before Taxes		3.1	3.4	2.4	2.4	.9
			RATIOS						
2.4 1.6 1.2	2.2 1.5 1.3	2.5 1.6 1.3	Current		3.3 1.6 1.3	3.7 2.2 1.4	2.1 1.6 1.3	2.2 1.5 1.3	2.4 1.5 1.3
1.0 (193) .6 .4	.9 .5 .3	1.1 .7 .4	Quick		1.2 .5 .2	2.0 .8 .5	1.0 .6 .3	1.1 .8 .5	1.1 .7 .4
20 18.3 49 7.4 84 4.3	18 20.7 42 8.7 68 5.4	11 34.3 48 7.7 77 4.7	Sales/Receivables	1 533.7 54 6.8 107 3.4	11 32.8 46 8.0 77 4.8	29 12.6 49 7.5 107 3.4	50 7.4 62 5.8 81 4.5	5 73.1 29 12.5 69 5.3
56 6.6 114 3.2 196 1.9	65 5.6 133 2.7 247 1.5	45 8.1 108 3.4 213 1.7	Cost of Sales/Inventory	134 2.7 180 2.0 559 .7	58 6.3 156 2.3 264 1.4	80 4.6 142 2.6 242 1.5	35 10.4 97 3.8 151 2.4	12 30.2 62 5.9 156 2.3
14 26.4 43 8.5 91 4.0	14 26.4 43 8.5 90 4.1	13 28.6 45 8.2 89 4.1	Cost of Sales/Payables	9 41.5 46 7.9 145 2.5	13 27.1 45 8.1 65 5.6	28 12.9 58 6.3 141 2.6	13 28.8 50 7.3 87 4.2	7 53.1 40 9.2 95 3.8
3.8 7.0 15.3	3.7 6.2 17.3	3.0 6.3 18.0	Sales/Working Capital		1.9 2.7 9.7	2.8 5.3 9.0	2.8 4.9 8.9	3.6 7.2 24.9	4.8 10.3 64.4
6.1 (178) 2.3 1.2	5.2 (201) 2.1 1.0	9.2 (175) 2.9 1.3	EBIT/Interest	(17) 7.6 3.7 -1.1	(23) 9.2 2.2 -.3	(33) 10.8 2.4 1.7	(42) 6.2 2.9 1.1	(56) 14.7 4.9 1.6
5.0 (20) 2.2 .4	20.5 (18) 1.6 .1	52.7 (14) 6.4 .1	Net Profit + Depr., Dep., Amort./Cur. Mat. L/T/D					
.0 .1 .4	.0 .1 .3	.0 .1 .2	Fixed/Worth		.0 .1 1.5	.0 .0 .1	.0 .1 .2	.0 .0 .2	.0 .1 .3
1.0 2.2 4.5	1.1 2.3 4.4	.9 2.1 5.4	Debt/Worth		1.0 2.5 9.7	.8 1.5 6.0	1.1 1.9 5.3	1.3 2.6 4.6	.9 2.3 3.7
27.9 (176) 14.0 3.6	26.8 (204) 6.6 .4	36.0 (196) 11.5 2.3	% Profit Before Taxes/Tangible Net Worth	(19) 32.8 16.1 1.3	(25) 25.6 6.6 -2.2	(50) 22.4 7.5 1.9	(57) 58.8 13.1 1.3	37.2 13.5 3.5
10.3 3.5 .8	7.9 2.1 .1	11.5 2.9 .6	% Profit Before Taxes/Total Assets		9.8 5.0 -3.2	14.4 3.0 .6	6.1 2.4 .7	11.6 3.5 .3	17.6 4.0 .8
539.5 113.5 28.5	462.4 120.4 30.3	721.5 126.9 36.4	Sales/Net Fixed Assets		597.4 44.7 16.6	UND 392.1 54.9	343.6 140.5 43.2	999.8 213.3 45.8	631.8 101.0 43.1
3.1 2.0 1.3	3.0 1.9 1.2	3.2 2.0 1.2	Sales/Total Assets		2.4 1.0 .7	3.0 2.0 1.1	2.5 1.6 .9	3.2 2.1 1.4	10.3 2.3 1.5
.1 (146) .2 .7	.1 (174) .3 .7	.1 (159) .2 .7	% Depr., Dep., Amort./Sales	(14) .3 .6 1.2	(18) .1 .2 .9	(34) .0 .2 .3	(37) .0 .2 .5	(51) .1 .2 .7
.8 (114) 2.1 4.6	1.1 (127) 2.4 5.1	1.4 (127) 2.8 5.1	% Officers', Directors' Owners' Comp/Sales	(15) 3.9 5.1 9.4	(18) 3.1 4.7 9.7	(28) 1.7 2.7 4.8	(36) 1.3 2.1 4.1	(26) .2 .6 2.2
11996294M	16616821M	21525980M	Net Sales ($)	4311M	39277M	108280M	305471M	784699M	20283942M
4168621M	4933873M	3793394M	Total Assets ($)	3178M	37259M	70572M	214148M	451212M	3017025M

© RMA 2010

M = $ thousand   MM = $ million
See Pages 9 through 22 for Explanation of Ratios and Data

Current Data Sorted by Assets   Comparative Historical Data

0-500M	500M-2MM	2-10MM	10-50MM	50-100MM	100-250MM	Type of Statement	4/1/05-3/31/06 ALL	4/1/06-3/31/07 ALL
2	2	14	29	10	6	Unqualified	43	49
2	15	63	22			Reviewed	92	107
6	41	38	12			Compiled	106	114
61	94	52	5			Tax Returns	119	129
24	76	96	46	5	4	Other	168	187
	102 (4/1-9/30/09)			623 (10/1/09-3/31/10)				
95	228	263	114	15	10	**NUMBER OF STATEMENTS**	528	586
%	%	%	%	%	%	**ASSETS**	%	%
23.4	11.1	9.0	7.2	3.9	5.5	Cash & Equivalents	8.8	8.3
28.6	32.5	30.9	30.6	25.6	24.0	Trade Receivables (net)	32.7	32.9
24.7	34.2	37.5	37.9	37.1	29.3	Inventory	35.6	35.8
2.1	2.9	3.0	2.5	4.9	6.9	All Other Current	2.1	2.7
78.8	80.7	80.5	78.2	71.5	65.8	Total Current	79.3	79.6
12.4	10.9	10.5	10.7	14.1	6.8	Fixed Assets (net)	11.7	12.2
2.7	2.9	3.7	5.5	11.5	25.7	Intangibles (net)	3.4	2.7
6.2	5.4	5.2	5.6	2.8	1.7	All Other Non-Current	5.6	5.4
100.0	100.0	100.0	100.0	100.0	100.0	Total	100.0	100.0
						LIABILITIES		
22.6	17.1	14.1	16.0	18.3	5.0	Notes Payable-Short Term	16.2	17.4
3.0	2.4	2.8	2.0	1.7	2.3	Cur. Mat.-L.T.D.	2.4	2.9
30.3	21.4	20.7	20.5	16.4	15.8	Trade Payables	25.4	22.4
.0	.1	.2	.1	.3	.1	Income Taxes Payable	.2	.2
12.6	11.2	8.2	9.4	9.8	6.8	All Other Current	10.3	9.9
68.5	52.1	45.9	48.0	46.6	30.0	Total Current	54.5	52.9
13.5	12.6	7.0	8.7	14.0	25.3	Long-Term Debt	9.5	11.1
.0	.0	.1	.3	.7	.8	Deferred Taxes	.1	.2
9.7	6.4	5.8	6.0	8.0	8.4	All Other Non-Current	5.5	6.0
8.3	28.9	41.1	36.9	30.7	35.5	Net Worth	30.4	29.8
100.0	100.0	100.0	100.0	100.0	100.0	Total Liabilties & Net Worth	100.0	100.0
						INCOME DATA		
100.0	100.0	100.0	100.0	100.0	100.0	Net Sales	100.0	100.0
35.1	34.4	30.9	27.7	26.7	30.3	Gross Profit	31.0	31.2
32.0	31.8	27.1	23.2	22.3	25.1	Operating Expenses	26.8	26.4
3.1	2.6	3.9	4.5	4.4	5.2	Operating Profit	4.2	4.8
.5	.5	.6	1.0	1.4	4.2	All Other Expenses (net)	.7	.8
2.6	2.1	3.3	3.5	3.0	1.1	Profit Before Taxes	3.6	4.0
						RATIOS		
2.8	2.9	2.8	2.8	2.1	3.0	Current	2.3	2.6
1.3	1.7	1.7	1.6	1.4	2.1		1.5	1.5
.7	1.1	1.3	1.2	1.3	1.7		1.1	1.1
1.5	1.4	1.6	1.2	1.1	1.3	Quick	1.3	1.4
.8	.9	.8	.8	.6	1.0		.8 (585)	.8
.3	.5	.5	.5	.3	.7		.5	.5
1 405.3	20 18.1	27 13.4	32 11.3	23 16.0	26 14.0	Sales/Receivables	24 15.3	24 15.4
22 17.0	33 11.1	40 9.0	44 8.4	48 7.6	43 8.6		40 9.1	37 9.8
37 9.7	52 7.1	55 6.7	61 6.0	63 5.8	61 6.0		54 6.7	53 6.8
0 UND	21 17.3	38 9.5	50 7.3	49 7.4	62 5.9	Cost of Sales/Inventory	30 12.3	25 14.5
19 18.9	52 7.0	77 4.7	82 4.5	89 4.1	80 4.6		59 6.2	58 6.3
77 4.7	114 3.2	126 2.9	139 2.6	146 2.5	129 2.8		107 3.4	115 3.2
0 UND	13 28.8	18 20.4	18 20.5	13 27.1	32 11.6	Cost of Sales/Payables	18 20.3	15 24.0
23 16.1	30 12.1	34 10.8	32 11.3	25 14.5	42 8.6		37 9.9	31 11.8
51 7.2	54 6.8	52 7.0	58 6.3	40 9.0	55 6.7		59 6.2	54 6.8
9.0	5.5	4.6	4.4	5.2	3.9	Sales/Working Capital	5.9	5.7
37.4	11.8	8.8	8.9	6.9	5.0		12.0	10.5
-22.7	49.5	20.8	22.1	12.8	6.6		45.8	46.2
12.7	9.7	16.0	14.7	5.9		EBIT/Interest	13.5	11.3
(69) 3.5	(200) 3.4	(240) 4.7	(107) 4.9	(13) 3.0			(467) 4.4	(525) 3.8
-1.3	.8	1.3	2.4	.0			1.6	1.5
		6.3	7.9	7.0	5.9	Net Profit + Depr., Dep., Amort./Cur. Mat. L/T/D	7.9	7.4
	(18) 1.6	(41) 3.1	(22) 3.4	(10) 2.9			(66) 2.3	(84) 2.2
		.3	.4	1.7	-1.4		.6	.9
.0	.0	.0	.1	.2	.0	Fixed/Worth	.1	.1
.3	.3	.1	.2	.8	.2		.2	.2
-1.8	1.9	.5	1.0	1.5	1.7		1.0	1.1
.9	.9	.7	.8	2.4	1.2	Debt/Worth	1.1	1.0
4.4	2.1	1.4	2.7	3.4	3.7		2.4	2.4
-7.0	17.6	4.5	6.4	7.8	NM		8.8	8.2
136.1	57.9	37.1	56.9	55.5		% Profit Before Taxes/Tangible Net Worth	65.2	64.8
(63) 49.2	(184) 14.9	(240) 15.8	(101) 24.7	(13) 28.1			(456) 28.8	(505) 31.4
12.5	.0	2.4	6.8	10.7			7.8	8.1
35.9	14.6	13.5	15.3	12.3	8.8	% Profit Before Taxes/Total Assets	17.6	18.2
9.7	4.9	5.0	7.0	6.4	5.5		7.2	8.0
-2.6	-1.0	.6	2.0	1.5	3.6		1.7	1.5
UND	233.4	195.3	150.7	69.4	90.1	Sales/Net Fixed Assets	170.6	153.4
146.7	56.3	66.6	45.2	15.1	37.6		56.3	52.8
26.3	20.5	18.3	14.0	4.7	19.5		21.2	19.6
7.4	4.8	3.5	3.0	2.4	2.4	Sales/Total Assets	4.1	4.1
4.6	3.0	2.5	2.4	1.8	1.5		3.1	3.0
2.8	2.1	1.8	1.6	1.4	1.1		2.1	2.1
.2	.2	.2	.2	.3	.5	% Depr., Dep., Amort./Sales	.3	.3
(50) .5	(148) .6	(207) .6	(95) .6	(14) 1.4			(395) .6	(443) .6
1.4	1.4	1.1	1.4	3.4			1.2	1.3
3.5	2.4	1.5	1.1			% Officers', Directors' Owners' Comp/Sales	1.7	1.6
(53) 6.7	(128) 4.1	(119) 3.2	(26) 2.3				(262) 3.6	(264) 3.4
12.7	7.0	5.9	3.3				7.1	6.3
155861M	944121M	3460720M	6063865M	2834486M	3104882M	Net Sales ($)	9564263M	12822273M
25965M	273427M	1250182M	2446606M	1118212M	1573305M	Total Assets ($)	3775717M	4682018M

M = $ thousand   MM = $ million
See Pages 9 through 22 for Explanation of Ratios and Data

Comparative Historical Data **Current Data Sorted by Sales**

			Type of Statement						
50	54	63	Unqualified	2		1	3	15	42
109	118	102	Reviewed	1	4	8	22	46	21
90	114	97	Compiled	5	21	15	25	22	9
143	188	212	Tax Returns	32	63	43	47	24	3
209	257	251	Other	15	47	34	45	52	58
4/1/07-3/31/08 ALL	4/1/08-3/31/09 ALL	4/1/09-3/31/10 ALL		102 (4/1-9/30/09)			623 (10/1/09-3/31/10)		
				0-1MM	1-3MM	3-5MM	5-10MM	10-25MM	25MM & OVER
601	731	725	**NUMBER OF STATEMENTS**	55	135	101	142	159	133
%	%	%	**ASSETS**	%	%	%	%	%	%
8.6	9.3	11.1	Cash & Equivalents	19.0	13.0	12.2	11.4	10.2	6.0
30.4	28.8	30.9	Trade Receivables (net)	26.2	25.6	31.8	33.8	31.7	33.2
37.1	38.1	34.7	Inventory	30.1	35.2	33.1	33.9	36.5	36.3
2.5	2.7	2.9	All Other Current	3.2	2.4	4.0	3.0	2.2	3.1
78.6	78.9	79.6	Total Current	78.4	76.2	81.1	82.0	80.6	78.7
11.2	12.1	10.9	Fixed Assets (net)	13.5	12.3	9.2	10.8	11.1	9.8
4.3	3.8	4.1	Intangibles (net)	5.3	2.8	5.2	1.9	3.9	6.6
5.9	5.2	5.4	All Other Non-Current	2.8	8.8	4.4	5.4	4.4	4.9
100.0	100.0	100.0	Total	100.0	100.0	100.0	100.0	100.0	100.0
			LIABILITIES						
17.2	18.3	16.4	Notes Payable-Short Term	27.7	18.8	14.9	14.2	13.9	15.8
3.1	2.9	2.5	Cur. Mat.-L.T.D.	3.5	1.8	2.9	3.0	3.0	1.5
22.6	21.0	22.0	Trade Payables	28.5	19.6	19.4	24.2	19.4	24.3
.1	.1	.1	Income Taxes Payable	.0	.0	.1	.2	.1	.2
10.4	9.7	9.9	All Other Current	11.7	11.4	8.4	10.4	8.6	10.1
53.4	52.0	51.0	Total Current	71.4	51.6	45.7	52.0	45.0	51.9
10.0	10.5	10.3	Long-Term Debt	13.7	16.7	9.6	8.6	6.8	8.9
.1	.1	.1	Deferred Taxes	.0	.0	.1	.0	.1	.4
6.9	5.9	6.6	All Other Non-Current	14.6	7.2	5.6	4.1	6.3	6.5
29.6	31.4	32.0	Net Worth	.4	24.5	39.0	35.2	41.8	32.4
100.0	100.0	100.0	Total Liabilities & Net Worth	100.0	100.0	100.0	100.0	100.0	100.0
			INCOME DATA						
100.0	100.0	100.0	Net Sales	100.0	100.0	100.0	100.0	100.0	100.0
33.0	31.9	32.0	Gross Profit	41.6	36.1	33.8	32.0	29.5	25.3
28.3	27.8	28.5	Operating Expenses	39.7	33.1	30.2	28.5	25.7	21.1
4.7	4.1	3.5	Operating Profit	1.9	3.0	3.7	3.5	3.8	4.2
.9	.8	.7	All Other Expenses (net)	1.0	.9	.3	.3	.7	1.0
3.7	3.3	2.8	Profit Before Taxes	.8	2.1	3.3	3.2	3.1	3.2
			RATIOS						
2.4	2.5	2.8		3.5	3.1	4.0	2.3	2.8	2.2
1.5	1.6	1.7	Current	1.3	1.6	1.7	1.6	1.9	1.5
1.1	1.1	1.1		.7	1.0	1.2	1.2	1.2	1.2
1.3	1.3	1.4		1.4	1.4	1.8	1.4	1.7	1.1
.8	.7	.8	Quick	.7	.7	.9	.9	.9	.8
.5	.4	.5		.3	.4	.6	.5	.5	.5
24 15.5	20 18.7	23 15.8		9 39.3	18 20.7	24 15.2	23 15.8	25 14.4	31 11.9
37 10.0	34 10.9	37 9.9	Sales/Receivables	32 11.4	32 11.6	36 10.2	39 9.2	38 9.5	41 9.0
52 7.0	48 7.6	54 6.8		68 5.4	49 7.5	61 6.0	54 6.8	54 6.7	53 6.9
30 12.1	29 12.4	26 14.0		0 UND	18 20.1	26 13.9	24 15.4	37 9.8	38 9.6
67 5.4	66 5.5	64 5.7	Cost of Sales/Inventory	50 7.3	73 5.0	59 6.2	52 7.1	64 5.7	66 5.5
117 3.1	129 2.8	119 3.1		230 1.6	156 2.3	119 3.1	121 3.0	116 3.2	108 3.4
16 22.6	13 28.1	15 25.0		5 73.1	9 39.1	14 25.6	15 23.6	16 22.5	18 20.0
33 11.1	28 13.2	31 11.8	Cost of Sales/Payables	34 10.6	30 12.3	28 13.2	38 9.7	29 12.8	33 11.1
56 6.6	52 7.0	54 6.8		83 4.4	58 6.3	44 8.3	56 6.5	47 7.7	52 7.1
5.6	5.2	5.1		3.9	4.9	4.8	5.7	4.6	5.6
11.4	10.2	9.9	Sales/Working Capital	15.7	9.5	8.9	10.8	9.4	9.7
49.2	46.1	34.9		-10.0	51.9	29.7	33.2	20.8	28.0
11.1	9.9	12.8		6.5	7.6	9.0	19.0	16.5	16.4
(533) 3.8	(651) 3.5	(638) 4.3	EBIT/Interest	(41) 1.5	(111) 2.1	(87) 3.8	(128) 5.4	(146) 5.0	(125) 5.3
1.5	1.2	1.2		-2.5	-.5	1.0	1.3	1.6	2.5
8.2	6.6	6.5					8.4	6.0	15.7
(75) 2.7	(102) 2.9	(98) 2.9	Net Profit + Depr., Dep., Amort./Cur. Mat. L/T/D				(19) 3.3	(30) 2.1	(34) 3.9
.6	.9	.7					1.3	.2	2.4
.1	.1	.0		.0	.0	.0	.1	.0	.1
.2	.2	.2	Fixed/Worth	1.3	.2	.2	.2	.1	.2
1.3	1.1	1.1		-.4	3.3	.7	.7	.5	1.4
1.1	.9	.8		1.5	.7	.6	.9	.6	1.1
2.5	2.4	2.1	Debt/Worth	22.0	2.1	1.8	1.8	1.4	2.8
9.5	9.7	8.9		-4.4	31.9	7.8	5.7	3.8	9.2
62.8	53.6	54.2		97.5	61.4	45.1	55.1	41.0	61.5
(502) 28.7	(612) 23.0	(609) 19.3	% Profit Before Taxes/Tangible Net Worth	(33) 21.0	(105) 16.1	(85) 15.3	(127) 16.3	(144) 16.4	(115) 28.2
9.2	4.0	2.9		-2.9	-4.8	1.4	5.3	2.5	11.2
18.1	16.3	15.5		17.5	17.7	14.8	14.5	15.1	16.6
6.9	5.3	5.5	% Profit Before Taxes/Total Assets	3.8	4.1	5.2	5.3	7.0	7.0
1.6	.6	.4		-8.5	-2.6	2.0	.8	1.0	2.5
159.2	200.6	233.1		UND	509.3	219.7	252.0	163.0	191.8
50.0	53.9	61.4	Sales/Net Fixed Assets	54.1	55.8	67.3	61.7	65.7	59.7
20.7	18.0	18.5		14.5	16.3	26.7	18.9	22.4	18.9
3.9	4.1	4.0		4.2	4.2	3.9	4.7	4.0	3.5
2.9	2.9	2.7	Sales/Total Assets	2.4	2.5	2.8	2.9	2.9	2.8
2.1	1.9	1.9		1.2	1.7	2.0	2.0	2.1	2.1
.2	.3	.2		.3	.3	.2	.2	.2	.3
(452) .6	(542) .7	(522) .6	% Depr., Dep., Amort./Sales	(30) 1.0	(80) 1.0	(69) .5	(106) .6	(125) .6	(112) .6
1.4	1.4	1.3		3.7	1.9	1.3	1.1	1.2	1.3
2.0	1.9	2.0		4.3	3.0	2.1	2.2	1.4	.8
(282) 3.7	(309) 3.4	(329) 3.8	% Officers', Directors' Owners' Comp/Sales	(29) 7.6	(63) 5.2	(57) 4.4	(85) 3.4	(70) 2.8	(25) 1.8
7.0	6.6	6.7		12.9	7.9	7.9	5.8	4.6	3.0
14313178M	15047492M	16563935M	Net Sales ($)	32940M	271698M	405774M	1035085M	2545782M	12272656M
5106697M	6243671M	6687697M	Total Assets ($)	20047M	127202M	181769M	408549M	1047797M	4902333M

M = $ thousand   MM = $ million
See Pages 9 through 22 for Explanation of Ratios and Data

Current Data Sorted by Assets   Comparative Historical Data

0-500M	500M-2MM	2-10MM	10-50MM	50-100MM	100-250MM	Type of Statement	4/1/05-3/31/06 ALL	4/1/06-3/31/07 ALL
		3	8	3	3	Unqualified	23	28
	1	15	6	1	1	Reviewed	22	21
	7	10	1			Compiled	16	20
7	7	13	1			Tax Returns	8	11
2	9	14	10	2	2	Other	39	46
	19 (4/1-9/30/09)		107 (10/1/09-3/31/10)					
9	24	55	26	6	6	NUMBER OF STATEMENTS	108	126
%	%	%	%	%	%	**ASSETS**	%	%
	8.7	5.7	5.4			Cash & Equivalents	4.8	4.6
	40.3	39.4	41.9			Trade Receivables (net)	43.0	39.6
	23.0	31.3	27.3			Inventory	25.5	25.7
	.5	1.1	1.5			All Other Current	1.8	2.5
	72.5	77.5	76.1			Total Current	75.0	72.4
	13.2	13.8	13.7			Fixed Assets (net)	13.8	14.6
	6.8	2.8	2.4			Intangibles (net)	5.2	3.1
	7.6	5.9	7.9			All Other Non-Current	5.9	9.8
	100.0	100.0	100.0			Total	100.0	100.0
						LIABILITIES		
	15.8	14.3	19.8			Notes Payable-Short Term	19.6	19.5
	4.0	2.2	1.5			Cur. Mat.-L.T.D.	3.1	3.2
	21.2	24.3	22.8			Trade Payables	25.9	25.1
	.0	.1	.0			Income Taxes Payable	.1	.1
	8.3	7.7	4.2			All Other Current	9.3	8.3
	49.2	48.5	48.4			Total Current	58.1	56.1
	7.8	14.2	15.9			Long-Term Debt	12.6	14.0
	.0	.1	.2			Deferred Taxes	.4	.2
	4.8	7.4	2.7			All Other Non-Current	5.2	4.7
	38.2	29.7	32.9			Net Worth	23.8	25.0
	100.0	100.0	100.0			Total Liabilties & Net Worth	100.0	100.0
						INCOME DATA		
	100.0	100.0	100.0			Net Sales	100.0	100.0
	28.1	21.3	17.7			Gross Profit	23.5	23.5
	23.5	20.8	16.2			Operating Expenses	20.9	21.2
	4.6	.6	1.6			Operating Profit	2.7	2.3
	1.2	.3	.6			All Other Expenses (net)	.5	.5
	3.4	.3	1.0			Profit Before Taxes	2.1	1.8
						RATIOS		
	2.8	2.5	3.0				1.9	2.0
	1.6	1.7	1.5			Current	1.3	1.3
	1.1	1.3	1.1				1.1	1.0
	2.0	1.4	1.5				1.3	1.1
	1.0	1.0	1.0			Quick	.8	.7
	.6	.6	.6				.6	.6
	28 12.8	27 13.4	35 10.4				30 12.2	30 12.1
	40 9.2	39 9.4	41 8.9			Sales/Receivables	41 8.9	39 9.3
	63 5.8	51 7.1	54 6.7				49 7.4	49 7.5
	5 67.5	24 15.4	20 18.2				12 29.5	13 28.4
	22 16.8	46 7.9	36 10.1			Cost of Sales/Inventory	29 12.8	32 11.4
	55 6.7	75 4.9	59 6.2				51 7.2	52 7.1
	9 39.2	15 24.2	18 20.3				19 19.4	17 22.1
	15 23.8	27 13.5	25 14.8			Cost of Sales/Payables	28 13.0	26 13.9
	41 9.0	47 7.8	37 9.9				40 9.0	44 8.2
	7.2	6.1	6.8				9.1	9.2
	16.2	11.0	11.4			Sales/Working Capital	20.9	23.2
	123.8	19.8	44.3				87.7	-999.8
	16.1	9.1	8.5				10.5	5.7
	(19) 4.9	(52) 2.5	(25) 3.0			EBIT/Interest	(103) 3.5	(118) 2.3
	1.7	.6	1.3				1.5	1.1
		4.4					10.5	3.5
	(12)	1.3				Net Profit + Depr., Dep., Amort./Cur. Mat. L/T/D	(19) 2.5	(20) 1.2
		-1.0					1.3	.4
	.0	.1	.1				.0	.1
	.1	.2	.3			Fixed/Worth	.3	.4
	1.2	1.6	1.0				1.3	2.0
	.5	.9	1.5				1.3	1.3
	2.5	2.0	2.8			Debt/Worth	3.2	3.0
	7.1	8.3	7.2				10.0	12.1
	57.5	37.5	22.9				53.7	38.2
	(21) 25.5	(50) 12.8	(25) 15.0			% Profit Before Taxes/Tangible Net Worth	(93) 20.1	(106) 19.2
	1.9	-.6	1.8				3.7	5.5
	16.0	11.1	6.7				13.1	11.3
	8.2	3.0	3.4			% Profit Before Taxes/Total Assets	4.3	3.9
	1.0	-.9	.6				1.2	.6
	592.5	259.0	226.3				286.7	210.4
	90.4	70.7	72.8			Sales/Net Fixed Assets	63.9	56.1
	25.5	11.4	12.1				21.8	15.8
	5.8	4.5	4.4				5.0	4.7
	3.2	3.2	3.2			Sales/Total Assets	4.0	3.6
	1.8	2.6	2.8				2.7	2.6
	.1	.1	.2				.2	.2
	(12) .6	(47) .4	(23) .4			% Depr., Dep., Amort./Sales	(81) .4	(93) .4
	1.4	1.5	.7				1.3	1.4
	1.9	1.2					.9	.8
	(13) 3.9	(32) 2.1				% Officers', Directors' Owners' Comp/Sales	(38) 3.2	(40) 2.3
	6.9	3.5					6.9	4.2
11497M	105133M	1043129M	1980284M	1753613M	2903379M	Net Sales ($)	8624322M	10792844M
1451M	28652M	279832M	556812M	429964M	963846M	Total Assets ($)	2133792M	2979746M

Comparative Historical Data   ## Current Data Sorted by Sales

			Type of Statement						
22	26	17	Unqualified				1	2	14
22	30	24	Reviewed				4	9	11
9	11	18	Compiled		3	3	4	7	1
11	27	28	Tax Returns	5	4	1	3	13	2
35	31	39	Other	1	4	6	3	7	18
4/1/07-3/31/08 ALL	4/1/08-3/31/09 ALL	4/1/09-3/31/10 ALL			19 (4/1-9/30/09)		107 (10/1/09-3/31/10)		
				0-1MM	1-3MM	3-5MM	5-10MM	10-25MM	25MM & OVER
99	125	126	NUMBER OF STATEMENTS	6	11	10	15	38	46
%	%	%	ASSETS	%	%	%	%	%	%
5.5	6.3	7.7	Cash & Equivalents		4.9	12.2	5.7	4.4	8.1
40.7	37.3	39.9	Trade Receivables (net)		25.0	43.4	27.3	43.8	43.6
29.5	27.7	27.3	Inventory		26.3	22.5	34.5	29.9	25.8
2.2	3.1	2.3	All Other Current		.8	.3	7.5	.6	3.1
77.9	74.4	77.1	Total Current		57.0	78.4	75.0	78.7	80.6
11.9	13.7	12.9	Fixed Assets (net)		15.4	9.3	21.2	13.4	10.1
4.1	3.4	3.7	Intangibles (net)		15.0	7.1	1.8	1.5	2.4
6.2	8.6	6.3	All Other Non-Current		12.5	5.2	2.0	6.5	6.9
100.0	100.0	100.0	Total		100.0	100.0	100.0	100.0	100.0
			LIABILITIES						
18.3	23.7	18.1	Notes Payable-Short Term		7.1	16.8	12.9	18.8	18.2
1.7	3.3	2.2	Cur. Mat.-L.T.D.		7.8	.9	2.8	2.2	.8
25.4	20.4	23.5	Trade Payables		18.4	19.3	22.1	26.0	23.3
.1	.2	.1	Income Taxes Payable		.0	.0	.0	.1	.1
8.0	9.3	9.0	All Other Current		8.1	7.6	6.4	7.8	7.4
53.5	56.9	52.8	Total Current		41.3	44.6	44.2	54.9	49.7
9.4	11.9	13.6	Long-Term Debt		11.7	8.0	11.5	16.5	8.7
.2	.2	.1	Deferred Taxes		.0	.0	.2	.1	.2
3.1	4.0	6.3	All Other Non-Current		12.1	12.2	1.8	4.4	6.3
33.9	27.1	27.2	Net Worth		34.9	35.2	42.4	24.1	35.0
100.0	100.0	100.0	Total Liabilties & Net Worth		100.0	100.0	100.0	100.0	100.0
			INCOME DATA						
100.0	100.0	100.0	Net Sales		100.0	100.0	100.0	100.0	100.0
22.0	21.5	21.8	Gross Profit		34.5	30.0	23.9	20.7	15.7
20.2	19.4	19.9	Operating Expenses		29.2	27.1	25.4	18.6	14.5
1.8	2.1	2.0	Operating Profit		5.4	2.9	-1.5	2.2	1.2
.4	.6	.5	All Other Expenses (net)		1.0	2.4	.7	.1	.3
1.4	1.4	1.4	Profit Before Taxes		4.3	.6	-2.2	2.0	.9
			RATIOS						
1.9	2.2	2.7			3.0	4.9	5.0	1.9	3.0
1.4	1.4	1.6	Current		2.0	1.7	1.7	1.5	1.6
1.2	1.0	1.1			1.0	1.3	1.1	1.2	1.1
1.2	1.3	1.5			2.1	2.1	1.4	1.3	1.6
.9	.8	1.0	Quick		.7	1.2	.6	1.0	1.0
.6	.6	.6			.6	1.0	.5	.6	.7
30 12.1	27 13.6	29 12.6		23 16.1	28 12.8	26 14.1	31 11.7	33 11.1
40 9.2	34 10.6	40 9.2	Sales/Receivables	43 8.6	38 9.7	36 10.2	41 8.8	40 9.1
49 7.4	43 8.5	52 7.0		65 5.6	55 6.7	54 6.9	53 6.9	52 7.1
17 21.2	16 23.5	15 23.9		12 30.3	20 17.9	23 16.1	24 15.0	12 30.0
36 10.1	32 11.4	35 10.4	Cost of Sales/Inventory	26 13.8	26 14.0	56 6.5	46 8.0	31 11.9
60 6.1	53 6.9	58 6.3		101 3.6	53 6.9	120 3.0	65 5.6	47 7.7
18 20.7	13 27.2	15 24.4		7 50.1	10 37.4	24 15.2	14 26.0	16 22.2
28 13.0	22 16.4	26 14.3	Cost of Sales/Payables	24 15.2	16 23.4	32 11.5	29 12.6	22 16.7
40 9.1	37 10.0	43 8.5		50 7.3	45 8.1	78 4.7	53 6.9	35 10.4
9.0	8.4	6.8		5.3	5.9	5.1	8.6	6.8
16.6	18.1	12.0	Sales/Working Capital	11.4	10.8	8.4	14.4	12.0
48.5	151.6	45.1		208.0	24.5	60.8	37.4	45.1
9.0	8.1	11.6				4.5	12.4	11.6
(91) 2.5	(120) 2.3	(113) 3.0	EBIT/Interest		(13) .6	(34) 3.0	(45) 3.3
1.2	1.1	1.1				-6.3	1.5	1.3
6.2	4.0	4.0						
(23) 1.4	(24) 1.1	(20) 1.9	Net Profit + Depr., Dep., Amort./Cur. Mat. L/T/D				
.6	.0	-.2					
.1	.1	.1		.0	.0	.0	.0	.1
.3	.4	.2	Fixed/Worth	.3	.2	.5	.2	.2
.8	1.2	1.3		10.1	NM	1.7	2.4	.6
1.1	1.1	.8		.2	.7	.2	1.1	.6
2.3	2.7	2.3	Debt/Worth	3.0	1.9	1.9	2.9	2.1
6.0	14.1	8.9		-4.6	NM	5.4	17.1	6.8
32.8	31.3	35.1				14.8	43.9	26.8
(92) 14.1	(104) 15.9	(110) 14.6	% Profit Before Taxes/Tangible Net Worth		-2.5	(33) 22.2	(44) 14.6
3.1	4.4	1.5				-11.5	3.6	2.2
9.6	8.8	11.5		11.5	22.3	5.2	11.9	7.1
3.6	3.3	3.4	% Profit Before Taxes/Total Assets	3.2	7.5	-.9	4.8	3.2
.5	.2	.4		.8	-4.1	-9.3	1.6	.8
183.4	203.6	288.6		252.0	576.4	178.0	386.3	235.9
57.9	69.4	77.2	Sales/Net Fixed Assets	52.5	111.6	16.6	105.8	72.8
18.6	15.7	14.9		6.2	35.4	4.4	14.3	19.8
4.9	4.7	4.7		3.4	6.3	4.0	4.5	4.9
3.9	3.9	3.3	Sales/Total Assets	1.9	3.3	2.6	3.6	3.6
2.8	2.7	2.6		1.4	2.5	1.5	2.8	2.8
.1	.2	.2				.3	.1	.2
(83) .5	(99) .4	(98) .4	% Depr., Dep., Amort./Sales		(13) 1.3	(31) .5	(41) .3
.9	1.1	.9				5.7	.9	.5
.9	1.1	1.3					1.2	.4
(39) 2.8	(52) 2.7	(56) 2.5	% Officers', Directors' Owners' Comp/Sales			(25) 2.1	(12) 1.4
5.2	4.7	5.3					3.0	3.8
8427830M	8392298M	7797035M	Net Sales ($)	3011M	19499M	40521M	100586M	643481M	6989937M
2172061M	2415288M	2260557M	Total Assets ($)	620M	10986M	13232M	43190M	201495M	1991034M

© RMA 2010   M = $ thousand   MM = $ million
See Pages 9 through 22 for Explanation of Ratios and Data

Current Data Sorted by Assets   Comparative Historical Data

0-500M	500M-2MM	2-10MM	10-50MM	50-100MM	100-250MM	Type of Statement	4/1/05-3/31/06 ALL	4/1/06-3/31/07 ALL
	2		5	1	1	Unqualified	15	10
1	5	33	8			Reviewed	31	40
2	10	9	1			Compiled	20	26
5	5	2				Tax Returns	15	16
6	13	11	13	2	2	Other	48	40
	28 (4/1-9/30/09)		109 (10/1/09-3/31/10)					
14	35	55	27	3	3	NUMBER OF STATEMENTS	129	132
%	%	%	%	%	%	ASSETS	%	%
7.7	8.2	8.4	4.0			Cash & Equivalents	7.3	6.2
38.1	39.1	37.2	34.1			Trade Receivables (net)	37.2	42.2
23.9	30.9	29.4	27.5			Inventory	27.2	28.2
3.5	3.6	3.1	5.4			All Other Current	2.5	2.0
73.2	81.9	78.0	71.0			Total Current	74.3	78.5
14.7	9.4	10.9	15.2			Fixed Assets (net)	13.2	12.0
3.5	4.6	5.6	11.0			Intangibles (net)	6.9	4.7
8.6	4.1	5.6	2.8			All Other Non-Current	5.6	4.8
100.0	100.0	100.0	100.0			Total	100.0	100.0
						LIABILITIES		
29.9	13.3	18.5	15.7			Notes Payable-Short Term	16.0	16.2
3.7	5.5	2.4	2.8			Cur. Mat.-L.T.D.	3.9	2.5
48.0	28.9	23.4	19.5			Trade Payables	24.1	26.6
.3	.1	.2	.1			Income Taxes Payable	.1	.3
9.5	9.5	8.6	11.7			All Other Current	10.2	10.1
91.3	57.4	53.1	49.8			Total Current	54.4	55.7
14.7	10.3	8.8	10.9			Long-Term Debt	12.1	11.2
.0	.1	.1	.8			Deferred Taxes	.3	.3
17.7	1.3	2.6	13.2			All Other Non-Current	7.5	6.1
-23.7	31.0	35.4	25.3			Net Worth	25.7	26.6
100.0	100.0	100.0	100.0			Total Liabilities & Net Worth	100.0	100.0
						INCOME DATA		
100.0	100.0	100.0	100.0			Net Sales	100.0	100.0
39.8	33.3	31.6	28.8			Gross Profit	32.7	31.6
38.9	32.7	29.3	27.5			Operating Expenses	30.6	28.0
.9	.6	2.3	1.3			Operating Profit	2.1	3.6
-.1	.1	.9	.9			All Other Expenses (net)	.8	.9
1.0	.5	1.4	.4			Profit Before Taxes	1.3	2.6
						RATIOS		
1.3	2.5	1.9	2.2				2.1	2.0
.8	1.5	1.5	1.6			Current	1.5	1.4
.5	1.0	1.2	1.0				1.1	1.1
1.0	1.4	1.3	1.2				1.3	1.3
.5	.8	.8	.7			Quick	.8	.9
.2	.6	.6	.6				.6	.6
18 20.3	22 16.6	33 11.1	30 12.2				30 12.0	30 12.3
28 13.1	31 11.8	40 9.0	39 9.4			Sales/Receivables	40 9.2	38 9.6
34 10.7	40 9.0	51 7.2	47 7.8				53 6.8	51 7.2
0 UND	7 54.0	22 16.8	16 22.4				16 23.5	15 24.9
17 22.0	39 9.4	48 7.7	46 7.9			Cost of Sales/Inventory	38 9.5	33 11.2
116 3.2	82 4.4	83 4.4	89 4.1				100 3.7	76 4.8
26 14.0	17 21.3	19 18.7	17 21.3				22 17.0	19 19.3
40 9.1	27 13.3	33 11.1	34 10.9			Cost of Sales/Payables	33 11.1	30 12.1
62 5.9	47 7.7	50 7.3	41 8.8				51 7.2	46 8.0
33.9	6.5	8.3	7.0				7.5	8.9
-78.0	13.8	12.9	13.0			Sales/Working Capital	17.0	16.9
-12.3	-123.9	29.2	-479.0				125.3	55.6
12.9	4.8	6.2	5.3				4.9	6.2
(10) 1.8	(29) 1.5	(49) 2.7	3.4			EBIT/Interest	(115) 2.7	(115) 2.9
-4.5	-3.0	.6	1.1				1.1	1.1
		3.5	3.7				8.9	11.6
		(19) 2.0	(11) 2.6			Net Profit + Depr., Dep., Amort./Cur. Mat. L/T/D	(35) 2.4	(34) 3.3
		1.5	1.1				.7	1.1
.3	.1	.1	.3				.1	.1
-1.8	.4	.3	.9			Fixed/Worth	.4	.4
-.1	-2.3	.7	-7.7				2.1	1.5
4.0	.8	1.1	1.5				1.1	1.4
-74.9	2.2	2.3	3.3			Debt/Worth	2.8	2.6
-2.3	-12.3	5.1	-23.8				11.1	7.2
	39.5	22.5	34.0				40.9	46.7
	(25) 4.6	(49) 10.5	(20) 18.4			% Profit Before Taxes/Tangible Net Worth	(102) 12.3	(111) 21.5
	-2.1	-1.0	1.5				3.8	6.0
14.3	9.3	8.3	12.3				9.7	12.8
3.6	1.2	2.7	4.4			% Profit Before Taxes/Total Assets	4.3	5.6
-10.5	-3.0	-1.2	.4				.8	.3
451.8	158.8	153.7	83.7				83.5	123.9
179.2	60.4	46.2	33.5			Sales/Net Fixed Assets	34.2	56.9
10.1	32.9	18.1	9.5				15.9	19.8
10.2	6.4	3.7	4.3				4.7	5.4
5.6	4.2	3.1	3.2			Sales/Total Assets	3.4	3.8
2.6	2.4	2.2	2.4				2.2	2.7
	.4	.4	.5				.4	.4
	(20) .7	(50) .8	(23) .9			% Depr., Dep., Amort./Sales	(106) .8	(105) .7
	1.3	1.1	1.4				1.4	1.3
	3.3	1.0					1.5	1.4
	(18) 5.9	(30) 1.7				% Officers', Directors' Owners' Comp/Sales	(59) 2.9	(59) 3.4
	10.2	4.5					6.3	6.7
26473M	334565M	803949M	1844692M	470256M	1212671M	Net Sales ($)	4244765M	5714360M
3934M	41238M	264959M	561232M	186880M	457505M	Total Assets ($)	1527075M	1677941M

M = $ thousand   MM = $ million
See Pages 9 through 22 for Explanation of Ratios and Data

Comparative Historical Data | **Current Data Sorted by Sales**

4/1/07-3/31/08 ALL	4/1/08-3/31/09 ALL	4/1/09-3/31/10 ALL	Type of Statement	0-1MM	1-3MM	3-5MM	5-10MM	10-25MM	25MM & OVER
12	12	9	Unqualified				1	1	7
33	44	47	Reviewed	1	2	1	12	22	9
18	22	22	Compiled		4	1	10	4	3
13	22	12	Tax Returns	2	6	1	2	1	
38	45	47	Other	3	4	4	10	10	16
					28 (4/1-9/30/09)		109 (10/1/09-3/31/10)		
114	145	137	NUMBER OF STATEMENTS	6	16	7	35	38	35
%	%	%	ASSETS	%	%	%	%	%	%
6.8	6.6	7.4	Cash & Equivalents		10.3		11.1	3.9	6.1
38.4	39.7	37.2	Trade Receivables (net)		31.1		37.3	41.3	35.7
29.0	29.6	28.7	Inventory		31.7		28.6	26.5	28.5
3.0	2.5	3.9	All Other Current		1.9		4.0	2.2	7.0
77.1	78.3	77.1	Total Current		75.0		81.0	74.0	77.4
11.1	12.0	11.6	Fixed Assets (net)		11.3		9.1	12.5	12.7
6.2	5.1	6.4	Intangibles (net)		7.7		5.1	7.6	7.3
5.6	4.6	4.9	All Other Non-Current		6.0		4.8	5.9	2.7
100.0	100.0	100.0	Total		100.0		100.0	100.0	100.0
			LIABILITIES						
20.6	19.1	17.8	Notes Payable-Short Term		14.4		11.1	20.1	18.2
2.7	3.7	3.5	Cur. Mat.-L.T.D.		7.6		1.6	3.0	3.0
23.5	23.3	26.5	Trade Payables		28.0		27.8	23.1	22.2
.2	.3	.2	Income Taxes Payable		.0		.2	.1	.2
11.4	8.8	9.7	All Other Current		9.7		7.3	10.0	12.6
58.3	55.1	57.6	Total Current		59.7		48.1	56.3	56.1
11.0	10.5	9.9	Long-Term Debt		9.2		11.8	7.6	8.1
.2	.3	.3	Deferred Taxes		.0		.0	.3	.6
5.8	8.0	5.9	All Other Non-Current		2.9		2.4	3.3	9.9
24.6	26.1	26.3	Net Worth		28.2		37.7	32.6	25.3
100.0	100.0	100.0	Total Liabilities & Net Worth		100.0		100.0	100.0	100.0
			INCOME DATA						
100.0	100.0	100.0	Net Sales		100.0		100.0	100.0	100.0
31.3	30.3	32.6	Gross Profit		39.0		30.6	31.3	29.1
28.6	27.9	31.0	Operating Expenses		39.6		28.8	29.4	27.1
2.7	2.5	1.6	Operating Profit		-.6		1.8	2.0	2.0
.9	.9	.6	All Other Expenses (net)		.2		-.1	1.4	.8
1.8	1.6	1.0	Profit Before Taxes		-.8		2.0	.6	1.2
			RATIOS						
2.2	2.0	2.0	Current		2.4		2.7	1.8	2.1
1.4	1.4	1.5			1.2		1.7	1.4	1.3
1.1	1.1	1.0			.8		1.3	1.1	1.0
1.4	1.3	1.2	Quick		1.1		1.6	1.0	1.2
.8	.8	.7			.9		1.1	.7	.7
.6	.6	.6			.3		.7	.6	.5
28 13.2	28 12.9	27 13.7	Sales/Receivables	20 17.8		24 15.0	36 10.1	30 12.2	
39 9.5	38 9.5	38 9.5		28 12.9		35 10.6	44 8.4	39 9.4	
49 7.5	48 7.6	47 7.8		39 9.4		42 8.7	54 6.8	45 8.0	
20 18.4	18 20.8	16 22.6	Cost of Sales/Inventory	12 30.6		12 30.4	19 19.3	19 18.9	
39 9.4	35 10.5	43 8.5		49 7.5		42 8.7	33 11.2	48 7.7	
80 4.6	84 4.4	83 4.4		152 2.4		80 4.6	82 4.7	78 4.7	
18 19.9	18 20.3	20 18.5	Cost of Sales/Payables	26 14.1		21 17.2	19 19.1	17 21.3	
28 12.9	29 12.8	34 10.9		32 11.4		30 12.0	35 10.5	35 10.6	
44 8.4	45 8.2	49 7.4		53 6.9		50 7.3	49 7.4	46 8.0	
8.5	8.9	7.4	Sales/Working Capital		5.1		6.5	10.0	7.0
16.3	15.5	14.2			26.9		12.6	14.5	17.7
120.3	48.9	251.0			-36.7		23.2	72.1	134.2
7.4	6.0	5.6	EBIT/Interest		7.4		9.3	6.2	5.3
(104) 2.4	(134) 2.7	(121) 2.7		(12) 1.9		(28) 2.0	(36) 3.4	3.4	
1.1	1.0	-.2			-3.2		-.5	.6	1.4
6.5	6.0	3.7	Net Profit + Depr., Dep., Amort./Cur. Mat. L/T/D					2.3	10.9
(30) 2.6	(33) 2.4	(41) 2.0					(14) 1.9	(15) 3.6	
1.3	1.1	.6						1.5	1.3
.1	.1	.1	Fixed/Worth		.1		.1	.2	.2
.4	.4	.4			.7		.3	.4	.6
1.3	1.7	2.4			-2.5		.7	1.2	2.1
1.2	1.3	1.1	Debt/Worth		.9		.7	1.2	1.7
2.9	3.0	2.8			5.3		1.8	2.3	3.3
15.8	18.3	23.5			-21.5		5.4	6.3	19.1
45.2	42.6	31.4	% Profit Before Taxes/Tangible Net Worth		28.9		25.7	30.3	38.3
(91) 23.6	(119) 14.5	(106) 11.4		(10) 6.2		(30) 9.4	(31) 11.9	(29) 16.9	
7.7	1.9	-.1			-73.3		1.1	.3	1.1
13.4	12.1	10.0	% Profit Before Taxes/Total Assets		10.4		11.2	7.9	12.3
4.2	3.7	2.7			1.7		2.2	3.2	4.4
.4	.3	-1.8			-6.2		-1.3	-1.3	.4
139.3	97.0	165.6	Sales/Net Fixed Assets		181.1		201.5	86.3	84.6
53.5	44.3	43.4			37.8		77.2	43.4	35.5
21.8	20.9	18.1			12.8		32.7	16.1	14.7
4.8	5.0	4.8	Sales/Total Assets		5.7		5.7	4.4	4.3
3.9	3.7	3.4			2.8		3.7	3.3	3.6
2.5	2.5	2.3			1.9		2.2	2.4	2.8
.3	.3	.4	% Depr., Dep., Amort./Sales				.4	.5	
(88) .7	(117) .6	(106) .7					(24) .5	(36) .8	(30) .8
1.5	1.3	1.3					1.3	1.2	1.5
1.6	1.4	1.3	% Officers', Directors' Owners' Comp/Sales				2.4	.8	
(51) 3.4	(59) 3.2	(61) 3.3					(20) 4.5	(18) 1.5	
6.2	6.9	6.3					7.3	3.7	
5511059M	5843959M	4692606M	Net Sales ($)	2599M	30759M	27955M	259881M	615071M	3756341M
1673556M	1851895M	1515748M	Total Assets ($)	2239M	11201M	5246M	83629M	229219M	1184214M

M = $ thousand   MM = $ million
See Pages 9 through 22 for Explanation of Ratios and Data

Current Data Sorted by Assets | Comparative Historical Data

	0-500M	500M-2MM	2-10MM	10-50MM	50-100MM	100-250MM	Type of Statement	4/1/05-3/31/06 ALL	4/1/06-3/31/07 ALL
		1	5	9	6	4	Unqualified	35	24
		7	35	23			Reviewed	73	57
	3	12	17	3			Compiled	32	35
	7	12	8	1			Tax Returns	21	16
		11	26	21	3	6	Other	56	71
		52 (4/1-9/30/09)		168 (10/1/09-3/31/10)					
NUMBER OF STATEMENTS	10	43	91	57	9	10		217	203
	%	%	%	%	%	%	**ASSETS**	%	%
	3.6	6.2	8.5	6.9		2.0	Cash & Equivalents	4.5	4.9
	31.5	38.2	36.3	34.5		42.9	Trade Receivables (net)	42.3	41.8
	39.1	35.8	29.5	25.8		24.9	Inventory	31.5	30.2
	3.9	3.9	2.3	4.5		3.7	All Other Current	1.9	2.4
	78.2	84.1	76.5	71.6		73.5	Total Current	80.2	79.3
	6.1	10.4	14.6	17.4		17.8	Fixed Assets (net)	12.7	12.4
	8.7	2.8	3.2	4.5		5.8	Intangibles (net)	2.4	3.0
	6.9	2.7	5.6	6.5		2.9	All Other Non-Current	4.7	5.3
	100.0	100.0	100.0	100.0		100.0	Total	100.0	100.0
							LIABILITIES		
	25.1	19.7	13.6	16.8		15.8	Notes Payable-Short Term	16.1	17.9
	5.6	1.7	2.2	2.5		1.3	Cur. Mat.-L.T.D.	2.3	2.1
	22.9	29.3	23.4	23.3		26.8	Trade Payables	27.5	28.3
	.1	.1	.2	.1		1.6	Income Taxes Payable	.2	.4
	11.1	6.5	7.6	8.0		6.3	All Other Current	7.8	7.4
	64.8	57.3	47.1	50.8		51.8	Total Current	53.7	56.1
	9.4	9.1	9.6	9.2		21.3	Long-Term Debt	11.3	9.5
	.0	.1	.2	.5		.9	Deferred Taxes	.1	.1
	6.5	6.3	4.7	4.8		1.9	All Other Non-Current	4.3	4.3
	19.3	27.2	38.3	34.7		24.1	Net Worth	30.6	30.0
	100.0	100.0	100.0	100.0		100.0	Total Liabilities & Net Worth	100.0	100.0
							INCOME DATA		
	100.0	100.0	100.0	100.0		100.0	Net Sales	100.0	100.0
	33.2	23.7	24.6	23.2		19.2	Gross Profit	23.2	22.7
	27.7	23.3	22.8	20.5		14.0	Operating Expenses	20.6	19.8
	5.6	.4	1.7	2.7		5.2	Operating Profit	2.7	2.9
	1.0	.2	.5	.5		.9	All Other Expenses (net)	.4	.7
	4.6	.3	1.2	2.2		4.4	Profit Before Taxes	2.3	2.3
							RATIOS		
	1.7	2.5	2.5	1.8		2.3	Current	2.1	2.1
	1.2	1.6	1.6	1.3		1.3		1.5	1.4
	.9	1.2	1.2	1.1		1.1		1.2	1.1
	1.0	1.4	1.5	1.4		1.3	Quick	1.3	1.3
	.5	.8	.9	.8		.8		.9	.8
	.3	.5	.6	.6		.7		.6	.6
	14 25.5	25 14.3	28 13.1	29 12.5		35 10.3	Sales/Receivables	32 11.4	31 11.7
	40 9.1	31 11.8	34 10.8	37 9.8		45 8.0		39 9.3	38 9.6
	51 7.2	42 8.7	43 8.5	46 7.9		53 6.9		49 7.5	46 7.9
	1 268.2	26 14.1	25 14.4	26 13.8		15 25.0	Cost of Sales/Inventory	27 13.8	25 14.8
	81 4.5	39 9.4	39 9.4	39 9.5		36 10.1		42 8.6	40 9.1
	150 2.4	70 5.2	64 5.7	50 7.3		87 4.2		58 6.3	55 6.6
	0 UND	14 26.8	18 20.2	16 22.5		21 17.1	Cost of Sales/Payables	21 17.7	19 19.5
	42 8.8	27 13.5	27 13.3	33 11.1		26 14.1		30 12.0	30 12.1
	78 4.7	40 9.0	46 8.0	48 7.7		40 9.1		47 7.8	46 8.0
	5.5	8.5	7.1	8.5		7.0	Sales/Working Capital	7.9	8.3
	51.3	14.0	12.7	15.9		26.1		14.4	17.4
	-57.6	44.8	28.3	76.8		295.3		29.3	59.6
		5.0	9.8	13.1			EBIT/Interest	12.6	10.0
	(38) 1.5	(81) 3.3		4.9				(207) 4.3	(190) 3.1
	-1.1	1.1	2.0					1.8	1.4
			4.3	6.5			Net Profit + Depr., Dep., Amort./Cur. Mat. L/T/D	9.5	6.2
		(23) 1.4	(25) 2.7					(53) 2.4	(45) 2.8
		.1	1.2					1.2	.8
	.0	.0	.1	.2		.2	Fixed/Worth	.1	.1
	.1	.2	.2	.4		.8		.3	.4
	-1.6	1.1	.9	.9		NM		.9	1.2
	2.5	.7	.8	1.4		2.0	Debt/Worth	1.1	1.2
	18.3	3.0	1.7	2.4		4.6		2.4	2.8
	-9.2	7.1	4.0	5.3		NM		6.1	8.5
		19.9	23.8	39.2			% Profit Before Taxes/Tangible Net Worth	41.7	48.0
		(36) 5.5	(82) 8.6	(55) 19.2				(194) 19.6	(178) 21.1
		-1.8	.2	6.3				7.9	7.1
	34.5	6.8	9.0	11.5		10.7	% Profit Before Taxes/Total Assets	13.1	13.6
	11.6	1.3	3.2	5.2		7.7		5.8	5.7
	-3.9	-3.0	.0	2.1		6.2		2.0	1.2
	UND	277.6	137.7	79.1		200.6	Sales/Net Fixed Assets	127.2	147.6
	207.6	87.1	44.5	40.0		31.6		57.0	58.8
	21.5	27.0	17.4	8.5		9.6		19.8	18.6
	5.5	6.0	4.4	4.1		5.3	Sales/Total Assets	4.5	4.7
	2.7	4.2	3.5	3.4		3.7		3.7	3.7
	1.6	3.1	2.7	2.6		1.9		2.9	2.9
		.1	.3	.3		.1	% Depr., Dep., Amort./Sales	.2	.2
		(33) .4	(76) .7	(52) .6		.5		(179) .5	(169) .5
		1.1	1.4	1.2		1.8		1.0	.9
		1.7	1.2	1.0			% Officers', Directors' Owners' Comp/Sales	1.7	1.2
		(26) 2.8	(43) 2.8	(19) 1.6				(88) 2.7	(84) 2.7
		4.7	3.9	2.9				4.4	4.8
	10548M	228424M	1501657M	3817064M	1889926M	5049904M	Net Sales ($)	8976426M	12404359M
	3398M	52353M	427781M	1201667M	663997M	1291860M	Total Assets ($)	2486859M	3057303M

Comparative Historical Data | | | | Current Data Sorted by Sales

4/1/07-3/31/08 ALL	4/1/08-3/31/09 ALL	4/1/09-3/31/10 ALL	Type of Statement	0-1MM	1-3MM	3-5MM	5-10MM	10-25MM	25MM & OVER
24	23	25	Unqualified		1		1	1	22
60	66	65	Reviewed			2	9	29	25
26	31	35	Compiled	2	4	3	9	11	6
20	24	28	Tax Returns	5	5	2	9	6	1
75	84	67	Other	1	4	4	11	12	35
					52 (4/1-9/30/09)		168 (10/1/09-3/31/10)		
205	228	220	NUMBER OF STATEMENTS	8	14	11	39	59	89
%	%	%	**ASSETS**	%	%	%	%	%	%
5.6	4.7	7.0	Cash & Equivalents		5.1	6.2	5.9	8.9	7.0
40.8	39.4	36.1	Trade Receivables (net)		29.7	29.5	38.9	37.9	36.9
29.9	30.8	30.0	Inventory		32.5	37.3	34.0	28.4	27.0
2.3	2.9	3.4	All Other Current		4.0	8.8	1.5	2.3	4.1
78.7	77.8	76.6	Total Current		71.3	81.7	80.3	77.5	74.9
13.6	13.9	14.4	Fixed Assets (net)		15.6	13.4	14.1	13.9	15.4
2.5	3.2	3.9	Intangibles (net)		6.4	.7	2.5	3.4	4.2
5.2	5.0	5.2	All Other Non-Current		6.7	4.2	3.1	5.2	5.5
100.0	100.0	100.0	Total		100.0	100.0	100.0	100.0	100.0
			LIABILITIES						
18.3	19.3	16.5	Notes Payable-Short Term		28.6	21.3	13.2	12.8	17.2
2.7	3.0	2.4	Cur. Mat.-L.T.D.		.7	2.4	2.5	2.4	2.1
28.7	25.2	24.4	Trade Payables		21.8	30.7	26.6	25.5	23.6
.2	.1	.2	Income Taxes Payable		.0	.1	.2	.2	.3
8.1	7.3	7.8	All Other Current		7.9	7.7	7.6	7.3	7.6
58.0	54.9	51.3	Total Current		58.9	62.1	50.0	48.1	50.8
11.3	11.5	10.0	Long-Term Debt		10.1	12.1	10.6	8.2	9.8
.2	.3	.3	Deferred Taxes		.1	.1	.3	.1	.5
3.3	5.8	5.0	All Other Non-Current		8.2	5.1	5.2	4.3	4.5
27.2	27.5	33.5	Net Worth		22.7	20.6	33.8	39.2	34.4
100.0	100.0	100.0	Total Liabilities & Net Worth		100.0	100.0	100.0	100.0	100.0
			INCOME DATA						
100.0	100.0	100.0	Net Sales		100.0	100.0	100.0	100.0	100.0
23.3	23.7	23.9	Gross Profit		22.4	28.2	25.8	22.2	22.1
20.8	21.3	21.7	Operating Expenses		21.0	28.6	24.5	20.6	19.2
2.6	2.4	2.2	Operating Profit		1.3	-.3	1.3	1.6	3.0
.5	.5	.5	All Other Expenses (net)		.0	.8	.5	.3	.5
2.0	2.0	1.6	Profit Before Taxes		1.3	-1.2	.7	1.3	2.5
			RATIOS						
2.0	2.0	2.3	Current		2.7	2.9	2.4	2.3	2.0
1.4	1.4	1.5			1.2	1.5	1.8	1.6	1.4
1.1	1.1	1.1			.9	1.1	1.2	1.2	1.1
1.3	1.2	1.4	Quick		1.3	1.2	1.4	1.4	1.5
.8	.8	.8			.7	.6	.9	.9	.8
.6	.5	.6			.4	.3	.6	.7	.6
29 12.5	28 13.0	28 13.2	Sales/Receivables	26 14.3	26 14.1	25 14.3	28 13.1	29 12.5	
37 9.9	34 10.6	35 10.4		33 11.2	32 11.5	33 11.1	34 10.8	37 9.9	
47 7.8	42 8.7	45 8.2		68 5.4	42 8.7	45 8.1	42 8.6	46 7.9	
25 14.9	24 15.2	26 14.2	Cost of Sales/Inventory	22 16.7	26 14.0	27 13.3	24 15.4	25 14.6	
39 9.3	39 9.4	39 9.5		71 5.1	55 6.7	46 8.0	36 10.2	37 9.8	
57 6.4	55 6.6	61 6.0		125 2.9	106 3.5	66 5.6	52 7.0	51 7.1	
20 18.3	17 22.0	17 21.5	Cost of Sales/Payables	10 36.3	15 24.7	17 21.6	19 19.2	16 23.2	
30 12.1	27 13.5	28 13.2		24 14.9	23 15.7	33 11.2	28 13.2	25 14.5	
44 8.3	40 9.1	46 7.9		73 5.0	60 6.1	49 7.5	41 8.8	42 8.6	
9.1	8.8	8.0	Sales/Working Capital		5.5	6.5	7.8	7.9	8.2
18.2	17.9	13.9			17.6	15.4	12.8	13.6	14.5
61.8	49.1	47.0			-36.2	56.4	23.8	30.0	61.1
6.9	7.2	10.1	EBIT/Interest		6.9	25.5	5.6	9.8	12.6
(198) 2.3	(212) 3.1	(203) 3.3			(11) 1.3	(10) .0	(37) 1.5	(53) 3.6	(85) 4.9
1.2	1.3	1.2			-1.0	-4.4	-.1	1.3	2.1
3.9	4.7	5.2	Net Profit + Depr., Dep., Amort./Cur. Mat. L/T/D					5.9	5.6
(54) 2.5	(55) 2.1	(55) 1.9						(15) 2.2	(31) 2.7
1.2	1.0	.3						.9	.7
.1	.1	.1	Fixed/Worth		.0	.1	.1	.0	.1
.4	.4	.3			.7	.4	.3	.2	.3
1.0	1.2	1.0			-.1	2.2	.7	.9	.9
1.2	1.2	1.0	Debt/Worth		.3	.4	1.0	.8	1.3
3.0	2.8	2.2			3.9	5.6	1.9	1.7	2.4
7.4	8.0	5.9			-4.3	11.9	4.2	3.7	5.6
36.8	32.6	32.9	% Profit Before Taxes/Tangible Net Worth		46.7		7.5	23.4	40.1
(182) 17.8	(195) 16.4	(196) 14.7			(10) 3.8		(35) 3.8	(54) 9.6	(85) 21.9
4.6	4.8	3.1			-6.1		-9.2	3.0	10.2
11.7	10.4	10.1	% Profit Before Taxes/Total Assets		11.2	16.3	3.3	7.8	11.0
4.0	4.5	3.5			1.2	-.1	1.2	3.3	6.7
.7	.8	.4			-4.6	-11.8	-3.0	.6	2.4
142.0	180.5	143.2	Sales/Net Fixed Assets		199.3	111.9	152.1	191.9	112.3
51.1	52.4	47.2			63.3	27.0	45.4	61.2	41.9
21.4	17.7	16.3			12.4	12.4	17.8	17.7	14.8
5.0	5.2	4.5	Sales/Total Assets		4.4	6.3	5.3	4.8	4.3
3.9	3.8	3.5			2.0	3.9	3.9	3.7	3.5
2.7	2.8	2.5			1.5	2.3	2.8	2.8	2.6
.2	.2	.3	% Depr., Dep., Amort./Sales		.3		.2	.2	.3
(180) .5	(179) .6	(182) .6			(10) 1.0		(35) .5	(47) .6	(77) .6
1.0	1.1	1.3			3.1		1.3	1.1	1.1
1.3	1.2	1.2	% Officers', Directors' Owners' Comp/Sales				1.7	.9	.9
(91) 2.5	(87) 2.5	(98) 2.5					(22) 3.2	(32) 2.6	(28) 1.5
4.8	3.9	4.0					5.3	3.9	2.8
14037694M	14529538M	12497523M	Net Sales ($)	4738M	27046M	42906M	292007M	900612M	11230214M
3802187M	3458210M	3641056M	Total Assets ($)	4734M	11634M	13772M	88744M	279938M	3242234M

M = $ thousand   MM = $ million
See Pages 9 through 22 for Explanation of Ratios and Data

Current Data Sorted by Assets   Comparative Historical Data

						Type of Statement		
1	1	5	35	6	9	Unqualified	42	43
1	7	30	22	1	1	Reviewed	35	33
1	7	9	2			Compiled	21	27
4	19	13	2			Tax Returns	23	25
4	6	44	29	8	6	Other	73	82
	37 (4/1-9/30/09)			228 (10/1/09-3/31/10)			4/1/05-3/31/06	4/1/06-3/31/07
0-500M	500M-2MM	2-10MM	10-50MM	50-100MM	100-250MM		ALL	ALL
10	33	101	90	15	16	NUMBER OF STATEMENTS	194	210
%	%	%	%	%	%	ASSETS	%	%
24.3	17.9	8.8	9.7	5.1	9.2	Cash & Equivalents	10.9	10.1
22.6	30.2	33.2	27.7	28.3	19.3	Trade Receivables (net)	33.1	35.3
38.3	29.6	33.6	33.1	25.0	24.9	Inventory	32.0	30.4
1.1	3.4	3.3	3.8	4.9	4.2	All Other Current	3.2	3.5
86.3	81.0	78.9	74.3	63.4	57.6	Total Current	79.2	79.3
7.0	10.4	9.7	9.2	15.1	12.4	Fixed Assets (net)	9.7	9.7
4.5	3.2	4.7	11.7	14.5	22.1	Intangibles (net)	4.7	6.4
2.1	5.4	6.7	4.8	7.1	7.9	All Other Non-Current	6.5	4.5
100.0	100.0	100.0	100.0	100.0	100.0	Total	100.0	100.0
						LIABILITIES		
8.8	14.6	15.8	12.0	10.6	7.3	Notes Payable-Short Term	15.0	14.9
5.3	2.7	1.7	2.7	4.5	.6	Cur. Mat.-L.T.D.	1.9	2.6
17.9	26.2	23.5	22.9	21.1	16.2	Trade Payables	25.0	25.6
.0	.0	.1	.1	.1	1.3	Income Taxes Payable	.2	.3
1.5	20.0	10.3	8.7	8.8	8.4	All Other Current	10.1	9.2
33.5	63.6	51.4	46.4	45.1	33.8	Total Current	52.2	52.7
9.7	7.6	7.6	8.2	6.8	14.8	Long-Term Debt	11.1	11.2
.0	.0	.4	.3	.4	.0	Deferred Taxes	.2	.1
24.8	6.4	7.9	5.2	4.3	12.7	All Other Non-Current	8.7	4.3
32.0	22.4	32.6	39.9	43.4	38.7	Net Worth	27.9	31.7
100.0	100.0	100.0	100.0	100.0	100.0	Total Liabilities & Net Worth	100.0	100.0
						INCOME DATA		
100.0	100.0	100.0	100.0	100.0	100.0	Net Sales	100.0	100.0
39.8	32.0	31.9	30.7	28.4	33.9	Gross Profit	27.4	32.4
36.7	29.0	27.8	24.3	23.4	26.4	Operating Expenses	22.3	26.0
3.1	3.0	4.1	6.5	5.0	7.5	Operating Profit	5.1	6.3
.7	-.2	.6	1.2	1.1	2.0	All Other Expenses (net)	.6	.6
2.4	3.3	3.5	5.2	3.9	5.5	Profit Before Taxes	4.6	5.7
						RATIOS		
13.8	2.5	2.1	2.3	1.6	2.1	Current	2.2	2.4
4.1	1.6	1.5	1.5	1.4	1.8		1.6	1.5
1.4	1.2	1.2	1.2	1.2	1.2		1.1	1.2
8.6	1.7	1.2	1.1	1.0	1.8	Quick	1.4	1.4
1.7	.8	.8	.8	.7	.9		.8	.8
.6	.6	.5	.5	.5	.5		.6	.6
12 31.1	9 40.5	28 12.9	28 13.0	34 10.6	16 23.5	Sales/Receivables	21 17.1	26 14.1
16 22.6	24 15.3	41 8.9	38 9.6	40 9.1	30 12.0		33 10.9	38 9.7
26 14.2	41 8.8	56 6.5	51 7.2	55 6.7	42 8.7		47 7.7	56 6.5
22 16.5	8 44.4	31 11.8	35 10.5	22 16.8	17 22.1	Cost of Sales/Inventory	21 17.2	22 16.3
72 5.1	28 13.1	63 5.8	78 4.7	51 7.2	50 7.3		44 8.2	49 7.4
260 1.4	61 6.0	111 3.3	129 2.8	122 3.0	99 3.7		84 4.3	91 4.0
11 32.8	11 32.2	22 16.6	25 14.4	25 14.8	20 18.2	Cost of Sales/Payables	15 24.6	18 20.0
18 20.2	20 18.3	38 9.7	39 9.3	30 12.1	39 9.4		30 12.3	36 10.0
155 2.4	40 9.1	75 4.9	58 6.3	40 9.2	59 6.2		52 7.1	58 6.3
3.1	8.3	6.1	5.0	7.6	5.9	Sales/Working Capital	7.4	6.4
9.6	17.3	12.8	9.4	14.7	10.7		13.6	14.1
17.4	90.6	26.1	25.1	23.3	29.8		40.2	35.5
	12.8	23.3	25.1	13.3	4.7	EBIT/Interest	13.7	17.6
	(27) 2.0	(87) 6.0	(80) 7.3	(14) 4.2	(11) 3.3		(161) 4.9	(177) 4.8
	-.8	2.3	3.2	1.6	2.5		1.5	2.0
		17.6	10.4			Net Profit + Depr., Dep.,	6.6	6.9
	(15) 4.0	(22) 3.9				Amort./Cur. Mat. L/T/D	(35) 3.4	(30) 3.6
	1.1	.8					1.3	1.6
.0	.1	.0	.0	.1	.1	Fixed/Worth	.0	.1
.0	.2	.1	.2	.5	.7		.2	.2
NM	.5	.7	.8	.9	NM		.8	1.0
.1	.9	1.1	1.0	1.2	1.1	Debt/Worth	1.0	1.0
1.4	2.5	2.4	1.9	2.1	3.8		2.4	2.8
-4.8	12.9	5.2	4.0	5.5	NM		9.4	9.1
	96.5	62.4	58.0	34.7	85.2	% Profit Before Taxes/Tangible Net Worth	63.3	83.8
	(29) 22.8	(91) 26.4	(80) 31.0	(14) 27.2	(12) 39.3		(163) 32.9	(183) 35.2
	3.5	9.3	12.7	15.8	13.8		11.8	13.7
19.4	26.7	16.0	16.1	12.6	14.5	% Profit Before Taxes/Total Assets	20.5	22.2
6.4	4.2	6.2	7.7	6.1	4.8		9.3	8.9
-1.3	-.2	2.6	4.0	1.9	3.6		1.6	3.2
UND	531.8	522.6	163.7	62.5	138.8	Sales/Net Fixed Assets	276.1	236.7
476.5	87.6	110.7	53.3	34.4	30.7		80.2	69.0
16.6	37.1	26.1	18.1	5.4	7.2		30.2	26.7
5.6	7.1	3.7	3.5	3.7	4.2	Sales/Total Assets	5.0	4.8
3.5	4.5	2.8	2.5	1.9	2.4		3.3	3.4
1.0	3.6	2.1	1.7	1.1	1.0		2.3	2.0
	.3	.2	.2	.1	.1	% Depr., Dep., Amort./Sales	.1	.1
	(20) .6	(60) .5	(71) .7	(10) .5	(13) .6		(150) .4	(164) .4
	1.5	1.2	1.6	5.3	3.7		.9	1.1
	1.7	1.0	.5			% Officers', Directors' Owners' Comp/Sales	1.4	1.3
	(24) 3.9	(47) 2.1	(17) 1.1				(68) 2.8	(67) 2.2
	5.4	3.9	2.2				4.2	5.4
12706M	208861M	1560864M	5325762M	2557342M	7849592M	Net Sales ($)	14532182M	17793121M
3025M	34562M	514870M	1984052M	1042608M	2579819M	Total Assets ($)	4310856M	5177806M

M = $ thousand   MM = $ million
See Pages 9 through 22 for Explanation of Ratios and Data

Comparative Historical Data   **Current Data Sorted by Sales**

			Type of Statement	0-1MM	1-3MM	3-5MM	5-10MM	10-25MM	25MM & OVER
27	53	55	Unqualified			3	8	6	46
37	47	56	Reviewed	1		3	8	16	28
22	21	19	Compiled	1	2	3	6	5	2
28	37	38	Tax Returns	2	5	8	11	10	2
108	101	97	Other	2	4	3	17	27	44
4/1/07-3/31/08 ALL	4/1/08-3/31/09 ALL	4/1/09-3/31/10 ALL			37 (4/1-9/30/09)		228 (10/1/09-3/31/10)		
222	259	265	**NUMBER OF STATEMENTS**	6	11	17	45	64	122
%	%	%	**ASSETS**	%	%	%	%	%	%
9.0	10.1	10.6	Cash & Equivalents		11.5	14.2	12.6	10.9	8.6
30.8	30.6	29.4	Trade Receivables (net)		30.5	28.3	27.4	32.1	29.5
32.8	31.8	32.1	Inventory		33.7	28.9	31.5	29.9	33.6
3.2	3.7	3.6	All Other Current		3.5	1.8	2.9	4.0	3.9
75.9	76.2	75.7	Total Current		79.3	73.3	74.4	76.8	75.5
11.0	9.7	10.0	Fixed Assets (net)		9.9	18.2	9.5	7.1	10.3
7.5	8.2	8.5	Intangibles (net)		.8	3.3	8.3	11.9	8.2
5.6	5.9	5.8	All Other Non-Current		10.0	5.2	7.7	4.2	5.9
100.0	100.0	100.0	Total		100.0	100.0	100.0	100.0	100.0
			LIABILITIES						
15.6	15.5	13.3	Notes Payable-Short Term		24.5	15.7	12.5	13.2	12.8
2.1	2.4	2.4	Cur. Mat.-L.T.D.		7.5	2.0	1.6	2.6	2.3
24.2	24.3	22.8	Trade Payables		19.6	22.5	18.2	23.0	25.4
.2	.2	.2	Income Taxes Payable		.0	.0	.2	.1	.3
9.1	8.6	10.4	All Other Current		39.8	8.5	13.6	7.5	8.9
51.1	50.9	49.1	Total Current		91.4	48.7	46.1	46.3	49.6
11.5	12.3	8.3	Long-Term Debt		7.9	18.6	8.2	5.2	8.7
.2	.5	.3	Deferred Taxes		.0	.0	.1	.5	.3
5.0	5.0	7.5	All Other Non-Current		11.5	6.4	8.5	9.8	4.1
32.2	31.4	34.8	Net Worth		-10.7	26.3	37.0	38.2	37.3
100.0	100.0	100.0	Total Liabilities & Net Worth		100.0	100.0	100.0	100.0	100.0
			INCOME DATA						
100.0	100.0	100.0	Net Sales		100.0	100.0	100.0	100.0	100.0
33.3	31.3	31.7	Gross Profit		41.1	38.1	37.6	32.2	26.8
27.4	26.0	26.8	Operating Expenses		41.1	37.7	32.0	25.1	22.2
5.9	5.2	5.0	Operating Profit		.0	.4	5.6	7.0	4.6
.8	1.0	.8	All Other Expenses (net)		.8	.6	1.4	.7	.8
5.1	4.2	4.1	Profit Before Taxes		-.9	-.2	4.2	6.4	3.8
			RATIOS						
2.3	2.3	2.3	Current		5.0	2.1	2.6	2.3	1.9
1.5	1.5	1.5			1.7	1.4	1.6	1.7	1.5
1.2	1.1	1.2			.9	1.2	1.1	1.3	1.2
1.2	1.3	1.2	Quick		1.5	1.5	1.6	1.4	1.0
.7	.8	.8			.6	.8	.8	.9	.7
.5	.5	.5			.4	.4	.5	.6	.5
22 16.4	25 14.7	25 14.7	Sales/Receivables		18 20.2	22 16.8	19 19.1	32 11.4	25 14.6
35 10.4	38 9.5	38 9.6			28 13.0	29 12.8	40 9.0	41 8.9	36 10.0
49 7.4	50 7.3	51 7.2			45 8.2	49 7.4	54 6.8	61 6.0	47 7.8
27 13.5	23 16.0	28 13.3	Cost of Sales/Inventory		9 42.7	21 17.0	31 11.9	26 14.2	28 13.2
53 6.9	52 7.1	61 6.0			55 6.6	70 5.2	67 5.5	66 5.5	54 6.8
104 3.5	112 3.2	119 3.1			166 2.2	150 2.4	132 2.8	110 3.3	94 3.9
20 18.3	21 17.3	20 18.2	Cost of Sales/Payables		10 35.4	24 15.5	17 21.3	20 18.2	23 16.0
39 9.4	37 9.9	34 10.6			18 20.0	34 10.7	38 9.6	34 10.8	36 10.0
58 6.3	57 6.4	59 6.2			84 4.4	107 3.4	70 5.2	73 5.0	54 6.7
6.4	5.7	6.1	Sales/Working Capital		5.9	9.7	5.2	4.9	6.5
13.5	12.6	11.6			16.5	16.4	10.2	9.4	13.2
34.1	41.8	26.5			-22.9	24.5	32.9	20.5	27.2
13.9	22.1	18.6	EBIT/Interest		8.0	8.1	30.4	28.4	20.6
(194) 4.6	(236) 6.0	(227) 5.8			1.2	(14) 3.1	(37) 7.0	(54) 6.5	(107) 6.5
2.0	2.3	2.2			-7.2	-.3	1.3	3.0	2.8
14.8	11.1	11.3	Net Profit + Depr., Dep., Amort./Cur. Mat. L/T/D					19.0	12.0
(43) 5.0	(40) 1.5	(49) 3.5						(10) 8.7	(32) 3.6
1.7	.2	-1.0						1.1	1.0
.1	.0	.0	Fixed/Worth		.0	.0	.0	.0	.1
.3	.3	.2			.1	.3	.2	.1	.3
1.2	1.0	.9			.5	4.3	1.3	.4	.9
1.1	1.1	1.0	Debt/Worth		1.3	1.2	.5	1.0	1.2
2.5	2.9	2.3			1.4	3.6	1.8	2.3	2.4
10.3	12.1	5.4			-7.5	10.1	7.9	5.1	4.6
76.6	78.9	62.5	% Profit Before Taxes/Tangible Net Worth			57.4	64.8	85.5	54.5
(188) 36.4	(213) 35.4	(233) 27.3				(16) 13.5	(37) 16.8	(58) 37.0	(110) 27.3
11.3	10.4	11.1				1.8	8.4	16.1	12.2
25.0	18.1	16.4	% Profit Before Taxes/Total Assets		16.5	8.6	18.6	20.7	14.6
9.6	7.5	6.8			.6	2.4	5.8	9.4	6.8
2.6	1.9	2.5			-11.9	-1.0	.7	4.4	3.0
204.5	245.5	275.0	Sales/Net Fixed Assets		801.3	567.0	304.5	346.3	202.1
54.9	68.8	66.5			151.8	54.8	66.5	110.9	57.6
22.4	23.1	19.4			18.5	8.9	31.1	25.6	15.9
4.4	4.3	4.0	Sales/Total Assets		4.2	4.9	4.5	3.6	4.2
3.2	3.0	2.8			3.7	3.2	2.5	2.7	3.0
1.9	1.8	1.9			2.3	1.3	1.5	2.0	1.9
.2	.2	.2	% Depr., Dep., Amort./Sales			.3	.3	.2	.2
(166) .6	(187) .5	(176) .5				(11) .5	(25) .7	(37) .5	(97) .5
1.1	1.4	1.5				5.8	1.4	1.5	1.4
1.0	1.1	1.0	% Officers', Directors' Owners' Comp/Sales				1.5	.6	.8
(78) 2.4	(88) 2.1	(95) 2.2					(23) 3.6	(29) 1.3	(25) 1.3
6.3	4.4	4.3					4.7	3.1	2.9
13324737M	16340606M	17515127M	Net Sales ($)	3013M	22562M	68411M	333103M	1057422M	16030616M
5057294M	6330924M	6158936M	Total Assets ($)	1728M	7111M	32524M	170481M	527456M	5419636M

© RMA 2010

M = $ thousand   MM = $ million
See Pages 9 through 22 for Explanation of Ratios and Data

Current Data Sorted by Assets   **Comparative Historical Data**

0-500M	500M-2MM	2-10MM	10-50MM	50-100MM	100-250MM	Type of Statement	4/1/05-3/31/06 ALL	4/1/06-3/31/07 ALL
		6	11	5		Unqualified	28	25
	3	30	11			Reviewed	49	48
	8	14	2			Compiled	28	26
11	17	6	2		1	Tax Returns	11	20
2	9	20	13	4		Other	36	46
	27 (4/1-9/30/09)		148 (10/1/09-3/31/10)					
13	37	76	39	9	1	NUMBER OF STATEMENTS	152	165
%	%	%	%	%	%	**ASSETS**	%	%
16.0	15.3	7.7	7.5			Cash & Equivalents	8.1	8.3
27.6	27.5	31.1	29.5			Trade Receivables (net)	31.0	30.7
39.8	38.2	42.7	43.0			Inventory	38.1	37.2
.4	3.4	3.7	3.1			All Other Current	2.0	3.8
83.8	84.4	85.2	83.1			Total Current	79.3	80.0
8.8	4.3	6.2	7.7			Fixed Assets (net)	10.1	10.3
1.0	4.4	3.4	3.8			Intangibles (net)	3.1	3.1
6.5	6.9	5.2	5.4			All Other Non-Current	7.5	6.6
100.0	100.0	100.0	100.0			Total	100.0	100.0
						LIABILITIES		
25.4	19.1	15.8	17.4			Notes Payable-Short Term	16.9	16.7
.5	6.1	2.4	3.2			Cur. Mat.-L.T.D.	2.4	1.9
23.6	24.3	20.3	15.7			Trade Payables	21.3	21.6
.0	.0	.1	.1			Income Taxes Payable	.1	.3
10.2	8.2	10.6	7.0			All Other Current	7.7	8.7
59.7	57.7	49.2	43.4			Total Current	48.4	49.2
6.9	7.6	8.0	8.0			Long-Term Debt	8.8	7.5
.0	.0	.0	.6			Deferred Taxes	.1	.1
51.3	3.1	8.6	2.2			All Other Non-Current	4.5	5.3
-17.9	31.6	34.2	45.8			Net Worth	38.2	37.9
100.0	100.0	100.0	100.0			Total Liabilties & Net Worth	100.0	100.0
						INCOME DATA		
100.0	100.0	100.0	100.0			Net Sales	100.0	100.0
44.5	36.4	28.9	28.9			Gross Profit	30.9	30.4
36.2	30.5	26.9	24.9			Operating Expenses	27.6	26.0
8.4	5.9	1.9	3.9			Operating Profit	3.4	4.3
1.7	.7	.4	1.1			All Other Expenses (net)	1.0	1.0
6.7	5.2	1.5	2.9			Profit Before Taxes	2.4	3.4
						RATIOS		
3.7	2.2	3.4	4.2			Current	2.4	2.7
1.1	1.5	1.8	1.9				1.7	1.7
1.0	1.0	1.3	1.3				1.2	1.2
2.0	1.5	1.4	2.1			Quick	1.2	1.3
.8	.6	.8	.8				.8	.8
.1	.3	.5	.4				.5	.5
0 UND	14 25.9	32 11.3	30 12.3			Sales/Receivables	27 13.6	22 16.3
25 14.8	29 12.8	46 7.9	39 9.2				43 8.6	42 8.6
42 8.8	49 7.5	66 5.5	64 5.7				59 6.2	64 5.7
8 46.1	43 8.5	50 7.3	54 6.8			Cost of Sales/Inventory	42 8.7	38 9.6
103 3.6	88 4.1	94 3.9	111 3.3				76 4.8	80 4.5
350 1.0	146 2.5	146 2.5	151 2.4				150 2.4	144 2.5
0 UND	10 38.3	20 18.4	19 19.2			Cost of Sales/Payables	20 17.9	15 23.8
30 12.3	34 10.8	34 10.8	32 11.4				39 9.4	37 9.9
102 3.6	50 7.4	55 6.6	47 7.7				61 6.0	64 5.7
8.9	4.0	3.8	3.6			Sales/Working Capital	5.0	4.5
15.9	12.8	6.1	5.7				9.0	8.4
205.4	584.2	13.1	13.3				20.1	21.8
	20.1	11.2	15.7			EBIT/Interest	7.4	9.3
	(28) 3.6	(68) 2.5	(36) 2.9				(134) 3.4	(147) 3.5
	1.6	1.4	1.2				1.6	1.2
			2.6			Net Profit + Depr., Dep., Amort./Cur. Mat. L/T/D	9.7	13.8
		(10) 1.0					(28) 4.2	(20) 4.4
			-.9				1.3	.6
.0	.0	.0	.0			Fixed/Worth	.0	.0
.2	.1	.1	.1				.1	.1
2.8	.4	.4	.5				.5	.5
1.9	1.1	.8	.7			Debt/Worth	.9	.8
8.4	2.9	1.7	1.8				1.8	1.8
NM	8.7	4.9	3.3				4.1	4.1
120.2	81.7	26.1	35.1			% Profit Before Taxes/Tangible Net Worth	37.6	40.8
(10) 49.1	(31) 39.7	(64) 9.3	(38) 12.9				(142) 11.7	(150) 15.6
1.2	7.6	1.9	1.8				3.0	4.9
28.9	31.7	9.2	16.2			% Profit Before Taxes/Total Assets	11.6	14.9
3.4	7.4	2.7	4.1				4.8	5.4
-1.3	2.5	.7	.4				1.0	.9
627.5	999.8	372.8	230.8			Sales/Net Fixed Assets	262.9	241.0
127.0	214.9	80.8	36.6				63.5	69.9
27.4	40.3	33.9	20.2				20.2	20.2
4.5	4.1	3.0	2.6			Sales/Total Assets	3.5	3.2
3.0	2.8	2.2	2.0				2.5	2.4
1.2	1.8	1.7	1.8				1.9	1.8
	.2	.1	.2			% Depr., Dep., Amort./Sales	.2	.2
	(23) .5	(59) .4	(32) .5				(123) .5	(130) .4
	.8	1.2	.9				1.3	1.2
3.6	1.5	1.9	1.3			% Officers', Directors' Owners' Comp/Sales	2.5	1.8
(10) 5.5	(22) 3.3	(35) 3.7	(18) 1.7				(81) 3.9	(89) 3.3
9.7	7.6	7.0	4.6				5.8	5.2
10675M	139431M	876230M	2060101M	1461608M	92101M	Net Sales ($)	4452092M	4115955M
2975M	44170M	366414M	830595M	615728M	111181M	Total Assets ($)	1801631M	1868694M

M = $ thousand   MM = $ million
See Pages 9 through 22 for Explanation of Ratios and Data

Comparative Historical Data | | | | Current Data Sorted by Sales

			Type of Statement						
15	18	22	Unqualified			1	1	5	15
51	55	44	Reviewed			3	11	22	8
30	30	24	Compiled		7	1	8	7	1
26	25	37	Tax Returns	5	16	6	5	2	3
46	52	48	Other	1	4	5	11	13	14
4/1/07-3/31/08	4/1/08-3/31/09	4/1/09-3/31/10			27 (4/1-9/30/09)		148 (10/1/09-3/31/10)		
ALL	ALL	ALL		0-1MM	1-3MM	3-5MM	5-10MM	10-25MM	25MM & OVER
168	180	175	NUMBER OF STATEMENTS	6	27	16	36	49	41
%	%	%	**ASSETS**	%	%	%	%	%	%
7.9	10.0	9.9	Cash & Equivalents		15.7	8.1	12.1	7.8	7.5
30.5	27.1	29.8	Trade Receivables (net)		26.2	32.6	31.2	28.8	34.4
39.7	42.7	41.2	Inventory		35.6	37.7	41.5	44.3	39.5
3.0	3.3	3.5	All Other Current		3.9	1.1	4.4	3.8	3.4
81.2	83.2	84.4	Total Current		81.5	79.4	89.2	84.7	84.8
8.6	8.4	6.6	Fixed Assets (net)		5.6	9.3	5.5	5.3	8.2
3.1	2.4	3.4	Intangibles (net)		5.4	4.5	2.7	3.3	3.0
7.1	6.0	5.6	All Other Non-Current		7.6	6.7	2.7	6.6	4.0
100.0	100.0	100.0	Total		100.0	100.0	100.0	100.0	100.0
			LIABILITIES						
17.1	18.9	17.6	Notes Payable-Short Term		19.2	15.8	14.8	17.9	15.1
1.6	2.2	3.1	Cur. Mat.-L.T.D.		7.0	2.8	2.4	3.3	1.4
19.3	17.2	20.1	Trade Payables		22.7	17.7	24.4	19.2	18.2
.1	.1	.1	Income Taxes Payable		.0	.1	.1	.1	.2
7.0	9.2	9.3	All Other Current		11.3	8.4	5.2	12.3	8.6
45.1	47.7	50.2	Total Current		60.2	44.8	46.8	52.8	43.5
6.4	7.8	7.6	Long-Term Debt		10.3	14.8	3.9	7.1	6.8
.2	.1	.2	Deferred Taxes		.0	.0	.0	.0	.6
7.2	5.6	8.8	All Other Non-Current		4.4	11.1	7.4	6.0	2.1
41.1	38.9	33.2	Net Worth		25.1	29.3	41.8	34.1	46.9
100.0	100.0	100.0	Total Liabilties & Net Worth		100.0	100.0	100.0	100.0	100.0
			INCOME DATA						
100.0	100.0	100.0	Net Sales		100.0	100.0	100.0	100.0	100.0
30.4	32.0	31.7	Gross Profit		37.6	35.1	33.2	28.0	26.3
26.6	28.9	27.9	Operating Expenses		32.8	33.2	30.1	24.5	22.8
3.8	3.2	3.8	Operating Profit		4.8	1.9	3.1	3.5	3.5
.9	.9	.7	All Other Expenses (net)		.8	-.5	1.1	.5	.6
2.8	2.3	3.0	Profit Before Taxes		3.9	2.4	2.0	3.1	2.9
			RATIOS						
2.9	2.8	3.0	Current		2.1	3.7	3.6	2.4	3.4
1.6	1.7	1.7			1.4	2.2	1.9	1.6	1.9
1.3	1.3	1.2			1.0	1.1	1.3	1.2	1.4
1.3	1.2	1.4	Quick		1.3	1.6	2.0	1.2	1.8
.9	.7	.8			.6	1.0	.8	.7	.8
.5	.4	.4			.2	.5	.5	.4	.6
26 14.0	22 16.6	26 14.2	Sales/Receivables	17 21.6	35 10.4	28 13.2	25 14.6	31 11.7	
41 8.8	40 9.2	40 9.1		29 12.8	50 7.4	47 7.8	39 9.4	49 7.4	
57 6.4	59 6.2	62 5.9		50 7.2	84 4.4	63 5.8	66 5.6	61 6.0	
42 8.6	47 7.8	48 7.5	Cost of Sales/Inventory	39 9.3	60 6.1	43 8.5	52 7.0	48 7.7	
86 4.2	101 3.6	94 3.9		120 3.0	84 4.3	92 3.9	94 3.9	79 4.6	
149 2.4	157 2.3	147 2.5		149 2.4	171 2.1	145 2.5	145 2.5	121 3.0	
16 22.7	15 25.0	18 20.8	Cost of Sales/Payables	0 UND	19 18.8	21 17.3	17 21.6	19 18.9	
33 11.0	29 12.6	34 10.9		41 8.9	33 10.9	36 10.1	31 11.9	30 12.1	
55 6.6	51 7.2	53 6.9		77 4.7	52 7.0	65 5.6	48 7.6	46 7.9	
4.0	3.8	3.9	Sales/Working Capital		3.3	4.0	3.1	4.3	4.3
7.1	7.3	7.1			15.9	5.6	5.9	7.3	6.6
18.3	15.5	16.5			-147.5	30.4	13.0	18.2	13.1
7.0	6.3	13.4	EBIT/Interest		11.9	5.2	11.0	16.7	16.5
(145) 2.8	(153) 2.8	(151) 2.8		(20) 1.9	(12) 2.9	(32) 2.1	(44) 2.8	(39) 7.5	
1.2	.6	1.3			-.1	1.7	1.1	1.7	1.5
21.2	7.3	2.6	Net Profit + Depr., Dep., Amort./Cur. Mat. L/T/D						11.1
(17) 3.0	(22) 2.5	(19) 1.7						(10) 1.8	
2.1	.4	-.3							-.9
.0	.0	.0	Fixed/Worth		.0	.0	.0	.0	.0
.1	.1	.1			.2	.1	.1	.1	.1
.4	.4	.4			-17.0	.8	.2	.5	.3
.5	.8	.8	Debt/Worth		1.1	1.1	.7	.8	.6
1.7	1.8	2.0			3.8	3.6	1.7	1.8	1.6
4.5	3.6	4.7			-327.5	8.6	4.6	3.8	3.2
33.7	33.3	39.8	% Profit Before Taxes/Tangible Net Worth		75.0	76.9	40.3	29.1	36.5
(153) 14.1	(165) 13.5	(153) 15.3		(20) 50.2	(13) 21.3	(34) 8.5	(42) 15.1	20.3	
2.2	1.6	2.3			.7	5.1	.1	4.9	3.3
13.1	10.5	13.5	% Profit Before Taxes/Total Assets		26.5	10.8	7.0	12.6	16.8
5.0	4.4	4.3			4.4	5.4	1.9	4.1	8.5
.9	.3	.8			.0	2.2	.3	1.3	1.1
302.7	365.5	440.0	Sales/Net Fixed Assets		999.8	999.8	655.0	358.7	260.1
68.8	74.3	76.9			106.1	71.9	89.0	94.5	45.4
23.2	20.4	32.0			30.2	10.2	40.0	33.8	23.5
3.3	3.1	3.2	Sales/Total Assets		3.9	2.7	3.4	3.1	3.2
2.4	2.3	2.2			2.1	2.2	2.3	2.3	2.3
1.7	1.6	1.7			1.4	1.5	1.7	1.8	1.9
.2	.2	.2	% Depr., Dep., Amort./Sales		.2	.4	.1	.1	.2
(116) .4	(133) .4	(129) .4		(17) .5	(10) 1.2	(24) .3	(40) .5	(34) .4	
1.1	.9	1.0			.8	2.1	.7	1.1	.9
2.2	1.7	1.6	% Officers', Directors', Owners' Comp/Sales		2.7	2.0	1.0	1.2	1.5
(90) 4.0	(93) 3.4	(89) 3.4		(19) 5.0	(11) 4.4	(18) 3.3	(21) 2.7	(16) 2.1	
6.5	6.9	7.0			9.7	12.1	7.4	4.8	5.0
6295508M	4951055M	4640146M	Net Sales ($)	1209M	48068M	64428M	244268M	796540M	3485633M
2559889M	1976343M	1971063M	Total Assets ($)	980M	25936M	32918M	113230M	360330M	1437669M

© RMA 2010

M = $ thousand   MM = $ million
See Pages 9 through 22 for Explanation of Ratios and Data

Current Data Sorted by Assets | **Comparative Historical Data**

0-500M	500M-2MM	2-10MM	10-50MM	50-100MM	100-250MM	Type of Statement	4/1/05-3/31/06 ALL	4/1/06-3/31/07 ALL
		5	18	9	2	Unqualified	27	23
	11	25	16			Reviewed	33	39
1	2	6	2			Compiled	9	18
4	5	6	2			Tax Returns	12	11
1	6	17	19	3		Other	44	35
	11 (4/1-9/30/09)		149 (10/1/09-3/31/10)					
6	24	59	57	12	2	**NUMBER OF STATEMENTS**	125	126
%	%	%	%	%	%	**ASSETS**	%	%
	14.6	11.5	8.3	9.7		Cash & Equivalents	9.2	7.1
	33.5	27.3	34.0	30.1		Trade Receivables (net)	32.0	31.3
	31.1	38.7	37.0	36.3		Inventory	39.7	41.2
	8.3	4.4	3.3	3.5		All Other Current	3.1	2.9
	87.6	81.8	82.6	79.6		Total Current	84.1	82.6
	6.3	11.2	6.2	7.1		Fixed Assets (net)	8.9	10.1
	1.8	1.3	4.2	8.6		Intangibles (net)	1.7	2.5
	4.3	5.6	7.0	4.6		All Other Non-Current	5.2	4.7
	100.0	100.0	100.0	100.0		Total	100.0	100.0
						LIABILITIES		
	14.3	17.4	19.9	9.2		Notes Payable-Short Term	18.0	20.6
	.1	.9	2.5	5.6		Cur. Mat.-L.T.D.	1.6	1.2
	16.4	18.9	16.9	11.0		Trade Payables	19.0	17.3
	.0	.1	.1	.5		Income Taxes Payable	.3	.2
	9.2	12.0	11.3	8.0		All Other Current	12.3	7.2
	40.1	49.2	50.6	34.3		Total Current	51.1	46.5
	4.8	8.4	2.5	1.9		Long-Term Debt	9.3	5.8
	.1	.0	.3	.1		Deferred Taxes	.1	.1
	3.9	9.0	4.6	2.3		All Other Non-Current	6.3	7.0
	51.2	33.4	42.1	61.3		Net Worth	33.1	40.6
	100.0	100.0	100.0	100.0		Total Liabilities & Net Worth	100.0	100.0
						INCOME DATA		
	100.0	100.0	100.0	100.0		Net Sales	100.0	100.0
	34.5	33.9	29.8	33.6		Gross Profit	31.0	32.4
	31.0	30.8	24.9	27.3		Operating Expenses	27.0	28.2
	3.6	3.1	4.9	6.4		Operating Profit	3.9	4.2
	.4	.7	.6	.8		All Other Expenses (net)	.9	.9
	3.2	2.4	4.3	5.5		Profit Before Taxes	3.0	3.3
						RATIOS		
	4.9	4.0	2.6	5.1		Current	3.3	2.9
	2.6	2.0	1.6	3.1			1.8	1.8
	1.3	1.3	1.2	1.5			1.3	1.2
	3.0	1.6	1.4	3.2		Quick	1.4	1.4
	1.2	.9	.9	1.4			.9	.8
	.6	.3	.4	.5			.5	.4
22	16.7	17 21.5	36 10.2	37 9.9		Sales/Receivables	31 11.7	29 12.6
35	10.5	40 9.2	48 7.6	51 7.1			49 7.4	47 7.8
47	7.7	57 6.4	75 4.9	68 5.3			74 4.9	64 5.7
18	19.8	41 9.0	45 8.0	55 6.7		Cost of Sales/Inventory	55 6.6	48 7.6
72	5.1	88 4.1	102 3.6	112 3.3			101 3.6	96 3.8
91	4.0	149 2.4	137 2.7	138 2.6			146 2.5	150 2.4
9	40.6	13 27.9	13 28.1	14 26.2		Cost of Sales/Payables	20 18.3	16 23.0
19	19.6	30 12.2	25 14.9	31 11.7			33 11.2	31 11.8
44	8.3	61 6.0	63 5.8	44 8.2			58 6.3	51 7.2
	5.3	3.7	3.4	3.1		Sales/Working Capital	3.6	3.9
	6.7	6.6	7.8	4.7			7.1	6.6
	10.9	15.0	15.3	12.5			13.7	18.6
	22.6	8.2	19.0	101.5		EBIT/Interest	7.4	10.4
(17)	3.9	(50) 3.0	(54) 6.5	(11) 9.9			(109) 3.7	(111) 3.1
	1.3	1.3	3.0	4.8			1.8	1.4
						Net Profit + Depr., Dep., Amort./Cur. Mat. L/T/D	15.7	16.0
							(23) 5.0	(25) 4.9
							2.9	2.6
	.0	.0	.0	.0		Fixed/Worth	.0	.0
	.1	.1	.1	.1			.1	.1
	.3	.6	.3	.3			.4	.4
	.3	.4	.7	.3		Debt/Worth	.6	.5
	.7	1.4	1.3	.5			1.4	1.5
	3.2	3.5	4.1	2.6			5.2	4.2
	26.4	37.7	40.1	34.2		% Profit Before Taxes/Tangible Net Worth	40.9	37.9
(23)	10.5	(52) 12.9	(52) 19.6	25.9			(116) 17.9	(116) 15.8
	3.0	1.2	3.6	13.3			5.9	3.9
	18.0	12.5	17.9	19.7		% Profit Before Taxes/Total Assets	12.8	13.2
	5.1	5.2	9.3	8.5			6.2	6.3
	1.0	.3	2.1	4.9			1.4	1.3
	UND	164.2	211.4	93.8		Sales/Net Fixed Assets	197.5	159.7
	58.3	56.9	77.8	45.3			68.1	56.2
	31.3	21.7	26.0	18.4			20.5	20.1
	4.1	3.1	3.0	2.7		Sales/Total Assets	3.0	3.1
	3.4	2.4	2.3	2.1			2.2	2.4
	2.6	1.5	1.7	1.7			1.5	1.7
	.2	.2	.3	.6		% Depr., Dep., Amort./Sales	.2	.3
(15)	.5	(47) .4	(46) .5	(10) 1.0			(99) .5	(103) .5
	.8	.9	1.0	2.0			.9	.9
	3.4	1.7	.6			% Officers', Directors' Owners' Comp/Sales	1.4	1.5
(12)	4.5	(25) 2.5	(19) 1.5				(58) 2.9	(57) 3.2
	8.3	4.3	12.0				6.2	6.3
5608M	114972M	686179M	2961864M	1702995M	546179M	Net Sales ($)	4297571M	4639333M
1943M	33086M	286740M	1258044M	771911M	430959M	Total Assets ($)	2135062M	2390595M

M = $ thousand   MM = $ million
See Pages 9 through 22 for Explanation of Ratios and Data

Comparative Historical Data — Current Data Sorted by Sales

Type of Statement counts and data periods:
- Left historical columns: 4/1/07-3/31/08 ALL, 4/1/08-3/31/09 ALL, 4/1/09-3/31/10 ALL
- Current data sorted by sales periods: 11 (4/1-9/30/09) and 149 (10/1/09-3/31/10)

4/1/07-3/31/08 ALL	4/1/08-3/31/09 ALL	4/1/09-3/31/10 ALL		0-1MM	1-3MM	3-5MM	5-10MM	10-25MM	25MM & OVER
			Type of Statement						
26	32	34	Unqualified				1	4	29
36	51	52	Reviewed		3	5	15	16	13
9	16	11	Compiled		4	2	2	2	1
8	15	17	Tax Returns	4	2	4	4	2	1
42	50	46	Other	2	4	1	6	14	19
121	164	160	**NUMBER OF STATEMENTS**	6	13	12	28	38	63
%	%	%	**ASSETS**	%	%	%	%	%	%
8.5	8.6	11.3	Cash & Equivalents		18.2	9.5	13.8	12.7	8.1
32.7	30.0	29.8	Trade Receivables (net)		20.5	22.3	30.7	31.2	34.4
39.6	43.2	36.3	Inventory		25.6	42.7	37.3	38.5	36.0
4.4	3.1	4.4	All Other Current		2.4	11.4	4.6	4.4	3.8
85.2	84.9	81.8	Total Current		66.7	86.0	86.4	86.8	82.4
7.1	7.2	8.9	Fixed Assets (net)		17.6	8.3	6.7	7.4	7.3
2.8	2.7	3.0	Intangibles (net)		1.6	3.4	.3	2.8	4.5
4.9	5.2	6.3	All Other Non-Current		14.2	2.3	6.6	3.1	5.8
100.0	100.0	100.0	Total		100.0	100.0	100.0	100.0	100.0
			LIABILITIES						
20.7	18.7	16.7	Notes Payable-Short Term		12.4	19.8	16.8	16.8	17.7
2.1	2.2	1.8	Cur. Mat.-L.T.D.		2.3	.0	.4	2.5	2.4
17.1	17.0	16.7	Trade Payables		14.0	10.0	16.1	19.8	17.6
.2	.1	.1	Income Taxes Payable		.0	.0	.1	.1	.2
7.6	8.4	10.8	All Other Current		7.5	7.1	15.4	8.4	11.5
47.6	46.4	46.2	Total Current		36.3	36.9	48.7	47.5	49.4
5.4	4.9	5.4	Long-Term Debt		14.8	7.4	8.1	4.0	3.1
.1	.2	.1	Deferred Taxes		.0	.0	.1	.1	.2
6.2	6.1	6.6	All Other Non-Current		6.6	11.2	12.4	5.3	3.1
40.7	42.4	41.6	Net Worth		42.3	44.5	30.7	43.1	44.1
100.0	100.0	100.0	Total Liabilities & Net Worth		100.0	100.0	100.0	100.0	100.0
			INCOME DATA						
100.0	100.0	100.0	Net Sales		100.0	100.0	100.0	100.0	100.0
30.0	30.6	33.5	Gross Profit		49.4	36.2	32.1	28.6	31.0
26.3	27.2	29.2	Operating Expenses		45.4	35.9	29.6	25.2	25.0
3.8	3.5	4.3	Operating Profit		4.0	.3	2.5	3.4	6.0
1.0	.5	.6	All Other Expenses (net)		.7	.6	1.2	.7	.5
2.8	3.0	3.7	Profit Before Taxes		3.3	-.3	1.3	2.7	5.5
			RATIOS						
3.2	3.5	4.3	Current		3.3	4.9	4.7	4.4	3.0
1.8	1.9	1.9			2.2	3.3	2.1	1.5	1.8
1.3	1.4	1.3			1.0	1.8	1.4	1.3	1.2
1.5	1.5	1.8	Quick		2.1	2.6	3.2	1.7	1.7
.9	.8	.9			.7	1.0	.9	.9	1.0
.5	.5	.4			.3	.5	.4	.5	.4
30 12.1	24 15.1	25 14.6	Sales/Receivables		6 60.1	10 36.1	30 12.2	19 19.1	34 10.6
39 9.3	41 8.9	43 8.5			25 14.6	39 9.3	45 8.1	38 9.6	47 7.8
68 5.4	61 6.0	63 5.8			55 6.6	55 6.6	51 7.1	72 5.1	68 5.4
44 8.2	51 7.1	41 8.9	Cost of Sales/Inventory		1 461.7	64 5.7	36 10.3	37 9.8	47 7.8
97 3.7	102 3.6	88 4.2			83 4.4	89 4.1	83 4.4	93 3.9	88 4.2
146 2.5	160 2.3	138 2.6			250 1.5	167 2.2	154 2.4	138 2.6	126 2.9
11 32.9	10 35.8	12 31.0	Cost of Sales/Payables		12 31.3	4 94.1	12 31.4	9 40.9	16 23.4
23 16.2	23 15.6	26 14.0			41 8.9	10 36.7	21 17.6	28 13.3	28 12.9
53 6.9	46 7.9	54 6.8			90 4.0	38 9.7	40 9.2	56 6.6	59 6.2
3.8	3.3	3.8	Sales/Working Capital		2.8	3.7	3.8	3.8	4.1
7.2	7.0	6.9			9.2	5.7	6.3	6.3	7.4
13.2	14.2	14.9			NM	7.6	10.5	14.7	15.4
6.3	8.9	18.3	EBIT/Interest		84.2		15.8	7.5	25.4
(110) 2.5	(142) 4.0	(137) 5.8			(10) 1.4		(22) 2.9	(35) 3.8	(59) 8.5
1.3	1.3	1.6			-1.5		1.3	1.8	4.5
12.5	26.4	17.5	Net Profit + Depr., Dep., Amort./Cur. Mat. L/T/D						93.6
(19) 8.5	(24) 8.7	(19) 7.0							(11) 10.4
1.4	2.5	1.7							1.5
.0	.0	.0	Fixed/Worth		.0	.0	.0	.1	.0
.1	.1	.1			.1	.1	.1	.1	.1
.4	.3	.3			1.4	.4	.2	.3	.3
.5	.6	.4	Debt/Worth		.4	.3	.3	.4	.4
1.5	1.5	1.1			.6	.8	1.1	1.8	1.1
4.1	3.6	3.5			5.2	6.9	4.6	3.1	3.6
34.1	41.8	37.9	% Profit Before Taxes/Tangible Net Worth		58.9	10.1	36.8	38.6	42.0
(109) 13.6	(151) 15.5	(146) 15.5			(12) 5.7	(11) 4.2	(24) 10.5	(35) 17.6	(58) 21.6
1.5	2.8	3.0			-4.6	-3.0	2.6	5.0	10.9
14.2	13.6	16.5	% Profit Before Taxes/Total Assets		26.2	5.5	19.3	12.6	20.2
5.4	5.1	6.6			.8	1.6	4.8	5.7	9.8
.8	.8	1.1			-3.4	-1.9	1.0	1.0	3.5
167.6	225.6	200.2	Sales/Net Fixed Assets		338.4	119.4	285.5	146.4	209.3
88.9	70.0	61.0			39.6	50.3	92.1	53.0	78.0
28.0	25.7	23.4			12.4	22.6	29.4	22.6	28.1
3.1	3.4	3.2	Sales/Total Assets		3.3	3.6	3.5	3.4	3.0
2.3	2.3	2.4			1.8	3.0	2.6	2.4	2.3
1.8	1.6	1.7			.9	1.4	1.8	1.7	1.9
.2	.2	.3	% Depr., Dep., Amort./Sales				.2	.2	.2
(98) .4	(128) .4	(124) .5					(22) .4	(32) .4	(49) .5
.8	1.0	1.0					.8	.9	1.3
1.6	1.7	1.5	% Officers', Directors' Owners' Comp/Sales				1.6	1.4	.4
(54) 3.1	(69) 3.0	(61) 3.3					(11) 4.7	(13) 1.9	(19) 2.0
5.1	5.0	6.6					6.7	2.3	8.1
6052756M	6184835M	6017797M	Net Sales ($)	3609M	29700M	49832M	206907M	617697M	5110052M
2790167M	2668616M	2782683M	Total Assets ($)	4614M	22053M	31030M	104115M	286802M	2334069M

© RMA 2010

M = $ thousand   MM = $ million
See Pages 9 through 22 for Explanation of Ratios and Data

Current Data Sorted by Assets | Comparative Historical Data

						Type of Statement		
	2	10	26	7	2	Unqualified	42	29
	6	35	16			Reviewed	46	44
1	8	1	1			Compiled	15	10
5	29	8	1			Tax Returns	17	21
3	2	22	25	6	2	Other	48	43
0-500M	25 (4/1-9/30/09) 500M-2MM	2-10MM	193 (10/1/09-3/31/10) 10-50MM	50-100MM	100-250MM		4/1/05-3/31/06 ALL	4/1/06-3/31/07 ALL
9	47	76	69	13	4	NUMBER OF STATEMENTS	168	147
%	%	%	%	%	%	ASSETS	%	%
	12.7	13.4	9.5	10.3		Cash & Equivalents	11.3	13.0
	28.5	37.5	34.2	30.3		Trade Receivables (net)	32.5	30.4
	39.0	30.8	33.0	24.3		Inventory	35.7	36.0
	4.1	4.6	7.0	4.8		All Other Current	3.0	4.1
	84.3	86.2	83.7	69.6		Total Current	82.6	83.6
	9.1	4.3	7.3	14.5		Fixed Assets (net)	7.0	7.1
	1.5	3.7	3.4	11.4		Intangibles (net)	2.4	1.8
	5.1	5.8	5.5	4.5		All Other Non-Current	8.0	7.5
	100.0	100.0	100.0	100.0		Total	100.0	100.0
						LIABILITIES		
	18.2	22.1	22.8	8.9		Notes Payable-Short Term	19.3	18.5
	3.9	.6	1.7	5.4		Cur. Mat.-L.T.D.	1.6	1.5
	23.0	23.7	21.5	13.3		Trade Payables	17.9	19.1
	.2	.0	.1	.2		Income Taxes Payable	.2	.3
	5.3	7.9	10.1	12.8		All Other Current	8.7	8.1
	50.6	54.2	56.2	40.7		Total Current	47.6	47.5
	6.8	2.7	2.7	11.9		Long-Term Debt	6.5	4.8
	.0	.0	.0	1.7		Deferred Taxes	.1	.1
	9.3	5.9	14.8	14.6		All Other Non-Current	3.3	4.8
	33.2	37.2	26.3	31.2		Net Worth	42.5	42.8
	100.0	100.0	100.0	100.0		Total Liabilities & Net Worth	100.0	100.0
						INCOME DATA		
	100.0	100.0	100.0	100.0		Net Sales	100.0	100.0
	32.9	32.1	29.7	33.4		Gross Profit	31.5	33.7
	29.1	27.3	24.8	30.2		Operating Expenses	27.4	28.8
	3.8	4.8	4.9	3.2		Operating Profit	4.1	4.9
	1.0	1.3	.9	2.3		All Other Expenses (net)	.7	.6
	2.8	3.5	4.0	.9		Profit Before Taxes	3.4	4.3
						RATIOS		
	3.7	2.7	2.1	3.3			2.9	2.8
	1.9	1.7	1.5	1.7		Current	1.7	1.8
	1.1	1.2	1.2	1.2			1.3	1.3
	2.0	1.7	1.3	1.3			1.8	1.5
	.9	.8	.7	.9		Quick	.9	.9
	.5	.5	.6	.7			.5	.5
	17 21.0	27 13.3	28 13.3	38 9.6			22 16.8	22 16.3
	26 14.0	45 8.1	49 7.5	44 8.2		Sales/Receivables	45 8.1	43 8.4
	46 7.9	63 5.7	70 5.2	80 4.6			68 5.3	63 5.8
	30 12.3	20 17.9	35 10.4	40 9.1			30 12.0	39 9.2
	52 7.0	46 7.9	66 5.5	61 6.0		Cost of Sales/Inventory	67 5.5	75 4.9
	100 3.7	82 4.4	92 4.0	100 3.7			126 2.9	129 2.8
	11 34.1	18 19.7	18 19.9	22 16.7			11 34.3	14 25.8
	23 16.1	34 10.7	32 11.5	29 12.8		Cost of Sales/Payables	23 15.8	28 13.1
	52 7.0	55 6.6	65 5.6	41 8.9			45 8.2	56 6.5
	5.6	4.8	5.6	4.6			4.1	3.8
	9.8	10.8	8.7	7.5		Sales/Working Capital	8.1	7.8
	53.9	32.1	24.5	20.6			20.8	15.8
	11.0	15.5	30.1	10.4			13.5	9.0
	(39) 3.0	(62) 4.9	(64) 6.4	3.2		EBIT/Interest	(149) 3.9	(125) 4.4
	1.2	1.9	2.1	-3.2			1.4	1.9
			28.1				13.3	27.0
			(16) 2.0			Net Profit + Depr., Dep., Amort./Cur. Mat. L/T/D	(27) 5.2	(22) 5.4
			.3				1.3	2.8
	.0	.0	.0	.2			.0	.0
	.1	.0	.1	.2		Fixed/Worth	.1	.1
	.4	.2	.5	NM			.3	.3
	.7	.7	.8	.8			.6	.6
	1.9	1.7	2.0	2.0		Debt/Worth	1.4	1.3
	6.5	5.3	4.7	NM			3.4	3.2
	62.0	52.2	77.0	61.4			48.9	51.8
	(43) 27.6	(66) 23.3	(62) 33.7	(10) 26.0		% Profit Before Taxes/Tangible Net Worth	(156) 20.0	(139) 19.4
	3.8	9.1	11.8	-9.6			3.6	5.8
	18.2	21.1	23.1	12.0			18.0	18.2
	6.3	8.4	8.7	5.8		% Profit Before Taxes/Total Assets	6.0	8.0
	.9	3.0	2.1	-8.5			1.5	2.5
	769.3	697.2	197.4	82.2			300.1	286.4
	105.2	189.5	102.1	34.6		Sales/Net Fixed Assets	93.1	91.7
	33.8	69.8	35.4	9.7			33.4	29.3
	5.3	4.2	3.4	2.6			3.5	3.4
	3.2	2.8	2.5	1.9		Sales/Total Assets	2.6	2.5
	2.4	2.2	1.9	1.7			1.9	1.8
	.1	.1	.2				.2	.1
	(34) .4	(45) .3	(48) .4			% Depr., Dep., Amort./Sales	(131) .4	(109) .4
	.7	.6	1.1				.8	.9
	1.8	1.4	.6				1.5	1.5
	(34) 3.0	(38) 2.6	(25) 1.0			% Officers', Directors' Owners' Comp/Sales	(78) 2.9	(68) 2.9
	6.9	5.6	3.0				6.6	6.2
12520M	218260M	1344006M	4757808M	1856207M	926925M	Net Sales ($)	8657488M	5789653M
2048M	54808M	412407M	1712260M	920762M	522839M	Total Assets ($)	3479553M	2680493M

M = $ thousand   MM = $ million
See Pages 9 through 22 for Explanation of Ratios and Data

Comparative Historical Data
Current Data Sorted by Sales

4/1/07-3/31/08 ALL	4/1/08-3/31/09 ALL	4/1/09-3/31/10 ALL	Type of Statement	0-1MM	1-3MM	3-5MM	5-10MM	10-25MM	25MM & OVER
26	28	47	Unqualified		1	1	3	4	38
31	31	57	Reviewed		2	6	6	23	20
13	14	11	Compiled	1	1	6	1	1	1
31	19	43	Tax Returns	5	15	10	4	7	2
68	69	60	Other	4			5	15	36
				25 (4/1-9/30/09)	193 (10/1/09-3/31/10)				
169	161	218	**NUMBER OF STATEMENTS**	10	19	23	19	50	97
%	%	%	**ASSETS**	%	%	%	%	%	%
9.5	10.6	12.2	Cash & Equivalents	20.4	12.4	10.9	15.7	16.0	8.9
32.6	30.2	33.3	Trade Receivables (net)	10.4	26.9	33.8	33.7	36.8	34.9
37.4	36.8	33.0	Inventory	42.7	42.6	35.5	26.4	31.0	31.8
4.5	4.1	5.1	All Other Current	2.3	2.8	3.7	7.1	3.7	6.4
84.0	81.7	83.6	Total Current	75.9	84.7	83.9	83.0	87.6	82.1
8.0	7.0	7.2	Fixed Assets (net)	14.7	9.7	8.8	6.5	2.2	8.4
2.3	4.0	3.7	Intangibles (net)	.4	1.0	2.2	7.7	2.3	4.8
5.6	7.2	5.5	All Other Non-Current	9.1	4.6	5.1	2.7	8.0	4.7
100.0	100.0	100.0	Total	100.0	100.0	100.0	100.0	100.0	100.0
			LIABILITIES						
22.9	20.7	20.6	Notes Payable-Short Term	47.5	17.1	16.2	11.8	21.0	21.2
1.0	1.4	2.0	Cur. Mat.-L.T.D.	7.5	3.3	.2	3.3	.9	2.0
18.7	18.6	22.0	Trade Payables	11.8	23.2	17.2	22.2	26.1	21.7
.2	.1	.1	Income Taxes Payable	.0	.0	.4	.0	.0	.1
8.6	9.6	8.9	All Other Current	.6	12.6	6.9	7.7	8.1	10.1
51.4	50.4	53.6	Total Current	67.3	56.3	40.9	45.0	56.2	55.1
7.4	6.9	5.0	Long-Term Debt	13.4	16.3	4.7	2.4	2.6	3.7
.1	.2	.2	Deferred Taxes	.0	.0	.0	.0	.0	.4
5.1	7.6	10.1	All Other Non-Current	9.6	18.7	2.5	13.9	4.6	12.3
36.0	34.9	31.1	Net Worth	9.6	8.8	51.9	38.6	36.6	28.5
100.0	100.0	100.0	Total Liabilities & Net Worth	100.0	100.0	100.0	100.0	100.0	100.0
			INCOME DATA						
100.0	100.0	100.0	Net Sales	100.0	100.0	100.0	100.0	100.0	100.0
34.0	32.7	31.7	Gross Profit	50.7	35.6	31.5	34.7	29.7	29.5
28.5	28.6	27.0	Operating Expenses	37.1	31.6	28.2	31.3	25.0	25.0
5.5	4.1	4.7	Operating Profit	13.6	4.0	3.3	3.4	4.7	4.5
1.3	1.3	1.2	All Other Expenses (net)	6.3	1.3	.4	.3	.6	1.3
4.1	2.7	3.5	Profit Before Taxes	7.3	2.7	2.9	3.1	4.1	3.1
			RATIOS						
3.0	2.6	2.8	Current	3.5	5.4	5.0	6.9	2.7	2.0
1.8	1.7	1.7		1.8	2.0	2.4	1.6	1.8	1.5
1.3	1.2	1.2		.5	1.0	1.3	1.1	1.1	1.2
1.4	1.6	1.6	Quick	1.7	1.3	2.6	3.8	1.9	1.3
.9	.8	.8		.6	1.0	1.6	.8	.9	.8
.5	.5	.6		.2	.4	.6	.5	.6	.6
24 15.5	24 15.3	22 16.2	Sales/Receivables	0 UND	17 21.0	24 15.3	18 20.1	21 17.1	28 13.3
46 7.9	41 9.0	41 8.8		15 24.2	31 11.9	30 12.3	53 6.9	39 9.3	44 8.2
68 5.4	56 6.5	63 5.8		38 9.7	61 5.9	53 6.9	70 5.2	62 5.9	66 5.5
46 7.9	38 9.6	30 12.1	Cost of Sales/Inventory	0 UND	48 7.5	33 11.1	15 24.0	17 21.0	33 11.1
81 4.5	75 4.8	57 6.4		159 2.3	95 3.8	52 7.0	75 4.9	43 8.4	57 6.4
140 2.6	131 2.8	91 4.0		377 1.0	153 2.4	66 5.5	130 2.8	72 5.0	87 4.2
16 23.2	13 28.9	15 24.4	Cost of Sales/Payables	0 UND	14 25.2	7 50.6	10 38.1	19 19.6	20 18.1
32 11.3	30 12.2	31 11.9		12 29.2	44 8.3	15 23.6	39 9.3	32 11.3	31 11.9
50 7.3	55 6.6	57 6.4		54 6.8	87 4.2	40 9.1	79 4.6	49 7.4	56 6.6
4.3	4.9	5.2	Sales/Working Capital	2.9	3.7	4.9	2.8	5.8	6.4
6.9	8.2	8.9		9.1	8.2	7.4	8.0	10.8	9.6
16.2	18.9	24.4		-3.8	-79.3	14.4	40.5	35.7	23.0
9.3	8.1	15.2	EBIT/Interest		2.8	10.2	18.7	17.6	22.9
(148) 3.7	(141) 2.8	(188) 4.4		(16) 1.2	(21) 3.9	(15) 5.2	(42) 5.2	(88) 5.3	
1.5	.9	1.8		-1.6	2.7	1.8	2.1	1.8	
60.6	6.5	22.4	Net Profit + Depr., Dep., Amort./Cur. Mat. L/T/D						27.0
(25) 9.5	(21) 1.7	(28) 2.7						(22) 5.4	
1.0	.0	.3						.3	
.0	.0	.0	Fixed/Worth	.0	.0	.0	.0	.0	.1
.1	.1	.1		.1	.1	.1	.1	.0	.2
.3	.4	.4		NM	41.6	.4	.6	.1	.5
.7	.6	.7	Debt/Worth	.3	1.1	.2	.3	.7	.8
1.6	1.7	1.9		2.9	3.0	.9	2.0	1.4	2.0
5.3	5.0	5.7		-2.6	345.0	3.9	9.9	5.2	5.2
57.4	52.1	62.8	% Profit Before Taxes/Tangible Net Worth		96.0	38.4	93.5	53.6	64.5
(152) 23.2	(142) 18.4	(191) 27.0		(15) 29.4	10.6	(15) 27.6	(46) 25.9	(85) 30.8	
5.7	1.3	8.4		-9.6	3.5	4.4	12.2	13.0	
18.6	16.9	20.4	% Profit Before Taxes/Total Assets	24.2	7.1	14.1	21.5	24.7	22.8
6.4	5.2	7.8		7.0	.9	6.7	9.4	10.5	8.3
1.3	-.2	1.7		-5.7	-4.4	2.0	.7	3.0	2.3
269.6	191.4	438.7	Sales/Net Fixed Assets	UND	999.8	477.2	544.0	999.8	151.1
85.5	73.1	114.8		29.8	105.2	97.4	115.0	430.0	81.1
29.0	30.2	40.9		13.8	52.7	41.8	62.2	110.8	30.8
3.2	3.8	3.9	Sales/Total Assets	2.8	3.3	4.3	3.2	5.4	3.8
2.4	2.6	2.8		1.8	2.7	3.2	2.7	3.2	2.8
1.7	1.8	1.9		1.2	1.6	2.4	1.5	2.3	1.9
.2	.2	.2	% Depr., Dep., Amort./Sales		.2	.2	.1	.1	.3
(127) .4	(111) .4	(143) .4		(12) .4	(20) .4	(11) .3	(30) .1	(66) .5	
.8	1.0	.8		.8	.9	.4	.4	1.1	
1.8	1.4	1.0	% Officers', Directors' Owners' Comp/Sales		2.1	2.3	1.4	1.2	.6
(82) 3.0	(65) 3.1	(107) 2.5		(17) 4.8	(14) 3.2	(10) 3.0	(25) 2.3	(37) 1.1	
5.0	5.4	5.0		7.8	5.7	4.5	5.6	3.0	
7515694M	7810144M	9115726M	Net Sales ($)	6563M	41241M	97682M	145751M	828408M	7996081M
3452492M	3518063M	3625124M	Total Assets ($)	7592M	19363M	31122M	74433M	288933M	3203681M

M = $ thousand   MM = $ million
See Pages 9 through 22 for Explanation of Ratios and Data

© RMA 2010

Current Data Sorted by Assets | **Comparative Historical Data**

0-500M	500M-2MM	2-10MM	10-50MM	50-100MM	100-250MM	Type of Statement	4/1/05-3/31/06 ALL	4/1/06-3/31/07 ALL
		2	7	5	4	Unqualified	9	13
	4	18	8	1		Reviewed	24	21
1	1	6	3			Compiled	11	5
1	3	3				Tax Returns	4	8
2	2	13	12	5	1	Other	32	30
	16 (4/1-9/30/09)		86 (10/1/09-3/31/10)					
4	10	42	30	11	5	NUMBER OF STATEMENTS	80	77
%	%	%	%	%	%	**ASSETS**	%	%
	15.5	9.6	7.5	23.2		Cash & Equivalents	8.1	11.1
	35.4	38.6	28.6	26.5		Trade Receivables (net)	33.6	33.4
	41.7	37.6	42.1	25.3		Inventory	40.3	39.5
	.6	1.7	5.5	5.5		All Other Current	3.3	2.8
	93.2	87.5	83.7	80.4		Total Current	85.3	86.9
	2.6	4.8	9.3	10.3		Fixed Assets (net)	7.1	5.4
	.1	3.7	2.5	3.1		Intangibles (net)	2.9	3.0
	4.1	4.0	4.5	6.2		All Other Non-Current	4.8	4.8
	100.0	100.0	100.0	100.0		Total	100.0	100.0
						LIABILITIES		
	12.1	18.3	21.1	7.9		Notes Payable-Short Term	18.9	17.1
	.4	2.6	1.6	.3		Cur. Mat.-L.T.D.	1.0	.4
	20.1	16.2	21.5	18.3		Trade Payables	19.8	21.2
	.0	.1	.9	.0		Income Taxes Payable	.1	.2
	14.3	10.9	9.5	13.0		All Other Current	8.2	10.7
	47.0	48.0	54.5	39.5		Total Current	48.0	49.5
	7.5	4.8	7.0	1.5		Long-Term Debt	3.1	3.3
	.0	.1	.2	.9		Deferred Taxes	.0	.1
	2.9	5.9	4.4	12.1		All Other Non-Current	5.7	5.7
	42.7	41.1	33.9	45.9		Net Worth	43.1	41.3
	100.0	100.0	100.0	100.0		Total Liabilities & Net Worth	100.0	100.0
						INCOME DATA		
	100.0	100.0	100.0	100.0		Net Sales	100.0	100.0
	26.2	32.1	32.9	32.3		Gross Profit	32.9	31.9
	25.0	29.0	27.4	28.6		Operating Expenses	29.9	28.7
	1.3	3.2	5.5	3.8		Operating Profit	3.0	3.2
	.2	-.1	1.3	.5		All Other Expenses (net)	.7	.7
	1.1	3.3	4.2	3.2		Profit Before Taxes	2.3	2.4
						RATIOS		
	6.8	3.0	2.3	2.6		Current	3.1	3.0
	2.1	1.9	1.6	2.0			1.8	1.9
	1.3	1.3	1.2	1.6			1.3	1.3
	3.1	1.7	1.1	1.5		Quick	1.3	1.5
	1.1	1.2	.8	1.2			.9	.9
	.4	.6	.3	1.0			.5	.6
	35 10.5	37 9.9	25 14.5	25 14.4		Sales/Receivables	30 12.3	35 10.3
	59 6.2	51 7.1	48 7.5	41 9.0			50 7.3	52 7.1
	92 4.0	73 5.0	69 5.3	67 5.4			72 5.1	72 5.1
	29 12.5	47 7.8	72 5.1	26 14.2		Cost of Sales/Inventory	47 7.7	56 6.5
	77 4.7	91 4.0	114 3.2	68 5.4			101 3.6	88 4.1
	227 1.6	142 2.6	154 2.4	90 4.0			137 2.7	126 2.9
	0 UND	10 37.1	16 23.3	28 13.1		Cost of Sales/Payables	12 29.5	12 29.4
	30 12.1	23 15.6	34 10.8	30 12.4			32 11.5	27 13.6
	88 4.1	50 7.3	59 6.2	67 5.5			70 5.2	71 5.2
	2.5	4.0	3.8	3.5		Sales/Working Capital	4.0	3.7
	3.7	6.5	8.5	6.4			6.5	6.1
	29.4	16.2	15.7	10.7			15.8	12.0
	44.5	8.7	13.1			EBIT/Interest	6.8	5.7
	3.3	(36) 3.8	(29) 4.9				(65) 2.4	(64) 2.3
	-4.5	1.4	1.4				1.0	.7
						Net Profit + Depr., Dep., Amort./Cur. Mat. L/T/D		
	.0	.0	.1	.1		Fixed/Worth	.0	.0
	.0	.1	.2	.2			.1	.1
	.1	.3	.4	.4			.4	.2
	.3	.5	.8	.6		Debt/Worth	.5	.4
	1.9	1.4	2.0	1.3			1.6	1.4
	7.9	4.2	9.0	2.2			4.5	4.1
		29.8	60.9	25.7		% Profit Before Taxes/Tangible Net Worth	42.0	32.8
	(39) 12.6	(26) 23.6	(10) 12.4				(74) 14.9	(70) 12.3
	4.8	6.3	-5.1				2.9	1.3
	12.9	15.3	16.0	8.9		% Profit Before Taxes/Total Assets	12.1	14.5
	2.3	4.8	5.6	6.4			4.5	4.2
	-7.7	.7	.8	-1.3			.6	.2
	UND	381.7	124.5	114.6		Sales/Net Fixed Assets	244.0	265.5
	344.5	74.5	55.3	29.8			69.7	86.9
	46.7	36.2	25.9	18.4			26.4	34.8
	4.2	3.2	3.1	3.0		Sales/Total Assets	3.1	3.2
	1.9	2.4	2.2	2.5			2.3	2.3
	1.3	2.0	1.7	1.8			1.8	1.8
		.2	.3	.4		% Depr., Dep., Amort./Sales	.2	.2
	(33) .4	(27) .7	(10) .8				(60) .5	(59) .5
	1.2	.9	1.5				1.1	.8
		1.4				% Officers', Directors' Owners' Comp/Sales	1.9	1.7
	(21) 2.4						(29) 3.3	(26) 3.9
	5.6						5.7	12.7
7179M	33694M	537475M	1383591M	1632009M	975952M	Net Sales ($)	2623434M	2620222M
962M	12107M	203166M	576243M	740583M	936749M	Total Assets ($)	1279688M	1323369M

M = $ thousand   MM = $ million
See Pages 9 through 22 for Explanation of Ratios and Data

Comparative Historical Data

Current Data Sorted by Sales

				Type of Statement						
10		11	18	Unqualified			1		1	16
27		17	31	Reviewed	1	1	1	9	11	8
9		7	11	Compiled		2	1	2	5	1
6		11	7	Tax Returns	1	3		3		
41		52	35	Other	2		2	6	9	16
4/1/07-		4/1/08-	4/1/09-		16 (4/1-9/30/09)			86 (10/1/09-3/31/10)		
3/31/08		3/31/09	3/31/10		0-1MM	1-3MM	3-5MM	5-10MM	10-25MM	25MM & OVER
ALL		ALL	ALL							
93		98	102	NUMBER OF STATEMENTS	4	6	5	20	26	41
%		%	%	ASSETS	%	%	%	%	%	%
7.3		7.7	11.9	Cash & Equivalents				14.1	7.4	13.0
33.0		28.7	32.7	Trade Receivables (net)				37.0	37.1	27.2
39.4		43.3	35.9	Inventory				38.5	36.4	33.8
2.9		4.1	4.1	All Other Current				.9	2.1	5.6
82.6		83.8	84.5	Total Current				90.6	83.0	79.7
7.1		7.1	6.6	Fixed Assets (net)				3.0	8.2	8.2
4.1		4.7	4.2	Intangibles (net)				1.4	5.2	6.4
6.1		4.4	4.7	All Other Non-Current				5.0	3.7	5.7
100.0		100.0	100.0	Total				100.0	100.0	100.0
				LIABILITIES						
20.0		18.7	16.4	Notes Payable-Short Term				15.7	23.2	13.0
1.0		1.6	1.6	Cur. Mat.-L.T.D.				.1	.8	1.2
15.9		17.1	17.5	Trade Payables				13.2	19.2	19.8
.2		.1	.3	Income Taxes Payable				.1	.0	.7
8.6		7.8	11.8	All Other Current				11.9	10.7	10.5
45.7		45.3	47.7	Total Current				40.9	53.9	45.1
4.5		5.5	5.3	Long-Term Debt				1.6	10.5	3.8
.1		.2	.2	Deferred Taxes				.0	.2	.5
4.2		10.5	5.6	All Other Non-Current				7.7	4.4	6.7
45.6		38.5	41.1	Net Worth				49.8	31.0	43.9
100.0		100.0	100.0	Total Liabilties & Net Worth				100.0	100.0	100.0
				INCOME DATA						
100.0		100.0	100.0	Net Sales				100.0	100.0	100.0
34.1		32.8	31.6	Gross Profit				34.2	30.4	34.1
29.6		30.1	27.8	Operating Expenses				30.8	26.8	28.7
4.5		2.7	3.8	Operating Profit				3.4	3.6	5.4
1.0		1.0	.4	All Other Expenses (net)				-.2	.1	.8
3.5		1.7	3.4	Profit Before Taxes				3.6	3.5	4.6
				RATIOS						
2.8		3.2	2.9					3.2	2.6	2.7
1.8		1.9	1.8	Current				2.8	1.5	1.8
1.3		1.4	1.4					1.3	1.1	1.5
1.5		1.4	1.8					2.3	1.6	1.5
.9		.8	1.0	Quick				1.6	.9	1.0
.6		.6	.5					.7	.5	.6

38	9.6	30	12.2	33	11.0	Sales/Receivables				35	10.4	36	10.1	26	14.2
53	6.9	50	7.3	50	7.3					53	6.9	57	6.4	41	8.9
75	4.9	65	5.6	69	5.3					75	4.9	69	5.3	65	5.6
59	6.2	71	5.2	44	8.3	Cost of Sales/Inventory				45	8.1	45	8.0	43	8.4
95	3.9	103	3.6	91	4.0					90	4.0	94	3.9	86	4.2
157	2.3	167	2.2	142	2.6					137	2.7	160	2.3	126	2.9
13	29.0	10	36.7	11	31.9	Cost of Sales/Payables				6	61.3	9	39.5	25	14.5
34	10.8	28	12.8	30	12.4					18	20.4	25	14.8	32	11.5
58	6.3	57	6.4	55	6.7					48	7.5	54	6.5	56	6.5

3.8		3.6	3.8	Sales/Working Capital				4.0	4.4	3.8
6.3		6.0	6.2					5.2	9.4	6.4
10.9		10.8	15.1					13.7	17.9	11.7
	7.4		7.1		11.2	EBIT/Interest			9.4		7.8		16.3
(85)	3.0	(85)	2.6	(88)	4.1		(19)	4.3	(22)	3.8	(35)	5.5
	1.3		1.5		1.5			1.8		1.5		2.4
	75.5		11.7		12.2	Net Profit + Depr., Dep.,					
(14)	8.1	(18)	4.1	(20)	5.3	Amort./Cur. Mat. L/T/D					
	2.2		1.6		2.3						
	.0		.1		.0	Fixed/Worth			.0		.0		.1
	.1		.1		.1				.0		.1		.2
	.3		.5		.4				.1		.6		.4
	.5		.7		.6	Debt/Worth			.4		.9		.7
	1.3		1.9		1.4				.7		2.2		1.4
	3.0		4.5		4.2				4.0		10.1		2.7
	36.7		34.2		32.5	% Profit Before Taxes/Tangible			22.7		42.0		53.9
(89)	12.9	(87)	14.4	(92)	16.6	Net Worth		(92)	11.8	(22)	21.5	(37)	17.9
	4.1		3.6		4.1				4.3		3.6		5.9
	14.1		10.6		14.3	% Profit Before Taxes/Total			12.2		15.7		16.1
	5.3		4.0		5.0	Assets			5.0		3.5		6.6
	.9		.4		.6				2.5		.6		2.3
	181.4		100.6		209.5	Sales/Net Fixed Assets			902.6		191.3		118.5
	63.8		47.9		63.9				106.3		48.1		44.3
	25.4		26.7		29.1				48.2		25.9		19.8
	3.1		3.1		3.1	Sales/Total Assets			3.3		2.8		3.1
	2.1		2.2		2.3				2.4		2.1		2.4
	1.6		1.6		1.7				2.1		1.8		1.8
	.2		.3		.2	% Depr., Dep., Amort./Sales			.1		.2		.4
(69)	.5	(78)	.5	(81)	.5		(13)	.3	(22)	.4	(36)	.8
	1.1		.9		1.1				1.1		.9		1.2
	1.1		.8		1.3	% Officers', Directors'					.6	
(38)	2.6	(37)	2.1	(34)	2.4	Owners' Comp/Sales				(12)	2.0	
	6.8		4.8		5.3						6.2	

3731593M	4485191M	4569900M	Net Sales ($)	2301M	12386M	19783M	152294M	435454M	3947682M
2056942M	2223321M	2469810M	Total Assets ($)	1727M	8472M	8385M	65533M	200927M	2184766M

M = $ thousand   MM = $ million
See Pages 9 through 22 for Explanation of Ratios and Data

Current Data Sorted by Assets						Type of Statement	Comparative Historical Data	
1			11	40	12	18	Unqualified	81	81
1	4		43	37	1		Reviewed	76	89
6	16		36	9			Compiled	62	83
15	33		33	3		1	Tax Returns	35	53
8	19		40	48	10	11	Other	123	122

0-500M	500M-2MM	2-10MM	10-50MM	50-100MM	100-250MM		4/1/05-3/31/06 ALL	4/1/06-3/31/07 ALL
	99 (4/1-9/30/09)			357 (10/1/09-3/31/10)				
31	72	163	137	23	30	NUMBER OF STATEMENTS	377	428
%	%	%	%	%	%	ASSETS	%	%
14.4	12.7	7.7	7.2	9.1	7.3	Cash & Equivalents	6.7	7.7
21.6	26.3	35.9	29.9	23.8	23.1	Trade Receivables (net)	31.0	30.5
31.0	33.2	31.2	30.1	22.5	27.4	Inventory	31.7	30.8
4.7	2.3	3.0	2.8	8.1	5.8	All Other Current	2.7	2.7
71.8	74.5	77.8	69.9	63.5	63.5	Total Current	72.0	71.6
21.3	17.6	13.8	22.0	26.1	24.9	Fixed Assets (net)	19.1	19.3
2.7	3.2	2.8	3.1	3.9	3.9	Intangibles (net)	2.4	2.3
4.1	4.7	5.6	5.0	6.5	7.6	All Other Non-Current	6.5	6.8
100.0	100.0	100.0	100.0	100.0	100.0	Total	100.0	100.0
						LIABILITIES		
15.0	10.7	14.4	15.6	8.5	9.4	Notes Payable-Short Term	16.9	14.0
9.5	3.3	2.6	2.3	2.5	1.6	Cur. Mat.-L.T.D.	2.3	2.9
29.5	24.6	26.7	20.7	21.0	19.3	Trade Payables	24.1	25.5
.0	.0	.2	.2	2.0	.3	Income Taxes Payable	.3	.3
24.9	7.1	8.9	7.5	8.5	12.8	All Other Current	8.4	8.9
78.9	45.7	52.8	46.3	42.4	43.4	Total Current	51.9	51.6
22.3	14.3	8.2	14.1	15.0	15.9	Long-Term Debt	13.2	13.9
.1	.0	.2	.4	.3	1.3	Deferred Taxes	.3	.3
3.3	6.8	4.8	4.5	5.7	4.3	All Other Non-Current	5.1	5.4
-4.6	33.1	34.0	34.8	36.6	35.2	Net Worth	29.5	28.8
100.0	100.0	100.0	100.0	100.0	100.0	Total Liabilties & Net Worth	100.0	100.0
						INCOME DATA		
100.0	100.0	100.0	100.0	100.0	100.0	Net Sales	100.0	100.0
25.6	22.0	17.8	17.9	15.8	18.3	Gross Profit	18.9	18.7
24.7	20.0	16.4	15.5	12.9	15.1	Operating Expenses	17.2	16.6
.9	2.1	1.4	2.4	2.9	3.2	Operating Profit	1.6	2.1
1.5	.2	.0	.3	.3	.7	All Other Expenses (net)	.2	.4
-.6	1.8	1.4	2.1	2.7	2.5	Profit Before Taxes	1.5	1.8
						RATIOS		
2.6	3.1	2.4	2.1	2.2	1.8		1.9	2.0
1.6	1.8	1.5	1.5	1.5	1.4	Current	1.4	1.4
.6	1.3	1.1	1.2	1.1	1.1		1.1	1.1
1.5	1.6	1.4	1.1	1.3	1.0		1.0	1.1
.5	.9	.9	.8	.6	.7	Quick	.7	.7
.2	.6	.5	.5	.4	.5		.5	.5

0	UND	2	189.1	16	23.1	16	22.9	11	34.3	8	43.8	Sales/Receivables	11 33.6 / 22 16.4 / 33 11.0	12 31.3 / 16 16.7 / 34 10.6
9	40.7	18	20.5	25	14.8	25	14.9	18	20.0	20	18.1			
25	14.8	33	11.0	37	9.8	35	10.3	25	14.3	29	12.5			
5	67.7	15	24.2	14	26.0	15	24.8	17	22.0	21	17.7	Cost of Sales/Inventory	16 23.2 / 26 14.0 / 40 9.0	15 25.0 / 25 14.4 / 40 9.1
20	18.4	27	13.6	26	14.0	27	13.7	20	18.1	27	13.7			
34	10.8	56	6.5	44	8.3	45	8.2	32	11.3	32	11.3			
0	UND	7	50.9	10	36.7	11	33.0	11	32.9	13	27.2	Cost of Sales/Payables	11 34.5 / 18 20.5 / 32 11.4	10 35.1 / 18 19.8 / 35 10.5
15	24.7	15	24.1	21	17.3	18	20.4	17	21.4	21	17.4			
41	8.9	35	10.5	32	11.3	31	11.8	31	11.9	25	14.5			

0-500M	500M-2MM	2-10MM	10-50MM	50-100MM	100-250MM		4/1/05-3/31/06	4/1/06-3/31/07
11.3	8.7	9.4	9.8	11.2	14.3	Sales/Working Capital	13.3	12.3
74.4	18.5	22.0	21.5	31.7	25.3		28.3	26.6
-21.3	43.3	92.5	53.8	59.2	72.5		74.1	87.6
8.0	12.0	12.4	16.4	45.7	9.8	EBIT/Interest	9.9	9.2
(24) 2.9	(59) 4.8	(144) 3.7	(127) 5.4	(20) 5.4	(26) 4.2		(341) 3.0	(380) 3.0
.1	1.2	1.9	2.6	3.4	2.6		1.5	1.5
	8.0	11.9	5.4	34.2		Net Profit + Depr., Dep., Amort./Cur. Mat. L/T/D	5.8	5.0
	(25) 3.1	(46) 3.6	(12) 1.9	(10) 3.6			(112) 2.9	(108) 3.0
	1.0	1.5	1.4	1.9			1.5	1.3
.1	.1	.1	.2	.4	.3	Fixed/Worth	.2	.1
.9	.3	.3	.6	.7	1.0		.5	.5
-.8	1.5	.9	1.6	1.8	1.7		1.5	1.4
1.1	.9	1.0	1.1	1.3	1.0	Debt/Worth	1.2	1.1
17.1	2.9	2.3	2.6	1.8	2.4		2.5	2.4
-3.9	9.5	4.8	5.5	3.8	6.1		5.5	5.4
73.7	59.0	39.2	46.3	36.5	50.2	% Profit Before Taxes/Tangible Net Worth	34.3	40.4
(16) 18.0	(62) 22.7	(150) 13.5	(128) 24.6	(22) 25.5	(29) 24.8		(336) 15.2	(384) 18.2
-10.9	6.2	4.9	13.1	13.2	13.0		5.5	6.7
32.4	16.3	10.7	14.0	10.1	13.7	% Profit Before Taxes/Total Assets	10.8	11.9
7.6	5.9	4.2	7.1	8.2	6.9		4.1	4.9
-1.6	.8	1.5	4.0	4.9	1.8		1.4	1.5
517.5	314.9	186.4	94.9	48.1	59.5	Sales/Net Fixed Assets	127.8	128.9
61.0	92.8	63.5	24.8	19.1	18.3		41.9	42.8
36.1	15.7	24.1	11.7	11.1	11.1		14.7	14.3
12.3	7.6	6.9	6.0	6.1	5.8	Sales/Total Assets	7.2	6.9
8.1	5.6	4.8	4.2	4.5	4.7		5.1	5.1
3.7	3.0	3.2	2.8	2.9	3.6		3.5	3.5
.2	.1	.2	.2	.4	.5	% Depr., Dep., Amort./Sales	.3	.2
(18) .5	(50) .5	(140) .4	(121) .6	(21) .6	(21) .7		(315) .5	(353) .6
1.9	2.3	.8	1.1	1.1	1.1		1.0	1.1
1.5	.6	.6	.6			% Officers', Directors' Owners' Comp/Sales	.7	.5
(10) 2.6	(41) 1.5	(74) 1.5	(38) 1.0				(135) 1.6	(174) 1.5
3.9	3.7	3.7	1.9				3.0	2.9
74744M	504494M	4193885M	14871228M	7959073M	21538925M	Net Sales ($)	43993041M	43168750M
8352M	88471M	805018M	2899938M	1603190M	4661526M	Total Assets ($)	8484342M	8671036M

M = $ thousand   MM = $ million
See Pages 9 through 22 for Explanation of Ratios and Data

Comparative Historical Data | Current Data Sorted by Sales

79 / 71 / 56 / 50 / 128	82 / 90 / 44 / 73 / 132	82 / 86 / 67 / 85 / 136	Type of Statement	0-1MM	1-3MM	3-5MM	5-10MM	10-25MM	25MM & OVER
			Unqualified		1		1	6	74
			Reviewed		3	1	2	20	60
			Compiled	1	4	5	15	19	23
			Tax Returns	8	11	9	15	29	13
			Other	2	10	6	12	20	86
4/1/07-3/31/08 ALL	4/1/08-3/31/09 ALL	4/1/09-3/31/10 ALL		99 (4/1-9/30/09)			357 (10/1/09-3/31/10)		
384	421	456	**NUMBER OF STATEMENTS**	11	29	21	45	94	256
%	%	%	**ASSETS**	%	%	%	%	%	%
7.7	7.1	8.9	Cash & Equivalents	18.3	12.9	14.4	9.2	9.9	7.1
29.9	31.9	30.1	Trade Receivables (net)	12.7	26.2	25.9	28.1	30.2	32.0
31.0	32.6	30.5	Inventory	25.4	33.1	26.5	32.1	33.3	29.4
3.8	3.2	3.4	All Other Current	.1	5.6	4.2	3.2	2.9	3.4
72.5	74.8	72.9	Total Current	56.5	77.8	71.1	72.7	76.3	71.9
18.8	17.4	18.7	Fixed Assets (net)	36.8	18.7	19.2	17.7	15.2	19.4
2.9	2.8	3.1	Intangibles (net)	2.6	1.9	1.7	3.2	3.7	3.1
5.8	5.1	5.3	All Other Non-Current	4.1	1.7	8.0	6.4	4.8	5.6
100.0	100.0	100.0	Total	100.0	100.0	100.0	100.0	100.0	100.0
			LIABILITIES						
15.0	15.1	13.6	Notes Payable-Short Term	5.4	10.3	16.7	11.8	12.4	14.8
2.9	2.7	3.0	Cur. Mat.-L.T.D.	7.7	5.8	4.1	3.6	2.0	2.6
23.8	24.0	24.0	Trade Payables	14.2	24.8	30.9	24.0	26.2	22.9
.3	.2	.3	Income Taxes Payable	.0	.0	.0	.1	.2	.4
8.3	9.1	9.6	All Other Current	53.7	10.9	7.2	4.8	8.6	8.9
50.4	51.1	50.4	Total Current	81.0	51.9	58.9	44.5	49.4	49.6
13.0	12.7	12.7	Long-Term Debt	23.6	15.9	31.4	12.9	8.5	11.9
.2	.3	.3	Deferred Taxes	.0	.1	.0	.1	.1	.4
5.6	4.4	4.9	All Other Non-Current	6.5	1.9	6.6	5.4	6.2	4.5
30.8	31.4	31.7	Net Worth	-11.0	30.2	3.2	37.2	35.8	33.6
100.0	100.0	100.0	Total Liabilities & Net Worth	100.0	100.0	100.0	100.0	100.0	100.0
			INCOME DATA						
100.0	100.0	100.0	Net Sales	100.0	100.0	100.0	100.0	100.0	100.0
18.6	17.4	19.0	Gross Profit	33.8	27.0	27.8	22.3	18.4	16.3
16.5	15.5	17.0	Operating Expenses	36.0	24.4	24.8	20.4	17.4	13.9
2.0	1.9	2.0	Operating Profit	-2.2	2.6	3.0	1.9	1.0	2.4
.4	.3	.3	All Other Expenses (net)	4.4	.8	.0	-.1	.2	.2
1.7	1.5	1.7	Profit Before Taxes	-6.6	1.8	3.0	2.0	.8	2.1
			RATIOS						
2.2	2.1	2.3	Current	3.1	3.9	3.4	3.0	2.6	2.0
1.4	1.4	1.5		.7	2.0	1.6	1.8	1.6	1.4
1.1	1.1	1.1		.3	1.2	1.1	1.2	1.2	1.1
1.1	1.1	1.3	Quick	3.1	1.6	2.5	1.7	1.4	1.1
.7	.7	.8		.4	1.0	.7	1.0	.8	.7
.5	.5	.5		.3	.5	.5	.5	.5	.5
13 27.6	15 24.0	12 30.2	Sales/Receivables	0 UND	3 108.8	4 102.5	6 56.9	15 25.2	13 27.9
23 16.1	24 15.2	23 15.7		15 23.9	15 24.4	23 16.0	23 15.5	24 14.9	23 15.8
33 11.0	35 10.4	34 10.7		57 6.4	43 8.5	39 9.5	41 8.9	37 10.0	33 11.1
16 22.9	16 23.3	15 24.5	Cost of Sales/Inventory	11 32.0	14 26.1	0 UND	15 23.6	16 22.7	14 26.7
27 13.5	27 13.6	26 14.1		52 7.0	34 10.8	29 12.6	28 13.1	30 12.1	24 15.0
43 8.5	44 8.3	44 8.4		224 1.6	76 4.8	57 6.4	68 5.3	47 7.8	38 9.7
10 35.3	10 37.2	10 35.6	Cost of Sales/Payables	0 UND	1 373.6	8 48.2	9 40.4	10 35.3	11 34.2
19 19.2	19 19.7	18 19.8		27 13.8	15 24.7	24 15.1	19 19.0	22 17.0	18 20.5
34 10.7	30 12.2	32 11.5		58 6.3	39 9.3	42 8.7	45 8.2	32 11.4	28 13.0
11.6	11.0	10.0	Sales/Working Capital	3.0	5.6	6.4	6.8	10.0	12.4
25.7	25.1	22.4		-57.0	11.3	21.0	14.9	19.9	27.0
62.4	80.8	72.9		-2.5	39.1	343.0	42.9	62.2	82.4
8.5	9.0	12.8	EBIT/Interest		8.8	5.6	16.6	10.2	17.3
(346) 2.9	(380) 3.6	(400) 4.6		(18) 2.6	(18) 2.7	(42) 6.9	(82) 3.0	(231) 5.3	
1.4	1.7	1.9			.5	1.2	1.9	1.4	2.7
7.6	7.0	8.9	Net Profit + Depr., Dep., Amort./Cur. Mat. L/T/D					11.7	9.7
(100) 2.4	(95) 3.7	(98) 3.2					(10) 3.3	(81) 3.4	
.9	1.5	1.5						.8	1.6
.1	.1	.1	Fixed/Worth	.0	.1	.1	.1	.1	.1
.5	.4	.4		2.8	.4	.5	.4	.3	.5
1.6	1.4	1.5		-6.5	NM	NM	1.0	1.0	1.6
1.1	1.3	1.1	Debt/Worth	1.0	.7	1.1	.6	1.1	1.2
2.7	2.7	2.4		-21.6	3.3	3.9	1.6	2.1	2.5
6.7	6.1	6.0		-3.0	NM	-34.4	4.5	4.9	5.7
41.1	42.3	42.2	% Profit Before Taxes/Tangible Net Worth		59.0	86.3	38.3	39.0	45.8
(344) 18.5	(378) 19.3	(407) 22.0		(22) 17.1	(15) 20.3	(39) 11.7	(88) 12.4	(238) 25.4	
6.3	7.2	8.3			3.6	4.1	4.6	3.7	12.6
11.0	11.3	13.4	% Profit Before Taxes/Total Assets	7.3	14.8	12.0	18.9	8.8	13.8
5.2	5.8	6.1		-.8	6.4	5.3	5.9	4.2	7.1
1.1	1.6	2.0		-4.4	.1	1.2	1.8	1.0	3.4
113.6	152.2	153.8	Sales/Net Fixed Assets	UND	368.5	301.1	140.8	140.1	153.5
39.5	50.5	47.5		4.1	58.8	54.8	48.9	50.2	39.2
13.7	16.7	14.8		1.0	15.1	12.6	15.2	21.1	14.5
6.7	6.9	6.9	Sales/Total Assets	4.1	6.9	7.3	6.6	6.5	7.1
4.7	5.0	4.7		1.7	3.4	4.7	4.5	4.7	5.0
3.1	3.2	3.0		.7	1.8	2.6	2.4	3.0	3.4
.2	.2	.2	% Depr., Dep., Amort./Sales		.1	.3	.3	.2	.2
(329) .5	(348) .5	(371) .5		(19) .5	(13) .8	(35) .8	(82) .5	(216) .5	
1.0	.9	1.0			1.3	2.6	2.1	.9	1.0
.6	.8	.6	% Officers', Directors' Owners' Comp/Sales			1.0	1.1	.6	.5
(134) 1.4	(144) 1.6	(169) 1.4				(12) 2.4	(23) 1.5	(51) 1.4	(71) .9
2.8	2.8	3.2				5.4	4.3	3.3	2.0
44906671M	47154033M	49142349M	Net Sales ($)	4273M	55360M	86210M	339521M	1520458M	47136527M
9537092M	9534459M	10066495M	Total Assets ($)	3836M	19824M	22918M	103705M	386623M	9529589M

© RMA 2010

M = $ thousand   MM = $ million
See Pages 9 through 22 for Explanation of Ratios and Data

Current Data Sorted by Assets | Comparative Historical Data

Current data date groups: **33 (4/1-9/30/09)**, **122 (10/1/09-3/31/10)**

	0-500M	500M-2MM	2-10MM	10-50MM	50-100MM	100-250MM		4/1/05-3/31/06 ALL	4/1/06-3/31/07 ALL
Type of Statement									
Unqualified			3	18	4	4		27	27
Reviewed			17	9	1			20	26
Compiled		7	13	1				10	11
Tax Returns	1	10	7	1				5	9
Other		7	13	26	10	3		48	51
NUMBER OF STATEMENTS	1	24	53	55	15	7		110	124
	%	%	%	%	%	%	ASSETS	%	%
		10.1	9.6	5.0	1.7		Cash & Equivalents	6.3	6.4
		40.9	34.1	32.9	25.6		Trade Receivables (net)	33.5	32.6
		22.9	31.9	31.0	37.6		Inventory	29.3	32.2
		4.7	1.5	3.1	3.0		All Other Current	2.0	2.5
		78.6	77.1	72.1	67.9		Total Current	71.1	73.7
		16.6	14.6	16.9	25.4		Fixed Assets (net)	19.4	16.5
		1.5	2.7	7.6	2.8		Intangibles (net)	2.7	4.0
		3.3	5.6	3.4	3.9		All Other Non-Current	6.9	5.7
		100.0	100.0	100.0	100.0		Total	100.0	100.0
							LIABILITIES		
		10.2	17.0	20.8	17.6		Notes Payable-Short Term	17.7	20.0
		2.6	2.4	1.9	2.2		Cur. Mat.-L.T.D.	2.7	2.8
		24.6	25.5	20.3	14.0		Trade Payables	21.8	22.0
		.0	.1	.3	.1		Income Taxes Payable	.2	.3
		12.6	7.3	5.5	7.7		All Other Current	7.7	7.4
		50.1	52.3	48.8	41.6		Total Current	50.2	52.4
		15.3	9.3	12.2	18.3		Long-Term Debt	13.9	12.1
		.0	.2	.3	.5		Deferred Taxes	.3	.5
		1.3	5.2	4.2	9.3		All Other Non-Current	5.4	3.7
		33.3	33.1	34.4	30.4		Net Worth	30.3	31.3
		100.0	100.0	100.0	100.0		Total Liabilities & Net Worth	100.0	100.0
							INCOME DATA		
		100.0	100.0	100.0	100.0		Net Sales	100.0	100.0
		26.0	17.8	16.0	15.3		Gross Profit	20.9	19.4
		21.1	15.2	13.9	12.8		Operating Expenses	18.2	16.7
		4.9	2.6	2.1	2.5		Operating Profit	2.7	2.6
		.5	.4	.8	.8		All Other Expenses (net)	.5	.4
		4.4	2.2	1.3	1.7		Profit Before Taxes	2.2	2.2
							RATIOS		
		2.3	2.2	1.8	2.5			2.0	2.4
		1.7	1.5	1.4	1.4	Current		1.3	1.4
		1.2	1.1	1.2	1.3			1.1	1.1
		1.8	1.3	1.1	1.4			1.4	1.5
		1.0	.7	.7	.8	Quick		.7	.7
		.6	.6	.5	.4			.5	.5
	19 19.5	**20** 18.0	**18** 20.6	**16** 22.7				**19** 19.1	**18** 20.3
	25 14.4	**29** 12.5	**28** 13.2	**27** 13.5		Sales/Receivables		**26** 14.2	**24** 15.5
	37 9.8	**41** 9.0	**34** 10.6	**39** 9.4				**40** 9.2	**36** 10.0
	13 28.2	**20** 18.7	**20** 18.2	**22** 17.0				**16** 23.3	**18** 20.8
	23 15.7	**37** 9.8	**27** 13.4	**59** 6.2		Cost of Sales/Inventory		**28** 12.8	**30** 12.3
	41 8.9	**59** 6.2	**41** 8.8	**61** 6.0				**48** 7.6	**54** 6.8
	6 60.5	**11** 33.6	**14** 25.4	**8** 45.4				**13** 28.0	**12** 30.0
	20 18.2	**25** 14.5	**21** 17.7	**19** 19.5		Cost of Sales/Payables		**22** 16.5	**20** 18.6
	33 11.0	**45** 8.2	**28** 13.0	**23** 15.6				**35** 10.5	**32** 11.4
		7.2	10.5	11.2	8.0			8.8	9.3
		18.8	19.1	19.8	11.4	Sales/Working Capital		25.2	18.8
		40.9	63.3	68.0	27.8			90.9	98.4
		20.6	8.6	9.0	5.4			7.6	8.2
	(21)	6.7	(50) 3.7	(52) 3.3	3.1	EBIT/Interest	(100)	3.2	(113) 3.3
		2.5	1.6	1.3	1.7			1.5	1.4
				10.4					9.2	10.4
			(18) 2.8			Net Profit + Depr., Dep., Amort./Cur. Mat. L/T/D	(35)	3.8	(42) 5.4
				1.3				1.1	1.7
		.0	.0	.2	.3			.2	.1
		.3	.4	.6	.9	Fixed/Worth		.6	.5
		1.5	1.6	1.9	1.1			1.4	1.1
		.6	1.0	1.3	1.8			1.0	.8
		2.0	2.6	3.2	2.2	Debt/Worth		3.2	2.9
		4.7	7.0	5.7	3.4			8.3	8.1
		57.7	43.7	68.8	31.3			34.9	37.8
	(21)	32.9	(46) 23.9	(50) 20.6	(14) 19.3	% Profit Before Taxes/Tangible Net Worth	(97)	17.6	(109) 21.5
		14.0	4.8	3.4	6.1			7.8	7.0
		24.6	11.9	12.2	9.2			9.6	14.3
		10.9	4.2	5.3	6.5	% Profit Before Taxes/Total Assets		4.8	5.6
		4.7	1.8	.8	1.7			1.6	1.5
		791.5	469.8	133.1	43.2			130.2	126.0
		41.9	51.3	29.1	21.3	Sales/Net Fixed Assets		39.4	38.1
		16.1	16.8	17.0	4.2			13.8	15.5
		7.2	6.7	5.8	6.4			6.1	6.1
		4.3	4.3	4.2	2.9	Sales/Total Assets		4.0	4.1
		2.8	2.3	2.4	1.8			2.4	2.7
		.2	.1	.2	.3			.3	.2
	(16)	.6	(42) .5	(48) .6	.6	% Depr., Dep., Amort./Sales	(91)	.6	(104) .5
		1.4	1.4	.9	1.1			1.7	1.0
		1.7	1.5	.8				.7	.7
	(12)	2.3	(19) 2.0	(16) 1.1		% Officers', Directors', Owners' Comp/Sales	(34)	1.7	(41) 1.4
		2.9	3.6	3.0				2.9	2.7
	3658M	156643M	1254550M	5572650M	4011649M	5552976M	Net Sales ($)	10650820M	13551278M
	267M	30142M	274093M	1217955M	1025780M	1065997M	Total Assets ($)	2445646M	2991634M

M = $ thousand   MM = $ million
See Pages 9 through 22 for Explanation of Ratios and Data

Comparative Historical Data

Current Data Sorted by Sales

					Type of Statement							
	30		45		29	Unqualified				1	2	27
	20		30		27	Reviewed					10	16
	12		18		21	Compiled		2	1	8	5	5
	11		20		19	Tax Returns		3	4	5	4	3
	53		50		59	Other		2	2	5	8	42
	4/1/07-		4/1/08-		4/1/09-			33 (4/1-9/30/09)		122 (10/1/09-3/31/10)		
	3/31/08		3/31/09		3/31/10							
	ALL		ALL		ALL		0-1MM	1-3MM	3-5MM	5-10MM	10-25MM	25MM & OVER
	126		163		155	NUMBER OF STATEMENTS		7	7	19	29	93
	%		%		%	ASSETS	%	%	%	%	%	%
	6.7		7.0		6.9	Cash & Equivalents				15.7	3.0	6.2
	34.5		32.3		33.4	Trade Receivables (net)	D			30.2	41.8	30.8
	30.4		32.1		30.5	Inventory	A			24.2	31.5	32.2
	2.9		3.1		2.9	All Other Current	T			3.1	2.7	2.9
	74.6		74.5		73.7	Total Current	A			73.1	79.1	72.0
	17.9		16.4		17.1	Fixed Assets (net)				18.1	13.8	17.7
	2.1		2.6		4.7	Intangibles (net)	N			2.2	4.0	5.9
	5.4		6.5		4.5	All Other Non-Current	O			6.7	3.0	4.4
	100.0		100.0		100.0	Total	T			100.0	100.0	100.0
					LIABILITIES	A					
	20.6		21.5		17.1	Notes Payable-Short Term	V			9.4	23.0	16.7
	2.1		2.4		2.3	Cur. Mat.-L.T.D.	A			2.8	2.2	2.1
	24.4		22.8		22.2	Trade Payables	I			22.4	25.7	21.1
	.1		.1		.2	Income Taxes Payable	L			.1	.4	.1
	8.7		7.9		7.6	All Other Current	A			5.1	7.8	7.1
	56.0		54.7		49.4	Total Current	B			39.8	59.1	47.1
	12.9		10.1		12.6	Long-Term Debt	L			25.9	7.7	12.7
	.2		.3		.2	Deferred Taxes	E			.1	.3	.1
	8.4		4.5		4.5	All Other Non-Current				2.9	5.8	4.8
	22.5		30.4		33.3	Net Worth				31.3	27.1	35.1
	100.0		100.0		100.0	Total Liabilties & Net Worth				100.0	100.0	100.0
					INCOME DATA						
	100.0		100.0		100.0	Net Sales				100.0	100.0	100.0
	19.5		17.2		18.3	Gross Profit				25.1	19.0	15.5
	16.3		14.6		15.5	Operating Expenses				20.4	17.0	13.2
	3.2		2.6		2.8	Operating Profit				4.7	2.1	2.3
	.8		.5		.6	All Other Expenses (net)				.6	.5	.6
	2.4		2.2		2.2	Profit Before Taxes				4.1	1.5	1.7
					RATIOS						
	2.1		1.8		2.1					4.5	1.5	2.1
	1.3		1.3		1.4	Current				1.8	1.2	1.5
	1.0		1.1		1.2					1.2	1.1	1.2
	1.2		1.1		1.2					3.5	.9	1.2
	.7		.6		.7	Quick				.8	.7	.7
	.4		.4		.5					.6	.4	.5
19	18.8	17	21.5	18	19.8					20 18.3	26 14.2	16 22.9
27	13.6	27	13.7	27	13.4	Sales/Receivables				30 12.1	30 12.2	24 15.2
40	9.1	36	10.2	36	10.1					42 8.6	45 8.1	34 10.8
16	22.4	18	20.6	19	18.8					14 25.8	16 22.5	19 18.7
29	12.5	29	12.4	29	12.4	Cost of Sales/Inventory				40 9.0	41 8.9	27 13.4
53	6.9	53	6.9	54	6.8					63 5.8	62 5.9	41 8.9
14	25.2	13	29.0	11	31.9					10 36.4	14 25.9	10 35.4
22	16.5	20	18.0	21	17.7	Cost of Sales/Payables				25 14.5	26 13.8	19 19.0
37	9.8	30	12.1	30	12.0					51 7.1	43 8.5	26 14.3
	11.3		11.7		9.6					6.2	12.9	11.1
	27.1		25.3		19.1	Sales/Working Capital				14.2	24.2	19.8
	106.6		112.2		65.0					21.1	60.5	65.9
	7.2		7.9		8.4					14.4	6.5	8.4
(118)	2.7	(155)	2.8	(144)	3.7	EBIT/Interest		(17)		2.7	3.3 (88)	3.8
	1.3		1.4		1.8					1.6	1.6	1.7
	10.7		5.3		8.2							10.4
(32)	3.6	(45)	2.2	(35)	2.6	Net Profit + Depr., Dep., Amort./Cur. Mat. L/T/D						(27) 5.1
	1.3		1.0		1.7							1.7
	.1		.1		.1					.1	.1	.1
	.5		.4		.5	Fixed/Worth				.8	.4	.5
	1.5		1.2		1.6					-1.5	1.8	1.3
	1.5		1.5		1.0					.5	2.4	1.2
	3.2		3.0		2.9	Debt/Worth				1.5	3.8	2.4
	7.0		7.1		5.7					-18.3	7.0	4.7
	50.1		50.3		52.0	% Profit Before Taxes/Tangible Net Worth				56.1	45.2	52.4
(109)	22.1	(149)	18.1	(138)	22.1			(14)		25.5 (25)	24.8 (86)	20.9
	8.6		7.1		6.5					11.0	3.0	6.1
	12.2		11.2		12.7					24.5	7.6	11.5
	4.1		4.3		6.0	% Profit Before Taxes/Total Assets				7.2	4.2	6.2
	1.5		1.4		1.9					2.7	1.1	2.0
	146.2		252.4		184.7					65.2	258.2	154.7
	35.4		45.3		34.3	Sales/Net Fixed Assets				34.2	59.9	31.6
	14.7		16.9		15.1					15.4	16.4	15.8
	5.7		6.3		6.3					5.2	6.8	6.9
	4.1		4.6		4.2	Sales/Total Assets				3.2	3.2	4.6
	2.6		2.4		2.4					2.2	2.1	2.8
	.3		.2		.2					.5	.1	.2
(97)	.5	(139)	.5	(126)	.6	% Depr., Dep., Amort./Sales		(15)		.9 (23)	.5 (81)	.6
	1.1		.9		1.1					1.4	1.3	1.0
	1.1		.8		1.2					1.5	1.1	.9
(39)	1.8	(52)	1.6	(48)	1.9	% Officers', Directors' Owners' Comp/Sales		(11)		1.9 (11)	2.2 (21)	1.6
	3.2		2.4		2.9					2.8	3.0	3.0
	13864858M		18021918M		16552126M	Net Sales ($)		15842M	29789M	139720M	496010M	15870765M
	3550459M		3751837M		3614234M	Total Assets ($)		7756M	13310M	47866M	171054M	3374248M

© RMA 2010

M = $ thousand   MM = $ million
See Pages 9 through 22 for Explanation of Ratios and Data

Current Data Sorted by Assets | Comparative Historical Data

						Type of Statement		
		4	10	3	7	Unqualified	15	16
		16	6	1		Reviewed	20	18
1	3	10	1			Compiled	12	21
1	3	3				Tax Returns	7	10
1	3	13	10	2	1	Other	25	33
	21 (4/1-9/30/09)		78 (10/1/09-3/31/10)				4/1/05-3/31/06	4/1/06-3/31/07
0-500M	500M-2MM	2-10MM	10-50MM	50-100MM	100-250MM		ALL	ALL
3	9	46	27	6	8	NUMBER OF STATEMENTS	79	98

0-500M %	500M-2MM %	2-10MM %	10-50MM %	50-100MM %	100-250MM %		ALL %	ALL %
						ASSETS		
		8.0	7.6			Cash & Equivalents	7.5	9.1
		37.0	32.6			Trade Receivables (net)	37.0	36.6
		24.6	26.5			Inventory	23.6	21.5
		2.0	4.0			All Other Current	2.7	2.6
		71.6	70.7			Total Current	70.9	69.8
		21.1	19.4			Fixed Assets (net)	22.5	19.9
		1.7	5.4			Intangibles (net)	2.6	4.8
		5.6	4.6			All Other Non-Current	4.0	5.4
		100.0	100.0			Total	100.0	100.0
						LIABILITIES		
		14.4	6.1			Notes Payable-Short Term	9.7	11.3
		2.6	3.9			Cur. Mat.-L.T.D.	2.5	2.1
		30.3	30.8			Trade Payables	32.8	32.9
		.3	.1			Income Taxes Payable	.1	.1
		7.3	9.8			All Other Current	7.8	8.2
		54.8	50.7			Total Current	53.0	54.7
		10.0	12.1			Long-Term Debt	13.6	11.8
		.1	.4			Deferred Taxes	.2	.2
		3.8	2.7			All Other Non-Current	3.6	3.3
		31.3	34.0			Net Worth	29.7	29.9
		100.0	100.0			Total Liabilities & Net Worth	100.0	100.0
						INCOME DATA		
		100.0	100.0			Net Sales	100.0	100.0
		21.4	18.2			Gross Profit	18.4	17.9
		18.7	15.1			Operating Expenses	15.2	15.5
		2.7	3.0			Operating Profit	3.2	2.4
		.4	.3			All Other Expenses (net)	.8	.3
		2.3	2.7			Profit Before Taxes	2.4	2.1
						RATIOS		
		1.9	1.7				1.8	1.7
		1.3	1.3			Current	1.3	1.3
		1.0	1.2				1.0	.9
		1.3	.9				1.2	1.2
		.8	.8			Quick	.8	.8
		.6	.7				.5	.5
		18 20.1	20 18.7				20 18.6	19 18.8
		31 11.8	27 13.6			Sales/Receivables	26 14.2	25 14.5
		37 9.8	33 11.2				33 11.2	37 9.8
		9 40.7	13 28.0				8 44.9	7 51.4
		14 25.3	23 15.9			Cost of Sales/Inventory	17 21.3	19 18.9
		49 7.5	52 7.0				35 10.4	32 11.4
		12 30.1	21 17.6				19 19.5	18 20.6
		24 15.0	27 13.4			Cost of Sales/Payables	25 14.8	26 14.2
		35 10.5	41 8.9				42 8.8	41 8.9
		12.8	11.6				11.8	14.7
		28.3	23.7			Sales/Working Capital	29.3	30.9
		-199.7	42.6				-999.8	-104.6
		11.2	20.7				11.3	16.3
		(40) 3.1	10.6			EBIT/Interest	(70) 3.1	(85) 3.8
		1.7	3.5				1.4	1.7
			12.5			Net Profit + Depr., Dep.,	7.6	10.1
			(12) 3.7			Amort./Cur. Mat. L/T/D	(19) 2.2	(18) 2.2
			3.0				.5	1.2
		.0	.2				.1	.1
		.6	.7			Fixed/Worth	.8	.7
		2.1	1.9				2.4	1.9
		.9	1.2				1.5	1.2
		2.3	2.7			Debt/Worth	2.8	3.6
		9.2	4.1				8.3	8.4
		39.9	77.6				39.9	49.8
		(39) 20.4	(26) 28.9			% Profit Before Taxes/Tangible Net Worth	(72) 11.4	(86) 22.5
		5.4	17.7				3.4	6.9
		13.8	14.5				10.8	14.0
		5.8	9.8			% Profit Before Taxes/Total Assets	3.5	5.9
		1.7	5.1				.7	2.0
		713.5	71.1				204.8	316.1
		31.0	20.9			Sales/Net Fixed Assets	31.5	31.6
		10.9	11.4				10.2	11.7
		6.5	5.6				6.1	6.2
		4.2	4.4			Sales/Total Assets	4.9	4.9
		3.0	2.8				3.1	2.6
		.2	.5				.3	.2
		(36) .7	(24) 1.1			% Depr., Dep., Amort./Sales	(64) .7	(77) .8
		2.5	2.1				1.5	1.6
		1.5	.5				.5	.6
		(17) 2.5	(11) 1.6			% Officers', Directors' Owners' Comp/Sales	(29) 1.4	(37) 2.0
		4.4	5.0				3.3	3.4
765M	66273M	1045891M	2814792M	2453551M	4985135M	Net Sales ($)	7493706M	9416886M
566M	9982M	222947M	688089M	448862M	1083126M	Total Assets ($)	1579367M	2360896M

M = $ thousand   MM = $ million
See Pages 9 through 22 for Explanation of Ratios and Data

Comparative Historical Data / Current Data Sorted by Sales

			Type of Statement	0-1MM	1-3MM	3-5MM	5-10MM	10-25MM	25MM & OVER
17	16	24	Unqualified				1		23
27	32	23	Reviewed			1	4	5	13
12	14	15	Compiled	1	1		2	5	6
7	13	7	Tax Returns	1		1	1	2	2
31	24	30	Other	1		1	4	9	15
4/1/07-3/31/08 ALL	4/1/08-3/31/09 ALL	4/1/09-3/31/10 ALL			21 (4/1-9/30/09)		78 (10/1/09-3/31/10)		
94	99	99	**NUMBER OF STATEMENTS**	3	1	3	12	21	59
%	%	%	**ASSETS**	%	%	%	%	%	%
8.1	12.3	9.0	Cash & Equivalents				6.3	7.2	8.1
37.6	35.3	35.0	Trade Receivables (net)				31.1	42.4	34.3
20.8	21.0	24.0	Inventory				26.4	20.7	23.8
2.0	2.7	3.1	All Other Current				8.3	1.3	3.1
68.5	71.3	71.1	Total Current				72.1	71.5	69.3
22.2	20.6	20.3	Fixed Assets (net)				19.3	18.5	22.1
3.6	3.8	3.0	Intangibles (net)				1.5	2.1	3.8
5.7	4.3	5.6	All Other Non-Current				7.1	7.9	4.8
100.0	100.0	100.0	Total				100.0	100.0	100.0
			LIABILITIES						
11.0	16.1	15.7	Notes Payable-Short Term				8.4	12.7	9.7
3.5	2.3	2.7	Cur. Mat.-L.T.D.				3.7	2.7	2.8
37.8	29.7	30.2	Trade Payables				22.5	35.6	30.8
.1	.1	.2	Income Taxes Payable				.4	.3	.1
9.1	9.0	8.5	All Other Current				9.1	5.3	10.4
61.5	57.2	57.3	Total Current				44.1	56.6	53.8
11.4	10.0	10.9	Long-Term Debt				9.9	10.4	11.3
.5	.3	.3	Deferred Taxes				.5	.0	.3
3.5	4.1	5.1	All Other Non-Current				7.8	3.8	3.1
23.0	28.4	26.4	Net Worth				37.8	29.1	31.5
100.0	100.0	100.0	Total Liabilities & Net Worth				100.0	100.0	100.0
			INCOME DATA						
100.0	100.0	100.0	Net Sales				100.0	100.0	100.0
15.9	17.1	19.8	Gross Profit				24.4	21.8	16.1
14.3	15.7	16.8	Operating Expenses				20.3	18.8	13.7
1.6	1.4	3.0	Operating Profit				4.1	3.0	2.4
.3	.4	.5	All Other Expenses (net)				.7	.5	.2
1.2	1.0	2.6	Profit Before Taxes				3.4	2.5	2.3
			RATIOS						
1.5	1.9	1.7	Current				2.8	2.1	1.6
1.1	1.3	1.3					1.8	1.2	1.3
.9	1.0	1.1					.9	1.0	1.1
1.0	1.3	1.1	Quick				1.6	1.7	1.0
.7	.8	.8					.8	.9	.8
.5	.6	.6					.3	.6	.6
18 19.9	16 22.6	18 20.3	Sales/Receivables				21 17.3	21 17.6	17 21.7
27 13.7	22 16.3	27 13.6					34 10.7	28 12.9	26 14.1
37 9.8	30 12.0	37 9.9					45 8.2	37 9.8	33 10.9
7 48.8	8 46.0	9 41.9	Cost of Sales/Inventory				10 35.9	8 44.3	9 38.7
16 22.6	15 23.8	15 23.7					21 17.3	14 26.5	16 23.4
34 10.6	28 13.0	48 7.6					74 4.9	41 8.9	39 9.5
21 17.8	14 26.9	14 26.6	Cost of Sales/Payables				13 29.2	12 30.1	18 20.4
29 12.6	19 19.6	25 14.7					21 17.7	25 14.6	24 15.1
44 8.4	29 12.7	37 9.9					32 11.3	49 7.4	35 10.6
17.5	13.8	12.6	Sales/Working Capital				8.2	14.7	16.7
121.6	39.0	29.7					12.9	39.2	31.2
-90.3	966.6	236.7					NM	NM	150.2
8.8	12.5	15.0	EBIT/Interest				6.0	12.1	18.1
(85) 3.2	(88) 4.9	(89) 6.0					(11) 2.9	(18) 5.4	(54) 8.0
1.3	1.6	2.2					1.1	2.2	2.7
3.6	3.6	8.0	Net Profit + Depr., Dep., Amort./Cur. Mat. L/T/D						13.4
(23) 2.0	(19) 2.4	(26) 3.5							(21) 3.9
.7	1.4	2.0							2.5
.2	.1	.0	Fixed/Worth				.0	.0	.2
1.0	.6	.7					.5	.5	.7
5.0	2.0	2.1					2.9	5.7	2.0
1.7	1.0	1.0	Debt/Worth				.5	1.0	1.2
4.6	2.4	2.7					1.4	2.5	2.7
13.0	6.4	6.4					55.6	13.6	4.5
49.2	44.8	50.6	% Profit Before Taxes/Tangible Net Worth				62.2	72.2	48.6
(80) 22.0	(85) 19.7	(85) 24.5					(11) 25.8	(17) 20.4	(53) 25.2
6.0	7.0	8.5					7.9	11.4	9.5
10.2	12.2	13.8	% Profit Before Taxes/Total Assets				18.0	20.5	13.6
4.2	6.3	7.4					5.2	7.8	8.6
.7	1.9	1.9					1.1	2.5	3.9
222.4	270.8	377.3	Sales/Net Fixed Assets				982.1	617.4	71.1
30.0	31.7	29.1					108.5	80.2	21.3
9.7	12.4	11.5					8.0	12.5	12.4
6.4	7.2	6.1	Sales/Total Assets				5.2	6.9	6.4
4.7	5.3	4.3					2.9	4.9	4.7
2.7	3.4	2.8					2.0	3.1	3.4
.3	.2	.4	% Depr., Dep., Amort./Sales					.1	.4
(79) .8	(80) .6	(78) .8						(16) .6	(52) .7
1.6	1.7	2.0						2.2	1.7
.7	1.1	.9	% Officers', Directors' Owners' Comp/Sales						.5
(32) 1.2	(47) 1.7	(34) 2.1							(22) 1.8
2.6	3.0	4.6							4.4
11461123M	9245984M	11366407M	Net Sales ($)	765M	1773M	11997M	88169M	325717M	10937986M
2643801M	2162218M	2453572M	Total Assets ($)	566M	572M	5271M	31232M	73799M	2342132M

© RMA 2010   M = $ thousand   MM = $ million
See Pages 9 through 22 for Explanation of Ratios and Data

Current Data Sorted by Assets   Comparative Historical Data

0-500M	500M-2MM	2-10MM	10-50MM	50-100MM	100-250MM	Type of Statement	4/1/05-3/31/06 ALL	4/1/06-3/31/07 ALL
		2	5	1	1	Unqualified	16	12
	2	6	5			Reviewed	11	15
1	1	5	2			Compiled	5	6
3	2	2				Tax Returns	4	4
	4	4	8	2	2	Other	14	12
	13 (4/1-9/30/09)		43 (10/1/09-3/31/10)					
4	9	19	18	3	3	NUMBER OF STATEMENTS	50	49
%	%	%	%	%	%	**ASSETS**	%	%
		6.4	6.1			Cash & Equivalents	4.1	6.4
		48.9	33.9			Trade Receivables (net)	34.8	43.6
		18.1	22.8			Inventory	20.9	18.7
		2.7	6.0			All Other Current	3.5	4.7
		76.1	68.8			Total Current	63.4	73.4
		13.2	17.7			Fixed Assets (net)	25.0	18.2
		1.9	2.5			Intangibles (net)	2.5	2.5
		8.9	11.0			All Other Non-Current	9.1	5.9
		100.0	100.0			Total	100.0	100.0
						LIABILITIES		
		17.8	11.5			Notes Payable-Short Term	18.3	14.9
		3.7	1.0			Cur. Mat.-L.T.D.	3.2	4.0
		31.7	27.4			Trade Payables	19.2	25.3
		.2	.3			Income Taxes Payable	.2	.1
		4.7	12.3			All Other Current	9.5	8.3
		58.1	52.5			Total Current	50.4	52.6
		9.2	7.1			Long-Term Debt	16.2	8.5
		.0	.2			Deferred Taxes	.0	.0
		3.7	2.3			All Other Non-Current	3.8	2.2
		28.9	37.9			Net Worth	29.5	36.7
		100.0	100.0			Total Liabilities & Net Worth	100.0	100.0
						INCOME DATA		
		100.0	100.0			Net Sales	100.0	100.0
		12.0	9.4			Gross Profit	16.5	16.9
		9.8	8.3			Operating Expenses	13.3	14.1
		2.2	1.1			Operating Profit	3.2	2.8
		.5	-.3			All Other Expenses (net)	.2	.3
		1.7	1.4			Profit Before Taxes	3.0	2.5
						RATIOS		
		1.7	1.9				1.9	2.2
		1.3	1.2			Current	1.4	1.5
		1.0	1.0				1.0	1.1
		1.4	1.0				1.3	1.5
		1.0	.7			Quick	.8	1.0
		.6	.3				.5	.6
		15 24.9	9 40.7				19 19.4	16 22.9
		21 17.8	16 22.8			Sales/Receivables	24 15.0	22 16.7
		29 12.5	24 15.1				34 10.7	29 12.6
		1 248.6	7 54.5				7 54.4	6 63.9
		7 54.7	8 43.4			Cost of Sales/Inventory	13 27.1	10 35.4
		26 14.3	27 13.4				40 9.1	24 15.4
		10 35.3	9 38.7				7 55.0	8 45.7
		14 25.4	13 27.3			Cost of Sales/Payables	15 24.2	15 24.8
		22 16.8	19 19.7				27 13.7	25 14.9
		19.6	17.8				11.5	16.4
		52.6	44.7			Sales/Working Capital	34.1	31.6
		282.1	-301.8				999.8	93.2
		36.5	89.7				11.9	7.3
		(17) 5.3	(15) 8.8			EBIT/Interest	(45) 4.5	(46) 2.4
		1.2	1.8				1.6	1.2
						Net Profit + Depr., Dep., Amort./Cur. Mat. L/T/D		
		.1	.1				.1	.0
		.4	.3			Fixed/Worth	.5	.2
		2.3	1.8				1.4	1.3
		.7	.8				1.1	.8
		3.6	2.6			Debt/Worth	2.2	1.9
		17.0	4.9				4.3	5.0
		82.8	44.5				44.3	37.5
		(16) 42.3	(17) 33.9			% Profit Before Taxes/Tangible Net Worth	(41) 23.3	(45) 15.7
		5.7	9.9				6.3	1.9
		25.5	19.7				14.3	17.5
		9.8	9.4			% Profit Before Taxes/Total Assets	7.5	4.5
		.9	3.7				1.4	.7
		517.9	207.7				277.5	999.8
		60.5	61.1			Sales/Net Fixed Assets	44.9	66.8
		29.0	18.9				4.7	14.0
		11.4	10.5				8.4	10.2
		7.7	7.1			Sales/Total Assets	5.2	7.0
		5.2	4.6				2.3	4.0
		.1	.0				.2	.1
		(17) .2	(15) .1			% Depr., Dep., Amort./Sales	(37) .8	(38) .4
		1.1	.7				2.9	1.7
		.2					.4	.5
		(10) .5				% Officers', Directors' Owners' Comp/Sales	(14) 1.1	(18) 1.2
		1.3					5.9	3.2
7039M	82587M	733151M	3040854M	1519133M	984069M	Net Sales ($)	3747196M	3555839M
1032M	10044M	91556M	416817M	259781M	579617M	Total Assets ($)	1200966M	1021766M

© RMA 2010

M = $ thousand   MM = $ million
See Pages 9 through 22 for Explanation of Ratios and Data

Comparative Historical Data | Current Data Sorted by Sales

					Type of Statement						
	12		13		9	Unqualified				1	1	7
	9		14		13	Reviewed				2	4	7
	9		9		7	Compiled					3	3
	2		2		7	Tax Returns	1	2	1	1	1	1
	17		19		20	Other	1			3	1	16
	4/1/07-		4/1/08-		4/1/09-			13 (4/1-9/30/09)		43 (10/1/09-3/31/10)		
	3/31/08		3/31/09		3/31/10		0-1MM	1-3MM	3-5MM	5-10MM	10-25MM	25MM & OVE
	ALL		ALL		ALL							
	49		57		56	NUMBER OF STATEMENTS	2	2	1	7	10	34
	%		%		%	ASSETS	%	%	%	%	%	%
	5.9		7.7		6.5	Cash & Equivalents					7.7	6.2
	43.2		40.3		39.9	Trade Receivables (net)					45.7	41.1
	20.4		22.5		20.2	Inventory					21.9	20.7
	3.1		3.6		4.9	All Other Current					.2	4.0
	72.6		74.2		71.5	Total Current					75.6	72.1
	19.7		18.9		18.1	Fixed Assets (net)					11.0	19.2
	2.6		2.3		2.0	Intangibles (net)					.9	2.2
	5.0		4.6		8.5	All Other Non-Current					12.6	6.5
	100.0		100.0		100.0	Total					100.0	100.0
						LIABILITIES						
	15.1		21.1		16.3	Notes Payable-Short Term					19.6	14.4
	3.4		2.4		2.9	Cur. Mat.-L.T.D.					1.3	2.5
	24.8		24.7		26.7	Trade Payables					28.1	28.2
	.1		.4		.2	Income Taxes Payable					.0	.3
	6.5		6.2		8.3	All Other Current					3.3	8.7
	49.9		54.8		54.4	Total Current					52.3	54.2
	11.1		10.2		10.4	Long-Term Debt					3.5	10.2
	.0		.1		.3	Deferred Taxes					.2	.4
	2.7		1.8		3.8	All Other Non-Current					10.8	1.6
	36.3		33.1		31.1	Net Worth					33.2	33.6
	100.0		100.0		100.0	Total Liabilties & Net Worth					100.0	100.0
						INCOME DATA						
	100.0		100.0		100.0	Net Sales					100.0	100.0
	15.8		13.3		13.9	Gross Profit					12.5	10.0
	13.0		11.3		11.8	Operating Expenses					11.2	8.1
	2.8		2.0		2.1	Operating Profit					1.4	1.9
	.2		.2		.2	All Other Expenses (net)					.3	.2
	2.6		1.8		1.9	Profit Before Taxes					1.1	1.7
						RATIOS						
	1.9		2.0		2.2						2.2	1.8
	1.4		1.2		1.3	Current					1.6	1.3
	1.1		1.0		1.0						1.1	1.0
	1.5		1.3		1.3						1.7	1.0
	1.0		.8		.8	Quick					1.1	.8
	.7		.7		.5						.6	.5
15	24.0	15	23.6	13	29.0					17	20.9	12	29.9
21	17.3	21	17.4	20	18.2	Sales/Receivables				25	14.6	18	20.1
29	12.5	29	12.6	29	12.7					37	9.8	25	14.5
6	65.5	6	62.3	5	71.8					2	219.0	6	63.8
10	35.2	14	26.4	10	37.0	Cost of Sales/Inventory				12	29.6	9	40.5
23	15.8	22	16.4	25	14.8					53	6.9	23	16.1
9	42.4	8	45.9	10	35.0					7	49.0	11	32.6
13	27.4	13	28.1	14	25.9	Cost of Sales/Payables				20	18.7	14	26.0
21	17.4	19	18.9	24	15.4					42	8.8	18	20.5
	21.5		21.3		14.5						13.0	19.7
	35.7		36.6		37.0	Sales/Working Capital					23.6	44.7
	97.2		254.3		271.7						92.7	NM
	9.5		8.3		22.6						17.1	32.3
(46)	3.8	(53)	4.9	(49)	6.3	EBIT/Interest					1.2	(29)	6.8
	1.7		1.8		1.2						-2.4	3.5
			24.3									
		(12)	9.4			Net Profit + Depr., Dep., Amort./Cur. Mat. L/T/D						
			3.9									
	.1		.1		.0						.0	.1
	.3		.4		.4	Fixed/Worth					.2	.7
	1.6		1.4		1.8						.9	1.9
	1.1		1.1		.9						.8	.8
	2.1		2.3		3.1	Debt/Worth					1.3	3.2
	4.2		4.6		6.8						6.9	5.5
	55.2		43.3		57.6							47.4
(47)	24.1	(51)	24.7	(49)	33.6	% Profit Before Taxes/Tangible Net Worth						(31)	33.9
	8.9		8.3		10.8							13.0
	18.1		15.4		19.3						22.3	18.5
	8.2		5.9		9.0	% Profit Before Taxes/Total Assets					.4	9.0
	2.9		1.2		1.3						-2.5	4.5
	690.3		668.2		736.2						999.8	590.7
	66.7		61.7		64.0	Sales/Net Fixed Assets					59.3	69.3
	12.3		18.8		16.4						23.1	17.9
	10.0		9.7		10.5						10.4	11.3
	6.9		7.2		7.0	Sales/Total Assets					6.5	7.2
	4.6		5.0		4.7						3.7	5.4
	.1		.1		.0							.0
(34)	.5	(45)	.3	(44)	.2	% Depr., Dep., Amort./Sales						(26)	.2
	1.7		.7		1.1							.6
	.3		.4		.3							.1
(15)	1.4	(14)	.9	(18)	1.1	% Officers', Directors' Owners' Comp/Sales						(10)	.4
	2.8		1.9		3.2							.7
4143212M		6232383M		6366833M		Net Sales ($)	1537M	2624M	4057M	63169M	153323M	6142123M
990984M		1228841M		1358847M		Total Assets ($)	353M	789M	415M	22043M	44504M	1290743M

© RMA 2010

M = $ thousand   MM = $ million
See Pages 9 through 22 for Explanation of Ratios and Data

Current Data Sorted by Assets							Comparative Historical Data	
	1	1	8		1	**Type of Statement** Unqualified	10	3
		16	4			Reviewed	15	15
	4	10	3			Compiled	22	18
2	7	4				Tax Returns	7	15
	4	6	5		1	Other	23	20
	24 (4/1-9/30/09)		53 (10/1/09-3/31/10)				4/1/05-3/31/06 ALL	4/1/06-3/31/07 ALL
0-500M	500M-2MM	2-10MM	10-50MM	50-100MM	100-250MM			
2	16	37	20		2	NUMBER OF STATEMENTS	77	71
%	%	%	%	%	%	**ASSETS**	%	%
	9.1	7.5	3.8	DATA NOT AVAILABLE		Cash & Equivalents	7.5	8.0
	28.5	25.7	33.4			Trade Receivables (net)	27.6	25.3
	34.7	35.1	32.8			Inventory	36.4	37.4
	1.8	2.2	2.0			All Other Current	1.5	2.1
	74.2	70.5	72.0			Total Current	72.9	72.8
	20.7	21.4	19.7			Fixed Assets (net)	19.1	19.5
	1.5	3.2	3.5			Intangibles (net)	2.9	2.8
	3.6	4.9	4.8			All Other Non-Current	5.0	4.8
	100.0	100.0	100.0			Total	100.0	100.0
						LIABILITIES		
	17.6	16.1	19.1			Notes Payable-Short Term	24.1	18.7
	.9	1.9	3.2			Cur. Mat.-L.T.D.	3.1	2.1
	16.8	20.1	18.7			Trade Payables	17.3	19.4
	.1	.2	.2			Income Taxes Payable	.2	.2
	4.8	5.2	4.5			All Other Current	5.8	10.1
	40.2	43.5	45.7			Total Current	50.5	50.4
	14.7	14.9	8.9			Long-Term Debt	9.5	13.4
	.1	.1	.7			Deferred Taxes	.4	.2
	6.2	9.3	2.4			All Other Non-Current	4.5	7.0
	38.9	32.2	42.3			Net Worth	35.1	29.0
	100.0	100.0	100.0			Total Liabilities & Net Worth	100.0	100.0
						INCOME DATA		
	100.0	100.0	100.0			Net Sales	100.0	100.0
	29.3	24.3	16.3			Gross Profit	23.3	24.7
	28.7	21.6	13.1			Operating Expenses	21.2	22.6
	.6	2.7	3.2			Operating Profit	2.1	2.1
	.8	.5	-.1			All Other Expenses (net)	.9	.6
	-.2	2.2	3.3			Profit Before Taxes	1.3	1.4
						RATIOS		
	3.5	2.3	2.1				2.6	2.6
	1.9	1.6	1.5			Current	1.3	1.4
	1.1	1.2	1.2				1.1	1.1
	1.5	1.1	1.2				1.3	1.0
	.9	.8	.7			Quick	.6	.6
	.6	.5	.6				.4	.5
	13 27.7	**18** 20.0	**24** 15.4				**18** 20.4	**13** 27.4
	19 19.5	**26** 13.8	**30** 12.2			Sales/Receivables	**29** 12.8	**26** 14.0
	34 10.6	**38** 9.7	**40** 9.1				**39** 9.5	**37** 9.8
	20 18.2	**33** 11.2	**19** 19.1				**27** 13.4	**25** 14.3
	37 9.8	**56** 6.5	**41** 8.9			Cost of Sales/Inventory	**51** 7.1	**51** 7.1
	60 6.1	**72** 5.1	**57** 6.4				**69** 5.3	**82** 4.5
	7 49.6	**12** 29.5	**7** 52.3				**9** 41.1	**9** 39.8
	19 18.8	**28** 13.2	**15** 24.2			Cost of Sales/Payables	**20** 18.5	**22** 16.3
	34 10.8	**40** 9.2	**31** 11.8				**33** 11.0	**35** 10.4
	8.3	7.0	9.1				8.0	8.6
	13.7	15.4	17.9			Sales/Working Capital	13.6	16.8
	58.8	41.3	33.3				56.1	72.2
	7.0	10.5	17.0				4.8	7.2
	1.5	(34) 3.8	6.7			EBIT/Interest	(72) 2.1	(67) 2.5
	-.4	1.4	4.0				1.1	.3
		13.2					3.3	9.8
		(10) 4.4				Net Profit + Depr., Dep., Amort./Cur. Mat. L/T/D	(24) 1.5	(16) 3.2
		1.0					.2	1.0
	.1	.1	.2				.1	.2
	.3	.5	.4			Fixed/Worth	.5	.4
	1.4	1.8	.9				1.5	1.3
	.6	.9	.9				.8	.7
	1.8	2.8	1.8			Debt/Worth	2.3	2.4
	7.4	7.2	2.3				4.6	5.7
	36.1	28.7	42.7				28.7	49.8
	(15) 5.4	(32) 17.2	(19) 28.2			% Profit Before Taxes/Tangible Net Worth	(74) 11.1	(64) 17.6
	-16.0	7.3	14.8				1.6	-.1
	7.4	11.1	15.5				7.2	10.1
	1.3	5.8	11.7			% Profit Before Taxes/Total Assets	3.0	4.5
	-2.9	1.7	5.3				.2	-2.4
	104.4	106.4	189.7				84.7	72.3
	53.8	25.1	24.9			Sales/Net Fixed Assets	27.5	26.5
	10.5	9.3	9.2				9.9	10.9
	5.0	4.4	5.4				4.7	5.3
	3.8	3.1	3.5			Sales/Total Assets	3.5	3.4
	3.0	2.3	2.4				2.1	2.4
	.1	.2	.2				.4	.3
	(13) .6	(34) .6	(16) .5			% Depr., Dep., Amort./Sales	(64) .8	(65) .9
	1.8	1.8	1.4				1.6	2.1
	1.5	1.4					1.0	.8
	(12) 2.9	(25) 2.5				% Officers', Directors' Owners' Comp/Sales	(35) 1.9	(38) 2.1
	5.5	5.1					4.3	4.2
1286M	**89166M**	**746649M**	**1752077M**		**313217M**	Net Sales ($)	**2998040M**	**1714281M**
513M	**19306M**	**195722M**	**407491M**		**271355M**	Total Assets ($)	**904151M**	**514728M**

M = $ thousand MM = $ million
See Pages 9 through 22 for Explanation of Ratios and Data

Comparative Historical Data   Current Data Sorted by Sales

	7 18 15 12 21 4/1/07- 3/31/08 ALL	8 16 17 9 27 4/1/08- 3/31/09 ALL	11 20 17 13 16 4/1/09- 3/31/10 ALL	Type of Statement	0-1MM	1-3MM	3-5MM	5-10MM	10-25MM	25MM & OVE
Unqualified						2	1	1	1	9
Reviewed						1	4	3	9	8
Compiled							1	3	8	3
Tax Returns					2	1		4	1	1
Other								3	4	7
					24 (4/1-9/30/09)			53 (10/1/09-3/31/10)		
NUMBER OF STATEMENTS	73	77	77		2	4	6	14	23	28
	%	%	%		%	%	%	%	%	%
ASSETS										
Cash & Equivalents	7.4	6.7	6.6					10.2	6.1	4.4
Trade Receivables (net)	27.3	29.8	27.3					26.9	27.8	32.8
Inventory	37.3	36.4	33.7					36.2	32.8	32.9
All Other Current	3.0	3.4	3.0					1.3	2.3	4.3
Total Current	75.0	76.3	70.7					74.6	68.9	74.4
Fixed Assets (net)	18.2	16.3	21.2					20.0	21.6	16.8
Intangibles (net)	2.3	3.2	3.2					.7	3.8	3.6
All Other Non-Current	4.5	4.2	4.9					4.8	5.6	5.1
Total	100.0	100.0	100.0					100.0	100.0	100.0
LIABILITIES										
Notes Payable-Short Term	15.7	16.9	18.2					17.0	15.9	18.5
Cur. Mat.-L.T.D.	3.4	1.2	2.0					1.4	2.0	2.7
Trade Payables	18.3	19.9	18.8					17.1	18.0	21.3
Income Taxes Payable	.1	.1	.2					.0	.3	.2
All Other Current	12.8	10.2	8.8					3.1	7.2	7.3
Total Current	50.1	48.3	47.9					38.6	43.4	50.1
Long-Term Debt	13.0	9.5	12.5					10.9	11.9	10.4
Deferred Taxes	.4	.2	.2					.0	.2	.5
All Other Non-Current	12.1	3.1	6.5					18.6	6.3	2.7
Net Worth	24.4	38.9	32.8					31.8	38.2	36.3
Total Liabilities & Net Worth	100.0	100.0	100.0					100.0	100.0	100.0
INCOME DATA										
Net Sales	100.0	100.0	100.0					100.0	100.0	100.0
Gross Profit	27.1	22.2	23.1					21.8	28.7	15.4
Operating Expenses	24.4	19.3	20.8					20.0	25.6	12.7
Operating Profit	2.7	3.0	2.3					1.8	3.1	2.7
All Other Expenses (net)	.6	.3	.5					.8	.1	.2
Profit Before Taxes	2.2	2.7	1.8					1.0	3.0	2.5
RATIOS										
Current	3.1	2.7	2.6					5.0	2.2	2.0
	1.5	1.5	1.6					1.6	1.6	1.4
	1.1	1.2	1.2					1.1	1.2	1.2
Quick	1.1	1.2	1.2					3.5	1.2	1.1
	.6	.7	.8					.8	.8	.7
	.4	.5	.5					.5	.5	.5
Sales/Receivables	16 22.5	18 19.9	17 21.3					16 23.3	20 18.2	17 21.5
	25 14.3	27 13.7	27 13.7					26 13.8	27 13.3	29 12.4
	36 10.1	34 10.8	37 9.9					44 8.2	38 9.7	38 9.5
Cost of Sales/Inventory	29 12.8	27 13.7	25 14.8					32 11.3	20 18.4	16 22.3
	53 6.9	48 7.7	46 7.9					53 6.9	46 7.9	40 9.1
	73 5.0	70 5.2	66 5.5					76 4.8	67 5.4	57 6.4
Cost of Sales/Payables	9 38.6	9 42.5	10 36.8					11 34.7	9 41.0	8 43.3
	22 16.8	19 19.7	22 16.9					21 17.6	28 12.9	18 20.5
	41 9.0	36 10.0	37 9.8					42 8.7	38 9.6	31 11.8
Sales/Working Capital	8.3	8.3	8.4					3.8	8.9	9.4
	15.4	15.0	16.7					12.7	15.4	21.5
	36.0	31.2	41.7					48.3	39.1	41.8
EBIT/Interest	9.2	9.0	9.6					8.2	10.6	17.0
	(68) 2.6	(72) 3.8	(74) 4.0					(12) 1.9	(22) 6.1	5.8
	1.2	1.5	1.3					-6.1	1.7	2.1
Net Profit + Depr., Dep., Amort./Cur. Mat. L/T/D	4.0	2.9	15.1							
	(17) 2.0	(15) 2.0	(17) 3.2							
	1.2	.5	1.0							
Fixed/Worth	.1	.1	.1					.1	.2	.1
	.4	.4	.4					.3	.4	.4
	2.0	.8	1.3					1.9	1.0	.9
Debt/Worth	.8	.7	.9					.5	.8	1.0
	2.2	1.8	1.9					1.6	1.8	1.9
	9.8	4.7	4.9					19.4	7.2	3.2
% Profit Before Taxes/Tangible Net Worth	40.7	43.3	34.8					39.9	42.8	39.9
	(60) 14.0	(71) 15.3	(68) 17.5					(13) 10.3	(21) 25.9	(25) 19.8
	5.3	5.0	5.7					-7.2	7.8	9.5
% Profit Before Taxes/Total Assets	14.2	14.8	12.1					11.8	12.4	12.6
	4.1	6.5	6.3					3.7	7.8	7.9
	.6	1.0	.9					-5.0	2.2	2.8
Sales/Net Fixed Assets	93.9	165.8	106.9					88.9	105.8	246.3
	46.1	40.6	30.1					32.9	33.6	28.8
	10.8	13.0	9.3					5.4	9.4	16.0
Sales/Total Assets	5.2	5.0	4.6					4.7	4.0	6.1
	3.5	3.7	3.3					2.8	3.2	4.3
	2.4	2.5	2.4					1.6	2.5	2.6
% Depr., Dep., Amort./Sales	.3	.2	.2					.3	.2	.1
	(62) .6	(69) .6	(67) .6					(12) 1.0	(20) .8	(24) .5
	2.0	1.3	1.6					2.0	1.9	1.3
% Officers', Directors' Owners' Comp/Sales	1.4	1.0	1.1						1.5	.7
	(33) 2.4	(31) 2.2	(45) 2.2					(16)	3.2	(13) 1.1
	4.8	4.2	4.8						5.5	1.8
Net Sales ($)	2147674M	3159738M	2902395M		1286M	8222M	25203M	109511M	363855M	2394318M
Total Assets ($)	661605M	998253M	894387M		513M	3305M	8861M	44755M	117616M	719337M

M = $ thousand   MM = $ million
See Pages 9 through 22 for Explanation of Ratios and Data

| Current Data Sorted by Assets | | | | | | | | Comparative Historical Data | |

	0-500M	500M-2MM	2-10MM	10-50MM	50-100MM	100-250MM	Type of Statement	4/1/05-3/31/06 ALL	4/1/06-3/31/07 ALL
			6	20	7	2	Unqualified	41	42
	1	4	44	12	1		Reviewed	49	55
	1	10	16	2	1		Compiled	40	34
	4	14	17				Tax Returns	31	26
		14	30	33	11	7	Other	77	82
		56 (4/1-9/30/09)		201 (10/1/09-3/31/10)					
NUMBER OF STATEMENTS	6	42	113	67	20	9		238	239
	%	%	%	%	%	%	**ASSETS**	%	%
		12.3	6.4	2.8	3.2		Cash & Equivalents	5.5	5.6
		38.0	40.0	31.4	22.9		Trade Receivables (net)	35.4	37.2
		26.6	31.7	43.9	37.8		Inventory	34.9	34.8
		1.0	1.3	3.3	3.6		All Other Current	3.3	2.5
		78.0	79.4	81.4	67.5		Total Current	79.1	80.0
		11.9	14.0	12.0	23.0		Fixed Assets (net)	14.2	13.4
		1.3	2.6	3.9	5.8		Intangibles (net)	1.9	2.1
		8.8	4.0	2.7	3.8		All Other Non-Current	4.7	4.5
		100.0	100.0	100.0	100.0		Total	100.0	100.0
							LIABILITIES		
		12.6	20.5	27.7	28.9		Notes Payable-Short Term	25.4	26.9
		1.5	3.7	1.9	1.7		Cur. Mat.-L.T.D.	1.7	2.1
		26.8	25.8	21.4	16.2		Trade Payables	22.9	23.8
		.1	.0	.1	.1		Income Taxes Payable	.2	.1
		6.3	6.9	5.6	3.6		All Other Current	5.5	8.0
		47.3	56.9	56.7	50.5		Total Current	55.7	60.8
		9.4	8.9	8.3	9.1		Long-Term Debt	8.5	6.7
		.0	.2	.3	.0		Deferred Taxes	.3	.3
		9.0	4.3	6.8	1.4		All Other Non-Current	6.7	6.1
		34.3	29.7	28.0	39.0		Net Worth	28.9	26.1
		100.0	100.0	100.0	100.0		Total Liabilities & Net Worth	100.0	100.0
							INCOME DATA		
		100.0	100.0	100.0	100.0		Net Sales	100.0	100.0
		16.1	14.6	11.6	19.1		Gross Profit	14.4	14.3
		14.3	13.0	8.7	16.8		Operating Expenses	12.8	12.0
		1.9	1.5	2.9	2.3		Operating Profit	1.6	2.4
		.3	.5	.7	1.0		All Other Expenses (net)	.5	.8
		1.6	1.0	2.2	1.3		Profit Before Taxes	1.1	1.6
							RATIOS		
		2.2	2.0	1.8	1.7		Current	1.9	1.7
		1.6	1.4	1.3	1.4			1.4	1.3
		1.1	1.1	1.2	1.1			1.1	1.1
		1.6	1.2	.7	.8		Quick	1.1	1.0
		1.1	.8	.6	.5			.7	.7
		.7	.6	.6	.4			.5	.5
		15 24.2	24 15.0	26 14.0	26 14.2		Sales/Receivables	22 16.9	24 15.3
		23 15.6	29 12.4	31 11.8	34 10.9			32 11.3	34 10.9
		42 8.6	39 9.3	39 9.3	37 9.9			41 8.8	42 8.7
		6 62.2	11 31.9	33 11.1	32 11.4		Cost of Sales/Inventory	14 26.6	16 22.5
		20 18.6	31 11.8	48 7.6	54 6.7			36 10.3	38 9.6
		46 7.9	55 6.7	77 4.8	96 3.8			70 5.2	68 5.4
		9 38.5	13 27.8	12 31.7	19 18.8		Cost of Sales/Payables	9 41.0	11 32.7
		21 17.1	22 16.9	24 15.0	27 13.5			21 17.1	24 15.3
		33 10.9	33 11.2	37 9.9	39 9.4			31 11.9	37 9.8
		10.2	10.9	9.2	10.2		Sales/Working Capital	9.8	10.5
		17.1	20.2	15.9	18.5			18.7	21.9
		72.7	61.5	40.0	89.2			63.4	81.3
		16.3	11.5	6.6	3.9		EBIT/Interest	7.3	5.0
		(39) 2.8	(104) 3.2	(66) 3.8	(19) 2.7			(222) 2.7	(228) 2.4
		1.2	1.0	2.0	1.1			1.4	1.1
			19.3	6.7			Net Profit + Depr., Dep., Amort./Cur. Mat. L/T/D	8.9	11.9
		(20) 2.0	(29) 4.5					(48) 3.7	(61) 4.3
		.9	2.7					1.4	1.5
		.0	.0	.0	.1		Fixed/Worth	.0	.1
		.1	.2	.2	.6			.2	.3
		.8	.9	1.1	.9			1.0	.9
		.9	1.3	1.7	1.1		Debt/Worth	1.3	1.5
		2.0	2.9	3.3	2.0			3.1	3.3
		5.9	8.5	5.8	8.3			6.7	8.0
		46.9	42.7	39.9	18.5		% Profit Before Taxes/Tangible Net Worth	37.4	35.8
		(38) 13.0	(102) 15.4	(61) 21.0	(19) 10.5			(220) 18.2	(216) 18.1
		5.6	1.3	9.0	.5			4.5	4.0
		11.9	10.6	11.0	4.2		% Profit Before Taxes/Total Assets	10.6	9.4
		3.6	3.4	4.7	2.0			3.9	4.7
		1.4	.1	2.2	.3			.8	.7
		750.7	337.2	573.9	238.7		Sales/Net Fixed Assets	508.9	351.4
		84.6	82.1	77.6	22.0			81.4	79.0
		25.1	24.2	24.8	4.3			20.3	22.4
		6.9	5.8	4.6	3.2		Sales/Total Assets	5.9	5.6
		5.3	4.3	3.8	2.7			4.0	3.9
		3.4	3.2	2.5	1.3			2.6	2.7
		.2	.1	.1	.1		% Depr., Dep., Amort./Sales	.1	.1
		(32) .5	(91) .4	(59) .3	(17) .5			(190) .4	(197) .4
		1.0	.8	.8	2.3			1.0	.9
		.9	.9	.5			% Officers', Directors' Owners' Comp/Sales	.8	.7
		(26) 1.5	(54) 1.7	(20) .9				(100) 1.6	(97) 1.6
		3.9	2.3	1.8				2.9	3.1
	21108M	282489M	2529884M	5591046M	3834933M	3371096M	Net Sales ($)	11902660M	12728433M
	1801M	51592M	565185M	1587298M	1564745M	1403503M	Total Assets ($)	3912246M	4429787M

M = $ thousand   MM = $ million
See Pages 9 through 22 for Explanation of Ratios and Data

Comparative Historical Data | Current Data Sorted by Sales

Type of Statement	4/1/07-3/31/08 ALL	4/1/08-3/31/09 ALL	4/1/09-3/31/10 ALL	0-1MM	1-3MM	3-5MM	5-10MM	10-25MM	25MM & OVER
Unqualified	40	42	35		1	1	2	1	30
Reviewed	47	59	62				6	30	26
Compiled	30	31	30		3	1	7	11	8
Tax Returns	21	33	35	1	4	6	8	13	3
Other	104	112	95	1	3		13	17	61
				_____56 (4/1-9/30/09)_____			_____201 (10/1/09-3/31/10)_____		
NUMBER OF STATEMENTS	242	277	257	2	11	8	36	72	128

ASSETS

	'07-'08 ALL %	'08-'09 ALL %	'09-'10 ALL %	0-1MM %	1-3MM %	3-5MM %	5-10MM %	10-25MM %	25MM & OVER %
Cash & Equivalents	6.2	8.0	6.2		13.5		9.3	8.3	3.5
Trade Receivables (net)	36.3	32.8	35.3		20.8		33.8	38.7	35.1
Inventory	35.7	34.4	35.0		30.7		28.6	29.3	40.3
All Other Current	2.8	2.4	2.0		1.4		1.0	1.7	2.6
Total Current	81.1	77.6	78.5		66.4		72.7	78.0	81.4
Fixed Assets (net)	13.1	15.3	14.0		17.1		18.8	14.0	12.1
Intangibles (net)	2.2	2.7	2.9		.3		2.1	3.2	3.1
All Other Non-Current	3.6	4.4	4.6		16.2		6.4	4.8	3.3
Total	100.0	100.0	100.0		100.0		100.0	100.0	100.0

LIABILITIES

	'07-'08 ALL	'08-'09 ALL	'09-'10 ALL	0-1MM	1-3MM	3-5MM	5-10MM	10-25MM	25MM & OVER
Notes Payable-Short Term	24.3	24.0	22.1		23.8		16.5	16.2	27.8
Cur. Mat.-L.T.D.	2.8	2.0	3.1		7.1		5.6	3.2	2.0
Trade Payables	25.1	23.0	23.7		14.9		19.4	27.2	23.7
Income Taxes Payable	.1	.1	.1		.2		.1	.0	.1
All Other Current	8.0	8.4	6.2		9.1		7.5	5.2	6.3
Total Current	60.3	57.5	55.1		55.1		49.0	51.9	59.8
Long-Term Debt	7.2	9.1	9.8		11.5		12.1	10.9	6.0
Deferred Taxes	.3	.2	.2		.0		.5	.2	.2
All Other Non-Current	5.8	4.5	5.5		6.7		8.2	4.4	4.2
Net Worth	26.4	28.7	29.4		26.7		30.2	32.7	29.7
Total Liabilities & Net Worth	100.0	100.0	100.0		100.0		100.0	100.0	100.0

INCOME DATA

	'07-'08 ALL	'08-'09 ALL	'09-'10 ALL	0-1MM	1-3MM	3-5MM	5-10MM	10-25MM	25MM & OVER
Net Sales	100.0	100.0	100.0		100.0		100.0	100.0	100.0
Gross Profit	14.6	15.2	14.5		25.7		15.6	14.8	12.0
Operating Expenses	12.4	13.1	12.5		24.0		14.4	12.9	9.8
Operating Profit	2.2	2.1	2.0		1.7		1.2	1.8	2.2
All Other Expenses (net)	.8	.6	.5		-.1		.8	.4	.6
Profit Before Taxes	1.4	1.5	1.5		1.9		.4	1.4	1.6

RATIOS

	'07-'08 ALL	'08-'09 ALL	'09-'10 ALL	0-1MM	1-3MM	3-5MM	5-10MM	10-25MM	25MM & OVER
Current	1.8	1.8	1.8		2.0		2.8	2.1	1.6
	1.3	1.4	1.4		1.4		1.4	1.5	1.3
	1.1	1.1	1.1		.9		1.0	1.2	1.1
Quick	1.0	1.0	1.1		1.0		1.4	1.4	.8
	.6	.7	.7		.6		1.0	.8	.6
	.5	.5	.5		.4		.6	.6	.4
Sales/Receivables	23 16.0	22 16.9	23 15.8		13 27.2		20 18.4	24 15.4	25 14.9
	31 11.6	29 12.8	29 12.4		20 18.4		25 14.6	32 11.5	30 12.3
	40 9.1	37 9.7	39 9.4		33 11.2		44 8.4	43 8.4	36 10.0
Cost of Sales/Inventory	14 25.3	14 25.3	16 22.7		27 13.6		6 65.5	10 35.3	24 15.1
	37 9.8	35 10.5	39 9.5		46 7.9		30 12.0	29 12.7	43 8.6
	66 5.5	59 6.2	58 6.3		133 2.7		53 6.8	54 6.7	61 6.0
Cost of Sales/Payables	13 29.1	12 29.5	13 27.8		11 33.1		4 96.4	17 22.1	16 22.7
	23 15.7	22 17.0	22 16.3		21 17.4		20 18.7	22 16.8	24 15.0
	36 10.0	31 11.9	33 11.0		39 9.3		33 11.1	34 10.7	32 11.3
Sales/Working Capital	10.7	10.6	10.3		7.1		5.7	11.1	11.0
	21.2	18.9	17.5		15.7		20.2	16.9	19.5
	70.0	57.0	56.4		-17.5		NM	36.7	52.0
EBIT/Interest	5.6	6.4	7.8		11.4		5.4	9.9	7.6
	(228) 2.6	(257) 2.5	(243) 3.1		(10) 3.7		(35) 1.4	(64) 3.3	(124) 3.2
	1.4	1.2	1.3		-.4		-.3	1.1	1.6
Net Profit + Depr., Dep., Amort./Cur. Mat. L/T/D	8.5	12.4	7.5					21.5	7.4
	(57) 4.9	(70) 2.9	(64) 3.9					(15) 2.0	(41) 4.5
	1.6	1.5	1.0					1.0	1.5
Fixed/Worth	.1	.1	.0		.1		.1	.0	.0
	.3	.3	.3		.5		.4	.1	.3
	.9	1.1	1.0		.8		3.9	.9	.9
Debt/Worth	1.5	1.3	1.4		.7		.8	1.2	1.5
	3.4	2.7	2.9		2.6		2.2	2.7	3.0
	7.7	7.5	7.7		34.0		20.4	6.0	6.4
% Profit Before Taxes/Tangible Net Worth	35.5	38.8	39.3				31.2	33.2	37.8
	(218) 19.4	(250) 14.9	(232) 15.3				(28) 5.7	(68) 10.7	(119) 18.5
	7.6	5.0	4.5				.4	3.3	6.5
% Profit Before Taxes/Total Assets	10.1	10.2	10.4		15.1		9.7	11.6	9.9
	4.1	3.9	3.8		2.8		1.6	3.4	4.2
					-.5		-4.0	.4	1.6
Sales/Net Fixed Assets	339.4	315.4	385.6		999.8		215.6	341.7	540.3
	74.7	64.3	79.9		27.4		56.0	125.5	79.0
	24.6	18.2	20.8		8.1		11.8	28.1	24.8
Sales/Total Assets	5.6	5.5	5.3		4.4		6.2	5.7	5.0
	4.0	3.9	4.1		2.0		3.9	4.3	4.0
	2.9	2.8	2.7		1.3		2.7	3.1	2.8
% Depr., Dep., Amort./Sales	.1	.1	.1				.2	.1	.1
	(203) .3	(231) .4	(212) .4				(30) .5	(61) .3	(104) .3
	.8	1.0	.9				1.1	.9	.4
% Officers', Directors' Owners' Comp/Sales	.7	.8	.8				1.0	.9	.5
	(89) 1.5	(108) 1.5	(110) 1.3				(18) 1.6	(42) 1.6	(36) 1.6
	3.9	2.9	2.4				3.3	2.1	1.8
Net Sales ($)	12960161M	16806383M	15630556M	1354M	21734M	30456M	267304M	1182737M	14126971M
Total Assets ($)	3992636M	5148197M	5174124M	644M	11597M	10032M	90314M	393983M	4667554M

M = $ thousand   MM = $ million
See Pages 9 through 22 for Explanation of Ratios and Data

Current Data Sorted by Assets   Comparative Historical Data

Type of Statement	0-500M	500M-2MM	2-10MM	10-50MM	50-100MM	100-250MM		4/1/05-3/31/06 ALL	4/1/06-3/31/07 ALL
Unqualified			7	14	6	5		29	27
Reviewed		2	39	11				43	56
Compiled	5	12	24	4				48	38
Tax Returns	2	10	8					12	14
Other	2	12	24	18	9	4		78	60
		33 (4/1-9/30/09)		185 (10/1/09-3/31/10)					
NUMBER OF STATEMENTS	9	36	102	47	15	9		210	195
ASSETS	%	%	%	%	%	%		%	%
Cash & Equivalents		13.8	6.2	8.6	1.7			6.6	8.3
Trade Receivables (net)		41.6	39.3	34.2	29.8			41.0	37.4
Inventory		19.1	29.5	22.7	30.2			26.3	24.8
All Other Current		2.0	3.0	1.8	5.5			1.9	1.7
Total Current		76.5	78.0	67.3	67.2			75.7	72.4
Fixed Assets (net)		14.4	14.6	22.4	19.0			16.9	19.1
Intangibles (net)		6.3	3.4	4.9	11.0			2.9	3.6
All Other Non-Current		2.8	4.1	5.4	2.8			4.5	5.0
Total		100.0	100.0	100.0	100.0			100.0	100.0
LIABILITIES									
Notes Payable-Short Term		9.3	20.6	19.0	11.9			21.4	16.9
Cur. Mat.-L.T.D.		1.4	1.8	1.9	1.5			2.4	2.5
Trade Payables		19.2	19.8	14.4	20.8			23.6	22.2
Income Taxes Payable		.5	.3	.1	.0			.1	.2
All Other Current		8.1	6.7	8.4	8.9			8.3	8.3
Total Current		38.4	49.2	43.9	43.2			55.7	50.2
Long-Term Debt		19.5	5.2	14.4	19.6			8.8	12.2
Deferred Taxes		.1	.1	.1	.5			.1	.1
All Other Non-Current		14.0	7.0	4.8	2.2			4.8	4.1
Net Worth		28.0	38.4	36.7	34.5			30.5	33.4
Total Liabilities & Net Worth		100.0	100.0	100.0	100.0			100.0	100.0
INCOME DATA									
Net Sales		100.0	100.0	100.0	100.0			100.0	100.0
Gross Profit		19.2	14.8	16.7	12.0			14.7	15.1
Operating Expenses		17.3	12.5	13.6	8.9			13.3	13.3
Operating Profit		2.0	2.3	3.1	3.1			1.4	1.8
All Other Expenses (net)		-.1	.2	.5	.7			.2	.2
Profit Before Taxes		2.1	2.1	2.7	2.3			1.2	1.6
RATIOS									
Current		4.1	2.6	2.6	3.2			1.8	2.2
		2.1	1.5	1.4	1.5			1.3	1.4
		1.3	1.2	1.1	1.2			1.1	1.1
Quick		3.0	1.4	1.6	1.2			1.2	1.4
		1.4	.9	.9	.8			.8	.9
		.8	.6	.6	.4			.6	.6
Sales/Receivables	10 35.9	15 24.4	17 21.0	17 20.9				17 21.9	15 23.7
	21 17.8	22 17.0	21 17.4	22 16.7				23 15.8	22 16.8
	28 13.3	29 12.7	27 13.5	35 10.5				32 11.3	31 11.8
Cost of Sales/Inventory	2 155.5	9 39.3	7 51.7	18 20.4				10 37.7	8 48.5
	10 37.4	18 19.7	18 20.0	25 14.3				17 21.1	17 21.3
	18 20.8	35 10.3	30 12.3	53 6.8				30 12.2	31 11.9
Cost of Sales/Payables	6 65.3	7 49.4	7 50.0	11 33.7				8 45.4	7 49.3
	9 42.5	12 31.0	12 30.2	12 29.3				13 27.3	13 27.4
	18 20.0	18 20.7	17 21.3	26 14.0				21 17.2	21 17.5
Sales/Working Capital		12.5	11.3	12.5	9.1			16.0	14.1
		24.2	22.2	25.6	18.5			30.4	30.0
		78.7	65.0	81.3	53.0			89.7	82.1
EBIT/Interest		29.8	16.1	13.5	12.8			6.8	6.2
	(33) 12.1	(88) 3.5	(46) 5.6	6.5				(197) 3.5	(164) 2.8
		1.6	1.9	2.0	4.4			1.6	1.5
Net Profit + Depr., Dep., Amort./Cur. Mat. L/T/D			14.4	29.0				6.7	9.1
		(21) 3.6	(12) 8.5					(38) 2.8	(39) 6.1
			.8	3.0				1.1	1.4
Fixed/Worth		.0	.1	.1	.4			.1	.1
		.3	.3	.5	.8			.4	.5
		3.8	1.0	1.7	1.5			1.3	1.6
Debt/Worth		.6	.9	.7	1.5			1.4	1.0
		1.7	1.9	2.0	3.2			3.0	2.5
		18.8	3.8	5.9	7.1			6.4	6.2
% Profit Before Taxes/Tangible Net Worth		84.3	50.5	48.9	47.5			38.6	47.2
	(28) 40.1	(94) 25.4	(41) 22.0	(13) 30.4				(188) 17.4	(174) 22.0
		14.9	6.7	13.2	21.5			5.6	6.0
% Profit Before Taxes/Total Assets		23.8	17.8	17.0	11.7			10.0	13.3
		13.7	7.2	6.4	10.1			5.0	6.0
		2.0	2.1	3.1	4.5			1.2	1.2
Sales/Net Fixed Assets		985.4	226.9	464.4	155.8			331.9	238.1
		80.4	77.8	35.7	25.1			62.7	57.5
		27.8	25.7	10.2	8.3			18.5	14.4
Sales/Total Assets		10.8	8.2	7.5	7.4			8.4	8.3
		6.6	5.6	4.5	5.4			5.8	5.8
		4.7	4.3	3.0	2.4			4.2	3.7
% Depr., Dep., Amort./Sales		.1	.1	.1	.3			.1	.1
	(25) .4	(86) .3	(41) .6	(12) .4				(179) .4	(167) .4
		1.6	.7	1.7	.9			.9	.9
% Officers', Directors' Owners' Comp/Sales		1.4	.6	1.0				.6	.5
	(20) 1.9	(52) 1.4	(11) 2.3					(86) 1.2	(82) 1.2
		3.7	2.8	4.7				2.8	2.3
Net Sales ($)	12591M	336929M	3194255M	5197990M	5747009M	6124109M		14223508M	13119561M
Total Assets ($)	2140M	43409M	491525M	1035927M	1122223M	1299149M		2252020M	2486896M

M = $ thousand   MM = $ million
See Pages 9 through 22 for Explanation of Ratios and Data

Comparative Historical Data | Current Data Sorted by Sales

4/1/07-3/31/08 ALL	4/1/08-3/31/09 ALL	4/1/09-3/31/10 ALL	Type of Statement	0-1MM	1-3MM	3-5MM	5-10MM	10-25MM	25MM & OV
25	32	32	Unqualified				3	2	30
52	53	52	Reviewed				3	16	33
29	35	45	Compiled	3	4	3	3	18	14
18	27	20	Tax Returns	1		2	9	6	2
52	60	69	Other	2	2	3	5	18	39
				33 (4/1-9/30/09)			185 (10/1/09-3/31/10)		
176	207	218	**NUMBER OF STATEMENTS**	6	6	8	20	60	118
%	%	%	**ASSETS**	%	%	%	%	%	%
6.9	7.7	8.4	Cash & Equivalents				8.8	8.2	6.6
37.5	38.1	37.0	Trade Receivables (net)				35.2	39.5	37.7
25.7	26.8	25.7	Inventory				24.0	25.8	27.6
2.4	2.4	2.8	All Other Current				1.2	3.8	2.6
72.6	75.0	73.9	Total Current				69.2	77.4	74.6
18.0	16.7	17.3	Fixed Assets (net)				24.0	14.3	17.4
5.0	3.5	4.9	Intangibles (net)				2.2	3.4	4.4
4.4	4.9	4.0	All Other Non-Current				4.6	5.0	3.7
100.0	100.0	100.0	Total				100.0	100.0	100.0
			LIABILITIES						
18.6	18.0	17.4	Notes Payable-Short Term				7.7	19.4	18.0
2.6	1.9	1.8	Cur. Mat.-L.T.D.				2.8	1.9	1.6
21.4	21.1	18.7	Trade Payables				19.6	18.0	19.6
.1	.1	.2	Income Taxes Payable				.0	.3	.3
7.5	7.5	7.6	All Other Current				4.5	7.5	8.1
50.1	48.7	45.7	Total Current				34.6	47.1	47.6
12.5	10.3	11.7	Long-Term Debt				27.6	5.1	10.8
.1	.1	.1	Deferred Taxes				.1	.1	.1
5.2	6.0	9.8	All Other Non-Current				13.7	9.9	5.2
32.2	34.9	32.7	Net Worth				23.9	37.8	36.3
100.0	100.0	100.0	Total Liabilties & Net Worth				100.0	100.0	100.0
			INCOME DATA						
100.0	100.0	100.0	Net Sales				100.0	100.0	100.0
14.0	14.6	16.5	Gross Profit				19.8	15.4	13.7
11.7	12.4	13.9	Operating Expenses				19.6	12.4	11.0
2.3	2.2	2.6	Operating Profit				.2	3.0	2.6
.7	.4	.3	All Other Expenses (net)				.2	.1	.4
1.6	1.8	2.3	Profit Before Taxes				.0	2.9	2.3
			RATIOS						
2.1	2.3	2.8	Current				4.5	2.9	2.2
1.4	1.5	1.6					2.4	1.5	1.5
1.1	1.2	1.2					1.2	1.2	1.2
1.3	1.5	1.6	Quick				3.9	2.0	1.3
.9	.9	.9					1.1	1.0	.9
.6	.6	.6					.8	.6	.6
15 24.0	14 26.4	15 24.8	Sales/Receivables				11 34.3	17 21.5	15 24.8
20 18.5	19 19.0	21 17.5					22 16.8	23 16.0	20 18.3
27 13.7	27 13.6	29 12.8					31 11.9	30 12.2	25 14.5
8 45.1	8 48.0	8 43.6	Cost of Sales/Inventory				11 34.5	9 41.9	9 40.9
16 22.9	16 22.4	18 20.4					13 27.7	20 18.4	18 20.5
28 12.9	30 12.3	31 11.6					31 11.7	37 9.9	28 13.1
8 48.3	7 53.3	7 49.4	Cost of Sales/Payables				6 59.7	7 49.6	7 49.0
13 28.3	12 31.4	12 31.0					9 40.3	13 28.7	12 31.5
18 19.8	20 18.4	18 20.0					18 19.8	21 17.5	17 21.3
15.9	15.0	11.2	Sales/Working Capital				8.1	11.3	14.3
28.0	30.1	23.2					20.8	21.2	25.5
100.8	74.8	68.2					90.4	66.8	65.8
6.4	9.3	16.5	EBIT/Interest				11.4	20.4	16.6
(158) 2.7	(185) 3.7	(195) 5.2					2.2	(52) 4.1	(110) 6.2
1.4	1.5	2.0					.1	1.8	2.4
15.5	5.9	15.5	Net Profit + Depr., Dep., Amort./Cur. Mat. L/T/D						16.0
(35) 3.9	(35) 2.8	(39) 4.7						(26)	5.9
1.2	1.0	1.5							2.7
.1	.1	.1	Fixed/Worth				.1	.1	.1
.4	.4	.4					.8	.2	.5
1.4	1.0	1.7					2.7	1.0	1.2
1.2	1.0	.8	Debt/Worth				.6	.7	.9
2.8	2.2	2.2					2.7	1.8	2.1
5.4	4.5	7.1					16.4	3.8	6.0
41.3	47.2	55.1	% Profit Before Taxes/Tangible Net Worth				67.4	55.6	54.3
(160) 20.1	(191) 23.4	(188) 27.9				(16)	21.6	(55) 28.8	(106) 27.9
7.0	7.1	12.3					4.0	6.5	14.4
10.5	14.2	18.2	% Profit Before Taxes/Total Assets				13.9	26.9	15.7
5.0	6.2	8.2					2.8	7.1	8.8
1.4	2.1	2.5					-2.2	1.4	3.3
238.8	316.7	234.6	Sales/Net Fixed Assets				229.6	229.8	256.0
64.1	81.0	67.9					40.0	74.6	77.2
18.9	21.8	15.6					9.5	22.3	15.6
8.4	9.4	8.1	Sales/Total Assets				6.9	7.0	8.8
6.0	6.2	5.6					5.8	5.3	6.3
3.9	4.2	3.7					4.4	3.7	4.1
.1	.1	.1	% Depr., Dep., Amort./Sales				.2	.1	.1
(148) .4	(167) .4	(176) .4				(16)	.7	(46) .4	(102) .4
.8	.9	.8					1.4	.7	.8
.5	.5	.7	% Officers', Directors' Owners' Comp/Sales				1.9	.7	1.3
(74) 1.2	(93) 1.0	(86) 1.6				(13)	2.9	(33) 1.4	(34) 1.3
2.2	2.1	3.0					3.3	2.5	2.9
16572918M	19013536M	20612883M	Net Sales ($)	3410M	12566M	35283M	155556M	1027110M	19378958M
3163148M	3607430M	3994373M	Total Assets ($)	2925M	3746M	11699M	35224M	222441M	3718338M

© RMA 2010

M = $ thousand   MM = $ million
See Pages 9 through 22 for Explanation of Ratios and Data

Current Data Sorted by Assets   Comparative Historical Data

	0-500M	500M-2MM	2-10MM	10-50MM	50-100MM	100-250MM	Type of Statement	4/1/05-3/31/06 ALL	4/1/06-3/31/07 ALL
		2	7	19	9	5	Unqualified	44	41
		8	43	22	3		Reviewed	51	75
	3	15	44	13	1		Compiled	49	70
	6	17	17	2		1	Tax Returns	22	24
		10	45	34	9	3	Other	78	64
		98 (4/1-9/30/09)		240 (10/1/09-3/31/10)					
NUMBER OF STATEMENTS	9	52	156	90	22	9		244	274
	%	%	%	%	%	%	ASSETS	%	%
		14.7	11.8	8.8	6.7		Cash & Equivalents	10.4	8.9
		41.0	46.3	38.6	25.7		Trade Receivables (net)	40.4	41.7
		11.7	8.7	8.7	13.6		Inventory	10.2	9.6
		6.2	5.1	4.5	5.5		All Other Current	4.0	3.7
		73.6	72.0	60.6	51.5		Total Current	65.0	63.9
		16.7	16.7	29.9	33.9		Fixed Assets (net)	25.0	25.0
		1.4	2.5	2.7	7.3		Intangibles (net)	2.6	3.1
		8.3	8.8	6.9	7.3		All Other Non-Current	7.5	8.0
		100.0	100.0	100.0	100.0		Total	100.0	100.0
							LIABILITIES		
		9.7	8.6	8.6	5.8		Notes Payable-Short Term	9.7	9.9
		3.1	1.7	3.0	3.3		Cur. Mat.-L.T.D.	2.2	2.6
		32.9	36.9	27.3	16.4		Trade Payables	30.4	32.5
		.3	.1	.2	.0		Income Taxes Payable	.2	.1
		9.9	8.4	9.1	9.9		All Other Current	10.7	9.7
		56.0	55.7	48.2	35.5		Total Current	53.2	54.8
		6.9	8.5	16.7	24.7		Long-Term Debt	11.2	12.7
		.1	.2	.3	1.2		Deferred Taxes	.5	.6
		4.6	3.7	2.7	2.8		All Other Non-Current	4.4	3.7
		32.4	31.9	32.1	35.8		Net Worth	30.7	28.3
		100.0	100.0	100.0	100.0		Total Liabilties & Net Worth	100.0	100.0
							INCOME DATA		
		100.0	100.0	100.0	100.0		Net Sales	100.0	100.0
		16.8	19.1	20.9	18.6		Gross Profit	20.4	20.3
		16.0	16.4	17.6	14.7		Operating Expenses	17.0	17.5
		.8	2.7	3.3	4.0		Operating Profit	3.3	2.8
		-.1	.2	.0	.7		All Other Expenses (net)	.5	.9
		.9	2.4	3.3	3.3		Profit Before Taxes	2.8	1.9
							RATIOS		
		2.3	1.8	1.7	1.8		Current	1.7	1.7
		1.5	1.2	1.3	1.4			1.2	1.2
		1.0	1.0	1.0	1.2			1.0	1.0
		1.5	1.5	1.4	1.2		Quick	1.3	1.3
		1.0	1.0	1.0	1.0			1.0	.9
		.7	.8	.7	.5			.7	.7
		10 36.3	21 17.3	25 14.4	27 13.5		Sales/Receivables	20 18.1	21 17.4
		18 19.9	29 12.4	31 12.0	31 11.8			29 12.4	28 12.9
		29 12.5	38 9.6	43 8.5	40 9.1			37 9.9	37 9.9
		1 632.5	1 293.5	3 125.1	6 61.7		Cost of Sales/Inventory	3 135.5	2 176.5
		6 63.8	5 73.1	7 50.8	8 47.9			6 59.1	6 60.0
		8 44.0	9 39.9	14 25.9	45 8.1			14 25.8	12 30.9
		6 62.3	17 21.2	18 20.1	13 27.2		Cost of Sales/Payables	15 24.2	16 22.9
		19 19.2	26 14.0	26 14.0	23 16.2			25 14.4	24 14.9
		31 11.7	39 9.4	42 8.7	32 11.6			34 10.8	37 9.8
		15.0	15.6	12.4	10.2		Sales/Working Capital	18.5	18.7
		32.3	45.2	34.8	18.9			50.0	53.9
		NM	347.3	999.8	39.5			NM	-255.9
		16.5	22.1	16.1	10.9		EBIT/Interest	13.9	12.3
	(40) 3.1	(141) 6.7	(82) 7.1	(20) 4.0			(217) 4.5	(251) 3.8
		-3.4	1.9	2.4	1.9			2.0	1.3
			11.2	7.8			Net Profit + Depr., Dep., Amort./Cur. Mat. L/T/D	8.3	8.2
		(33) 2.6	(29) 3.5				(68) 3.8	(72) 4.1
			1.4	2.1				1.6	1.5
		.1	.1	.3	.5		Fixed/Worth	.3	.3
		.3	.4	.9	1.6			.7	.7
		.9	1.1	2.1	2.3			1.7	1.8
		.8	1.0	1.4	1.2		Debt/Worth	1.2	1.2
		1.4	2.8	2.4	2.7			2.4	2.4
		6.7	7.1	4.0	5.1			5.0	5.3
		52.7	49.7	52.7	37.2		% Profit Before Taxes/Tangible Net Worth	43.9	43.6
	(45) 16.0	(144) 18.0	(83) 21.7	(20) 20.8			(221) 19.0	(247) 17.8
		1.1	5.1	11.6	5.5			6.7	4.8
		22.8	15.3	14.4	15.0		% Profit Before Taxes/Total Assets	13.5	12.5
		3.9	4.6	5.9	8.9			5.6	5.4
		-2.8	1.3	2.2	2.9			1.4	.7
		234.3	179.2	65.9	16.1		Sales/Net Fixed Assets	92.4	103.2
		64.5	51.1	14.9	10.3			27.0	26.5
		23.5	18.5	5.2	3.5			9.5	10.1
		8.9	7.7	5.6	5.0		Sales/Total Assets	7.5	7.8
		7.3	5.7	3.9	2.6			5.4	5.4
		5.2	3.9	2.1	1.1			3.0	3.2
		.2	.2	.4	1.0		% Depr., Dep., Amort./Sales	.3	.3
	(41) .5	(130) .5	(78) 1.2	(20) 1.3			(216) .7	(247) .7
		1.0	1.3	2.4	4.0			1.4	1.4
		1.6	.7	.4			% Officers', Directors' Owners' Comp/Sales	1.1	.9
	(29) 2.1	(71) 1.7	(17) .8				(99) 1.7	(113) 1.7
		3.7	2.5	2.3				3.0	2.5
	35308M	534272M	4426184M	7568965M	4338480M	4927812M	Net Sales ($)	13390948M	15638859M
	2588M	69650M	768917M	1873818M	1469863M	1491983M	Total Assets ($)	3731487M	3771877M

M = $ thousand   MM = $ million

See Pages 9 through 22 for Explanation of Ratios and Data

© RMA 2010

Comparative Historical Data / Current Data Sorted by Sales

Type of Statement	07/08	08/09	09/10	0-1MM	1-3MM	3-5MM	5-10MM	10-25MM	25MM & OV
Unqualified	36	38	42	1			1	4	37
Reviewed	70	73	76		1	1	5	24	45
Compiled	75	67	76		4	5	11	21	34
Tax Returns	22	40	43			6	10	20	5
Other	85	93	101		2	2	9	29	60
(Date Range)	4/1/07-3/31/08 ALL	4/1/08-3/31/09 ALL	4/1/09-3/31/10 ALL	98 (4/1-9/30/09)			240 (10/1/09-3/31/10)		
NUMBER OF STATEMENTS	288	311	338	1	8	14	36	98	181

ASSETS (%)

	07/08	08/09	09/10	3-5MM	5-10MM	10-25MM	25MM & OV
Cash & Equivalents	10.1	9.7	11.3	21.2	12.9	11.9	9.6
Trade Receivables (net)	41.6	40.6	41.2	35.2	36.2	43.0	42.5
Inventory	8.1	10.0	9.5	12.1	10.1	10.0	8.9
All Other Current	5.9	5.7	5.3	6.8	3.7	5.0	5.4
Total Current	65.7	66.0	67.3	75.4	62.9	69.9	66.4
Fixed Assets (net)	23.8	22.7	22.0	18.9	20.3	20.1	23.2
Intangibles (net)	3.0	3.0	2.7	.4	2.0	1.5	3.7
All Other Non-Current	7.6	8.3	8.0	5.4	14.9	8.5	6.8
Total	100.0	100.0	100.0	100.0	100.0	100.0	100.0

LIABILITIES

	07/08	08/09	09/10	3-5MM	5-10MM	10-25MM	25MM & OV
Notes Payable-Short Term	10.3	9.6	9.3	23.1	7.8	8.8	7.9
Cur. Mat.-L.T.D.	2.4	2.2	2.5	6.6	2.6	2.4	1.9
Trade Payables	31.2	32.7	31.8	34.2	24.5	33.4	32.4
Income Taxes Payable	.2	.2	.2	1.1	.0	.1	.2
All Other Current	9.0	9.3	8.9	3.2	6.5	8.7	8.8
Total Current	53.1	53.9	52.5	68.2	41.4	53.4	51.2
Long-Term Debt	12.0	12.8	12.6	8.2	10.6	9.1	13.9
Deferred Taxes	.4	.4	.3	.0	.1	.2	.4
All Other Non-Current	3.2	5.4	3.8	2.3	5.8	4.3	3.4
Net Worth	31.4	27.5	30.8	21.3	42.1	33.0	30.9
Total Liabilities & Net Worth	100.0	100.0	100.0	100.0	100.0	100.0	100.0

INCOME DATA

	07/08	08/09	09/10	3-5MM	5-10MM	10-25MM	25MM & OV
Net Sales	100.0	100.0	100.0	100.0	100.0	100.0	100.0
Gross Profit	20.0	20.0	19.1	23.8	21.5	21.3	16.6
Operating Expenses	16.3	17.1	16.3	24.4	20.0	17.6	13.8
Operating Profit	3.7	2.9	2.9	-.6	1.5	3.8	2.9
All Other Expenses (net)	.3	.4	.2	-.6	.4	.3	.1
Profit Before Taxes	3.4	2.6	2.7	-.1	1.0	3.5	2.8

RATIOS

	07/08	08/09	09/10	3-5MM	5-10MM	10-25MM	25MM & OV
Current	1.7	1.6	1.9	2.8	2.9	2.1	1.7
	1.2	1.2	1.3	1.3	1.5	1.2	1.3
	1.0	1.0	1.0	.7	1.0	1.0	1.1
Quick	1.3	1.3	1.4	1.6	2.0	1.5	1.4
	.9	.9	1.0	1.0	1.1	1.0	1.0
	.7	.7	.7	.4	.7	.7	.7
Sales/Receivables	20 18.2	20 18.0	21 17.7	0 UND	14 26.9	19 19.2	24 15.4
	28 13.1	28 13.2	29 12.6	29 12.7	23 15.6	29 12.6	29 12.4
	39 9.4	37 9.9	37 9.7	55 6.7	38 9.7	41 9.0	36 10.2
Cost of Sales/Inventory	1 506.6	2 214.3	2 199.3	0 UND	3 124.5	2 184.9	2 185.9
	5 76.4	6 66.3	6 61.8	6 60.9	6 63.2	6 57.1	6 61.8
	10 37.3	12 31.6	11 34.3	22 16.3	19 19.2	11 34.1	10 36.0
Cost of Sales/Payables	15 23.7	15 24.7	15 24.3	0 UND	7 55.8	15 23.7	17 21.4
	25 14.7	25 14.7	25 14.8	20 18.2	23 15.8	25 14.8	25 14.8
	36 10.2	36 10.1	37 9.8	50 7.3	40 9.2	39 9.5	35 10.3
Sales/Working Capital	18.8	19.9	14.7	4.3	10.8	15.0	15.1
	53.8	43.2	35.3	15.9	26.1	36.3	35.4
	-999.8	999.8	725.5	-35.7	NM	NM	195.0
EBIT/Interest	14.2	14.3	16.2	5.0	25.7	21.9	14.3
	(258) 5.0	(283) 4.4	(298) 6.1	(30) 2.3	(86) 2.2	(161) 7.5	6.7
	1.8	1.8	1.7	-13.2	-2.7	1.6	2.1
Net Profit + Depr., Dep., Amort./Cur. Mat. L/T/D	10.5	6.6	8.8			2.6	9.6
	(70) 3.4	(76) 2.8	(82) 3.0		(16)	1.8	(58) 3.6
	1.7	1.5	1.4			.6	2.0
Fixed/Worth	.2	.2	.2	.1	.2	.1	.2
	.6	.6	.6	.3	.4	.5	.7
	2.0	1.8	1.8	19.3	1.0	1.1	2.0
Debt/Worth	1.3	1.3	1.0	.3	.5	1.0	1.3
	2.4	2.7	2.4	4.0	1.1	2.4	2.6
	5.0	7.1	6.0	NM	2.7	5.3	5.6
% Profit Before Taxes/Tangible Net Worth	50.7	50.7	50.1	15.5	55.4	48.6	50.1
	(257) 20.0	(274) 20.0	(303) 20.3	(11) 4.9	(31) 13.0	(89) 18.8	(167) 23.1
	8.2	4.9	5.1	-24.6	-1.6	5.7	7.5
% Profit Before Taxes/Total Assets	16.0	13.5	15.2	5.6	22.2	18.2	14.6
	6.0	5.5	5.0	2.2	3.8	4.9	5.4
	1.4	1.0	1.4	-7.7	-2.2	1.4	1.9
Sales/Net Fixed Assets	119.4	120.4	161.0	100.1	74.3	183.1	172.2
	29.7	35.3	34.9	37.2	27.5	40.6	37.6
	10.6	12.0	10.2	10.7	11.9	15.8	9.3
Sales/Total Assets	7.9	7.7	7.5	7.7	7.3	7.7	7.6
	5.2	5.6	5.3	5.0	4.5	5.5	5.4
	2.7	3.0	3.0	1.4	2.2	3.3	3.1
% Depr., Dep., Amort./Sales	.2	.2	.2	.2	.3	.2	.2
	(255) .7	(263) .6	(278) .7	(11) .6	(30) .8	(83) .6	(147) .7
	1.4	1.4	1.6	3.0	1.9	1.4	1.4
% Officers', Directors' Owners' Comp/Sales	.6	.6	.8		1.9	.8	.5
	(110) 1.7	(118) 1.5	(125) 1.7		(21) 2.7	(42) 1.9	(52) 1.0
	2.6	2.6	3.1		3.7	2.7	1.9

	07/08	08/09	09/10	0-1MM	1-3MM	3-5MM	5-10MM	10-25MM	25MM & OV
Net Sales ($)	20524342M	19652929M	21831021M	13M	16923M	58063M	272190M	1628623M	19855209M
Total Assets ($)	4886626M	5352042M	5676819M	5M	8659M	27287M	98666M	426124M	5116078M

M = $ thousand   MM = $ million

See Pages 9 through 22 for Explanation of Ratios and Data

Current Data Sorted by Assets | Comparative Historical Data

Type of Statement

Type of Statement	0-500M	500M-2MM	2-10MM	10-50MM	50-100MM	100-250MM	ALL 4/1/05-3/31/06	ALL 4/1/06-3/31/07
Unqualified		1	11	40	20	8	56	76
Reviewed		5	56	34	5		80	71
Compiled	1	12	29	7		8	46	58
Tax Returns	9	33	20	3	1		29	43
Other	6	24	60	51	8	8	116	115
		97 (4/1-9/30/09)		355 (10/1/09-3/31/10)				
NUMBER OF STATEMENTS	16	75	176	135	34	16	327	363

ASSETS

	0-500M %	500M-2MM %	2-10MM %	10-50MM %	50-100MM %	100-250MM %	ALL %	ALL %
Cash & Equivalents	8.5	9.9	7.7	6.3	9.1	11.5	6.9	8.4
Trade Receivables (net)	25.2	31.2	31.8	29.8	28.2	19.1	29.3	28.7
Inventory	32.5	30.4	31.3	32.5	26.6	23.0	29.5	29.7
All Other Current	.9	3.4	2.8	3.1	3.0	6.5	2.7	2.6
Total Current	67.1	74.8	73.6	71.7	66.9	60.0	68.4	69.5
Fixed Assets (net)	16.0	16.7	16.5	18.8	22.6	20.8	20.7	19.8
Intangibles (net)	9.5	4.4	3.5	5.1	5.2	12.4	4.9	4.8
All Other Non-Current	7.1	4.1	6.4	4.5	5.3	6.7	6.0	6.0
Total	100.0	100.0	100.0	100.0	100.0	100.0	100.0	100.0

LIABILITIES

	0-500M	500M-2MM	2-10MM	10-50MM	50-100MM	100-250MM	ALL	ALL
Notes Payable-Short Term	24.7	17.2	16.4	15.0	10.7	12.0	14.9	17.1
Cur. Mat.-L.T.D.	8.3	3.5	2.5	2.5	1.6	2.1	2.6	2.7
Trade Payables	25.3	26.7	24.3	20.4	20.9	10.9	22.4	22.5
Income Taxes Payable	.1	.0	.4	.3	.2	.4	.2	.2
All Other Current	12.4	5.8	8.4	9.7	10.5	18.7	8.7	9.1
Total Current	70.9	53.3	52.0	47.8	43.8	44.1	48.8	51.7
Long-Term Debt	14.2	13.7	11.4	11.4	16.4	11.8	14.3	13.9
Deferred Taxes	.0	.0	.3	.3	.4	.9	.4	.4
All Other Non-Current	11.6	6.9	4.3	3.0	3.2	4.1	5.9	4.6
Net Worth	3.5	26.1	32.0	37.4	36.3	39.0	30.6	29.3
Total Liabilities & Net Worth	100.0	100.0	100.0	100.0	100.0	100.0	100.0	100.0

INCOME DATA

	0-500M	500M-2MM	2-10MM	10-50MM	50-100MM	100-250MM	ALL	ALL
Net Sales	100.0	100.0	100.0	100.0	100.0	100.0	100.0	100.0
Gross Profit	35.8	27.2	21.7	21.4	20.6	37.7	24.6	25.7
Operating Expenses	30.0	25.4	19.0	16.7	16.1	28.0	22.0	22.3
Operating Profit	5.8	1.8	2.7	4.7	4.5	9.6	2.6	3.3
All Other Expenses (net)	1.7	.0	.3	.7	.4	.5	.5	.7
Profit Before Taxes	4.1	1.8	2.4	4.1	4.1	9.1	2.2	2.6

RATIOS

	0-500M	500M-2MM	2-10MM	10-50MM	50-100MM	100-250MM	ALL	ALL
Current	3.4	2.8	2.0	2.0	2.4	2.5	2.1	2.0
	1.6	1.5	1.5	1.5	1.6	1.4	1.3	1.4
	.9	1.0	1.1	1.2	1.1	1.1	1.1	1.1
Quick	1.4	1.4	1.1	1.1	1.3	1.3	1.2	1.2
	.6	.8	.7	.7	.8	.7	.7	.7
	.4	.5	.5	.5	.5	.4	.5	.4
Sales/Receivables	16 22.4	12 30.3	20 18.5	22 16.4	18 20.0	14 26.7	19 19.6	18 20.2
	26 14.0	23 16.2	27 13.5	30 12.1	24 15.2	30 12.3	27 13.3	28 12.9
	39 9.3	34 10.6	40 9.2	39 9.4	35 10.5	35 10.5	38 9.6	39 9.5
Cost of Sales/Inventory	16 23.2	7 51.4	19 18.9	22 16.6	17 22.1	27 13.7	20 18.6	18 19.8
	45 8.0	32 11.5	32 11.6	45 8.1	25 14.7	48 7.6	34 10.8	36 10.2
	120 3.0	64 5.7	56 6.6	69 5.3	53 6.9	101 3.6	62 5.9	67 5.5
Cost of Sales/Payables	13 28.3	14 26.4	17 22.0	14 25.4	15 24.7	13 27.2	14 26.5	15 24.8
	25 14.4	21 17.6	26 13.9	26 14.3	22 17.0	21 17.0	25 14.4	26 14.2
	48 7.6	42 8.7	39 9.4	36 10.1	32 11.3	34 10.7	41 9.0	38 9.5
Sales/Working Capital	6.5	8.3	10.0	7.6	7.2	11.5	10.4	9.9
	12.6	17.3	17.8	17.0	17.0	20.8	19.7	22.0
	-156.0	363.1	85.9	43.0	142.7	90.0	72.5	101.8
EBIT/Interest	6.0	10.2	15.5	20.1	66.4	11.4	9.6	10.2
	(13) 2.0	(65) 4.2	(165) 5.6	(128) 5.4	(32) 9.2	(13) 5.0	(304) 3.3	(330) 3.1
	.3	1.1	2.0	2.8	2.7	2.2	1.3	1.3
Net Profit + Depr., Dep., Amort./Cur. Mat. L/T/D		9.8	8.8	5.5	16.7		6.1	10.4
		(12) 2.9	(39) 3.2	(40) 3.9	(14) 8.5		(94) 3.2	(96) 4.3
		.5	1.5	2.0	4.8		1.4	1.5
Fixed/Worth	.1	.1	.1	.1	.2	.2	.1	.1
	.4	.5	.4	.4	.6	.9	.6	.5
	NM	3.0	1.3	1.4	2.6	1.5	2.0	1.9
Debt/Worth	.6	.9	1.1	1.0	.7	1.0	1.1	1.1
	5.5	2.5	2.4	2.0	2.5	2.4	2.7	2.7
	-12.8	12.6	6.1	5.1	9.6	28.5	6.8	7.9
% Profit Before Taxes/Tangible Net Worth	53.8	43.6	45.0	48.6	42.1	78.4	47.3	47.0
	(11) 19.0	(59) 14.1	(162) 25.4	(123) 26.7	(28) 33.4	(14) 25.4	(281) 18.3	(305) 19.6
	4.1	3.3	9.4	14.6	17.9	15.9	5.1	7.4
% Profit Before Taxes/Total Assets	13.0	12.6	12.9	15.5	19.7	15.9	13.1	14.3
	6.2	4.9	7.0	7.4	13.7	8.9	5.3	6.3
	-.8	.2	2.0	3.2	4.5	2.7	1.0	1.4
Sales/Net Fixed Assets	364.1	213.6	158.9	191.2	64.7	65.3	118.2	134.9
	35.0	47.0	47.0	25.8	20.0	13.9	31.3	32.4
	17.1	17.7	13.0	9.0	9.2	7.5	10.0	10.5
Sales/Total Assets	4.4	7.6	5.6	4.8	6.3	4.2	5.6	5.5
	3.6	4.2	3.6	3.2	3.8	2.8	3.4	3.4
	2.2	2.9	2.5	2.2	2.0	1.2	2.3	2.4
% Depr., Dep., Amort./Sales	.6	.2	.2	.3	.3	.1	.3	.3
	(10) 1.4	(56) .6	(144) .5	(113) .8	(28) 1.0	(13) .8	(267) .7	(303) .7
	2.4	1.7	1.5	1.9	1.8	1.6	1.9	2.0
% Officers', Directors' Owners' Comp/Sales		.9	.9	.7			.9	.9
		(48) 1.9	(69) 1.6	(39) 1.9			(108) 1.9	(126) 2.3
		3.4	3.9	3.0			4.6	4.0
Net Sales ($)	26725M	505722M	3706879M	11061790M	11044492M	7718362M	17114570M	24191539M
Total Assets ($)	4712M	95250M	887094M	3119434M	2363891M	2637115M	5249636M	7185386M

M = $ thousand   MM = $ million
See Pages 9 through 22 for Explanation of Ratios and Data

Comparative Historical Data | Current Data Sorted by Sales

Type of Statement	4/1/07-3/31/08 ALL	4/1/08-3/31/09 ALL	4/1/09-3/31/10 ALL	0-1MM	1-3MM	3-5MM	5-10MM	10-25MM	25MM & OVER
Unqualified	78	63	80			1	3	4	72
Reviewed	65	90	100			1	8	33	58
Compiled	51	51	49		3	6	11	15	14
Tax Returns	47	54	66	5	12	9	17	18	5
Other	115	150	157	4	8	5	19	46	75
					97 (4/1-9/30/09)		355 (10/1/09-3/31/10)		
NUMBER OF STATEMENTS	356	408	452	9	23	22	58	116	224
ASSETS	%	%	%	%	%	%	%	%	%
Cash & Equivalents	7.9	7.1	7.9		9.3	8.1	8.8	7.2	7.7
Trade Receivables (net)	28.3	29.2	30.2		31.8	21.0	31.2	30.5	30.8
Inventory	29.9	31.5	30.9		32.5	34.0	31.0	30.1	31.0
All Other Current	3.5	4.0	3.1		1.5	4.9	3.1	2.9	3.2
Total Current	69.6	71.8	72.0		75.1	68.0	74.2	70.6	72.7
Fixed Assets (net)	19.4	18.0	17.8		17.4	20.4	14.4	19.3	17.2
Intangibles (net)	4.4	4.2	4.8		3.4	5.3	4.6	4.2	5.1
All Other Non-Current	6.6	6.1	5.4		4.2	6.3	6.8	5.9	5.0
Total	100.0	100.0	100.0		100.0	100.0	100.0	100.0	100.0
LIABILITIES									
Notes Payable-Short Term	17.0	17.4	15.8		17.6	24.6	16.0	16.3	14.3
Cur. Mat.-L.T.D.	2.5	2.9	2.8		5.7	7.7	2.9	2.1	2.2
Trade Payables	22.2	21.9	22.8		21.7	17.3	24.6	25.8	21.7
Income Taxes Payable	.2	.2	.3		.1	.0	.4	.3	.3
All Other Current	8.9	9.0	9.0		6.9	5.3	8.2	8.3	10.4
Total Current	50.9	51.3	50.7		52.0	55.0	52.1	52.9	48.9
Long-Term Debt	15.7	12.5	12.3		12.6	20.0	14.9	10.9	11.2
Deferred Taxes	.2	.3	.3		.0	.0	.0	.3	.4
All Other Non-Current	4.8	4.0	4.5		10.5	5.1	5.0	5.2	3.2
Net Worth	28.4	31.9	32.2		25.0	19.9	28.0	30.8	36.5
Total Liabilities & Net Worth	100.0	100.0	100.0		100.0	100.0	100.0	100.0	100.0
INCOME DATA									
Net Sales	100.0	100.0	100.0		100.0	100.0	100.0	100.0	100.0
Gross Profit	24.6	22.9	23.5		31.4	33.1	27.3	21.3	21.1
Operating Expenses	21.4	20.1	19.9		26.4	31.3	24.3	18.8	16.8
Operating Profit	3.2	2.8	3.6		5.0	1.8	3.0	2.5	4.4
All Other Expenses (net)	.7	.7	.4		.7	.4	.4	.1	.5
Profit Before Taxes	2.5	2.1	3.2		4.3	1.4	2.6	2.3	3.9
RATIOS									
Current	2.2	2.2	2.1		3.1	3.0	2.0	2.1	2.1
	1.4	1.4	1.5		1.5	1.8	1.5	1.4	1.5
	1.1	1.1	1.1		1.0	.8	.9	1.1	1.1
Quick	1.3	1.2	1.1		1.5	1.1	1.2	1.1	1.2
	(355) .7	.7	.8		.8	.6	.7	.7	.8
	.4	.5	.5		.6	.5	.5	.5	.5
Sales/Receivables	18 20.7	18 20.0	19 19.1		17 21.2	16 22.3	21 17.4	18 19.8	20 18.5
	26 13.9	27 13.5	27 13.3		28 13.2	22 16.8	31 11.9	27 13.5	27 13.5
	37 9.8	37 9.8	38 9.6		56 6.5	41 9.0	41 8.9	39 9.4	36 10.2
Cost of Sales/Inventory	18 20.5	19 19.5	19 19.5		19 19.6	30 12.0	16 22.2	17 21.2	19 19.4
	34 10.8	33 11.2	37 9.9		54 6.8	59 6.2	42 8.6	31 11.8	35 10.3
	62 5.9	63 5.8	62 5.9		124 2.9	106 3.4	73 5.0	55 6.6	57 6.4
Cost of Sales/Payables	13 28.7	14 26.7	15 24.7		12 29.5	18 20.3	17 21.6	17 22.0	14 26.6
	25 14.5	23 15.9	24 15.2		21 17.6	32 11.5	30 12.2	27 13.7	22 16.4
	37 10.0	36 10.2	38 9.7		36 10.3	49 7.4	51 7.2	38 9.6	34 10.8
Sales/Working Capital	9.7	9.0	8.9		6.4	4.0	8.1	10.1	9.9
	19.8	18.9	17.6		11.1	11.5	14.8	19.4	17.9
	79.7	65.2	69.6		172.3	-21.3	-152.6	108.2	48.2
EBIT/Interest	(320) 10.7	(376) 11.5	(416) 16.4		(19) 12.3	(20) 10.5	(52) 9.8	(109) 11.7	(208) 26.2
	3.2	3.6	5.2		4.3	1.4	4.0	5.4	6.2
	1.4	1.4	2.0		3.2	.4	1.5	2.0	2.7
Net Profit + Depr., Dep., Amort./Cur. Mat. L/T/D	(85) 17.6	(91) 11.7	(112) 9.6				(11) 5.6	(24) 15.8	(70) 9.7
	6.0	5.0	4.0				1.6	3.1	4.7
	2.0	1.7	1.8				1.0	1.7	2.2
Fixed/Worth	.1	.1	.1		.1	.0	.1	.1	.1
	.5	.4	.4		.5	.7	.5	.4	.4
	1.7	1.5	1.7		-.7	-2.5	2.0	1.9	1.2
Debt/Worth	1.1	1.0	1.0		.5	.8	1.2	.9	1.0
	2.4	2.5	2.4		2.2	2.1	3.1	2.4	2.1
	8.1	6.9	6.4		-15.5	-14.0	7.7	6.0	5.4
% Profit Before Taxes/Tangible Net Worth	(308) 45.1	(352) 41.2	(397) 45.3		(17) 36.9	(16) 16.3	(48) 44.3	(107) 45.4	(202) 49.6
	21.6	19.7	25.1		19.0	11.5	16.4	26.1	27.3
	7.8	6.6	11.1		11.4	.2	6.0	9.3	16.5
% Profit Before Taxes/Total Assets	14.0	13.0	14.9		15.8	7.7	11.3	12.9	16.9
	6.2	6.1	7.2		8.8	.9	4.3	6.7	8.7
	1.3	1.1	2.5		4.0	-1.8	1.3	1.9	3.4
Sales/Net Fixed Assets	140.7	188.5	162.0		365.7	145.0	153.2	189.3	166.5
	34.6	41.0	39.5		37.8	33.7	40.6	45.0	40.1
	11.7	11.6	11.6		12.5	9.8	17.5	9.8	11.4
Sales/Total Assets	5.3	5.1	5.4		4.5	3.3	5.3	5.7	5.6
	3.5	3.5	3.5		3.6	2.9	3.5	3.5	3.8
	2.6	2.5	2.4		2.1	1.9	2.4	2.6	2.4
% Depr., Dep., Amort./Sales	(288) .3	(324) .2	(364) .2		(16) .7	(16) .4	(44) .2	(98) .2	(186) .2
	.7	.6	.7		1.4	1.6	.6	.6	.6
	1.5	1.5	1.6		2.1	4.1	1.7	1.5	1.4
% Officers', Directors' Owners' Comp/Sales	(137) .9	(145) .9	(170) .8		(11) 2.1	(14) 1.0	(32) 1.2	(55) .8	(54) .5
	1.8	1.5	1.8		3.7	2.5	1.8	1.3	1.6
	4.4	3.2	3.7		6.2	3.6	3.1		
Net Sales ($)	25557364M	32108238M	34063970M	5495M	45381M	83996M	411498M	1937461M	31580139M
Total Assets ($)	7713201M	8755269M	9107496M	3112M	16761M	34687M	143757M	593194M	8315985M

© RMA 2010

M = $ thousand   MM = $ million
See Pages 9 through 22 for Explanation of Ratios and Data

WHOLESALE—Grain and Field Bean Merchant Wholesalers NAICS 424510

| Current Data Sorted by Assets | | | | | | | Comparative Historical Data | |

0-500M	500M-2MM	2-10MM	10-50MM	50-100MM	100-250MM	Type of Statement		
1	6	44	66	29	25	Unqualified	169	197
	10	38	16	1		Reviewed	59	89
1	3	4	3			Compiled	11	18
1	8	10				Tax Returns	11	9
5	19	16	6	4		Other	44	57
	167 (4/1-9/30/09)		149 (10/1/09-3/31/10)				4/1/05-3/31/06 ALL	4/1/06-3/31/07 ALL
3	32	115	101	36	29	NUMBER OF STATEMENTS	294	370
%	%	%	%	%	%	ASSETS	%	%
	15.7	12.1	8.9	7.4	3.7	Cash & Equivalents	7.6	7.0
	29.8	19.9	15.6	16.8	19.5	Trade Receivables (net)	18.1	17.6
	22.6	31.8	37.4	38.0	45.4	Inventory	32.7	36.2
	2.3	4.5	6.0	4.6	6.6	All Other Current	7.3	7.6
	70.4	68.2	67.9	66.7	75.2	Total Current	65.9	68.5
	21.2	23.3	25.9	24.6	19.0	Fixed Assets (net)	27.5	24.8
	.4	.5	.4	.3	.1	Intangibles (net)	.4	.7
	8.0	8.0	5.7	8.4	5.8	All Other Non-Current	6.2	6.0
	100.0	100.0	100.0	100.0	100.0	Total	100.0	100.0
						LIABILITIES		
	8.6	11.0	14.6	14.2	25.6	Notes Payable-Short Term	17.6	20.5
	4.4	2.3	1.8	1.2	1.9	Cur. Mat.-L.T.D.	1.6	1.7
	22.2	19.9	17.5	18.8	17.3	Trade Payables	19.1	16.7
	.1	.5	.5	.2	.3	Income Taxes Payable	.3	.3
	9.3	12.7	12.5	10.3	10.5	All Other Current	9.3	10.6
	44.6	46.4	46.9	44.7	55.6	Total Current	47.9	49.8
	17.3	9.2	13.0	11.6	11.4	Long-Term Debt	9.5	10.0
	.4	1.5	1.4	1.8	.7	Deferred Taxes	1.4	1.1
	1.6	2.5	2.0	1.6	2.4	All Other Non-Current	1.3	2.1
	36.2	40.4	36.8	40.3	29.9	Net Worth	39.8	36.9
	100.0	100.0	100.0	100.0	100.0	Total Liabilities & Net Worth	100.0	100.0
						INCOME DATA		
	100.0	100.0	100.0	100.0	100.0	Net Sales	100.0	100.0
	12.3	13.0	9.3	7.1	9.4	Gross Profit	10.5	11.4
	11.3	9.3	6.1	4.4	6.5	Operating Expenses	8.8	9.1
	1.0	3.7	3.1	2.6	2.9	Operating Profit	1.8	2.4
	.0	-.1	.1	-.4	-.1	All Other Expenses (net)	.3	.5
	1.0	3.8	3.0	3.0	3.0	Profit Before Taxes	1.5	1.9
						RATIOS		
	2.8	2.1	1.8	1.9	1.5	Current	1.7	1.7
	1.5	1.5	1.4	1.4	1.3		1.3	1.3
	1.3	1.1	1.2	1.2	1.2		1.1	1.1
	2.1	1.1	.8	.9	.7	Quick	.8	.8
	1.2	(100) .6	.5	.5	.3	(293)	.5	.4
	.8	.4	.2	.3	.2		.2	.2
	5 67.7	7 53.6	5 79.0	6 56.8	9 42.7	Sales/Receivables	3 145.7	4 91.7
	19 18.9	17 21.4	9 39.5	12 31.1	19 19.1		14 25.5	17 22.1
	43 8.6	29 12.6	23 16.1	23 15.8	33 11.2		32 11.5	31 11.9
	5 74.6	13 27.7	21 17.2	23 15.7	29 12.7	Cost of Sales/Inventory	19 19.2	24 15.0
	12 31.5	35 10.4	40 9.1	41 8.8	58 6.3		39 9.3	49 7.4
	46 7.9	67 5.5	72 5.0	63 5.8	80 4.6		69 5.3	90 4.0
	3 144.4	7 54.9	6 63.1	7 52.7	9 38.7	Cost of Sales/Payables	8 46.6	6 58.7
	12 29.9	16 23.2	18 20.8	16 23.2	17 21.4		17 21.7	15 24.9
	23 16.2	32 11.5	34 10.7	29 12.7	24 15.4		35 10.5	37 10.0
	7.4	9.2	11.6	12.7	9.2	Sales/Working Capital	11.1	10.5
	25.1	19.6	18.0	19.3	14.2		21.8	20.3
	54.6	42.1	33.8	29.3	33.7		41.3	41.3
	34.3	15.1	14.5	12.4	5.5	EBIT/Interest	8.1	5.3
	(24) 3.6	(107) 5.7	(98) 6.9	7.3	(27) 3.7	(279)	3.5	(351) 2.7
	1.0	2.3	3.7	3.4	2.7		1.6	1.5
		10.3	10.6	13.9	5.9	Net Profit + Depr., Dep., Amort./Cur. Mat. L/T/D	6.7	8.9
		(33) 5.7	(46) 6.6	(12) 7.0	(11) 3.0	(104)	3.6	(131) 3.9
		2.6	3.9	2.3	1.6		1.9	2.3
	.1	.2	.4	.4	.4	Fixed/Worth	.4	.4
	.5	.5	.8	.6	.6		.7	.7
	1.6	1.0	1.0	.9	1.0		1.0	1.1
	.5	.9	1.1	.9	1.9	Debt/Worth	.8	1.0
	1.5	1.4	1.8	1.6	2.6		1.6	1.8
	7.7	3.0	3.0	2.5	4.6		3.5	4.0
	43.0	32.5	43.1	39.0	34.3	% Profit Before Taxes/Tangible Net Worth	18.1	21.4
	(27) 18.6	(113) 21.0	29.8	18.2	22.8	(287)	9.4	(360) 11.7
	1.6	8.8	17.0	8.6	11.4		3.5	4.8
	15.2	13.9	15.9	14.5	7.5	% Profit Before Taxes/Total Assets	7.0	8.1
	7.7	7.4	10.8	7.3	5.8		3.6	4.0
	-.7	2.5	5.0	4.0	3.9		1.3	1.3
	165.5	41.4	24.5	33.5	28.9	Sales/Net Fixed Assets	26.0	27.3
	17.3	16.6	14.6	13.9	16.4		11.5	11.8
	10.6	9.2	9.0	9.6	11.3		6.8	7.2
	7.7	4.7	4.7	4.2	4.1	Sales/Total Assets	4.5	4.0
	5.2	3.4	3.5	3.2	3.2		3.0	2.8
	2.3	2.3	2.5	2.8	2.2		2.2	2.0
	.4	.4	.5	.4	.3	% Depr., Dep., Amort./Sales	.7	.7
	(23) .7	(110) .8	(97) .9	(35) .6	(28) .8	(274)	1.3	(344) 1.2
	1.5	1.2	1.3	1.0	1.1		1.7	1.7
	.5	.4				% Officers', Directors' Owners' Comp/Sales	.7	.6
	(13) 1.5	(29) .8				(45)	1.3	(59) 1.3
	3.9	2.7					3.4	2.8
3597M	228743M	2506132M	8785280M	9591709M	17911034M	Net Sales ($)	23579690M	30036924M
464M	40658M	628325M	2311755M	2540996M	4818882M	Total Assets ($)	5232804M	7562133M

M = $ thousand   MM = $ million
See Pages 9 through 22 for Explanation of Ratios and Data

Comparative Historical Data   Current Data Sorted by Sales

4/1/07-3/31/08 ALL	4/1/08-3/31/09 ALL	4/1/09-3/31/10 ALL	Type of Statement	0-1MM	1-3MM	3-5MM	5-10MM	10-25MM	25MM & OVER
220	174	171	Unqualified	1			7	27	136
92	73	65	Reviewed	2	5	4	8	20	26
17	17	11	Compiled		2	1	1	3	4
11	18	19	Tax Returns	1	5		5	6	2
79	76	50	Other		1		11	13	25
					167 (4/1-9/30/09)		149 (10/1/09-3/31/10)		
419	358	316	NUMBER OF STATEMENTS	4	13	5	32	69	193
%	%	%	**ASSETS**	%	%	%	%	%	%
7.3	8.1	10.1	Cash & Equivalents		11.3		13.1	13.2	8.1
17.8	19.0	19.2	Trade Receivables (net)		26.7		18.1	16.7	19.5
38.9	39.1	34.4	Inventory		23.7		29.5	32.1	37.1
8.1	9.8	4.9	All Other Current		.6		4.5	5.2	5.3
72.2	76.1	68.7	Total Current		62.4		65.3	67.2	70.0
21.2	17.8	23.8	Fixed Assets (net)		25.9		24.3	24.2	23.5
.4	.5	.4	Intangibles (net)		.1		1.5	.3	.3
6.1	5.6	7.1	All Other Non-Current		11.7		8.8	8.2	6.2
100.0	100.0	100.0	Total		100.0		100.0	100.0	100.0
			LIABILITIES						
27.1	26.0	13.6	Notes Payable-Short Term		4.8		9.2	11.3	15.8
1.6	2.2	2.2	Cur. Mat.-L.T.D.		8.1		1.4	3.3	1.5
16.2	17.6	19.2	Trade Payables		19.8		20.2	17.6	19.9
.3	.4	.4	Income Taxes Payable		.1		.0	.5	.5
10.0	12.5	11.8	All Other Current		15.3		14.8	12.0	11.2
55.4	58.6	47.2	Total Current		48.1		45.6	44.6	48.8
9.1	7.9	11.6	Long-Term Debt		25.6		10.4	10.2	11.0
1.1	.8	1.3	Deferred Taxes		.0		.4	1.3	1.6
1.2	1.6	2.1	All Other Non-Current		3.3		3.2	.7	2.3
33.2	31.0	37.8	Net Worth		23.0		40.4	43.2	36.3
100.0	100.0	100.0	Total Liabilities & Net Worth		100.0		100.0	100.0	100.0
			INCOME DATA						
100.0	100.0	100.0	Net Sales		100.0		100.0	100.0	100.0
10.9	10.1	10.6	Gross Profit		18.0		17.2	12.3	8.1
7.9	7.1	7.7	Operating Expenses		12.7		13.6	8.5	5.4
3.0	3.1	3.0	Operating Profit		5.3		3.6	3.9	2.8
.6	.4	-.1	All Other Expenses (net)		-1.5		.8	-.2	.0
2.5	2.6	3.1	Profit Before Taxes		6.7		2.8	4.1	2.8
			RATIOS						
1.6	1.6	1.9	Current		1.8		2.2	2.2	1.8
1.2	1.2	1.4			1.3		1.3	1.6	1.4
1.1	1.1	1.2			.8		1.1	1.2	1.2
.8	.8	1.0	Quick		1.2		1.4	1.4	.8
.4	.4	(315) .6			.9		.7	(192) .6	.5
.2	.2	.3			.3		.3	.3	.2
7 51.1	6 57.4	6 60.6	Sales/Receivables		9 41.9		8 47.9	6 64.5	6 63.6
17 21.5	15 24.0	13 27.3			24 15.1		21 17.4	12 29.3	12 30.9
33 11.2	31 11.8	28 13.1			84 4.3		36 10.1	26 14.2	26 13.8
29 12.4	24 15.3	16 22.4	Cost of Sales/Inventory		0 UND		5 74.6	13 28.0	20 18.5
55 6.6	49 7.4	37 9.9			29 12.6		52 7.0	35 10.4	36 10.0
92 4.0	87 4.2	67 5.5			135 2.7		118 3.1	84 4.4	60 6.0
7 54.6	5 74.5	6 60.6	Cost of Sales/Payables		0 UND		9 38.9	5 74.3	7 53.6
16 23.5	13 28.8	16 22.4			8 44.0		17 21.2	16 22.6	16 22.4
34 10.9	31 11.9	30 12.3			44 8.4		59 6.2	35 10.4	27 13.6
12.2	12.7	10.5	Sales/Working Capital		5.5		5.7	7.9	13.4
20.7	23.1	19.4			12.1		24.8	13.0	20.8
37.8	51.4	37.4			-57.5		75.7	34.0	36.6
3.9	6.4	13.6	EBIT/Interest		38.9		24.5	15.6	12.7
(400) 2.4	(343) 2.7	(295) 5.5			(11) 2.4		(27) 2.8	(64) 7.6	(186) 5.7
1.5	1.6	2.7			-1.8		1.4	2.8	3.2
6.7	9.6	9.9	Net Profit + Depr., Dep., Amort./Cur. Mat. L/T/D					13.2	8.6
(148) 4.2	(144) 4.4	(107) 5.9						(18) 5.8	(83) 5.9
2.4	2.5	2.8						2.4	2.9
.4	.3	.3	Fixed/Worth		.3		.2	.2	.4
.7	.6	.6			.6		.5	.5	.7
1.1	1.0	1.0			1.8		1.4	.9	1.0
1.2	1.5	1.0	Debt/Worth		.7		.8	.6	1.1
2.3	2.7	1.7			3.0		2.0	1.4	1.7
5.0	5.1	3.4			11.5		3.7	2.5	3.5
25.1	34.4	37.1	% Profit Before Taxes/Tangible Net Worth		58.2		21.7	34.7	40.3
(411) 14.8	(349) 21.0	(309) 23.2			(12) 19.9		(30) 13.4	(68) 22.4	(192) 28.2
7.6	9.1	10.1			-11.6		5.3	6.1	15.0
7.1	10.3	14.4	% Profit Before Taxes/Total Assets		18.1		7.8	15.7	14.7
4.1	5.3	7.8			4.1		3.7	9.0	8.4
1.8	2.0	3.3			-4.7		1.1	3.1	4.4
28.2	45.8	32.3	Sales/Net Fixed Assets		22.4		31.1	51.2	32.4
14.1	18.2	15.6			8.9		12.9	16.3	16.5
9.2	10.9	9.3			4.6		6.2	8.3	10.7
3.9	4.5	4.9	Sales/Total Assets		3.1		4.1	4.6	5.5
2.7	3.1	3.4			2.3		2.2	3.1	3.8
1.9	2.1	2.5			1.2		1.7	2.2	2.8
.6	.4	.4	% Depr., Dep., Amort./Sales		.6		.7	.4	.4
(394) 1.0	(326) .7	(294) .8			(10) 1.4	(26) 1.2		(62) .8	(187) .8
1.4	1.0	1.2			5.1		1.7	1.3	1.1
.5	.3	.3	% Officers', Directors' Owners' Comp/Sales					.5	.3
(57) 1.4	(60) 1.0	(55) .8						(16) .7	(25) .5
3.1	1.7	2.4						2.3	1.7
28552463M	49371391M	39026495M	Net Sales ($)	1783M	29730M	20749M	242690M	1132515M	37599028M
11187017M	12476073M	10341080M	Total Assets ($)	2109M	18467M	7821M	134540M	509830M	9668313M

M = $ thousand   MM = $ million
See Pages 9 through 22 for Explanation of Ratios and Data

Current Data Sorted by Assets							Type of Statement	Comparative Historical Data	
		1	2	1			Unqualified	4	5
		3					Reviewed	2	2
1			1				Compiled	9	7
1	2						Tax Returns	7	8
3	7	1					Other	8	17
		2	4	1				4/1/05-	4/1/06-
	7 (4/1-9/30/09)		23 (10/1/09-3/31/10)					3/31/06	3/31/07
0-500M	500M-2MM	2-10MM	10-50MM	50-100MM	100-250MM		NUMBER OF STATEMENTS	ALL	ALL
5	9	7	7	2				30	39
%	%	%	%	%	%		ASSETS	%	%
						D	Cash & Equivalents	4.3	9.9
						A	Trade Receivables (net)	26.3	25.8
						T	Inventory	26.7	21.7
						A	All Other Current	7.6	6.6
							Total Current	64.9	64.1
						N	Fixed Assets (net)	25.2	24.5
						O	Intangibles (net)	3.1	2.2
						T	All Other Non-Current	6.8	9.2
							Total	100.0	100.0
						A	LIABILITIES		
						V	Notes Payable-Short Term	18.6	20.0
						A	Cur. Mat.-L.T.D.	4.5	2.4
						I	Trade Payables	10.0	15.9
						L	Income Taxes Payable	.1	.1
						A	All Other Current	16.7	17.8
						B	Total Current	49.9	56.2
						L	Long-Term Debt	12.1	20.4
						E	Deferred Taxes	.2	.1
							All Other Non-Current	1.2	.9
							Net Worth	36.7	22.3
							Total Liabilties & Net Worth	100.0	100.0
							INCOME DATA		
							Net Sales	100.0	100.0
							Gross Profit	23.7	18.8
							Operating Expenses	23.4	17.4
							Operating Profit	.3	1.4
							All Other Expenses (net)	-.6	.6
							Profit Before Taxes	.9	.9
							RATIOS		
								1.6	1.8
							Current	1.3	1.1
								1.0	.9
								1.0	1.1
							Quick	(29) .6	.8
								.4	.5
								2 242.2	5 73.2
							Sales/Receivables	16 22.2	13 27.5
								26 14.3	24 15.2
								3 108.6	2 194.8
							Cost of Sales/Inventory	17 21.4	6 57.9
								60 6.1	25 14.4
								0 UND	0 974.6
							Cost of Sales/Payables	4 83.7	4 81.5
								24 15.2	14 25.8
								16.1	26.7
							Sales/Working Capital	84.8	178.7
								392.0	-202.0
								7.6	8.8
							EBIT/Interest	(28) 3.4	(37) 2.7
								.1	.6
							Net Profit + Depr., Dep., Amort./Cur. Mat. L/T/D		
								.5	.2
							Fixed/Worth	.8	.7
								1.7	1.9
								1.0	1.6
							Debt/Worth	1.9	4.4
								7.6	8.7
								65.4	63.4
							% Profit Before Taxes/Tangible Net Worth	(27) 12.9	(35) 15.7
								1.0	-4.2
								15.1	17.4
							% Profit Before Taxes/Total Assets	3.7	5.1
								-2.6	-1.1
								73.2	285.9
							Sales/Net Fixed Assets	24.5	39.1
								8.2	13.3
								11.1	14.9
							Sales/Total Assets	4.3	8.1
								2.4	3.0
								.5	.2
							% Depr., Dep., Amort./Sales	(27) .9	(35) .5
								2.0	1.2
								.6	.4
							% Officers', Directors' Owners' Comp/Sales	(11) 1.0	(14) 1.2
								1.6	1.9
6901M	214709M	91250M	755138M	2582856M			Net Sales ($)	2267467M	3521343M
1370M	11040M	23845M	157765M	151527M			Total Assets ($)	441786M	422192M

M = $ thousand   MM = $ million
See Pages 9 through 22 for Explanation of Ratios and Data

Comparative Historical Data   Current Data Sorted by Sales

Type of Statement

	4/1/07-3/31/08 ALL	4/1/08-3/31/09 ALL	4/1/09-3/31/10 ALL	0-1MM	1-3MM	3-5MM	5-10MM	10-25MM	25MM & OVER
Unqualified	3	9	4		2	1		1	3
Reviewed	3	3	4		1			1	1
Compiled	2	4	4		3		1	1	1
Tax Returns	9	5	11				2		2
Other	17	8	7	2			2	2	4
	4/1/07-3/31/08	4/1/08-3/31/09	4/1/09-3/31/10		7 (4/1-9/30/09)			23 (10/1/09-3/31/10)	
NUMBER OF STATEMENTS	34	29	30	2	6	1	5	5	11

Main Data (values in %, three-value ratio rows shown as a / b / c)

	07/08 ALL %	08/09 ALL %	09/10 ALL %	25MM & OVER %
ASSETS				
Cash & Equivalents	13.1	10.2	12.4	8.9
Trade Receivables (net)	23.7	24.0	27.0	34.2
Inventory	20.1	25.7	24.9	19.6
All Other Current	7.3	4.4	3.6	7.9
Total Current	64.2	64.3	67.9	70.5
Fixed Assets (net)	23.8	24.4	21.6	20.2
Intangibles (net)	.2	3.2	1.4	.5
All Other Non-Current	11.7	8.1	9.1	8.9
Total	100.0	100.0	100.0	100.0
LIABILITIES				
Notes Payable-Short Term	23.8	24.6	16.5	18.2
Cur. Mat.-L.T.D.	2.1	2.7	4.3	6.9
Trade Payables	11.5	9.6	13.0	13.9
Income Taxes Payable	.1	.9	.2	.4
All Other Current	12.8	16.7	21.5	21.7
Total Current	50.2	54.4	55.5	61.0
Long-Term Debt	21.2	12.3	15.5	9.8
Deferred Taxes	.1	.0	.0	.0
All Other Non-Current	1.2	3.6	2.4	4.2
Net Worth	27.3	29.7	26.6	24.9
Total Liabilties & Net Worth	100.0	100.0	100.0	100.0
INCOME DATA				
Net Sales	100.0	100.0	100.0	100.0
Gross Profit	19.2	23.6	26.5	9.4
Operating Expenses	19.5	21.5	25.3	8.8
Operating Profit	-.3	2.1	1.3	.7
All Other Expenses (net)	-.5	-.2	-.5	-.9
Profit Before Taxes	.2	2.4	1.7	1.6
RATIOS				
Current	2.2 / 1.1 / .9	2.1 / 1.3 / .9	2.1 / 1.4 / 1.0	1.5 / 1.1 / 1.0
Quick	1.7 / .9 / .3	1.2 / .6 / .3	1.0 / .8 / .5	.8 / .6 / .5
Sales/Receivables	0 UND / 6 58.6 / 18 20.7	1 486.4 / 9 40.0 / 21 17.3	4 88.7 / 15 23.6 / 23 15.9	5 72.9 / 17 22.1 / 20 18.1
Cost of Sales/Inventory	1 459.4 / 4 87.2 / 28 12.9	2 156.3 / 19 19.1 / 46 7.9	3 140.7 / 18 20.4 / 62 5.9	3 144.7 / 3 132.0 / 26 14.0
Cost of Sales/Payables	0 UND / 3 126.5 / 14 26.5	1 505.2 / 4 103.0 / 21 17.5	0 UND / 9 42.3 / 19 18.9	1 295.6 / 7 52.8 / 18 19.8
Sales/Working Capital	22.3 / 127.3 / -130.1	18.3 / 63.6 / NM	13.7 / 35.7 / -573.5	19.0 / 136.7 / -498.2
EBIT/Interest	11.2 / (30) 2.2 / 1.0	12.6 / (23) 1.9 / .8	13.1 / (26) 3.5 / 1.3	11.8 / 4.2 / 1.7
Net Profit + Depr., Dep., Amort./Cur. Mat. L/T/D				
Fixed/Worth	.3 / .9 / 1.8	.3 / .8 / 3.1	.1 / .8 / 2.5	.1 / .6 / 1.7
Debt/Worth	1.0 / 3.8 / 12.0	.7 / 3.2 / 11.9	1.1 / 3.9 / 18.9	1.4 / 4.0 / 18.2
% Profit Before Taxes/Tangible Net Worth	64.9 / (30) 20.7 / -.1	51.6 / (24) 22.4 / 2.7	57.6 / (27) 17.0 / 7.1	91.4 / 24.4 / 10.0
% Profit Before Taxes/Total Assets	14.0 / 2.5 / -.2	28.4 / 4.9 / .5	13.0 / 4.8 / .9	21.0 / 8.6 / 2.0
Sales/Net Fixed Assets	175.6 / 35.5 / 14.9	173.8 / 35.6 / 17.8	249.0 / 28.1 / 11.8	743.9 / 30.8 / 18.3
Sales/Total Assets	15.3 / 7.2 / 3.9	12.4 / 6.5 / 3.9	11.7 / 5.2 / 3.3	17.2 / 7.2 / 4.8
% Depr., Dep., Amort./Sales	(32) .2 / .5 / .8	(26) .3 / .5 / 1.7	(26) .2 / .7 / 2.5	(10) .0 / .5 / 1.2
% Officers', Directors' Owners' Comp/Sales	(13) .3 / 1.1 / 2.2	(12) 1.1	.3 / 1.1 / 5.4	

Net Sales ($) / Total Assets ($)

	07/08 ALL	08/09 ALL	09/10 ALL	0-1MM	1-3MM	3-5MM	5-10MM	10-25MM	25MM & OVER
Net Sales ($)	906105M	1094056M	3650854M	1823M	11719M	4933M	36412M	83059M	3512908M
Total Assets ($)	146092M	201868M	345547M	682M	4660M	5859M	18476M	29716M	286154M

© RMA 2010

M = $ thousand   MM = $ million
See Pages 9 through 22 for Explanation of Ratios and Data

WHOLESALE—Other Farm Product Raw Material Merchant Wholesalers NAICS 424590

Current Data Sorted by Assets							Comparative Historical Data	
	2	3	11	4	2	Type of Statement — Unqualified	28	32
		15	9	3		Reviewed	23	25
	5	8	1			Compiled	10	11
	7	6	2			Tax Returns	13	15
1	7	10	8	6	1	Other	31	32
	40 (4/1-9/30/09)		71 (10/1/09-3/31/10)				4/1/05-3/31/06 ALL	4/1/06-3/31/07 ALL
0-500M	500M-2MM	2-10MM	10-50MM	50-100MM	100-250M			
1	21	42	31	13	3	NUMBER OF STATEMENTS	105	115
%	%	%	%	%	%	**ASSETS**	%	%
	18.6	8.5	7.2	5.2		Cash & Equivalents	8.8	7.3
	46.6	42.9	32.6	18.2		Trade Receivables (net)	33.1	33.7
	14.9	24.2	37.0	49.3		Inventory	28.3	31.7
	3.5	5.9	5.2	4.8		All Other Current	4.2	6.1
	83.5	81.5	82.1	77.4		Total Current	74.4	78.8
	8.8	14.4	13.4	14.9		Fixed Assets (net)	17.8	14.5
	.9	1.0	.7	.2		Intangibles (net)	1.4	1.2
	6.8	3.1	3.9	7.4		All Other Non-Current	6.5	5.6
	100.0	100.0	100.0	100.0		Total	100.0	100.0
						LIABILITIES		
	16.0	18.5	19.4	25.7		Notes Payable-Short Term	17.9	21.5
	.4	1.0	1.2	1.3		Cur. Mat.-L.T.D.	1.4	1.3
	18.7	23.6	26.6	18.8		Trade Payables	19.4	21.3
	.0	.1	.5	.3		Income Taxes Payable	.3	.2
	23.8	10.2	10.0	16.4		All Other Current	10.7	11.4
	58.9	53.4	57.6	62.5		Total Current	49.5	55.6
	5.5	7.5	7.6	5.5		Long-Term Debt	10.1	7.9
	.0	.1	.2	.8		Deferred Taxes	.2	.2
	3.7	1.7	4.2	2.3		All Other Non-Current	3.8	3.1
	31.8	37.3	30.4	29.0		Net Worth	36.3	33.1
	100.0	100.0	100.0	100.0		Total Liabilties & Net Worth	100.0	100.0
						INCOME DATA		
	100.0	100.0	100.0	100.0		Net Sales	100.0	100.0
	18.6	18.3	13.5	13.8		Gross Profit	18.4	17.3
	16.3	14.1	9.5	10.5		Operating Expenses	15.4	14.9
	2.3	4.2	4.0	3.3		Operating Profit	3.1	2.4
	-.2	1.8	.4	-.2		All Other Expenses (net)	.4	.8
	2.5	2.5	3.6	3.6		Profit Before Taxes	2.6	1.7
						RATIOS		
	2.2	1.9	1.9	1.7		Current	2.2	2.3
	1.3	1.4	1.3	1.2			1.4	1.3
	1.1	1.2	1.1	.9			1.1	1.1
	1.8	1.7	1.1	.5		Quick	1.3	1.1
	1.0	1.1	.7	.4			.8 (114)	.6
	.8	.5	.5	.2			.5	.4
17 21.7	24 15.1	24 15.1	8 43.8			Sales/Receivables	19 19.5	19 19.3
31 11.9	35 10.3	44 8.4	29 12.4				30 12.1	30 12.0
49 7.4	62 5.9	59 6.2	54 6.8				48 7.6	48 7.6
0 UND	0 UND	25 14.6	43 8.5			Cost of Sales/Inventory	10 37.0	10 36.8
4 89.4	16 22.8	52 7.0	59 6.2				35 10.4	45 8.2
40 9.1	61 5.9	100 3.6	162 2.3				69 5.3	85 4.3
0 757.0	15 24.8	17 20.9	9 38.5			Cost of Sales/Payables	8 47.0	9 40.6
9 40.8	26 14.1	36 10.2	29 12.5				19 19.0	20 18.0
31 11.7	42 8.7	82 4.5	46 7.9				39 9.4	38 9.6
	9.3	8.3	6.9	6.2		Sales/Working Capital	7.6	8.1
	15.5	18.2	16.1	28.8			17.1	20.0
	226.9	35.9	34.4	-23.2			37.5	54.5
	32.1	26.3	20.4	22.3		EBIT/Interest	8.0	5.4
	(19) 8.5	(40) 5.4	(30) 7.0	6.9			(97) 4.1	(109) 2.4
	2.0	1.4	1.7	3.1			1.6	1.2
						Net Profit + Depr., Dep., Amort./Cur. Mat. L/T/D	15.3	8.5
							(24) 5.5	(18) 4.7
							3.0	2.8
	.0	.0	.1	.2		Fixed/Worth	.1	.0
	.0	.2	.4	.4			.3	.2
	1.0	.6	.8	1.5			.9	.9
	1.1	.8	1.5	1.4		Debt/Worth	1.3	1.1
	3.0	2.2	2.8	2.4			2.2	2.5
	14.5	4.1	5.1	7.6			4.0	5.2
	98.3	42.0	64.8	81.5		% Profit Before Taxes/Tangible Net Worth	44.0	39.8
	(18) 40.2	(39) 17.3	(30) 33.1	25.9			(101) 21.7	(109) 14.4
	2.3	2.5	9.2	18.1			5.5	2.9
	31.2	13.2	17.2	11.9		% Profit Before Taxes/Total Assets	11.0	10.1
	8.2	6.6	8.2	8.6			5.8	4.0
	-.5	.9	1.8	3.4			1.5	.8
	UND	999.8	186.5	76.0		Sales/Net Fixed Assets	129.1	379.7
	574.0	54.4	23.1	23.8			29.1	46.0
	37.3	11.2	10.2	5.0			10.1	11.1
	7.2	5.0	3.2	3.7		Sales/Total Assets	4.6	5.0
	4.4	3.1	2.8	1.5			3.1	3.4
	3.1	2.0	1.8	1.2			2.0	2.3
	.5	.1	.3	.2		% Depr., Dep., Amort./Sales	.3	.1
	(10) .8	(31) .6	(26) .8	(12) 1.0			(93) .7	(90) .5
	1.3	1.9	1.3	2.2			1.8	1.8
		1.1				% Officers', Directors' Owners' Comp/Sales	.5	.6
		(12) 1.7					(32) 1.3	(29) 1.4
		4.0					2.7	3.5
723M	162966M	967946M	2214838M	2525781M	833734M	Net Sales ($)	7943389M	9101429M
452M	25388M	209764M	761583M	974210M	530540M	Total Assets ($)	2371832M	2429252M

M = $ thousand   MM = $ million

See Pages 9 through 22 for Explanation of Ratios and Data

Comparative Historical Data   **Current Data Sorted by Sales**

4/1/07- 3/31/08 ALL	4/1/08- 3/31/09 ALL	4/1/09- 3/31/10 ALL	Type of Statement	0-1MM	1-3MM	3-5MM	5-10MM	10-25MM	25MM & OVER
29	25	22	Unqualified		1		1	1	19
21	26	27	Reviewed		3		3	9	15
16	19	14	Compiled		1	1	4	3	3
11	21	15	Tax Returns		2	5	1	5	3
51	45	33	Other	1		1	5	7	17
					40 (4/1-9/30/09)		71 (10/1/09-3/31/10)		
128	136	111	**NUMBER OF STATEMENTS**	1	7	7	14	25	57
%	%	%		%	%	%	%	%	%
			ASSETS						
7.4	8.7	9.7	Cash & Equivalents				12.1	9.8	7.4
34.6	34.5	37.5	Trade Receivables (net)				42.7	47.6	33.0
32.5	30.5	29.7	Inventory				19.1	22.5	36.1
5.9	5.6	5.0	All Other Current				.8	7.3	5.7
80.4	79.4	81.8	Total Current				74.6	87.2	82.1
14.2	14.2	12.9	Fixed Assets (net)				19.5	8.9	12.6
1.3	1.5	.8	Intangibles (net)				.0	.4	1.0
4.2	4.8	4.6	All Other Non-Current				5.9	3.5	4.3
100.0	100.0	100.0	Total				100.0	100.0	100.0
			LIABILITIES						
23.5	24.2	19.8	Notes Payable-Short Term				14.3	21.4	20.7
1.3	1.6	1.0	Cur. Mat.-L.T.D.				1.5	.8	1.1
20.5	23.4	22.6	Trade Payables				15.0	25.9	24.9
.1	.2	.2	Income Taxes Payable				.0	.4	.2
11.5	8.8	13.1	All Other Current				16.7	9.2	14.5
56.9	58.1	56.7	Total Current				47.6	57.7	61.4
7.4	6.7	6.8	Long-Term Debt				9.2	3.5	5.9
.2	.1	.2	Deferred Taxes				.1	.0	.3
4.4	2.8	2.8	All Other Non-Current				1.3	3.0	3.1
31.2	32.2	33.4	Net Worth				41.9	35.9	29.3
100.0	100.0	100.0	Total Liabilities & Net Worth				100.0	100.0	100.0
			INCOME DATA						
100.0	100.0	100.0	Net Sales				100.0	100.0	100.0
16.5	16.2	16.4	Gross Profit				14.6	18.1	12.0
12.5	13.0	12.4	Operating Expenses				10.8	14.0	8.4
3.9	3.2	4.0	Operating Profit				3.8	4.1	3.6
1.1	.9	.8	All Other Expenses (net)				.3	1.3	.9
2.8	2.4	3.2	Profit Before Taxes				3.5	2.7	2.8
			RATIOS						
1.9	1.9	1.9	Current				2.3	1.9	1.7
1.3	1.3	1.3					1.5	1.4	1.3
1.1	1.1	1.1					1.1	1.2	1.1
1.1	1.2	1.2	Quick				2.0	1.8	1.1
.8	.8	.8					1.1	1.0	.6
.5	.4	.5					.9	.6	.3
17 21.2	19 19.2	23 15.8	Sales/Receivables				24 15.4	23 15.6	20 18.6
34 10.8	30 12.1	37 9.9					35 10.5	37 9.8	37 9.9
45 8.0	47 7.8	59 6.2					84 4.4	73 5.0	51 7.2
9 40.7	8 48.2	3 140.5	Cost of Sales/Inventory				0 UND	0 UND	16 23.3
42 8.7	34 10.6	33 11.2					16 23.4	10 38.3	47 7.8
90 4.0	86 4.2	86 4.2					63 5.8	71 5.1	102 3.6
9 41.3	9 39.7	9 40.8	Cost of Sales/Payables				7 48.8	11 33.4	10 35.9
21 17.5	23 15.8	27 13.5					18 20.3	32 11.3	28 13.2
42 8.7	51 7.1	49 7.5					39 9.4	52 7.0	50 7.3
10.2	10.1	7.8	Sales/Working Capital				7.5	8.3	9.3
18.9	21.2	16.1					20.0	14.3	22.2
37.7	44.4	37.9					39.5	24.5	57.9
7.3	7.8	24.8	EBIT/Interest				32.1	25.0	25.3
(122) 2.8	(129) 3.5	(105) 6.2					(11) 5.0	2.0	(56) 8.1
1.6	1.3	1.7					3.2	.0	2.8
16.0	7.9	9.5	Net Profit + Depr., Dep., Amort./Cur. Mat. L/T/D						13.1
(27) 5.4	(22) 4.0	(19) 4.5							(12) 6.8
2.1	2.2	1.8							1.7
.0	.1	.0	Fixed/Worth				.0	.0	.0
.2	.3	.2					.1	.1	.4
.7	1.0	.8					.9	.4	.9
1.3	1.1	1.2	Debt/Worth				.7	1.1	1.6
2.7	2.6	2.4					2.2	2.2	2.8
5.2	5.6	4.9					3.5	4.0	6.5
37.8	39.1	60.7	% Profit Before Taxes/Tangible Net Worth				51.8	51.0	69.6
(122) 16.8	(127) 18.1	(104) 25.1					23.9	(22) 12.1	(55) 32.2
6.2	2.6	7.6					6.6	1.2	12.3
10.4	11.5	15.2	% Profit Before Taxes/Total Assets				15.4	18.4	15.6
4.4	5.0	7.8					7.5	1.7	9.0
1.7	.5	1.5					4.8	-2.2	3.4
410.3	286.1	574.0	Sales/Net Fixed Assets				925.5	838.9	264.8
46.6	47.6	38.6					13.1	93.8	31.6
11.1	11.2	11.5					6.5	28.5	10.9
4.8	5.3	4.6	Sales/Total Assets				5.6	5.4	4.7
3.3	3.3	3.0					2.7	3.6	2.9
2.1	2.0	1.9					1.8	2.3	1.7
.1	.2	.3	% Depr., Dep., Amort./Sales					.1	.2
(103) .5	(106) .6	(82) .8					(18)	.6	(46) .7
1.5	1.9	1.6						1.2	1.5
.6	.4	.6	% Officers', Directors' Owners' Comp/Sales						.3
(36) 1.4	(40) .9	(31) 1.5							(14) .8
3.3	3.1	2.4							1.9
9391871M	9129058M	6705988M	Net Sales ($)	723M	15828M	30496M	107134M	376505M	6175302M
3135412M	2867251M	2501937M	Total Assets ($)	452M	7267M	14082M	45319M	129022M	2305795M

M = $ thousand   MM = $ million
See Pages 9 through 22 for Explanation of Ratios and Data

WHOLESALE—Plastics Materials and Basic Forms and Shapes Merchant Wholesalers NAICS 424610

Current Data Sorted by Assets | Comparative Historical Data

Type of Statement							4/1/05-3/31/06 ALL	4/1/06-3/31/07 ALL
Unqualified	1	7	13	4	1		17	16
Reviewed	1	16	15		1		34	46
Compiled	4	10	2				19	28
Tax Returns	11	10	10				14	16
Other	14	23	18	1	3		49	62

(0-500M: 5 / 4; 50-100MM: 4 / ... / 1; 100-250MM: 1 / ... / 3)
22 (4/1-9/30/09) 142 (10/1/09-3/31/10)

0-500M	500M-2MM	2-10MM	10-50MM	50-100MM	100-250MM		4/1/05-3/31/06 ALL	4/1/06-3/31/07 ALL
9	31	66	48	6	4	**NUMBER OF STATEMENTS**	133	168
%	%	%	%	%	%	**ASSETS**	%	%
	8.1	9.5	4.5			Cash & Equivalents	7.1	7.0
	44.9	38.2	41.8			Trade Receivables (net)	42.6	39.5
	25.6	30.5	27.6			Inventory	28.1	30.5
	1.9	1.8	2.3			All Other Current	1.8	1.8
	80.5	80.0	76.2			Total Current	79.6	78.8
	5.9	11.3	15.4			Fixed Assets (net)	12.6	12.5
	1.3	2.9	4.2			Intangibles (net)	2.6	2.4
	12.3	5.8	4.2			All Other Non-Current	5.2	6.3
	100.0	100.0	100.0			Total	100.0	100.0
						LIABILITIES		
	16.5	15.0	21.1			Notes Payable-Short Term	18.1	17.7
	1.4	1.3	2.4			Cur. Mat.-L.T.D.	2.3	2.0
	29.5	28.2	26.8			Trade Payables	27.1	24.7
	.7	.1	.1			Income Taxes Payable	.4	.3
	4.0	7.8	5.9			All Other Current	10.0	8.2
	52.2	52.4	56.3			Total Current	58.0	52.9
	7.8	8.5	10.4			Long-Term Debt	8.6	7.4
	.1	.2	.4			Deferred Taxes	.3	.1
	9.8	4.0	4.9			All Other Non-Current	3.6	4.7
	30.1	34.9	28.1			Net Worth	29.5	34.9
	100.0	100.0	100.0			Total Liabilities & Net Worth	100.0	100.0
						INCOME DATA		
	100.0	100.0	100.0			Net Sales	100.0	100.0
	27.5	21.6	17.6			Gross Profit	23.2	24.6
	24.0	18.8	14.0			Operating Expenses	19.4	19.9
	3.5	2.7	3.6			Operating Profit	3.8	4.7
	.0	.6	.8			All Other Expenses (net)	.6	.7
	3.5	2.2	2.8			Profit Before Taxes	3.3	3.9
						RATIOS		
	2.9	2.4	1.9				1.9	2.2
	1.9	1.5	1.3			Current	1.3	1.4
	1.1	1.2	1.1				1.1	1.2
	1.8	1.5	1.1				1.2	1.2
	1.1	.9	.8			Quick	.8	.8
	.6	.6	.6				.6	.6
	39 9.4	31 11.9	39 9.3				36 10.1	35 10.5
	46 8.0	40 9.0	47 7.7			Sales/Receivables	48 7.6	45 8.2
	66 5.5	52 7.0	67 5.4				61 6.0	55 6.6
	6 62.1	14 27.0	25 14.8				18 20.3	22 16.7
	49 7.5	45 8.1	44 8.3			Cost of Sales/Inventory	45 8.2	48 7.5
	78 4.7	80 4.6	66 5.5				71 5.1	74 4.9
	23 15.7	18 20.0	25 14.7				23 15.7	22 16.9
	39 9.4	34 10.8	41 8.9			Cost of Sales/Payables	42 8.7	35 10.4
	67 5.5	54 6.7	54 6.8				55 6.6	48 7.6
	5.5	7.0	6.7				7.9	7.4
	7.2	13.0	15.8			Sales/Working Capital	15.8	12.2
	49.2	32.8	42.9				53.5	27.6
	23.4	13.9	9.9				16.0	17.2
	(27) 12.1	(56) 5.6	(47) 5.0			EBIT/Interest	(119) 5.6	(155) 4.5
	3.3	1.3	1.2				2.3	2.1
		3.8	11.8				19.7	13.0
		(11) 3.2	(14) 3.6			Net Profit + Depr., Dep., Amort./Cur. Mat. L/T/D	(21) 8.3	(36) 6.5
		.8	1.9				1.6	3.0
	.0	.0	.0				.1	.1
	.2	.2	.3			Fixed/Worth	.2	.2
	1.0	.7	2.4				1.0	.7
	.6	.9	1.3				1.2	.9
	3.4	1.9	4.0			Debt/Worth	2.7	2.0
	17.5	3.9	7.3				7.1	5.6
	96.6	49.3	45.5				67.6	47.0
	(27) 34.3	(62) 20.4	(41) 28.2			% Profit Before Taxes/Tangible Net Worth	(120) 35.5	(153) 25.2
	15.8	1.2	7.5				12.0	11.6
	18.5	16.2	12.5				19.0	19.6
	13.0	5.9	5.0			% Profit Before Taxes/Total Assets	7.5	8.4
	3.4	.6	1.2				3.5	3.1
	999.8	339.8	383.3				256.1	296.2
	98.8	67.5	80.3			Sales/Net Fixed Assets	71.9	64.9
	34.7	11.7	10.1				15.7	15.2
	4.0	4.7	3.3				4.0	3.9
	3.3	3.3	2.6			Sales/Total Assets	3.0	3.1
	2.3	2.3	2.0				2.4	2.4
	.3	.2	.1				.2	.2
	(13) .6	(48) .7	(39) .4			% Depr., Dep., Amort./Sales	(108) .6	(138) .6
	2.6	2.0	1.5				1.1	1.1
	1.2	.7	.5				1.3	1.3
	(17) 2.8	(28) 1.7	(17) .6			% Officers', Directors' Owners' Comp/Sales	(54) 2.4	(77) 2.7
	6.8	3.4	3.3				4.8	6.2
7532M	121426M	1123024M	3183632M	1223948M	1085952M	Net Sales ($)	6449963M	5927417M
2082M	39744M	308817M	1055631M	430119M	524961M	Total Assets ($)	2145217M	1792775M

M = $ thousand   MM = $ million
See Pages 9 through 22 for Explanation of Ratios and Data

Comparative Historical Data — **Current Data Sorted by Sales**

4/1/07-3/31/08 ALL	4/1/08-3/31/09 ALL	4/1/09-3/31/10 ALL	Type of Statement	0-1MM	1-3MM	3-5MM	5-10MM	10-25MM	25MM & OVER
20	25	26	Unqualified			1		5	19
35	31	33	Reviewed		2	1	8	9	21
25	10	16	Compiled		1	2	7	2	3
18	17	26	Tax Returns	4	3	7	5	6	1
62	49	63	Other	1	7	9	4	14	22
						22 (4/1-9/30/09)		142 (10/1/09-3/31/10)	
160	132	164	NUMBER OF STATEMENTS	5	13	20	24	36	66
%	%	%	**ASSETS**	%	%	%	%	%	%
6.4	7.6	8.3	Cash & Equivalents		10.4	4.7	7.1	8.2	9.8
40.1	40.1	40.2	Trade Receivables (net)		37.8	44.3	39.7	39.7	39.9
30.4	30.0	28.4	Inventory		17.9	29.0	29.6	32.5	27.2
2.5	2.3	1.9	All Other Current		3.2	.9	1.5	1.4	2.5
79.5	80.0	78.8	Total Current		69.4	78.9	77.9	81.8	79.4
11.7	11.4	11.1	Fixed Assets (net)		6.6	11.5	13.2	8.2	13.1
2.4	2.3	3.2	Intangibles (net)		2.7	1.0	3.2	4.8	2.8
6.4	6.4	6.9	All Other Non-Current		21.3	8.6	5.7	5.2	4.7
100.0	100.0	100.0	Total		100.0	100.0	100.0	100.0	100.0
			LIABILITIES						
17.2	21.4	17.4	Notes Payable-Short Term		5.4	22.1	20.3	15.9	17.2
2.4	1.9	1.6	Cur. Mat.-L.T.D.		2.3	1.8	1.2	1.0	2.0
27.8	24.7	28.0	Trade Payables		32.6	29.5	25.7	27.8	28.6
.1	.1	.2	Income Taxes Payable		1.3	.2	.1	.1	.1
9.2	7.9	6.4	All Other Current		4.0	5.5	6.6	7.5	6.0
56.7	56.0	53.6	Total Current		45.6	59.1	53.9	52.4	53.9
8.6	8.5	9.3	Long-Term Debt		15.8	9.7	7.8	6.6	10.1
.2	.1	.3	Deferred Taxes		.2	.0	.3	.2	.4
4.6	6.8	6.3	All Other Non-Current		21.3	4.9	10.4	2.1	4.4
29.8	28.6	30.5	Net Worth		17.1	26.2	27.6	38.7	31.3
100.0	100.0	100.0	Total Liabilities & Net Worth		100.0	100.0	100.0	100.0	100.0
			INCOME DATA						
100.0	100.0	100.0	Net Sales		100.0	100.0	100.0	100.0	100.0
23.0	22.0	21.5	Gross Profit		25.6	27.0	26.2	22.3	15.9
19.0	20.1	18.1	Operating Expenses		21.0	26.2	22.9	19.0	12.0
4.0	1.9	3.4	Operating Profit		4.6	.8	3.3	3.3	3.9
.8	.8	.6	All Other Expenses (net)		-.5	.6	.7	.3	.9
3.1	1.1	2.8	Profit Before Taxes		5.1	.2	2.7	3.0	3.0
			RATIOS						
2.0	2.1	2.4	Current		2.9	2.3	2.8	2.5	2.3
1.4	1.4	1.5			1.7	1.3	1.6	1.6	1.4
1.1	1.1	1.1			1.1	1.0	1.1	1.2	1.2
1.2	1.2	1.4	Quick		1.7	1.2	1.6	1.6	1.3
.8	.8	.9			1.1	.9	.9	.9	1.0
.6	.5	.6			.7	.5	.5	.6	.6
33 11.2	31 11.8	35 10.6	Sales/Receivables		39 9.3	38 9.7	38 9.7	31 11.8	32 11.2
43 8.4	37 9.8	44 8.3			41 8.9	54 6.7	43 8.4	39 9.3	44 8.3
56 6.6	51 7.2	58 6.3			63 5.8	80 4.6	64 5.7	50 7.3	59 6.2
23 16.1	16 23.4	17 21.4	Cost of Sales/Inventory		0 UND	19 19.1	12 29.7	17 22.1	21 17.7
48 7.6	40 9.1	47 7.8			52 7.1	54 6.7	56 6.6	49 7.4	41 8.9
85 4.3	77 4.7	75 4.9			71 5.2	94 3.9	82 4.4	83 4.4	54 6.8
25 14.4	17 21.6	21 17.6	Cost of Sales/Payables		20 18.6	32 11.2	14 26.6	19 18.9	20 17.9
39 9.4	31 11.7	37 9.8			28 13.1	41 8.9	35 10.4	33 11.2	39 9.4
55 6.6	41 8.8	55 6.7			64 5.7	67 5.4	69 5.3	52 7.0	51 7.2
7.9	8.2	6.2	Sales/Working Capital		4.6	5.7	6.1	7.1	6.8
12.8	15.0	12.7			7.1	16.5	8.9	12.8	15.5
34.6	67.3	40.6			181.7	78.7	94.6	31.3	34.8
9.7	7.9	16.1	EBIT/Interest			27.9	11.9	13.7	15.7
(143) 2.9	(119) 3.3	(146) 6.0				(20) 5.7	(31) 7.5	(62) 6.3	5.1
1.6	1.1	1.6				-1.0	1.0	3.1	1.2
7.3	9.0	5.3	Net Profit + Depr., Dep., Amort./Cur. Mat. L/T/D						25.9
(30) 4.0	(26) 3.2	(32) 2.5						(16) 4.2
1.6	1.4	1.1							1.9
.0	.0	.0	Fixed/Worth		.0	.0	.0	.1	.0
.2	.2	.2			.4	.4	.3	.2	.1
.9	1.0	1.0			NM	1.5	1.4	.4	1.1
1.1	1.2	1.1	Debt/Worth		.4	1.1	.7	.9	1.3
2.8	2.7	2.6			5.2	4.0	2.7	1.8	2.7
7.6	7.0	7.3			-15.1	16.9	11.5	4.0	6.5
42.7	39.5	53.6	% Profit Before Taxes/Tangible Net Worth			70.9	54.1	32.8	63.2
(139) 25.5	(115) 19.0	(146) 27.4				(19) 23.8	(21) 15.0	(32) 23.7	(61) 31.0
9.4	4.9	5.8				-45.5	-4.6	6.9	7.5
14.7	11.0	15.3	% Profit Before Taxes/Total Assets		24.9	15.0	19.5	14.1	14.8
6.0	5.5	6.0			5.9	6.1	7.4	7.5	5.8
2.2	.7	1.2			1.4	-7.3	.1	2.7	1.2
298.8	517.3	548.2	Sales/Net Fixed Assets		UND	821.6	381.4	266.3	639.7
68.8	82.0	85.4			98.6	52.9	33.9	72.6	143.3
14.7	18.5	14.5			21.2	10.6	8.6	21.1	12.4
3.9	4.4	3.9	Sales/Total Assets		4.0	3.7	3.7	4.8	3.9
3.0	3.4	2.9			2.6	2.9	2.6	3.5	2.9
2.3	2.6	2.2			1.4	2.0	2.0	2.7	2.1
.2	.1	.1	% Depr., Dep., Amort./Sales			.4	.3	.2	.1
(123) .6	(105) .5	(111) .7				(12) 1.2	(15) 2.0	(24) .6	(52) .3
1.3	1.3	2.0				2.6	4.6	1.1	1.4
.9	1.0	.6	% Officers', Directors' Owners' Comp/Sales			1.9	1.0	.7	.5
(73) 2.6	(60) 2.6	(67) 1.7				(13) 2.8	(12) 2.9	(16) 1.3	(22) .7
5.4	5.3	4.5				6.8	5.1	3.5	2.8
6421253M	8024058M	6745514M	Net Sales ($)	2624M	24254M	79215M	176832M	603580M	5859009M
2296577M	2233752M	2361354M	Total Assets ($)	1130M	11388M	35144M	75776M	193713M	2044203M

M = $ thousand   MM = $ million
See Pages 9 through 22 for Explanation of Ratios and Data

WHOLESALE—Other Chemical and Allied Products Merchant Wholesalers   NAICS 424690

Current Data Sorted by Assets   **Comparative Historical Data**

	0-500M	500M-2MM	2-10MM	10-50MM	50-100MM	100-250MM	Type of Statement	4/1/05-3/31/06 ALL	4/1/06-3/31/07 ALL
	1		15	36	14	7	Unqualified	66	68
		6	54	29			Reviewed	89	93
	1	13	27	5	1		Compiled	46	54
	13	25	14	1			Tax Returns	21	33
	9	24	50	47	14	8	Other	105	112
		70 (4/1-9/30/09)		344 (10/1/09-3/31/10)					
NUMBER OF STATEMENTS	24	68	160	118	29	15		327	360
	%	%	%	%	%	%	**ASSETS**	%	%
Cash & Equivalents	16.2	16.2	8.2	9.2	6.1	9.9		6.4	7.3
Trade Receivables (net)	34.0	34.3	35.6	33.5	26.7	32.9		41.1	38.1
Inventory	30.3	25.9	32.7	28.9	21.5	19.4		27.1	27.5
All Other Current	3.5	2.0	3.0	2.1	2.5	9.5		2.0	1.9
Total Current	84.0	78.5	79.5	73.6	56.8	71.6		76.5	74.9
Fixed Assets (net)	9.7	12.3	13.2	17.7	22.0	22.7		15.2	16.0
Intangibles (net)	3.3	2.7	3.0	4.8	9.5	2.8		3.0	2.5
All Other Non-Current	2.9	6.6	4.3	4.0	11.7	2.9		5.3	6.6
Total	100.0	100.0	100.0	100.0	100.0	100.0		100.0	100.0
							LIABILITIES		
Notes Payable-Short Term	11.8	13.3	14.9	15.0	12.9	6.7		17.8	16.2
Cur. Mat.-L.T.D.	3.1	1.9	2.2	1.8	3.6	1.3		2.2	2.3
Trade Payables	28.9	22.5	25.1	19.5	15.5	17.1		27.3	25.7
Income Taxes Payable	.0	.4	.3	.3	.2	.0		.4	.3
All Other Current	7.0	9.4	7.1	9.0	10.5	14.7		9.6	9.7
Total Current	50.9	47.4	49.7	45.6	42.6	39.9		57.3	54.2
Long-Term Debt	14.0	10.8	7.1	9.8	15.4	11.1		8.3	9.8
Deferred Taxes	.0	.1	.3	.4	1.5	1.0		.3	.4
All Other Non-Current	3.7	4.6	2.9	1.8	4.2	3.8		4.0	4.0
Net Worth	31.8	37.2	40.1	42.4	36.3	44.2		30.1	31.6
Total Liabilities & Net Worth	100.0	100.0	100.0	100.0	100.0	100.0		100.0	100.0
							INCOME DATA		
Net Sales	100.0	100.0	100.0	100.0	100.0	100.0		100.0	100.0
Gross Profit	33.4	32.0	26.8	22.2	24.6	20.6		26.0	25.0
Operating Expenses	28.0	28.1	23.0	17.7	19.4	11.4		22.2	21.4
Operating Profit	5.4	3.9	3.8	4.5	5.2	9.2		3.7	3.6
All Other Expenses (net)	.1	.7	.3	.3	.5	.0		.7	.5
Profit Before Taxes	5.2	3.3	3.5	4.2	4.7	9.2		3.0	3.2
							RATIOS		
Current	3.3	2.8	2.5	2.3	2.3	3.6		1.8	1.9
	2.2	1.8	1.6	1.5	1.4	1.9		1.3	1.4
	.9	1.2	1.3	1.2	1.0	1.3		1.1	1.1
Quick	2.4	1.9	1.3	1.5	1.6	1.9		1.1	1.2
	1.0	1.1	.9	1.0	.7	1.5		.8	.8
	.4	.7	.6	.6	.5	.7		.6	.6
Sales/Receivables	16 23.1	19 18.9	33 11.0	34 10.8	35 10.5	39 9.4		38 9.7	34 10.9
	30 12.3	38 9.5	41 8.9	44 8.3	44 8.4	50 7.3		47 7.8	43 8.6
	41 8.8	53 6.9	51 7.1	58 6.3	53 6.9	61 6.0		58 6.3	53 6.9
Cost of Sales/Inventory	1 311.1	10 36.3	35 10.3	28 13.1	25 14.7	13 28.0		21 17.3	22 16.3
	43 8.6	38 9.6	57 6.4	47 7.8	46 7.9	27 13.7		42 8.8	43 8.4
	81 4.5	81 4.5	86 4.2	80 4.6	83 4.4	74 4.9		72 5.1	61 5.9
Cost of Sales/Payables	24 15.1	12 29.4	24 15.0	23 16.0	24 15.4	16 22.7		27 13.3	22 16.6
	36 10.3	33 11.2	35 10.4	32 11.6	33 11.0	28 13.0		42 8.8	36 10.2
	58 6.3	47 7.8	57 6.4	46 8.0	42 8.8	38 9.5		60 6.1	53 6.9
Sales/Working Capital	7.2	5.5	6.2	6.4	6.0	3.4		8.7	8.2
	10.2	11.4	10.8	10.0	12.6	6.1		17.2	15.7
	-176.0	24.0	16.9	21.5	-95.9	13.8		53.7	54.2
EBIT/Interest	20.0	16.5	14.7	18.4	12.7	86.7		9.6	9.5
	(16) 4.6	(60) 2.9	(143) 4.3	(109) 8.0	(28) 3.7	(13) 15.9		(292) 4.2	(327) 3.7
	-1.0	.6	2.0	3.0	2.6	2.3		1.7	1.8
Net Profit + Depr., Dep., Amort./Cur. Mat. L/T/D			6.3	10.8	14.0			7.6	8.2
		(35) 2.3	(33) 4.5	(14) 3.9				(82) 2.6	(96) 4.0
			1.6	1.5	1.5			1.2	1.7
Fixed/Worth	.0	.0	.1	.1	.2	.1		.1	.1
	.2	.2	.2	.3	.4	.6		.3	.3
	NM	.9	.6	1.0	2.5	1.0		1.1	1.3
Debt/Worth	.5	.8	.8	.9	1.2	.6		1.2	1.0
	2.2	2.0	1.7	1.8	2.7	1.4		2.7	2.4
	-15.6	5.6	3.7	3.0	9.6	3.9		6.0	6.7
% Profit Before Taxes/Tangible Net Worth	107.1	52.3	46.8	45.2	54.2	100.0		50.6	50.8
	(17) 45.8	(62) 15.8	(154) 23.0	(113) 26.4	(26) 26.9	33.6		(297) 23.1	(328) 26.4
	4.2	.9	5.6	13.3	10.1	9.9		8.0	10.4
% Profit Before Taxes/Total Assets	44.0	16.0	15.9	16.9	8.2	30.6		13.9	15.0
	11.4	4.0	7.0	9.0	6.1	9.1		6.0	6.7
	-2.9	.2	1.8	3.7	4.5	3.6		1.9	2.4
Sales/Net Fixed Assets	UND	234.8	157.7	186.2	52.3	92.5		174.6	150.4
	153.3	71.8	49.1	24.1	13.2	8.6		36.7	38.1
	36.2	19.7	14.4	7.6	6.5	5.0		13.4	11.7
Sales/Total Assets	5.3	4.5	3.7	3.6	2.9	3.0		3.9	4.2
	3.6	3.1	2.9	2.6	1.9	2.0		3.0	3.2
	3.0	2.5	2.3	1.8	1.1	1.5		2.2	2.2
% Depr., Dep., Amort./Sales		.3	.2	.3	.6	.1		.3	.3
		(41) .7	(135) .6	(100) .8	(25) 1.7	(14) 1.3		(275) .7	(302) .7
		2.1	1.2	2.9	3.9	2.6		1.6	1.7
% Officers', Directors' Owners' Comp/Sales	3.7	2.7	1.6	.7				1.2	1.4
	(13) 5.3	(39) 4.5	(71) 2.7	(22) 2.0				(109) 2.7	(123) 3.0
	8.1	9.2	5.1	4.4				6.3	5.8
Net Sales ($)	30964M	271971M	2450268M	7325468M	4174606M	7098475M		14804128M	17665194M
Total Assets ($)	6861M	79361M	791370M	2623245M	2021540M	2253455M		5032572M	6597703M

M = $ thousand   MM = $ million
See Pages 9 through 22 for Explanation of Ratios and Data

Comparative Historical Data / Current Data Sorted by Sales

			Type of Statement						
69	71	73	Unqualified	1		1	3	12	56
84	84	89	Reviewed		1	4	16	41	27
48	47	47	Compiled	1	5	4	14	16	7
37	52	53	Tax Returns	6	17	15	9	6	
110	156	152	Other	4	19	5	16	38	70
4/1/07-3/31/08 ALL	4/1/08-3/31/09 ALL	4/1/09-3/31/10 ALL		0-1MM	70 (4/1-9/30/09) 1-3MM	3-5MM	5-10MM	344 (10/1/09-3/31/10) 10-25MM	25MM & OVER
348	410	414	**NUMBER OF STATEMENTS**	12	42	29	58	113	160
%	%	%	**ASSETS**	%	%	%	%	%	%
8.2	7.8	10.2	Cash & Equivalents	15.8	17.4	18.2	7.2	8.7	8.5
37.2	37.5	34.0	Trade Receivables (net)	23.5	29.6	28.8	37.0	34.3	35.5
27.8	31.4	29.1	Inventory	16.8	29.3	23.9	30.8	33.8	27.0
2.3	2.3	2.8	All Other Current	4.8	4.5	1.1	2.4	2.6	2.8
75.4	78.9	76.0	Total Current	61.0	80.9	72.1	77.5	79.4	73.7
16.1	13.6	15.1	Fixed Assets (net)	26.8	12.0	15.4	13.9	13.8	16.3
3.0	2.7	3.9	Intangibles (net)	6.1	3.8	2.7	3.7	2.8	4.9
5.5	4.8	5.0	All Other Non-Current	6.0	3.3	9.8	5.0	4.0	5.1
100.0	100.0	100.0	Total	100.0	100.0	100.0	100.0	100.0	100.0
			LIABILITIES						
16.9	17.6	14.1	Notes Payable-Short Term	7.0	14.1	11.9	15.1	16.3	13.0
3.2	2.2	2.2	Cur. Mat.-L.T.D.	6.3	1.4	2.3	2.6	2.4	1.7
25.2	24.4	22.3	Trade Payables	19.3	20.1	18.8	26.3	24.7	20.6
.2	.2	.3	Income Taxes Payable	.0	.2	.8	.1	.3	.3
8.7	8.3	8.5	All Other Current	7.9	10.1	5.9	8.5	7.1	9.7
54.3	52.7	47.3	Total Current	40.5	45.8	39.7	52.6	50.8	45.3
10.3	8.8	9.6	Long-Term Debt	24.1	13.8	8.5	10.2	5.8	10.1
.3	.3	.4	Deferred Taxes	.0	.1	.0	.2	.3	.7
3.8	3.7	3.0	All Other Non-Current	1.9	3.5	5.8	4.5	2.6	2.3
31.4	34.5	39.7	Net Worth	34.2	36.9	46.0	32.5	40.6	41.6
100.0	100.0	100.0	Total Liabilities & Net Worth	100.0	100.0	100.0	100.0	100.0	100.0
			INCOME DATA						
100.0	100.0	100.0	Net Sales	100.0	100.0	100.0	100.0	100.0	100.0
25.4	24.1	26.4	Gross Profit	40.3	34.6	28.8	33.0	25.9	20.6
20.9	19.4	21.9	Operating Expenses	27.2	32.1	26.7	28.5	22.1	15.5
4.4	4.7	4.4	Operating Profit	13.2	2.5	2.1	4.5	3.8	5.1
.6	.5	.4	All Other Expenses (net)	2.7	.4	.4	.3	.3	.2
3.9	4.2	4.1	Profit Before Taxes	10.5	2.1	1.7	4.2	3.4	4.9
			RATIOS						
2.0	2.1	2.5	Current	2.7	3.7	3.2	2.3	2.3	2.6
1.4	1.5	1.6		1.9	2.2	1.8	1.6	1.5	1.6
1.1	1.2	1.2		1.0	1.2	1.3	1.2	1.2	1.2
1.2	1.3	1.6	Quick	2.2	2.3	1.8	1.4	1.3	1.6
(347) .8	.8	1.0		1.1	1.0	1.2	.8	.8	1.0
.6	.6	.6		.8	.8	.8	.6	.5	.6
33 11.0	30 12.1	32 11.4	Sales/Receivables	10 35.4	17 21.6	16 22.2	36 10.2	34 10.9	34 10.7
43 8.5	39 9.3	41 8.8		35 10.5	33 11.1	33 10.9	44 8.3	41 8.8	43 8.5
52 7.0	50 7.2	53 6.9		58 6.3	50 7.3	52 7.0	57 6.4	54 6.7	51 7.1
24 15.3	22 16.4	26 14.0	Cost of Sales/Inventory	0 UND	18 20.7	11 34.7	30 12.2	38 9.5	25 14.8
45 8.2	47 7.8	48 7.6		31 11.9	35 6.7	44 8.3	56 6.5	58 6.3	43 8.5
65 5.6	76 4.8	82 4.4		76 4.8	85 4.3	81 4.5	87 4.2	91 4.0	68 5.3
24 15.5	18 20.4	23 16.1	Cost of Sales/Payables	25 14.8	15 24.6	10 36.3	29 12.6	25 14.6	22 16.6
36 10.2	28 12.8	33 11.0		32 11.3	24 10.9	28 13.1	39 9.3	35 10.3	30 12.3
54 6.8	47 7.8	48 7.6		78 4.7	61 5.9	43 8.5	66 5.6	60 6.1	40 9.1
8.3	7.4	6.1	Sales/Working Capital	5.7	5.2	5.2	6.1	6.9	6.1
15.2	12.6	10.5		9.3	8.7	8.2	11.6	10.8	10.7
41.9	31.9	21.3		NM	26.4	15.5	25.7	17.4	26.4
9.3	13.3	16.3	EBIT/Interest		15.8	12.0	12.9	14.2	18.9
(313) 3.8	(363) 5.7	(369) 4.8		(36) 2.6	(26) 1.9	(53) 3.1	(104) 4.6	(145) 8.1	
2.0	2.0	2.1		.0	-.6	1.6	2.2	3.2	
7.1	12.6	9.0	Net Profit + Depr., Dep.,					6.1	14.5
(97) 3.2	(93) 4.1	(95) 3.2	Amort./Cur. Mat. L/T/D				(33) 2.3	(48) 6.4	
1.2	1.7	1.4						1.3	2.1
.1	.0	.0	Fixed/Worth	.0	.0	.0	.1	.1	.0
.3	.2	.2		.9	.3	.2	.3	.2	.3
1.1	.8	.9		27.5	1.9	.8	1.0	.7	.9
1.1	.9	.8	Debt/Worth	.4	.7	.3	.8	.8	.9
2.5	2.4	1.8		2.6	1.7	1.1	3.1	1.8	1.7
6.9	5.0	3.9		NM	8.2	2.8	14.4	3.1	3.5
53.6	55.0	49.2	% Profit Before Taxes/Tangible		64.4	13.0	59.3	42.5	55.4
(312) 28.5	(375) 28.7	(387) 24.7	Net Worth	(34) 21.6	(28) 3.2	(51) 18.4	(111) 24.9	(154) 30.7	
10.3	9.3	8.4			3.0	-7.2	3.1	8.1	13.6
15.4	17.3	17.1	% Profit Before Taxes/Total	40.5	19.4	8.6	16.1	13.6	19.7
8.6	8.7	7.2	Assets	5.6	7.1	.9	5.1	7.5	8.8
2.9	2.5	2.3		-8.5	-.8	-1.7	1.2	2.2	4.4
138.4	284.7	189.2	Sales/Net Fixed Assets	UND	203.1	329.1	198.3	162.8	191.9
39.1	50.7	40.7		20.1	53.4	53.6	51.6	40.1	32.7
11.1	14.7	11.7		4.6	11.7	10.3	15.1	13.8	8.7
4.0	4.4	3.8	Sales/Total Assets	3.4	3.7	4.7	3.8	3.7	3.9
3.1	3.3	2.8		2.7	2.9	3.0	2.8	2.8	2.8
2.1	2.3	2.1		.9	2.4	2.0	2.4	2.1	2.0
.3	.2	.3	% Depr., Dep., Amort./Sales		.3	.3	.3	.3	.2
(291) .7	(333) .5	(323) .8		(20) 1.3	(21) 1.1	(45) .7	(99) .7	(133) .8	
1.8	1.4	2.0			2.1	3.2	1.1	1.3	2.3
1.5	1.2	1.6	% Officers', Directors'		4.1	2.1	1.9	1.5	.6
(119) 2.9	(149) 3.0	(148) 3.3	Owners' Comp/Sales	(20) 7.4	(20) 4.4	(31) 3.5	(45) 2.8	(28) 1.8	
5.7	5.6	6.0			10.9	6.6	6.6	4.6	3.6
17186747M	25017181M	21351752M	Net Sales ($)	5611M	81883M	116182M	437689M	1864475M	18845912M
6129167M	7669498M	7775832M	Total Assets ($)	5282M	37528M	46139M	165244M	781055M	6740584M

© RMA 2010

M = $ thousand   MM = $ million
See Pages 9 through 22 for Explanation of Ratios and Data

WHOLESALE—Petroleum Bulk Stations and Terminals NAICS 424710

Current Data Sorted by Assets						Comparative Historical Data		
						Type of Statement		
1	1	10	24	8	12	Unqualified	35	36
	5	44	47			Reviewed	71	88
3	18	31	11		1	Compiled	68	83
3	14	17	3	6	7	Tax Returns	19	30
2	8	30	45			Other	88	60
	105 (4/1-9/30/09)		246 (10/1/09-3/31/10)				4/1/05-3/31/06 ALL	4/1/06-3/31/07 ALL
0-500M	500M-2MM	2-10MM	10-50MM	50-100MM	100-250MM			
9	46	132	130	14	20	**NUMBER OF STATEMENTS**	281	297
%	%	%	%	%	%	**ASSETS**	%	%
	12.6	11.8	9.6	5.0	7.1	Cash & Equivalents	9.7	9.2
	32.3	33.5	24.9	26.7	20.4	Trade Receivables (net)	34.0	35.4
	12.4	14.2	12.1	15.8	22.2	Inventory	13.5	14.3
	3.3	1.6	3.6	.8	3.5	All Other Current	2.7	3.2
	60.6	61.1	50.2	48.2	53.1	Total Current	59.9	62.1
	28.9	27.3	36.8	41.5	35.7	Fixed Assets (net)	29.9	28.3
	1.9	3.6	4.6	3.8	6.8	Intangibles (net)	3.7	3.2
	8.7	8.0	8.3	6.4	4.4	All Other Non-Current	6.5	6.4
	100.0	100.0	100.0	100.0	100.0	Total	100.0	100.0
						LIABILITIES		
	9.8	8.0	9.4	12.8	8.4	Notes Payable-Short Term	11.3	12.0
	6.4	3.2	3.9	3.3	2.4	Cur. Mat.-L.T.D.	3.4	3.4
	23.0	28.3	22.3	18.5	16.2	Trade Payables	26.8	28.8
	.3	.3	.2	.1	.2	Income Taxes Payable	.2	.2
	14.4	8.1	7.1	9.2	10.1	All Other Current	7.7	7.6
	53.9	48.0	42.9	43.8	37.3	Total Current	49.4	52.0
	18.5	17.9	20.0	20.7	21.1	Long-Term Debt	17.6	16.5
	.4	.4	.8	.9	1.7	Deferred Taxes	.9	.9
	2.7	1.7	2.3	6.2	2.4	All Other Non-Current	3.7	3.1
	24.5	32.0	34.0	28.5	37.4	Net Worth	28.3	27.6
	100.0	100.0	100.0	100.0	100.0	Total Liabilities & Net Worth	100.0	100.0
						INCOME DATA		
	100.0	100.0	100.0	100.0	100.0	Net Sales	100.0	100.0
	16.4	10.5	12.7	8.7	9.2	Gross Profit	11.0	10.7
	14.4	9.7	10.7	8.2	7.8	Operating Expenses	10.0	9.5
	2.0	.8	2.0	.5	1.5	Operating Profit	.9	1.2
	.1	.0	.0	-.1	.5	All Other Expenses (net)	.0	.0
	1.9	.9	2.0	.6	1.0	Profit Before Taxes	.9	1.1
						RATIOS		
	1.7	1.7	1.5	1.3	1.8		1.6	1.6
	1.1	1.3	1.2	1.0	1.5	Current	1.2	1.2
	.8	1.0	.9	.8	1.1		1.0	1.0
	1.4	1.3	1.1	1.1	1.1		1.2	1.1
	.8	.9	.8	.6	.7	Quick	.9	.9
	.6	.7	.5	.4	.5		.6	.6
10 36.1	9 40.6	8 48.2	6 60.3	11 32.4		Sales/Receivables	11 34.4	9 38.4
19 19.7	15 25.0	15 24.3	16 23.4	17 22.1			18 20.6	16 23.3
27 13.7	26 14.2	23 15.9	40 9.1	25 14.6			28 12.9	26 14.1
2 224.1	3 139.9	3 109.1	4 87.9	9 40.1		Cost of Sales/Inventory	3 106.5	3 126.5
7 53.2	7 53.8	6 58.7	8 43.9	17 21.3			7 52.0	7 55.7
16 23.0	14 25.9	13 28.9	20 17.9	39 9.4			13 28.8	11 32.3
8 47.1	10 35.4	11 34.7	9 41.6	10 35.4		Cost of Sales/Payables	11 33.3	10 38.0
13 29.1	13 27.2	14 26.8	12 30.2	14 26.6			15 24.5	13 27.3
21 17.3	21 17.0	18 20.1	19 18.9	30 12.3			19 18.8	18 20.2
	18.2	21.6	34.0	56.7	9.5	Sales/Working Capital	27.6	32.8
	164.9	56.7	85.7	169.4	27.4		67.4	76.5
	-82.3	978.4	-136.0	-155.2	323.3		-374.0	-619.0
	8.3	6.1	9.1	8.8	8.4	EBIT/Interest	5.7	6.5
(42)	3.7	(120) 2.6	(127) 3.2	2.0	4.5		(268) 3.1	(282) 2.8
	1.4	1.3	1.7	.7	1.4		1.6	1.4
		6.3	4.4		9.4	Net Profit + Depr., Dep., Amort./Cur. Mat. L/T/D	4.5	3.9
	(37)	2.3	(49) 2.4	(10) 3.3			(92) 2.1	(119) 2.3
		1.2	1.3		1.3		1.0	1.3
	.5	.4	.7	.8	.6	Fixed/Worth	.5	.5
	1.3	.8	1.3	2.3	.9		1.1	1.0
	32.4	2.2	2.7	3.0	3.1		2.3	2.0
	1.4	1.2	1.2	1.6	1.2	Debt/Worth	1.6	1.5
	3.2	2.4	2.4	3.4	2.5		3.3	2.9
	999.8	6.1	5.8	6.8	5.9		6.8	6.8
	56.6	35.6	36.1	24.7	35.4	% Profit Before Taxes/Tangible Net Worth	36.7	35.1
(36)	18.8	(126) 13.4	(118) 17.8	(12) 9.4	18.8		(254) 16.2	(269) 16.2
	5.2	2.2	8.5	4.8	3.6		6.4	5.2
	11.8	8.0	9.4	7.0	9.0	% Profit Before Taxes/Total Assets	8.4	8.7
	5.2	2.8	4.9	1.9	4.9		4.1	4.5
	1.2	.7	1.8	-.5	.8		1.5	1.1
	66.6	75.1	41.0	22.3	19.5	Sales/Net Fixed Assets	56.7	69.9
	36.1	29.6	16.9	10.6	10.3		25.5	31.4
	11.0	13.9	8.5	8.2	5.4		12.1	14.5
	8.9	11.3	8.3	6.2	4.8	Sales/Total Assets	9.7	11.0
	5.8	6.6	6.3	5.2	3.3		6.4	7.5
	3.1	4.4	3.8	3.9	2.5		4.2	5.0
	.3	.4	.5	.8	.5	% Depr., Dep., Amort./Sales	.4	.3
(42)	.8	(114) .8	(125) .8	(13) 1.2	(17) 1.0		(254) .7	(279) .6
	1.3	1.3	1.4	1.6	1.5		1.2	1.0
	.4	.3	.2			% Officers', Directors' Owners' Comp/Sales	.3	.2
(24)	1.4	(54) .5	(31) .4				(99) .6	(104) .5
	2.4	1.0	1.2				1.6	1.2
20542M	492053M	5908085M	18696386M	4789792M	13461647M	Net Sales ($)	36300976M	43541526M
2600M	62850M	741343M	2958480M	890217M	3140314M	Total Assets ($)	4808363M	5002308M

M = $ thousand   MM = $ million
See Pages 9 through 22 for Explanation of Ratios and Data

Comparative Historical Data | Current Data Sorted by Sales

Type of Statement	4/1/07-3/31/08 ALL	4/1/08-3/31/09 ALL	4/1/09-3/31/10 ALL	0-1MM	1-3MM	3-5MM	5-10MM	10-25MM	25MM & OVER
Unqualified	57	41	56		1	2		8	45
Reviewed	68	87	96	1	3	2	3	11	80
Compiled	83	48	63	2	3	5	4	16	34
Tax Returns	26	28	38	1		3	6	8	16
Other	86	97	98			6	7	12	72
				105 (4/1-9/30/09)			246 (10/1/09-3/31/10)		
NUMBER OF STATEMENTS	320	301	351	4	7	18	20	55	247
ASSETS	%	%	%	%	%	%	%	%	%
Cash & Equivalents	8.2	10.2	10.8			14.8	18.1	10.5	9.9
Trade Receivables (net)	35.3	30.2	28.6			29.2	24.4	28.2	29.8
Inventory	14.5	14.1	14.0			14.0	13.0	15.4	13.6
All Other Current	2.9	3.4	2.6			1.0	2.8	1.2	2.8
Total Current	60.9	57.8	56.1			59.0	58.3	55.3	56.0
Fixed Assets (net)	30.3	33.3	32.0			32.0	28.8	30.1	32.8
Intangibles (net)	3.2	3.2	4.1			2.4	7.7	4.0	3.9
All Other Non-Current	5.6	5.8	7.9			6.6	5.2	10.5	7.3
Total	100.0	100.0	100.0			100.0	100.0	100.0	100.0
LIABILITIES									
Notes Payable-Short Term	12.9	10.5	9.0			12.3	10.4	9.7	8.8
Cur. Mat.-L.T.D.	3.8	3.9	3.8			3.1	4.0	3.8	3.5
Trade Payables	27.4	23.1	24.0			13.5	20.8	18.9	26.7
Income Taxes Payable	.1	.2	.2			1.3	.0	.1	.2
All Other Current	6.1	7.3	9.6			15.8	24.4	8.3	7.7
Total Current	50.3	44.9	46.6			45.9	59.6	40.7	46.9
Long-Term Debt	17.1	17.0	19.1			24.5	15.5	20.1	19.0
Deferred Taxes	.8	.6	.6			.7	.4	.3	.8
All Other Non-Current	3.3	3.0	2.8			8.0	3.7	1.7	2.2
Net Worth	28.5	34.5	30.8			20.8	20.9	37.1	31.1
Total Liabilities & Net Worth	100.0	100.0	100.0			100.0	100.0	100.0	100.0
INCOME DATA									
Net Sales	100.0	100.0	100.0			100.0	100.0	100.0	100.0
Gross Profit	10.7	9.2	12.2			24.1	24.4	17.5	8.7
Operating Expenses	9.6	8.0	10.8			19.2	20.9	15.5	7.8
Operating Profit	1.1	1.2	1.4			4.9	3.5	2.0	.9
All Other Expenses (net)	.1	.1	.0			1.0	.3	-.3	.0
Profit Before Taxes	1.0	1.1	1.4			3.8	3.2	2.3	.9
RATIOS									
Current	1.6	1.7	1.7			1.8	2.1	2.0	1.6
	1.2	1.3	1.2			1.3	1.1	1.4	1.2
	1.0	1.0	.9			.9	.7	1.1	.9
Quick	1.1	1.3	1.2			1.4	1.6	1.3	1.1
	.9	.8	.8			1.0	.8	.9	.8
	.7	.6	.6			.8	.4	.6	.6
Sales/Receivables	11 33.2	6 63.1	8 45.3			11 32.3	12 31.3	14 25.5	8 47.9
	18 20.5	11 33.1	15 24.2			26 14.2	21 17.2	23 15.9	14 26.2
	28 13.0	20 18.1	25 14.7			47 7.8	28 12.9	31 11.8	20 17.9
Cost of Sales/Inventory	3 116.1	2 152.9	3 113.4			4 81.7	2 225.8	7 54.5	3 140.2
	7 53.9	5 72.0	7 51.7			12 30.4	13 28.0	13 27.5	6 61.3
	13 27.8	10 37.9	15 23.6			25 14.4	22 16.8	25 14.8	11 32.2
Cost of Sales/Payables	11 34.1	6 61.3	10 36.5			9 40.5	8 44.0	9 40.2	10 35.7
	14 26.5	9 40.9	13 27.4			16 23.0	18 20.7	17 20.9	13 28.7
	20 18.5	14 26.5	20 18.3			26 13.8	32 11.5	32 11.5	17 21.0
Sales/Working Capital	27.2	32.1	24.3			12.5	16.7	11.5	34.0
	82.1	81.1	70.6			23.7	159.5	30.8	89.1
	-999.8	-999.8	-172.6			-139.2	-21.8	200.4	-173.6
EBIT/Interest	(302) 5.0	(290) 7.1	(329) 8.0			(17) 13.6	(19) 8.2	(52) 6.4	(234) 7.7
	2.5	3.3	3.0			3.6	5.1	2.5	2.9
	1.3	1.6	1.5			1.2	1.9	1.7	1.5
Net Profit + Depr., Dep., Amort./Cur. Mat. L/T/D	(109) 4.3	(107) 5.1	(108) 5.5					(15) 2.6	(86) 6.2
	1.9	2.5	2.4					2.1	2.6
	1.0	1.4	1.4					1.2	1.3
Fixed/Worth	.5	.5	.5			.3	.7	.5	.6
	1.2	1.0	1.2			1.2	1.3	.8	1.2
	2.3	2.0	2.7			5.8	67.6	2.2	2.6
Debt/Worth	1.5	1.1	1.3			1.1	1.2	.9	1.4
	3.3	2.5	2.6			2.3	3.2	1.9	2.7
	6.4	4.8	6.9			23.0	NM	5.8	6.2
% Profit Before Taxes/Tangible Net Worth	(291) 33.0	(281) 36.7	(317) 37.7			(15) 57.8	(15) 64.8	(51) 27.9	(228) 35.5
	13.7	19.4	16.6			28.9	21.9	9.9	16.8
	4.3	5.9	4.6			15.3	7.8	3.0	4.6
% Profit Before Taxes/Total Assets	8.0	11.3	8.7			22.4	11.3	8.1	8.6
	3.2	4.7	4.2			7.2	5.1	3.8	3.9
	.9	1.5	1.1			-.7	2.4	1.4	1.0
Sales/Net Fixed Assets	63.2	77.2	58.6			43.8	51.8	60.1	59.8
	27.8	31.1	24.4			20.4	24.1	18.8	25.0
	12.4	13.5	9.8			6.0	6.9	6.4	11.3
Sales/Total Assets	9.8	12.7	9.0			6.0	6.3	6.3	10.4
	6.8	8.7	6.1			3.6	4.9	3.8	7.1
	4.5	5.6	3.6			2.3	2.2	2.1	4.7
% Depr., Dep., Amort./Sales	(291) .4	(280) .3	(318) .5			(17) .6	(17) .6	(50) .6	(225) .4
	.6	.5	.8			1.3	1.0	1.0	.8
	1.2	1.0	1.4			2.7	2.6	2.4	1.2
% Officers', Directors' Owners' Comp/Sales	(112) .2	(98) .2	(114) .3					(19) .3	(75) .2
	.6	.4	.6					1.1	.3
	1.2	1.0	1.3					1.9	.8
Net Sales ($)	58700713M	66936986M	43368505M	3123M	12371M	69991M	154822M	890117M	42238081M
Total Assets ($)	7566895M	6682355M	7795804M	1804M	5710M	32471M	56624M	298706M	7400489M

M = $ thousand   MM = $ million
See Pages 9 through 22 for Explanation of Ratios and Data

WHOLESALE—Petroleum and Petroleum Products Merchant Wholesalers (except Bulk Stations and Terminals) NAICS 424720

Current Data Sorted by Assets **Comparative Historical Data**

						Type of Statement		
		3	8	53	23	20	Unqualified	101	109
1	9	86	84	3	1	Reviewed	154	185
3	27	58	17	1	1	Compiled	107	135
3	27	27	2			Tax Returns	46	39
2	23	72	99	28	26	Other	170	166

	185 (4/1-9/30/09)		522 (10/1/09-3/31/10)				4/1/05-3/31/06 ALL	4/1/06-3/31/07 ALL

0-500M	500M-2MM	2-10MM	10-50MM	50-100MM	100-250MM	NUMBER OF STATEMENTS		
9	89	251	255	55	48		578	634
%	%	%	%	%	%	**ASSETS**	%	%
	20.5	13.2	8.9	5.5	7.1	Cash & Equivalents	9.0	9.2
	29.2	36.5	30.0	27.8	25.6	Trade Receivables (net)	36.3	36.4
	15.6	12.7	14.2	15.3	14.3	Inventory	13.3	14.2
	1.7	3.7	4.2	2.1	6.8	All Other Current	3.2	3.5
	67.1	66.1	57.4	50.7	53.9	Total Current	61.8	63.3
	22.7	22.5	31.6	37.0	32.6	Fixed Assets (net)	27.3	26.2
	1.4	4.0	3.5	6.0	7.5	Intangibles (net)	3.3	3.2
	8.9	7.5	7.6	6.4	6.0	All Other Non-Current	7.6	7.3
	100.0	100.0	100.0	100.0	100.0	Total	100.0	100.0
						LIABILITIES		
	7.4	9.7	10.2	9.8	6.8	Notes Payable-Short Term	11.6	11.1
	3.0	3.2	3.2	2.3	2.4	Cur. Mat.-L.T.D.	3.2	3.1
	23.2	31.5	25.3	25.2	23.1	Trade Payables	29.8	31.1
	.2	.3	.2	.1	.1	Income Taxes Payable	.2	.3
	9.5	8.6	7.0	5.4	8.6	All Other Current	7.7	7.6
	43.4	53.3	45.8	42.8	41.0	Total Current	52.4	53.3
	19.7	12.5	17.5	21.3	20.0	Long-Term Debt	16.7	15.3
	.1	.5	.7	.5	.7	Deferred Taxes	.6	.7
	2.7	3.2	3.0	2.8	5.5	All Other Non-Current	3.9	4.0
	34.1	30.5	33.1	32.7	32.8	Net Worth	26.4	26.8
	100.0	100.0	100.0	100.0	100.0	Total Liabilities & Net Worth	100.0	100.0
						INCOME DATA		
	100.0	100.0	100.0	100.0	100.0	Net Sales	100.0	100.0
	17.9	11.3	10.2	8.1	6.8	Gross Profit	11.6	10.5
	16.6	10.4	8.7	6.9	5.2	Operating Expenses	10.4	9.2
	1.2	.9	1.5	1.3	1.6	Operating Profit	1.3	1.3
	-.3	-.2	.0	.3	.2	All Other Expenses (net)	.0	.1
	1.6	1.1	1.5	.9	1.4	Profit Before Taxes	1.3	1.2
						RATIOS		
	2.3	1.6	1.5	1.6	1.5	Current	1.5	1.5
	1.5	1.2	1.2	1.1	1.3		1.2	1.2
	1.2	1.0	1.0	.8	1.0		1.0	.9
	1.8	1.2	1.1	1.1	1.1	Quick	1.1	1.2
	1.1	.9	.8	.7	.8		.9	.9
	.6	.7	.6	.5	.5		.6	.6
	6 58.8	9 40.9	10 38.1	8 43.3	7 50.4	Sales/Receivables	10 35.3	10 36.3
	18 20.6	16 22.4	16 22.6	16 23.3	12 31.0		20 18.6	18 20.3
	31 11.8	29 12.7	28 13.2	29 12.7	22 16.8		31 11.9	29 12.6
	2 221.6	1 291.2	3 117.7	3 123.0	3 139.0	Cost of Sales/Inventory	2 155.7	2 162.6
	9 39.2	5 70.5	7 51.8	7 54.2	6 56.2		6 57.0	6 61.6
	20 18.2	12 30.9	15 24.3	19 19.6	13 28.7		13 27.6	14 26.0
	7 54.5	10 34.9	11 34.7	10 36.1	9 41.6	Cost of Sales/Payables	11 32.8	10 34.9
	13 27.5	14 26.4	14 26.5	15 24.1	13 27.4		15 23.6	14 25.5
	28 12.9	22 16.9	19 19.0	22 16.3	17 21.6		24 15.5	23 15.6
	14.9	25.5	24.7	22.6	31.1	Sales/Working Capital	28.0	26.8
	30.5	73.1	76.2	124.7	44.6		82.6	82.6
	162.2	-590.7	-999.8	-95.9	NM		-439.2	-241.7
	12.0	11.1	10.1	5.5	8.2	EBIT/Interest	7.3	6.9
	(74) 3.2	(229) 3.4	(248) 3.9	3.3	(45) 3.8		(539) 3.3	(596) 3.1
	1.1	1.2	2.0	2.0	2.7		1.7	1.6
	5.0	5.5	5.9	20.2	6.7	Net Profit + Depr., Dep., Amort./Cur. Mat. L/T/D	4.3	5.1
	(17) 2.5	(65) 2.3	(94) 2.2	(19) 5.6	(13) 2.2		(193) 2.3	(212) 2.4
	1.0	1.0	1.4	2.6	.7		1.4	1.3
	.1	.2	.5	.6	.4	Fixed/Worth	.4	.4
	.5	.8	1.1	1.5	.9		1.0	1.0
	1.8	1.9	2.2	3.2	2.6		2.4	2.4
	.8	1.4	1.3	1.6	1.8	Debt/Worth	1.7	1.6
	1.7	2.6	2.5	2.7	3.1		3.4	3.3
	14.2	7.8	5.0	6.7	7.0		6.5	7.1
	33.7	38.0	38.3	28.1	49.2	% Profit Before Taxes/Tangible Net Worth	39.0	40.1
	(76) 10.0	(226) 15.9	(241) 20.9	(52) 14.2	(46) 20.1		(517) 19.4	(571) 20.3
	1.3	4.0	7.8	6.4	7.8		7.8	8.9
	11.6	10.0	10.0	6.8	7.7	% Profit Before Taxes/Total Assets	9.1	9.5
	4.6	3.6	5.2	3.2	6.0		4.5	4.8
	.6	.5	2.1	1.8	2.1		1.6	1.8
	157.5	129.2	52.2	46.9	170.4	Sales/Net Fixed Assets	77.7	81.7
	40.5	46.8	22.3	14.1	16.7		28.9	36.3
	13.1	16.9	10.7	8.3	6.7		12.7	14.9
	8.8	11.5	8.9	8.3	9.7	Sales/Total Assets	9.3	10.0
	5.9	7.0	5.7	5.3	5.0		6.3	7.0
	3.2	4.5	3.9	3.7	2.8		4.2	4.4
	.4	.2	.4	.4	.1	% Depr., Dep., Amort./Sales	.3	.3
	(66) .7	(213) .5	(240) .8	(53) .9	(41) .6		(527) .6	(569) .6
	2.3	1.1	1.3	1.4	1.2		1.2	1.0
	.7	.2	.1			% Officers', Directors' Owners' Comp/Sales	.3	.3
	(42) 1.5	(101) .4	(69) .3				(200) .6	(201) .6
	2.9	1.0	.8				1.3	1.3
16389M	891341M	11928789M	37922713M	23159270M	50036415M	Net Sales ($)	76839726M	100603833M
2553M	112530M	1357095M	5782643M	3854997M	7444392M	Total Assets ($)	11422166M	13991713M

M = $ thousand   MM = $ million
See Pages 9 through 22 for Explanation of Ratios and Data

WHOLESALE—Petroleum and Petroleum Products Merchant Wholesalers (except Bulk Stations and Terminals) NAICS 424720

Comparative Historical Data | Current Data Sorted by Sales

4/1/07-3/31/08 ALL	4/1/08-3/31/09 ALL	4/1/09-3/31/10 ALL	Type of Statement	0-1MM	1-3MM	3-5MM	5-10MM	10-25MM	25MM & OVER
95	109	107	Unqualified			1	2	3	101
180	197	184	Reviewed		2	2	6	37	137
127	112	107	Compiled	1	7	6	10	27	56
44	50	59	Tax Returns		5	8	13	10	21
198	232	250	Other	2	5	10	10	26	199
					185 (4/1-9/30/09)		522 (10/1/09-3/31/10)		
644	700	707	**NUMBER OF STATEMENTS**	3	19	27	41	103	514
%	%	%	**ASSETS**	%	%	%	%	%	%
8.4	11.3	11.5	Cash & Equivalents		11.2	14.7	19.1	15.0	10.1
37.9	33.0	31.8	Trade Receivables (net)		21.2	27.1	25.3	32.9	32.8
13.9	13.5	13.9	Inventory		17.9	19.4	16.3	12.9	13.6
3.2	3.5	3.7	All Other Current		.6	1.8	1.7	2.8	4.2
63.4	61.4	60.8	Total Current		51.0	62.9	62.3	63.6	60.7
26.5	27.1	27.8	Fixed Assets (net)		34.5	26.4	27.5	24.6	28.1
2.7	3.6	3.8	Intangibles (net)		.3	5.2	2.1	4.0	4.0
7.3	7.9	7.6	All Other Non-Current		14.2	5.5	8.1	7.8	7.3
100.0	100.0	100.0	Total		100.0	100.0	100.0	100.0	100.0
			LIABILITIES						
12.8	11.2	9.4	Notes Payable-Short Term		7.0	9.3	8.5	9.4	9.6
3.1	3.5	3.0	Cur. Mat.-L.T.D.		2.1	4.3	4.6	3.3	2.8
29.5	26.4	27.0	Trade Payables		18.6	19.4	20.7	24.7	28.8
.3	.2	.2	Income Taxes Payable		.0	.2	.1	.6	.2
7.3	8.3	8.0	All Other Current		8.0	9.8	7.9	7.7	7.7
52.9	49.7	47.7	Total Current		35.9	43.0	41.8	45.6	49.1
15.6	16.0	16.7	Long-Term Debt		31.7	19.6	22.1	15.4	15.7
.6	.6	.5	Deferred Taxes		.3	.1	.3	.6	.6
3.7	3.5	3.4	All Other Non-Current		11.5	4.2	3.8	3.3	3.1
27.2	30.3	31.7	Net Worth		20.7	33.0	32.1	35.2	31.5
100.0	100.0	100.0	Total Liabilities & Net Worth		100.0	100.0	100.0	100.0	100.0
			INCOME DATA						
100.0	100.0	100.0	Net Sales		100.0	100.0	100.0	100.0	100.0
9.7	9.1	11.5	Gross Profit		29.1	34.5	20.8	13.5	8.3
8.6	8.0	10.2	Operating Expenses		26.8	32.2	17.9	12.5	7.2
1.1	1.2	1.3	Operating Profit		2.3	2.4	2.9	1.0	1.1
.1	.0	-.1	All Other Expenses (net)		-.2	-.4	-.1	-.3	.0
1.0	1.2	1.4	Profit Before Taxes		2.6	2.8	3.0	1.3	1.1
			RATIOS						
1.5 / 1.2 / 1.0	1.6 / 1.2 / 1.0	1.6 / 1.2 / 1.0	Current		3.7 / 1.4 / 1.0	2.0 / 1.6 / 1.3	2.4 / 1.4 / 1.0	2.0 / 1.3 / 1.0	1.5 / 1.2 / 1.0
1.1 / (643) .9 / .6	1.2 / .9 / .6	1.2 / .9 / .6	Quick		2.2 / 1.0 / .3	1.5 / .9 / .6	1.8 / .8 / .5	1.5 / 1.1 / .6	1.2 / .8 / .6
10 36.3 / 18 20.0 / 30 12.1	5 66.5 / 12 30.4 / 23 16.0	9 42.9 / 16 23.1 / 28 13.1	Sales/Receivables		5 69.1 / 21 17.1 / 40 9.2	13 28.4 / 24 15.3 / 43 8.6	10 36.3 / 22 16.8 / 42 8.6	9 39.9 / 22 16.5 / 38 9.7	8 43.8 / 15 25.2 / 24 15.1
2 167.7 / 6 61.3 / 12 29.4	1 246.7 / 4 85.1 / 10 36.9	2 165.3 / 6 56.9 / 15 25.2	Cost of Sales/Inventory		5 80.0 / 11 33.9 / 51 7.1	8 46.1 / 18 20.0 / 54 6.8	5 71.0 / 10 37.6 / 34 10.6	2 168.9 / 8 44.0 / 16 23.2	2 181.1 / 5 67.0 / 12 31.3
10 36.6 / 14 26.9 / 21 17.5	6 59.8 / 9 39.5 / 16 23.0	10 36.8 / 14 26.5 / 21 17.6	Cost of Sales/Payables		7 52.3 / 14 26.7 / 48 7.6	10 36.7 / 31 11.9 / 53 6.9	9 42.6 / 17 21.6 / 40 9.0	9 39.3 / 16 23.1 / 27 13.5	10 35.8 / 13 27.1 / 18 20.4
29.9 / 86.4 / -306.4	32.2 / 107.6 / -421.8	22.5 / 67.8 / -999.8	Sales/Working Capital		6.5 / 21.7 / UND	10.2 / 17.3 / 67.2	11.4 / 25.5 / NM	17.8 / 39.1 / -999.8	30.6 / 89.7 / -457.5
(606) 5.8 / 2.6 / 1.4	(666) 7.2 / 3.4 / 1.7	(657) 9.8 / 3.5 / 1.7	EBIT/Interest		(14) 7.7 / 3.0 / -.3	(24) 13.4 / 4.1 / 1.0	(37) 14.0 / 3.0 / 1.2	(96) 8.9 / 3.5 / 1.4	(483) 9.9 / 3.6 / 1.8
(208) 4.5 / 2.4 / 1.3	(225) 5.9 / 2.6 / 1.6	(208) 5.9 / 2.5 / 1.3	Net Profit + Depr., Dep., Amort./Cur. Mat. L/T/D					(30) 6.0 / 2.2 / 1.0	(168) 5.9 / 2.5 / 1.3
.4 / 1.0 / 2.2	.4 / 1.0 / 2.3	.3 / .9 / 1.3	Fixed/Worth		.1 / .8 / 17.8	.3 / .7 / 3.6	.2 / .8 / 2.8	.2 / .7 / 2.3	.4 / 1.0 / 2.2
1.7 / 3.4 / 6.6	1.4 / 3.0 / 6.4	1.3 / 2.5 / 6.3	Debt/Worth		1.0 / 2.1 / -85.0	.8 / 1.7 / 7.9	1.0 / 2.6 / 6.3	.9 / 2.0 / 10.0	1.4 / 2.7 / 5.9
(582) 34.8 / 17.4 / 6.1	(640) 41.4 / 21.3 / 8.3	(645) 37.4 / 17.3 / 5.3	% Profit Before Taxes/Tangible Net Worth		(14) 76.9 / 13.8 / 5.3	(23) 54.7 / 8.1 / 1.1	(37) 57.8 / 12.8 / 1.5	(88) 34.3 / 14.3 / 3.7	(481) 37.1 / 18.8 / 6.7
8.2 / 3.9 / 1.2	11.0 / 5.4 / 1.6	10.0 / 4.5 / 1.3	% Profit Before Taxes/Total Assets		12.4 / 6.2 / -2.6	17.3 / 4.6 / .5	11.9 / 3.8 / .7	10.7 / 4.3 / .6	9.5 / 4.5 / 1.6
85.2 / 35.2 / 14.9	117.1 / 42.5 / 16.2	85.7 / 29.9 / 11.9	Sales/Net Fixed Assets		53.5 / 17.4 / 4.4	70.9 / 20.2 / 7.1	93.8 / 19.2 / 10.5	90.1 / 32.8 / 10.8	95.2 / 31.7 / 12.7
10.5 / 7.0 / 4.6	13.9 / 8.8 / 5.0	9.7 / 6.1 / 3.9	Sales/Total Assets		6.1 / 2.8 / 1.5	5.4 / 3.6 / 2.6	6.1 / 3.9 / 2.0	8.0 / 4.9 / 3.4	10.7 / 6.8 / 4.6
(573) .3 / .5 / .9	(627) .2 / .5 / .9	(620) .3 / .7 / 1.2	% Depr., Dep., Amort./Sales		(16) .7 / 2.7 / 3.3	(19) .6 / 1.2 / 3.5	(30) .6 / 1.1 / 1.9	(85) .4 / .8 / 1.8	(467) .3 / .6 / 1.1
(216) .2 / .5 / .9	(200) .2 / .5 / .9	(222) .2 / .5 / 1.2	% Officers', Directors', Owners' Comp/Sales			(11) 1.0 / 2.6 / 7.7	(24) 1.2 / 1.7 / 3.8	(42) .5 / .9 / 1.5	(141) .1 / .3 / .7
126804496M	182793373M	123954917M	Net Sales ($)	1286M	34684M	104721M	298195M	1742298M	121773733M
16476615M	18605472M	18554210M	Total Assets ($)	1804M	14399M	40568M	115403M	458074M	17923962M

M = $ thousand   MM = $ million
See Pages 9 through 22 for Explanation of Ratios and Data

WHOLESALE—Beer and Ale Merchant Wholesalers NAICS 424810

Current Data Sorted by Assets   **Comparative Historical Data**

0-500M	500M-2MM	2-10MM	10-50MM	50-100MM	100-250MM	Type of Statement	4/1/05-3/31/06 ALL	4/1/06-3/31/07 ALL
1	1	15	65	24	13	Unqualified	112	114
	10	35	56	3	1	Reviewed	102	109
	14	31	6	1		Compiled	50	66
6	4	9	3			Tax Returns	14	18
4	10	41	95	26	19	Other	134	146
	54 (4/1-9/30/09)			439 (10/1/09-3/31/10)				
11	39	131	225	54	33	**NUMBER OF STATEMENTS**	412	453
%	%	%	%	%	%	**ASSETS**	%	%
23.4	14.2	14.1	8.5	4.7	5.0	Cash & Equivalents	12.2	12.1
2.6	7.4	8.7	9.6	6.8	5.4	Trade Receivables (net)	9.4	10.1
42.6	37.3	24.2	16.5	10.6	14.1	Inventory	20.1	19.8
.1	2.1	2.6	2.7	1.7	1.6	All Other Current	2.5	2.5
68.7	60.9	49.5	37.2	23.8	26.1	Total Current	44.2	44.5
18.2	21.1	19.7	19.9	22.4	15.2	Fixed Assets (net)	24.0	23.0
2.7	10.1	20.5	32.4	45.0	48.3	Intangibles (net)	22.5	24.2
10.3	7.9	10.3	10.5	8.7	10.4	All Other Non-Current	9.3	8.3
100.0	100.0	100.0	100.0	100.0	100.0	Total	100.0	100.0
						LIABILITIES		
13.8	11.5	7.9	4.3	4.4	4.8	Notes Payable-Short Term	7.3	7.4
5.7	3.7	3.2	3.7	2.7	2.6	Cur. Mat.-L.T.D.	4.0	3.4
4.2	10.5	11.9	8.1	6.1	6.1	Trade Payables	10.9	11.5
.0	.2	.2	.1	.1	.0	Income Taxes Payable	.1	.1
19.3	7.7	8.4	6.2	5.3	5.3	All Other Current	7.8	7.6
43.1	33.7	31.6	22.3	18.6	18.9	Total Current	30.1	30.0
6.6	14.0	17.8	28.6	39.2	34.5	Long-Term Debt	23.9	24.0
.0	.0	.4	.6	.4	.1	Deferred Taxes	.4	.4
64.1	2.4	4.2	4.9	3.7	3.3	All Other Non-Current	3.5	3.0
-13.8	49.9	46.0	43.6	38.1	43.3	Net Worth	42.0	42.7
100.0	100.0	100.0	100.0	100.0	100.0	Total Liabilities & Net Worth	100.0	100.0
						INCOME DATA		
100.0	100.0	100.0	100.0	100.0	100.0	Net Sales	100.0	100.0
14.7	24.1	26.0	25.1	25.2	26.5	Gross Profit	25.2	25.1
16.8	21.6	21.8	19.9	19.5	20.4	Operating Expenses	21.8	21.6
-2.1	2.5	4.2	5.2	5.7	6.1	Operating Profit	3.4	3.5
.2	.4	.2	.4	.8	.1	All Other Expenses (net)	.3	.4
-2.3	2.1	4.0	4.8	4.9	6.0	Profit Before Taxes	3.1	3.1
						RATIOS		
3.6	3.8	3.1	2.8	1.9	2.3	Current	2.3	2.5
2.4	2.1	1.7	1.6	1.4	1.6		1.5	1.6
.9	1.2	1.1	1.0	.9	1.2		1.0	1.0
1.2	1.2	1.5	1.3	.9	.9	Quick	1.4	1.3
.3	.6	.7	.7	.6	.6		.6	.7
.0	.3	.3	.3	.3	.3		.3	.3
0 UND	0 UND	1 411.3	2 213.1	2 183.0	3 132.9	Sales/Receivables	1 291.2	2 235.5
0 UND	1 319.8	2 150.2	4 91.9	5 72.7	4 84.6		4 100.4	5 79.2
0 UND	10 34.9	15 24.6	21 17.1	18 20.5	15 25.1		18 20.2	18 19.8
14 27.0	21 17.2	18 20.0	19 19.3	19 18.8	21 17.3	Cost of Sales/Inventory	13 27.9	13 28.0
26 13.8	29 12.7	23 16.1	22 16.4	22 16.2	30 12.4		21 17.5	23 16.1
37 9.7	33 11.1	31 11.8	30 12.0	28 12.9	37 9.9		30 12.3	31 11.9
0 UND	0 UND	4 82.6	7 49.5	8 46.7	7 53.7	Cost of Sales/Payables	7 49.4	7 52.0
1 443.5	6 61.5	10 37.4	12 30.4	14 26.8	14 27.0		12 29.9	13 28.9
9 42.9	11 32.1	15 24.4	16 22.2	17 21.9	18 20.3		18 20.7	19 19.0
9.7	14.0	11.1	12.9	20.6	13.8	Sales/Working Capital	13.5	13.3
27.8	21.5	23.2	23.6	29.3	22.8		28.7	26.4
-299.3	72.4	153.0	252.3	-263.9	58.2		-419.6	999.8
	23.2	18.1	14.1	10.1	17.5	EBIT/Interest	11.3	11.0
	(34) 5.3	(115) 6.3	(204) 6.7	(53) 5.4	(31) 6.0		(369) 4.7	(410) 4.6
	1.4	3.2	3.9	3.2	4.2		2.3	2.0
		5.8	8.7	25.0		Net Profit + Depr., Dep., Amort./Cur. Mat. L/T/D	7.5	5.4
		(21) 3.1	(51) 4.1	(13) 3.1			(89) 3.0	(84) 2.3
		1.3	2.1	2.4			1.4	1.2
.1	.2	.2	.4	1.4	.6	Fixed/Worth	.4	.4
.4	.5	.6	1.7	-1.9	-4.4		1.3	1.1
-1.7	1.3	-12.7	-1.0	-.3	-.4		-2.6	-2.0
.4	.4	.5	1.1	2.6	2.0	Debt/Worth	.8	.7
2.0	1.1	1.6	3.2	-5.2	-28.9		2.4	2.7
-11.6	4.3	-43.1	-3.0	-1.9	-2.3		-10.0	-9.0
	64.8	59.0	63.4	85.3	90.7	% Profit Before Taxes/Tangible Net Worth	51.6	57.6
	(35) 28.8	(97) 32.8	(134) 40.9	(23) 62.7	(15) 61.3		(283) 27.7	(312) 26.2
	3.8	17.0	24.7	21.2	35.7		11.1	11.8
22.5	22.3	20.8	18.2	12.6	12.5	% Profit Before Taxes/Total Assets	16.2	16.5
2.0	10.2	12.5	12.8	10.3	10.8		9.4	9.3
-17.8	.6	5.9	7.3	6.7	8.8		4.2	3.9
558.4	96.4	66.0	49.8	26.9	46.8	Sales/Net Fixed Assets	38.9	42.0
37.6	33.9	30.1	20.3	11.1	17.5		21.7	21.4
19.0	18.0	13.3	9.4	6.4	8.5		10.4	10.2
8.7	7.7	5.4	3.6	2.7	2.7	Sales/Total Assets	5.0	4.9
5.7	6.5	4.1	2.8	2.2	1.9		3.7	3.5
4.2	4.7	3.0	2.1	1.5	1.4		2.6	2.5
	.4	.6	.7	.8	.5	% Depr., Dep., Amort./Sales	.7	.7
	(30) 1.0	(109) .9	(197) 1.0	(51) 1.3	(27) .8		(383) 1.0	(413) 1.1
	1.6	1.5	1.4	1.7	1.3		1.5	1.6
	1.8	1.1	.6			% Officers', Directors' Owners' Comp/Sales	.9	1.1
	(23) 2.9	(53) 2.0	(50) 1.0				(148) 1.9	(160) 1.8
	5.1	3.3	1.6				3.2	3.0
18042M	346576M	3005632M	15435259M	7767537M	10144315M	Net Sales ($)	23153407M	27454232M
3117M	53400M	702246M	5468449M	3604821M	4893272M	Total Assets ($)	7392936M	8925421M

M = $ thousand   MM = $ million
See Pages 9 through 22 for Explanation of Ratios and Data

Comparative Historical Data / Current Data Sorted by Sales

Type of Statement	4/1/07-3/31/08 ALL	4/1/08-3/31/09 ALL	4/1/09-3/31/10 ALL	0-1MM	1-3MM	3-5MM	5-10MM	10-25MM	25MM & OVE
Unqualified	108	100	118				1	8	109
Reviewed	110	129	106		1	2	8	24	71
Compiled	56	64	52	1		2	11	24	16
Tax Returns	18	22	22	1	4	2 / 3	3	4	8
Other	157	185	195	2	4	3	8	25	153
					54 (4/1-9/30/09)			439 (10/1/09-3/31/10)	
NUMBER OF STATEMENTS	449	500	493	4	9	7	31	85	357
	%	%	%	%	%	%	%	%	%
ASSETS									
Cash & Equivalents	10.8	10.4	10.1				12.7	15.8	8.1
Trade Receivables (net)	9.7	9.3	8.5				11.7	7.2	8.8
Inventory	20.3	19.2	19.9				34.1	21.2	17.4
All Other Current	3.1	2.6	2.3				1.4	3.9	2.2
Total Current	43.8	41.5	40.8				59.9	48.2	36.4
Fixed Assets (net)	21.7	20.7	19.9				14.8	21.2	19.8
Intangibles (net)	25.8	29.1	29.3				18.9	19.4	33.8
All Other Non-Current	8.7	8.8	10.0				6.3	11.2	9.9
Total	100.0	100.0	100.0				100.0	100.0	100.0
LIABILITIES									
Notes Payable-Short Term	7.0	6.8	6.1				9.6	8.5	4.8
Cur. Mat.-L.T.D.	3.6	3.6	3.4				2.8	3.7	3.3
Trade Payables	10.7	9.5	8.9				13.7	10.3	8.2
Income Taxes Payable	.1	.1	.1				.0	.3	.1
All Other Current	7.2	6.2	7.0				6.5	5.8	6.9
Total Current	28.6	26.2	25.5				32.6	28.6	23.3
Long-Term Debt	24.9	26.8	25.6				15.5	21.1	28.4
Deferred Taxes	.4	.4	.4				.4	.3	.5
All Other Non-Current	4.6	3.9	5.6				4.0	4.9	4.2
Net Worth	41.5	42.8	42.8				47.4	45.0	43.6
Total Liabilities & Net Worth	100.0	100.0	100.0				100.0	100.0	100.0
INCOME DATA									
Net Sales	100.0	100.0	100.0				100.0	100.0	100.0
Gross Profit	25.3	25.3	25.1				26.5	25.5	25.2
Operating Expenses	21.3	21.1	20.5				23.9	20.9	20.2
Operating Profit	4.1	4.2	4.7				2.6	4.6	5.0
All Other Expenses (net)	.2	.4	.4				.5	.2	.4
Profit Before Taxes	3.8	3.8	4.3				2.1	4.5	4.6
RATIOS									
Current	2.5	2.5	2.8				3.6	3.8	2.6
	1.4	1.6	1.6				1.9	1.7	1.6
	1.0	1.1	1.1				1.2	1.2	1.0
Quick	1.3	1.3	1.2				1.2	2.0	1.1
	.6	.7	.7				.7	.8	.7
	.3	.3	.3				.4	.3	.3
Sales/Receivables	2 209.5	2 222.8	1 273.0				1 364.0	0 999.8	2 213.1
	5 71.5	5 79.3	4 101.5				5 66.6	2 215.1	4 92.2
	18 20.5	18 20.8	17 21.3				20 18.1	15 24.4	18 20.3
Cost of Sales/Inventory	16 22.7	18 20.6	19 19.0				22 16.6	18 19.8	19 19.3
	24 15.1	24 15.0	23 15.8				33 11.1	22 16.3	23 16.1
	32 11.4	32 11.5	31 11.6				50 7.3	28 13.2	31 11.9
Cost of Sales/Payables	7 54.4	7 51.9	6 62.1				4 92.7	2 170.6	7 53.4
	13 29.1	12 30.4	11 32.8				11 33.0	8 46.3	12 30.1
	19 19.3	18 20.7	16 22.7				26 14.3	12 29.4	16 22.5
Sales/Working Capital	12.5	12.9	13.1				12.8	11.0	13.6
	27.7	24.1	25.1				19.8	21.6	25.9
	562.1	116.9	181.1				63.4	81.5	906.0
EBIT/Interest	(404) 10.9	(457) 12.2	(445) 14.1				(29) 10.0	(71) 14.4	(329) 14.6
	4.7	4.8	6.3				5.1	6.3	6.6
	2.3	2.5	3.3				2.8	3.5	3.7
Net Profit + Depr., Dep., Amort./Cur. Mat. L/T/D	(100) 6.6	(115) 7.9	(94) 8.7						10.3
	3.0	2.6	3.3					(78) 3.7	3.7
	2.0	1.6	1.9						2.1
Fixed/Worth	.4	.3	.3				.2	.2	.4
	1.2	1.4	1.4				.5	.7	1.7
	-1.5	-1.1	-1.1				9.8	7.2	-.8
Debt/Worth	.9	.8	.8				.5	.4	1.1
	3.0	3.1	3.1				1.6	1.7	4.2
	-6.0	-4.0	-4.3				29.3	14.3	-3.1
% Profit Before Taxes/Tangible Net Worth	65.3	67.6	67.7				50.9	59.0	72.5
	(302) 33.9	(325) 32.5	(312) 38.7				(24) 20.1	(65) 33.5	(208) 43.2
	18.5	13.9	20.9				3.5	18.0	24.9
% Profit Before Taxes/Total Assets	18.1	16.4	17.6				13.3	21.3	17.4
	10.5	9.5	11.7				7.3	12.5	12.0
	5.5	4.6	6.6				1.9	6.1	7.3
Sales/Net Fixed Assets	44.0	43.3	51.1				66.0	65.9	45.7
	20.9	21.5	22.5				30.1	30.9	21.1
	10.4	10.1	10.4				17.6	11.1	9.3
Sales/Total Assets	4.6	4.5	4.5				5.9	5.8	3.9
	3.3	3.1	3.0				4.1	4.0	2.8
	2.5	2.3	2.2				2.2	2.6	2.1
% Depr., Dep., Amort./Sales	(399) .7	(437) .7	(423) .7				(25) .3	(71) .6	(312) .7
	1.1	1.1	1.0				1.0	.9	1.0
	1.6	1.6	1.4				1.6	1.4	1.4
% Officers', Directors' Owners' Comp/Sales	(140) .8	(132) .9	(135) .8				(18) 2.0	(35) 1.3	(75) .6
	1.5	1.6	1.6				2.9	1.9	1.1
	2.9	3.0	2.9				6.8	2.5	2.1
Net Sales ($)	30407156M	32256216M	36717361M	2117M	18544M	27940M	231366M	1439306M	34998088M
Total Assets ($)	10654488M	12604666M	14725305M	3305M	4311M	6215M	73283M	465341M	14172850M

M = $ thousand   MM = $ million
See Pages 9 through 22 for Explanation of Ratios and Data

WHOLESALE—Wine and Distilled Alcoholic Beverage Merchant Wholesalers NAICS 424820

Current Data Sorted by Assets | **Comparative Historical Data**

						Type of Statement	37	46
1	2	3	17	7	21	Unqualified	37	46
	1	17	11	4	2	Reviewed	21	22
	2	14	2			Compiled	18	14
4	7	3	3			Tax Returns	14	11
1	9	15	16	13	13	Other	57	50
	37 (4/1-9/30/09)		151 (10/1/09-3/31/10)				4/1/05-3/31/06 ALL	4/1/06-3/31/07 ALL
0-500M	500M-2MM	2-10MM	10-50MM	50-100MM	100-250MM	NUMBER OF STATEMENTS	147	143
6	21	52	49	24	36			
%	%	%	%	%	%	**ASSETS**	%	%
	6.3	7.2	6.8	5.4	4.6	Cash & Equivalents	7.9	5.5
	20.0	25.0	20.8	21.9	20.2	Trade Receivables (net)	24.6	22.0
	52.2	47.1	37.2	39.3	32.6	Inventory	40.0	42.3
	2.5	1.6	3.3	2.5	4.1	All Other Current	2.9	2.7
	81.0	81.0	68.1	69.2	61.5	Total Current	75.5	72.5
	12.1	9.6	12.9	8.5	11.3	Fixed Assets (net)	8.9	11.0
	2.9	3.6	13.0	19.6	13.7	Intangibles (net)	9.0	9.9
	4.1	5.8	5.9	2.7	13.4	All Other Non-Current	6.6	6.6
	100.0	100.0	100.0	100.0	100.0	Total	100.0	100.0
						LIABILITIES		
	17.1	19.6	10.8	15.7	8.1	Notes Payable-Short Term	13.6	14.3
	2.2	1.2	1.8	1.0	2.2	Cur. Mat.-L.T.D.	2.2	1.8
	32.3	24.8	20.0	17.4	19.4	Trade Payables	25.6	23.7
	.0	.0	.3	.0	.0	Income Taxes Payable	.1	.2
	8.7	8.1	9.9	10.2	9.4	All Other Current	9.4	11.4
	60.3	53.8	42.6	44.3	39.1	Total Current	50.9	51.4
	25.4	5.1	11.2	17.1	19.1	Long-Term Debt	10.5	12.2
	.2	.2	.3	.7	.2	Deferred Taxes	.2	.2
	7.2	3.9	4.3	3.0	3.3	All Other Non-Current	5.2	4.4
	6.9	37.1	41.6	34.9	38.3	Net Worth	33.1	31.8
	100.0	100.0	100.0	100.0	100.0	Total Liabilities & Net Worth	100.0	100.0
						INCOME DATA		
	100.0	100.0	100.0	100.0	100.0	Net Sales	100.0	100.0
	32.9	27.1	24.9	24.7	25.6	Gross Profit	26.7	25.9
	29.0	25.2	21.6	19.8	20.6	Operating Expenses	22.8	22.2
	3.9	1.9	3.3	4.8	5.1	Operating Profit	4.0	3.7
	.8	-.2	.9	.4	.5	All Other Expenses (net)	.3	.6
	3.0	2.1	2.3	4.4	4.6	Profit Before Taxes	3.7	3.1
						RATIOS		
	2.0	2.1	2.4	2.2	2.0		2.3	1.9
	1.6	1.5	1.5	1.6	1.7	Current	1.5	1.3
	1.0	1.2	1.1	1.1	1.4		1.1	1.1
	.7	.8	1.0	.9	1.0		1.0	.8
	.4	.5	.6	.7	.6	Quick	.6	.5
	.1	.3	.4	.4	.4		.4	.4
1 624.5	13 27.3	11 32.5	7 49.7	18 20.4		Sales/Receivables	10 35.0	8 44.1
28 12.9	37 9.9	28 13.2	36 10.0	29 12.4			32 11.3	30 12.2
51 7.2	50 7.3	40 9.2	40 9.2	41 9.0			53 6.8	48 7.6
38 9.6	45 8.2	31 11.9	51 7.1	34 10.9		Cost of Sales/Inventory	41 8.9	44 8.3
93 3.9	86 4.2	55 6.7	58 6.3	57 6.4			61 6.0	62 5.9
116 3.2	119 3.1	89 4.1	77 4.8	80 4.5			87 4.2	93 3.9
12 30.5	16 22.3	17 21.3	18 20.2	25 14.7		Cost of Sales/Payables	22 16.6	23 16.2
38 9.5	33 11.2	29 12.4	33 11.2	34 10.8			37 9.8	32 11.3
80 4.6	72 5.1	48 7.6	41 8.9	48 7.5			58 6.3	53 6.8
	5.7	5.9	7.4	6.0	7.9	Sales/Working Capital	6.2	7.5
	9.2	11.2	12.6	9.7	10.6		13.2	16.0
	-624.7	24.4	35.4	35.6	33.1		49.6	86.7
	38.1	9.4	16.0	15.6	28.0	EBIT/Interest	18.2	13.0
	(18) 5.6	(42) 4.3	(41) 6.9	(23) 8.5	(35) 6.9		(137) 5.0	(134) 4.5
	.3	1.1	2.1	3.7	1.9		2.1	1.6
		10.3	3.9		6.0	Net Profit + Depr., Dep.,	11.0	24.4
		(10) 6.0	(12) 1.7		(11) 2.8	Amort./Cur. Mat. L/T/D	(25) 5.0	(22) 6.6
		1.4	.7		1.4		2.4	2.3
	.0	.0	.1	.2	.1	Fixed/Worth	.1	.1
	.3	.2	.2	.6	.5		.3	.3
	NM	.6	1.8	-.4	2.5		1.0	1.8
	1.0	.8	.8	1.2	1.2	Debt/Worth	1.1	1.4
	3.3	1.8	2.1	4.1	2.7		2.5	2.6
	-22.8	5.1	5.5	-9.3	16.7		13.8	56.6
	64.9	38.1	63.5	32.4	52.8	% Profit Before Taxes/Tangible	53.5	46.4
	(15) 46.1	(47) 15.7	(38) 28.8	(15) 15.5	(29) 33.2	Net Worth	(118) 23.5	(110) 18.9
	-9.6	1.4	8.8	1.4	12.3		6.5	5.7
	26.5	11.5	15.1	15.5	15.3	% Profit Before Taxes/Total	14.7	16.4
	11.0	5.3	7.5	8.9	9.7	Assets	7.5	7.0
	-3.1	.5	3.1	3.5	3.5		2.3	1.3
	278.1	479.5	138.3	97.3	103.6	Sales/Net Fixed Assets	159.4	151.9
	92.0	86.6	47.5	50.5	39.0		62.6	52.9
	30.5	25.7	23.4	18.5	13.5		31.3	22.8
	4.6	4.0	4.0	3.5	3.4	Sales/Total Assets	4.1	4.1
	3.3	3.0	3.1	3.0	2.5		3.0	2.9
	1.9	1.9	2.2	1.7	1.6		2.1	2.0
	.1	.2	.3	.4	.4	% Depr., Dep., Amort./Sales	.3	.3
	(14) .2	(39) .6	(43) .6	(21) .8	(31) .6		(117) .5	(114) .5
	1.4	1.1	1.2	1.8	1.6		.9	.9
	2.0	1.5	1.0			% Officers', Directors'	1.3	1.8
	(14) 2.9	(18) 3.4	(11) 1.3			Owners' Comp/Sales	(40) 2.4	(36) 3.4
	5.9	6.4	2.8				5.5	7.7
13419M	86521M	789456M	3726796M	4608519M	13554420M	Net Sales ($)	12507298M	14844663M
1092M	24309M	268609M	1180981M	1628597M	5596538M	Total Assets ($)	5022957M	5859229M

M = $ thousand   MM = $ million
See Pages 9 through 22 for Explanation of Ratios and Data

Comparative Historical Data | Current Data Sorted by Sales

4/1/07-3/31/08 ALL	4/1/08-3/31/09 ALL	4/1/09-3/31/10 ALL	Type of Statement	0-1MM	1-3MM	3-5MM	5-10MM	10-25MM	25MM & OVER
46	54	51	Unqualified	1		2	1	2	45
18	24	35	Reviewed			1	2	12	20
17	24	18	Compiled		1		7	7	3
25	22	17	Tax Returns	4	3	3	4	1	2
63	68	67	Other	2	4	4	6	9	42
					37 (4/1-9/30/09)		151 (10/1/09-3/31/10)		
169	192	188	**NUMBER OF STATEMENTS**	7	8	10	20	31	112
%	%	%	**ASSETS**	%	%	%	%	%	%
6.5	6.8	6.5	Cash & Equivalents			4.8	5.2	7.0	6.0
22.0	21.2	21.7	Trade Receivables (net)			35.4	13.6	29.3	21.2
42.5	41.8	41.5	Inventory			47.0	54.0	44.8	37.3
3.4	2.9	2.7	All Other Current			2.3	1.5	1.8	3.3
74.5	72.8	72.4	Total Current			89.5	74.4	83.0	67.8
9.9	11.3	11.2	Fixed Assets (net)			3.2	15.4	7.2	10.3
9.9	10.9	9.9	Intangibles (net)			4.2	1.9	5.2	14.4
5.8	5.1	6.5	All Other Non-Current			3.1	8.4	4.5	7.5
100.0	100.0	100.0	Total			100.0	100.0	100.0	100.0
			LIABILITIES						
13.7	15.4	13.8	Notes Payable-Short Term			17.1	24.0	18.2	10.6
1.7	2.0	1.6	Cur. Mat.-L.T.D.			2.6	1.9	1.3	1.7
24.4	23.5	23.1	Trade Payables			38.4	22.6	30.5	19.6
.1	.2	.1	Income Taxes Payable			.0	.0	.1	.1
9.9	9.4	9.5	All Other Current			10.5	6.1	7.3	10.0
49.8	50.6	48.2	Total Current			68.5	54.6	57.4	42.1
11.7	11.8	14.5	Long-Term Debt			36.2	10.2	5.8	13.8
.4	.3	.3	Deferred Taxes			.0	.4	.1	.3
5.9	4.0	4.0	All Other Non-Current			6.6	6.4	1.7	3.6
32.1	33.2	33.1	Net Worth			-11.3	28.4	35.0	40.3
100.0	100.0	100.0	Total Liabilities & Net Worth			100.0	100.0	100.0	100.0
			INCOME DATA						
100.0	100.0	100.0	Net Sales			100.0	100.0	100.0	100.0
26.8	27.1	26.6	Gross Profit			26.9	28.7	26.2	24.8
22.6	24.1	23.2	Operating Expenses			25.5	26.2	24.4	20.2
4.1	3.0	3.4	Operating Profit			1.4	2.6	1.8	4.6
.5	.5	.5	All Other Expenses (net)			-.1	1.1	.5	.3
3.6	2.6	2.9	Profit Before Taxes			1.4	1.5	1.3	4.3
			RATIOS						
2.1	2.2	2.1	Current			1.8	1.9	2.1	2.2
1.5	1.5	1.5				1.5	1.5	1.4	1.6
1.2	1.1	1.2				1.3	1.1	1.1	1.2
.9	.9	.9	Quick			.9	.5	.8	1.0
.6	.6	.6				.6	.4	.6	.6
.4	.4	.4				.3	.1	.3	.4
9 40.0	10 37.2	10 35.2	Sales/Receivables	31 11.6	1 250.9	20 18.0			12 29.9
31 11.7	31 11.8	30 12.4		46 7.9	11 33.5	36 10.2			28 12.9
45 8.1	43 8.6	44 8.3		67 5.5	53 6.9	50 7.2			40 9.2
41 9.0	41 8.9	39 9.4	Cost of Sales/Inventory	64 5.7	66 5.5	38 9.6			36 10.1
60 6.1	67 5.5	67 5.5		90 4.1	103 3.6	65 5.6			57 6.4
101 3.6	100 3.6	102 3.6		126 2.9	174 2.1	102 3.6			80 4.5
21 17.0	21 17.4	18 20.3	Cost of Sales/Payables	23 16.0	16 22.8	17 21.5			19 18.9
35 10.5	34 10.9	32 11.3		69 5.3	38 9.6	33 11.1			30 12.2
66 5.6	60 6.1	56 6.5		91 4.0	72 5.1	87 4.2			43 8.5
6.8	7.0	6.5	Sales/Working Capital			5.2	5.5	7.3	7.8
13.5	12.7	11.3				7.9	16.0	14.8	11.3
36.3	49.4	32.3				NM	33.8	48.3	31.5
15.0	9.3	18.9	EBIT/Interest				7.1	12.3	21.7
(158) 4.9	(169) 3.7	(164) 5.9				(17) 5.3	(27) 3.3	(99) 7.3	
2.0	1.2	1.8				.2	1.1	2.6	
10.9	8.1	7.5	Net Profit + Depr., Dep., Amort./Cur. Mat. L/T/D						4.5
(33) 4.5	(42) 3.5	(41) 2.9						(30) 2.7	
1.7	1.1	1.3							1.3
.1	.1	.1	Fixed/Worth			.0	.2	.0	.1
.3	.3	.3				.0	.5	.2	.4
1.8	2.6	1.9				NM	1.5	.6	2.5
1.4	1.2	1.0	Debt/Worth			1.5	.9	.8	.9
2.9	3.4	2.3				3.1	2.5	2.2	2.2
15.4	23.0	20.2				-23.9	17.5	9.2	33.2
82.5	45.6	51.2	% Profit Before Taxes/Tangible Net Worth				45.4	51.2	53.0
(141) 28.9	(149) 22.0	(148) 22.6				(17) 15.7	(27) 16.1	(86) 28.7	
10.3	5.2	5.5					-13.5	1.4	9.4
15.5	13.4	15.3	% Profit Before Taxes/Total Assets			15.8	12.5	11.7	15.8
8.5	6.1	7.5				6.8	6.4	4.5	8.4
2.7	.8	2.0				-7.9	-2.1	.2	3.9
171.3	116.6	154.2	Sales/Net Fixed Assets			999.8	177.6	544.5	111.1
57.0	55.0	58.6				253.2	47.0	111.1	48.4
22.3	19.5	22.6				78.4	19.7	39.5	20.4
4.1	3.7	3.8	Sales/Total Assets			3.8	4.3	4.7	3.8
2.9	2.9	3.0				2.2	2.6	3.3	3.1
2.1	2.0	1.9				1.8	1.4	2.2	2.1
.3	.3	.3	% Depr., Dep., Amort./Sales				.3	.2	.4
(130) .5	(154) .6	(151) .6				(16) .6	(22) .7	(98) .6	
1.0	1.3	1.3					1.7	1.0	1.3
1.5	1.3	1.2	% Officers', Directors' Owners' Comp/Sales				1.6	1.0	.2
(45) 2.7	(42) 2.6	(47) 2.1				(11) 2.0	(10) 3.2	(13) 1.2	
4.4	4.7	4.6					3.5	6.6	2.4
16833017M	22478097M	22779131M	Net Sales ($)	3429M	16152M	40989M	146221M	506092M	22066248M
6474514M	8649454M	8700126M	Total Assets ($)	2218M	27844M	18628M	94371M	162256M	8394809M

M = $ thousand   MM = $ million
See Pages 9 through 22 for Explanation of Ratios and Data

WHOLESALE—Farm Supplies Merchant Wholesalers NAICS 424910

Current Data Sorted by Assets | **Comparative Historical Data**

Type of Statement	0-500M	500M-2MM	2-10MM	10-50MM	50-100MM	100-250MM	4/1/05-3/31/06 ALL	4/1/06-3/31/07 ALL
Unqualified	1	23	174	242	54	32	649	608
Reviewed	1	10	61	15	1		63	78
Compiled	1	21	29	7	2		56	49
Tax Returns	7	11	11	1			22	34
Other	2	20	48	51	11	10	124	118
		365 (4/1-9/30/09)		481 (10/1/09-3/31/10)				
NUMBER OF STATEMENTS	12	85	323	316	68	42	914	887
	%	%	%	%	%	%	%	%
ASSETS								
Cash & Equivalents	10.8	9.3	9.0	6.3	6.4	6.7	5.8	5.8
Trade Receivables (net)	16.8	22.8	22.7	21.0	20.2	21.4	17.5	18.3
Inventory	30.1	33.2	30.0	30.7	31.4	34.8	30.0	30.8
All Other Current	7.4	2.2	4.1	5.9	6.1	8.6	8.2	8.6
Total Current	65.0	67.5	65.8	63.9	64.1	71.6	61.6	63.5
Fixed Assets (net)	28.8	19.9	20.6	21.2	20.4	18.9	23.2	22.5
Intangibles (net)	2.1	1.6	.8	.8	.9	.6	.8	.8
All Other Non-Current	4.2	10.9	12.8	14.0	14.7	8.9	14.4	13.2
Total	100.0	100.0	100.0	100.0	100.0	100.0	100.0	100.0
LIABILITIES								
Notes Payable-Short Term	22.9	14.9	13.5	15.5	13.5	18.8	17.2	17.9
Cur. Mat.-L.T.D.	8.2	1.5	1.6	1.6	2.0	1.1	2.0	1.8
Trade Payables	23.0	16.4	18.7	21.6	21.6	20.4	17.6	17.5
Income Taxes Payable	.0	.1	.3	.4	.3	.4	.4	.4
All Other Current	17.7	7.0	7.7	7.5	10.1	8.2	6.8	7.6
Total Current	71.7	39.8	41.7	46.7	47.5	48.8	44.0	45.1
Long-Term Debt	20.5	7.8	5.8	8.6	9.8	10.3	8.2	8.1
Deferred Taxes	.0	.2	.3	.6	.5	.4	.3	.4
All Other Non-Current	4.3	4.2	1.2	1.9	3.2	6.5	1.7	1.8
Net Worth	3.5	48.0	50.9	42.2	39.0	34.1	45.8	44.6
Total Liabilities & Net Worth	100.0	100.0	100.0	100.0	100.0	100.0	100.0	100.0
INCOME DATA								
Net Sales	100.0	100.0	100.0	100.0	100.0	100.0	100.0	100.0
Gross Profit	28.8	21.9	16.4	12.5	10.8	14.6	15.5	16.1
Operating Expenses	29.6	20.7	14.4	10.4	9.4	11.5	14.0	14.2
Operating Profit	-.8	1.2	2.0	2.1	1.4	3.2	1.5	1.8
All Other Expenses (net)	.7	-.4	-.9	-1.0	-1.4	.1	-.6	-.6
Profit Before Taxes	-1.5	1.6	2.9	3.1	2.8	3.0	2.1	2.4
RATIOS								
Current	1.7	3.3	2.3	1.6	1.7	1.9	1.8	1.8
	1.1	2.0	1.6	1.3	1.3	1.4	1.3	1.3
	.7	1.2	1.3	1.2	1.2	1.2	1.2	1.2
Quick	1.2	1.6	1.2	.8	.7	.8	.8	.8
	.5	.9	.8	.6	.6	.5	(913) .5	.5
	.2	.4	.5	.4	.4	.3	.3	.3
Sales/Receivables	0 UND	12 31.0	19 19.3	17 20.9	15 23.9	17 22.0	13 27.1	13 27.9
	7 49.8	21 17.6	28 13.1	26 13.9	25 14.7	29 12.6	23 15.9	23 15.6
	23 15.6	37 9.9	41 9.0	41 8.9	40 9.1	40 9.1	34 10.6	35 10.3
Cost of Sales/Inventory	5 80.0	24 15.1	29 12.7	32 11.5	29 12.5	28 13.1	35 10.5	34 10.8
	44 8.4	56 6.6	46 8.0	50 7.3	47 7.8	55 6.6	52 7.0	53 6.9
	84 4.3	90 4.1	77 4.7	79 4.6	71 5.1	101 3.6	77 4.8	81 4.5
Cost of Sales/Payables	4 81.5	6 57.8	14 25.9	17 21.4	19 19.0	19 18.8	17 21.6	15 23.7
	13 28.8	16 22.6	25 14.6	31 11.7	28 13.2	30 12.3	28 13.3	26 13.9
	37 9.8	31 11.6	43 8.6	54 6.8	50 7.2	54 6.7	43 8.5	44 8.3
Sales/Working Capital	7.8	5.2	6.7	9.9	11.6	7.5	9.1	8.9
	120.1	10.0	11.7	15.5	18.2	13.3	16.4	16.1
	-21.6	30.4	20.8	25.3	32.3	22.6	28.4	28.0
EBIT/Interest	12.7	16.5	18.4	13.2	10.2	7.9	6.7	5.7
	(10) 1.6	(72) 3.2	(295) 6.1	(311) 6.6	(65) 6.5	(40) 4.6	(861) 3.6	(830) 3.1
	.6	.3	2.2	3.4	4.1	1.7	2.0	1.8
Net Profit + Depr., Dep., Amort./Cur. Mat. L/T/D			9.9	10.4	14.1	13.4	7.7	7.0
		(112)	5.4	(195) 5.7	(41) 7.5	(28) 8.4	(438) 4.3	(401) 4.5
			2.3	2.8	5.4	3.4	2.8	2.7
Fixed/Worth	.1	.1	.2	.3	.4	.5	.3	.3
	1.6	.3	.4	.5	.5	.6	.5	.5
	-1.4	.8	.6	.7	.7	.8	.7	.7
Debt/Worth	1.6	.3	.5	.9	1.0	1.1	.6	.6
	7.7	.9	.9	1.4	1.5	2.2	1.2	1.3
	-4.4	2.8	1.8	2.3	2.8	3.6	2.0	2.4
% Profit Before Taxes/Tangible Net Worth		18.2	24.2	27.2	31.1	28.1	16.8	18.2
	(75)	7.4	(318) 14.5	(309) 18.9	(67) 22.2	18.0	(891) 10.1	(868) 11.2
		-.2	5.5	9.9	13.5	9.0	4.9	5.4
% Profit Before Taxes/Total Assets	11.0	10.4	12.3	11.5	12.3	9.2	7.3	8.2
	.9	4.0	7.1	7.5	7.7	5.2	4.6	4.7
	-2.4	-1.1	2.1	3.8	4.0	2.2	1.9	2.2
Sales/Net Fixed Assets	129.4	41.0	24.9	19.0	19.6	18.5	16.3	17.8
	48.5	20.1	13.1	12.4	13.6	13.3	10.3	11.0
	7.0	9.6	8.5	8.4	9.8	9.3	7.4	7.5
Sales/Total Assets	6.8	4.2	3.3	3.1	3.4	3.1	2.9	3.0
	4.3	3.1	2.5	2.4	2.6	2.3	2.3	2.2
	1.8	2.0	1.8	1.8	1.9	1.8	1.8	1.8
% Depr., Dep., Amort./Sales		.7	.7	.8	.8	.8	1.1	1.0
	(70)	1.0	(309) 1.2	(309) 1.2	(65) 1.0	(40) 1.1	(887) 1.5	(852) 1.4
		2.0	1.8	1.6	1.4	1.5	2.0	2.0
% Officers', Directors' Owners' Comp/Sales		1.4	1.1	.4			1.1	1.1
	(23)	3.3	(48) 1.8	(20) 1.1			(89) 2.2	(91) 2.0
		7.4	3.9	3.7			4.8	4.6
Net Sales ($)	20581M	386306M	4875888M	18796511M	13854897M	16940679M	35560087M	37554454M
Total Assets ($)	4472M	108299M	1725649M	7223422M	4902693M	6498727M	15014549M	15683424M

M = $ thousand   MM = $ million
See Pages 9 through 22 for Explanation of Ratios and Data

Comparative Historical Data

Current Data Sorted by Sales

Comparative Historical Data			Type of Statement	Current Data Sorted by Sales					
587	519	526	Unqualified	8	22	58	132	305	
74	81	88	Reviewed	6	11	12	34	25	
65	71	60	Compiled	9	8	15	20	8	
44	33	30	Tax Returns	8	5	7	5	3	
120	148	142	Other	9	8	20	35	68	
4/1/07-3/31/08 ALL	4/1/08-3/31/09 ALL	4/1/09-3/31/10 ALL		365 (4/1-9/30/09)		481 (10/1/09-3/31/10)			
				0-1MM	1-3MM	3-5MM	5-10MM	10-25MM	25MM & OVER
890	852	846	NUMBER OF STATEMENTS	5	40	54	112	226	409
%	%	%	ASSETS	%	%	%	%	%	%
6.9	6.6	7.7	Cash & Equivalents	9.6	9.7	9.1	8.6	6.4	
22.2	21.6	21.7	Trade Receivables (net)	16.1	20.2	20.7	23.2	22.1	
32.3	34.4	30.9	Inventory	32.8	32.8	31.5	29.9	30.9	
5.9	7.0	5.0	All Other Current	3.0	2.7	3.5	4.6	6.1	
67.3	69.6	65.4	Total Current	61.5	65.5	64.9	66.3	65.5	
19.8	18.8	20.8	Fixed Assets (net)	22.2	20.8	20.5	20.7	20.6	
.7	.8	.9	Intangibles (net)	3.6	.9	.4	1.1	.8	
12.3	10.8	12.9	All Other Non-Current	12.7	12.8	14.2	11.9	13.2	
100.0	100.0	100.0	Total	100.0	100.0	100.0	100.0	100.0	
			LIABILITIES						
20.6	18.5	14.8	Notes Payable-Short Term	17.1	13.3	14.1	14.3	15.2	
1.9	1.9	1.7	Cur. Mat.-L.T.D.	3.1	1.6	2.0	1.4	1.6	
17.7	20.0	19.9	Trade Payables	10.2	19.5	14.8	20.5	22.0	
.6	.5	.3	Income Taxes Payable	.1	.1	.2	.3	.4	
7.9	9.1	7.9	All Other Current	5.7	10.0	6.1	8.4	8.1	
48.7	50.0	44.6	Total Current	36.1	44.5	37.2	44.9	47.4	
8.0	7.9	7.8	Long-Term Debt	12.2	6.7	7.7	6.0	8.4	
.3	.3	.4	Deferred Taxes	.1	.2	.3	.3	.6	
2.0	1.7	2.2	All Other Non-Current	5.4	2.3	1.5	1.6	2.4	
41.0	40.1	44.9	Net Worth	46.2	46.4	53.3	47.2	41.3	
100.0	100.0	100.0	Total Liabilities & Net Worth	100.0	100.0	100.0	100.0	100.0	
			INCOME DATA						
100.0	100.0	100.0	Net Sales	100.0	100.0	100.0	100.0	100.0	
15.6	15.5	15.1	Gross Profit	27.8	22.0	20.3	15.1	11.4	
13.3	12.4	13.2	Operating Expenses	26.7	21.4	18.2	12.6	9.6	
2.3	3.1	1.9	Operating Profit	1.1	.5	2.1	2.5	1.8	
-.6	-.6	-.9	All Other Expenses (net)	-.3	-.5	-.9	-1.1	-.9	
2.9	3.7	2.8	Profit Before Taxes	1.4	1.1	3.0	3.6	2.7	
			RATIOS						
1.7	1.7	1.9		3.9	2.7	2.6	2.0	1.7	
1.3	1.3	1.4	Current	2.0	1.5	1.7	1.5	1.4	
1.1	1.2	1.2		1.1	1.2	1.3	1.2	1.2	
.9	.9	1.0		1.6	1.6	1.3	1.1	.8	
.6 (851)	.5	.6	Quick	.9	.7	.8	.7	.6	
.4	.3	.4		.3	.4	.5	.4	.4	
19 · 19.5	16 · 23.0	17 · 21.3		7 · 54.8	18 · 20.7	19 · 19.5	20 · 17.9	16 · 22.8	
30 · 12.2	26 · 14.2	26 · 13.9	Sales/Receivables	21 · 17.4	26 · 14.0	27 · 13.3	29 · 12.5	25 · 14.8	
45 · 8.2	39 · 9.4	40 · 9.2		38 · 9.6	49 · 7.4	41 · 8.9	42 · 8.6	38 · 9.6	
36 · 10.1	34 · 10.8	29 · 12.7		29 · 12.4	35 · 10.5	35 · 10.6	32 · 11.5	26 · 14.1	
58 · 6.3	57 · 6.5	49 · 7.5	Cost of Sales/Inventory	75 · 4.9	69 · 5.3	63 · 5.8	48 · 7.7	43 · 8.5	
85 · 4.3	85 · 4.3	81 · 4.5		111 · 3.3	100 · 3.7	83 · 4.4	81 · 4.5	70 · 5.3	
15 · 23.9	15 · 23.7	15 · 24.0		8 · 43.6	14 · 26.5	12 · 29.5	16 · 23.4	16 · 22.7	
28 · 13.0	28 · 13.1	26 · 14.0	Cost of Sales/Payables	16 · 23.2	27 · 13.3	28 · 12.9	26 · 13.9	27 · 13.8	
47 · 7.8	46 · 8.0	47 · 7.8		27 · 13.7	48 · 7.6	45 · 8.2	48 · 7.6	49 · 7.4	
8.5	9.5	8.1		4.5	4.5	6.0	7.7	11.2	
15.1	16.3	13.7	Sales/Working Capital	6.9	8.9	9.5	12.5	17.0	
28.4	27.7	24.8		43.0	27.1	13.4	20.9	27.9	
6.4	10.1	13.5		12.5	12.6	15.0	18.8	11.7	
(833) 3.4	(794) 5.1	(793) 6.0	EBIT/Interest	(33) 2.7	(47) 1.8	(102) 4.4	(211) 7.2	(397) 6.3	
2.1	2.8	2.4		.2	-1.6	1.8	2.6	3.3	
9.9	12.7	10.9				8.2	9.8	12.4	
(427) 5.8	(383) 6.6	(384) 6.0	Net Profit + Depr., Dep., Amort./Cur. Mat. L/T/D		(27) 5.3	(102) 5.5	(246) 6.7		
3.5	3.8	3.0				2.0	2.3	3.5	
.3	.3	.3		.1	.2	.2	.3	.3	
.5	.4	.4	Fixed/Worth	.4	.3	.3	.4	.5	
.7	.7	.7		97.0	.9	.5	.6	.7	
.8	.8	.6		.2	.3	.4	.6	.9	
1.5	1.7	1.2	Debt/Worth	.7	1.0	.8	1.1	1.4	
2.9	3.0	2.3		486.6	2.9	1.9	2.1	2.3	
23.9	34.3	25.9		16.0	18.2	23.2	24.0	27.9	
(868) 15.3	(834) 22.0	(818) 16.4	% Profit Before Taxes/Tangible Net Worth	(31) 5.8	(49) 6.9	(220) 10.4	(402) 15.1	19.8	
8.7	12.0	6.6		-4.2	-2.1	3.0	7.6	11.1	
9.6	12.5	11.5		10.9	8.2	10.5	12.3	11.7	
5.9	7.8	6.9	% Profit Before Taxes/Total Assets	4.8	2.7	5.6	7.4	7.6	
3.3	4.5	2.5		-2.2	-2.2	1.6	2.5	3.9	
21.1	27.0	22.8		39.2	24.6	26.7	21.5	20.7	
13.0	15.6	13.2	Sales/Net Fixed Assets	12.8	12.6	14.5	12.0	13.9	
8.4	10.2	8.7		5.8	6.8	7.9	8.0	9.8	
2.9	3.4	3.3		3.4	3.0	3.0	3.2	3.5	
2.3	2.5	2.5	Sales/Total Assets	2.2	1.9	2.3	2.4	2.7	
1.7	1.9	1.9		1.5	1.4	1.7	1.8	2.1	
.8	.7	.8		.6	.8	.8	.8	.8	
(844) 1.2	(803) 1.0	(800) 1.1	% Depr., Dep., Amort./Sales	(33) 1.1	(48) 1.5	(108) 1.3	(216) 1.3	(393) 1.1	
1.7	1.5	1.7		3.0	2.4	1.9	1.9	1.5	
1.1	1.0	1.0		2.2	.4	1.1	1.0	.5	
(107) 2.2	(105) 2.1	(100) 2.0	% Officers', Directors' Owners' Comp/Sales	(14) 5.1	(10) 2.8	(20) 1.8	(29) 2.3	(25) 1.1	
4.8	4.0	4.6		10.1	3.8	3.3	4.1		
46797126M	62130173M	54874862M	Net Sales ($)	2591M	82253M	214511M	853319M	3733469M	49988719M
20583502M	22981696M	20463262M	Total Assets ($)	1899M	39908M	129203M	408742M	1917659M	17965851M

M = $ thousand   MM = $ million

See Pages 9 through 22 for Explanation of Ratios and Data

WHOLESALE—Book, Periodical, and Newspaper Merchant Wholesalers   NAICS 424920

Current Data Sorted by Assets | **Comparative Historical Data**

0-500M	500M-2MM	2-10MM	10-50MM	50-100MM	100-250MM		4/1/05-3/31/06 ALL	4/1/06-3/31/07 ALL
						Type of Statement		
	2	1	5	1		Unqualified	12	14
	3	7	2			Reviewed	7	9
1	4	4	1	1		Compiled	6	9
7		1	1			Tax Returns	6	6
1	5	11	10		1	Other	15	16
		14 (4/1-9/30/09)		54 (10/1/09-3/31/10)				
9	14	24	19	2		**NUMBER OF STATEMENTS**	46	54
%	%	%	%	%		**ASSETS**	%	%
	9.2	7.1	11.4			Cash & Equivalents	8.3	11.2
	20.5	28.9	24.7			Trade Receivables (net)	30.8	26.4
	37.2	32.7	33.0			Inventory	29.4	33.1
	1.8	3.2	9.6	D		All Other Current	4.5	3.7
	68.7	71.9	78.7	A		Total Current	73.0	74.5
	12.7	17.9	12.6	T		Fixed Assets (net)	16.1	15.0
	6.1	4.5	3.2	A		Intangibles (net)	6.1	3.3
	12.5	5.7	5.5			All Other Non-Current	4.8	7.2
	100.0	100.0	100.0	N		Total	100.0	100.0
				O		**LIABILITIES**		
	12.4	7.9	10.5	T		Notes Payable-Short Term	16.0	9.1
	1.6	3.5	1.8			Cur. Mat.-L.T.D.	2.5	.9
	25.6	24.3	33.2	A		Trade Payables	23.5	27.5
	.0	.1	.3	V		Income Taxes Payable	.3	.3
	19.3	11.9	10.1	A		All Other Current	8.5	9.1
	58.8	47.8	55.9	I		Total Current	50.8	47.0
	10.9	14.2	7.3	L		Long-Term Debt	12.2	10.7
	.0	.1	.1	A		Deferred Taxes	.3	.1
	.0	7.1	1.1	B		All Other Non-Current	5.5	5.3
	30.3	30.9	35.6	L		Net Worth	31.1	36.9
	100.0	100.0	100.0	E		Total Liabilities & Net Worth	100.0	100.0
						INCOME DATA		
	100.0	100.0	100.0			Net Sales	100.0	100.0
	38.5	36.2	36.6			Gross Profit	36.0	35.4
	33.9	30.4	34.2			Operating Expenses	34.0	31.8
	4.6	5.9	2.4			Operating Profit	2.0	3.6
	-.2	1.6	.5			All Other Expenses (net)	.5	.5
	4.8	4.2	1.9			Profit Before Taxes	1.5	3.1
						RATIOS		
	2.3	2.6	2.0				2.4	3.4
	1.3	1.5	1.2			Current	1.4	1.6
	.6	1.1	1.1				1.0	1.0
	1.1	1.4	.9				1.3	1.4
	.4	.7	.7			Quick	.8	.8
	.2	.5	.3				.4	.5
(7) 52.8	(21) 17.5	(28) 12.9				Sales/Receivables	(19) 19.6	(16) 23.4
(13) 27.4	(36) 10.1	(37) 9.9					(35) 10.5	(34) 10.8
(47) 7.7	(67) 5.5	(56) 6.5					(65) 5.6	(61) 6.0
(9) 40.0	(27) 13.6	(43) 8.5				Cost of Sales/Inventory	(12) 29.7	(31) 11.6
(51) 7.2	(96) 3.8	(89) 4.1					(57) 6.4	(62) 5.9
(200) 1.8	(138) 2.7	(170) 2.1					(121) 3.0	(156) 2.3
(8) 45.0	(24) 15.3	(45) 8.0				Cost of Sales/Payables	(13) 27.5	(23) 15.8
(62) 5.9	(47) 7.8	(63) 5.8					(45) 8.2	(58) 6.3
(102) 3.6	(69) 5.3	(118) 3.1					(79) 4.6	(97) 3.8
2.7	3.8	3.5				Sales/Working Capital	5.8	4.0
18.0	11.8	14.4					17.7	10.0
-14.9	35.1	40.2					167.8	NM
5.2	34.2	23.0				EBIT/Interest	10.3	14.2
(11) 3.5	(21) 9.0	(16) 3.4					(42) 4.0	(43) 5.4
1.3	1.2	.7					1.2	1.9
						Net Profit + Depr., Dep., Amort./Cur. Mat. L/T/D	34.9	24.1
							(10) 7.4	(10) 5.0
							1.0	1.0
.0	.1	.1				Fixed/Worth	.2	.1
.4	.7	.4					.4	.4
94.4	NM	.8					2.3	1.3
1.5	.5	1.3				Debt/Worth	1.0	.6
3.8	3.0	2.8					3.3	2.4
391.9	NM	4.6					7.3	6.6
112.9	54.2	20.7				% Profit Before Taxes/Tangible Net Worth	50.2	42.3
(12) 21.8	(18) 29.3	10.6					(38) 20.0	(49) 17.9
3.3	2.1	1.4					6.0	4.4
11.3	19.3	7.2				% Profit Before Taxes/Total Assets	11.4	12.2
4.2	11.8	1.6					5.7	5.9
-.6	-.2	.3					1.1	1.6
221.9	76.7	47.2				Sales/Net Fixed Assets	58.8	51.5
51.9	35.7	24.1					42.2	23.5
22.1	12.3	9.9					14.2	11.0
4.6	3.6	3.5				Sales/Total Assets	5.2	4.6
2.4	2.6	2.1					2.2	2.2
1.3	1.6	1.5					1.7	1.4
.2	.6	.7				% Depr., Dep., Amort./Sales	.5	.5
(11) 1.2	(18) .9	(16) 1.4					(39) .9	(46) .9
3.1	1.5	1.9					1.6	1.5
						% Officers', Directors' Owners' Comp/Sales	1.9	2.2
							(16) 5.6	(12) 4.2
							16.2	10.6
14659M	46674M	376349M	993593M	339921M		Net Sales ($)	2070723M	2888461M
3011M	15603M	121795M	428612M	141349M		Total Assets ($)	930918M	1567954M

M = $ thousand   MM = $ million
See Pages 9 through 22 for Explanation of Ratios and Data

Comparative Historical Data — Current Data Sorted by Sales

4/1/07-3/31/08 ALL	4/1/08-3/31/09 ALL	4/1/09-3/31/10 ALL	Type of Statement	0-1MM	1-3MM	3-5MM	5-10MM	10-25MM	25MM & OVER
9	9	7	Unqualified					1	5
9	7	11	Reviewed			1	1	6	3
6	8	9	Compiled		3	2	2	1	1
8	13	13	Tax Returns	5	5			3	
22	23	28	Other	1	5	3	3	5	12
				14 (4/1-9/30/09)			54 (10/1/09-3/31/10)		
54	60	68	**NUMBER OF STATEMENTS**	6	13	6	6	16	21
%	%	%	**ASSETS**	%	%	%	%	%	%
8.7	10.3	10.0	Cash & Equivalents		11.0			7.6	9.7
28.9	28.5	26.5	Trade Receivables (net)		20.5			26.4	29.0
32.4	31.3	33.1	Inventory		35.4			33.1	32.1
4.1	4.7	4.2	All Other Current		.3			1.8	10.7
74.0	74.8	73.7	Total Current		67.1			69.0	81.5
12.1	15.0	14.0	Fixed Assets (net)		16.0			15.0	13.7
3.7	4.1	4.0	Intangibles (net)		6.5			6.0	1.7
10.1	6.1	8.3	All Other Non-Current		10.3			10.0	3.1
100.0	100.0	100.0	Total		100.0			100.0	100.0
			LIABILITIES						
15.2	13.9	9.5	Notes Payable-Short Term		7.8			14.6	7.3
1.7	3.2	4.6	Cur. Mat.-L.T.D.		6.7			3.0	1.4
33.2	32.8	28.7	Trade Payables		24.9			18.9	37.1
.3	.2	.1	Income Taxes Payable		.1			.0	.3
11.8	14.1	12.5	All Other Current		10.6			12.2	10.8
62.2	64.3	55.5	Total Current		50.0			48.7	56.8
8.6	9.8	11.6	Long-Term Debt		13.9			13.9	6.3
.0	.0	.1	Deferred Taxes		.0			.1	.1
3.8	5.7	4.6	All Other Non-Current		8.6			9.7	.7
25.4	20.2	28.3	Net Worth		27.5			27.6	36.1
100.0	100.0	100.0	Total Liabilities & Net Worth		100.0			100.0	100.0
			INCOME DATA						
100.0	100.0	100.0	Net Sales		100.0			100.0	100.0
33.6	36.7	36.0	Gross Profit		42.0			37.7	30.1
31.2	34.1	32.3	Operating Expenses		35.9			34.5	26.9
2.4	2.6	3.7	Operating Profit		6.1			3.2	3.2
.6	.2	.5	All Other Expenses (net)		-.6			.6	.2
1.8	2.4	3.2	Profit Before Taxes		6.8			2.6	3.0
			RATIOS						
2.0	1.8	2.3			2.0			2.5	2.1
1.2	1.2	1.3	Current		1.5			1.4	1.2
1.0	1.0	1.0			.8			1.0	1.1
1.0	.9	1.1			.9			1.3	1.0
.6	(59) .6	.6	Quick		.4			.6	.8
.4	.4	.3			.3			.3	.3
21 17.6	18 19.9	17 21.7		11 34.7			21 17.5	23 16.0	
43 8.6	37 9.9	34 10.6	Sales/Receivables	18 20.7			34 10.6	34 10.9	
62 5.9	65 5.6	59 6.2		53 6.8			59 6.2	49 7.5	
34 10.9	19 19.4	18 20.1		18 19.9			19 18.9	19 19.4	
59 6.1	56 6.5	74 4.9	Cost of Sales/Inventory	87 4.2			102 3.6	64 5.7	
152 2.4	127 2.9	152 2.4		216 1.7			176 2.1	97 3.8	
25 14.5	19 19.4	28 13.0		3 127.9			20 18.3	32 11.5	
60 6.0	67 5.5	53 6.8	Cost of Sales/Payables	67 5.5			37 9.8	62 5.9	
104 3.5	103 3.5	88 4.1		98 3.7			64 5.7	94 3.9	
6.4	6.6	3.9			3.1			5.0	7.1
20.6	23.8	13.0	Sales/Working Capital		22.4			14.0	14.4
-98.8	-162.8	NM			-122.9			NM	75.3
11.8	11.2	19.6			8.2			11.3	49.0
(47) 3.7	(49) 4.2	(54) 3.7	EBIT/Interest		(10) 3.3			2.6	(17) 9.0
1.1	.8	1.2			.1			.6	1.9
35.8									
(10) 7.2			Net Profit + Depr., Dep., Amort./Cur. Mat. L/T/D						
1.3									
.2	.1	.1			.0			.2	.2
.4	.5	.5	Fixed/Worth		.4			.8	.4
2.1	3.5	2.3			-10.0			74.8	1.0
1.1	1.3	1.5			1.5			1.5	.9
4.0	3.3	3.1	Debt/Worth		1.7			4.1	2.8
17.6	28.3	17.1			-76.6			754.5	6.1
54.0	48.8	44.9						46.2	42.7
(44) 14.1	(47) 15.7	(56) 20.3	% Profit Before Taxes/Tangible Net Worth					(13) 13.2	(20) 15.5
3.7	1.3	2.7						-8.6	6.9
11.1	13.1	14.2			14.3			11.8	17.7
3.4	4.4	3.5	% Profit Before Taxes/Total Assets		2.8			2.8	3.6
.2	-.8	.0			-1.4			-1.5	1.3
175.2	95.0	102.0			335.2			81.1	52.5
30.7	39.2	31.8	Sales/Net Fixed Assets		47.9			26.4	30.4
15.1	15.9	14.4			15.1			10.9	14.6
4.1	4.1	3.8			4.1			3.8	4.9
2.4	2.5	2.4	Sales/Total Assets		3.0			2.6	2.5
1.5	1.6	1.6			1.2			1.6	2.2
.4	.5	.6			.2			.7	.6
(40) .9	(44) .9	(52) 1.1	% Depr., Dep., Amort./Sales		(10) 1.3			(13) .9	(19) .8
1.6	1.4	1.7			2.0			1.5	1.6
1.3	1.8	1.8							
(16) 2.6	(21) 2.4	(21) 2.6	% Officers', Directors' Owners' Comp/Sales						
6.2	3.6	4.4							
2418762M	2138924M	1771196M	Net Sales ($)	3083M	23845M	24709M	41183M	249318M	1429058M
1199469M	1069132M	710370M	Total Assets ($)	3271M	15985M	14084M	20112M	118225M	538693M

© RMA 2010

M = $ thousand   MM = $ million
See Pages 9 through 22 for Explanation of Ratios and Data

Current Data Sorted by Assets | Comparative Historical Data

Type of Statement	0-500M	500M-2MM	2-10MM	10-50MM	50-100MM	100-250MM	4/1/05-3/31/06 ALL	4/1/06-3/31/07 ALL
Unqualified			2	9	3		12	19
Reviewed		6	14	6			22	26
Compiled	5	8	13	1			34	41
Tax Returns	2	15	12				20	25
Other	5	13	16	11	1	1	30	33
		41 (4/1-9/30/09)		102 (10/1/09-3/31/10)				
NUMBER OF STATEMENTS	12	42	57	27	4	1	118	144
	%	%	%	%	%	%	%	%
ASSETS								
Cash & Equivalents	6.3	10.6	9.6	5.9			6.3	9.4
Trade Receivables (net)	23.3	26.2	22.5	27.0			27.0	25.1
Inventory	37.7	26.5	31.1	25.0			27.4	28.6
All Other Current	.1	1.3	4.6	4.7			3.0	3.1
Total Current	67.3	64.5	67.9	62.7			63.7	66.1
Fixed Assets (net)	27.3	24.1	24.5	22.0			25.5	23.5
Intangibles (net)	3.7	3.5	3.1	3.3			2.9	3.5
All Other Non-Current	1.6	7.9	4.5	12.0			7.9	6.9
Total	100.0	100.0	100.0	100.0			100.0	100.0
LIABILITIES								
Notes Payable-Short Term	15.2	13.8	11.8	11.9			19.0	21.3
Cur. Mat.-L.T.D.	5.0	3.5	3.4	2.3			2.7	3.9
Trade Payables	24.3	19.3	13.1	15.7			16.8	18.3
Income Taxes Payable	.0	.6	.2	.5			.3	.4
All Other Current	8.9	3.4	6.5	6.4			6.9	9.4
Total Current	53.4	40.6	35.0	36.8			45.7	53.4
Long-Term Debt	38.9	18.3	13.8	16.8			16.9	15.1
Deferred Taxes	.0	.0	.3	.0			.4	.5
All Other Non-Current	25.4	10.1	7.9	6.2			10.1	7.9
Net Worth	-17.6	30.9	43.0	40.2			26.9	23.1
Total Liabilities & Net Worth	100.0	100.0	100.0	100.0			100.0	100.0
INCOME DATA								
Net Sales	100.0	100.0	100.0	100.0			100.0	100.0
Gross Profit	52.1	37.1	35.6	28.6			36.2	34.4
Operating Expenses	55.3	35.0	33.5	28.7			34.6	32.6
Operating Profit	-3.2	2.1	2.1	-.1			1.6	1.8
All Other Expenses (net)	1.4	1.7	.7	1.5			1.1	.7
Profit Before Taxes	-4.6	.4	1.5	-1.6			.5	1.0
RATIOS								
Current	4.7	3.4	3.5	3.0			2.4	2.1
	1.1	1.9	2.0	2.1			1.4	1.4
	.8	1.1	1.4	1.0			1.0	.9
Quick	1.3	2.0	1.8	1.4			1.2	1.1
	.7	.9	1.0	.8			(117) .7	(143) .7
	.1	.4	.4	.4			.4	.3
Sales/Receivables	0 736.8	11 33.9	18 20.0	25 14.5			18 20.7	12 29.4
	11 33.1	27 13.5	31 11.6	32 11.5			33 10.9	29 12.8
	27 13.4	37 9.9	39 9.3	62 5.9			51 7.2	42 8.8
Cost of Sales/Inventory	34 10.7	2 229.1	15 24.6	12 29.6			15 24.6	14 25.4
	55 6.6	31 11.8	58 6.3	48 7.7			49 7.4	44 8.2
	130 2.8	113 3.2	209 1.7	128 2.9			124 2.9	118 3.1
Cost of Sales/Payables	0 UND	3 115.3	10 36.4	15 25.1			15 24.0	10 37.1
	27 13.8	18 19.8	22 16.8	29 12.6			29 12.4	29 12.7
	55 6.7	47 7.8	45 8.2	43 8.6			54 6.8	53 6.9
Sales/Working Capital	7.9	6.8	3.7	4.6			5.6	6.4
	74.2	12.2	8.2	6.9			15.2	17.0
	-14.8	38.2	21.0	85.4			NM	-62.7
EBIT/Interest	4.9	6.4	19.5	4.6			3.8	7.9
	(10) 1.1	(40) 1.8	(49) 3.0	1.6			(106) 1.5	(135) 2.2
	-3.2	.0	.5	1.0			-.2	.3
Net Profit + Depr., Dep., Amort./Cur. Mat. L/T/D			6.3	3.9			7.4	5.7
		(16) 2.7	(11) 2.2			(26) 2.7	(30) 3.8
			1.6	.9			.0	1.5
Fixed/Worth	.5	.1	.1	.3			.2	.2
	NM	.9	.4	.6			.8	.9
	-.3	3.9	1.2	.9			6.3	3.6
Debt/Worth	1.8	.7	.5	.7			1.1	1.0
	NM	3.1	1.1	1.7			2.7	2.6
	-3.1	16.0	4.0	4.1			14.9	13.6
% Profit Before Taxes/Tangible Net Worth		42.8	26.3	11.3			19.9	41.1
	(35) 8.7	(49) 11.6	(22) 2.6			(92) 7.6	(112) 15.0
		-10.0	1.7	-.1			.1	3.9
% Profit Before Taxes/Total Assets	14.6	13.4	13.2	3.4			5.7	13.1
	.7	2.4	3.5	1.6			1.8	3.6
	-19.8	-3.6	-.5	.2			-3.5	-2.6
Sales/Net Fixed Assets	62.1	102.8	46.2	53.0			34.3	47.1
	24.8	22.9	12.7	12.6			16.6	19.8
	6.0	6.5	4.4	3.8			5.0	7.8
Sales/Total Assets	6.0	4.5	4.3	3.1			3.7	4.2
	3.7	2.8	2.4	2.4			2.6	3.0
	2.6	1.9	1.6	1.2			1.9	2.0
% Depr., Dep., Amort./Sales	.3	.6	.7	.7			.7	.6
	(10) 1.4	(33) 1.3	(53) 1.6	(25) 1.2			(102) 1.3	(134) 1.2
	3.9	4.0	3.2	3.3			2.8	2.1
% Officers', Directors' Owners' Comp/Sales		2.2	1.5				2.1	1.8
	(22) 3.8	(21) 2.4			(57) 4.4	(68) 2.9
		6.9	4.9				6.8	6.3
Net Sales ($)	15576M	157559M	717396M	1348396M	231739M	393400M	2674683M	2553893M
Total Assets ($)	3411M	46132M	256890M	628548M	258951M	180789M	1259142M	1044025M

M = $ thousand   MM = $ million
See Pages 9 through 22 for Explanation of Ratios and Data

Comparative Historical Data / Current Data Sorted by Sales

Type of Statement	4/1/07-3/31/08 ALL	4/1/08-3/31/09 ALL	4/1/09-3/31/10 ALL		0-1MM	1-3MM	3-5MM	5-10MM	10-25MM	25MM & OVER
Unqualified	13	9	14					1	3	10
Reviewed	34	34	26		1	1	5	8	7	4
Compiled	31	28	27		4	8	2	3	10	
Tax Returns	16	23	29		5	6	7	8	2	1
Other	40	50	47		2	9	5	9	8	14
					41 (4/1-9/30/09)		102 (10/1/09-3/31/10)			
NUMBER OF STATEMENTS	134	144	143		12	24	19	29	30	29
	%	%	%		%	%	%	%	%	%
ASSETS										
Cash & Equivalents	7.9	6.0	8.7		5.6	3.5	10.2	10.2	14.3	5.8
Trade Receivables (net)	25.1	26.4	24.1		15.1	14.8	17.7	26.3	26.1	35.3
Inventory	28.2	27.5	29.2		33.9	41.3	34.3	29.5	25.3	17.7
All Other Current	4.0	4.5	3.1		.9	1.2	1.9	2.4	5.5	4.9
Total Current	65.1	64.4	65.1		55.6	60.8	64.1	68.4	71.1	63.7
Fixed Assets (net)	21.9	24.8	24.5		38.8	27.8	24.7	23.3	20.6	21.1
Intangibles (net)	4.7	3.4	3.7		5.0	2.9	4.9	3.0	2.2	5.1
All Other Non-Current	8.2	7.5	6.7		.6	8.5	6.4	5.3	6.1	10.1
Total	100.0	100.0	100.0		100.0	100.0	100.0	100.0	100.0	100.0
LIABILITIES										
Notes Payable-Short Term	14.4	15.7	12.6		4.4	20.7	9.1	17.1	8.1	11.8
Cur. Mat.-L.T.D.	3.6	3.7	3.7		11.1	4.1	1.7	3.3	1.9	4.1
Trade Payables	17.0	16.4	16.2		13.3	10.5	19.8	15.0	19.8	17.2
Income Taxes Payable	.6	.3	.3		.0	.2	1.0	.2	.1	.5
All Other Current	7.4	7.4	5.8		5.9	4.3	3.3	3.8	8.9	7.5
Total Current	43.0	43.4	38.7		34.7	39.8	34.9	39.3	38.8	41.0
Long-Term Debt	12.3	14.8	18.1		51.9	18.8	22.7	12.9	9.6	14.7
Deferred Taxes	.4	.2	.1		.0	.0	.1	.1	.4	.1
All Other Non-Current	7.6	8.4	9.5		13.3	13.4	5.0	11.6	4.5	10.5
Net Worth	36.6	33.3	33.6		.1	27.9	37.3	36.1	46.6	33.7
Total Liabilities & Net Worth	100.0	100.0	100.0		100.0	100.0	100.0	100.0	100.0	100.0
INCOME DATA										
Net Sales	100.0	100.0	100.0		100.0	100.0	100.0	100.0	100.0	100.0
Gross Profit	33.6	36.8	36.2		49.3	44.5	41.1	34.5	29.7	29.3
Operating Expenses	30.4	35.1	34.8		51.8	42.0	40.0	33.6	27.8	26.7
Operating Profit	3.2	1.8	1.5		-2.5	2.5	1.1	.8	1.9	2.7
All Other Expenses (net)	1.0	.9	1.4		3.7	1.8	1.6	.8	.7	1.0
Profit Before Taxes	2.2	.9	.1		-6.2	.7	-.5	.0	1.1	1.7
RATIOS										
Current	3.1 / 1.6 / 1.1	2.9 / 1.5 / 1.0	3.4 / 1.9 / 1.1		7.0 / 1.3 / .9	3.4 / 1.9 / 1.1	4.0 / 1.9 / 1.4	3.5 / 2.0 / 1.4	4.3 / 2.0 / 1.1	2.5 / 1.7 / 1.1
Quick	1.3 / .8 / .4	1.4 / .8 / .4	1.5 / .9 / .4		3.2 / .6 / .3	1.0 / .3 / .1	2.2 / .9 / .3	2.1 / .8 / .6	1.8 / 1.1 / .5	1.6 / 1.0 / .6
Sales/Receivables	13 27.2 / 27 13.5 / 43 8.4	17 21.6 / 29 12.8 / 44 8.3	12 30.4 / 29 12.4 / 40 9.0		0 UND / 12 31.3 / 27 13.4	0 736.8 / 26 13.8 / 38 9.7	12 30.7 / 25 14.6 / 35 10.3	19 18.9 / 31 11.9 / 47 7.7	17 21.6 / 31 11.8 / 37 9.9	26 14.1 / 34 10.8 / 61 5.9
Cost of Sales/Inventory	15 25.0 / 47 7.8 / 108 3.4	13 29.0 / 43 8.5 / 127 2.9	12 31.4 / 48 7.6 / 156 2.3		34 10.6 / 65 5.6 / 222 1.6	24 15.0 / 125 2.9 / 261 1.4	16 23.3 / 79 4.6 / 313 1.2	8 44.8 / 70 5.2 / 209 1.7	2 217.8 / 34 10.6 / 113 3.2	4 90.4 / 32 11.4 / 72 5.1
Cost of Sales/Payables	12 29.2 / 26 14.2 / 46 8.0	11 33.8 / 24 15.3 / 41 8.9	10 38.1 / 23 15.6 / 45 8.1		0 UND / 20 18.2 / 40 9.0	0 UND / 11 32.4 / 45 8.1	10 38.1 / 44 8.3 / 63 5.8	10 37.8 / 18 19.9 / 43 8.6	14 25.8 / 26 14.1 / 45 8.2	18 20.5 / 29 12.4 / 41 9.0
Sales/Working Capital	4.6 / 13.1 / 75.2	5.0 / 15.8 / 146.9	5.0 / 10.2 / 32.8		5.2 / 12.5 / NM	3.8 / 11.6 / 82.4	5.5 / 8.5 / 21.4	3.5 / 5.5 / 21.0	6.4 / 10.7 / 38.4	6.2 / 10.6 / 57.1
EBIT/Interest	7.5 / (124) 2.0 / 1.0	6.0 / (132) 1.7 / -.4	7.1 / (131) 1.8 / .2		4.8 / (11) .2 / -1.3	3.5 / (22) 1.5 / -2.8	3.7 / (18) 1.0 / -2.4	19.1 / (27) 1.6 / .7	35.0 / (26) 9.1 / 1.0	6.1 / (27) 2.1 / 1.4
Net Profit + Depr., Dep., Amort./Cur. Mat. L/T/D	5.1 / (33) 2.9 / 1.0	4.1 / (38) 1.9 / .7	4.2 / (35) 1.7 / .9							6.7 / (12) 3.0 / 1.0
Fixed/Worth	.2 / .6 / 1.9	.2 / .6 / 3.0	.2 / .6 / 3.3		.4 / 7.7 / -1.9	.5 / 1.0 / 22.3	.1 / .4 / 2.6	.1 / .4 / 4.7	.1 / .4 / .9	.2 / .6 / 3.8
Debt/Worth	.8 / 1.8 / 6.9	.8 / 1.9 / 9.2	.7 / 1.6 / 7.5		1.1 / 9.5 / -4.7	.7 / 4.4 / 151.3	.3 / 1.7 / 4.2	.4 / 1.1 / NM	.6 / 1.3 / 3.8	.7 / 1.7 / 6.3
% Profit Before Taxes/Tangible Net Worth	32.1 / (115) 11.1 / 1.6	25.9 / (117) 7.8 / -1.6	27.4 / (116) 8.8 / -.9			27.4 / (19) 8.8 / -11.7	24.6 / (16) 1.8 / -5.1	24.0 / (22) 11.1 / -2.5	45.0 / (28) 17.4 / 2.3	27.2 / (23) 8.9 / 1.7
% Profit Before Taxes/Total Assets	10.6 / 3.7 / -.2	7.9 / 2.0 / -3.5	10.1 / 2.6 / -2.4		12.1 / -4.9 / -19.8	7.4 / 2.1 / -6.0	9.0 / .2 / -3.3	15.9 / 3.0 / -.9	17.1 / 5.1 / .8	8.3 / 2.7 / .8
Sales/Net Fixed Assets	48.8 / 22.5 / 6.1	50.3 / 17.5 / 7.0	56.4 / 15.6 / 5.2		27.5 / 8.2 / 1.2	24.2 / 8.0 / 4.7	61.9 / 26.5 / 3.1	80.1 / 11.4 / 6.2	68.9 / 24.7 / 7.0	68.2 / 17.7 / 7.5
Sales/Total Assets	3.9 / 2.7 / 1.7	4.1 / 2.8 / 1.9	4.2 / 2.5 / 1.7		3.5 / 1.8 / .9	2.6 / 2.1 / 1.4	3.2 / 2.9 / 1.7	4.4 / 2.2 / 1.6	4.9 / 3.2 / 1.8	4.3 / 2.8 / 2.2
% Depr., Dep., Amort./Sales	.5 / (123) 1.1 / 2.2	.6 / (127) 1.2 / 2.6	.7 / (126) 1.4 / 3.5		.4 / (11) 2.4 / 11.0	1.1 / (19) 2.6 / 5.6	.6 / (18) 1.3 / 4.0	.4 / (24) 1.3 / 3.0	.7 / (27) 1.2 / 3.5	.7 / (27) 1.2 / 2.5
% Officers', Directors' Owners' Comp/Sales	2.1 / (51) 3.5 / 5.6	2.2 / (55) 3.2 / 6.9	1.8 / (59) 2.9 / 6.4			3.8 / (12) 6.1 / 8.6	1.9 / (11) 3.8 / 5.2	2.0 / (13) 2.3 / 2.6		
Net Sales ($)	2508432M	2974366M	2864066M		8340M	46519M	73880M	206633M	487284M	2041410M
Total Assets ($)	1091134M	1236129M	1374721M		8013M	33804M	39405M	132462M	259364M	901673M

© RMA 2010

M = $ thousand   MM = $ million
See Pages 9 through 22 for Explanation of Ratios and Data

Current Data Sorted by Assets   Comparative Historical Data

0-500M	500M-2MM	2-10MM	10-50MM	50-100MM	100-250MM	Type of Statement	4/1/05-3/31/06 ALL	4/1/06-3/31/07 ALL
		6	10	7	4	Unqualified	34	25
	2	29	13		1	Reviewed	38	42
1	5	13	3			Compiled	16	19
3	6	10	1			Tax Returns	13	14
1	4	11	15	3	3	Other	25	29
	35 (4/1-9/30/09)		116 (10/1/09-3/31/10)					
5	17	69	42	10	8	NUMBER OF STATEMENTS	126	129
%	%	%	%	%	%	**ASSETS**	%	%
	6.8	10.6	6.7	7.4		Cash & Equivalents	9.2	8.7
	24.4	33.1	35.2	40.8		Trade Receivables (net)	31.8	34.2
	55.5	39.5	31.7	26.1		Inventory	34.1	35.8
	.8	2.3	3.7	2.0		All Other Current	4.0	2.5
	87.5	85.4	77.4	76.4		Total Current	79.1	81.3
	7.0	7.4	15.7	11.5		Fixed Assets (net)	10.8	10.5
	2.1	.9	2.1	1.7		Intangibles (net)	2.2	1.3
	3.3	6.3	4.9	10.4		All Other Non-Current	7.8	6.9
	100.0	100.0	100.0	100.0		Total	100.0	100.0
						LIABILITIES		
	15.0	17.2	25.1	24.5		Notes Payable-Short Term	20.2	25.0
	.9	1.9	2.8	1.0		Cur. Mat.-L.T.D.	3.3	2.0
	24.9	18.8	18.3	20.6		Trade Payables	17.8	19.2
	.1	.1	.6	1.0		Income Taxes Payable	.3	.1
	7.4	8.2	6.2	6.5		All Other Current	6.8	6.9
	48.3	46.2	52.9	53.6		Total Current	48.3	53.1
	12.8	5.4	7.2	6.5		Long-Term Debt	12.3	9.1
	.0	.2	.0	.2		Deferred Taxes	.2	.2
	10.6	2.4	6.2	5.2		All Other Non-Current	3.4	4.1
	28.4	45.7	33.7	34.6		Net Worth	35.9	33.5
	100.0	100.0	100.0	100.0		Total Liabilties & Net Worth	100.0	100.0
						INCOME DATA		
	100.0	100.0	100.0	100.0		Net Sales	100.0	100.0
	13.0	9.2	9.2	11.2		Gross Profit	8.9	9.6
	10.2	7.7	7.9	6.8		Operating Expenses	7.5	8.2
	2.8	1.5	1.2	4.4		Operating Profit	1.5	1.4
	-.4	.0	.1	.6		All Other Expenses (net)	.4	.1
	3.2	1.6	1.1	3.7		Profit Before Taxes	1.1	1.3
						RATIOS		
	3.1	3.0	2.1	3.2		Current	2.5	2.5
	1.7	1.8	1.4	1.2			1.5	1.4
	1.4	1.3	1.1	1.1			1.2	1.1
	1.3	1.8	1.0	1.7		Quick	1.3	1.4
	.7	.9	.8	.9			(125) .8	.8
	.3	.6	.6	.7			.6	.5
5 75.6	8 43.8	10 35.6	14 25.7			Sales/Receivables	10 38.3	11 34.7
10 37.3	13 27.4	17 22.1	20 18.0				15 23.8	16 23.5
14 25.6	21 17.8	21 17.5	30 12.3				22 16.7	22 16.6
13 27.3	10 34.9	10 35.9	8 48.4			Cost of Sales/Inventory	10 35.4	11 33.9
27 13.7	18 20.0	14 25.5	13 28.1				16 23.4	17 21.3
51 7.1	30 12.3	21 17.6	22 16.4				26 14.1	33 11.2
5 70.8	2 181.7	3 133.4	7 51.2			Cost of Sales/Payables	4 100.0	4 98.4
9 41.8	7 50.1	7 55.6	10 37.6				7 48.8	7 51.0
16 23.2	14 26.1	14 25.5	15 24.5				13 27.4	16 23.3
	13.5	13.9	19.6	10.9		Sales/Working Capital	15.6	14.2
	27.0	24.7	37.3	67.4			32.6	33.2
	54.9	48.6	103.6	134.1			57.3	78.7
	13.3	38.4	16.3	16.6		EBIT/Interest	9.9	9.7
(15) 4.8	(61) 6.6	(40) 4.5	6.1				(114) 2.8	(120) 2.2
	1.7	2.7	2.4	2.9			1.3	1.1
		6.5	38.1			Net Profit + Depr., Dep., Amort./Cur. Mat. L/T/D	8.3	5.8
	(17) 3.5	(12) 14.5					(43) 3.3	(38) 2.7
	2.4	6.3					1.5	1.0
	.0	.0	.1	.2		Fixed/Worth	.1	.1
	.3	.1	.3	.4			.2	.3
	1.6	.3	1.1	.7			.7	.8
	1.4	.5	.8	1.1		Debt/Worth	.8	.8
	3.1	1.2	2.8	3.2			1.8	2.2
	12.1	3.2	6.7	3.7			4.5	6.9
	193.7	33.1	41.7	52.2		% Profit Before Taxes/Tangible Net Worth	25.4	30.4
(15) 29.1	(68) 17.4	(40) 25.4	24.1				(119) 11.1	(119) 12.0
	7.6	7.2	11.7	12.7			5.2	4.1
	15.8	13.0	12.4	12.5		% Profit Before Taxes/Total Assets	6.8	9.8
	7.2	7.5	6.4	6.9			4.2	4.3
	3.1	3.1	4.0	2.6			1.2	.4
	959.4	638.0	215.7	152.4		Sales/Net Fixed Assets	356.3	332.2
	327.5	199.0	72.6	104.5			113.7	105.4
	83.5	75.5	29.5	21.0			40.8	47.7
	14.2	11.8	11.4	10.6		Sales/Total Assets	11.1	10.2
	8.4	8.4	8.7	10.1			8.3	7.7
	4.8	6.1	5.7	4.2			5.0	4.9
	.1	.1	.1			% Depr., Dep., Amort./Sales	.1	.1
(13)	.2	(54) .2	(39) .2				(108) .2	(106) .2
	.5	.3	.4				.4	.4
	.4	.3	.1			% Officers', Directors' Owners' Comp/Sales	.3	.3
(11)	.9	(41) .6	(12) .3				(47) .6	(48) .7
	3.9	1.3	1.0				1.3	1.9
16611M	228173M	3045900M	7036820M	5074830M	4408842M	Net Sales ($)	16891458M	13221136M
1400M	22406M	340853M	875090M	709328M	1024345M	Total Assets ($)	2523983M	2046171M

M = $ thousand   MM = $ million
See Pages 9 through 22 for Explanation of Ratios and Data

Comparative Historical Data

Current Data Sorted by Sales

4/1/07-3/31/08 ALL	4/1/08-3/31/09 ALL	4/1/09-3/31/10 ALL	Type of Statement	0-1MM	1-3MM	3-5MM	5-10MM	10-25MM	25MM & OVER
27	25	27	Unqualified				1	1	25
36	35	45	Reviewed					7	38
9	14	22	Compiled		1			9	11
10	17	20	Tax Returns		1	1	4	2	11
26	29	37	Other		2	1	2	4	29
					35 (4/1-9/30/09)			116 (10/1/09-3/31/10)	
108	120	151	**NUMBER OF STATEMENTS**		5	2	7	23	114

(In the Assets/Liabilities/Income % breakdowns below the center columns are marked vertically "DATA NOT AVAILABLE"; only the 10-25MM and 25MM & OVER columns are reported.)

%	%	%	ASSETS					%	%
8.2	8.4	9.0	Cash & Equivalents					7.2	8.7
31.5	31.1	32.0	Trade Receivables (net)					29.6	34.2
36.9	37.3	37.7	Inventory					45.8	34.7
2.9	2.8	2.7	All Other Current					.5	3.4
79.4	79.5	81.5	Total Current					83.2	81.0
11.1	12.8	10.3	Fixed Assets (net)					9.4	10.9
1.6	1.4	1.6	Intangibles (net)					.9	1.5
7.9	6.3	6.6	All Other Non-Current					6.5	6.6
100.0	100.0	100.0	Total					100.0	100.0

			LIABILITIES						
23.5	20.2	18.4	Notes Payable-Short Term					14.6	20.2
1.8	2.5	2.0	Cur. Mat.-L.T.D.					1.5	2.1
17.5	20.2	19.2	Trade Payables					24.2	18.0
.2	.1	.4	Income Taxes Payable					.0	.5
6.6	7.3	8.4	All Other Current					5.5	8.8
49.5	50.5	48.4	Total Current					45.9	49.6
9.6	11.1	7.2	Long-Term Debt					11.9	6.1
.2	.1	.1	Deferred Taxes					.0	.2
3.5	3.5	4.6	All Other Non-Current					11.3	3.2
37.2	34.9	39.7	Net Worth					31.0	40.9
100.0	100.0	100.0	Total Liabilities & Net Worth					100.0	100.0

			INCOME DATA						
100.0	100.0	100.0	Net Sales					100.0	100.0
9.6	11.1	10.3	Gross Profit					12.9	9.0
7.9	10.2	8.2	Operating Expenses					9.9	7.3
1.7	.9	2.1	Operating Profit					3.0	1.7
-.1	.4	.0	All Other Expenses (net)					.0	.0
1.8	.5	2.1	Profit Before Taxes					3.0	1.7

			RATIOS						
2.5	2.7	2.6						3.1	2.3
1.5	1.6	1.7	Current					1.8	1.6
1.1	1.2	1.2						1.4	1.2
1.3	1.4	1.5						1.6	1.3
.7	.8	.8	Quick					.6	.8
.5	.5	.5						.4	.6
9 42.2	9 40.8	8 44.3						12 30.3	8 44.3
15 24.6	15 25.0	14 25.7	Sales/Receivables					17 21.6	14 26.1
21 17.4	22 16.5	19 19.0						31 11.9	19 19.5
11 33.1	11 34.3	11 32.6						16 23.1	10 38.3
18 20.3	16 23.5	17 21.3	Cost of Sales/Inventory					27 13.7	14 25.7
27 13.3	30 12.0	29 12.7						45 8.1	22 16.6
4 102.9	4 84.4	3 126.1						6 57.3	2 172.7
8 45.1	9 42.3	8 47.2	Cost of Sales/Payables					13 27.3	7 54.0
15 23.7	16 22.7	14 26.2						24 15.0	12 30.3
14.4	14.6	14.6						10.1	17.2
32.3	32.2	28.5	Sales/Working Capital					16.4	33.6
92.9	99.1	64.2						45.6	68.2
6.5	7.0	17.9						50.7	16.9
(102) 2.5	(110) 2.6	(136) 5.9	EBIT/Interest					(20) 10.2	(105) 5.8
1.5	1.4	2.6						1.3	2.8
5.8	6.0	15.8	Net Profit + Depr., Dep.,						15.8
(35) 2.9	(28) 2.0	(35) 6.7	Amort./Cur. Mat. L/T/D						(32) 7.5
1.4	.3	2.9							2.9
.1	.1	.1						.0	.1
.2	.3	.2	Fixed/Worth					.1	.2
.8	.8	.6						.7	.6
.8	.8	.7						.7	.7
2.4	2.2	1.8	Debt/Worth					3.1	1.8
4.9	4.8	4.3						13.4	4.1
26.2	25.8	44.5	% Profit Before Taxes/Tangible					82.1	36.9
(102) 12.4	(111) 14.2	(145) 20.2	Net Worth					(21) 31.0	(111) 18.8
4.3	3.8	9.3						4.7	9.4
7.7	9.1	14.3	% Profit Before Taxes/Total					33.1	12.1
3.9	3.4	7.2	Assets					10.3	6.4
1.6	1.1	3.3						1.3	3.8
229.6	243.1	386.3						999.8	324.2
120.7	95.5	130.4	Sales/Net Fixed Assets					142.6	129.4
47.3	41.5	55.2						104.2	52.3
9.5	10.3	11.5						8.4	11.9
7.9	8.3	8.4	Sales/Total Assets					6.4	9.5
5.4	5.4	5.7						4.3	6.4
.1	.1	.1						.0	.1
(100) .2	(105) .2	(125) .2	% Depr., Dep., Amort./Sales					(18) .1	(99) .2
.4	.4	.4						.5	.4
.3	.4	.3						.5	.2
(37) .6	(51) .8	(68) .6	% Officers', Directors' Owners' Comp/Sales					(11) .9	(49) .5
1.8	1.4	1.3						1.4	1.0
19840027M	14055654M	19811176M	Net Sales ($)		10742M	7056M	47257M	385491M	19360630M
2550502M	1868636M	2973422M	Total Assets ($)		3400M	836M	91421M	101856M	2775909M

M = $ thousand   MM = $ million
See Pages 9 through 22 for Explanation of Ratios and Data

Current Data Sorted by Assets   Comparative Historical Data

0-500M	500M-2MM	2-10MM	10-50MM	50-100MM	100-250MM	Type of Statement	4/1/05-3/31/06 ALL	4/1/06-3/31/07 ALL
	1	1		3		Unqualified	2	11
	1	8	2			Reviewed	12	17
3	4	5	1			Compiled	8	8
	5	1				Tax Returns	12	14
2	5	7	7		1	Other	17	13
	7 (4/1-9/30/09)		50 (10/1/09-3/31/10)					
5	16	22	10	3	1	NUMBER OF STATEMENTS	51	63
%	%	%	%	%	%	**ASSETS**	%	%
	5.8	6.4	8.0			Cash & Equivalents	5.5	6.4
	37.2	33.0	22.7			Trade Receivables (net)	32.2	31.8
	37.2	39.0	44.9			Inventory	38.5	36.8
	2.0	5.1	3.8			All Other Current	2.0	2.5
	82.1	83.5	79.4			Total Current	78.3	77.5
	9.1	10.4	9.6			Fixed Assets (net)	11.3	13.6
	2.2	2.2	5.9			Intangibles (net)	4.8	3.6
	6.6	3.8	5.1			All Other Non-Current	5.7	5.3
	100.0	100.0	100.0			Total	100.0	100.0
						LIABILITIES		
	15.1	12.2	10.5			Notes Payable-Short Term	12.8	13.4
	3.2	1.5	1.8			Cur. Mat.-L.T.D.	3.2	1.9
	33.2	26.6	23.6			Trade Payables	25.0	25.5
	.0	.1	.2			Income Taxes Payable	.3	.3
	1.7	5.0	8.2			All Other Current	10.2	7.8
	53.3	45.3	44.2			Total Current	51.5	48.9
	8.2	13.3	22.6			Long-Term Debt	8.8	10.5
	.0	.3	.5			Deferred Taxes	.2	.2
	7.6	3.5	4.9			All Other Non-Current	5.1	3.5
	30.9	37.6	27.8			Net Worth	34.5	36.9
	100.0	100.0	100.0			Total Liabilities & Net Worth	100.0	100.0
						INCOME DATA		
	100.0	100.0	100.0			Net Sales	100.0	100.0
	34.4	29.7	34.3			Gross Profit	31.2	30.6
	31.6	28.9	29.3			Operating Expenses	28.1	26.8
	2.9	.8	5.0			Operating Profit	3.1	3.7
	.3	-.7	.2			All Other Expenses (net)	.2	-.2
	2.6	1.5	4.8			Profit Before Taxes	2.9	3.9
						RATIOS		
	2.4	2.8	3.4			Current	2.4	2.5
	1.5	1.8	1.8			Current	1.6	1.6
	1.2	1.4	1.3			Current	1.2	1.2
	1.4	1.7	1.7			Quick	1.2	1.3
	.6	.9	.6			Quick	.7	.8
	.5	.5	.4			Quick	.5	.5
	34 10.8	24 15.5	30 12.2			Sales/Receivables	27 13.6	31 11.7
	46 8.0	37 9.8	38 9.6			Sales/Receivables	37 9.8	39 9.3
	58 6.3	44 8.3	62 5.9			Sales/Receivables	46 8.0	49 7.5
	57 6.4	39 9.4	74 4.9			Cost of Sales/Inventory	44 8.2	44 8.2
	70 5.2	72 5.1	108 3.4			Cost of Sales/Inventory	70 5.2	73 5.0
	109 3.3	118 3.1	206 1.8			Cost of Sales/Inventory	91 4.0	101 3.6
	42 8.7	20 18.3	22 16.6			Cost of Sales/Payables	22 16.4	25 14.9
	68 5.3	41 9.0	49 7.5			Cost of Sales/Payables	38 9.6	44 8.4
	109 3.4	68 5.4	90 4.1			Cost of Sales/Payables	60 6.1	64 5.7
	6.2	5.1	3.5			Sales/Working Capital	7.4	6.4
	9.4	8.0	6.9			Sales/Working Capital	9.9	9.9
	19.3	15.2	11.0			Sales/Working Capital	20.2	17.5
	11.1	8.1				EBIT/Interest	14.7	10.3
	6.0	(18) 1.6				EBIT/Interest	(48) 5.3	(58) 5.7
	1.4	-.9				EBIT/Interest	2.2	1.9
						Net Profit + Depr., Dep.,	13.3	15.2
						Amort./Cur. Mat. L/T/D	(14) 7.4	(17) 5.9
							1.7	2.0
	.2	.0	.1			Fixed/Worth	.1	.1
	.3	.2	.4			Fixed/Worth	.2	.3
	.6	.7	2.1			Fixed/Worth	.6	.9
	1.6	.7	1.2			Debt/Worth	.7	.7
	3.1	2.1	7.5			Debt/Worth	1.8	1.8
	5.3	4.5	15.8			Debt/Worth	7.8	6.3
	47.4	19.3				% Profit Before Taxes/Tangible	37.7	38.7
	(15) 17.8	(21) 3.7				Net Worth	(43) 21.0	(55) 22.8
	7.4	-8.0					11.1	11.8
	11.9	10.2	10.7			% Profit Before Taxes/Total	13.1	14.5
	5.1	1.0	7.0			Assets	8.1	8.8
	.7	-3.1	1.1				3.4	3.6
	50.4	196.2	110.6			Sales/Net Fixed Assets	125.1	88.8
	29.0	35.3	30.4			Sales/Net Fixed Assets	48.2	36.6
	13.2	17.3	18.9			Sales/Net Fixed Assets	27.2	16.1
	3.5	4.3	2.3			Sales/Total Assets	4.0	3.6
	2.4	3.2	1.9			Sales/Total Assets	3.0	2.9
	2.0	2.0	1.5			Sales/Total Assets	2.5	2.2
	.6	.3				% Depr., Dep., Amort./Sales	.3	.4
	(11) 1.0	(19) .5				% Depr., Dep., Amort./Sales	(42) .6	(51) .7
	1.9	1.1				% Depr., Dep., Amort./Sales	1.0	1.3
						% Officers', Directors'	2.0	1.8
						Owners' Comp/Sales	(21) 4.2	(29) 3.0
							7.0	3.9
4690M	49697M	309027M	524321M	359688M	167383M	Net Sales ($)	1730077M	1832196M
1929M	20536M	92737M	289498M	172027M	136481M	Total Assets ($)	663509M	666079M

Comparative Historical Data | Current Data Sorted by Sales

			Type of Statement	0-1MM	1-3MM	3-5MM	5-10MM	10-25MM	25MM & OVER
			Unqualified			1		1	3
			Reviewed				4	5	2
			Compiled	2	2	4		1	4
			Tax Returns		2	3		1	
			Other	4	1	4	4	1	8
9/9/5/14/17	7/10/9/12/19	5/11/13/6/22				7 (4/1-9/30/09)	50 (10/1/09-3/31/10)		
4/1/07- 3/31/08 ALL	4/1/08- 3/31/09 ALL	4/1/09- 3/31/10 ALL							
54	57	57	NUMBER OF STATEMENTS	6	6	12	8	9	17
%	%	%	ASSETS	%	%	%	%	%	%
5.8	4.5	6.1	Cash & Equivalents			5.5			7.0
30.9	30.6	31.4	Trade Receivables (net)			29.1			28.9
38.4	40.4	39.5	Inventory			42.2			40.2
4.1	3.6	3.9	All Other Current			2.5			5.6
79.2	79.1	80.9	Total Current			79.4			81.7
10.9	11.0	10.0	Fixed Assets (net)			12.4			7.5
3.1	4.2	4.5	Intangibles (net)			2.1			6.5
6.8	5.6	4.6	All Other Non-Current			6.1			4.3
100.0	100.0	100.0	Total			100.0			100.0
			LIABILITIES						
14.3	16.8	15.5	Notes Payable-Short Term			15.2			11.2
2.3	2.8	2.2	Cur. Mat.-L.T.D.			1.2			1.5
28.1	27.0	28.6	Trade Payables			31.6			28.4
.2	.1	.1	Income Taxes Payable			.0			.4
9.9	7.0	4.4	All Other Current			3.5			6.3
54.9	53.7	50.8	Total Current			51.5			47.8
11.6	11.6	14.8	Long-Term Debt			12.9			19.2
.3	.2	.3	Deferred Taxes			.0			.7
5.6	7.0	5.3	All Other Non-Current			5.2			3.5
27.6	27.5	28.8	Net Worth			30.4			28.8
100.0	100.0	100.0	Total Liabilties & Net Worth			100.0			100.0
			INCOME DATA						
100.0	100.0	100.0	Net Sales			100.0			100.0
30.2	31.4	31.8	Gross Profit			31.1			29.8
27.2	29.3	29.7	Operating Expenses			30.2			26.6
3.1	2.1	2.1	Operating Profit			.9			3.2
.3	.7	.0	All Other Expenses (net)			-1.2			.0
2.8	1.4	2.1	Profit Before Taxes			2.1			3.2
			RATIOS						
2.0	2.2	2.5	Current			2.1			2.7
1.4	1.4	1.6				1.5			2.0
1.1	1.2	1.2				1.3			1.3
.9	.9	1.4	Quick			1.0			1.4
.6	.6	.7				.6			.8
.4	.5	.5				.5			.4
28 13.0	32 11.4	32 11.6	Sales/Receivables			29 12.5			37 9.9
36 10.0	41 8.9	39 9.5				40 9.2			39 9.5
49 7.4	51 7.1	52 7.1				49 7.5			55 6.6
51 7.1	54 6.8	60 6.1	Cost of Sales/Inventory			60 6.1			62 5.9
66 5.5	85 4.3	80 4.6				87 4.2			89 4.1
111 3.3	114 3.2	127 2.9				156 2.3			147 2.5
26 14.1	27 13.5	28 13.0	Cost of Sales/Payables			42 8.7			24 14.9
39 9.5	44 8.2	57 6.4				63 5.8			53 6.8
76 4.8	76 4.8	78 4.7				103 3.6			69 5.3
6.9	6.6	5.8	Sales/Working Capital			6.5			3.6
12.3	11.2	8.5				8.8			7.0
29.9	24.8	19.3				14.3			12.1
9.6	6.6	10.9	EBIT/Interest			9.9			13.9
(52) 3.3	(53) 1.6	(49) 2.6				2.0		(13) 2.6	
1.5	-.3	.6				.9			.5
13.6	7.1		Net Profit + Depr., Dep., Amort./Cur. Mat. L/T/D						
(15) 3.9	(15) 2.3								
1.7	1.3								
.1	.2	.1	Fixed/Worth			.2			.1
.3	.4	.3				.4			.3
1.8	1.3	1.2				.8			2.5
1.2	1.5	1.4	Debt/Worth			1.7			1.2
3.0	3.4	3.4				3.1			4.4
11.5	13.6	10.2				5.3			17.5
38.3	44.0	49.8	% Profit Before Taxes/Tangible Net Worth			37.5			87.7
(44) 23.1	(47) 14.0	(49) 14.9				13.1		(14) 12.7	
11.0	.7	-.7				-13.2			-.2
12.2	11.4	10.2	% Profit Before Taxes/Total Assets			10.6			8.3
5.5	2.6	4.0				4.2			2.8
1.4	-3.3	-1.6				-.4			-1.5
117.9	65.2	78.8	Sales/Net Fixed Assets			36.5			133.4
41.8	31.5	29.9				25.0			30.9
17.9	19.3	16.1				13.2			19.8
3.4	3.5	3.6	Sales/Total Assets			3.4			2.9
2.9	2.5	2.3				2.2			2.2
2.3	2.0	1.9				2.0			1.6
.4	.5	.5	% Depr., Dep., Amort./Sales						.5
(48) .6	(52) 1.0	(44) .9						(11) 1.2	
1.0	1.4	1.7							1.4
1.7	1.7	2.4	% Officers', Directors' Owners' Comp/Sales						
(25) 3.4	(25) 3.0	(23) 3.3							
5.7	3.7	5.2							
2141153M	1486125M	1414806M	Net Sales ($)	4106M	9557M	45309M	61720M	143608M	1150506M
847571M	609115M	713208M	Total Assets ($)	3810M	4971M	19890M	24572M	43895M	616070M

M = $ thousand   MM = $ million
See Pages 9 through 22 for Explanation of Ratios and Data

WHOLESALE—Other Miscellaneous Nondurable Goods Merchant Wholesalers NAICS 424990

Current Data Sorted by Assets | Comparative Historical Data

Type of Statement	0-500M	500M-2MM	2-10MM	10-50MM	50-100MM	100-250MM		4/1/05-3/31/06 ALL	4/1/06-3/31/07 ALL
Unqualified		3	16	19	9	8		61	81
Reviewed		25	95	33	3			105	117
Compiled	9	26	57	10				70	93
Tax Returns	42	97	58	2				84	138
Other	11	58	119	64	14	3		200	177
		140 (4/1-9/30/09)		641 (10/1/09-3/31/10)					
NUMBER OF STATEMENTS	62	209	345	128	26	11		520	606
ASSETS	%	%	%	%	%	%		%	%
Cash & Equivalents	14.5	10.8	10.0	6.4	16.0	8.8		8.9	9.1
Trade Receivables (net)	26.5	33.6	31.6	28.8	23.4	17.6		32.9	32.9
Inventory	28.2	30.0	33.6	35.7	26.8	14.2		33.3	32.7
All Other Current	3.0	2.9	2.9	4.1	5.1	3.8		2.8	2.7
Total Current	72.2	77.4	78.1	75.0	71.4	44.5		77.9	77.3
Fixed Assets (net)	14.6	13.1	11.1	14.0	12.7	21.5		13.1	13.4
Intangibles (net)	3.1	4.1	3.9	6.2	10.1	29.1		3.2	3.7
All Other Non-Current	10.1	5.5	6.9	4.8	5.9	4.9		5.9	5.7
Total	100.0	100.0	100.0	100.0	100.0	100.0		100.0	100.0
LIABILITIES									
Notes Payable-Short Term	21.7	14.3	15.4	16.7	9.4	7.3		17.6	17.4
Cur. Mat.-L.T.D.	3.6	3.5	2.3	2.4	1.4	4.3		2.4	2.8
Trade Payables	26.5	24.9	22.0	21.1	14.5	6.1		22.5	21.2
Income Taxes Payable	.0	.1	.4	.2	.1	.4		.2	.2
All Other Current	11.8	8.4	6.6	8.4	16.3	9.3		9.0	10.3
Total Current	63.5	51.2	46.8	48.9	41.7	27.4		51.7	52.0
Long-Term Debt	24.6	10.7	9.1	9.5	10.6	12.5		10.2	11.1
Deferred Taxes	.1	.1	.1	.4	.5	1.5		.1	.1
All Other Non-Current	15.2	6.4	5.6	6.9	4.1	7.7		7.6	6.3
Net Worth	-3.4	31.6	38.3	34.3	43.0	51.0		30.4	30.5
Total Liabilities & Net Worth	100.0	100.0	100.0	100.0	100.0	100.0		100.0	100.0
INCOME DATA									
Net Sales	100.0	100.0	100.0	100.0	100.0	100.0		100.0	100.0
Gross Profit	34.6	32.0	30.8	29.7	36.6	41.0		31.7	32.4
Operating Expenses	31.7	29.3	26.5	25.2	25.2	35.5		27.6	27.9
Operating Profit	2.9	2.8	4.3	4.6	11.4	5.5		4.0	4.5
All Other Expenses (net)	1.3	.6	.6	1.0	.6	2.6		.7	1.1
Profit Before Taxes	1.6	2.2	3.7	3.6	10.7	2.9		3.3	3.3
RATIOS									
Current	2.6 / 1.2 / .7	2.8 / 1.5 / 1.1	2.9 / 1.6 / 1.2	2.3 / 1.6 / 1.2	2.8 / 1.8 / 1.2	2.3 / 1.5 / .9		2.4 / 1.5 / 1.1	2.5 / 1.5 / 1.2
Quick	1.3 / .7 / .4	1.5 / .9 / .5	1.5 / .8 / .6	1.0 / .7 / .5	1.7 / .9 / .5	1.2 / .9 / .3		(519) 1.3 / .8 / .5	(605) 1.4 / .8 / .5
Sales/Receivables	3 129.1 / 20 18.1 / 38 9.6	20 17.9 / 36 10.2 / 54 6.7	25 14.6 / 37 9.8 / 54 6.7	27 13.6 / 41 8.9 / 58 6.3	16 22.9 / 42 8.7 / 47 7.7	15 24.1 / 42 8.6 / 65 5.6		24 15.2 / 38 9.6 / 55 6.6	24 15.1 / 38 9.7 / 54 6.8
Cost of Sales/Inventory	0 UND / 29 12.6 / 84 4.4	16 22.6 / 41 8.9 / 82 4.4	27 13.4 / 63 5.8 / 118 3.1	42 8.8 / 74 4.9 / 118 3.1	16 23.0 / 87 4.2 / 128 2.8	16 22.7 / 58 6.3 / 155 2.4		25 14.4 / 56 6.5 / 106 3.4	26 13.9 / 56 6.5 / 107 3.4
Cost of Sales/Payables	0 UND / 23 16.1 / 47 7.8	13 28.3 / 32 11.4 / 57 6.4	15 24.1 / 30 12.0 / 57 6.4	20 18.0 / 35 10.4 / 55 6.6	12 30.2 / 33 11.1 / 50 7.3	14 25.2 / 29 12.8 / 52 7.0		15 25.1 / 31 11.8 / 54 6.7	15 23.7 / 31 11.7 / 53 6.9
Sales/Working Capital	10.0 / 36.0 / -26.7	6.1 / 13.1 / 100.5	5.2 / 9.8 / 30.4	5.3 / 10.4 / 20.3	3.7 / 7.4 / 25.8	3.9 / 12.7 / -46.6		5.3 / 11.7 / 39.4	5.5 / 11.6 / 32.5
EBIT/Interest	13.1 / (47) 2.0 / -1.0	11.2 / (170) 3.5 / 1.0	18.3 / (307) 5.3 / 1.6	10.8 / (118) 4.4 / 1.7	33.4 / (24) 9.7 / 5.0	30.9 / 2.3 / .7		11.8 / (470) 3.9 / 1.5	10.7 / (539) 3.4 / 1.4
Net Profit + Depr., Dep., Amort./Cur. Mat. L/T/D		3.5 / (16) 1.3 / .2	6.9 / (59) 2.2 / .5	11.6 / (39) 2.6 / 2.1				10.7 / (95) 3.7 / 1.4	11.7 / (94) 3.0 / 1.0
Fixed/Worth	.0 / .6 / -.6	.0 / .2 / 1.5	.1 / .2 / .8	.1 / .4 / 1.2	.1 / .4 / 1.5	.3 / .4 / -.3		.1 / .2 / 1.2	.1 / .3 / 1.1
Debt/Worth	.8 / 3.2 / -6.3	.9 / 2.5 / 11.4	.6 / 2.1 / 5.6	1.0 / 2.2 / 4.7	.6 / 2.3 / 18.3	.6 / 2.0 / -4.5		.9 / 2.4 / 7.3	.9 / 2.3 / 7.1
% Profit Before Taxes/Tangible Net Worth	101.6 / (43) 39.2 / -6.5	41.1 / (171) 17.8 / 3.1	53.3 / (310) 20.3 / 5.2	41.9 / (113) 16.7 / 7.6	59.3 / (21) 35.2 / 19.0			54.2 / (445) 20.3 / 6.1	54.7 / (517) 23.0 / 7.2
% Profit Before Taxes/Total Assets	27.9 / 10.8 / -4.3	14.0 / 4.9 / .1	17.9 / 5.9 / 1.4	11.6 / 5.6 / 2.3	18.7 / 12.7 / 6.7	14.0 / 3.6 / -.8		14.4 / 6.1 / 1.5	16.1 / 7.1 / 1.6
Sales/Net Fixed Assets	854.3 / 82.8 / 20.3	262.1 / 60.0 / 19.4	212.4 / 54.9 / 19.8	103.7 / 39.1 / 11.1	73.7 / 22.6 / 10.3	71.7 / 13.7 / 6.7		128.9 / 47.8 / 15.8	151.7 / 48.1 / 16.9
Sales/Total Assets	6.0 / 4.4 / 2.9	4.6 / 3.3 / 2.3	4.1 / 2.6 / 1.8	3.3 / 2.3 / 1.8	3.8 / 1.9 / 1.4	1.9 / 1.3 / .7		4.1 / 2.9 / 1.9	4.0 / 2.8 / 2.0
% Depr., Dep., Amort./Sales	.2 / (32) .8 / 1.5	.2 / (134) .7 / 1.6	.2 / (260) .5 / 1.2	.3 / (114) .8 / 1.6	.5 / (21) 1.5 / 2.6			.3 / (400) .7 / 1.5	.3 / (477) .7 / 1.4
% Officers', Directors' Owners' Comp/Sales	2.9 / (28) 5.0 / 11.5	2.0 / (125) 3.6 / 6.7	1.1 / (161) 2.3 / 4.6	.6 / (33) 1.1 / 2.5				1.7 / (228) 3.3 / 5.8	1.6 / (285) 3.2 / 5.7
Net Sales ($)	101617M	1030460M	4851671M	8358966M	4962331M	2565983M		17535170M	19252812M
Total Assets ($)	18776M	261896M	1583652M	2791853M	1883848M	1741840M		6016377M	7017098M

M = $ thousand   MM = $ million
See Pages 9 through 22 for Explanation of Ratios and Data

Comparative Historical Data

Current Data Sorted by Sales

			Type of Statement						
80	55	55	Unqualified	1	4	2	4	10	39
116	138	156	Reviewed			15	35	63	38
107	103	102	Compiled	7	17	15	18	28	17
138	162	199	Tax Returns	23	49	50	37	31	9
224	233	269	Other	4	29	36	60	58	82
4/1/07-3/31/08 ALL	4/1/08-3/31/09 ALL	4/1/09-3/31/10 ALL		140 (4/1-9/30/09)			641 (10/1/09-3/31/10)		
				0-1MM	1-3MM	3-5MM	5-10MM	10-25MM	25MM & OVER
665	691	781	NUMBER OF STATEMENTS	35	99	118	154	190	185
%	%	%	ASSETS	%	%	%	%	%	%
9.7	9.1	10.2	Cash & Equivalents	10.0	11.3	10.6	9.4	10.3	9.9
30.9	29.8	30.8	Trade Receivables (net)	22.9	27.5	27.4	32.4	33.8	31.7
33.8	36.3	32.1	Inventory	33.6	31.9	31.3	31.1	33.4	31.7
2.8	3.2	3.2	All Other Current	1.1	3.4	2.7	3.2	2.6	4.4
77.1	78.3	76.2	Total Current	67.6	74.1	72.0	76.1	80.2	77.7
13.1	12.1	12.6	Fixed Assets (net)	16.1	15.2	14.5	11.8	11.2	11.3
4.0	4.2	4.8	Intangibles (net)	6.8	3.9	5.3	3.4	3.8	6.9
5.8	5.4	6.4	All Other Non-Current	9.5	6.8	8.2	8.7	4.8	4.1
100.0	100.0	100.0	Total	100.0	100.0	100.0	100.0	100.0	100.0
			LIABILITIES						
16.5	18.2	15.5	Notes Payable-Short Term	14.2	17.8	16.8	14.1	15.8	14.6
2.5	2.7	2.8	Cur. Mat.-L.T.D.	3.6	2.8	4.9	2.5	2.3	1.9
21.4	21.0	22.5	Trade Payables	19.2	22.4	19.5	21.6	25.0	23.5
.3	.2	.2	Income Taxes Payable	.0	.1	.0	.2	.6	.2
9.1	9.6	8.2	All Other Current	16.7	6.6	7.4	8.5	6.8	9.1
49.9	51.7	49.2	Total Current	53.7	49.8	48.6	46.8	50.4	49.2
10.7	9.4	10.9	Long-Term Debt	28.3	18.9	10.8	9.3	6.8	9.1
.1	.2	.2	Deferred Taxes	.0	.1	.1	.1	.2	.4
6.0	6.9	6.8	All Other Non-Current	15.2	7.4	7.2	7.1	6.0	5.1
33.3	31.9	32.9	Net Worth	2.7	23.8	33.3	36.6	36.6	36.1
100.0	100.0	100.0	Total Liabilities & Net Worth	100.0	100.0	100.0	100.0	100.0	100.0
			INCOME DATA						
100.0	100.0	100.0	Net Sales	100.0	100.0	100.0	100.0	100.0	100.0
32.5	30.7	31.6	Gross Profit	41.9	35.8	34.9	33.1	28.2	27.5
28.7	27.5	27.5	Operating Expenses	39.7	32.8	31.4	28.2	23.9	23.1
3.9	3.3	4.1	Operating Profit	2.2	3.0	3.5	4.9	4.3	4.4
.9	.8	.8	All Other Expenses (net)	2.4	1.4	.7	.5	.3	.8
2.9	2.4	3.3	Profit Before Taxes	-.2	1.5	2.8	4.4	4.0	3.6
			RATIOS						
2.7	2.5	2.6	Current	4.5	3.3	2.5	3.1	2.5	2.3
1.5	1.5	1.5		1.9	1.7	1.5	1.6	1.6	1.5
1.2	1.2	1.2		.6	1.0	1.0	1.2	1.2	1.2
1.4	1.3	1.4	Quick	1.6	1.7	1.1	1.6	1.4	1.2
.8	.7	.8		.7	.9	.8	.8	.8	.8
.5	.5	.5		.3	.5	.4	.6	.6	.6
22 16.5	20 17.9	22 16.7	Sales/Receivables	8 47.4	19 19.5	16 22.4	25 14.6	23 15.7	23 15.9
37 9.9	33 10.9	36 10.0		36 10.1	35 10.4	40 9.1	36 10.1	36 10.1	37 9.7
53 6.9	48 7.6	53 6.9		72 5.1	66 5.5	59 6.2	50 7.4	52 7.0	50 7.3
27 13.3	25 14.7	24 15.2	Cost of Sales/Inventory	0 UND	19 19.5	30 12.3	26 14.1	24 15.1	21 17.1
58 6.3	63 5.8	56 6.5		85 4.3	62 5.9	60 6.1	59 6.2	54 6.8	53 6.9
115 3.2	119 3.1	108 3.4		215 1.7	122 3.0	134 2.7	100 3.7	108 3.4	92 4.0
15 24.6	13 27.8	15 24.6	Cost of Sales/Payables	4 97.8	7 53.6	15 24.9	15 25.0	16 23.0	15 23.6
30 12.0	28 12.9	31 11.8		25 14.6	35 10.5	33 11.2	32 11.6	29 12.5	31 11.8
53 6.8	51 7.2	56 6.6		78 4.7	75 4.8	60 6.1	59 6.2	52 7.0	47 7.7
5.4	5.8	5.4	Sales/Working Capital	2.2	4.1	5.6	5.4	6.1	6.4
11.6	11.8	11.6		8.3	13.2	9.8	10.1	12.0	12.9
34.9	32.3	38.4		-8.4	840.0	103.2	35.3	33.2	27.9
8.3	9.4	14.4	EBIT/Interest	2.3	7.6	12.3	14.6	19.9	16.4
(577) 3.0	(603) 3.0	(677) 4.3		(25) .3	(83) 2.0	(105) 4.0	(126) 4.0	(173) 5.7	(165) 6.3
1.3	1.2	1.4		-5.9	-.8	1.4	1.2	2.2	2.1
8.5	6.1	7.3	Net Profit + Depr., Dep., Amort./Cur. Mat. L/T/D			4.7	3.6	10.3	14.9
(103) 3.4	(109) 2.8	(125) 2.6			(10) 1.4	(28) 1.1	(37) 2.9	(46) 3.7	
.9	1.3	.8				.3	.0	1.0	2.3
.1	.1	.1	Fixed/Worth	.0	.0	.0	.1	.1	.1
.2	.2	.3		.6	.4	.2	.2	.2	.3
.9	1.0	1.2		-.5	7.5	1.4	.9	.9	.9
.9	1.0	.8	Debt/Worth	1.0	.8	.9	.6	.7	1.0
2.3	2.2	2.2		3.3	2.3	2.5	1.9	2.3	2.3
6.7	6.4	7.4		-6.8	51.8	7.3	4.7	7.5	5.3
46.3	41.7	50.0	% Profit Before Taxes/Tangible Net Worth	50.0	48.9	36.6	41.4	60.3	48.1
(575) 18.0	(595) 16.8	(666) 20.0		(23) -.2	(79) 15.8	(101) 16.7	(134) 17.8	(169) 24.0	(160) 25.2
4.4	2.8	5.1		-13.2	-3.1	3.3	1.6	6.8	11.7
14.6	12.6	16.2	% Profit Before Taxes/Total Assets	15.4	14.9	12.3	16.7	20.1	15.9
5.5	4.7	5.9		-.1	3.7	4.8	5.1	7.9	8.3
.9	.5	1.1		-8.6	-3.3	.6	.5	2.5	2.9
142.9	198.8	177.8	Sales/Net Fixed Assets	363.0	322.4	164.1	178.8	169.6	152.7
51.1	58.1	53.7		59.2	48.4	42.4	49.3	64.9	58.6
16.5	18.8	16.7		8.0	13.8	11.2	19.4	20.5	15.5
4.0	4.3	4.2	Sales/Total Assets	3.2	4.2	3.5	3.8	4.6	4.9
2.8	2.9	2.8		2.0	2.6	2.6	2.9	3.1	3.0
1.9	2.0	1.9		1.1	1.6	1.6	1.9	2.1	2.0
.3	.2	.3	% Depr., Dep., Amort./Sales	.3	.3	.3	.3	.2	.3
(516) .6	(527) .6	(568) .6		(25) 1.4	(56) .9	(73) 1.1	(114) .6	(151) .5	(149) .6
1.4	1.4	1.5		4.8	1.9	2.5	1.3	1.2	1.5
1.6	1.3	1.3	% Officers', Directors' Owners' Comp/Sales	7.1	2.8	1.9	1.7	1.1	.5
(313) 3.0	(322) 2.8	(350) 2.9		(10) 8.1	(52) 4.1	(71) 4.0	(80) 3.0	(89) 2.0	(48) 1.0
5.4	5.3	5.2		17.7	7.1	7.1	4.6	3.9	2.3
19693554M	22453908M	21871028M	Net Sales ($)	21505M	196962M	465267M	1115562M	3008959M	17062773M
7432726M	7840976M	8281865M	Total Assets ($)	19622M	96540M	235454M	495493M	1112770M	6321986M

© RMA 2010

M = $ thousand   MM = $ million
See Pages 9 through 22 for Explanation of Ratios and Data

Current Data Sorted by Assets							Comparative Historical Data	

Type of Statement

0-500M	500M-2MM	2-10MM	10-50MM	50-100MM	100-250MM		4/1/05-3/31/06 ALL	4/1/06-3/31/07 ALL
		1	2			Unqualified	12	5
	1	2				Reviewed	8	8
	1	2				Compiled	6	7
1	3	2				Tax Returns	3	4
	5	5	4			Other	5	11
	3 (4/1-9/30/09)		26 (10/1/09-3/31/10)					
1	10	12	6			NUMBER OF STATEMENTS	34	35
%	%	%	%	%	%	**ASSETS**	%	%
	19.8	12.5				Cash & Equivalents	8.8	10.9
	37.6	33.1				Trade Receivables (net)	32.7	32.9
	22.8	30.2				Inventory	28.3	34.3
	2.0	5.9				All Other Current	1.0	1.4
	82.1	81.8				Total Current	70.9	79.5
	8.3	9.1	D	D		Fixed Assets (net)	18.2	13.3
	5.4	4.5	A	A		Intangibles (net)	8.0	4.9
	4.1	4.6	T	T		All Other Non-Current	2.9	2.3
	100.0	100.0	A	A		Total	100.0	100.0
						LIABILITIES		
	11.3	10.7	N	N		Notes Payable-Short Term	17.1	13.9
	3.2	3.0	O	O		Cur. Mat.-L.T.D.	2.5	3.4
	22.2	28.2	T	T		Trade Payables	17.7	23.3
	.1	.8				Income Taxes Payable	.2	.2
	4.6	14.8	A	A		All Other Current	14.6	9.5
	41.5	57.5	V	V		Total Current	52.1	50.3
	2.7	2.5	A	A		Long-Term Debt	11.7	11.0
	.0	.0	I	I		Deferred Taxes	.1	.0
	6.6	5.0	L	L		All Other Non-Current	1.6	4.7
	49.2	35.1	A	A		Net Worth	34.5	33.9
	100.0	100.0	B	B		Total Liabilties & Net Worth	100.0	100.0
			L	L		**INCOME DATA**		
	100.0	100.0	E	E		Net Sales	100.0	100.0
	35.3	32.3				Gross Profit	33.0	30.7
	33.3	29.5				Operating Expenses	30.3	28.0
	2.0	2.8				Operating Profit	2.7	2.7
	-.1	.1				All Other Expenses (net)	.7	.4
	2.1	2.7				Profit Before Taxes	2.0	2.3
						RATIOS		
	6.0	1.7					1.9	2.3
	3.3	1.4				Current	1.3	1.6
	1.1	1.2					1.0	1.2
	4.6	.8					1.2	1.3
	1.4	.8				Quick	.8	.9
	.7	.5					.5	.6
18	20.8	19	19.3				29	12.6	18	20.7
26	14.3	38	9.6			Sales/Receivables	45	8.1	42	8.7
44	8.4	49	7.4				59	6.2	54	6.8
0	UND	19	18.8				13	28.6	18	20.6
9	41.5	31	11.8			Cost of Sales/Inventory	46	7.9	50	7.3
101	3.6	149	2.4				79	4.6	74	5.0
6	58.8	28	12.8				8	48.3	15	24.1
13	28.5	39	9.4			Cost of Sales/Payables	33	11.0	38	9.7
38	9.7	49	7.4				53	6.8	69	5.3
	4.4	6.1					8.4	6.7
	7.6	18.4				Sales/Working Capital	15.9	12.7
	NM	49.7					NM	33.7
		114.6					10.1	7.1
	(10)	8.5				EBIT/Interest	(32) 3.0	(31) 2.6
		2.7					.3	1.4
						Net Profit + Depr., Dep., Amort./Cur. Mat. L/T/D		
	.1	.1					.1	.2
	.1	.3				Fixed/Worth	.6	.3
	NM	.8					3.8	1.2
	.2	1.3					.9	1.0
	1.2	2.2				Debt/Worth	2.5	2.2
	NM	3.9					7.4	11.1
		49.7				% Profit Before Taxes/Tangible Net Worth	37.0	51.5
	(11)	13.5					(28) 21.3	(30) 15.2
		5.3					6.3	4.0
	19.5	16.6				% Profit Before Taxes/Total Assets	10.7	17.6
	.6	6.7					4.5	4.0
	-7.7	1.5					-.7	.7
	548.2	223.2					73.3	112.6
	54.2	36.8				Sales/Net Fixed Assets	20.8	34.0
	30.8	18.8					7.9	16.9
	6.4	5.4					3.9	4.5
	3.8	3.2				Sales/Total Assets	3.1	3.3
	2.7	1.9					1.9	2.3
							.6	.4
						% Depr., Dep., Amort./Sales	(30) 1.2	(27) .9
							2.4	1.4
							1.3	1.7
						% Officers', Directors' Owners' Comp/Sales	(10) 6.7	(12) 5.7
							14.1	8.0
1016M	65423M	273845M	261273M			Net Sales ($)	1172424M	1091543M
332M	11079M	68915M	98805M			Total Assets ($)	464211M	311113M

© RMA 2010

M = $ thousand   MM = $ million
See Pages 9 through 22 for Explanation of Ratios and Data

Comparative Historical Data   Current Data Sorted by Sales

			Type of Statement	0-1MM	1-3MM	3-5MM	5-10MM	10-25MM	25MM & OVER
6	5	3	Unqualified					1	2
13	3	3	Reviewed					1	1
2	4	3	Compiled		1		1	1	
6	2	6	Tax Returns		2	1	2	2	1
20	17	14	Other		2	2	2	3	5
4/1/07-3/31/08 ALL	4/1/08-3/31/09 ALL	4/1/09-3/31/10 ALL			3 (4/1-9/30/09)		26 (10/1/09-3/31/10)		
47	31	29	**NUMBER OF STATEMENTS**	6	3	3	8	9	

%	%	%		%	%	%	%	%	%
			ASSETS						
14.3	12.0	15.5	Cash & Equivalents	D					
43.2	29.5	33.1	Trade Receivables (net)	A					
17.9	29.4	28.8	Inventory	T					
6.4	5.9	3.5	All Other Current	A					
81.9	76.8	80.9	Total Current						
9.4	12.7	9.6	Fixed Assets (net)	N					
5.3	5.6	4.9	Intangibles (net)	O					
3.5	5.0	4.6	All Other Non-Current	T					
100.0	100.0	100.0	Total						
			LIABILITIES	A					
9.9	23.6	11.8	Notes Payable-Short Term	V					
1.7	1.1	3.4	Cur. Mat.-L.T.D.	A					
28.7	24.9	23.6	Trade Payables	I					
.2	.3	.4	Income Taxes Payable	L					
16.6	8.4	11.5	All Other Current	A					
57.0	58.3	50.6	Total Current	B					
4.6	7.0	2.7	Long-Term Debt	L					
.1	.3	.0	Deferred Taxes	E					
3.6	3.1	5.4	All Other Non-Current						
34.6	31.2	41.2	Net Worth						
100.0	100.0	100.0	Total Liabilities & Net Worth						
			INCOME DATA						
100.0	100.0	100.0	Net Sales						
32.4	33.2	33.2	Gross Profit						
29.4	32.2	30.5	Operating Expenses						
2.9	1.0	2.7	Operating Profit						
.3	.5	.7	All Other Expenses (net)						
2.6	.5	2.0	Profit Before Taxes						
			RATIOS						
2.0	2.1	3.0							
1.7	1.4	1.5	Current						
1.1	1.1	1.2							
1.6	1.2	1.6							
1.1	.7	.8	Quick						
.8	.4	.5							
(26) 14.3	(18) 20.3	(20) 18.4							
(49) 7.5	(37) 9.8	(35) 10.5	Sales/Receivables						
(65) 5.6	(50) 7.3	(49) 7.5							
(4) 96.8	(16) 22.9	(12) 31.6							
(24) 15.2	(54) 6.8	(56) 6.5	Cost of Sales/Inventory						
(58) 6.3	(89) 4.1	(144) 2.5							
(15) 24.9	(11) 34.3	(11) 32.8							
(38) 9.6	(37) 10.0	(31) 11.9	Cost of Sales/Payables						
(67) 5.5	(76) 4.8	(49) 7.4							
5.9	6.0	4.8							
10.1	15.4	11.2	Sales/Working Capital						
33.3	81.5	68.2							
15.8	18.4	34.2							
(40) 7.0	(28) 4.3	(24) 5.2	EBIT/Interest						
2.4	1.8	-1.2							
6.6			Net Profit + Depr., Dep.,						
(11) 3.6			Amort./Cur. Mat. L/T/D						
1.5									
.1	.1	.1							
.3	.4	.2	Fixed/Worth						
.6	1.3	.7							
1.0	1.1	.7							
2.0	3.2	1.9	Debt/Worth						
6.7	9.6	5.2							
44.3	70.0	47.0	% Profit Before Taxes/Tangible						
(42) 22.4	(26) 11.3	(25) 6.1	Net Worth						
7.1	3.9	-7.0							
18.5	18.5	14.2	% Profit Before Taxes/Total						
8.9	4.4	3.6	Assets						
3.7	1.4	-2.7							
93.8	85.9	211.3							
57.3	34.7	47.2	Sales/Net Fixed Assets						
19.7	18.6	20.1							
4.3	4.3	5.2							
3.3	3.0	3.2	Sales/Total Assets						
2.5	1.9	2.2							
.2	.2	.4							
(38) .7	(23) .6	(18) 1.3	% Depr., Dep., Amort./Sales						
1.2	1.7	2.0							
2.9		.6	% Officers', Directors'						
(13) 6.4		(11) 4.2	Owners' Comp/Sales						
11.1		5.3							
2020937M	1001021M	601557M	Net Sales ($)		12488M	9933M	25997M	131311M	421828M
677858M	343230M	179131M	Total Assets ($)		6434M	5508M	5223M	49572M	112394M

M = $ thousand   MM = $ million
See Pages 9 through 22 for Explanation of Ratios and Data

Current Data Sorted by Assets   Comparative Historical Data

0-500M	500M-2MM	2-10MM	10-50MM	50-100MM	100-250MM	Type of Statement	4/1/05-3/31/06 ALL	4/1/06-3/31/07 ALL
1		5	9	3	1	Unqualified	40	30
	1	14	8			Reviewed	38	33
	12	13	4			Compiled	32	22
13	14	12	1			Tax Returns	31	38
4	16	25	15	1	3	Other	47	67
_____32 (4/1-9/30/09)_____			____143 (10/1/09-3/31/10)____					
18	43	69	37	4	4	NUMBER OF STATEMENTS	188	190

%	%	%	%	%	%		%	%
						ASSETS		
23.0	14.3	9.3	11.3			Cash & Equivalents	7.6	9.8
21.2	37.0	41.4	32.9			Trade Receivables (net)	33.8	37.0
22.8	25.1	28.7	18.4			Inventory	32.5	26.9
5.8	5.1	3.8	7.7			All Other Current	1.9	3.1
72.8	81.5	83.1	70.3			Total Current	75.7	76.8
17.1	11.2	6.9	12.5			Fixed Assets (net)	13.4	12.3
3.5	1.1	2.5	3.2			Intangibles (net)	4.2	3.9
6.5	6.3	7.5	14.0			All Other Non-Current	6.7	7.0
100.0	100.0	100.0	100.0			Total	100.0	100.0
						LIABILITIES		
12.2	16.8	17.6	17.4			Notes Payable-Short Term	19.6	21.4
7.0	7.5	2.3	.9			Cur. Mat.-L.T.D.	2.9	2.3
28.4	24.9	25.4	21.7			Trade Payables	24.6	22.1
.4	.0	.1	.1			Income Taxes Payable	.2	.3
13.5	5.9	10.0	15.6			All Other Current	8.7	8.8
61.5	55.1	55.4	55.6			Total Current	56.1	55.0
23.9	8.5	4.9	8.0			Long-Term Debt	12.3	11.0
.0	.0	.1	.1			Deferred Taxes	.3	.2
1.3	6.6	4.7	3.9			All Other Non-Current	6.0	5.7
13.3	29.7	34.8	32.5			Net Worth	25.3	28.2
100.0	100.0	100.0	100.0			Total Liabilities & Net Worth	100.0	100.0
						INCOME DATA		
100.0	100.0	100.0	100.0			Net Sales	100.0	100.0
31.1	30.6	21.0	31.6			Gross Profit	25.5	25.2
26.5	26.3	18.7	25.6			Operating Expenses	22.1	21.0
4.6	4.3	2.3	6.0			Operating Profit	3.4	4.1
1.7	1.0	.1	.6			All Other Expenses (net)	.5	.5
2.9	3.4	2.2	5.5			Profit Before Taxes	3.0	3.6
						RATIOS		
3.8	2.6	2.1	2.0			Current	2.0	2.3
1.4	1.7	1.5	1.3				1.4	1.4
.9	1.2	1.1	1.0				1.1	1.1
2.2	1.8	1.5	1.3			Quick	1.2	1.5
.9	1.2	.9	.9				.7	.9
.4	.6	.6	.5				.4	.5
0 UND	14 26.1	17 21.8	25 14.8			Sales/Receivables	22 16.5	19 19.3
14 25.8	27 13.5	33 11.0	48 7.6				35 10.5	34 10.7
40 9.0	49 7.4	61 6.0	72 5.1				49 7.4	49 7.6
0 UND	0 UND	6 63.4	0 UND			Cost of Sales/Inventory	19 18.8	4 86.1
8 46.4	37 9.9	33 11.2	7 50.2				49 7.4	29 12.7
65 5.6	99 3.7	72 5.0	56 6.5				97 3.8	77 4.8
0 UND	5 75.4	14 26.1	11 31.8			Cost of Sales/Payables	14 25.9	8 44.6
7 55.5	23 15.9	25 14.4	38 9.6				31 11.7	25 14.7
49 7.5	54 6.8	45 8.0	69 5.3				51 7.1	47 7.8
9.7	6.1	6.4	6.7			Sales/Working Capital	6.9	6.9
25.3	14.0	17.2	13.0				20.3	15.5
-129.1	33.0	41.0	NM				98.5	77.2
13.9	13.9	16.5	14.4			EBIT/Interest	9.3	14.0
(13) 4.5	(33) 4.9	(61) 4.2	(31) 4.8				(169) 3.5	(162) 3.7
3.0	1.9	1.6	1.0				1.5	1.7
		6.3				Net Profit + Depr., Dep., Amort./Cur. Mat. L/T/D	9.1	5.7
	(10) 2.1						(44) 3.2	(36) 3.4
		.8					1.1	1.4
.1	.0	.0	.1			Fixed/Worth	.1	.1
.7	.2	.1	.2				.4	.2
NM	.6	.3	1.1				1.3	1.0
.9	.6	.9	.9			Debt/Worth	1.3	1.0
2.9	2.1	2.4	2.1				2.6	2.8
NM	7.6	6.9	5.3				9.0	8.0
145.0	63.7	48.1	76.5			% Profit Before Taxes/Tangible Net Worth	53.6	61.3
(14) 32.6	(38) 26.8	(63) 15.7	(34) 25.2				(158) 21.7	(163) 25.8
3.5	7.4	2.8	9.1				5.8	7.3
28.5	24.2	12.4	19.1			% Profit Before Taxes/Total Assets	12.1	18.9
6.7	7.8	4.2	7.2				4.9	6.7
2.4	1.9	1.7	.4				1.4	2.1
366.3	416.5	930.5	267.8			Sales/Net Fixed Assets	150.6	309.4
64.8	99.0	113.3	27.7				44.9	57.1
28.0	22.8	24.8	9.3				15.1	23.1
10.0	5.2	6.1	3.5			Sales/Total Assets	5.0	5.6
5.5	3.4	3.6	2.1				3.1	3.5
3.0	2.5	2.4	1.0				1.9	2.0
.1	.3	.1	.2			% Depr., Dep., Amort./Sales	.3	.2
(11) .6	(25) .8	(54) .2	(29) .5				(149) .6	(131) .6
3.5	1.1	.9	1.7				1.3	1.2
1.1	1.2	1.3				% Officers', Directors' Owners' Comp/Sales	1.2	1.0
(11) 5.3	(29) 2.4	(29) 2.7					(69) 2.5	(75) 2.6
11.4	4.7	4.9					4.8	6.2
34887M	261156M	1615289M	2179036M	1491766M	7092997M	Net Sales ($)	9144804M	11566708M
4957M	51775M	333734M	742510M	266758M	577285M	Total Assets ($)	2987229M	2864403M

M = $ thousand   MM = $ million
See Pages 9 through 22 for Explanation of Ratios and Data

Comparative Historical Data

Current Data Sorted by Sales

Type of Statement — right-side period groupings: 32 (4/1-9/30/09) and 143 (10/1/09-3/31/10)

4/1/07-3/31/08 ALL	4/1/08-3/31/09 ALL	4/1/09-3/31/10 ALL		0-1MM	1-3MM	3-5MM	5-10MM	10-25MM	25MM & OVER
17	15	19	Unqualified	1			1	1	16
31	36	23	Reviewed				4	9	9
27	24	29	Compiled			1	5	8	4
30	47	40	Tax Returns	2	14	7	6	10	1
55	57	64	Other	2	7	7	10	17	21
160	179	175	**NUMBER OF STATEMENTS**	9	24	20	26	45	51
%	%	%	**ASSETS**	%	%	%	%	%	%
9.0	12.0	12.2	Cash & Equivalents	19.2	14.8	8.3	10.3		9.9
37.3	38.1	36.0	Trade Receivables (net)	26.9	25.3	32.9	39.7		46.1
28.8	24.2	25.2	Inventory	23.6	34.4	27.1	22.1		24.3
3.4	4.4	5.1	All Other Current	4.9	4.6	5.2	8.4		3.3
78.5	78.8	78.5	Total Current	74.6	79.0	73.5	80.5		83.6
12.8	10.8	10.7	Fixed Assets (net)	16.6	7.7	13.2	8.9		8.0
2.6	2.6	2.3	Intangibles (net)	2.7	1.3	4.8	1.1		2.2
6.2	7.9	8.5	All Other Non-Current	6.0	12.0	8.5	9.5		6.2
100.0	100.0	100.0	Total	100.0	100.0	100.0	100.0		100.0
			LIABILITIES						
19.1	17.8	16.7	Notes Payable-Short Term	9.8	17.8	14.5	18.3		19.8
1.8	3.9	3.8	Cur. Mat.-L.T.D.	14.1	3.2	4.1	1.1		1.7
22.5	24.4	24.5	Trade Payables	31.9	15.7	22.3	29.7		24.3
.1	.1	.1	Income Taxes Payable	.1	.0	.2	.0		.1
8.4	11.2	10.5	All Other Current	18.3	9.5	7.2	10.4		9.4
51.9	57.4	55.6	Total Current	74.1	46.2	48.4	59.5		55.2
11.4	7.9	8.8	Long-Term Debt	26.5	2.2	7.6	4.2		5.9
.1	.1	.1	Deferred Taxes	.0	.0	.0	.0		.2
4.4	3.5	4.6	All Other Non-Current	2.3	13.0	3.7	4.3		3.6
32.2	31.1	31.0	Net Worth	-2.9	38.6	40.3	32.0		35.0
100.0	100.0	100.0	Total Liabilities & Net Worth	100.0	100.0	100.0	100.0		100.0
			INCOME DATA						
100.0	100.0	100.0	Net Sales	100.0	100.0	100.0	100.0		100.0
24.2	23.3	26.4	Gross Profit	35.2	32.6	28.7	25.3		15.4
19.8	20.1	22.7	Operating Expenses	33.7	27.8	25.6	19.8		13.3
4.4	3.2	3.8	Operating Profit	1.5	4.8	3.1	5.6		2.0
1.0	.4	.6	All Other Expenses (net)	.4	.9	.6	-.2		.4
3.4	2.8	3.2	Profit Before Taxes	1.1	3.9	2.5	5.8		1.6
			RATIOS						
2.3	2.2	2.3		3.6	3.3	2.2	1.9		2.0
1.5	1.4	1.5	Current	1.5	2.2	1.4	1.3		1.5
1.2	1.1	1.1		.7	1.2	1.1	1.0		1.2
1.5	1.4	1.6		2.2	1.9	1.3	1.2		1.6
.9	.9	.9	Quick	.9	1.1	.9	.8		1.0
.5	.6	.6		.5	.4	.6	.5		.7
18 20.7	18 20.4	14 25.3		0 UND	3 145.5	35 10.3	20 18.4		15 23.8
34 10.8	33 11.0	35 10.5	Sales/Receivables	28 12.9	18 20.1	44 8.2	40 9.1		30 12.1
51 7.2	52 7.0	59 6.2		46 7.9	57 6.4	66 5.5	65 5.5		47 7.8
7 50.4	0 999.8	2 240.2		0 UND	0 UND	10 36.4	0 UND		0 999.8
31 11.8	18 19.8	28 13.2	Cost of Sales/Inventory	15 24.5	49 7.5	46 7.9	18 20.7		10 36.6
76 4.8	64 5.7	69 5.3		103 3.5	160 2.3	75 4.9	70 5.2		40 9.2
8 44.7	10 36.5	9 39.4		6 56.2	5 74.6	11 32.9	16 23.0		6 60.0
24 15.0	24 15.0	25 14.5	Cost of Sales/Payables	29 12.6	24 15.2	39 9.5	29 12.6		17 21.8
46 7.9	44 8.3	51 7.1		75 4.9	48 7.7	64 5.7	57 6.4		34 10.7
7.5	8.4	6.5		5.5	4.7	6.5	5.9		9.6
16.3	19.1	15.0	Sales/Working Capital	18.7	10.1	13.4	21.8		21.3
49.7	97.7	77.8		NM	18.9	67.6	NM		63.2
10.2	16.5	13.5		13.0	11.7	7.6	25.5		12.3
(140) 3.7	(148) 4.5	(145) 4.3	EBIT/Interest	(20) 3.4	(15) 5.8	(23) 3.2	(37) 8.0		(46) 4.2
1.5	1.6	1.8		.0	1.0	1.5	2.5		1.8
9.5	8.3	4.3	Net Profit + Depr., Dep.,						5.0
(30) 3.7	(24) 2.9	(20) 1.7	Amort./Cur. Mat. L/T/D					(10)	1.7
1.3	1.7	.7							.5
.1	.0	.0		.1	.1	.1	.1		.0
.2	.2	.2	Fixed/Worth	.7	.2	.2	.2		.1
.8	.6	.9		33.5	.5	.9	.5		.5
1.0	.9	.9		1.9	.6	.7	1.1		1.0
2.6	2.2	2.4	Debt/Worth	4.1	2.1	2.1	2.5		1.9
7.2	6.7	6.2		124.8	7.1	5.4	5.2		5.8
62.9	58.4	56.1	% Profit Before Taxes/Tangible	77.3	50.1	57.6	74.3		48.9
(141) 24.2	(154) 20.0	(157) 18.9	Net Worth	(19) 23.5	(18) 19.5	(23) 9.7	(44) 26.5		(46) 16.9
6.6	8.9	4.6		7.7	5.5	2.5	10.7		4.7
19.3	16.0	14.9	% Profit Before Taxes/Total	20.7	14.7	11.6	18.3		13.5
7.6	6.7	6.7	Assets	6.2	9.3	3.4	9.1		4.8
1.7	1.4	1.8		2.1	1.0	1.8	2.2		1.6
290.5	759.5	420.0		168.1	417.5	474.8	161.7		999.8
66.2	74.9	75.8	Sales/Net Fixed Assets	42.1	59.1	50.2	61.8		200.8
20.6	22.1	18.5		16.5	24.6	10.8	18.8		27.7
6.2	5.9	6.1		6.3	3.9	4.1	4.8		9.7
3.6	3.6	3.3	Sales/Total Assets	3.2	2.8	2.7	3.4		5.6
2.4	2.3	2.0		2.0	1.8	1.1	2.0		2.9
.1	.2	.1		.1	.3	.2	.1		.1
(121) .4	(121) .4	(125) .5	% Depr., Dep., Amort./Sales	(15) .6	(13) .8	(19) .6	(36) .5	(37)	.2
1.1	1.0	1.1		1.8	1.1	2.4	1.1		.8
1.0	1.0	1.2	% Officers', Directors'	1.5	2.4	.9	1.2		.7
(71) 2.4	(90) 3.1	(78) 2.4	Owners' Comp/Sales	(14) 3.9	(12) 3.8	(14) 1.6	(18) 2.9	(16)	1.4
3.6	6.0	5.1		5.9	4.7	3.0	5.5		2.3
11016257M	9055793M	12675131M	Net Sales ($)	5363M	51947M	81856M	189555M	723994M	11622416M
2604440M	2169101M	1977019M	Total Assets ($)	5981M	27973M	46151M	113116M	310326M	1473472M

RETAIL TRADE

Current Data Sorted by Assets · Comparative Historical Data

Type of Statement	0-500M	500M-2MM	2-10MM	10-50MM	50-100MM	100-250MM	4/1/05-3/31/06 ALL	4/1/06-3/31/07 ALL
Unqualified	1	1	44	43	14	12	152	169
Reviewed		8	193	155	16	8	359	404
Compiled	2	15	66	25	2	3	135	142
Tax Returns	9	49	220	56	1		206	277
Other	20	110	1025	542	30	20	2315	2049
	146 (4/1-9/30/09)		2,544 (10/1/09-3/31/10)					
NUMBER OF STATEMENTS	32	183	1548	821	63	43	3167	3041

	0-500M %	500M-2MM %	2-10MM %	10-50MM %	50-100MM %	100-250MM %	Hist ALL %	Hist ALL %
ASSETS								
Cash & Equivalents	10.2	12.8	11.7	13.5	11.9	9.7	10.9	10.1
Trade Receivables (net)	7.8	7.5	7.7	8.0	7.4	6.9	5.9	7.2
Inventory	47.3	62.1	59.0	47.3	39.6	35.2	62.9	62.8
All Other Current	3.5	2.0	2.3	2.4	4.8	2.5	3.7	2.5
Total Current	68.8	84.5	80.8	71.2	63.8	54.3	83.4	82.5
Fixed Assets (net)	14.7	8.6	9.2	15.0	18.7	28.2	8.9	9.5
Intangibles (net)	3.6	2.0	3.4	4.9	7.0	8.2	3.7	2.3
All Other Non-Current	12.9	4.9	6.5	8.9	10.5	9.3	4.1	5.7
Total	100.0	100.0	100.0	100.0	100.0	100.0	100.0	100.0
LIABILITIES								
Notes Payable-Short Term	33.2	40.8	49.3	42.6	38.5	34.0	53.0	52.3
Cur. Mat.-L.T.D.	1.2	2.5	1.6	1.7	3.1	3.0	1.5	1.7
Trade Payables	31.8	6.7	4.8	4.2	4.2	4.7	4.2	4.3
Income Taxes Payable	.2	.0	.1	.1	.1	.0	.1	.1
All Other Current	26.4	16.3	10.7	9.9	9.5	8.2	13.8	12.6
Total Current	92.8	66.3	66.6	58.5	55.4	49.9	72.6	70.9
Long-Term Debt	23.3	9.4	7.7	11.1	14.3	18.0	6.0	7.2
Deferred Taxes	.1	.1	.1	.2	.3	.2	.1	.1
All Other Non-Current	13.4	7.8	5.0	3.6	3.8	3.0	3.4	3.8
Net Worth	-29.5	16.4	20.7	26.6	26.2	28.9	17.8	18.0
Total Liabilities & Net Worth	100.0	100.0	100.0	100.0	100.0	100.0	100.0	100.0
INCOME DATA								
Net Sales	100.0	100.0	100.0	100.0	100.0	100.0	100.0	100.0
Gross Profit	22.5	16.1	13.4	14.0	16.3	16.1	12.9	12.8
Operating Expenses	22.6	18.6	14.1	13.5	14.8	14.2	12.6	12.6
Operating Profit	-.1	-2.5	-.7	.6	1.6	1.9	.2	.2
All Other Expenses (net)	.0	-.5	-1.1	-.8	.2	-.3	-.4	-.3
Profit Before Taxes	.0	-2.0	.4	1.4	1.3	2.2	.6	.5

RATIOS

Ratio	0-500M	500M-2MM	2-10MM	10-50MM	50-100MM	100-250MM	Hist ALL	Hist ALL
Current	2.1	1.9	1.4	1.4	1.3	1.2	1.3	1.3
	1.3	1.3	1.2	1.2	1.2	1.1	1.1	1.1
	.7	1.0	1.1	1.0	1.0	.9	1.0	1.0
Quick	.7	.5	.4	.5	.5	.4	.3	.3
	.2	(182) .3	(1547) .3	.3	.4	.3	(3162) .2	(3034) .2
	.0	.1	.2	.2	.2	.2	.1	.1
Sales/Receivables	0 UND	2 207.7	3 121.0	4 87.2	4 93.4	4 89.6	1 287.9	3 120.4
	1 574.4	4 86.1	5 68.1	7 52.0	7 49.6	9 41.6	4 96.2	5 66.6
	9 41.4	9 41.6	9 39.1	11 32.9	13 29.1	16 23.0	8 46.0	9 38.5
Cost of Sales/Inventory	9 38.9	50 7.3	53 6.9	48 7.6	50 7.3	50 7.2	53 6.8	55 6.7
	50 7.3	76 4.8	68 5.4	62 5.9	64 5.7	58 6.3	71 5.1	71 5.1
	76 4.8	100 3.6	87 4.2	80 4.6	78 4.7	66 5.5	92 4.0	94 3.9
Cost of Sales/Payables	0 UND	2 213.3	2 172.4	2 153.9	3 139.9	3 106.4	2 223.1	3 207.3
	5 79.2	4 83.7	4 101.6	4 88.9	4 83.4	5 77.7	3 119.6	3 113.5
	15 24.4	9 39.0	6 60.4	7 53.1	7 52.6	9 40.1	5 70.0	6 66.1
Sales/Working Capital	11.0	9.0	14.2	14.1	18.2	21.0	19.6	18.3
	39.4	17.7	26.0	29.4	37.2	51.5	36.1	34.7
	-38.0	86.5	72.2	118.1	-999.8	-97.5	179.1	132.9
EBIT/Interest	9.3	2.1	5.5	9.2	10.9	7.5	4.4	4.0
	(18) 4.6	(131) .4	(1022) 2.0	(577) 3.1	(47) 4.5	(35) 3.6	(2661) 1.8	(2307) 1.7
	1.2	-2.4	.4	1.4	1.8	1.7	.8	.6
Net Profit + Depr., Dep., Amort./Cur. Mat. L/T/D			5.4	4.4	2.7	2.7	6.8	5.1
		(62) 2.0	(64) 1.7	(15) 1.2	(10) 2.1		(191) 2.3	(199) 2.1
			.7	.6	.2	.8	.7	.8
Fixed/Worth	.1	.1	.1	.2	.3	.9	.2	.2
	.7	.4	.4	.5	.7	1.3	.5	.5
	-.8	-12.8	1.6	1.8	2.5	2.6	1.8	1.7
Debt/Worth	1.0	1.6	2.2	2.0	2.2	2.1	3.0	2.8
	14.6	4.4	4.5	3.8	4.2	3.2	5.9	5.6
	-8.0	-121.2	15.0	9.2	8.9	19.4	18.0	14.9
% Profit Before Taxes/Tangible Net Worth	58.6	19.3	32.0	40.9	36.4	52.7	42.8	36.3
	(21) 22.2	(136) .3	(1297) 12.6	(734) 18.3	(57) 21.0	(38) 25.4	(2678) 18.0	(2596) 15.3
	.0	-28.5	.1	5.7	7.3	9.3	1.4	.4
% Profit Before Taxes/Total Assets	15.2	2.8	6.2	8.0	7.4	10.2	7.0	6.3
	5.3	-1.0	2.3	3.8	3.6	5.2	2.4	2.1
	-4.5	-10.6	-.9	.9	1.5	2.4	-.5	-1.0
Sales/Net Fixed Assets	UND	171.6	153.8	89.8	38.9	24.3	156.2	144.5
	82.0	88.7	65.4	38.8	23.2	8.7	74.7	67.3
	28.8	41.4	31.0	13.1	7.4	5.6	33.3	29.6
Sales/Total Assets	8.8	5.0	4.5	4.0	3.7	3.1	4.6	4.5
	5.2	3.8	3.6	3.1	2.6	2.5	3.7	3.6
	2.9	2.8	2.8	2.4	1.7	1.9	2.9	2.8
% Depr., Dep., Amort./Sales	.2	.2	.2	.2	.3	.6	.1	.1
	(15) .8	(150) .3	(1310) .3	(749) .3	(59) .5	(36) .7	(2737) .2	(2637) .2
	1.0	.6	.5	.6	.8	1.1	.4	.4
% Officers', Directors' Owners' Comp/Sales		.7	.4	.2	.2		.3	.3
	(103)	1.3	(932) .6	(464) .5	(25) .4		(2074) .5	(1793) .5
		2.2	1.2	.9	1.2		.9	1.0
Net Sales ($)	57405M	1071188M	31847760M	47347726M	11119855M	16093887M	155070896M	150864002M
Total Assets ($)	7451M	248891M	8651448M	15246570M	4196164M	6201349M	41872549M	42067557M

© RMA 2010

M = $ thousand   MM = $ million
See Pages 9 through 22 for Explanation of Ratios and Data

Comparative Historical Data | Current Data Sorted by Sales

Type of Statement

4/1/07-3/31/08 ALL	4/1/08-3/31/09 ALL	4/1/09-3/31/10 ALL	Type of Statement	0-1MM	1-3MM	3-5MM	5-10MM	10-25MM	25MM & OVER
91	86	115	Unqualified		3	2	7	26	77
337	322	380	Reviewed	1		3	26	106	244
118	126	113	Compiled	1	5	8	11	41	47
230	265	335	Tax Returns	5	21	15	46	138	110
1699	1860	1747	Other	14	31	51	181	616	854

Right-side period groupings: 146 (4/1-9/30/09); 2,544 (10/1/09-3/31/10)

4/1/07-3/31/08 ALL	4/1/08-3/31/09 ALL	4/1/09-3/31/10 ALL		0-1MM	1-3MM	3-5MM	5-10MM	10-25MM	25MM & OVER
2475	2659	2690	**NUMBER OF STATEMENTS**	21	60	79	271	927	1332

ASSETS (%)

Hist 1	Hist 2	Hist 3	Item	0-1MM	1-3MM	3-5MM	5-10MM	10-25MM	25MM & OVER
9.9	9.9	12.3	Cash & Equivalents	16.1	11.7	11.3	10.7	10.8	13.7
7.0	6.6	7.7	Trade Receivables (net)	10.6	10.1	8.1	7.6	7.6	7.7
62.8	61.7	54.7	Inventory	36.3	50.5	54.2	62.0	57.7	51.7
2.4	2.2	2.4	All Other Current	1.2	4.0	2.2	1.7	2.3	2.6
82.1	80.3	77.1	Total Current	64.2	76.3	75.6	82.0	78.4	75.6
9.6	10.4	11.5	Fixed Assets (net)	16.5	10.6	13.2	9.0	10.7	12.5
2.7	3.1	3.9	Intangibles (net)	6.1	3.8	3.0	2.7	4.1	4.1
5.6	6.2	7.4	All Other Non-Current	13.3	9.3	8.2	6.3	6.8	7.8
100.0	100.0	100.0	Total	100.0	100.0	100.0	100.0	100.0	100.0

LIABILITIES (%)

Hist 1	Hist 2	Hist 3	Item	0-1MM	1-3MM	3-5MM	5-10MM	10-25MM	25MM & OVER
50.9	51.7	46.0	Notes Payable-Short Term	25.9	34.5	36.6	46.3	48.3	45.7
2.3	1.9	1.8	Cur. Mat.-L.T.D.	2.7	2.1	2.7	2.5	1.6	1.7
4.5	4.2	5.1	Trade Payables	4.5	11.3	12.6	5.4	4.5	4.7
.1	.1	.1	Income Taxes Payable	.2	.0	.0	.0	.0	.1
13.0	11.8	11.0	All Other Current	27.6	16.1	10.5	12.8	11.0	10.1
70.7	69.8	63.9	Total Current	60.8	64.1	62.4	67.2	65.5	62.2
7.6	8.1	9.3	Long-Term Debt	16.2	14.5	15.4	9.8	9.1	8.7
.1	.1	.1	Deferred Taxes	.6	.1	.2	.1	.1	.1
3.6	4.1	4.8	All Other Non-Current	9.7	11.5	9.7	7.9	4.7	3.6
18.0	18.0	21.9	Net Worth	12.7	9.8	12.3	15.0	20.7	25.3
100.0	100.0	100.0	Total Liabilities & Net Worth	100.0	100.0	100.0	100.0	100.0	100.0

INCOME DATA (%)

Hist 1	Hist 2	Hist 3	Item	0-1MM	1-3MM	3-5MM	5-10MM	10-25MM	25MM & OVER
100.0	100.0	100.0	Net Sales	100.0	100.0	100.0	100.0	100.0	100.0
13.1	13.4	14.0	Gross Profit	33.1	21.2	15.5	14.7	13.6	13.4
12.9	14.2	14.3	Operating Expenses	34.9	23.7	18.6	15.8	14.3	13.0
.2	-.8	-.3	Operating Profit	-1.8	-2.5	-3.0	-1.2	-.7	.4
-.4	-.6	-.9	All Other Expenses (net)	.8	.3	-.8	-.8	-1.1	-.9
.6	-.2	.6	Profit Before Taxes	-2.6	-2.7	-2.3	-.3	.4	1.3

RATIOS

Current

Hist 1	Hist 2	Hist 3	0-1MM	1-3MM	3-5MM	5-10MM	10-25MM	25MM & OVER
1.3	1.3	1.4	2.9	1.9	2.0	1.5	1.4	1.4
1.1	1.1	1.2	1.4	1.4	1.3	1.3	1.2	1.2
1.0	1.0	1.1	.8	1.1	1.1	1.0	1.1	1.0

Quick

Hist 1	Hist 2	Hist 3	0-1MM	1-3MM	3-5MM	5-10MM	10-25MM	25MM & OVER
.3	.3	.4	1.0	.7	.7	.4	.4	.5
(2472) .2	(2657) .2	(2688) .3	.4	.3	.2	(270) .2	(926) .2	.3
.1	.1	.2	.1	.1	.1	.1	.2	.2

Sales/Receivables

Hist 1	Hist 2	Hist 3	0-1MM	1-3MM	3-5MM	5-10MM	10-25MM	25MM & OVER
3 131.4	3 131.5	3 114.4	0 UND	1 681.2	1 330.8	3 133.3	3 116.8	4 103.4
5 70.3	5 68.1	6 63.5	6 59.5	8 47.7	5 72.8	5 71.5	6 66.2	6 60.2
9 39.5	9 38.7	10 36.1	19 19.5	24 15.5	11 33.7	9 38.4	10 36.2	10 36.8

Cost of Sales/Inventory

Hist 1	Hist 2	Hist 3	0-1MM	1-3MM	3-5MM	5-10MM	10-25MM	25MM & OVER
57 6.4	60 6.0	51 7.2	20 18.0	55 6.6	64 5.7	68 5.4	57 6.4	47 7.8
73 5.0	77 4.7	66 5.6	59 6.2	102 3.6	94 3.9	86 4.2	71 5.1	59 6.2
93 3.9	99 3.7	85 4.3	148 2.5	191 1.9	130 2.8	110 3.3	88 4.1	74 5.0

Cost of Sales/Payables

Hist 1	Hist 2	Hist 3	0-1MM	1-3MM	3-5MM	5-10MM	10-25MM	25MM & OVER
2 205.0	2 201.8	2 165.4	0 UND	3 136.6	2 213.2	2 184.5	2 175.6	2 155.9
3 111.0	3 113.9	4 95.6	6 60.0	10 34.9	6 64.8	4 86.3	4 101.4	4 94.9
6 66.2	6 66.1	7 56.0	16 23.4	19 19.4	12 29.5	8 44.0	6 60.9	6 58.9

Sales/Working Capital

Hist 1	Hist 2	Hist 3	0-1MM	1-3MM	3-5MM	5-10MM	10-25MM	25MM & OVER
18.1	17.4	14.0	3.9	4.7	6.4	9.7	14.7	16.6
34.2	34.7	26.8	11.0	8.3	13.7	19.2	26.7	30.5
129.1	230.1	99.1	UND	49.4	62.9	106.7	75.4	115.5

EBIT/Interest

Hist 1	Hist 2	Hist 3	0-1MM	1-3MM	3-5MM	5-10MM	10-25MM	25MM & OVER
3.7	3.2	6.3		4.2	1.9	3.6	4.6	9.7
(1933) 1.7	(1975) 1.2	(1830) 2.3		(38) 1.5	(55) -.2	(193) 1.2	(626) 1.8	(909) 3.4
.8	-.4	.8		-.2	-3.3	-1.0	.2	1.5

Net Profit + Depr., Dep., Amort./Cur. Mat. L/T/D

Hist 1	Hist 2	Hist 3	0-1MM	1-3MM	3-5MM	5-10MM	10-25MM	25MM & OVER
5.9	3.7	4.3					4.8	4.3
(166) 2.0	(145) 1.6	(157) 1.8				(42)	1.5	(104) 2.1
.6	.4	.5					.3	.7

Fixed/Worth

Hist 1	Hist 2	Hist 3	0-1MM	1-3MM	3-5MM	5-10MM	10-25MM	25MM & OVER
.2	.2	.1	.0	.1	.2	.1	.1	.2
.5	.5	.4	.4	.4	.6	.3	.4	.4
1.7	2.2	1.8	UND	1.7	25.8	4.5	2.3	1.4

Debt/Worth

Hist 1	Hist 2	Hist 3	0-1MM	1-3MM	3-5MM	5-10MM	10-25MM	25MM & OVER
2.8	2.8	2.1	.9	1.5	1.4	2.0	2.3	2.0
5.6	5.4	4.3	5.6	3.1	6.1	4.6	4.8	4.0
16.9	18.4	12.6	UND	15.7	-198.3	98.8	18.8	8.8

% Profit Before Taxes/Tangible Net Worth

Hist 1	Hist 2	Hist 3	0-1MM	1-3MM	3-5MM	5-10MM	10-25MM	25MM & OVER
36.2	24.6	34.5	86.4	11.2	7.9	19.3	26.6	44.3
(2116) 15.7	(2203) 6.2	(2283) 14.3	(17) 15.1	(47) 1.7	(59) -7.9	(207) 5.7	(765) 8.9	(1188) 21.3
1.5	-9.3	1.0	-1.7	-22.4	-38.4	-10.3	-3.0	6.7

% Profit Before Taxes/Total Assets

Hist 1	Hist 2	Hist 3	0-1MM	1-3MM	3-5MM	5-10MM	10-25MM	25MM & OVER
6.0	4.0	6.9	14.2	3.0	1.7	3.4	5.2	8.6
2.1	.5	2.7	.0	.2	-3.3	.7	1.5	4.3
-.7	-3.2	-.4	-3.2	-8.5	-10.4	-4.0	-1.3	1.2

Sales/Net Fixed Assets

Hist 1	Hist 2	Hist 3	0-1MM	1-3MM	3-5MM	5-10MM	10-25MM	25MM & OVER
142.4	129.0	130.2	UND	141.2	117.8	162.1	139.2	115.6
67.7	60.4	57.4	70.0	47.6	40.2	74.3	61.4	53.4
28.9	25.4	23.2	9.2	16.3	15.8	31.2	25.8	21.6

Sales/Total Assets

Hist 1	Hist 2	Hist 3	0-1MM	1-3MM	3-5MM	5-10MM	10-25MM	25MM & OVER
4.5	4.1	4.3	3.6	3.6	3.6	3.9	4.2	4.6
3.6	3.3	3.4	1.4	1.8	2.6	3.0	3.4	3.7
2.8	2.6	2.6	.4	.9	1.5	2.4	2.6	2.8

% Depr., Dep., Amort./Sales

Hist 1	Hist 2	Hist 3	0-1MM	1-3MM	3-5MM	5-10MM	10-25MM	25MM & OVER
.1	.2	.2		.2	.2	.2	.2	.2
(2150) .2	(2297) .3	(2319) .3		(42) .6	(61) .4	(208) .3	(794) .3	(1206) .3
.4	.5	.6		1.0	.8	.5	.5	.6

% Officers', Directors' Owners' Comp/Sales

Hist 1	Hist 2	Hist 3	0-1MM	1-3MM	3-5MM	5-10MM	10-25MM	25MM & OVER
.3	.3	.3		.6	.6	.4	.4	.3
(1514) .5	(1558) .5	(1541) .6		(25) 2.3	(43) 1.2	(136) .9	(569) .7	(761) .5
1.0	1.0	1.2		5.5	2.3	1.5	1.3	.9

Net Sales ($) / Total Assets ($)

Hist 1	Hist 2	Hist 3		0-1MM	1-3MM	3-5MM	5-10MM	10-25MM	25MM & OVER
126662900M	118960218M	107537821M	Net Sales ($)	8750M	118094M	318452M	2074878M	15749398M	89268249M
35620298M	36681715M	34551873M	Total Assets ($)	21916M	85741M	180927M	894414M	5247509M	28121366M

© RMA 2010   M = $ thousand   MM = $ million
See Pages 9 through 22 for Explanation of Ratios and Data

Current Data Sorted by Assets   Comparative Historical Data

						Type of Statement		
	2	8	10	3	2	Unqualified	14	17
2	3	24	5	1		Reviewed	23	43
19	46	30	4			Compiled	134	119
92	106	33	1		3	Tax Returns	214	256
18	46	70	12	1		Other	181	188
0-500M	55 (4/1-9/30/09) 500M-2MM	2-10MM	486 (10/1/09-3/31/10) 10-50MM	50-100MM	100-250MM		4/1/05-3/31/06 ALL	4/1/06-3/31/07 ALL
131	203	165	32	5	5	NUMBER OF STATEMENTS	566	623
%	%	%	%	%	%	**ASSETS**	%	%
11.2	8.2	6.9	6.1			Cash & Equivalents	8.6	7.8
6.7	12.3	18.1	47.1			Trade Receivables (net)	12.7	13.9
66.9	62.9	51.7	23.9			Inventory	58.4	59.9
1.6	2.1	3.4	4.5			All Other Current	2.5	2.1
86.5	85.4	80.0	81.6			Total Current	82.2	83.7
9.1	9.4	11.2	12.5			Fixed Assets (net)	11.4	11.1
1.5	.7	1.8	1.5			Intangibles (net)	1.2	1.0
2.9	4.4	7.0	4.4			All Other Non-Current	5.3	4.1
100.0	100.0	100.0	100.0			Total	100.0	100.0
						LIABILITIES		
43.7	36.9	39.9	39.9			Notes Payable-Short Term	36.5	38.7
5.4	4.2	1.6	2.5			Cur. Mat.-L.T.D.	2.1	3.2
5.7	6.2	3.9	3.8			Trade Payables	5.3	5.3
.2	.0	.1	.2			Income Taxes Payable	.1	.2
13.7	12.3	12.9	9.7			All Other Current	11.5	10.3
68.6	59.7	58.3	56.1			Total Current	55.5	57.7
18.5	10.3	9.0	6.9			Long-Term Debt	12.1	11.4
.0	.0	.1	.1			Deferred Taxes	.0	.1
13.3	13.0	8.7	7.1			All Other Non-Current	7.2	8.3
-.4	17.0	23.8	29.9			Net Worth	25.1	22.4
100.0	100.0	100.0	100.0			Total Liabilities & Net Worth	100.0	100.0
						INCOME DATA		
100.0	100.0	100.0	100.0			Net Sales	100.0	100.0
18.6	18.9	20.0	32.3			Gross Profit	19.5	19.2
18.2	18.3	17.6	25.9			Operating Expenses	17.2	17.0
.4	.7	2.4	6.4			Operating Profit	2.3	2.2
.9	.5	.9	1.7			All Other Expenses (net)	.6	.7
-.4	.2	1.5	4.7			Profit Before Taxes	1.7	1.5
						RATIOS		
2.9	2.9	2.0	1.8				2.5	2.4
1.3	1.5	1.3	1.4			Current	1.4	1.3
1.0	1.1	1.1	1.2				1.1	1.1
.6	.7	.7	1.2				.8	.8
(130) .2	(201) .2	.3	1.1			Quick	(563) .3	(620) .2
.1	.1	.1	.3				.1	.1
0 UND	0 UND	1 251.8	3 124.1				0 UND	0 UND
0 UND	3 119.1	7 55.7	151 2.4			Sales/Receivables	3 138.9	3 111.9
3 109.5	13 27.6	16 22.2	331 1.1				11 32.8	12 29.4
34 10.8	46 7.9	47 7.7	38 9.5				40 9.2	40 9.2
59 6.1	76 4.8	65 5.6	54 6.8			Cost of Sales/Inventory	60 6.0	62 5.9
97 3.8	110 3.3	94 3.9	68 5.4				90 4.0	93 3.9
0 UND	0 UND	1 409.6	3 117.7				0 UND	0 UND
0 UND	2 158.6	3 121.1	7 52.9			Cost of Sales/Payables	2 169.9	2 174.3
3 122.2	7 50.8	7 52.9	17 22.0				7 52.4	7 55.3
9.4	6.0	7.9	3.6				8.1	7.9
29.3	14.3	17.0	5.5			Sales/Working Capital	19.3	18.9
-112.4	75.4	81.2	16.5				75.2	87.2
4.8	4.9	5.6	4.0				4.6	3.8
(114) 1.7	(175) 1.7	(147) 2.6	(28) 3.1			EBIT/Interest	(489) 2.1	(542) 1.8
-.5	.7	1.1	1.9				1.0	1.0
		6.1					5.9	5.0
	(11) 1.3					Net Profit + Depr., Dep., Amort./Cur. Mat. L/T/D	(20) 2.7	(24) 1.7
		.1					1.0	.8
.0	.0	.1	.0				.0	.0
.3	.2	.3	.2			Fixed/Worth	.2	.3
-2.1	1.9	2.4	.7				1.5	1.7
1.6	1.2	1.5	1.7				1.2	1.4
20.8	4.2	3.3	2.7			Debt/Worth	3.9	4.2
-4.5	56.3	13.9	4.0				16.2	18.2
104.0	39.3	33.1	36.1			% Profit Before Taxes/Tangible	55.6	56.6
(77) 24.5	(156) 14.4	(141) 14.5	24.1			Net Worth	(471) 22.0	(525) 21.2
-7.2	2.2	3.5	18.3				4.9	3.7
14.1	8.0	8.2	8.6			% Profit Before Taxes/Total	12.4	10.8
1.6	3.1	3.9	6.4			Assets	4.4	4.2
-9.6	-.7	.2	4.3				.2	.1
UND	555.0	189.7	105.9				426.7	461.7
240.5	108.6	58.5	36.6			Sales/Net Fixed Assets	97.7	94.7
33.5	30.1	25.0	8.4				29.2	26.1
8.9	5.1	4.6	3.3				6.1	6.3
5.0	3.7	3.3	1.3			Sales/Total Assets	4.1	4.2
3.1	2.4	1.8	.9				2.5	2.5
.2	.1	.1	.3				.1	.1
(69) .4	(142) .2	(127) .2	(27) .5			% Depr., Dep., Amort./Sales	(383) .2	(440) .2
1.0	.6	.5	1.0				.6	.5
1.4	1.0	.6					.8	.8
(77) 2.4	(118) 2.0	(87) 1.0				% Officers', Directors' Owners' Comp/Sales	(326) 1.6	(344) 1.5
4.2	3.1	2.3					3.2	2.9
236818M	816917M	2388580M	1479898M	305099M	4072000M	Net Sales ($)	9235241M	9367490M
36031M	209415M	690789M	751669M	377351M	879784M	Total Assets ($)	2652755M	2910959M

© RMA 2010

M = $ thousand   MM = $ million
See Pages 9 through 22 for Explanation of Ratios and Data

Comparative Historical Data   Current Data Sorted by Sales

			Type of Statement						
20	17	25	Unqualified	1	1	1	2	4	17
25	27	35	Reviewed	1	3	3	11	13	4
102	108	99	Compiled	7	32	23	19	10	8
212	224	235	Tax Returns	45	79	46	40	19	6
189	192	147	Other	8	29	24	27	38	21
4/1/07-3/31/08 ALL	4/1/08-3/31/09 ALL	4/1/09-3/31/10 ALL		55 (4/1-9/30/09)			486 (10/1/09-3/31/10)		
548	568	541	NUMBER OF STATEMENTS	0-1MM 61	1-3MM 144	3-5MM 97	5-10MM 99	10-25MM 84	25MM & OVER 56
%	%	%	**ASSETS**	%	%	%	%	%	%
7.5	7.7	8.3	Cash & Equivalents	9.8	8.5	8.2	8.4	7.3	8.1
13.1	14.3	15.1	Trade Receivables (net)	13.4	15.7	10.0	15.5	14.0	25.2
59.1	56.8	57.5	Inventory	59.4	58.6	64.5	56.6	55.0	45.7
3.8	2.6	2.6	All Other Current	1.6	2.3	3.2	2.5	3.3	3.0
83.5	81.5	83.6	Total Current	84.3	85.0	86.0	83.0	79.5	82.0
10.6	11.8	10.2	Fixed Assets (net)	11.3	10.5	6.9	11.1	10.6	11.6
.8	1.1	1.2	Intangibles (net)	1.1	1.6	.4	1.0	1.6	1.7
5.1	5.7	5.0	All Other Non-Current	3.3	2.8	6.7	4.9	8.4	4.7
100.0	100.0	100.0	Total	100.0	100.0	100.0	100.0	100.0	100.0
			LIABILITIES						
37.7	42.3	39.8	Notes Payable-Short Term	38.6	41.0	39.4	37.4	40.6	41.9
3.2	2.2	3.6	Cur. Mat.-L.T.D.	3.1	5.6	3.3	3.4	1.8	2.0
5.6	5.0	5.2	Trade Payables	3.8	5.1	6.8	5.9	3.7	5.4
.1	.1	.1	Income Taxes Payable	.2	.1	.1	.1	.2	.1
10.8	12.3	12.7	All Other Current	8.6	12.7	11.6	14.9	15.1	11.2
57.4	61.9	61.3	Total Current	54.3	64.5	61.1	61.6	61.4	60.5
11.7	11.7	11.8	Long-Term Debt	16.1	17.8	9.6	8.8	7.3	7.0
.0	.0	.1	Deferred Taxes	.0	.0	.0	.1	.0	.1
8.2	8.5	11.3	All Other Non-Current	21.7	10.8	11.7	8.5	9.8	7.3
22.7	17.9	15.6	Net Worth	7.8	6.8	17.5	21.0	21.5	25.0
100.0	100.0	100.0	Total Liabilities & Net Worth	100.0	100.0	100.0	100.0	100.0	100.0
			INCOME DATA						
100.0	100.0	100.0	Net Sales	100.0	100.0	100.0	100.0	100.0	100.0
19.6	20.2	20.2	Gross Profit	25.6	21.3	18.1	18.9	16.8	22.6
17.4	18.5	18.6	Operating Expenses	26.2	20.0	16.7	16.7	15.3	18.7
2.2	1.7	1.6	Operating Profit	-.5	1.3	1.4	2.2	1.6	3.9
.8	.9	.8	All Other Expenses (net)	1.4	.5	1.1	1.0	.3	.8
1.4	.8	.8	Profit Before Taxes	-1.9	.8	.3	1.3	1.3	3.2
			RATIOS						
2.3	2.1	2.4	Current	6.4	3.0	2.9	1.8	1.9	1.7
1.4	1.3	1.4		1.6	1.5	1.4	1.3	1.3	1.3
1.1	1.0	1.1		1.1	1.0	1.1	1.1	1.0	1.1
.7	.8	.7	Quick	1.4	1.0	.5	.7	.6	1.1
(546) .2	(566) .2	(538) .3		(60) .2	(143) .3	(96) .2	.3	.3	.4
.1	.1	.1		.1	.1	.1	.1	.1	.2
0 UND	0 UND	0 UND	Sales/Receivables	0 UND	0 UND	0 UND	0 999.8	0 896.1	2 196.1
3 117.3	3 138.4	3 119.8		0 UND	2 149.3	2 214.1	5 70.4	4 92.0	10 35.3
15 24.8	14 26.5	15 25.1		23 15.9	26 14.2	7 55.6	13 27.4	12 30.0	53 6.9
41 8.9	40 9.0	43 8.5	Cost of Sales/Inventory	62 5.9	44 8.2	43 8.6	42 8.7	39 9.4	36 10.0
65 5.6	65 5.6	65 5.6		107 3.4	77 4.7	67 5.4	60 6.1	60 6.1	49 7.5
97 3.8	101 3.6	100 3.6		160 2.3	115 3.2	103 3.6	88 4.1	74 4.9	67 5.5
0 UND	0 UND	0 UND	Cost of Sales/Payables	0 UND	0 UND	0 UND	1 422.2	1 366.7	2 242.4
2 172.2	2 167.9	2 181.9		0 UND	1 483.3	2 185.4	3 116.2	2 149.8	4 85.0
7 49.2	7 53.2	7 52.0		4 90.3	6 59.7	6 62.3	7 50.2	6 60.1	9 39.8
6.9	7.1	6.7	Sales/Working Capital	3.0	4.7	8.1	7.9	10.0	5.8
18.9	19.6	15.9		12.6	13.9	15.7	19.9	19.2	17.7
77.1	214.4	102.0		45.4	150.7	87.1	110.8	128.4	68.0
4.5	4.0	4.9	EBIT/Interest	3.2	5.6	4.4	3.5	5.4	9.0
(485) 1.9	(491) 1.5	(472) 2.1		(47) 1.1	(127) 2.0	(88) 1.8	(92) 1.8	(71) 2.8	(47) 3.1
1.0	.1	.7		-1.0	.0	.9	.9	1.3	2.1
11.8	14.1	6.4	Net Profit + Depr., Dep., Amort./Cur. Mat. L/T/D						
(16) 2.0	(16) 3.1	(21) 3.4							
1.0	.9	.5							
.0	.0	.0	Fixed/Worth	.0	.0	.0	.1	.1	.1
.2	.3	.3		.2	.3	.2	.3	.3	.3
1.4	3.8	4.0		-13.7	-3.3	1.9	4.9	2.5	.9
1.5	1.6	1.4	Debt/Worth	1.4	1.2	1.0	1.7	1.4	1.9
3.9	4.3	4.1		12.4	5.3	3.6	4.0	3.4	3.2
16.0	33.7	189.5		-6.2	-9.8	62.9	42.1	18.4	5.5
48.1	39.9	39.4	% Profit Before Taxes/Tangible Net Worth	39.2	37.9	50.8	29.3	37.0	42.7
(461) 20.2	(445) 13.9	(414) 17.7		(37) 10.3	(99) 17.7	(77) 18.6	(77) 11.4	(72) 17.1	(52) 25.5
3.8	-5.3	2.8		-11.8	.2	.9	.9	5.6	16.3
12.2	8.9	9.1	% Profit Before Taxes/Total Assets	6.4	11.8	9.8	6.0	9.1	10.5
3.9	2.2	3.9		.0	4.0	3.5	2.6	5.0	6.3
.1	-4.0	-.8		-10.4	-3.5	-.7	-.5	1.1	3.4
526.3	408.0	463.8	Sales/Net Fixed Assets	UND	667.0	999.8	273.8	182.2	221.8
97.5	79.5	90.7		174.0	100.0	189.0	64.0	80.6	58.0
25.1	23.7	26.1		13.4	20.0	42.2	26.2	34.1	14.3
5.9	5.5	5.3	Sales/Total Assets	3.8	5.2	5.6	5.9	5.1	6.1
3.8	3.5	3.6		2.5	3.4	4.0	3.7	4.1	4.2
2.4	2.2	2.1		1.2	1.8	2.6	2.2	3.0	1.1
.1	.1	.1	% Depr., Dep., Amort./Sales	.4	.1	.1	.1	.1	.1
(367) .3	(383) .3	(372) .3		(30) .9	(91) .4	(64) .2	(78) .3	(68) .2	(41) .3
.5	.6	.7		1.8	.8	.5	.5	.4	.8
.8	.8	.9	% Officers', Directors' Owners' Comp/Sales	2.0	1.6	1.1	.7	.5	.5
(301) 1.6	(295) 1.7	(294) 1.8		(24) 4.2	(88) 2.8	(53) 2.0	(58) 1.5	(46) .8	(25) 1.2
3.0	3.5	3.2		7.1	4.2	3.0	2.4	1.5	2.5
7942528M	6177684M	9299312M	Net Sales ($)	31801M	272269M	374175M	709186M	1314301M	6597580M
2621151M	2311390M	2945039M	Total Assets ($)	19538M	123169M	120887M	256833M	429659M	1994953M

© RMA 2010

M = $ thousand   MM = $ million
See Pages 9 through 22 for Explanation of Ratios and Data

Current Data Sorted by Assets   Comparative Historical Data

Current date sub-headers: 47 (4/1-9/30/09)   350 (10/1/09-3/31/10)

Type of Statement	0-500M	500M-2MM	2-10MM	10-50MM	50-100MM	100-250MM		4/1/05-3/31/06 ALL	4/1/06-3/31/07 ALL
Unqualified		1	4	5		2		6	6
Reviewed		8	26	8				40	45
Compiled	5	45	52	6				108	89
Tax Returns	13	38	29	1				60	78
Other	4	41	79	30				115	123
NUMBER OF STATEMENTS	22	133	190	50		2		329	341

0-500M	500M-2MM	2-10MM	10-50MM	50-100MM	100-250MM		4/1/05-3/31/06 ALL	4/1/06-3/31/07 ALL
%	%	%	%	%	%	**ASSETS**	%	%
15.7	8.7	7.8	11.5			Cash & Equivalents	8.6	7.2
1.9	1.9	3.2	4.9			Trade Receivables (net)	4.3	2.7
63.0	76.5	71.7	60.9			Inventory	73.5	76.2
1.0	.4	.8	1.2			All Other Current	1.2	.8
81.6	87.6	83.5	78.5			Total Current	87.6	86.9
13.4	8.9	11.3	12.3			Fixed Assets (net)	9.3	9.7
4.0	1.8	3.0	5.9			Intangibles (net)	2.0	1.9
1.1	1.7	2.2	3.3			All Other Non-Current	1.1	1.5
100.0	100.0	100.0	100.0			Total	100.0	100.0
						LIABILITIES		
31.4	47.3	46.9	44.8			Notes Payable-Short Term	51.2	51.9
2.1	3.1	4.2	.6			Cur. Mat.-L.T.D.	2.0	2.5
10.4	5.7	5.9	7.9			Trade Payables	6.3	6.4
.0	.0	.1	.3			Income Taxes Payable	.1	.1
15.1	7.1	8.1	6.5			All Other Current	6.8	7.7
59.0	63.3	65.1	60.1			Total Current	66.4	68.6
29.0	8.4	9.0	8.1			Long-Term Debt	6.1	6.4
.0	.0	.1	.0			Deferred Taxes	.0	.0
4.0	5.9	3.4	5.0			All Other Non-Current	3.2	3.5
8.1	22.4	22.5	26.9			Net Worth	24.2	21.5
100.0	100.0	100.0	100.0			Total Liabilities & Net Worth	100.0	100.0
						INCOME DATA		
100.0	100.0	100.0	100.0			Net Sales	100.0	100.0
29.9	22.5	20.3	19.2			Gross Profit	20.1	20.8
35.6	22.2	19.4	17.5			Operating Expenses	17.4	18.3
-5.7	.4	.9	1.7			Operating Profit	2.7	2.5
.9	1.3	1.4	.9			All Other Expenses (net)	1.0	1.5
-6.6	-.9	-.5	.8			Profit Before Taxes	1.7	.9

(Columns 50-100MM shown as "DATA NOT AVAILABLE")

RATIOS

0-500M	500M-2MM	2-10MM	10-50MM	50-100MM	100-250MM		4/1/05-3/31/06 ALL	4/1/06-3/31/07 ALL
7.0	1.9	1.6	1.4			Current	1.5	1.4
1.7	1.3	1.3	1.2				1.2	1.2
1.1	1.1	1.1	1.1				1.1	1.1
1.1	.3	.3	.4			Quick	.3	.2
.2	.1	.1	.1				(328) .1	.1
.0	.0	.0	.1				.1	.1
0 UND	0 UND	1 378.1	2 239.7			Sales/Receivables	0 999.8	0 999.8
0 UND	1 344.2	3 120.1	4 86.1				2 237.9	2 211.6
5 69.7	3 125.6	7 55.1	10 36.0				5 66.5	4 85.1
52 7.0	113 3.2	113 3.2	101 3.6			Cost of Sales/Inventory	101 3.6	110 3.3
132 2.8	160 2.3	149 2.4	141 2.6				135 2.7	147 2.5
200 1.8	239 1.5	196 1.9	180 2.0				184 2.0	203 1.8
0 UND	0 UND	1 256.2	4 100.3			Cost of Sales/Payables	1 412.2	1 410.4
3 114.1	2 177.1	4 88.7	7 48.8				3 123.5	3 114.9
17 21.2	6 61.2	11 34.7	15 24.3				7 50.5	9 41.3
3.2	4.8	7.5	8.7			Sales/Working Capital	8.3	8.5
7.4	10.3	13.7	14.0				16.6	17.0
NM	27.1	34.6	27.1				37.9	36.9
.9	2.5	2.7	3.2			EBIT/Interest	3.3	2.4
(19) -.2	(127) 1.0	(182) 1.2	(47) 1.3				(308) 1.6	(317) 1.4
-5.4	.0	.3	.1				1.0	.9
		6.6				Net Profit + Depr., Dep., Amort./Cur. Mat. L/T/D	7.2	17.9
	(10) 1.3						(42) 3.5	(28) 6.0
	.0						.9	2.9
.1	.1	.1	.1			Fixed/Worth	.1	.1
.9	.2	.3	.4				.3	.3
-.4	1.0	1.3	1.5				.8	1.1
2.1	1.4	2.1	2.0			Debt/Worth	2.4	2.5
10.8	3.7	3.8	4.1				4.3	5.2
-3.6	11.5	9.3	8.3				9.7	11.5
35.2	20.5	23.2	29.2			% Profit Before Taxes/Tangible Net Worth	37.4	30.9
(13) -8.3	(108) 1.5	(162) 5.4	(47) 7.4				(303) 14.0	(307) 11.0
-91.4	-16.8	-4.0	-16.3				2.5	.0
.2	4.3	5.0	4.7			% Profit Before Taxes/Total Assets	7.0	5.7
-7.2	.1	.9	1.4				2.5	2.1
-11.4	-4.3	-2.8	-2.6				.3	-.4
175.2	151.5	146.1	104.5			Sales/Net Fixed Assets	155.6	142.4
43.8	49.8	40.4	38.8				57.5	52.8
13.6	17.8	13.5	10.6				21.2	20.6
4.3	3.0	2.8	2.6			Sales/Total Assets	3.2	3.0
2.6	2.2	2.3	2.1				2.6	2.3
1.5	1.6	1.6	1.7				1.8	1.7
.6	.2	.2	.3			% Depr., Dep., Amort./Sales	.2	.2
(17) 1.4	(102) .6	(140) .5	(39) .5				(270) .3	(269) .4
2.7	1.1	1.2	1.0				.8	.8
2.2	1.5	.8	.3			% Officers', Directors' Owners' Comp/Sales	.9	.9
(14) 5.0	(77) 2.5	(115) 1.5	(22) .7				(196) 1.7	(190) 1.9
8.0	4.5	2.5	1.0				2.9	3.3
18208M	385270M	2004979M	2379499M		795666M	Net Sales ($)	7464842M	8876393M
6497M	163888M	877427M	1114482M		277746M	Total Assets ($)	2614240M	2568536M

M = $ thousand   MM = $ million
See Pages 9 through 22 for Explanation of Ratios and Data

Comparative Historical Data | Current Data Sorted by Sales

			Type of Statement						
9	11	12	Unqualified			1	2	3	6
52	52	42	Reviewed		5	8	8	12	9
96	106	108	Compiled	7	29	19	26	22	5
74	96	81	Tax Returns	10	22	20	19	9	1
123	158	154	Other	11	23	19	32	42	27
4/1/07-3/31/08 ALL	4/1/08-3/31/09 ALL	4/1/09-3/31/10 ALL		47 (4/1-9/30/09)			350 (10/1/09-3/31/10)		
				0-1MM	1-3MM	3-5MM	5-10MM	10-25MM	25MM & OVER
354	423	397	NUMBER OF STATEMENTS	28	79	67	87	88	48
%	%	%	ASSETS	%	%	%	%	%	%
6.0	6.3	9.0	Cash & Equivalents	9.6	9.4	8.6	6.4	9.6	12.1
2.8	2.7	2.9	Trade Receivables (net)	2.9	1.1	2.4	2.8	3.6	5.6
77.4	75.8	71.3	Inventory	68.0	75.2	71.8	73.6	71.3	62.5
.8	.5	.7	All Other Current	1.0	.2	.5	.9	1.0	1.1
87.0	85.4	84.0	Total Current	81.4	85.9	83.2	83.7	85.5	81.3
8.9	10.0	10.8	Fixed Assets (net)	14.6	10.3	12.6	10.6	9.1	10.5
2.5	3.1	3.1	Intangibles (net)	2.1	2.2	2.8	2.9	2.8	6.5
1.6	1.6	2.1	All Other Non-Current	2.0	1.7	1.3	2.8	2.7	1.7
100.0	100.0	100.0	Total	100.0	100.0	100.0	100.0	100.0	100.0
			LIABILITIES						
55.9	53.9	45.8	Notes Payable-Short Term	37.8	43.9	46.7	48.0	46.4	46.8
1.8	2.0	3.2	Cur. Mat.-L.T.D.	4.4	2.7	4.5	3.2	3.8	.6
6.5	4.9	6.3	Trade Payables	7.1	7.5	3.6	5.7	7.1	7.6
.1	.1	.1	Income Taxes Payable	.0	.0	.0	.0	.2	.1
5.9	7.9	8.0	All Other Current	17.0	5.7	6.3	9.2	8.0	6.9
70.2	68.8	63.4	Total Current	66.3	59.9	61.0	66.2	65.4	62.0
6.9	9.2	9.7	Long-Term Debt	32.4	10.0	7.2	9.4	7.3	4.8
.0	.0	.0	Deferred Taxes	.0	.0	.0	.0	.1	.1
3.0	2.9	4.5	All Other Non-Current	3.5	7.4	6.0	3.4	2.2	4.6
20.0	19.0	22.3	Net Worth	-2.2	22.7	25.7	21.0	25.0	28.6
100.0	100.0	100.0	Total Liabilities & Net Worth	100.0	100.0	100.0	100.0	100.0	100.0
			INCOME DATA						
100.0	100.0	100.0	Net Sales	100.0	100.0	100.0	100.0	100.0	100.0
20.1	21.2	21.4	Gross Profit	31.8	23.7	19.5	21.3	19.6	17.8
17.5	20.7	20.9	Operating Expenses	37.0	22.9	19.9	20.5	18.1	15.6
2.6	.5	.4	Operating Profit	-5.3	.7	-.4	.7	1.5	2.2
1.9	1.7	1.3	All Other Expenses (net)	1.9	1.5	1.5	1.2	.9	.8
.8	-1.2	-.8	Profit Before Taxes	-7.1	-.8	-1.9	-.5	.6	1.4
			RATIOS						
1.3	1.4	1.6		2.1	2.1	1.8	1.6	1.5	1.5
1.2	1.2	1.3	Current	1.4	1.3	1.3	1.3	1.3	1.3
1.1	1.1	1.1		.9	1.1	1.1	1.0	1.1	1.1
.2	.2	.3		.7	.4	.3	.2	.3	.4
.1	(421) .1	.1	Quick	.1	.1	.1	.1	.2	.2
.0	.0	.0		.0	.0	.0	.1	.1	.1
1 711.0	0 929.6	0 999.8		0 UND	0 UND	0 991.4	1 627.0	1 396.8	2 206.7
2 172.3	2 164.1	2 172.9	Sales/Receivables	1 575.5	1 404.5	2 189.2	3 134.0	3 120.4	5 78.4
5 73.8	6 61.1	6 64.8		11 32.1	3 115.1	5 67.2	6 62.0	7 48.7	10 36.8
117 3.1	121 3.0	109 3.4		164 2.2	126 2.9	116 3.1	112 3.3	104 3.5	82 4.5
152 2.4	173 2.1	148 2.5	Cost of Sales/Inventory	256 1.4	187 2.0	159 2.3	152 2.4	130 2.8	113 3.2
195 1.9	236 1.5	210 1.7		454 .8	270 1.4	211 1.7	186 2.0	160 2.3	148 2.5
1 359.6	1 429.6	1 319.8		0 UND	0 UND	1 554.8	1 339.9	2 179.3	3 116.7
4 102.9	3 125.1	4 100.8	Cost of Sales/Payables	0 UND	3 134.3	3 121.1	3 134.3	5 69.0	6 63.4
8 43.3	8 46.9	11 34.1		17 21.2	8 44.9	7 51.5	10 38.0	11 32.1	13 28.1
10.7	8.1	6.3		2.7	4.0	5.4	7.6	8.3	9.8
20.0	15.6	12.5	Sales/Working Capital	6.1	9.5	9.6	14.4	14.6	14.8
43.9	48.1	30.0		NM	22.0	32.4	54.7	25.7	25.9
1.9	1.9	2.7		1.0	2.4	1.4	2.9	3.2	4.0
(339) 1.3	(398) 1.1	(377) 1.1	EBIT/Interest	(22) -.3	(77) 1.0	(64) .7	(83) 1.3	(84) 1.6	(47) 2.0
.9	-.1	.1		-4.4	-.1	-.7	.3	.5	.5
8.1	8.7	4.8	Net Profit + Depr., Dep.,						
(34) 2.2	(27) 1.7	(19) 1.4	Amort./Cur. Mat. L/T/D						
.1	.0	.0							
.1	.1	.1		.2	.1	.1	.1	.1	.1
.3	.3	.3	Fixed/Worth	5.9	.3	.5	.4	.2	.3
1.1	1.6	1.5		-.4	1.3	2.9	2.0	.6	1.4
3.0	2.6	1.9		2.3	1.4	1.7	2.1	2.1	1.9
5.4	5.2	3.8	Debt/Worth	144.9	3.7	3.7	4.0	3.5	3.9
13.3	15.5	11.3		-4.0	20.0	14.5	10.5	7.1	7.2
28.9	18.4	23.2	% Profit Before Taxes/Tangible	51.4	12.8	13.7	26.3	24.8	46.0
(318) 8.8	(358) 3.2	(332) 5.0	Net Worth	(15) -8.3	(63) 1.3	(54) -2.5	(74) 8.4	(80) 9.7	(46) 13.1
-1.4	-16.4	-9.9		-55.7	-7.3	-25.3	-4.0	-2.0	-6.1
4.2	3.1	4.5	% Profit Before Taxes/Total	.4	3.1	2.5	5.3	6.3	5.9
1.5	.2	.4	Assets	-6.0	.2	-1.5	1.0	2.0	3.0
-.7	-4.5	-3.9		-15.1	-4.7	-5.0	-2.6	-1.6	-1.3
137.0	142.5	132.9		45.4	127.7	125.7	136.6	234.7	123.8
56.3	52.5	42.3	Sales/Net Fixed Assets	15.3	33.8	50.4	36.0	64.4	60.2
21.4	16.9	13.6		6.2	14.1	12.8	15.3	17.2	13.8
2.9	2.7	2.9		2.1	2.6	2.8	3.1	3.1	2.9
2.4	2.1	2.2	Sales/Total Assets	1.1	1.9	2.0	2.3	2.6	2.4
1.8	1.5	1.6		.8	1.4	1.6	1.7	1.9	2.1
.2	.2	.3		.7	.3	.3	.3	.2	.3
(281) .4	(323) .5	(300) .5	% Depr., Dep., Amort./Sales	(21) 1.7	(61) .8	(50) .5	(63) .5	(67) .3	(38) .5
.7	.9	1.2		3.2	1.4	1.1	1.2	.7	.9
.9	.8	.9		2.3	2.0	1.3	.7	.8	.3
(197) 1.7	(233) 1.6	(228) 1.8	% Officers', Directors' Owners' Comp/Sales	(14) 5.6	(48) 3.4	(42) 2.2	(49) 1.7	(51) 1.1	(24) .7
3.0	2.8	3.2		7.7	5.1	3.0	2.8	1.9	1.0
7492176M	7551120M	5583622M	Net Sales ($)	16828M	156483M	259826M	632006M	1334901M	3183578M
3193218M	3637674M	2440040M	Total Assets ($)	16245M	88361M	144276M	304749M	593620M	1292789M

M = $ thousand   MM = $ million
See Pages 9 through 22 for Explanation of Ratios and Data

Current Data Sorted by Assets   Comparative Historical Data

0-500M	500M-2MM	2-10MM	10-50MM	50-100MM	100-250MM	Type of Statement	4/1/05-3/31/06 ALL	4/1/06-3/31/07 ALL
		1	4	1		Unqualified	2	13
	3	38	10			Reviewed	44	45
3	16	65	6			Compiled	90	78
8	17	43				Tax Returns	58	68
2	21	68	18		1	Other	98	143
39 (4/1-9/30/09)		286 (10/1/09-3/31/10)						
13	57	215	38	1	1	NUMBER OF STATEMENTS	292	347
%	%	%	%	%	%	ASSETS	%	%
6.2	7.4	7.7	5.8			Cash & Equivalents	8.7	6.4
.2	4.3	3.7	4.1			Trade Receivables (net)	3.9	3.5
67.4	75.4	61.2	38.3			Inventory	66.9	66.6
1.2	.8	2.0	1.5			All Other Current	1.0	1.3
74.9	87.9	74.6	49.7			Total Current	80.6	77.8
20.0	8.8	13.0	31.1			Fixed Assets (net)	12.1	13.8
1.9	1.8	7.3	14.1			Intangibles (net)	4.9	6.1
3.2	1.6	5.1	4.5			All Other Non-Current	2.4	2.3
100.0	100.0	100.0	100.0			Total	100.0	100.0
						LIABILITIES		
41.3	42.9	30.6	20.7			Notes Payable-Short Term	34.7	34.2
2.0	5.0	5.1	2.8			Cur. Mat.-L.T.D.	2.4	3.4
4.2	12.8	9.4	5.8			Trade Payables	12.7	11.1
.0	.0	.1	.0			Income Taxes Payable	.2	.1
3.9	14.6	11.2	7.8			All Other Current	8.2	9.3
51.5	75.2	56.4	37.1			Total Current	58.2	58.0
23.4	10.8	12.1	21.7			Long-Term Debt	10.5	11.8
.0	.0	.0	.2			Deferred Taxes	.0	.1
4.1	6.7	5.2	3.9			All Other Non-Current	4.4	4.8
20.9	7.3	26.3	37.1			Net Worth	26.8	25.3
100.0	100.0	100.0	100.0			Total Liabilities & Net Worth	100.0	100.0
						INCOME DATA		
100.0	100.0	100.0	100.0			Net Sales	100.0	100.0
35.4	21.8	23.3	25.3			Gross Profit	23.0	22.2
36.0	23.3	23.9	23.8			Operating Expenses	19.8	19.6
-.6	-1.5	-.6	1.5			Operating Profit	3.2	2.6
.5	1.2	.6	.5			All Other Expenses (net)	.5	.6
-1.1	-2.7	-1.2	1.0			Profit Before Taxes	2.7	2.1
						RATIOS		
5.5	1.7	1.8	1.7			Current	1.7	1.6
1.8	1.2	1.3	1.3				1.3	1.3
1.0	.9	1.0	1.0				1.1	1.1
.3	.2	.3	.5			Quick	.4	.3
(12) .0	.1	.1	.2				.2 (345)	.1
.0	.1	.1	.1				.1	.1
0 UND	0 999.8	1 260.9	2 213.2			Sales/Receivables	1 386.0	1 289.0
0 UND	3 137.1	3 113.2	4 89.7				3 116.3	4 99.1
0 UND	6 62.2	8 47.6	9 38.8				7 54.4	6 56.4
75 4.8	92 4.0	93 3.9	82 4.5			Cost of Sales/Inventory	88 4.1	99 3.7
166 2.2	165 2.2	126 2.9	107 3.4				117 3.1	130 2.8
182 2.0	217 1.7	185 2.0	166 2.2				154 2.4	170 2.1
0 UND	3 138.2	5 71.7	5 66.5			Cost of Sales/Payables	5 80.4	4 85.4
0 UND	8 45.0	10 37.8	12 31.4				11 34.3	9 40.6
1 384.5	17 21.0	20 18.4	19 19.0				24 15.5	21 17.2
6.8	7.0	6.2	7.4			Sales/Working Capital	8.3	8.7
12.4	18.7	13.8	16.0				14.1	14.5
UND	-50.8	72.9	-786.3				33.5	29.5
	.9	2.3	6.4			EBIT/Interest	7.0	5.2
(49) -.5		(201) .7	(35) 1.3				(275) 2.6	(321) 2.1
	-1.4	-1.1	.0				1.2	1.0
		.2				Net Profit + Depr., Dep., Amort./Cur. Mat. L/T/D	7.6	4.7
	(13) -.2						(32) 3.0	(24) 2.5
	-1.9						.2	.8
.1	.1	.2	.6			Fixed/Worth	.2	.2
1.3	.5	.5	2.1				.5	.5
UND	-1.2	2.3	-20.9				1.6	3.5
.8	2.2	1.5	1.1			Debt/Worth	1.4	1.8
2.0	6.2	4.0	4.1				3.6	4.2
UND	-13.5	20.4	-56.0				13.0	22.9
418.9	8.9	17.0	13.4			% Profit Before Taxes/Tangible Net Worth	57.0	49.4
(11) 36.1	(39) -12.2	(169) .5	(28) 1.1				(241) 22.7	(286) 21.6
.0	-61.8	-17.2	-18.1				7.4	3.5
16.3	.1	3.2	6.7			% Profit Before Taxes/Total Assets	12.6	10.7
.0	-4.7	-.7	1.8				4.9	4.5
-1.7	-10.1	-5.5	-2.2				1.0	-.1
565.2	116.4	66.9	31.1			Sales/Net Fixed Assets	81.5	81.5
49.2	70.3	27.8	5.4				35.4	29.3
7.7	25.2	12.0	2.2				15.8	13.5
4.6	3.3	2.9	2.3			Sales/Total Assets	3.4	3.1
3.2	2.3	2.2	1.4				2.6	2.3
1.9	1.7	1.5	1.1				2.0	1.8
	.2	.4	1.0			% Depr., Dep., Amort./Sales	.3	.4
	(40) .4	(181) .8	(37) 1.6				(244) .6	(275) .7
	1.1	1.3	2.4				1.0	1.2
	1.6	1.1	.8			% Officers', Directors' Owners' Comp/Sales	.9	.9
	(25) 2.7	(108) 2.0	(15) 1.1				(155) 1.6	(176) 1.4
	4.7	3.3	1.9				3.2	2.8
11126M	204833M	2238186M	1135133M	122918M	428740M	Net Sales ($)	4211764M	4993151M
2595M	75571M	996299M	641383M	58627M	168483M	Total Assets ($)	1615763M	2271006M

© RMA 2010

M = $ thousand   MM = $ million
See Pages 9 through 22 for Explanation of Ratios and Data

Comparative Historical Data | | | | **Current Data Sorted by Sales**

Type of Statement

4/1/07-3/31/08	4/1/08-3/31/09	4/1/09-3/31/10	Type of Statement	0-1MM	1-3MM	3-5MM	5-10MM	10-25MM	25MM & OVER
10	9	6	Unqualified			1	16	27	5
43	35	51	Reviewed						7
57	79	90	Compiled	2	8	16	32	28	4
86	100	68	Tax Returns	6	13	12	24	10	3
127	132	110	Other	2	19	15	25	38	11
ALL	ALL	ALL		39 (4/1-9/30/09)			286 (10/1/09-3/31/10)		
323	355	325	NUMBER OF STATEMENTS	10	40	44	97	104	30

ASSETS

07-08	08-09	09-10		0-1MM	1-3MM	3-5MM	5-10MM	10-25MM	25MM & OVER
%	%	%		%	%	%	%	%	%
6.2	6.8	7.3	Cash & Equivalents	.7	7.1	6.1	7.1	8.7	7.6
3.8	4.4	3.7	Trade Receivables (net)	.0	3.9	3.5	3.5	3.7	5.9
64.8	63.4	61.2	Inventory	69.3	70.7	71.5	61.2	56.8	46.1
1.5	1.3	1.7	All Other Current	2.7	1.9	1.6	1.1	2.0	2.0
76.3	75.8	73.9	Total Current	72.8	83.6	82.8	72.8	71.2	61.6
13.8	14.9	14.9	Fixed Assets (net)	23.3	11.3	11.5	15.0	14.2	24.0
7.1	6.0	6.9	Intangibles (net)	3.3	1.2	3.5	7.5	10.0	8.2
2.8	3.2	4.3	All Other Non-Current	.7	3.9	2.3	4.7	4.6	6.3
100.0	100.0	100.0	Total	100.0	100.0	100.0	100.0	100.0	100.0

LIABILITIES

07-08	08-09	09-10		0-1MM	1-3MM	3-5MM	5-10MM	10-25MM	25MM & OVER
33.6	31.3	32.1	Notes Payable-Short Term	49.4	40.6	42.4	32.2	25.7	21.6
3.6	3.7	4.7	Cur. Mat.-L.T.D.	2.7	9.4	1.6	4.2	4.1	6.9
11.7	12.0	9.4	Trade Payables	3.8	7.7	9.0	11.7	8.7	9.0
.1	.1	.0	Income Taxes Payable	.0	.1	.0	.1	.0	.0
9.7	11.8	11.1	All Other Current	2.1	16.2	13.1	9.9	10.6	10.2
58.7	58.8	57.3	Total Current	57.9	73.9	66.1	58.0	49.1	47.8
13.7	11.5	13.5	Long-Term Debt	48.1	18.1	10.0	10.9	11.7	15.6
.0	.0	.0	Deferred Taxes	.0	.0	.0	.0	.0	.0
4.2	3.8	5.2	All Other Non-Current	3.3	8.2	3.1	3.4	7.8	2.0
23.4	25.8	24.0	Net Worth	-9.4	-.2	20.7	27.7	31.4	34.5
100.0	100.0	100.0	Total Liabilties & Net Worth	100.0	100.0	100.0	100.0	100.0	100.0

INCOME DATA

07-08	08-09	09-10		0-1MM	1-3MM	3-5MM	5-10MM	10-25MM	25MM & OVER
100.0	100.0	100.0	Net Sales	100.0	100.0	100.0	100.0	100.0	100.0
23.1	23.1	23.8	Gross Profit	30.6	25.2	22.9	22.9	23.9	23.6
21.0	21.7	24.3	Operating Expenses	35.5	26.6	24.4	24.0	23.1	22.7
2.1	1.4	-.5	Operating Profit	-5.0	-1.4	-1.4	-1.1	.8	.8
.5	.4	.7	All Other Expenses (net)	1.4	2.7	.7	.5	.3	-.2
1.6	1.0	-1.2	Profit Before Taxes	-6.3	-4.1	-2.1	-1.6	.5	1.0

RATIOS

07-08	08-09	09-10		0-1MM	1-3MM	3-5MM	5-10MM	10-25MM	25MM & OVER
1.6 / 1.3 / 1.1	1.7 / 1.3 / 1.0	1.8 / 1.2 / 1.0	Current	4.2 / 1.0 / .9	1.5 / 1.1 / .9	1.9 / 1.2 / 1.1	1.6 / 1.2 / 1.0	2.0 / 1.5 / 1.1	1.8 / 1.2 / 1.0
.3 / (322) .1 / .1	.3 / (354) .1 / .1	.3 / (324) .1 / .1	Quick	.2 / .1 / .0	.3 / .1 / .0	.2 / .1 / .1	.4 / .2 / .1	.7 / .2 / .1	
2 213.4 / 4 95.4 / 7 51.6	1 282.9 / 4 97.9 / 7 44.7	1 360.7 / 3 119.2 / 7 50.8	Sales/Receivables	0 UND / 0 UND / 0 UND	0 UND / 3 114.1 / 10 35.8	1 441.0 / 3 120.9 / 6 60.0	1 282.9 / 3 108.1 / 7 49.8	1 279.9 / 3 114.4 / 7 50.0	2 202.8 / 4 83.5 / 9 38.8
94 3.9 / 124 2.9 / 159 2.3	94 3.9 / 120 3.0 / 163 2.2	92 4.0 / 127 2.9 / 186 2.0	Cost of Sales/Inventory	161 2.3 / 182 2.0 / 256 1.4	164 2.2 / 223 1.6 / 290 1.3	130 2.8 / 182 2.0 / 258 1.4	106 3.5 / 134 2.7 / 179 2.0	83 4.4 / 102 3.6 / 131 2.8	66 5.5 / 79 4.6 / 107 3.4
4 82.6 / 9 41.9 / 19 19.3	5 76.5 / 9 40.2 / 22 16.8	5 79.7 / 9 39.1 / 19 19.2	Cost of Sales/Payables	0 UND / 0 UND / 1 555.4	1 386.6 / 10 36.6 / 26 14.0	5 78.4 / 9 42.1 / 18 20.7	6 62.5 / 10 37.8 / 25 14.7	5 78.9 / 10 37.5 / 18 20.3	4 96.3 / 10 36.0 / 16 23.3
8.5 / 15.0 / 44.8	8.1 / 16.5 / 78.5	6.8 / 15.2 / 502.6	Sales/Working Capital	4.8 / UND / UND	5.7 / 20.5 / -17.1	5.5 / 10.4 / 59.1	7.2 / 15.5 / 464.1	6.8 / 12.8 / 51.5	9.3 / 28.1 / -121.3
4.5 / (293) 1.6 / .8	4.9 / (328) 1.5 / .4	2.6 / (295) .6 / -1.0	EBIT/Interest		.9 / (37) .1 / -1.1	1.4 / (37) .4 / -1.2	1.5 / (93) .2 / -1.5	5.1 / (93) 1.4 / -.9	11.4 / 1.6 / -.1
11.1 / (20) 1.5 / .2	8.7 / (27) 1.6 / .7	.5 / (21) .0 / -1.0	Net Profit + Depr., Dep., Amort./Cur. Mat. L/T/D						
.2 / .6 / 4.0	.2 / .5 / 3.6	.2 / .6 / 5.2	Fixed/Worth	.4 / 44.0 / -.4	.1 / .9 / -1.8	.1 / .5 / 4.1	.2 / .6 / 2.5	.2 / .6 / -7.0	.3 / 1.2 / 6.6
2.0 / 4.5 / 21.6	1.5 / 3.8 / 20.2	1.5 / 4.3 / 89.2	Debt/Worth	1.8 / 105.0 / -2.6	3.5 / 8.6 / -8.8	1.4 / 4.6 / 16.0	1.7 / 3.9 / 14.0	1.1 / 3.1 / -26.5	1.1 / 3.7 / 35.9
44.2 / (257) 15.7 / 1.2	31.8 / (286) 9.9 / -2.1	15.9 / (249) -.2 / -19.5	% Profit Before Taxes/Tangible Net Worth		11.6 / (24) -11.9 / -44.5	3.6 / (36) -5.1 / -30.3	7.5 / (81) -5.2 / -31.2	34.3 / (77) 8.4 / -4.2	23.5 / (24) 5.3 / -21.0
10.1 / 2.7 / -.6	7.6 / 1.8 / -2.1	3.8 / -.9 / -5.8	% Profit Before Taxes/Total Assets	2.1 / .0 / -12.5	.0 / -4.2 / -10.0	.6 / -2.3 / -8.0	2.1 / -2.2 / -6.9	7.9 / 1.8 / -3.5	9.1 / 2.5 / -2.8
74.5 / 29.5 / 13.1	88.1 / 33.1 / 13.7	77.7 / 28.8 / 10.0	Sales/Net Fixed Assets	UND / 23.3 / 3.6	130.4 / 37.5 / 5.6	86.1 / 33.2 / 9.7	61.1 / 22.2 / 10.2	82.8 / 29.3 / 12.7	63.5 / 19.0 / 4.7
3.2 / 2.5 / 1.7	3.1 / 2.4 / 1.8	2.9 / 2.2 / 1.5	Sales/Total Assets	2.7 / 1.9 / 1.1	2.3 / 1.6 / 1.0	2.4 / 1.9 / 1.2	2.8 / 2.0 / 1.5	3.3 / 2.5 / 1.8	3.5 / 2.6 / 2.1
.4 / (271) .7 / 1.3	.4 / (278) .7 / 1.2	.4 / (266) .8 / 1.5	% Depr., Dep., Amort./Sales		.3 / (25) 1.0 / 1.8	.3 / (36) .5 / 1.0	.4 / (83) .8 / 1.3	.4 / (89) .8 / 1.4	.6 / (28) 1.3 / 2.3
.8 / (158) 1.4 / 2.9	1.0 / (193) 1.7 / 2.8	1.1 / (153) 2.0 / 3.9	% Officers', Directors' Owners' Comp/Sales		2.2 / (20) 4.2 / 5.0	1.2 / (20) 2.0 / 4.3	1.1 / (55) 2.0 / 3.5	.8 / (46) 1.6 / 2.7	.7 / (11) 2.2 / 4.6
4427901M	5538136M	4140936M	Net Sales ($)	3825M	79830M	175901M	718920M	1449448M	1713012M
2021485M	2578095M	1942958M	Total Assets ($)	2372M	64328M	105545M	410841M	648979M	710893M

© RMA 2010

M = $ thousand   MM = $ million
See Pages 9 through 22 for Explanation of Ratios and Data

RETAIL—Boat Dealers NAICS 441222

Current Data Sorted by Assets

Comparative Historical Data

Type of Statement	0-500M	500M-2MM	2-10MM	10-50MM	50-100MM	100-250MM		7	3
Unqualified									
Reviewed		7	15	8	1	1		39	41
Compiled	3	25	21	4				63	77
Tax Returns	11	28	14					55	61
Other	4	29	44	14				104	83
		32 (4/1-9/30/09)		201 (10/1/09-3/31/10)				4/1/05-3/31/06 ALL	4/1/06-3/31/07 ALL
NUMBER OF STATEMENTS	18	89	95	29	1	1		268	265
ASSETS	%	%	%	%	%	%		%	%
Cash & Equivalents	17.0	8.8	6.9	7.8				6.2	6.9
Trade Receivables (net)	7.7	3.6	4.8	8.8				3.9	3.3
Inventory	41.6	68.4	64.0	52.8				72.9	73.0
All Other Current	2.6	1.1	1.5	1.2				1.5	1.5
Total Current	68.8	81.9	77.2	70.6				84.5	84.7
Fixed Assets (net)	18.2	14.9	16.8	21.8				12.2	11.2
Intangibles (net)	.5	1.7	3.8	5.1				1.8	1.7
All Other Non-Current	12.5	1.5	2.2	2.5				1.5	2.3
Total	100.0	100.0	100.0	100.0				100.0	100.0
LIABILITIES									
Notes Payable-Short Term	17.7	40.1	40.2	44.8				48.1	45.9
Cur. Mat.-L.T.D.	.7	4.5	2.7	1.1				1.7	2.5
Trade Payables	10.6	5.1	5.6	6.8				7.5	6.6
Income Taxes Payable	.1	.1	.2	.0				.1	.1
All Other Current	21.4	10.3	11.7	6.2				10.3	10.1
Total Current	50.5	60.1	60.4	58.9				67.8	65.2
Long-Term Debt	23.5	16.2	15.5	14.1				11.6	11.7
Deferred Taxes	.0	.1	.1	.1				.3	.1
All Other Non-Current	18.9	5.9	2.0	3.6				3.1	4.0
Net Worth	7.1	17.8	22.1	23.4				17.2	19.0
Total Liabilities & Net Worth	100.0	100.0	100.0	100.0				100.0	100.0
INCOME DATA									
Net Sales	100.0	100.0	100.0	100.0				100.0	100.0
Gross Profit	35.2	28.1	24.4	20.3				23.9	23.6
Operating Expenses	37.7	26.3	23.2	20.0				20.6	20.5
Operating Profit	-2.5	1.9	1.1	.3				3.2	3.2
All Other Expenses (net)	.7	2.6	2.3	1.7				1.4	1.8
Profit Before Taxes	-3.2	-.7	-1.2	-1.4				1.8	1.4
RATIOS									
Current	4.9	2.0	1.6	1.3				1.4	1.6
	1.5	1.4	1.2	1.2				1.2	1.2
	.8	1.1	1.0	1.1				1.0	1.1
Quick	1.1	.5	.3	.5				.2	.3
	.5	.2	.1	.2				.1 (264)	.1
	.2	.0	.1	.1				.0	.0
Sales/Receivables	0 UND	0 999.8	2 221.4	4 88.8				1 581.1	1 394.9
	1 313.3	3 145.0	6 66.2	8 47.1				3 112.5	3 109.8
	9 39.5	10 35.2	15 24.5	13 27.3				8 44.9	8 47.7
Cost of Sales/Inventory	0 UND	98 3.7	135 2.7	105 3.5				133 2.7	132 2.8
	37 9.8	184 2.0	213 1.7	198 1.8				185 2.0	196 1.9
	63 5.8	284 1.3	320 1.1	333 1.1				241 1.5	259 1.4
Cost of Sales/Payables	0 UND	0 UND	2 192.7	2 184.6				1 300.4	1 411.8
	0 UND	3 115.9	8 44.4	9 40.8				5 79.3	4 99.8
	13 28.6	10 36.2	17 21.2	17 21.4				15 24.7	11 32.1
Sales/Working Capital	7.6	4.2	5.4	6.4				7.5	6.7
	20.3	7.5	8.8	11.1				16.2	13.1
	-24.5	36.7	110.8	33.1				58.9	49.3
EBIT/Interest	1.8	2.6	2.2	1.3				3.4	3.0
	(14) -1.4	(85) 1.1	(92) 1.1	(28) .8				(256) 1.6	(253) 1.5
	-5.5	.1	.1	-1.8				1.1	1.0
Net Profit + Depr., Dep., Amort./Cur. Mat. L/T/D			1.4					5.5	5.1
		(15) .6						(42) 2.4	(30) 1.8
			-.6					1.3	.7
Fixed/Worth	.1	.2	.2	.4				.2	.2
	.8	.5	.8	1.2				.6	.4
	-.4	-3.7	4.6	3.3				3.2	2.1
Debt/Worth	.3	1.4	2.2	2.5				2.9	2.6
	7.0	3.4	4.8	7.5				7.3	6.3
	-3.9	-46.4	24.3	14.8				21.4	28.8
% Profit Before Taxes/Tangible Net Worth	31.9	31.0	17.7	6.7				44.7	38.8
	(11) -2.7	(65) 4.5	(79) 5.3	-7.7				(222) 17.5	(224) 19.5
	-42.6	-6.5	-11.8	-36.3				4.9	1.1
% Profit Before Taxes/Total Assets	20.3	7.5	3.4	.8				6.7	7.1
	-6.4	.6	.5	-1.2				2.1	2.0
	-37.9	-5.4	-3.3	-5.1				.2	-.2
Sales/Net Fixed Assets	142.1	74.4	60.4	39.5				88.4	94.0
	55.7	26.0	18.3	8.9				36.0	35.8
	14.0	9.2	5.6	3.1				11.2	12.9
Sales/Total Assets	8.5	2.8	2.0	1.6				2.5	2.5
	4.9	1.8	1.4	1.1				1.9	1.8
	2.5	1.3	1.0	.9				1.5	1.4
% Depr., Dep., Amort./Sales	.4	.4	.5	.5				.4	.3
	(15) 1.0	(70) .8	(77) .9	(25) .7				(208) .7	(219) .6
	1.6	1.7	1.8	2.0				1.2	1.0
% Officers', Directors' Owners' Comp/Sales	2.5	2.0	1.0	1.2				1.0	1.0
	(11) 5.1	(48) 3.6	(45) 2.0	(11) 1.5				(138) 1.8	(148) 1.8
	8.3	6.8	3.2	2.2				3.9	3.5
Net Sales ($)	17821M	215415M	641428M	742257M	63218M	275842M		4519886M	6116936M
Total Assets ($)	3955M	94702M	410222M	513349M	86920M	179641M		2000518M	1977268M

© RMA 2010

M = $ thousand   MM = $ million
See Pages 9 through 22 for Explanation of Ratios and Data

Comparative Historical Data | Current Data Sorted by Sales

8	6	6	Type of Statement					3	3
8	6	6	Unqualified					3	3
41	25	30	Reviewed		8	6	7	5	4
63	73	53	Compiled	5	23	10	9	4	2
55	54	53	Tax Returns	13	24	10	4	2	
94	97	91	Other	7	21	17	25	17	4
4/1/07-3/31/08 ALL	4/1/08-3/31/09 ALL	4/1/09-3/31/10 ALL		0-1MM	32 (4/1-9/30/09) 1-3MM	3-5MM	201 (10/1/09-3/31/10) 5-10MM	10-25MM	25MM & OVER
261	255	233	NUMBER OF STATEMENTS	25	76	43	45	31	13
%	%	%	ASSETS	%	%	%	%	%	%
6.4	6.0	8.5	Cash & Equivalents	8.5	9.6	9.2	7.6	6.2	9.2
4.3	4.3	5.0	Trade Receivables (net)	4.7	3.6	4.0	4.3	6.5	16.4
71.9	72.2	62.5	Inventory	55.0	65.0	68.6	63.6	58.2	48.3
2.1	.7	1.4	All Other Current	2.9	.7	1.8	1.1	1.8	1.9
84.8	83.3	77.4	Total Current	71.0	78.9	83.5	76.6	72.7	75.7
10.9	12.3	16.8	Fixed Assets (net)	21.9	16.2	11.5	17.5	19.8	19.4
1.9	1.9	2.9	Intangibles (net)	.8	2.6	2.5	3.5	5.0	2.8
2.3	2.5	2.8	All Other Non-Current	6.3	2.4	2.4	2.5	2.5	2.1
100.0	100.0	100.0	Total	100.0	100.0	100.0	100.0	100.0	100.0
			LIABILITIES						
42.9	47.3	39.0	Notes Payable-Short Term	35.2	35.3	43.9	42.8	38.6	40.1
5.0	3.1	3.0	Cur. Mat.-L.T.D.	2.2	4.9	1.9	3.4	1.1	.8
7.7	6.8	5.9	Trade Payables	7.3	5.4	6.3	5.3	3.5	13.1
.1	.1	.2	Income Taxes Payable	.1	.1	.0	.4	.1	.9
10.2	9.0	11.1	All Other Current	12.6	12.7	12.6	7.3	9.5	11.3
65.9	66.3	59.3	Total Current	57.4	58.5	64.8	59.1	52.7	66.2
11.0	13.0	16.2	Long-Term Debt	17.5	19.4	13.6	15.9	12.0	15.0
.1	.0	.1	Deferred Taxes	.0	.0	.0	.1	.2	.0
4.6	3.5	5.0	All Other Non-Current	10.7	7.2	2.5	3.1	2.6	.8
18.4	17.1	19.4	Net Worth	14.4	14.8	19.1	21.8	32.5	18.1
100.0	100.0	100.0	Total Liabilties & Net Worth	100.0	100.0	100.0	100.0	100.0	100.0
			INCOME DATA						
100.0	100.0	100.0	Net Sales	100.0	100.0	100.0	100.0	100.0	100.0
22.7	24.2	26.2	Gross Profit	39.7	27.8	25.4	20.9	22.2	21.4
20.2	23.4	25.2	Operating Expenses	37.9	27.5	23.4	19.3	21.8	21.0
2.5	.8	1.0	Operating Profit	1.7	.3	2.0	1.6	.3	.4
1.7	1.8	2.2	All Other Expenses (net)	4.2	2.9	1.4	1.6	1.2	1.5
.8	-.9	-1.2	Profit Before Taxes	-2.5	-2.6	.6	-.1	-.8	-1.1
			RATIOS						
1.5	1.5	1.7	Current	3.0	1.9	1.7	1.6	1.9	1.3
1.2	1.2	1.3		1.4	1.4	1.2	1.3	1.2	1.1
1.0	1.0	1.0		.8	1.1	1.0	1.0	1.1	1.0
.3	.3	.4	Quick	.6	.3	.4	.3	.5	.4
(260) .1	(254) .1	.2		.3	.2	.1	.1	.2	.2
.0	.0	.1		.0	.1	.0	.1	.1	.1
1 488.3	1 465.5	1 415.0	Sales/Receivables	0 UND	0 987.7	0 999.8	2 240.2	2 147.8	3 117.4
4 95.8	4 91.0	5 73.8		4 100.6	4 93.4	3 114.0	4 84.4	8 46.5	6 59.7
10 37.1	11 32.8	12 29.8		12 30.7	13 28.6	10 36.5	14 26.6	15 23.9	25 14.3
133 2.7	146 2.5	103 3.5	Cost of Sales/Inventory	50 7.4	134 2.7	97 3.8	105 3.5	110 3.3	74 4.9
188 1.9	219 1.7	189 1.9		287 1.3	210 1.7	199 1.8	146 2.5	187 1.9	149 2.4
253 1.4	312 1.2	300 1.2		542 .7	275 1.3	349 1.0	215 1.7	257 1.5	237 1.5
1 383.6	1 371.9	1 440.8	Cost of Sales/Payables	0 UND	0 UND	1 492.8	1 271.1	2 185.2	8 44.4
4 91.2	4 93.6	5 71.4		0 UND	5 70.5	9 42.7	4 84.5	8 46.0	14 25.3
15 24.8	12 29.3	15 24.5		15 24.1	15 24.7	16 22.3	9 40.8	16 23.2	25 14.5
6.5	5.8	4.8	Sales/Working Capital	3.2	4.0	4.9	6.1	5.9	9.4
14.2	12.7	9.4		7.1	7.1	10.1	10.0	11.8	33.4
48.6	56.8	77.4		-39.7	67.9	-69.8	71.5	25.0	-730.6
2.5	1.7	2.2	EBIT/Interest	1.4	2.5	2.2	2.3	2.4	1.8
(252) 1.3	(239) 1.0	(221) 1.0		(22) .6	(74) 1.0	(39) 1.1	1.3	(28) 1.1	.8
.7	-.1	-.3		-1.3	-.4	.1	.4	-1.0	-2.0
4.4	2.3	1.6	Net Profit + Depr., Dep., Amort./Cur. Mat. L/T/D						
(33) 2.3	(20) 1.3	(30) .4							
.4	.2	-1.0							
.1	.1	.2	Fixed/Worth	.1	.2	.2	.1	.3	.5
.5	.6	.8		.8	.9	.8	.6	.5	1.9
2.4	3.5	5.9		NM	-5.0	-3.8	3.5	1.7	4.2
2.4	2.6	1.7	Debt/Worth	1.0	1.4	2.0	2.1	1.7	3.4
5.4	5.3	4.8		5.7	4.0	5.0	4.4	3.5	7.8
24.8	30.3	36.4		-42.7	-11.4	-165.0	28.0	11.3	20.8
29.5	16.7	18.5	% Profit Before Taxes/Tangible Net Worth	25.2	20.0	17.8	20.4	16.0	19.1
(221) 9.6	(206) 3.1	(186) 3.7		(18) -1.2	(53) 3.0	(32) 4.4	(40) 6.2	(30) 4.1	-16.3
-3.0	-13.5	-16.1		-14.0	-8.0	-8.5	-16.3	-17.4	-101.5
5.2	2.9	4.3	% Profit Before Taxes/Total Assets	4.4	6.0	5.2	3.5	5.6	1.8
1.4	.3	.2		-1.7	.0	.5	.7	.1	-.8
-1.6	-3.9	-4.9		-6.8	-6.6	-3.9	-2.9	-4.2	-9.4
95.6	78.9	69.4	Sales/Net Fixed Assets	79.2	87.7	90.7	77.1	45.1	29.4
36.3	29.8	20.9		15.1	21.9	35.8	33.2	11.6	12.5
12.3	11.0	6.4		4.5	6.4	13.5	4.3	4.8	4.7
2.5	2.3	2.5	Sales/Total Assets	3.3	2.4	2.6	2.4	2.6	2.8
1.8	1.6	1.7		1.2	1.7	1.7	1.8	1.4	1.9
1.4	1.1	1.1		.7	1.1	1.0	1.3	1.0	1.0
.3	.4	.5	% Depr., Dep., Amort./Sales	.3	.5	.3	.4	.4	.5
(212) .5	(205) .8	(189) .9		(22) 1.3	(62) 1.0	(31) .7	(35) .7	(27) .7	(12) .6
1.0	1.3	1.7		3.2	1.6	1.7	2.4	1.9	1.0
1.1	1.3	1.4	% Officers', Directors' Owners' Comp/Sales	4.8	1.9	1.4	.6	.7	
(119) 1.9	(130) 2.4	(115) 2.6		(12) 8.0	(41) 3.9	(23) 2.2	(20) 1.6	(16) 1.6	
4.0	4.8	4.7		8.4	6.0	3.5	2.6	3.3	
4211309M	2783410M	1955981M	Net Sales ($)	16568M	140025M	166255M	325565M	485044M	822524M
2278530M	1804974M	1288789M	Total Assets ($)	15629M	106046M	114576M	217899M	339180M	495459M

© RMA 2010

M = $ thousand   MM = $ million
See Pages 9 through 22 for Explanation of Ratios and Data

Current Data Sorted by Assets   Comparative Historical Data

0-500M	500M-2MM	2-10MM	10-50MM	50-100MM	100-250MM	Type of Statement	4/1/05-3/31/06 ALL	4/1/06-3/31/07 ALL
		6	21	4	3	Unqualified	31	42
	3	42	18	2	1	Reviewed	36	50
4	12	21	6			Compiled	48	59
14	38	20	5	2	1	Tax Returns	52	67
8	19	47	27			Other	100	103
	50 (4/1-9/30/09)		274 (10/1/09-3/31/10)					
26	72	136	77	8	5	**NUMBER OF STATEMENTS**	267	321
%	%	%	%	%	%	**ASSETS**	%	%
11.9	7.2	9.0	7.1			Cash & Equivalents	8.3	9.0
6.4	12.1	13.1	14.3			Trade Receivables (net)	13.6	10.9
52.8	58.2	54.3	44.5			Inventory	52.5	55.0
4.9	1.1	1.9	3.2			All Other Current	2.6	2.4
76.0	78.6	78.3	69.2			Total Current	77.0	77.4
18.2	13.1	15.5	21.2			Fixed Assets (net)	16.6	16.3
1.9	2.8	1.3	2.4			Intangibles (net)	1.4	1.1
3.9	5.5	4.9	7.1			All Other Non-Current	5.0	5.2
100.0	100.0	100.0	100.0			Total	100.0	100.0
						LIABILITIES		
46.8	33.8	34.5	31.5			Notes Payable-Short Term	32.6	38.8
4.2	5.0	3.0	4.6			Cur. Mat.-L.T.D.	3.6	3.5
11.7	10.4	10.4	9.5			Trade Payables	13.1	9.6
.0	.1	.0	.1			Income Taxes Payable	.1	.1
15.1	11.1	8.3	10.4			All Other Current	9.4	9.8
77.8	60.3	56.1	56.0			Total Current	58.7	61.8
27.5	9.5	10.9	14.8			Long-Term Debt	11.8	13.5
.0	.0	.1	.3			Deferred Taxes	.4	.2
5.8	24.4	5.4	2.5			All Other Non-Current	4.6	2.9
-11.0	5.8	27.5	26.4			Net Worth	24.5	21.7
100.0	100.0	100.0	100.0			Total Liabilities & Net Worth	100.0	100.0
						INCOME DATA		
100.0	100.0	100.0	100.0			Net Sales	100.0	100.0
30.7	26.6	21.3	20.1			Gross Profit	20.9	21.0
30.4	25.5	20.6	18.9			Operating Expenses	17.7	18.2
.3	1.1	.7	1.2			Operating Profit	3.2	2.8
1.2	1.0	.5	.6			All Other Expenses (net)	.7	.7
-.9	.2	.2	.6			Profit Before Taxes	2.5	2.1
						RATIOS		
2.1	2.4	1.8	1.5				1.7	1.6
1.3	1.3	1.3	1.2			Current	1.3	1.2
.7	1.0	1.1	1.0				1.1	1.0
.5	.8	.7	.6				.6	.5
.2	.3	.4	.4			Quick	(266) .3	.3
.0	.1	.1	.2				.2	.1
0 UND	0 868.8	5 69.7	12 30.5				4 98.1	4 97.9
0 953.9	7 51.4	15 24.9	19 19.7			Sales/Receivables	12 31.3	10 38.0
13 27.7	25 14.6	27 13.5	32 11.3				24 15.3	19 18.9
31 11.7	45 8.1	63 5.8	50 7.3				47 7.7	49 7.5
73 5.0	93 3.9	96 3.8	76 4.8			Cost of Sales/Inventory	77 4.7	87 4.2
137 2.7	169 2.2	168 2.2	110 3.3				114 3.2	133 2.7
0 UND	2 217.4	6 63.8	8 47.6				4 100.2	2 164.8
3 128.7	6 60.0	13 28.2	14 25.6			Cost of Sales/Payables	10 38.3	8 45.3
20 18.2	25 14.7	24 15.0	21 17.5				24 15.3	19 19.2
8.5	5.1	5.8	10.3				8.9	10.0
25.7	18.3	10.3	23.2			Sales/Working Capital	19.3	22.5
-16.2	UND	33.4	92.7				72.7	151.2
3.2	3.2	4.4	3.5				6.1	4.7
(16) .7	(60) 1.5	(127) 1.9	(70) 1.9			EBIT/Interest	(248) 2.9	(295) 2.2
-3.0	-1.1	.6	.6				1.6	1.3
		7.5	1.6				5.7	6.1
	(23) 2.3		(19) 1.1			Net Profit + Depr., Dep., Amort./Cur. Mat. L/T/D	(42) 2.2	(49) 2.4
		1.1	.5				1.2	1.1
.1	.1	.1	.2				.1	.2
.6	.4	.4	.9			Fixed/Worth	.4	.5
-.2	-3.0	1.3	1.8				1.6	1.7
1.1	1.4	1.3	2.1				1.6	1.8
5.0	6.8	2.8	3.3			Debt/Worth	3.6	4.8
-3.3	-18.5	8.5	6.1				9.3	10.7
38.9	46.1	24.9	25.9				48.8	48.0
(18) .0	(51) 8.8	(124) 7.7	(72) 11.2			% Profit Before Taxes/Tangible Net Worth	(241) 24.0	(284) 25.0
-57.3	-5.9	-5.1	-.5				10.5	8.5
12.8	8.0	6.3	5.4				11.0	9.1
-1.6	1.9	2.0	2.2			% Profit Before Taxes/Total Assets	5.1	4.6
-21.5	-4.5	-1.7	-.6				1.6	.9
162.9	143.2	76.4	53.2				128.0	111.9
44.9	36.2	27.4	13.5			Sales/Net Fixed Assets	44.2	35.6
9.6	13.7	9.9	5.9				12.3	12.1
6.3	4.6	3.4	3.1				4.2	3.8
2.8	2.7	2.5	2.3			Sales/Total Assets	2.9	2.8
2.0	1.7	1.6	1.6				2.0	1.9
.4	.4	.4	.5				.3	.2
(15) .6	(53) .8	(118) .8	(72) .9			% Depr., Dep., Amort./Sales	(201) .6	(269) .6
8.5	2.3	2.0	3.5				1.6	1.8
3.5	1.8	.7	.5				.6	.5
(12) 5.9	(44) 2.7	(64) 1.5	(17) 1.2			% Officers', Directors' Owners' Comp/Sales	(98) 1.4	(125) 1.3
9.2	5.9	2.7	2.2				2.8	2.7
27747M	292923M	1566081M	4069433M	1225068M	1304456M	Net Sales ($)	9741178M	12560940M
7151M	79227M	610729M	1692782M	635945M	745598M	Total Assets ($)	3537518M	4511508M

M = $ thousand   MM = $ million
See Pages 9 through 22 for Explanation of Ratios and Data

Comparative Historical Data

Current Data Sorted by Sales

						Type of Statement						
	42		37		34	Unqualified		1			9	24
	44		52		66	Reviewed		1	4	18	23	20
	53		46		43	Compiled	8	5	6	7	13	4
	71		56		77	Tax Returns	15	24	11	13	10	4
	120		117		104	Other	9	8	11	22	25	29
	4/1/07-		4/1/08-		4/1/09-			50 (4/1-9/30/09)		274 (10/1/09-3/31/10)		
	3/31/08		3/31/09		3/31/10		0-1MM	1-3MM	3-5MM	5-10MM	10-25MM	25MM & OVER
	ALL		ALL		ALL							
	330		308		324	NUMBER OF STATEMENTS	32	38	33	60	80	81
	%		%		%	ASSETS	%	%	%	%	%	%
	7.9		7.8		8.3	Cash & Equivalents	8.3	9.4	8.5	7.3	7.6	9.1
	11.5		11.2		12.4	Trade Receivables (net)	9.9	10.3	6.5	12.0	15.1	14.6
	52.2		52.5		51.7	Inventory	49.7	57.0	57.4	59.7	49.7	43.7
	3.0		2.1		2.4	All Other Current	1.8	3.1	4.3	.8	1.7	3.3
	74.7		73.5		74.8	Total Current	69.7	79.7	76.8	79.8	74.1	70.6
	17.7		18.0		17.3	Fixed Assets (net)	20.5	13.7	15.9	13.9	17.6	20.5
	1.5		2.1		2.0	Intangibles (net)	1.4	3.0	1.5	2.1	1.5	2.3
	6.0		6.4		5.9	All Other Non-Current	8.5	3.6	5.7	4.2	6.8	6.5
	100.0		100.0		100.0	Total	100.0	100.0	100.0	100.0	100.0	100.0
						LIABILITIES						
	31.4		32.2		34.0	Notes Payable-Short Term	37.6	34.1	38.5	33.7	32.9	32.1
	4.7		4.4		4.2	Cur. Mat.-L.T.D.	4.2	8.5	2.3	3.7	2.2	5.3
	10.4		8.6		10.1	Trade Payables	8.8	9.3	9.6	11.5	10.8	9.5
	.1		.1		.0	Income Taxes Payable	.1	.0	.0	.0	.1	.1
	10.4		9.4		9.8	All Other Current	17.7	6.3	4.4	12.4	8.0	10.4
	57.0		54.7		58.2	Total Current	68.3	58.3	54.7	61.4	54.0	57.4
	14.1		15.4		13.5	Long-Term Debt	24.1	12.1	16.6	10.8	9.4	14.8
	.3		.3		.2	Deferred Taxes	.0	.0	.3	.0	.0	.4
	3.5		5.0		8.8	All Other Non-Current	23.7	26.3	5.2	5.9	5.1	2.0
	25.1		24.5		19.3	Net Worth	-16.2	3.3	23.1	21.9	31.4	25.4
	100.0		100.0		100.0	Total Liabilties & Net Worth	100.0	100.0	100.0	100.0	100.0	100.0
						INCOME DATA						
	100.0		100.0		100.0	Net Sales	100.0	100.0	100.0	100.0	100.0	100.0
	22.0		22.2		23.4	Gross Profit	34.8	29.2	26.1	20.1	20.1	20.7
	19.5		20.8		22.3	Operating Expenses	34.1	28.1	24.7	20.5	19.0	18.5
	2.5		1.4		1.1	Operating Profit	.7	1.1	1.4	-.4	1.1	2.2
	.7		.7		.8	All Other Expenses (net)	2.5	.9	1.4	.3	.0	.8
	1.8		.7		.3	Profit Before Taxes	-1.8	.2	.0	-.7	1.1	1.5
						RATIOS						
	1.8		1.7		1.8		4.2	4.2	1.9	1.8	1.8	1.4
	1.3		1.3		1.3	Current	1.2	1.5	1.3	1.3	1.3	1.2
	1.1		1.0		1.1		.8	1.1	1.1	1.1	1.1	1.0
	.6		.6		.7		.7	1.4	.5	.5	.7	.6
(327)	.3		.3		.3	Quick	.1	.4	.2	.3	.4	.4
	.1		.1		.1		.0	.1	.1	.1	.1	.2
4	104.2	5	79.3	5	77.5		0 UND	1 331.4	0 736.5	3 111.5	7 49.0	10 35.2
11	32.7	12	29.8	14	25.4	Sales/Receivables	1 264.4	13 27.6	6 60.0	12 30.8	15 24.1	18 19.9
22	17.0	25	14.6	27	13.8		35 10.4	24 15.4	24 15.4	27 13.6	26 14.0	28 12.9
50	7.3	53	6.8	51	7.2		49 7.5	74 4.9	81 4.5	50 7.3	42 8.7	49 7.4
79	4.6	82	4.4	86	4.3	Cost of Sales/Inventory	131 2.8	117 3.1	162 2.3	106 3.4	75 4.9	66 5.6
124	2.9	135	2.7	145	2.5		415 .9	222 1.6	241 1.5	162 2.2	112 3.3	91 4.0
3	145.3	3	125.6	4	85.4		0 UND	2 181.7	1 475.7	6 63.0	6 57.4	7 51.9
8	44.6	9	41.3	12	30.3	Cost of Sales/Payables	6 57.5	6 65.6	10 36.7	14 26.5	13 28.4	12 29.5
19	19.2	19	18.9	24	15.3		43 8.5	27 13.8	35 10.6	27 13.3	23 15.8	20 18.2
	8.4		8.5		7.1		2.9	4.0	5.2	6.6	8.9	12.4
	18.5		18.6		17.2	Sales/Working Capital	18.4	10.1	10.5	10.8	19.1	28.6
	80.3		128.3		88.1		-11.5	52.7	67.6	54.8	44.0	292.8
	4.6		3.7		3.8		1.6	4.3	2.6	2.2	6.2	4.2
(302)	2.1	(277)	1.7	(286)	1.7	EBIT/Interest	(22) -.1	(31) 1.6	(31) 1.5	(55) 1.2	(73) 2.9	(74) 2.2
	1.2		.9		.4		-2.5	-.3	-.3	.5	1.1	1.1
	7.0		3.9		3.5						5.1	1.9
(48)	1.4	(47)	1.5	(47)	1.2	Net Profit + Depr., Dep., Amort./Cur. Mat. L/T/D				(16) 1.2	(19) 1.2
	.8		.8		.7						.7	.5
	.2		.2		.1		.2	.1	.1	.2	.1	.2
	.5		.6		.5	Fixed/Worth	1.6	.4	.6	.4	.5	.9
	1.6		2.5		2.1		-.3	-17.2	3.7	1.6	1.3	1.7
	1.5		1.7		1.6		1.2	.8	1.3	1.9	1.2	2.0
	3.4		3.7		3.2	Debt/Worth	10.8	4.7	4.5	2.9	2.7	3.3
	8.7		11.9		10.9		-2.6	-43.5	32.9	18.5	5.9	6.1
	40.0		31.0		27.0	% Profit Before Taxes/Tangible Net Worth	58.3	17.3	25.3	19.7	28.0	32.6
(294)	18.7	(272)	11.0	(278)	9.6		(19) 4.5	(28) 5.1	(30) 5.7	(51) 1.9	(73) 9.9	(77) 16.0
	5.1		.0		-5.0		-50.0	-10.4	-27.5	-7.7	1.7	3.6
	9.8		7.8		6.5	% Profit Before Taxes/Total Assets	5.2	10.6	6.0	3.1	8.0	7.3
	4.1		2.0		2.0		-2.9	1.6	1.1	.5	3.6	2.9
	.5		-.6		-1.8		-18.1	-5.3	-4.1	-1.8	-.3	.5
	84.4		67.1		79.8	Sales/Net Fixed Assets	98.4	91.6	95.0	102.6	79.5	68.4
	27.8		28.6		27.3		9.1	31.0	16.5	33.6	29.9	24.1
	9.6		8.4		8.1		2.7	14.4	7.2	14.1	8.0	6.8
	3.6		3.5		3.6	Sales/Total Assets	2.3	3.5	2.6	3.9	4.2	3.6
	2.7		2.5		2.5		1.3	2.4	1.7	2.5	2.8	2.6
	2.0		1.7		1.6		.7	1.7	1.4	1.7	1.8	1.9
	.3		.4		.4		.6	.5	.4	.4	.3	.4
(275)	.7	(251)	.9	(267)	.8	% Depr., Dep., Amort./Sales	(23) 3.5	(30) .9	(23) .9	(49) .8	(72) .7	(70) .8
	2.0		2.6		2.7		8.5	2.1	3.0	1.2	2.3	3.3
	.7		1.0		1.0		2.5	2.0	2.0	1.0	.7	.4
(120)	1.6	(124)	1.8	(138)	2.1	% Officers', Directors' Owners' Comp/Sales	(13) 5.9	(27) 3.5	(14) 2.5	(33) 1.7	(33) 1.2	(18) .8
	4.1		3.7		3.9		10.3	6.0	4.3	3.1	2.1	2.2
	11361900M		9663951M		8485708M	Net Sales ($)	19157M	73861M	132311M	443239M	1285188M	6531952M
	4631918M		4272693M		3771432M	Total Assets ($)	19370M	39732M	73794M	201169M	543496M	2893871M

© RMA 2010

M = $ thousand   MM = $ million
See Pages 9 through 22 for Explanation of Ratios and Data

Current Data Sorted by Assets   **Comparative Historical Data**

						Type of Statement		
1		4	7	5	3	Unqualified	24	23
2	9	33	9	2		Reviewed	42	59
9	34	29	5			Compiled	84	95
61	67	28	2			Tax Returns	101	114
13	42	31	20	5	5	Other	125	95
	60 (4/1-9/30/09)		366 (10/1/09-3/31/10)				4/1/05-3/31/06	4/1/06-3/31/07
0-500M	500M-2MM	2-10MM	10-50MM	50-100MM	100-250MM		ALL	ALL
86	152	125	43	12	8	**NUMBER OF STATEMENTS**	376	386
%	%	%	%	%	%	**ASSETS**	%	%
10.7	7.1	6.1	5.4	6.8		Cash & Equivalents	7.8	6.8
11.8	13.7	15.6	16.1	15.4		Trade Receivables (net)	17.8	17.0
44.7	49.3	47.5	39.4	40.2		Inventory	46.4	47.3
1.1	1.9	2.5	1.6	2.4		All Other Current	1.9	2.5
68.3	71.9	71.7	62.4	64.8		Total Current	73.8	73.6
21.9	19.5	17.1	21.3	17.6		Fixed Assets (net)	18.5	17.6
4.6	3.1	4.2	8.9	12.0		Intangibles (net)	2.8	3.4
5.2	5.4	7.0	7.4	5.6		All Other Non-Current	4.9	5.4
100.0	100.0	100.0	100.0	100.0		Total	100.0	100.0
						LIABILITIES		
14.7	12.1	11.0	11.1	10.1		Notes Payable-Short Term	11.7	12.8
3.7	2.6	2.7	4.6	.9		Cur. Mat.-L.T.D.	4.0	4.5
29.2	16.3	19.2	19.8	16.0		Trade Payables	23.4	20.7
.1	.1	.1	.3	.0		Income Taxes Payable	.2	.2
14.2	6.3	7.4	9.6	17.6		All Other Current	9.8	7.9
61.8	37.4	40.4	45.4	44.5		Total Current	49.2	46.1
26.5	23.5	18.7	16.9	11.0		Long-Term Debt	20.1	21.0
.0	.0	.1	.6	.8		Deferred Taxes	.1	.1
12.2	4.9	7.1	4.3	6.4		All Other Non-Current	5.7	5.2
-.5	34.2	33.6	32.8	37.3		Net Worth	24.9	27.6
100.0	100.0	100.0	100.0	100.0		Total Liabilities & Net Worth	100.0	100.0
						INCOME DATA		
100.0	100.0	100.0	100.0	100.0		Net Sales	100.0	100.0
41.1	37.6	35.4	35.2	31.4		Gross Profit	37.1	37.4
37.9	35.6	33.5	32.9	26.1		Operating Expenses	34.3	33.8
3.3	2.0	1.9	2.3	5.3		Operating Profit	2.8	3.6
1.6	.9	.3	.0	1.8		All Other Expenses (net)	.5	.6
1.6	1.1	1.6	2.4	3.6		Profit Before Taxes	2.3	3.0
						RATIOS		
3.6	4.0	2.9	2.2	1.6			2.8	3.0
1.5	2.1	1.7	1.5	1.4		Current	1.7	1.7
.9	1.3	1.2	1.0	1.2			1.2	1.2
.9	1.1	1.0	.8	.6			.9	.9
.5	.6	.5	.4	.5		Quick	(375) .5	.5
.2	.3	.3	.3	.2			.3	.3
0 UND	5 75.3	14 25.9	9 41.0	9 39.9			10 38.3	8 48.0
9 42.5	20 18.3	24 14.9	24 15.4	30 12.3		Sales/Receivables	21 17.1	22 16.9
26 14.3	31 11.6	34 10.9	42 8.7	43 8.4			33 11.2	33 11.0
21 17.1	63 5.8	67 5.4	56 6.5	67 5.5			46 7.9	55 6.7
71 5.2	115 3.2	111 3.3	104 3.5	103 3.5		Cost of Sales/Inventory	84 4.4	95 3.8
204 1.8	187 1.9	176 2.1	178 2.1	180 2.0			132 2.8	161 2.3
9 42.9	16 23.5	25 14.4	30 12.0	30 12.3			21 17.5	19 19.7
28 12.9	36 10.1	42 8.7	49 7.5	34 10.6		Cost of Sales/Payables	40 9.1	36 10.0
55 6.6	51 7.1	63 5.8	71 5.1	66 5.5			63 5.8	60 6.1
5.9	3.8	4.5	4.1	4.8			5.4	4.9
18.5	6.6	7.7	11.8	12.8		Sales/Working Capital	11.1	9.5
-43.9	22.8	21.2	83.5	23.2			40.1	33.3
6.4	5.5	5.5	12.1	16.8			9.7	7.4
(65) 2.7	(139) 2.4	(116) 2.2	(41) 3.7	3.0		EBIT/Interest	(320) 3.3	(343) 2.6
.3	.5	1.0	1.8	1.4			1.3	1.3
		1.8	5.6	4.5		Net Profit + Depr., Dep.,	9.1	7.2
	(12) .8	(24) 3.0	(14) 2.6			Amort./Cur. Mat. L/T/D	(64) 3.4	(61) 2.3
		-.6	.3	.7			1.4	1.3
.1	.1	.2	.2	.3			.2	.1
1.2	.3	.3	.8	.7		Fixed/Worth	.4	.4
-.8	1.6	1.8	3.1	NM			1.9	1.5
1.0	.9	.9	1.3	1.4			.9	.9
6.3	1.8	1.9	4.4	3.0		Debt/Worth	2.3	2.0
-5.6	6.6	6.7	14.6	NM			11.8	6.9
42.2	27.6	27.6	42.8			% Profit Before Taxes/Tangible	43.6	41.2
(52) 15.3	(131) 8.9	(109) 11.0	(35) 18.0			Net Worth	(312) 18.8	(327) 16.0
.0	-.9	.9	2.7				5.6	4.6
13.1	9.0	9.4	8.8	13.6			13.9	14.0
3.4	3.1	3.9	3.4	4.0		% Profit Before Taxes/Total Assets	5.3	4.8
-3.1	-1.5	.1	.5	.9			.8	1.0
152.4	72.4	52.5	30.7	39.8			58.8	62.3
39.3	26.5	24.5	16.5	16.4		Sales/Net Fixed Assets	26.0	25.8
10.0	10.0	10.0	6.0	6.6			12.7	11.8
5.2	3.2	3.1	2.6	3.7			4.0	3.9
3.3	2.4	2.3	2.0	1.8		Sales/Total Assets	2.9	2.8
2.2	1.7	1.7	1.4	1.3			2.1	1.9
.4	.5	.6	1.1	.9			.6	.5
(53) .8	(123) .9	(109) 1.1	(39) 1.4	(10) 1.2		% Depr., Dep., Amort./Sales	(320) 1.2	(306) 1.1
1.8	1.7	1.9	1.9	1.7			1.8	1.7
2.8	2.3	1.3	.9			% Officers', Directors'	1.9	2.0
(48) 4.4	(93) 3.3	(68) 2.2	(13) 1.6			Owners' Comp/Sales	(182) 3.9	(187) 3.2
8.2	5.8	4.3	3.0				7.2	5.4
91030M	460426M	1364470M	2139840M	2102719M	1792237M	Net Sales ($)	8226328M	8783395M
23249M	174945M	545813M	1088048M	931873M	1087690M	Total Assets ($)	2641113M	3195924M

M = $ thousand   MM = $ million
See Pages 9 through 22 for Explanation of Ratios and Data

Comparative Historical Data / Current Data Sorted by Sales

Hist 1	Hist 2	Hist 3	Type of Statement	0-1MM	1-3MM	3-5MM	5-10MM	10-25MM	25MM & OVER
15	20	20	Unqualified	1			3	1	15
29	45	55	Reviewed	2	7	4	10	21	11
74	80	77	Compiled	9	19	14	16	15	4
113	133	158	Tax Returns	40	60	29	12	17	4
106	98	116	Other	17	29	13	15	14	28
4/1/07-3/31/08 ALL	4/1/08-3/31/09 ALL	4/1/09-3/31/10 ALL		60 (4/1-9/30/09)			366 (10/1/09-3/31/10)		
337	376	426	**NUMBER OF STATEMENTS**	69	115	60	56	68	58
%	%	%	**ASSETS**	%	%	%	%	%	%
6.8	6.7	7.5	Cash & Equivalents	10.5	6.9	6.9	6.5	6.4	7.6
15.4	16.7	14.1	Trade Receivables (net)	10.2	12.0	16.1	18.0	15.6	15.2
48.2	48.2	46.2	Inventory	45.5	48.5	49.8	45.8	48.2	37.1
2.7	1.8	1.9	All Other Current	1.2	1.4	3.0	2.2	2.4	1.8
73.1	73.4	69.7	Total Current	67.4	68.8	75.8	72.5	72.7	61.7
17.7	17.8	19.6	Fixed Assets (net)	26.1	20.4	13.9	17.2	17.5	21.1
3.3	3.0	4.6	Intangibles (net)	4.8	4.1	4.3	3.1	2.4	9.8
5.9	5.8	6.1	All Other Non-Current	1.8	6.6	6.0	7.2	7.5	7.5
100.0	100.0	100.0	Total	100.0	100.0	100.0	100.0	100.0	100.0
			LIABILITIES						
10.4	11.2	12.1	Notes Payable-Short Term	16.4	12.5	10.2	12.2	9.9	10.7
4.2	3.2	3.0	Cur. Mat.-L.T.D.	4.0	2.4	2.9	2.7	2.6	3.4
18.8	20.8	20.1	Trade Payables	23.0	17.4	20.9	21.0	20.6	19.6
.1	.1	.1	Income Taxes Payable	.1	.1	.0	.1	.1	.1
8.6	10.5	8.9	All Other Current	12.9	7.5	6.3	7.5	8.7	11.6
42.1	45.8	44.2	Total Current	56.3	39.8	40.3	43.6	42.0	45.4
21.5	19.9	21.6	Long-Term Debt	34.9	24.3	17.9	17.2	13.6	18.3
.1	.2	.1	Deferred Taxes	.0	.0	.0	.0	.2	.7
7.0	5.4	7.1	All Other Non-Current	11.6	6.5	6.4	7.6	5.4	4.9
29.3	28.6	27.0	Net Worth	-2.9	29.4	35.5	31.6	38.9	30.7
100.0	100.0	100.0	Total Liabilities & Net Worth	100.0	100.0	100.0	100.0	100.0	100.0
			INCOME DATA						
100.0	100.0	100.0	Net Sales	100.0	100.0	100.0	100.0	100.0	100.0
37.0	36.5	37.3	Gross Profit	44.1	37.2	38.2	33.4	33.5	36.8
34.1	33.8	34.9	Operating Expenses	40.6	35.5	35.7	31.7	31.8	33.1
2.9	2.6	2.4	Operating Profit	3.5	1.8	2.5	1.7	1.7	3.7
.6	.9	.8	All Other Expenses (net)	2.6	.8	.3	.4	-.1	.6
2.3	1.8	1.6	Profit Before Taxes	.9	.9	2.2	1.3	1.8	3.1
			RATIOS						
3.1 / 1.9 / 1.2	3.1 / 1.8 / 1.2	3.3 / 1.7 / 1.1	Current	3.9 / 1.8 / .9	4.1 / 2.0 / 1.2	4.0 / 2.3 / 1.2	3.0 / 1.7 / 1.1	2.7 / 1.7 / 1.3	1.8 / 1.4 / 1.1
1.0 / .5 / .3	1.0 / .5 / .3	1.0 / .5 / .3	Quick	1.0 / .6 / .2	.9 / .5 / .2	1.0 / .6 / .3	1.0 / .5 / .3	1.1 / .4 / .3	.8 / .4 / .3
8 48.5 / 22 16.8 / 32 11.3	8 48.0 / 21 17.2 / 33 11.1	6 60.4 / 20 18.2 / 33 11.2	Sales/Receivables	0 UND / 14 26.6 / 32 11.6	4 102.3 / 14 26.7 / 29 12.4	11 34.0 / 26 14.1 / 35 10.4	14 26.9 / 24 15.1 / 29 12.4	12 31.5 / 21 17.8 / 42 8.7	8 47.7 / 24 15.2 / 42 8.7
62 5.9 / 104 3.5 / 168 2.2	53 6.9 / 97 3.8 / 172 2.1	55 6.7 / 104 3.5 / 187 2.0	Cost of Sales/Inventory	45 8.1 / 143 2.6 / 241 1.5	57 6.4 / 115 3.2 / 187 2.0	69 5.3 / 131 2.8 / 203 1.8	51 7.2 / 90 4.0 / 137 2.7	55 6.7 / 94 3.9 / 154 2.4	49 7.4 / 88 4.1 / 176 2.1
17 21.5 / 34 10.6 / 61 6.0	19 19.4 / 35 10.4 / 57 6.4	21 17.2 / 37 9.7 / 59 6.2	Cost of Sales/Payables	0 UND / 29 12.5 / 53 6.9	16 22.6 / 34 10.8 / 54 6.8	23 15.9 / 39 9.2 / 69 5.3	26 14.1 / 38 9.7 / 52 7.1	26 14.1 / 38 9.6 / 60 6.1	29 12.5 / 51 7.2 / 71 5.2
4.0 / 8.3 / 25.6	4.2 / 9.1 / 31.4	4.2 / 8.0 / 39.4	Sales/Working Capital	3.3 / 7.7 / UND	3.9 / 7.0 / 38.2	3.0 / 5.3 / 16.3	5.5 / 8.8 / 41.6	5.1 / 9.3 / 21.7	5.8 / 13.5 / 41.6
5.8 / (300) 2.3 / 1.1	7.7 / (339) 2.9 / 1.0	6.1 / (381) 2.6 / 1.0	EBIT/Interest	4.2 / (51) 1.8 / .0	7.6 / (107) 2.4 / .6	4.3 / (55) 2.1 / .8	5.5 / (50) 2.1 / .6	7.1 / (63) 3.4 / 1.2	10.0 / (55) 3.7 / 1.8
4.4 / (55) 1.5 / .5	5.2 / (64) 2.0 / .8	4.8 / (62) 2.1 / .6	Net Profit + Depr., Dep., Amort./Cur. Mat. L/T/D					5.5 / (16) 3.2 / 1.1	5.5 / (22) 2.6 / 1.1
.1 / .4 / 1.7	.1 / .4 / 1.7	.1 / .4 / 3.3	Fixed/Worth	.1 / 1.3 / -.9	.1 / .4 / 4.9	.1 / .2 / 1.2	.1 / .3 / .9	.2 / .4 / .9	.3 / .9 / 4.8
.9 / 2.2 / 8.8	.9 / 2.3 / 8.2	1.0 / 2.3 / 13.8	Debt/Worth	1.1 / 6.5 / -5.5	1.0 / 2.1 / 12.8	.6 / 2.2 / 5.9	.9 / 1.7 / 5.7	.7 / 1.6 / 5.2	1.4 / 3.7 / 17.9
42.2 / (285) 15.5 / 4.4	34.5 / (312) 13.9 / 2.3	30.8 / (343) 11.4 / .4	% Profit Before Taxes/Tangible Net Worth	29.1 / (43) 13.6 / -1.6	27.0 / (89) 8.5 / -3.4	35.9 / (54) 11.9 / 2.3	26.2 / (50) 9.4 / -1.1	25.8 / (62) 10.4 / 2.0	44.7 / (45) 21.3 / 7.8
11.6 / 4.3 / .6	11.0 / 4.2 / .0	9.9 / 3.5 / -.2	% Profit Before Taxes/Total Assets	10.0 / 1.9 / -5.3	11.0 / 3.3 / -1.6	8.9 / 3.3 / .1	9.0 / 3.7 / -.6	9.8 / 3.6 / .6	10.5 / 5.5 / 2.5
60.2 / 24.8 / 11.7	67.2 / 26.9 / 12.3	65.1 / 23.6 / 8.9	Sales/Net Fixed Assets	120.9 / 22.8 / 5.3	91.8 / 23.7 / 8.2	69.4 / 34.6 / 13.1	62.4 / 28.1 / 12.8	45.4 / 24.0 / 11.3	36.1 / 14.7 / 6.5
3.6 / 2.5 / 1.8	3.8 / 2.6 / 1.9	3.4 / 2.4 / 1.7	Sales/Total Assets	4.1 / 2.3 / 1.2	3.3 / 2.4 / 1.6	3.7 / 2.0 / 1.7	3.7 / 2.8 / 1.9	3.8 / 2.7 / 2.1	2.8 / 2.1 / 1.5
.5 / (272) 1.0 / 1.7	.5 / (307) 1.0 / 1.9	.6 / (342) 1.1 / 1.8	% Depr., Dep., Amort./Sales	.3 / (41) 1.0 / 3.0	.5 / (86) .9 / 1.9	.4 / (53) .9 / 1.6	.5 / (50) 1.1 / 2.0	.8 / (60) 1.1 / 1.5	.9 / (52) 1.3 / 1.7
1.5 / (185) 3.3 / 5.9	1.6 / (183) 3.1 / 5.6	1.8 / (222) 3.2 / 6.2	% Officers', Directors' Owners' Comp/Sales	2.9 / (31) 5.7 / 8.4	2.4 / (70) 4.2 / 6.7	2.3 / (43) 3.2 / 6.5	1.3 / (30) 2.0 / 3.7	1.2 / (38) 1.7 / 2.6	.7 / (10) 2.3 / 3.2
6929065M	9273020M	7950722M	Net Sales ($)	40326M	224033M	234786M	392200M	1036660M	6022717M
3011706M	3884791M	3851618M	Total Assets ($)	22043M	105543M	115490M	166079M	437395M	3005068M

M = $ thousand   MM = $ million
See Pages 9 through 22 for Explanation of Ratios and Data

RETAIL—Tire Dealers NAICS 441320

Current Data Sorted by Assets — Comparative Historical Data

0-500M	500M-2MM	2-10MM	10-50MM	50-100MM	100-250MM	Type of Statement	4/1/05-3/31/06 ALL	4/1/06-3/31/07 ALL
	1	1	9	3	3	Unqualified	11	13
	6	20	7			Reviewed	11	29
7	4	17	3	1		Compiled	43	37
16	23	8	2			Tax Returns	15	36
8	7	14	5	3	2	Other	35	25
	35 (4/1-9/30/09)		135 (10/1/09-3/31/10)					
31	41	60	26	7	5	NUMBER OF STATEMENTS	115	140
%	%	%	%	%	%	ASSETS	%	%
11.1	11.9	10.2	3.4			Cash & Equivalents	7.9	6.4
13.9	19.5	19.7	21.0			Trade Receivables (net)	18.9	20.5
42.3	35.8	36.5	44.6			Inventory	38.2	40.5
1.6	2.8	4.1	1.2			All Other Current	2.8	2.4
69.0	70.0	70.5	70.2			Total Current	67.9	69.9
14.3	16.2	23.4	21.0			Fixed Assets (net)	24.2	21.8
7.7	5.5	1.6	4.6			Intangibles (net)	2.5	1.9
8.7	8.4	4.5	4.1			All Other Non-Current	5.4	6.4
100.0	100.0	100.0	100.0			Total	100.0	100.0
						LIABILITIES		
14.3	7.3	10.0	7.8			Notes Payable-Short Term	13.0	10.9
5.0	3.6	2.0	2.3			Cur. Mat.-L.T.D.	3.0	2.9
36.5	34.1	29.2	34.0			Trade Payables	31.9	30.9
.0	.0	.1	.1			Income Taxes Payable	.3	.2
7.3	8.4	6.8	7.0			All Other Current	10.8	7.3
63.1	53.4	48.1	51.2			Total Current	59.0	52.1
34.1	16.3	11.2	9.9			Long-Term Debt	19.5	15.1
.0	.1	.3	.6			Deferred Taxes	.1	.2
4.5	4.1	2.0	2.0			All Other Non-Current	4.5	5.0
-1.7	26.3	38.4	36.4			Net Worth	16.8	27.6
100.0	100.0	100.0	100.0			Total Liabilities & Net Worth	100.0	100.0
						INCOME DATA		
100.0	100.0	100.0	100.0			Net Sales	100.0	100.0
44.2	37.3	32.1	29.7			Gross Profit	37.0	34.4
41.4	35.3	29.7	27.9			Operating Expenses	35.2	31.7
2.8	1.9	2.4	1.7			Operating Profit	1.8	2.8
.9	.3	-.4	.3			All Other Expenses (net)	.4	.1
1.9	1.7	2.8	1.4			Profit Before Taxes	1.4	2.7
						RATIOS		
1.9	2.3	2.1	1.7				1.8	2.0
1.2	1.5	1.4	1.3			Current	1.2	1.4
.7	1.0	1.2	1.1				.9	1.0
.8	1.2	.9	.6				.8	.8
(30) .4	.7	.6	.5			Quick	.4	.5
.2	.3	.4	.3				.3	.3
2 227.1	8 46.8	12 31.5	16 23.5				9 41.8	11 33.7
8 45.7	14 25.7	21 17.2	29 12.6			Sales/Receivables	19 19.6	22 16.9
21 17.7	29 12.5	34 10.6	37 9.8				32 11.2	36 10.0
43 8.5	29 12.8	52 7.1	54 6.8				48 7.7	50 7.3
52 7.0	50 7.3	65 5.7	92 3.9			Cost of Sales/Inventory	64 5.7	70 5.2
70 5.2	91 4.0	100 3.7	105 3.5				90 4.0	98 3.7
8 45.0	32 11.3	33 10.9	41 8.9				33 11.0	33 11.0
46 7.9	44 8.3	51 7.2	60 6.1			Cost of Sales/Payables	58 6.3	49 7.4
71 5.1	58 6.3	69 5.3	72 5.1				77 4.7	74 4.9
12.1	6.2	7.5	10.1				9.4	7.5
30.2	16.6	13.3	16.3			Sales/Working Capital	28.0	16.6
-20.6	851.4	42.9	52.9				-45.3	-582.0
11.2	14.3	9.9	10.9				7.7	7.8
(21) 1.8	(34) 3.8	(54) 4.2	4.2			EBIT/Interest	(111) 3.5	(129) 3.5
-.1	.8	1.7	1.2				1.3	1.8
		5.0	5.4				5.8	5.5
		(13) 3.1	(15) 3.9			Net Profit + Depr., Dep., Amort./Cur. Mat. L/T/D	(34) 3.3	(40) 2.6
		2.1	1.9				1.4	1.0
.2	.1	.2	.3				.4	.3
.8	.6	.6	.6			Fixed/Worth	1.1	.7
-.5	4.4	1.2	1.2				6.2	1.8
1.0	.9	.9	1.4				1.5	1.0
4.6	1.7	1.8	2.0			Debt/Worth	3.6	2.8
-5.3	NM	3.7	3.4				26.4	7.6
154.6	24.0	28.6	27.3				45.5	38.7
(19) 50.0	(31) 12.3	(57) 15.6	(25) 12.1			% Profit Before Taxes/Tangible Net Worth	(91) 19.8	(120) 21.1
15.3	1.1	3.3	1.6				6.9	6.8
17.7	10.5	9.9	7.5				10.1	12.6
8.3	4.8	5.1	3.3			% Profit Before Taxes/Total Assets	4.8	5.3
-2.4	-.5	1.3	.3				1.1	1.7
133.6	110.6	38.0	27.8				36.4	47.8
39.6	21.2	18.0	14.9			Sales/Net Fixed Assets	19.3	17.9
22.1	15.0	8.8	9.2				9.0	9.0
7.5	4.4	3.6	3.8				4.4	3.8
4.2	3.5	2.8	3.0			Sales/Total Assets	3.3	3.1
3.4	2.5	2.1	2.0				2.5	2.4
.4	.7	.9	.7				.7	.6
(21) .8	(32) 1.3	(53) 1.3	(25) 1.1			% Depr., Dep., Amort./Sales	(108) 1.4	(128) 1.3
1.9	1.7	1.9	1.6				1.9	1.8
1.7	2.1	1.0					1.3	1.3
(17) 3.2	(22) 5.1	(29) 3.0				% Officers', Directors' Owners' Comp/Sales	(44) 2.8	(76) 3.0
9.3	6.8	6.3					4.7	5.7
35175M	145705M	844350M	1927884M	1239136M	2124682M	Net Sales ($)	5403026M	5316430M
7712M	39299M	295380M	671449M	481326M	761332M	Total Assets ($)	1758442M	1730625M

© RMA 2010

M = $ thousand   MM = $ million
See Pages 9 through 22 for Explanation of Ratios and Data

Comparative Historical Data / Current Data Sorted by Sales

Row	Type of Statement	4/1/07-3/31/08 ALL	4/1/08-3/31/09 ALL	4/1/09-3/31/10 ALL	0-1MM	1-3MM	3-5MM	5-10MM	10-25MM	25MM & OVER
	Unqualified	15	16	17		1			2	14
	Reviewed	40	46	33		3	1	8	13	8
	Compiled	42	37	32	2	7	2	9	6	6
	Tax Returns	42	32	49	10	17	8	9	2	3
	Other	33	44	39	7	5	8	6	13
					35 (4/1-9/30/09)			135 (10/1/09-3/31/10)		
NUMBER OF STATEMENTS		172	175	170	19	33	11	34	29	44
	ASSETS	%	%	%	%	%	%	%	%	%
	Cash & Equivalents	7.9	7.2	9.1	12.2	10.3	16.9	11.8	6.3	4.8
	Trade Receivables (net)	20.4	19.4	18.7	12.3	16.7	20.7	20.6	19.7	20.2
	Inventory	38.0	42.0	38.7	35.0	41.2	30.4	34.0	40.7	43.0
	All Other Current	2.5	3.1	2.7	.6	1.7	3.6	6.0	3.2	1.4
	Total Current	68.8	71.7	69.3	60.1	69.9	71.8	72.4	69.9	69.3
	Fixed Assets (net)	23.9	20.3	20.4	19.1	13.5	22.3	19.8	22.3	24.9
	Intangibles (net)	.9	2.2	4.2	8.8	7.9	1.0	1.8	4.1	2.2
	All Other Non-Current	6.5	5.8	6.0	11.5	8.8	5.0	5.9	3.7	3.6
	Total	100.0	100.0	100.0	100.0	100.0	100.0	100.0	100.0	100.0
	LIABILITIES									
	Notes Payable-Short Term	9.2	10.4	9.8	15.8	7.8	9.4	6.6	14.8	7.8
	Cur. Mat.-L.T.D.	4.0	3.3	3.1	6.1	4.0	2.8	2.2	2.3	2.5
	Trade Payables	33.2	30.0	32.2	33.0	29.4	54.7	27.6	30.5	33.0
	Income Taxes Payable	.2	.1	.1	.0	.0	.0	.0	.2	.1
	All Other Current	8.3	8.9	7.2	6.2	9.8	3.9	9.5	4.3	6.7
	Total Current	54.9	52.7	52.3	61.0	51.0	70.8	46.0	52.1	50.0
	Long-Term Debt	17.9	11.3	17.4	53.3	14.2	9.4	12.8	11.6	13.7
	Deferred Taxes	.2	.3	.2	.0	.0	.0	.3	.1	.5
	All Other Non-Current	5.9	6.9	3.0	2.2	3.7	1.5	3.7	3.8	2.1
	Net Worth	20.9	28.8	27.1	-16.5	31.2	18.3	37.3	32.5	33.8
	Total Liabilities & Net Worth	100.0	100.0	100.0	100.0	100.0	100.0	100.0	100.0	100.0
	INCOME DATA									
	Net Sales	100.0	100.0	100.0	100.0	100.0	100.0	100.0	100.0	100.0
	Gross Profit	34.5	33.5	34.9	43.5	40.9	30.4	33.2	32.8	30.4
	Operating Expenses	31.6	31.0	32.4	41.1	37.6	30.1	30.0	31.5	27.8
	Operating Profit	2.9	2.5	2.5	2.4	3.2	.3	3.3	1.3	2.6
	All Other Expenses (net)	.3	.0	.2	1.4	.6	-.6	-.2	-.5	.4
	Profit Before Taxes	2.7	2.4	2.3	1.0	2.6	1.0	3.5	1.8	2.2
	RATIOS									
	Current	2.0	2.1	1.9	1.9	2.6	2.3	2.3	1.8	1.7
		1.4	1.4	1.4	1.1	1.6	1.4	1.6	1.2	1.4
		1.0	1.1	1.0	.6	.9	.7	1.1	1.1	1.2
	Quick	.8	.7	.9	1.1	1.1	1.0	1.2	.8	.7
		.5	.5	(169) .5	.4	(32) .5	.7	.7	.4	.5
		.3	.3	.3	.2	.3	.2	.4	.3	.4
	Sales/Receivables	9 38.7	10 37.8	7 51.5	3 107.0	4 94.6	11 34.4	12 31.6	10 37.9	9 41.5
		20 18.2	19 18.8	18 20.8	10 35.9	9 41.3	20 18.6	26 14.0	18 20.2	28 12.9
		34 10.8	33 11.1	33 11.1	21 17.1	26 13.8	28 12.9	35 10.4	32 11.4	36 10.0
	Cost of Sales/Inventory	43 8.5	48 7.6	45 8.1	43 8.5	29 12.4	30 12.0	35 10.3	49 7.5	55 6.6
		65 5.6	68 5.4	65 5.6	59 6.2	55 6.6	41 8.9	67 5.5	65 5.6	73 5.0
		90 4.1	100 3.6	94 3.9	104 3.5	93 3.9	50 7.3	102 3.6	93 3.9	95 3.9
	Cost of Sales/Payables	32 11.4	33 11.1	35 10.4	8 45.0	23 16.0	36 10.1	36 10.1	30 12.3	44 8.3
		49 7.4	49 7.5	49 7.4	41 9.0	47 7.8	56 6.5	44 8.3	49 7.5	58 6.3
		69 5.3	66 5.5	66 5.5	71 5.1	63 5.8	74 5.0	64 5.7	69 5.3	67 5.4
	Sales/Working Capital	8.4	8.5	9.3	10.0	8.3	9.2	6.9	10.1	10.7
		19.4	16.7	15.6	84.2	13.2	20.5	10.7	15.8	15.7
		75.8	77.8	221.5	-19.8	-110.2	-23.9	72.4	133.8	39.3
	EBIT/Interest	8.3	10.2	10.7	9.5	12.8		10.7	9.5	10.9
		(153) 3.5	(157) 4.7	(147) 4.1	(10) 1.1	(28) 3.2		(30) 5.6	(28) 2.7	(42) 4.7
		1.9	1.8	1.4	-.8	.7		2.9	1.0	2.1
	Net Profit + Depr., Dep., Amort./Cur. Mat. L/T/D	9.4	7.6	5.0					6.1	5.4
		(34) 4.1	(42) 2.8	(37) 2.8					(10) 2.6	(23) 3.1
		2.2	1.3	1.8					.7	2.1
	Fixed/Worth	.2	.2	.2	.2	.1	.3	.1	.2	.3
		.7	.6	.6	2.0	.4	.9	.3	.8	.8
		2.0	1.5	1.5	-.5	-4.9	5.6	1.0	1.4	1.3
	Debt/Worth	1.0	1.1	1.0	2.2	.7	.5	.9	1.1	1.6
		2.1	2.2	2.1	18.9	1.3	5.1	1.7	1.9	2.3
		7.2	5.2	5.3	-2.7	-27.4	69.0	3.8	6.9	3.5
	% Profit Before Taxes/Tangible Net Worth	37.3	33.0	35.8	327.3	55.5		40.8	23.6	33.8
		(146) 20.9	(150) 16.1	(144) 15.5	(11) 50.0	(24) 22.5		(30) 12.3	(26) 10.8	16.4
		8.7	4.8	6.1	15.3	11.7		5.8	.5	6.9
	% Profit Before Taxes/Total Assets	13.0	12.2	11.8	16.6	15.4	10.0	10.4	8.1	10.4
		5.5	5.3	5.1	4.8	6.8	5.0	5.2	3.7	5.2
		2.2	1.5	.6	-4.0	-.6	-2.9	2.6	.0	1.9
	Sales/Net Fixed Assets	46.9	44.2	56.6	151.0	87.9	57.5	49.3	62.3	28.9
		19.3	20.6	20.3	31.2	30.9	17.2	22.7	18.4	12.8
		9.7	11.8	10.2	10.3	17.5	10.2	11.6	8.9	8.8
	Sales/Total Assets	4.4	4.2	4.2	5.0	5.4	4.6	3.5	3.9	3.9
		3.3	3.2	3.2	3.0	3.8	3.9	2.8	3.3	3.0
		2.4	2.5	2.2	1.8	2.5	2.8	2.0	2.2	2.3
	% Depr., Dep., Amort./Sales	.7	.7	.7	.5	.4		.7	.8	.7
		(155) 1.2	(157) 1.2	(143) 1.2	(12) 1.6	(26) 1.3		(27) 1.2	(26) 1.3	(43) 1.2
		1.9	1.8	1.8	2.4	1.6		1.9	2.1	1.9
	% Officers', Directors' Owners' Comp/Sales	1.2	.7	1.2	2.0	1.2		1.7	.8	.7
		(94) 3.1	(67) 1.7	(79) 3.0	(10) 5.2	(19) 3.8		(19) 3.3	(11) 1.7	(13) 1.1
		5.9	5.3	6.3	9.7	7.8		6.3	6.9	1.4
	Net Sales ($)	6816057M	7102577M	6316932M	13088M	61006M	42269M	235591M	477841M	5487137M
	Total Assets ($)	2124796M	2255184M	2256498M	5875M	18423M	14117M	100313M	163068M	1954702M

© RMA 2010

M = $ thousand   MM = $ million
See Pages 9 through 22 for Explanation of Ratios and Data

RETAIL—Furniture Stores NAICS 442110

	Current Data Sorted by Assets						Type of Statement	Comparative Historical Data	
	1	2	15	27	13	12	Unqualified	46	52
	1	16	46	40	1	1	Reviewed	80	97
	26	55	56	9		2	Compiled	127	168
	50	84	40	2			Tax Returns	117	149
	15	67	81	44	8	15	Other	203	225
		138 (4/1-9/30/09)			591 (10/1/09-3/31/10)			4/1/05-3/31/06	4/1/06-3/31/07
	0-500M	500M-2MM	2-10MM	10-50MM	50-100MM	100-250MM		ALL	ALL
	93	224	238	122	22	30	NUMBER OF STATEMENTS	573	691
	%	%	%	%	%	%	ASSETS	%	%
	14.5	9.3	9.5	6.8	10.9	7.4	Cash & Equivalents	9.0	8.9
	10.2	10.9	12.9	13.1	4.6	15.0	Trade Receivables (net)	12.4	12.7
	52.4	52.3	43.8	36.8	30.2	23.8	Inventory	48.9	48.9
	2.8	1.2	2.4	2.8	3.3	2.0	All Other Current	2.3	2.5
	80.0	73.8	68.5	59.5	48.8	48.2	Total Current	72.6	73.0
	13.2	16.5	22.7	31.2	41.6	39.5	Fixed Assets (net)	18.9	19.5
	1.3	2.6	3.2	3.8	6.8	5.4	Intangibles (net)	2.1	2.2
	5.6	7.1	5.6	5.5	2.7	7.0	All Other Non-Current	6.4	5.2
	100.0	100.0	100.0	100.0	100.0	100.0	Total	100.0	100.0
							LIABILITIES		
	21.0	11.7	9.4	8.4	4.2	7.4	Notes Payable-Short Term	12.0	11.9
	2.1	2.7	2.9	2.7	5.2	1.7	Cur. Mat.-L.T.D.	2.4	2.6
	19.7	19.3	19.8	15.4	13.2	11.4	Trade Payables	19.4	19.1
	.0	.1	.2	.2	.2	.9	Income Taxes Payable	.3	.2
	25.1	21.1	18.2	18.6	17.9	11.5	All Other Current	18.8	17.9
	67.9	54.9	50.6	45.4	40.8	32.8	Total Current	52.9	51.7
	14.4	13.5	14.7	15.1	23.6	24.7	Long-Term Debt	14.2	14.3
	.0	.1	.0	.1	.2	.5	Deferred Taxes	.1	.1
	11.0	7.1	5.9	5.8	6.2	10.0	All Other Non-Current	6.3	5.4
	6.7	24.4	28.7	33.7	29.2	32.1	Net Worth	26.5	28.5
	100.0	100.0	100.0	100.0	100.0	100.0	Total Liabilties & Net Worth	100.0	100.0
							INCOME DATA		
	100.0	100.0	100.0	100.0	100.0	100.0	Net Sales	100.0	100.0
	43.2	40.9	42.0	41.9	46.1	46.0	Gross Profit	42.3	41.7
	42.7	41.2	40.2	39.6	42.5	45.5	Operating Expenses	40.1	39.6
	.5	-.2	1.9	2.3	3.6	.5	Operating Profit	2.2	2.1
	.2	.3	.6	.9	.9	-.2	All Other Expenses (net)	.7	.5
	.3	-.5	1.3	1.4	2.7	.7	Profit Before Taxes	1.4	1.6
							RATIOS		
	3.4	2.5	2.1	2.1	2.1	2.2		2.2	2.4
	1.3	1.5	1.3	1.3	1.2	1.3	Current	1.4	1.4
	.9	1.0	1.1	1.0	1.0	1.0		1.0	1.1
	.9	.8	.8	.8	.9	1.2		.8	.8
	.3 (220)	.3 (237)	.3	.3	.3	.3	Quick	.3 (571)	.3 (684)
	.1	.1	.1	.1	.1	.2		.1	.1
	0 UND	0 UND	0 999.8	1 340.6	1 396.0	0 862.2		0 999.8	0 999.8
	0 746.0	3 104.9	3 113.6	4 101.9	2 187.6	8 44.0	Sales/Receivables	4 86.8	4 86.2
	16 23.4	16 22.2	25 14.9	30 12.0	4 104.2	67 5.4		18 20.8	23 15.9
	42 8.7	54 6.8	61 5.9	67 5.5	56 6.5	67 5.4		66 5.5	67 5.4
	90 4.1	113 3.2	99 3.7	101 3.6	107 3.4	96 3.8	Cost of Sales/Inventory	106 3.4	111 3.3
	131 2.8	194 1.9	151 2.4	135 2.7	119 3.1	120 3.0		152 2.4	160 2.3
	0 UND	17 22.0	21 17.7	18 20.6	30 12.2	33 11.0		20 18.2	19 19.0
	18 19.8	32 11.5	34 10.7	32 11.4	41 8.9	48 7.7	Cost of Sales/Payables	36 10.2	34 10.7
	49 7.4	54 6.8	56 6.5	51 7.2	49 7.5	60 6.0		56 6.5	54 6.7
	6.9	6.2	7.4	7.4	7.4	4.9		6.6	6.1
	31.3	15.1	15.6	16.9	28.3	19.3	Sales/Working Capital	14.7	13.8
	-28.8	465.3	144.6	-210.1	731.0	NM		209.3	95.2
	5.9	6.1	8.6	10.1	6.5	4.5		7.7	7.2
	1.4 (66)	1.8 (178)	2.1 (208)	3.1 (113)	2.2 (19)	2.3 (27)	EBIT/Interest	2.5 (497)	2.3 (586)
	-6.6	-2.1	.5	1.1	1.1	.7		.5	.7
		5.5	5.9	17.4		6.1		6.5	9.1
		2.1 (13)	1.9 (36)	2.0 (35)		4.6 (10)	Net Profit + Depr., Dep., Amort./Cur. Mat. L/T/D	2.5 (93)	1.9 (106)
		.0	-.3	.6		1.8		.5	.5
	.1	.2	.2	.4	.7	.7		.2	.2
	.8	.6	.6	.9	2.2	1.7	Fixed/Worth	.6	.6
	-.7	27.9	3.4	3.0	3.4	2.6		2.7	2.6
	.6	.9	1.0	.9	1.1	1.0		1.0	1.0
	6.7	2.9	2.6	2.5	2.4	1.9	Debt/Worth	2.7	2.5
	-5.1	-260.5	11.6	8.2	5.9	5.3		12.3	9.8
	64.8	32.3	29.7	26.9	31.9	20.1		48.4	37.9
	13.5 (59)	6.7 (167)	11.9 (199)	10.5 (104)	17.6 (18)	12.3 (25)	% Profit Before Taxes/Tangible Net Worth	15.0 (477)	12.5 (580)
	-9.7	-16.7	.5	.7	8.9	-.2		.3	.6
	12.2	8.0	10.8	7.8	8.8	6.8		11.4	11.9
	2.0	1.5	2.5	3.6	4.3	3.6	% Profit Before Taxes/Total Assets	4.0	3.5
	-9.9	-8.9	-.2	.0	1.1	-1.0		-1.0	-1.0
	270.8	83.8	49.8	33.9	13.2	6.1		60.1	59.6
	47.5	29.0	20.8	10.5	6.0	3.9	Sales/Net Fixed Assets	23.2	22.7
	21.6	11.9	8.2	4.7	2.3	2.0		10.2	9.7
	6.1	4.5	4.2	3.8	3.2	2.0		4.1	3.9
	4.0	2.9	2.8	2.5	1.9	1.5	Sales/Total Assets	2.9	2.8
	2.8	2.0	1.8	1.4	1.4	.9		2.0	1.9
	.4	.4	.4	.8	1.9	1.2		.4	.4
	.6 (60)	.7 (176)	.9 (204)	1.4 (113)	2.4 (19)	2.3 (22)	% Depr., Dep., Amort./Sales	.8 (471)	.8 (558)
	1.3	1.4	1.5	2.1	2.9	3.1		1.3	1.3
	2.7	2.0	1.3	1.0				1.7	1.4
	4.4 (51)	4.2 (119)	2.1 (109)	1.6 (26)			% Officers', Directors' Owners' Comp/Sales	3.2 (294)	3.2 (317)
	6.8	6.6	3.9	2.6				5.6	6.0
	113303M	860625M	3464480M	6735897M	3559797M	9341301M	Net Sales ($)	18232096M	20241115M
	24488M	259405M	1143661M	2631298M	1659634M	4879785M	Total Assets ($)	7495661M	8663545M

M = $ thousand   MM = $ million
See Pages 9 through 22 for Explanation of Ratios and Data

Comparative Historical Data | Current Data Sorted by Sales

			Type of Statement						
52	46	70	Unqualified	1	2	2	4	9	52
90	83	105	Reviewed		2	5	19	31	48
132	126	148	Compiled	16	42	26	26	26	12
164	163	176	Tax Returns	36	64	31	27	14	4
198	238	230	Other	12	28	36	39	43	72
4/1/07-3/31/08 ALL	4/1/08-3/31/09 ALL	4/1/09-3/31/10 ALL		138 (4/1-9/30/09)			591 (10/1/09-3/31/10)		
				0-1MM	1-3MM	3-5MM	5-10MM	10-25MM	25MM & OVER
636	656	729	NUMBER OF STATEMENTS	65	138	100	115	123	188
%	%	%	**ASSETS**	%	%	%	%	%	%
9.2	9.3	9.6	Cash & Equivalents	12.3	9.3	8.4	11.2	10.6	7.9
12.5	12.4	11.8	Trade Receivables (net)	7.7	9.4	12.5	12.8	13.6	12.9
47.5	45.0	45.1	Inventory	50.6	51.4	50.6	45.2	43.4	36.7
2.7	2.8	2.2	All Other Current	2.4	1.6	.8	1.7	3.2	2.9
71.8	69.5	68.7	Total Current	73.0	71.6	72.2	70.9	70.8	60.4
20.3	22.1	22.2	Fixed Assets (net)	20.4	18.5	19.2	19.0	21.9	29.4
1.9	3.1	3.1	Intangibles (net)	1.3	2.5	2.4	3.2	3.1	4.3
5.9	5.3	6.0	All Other Non-Current	5.3	7.4	6.2	6.9	4.1	5.9
100.0	100.0	100.0	Total	100.0	100.0	100.0	100.0	100.0	100.0
			LIABILITIES						
11.7	13.8	11.2	Notes Payable-Short Term	20.3	14.0	11.0	8.8	10.1	8.2
2.5	3.3	2.7	Cur. Mat.-L.T.D.	2.4	2.2	2.8	3.6	3.1	2.4
18.3	16.3	18.4	Trade Payables	14.9	15.0	17.9	22.1	21.1	18.2
.2	.2	.2	Income Taxes Payable	.0	.0	.2	.0	.3	.3
18.7	16.7	19.8	All Other Current	24.7	18.7	16.6	22.1	18.7	19.8
51.4	50.4	52.2	Total Current	62.3	49.9	48.5	56.7	53.3	48.9
14.5	17.1	15.0	Long-Term Debt	17.9	18.4	15.1	13.6	12.0	14.4
.0	.1	.1	Deferred Taxes	.0	.1	.0	.0	.0	.2
6.7	7.0	7.1	All Other Non-Current	13.2	8.0	6.3	3.9	6.4	7.1
27.3	25.5	25.6	Net Worth	6.6	23.6	30.0	25.7	28.3	29.4
100.0	100.0	100.0	Total Liabilties & Net Worth	100.0	100.0	100.0	100.0	100.0	100.0
			INCOME DATA						
100.0	100.0	100.0	Net Sales	100.0	100.0	100.0	100.0	100.0	100.0
42.5	42.4	42.1	Gross Profit	45.6	42.6	43.2	40.3	40.1	42.4
40.4	41.3	41.0	Operating Expenses	46.1	42.9	42.6	38.1	38.4	40.4
2.1	1.1	1.1	Operating Profit	-.5	-.3	.6	2.2	1.7	1.9
.5	.6	.5	All Other Expenses (net)	1.2	.3	.5	.2	.5	.5
1.7	.5	.6	Profit Before Taxes	-1.8	-.6	.1	2.0	1.2	1.5
			RATIOS						
2.3	2.4	2.3	Current	4.5	3.1	2.5	2.0	2.1	1.8
1.4	1.4	1.4		1.6	1.6	1.6	1.2	1.4	1.2
1.0	1.0	1.0		.8	1.0	1.1	.9	1.1	1.0
.9	.8	.8	Quick	1.3	.8	.8	.7	.9	.7
(632) .3	(654) .3	(724) .3		.3	(137) .3	(98) .3	(114) .3	(122) .4	.3
.1	.1	.1		.1	.1	.1	.2	.1	.1
0 999.8	0 999.8	0 UND	Sales/Receivables	0 UND	0 UND	0 UND	1 678.5	0 999.8	1 403.3
4 99.5	3 110.6	3 118.6		0 746.0	4 85.1	3 138.3	5 78.1	3 118.6	3 117.1
19 19.1	19 19.6	20 18.4		16 23.4	16 22.5	20 18.0	20 18.2	27 13.8	18 20.1
65 5.6	56 6.5	59 6.2	Cost of Sales/Inventory	63 5.8	64 5.7	83 4.4	48 7.6	53 6.8	59 6.2
104 3.5	101 3.6	102 3.6		131 2.8	117 3.1	132 2.8	87 4.2	90 4.0	88 4.2
156 2.4	154 2.4	150 2.4		266 1.4	210 1.7	186 2.0	142 2.6	129 2.8	118 3.1
17 22.1	14 26.0	17 21.1	Cost of Sales/Payables	0 UND	9 38.7	21 17.2	19 19.5	20 18.4	23 15.8
32 11.3	28 13.0	33 11.2		25 14.5	26 13.9	40 9.1	34 10.8	32 11.3	36 10.2
51 7.2	49 7.5	53 6.9		53 6.9	51 7.2	56 6.5	62 5.9	52 7.1	53 6.9
5.9	6.4	6.6	Sales/Working Capital	2.8	5.1	5.7	8.0	8.4	9.3
16.0	15.7	16.5		11.8	11.9	12.5	23.2	19.1	25.4
-446.3	114.4	UND		-18.0	UND	43.7	-72.0	112.0	NM
6.4	5.8	7.1	EBIT/Interest	4.0	3.8	6.4	9.7	11.2	7.6
(524) 2.4	(560) 1.6	(611) 2.1		(49) .8	(106) .7	(84) 1.7	(100) 2.5	(104) 2.6	(168) 3.0
.3	-.5	-.5		-6.4	-2.2	-2.2	.5	.9	1.1
8.1	5.0	5.6	Net Profit + Depr., Dep.,				5.8	5.9	9.3
(87) 2.6	(86) 2.0	(104) 2.1	Amort./Cur. Mat. L/T/D				(12) 1.3	(20) 2.0	(57) 2.9
.4	.2	.4					-2.3	.5	1.1
.2	.2	.2	Fixed/Worth	.1	.2	.2	.2	.2	.4
.7	.8	.8		.8	.7	.4	.6	.6	1.0
3.4	5.2	5.5		-.7	-19.3	3.4	7.3	2.1	3.4
1.0	1.0	1.0	Debt/Worth	.6	.7	1.0	.9	1.3	1.0
2.7	2.9	2.6		4.7	3.1	2.1	3.0	2.4	2.6
12.5	17.0	21.3		-4.9	-57.2	15.3	51.9	9.9	9.3
40.7	31.8	32.7	% Profit Before Taxes/Tangible	38.9	20.5	25.9	47.2	38.2	33.8
(516) 14.1	(522) 7.3	(572) 10.6	Net Worth	(39) 8.3	(101) 1.9	(81) 3.9	(89) 14.1	(105) 11.7	(157) 14.6
1.3	-5.0	-.8		-9.7	-18.5	-20.7	.6	1.1	2.6
12.2	9.0	9.4	% Profit Before Taxes/Total	10.4	5.6	6.1	14.2	10.9	8.1
4.0	1.6	2.7	Assets	-.3	.3	1.8	3.7	3.2	4.0
-1.6	-4.2	-4.0		-11.5	-8.5	-6.7	-.9	-1.0	.4
60.1	57.0	58.7	Sales/Net Fixed Assets	107.8	99.1	81.2	103.6	56.0	33.7
22.4	20.9	22.4		23.2	26.4	30.4	24.6	29.2	12.6
9.1	8.4	8.0		8.6	10.3	11.1	10.3	7.5	5.0
4.0	4.3	4.3	Sales/Total Assets	3.8	4.0	3.8	4.6	5.0	4.1
2.9	2.8	2.8		2.1	2.5	2.7	3.1	3.3	2.9
1.9	1.8	1.7		1.4	1.7	1.8	2.3	1.7	1.7
.4	.4	.5	% Depr., Dep., Amort./Sales	.5	.4	.3	.4	.5	.8
(505) .8	(520) 1.0	(594) 1.0		(45) 1.1	(108) .9	(78) .6	(93) .7	(108) .9	(162) 1.4
1.5	1.6	1.7		1.9	1.7	1.3	1.2	1.6	2.2
1.6	1.6	1.6	% Officers', Directors'	3.9	2.1	2.3	1.3	1.2	1.6
(280) 3.5	(292) 3.1	(308) 3.0	Owners' Comp/Sales	(33) 5.4	(80) 3.9	(57) 3.9	(58) 2.0	(51) 1.8	(29) 1.6
5.9	5.5	5.4		7.9	6.8	5.4	4.2	2.9	2.8
21887143M	21661544M	24075403M	Net Sales ($)	40857M	259907M	395617M	828138M	1957564M	20593320M
8771758M	9445744M	10598271M	Total Assets ($)	27094M	132352M	209235M	326847M	826436M	9076307M

M = $ thousand   MM = $ million
See Pages 9 through 22 for Explanation of Ratios and Data

Current Data Sorted by Assets   Comparative Historical Data

0-500M	500M-2MM	2-10MM	10-50MM	50-100MM	100-250MM	Type of Statement	11 / 47 / 83 / 93 / 115	17 / 49 / 91 / 92 / 109
		1	6	1	1	Unqualified	11	17
3	14	33	1	1		Reviewed	47	49
14	24	14	1			Compiled	83	91
45	56	14	3		3	Tax Returns	93	92
23	48	35	13	5		Other	115	109
	64 (4/1-9/30/09)		295 (10/1/09-3/31/10)				4/1/05-3/31/06 ALL	4/1/06-3/31/07 ALL
85	142	97	24	7	4	NUMBER OF STATEMENTS	349	358
%	%	%	%	%	%	**ASSETS**	%	%
11.2	10.5	10.3	5.5			Cash & Equivalents	7.5	8.5
15.4	24.1	23.0	20.9			Trade Receivables (net)	29.0	31.1
35.4	34.7	30.8	38.3			Inventory	36.2	32.2
3.3	3.9	3.9	2.5			All Other Current	2.4	2.8
65.4	73.1	68.0	67.1			Total Current	75.1	74.6
21.8	14.6	20.2	17.1			Fixed Assets (net)	15.6	16.4
2.9	4.0	3.2	8.8			Intangibles (net)	3.0	2.6
9.9	8.3	8.7	7.0			All Other Non-Current	6.3	6.4
100.0	100.0	100.0	100.0			Total	100.0	100.0
						LIABILITIES		
20.4	15.9	11.0	10.5			Notes Payable-Short Term	12.0	13.9
4.4	5.2	2.1	4.3			Cur. Mat.-L.T.D.	1.9	2.8
26.3	16.3	17.0	19.1			Trade Payables	21.3	19.8
.1	.3	.4	.1			Income Taxes Payable	.4	.2
21.5	16.5	17.2	13.2			All Other Current	15.7	15.7
72.7	54.2	47.8	47.1			Total Current	51.2	52.3
24.8	10.8	10.6	11.0			Long-Term Debt	12.9	12.0
.0	.0	.1	.7			Deferred Taxes	.1	.1
19.3	5.9	5.8	8.5			All Other Non-Current	4.5	4.6
-16.8	29.1	35.7	32.7			Net Worth	31.4	31.0
100.0	100.0	100.0	100.0			Total Liabilities & Net Worth	100.0	100.0
						INCOME DATA		
100.0	100.0	100.0	100.0			Net Sales	100.0	100.0
39.4	36.5	37.9	33.4			Gross Profit	35.3	33.9
40.7	36.3	37.6	33.6			Operating Expenses	32.5	30.7
-1.3	.2	.3	-.2			Operating Profit	2.8	3.1
.6	.4	.6	1.3			All Other Expenses (net)	.2	.4
-1.9	-.2	-.3	-1.4			Profit Before Taxes	2.6	2.7
						RATIOS		
2.4	2.5	2.8	1.7				2.4	2.4
1.2	1.4	1.4	1.4			Current	1.5	1.5
.6	.9	1.1	1.2				1.1	1.1
1.2	1.4	1.3	.7				1.3	1.4
(84) .5	.6	.6	.5			Quick	(348) .7	.7
.1	.3	.3	.3				.4	.4
0 UND	9 39.4	9 38.7	8 47.7				11 33.9	12 30.8
10 36.4	23 15.7	23 16.1	22 16.3			Sales/Receivables	25 14.5	26 13.9
21 17.1	37 10.0	44 8.3	42 8.6				42 8.6	43 8.5
15 24.1	24 15.2	26 14.1	35 10.4				24 15.4	20 18.5
42 8.8	49 7.5	51 7.1	83 4.4			Cost of Sales/Inventory	50 7.3	38 9.5
79 4.6	92 4.0	97 3.8	189 1.9				89 4.1	77 4.8
7 55.1	13 27.7	15 24.2	20 17.9				16 22.9	13 27.9
21 17.6	22 16.4	26 13.8	31 11.9			Cost of Sales/Payables	29 12.8	24 15.0
45 8.2	37 9.9	46 7.9	58 6.2				47 7.8	40 9.2
11.3	5.7	6.2	7.2				7.2	7.7
53.6	16.6	13.0	10.4			Sales/Working Capital	15.8	14.3
-17.5	-54.4	80.1	42.0				81.0	71.5
6.0	6.0	4.7	4.0				13.7	14.9
(67) 1.0	(117) 1.0	(83) 1.1	(22) .7			EBIT/Interest	(303) 4.0	(320) 4.2
-8.3	-3.6	-3.9	-4.3				1.4	1.4
	4.1	9.0					7.3	5.0
	(11) 1.7	(15) 1.8				Net Profit + Depr., Dep., Amort./Cur. Mat. L/T/D	(43) 2.8	(49) 2.9
	-.2	-.1					1.4	1.0
.3	.1	.1	.4				.1	.1
2.0	.5	.5	.6			Fixed/Worth	.4	.4
-.3	49.6	1.4	1.5				1.5	1.6
.9	.8	.7	.9				.8	.9
10.2	2.3	1.6	1.9			Debt/Worth	2.2	2.1
-2.3	168.9	5.8	5.1				8.3	6.1
68.2	30.3	19.7	12.1				53.1	59.9
(49) 11.1	(108) 5.0	(86) 2.6	(19) 3.1			% Profit Before Taxes/Tangible Net Worth	(299) 21.1	(318) 25.2
-9.6	-26.4	-15.4	-4.2				3.3	7.2
10.9	8.6	6.7	4.5				16.2	19.2
.0	1.5	.9	-.1			% Profit Before Taxes/Total Assets	5.9	7.7
-35.7	-8.2	-4.7	-12.5				1.0	1.8
97.2	73.4	50.2	43.4				78.9	89.6
27.0	35.3	20.3	13.5			Sales/Net Fixed Assets	34.8	37.4
14.3	18.1	7.3	6.9				17.2	17.3
7.3	4.6	3.5	3.7				4.6	5.1
4.5	3.4	2.7	2.1			Sales/Total Assets	3.6	3.8
2.7	2.2	1.8	1.6				2.7	2.8
.5	.4	.5	.8				.4	.3
(63) 1.0	(111) .7	(82) .9	(19) 1.1			% Depr., Dep., Amort./Sales	(288) .6	(293) .7
1.8	1.4	1.8	1.6				1.1	1.2
3.3	2.1	1.4					2.0	1.7
(44) 5.9	(87) 3.9	(51) 3.3				% Officers', Directors' Owners' Comp/Sales	(216) 3.6	(221) 3.3
9.1	5.9	7.2					6.7	5.9
92532M	532954M	1100202M	1689826M	2096393M	2454988M	Net Sales ($)	5309673M	5433190M
21065M	151315M	399546M	504385M	573444M	692636M	Total Assets ($)	1374048M	1528665M

M = $ thousand   MM = $ million
See Pages 9 through 22 for Explanation of Ratios and Data

Comparative Historical Data | Current Data Sorted by Sales

Type of Statement

4/1/07-3/31/08 ALL	4/1/08-3/31/09 ALL	4/1/09-3/31/10 ALL	Type of Statement	0-1MM	1-3MM	3-5MM	5-10MM	10-25MM	25MM & OVER
13	11	9	Unqualified	1	6	7	23	12	9
52	49	52	Reviewed						
70	78	53	Compiled	12	16	10	8	5	3
88	110	121	Tax Returns	33	46	16	14	7	5
114	118	124	Other	12	32	21	22	18	19
					64 (4/1-9/30/09)		295 (10/1/09-3/31/10)		
337	366	359	NUMBER OF STATEMENTS	58	100	54	67	42	38

%	%	%	ASSETS	%	%	%	%	%	%
9.4	8.3	10.3	Cash & Equivalents	8.4	12.1	12.7	9.8	9.3	6.9
28.7	25.2	21.1	Trade Receivables (net)	12.1	17.9	23.6	30.0	23.6	21.8
31.9	34.4	33.7	Inventory	40.8	39.1	26.7	25.0	33.8	34.2
4.0	2.8	3.6	All Other Current	3.8	2.2	5.9	4.8	2.2	3.2
73.9	70.7	68.8	Total Current	65.1	71.4	68.8	69.5	68.9	66.0
16.9	17.6	18.3	Fixed Assets (net)	21.3	17.6	16.1	18.2	18.5	18.3
2.4	3.9	4.2	Intangibles (net)	3.9	3.4	4.9	2.4	4.6	8.0
6.8	7.8	8.8	All Other Non-Current	9.7	7.6	10.2	9.9	8.1	7.7
100.0	100.0	100.0	Total	100.0	100.0	100.0	100.0	100.0	100.0

			LIABILITIES						
14.4	15.6	15.2	Notes Payable-Short Term	15.9	15.9	13.9	18.0	13.3	11.5
3.0	4.7	4.1	Cur. Mat.-L.T.D.	5.2	6.2	3.1	2.1	1.9	4.3
19.4	19.4	19.4	Trade Payables	25.9	16.9	16.6	18.2	19.4	21.6
.3	.1	.3	Income Taxes Payable	.1	.1	.7	.5	.1	.2
14.7	17.3	17.7	All Other Current	18.9	19.5	17.8	13.0	12.8	25.2
51.8	57.1	56.7	Total Current	66.1	58.6	52.2	51.8	47.4	62.8
14.5	13.0	14.7	Long-Term Debt	28.2	16.0	9.4	8.2	9.7	15.5
.1	.1	.1	Deferred Taxes	.0	.0	.0	.0	.2	.0
5.3	6.8	9.5	All Other Non-Current	15.0	12.2	6.3	6.0	4.6	10.3
28.3	23.0	19.0	Net Worth	-9.3	13.2	32.1	33.9	38.1	11.0
100.0	100.0	100.0	Total Liabilities & Net Worth	100.0	100.0	100.0	100.0	100.0	100.0

			INCOME DATA						
100.0	100.0	100.0	Net Sales	100.0	100.0	100.0	100.0	100.0	100.0
35.3	34.7	37.5	Gross Profit	42.0	40.4	35.9	34.7	32.9	35.7
32.7	34.0	37.6	Operating Expenses	44.0	40.1	35.1	35.5	32.0	34.8
2.6	.8	-.1	Operating Profit	-2.1	.3	.8	-.9	1.0	.9
.4	.4	.6	All Other Expenses (net)	1.4	.7	.0	.4	.1	.9
2.2	.4	-.7	Profit Before Taxes	-3.4	-.4	.8	-1.3	.9	-.1

			RATIOS						
2.5	2.2	2.4	Current	3.6	3.5	3.9	2.1	2.0	1.7
1.5	1.4	1.4		1.2	1.4	1.4	1.4	1.4	1.3
1.1	1.0	.9		.6	.8	.9	1.0	1.2	1.0
1.3	1.2	1.2	Quick	1.1	1.5	1.5	1.3	1.1	.9
.7	(365) .6	(358) .6		(57) .4	.5	.8	.7	.5	.5
.4	.3	.2		.1	.2	.3	.4	.3	.2
11 33.1	8 48.4	6 57.0	Sales/Receivables	0 UND	5 78.1	9 40.3	18 20.4	9 39.1	5 77.9
25 14.4	23 15.6	20 18.5		9 41.1	14 25.3	22 16.5	28 13.2	21 17.3	20 18.6
43 8.5	39 9.4	32 11.3		26 14.1	27 13.6	38 9.5	39 9.4	38 9.6	41 8.9
19 19.3	22 16.8	24 15.4	Cost of Sales/Inventory	26 13.8	24 15.3	20 18.3	14 26.1	26 14.1	30 12.0
41 8.9	45 8.1	49 7.4		85 4.3	56 6.5	41 8.9	35 10.4	45 8.2	60 6.0
76 4.8	94 3.9	92 4.0		243 1.5	126 2.9	72 5.1	62 5.9	79 4.6	110 3.3
13 27.3	13 27.8	14 26.9	Cost of Sales/Payables	6 61.7	14 26.7	13 27.2	15 24.0	14 26.2	18 20.5
24 15.4	23 15.9	25 14.8		20 17.8	26 13.9	22 16.6	25 14.9	24 15.2	33 11.2
43 8.5	40 9.0	43 8.5		69 5.3	44 8.3	35 10.4	40 9.2	38 9.5	62 5.9
7.5	8.4	6.7	Sales/Working Capital	3.9	5.7	5.7	8.6	8.2	7.8
14.4	18.5	17.2		18.7	17.8	18.9	20.9	14.8	17.3
109.4	-230.7	-50.2		-9.8	-28.6	-48.9	-415.3	42.3	-130.8
11.0	6.4	5.3	EBIT/Interest	2.4	5.1	15.2	3.7	4.5	5.7
(293) 3.3	(315) 1.8	(299) 1.0		(41) -.5	(87) 1.2	(43) 2.6	(58) .9	(34) 1.5	(36) .9
1.2	-.7	-4.1		-8.6	-3.8	-1.8	-6.2	-3.9	-3.5
4.4	4.7	3.9	Net Profit + Depr., Dep., Amort./Cur. Mat. L/T/D				7.1		
(41) 1.8	(44) 1.5	(37) 1.7					(10) 1.7		
.6	-.2	-.2					.0		
.1	.2	.2	Fixed/Worth	.2	.2	.2	.1	.2	.2
.4	.5	.6		.7	1.1	.4	.5	.5	.7
1.4	6.3	165.0		-.4	-3.0	NM	1.6	1.4	NM
1.0	.9	.8	Debt/Worth	.7	.7	.8	.7	1.1	1.0
2.3	2.5	2.4		9.0	4.0	2.0	1.6	1.7	2.5
7.2	26.5	-70.7		-2.6	-9.1	NM	6.2	7.9	-4.7
52.2	36.5	26.1	% Profit Before Taxes/Tangible Net Worth	18.2	32.4	40.5	27.3	26.3	21.6
(288) 21.5	(292) 12.2	(268) 5.6		(36) 5.1	(69) 5.5	(41) 6.6	(56) 4.8	(38) 7.1	(28) 4.6
4.4	-5.6	-12.7		-27.6	-25.1	-11.7	-7.2	-6.7	-5.0
16.3	9.2	8.6	% Profit Before Taxes/Total Assets	6.9	9.7	11.6	6.2	10.7	5.7
5.8	2.3	.9		-2.4	.7	3.3	.7	2.3	-.1
.6	-4.2	-9.3		-23.7	-7.8	-8.2	-9.6	-5.0	-9.0
86.5	76.8	65.7	Sales/Net Fixed Assets	103.9	60.9	66.4	58.3	68.0	61.9
33.1	32.4	28.1		21.5	25.7	42.7	29.3	34.3	21.1
15.3	15.4	12.0		5.5	13.3	14.3	12.1	11.3	8.1
4.8	5.1	4.7	Sales/Total Assets	4.5	5.1	4.8	4.5	4.9	4.7
3.7	3.6	3.3		2.0	3.4	3.2	3.6	3.3	3.0
2.5	2.3	2.1		1.0	2.2	2.2	2.6	2.6	1.8
.4	.4	.4	% Depr., Dep., Amort./Sales	.4	.5	.4	.4	.4	.6
(274) .7	(288) .7	(280) .9		(43) 1.1	(77) .9	(42) .7	(56) .9	(36) .8	(26) 1.1
1.2	1.2	1.6		3.6	1.7	1.2	1.8	1.1	1.7
1.9	1.7	2.1	% Officers', Directors' Owners' Comp/Sales	4.6	2.8	2.1	1.7	1.0	.9
(202) 3.6	(210) 3.3	(193) 3.9		(26) 4.6	(65) 5.5	(34) 3.1	(36) 2.7	(21) 2.2	(11) 2.4
6.6	6.3	7.2		12.7	8.5	6.1	5.1	4.1	2.6
5731901M	5396098M	7966895M	Net Sales ($)	35484M	188780M	203567M	474691M	664700M	6399673M
1653845M	1749744M	2342391M	Total Assets ($)	30519M	88016M	74506M	151663M	215598M	1782089M

M = $ thousand   MM = $ million
See Pages 9 through 22 for Explanation of Ratios and Data

Current Data Sorted by Assets

Comparative Historical Data

0-500M	500M-2MM	2-10MM	10-50MM	50-100MM	100-250MM	Type of Statement	4/1/05-3/31/06 ALL	4/1/06-3/31/07 ALL
	1	1	1	5	5	Unqualified	11	9
	1	11	2			Reviewed	15	15
3	13	9	2			Compiled	33	30
34	21	6	2		1	Tax Returns	57	60
15	24	17	10	1	2	Other	49	52
	27 (4/1-9/30/09)		159 (10/1/09-3/31/10)					
52	59	44	17	6	8	NUMBER OF STATEMENTS	165	166
%	%	%	%	%	%	**ASSETS**	%	%
18.4	10.9	9.5	13.9			Cash & Equivalents	10.8	10.2
9.7	12.4	14.0	9.7			Trade Receivables (net)	11.9	12.1
43.2	49.6	40.0	42.1			Inventory	47.3	49.9
1.6	1.5	5.9	3.5			All Other Current	1.5	2.6
72.9	74.4	69.3	69.1			Total Current	71.5	74.8
14.5	14.9	18.8	22.9			Fixed Assets (net)	18.4	16.9
3.1	3.0	2.5	.4			Intangibles (net)	3.5	3.4
9.5	7.6	9.4	7.6			All Other Non-Current	6.7	4.8
100.0	100.0	100.0	100.0			Total	100.0	100.0
						LIABILITIES		
22.6	12.3	8.6	9.8			Notes Payable-Short Term	11.9	13.4
2.6	3.8	2.7	2.7			Cur. Mat.-L.T.D.	3.6	4.0
16.7	22.3	13.6	14.1			Trade Payables	15.6	18.5
.2	.0	.2	.6			Income Taxes Payable	.2	.2
17.8	17.0	19.0	9.8			All Other Current	13.0	14.0
59.9	55.4	44.0	37.1			Total Current	44.3	50.2
24.4	14.7	13.9	20.8			Long-Term Debt	18.1	17.2
.0	.0	.0	.1			Deferred Taxes	.1	.0
11.2	10.3	5.7	7.9			All Other Non-Current	7.8	6.4
4.4	19.6	36.3	34.1			Net Worth	29.7	26.3
100.0	100.0	100.0	100.0			Total Liabilities & Net Worth	100.0	100.0
						INCOME DATA		
100.0	100.0	100.0	100.0			Net Sales	100.0	100.0
46.0	42.6	44.9	38.6			Gross Profit	44.9	44.7
42.8	41.1	41.5	38.6			Operating Expenses	41.4	41.5
3.2	1.5	3.4	.0			Operating Profit	3.5	3.2
.7	.4	.3	.9			All Other Expenses (net)	1.2	1.1
2.6	1.1	3.1	-1.0			Profit Before Taxes	2.3	2.1
						RATIOS		
2.6	2.6	3.6	4.0				2.8	2.4
1.7	1.4	1.5	1.8			Current	1.9	1.6
.8	1.0	1.0	1.1				1.1	1.1
1.5	.9	1.3	1.2				1.0	.7
.5	.4	.5	.4			Quick	(162) .5	(165) .4
.2	.1	.1	.3				.2	.2
0 UND	0 999.8	0 836.5	0 UND				0 UND	0 UND
1 249.5	11 34.4	9 39.9	7 51.2			Sales/Receivables	8 48.3	8 45.4
17 21.6	29 12.5	26 14.1	27 13.8				25 14.8	27 13.6
23 15.7	85 4.3	53 6.9	76 4.8				67 5.4	68 5.4
104 3.5	127 2.9	120 3.0	139 2.6			Cost of Sales/Inventory	117 3.1	117 3.1
182 2.0	173 2.1	198 1.8	203 1.8				189 1.9	192 1.9
3 125.5	21 17.5	17 20.9	20 18.6				12 29.3	17 21.2
27 13.6	36 10.3	34 10.9	34 10.8			Cost of Sales/Payables	30 12.1	41 8.8
61 6.0	66 5.5	46 7.9	66 5.5				56 6.5	64 5.7
6.1	4.6	3.7	3.3				4.6	5.0
15.5	9.8	9.1	6.2			Sales/Working Capital	9.7	10.3
-42.5	-122.2	NM	524.7				36.0	56.0
8.7	4.9	11.2	13.2				11.6	10.0
(34) 2.0	(49) 1.7	(38) 4.0	(15) .9			EBIT/Interest	(141) 2.8	(150) 2.9
-1.6	-.4	1.5	-1.8				.7	.9
						Net Profit + Depr., Dep., Amort./Cur. Mat. L/T/D	9.0	12.5
							(20) 2.5	(14) 3.3
							1.3	.9
.1	.2	.1	.2				.1	.1
.6	.7	.3	.4			Fixed/Worth	.4	.4
-.6	-5.4	2.9	1.2				2.8	4.5
.7	1.6	.7	.5				.9	1.1
5.1	3.2	1.9	1.5			Debt/Worth	2.1	2.4
-3.5	-58.7	7.8	3.5				16.1	20.4
102.1	51.8	39.7	14.6				49.3	59.2
(29) 25.6	(44) 18.0	(38) 15.3	(15) -2.4			% Profit Before Taxes/Tangible Net Worth	(132) 16.2	(133) 18.5
-2.7	4.7	3.5	-29.4				2.8	3.7
20.7	12.5	17.1	13.6				16.1	14.7
8.1	3.7	4.0	-.9			% Profit Before Taxes/Total Assets	3.9	4.9
-11.8	-1.7	.8	-8.2				-1.4	-.1
192.8	67.6	57.1	22.3				69.7	62.6
49.3	29.7	25.5	16.7			Sales/Net Fixed Assets	29.1	24.4
10.9	12.0	7.0	6.0				10.5	12.0
5.4	3.5	3.2	2.9				3.9	3.7
3.5	2.5	2.4	2.2			Sales/Total Assets	2.7	2.7
2.1	1.8	1.8	1.4				1.8	1.9
.3	.5	.5	.7				.4	.4
(32) .8	(44) .9	(33) 1.0	(16) 1.3			% Depr., Dep., Amort./Sales	(128) 1.0	(123) 1.0
2.3	1.4	1.6	2.0				1.7	1.6
4.1	2.2	1.2					3.3	2.6
(28) 6.1	(36) 3.9	(22) 3.7				% Officers', Directors' Owners' Comp/Sales	(89) 4.7	(92) 4.1
7.8	7.0	9.1					9.3	8.0
50428M	171179M	514277M	1162146M	1158987M	2027209M	Net Sales ($)	3664031M	3614861M
14035M	63463M	202863M	391357M	483848M	1043361M	Total Assets ($)	1323335M	1408024M

Comparative Historical Data | Current Data Sorted by Sales

Type of Statement	4/1/07-3/31/08 ALL	4/1/08-3/31/09 ALL	4/1/09-3/31/10 ALL	27 (4/1-9/30/09) 0-1MM	1-3MM	3-5MM	159 (10/1/09-3/31/10) 5-10MM	10-25MM	25MM & OVER
Unqualified	12	7	12				1		11
Reviewed	14	15	14		1	1	3	7	2
Compiled	24	32	28	3	9	4	5	4	3
Tax Returns	69	65	63	21	28	6	3	4	1
Other	49	67	69	11	22	6	7	11	12
NUMBER OF STATEMENTS	168	186	186	35	60	17	19	26	29
ASSETS	%	%	%	%	%	%	%	%	%
Cash & Equivalents	8.7	9.2	13.0	13.0	14.3	10.7	10.4	13.1	13.3
Trade Receivables (net)	9.2	11.7	11.1	7.9	12.7	10.4	12.4	16.6	5.9
Inventory	53.6	49.6	44.5	48.4	43.4	56.3	44.4	34.2	44.9
All Other Current	1.9	3.5	3.0	1.8	1.3	2.0	7.6	3.3	5.1
Total Current	73.3	73.9	71.6	71.0	71.7	79.4	74.8	67.2	69.2
Fixed Assets (net)	19.1	17.7	16.7	16.3	14.2	15.6	17.7	19.4	19.9
Intangibles (net)	3.1	3.5	3.6	4.5	1.7	1.3	4.6	3.0	7.4
All Other Non-Current	4.6	4.9	8.2	8.1	12.4	3.7	2.9	10.4	3.5
Total	100.0	100.0	100.0	100.0	100.0	100.0	100.0	100.0	100.0
LIABILITIES									
Notes Payable-Short Term	14.0	13.1	13.9	16.3	18.8	12.1	8.9	7.7	10.3
Cur. Mat.-L.T.D.	4.4	3.2	2.9	3.5	3.5	2.3	3.6	1.6	2.9
Trade Payables	20.0	21.1	17.7	13.0	19.6	20.3	19.9	16.9	17.3
Income Taxes Payable	.3	.1	.2	.3	.1	.0	.2	.1	.6
All Other Current	16.3	15.9	16.8	23.6	11.2	22.6	25.1	14.3	13.4
Total Current	55.1	53.3	51.4	56.7	53.2	57.3	57.6	40.6	43.6
Long-Term Debt	15.1	19.7	17.1	28.4	18.2	6.6	15.9	14.2	10.6
Deferred Taxes	.1	.1	.2	.0	.0	.0	.1	.0	1.1
All Other Non-Current	9.1	12.4	8.9	12.2	11.5	8.6	5.4	2.3	7.9
Net Worth	20.8	14.6	22.4	2.6	17.1	27.5	21.0	43.0	36.8
Total Liabilities & Net Worth	100.0	100.0	100.0	100.0	100.0	100.0	100.0	100.0	100.0
INCOME DATA									
Net Sales	100.0	100.0	100.0	100.0	100.0	100.0	100.0	100.0	100.0
Gross Profit	44.7	43.2	44.0	47.4	45.6	40.3	42.5	40.5	43.0
Operating Expenses	41.4	41.7	41.5	46.1	42.2	39.5	40.7	36.6	40.5
Operating Profit	3.3	1.5	2.6	1.3	3.5	.8	1.8	4.0	2.4
All Other Expenses (net)	1.1	.5	.6	.7	.8	-.2	-.5	.0	1.8
Profit Before Taxes	2.2	1.0	1.9	.6	2.7	1.0	2.3	3.9	.6
RATIOS									
Current	2.3	2.6	2.8	3.6	2.6	2.7	3.1	3.5	2.6
	1.4	1.5	1.6	1.6	1.7	1.4	1.2	1.6	1.6
	.9	1.0	1.0	.9	1.0	.9	.8	1.2	1.1
Quick	.6	.9	1.1	1.0	1.6	.7	1.3	1.3	.8
	(166) .3	(184) .4	.4	.4	.5	.4	.2	.6	.3
	.1	.1	.1	.1	.1	.1	.3	.1	.1
Sales/Receivables	0 UND	0 UND	0 UND	0 UND	0 UND	0 999.8	0 999.8	0 UND	0 UND
	4 103.2	5 80.9	6 58.9	2 155.0	7 49.4	8 45.7	11 34.8	8 44.8	4 101.4
	19 19.5	21 17.7	23 15.7	17 21.2	22 16.4	23 15.6	21 17.2	39 9.3	16 23.4
Cost of Sales/Inventory	70 5.2	54 6.8	63 5.8	103 3.6	59 6.2	84 4.3	46 7.9	28 12.9	67 5.5
	111 3.3	114 3.2	119 3.1	169 2.2	108 3.4	130 2.8	108 3.4	88 4.1	123 3.0
	171 2.1	193 1.9	188 1.9	283 1.3	171 2.1	199 1.8	187 2.0	143 2.6	189 1.9
Cost of Sales/Payables	20 17.9	16 22.7	17 21.5	3 128.0	13 27.7	25 14.5	25 14.5	17 21.7	25 14.7
	40 9.1	34 10.7	34 10.8	46 8.0	28 13.1	33 11.0	33 11.0	37 9.8	34 10.8
	63 5.8	64 5.7	61 6.0	67 5.5	60 6.1	64 5.7	56 6.5	48 7.6	78 4.7
Sales/Working Capital	6.5	5.2	5.0	5.5	4.5	6.9	4.4	4.9	4.7
	15.3	11.4	11.4	9.5	11.2	13.5	39.1	9.1	7.3
	-87.4	-104.1	-119.1	-38.6	-191.9	-72.5	-16.0	42.4	74.2
EBIT/Interest	6.8	7.5	7.6	6.6	5.5	5.0	12.6	26.3	13.7
	(146) 2.6	(158) 2.5	(149) 2.8	(23) 1.7	(49) 1.7	(13) 1.4	(14) 3.3	(24) 5.9	(26) 2.9
	.8	-.7	.3	-1.8	.1	-2.5	.1	1.6	.8
Net Profit + Depr., Dep., Amort./Cur. Mat. L/T/D	43.8	6.7	17.3						60.1
	(18) 6.1	(14) 1.2	(21) 2.1						(10) 10.4
	1.8	-.3	.0						-7.3
Fixed/Worth	.2	.2	.1	.1	.1	.1	.2	.1	.2
	.6	.7	.6	1.0	.5	.9	2.3	.3	.5
	10.3	11.3	UND	-.5	UND	NM	-.8	1.3	1.5
Debt/Worth	1.3	1.1	.9	1.1	.9	.9	.8	.7	.7
	2.7	2.9	2.4	9.8	2.6	1.9	9.9	1.4	1.5
	31.0	NM	-52.2	-3.2	UND	NM	-8.2	3.3	4.9
% Profit Before Taxes/Tangible Net Worth	57.9	45.9	46.1	83.9	68.3	47.1	54.7	40.2	22.6
	(130) 18.0	(140) 12.1	(138) 14.7	(19) 13.2	(45) 24.4	(13) 4.7	(11) 28.4	(25) 14.7	(25) 5.6
	1.5	-.5	1.2	-19.8	8.2	-12.3	-9.5	3.8	-5.2
% Profit Before Taxes/Total Assets	17.2	11.6	15.4	16.8	15.5	6.9	17.2	18.4	9.8
	4.7	2.8	4.0	4.2	5.7	2.9	2.3	6.4	2.1
	-.8	-5.2	-2.6	-12.8	-.1	-6.3	-4.8	1.4	-2.0
Sales/Net Fixed Assets	63.1	67.7	69.2	102.0	86.3	98.8	50.8	95.0	22.3
	25.0	26.9	24.4	29.4	35.9	33.1	21.2	36.7	11.4
	12.5	9.7	8.3	7.3	12.2	8.2	9.5	11.1	6.7
Sales/Total Assets	4.1	3.9	3.7	3.8	4.0	3.5	4.1	4.2	3.0
	2.9	2.7	2.5	2.1	2.6	2.6	2.7	2.7	2.4
	2.0	1.9	1.8	1.3	1.7	2.1	2.0	2.0	1.5
% Depr., Dep., Amort./Sales	.4	.5	.5	.5	.5	.2	.3	.6	.8
	(130) .9	(132) 1.1	(137) 1.0	(21) 1.1	(41) .9	(15) .6	(14) 1.1	(21) .9	(25) 1.7
	1.6	1.8	2.0	2.5	1.6	1.3	2.5	1.2	2.6
% Officers', Directors' Owners' Comp/Sales	2.2	1.8	2.0	6.5	3.0	.9	2.1	1.1	
	(80) 4.0	(87) 3.7	(96) 4.6	(11) 8.4	(39) 4.5	(12) 3.7	(11) 3.4	(15) 4.6	
	6.4	7.3	7.4	12.9	6.7	9.2	4.3	9.6	
Net Sales ($)	4483701M	5787317M	5084226M	20133M	108371M	67121M	144159M	413100M	4331342M
Total Assets ($)	1645637M	2293305M	2198927M	10049M	53065M	28136M	60450M	168042M	1879185M

© RMA 2010

M = $ thousand   MM = $ million

See Pages 9 through 22 for Explanation of Ratios and Data

RETAIL—Household Appliance Stores NAICS 443111

| Current Data Sorted by Assets | | | | | | | Comparative Historical Data | | |

							Type of Statement		
							Unqualified	8	8
		1		2		2	Reviewed	12	13
		4	8	5			Compiled	33	29
4		12	7				Tax Returns	26	35
17		18	9	1			Other	36	38
4		12	17	8		1		4/1/05-3/31/06	4/1/06-3/31/07
	18 (4/1-9/30/09)			114 (10/1/09-3/31/10)				ALL	ALL
0-500M	500M-2MM	2-10MM	10-50MM	50-100MM	100-250MM		NUMBER OF STATEMENTS		
25	47	41	16		3			115	123
%	%	%	%	%	%		ASSETS	%	%
16.0	9.3	10.1	11.2				Cash & Equivalents	10.4	10.8
9.5	14.5	15.4	7.9				Trade Receivables (net)	19.4	15.8
39.7	44.9	48.5	47.6				Inventory	43.8	47.7
1.7	1.9	3.3	1.9				All Other Current	3.1	2.9
66.9	70.6	77.3	68.6				Total Current	76.7	77.2
19.1	19.1	15.9	26.1				Fixed Assets (net)	16.0	15.9
3.1	4.9	1.4	3.0				Intangibles (net)	2.9	1.8
11.0	5.5	5.4	2.3				All Other Non-Current	4.3	5.2
100.0	100.0	100.0	100.0				Total	100.0	100.0
							LIABILITIES		
22.1	13.4	10.9	18.6				Notes Payable-Short Term	11.5	12.3
12.3	3.2	1.7	1.1				Cur. Mat.-L.T.D.	3.1	2.7
23.4	20.0	22.1	18.7				Trade Payables	24.7	22.1
.0	.1	.1	.0				Income Taxes Payable	.1	.1
25.7	14.8	16.4	11.0				All Other Current	16.6	17.2
83.5	51.5	51.2	49.4				Total Current	56.0	54.4
19.6	20.2	10.5	13.7				Long-Term Debt	14.2	12.1
.0	.0	.2	.0				Deferred Taxes	.1	.1
15.4	7.8	6.3	3.0				All Other Non-Current	5.7	7.8
-18.5	20.6	31.7	33.8				Net Worth	24.0	25.6
100.0	100.0	100.0	100.0				Total Liabilties & Net Worth	100.0	100.0
							INCOME DATA		
100.0	100.0	100.0	100.0				Net Sales	100.0	100.0
40.1	31.0	31.3	33.5				Gross Profit	34.0	34.3
40.8	29.5	29.6	30.8				Operating Expenses	31.2	31.3
-.8	1.5	1.7	2.7				Operating Profit	2.9	3.0
.5	.8	-.2	-.2				All Other Expenses (net)	.5	.3
-1.3	.7	1.9	2.9				Profit Before Taxes	2.3	2.7
							RATIOS		
1.5	2.1	2.2	1.8					2.2	2.3
1.1	1.4	1.5	1.5				Current	1.3	1.5
.5	1.1	1.1	1.0					1.1	1.1
.7	.9	.8	.5					.9	.9
.4	.4	.4	.3				Quick	.5	.4
.1	.2	.3	.2					.3	.3
0 UND	3 117.6	5 74.2	6 63.2					6 64.5	5 69.6
6 56.4	9 39.4	16 23.2	8 47.8				Sales/Receivables	17 21.6	12 30.4
17 21.9	23 16.1	26 14.3	15 25.2					30 12.3	23 15.7
36 10.1	42 8.7	60 6.1	66 5.5					48 7.6	49 7.5
46 7.9	69 5.3	84 4.3	87 4.2				Cost of Sales/Inventory	82 4.4	75 4.9
90 4.0	114 3.2	119 3.1	114 3.2					112 3.2	118 3.1
2 218.8	13 28.9	20 18.1	22 16.9					23 16.2	16 22.2
23 15.6	29 12.6	33 11.2	31 11.7				Cost of Sales/Payables	41 8.8	33 11.1
61 6.0	48 7.6	59 6.2	54 6.7					65 5.6	57 6.4
17.4	6.7	6.0	7.7					6.7	7.5
53.8	18.5	12.3	13.3				Sales/Working Capital	14.1	15.1
-11.6	51.1	43.4	NM					129.7	84.3
9.1	6.3	11.5	13.0					11.3	9.7
(21) 1.6	(42) 1.9	(37) 3.3	(14) 4.8				EBIT/Interest	(106) 3.3	(100) 3.5
-3.1	.1	-.1	1.2					1.4	1.2
	6.2						Net Profit + Depr., Dep.,		9.4 / 25.1
	(10) 1.8						Amort./Cur. Mat. L/T/D	(14) 4.2	(13) 4.8
	1.1							1.0	2.1
.2	.2	.2	.3					.2	.2
1.2	.5	.5	1.0				Fixed/Worth	.5	.5
-.6	-4.7	1.2	3.5					2.6	4.0
1.6	1.1	1.2	1.2					1.4	1.4
32.7	2.4	2.4	1.7				Debt/Worth	3.6	3.1
-3.0	-68.0	8.0	24.7					15.5	16.0
178.1	34.7	45.0	17.7				% Profit Before Taxes/Tangible	49.1	55.8
(13) 12.4	(34) 16.6	(38) 10.7	(14) 5.4				Net Worth	(91) 24.9	(99) 22.2
4.1	3.8	-4.7	.1					10.5	8.1
16.0	9.1	9.4	11.1				% Profit Before Taxes/Total	12.2	14.7
2.4	3.2	2.3	1.5				Assets	6.3	5.5
-7.5	-1.1	-.9	-.3					.8	1.0
194.1	77.8	80.5	25.4					73.9	102.7
40.1	28.4	28.3	18.8				Sales/Net Fixed Assets	38.4	38.0
11.5	11.9	11.8	6.2					15.7	14.1
6.2	4.8	3.7	3.3					4.2	4.5
4.5	3.2	2.8	2.7				Sales/Total Assets	3.1	3.4
3.0	2.1	2.2	2.2					2.1	2.4
.3	.4	.4	.7					.4	.4
(15) .8	(33) 1.0	(35) .6	.8				% Depr., Dep., Amort./Sales	(98) .8	(98) .8
1.4	1.4	1.1	1.3					1.3	1.6
1.8	1.6	.9					% Officers', Directors'	1.5	1.3
(14) 6.8	(28) 3.0	(15) 2.1					Owners' Comp/Sales	(56) 2.5	(60) 2.7
13.3	4.3	3.4						6.4	6.1
35360M	208761M	716129M	935359M		773922M		Net Sales ($)	2031450M	2108692M
7092M	54409M	207498M	355977M		314457M		Total Assets ($)	854460M	676697M

(Columns 50-100MM and 100-250MM: DATA NOT AVAILABLE)

M = $ thousand   MM = $ million
See Pages 9 through 22 for Explanation of Ratios and Data

Comparative Historical Data   Current Data Sorted by Sales

4/1/07-3/31/08 ALL	4/1/08-3/31/09 ALL	4/1/09-3/31/10 ALL	Type of Statement	0-1MM	1-3MM	3-5MM	5-10MM	10-25MM	25MM & OVER
6	6	5	Unqualified		1				4
13	18	17	Reviewed		1	3	1	5	7
29	29	23	Compiled	2	5	5	5	4	2
29	40	45	Tax Returns	12	13	10	7	2	1
41	39	42	Other	2	7	4	7	10	12
					18 (4/1-9/30/09)		114 (10/1/09-3/31/10)		
118	132	132	NUMBER OF STATEMENTS	16	27	22	20	21	26
%	%	%	ASSETS	%	%	%	%	%	%
12.6	10.5	10.9	Cash & Equivalents	12.6	10.4	13.6	10.0	7.9	11.1
17.9	13.7	13.4	Trade Receivables (net)	7.5	16.8	12.1	14.8	14.8	12.6
44.6	48.2	45.1	Inventory	33.8	41.5	46.3	49.8	50.1	47.0
2.4	2.3	2.3	All Other Current	.6	1.8	.9	4.2	3.8	2.2
77.5	74.6	71.7	Total Current	54.5	70.5	72.9	78.9	76.6	72.9
14.1	18.0	18.7	Fixed Assets (net)	35.8	15.5	15.2	15.1	15.0	20.4
3.0	2.2	3.6	Intangibles (net)	6.9	5.3	2.9	.5	1.8	4.2
5.5	5.1	6.0	All Other Non-Current	2.8	8.8	9.1	5.5	6.7	2.5
100.0	100.0	100.0	Total	100.0	100.0	100.0	100.0	100.0	100.0
			LIABILITIES						
13.4	15.1	15.3	Notes Payable-Short Term	13.5	27.3	9.9	6.5	13.1	16.9
3.1	4.3	4.1	Cur. Mat.-L.T.D.	5.9	6.6	6.9	3.7	1.3	.8
19.6	18.9	21.1	Trade Payables	15.6	19.6	22.8	24.1	20.4	22.8
.1	.1	.1	Income Taxes Payable	.0	.0	.2	.0	.1	.2
14.2	14.9	16.8	All Other Current	27.3	10.9	15.5	23.4	13.6	14.8
50.5	53.3	57.3	Total Current	62.2	64.4	55.3	57.7	48.5	55.5
13.7	15.8	16.0	Long-Term Debt	41.9	18.9	11.7	8.4	11.6	9.8
.0	.0	.1	Deferred Taxes	.0	.0	.0	.0	.3	.0
6.4	4.1	8.2	All Other Non-Current	1.9	21.0	2.1	7.1	10.3	3.3
29.3	26.9	18.4	Net Worth	-6.0	-4.3	30.8	26.8	29.2	31.3
100.0	100.0	100.0	Total Liabilities & Net Worth	100.0	100.0	100.0	100.0	100.0	100.0
			INCOME DATA						
100.0	100.0	100.0	Net Sales	100.0	100.0	100.0	100.0	100.0	100.0
32.9	35.0	33.5	Gross Profit	39.1	38.6	29.5	29.2	28.6	35.5
29.6	33.2	32.1	Operating Expenses	39.8	39.7	27.6	26.7	26.8	31.9
3.2	1.8	1.4	Operating Profit	-.6	-1.1	2.0	2.4	1.9	3.6
.5	.2	.4	All Other Expenses (net)	2.3	.3	-.3	.0	.4	.0
2.7	1.6	1.0	Profit Before Taxes	-2.9	-1.5	2.3	2.4	1.5	3.6
			RATIOS						
2.5	2.6	2.0	Current	3.2	2.1	2.0	1.7	2.4	1.7
1.4	1.5	1.4		1.2	1.3	1.4	1.4	1.7	1.3
1.1	1.1	1.0		.6	.9	1.0	1.1	1.1	1.0
1.1	.9	.8	Quick	.9	1.0	.7	.7	.8	.7
.6	.4	.4		.5	.4	.5	.4	.3	.3
.2	.2	.2		.2	.1	.2	.2	.3	.3
5 72.5	3 107.9	4 85.4	Sales/Receivables	0 UND	3 139.2	4 99.7	5 73.7	4 85.4	6 65.4
14 25.2	9 39.8	10 35.5		7 52.3	13 28.3	9 41.9	11 31.9	16 22.2	8 47.8
31 11.9	22 16.4	20 17.9		17 21.7	36 10.1	21 17.3	22 16.7	22 16.3	16 22.2
45 8.1	53 6.9	46 8.0	Cost of Sales/Inventory	40 9.0	46 7.9	38 9.7	29 12.5	62 5.9	62 5.9
69 5.3	76 4.8	76 4.8		96 3.8	83 4.4	63 5.8	60 6.1	86 4.3	77 4.7
105 3.5	114 3.2	111 3.3		159 2.3	156 2.3	94 3.9	87 4.2	100 3.7	97 3.7
12 29.9	14 27.0	16 23.5	Cost of Sales/Payables	0 UND	17 21.4	16 23.1	11 32.6	15 24.6	21 17.5
27 13.6	28 13.2	30 12.0		41 8.9	30 12.0	28 13.2	23 15.6	29 12.6	35 10.5
49 7.4	44 8.3	55 6.6		60 6.0	60 6.1	50 7.3	47 7.7	48 7.6	63 5.8
6.6	7.3	7.4	Sales/Working Capital	5.5	3.6	11.5	12.8	6.0	8.0
13.8	12.6	18.2		52.3	18.3	18.0	20.7	10.9	19.5
67.7	89.8	810.3		-10.4	-74.1	307.0	39.3	NM	NM
7.0	9.0	8.9	EBIT/Interest	2.3	4.5	19.6	19.2	7.4	13.5
(99) 3.2	(109) 2.6	(117) 2.5		(14) .5	(25) 1.7	(19) 2.5	(15) 3.7	2.4	(23) 5.1
1.5	.7	.4		-4.2	-.9	1.6	1.7	-1.4	1.4
5.7	3.2	12.2	Net Profit + Depr., Dep., Amort./Cur. Mat. L/T/D						
(16) 2.5	(15) 1.1	(25) 3.1							
.4	.4	1.1							
.1	.2	.2	Fixed/Worth	.3	.1	.2	.2	.2	.3
.4	.5	.6		2.6	.7	.5	.4	.5	.9
1.5	4.4	5.0		-1.5	-.8	2.0	2.8	3.5	1.4
.9	.8	1.3	Debt/Worth	1.7	1.7	.8	.8	1.4	1.3
2.3	2.0	3.0		NM	3.2	2.0	2.4	2.2	2.5
12.0	26.2	48.3		-2.3	-5.3	17.2	26.4	15.5	10.4
48.1	36.6	37.2	% Profit Before Taxes/Tangible Net Worth		35.4	34.3	89.8	34.1	43.5
(96) 26.5	(106) 16.4	(101) 13.5			(17) 9.5	(18) 17.6	(17) 23.0	(18) 14.2	(23) 7.6
8.5	5.8	1.8			-9.5	6.8	11.4	-6.9	.6
16.1	13.3	10.5	% Profit Before Taxes/Total Assets	4.3	6.1	14.0	10.9	9.9	12.9
6.9	4.4	2.6		-1.5	1.0	4.5	4.9	2.6	1.8
1.7	-.5	-1.1		-20.6	-8.5	2.3		-2.2	.0
87.9	68.9	73.9	Sales/Net Fixed Assets	63.4	80.0	75.8	158.2	71.7	44.6
34.9	25.8	27.1		10.3	34.2	39.5	42.4	19.9	22.4
15.3	12.3	11.8		3.1	12.5	13.2	25.3	11.7	11.9
4.7	4.5	4.3	Sales/Total Assets	4.7	4.2	4.3	5.2	3.6	4.1
3.5	3.3	3.1		2.4	2.9	3.5	4.1	2.8	3.0
2.4	2.3	2.3		1.4	1.9	2.4	3.0	2.4	2.3
.3	.4	.4	% Depr., Dep., Amort./Sales	.7	.4	.4	.2	.4	.6
(91) .7	(107) .6	(102) .8		(12) 1.0	(16) 1.1	(17) .6	(13) .4	(18) .7	.8
1.2	1.2	1.3		2.0	1.8	1.1	1.1	1.3	1.2
1.6	1.5	1.4	% Officers', Directors' Owners' Comp/Sales		1.9	2.5	1.1		
(56) 2.8	(74) 3.1	(61) 2.8			(15) 3.2	(14) 3.2	(13) 3.0		
4.2	5.3	4.9			5.6	5.1	4.9		
2348291M	3979457M	2669531M	Net Sales ($)	10271M	49545M	82890M	156939M	332620M	2037266M
738055M	1060507M	939433M	Total Assets ($)	5644M	22938M	27672M	42649M	112165M	728365M

© RMA 2010

M = $ thousand   MM = $ million
See Pages 9 through 22 for Explanation of Ratios and Data

RETAIL—Radio, Television, and Other Electronics Stores NAICS 443112

Current Data Sorted by Assets | **Comparative Historical Data**

0-500M	500M-2MM	2-10MM	10-50MM	50-100MM	100-250MM	Type of Statement	4/1/05-3/31/06 ALL	4/1/06-3/31/07 ALL
		4	5	3	3	Unqualified	15	18
	4	15	1			Reviewed	16	14
3	9	13				Compiled	12	22
14	19	6	8			Tax Returns	31	30
10	16	20			5	Other	42	53
	33 (4/1-9/30/09)		125 (10/1/09-3/31/10)					
27	48	58	14	3	8	**NUMBER OF STATEMENTS**	116	137
%	%	%	%	%	%	**ASSETS**	%	%
16.2	15.2	12.5	10.1			Cash & Equivalents	11.7	12.3
16.0	22.7	23.4	19.9			Trade Receivables (net)	20.3	24.8
40.3	36.3	31.4	40.2			Inventory	40.2	36.4
3.5	2.4	3.1	3.2			All Other Current	2.1	3.5
76.0	76.6	70.4	73.3			Total Current	74.2	77.0
13.3	15.8	20.0	9.9			Fixed Assets (net)	17.4	15.7
4.7	3.1	2.4	5.9			Intangibles (net)	2.3	1.7
5.9	4.5	7.2	10.9			All Other Non-Current	6.1	5.6
100.0	100.0	100.0	100.0			Total	100.0	100.0
						LIABILITIES		
18.4	14.0	8.4	19.3			Notes Payable-Short Term	13.8	12.0
5.5	3.0	2.9	1.2			Cur. Mat.-L.T.D.	4.3	1.7
25.2	26.5	24.0	22.2			Trade Payables	25.9	26.5
.0	.5	.1	.2			Income Taxes Payable	.1	.2
26.8	12.6	13.7	9.1			All Other Current	11.5	16.0
75.9	56.6	49.1	52.0			Total Current	55.7	56.5
36.8	14.6	10.8	7.2			Long-Term Debt	10.4	9.8
.0	.1	.2	.0			Deferred Taxes	.1	.1
13.0	6.4	2.9	7.1			All Other Non-Current	7.7	6.5
-25.7	22.3	36.9	33.7			Net Worth	26.0	27.1
100.0	100.0	100.0	100.0			Total Liabilities & Net Worth	100.0	100.0
						INCOME DATA		
100.0	100.0	100.0	100.0			Net Sales	100.0	100.0
43.7	35.9	35.3	30.5			Gross Profit	35.8	36.9
40.8	32.6	31.5	27.6			Operating Expenses	32.8	33.2
2.9	3.2	3.8	2.9			Operating Profit	2.9	3.8
.1	-.2	.2	1.1			All Other Expenses (net)	.6	.4
2.8	3.4	3.6	1.9			Profit Before Taxes	2.3	3.3
						RATIOS		
3.7	2.2	2.5	2.3				2.3	2.0
1.4	1.5	1.4	1.4			Current	1.5	1.4
.6	.9	1.0	1.0				1.1	1.1
1.2	1.2	1.2	1.1				1.2	1.2
.4	.7	.7	.6			Quick	.6 (136)	.7
.2	.4	.3	.3				.3	.3
0 UND	6 62.9	9 41.4	12 30.2				5 81.1	6 56.2
7 52.0	21 17.4	30 12.1	24 15.3			Sales/Receivables	20 18.6	18 20.2
20 17.9	36 10.1	48 7.6	33 11.1				37 9.8	35 10.6
14 26.0	24 15.1	21 17.0	26 13.9				32 11.4	21 17.0
58 6.3	55 6.7	49 7.4	61 6.0			Cost of Sales/Inventory	70 5.2	47 7.8
116 3.1	92 4.0	98 3.7	92 4.0				122 3.0	90 4.0
1 320.8	16 22.9	24 14.9	17 21.8				21 17.1	18 20.1
30 12.3	31 11.7	45 8.1	26 14.1			Cost of Sales/Payables	39 9.3	38 9.7
48 7.5	65 5.6	60 6.1	49 7.4				70 5.2	65 5.6
5.6	8.6	6.2	7.9				6.7	8.3
12.4	12.9	16.9	14.5			Sales/Working Capital	14.7	17.4
-28.1	-101.0	371.7	NM				85.7	122.3
8.0	24.1	14.7	14.5				8.2	16.5
(17) 1.3	(40) 6.1	(50) 4.5	(12) 5.1			EBIT/Interest	(98) 3.1	(111) 3.7
-1.3	1.7	1.6	.6				.9	1.4
						Net Profit + Depr., Dep.,	5.4	14.3
						Amort./Cur. Mat. L/T/D	(19) 2.2	(16) 4.9
							.6	1.3
.0	.1	.2	.1				.2	.2
.4	.5	.5	.3			Fixed/Worth	.4	.5
-.3	2.9	1.6	1.6				2.7	1.5
2.1	1.1	.9	.9				.9	1.0
UND	2.7	1.7	3.0			Debt/Worth	2.3	2.7
-2.1	23.8	7.6	7.6				12.0	8.9
999.8	96.6	53.2	88.7			% Profit Before Taxes/Tangible	40.4	75.8
(14) 123.1	(38) 34.1	(53) 20.7	(12) 45.9			Net Worth	(94) 18.3	(117) 30.2
32.9	2.4	2.0	14.6				1.7	6.8
39.1	22.2	14.1	17.1			% Profit Before Taxes/Total	14.7	22.1
15.1	7.5	6.3	10.1			Assets	5.1	8.5
-2.2	.6	.7	.1				.4	1.4
UND	132.6	63.9	225.1				77.4	70.6
75.2	29.3	21.0	38.5			Sales/Net Fixed Assets	24.3	32.4
19.4	14.6	9.1	22.4				13.0	15.6
4.6	4.8	3.8	4.1				4.2	5.0
3.8	3.7	3.0	3.0			Sales/Total Assets	3.2	3.7
3.0	2.6	2.1	1.9				2.3	2.8
.2	.4	.3	.1				.4	.4
(14) .6	(34) .8	(50) .9	(10) .6			% Depr., Dep., Amort./Sales	(97) .8	(112) .7
1.3	1.5	1.6	1.4				1.5	1.3
3.0	.9	1.2				% Officers', Directors'	1.9	1.6
(16) 4.9	(25)	(20) 2.6				Owners' Comp/Sales	(57) 4.2	(62) 3.4
8.3	6.3	5.3					6.9	7.2
25254M	210806M	876246M	1170783M	952135M	4519856M	Net Sales ($)	3491071M	4754800M
6344M	53106M	259964M	374482M	250543M	1270433M	Total Assets ($)	1076065M	1268527M

M = $ thousand   MM = $ million
See Pages 9 through 22 for Explanation of Ratios and Data

Comparative Historical Data   ## Current Data Sorted by Sales

4/1/07-3/31/08 ALL	4/1/08-3/31/09 ALL	4/1/09-3/31/10 ALL	Type of Statement	0-1MM	1-3MM	3-5MM	5-10MM	10-25MM	25MM & OVR
20	13	15	Unqualified					3	12
20	29	20	Reviewed		2	2	6	5	5
18	21	25	Compiled	1	5	7	7	5	
30	33	39	Tax Returns	7	17	7	4	4	
53	59	59	Other	8	6	5	15	9	16
					33 (4/1-9/30/09)		125 (10/1/09-3/31/10)		
141	155	158	**NUMBER OF STATEMENTS**	16	30	21	32	26	33
%	%	%	**ASSETS**	%	%	%	%	%	%
12.4	12.2	13.7	Cash & Equivalents	12.9	12.6	11.7	18.5	13.8	11.8
23.9	20.7	21.0	Trade Receivables (net)	14.0	22.8	26.3	21.6	16.8	22.1
36.6	37.3	36.3	Inventory	38.3	41.2	24.9	31.7	39.2	40.2
3.7	3.9	2.9	All Other Current	5.2	1.3	2.0	3.7	3.2	2.8
76.6	74.1	73.9	Total Current	70.4	77.8	64.9	75.3	72.9	77.0
14.8	15.4	16.8	Fixed Assets (net)	19.6	12.0	24.4	18.1	14.0	16.1
3.4	3.5	3.2	Intangibles (net)	1.8	5.7	3.3	1.7	3.3	2.9
5.3	6.9	6.1	All Other Non-Current	8.3	4.5	7.5	4.9	9.8	3.9
100.0	100.0	100.0	Total	100.0	100.0	100.0	100.0	100.0	100.0
			LIABILITIES						
14.2	11.9	13.7	Notes Payable-Short Term	19.5	16.9	13.5	9.4	7.2	17.6
1.4	2.4	3.1	Cur. Mat.-L.T.D.	6.4	2.5	5.7	2.9	2.1	1.2
25.1	27.6	24.9	Trade Payables	28.9	15.8	26.6	30.4	24.5	25.4
.1	.1	.3	Income Taxes Payable	.0	.1	.6	.4	.1	.3
14.9	14.2	15.1	All Other Current	27.7	16.1	10.1	16.1	14.5	11.0
55.7	56.1	57.2	Total Current	82.4	51.3	56.4	59.2	48.5	55.4
9.7	9.4	15.9	Long-Term Debt	48.6	17.2	18.0	10.5	11.2	6.2
.1	.1	.1	Deferred Taxes	.0	.1	.3	.1	.2	.1
7.9	7.7	6.2	All Other Non-Current	8.4	16.3	3.4	2.4	1.9	4.8
26.6	26.6	20.7	Net Worth	-39.5	15.0	21.8	27.9	38.1	33.5
100.0	100.0	100.0	Total Liabilities & Net Worth	100.0	100.0	100.0	100.0	100.0	100.0
			INCOME DATA						
100.0	100.0	100.0	Net Sales	100.0	100.0	100.0	100.0	100.0	100.0
34.9	36.3	35.7	Gross Profit	45.8	37.8	38.1	35.8	34.0	28.7
32.5	33.7	32.5	Operating Expenses	43.1	34.8	36.4	30.9	30.4	25.9
2.3	2.7	3.3	Operating Profit	2.7	3.1	1.7	4.9	3.6	2.8
.6	.6	.2	All Other Expenses (net)	-.1	.0	.1	.1	.4	.4
1.8	2.1	3.1	Profit Before Taxes	2.8	3.0	1.6	4.7	3.3	2.4
			RATIOS						
2.4	1.9	2.3	Current	3.3	2.7	1.9	2.4	2.1	2.3
1.4	1.4	1.4		1.1	2.0	1.3	1.3	1.4	1.3
1.0	1.0	1.0		.3	1.2	.7	.9	1.1	1.0
1.3	1.0	1.1	Quick	.9	1.4	1.2	1.1	1.0	1.1
.7	.6	.6		.3	.8	.7	.7	.7	.6
.3	.3	.2		.0	.4	.3	.4	.2	.2
6 57.9	6 59.0	5 72.3	Sales/Receivables	0 UND	7 53.0	22 16.3	10 37.7	2 216.1	5 68.5
22 16.9	16 22.2	20 18.2		5 80.8	20 18.6	29 12.7	25 14.7	9 42.8	19 19.6
40 9.1	34 10.6	37 9.8		18 20.5	41 9.0	47 7.8	40 9.1	31 11.8	33 11.0
27 13.8	26 13.9	25 14.4	Cost of Sales/Inventory	5 80.5	31 12.0	14 25.8	26 13.8	29 12.6	28 13.3
48 7.6	61 6.0	56 6.5		56 6.5	87 4.2	38 9.6	46 8.0	69 5.3	59 6.2
94 3.9	93 3.9	98 3.7		139 2.6	118 3.1	105 3.5	65 5.6	92 4.0	93 3.9
17 21.4	20 18.6	19 18.8	Cost of Sales/Payables	20 18.6	7 55.4	23 15.5	18 20.4	26 14.2	19 19.2
32 11.5	37 9.9	34 10.8		47 7.8	22 16.7	46 7.9	49 7.5	34 10.6	30 12.2
61 6.0	61 6.0	57 6.4		64 5.7	35 10.6	64 5.7	69 5.3	58 6.3	50 7.3
7.0	8.8	7.2	Sales/Working Capital	4.1	4.9	9.0	9.1	7.4	8.3
20.1	20.0	17.7		174.3	9.7	13.2	22.7	22.5	19.0
204.6	-284.6	-158.6		-6.2	21.1	-17.9	-60.7	59.7	-999.8
10.3	10.8	14.6	EBIT/Interest		14.8	17.9	34.8	10.5	15.3
(109) 3.5	(123) 3.7	(129) 4.8		(23) 3.8	(20) 2.4	(27) 5.7	(22) 4.4	(28) 5.2	
1.4	.9	1.2			1.1	-.4	3.6	1.1	1.3
12.9	10.2	9.7	Net Profit + Depr., Dep., Amort./Cur. Mat. L/T/D						
(19) 7.6	(27) 2.4	(23) 2.4							
1.8	1.0	1.0							
.2	.1	.1	Fixed/Worth	.0	.0	.2	.2	.1	.2
.5	.5	.5		NM	.4	1.1	1.0	.4	.4
2.1	2.0	2.5		-.4	3.8	5.2	8.0	1.0	1.9
1.0	1.2	1.1	Debt/Worth	4.5	.9	1.3	1.1	1.0	.8
2.7	3.5	2.7		NM	2.8	3.3	2.0	1.8	2.9
13.9	10.8	27.9		-2.8	-5.6	19.1	42.5	5.0	7.8
57.8	70.0	94.4	% Profit Before Taxes/Tangible Net Worth		133.1	50.8	96.6	53.3	91.3
(111) 26.7	(124) 21.5	(127) 27.8		(22) 29.7	(17) 31.3	(26) 33.5	(24) 21.5	(30) 28.9	
6.1	3.5	4.5			1.6	-19.4	12.9	.8	6.2
16.1	17.6	19.6	% Profit Before Taxes/Total Assets	36.8	39.3	18.7	26.1	13.6	15.8
5.7	5.6	8.0		12.1	3.7	4.6	11.4	8.0	9.8
.5	-.6	.6		-1.5	.2	-7.7	3.4	.5	1.1
89.9	97.5	89.7	Sales/Net Fixed Assets	UND	464.3	54.2	132.6	78.8	52.7
34.1	37.3	27.2		40.1	25.1	26.8	25.0	42.0	26.7
17.3	16.9	13.2		7.5	15.8	5.7	9.4	19.5	15.8
4.9	5.0	4.5	Sales/Total Assets	4.6	4.2	4.4	4.7	4.4	4.7
3.4	3.5	3.3		3.7	3.4	2.8	3.5	3.1	3.6
2.6	2.6	2.4		1.6	2.4	2.1	2.1	2.7	2.7
.4	.4	.4	% Depr., Dep., Amort./Sales		.3	.8	.4	.3	.3
(116) .6	(116) .7	(117) .8		(21) .6	(14) 1.5	(24) 1.0	(24) .7	(26) .6	
1.4	1.3	1.4			1.2	3.7	1.4	1.5	1.3
1.5	1.1	1.4	% Officers', Directors' Owners' Comp/Sales		2.5	1.3	1.1		
(60) 3.8	(64) 2.6	(64) 3.0		(22) 3.8	(10) 2.3	(12) 3.1			
6.7	5.4	6.5			6.9	6.2	5.3		
6068803M	7083331M	7755080M	Net Sales ($)	7428M	57353M	89370M	231877M	379863M	6989189M
1752022M	1918894M	2214872M	Total Assets ($)	3072M	20830M	36586M	81441M	124375M	1948568M

M = $ thousand   MM = $ million
See Pages 9 through 22 for Explanation of Ratios and Data

Current Data Sorted by Assets | Comparative Historical Data

Type of Statement							4/1/05-3/31/06 ALL	4/1/06-3/31/07 ALL
Unqualified	1	5	2	1		2	15	11
Reviewed	3	10	1				14	14
Compiled	6	4	1				13	17
Tax Returns	15	12	9				27	33
Other	10	16	17	6	1	2	44	36
	12 (4/1-9/30/09)			112 (10/1/09-3/31/10)				

	0-500M	500M-2MM	2-10MM	10-50MM	50-100MM	100-250MM	4/1/05-3/31/06 ALL	4/1/06-3/31/07 ALL
NUMBER OF STATEMENTS	25	38	45	10	2	4	113	111
	%	%	%	%	%	%	%	%
ASSETS								
Cash & Equivalents	18.4	14.6	15.1	19.9			14.6	10.3
Trade Receivables (net)	29.7	33.0	40.6	35.5			37.9	37.3
Inventory	24.6	19.7	20.6	12.2			18.7	21.6
All Other Current	2.7	2.8	2.0	4.8			2.4	2.1
Total Current	75.4	70.1	78.2	72.4			73.6	71.4
Fixed Assets (net)	14.0	14.5	10.6	14.2			15.3	13.2
Intangibles (net)	3.8	6.1	4.5	8.0			5.6	9.2
All Other Non-Current	6.8	9.2	6.7	5.4			5.5	6.1
Total	100.0	100.0	100.0	100.0			100.0	100.0
LIABILITIES								
Notes Payable-Short Term	13.6	9.3	9.4	2.5			17.8	16.7
Cur. Mat.-L.T.D.	8.1	2.5	1.7	.7			2.6	2.3
Trade Payables	18.1	27.7	34.5	23.3			31.8	26.6
Income Taxes Payable	.0	.1	1.1	.3			.7	.3
All Other Current	17.5	9.5	14.2	23.3			17.2	18.1
Total Current	57.3	49.1	61.0	50.1			70.1	64.0
Long-Term Debt	11.6	14.4	7.7	15.7			12.2	14.3
Deferred Taxes	.0	.1	.1	.0			.4	.2
All Other Non-Current	18.8	3.4	4.2	5.3			7.2	8.5
Net Worth	12.3	33.0	27.0	28.9			10.1	12.9
Total Liabilties & Net Worth	100.0	100.0	100.0	100.0			100.0	100.0
INCOME DATA								
Net Sales	100.0	100.0	100.0	100.0			100.0	100.0
Gross Profit	47.6	40.5	29.0	39.3			37.7	36.6
Operating Expenses	42.1	37.2	24.5	31.5			35.2	32.7
Operating Profit	5.5	3.2	4.5	7.8			2.6	3.9
All Other Expenses (net)	.9	.5	.4	2.8			1.3	1.0
Profit Before Taxes	4.6	2.7	4.2	5.0			1.3	3.0
RATIOS								
Current	3.0	3.4	1.9	1.8			1.8	1.8
	1.5	1.4	1.2	1.2			1.2	1.2
	.9	1.0	1.0	1.1			.9	.9
Quick	1.8	1.9	1.3	1.5			1.3	1.4
	.8	.9	.9	1.1			.9	.8
	.3	.4	.6	.7			.4	.5
Sales/Receivables	0 UND	12 31.5	19 18.8	20 17.8			13 27.3	15 24.0
	29 12.7	31 12.0	46 7.9	50 7.4			31 11.9	38 9.7
	38 9.7	46 7.9	60 6.1	69 5.3			59 6.2	60 6.1
Cost of Sales/Inventory	0 UND	3 141.4	1 318.9	0 UND			1 397.8	6 63.1
	31 11.7	20 18.6	15 23.8	12 29.8			16 22.6	26 14.0
	55 6.6	62 5.9	50 7.3	27 13.6			35 10.5	53 6.9
Cost of Sales/Payables	4 95.9	16 22.7	20 18.2	17 22.0			16 22.5	23 15.5
	31 11.9	38 9.6	48 7.5	30 12.2			31 11.7	36 10.2
	45 8.1	54 6.7	58 6.3	50 7.3			59 6.2	52 7.0
Sales/Working Capital	6.4	7.0	11.3	9.4			12.3	11.6
	24.2	24.7	26.2	17.2			35.4	32.3
	-109.4	NM	-84.9	42.9			-47.6	-42.7
EBIT/Interest	12.1	11.7	48.5				14.2	9.2
	(18) 4.1	(29) 3.2	(42) 9.0				(90) 3.5	(95) 3.5
	2.2	.9	2.4				1.0	1.0
Net Profit + Depr., Dep., Amort./Cur. Mat. L/T/D							7.2	8.4
							(15) 3.4	(15) 4.7
							1.7	2.1
Fixed/Worth	.0	.2	.1	.1			.2	.1
	.4	.5	.3	.7			.6	.8
	3.5	NM	1.6	1.0			UND	-1.2
Debt/Worth	1.3	1.2	1.3	.4			1.7	1.6
	3.6	2.3	4.2	4.5			4.1	4.9
	-9.1	NM	14.0	18.3			-72.6	-10.1
% Profit Before Taxes/Tangible Net Worth	112.7	53.4	70.4				70.0	73.8
	(18) 37.5	(29) 25.6	(37) 37.4				(83) 27.9	(76) 34.8
	17.4	1.7	13.9				4.2	9.7
% Profit Before Taxes/Total Assets	23.4	16.8	18.5	25.0			20.4	18.3
	10.2	6.0	9.2	9.8			5.5	7.0
	2.8	.5	3.2	-2.4			.1	.5
Sales/Net Fixed Assets	UND	145.5	283.5	426.2			181.5	123.7
	64.4	48.5	81.6	64.9			41.0	41.1
	15.5	14.3	29.5	15.2			16.2	17.3
Sales/Total Assets	5.6	5.7	4.6	4.5			6.4	5.3
	4.4	3.8	3.6	2.6			3.9	3.6
	2.8	2.6	2.8	1.3			2.6	2.3
% Depr., Dep., Amort./Sales	.4	.2	.2				.3	.3
	(12) 1.3	(26) .7	(31) .3				(78) .8	(88) .7
	2.1	1.6	.7				1.5	1.3
% Officers', Directors' Owners' Comp/Sales	3.2	2.5	1.5				2.6	1.6
	(10) 6.9	(21) 3.9	(17) 5.6				(48) 5.0	(57) 3.6
	14.6	5.6	7.9				9.4	7.3
Net Sales ($)	24842M	191595M	815353M	699100M	352151M	1976716M	3304183M	7129277M
Total Assets ($)	6048M	41143M	208648M	263455M	149688M	631677M	809377M	1557083M

M = $ thousand   MM = $ million
See Pages 9 through 22 for Explanation of Ratios and Data

Comparative Historical Data / Current Data Sorted by Sales

	Hist 1	Hist 2	Hist 3	Type of Statement	0-1MM	1-3MM	3-5MM	5-10MM	10-25MM	25MM & OVER
	10	8	11	Unqualified			1	2	1	7
	8	12	14	Reviewed			1	3	7	3
	5	14	11	Compiled	1	1	2	2	3	2
	24	35	36	Tax Returns	10	10	5	6	5	
	43	48	52	Other	6	6	6	7	11	11
	4/1/07-3/31/08 ALL	4/1/08-3/31/09 ALL	4/1/09-3/31/10 ALL		12 (4/1-9/30/09)			112 (10/1/09-3/31/10)		
	90	117	124	NUMBER OF STATEMENTS	17	22	15	20	27	23
	%	%	%	ASSETS	%	%	%	%	%	%
	14.0	13.8	15.8	Cash & Equivalents	23.5	11.1	14.3	12.0	19.7	14.2
	36.0	35.8	35.5	Trade Receivables (net)	17.1	33.4	37.7	39.8	41.0	39.5
	18.2	18.0	20.3	Inventory	23.3	21.0	18.2	20.8	20.8	17.8
	3.4	2.6	2.8	All Other Current	2.8	4.3	1.0	3.3	1.2	3.8
	71.6	70.2	74.4	Total Current	66.8	69.9	71.2	75.9	82.7	75.3
	13.6	17.0	12.5	Fixed Assets (net)	16.1	19.0	12.6	11.7	8.7	8.6
	8.5	6.2	5.6	Intangibles (net)	9.2	3.8	4.9	5.8	3.4	7.5
	6.3	6.6	7.5	All Other Non-Current	7.9	7.3	11.2	6.6	5.2	8.6
	100.0	100.0	100.0	Total	100.0	100.0	100.0	100.0	100.0	100.0
				LIABILITIES						
	13.0	13.8	9.7	Notes Payable-Short Term	11.4	13.4	8.9	12.9	6.9	5.6
	3.6	2.9	3.1	Cur. Mat.-L.T.D.	9.9	4.5	1.7	1.1	1.9	.8
	27.0	27.3	28.3	Trade Payables	9.7	22.4	19.9	39.3	34.6	36.2
	.2	.9	.5	Income Taxes Payable	.0	.1	.1	.2	1.0	1.0
	19.0	13.8	14.3	All Other Current	17.8	11.2	11.0	11.5	16.7	16.2
	62.8	58.7	55.8	Total Current	48.8	51.6	41.7	65.0	61.1	59.8
	11.3	10.3	10.9	Long-Term Debt	19.0	14.9	11.6	5.2	6.2	11.2
	.3	.4	.1	Deferred Taxes	.0	.0	.0	.0	.2	.4
	4.2	7.1	7.4	All Other Non-Current	22.4	5.7	4.2	3.3	5.0	6.4
	21.5	23.6	25.8	Net Worth	9.8	27.8	42.5	26.5	27.5	22.3
	100.0	100.0	100.0	Total Liabilties & Net Worth	100.0	100.0	100.0	100.0	100.0	100.0
				INCOME DATA						
	100.0	100.0	100.0	Net Sales	100.0	100.0	100.0	100.0	100.0	100.0
	39.2	38.4	36.4	Gross Profit	55.2	47.5	39.9	35.2	27.5	21.2
	35.6	35.6	31.9	Operating Expenses	50.0	43.6	33.5	30.7	22.3	18.5
	3.7	2.8	4.5	Operating Profit	5.2	4.0	6.4	4.5	5.2	2.7
	.8	1.2	.7	All Other Expenses (net)	2.4	.6	.1	.2	.1	1.3
	2.9	1.6	3.8	Profit Before Taxes	2.8	3.4	6.3	4.3	5.1	1.3
				RATIOS						
	2.0	2.0	2.1	Current	3.3	3.4	7.0	1.7	2.2	1.3
	1.2	1.3	1.2		1.5	1.6	1.5	1.1	1.4	1.1
	.9	.9	1.0		.9	.9	1.1	1.0	.9	1.1
	1.3	1.3	1.5	Quick	1.7	1.9	6.4	1.1	1.6	1.1
	.9	.8	.9		.6	.6	1.1	.8	1.1	.8
	.5	.6	.5		.4	.4	.5	.5	.7	.6
	19 19.3	12 31.0	11 32.4	Sales/Receivables	0 UND	10 36.8	16 22.6	30 12.3	9 41.4	19 19.4
	37 9.8	27 13.3	34 10.8		12 31.1	30 12.2	35 10.4	40 9.2	37 9.8	42 8.7
	58 6.3	48 7.7	55 6.6		40 9.2	46 7.9	67 5.5	56 6.5	60 6.1	66 5.5
	0 964.7	1 585.8	0 848.8	Cost of Sales/Inventory	0 UND	0 UND	0 UND	2 153.4	1 341.7	0 999.8
	18 20.7	15 24.1	18 20.1		38 9.7	32 11.3	13 27.1	18 20.6	12 31.1	14 25.8
	47 7.8	44 8.2	55 6.7		168 2.2	70 5.2	42 8.6	61 5.9	39 9.3	38 9.7
	21 17.5	15 25.0	18 20.6	Cost of Sales/Payables	4 95.9	14 27.0	3 140.6	29 12.6	17 21.9	21 17.2
	37 10.0	32 11.4	38 9.6		34 10.9	38 9.6	18 20.2	48 7.5	36 10.1	32 11.5
	57 6.4	55 6.6	57 6.4		62 5.8	66 5.5	39 9.3	54 6.7	52 7.0	59 6.2
	8.8	12.0	8.4	Sales/Working Capital	5.6	6.2	5.2	16.1	11.1	13.9
	24.5	32.0	25.1		25.3	14.9	17.4	52.6	21.1	39.3
	-55.1	-62.2	442.9		-109.4	-59.8	59.4	-264.5	-84.6	83.9
	10.1	13.1	27.9	EBIT/Interest	10.1	10.5	86.5	10.3	101.3	105.8
	(75) 3.6	(99) 4.2	(102) 6.0		(12) 2.3	(16) 3.9	(14) 7.7	(17) 2.3	(25) 16.1	(18) 5.5
	1.8	.8	2.0		1.5	1.8	.9	.4	5.9	-1.4
	3.1	3.7		Net Profit + Depr., Dep., Amort./Cur. Mat. L/T/D						
	(12) 1.6	(11) 1.8								
	.8	.4								
	.2	.1	.1	Fixed/Worth	.2	.0	.1	.1	.1	.1
	.5	.4	.4		.7	.8	.3	.4	.3	.4
	3.1	2.3	2.7		-.2	3.2	.8	NM	1.1	1.1
	1.3	1.4	1.2	Debt/Worth	1.3	1.2	.4	1.9	1.2	1.4
	4.1	3.4	3.6		10.4	2.3	1.6	4.9	2.2	6.0
	NM	14.9	25.1		-2.6	10.8	11.5	NM	6.6	23.4
	81.8	74.8	63.5	% Profit Before Taxes/Tangible Net Worth	174.6	44.9	74.5	74.0	59.9	62.2
	(68) 34.4	(93) 27.8	(97) 31.4		(10) 32.7	(19) 25.6	(12) 34.1	(15) 20.7	(22) 43.4	(19) 27.7
	13.6	2.2	11.4		2.5	6.4	11.7	4.6	22.0	6.8
	18.0	14.9	17.6	% Profit Before Taxes/Total Assets	11.1	16.9	33.5	15.8	31.2	14.2
	7.9	6.2	7.9		6.6	10.6	9.1	6.5	11.2	5.2
	1.9	-1.2	1.9		-4.1	1.7	1.7	1.0	4.2	.9
	106.0	174.8	226.1	Sales/Net Fixed Assets	157.1	422.6	252.2	273.8	188.2	287.2
	39.8	47.1	66.7		38.0	26.1	52.1	57.7	92.1	96.4
	16.5	16.8	18.4		10.7	11.5	15.8	28.9	36.9	28.6
	5.1	6.0	5.2	Sales/Total Assets	4.3	5.2	4.7	5.7	5.7	4.4
	3.6	4.1	3.6		2.8	3.2	3.7	3.4	3.9	3.9
	2.0	2.8	2.6		1.5	2.5	2.9	2.2	3.3	2.5
	.4	.3	.2	% Depr., Dep., Amort./Sales		.7	.1	.1	.1	.2
	(61) .7	(84) .7	(76) .6		(14) 1.2	(10) .7	(12) .2	(21) .4	(11) .5	
	1.8	1.5	1.3		2.0	1.5	.7	.6	.8	
	1.6	2.8	2.4	% Officers', Directors' Owners' Comp/Sales		3.2		3.8	1.0	
	(39) 4.0	(49) 4.2	(50) 4.2			(12) 4.7		(11) 5.1	(11) 3.1	
	9.2	7.0	7.8			7.8		5.8	7.4	
	2568355M	3206435M	4059757M	Net Sales ($)	9978M	42304M	60667M	157089M	449757M	3339962M
	1153130M	1037608M	1300659M	Total Assets ($)	7175M	13934M	16519M	69505M	107960M	1085566M

M = $ thousand   MM = $ million
See Pages 9 through 22 for Explanation of Ratios and Data

Current Data Sorted by Assets　　　　Comparative Historical Data

Type of Statement	0-500M	500M-2MM	2-10MM	10-50MM	50-100MM	100-250MM		4/1/05-3/31/06 ALL	4/1/06-3/31/07 ALL
Unqualified		1	10	16	5	1		64	66
Reviewed	2	15	62	20	2	1		150	137
Compiled	1	27	41	5	1			123	123
Tax Returns	8	23	13	1				50	64
Other	4	18	45	30	3	2		160	127
		41 (4/1-9/30/09)		316 (10/1/09-3/31/10)					
NUMBER OF STATEMENTS	15	84	171	72	11	4		547	517
ASSETS	%	%	%	%	%	%		%	%
Cash & Equivalents	5.2	10.1	7.7	5.6	3.6			6.3	7.0
Trade Receivables (net)	19.1	20.8	24.1	18.7	21.2			29.9	28.4
Inventory	48.7	38.8	32.5	26.2	32.4			34.5	33.3
All Other Current	1.4	3.6	1.8	2.1	1.9			2.3	2.3
Total Current	74.3	73.4	66.3	52.6	59.1			73.0	71.0
Fixed Assets (net)	14.7	16.4	21.4	33.2	28.1			18.9	19.7
Intangibles (net)	1.7	.7	1.5	5.4	4.6			1.8	2.7
All Other Non-Current	9.2	9.5	10.9	8.9	8.2			6.3	6.7
Total	100.0	100.0	100.0	100.0	100.0			100.0	100.0
LIABILITIES									
Notes Payable-Short Term	18.5	14.4	12.6	11.1	2.6			14.0	14.7
Cur. Mat.-L.T.D.	2.3	2.0	3.7	3.7	4.4			2.7	2.7
Trade Payables	13.7	15.0	12.9	9.3	13.7			16.0	15.1
Income Taxes Payable	.2	.1	.1	.1	.0			.2	.1
All Other Current	6.2	7.6	5.4	5.3	6.7			8.3	8.4
Total Current	40.9	39.1	34.7	29.6	27.4			41.3	41.1
Long-Term Debt	19.7	16.3	14.2	18.4	18.8			12.7	15.2
Deferred Taxes	.0	.2	.3	.2	.1			.3	.2
All Other Non-Current	17.2	5.4	5.1	5.7	5.3			4.5	4.2
Net Worth	22.2	39.0	45.6	46.2	48.4			41.3	39.3
Total Liabilties & Net Worth	100.0	100.0	100.0	100.0	100.0			100.0	100.0
INCOME DATA									
Net Sales	100.0	100.0	100.0	100.0	100.0			100.0	100.0
Gross Profit	33.9	30.5	27.2	28.2	29.3			26.6	27.5
Operating Expenses	33.0	30.4	29.0	29.4	28.9			23.3	24.5
Operating Profit	.9	.1	-1.8	-1.2	.4			3.3	3.0
All Other Expenses (net)	.5	-.1	.0	.2	-.2			.1	.3
Profit Before Taxes	.4	.2	-1.8	-1.4	.6			3.2	2.7
RATIOS									
Current	3.4	3.9	3.5	3.7	2.8			2.8	3.2
	2.1	2.2	2.2	1.8	2.2			1.8	1.8
	1.1	1.4	1.4	1.0	1.9			1.4	1.3
Quick	1.1	1.3	1.8	1.9	1.4			1.4	1.5
	.8	.8	1.0	.6	.7			.9	.9
	.2	.4	.6	.4	.6			.6	.6
Sales/Receivables	19　19.3	15　25.1	28　13.3	25　14.6	26　13.9			26　14.1	25　14.8
	22　16.5	26　14.1	36　10.1	38　9.6	29　12.6			36　10.1	33　11.0
	28　12.8	42　8.8	48　7.6	52　7.1	40　9.2			47　7.7	46　8.0
Cost of Sales/Inventory	45　8.1	39　9.5	51　7.2	49　7.5	59　6.2			38　9.7	34　10.7
	89　4.1	78　4.7	68　5.3	68　5.4	71　5.1			55　6.6	54　6.8
	226　1.6	126　2.9	96　3.8	102　3.6	94　3.9			81　4.5	81　4.5
Cost of Sales/Payables	0　UND	12　30.9	15　25.0	16　22.4	17　21.3			15　24.2	14　26.3
	23　15.8	22　16.5	21　17.2	22　16.6	27　13.4			22　16.9	21　17.6
	56　6.5	35　10.5	34　10.9	33　11.0	42　8.7			32　11.2	33　11.0
Sales/Working Capital	5.0	4.6	4.6	4.1	5.2			6.2	5.7
	8.3	6.8	6.8	8.3	6.3			9.6	9.8
	100.1	21.4	12.4	704.9	9.9			16.4	20.3
EBIT/Interest	2.3	4.1	2.1	3.3	9.4			10.6	9.4
	(11) .6	(71) 1.0	(158) .2	(68) 1.0	1.9			(502) 4.3	(489) 3.0
	-3.5	-1.2	-3.9	-1.4	-1.3			2.0	1.4
Net Profit + Depr., Dep., Amort./Cur. Mat. L/T/D			2.6	4.1				6.7	7.2
			(51) 1.2	(21) 1.1				(159) 3.3	(147) 3.3
			-.5	.4				1.4	1.2
Fixed/Worth	.0	.1	.2	.4	.2			.2	.2
	.2	.4	.4	.8	.6			.4	.4
	9.9	1.0	1.0	2.3	1.3			.9	1.0
Debt/Worth	.7	.4	.4	.5	.6			.7	.7
	1.4	1.2	1.1	1.3	1.1			1.4	1.5
	-8.3	4.4	3.4	3.5	2.0			3.3	3.5
% Profit Before Taxes/Tangible Net Worth	60.0	17.1	5.5	5.8	9.8			35.5	36.4
	(10) 6.6	(71) .4	(158) -2.0	(65) .1	3.7			(509) 19.1	(471) 15.1
	-11.4	-8.0	-18.7	-16.1	-9.3			7.8	3.8
% Profit Before Taxes/Total Assets	12.1	7.8	2.3	2.9	4.1			15.5	14.3
	-1.2	.1	-1.2	.0	1.9			7.2	5.0
	-14.6	-5.2	-8.6	-5.9	-5.2			2.6	1.2
Sales/Net Fixed Assets	999.8	53.8	23.3	10.2	25.0			42.4	36.9
	88.9	20.4	11.9	6.0	10.5			18.5	18.0
	9.7	9.1	6.5	3.3	3.4			9.8	9.3
Sales/Total Assets	4.9	3.6	2.9	2.3	2.9			3.6	3.7
	2.2	2.6	2.2	1.8	2.0			2.9	2.9
	1.6	1.8	1.6	1.3	1.9			2.3	2.2
% Depr., Dep., Amort./Sales	.4	.8	1.0	1.4				.6	.6
	(10) .9	(65) 1.2	(163) 1.5	(69) 1.9				(485) 1.0	(466) 1.0
	2.3	1.7	2.4	3.1				1.5	1.6
% Officers', Directors' Owners' Comp/Sales		2.2	1.3	.6				1.4	1.1
		(50) 4.0	(75) 2.4	(22) 1.1				(240) 2.6	(218) 2.2
		6.3	4.0	2.4				4.3	4.1
Net Sales ($)	13092M	294291M	1945861M	3132923M	1630981M	1116710M		16576687M	18296483M
Total Assets ($)	4364M	101817M	830315M	1770146M	731133M	534178M		5767767M	6780137M

© RMA 2010

M = $ thousand　　MM = $ million
See Pages 9 through 22 for Explanation of Ratios and Data

Comparative Historical Data | Current Data Sorted by Sales

Type of Statement

Type of Statement	4/1/07-3/31/08 ALL	4/1/08-3/31/09 ALL	4/1/09-3/31/10 ALL	0-1MM	1-3MM	3-5MM	5-10MM	10-25MM	25MM & OVER
Unqualified	56	39	33			1	1	11	20
Reviewed	118	114	102	1	12	5	34	31	19
Compiled	92	69	75	3	14	15	23	18	2
Tax Returns	49	44	45	5	15	11	12	2	
Other	117	102	102	4	12	10	15	29	32
				41 (4/1-9/30/09)		316 (10/1/09-3/31/10)			
NUMBER OF STATEMENTS	432	368	357	13	53	42	85	91	73

ASSETS (%)

	08	09	10	0-1MM	1-3MM	3-5MM	5-10MM	10-25MM	25MM & OVER
Cash & Equivalents	7.1	7.3	7.6	2.3	6.6	10.6	8.8	7.5	6.2
Trade Receivables (net)	27.0	23.9	21.8	9.5	20.2	19.2	24.4	22.7	22.7
Inventory	33.6	33.7	33.3	52.6	39.8	34.7	31.1	31.6	29.3
All Other Current	2.6	2.4	2.3	.8	4.5	1.9	2.2	2.0	1.8
Total Current	70.3	67.4	65.1	65.2	71.2	66.4	66.5	63.8	59.9
Fixed Assets (net)	21.1	21.8	22.8	18.1	19.0	19.5	21.7	22.4	29.9
Intangibles (net)	1.9	2.3	2.2	.6	1.0	1.5	1.1	3.8	2.9
All Other Non-Current	6.7	8.6	10.0	16.0	8.9	12.6	10.6	10.0	7.3
Total	100.0	100.0	100.0	100.0	100.0	100.0	100.0	100.0	100.0

LIABILITIES

	08	09	10	0-1MM	1-3MM	3-5MM	5-10MM	10-25MM	25MM & OVER
Notes Payable-Short Term	12.9	14.7	12.6	20.1	13.7	13.1	13.1	10.6	12.2
Cur. Mat.-L.T.D.	3.5	3.4	3.2	1.1	2.5	3.0	3.9	3.6	3.0
Trade Payables	13.9	12.3	12.7	10.1	13.6	12.3	13.4	13.3	11.3
Income Taxes Payable	.1	.1	.1	.0	.2	.0	.1	.0	.1
All Other Current	7.0	7.0	6.0	2.1	7.4	4.9	6.9	5.4	6.0
Total Current	37.4	37.5	34.6	33.5	37.3	33.4	37.4	32.8	32.7
Long-Term Debt	14.2	14.8	16.0	22.5	20.2	16.1	15.1	13.3	16.2
Deferred Taxes	.2	.3	.3	.0	.4	.2	.2	.3	.3
All Other Non-Current	4.4	6.1	5.8	8.8	9.2	3.4	4.5	6.8	4.4
Net Worth	43.9	41.3	43.3	35.3	33.0	46.9	42.8	46.7	46.3
Total Liabilties & Net Worth	100.0	100.0	100.0	100.0	100.0	100.0	100.0	100.0	100.0

INCOME DATA

	08	09	10	0-1MM	1-3MM	3-5MM	5-10MM	10-25MM	25MM & OVER
Net Sales	100.0	100.0	100.0	100.0	100.0	100.0	100.0	100.0	100.0
Gross Profit	27.4	27.7	28.5	36.8	32.3	29.8	27.5	27.2	26.4
Operating Expenses	25.5	27.7	29.5	34.5	33.2	31.4	28.9	28.3	27.2
Operating Profit	1.9	.1	-1.0	2.2	-.9	-1.6	-1.5	-1.1	-.7
All Other Expenses (net)	.1	.2	.0	-.6	-.1	.9	-.1	-.1	.2
Profit Before Taxes	1.7	-.2	-1.1	2.9	-.8	-2.5	-1.3	-1.0	-.9

RATIOS

	08	09	10	0-1MM	1-3MM	3-5MM	5-10MM	10-25MM	25MM & OVER
Current	3.4 / 2.0 / 1.4	3.5 / 2.0 / 1.3	3.5 / 2.1 / 1.3	3.8 / 3.0 / 1.0	3.4 / 2.0 / 1.3	4.1 / 2.7 / 1.5	3.1 / 1.9 / 1.3	3.5 / 2.2 / 1.4	3.5 / 1.9 / 1.3
Quick	1.7 / .9 / .5	1.6 / .8 / .5	1.6 / .9 / .5	1.0 / .6 / .1	1.1 / .8 / .4	2.0 / 1.0 / .4	1.6 / .9 / .6	2.0 / .9 / .5	1.7 / 1.0 / .5
Sales/Receivables	24 15.5 / 33 10.9 / 46 7.9	21 17.5 / 31 11.8 / 44 8.2	23 15.8 / 34 10.8 / 47 7.8	1 399.9 / 21 17.7 / 36 10.1	20 18.6 / 29 12.5 / 44 8.2	22 16.9 / 36 10.2 / 46 7.9	23 16.0 / 35 10.3 / 49 7.4	27 13.7 / 33 11.0 / 47 7.8	24 15.0 / 37 9.9 / 50 7.3
Cost of Sales/Inventory	39 9.3 / 58 6.3 / 84 4.3	42 8.7 / 64 5.7 / 91 4.0	49 7.4 / 70 5.3 / 101 3.6	117 3.1 / 185 2.0 / 274 1.3	58 6.3 / 98 3.7 / 138 2.7	40 9.1 / 76 4.8 / 108 3.4	47 7.8 / 63 5.8 / 82 4.4	46 7.9 / 70 5.2 / 96 3.8	48 7.6 / 62 5.8 / 81 4.5
Cost of Sales/Payables	13 28.1 / 20 18.3 / 31 11.9	11 34.6 / 17 21.2 / 30 12.1	14 25.9 / 22 16.6 / 35 10.5	0 UND / 26 14.0 / 66 5.5	10 35.1 / 24 15.5 / 39 9.4	11 32.1 / 19 18.9 / 32 11.3	14 26.8 / 22 16.6 / 36 10.2	15 24.4 / 23 16.2 / 32 11.5	17 21.9 / 21 17.4 / 32 11.6
Sales/Working Capital	5.3 / 8.3 / 15.7	4.9 / 8.1 / 18.5	4.5 / 7.0 / 16.4	3.1 / 4.4 / UND	3.8 / 6.5 / 12.6	4.1 / 6.1 / 14.8	4.6 / 7.7 / 17.4	4.7 / 7.2 / 12.4	5.1 / 8.6 / 22.4
EBIT/Interest	(404) 6.5 / 2.2 / .8	(347) 4.0 / 1.5 / -.9	(323) 3.0 / .8 / -2.8		(46) 3.3 / .8 / -5.9	(35) 2.0 / .5 / -2.0	(82) 3.7 / 1.0 / -1.5	(83) 2.7 / .8 / -4.0	(68) 3.4 / 1.0 / -1.4
Net Profit + Depr., Dep., Amort./Cur. Mat. L/T/D	(121) 7.7 / 2.0 / .9	(101) 3.4 / 1.7 / .3	(85) 3.2 / 1.2 / -.4				(24) 2.9 / 1.7 / -.3	(31) 2.6 / 1.2 / -.6	(22) 3.9 / 1.1 / .0
Fixed/Worth	.2 / .4 / 1.1	.2 / .5 / 1.1	.2 / .5 / 1.2	.0 / .2 / 5.4	.2 / .4 / 1.7	.1 / .5 / 1.6	.2 / .4 / 1.2	.2 / .5 / 1.0	.3 / .6 / 1.7
Debt/Worth	.6 / 1.3 / 2.7	.5 / 1.4 / 3.4	.4 / 1.2 / 3.6	.3 / 1.4 / NM	.4 / 1.2 / 5.1	.3 / .9 / 3.3	.4 / 1.4 / 3.7	.4 / 1.1 / 2.9	.4 / 1.3 / 3.1
% Profit Before Taxes/Tangible Net Worth	(398) 24.4 / 9.4 / -.3	(328) 12.3 / 3.0 / -8.3	(319) 7.0 / -.7 / -13.3	(10) 37.7 / -.2 / -14.1	(41) 24.1 / -1.3 / -11.2	(38) 3.7 / -1.3 / -12.8	(78) 5.9 / -.4 / -23.0	(83) 6.8 / -1.6 / -14.2	(69) 6.7 / .5 / -15.0
% Profit Before Taxes/Total Assets	9.7 / 3.1 / -.6	5.6 / 1.1 / -4.9	3.1 / -.5 / -6.9	11.8 / -1.2 / -10.8	9.6 / -.5 / -8.1	1.7 / -1.4 / -8.1	3.0 / -.2 / -7.4	3.1 / -.6 / -5.6	3.5 / .0 / -6.9
Sales/Net Fixed Assets	31.9 / 14.7 / 7.5	28.7 / 14.3 / 7.5	24.9 / 11.0 / 6.0	260.3 / 11.6 / 4.8	24.6 / 11.3 / 7.2	46.5 / 15.6 / 6.2	28.8 / 12.7 / 6.2	24.3 / 10.0 / 6.0	14.9 / 7.6 / 4.8
Sales/Total Assets	3.5 / 2.7 / 2.0	3.3 / 2.5 / 1.9	2.9 / 2.2 / 1.6	1.8 / 1.6 / 1.4	2.9 / 2.1 / 1.6	3.2 / 2.1 / 1.5	3.2 / 2.3 / 1.7	2.9 / 2.2 / 1.6	2.7 / 2.3 / 1.7
% Depr., Dep., Amort./Sales	(398) .7 / 1.2 / 1.8	(329) .8 / 1.4 / 2.1	(318) 1.0 / 1.5 / 2.4		(43) .9 / 1.3 / 2.4	(36) .8 / 1.2 / 2.7	(80) .9 / 1.5 / 2.5	(84) 1.0 / 1.5 / 2.4	(67) 1.1 / 1.8 / 2.5
% Officers', Directors' Owners' Comp/Sales	(174) 1.3 / 2.3 / 4.3	(156) 1.4 / 2.3 / 4.5	(156) 1.5 / 2.8 / 4.4		(29) 3.1 / 4.1 / 6.5	(22) 1.8 / 3.1 /	(49) 2.1 / 3.0 / 4.6	(31) .9 / 1.5 / 3.2	(18) .5 / .8 / 2.4
Net Sales ($)	14652606M	11505635M	8133858M	8038M	110440M	168494M	603412M	1520775M	5722699M
Total Assets ($)	5602496M	4524109M	3971953M	7067M	58407M	92214M	305443M	791117M	2717705M

M = $ thousand   MM = $ million
See Pages 9 through 22 for Explanation of Ratios and Data

Current Data Sorted by Assets

Comparative Historical Data

Type of Statement								
	2	1	1			Unqualified	6	2
	1	3	1			Reviewed	19	13
4		5				Compiled	10	11
2	8					Tax Returns	17	21
1	1	3			1	Other	11	3
	4 (4/1-9/30/09)		30 (10/1/09-3/31/10)				4/1/05-3/31/06	4/1/06-3/31/07
0-500M	500M-2MM	2-10MM	10-50MM	50-100MM	100-250MM	NUMBER OF STATEMENTS	ALL	ALL
7	12	12	3				63	50

0-500M %	500M-2MM %	2-10MM %	10-50MM %	50-100MM %	100-250MM %		%	%
						ASSETS		
	10.5	4.2				Cash & Equivalents	7.4	7.1
	23.8	23.8				Trade Receivables (net)	26.0	24.1
	34.3	36.0	D	D		Inventory	31.2	41.3
	4.5	1.1	A	A		All Other Current	2.8	.8
	73.2	65.1	T	T		Total Current	67.4	73.2
	15.0	22.2	A	A		Fixed Assets (net)	16.1	13.6
	7.5	3.6				Intangibles (net)	2.9	2.3
	4.3	9.1	N	N		All Other Non-Current	13.6	10.9
	100.0	100.0	O	O		Total	100.0	100.0
			T	T		**LIABILITIES**		
	10.0	15.2				Notes Payable-Short Term	8.5	12.1
	5.1	1.7	A	A		Cur. Mat.-L.T.D.	1.5	3.4
	24.4	12.7	V	V		Trade Payables	21.2	19.9
	.0	.7	A	A		Income Taxes Payable	.5	.3
	8.9	6.3	I	I		All Other Current	11.6	11.9
	48.3	36.6	L	L		Total Current	43.5	47.6
	40.1	14.9	A	A		Long-Term Debt	23.9	14.9
	.0	.7	B	B		Deferred Taxes	.1	.3
	1.9	3.1	L	L		All Other Non-Current	15.6	9.0
	9.6	44.7	E	E		Net Worth	16.9	28.2
	100.0	100.0				Total Liabilties & Net Worth	100.0	100.0
						INCOME DATA		
	100.0	100.0				Net Sales	100.0	100.0
	33.7	33.5				Gross Profit	34.1	35.7
	36.9	31.4				Operating Expenses	32.2	34.5
	-3.3	2.1				Operating Profit	2.0	1.2
	.8	.7				All Other Expenses (net)	.5	.4
	-4.1	1.5				Profit Before Taxes	1.5	.8
						RATIOS		
	2.2	2.2					2.7	2.5
	1.5	1.8				Current	1.6	1.7
	1.0	1.6					1.1	1.1
	1.5	1.1					1.4	1.4
	.9	.8				Quick	.8	.6
	.3	.3					.4	.4
	15 24.5	10 36.0					15 23.6	20 17.9
	27 13.6	37 9.9				Sales/Receivables	30 12.0	34 10.8
	44 8.3	52 7.0					42 8.8	50 7.3
	30 12.0	44 8.3					25 14.4	58 6.3
	77 4.7	69 5.3				Cost of Sales/Inventory	56 6.5	80 4.6
	88 4.1	104 3.5					108 3.4	130 2.8
	26 14.0	9 39.2					21 17.4	17 21.6
	43 8.6	26 13.8				Cost of Sales/Payables	31 11.9	37 9.7
	74 4.9	51 7.2					71 5.1	63 5.8
	4.7	6.1					6.7	6.0
	13.8	8.8				Sales/Working Capital	12.1	9.3
	NM	13.3					32.9	28.7
	8.6	7.9					8.8	8.9
	-1.9	1.5				EBIT/Interest	(57) 2.6	(48) 2.3
	-4.1	.8					.9	.6
							13.7	7.2
						Net Profit + Depr., Dep., Amort./Cur. Mat. L/T/D	(18) 1.4	(10) 1.6
							-.4	-.6
	.2	.1					.2	.2
	1.6	.3				Fixed/Worth	.5	.6
	-1.3	.9					3.7	NM
	1.3	.9					1.0	.9
	6.6	1.9				Debt/Worth	3.1	2.6
	-8.9	2.5					62.6	NM
		6.7					47.7	27.5
		4.0				% Profit Before Taxes/Tangible Net Worth	(48) 10.9	(38) 10.3
		-2.8					2.6	1.2
	8.9	1.8					13.1	7.4
	-3.7	1.0				% Profit Before Taxes/Total Assets	2.7	2.8
	-19.4	-.8					.0	-1.9
	171.3	77.0					65.9	63.4
	24.7	16.3				Sales/Net Fixed Assets	23.2	24.8
	11.4	9.1					13.1	12.3
	3.5	3.4					4.1	3.3
	2.9	2.5				Sales/Total Assets	3.0	2.7
	1.9	2.0					1.8	1.8
	.9	.7					.5	.7
	(10) 1.1	(11) 1.7				% Depr., Dep., Amort./Sales	(50) 1.0	(37) 1.0
	2.7	3.2					1.7	1.5
							1.8	2.4
						% Officers', Directors' Owners' Comp/Sales	(33) 3.6	(27) 3.6
							6.4	8.0
6869M	38260M	122037M	95943M			Net Sales ($)	847564M	368017M
2554M	13201M	48957M	55435M			Total Assets ($)	463265M	230624M

M = $ thousand   MM = $ million
See Pages 9 through 22 for Explanation of Ratios and Data

Comparative Historical Data / Current Data Sorted by Sales

	4/1/07-3/31/08 ALL	4/1/08-3/31/09 ALL	4/1/09-3/31/10 ALL	0-1MM	1-3MM	3-5MM	5-10MM	10-25MM	25MM & OVER
Type of Statement				4 (4/1-9/30/09)			30 (10/1/09-3/31/10)		
Unqualified	4	3	4				2	2	
Reviewed	8	11	5		2		2		1
Compiled	7	6	9	2	2	1	2	2	
Tax Returns	15	11	10	1	4	4	1		
Other	9	6	6	1	1		3		1
NUMBER OF STATEMENTS	43	37	34	4	9	5	8	6	2
	%	%	%	%	%	%	%	%	%
ASSETS									
Cash & Equivalents	8.7	10.0	7.7						
Trade Receivables (net)	26.9	26.3	21.2						
Inventory	38.2	37.2	38.8						
All Other Current	1.0	2.0	2.9						
Total Current	74.8	75.4	70.6						
Fixed Assets (net)	17.9	16.9	18.1						
Intangibles (net)	1.6	3.1	5.1						
All Other Non-Current	5.7	4.6	6.2						
Total	100.0	100.0	100.0						
LIABILITIES									
Notes Payable-Short Term	12.4	11.2	12.7						
Cur. Mat.-L.T.D.	2.8	1.2	3.9						
Trade Payables	19.7	18.5	17.0						
Income Taxes Payable	.0	.0	.2						
All Other Current	9.0	6.8	8.5						
Total Current	43.9	37.7	42.3						
Long-Term Debt	19.5	14.6	27.9						
Deferred Taxes	.0	.1	.3						
All Other Non-Current	7.8	9.6	3.0						
Net Worth	28.8	38.0	26.6						
Total Liabilities & Net Worth	100.0	100.0	100.0						
INCOME DATA									
Net Sales	100.0	100.0	100.0						
Gross Profit	34.7	38.1	34.4						
Operating Expenses	31.9	36.9	36.6						
Operating Profit	2.8	1.2	-2.2						
All Other Expenses (net)	-.4	.0	.3						
Profit Before Taxes	3.3	1.2	-2.5						
RATIOS									
Current	3.1	3.9	2.4						
	1.7	2.4	1.8						
	1.2	1.4	1.3						
Quick	1.2	2.0	1.1						
	.7	1.0	.7						
	.4	.5	.3						
Sales/Receivables	17 21.9	12 29.7	15 24.3						
	25 14.3	25 14.6	26 14.2						
	42 8.6	44 8.4	44 8.3						
Cost of Sales/Inventory	36 10.1	36 10.1	53 6.9						
	60 6.0	62 5.9	79 4.6						
	102 3.6	112 3.3	122 3.0						
Cost of Sales/Payables	17 21.8	16 22.7	17 21.3						
	33 10.9	22 16.8	33 11.1						
	49 7.5	57 6.4	57 6.4						
Sales/Working Capital	6.3	5.7	4.9						
	10.4	7.4	9.2						
	32.2	17.7	21.2						
EBIT/Interest	18.1	7.1	4.1						
	(39) 4.7	(32) 3.0	(32) .8						
	.9	1.0	-4.0						
Net Profit + Depr., Dep., Amort./Cur. Mat. L/T/D	12.6								
	(10) 2.3								
	-.6								
Fixed/Worth	.1	.1	.1						
	.4	.3	.4						
	1.8	1.7	3.4						
Debt/Worth	.8	.5	.8						
	2.4	1.9	2.0						
	5.4	5.3	7.1						
% Profit Before Taxes/Tangible Net Worth	83.5	36.3	13.6						
	(37) 30.9	(31) 12.0	(27) .6						
	2.9	-.5	-14.2						
% Profit Before Taxes/Total Assets	22.3	11.8	2.2						
	6.8	2.8	-.6						
	-.9	-.3	-12.1						
Sales/Net Fixed Assets	86.2	50.5	72.6						
	19.6	23.6	22.4						
	11.8	15.1	9.9						
Sales/Total Assets	3.8	3.8	3.4						
	3.2	3.3	2.5						
	2.7	2.9	1.9						
% Depr., Dep., Amort./Sales	.4	.6	.8						
	(35) 1.0	(32) 1.0	(30) 1.4						
	1.4	1.5	2.2						
% Officers', Directors' Owners' Comp/Sales	.8	1.7	1.8						
	(20) 2.9	(19) 3.5	(20) 2.9						
	5.3	7.6	5.9						
Net Sales ($)	1170240M	335637M	263109M	2963M	14073M	20210M	56026M	93789M	76048M
Total Assets ($)	329700M	132593M	120147M	1336M	6172M	8058M	24970M	47947M	31664M

© RMA 2010

M = $ thousand   MM = $ million
See Pages 9 through 22 for Explanation of Ratios and Data

RETAIL—Hardware Stores NAICS 444130

Current Data Sorted by Assets | **Comparative Historical Data**

0-500M	500M-2MM	2-10MM	10-50MM	50-100MM	100-250MM	Type of Statement	4/1/05-3/31/06 ALL	4/1/06-3/31/07 ALL
		1	4		1	Unqualified	12	10
1	16	26	5			Reviewed	51	50
10	36	17	1			Compiled	81	94
31	67	23	1			Tax Returns	77	77
12	47	27	10		2	Other	86	95
	57 (4/1-9/30/09)		280 (10/1/09-3/31/10)				307	326
54	166	94	20		3	**NUMBER OF STATEMENTS**	307	326
%	%	%	%	%	%	**ASSETS**	%	%
11.4	6.8	6.3	4.1			Cash & Equivalents	6.1	6.0
9.2	8.6	12.7	10.3			Trade Receivables (net)	14.6	12.6
52.3	53.1	47.3	48.9			Inventory	51.3	52.2
1.6	1.5	1.9	2.8			All Other Current	2.4	2.0
74.4	70.0	68.3	66.1			Total Current	74.4	72.9
9.9	13.7	19.0	24.2	D		Fixed Assets (net)	14.3	16.1
4.6	4.2	2.9	2.4	A		Intangibles (net)	2.6	2.0
11.1	12.1	9.8	7.3	T		All Other Non-Current	8.7	8.9
100.0	100.0	100.0	100.0	A		Total	100.0	100.0
						LIABILITIES		
9.6	8.3	8.6	13.7	N		Notes Payable-Short Term	11.7	9.9
5.1	3.2	3.0	3.7	O		Cur. Mat.-L.T.D.	3.3	3.2
13.4	11.5	12.2	10.7	T		Trade Payables	15.2	13.7
.5	.1	.1	.0			Income Taxes Payable	.2	.2
7.5	5.9	7.0	6.6	A		All Other Current	7.3	6.9
36.0	29.0	30.9	34.7	V		Total Current	37.7	33.8
28.5	24.0	18.2	15.1	A		Long-Term Debt	19.5	20.3
.0	.1	.2	.3	I		Deferred Taxes	.2	.1
17.6	9.4	6.4	3.9	L		All Other Non-Current	7.4	7.6
17.9	37.6	44.2	46.1	A		Net Worth	35.3	38.2
100.0	100.0	100.0	100.0	B		Total Liabilities & Net Worth	100.0	100.0
				L		**INCOME DATA**		
100.0	100.0	100.0	100.0	E		Net Sales	100.0	100.0
42.3	39.5	36.6	37.5			Gross Profit	36.0	36.7
40.2	38.1	34.9	34.8			Operating Expenses	34.1	34.2
2.2	1.4	1.7	2.8			Operating Profit	2.0	2.5
.2	-.3	.4	-.1			All Other Expenses (net)	-.1	.2
2.0	1.7	1.4	2.8			Profit Before Taxes	2.1	2.3
						RATIOS		
5.0	5.3	4.4	2.6				3.5	3.9
2.5	3.0	2.7	1.9			Current	2.1	2.5
1.6	1.7	1.5	1.6				1.5	1.6
1.3	1.1	1.2	.9				1.0	1.1
.5	.6	.5	.4			Quick	.5	.5
.3	.2	.3	.2				.2	.2
2 149.4	4 88.3	8 46.8	5 72.3				7 55.3	7 50.5
7 48.7	9 40.8	16 22.5	13 27.6			Sales/Receivables	14 26.3	13 28.6
15 24.5	17 21.3	29 12.6	20 18.1				31 11.8	25 14.6
59 6.1	102 3.6	83 4.4	102 3.6				79 4.6	92 4.0
136 2.7	145 2.5	137 2.7	139 2.6			Cost of Sales/Inventory	121 3.0	136 2.7
248 1.5	199 1.8	189 1.9	174 2.1				178 2.0	187 2.0
9 39.2	13 29.0	15 25.1	14 26.5				17 21.6	15 24.5
21 17.4	24 15.5	24 15.1	26 14.3			Cost of Sales/Payables	27 13.3	27 13.7
43 8.6	35 10.4	37 9.8	40 9.1				45 8.1	43 8.6
3.4	3.7	3.7	4.5				4.1	3.9
6.1	5.3	5.2	6.8			Sales/Working Capital	6.6	5.5
12.5	8.2	9.7	10.0				12.1	9.7
6.3	6.4	6.0	12.3				8.5	7.2
(40) 2.6	(147) 2.6	(86) 2.0	(19) 7.2			EBIT/Interest	(282) 3.1	(304) 3.0
.2	.5	.1	1.5				1.3	1.3
	3.9	4.1					3.8	2.9
	(20) 1.1	(21) 1.8				Net Profit + Depr., Dep., Amort./Cur. Mat. L/T/D	(56) 1.6	(63) 1.5
	.5	.5					.6	.8
.1	.1	.1	.1				.1	.1
.3	.3	.4	.4			Fixed/Worth	.4	.3
-1.0	2.5	.9	.9				.9	1.0
.7	.5	.6	.7				.8	.7
2.6	1.7	1.3	1.8			Debt/Worth	1.7	1.5
-10.2	11.2	3.8	2.5				4.5	3.8
41.6	27.0	18.1	21.5				29.7	32.3
(38) 26.3	(131) 11.0	(89) 6.4	13.6			% Profit Before Taxes/Tangible Net Worth	(269) 13.5	(287) 12.3
4.3	3.5	-3.4	3.1				3.7	4.3
15.0	10.0	6.5	9.5				10.5	11.1
6.0	4.1	3.3	6.1			% Profit Before Taxes/Total Assets	5.3	4.8
-3.4	.2	-2.1	1.5				.7	1.0
142.8	56.9	31.4	48.0				59.6	52.0
44.0	25.5	17.5	15.5			Sales/Net Fixed Assets	22.9	20.3
18.9	11.0	6.1	3.8				10.7	9.8
3.4	2.9	2.5	2.6				3.1	2.8
2.5	2.3	2.1	2.0			Sales/Total Assets	2.5	2.4
1.8	1.7	1.6	1.7				1.9	1.7
.5	.6	.7	.8				.5	.7
(32) 1.2	(138) 1.2	(80) 1.3	(18) 1.8			% Depr., Dep., Amort./Sales	(262) 1.0	(274) 1.2
2.5	2.5	2.1	2.0				1.9	2.0
3.5	2.3	1.3					2.0	1.8
(32) 4.7	(105) 3.9	(58) 2.5				% Officers', Directors' Owners' Comp/Sales	(187) 3.4	(193) 3.2
8.4	5.9	4.5					5.7	5.3
52396M	419997M	910321M	955871M		895914M	Net Sales ($)	5361226M	4969626M
17966M	176724M	424974M	454592M		422062M	Total Assets ($)	1926895M	1977145M

© RMA 2010

M = $ thousand   MM = $ million
See Pages 9 through 22 for Explanation of Ratios and Data

Comparative Historical Data | Current Data Sorted by Sales

Type of Statement	4/1/07-3/31/08 ALL	4/1/08-3/31/09 ALL	4/1/09-3/31/10 ALL	0-1MM	1-3MM	3-5MM	5-10MM	10-25MM	25MM & OVER
Unqualified	10	12	6	2	7	11	9	15	5
Reviewed	47	33	48	5	27	10	18	4	4
Compiled	90	83	64	29	55	18	15	4	
Tax Returns	69	106	121	10	39	15	9		12
Other	89	103	98					1	
				57 (4/1-9/30/09)			280 (10/1/09-3/31/10)		
NUMBER OF STATEMENTS	305	337	337	46	128	54	55	33	21

ASSETS

	%	%	%	%	%	%	%	%	%
Cash & Equivalents	6.4	6.4	7.2	10.1	6.7	8.6	6.5	6.7	3.5
Trade Receivables (net)	12.8	10.3	10.0	6.1	7.7	10.3	13.5	15.9	12.8
Inventory	51.0	53.7	51.0	53.9	53.4	47.2	47.7	51.1	47.8
All Other Current	2.2	2.6	1.7	2.0	1.5	1.5	1.6	2.0	3.1
Total Current	72.4	73.0	69.9	72.1	69.4	67.6	69.3	75.7	67.3
Fixed Assets (net)	16.3	14.4	15.3	13.0	13.6	16.0	18.2	14.4	22.3
Intangibles (net)	1.8	2.3	3.9	4.9	4.8	2.7	3.4	1.7	3.6
All Other Non-Current	9.6	10.2	10.9	10.0	12.2	13.7	9.1	8.1	6.8
Total	100.0	100.0	100.0	100.0	100.0	100.0	100.0	100.0	100.0

LIABILITIES

Notes Payable-Short Term	10.3	12.1	8.9	4.8	10.5	6.0	7.5	13.5	11.4
Cur. Mat.-L.T.D.	3.4	3.0	3.5	4.4	3.8	3.3	3.0	2.1	3.2
Trade Payables	13.8	13.2	12.0	9.8	10.7	13.2	14.6	13.0	12.7
Income Taxes Payable	.2	.1	.2	.5	.1	.1	.1	.3	.0
All Other Current	7.5	7.0	6.5	8.5	6.6	4.9	5.7	6.0	8.6
Total Current	35.2	35.4	30.9	28.0	31.7	27.5	30.8	34.9	35.9
Long-Term Debt	21.0	19.8	22.7	34.2	23.9	24.4	16.8	13.9	15.5
Deferred Taxes	.1	.1	.1	.0	.0	.1	.3	.3	.5
All Other Non-Current	6.6	7.8	9.5	20.6	10.8	4.2	6.6	5.9	3.9
Net Worth	37.1	36.9	36.7	17.2	33.6	43.8	45.5	45.0	44.2
Total Liabilities & Net Worth	100.0	100.0	100.0	100.0	100.0	100.0	100.0	100.0	100.0

INCOME DATA

Net Sales	100.0	100.0	100.0	100.0	100.0	100.0	100.0	100.0	100.0
Gross Profit	36.7	36.4	38.9	44.3	40.2	38.1	35.5	36.6	33.9
Operating Expenses	34.4	34.7	37.2	41.6	39.1	35.7	33.9	35.0	31.6
Operating Profit	2.3	1.7	1.7	2.7	1.1	2.4	1.6	1.6	2.3
All Other Expenses (net)	.2	.0	.0	.6	-.4	-.1	.1	.2	.1
Profit Before Taxes	2.0	1.7	1.8	2.1	1.5	2.5	1.5	1.3	-2.2

RATIOS

Current	4.1	4.2	4.9	6.0	5.1	5.4	4.0	4.3	2.6
	2.4	2.6	2.8	3.1	2.9	2.9	2.7	2.4	1.7
	1.5	1.6	1.6	1.9	1.7	1.7	1.5	1.5	1.5
Quick	1.1	1.0	1.1	1.4	1.1	1.2	1.3	1.1	.9
	(304) .5	.5	.5	.5	.5	.7	.5	.6	.5
	.3	.2	.2	.2	.2	.3	.3	.2	.2
Sales/Receivables	6 56.4	4 81.5	5 78.7	2 152.1	4 92.8	5 72.7	6 56.2	8 43.5	7 54.7
	12 29.3	9 39.4	10 36.7	8 45.3	8 46.3	11 34.0	14 25.5	15 25.9	15 24.1
	29 12.6	22 16.4	20 18.0	17 21.3	15 24.3	22 16.6	29 12.5	30 12.1	22 16.4
Cost of Sales/Inventory	85 4.3	94 3.9	95 3.8	131 2.8	109 3.3	83 4.4	77 4.8	72 5.1	89 4.1
	126 2.9	138 2.7	141 2.6	221 1.6	155 2.4	116 3.1	115 3.2	151 2.4	109 3.4
	173 2.1	185 2.0	200 1.8	287 1.3	200 1.8	158 2.3	166 2.2	187 2.0	152 2.4
Cost of Sales/Payables	15 24.3	14 26.4	14 26.6	4 92.8	12 29.3	16 22.7	14 25.3	16 23.5	16 22.9
	26 14.3	24 15.0	24 15.4	20 18.1	22 16.5	28 12.8	26 14.1	24 15.4	24 15.2
	42 8.6	38 9.5	37 9.8	43 8.6	34 10.9	39 9.3	38 9.6	35 10.4	34 10.8
Sales/Working Capital	4.2	3.8	3.7	2.6	3.7	3.8	4.5	4.1	5.9
	5.9	5.6	5.5	3.9	5.3	6.2	5.6	5.1	8.1
	11.7	10.5	9.2	6.3	9.0	10.4	9.7	11.5	11.7
EBIT/Interest	5.2	6.5	6.7	3.2	6.6	5.9	7.4	6.0	11.8
	(281) 2.4	(306) 2.4	(295) 2.6	(34) 2.4	(111) 2.8	(50) 2.2	(49) 3.0	(30) 1.7	7.2
	1.0	.9	.5	.6	.4	.3	1.0	-.2	1.3
Net Profit + Depr., Dep., Amort./Cur. Mat. L/T/D	4.3	4.1	4.2		3.4	3.2		4.9	
	(61) 1.9	(54) 1.7	(50) 1.6		(10) 1.0	(11) 1.6		(10) 2.8	
	.7	.4	.5		.5	.7		.1	
Fixed/Worth	.1	.1	.1	.0	.1	.1	.1	.1	.2
	.4	.3	.3	.4	.4	.3	.3	.2	.5
	1.0	1.1	1.6	-.9	-9.8	.9	1.0	.6	.9
Debt/Worth	.7	.6	.6	.7	.5	.4	.6	.6	.7
	1.6	1.6	1.7	3.1	1.8	1.5	1.3	1.7	1.4
	4.7	4.6	7.3	-11.4	-45.7	3.5	3.1	3.4	2.5
% Profit Before Taxes/Tangible Net Worth	25.1	25.4	26.9	47.6	30.6	23.0	20.0	20.5	24.0
	(269) 9.7	(289) 12.2	(280) 11.0	(33) 19.5	(95) 11.4	(46) 7.9	(54) 8.4	(32) 6.1	(20) 14.1
	1.6	1.5	1.9	3.5	2.9	1.1	.8	-3.0	.6
% Profit Before Taxes/Total Assets	9.0	9.8	9.9	11.4	11.6	7.7	9.0	9.8	9.4
	3.5	4.2	4.1	4.2	4.3	3.6	4.1	2.5	6.2
	.3	-.2	-.5	-2.2	-1.3	-2.2	.1	-1.0	1.0
Sales/Net Fixed Assets	53.3	73.0	56.5	146.1	53.4	54.2	59.3	34.3	47.6
	23.1	26.0	24.4	36.8	27.2	19.7	25.5	24.1	14.1
	10.2	10.2	9.7	9.1	11.4	9.1	6.3	16.0	6.4
Sales/Total Assets	2.9	3.0	2.9	2.3	2.9	3.1	3.1	3.0	3.1
	2.4	2.4	2.2	1.7	2.3	2.3	2.2	2.4	2.3
	1.8	1.8	1.7	1.4	1.7	1.8	1.7	1.9	1.7
% Depr., Dep., Amort./Sales	.5	.6	.6	.6	.6	.7	.6	.6	.7
	(256) 1.2	(269) 1.2	(270) 1.3	(29) 1.3	(103) 1.3	(47) 1.3	(45) 1.1	(29) 1.1	(17) 1.8
	1.8	2.0	2.2	3.4	2.6	2.0	2.1	1.5	2.0
% Officers', Directors' Owners' Comp/Sales	2.3	1.7	1.9	3.5	2.3	2.4	1.1	1.2	
	(172) 4.0	(197) 3.1	(201) 3.5	(26) 5.7	(75) 3.9	(40) 3.8	(39) 2.0	(16) 2.8	
	6.4	5.4	5.6	9.2	5.3	5.4	5.6	3.8	
Net Sales ($)	4482123M	5286386M	3234499M	28058M	237156M	211693M	386738M	522395M	1848459M
Total Assets ($)	1909677M	2072674M	1496318M	21422M	112110M	99184M	192442M	228535M	842625M

M = $ thousand   MM = $ million
See Pages 9 through 22 for Explanation of Ratios and Data

Current Data Sorted by Assets · Comparative Historical Data

0-500M	500M-2MM	2-10MM	10-50MM	50-100MM	100-250MM		4/1/05-3/31/06 ALL	4/1/06-3/31/07 ALL
						Type of Statement		
1	1	7	17	6	5	Unqualified	35	34
3	22	44	22	2	1	Reviewed	85	99
10	33	30	1			Compiled	75	90
45	63	27				Tax Returns	68	128
22	47	45	23	2	4	Other	93	121
	57 (4/1-9/30/09)		426 (10/1/09-3/31/10)					
81	166	153	63	10	10	**NUMBER OF STATEMENTS**	356	472
%	%	%	%	%	%	**ASSETS**	%	%
12.0	8.3	9.0	7.9	4.0	5.0	Cash & Equivalents	7.2	7.2
23.6	27.0	25.1	24.3	17.6	18.3	Trade Receivables (net)	32.9	30.2
28.1	36.8	33.9	28.9	27.2	29.2	Inventory	32.5	32.8
3.1	2.6	1.8	2.3	2.4	3.0	All Other Current	2.1	2.4
66.8	74.7	69.9	63.4	51.2	55.4	Total Current	74.7	72.6
17.7	17.0	18.5	23.6	29.9	29.3	Fixed Assets (net)	18.3	18.4
6.3	1.5	3.6	3.9	3.3	8.9	Intangibles (net)	1.4	2.8
9.2	6.8	8.1	9.2	15.7	6.4	All Other Non-Current	5.6	6.3
100.0	100.0	100.0	100.0	100.0	100.0	Total	100.0	100.0
						LIABILITIES		
22.0	14.5	11.4	11.2	13.5	3.0	Notes Payable-Short Term	14.1	13.7
4.9	3.1	3.3	3.6	4.4	1.6	Cur. Mat.-L.T.D.	2.4	3.6
24.8	19.1	14.6	13.2	8.0	16.6	Trade Payables	20.8	17.8
.0	.1	.1	.1	.3	.6	Income Taxes Payable	.3	.3
22.3	9.8	8.8	8.3	7.2	6.9	All Other Current	8.7	10.7
74.1	46.6	38.2	36.3	33.4	28.7	Total Current	46.3	46.0
22.1	18.2	13.7	16.3	17.9	20.8	Long-Term Debt	13.1	15.3
.0	.2	.2	1.0	.2	1.8	Deferred Taxes	.2	.2
19.9	6.1	7.1	6.9	3.1	1.2	All Other Non-Current	6.3	7.8
-16.0	29.0	40.8	39.5	45.3	47.5	Net Worth	34.1	30.6
100.0	100.0	100.0	100.0	100.0	100.0	Total Liabilities & Net Worth	100.0	100.0
						INCOME DATA		
100.0	100.0	100.0	100.0	100.0	100.0	Net Sales	100.0	100.0
37.2	30.3	28.8	29.7	29.4	21.0	Gross Profit	28.7	30.1
37.7	30.4	28.7	29.1	24.9	20.2	Operating Expenses	25.6	27.0
-.5	-.1	.2	.6	4.5	.8	Operating Profit	3.2	3.1
.4	.5	.2	.9	.9	.7	All Other Expenses (net)	.3	.4
-.9	-.6	.0	-.3	3.5	.1	Profit Before Taxes	2.9	2.7
						RATIOS		
2.6	3.0	3.2	2.9	2.4	3.0		2.4	2.5
1.3	1.8	2.0	1.7	1.5	2.2	Current	1.7	1.7
.6	1.1	1.3	1.3	1.1	1.4		1.2	1.2
1.2	1.4	1.8	1.4	.9	1.5		1.3	1.4
(80) .6	.8	.9	1.0	.6	.8	Quick	(355) .9	.8
.2	.4	.5	.6	.5	.5		.5	.5
1 282.3	19 18.9	23 16.1	27 13.5	30 12.2	22 16.4		24 15.1	22 16.7
16 22.2	30 12.3	33 11.0	39 9.3	33 11.1	36 10.3	Sales/Receivables	36 10.2	34 10.9
33 11.0	44 8.3	45 8.1	53 6.9	40 9.1	51 7.1		48 7.6	47 7.7
6 57.5	35 10.4	41 8.9	42 8.7	53 6.9	41 9.0		28 13.2	27 13.7
26 13.8	66 5.5	72 5.1	66 5.5	60 6.1	51 7.2	Cost of Sales/Inventory	47 7.8	54 6.7
67 5.5	105 3.5	103 3.5	111 3.3	87 4.2	109 3.4		80 4.6	85 4.3
0 UND	16 22.6	15 24.4	17 20.9	14 26.6	22 16.7		17 22.1	14 26.1
18 20.2	26 14.1	24 15.0	29 12.7	21 17.3	28 13.0	Cost of Sales/Payables	27 13.4	24 15.5
44 8.2	48 7.7	41 9.0	42 8.6	29 12.6	41 9.0		43 8.4	40 9.1
8.0	4.9	4.5	4.8	7.6	4.0		6.8	6.6
43.2	11.2	7.1	9.2	9.5	7.0	Sales/Working Capital	11.3	10.8
-11.9	68.1	16.5	15.5	NM	15.5		29.9	29.6
7.3	8.1	5.8	4.8		72.6		11.0	8.1
(59) .5	(145) 1.7	(134) 1.6	(58) 1.5		2.0	EBIT/Interest	(322) 4.0	(418) 3.3
-5.6	-1.4	-.9	-1.9		-4.2		1.6	1.2
	2.4	3.9	2.8			Net Profit + Depr., Dep.,	6.0	9.2
	(18) 1.7	(27) 2.0	(19) 1.7			Amort./Cur. Mat. L/T/D	(84) 3.1	(91) 3.0
	.2	-1.1	.0				1.4	.9
.0	.1	.2	.2	.4	.3		.2	.2
.8	.4	.4	.6	.6	.6	Fixed/Worth	.5	.5
-.4	2.2	1.2	1.5	1.2	1.5		1.1	1.5
.8	.7	.6	.6	1.1	.4		.9	.8
17.7	1.9	1.3	1.3	1.3	2.0	Debt/Worth	1.9	2.0
-2.2	17.1	4.8	4.2	2.0	2.2		4.0	6.0
67.0	26.3	18.8	11.0	34.1		% Profit Before Taxes/Tangible	43.8	49.7
(45) 32.3	(133) 4.0	(135) 4.1	(56) 3.7	3.2		Net Worth	(317) 22.3	(406) 19.1
-17.6	-9.4	-8.4	-8.7	.0			7.1	6.5
23.6	6.2	7.1	4.0	12.9	10.7	% Profit Before Taxes/Total	15.8	14.8
1.7	.7	1.6	1.6	2.1	1.7	Assets	6.7	6.4
-23.7	-7.5	-3.8	-6.4	.0	-10.6		1.1	.9
457.8	67.1	42.5	24.3	17.4	41.0		54.4	57.5
46.1	26.1	22.5	11.8	7.8	13.1	Sales/Net Fixed Assets	24.6	25.6
14.3	12.5	9.2	4.6	2.4	2.4		11.9	10.7
6.2	3.9	3.1	2.7	2.5	3.1		4.3	4.1
3.8	3.0	2.5	2.0	2.1	1.5	Sales/Total Assets	3.3	3.1
2.4	2.1	1.8	1.4	1.2	1.3		2.4	2.3
.3	.5	.6	.8	1.0			.5	.5
(51) .9	(133) 1.2	(139) 1.2	(59) 1.7	1.5		% Depr., Dep., Amort./Sales	(304) 1.0	(405) 1.0
2.1	2.0	1.9	2.7	2.8			1.5	1.5
3.8	2.1	1.4	.9			% Officers', Directors'	1.4	1.5
(42) 6.0	(88) 3.6	(77) 2.2	(14) 1.5			Owners' Comp/Sales	(183) 2.8	(210) 3.1
12.5	6.3	4.6	2.5				5.5	5.2
103198M	602962M	1736589M	2601077M	1147020M	2807351M	Net Sales ($)	8239317M	10116751M
21987M	195790M	691204M	1229604M	602254M	1369857M	Total Assets ($)	3150716M	3861566M

M = $ thousand   MM = $ million
See Pages 9 through 22 for Explanation of Ratios and Data

Comparative Historical Data

Current Data Sorted by Sales

			Type of Statement						
30	38	37	Unqualified	1	1	1	1	7	26
87	110	94	Reviewed	2	3	13	25	31	20
80	66	74	Compiled	6	19	17	15	17	
133	130	135	Tax Returns	31	55	17	21	11	
144	147	143	Other	16	31	20	26	11	18
4/1/07-3/31/08 ALL	4/1/08-3/31/09 ALL	4/1/09-3/31/10 ALL		57 (4/1-9/30/09)			426 (10/1/09-3/31/10)		
				0-1MM	1-3MM	3-5MM	5-10MM	10-25MM	25MM & OVER
474	491	483	NUMBER OF STATEMENTS	56	109	68	88	98	64
%	%	%	**ASSETS**	%	%	%	%	%	%
7.8	8.2	8.9	Cash & Equivalents	12.9	8.6	8.2	8.6	8.8	7.5
27.6	26.0	25.1	Trade Receivables (net)	17.6	23.3	26.9	26.3	27.6	27.2
32.1	34.5	33.0	Inventory	28.7	35.2	34.6	33.7	33.6	29.8
3.0	2.3	2.4	All Other Current	2.8	2.0	4.2	2.0	1.8	2.5
70.4	70.9	69.5	Total Current	62.0	69.0	73.9	70.7	71.7	67.0
19.3	19.1	19.0	Fixed Assets (net)	21.3	17.1	18.4	18.4	18.3	22.4
3.4	2.3	3.4	Intangibles (net)	5.9	4.2	2.4	2.5	3.0	3.2
6.9	7.7	8.1	All Other Non-Current	10.7	9.6	5.2	8.5	7.1	7.4
100.0	100.0	100.0	Total	100.0	100.0	100.0	100.0	100.0	100.0
			LIABILITIES						
12.3	18.0	14.1	Notes Payable-Short Term	20.5	11.8	15.4	14.3	14.7	9.9
4.1	3.6	3.5	Cur. Mat.-L.T.D.	5.2	4.4	2.5	3.7	2.7	2.9
17.5	15.9	17.6	Trade Payables	19.0	20.0	18.5	16.2	16.5	14.8
.1	.2	.1	Income Taxes Payable	.0	.0	.1	.1	.1	.2
10.8	10.4	11.3	All Other Current	22.1	13.9	6.7	10.8	7.5	8.6
44.9	48.2	46.6	Total Current	66.7	50.2	43.1	45.0	41.5	36.2
16.2	17.2	17.2	Long-Term Debt	18.5	21.0	21.3	16.9	10.8	15.5
.2	.3	.3	Deferred Taxes	.2	.0	.1	.2	.5	.7
8.1	5.9	8.7	All Other Non-Current	25.7	6.5	9.6	6.0	6.4	3.7
30.6	28.4	27.3	Net Worth	-11.0	22.2	25.8	31.8	40.8	43.8
100.0	100.0	100.0	Total Liabilities & Net Worth	100.0	100.0	100.0	100.0	100.0	100.0
			INCOME DATA						
100.0	100.0	100.0	Net Sales	100.0	100.0	100.0	100.0	100.0	100.0
31.1	30.0	30.7	Gross Profit	41.0	31.9	28.8	30.5	27.8	26.3
28.5	29.2	30.6	Operating Expenses	43.7	31.9	28.2	30.7	27.1	24.5
2.6	.8	.1	Operating Profit	-2.7	.0	.6	-.2	.8	1.7
.7	.5	.4	All Other Expenses (net)	1.0	.3	.3	.5	.2	.6
2.0	.3	-.3	Profit Before Taxes	-3.7	-.3	.3	-.7	.5	1.2
			RATIOS						
2.9	2.9	3.1		2.7	3.2	3.0	3.2	2.8	2.9
1.7	1.8	1.7	Current	1.3	1.7	1.9	1.9	1.7	1.7
1.1	1.1	1.1		.6	.9	1.2	1.2	1.2	1.4
1.5	1.5	1.5		1.2	1.4	1.6	2.0	1.5	1.4
.8	.8 (482)	.8	Quick	(55) .6	.7	.9	.9	.9	1.0
.5	.4	.4		.1	.4	.4	.4	.5	.6
21 17.2	16 22.5	19 19.5		0 UND	13 28.9	20 18.5	22 16.8	24 15.3	28 13.0
31 11.7	30 12.2	31 11.8	Sales/Receivables	17 21.5	26 14.0	31 11.9	32 11.5	36 10.2	35 10.5
46 7.9	44 8.3	44 8.3		45 8.2	38 9.5	43 8.5	45 8.1	50 7.4	48 7.6
26 14.3	30 12.3	32 11.2		6 64.7	29 12.6	29 12.6	40 9.1	35 10.4	39 9.3
53 6.8	56 6.5	61 6.0	Cost of Sales/Inventory	48 7.6	59 6.2	70 5.2	62 5.9	66 5.5	56 6.6
86 4.2	92 4.0	101 3.6		150 2.4	109 3.3	103 3.6	83 4.4	95 3.8	89 4.1
14 26.6	11 34.0	15 25.2		0 UND	13 27.7	19 19.5	14 25.5	15 23.8	18 20.6
25 14.6	21 17.5	25 14.4	Cost of Sales/Payables	19 19.6	28 13.2	25 14.9	24 15.1	26 14.0	27 13.8
42 8.7	37 9.8	42 8.6		63 5.8	49 7.4	43 8.4	40 9.0	41 8.9	35 10.4
5.9	5.9	4.9		4.3	4.1	5.6	5.1	5.1	4.9
10.3	10.8	9.5	Sales/Working Capital	20.1	13.2	10.3	8.4	9.0	9.5
43.5	69.4	39.5		-7.0	-45.6	23.8	27.5	19.1	15.9
7.3	6.6	5.9		4.5	11.3	3.1	2.8	8.4	5.9
(431) 2.5	(443) 2.0	(415) 1.6	EBIT/Interest	(36) -1.7	(91) 2.2	(60) 1.4	(77) 1.3	(92) 1.8	(59) 1.7
.4	-.5	-1.6		-7.0	-2.6	-.6	-.8	-.8	-.6
4.4	5.7	3.1				2.0	2.6	4.0	4.1
(78) 1.5	(83) 1.7	(73) 1.7	Net Profit + Depr., Dep., Amort./Cur. Mat. L/T/D		(11) .4	(13) 1.2	(22) 2.6	(21) 2.2	
.3	.2	.0				-1.0	-.6	-.5	.4
.2	.2	.1		.0	.1	.1	.2	.2	.2
.5	.5	.4	Fixed/Worth	1.0	.4	.5	.5	.4	.5
1.9	1.7	2.0		-.6	-6.3	2.6	2.7	1.3	1.1
.9	.7	.7		.7	.6	.7	.6	.6	.6
1.9	2.0	1.9	Debt/Worth	8.7	2.0	2.1	2.0	1.4	1.2
8.4	8.4	13.9		-2.6	-10.5	13.7	14.0	4.6	2.2
36.4	27.2	23.9		53.1	39.8	28.0	17.2	19.6	14.2
(388) 13.9	(402) 7.9	(388) 4.7	% Profit Before Taxes/Tangible Net Worth	(35) 1.0	(78) 5.4	(55) 8.5	(70) 3.0	(90) 5.4	(60) 4.3
.7	-4.2	-8.7		-35.4	-9.1	-10.7	-10.8	-7.6	-3.7
12.4	10.5	7.7		10.0	15.1	6.7	5.2	8.1	6.4
4.5	2.6	1.4	% Profit Before Taxes/Total Assets	-4.4	1.5	1.0	1.0	1.6	2.3
-1.7	-4.3	-7.1		-29.7	-9.0	-8.3	-5.9	-2.8	-2.0
52.7	55.6	56.9		220.2	66.6	62.5	44.4	49.0	31.4
21.9	24.0	23.1	Sales/Net Fixed Assets	32.0	30.1	23.6	26.6	22.8	14.9
9.6	10.1	9.7		6.4	13.4	11.2	10.3	7.8	5.6
4.0	4.0	3.7		4.6	3.8	3.8	3.7	3.5	3.1
2.8	2.9	2.7	Sales/Total Assets	2.4	2.9	3.0	2.7	2.5	2.5
2.1	2.1	1.8		1.3	1.7	2.0	2.1	1.8	1.6
.6	.6	.6		.6	.5	.5	.7	.6	.8
(395) 1.1	(395) 1.1	(399) 1.2	% Depr., Dep., Amort./Sales	(32) 2.2	(86) 1.2	(55) 1.3	(75) 1.3	(92) 1.1	(59) 1.2
2.0	2.1	2.2		4.9	2.1	2.1	2.0	1.8	2.4
1.8	1.7	1.9		5.2	2.7	2.0	1.8	1.2	.7
(238) 3.2	(225) 3.2	(224) 3.2	% Officers', Directors' Owners' Comp/Sales	(26) 10.5	(58) 4.1	(40) 3.2	(38) 2.8	(43) 2.0	(19) 1.5
5.7	5.8	6.1		17.8	6.2	5.5	3.7	2.8	
9650983M	10117302M	8998197M	Net Sales ($)	30820M	221685M	267299M	613121M	1569635M	6295637M
3663549M	4200071M	4110696M	Total Assets ($)	20539M	95365M	103415M	286673M	754733M	2849971M

M = $ thousand   MM = $ million
See Pages 9 through 22 for Explanation of Ratios and Data

RETAIL—Outdoor Power Equipment Stores   NAICS 444210

Current Data Sorted by Assets							Comparative Historical Data	

0-500M	500M-2MM	2-10MM	10-50MM	50-100MM	100-250MM	Type of Statement	1 4/1/05-3/31/06 ALL	1 4/1/06-3/31/07 ALL
		1	1		1	Unqualified	1	1
	2	13	2			Reviewed	13	16
7	6	11	2			Compiled	24	26
10	11	11	3			Tax Returns	12	20
4	2	12	4			Other	13	27
	16 (4/1-9/30/09)		87 (10/1/09-3/31/10)					
21	21	48	12		1	NUMBER OF STATEMENTS	63	90
%	%	%	%	%	%		%	%
						ASSETS		
10.0	8.8	4.7	7.6			Cash & Equivalents	5.5	6.2
17.7	9.0	11.2	10.5			Trade Receivables (net)	13.3	12.7
49.1	61.9	62.8	58.5			Inventory	60.8	59.4
.7	.4	1.0	2.2			All Other Current	1.7	1.8
77.5	80.1	79.7	78.8			Total Current	81.2	80.1
13.1	16.3	15.2	12.2			Fixed Assets (net)	12.7	15.3
1.3	.4	.9	6.3			Intangibles (net)	1.8	1.8
7.9	3.2	4.2	2.8			All Other Non-Current	4.2	2.8
100.0	100.0	100.0	100.0			Total	100.0	100.0
						LIABILITIES		
15.5	14.7	23.2	13.2			Notes Payable-Short Term	17.2	23.0
4.0	4.6	3.2	1.9			Cur. Mat.-L.T.D.	5.3	3.0
24.6	15.8	22.3	27.9			Trade Payables	21.5	24.0
.0	.1	.1	.4			Income Taxes Payable	.1	.3
14.0	9.2	11.7	7.8			All Other Current	9.6	8.3
58.0	44.4	60.5	51.1			Total Current	53.7	58.6
20.0	18.5	9.6	7.4			Long-Term Debt	13.9	13.3
.0	.1	.2	.1			Deferred Taxes	.4	.2
13.9	4.5	4.4	.8			All Other Non-Current	5.8	5.4
8.0	32.5	25.3	40.6			Net Worth	26.2	22.5
100.0	100.0	100.0	100.0			Total Liabilities & Net Worth	100.0	100.0
						INCOME DATA		
100.0	100.0	100.0	100.0			Net Sales	100.0	100.0
30.2	33.1	27.6	22.5			Gross Profit	24.6	27.7
32.2	31.1	27.4	20.3			Operating Expenses	22.3	25.8
-2.0	2.0	.2	2.2			Operating Profit	2.3	1.8
1.1	.9	.7	-.2			All Other Expenses (net)	.2	.8
-3.1	1.1	-.5	2.4			Profit Before Taxes	2.1	1.0
						RATIOS		
2.7	2.9	1.8	2.3				2.0	1.8
2.0	1.9	1.4	1.5			Current	1.4	1.4
.9	1.2	1.2	1.2				1.2	1.1
1.4	1.0	.4	.7				.7	.5
.2	.3	.2	.2			Quick	.3	.3
.1	.1	.1	.1				.2	.1
2 146.7	4 100.3	6 59.1	3 124.6				5 72.5	3 106.7
10 37.6	9 40.2	12 31.0	7 49.2			Sales/Receivables	11 32.0	11 33.9
32 11.4	21 17.1	25 14.5	30 12.2				26 14.2	24 15.5
25 14.7	81 4.5	94 3.9	82 4.4				87 4.2	76 4.8
79 4.6	182 2.0	127 2.9	119 3.1			Cost of Sales/Inventory	117 3.1	120 3.0
196 1.9	276 1.3	197 1.9	139 2.6				176 2.1	178 2.1
0 UND	9 38.9	12 29.6	14 26.9				6 61.2	9 39.7
30 12.2	22 16.9	39 9.5	51 7.2			Cost of Sales/Payables	23 16.1	34 10.6
77 4.7	62 5.9	75 4.9	70 5.2				67 5.5	76 4.8
5.1	3.3	6.7	5.4				5.6	6.2
11.3	6.5	10.2	9.3			Sales/Working Capital	11.4	10.6
NM	15.9	17.8	20.2				20.6	193.7
2.5	5.2	3.8	12.6				5.4	4.7
(19) 1.3	(19) 2.4	1.8	(11) 5.6			EBIT/Interest	(61) 3.1	(87) 1.9
-5.3	1.4	-.1	1.6				1.7	.9
							9.2	8.0
						Net Profit + Depr., Dep., Amort./Cur. Mat. L/T/D	(14) 4.9	(15) 3.5
							1.6	1.5
.0	.2	.1	.1				.1	.1
.5	.6	.4	.2			Fixed/Worth	.4	.3
-.3	1.2	1.7	.4				1.6	2.0
.7	.9	1.7	.8				1.6	1.6
10.3	1.9	3.9	2.1			Debt/Worth	3.5	3.1
-4.8	6.6	9.6	3.4				11.1	14.7
21.3	24.0	20.4	28.7				38.4	28.0
(13) 4.3	(18) 10.2	(43) 9.7	(11) 17.4			% Profit Before Taxes/Tangible Net Worth	(59) 19.1	(77) 14.6
-10.5	4.3	.5	6.3				10.3	1.4
6.1	4.8	4.8	10.5				10.0	7.5
.3	3.5	2.0	4.2			% Profit Before Taxes/Total Assets	3.8	2.9
-17.7	.8	-2.8	2.1				1.6	-.4
321.9	58.2	72.3	72.6				72.6	71.7
64.6	15.3	33.9	32.5			Sales/Net Fixed Assets	40.2	30.0
12.9	8.6	12.6	23.2				13.1	12.7
4.6	3.4	3.3	2.9				3.1	3.4
2.6	1.9	2.0	2.4			Sales/Total Assets	2.4	2.5
2.1	1.5	1.5	2.2				1.8	1.6
.3	.5	.5	.4				.4	.5
(14) 1.2	(19) 1.0	(44) .8	(10) .7			% Depr., Dep., Amort./Sales	(54) .8	(67) 1.2
2.0	3.3	2.1	1.2				1.8	1.8
3.8	1.7	.8					.9	1.1
(13) 5.7	(12) 4.4	(24) 1.5				% Officers', Directors' Owners' Comp/Sales	(35) 2.5	(46) 2.1
7.4	5.7	3.3					4.9	3.5
23787M	55273M	506609M	657402M		262061M	Net Sales ($)	674004M	767047M
6530M	22554M	204819M	270441M		230498M	Total Assets ($)	272317M	319605M

(Column 50-100MM: DATA NOT AVAILABLE)

© RMA 2010

M = $ thousand   MM = $ million
See Pages 9 through 22 for Explanation of Ratios and Data

Comparative Historical Data   Current Data Sorted by Sales

Type of Statement

Type of Statement	4/1/07-3/31/08 ALL	4/1/08-3/31/09 ALL	4/1/09-3/31/10 ALL	0-1MM	1-3MM	3-5MM	5-10MM	10-25MM	25MM & OVER
Unqualified	1	3	3				1		2
Reviewed	6	10	17		2	3	4	6	2
Compiled	22	21	26	4	6	4	5	4	3
Tax Returns	22	24	35	10	9	5	5	4	2
Other	29	25	22	3	3	1	5	4	5
	80	83	103	16 (4/1-9/30/09)			87 (10/1/09-3/31/10)		

	07-08 ALL	08-09 ALL	09-10 ALL	0-1MM	1-3MM	3-5MM	5-10MM	10-25MM	25MM & OVER
NUMBER OF STATEMENTS	80	83	103	17	20	13	20	19	14
	%	%	%	%	%	%	%	%	%
ASSETS									
Cash & Equivalents	5.3	6.4	6.9	7.1	7.4	8.4	8.1	4.0	6.9
Trade Receivables (net)	10.3	10.6	12.0	17.6	9.6	11.8	7.6	15.8	10.1
Inventory	61.7	61.6	59.2	52.1	61.2	57.5	60.5	60.0	64.0
All Other Current	1.3	.6	1.0	.0	1.1	.9	.7	1.2	2.0
Total Current	78.6	79.2	79.1	76.8	79.3	78.7	76.9	80.9	82.9
Fixed Assets (net)	17.2	14.4	14.8	13.1	15.9	18.8	16.3	11.8	13.4
Intangibles (net)	1.7	1.5	1.5	1.7	.2	-1.5	.7	4.0	.8
All Other Non-Current	2.6	4.9	4.6	8.4	4.6	1.1	6.1	3.2	2.8
Total	100.0	100.0	100.0	100.0	100.0	100.0	100.0	100.0	100.0
LIABILITIES									
Notes Payable-Short Term	19.8	23.6	19.0	13.0	19.8	21.9	22.3	21.1	14.8
Cur. Mat.-L.T.D.	4.8	2.4	3.5	7.1	3.2	5.8	2.4	.9	2.3
Trade Payables	24.3	19.5	21.9	21.0	21.0	22.4	20.7	18.4	30.3
Income Taxes Payable	.1	.3	.1	.0	.0	.1	.0	.1	.4
All Other Current	11.3	10.5	11.1	6.9	22.8	5.9	10.7	10.2	6.5
Total Current	60.4	56.3	55.6	48.0	66.9	56.0	56.1	50.8	54.3
Long-Term Debt	16.1	12.9	13.3	24.6	18.7	11.1	10.6	4.1	9.8
Deferred Taxes	.4	.2	.1	.0	.0	.2	.2	.1	.3
All Other Non-Current	4.7	3.4	5.9	11.9	8.2	4.8	4.2	4.2	.9
Net Worth	18.5	27.2	25.1	15.4	6.1	27.8	28.9	40.7	34.8
Total Liabilities & Net Worth	100.0	100.0	100.0	100.0	100.0	100.0	100.0	100.0	100.0
INCOME DATA									
Net Sales	100.0	100.0	100.0	100.0	100.0	100.0	100.0	100.0	100.0
Gross Profit	28.3	28.6	28.6	31.8	32.6	33.2	28.8	23.6	21.4
Operating Expenses	26.5	26.5	28.3	33.3	33.8	30.9	27.9	23.0	19.5
Operating Profit	1.8	2.0	.4	-1.5	-1.3	2.3	1.0	.7	1.9
All Other Expenses (net)	.9	1.2	.7	1.5	1.4	1.8	-.1	.0	.0
Profit Before Taxes	.9	.8	-.3	-3.0	-2.7	.6	1.1	.7	2.0
RATIOS									
Current	1.6 / 1.3 / 1.1	2.2 / 1.5 / 1.1	2.3 / 1.5 / 1.1	2.9 / 2.0 / 1.1	2.2 / 1.2 / .8	2.2 / 1.3 / 1.2	1.8 / 1.5 / 1.2	2.4 / 1.6 / 1.2	2.4 / 1.5 / 1.2
Quick	(79) .4 / .2 / .1	(82) .6 / .2 / .1	.5 / .2 / .1	1.3 / .4 / .1	.3 / .2 / .1	.8 / .2 / .1	.4 / .3 / .2	.7 / .3 / .2	.6 / .2 / .2
Sales/Receivables	3 138.1 / 9 42.4 / 21 17.4	4 95.9 / 10 37.9 / 23 16.0	5 77.3 / 11 32.7 / 26 14.3	0 UND / 10 37.6 / 47 7.7	4 84.8 / 9 41.8 / 25 14.7	6 57.1 / 18 19.8 / 24 15.4	6 59.0 / 11 32.5 / 23 15.8	6 61.3 / 12 31.1 / 32 11.4	3 125.7 / 7 49.2 / 32 11.4
Cost of Sales/Inventory	78 4.7 / 118 3.1 / 203 1.8	81 4.5 / 129 2.8 / 213 1.7	79 4.6 / 126 2.9 / 201 1.8	76 4.8 / 182 2.0 / 310 1.2	82 4.5 / 179 2.0 / 244 1.5	58 6.3 / 136 2.7 / 277 1.3	87 4.2 / 152 2.4 / 218 1.7	65 5.6 / 108 3.4 / 126 2.9	77 4.7 / 119 3.1 / 140 2.6
Cost of Sales/Payables	12 30.0 / 29 12.7 / 72 5.1	8 48.4 / 23 15.5 / 63 5.8	12 29.3 / 38 9.5 / 70 5.2	9 41.9 / 63 5.8 / 87 4.2	12 30.6 / 29 12.5 / 75 4.8	7 50.4 / 46 7.9 / 93 3.9	9 41.4 / 44 8.2 / 80 4.6	12 31.0 / 15 23.7 / 54 6.7	13 28.1 / 51 7.2 / 75 4.9
Sales/Working Capital	8.4 / 14.5 / 80.7	5.5 / 10.6 / 20.9	5.8 / 10.1 / 18.5	3.1 / 5.9 / 34.4	5.0 / 11.2 / -219.6	7.0 / 10.4 / 37.6	6.5 / 10.2 / 15.9	6.8 / 10.8 / 17.9	7.3 / 9.8 / 15.0
EBIT/Interest	(78) 5.1 / 1.6 / .9	(74) 4.5 / 2.0 / .9	(98) 4.4 / 2.1 / 1.1	(15) 2.4 / 1.3 / -5.3	3.5 / 1.9 / -.4	(12) 2.8 / 2.4 / 1.4	(19) 3.0 / 1.7 / -.4	13.6 / 3.7 / 1.1	(13) 9.8 / 3.8 / 1.6
Net Profit + Depr., Dep., Amort./Cur. Mat. L/T/D	(14) 8.0 / 1.8 / 1.2	(13) 16.1 / 6.5 / 2.5	(15) 5.5 / 2.9 / 1.1						
Fixed/Worth	.2 / .5 / 3.4	.1 / .3 / 1.7	.1 / .4 / 1.8	.1 / .4 / 2.9	.2 / 1.3 / -.5	.1 / .4 / 2.0	.2 / .4 / 1.4	.1 / .2 / .5	.1 / .2 / .8
Debt/Worth	1.9 / 3.7 / 13.8	1.3 / 2.5 / 9.5	1.3 / 2.9 / 12.0	.9 / 3.9 / NM	1.5 / 7.3 / -5.3	1.4 / 3.6 / 17.2	1.5 / 4.3 / 9.6	.7 / 1.7 / 4.1	1.0 / 2.4 / 3.6
% Profit Before Taxes/Tangible Net Worth	(67) 34.7 / 10.5 / 1.8	(73) 34.4 / 10.2 / 2.1	(86) 21.4 / 9.7 / 2.2	(13) 20.9 / 4.3 / -10.5	(12) 25.4 / 8.7 / 2.8	(12) 65.1 / 9.8 / -11.3	(18) 24.3 / 9.6 / -15.1	15.1 / 10.0 / 2.5	(13) 24.7 / 17.4 / 7.2
% Profit Before Taxes/Total Assets	6.9 / 1.6 / -.7	6.6 / 2.8 / .0	4.9 / 2.4 / .1	2.6 / .3 / -15.1	4.7 / 2.5 / -7.8	5.4 / 3.2 / -1.1	5.2 / 1.7 / -3.7	6.2 / 3.8 / .4	7.4 / 4.2 / 2.2
Sales/Net Fixed Assets	77.7 / 27.4 / 10.7	89.2 / 35.6 / 11.4	78.6 / 33.3 / 11.6	251.9 / 19.3 / 6.9	83.1 / 24.1 / 9.9	115.5 / 42.9 / 14.3	68.8 / 33.5 / 8.9	70.2 / 33.4 / 18.3	84.0 / 32.6 / 21.1
Sales/Total Assets	3.8 / 2.6 / 1.7	3.3 / 2.3 / 1.6	3.2 / 2.3 / 1.6	2.7 / 2.0 / 1.2	3.1 / 2.0 / 1.4	3.6 / 1.8 / 1.5	3.5 / 1.9 / 1.5	3.9 / 3.1 / 2.3	3.1 / 2.5 / 2.2
% Depr., Dep., Amort./Sales	(65) .5 / 1.0 / 1.7	(60) .5 / .9 / 2.1	(87) .5 / .9 / 1.9	(10) .3 / 1.4 / 4.6	(19) .5 / 1.1 / 2.8	(12) .3 / 1.3 / 3.4	(18) .5 / 1.0 / 2.0	(10) .4 / .7 / 1.3	.4 / .5 / 1.0
% Officers', Directors' Owners' Comp/Sales	(46) 1.0 / 2.4 / 3.6	(46) 1.3 / 2.4 / 4.6	(53) 1.2 / 2.3 / 5.6	(10) 4.0 / 5.9 / 8.9	(10) 1.9 / 4.6 / 5.1	(13) 1.1 / 1.8 / 6.6	(11) 1.1 / 1.3 / 2.7		
Net Sales ($)	1033121M	1400995M	1505132M	10749M	38434M	49500M	138974M	306181M	961294M
Total Assets ($)	419118M	597394M	734842M	5998M	21518M	27633M	69696M	107455M	502542M

© RMA 2010

M = $ thousand   MM = $ million

See Pages 9 through 22 for Explanation of Ratios and Data

RETAIL—Nursery, Garden Center, and Farm Supply Stores NAICS 444220

	Current Data Sorted by Assets						Comparative Historical Data	

Type of Statement

	0-500M	500M-2MM	2-10MM	10-50MM	50-100MM	100-250MM	4/1/05-3/31/06 ALL	4/1/06-3/31/07 ALL
Unqualified		3	5	7	1	1	10	9
Reviewed	1	6	20	6			47	41
Compiled	4	28	13	3			65	79
Tax Returns	23	31	5	1			50	52
Other	10	20	18	15		1	65	63
		40 (4/1-9/30/09)		182 (10/1/09-3/31/10)				
NUMBER OF STATEMENTS	38	88	61	32	1	2	237	244
ASSETS	%	%	%	%	%	%	%	%
Cash & Equivalents	11.5	8.7	5.5	5.0			7.7	7.4
Trade Receivables (net)	10.6	11.0	10.1	14.3			13.0	12.7
Inventory	41.2	39.1	37.2	32.2			38.0	35.0
All Other Current	.6	1.7	1.6	3.4			1.6	2.8
Total Current	63.9	60.5	54.5	54.9			60.3	57.9
Fixed Assets (net)	31.1	31.8	34.7	32.2			29.4	31.8
Intangibles (net)	1.6	3.0	2.3	5.3			2.1	2.9
All Other Non-Current	3.4	4.6	8.5	7.6			8.2	7.4
Total	100.0	100.0	100.0	100.0			100.0	100.0
LIABILITIES								
Notes Payable-Short Term	26.3	11.4	12.6	12.5			15.1	13.9
Cur. Mat.-L.T.D.	2.9	5.5	5.2	4.4			5.2	5.1
Trade Payables	24.3	13.4	16.3	16.6			16.6	16.8
Income Taxes Payable	.0	.0	.2	.3			.3	.2
All Other Current	40.1	11.0	9.2	6.7			10.5	11.6
Total Current	93.6	41.4	43.5	40.4			47.7	47.6
Long-Term Debt	28.3	22.3	19.5	15.2			19.4	22.9
Deferred Taxes	.0	.4	.6	.8			.5	.4
All Other Non-Current	17.6	6.0	3.4	6.4			9.7	7.8
Net Worth	-39.4	29.9	33.0	37.2			22.7	21.3
Total Liabilities & Net Worth	100.0	100.0	100.0	100.0			100.0	100.0
INCOME DATA								
Net Sales	100.0	100.0	100.0	100.0			100.0	100.0
Gross Profit	42.6	39.1	37.5	31.1			37.0	37.6
Operating Expenses	43.2	38.2	36.2	28.9			34.8	34.8
Operating Profit	-.6	.9	1.3	2.2			2.2	2.9
All Other Expenses (net)	.6	.9	.7	.7			.8	1.0
Profit Before Taxes	-1.2	.0	.6	1.4			1.4	1.8
RATIOS								
Current	2.3	2.7	2.0	1.9			2.2	2.2
	1.1	1.5	1.5	1.3			1.3	1.3
	.4	1.0	.9	1.0			1.0	.8
Quick	.7	.9	.6	.9			.9	.9
	.2	.5	.3	.4			.4	.3
	.1	.1	.1	.2			.2	.1
Sales/Receivables	0 UND	3 129.4	3 128.7	2 150.6			3 134.7	2 180.2
	4 85.0	9 39.2	10 35.7	18 20.3			10 37.2	9 40.3
	12 31.0	23 16.2	33 11.0	36 10.2			26 14.1	24 15.4
Cost of Sales/Inventory	18 20.7	45 8.1	59 6.2	44 8.3			37 9.9	33 11.0
	51 7.2	74 4.9	89 4.1	66 5.5			71 5.2	70 5.2
	117 3.1	149 2.5	142 2.6	127 2.9			117 3.1	118 3.1
Cost of Sales/Payables	0 UND	8 47.8	10 35.3	15 24.9			11 34.6	9 42.3
	15 24.7	18 20.1	30 12.0	33 11.2			26 13.8	28 13.3
	47 7.8	42 8.7	63 5.8	59 6.2			49 7.5	47 7.8
Sales/Working Capital	10.7	6.5	6.0	9.3			7.4	8.2
	UND	12.9	14.2	16.6			18.3	20.4
	-8.8	NM	-55.8	NM			-201.8	-31.8
EBIT/Interest	2.9	6.2	5.4	5.7			6.9	5.6
	(33) .9	(83) 2.1	(58) 1.9	(29) 2.5			(224) 2.9	(233) 2.1
	-1.7	.7	-.5	.7			.8	.8
Net Profit + Depr., Dep., Amort./Cur. Mat. L/T/D		3.5	5.1	9.3			3.8	3.4
		(12) 1.6	(13) 1.5	(11) 5.6			(43) 2.4	(46) 2.3
		.5	.2	.9			1.0	1.2
Fixed/Worth	.5	.4	.4	.5			.3	.4
	UND	.9	1.2	1.1			.9	1.0
	-.2	7.1	5.0	3.2			3.4	3.9
Debt/Worth	1.6	.8	.9	1.2			1.1	.9
	UND	1.9	2.0	2.5			2.4	2.6
	-1.9	31.4	8.2	5.4			9.5	9.8
% Profit Before Taxes/Tangible Net Worth	40.8	25.6	25.3	22.9			37.3	36.8
	(20) .2	(71) 9.0	(51) 7.2	(28) 6.3			(193) 13.6	(198) 14.2
	-15.8	.3	-4.3	-6.4			1.0	.9
% Profit Before Taxes/Total Assets	9.2	8.4	8.6	7.2			11.6	11.6
	.0	2.7	1.4	2.5			4.4	3.6
	-7.3	-1.3	-2.1	-.4			-1.2	-.3
Sales/Net Fixed Assets	46.6	28.5	17.7	14.5			28.4	25.4
	17.7	11.0	6.7	7.8			12.1	10.8
	7.2	4.7	4.2	3.4			5.5	4.9
Sales/Total Assets	6.3	3.6	2.9	2.6			4.1	4.0
	4.0	2.5	2.2	1.8			2.8	2.8
	2.1	1.8	1.4	1.6			1.9	1.9
% Depr., Dep., Amort./Sales	.8	1.0	.8	1.0			.9	.9
	(26) 2.0	(79) 2.0	(57) 1.8	(30) 1.7			(204) 1.6	(216) 1.5
	3.0	4.2	3.6	3.2			3.2	2.6
% Officers', Directors' Owners' Comp/Sales	2.9	2.6	1.0	.3			1.9	1.7
	(19) 7.3	(61) 4.6	(24) 2.1	(10) 1.0			(130) 3.4	(129) 3.7
	10.2	6.2	3.3	1.5			6.0	6.2
Net Sales ($)	43735M	271202M	625930M	1607535M	120448M	679357M	2443870M	4216116M
Total Assets ($)	10988M	95986M	266139M	746371M	55184M	254661M	984696M	1587781M

M = $ thousand   MM = $ million
See Pages 9 through 22 for Explanation of Ratios and Data

Comparative Historical Data
Current Data Sorted by Sales

19	16	17	Type of Statement						
37	46	33	Unqualified	1	2	1	1	4	9
69	60	48	Reviewed	1	2	7	10	10	3
49	54	60	Compiled	1	25	10	4	10	3
70	62	64	Tax Returns	18	24	10	3	5	3
4/1/07-3/31/08	4/1/08-3/31/09	4/1/09-3/31/10	Other	4	19	9	9	4	14
ALL	ALL	ALL		40 (4/1-9/30/09)			182 (10/1/09-3/31/10)		
				0-1MM	1-3MM	3-5MM	5-10MM	10-25MM	25MM & OVER
244	238	222	NUMBER OF STATEMENTS	24	72	37	27	32	30
%	%	%	**ASSETS**	%	%	%	%	%	%
8.0	8.1	7.7	Cash & Equivalents	10.2	8.9	8.3	8.0	5.7	4.0
14.7	12.5	11.3	Trade Receivables (net)	9.0	10.1	9.6	15.8	13.1	11.9
35.9	36.7	37.9	Inventory	39.9	38.2	38.8	37.8	38.3	33.7
2.3	1.9	1.8	All Other Current	.3	1.3	1.0	3.6	2.2	3.4
60.9	59.3	58.7	Total Current	59.4	58.5	57.7	65.3	59.3	53.0
30.2	31.9	32.4	Fixed Assets (net)	31.5	34.0	34.9	26.4	30.0	34.0
2.7	2.0	2.9	Intangibles (net)	4.1	2.6	2.2	1.3	2.3	5.4
6.2	6.9	6.1	All Other Non-Current	5.0	4.8	5.2	7.0	8.4	7.7
100.0	100.0	100.0	Total	100.0	100.0	100.0	100.0	100.0	100.0
			LIABILITIES						
15.3	14.7	14.5	Notes Payable-Short Term	26.2	13.2	14.2	13.4	12.6	11.8
5.0	4.8	4.7	Cur. Mat.-L.T.D.	2.9	5.3	5.4	3.9	5.8	3.6
14.1	15.2	16.6	Trade Payables	20.3	12.6	15.5	19.8	20.5	17.4
.2	.4	.1	Income Taxes Payable	.0	.0	.1	.2	.2	.3
7.9	9.2	14.8	All Other Current	49.2	12.6	8.5	11.1	11.5	7.1
42.6	44.3	50.8	Total Current	98.6	43.7	43.9	48.3	50.7	40.3
21.7	22.8	21.3	Long-Term Debt	39.1	25.9	22.1	9.6	12.7	15.0
.4	.4	.4	Deferred Taxes	.0	.0	1.0	.2	.3	.9
6.0	6.0	7.3	All Other Non-Current	21.7	7.3	3.8	4.5	4.7	5.4
29.2	26.5	20.2	Net Worth	-59.4	22.8	29.2	37.4	31.7	38.4
100.0	100.0	100.0	Total Liabilities & Net Worth	100.0	100.0	100.0	100.0	100.0	100.0
			INCOME DATA						
100.0	100.0	100.0	Net Sales	100.0	100.0	100.0	100.0	100.0	100.0
38.0	37.6	37.8	Gross Profit	42.5	41.0	37.9	36.1	33.5	32.1
35.1	35.9	36.8	Operating Expenses	41.5	41.2	36.2	35.2	31.8	30.2
3.0	1.7	.9	Operating Profit	1.0	-.2	1.7	.9	1.7	1.9
.9	.9	.7	All Other Expenses (net)	2.4	.9	.7	-.2	.2	.5
2.0	.8	.2	Profit Before Taxes	-1.4	-1.1	1.0	1.1	1.5	1.4
			RATIOS						
2.6	2.3	2.3		3.1	3.1	2.3	2.2	1.8	2.0
1.4	1.4	1.4	Current	1.3	1.5	1.4	1.5	1.4	1.3
1.0	1.0	.9		.3	.8	1.0	.9	1.0	1.0
1.1	.9	.8		.6	.9	.8	1.0	.6	.8
.4	(237) .4	.4	Quick	.2	.4	.4	.5	.3	.3
.2	.1	.1		.1	.1	.2	.1	.1	.1
3 104.9	2 150.6	2 166.8		0 UND	4 88.1	1 408.5	5 77.2	2 149.3	2 202.8
13 28.4	10 36.8	9 41.7	Sales/Receivables	2 173.1	10 36.1	7 55.0	20 17.9	10 36.9	8 43.1
30 12.1	25 14.5	24 15.0		14 25.5	23 16.0	24 15.4	33 11.1	31 11.7	24 15.3
39 9.3	39 9.4	44 8.4		14 26.7	37 10.0	53 6.9	46 7.9	37 9.8	44 8.3
75 4.9	75 4.9	72 5.1	Cost of Sales/Inventory	67 5.4	81 4.5	74 4.9	68 5.4	74 4.9	64 5.7
136 2.7	138 2.6	128 2.8		190 1.9	196 1.9	115 3.2	139 2.6	127 2.9	121 3.0
9 39.7	10 36.5	9 41.3		0 UND	7 51.2	5 69.7	19 19.0	17 21.5	17 22.0
26 14.3	24 15.1	23 15.8	Cost of Sales/Payables	12 31.0	19 19.6	13 29.1	30 12.0	33 11.1	30 12.2
49 7.4	50 7.3	51 7.2		56 6.5	39 9.4	53 6.9	52 7.0	66 5.5	49 7.5
6.1	7.5	7.1		5.2	5.6	8.9	6.4	10.6	12.6
14.5	17.1	15.6	Sales/Working Capital	42.0	12.5	13.8	11.7	19.5	19.4
999.8	-901.5	-64.6		-6.9	-20.3	299.2	-55.1	-112.9	NM
5.8	5.6	5.7		2.7	5.1	6.0	14.1	7.1	5.7
(228) 2.0	(220) 1.9	(206) 1.8	EBIT/Interest	(21) .9	(67) 1.5	(35) 1.7	(25) 2.4	(29) 3.5	(29) 3.3
.9	.3	.1		-2.3	-.6	.1	-.2	1.1	.9
3.7	4.6	5.7	Net Profit + Depr., Dep.,						10.4
(37) 2.1	(54) 1.8	(37) 2.9	Amort./Cur. Mat. L/T/D					(12)	5.6
1.0	.4	.4							1.8
.3	.4	.4		1.0	.4	.5	.3	.4	.4
.9	1.0	1.2	Fixed/Worth	-12.6	1.2	.9	.5	1.1	1.0
3.2	3.2	14.9		-.1	UND	9.3	2.0	4.1	2.7
.9	1.0	.9		2.1	.8	.9	.9	.7	.8
2.7	2.7	2.2	Debt/Worth	-31.5	2.1	1.9	1.6	1.9	2.3
7.4	6.9	38.0		-1.8	UND	21.1	5.7	12.4	4.6
34.8	28.2	25.2	% Profit Before Taxes/Tangible	48.1	26.9	15.2	25.3	28.1	26.4
(206) 12.7	(197) 9.5	(173) 8.4	Net Worth	(11) .5	(54) 7.2	(29) 5.7	5.8	(25) 16.4	(27) 9.8
.7	-4.8	-4.1		-8.1	-4.6	-2.6	-9.4	1.0	-1.8
10.5	7.8	8.3	% Profit Before Taxes/Total	7.7	8.2	7.5	15.2	10.5	8.8
3.1	2.5	1.6	Assets	-.3	1.2	1.4	1.8	5.0	3.0
-.4	-2.8	-2.2		-9.9	-4.4	-1.3	-2.0	.6	-.2
27.6	26.0	25.0		50.9	26.6	22.2	28.6	23.3	15.4
10.6	9.9	10.1	Sales/Net Fixed Assets	13.0	11.1	6.7	13.0	10.2	8.2
4.8	4.6	4.7		4.6	3.1	4.0	6.6	5.3	4.9
3.6	3.7	3.6		4.5	3.8	3.3	4.2	3.7	3.2
2.5	2.6	2.4	Sales/Total Assets	2.2	2.2	2.7	2.9	2.5	2.3
1.6	1.8	1.7		1.9	1.6	1.6	1.5	1.9	1.6
.9	.8	1.0		1.1	1.2	1.2	.7	.6	.8
(212) 1.6	(206) 1.5	(195) 1.8	% Depr., Dep., Amort./Sales	(17) 2.5	(62) 2.8	(34) 1.8	(24) 1.8	(28) 1.5	1.6
3.1	3.6	3.6		3.0	4.6	4.3	2.9	2.4	2.2
1.6	1.9	1.5		6.2	3.0	2.0	.7	1.0	
(116) 3.4	(116) 3.5	(114) 3.3	% Officers', Directors' Owners' Comp/Sales	(10) 7.4	(43) 5.4	(26) 3.2	(16)	(11) 1.5	
5.7	6.9	6.2		11.5	7.3	4.9	3.1	2.8	
2626085M	4104721M	3348207M	Net Sales ($)	14736M	136007M	142116M	191571M	515294M	2348483M
1140757M	1832240M	1429329M	Total Assets ($)	6664M	70237M	68343M	83124M	219243M	981718M

M = $ thousand   MM = $ million
See Pages 9 through 22 for Explanation of Ratios and Data

Current Data Sorted by Assets | Comparative Historical Data

Type of Statement	0-500M	500M-2MM	2-10MM	10-50MM	50-100MM	100-250MM		4/1/05-3/31/06 ALL	4/1/06-3/31/07 ALL
Unqualified		1	10	33	13	18		74	82
Reviewed		11	34	40	7	1		104	95
Compiled	21	66	58	13	3			135	159
Tax Returns	59	120	55	8				188	192
Other	20	74	97	51	20	25		222	223
		159 (4/1-9/30/09)		699 (10/1/09-3/31/10)					
NUMBER OF STATEMENTS	100	272	254	145	43	44		723	751
ASSETS	%	%	%	%	%	%		%	%
Cash & Equivalents	14.3	13.7	15.7	13.2	12.8	8.0		13.0	12.5
Trade Receivables (net)	3.8	3.0	4.2	3.8	5.4	5.9		4.8	4.5
Inventory	46.7	36.8	26.8	22.5	19.3	21.3		29.5	30.3
All Other Current	2.1	2.5	2.7	4.1	3.9	3.1		2.0	2.6
Total Current	66.8	56.0	49.4	43.6	41.5	38.2		49.3	49.8
Fixed Assets (net)	22.6	27.5	34.6	42.9	44.6	46.7		36.7	36.0
Intangibles (net)	4.8	6.3	6.2	4.3	5.1	4.7		4.7	5.3
All Other Non-Current	5.8	10.2	9.8	9.2	8.8	10.4		9.3	8.8
Total	100.0	100.0	100.0	100.0	100.0	100.0		100.0	100.0
LIABILITIES									
Notes Payable-Short Term	12.1	5.2	4.2	2.5	3.7	2.8		3.9	4.6
Cur. Mat.-L.T.D.	4.7	3.3	4.1	4.8	3.2	2.7		3.8	4.1
Trade Payables	17.6	20.7	19.2	18.9	16.3	16.8		19.0	18.1
Income Taxes Payable	.0	.2	.1	.1	.1	.1		.1	.2
All Other Current	13.9	9.9	9.7	9.4	11.4	11.3		10.8	11.1
Total Current	48.2	39.2	37.3	35.9	34.7	33.8		37.7	38.1
Long-Term Debt	21.8	24.8	25.8	24.8	18.7	22.2		26.2	26.1
Deferred Taxes	.0	.1	.2	.5	.6	.5		.4	.2
All Other Non-Current	14.8	9.5	6.5	5.5	5.3	9.1		8.6	7.2
Net Worth	15.2	26.4	30.3	33.3	40.8	34.4		27.1	28.4
Total Liabilities & Net Worth	100.0	100.0	100.0	100.0	100.0	100.0		100.0	100.0
INCOME DATA									
Net Sales	100.0	100.0	100.0	100.0	100.0	100.0		100.0	100.0
Gross Profit	27.3	26.0	26.9	26.4	27.6	26.4		25.7	25.2
Operating Expenses	25.4	24.6	25.2	24.8	24.7	24.3		24.1	23.9
Operating Profit	1.9	1.4	1.7	1.7	2.9	2.1		1.5	1.3
All Other Expenses (net)	-.4	-.4	-.3	-.1	.0	.5		-.2	-.3
Profit Before Taxes	2.2	1.8	2.0	1.8	2.9	1.6		1.7	1.5
RATIOS									
Current	4.2	3.7	2.3	1.6	1.5	1.5		2.3	2.4
	2.1	1.7	1.4	1.2	1.2	1.0		1.5	1.4
	1.1	1.0	.9	.9	.8	.8		.9	1.0
Quick	1.1	1.1	1.0	.7	1.0	.5		.9	.9
	(99) .4	(271) .4	.5	(144) .4	.4	.3		(715) .5	(749) .4
	.1	.1	.2	.2	.2	.2		.2	.2
Sales/Receivables	0 UND	0 UND	0 999.8	1 548.9	1 337.4	2 149.0		0 999.8	0 999.8
	0 UND	1 549.7	2 266.4	2 169.7	3 137.9	4 89.9		1 296.5	1 243.4
	2 242.0	2 184.3	3 132.4	4 96.1	5 72.7	6 58.7		3 110.0	3 107.3
Cost of Sales/Inventory	17 21.4	18 20.0	18 20.4	17 21.9	15 23.7	17 21.5		16 23.3	17 22.1
	30 12.4	26 13.9	24 15.5	23 16.2	22 16.8	21 17.5		23 15.9	24 15.2
	43 8.4	36 10.2	30 12.0	31 11.7	29 12.5	29 12.6		31 11.8	33 11.1
Cost of Sales/Payables	0 UND	5 68.2	9 42.4	13 27.7	14 26.8	14 26.4		8 45.8	7 49.1
	5 68.3	11 33.8	15 24.5	18 20.2	19 19.4	19 19.2		14 25.7	14 26.0
	13 28.6	19 19.4	22 16.6	26 14.3	28 12.8	25 14.5		21 17.0	21 17.2
Sales/Working Capital	10.9	14.8	17.2	24.8	26.3	28.9		18.0	17.8
	24.9	30.9	35.4	85.3	51.2	199.1		40.1	42.9
	241.6	524.8	-135.9	-143.3	-82.4	-63.4		-207.8	-478.2
EBIT/Interest	11.0	13.4	14.1	10.5	20.3	11.4		9.1	8.6
	(66) 4.1	(211) 4.4	(221) 5.0	(138) 5.0	(41) 5.8	(40) 2.9		(611) 3.4	(647) 3.5
	.9	1.0	1.9	1.7	1.9	1.9		1.0	1.3
Net Profit + Depr., Dep., Amort./Cur. Mat. L/T/D		3.8	12.1	4.8	6.4	16.2		4.9	6.8
		(13) 2.4	(50) 2.6	(57) 2.8	(18) 2.9	(11) 5.0		(130) 2.3	(131) 2.6
		.9	1.2	1.6	1.6	1.3		1.4	1.2
Fixed/Worth	.1	.3	.5	.8	.6	1.1		.5	.5
	.7	1.0	1.4	1.4	1.1	1.7		1.5	1.4
	-2.1	-6.1	NM	4.2	1.8	3.6		7.8	7.2
Debt/Worth	.5	.6	.8	1.0	1.0	1.2		1.0	1.0
	2.5	2.6	2.4	2.4	1.6	2.9		2.5	2.4
	-7.0	-14.0	NM	5.5	2.3	4.8		16.8	15.7
% Profit Before Taxes/Tangible Net Worth	88.8	64.9	60.1	39.8	39.4	32.3		52.8	48.4
	(68) 35.2	(192) 26.2	(191) 28.5	(126) 19.9	(40) 18.9	(40) 20.4		(577) 23.7	(588) 21.7
	10.1	9.1	9.4	7.3	8.5	9.3		5.6	7.0
% Profit Before Taxes/Total Assets	30.9	18.9	16.6	10.6	15.7	10.5		15.6	15.2
	11.2	7.7	8.0	6.4	7.8	5.4		6.2	6.4
	1.1	1.3	2.5	2.2	2.5	3.0		.5	.9
Sales/Net Fixed Assets	158.5	74.8	38.2	18.7	15.7	13.3		39.7	40.1
	45.4	34.7	18.6	11.2	8.2	8.9		16.6	16.7
	20.7	13.8	8.3	7.0	6.3	6.6		8.1	8.5
Sales/Total Assets	11.6	9.3	7.1	6.1	5.8	5.0		7.8	7.6
	7.9	6.6	5.1	4.9	4.1	4.3		5.4	5.3
	4.2	4.2	3.5	3.3	2.9	3.7		3.7	3.7
% Depr., Dep., Amort./Sales	.2	.4	.6	.9	1.1	.9		.6	.6
	(74) .6	(222) .8	(239) 1.1	(136) 1.2	(38) 1.5	(18) 1.1		(638) 1.0	(656) 1.0
	1.5	1.4	1.5	1.6	2.0	1.6		1.6	1.7
% Officers', Directors' Owners' Comp/Sales	1.6	.8	.4	.3				.8	.7
	(53) 3.0	(122) 1.2	(102) 1.0	(37) .9				(279) 1.4	(282) 1.3
	4.9	2.0	2.4	1.6				2.4	2.6
Net Sales ($)	281381M	2212953M	6734867M	16779415M	13197071M	30867235M		54414670M	67025180M
Total Assets ($)	30783M	311251M	1240298M	3399745M	3049167M	7273347M		11957628M	13939925M

M = $ thousand   MM = $ million
See Pages 9 through 22 for Explanation of Ratios and Data

Comparative Historical Data

Current Data Sorted by Sales

Hist 1	Hist 2	Hist 3	Type of Statement	0-1MM	1-3MM	3-5MM	5-10MM	10-25MM	25MM & OVER
78	77	75	Unqualified			1	1	5	68
93	93	93	Reviewed		1	3	11	14	64
161	136	161	Compiled	4	12	19	32	55	39
185	254	242	Tax Returns	14	49	38	63	50	28
284	279	287	Other	9	20	16		82	132
4/1/07-3/31/08 ALL	4/1/08-3/31/09 ALL	4/1/09-3/31/10 ALL		159 (4/1-9/30/09)			699 (10/1/09-3/31/10)		
801	839	858	**NUMBER OF STATEMENTS**	27	82	77	135	206	331
%	%	%	**ASSETS**	%	%	%	%	%	%
13.8	13.9	14.0	Cash & Equivalents	11.0	16.7	11.7	13.1	15.4	13.5
4.1	4.2	3.8	Trade Receivables (net)	.6	3.4	3.7	3.1	3.7	4.6
30.6	29.8	30.9	Inventory	38.1	35.1	36.6	34.8	32.7	25.3
3.2	3.2	2.9	All Other Current	1.3	2.4	2.2	3.0	2.5	3.5
51.7	51.1	51.6	Total Current	51.1	57.6	54.3	54.1	54.2	46.8
35.5	34.0	33.5	Fixed Assets (net)	32.8	28.4	29.0	27.5	31.4	39.5
4.9	4.9	5.6	Intangibles (net)	12.5	8.1	6.0	6.6	5.2	4.2
7.8	10.0	9.3	All Other Non-Current	3.7	5.9	10.7	11.8	9.2	9.4
100.0	100.0	100.0	Total	100.0	100.0	100.0	100.0	100.0	100.0
			LIABILITIES						
4.0	4.9	5.0	Notes Payable-Short Term	6.1	6.5	7.1	6.3	6.1	2.9
3.7	3.1	3.9	Cur. Mat.-L.T.D.	11.6	4.3	2.6	2.7	3.4	4.3
18.8	18.1	19.2	Trade Payables	5.4	12.1	17.1	18.9	22.7	20.4
.2	.1	.1	Income Taxes Payable	.0	.0	.3	.1	.0	.2
10.2	11.2	10.4	All Other Current	9.3	8.3	8.4	10.2	12.2	10.4
36.9	37.4	38.6	Total Current	32.4	31.2	35.6	38.2	44.5	38.2
24.4	24.0	24.3	Long-Term Debt	30.6	26.9	30.1	23.7	22.6	23.1
.2	.2	.2	Deferred Taxes	.0	.0	.1	.0	.2	.4
8.4	8.3	8.3	All Other Non-Current	11.0	18.1	8.3	8.8	8.3	5.5
30.1	30.2	28.5	Net Worth	26.1	23.8	25.8	29.2	24.5	32.8
100.0	100.0	100.0	Total Liabilities & Net Worth	100.0	100.0	100.0	100.0	100.0	100.0
			INCOME DATA						
100.0	100.0	100.0	Net Sales	100.0	100.0	100.0	100.0	100.0	100.0
25.3	25.4	26.6	Gross Profit	34.3	29.0	23.9	26.3	26.7	26.0
24.0	24.2	24.9	Operating Expenses	30.4	27.5	22.8	24.7	25.0	24.3
1.3	1.2	1.7	Operating Profit	4.0	1.5	1.1	1.6	1.7	1.7
-.2	-.3	-.3	All Other Expenses (net)	.0	-.4	-.6	-.2	-.4	-.1
1.5	1.5	2.0	Profit Before Taxes	3.9	1.9	1.7	1.8	2.2	1.8
			RATIOS						
2.5	2.4	2.6	Current	8.3	9.5	4.8	3.2	2.4	1.8
1.4	1.4	1.4		3.2	2.7	1.8	1.7	1.4	1.2
1.0	.9	.9		1.2	1.3	.9	1.1	.9	.9
.9	.9	1.0	Quick	1.7	3.2	1.7	1.0	1.0	.8
(799) .4	(837) .4	(855) .4		.5	.5	(76) .4	.4	(204) .4	.4
.2	.2	.2		.2	.2	.2	.1	.1	.2
0 UND	0 999.8	0 999.8	Sales/Receivables	0 UND	0 UND	0 UND	0 UND	0 999.8	1 424.1
1 326.2	1 344.0	1 307.2		0 UND	0 999.8	0 730.2	1 422.9	1 416.2	2 165.2
3 128.8	3 117.2	3 122.0		0 UND	2 187.3	3 129.7	2 187.6	2 146.0	4 89.4
17 22.1	17 21.2	17 20.9	Cost of Sales/Inventory	31 11.8	25 14.5	18 20.0	18 20.2	17 21.7	17 21.7
24 15.4	24 15.2	24 15.0		48 7.7	36 10.1	28 13.0	26 14.3	23 15.6	22 16.8
33 11.1	34 10.8	34 10.8		138 2.7	68 5.4	38 9.7	33 11.0	29 12.4	28 13.0
7 53.2	7 52.5	7 50.5	Cost of Sales/Payables	0 UND	0 UND	3 110.6	6 63.4	9 42.4	12 30.5
14 25.8	14 26.1	14 26.5		0 UND	6 62.6	7 49.2	11 32.5	14 25.8	17 22.0
22 16.9	22 16.9	22 16.5		3 108.3	17 21.5	19 19.3	18 19.8	21 17.6	24 15.1
17.1	16.9	16.7	Sales/Working Capital	6.6	7.5	13.8	16.7	17.2	24.6
40.1	41.9	40.8		13.2	14.2	25.4	28.8	45.3	62.5
-436.9	-293.1	-204.5		56.2	47.8	-220.9	280.3	-110.1	-119.7
9.8	10.7	12.9	EBIT/Interest	7.4	10.5	8.6	15.9	12.7	16.6
(663) 3.7	(691) 3.6	(717) 4.6		(16) 3.9	(60) 3.1	(58) 3.3	(107) 5.7	(166) 4.6	(310) 5.2
1.1	1.3	1.6		1.6	.7	.7	1.3	1.2	2.2
4.9	4.7	6.8	Net Profit + Depr., Dep., Amort./Cur. Mat. L/T/D				4.2	12.0	7.1
(119) 2.3	(123) 2.4	(150) 2.8				(13) 2.3	(31) 3.5	(102) 2.7	
1.4	1.3	1.3					1.7	.9	1.5
.5	.5	.4	Fixed/Worth	.2	.2	.3	.3	.4	.7
1.3	1.3	1.3		1.2	1.1	1.0	.9	1.5	1.3
9.4	5.9	15.3		-1.4	-8.1	-3.8	-152.5	-4.3	3.5
.8	.8	.8	Debt/Worth	.2	.6	.5	.7	.8	1.0
2.3	2.4	2.3		2.2	3.7	2.2	1.9	3.6	2.2
19.5	14.7	64.9		-3.1	-10.7	-8.8	-307.8	-16.0	6.0
44.9	55.2	55.2	% Profit Before Taxes/Tangible Net Worth	90.7	55.6	42.1	67.1	62.2	49.0
(625) 21.2	(669) 24.8	(657) 23.1		(19) 38.8	(56) 21.4	(50) 14.1	(101) 28.5	(145) 22.0	(286) 22.8
6.7	7.6	9.0		14.4	4.1	4.8	10.3	3.2	10.7
15.7	16.0	16.9	% Profit Before Taxes/Total Assets	27.9	15.9	16.4	21.9	17.9	15.1
6.7	6.4	7.6		11.6	7.0	6.1	8.9	7.6	7.5
.6	1.0	2.0		.4	-.1	-1.2	2.3	1.4	3.3
47.8	47.1	47.2	Sales/Net Fixed Assets	37.0	63.7	76.9	89.4	57.1	25.9
17.8	17.3	19.5		20.8	19.0	35.4	31.0	26.8	13.2
8.5	8.1	8.6		4.5	7.0	12.8	13.0	10.0	8.0
7.8	7.8	7.7	Sales/Total Assets	5.2	5.8	9.2	9.2	9.2	6.6
5.3	5.1	5.5		3.3	3.9	6.0	6.5	6.1	5.2
3.6	3.7	3.7		1.2	2.6	3.8	4.2	3.9	3.9
.6	.6	.6	% Depr., Dep., Amort./Sales	1.2	.4	.3	.4	.5	.8
(683) 1.0	(719) 1.0	(727) 1.0		(17) 1.8	(61) 1.0	(66) .8	(113) .9	(181) .9	(289) 1.1
1.6	1.6	1.5		2.4	1.9	1.3	1.4	1.4	1.6
.8	.7	.6	% Officers', Directors' Owners' Comp/Sales		1.2	1.2	.8	.5	.3
(313) 1.4	(331) 1.3	(322) 1.2			(45) 2.7	(35) 1.6	(70) 1.2	(90) 1.0	(74) .8
2.4	2.7	2.5			4.2	2.7	2.3	2.4	1.4
71166362M	74780490M	70072922M	Net Sales ($)	15349M	167639M	310071M	1009508M	3273994M	65296361M
15402235M	16330138M	15304591M	Total Assets ($)	7029M	51364M	67779M	207976M	729200M	14241243M

M = $ thousand   MM = $ million
See Pages 9 through 22 for Explanation of Ratios and Data

RETAIL—Convenience Stores   NAICS 445120

Current Data Sorted by Assets | **Comparative Historical Data**

Type of Statement	0-500M	500M-2MM	2-10MM	10-50MM	50-100MM	100-250MM		4/1/05-3/31/06 ALL	4/1/06-3/31/07 ALL
Unqualified		1	7	2	3	3		9	20
Reviewed				6	2			11	10
Compiled	7	13	8	2				27	26
Tax Returns	100	64	15	2		3		83	109
Other	23	17	12	10	3	5		34	51
	23 (4/1-9/30/09)			285 (10/1/09-3/31/10)					
NUMBER OF STATEMENTS	130	95	42	22	8	11		164	216
	%	%	%	%	%	%		%	%

ASSETS

	0-500M	500M-2MM	2-10MM	10-50MM	50-100MM	100-250MM		4/1/05-3/31/06	4/1/06-3/31/07
Cash & Equivalents	14.9	9.6	10.3	8.8		6.6		10.5	12.1
Trade Receivables (net)	1.8	2.1	4.0	8.9		3.1		3.5	4.8
Inventory	43.2	20.8	17.4	19.3		13.7		31.9	28.2
All Other Current	1.7	.6	1.4	2.3		3.0		2.0	1.8
Total Current	61.7	33.0	33.1	39.3		26.4		47.9	47.0
Fixed Assets (net)	19.5	55.0	55.7	49.9		62.5		35.7	40.6
Intangibles (net)	12.1	5.7	3.3	6.0		9.3		10.0	7.6
All Other Non-Current	6.7	6.2	7.9	4.8		1.8		6.4	4.8
Total	100.0	100.0	100.0	100.0		100.0		100.0	100.0

LIABILITIES

	0-500M	500M-2MM	2-10MM	10-50MM	50-100MM	100-250MM		4/1/05-3/31/06	4/1/06-3/31/07
Notes Payable-Short Term	9.4	3.9	4.5	7.7		1.9		4.8	3.3
Cur. Mat.-L.T.D.	1.9	3.3	1.9	4.4		2.9		2.9	3.4
Trade Payables	9.3	11.4	10.5	18.4		10.2		14.1	12.9
Income Taxes Payable	.1	.0	.0	.1		.5		.1	.1
All Other Current	14.0	12.4	8.6	11.8		7.5		10.0	13.7
Total Current	34.7	30.9	25.5	42.5		23.0		31.8	33.4
Long-Term Debt	24.3	48.7	42.8	33.4		41.9		36.5	31.9
Deferred Taxes	.0	.0	.1	.0		2.7		.2	.2
All Other Non-Current	15.0	6.7	5.5	2.1		2.9		10.8	10.0
Net Worth	25.9	13.7	26.1	22.1		29.6		20.6	24.6
Total Liabilties & Net Worth	100.0	100.0	100.0	100.0		100.0		100.0	100.0

INCOME DATA

	0-500M	500M-2MM	2-10MM	10-50MM	50-100MM	100-250MM		4/1/05-3/31/06	4/1/06-3/31/07
Net Sales	100.0	100.0	100.0	100.0		100.0		100.0	100.0
Gross Profit	23.1	19.0	16.6	17.6		18.0		22.0	19.2
Operating Expenses	21.6	17.0	15.4	16.0		16.1		19.9	17.2
Operating Profit	1.4	2.1	1.3	1.6		1.9		2.1	2.0
All Other Expenses (net)	-1.4	-.2	.0	1.4		.2		-.2	.2
Profit Before Taxes	2.8	2.3	1.2	.2		1.7		2.3	1.8

RATIOS

	0-500M	500M-2MM	2-10MM	10-50MM	50-100MM	100-250MM		4/1/05-3/31/06	4/1/06-3/31/07
Current	15.1	3.5	2.6	1.3		1.5		5.1	3.3
	3.4	1.4	1.5	1.0		1.0		1.8	1.4
	1.4	.7	1.0	.7		.6		1.0	.8
Quick	3.0	1.0	1.2	.7		.7		1.3	1.4
	(129) .7	.4	.6	.5		.4		(162) .5	(213) .5
	.2	.1	.3	.3		.2		.2	.2
Sales/Receivables	0 UND	0 UND	0 UND	1 394.4		0 UND		0 UND	0 UND
	0 UND	0 UND	1 369.6	3 105.0		2 149.5		0 UND	0 999.8
	0 UND	1 554.8	3 114.0	6 63.9		4 84.0		2 217.6	3 127.4
Cost of Sales/Inventory	13 27.9	10 36.1	7 54.2	5 74.2		8 47.7		9 42.0	9 41.9
	25 14.8	18 20.8	12 30.2	12 30.5		12 31.7		18 20.7	13 27.3
	48 7.5	28 13.1	26 14.2	24 15.2		13 27.6		40 9.2	31 11.8
Cost of Sales/Payables	0 UND	0 UND	3 127.6	8 45.9		0 UND		0 UND	0 UND
	0 UND	3 104.6	7 50.3	13 27.1		11 32.7		4 97.0	4 87.0
	6 65.3	13 28.0	13 28.1	21 17.1		19 19.0		14 26.0	14 26.2
Sales/Working Capital	8.3	17.8	25.7	29.8		68.5		12.9	20.8
	20.3	78.5	55.3	777.2		-999.8		37.0	65.3
	79.3	-36.2	-554.7	-47.7		-37.4		999.8	-100.3
EBIT/Interest	8.0	6.6	6.0	6.1		5.9		6.0	6.0
	(67) 3.2	(85) 2.0	(41) 2.9	2.9		(10) 2.8		(119) 2.9	(158) 2.4
	.9	1.1	1.0	1.1		1.7		1.2	.7
Net Profit + Depr., Dep., Amort./Cur. Mat. L/T/D								5.1	3.0
								(13) 1.6	(17) 2.1
								1.4	1.0
Fixed/Worth	.0	1.3	1.1	1.4		2.0		.4	.4
	.4	5.9	2.5	2.8		4.1		3.0	2.5
	-8.3	-50.7	30.3	14.8		6.0		-10.5	-179.0
Debt/Worth	.4	1.9	1.1	1.9		1.8		1.1	1.3
	2.3	6.0	3.7	4.3		4.3		5.8	4.1
	-4.7	-51.7	47.4	142.3		6.6		-10.3	-65.1
% Profit Before Taxes/Tangible Net Worth	97.7	84.2	51.5	61.6		40.0		76.3	67.4
	(89) 47.8	(67) 29.8	(33) 23.3	(18) 28.0		(10) 22.3		(108) 38.1	(157) 28.8
	16.4	6.5	7.4	11.5		8.4		14.6	8.0
% Profit Before Taxes/Total Assets	28.0	12.1	10.1	10.3		10.3		18.8	17.3
	12.0	3.7	5.3	5.4		3.6		7.1	5.5
	.6	.7	.3	.2		2.0		1.1	.2
Sales/Net Fixed Assets	UND	22.3	21.7	18.1		10.0		121.6	90.2
	70.8	5.6	7.7	12.8		7.1		17.9	17.0
	15.7	2.3	2.7	6.1		5.0		6.0	5.3
Sales/Total Assets	12.9	6.4	6.4	7.3		5.4		10.6	9.4
	6.2	3.2	3.9	5.4		4.6		4.7	5.4
	2.7	1.8	2.1	1.6		4.1		2.7	3.1
% Depr., Dep., Amort./Sales	.3	.8	.8	.8				.4	.6
	(70) .8	(84) 1.5	(38) 1.2	(20) 1.2				(121) 1.0	(170) 1.1
	1.7	2.8	2.0	2.3				1.7	1.7
% Officers', Directors', Owners' Comp/Sales	1.1	.9	.4					.8	.9
	(76) 2.7	(43) 1.4	(22) .7					(69) 2.2	(80) 1.7
	4.4	2.6	1.0					4.6	3.6
Net Sales ($)	221589M	451901M	980057M	2573604M	2716427M	7908778M		9480645M	24526929M
Total Assets ($)	30276M	98336M	187154M	531353M	567057M	1596445M		1359663M	2851434M

M = $ thousand   MM = $ million
See Pages 9 through 22 for Explanation of Ratios and Data

Comparative Historical Data / Current Data Sorted by Sales

Type of Statement	4/1/07-3/31/08 ALL	4/1/08-3/31/09 ALL	4/1/09-3/31/10 ALL	0-1MM	1-3MM	3-5MM	5-10MM	10-25MM	25MM & OVER
Unqualified	19	16	9	1		1	1	1	8
Reviewed	11	20	15	6	4	6	5	4	12
Compiled	27	20	30	51	61	32	16	15	5
Tax Returns	122	152	184	16	14	7	5	7	9
Other	56	57	70						21
				23 (4/1-9/30/09)			285 (10/1/09-3/31/10)		
NUMBER OF STATEMENTS	235	265	308	74	79	46	27	27	55
ASSETS	%	%	%	%	%	%	%	%	%
Cash & Equivalents	12.4	12.8	11.7	13.7	9.7	11.4	15.4	13.7	9.6
Trade Receivables (net)	4.0	3.8	2.8	.2	2.3	3.6	1.2	3.5	6.7
Inventory	27.9	26.4	29.2	33.3	34.3	23.6	29.2	32.4	19.3
All Other Current	1.8	1.6	1.5	1.8	1.4	.2	.1	1.6	2.9
Total Current	46.1	44.6	45.2	49.0	47.8	38.8	45.9	51.1	38.5
Fixed Assets (net)	39.1	39.4	40.1	29.5	38.1	48.7	43.5	34.0	51.3
Intangibles (net)	8.9	10.4	8.2	15.4	7.8	5.2	5.0	4.8	4.8
All Other Non-Current	6.0	5.7	6.5	6.1	6.3	7.2	5.5	10.1	5.5
Total	100.0	100.0	100.0	100.0	100.0	100.0	100.0	100.0	100.0
LIABILITIES									
Notes Payable-Short Term	4.8	2.9	6.5	5.1	10.7	3.5	5.7	4.9	5.9
Cur. Mat.-L.T.D.	3.0	2.8	2.5	2.0	2.8	2.4	2.0	2.4	3.3
Trade Payables	12.2	10.5	11.0	4.0	8.5	9.1	16.9	22.9	16.8
Income Taxes Payable	.1	.0	.1	.1	.1	.0	.0	.0	.2
All Other Current	12.5	11.4	12.2	15.3	9.5	7.5	22.1	14.2	10.0
Total Current	32.7	27.5	32.3	26.5	31.6	22.5	46.7	44.4	36.2
Long-Term Debt	31.9	36.3	35.8	33.5	37.0	42.0	38.8	29.3	33.7
Deferred Taxes	.2	.2	.2	.0	.0	.0	.0	.0	.9
All Other Non-Current	11.1	12.1	9.5	16.6	11.5	4.9	12.5	2.6	2.9
Net Worth	24.2	23.8	22.2	23.4	19.9	30.5	2.0	23.6	26.3
Total Liabilities & Net Worth	100.0	100.0	100.0	100.0	100.0	100.0	100.0	100.0	100.0
INCOME DATA									
Net Sales	100.0	100.0	100.0	100.0	100.0	100.0	100.0	100.0	100.0
Gross Profit	19.4	19.0	20.2	27.8	20.3	15.5	18.3	18.3	15.6
Operating Expenses	17.3	17.8	18.6	25.5	18.9	13.9	16.3	17.6	14.1
Operating Profit	2.1	1.2	1.6	2.2	1.4	1.5	2.0	.7	1.5
All Other Expenses (net)	-.2	-.3	-.5	-1.8	-.5	.0	-.2	-.7	.6
Profit Before Taxes	2.3	1.5	2.2	4.0	2.0	1.6	2.2	1.4	.9
RATIOS									
Current	4.0	4.9	4.9	23.8	8.5	4.7	3.3	1.8	1.4
	1.6	1.9	1.7	4.6	2.4	1.9	2.1	1.2	1.0
	.8	.9	.9	1.3	.8	.9	1.0	.8	.8
Quick	1.4	1.7	1.8	4.7	2.5	1.9	1.8	.7	.7
	(232) .5	(261) .6	(307) .5	(73) .7	.4	.6	.6	.5	.5
	.2	.2	.2	.1	.1	.2	.1	.3	.2
Sales/Receivables	0 UND	0 UND	0 UND	0 UND	0 UND	0 UND	0 UND	0 UND	1 361.9
	0 999.8	0 UND	0 UND	0 UND	0 UND	0 UND	0 UND	0 777.9	3 121.4
	3 117.4	2 212.7	2 230.3	0 UND	1 622.5	1 543.2	1 436.7	2 241.5	5 79.2
Cost of Sales/Inventory	9 39.1	7 50.6	10 37.2	21 17.4	15 24.9	8 46.1	7 56.1	7 54.1	7 49.2
	15 24.1	13 27.3	18 20.1	39 9.4	22 16.6	11 33.4	12 31.6	16 22.3	12 30.9
	34 10.8	34 10.8	35 10.3	76 4.8	37 9.9	21 17.0	25 14.7	25 14.8	16 22.2
Cost of Sales/Payables	0 UND	0 UND	0 UND	0 UND	0 UND	0 UND	0 UND	0 999.8	7 54.1
	4 101.9	3 119.5	4 103.2	0 UND	1 422.8	2 204.5	6 57.8	7 51.5	7 32.7
	12 29.8	10 38.3	13 29.0	9 40.9	9 40.5	6 61.8	12 30.1	17 21.5	17 21.6
Sales/Working Capital	13.7	15.5	14.5	5.2	10.3	22.2	17.9	27.1	48.0
	48.3	45.1	42.6	13.3	31.5	39.9	50.0	112.1	571.6
	-106.6	-418.2	-256.6	77.3	-171.3	-259.8	-999.8	-87.3	-100.2
EBIT/Interest	5.1	6.0	6.6	7.7	3.3	6.2	12.1	9.7	6.1
	(170) 2.4	(191) 2.4	(233) 2.7	(41) 3.3	(58) 1.3	(36) 2.5	(20) 4.9	(25) 4.1	(53) 3.2
	1.0	1.1	1.1	1.2	.7	1.0	1.7	1.9	1.8
Net Profit + Depr., Dep., Amort./Cur. Mat. L/T/D	4.3	5.4	4.2						4.2
	(20) 2.4	(17) 2.4	(20) 2.0					(12)	2.2
	1.4	1.3	1.4						1.5
Fixed/Worth	.3	.4	.3	.1	.1	.5	.2	.3	1.3
	2.3	2.5	2.1	1.4	2.2	2.6	1.4	2.6	2.7
	-22.7	-50.9	195.4	-1.5	-16.7	NM	6.7	50.5	6.0
Debt/Worth	1.0	1.0	1.1	.5	1.1	.7	1.0	1.8	1.7
	3.9	4.3	3.9	2.7	4.4	4.3	2.7	4.8	3.5
	-24.1	-42.0	-66.7	-3.1	-13.3	NM	-3.9	81.9	9.0
% Profit Before Taxes/Tangible Net Worth	67.7	73.6	75.3	94.1	96.8	77.0	57.1	136.4	46.5
	(166) 33.7	(194) 31.4	(224) 29.8	(48) 33.8	(52) 20.5	(35) 40.9	(19) 30.2	(23) 50.2	(47) 23.3
	11.3	8.8	11.3	17.1	4.5	10.4	16.2	18.3	8.5
% Profit Before Taxes/Total Assets	16.7	16.5	15.2	20.9	14.6	18.9	18.4	11.7	10.2
	7.4	6.8	6.4	9.7	2.8	8.4	8.7	8.5	5.1
	.7	1.0	.7	.8	-.4	.5	1.9	3.0	2.0
Sales/Net Fixed Assets	64.1	86.0	71.1	155.0	352.0	47.9	131.5	94.6	23.1
	16.0	17.0	15.3	22.7	15.2	9.6	19.4	27.3	11.0
	6.3	5.9	4.8	3.9	2.8	4.2	5.4	7.5	6.5
Sales/Total Assets	10.1	9.5	9.1	5.4	9.6	10.1	14.7	10.9	8.7
	4.9	5.1	4.4	2.5	3.6	5.0	6.6	7.1	5.4
	2.5	2.8	2.4	1.5	2.2	2.6	3.3	4.3	3.6
% Depr., Dep., Amort./Sales	.5	.4	.5	.6	.6	.7	.3	.2	.6
	(173) 1.0	(195) .9	(223) 1.1	(42) 1.8	(57) 1.4	(36) 1.2	(22) .8	(23) .8	(43) 1.0
	1.7	1.9	2.0	4.4	2.5	2.4	2.0	1.6	1.5
% Officers', Directors' Owners' Comp/Sales	1.0	.7	.8	2.2	.9	.8	.6	.6	.2
	(95) 2.0	(111) 1.6	(149) 1.7	(39) 3.4	(39) 2.6	(24) 1.3	(16) .9	(14) .9	(17) .7
	4.7	3.0	3.6	4.7	4.2	2.2	2.0	1.2	1.2
Net Sales ($)	20740848M	14585502M	14852356M	47077M	135727M	179842M	194488M	404983M	13890239M
Total Assets ($)	2501821M	2680062M	3010621M	24280M	46838M	47366M	46211M	78175M	2767751M

© RMA 2010

M = $ thousand   MM = $ million
See Pages 9 through 22 for Explanation of Ratios and Data

RETAIL—Meat Markets NAICS 445210

Current Data Sorted by Assets							Comparative Historical Data	

Type of Statement

0-500M	500M-2MM	2-10MM	10-50MM	50-100MM	100-250MM		4/1/05-3/31/06 ALL	4/1/06-3/31/07 ALL
				1		Unqualified	3	4
		3	1			Reviewed	3	6
4	6	1				Compiled	10	10
14	8	1				Tax Returns	8	13
8		5	2		1	Other	11	6
	9 (4/1-9/30/09)		57 (10/1/09-3/31/10)					
26	25	10	3	1	1	NUMBER OF STATEMENTS	35	39

0-500M %	500M-2MM %	2-10MM %	10-50MM %	50-100MM %	100-250MM %		%	%
						ASSETS		
12.5	15.0	5.5				Cash & Equivalents	10.2	13.4
4.2	8.3	12.2				Trade Receivables (net)	20.7	17.9
27.1	15.9	21.9				Inventory	21.6	23.8
1.5	2.2	.6				All Other Current	3.5	1.8
45.3	41.4	40.2				Total Current	56.0	56.9
38.8	43.4	31.7				Fixed Assets (net)	31.9	26.2
7.1	10.4	15.2				Intangibles (net)	3.9	9.2
8.8	4.8	12.9				All Other Non-Current	8.3	7.7
100.0	100.0	100.0				Total	100.0	100.0
						LIABILITIES		
11.7	2.4	9.0				Notes Payable-Short Term	11.5	9.9
3.9	3.0	1.0				Cur. Mat.-L.T.D.	1.7	1.8
19.3	16.2	15.0				Trade Payables	23.7	18.1
.2	.0	.1				Income Taxes Payable	.0	.0
22.9	3.1	20.5				All Other Current	9.5	8.7
58.1	24.6	45.8				Total Current	46.4	38.6
33.5	31.5	20.6				Long-Term Debt	29.9	22.8
.0	.0	.2				Deferred Taxes	.1	.1
21.8	11.4	17.6				All Other Non-Current	7.5	2.5
-13.4	32.5	15.8				Net Worth	16.1	35.9
100.0	100.0	100.0				Total Liabilities & Net Worth	100.0	100.0
						INCOME DATA		
100.0	100.0	100.0				Net Sales	100.0	100.0
36.1	32.9	37.9				Gross Profit	31.5	32.2
36.0	27.5	33.5				Operating Expenses	28.7	28.9
.1	5.4	4.4				Operating Profit	2.8	3.3
.4	.7	1.1				All Other Expenses (net)	.8	.7
-.3	4.7	3.2				Profit Before Taxes	2.0	2.6
						RATIOS		
2.0	3.1	1.8				Current	2.0	3.4
.7	1.6	1.2					1.2	1.6
.3	1.0	1.0					.8	1.0
.7	2.1	.9				Quick	1.3	2.1
(25) .2	.9	.7					.7 (38)	.8
.0	.3	.1					.2	.3
0 UND	0 UND	1 551.7				Sales/Receivables	1 269.1	0 999.8
0 UND	0 999.8	10 36.3					7 55.5	8 44.0
2 224.1	9 39.2	25 14.8					26 14.3	25 14.5
6 61.6	7 51.0	0 UND				Cost of Sales/Inventory	12 31.4	11 32.2
20 17.8	18 20.5	19 19.0					19 18.7	23 15.7
26 13.8	35 10.5	109 3.3					33 11.0	61 6.0
0 UND	1 720.7	11 32.8				Cost of Sales/Payables	10 36.8	8 47.4
7 50.4	17 22.1	17 22.1					14 26.3	18 19.8
21 17.5	30 12.1	42 8.7					32 11.5	31 11.6
28.9	9.4	19.3				Sales/Working Capital	17.0	9.3
-71.6	32.2	66.8					61.8	33.0
-16.9	NM	UND					-33.8	-424.8
4.2	12.7					EBIT/Interest	11.0	11.8
(20) .8	(18) 5.0						(31) 4.2	(34) 3.5
-5.5	1.2						1.2	1.1
						Net Profit + Depr., Dep., Amort./Cur. Mat. L/T/D		
.5	.7	.4				Fixed/Worth	.3	.2
18.5	1.8	1.2					2.6	1.1
-.5	112.0	NM					-5.1	3.2
2.4	1.0	1.8				Debt/Worth	1.6	.8
90.8	2.9	3.3					4.4	2.2
-2.2	120.4	-30.2					-38.0	21.7
81.4	128.7					% Profit Before Taxes/Tangible Net Worth	37.6	32.5
(14) 21.5	(20) 61.0						(25) 16.4	(31) 18.1
-19.3	1.5						2.5	8.7
17.9	25.4	12.6				% Profit Before Taxes/Total Assets	12.3	13.8
-.6	10.4	6.0					5.5	6.3
-22.5	.9	-2.2					.6	.6
79.3	19.0	94.8				Sales/Net Fixed Assets	200.3	141.0
29.9	9.9	21.7					19.5	15.2
11.7	3.9	3.3					7.2	7.9
12.6	6.5	4.4				Sales/Total Assets	7.4	6.8
8.1	3.5	3.3					4.9	3.5
4.7	1.7	1.3					2.7	2.2
.5	.9					% Depr., Dep., Amort./Sales	.2	.4
(24) 1.2	(16) 2.4						(31) 1.2	(30) 1.0
2.6	4.5						2.4	3.0
2.6	.9					% Officers', Directors' Owners' Comp/Sales	1.2	1.1
(18) 5.3	(14) 2.5						(16) 3.2	(19) 2.0
7.4	5.6						7.3	5.6
52211M	156639M	137614M	137536M	138234M	521932M	Net Sales ($)	931213M	1037739M
5974M	28314M	47395M	59152M	83240M	118578M	Total Assets ($)	174136M	311661M

© RMA 2010

M = $ thousand   MM = $ million

See Pages 9 through 22 for Explanation of Ratios and Data

Comparative Historical Data

Current Data Sorted by Sales

4	4	1	Type of Statement						
			Unqualified					2	1
3	4	4	Reviewed					2	2
5	9	11	Compiled	3	3	1	2	2	
24	17	23	Tax Returns	6	10	3		3	1
20	20	27	Other	2	10	3	7	3	2
4/1/07-3/31/08 ALL	4/1/08-3/31/09 ALL	4/1/09-3/31/10 ALL		0-1MM	9 (4/1-9/30/09) 1-3MM	3-5MM	5-10MM	57 (10/1/09-3/31/10) 10-25MM	25MM & OVER
56	54	66	**NUMBER OF STATEMENTS**	11	23	7	9	10	6
%	%	%	**ASSETS**	%	%	%	%	%	%
12.4	12.8	11.9	Cash & Equivalents	15.2	10.3			16.9	
7.8	9.6	7.4	Trade Receivables (net)	1.7	4.4			17.6	
25.1	21.2	21.8	Inventory	15.2	22.7			25.9	
1.0	3.1	1.6	All Other Current	.1	4.0			.4	
46.3	46.7	42.8	Total Current	32.1	41.5			60.7	
37.9	36.8	38.7	Fixed Assets (net)	48.3	42.8			35.0	
9.5	10.4	11.0	Intangibles (net)	11.9	7.9			.5	
6.3	6.0	7.5	All Other Non-Current	7.7	7.8			3.8	
100.0	100.0	100.0	Total	100.0	100.0			100.0	
			LIABILITIES						
5.4	10.4	7.5	Notes Payable-Short Term	15.0	5.6			8.2	
3.8	4.8	3.0	Cur. Mat.-L.T.D.	5.2	3.1			4.5	
12.3	14.0	16.6	Trade Payables	19.4	10.5			27.1	
.1	.0	.1	Income Taxes Payable	.3	.1			.1	
13.6	9.1	14.0	All Other Current	7.6	25.0			5.8	
35.2	38.5	41.2	Total Current	47.5	44.3			45.7	
26.9	20.2	29.3	Long-Term Debt	54.3	33.1			16.8	
.1	.1	.0	Deferred Taxes	.0	.0			.0	
11.6	9.1	15.9	All Other Non-Current	1.2	22.1			3.9	
26.2	32.2	13.6	Net Worth	-2.9	.5			33.6	
100.0	100.0	100.0	Total Liabilities & Net Worth	100.0	100.0			100.0	
			INCOME DATA						
100.0	100.0	100.0	Net Sales	100.0	100.0			100.0	
36.1	33.4	35.2	Gross Profit	48.4	39.9			29.5	
35.5	30.7	31.9	Operating Expenses	44.9	36.4			26.2	
.6	2.7	3.3	Operating Profit	3.5	3.5			3.3	
1.1	.5	.6	All Other Expenses (net)	1.3	.6			.4	
-.5	2.2	2.7	Profit Before Taxes	2.2	2.8			2.9	
			RATIOS						
3.5	2.6	2.4		2.8	3.1			1.8	
1.7	1.5	1.3	Current	.9	1.4			1.4	
.6	.7	.7		.2	.5			1.1	
1.7	1.4	1.1		1.9	2.6			1.1	
(55) .5	.5	(65) .5	Quick	.7	(22) .2			.8	
.1	.2	.1		.1	.0			.3	
0 UND	0 UND	0 UND		0 UND	0 UND			0 UND	
2 189.0	1 666.9	1 382.9	Sales/Receivables	0 UND	0 UND			5 66.7	
8 43.7	15 24.1	8 47.7		2 181.7	8 47.4			26 13.9	
14 26.6	8 47.6	6 59.7		20 18.4	6 59.1			13 27.2	
20 18.6	20 18.0	20 18.2	Cost of Sales/Inventory	25 14.5	26 14.1			19 18.8	
44 8.4	40 9.1	32 11.5		27 13.6	44 8.3			37 9.8	
3 107.0	1 605.1	2 187.7		0 UND	0 UND			12 31.7	
14 26.3	10 36.4	16 23.5	Cost of Sales/Payables	17 22.1	10 38.2			22 16.9	
24 15.4	30 12.0	28 13.0		50 7.3	28 13.2			38 9.7	
11.7	14.5	16.8		15.8	10.6			17.0	
55.7	48.7	69.6	Sales/Working Capital	-119.1	33.9			36.7	
-22.7	-34.1	-48.5		-13.3	-22.7			UND	
6.9	10.1	8.5			9.8				
(42) 1.4	(45) 3.7	(52) 3.1	EBIT/Interest		(19) 4.5				
-.9	.3	.2			.3				
			Net Profit + Depr., Dep., Amort./Cur. Mat. L/T/D						
.2	.3	.5		.5	.6			.3	
1.3	1.6	1.8	Fixed/Worth	2.7	2.1			.8	
-5.3	UND	-3.2		-.9	-1.4			1.4	
.7	.8	1.2		2.5	1.1			1.0	
2.5	3.0	4.5	Debt/Worth	5.0	5.8			1.8	
-7.7	-34.0	-5.0		-2.3	-2.2			3.2	
42.8	42.2	82.7			76.0				
(39) 14.3	(39) 9.2	(45) 21.0	% Profit Before Taxes/Tangible Net Worth		(16) 36.5				
-2.4	-3.7	-6.0			-10.0				
19.7	19.5	19.0		15.1	18.9			29.3	
2.3	4.9	7.5	% Profit Before Taxes/Total Assets	3.2	7.5			7.6	
-4.6	-1.9	-3.3		-6.7	-3.7			2.0	
73.1	64.6	61.1		60.6	32.3			84.0	
16.0	16.1	16.3	Sales/Net Fixed Assets	5.5	12.2			21.4	
4.0	5.3	5.2		3.3	3.9			7.1	
6.8	7.5	8.8		7.0	9.1			7.9	
4.9	5.0	4.6	Sales/Total Assets	3.0	3.8			5.7	
2.3	1.9	2.3		1.6	2.3			3.7	
.6	.5	.6		1.8	1.0				
(42) 1.8	(42) 1.2	(50) 1.6	% Depr., Dep., Amort./Sales	(10) 3.2	(18) 1.6				
4.4	2.9	3.3		7.1	2.9				
1.4	1.0	1.3			2.6				
(30) 3.3	(26) 2.7	(36) 3.2	% Officers', Directors' Owners' Comp/Sales		(15) 4.3				
5.7	5.5	6.9			6.7				
1098310M	998220M	1144166M	Net Sales ($)	8749M	40623M	26798M	68640M	144904M	854452M
457387M	401978M	342653M	Total Assets ($)	3330M	15033M	4381M	35252M	38042M	246615M

© RMA 2010

M = $ thousand   MM = $ million

See Pages 9 through 22 for Explanation of Ratios and Data

RETAIL—Fruit and Vegetable Markets NAICS 445230

Current Data Sorted by Assets							Comparative Historical Data	

0-500M	500M-2MM	2-10MM	10-50MM	50-100MM	100-250MM	Type of Statement	4/1/05-3/31/06 ALL	4/1/06-3/31/07 ALL
		1	1			Unqualified	2	1
		1	3			Reviewed	3	2
1	6	5				Compiled	7	7
7	8	1				Tax Returns	12	10
1	1	5	2		1	Other	6	5
	10 (4/1-9/30/09)		34 (10/1/09-3/31/10)					
9	15	13	6		1	NUMBER OF STATEMENTS	30	25
%	%	%	%		%	**ASSETS**	%	%
	15.2	14.8		D		Cash & Equivalents	12.9	17.0
	22.4	22.0		A		Trade Receivables (net)	18.4	19.2
	16.9	18.6		T		Inventory	19.6	20.7
	.6	1.6		A		All Other Current	3.3	2.3
	55.0	56.9				Total Current	54.3	59.3
	29.3	31.9		N		Fixed Assets (net)	32.2	25.2
	7.9	.8		O		Intangibles (net)	8.3	3.0
	7.8	10.4		T		All Other Non-Current	5.2	12.5
	100.0	100.0				Total	100.0	100.0
				A		**LIABILITIES**		
	5.0	10.3		V		Notes Payable-Short Term	12.0	9.4
	10.0	.8		A		Cur. Mat.-L.T.D.	1.4	.3
	33.1	37.9		I		Trade Payables	29.1	30.5
	1.4	.2		L		Income Taxes Payable	.4	.6
	11.8	4.9		A		All Other Current	12.6	21.6
	61.2	54.2		B		Total Current	55.5	62.4
	16.6	26.9		L		Long-Term Debt	10.4	11.0
	.0	.0		E		Deferred Taxes	.4	.0
	6.7	3.6				All Other Non-Current	10.4	3.6
	15.5	15.3				Net Worth	23.4	23.0
	100.0	100.0				Total Liabilities & Net Worth	100.0	100.0
						INCOME DATA		
	100.0	100.0				Net Sales	100.0	100.0
	27.4	33.9				Gross Profit	26.7	26.2
	24.3	31.9				Operating Expenses	24.6	24.9
	3.1	2.0				Operating Profit	2.1	1.3
	.6	.2				All Other Expenses (net)	.2	-.6
	2.4	1.8				Profit Before Taxes	2.0	2.0
						RATIOS		
	3.4	2.2					1.8	1.7
	1.1	1.2				Current	1.1	1.1
	.2	.5					.7	.7
	2.6	1.3					1.3	1.1
	(14) .9	.5				Quick	(27) .9	.7
	.2	.4					.0	.1
0 UND	0 UND	0 847.1					0 UND	0 UND
3 118.0	3 118.0	20 18.0				Sales/Receivables	1 354.7	2 187.0
26 14.0	26 14.0	39 9.5					21 17.0	24 14.9
4 86.0	4 86.0	4 83.4					5 69.1	4 82.2
7 54.4	7 54.4	21 17.7				Cost of Sales/Inventory	10 37.6	8 46.8
14 26.5	14 26.5	29 12.8					22 16.3	19 18.9
1 485.7	1 485.7	15 23.9					7 51.7	0 UND
17 20.9	17 20.9	34 10.7				Cost of Sales/Payables	19 19.4	13 28.4
41 8.9	41 8.9	83 4.4					35 10.4	36 10.3
	22.7	10.5					26.7	43.0
	160.8	60.5				Sales/Working Capital	544.3	114.8
	-32.5	-15.7					-49.8	-40.5
	6.3						13.6	22.5
	(12) 3.0					EBIT/Interest	(22) 3.0	(17) 4.4
	.6						-.7	-1.7
						Net Profit + Depr., Dep., Amort./Cur. Mat. L/T/D		
	.3	.2					.5	.3
	2.9	.7				Fixed/Worth	1.5	1.1
	-8.9	NM					-2.7	UND
	.8	1.2					1.1	1.3
	19.6	3.9				Debt/Worth	2.8	4.4
	-10.7	NM					-8.1	UND
	193.2	92.1				% Profit Before Taxes/Tangible Net Worth	87.6	109.7
	(11) 32.2	(10) 18.4					(21) 30.7	(19) 34.9
	19.5	8.5					1.4	6.7
	20.5	11.2				% Profit Before Taxes/Total Assets	25.8	23.2
	7.2	8.0					7.7	11.9
	-.1	2.6					-1.6	-2.2
	125.4	69.6					67.0	117.1
	54.5	12.7				Sales/Net Fixed Assets	31.9	33.1
	24.7	5.5					9.5	15.0
	10.4	5.9					8.8	9.2
	7.5	3.8				Sales/Total Assets	6.3	7.0
	3.7	2.5					4.4	5.0
	.4	.5					.2	.3
	(14) .6	(12) 1.2				% Depr., Dep., Amort./Sales	(27) .6	(22) .5
	1.4	3.3					1.3	1.2
	1.0						.7	1.0
	(11) 1.9					% Officers', Directors' Owners' Comp/Sales	(16) 1.1	(10) 2.5
	3.0						2.6	5.8
22242M	105800M	271337M	397223M		348823M	Net Sales ($)	1009945M	473860M
2102M	16708M	47863M	125427M		106920M	Total Assets ($)	225199M	73483M

© RMA 2010

M = $ thousand   MM = $ million
See Pages 9 through 22 for Explanation of Ratios and Data

Comparative Historical Data / Current Data Sorted by Sales

Type of Statement	07-08	08-09	09-10	0-1MM	1-3MM	3-5MM	5-10MM	10-25MM	25MM & OVER
Unqualified	1	2	2						2
Reviewed	1	2	4	4		1	6	5	4
Compiled	13	9	12	2	4	1	7		
Tax Returns	13	8	16					5	3
Other	5	4	10						
	4/1/07-3/31/08 ALL	4/1/08-3/31/09 ALL	4/1/09-3/31/10 ALL	0-1MM	10 (4/1-9/30/09) 1-3MM	3-5MM	5-10MM	34 (10/1/09-3/31/10) 10-25MM	25MM & OVER
NUMBER OF STATEMENTS	33	25	44	6	4	2	13	10	9
	%	%	%	%	%	%	%	%	%
ASSETS									
Cash & Equivalents	14.5	11.3	17.0				8.8	17.6	
Trade Receivables (net)	11.8	15.8	19.0				26.5	19.2	
Inventory	21.5	17.1	17.2				19.9	22.1	
All Other Current	2.5	1.5	.9				1.4	.8	
Total Current	50.3	45.7	54.0				56.7	59.8	
Fixed Assets (net)	36.3	30.8	34.0				25.4	32.6	
Intangibles (net)	8.1	12.6	5.3				9.1	.9	
All Other Non-Current	5.3	10.9	6.7				8.8	6.7	
Total	100.0	100.0	100.0				100.0	100.0	
LIABILITIES									
Notes Payable-Short Term	8.6	7.2	6.1				5.9	5.8	
Cur. Mat.-L.T.D.	2.1	4.9	5.7				10.3	.6	
Trade Payables	29.8	24.8	29.5				35.6	44.9	
Income Taxes Payable	.7	.1	.6				1.6	.0	
All Other Current	16.2	28.2	11.9				8.1	10.6	
Total Current	57.4	65.1	53.8				61.5	61.8	
Long-Term Debt	20.2	21.1	16.4				19.1	23.4	
Deferred Taxes	.0	.0	.0				.0	.0	
All Other Non-Current	2.6	4.2	6.9				8.8	3.3	
Net Worth	19.7	9.5	22.8				10.6	11.4	
Total Liabilities & Net Worth	100.0	100.0	100.0				100.0	100.0	
INCOME DATA									
Net Sales	100.0	100.0	100.0				100.0	100.0	
Gross Profit	29.4	30.2	29.2				28.0	25.5	
Operating Expenses	28.0	28.9	26.9				26.6	23.2	
Operating Profit	1.4	1.3	2.3				1.4	2.3	
All Other Expenses (net)	.6	.1	.2				.5	.0	
Profit Before Taxes	.9	1.2	2.1				.9	2.3	
RATIOS									
Current	1.9 / 1.1 / .5	1.6 / .8 / .3	2.2 / 1.1 / .6				2.7 / 1.2 / .4	3.1 / 1.1 / .5	
Quick	1.2 / (32) .5 / .1	1.0 / .4 / .1	2.0 / (43) .9 / .3				1.9 / (12) .9 / .4	1.7 / .7 / .3	
Sales/Receivables	0 UND / 0 999.8 / 9 41.0	0 UND / 6 64.5 / 20 17.9	0 UND / 3 135.5 / 27 13.3				0 UND / 16 23.0 / 33 11.1	0 UND / 2 175.9 / 26 14.2	
Cost of Sales/Inventory	5 66.8 / 9 42.4 / 22 16.6	5 77.6 / 9 40.5 / 20 18.6	4 83.7 / 8 44.9 / 22 16.9				4 81.5 / 10 35.7 / 25 14.5	6 61.6 / 11 32.1 / 22 16.5	
Cost of Sales/Payables	3 125.6 / 23 16.0 / 41 9.0	0 UND / 17 21.4 / 38 9.5	3 106.8 / 18 20.4 / 40 9.1				0 UND / 18 19.8 / 45 8.2	7 49.8 / 30 12.2 / 44 8.4	
Sales/Working Capital	28.9 / 116.9 / -23.4	46.6 / -57.1 / -7.6	17.4 / 127.2 / -24.0				14.8 / 129.8 / -27.9	21.6 / 142.7 / -20.8	
EBIT/Interest	26.2 / (26) 5.5 / .2	14.5 / (19) 1.6 / -.2	5.7 / (29) 3.4 / .7				4.0 / (10) 1.5 / -.6		
Net Profit + Depr., Dep., Amort./Cur. Mat. L/T/D									
Fixed/Worth	.4 / 1.0 / -.9	.5 / 1.4 / -2.4	.3 / 1.4 / 15.6				.4 / 2.9 / NM	.4 / 3.5 / -1.7	
Debt/Worth	.6 / 3.6 / -16.5	1.6 / 7.8 / -5.8	.8 / 2.6 / NM				1.4 / 19.6 / NM	1.4 / 5.2 / -7.5	
% Profit Before Taxes/Tangible Net Worth	47.8 / (23) 23.7 / 10.2	37.2 / (16) 9.1 / -28.4	92.4 / (33) 29.5 / 11.7				211.2 / (10) 28.1 / 11.5		
% Profit Before Taxes/Total Assets	19.9 / 9.5 / -.6	23.3 / 7.2 / -1.9	15.5 / 8.8 / 3.3				10.9 / 5.2 / -4.5	30.9 / 10.9 / 5.1	
Sales/Net Fixed Assets	66.9 / 22.3 / 8.3	74.3 / 28.3 / 8.6	76.9 / 26.6 / 6.3				151.7 / 74.5 / 8.8	55.5 / 26.6 / 9.4	
Sales/Total Assets	9.7 / 5.7 / 3.8	10.8 / 5.2 / 3.5	9.3 / 4.5 / 2.6				10.3 / 6.2 / 2.8	8.3 / 5.9 / 4.0	
% Depr., Dep., Amort./Sales	.3 / (26) 1.2 / 3.2	.5 / (21) .9 / 2.7	.5 / (39) 1.1 / 2.5				.5 / (11) .6 / 2.0		
% Officers', Directors' Owners' Comp/Sales	1.3 / (15) 2.0 / 5.9	1.7 / (14) 2.5 / 3.7	1.2 / (21) 2.1 / 4.1						
Net Sales ($)	560644M	421864M	1145425M	4124M	8705M	8557M	93767M	151366M	878906M
Total Assets ($)	93666M	76698M	299020M	2346M	3318M	1311M	19770M	28155M	244120M

© RMA 2010

M = $ thousand   MM = $ million

See Pages 9 through 22 for Explanation of Ratios and Data

RETAIL—Baked Goods Stores NAICS 445291

Current Data Sorted by Assets

Comparative Historical Data

Type of Statement	0-500M	500M-2MM	2-10MM	10-50MM	50-100MM	100-250MM		4/1/05-3/31/06 ALL	4/1/06-3/31/07 ALL
Unqualified			1			1		1	1
Reviewed									1
Compiled			2					2	
Tax Returns	24	9	1	1				7	20
Other	5	2	1			2		2	2
		4 (4/1-9/30/09)		45 (10/1/09-3/31/10)					
NUMBER OF STATEMENTS	29	11	5	1		3		12	24

Columns 2-10MM, 10-50MM, 50-100MM and 100-250MM: **DATA NOT AVAILABLE**

	0-500M %	500M-2MM %	2-10MM %	10-50MM %	50-100MM %	100-250MM %		4/1/05-3/31/06 ALL %	4/1/06-3/31/07 ALL %
ASSETS									
Cash & Equivalents	7.4	7.0						16.8	13.9
Trade Receivables (net)	6.9	5.2						11.0	9.6
Inventory	5.4	4.8						4.8	5.4
All Other Current	2.1	.8						.5	.6
Total Current	21.8	17.7						33.0	29.6
Fixed Assets (net)	47.0	28.3						37.8	42.0
Intangibles (net)	17.8	36.9						12.2	10.1
All Other Non-Current	13.5	17.0						17.0	18.4
Total	100.0	100.0						100.0	100.0
LIABILITIES									
Notes Payable-Short Term	1.1	8.5						4.7	3.7
Cur. Mat.-L.T.D.	3.4	.7						8.0	4.6
Trade Payables	10.8	7.3						11.7	10.7
Income Taxes Payable	.0	.5						.0	.0
All Other Current	36.5	20.3						13.9	41.6
Total Current	51.8	37.3						38.3	60.6
Long-Term Debt	48.5	46.2						17.1	39.1
Deferred Taxes	.0	.0						.8	.3
All Other Non-Current	31.7	20.2						7.4	2.5
Net Worth	-32.1	-3.7						36.4	-2.5
Total Liabilities & Net Worth	100.0	100.0						100.0	100.0
INCOME DATA									
Net Sales	100.0	100.0						100.0	100.0
Gross Profit	61.5	51.2						59.0	61.6
Operating Expenses	59.9	46.0						51.6	54.2
Operating Profit	1.6	5.2						7.4	7.4
All Other Expenses (net)	1.5	2.7						.5	2.8
Profit Before Taxes	.1	2.5						6.8	4.6

RATIOS

Ratio	0-500M	500M-2MM	2-10MM	10-50MM	50-100MM	100-250MM	4/1/05-3/31/06 ALL	4/1/06-3/31/07 ALL
Current	1.2	1.1					2.3	2.2
	.5	.5					.7	.5
	.1	.2					.3	.1
Quick	.8	.7					1.7	1.5
	.3	.4					.5	.4
	.1	.1					.2	.0
Sales/Receivables	0 UND	0 UND					0 UND	0 UND
	0 UND	0 UND					0 UND	0 UND
	3 129.4	16 22.6					7 50.5	2 174.5
Cost of Sales/Inventory	3 134.7	2 177.0					1 284.2	3 115.8
	6 61.0	5 68.8					6 65.5	6 63.6
	11 34.2	8 48.6					26 14.0	10 38.3
Cost of Sales/Payables	0 UND	0 UND					3 137.1	9 41.2
	17 21.6	14 26.6					21 17.7	23 15.7
	39 9.5	44 8.3					37 9.8	39 9.5
Sales/Working Capital	102.3	156.6					20.4	17.6
	-36.8	-14.4					-51.0	-41.8
	-4.1	-7.9					-7.7	-8.4
EBIT/Interest	6.7	3.2						9.8
	(22) 1.6	(10) 1.4					(19) 6.2	
	-.3	1.1						.2
Net Profit + Depr., Dep., Amort./Cur. Mat. L/T/D								
Fixed/Worth	.7	1.3					.6	.7
	-2.4	-.7					3.0	4.8
	-.6	-.1					-6.7	-1.1
Debt/Worth	NM	7.3					1.1	1.1
	-3.6	-2.0					4.3	11.1
	-1.8	-1.3					-17.9	-3.4
% Profit Before Taxes/Tangible Net Worth								137.8
							(14)	57.2
								24.2
% Profit Before Taxes/Total Assets	34.2	14.9					40.5	34.9
	6.0	2.0					15.8	14.9
	-9.9	.3					.7	-4.9
Sales/Net Fixed Assets	24.3	20.7					53.1	26.4
	8.0	6.5					10.8	9.1
	2.8	5.8					5.6	4.2
Sales/Total Assets	4.8	2.4					5.5	4.3
	3.6	2.0					4.2	3.1
	1.8	1.3					2.8	2.4
% Depr., Dep., Amort./Sales	1.0						1.3	1.4
	(24) 5.4						(11) 2.6	(21) 3.4
	9.0						4.7	4.7
% Officers', Directors' Owners' Comp/Sales								2.9
								(11) 4.8
								12.5

	0-500M	500M-2MM	2-10MM	10-50MM	50-100MM	100-250MM		4/1/05-3/31/06 ALL	4/1/06-3/31/07 ALL
Net Sales ($)	27926M	15635M	64159M	19096M		3049856M		37797M	57839M
Total Assets ($)	8248M	8312M	27624M	11116M		402686M		11053M	18268M

M = $ thousand   MM = $ million
See Pages 9 through 22 for Explanation of Ratios and Data

Comparative Historical Data   Current Data Sorted by Sales

			Type of Statement						
1	2	2	Unqualified					1	1
			Reviewed						
4	11	2	Compiled				1	1	
18	23	36	Tax Returns	20	13	1			2
7	9	9	Other	3	3	1		2	
4/1/07-3/31/08	4/1/08-3/31/09	4/1/09-3/31/10			4 (4/1-9/30/09)		45 (10/1/09-3/31/10)		
ALL	ALL	ALL		0-1MM	1-3MM	3-5MM	5-10MM	10-25MM	25MM & OVER
30	45	49	NUMBER OF STATEMENTS	23	16	2	1	4	3
%	%	%	ASSETS	%	%	%	%	%	%
9.0	6.7	7.9	Cash & Equivalents	8.5	6.3				
3.7	6.6	5.7	Trade Receivables (net)	3.3	9.5				
5.1	3.9	5.2	Inventory	4.1	4.6				
3.7	5.7	1.6	All Other Current	1.8	1.7				
21.5	22.9	20.4	Total Current	17.7	22.1				
55.3	50.5	41.2	Fixed Assets (net)	43.4	38.6				
13.2	11.9	22.0	Intangibles (net)	27.8	18.7				
10.0	14.8	16.4	All Other Non-Current	11.1	20.6				
100.0	100.0	100.0	Total	100.0	100.0				
			LIABILITIES						
2.8	3.7	2.7	Notes Payable-Short Term	1.1	4.1				
4.6	3.6	2.8	Cur. Mat.-L.T.D.	4.1	.6				
5.6	7.9	10.1	Trade Payables	9.3	10.7				
.1	.0	.1	Income Taxes Payable	.0	.3				
11.1	21.0	28.5	All Other Current	44.0	16.0				
24.2	36.3	44.3	Total Current	58.6	31.6				
57.8	39.5	50.9	Long-Term Debt	38.2	68.5				
.2	.1	.1	Deferred Taxes	.0	.0				
13.5	14.9	24.3	All Other Non-Current	29.4	28.4				
4.3	9.2	-19.6	Net Worth	-26.2	-28.6				
100.0	100.0	100.0	Total Liabilities & Net Worth	100.0	100.0				
			INCOME DATA						
100.0	100.0	100.0	Net Sales	100.0	100.0				
54.5	53.7	57.7	Gross Profit	58.8	62.9				
52.1	49.6	54.4	Operating Expenses	59.2	55.7				
2.4	4.1	3.3	Operating Profit	-.4	7.2				
2.6	3.2	2.0	All Other Expenses (net)	1.8	2.0				
-.2	.8	1.4	Profit Before Taxes	-2.2	5.2				
			RATIOS						
2.6	1.3	1.1	Current	.8	1.2				
.5	.6	.5		.5	.6				
.3	.2	.2		.1	.2				
1.7	.7	.7	Quick	.8	1.0				
.4	.4	.3		.2	.4				
.2	.1	.1		.0	.1				
0 UND	0 UND	0 UND	Sales/Receivables	0 UND	0 UND				
0 UND	0 UND	0 UND		0 UND	0 UND				
0 UND	4 83.2	3 129.4		0 UND	12 31.4				
3 128.8	3 124.2	3 123.8	Cost of Sales/Inventory	3 132.0	2 175.9				
7 48.8	5 71.8	6 63.7		6 62.8	4 87.3				
15 23.6	10 38.0	10 34.9		9 40.7	9 41.5				
0 UND	0 UND	0 UND	Cost of Sales/Payables	0 UND	0 UND				
17 21.7	12 29.4	15 23.8		9 39.8	20 17.8				
34 10.6	36 10.0	33 10.9		43 8.6	42 8.8				
33.2	64.7	137.2	Sales/Working Capital	-131.3	127.5				
-29.0	-41.3	-31.0		-16.5	-61.7				
-11.0	-15.3	-7.6		-2.6	-11.8				
4.2	4.4	4.8	EBIT/Interest	2.1	7.1				
(28) 2.1	(36) 2.1	(40) 1.7		(17) 1.2	(14) 2.3				
.3	.6	.8		-1.4	1.1				
			Net Profit + Depr., Dep., Amort./Cur. Mat. L/T/D						
2.5	1.5	1.0	Fixed/Worth	-130.5	1.1				
NM	8.8	-4.1		-2.0	-1.6				
-2.1	-2.3	-.3		-.1	-.3				
2.5	2.1	6.0	Debt/Worth	-9.2	5.6				
NM	269.0	-5.0		-2.9	-5.3				
-3.6	-3.5	-1.6		-1.4	-1.5				
151.1	73.8	87.3	% Profit Before Taxes/Tangible Net Worth						
(15) 47.8	(23) 42.0	(15) 28.7							
2.4	6.1	2.6							
14.7	15.0	28.8	% Profit Before Taxes/Total Assets	17.4	32.7				
2.8	5.0	5.6		3.2	12.5				
-8.2	-1.9	-.7		-9.7	1.8				
7.4	9.3	18.2	Sales/Net Fixed Assets	38.7	13.5				
3.7	4.9	7.9		6.7	9.6				
2.0	3.0	4.1		2.2	6.5				
3.5	4.0	4.2	Sales/Total Assets	4.1	4.3				
1.9	2.1	2.5		2.4	2.7				
1.1	1.6	1.6		1.5	2.0				
2.3	1.8	1.5	% Depr., Dep., Amort./Sales	1.5	1.3				
(29) 5.2	(44) 3.2	(37) 5.0		(18) 5.9	(13) 5.0				
7.8	5.1	7.9		9.7	6.8				
1.5	3.1	2.7	% Officers', Directors' Owners' Comp/Sales						
(10) 3.7	(14) 4.7	(14) 4.2							
5.0	8.1	6.4							
125132M	1635888M	3176672M	Net Sales ($)	15486M	22915M	6499M	8940M	72976M	3049856M
43793M	361438M	457986M	Total Assets ($)	7869M	10475M	1124M	8116M	27716M	402686M

© RMA 2010

M = $ thousand   MM = $ million
See Pages 9 through 22 for Explanation of Ratios and Data

Current Data Sorted by Assets   Comparative Historical Data

						Type of Statement		
		2	2	1	1	Unqualified	2	4
						Reviewed	3	1
6	5	2				Compiled	10	5
11	6	4				Tax Returns	6	13
	2	2	1	1		Other	7	8
	10 (4/1-9/30/09)		36 (10/1/09-3/31/10)				4/1/05-3/31/06	4/1/06-3/31/07
0-500M	500M-2MM	2-10MM	10-50MM	50-100MM	100-250MM		ALL	ALL
17	13	10	3	2	1	NUMBER OF STATEMENTS	28	31
%	%	%	%	%	%	ASSETS	%	%
22.5	23.6	7.9				Cash & Equivalents	12.4	19.7
3.7	7.0	12.6				Trade Receivables (net)	12.2	8.4
6.3	25.8	17.6				Inventory	24.4	17.0
.3	3.1	.5				All Other Current	3.7	2.2
32.8	59.4	38.6				Total Current	52.6	47.4
35.8	28.8	49.3				Fixed Assets (net)	34.6	39.2
5.5	5.4	1.3				Intangibles (net)	6.3	7.2
25.8	6.4	10.8				All Other Non-Current	6.5	6.2
100.0	100.0	100.0				Total	100.0	100.0
						LIABILITIES		
.7	2.3	8.8				Notes Payable-Short Term	16.0	10.1
3.6	1.7	4.8				Cur. Mat.-L.T.D.	3.7	4.0
10.0	9.0	5.6				Trade Payables	13.4	11.7
.0	.1	1.8				Income Taxes Payable	.4	.1
11.3	17.6	11.1				All Other Current	9.4	11.1
25.5	30.7	32.1				Total Current	42.9	37.0
34.0	31.5	52.5				Long-Term Debt	21.9	29.9
.0	.0	.5				Deferred Taxes	.2	.0
5.7	37.2	2.7				All Other Non-Current	16.7	.6
34.8	.6	12.3				Net Worth	18.3	32.6
100.0	100.0	100.0				Total Liabilties & Net Worth	100.0	100.0
						INCOME DATA		
100.0	100.0	100.0				Net Sales	100.0	100.0
64.3	53.6	51.8				Gross Profit	45.8	49.0
56.9	50.9	44.2				Operating Expenses	42.3	40.0
7.4	2.7	7.6				Operating Profit	3.5	8.9
.9	.9	1.7				All Other Expenses (net)	.7	1.2
6.5	1.8	5.9				Profit Before Taxes	2.8	7.8
						RATIOS		
5.3	4.4	7.6					2.1	3.3
1.0	2.8	1.6				Current	1.4	1.4
.4	1.1	.4					1.0	.9
3.7	2.7	3.0					1.2	1.8
.8	1.2	.5				Quick	.6	.7
.2	.4	.1					.2	.3

0	UND	0	UND	0	UND				0	UND	0	UND
0	UND	1	329.0	2	182.4		Sales/Receivables		4	84.7	0	UND
1	480.1	5	81.0	13	29.1				21	17.0	9	39.3
0	UND	17	21.3	14	25.9				24	15.4	8	47.2
9	39.0	67	5.5	45	8.1		Cost of Sales/Inventory		50	7.3	35	10.5
32	11.5	99	3.7	85	4.3				89	4.1	59	6.2
0	UND	0	UND	7	53.6				6	56.2	0	UND
5	73.3	20	18.5	14	26.5		Cost of Sales/Payables		20	18.4	9	39.7
26	14.0	34	10.8	24	15.3				47	7.8	39	9.4

7.1	3.5	4.1					11.2	7.7
-486.7	6.5	NM				Sales/Working Capital	26.9	44.4
-19.6	45.5	-12.5					NM	-56.2
	8.9						13.1	13.4
	(11) 5.2					EBIT/Interest	(25) 3.4	(26) 3.1
	2.5						1.3	1.4
						Net Profit + Depr., Dep., Amort./Cur. Mat. L/T/D		
.1	.6	.3					.4	.3
.7	.9	1.8				Fixed/Worth	1.6	1.1
-2.8	-.8	3.0					NM	25.1
.4	1.3	.6					1.2	.4
1.6	-175.0	2.3				Debt/Worth	3.3	1.5
-5.5	-3.6	2.8					NM	92.0
100.0						% Profit Before Taxes/Tangible Net Worth	46.1	84.5
(11) 49.5							(21) 26.2	(24) 38.4
40.9							5.9	2.4
40.1	17.3	12.5				% Profit Before Taxes/Total Assets	15.0	39.7
26.1	4.2	6.6					6.0	10.7
4.4	-6.5	-1.7					1.1	1.0
207.0	28.9	6.4				Sales/Net Fixed Assets	36.8	56.9
12.6	8.1	3.9					8.4	5.9
4.0	4.1	3.1					4.7	2.8
4.9	3.5	3.0				Sales/Total Assets	4.0	4.4
3.5	2.0	2.2					2.9	2.3
1.9	1.5	1.6					1.8	1.6
.8	.9					% Depr., Dep., Amort./Sales	.9	.8
(12) 3.4	(11) 1.1						(20) 2.0	(23) 2.0
6.1	3.0						3.7	4.3
						% Officers', Directors' Owners' Comp/Sales	2.6	2.3
							(15) 3.9	(11) 4.0
							8.0	8.2
15094M	32375M	86613M	128131M	323273M	128918M	Net Sales ($)	691134M	962281M
4839M	14068M	39473M	78325M	105684M	116587M	Total Assets ($)	218982M	373117M

M = $ thousand   MM = $ million
See Pages 9 through 22 for Explanation of Ratios and Data

Comparative Historical Data | Current Data Sorted by Sales

			Type of Statement						
3	2	6	Unqualified	1			1		4
4	4		Reviewed						
7	7	13	Compiled	3	6	3	1		
9	17	21	Tax Returns	10	5	2	3	1	
5	8	6	Other		2	1		2	1
4/1/07-3/31/08 ALL	4/1/08-3/31/09 ALL	4/1/09-3/31/10 ALL		10 (4/1-9/30/09)			36 (10/1/09-3/31/10)		
28	38	46	NUMBER OF STATEMENTS	13	14	6	5	3	5
%	%	%	**ASSETS**	%	%	%	%	%	%
15.3	10.9	17.6	Cash & Equivalents	21.8	22.3				
6.8	7.1	9.2	Trade Receivables (net)	6.6	12.8				
25.8	23.9	16.4	Inventory	5.6	13.4				
1.9	3.4	2.3	All Other Current	.4	.7				
49.8	45.3	45.4	Total Current	34.3	49.3				
34.5	38.0	36.5	Fixed Assets (net)	32.9	35.0				
9.6	9.1	4.1	Intangibles (net)	9.8	1.2				
6.1	7.6	13.9	All Other Non-Current	23.1	14.6				
100.0	100.0	100.0	Total	100.0	100.0				
			LIABILITIES						
19.0	6.4	3.4	Notes Payable-Short Term	.9	1.7				
8.2	4.4	3.0	Cur. Mat.-L.T.D.	5.0	1.2				
11.3	13.2	9.5	Trade Payables	6.7	7.5				
.4	.1	.4	Income Taxes Payable	.0	.0				
12.5	14.0	16.7	All Other Current	15.8	20.8				
51.5	38.1	33.1	Total Current	28.4	31.2				
23.8	32.1	36.4	Long-Term Debt	39.2	22.8				
.1	.1	.1	Deferred Taxes	.0	.0				
1.6	22.1	13.2	All Other Non-Current	2.7	20.4				
23.0	7.6	17.2	Net Worth	29.6	25.5				
100.0	100.0	100.0	Total Liabilities & Net Worth	100.0	100.0				
			INCOME DATA						
100.0	100.0	100.0	Net Sales	100.0	100.0				
47.4	55.0	54.5	Gross Profit	64.9	61.7				
42.2	52.1	49.1	Operating Expenses	59.2	52.7				
5.2	3.0	5.4	Operating Profit	5.8	9.0				
1.9	1.6	1.7	All Other Expenses (net)	.8	1.2				
3.3	1.4	3.8	Profit Before Taxes	4.9	7.9				
			RATIOS						
2.9	2.7	4.3	Current	4.8	7.7				
1.1	1.3	1.6		1.4	1.6				
.5	.7	.6		.5	.4				
1.4	1.1	2.3	Quick	3.5	4.3				
.4	.5	.7		.8	1.4				
.2	.1	.2		.4	.2				
0 UND	0 UND	0 UND	Sales/Receivables	0 UND	0 UND				
0 999.8	1 370.1	1 595.6		0 UND	1 290.2				
11 33.6	17 21.0	12 30.4		4 91.8	7 49.6				
33 11.0	13 27.6	9 40.3	Cost of Sales/Inventory	0 UND	9 42.4				
71 5.1	44 8.3	35 10.5		9 41.3	24 15.3				
114 3.2	76 4.8	68 5.4		27 13.5	83 4.4				
4 103.5	0 UND	0 UND	Cost of Sales/Payables	0 UND	0 UND				
16 22.5	10 35.0	13 27.6		0 UND	12 31.7				
56 6.5	42 8.6	31 11.9		10 34.9	23 16.2				
7.5	13.2	5.9	Sales/Working Capital	5.1	3.1				
143.8	25.6	18.6		42.0	33.5				
-11.7	-23.7	-17.1		-14.3	-19.2				
10.6	6.1	8.9	EBIT/Interest						
(26) 2.6	(32) 2.2	(35) 3.8							
.8	-1.5	1.3							
			Net Profit + Depr., Dep., Amort./Cur. Mat. L/T/D						
.5	.6	.3	Fixed/Worth	.2	.2				
1.6	2.0	.9		4.4	.8				
-.8	-2.5	-2.9		-1.8	-3.8				
.3	1.7	.6	Debt/Worth	.5	.6				
3.4	4.9	2.4		5.4	1.5				
-4.0	-5.2	-5.3		-4.5	-5.2				
30.3	75.7	47.9	% Profit Before Taxes/Tangible Net Worth						
(20) 24.0	(25) 20.4	(30) 26.6							
1.3	-2.5	2.8							
18.5	18.0	20.4	% Profit Before Taxes/Total Assets	34.0	38.8				
5.5	3.0	7.7		6.0	18.9				
-1.1	-6.3	.7		1.6	-2.7				
25.5	27.5	17.8	Sales/Net Fixed Assets	UND	27.3				
8.6	7.0	5.8		4.1	6.7				
3.1	3.4	3.9		3.6	3.9				
3.7	4.2	3.9	Sales/Total Assets	4.2	4.1				
2.3	2.3	2.5		2.1	2.3				
1.5	1.5	1.6		1.4	1.4				
1.3	1.1	1.1	% Depr., Dep., Amort./Sales		.5				
(22) 1.9	(32) 2.2	(35) 2.0			(11) 1.7				
3.6	4.6	4.8			3.9				
2.4	2.7	3.0	% Officers', Directors' Owners' Comp/Sales						
(12) 3.8	(17) 4.3	(18) 5.2							
9.0	11.3	7.3							
529913M	300326M	714404M	Net Sales ($)	7915M	22983M	23182M	37262M	44008M	579054M
252936M	119602M	358976M	Total Assets ($)	3936M	29944M	7950M	19603M	13650M	283893M

M = $ thousand   MM = $ million
See Pages 9 through 22 for Explanation of Ratios and Data

Current Data Sorted by Assets   Comparative Historical Data

Type of Statement

0-500M	500M-2MM	2-10MM	10-50MM	50-100MM	100-250MM	Type of Statement	4/1/05-3/31/06 ALL	4/1/06-3/31/07 ALL
2		4	6	4	4	Unqualified	8	12
1	2	14	7	2		Reviewed	13	18
6	10	5	1			Compiled	19	24
71	41	11			1	Tax Returns	90	113
17	14	24	3	4	1	Other	41	56
	26 (4/1-9/30/09)		229 (10/1/09-3/31/10)					

0-500M	500M-2MM	2-10MM	10-50MM	50-100MM	100-250MM		4/1/05-3/31/06 ALL	4/1/06-3/31/07 ALL
97	67	58	17	10	6	**NUMBER OF STATEMENTS**	171	223
%	%	%	%	%	%	**ASSETS**	%	%
21.1	13.5	10.7	8.2	12.7		Cash & Equivalents	13.8	12.8
3.0	6.7	10.5	16.7	19.0		Trade Receivables (net)	6.8	6.1
16.8	15.3	27.9	15.8	8.9		Inventory	17.3	16.0
1.1	2.1	4.4	5.1	3.2		All Other Current	2.3	3.5
42.0	37.6	53.5	45.9	43.8		Total Current	40.2	38.4
37.1	40.5	31.9	30.0	27.0		Fixed Assets (net)	37.2	39.8
13.5	14.2	6.7	15.3	18.6		Intangibles (net)	15.7	13.8
7.4	7.8	7.9	8.8	10.5		All Other Non-Current	6.9	8.0
100.0	100.0	100.0	100.0	100.0		Total	100.0	100.0
						LIABILITIES		
9.7	4.5	8.2	10.9	1.6		Notes Payable-Short Term	8.9	7.5
5.2	3.0	5.1	7.6	6.8		Cur. Mat.-L.T.D.	5.7	5.4
7.3	10.1	19.7	17.8	9.3		Trade Payables	16.0	13.3
.1	.1	.1	.3	.1		Income Taxes Payable	.4	.2
22.9	10.4	10.7	8.3	12.9		All Other Current	16.4	14.9
45.1	28.1	43.7	44.9	30.7		Total Current	47.3	41.4
31.0	36.0	19.4	18.4	30.6		Long-Term Debt	26.1	29.8
.0	.0	.2	.1	.1		Deferred Taxes	.2	.1
12.9	8.1	2.2	4.6	6.4		All Other Non-Current	10.9	13.0
11.0	27.8	34.5	32.1	32.2		Net Worth	15.5	15.5
100.0	100.0	100.0	100.0	100.0		Total Liabilities & Net Worth	100.0	100.0
						INCOME DATA		
100.0	100.0	100.0	100.0	100.0		Net Sales	100.0	100.0
55.8	45.9	37.4	38.4	37.5		Gross Profit	50.2	51.3
51.4	42.9	33.9	35.0	33.2		Operating Expenses	45.9	47.8
4.5	3.0	3.6	3.4	4.3		Operating Profit	4.3	3.5
.6	.8	.5	1.6	2.6		All Other Expenses (net)	1.1	1.2
3.9	2.2	3.1	1.8	1.7		Profit Before Taxes	3.1	2.3
						RATIOS		
5.7	3.1	1.8	1.8	1.6			2.1	2.0
1.4	1.4	1.3	1.3	1.2		Current	1.1	1.2
.5	.7	.8	.6	1.0			.4	.4
3.2	2.1	.9	1.2	1.4			1.2	1.2
.7	.8	.4	.7	.9		Quick	.5	.5
.1	.3	.1	.1	.3			.1 (220)	.1
0 UND	0 UND	0 UND	3 106.4	0 UND			0 UND	0 UND
0 UND	0 UND	3 122.3	8 47.4	4 83.4		Sales/Receivables	0 UND	0 UND
0 UND	6 58.1	27 13.5	44 8.2	23 15.6			6 64.3	5 70.2
4 102.3	6 56.9	13 27.4	19 19.1	2 146.7			6 56.9	7 49.7
12 30.7	18 20.3	45 8.1	25 14.6	16 23.5		Cost of Sales/Inventory	16 23.0	16 23.2
28 12.9	38 9.6	82 4.4	47 7.8	52 7.0			39 9.4	45 8.1
0 UND	0 UND	12 30.1	22 16.5	10 38.0			3 141.0	0 UND
3 118.0	15 23.6	26 14.0	32 11.4	15 23.7		Cost of Sales/Payables	18 20.3	13 27.3
20 17.9	27 13.4	60 6.1	48 7.6	35 10.4			43 8.6	35 10.4
14.4	10.5	9.1	13.8	14.1			19.1	15.9
53.3	27.8	29.9	19.9	42.4		Sales/Working Capital	223.5	126.8
-13.1	-50.7	-61.1	-15.5	NM			-13.6	-15.8
15.2	19.6	16.1	4.3				8.5	8.3
(64) 3.8	(56) 3.1	(50) 4.8	(15) 3.0			EBIT/Interest	(133) 3.1	(177) 2.8
.0	.8	2.0	1.5				.8	.6
		6.0					6.3	3.0
	(14) 1.5					Net Profit + Depr., Dep., Amort./Cur. Mat. L/T/D	(17) 1.5	(14) 1.9
		.9					.7	1.2
.5	.5	.3	.3	.2			.7	.6
2.9	1.9	.9	1.6	.9		Fixed/Worth	3.3	3.9
-1.1	-4.6	1.9	NM	NM			-1.4	-1.9
.4	.8	.8	1.5	1.2			1.0	1.2
7.8	3.2	2.3	2.7	1.6		Debt/Worth	5.9	7.2
-3.2	-4.5	6.1	-15.9	-3.9			-3.7	-3.8
281.8	75.2	40.7	19.0				95.8	117.6
(54) 68.9	(44) 32.2	(50) 20.8	(12) 9.8			% Profit Before Taxes/Tangible Net Worth	(103) 32.4	(135) 34.7
29.1	11.8	9.9	2.6				13.9	9.8
54.1	21.8	18.6	8.5	7.3			23.7	23.4
13.4	8.8	7.9	4.8	3.3		% Profit Before Taxes/Total Assets	7.8	6.7
.0	-.1	2.1	.8	-.7			-.7	-1.8
50.3	25.8	29.5	54.1	138.6			35.0	27.7
17.9	9.4	11.6	9.3	10.4		Sales/Net Fixed Assets	15.0	11.2
6.0	3.8	6.3	5.2	3.7			5.1	3.9
7.8	4.8	4.9	3.7	4.8			6.4	5.1
4.2	3.3	3.0	2.6	2.3		Sales/Total Assets	3.3	3.2
2.7	1.6	2.0	1.5	1.3			1.9	1.8
.8	1.3	.6	.4				.7	1.2
(76) 2.0	(53) 2.4	(52) 1.5	(16) 1.7			% Depr., Dep., Amort./Sales	(142) 1.9	(175) 2.1
4.7	4.4	2.1	4.2				4.2	4.1
2.2	1.3	.1					2.4	1.3
(40) 4.7	(32) 4.2	(34) 1.6				% Officers', Directors' Owners' Comp/Sales	(80) 4.1	(94) 3.0
9.1	5.7	3.2					7.3	8.2
95844M	281644M	1033780M	898340M	2166811M	4443456M	Net Sales ($)	4335941M	2575641M
19965M	70337M	292970M	338361M	701116M	1032923M	Total Assets ($)	1219144M	1015132M

M = $ thousand   MM = $ million
See Pages 9 through 22 for Explanation of Ratios and Data

Comparative Historical Data | Current Data Sorted by Sales

4/1/07-3/31/08 ALL	4/1/08-3/31/09 ALL	4/1/09-3/31/10 ALL	Type of Statement	0-1MM	1-3MM	3-5MM	5-10MM	10-25MM	25MM & OVER
14	20	20	Unqualified	2	1		1	3	13
15	20	26	Reviewed	1	2	1	2	9	11
20	26	22	Compiled	3	8	3	2	3	3
107	120	124	Tax Returns	59	34	8	18	3	2
55	56	63	Other	10	14	3	10	14	12
				26 (4/1-9/30/09)			229 (10/1/09-3/31/10)		
211	242	255	NUMBER OF STATEMENTS	75	59	15	33	32	41
%	%	%	ASSETS	%	%	%	%	%	%
11.1	12.2	15.5	Cash & Equivalents	19.9	15.1	12.6	16.4	11.8	11.2
7.6	7.7	7.2	Trade Receivables (net)	1.4	6.1	9.3	10.3	9.5	14.1
16.2	16.6	18.4	Inventory	12.1	19.7	19.5	19.2	28.6	19.2
3.4	3.2	2.5	All Other Current	1.1	2.2	1.5	.8	4.0	6.0
38.3	39.6	43.6	Total Current	34.5	43.2	42.9	46.7	54.0	50.4
39.3	40.6	36.5	Fixed Assets (net)	42.3	33.5	39.8	34.8	30.5	35.1
13.1	13.5	12.2	Intangibles (net)	19.1	12.0	6.0	9.6	8.6	7.0
9.3	6.3	7.7	All Other Non-Current	4.1	11.3	11.3	8.9	6.9	7.4
100.0	100.0	100.0	Total	100.0	100.0	100.0	100.0	100.0	100.0
			LIABILITIES						
7.0	9.0	7.6	Notes Payable-Short Term	6.7	11.3	3.8	7.4	6.0	6.5
4.9	3.5	4.8	Cur. Mat.-L.T.D.	3.5	5.4	5.4	4.4	5.4	5.9
12.2	12.9	11.7	Trade Payables	4.6	8.2	17.0	18.3	17.4	18.1
.1	.1	.1	Income Taxes Payable	.1	.0	.0	.2	.2	.2
12.8	13.0	15.2	All Other Current	24.5	14.2	6.0	9.2	9.7	12.0
37.0	38.5	39.4	Total Current	39.4	39.2	32.1	39.5	38.7	42.6
28.8	32.4	29.1	Long-Term Debt	37.9	27.8	34.0	28.9	17.7	21.7
.1	.1	.1	Deferred Taxes	.0	.0	.0	.2	.1	.2
10.0	9.4	8.3	All Other Non-Current	14.9	8.3	8.6	2.8	1.5	6.0
24.1	19.6	23.2	Net Worth	7.8	24.7	25.3	28.6	42.0	29.5
100.0	100.0	100.0	Total Liabilties & Net Worth	100.0	100.0	100.0	100.0	100.0	100.0
			INCOME DATA						
100.0	100.0	100.0	Net Sales	100.0	100.0	100.0	100.0	100.0	100.0
48.7	47.5	46.6	Gross Profit	59.0	49.5	37.6	42.8	39.6	31.9
45.1	43.5	42.8	Operating Expenses	57.0	42.9	34.9	39.3	34.5	28.9
3.6	4.1	3.8	Operating Profit	2.0	6.6	2.7	3.6	5.0	2.9
1.1	1.4	.8	All Other Expenses (net)	1.2	.7	.0	.2	.1	1.3
2.4	2.6	3.0	Profit Before Taxes	.7	5.8	2.6	3.3	4.9	1.6
			RATIOS						
2.4	2.4	2.7	Current	4.9	5.2	2.0	2.0	1.8	1.8
1.2	1.2	1.3		1.6	1.4	1.3	1.1	1.4	1.3
.6	.5	.7		.4	.6	1.2	.5	1.1	.8
1.5	1.2	1.7	Quick	2.8	2.4	1.0	1.5	1.0	1.3
(210) .4	.5	.6		.8	.7	.7	.5	.5	.5
.2	.2	.2		.1	.2	.5	.2	.1	.1
0 UND	0 UND	0 UND	Sales/Receivables	0 UND	0 UND	0 UND	0 UND	0 UND	0 791.1
0 UND	0 999.8	0 UND		0 UND	0 UND	4 91.8	2 174.0	2 153.0	3 113.7
8 45.8	10 36.0	6 58.1		0 UND	4 86.1	12 31.0	34 10.8	25 14.3	23 15.7
7 52.5	7 53.9	7 51.4	Cost of Sales/Inventory	4 103.5	7 51.2	16 22.7	4 82.2	15 25.0	9 40.2
14 25.5	16 23.5	17 20.9		11 34.0	16 22.7	21 17.2	14 26.3	45 8.0	24 15.0
43 8.6	37 9.7	47 7.7		29 12.6	42 8.7	33 11.0	83 4.4	77 4.7	47 7.7
0 UND	1 597.1	0 UND	Cost of Sales/Payables	0 UND	0 UND	10 36.9	6 56.3	15 23.7	11 33.0
14 25.2	18 20.4	15 24.3		3 105.4	4 88.5	19 19.1	26 13.9	28 13.3	20 18.7
35 10.5	38 9.7	32 11.4		22 16.7	20 18.4	26 13.9	55 6.6	42 8.7	34 10.8
15.4	14.3	12.8	Sales/Working Capital	13.9	9.9	17.4	9.9	9.5	16.8
82.2	70.6	32.9		40.4	32.9	38.1	32.1	20.1	54.4
-27.0	-29.6	-38.7		-9.3	-38.0	90.6	-27.4	75.5	-60.4
5.6	8.5	13.9	EBIT/Interest	10.8	22.9	8.0	21.2	21.5	7.3
(161) 2.1	(186) 2.4	(200) 3.7		(50) 2.1	(45) 3.6	(11) 3.9	(29) 6.9	(29) 5.6	(36) 3.1
.8	.7	1.1		-1.8	1.0	.5	2.3	2.8	1.2
6.1	9.2	5.0	Net Profit + Depr., Dep., Amort./Cur. Mat. L/T/D					18.8	5.9
(20) 4.0	(22) 2.5	(33) 1.6						(10) 1.4	(17) 2.0
1.2	1.8	.8						.8	.2
.7	.6	.5	Fixed/Worth	.6	.5	.5	.3	.3	.5
1.9	2.3	1.4		55.8	1.6	.9	1.0	.8	1.4
-3.4	-3.4	-4.6		-1.1	-2.0	-4.6	5.2	3.0	3.2
1.1	1.1	.8	Debt/Worth	.5	.8	.5	1.1	.7	1.2
3.5	4.5	2.8		UND	5.3	1.2	2.6	1.7	2.3
-8.8	-5.1	-5.1		-2.7	-4.4	-9.8	-18.2	4.6	6.0
95.4	84.7	75.3	% Profit Before Taxes/Tangible Net Worth	132.8	183.3	42.8	58.2	68.6	32.2
(143) 25.5	(154) 27.1	(171) 30.0		(38) 50.0	(38) 57.0	(11) 23.5	(24) 31.4	(27) 24.9	(33) 13.8
.7	6.7	10.5		9.2	20.5	-4.4	17.8	12.2	5.8
21.9	20.7	24.4	% Profit Before Taxes/Total Assets	26.3	48.2	20.7	19.4	23.6	12.7
5.1	6.9	9.0		9.2	13.4	13.7	10.7	9.5	5.1
-1.3	-.9	.7		-3.6	1.2	-1.7	1.4	3.6	.2
30.8	32.3	32.8	Sales/Net Fixed Assets	26.7	38.6	25.8	35.0	35.0	55.4
14.4	10.5	11.9		7.3	19.5	9.4	12.2	14.8	12.8
4.5	4.3	5.0		3.1	6.2	4.6	5.6	6.6	5.1
6.5	5.5	5.5	Sales/Total Assets	4.6	7.2	5.3	4.9	5.1	6.4
3.7	2.9	3.4		2.9	4.0	3.6	3.3	3.4	3.5
1.8	1.8	2.0		1.6	2.2	2.1	2.0	2.3	2.5
.9	1.2	.9	% Depr., Dep., Amort./Sales	2.2	.7	.7	.8	.3	.3
(177) 1.8	(197) 2.5	(208) 1.8		(59) 4.1	(46) 1.1	(14) 1.9	(26) 1.7	(28) 1.5	(35) 1.4
3.4	4.5	3.5		8.3	2.5	2.5	2.6	2.0	2.7
1.6	1.6	.9	% Officers', Directors' Owners' Comp/Sales	3.9	1.4		1.3	.1	.1
(85) 2.7	(106) 2.9	(116) 3.3		(28) 7.0	(30) 4.3		(20) 2.1	(16) .5	(16) .3
5.6	6.1	5.7		13.8	5.2		4.7	2.6	3.2
5016147M	5038173M	8919875M	Net Sales ($)	42261M	113101M	54734M	247383M	512927M	7949469M
1769575M	1505936M	2455672M	Total Assets ($)	19655M	39503M	17610M	109854M	184188M	2084862M

© RMA 2010

M = $ thousand   MM = $ million
See Pages 9 through 22 for Explanation of Ratios and Data

Current Data Sorted by Assets   Comparative Historical Data

	0-500M	500M-2MM	2-10MM	10-50MM	50-100MM	100-250MM	Type of Statement	4/1/05-3/31/06 ALL	4/1/06-3/31/07 ALL
	3	1	3	7		1	Unqualified	10	14
		5	11	4			Reviewed	22	19
	15	29	15	1			Compiled	50	55
	112	81	30	1			Tax Returns	121	158
	11	21	14	7	3	1	Other	47	52
		36 (4/1-9/30/09)		340 (10/1/09-3/31/10)					
NUMBER OF STATEMENTS	141	137	73	19	4	2		250	298
	%	%	%	%	%	%	ASSETS	%	%
	10.6	12.9	11.2	10.7			Cash & Equivalents	10.6	11.7
	1.3	1.3	3.1	2.1			Trade Receivables (net)	1.8	2.5
	51.7	45.2	42.7	42.0			Inventory	47.9	46.8
	1.8	1.7	3.1	1.8			All Other Current	1.8	2.0
	65.3	61.1	60.1	56.6			Total Current	62.1	63.0
	16.3	16.6	19.9	19.0			Fixed Assets (net)	17.9	17.1
	15.7	15.0	14.7	13.4			Intangibles (net)	13.5	13.5
	2.7	7.3	5.4	11.0			All Other Non-Current	6.5	6.3
	100.0	100.0	100.0	100.0			Total	100.0	100.0
							LIABILITIES		
	9.1	4.3	6.4	6.1			Notes Payable-Short Term	7.4	7.7
	2.9	2.9	3.3	3.3			Cur. Mat.-L.T.D.	3.6	3.3
	7.9	18.0	20.2	19.7			Trade Payables	17.8	18.5
	.2	.1	.1	.0			Income Taxes Payable	.1	.2
	11.5	10.3	7.2	10.7			All Other Current	11.5	12.0
	31.5	35.5	37.2	39.8			Total Current	40.5	41.8
	20.4	26.6	26.6	14.6			Long-Term Debt	22.1	21.6
	.0	.0	.0	.0			Deferred Taxes	.0	.2
	17.9	11.5	6.5	3.1			All Other Non-Current	8.4	6.7
	30.2	26.4	29.7	42.5			Net Worth	29.0	29.8
	100.0	100.0	100.0	100.0			Total Liabilties & Net Worth	100.0	100.0
							INCOME DATA		
	100.0	100.0	100.0	100.0			Net Sales	100.0	100.0
	24.1	22.4	21.1	24.9			Gross Profit	22.9	23.8
	22.8	20.5	19.2	20.6			Operating Expenses	21.4	21.4
	1.3	1.8	1.9	4.2			Operating Profit	1.4	2.4
	-1.4	-.2	.4	.7			All Other Expenses (net)	-.1	.1
	2.7	2.0	1.5	3.6			Profit Before Taxes	1.6	2.3
							RATIOS		
	16.1	3.8	2.7	3.2				3.3	3.4
	3.3	2.0	1.5	1.9			Current	1.8	1.6
	1.6	1.2	1.1	1.2				1.0	1.1
	2.2	1.0	.7	.8				.8	.8
	(138) .6	(135) .4	(72) .3	.3			Quick	(249) .3	(296) .3
	.1	.2	.1	.1				.1	.1
	0 UND	0 UND	0 UND	0 UND				0 UND	0 UND
	0 UND	0 UND	1 596.3	0 999.8			Sales/Receivables	0 UND	0 UND
	0 UND	0 999.8	4 83.1	6 66.2				1 400.8	1 335.1
	34 10.7	47 7.8	40 9.2	52 7.1				38 9.5	40 9.0
	55 6.6	66 5.5	64 5.7	75 4.9			Cost of Sales/Inventory	57 6.4	59 6.1
	83 4.4	89 4.1	87 4.2	106 3.4				79 4.6	82 4.4
	0 UND	0 UND	9 42.1	20 17.9				2 206.3	1 350.6
	1 720.0	22 16.9	30 12.2	27 13.4			Cost of Sales/Payables	21 17.6	21 17.7
	11 31.8	40 9.2	42 8.6	39 9.4				34 10.7	39 9.3
	5.2	5.8	7.2	5.3				8.5	8.4
	10.1	11.5	16.9	16.7			Sales/Working Capital	16.8	16.3
	29.6	31.5	54.8	34.1				370.9	106.3
	13.0	8.1	6.4	11.6				8.2	8.0
	(84) 3.2	(107) 2.7	(66) 3.4	(13) 4.9			EBIT/Interest	(206) 3.7	(240) 3.5
	.6	1.1	1.2	3.3				1.3	1.0
			6.7				Net Profit + Depr., Dep.,	4.2	11.4
		(10) 2.1					Amort./Cur. Mat. L/T/D	(21) 1.5	(19) 3.7
			1.1					.6	1.0
	.0	.1	.4	.4				.1	.2
	.6	1.1	1.1	.8			Fixed/Worth	.8	.7
	-1.7	-.8	-6.2	3.6				-4.0	-2.0
	.5	.9	1.5	.4				.8	.9
	2.7	5.0	4.3	2.8			Debt/Worth	3.5	3.1
	-4.7	-4.3	-9.9	33.0				-12.8	-7.0
	94.6	41.9	56.7	45.9			% Profit Before Taxes/Tangible	43.0	46.7
	(94) 27.8	(83) 18.9	(51) 16.9	(15) 26.2			Net Worth	(172) 20.1	(203) 18.6
	12.5	8.0	3.7	19.5				7.8	5.9
	21.0	12.9	9.6	13.1			% Profit Before Taxes/Total	11.4	14.2
	8.2	4.8	4.4	9.5			Assets	5.6	6.3
	1.4	.5	.8	4.4				1.0	.2
	413.5	109.7	62.2	35.6				137.6	115.3
	65.2	32.0	30.7	26.8			Sales/Net Fixed Assets	39.0	36.1
	19.7	11.5	10.1	11.4				14.3	13.9
	6.6	4.4	4.4	3.6				5.2	5.0
	3.9	2.8	3.1	2.7			Sales/Total Assets	3.8	3.5
	2.6	1.9	1.9	1.8				2.7	2.5
	.3	.4	.4	.4				.3	.3
	(81) 1.2	(98) .9	(60) .7	(17) .8			% Depr., Dep., Amort./Sales	(180) .8	(230) .8
	2.2	2.4	1.3	1.0				1.4	1.6
	1.7	1.2	.9				% Officers', Directors'	1.5	1.5
	(83) 2.9	(78) 2.2	(32) 1.8				Owners' Comp/Sales	(134) 2.5	(162) 2.8
	4.3	4.2	2.6					4.4	4.2
Net Sales ($)	160934M	442743M	1037594M	1187595M	850376M	1260833M		4450747M	4992693M
Total Assets ($)	37801M	133353M	281091M	427409M	310347M	399746M		1279135M	1604254M

© RMA 2010

M = $ thousand   MM = $ million
See Pages 9 through 22 for Explanation of Ratios and Data

Comparative Historical Data / Current Data Sorted by Sales

4/1/07-3/31/08 ALL	4/1/08-3/31/09 ALL	4/1/09-3/31/10 ALL	Type of Statement	0-1MM	1-3MM	3-5MM	5-10MM	10-25MM	25MM & OVER
12	17	15	Unqualified	3		1	1	4	6
25	29	20	Reviewed			1	6	5	8
69	49	60	Compiled	6	19	8	14	9	4
194	171	224	Tax Returns	73	94	30	14	12	1
59	63	57	Other	10	14	6	9	5	13
				36 (4/1-9/30/09)		340 (10/1/09-3/31/10)			
359	329	376	**NUMBER OF STATEMENTS**	92	127	46	44	35	32
%	%	%	**ASSETS**	%	%	%	%	%	%
11.4	11.0	11.4	Cash & Equivalents	9.3	13.0	11.3	11.3	14.5	7.7
2.3	1.0	1.7	Trade Receivables (net)	.9	1.5	2.4	1.0	2.3	4.4
45.5	45.8	46.8	Inventory	46.3	46.7	51.7	48.4	46.3	40.3
2.4	1.5	2.0	All Other Current	2.6	1.1	2.1	2.8	2.5	2.1
61.6	59.3	61.9	Total Current	59.1	62.3	67.4	63.5	65.6	54.6
19.1	18.2	17.6	Fixed Assets (net)	19.7	15.6	13.4	19.2	18.2	22.3
13.8	15.4	15.0	Intangibles (net)	15.9	18.2	13.8	11.8	8.9	12.1
5.6	7.0	5.5	All Other Non-Current	5.4	3.9	5.4	5.6	7.3	11.0
100.0	100.0	100.0	Total	100.0	100.0	100.0	100.0	100.0	100.0
			LIABILITIES						
6.7	8.5	6.6	Notes Payable-Short Term	10.9	3.3	7.6	6.3	8.0	4.9
2.0	4.4	3.0	Cur. Mat.-L.T.D.	2.4	3.3	2.7	1.9	3.1	4.9
15.5	12.7	14.6	Trade Payables	7.2	10.1	23.6	21.4	22.6	22.7
.1	.0	.1	Income Taxes Payable	.1	.2	.3	.0	.0	.0
9.8	10.9	10.3	All Other Current	9.5	10.5	13.9	9.4	8.8	9.2
34.1	36.5	34.6	Total Current	30.0	27.4	48.1	39.0	42.6	41.8
23.0	25.2	23.6	Long-Term Debt	23.2	26.6	29.1	18.7	19.8	16.3
.0	.0	.0	Deferred Taxes	.0	.0	.0	.0	.0	.0
14.0	11.7	12.5	All Other Non-Current	21.1	14.3	8.3	6.1	4.3	4.5
28.9	26.5	29.3	Net Worth	25.7	31.7	14.5	36.2	33.3	37.4
100.0	100.0	100.0	Total Liabilties & Net Worth	100.0	100.0	100.0	100.0	100.0	100.0
			INCOME DATA						
100.0	100.0	100.0	Net Sales	100.0	100.0	100.0	100.0	100.0	100.0
23.5	23.9	23.0	Gross Profit	24.3	23.3	21.7	21.4	22.7	23.0
21.6	21.8	21.2	Operating Expenses	23.4	21.5	19.8	18.9	20.7	19.2
1.9	2.1	1.9	Operating Profit	.9	1.8	1.9	2.5	2.0	3.9
-.6	-.2	-.5	All Other Expenses (net)	-1.7	-.6	.4	.3	.2	.5
2.5	2.2	2.3	Profit Before Taxes	2.6	2.4	1.5	2.2	1.8	3.3
			RATIOS						
5.5	6.0	5.3	Current	19.0	6.8	2.2	2.5	2.2	2.3
2.2	2.0	2.1		5.7	2.9	1.5	1.5	1.5	1.3
1.2	1.1	1.2		1.9	1.6	1.1	1.2	1.2	.9
.9	1.2	1.2	Quick	2.7	1.6	.5	.5	.8	.6
(354) .4	(325) .3	(370) .4		(90) .9	(126) .5	(44) .4	.3	.3	(31) .3
.1	.1	.1		.1	.2	.1	.1	.1	.1
0 UND	0 UND	0 UND	Sales/Receivables	0 UND	0 UND	0 UND	0 UND	0 UND	0 UND
0 UND	0 UND	0 UND		0 UND	0 UND	0 UND	0 UND	0 UND	1 465.2
1 547.4	0 759.0	1 552.4		0 UND	9 999.8	2 175.5	4 237.3	5 85.8	5 70.2
37 10.0	38 9.7	40 9.2	Cost of Sales/Inventory	49 7.5	36 10.1	52 7.0	30 12.3	39 9.3	25 14.7
60 6.1	62 5.9	63 5.8		74 4.9	57 6.4	67 5.4	62 5.8	52 7.0	51 7.1
86 4.3	93 3.9	88 4.1		103 3.5	87 4.2	79 4.6	84 4.4	69 5.3	74 4.9
0 UND	0 UND	0 UND	Cost of Sales/Payables	0 UND	0 UND	10 36.9	2 165.5	11 33.8	14 26.6
15 25.2	11 32.2	12 30.1		1 349.0	3 108.3	33 11.1	29 12.5	33 11.1	23 15.6
34 10.7	28 13.0	33 11.0		11 31.8	26 14.0	51 7.2	41 8.8	45 8.2	30 12.1
6.6	6.4	5.8	Sales/Working Capital	4.2	5.8	9.3	9.4	7.4	12.3
12.7	14.6	12.1		6.8	10.1	18.3	23.7	18.5	32.2
43.5	106.0	32.9		17.5	25.4	51.8	40.4	35.2	-243.7
7.5	8.6	8.0	EBIT/Interest	5.2	12.1	6.1	14.5	8.4	15.9
(284) 3.4	(264) 3.6	(276) 3.2		(59) 2.5	(87) 2.7	(36) 2.7	(37) 3.9	(31) 4.0	(26) 6.6
1.5	1.1	1.1		.0	.6	1.3	1.4	2.1	3.1
13.9	5.7	7.5	Net Profit + Depr., Dep., Amort./Cur. Mat. L/T/D						
(20) 6.8	(19) 1.4	(21) 2.2							
1.8	.1	1.0							
.2	.1	.1	Fixed/Worth	.0	.1	.2	.2	.4	.4
.9	.9	.9		1.0	.7	NM	.6	.8	.9
-1.8	-1.3	-1.7		-1.8	-.5	-.3	NM	3.1	3.1
.9	.9	.8	Debt/Worth	.6	.6	2.7	.6	1.0	1.2
4.3	4.7	3.8		8.0	2.9	-242.9	2.3	2.8	3.2
-6.4	-4.7	-7.4		-3.8	-3.5	-4.1	NM	8.1	30.5
60.9	57.1	63.5	% Profit Before Taxes/Tangible Net Worth	86.0	78.5	50.9	43.8	49.9	76.7
(243) 28.4	(215) 25.5	(249) 22.7		(56) 23.4	(83) 23.9	(22) 18.9	(33) 21.1	(29) 17.4	(26) 24.8
10.2	9.8	9.3		6.1	9.4	12.7	5.1	4.7	13.1
14.0	15.5	14.1	% Profit Before Taxes/Total Assets	13.3	17.8	10.1	17.2	11.7	16.4
7.0	6.7	6.1		5.2	6.4	3.9	6.9	4.4	9.2
2.1	.4	.8		.0	.4	.6	1.0	1.2	4.6
108.7	126.0	127.8	Sales/Net Fixed Assets	663.5	173.4	138.9	73.2	105.4	45.9
35.8	33.0	37.1		31.6	47.1	50.8	53.7	32.8	27.5
11.5	10.6	11.6		10.3	13.5	17.9	11.5	10.6	10.5
5.0	4.8	4.8	Sales/Total Assets	3.9	5.3	5.2	5.1	5.3	5.4
3.4	3.4	3.1		2.6	3.1	3.2	3.9	3.9	3.7
2.2	2.1	2.1		1.8	2.2	1.9	2.7	2.9	2.5
.3	.4	.4	% Depr., Dep., Amort./Sales	.9	.3	.3	.2	.4	.3
(273) .8	(223) .9	(261) .8		(53) 1.6	(81) 1.2	(33) .7	(35) .4	(31) .6	(28) .7
1.7	1.9	1.9		2.9	2.5	1.6	.9	1.2	.9
1.5	1.5	1.3	% Officers', Directors' Owners' Comp/Sales	1.8	1.6	1.2	1.0	.7	
(208) 2.7	(175) 2.9	(199) 2.5		(46) 3.3	(80) 2.7	(26) 1.8	(25) 1.9	(13) 1.8	
4.3	5.0	4.1		4.2	4.8	3.4	3.2	2.4	
6588970M	6774982M	4940075M	Net Sales ($)	63876M	224601M	177021M	299145M	514134M	3661298M
1912616M	1957276M	1589747M	Total Assets ($)	29271M	75958M	67188M	97811M	172014M	1147505M

M = $ thousand   MM = $ million
See Pages 9 through 22 for Explanation of Ratios and Data

Current Data Sorted by Assets   Comparative Historical Data

						Type of Statement		
		5	8	6		Unqualified	19	12
3	8	19	2			Reviewed	22	27
11	35	27				Compiled	64	73
46	87	27				Tax Returns	97	135
21	38	34	13	2	6	Other	96	84
	58 (4/1-9/30/09)		340 (10/1/09-3/31/10)				4/1/05-3/31/06 ALL	4/1/06-3/31/07 ALL
0-500M	500M-2MM	2-10MM	10-50MM	50-100MM	100-250MM	NUMBER OF STATEMENTS		
81	168	112	23	8	6		298	331
%	%	%	%	%	%	ASSETS	%	%
17.7	11.5	9.4	5.5			Cash & Equivalents	11.6	11.3
18.8	22.9	32.5	25.7			Trade Receivables (net)	24.5	26.2
38.4	35.5	26.0	27.5			Inventory	36.6	34.6
.9	1.4	1.2	3.5			All Other Current	2.6	2.6
75.7	71.2	69.1	62.2			Total Current	75.3	74.7
12.0	10.4	13.5	21.3			Fixed Assets (net)	13.3	12.8
5.8	6.8	8.0	11.0			Intangibles (net)	5.7	6.1
6.4	11.6	9.4	5.5			All Other Non-Current	5.7	6.4
100.0	100.0	100.0	100.0			Total	100.0	100.0
						LIABILITIES		
17.7	9.3	10.5	8.6			Notes Payable-Short Term	10.0	9.4
4.0	3.4	3.2	3.6			Cur. Mat.-L.T.D.	3.5	3.7
27.9	26.7	28.0	25.3			Trade Payables	24.5	25.5
.1	.1	.1	.0			Income Taxes Payable	.1	.2
14.9	6.4	8.6	8.7			All Other Current	7.3	7.0
64.7	45.9	50.4	46.3			Total Current	45.5	45.8
18.5	14.1	12.8	23.0			Long-Term Debt	16.0	15.9
.0	.0	.1	.6			Deferred Taxes	.1	.1
8.7	5.4	4.7	1.2			All Other Non-Current	5.7	6.2
8.1	34.6	32.0	28.8			Net Worth	32.7	32.0
100.0	100.0	100.0	100.0			Total Liabilties & Net Worth	100.0	100.0
						INCOME DATA		
100.0	100.0	100.0	100.0			Net Sales	100.0	100.0
30.3	24.2	28.3	25.8			Gross Profit	25.8	24.9
26.4	21.6	24.7	23.8			Operating Expenses	23.2	22.6
3.9	2.7	3.6	1.9			Operating Profit	2.5	2.4
.3	.0	.2	.7			All Other Expenses (net)	.2	.1
3.6	2.7	3.4	1.3			Profit Before Taxes	2.3	2.2
						RATIOS		
3.2	3.2	2.1	1.8				3.1	2.7
1.7	1.7	1.4	1.4			Current	1.8	1.8
.9	1.1	1.1	1.2				1.3	1.2
1.5	1.6	1.4	1.0				1.6	1.4
.7	.8	.8	.8			Quick	(297) .9	.9
.3	.4	.5	.5				.5	.5
0 UND	7 51.5	18 20.0	23 15.9				10 38.1	10 38.0
7 49.4	17 21.6	26 13.8	29 12.7			Sales/Receivables	18 20.6	19 19.6
20 18.0	24 14.9	37 10.0	39 9.4				26 14.3	28 13.2
17 21.0	21 17.0	18 20.0	25 14.4				23 15.9	22 16.5
29 12.4	31 11.8	28 12.9	40 9.1			Cost of Sales/Inventory	34 10.8	32 11.5
46 7.9	43 8.5	36 10.1	54 6.7				49 7.4	44 8.2
4 81.2	13 29.0	15 24.8	32 11.4				13 29.0	13 27.4
17 21.4	19 19.0	27 13.3	41 8.9			Cost of Sales/Payables	20 18.5	21 17.0
30 12.1	36 10.2	44 8.3	50 7.3				32 11.3	36 10.3
11.2	9.8	11.6	9.0				9.3	10.1
21.3	18.1	23.8	19.7			Sales/Working Capital	14.6	16.3
-212.4	60.0	112.8	41.8				38.6	44.0
20.2	22.0	22.0	6.6				14.2	12.2
(49) 4.8	(133) 4.9	(103) 6.0	(22) 2.6			EBIT/Interest	(243) 4.8	(261) 3.9
.9	1.4	2.4	.1				1.9	1.3
	3.9	2.0					5.2	4.1
	(12) 1.6	(15) .9				Net Profit + Depr., Dep., Amort./Cur. Mat. L/T/D	(42) 1.8	(43) 1.4
	.9	.4					1.2	.8
.0	.1	.2	.4				.1	.1
.3	.2	.5	1.2			Fixed/Worth	.4	.4
5.1	1.7	3.3	-12.9				1.9	2.4
.8	.8	1.0	1.8				.8	.9
4.1	2.2	3.4	4.2			Debt/Worth	1.9	2.3
-7.7	13.1	35.6	-31.1				9.4	25.1
177.8	81.6	76.1	60.2				68.6	73.4
(57) 61.3	(135) 26.7	(89) 34.8	(17) 24.5			% Profit Before Taxes/Tangible Net Worth	(244) 27.8	(265) 21.4
23.5	6.8	11.9	-4.8				9.6	6.8
38.4	22.9	21.4	9.6				20.2	16.7
14.6	9.4	9.2	2.5			% Profit Before Taxes/Total Assets	9.0	7.2
.1	.6	3.0	-1.8				2.3	1.0
571.8	280.2	88.7	45.1				125.9	136.4
155.5	75.1	48.4	24.1			Sales/Net Fixed Assets	60.2	51.4
33.3	34.8	23.6	10.0				26.5	24.4
8.8	6.5	5.5	4.1				6.4	6.6
6.4	4.9	4.4	3.4			Sales/Total Assets	4.9	4.7
4.1	3.7	3.3	2.2				3.5	3.5
.1	.2	.3	.7				.3	.3
(45) .3	(115) .5	(97) .6	(18) 1.2			% Depr., Dep., Amort./Sales	(239) .5	(263) .5
1.1	1.0	1.0	1.7				1.0	.9
2.1	1.7	1.1					1.7	1.7
(44) 3.7	(121) 2.9	(49) 2.1				% Officers', Directors' Owners' Comp/Sales	(156) 3.1	(181) 3.0
8.0	4.3	3.6					5.2	4.9
190122M	962582M	2080258M	1593505M	1520168M	2394672M	Net Sales ($)	7393566M	8264219M
25868M	180376M	474813M	551858M	511925M	851637M	Total Assets ($)	2048709M	2117197M

M = $ thousand   MM = $ million
See Pages 9 through 22 for Explanation of Ratios and Data

Comparative Historical Data   Current Data Sorted by Sales

			Type of Statement						
21	22	19	Unqualified			2	1	3	15
30	27	32	Reviewed		11	14	6	14	8
59	78	73	Compiled	2		14	21	20	5
116	165	160	Tax Returns	5	51	37	43	20	4
91	97	114	Other		28	13	22	23	28
4/1/07-	4/1/08-	4/1/09-			58 (4/1-9/30/09)		340 (10/1/09-3/31/10)		
3/31/08	3/31/09	3/31/10							
ALL	ALL	ALL		0-1MM	1-3MM	3-5MM	5-10MM	10-25MM	25MM & OVER
317	389	398	**NUMBER OF STATEMENTS**	9	90	66	93	80	60
%	%	%	**ASSETS**	%	%	%	%	%	%
10.9	12.1	11.9	Cash & Equivalents		12.4	12.4	13.5	9.6	7.9
24.8	25.0	24.8	Trade Receivables (net)		20.2	20.4	25.1	30.2	31.2
34.1	33.3	32.6	Inventory		33.8	37.3	33.5	30.9	26.6
2.0	2.1	1.4	All Other Current		.8	1.4	2.1	1.1	1.6
71.8	72.5	70.7	Total Current		67.1	71.5	74.2	71.7	67.3
14.5	12.9	12.4	Fixed Assets (net)		11.6	9.4	11.8	13.9	14.1
7.1	7.5	7.6	Intangibles (net)		9.7	6.9	6.0	5.8	11.3
6.6	7.2	9.4	All Other Non-Current		11.6	12.3	8.1	8.6	7.3
100.0	100.0	100.0	Total		100.0	100.0	100.0	100.0	100.0
			LIABILITIES						
12.1	9.8	11.2	Notes Payable-Short Term		10.2	16.0	8.0	9.3	10.5
4.4	4.5	3.4	Cur. Mat.-L.T.D.		4.0	3.4	3.2	3.0	3.3
23.4	25.3	27.0	Trade Payables		22.8	27.0	28.5	32.1	25.0
.1	.1	.1	Income Taxes Payable		.1	.2	.1	.1	.1
8.3	9.5	9.1	All Other Current		9.4	6.0	5.6	10.9	9.6
48.2	49.2	50.9	Total Current		46.5	52.7	45.4	55.3	48.4
16.4	16.7	15.1	Long-Term Debt		18.2	16.3	17.4	9.9	14.0
.1	.1	.1	Deferred Taxes		.0	.0	.0	.1	.4
6.2	4.5	5.7	All Other Non-Current		9.0	3.1	5.3	5.9	2.7
29.0	29.6	28.2	Net Worth		26.3	28.0	31.9	28.7	34.5
100.0	100.0	100.0	Total Liabilties & Net Worth		100.0	100.0	100.0	100.0	100.0
			INCOME DATA						
100.0	100.0	100.0	Net Sales		100.0	100.0	100.0	100.0	100.0
26.0	25.2	26.8	Gross Profit		29.8	24.3	24.6	25.7	26.4
23.9	22.7	23.7	Operating Expenses		25.3	22.0	21.2	22.6	24.3
2.1	2.4	3.1	Operating Profit		4.5	2.3	3.3	3.1	2.1
.3	.2	.2	All Other Expenses (net)		.5	.0	.1	.0	.3
1.7	2.2	2.9	Profit Before Taxes		4.0	2.3	3.3	3.1	1.8
			RATIOS						
2.5	2.7	2.6			3.6	3.4	3.0	1.9	2.2
1.6	1.6	1.6	Current		1.8	1.7	1.7	1.5	1.4
1.1	1.1	1.1			1.0	1.0	1.2	1.1	1.1
1.2	1.5	1.4			1.7	1.7	1.4	1.2	1.0
(316) .8	.8	.8	Quick		.7	.8	.8	.8	.8
.5	.5	.5			.3	.4	.4	.4	.5
11 34.0	9 40.7	8 46.2		3 141.0	3 143.7	8 46.8	11 33.3	20 18.3	
19 18.8	19 18.9	19 18.7	Sales/Receivables	17 21.0	15 24.9	19 19.2	20 18.6	27 13.5	
28 13.0	27 13.4	28 12.8		26 13.8	24 15.4	28 13.2	32 11.3	39 9.4	
22 16.2	21 17.5	20 18.0		25 14.8	18 20.2	21 17.8	17 21.4	21 17.2	
33 11.1	31 11.9	31 11.9	Cost of Sales/Inventory	39 9.4	29 12.6	30 12.1	26 14.2	33 11.2	
47 7.7	42 8.7	45 8.1		51 7.1	39 9.4	39 9.5	36 10.2	49 7.4	
14 26.1	14 25.9	13 27.1		12 30.3	4 95.8	15 25.1	14 26.6	19 19.1	
21 17.5	21 17.4	23 15.6	Cost of Sales/Payables	18 20.2	18 20.5	20 18.2	27 13.5	32 11.4	
35 10.3	35 10.5	41 8.9		42 8.7	36 10.2	37 9.8	42 8.8	42 8.6	
11.0	10.2	10.3			9.0	11.2	10.2	13.7	10.3
19.4	20.0	20.8	Sales/Working Capital		16.0	21.5	16.0	27.0	23.3
93.3	71.6	111.4			118.8	UND	46.0	224.9	97.9
9.9	13.2	18.5			11.4	13.1	26.0	26.4	10.5
(269) 3.5	(317) 4.3	(319) 4.9	EBIT/Interest	(64) 3.5	(50) 5.2	(72) 5.2	(74) 7.0	(55) 4.2	
1.1	1.1	1.4			1.0	.7	1.1	2.7	2.2
6.2	4.8	4.6							8.1
(48) 1.8	(44) 1.4	(45) 1.4	Net Profit + Depr., Dep., Amort./Cur. Mat. L/T/D					(21) 2.0	
.5	.4	.7							.8
.2	.1	.1			.0	.0	.1	.1	.3
.5	.5	.4	Fixed/Worth		.3	.3	.2	.4	.6
3.4	6.0	3.9			6.0	2.4	2.3	2.9	15.0
.9	.9	.9			.6	.7	.8	1.2	.9
2.4	2.5	2.8	Debt/Worth		2.3	2.7	2.0	3.1	3.7
22.9	257.1	44.6			-275.6	44.6	UND	18.9	94.1
57.1	64.8	88.1			95.3	110.1	72.2	84.0	82.0
(252) 22.4	(296) 27.0	(305) 33.5	% Profit Before Taxes/Tangible Net Worth	(67) 33.0	(52) 34.6	(70) 28.9	(65) 37.2	(46) 31.7	
5.9	7.8	10.6			17.2	6.8	5.9	9.5	11.3
18.2	19.9	22.6			23.7	25.9	28.8	24.3	13.0
5.6	7.6	9.3	% Profit Before Taxes/Total Assets		10.2	10.1	9.6	10.4	6.0
.7	.9	1.3			2.4	2.8	1.3	2.8	1.3
121.7	149.5	180.2			262.0	515.5	253.4	113.4	59.5
48.6	59.4	58.0	Sales/Net Fixed Assets		74.1	102.9	71.7	58.6	30.8
21.0	27.4	25.3			28.4	41.2	25.0	28.0	19.9
6.4	6.7	6.5			5.5	8.1	6.8	7.3	5.0
4.7	4.8	4.6	Sales/Total Assets		4.1	5.9	4.7	5.1	4.0
3.3	3.4	3.5			3.3	4.1	3.7	3.9	2.7
.3	.3	.2			.2	.2	.3	.2	.6
(261) .6	(297) .6	(288) .6	% Depr., Dep., Amort./Sales	(56) .5	(41) .3	(69) .7	(64) .5	(54) .8	
1.2	1.1	1.1			1.3	1.1	1.0	.8	1.2
1.6	1.7	1.5			2.8	1.8	1.4	1.1	1.2
(162) 3.0	(210) 3.1	(218) 2.8	% Officers', Directors' Owners' Comp/Sales	(50) 4.2	(49) 2.9	(63) 2.4	(41) 2.1	(11) 1.6	
5.1	5.3	4.3			6.3	4.2	3.7	3.6	2.6
9487431M	10579641M	8741307M	Net Sales ($)	3877M	185861M	259211M	658067M	1283055M	6351236M
2354203M	2839091M	2596477M	Total Assets ($)	1145M	50303M	52084M	154644M	291733M	2046568M

M = $ thousand   MM = $ million
See Pages 9 through 22 for Explanation of Ratios and Data

Current Data Sorted by Assets   Comparative Historical Data

	0-500M	500M-2MM	2-10MM	10-50MM	50-100MM	100-250MM		5 1 6 8 14 / 4/1/05-3/31/06 ALL	6 2 4 20 7 / 4/1/06-3/31/07 ALL
Type of Statement									
Unqualified			2	7	1			5	6
Reviewed		1	3	1				1	2
Compiled	1	6	5					6	4
Tax Returns	6	9	5					8	20
Other	3	6	7	7	2			14	7
		16 (4/1-9/30/09)		56 (10/1/09-3/31/10)					
NUMBER OF STATEMENTS	10	22	22	15	3			34	39
	%	%	%	%	%	%		%	%
ASSETS									
Cash & Equivalents	6.4	16.7	14.1	7.6			D	4.5	8.1
Trade Receivables (net)	3.9	12.6	18.6	11.0			A	17.3	17.5
Inventory	53.2	50.6	47.3	30.5			T	47.9	45.3
All Other Current	10.1	1.3	1.8	2.4			A	3.0	4.0
Total Current	73.7	81.3	81.8	51.5				72.7	74.8
Fixed Assets (net)	14.1	8.3	13.0	36.5			N	13.3	14.0
Intangibles (net)	5.7	2.0	2.2	7.4			O	5.9	3.9
All Other Non-Current	6.5	8.4	3.0	4.6			T	8.1	7.4
Total	100.0	100.0	100.0	100.0				100.0	100.0
LIABILITIES							A		
Notes Payable-Short Term	26.6	7.8	9.3	8.8			V	17.3	19.8
Cur. Mat.-L.T.D.	3.8	2.3	1.6	1.9			A	1.5	3.3
Trade Payables	17.4	23.7	22.2	15.4			I	23.0	20.8
Income Taxes Payable	.0	.0	.1	.3			L	.2	.4
All Other Current	22.1	13.2	8.4	10.0			A	7.0	9.9
Total Current	69.9	47.1	41.7	36.5			B	49.0	54.3
Long-Term Debt	9.5	11.7	10.7	28.2			L	16.8	13.9
Deferred Taxes	.0	.0	.3	.2			E	.0	.0
All Other Non-Current	19.2	3.3	5.0	12.5				7.2	10.4
Net Worth	1.5	37.9	42.4	22.5				27.0	21.4
Total Liabilities & Net Worth	100.0	100.0	100.0	100.0				100.0	100.0
INCOME DATA									
Net Sales	100.0	100.0	100.0	100.0				100.0	100.0
Gross Profit	48.1	46.7	42.3	52.8				40.8	42.6
Operating Expenses	50.6	44.2	34.2	52.6				36.3	39.5
Operating Profit	-2.6	2.6	8.1	.1				4.6	3.2
All Other Expenses (net)	.6	.5	.4	-.1				1.1	1.1
Profit Before Taxes	-3.2	2.1	7.8	.2				3.5	2.1
RATIOS									
Current	8.3	4.6	4.1	2.3				3.8	3.1
	2.9	2.3	1.8	1.4				1.4	1.5
	.8	1.0	1.2	1.0				1.1	1.0
Quick	1.1	1.9	1.4	.9				.8	.9
	.2	.7	.8	.4				.3 (38)	.5
	.0	.4	.2	.2				.2	.2
Sales/Receivables	0 UND	0 UND	0 UND	5 70.4				3 121.9	0 UND
	0 UND	7 55.5	16 23.2	10 38.2				19 18.9	10 35.3
	2 213.6	25 14.3	48 7.5	47 7.8				53 6.9	32 11.3
Cost of Sales/Inventory	0 UND	52 7.0	71 5.1	71 5.1				70 5.2	46 8.0
	138 2.6	118 3.1	119 3.1	97 3.8				122 3.0	89 4.1
	231 1.6	158 2.3	175 2.1	167 2.2				209 1.7	194 1.9
Cost of Sales/Payables	0 UND	27 13.7	32 11.5	25 14.6				21 17.6	9 42.8
	26 14.1	36 10.2	33 11.0	50 7.3				42 8.8	37 10.0
	46 7.9	80 4.6	42 8.6	87 4.2				125 2.9	83 4.4
Sales/Working Capital	4.0	4.1	3.7	5.4				5.9	4.5
	4.6	11.6	9.1	27.6				12.4	15.3
	-22.8	NM	24.2	249.3				27.5	89.0
EBIT/Interest		9.9	39.7	7.2				7.0	5.7
	(16) 3.6	(16) 4.9	(11) 1.3					(30) 2.8	(30) 3.3
	-4.8	1.1	-.2					1.8	1.2
Net Profit + Depr., Dep., Amort./Cur. Mat. L/T/D									
Fixed/Worth	.0	.0	.0	.4				.1	.06
	.2	.1	.1	1.7				.4	.3
	-.4	.7	.9	-1.5				2.9	5.4
Debt/Worth	.3	.3	.6	.8				1.4	.8
	3.7	1.2	1.6	3.1				3.6	3.0
	-2.5	NM	4.9	-6.7				23.3	-7.5
% Profit Before Taxes/Tangible Net Worth		47.3	99.2					32.7	46.8
	(17) 19.0	27.3						(28) 21.2	(28) 26.4
	1.9	1.9						6.8	13.9
% Profit Before Taxes/Total Assets	10.2	18.0	39.1	5.2				10.9	14.6
	1.7	6.7	10.2	-1.3				4.8	5.0
	-15.3	-5.7	.3	-9.3				2.4	.4
Sales/Net Fixed Assets	157.3	831.9	268.9	16.5				108.4	192.0
	69.8	108.9	64.3	6.0				38.6	73.3
	6.5	43.9	15.9	4.7				11.6	16.1
Sales/Total Assets	3.1	4.3	3.7	3.2				3.2	5.1
	2.4	3.3	2.8	2.5				2.5	2.6
	1.5	2.2	2.1	1.4				1.8	1.7
% Depr., Dep., Amort./Sales		.1	.2	1.3				.3	.3
	(11) .1	(14) .7	(13) 3.8					(29) .6	(27) .8
	1.3	1.7	5.3					.9	1.7
% Officers', Directors' Owners' Comp/Sales								1.5	1.5
								(19) 2.5	(19) 1.9
								5.6	5.1
Net Sales ($)	7053M	74600M	308735M	904394M	419425M			813463M	1832206M
Total Assets ($)	3039M	22601M	102432M	433528M	204114M			380099M	791503M

M = $ thousand   MM = $ million
See Pages 9 through 22 for Explanation of Ratios and Data

Comparative Historical Data | Current Data Sorted by Sales

4/1/07-3/31/08 ALL	4/1/08-3/31/09 ALL	4/1/09-3/31/10 ALL		0-1MM	16 (4/1-9/30/09) 1-3MM	3-5MM	5-10MM	56 (10/1/09-3/31/10) 10-25MM	25MM & OVER
			Type of Statement						
7	7	10	Unqualified			1	1	2	7
8	6	5	Reviewed				1	1	2
6	12	12	Compiled		5	1	3	3	
12	19	20	Tax Returns	5	6	1	6	2	
16	24	25	Other	3	4	1	4	2	11
49	68	72	**NUMBER OF STATEMENTS**	8	15	4	15	10	20
%	%	%	**ASSETS**	%	%	%	%	%	%
11.0	11.5	12.6	Cash & Equivalents		18.2		13.2	14.4	10.2
16.8	13.4	13.1	Trade Receivables (net)		7.8		13.7	19.2	15.6
46.9	44.6	44.4	Inventory		57.2		48.1	48.7	29.3
2.6	2.8	3.4	All Other Current		1.5		1.0	.8	4.9
77.3	72.4	73.5	Total Current		84.8		76.1	83.1	60.1
10.7	16.6	16.9	Fixed Assets (net)		4.6		15.0	10.1	29.2
4.0	6.5	3.8	Intangibles (net)		2.7		1.4	4.4	5.9
8.0	4.5	5.8	All Other Non-Current		8.0		7.5	2.4	4.8
100.0	100.0	100.0	Total		100.0		100.0	100.0	100.0
			LIABILITIES						
14.3	16.6	11.0	Notes Payable-Short Term		10.4		10.8	7.0	8.9
1.2	1.5	2.2	Cur. Mat.-L.T.D.		3.1		1.4	.5	2.2
20.4	18.3	19.9	Trade Payables		18.2		17.6	23.3	19.2
.1	.0	.1	Income Taxes Payable		.0		.0	.0	.5
16.4	10.1	12.4	All Other Current		14.6		12.5	5.0	11.9
52.3	46.6	45.7	Total Current		46.3		42.3	35.8	42.8
11.7	19.3	14.3	Long-Term Debt		4.6		21.0	6.3	22.6
.3	.2	.2	Deferred Taxes		.0		.0	.4	.7
8.0	16.0	8.1	All Other Non-Current		2.3		2.5	7.5	10.3
27.8	17.7	31.7	Net Worth		46.9		34.2	49.9	23.6
100.0	100.0	100.0	Total Liabilities & Net Worth		100.0		100.0	100.0	100.0
			INCOME DATA						
100.0	100.0	100.0	Net Sales		100.0		100.0	100.0	100.0
45.3	43.7	47.7	Gross Profit		45.5		49.8	32.7	52.2
40.1	38.5	43.5	Operating Expenses		44.3		41.8	26.1	47.2
5.2	5.2	4.1	Operating Profit		1.2		8.0	6.6	5.0
.6	1.4	.8	All Other Expenses (net)		.7		.5	.2	1.7
4.6	3.8	3.3	Profit Before Taxes		.5		7.5	6.4	3.2
			RATIOS						
3.5	3.6	4.1	Current		5.0		3.6	5.5	2.2
1.8	1.8	1.7			2.6		1.5	3.2	1.4
1.0	1.1	1.1			1.0		1.1	1.4	1.1
1.6	1.3	1.3	Quick		1.8		1.4	1.7	.9
.5	.4	.6			.6		.5	1.2	.5
.3	.2	.2			.1		.2	.5	.2
2 241.7	2 153.9	0 UND	Sales/Receivables	0 UND	0 UND		0 UND	0 UND	6 61.4
21 17.7	12 31.0	7 54.1		1 266.8			6 57.9	22 16.8	11 32.8
47 7.8	28 13.1	32 11.3		15 23.7			29 12.4	48 7.5	41 8.8
78 4.7	63 5.8	68 5.3	Cost of Sales/Inventory	56 6.5			92 4.0	71 5.2	56 6.5
134 2.7	117 3.1	112 3.3		139 2.6			116 3.2	111 3.3	85 4.3
201 1.8	202 1.8	165 2.2		212 1.7			210 1.7	160 2.3	138 2.6
22 16.3	15 24.7	26 14.2	Cost of Sales/Payables	30 12.1			24 15.4	19 19.6	29 12.7
46 7.9	34 10.6	34 10.7		37 10.0			33 11.1	32 11.3	52 7.1
79 4.6	61 6.0	56 6.5		78 4.7			56 6.5	34 10.6	86 4.3
4.2	4.0	4.0	Sales/Working Capital		3.6		3.8	3.4	5.5
7.1	7.0	9.9			6.1		13.9	4.7	21.8
289.9	41.3	56.0			603.7		40.7	18.7	94.0
19.7	6.7	10.9	EBIT/Interest		14.3		22.1		50.7
(43) 6.0	(55) 2.3	(53) 3.2		(10) 3.6			(13) 4.0		(17) 2.0
1.7	-1.6	-.4			-24.0		.6		-.4
			Net Profit + Depr., Dep., Amort./Cur. Mat. L/T/D						
.1	.0	.0	Fixed/Worth		.0		.0	.0	.3
.3	.3	.3			.1		.3	.1	1.2
1.0	3.1	1.3			.5		.9	.4	-29.8
.7	.8	.6	Debt/Worth		.3		.6	.5	.8
2.5	2.1	1.6			.6		2.5	1.3	2.5
39.4	19.5	8.2			220.7		7.0	3.3	-59.4
57.7	39.5	54.3	% Profit Before Taxes/Tangible Net Worth		39.8		99.2	76.9	89.5
(38) 31.0	(53) 13.6	(57) 16.7		(12) 17.3			(14) 16.6	38.4	(14) 22.1
14.3	-1.6	.5			4.9		-9.7	5.1	-13.0
22.2	14.5	19.9	% Profit Before Taxes/Total Assets		20.8		66.3	33.2	16.0
9.8	4.9	5.3			6.8		5.9	12.3	-.2
1.1	-4.8	-4.2			-16.4		-1.8	5.1	-8.8
120.6	150.3	179.8	Sales/Net Fixed Assets		771.0		497.3	284.2	23.2
43.4	39.3	44.0			86.2		44.5	70.1	9.0
13.7	10.6	7.0			42.4		6.9	49.9	5.0
3.2	3.7	3.5	Sales/Total Assets		3.3		5.5	3.9	3.2
2.5	2.4	2.7			3.0		2.8	3.0	2.6
1.6	1.6	1.9			1.9		2.1	2.3	1.6
.3	.3	.2	% Depr., Dep., Amort./Sales						.8
(39) .8	(50) 1.1	(46) 1.3							(18) 1.9
1.4	2.1	3.2							4.0
1.8	1.5	1.3	% Officers', Directors' Owners' Comp/Sales						
(21) 2.7	(30) 2.9	(26) 3.4							
8.4	5.7	7.7							
1216371M	1431678M	1714207M	Net Sales ($)	4113M	28143M	16650M	107565M	159442M	1398294M
605558M	751535M	765714M	Total Assets ($)	2858M	11451M	5698M	39438M	86190M	620079M

M = $ thousand   MM = $ million
See Pages 9 through 22 for Explanation of Ratios and Data

Current Data Sorted by Assets

Comparative Historical Data

0-500M	500M-2MM	2-10MM	10-50MM	50-100MM	100-250MM	Type of Statement	4/1/05-3/31/06 ALL	4/1/06-3/31/07 ALL
		1	1			Unqualified	1	4
		1	1			Reviewed	1	5
2	1	2				Compiled	9	10
12	8	2				Tax Returns	24	18
9	6	4	1	.	1	Other	20	9
	7 (4/1-9/30/09)		45 (10/1/09-3/31/10)					
23	15	10	3		1	**NUMBER OF STATEMENTS**	55	46
%	%	%	%	%	%	**ASSETS**	%	%
20.4	8.9	5.8				Cash & Equivalents	13.9	13.8
2.5	7.7	21.5				Trade Receivables (net)	11.5	11.9
28.8	33.5	13.9				Inventory	29.8	29.7
2.3	3.4	1.5				All Other Current	1.4	2.0
54.0	53.5	42.7				Total Current	56.6	57.4
26.3	17.7	32.2				Fixed Assets (net)	24.0	23.6
12.3	9.4	7.4				Intangibles (net)	6.5	11.3
7.5	19.4	17.7				All Other Non-Current	12.8	7.8
100.0	100.0	100.0				Total	100.0	100.0
						LIABILITIES		
2.7	10.6	5.3				Notes Payable-Short Term	6.5	6.9
6.1	1.8	18.0				Cur. Mat.-L.T.D.	8.3	4.8
16.2	21.6	26.3				Trade Payables	14.9	20.3
.0	.0	.1				Income Taxes Payable	.1	.0
17.0	4.6	63.1				All Other Current	16.9	15.0
42.0	38.6	112.8				Total Current	46.7	47.0
12.1	25.5	15.1				Long-Term Debt	22.2	34.1
.0	.0	.1				Deferred Taxes	.2	.1
14.8	5.5	1.5				All Other Non-Current	13.9	8.3
31.0	30.4	-29.5				Net Worth	17.0	10.6
100.0	100.0	100.0				Total Liabilities & Net Worth	100.0	100.0
						INCOME DATA		
100.0	100.0	100.0				Net Sales	100.0	100.0
63.4	58.1	47.4				Gross Profit	52.2	57.1
56.2	53.3	45.9				Operating Expenses	47.0	50.1
7.2	4.8	1.5				Operating Profit	5.2	7.1
.4	.3	.5				All Other Expenses (net)	1.6	1.5
6.8	4.5	.9				Profit Before Taxes	3.6	5.5
						RATIOS		
2.2	2.8	1.4					2.5	2.6
1.3	1.4	1.0				Current	1.5	1.5
1.0	.8	.7					.8	.8
.6	.6	.9					1.4	1.4
.3	.4	.3				Quick	(53) .6	(44) .8
.1	.0	.1					.2	.3
0 UND	0 UND	1 260.3					2 167.1	0 UND
0 UND	1 371.6	7 50.0				Sales/Receivables	8 47.0	9 41.3
2 156.8	16 22.4	33 11.1					19 18.9	22 16.7
45 8.1	43 8.4	6 56.6					47 7.7	41 8.9
129 2.8	91 4.0	40 9.0				Cost of Sales/Inventory	74 4.9	64 5.7
181 2.0	201 1.8	193 1.9					140 2.6	99 3.7
16 22.9	22 16.8	20 18.1					6 59.0	19 19.3
38 9.6	45 8.2	44 8.4				Cost of Sales/Payables	32 11.5	31 11.7
141 2.6	138 2.7	103 3.5					52 7.0	77 4.7
10.4	14.6	65.3					6.7	8.9
20.4	23.8	-211.7				Sales/Working Capital	14.4	27.3
UND	-24.9	-9.8					-20.4	-18.4
45.5	29.6						10.9	13.5
(10) 6.3	(13) 3.5					EBIT/Interest	(44) 4.0	(37) 2.5
2.2	1.5						.5	.5
						Net Profit + Depr., Dep., Amort./Cur. Mat. L/T/D		
.3	.2	.6					.1	.2
.8	.5	1.6				Fixed/Worth	.9	1.2
-1.4	-2.8	NM					UND	-1.1
.7	1.1	.5					1.0	1.0
1.7	4.1	8.9				Debt/Worth	6.3	5.9
-6.7	-9.0	NM					-20.9	-4.2
150.0	105.3						78.3	115.4
(15) 94.6	(11) 42.0					% Profit Before Taxes/Tangible Net Worth	(39) 31.9	(29) 49.4
30.7	36.1						6.1	9.5
43.1	34.1	8.8					24.4	26.1
26.6	9.2	4.2				% Profit Before Taxes/Total Assets	9.7	7.3
.0	1.8	-.6					1.1	-.4
235.0	120.9	25.8					50.8	93.3
12.3	25.6	6.4				Sales/Net Fixed Assets	17.4	25.5
5.6	9.4	3.5					7.7	7.5
4.8	3.8	3.6					3.4	5.3
2.6	2.4	2.3				Sales/Total Assets	2.8	3.2
1.8	1.4	1.7					1.9	2.2
	.4						.8	.8
	(10) .7					% Depr., Dep., Amort./Sales	(45) 1.5	(32) 1.6
	3.0						2.9	2.5
							2.4	2.2
						% Officers', Directors' Owners' Comp/Sales	(23) 4.6	(22) 7.0
							8.5	15.8
20920M	48359M	177819M	250625M		229685M	Net Sales ($)	1080128M	915311M
5504M	15019M	53070M	63005M		112221M	Total Assets ($)	435705M	551932M

Note: The 50-100MM column is marked "DATA NOT AVAILABLE."

M = $ thousand   MM = $ million
See Pages 9 through 22 for Explanation of Ratios and Data

Comparative Historical Data

Current Data Sorted by Sales

			Type of Statement						
	1	2	Unqualified				1		1
3	5	2	Reviewed				1		1
7	3	5	Compiled	2	2		1		
20	12	22	Tax Returns	8	6	3	4	1	
13	15	21	Other	9	3	3	1	1	4
4/1/07-3/31/08 ALL	4/1/08-3/31/09 ALL	4/1/09-3/31/10 ALL		0-1MM	1-3MM	3-5MM	5-10MM	10-25MM	25MM & OVER
				7 (4/1-9/30/09)			45 (10/1/09-3/31/10)		
43	36	52	NUMBER OF STATEMENTS	19	11	6	8	2	6
%	%	%	ASSETS	%	%	%	%	%	%
11.9	13.2	13.4	Cash & Equivalents	15.6	8.8				
14.4	15.5	9.1	Trade Receivables (net)	4.0	3.9				
25.3	26.1	26.3	Inventory	30.7	27.2				
3.1	2.5	2.5	All Other Current	2.7	.0				
54.6	57.3	51.3	Total Current	53.0	40.0				
25.4	25.9	25.7	Fixed Assets (net)	22.8	24.5				
11.0	8.4	10.3	Intangibles (net)	13.9	11.5				
8.9	8.4	12.6	All Other Non-Current	10.3	24.0				
100.0	100.0	100.0	Total	100.0	100.0				
			LIABILITIES						
13.1	8.5	5.8	Notes Payable-Short Term	3.9	8.3				
5.5	6.1	7.1	Cur. Mat.-L.T.D.	6.5	1.8				
25.6	15.2	19.9	Trade Payables	18.2	14.3				
.0	.2	.0	Income Taxes Payable	.0	.0				
13.9	19.1	21.8	All Other Current	17.1	7.3				
58.2	49.1	54.7	Total Current	45.8	31.8				
22.4	21.9	17.3	Long-Term Debt	10.9	30.8				
.0	.0	.1	Deferred Taxes	.0	.0				
9.1	10.6	8.6	All Other Non-Current	19.1	3.2				
10.3	18.4	19.3	Net Worth	24.3	34.2				
100.0	100.0	100.0	Total Liabilties & Net Worth	100.0	100.0				
			INCOME DATA						
100.0	100.0	100.0	Net Sales	100.0	100.0				
58.9	56.1	58.5	Gross Profit	61.9	58.5				
52.8	49.3	52.9	Operating Expenses	55.4	51.8				
6.1	6.8	5.6	Operating Profit	6.5	6.7				
1.3	1.7	.5	All Other Expenses (net)	.4	.8				
4.8	5.1	5.1	Profit Before Taxes	6.1	5.9				
			RATIOS						
2.2	2.7	2.2	Current	2.2	2.7				
1.1	1.2	1.3		1.2	1.3				
.6	.8	.9		.9	.8				
1.3	1.1	.8	Quick	.4	.5				
.6	.6	.4		.2	.3				
.1	.2	.1		.1	.0				
0 UND	1 495.8	0 UND	Sales/Receivables	0 UND	0 UND				
9 39.6	12 31.4	1 404.6		0 UND	1 500.5				
21 17.5	22 16.9	16 23.2		7 54.3	14 26.9				
22 16.6	32 11.3	35 10.5	Cost of Sales/Inventory	71 5.2	57 6.4				
63 5.8	76 4.8	90 4.0		144 2.5	117 3.1				
107 3.4	128 2.9	183 2.0		242 1.5	201 1.8				
15 24.7	2 189.7	21 17.4	Cost of Sales/Payables	16 22.9	22 16.8				
36 10.0	28 13.2	46 8.0		80 4.6	38 9.5				
70 5.3	46 7.9	122 3.0		149 2.5	104 3.5				
12.7	11.6	12.6	Sales/Working Capital	9.2	18.5				
82.0	31.3	30.3		18.5	39.3				
-22.0	-27.8	-38.8		-33.6	-16.4				
11.5	12.1	27.6	EBIT/Interest						
(33) 3.3	(28) 3.4	(36) 4.4							
1.0	1.5	2.3							
			Net Profit + Depr., Dep., Amort./Cur. Mat. L/T/D						
.3	.3	.3	Fixed/Worth	.2	.1				
1.4	.9	.8		.8	.8				
-.8	-1.7	NM		-1.4	-2.6				
1.1	.7	.8	Debt/Worth	1.1	.7				
3.4	6.4	3.3		6.4	4.1				
-3.0	-5.2	-11.6		-3.5	-7.8				
72.6	77.8	145.1	% Profit Before Taxes/Tangible Net Worth	142.0					
(28) 24.8	(23) 47.6	(38) 66.4		(12) 98.2					
2.0	7.3	30.5		34.5					
33.3	31.4	30.0	% Profit Before Taxes/Total Assets	28.2	42.8				
9.5	10.2	9.3		12.0	7.5				
.0	2.7	1.6		.0	-3.6				
101.4	70.3	69.5	Sales/Net Fixed Assets	235.0	44.9				
21.8	16.7	13.2		11.0	14.2				
8.8	6.8	5.5		4.3	3.9				
6.1	5.6	3.8	Sales/Total Assets	3.7	3.1				
3.6	2.6	2.5		2.1	1.9				
2.4	1.8	1.7		1.5	1.3				
.4	.5	.5	% Depr., Dep., Amort./Sales						
(29) 1.3	(25) 1.9	(30) 1.2							
2.4	5.1	2.7							
1.9	7.0	2.7	% Officers', Directors' Owners' Comp/Sales						
(21) 4.5	(13) 9.6	(23) 6.9							
7.0	12.4	12.3							
747487M	629321M	727408M	Net Sales ($)	9516M	16190M	22202M	52720M	37001M	589779M
406937M	285235M	248819M	Total Assets ($)	5213M	12422M	7724M	21788M	14089M	187583M

© RMA 2010

M = $ thousand   MM = $ million
See Pages 9 through 22 for Explanation of Ratios and Data

Current Data Sorted by Assets							Comparative Historical Data	
						Type of Statement		
		1	2		2	Unqualified	2	4
		2				Reviewed		
	2	1				Compiled	1	1
8	3	3				Tax Returns	3	4
5	6	2	2	1		Other	4	4
	1 (4/1-9/30/09)		39 (10/1/09-3/31/10)					
0-500M	**500M-2MM**	**2-10MM**	**10-50MM**	**50-100MM**	**100-250MM**		**4/1/05-3/31/06 ALL**	**4/1/06-3/31/07 ALL**
13	11	9	4	1	2	**NUMBER OF STATEMENTS**	10	13
%	%	%	%	%	%	**ASSETS**	%	%
13.0	6.7					Cash & Equivalents	10.9	7.0
6.5	18.0					Trade Receivables (net)	23.4	17.5
30.3	22.3					Inventory	35.0	39.5
10.1	.3					All Other Current	1.4	5.3
59.9	47.3					Total Current	70.8	69.3
27.6	13.9					Fixed Assets (net)	19.1	21.3
8.2	16.5					Intangibles (net)	6.6	5.2
4.3	22.3					All Other Non-Current	3.5	4.2
100.0	100.0					Total	100.0	100.0
						LIABILITIES		
10.8	12.2					Notes Payable-Short Term	10.3	15.0
11.0	3.5					Cur. Mat.-L.T.D.	3.4	2.7
27.9	31.1					Trade Payables	15.0	22.5
.0	.0					Income Taxes Payable	1.2	.8
6.0	21.7					All Other Current	30.2	8.7
55.6	68.6					Total Current	60.1	49.7
40.5	15.1					Long-Term Debt	19.2	29.0
.0	.0					Deferred Taxes	.5	.4
36.2	5.9					All Other Non-Current	9.7	5.7
-32.0	10.5					Net Worth	10.6	15.3
100.0	100.0					Total Liabilties & Net Worth	100.0	100.0
						INCOME DATA		
100.0	100.0					Net Sales	100.0	100.0
64.4	46.5					Gross Profit	41.9	44.4
58.9	42.9					Operating Expenses	33.9	38.7
5.5	3.6					Operating Profit	8.0	5.7
1.2	1.5					All Other Expenses (net)	.9	1.5
4.3	2.1					Profit Before Taxes	7.1	4.2
						RATIOS		
3.0	2.8						2.5	1.9
1.7	1.0					Current	1.7	1.4
.7	.2						1.0	1.0
1.3	1.0						1.7	.9
.3	.4					Quick	.7	.4
.1	.1						.1	.2
0 UND	**0** UND						**0** UND	**1** 357.4
0 UND	**2** 149.1					Sales/Receivables	**16** 23.5	**14** 26.6
0 UND	**30** 12.3						**33** 11.2	**37** 9.9
28 12.9	**7** 54.5						**3** 143.8	**39** 9.3
91 4.0	**49** 7.5					Cost of Sales/Inventory	**31** 11.8	**65** 5.6
126 2.9	**60** 6.1						**101** 3.6	**156** 2.3
0 UND	**10** 35.4						**9** 39.8	**17** 21.1
4 103.0	**53** 6.8					Cost of Sales/Payables	**17** 21.2	**39** 9.3
46 8.0	**79** 4.6						**40** 9.2	**82** 4.5
9.4	11.7						7.2	8.6
50.0	296.3					Sales/Working Capital	11.3	22.0
-20.6	-4.5						NM	177.9
								7.5
						EBIT/Interest		(11) 2.2
								-3.1
						Net Profit + Depr., Dep., Amort./Cur. Mat. L/T/D		
.7	.2						.1	.3
2.7	.5					Fixed/Worth	.3	2.2
-.2	-.4						-1.1	-1.4
.9	1.7						.8	1.5
-2.9	2.7					Debt/Worth	2.7	8.5
-1.7	-1.9						-5.0	-6.2
						% Profit Before Taxes/Tangible Net Worth		
19.1	21.5						60.3	26.5
16.3	5.6					% Profit Before Taxes/Total Assets	16.6	11.5
-.4	-.8						9.5	-6.7
204.9	105.5						128.5	73.5
23.2	29.6					Sales/Net Fixed Assets	52.8	12.7
9.4	14.7						16.8	10.6
9.1	7.1						5.6	4.3
4.7	3.6					Sales/Total Assets	3.8	3.3
2.3	1.7						2.8	2.3
								.3
						% Depr., Dep., Amort./Sales		1.1
								1.7
						% Officers', Directors' Owners' Comp/Sales		
12640M	**44855M**	**293698M**	**430333M**	**86817M**	**487534M**	Net Sales ($)	**543992M**	**640153M**
2578M	**10468M**	**49023M**	**115292M**	**58830M**	**208209M**	Total Assets ($)	**167366M**	**203043M**

M = $ thousand MM = $ million

See Pages 9 through 22 for Explanation of Ratios and Data

Comparative Historical Data · Current Data Sorted by Sales

		Comparative Historical Data		Type of Statement			Current Data Sorted by Sales			
				Unqualified	3	5	5			
				Reviewed	2	2	2			
				Compiled	1	2	3			
				Tax Returns	6	3	14			
				Other	4	10	16			

	4/1/07-3/31/08 ALL	4/1/08-3/31/09 ALL	4/1/09-3/31/10 ALL		0-1MM	1-3MM	3-5MM	5-10MM	10-25MM	25MM & OVER
Type of Statement						1 (4/1-9/30/09)		39 (10/1/09-3/31/10)		
Unqualified						1		1	2	5
Reviewed										
Compiled										1
Tax Returns					8	2	1	1	1	1
Other					2	5	2	2		5
NUMBER OF STATEMENTS	16	22	40		10	8	3	4	3	12
ASSETS	%	%	%		%	%	%	%	%	%
Cash & Equivalents	10.8	11.9	13.3		9.2					22.8
Trade Receivables (net)	10.1	13.8	12.5		8.4					9.0
Inventory	33.6	31.5	27.5		29.6					28.2
All Other Current	6.1	12.3	7.0		10.4					11.3
Total Current	60.6	69.6	60.3		57.7					71.4
Fixed Assets (net)	19.9	21.7	20.7		26.0					19.3
Intangibles (net)	6.7	5.6	9.2		10.0					2.1
All Other Non-Current	12.8	3.1	9.8		6.4					7.3
Total	100.0	100.0	100.0		100.0					100.0
LIABILITIES										
Notes Payable-Short Term	12.6	11.4	9.2		3.3					2.5
Cur. Mat.-L.T.D.	.9	3.1	5.5		13.6					3.3
Trade Payables	17.3	18.0	23.7		8.3					14.7
Income Taxes Payable	.2	.8	.0		.0					.1
All Other Current	9.8	18.8	15.8		5.8					24.5
Total Current	40.8	52.1	54.3		31.0					45.2
Long-Term Debt	25.4	35.7	21.1		51.8					8.5
Deferred Taxes	.0	.3	.0		.0					.0
All Other Non-Current	26.1	15.8	17.3		36.1					6.8
Net Worth	7.7	-3.8	7.3		-18.5					39.5
Total Liabilities & Net Worth	100.0	100.0	100.0		100.0					100.0
INCOME DATA										
Net Sales	100.0	100.0	100.0		100.0					100.0
Gross Profit	51.3	48.5	54.7		59.0					58.3
Operating Expenses	50.5	41.1	48.7		54.8					48.7
Operating Profit	.8	7.4	6.1		4.2					9.6
All Other Expenses (net)	1.7	1.3	1.2		1.4					1.0
Profit Before Taxes	-.9	6.1	4.9		2.8					8.6
RATIOS										
Current	3.1	2.2	3.0		5.4					3.3
	1.5	1.4	1.5		2.6					1.5
	1.0	.9	.9		1.3					1.3
Quick	1.0	1.2	1.5		2.2					1.6
	.3	.4	.5		.5					.9
	.1	.1	.1		.1					.1
Sales/Receivables	0 UND	1 561.1	0 UND		0 UND					2 239.0
	2 165.7	8 45.1	3 136.8		0 UND					7 50.4
	19 18.8	47 7.8	17 21.0		14 26.1					15 24.7
Cost of Sales/Inventory	25 14.4	47 7.7	26 13.9		44 8.3					34 10.6
	73 5.0	81 4.5	59 6.2		111 3.3					82 4.5
	153 2.4	101 3.6	104 3.5		130 2.8					101 3.6
Cost of Sales/Payables	21 17.0	11 32.6	4 103.1		0 UND					18 20.8
	34 10.6	32 11.4	24 15.2		0 UND					24 15.4
	60 6.1	62 5.9	60 6.1		42 8.7					61 6.0
Sales/Working Capital	5.4	6.2	11.2		4.3					5.8
	19.5	18.0	27.2		14.4					14.2
	NM	-70.3	-48.1		NM					35.4
EBIT/Interest	7.3	19.1	20.0							164.5
	(14) 1.6	(15) 4.8	(30) 3.6						(10)	23.0
	-9.6	.6	1.2							4.5
Net Profit + Depr., Dep., Amort./Cur. Mat. L/T/D										
Fixed/Worth	.2	.2	.2		.3					.2
	.4	1.3	1.0		2.0					.4
	NM	-.8	-.5		-.3					1.1
Debt/Worth	1.0	1.3	.9		.8					.4
	4.0	1.7	2.5		NM					1.7
	NM	-4.7	-2.3		-1.7					2.9
% Profit Before Taxes/Tangible Net Worth	248.7	112.8	105.3							160.5
	(12) 31.0	(13) 50.7	(25) 45.0						(11)	51.6
	-7.4	21.8	18.7							45.0
% Profit Before Taxes/Total Assets	21.4	39.4	32.7		18.6					44.5
	3.6	17.2	16.8		11.2					30.2
	-10.9	1.7	.6		-6.1					10.3
Sales/Net Fixed Assets	73.3	95.1	104.0		UND					99.3
	24.8	13.3	25.9		20.0					13.4
	6.6	7.9	10.5		8.1					8.8
Sales/Total Assets	4.9	5.1	7.1		6.2					6.5
	2.6	3.2	4.0		3.7					3.2
	1.2	2.3	2.4		1.6					2.6
% Depr., Dep., Amort./Sales	.3	.4	.5							.5
	(12) 1.1	(16) 1.0	(26) 1.0						(10)	.9
	2.9	2.5	2.3							1.8
% Officers', Directors' Owners' Comp/Sales			2.7							
		(14)	9.8							
			14.6							
Net Sales ($)	710699M	2716142M	1355877M		4485M	15740M	13125M	32898M	50538M	1239091M
Total Assets ($)	341564M	963324M	444400M		1868M	5857M	1621M	6642M	10249M	418163M

© RMA 2010

M = $ thousand   MM = $ million
See Pages 9 through 22 for Explanation of Ratios and Data

Current Data Sorted by Assets   Comparative Historical Data

0-500M	500M-2MM	2-10MM	10-50MM	50-100MM	100-250MM	Type of Statement	4/1/05-3/31/06 ALL	4/1/06-3/31/07 ALL
						Unqualified	3	4
						Reviewed	2	
	2	3				Compiled	5	3
4	5	3				Tax Returns	7	3
1	4	3	1	1	1	Other	7	5
		7 (4/1-9/30/09)		24 (10/1/09-3/31/10)				
6	11	8	3	2	1	NUMBER OF STATEMENTS	24	15
%	%	%	%	%	%	**ASSETS**	%	%
	8.1					Cash & Equivalents	10.5	11.6
	30.7					Trade Receivables (net)	32.5	41.0
	24.1					Inventory	24.1	23.8
	.6					All Other Current	1.4	1.0
	63.5					Total Current	68.5	77.4
	29.0					Fixed Assets (net)	18.4	12.4
	6.0					Intangibles (net)	6.3	2.9
	1.4					All Other Non-Current	6.8	7.2
	100.0					Total	100.0	100.0
						LIABILITIES		
	5.0					Notes Payable-Short Term	12.8	11.5
	2.5					Cur. Mat.-L.T.D.	4.9	6.0
	29.2					Trade Payables	23.0	17.3
	3.2					Income Taxes Payable	.6	1.3
	16.5					All Other Current	9.0	8.4
	56.5					Total Current	50.4	44.5
	22.3					Long-Term Debt	15.3	9.4
	.0					Deferred Taxes	.0	.2
	12.9					All Other Non-Current	3.2	6.8
	8.4					Net Worth	31.1	39.1
	100.0					Total Liabilities & Net Worth	100.0	100.0
						INCOME DATA		
	100.0					Net Sales	100.0	100.0
	51.1					Gross Profit	48.0	50.4
	47.2					Operating Expenses	42.4	45.0
	3.9					Operating Profit	5.5	5.5
	1.3					All Other Expenses (net)	1.0	-.1
	2.6					Profit Before Taxes	4.5	5.5
						RATIOS		
	2.2					Current	2.7	3.7
	1.5						1.3	1.4
	.8						1.0	1.2
	1.3					Quick	1.4	3.1
	.9						.8	1.1
	.6						.6	.7
	21 17.5					Sales/Receivables	14 26.0	30 12.1
	53 6.9						37 9.9	44 8.3
	59 6.2						57 6.4	78 4.7
	2 175.0					Cost of Sales/Inventory	18 20.1	23 16.2
	43 8.5						33 11.2	46 7.9
	52 7.0						95 3.8	110 3.3
	19 19.6					Cost of Sales/Payables	21 17.6	12 31.0
	49 7.5						43 8.4	28 13.1
	74 4.9						67 5.5	67 5.5
	8.9					Sales/Working Capital	9.1	6.1
	17.3						24.3	9.7
	-21.3						NM	27.4
	59.7					EBIT/Interest	13.5	17.2
(10)	3.2						(21) 6.7	(13) 5.9
	1.3						1.0	3.9
						Net Profit + Depr., Dep., Amort./Cur. Mat. L/T/D		
	.2					Fixed/Worth	.2	.1
	-22.3						.8	.2
	-3.0						7.8	.7
	2.0					Debt/Worth	1.1	.7
	-58.9						2.5	2.5
	-6.9						32.0	6.1
						% Profit Before Taxes/Tangible Net Worth	76.0	46.6
							(20) 39.8	(14) 27.1
							16.9	9.4
	12.5					% Profit Before Taxes/Total Assets	21.6	23.4
	8.0						11.4	12.4
	.0						.2	5.5
	67.1					Sales/Net Fixed Assets	49.9	106.0
	15.4						24.7	38.4
	5.0						13.9	12.8
	4.3					Sales/Total Assets	4.2	4.8
	2.8						3.3	3.2
	2.2						2.3	2.1
						% Depr., Dep., Amort./Sales	.8	.4
							(19) 1.4	(10) 1.3
							2.6	3.3
						% Officers', Directors' Owners' Comp/Sales	3.8	
							(14) 5.9	
							9.7	
8672M	41777M	107258M	289999M	197086M	421778M	Net Sales ($)	942222M	320112M
2100M	12823M	37609M	68339M	164231M	120209M	Total Assets ($)	385352M	141629M

M = $ thousand   MM = $ million
See Pages 9 through 22 for Explanation of Ratios and Data

Comparative Historical Data · Current Data Sorted by Sales

			Type of Statement	0-1MM	1-3MM	3-5MM	5-10MM	10-25MM	25MM & OVER
2	6	4	Unqualified				1	1	3
1	1.	2	Reviewed		1			1	
6	5	5	Compiled		1		3	1	
2	8	9	Tax Returns	2	4	3	2		
11	12	11	Other	1	1	2		2	2
4/1/07-3/31/08 ALL	4/1/08-3/31/09 ALL	4/1/09-3/31/10 ALL		7 (4/1-9/30/09)			24 (10/1/09-3/31/10)		
22	32	31	NUMBER OF STATEMENTS	3	7	5	6	5	5
%	%	%	ASSETS	%	%	%	%	%	%
7.5	7.7	8.6	Cash & Equivalents						
33.5	28.8	32.5	Trade Receivables (net)						
20.5	17.9	22.8	Inventory						
2.7	4.6	6.2	All Other Current						
64.2	59.0	70.1	Total Current						
18.9	16.8	18.8	Fixed Assets (net)						
9.6	17.0	5.2	Intangibles (net)						
7.3	7.2	5.9	All Other Non-Current						
100.0	100.0	100.0	Total						
			LIABILITIES						
25.7	13.0	7.9	Notes Payable-Short Term						
4.1	3.4	3.9	Cur. Mat.-L.T.D.						
20.3	21.0	29.2	Trade Payables						
1.1	1.0	1.5	Income Taxes Payable						
9.5	9.2	17.4	All Other Current						
60.7	47.5	59.8	Total Current						
12.1	11.2	17.1	Long-Term Debt						
.4	.6	.3	Deferred Taxes						
5.2	3.5	6.0	All Other Non-Current						
21.6	37.1	16.8	Net Worth						
100.0	100.0	100.0	Total Liabilities & Net Worth						
			INCOME DATA						
100.0	100.0	100.0	Net Sales						
53.9	54.9	52.9	Gross Profit						
50.4	49.2	47.6	Operating Expenses						
3.5	5.7	5.2	Operating Profit						
1.5	1.0	1.6	All Other Expenses (net)						
1.9	4.7	3.7	Profit Before Taxes						
			RATIOS						
2.4	1.7	2.3							
1.1	1.2	1.4	Current						
.9	.9	1.0							
1.3	1.3	1.2							
.9	.9 (30)	.8	Quick						
.4	.5	.5							
22 16.8	12 30.2	15 24.3							
37 9.9	42 8.7	52 7.0	Sales/Receivables						
71 5.1	56 6.5	61 5.9							
26 13.8	20 18.3	14 26.6							
37 9.7	40 9.0	43 8.5	Cost of Sales/Inventory						
81 4.5	55 6.7	63 5.8							
24 14.9	27 13.6	26 14.1							
57 6.5	60 6.1	50 7.3	Cost of Sales/Payables						
107 3.4	81 4.5	99 3.7							
8.1	9.1	7.9							
68.6	24.0	17.4	Sales/Working Capital						
-76.5	-48.0	-135.8							
22.6	34.0	14.9							
(21) 4.8	(27) 5.9	(25) 4.1	EBIT/Interest						
-.5	2.1	1.7							
			Net Profit + Depr., Dep., Amort./Cur. Mat. L/T/D						
.3	.3	.2							
.8	.8	.9	Fixed/Worth						
NM	-.9	-3.0							
1.1	1.0	1.3							
3.0	2.6	4.3	Debt/Worth						
NM	-11.7	-13.8							
57.2	90.6	95.8	% Profit Before Taxes/Tangible Net Worth						
(17) 40.8	(23) 28.7	(21) 36.5							
-8.9	15.6	13.4							
20.5	24.7	23.3	% Profit Before Taxes/Total Assets						
5.2	7.7	8.9							
-5.6	2.6	.4							
52.0	97.9	82.3							
18.3	26.3	26.6	Sales/Net Fixed Assets						
9.0	9.3	13.3							
4.0	3.8	4.5							
2.9	2.7	3.4	Sales/Total Assets						
2.0	2.0	2.0							
.7	.7	.6							
(19) 1.5	(21) 1.1	(23) 1.2	% Depr., Dep., Amort./Sales						
4.0	4.3	5.8							
	2.3	3.7	% Officers', Directors' Owners' Comp/Sales						
	(16) 7.0	(16) 5.7							
	18.8	11.9							
331576M	1014568M	1066570M	Net Sales ($)	1583M	14897M	21185M	40604M	98619M	889682M
171495M	422442M	405311M	Total Assets ($)	1438M	4413M	6865M	15949M	35628M	341018M

M = $ thousand   MM = $ million
See Pages 9 through 22 for Explanation of Ratios and Data

Current Data Sorted by Assets						Type of Statement	Comparative Historical Data	
1	24	7 42	45 42	20 5	20 2	Unqualified Reviewed	68 71	93 107
7 47	47	53	26	2		Compiled	133	179
293	214	87	6		3	Tax Returns	215	376
70	72	78	69	19	14	Other	153	254
	160 (4/1-9/30/09)		1,155 (10/1/09-3/31/10)				4/1/05- 3/31/06	4/1/06- 3/31/07
0-500M	500M-2MM	2-10MM	10-50MM	50-100MM	100-250MM		ALL	ALL
418	357	267	188	46	39	**NUMBER OF STATEMENTS**	640	1009
%	%	%	%	%	%	**ASSETS**	%	%
16.7	10.4	9.5	9.8	10.5	7.2	Cash & Equivalents	11.1	11.7
4.1	3.8	7.2	8.3	9.0	4.6	Trade Receivables (net)	7.4	7.4
38.0	14.4	11.7	12.5	10.2	9.0	Inventory	20.7	18.9
2.2	1.9	1.8	2.6	2.2	1.8	All Other Current	2.6	2.7
61.0	30.4	30.2	33.2	31.9	22.5	Total Current	41.7	40.7
22.3	54.1	55.9	52.7	58.0	65.2	Fixed Assets (net)	46.6	47.0
10.5	7.4	5.7	4.5	3.6	4.5	Intangibles (net)	5.6	7.2
6.2	8.0	8.2	9.6	6.5	7.8	All Other Non-Current	6.1	5.2
100.0	100.0	100.0	100.0	100.0	100.0	Total	100.0	100.0
						LIABILITIES		
4.1	5.4	4.5	3.5	3.8	2.5	Notes Payable-Short Term	3.6	4.6
1.9	2.8	3.6	4.2	4.0	3.3	Cur. Mat.-L.T.D.	3.0	3.0
19.8	10.5	14.1	19.4	16.5	14.1	Trade Payables	17.2	17.7
.1	.0	.1	.2	.2	.3	Income Taxes Payable	.2	.2
16.1	9.3	7.9	7.5	7.9	6.3	All Other Current	9.3	10.9
42.0	28.0	30.3	35.0	32.4	26.4	Total Current	33.3	36.3
21.7	49.6	43.6	31.9	31.3	35.4	Long-Term Debt	36.6	36.8
.0	.2	.2	.9	.8	.5	Deferred Taxes	.5	.2
21.5	8.5	4.2	3.7	5.0	6.3	All Other Non-Current	10.3	9.0
14.8	13.7	21.7	28.5	30.4	31.3	Net Worth	19.4	17.7
100.0	100.0	100.0	100.0	100.0	100.0	Total Liabilities & Net Worth	100.0	100.0
						INCOME DATA		
100.0	100.0	100.0	100.0	100.0	100.0	Net Sales	100.0	100.0
13.7	14.2	14.1	12.2	12.3	9.5	Gross Profit	13.4	12.5
13.6	12.6	13.2	11.5	10.8	8.3	Operating Expenses	12.5	11.7
.2	1.5	.9	.7	1.6	1.2	Operating Profit	.8	.7
-.4	.6	.4	-.1	-.1	.0	All Other Expenses (net)	.1	.1
.6	.9	.5	.8	1.6	1.2	Profit Before Taxes	.8	.6
						RATIOS		
4.7	3.1	1.8	1.3	1.2	1.0		2.5	2.1
2.0	1.5	1.1	.9	.9	.8	Current	1.3	1.2
1.0	.8	.7	.7	.7	.5		.8	.7
1.5	1.3	1.0	.8	.7	.6		1.1	1.0
.5	(355) .6	.5	.5	.5	.3	Quick	(634) .6	(1004) .5
.2	.2	.2	.3	.4	.2		.3	.2
0 UND	0 UND	0 UND	2 170.6	3 136.4	2 204.0		0 UND	0 UND
0 UND	0 999.8	2 210.9	4 101.9	4 84.2	3 126.0	Sales/Receivables	2 212.5	2 223.1
1 380.5	2 190.7	5 75.5	6 57.1	6 57.6	5 78.7		5 73.8	5 76.7
6 61.6	6 60.7	6 66.8	5 67.1	5 76.7	4 83.8		6 63.1	5 75.5
10 37.4	10 38.1	8 45.0	9 40.1	8 43.0	8 46.5	Cost of Sales/Inventory	9 40.9	8 47.1
16 22.6	16 23.5	13 28.5	13 29.0	11 31.8	10 36.6		13 27.9	12 30.8
0 UND	0 UND	2 212.1	9 39.7	10 35.8	11 33.9		2 203.8	2 168.0
3 111.1	4 86.6	8 47.9	13 28.0	13 27.7	13 29.1	Cost of Sales/Payables	8 46.8	7 49.9
7 51.1	10 37.3	13 27.3	16 22.7	16 22.7	16 22.5		14 26.1	13 28.8
26.8	26.1	37.9	59.7	112.2	-999.8		31.5	37.6
61.0	76.5	147.2	-386.8	-210.5	-86.0	Sales/Working Capital	104.7	163.6
999.8	-94.0	-51.5	-45.7	-61.7	-29.8		-131.8	-85.0
7.5	3.2	4.3	5.9	4.3	7.4		4.7	4.0
(190) 2.2	(304) 1.7	(250) 1.9	(180) 2.3	(45) 3.0	(37) 3.0	EBIT/Interest	(514) 2.1	(809) 1.7
.0	.7	1.0	1.1	2.2	1.5		1.0	.7
	3.4	4.4	3.9	3.2			3.3	5.3
(18)	1.8	(37) 2.0	(67) 2.1	(19) 1.8		Net Profit + Depr., Dep., Amort./Cur. Mat. L/T/D	(85) 2.0	(107) 3.0
	1.1	1.2	1.1	1.5			1.3	1.7
.0	1.2	1.4	1.1	1.7	1.7		.8	.9
.7	5.2	3.6	2.0	2.3	2.4	Fixed/Worth	2.7	3.2
-1.3	-5.1	-999.0	5.5	3.9	3.9		30.4	-14.5
.6	1.8	2.0	1.4	1.7	1.6		1.6	1.6
4.3	9.3	4.6	2.8	2.9	2.4	Debt/Worth	4.2	5.6
-5.1	-8.0	-999.8	7.3	6.7	6.3		565.8	-16.0
76.7	55.6	42.8	25.1	34.9	30.0		54.0	44.8
(272) 33.9	(234) 20.9	(200) 15.2	(159) 13.0	(43) 24.9	(35) 20.6	% Profit Before Taxes/Tangible Net Worth	(482) 23.9	(707) 19.2
9.3	4.9	2.1	4.5	11.4	3.8		6.0	3.6
22.7	8.8	7.6	7.1	8.0	6.4		11.3	9.4
8.9	3.3	2.7	3.3	5.2	3.9	% Profit Before Taxes/Total Assets	4.5	3.3
-1.2	-1.1	-.2	.2	2.7	.5		.3	-1.3
999.8	29.2	24.0	17.4	11.8	7.8		69.6	68.9
134.8	7.2	7.3	10.0	7.3	6.0	Sales/Net Fixed Assets	12.3	14.6
34.8	3.5	2.8	5.8	5.1	4.0		5.7	5.3
23.7	7.8	8.1	7.8	6.3	5.1		11.9	12.8
14.3	4.2	4.0	5.3	4.7	4.3	Sales/Total Assets	6.1	6.3
8.2	2.5	2.1	3.2	3.2	3.0		3.7	3.5
.2	.7	.7	.7	.9	.8		.5	.5
(247) .5	(304) 1.2	(236) 1.3	(180) 1.0	(45) 1.2	(25) 1.0	% Depr., Dep., Amort./Sales	(529) 1.0	(832) .9
1.1	2.1	2.3	1.5	1.8	1.4		1.5	1.5
.5	.6	.3	.2				.4	.4
(234) 1.0	(169) 1.0	(99) .5	(58) .3			% Officers', Directors' Owners' Comp/Sales	(250) .8	(398) .8
1.6	1.8	1.5	.6				1.6	1.7
1458270M	2282010M	7410747M	24723187M	17120853M	31861148M	Net Sales ($)	48476855M	82182727M
102880M	385363M	1206371M	4402610M	3255682M	6438913M	Total Assets ($)	7344544M	12523505M

© RMA 2010

Comparative Historical Data | Current Data Sorted by Sales

4/1/07-3/31/08 ALL	4/1/08-3/31/09 ALL	4/1/09-3/31/10 ALL	Type of Statement	0-1MM	1-3MM	3-5MM	5-10MM	10-25MM	25MM & OVER
					160 (4/1-9/30/09)		1,155 (10/1/09-3/31/10)		
72	108	93	Unqualified		1			2	90
75	130	122	Reviewed	1	5	10	10	18	78
170	189	175	Compiled	7	28	33	33	20	54
366	433	603	Tax Returns	37	208	150	126	52	30
286	362	322	Other	6	48	53	54	31	130
969	**1222**	**1315**	**NUMBER OF STATEMENTS**	**51**	**290**	**246**	**223**	**123**	**382**
%	%	%	**ASSETS**	%	%	%	%	%	%
11.1	12.6	12.0	Cash & Equivalents	11.1	11.6	12.5	13.0	14.7	10.8
7.1	6.5	5.4	Trade Receivables (net)	3.1	2.3	3.4	4.5	7.2	9.5
19.8	17.4	20.8	Inventory	19.6	28.0	24.7	19.2	18.6	14.5
2.0	2.4	2.0	All Other Current	2.9	1.6	2.0	1.8	2.3	2.4
40.0	38.9	40.3	Total Current	36.7	43.5	42.5	38.5	42.7	37.2
47.0	47.2	44.6	Fixed Assets (net)	49.9	41.5	43.1	42.7	40.8	49.6
6.5	6.7	7.4	Intangibles (net)	11.7	9.6	6.7	9.8	7.5	4.2
6.5	7.2	7.7	All Other Non-Current	1.7	5.4	7.7	8.9	9.0	9.0
100.0	100.0	100.0	Total	100.0	100.0	100.0	100.0	100.0	100.0
			LIABILITIES						
4.7	4.4	4.4	Notes Payable-Short Term	3.5	4.2	4.0	4.9	5.0	4.5
3.2	3.3	2.9	Cur. Mat.-L.T.D.	4.7	2.2	2.3	2.6	3.5	3.7
18.2	14.7	15.8	Trade Payables	13.9	10.2	14.2	13.1	20.1	21.5
.2	.1	.1	Income Taxes Payable	.2	.0	.1	.0	.0	.2
8.8	10.2	10.8	All Other Current	16.0	12.5	10.8	12.6	8.9	8.3
35.1	32.8	34.0	Total Current	38.3	29.0	31.5	33.2	37.6	38.2
38.0	37.4	35.9	Long-Term Debt	46.4	40.0	37.2	38.9	34.0	29.5
.2	.2	.3	Deferred Taxes	.0	.0	.0	.3	.1	.7
11.0	9.0	10.9	All Other Non-Current	19.1	19.9	13.0	9.0	7.0	4.0
15.6	20.7	18.9	Net Worth	-3.9	11.1	18.4	18.7	21.4	27.5
100.0	100.0	100.0	Total Liabilities & Net Worth	100.0	100.0	100.0	100.0	100.0	100.0
			INCOME DATA						
100.0	100.0	100.0	Net Sales	100.0	100.0	100.0	100.0	100.0	100.0
12.7	12.3	13.5	Gross Profit	31.0	15.6	12.4	12.5	12.8	11.1
11.8	10.8	12.7	Operating Expenses	29.8	15.1	11.4	11.2	12.3	10.4
.9	1.4	.8	Operating Profit	1.2	.5	1.0	1.3	.6	.7
.3	.4	.1	All Other Expenses (net)	1.8	.0	.0	.3	-.1	-.1
.6	1.1	.8	Profit Before Taxes	-.6	.5	1.0	1.0	.6	.9
			RATIOS						
2.2	2.5	2.5		5.1	5.8	3.4	3.4	1.9	1.3
1.2	1.2	1.3	Current	1.5	2.0	1.7	1.7	1.2	1.0
.8	.8	.8		.7	.9	.8	.8	.9	.7
1.0	1.2	1.1		1.6	1.6	1.4	1.4	1.0	.8
(967) .5	(1219) .6	(1313) .5	Quick	.4	.5	.5	(221) .7	.6	.5
.2	.2	.2		.1	.1	.2	.3	.3	.3
0 UND	0 UND	0 UND		0 UND	0 UND	0 UND	0 UND	0 999.8	2 200.8
1 299.5	1 371.5	1 478.2	Sales/Receivables	0 UND	0 UND	0 UND	0 999.8	2 240.9	3 105.5
5 80.1	3 107.8	3 105.5		4 91.0	1 500.1	2 238.4	2 170.4	4 101.4	6 59.3
5 69.2	4 89.8	6 65.3		13 28.5	10 37.2	6 60.1	5 78.7	4 99.0	5 74.1
8 45.1	7 56.1	9 40.0	Cost of Sales/Inventory	29 12.5	13 27.5	9 42.2	7 50.2	7 51.4	8 44.4
12 29.3	10 35.7	14 26.1		46 7.9	19 18.8	12 29.6	10 38.1	11 32.8	11 31.8
2 227.7	1 308.5	1 406.0		0 UND	0 UND	0 UND	0 999.8	3 107.3	9 41.8
7 49.8	5 71.9	6 59.1	Cost of Sales/Payables	4 92.0	3 132.5	3 122.6	3 124.9	8 48.6	12 29.3
13 28.6	9 38.9	12 29.3		16 22.3	8 44.9	8 46.3	7 49.9	13 27.6	16 23.1
40.1	40.2	32.2		8.4	21.2	30.2	34.1	44.2	62.1
154.4	150.3	109.2	Sales/Working Capital	20.9	44.9	68.6	83.0	146.8	-495.6
-83.3	-100.9	-77.9		-11.4	-213.7	-139.9	-170.7	-171.2	-50.4
3.6	5.7	4.7		2.1	3.1	6.0	4.8	5.8	6.1
(776) 1.7	(999) 2.4	(1006) 2.0	EBIT/Interest	(32) .7	(186) 1.5	(165) 2.0	(167) 2.0	(99) 1.9	(357) 2.6
.7	1.1	.9		-1.0	.2	.8	1.0	.5	1.3
5.3	4.3	3.4					7.5	4.1	3.3
(118) 2.6	(151) 2.4	(150) 2.0	Net Profit + Depr., Dep., Amort./Cur. Mat. L/T/D			(11) 3.1	(15) 2.1	(112) 1.9
1.3	1.3	1.3					1.3	1.0	1.3
.9	.8	.7		1.1	.3	.3	.4	.7	1.1
3.4	2.6	2.7	Fixed/Worth	28.2	4.7	2.5	2.6	2.5	2.2
-14.1	UND	-15.3		-1.2	-3.5	-7.6	-6.1	-6.5	5.5
1.7	1.4	1.3		2.0	.7	.9	1.0	1.5	1.5
5.5	3.9	4.1	Debt/Worth	63.0	11.7	4.2	3.7	4.1	2.9
-18.6	-80.2	-19.4		-3.2	-6.0	-12.7	-8.6	-19.4	9.9
44.2	56.5	47.8		67.8	72.3	58.1	60.3	52.6	31.3
(678) 18.7	(903) 23.8	(943) 20.9	% Profit Before Taxes/Tangible Net Worth	(26) 28.6	(184) 20.0	(170) 26.9	(153) 29.3	(87) 20.7	(323) 15.6
4.7	7.3	4.9		-12.9	1.4	7.9	8.3	2.4	4.9
9.1	13.2	10.9		10.7	11.3	15.1	17.5	12.5	7.4
3.0	5.1	3.9	% Profit Before Taxes/Total Assets	.1	3.4	4.6	5.1	3.4	3.6
-.9	.3	.0		-10.3	-2.9	.1	.5	-.4	.7
70.6	65.9	84.6		51.5	163.0	200.2	147.1	97.9	27.8
13.8	15.6	13.6	Sales/Net Fixed Assets	3.3	18.8	22.7	16.1	23.0	11.6
5.5	6.2	4.9		1.2	3.7	4.5	4.8	5.6	6.1
12.3	13.0	12.2		2.9	12.4	16.8	17.6	13.7	9.2
6.4	7.2	5.9	Sales/Total Assets	1.7	5.3	8.2	6.0	7.6	5.9
3.5	3.9	3.1		1.0	2.5	3.2	3.2	3.9	4.0
.5	.4	.5		1.2	.5	.3	.5	.4	.6
(801) .9	(981) .8	(1037) 1.0	% Depr., Dep., Amort./Sales	(39) 3.4	(208) 1.2	(176) .9	(168) 1.1	(97) 1.0	(349) .9
1.5	1.4	1.8		5.6	2.2	2.0	1.9	1.7	1.4
.3	.3	.4		1.1	.8	.5	.4	.3	.2
(389) .7	(467) .6	(572) .8	% Officers', Directors' Owners' Comp/Sales	(22) 2.9	(157) 1.2	(125) 1.2	(102) .7	(59) .8	(107) .6
1.6	1.3	1.6		5.3	1.8	1.4	1.4	1.5	.6
67922918M	125639612M	84856215M	Net Sales ($)	30224M	591116M	941637M	1520315M	1904891M	79868032M
11583578M	17069698M	15791819M	Total Assets ($)	24782M	175913M	210360M	329982M	385050M	14665732M

M = $ thousand   MM = $ million
See Pages 9 through 22 for Explanation of Ratios and Data

Current Data Sorted by Assets   Comparative Historical Data

	0-500M	500M-2MM	2-10MM	10-50MM	50-100MM	100-250MM	Type of Statement	ALL 4/1/05-3/31/06	ALL 4/1/06-3/31/07
		1	3	9	6	6	Unqualified	49	46
		1	9	19	1		Reviewed	79	54
	7	12	16	9		1	Compiled	87	49
	32	18	14	3			Tax Returns	168	106
	11	26	29	22	9	10	Other	168	86
		39 (4/1-9/30/09)		235 (10/1/09-3/31/10)					
NUMBER OF STATEMENTS	50	58	71	62	16	17		551	341
	%	%	%	%	%	%	**ASSETS**	%	%
Cash & Equivalents	18.4	11.9	10.3	8.5	12.2	5.3		12.6	11.1
Trade Receivables (net)	8.0	10.4	9.7	11.3	9.3	8.2		8.5	9.9
Inventory	30.5	14.8	8.8	9.7	9.3	8.1		15.6	14.6
All Other Current	3.2	3.3	2.6	2.8	1.2	3.6		2.6	1.9
Total Current	60.1	40.5	31.4	32.2	32.0	25.1		39.2	37.5
Fixed Assets (net)	20.0	45.5	54.4	53.0	59.0	56.5		48.2	48.3
Intangibles (net)	13.9	7.6	4.4	3.4	4.7	7.9		6.5	6.3
All Other Non-Current	6.0	6.4	9.8	11.3	4.4	10.4		6.0	7.8
Total	100.0	100.0	100.0	100.0	100.0	100.0		100.0	100.0
							LIABILITIES		
Notes Payable-Short Term	4.7	7.1	3.0	4.4	.4	2.0		4.7	4.4
Cur. Mat.-L.T.D.	6.2	3.4	2.7	4.2	2.4	5.6		3.3	4.2
Trade Payables	13.6	14.2	11.4	18.9	15.2	11.5		17.3	18.3
Income Taxes Payable	.0	.0	.1	.3	.0	.0		.1	.1
All Other Current	24.0	8.8	4.9	5.2	5.8	10.6		10.0	8.8
Total Current	48.5	33.6	22.0	32.9	23.8	29.6		35.4	35.9
Long-Term Debt	29.4	37.4	42.7	32.6	28.4	35.0		35.7	34.5
Deferred Taxes	.2	.1	1.4	.8	.8	.2		.2	.3
All Other Non-Current	11.2	9.0	4.8	5.1	1.4	11.8		9.4	7.1
Net Worth	10.8	19.9	29.1	28.6	45.7	23.4		19.3	22.2
Total Liabilties & Net Worth	100.0	100.0	100.0	100.0	100.0	100.0		100.0	100.0
							INCOME DATA		
Net Sales	100.0	100.0	100.0	100.0	100.0	100.0		100.0	100.0
Gross Profit	16.7	15.4	15.1	10.7	13.3	11.0		14.4	12.9
Operating Expenses	16.2	13.7	13.0	8.9	11.3	8.8		12.8	11.5
Operating Profit	.5	1.7	2.1	1.9	2.0	2.2		1.6	1.5
All Other Expenses (net)	-.2	.2	.6	.3	.4	1.2		.3	.3
Profit Before Taxes	.7	1.5	1.5	1.6	1.6	.9		1.4	1.2
							RATIOS		
Current	4.2	3.7	2.5	1.2	1.9	1.2		2.1	1.8
	1.8	1.6	1.5	.9	1.1	.7		1.2	1.0
	.7	.7	.9	.7	.8	.6		.8	.7
Quick	2.2	1.7	1.6	.9	1.6	.8		1.2	1.0
	.6	.8	1.0	.5	.5	.4		(550) .6	.6
	.2	.2	.4	.3	.3	.2		.3	.3
Sales/Receivables	0 UND	0 UND	0 829.0	2 178.3	2 193.9	4 90.9		0 999.8	0 999.8
	0 999.8	2 234.2	2 146.6	4 95.1	4 85.7	5 70.8		2 149.9	3 120.2
	2 147.4	8 52.2	8 46.7	9 40.4	9 42.6	9 40.4		6 59.6	6 53.9
Cost of Sales/Inventory	5 73.2	6 64.7	5 77.6	4 91.3	5 78.2	4 89.2		5 75.7	4 89.3
	8 46.9	10 37.7	8 43.7	7 53.2	8 46.7	7 51.8		7 48.9	7 52.5
	14 26.6	15 24.3	12 29.8	9 38.9	12 30.6	11 32.7		12 30.5	11 32.9
Cost of Sales/Payables	0 UND	1 694.1	2 158.4	9 42.6	9 42.4	10 38.0		3 107.2	4 99.6
	1 546.0	6 64.9	8 43.5	12 30.4	11 33.0	12 31.4		9 38.9	9 39.9
	7 54.0	15 25.0	13 27.1	16 22.6	16 22.8	16 23.5		15 24.5	14 25.4
Sales/Working Capital	21.1	27.4	21.9	98.5	28.5	93.7		34.4	48.6
	88.0	60.1	60.0	-376.5	553.9	-58.2		147.1	580.0
	-130.4	-43.0	-234.4	-59.2	-137.0	-36.5		-78.9	-67.7
EBIT/Interest	13.8	6.0	5.4	4.9	14.4	4.4		5.7	4.7
	(32) 2.4	(50) 2.1	(67) 2.4	(61) 2.6	4.5	2.4		(455) 2.4	(292) 2.1
	-.2	1.0	1.1	1.2	2.8	.8		1.2	1.0
Net Profit + Depr., Dep., Amort./Cur. Mat. L/T/D				3.0				4.3	4.6
				(20) 2.1				(71) 2.2	(57) 2.3
				1.6				1.4	1.6
Fixed/Worth	.1	.8	.9	1.3	1.1	1.9		.8	1.0
	.9	3.9	2.1	2.1	1.5	5.1		2.6	2.5
	-1.0	-4.1	10.0	3.5	2.2	12.3		38.5	UND
Debt/Worth	.4	1.6	1.4	1.6	.8	2.2		1.5	1.7
	2.3	7.8	2.4	2.8	1.3	6.9		3.7	4.1
	-3.3	-6.5	22.8	5.0	2.3	16.2		UND	-252.0
% Profit Before Taxes/Tangible Net Worth	110.6	74.2	44.4	21.8	26.8	37.4		49.2	45.8
	(34) 29.0	(37) 19.4	(61) 15.8	(54) 13.0	13.3	(15) 19.7		(415) 23.5	(254) 20.1
	-.5	5.0	1.1	3.6	8.3	8.2		9.8	5.8
% Profit Before Taxes/Total Assets	20.4	8.2	8.8	5.6	10.7	6.1		11.1	10.5
	4.7	4.6	4.0	3.5	6.0	3.6		5.2	4.3
	-9.6	-.3	.0	.6	2.9	-.7		1.1	.2
Sales/Net Fixed Assets	803.0	41.5	22.0	25.6	13.4	9.9		44.6	41.2
	98.7	11.4	7.1	9.5	7.5	7.7		11.6	13.0
	39.6	4.4	3.6	5.5	4.1	5.7		4.8	5.7
Sales/Total Assets	19.7	8.9	7.0	8.4	5.5	5.6		10.1	11.2
	12.8	4.9	4.0	5.3	4.5	3.3		5.8	6.0
	8.3	3.0	2.5	3.5	2.8	2.9		3.3	3.6
% Depr., Dep., Amort./Sales	.3	.6	.7	.6	.8	.7		.6	.6
	(28) .5	(46) 1.0	(59) 1.0	(59) .9	1.3	(10) 1.0		(458) 1.0	(300) .9
	1.0	1.8	1.8	1.5	1.9	1.6		1.7	1.4
% Officers', Directors' Owners' Comp/Sales	.6	.2	.6	.2				.4	.3
	(27) 1.1	(27) .9	(24) 1.0	(19) .4				(212) .9	(142) .8
	2.5	1.7	2.1	1.3				1.9	1.8
Net Sales ($)	178602M	582618M	2003750M	8702487M	5033982M	10691924M		56564921M	29704678M
Total Assets ($)	12550M	64608M	346641M	1431494M	1037228M	2608687M		8015447M	4859743M

M = $ thousand   MM = $ million
See Pages 9 through 22 for Explanation of Ratios and Data

Comparative Historical Data | Current Data Sorted by Sales

Right-side columns grouped as: **39 (4/1-9/30/09)** and **235 (10/1/09-3/31/10)**

4/1/07-3/31/08 ALL	4/1/08-3/31/09 ALL	4/1/09-3/31/10 ALL	Type of Statement	0-1MM	1-3MM	3-5MM	5-10MM	10-25MM	25MM & OVER
39	13	25	Unqualified		1			1	23
56	10	31	Reviewed			1		5	25
47	20	44	Compiled	3	4	8	8	7	14
83	61	67	Tax Returns	4	18	10	19	11	5
82	38	107	Other		13	13	17	14	50
307	142	274	NUMBER OF STATEMENTS	7	36	32	44	38	117
%	%	%	**ASSETS**	%	%	%	%	%	%
10.2	12.1	11.5	Cash & Equivalents		12.0	9.8	11.6	14.6	10.3
12.4	10.1	9.8	Trade Receivables (net)		2.7	5.4	9.7	8.7	12.7
14.6	17.9	14.2	Inventory		24.9	17.2	14.5	11.0	10.5
2.2	2.3	2.9	All Other Current		3.8	3.0	.8	1.6	3.8
39.4	42.4	38.4	Total Current		43.3	35.3	36.5	35.9	37.2
47.8	43.3	46.3	Fixed Assets (net)		35.4	52.6	43.4	47.1	50.2
5.7	5.0	6.8	Intangibles (net)		14.7	8.0	7.7	6.8	3.9
7.1	9.3	8.5	All Other Non-Current		6.6	4.1	12.4	10.2	8.7
100.0	100.0	100.0	Total		100.0	100.0	100.0	100.0	100.0
			LIABILITIES						
4.2	6.6	4.3	Notes Payable-Short Term		2.3	4.4	5.4	4.0	3.7
3.5	3.8	4.0	Cur. Mat.-L.T.D.		5.6	1.3	6.7	2.7	3.9
17.7	15.3	14.3	Trade Payables		9.6	11.2	9.8	13.5	18.9
.1	.1	.1	Income Taxes Payable		.0	.0	.0	.0	.2
8.3	12.5	9.7	All Other Current		20.1	11.0	7.1	11.0	6.8
33.9	38.1	32.3	Total Current		37.6	27.9	29.0	31.1	33.4
33.7	35.3	35.5	Long-Term Debt		37.8	43.5	36.6	38.9	27.9
.2	.1	.7	Deferred Taxes		2.1	.1	.3	.3	.7
5.7	9.2	7.1	All Other Non-Current		9.2	5.6	10.7	3.1	6.0
26.6	17.2	24.3	Net Worth		13.3	23.0	23.5	26.5	32.0
100.0	100.0	100.0	Total Liabilities & Net Worth		100.0	100.0	100.0	100.0	100.0
			INCOME DATA						
100.0	100.0	100.0	Net Sales		100.0	100.0	100.0	100.0	100.0
12.2	12.8	14.1	Gross Profit		22.3	18.2	13.2	13.2	10.1
10.6	11.7	12.4	Operating Expenses		20.3	14.3	11.3	11.7	9.1
1.5	1.1	1.7	Operating Profit		2.0	3.9	1.9	1.5	1.0
.3	.3	.3	All Other Expenses (net)		.4	.6	.3	.3	.2
1.3	.7	1.3	Profit Before Taxes		1.6	3.3	1.6	1.2	.8
			RATIOS						
1.9	2.5	2.2	Current		4.1	4.2	3.1	2.4	1.4
1.1	1.2	1.2			1.7	2.0	1.5	1.4	1.0
.8	.8	.7			.6	.7	.8	.9	.7
1.0	1.4	1.3	Quick		2.6	1.9	1.7	1.5	1.0
(306) .6	.6	.6			.5	.9	.8	.9	.5
.3	.3	.3			.1	.2	.4	.3	.3
0 999.8	0 UND	0 734.2	Sales/Receivables		0 UND	0 UND	0 UND	1 668.5	2 180.8
3 104.3	2 216.7	3 137.8			0 872.4	1 311.4	1 515.7	3 127.0	4 89.0
9 39.3	6 60.4	7 51.6			2 163.9	10 37.9	8 44.2	7 50.6	9 41.4
4 91.5	4 99.4	5 75.6	Cost of Sales/Inventory		6 61.6	7 50.4	4 86.1	4 91.2	4 93.8
7 53.3	6 65.3	8 46.7			13 28.7	11 34.4	7 53.1	7 49.9	7 53.8
10 35.4	10 35.6	12 29.8			24 15.3	14 25.4	10 34.9	12 29.3	10 37.9
4 98.7	1 320.9	2 198.4	Cost of Sales/Payables		0 UND	0 UND	0 795.1	1 244.4	9 42.5
9 38.9	5 76.4	9 41.6			3 136.6	4 93.5	3 116.2	6 56.6	12 31.4
14 26.0	10 38.2	14 26.4			9 39.2	9 41.0	13 27.9	13 28.3	15 24.0
47.0	39.9	30.4	Sales/Working Capital		17.9	21.0	28.0	25.1	60.2
205.4	145.6	132.1			51.5	44.9	89.4	90.9	999.8
-82.2	-125.7	-73.6			-30.6	-42.1	-186.1	-204.2	-67.5
4.9	7.0	5.8	EBIT/Interest		6.3	3.4	7.0	5.5	5.6
(263) 2.1	(121) 2.3	(243) 2.6		(28) 2.0	(27) 1.9	(35) 2.7	(34) 2.0	(114) 2.9
1.2	1.2	1.1			.4	.6	1.2	.7	1.2
4.4	12.6	3.6	Net Profit + Depr., Dep., Amort./Cur. Mat. L/T/D						3.8
(53) 2.0	(18) 5.6	(39) 2.2						(34) 2.2
.9	2.3	1.5							1.4
.9	.6	.9	Fixed/Worth		.6	.8	.7	.7	1.2
2.2	1.9	2.1			33.3	4.9	2.9	2.1	1.8
12.2	36.1	21.9			-1.9	-2.7	28.6	33.6	3.6
1.4	1.1	1.4	Debt/Worth		1.7	.7	1.5	1.1	1.4
3.4	4.1	3.0			60.6	7.1	3.7	2.4	2.3
26.6	291.7	34.6			-3.9	-5.3	44.9	43.6	5.2
39.7	54.3	39.6	% Profit Before Taxes/Tangible Net Worth		161.3	42.4	99.7	50.5	25.0
(244) 17.7	(109) 21.6	(217) 16.0		(21) 31.6	(19) 16.4	(35) 31.9	(31) 14.8	(107) 13.1
6.0	7.9	4.3			3.6	-2.3	5.0	.1	5.1
10.1	13.2	8.7	% Profit Before Taxes/Total Assets		10.3	11.2	18.9	9.5	6.5
4.6	5.2	3.9			3.5	4.6	6.5	4.2	3.7
.7	.9	.0			-5.7	-1.2	.1	-.2	.8
44.3	87.4	40.3	Sales/Net Fixed Assets		178.0	32.1	53.7	28.7	25.9
12.2	21.2	10.9			46.5	7.2	12.5	11.6	10.2
5.3	6.9	5.7			4.3	3.0	6.3	3.8	6.7
11.0	15.4	9.5	Sales/Total Assets		10.8	8.8	13.3	8.9	8.9
6.4	7.5	5.4			7.3	3.6	4.9	4.7	5.5
3.7	4.3	3.1			2.0	1.8	2.7	2.6	3.8
.4	.4	.6	% Depr., Dep., Amort./Sales		.4	.5	.6	.6	.6
(265) .9	(120) .7	(218) 1.0		(22) .9	(25) 1.5	(31) 1.0	(32) 1.2	(103) .9
1.3	1.3	1.6			1.6	2.5	1.8	1.8	1.3
.3	.3	.4	% Officers', Directors' Owners' Comp/Sales		.6	.6	.6	.2	.2
(116) .7	(55) .6	(99) .8		(17) 1.4	(10) 1.5	(23) 1.0	(16)	(29) .4
1.2	1.0	2.0			2.2	2.9	1.9	1.7	.8
36904497M	17696951M	27193363M	Net Sales ($)	4522M	72122M	124150M	326731M	649187M	26016651M
5883973M	2383327M	5501208M	Total Assets ($)	1584M	22131M	56238M	91155M	162200M	5167900M

© RMA 2010

M = $ thousand   MM = $ million
See Pages 9 through 22 for Explanation of Ratios and Data

Current Data Sorted by Assets   Comparative Historical Data

Type of Statement	0-500M	500M-2MM	2-10MM	10-50MM	50-100MM	100-250MM		4/1/05-3/31/06 ALL	4/1/06-3/31/07 ALL
Unqualified				2		2		9	6
Reviewed			5	2				7	13
Compiled	4	4	2					21	13
Tax Returns	5	8	2					13	16
Other	3	6	4	2		3		31	27
			14 (4/1-9/30/09)	40 (10/1/09-3/31/10)					
NUMBER OF STATEMENTS	12	18	13	6		5		81	75
ASSETS	%	%	%	%	%	%		%	%
Cash & Equivalents	6.3	19.7	7.0		D			12.6	10.6
Trade Receivables (net)	4.8	7.8	6.8		A			5.7	10.0
Inventory	66.0	44.6	57.8		T			50.6	50.1
All Other Current	1.2	3.5	3.1		A			2.7	1.7
Total Current	78.3	75.6	74.6					71.6	72.4
Fixed Assets (net)	10.1	15.7	13.7		N			20.1	19.1
Intangibles (net)	5.0	.2	2.3		O			1.2	2.2
All Other Non-Current	6.6	8.5	9.4		T			7.1	6.3
Total	100.0	100.0	100.0					100.0	100.0
LIABILITIES					A				
Notes Payable-Short Term	14.3	4.8	13.7		V			11.1	13.9
Cur. Mat.-L.T.D.	3.1	3.2	3.2		A			1.9	2.9
Trade Payables	20.4	27.4	17.9		I			18.9	23.1
Income Taxes Payable	.0	.0	.2		L			.1	.1
All Other Current	32.5	7.6	10.7		A			11.0	8.7
Total Current	70.4	43.0	45.8		B			43.1	48.6
Long-Term Debt	29.6	10.5	2.3		L			12.3	18.4
Deferred Taxes	.0	.0	.1		E			.0	.1
All Other Non-Current	1.8	.4	2.2					4.6	7.4
Net Worth	-1.8	46.1	49.6					40.0	25.4
Total Liabilities & Net Worth	100.0	100.0	100.0					100.0	100.0
INCOME DATA									
Net Sales	100.0	100.0	100.0					100.0	100.0
Gross Profit	48.2	39.9	42.3					47.5	45.7
Operating Expenses	49.2	37.7	40.9					44.7	42.3
Operating Profit	-1.0	2.3	1.4					2.8	3.4
All Other Expenses (net)	1.1	.4	-1.1					.1	.5
Profit Before Taxes	-2.1	1.9	2.5					2.7	2.8
RATIOS									
Current	3.3	4.5	2.5					2.6	3.2
	1.2	2.1	1.9					1.9	1.8
	.8	1.2	1.3					1.2	1.2
Quick	.3	1.1	.7					.8	1.1
	.1	.7	.2					.3	.3
	.1	.2	.1					.1	.1
Sales/Receivables	0 UND	0 UND	0 UND					0 UND	0 UND
	1 519.3	3 132.1	4 87.2					3 145.5	5 68.6
	8 46.8	19 18.8	18 20.5					14 26.4	22 16.5
Cost of Sales/Inventory	94 3.9	51 7.2	121 3.0					91 4.0	84 4.4
	143 2.5	105 3.5	171 2.1					141 2.6	148 2.5
	284 1.3	186 2.0	367 1.0					232 1.6	209 1.7
Cost of Sales/Payables	26 14.1	22 16.8	37 9.9					30 12.3	33 11.2
	43 8.5	46 7.9	49 7.5					49 7.4	50 7.3
	80 4.5	89 4.1	75 4.8					81 4.5	89 4.1
Sales/Working Capital	5.2	3.7	3.4					4.1	4.7
	12.2	7.5	7.0					7.6	7.5
	-18.2	38.4	14.4					36.1	26.3
EBIT/Interest	.3	40.3	6.0					8.4	11.5
	(10) -.6	(15) 4.1	(10) 2.9					(66) 3.1	(65) 2.7
	-3.5	.8	-9.1					.0	.8
Net Profit + Depr., Dep., Amort./Cur. Mat. L/T/D									
Fixed/Worth	.3	.1	.1					.1	.1
	-1.7	.2	.2					.4	.4
	-.3	1.2	.5					1.2	1.4
Debt/Worth	2.1	.4	.6					.6	.7
	-31.4	1.3	.9					1.2	1.8
	-3.8	7.1	2.3					3.6	5.6
% Profit Before Taxes/Tangible Net Worth		45.5	22.0					29.8	33.3
	(16) 12.8	(12) 9.4						(74) 11.7	(63) 13.1
		1.6	-12.7					.4	2.4
% Profit Before Taxes/Total Assets	-1.3	17.7	11.6					12.0	14.5
	-4.9	6.3	4.5					4.6	5.3
	-9.1	.4	-5.6					-.3	-.1
Sales/Net Fixed Assets	71.9	75.9	35.7					41.3	71.3
	46.0	23.6	15.8					16.6	16.6
	13.3	5.9	8.6					7.9	8.0
Sales/Total Assets	3.2	3.4	2.6					3.0	3.2
	2.5	2.6	2.1					2.4	2.4
	1.4	2.1	1.1					1.6	1.8
% Depr., Dep., Amort./Sales	.4	.2	.4					.5	.4
	(10) .7	(13) .5	(11) 1.6					(70) 1.1	(61) 1.1
	.9	1.3	2.2					1.7	1.6
% Officers', Directors' Owners' Comp/Sales								3.6	2.6
								(49) 5.6	(46) 6.5
								7.9	11.4
Net Sales ($)	10117M	52921M	108483M	379716M		2046294M		3064975M	2053029M
Total Assets ($)	4001M	20087M	51069M	172477M		837183M		1388097M	783013M

M = $ thousand   MM = $ million
See Pages 9 through 22 for Explanation of Ratios and Data

Comparative Historical Data

Current Data Sorted by Sales

				Type of Statement						
				Unqualified						4
				Reviewed			3		1	3
				Compiled			3			
6		10	4		2	3	3	2		
12		9	7	Tax Returns	6	5	4			
10		10	10	Other	3	3	5	1	2	4
11		16	15							
18		21	18			14 (4/1-9/30/09)		40 (10/1/09-3/31/10)		
4/1/07-3/31/08 ALL		4/1/08-3/31/09 ALL	4/1/09-3/31/10 ALL		0-1MM	1-3MM	3-5MM	5-10MM	10-25MM	25MM & OVER
57		66	54	**NUMBER OF STATEMENTS**	11	11	15	3	3	11
%		%	%	**ASSETS**	%	%	%	%	%	%
12.0		11.1	12.4	Cash & Equivalents	5.4	9.9	14.8			15.5
6.8		7.1	6.4	Trade Receivables (net)	3.3	5.7	10.7			6.8
53.2		47.2	50.1	Inventory	64.9	54.0	49.0			36.3
2.8		2.6	2.6	All Other Current	1.9	6.3	1.6			2.3
74.7		68.0	71.5	Total Current	75.5	75.9	76.1			60.9
18.7		19.5	17.4	Fixed Assets (net)	13.2	10.3	16.7			24.7
1.4		3.7	3.0	Intangibles (net)	5.4	.1	.1			6.8
5.2		8.8	8.1	All Other Non-Current	5.8	13.7	7.1			7.6
100.0		100.0	100.0	Total	100.0	100.0	100.0			100.0
				LIABILITIES						
10.5		8.7	8.4	Notes Payable-Short Term	16.1	4.7	9.2			2.4
2.4		2.3	3.0	Cur. Mat.-L.T.D.	3.4	1.5	3.4			2.0
26.1		24.2	23.6	Trade Payables	18.1	19.4	28.5			28.9
1.2		.2	.2	Income Taxes Payable	.0	.0	.0			1.1
10.1		10.8	13.8	All Other Current	16.7	22.2	12.8			8.2
50.4		46.2	49.0	Total Current	54.2	47.7	53.9			42.6
16.7		20.2	15.1	Long-Term Debt	34.1	2.4	11.0			14.0
.1		.0	.1	Deferred Taxes	.0	.0	.0			.4
9.3		6.0	2.9	All Other Non-Current	1.5	2.3	1.0			9.2
23.6		27.6	32.8	Net Worth	10.1	47.7	34.1			33.9
100.0		100.0	100.0	Total Liabilities & Net Worth	100.0	100.0	100.0			100.0
				INCOME DATA						
100.0		100.0	100.0	Net Sales	100.0	100.0	100.0			100.0
46.0		48.2	44.6	Gross Profit	48.2	42.9	39.7			47.7
44.0		45.5	42.6	Operating Expenses	47.7	41.0	39.8			42.0
2.0		2.7	1.9	Operating Profit	.5	2.0	-.1			5.7
1.1		.7	.5	All Other Expenses (net)	1.3	-.7	-.7			1.6
.9		2.0	1.4	Profit Before Taxes	-.8	2.7	.5			4.1
				RATIOS						
2.2		2.5	3.0		3.3	3.9	2.2			1.9
1.5		1.8	1.7	Current	1.2	3.5	1.5			1.6
1.1		1.1	1.1		.9	1.7	1.1			1.2
.6		.8	.8		.3	.8	.9			.8
.2		.3	.3	Quick	.1	.5	.3			.4
.1		.1	.1		.1	.2	.1			.2
0 UND		0 UND	0 UND		0 UND	0 UND	1 397.8		2 158.4	
2 186.3		1 250.7	3 118.0	Sales/Receivables	2 157.7	3 114.9	6 57.9		4 90.8	
16 22.4		12 30.1	12 30.0		12 30.0	6 64.2	20 18.4		23 15.9	
96 3.8		85 4.3	83 4.4		118 3.1	87 4.2	53 6.9		79 4.6	
137 2.7		138 2.6	143 2.5	Cost of Sales/Inventory	230 1.6	165 2.2	120 3.0		117 3.1	
196 1.9		204 1.8	229 1.6		545 .7	233 1.6	194 1.9		149 2.5	
40 9.2		33 11.0	32 11.2		42 8.8	26 14.2	22 16.4		38 9.5	
61 6.0		59 6.2	49 7.5	Cost of Sales/Payables	47 7.7	39 9.3	49 7.4		71 5.2	
97 3.8		103 3.5	89 4.1		86 4.2	81 4.5	120 3.0		113 3.2	
6.1		4.5	4.3		1.4	3.0	5.7			7.0
11.2		9.4	9.0	Sales/Working Capital	9.7	4.8	13.7			10.6
125.9		24.2	35.6		-36.8	8.3	37.3			24.3
4.9		5.7	6.1		1.5		7.5			
(45) 2.0		(55) 2.1	(45) 3.0	EBIT/Interest	(10) -.1		4.1			
.0		-.5	-.6		-2.7		-4.1			
				Net Profit + Depr., Dep., Amort./Cur. Mat. L/T/D						
.1		.1	.1		.4	.0	.2			.2
.5		.6	.5	Fixed/Worth	-2.4	.1	.5			.7
2.2		2.6	UND		-.5	.8	1.1			1.3
1.1		.8	.7		2.1	.3	.8			.9
1.6		2.0	1.4	Debt/Worth	-55.6	.4	1.9			1.5
20.3		30.3	UND		-4.2	1.4	6.5			1.9
25.5		33.6	24.5	% Profit Before Taxes/Tangible Net Worth		32.2	35.9			
(44) 9.4		(51) 12.0	(41) 13.0		(10)	5.7	(13) 13.0			
.5		-2.2	.6			-5.8	-8.3			
12.0		10.1	9.8	% Profit Before Taxes/Total Assets	-.1	16.9	8.7			17.4
3.1		4.5	4.4		-3.7	3.6	2.7			7.4
-.3		-4.5	-4.6		-7.5	-15.3	-11.8			6.6
72.0		44.6	53.3		50.8	72.5	80.5			29.3
19.9		14.7	17.8	Sales/Net Fixed Assets	15.7	56.8	18.0			8.1
7.9		7.7	7.4		3.2	17.6	7.6			6.9
3.8		3.0	3.2		2.7	3.3	3.5			3.2
2.6		2.2	2.3	Sales/Total Assets	1.8	2.3	2.4			2.2
2.0		1.7	1.5		.9	1.0	1.8			1.7
.3		.4	.4			.2	.3			
(42) 1.0		(58) 1.0	(43) .7	% Depr., Dep., Amort./Sales	(10) .3	(12) .7				
1.6		1.9	1.9			.5	1.9			
1.6		3.0	1.9							
(25) 5.4		(25) 6.3	(21) 5.0	% Officers', Directors' Owners' Comp/Sales						
7.9		12.7	7.7							
3671737M		4100298M	2597531M	Net Sales ($)	7099M	19677M	61234M	22998M	43304M	2443219M
1204920M		1725007M	1084817M	Total Assets ($)	4679M	12205M	27998M	19918M	14643M	1005374M

M = $ thousand   MM = $ million
See Pages 9 through 22 for Explanation of Ratios and Data

Current Data Sorted by Assets   Comparative Historical Data

0-500M	500M-2MM	2-10MM	10-50MM	50-100MM	100-250MM	Type of Statement	ALL 4/1/05-3/31/06	ALL 4/1/06-3/31/07
		1	8	4	3	Unqualified	13	17
		5	6			Reviewed	12	11
3	3	2			1	Compiled	20	10
23	11	2			2	Tax Returns	13	27
6	6	5	7	6	5	Other	32	33
	15 (4/1-9/30/09)		94 (10/1/09-3/31/10)					
32	20	15	21	10	11	NUMBER OF STATEMENTS	90	98
%	%	%	%	%	%	ASSETS	%	%
12.9	13.6	14.2	17.7	14.9	15.1	Cash & Equivalents	14.4	14.4
1.6	6.0	5.9	7.8	9.3	1.6	Trade Receivables (net)	6.1	8.5
59.3	43.2	32.6	27.5	27.4	36.5	Inventory	49.3	49.6
4.7	7.0	6.5	3.6	10.2	3.9	All Other Current	2.6	2.5
78.6	69.8	59.1	56.6	61.7	57.1	Total Current	72.4	75.1
17.9	20.6	30.5	31.1	26.7	22.1	Fixed Assets (net)	19.5	17.4
.4	3.4	2.5	3.9	6.2	15.0	Intangibles (net)	1.9	1.8
3.1	6.3	7.9	8.5	5.3	5.8	All Other Non-Current	6.2	5.6
100.0	100.0	100.0	100.0	100.0	100.0	Total	100.0	100.0
						LIABILITIES		
13.7	13.3	5.2	4.4	1.8	5.9	Notes Payable-Short Term	10.6	10.7
10.6	1.9	2.2	1.1	3.7	5.2	Cur. Mat.-L.T.D.	1.8	4.8
5.9	11.4	22.0	19.4	20.0	12.2	Trade Payables	19.2	17.1
.0	.0	.2	.4	.0	.2	Income Taxes Payable	.5	.3
21.3	13.0	6.3	16.6	13.0	12.3	All Other Current	12.9	10.0
51.5	39.6	35.9	42.0	38.6	35.7	Total Current	45.1	42.8
15.4	14.9	9.6	17.4	10.6	29.6	Long-Term Debt	8.6	10.7
.0	.0	.0	1.2	.2	2.3	Deferred Taxes	.2	.2
8.4	9.6	10.0	6.9	5.5	5.9	All Other Non-Current	8.3	4.1
24.6	35.9	44.5	32.5	45.0	26.5	Net Worth	37.8	42.1
100.0	100.0	100.0	100.0	100.0	100.0	Total Liabilities & Net Worth	100.0	100.0
						INCOME DATA		
100.0	100.0	100.0	100.0	100.0	100.0	Net Sales	100.0	100.0
48.3	49.5	48.1	41.3	51.3	37.5	Gross Profit	44.6	43.1
45.3	47.6	45.4	42.8	46.0	39.7	Operating Expenses	41.9	39.5
3.0	1.9	2.7	-1.5	5.3	-2.2	Operating Profit	2.7	3.5
.8	.2	-.1	1.4	.9	2.8	All Other Expenses (net)	.6	1.2
2.3	1.7	2.8	-2.9	4.4	-5.1	Profit Before Taxes	2.0	2.3
						RATIOS		
5.6	6.6	4.2	2.1	2.9	1.9		2.6	5.3
2.3	2.5	1.7	1.6	1.4	1.5	Current	1.7	1.9
1.2	1.1	1.0	.9	1.1	1.2		1.3	1.1
.9	1.4	1.4	.9	1.7	.8		.9	1.5
.2	.5	.5	.6	.4	.3	Quick	.4 (97)	.4
.1	.0	.2	.3	.3	.1		.1	.1
0 UND	0 UND	0 UND	0 999.8	0 UND	0 UND		0 UND	0 UND
0 UND	0 UND	0 836.3	3 117.1	1 316.5	2 232.8	Sales/Receivables	0 786.6	2 235.2
0 UND	5 81.1	3 138.9	6 56.9	33 11.2	4 81.4		6 65.3	16 23.3
72 5.1	65 5.6	45 8.1	36 10.0	48 7.6	52 7.1		65 5.7	66 5.5
124 3.0	130 2.8	63 5.8	53 6.9	83 4.4	80 4.6	Cost of Sales/Inventory	99 3.7	100 3.6
211 1.7	194 1.9	114 3.2	91 4.0	109 3.4	116 3.2		186 2.0	155 2.3
0 UND	9 39.4	12 30.9	15 23.7	37 10.0	19 19.4		18 19.8	9 41.9
5 67.7	23 15.8	37 9.8	28 13.0	67 5.5	24 15.2	Cost of Sales/Payables	35 10.4	30 12.3
20 18.1	52 7.1	93 3.9	60 6.1	75 4.8	45 8.2		65 5.6	60 6.0
4.9	3.2	5.8	8.8	5.7	7.8		5.7	4.6
7.5	7.3	11.1	15.9	23.1	13.0	Sales/Working Capital	9.8	9.3
28.6	121.2	588.7	-63.1	NM	24.3		24.6	75.6
2.5	15.5	27.5	7.4		9.1		27.6	23.4
(17) 1.4	(17) .7	(11) 9.8	(17) -.7		-1.8	EBIT/Interest	(70) 3.8	(80) 4.3
-1.0	-7.1	2.3	-9.5		-20.1		.1	-.5
						Net Profit + Depr., Dep., Amort./Cur. Mat. L/T/D	25.6	8.4
							(13) 2.7 (13)	2.4
							1.0	.1
.1	.1	.2	.3	.3	.4		.2	.1
.4	.5	.4	.7	1.0	.6	Fixed/Worth	.4	.3
60.6	1.8	1.6	2.4	2.9	-.3		.9	.9
.3	.4	.2	.6	.5	.7		.6	.5
1.9	1.4	1.4	1.4	1.5	1.8	Debt/Worth	1.5	1.3
NM	13.2	2.6	3.4	15.2	-3.0		3.8	3.2
55.9	40.3	31.9	13.6				40.5	45.5
(24) 16.1	(17) 12.7	(14) 15.9	(18) 4.3			% Profit Before Taxes/Tangible Net Worth	(79) 9.8 (86)	19.3
2.4	-17.8	.5	-22.1				-2.5	-.2
24.8	8.8	19.1	7.3	11.7	7.3		16.5	21.9
4.1	1.7	9.0	-1.6	7.1	-12.9	% Profit Before Taxes/Total Assets	5.2	7.1
-2.4	-7.4	.6	-11.4	3.2	-24.3		-1.7	-4.2
147.6	53.7	27.3	33.6	15.9	18.3		49.8	88.2
31.3	15.0	8.0	14.3	10.4	8.5	Sales/Net Fixed Assets	19.2	26.1
12.6	5.3	6.6	5.1	6.1	7.2		9.2	7.8
4.6	2.6	3.8	4.7	3.0	3.0		4.1	4.3
3.6	2.1	2.9	2.8	2.5	2.5	Sales/Total Assets	2.8	3.1
2.2	1.6	2.5	2.2	2.2	2.0		1.9	2.0
.5	.2	.5	1.1				.5	.4
(18) 1.3	(16) .6	(13) 1.0	(20) 2.3			% Depr., Dep., Amort./Sales	(69) 1.1 (72)	.9
2.0	1.3	2.1	4.3				1.9	2.0
3.1	2.5						2.2	1.9
(15) 5.2	(12) 3.9					% Officers', Directors' Owners' Comp/Sales	(33) 4.4 (45)	4.7
7.3	6.2						6.8	7.5
21750M	46104M	240565M	1652085M	2111183M	4292085M	Net Sales ($)	4440743M	4718795M
6165M	20290M	73193M	489625M	796557M	1743118M	Total Assets ($)	1636060M	1754615M

© RMA 2010

M = $ thousand   MM = $ million
See Pages 9 through 22 for Explanation of Ratios and Data

Comparative Historical Data / Current Data Sorted by Sales

4/1/07-3/31/08 ALL	4/1/08-3/31/09 ALL	4/1/09-3/31/10 ALL	Type of Statement	0-1MM	1-3MM	3-5MM	5-10MM	10-25MM	25MM & OVER
15	19	16	Unqualified					2	14
12	15	11	Reviewed		1		1	2	7
12	15	9	Compiled	3	3		1	1	1
14	23	38	Tax Returns	19	11	3	2	1	2
31	31	35	Other	7	5		2	4	17
				15 (4/1-9/30/09)		94 (10/1/09-3/31/10)			
84	**103**	**109**	**NUMBER OF STATEMENTS**	**29**	**20**	**3**	**6**	**10**	**41**
%	%	%	**ASSETS**	%	%	%	%	%	%
12.8	11.7	14.5	Cash & Equivalents	11.1	12.0			10.8	16.8
6.5	8.2	4.9	Trade Receivables (net)	3.5	3.5			5.5	6.7
51.2	42.0	41.3	Inventory	60.7	40.5			27.5	30.9
3.4	4.1	5.5	All Other Current	3.6	11.6			4.0	5.2
73.9	66.1	66.3	Total Current	79.0	67.6			47.7	59.5
17.9	21.7	23.9	Fixed Assets (net)	15.3	26.0			32.4	27.6
2.9	3.4	3.9	Intangibles (net)	1.5	2.0			7.4	6.1
5.3	8.8	5.9	All Other Non-Current	4.2	4.4			12.4	6.8
100.0	100.0	100.0	Total	100.0	100.0			100.0	100.0
			LIABILITIES						
12.4	13.0	8.8	Notes Payable-Short Term	15.2	13.3			3.3	4.2
6.4	3.6	4.8	Cur. Mat.-L.T.D.	10.8	2.4			3.8	2.7
19.6	15.5	13.7	Trade Payables	6.0	9.5			23.0	18.8
.4	.4	.1	Income Taxes Payable	.0	.0			.2	.2
12.4	12.0	15.1	All Other Current	24.2	10.5			6.9	15.0
51.3	44.6	42.6	Total Current	56.3	35.7			37.3	41.1
14.0	13.3	15.9	Long-Term Debt	17.3	12.1			8.9	19.5
.1	.3	.5	Deferred Taxes	.0	.0			.6	1.1
7.9	6.2	8.0	All Other Non-Current	10.4	6.5			6.5	8.0
26.7	35.6	33.0	Net Worth	16.0	45.6			46.6	30.3
100.0	100.0	100.0	Total Liabilities & Net Worth	100.0	100.0			100.0	100.0
			INCOME DATA						
100.0	100.0	100.0	Net Sales	100.0	100.0			100.0	100.0
44.3	46.7	46.4	Gross Profit	48.7	48.6			53.7	41.1
41.8	44.5	44.8	Operating Expenses	45.9	47.5			52.5	40.5
2.5	2.2	1.6	Operating Profit	2.9	1.1			1.2	.5
.9	.8	.9	All Other Expenses (net)	.5	.8			.8	1.5
1.6	1.4	.7	Profit Before Taxes	2.4	.4			.4	-.9
			RATIOS						
2.5	3.3	3.6	Current	4.9	7.3			2.0	2.0
1.5	1.7	1.7		2.1	3.1			1.3	1.4
1.2	1.0	1.1		1.2	1.1			.8	1.0
.8	1.0	1.0	Quick	1.2	.9			1.0	.9
.3	(101) .4	.4		.2	.7			.5	.4
.1	.1	.2		.1	.2			.2	.2
0 UND	0 UND	0 UND	Sales/Receivables	0 UND	0 UND			0 UND	0 UND
2 199.9	1 479.8	0 999.8		0 UND	0 UND			1 530.6	2 218.5
8 47.4	15 24.3	4 94.9		3 137.5	2 158.7			3 133.5	6 64.5
76 4.8	56 6.5	50 7.2	Cost of Sales/Inventory	104 3.5	42 8.6			42 8.7	45 8.1
112 3.3	98 3.7	84 4.3		147 2.5	83 4.4			68 5.4	73 5.0
184 2.0	173 2.1	148 2.5		244 1.5	194 1.9			91 4.0	98 3.7
21 17.1	9 38.7	8 43.6	Cost of Sales/Payables	0 UND	2 151.1			29 12.4	19 18.8
36 10.0	31 11.8	22 17.0		9 40.6	15 24.7			61 6.0	31 11.9
69 5.3	53 6.9	53 6.9		21 17.4	47 7.8			81 4.5	63 5.8
6.0	5.4	5.6	Sales/Working Capital	3.5	4.1			9.0	7.6
13.7	13.1	12.4		6.2	8.6			38.3	15.9
32.2	304.4	58.2		27.2	114.3			-79.7	-168.7
7.7	4.9	8.8	EBIT/Interest	1.9	2.6				8.6
(73) 1.8	(78) 1.2	(81) 1.4		(16) 1.1	(15) .7			(34) .8	
-1.2	-1.1	-5.1		-1.1	-7.7				-6.2
19.4	6.2	22.3	Net Profit + Depr., Dep., Amort./Cur. Mat. L/T/D						24.1
(12) 2.6	(15) 1.4	(14) 1.9						(10) 11.7	
1.6	.8	-.3							1.2
.2	.1	.2	Fixed/Worth	.0	.1			.3	.4
.6	.6	.6		.4	.6			.7	.7
1.6	2.5	2.0		NM	1.8			1.8	2.5
.9	.5	.5	Debt/Worth	1.0	.1			.7	.7
2.0	1.2	1.5		2.1	.6			1.4	1.5
10.8	10.3	8.0		-7.3	13.2			3.0	4.7
47.3	29.3	33.5	% Profit Before Taxes/Tangible Net Worth	68.4	37.7			31.9	17.5
(67) 16.0	(80) 8.5	(90) 12.0		(21) 14.9	(17) 11.1			16.1	(33) 10.6
-.6	-4.8	-7.2		.8	-4.4			-47.2	-12.5
19.0	14.2	13.8	% Profit Before Taxes/Total Assets	13.7	19.8			17.7	10.7
3.5	1.7	3.2		3.2	3.6			7.9	2.7
-3.6	-4.5	-6.9		-4.1	-2.8			-8.9	-11.2
51.0	42.0	44.9	Sales/Net Fixed Assets	UND	74.7			43.3	22.2
21.0	16.0	15.1		22.2	13.7			8.0	12.0
9.4	7.4	7.3		11.0	5.1			6.6	6.5
4.2	4.1	3.9	Sales/Total Assets	3.9	4.4			3.6	4.2
2.7	2.8	2.8		2.9	2.4			3.0	2.8
2.0	1.8	2.1		1.7	1.8			1.9	2.3
.5	.4	.6	% Depr., Dep., Amort./Sales	.6	.3				.9
(58) 1.2	(74) 1.1	(80) 1.5		(15) 1.0	(15) .6			(32) 2.2	
2.1	2.0	2.6		2.0	1.7				3.6
1.7	2.0	1.8	% Officers', Directors' Owners' Comp/Sales	2.7	2.9				
(30) 3.6	(43) 3.0	(43) 4.0		(13) 5.2	(10) 4.4				
5.4	5.2	6.1		6.8	7.2				
4032536M	5455843M	8363772M	Net Sales ($)	13888M	35625M	10835M	43419M	180777M	8079228M
1531599M	2384260M	3128948M	Total Assets ($)	6423M	19249M	4273M	17044M	71823M	3010136M

M = $ thousand   MM = $ million
See Pages 9 through 22 for Explanation of Ratios and Data

Current Data Sorted by Assets | Comparative Historical Data

Date ranges: 500M-2MM column = 15 (4/1-9/30/09); 10-50MM column = 83 (10/1/09-3/31/10)

	0-500M	500M-2MM	2-10MM	10-50MM	50-100MM	100-250MM	Type of Statement	4/1/05-3/31/06 ALL	4/1/06-3/31/07 ALL
				8	3		Unqualified	12	7
	2	6	9	3			Reviewed	12	16
	1	6	5	1			Compiled	19	11
	11	6	7				Tax Returns	18	19
	7	4	13	1	3	2	Other	17	19
	21	22	34	13	6	2	**NUMBER OF STATEMENTS**	78	72
	%	%	%	%	%	%	**ASSETS**	%	%
	23.2	10.1	12.9	13.8			Cash & Equivalents	13.7	11.6
	9.8	4.6	12.2	3.2			Trade Receivables (net)	4.8	5.1
	49.0	53.0	42.9	43.6			Inventory	49.8	55.8
	2.3	.8	2.5	.8			All Other Current	1.4	1.5
	84.3	68.5	70.6	61.4			Total Current	69.7	74.0
	10.5	15.3	18.5	26.6			Fixed Assets (net)	21.7	18.1
	2.1	1.7	4.8	4.5			Intangibles (net)	2.2	2.2
	3.2	14.5	6.2	7.4			All Other Non-Current	6.5	5.7
	100.0	100.0	100.0	100.0			Total	100.0	100.0
							LIABILITIES		
	8.7	2.6	11.8	5.1			Notes Payable-Short Term	8.5	8.7
	2.3	2.9	4.1	1.7			Cur. Mat.-L.T.D.	3.4	3.0
	11.1	19.2	18.6	13.4			Trade Payables	15.1	16.5
	.1	.0	.2	.3			Income Taxes Payable	.3	.3
	19.9	9.8	11.7	14.3			All Other Current	9.6	12.2
	41.9	34.5	46.4	34.7			Total Current	36.8	40.8
	14.5	15.3	15.5	12.0			Long-Term Debt	17.1	14.0
	.3	.0	.0	.1			Deferred Taxes	.1	.0
	15.1	5.0	1.8	5.9			All Other Non-Current	5.3	5.6
	28.2	45.2	36.2	47.2			Net Worth	40.7	39.6
	100.0	100.0	100.0	100.0			Total Liabilities & Net Worth	100.0	100.0
							INCOME DATA		
	100.0	100.0	100.0	100.0			Net Sales	100.0	100.0
	49.0	40.2	42.8	45.7			Gross Profit	42.7	41.1
	44.4	38.0	41.9	40.3			Operating Expenses	40.7	39.2
	4.6	2.2	.9	5.3			Operating Profit	2.0	2.0
	.2	.6	-.2	1.0			All Other Expenses (net)	.1	.4
	4.4	1.7	1.1	4.4			Profit Before Taxes	1.9	1.6
							RATIOS		
	11.1	4.7	3.3	2.8			Current	3.7	3.8
	2.6	2.5	1.9	1.6				2.1	1.8
	1.4	1.3	1.0	1.2				1.3	1.3
	5.9	.9	1.7	.8			Quick	1.2	.9
	.7	.3	.6	.4				(77) .4	.3
	.4	.1	.1	.2				.1	.2
	0 UND	0 UND	0 UND	0 UND			Sales/Receivables	0 UND	0 UND
	0 UND	0 UND	2 188.2	1 271.5				1 373.7	1 277.1
	4 91.0	13 27.5	20 18.3	6 58.7				8 46.4	8 43.4
	53 6.9	74 4.9	75 4.8	81 4.5			Cost of Sales/Inventory	82 4.5	75 4.8
	85 4.3	110 3.3	111 3.3	124 2.9				117 3.1	115 3.2
	149 2.4	209 1.7	183 2.0	178 2.1				209 1.7	187 1.9
	0 UND	19 19.5	12 30.7	26 14.0			Cost of Sales/Payables	16 22.6	10 35.4
	7 49.2	41 8.9	35 10.4	42 8.7				28 13.0	24 15.1
	31 11.8	52 7.0	60 6.0	58 6.3				53 6.9	59 6.2
	5.2	2.9	3.7	4.7			Sales/Working Capital	4.3	5.0
	9.3	7.4	9.9	14.9				8.0	8.8
	18.7	33.9	NM	46.9				18.1	22.9
	8.4	9.2	12.7	16.7			EBIT/Interest	10.7	11.9
	(10) 2.1	(15) 2.8	(29) 2.7	(12) 7.9				(68) 2.5	(58) 3.0
	1.5	1.2	-1.4	3.2				.8	.3
							Net Profit + Depr., Dep., Amort./Cur. Mat. L/T/D	5.5	3.9
								(17) 1.9	(19) 2.6
								1.2	1.2
	.0	.1	.1	.3			Fixed/Worth	.1	.2
	.3	.3	.5	.4				.3	.5
	.7	1.7	3.1	1.3				1.0	1.4
	.3	.3	.6	.7			Debt/Worth	.6	.6
	1.2	1.2	1.6	.9				1.1	1.3
	NM	5.4	18.7	4.3				4.2	4.2
	99.0	26.0	42.7	32.2			% Profit Before Taxes/Tangible Net Worth	37.1	41.1
	(16) 68.2	(20) 6.5	(28) 7.7	(12) 19.1				(69) 12.2	(63) 12.1
	29.1	3.5	-2.7	8.7				.0	-3.2
	48.5	5.3	11.3	14.6			% Profit Before Taxes/Total Assets	15.0	14.1
	18.4	3.0	2.9	10.6				3.0	4.9
	5.9	-2.0	-4.3	4.2				-.9	-1.8
	UND	66.4	146.6	28.4			Sales/Net Fixed Assets	50.4	46.4
	46.4	21.9	18.8	14.8				15.9	17.1
	18.5	13.4	7.9	4.6				7.5	9.9
	5.0	4.3	3.1	4.4			Sales/Total Assets	3.5	3.9
	3.9	2.7	2.4	2.7				2.4	2.7
	2.9	1.4	1.6	1.3				1.8	2.1
		.5	.4	.8			% Depr., Dep., Amort./Sales	.6	.5
		(16) .6	(28) 1.0	(11) 1.1				(64) 1.1	(61) .8
		1.6	1.6	4.4				1.9	1.3
		4.3	1.5	.8			% Officers', Directors' Owners' Comp/Sales	3.2	2.0
		(11) 8.9	(12) 3.3	(12) 1.7				(29) 7.0	(30) 3.8
		10.3	6.1	4.6				11.7	8.3
	24410M	70014M	364240M	1074360M	1769700M	592187M	Net Sales ($)	3627082M	3614967M
	5557M	23967M	147446M	352444M	502054M	327495M	Total Assets ($)	1382919M	1410220M

M = $ thousand   MM = $ million
See Pages 9 through 22 for Explanation of Ratios and Data

Comparative Historical Data

Current Data Sorted by Sales

4/1/07-3/31/08 ALL	4/1/08-3/31/09 ALL	4/1/09-3/31/10 ALL	Type of Statement	0-1MM	1-3MM	3-5MM	5-10MM	10-25MM	25MM & OVER
9	10	11	Unqualified						11
10	10	20	Reviewed	2	3	7	3	1	4
6	11	13	Compiled	3	1	4	2	2	1
16	27	24	Tax Returns	5	10	1	5	3	
31	35	30	Other	4	4	3	10	3	6
				15 (4/1-9/30/09)			83 (10/1/09-3/31/10)		
72	93	98	NUMBER OF STATEMENTS	14	18	15	20	9	22
%	%	%	ASSETS	%	%	%	%	%	%
10.6	11.0	14.8	Cash & Equivalents	17.9	16.8	9.4	15.6		15.5
7.1	9.0	8.2	Trade Receivables (net)	8.0	4.9	7.1	8.6		4.0
49.2	46.0	46.5	Inventory	45.1	54.0	49.5	45.8		43.7
2.5	3.0	2.4	All Other Current	.8	2.6	.7	.8		4.9
69.3	69.0	71.9	Total Current	71.8	78.3	66.6	70.9		68.2
20.8	20.3	17.2	Fixed Assets (net)	16.6	12.7	17.8	15.3		22.1
3.0	1.9	3.3	Intangibles (net)	2.9	1.7	2.0	6.4		4.3
6.9	8.8	7.6	All Other Non-Current	8.8	7.3	13.5	7.4		5.5
100.0	100.0	100.0	Total	100.0	100.0	100.0	100.0		100.0
			LIABILITIES						
8.5	7.9	7.4	Notes Payable-Short Term	9.1	3.2	4.8	12.8		5.6
3.0	2.5	2.9	Cur. Mat.-L.T.D.	2.2	3.1	3.0	1.4		1.6
17.2	19.0	16.3	Trade Payables	8.6	9.8	22.7	18.5		16.1
.3	.2	.3	Income Taxes Payable	.0	.1	.0	.3		1.2
12.3	13.0	13.4	All Other Current	21.0	8.7	16.4	12.3		13.4
41.2	42.6	40.3	Total Current	41.0	25.0	46.9	45.3		37.8
15.5	12.6	14.3	Long-Term Debt	9.8	23.6	14.0	18.9		8.2
.4	.0	.1	Deferred Taxes	.0	.6	.0	.0		.1
7.2	6.9	6.2	All Other Non-Current	20.8	6.4	3.0	2.4		4.5
35.8	37.9	39.2	Net Worth	28.5	44.7	36.0	33.4		49.4
100.0	100.0	100.0	Total Liabilities & Net Worth	100.0	100.0	100.0	100.0		100.0
			INCOME DATA						
100.0	100.0	100.0	Net Sales	100.0	100.0	100.0	100.0		100.0
43.5	44.3	44.0	Gross Profit	47.6	51.3	43.8	38.3		45.8
40.2	41.1	40.9	Operating Expenses	44.6	47.5	41.8	36.8		40.8
3.3	3.2	3.1	Operating Profit	3.0	3.8	2.0	1.5		5.0
.8	.7	.2	All Other Expenses (net)	.3	.5	.7	-.2		.1
2.4	2.6	2.8	Profit Before Taxes	2.7	3.3	1.3	1.7		4.9
			RATIOS						
3.0	3.2	4.3	Current	16.7	5.0	3.8	4.0		3.2
1.7	1.8	2.0		2.7	3.8	1.2	1.9		1.9
1.3	1.1	1.2		1.4	2.3	.9	1.1		1.2
.9	1.0	1.2	Quick	4.3	1.3	.5	1.5		1.1
.3	.5	.6		.9	.7	.3	.6		.5
.1	.1	.2		.5	.2	.0	.2		.2
0 UND	0 UND	0 UND	Sales/Receivables	0 UND	0 UND	0 UND	0 UND		0 999.8
1 271.7	1 280.9	0 973.0		0 UND	0 UND	0 UND	1 633.8		1 253.7
10 35.3	12 29.7	13 28.1		8 47.6	11 33.3	20 18.4	14 26.0		4 84.3
64 5.7	60 6.0	73 5.0	Cost of Sales/Inventory	74 5.0	103 3.5	74 4.9	67 5.5		68 5.4
114 3.2	105 3.5	109 3.4		91 4.0	177 2.1	80 4.6	118 3.1		113 3.2
154 2.4	164 2.2	179 2.0		233 1.6	392 .9	164 2.2	168 2.2		150 2.4
14 25.6	21 17.4	11 32.7	Cost of Sales/Payables	0 UND	9 39.4	33 11.0	8 46.0		25 14.7
36 10.2	38 9.7	34 10.8		2 162.1	24 15.2	51 7.1	28 13.2		40 9.1
66 5.5	62 5.9	53 6.9		22 16.8	65 5.6	57 6.5	51 7.2		60 6.1
6.0	6.0	4.3	Sales/Working Capital	2.8	2.4	6.6	4.1		5.3
10.6	12.4	9.0		7.3	3.9	33.3	9.6		8.2
26.7	45.2	29.8		18.2	7.7	-26.2	NM		23.8
4.7	12.4	12.7	EBIT/Interest		7.6	7.3	7.7		17.0
(60) 1.8	(75) 3.3	(73) 4.0		(13) 2.2	(12) 1.8	(14) 2.9		(19) 8.1	
.4	.6	1.2			1.3	-8.8	-.1		5.4
2.5	14.1	8.3	Net Profit + Depr., Dep., Amort./Cur. Mat. L/T/D						
(15) .2	(10) 2.3	(12) 1.5							
-1.3	-1.0	-3.9							
.3	.1	.1	Fixed/Worth	.0	.1	.1	.0		.3
.5	.4	.4		.4	.3	.3	.5		.4
1.9	1.0	1.1		1.1	.7	3.4	9.8		1.1
.8	.7	.5	Debt/Worth	.2	.5	.4	.5		.4
1.7	1.4	1.2		1.1	.7	2.2	3.3		.9
7.2	2.6	5.4		NM	5.1	15.1	28.7		2.8
32.9	53.2	58.0	% Profit Before Taxes/Tangible Net Worth	100.0	49.1	57.0	60.0		45.0
(62) 7.9	(83) 13.5	(84) 15.2		(11) 66.7	(16) 9.0	(12) 15.5	(16) 8.8		(21) 22.0
1.0	1.1	4.0		-1.1	5.0	-8.7	-6.7		12.6
9.6	18.7	16.7	% Profit Before Taxes/Total Assets	44.6	11.5	18.4	9.2		19.2
2.8	5.8	5.4		6.8	4.9	3.1	3.4		11.1
-3.0	-.3	.7		-6.7	2.5	-10.7	-3.4		4.4
31.8	55.5	114.0	Sales/Net Fixed Assets	318.8	45.2	233.9	275.5		34.5
15.3	18.3	21.1		41.4	22.5	18.6	23.4		16.1
8.7	9.0	10.5		8.9	13.4	8.5	14.6		7.8
3.9	4.1	4.2	Sales/Total Assets	4.1	3.8	6.3	3.1		4.2
2.7	2.6	2.8		2.7	2.7	2.8	2.4		2.8
2.0	2.0	1.7		1.4	1.2	1.8	1.6		1.9
.6	.6	.5	% Depr., Dep., Amort./Sales		.6	.5	.4		.8
(60) 1.0	(66) 1.2	(68) 1.1		(14) 1.1	(12) 1.0	(12) .7		(16) 1.2	
2.0	2.2	1.6			2.1	2.2	1.5		1.6
2.2	2.1	1.3	% Officers', Directors' Owners' Comp/Sales		3.9				
(26) 3.3	(40) 4.1	(37) 3.8		(12) 5.7					
6.4	7.7	6.7			9.0				
5269706M	5043540M	3894911M	Net Sales ($)	8200M	29007M	58707M	147432M	160703M	3490862M
1986777M	1671505M	1358963M	Total Assets ($)	4847M	22762M	32356M	68943M	40964M	1189091M

M = $ thousand   MM = $ million
See Pages 9 through 22 for Explanation of Ratios and Data

Current Data Sorted by Assets   Comparative Historical Data

Type of Statement

	0-500M	500M-2MM	2-10MM	10-50MM	50-100MM	100-250MM	4/1/05-3/31/06 ALL	4/1/06-3/31/07 ALL
Unqualified			2		1	1	5	2
Reviewed	1	2	3				14	8
Compiled	1	1	1				8	16
Tax Returns	16	12	7				12	18
Other	7	4	7	3	1		18	21
	10 (4/1-9/30/09)			60 (10/1/09-3/31/10)				
NUMBER OF STATEMENTS	25	19	20	3	2	1	57	65

Main Table

0-500M	500M-2MM	2-10MM	10-50MM	50-100MM	100-250MM		4/1/05-3/31/06 ALL	4/1/06-3/31/07 ALL
%	%	%	%	%	%	**ASSETS**	%	%
12.4	10.3	12.6				Cash & Equivalents	11.6	15.4
7.8	14.3	14.3				Trade Receivables (net)	12.0	12.6
59.4	54.4	33.8				Inventory	46.1	42.7
.9	1.0	2.8				All Other Current	3.6	2.3
80.4	80.0	63.4				Total Current	73.3	73.0
10.9	13.8	17.4				Fixed Assets (net)	16.8	13.1
3.2	3.0	6.1				Intangibles (net)	3.4	4.2
5.4	3.2	13.1				All Other Non-Current	6.5	9.6
100.0	100.0	100.0				Total	100.0	100.0
						LIABILITIES		
26.3	8.7	6.6				Notes Payable-Short Term	13.2	9.9
3.5	1.3	3.5				Cur. Mat.-L.T.D.	1.6	.8
30.3	14.2	29.4				Trade Payables	18.3	20.8
.3	.0	.7				Income Taxes Payable	.1	.2
6.9	12.6	7.2				All Other Current	8.8	12.3
67.4	36.9	47.5				Total Current	42.1	44.1
14.4	15.4	11.8				Long-Term Debt	12.0	10.6
.0	.0	.1				Deferred Taxes	.2	.1
9.9	3.6	2.3				All Other Non-Current	10.1	7.4
8.3	44.1	38.3				Net Worth	35.6	37.8
100.0	100.0	100.0				Total Liabilities & Net Worth	100.0	100.0
						INCOME DATA		
100.0	100.0	100.0				Net Sales	100.0	100.0
51.9	48.2	42.4				Gross Profit	47.7	45.1
50.2	44.7	40.8				Operating Expenses	42.8	41.7
1.7	3.5	1.6				Operating Profit	4.9	3.5
.8	1.0	.4				All Other Expenses (net)	1.4	.6
.9	2.6	1.2				Profit Before Taxes	3.5	2.9
						RATIOS		
3.6	12.2	1.7				Current	3.2	2.9
2.2	2.9	1.2					1.7	2.0
.9	1.3	.9					1.3	1.3
.9	1.5	.8				Quick	1.1	1.3
(24) .3	.5	.3					.5	.6
.1	.3	.1					.1	.2
0 UND	0 UND	0 UND				Sales/Receivables	0 UND	0 UND
0 UND	5 68.4	8 46.0					3 117.9	3 109.2
7 56.0	34 10.6	28 13.0					37 9.9	36 10.2
58 6.3	95 3.8	57 6.4				Cost of Sales/Inventory	68 5.4	58 6.3
167 2.2	219 1.7	96 3.8					104 3.5	107 3.4
369 1.0	287 1.3	129 2.8					219 1.7	215 1.7
0 UND	12 31.6	37 9.9				Cost of Sales/Payables	19 19.5	21 17.7
19 19.3	22 16.6	74 4.9					34 10.9	50 7.3
64 5.7	53 6.9	83 4.4					75 4.8	75 4.9
3.3	2.5	7.8				Sales/Working Capital	4.5	5.1
7.4	4.0	34.0					9.4	7.4
-95.7	14.9	-29.6					19.9	24.1
29.0	28.8	9.3				EBIT/Interest	8.8	22.0
(17) 3.1	(15) 5.9	(17) 6.0					(44) 4.6	(56) 4.1
-2.4	-.3	2.7					1.4	.7
						Net Profit + Depr., Dep., Amort./Cur. Mat. L/T/D		
.1	.0	.1				Fixed/Worth	.1	.1
.4	.3	.4					.3	.2
-.6	.9	3.5					.9	1.4
.3	.2	.7				Debt/Worth	.5	.7
7.0	1.2	2.6					1.3	1.4
-5.3	18.3	7.8					3.4	7.4
97.4	38.0	57.6				% Profit Before Taxes/Tangible Net Worth	55.7	66.3
(18) 23.8	(15) 13.7	(16) 26.3					(50) 14.8	(56) 18.3
-18.0	-9.9	7.2					5.5	4.3
31.7	30.4	11.7				% Profit Before Taxes/Total Assets	15.4	23.5
8.2	5.7	8.4					7.3	6.1
-11.7	-3.1	2.1					.9	-.1
142.2	145.8	68.0				Sales/Net Fixed Assets	72.9	107.8
48.2	35.7	23.6					21.0	26.8
15.4	14.8	7.5					11.3	14.8
5.5	3.5	3.7				Sales/Total Assets	3.7	3.9
3.0	2.3	2.7					2.7	2.6
1.5	1.8	1.4					1.7	1.6
.4	.3	.4				% Depr., Dep., Amort./Sales	.6	.4
(17) .7	(14) .6	(18) .9					(43) .9	(50) .9
2.8	.8	2.0					1.6	1.5
5.0	1.4					% Officers', Directors' Owners' Comp/Sales	2.5	2.2
(11) 5.3	(12) 4.1						(27) 3.8	(33) 4.4
16.9	9.7						13.4	9.2
20756M	61996M	242853M	129319M	285062M	176206M	Net Sales ($)	1333393M	1518311M
5685M	20720M	95391M	56795M	141199M	206436M	Total Assets ($)	659028M	725533M

M = $ thousand   MM = $ million
See Pages 9 through 22 for Explanation of Ratios and Data

Comparative Historical Data   ## Current Data Sorted by Sales

			Type of Statement						
11	5	4	Unqualified				1	3	3
7	7	6	Reviewed	1	1		1		
7	7	3	Compiled	1			1	1	
18	17	35	Tax Returns	11	15	3	5	1	
9	20	22	Other	5	4	2	4	4	3
4/1/07-3/31/08 ALL	4/1/08-3/31/09 ALL	4/1/09-3/31/10 ALL		0-1MM	1-3MM	3-5MM	5-10MM	10-25MM	25MM & OVER
					10 (4/1-9/30/09)		60 (10/1/09-3/31/10)		
52	56	70	NUMBER OF STATEMENTS	18	20	5	12	9	6
%	%	%	ASSETS	%	%	%	%	%	%
13.4	12.9	12.0	Cash & Equivalents	7.8	12.9		12.0		
14.3	10.7	11.0	Trade Receivables (net)	5.0	11.3		13.3		
44.1	42.3	48.1	Inventory	65.6	51.6		38.9		
1.9	3.7	2.4	All Other Current	.7	.9		.6		
73.7	69.6	73.4	Total Current	79.1	76.8		64.9		
14.3	17.4	14.7	Fixed Assets (net)	10.7	11.6		23.6		
5.9	3.7	4.3	Intangibles (net)	4.7	5.3		2.0		
6.2	9.4	7.6	All Other Non-Current	5.5	6.3		9.5		
100.0	100.0	100.0	Total	100.0	100.0		100.0		
			LIABILITIES						
9.5	8.7	14.1	Notes Payable-Short Term	31.3	9.9		4.8		
2.2	2.2	2.6	Cur. Mat.-L.T.D.	2.6	3.6		3.4		
22.2	16.3	24.3	Trade Payables	26.1	21.1		29.6		
.5	.1	.3	Income Taxes Payable	.5	.0		.3		
10.0	9.6	8.7	All Other Current	6.9	7.5		14.3		
44.4	36.9	50.1	Total Current	67.3	42.1		52.5		
10.6	12.9	13.3	Long-Term Debt	17.1	15.0		8.9		
.3	.2	.3	Deferred Taxes	.0	.0		.0		
7.0	8.1	10.5	All Other Non-Current	10.5	5.6		3.2		
37.7	42.0	25.8	Net Worth	5.0	37.3		35.5		
100.0	100.0	100.0	Total Liabilities & Net Worth	100.0	100.0		100.0		
			INCOME DATA						
100.0	100.0	100.0	Net Sales	100.0	100.0		100.0		
45.7	48.9	48.0	Gross Profit	53.2	50.3		43.9		
40.7	47.1	45.7	Operating Expenses	53.2	47.1		38.8		
5.1	1.7	2.4	Operating Profit	.1	3.2		5.2		
1.0	.5	.7	All Other Expenses (net)	.9	1.0		.6		
4.1	1.3	1.6	Profit Before Taxes	-.8	2.3		4.6		
			RATIOS						
2.8	4.4	3.4	Current	4.5	6.1		2.1		
1.9	2.3	1.7		2.6	2.5		1.6		
1.2	1.2	.9		.9	.9		.7		
1.2	1.0	.9	Quick	.8	1.9		.8		
.5	.5	(69) .4		(17) .2	.5		.4		
.2	.2	.1		.1	.2		.2		
0 UND	0 UND	0 UND	Sales/Receivables	0 UND	0 UND		0 809.2		
7 49.3	4 85.5	2 152.9		0 UND	7 54.0		4 86.7		
32 11.5	28 13.2	20 18.6		0 UND	31 11.7		23 15.9		
74 5.0	80 4.6	61 6.0	Cost of Sales/Inventory	84 4.4	58 6.3		15 24.2		
110 3.3	119 3.1	124 2.9		289 1.3	162 2.3		102 3.6		
190 1.9	197 1.9	268 1.4		600 .6	271 1.3		140 2.6		
17 21.7	7 54.5	11 33.0	Cost of Sales/Payables	0 UND	15 24.2		34 10.8		
54 6.8	24 15.3	38 9.5		9 40.5	53 6.9		54 6.8		
69 5.3	55 6.7	76 4.8		41 8.9	68 5.4		83 4.4		
4.7	4.4	3.6	Sales/Working Capital	2.0	3.3		8.5		
9.2	6.9	8.5		5.1	8.0		12.8		
19.6	50.1	-82.0		-137.6	-28.8		-22.8		
13.9	17.4	10.1	EBIT/Interest	12.1	48.3		9.0		
(44) 4.1	(43) 2.1	(53) 3.1		(12) 1.3	(15) 1.8		(11) 6.3		
1.5	-2.1	-.6		-3.1	-8.9		4.8		
			Net Profit + Depr., Dep., Amort./Cur. Mat. L/T/D						
.1	.1	.1	Fixed/Worth	.1	.1		.1		
.3	.4	.4		.5	.3		.4		
2.4	1.0	NM		-.4	NM		NM		
.5	.4	.5	Debt/Worth	.3	.3		.7		
1.8	1.0	2.2		7.9	2.1		1.2		
10.6	12.9	NM		-6.2	NM		NM		
57.3	47.5	57.2	% Profit Before Taxes/Tangible Net Worth	73.2	44.6				
(44) 17.5	(47) 22.2	(53) 20.0		(13) -3.6	(15) 32.5				
5.6	-13.3	-4.7		-37.9	3.8				
22.9	26.1	24.6	% Profit Before Taxes/Total Assets	32.0	29.3		26.4		
6.6	3.6	6.5		-1.9	5.4		10.7		
1.3	-7.7	-3.6		-12.9	-6.0		6.4		
72.8	60.8	103.1	Sales/Net Fixed Assets	176.9	138.0		50.9		
26.0	17.6	30.9		46.2	50.9		23.6		
12.2	9.1	11.8		12.7	16.3		12.6		
3.7	3.7	4.1	Sales/Total Assets	5.9	4.3		5.3		
2.6	2.4	2.4		1.9	2.4		3.6		
1.8	1.7	1.7		1.1	1.7		1.9		
.6	.3	.4	% Depr., Dep., Amort./Sales	.6	.3		.5		
(39) .9	(42) 1.5	(52) .7		(11) 1.9	(15) .5		.9		
2.1	2.9	1.9		3.3	.7		1.8		
2.2	2.0	1.9	% Officers', Directors' Owners' Comp/Sales		.9				
(17) 3.1	(22) 3.5	(30) 5.0			(11) 5.1				
7.6	5.5	10.3			10.3				
1541693M	1746798M	916192M	Net Sales ($)	8023M	39490M	17513M	86523M	165871M	598772M
740768M	1001515M	526226M	Total Assets ($)	3230M	18365M	16942M	31432M	54773M	401484M

© RMA 2010

M = $ thousand   MM = $ million
See Pages 9 through 22 for Explanation of Ratios and Data

Current Data Sorted by Assets   Comparative Historical Data

Type of Statement		
Unqualified	11	12
Reviewed	23	21
Compiled	25	24
Tax Returns	50	56
Other	40	44

Type of Statement counts (current data):

	1		7	9	2	
		1	12	6	1	
	2	13	6	1		
	28	19	5	1		1
	9	15	17	10	3	1

23 (4/1-9/30/09)   146 (10/1/09-3/31/10)   4/1/05-3/31/06 ALL   4/1/06-3/31/07 ALL

0-500M	500M-2MM	2-10MM	10-50MM	50-100MM	100-250MM		4/1/05-3/31/06 ALL	4/1/06-3/31/07 ALL
40	48	47	27	5	2	NUMBER OF STATEMENTS	149	157
%	%	%	%	%	%	**ASSETS**	%	%
12.5	12.2	8.9	13.2			Cash & Equivalents	9.0	9.5
4.9	14.3	12.7	11.5			Trade Receivables (net)	10.9	9.4
55.8	40.9	40.9	39.3			Inventory	48.9	51.9
1.3	1.0	2.4	3.5			All Other Current	1.9	2.2
74.5	68.4	64.8	67.6			Total Current	70.7	73.0
11.1	20.2	24.9	20.6			Fixed Assets (net)	20.9	18.1
6.5	4.5	2.9	7.2			Intangibles (net)	3.3	3.1
8.0	6.9	7.4	4.6			All Other Non-Current	5.0	5.8
100.0	100.0	100.0	100.0			Total	100.0	100.0
						LIABILITIES		
20.4	13.2	9.3	11.6			Notes Payable-Short Term	13.1	14.7
6.6	2.4	2.8	2.6			Cur. Mat.-L.T.D.	3.2	2.7
19.1	19.6	20.0	15.8			Trade Payables	20.3	18.8
.1	.1	.2	.0			Income Taxes Payable	.2	.3
9.7	6.7	9.1	13.1			All Other Current	10.2	11.1
55.9	42.0	41.4	43.2			Total Current	46.9	47.7
17.1	18.4	14.5	19.4			Long-Term Debt	21.2	12.2
.0	.0	.0	.3			Deferred Taxes	.1	.1
28.3	7.7	6.1	11.2			All Other Non-Current	9.5	4.0
-1.5	31.9	38.0	26.0			Net Worth	22.3	35.9
100.0	100.0	100.0	100.0			Total Liabilities & Net Worth	100.0	100.0
						INCOME DATA		
100.0	100.0	100.0	100.0			Net Sales	100.0	100.0
46.0	43.5	47.7	48.6			Gross Profit	46.6	46.2
42.9	39.6	44.4	44.4			Operating Expenses	42.3	41.4
3.0	3.9	3.3	4.1			Operating Profit	4.2	4.7
1.5	1.4	.3	1.4			All Other Expenses (net)	.7	.8
1.6	2.5	3.0	2.8			Profit Before Taxes	3.5	3.9
						RATIOS		
3.3	5.2	2.3	2.8			Current	2.9	3.0
1.6	1.7	2.0	1.4				1.8	1.6
1.0	1.1	1.1	1.1				1.3	1.1
.8	1.6	1.3	1.1			Quick	1.0	.7
.2	(47) .5	.5	.3				.4 (156)	.3
.0	.2	.1	.2				.1	.1
0 UND	0 UND	0 UND	2 219.6			Sales/Receivables	0 UND	0 UND
0 UND	8 43.5	5 72.1	5 73.7				3 120.8	2 196.0
5 71.5	36 10.2	36 10.2	28 13.0				29 12.5	25 14.8
74 4.9	52 7.0	77 4.7	93 3.9			Cost of Sales/Inventory	65 5.7	74 4.9
121 3.0	124 2.9	104 3.5	130 2.8				132 2.8	125 2.9
153 2.4	260 1.4	173 2.1	205 1.8				208 1.8	191 1.9
3 134.8	18 20.1	27 13.6	24 15.4			Cost of Sales/Payables	20 18.6	14 25.8
18 19.8	41 8.8	55 6.7	40 9.1				37 9.8	37 10.0
60 6.1	69 5.3	92 3.9	67 5.4				69 5.3	59 6.2
6.3	3.5	4.9	4.2			Sales/Working Capital	4.7	4.9
15.8	9.0	8.6	16.9				9.4	10.1
NM	57.8	27.5	49.8				26.0	56.7
11.6	22.3	9.7	7.9			EBIT/Interest	12.7	11.6
(26) 3.2	(37) 1.8	(42) 4.0	(24) 4.9				(134) 4.4	(136) 3.8
.4	.0	1.2	1.1				1.0	1.4
						Net Profit + Depr., Dep., Amort./Cur. Mat. L/T/D	6.8	6.3
							(16) 2.3	(19) 3.7
							1.2	1.1
.1	.1	.1	.2			Fixed/Worth	.1	.1
.4	.5	.4	.6				.4	.4
-.9	14.5	1.4	1.7				1.9	1.6
.9	.5	.6	.8			Debt/Worth	.8	.6
12.1	2.6	1.2	2.2				2.1	1.8
-3.1	34.9	6.5	3.7				8.7	6.0
229.5	56.2	28.2	49.5			% Profit Before Taxes/Tangible Net Worth	52.7	69.3
(25) 34.8	(38) 11.3	(41) 15.5	(23) 14.9				(122) 27.9	(134) 27.2
-3.0	-6.6	3.6	1.1				7.5	4.0
24.0	20.5	11.5	16.5			% Profit Before Taxes/Total Assets	19.4	19.4
9.4	3.9	6.8	5.1				8.8	6.8
-3.2	-2.8	.8	.3				.2	.9
516.0	242.9	43.5	45.0			Sales/Net Fixed Assets	62.5	65.6
55.0	19.0	14.0	21.7				20.0	25.4
19.9	6.4	5.4	8.4				9.4	10.3
5.0	3.1	3.0	3.2			Sales/Total Assets	3.6	3.7
3.5	2.1	2.1	2.1				2.6	2.8
2.5	1.1	1.6	1.7				1.8	1.8
.2	.4	.6	.8			% Depr., Dep., Amort./Sales	.5	.4
(22) .5	(27) .9	(43) 1.0	(25) 1.3				(118) 1.1	(125) 1.0
1.4	3.2	1.9	2.3				2.0	1.9
3.2	3.5	1.9				% Officers', Directors' Owners' Comp/Sales	2.3	2.2
(24) 4.5	(26) 5.3	(29) 3.4					(81) 5.2	(79) 4.5
7.9	6.9	5.4					8.1	6.5
38346M	141453M	511266M	1423518M	411305M	1263444M	Net Sales ($)	3891456M	1693187M
9968M	53157M	216799M	579815M	375821M	308538M	Total Assets ($)	1359770M	701886M

M = $ thousand   MM = $ million
See Pages 9 through 22 for Explanation of Ratios and Data

Comparative Historical Data / Current Data Sorted by Sales

4/1/07-3/31/08 ALL	4/1/08-3/31/09 ALL	4/1/09-3/31/10 ALL	Type of Statement	0-1MM	1-3MM	3-5MM	5-10MM	10-25MM	25MM & OVER
11	16	19	Unqualified	1	1	1	1	5	10
17	21	19	Reviewed			2	3	9	5
20	17	22	Compiled	3	9	2	4	2	2
45	34	54	Tax Returns	24	15	6	2	4	3
56	42	55	Other	8	11	8	10	6	12
				23 (4/1-9/30/09)		146 (10/1/09-3/31/10)			
149	130	169	**NUMBER OF STATEMENTS**	36	36	19	20	26	32
%	%	%	**ASSETS**	%	%	%	%	%	%
8.7	8.4	11.1	Cash & Equivalents	11.6	9.3	14.1	12.1	10.3	10.7
10.3	12.7	10.9	Trade Receivables (net)	6.1	9.0	17.4	11.4	16.1	10.3
48.7	46.4	44.2	Inventory	46.4	52.3	38.8	37.9	40.8	42.5
2.8	2.4	2.0	All Other Current	.5	.9	2.8	1.7	3.0	3.9
70.5	69.9	68.2	Total Current	64.6	71.5	73.1	63.1	70.2	67.4
18.8	19.3	19.9	Fixed Assets (net)	18.2	15.7	22.7	26.9	18.6	21.6
4.8	4.6	5.0	Intangibles (net)	6.9	5.9	.4	3.5	4.4	6.2
6.0	6.2	6.8	All Other Non-Current	10.3	6.9	3.8	6.5	6.8	4.8
100.0	100.0	100.0	Total	100.0	100.0	100.0	100.0	100.0	100.0
			LIABILITIES						
14.6	13.6	13.6	Notes Payable-Short Term	18.6	16.2	9.0	12.1	9.1	12.7
3.5	3.6	3.5	Cur. Mat.-L.T.D.	7.0	3.0	1.0	3.4	2.2	2.6
16.7	21.5	19.1	Trade Payables	18.0	14.6	20.7	19.1	22.0	22.3
.1	.1	.1	Income Taxes Payable	.2	.0	.4	.0	.3	.0
11.9	11.8	9.4	All Other Current	9.1	6.7	6.8	13.3	6.9	13.7
46.8	50.6	45.7	Total Current	52.9	40.5	37.9	47.9	40.4	51.3
16.3	14.3	17.8	Long-Term Debt	24.5	17.3	11.5	18.2	9.0	21.3
.3	.1	.1	Deferred Taxes	.0	.0	.0	.0	.1	.2
8.7	7.5	12.7	All Other Non-Current	34.6	6.0	5.4	4.5	4.9	11.6
27.9	27.5	23.6	Net Worth	-12.1	36.1	45.2	29.4	45.7	15.5
100.0	100.0	100.0	Total Liabilities & Net Worth	100.0	100.0	100.0	100.0	100.0	100.0
			INCOME DATA						
100.0	100.0	100.0	Net Sales	100.0	100.0	100.0	100.0	100.0	100.0
45.7	45.0	46.2	Gross Profit	46.7	44.0	47.4	48.8	44.8	47.0
42.1	42.4	42.7	Operating Expenses	45.0	38.6	44.2	45.1	41.1	43.5
3.6	2.6	3.6	Operating Profit	1.7	5.4	3.2	3.7	3.7	3.5
1.4	1.5	1.2	All Other Expenses (net)	2.3	1.0	-.1	1.0	.1	1.7
2.2	1.1	2.4	Profit Before Taxes	-.6	4.4	3.3	2.7	3.6	1.8
			RATIOS						
3.0	2.5	2.5	Current	3.3	4.7	4.0	2.4	2.4	2.1
1.7	1.5	1.7		1.4	1.9	2.0	1.5	1.8	1.2
1.1	1.0	1.1		.8	1.3	1.5	.7	1.2	1.0
.8	.8	1.1	Quick	.8	1.1	1.8	1.1	1.3	.7
(148) .3	.3	(168) .4		(35) .2	.4	.9	.3	.6	.3
.1	.1	.1		.1	.1	.3	.1	.2	.1
0 UND	0 UND	0 UND	Sales/Receivables	0 UND	0 UND	0 999.8	0 UND	0 UND	1 352.4
2 155.9	5 66.9	4 94.4		0 UND	1 686.9	24 15.2	2 206.2	9 41.0	5 75.2
28 13.2	32 11.5	29 12.8		22 16.6	15 25.0	39 9.4	23 16.1	30 12.0	27 13.3
81 4.5	77 4.7	74 4.9	Cost of Sales/Inventory	101 3.6	88 4.1	46 8.0	51 7.2	60 6.1	87 4.2
139 2.6	113 3.2	120 3.0		133 2.7	123 3.0	95 3.8	100 3.6	100 3.6	115 3.2
222 1.6	215 1.7	200 1.8		226 1.6	201 1.8	222 1.6	172 2.1	148 2.5	188 1.9
14 26.4	20 18.0	17 21.5	Cost of Sales/Payables	0 UND	11 34.0	20 18.5	29 12.6	16 22.2	33 11.0
36 10.1	42 8.6	42 8.8		28 12.9	21 17.0	37 9.9	57 6.5	35 10.3	48 7.7
68 5.4	77 4.7	75 4.9		85 4.3	60 6.1	70 5.2	88 4.2	68 5.4	81 4.5
4.9	5.8	4.7	Sales/Working Capital	4.5	4.2	3.3	6.5	5.7	5.5
10.0	11.7	10.1		15.8	8.4	5.9	13.3	9.5	18.2
65.7	140.6	64.2		-34.1	26.5	18.1	-11.1	32.0	-134.7
8.0	6.7	8.9	EBIT/Interest	6.4	8.8	36.7	19.3	14.6	7.1
(132) 2.4	(108) 2.2	(136) 3.3		(25) .6	(27) 2.5	(16) 2.3	(16) 3.4	(23) 4.6	(29) 1.4
.8	-.4	.6		-.9	1.0	1.0	1.2	3.0	-.1
10.9	6.2	11.2	Net Profit + Depr., Dep., Amort./Cur. Mat. L/T/D						
(24) 2.4	(14) 2.8	(19) 2.7							
1.2	.7	1.1							
.2	.1	.1	Fixed/Worth	.1	.1	.1	.1	.1	.3
.6	.6	.5		2.1	.4	.4	.5	.3	1.1
10.5	3.4	9.9		-.5	4.6	.8	NM	1.2	-7.1
.8	1.0	.7	Debt/Worth	1.1	.4	.4	.6	.7	1.4
3.1	2.5	2.3		32.4	2.4	1.3	2.1	1.3	3.1
59.1	11.8	45.9		-2.2	44.5	7.0	NM	3.0	-45.3
54.1	43.1	45.7	% Profit Before Taxes/Tangible Net Worth	65.8	110.5	39.2	36.3	26.6	57.9
(118) 21.0	(105) 14.1	(130) 15.5		(21) 6.0	(28) 23.3	(15) 6.0	(24) 15.5	17.6	(23) 16.0
3.1	.2	1.2		-22.8	2.7	-.1	7.8	6.3	.1.9
15.7	14.8	16.5	% Profit Before Taxes/Total Assets	19.5	22.0	14.9	9.0	14.9	15.6
6.5	3.4	5.5		.4	6.9	1.2	3.7	8.8	4.3
-.7	-3.9	-1.3		-6.1	.4	.0	.3	2.1	-7.3
44.6	60.4	86.9	Sales/Net Fixed Assets	516.0	385.6	130.6	81.0	50.1	45.3
19.7	19.6	21.7		23.2	43.5	11.6	14.8	22.8	21.0
8.7	8.6	8.0		7.9	9.4	6.4	5.0	9.6	7.8
3.5	3.6	3.5	Sales/Total Assets	4.2	3.6	3.2	3.4	3.4	3.8
2.5	2.4	2.4		2.2	2.5	2.4	2.4	2.5	2.5
1.7	1.7	1.6		1.1	1.3	1.6	1.5	1.8	1.7
.5	.6	.4	% Depr., Dep., Amort./Sales	.5	.2	.3	.7	.5	.7
(115) 1.0	(101) 1.2	(122) 1.0		(20) 1.4	(20) .8	(13) .7	(16) 1.1	(25) 1.2	(28) 1.2
1.8	2.1	2.1		3.1	1.8	3.0	2.6	1.7	2.3
2.3	2.0	2.4	% Officers', Directors' Owners' Comp/Sales	3.4	3.9	2.1	2.7	1.3	1.6
(78) 4.0	(63) 3.7	(90) 4.0		(20) 4.8	(19) 6.2	(14) 3.0	(11) 4.0	(13) 3.5	(13) 2.0
6.7	6.2	6.5		9.7	8.1	5.2	6.2	5.7	4.6
3091418M	3048118M	3789332M	Net Sales ($)	20789M	58367M	72666M	149201M	386835M	3101474M
1344396M	1584245M	1544098M	Total Assets ($)	14886M	32084M	38742M	85668M	239423M	1133295M

© RMA 2010

M = $ thousand   MM = $ million
See Pages 9 through 22 for Explanation of Ratios and Data

Current Data Sorted by Assets   Comparative Historical Data

0-500M	500M-2MM	2-10MM	10-50MM	50-100MM	100-250MM		ALL 4/1/05-3/31/06	ALL 4/1/06-3/31/07
						Type of Statement		
			2	1	1	Unqualified	7	10
	4	2	2			Reviewed	11	7
3	7	4	3			Compiled	9	12
13	9	7	1		1	Tax Returns	24	18
13	6	13	3	3		Other	24	32
17 (4/1-9/30/09)			81 (10/1/09-3/31/10)					
29	26	26	11	4	2	**NUMBER OF STATEMENTS**	75	79
%	%	%	%	%	%	**ASSETS**	%	%
8.5	10.0	8.6	17.2			Cash & Equivalents	9.5	9.8
3.2	5.2	7.7	3.4			Trade Receivables (net)	4.1	5.9
66.6	65.7	56.7	40.8			Inventory	61.9	65.5
4.0	.7	1.5	1.2			All Other Current	2.8	1.6
82.2	81.6	74.4	62.7			Total Current	78.3	82.8
11.4	12.7	10.7	24.5			Fixed Assets (net)	13.1	11.3
4.4	2.0	3.9	.4			Intangibles (net)	2.1	2.6
2.0	3.7	10.9	12.5			All Other Non-Current	6.5	3.4
100.0	100.0	100.0	100.0			Total	100.0	100.0
						LIABILITIES		
14.8	10.1	8.5	5.3			Notes Payable-Short Term	11.2	14.0
6.8	1.7	1.1	9.7			Cur. Mat.-L.T.D.	4.2	2.9
7.4	20.5	33.1	13.4			Trade Payables	21.6	22.8
.7	.1	.0	.0			Income Taxes Payable	.2	.1
49.7	5.6	13.3	11.3			All Other Current	13.4	10.1
79.4	38.0	56.1	39.7			Total Current	50.5	49.8
12.4	17.9	4.4	16.0			Long-Term Debt	13.6	15.2
.0	.0	.0	.0			Deferred Taxes	.1	
1.0	1.8	2.6	2.0			All Other Non-Current	8.5	4.3
7.1	42.4	37.0	42.3			Net Worth	27.3	30.6
100.0	100.0	100.0	100.0			Total Liabilties & Net Worth	100.0	100.0
						INCOME DATA		
100.0	100.0	100.0	100.0			Net Sales	100.0	100.0
47.9	43.4	43.7	46.6			Gross Profit	43.3	42.2
46.7	39.7	40.1	39.2			Operating Expenses	42.2	38.7
1.2	3.7	3.5	7.4			Operating Profit	1.1	3.5
3.3	.3	.4	2.3			All Other Expenses (net)	.7	.9
-2.1	3.3	3.2	5.1			Profit Before Taxes	.5	2.6
						RATIOS		
2.8	3.2	2.1	5.1			Current	2.8	2.9
1.4	2.3	1.4	1.9				1.6	2.0
.8	1.6	1.2	.6				1.1	1.3
.6	.7	.5	1.4			Quick	.6	.8
.1	.2	.2	.9				(73) .2	.1
.0	.1	.0	.2				.1	.1
0 UND	0 UND	0 999.8	0 999.8			Sales/Receivables	0 UND	0 UND
0 UND	0 UND	0 999.8	3 133.6				1 378.1	1 558.5
2 165.1	11 32.8	4 82.5	11 32.9				6 58.7	4 92.5
103 3.5	88 4.2	93 3.9	56 6.5			Cost of Sales/Inventory	115 3.2	109 3.3
189 1.9	196 1.9	139 2.6	133 2.7				176 2.1	184 2.0
261 1.4	290 1.3	218 1.7	257 1.4				249 1.5	232 1.6
0 UND	25 14.7	42 8.7	15 24.8			Cost of Sales/Payables	27 13.4	26 13.9
5 69.5	47 7.7	70 5.2	28 13.0				47 7.7	44 8.2
37 9.8	77 4.8	102 3.6	75 4.9				72 5.1	73 5.0
3.5	3.4	6.5	3.2			Sales/Working Capital	4.0	3.7
13.9	6.0	10.9	4.4				7.0	6.3
-16.9	11.8	30.7	-13.0				37.5	20.0
7.4	11.7	46.7				EBIT/Interest	5.5	7.6
(17) .0	(22) 4.4	(24) 4.2					(67) 2.1	(73) 2.5
-3.5	1.1	1.0					.8	.4
						Net Profit + Depr., Dep., Amort./Cur. Mat. L/T/D	4.1	13.4
							(10) 2.4	(14) 3.0
							.2	1.4
.0	.1	.1	.2			Fixed/Worth	.1	.1
.4	.3	.2	.4				.3	.3
-1.2	.7	.6	10.8				2.0	.9
.6	.6	.6	.2			Debt/Worth	.6	.8
2.8	1.2	2.0	1.0				2.4	1.9
-7.1	3.6	4.4	16.5				8.5	5.1
59.0	34.9	38.3	21.2			% Profit Before Taxes/Tangible Net Worth	27.4	33.0
(17) 17.7	(24) 16.9	(24) 16.3	(10) 18.9				(60) 9.2	(68) 14.4
-.9	2.7	.5	-4.6				1.2	.7
20.5	19.5	12.6	18.5			% Profit Before Taxes/Total Assets	9.1	11.5
-.3	7.0	7.2	9.8				1.6	3.8
-19.0	.5	-.1	2.3				-2.5	-1.0
231.4	61.8	122.2	18.5			Sales/Net Fixed Assets	74.1	107.0
31.4	29.6	51.8	11.9				24.4	34.5
11.8	17.7	9.8	7.5				11.9	14.2
3.4	3.8	3.4	3.1			Sales/Total Assets	3.2	3.5
2.4	2.4	2.9	2.1				2.3	2.4
1.9	1.7	1.5	1.3				1.7	1.8
.4	.3	.2	.8			% Depr., Dep., Amort./Sales	.5	.5
(21) .9	(19) .6	(19) .6	(10) 1.0				(61) .9	(60) .7
2.0	1.3	1.0	2.8				1.5	1.3
2.9	2.9	1.6				% Officers', Directors' Owners' Comp/Sales	2.1	1.9
(22) 5.8	(14) 4.4	(13) 2.2					(43) 4.1	(45) 4.7
16.0	7.0	5.3					9.4	9.0
23292M	90303M	336674M	619364M	532258M	633682M	Net Sales ($)	1892433M	3391706M
8558M	32255M	119248M	263306M	301875M	286336M	Total Assets ($)	914077M	1562172M

M = $ thousand   MM = $ million
See Pages 9 through 22 for Explanation of Ratios and Data

Comparative Historical Data | Current Data Sorted by Sales

Type of Statement	4/1/07-3/31/08	4/1/08-3/31/09	4/1/09-3/31/10		0-1MM	1-3MM	3-5MM	5-10MM	10-25MM	25MM & OVER
Unqualified	6	7	4			2	1	1	2	4
Reviewed	12	9	8		2	5	1	5	2	2
Compiled	16	14	17		11	8	4	5	2	2
Tax Returns	22	29	31		9	9	1	4	8	1
Other	29	31	38							7
	ALL	ALL	ALL		17 (4/1-9/30/09)			81 (10/1/09-3/31/10)		
NUMBER OF STATEMENTS	85	90	98		22	24	7	15	14	16

	%	%	%		%	%	%	%	%	%
ASSETS										
Cash & Equivalents	9.3	13.3	11.0		8.7	7.6		9.0	9.2	21.1
Trade Receivables (net)	5.3	4.3	5.3		4.1	4.5		10.1	2.7	5.3
Inventory	61.1	58.0	58.7		62.6	66.7		56.5	63.7	43.8
All Other Current	2.4	2.2	2.3		4.8	1.0		.9	2.2	3.0
Total Current	78.1	77.9	77.3		80.2	79.8		76.4	77.9	73.3
Fixed Assets (net)	14.7	14.5	13.1		13.0	11.9		9.8	13.5	16.8
Intangibles (net)	1.3	2.8	3.5		5.8	1.1		1.8	1.7	3.8
All Other Non-Current	5.9	4.8	6.2		1.1	7.2		11.9	6.9	6.2
Total	100.0	100.0	100.0		100.0	100.0		100.0	100.0	100.0
LIABILITIES										
Notes Payable-Short Term	9.9	11.5	10.1		14.8	10.3		9.3	10.2	4.6
Cur. Mat.-L.T.D.	3.7	3.3	3.9		8.4	1.1		1.4	1.1	6.5
Trade Payables	23.0	22.7	18.6		6.3	16.0		23.6	36.7	16.2
Income Taxes Payable	.0	.1	.2		.2	.0		.1	.1	.2
All Other Current	10.4	9.4	21.5		50.2	19.9		17.5	6.3	9.3
Total Current	47.0	47.0	54.3		79.9	47.3		51.8	54.3	36.8
Long-Term Debt	7.0	14.5	12.1		10.0	21.6		8.0	1.1	10.3
Deferred Taxes	.0	.0	.0		.0	.0		.0	.1	.0
All Other Non-Current	5.7	6.0	2.5		1.3	1.9		2.0	2.8	6.3
Net Worth	40.2	32.4	31.0		8.7	29.2		38.1	41.7	46.6
Total Liabilities & Net Worth	100.0	100.0	100.0		100.0	100.0		100.0	100.0	100.0
INCOME DATA										
Net Sales	100.0	100.0	100.0		100.0	100.0		100.0	100.0	100.0
Gross Profit	43.1	41.9	45.0		48.0	50.2		43.2	37.9	40.6
Operating Expenses	39.6	39.2	41.9		48.0	45.4		37.2	36.5	36.9
Operating Profit	3.4	2.7	3.1		-.1	4.8		6.0	1.4	3.7
All Other Expenses (net)	.8	.8	1.5		3.0	3.2		-.2	.2	.7
Profit Before Taxes	2.7	1.9	1.6		-3.1	1.6		6.1	1.1	3.0
RATIOS										
Current	3.5	3.2	3.0		3.3	4.0		3.0	1.9	7.1
	1.7	1.7	1.8		1.5	2.0		1.9	1.4	2.5
	1.2	1.2	1.2		.7	1.3		1.5	1.1	1.4
Quick	.7	.9	.8		.9	.4		.9	.4	1.6
	.3	.2	.2		.1	.1		.3	.1	.9
	.1	.1	.0		.0	.0		.0	.0	.2
Sales/Receivables	0 UND	0 UND	0 UND		0 UND	0 UND		0 999.8	0 UND	0 999.8
	1 389.0	0 UND	0 999.8		0 UND	0 UND		0 999.8	0 999.8	3 118.0
	6 60.2	4 95.0	6 56.5		9 42.3	3 144.4		26 14.1	1 291.2	19 19.1
Cost of Sales/Inventory	98 3.7	81 4.5	88 4.2		101 3.6	151 2.4		85 4.3	71 5.1	57 6.4
	167 2.2	159 2.3	163 2.2		210 1.7	242 1.5		133 2.7	116 3.2	94 3.9
	219 1.7	232 1.6	255 1.4		366 1.0	393 .9		219 1.7	151 2.4	183 2.0
Cost of Sales/Payables	22 16.7	22 17.0	15 24.6		0 UND	5 68.2		25 14.3	42 8.7	16 22.4
	42 8.6	40 9.0	40 9.2		9 39.6	60 6.1		45 8.2	45 8.1	29 12.7
	82 4.4	76 4.8	75 4.9		46 7.9	94 3.9		85 4.3	97 3.8	41 8.8
Sales/Working Capital	4.0	3.9	3.6		3.2	2.9		5.6	8.9	3.3
	7.2	7.6	8.3		9.8	6.0		7.7	15.4	5.6
	21.2	41.0	24.2		-5.2	15.1		10.7	41.5	-20.9
EBIT/Interest	9.6	11.6	23.3		4.4	11.4		38.8	46.0	40.8
	(66) 2.9	(76) 3.0	(76) 4.2		(15) -.8	(15) 5.2		(14) 4.1	(13) 4.3	(13) 12.9
	.8	.2	.6		-4.0	.1		2.0	.6	1.7
Net Profit + Depr., Dep., Amort./Cur. Mat. L/T/D	2.5	1.9	3.9							
	(14) .7	(14) 1.4	(13) 2.1							
	-22.3	.0	1.2							
Fixed/Worth	.1	.1	.1		.0	.0		.1	.1	.2
	.3	.3	.3		.5	.2		.2	.3	.3
	.9	1.7	1.2		-1.6	1.6		.3	.8	9.0
Debt/Worth	.6	.6	.5		.5	.6		.6	.8	.2
	1.5	1.7	1.6		2.5	1.5		1.4	1.7	1.0
	5.2	8.1	6.9		-7.9	6.8		2.0	4.4	17.0
% Profit Before Taxes/Tangible Net Worth	39.1	46.0	36.8		48.7	24.1		70.7	37.7	24.0
	(78) 17.5	(74) 15.5	(79) 16.7		(12) 10.6	(20) 10.8		(14) 21.2	14.8	(13) 18.4
	.7	2.0	.2		-.3	-1.0		9.8	-2.0	-2.1
% Profit Before Taxes/Total Assets	14.5	13.6	17.6		20.4	10.7		21.6	13.9	18.2
	5.2	4.1	5.5		-1.8	2.0		9.0	6.7	6.6
	-1.1	-2.3	-1.6		-24.3	-2.6		1.3	-.5	2.6
Sales/Net Fixed Assets	79.5	71.7	93.7		232.8	152.1		90.1	103.4	68.0
	25.6	26.9	25.6		17.7	45.8		34.4	73.1	13.7
	11.8	11.4	11.6		9.5	16.4		10.0	12.9	9.4
Sales/Total Assets	3.6	3.5	3.4		2.6	3.0		3.7	3.9	3.2
	2.5	2.4	2.4		2.3	1.9		2.9	3.3	2.1
	1.9	1.8	1.7		1.5	1.5		1.5	2.8	1.9
% Depr., Dep., Amort./Sales	.5	.5	.4		.6	.3		.2		.5
	(68) .9	(71) .9	(73) .7		(15) 1.1	(18) .7		(13) .5	(13) .9	
	1.8	1.9	1.5		2.0	1.4		1.2		2.0
% Officers', Directors' Owners' Comp/Sales	1.6	1.7	2.1		3.4	2.9				
	(39) 3.4	(47) 4.3	(56) 4.1		(17) 7.5	(14) 3.7				
	7.3	7.4	7.9		17.4	7.8				
Net Sales ($)	4221032M	1950471M	2235573M		11882M	42276M	26383M	100931M	238483M	1815618M
Total Assets ($)	1726681M	951869M	1011578M		6074M	37009M	10325M	53326M	71702M	833142M

© RMA 2010

M = $ thousand   MM = $ million
See Pages 9 through 22 for Explanation of Ratios and Data

RETAIL—Jewelry Stores NAICS 448310

| Current Data Sorted by Assets | | | | | | | Comparative Historical Data | |

0-500M	500M-2MM	2-10MM	10-50MM	50-100MM	100-250MM	Type of Statement	4/1/05-3/31/06 ALL	4/1/06-3/31/07 ALL
1	4	16	8	3	4	Unqualified	16	12
4	25	23	11			Reviewed	42	45
28	41	22	4			Compiled	72	66
5	24	31	1			Tax Returns	68	79
			17	2	2	Other	77	70
68 (4/1-9/30/09)			208 (10/1/09-3/31/10)					
38	94	92	41	5	6	NUMBER OF STATEMENTS	275	272
%	%	%	%	%	%	ASSETS	%	%
15.9	8.2	4.9	4.3			Cash & Equivalents	6.3	6.8
1.8	6.5	8.8	12.0			Trade Receivables (net)	7.9	8.1
64.0	66.6	66.1	65.8			Inventory	69.5	68.5
.8	1.1	2.5	.9			All Other Current	.6	1.2
82.5	82.5	82.4	82.9			Total Current	84.3	84.5
8.1	10.7	10.7	10.2			Fixed Assets (net)	9.4	10.3
4.7	2.4	.8	3.0			Intangibles (net)	1.1	1.3
4.7	4.4	6.2	3.8			All Other Non-Current	5.2	3.8
100.0	100.0	100.0	100.0			Total	100.0	100.0
						LIABILITIES		
13.3	15.6	13.3	16.6			Notes Payable-Short Term	14.6	14.2
4.7	1.9	1.7	3.0			Cur. Mat.-L.T.D.	2.7	2.3
13.8	19.6	18.9	13.1			Trade Payables	21.6	22.9
.1	.0	.2	.5			Income Taxes Payable	.2	.1
14.0	7.7	8.4	9.2			All Other Current	8.2	9.4
46.0	44.9	42.4	42.4			Total Current	47.3	48.9
18.0	15.1	9.0	8.0			Long-Term Debt	9.5	9.5
.0	.0	.0	.2			Deferred Taxes	.2	.0
10.2	8.1	7.9	8.8			All Other Non-Current	6.6	5.6
25.9	32.0	40.6	40.5			Net Worth	36.4	36.0
100.0	100.0	100.0	100.0			Total Liabilities & Net Worth	100.0	100.0
						INCOME DATA		
100.0	100.0	100.0	100.0			Net Sales	100.0	100.0
48.1	44.8	38.9	41.8			Gross Profit	43.6	42.7
43.0	41.6	36.2	37.5			Operating Expenses	39.4	38.1
5.1	3.2	2.6	4.3			Operating Profit	4.3	4.6
1.2	1.6	1.2	.8			All Other Expenses (net)	1.1	1.3
3.9	1.6	1.5	3.5			Profit Before Taxes	3.1	3.3
						RATIOS		
3.9	4.8	3.1	2.9			Current	2.8	2.6
1.9	2.0	1.9	2.0				1.8	1.7
1.3	1.2	1.4	1.4				1.4	1.3
.6	.7	.5	.6			Quick	.5	.6
.3	.2	.3	.3				(274) .2	.2
.1	.1	.1	.1				.1	.1
0 UND	0 UND	1 340.5	2 161.6			Sales/Receivables	0 UND	0 UND
0 UND	5 77.4	9 39.5	16 23.3				6 64.6	5 67.7
2 158.3	14 26.0	30 12.3	48 7.6				24 15.5	22 16.8
61 6.0	201 1.8	192 1.9	200 1.8			Cost of Sales/Inventory	203 1.8	189 1.9
255 1.4	347 1.1	308 1.2	363 1.0				292 1.3	290 1.3
653 .6	540 .7	453 .8	494 .7				388 .9	374 1.0
0 UND	20 18.4	33 11.2	27 13.6			Cost of Sales/Payables	36 10.1	40 9.1
33 11.0	51 7.2	66 5.5	60 6.0				69 5.3	77 4.7
83 4.4	113 3.2	102 3.6	88 4.1				125 2.9	132 2.8
2.3	1.9	2.2	1.9			Sales/Working Capital	2.8	2.6
6.3	4.1	3.2	3.4				4.6	4.8
26.3	8.7	6.6	5.4				8.0	8.1
12.5	5.6	7.9	9.2			EBIT/Interest	6.6	6.4
(27) 3.5	(86) 2.3	(88) 2.5	(38) 3.0				(254) 2.6	(243) 2.6
1.0	-.1	1.3	1.2				1.1	1.1
		1.2	10.9			Net Profit + Depr., Dep., Amort./Cur. Mat. L/T/D	6.5	3.3
	(13) .8	(12) 3.6					(47) 2.2	(43) 1.3
	.1	1.3					.9	.6
.0	.0	.0	.1			Fixed/Worth	.1	.1
.1	.2	.2	.2				.2	.2
-4.3	1.0	.5	.4				.5	.6
.5	.7	.8	.6			Debt/Worth	.9	.9
2.5	2.0	1.5	1.0				1.7	1.8
-11.5	15.4	3.7	2.7				4.0	3.7
115.1	27.1	19.6	15.8			% Profit Before Taxes/Tangible Net Worth	26.5	29.5
(26) 19.5	(75) 7.2	(90) 8.3	(37) 6.4				(254) 10.6	(244) 11.2
5.2	2.4	1.4	.6				2.3	3.0
17.3	7.0	6.9	7.6			% Profit Before Taxes/Total Assets	9.8	10.7
9.4	2.2	2.8	2.7				3.2	4.4
.2	-2.2	.6	.3				.2	.5
UND	92.0	57.8	27.8			Sales/Net Fixed Assets	89.3	71.8
44.6	22.3	21.7	18.1				26.3	24.6
13.5	8.2	8.5	8.4				11.5	10.7
3.6	2.0	1.9	1.7			Sales/Total Assets	2.1	2.1
2.1	1.3	1.3	1.2				1.6	1.6
1.2	.9	.9	1.0				1.2	1.2
.3	.4	.4	.7			% Depr., Dep., Amort./Sales	.4	.4
(20) 1.4	(64) 1.1	(79) .8	(34) 1.2				(220) .8	(224) .8
2.5	2.2	1.8	1.9				1.6	1.6
4.2	4.0	2.0	2.0			% Officers', Directors' Owners' Comp/Sales	3.0	3.1
(28) 8.9	(48) 7.2	(37) 3.3	(11) 2.3				(152) 5.6	(152) 5.3
13.4	11.0	5.9	3.6				8.8	8.3
40375M	175124M	648935M	1331042M	752809M	1521105M	Net Sales ($)	4749367M	4775457M
10570M	98401M	455297M	950982M	275061M	986124M	Total Assets ($)	3186932M	3206450M

© RMA 2010

M = $ thousand   MM = $ million
See Pages 9 through 22 for Explanation of Ratios and Data

Comparative Historical Data   Current Data Sorted by Sales

Type of Statement	4/1/07-3/31/08 ALL	4/1/08-3/31/09 ALL	4/1/09-3/31/10 ALL	68 (4/1-9/30/09) 0-1MM	1-3MM	3-5MM	208 (10/1/09-3/31/10) 5-10MM	10-25MM	25MM & OVER
Unqualified	14	12	16	1	4	1	8	2	13
Reviewed	45	36	31	3				8	7
Compiled	55	73	56	13	16	9	12	6	
Tax Returns	73	68	92	38	28	8	13	5	
Other	89	90	81	11	17	14	7	20	12
NUMBER OF STATEMENTS	276	279	276	66	65	32	40	41	32
ASSETS	%	%	%	%	%	%	%	%	%
Cash & Equivalents	5.8	5.6	7.8	10.7	6.7	6.1	6.3	8.1	7.1
Trade Receivables (net)	8.1	7.3	7.4	2.3	4.9	8.2	11.3	11.3	12.8
Inventory	68.7	68.6	65.5	66.4	69.4	72.0	61.9	63.2	56.7
All Other Current	1.5	1.5	1.7	1.3	1.3	1.2	2.5	1.6	2.6
Total Current	84.1	83.0	82.4	80.6	82.3	87.5	82.0	84.2	79.2
Fixed Assets (net)	10.2	10.1	10.5	8.1	13.7	7.4	8.7	12.0	12.3
Intangibles (net)	1.6	2.0	2.3	5.3	.8	.9	.5	.8	4.4
All Other Non-Current	4.1	4.9	4.9	6.0	3.2	4.1	8.7	3.1	4.0
Total	100.0	100.0	100.0	100.0	100.0	100.0	100.0	100.0	100.0
LIABILITIES									
Notes Payable-Short Term	15.1	15.1	14.5	15.7	14.8	13.0	12.8	15.5	13.9
Cur. Mat.-L.T.D.	2.3	3.7	2.4	3.1	2.0	3.3	1.0	1.4	3.8
Trade Payables	20.9	19.1	17.7	15.3	16.3	20.2	21.1	16.8	19.6
Income Taxes Payable	.1	.1	.2	.1	.1	.4	.1	.0	.7
All Other Current	9.1	8.8	9.0	9.9	8.6	10.5	7.7	9.7	7.5
Total Current	47.4	46.8	43.8	44.1	41.7	47.3	42.6	43.4	45.5
Long-Term Debt	13.5	12.8	12.4	18.7	14.5	9.9	5.5	9.6	10.3
Deferred Taxes	.1	.1	.1	.0	.0	.0	.0	.1	.8
All Other Non-Current	7.9	8.7	8.3	9.2	11.4	5.7	5.3	6.2	8.9
Net Worth	31.1	31.6	35.4	28.0	32.3	37.0	46.6	40.8	34.4
Total Liabilities & Net Worth	100.0	100.0	100.0	100.0	100.0	100.0	100.0	100.0	100.0
INCOME DATA									
Net Sales	100.0	100.0	100.0	100.0	100.0	100.0	100.0	100.0	100.0
Gross Profit	43.1	43.6	42.7	50.9	43.8	39.4	34.5	41.3	38.7
Operating Expenses	39.0	40.7	39.4	47.3	40.4	34.7	31.2	39.9	35.0
Operating Profit	4.1	3.0	3.3	3.7	3.4	4.6	3.3	1.4	3.7
All Other Expenses (net)	1.9	1.5	1.3	1.5	2.0	2.0	.5	-.3	1.5
Profit Before Taxes	2.2	1.5	2.1	2.2	1.4	2.7	2.8	1.7	2.2
RATIOS									
Current	2.9	3.1	3.4	4.9	3.9	2.8	3.1	3.2	2.8
	1.9	1.9	2.0	2.0	2.0	2.1	1.9	1.9	1.8
	1.3	1.4	1.4	1.2	1.5	1.3	1.4	1.4	1.3
Quick	.6	.5	.6	.6	.6	.4	.8	.7	.6
	.2	(277) .2	.3	.2	.2	.1	.3	.4	.3
	.1	.1	.1	.1	.1	.0	.1	.2	.1
Sales/Receivables	0 UND	0 UND	0 UND	0 UND	0 UND	0 UND	2 163.8	2 193.1	3 111.0
	6 60.5	5 68.4	5 68.2	0 UND	4 99.4	6 65.1	10 35.5	16 23.0	9 42.6
	20 18.2	18 20.2	18 20.2	7 50.4	15 24.8	15 25.2	20 18.6	35 10.5	36 10.1
Cost of Sales/Inventory	189 1.9	193 1.9	185 2.0	282 1.3	210 1.7	190 1.9	132 2.8	197 1.9	104 3.5
	304 1.2	312 1.2	308 1.2	513 .7	330 1.1	302 1.2	252 1.4	279 1.3	215 1.7
	438 .8	479 .8	496 .7	822 .4	505 .7	421 .9	440 .8	484 .8	307 1.2
Cost of Sales/Payables	30 12.2	28 12.8	24 14.9	5 77.9	18 20.6	22 16.4	25 14.6	33 11.2	29 12.4
	68 5.4	58 6.3	54 6.7	55 6.6	49 7.5	55 6.7	62 5.8	53 6.9	56 6.5
	126 2.9	118 3.1	102 3.6	114 3.2	118 3.1	111 3.3	87 4.2	80 4.6	98 3.7
Sales/Working Capital	2.5	2.5	2.0	1.5	2.1	2.2	2.6	1.9	3.1
	4.4	4.4	3.9	4.0	3.2	3.7	3.9	3.9	4.5
	7.6	8.7	8.4	9.2	6.3	14.5	8.5	9.0	9.7
EBIT/Interest	5.3	5.9	8.1	5.6	4.7	7.2	10.1	13.9	8.8
	(258) 2.1	(261) 1.7	(249) 2.8	(51) 1.8	(61) 1.9	(30) 3.0	(38) 3.3	(38) 3.3	(31) 2.7
	1.0	.5	1.0	-.1	.1	1.5	1.3	.6	.7
Net Profit + Depr., Dep., Amort./Cur. Mat. L/T/D	4.7	1.9	6.8		2.5				11.6
	(50) 1.7	(47) .7	(36) 1.4		(10) 1.2			(11) 5.4	
	.4	.0	.7		.7				.8
Fixed/Worth	.1	.1	.0	.0	.0	.1	.0	.1	.1
	.2	.2	.2	.2	.3	.1	.1	.3	.2
	.7	.7	.6	NM	1.5	.4	.4	.5	.6
Debt/Worth	.9	.8	.7	.7	.6	.8	.6	.5	.7
	2.0	1.9	1.8	2.3	1.9	1.5	1.2	1.5	1.7
	5.9	5.6	5.9	-12.2	10.9	3.9	2.0	5.2	3.0
% Profit Before Taxes/Tangible Net Worth	26.2	22.1	20.7	29.6	19.1	17.8	27.0	24.0	13.0
	(237) 9.2	(243) 7.6	(237) 8.2	(46) 7.1	(54) 7.2	(31) 11.0	(39) 9.2	(27) 8.0	7.7
	1.2	-.7	1.7	-1.2	.5	3.8	1.9	-2.4	.2
% Profit Before Taxes/Total Assets	8.4	7.2	8.1	11.1	6.2	5.8	8.8	9.7	7.6
	2.9	1.9	2.8	2.2	2.1	3.0	4.3	3.5	3.5
	-.2	-1.6	-.2	-2.8	-2.0	1.7	.7	-1.8	-.5
Sales/Net Fixed Assets	79.9	80.4	68.2	103.6	66.2	88.1	117.1	30.4	30.7
	23.7	25.4	21.2	21.4	22.3	36.3	37.7	15.5	18.3
	10.4	10.1	8.5	8.4	6.7	15.3	8.5	8.6	9.1
Sales/Total Assets	2.0	2.1	2.0	1.6	2.0	2.2	2.2	2.3	2.1
	1.5	1.5	1.4	1.1	1.3	1.5	1.5	1.3	1.7
	1.2	1.1	1.0	.7	1.0	.9	1.0	1.0	1.3
% Depr., Dep., Amort./Sales	.4	.3	.5	.7	.4	.2	.2	.6	.7
	(217) .9	(212) .9	(207) 1.1	(35) 1.5	(54) 1.1	(23) .8	(35) .6	(33) 1.2	(27) 1.5
	1.7	1.9	2.0	2.6	2.5	1.0	1.2	2.0	2.3
% Officers', Directors' Owners' Comp/Sales	2.9	3.1	2.7	5.6	4.4	2.3	1.6	1.0	
	(147) 5.2	(138) 5.5	(124) 5.3	(38) 9.2	(32) 6.2	(15) 6.2	(21) 3.6	(13) 2.3	
	8.5	9.7	9.3	13.1	9.9	7.9	5.8	3.0	
Net Sales ($)	7046532M	5279892M	4469390M	38960M	116478M	120155M	275742M	626605M	3291450M
Total Assets ($)	3982732M	3232773M	2776435M	47482M	102685M	93491M	197846M	503329M	1831602M

© RMA 2010

M = $ thousand   MM = $ million
See Pages 9 through 22 for Explanation of Ratios and Data

Current Data Sorted by Assets — Comparative Historical Data

Type of Statement

Type of Statement	0-500M	500M-2MM	2-10MM	10-50MM	50-100MM	100-250MM	4/1/05-3/31/06 ALL	4/1/06-3/31/07 ALL
Unqualified			2	10	5	3	11	13
Reviewed	1	9	18	6			37	40
Compiled	4	22	34	5		2	53	73
Tax Returns	36	44	17	2		5	81	96
Other	19	45	37	16	3		96	109

56 (4/1-9/30/09) · 289 (10/1/09-3/31/10)

0-500M	500M-2MM	2-10MM	10-50MM	50-100MM	100-250MM		4/1/05-3/31/06 ALL	4/1/06-3/31/07 ALL
60	120	108	39	8	10	**NUMBER OF STATEMENTS**	278	331
%	%	%	%	%	%	**ASSETS**	%	%
10.8	11.6	8.6	5.9		7.3	Cash & Equivalents	8.0	9.0
4.7	5.7	5.9	4.0		9.2	Trade Receivables (net)	7.3	7.3
64.5	56.2	60.1	49.4		50.5	Inventory	59.7	57.8
.8	1.5	1.6	6.4		2.2	All Other Current	1.8	1.6
80.7	74.9	76.2	65.7		69.2	Total Current	76.7	75.7
11.7	16.8	15.4	21.5		19.1	Fixed Assets (net)	15.9	15.9
3.5	3.9	4.2	7.0		10.0	Intangibles (net)	2.8	3.2
4.1	4.3	4.2	5.8		1.7	All Other Non-Current	4.5	5.2
100.0	100.0	100.0	100.0		100.0	Total	100.0	100.0
						LIABILITIES		
14.1	13.2	13.5	11.2		3.3	Notes Payable-Short Term	15.5	14.0
5.8	2.5	3.6	5.3		1.4	Cur. Mat.-L.T.D.	2.8	2.5
29.5	25.1	25.2	21.7		24.2	Trade Payables	25.2	24.3
.0	.1	.4	.2		.7	Income Taxes Payable	.2	.2
14.1	15.6	8.8	11.2		8.5	All Other Current	9.1	8.6
63.5	56.5	51.4	49.6		38.1	Total Current	52.8	49.6
16.0	13.9	11.9	16.7		27.6	Long-Term Debt	13.2	14.9
.0	.0	.1	.0		.2	Deferred Taxes	.1	.2
7.9	7.8	3.9	4.3		11.5	All Other Non-Current	8.5	8.2
12.6	21.8	32.7	29.4		22.6	Net Worth	25.3	27.1
100.0	100.0	100.0	100.0		100.0	Total Liabilities & Net Worth	100.0	100.0
						INCOME DATA		
100.0	100.0	100.0	100.0		100.0	Net Sales	100.0	100.0
40.9	38.1	33.2	37.3		36.1	Gross Profit	38.2	37.3
39.9	35.6	31.0	34.7		33.6	Operating Expenses	36.4	34.4
1.1	2.5	2.2	2.6		2.6	Operating Profit	1.8	2.8
.8	1.0	.6	.8		1.9	All Other Expenses (net)	1.0	1.4
.2	1.5	1.5	1.8		.7	Profit Before Taxes	.8	1.4
						RATIOS		
2.8	2.9	2.2	2.1		2.8	Current	2.3	2.4
1.6	1.6	1.5	1.4		1.8		1.6	1.6
1.0	1.0	1.1	.9		1.3		1.1	1.1
.6	.9	.6	.4		.6	Quick	.5	.6
(119) .2	.2	(107) .2	.2		.1		(274) .2	(328) .2
.1	.1	.1	.0		.0		.1	.1
0 UND	0 UND	0 UND	1 510.3		0 UND	Sales/Receivables	0 UND	0 UND
0 813.4	1 325.4	2 191.1	2 185.0		2 192.2		2 149.9	2 174.1
8 45.7	8 44.1	8 43.6	9 41.5		4 81.4		14 26.7	14 25.3
78 4.7	86 4.3	94 3.9	95 3.8		47 7.8	Cost of Sales/Inventory	98 3.7	90 4.1
171 2.1	134 2.7	140 2.6	147 2.5		135 2.7		150 2.4	134 2.7
254 1.4	206 1.8	206 1.8	195 1.9		210 1.7		202 1.8	199 1.8
6 56.3	19 18.8	32 11.5	24 15.4		40 9.1	Cost of Sales/Payables	27 13.7	25 14.7
45 8.0	46 7.9	49 7.5	49 7.5		43 8.6		53 6.9	50 7.3
105 3.5	93 3.9	75 4.9	81 4.5		87 4.2		87 4.2	84 4.3
4.9	4.4	5.5	5.1		6.6	Sales/Working Capital	5.7	4.9
12.6	9.0	9.6	12.9		9.8		10.3	9.6
-288.1	NM	26.9	-61.1		17.7		41.1	35.5
4.7	11.2	8.5	9.2			EBIT/Interest	6.4	6.4
(47) 1.0	(95) 2.6	(104) 2.7	2.2				(248) 2.4	(287) 2.4
-3.0	.5	.8	-.1				.4	1.0
		(25) 6.4				Net Profit + Depr., Dep., Amort./Cur. Mat. L/T/D	(35) 13.2	(43) 6.0
		2.0					4.5	2.5
		.4					1.1	1.0
.1	.1	.2	.2		.4	Fixed/Worth	.2	.1
.8	.4	.3	1.1		1.2		.5	.4
-1.0	-7.0	1.4	6.5		-.5		2.3	1.6
1.1	.8	1.1	1.2		1.4	Debt/Worth	1.0	1.0
5.3	3.1	2.5	3.7		2.2		2.7	2.3
-7.1	-20.3	6.4	14.5		-3.5		13.8	10.3
57.6	32.1	29.8	49.6			% Profit Before Taxes/Tangible Net Worth	37.3	41.1
(40) 12.1	(84) 15.9	(96) 12.7	(30) 17.5				(229) 14.2	(271) 14.7
-10.0	1.1	.7	-7.6				-2.2	2.3
11.2	10.9	7.8	11.1		9.1	% Profit Before Taxes/Total Assets	10.5	11.4
.1	3.9	3.5	4.0		1.9		3.0	4.0
-9.7	-2.3	.0	-4.6		-3.7		-2.2	-.2
142.1	91.8	58.5	86.2		50.6	Sales/Net Fixed Assets	65.5	75.2
37.1	30.8	25.6	20.7		13.0		26.5	27.8
19.1	9.2	12.7	4.5		8.4		10.6	11.2
3.9	3.1	3.2	2.5		4.0	Sales/Total Assets	3.3	3.4
2.6	2.4	2.3	1.9		2.4		2.5	2.4
2.2	1.7	1.7	1.2		1.9		1.7	1.7
.5	.3	.3	.8			% Depr., Dep., Amort./Sales	.5	.4
(35) 1.1	(82) .7	(92) .7	(34) 1.1				(227) .8	(267) .9
2.5	1.7	1.4	2.8				1.6	1.6
3.0	2.4	1.3	.4			% Officers', Directors' Owners' Comp/Sales	2.0	2.0
(37) 5.7	(67) 3.5	(51) 2.3	(10) 1.2				(131) 3.9	(175) 3.5
	6.7	4.3	3.4				6.6	6.5
54260M	336636M	1249325M	1493023M	1134183M	4763773M	Net Sales ($)	4165929M	6035112M
16964M	134384M	465840M	720975M	544931M	1533783M	Total Assets ($)	1809951M	2809946M

M = $ thousand   MM = $ million
See Pages 9 through 22 for Explanation of Ratios and Data

Comparative Historical Data / Current Data Sorted by Sales

4/1/07-3/31/08 ALL	4/1/08-3/31/09 ALL	4/1/09-3/31/10 ALL	Type of Statement	0-1MM	1-3MM	3-5MM	5-10MM	10-25MM	25MM & OVER
14	23	20	Unqualified	2	4	7	12	6	14
34	24	34	Reviewed					6	3
65	59	65	Compiled	3	14	8	21	12	7
101	106	101	Tax Returns	31	33	19	11	2	5
94	111	125	Other	18	32	16	15	22	22
				56 (4/1-9/30/09)			**289 (10/1/09-3/31/10)**		
308	323	345	**NUMBER OF STATEMENTS**	54	83	50	59	48	51
%	%	%	**ASSETS**	%	%	%	%	%	%
9.8	8.8	9.6	Cash & Equivalents	5.9	12.6	11.9	9.7	9.0	7.1
6.2	6.2	5.5	Trade Receivables (net)	3.0	6.9	4.6	5.8	7.1	4.7
57.3	59.5	58.0	Inventory	64.6	57.3	53.4	60.8	56.5	55.0
2.0	1.8	2.1	All Other Current	.8	1.5	1.0	1.2	2.8	5.6
75.3	76.3	75.2	Total Current	74.3	78.3	70.9	77.6	75.4	72.4
16.3	15.3	16.0	Fixed Assets (net)	18.0	12.9	19.4	13.7	17.5	16.8
3.5	3.3	4.5	Intangibles (net)	2.5	5.4	3.6	4.5	3.3	7.0
4.9	5.1	4.3	All Other Non-Current	5.3	3.5	6.1	4.2	3.7	3.9
100.0	100.0	100.0	Total	100.0	100.0	100.0	100.0	100.0	100.0
			LIABILITIES						
13.7	14.5	12.8	Notes Payable-Short Term	17.3	12.8	11.7	12.3	13.8	9.1
2.0	2.5	3.8	Cur. Mat.-L.T.D.	2.1	5.1	5.9	3.4	1.8	3.5
23.7	24.4	25.4	Trade Payables	25.8	27.0	25.1	24.7	25.0	24.0
.1	.2	.2	Income Taxes Payable	.0	.1	.1	.3	.4	.3
12.1	11.2	12.3	All Other Current	14.6	17.2	10.4	7.3	10.3	11.7
51.6	52.8	54.6	Total Current	59.7	62.3	53.2	48.1	51.3	48.5
15.4	15.9	14.4	Long-Term Debt	19.7	13.0	13.5	10.4	13.8	16.8
.0	.0	.1	Deferred Taxes	.0	.1	.0	.0	.1	.2
9.3	6.3	6.2	All Other Non-Current	6.4	8.7	7.1	4.6	2.8	5.8
23.7	25.0	24.8	Net Worth	14.2	15.9	26.2	36.8	32.0	28.6
100.0	100.0	100.0	Total Liabilities & Net Worth	100.0	100.0	100.0	100.0	100.0	100.0
			INCOME DATA						
100.0	100.0	100.0	Net Sales	100.0	100.0	100.0	100.0	100.0	100.0
38.5	37.6	36.9	Gross Profit	43.5	36.6	35.4	35.3	35.7	34.8
35.7	35.7	34.8	Operating Expenses	42.5	34.1	33.5	32.6	34.2	32.2
2.9	1.9	2.1	Operating Profit	1.0	2.6	1.9	2.7	1.5	2.6
1.4	1.1	.8	All Other Expenses (net)	1.4	1.0	.8	.4	.5	.9
1.5	.8	1.2	Profit Before Taxes	-.4	1.6	1.1	2.3	1.0	1.7
			RATIOS						
2.3	2.4	2.6		2.8	3.3	2.4	2.5	2.2	2.1
1.6	1.6	1.5	Current	1.5	1.6	1.5	1.7	1.4	1.4
1.1	1.0	1.1		.9	1.0	1.0	1.3	1.1	1.2
.6	.6	.6		.3	.9	.7	.8	.6	.3
(305) .2	(320) .2	(343) .2	Quick	(53) .1	.3	.2	(58) .3	.2	.1
.1	.1	.1		.0	.1	.1	.1	.1	.1
0 UND	0 UND	0 UND		0 UND	0 UND	0 UND	0 UND	1 395.4	1 574.2
2 222.5	1 309.4	2 219.6	Sales/Receivables	0 UND	3 140.6	0 895.6	1 348.1	4 103.5	2 191.7
11 34.5	9 39.3	8 43.6		6 61.9	10 36.8	11 34.4	7 51.0	15 24.3	6 57.3
87 4.2	91 4.0	91 4.0		139 2.6	71 5.1	73 5.0	89 4.1	92 4.0	80 4.6
146 2.5	136 2.7	144 2.5	Cost of Sales/Inventory	235 1.6	136 2.7	120 3.0	152 2.4	126 2.9	123 3.0
205 1.8	199 1.8	209 1.7		299 1.2	200 1.8	179 2.0	214 1.7	163 2.2	183 2.0
27 13.5	23 16.1	25 14.8		2 157.8	23 15.6	21 17.6	28 12.8	33 11.1	29 12.4
50 7.3	46 7.9	48 7.5	Cost of Sales/Payables	56 6.6	54 6.7	39 9.3	49 7.5	48 7.7	48 7.5
79 4.6	79 4.6	84 4.4		131 2.8	85 4.3	96 3.8	78 4.7	69 5.3	80 4.6
5.6	5.6	4.9		3.3	4.3	4.9	5.2	5.8	7.2
9.3	11.0	10.1	Sales/Working Capital	7.4	11.2	10.5	7.7	12.7	11.7
44.7	154.8	51.1		-36.5	-999.8	-196.5	17.4	-41.8	27.2
5.6	6.7	7.1		5.0	5.7	6.8	10.2	6.2	10.4
(267) 2.2	(275) 2.2	(301) 2.1	EBIT/Interest	(46) 1.0	(62) 2.0	(41) 1.8	(57) 3.0	(47) 2.0	(48) 2.8
.7	-.3	.1		-2.2	.1	-.2	.8	.7	.4
7.7	10.0	8.1	Net Profit + Depr., Dep.,				18.7	5.0	13.1
(36) 1.9	(38) 2.0	(47) 1.6	Amort./Cur. Mat. L/T/D				(13) 3.7	(11) 1.6	(13) 1.3
.6	.5	.3					.0	1.1	.0
.1	.1	.1		.1	.1	.1	.1	.1	.2
.5	.5	.4	Fixed/Worth	1.0	.6	.4	.3	.4	.6
4.1	3.6	6.3		-.5	-3.0	NM	1.0	2.0	6.5
1.1	1.1	1.0		1.1	.9	.8	.8	1.1	1.4
2.8	3.2	2.9	Debt/Worth	4.5	4.6	2.9	2.0	2.9	2.5
20.0	21.4	26.3		-6.6	-16.5	NM	4.6	6.7	14.3
40.9	36.7	31.3	% Profit Before Taxes/Tangible	47.9	29.9	35.0	37.0	25.7	31.4
(247) 16.1	(259) 13.8	(264) 12.7	Net Worth	(36) 12.0	(55) 16.1	(38) 11.2	(54) 12.7	(42) 8.4	(39) 17.1
.8	-3.8	-.3		-6.8	-2.4	-1.0	.3	-.9	-.9
9.5	10.8	9.3	% Profit Before Taxes/Total	9.6	11.7	8.5	10.3	7.7	10.7
3.4	3.0	3.4	Assets	1.0	3.8	3.4	3.6	2.4	4.5
-1.5	-3.2	-2.3		-10.4	-2.3	-4.0	-.3	-.3	-1.6
86.1	85.7	80.3		93.4	102.4	61.9	69.4	61.8	65.0
29.4	29.5	27.2	Sales/Net Fixed Assets	22.9	36.7	25.6	30.1	26.2	21.6
10.7	12.2	10.8		8.6	14.5	11.2	16.1	9.7	10.0
3.3	3.4	3.2		2.4	3.3	3.2	3.1	3.8	3.6
2.4	2.5	2.3	Sales/Total Assets	2.0	2.4	2.5	2.3	2.6	2.5
1.7	1.8	1.7		1.3	1.9	1.7	1.8	1.7	1.9
.5	.4	.4		.7	.4	.4	.3	.3	.5
(218) .9	(232) .8	(256) .8	% Depr., Dep., Amort./Sales	(31) 1.3	(53) .8	(37) .9	(51) .6	(43) .8	(41) .9
2.0	1.5	1.7		2.8	1.8	1.9	1.3	1.7	2.0
2.1	2.0	1.8	% Officers', Directors'	4.3	1.9	2.0	1.2	1.9	.4
(144) 4.1	(141) 3.5	(166) 3.3	Owners' Comp/Sales	(31) 6.6	(48) 3.3	(32) 3.7	(31) 2.0	(13) 3.2	(11) 1.1
6.9	6.1	6.2		9.7	5.8	5.7	3.1	7.5	5.3
6858998M	8895047M	9031200M	Net Sales ($)	33255M	160414M	194624M	414318M	751733M	7476856M
3188658M	3554149M	3416877M	Total Assets ($)	22820M	73248M	98127M	196378M	357783M	2668521M

© RMA 2010

M = $ thousand   MM = $ million
See Pages 9 through 22 for Explanation of Ratios and Data

RETAIL—Hobby, Toy, and Game Stores NAICS 451120

Current Data Sorted by Assets							Comparative Historical Data	

0-500M	500M-2MM	2-10MM	10-50MM	50-100MM	100-250MM	Type of Statement	4/1/05-3/31/06 ALL	4/1/06-3/31/07 ALL
		1	1	1		Unqualified	4	4
1	3	3	1			Reviewed	5	7
12	11	4				Compiled	12	8
8	3	4				Tax Returns	14	18
					4	Other	14	21
	9 (4/1-9/30/09)		51 (10/1/09-3/31/10)					
21	18	14	2	1	4	NUMBER OF STATEMENTS	49	58
%	%	%	%	%	%	ASSETS	%	%
8.8	11.3	6.5				Cash & Equivalents	11.1	10.3
3.1	3.7	10.7				Trade Receivables (net)	5.7	7.9
65.1	61.9	51.7				Inventory	60.3	55.6
1.5	.8	3.3				All Other Current	1.5	2.0
78.5	77.7	72.3				Total Current	78.5	75.8
14.7	12.4	13.2				Fixed Assets (net)	15.1	16.0
5.6	6.9	6.2				Intangibles (net)	3.6	3.6
1.2	3.0	8.3				All Other Non-Current	2.8	4.5
100.0	100.0	100.0				Total	100.0	100.0
						LIABILITIES		
12.0	7.7	6.7				Notes Payable-Short Term	14.8	10.1
1.2	3.1	1.7				Cur. Mat.-L.T.D.	3.3	3.7
17.1	14.4	16.0				Trade Payables	14.1	21.1
.0	.1	.0				Income Taxes Payable	.6	.8
18.0	10.4	7.3				All Other Current	11.9	6.3
48.4	35.7	31.7				Total Current	44.7	41.9
33.2	24.7	22.9				Long-Term Debt	23.5	26.0
.0	.0	.5				Deferred Taxes	.2	.3
.6	12.4	2.3				All Other Non-Current	9.0	6.9
17.9	27.1	42.6				Net Worth	22.7	25.0
100.0	100.0	100.0				Total Liabilities & Net Worth	100.0	100.0
						INCOME DATA		
100.0	100.0	100.0				Net Sales	100.0	100.0
48.2	42.5	42.4				Gross Profit	44.4	44.0
47.5	39.7	37.4				Operating Expenses	42.2	41.3
.8	2.8	5.0				Operating Profit	2.2	2.6
2.0	1.0	.8				All Other Expenses (net)	1.2	1.6
-1.3	1.7	4.1				Profit Before Taxes	1.0	1.1
						RATIOS		
5.9	4.9	3.7				Current	4.1	3.7
1.8	2.2	2.5					1.9	2.0
1.1	1.4	1.5					1.3	1.2
.6	1.2	1.6				Quick	1.0	1.0
(20) .2	.3	.4					.5 (57)	.4
.1	.2	.2					.1	.1
0 UND	0 UND	1 414.5				Sales/Receivables	0 UND	0 UND
0 UND	1 661.3	11 32.9					0 999.8	1 297.1
6 65.4	10 35.2	48 7.6					11 33.0	14 25.8
119 3.1	104 3.5	76 4.8				Cost of Sales/Inventory	86 4.2	74 5.0
182 2.0	168 2.2	113 3.2					137 2.7	131 2.8
369 1.0	235 1.6	245 1.5					240 1.5	215 1.7
3 108.9	0 UND	31 11.9				Cost of Sales/Payables	15 23.9	14 25.9
36 10.3	32 11.6	47 7.8					34 10.8	40 9.1
70 5.2	53 6.9	61 6.0					49 7.5	70 5.2
2.9	4.4	2.7				Sales/Working Capital	3.9	4.6
5.9	8.1	5.1					7.1	7.4
57.4	12.7	17.6					17.7	31.0
6.3	13.8	7.7				EBIT/Interest	4.5	4.1
(17) .1	(17) 1.3	(13) 4.7					(43) 1.8	(52) 2.1
-2.5	-.1	2.1					.4	1.0
						Net Profit + Depr., Dep., Amort./Cur. Mat. L/T/D		
.1	.1	.0				Fixed/Worth	.1	.1
.3	.5	.1					.9	.4
NM	1.7	2.9					-24.3	3.0
.6	.5	.7				Debt/Worth	1.0	1.0
4.8	3.2	1.2					4.6	3.2
-25.9	21.6	11.0					-33.9	81.4
100.0	32.1	74.9				% Profit Before Taxes/Tangible Net Worth	43.2	68.1
(15) 15.9	(15) 12.0	(13) 33.9					(36) 13.6	(45) 23.5
-35.1	-15.6	7.5					.1	6.7
13.3	10.7	9.4				% Profit Before Taxes/Total Assets	9.5	10.4
2.4	.5	6.9					2.5	5.1
-10.6	-6.4	3.5					-2.8	.0
106.1	155.4	305.4				Sales/Net Fixed Assets	74.7	88.4
28.0	27.6	52.0					32.6	36.5
8.7	12.5	7.5					15.6	10.0
3.6	3.4	2.6				Sales/Total Assets	3.6	3.9
2.4	2.2	1.9					2.4	2.5
1.0	2.0	1.5					1.6	1.5
.4	.5	.3				% Depr., Dep., Amort./Sales	.4	.5
(11) .5	(14) .8	(10) .6					(39) .8	(40) .9
4.4	2.2	2.3					1.5	1.7
		1.9				% Officers', Directors' Owners' Comp/Sales	3.9	1.9
	(15) 3.2						(23) 7.1	(27) 3.1
	6.5						10.9	6.7
13212M	55507M	120174M	86480M	125135M	943116M	Net Sales ($)	2578830M	1792483M
5348M	16956M	58898M	37551M	56274M	604575M	Total Assets ($)	1042095M	921054M

M = $ thousand   MM = $ million
See Pages 9 through 22 for Explanation of Ratios and Data

Comparative Historical Data   Current Data Sorted by Sales

Type of Statement				0-1MM	1-3MM	3-5MM	5-10MM	10-25MM	25MM & OV
Unqualified	4	4	6			1	1	3	2
Reviewed	4	6	4		1		2	2	1
Compiled	10	6	4	1	2	1	1		
Tax Returns	23	18	27	14	4	5	2		
Other	18	8	19	7	4		2		4
	4/1/07-3/31/08 ALL	4/1/08-3/31/09 ALL	4/1/09-3/31/10 ALL	9 (4/1-9/30/09)			51 (10/1/09-3/31/10)		
NUMBER OF STATEMENTS	59	42	60	22	11	7	8	5	7
	%	%	%	%	%	%	%	%	%
ASSETS									
Cash & Equivalents	11.4	8.8	9.0	7.7	12.8				
Trade Receivables (net)	5.8	6.3	6.7	3.3	3.5				
Inventory	54.2	62.3	57.9	66.8	57.2				
All Other Current	3.0	1.4	2.1	1.3	.6				
Total Current	74.3	78.8	75.7	79.2	74.0				
Fixed Assets (net)	16.6	11.4	14.0	13.3	15.4				
Intangibles (net)	2.3	4.0	6.3	6.3	8.5				
All Other Non-Current	6.8	5.8	4.0	1.2	2.0				
Total	100.0	100.0	100.0	100.0	100.0				
LIABILITIES									
Notes Payable-Short Term	13.3	13.5	8.9	11.0	9.6				
Cur. Mat.-L.T.D.	4.1	2.1	2.0	2.3	1.8				
Trade Payables	17.5	15.8	15.4	13.8	12.4				
Income Taxes Payable	.2	.0	.1	.0	.0				
All Other Current	10.4	11.7	11.9	20.7	4.2				
Total Current	45.5	43.1	38.2	47.8	28.0				
Long-Term Debt	18.2	24.7	26.1	29.6	16.2				
Deferred Taxes	.2	.3	.1	.0	.0				
All Other Non-Current	6.0	7.1	5.0	.7	15.8				
Net Worth	30.1	24.8	30.6	21.8	40.1				
Total Liabilties & Net Worth	100.0	100.0	100.0	100.0	100.0				
INCOME DATA									
Net Sales	100.0	100.0	100.0	100.0	100.0				
Gross Profit	41.4	42.4	45.3	48.4	45.9				
Operating Expenses	37.6	39.9	41.8	48.1	41.0				
Operating Profit	3.8	2.5	3.5	.3	4.9				
All Other Expenses (net)	1.7	1.5	1.3	2.1	.9				
Profit Before Taxes	2.1	1.0	2.2	-1.7	4.0				
RATIOS									
Current	3.6	3.9	4.3	5.9	11.7				
	1.8	2.3	2.2	1.9	2.7				
	1.1	1.3	1.4	1.1	1.5				
Quick	.6	.8	1.1	.6	3.1				
	.3	.3 (59)	.3	(21) .2	.3				
	.1	.1	.2	.1	.2				
Sales/Receivables	0 UND	0 UND	0 UND	0 UND	0 UND				
	0 910.5	1 388.9	2 216.8	0 UND	1 352.0				
	7 53.9	17 22.1	15 23.9	5 67.6	9 40.2				
Cost of Sales/Inventory	90 4.1	88 4.2	96 3.8	128 2.9	96 3.8				
	126 2.9	164 2.2	168 2.2	211 1.7	158 2.3				
	180 2.0	229 1.6	243 1.5	439 .8	248 1.5				
Cost of Sales/Payables	14 25.4	14 25.7	23 15.9	0 UND	0 UND				
	32 11.6	25 14.5	37 9.8	37 9.8	31 11.7				
	52 7.0	45 8.2	57 6.5	71 5.1	54 6.7				
Sales/Working Capital	4.6	4.2	3.1	2.7	2.4				
	10.3	5.8	5.9	5.7	5.3				
	82.2	21.8	16.4	25.4	13.3				
EBIT/Interest	7.0	7.3	10.0	4.3	11.6				
	(45) 2.4	(40) 2.5	(53) 3.2	(18) -.6	(10) 4.5				
	.7	-.5	-.1	-3.5	.2				
Net Profit + Depr., Dep., Amort./Cur. Mat. L/T/D									
Fixed/Worth	.1	.1	.1	.1	.0				
	.3	.2	.3	.3	.5				
	3.5	4.8	2.0	NM	1.6				
Debt/Worth	.6	.7	.6	.6	.3				
	2.0	2.4	2.3	3.3	2.9				
	15.2	-16.8	10.4	-29.6	7.0				
% Profit Before Taxes/Tangible Net Worth	45.7	40.1	71.2	50.3	89.7				
	(50) 15.2	(31) 12.5	(50) 17.5	(16) 5.6	(10) 20.2				
	-4.8	-6.7	-5.2	-29.1	-15.8				
% Profit Before Taxes/Total Assets	15.4	14.1	12.2	8.8	13.5				
	4.6	3.4	6.3	-2.9	6.8				
	-1.1	-5.2	-3.8	-10.3	-6.4				
Sales/Net Fixed Assets	111.0	119.7	112.9	104.0	103.4				
	48.0	40.9	31.7	31.9	26.0				
	11.5	21.2	9.7	8.8	12.6				
Sales/Total Assets	4.2	3.1	3.0	3.3	2.9				
	2.7	2.3	2.1	1.6	2.2				
	1.6	2.0	1.5	1.0	2.0				
% Depr., Dep., Amort./Sales	.4	.5	.5	.4					
	(42) .8	(29) .9	(42) .8	(13) .9					
	2.5	1.6	2.7	4.1					
% Officers', Directors' Owners' Comp/Sales	2.3	2.0	1.3	3.0					
	(33) 3.7	(20) 2.8	(31) 3.1	(10) 6.3					
	5.8	5.3	6.5	7.5					
Net Sales ($)	505075M	789892M	1343624M	11178M	21706M	25738M	55951M	74320M	1154731M
Total Assets ($)	246125M	351167M	779602M	6253M	10874M	9876M	34007M	20192M	698400M

© RMA 2010

M = $ thousand   MM = $ million
See Pages 9 through 22 for Explanation of Ratios and Data

Current Data Sorted by Assets   Comparative Historical Data

Type of Statement								4/1/05-3/31/06 ALL	4/1/06-3/31/07 ALL
Unqualified								2	2
Reviewed								25	19
Compiled								19	20
Tax Returns								17	21
Other								27	20

Current Data column period labels: 22 (4/1-9/30/09) ; 53 (10/1/09-3/31/10)

	0-500M	500M-2MM	2-10MM	10-50MM	50-100MM	100-250MM		4/1/05-3/31/06 ALL	4/1/06-3/31/07 ALL
NUMBER OF STATEMENTS	11	25	30	6	1	2		90	82
ASSETS	%	%	%	%	%	%		%	%
Cash & Equivalents	10.5	9.0	2.9					5.9	5.3
Trade Receivables (net)	2.0	10.5	10.7					13.5	13.7
Inventory	72.5	59.6	66.1					60.6	58.2
All Other Current	1.0	.6	3.3					2.3	2.7
Total Current	86.0	79.7	83.0					82.3	79.9
Fixed Assets (net)	11.4	14.4	12.1					11.8	13.1
Intangibles (net)	1.6	2.6	1.6					1.2	2.0
All Other Non-Current	1.0	3.3	3.3					4.7	5.1
Total	100.0	100.0	100.0					100.0	100.0
LIABILITIES									
Notes Payable-Short Term	13.9	17.3	19.0					17.5	22.6
Cur. Mat.-L.T.D.	1.5	3.2	3.8					2.7	4.7
Trade Payables	14.2	11.9	18.7					18.9	13.6
Income Taxes Payable	.0	.1	.3					.2	.2
All Other Current	9.2	6.1	7.3					11.1	7.4
Total Current	38.7	38.6	49.1					50.3	48.5
Long-Term Debt	12.4	13.4	9.4					12.1	12.5
Deferred Taxes	.0	.0	.2					.2	.2
All Other Non-Current	15.5	12.0	6.7					8.5	5.0
Net Worth	33.4	36.0	34.6					28.9	33.8
Total Liabilities & Net Worth	100.0	100.0	100.0					100.0	100.0
INCOME DATA									
Net Sales	100.0	100.0	100.0					100.0	100.0
Gross Profit	52.2	40.9	42.6					41.2	42.5
Operating Expenses	49.6	39.6	41.7					38.4	39.8
Operating Profit	2.5	1.2	1.0					2.8	2.7
All Other Expenses (net)	1.6	.4	.1					1.3	2.0
Profit Before Taxes	1.0	.8	.8					1.5	.7
RATIOS									
Current	5.0 / 1.9 / 1.5	3.3 / 2.2 / 1.4	3.3 / 1.7 / 1.2					2.2 / 1.7 / 1.3	2.3 / 1.7 / 1.3
Quick	.5 / .2 / .0	.9 / .4 / .2	.4 / .2 / .1					.7 / .3 / .1 (81)	.8 / .3 / .1
Sales/Receivables	0 UND / 3 107.9 / 10 34.9	2 203.3 / 14 25.4 / 23 15.8	3 108.4 / 12 31.1 / 24 15.4					5 73.0 / 14 26.7 / 29 12.4	5 71.5 / 13 29.1 / 34 10.6
Cost of Sales/Inventory	178 2.0 / 386 .9 / 621 .6	111 3.3 / 177 2.1 / 251 1.5	148 2.5 / 246 1.5 / 398 .9					133 2.7 / 180 2.0 / 265 1.4	134 2.7 / 192 1.9 / 277 1.3
Cost of Sales/Payables	11 32.6 / 38 9.7 / 102 3.6	13 29.2 / 28 13.1 / 47 7.8	22 16.4 / 47 7.8 / 81 4.5					19 19.3 / 44 8.3 / 77 4.7	19 18.8 / 36 10.1 / 76 4.8
Sales/Working Capital	2.4 / 3.2 / 5.7	3.1 / 5.9 / 10.6	3.4 / 5.6 / 24.1					3.6 / 6.4 / 14.4	3.6 / 6.1 / 11.5
EBIT/Interest		(23) 4.4 / 1.4 / .6	(29) 5.8 / 1.5 / .7					(85) 3.4 / 1.6 / .8	(77) 2.6 / 1.4 / .4
Net Profit + Depr., Dep., Amort./Cur. Mat. L/T/D								(18) 3.2 / .9 / .1	(20) 2.1 / .4 / -.3
Fixed/Worth	.0 / .2 / 1.5	.1 / .2 / 1.9	.1 / .2 / 1.3					.1 / .3 / .8	.1 / .3 / .8
Debt/Worth	.5 / 2.3 / 4.3	.8 / 1.7 / 6.0	1.0 / 2.5 / 5.3					1.3 / 2.2 / 6.3	1.0 / 2.1 / 4.6
% Profit Before Taxes/Tangible Net Worth	(10) 80.4 / 3.3 / 1.4	(21) 31.3 / 3.5 / -3.7	(28) 16.5 / 7.3 / -3.4					(82) 19.9 / 7.0 / -2.1	(76) 16.5 / 5.3 / -8.5
% Profit Before Taxes/Total Assets	2.3 / 1.2 / .0	6.1 / .3 / -2.5	4.6 / 2.3 / -1.2					5.2 / 1.9 / -.7	5.7 / 1.8 / -2.4
Sales/Net Fixed Assets	121.7 / 49.7 / 9.6	83.7 / 22.4 / 9.2	121.5 / 26.6 / 7.3					64.4 / 24.3 / 13.9	50.3 / 21.8 / 11.3
Sales/Total Assets	3.5 / 1.7 / 1.0	2.9 / 2.1 / 1.4	2.3 / 1.7 / 1.3					2.8 / 1.9 / 1.3	2.6 / 1.8 / 1.3
% Depr., Dep., Amort./Sales		(20) .4 / .8 / 1.7	(27) .5 / 1.2 / 4.9					(78) .5 / .8 / 1.6	(65) .5 / 1.0 / 2.0
% Officers', Directors' Owners' Comp/Sales		(17) 1.6 / 4.3 / 6.1	(14) 1.0 / 3.1 / 6.9					(47) 2.3 / 3.6 / 7.2	(40) 2.0 / 3.2 / 6.1
Net Sales ($)	6434M	64580M	259083M	243113M	34650M	607691M		1020790M	657976M
Total Assets ($)	3807M	29334M	126006M	105695M	98324M	250014M		651658M	441559M

© RMA 2010

M = $ thousand   MM = $ million
See Pages 9 through 22 for Explanation of Ratios and Data

Comparative Historical Data — Current Data Sorted by Sales

13 / 22 / 16 / 23	2 / 13 / 19 / 21 / 22	6 / 12 / 20 / 25 / 12	Type of Statement	1 / / 1 / 9 / 1	2 / / 7 / 8 / 1	1 / / 7 / 5 / 5	3 / / 2 / 3 / 2	1 / 4 / 3 / / 1	4 / 2 / / / 2
			Unqualified						
13	13	12	Reviewed					4	2
22	19	20	Compiled	1	7	7	2	3	
16	21	25	Tax Returns	9	8	5	3		
23	22	12	Other	1	1	5	2	1	2
4/1/07-3/31/08 ALL	4/1/08-3/31/09 ALL	4/1/09-3/31/10 ALL		0-1MM	1-3MM 22 (4/1-9/30/09)	3-5MM	5-10MM 53 (10/1/09-3/31/10)	10-25MM	25MM & OV
74	**77**	**75**	**NUMBER OF STATEMENTS**	**12**	**18**	**18**	**10**	**9**	**8**
%	%	%		%	%	%	%	%	%
			ASSETS						
6.7	7.5	6.3	Cash & Equivalents	12.8	6.1	3.7	5.9		
13.0	12.0	10.9	Trade Receivables (net)	2.8	11.8	9.6	8.4		
55.7	60.7	62.2	Inventory	69.6	58.2	69.0	60.6		
1.8	1.7	2.4	All Other Current	.3	.7	3.0	3.4		
77.2	81.9	81.8	Total Current	85.5	76.8	85.3	78.2		
14.4	13.5	12.3	Fixed Assets (net)	12.0	15.6	11.6	14.9		
2.1	.9	1.9	Intangibles (net)	1.4	4.3	.2	1.1		
6.3	3.7	4.0	All Other Non-Current	1.0	3.3	2.9	5.8		
100.0	100.0	100.0	Total	100.0	100.0	100.0	100.0		
			LIABILITIES						
19.4	17.0	17.2	Notes Payable-Short Term	14.0	20.1	18.2	22.5		
4.1	3.7	2.8	Cur. Mat.-L.T.D.	.9	4.3	.7	4.1		
17.2	18.6	14.8	Trade Payables	13.1	13.9	13.7	14.8		
.3	.5	.1	Income Taxes Payable	.0	.1	.2	.0		
7.3	8.7	7.5	All Other Current	7.7	7.9	6.1	6.2		
48.2	48.4	42.4	Total Current	35.7	46.3	38.8	47.6		
17.4	14.4	12.0	Long-Term Debt	12.0	16.0	10.3	9.0		
.1	.1	.1	Deferred Taxes	.0	.0	.0	.2		
5.6	4.0	9.3	All Other Non-Current	18.9	10.4	12.9	1.1		
28.7	33.1	36.1	Net Worth	33.4	27.4	38.0	42.1		
100.0	100.0	100.0	Total Liabilties & Net Worth	100.0	100.0	100.0	100.0		
			INCOME DATA						
100.0	100.0	100.0	Net Sales	100.0	100.0	100.0	100.0		
41.8	41.9	43.5	Gross Profit	50.6	44.5	44.9	39.6		
37.9	39.8	42.0	Operating Expenses	47.5	43.6	45.2	37.4		
3.9	2.1	1.5	Operating Profit	3.1	.9	-.2	2.3		
1.6	1.0	.5	All Other Expenses (net)	1.3	1.6	-1.1	.1		
2.4	1.1	1.0	Profit Before Taxes	1.7	-.6	.8	2.1		
			RATIOS						
2.0	2.7	3.5		5.0	2.4	3.8	6.1		
1.6	1.8	1.9	Current	2.7	1.8	2.1	1.6		
1.2	1.3	1.3		1.5	1.2	1.4	.9		
.7	.8	.7		1.5	.7	.4	1.3		
.3	.3	.3	Quick	.4	.3	.3	.1		
.1	.1	.1		.1	.1	.3	.0		
2 146.4	1 282.8	2 147.7		0 UND	3 142.0	1 248.8	2 181.2		
11 32.4	11 32.6	11 32.2	Sales/Receivables	4 97.6	9 42.5	13 28.6	7 53.1		
31 11.9	26 14.0	24 15.5		13 28.4	27 13.4	22 16.5	48 7.5		
105 3.5	119 3.1	142 2.6		200 1.8	154 2.4	186 2.0	109 3.3		
181 2.0	190 1.9	227 1.6	Cost of Sales/Inventory	337 1.1	201 1.8	273 1.3	266 1.4		
270 1.4	310 1.2	321 1.1		584 .6	284 1.3	398 .9	341 1.1		
16 23.0	15 23.7	16 22.8		14 27.0	10 35.2	16 23.0	13 27.4		
37 9.8	40 9.1	36 10.2	Cost of Sales/Payables	38 9.6	42 8.7	34 10.8	35 10.4		
85 4.3	76 4.8	55 6.7		86 4.3	50 7.3	73 5.0	89 4.1		
3.6	4.0	2.8		2.2	3.3	2.6	3.9		
8.8	6.8	5.0	Sales/Working Capital	2.9	6.5	4.4	8.2		
22.8	14.4	11.1		5.3	27.8	7.0	-39.7		
3.1	5.1	5.3		3.0	2.4	5.7			
(69) 1.8	(69) 2.0	(70) 1.5	EBIT/Interest	(10) 1.5	(17) 1.0	(17) 1.4			
1.2	.4	.6		.8	-1.6	.7			
13.9	17.7	29.6	Net Profit + Depr., Dep.,						
(15) 3.3	(19) 4.0	(15) 5.5	Amort./Cur. Mat. L/T/D						
1.6	.5	.4							
.1	.1	.1		.0	.1	.1	.1		
.3	.2	.2	Fixed/Worth	.2	.5	.2	.4		
1.7	.8	1.1		2.6	3.5	.8	1.3		
1.1	.8	.9		.6	1.3	.9	.4		
2.3	1.8	2.1	Debt/Worth	2.6	2.1	2.0	2.2		
7.8	4.5	4.2		7.1	NM	3.7	6.0		
30.6	18.3	19.2	% Profit Before Taxes/Tangible	75.0	17.1	15.9			
(62) 8.6	(70) 4.8	(68) 4.4	Net Worth	(11) 4.5	(14) 2.4	.8			
1.2	-4.1	-3.6		1.8	-19.4	-3.9			
8.3	6.6	5.8	% Profit Before Taxes/Total	5.3	3.3	4.6	9.5		
2.9	2.1	1.3	Assets	1.2	-.1	.5	3.3		
.5	-1.9	-1.7		.2	-6.4	-1.3	-2.2		
57.4	73.5	87.6		118.2	81.8	85.2	283.1		
24.6	26.3	26.1	Sales/Net Fixed Assets	32.0	15.5	26.9	22.0		
10.6	10.1	12.1		5.5	6.2	13.0	5.9		
3.0	2.9	2.7		2.0	2.3	2.5	2.9		
1.9	2.1	1.8	Sales/Total Assets	1.3	1.6	1.7	1.7		
1.4	1.4	1.3		1.0	1.3	1.3	1.2		
.4	.6	.5			.4	.4			
(60) .9	(62) 1.1	(63) 1.0	% Depr., Dep., Amort./Sales		(15) .8	(16) .9			
1.9	2.1	2.1			2.3	1.6			
2.0	2.5	2.2	% Officers', Directors'		1.5	3.8			
(38) 4.5	(35) 3.7	(38) 4.5	Owners' Comp/Sales		(11) 4.2	(12) 6.4			
6.2	6.4	8.2			4.5	9.6			
604247M	1043948M	1215551M	Net Sales ($)	6735M	33928M	72841M	72476M	132697M	896874M
377513M	543393M	613180M	Total Assets ($)	4649M	21857M	42860M	47785M	57231M	438798M

© RMA 2010

M = $ thousand   MM = $ million
See Pages 9 through 22 for Explanation of Ratios and Data

RETAIL—Book Stores NAICS 451211

Current Data Sorted by Assets							Comparative Historical Data	

Type of Statement

	0-500M	500M-2MM	2-10MM	10-50MM	50-100MM	100-250MM	Type of Statement	4/1/05-3/31/06 ALL	4/1/06-3/31/07 ALL
Unqualified	1	1	1	5			Unqualified	12	10
Reviewed			3	1			Reviewed	7	9
Compiled		3	4				Compiled	12	11
Tax Returns	14	5	3				Tax Returns	9	14
Other	1	3	7	5	1	1	Other	24	19
	21 (4/1-9/30/09)		38 (10/1/09-3/31/10)						
NUMBER OF STATEMENTS	16	12	18	11	1	1	NUMBER OF STATEMENTS	64	63
ASSETS	%	%	%	%	%	%	**ASSETS**	%	%
Cash & Equivalents	18.7	8.4	13.6	13.6			Cash & Equivalents	9.0	12.6
Trade Receivables (net)	2.2	5.5	7.2	5.7			Trade Receivables (net)	6.7	7.9
Inventory	52.7	56.3	55.4	35.4			Inventory	51.9	47.1
All Other Current	.0	1.9	2.0	4.7			All Other Current	3.2	2.0
Total Current	73.7	72.1	78.2	59.4			Total Current	70.7	69.5
Fixed Assets (net)	12.3	14.3	15.9	29.4			Fixed Assets (net)	20.5	22.8
Intangibles (net)	5.1	1.5	.0	5.5			Intangibles (net)	1.2	2.3
All Other Non-Current	8.9	12.0	5.9	5.6			All Other Non-Current	7.6	5.3
Total	100.0	100.0	100.0	100.0			Total	100.0	100.0
LIABILITIES							**LIABILITIES**		
Notes Payable-Short Term	22.8	18.0	13.9	3.9			Notes Payable-Short Term	11.4	13.9
Cur. Mat.-L.T.D.	2.7	6.0	2.3	1.5			Cur. Mat.-L.T.D.	2.6	2.1
Trade Payables	29.6	29.7	13.9	17.0			Trade Payables	25.8	21.8
Income Taxes Payable	1.6	.0	.3	.1			Income Taxes Payable	.1	.3
All Other Current	25.6	14.1	7.4	12.7			All Other Current	11.6	12.4
Total Current	82.3	67.8	37.9	35.3			Total Current	51.4	50.4
Long-Term Debt	41.3	4.7	9.4	12.5			Long-Term Debt	9.6	9.0
Deferred Taxes	.0	.0	.9	.0			Deferred Taxes	.2	.3
All Other Non-Current	3.1	6.2	2.8	5.0			All Other Non-Current	11.0	6.7
Net Worth	-26.7	21.3	49.0	47.3			Net Worth	27.8	33.5
Total Liabilties & Net Worth	100.0	100.0	100.0	100.0			Total Liabilties & Net Worth	100.0	100.0
INCOME DATA							**INCOME DATA**		
Net Sales	100.0	100.0	100.0	100.0			Net Sales	100.0	100.0
Gross Profit	35.8	40.5	45.2	41.7			Gross Profit	40.4	40.5
Operating Expenses	32.6	38.2	40.2	39.6			Operating Expenses	38.4	39.1
Operating Profit	3.3	2.3	5.1	2.0			Operating Profit	2.0	1.3
All Other Expenses (net)	1.1	.6	1.2	.3			All Other Expenses (net)	.9	1.0
Profit Before Taxes	2.1	1.6	3.9	1.7			Profit Before Taxes	1.1	.4
RATIOS							**RATIOS**		
Current	2.1 / 1.5 / .8	1.9 / 1.0 / .8	4.0 / 2.1 / 1.4	2.8 / 2.2 / 1.4			Current	2.3 / 1.6 / 1.2	2.8 / 1.6 / 1.0
Quick	.8 / .2 / .1	.5 / .2 / .0	1.1 / .5 / .2	1.6 / .4 / .3			Quick	.6 / .3 / .1	.7 / .3 / .1
Sales/Receivables	0 UND / 0 UND / 5 77.2	0 UND / 2 237.0 / 32 11.4	0 999.8 / 9 40.8 / 21 17.8	2 177.6 / 7 55.5 / 18 19.8			Sales/Receivables	1 280.7 / 4 103.2 / 14 26.1	1 311.1 / 3 107.2 / 13 27.3
Cost of Sales/Inventory	77 4.7 / 112 3.3 / 155 2.4	105 3.5 / 122 3.0 / 158 2.3	104 3.5 / 145 2.5 / 277 1.3	87 4.2 / 96 3.8 / 153 2.4			Cost of Sales/Inventory	79 4.6 / 108 3.4 / 167 2.2	69 5.3 / 103 3.5 / 162 2.2
Cost of Sales/Payables	9 42.5 / 43 8.4 / 105 3.5	56 6.5 / 66 5.5 / 97 3.8	6 56.7 / 57 6.4 / 85 4.3	18 20.7 / 31 11.8 / 46 7.9			Cost of Sales/Payables	30 12.2 / 44 8.3 / 85 4.3	15 23.6 / 46 8.0 / 82 4.4
Sales/Working Capital	5.6 / 14.1 / -41.1	8.1 / 284.1 / -10.3	2.2 / 6.6 / 15.2	4.8 / 6.1 / 15.1			Sales/Working Capital	6.4 / 9.8 / 30.4	5.9 / 10.3 / -191.6
EBIT/Interest	31.2 / (11) 2.8 / -1.4	19.0 / (10) 1.7 / -5.8	22.7 / (14) 9.2 / 1.6				EBIT/Interest	9.0 / (55) 2.3 / .2	11.3 / (53) 3.0 / 1.0
Net Profit + Depr., Dep., Amort./Cur. Mat. L/T/D							Net Profit + Depr., Dep., Amort./Cur. Mat. L/T/D	9.2 / (12) 3.9 / .5	9.4 / (11) 3.8 / 1.7
Fixed/Worth	.0 / .3 / -.7	.0 / 1.0 / -2.8	.1 / .2 / .5	.2 / .4 / 1.8			Fixed/Worth	.2 / .5 / 3.0	.2 / .6 / 4.7
Debt/Worth	1.2 / NM / -5.5	.7 / 35.4 / -15.0	.5 / 1.2 / 2.1	.5 / 1.3 / 4.1			Debt/Worth	.6 / 1.6 / 11.6	.5 / 1.6 / 100.8
% Profit Before Taxes/Tangible Net Worth			38.9 / 10.1 / 2.4	35.4 / (10) 2.4 / .6			% Profit Before Taxes/Tangible Net Worth	28.2 / (51) 8.8 / .1	24.3 / (51) 8.8 / 1.2
% Profit Before Taxes/Total Assets	27.4 / 7.3 / -4.6	10.9 / 2.2 / -4.7	15.2 / 5.8 / .9	7.0 / .8 / .4			% Profit Before Taxes/Total Assets	8.9 / 4.2 / -.4	9.2 / 3.6 / -1.3
Sales/Net Fixed Assets	UND / 86.5 / 12.3	783.6 / 48.9 / 13.5	34.0 / 15.1 / 9.8	22.8 / 10.4 / 3.8			Sales/Net Fixed Assets	40.7 / 20.6 / 6.5	47.5 / 16.7 / 6.0
Sales/Total Assets	4.7 / 3.2 / 2.1	3.3 / 2.7 / 1.5	2.9 / 2.4 / 1.4	2.8 / 2.1 / 1.6			Sales/Total Assets	3.5 / 2.4 / 1.8	3.6 / 2.4 / 1.9
% Depr., Dep., Amort./Sales			.8 / (13) 1.6 / 2.4				% Depr., Dep., Amort./Sales	.5 / (52) 1.0 / 1.9	.9 / (54) 1.3 / 2.3
% Officers', Directors' Owners' Comp/Sales							% Officers', Directors' Owners' Comp/Sales	2.5 / (15) 4.2 / 7.0	1.9 / (23) 4.0 / 6.4
Net Sales ($)	11483M	31152M	217937M	642175M	210807M	531346M	Net Sales ($)	1401615M	1246712M
Total Assets ($)	3855M	11872M	89965M	305722M	89111M	238800M	Total Assets ($)	679312M	544870M

M = $ thousand   MM = $ million
See Pages 9 through 22 for Explanation of Ratios and Data

Comparative Historical Data   Current Data Sorted by Sales

			Type of Statement						
14	13	8	Unqualified	1			1		6
4	3	4	Reviewed				2		2
9	10	7	Compiled		2	1	1	3	
13	16	22	Tax Returns	12	7	1	1	1	
17	17	18	Other	3	4	1	1	1	9
4/1/07-3/31/08 ALL	4/1/08-3/31/09 ALL	4/1/09-3/31/10 ALL		0-1MM	21 (4/1-9/30/09) 1-3MM	3-5MM	38 (10/1/09-3/31/10) 5-10MM	10-25MM	25MM & OVR
57	59	59	**NUMBER OF STATEMENTS**	16	13	2	6	5	17
%	%	%	**ASSETS**	%	%	%	%	%	%
14.5	13.3	14.0	Cash & Equivalents	16.7	8.6				13.2
6.4	6.7	5.0	Trade Receivables (net)	3.3	6.4				6.3
50.6	44.9	50.7	Inventory	53.0	52.0				40.8
1.7	2.4	2.2	All Other Current	.1	1.2				5.2
73.2	67.2	71.9	Total Current	73.2	68.2				65.4
19.5	23.3	17.6	Fixed Assets (net)	14.3	12.5				26.9
2.7	1.7	2.8	Intangibles (net)	3.6	3.3				3.6
4.6	7.8	7.7	All Other Non-Current	8.8	16.0				4.1
100.0	100.0	100.0	Total	100.0	100.0				100.0
			LIABILITIES						
15.8	9.7	14.8	Notes Payable-Short Term	25.9	11.4				4.9
2.3	1.8	2.9	Cur. Mat.-L.T.D.	3.0	7.2				1.3
28.6	28.6	22.0	Trade Payables	24.7	31.5				14.5
2.1	.7	.6	Income Taxes Payable	1.5	.1				.3
14.4	21.2	14.7	All Other Current	11.4	31.6				12.5
63.1	62.1	55.1	Total Current	66.5	81.7				33.5
10.6	11.1	17.6	Long-Term Debt	41.6	10.2				9.4
.2	.1	.3	Deferred Taxes	.0	.0				.7
4.9	11.0	3.9	All Other Non-Current	3.1	4.1				3.9
21.2	15.6	23.1	Net Worth	-11.3	3.9				52.5
100.0	100.0	100.0	Total Liabilities & Net Worth	100.0	100.0				100.0
			INCOME DATA						
100.0	100.0	100.0	Net Sales	100.0	100.0				100.0
37.6	43.5	41.3	Gross Profit	37.5	40.2				46.2
36.2	40.9	37.9	Operating Expenses	33.1	37.1				43.4
1.4	2.6	3.4	Operating Profit	4.4	3.1				2.8
1.1	.9	.9	All Other Expenses (net)	1.4	.9				.2
.4	1.7	2.6	Profit Before Taxes	3.0	2.3				2.6
			RATIOS						
2.6	2.4	2.8	Current	2.2	2.1				4.0
1.5	1.5	1.8		1.5	1.1				2.5
.8	.9	1.0		.7	.8				1.7
.8	.9	1.0	Quick	.5	.5				1.6
.3	.4	.4		.2	.2				1.0
.1	.1	.2		.1	.0				.2
1 477.1	0 754.0	0 UND	Sales/Receivables	0 UND	0 UND				2 220.0
3 107.2	2 166.8	3 142.9		0 UND	5 73.0				7 55.5
14 25.2	11 32.6	17 21.2		11 34.3	24 14.9				18 20.0
77 4.7	70 5.2	92 4.0	Cost of Sales/Inventory	86 4.3	83 4.4				91 4.0
115 3.2	113 3.2	123 3.0		151 2.4	106 3.4				111 3.3
146 2.5	153 2.4	161 2.3		293 1.2	147 2.5				142 2.6
27 13.4	26 14.1	21 17.5	Cost of Sales/Payables	9 42.5	53 6.9				11 33.5
44 8.2	53 6.9	47 7.8		58 6.3	68 5.4				29 12.6
78 4.7	98 3.7	79 4.6		160 2.3	110 3.3				46 7.9
6.5	6.4	4.8	Sales/Working Capital	2.5	9.3				4.8
14.4	12.0	9.0		14.1	93.5				6.0
-22.3	-23.1	474.7		-12.2	-10.6				12.0
10.3	12.7	15.7	EBIT/Interest	27.3	35.3				18.4
(48) 1.8	(51) 3.2	(46) 3.9		(12) 4.4	(10) 2.5			(14)	7.0
.5	-.1	.7		-4.1	-1.3				1.7
			Net Profit + Depr., Dep., Amort./Cur. Mat. L/T/D						
.2	.2	.1	Fixed/Worth	.0	.1				.2
.6	.5	.4		.2	1.1				.4
-1.0	-5.7	1.8		NM	-.5				.9
.5	.6	.5	Debt/Worth	.9	1.3				.3
3.3	2.1	1.7		95.3	3.2				.6
-5.4	-12.5	64.1		-5.6	-7.4				2.3
14.4	38.7	38.9	% Profit Before Taxes/Tangible Net Worth						19.1
(40) 5.7	(42) 13.2	(46) 9.3						(16)	9.7
-1.3	1.0	.8							1.1
7.9	13.1	14.9	% Profit Before Taxes/Total Assets	25.8	12.7				13.9
1.7	6.8	3.2		2.0	7.2				5.2
-2.1	-2.3	.2		-5.9	-.7				.5
55.2	51.5	139.7	Sales/Net Fixed Assets	UND	107.9				27.1
15.2	13.0	20.8		73.1	26.4				9.9
7.6	7.7	8.7		8.7	11.1				5.0
3.6	3.3	3.3	Sales/Total Assets	4.7	3.4				3.0
2.6	2.6	2.5		2.3	2.8				2.4
1.7	2.2	1.7		1.1	1.2				1.9
.8	.7	.7	% Depr., Dep., Amort./Sales						1.2
(46) 1.4	(47) 1.1	(39) 1.3						(13)	1.6
1.9	1.9	2.2							2.4
2.2	1.8	2.8	% Officers', Directors' Owners' Comp/Sales						
(12) 4.2	(22) 3.0	(22) 4.6							
8.1	3.8	8.2							
2483349M	1265366M	1644900M	Net Sales ($)	8658M	23324M	7780M	49547M	61868M	1493723M
948334M	538209M	739325M	Total Assets ($)	7167M	19666M	2907M	21691M	22957M	664937M

© RMA 2010

M = $ thousand   MM = $ million
See Pages 9 through 22 for Explanation of Ratios and Data

Current Data Sorted by Assets

Comparative Historical Data

						Type of Statement		
						Unqualified	7	7
			5			Reviewed	6	6
		4	5	2	3	Compiled	9	8
1	6	2				Tax Returns		6
3	3	2	1			Other	15	14
5	5	5			1		4/1/05-	4/1/06-
	7 (4/1-9/30/09)		46 (10/1/09-3/31/10)				3/31/06	3/31/07
0-500M	500M-2MM	2-10MM	10-50MM	50-100MM	100-250MM		ALL	ALL
4	14	13	16	2	4	NUMBER OF STATEMENTS	37	41
%	%	%	%	%	%	**ASSETS**	%	%
	18.6	7.5	17.0			Cash & Equivalents	15.5	9.9
	6.7	11.1	3.3			Trade Receivables (net)	9.4	11.8
	48.3	56.0	39.7			Inventory	32.8	46.0
	.9	1.1	3.1			All Other Current	2.2	1.6
	74.5	75.7	63.0			Total Current	60.0	69.3
	19.4	19.1	28.4			Fixed Assets (net)	23.3	21.1
	.6	.2	3.9			Intangibles (net)	8.3	3.8
	5.5	5.1	4.6			All Other Non-Current	8.4	5.7
	100.0	100.0	100.0			Total	100.0	100.0
						LIABILITIES		
	11.6	7.6	4.8			Notes Payable-Short Term	8.7	10.0
	2.0	2.6	2.5			Cur. Mat.-L.T.D.	3.7	1.9
	15.0	25.5	12.6			Trade Payables	15.7	18.9
	.6	.8	.2			Income Taxes Payable	.3	.5
	6.0	7.9	9.1			All Other Current	11.4	8.5
	35.0	44.3	29.1			Total Current	39.7	39.9
	18.7	14.2	17.9			Long-Term Debt	18.0	22.3
	.5	.2	.9			Deferred Taxes	.5	.4
	9.3	3.6	8.1			All Other Non-Current	6.7	4.5
	36.6	37.7	44.0			Net Worth	35.0	33.0
	100.0	100.0	100.0			Total Liabilities & Net Worth	100.0	100.0
						INCOME DATA		
	100.0	100.0	100.0			Net Sales	100.0	100.0
	41.3	40.1	39.6			Gross Profit	37.1	37.4
	39.3	35.8	31.6			Operating Expenses	34.3	35.7
	2.0	4.2	8.1			Operating Profit	2.8	1.7
	.7	.3	6.8			All Other Expenses (net)	.8	.6
	1.3	3.9	1.3			Profit Before Taxes	2.0	1.1
						RATIOS		
	3.4	2.8	4.6			Current	2.6	3.7
	2.7	1.8	2.3				1.6	2.0
	1.1	1.4	1.5				1.1	1.3
	1.2	1.2	1.5			Quick	1.4	1.1
	.8	.5	1.0				.5	.4
	.1	.0	.5				.2	.1
0 UND		0 UND	0 UND			Sales/Receivables	0 UND	0 UND
0 UND		3 126.2	4 83.6				2 151.3	4 86.3
3 117.2		48 7.5	14 26.9				16 22.4	21 17.2
32 11.3		76 4.8	50 7.3			Cost of Sales/Inventory	9 39.2	52 7.1
90 4.0		121 3.0	109 3.3				60 6.1	118 3.1
187 1.9		174 2.1	120 3.0				115 3.2	197 1.9
3 125.3		19 19.6	12 30.2			Cost of Sales/Payables	11 33.1	18 20.4
19 19.1		35 10.5	28 13.2				26 14.3	42 8.7
30 12.1		112 3.2	42 8.8				44 8.4	62 5.9
5.3		5.4	3.7			Sales/Working Capital	6.7	4.0
10.1		7.7	6.3				13.2	6.6
45.6		13.4	13.7				74.7	39.2
30.6		55.9	20.8			EBIT/Interest	17.5	5.4
(10) 3.0		(12) 4.6	(14) 6.2				(33) 3.0	(34) 2.8
.5		1.2	2.4				1.3	1.4
			20.5			Net Profit + Depr., Dep.,	12.9	6.3
			(10) 4.2			Amort./Cur. Mat. L/T/D	(10) 4.6	(10) 3.3
			.0				2.9	.9
.0		.1	.3			Fixed/Worth	.2	.2
.2		.3	.7				.6	.5
NM		2.0	1.5				NM	3.6
.5		.5	.3			Debt/Worth	.9	.7
1.7		1.7	1.0				1.9	1.7
NM		6.8	45.2				NM	13.0
32.7		45.6	21.0			% Profit Before Taxes/Tangible	30.2	33.0
(11) 18.6		(12) 18.4	(14) 9.0			Net Worth	(28) 15.2	(35) 11.3
5.8		1.3	5.7				2.4	4.2
14.9		18.5	12.0			% Profit Before Taxes/Total	13.1	10.4
7.2		4.4	4.1			Assets	6.0	4.4
-.4		.7	2.5				.7	1.6
308.4		130.5	42.2			Sales/Net Fixed Assets	80.7	75.4
48.8		24.6	12.7				22.2	18.3
8.7		11.7	2.8				5.4	7.1
5.2		3.6	3.4			Sales/Total Assets	4.6	4.0
3.5		2.7	2.4				3.0	2.2
1.8		2.1	1.3				1.7	1.6
.1		.6	.5			% Depr., Dep., Amort./Sales	.3	.4
(10) .4		(11) .7	1.6				(33) .9	(33) .9
2.2		1.4	2.9				2.0	2.2
						% Officers', Directors'	2.7	3.7
						Owners' Comp/Sales	(12) 4.2	(14) 4.5
							7.0	7.7
11510M	63678M	160739M	900168M	526282M	1410599M	Net Sales ($)	3631239M	3123374M
777M	15161M	55311M	336491M	146452M	639399M	Total Assets ($)	1141378M	1030968M

© RMA 2010

M = $ thousand   MM = $ million
See Pages 9 through 22 for Explanation of Ratios and Data

Comparative Historical Data | Current Data Sorted by Sales

6	13	10	Type of Statement						
4	4	9	Unqualified	1	1		1	1	9
3	4	9	Reviewed		2		4	2	4
9	8	9	Compiled		2	2	4	1	
17	6	16	Tax Returns		3	1			1
			Other	1	2	2	5		4
4/1/07-3/31/08 ALL	4/1/08-3/31/09 ALL	4/1/09-3/31/10 ALL		7 (4/1-9/30/09)			46 (10/1/09-3/31/10)		
				0-1MM	1-3MM	3-5MM	5-10MM	10-25MM	25MM & OVER
39	35	53	NUMBER OF STATEMENTS	2	8	5	11	9	18
%	%	%		%	%	%	%	%	%
			ASSETS						
7.1	9.8	15.0	Cash & Equivalents				21.6		13.8
9.5	5.4	9.2	Trade Receivables (net)				11.0		9.4
48.2	50.4	45.0	Inventory				51.6		46.8
2.7	1.1	1.7	All Other Current				1.3		3.2
67.6	66.7	71.0	Total Current				85.5		73.3
21.7	24.5	21.6	Fixed Assets (net)				11.3		18.4
3.3	2.5	2.4	Intangibles (net)				.0		3.7
7.4	6.4	5.0	All Other Non-Current				3.1		4.6
100.0	100.0	100.0	Total				100.0		100.0
			LIABILITIES						
7.1	9.7	10.3	Notes Payable-Short Term				11.4		9.2
2.1	1.7	2.1	Cur. Mat.-L.T.D.				1.9		1.7
16.5	13.8	16.4	Trade Payables				28.4		16.9
.1	.1	.5	Income Taxes Payable				1.3		.3
8.8	9.9	7.9	All Other Current				5.2		10.5
34.6	35.3	37.2	Total Current				48.2		38.7
16.3	17.7	14.5	Long-Term Debt				14.7		9.8
.4	.5	.5	Deferred Taxes				.2		.1
5.2	8.2	9.3	All Other Non-Current				14.4		7.0
43.5	38.3	38.6	Net Worth				22.6		44.4
100.0	100.0	100.0	Total Liabilities & Net Worth				100.0		100.0
			INCOME DATA						
100.0	100.0	100.0	Net Sales				100.0		100.0
40.1	42.7	41.1	Gross Profit				36.1		40.2
36.5	38.1	35.9	Operating Expenses				33.6		36.5
3.6	4.6	5.2	Operating Profit				2.6		3.7
.7	1.7	2.5	All Other Expenses (net)				.4		.4
2.9	3.0	2.7	Profit Before Taxes				2.1		3.2
			RATIOS						
3.5	3.8	3.1					3.8		3.8
2.4	2.1	2.1	Current				1.8		1.9
1.5	1.3	1.3					1.1		1.4
1.3	1.2	1.2					1.3		1.5
.4	.3	.8	Quick				1.0		.9
.1	.1	.2					.0		.2
0 UND	0 UND	0 UND					0 UND		0 UND
4 93.2	2 228.1	2 216.7	Sales/Receivables				0 UND		2 187.0
18 20.2	15 24.8	15 24.1					32 11.3		15 24.2
56 6.6	94 3.9	54 6.8					35 10.3		65 5.7
118 3.1	124 2.9	104 3.5	Cost of Sales/Inventory				108 3.4		116 3.1
200 1.8	215 1.7	155 2.4					157 2.3		134 2.7
14 25.4	12 30.9	8 43.0					20 18.4		22 16.3
29 12.8	29 12.7	26 14.2	Cost of Sales/Payables				29 12.7		34 10.8
53 6.8	54 6.8	42 8.7					111 3.3		60 6.1
3.6	3.9	5.4					6.4		4.6
6.3	6.2	7.7	Sales/Working Capital				7.7		8.4
14.3	18.3	19.3					66.5		14.9
8.3	8.7	25.9							30.2
(34) 3.1	(34) 1.9	(44) 5.3	EBIT/Interest					(17)	16.6
1.3	-.2	1.8							3.2
3.5		8.9	Net Profit + Depr., Dep.,						14.9
(10) 1.9	(18) 3.4	3.4	Amort./Cur. Mat. L/T/D					(11)	4.2
.6		.1							.0
.1	.2	.1					.1		.3
.4	.5	.4	Fixed/Worth				.2		.4
1.1	1.7	1.2					2.9		.8
.4	.7	.5					.6		.4
1.2	2.0	1.6	Debt/Worth				2.7		1.1
2.9	3.7	6.3					29.6		3.0
15.2	34.2	41.6	% Profit Before Taxes/Tangible						37.2
(34) 5.5	(32) 7.8	(46) 17.5	Net Worth					(17)	11.0
1.0	-7.4	5.7							5.3
8.8	9.1	16.6	% Profit Before Taxes/Total				24.5		18.9
3.1	3.5	8.0	Assets				4.4		8.4
.3	-2.4	1.7					.5		2.7
71.8	37.8	88.3					193.0		44.8
16.4	12.9	24.3	Sales/Net Fixed Assets				66.8		19.0
5.8	5.0	7.9					24.3		10.7
3.6	3.1	4.2					5.2		4.1
2.3	2.3	2.7	Sales/Total Assets				3.7		2.6
1.5	1.5	1.8					2.4		2.0
.4	.6	.3							.5
(30) 1.2	(27) 1.5	(46) .9	% Depr., Dep., Amort./Sales						1.2
3.4	2.3	2.0							1.7
1.4	1.1	1.8	% Officers', Directors'						
(10) 2.8	(11) 4.1	(24) 3.3	Owners' Comp/Sales						
8.5	7.3	5.5							
3396186M	2906528M	3072976M	Net Sales ($)	973M	12930M	19713M	82738M	156762M	2799860M
1426787M	1277213M	1193591M	Total Assets ($)	4106M	18262M	7217M	23128M	82043M	1058835M

M = $ thousand   MM = $ million
See Pages 9 through 22 for Explanation of Ratios and Data

RETAIL—All Other General Merchandise Stores NAICS 452990

Current Data Sorted by Assets

Comparative Historical Data

	0-500M	500M-2MM	2-10MM	10-50MM	50-100MM	100-250MM	Type of Statement	4/1/05-3/31/06 ALL	4/1/06-3/31/07 ALL
	1		2	10	1	6	Unqualified	15	12
			11	7	1		Reviewed	19	23
	2	5	6	1		1	Compiled	26	23
	29	24	7	15	1		Tax Returns	54	44
	10	11	15	19		2	Other	40	45
		21 (4/1-9/30/09)		156 (10/1/09-3/31/10)					
NUMBER OF STATEMENTS	42	40	41	37	8	9		154	147
ASSETS	%	%	%	%	%	%		%	%
Cash & Equivalents	17.0	15.3	9.2	8.5				10.8	12.9
Trade Receivables (net)	6.0	10.6	10.1	6.9				6.8	7.3
Inventory	43.8	44.7	47.9	41.6				47.4	43.6
All Other Current	1.8	2.8	3.0	3.9				2.6	2.5
Total Current	68.6	73.4	70.3	60.8				67.7	66.4
Fixed Assets (net)	19.4	14.9	17.9	27.6				22.3	24.4
Intangibles (net)	7.4	4.4	5.8	5.4				3.8	3.4
All Other Non-Current	4.5	7.2	5.9	6.2				6.3	5.8
Total	100.0	100.0	100.0	100.0				100.0	100.0
LIABILITIES									
Notes Payable-Short Term	11.9	8.1	11.8	8.5				9.0	9.4
Cur. Mat.-L.T.D.	2.8	3.1	2.7	1.7				1.9	2.7
Trade Payables	15.4	13.7	14.2	16.4				16.2	19.1
Income Taxes Payable	.0	.0	.1	.3				.2	.1
All Other Current	8.3	12.7	9.4	13.3				12.4	12.3
Total Current	38.4	37.5	38.0	40.2				39.7	43.6
Long-Term Debt	29.6	21.1	15.0	12.0				19.0	19.6
Deferred Taxes	.0	.0	.1	.1				.2	.1
All Other Non-Current	22.6	15.0	6.7	2.4				7.2	9.4
Net Worth	9.5	26.4	40.2	45.2				34.0	27.3
Total Liabilities & Net Worth	100.0	100.0	100.0	100.0				100.0	100.0
INCOME DATA									
Net Sales	100.0	100.0	100.0	100.0				100.0	100.0
Gross Profit	45.1	38.8	39.4	37.6				39.3	40.3
Operating Expenses	42.2	37.0	36.0	33.7				36.8	36.6
Operating Profit	2.8	1.8	3.4	3.9				2.4	3.7
All Other Expenses (net)	1.3	.4	.3	.9				.8	.8
Profit Before Taxes	1.5	1.4	3.1	3.0				1.7	2.9
RATIOS									
Current	5.6	5.5	3.8	3.2				3.5	2.9
	2.7	3.0	1.7	1.5				2.0	1.7
	1.2	1.4	1.3	1.1				1.2	1.2
Quick	2.2	2.0	.9	1.0				1.1	1.1
	.7	.5	.4	(36) .3			(153)	.4	.4
	.1	.3	.1	.0				.1	.1
Sales/Receivables	0 UND	0 UND	0 999.8	1 247.8			0	UND	0 UND
	0 UND	2 221.4	3 129.1	3 117.7			1	246.8	1 324.0
	12 30.4	16 22.7	20 18.4	6 59.2			9	40.3	10 36.5
Cost of Sales/Inventory	31 11.9	25 14.8	62 5.9	29 12.6			65	5.6	40 9.2
	72 5.1	85 4.3	101 3.6	113 3.2			112	3.3	89 4.1
	177 2.1	248 1.5	181 2.0	197 1.9			173	2.1	168 2.2
Cost of Sales/Payables	0 UND	4 92.6	14 26.9	21 17.0			10	36.3	8 43.6
	10 35.4	12 30.4	33 11.1	34 10.6			25	14.7	23 15.8
	36 10.2	34 10.7	43 8.4	61 6.0			43	8.4	51 7.1
Sales/Working Capital	4.3	3.1	4.6	5.0				4.8	5.5
	8.2	7.2	9.0	10.2				8.7	9.7
	32.3	23.3	24.0	57.2				25.5	45.4
EBIT/Interest	27.4	10.5	13.9	16.9				7.5	6.7
	(24) 2.4	(32) 2.4	(37) 4.0	(35) 6.7			(125)	2.9	(129) 2.7
	-.2	-.3	1.4	1.5				1.4	1.1
Net Profit + Depr., Dep., Amort./Cur. Mat. L/T/D								9.0	10.0
							(29)	3.2	(19) 2.9
								1.9	1.6
Fixed/Worth	.1	.0	.1	.3				.2	.2
	1.0	.2	.4	.5				.5	.7
	-.5	14.8	1.3	1.1				3.0	3.9
Debt/Worth	.4	.8	.8	.6				.7	.7
	3.5	2.6	1.8	1.4				1.8	2.0
	-5.8	NM	4.0	3.0				14.7	21.5
% Profit Before Taxes/Tangible Net Worth	90.5	51.0	38.8	33.6				33.0	38.2
	(27) 24.4	(30) 13.4	(36) 12.0	(34) 19.8			(124)	13.9	(116) 18.7
	8.9	-.4	4.5	3.2				2.6	4.8
% Profit Before Taxes/Total Assets	36.7	12.3	13.1	19.2				13.0	15.6
	7.3	5.6	4.3	6.6				4.4	4.8
	-7.1	-4.2	-.5	.8				-.1	.0
Sales/Net Fixed Assets	137.5	495.7	47.9	30.1				39.2	46.3
	34.8	32.3	20.7	11.7				18.1	20.1
	10.4	8.9	11.9	6.7				8.6	7.3
Sales/Total Assets	5.8	4.8	3.5	3.2				3.9	4.2
	2.7	2.9	2.6	2.4				2.6	2.6
	1.7	1.5	2.0	1.6				1.7	1.9
% Depr., Dep., Amort./Sales	.5	.6	.6	.7				.5	.5
	(27) 1.1	(23) 1.4	(36) 1.1	(32) 1.1			(142)	1.0	(123) 1.0
	3.4	2.5	1.8	1.9				1.9	1.7
% Officers', Directors' Owners' Comp/Sales	2.7	2.1	1.2					2.3	1.7
	(26) 5.3	(25) 4.1	(14) 1.6				(69)	4.2	(61) 3.9
	7.1	8.6	2.2					8.2	8.3
Net Sales ($)	38848M	125709M	542434M	2234812M	1609609M	3951771M		7210071M	5002651M
Total Assets ($)	10893M	39960M	192905M	800169M	576628M	1521548M		2457693M	1797338M

M = $ thousand   MM = $ million
See Pages 9 through 22 for Explanation of Ratios and Data

Comparative Historical Data | | Current Data Sorted by Sales

			Type of Statement						
10	12	20	Unqualified	1				2	17
18	17	19	Reviewed			1	3	10	5
25	15	15	Compiled	1	2	3	4	2	3
42	49	61	Tax Returns	23	21	6	6	4	1
44	45	62	Other	10	10	3	7	9	23
4/1/07-3/31/08	4/1/08-3/31/09	4/1/09-3/31/10		0-1MM	21 (4/1-9/30/09) 1-3MM	3-5MM	5-10MM	156 (10/1/09-3/31/10) 10-25MM	25MM & OVE
ALL	ALL	ALL							
139	138	177	**NUMBER OF STATEMENTS**	35	33	13	20	27	49
%	%	%	**ASSETS**	%	%	%	%	%	%
10.9	11.0	12.3	Cash & Equivalents	14.0	15.8	18.4	8.7	10.5	9.5
9.5	8.7	8.8	Trade Receivables (net)	8.0	7.0	12.1	11.0	8.9	8.7
43.9	47.9	43.9	Inventory	43.3	46.8	35.6	48.3	46.4	41.4
3.2	5.1	2.8	All Other Current	1.9	1.9	.7	2.5	4.8	3.8
67.4	72.6	67.8	Total Current	67.1	71.5	66.7	70.4	70.6	63.4
21.4	16.2	20.0	Fixed Assets (net)	18.7	21.1	18.7	16.6	17.3	23.5
4.8	4.3	6.1	Intangibles (net)	8.2	4.0	4.9	3.3	4.6	8.4
6.3	6.9	6.1	All Other Non-Current	5.9	3.3	9.7	9.6	7.5	4.8
100.0	100.0	100.0	Total	100.0	100.0	100.0	100.0	100.0	100.0
			LIABILITIES						
8.6	10.9	9.9	Notes Payable-Short Term	6.7	13.1	12.3	7.5	12.5	9.0
2.4	3.5	2.6	Cur. Mat.-L.T.D.	2.8	2.4	1.0	5.4	1.9	2.2
16.7	15.2	14.9	Trade Payables	16.9	9.7	15.5	12.3	14.5	18.1
.2	.1	.1	Income Taxes Payable	.0	.0	.0	.1	.1	.3
8.0	11.3	10.6	All Other Current	13.6	8.8	3.6	16.0	10.7	9.4
35.9	40.9	38.2	Total Current	40.2	34.0	32.4	41.3	39.7	39.0
20.7	16.1	20.0	Long-Term Debt	22.2	30.8	27.7	15.3	12.0	15.5
.1	.1	.1	Deferred Taxes	.0	.0	.0	.1	.0	.4
9.5	10.2	11.1	All Other Non-Current	34.9	5.5	1.6	13.3	5.6	2.6
33.9	32.7	30.5	Net Worth	2.8	29.7	38.2	30.1	42.7	42.4
100.0	100.0	100.0	Total Liabilities & Net Worth	100.0	100.0	100.0	100.0	100.0	100.0
			INCOME DATA						
100.0	100.0	100.0	Net Sales	100.0	100.0	100.0	100.0	100.0	100.0
41.5	39.4	40.1	Gross Profit	46.3	40.8	41.4	34.4	43.5	35.4
37.7	35.3	37.0	Operating Expenses	44.8	36.8	39.4	32.7	40.2	31.0
3.8	4.1	3.1	Operating Profit	1.5	4.0	2.0	1.7	3.3	4.4
.9	1.2	.8	All Other Expenses (net)	2.3	.1	-.3	.5	.3	1.0
2.8	2.8	2.3	Profit Before Taxes	-.8	3.9	2.3	1.2	3.0	3.5
			RATIOS						
3.6	4.0	4.1	Current	14.1	3.8	6.2	4.3	4.2	2.6
2.0	2.0	2.1		2.7	2.7	4.2	2.3	2.1	1.5
1.3	1.3	1.2		1.2	1.3	.9	1.4	1.2	1.2
1.2	1.1	1.2	Quick	2.1	1.3	3.7	.7	1.2	1.0
.4 (137)	.4 (176)	.4		.7	.4	.5	.4	.4 (48)	.3
.1	.1	.1		.2	.1	.2	.2	.1	.1
0 UND	0 UND	0 UND	Sales/Receivables	0 UND	0 UND	0 UND	0 UND	0 999.8	1 327.3
2 178.4	2 183.7	2 184.8		0 UND	0 UND	1 325.3	3 109.0	3 129.1	3 117.7
17 21.0	18 20.5	12 29.4		22 16.5	7 53.9	6 61.0	18 20.7	15 24.4	7 54.8
41 9.0	47 7.7	36 10.2	Cost of Sales/Inventory	62 5.8	26 14.2	25 14.8	41 8.9	57 6.5	30 12.0
103 3.6	96 3.8	99 3.7		120 3.1	97 3.8	60 6.1	109 3.4	101 3.6	105 3.5
167 2.2	166 2.2	181 2.0		281 1.3	218 1.7	71 5.2	178 2.0	191 1.9	146 2.5
9 41.0	4 94.5	6 56.4	Cost of Sales/Payables	0 UND	1 707.8	11 32.4	8 45.2	17 21.4	22 16.8
27 13.3	22 16.8	23 15.7		12 29.2	5 70.8	18 19.8	28 13.2	33 11.1	33 11.0
52 7.1	42 8.7	48 7.7		56 6.5	25 14.8	37 9.9	40 9.2	46 8.0	53 6.8
4.2	4.4	4.5	Sales/Working Capital	2.3	4.3	5.0	4.6	4.9	5.3
9.2	8.6	8.0		7.2	8.0	9.6	7.4	10.0	10.2
28.3	28.7	31.1		24.2	15.0	-190.9	14.8	30.6	41.4
8.0	12.9	15.9	EBIT/Interest	3.3	33.5	12.5	9.3	17.8	18.3
(119) 2.5	(118) 3.7	(144) 3.9		(17) 1.0	(29) 4.5	(10) 1.4	(19) 1.6	(22) 4.9	(47) 7.2
1.2	.7	.6		-1.1	-.2	-.1	.4	1.5	2.4
18.9	16.9	9.0	Net Profit + Depr., Dep., Amort./Cur. Mat. L/T/D						14.2
(23) 3.1	(18) 3.0	(25) 3.7						(19)	4.2
1.2	1.5	2.2							2.4
.2	.1	.1	Fixed/Worth	.1	.1	.0	.1	.1	.3
.7	.4	.5		1.7	.5	.2	.3	.4	.5
8.4	1.9	2.7		-.4	2.1	11.3	NM	1.4	1.1
.6	.7	.7	Debt/Worth	1.0	.5	.2	.7	.6	.8
2.0	1.6	2.1		5.5	1.6	2.5	2.2	1.3	1.8
17.4	7.3	8.5		-2.4	6.5	NM	NM	5.1	3.6
38.1	48.9	50.9	% Profit Before Taxes/Tangible Net Worth	68.7	92.1	24.2	39.5	35.4	51.1
(107) 14.5	(115) 13.7	(143) 19.5		(22) 18.4	(27) 24.3	(10) 11.2	(15) 11.4	(22) 13.5	(47) 24.9
3.8	2.0	4.4		3.6	2.5	1.1	3.0	5.0	3.7
13.3	18.7	16.3	% Profit Before Taxes/Total Assets	15.1	35.0	14.7	16.7	11.9	19.2
4.3	4.5	6.1		5.8	8.6	2.3	1.9	6.1	7.4
.8	-.8	-.9		-9.1	-2.0	-6.9	-2.0	-.7	1.2
45.7	71.6	56.2	Sales/Net Fixed Assets	196.0	109.6	UND	43.6	53.1	30.1
21.4	29.6	21.4		19.1	25.9	69.4	19.6	22.5	17.9
7.5	12.4	8.6		7.3	8.4	10.5	12.2	10.6	8.6
3.8	4.4	3.8	Sales/Total Assets	2.8	5.2	5.2	4.1	3.6	3.4
2.4	2.8	2.5		1.9	3.1	3.6	2.6	2.5	2.5
1.4	2.0	1.8		1.1	1.6	2.5	2.1	1.8	2.0
.6	.4	.7	% Depr., Dep., Amort./Sales	.7	.6			.7	.5	.8
(110) 1.2	(101) .9	(133) 1.2		(22) 2.0	(23) 1.1		(15) 1.0	(24) 1.3	(42) 1.1
2.0	1.6	2.0		4.2	2.1		1.5	1.8	1.9
2.0	1.9	1.8	% Officers', Directors' Owners' Comp/Sales	2.8	2.7				
(64) 3.6	(59) 4.0	(70) 3.9		(20) 6.4	(19) 4.1				
9.5	8.9	9.8		11.0	5.6				
5651576M	5301191M	8503183M	Net Sales ($)	17966M	66439M	52454M	138333M	452107M	7775884M
2374406M	1992501M	3142103M	Total Assets ($)	10690M	40874M	17397M	64408M	185617M	2823117M

© RMA 2010

M = $ thousand   MM = $ million
See Pages 9 through 22 for Explanation of Ratios and Data

RETAIL—Florists NAICS 453110

Current Data Sorted by Assets							Comparative Historical Data	
0-500M	500M-2MM	2-10MM	10-50MM	50-100MM	100-250MM	Type of Statement		
	7 (4/1-9/30/09)		45 (10/1/09-3/31/10)			Unqualified		
	1	2	1			Reviewed	6	8
3	7	2 4				Compiled	17	13
16	5	2 3				Tax Returns	29	33
6						Other	19	15
							4/1/05-3/31/06 ALL	4/1/06-3/31/07 ALL
25	13	13	1			NUMBER OF STATEMENTS	71	69
%	%	%	%	%	%	ASSETS	%	%
13.1	7.5	13.7				Cash & Equivalents	9.4	10.8
15.0	13.1	17.4				Trade Receivables (net)	12.2	13.0
17.7	28.5	19.8		D A T A	D A T A	Inventory	23.6	20.9
4.4	4.2	1.5				All Other Current	.9	2.2
50.2	53.3	52.5		N O T	N O T	Total Current	46.0	46.9
40.5	33.9	30.7				Fixed Assets (net)	35.3	37.9
7.8	5.0	7.3		A V A I L A B L E	A V A I L A B L E	Intangibles (net)	9.6	7.9
1.5	7.8	9.5				All Other Non-Current	9.0	7.2
100.0	100.0	100.0				Total	100.0	100.0
						LIABILITIES		
14.3	10.4	5.4				Notes Payable-Short Term	16.6	8.2
5.5	5.0	3.0				Cur. Mat.-L.T.D.	10.7	4.9
43.0	13.9	14.7				Trade Payables	15.8	14.5
.0	.2	.0				Income Taxes Payable	.1	.0
24.0	15.3	9.8				All Other Current	10.7	14.4
86.7	44.7	32.9				Total Current	53.9	42.1
51.6	31.9	26.8				Long-Term Debt	34.7	35.4
.0	.0	.0				Deferred Taxes	.1	.3
17.2	11.8	13.2				All Other Non-Current	8.2	12.0
-55.5	11.5	27.1				Net Worth	3.2	10.3
100.0	100.0	100.0				Total Liabilities & Net Worth	100.0	100.0
						INCOME DATA		
100.0	100.0	100.0				Net Sales	100.0	100.0
59.7	51.0	48.4				Gross Profit	56.7	53.3
59.7	49.4	46.0				Operating Expenses	53.6	52.1
.0	1.6	2.4				Operating Profit	3.0	1.2
.7	.9	-.7				All Other Expenses (net)	1.2	1.6
-.7	.7	3.1				Profit Before Taxes	1.9	-.3
						RATIOS		
1.4	1.8	3.0				Current	2.2	2.6
1.1	1.1	1.7					1.1	1.7
.7	.9	.9					.6	.7
.9	.5	2.0				Quick	1.2	1.4
.5	.3	.8					.5	.6
.1	.2	.5					.2	.2
4 98.9	1 469.1	13 27.2				Sales/Receivables	4 85.1	6 60.9
11 32.9	13 28.3	26 13.9					10 35.1	11 33.7
15 24.5	22 16.6	37 9.8					20 18.4	24 15.2
20 18.6	28 13.1	25 14.8				Cost of Sales/Inventory	19 19.4	20 18.3
31 11.9	54 6.7	48 7.6					46 8.0	56 6.5
87 4.2	150 2.4	119 3.1					97 3.8	105 3.5
0 UND	5 80.4	31 11.9				Cost of Sales/Payables	6 56.4	2 197.8
50 7.3	19 19.3	42 8.7					23 15.7	29 12.4
138 2.7	54 6.8	51 7.2					54 6.7	59 6.2
25.0	12.8	4.3				Sales/Working Capital	10.6	8.8
95.9	72.5	10.5					80.4	22.1
-12.6	-83.0	NM					-17.0	-24.7
6.0	4.7	6.0				EBIT/Interest	7.7	4.9
(21) .1	(12) 1.5	(11) 2.7					(58) 2.2	(61) 1.5
-1.5	.8	1.0					.2	.3
						Net Profit + Depr., Dep., Amort./Cur. Mat. L/T/D		
.7	1.3	.2				Fixed/Worth	.6	.7
-3.2	7.1	.8					1.9	1.8
-.4	-2.5	29.2					-2.1	-1.1
3.7	4.3	.4				Debt/Worth	.6	.9
-6.5	14.5	4.4					5.3	2.9
-2.0	-7.3	49.7					-5.1	-3.2
284.4		55.3				% Profit Before Taxes/Tangible Net Worth	64.1	36.3
(11) 64.7		(11) 24.3					(46) 13.4	(40) 10.3
14.3		-4.9					-6.2	.1
35.8	9.0	13.5				% Profit Before Taxes/Total Assets	12.9	12.6
4.5	.5	2.0					4.2	3.5
-26.8	-3.7	-2.0					-3.2	-3.6
35.3	53.7	69.5				Sales/Net Fixed Assets	30.2	18.1
12.2	14.5	13.2					11.9	8.9
3.1	3.3	3.8					5.4	4.0
6.1	4.0	3.3				Sales/Total Assets	5.4	4.5
4.5	2.5	2.3					3.1	2.5
2.0	1.7	1.5					1.8	1.7
1.1	1.3	.7				% Depr., Dep., Amort./Sales	1.1	1.3
(17) 2.8	(10) 2.1	(12) 2.3					(57) 1.7	(61) 2.1
4.3	3.5	4.0					2.6	3.3
3.7						% Officers', Directors' Owners' Comp/Sales	2.3	3.1
(15) 6.8							(42) 4.5	(36) 5.3
12.1							8.4	9.4
18539M	31838M	96577M	10440M			Net Sales ($)	1685102M	1858561M
4588M	11386M	40694M	12912M			Total Assets ($)	544503M	370771M

M = $ thousand   MM = $ million
See Pages 9 through 22 for Explanation of Ratios and Data

Comparative Historical Data

Current Data Sorted by Sales

							Type of Statement								
	2		1		2		Unqualified				1			1	
	3		4		3		Reviewed				1	2		2	
	13		18		7		Compiled	3			2	2			
	31		30		25		Tax Returns	14	7		2	2			
	22		8		15		Other	5	6		1	1		2	
	4/1/07-3/31/08 ALL		4/1/08-3/31/09 ALL		4/1/09-3/31/10 ALL			0-1MM	7 (4/1-9/30/09) 1-3MM	3-5MM	45 (10/1/09-3/31/10) 5-10MM	10-25MM		25MM & OVER	
	71		61		52		NUMBER OF STATEMENTS	22	13	7	5	5		5	
	%		%		%		ASSETS	%	%	%	%	%		%	
	10.2		7.7		11.7		Cash & Equivalents	9.7	15.8						D
	15.8		13.5		14.9		Trade Receivables (net)	13.0	15.7						A
	23.2		23.0		20.6		Inventory	24.3	13.2						T
	2.6		2.0		3.6		All Other Current	.2	9.5						A
	51.8		46.3		50.8		Total Current	47.1	54.2						
	34.7		32.9		36.2		Fixed Assets (net)	45.4	34.9						N
	6.8		13.4		6.8		Intangibles (net)	6.5	8.3						O
	6.7		7.5		6.2		All Other Non-Current	1.0	2.6						T
	100.0		100.0		100.0		Total	100.0	100.0						
							LIABILITIES								A
	17.4		12.3		10.8		Notes Payable-Short Term	8.9	18.1						V
	5.3		4.7		4.7		Cur. Mat.-L.T.D.	7.0	2.9						A
	19.5		13.6		27.9		Trade Payables	29.5	39.1						I
	.1		.0		.1		Income Taxes Payable	.0	.0						L
	11.7		11.2		17.9		All Other Current	29.0	9.2						A
	53.9		41.8		61.3		Total Current	74.4	69.3						B
	42.9		34.6		40.8		Long-Term Debt	60.4	30.4						L
	.1		.2		.0		Deferred Taxes	.0	.0						E
	12.8		9.8		14.6		All Other Non-Current	14.2	20.9						
	-9.8		13.6		-16.6		Net Worth	-48.9	-20.5						
	100.0		100.0		100.0		Total Liabilities & Net Worth	100.0	100.0						
							INCOME DATA								
	100.0		100.0		100.0		Net Sales	100.0	100.0						
	53.7		53.4		54.4		Gross Profit	58.0	61.7						
	52.3		52.4		53.3		Operating Expenses	59.7	56.7						
	1.4		1.0		1.1		Operating Profit	-1.7	5.1						
	1.2		.4		.4		All Other Expenses (net)	.9	.9						
	.2		.6		.7		Profit Before Taxes	-2.6	4.1						
							RATIOS								
	2.6		2.1		1.8			1.8	2.1						
	1.3		1.2		1.2		Current	1.0	1.2						
	.8		.7		.8			.7	.8						
	1.3		1.0		.9			.8	1.0						
	.6		.6		.5		Quick	.4	.6						
	.2		.2		.2			.2	.2						
5	77.2	4	88.3	7	49.4			0 UND	6 62.5						
13	28.8	12	30.7	13	27.6		Sales/Receivables	13 27.6	11 32.9						
26	14.2	20	18.6	22	16.6			18 20.7	15 23.6						
21	17.1	19	19.5	22	16.2			26 14.0	6 64.4						
53	6.9	36	10.2	38	9.6		Cost of Sales/Inventory	70 5.2	25 14.5						
90	4.0	93	3.9	104	3.5			126 2.9	90 4.0						
8	47.8	10	35.8	9	39.7			0 UND	10 37.7						
34	10.9	34	10.8	42	8.7		Cost of Sales/Payables	47 7.7	48 7.6						
58	6.3	53	6.8	66	5.5			138 2.7	85 4.3						
	9.7		10.1		11.0			21.8	15.3						
	34.6		66.8		50.6		Sales/Working Capital	-171.0	52.0						
	-22.6		-33.5		-25.7			-14.2	NM						
	5.8		4.6		5.6			4.3	14.4						
(58)	1.5	(57)	1.8	(45)	1.4		EBIT/Interest	(20) .1	(10) 4.8						
	.0		-.1		-.4			-1.3	-.8						
							Net Profit + Depr., Dep., Amort./Cur. Mat. L/T/D								
	.4		.5		.6			6.3	.5						
	2.0		1.9		7.2		Fixed/Worth	-3.1	5.7						
	-.8		-1.3		-1.7			-.6	-1.1						
	.8		1.6		3.1			10.4	1.9						
	4.0		6.6		15.3		Debt/Worth	-6.5	10.8						
	-2.9		-3.7		-3.5			-3.1	-3.3						
	58.9		46.9		135.2		% Profit Before Taxes/Tangible Net Worth								
(41)	22.9	(38)	9.6	(31)	28.9										
	1.1		-5.2		2.6										
	13.1		9.1		16.7			5.8	46.3						
	1.7		3.0		1.6		% Profit Before Taxes/Total Assets	-3.3	15.8						
	-3.8		-4.7		-7.2			-24.4	-7.7						
	31.8		64.0		29.7			29.5	82.1						
	10.1		12.9		13.2		Sales/Net Fixed Assets	8.1	23.1						
	5.5		5.1		3.3			2.3	3.3						
	4.9		4.9		4.7			5.1	7.0						
	3.0		2.8		2.7		Sales/Total Assets	2.5	3.9						
	1.8		1.9		1.7			1.5	1.9						
	1.1		1.1		1.2			1.2							
(55)	2.0	(52)	1.9	(40)	2.2		% Depr., Dep., Amort./Sales	(16) 3.0							
	3.4		3.2		3.8			5.0							
	3.5		3.0		2.4			3.6							
(46)	6.0	(35)	5.3	(30)	5.4		% Officers', Directors' Owners' Comp/Sales	(15) 6.7							
	10.3		8.6		7.2			12.1							
	449284M		798579M		157394M		Net Sales ($)	11144M	22832M	28126M	30770M	64522M			
	195675M		169612M		69580M		Total Assets ($)	4933M	10993M	14203M	11508M	27943M			

© RMA 2010

M = $ thousand   MM = $ million
See Pages 9 through 22 for Explanation of Ratios and Data

Current Data Sorted by Assets | Comparative Historical Data

							Type of Statement		
		3	3		1		Unqualified	8	11
	5	5	2				Reviewed	16	23
2	15	7					Compiled	17	23
11	12	10					Tax Returns	26	42
6	14	10					Other	25	31
	24 (4/1-9/30/09)		89 (10/1/09-3/31/10)					4/1/05-	4/1/06-
								3/31/06	3/31/07
0-500M	500M-2MM	2-10MM	10-50MM	50-100MM	100-250MM			ALL	ALL
19	46	35	11	1	1		NUMBER OF STATEMENTS	92	130
%	%	%	%	%	%		ASSETS	%	%
10.5	7.7	9.1	9.7				Cash & Equivalents	6.7	8.8
24.9	31.0	28.8	30.3				Trade Receivables (net)	37.8	32.6
25.0	31.3	26.9	21.2				Inventory	28.9	27.8
1.9	2.9	3.6	4.1				All Other Current	1.8	2.6
62.2	72.9	68.3	65.3				Total Current	75.2	71.8
24.5	12.1	21.6	13.0				Fixed Assets (net)	16.4	16.4
6.0	4.3	3.6	18.2				Intangibles (net)	2.8	4.0
7.3	10.7	6.5	3.5				All Other Non-Current	5.7	7.8
100.0	100.0	100.0	100.0				Total	100.0	100.0
							LIABILITIES		
28.8	15.6	10.6	12.0				Notes Payable-Short Term	14.1	12.8
5.0	3.7	2.6	2.5				Cur. Mat.-L.T.D.	3.4	6.8
20.8	24.1	21.9	16.2				Trade Payables	23.9	23.3
.2	.1	.0	.0				Income Taxes Payable	.1	.2
6.3	11.9	9.3	16.3				All Other Current	12.9	12.3
61.1	55.4	44.5	47.1				Total Current	54.4	55.4
24.1	10.7	15.6	10.0				Long-Term Debt	13.4	11.3
.0	.1	.0	.6				Deferred Taxes	.2	.2
7.1	6.2	2.6	6.1				All Other Non-Current	5.4	5.8
7.8	27.6	37.4	36.3				Net Worth	26.6	27.2
100.0	100.0	100.0	100.0				Total Liabilities & Net Worth	100.0	100.0
							INCOME DATA		
100.0	100.0	100.0	100.0				Net Sales	100.0	100.0
47.0	36.4	37.1	37.5				Gross Profit	35.6	37.4
41.7	35.1	37.6	36.6				Operating Expenses	33.6	35.5
5.3	1.2	-.5	.9				Operating Profit	2.1	2.0
.9	.2	.1	.3				All Other Expenses (net)	.2	.4
4.4	1.1	-.6	.6				Profit Before Taxes	1.9	1.6
							RATIOS		
1.6	2.5	2.2	2.4					2.1	2.3
1.1	1.3	1.5	1.3				Current	1.4	1.5
.9	.8	1.3	1.1					1.1	1.1
1.1	1.1	1.3	1.0					1.2	1.3
.8	.7	.9	.8				Quick	.9	.9
.3	.5	.5	.5					.5	.5
7 54.9	23 16.1	21 17.1	33 11.1					28 13.2	23 16.1
21 17.2	31 11.6	30 12.3	40 9.1				Sales/Receivables	34 10.7	33 11.0
24 15.3	43 8.6	40 9.2	43 8.4					44 8.3	48 7.6
6 62.0	15 25.1	25 14.4	23 16.0					19 19.7	21 17.8
24 15.0	40 9.1	39 9.4	41 9.0				Cost of Sales/Inventory	46 7.9	46 8.0
50 7.3	115 3.2	63 5.8	116 3.1					78 4.7	90 4.0
0 UND	19 19.1	23 15.7	17 21.0					21 17.6	18 20.2
22 17.0	33 11.0	35 10.5	33 11.0				Cost of Sales/Payables	30 12.1	31 11.8
46 7.9	51 7.1	56 6.6	43 8.4					44 8.3	52 7.0
15.4	9.2	7.7	7.7					7.9	7.7
135.3	23.5	12.8	16.5				Sales/Working Capital	17.2	14.6
-61.9	-28.2	31.0	65.9					58.3	97.7
10.5	8.9	8.3	7.1					9.3	8.2
(17) 2.5	(42) 1.9	(33) 1.8	(10) 1.7				EBIT/Interest	(88) 2.5	(112) 2.5
.7	.5	-.4	-5.2					1.0	.9
							Net Profit + Depr., Dep.,	4.4	3.2
							Amort./Cur. Mat. L/T/D	(21) 1.6	(22) 1.5
								.9	1.0
.3	.2	.1	.6					.2	.1
1.9	.4	.4	.8				Fixed/Worth	.5	.4
-.7	-30.5	1.8	2.7					15.6	2.9
1.3	.7	1.0	1.0					1.0	.8
2.9	3.5	1.9	4.8				Debt/Worth	2.6	2.0
-3.1	-93.1	4.2	8.8					128.6	8.6
131.3	20.8	15.5					% Profit Before Taxes/Tangible	30.7	37.0
(11) 76.5	(34) 5.4	(31) 5.2					Net Worth	(71) 10.0	(105) 11.8
19.3	-6.0	-9.2						.0	1.9
32.7	8.0	6.7	8.4				% Profit Before Taxes/Total	9.9	10.8
17.3	2.4	1.6	.4				Assets	4.0	3.3
-.8	-1.2	-3.0	-3.3					.0	.0
176.0	117.8	50.9	38.1					73.0	75.7
41.2	41.6	27.2	23.3				Sales/Net Fixed Assets	34.4	35.6
6.6	18.3	7.6	10.2					14.0	13.6
6.4	5.3	4.3	4.0					5.5	4.7
4.6	3.7	3.2	2.8				Sales/Total Assets	3.7	3.3
2.4	2.2	2.3	1.8					2.7	2.3
.4	.4	.6						.4	.5
(11) 2.0	(39) .8	(31) 1.1					% Depr., Dep., Amort./Sales	(82) .8	(104) 1.0
4.0	1.6	2.2						1.7	1.9
5.8	2.6	1.1						2.0	2.2
(13) 7.7	(22) 3.1	(16) 1.8					% Officers', Directors' Owners' Comp/Sales	(51) 3.8	(73) 4.2
9.5	5.5	3.9						6.8	7.1
19424M	214672M	566684M	525410M	213590M	742720M		Net Sales ($)	1885602M	1763714M
4669M	54640M	173812M	223646M	65348M	199206M		Total Assets ($)	587469M	540121M

M = $ thousand   MM = $ million
See Pages 9 through 22 for Explanation of Ratios and Data

Comparative Historical Data | Current Data Sorted by Sales

7 15 28 20 37	3 14 30 29 40	7 12 24 33 37	Type of Statement	0-1MM	1-3MM	3-5MM	5-10MM	10-25MM	25MM & OVER
			Unqualified					1	6
			Reviewed	1	1	2	3	3	3
			Compiled	8	5	6	6	3	3
			Tax Returns	5	7	4	9	5	
			Other			3		7	8
4/1/07- 3/31/08 ALL	4/1/08- 3/31/09 ALL	4/1/09- 3/31/10 ALL		24 (4/1-9/30/09)			89 (10/1/09-3/31/10)		
107	116	113	NUMBER OF STATEMENTS	14	20	15	25	19	20
%	%	%	ASSETS	%	%	%	%	%	%
9.8	10.0	8.7	Cash & Equivalents	11.3	7.6	10.9	9.3	6.9	7.2
29.8	29.4	29.2	Trade Receivables (net)	15.6	26.3	34.2	31.6	27.3	36.7
32.1	29.2	27.8	Inventory	31.2	27.8	33.6	29.9	25.4	20.9
2.5	1.5	3.1	All Other Current	2.6	1.5	1.2	4.8	2.5	4.8
74.2	70.2	68.8	Total Current	60.7	63.1	79.8	75.7	62.1	69.5
13.4	17.6	17.4	Fixed Assets (net)	29.7	11.5	11.7	15.1	22.2	17.5
6.0	4.9	5.8	Intangibles (net)	3.0	6.5	5.3	2.4	7.1	10.2
6.4	7.3	8.0	All Other Non-Current	6.6	18.9	3.3	6.7	8.6	2.8
100.0	100.0	100.0	Total	100.0	100.0	100.0	100.0	100.0	100.0
			LIABILITIES						
13.2	17.3	16.0	Notes Payable-Short Term	32.7	8.8	27.7	13.6	7.8	13.6
4.9	5.1	3.4	Cur. Mat.-L.T.D.	2.9	5.3	1.7	4.3	3.3	2.2
27.2	26.0	22.4	Trade Payables	13.6	20.1	26.9	27.8	20.9	22.1
.1	.2	.1	Income Taxes Payable	.2	.0	.2	.0	.0	.2
13.9	12.1	10.5	All Other Current	5.7	12.3	11.6	9.1	11.7	11.9
59.3	60.7	52.4	Total Current	55.1	46.5	68.0	54.8	43.7	50.0
16.3	15.2	14.2	Long-Term Debt	25.3	21.1	5.0	10.2	17.3	8.7
.1	.1	.1	Deferred Taxes	.0	.0	.1	.0	.0	.3
6.0	3.8	5.2	All Other Non-Current	7.5	6.9	5.4	5.5	1.5	5.2
18.4	20.3	28.0	Net Worth	12.2	25.5	21.5	29.5	37.5	35.8
100.0	100.0	100.0	Total Liabilities & Net Worth	100.0	100.0	100.0	100.0	100.0	100.0
			INCOME DATA						
100.0	100.0	100.0	Net Sales	100.0	100.0	100.0	100.0	100.0	100.0
37.7	38.7	38.7	Gross Profit	47.3	44.1	38.1	35.3	34.5	35.8
35.8	37.1	37.3	Operating Expenses	42.3	42.1	37.5	34.9	34.2	35.1
1.9	1.7	1.3	Operating Profit	5.0	2.0	.5	.5	.3	.7
.4	.4	.3	All Other Expenses (net)	1.4	.5	.1	.1	-.1	.1
1.5	1.2	1.0	Profit Before Taxes	3.7	1.5	.5	.3	.4	.6
			RATIOS						
2.1	1.9	2.0	Current	2.1	2.5	1.7	2.1	2.2	1.9
1.5	1.2	1.3		1.3	1.0	1.3	1.5	1.4	1.4
1.0	.8	1.0		.4	.8	.8	.8	1.0	1.1
1.2	1.1	1.2	Quick	1.2	1.0	1.2	1.3	1.2	1.3
.7	.7	.8		.4	.8	.6	.7	.8	.8
.4	.4	.4		.2	.4	.4	.5	.4	.6
11 32.1	15 24.1	21 17.6	Sales/Receivables	0 UND	22 16.5	23 15.8	22 16.8	16 22.3	33 11.0
28 12.9	28 12.9	29 12.4		13 27.5	32 11.4	28 12.8	29 12.4	28 13.0	39 9.3
37 9.7	39 9.3	40 9.1		23 15.9	46 7.9	40 9.1	38 9.6	32 11.4	49 7.5
24 14.9	19 18.7	16 23.0	Cost of Sales/Inventory	7 49.4	9 41.6	29 12.8	13 28.3	17 22.1	19 19.3
50 7.3	40 9.1	39 9.4		41 8.9	70 5.2	55 6.6	40 9.1	37 9.8	34 10.6
95 3.8	106 3.4	93 3.9		200 1.8	166 2.2	93 3.9	64 5.7	57 6.4	62 5.8
19 18.7	18 20.7	20 18.7	Cost of Sales/Payables	0 UND	32 11.6	18 20.4	21 17.5	20 18.5	19 19.2
30 12.2	34 10.7	34 10.8		7 49.7	43 8.5	28 13.1	36 10.1	34 10.7	29 12.5
53 6.9	54 6.7	49 7.4		52 7.0	69 5.3	55 6.6	49 7.4	46 7.9	45 8.2
9.2	12.0	9.7	Sales/Working Capital	9.7	5.4	9.9	9.1	7.7	11.9
16.2	40.8	22.4		34.6	209.1	22.5	16.5	23.4	16.4
200.6	-26.3	-165.8		-11.2	-55.9	-23.2	-29.7	-148.1	65.6
6.9	5.8	7.6	EBIT/Interest	4.6	16.9	5.7	8.7	5.4	7.6
(97) 2.3	(107) 1.8	(104) 1.9		(11) 1.9	(19) 1.0	(13) 1.7	(24) 2.4	(18) 1.2	(19) 4.5
.7	-.6	.0		.8	-.8	.8	-.3	-.3	-5.1
6.3	5.0	5.7	Net Profit + Depr., Dep., Amort./Cur. Mat. L/T/D						
(18) 2.9	(15) 2.1	(18) 2.4							
1.6	1.7	-.6							
.1	.2	.2	Fixed/Worth	.2	.1	.2	.1	.2	.2
.4	.8	.7		1.3	.6	.7	.4	.7	.7
-4.0	-8.9	4.8		-1.5	NM	-.8	-19.3	1.7	1.7
.8	1.3	1.0	Debt/Worth	1.1	.5	2.0	.8	1.0	1.3
2.4	3.5	2.6		2.5	5.1	4.2	1.9	2.2	2.6
-22.6	-13.4	33.1		-5.1	-33.3	-6.4	-44.8	4.7	7.2
32.0	43.1	35.7	% Profit Before Taxes/Tangible Net Worth		118.6	15.4	32.3	19.3	43.3
(76) 13.2	(84) 14.3	(87) 5.8		(14)	7.3	(11) 5.3	(18) 7.2	(17) 1.3	(18) 11.2
2.4	-6.2	-1.7			-10.0	-5.9	-1.6	-17.1	-2.1
13.0	13.3	11.6	% Profit Before Taxes/Total Assets	26.7	19.3	6.0	6.4	8.5	10.9
3.4	1.9	2.3		16.9	-.3	1.9	3.2	.5	3.7
-.3	-3.9	-1.8		-.9	-5.0	-1.2	-1.8	-3.0	-1.4
90.6	71.5	75.4	Sales/Net Fixed Assets	84.0	160.1	106.9	117.0	46.0	53.6
40.4	34.7	35.2		14.9	25.4	38.6	44.5	27.2	29.3
18.5	13.0	10.7		4.6	12.3	12.0	22.1	9.1	9.9
5.3	5.2	4.8	Sales/Total Assets	5.6	3.1	4.3	5.4	5.7	4.5
3.4	3.4	3.4		2.8	2.3	3.7	4.1	3.6	3.6
2.5	2.3	2.2		2.0	1.4	2.4	3.0	2.5	2.6
.4	.4	.5	% Depr., Dep., Amort./Sales		.4	.3	.4	.4	.5
(82) .7	(96) .8	(91) 1.1		(16) 1.4	(12) 1.2	(21) .8	(18) 1.2	(16) 1.0	
1.6	1.7	2.2			2.6	2.3	1.4	2.2	1.5
2.0	1.7	1.8	% Officers', Directors' Owners' Comp/Sales		2.6		1.1		
(47) 3.3	(52) 2.9	(54) 3.3		(11) 5.2	(15) 2.8				
6.4	8.3	6.5			10.5		5.2		
1449974M	2184617M	2282500M	Net Sales ($)	7696M	37518M	58090M	175668M	289173M	1714355M
569719M	689537M	721321M	Total Assets ($)	3125M	20202M	17977M	48889M	96073M	535055M

© RMA 2010

M = $ thousand   MM = $ million
See Pages 9 through 22 for Explanation of Ratios and Data

RETAIL—Gift, Novelty, and Souvenir Stores NAICS 453220

Current Data Sorted by Assets | **Comparative Historical Data**

Type of Statement

Type of Statement	0-500M	500M-2MM	2-10MM	10-50MM	50-100MM	100-250MM	4/1/05-3/31/06 ALL	4/1/06-3/31/07 ALL
Unqualified				4			12	8
Reviewed		1	5	3			14	13
Compiled	12	16	7	2	3	3	25	33
Tax Returns	48	34	16	1	1	3	68	71
Other	18	30	26	4			46	53
	32 (4/1-9/30/09)			205 (10/1/09-3/31/10)				
NUMBER OF STATEMENTS	78	81	54	14	4	6	165	178

ASSETS (%)

	0-500M	500M-2MM	2-10MM	10-50MM	50-100MM	100-250MM	4/1/05-3/31/06 ALL	4/1/06-3/31/07 ALL
Cash & Equivalents	13.3	12.7	14.4	18.2			14.8	12.7
Trade Receivables (net)	3.7	6.4	7.3	6.8			6.0	8.4
Inventory	57.2	44.2	38.6	24.8			45.4	45.7
All Other Current	2.0	4.6	5.6	4.2			1.8	2.5
Total Current	76.2	68.0	65.9	53.9			68.0	69.3
Fixed Assets (net)	16.6	22.0	22.9	35.6			22.4	19.5
Intangibles (net)	3.1	2.7	1.9	4.6			2.9	3.6
All Other Non-Current	4.0	7.3	9.4	5.9			6.6	7.5
Total	100.0	100.0	100.0	100.0			100.0	100.0

LIABILITIES

	0-500M	500M-2MM	2-10MM	10-50MM	50-100MM	100-250MM	4/1/05-3/31/06 ALL	4/1/06-3/31/07 ALL
Notes Payable-Short Term	27.5	17.0	8.4	3.5			12.8	9.5
Cur. Mat.-L.T.D.	3.7	3.3	2.2	1.6			4.0	2.5
Trade Payables	17.6	19.7	14.0	17.7			18.2	16.1
Income Taxes Payable	.1	.1	.4	.0			.2	.2
All Other Current	17.1	7.3	11.7	9.7			14.4	12.2
Total Current	65.9	47.3	36.8	32.4			49.6	40.4
Long-Term Debt	23.1	16.2	16.1	15.5			20.1	18.1
Deferred Taxes	.0	.0	.1	.0			.0	.0
All Other Non-Current	19.7	11.4	8.8	.9			9.8	9.6
Net Worth	-8.8	25.1	38.3	51.2			20.5	31.8
Total Liabilities & Net Worth	100.0	100.0	100.0	100.0			100.0	100.0

INCOME DATA

	0-500M	500M-2MM	2-10MM	10-50MM	50-100MM	100-250MM	4/1/05-3/31/06 ALL	4/1/06-3/31/07 ALL
Net Sales	100.0	100.0	100.0	100.0			100.0	100.0
Gross Profit	51.3	49.2	47.6	42.7			50.8	49.1
Operating Expenses	49.2	45.9	42.6	37.5			47.6	44.9
Operating Profit	2.1	3.3	5.0	5.2			3.2	4.3
All Other Expenses (net)	1.2	.9	1.2	1.0			.9	.7
Profit Before Taxes	.9	2.4	3.8	4.2			2.3	3.5

RATIOS

Ratio	0-500M	500M-2MM	2-10MM	10-50MM	50-100MM	100-250MM	4/1/05-3/31/06 ALL	4/1/06-3/31/07 ALL
Current	4.3	3.1	3.1	2.9			3.0	4.0
	1.6	1.5	2.0	1.8			1.7	2.0
	.8	1.1	1.0	1.2			1.1	1.3
Quick	.7	.9	1.2	1.9			(164) 1.0	(177) 1.2
	.3	.4	.5	.6			.3	.4
	.1	.1	.2	.1			.1	.1
Sales/Receivables	0 UND	0 UND	0 UND	0 UND			0 UND	0 UND
	0 UND	0 UND	0 974.9	2 146.5			0 UND	0 UND
	0 UND	2 231.5	9 40.9	14 26.5			5 68.0	10 35.0
Cost of Sales/Inventory	90 4.0	79 4.6	40 9.2	21 17.8			58 6.3	57 6.4
	153 2.4	154 2.4	121 3.0	80 4.5			125 2.9	122 3.0
	238 1.5	244 1.5	194 1.9	103 3.6			212 1.7	209 1.7
Cost of Sales/Payables	0 UND	24 15.0	10 35.2	16 22.1			12 30.8	8 43.8
	17 20.9	55 6.7	30 12.1	31 11.7			39 9.4	36 10.0
	58 6.2	98 3.7	46 8.0	55 6.7			68 5.4	71 5.1
Sales/Working Capital	5.3	4.9	4.2	5.6			4.7	4.1
	13.0	9.9	8.2	13.2			9.4	8.2
	-18.9	36.3	-143.9	29.5			99.5	27.5
EBIT/Interest	10.1	6.7	10.5				6.7	10.1
	(61) 2.8	(60) 1.9	(45) 5.1				(141) 2.5	(152) 2.8
	-.1	-.7	1.2				.2	.9
Net Profit + Depr., Dep., Amort./Cur. Mat. L/T/D							4.0	7.7
							(19) 1.5	(19) 1.6
							.6	.4
Fixed/Worth	.0	.1	.1	.2			.2	.1
	.8	.5	.5	.5			.7	.4
	-.5	UND	1.7	2.1			8.3	2.4
Debt/Worth	.8	.7	.8	.4			.9	.6
	8.4	2.8	1.5	1.1			2.5	1.7
	-3.1	UND	5.9	3.0			52.0	9.2
% Profit Before Taxes/Tangible Net Worth	56.3	53.9	49.7	30.0			50.7	45.3
	(47) 27.7	(61) 14.9	(49) 22.7	(13) 23.3			(130) 17.3	(145) 18.5
	-1.7	1.3	2.6	9.9			1.7	1.4
% Profit Before Taxes/Total Assets	22.1	18.8	16.7	17.0			17.3	19.8
	4.3	3.5	7.7	11.6			4.2	6.4
	-6.8	-1.3	.4	1.7			-1.7	.2
Sales/Net Fixed Assets	376.3	68.9	73.0	28.3			51.8	66.7
	28.4	22.1	20.0	10.4			19.9	24.3
	13.5	8.8	7.7	2.5			6.3	9.7
Sales/Total Assets	4.5	3.1	3.5	3.9			3.5	3.6
	2.8	2.0	2.4	2.8			2.6	2.6
	2.0	1.3	1.5	1.3			1.7	1.8
% Depr., Dep., Amort./Sales	.5	.3	.6	1.6			.6	.6
	(51) 1.4	(69) .9	(47) 1.3	2.6			(135) 1.2	(131) 1.1
	2.4	1.9	2.2	3.4			2.4	1.9
% Officers', Directors' Owners' Comp/Sales	2.3	3.4	1.2				2.3	2.8
	(34) 6.4	(40) 4.6	(23) 2.2				(80) 5.2	(88) 5.7
	8.9	6.8	3.6				7.6	8.4
Net Sales ($)	74504M	188115M	701085M	650325M	451272M	1855885M	4243484M	3938594M
Total Assets ($)	21283M	79696M	259112M	240678M	257468M	934935M	1894125M	1294092M

M = $ thousand   MM = $ million
See Pages 9 through 22 for Explanation of Ratios and Data

Comparative Historical Data | Current Data Sorted by Sales

			Type of Statement						
8	11	11	Unqualified		1		1		10
20	21	8	Reviewed					4	3
29	30	37	Compiled	9	14	5	5	4	
77	83	100	Tax Returns	44	30	12	7	4	
57	49	81	Other	16	30	6	7	7	12
4/1/07-3/31/08 ALL	4/1/08-3/31/09 ALL	4/1/09-3/31/10 ALL		32 (4/1-9/30/09) 0-1MM	1-3MM	3-5MM	205 (10/1/09-3/31/10) 5-10MM	10-25MM	25MM & OVER
191	194	237	NUMBER OF STATEMENTS	69	75	23	19	26	25
%	%	%	ASSETS	%	%	%	%	%	%
14.4	12.3	14.2	Cash & Equivalents	10.0	15.3	14.0	10.4	17.1	22.1
6.5	5.8	5.8	Trade Receivables (net)	3.7	3.0	11.4	9.4	11.9	5.4
46.3	47.8	45.1	Inventory	50.2	52.1	36.3	36.8	37.0	33.2
3.4	2.9	3.9	All Other Current	1.8	5.1	3.4	4.3	5.9	3.6
70.6	68.8	68.9	Total Current	65.7	75.5	65.1	60.9	71.9	64.3
21.2	22.6	21.7	Fixed Assets (net)	26.5	14.3	27.1	28.2	17.5	25.2
2.8	2.7	2.9	Intangibles (net)	2.5	3.5	3.3	1.5	1.2	5.2
5.4	5.9	6.4	All Other Non-Current	5.4	6.7	4.4	9.4	9.4	5.3
100.0	100.0	100.0	Total	100.0	100.0	100.0	100.0	100.0	100.0
			LIABILITIES						
9.3	9.9	17.2	Notes Payable-Short Term	23.4	22.7	9.8	5.8	12.0	4.6
2.5	3.6	3.0	Cur. Mat.-L.T.D.	5.2	2.3	2.1	2.9	1.7	1.2
18.1	17.1	17.4	Trade Payables	12.7	22.7	15.0	14.5	15.6	20.6
.2	.1	.1	Income Taxes Payable	.0	.1	.1	.4	.2	.3
9.7	8.8	11.7	All Other Current	20.7	6.0	4.9	8.0	11.9	12.9
39.8	39.4	49.5	Total Current	62.0	53.9	32.0	31.7	41.4	39.6
21.6	18.4	18.5	Long-Term Debt	36.1	8.9	13.5	20.9	10.0	10.0
.0	.1	.1	Deferred Taxes	.0	.0	.0	.0	.1	.3
9.1	10.5	12.7	All Other Non-Current	16.7	14.6	13.6	6.9	7.5	4.6
29.5	31.7	19.3	Net Worth	-14.7	22.5	40.9	40.4	40.9	45.4
100.0	100.0	100.0	Total Liabilities & Net Worth	100.0	100.0	100.0	100.0	100.0	100.0
			INCOME DATA						
100.0	100.0	100.0	Net Sales	100.0	100.0	100.0	100.0	100.0	100.0
48.6	47.9	49.3	Gross Profit	53.9	48.9	44.2	51.6	43.8	46.6
43.7	45.1	45.8	Operating Expenses	51.8	45.8	38.2	45.9	39.5	42.7
4.9	2.8	3.5	Operating Profit	2.2	3.1	5.9	5.7	4.3	3.9
1.3	1.5	1.1	All Other Expenses (net)	1.7	.7	2.1	.5	.6	.3
3.6	1.3	2.5	Profit Before Taxes	.5	2.4	3.8	5.3	3.8	3.6
			RATIOS						
3.6 / 1.8 / 1.2	3.9 / 1.9 / 1.2	3.2 / 1.7 / 1.0	Current	4.1 / 1.5 / .6	3.1 / 1.5 / 1.0	4.8 / 2.4 / 1.5	4.0 / 2.3 / 1.5	3.0 / 1.9 / .9	2.6 / 1.6 / 1.2
(188) 1.1 / .5 / .2	(192) 1.0 / .4 / .1	.9 / .4 / .1	Quick	.7 / .2 / .1	.7 / .3 / .1	1.7 / .7 / .4	1.0 / .3 / .1	1.4 / .7 / .2	1.3 / .6 / .2
0 UND / 0 UND / 5 74.1	0 UND / 0 999.8 / 8 47.1	0 UND / 0 UND / 4 99.7	Sales/Receivables	0 UND / 0 UND / 0 UND	0 UND / 0 UND / 0 999.8	0 UND / 2 198.1 / 23 15.7	0 UND / 0 999.8 / 12 31.2	0 UND / 1 632.7 / 26 13.9	0 UND / 2 194.3 / 13 28.0
66 5.5 / 126 2.9 / 201 1.8	61 6.0 / 130 2.8 / 211 1.7	70 5.2 / 136 2.7 / 217 1.7	Cost of Sales/Inventory	115 3.2 / 208 1.8 / 354 1.0	80 4.6 / 148 2.5 / 209 1.7	32 11.4 / 80 4.5 / 192 1.9	30 12.4 / 114 3.2 / 154 2.4	37 9.8 / 91 4.0 / 141 2.6	23 16.2 / 88 4.1 / 150 2.4
5 72.4 / 31 11.8 / 67 5.5	7 51.8 / 28 12.9 / 63 5.8	9 39.0 / 35 10.4 / 74 4.9	Cost of Sales/Payables	0 UND / 18 20.5 / 63 5.8	22 16.7 / 59 6.2 / 97 3.8	4 86.8 / 32 11.3 / 45 8.2	5 77.9 / 34 10.7 / 70 5.2	17 21.0 / 30 12.3 / 42 8.6	30 12.3 / 48 7.7 / 70 5.2
4.7 / 8.4 / 26.0	4.8 / 8.9 / 38.1	5.0 / 10.6 / NM	Sales/Working Capital	4.1 / 12.9 / -12.9	5.6 / 10.7 / 78.3	3.3 / 6.4 / 19.2	6.4 / 10.4 / 26.3	4.5 / 9.5 / -61.8	6.4 / 12.3 / 43.2
(151) 10.6 / 3.1 / .8	(158) 8.3 / 2.5 / -.1	(185) 10.4 / 3.2 / .4	EBIT/Interest	(57) 4.4 / 1.4 / .1	(51) 16.0 / 3.5 / -1.2	(19) 3.9 / 1.8 / -.2	(17) 11.7 / 5.3 / 3.1	(22) 18.5 / 6.8 / 1.1	(19) 18.5 / 4.6 / 1.3
(17) 8.8 / 3.6 / .7	(15) 6.0 / 2.5 / .9	(19) 3.8 / 2.2 / -.2	Net Profit + Depr., Dep., Amort./Cur. Mat. L/T/D						
.1 / .5 / 2.3	.2 / .5 / 2.3	.1 / .6 / 23.2	Fixed/Worth	.2 / 5.8 / -1.2	.0 / .3 / -1.5	.1 / 1.1 / 1.7	.2 / .4 / 1.9	.0 / .4 / 1.9	.3 / .5 / 1.9
.8 / 2.0 / 9.3	.6 / 2.5 / 6.9	.8 / 2.3 / UND	Debt/Worth	1.6 / 21.3 / -4.6	.6 / 2.1 / -5.3	.5 / 1.5 / 5.1	.9 / 1.7 / 4.5	.6 / 1.3 / 10.0	.7 / 1.1 / 4.0
(156) 50.4 / 26.8 / 1.9	(166) 40.4 / 20.0 / .1	(178) 50.3 / 22.7 / 2.4	% Profit Before Taxes/Tangible Net Worth	(39) 56.3 / 10.3 / .0	(54) 50.8 / 26.1 / 2.9	(21) 46.2 / 6.9 / -9.4	47.1 / 14.4 / 2.5	(23) 51.0 / 25.2 / 3.4	(22) 73.2 / 23.0 / 16.4
19.9 / 7.3 / -.3	15.9 / 4.4 / -3.4	19.2 / 5.1 / -1.1	% Profit Before Taxes/Total Assets	16.6 / 1.1 / -4.3	21.1 / 5.6 / -4.8	21.0 / 2.4 / .0	17.5 / 4.7 / 1.5	15.9 / 8.6 / -.9	20.8 / 11.1 / 4.6
65.5 / 21.1 / 8.7	49.4 / 17.7 / 7.4	76.3 / 22.1 / 8.1	Sales/Net Fixed Assets	68.0 / 16.2 / 4.0	163.4 / 31.7 / 18.2	125.7 / 16.5 / 3.9	31.8 / 20.2 / 5.4	184.9 / 25.2 / 8.2	38.4 / 14.6 / 8.5
3.7 / 2.5 / 1.7	3.8 / 2.6 / 1.6	3.7 / 2.4 / 1.6	Sales/Total Assets	2.8 / 1.9 / 1.1	3.8 / 2.5 / 1.8	4.1 / 2.1 / 1.1	4.1 / 3.1 / 1.3	3.9 / 2.5 / 2.1	4.0 / 2.9 / 2.3
(147) .6 / 1.1 / 2.1	(156) .7 / 1.2 / 2.5	(186) .5 / 1.3 / 2.4	% Depr., Dep., Amort./Sales	(49) .5 / 2.1 / 3.4	(60) .3 / 1.0 / 1.6	(20) .5 / 1.2 / 2.4	(16) .7 / 1.1 / 2.5	(22) .3 / 1.0 / 1.8	(19) 1.3 / 1.8 / 3.1
(95) 2.5 / 4.8 / 7.1	(88) 2.1 / 3.9 / 7.0	(101) 2.1 / 3.8 / 6.9	% Officers', Directors' Owners' Comp/Sales	(30) 3.5 / 6.5 / 9.3	(30) 2.5 / 4.6 / 7.1	(14) 1.7 / 3.1 / 4.8	(13) 1.7 / 2.8 / 4.2	(11) 1.2 / 2.3 / 3.6	
4223496M	3462194M	3921186M	Net Sales ($)	35292M	135275M	87865M	156278M	392643M	3113833M
1770342M	1400336M	1793172M	Total Assets ($)	25404M	63182M	57731M	145728M	144637M	1356490M

RETAIL—Used Merchandise Stores   NAICS 453310

	Current Data Sorted by Assets						Comparative Historical Data	

14

Type of Statement	0-500M	500M-2MM	2-10MM	10-50MM	50-100MM	100-250MM	4/1/05-3/31/06 ALL	4/1/06-3/31/07 ALL
Unqualified			2	6	2		7	8
Reviewed		1	7	2			5	6
Compiled	4	2	4	1			18	17
Tax Returns	13	14	5	1			22	29
Other	3	8	7	2			34	23
		15 (4/1-9/30/09)		68 (10/1/09-3/31/10)				
NUMBER OF STATEMENTS	20	25	25	11	2		86	83
	%	%	%	%	%	%	%	%
ASSETS								
Cash & Equivalents	19.4	12.6	12.4	15.5			11.9	11.1
Trade Receivables (net)	3.8	17.6	17.6	12.0			9.8	13.8
Inventory	34.2	38.1	41.6	23.8		D	37.3	35.6
All Other Current	4.0	5.5	2.4	11.4		A	5.6	3.2
Total Current	61.4	73.7	74.1	62.7		T	64.6	63.7
Fixed Assets (net)	18.3	19.9	19.5	31.3		A	23.9	21.9
Intangibles (net)	8.4	1.5	1.3	1.0			4.4	5.4
All Other Non-Current	12.0	4.9	5.2	5.1		N	7.1	9.0
Total	100.0	100.0	100.0	100.0		O	100.0	100.0
LIABILITIES						T		
Notes Payable-Short Term	32.0	9.1	10.3	12.7			15.5	12.1
Cur. Mat.-L.T.D.	14.8	1.8	1.4	.8		A	2.6	3.2
Trade Payables	8.3	8.4	5.5	2.9		V	8.6	8.7
Income Taxes Payable	.0	.1	.2	.0		A	.1	.3
All Other Current	23.9	12.2	8.9	8.4		I	12.5	28.7
Total Current	79.0	31.7	26.3	24.8		L	39.2	52.9
Long-Term Debt	18.2	5.9	12.5	12.7		A	16.7	16.4
Deferred Taxes	.0	.0	.0	.1		B	.0	.1
All Other Non-Current	3.9	4.5	4.3	11.0		L	8.5	7.2
Net Worth	-1.2	58.0	56.8	51.4		E	35.6	23.4
Total Liabilties & Net Worth	100.0	100.0	100.0	100.0			100.0	100.0
INCOME DATA								
Net Sales	100.0	100.0	100.0	100.0			100.0	100.0
Gross Profit	58.6	62.8	55.1	51.2			46.9	55.8
Operating Expenses	58.3	54.6	48.5	43.5			41.8	50.4
Operating Profit	.4	8.2	6.6	7.7			5.0	5.4
All Other Expenses (net)	.5	1.1	.2	.8			.9	1.6
Profit Before Taxes	-.2	7.1	6.4	7.0			4.1	3.8
RATIOS								
Current	3.0	5.7	15.7	4.7			4.5	4.2
	1.3	2.3	2.9	2.1			2.0	2.0
	.5	1.7	1.6	1.7			1.1	.9
Quick	1.4	3.0	2.9	2.7			1.2	1.4
	.4	1.0	.8	1.1			(85) .6	.5
	.1	.3	.2	.3			.1	.1
Sales/Receivables	0 UND	1 422.1	0 UND	0 999.8			0 UND	0 UND
	0 UND	3 112.1	9 41.7	27 13.7			0 UND	6 63.3
	2 198.1	93 3.9	64 5.7	45 8.1			25 14.5	56 6.5
Cost of Sales/Inventory	19 19.1	54 6.8	51 7.2	31 11.9			29 12.7	50 7.3
	59 6.2	142 2.6	167 2.2	124 2.9			89 4.1	116 3.1
	146 2.5	285 1.3	392 .9	231 1.6			153 2.4	261 1.4
Cost of Sales/Payables	0 UND	0 UND	5 74.7	4 92.8			0 UND	3 127.8
	0 UND	20 17.9	18 19.9	11 33.6			10 36.4	17 22.1
	24 15.1	45 8.1	43 8.5	14 25.9			31 11.7	48 7.6
Sales/Working Capital	8.0	2.9	1.4	2.6			3.3	3.2
	45.7	5.3	3.4	5.8			9.7	6.3
	-10.0	20.6	9.6	8.9			146.0	-96.5
EBIT/Interest	8.9	65.6	29.0				6.9	9.2
	(14) 3.3	(18) 17.9	(21) 6.5				(75) 3.8	(71) 2.0
	-6.4	1.6	2.7				1.3	-.2
Net Profit + Depr., Dep., Amort./Cur. Mat. L/T/D								
Fixed/Worth	.0	.0	.0	.1			.1	.1
	.3	.2	.0	.5			.5	.4
	NM	.7	.9	1.7			2.6	6.1
Debt/Worth	.4	.2	.2	.2			.6	.5
	4.4	.8	.8	.8			1.5	1.4
	-1.9	1.6	1.5	1.6			8.5	UND
% Profit Before Taxes/Tangible Net Worth	67.4	76.5	48.4	25.4			49.9	47.0
	(12) 14.3	(24) 30.2	(24) 19.3	(10) 17.8			(70) 19.7	(63) 25.6
	-22.7	5.8	3.8	7.9			5.6	8.0
% Profit Before Taxes/Total Assets	29.4	38.6	31.0	17.8			15.9	17.8
	7.8	13.2	9.1	7.5			6.1	7.0
	-21.5	3.8	2.4	1.1			1.0	-1.1
Sales/Net Fixed Assets	460.3	113.2	176.7	16.8			84.0	49.6
	32.7	24.4	49.6	7.4			23.1	19.3
	13.8	11.9	7.9	3.1			6.7	8.7
Sales/Total Assets	10.1	4.1	3.9	1.7			3.8	3.5
	5.0	2.1	1.4	1.4			2.6	1.9
	2.4	1.3	.7	1.1			1.3	1.2
% Depr., Dep., Amort./Sales	.4	.2	.2	.8			.6	.3
	(14) 1.0	(18) 1.4	(20) .6	(10) 1.9			(68) 1.3	(67) 1.0
	1.6	2.4	1.2	3.0			2.5	2.3
% Officers', Directors' Owners' Comp/Sales	1.6	.8	2.4				2.0	2.7
	(13) 6.7	(15) 2.6	(10) 4.2				(38) 4.5	(40) 4.6
	9.7	5.0	13.3				7.5	9.8
Net Sales ($)	25571M	74141M	259620M	334131M	120460M		1036318M	1072961M
Total Assets ($)	4776M	25165M	104754M	228126M	108522M		481740M	530198M

M = $ thousand   MM = $ million
See Pages 9 through 22 for Explanation of Ratios and Data

Comparative Historical Data / Current Data Sorted by Sales

4/1/07-3/31/08 ALL	4/1/08-3/31/09 ALL	4/1/09-3/31/10 ALL	Type of Statement	0-1MM	1-3MM	3-5MM	5-10MM	10-25MM	25MM & OVER
10	9	10	Unqualified	5	3	3		2	7
3	6	10	Reviewed		2		1	2	1
11	8	10	Compiled			1	1	2	1
34	39	33	Tax Returns	9	12	5	5	1	
31	24	20	Other	7	5	1	2	2	3
				15 (4/1-9/30/09)			68 (10/1/09-3/31/10)		
89	86	83	NUMBER OF STATEMENTS	21	22	10	9	9	12
%	%	%	**ASSETS**	%	%	%	%	%	%
11.9	14.5	14.5	Cash & Equivalents	14.0	11.5	13.4			12.0
13.4	11.2	13.2	Trade Receivables (net)	9.9	15.3	22.7			5.5
40.0	34.4	35.4	Inventory	37.6	47.5	40.5			26.1
3.3	5.5	5.4	All Other Current	1.5	5.3	4.5			12.6
68.6	65.5	68.5	Total Current	63.0	79.6	81.0			56.3
21.9	23.0	21.3	Fixed Assets (net)	24.3	10.6	10.4			34.1
3.5	3.8	3.0	Intangibles (net)	5.9	3.7	.6			.8
6.0	7.7	7.2	All Other Non-Current	6.8	6.1	8.0			8.7
100.0	100.0	100.0	Total	100.0	100.0	100.0			100.0
			LIABILITIES						
13.3	13.3	15.4	Notes Payable-Short Term	30.0	10.4	12.6			15.2
3.3	3.0	4.9	Cur. Mat.-L.T.D.	6.0	9.1	.2			3.3
9.3	11.8	6.7	Trade Payables	7.9	6.3	7.3			7.0
.1	.1	.1	Income Taxes Payable	.0	.0	.3			.2
7.9	14.1	13.4	All Other Current	11.8	21.6	12.1			13.4
33.9	42.3	40.4	Total Current	55.8	47.4	32.6			39.2
17.0	16.6	12.1	Long-Term Debt	23.9	2.7	3.0			14.8
.1	.0	.0	Deferred Taxes	.0	.0	.0			.0
13.5	10.6	5.4	All Other Non-Current	4.5	2.6	.0			13.6
35.5	30.5	42.1	Net Worth	15.7	47.3	64.4			32.5
100.0	100.0	100.0	Total Liabilities & Net Worth	100.0	100.0	100.0			100.0
			INCOME DATA						
100.0	100.0	100.0	Net Sales	100.0	100.0	100.0			100.0
52.3	56.2	58.7	Gross Profit	57.8	61.2	53.1			65.0
47.6	51.5	52.7	Operating Expenses	55.6	55.4	46.3			58.6
4.7	4.7	6.0	Operating Profit	2.1	5.9	6.8			6.4
1.0	.8	.6	All Other Expenses (net)	1.8	.4	-.8			1.3
3.7	3.9	5.3	Profit Before Taxes	.3	5.4	7.6			5.1
			RATIOS						
6.0	8.8	5.7	Current	9.3	18.2	6.1			2.0
2.5	2.3	2.1		2.1	3.3	2.1			1.5
1.2	1.2	1.4		.9	1.6	1.7			1.0
1.8	2.4	2.2	Quick	2.2	3.3	1.4			.9
(88) .8	.7	.8		.4	.6	1.0			.4
.2	.2	.3		.1	.1	.7			.1
0 UND	0 UND	0 UND	Sales/Receivables	0 UND	0 UND	0 UND			0 UND
7 52.9	1 333.5	3 113.7		1 297.0	1 472.6	7 55.5			10 37.7
58 6.3	35 10.5	45 8.1		43 8.4	59 6.2	149 2.4			19 19.5
34 10.7	26 14.3	46 8.0	Cost of Sales/Inventory	49 7.4	60 6.1	52 7.0			30 12.1
119 3.1	97 3.8	124 2.9		166 2.2	148 2.5	167 2.2			89 4.1
314 1.2	225 1.6	254 1.4		476 .8	335 1.1	228 1.6			130 2.8
0 UND	0 UND	0 UND	Cost of Sales/Payables	0 UND	0 UND	0 UND			10 37.2
9 40.3	8 43.0	14 25.9		0 UND	20 18.2	16 23.4			22 16.4
42 8.7	30 12.2	36 10.1		36 10.3	37 9.9	28 13.0			84 4.4
2.4	3.2	2.6	Sales/Working Capital	2.3	1.8	2.3			4.7
6.3	9.3	6.2		6.2	4.0	6.1			12.5
37.8	59.2	22.6		NM	19.8	22.6			NM
10.5	15.2	31.8	EBIT/Interest	10.5	56.1	71.3			8.5
(77) 3.7	(71) 4.8	(64) 6.0		(12) 1.5	(18) 5.6	7.4		(11)	6.4
.7	1.1	1.2		-5.6	1.5	1.5			2.1
			Net Profit + Depr., Dep., Amort./Cur. Mat. L/T/D						
.0	.1	.0	Fixed/Worth	.0	.0	.0			.2
.4	.3	.2		.3	.1	.0			.9
2.6	2.4	1.0		2.0	.6	.3			1.7
.5	.4	.3	Debt/Worth	.4	.2	.4			.8
1.2	1.0	.9		3.2	.7	.6			1.7
9.7	15.4	2.7		NM	1.6	.8			5.3
52.7	48.6	49.3	% Profit Before Taxes/Tangible Net Worth	47.7	45.9	55.2			52.9
(72) 19.4	(68) 17.1	(72) 20.1		(16) 14.3	(18) 16.5	25.4		(10)	11.1
3.2	-1.3	4.6		-14.7	4.0	.9			5.9
21.4	23.5	28.6	% Profit Before Taxes/Total Assets	14.8	30.1	46.1			16.0
6.8	5.4	9.5		6.0	11.8	13.6			4.6
-.5	-4.1	1.8		-10.1	2.6	.3			1.5
95.3	96.8	118.6	Sales/Net Fixed Assets	143.5	203.9	212.8			19.9
23.3	22.0	24.4		21.2	39.4	88.4			8.9
6.1	9.8	10.4		1.3	17.1	22.7			5.0
3.7	5.0	4.5	Sales/Total Assets	5.1	4.2	5.5			4.4
1.8	2.6	2.0		1.7	2.1	2.1			2.2
1.1	1.5	1.2		.6	1.3	1.3			1.4
.4	.5	.3	% Depr., Dep., Amort./Sales	.4	.2	.1			1.1
(58) 1.1	(62) 1.2	(64) 1.0		(13) .7	(16) 1.0	.3		(10)	2.0
2.0	2.6	2.0		2.0	1.7	.7			3.0
2.4	2.0	1.2	% Officers', Directors' Owners' Comp/Sales	6.0	1.2				
(47) 4.2	(41) 3.2	(43) 3.4		(12) 8.4	(11) 2.6				
11.1	8.4	7.0		10.5	6.7				
1750442M	1199473M	813923M	Net Sales ($)	11331M	45168M	39364M	56818M	165944M	495298M
653642M	565723M	471343M	Total Assets ($)	12142M	29671M	20534M	31396M	94904M	282696M

M = $ thousand   MM = $ million
See Pages 9 through 22 for Explanation of Ratios and Data

RETAIL—Pet and Pet Supplies Stores NAICS 453910

Current Data Sorted by Assets   **Comparative Historical Data**

	0-500M	500M-2MM	2-10MM	10-50MM	50-100MM	100-250MM		4/1/05-3/31/06 ALL	4/1/06-3/31/07 ALL
Type of Statement									
Unqualified			5	2	3	1		3	2
Reviewed		3	3	1				4	3
Compiled	2	4	5					5	4
Tax Returns	16	7	5					9	17
Other	5	4	7	2		1		5	6
		13 (4/1-9/30/09)		58 (10/1/09-3/31/10)					
NUMBER OF STATEMENTS	23	18	20					26	32
	%	%	%	%	%	%		%	%
ASSETS									
Cash & Equivalents	10.1	10.2	5.5					8.6	12.8
Trade Receivables (net)	1.1	9.5	12.5					5.0	9.0
Inventory	49.4	46.9	46.7					55.0	51.2
All Other Current	3.8	.6	1.8					2.2	1.1
Total Current	64.4	67.2	66.5					70.8	74.0
Fixed Assets (net)	28.0	21.4	20.2					22.1	17.3
Intangibles (net)	2.5	6.3	5.9					.7	2.7
All Other Non-Current	5.0	5.0	7.4					6.4	6.0
Total	100.0	100.0	100.0					100.0	100.0
LIABILITIES									
Notes Payable-Short Term	11.7	15.9	14.2					11.5	10.6
Cur. Mat.-L.T.D.	.7	1.1	2.5					1.9	.9
Trade Payables	16.1	14.8	21.9					30.0	19.8
Income Taxes Payable	.1	.1	.1					.0	.0
All Other Current	10.7	9.0	7.6					12.7	11.6
Total Current	39.3	40.8	46.2					56.1	42.9
Long-Term Debt	46.1	18.6	12.8					16.6	19.9
Deferred Taxes	.0	.0	.3					.3	.0
All Other Non-Current	4.5	9.6	7.6					2.8	24.7
Net Worth	10.0	31.0	33.1					24.3	12.5
Total Liabilities & Net Worth	100.0	100.0	100.0					100.0	100.0
INCOME DATA									
Net Sales	100.0	100.0	100.0					100.0	100.0
Gross Profit	40.5	34.3	33.4					34.1	37.3
Operating Expenses	39.7	33.0	30.3					32.7	35.2
Operating Profit	.8	1.3	3.1					1.4	2.0
All Other Expenses (net)	1.3	-.1	.8					.9	.8
Profit Before Taxes	-.5	1.4	2.3					.5	1.2
RATIOS									
Current	3.7	3.4	1.7					2.0	3.7
	1.6	2.0	1.4					1.3	2.4
	.8	1.1	1.1					.9	1.2
Quick	1.4	.8	.6					.6	.9
	(22) .4	.5	.2					(25) .2	.4
	.0	.1	.1					.1	.1
Sales/Receivables	0 UND	0 UND	1 727.1					0 UND	0 UND
	0 UND	1 333.4	3 106.8					2 182.2	0 UND
	0 UND	12 29.3	33 11.2					6 64.2	6 61.5
Cost of Sales/Inventory	32 11.5	50 7.2	48 7.5					55 6.7	50 7.4
	52 7.0	64 5.7	65 5.6					66 5.6	65 5.6
	115 3.2	120 3.0	95 3.9					84 4.4	82 4.4
Cost of Sales/Payables	0 UND	5 69.3	24 15.3					13 27.9	13 27.3
	17 21.9	19 18.7	40 9.2					29 12.4	23 16.2
	35 10.3	33 11.0	57 6.4					52 7.0	41 8.9
Sales/Working Capital	8.2	5.5	10.3					14.4	8.5
	19.3	14.7	15.4					34.0	12.8
	-89.8	NM	58.7					-121.2	63.2
EBIT/Interest	16.9	15.8	7.4					20.5	7.4
	(20) 1.6	6.5	(18) 2.6					(24) 2.1	(26) 3.4
	.0	.6	1.0					1.0	1.0
Net Profit + Depr., Dep., Amort./Cur. Mat. L/T/D									
Fixed/Worth	.2	.1	.1					.3	.1
	4.2	.5	.4					.8	.6
	-.5	3.8	1.4					NM	NM
Debt/Worth	1.1	1.2	1.6					.7	.6
	4.8	2.7	2.3					2.3	2.6
	-4.1	8.5	5.0					NM	-131.4
% Profit Before Taxes/Tangible Net Worth	199.3	58.9	39.6					54.6	49.4
	(14) 48.7	(16) 21.0	(19) 31.3					(20) 14.2	(23) 20.0
	19.7	-1.3	.9					8.2	4.3
% Profit Before Taxes/Total Assets	18.8	20.2	14.0					17.5	16.7
	4.4	5.5	5.1					5.8	7.0
	-10.0	-1.4	.4					.6	-1.1
Sales/Net Fixed Assets	75.0	87.7	78.8					56.0	103.6
	42.4	24.4	29.6					25.1	37.3
	10.1	10.8	8.0					11.8	22.2
Sales/Total Assets	5.5	5.2	5.4					6.0	5.9
	3.9	3.0	3.1					4.8	4.8
	2.9	2.2	1.7					3.2	2.9
% Depr., Dep., Amort./Sales	.4	.4	.4					.6	.5
	(13) 1.2	(13) .9	(16) 1.2					(22) 1.1	(25) .9
	2.0	2.0	1.7					1.7	1.3
% Officers', Directors' Owners' Comp/Sales	3.0		1.1					1.7	1.4
	(12) 4.6		(10) 2.3					(12) 3.6	(10) 2.9
	10.1		3.4					7.1	10.5
Net Sales ($)	24501M	64127M	366323M	302241M	586008M	607933M		316195M	366346M
Total Assets ($)	5129M	18109M	101178M	88229M	197373M	279637M		92463M	91423M

M = $ thousand   MM = $ million
See Pages 9 through 22 for Explanation of Ratios and Data

Comparative Historical Data / Current Data Sorted by Sales

Type of Statement / Number of Statements

Type of Statement	4/1/07-3/31/08 ALL	4/1/08-3/31/09 ALL	4/1/09-3/31/10 ALL	0-1MM	1-3MM	3-5MM	5-10MM	10-25MM	25MM & OVER
Unqualified	3	3	6		3	3			6
Reviewed	4	6	8	1	9	1	1	3	1
Compiled	6	5	10	10	1		1	2	2
Tax Returns	10	14	28	6	3	3	2	3	1
Other	12	12	19		3	3		1	6
				13 (4/1-9/30/09)			58 (10/1/09-3/31/10)		
NUMBER OF STATEMENTS	**35**	**40**	**71**	**17**	**15**	**10**	**4**	**9**	**16**

ASSETS (%)

	08	09	10	0-1MM	1-3MM	3-5MM	5-10MM	10-25MM	25MM & OVER
Cash & Equivalents	9.4	11.1	9.7	8.5	8.9	12.3			13.6
Trade Receivables (net)	14.6	9.9	7.7	1.5	8.6	5.2			10.9
Inventory	45.2	47.1	46.5	45.8	44.8	58.2			46.1
All Other Current	4.2	1.6	2.2	4.6	.6	2.5			2.5
Total Current	73.4	69.7	66.2	60.5	62.9	78.1			73.1
Fixed Assets (net)	17.4	22.4	23.7	33.2	20.6	11.3			19.8
Intangibles (net)	4.1	2.9	4.8	3.8	9.5	3.9			4.0
All Other Non-Current	5.2	5.0	5.4	2.5	7.0	6.7			3.1
Total	100.0	100.0	100.0	100.0	100.0	100.0			100.0

LIABILITIES

	08	09	10	0-1MM	1-3MM	3-5MM	5-10MM	10-25MM	25MM & OVER
Notes Payable-Short Term	19.8	12.2	13.3	13.0	17.4	16.9			9.5
Cur. Mat.-L.T.D.	2.2	1.9	1.5	1.6	.3	2.2			1.4
Trade Payables	19.2	17.3	17.2	10.3	19.3	18.6			21.7
Income Taxes Payable	.0	.1	.1	.2	.0	.2			.2
All Other Current	11.2	7.4	9.3	3.5	15.1	12.5			9.1
Total Current	52.3	38.8	41.4	28.5	52.0	50.4			41.9
Long-Term Debt	15.9	20.3	24.3	60.3	20.6	4.9			7.6
Deferred Taxes	.0	.1	.1	.0	.0	.0			.1
All Other Non-Current	7.7	9.1	6.9	5.8	6.2	7.5			6.6
Net Worth	24.1	31.7	27.3	5.4	21.1	37.1			43.8
Total Liabilities & Net Worth	100.0	100.0	100.0	100.0	100.0	100.0			100.0

INCOME DATA

	08	09	10	0-1MM	1-3MM	3-5MM	5-10MM	10-25MM	25MM & OVER
Net Sales	100.0	100.0	100.0	100.0	100.0	100.0			100.0
Gross Profit	37.0	38.3	36.7	44.7	29.4	35.1			35.6
Operating Expenses	34.0	33.9	34.2	43.5	29.3	32.8			29.5
Operating Profit	3.0	4.3	2.5	1.2	.1	2.4			6.1
All Other Expenses (net)	.8	.6	.7	2.0	-.1	.4			.2
Profit Before Taxes	2.3	3.8	1.9	-.8	.2	2.0			5.9

RATIOS

	08	09	10	0-1MM	1-3MM	3-5MM	5-10MM	10-25MM	25MM & OVER
Current	2.7	2.7	2.9	11.0	2.5	1.9			2.5
	1.7	1.9	1.6	2.4	1.3	1.5			1.7
	1.2	1.3	1.1	.8	.7	1.1			1.2
Quick	.9	1.1	.8	1.8	.8	.7			.8
	.4	.4	(70) .4	(16) .5	.2	.2			.5
	.2	.1	.1	.0	.0	.1			.2
Sales/Receivables	0 999.8	0	0 UND	0 UND	0 UND	0 UND			0 876.9
	4 102.6	3 138.1	1 601.5	0 UND	0 UND	4 94.5			4 91.1
	24 15.2	19 19.2	8 46.9	0 UND	3 108.1	14 25.2			20 18.2
Cost of Sales/Inventory	37 9.9	49 7.5	48 7.6	37 9.8	52 7.1	42 8.6			56 6.6
	56 6.6	67 5.4	62 5.9	88 4.2	62 5.9	56 6.5			63 5.8
	102 3.6	106 3.4	95 3.8	119 3.1	95 3.8	216 1.7			83 4.4
Cost of Sales/Payables	4 103.6	12 29.6	12 30.8	0 UND	13 29.0	11 34.2			18 20.7
	23 15.7	21 17.2	24 14.9	8 45.0	24 14.9	23 15.8			29 12.4
	46 8.0	39 9.4	41 8.9	35 10.3	53 6.9	39 9.4			44 8.4
Sales/Working Capital	8.5	5.6	8.6	6.2	5.5	11.3			9.6
	12.8	13.7	15.6	12.1	20.7	15.8			15.3
	62.0	24.7	125.8	-370.4	-23.8	82.2			39.4
EBIT/Interest	13.9	11.6	16.2	5.9	12.0				31.1
	(27) 2.5	(34) 2.8	(65) 4.0	(16) 1.4	(14) 2.5			(13)	16.0
	1.1	.7	.9	.0	-.4				6.5
Net Profit + Depr., Dep., Amort./Cur. Mat. L/T/D									
Fixed/Worth	.1	.2	.2	.5	.1	.2			.1
	.6	.7	.8	4.6	2.3	.3			.5
	1.3	2.5	4.0	-.6	UND	.5			1.3
Debt/Worth	1.0	1.0	1.1	.9	2.2	1.0			.8
	2.8	2.6	2.9	4.8	3.8	2.1			1.5
	8.0	6.2	10.9	-2.5	-4.9	5.7			3.9
% Profit Before Taxes/Tangible Net Worth	48.3	70.2	61.4		120.0	68.7			69.8
	(28) 20.8	(37) 27.8	(58) 33.5	(11)	20.4	28.7		(15)	39.8
	2.7	1.1	9.1		-1.5	5.0			31.3
% Profit Before Taxes/Total Assets	18.1	17.5	18.8	16.7	11.5	41.3			26.0
	3.7	8.7	9.6	2.4	1.9	10.1			18.8
	.2	.1	-.1	-5.6	-6.1	1.5			12.0
Sales/Net Fixed Assets	112.3	44.9	66.6	119.0	84.9	100.9			55.7
	35.9	29.9	26.3	17.0	31.8	37.7			36.3
	12.7	10.0	8.1	3.7	11.7	21.0			7.2
Sales/Total Assets	5.4	5.6	5.1	4.3	4.6	7.2			5.3
	3.7	3.9	3.5	3.5	3.3	5.2			3.9
	2.6	2.3	2.3	1.5	2.3	1.6			2.2
% Depr., Dep., Amort./Sales	.4	.5	.4		.3				.4
	(26) .9	(31) 1.0	(52) 1.0	(10)	.7			(15)	1.0
	1.7	2.0	1.7		1.7				1.5
% Officers', Directors' Owners' Comp/Sales	2.3	1.3	2.3						
	(17) 3.4	(18) 3.0	(31) 3.6						
	5.7	5.4	6.4						
Net Sales ($)	608088M	981931M	1951133M	9722M	28612M	39712M	32151M	134247M	1706689M
Total Assets ($)	170063M	314951M	689655M	3347M	12050M	14996M	18935M	36180M	604147M

M = $ thousand   MM = $ million
See Pages 9 through 22 for Explanation of Ratios and Data

RETAIL—Art Dealers NAICS 453920

	Current Data Sorted by Assets							Comparative Historical Data	
Type of Statement	0-500M	500M-2MM	2-10MM	10-50MM	50-100MM	100-250MM			
Unqualified			1	2	1	1			
Reviewed		2	2	4	2			2	3
Compiled			2	2				9	9
Tax Returns	3	7		4				3	2
Other	1	6	5					5	4
								10	6
		7 (4/1-9/30/09)		38 (10/1/09-3/31/10)				4/1/05-3/31/06 ALL	4/1/06-3/31/07 ALL
NUMBER OF STATEMENTS	4	15	10	12	3	1		29	24
	%	%	%	%	%	%		%	%
ASSETS									
Cash & Equivalents		13.4	23.2	10.8				8.3	6.2
Trade Receivables (net)		11.4	10.6	8.0				13.3	11.7
Inventory		37.9	41.2	59.8				52.2	66.6
All Other Current		.8	.7	2.5				1.9	2.4
Total Current		63.4	75.7	81.1				75.7	86.9
Fixed Assets (net)		20.0	14.4	11.6				13.6	5.7
Intangibles (net)		4.4	2.0	.2				1.8	.9
All Other Non-Current		12.2	7.9	7.1				8.9	6.5
Total		100.0	100.0	100.0				100.0	100.0
LIABILITIES									
Notes Payable-Short Term		15.1	3.9	20.8				18.4	18.5
Cur. Mat.-L.T.D.		1.6	.9	.4				4.8	1.8
Trade Payables		9.0	18.6	6.2				20.9	12.4
Income Taxes Payable		.6	.3	.0				.1	.3
All Other Current		6.1	5.8	19.5				13.8	8.9
Total Current		32.4	29.6	46.9				58.0	41.8
Long-Term Debt		23.2	6.4	11.5				9.4	9.6
Deferred Taxes		.0	.0	.0				.0	.0
All Other Non-Current		6.5	15.7	10.6				15.7	17.2
Net Worth		37.9	48.3	31.0				16.9	31.3
Total Liabilities & Net Worth		100.0	100.0	100.0				100.0	100.0
INCOME DATA									
Net Sales		100.0	100.0	100.0				100.0	100.0
Gross Profit		42.2	42.6	38.7				43.0	37.3
Operating Expenses		43.3	37.7	26.8				37.1	30.7
Operating Profit		-1.1	4.9	11.9				5.9	6.6
All Other Expenses (net)		.5	1.0	5.2				2.2	1.2
Profit Before Taxes		-1.6	3.9	6.7				3.6	5.3
RATIOS									
Current		4.5	8.2	4.0				2.4	5.0
		2.5	2.3	1.8				1.5	1.8
		1.2	1.7	1.0				1.0	1.2
Quick		2.2	2.2	.9				.9	1.3
		.3	1.2	.5				.3	.4
		.1	.6	.2				.1	.1
Sales/Receivables	0 UND	2 160.9	8 45.9					1 551.4	1 629.0
	0 UND	39 9.3	55 6.6					17 21.1	11 32.2
	37 9.8	43 8.5	77 4.8					32 11.2	36 10.0
Cost of Sales/Inventory	14 26.7	90 4.1	87 4.2					52 7.0	150 2.4
	130 2.8	156 2.3	462 .8					211 1.7	259 1.4
	295 1.2	478 .8	1440 .3					450 .8	550 .7
Cost of Sales/Payables	0 999.8	6 61.9	17 20.9					11 32.7	7 48.7
	22 16.7	73 5.0	38 9.6					54 6.8	43 8.6
	56 6.5	112 3.3	88 4.1					114 3.2	84 4.4
Sales/Working Capital		3.3	1.7	1.2				2.9	1.2
		6.4	3.0	1.6				6.5	4.5
		48.0	13.1	288.9				-140.6	15.6
EBIT/Interest		7.0		26.3				15.4	8.3
		(13) 2.0		(10) 3.4				(27) 3.7	(19) 4.2
		-.8		1.2				1.1	.7
Net Profit + Depr., Dep., Amort./Cur. Mat. L/T/D									
Fixed/Worth		.1	.0	.0				.1	.0
		.5	.2	.7				.4	.1
		5.9	1.1	13.3				-3.1	.5
Debt/Worth		.7	.3	.9				.9	.7
		1.9	1.4	3.6				2.4	1.6
		15.1	6.0	158.4				-44.7	10.0
% Profit Before Taxes/Tangible Net Worth		50.6	55.4	29.8				59.9	46.0
		(14) 13.0	17.5	(10) 12.1				(20) 30.3	(21) 27.5
		-20.9	7.5	4.8				7.2	3.9
% Profit Before Taxes/Total Assets		9.2	11.0	8.0				17.7	17.1
		2.0	6.4	4.8				4.0	5.6
		-11.4	2.6	.4				.5	.9
Sales/Net Fixed Assets		77.9	120.3	48.0				97.5	124.8
		17.1	22.8	28.5				26.8	66.1
		6.9	5.7	10.5				8.7	29.2
Sales/Total Assets		3.1	1.7	1.5				4.0	2.3
		2.1	1.4	.7				1.4	1.5
		1.4	.5	.4				.7	.8
% Depr., Dep., Amort./Sales				.2				.3	.2
			(10) .8					(24) .8	(20) .5
				1.7				1.7	.9
% Officers', Directors' Owners' Comp/Sales								1.7	.9
								(14) 5.7	(13) 2.9
								14.7	11.8
Net Sales ($)	2392M	55697M	226878M	300907M	164694M	119697M		918400M	737161M
Total Assets ($)	717M	14600M	46608M	260252M	201765M	165674M		811601M	665893M

M = $ thousand   MM = $ million
See Pages 9 through 22 for Explanation of Ratios and Data

Comparative Historical Data / Current Data Sorted by Sales

			Type of Statement	0-1MM	1-3MM	3-5MM	5-10MM	10-25MM	25MM & OVER
2	4	4	Unqualified		1			1	2
7	6	7	Reviewed		2			3	2
4	3	6	Compiled		3	2	1		2
10	11	12	Tax Returns	5	7		4	1	1
10	16	16	Other	2					1
4/1/07-3/31/08 ALL	4/1/08-3/31/09 ALL	4/1/09-3/31/10 ALL			7 (4/1-9/30/09)		38 (10/1/09-3/31/10)		
33	40	45	**NUMBER OF STATEMENTS**	7	13	3	8	6	8
%	%	%	**ASSETS**	%	%	%	%	%	%
14.4	6.4	16.3	Cash & Equivalents		17.5				
10.4	10.7	8.8	Trade Receivables (net)		8.2				
53.4	47.2	49.2	Inventory		45.8				
3.9	.8	1.2	All Other Current		.8				
82.0	65.1	75.5	Total Current		72.3				
9.9	22.1	14.1	Fixed Assets (net)		20.7				
2.4	3.3	2.3	Intangibles (net)		5.0				
5.7	9.4	8.1	All Other Non-Current		2.1				
100.0	100.0	100.0	Total		100.0				
			LIABILITIES						
12.3	9.7	13.5	Notes Payable-Short Term		12.2				
5.2	2.2	.9	Cur. Mat.-L.T.D.		2.2				
17.9	20.3	9.3	Trade Payables		9.3				
.0	.0	.3	Income Taxes Payable		.3				
7.8	11.5	9.8	All Other Current		6.2				
43.2	43.6	33.7	Total Current		30.1				
13.7	17.3	12.8	Long-Term Debt		18.0				
.0	.0	.0	Deferred Taxes		.0				
7.8	20.0	9.5	All Other Non-Current		13.7				
35.2	19.0	43.9	Net Worth		38.1				
100.0	100.0	100.0	Total Liabilities & Net Worth		100.0				
			INCOME DATA						
100.0	100.0	100.0	Net Sales		100.0				
45.0	45.8	42.1	Gross Profit		45.4				
37.0	40.0	36.1	Operating Expenses		41.4				
7.9	5.8	6.0	Operating Profit		4.0				
-.3	3.2	1.6	All Other Expenses (net)		1.6				
8.2	2.6	4.4	Profit Before Taxes		2.5				
			RATIOS						
3.5	4.5	5.0	Current		6.1				
2.3	2.1	2.4			2.4				
1.2	1.0	1.4			1.6				
1.1	1.4	2.1	Quick		2.1				
.6	.4	.6			.6				
.2	.1	.2			.2				
0 UND	0 UND	0 UND	Sales/Receivables	0 UND					
15 24.2	12 31.1	13 27.6		37 9.8					
36 10.2	52 7.1	49 7.4		49 7.4					
69 5.3	96 3.8	69 5.3	Cost of Sales/Inventory	107 3.4					
170 2.2	222 1.6	247 1.5		137 2.7					
607 .6	443 .8	655 .6		375 1.0					
1 402.6	5 75.8	2 167.1	Cost of Sales/Payables	8 45.3					
58 6.3	31 11.9	25 14.5		25 14.5					
99 3.7	79 4.6	77 4.8		66 5.6					
1.9	2.2	1.5	Sales/Working Capital		2.1				
5.0	3.4	4.3			5.6				
21.9	313.3	20.0			9.0				
6.1	9.0	14.2	EBIT/Interest		4.2				
(21) 3.7	(31) 3.4	(35) 4.1		(11) 2.3					
1.5	1.2	1.6			.3				
			Net Profit + Depr., Dep., Amort./Cur. Mat. L/T/D						
.0	.1	.0	Fixed/Worth		.1				
.1	1.2	.2			1.8				
UND	12.0	2.0			7.5				
.6	.5	.4	Debt/Worth		.6				
1.6	2.2	1.6			2.5				
UND	79.2	6.8			15.4				
45.2	31.3	49.2	% Profit Before Taxes/Tangible Net Worth		98.6				
(26) 26.1	(31) 8.9	(41) 14.7		(12) 13.0					
6.0	2.0	4.6			-2.1				
21.5	10.3	11.0	% Profit Before Taxes/Total Assets		7.7				
10.3	3.3	5.8			4.0				
2.9	-1.5	.6			-2.6				
289.7	47.2	98.0	Sales/Net Fixed Assets		42.1				
48.0	16.1	22.0			13.4				
14.5	4.1	9.5			4.6				
3.0	2.5	2.5	Sales/Total Assets		2.5				
1.8	1.5	1.6			1.6				
.9	.8	.5			.7				
.3	.5	.2	% Depr., Dep., Amort./Sales						
(23) .6	(30) 1.2	(28) 1.2							
1.4	2.1	1.9							
2.1	2.8	2.0	% Officers', Directors' Owners' Comp/Sales						
(20) 4.9	(18) 4.7	(25) 3.2							
12.4	8.0	7.5							
944104M	662825M	870265M	Net Sales ($)	3851M	25486M	12330M	57051M	78886M	692661M
744445M	744966M	689616M	Total Assets ($)	3196M	24993M	42864M	80814M	128975M	408774M

M = $ thousand   MM = $ million
See Pages 9 through 22 for Explanation of Ratios and Data

RETAIL—Manufactured (Mobile) Home Dealers NAICS 453930

Current Data Sorted by Assets / Comparative Historical Data

Type of Statement

	0-500M	500M-2MM	2-10MM	10-50MM	50-100MM	100-250MM	4/1/05-3/31/06 ALL	4/1/06-3/31/07 ALL
Unqualified				5	1		5	4
Reviewed		5	6	3		1	11	9
Compiled	5	13	8	2			42	53
Tax Returns	8	14	4	2			31	31
Other	1	19	9				31	27
	15 (4/1-9/30/09)			91 (10/1/09-3/31/10)				
NUMBER OF STATEMENTS	14	51	27	12	1	1	120	124
	%	%	%	%	%	%	%	%
ASSETS								
Cash & Equivalents	8.3	10.5	6.3	8.8			9.8	9.8
Trade Receivables (net)	8.9	6.4	10.9	12.4			9.7	8.2
Inventory	53.8	55.0	51.2	25.4			56.8	59.8
All Other Current	.5	4.5	10.0	1.0			2.4	2.9
Total Current	71.5	76.5	78.5	47.5			78.8	80.7
Fixed Assets (net)	21.9	15.6	12.3	29.5			14.4	14.1
Intangibles (net)	.5	1.5	.9	2.3			.2	.8
All Other Non-Current	6.0	6.4	8.3	20.8			6.6	4.4
Total	100.0	100.0	100.0	100.0			100.0	100.0
LIABILITIES								
Notes Payable-Short Term	67.5	39.7	30.7	14.2			34.7	41.2
Cur. Mat.-L.T.D.	12.7	2.5	2.0	3.8			1.7	3.5
Trade Payables	3.5	4.6	5.9	8.9			5.7	6.2
Income Taxes Payable	.0	.1	.0	.2			.1	.1
All Other Current	7.5	13.8	14.3	16.1			13.2	13.2
Total Current	91.2	60.8	52.8	43.2			55.4	64.2
Long-Term Debt	35.6	12.7	10.9	18.9			10.6	7.7
Deferred Taxes	.0	.0	.1	.0			.0	.0
All Other Non-Current	11.6	9.4	8.6	6.8			6.6	2.9
Net Worth	-38.8	17.2	27.7	31.1			27.4	25.1
Total Liabilities & Net Worth	100.0	100.0	100.0	100.0			100.0	100.0
INCOME DATA								
Net Sales	100.0	100.0	100.0	100.0			100.0	100.0
Gross Profit	34.4	26.4	26.8	30.3			24.8	24.0
Operating Expenses	29.9	26.3	23.7	32.5			20.2	20.4
Operating Profit	4.5	.1	3.2	-2.2			4.5	3.6
All Other Expenses (net)	1.9	1.3	1.2	-.3			1.2	1.0
Profit Before Taxes	2.6	-1.2	1.9	-1.9			3.3	2.7
RATIOS								
Current	6.1	2.0	2.7	2.1			2.3	1.7
	1.1	1.3	1.4	1.0			1.4	1.2
	.5	.9	1.0	.5			1.0	1.0
Quick	.7	.5	.7	.8			.7	.5
	(13) .1	.2	.2	.3			(118) .3	(123) .2
	.0	.1	.1	.3			.1	.1
Sales/Receivables	0 UND	0 UND	0 UND	3 123.7			0 UND	0 UND
	0 UND	4 85.0	6 64.9	25 14.4			9 42.2	4 100.2
	0 UND	18 20.0	19 19.4	69 5.3			24 15.5	22 16.8
Cost of Sales/Inventory	26 13.8	115 3.2	75 4.9	35 10.4			91 4.0	85 4.3
	223 1.6	166 2.2	197 1.8	70 5.3			130 2.8	142 2.6
	348 1.0	224 1.6	376 1.0	202 1.8			213 1.7	201 1.8
Cost of Sales/Payables	0 UND	0 UND	4 94.3	9 38.9			1 417.4	0 UND
	0 UND	2 151.5	6 59.2	27 13.5			4 101.7	4 100.4
	9 40.7	15 24.5	24 15.1	68 5.4			13 27.3	11 34.4
Sales/Working Capital	6.5	4.9	2.1	5.1			4.9	5.7
	34.5	14.0	10.3	-138.6			11.3	13.5
	-2.2	-34.1	33.8	-16.6			59.9	121.9
EBIT/Interest	3.4	2.9	3.8	10.2			4.3	5.1
	1.4	1.1	1.3	(10) 2.4			(112) 2.2	(117) 2.1
	-.5	-1.2	-.2	-4.6			1.3	.8
Net Profit + Depr., Dep., Amort./Cur. Mat. L/T/D								
Fixed/Worth	.2	.1	.1	.4			.1	.1
	-3.7	.7	.6	1.0			.4	.4
	-.3	-3.3	1.0	2.1			1.2	1.6
Debt/Worth	3.1	2.5	1.5	.9			1.4	1.4
	-10.0	5.9	2.5	2.5			2.8	3.5
	-1.9	-22.9	13.2	7.1			9.5	16.7
% Profit Before Taxes/Tangible Net Worth		36.0	35.3	46.4			57.4	50.3
		(36) 13.0	(24) 8.0	(10) 11.0			(104) 15.6	(107) 18.1
		-12.4	-9.5	-4.6			4.1	1.3
% Profit Before Taxes/Total Assets	15.1	6.0	6.7	10.4			10.8	12.0
	2.2	.5	1.5	4.3			4.4	4.1
	-6.0	-11.6	-3.4	-3.2			.6	-.7
Sales/Net Fixed Assets	158.4	79.4	59.2	13.8			62.4	111.6
	22.3	19.7	14.4	5.5			30.5	32.8
	5.0	8.4	7.7	2.8			10.8	9.7
Sales/Total Assets	6.0	2.2	2.2	2.0			2.8	2.7
	1.9	1.9	1.2	1.5			2.0	2.0
	1.3	1.4	.8	1.1			1.4	1.6
% Depr., Dep., Amort./Sales		.6	.2	.8			.3	.3
		(36) .8	(23) .7	1.2			(97) .6	(96) .5
		1.3	1.6	2.7			1.2	1.0
% Officers', Directors' Owners' Comp/Sales		1.6					1.5	1.2
		(28) 2.7					(67) 2.6	(59) 2.5
		5.5					4.1	3.5
Net Sales ($)	8773M	102522M	183462M	543097M	52550M	443157M	666493M	779721M
Total Assets ($)	3739M	55987M	122096M	287877M	51527M	161639M	438567M	482506M

M = $ thousand   MM = $ million
See Pages 9 through 22 for Explanation of Ratios and Data

Comparative Historical Data / Current Data Sorted by Sales

Type of Statement

	4/1/07-3/31/08 ALL	4/1/08-3/31/09 ALL	4/1/09-3/31/10 ALL	Type of Statement	0-1MM	1-3MM	3-5MM	5-10MM 15 (4/1-9/30/09)	10-25MM 91 (10/1/09-3/31/10)	25MM & OVER
	4	9	6	Unqualified		5	3	1	1	4
	4	16	15	Reviewed		7	6	2	3	2
	44	33	26	Compiled	9	13	3	2	2	
	39	45	28	Tax Returns	8			2	2	
	24	36	31	Other	6	12	7	2	2	
	115	139	106	NUMBER OF STATEMENTS	23	37	19	9	12	6

Assets (%)

4/1/07-3/31/08	4/1/08-3/31/09	4/1/09-3/31/10	ASSETS	0-1MM	1-3MM	3-5MM	5-10MM	10-25MM	25MM & OVER
7.6	9.8	8.9	Cash & Equivalents	8.7	8.2	11.6		4.3	
8.4	7.8	8.6	Trade Receivables (net)	1.4	9.6	5.8		14.7	
56.5	53.9	49.7	Inventory	53.3	56.0	58.0		40.2	
4.2	3.4	4.9	All Other Current	4.5	5.9	4.6		2.7	
76.8	74.9	72.1	Total Current	67.9	79.7	80.0		62.0	
14.7	16.7	18.1	Fixed Assets (net)	21.5	14.6	10.9		24.1	
1.3	1.6	1.3	Intangibles (net)	1.3	.9	2.3		.2	
7.2	6.8	8.5	All Other Non-Current	9.2	4.8	6.7		13.7	
100.0	100.0	100.0	Total	100.0	100.0	100.0		100.0	

Liabilities

4/1/07-3/31/08	4/1/08-3/31/09	4/1/09-3/31/10	LIABILITIES	0-1MM	1-3MM	3-5MM	5-10MM	10-25MM	25MM & OVER
36.4	33.6	37.6	Notes Payable-Short Term	57.8	41.1	29.2		25.3	
3.0	4.8	3.9	Cur. Mat.-L.T.D.	1.8	5.1	6.0		.9	
8.7	5.1	5.3	Trade Payables	1.7	5.1	4.7		12.8	
.0	.1	.1	Income Taxes Payable	.0	.0	.3		.0	
11.9	13.6	13.2	All Other Current	16.7	11.8	9.3		17.2	
60.1	57.1	60.1	Total Current	77.9	63.1	49.6		56.2	
9.9	14.8	16.4	Long-Term Debt	25.5	13.0	11.6		9.5	
.0	.0	.0	Deferred Taxes	.0	.0	.0		.1	
5.1	5.8	9.0	All Other Non-Current	13.5	9.9	7.7		7.0	
24.9	22.3	14.4	Net Worth	-17.2	14.1	31.2		27.1	
100.0	100.0	100.0	Total Liabilities & Net Worth	100.0	100.0	100.0		100.0	

Income Data

4/1/07-3/31/08	4/1/08-3/31/09	4/1/09-3/31/10	INCOME DATA	0-1MM	1-3MM	3-5MM	5-10MM	10-25MM	25MM & OVER
100.0	100.0	100.0	Net Sales	100.0	100.0	100.0		100.0	
22.9	25.3	27.7	Gross Profit	38.0	23.6	25.9		22.4	
21.0	22.7	26.4	Operating Expenses	33.2	24.9	23.6		25.2	
1.8	2.6	1.2	Operating Profit	4.9	-1.3	2.3		-2.7	
1.1	1.2	1.2	All Other Expenses (net)	2.8	.8	1.0		.7	
.7	1.4	.1	Profit Before Taxes	2.1	-2.1	1.3		-3.4	

Ratios

4/1/07-3/31/08	4/1/08-3/31/09	4/1/09-3/31/10	RATIOS	0-1MM	1-3MM	3-5MM	5-10MM	10-25MM	25MM & OVER
2.0	2.4	2.2	Current	2.2	2.2	4.7		1.5	
1.2	1.3	1.3		1.2	1.3	1.5		1.1	
1.0	1.0	.9		.6	1.0	1.0		.7	
.6	.7	.6	Quick	.4	.4	.9		.4	
(113) .2	(105) .3	.2		(22) .1	.2	.3		.3	
.1	.1	.1		.0	.1	.1		.2	
0 999.8	0 UND	0 UND	Sales/Receivables	0 UND	0 UND	0 UND		4 82.9	
6 58.5	5 78.6	5 79.4		0 UND	4 85.0	5 73.9		21 17.3	
19 19.4	22 16.6	20 18.5		6 62.2	20 18.4	19 19.4		49 7.5	
96 3.8	83 4.4	73 5.0	Cost of Sales/Inventory	196 1.9	97 3.8	126 2.9		44 8.3	
141 2.6	141 2.6	159 2.3		297 1.2	144 2.5	166 2.2		84 4.4	
201 1.8	226 1.6	271 1.3		387 .9	227 1.6	369 1.0		168 2.2	
1 633.2	0 UND	0 UND	Cost of Sales/Payables	0 UND	0 UND	4 94.3		10 35.7	
4 81.3	4 82.9	6 64.8		0 UND	2 151.5	6 59.2		29 12.5	
15 24.2	15 24.3	18 20.4		9 41.0	12 29.2	15 24.5		57 6.4	
4.8	3.9	4.1	Sales/Working Capital	2.8	5.2	2.3		9.1	
11.8	13.2	17.1		43.0	17.6	8.1		NM	
UND	-73.6	-32.7		-3.1	NM	33.5		-17.3	
3.8	3.5	3.8	EBIT/Interest	4.1	2.1	3.1		5.4	
(109) 1.4	(132) 1.4	(104) 1.3		1.5	.5	1.1	(11)	2.2	
.6	.0	-.5		-.5	-1.6	.2		-7.9	
	6.3	6.2	Net Profit + Depr., Dep., Amort./Cur. Mat. L/T/D						
	(18) 2.5	(11) 3.5							
	.0	-3.2							
.1	.1	.2	Fixed/Worth	.2	.2	.1		.4	
.5	.5	.7		-44.0	.7	.3		1.0	
3.4	2.6	-4.4		-.8	-2.4	1.0		2.2	
1.2	1.2	1.8	Debt/Worth	3.7	2.4	1.4		1.1	
3.7	3.9	4.4		-21.5	6.2	2.5		3.4	
44.0	17.4	-23.2		-5.5	-22.5	10.8		6.5	
36.8	25.9	34.3	% Profit Before Taxes/Tangible Net Worth	30.8	26.9	41.2		34.6	
(94) 12.3	(112) 8.9	(76) 10.0		(10) 17.0	(24) 8.1	(18) 3.4	(10)	10.8	
-2.5	-5.8	-7.9		-.5	-12.4	-11.8		-27.2	
8.8	7.3	7.0	% Profit Before Taxes/Total Assets	7.4	4.5	6.0		7.4	
2.3	1.5	1.4		2.0	-1.1	.3		4.9	
-2.9	-4.1	-5.4		-5.9	-14.2	-3.0		-9.6	
67.7	76.0	46.8	Sales/Net Fixed Assets	50.3	62.5	135.9		17.7	
24.4	27.3	14.3		8.4	23.3	37.0		10.8	
9.2	7.1	5.1		2.3	11.6	9.9		3.9	
2.9	2.9	2.3	Sales/Total Assets	1.7	2.5	2.2		3.1	
2.1	1.8	1.7		1.3	1.9	2.0		1.5	
1.4	1.1	1.1		.7	1.4	1.0		1.2	
.4	.3	.6	% Depr., Dep., Amort./Sales	.8	.5	.3		.4	
(94) .7	(110) .7	(80) .9		(14) 1.4	(23) .6	(16) .7		.8	
1.4	1.7	1.9		2.9	1.3	.9		2.4	
1.4	1.5	1.3	% Officers', Directors' Owners' Comp/Sales		1.6				
(52) 2.6	(65) 2.4	(43) 2.5		(20) 2.8					
3.8	4.1	4.3			4.6				

Dollar Totals

4/1/07-3/31/08	4/1/08-3/31/09	4/1/09-3/31/10		0-1MM	1-3MM	3-5MM	5-10MM	10-25MM	25MM & OVER
891560M	1751751M	1333561M	Net Sales ($)	12325M	72355M	71630M	66560M	204180M	906511M
448878M	873106M	682865M	Total Assets ($)	15296M	46776M	51622M	79265M	121271M	368635M

© RMA 2010

M = $ thousand   MM = $ million
See Pages 9 through 22 for Explanation of Ratios and Data

RETAIL—Tobacco Stores   NAICS 453991

							Comparative Historical Data	

Current Data Sorted by Assets

	1		1 4		1	1	Type of Statement		
2 9 9	13 5		2 7 6	2	1 1 1	1	Unqualified		1
							Reviewed	2	2
							Compiled	8	10
	10 (4/1-9/30/09)			58 (10/1/09-3/31/10)			Tax Returns	13	5
							Other	4	1
0-500M	500M-2MM	2-10MM	10-50MM	50-100MM	100-250MM		4/1/05-3/31/06 ALL	4/1/06-3/31/07 ALL
20	19	20	4	3	2	NUMBER OF STATEMENTS	27	19
%	%	%	%	%	%	ASSETS	%	%
9.6	13.3	8.7				Cash & Equivalents	13.0	13.8
8.8	16.1	8.2				Trade Receivables (net)	11.1	9.0
36.2	39.6	42.9				Inventory	45.2	39.9
2.4	.6	5.6				All Other Current	2.3	4.7
56.9	69.5	65.4				Total Current	71.6	67.4
23.3	18.4	20.7				Fixed Assets (net)	21.4	24.5
8.1	1.7	7.5				Intangibles (net)	4.1	3.4
11.6	10.4	6.4				All Other Non-Current	2.9	4.7
100.0	100.0	100.0				Total	100.0	100.0
						LIABILITIES		
10.8	7.0	13.4				Notes Payable-Short Term	10.3	12.1
2.6	4.4	1.4				Cur. Mat.-L.T.D.	2.6	2.9
13.3	20.5	25.6				Trade Payables	23.4	12.4
.0	.0	.2				Income Taxes Payable	.1	.3
7.9	7.9	11.3				All Other Current	13.7	8.9
34.7	39.9	51.9				Total Current	50.2	36.7
28.7	13.4	21.2				Long-Term Debt	17.0	12.3
.0	.0	.0				Deferred Taxes	.0	.0
44.2	5.3	8.7				All Other Non-Current	3.2	5.2
-7.7	41.4	18.3				Net Worth	29.6	45.8
100.0	100.0	100.0				Total Liabilties & Net Worth	100.0	100.0
						INCOME DATA		
100.0	100.0	100.0				Net Sales	100.0	100.0
46.7	34.7	26.8				Gross Profit	20.7	13.8
48.0	32.7	29.4				Operating Expenses	19.5	11.4
-1.3	2.1	-2.6				Operating Profit	1.2	2.4
.2	-.8	2.2				All Other Expenses (net)	.5	.3
-1.5	2.9	-4.8				Profit Before Taxes	.7	2.2
						RATIOS		
4.2	3.5	2.1					3.0	4.4
2.3	1.7	1.3				Current	1.6	2.4
.6	1.3	1.0					.9	1.0
1.2	1.4	.8					1.2	2.0
.3	.4	.3				Quick	.4	.9
.1	.2	.1					.2	.1
0 UND	0 UND	2 237.0					0 UND	1 363.1
1 308.4	6 59.1	4 89.8				Sales/Receivables	1 244.0	2 157.1
22 16.7	31 11.9	9 38.6					7 51.2	6 57.9
15 24.5	14 25.5	16 23.1					11 32.8	13 27.7
22 16.5	71 5.2	59 6.1				Cost of Sales/Inventory	25 14.5	20 18.2
147 2.5	132 2.8	133 2.7					63 5.8	32 11.5
0 UND	8 47.1	8 43.6					0 UND	0 UND
32 11.4	23 15.5	32 11.3				Cost of Sales/Payables	9 40.0	8 44.9
58 6.3	62 5.9	64 5.7					32 11.2	14 25.6
6.7	3.9	8.7					9.6	11.7
14.3	12.6	27.5				Sales/Working Capital	26.4	22.2
-35.6	38.1	-230.5					-159.1	-278.2
12.5	18.9	9.1					5.3	8.7
(13) 1.7	(16) 8.6	(15) 1.4				EBIT/Interest	(21) 1.4	(16) 3.0
-10.6	.3	-1.0					-1.6	1.2
						Net Profit + Depr., Dep., Amort./Cur. Mat. L/T/D		
.2	.1	.2					.2	.1
8.9	.2	1.0				Fixed/Worth	.5	.5
-.4	1.8	NM					1.5	2.7
1.5	.8	2.2					.7	.3
UND	1.5	3.5				Debt/Worth	2.1	2.2
-3.2	6.8	NM					7.0	5.7
140.0	73.3	71.5					46.1	47.3
(11) 45.4	(18) 27.9	(15) 20.0				% Profit Before Taxes/Tangible Net Worth	(23) 15.7	(18) 23.4
2.0	-1.2	-8.2					2.0	4.2
25.7	24.0	14.3					12.5	22.8
2.2	6.6	1.5				% Profit Before Taxes/Total Assets	2.1	9.3
-21.3	-1.0	-5.6					-3.0	.9
296.4	66.5	118.0					123.6	153.8
28.6	36.0	29.2				Sales/Net Fixed Assets	36.4	35.4
12.3	21.4	7.9					17.4	19.8
5.2	5.6	5.8					11.3	9.6
2.9	2.7	3.3				Sales/Total Assets	6.8	7.3
2.0	1.7	1.7					4.2	5.7
1.3	.3	.2					.3	.2
(12) 2.8	(15) .5	(17) .8				% Depr., Dep., Amort./Sales	(22) .5	(18) .4
4.6	1.6	1.8					1.4	.7
								.5
						% Officers', Directors' Owners' Comp/Sales	(14) 1.2	
							4.7	
19956M	79124M	375637M	237496M	1448197M	537133M	Net Sales ($)	268058M	739801M
5068M	18473M	86312M	84055M	252045M	302561M	Total Assets ($)	42623M	160480M

M = $ thousand   MM = $ million
See Pages 9 through 22 for Explanation of Ratios and Data

Comparative Historical Data | Current Data Sorted by Sales

Type of Statement counts (Comparative Historical Data)

	4/1/07-3/31/08 ALL	4/1/08-3/31/09 ALL	4/1/09-3/31/10 ALL
Unqualified	1		1
Reviewed	2	3	7
Compiled	4	9	4
Tax Returns	3	3	33
Other	6	7	23

Type of Statement counts (Current Data Sorted by Sales) — 10 (4/1-9/30/09); 58 (10/1/09-3/31/10)

Type of Statement	0-1MM	1-3MM	3-5MM	5-10MM	10-25MM	25MM & OVER
Unqualified					1	1
Reviewed		2			3	3
Compiled	9	11	2	1	1	1
Tax Returns						7
Other	7	8		4	2	3

Main data table

4/1/07-3/31/08 ALL	4/1/08-3/31/09 ALL	4/1/09-3/31/10 ALL		0-1MM	1-3MM	3-5MM	5-10MM	10-25MM	25MM & OVER
16	22	68	**NUMBER OF STATEMENTS**	16	21	2	5	10	14
%	%	%	**ASSETS**	%	%	%	%	%	%
16.7	12.8	10.0	Cash & Equivalents	8.5	11.2			5.5	13.8
7.2	9.8	10.9	Trade Receivables (net)	4.3	17.3			8.7	9.7
44.9	45.3	39.7	Inventory	38.5	36.0			38.8	40.8
6.1	5.0	2.6	All Other Current	2.6	.5			9.4	1.9
74.7	72.9	63.2	Total Current	54.0	65.0			62.3	66.2
14.2	15.6	21.7	Fixed Assets (net)	26.8	16.9			24.7	23.4
5.0	2.5	5.2	Intangibles (net)	6.8	7.4			6.8	1.0
6.0	9.0	9.8	All Other Non-Current	12.3	10.7			6.2	9.4
100.0	100.0	100.0	Total	100.0	100.0			100.0	100.0
			LIABILITIES						
6.7	23.2	12.1	Notes Payable-Short Term	8.8	11.0			10.4	19.9
1.3	1.1	2.5	Cur. Mat.-L.T.D.	2.2	4.4			2.3	.4
18.8	15.0	18.3	Trade Payables	9.9	15.2			39.0	13.3
.1	.0	.1	Income Taxes Payable	.0	.0			.3	
9.9	6.6	10.1	All Other Current	9.0	6.1			13.9	15.8
36.8	46.0	43.0	Total Current	29.8	36.7			65.8	49.4
5.6	11.8	19.7	Long-Term Debt	31.0	21.2			18.0	9.9
.0	.0	.0	Deferred Taxes	.0	.0			.0	.0
3.4	3.7	17.4	All Other Non-Current	52.6	8.1			5.4	1.5
54.2	38.6	19.9	Net Worth	-13.6	34.1			10.8	39.1
100.0	100.0	100.0	Total Liabilities & Net Worth	100.0	100.0			100.0	100.0
			INCOME DATA						
100.0	100.0	100.0	Net Sales	100.0	100.0			100.0	100.0
15.9	17.5	35.5	Gross Profit	48.9	43.3			21.8	24.6
13.1	16.1	35.6	Operating Expenses	52.2	40.9			25.2	21.3
2.9	1.4	-.1	Operating Profit	-3.3	2.4			-3.5	3.3
.0	.2	.5	All Other Expenses (net)	-.2	1.9			.3	-.2
2.8	1.3	-.6	Profit Before Taxes	-3.1	.6			-3.8	3.4
			RATIOS						
7.5	3.0	2.9	Current	4.7	5.8			1.5	2.6
2.8	1.6	1.4		2.3	1.8			1.3	1.1
1.2	1.1	1.1		1.1	1.1			.7	1.0
2.3	.8	1.0	Quick	1.1	1.8			.3	.8
.8	(21) .5	.3		.1	.9			.3	.5
.1	.2	.1		.0	.2			.1	.1
0 UND	1 535.2	0 823.1	Sales/Receivables	0 UND	0 UND			0 UND	1 548.5
1 250.9	4 87.3	3 122.2		1 308.4	6 59.1			2 187.4	4 94.7
4 94.8	8 45.7	21 17.2		12 31.4	40 9.1			8 44.8	7 52.5
16 23.2	21 17.5	16 23.0	Cost of Sales/Inventory	22 16.7	14 26.3			0 UND	17 21.2
26 14.3	28 13.1	42 8.8		65 5.6	41 8.9			38 9.6	30 12.0
43 8.4	55 6.6	134 2.7		155 2.4	143 2.5			102 3.6	120 3.0
2 240.8	3 118.1	8 47.1	Cost of Sales/Payables	0 UND	5 76.9			8 46.5	8 45.5
11 32.2	11 34.0	21 17.5		36 10.1	33 11.0			45 8.2	10 35.5
21 17.0	17 22.0	57 6.3		69 5.3	64 5.7			70 5.2	16 23.2
10.4	18.0	6.7	Sales/Working Capital	4.0	4.3			17.3	19.0
23.4	27.5	19.1		11.4	12.4			62.3	49.9
70.5	115.4	106.9		NM	84.4			-98.6	NM
73.1	13.2	13.3	EBIT/Interest		13.6				
(12) 4.4	(18) 2.0	(50) 3.3			(19) 4.0				
.8	.0	.2			-.1				
			Net Profit + Depr., Dep., Amort./Cur. Mat. L/T/D						
.0	.1	.2	Fixed/Worth	.2	.1			.5	.2
.2	.3	.7		8.5	.2			1.0	.5
.6	.8	14.5		-.7	7.1			-1.1	1.1
.1	.5	1.2	Debt/Worth	1.5	.8			1.4	.7
.9	2.6	3.0		UND	3.7			2.9	2.3
5.3	8.6	UND		-4.2	40.2			-9.0	6.5
53.3	35.8	71.5	% Profit Before Taxes/Tangible Net Worth		48.4				58.6
(13) 36.6	(19) 16.4	(52) 25.4			(17) 14.2				(13) 35.0
4.2	4.2	2.1			-8.8				10.8
32.5	18.2	20.4	% Profit Before Taxes/Total Assets	15.5	21.4			20.9	23.2
17.0	2.9	3.2		.0	2.1			4.9	11.6
-.2	-2.4	-4.8		-21.3	-4.0			-6.4	2.9
333.5	152.1	101.4	Sales/Net Fixed Assets	40.5	105.5			111.7	109.6
94.6	70.9	30.0		18.9	46.3			29.2	28.7
26.7	23.2	9.5		5.0	21.4			8.0	10.2
9.9	7.5	5.4	Sales/Total Assets	3.4	4.4			7.4	7.0
7.1	5.6	2.9		2.0	2.3			4.5	4.3
5.7	4.9	1.9		1.6	1.3			3.1	2.6
.1	.1	.3	% Depr., Dep., Amort./Sales	1.2	.3				.3
(12) .3	(18) .3	(51) 1.0		(11) 2.5	(14) 1.5			(12)	.4
.6	.5	3.1		4.4	4.3				.7
		1.7	% Officers', Directors' Owners' Comp/Sales		3.5				
	(26) 3.8			(11) 5.2					
		7.2			7.2				
644183M	235669M	2697543M	Net Sales ($)	8448M	45330M	9222M	30093M	142940M	2461510M
163413M	43994M	748514M	Total Assets ($)	4467M	30044M	4015M	6498M	33498M	669992M

M = $ thousand   MM = $ million
See Pages 9 through 22 for Explanation of Ratios and Data

RETAIL—All Other Miscellaneous Store Retailers (except Tobacco Stores) NAICS 453998

Current Data Sorted by Assets   **Comparative Historical Data**

Type of Statement	0-500M	500M-2MM	2-10MM	10-50MM	50-100MM	100-250MM		4/1/05-3/31/06 ALL	4/1/06-3/31/07 ALL
Unqualified	3	4	6	21	6	8		35	36
Reviewed	13	11	37	16	2			63	52
Compiled	80	28	35	6				96	89
Tax Returns	32	71	35	1				189	152
Other		49	64	42	10	8		194	159
	95 (4/1-9/30/09)			493 (10/1/09-3/31/10)					
NUMBER OF STATEMENTS	128	163	177	86	18	16		577	488
	%	%	%	%	%	%		%	%
ASSETS									
Cash & Equivalents	14.1	12.5	9.6	9.9	11.9	16.7		10.8	10.9
Trade Receivables (net)	10.3	13.4	18.1	17.5	18.0	15.3		17.6	18.1
Inventory	38.6	41.5	36.4	34.8	23.0	24.6		38.5	37.8
All Other Current	1.0	1.8	3.1	4.8	6.6	6.0		2.8	2.6
Total Current	64.0	69.2	67.1	66.9	59.6	62.6		69.7	69.4
Fixed Assets (net)	19.9	19.2	20.8	20.5	22.8	21.0		20.7	20.6
Intangibles (net)	7.1	4.5	4.4	6.9	12.6	11.1		4.2	4.6
All Other Non-Current	8.9	7.1	7.7	5.7	5.0	5.3		5.3	5.5
Total	100.0	100.0	100.0	100.0	100.0	100.0		100.0	100.0
LIABILITIES									
Notes Payable-Short Term	15.2	11.1	12.9	15.5	5.8	10.4		12.8	14.0
Cur. Mat.-L.T.D.	5.6	3.2	2.9	3.7	5.1	1.4		3.0	2.7
Trade Payables	18.2	18.7	20.9	16.0	18.9	9.3		19.7	18.7
Income Taxes Payable	.1	.1	.3	.5	.6	.5		.4	.4
All Other Current	18.5	14.5	12.1	13.6	9.0	13.2		11.8	12.9
Total Current	57.7	47.5	49.1	49.3	39.4	34.7		47.8	48.8
Long-Term Debt	26.0	18.6	14.4	11.7	19.5	17.6		18.0	17.7
Deferred Taxes	.0	.3	.3	.4	1.2	1.8		.2	.2
All Other Non-Current	19.6	6.2	7.0	5.2	6.2	10.1		7.5	8.7
Net Worth	-3.2	27.3	29.1	33.4	33.8	35.8		26.6	24.6
Total Liabilties & Net Worth	100.0	100.0	100.0	100.0	100.0	100.0		100.0	100.0
INCOME DATA									
Net Sales	100.0	100.0	100.0	100.0	100.0	100.0		100.0	100.0
Gross Profit	48.3	40.1	36.9	32.6	33.2	36.9		39.5	39.4
Operating Expenses	46.6	37.7	33.5	27.8	27.5	29.6		35.4	35.9
Operating Profit	1.8	2.5	3.4	4.8	5.7	7.4		4.1	3.5
All Other Expenses (net)	1.0	.8	.9	.8	2.5	1.3		1.0	1.0
Profit Before Taxes	.8	1.7	2.5	4.1	3.2	6.1		3.1	2.5
RATIOS									
	3.8	3.0	2.4	1.9	2.2	2.7		2.6	2.4
Current	1.3	1.6	1.4	1.4	1.5	1.9		1.5	1.5
	.7	1.1	1.0	1.1	1.0	1.2		1.1	1.0
	1.3	1.3	.9	.9	1.4	1.6		1.1	1.1
Quick	(127) .4	.5	.5	.5	.8	1.0		(574) .6	(487) .6
	.1	.2	.2	.2	.4	.7		.2	.2
	0 UND	1 444.3	3 133.1	3 104.7	5 77.0	18 19.9		2 190.4	2 199.1
Sales/Receivables	0 848.9	9 42.3	18 20.4	26 14.1	41 9.0	38 9.6		14 26.1	16 23.1
	14 26.5	26 14.1	43 8.5	60 6.1	59 6.1	64 5.7		38 9.7	39 9.3
	14 25.9	29 12.4	30 12.3	30 12.2	24 15.3	45 8.1		26 13.8	29 12.5
Cost of Sales/Inventory	60 6.1	84 4.4	66 5.5	76 4.8	101 3.6	73 5.0		75 4.9	70 5.2
	125 2.9	160 2.3	118 3.1	158 2.3	149 2.5	149 2.5		138 2.6	137 2.7
	0 UND	11 34.3	16 23.3	18 20.6	25 14.4	10 35.8		11 34.2	11 34.2
Cost of Sales/Payables	18 20.1	30 12.0	33 10.9	32 11.4	46 7.9	30 12.3		31 11.7	31 11.8
	48 7.7	61 6.0	60 6.0	52 7.1	68 5.3	66 5.5		58 6.3	57 6.4
	7.6	5.4	7.1	5.9	3.5	2.8		5.7	5.5
Sales/Working Capital	37.2	12.4	15.5	11.5	7.8	4.4		12.4	13.5
	-21.3	65.2	-315.6	48.2	NM	22.3		62.0	195.3
	4.4	9.8	12.6	10.6	6.6	17.2		9.3	8.3
EBIT/Interest	(95) 1.1	(144) 2.7	(161) 4.0	(78) 3.8	(16) 3.5	(13) 6.3		(501) 3.5	(426) 2.6
	-3.2	.8	1.3	1.4	-.6	1.1		1.2	.9
		2.3	5.2	8.1	5.0	11.9		7.4	10.1
Net Profit + Depr., Dep., Amort./Cur. Mat. L/T/D		(11) .8	(43) 2.6	(30) 3.0	(11) .8	(10) 4.2		(79) 2.4	(54) 3.4
		.4	.6	.7	.1	1.9		1.3	1.3
	.2	.1	.2	.3	.4	.3		.2	.2
Fixed/Worth	1.7	.4	.7	.5	.8	.9		.6	.6
	-.6	24.8	2.2	2.0	NM	1.9		2.5	2.9
	.8	.8	1.0	1.0	1.2	.9		1.0	1.0
Debt/Worth	12.7	2.5	2.3	2.6	2.0	3.3		2.6	2.7
	-2.9	66.6	10.4	12.0	NM	7.5		10.0	12.1
	74.4	51.6	53.1	57.8	27.9	51.6		56.1	46.8
% Profit Before Taxes/Tangible Net Worth	(76) 13.1	(129) 13.1	(147) 18.2	(72) 16.9	(14) 18.9	(14) 16.6		(480) 22.1	(391) 18.8
	-11.5	.2	4.3	6.5	-.1	4.6		5.3	2.5
	20.0	15.4	12.7	13.2	7.3	15.1		15.1	15.2
% Profit Before Taxes/Total Assets	1.9	5.4	5.0	5.2	4.6	5.1		6.0	4.6
	-9.0	-.2	1.0	.9	-2.9	1.2		.6	-.2
	146.6	107.7	72.2	52.3	16.9	25.5		66.6	67.2
Sales/Net Fixed Assets	35.0	25.4	20.1	16.8	6.5	8.7		26.7	24.6
	9.5	9.0	7.7	5.8	4.3	3.5		9.1	8.8
	6.3	4.1	3.8	2.7	2.0	2.1		4.2	4.2
Sales/Total Assets	3.7	2.8	2.7	2.0	1.5	1.3		2.8	2.7
	2.1	1.9	1.8	1.5	1.2	.8		1.8	1.8
	.4	.3	.4	.5	1.6	1.0		.5	.5
% Depr., Dep., Amort./Sales	(80) 1.4	(115) 1.0	(150) .9	(74) 1.1	(17) 2.2	(11) 2.4		(457) 1.0	(378) 1.1
	2.7	2.0	2.1	2.6	4.2	3.8		2.0	2.5
	3.4		1.1	.9				1.6	1.9
% Officers', Directors' Owners' Comp/Sales	(68) 5.6	(89) 4.0	(66) 2.6	(13) 1.6				(259) 3.7	(214) 3.8
	9.6	6.7	4.1	6.3				7.3	8.0
Net Sales ($)	126416M	617862M	2564492M	4578763M	1964021M	5018167M		15439132M	14042309M
Total Assets ($)	30362M	181066M	827300M	2064334M	1230563M	2844474M		6067119M	6187560M

M = $ thousand   MM = $ million
See Pages 9 through 22 for Explanation of Ratios and Data

Comparative Historical Data | Current Data Sorted by Sales

			Type of Statement						
42	51	45	Unqualified	1	2	1	3	5	34
51	72	69	Reviewed		9	4	10	28	17
76	66	82	Compiled	7	24	7	18	16	10
128	184	187	Tax Returns	55	54	26	32	18	2
179	215	205	Other	33	36	20	22	35	59
4/1/07-3/31/08 ALL	4/1/08-3/31/09 ALL	4/1/09-3/31/10 ALL		95 (4/1-9/30/09)		493 (10/1/09-3/31/10)			
				0-1MM	1-3MM	3-5MM	5-10MM	10-25MM	25MM & OVER
476	588	588	NUMBER OF STATEMENTS	96	125	58	85	102	122
%	%	%	ASSETS	%	%	%	%	%	%
9.7	10.2	11.7	Cash & Equivalents	12.3	12.1	11.9	11.7	10.6	11.6
18.6	17.0	14.9	Trade Receivables (net)	7.8	12.4	13.1	17.3	20.7	17.4
37.9	38.5	37.3	Inventory	37.8	41.1	37.5	36.2	37.3	33.6
3.5	3.1	2.7	All Other Current	1.2	1.6	2.0	2.4	2.9	5.4
69.8	68.7	66.6	Total Current	59.1	67.3	64.5	67.8	71.5	68.0
19.1	20.8	20.2	Fixed Assets (net)	23.4	18.8	25.4	18.7	17.9	19.6
5.1	4.9	5.8	Intangibles (net)	7.6	6.4	3.2	4.8	4.0	7.3
6.0	5.6	7.3	All Other Non-Current	9.8	7.5	6.9	8.8	6.6	5.0
100.0	100.0	100.0	Total	100.0	100.0	100.0	100.0	100.0	100.0
			LIABILITIES						
13.8	17.3	13.0	Notes Payable-Short Term	13.0	13.4	10.3	14.2	14.6	11.6
3.5	3.7	3.7	Cur. Mat.-L.T.D.	4.2	5.3	3.5	2.6	4.0	2.3
21.5	17.8	18.6	Trade Payables	15.4	18.8	18.4	18.3	21.2	19.1
.4	.2	.2	Income Taxes Payable	.1	.1	.1	.2	.3	.6
12.1	11.6	14.3	All Other Current	15.3	18.9	10.3	13.3	10.5	14.6
51.3	50.5	49.9	Total Current	48.0	56.6	42.5	48.7	50.7	48.2
17.4	18.4	17.9	Long-Term Debt	28.3	22.5	16.8	14.0	12.6	12.9
.2	.3	.3	Deferred Taxes	.4	.0	.2	.0	.3	.8
8.5	7.8	9.3	All Other Non-Current	15.5	12.0	10.9	5.5	5.9	6.5
22.6	23.0	22.5	Net Worth	7.9	8.9	29.6	31.7	30.5	31.6
100.0	100.0	100.0	Total Liabilities & Net Worth	100.0	100.0	100.0	100.0	100.0	100.0
			INCOME DATA						
100.0	100.0	100.0	Net Sales	100.0	100.0	100.0	100.0	100.0	100.0
37.5	38.8	39.6	Gross Profit	53.0	45.2	40.1	38.8	31.9	29.9
33.8	35.1	36.4	Operating Expenses	50.3	42.7	38.6	34.8	28.2	25.8
3.7	3.7	3.2	Operating Profit	2.7	2.6	1.5	4.0	3.6	4.1
1.0	1.0	.9	All Other Expenses (net)	2.0	.8	.8	.4	1.1	.6
2.7	2.7	2.2	Profit Before Taxes	.6	1.8	.7	3.6	2.6	3.5
			RATIOS						
2.3	2.6	2.6		3.2	3.4	2.9	2.6	2.0	2.3
1.5	1.5	1.5	Current	1.3	1.7	1.7	1.4	1.4	1.4
1.0	1.1	1.0		.7	.9	1.0	1.0	1.1	1.1
1.1	1.1	1.1		1.0	1.5	1.1	1.2	.9	1.1
(474) .6	(587) .5	(587) .5	Quick	(95) .3	.4	.5	.6	.6	.6
.2	.2	.2		.1	.1	.2	.2	.3	.2
2 206.1	2 228.6	1 507.0		0 UND	0 UND	2 155.3	1 272.7	4 90.0	3 124.4
15 23.8	14 26.9	10 35.7	Sales/Receivables	1 440.8	6 66.1	15 25.0	12 29.6	25 14.4	21 17.2
39 9.4	35 10.5	36 10.1		17 21.4	26 14.2	26 14.1	34 10.6	46 7.9	50 7.3
24 15.0	26 14.2	28 13.0		31 11.9	26 14.1	21 17.4	26 14.0	37 9.9	25 14.6
70 5.2	75 4.9	70 5.2	Cost of Sales/Inventory	115 3.2	84 4.4	53 6.9	69 5.3	73 5.0	56 6.5
137 2.7	150 2.4	139 2.6		188 1.9	158 2.3	140 2.6	100 3.6	126 2.9	109 3.3
16 23.4	9 39.8	12 31.7		0 UND	9 41.3	11 32.8	12 29.7	19 18.9	15 24.7
34 10.6	30 12.0	29 12.4	Cost of Sales/Payables	26 14.1	24 14.9	35 10.4	25 14.8	32 11.4	32 11.3
60 6.0	56 6.5	57 6.5		70 5.2	60 6.1	66 5.5	52 7.0	49 7.4	54 6.8
6.2	6.0	6.2		4.4	5.4	6.2	6.9	7.3	6.3
13.9	14.1	14.5	Sales/Working Capital	19.1	12.2	13.3	16.7	14.4	14.2
106.1	96.5	-155.8		-15.1	-67.8	166.9	-251.4	54.3	54.8
11.0	7.1	9.5		3.7	8.8	5.0	13.8	13.0	15.6
(414) 3.1	(510) 2.8	(507) 2.8	EBIT/Interest	(70) .9	(106) 1.9	(50) 1.9	(77) 5.8	(97) 3.4	(107) 4.9
1.0	.7	.6		-2.5	-1.2	.2	1.6	1.3	1.5
10.8	7.2	5.7					5.4	7.3	7.7
(90) 2.9	(89) 2.5	(108) 2.3	Net Profit + Depr., Dep., Amort./Cur. Mat. L/T/D				(14) 2.3	(25) 3.0	(53) 2.4
1.1	1.2	.6					-.8	.9	.8
.2	.2	.2		.2	.1	.1	.2	.2	.3
.5	.6	.7	Fixed/Worth	1.9	.8	.5	.4	.6	.6
2.5	4.1	13.4		-.8	-2.3	3.5	2.1	2.2	2.0
1.1	1.0	.9		.7	.8	.9	.8	.9	1.2
2.9	2.8	2.8	Debt/Worth	12.7	3.0	1.9	2.5	2.3	2.9
11.9	24.8	100.8		-3.3	-9.3	22.2	13.1	10.1	8.8
50.7	49.5	53.3	% Profit Before Taxes/Tangible Net Worth	83.5	47.4	26.1	54.7	56.6	55.5
(394) 22.2	(464) 18.9	(452) 16.5		(60) 12.8	(85) 12.1	(50) 8.2	(70) 21.6	(85) 17.2	(102) 21.6
4.1	2.0	1.9		-10.0	-1.8	-5.9	4.1	4.6	7.0
15.7	14.8	14.0	% Profit Before Taxes/Total Assets	13.3	17.4	10.2	14.4	13.0	14.3
5.3	4.6	4.8		1.2	3.8	2.5	8.1	6.3	5.2
-.1	-.5	-.7		-8.3	-3.8	-.9	1.9	1.0	1.0
73.5	77.3	80.1		62.2	112.2	76.8	90.4	85.0	55.4
26.4	22.2	21.9	Sales/Net Fixed Assets	17.6	36.3	19.0	23.5	26.5	19.1
9.5	7.5	7.1		5.1	9.3	7.5	7.7	8.9	7.1
4.2	4.2	4.0		3.6	4.2	4.9	4.0	3.7	3.9
2.7	2.6	2.7	Sales/Total Assets	2.1	2.9	2.7	2.9	2.6	2.5
1.9	1.7	1.7		1.2	1.8	2.0	2.1	1.9	1.6
.4	.5	.5		.4	.5	.4	.5	.4	.5
(361) 1.1	(452) 1.1	(447) 1.1	% Depr., Dep., Amort./Sales	(52) 2.0	(92) 1.2	(45) 1.0	(67) 1.0	(87) .9	(104) 1.1
2.3	2.4	2.4		5.3	2.5	1.9	1.8	2.2	2.2
1.7	1.8	1.8		4.8	2.5	1.9	1.4	.8	.7
(188) 3.7	(222) 3.4	(238) 3.8	% Officers', Directors' Owners' Comp/Sales	(45) 8.0	(67) 4.1	(35) 4.1	(38) 2.7	(34) 2.3	(19) 1.1
6.7	5.9	6.5		10.9	7.6	5.7	5.8	3.1	1.8
16083622M	18080077M	14869721M	Net Sales ($)	48893M	231435M	226555M	613331M	1614794M	12134713M
7452913M	8120300M	7178099M	Total Assets ($)	34735M	110783M	103426M	279452M	834655M	5815048M

M = $ thousand   MM = $ million
See Pages 9 through 22 for Explanation of Ratios and Data

Current Data Sorted by Assets   Comparative Historical Data

Type of Statement

0-500M	500M-2MM	2-10MM	10-50MM	50-100MM	100-250MM	Type of Statement	4/1/05-3/31/06 ALL	4/1/06-3/31/07 ALL
		2	4	6	1	Unqualified	6	8
		2	2			Reviewed	5	4
	1	2				Compiled	5	3
1	7	4				Tax Returns	5	8
4	6	15	11	2	8	Other	16	22
	11 (4/1-9/30/09)		71 (10/1/09-3/31/10)					
9	14	25	17	8	9	NUMBER OF STATEMENTS	37	45
%	%	%	%	%	%		%	%

ASSETS

0-500M	500M-2MM	2-10MM	10-50MM	50-100MM	100-250MM		4/1/05-3/31/06	4/1/06-3/31/07
	7.8	20.7	16.9			Cash & Equivalents	11.6	13.5
	14.6	9.6	9.4			Trade Receivables (net)	12.7	13.4
	46.8	41.8	35.2			Inventory	40.8	40.7
	2.0	4.5	8.8			All Other Current	7.6	5.5
	71.3	76.6	70.3			Total Current	72.7	73.1
	19.1	12.3	17.0			Fixed Assets (net)	10.2	13.4
	6.7	6.2	10.0			Intangibles (net)	9.3	8.5
	3.0	4.9	2.7			All Other Non-Current	7.9	5.0
	100.0	100.0	100.0			Total	100.0	100.0

LIABILITIES

0-500M	500M-2MM	2-10MM	10-50MM	50-100MM	100-250MM		4/1/05-3/31/06	4/1/06-3/31/07
	12.9	8.1	6.5			Notes Payable-Short Term	11.4	11.8
	.9	3.5	.9			Cur. Mat.-L.T.D.	3.7	1.8
	28.2	21.7	22.2			Trade Payables	26.2	21.7
	.1	.3	.2			Income Taxes Payable	.2	.3
	6.2	19.4	14.3			All Other Current	16.0	14.4
	48.2	52.9	44.1			Total Current	57.5	50.0
	16.7	15.0	6.4			Long-Term Debt	11.9	13.0
	.0	.1	.4			Deferred Taxes	.1	.2
	3.1	2.8	.6			All Other Non-Current	11.8	3.4
	32.0	29.1	48.5			Net Worth	18.7	33.4
	100.0	100.0	100.0			Total Liabilities & Net Worth	100.0	100.0

INCOME DATA

0-500M	500M-2MM	2-10MM	10-50MM	50-100MM	100-250MM		4/1/05-3/31/06	4/1/06-3/31/07
	100.0	100.0	100.0			Net Sales	100.0	100.0
	37.3	42.0	35.7			Gross Profit	40.7	39.6
	32.2	36.5	32.9			Operating Expenses	39.7	36.0
	5.1	5.5	2.8			Operating Profit	1.0	3.6
	.5	1.2	.3			All Other Expenses (net)	1.0	.8
	4.6	4.3	2.5			Profit Before Taxes	.0	2.9

RATIOS

0-500M	500M-2MM	2-10MM	10-50MM	50-100MM	100-250MM		4/1/05-3/31/06	4/1/06-3/31/07
	2.3	2.7	2.2			Current	2.0	2.2
	1.5	1.6	1.5				1.3	1.5
	1.1	1.0	1.3				1.0	1.0
	.9	.9	.9			Quick	.7	1.0
	.3	.6	.6				.3	.5
	.1	.3	.3				.2	.2
	0 UND	0 UND	1 254.1			Sales/Receivables	1 314.5	1 279.4
	2 173.2	2 175.3	5 77.0				8 47.4	6 65.2
	10 37.4	12 30.6	14 26.5				15 23.6	22 16.6
	20 18.5	34 10.7	6 60.6			Cost of Sales/Inventory	29 12.5	42 8.7
	57 6.4	79 4.6	54 6.7				74 4.9	89 4.1
	89 4.1	132 2.8	88 4.2				107 3.4	130 2.8
	23 16.2	21 17.4	19 19.1			Cost of Sales/Payables	26 14.1	25 14.8
	32 11.2	31 11.7	24 14.9				37 9.9	40 9.1
	46 8.0	48 7.7	52 7.0				56 6.5	62 5.9
	7.5	6.8	9.3			Sales/Working Capital	9.6	7.2
	22.4	13.4	15.4				16.8	14.2
	311.0	NM	37.5				-304.9	586.1
	78.2	40.5	24.7			EBIT/Interest	3.2	10.6
	(12) 9.4	(21) 8.7	(11) 13.1				(32) 1.1	(38) 3.4
	3.8	1.1	3.3				-5.0	-2.2
						Net Profit + Depr., Dep., Amort./Cur. Mat. L/T/D		39.2
							(13)	7.4
								4.1
	.1	.1	.2			Fixed/Worth	.2	.2
	.3	.2	.4				.5	.4
	2.9	7.2	.7				-7.0	1.4
	1.6	.7	.9			Debt/Worth	1.4	1.2
	2.7	1.7	1.6				2.7	2.2
	5.7	45.2	2.0				-27.1	5.7
	147.6	95.8	58.5			% Profit Before Taxes/Tangible Net Worth	36.2	51.6
	(13) 55.0	(20) 31.0	36.3				(26) 5.2	(40) 18.2
	24.0	17.9	5.2				-7.9	-9.4
	28.9	28.0	22.1			% Profit Before Taxes/Total Assets	16.7	21.7
	19.8	12.5	14.6				.5	6.3
	3.7	1.8	1.6				-6.8	-4.4
	396.5	299.3	51.6			Sales/Net Fixed Assets	85.0	92.9
	62.9	45.6	28.4				43.1	33.8
	17.4	20.4	15.2				22.5	16.7
	6.3	4.5	4.3			Sales/Total Assets	4.7	4.9
	4.6	3.2	3.8				3.4	2.7
	2.9	2.3	2.8				2.4	2.0
		.3	.9			% Depr., Dep., Amort./Sales	.5	.5
		(17) .7	(14) 2.1				(30) .7	(39) .7
		1.9	2.9				1.3	1.5
		.7				% Officers', Directors' Owners' Comp/Sales	3.5	2.1
		(10) 3.0					(10) 5.8	(15) 4.2
		7.5					7.1	6.1
20685M	89729M	459901M	1345537M	1272579M	2819037M	Net Sales ($)	3385202M	4985701M
2208M	16154M	135152M	322149M	534227M	1487742M	Total Assets ($)	1444331M	2070103M

Comparative Historical Data | Current Data Sorted by Sales

	4/1/07-3/31/08 ALL	4/1/08-3/31/09 ALL	4/1/09-3/31/10 ALL	0-1MM	1-3MM	3-5MM	5-10MM	10-25MM	25MM & OVER
Type of Statement									
Unqualified	8	15	13					2	11
Reviewed	4	5	4		1			1	3
Compiled	5	6	4					3	
Tax Returns	11	14	15		3			2	1
Other	30	40	46	5	4	3	9	9	25
	11 (4/1-9/30/09)						71 (10/1/09-3/31/10)		
NUMBER OF STATEMENTS	58	80	82	5	8	3	9	17	40
	%	%	%	%	%	%	%	%	%
ASSETS									
Cash & Equivalents	19.2	15.0	16.9					16.7	19.4
Trade Receivables (net)	13.3	10.6	10.5					11.8	8.3
Inventory	39.4	37.7	36.3					48.5	31.2
All Other Current	5.4	7.4	4.9					4.1	7.1
Total Current	77.3	70.8	68.6					81.2	66.0
Fixed Assets (net)	13.0	14.4	15.4					15.8	14.8
Intangibles (net)	5.9	8.6	10.3					.3	16.1
All Other Non-Current	3.8	6.2	5.7					2.7	3.1
Total	100.0	100.0	100.0					100.0	100.0
LIABILITIES									
Notes Payable-Short Term	15.6	16.2	9.4					9.5	4.6
Cur. Mat.-L.T.D.	2.9	2.4	2.0					5.1	1.6
Trade Payables	22.5	25.6	22.1					27.7	21.1
Income Taxes Payable	.1	.4	.4					.3	.6
All Other Current	16.4	15.0	13.6					14.4	14.0
Total Current	57.5	59.7	47.5					57.0	41.9
Long-Term Debt	9.5	11.2	11.8					18.7	9.1
Deferred Taxes	.3	.2	.4					.2	.7
All Other Non-Current	10.1	6.6	5.0					2.2	1.8
Net Worth	22.7	22.4	35.3					21.8	46.6
Total Liabilities & Net Worth	100.0	100.0	100.0					100.0	100.0
INCOME DATA									
Net Sales	100.0	100.0	100.0					100.0	100.0
Gross Profit	38.6	40.6	39.2					37.3	37.6
Operating Expenses	33.4	37.5	34.8					33.2	33.9
Operating Profit	5.2	3.1	4.5					4.1	3.7
All Other Expenses (net)	.6	1.5	.8					.7	.7
Profit Before Taxes	4.6	1.6	3.6					3.3	3.0
RATIOS									
Current	2.2	2.1	2.3					2.6	2.1
	1.6	1.5	1.5					1.5	1.5
	1.0	1.0	1.1					1.1	1.2
Quick	1.1	1.0	1.1					1.0	1.1
	.5	.4	.6					.4	.7
	.2	.1	.2					.1	.2
Sales/Receivables	2 234.3	1 592.4	0 999.8					0 UND	2 186.4
	6 62.9	4 83.5	3 117.9					2 175.3	5 71.6
	14 25.2	13 27.3	14 25.7					24 15.4	14 26.3
Cost of Sales/Inventory	31 12.0	24 15.2	30 12.3					31 11.7	30 12.0
	71 5.2	68 5.4	61 6.0					58 6.3	61 6.0
	123 3.0	132 2.8	107 3.4					105 3.5	94 3.9
Cost of Sales/Payables	17 21.4	16 22.8	20 18.0					25 14.7	21 17.1
	25 14.3	32 11.3	34 10.7					30 12.3	43 8.6
	53 6.9	56 6.5	53 6.9					40 9.2	60 6.1
Sales/Working Capital	7.4	8.4	7.7					6.8	7.8
	13.6	18.9	17.3					15.7	14.4
	207.5	193.4	158.1					540.6	31.3
EBIT/Interest	14.5	13.5	56.2					49.1	50.6
	(47) 4.7	(61) 3.8	(65) 9.3					(15) 11.5	(33) 9.4
	1.6	-.5	1.7					4.1	1.7
Net Profit + Depr., Dep., Amort./Cur. Mat. L/T/D	44.5		146.8						214.2
	(11) 9.2		(13) 25.1						(10) 80.3
	1.6		2.8						2.2
Fixed/Worth	.1	.2	.1					.1	.2
	.5	.4	.4					.2	.5
	2.3	UND	2.1					5.9	.9
Debt/Worth	1.1	.8	.8					1.0	.8
	2.4	2.7	1.9					2.1	1.7
	8.5	UND	7.9					15.3	2.7
% Profit Before Taxes/Tangible Net Worth	71.1	65.4	76.4					121.9	57.9
	(50) 38.7	(60) 34.7	(70) 39.9					(14) 50.5	(35) 36.1
	-.2	7.7	15.6					20.2	10.3
% Profit Before Taxes/Total Assets	21.0	21.5	27.2					29.8	21.4
	11.1	7.5	11.8					12.5	8.5
	-.1	-3.5	2.1					9.5	.7
Sales/Net Fixed Assets	144.9	98.5	110.0					243.9	47.7
	40.9	32.6	31.3					45.6	23.9
	15.2	14.7	16.3					15.4	11.7
Sales/Total Assets	4.9	4.9	5.5					7.2	4.0
	3.6	3.2	3.4					4.0	3.2
	2.5	2.2	2.4					2.9	1.9
% Depr., Dep., Amort./Sales	.3	.4	.5					.2	.8
	(40) .8	(50) .7	(53) 1.2					(13) .5	(29) 1.9
	1.9	1.9	2.5					1.8	3.0
% Officers', Directors' Owners' Comp/Sales	.6	1.3	1.0						
	(18) 3.3	(15) 5.7	(21) 2.6						
	7.6	9.4	7.6						
Net Sales ($)	6637379M	7315087M	6007468M	2511M	20039M	11464M	60252M	290244M	5622958M
Total Assets ($)	2219788M	2432713M	2497632M	1514M	10387M	1530M	17960M	72444M	2393797M

M = $ thousand   MM = $ million
See Pages 9 through 22 for Explanation of Ratios and Data

Current Data Sorted by Assets   Comparative Historical Data

Type of Statement

	0-500M	500M-2MM	2-10MM	10-50MM	50-100MM	100-250MM		4/1/05-3/31/06 ALL	4/1/06-3/31/07 ALL
Unqualified		1	6	13	3	9		38	34
Reviewed			7	3	2			17	20
Compiled		2	6	2				10	16
Tax Returns	4	5	1	2				18	22
Other	1	7	21	16	7	6		60	53
		21 (4/1-9/30/09)		103 (10/1/09-3/31/10)					
NUMBER OF STATEMENTS	5	15	41	36	12	15		143	145

	0-500M %	500M-2MM %	2-10MM %	10-50MM %	50-100MM %	100-250MM %		ALL %	ALL %
ASSETS									
Cash & Equivalents		18.3	7.9	17.7	13.2	12.4		13.6	12.2
Trade Receivables (net)		13.1	14.4	10.4	10.1	18.1		13.9	12.5
Inventory		47.3	41.9	34.3	36.9	22.3		37.6	39.9
All Other Current		4.5	4.3	4.2	7.6	4.3		4.7	4.7
Total Current		83.2	68.5	66.6	67.9	57.1		69.8	69.1
Fixed Assets (net)		9.4	17.4	14.1	12.5	19.1		14.4	14.4
Intangibles (net)		1.7	3.8	10.5	14.3	19.8		8.1	7.7
All Other Non-Current		5.7	10.3	8.9	5.3	3.9		7.7	8.8
Total		100.0	100.0	100.0	100.0	100.0		100.0	100.0
LIABILITIES									
Notes Payable-Short Term		15.3	14.6	6.3	2.3	2.8		9.4	11.6
Cur. Mat.-L.T.D.		1.7	1.7	2.4	1.1	3.3		3.0	2.3
Trade Payables		18.4	23.2	21.2	19.8	15.5		26.1	27.2
Income Taxes Payable		.0	.4	.1	1.0	.1		.3	.3
All Other Current		4.8	9.7	14.5	14.5	9.6		13.3	15.1
Total Current		40.3	49.5	44.4	38.7	31.4		51.9	56.5
Long-Term Debt		3.5	10.7	13.6	15.7	8.7		13.1	11.3
Deferred Taxes		.0	.1	1.5	2.6	.9		.2	.4
All Other Non-Current		22.7	27.8	5.5	10.2	3.9		7.0	7.0
Net Worth		33.5	11.9	35.0	32.7	55.2		27.8	24.8
Total Liabilities & Net Worth		100.0	100.0	100.0	100.0	100.0		100.0	100.0
INCOME DATA									
Net Sales		100.0	100.0	100.0	100.0	100.0		100.0	100.0
Gross Profit		33.3	44.6	45.2	42.5	44.1		41.6	43.5
Operating Expenses		27.8	40.9	41.5	39.4	37.7		38.7	41.2
Operating Profit		5.4	3.7	3.7	3.1	6.4		2.9	2.4
All Other Expenses (net)		.2	.9	1.1	1.4	1.7		.6	.7
Profit Before Taxes		5.2	2.7	2.6	1.7	4.7		2.3	1.7
RATIOS									
Current		4.1	3.0	2.3	3.5	3.0		2.3	2.2
		2.6	1.5	1.7	1.9	1.8		1.4	1.3
		1.2	.9	1.1	1.1	1.4		1.0	1.0
Quick		1.6	1.4	1.1	1.1	1.5		1.0	.8
		.7	.2	.6	.8	1.0		.5	(144) .3
		.3	.1	.2	.2	.2		.1	.1
Sales/Receivables		1 344.4	3 105.8	2 177.2	2 201.3	4 82.8		2 227.0	1 438.6
		3 108.3	7 53.3	5 71.4	9 41.3	25 14.5		6 60.2	5 71.3
		21 17.3	17 21.1	10 34.9	31 11.9	48 7.7		22 16.8	14 25.3
Cost of Sales/Inventory		40 9.1	36 10.1	43 8.5	63 5.8	67 5.5		40 9.1	44 8.4
		69 5.3	86 4.2	76 4.8	100 3.7	77 4.7		74 4.9	78 4.7
		107 3.4	135 2.7	131 2.8	144 2.5	108 3.4		119 3.1	121 3.0
Cost of Sales/Payables		2 198.3	18 20.4	22 16.8	20 18.1	46 8.0		21 17.5	20 18.2
		13 28.0	38 9.5	35 10.4	35 10.6	53 6.9		42 8.7	42 8.6
		26 13.9	55 6.6	52 7.0	70 5.2	61 6.0		68 5.3	61 5.9
Sales/Working Capital		5.5	6.2	6.3	4.8	3.0		6.8	7.6
		10.2	16.3	10.8	6.8	9.1		19.1	21.8
		34.0	-73.3	40.1	NM	21.6		237.9	-132.0
EBIT/Interest		20.0	27.9	26.4		12.6		15.6	17.2
		(12) 5.3	(35) 6.6	(28) 5.7		(14) 5.3		(122) 5.5	(122) 5.1
		2.4	.9	-.4		2.1		1.2	1.0
Net Profit + Depr., Dep., Amort./Cur. Mat. L/T/D				21.1				13.7	15.9
				(11) 3.0				(23) 7.0	(21) 6.9
				.5				1.7	2.4
Fixed/Worth		.0	.1	.2	.1	.2		.2	.1
		.1	.3	.5	.9	.4		.5	.5
		.4	1.6	13.7	-.7	1.1		4.0	2.7
Debt/Worth		.4	.7	.9	.6	.5		.8	.9
		1.0	1.7	1.9	3.2	1.3		2.7	2.9
		12.1	5.7	729.9	-4.9	1.9		20.1	42.6
% Profit Before Taxes/Tangible Net Worth		369.3	45.9	84.7		34.8		66.7	62.0
		(13) 38.2	(33) 25.2	(28) 35.2		(13) 8.6		(110) 24.5	(110) 27.9
		16.9	9.0	12.8		.0		5.6	6.3
% Profit Before Taxes/Total Assets		43.6	16.0	21.1	13.1	12.6		18.0	17.5
		14.1	12.2	9.3	6.2	5.3		7.7	7.9
		2.5	-.3	-1.4	.9	1.2		.2	-.4
Sales/Net Fixed Assets		UND	67.6	63.2	49.0	69.9		89.0	95.7
		78.5	44.9	23.0	27.2	18.6		36.7	37.4
		25.4	17.6	12.4	11.4	5.6		14.0	17.2
Sales/Total Assets		7.0	5.3	4.0	3.1	2.7		4.8	5.3
		3.7	3.4	2.7	2.3	1.7		3.0	3.5
		2.9	2.8	1.7	1.5	1.2		2.3	2.6
% Depr., Dep., Amort./Sales			.5	.4		.9		.5	.5
		(29) .7	(30) .8	(10) 1.4	(10) 2.1			(109) .8	(109) .8
		1.5	1.6	1.6	2.8			1.4	1.5
% Officers', Directors' Owners' Comp/Sales								1.3	1.8
								(35) 3.2	(34) 3.2
								5.2	6.3
Net Sales ($)	8486M	120969M	835882M	3167926M	2118571M	5081231M		13141263M	11479835M
Total Assets ($)	983M	17891M	198261M	934721M	910277M	2540066M		4634463M	3830512M

M = $ thousand   MM = $ million
See Pages 9 through 22 for Explanation of Ratios and Data

Comparative Historical Data

Current Data Sorted by Sales

			Type of Statement						
34	30	31	Unqualified					3	28
19	11	13	Reviewed		2		1	5	5
16	15	10	Compiled		1		4	4	1
24	19	12	Tax Returns	3	2	1	2	1	3
53	62	58	Other	1	3	3	4	9	38
4/1/07-3/31/08 ALL	4/1/08-3/31/09 ALL	4/1/09-3/31/10 ALL		21 (4/1-9/30/09)			103 (10/1/09-3/31/10)		
				0-1MM	1-3MM	3-5MM	5-10MM	10-25MM	25MM & OVER
146	137	124	NUMBER OF STATEMENTS	4	5	7	11	22	75
%	%	%	ASSETS	%	%	%	%	%	%
16.1	11.6	13.3	Cash & Equivalents				8.6	11.2	15.1
11.1	11.4	12.8	Trade Receivables (net)				18.3	18.2	11.4
38.0	40.8	37.0	Inventory				48.2	34.7	34.4
4.8	4.4	4.4	All Other Current				2.5	4.6	4.8
69.9	68.1	67.5	Total Current				77.7	68.6	65.7
12.8	16.3	16.4	Fixed Assets (net)				11.9	19.2	15.1
9.5	8.0	8.4	Intangibles (net)				6.7	.4	11.5
7.8	7.7	7.7	All Other Non-Current				3.8	11.7	7.6
100.0	100.0	100.0	Total				100.0	100.0	100.0
			LIABILITIES						
11.6	15.4	10.0	Notes Payable-Short Term				22.5	13.2	5.8
3.1	3.0	2.0	Cur. Mat.-L.T.D.				2.3	1.2	2.1
22.5	21.5	21.2	Trade Payables				16.6	17.4	23.6
.3	.3	.3	Income Taxes Payable				.0	.1	.4
12.7	12.5	10.6	All Other Current				3.4	12.4	12.8
50.2	52.6	44.1	Total Current				44.9	44.2	44.7
11.8	11.8	11.8	Long-Term Debt				8.6	9.5	11.6
.6	.4	.8	Deferred Taxes				.0	.2	1.3
6.9	8.4	15.0	All Other Non-Current				1.8	3.6	19.1
30.6	26.7	28.3	Net Worth				44.7	42.5	23.3
100.0	100.0	100.0	Total Liabilities & Net Worth				100.0	100.0	100.0
			INCOME DATA						
100.0	100.0	100.0	Net Sales				100.0	100.0	100.0
43.1	44.2	43.4	Gross Profit				37.6	46.8	44.0
39.5	41.9	39.3	Operating Expenses				31.8	40.8	40.5
3.7	2.4	4.1	Operating Profit				5.9	6.0	3.5
.8	.9	1.0	All Other Expenses (net)				.9	.8	1.3
2.9	1.5	3.1	Profit Before Taxes				4.9	5.2	2.2
			RATIOS						
2.8	2.4	2.8	Current				4.1	3.3	2.6
1.5	1.5	1.7					1.8	1.6	1.7
1.1	.9	1.1					1.3	1.0	1.1
1.2	1.0	1.2	Quick				1.7	1.6	1.2
.4	.4	.6					.5	.4	.6
.1	.1	.2					.1	.2	.2
1 445.0	2 201.3	2 171.4	Sales/Receivables				1 344.4	5 78.3	2 170.0
5 67.6	6 59.6	7 55.9					9 42.4	8 47.9	6 57.4
15 24.4	19 19.3	21 17.4					49 7.4	20 18.1	21 17.6
39 9.3	35 10.4	45 8.0	Cost of Sales/Inventory				30 12.1	22 16.3	50 7.3
78 4.7	79 4.6	82 4.5					122 3.0	68 5.4	81 4.5
116 3.1	140 2.6	124 2.9					167 2.2	112 3.3	124 2.9
18 19.9	20 18.4	19 19.4	Cost of Sales/Payables				4 98.1	14 26.5	21 17.2
34 10.6	37 9.9	35 10.3					47 7.7	28 12.9	38 9.6
63 5.8	60 6.1	53 6.9					58 6.3	47 7.7	61 6.0
6.8	7.0	5.8	Sales/Working Capital				4.0	6.7	5.9
13.7	14.9	11.6					9.2	15.3	11.5
54.0	-77.9	76.7					34.0	NM	96.6
15.9	10.0	20.5	EBIT/Interest				24.8	33.3	25.2
(114) 3.9	(118) 3.5	(102) 5.1					(10) 4.2	(18) 5.4	(60) 5.4
1.4	-1.3	1.1					1.9	.6	.9
21.2	21.4	20.4	Net Profit + Depr., Dep., Amort./Cur. Mat. L/T/D						20.4
(21) 3.8	(27) 6.2	(26) 3.6						(22) 3.4
2.3	1.5	.9							.9
.1	.2	.1	Fixed/Worth				.0	.1	.2
.3	.5	.4					.1	.4	.4
2.0	3.7	1.9					.6	1.2	-1.9
.7	.9	.6	Debt/Worth				.4	.5	.7
1.7	2.2	1.7					1.2	1.7	1.8
19.5	27.6	7.5					7.5	2.9	-20.1
60.9	71.6	55.8	% Profit Before Taxes/Tangible Net Worth				111.3	53.6	57.4
(115) 31.1	(107) 20.5	(98) 24.6					(10) 31.2	(21) 27.2	(56) 24.2
9.4	2.8	10.3					7.8	5.0	10.5
20.5	13.6	17.4	% Profit Before Taxes/Total Assets				43.6	20.7	16.2
8.1	6.5	9.1					13.4	13.0	7.8
1.1	-2.2	1.3					3.4	.3	.3
121.9	84.5	69.0	Sales/Net Fixed Assets				104.1	58.2	65.9
37.6	30.9	28.6					59.1	30.9	26.6
14.9	11.3	13.3					25.4	11.3	12.2
4.5	4.4	4.8	Sales/Total Assets				3.5	4.5	4.7
3.2	3.1	3.1					3.1	3.3	2.8
2.2	2.2	1.9					2.0	2.6	1.7
.4	.6	.5	% Depr., Dep., Amort./Sales						.5
(103) .8	(102) 1.0	(90) .8					(17) .7	(58) 1.1
1.6	1.7	1.6						1.6	1.8
1.2	1.9	1.1	% Officers', Directors' Owners' Comp/Sales						
(37) 3.0	(35) 2.7	(21) 3.0							
7.4	6.2	5.6							
12385152M	11992022M	11333065M	Net Sales ($)	2657M	11848M	29190M	79151M	327189M	10883030M
5015679M	3847815M	4602199M	Total Assets ($)	1418M	3917M	9976M	26283M	110239M	4450366M

© RMA 2010

M = $ thousand   MM = $ million
See Pages 9 through 22 for Explanation of Ratios and Data

Current Data Sorted by Assets   Comparative Historical Data

0-500M	500M-2MM	2-10MM	10-50MM	50-100MM	100-250MM	Type of Statement	4/1/05-3/31/06 ALL	4/1/06-3/31/07 ALL
		1	4	1		Unqualified	4	8
	2	6	6			Reviewed	16	24
2	8	5				Compiled	23	27
8	8	1				Tax Returns	20	27
4	12	18	5			Other	37	27
	20 (4/1-9/30/09)		71 (10/1/09-3/31/10)					
14	30	31	15	1		**NUMBER OF STATEMENTS**	100	113
%	%	%	%	%	%	**ASSETS**	%	%
20.0	8.6	14.0	12.6			Cash & Equivalents	10.3	9.4
1.7	10.4	8.0	15.7			Trade Receivables (net)	7.2	6.5
22.6	13.9	15.0	10.1			Inventory	15.9	16.2
4.8	.6	2.1	1.7			All Other Current	2.3	2.1
49.0	33.5	39.1	40.0			Total Current	35.7	34.3
43.6	49.7	43.5	41.1			Fixed Assets (net)	49.9	50.8
6.9	11.1	9.4	12.4			Intangibles (net)	6.8	7.8
.6	5.7	8.0	6.6			All Other Non-Current	7.7	7.2
100.0	100.0	100.0	100.0			Total	100.0	100.0
						LIABILITIES		
14.5	5.4	4.8	6.7			Notes Payable-Short Term	9.1	7.4
6.2	7.5	9.8	10.7			Cur. Mat.-L.T.D.	7.5	9.5
5.7	13.4	11.9	12.7			Trade Payables	15.1	13.2
.1	.0	.3	.1			Income Taxes Payable	.1	.1
9.2	5.6	6.9	9.9			All Other Current	14.8	7.7
35.6	31.9	33.8	40.1			Total Current	46.6	37.9
37.8	32.0	28.5	22.2			Long-Term Debt	28.1	31.7
.0	.4	.0	1.0			Deferred Taxes	.3	.3
11.9	8.5	10.3	6.7			All Other Non-Current	10.0	9.3
14.7	27.2	27.5	30.1			Net Worth	15.0	20.9
100.0	100.0	100.0	100.0			Total Liabilities & Net Worth	100.0	100.0
						INCOME DATA		
100.0	100.0	100.0	100.0			Net Sales	100.0	100.0
38.7	43.6	50.1	47.0			Gross Profit	46.8	46.7
37.6	37.3	46.3	44.7			Operating Expenses	44.8	43.0
1.2	6.3	3.9	2.3			Operating Profit	2.0	3.8
.7	1.0	.4	.8			All Other Expenses (net)	.3	1.3
.5	5.3	3.4	1.6			Profit Before Taxes	1.7	2.4
						RATIOS		
3.0	1.8	2.4	1.2				1.8	1.5
1.3	1.0	1.2	1.0			Current	.8	.8
.6	.6	.7	.7				.5	.5
1.2	1.4	1.3	.8				.7	.7
.5	.5	(30) .5	.7			Quick	.4	.4
.2	.2	.3	.4				.1	.2
0 UND	0 UND	2 218.6	3 117.2				1 440.4	0 768.5
0 UND	3 135.3	4 81.4	12 29.5			Sales/Receivables	4 84.5	5 71.0
2 169.5	7 50.1	15 24.0	29 12.8				13 28.2	14 26.6
5 77.4	9 40.7	22 16.4	14 26.0				19 19.3	19 19.1
41 9.0	32 11.4	34 10.7	30 12.0			Cost of Sales/Inventory	29 12.4	31 11.7
54 6.7	48 7.6	49 7.4	40 9.2				44 8.3	46 8.0
0 UND	2 151.8	11 32.3	13 27.4				8 46.5	9 42.0
11 31.8	16 22.9	23 16.2	32 11.5			Cost of Sales/Payables	27 13.5	26 14.1
18 20.8	39 9.4	42 8.7	44 8.4				45 8.2	42 8.8
6.9	17.2	13.1	45.7				23.7	23.6
UND	313.5	53.2	-59.0			Sales/Working Capital	-54.7	-105.9
-34.0	-17.5	-17.4	-21.6				-11.5	-16.5
12.6	6.0	4.9	7.1				4.2	3.9
(12) 5.4	(28) 2.3	(29) 2.1	(14) 2.7			EBIT/Interest	(90) 1.3	(107) 1.9
-.6	.4	.7	1.6				.0	.7
						Net Profit + Depr., Dep.,	2.6	2.6
						Amort./Cur. Mat. L/T/D	(12) 1.8	(13) 2.2
							.8	1.1
.7	1.0	1.3	1.2				1.0	1.3
5.4	2.3	3.9	2.4			Fixed/Worth	3.2	3.0
-2.8	-10.7	-22.3	58.9				-6.2	-13.9
.6	1.1	2.0	1.3				1.3	1.3
6.7	3.3	6.5	3.9			Debt/Worth	4.5	3.3
-5.1	-20.3	-51.9	262.4				-9.3	-27.6
	70.9	78.7	102.0			% Profit Before Taxes/Tangible	38.7	36.4
	(22) 12.1	(22) 26.1	(13) 47.9			Net Worth	(72) 12.4	(82) 12.6
	-1.0	4.1	10.6				-1.8	-6.6
18.2	10.0	13.0	13.3			% Profit Before Taxes/Total	9.8	10.6
.7	3.3	4.5	3.8			Assets	1.9	4.3
-9.8	-1.2	-.2	2.5				-3.0	-1.4
20.3	11.0	12.8	11.5				10.9	9.6
11.0	5.2	6.7	6.4			Sales/Net Fixed Assets	6.5	6.5
5.5	2.1	3.5	4.1				3.8	4.3
5.5	4.2	3.3	3.7				4.3	4.1
3.9	2.5	2.9	2.9			Sales/Total Assets	3.1	3.0
2.4	1.3	1.7	2.0				2.1	2.2
	3.5	3.0	3.0				3.2	3.1
	(22) 5.5	(23) 4.5	4.3			% Depr., Dep., Amort./Sales	(91) 3.8	(104) 4.3
	7.3	5.7	6.6				5.6	6.7
	1.9					% Officers', Directors'	2.1	1.5
	(13) 3.4					Owners' Comp/Sales	(47) 4.1	(46) 3.2
	6.3						7.0	5.2
15633M	100068M	446738M	722955M	103803M		Net Sales ($)	1152762M	1519696M
3526M	32067M	137483M	249224M	71498M		Total Assets ($)	586358M	535289M

© RMA 2010

M = $ thousand   MM = $ million
See Pages 9 through 22 for Explanation of Ratios and Data

Comparative Historical Data   Current Data Sorted by Sales

Type of Statement	4/1/07-3/31/08 ALL	4/1/08-3/31/09 ALL	4/1/09-3/31/10 ALL	0-1MM	1-3MM	3-5MM	5-10MM	10-25MM	25MM & OVER
Unqualified	4	6	6				1		5
Reviewed	17	24	14		1			6	7
Compiled	17	23	15		4	6	2	3	
Tax Returns	17	17	17	6	6	4	1		
Other	31	32	39	5	13	1	8	7	5

Current data periods: 20 (4/1-9/30/09) ; 71 (10/1/09-3/31/10)

Item	07-08 ALL	08-09 ALL	09-10 ALL	0-1MM	1-3MM	3-5MM	5-10MM	10-25MM	25MM & OVER
NUMBER OF STATEMENTS	86	102	91	11	24	11	12	16	17
ASSETS	%	%	%	%	%	%	%	%	%
Cash & Equivalents	9.5	9.1	12.8	22.7	11.5	9.5	11.7	9.7	14.1
Trade Receivables (net)	6.5	8.6	9.0	.0	7.2	4.6	10.2	11.4	17.2
Inventory	15.6	17.7	14.9	16.9	13.2	13.3	14.9	18.7	13.2
All Other Current	2.7	2.4	1.9	4.1	.8	2.2	.7	1.3	3.5
Total Current	34.4	37.9	38.6	43.7	32.7	29.6	37.5	41.2	48.0
Fixed Assets (net)	51.9	47.8	45.3	40.0	49.9	61.0	46.5	37.1	39.1
Intangibles (net)	8.3	6.7	10.1	14.4	8.1	6.1	11.6	12.7	9.1
All Other Non-Current	5.4	7.6	6.0	2.0	9.3	3.4	4.4	9.0	3.8
Total	100.0	100.0	100.0	100.0	100.0	100.0	100.0	100.0	100.0
LIABILITIES									
Notes Payable-Short Term	8.2	7.9	7.2	9.3	8.5	6.0	4.5	6.7	7.1
Cur. Mat.-L.T.D.	7.3	8.3	8.5	3.4	5.1	11.7	11.3	8.8	12.3
Trade Payables	14.1	15.5	11.5	2.2	10.5	12.3	7.9	15.4	17.1
Income Taxes Payable	.1	.1	.1	.0	.0	.0	.0	.7	.1
All Other Current	8.8	10.2	7.4	9.9	3.8	11.6	4.9	4.8	12.3
Total Current	38.5	42.1	34.7	24.7	28.0	41.7	28.5	36.4	48.9
Long-Term Debt	29.4	30.0	29.7	47.9	32.4	22.2	37.4	26.1	17.0
Deferred Taxes	.4	.5	.3	.0	.0	1.1	.1	.0	.9
All Other Non-Current	10.5	8.9	10.6	11.2	8.5	10.7	7.6	10.7	15.0
Net Worth	21.1	18.6	24.7	16.2	31.1	24.3	26.4	26.8	18.2
Total Liabilities & Net Worth	100.0	100.0	100.0	100.0	100.0	100.0	100.0	100.0	100.0
INCOME DATA									
Net Sales	100.0	100.0	100.0	100.0	100.0	100.0	100.0	100.0	100.0
Gross Profit	46.8	43.0	45.4	48.3	48.7	36.7	51.1	45.1	40.8
Operating Expenses	45.0	41.5	41.4	39.7	42.0	35.0	47.8	43.2	39.4
Operating Profit	1.8	1.5	4.0	8.5	6.7	1.7	3.3	1.8	1.4
All Other Expenses (net)	1.1	.7	.8	1.1	1.7	.3	.1	.6	.3
Profit Before Taxes	.7	.8	3.2	7.4	5.0	1.5	3.2	1.2	1.1
RATIOS									
Current	1.3	1.5	1.8	4.4	2.8	1.1	2.3	2.7	1.3
	.9	1.0	1.1	1.7	1.1	.7	1.2	1.0	1.1
	.6	.6	.6	.6	.5	.4	.8	.7	.6
Quick	.6	.8	1.2	1.8	1.6	.5	1.3	1.5	.8
	.4	.4	.5 (90)	.8	.5	.4	.8	.5 (15)	.7
	.2	.2	.2	.3	.1	.2	.4	.4	.4
Sales/Receivables	1 391.2	2 231.5	0 999.8	0 UND	0 UND	2 235.7	2 191.1	2 159.3	7 54.3
	5 79.9	6 62.1	3 106.3	0 UND	1 277.5	3 133.3	4 89.0	5 71.7	14 26.6
	11 32.1	14 26.4	12 30.0	0 UND	7 52.7	5 66.9	25 14.5	11 34.4	22 16.4
Cost of Sales/Inventory	22 16.5	17 21.7	14 25.9	0 UND	19 19.5	6 61.4	23 15.6	24 15.1	13 27.9
	32 11.3	31 11.6	32 11.3	43 8.5	37 9.8	22 16.5	35 10.4	39 9.5	25 14.7
	43 8.5	45 8.0	47 7.8	75 4.8	50 7.3	36 10.1	59 6.1	52 7.0	33 11.0
Cost of Sales/Payables	13 27.1	11 33.5	7 53.7	0 UND	1 251.5	12 30.6	11 33.8	12 30.7	12 29.3
	29 12.7	24 15.1	17 21.3	0 UND	15 24.5	13 29.0	23 16.0	32 11.5	24 15.2
	44 8.2	42 8.6	37 9.9	19 19.5	63 5.8	30 12.1	27 13.5	61 6.0	42 8.6
Sales/Working Capital	36.4	26.8	16.5	3.9	16.7	129.2	13.3	12.6	35.8
	-73.1	-139.7	133.0	15.6	157.2	-28.8	39.8	NM	79.6
	-18.9	-15.3	-20.7	-25.6	-19.9	-17.1	NM	-21.8	-16.2
EBIT/Interest	4.1	3.6	6.1		9.5	4.5	4.8	2.6	6.3
	1.6 (82)	1.6 (99)	2.3 (84)	3.9 (23)	1.0	2.1 (10)	1.7 (15)	2.9 (16)	
	.5	.5	.8	-.4	-1.9	1.2	1.2	1.1	
Net Profit + Depr., Dep., Amort./Cur. Mat. L/T/D	3.5	5.2	2.7						
	1.9 (12)	2.0 (18)	2.1 (13)						
	1.3	1.2	1.4						
Fixed/Worth	1.2	1.3	1.0	.6	.9	1.6	1.2	1.9	1.3
	2.9	2.6	2.8	-6.6	1.9	3.9	3.4	5.6	2.4
	-63.5	-11.3	-13.3	-1.0	8.0	-13.0	-19.9	-9.3	141.1
Debt/Worth	1.5	1.5	1.3	.6	.8	1.5	2.0	2.8	2.3
	4.3	4.4	4.4	-17.6	3.0	3.2	7.0	13.9	3.9
	-90.8	-15.9	-24.2	-2.4	39.7	-24.2	-28.2	-18.6	315.3
% Profit Before Taxes/Tangible Net Worth	37.0	32.9	71.5		77.6			122.5	74.1
	16.8 (64)	16.4 (70)	19.0 (66)		25.9 (20)			16.8 (11)	47.7 (14)
	-1.9	-4.7	.9		-2.2			5.1	10.6
% Profit Before Taxes/Total Assets	9.6	8.5	11.9	20.7	15.6	6.0	18.9	5.2	13.1
	2.2	2.7	3.6	3.3	5.5	.1	4.1	2.3	4.6
	-1.5	-3.0	-.8	-10.3	-3.0	-3.3	.2	1.0	.9
Sales/Net Fixed Assets	8.9	13.5	12.4	15.2	10.8	11.1	11.7	15.1	16.2
	6.1	6.9	6.4	10.6	4.9	6.5	6.2	7.0	7.4
	3.6	5.0	3.6	2.7	1.9	4.3	3.9	3.7	5.7
Sales/Total Assets	3.9	5.0	4.1	4.3	2.8	5.5	3.2	4.8	5.4
	2.9	3.3	2.8	2.3	2.0	4.1	3.1	2.6	3.4
	2.1	2.4	1.7	.8	1.2	2.7	2.0	1.6	2.2
% Depr., Dep., Amort./Sales	3.3	2.9	3.0		3.7			3.0	2.7
	4.3 (79)	4.3 (92)	5.0 (68)		7.1 (17)			5.7 (15)	3.4 (15)
	6.5	5.7	6.6		10.6			6.4	5.1
% Officers', Directors' Owners' Comp/Sales	1.3	1.2	1.5						
	2.8 (34)	2.6 (43)	3.2 (31)						
	6.2	4.1	5.8						
Net Sales ($)	1703879M	1921358M	1389197M	5317M	43062M	43306M	93028M	246350M	958134M
Total Assets ($)	677679M	668637M	493798M	4576M	29522M	12353M	35106M	109165M	303076M

© RMA 2010
M = $ thousand MM = $ million
See Pages 9 through 22 for Explanation of Ratios and Data

Current Data Sorted by Assets   Comparative Historical Data

Type of Statement	0-500M	500M-2MM	2-10MM	10-50MM	50-100MM	100-250MM	4/1/05-3/31/06 ALL	4/1/06-3/31/07 ALL
Unqualified	1		4	16	3	2	31	30
Reviewed	2	12	57	25	1		89	106
Compiled	7	29	22	2		2	61	70
Tax Returns	9	20	5				31	36
Other	2	11	15	17	5	4	63	52
	134 (4/1-9/30/09)			139 (10/1/09-3/31/10)				
NUMBER OF STATEMENTS	21	72	103	60	9	8	275	294
	%	%	%	%	%	%	%	%
ASSETS								
Cash & Equivalents	27.6	19.3	18.2	15.2			16.5	14.9
Trade Receivables (net)	24.1	24.7	27.5	21.6			29.5	27.3
Inventory	13.3	10.5	10.3	11.1			11.1	12.4
All Other Current	2.0	4.6	3.1	3.5			2.2	2.2
Total Current	67.0	59.2	59.1	51.3			59.3	56.8
Fixed Assets (net)	22.0	22.1	24.5	29.6			26.4	25.7
Intangibles (net)	6.2	8.5	6.9	10.1			6.6	10.3
All Other Non-Current	4.8	10.3	9.6	9.0			7.7	7.2
Total	100.0	100.0	100.0	100.0			100.0	100.0
LIABILITIES								
Notes Payable-Short Term	11.6	13.0	8.7	7.7			10.7	9.8
Cur. Mat.-L.T.D.	6.1	6.3	3.6	2.6			4.6	4.6
Trade Payables	17.5	20.1	17.0	18.4			18.2	18.2
Income Taxes Payable	.2	.1	.3	.4			.2	.2
All Other Current	28.7	19.7	20.0	19.9			17.5	22.8
Total Current	64.0	59.2	49.6	49.1			51.2	55.6
Long-Term Debt	20.8	13.8	12.7	17.9			15.7	17.0
Deferred Taxes	.0	.1	.6	.6			.5	.4
All Other Non-Current	9.9	8.5	5.6	4.7			6.3	5.5
Net Worth	5.3	18.4	31.5	27.7			26.4	21.6
Total Liabilties & Net Worth	100.0	100.0	100.0	100.0			100.0	100.0
INCOME DATA								
Net Sales	100.0	100.0	100.0	100.0			100.0	100.0
Gross Profit	24.6	20.5	21.0	16.5			17.8	17.1
Operating Expenses	20.8	19.4	18.7	14.2			16.5	15.7
Operating Profit	3.8	1.0	2.3	2.2			1.3	1.4
All Other Expenses (net)	.3	.0	.0	.2			.1	.2
Profit Before Taxes	3.5	1.0	2.2	2.1			1.2	1.1
RATIOS								
Current	2.4	1.8	1.7	1.3			1.6	1.4
	1.4	1.0	1.2	1.0			1.1	1.0
	.6	.7	.9	.8			.9	.8
Quick	1.7	1.3	1.4	1.1			1.2	1.1
	.9	.8	.9	.7			.9	.7
	.5	.5	.6	.5			.6	.5
Sales/Receivables	1 407.6	6 57.2	11 32.7	8 45.1			13 28.7	10 35.4
	10 37.3	15 23.7	18 20.2	14 26.1			24 15.5	19 19.4
	20 18.4	27 13.3	30 12.0	27 13.7			32 11.4	28 13.0
Cost of Sales/Inventory	2 224.5	2 182.9	5 73.5	5 75.0			4 89.4	4 88.4
	6 60.0	7 54.8	10 37.1	9 38.5			8 44.8	8 44.0
	13 28.9	15 24.7	17 22.0	15 24.9			15 24.1	15 24.4
Cost of Sales/Payables	4 87.2	6 58.7	9 39.5	10 37.2			9 40.6	8 47.7
	9 39.5	16 22.7	16 23.4	13 28.7			15 24.8	13 27.4
	21 17.6	26 13.9	22 16.2	20 18.0			23 15.9	19 19.0
Sales/Working Capital	16.7	21.1	19.4	23.9			19.6	26.9
	30.4	253.8	43.6	999.8			89.2	564.1
	-31.0	-27.9	-118.6	-35.0			-56.8	-35.8
EBIT/Interest	34.0	13.2	11.3	9.1			6.7	5.2
	(19) 8.6	(62) 3.6	(93) 3.9	(56) 3.7			(260) 2.4	(280) 2.1
	2.0	-.8	1.8	1.7			1.1	.8
Net Profit + Depr., Dep., Amort./Cur. Mat. L/T/D			5.9	6.8			3.6	3.7
		(40) 2.6	(26) 3.1				(93) 1.9	(80) 2.0
			1.4	1.3			1.0	1.2
Fixed/Worth	.3	.4	.3	.6			.5	.5
	.8	1.6	.9	1.6			1.2	1.9
	-1.9	-2.0	4.1	16.0			5.8	-7.0
Debt/Worth	.8	1.3	1.1	1.7			1.4	1.8
	6.7	5.7	2.3	3.3			3.5	5.3
	-4.6	-9.2	11.8	226.6			19.8	-19.9
% Profit Before Taxes/Tangible Net Worth	99.6	73.1	50.2	41.2			45.1	35.2
	(12) 47.3	(50) 25.9	(82) 20.4	(46) 21.0			(221) 15.1	(204) 13.7
	21.3	-1.8	6.7	9.4			2.9	2.3
% Profit Before Taxes/Total Assets	32.1	13.9	13.2	12.6			8.2	7.6
	13.0	6.4	5.7	5.2			3.2	2.9
	2.9	-4.6	1.7	2.4			.1	-.3
Sales/Net Fixed Assets	81.6	67.3	39.1	64.8			44.1	51.0
	41.2	31.4	18.3	17.5			20.2	26.0
	21.7	15.5	10.9	9.6			10.8	11.6
Sales/Total Assets	9.3	6.7	5.4	6.8			6.5	6.9
	6.6	4.5	4.0	4.4			4.4	4.8
	4.5	3.6	3.1	3.1			3.1	3.3
% Depr., Dep., Amort./Sales	.5	.6	.7	.7			.7	.6
	(17) .7	(55) 1.3	(96) 1.2	(50) 1.3			(254) 1.1	(254) 1.1
	1.5	1.9	1.9	1.9			1.9	1.8
% Officers', Directors' Owners' Comp/Sales	2.3	1.4	1.3	.5			.9	.7
	(16) 3.7	(48) 2.3	(60) 1.8	(19) 1.2			(135) 1.6	(146) 1.7
	8.0	4.5	3.4	2.1			3.2	3.1
Net Sales ($)	57516M	470910M	2051298M	6309995M	2895800M	6012895M	12785794M	15926861M
Total Assets ($)	7301M	86814M	458821M	1250959M	673199M	1075711M	2933965M	3203639M

© RMA 2010

M = $ thousand   MM = $ million
See Pages 9 through 22 for Explanation of Ratios and Data

Comparative Historical Data   **Current Data Sorted by Sales**

4/1/07-3/31/08 ALL	4/1/08-3/31/09 ALL	4/1/09-3/31/10 ALL	Type of Statement	0-1MM	1-3MM	3-5MM	5-10MM	10-25MM	25MM & OVER
29	28	26	Unqualified		1			3	22
117	93	97	Reviewed		1	9	12	40	35
73	63	60	Compiled	1	5	13	19	16	6
37	31	36	Tax Returns		12	11	8	8	3
58	46	54	Other	1	1	1	8	16	27
					134 (4/1-9/30/09)			139 (10/1/09-3/31/10)	
314	261	273	**NUMBER OF STATEMENTS**	2	20	34	47	77	93
%	%	%	**ASSETS**	%	%	%	%	%	%
13.9	18.0	18.0	Cash & Equivalents		23.5	20.6	20.5	17.4	15.2
31.1	27.8	24.8	Trade Receivables (net)		18.5	27.7	24.1	28.0	22.9
11.3	10.3	10.9	Inventory		16.9	7.7	10.7	10.5	11.3
2.6	2.8	3.6	All Other Current		2.9	5.2	3.7	2.7	3.8
58.9	58.8	57.3	Total Current		61.8	61.2	58.9	58.6	53.2
25.8	24.4	25.6	Fixed Assets (net)		22.0	21.8	22.2	23.4	31.1
8.0	8.4	7.8	Intangibles (net)		9.0	8.9	8.8	7.6	7.0
7.3	8.4	9.2	All Other Non-Current		7.3	8.0	10.0	10.3	8.7
100.0	100.0	100.0	Total		100.0	100.0	100.0	100.0	100.0
			LIABILITIES						
13.2	13.3	9.8	Notes Payable-Short Term		14.6	10.4	11.5	10.6	7.3
4.0	3.4	4.2	Cur. Mat.-L.T.D.		11.3	7.3	3.8	3.5	2.4
19.0	16.9	17.8	Trade Payables		17.9	19.5	18.0	15.2	19.6
.2	.3	.2	Income Taxes Payable		.2	.1	.1	.3	.3
20.7	17.5	20.2	All Other Current		17.2	21.6	26.3	22.2	16.0
57.1	51.4	52.3	Total Current		61.1	59.0	59.7	51.8	45.6
15.6	15.3	15.1	Long-Term Debt		22.7	16.1	16.5	11.4	15.6
.4	.4	.5	Deferred Taxes		.1	.1	.2	.6	.8
5.1	7.9	6.9	All Other Non-Current		11.7	7.2	10.4	4.8	5.8
21.8	24.9	25.2	Net Worth		4.5	17.6	13.1	31.4	32.2
100.0	100.0	100.0	Total Liabilties & Net Worth		100.0	100.0	100.0	100.0	100.0
			INCOME DATA						
100.0	100.0	100.0	Net Sales		100.0	100.0	100.0	100.0	100.0
16.5	14.1	19.8	Gross Profit		25.7	22.1	23.0	20.4	15.0
15.4	13.2	17.8	Operating Expenses		25.2	19.7	20.9	18.4	13.1
1.1	.9	2.1	Operating Profit		.5	2.4	2.1	2.1	1.9
.2	.0	.1	All Other Expenses (net)		.3	.2	.1	.1	.0
.9	.9	2.0	Profit Before Taxes		.2	2.2	2.0	2.0	1.9
			RATIOS						
1.4 1.0 .8	1.6 1.1 .8	1.7 1.1 .8	Current		2.0 1.5 .7	1.5 1.0 .8	1.5 1.0 .7	1.7 1.2 .9	1.6 1.2 .9
1.1 .8 .5	1.3 .9 .6	1.3 .8 .5	Quick		1.7 .8 .5	1.4 .9 .4	1.3 .7 .4	1.4 .9 .6	1.1 .8 .5
11 31.7 20 18.2 33 11.0	9 39.5 16 22.6 26 13.9	8 43.4 16 23.0 28 12.9	Sales/Receivables		7 54.7 16 22.6 22 16.7	8 45.6 15 23.7 32 11.4	5 67.0 16 23.2 30 12.0	13 27.8 21 17.2 31 11.8	7 51.9 14 27.0 22 16.3
4 103.0 9 42.5 14 25.6	2 161.4 6 60.4 12 29.4	4 102.2 8 43.1 16 23.3	Cost of Sales/Inventory		4 81.7 12 29.9 35 10.3	1 288.3 6 63.5 15 23.6	3 109.2 9 42.3 17 21.8	4 92.9 10 38.2 16 22.8	5 78.1 8 48.1 14 25.4
9 42.0 14 26.7 21 17.4	7 52.3 11 34.4 16 23.4	8 43.0 14 26.2 24 15.3	Cost of Sales/Payables		7 55.3 18 20.1 29 12.6	6 56.4 14 26.6 27 13.4	11 33.4 18 20.5 26 14.2	8 47.6 13 27.8 22 16.3	9 38.7 13 27.8 21 17.7
22.8 214.7 -38.6	22.4 124.6 -63.6	19.7 72.1 -59.1	Sales/Working Capital		11.9 19.6 -20.7	21.3 NM -29.2	20.5 304.0 -26.0	19.7 46.8 -93.2	20.4 72.1 -115.9
5.1 (292) 2.2 .9	5.7 (246) 2.2 1.1	12.3 (247) 3.9 1.5	EBIT/Interest		14.0 (19) 2.1 -1.7	12.1 (29) 3.9 .6	16.7 (38) 4.4 .6	10.1 (73) 3.4 1.2	10.7 (86) 4.4 2.3
3.2 (99) 2.0 1.2	3.8 (85) 2.1 1.1	6.8 (82) 2.8 1.3	Net Profit + Depr., Dep., Amort./Cur. Mat. L/T/D					6.5 (29) 2.4 1.1	12.4 (41) 3.9 1.7
.6 1.5 -7.1	.5 1.2 9.5	.4 1.1 17.4	Fixed/Worth		.4 .9 -1.9	.2 1.2 -7.2	.5 2.1 -.6	.4 .8 4.2	.6 1.2 4.5
1.6 4.6 -27.2	1.4 3.8 48.5	1.2 3.2 324.7	Debt/Worth		1.1 4.4 -6.9	1.6 7.5 -13.0	1.5 6.0 -4.0	1.0 2.6 16.0	1.2 2.8 8.5
31.2 (226) 14.6 2.6	37.7 (199) 16.8 4.1	55.3 (206) 21.7 8.2	% Profit Before Taxes/Tangible Net Worth		47.5 (12) 16.6 -21.6	74.3 (23) 37.2 12.0	76.8 (28) 30.4 9.8	44.2 (63) 19.7 4.0	52.3 (78) 21.1 10.3
7.8 3.2 .0	8.3 3.3 .5	13.8 5.9 1.5	% Profit Before Taxes/Total Assets		15.3 4.0 -4.6	16.7 8.1 1.1	17.6 6.6 -1.1	13.1 4.8 .5	13.1 5.9 3.0
52.5 22.5 12.2	62.8 27.3 15.3	54.7 19.9 11.7	Sales/Net Fixed Assets		52.0 26.8 15.8	117.6 30.7 11.7	43.4 23.5 15.9	42.7 18.7 11.3	64.2 16.8 10.4
6.8 4.7 3.4	7.9 5.4 3.8	6.5 4.3 3.2	Sales/Total Assets		6.2 4.3 2.7	7.7 4.2 3.1	5.4 4.2 3.1	5.6 4.1 3.1	7.1 5.3 3.6
.6 (281) 1.1 1.7	.5 (233) .9 1.5	.6 (234) 1.2 1.9	% Depr., Dep., Amort./Sales		.7 (17) 1.3 3.0	.8 (25) 1.5 3.1	.7 (38) 1.3 1.8	.7 (72) 1.2 1.9	.6 (80) 1.0 1.6
.9 (154) 1.7 3.0	.7 (139) 1.3 2.7	1.2 (145) 2.0 4.0	% Officers', Directors' Owners' Comp/Sales		2.3 (14) 3.6 6.9	2.1 (27) 3.4 5.3	1.2 (28) 2.0 4.0	1.2 (47) 1.7 2.7	.4 (28) 1.1 2.1
19437758M 3997671M	19228617M 3468379M	17798414M 3552805M	Net Sales ($) Total Assets ($)	1222M 480M	40717M 11406M	143621M 36002M	345067M 82914M	1233118M 359117M	16034669M 3062886M

© RMA 2010

M = $ thousand   MM = $ million
See Pages 9 through 22 for Explanation of Ratios and Data

Current Data Sorted by Assets   Comparative Historical Data

Type of Statement	0-500M	500M-2MM	2-10MM	10-50MM	50-100MM	100-250MM		4/1/05-3/31/06 ALL	4/1/06-3/31/07 ALL
Unqualified		1		8	6			18	18
Reviewed		7	5	6				19	26
Compiled		5	6	1	1			27	24
Tax Returns	8	14	5					11	23
Other	2	7	12	8	2			22	18
		32 (4/1-9/30/09)		72 (10/1/09-3/31/10)					
NUMBER OF STATEMENTS	10	34	28	23	9			97	109
	%	%	%	%	%	%		%	%
ASSETS									
Cash & Equivalents	13.4	12.2	16.0	6.4				9.7	9.0
Trade Receivables (net)	19.4	21.2	20.7	17.8				22.8	23.5
Inventory	19.4	9.3	11.7	7.8				12.4	12.5
All Other Current	7.5	2.3	5.0	2.9				5.3	2.9
Total Current	59.7	45.1	53.5	34.8				50.2	47.9
Fixed Assets (net)	28.8	44.4	36.5	42.1			D	38.0	41.2
Intangibles (net)	6.2	3.1	3.6	17.2			A	5.6	5.3
All Other Non-Current	5.3	7.4	6.4	5.9			T	6.1	5.7
Total	100.0	100.0	100.0	100.0			A	100.0	100.0
LIABILITIES									
Notes Payable-Short Term	4.9	7.8	5.3	6.1			N	7.3	8.7
Cur. Mat.-L.T.D.	2.9	13.3	3.7	4.9			O	4.5	5.0
Trade Payables	17.3	15.6	12.4	10.5			T	17.3	18.5
Income Taxes Payable	.0	.0	.2	.3				.4	.3
All Other Current	11.3	12.8	13.1	10.6			A	9.8	8.9
Total Current	36.4	49.6	34.7	32.4			V	39.3	41.3
Long-Term Debt	27.1	33.5	15.2	22.6			A	20.9	24.6
Deferred Taxes	.0	.1	.9	2.7			I	1.0	.9
All Other Non-Current	.9	3.0	3.8	3.4			L	8.4	5.4
Net Worth	35.7	13.8	45.2	38.9			A	30.3	27.8
Total Liabilities & Net Worth	100.0	100.0	100.0	100.0			B	100.0	100.0
INCOME DATA							L		
Net Sales	100.0	100.0	100.0	100.0			E	100.0	100.0
Gross Profit	31.3	34.5	30.6	36.7				31.5	28.8
Operating Expenses	24.5	29.3	26.6	31.5				29.0	26.0
Operating Profit	6.9	5.2	4.0	5.1				2.5	2.8
All Other Expenses (net)	-.6	.3	.3	1.2				.3	.8
Profit Before Taxes	7.5	4.9	3.6	3.9				2.2	2.0
RATIOS									
Current	5.4	2.0	2.6	1.8				2.1	2.0
	2.1	1.1	1.3	1.3				1.3	1.3
	.9	.5	1.1	.7				.9	.8
Quick	3.9	1.8	1.9	1.6				1.3	1.4
	1.5	.7	1.0	.8				.8	.9
	.3	.4	.5	.3				.5	.6
Sales/Receivables	0 UND	17 21.0	13 28.6	12 30.2				16 22.3	16 22.4
	15 23.9	27 13.5	25 14.5	21 17.0				28 12.9	26 14.3
	42 8.8	35 10.3	33 10.9	37 10.0				44 8.4	41 8.9
Cost of Sales/Inventory	12 30.5	8 47.7	7 49.3	10 36.3				10 36.2	7 51.2
	27 13.5	15 24.0	15 24.8	17 20.9				21 17.7	16 23.1
	74 5.0	26 14.0	36 10.0	43 8.5				39 9.4	31 11.9
Cost of Sales/Payables	0 UND	4 86.5	12 31.7	11 32.7				15 24.9	12 31.5
	34 10.6	17 20.9	17 21.8	21 17.2				27 13.4	25 14.8
	42 8.7	53 6.8	32 11.4	29 12.5				43 8.5	42 8.7
Sales/Working Capital	5.6	8.9	9.3	9.3				10.2	10.1
	11.9	99.3	28.5	45.5				24.7	43.4
	-42.6	-9.0	93.8	-20.8				-71.1	-49.6
EBIT/Interest		18.5	30.3	15.3				6.9	7.1
		(32) 2.7	(26) 5.3	(20) 4.0				(89) 2.6	(104) 2.5
		.8	1.2	1.6				1.5	.9
Net Profit + Depr., Dep., Amort./Cur. Mat. L/T/D								4.1	6.0
								(33) 2.0	(24) 1.9
								1.2	1.0
Fixed/Worth	.0	.9	.4	.8				.5	.7
	.6	2.0	.8	2.0				1.6	1.9
	NM	-2.4	2.0	5.4				4.3	6.5
Debt/Worth	.5	.8	.7	1.0				1.2	1.1
	1.8	4.5	1.2	2.3				2.5	2.6
	NM	-5.5	2.4	8.1				9.4	12.8
% Profit Before Taxes/Tangible Net Worth		68.7	55.0	80.4				33.0	32.2
		(22) 45.5	(27) 20.3	(19) 20.9				(80) 15.5	(88) 16.0
		1.8	1.4	14.7				4.0	2.4
% Profit Before Taxes/Total Assets	22.0	23.0	17.0	16.8				9.4	11.5
	9.9	6.3	5.4	5.2				4.0	3.4
	2.9	-.8	1.0	1.7				.5	-.9
Sales/Net Fixed Assets	UND	19.3	21.7	10.7				18.0	20.0
	13.1	8.4	10.6	5.2				6.7	5.8
	4.2	2.5	3.6	3.3				3.8	3.2
Sales/Total Assets	4.7	4.2	4.2	3.3				3.5	4.1
	2.7	2.6	2.9	2.2				2.5	2.5
	1.9	1.4	2.1	1.1				1.7	1.7
% Depr., Dep., Amort./Sales		1.3	2.1	2.0				1.9	1.6
		(26) 3.1	(25) 3.2	(21) 3.2				(90) 3.5	(99) 3.2
		6.7	6.0	5.8				4.5	4.6
% Officers', Directors' Owners' Comp/Sales		1.9	1.2					1.1	1.3
		(10) 3.2	(14) 3.0					(40) 2.6	(45) 2.8
		6.8	6.7					4.3	4.4
Net Sales ($)	12524M	105652M	491090M	1579480M	1854840M			2494275M	3747511M
Total Assets ($)	3416M	37457M	139180M	522818M	621920M			1037985M	1602474M

© RMA 2010

M = $ thousand   MM = $ million
See Pages 9 through 22 for Explanation of Ratios and Data

Comparative Historical Data | Current Data Sorted by Sales

4/1/07-3/31/08 ALL	4/1/08-3/31/09 ALL	4/1/09-3/31/10 ALL	Type of Statement	0-1MM	1-3MM	3-5MM	5-10MM	10-25MM	25MM & OVER
18	22	15	Unqualified		1			3	11
17	17	18	Reviewed		3	2	4	5	4
18	22	13	Compiled		2	2	3	2	4
18	22	27	Tax Returns	5	12	5	3	1	1
35	23	31	Other	3	4	2	3	10	9
					32 (4/1-9/30/09)		72 (10/1/09-3/31/10)		
106	**106**	**104**	**NUMBER OF STATEMENTS**	**8**	**22**	**11**	**13**	**21**	**29**
%	%	%	**ASSETS**	%	%	%	%	%	%
8.1	11.0	11.6	Cash & Equivalents		13.3	17.1	9.4	12.5	9.2
24.5	23.1	20.4	Trade Receivables (net)		15.2	25.3	19.3	17.6	25.0
12.0	10.2	10.7	Inventory		11.8	8.0	13.4	9.1	9.6
3.6	3.7	3.8	All Other Current		3.8	5.4	3.2	5.6	2.9
48.2	48.0	46.5	Total Current		44.2	55.8	45.3	44.8	46.7
40.2	38.7	40.3	Fixed Assets (net)		40.8	33.7	38.0	37.8	41.7
4.2	5.7	6.9	Intangibles (net)		7.7	2.4	7.7	9.4	7.8
7.4	7.5	6.2	All Other Non-Current		7.4	8.2	9.0	7.9	3.8
100.0	100.0	100.0	Total		100.0	100.0	100.0	100.0	100.0
			LIABILITIES						
7.9	5.3	6.6	Notes Payable-Short Term		5.7	7.8	11.9	3.6	6.6
4.7	7.1	6.9	Cur. Mat.-L.T.D.		10.3	4.1	6.2	3.0	3.4
18.4	16.5	13.3	Trade Payables		13.8	21.6	10.2	11.5	12.7
.4	.1	.2	Income Taxes Payable		.0	.3	.0	.1	.4
12.2	12.2	11.8	All Other Current		11.2	10.9	19.6	13.2	7.5
43.6	41.3	38.7	Total Current		41.0	44.6	47.9	31.5	30.7
26.2	24.4	24.7	Long-Term Debt		32.8	22.4	21.3	18.2	19.8
1.2	1.0	1.4	Deferred Taxes		.0	.0	1.6	1.4	3.2
5.5	5.4	3.0	All Other Non-Current		.6	4.6	7.9	3.0	2.7
23.5	28.0	32.3	Net Worth		25.6	28.4	21.3	45.9	43.7
100.0	100.0	100.0	Total Liabilities & Net Worth		100.0	100.0	100.0	100.0	100.0
			INCOME DATA						
100.0	100.0	100.0	Net Sales		100.0	100.0	100.0	100.0	100.0
27.4	25.6	33.2	Gross Profit		38.9	29.7	34.4	39.1	25.0
24.9	23.0	28.4	Operating Expenses		35.4	22.0	31.0	32.4	21.7
2.5	2.6	4.9	Operating Profit		3.5	7.7	3.4	6.7	3.3
1.0	.7	.4	All Other Expenses (net)		.4	-.7	2.3	.5	.0
1.5	1.8	4.4	Profit Before Taxes		3.1	8.4	1.1	6.1	3.3
			RATIOS						
1.8	2.0	2.2	Current		3.4	2.1	1.9	3.2	2.8
1.2	1.2	1.3			1.2	1.7	1.0	1.4	1.5
.8	.7	.8			.5	1.1	.8	.9	1.1
1.3	1.4	1.9	Quick		2.5	2.1	1.2	2.0	1.9
.8	.8	.9			.6	1.1	.8	1.0	1.2
.5	.5	.4				.4	.4	.6	.6
18 19.8	14 25.6	15 25.1	Sales/Receivables	8 46.5	18 20.8	20 18.6	13 28.2	13 28.7	
30 12.4	27 13.7	26 14.2		28 13.2	24 15.2	24 15.2	24 15.1	25 14.8	
38 9.6	35 10.4	35 10.4		37 9.9	35 10.4	34 10.9	33 11.0	36 10.1	
8 47.0	6 61.0	9 40.8	Cost of Sales/Inventory	12 31.2	0 982.7	13 28.8	9 39.7	6 65.0	
16 22.4	14 27.0	18 20.0		23 15.6	8 46.0	37 9.8	22 16.9	11 32.7	
29 12.6	30 12.3	37 9.8		38 9.7	21 17.4	53 6.8	36 10.1	34 10.6	
14 25.9	9 41.2	10 38.4	Cost of Sales/Payables	4 95.8	10 35.2	14 25.5	13 29.1	10 37.8	
23 16.1	17 21.0	19 19.5		22 16.6	21 17.1	32 11.3	19 19.3	13 28.9	
36 10.2	30 12.0	34 10.8		42 8.7	77 4.7	38 9.6	32 11.4	22 16.6	
14.8	12.6	8.6	Sales/Working Capital		6.5	8.1	19.4	7.5	9.2
45.5	58.4	31.0			69.1	23.2	100.3	27.6	21.7
-34.4	-28.9	-33.4			-9.0	101.3	-20.4	NM	170.2
5.9	9.3	17.7	EBIT/Interest		28.7		6.5	30.8	16.8
(100) 2.4	(100) 3.0	(95) 3.5			(21) 3.6		2.8	(19) 9.0	(26) 2.9
1.1	1.1	1.4			.5		.9	1.7	1.5
6.0	5.3	21.7	Net Profit + Depr., Dep., Amort./Cur. Mat. L/T/D						24.4
(33) 2.0	(23) 3.1	(22) 3.8							(12) 12.4
1.3	1.1	1.5							1.3
.6	.6	.6	Fixed/Worth		.4	.5	.6	.6	.6
1.7	1.8	1.3			1.2	1.3	2.3	1.1	1.3
35.1	5.9	3.4			NM	4.2	-1.8	2.0	2.1
1.2	1.0	.8	Debt/Worth		.5	.8	1.2	.7	1.0
2.7	2.6	2.0			1.7	4.8	2.6	1.2	1.6
110.3	13.3	6.0			NM	7.0	-5.4	2.7	2.6
33.4	46.4	56.6	% Profit Before Taxes/Tangible Net Worth		65.7			86.3	37.8
(81) 17.2	(87) 23.1	(85) 23.1			(17) 24.1			(19) 21.6	(28) 20.6
4.1	6.9	5.1			.9			8.5	5.6
10.3	13.9	17.0	% Profit Before Taxes/Total Assets		21.1	41.5	6.7	20.3	16.8
4.9	4.6	6.3			6.8	9.1	3.2	11.6	6.3
.3	1.4	1.2			-1.9	5.5	-.4	1.4	1.5
15.7	18.7	18.3	Sales/Net Fixed Assets		15.5	21.8	17.8	17.9	22.6
7.3	8.3	6.8			8.0	13.5	5.2	7.9	6.4
3.3	3.6	3.4			2.5	5.8	2.5	2.9	4.1
4.7	4.7	3.8	Sales/Total Assets		3.5	5.1	3.2	3.9	5.1
2.6	2.9	2.6			2.3	4.1	2.6	2.7	3.0
1.9	1.8	1.7			1.4	1.9	.9	1.3	2.1
1.6	1.4	2.1	% Depr., Dep., Amort./Sales		1.8	3.0		2.5	1.9
(96) 3.2	(97) 3.0	(85) 3.2			(17) 4.1	(11) 4.7		(19) 3.2	(26) 2.5
4.6	4.7	5.9			8.6	7.7		5.6	4.3
1.6	1.0	1.5	% Officers', Directors' Owners' Comp/Sales						
(46) 3.1	(40) 2.1	(30) 3.0							
6.1	4.3	6.5							
4180002M	5726298M	4043586M	Net Sales ($)	5139M	42764M	42758M	77886M	347922M	3527117M
1492095M	1900396M	1324791M	Total Assets ($)	3752M	19726M	14034M	54808M	176438M	1056033M

M = $ thousand   MM = $ million
See Pages 9 through 22 for Explanation of Ratios and Data

RETAIL—Other Direct Selling Establishments NAICS 454390

Current Data Sorted by Assets | **Comparative Historical Data**

						Type of Statement		
		3	7	3	10	Unqualified	9	15
2	8	10	3			Reviewed	14	13
5	13	4	1			Compiled	28	31
46	30	13	2	1		Tax Returns	45	82
18	31	27	8	3	5	Other	53	65
	29 (4/1-9/30/09)		224 (10/1/09-3/31/10)				4/1/05-3/31/06	4/1/06-3/31/07
0-500M	500M-2MM	2-10MM	10-50MM	50-100MM	100-250MM		ALL	ALL
71	82	57	21	7	15	**NUMBER OF STATEMENTS**	149	206
%	%	%	%	%	%		%	%
						ASSETS		
18.7	11.6	12.4	24.1		15.0	Cash & Equivalents	12.6	14.1
21.0	26.7	20.9	17.6		10.5	Trade Receivables (net)	21.7	24.0
28.6	28.7	28.9	22.4		21.7	Inventory	22.6	24.6
2.6	2.3	4.9	2.3		6.0	All Other Current	3.7	3.3
70.9	69.4	67.1	66.3		53.2	Total Current	60.5	66.0
18.3	16.8	18.1	16.4		16.0	Fixed Assets (net)	25.0	19.8
4.4	5.9	8.3	8.0		15.9	Intangibles (net)	6.6	4.9
6.4	7.9	6.5	9.3		14.9	All Other Non-Current	7.9	9.3
100.0	100.0	100.0	100.0		100.0	Total	100.0	100.0
						LIABILITIES		
23.2	13.7	11.7	5.3		.1	Notes Payable-Short Term	16.1	15.2
2.6	4.8	3.8	1.7		1.5	Cur. Mat.-L.T.D.	5.3	2.8
17.0	17.1	21.7	11.5		9.7	Trade Payables	17.6	17.9
.2	.1	.2	.8		.4	Income Taxes Payable	.2	.3
20.3	8.5	20.5	20.5		15.0	All Other Current	12.2	12.6
63.3	44.2	57.9	39.8		26.7	Total Current	51.3	48.8
26.4	17.9	12.0	12.2		20.7	Long-Term Debt	21.0	18.1
.0	.0	.1	.0		1.0	Deferred Taxes	.2	.1
10.1	4.1	4.0	7.6		1.1	All Other Non-Current	8.1	6.2
.2	33.9	26.0	40.4		50.4	Net Worth	19.5	26.9
100.0	100.0	100.0	100.0		100.0	Total Liabilities & Net Worth	100.0	100.0
						INCOME DATA		
100.0	100.0	100.0	100.0		100.0	Net Sales	100.0	100.0
44.4	41.3	39.4	38.3		50.0	Gross Profit	43.7	43.5
41.6	35.7	34.7	31.4		37.9	Operating Expenses	38.6	37.2
2.8	5.6	4.7	6.9		12.0	Operating Profit	5.1	6.2
.7	.8	1.3	.6		1.7	All Other Expenses (net)	1.1	.7
2.1	4.8	3.4	6.3		10.3	Profit Before Taxes	4.0	5.6
						RATIOS		
2.7	3.5	1.8	4.2		2.9		2.2	2.5
1.3	1.5	1.2	1.7		1.9	Current	1.3	1.4
.8	1.0	.9	1.0		1.4		.8	.9
2.0	2.0	1.2	2.1		1.5		1.4	1.4
.6	.8	(55) .5	1.0		1.0	Quick	(148) .8	(205) .8
.2	.4	.2	.6		.7		.2	.3
0 UND	3 135.8	2 180.4	7 48.7		0 UND		2 229.8	1 306.8
9 38.9	28 12.8	16 23.5	18 20.4		13 27.8	Sales/Receivables	21 17.7	19 19.7
26 13.9	42 8.7	53 6.9	37 9.9		29 12.4		46 7.9	46 7.9
0 UND	9 42.5	11 33.7	6 56.3		41 8.9		8 43.8	6 58.0
22 16.4	40 9.2	38 9.7	46 7.9		77 4.7	Cost of Sales/Inventory	41 9.0	34 10.6
75 4.8	109 3.4	83 4.4	127 2.9		86 4.2		70 5.2	71 5.2
0 UND	10 37.3	18 20.4	9 41.8		17 21.2		9 41.6	4 94.6
7 52.7	27 13.8	28 12.9	22 16.6		26 14.0	Cost of Sales/Payables	25 14.4	27 13.3
36 10.0	49 7.5	81 4.5	42 8.7		44 8.4		58 6.3	56 6.5
11.3	6.0	8.6	4.5		5.5		8.7	8.0
39.6	16.1	22.8	9.9		11.0	Sales/Working Capital	16.9	18.7
-50.2	-104.7	-69.6	235.7		20.0		-49.7	-118.1
12.2	19.0	9.9	37.5		139.9		22.2	15.1
(51) 5.5	(70) 4.1	(43) 2.5	(17) 3.1		(14) 45.7	EBIT/Interest	(126) 4.8	(170) 5.2
-.2	1.4	.5	1.6		2.8		1.2	1.5
						Net Profit + Depr., Dep.,	4.5	4.5
						Amort./Cur. Mat. L/T/D	(14) 1.2	(21) 2.1
							.3	1.4
.1	.1	.2	.1		.2		.1	.1
.8	.5	.6	.6		.4	Fixed/Worth	.8	.7
-1.2	6.2	2.9	4.0		1.3		-9.8	11.9
1.4	.5	1.3	.9		.4		.9	1.0
19.7	3.0	3.5	2.7		1.0	Debt/Worth	3.0	2.7
-5.5	26.3	12.4	14.6		7.0		-22.4	122.3
235.3	78.7	89.6	204.1		157.8		100.8	114.2
(44) 85.9	(65) 30.1	(46) 26.4	(19) 19.3		(12) 26.0	% Profit Before Taxes/Tangible Net Worth	(109) 37.1	(162) 49.2
12.0	14.3	3.9	8.4		9.1		19.2	12.0
43.3	21.8	20.9	18.3		52.2		26.5	30.3
10.4	9.1	7.1	9.4		12.2	% Profit Before Taxes/Total Assets	10.7	11.2
-5.6		.3	2.4		5.0		.6	2.0
385.0	130.8	60.1	139.7		50.2		75.5	156.2
49.7	48.3	28.7	30.0		23.3	Sales/Net Fixed Assets	19.2	33.4
17.6	11.3	11.2	10.5		10.5		7.0	10.6
8.4	4.8	5.2	4.1		3.5		4.4	5.9
4.7	3.2	2.6	2.3		2.5	Sales/Total Assets	3.1	3.4
2.3	2.1	1.7	1.7		1.3		2.1	2.2
.4	.4	.6	.2				.7	.4
(38) 1.6	(49) 1.0	(44) 1.3	(18) 1.2			% Depr., Dep., Amort./Sales	(109) 1.4	(139) .9
3.1	2.0	2.2	3.3				4.2	2.3
2.8	1.9	1.7					3.0	1.7
(39) 6.5	(39) 3.0	(19) 2.7				% Officers', Directors' Owners' Comp/Sales	(71) 6.4	(100) 4.4
10.3	7.2	6.9					10.5	7.9
78585M	394436M	889478M	1743786M	1770776M	6296340M	Net Sales ($)	4023945M	5804759M
15715M	99684M	264954M	477239M	543060M	2699415M	Total Assets ($)	1383855M	2115109M

© RMA 2010

M = $ thousand   MM = $ million
See Pages 9 through 22 for Explanation of Ratios and Data

Comparative Historical Data | Current Data Sorted by Sales

4/1/07-3/31/08 ALL	4/1/08-3/31/09 ALL	4/1/09-3/31/10 ALL	Type of Statement	0-1MM	1-3MM	3-5MM	5-10MM	10-25MM	25MM & OVER
12	18	23	Unqualified			1		2	20
10	11	23	Reviewed	1	4	3	5	7	3
23	24	23	Compiled	1	8	4	7	2	1
80	86	92	Tax Returns	33	27	13	5	10	4
75	88	92	Other	11	14	17	13	20	17
				29 (4/1-9/30/09)			224 (10/1/09-3/31/10)		
200	227	253	**NUMBER OF STATEMENTS**	46	53	38	30	41	45
%	%	%	**ASSETS**	%	%	%	%	%	%
16.5	11.8	15.0	Cash & Equivalents	19.8	12.8	11.0	9.1	13.1	21.9
21.9	22.8	21.6	Trade Receivables (net)	14.6	25.3	25.5	31.8	23.3	12.7
28.2	30.3	27.9	Inventory	28.2	30.1	31.3	28.7	23.9	24.9
3.5	2.7	3.2	All Other Current	3.6	1.4	4.9	1.4	4.2	3.8
70.1	67.6	67.7	Total Current	66.3	69.6	72.8	71.0	64.5	63.3
17.8	18.5	17.8	Fixed Assets (net)	21.7	17.1	12.2	19.0	16.9	19.4
5.0	5.7	6.9	Intangibles (net)	4.9	5.8	11.0	3.2	7.8	8.4
7.2	8.1	7.6	All Other Non-Current	7.2	7.5	4.0	6.8	10.7	8.9
100.0	100.0	100.0	Total	100.0	100.0	100.0	100.0	100.0	100.0
			LIABILITIES						
13.3	17.2	14.2	Notes Payable-Short Term	27.4	14.0	12.2	13.3	13.2	4.2
4.0	4.0	3.4	Cur. Mat.-L.T.D.	2.5	4.0	6.8	4.6	1.7	1.5
20.0	17.7	17.2	Trade Payables	11.2	19.2	18.0	20.4	19.7	15.6
.3	.2	.2	Income Taxes Payable	.2	.1	.0	.5	.1	.5
16.3	17.3	16.0	All Other Current	21.9	11.0	10.4	8.6	17.1	24.8
54.0	56.5	51.0	Total Current	63.3	48.4	47.5	47.3	51.6	46.5
21.3	22.3	19.2	Long-Term Debt	28.6	23.5	16.2	15.3	9.8	18.3
.2	.2	.1	Deferred Taxes	.0	.0	.0	.0	.1	.5
5.7	8.9	6.1	All Other Non-Current	7.4	9.4	3.0	4.9	5.6	4.5
18.8	12.2	23.6	Net Worth	.8	18.8	33.3	32.5	32.9	30.1
100.0	100.0	100.0	Total Liabilities & Net Worth	100.0	100.0	100.0	100.0	100.0	100.0
			INCOME DATA						
100.0	100.0	100.0	Net Sales	100.0	100.0	100.0	100.0	100.0	100.0
42.6	40.1	42.0	Gross Profit	47.9	43.5	45.5	36.3	35.0	41.7
36.0	35.6	36.9	Operating Expenses	44.4	39.0	41.0	29.7	30.3	34.3
6.6	4.6	5.1	Operating Profit	3.5	4.5	4.4	6.6	4.7	7.4
.9	1.3	1.0	All Other Expenses (net)	1.3	.4	1.8	.9	.8	.9
5.7	3.3	4.1	Profit Before Taxes	2.2	4.2	2.7	5.7	4.0	6.5
			RATIOS						
3.0	2.0	2.7	Current	2.8	3.2	3.1	2.2	2.3	2.8
1.5	1.2	1.5		1.7	1.3	2.0	1.5	1.3	1.6
1.0	.8	1.0		.7	1.0	1.1	1.0	.9	1.0
1.6	1.1	1.6	Quick	2.1	1.8	2.1	1.9	1.4	1.2
.8	(226) .6	(251) .8		.5	.8	(37) .8	(29) .8	.8	.9
.3	.3	.3		.2	.3	.3	.3	.3	.3
1 374.3	3 127.8	1 343.1	Sales/Receivables	0 UND	3 145.9	3 110.3	8 48.4	1 397.7	1 471.7
18 20.2	22 16.6	15 24.8		6 60.0	25 14.7	30 12.3	34 10.7	18 20.4	8 47.2
41 8.9	39 9.4	39 9.4		27 13.7	9.0	45 8.1	56 6.5	41 9.0	28 13.1
5 66.6	11 34.5	8 45.4	Cost of Sales/Inventory	0 UND	15 24.4	6 57.1	12 29.4	4 83.7	12 30.0
38 9.6	43 8.4	40 9.1		27 13.4	49 7.5	36 10.0	40 9.2	21 17.1	44 8.4
89 4.1	102 3.6	92 4.0		161 2.3	104 3.5	106 3.4	85 4.3	79 4.6	81 4.5
8 46.7	9 38.8	6 58.2	Cost of Sales/Payables	0 UND	5 72.3	13 29.0	20 18.3	7 54.5	13 27.7
26 14.1	24 15.4	24 15.5		4 84.4	32 11.6	27 13.7	28 13.1	24 15.0	23 15.9
52 7.0	45 8.1	49 7.5		32 11.6	61 6.0	55 6.7	40 9.2	45 8.2	43 8.5
6.7	8.6	6.7	Sales/Working Capital	5.2	6.4	5.3	8.4	9.1	7.7
13.7	23.8	21.2		41.2	23.7	13.5	17.4	24.0	17.1
NM	-43.6	-150.5		-15.5	151.7	115.0	-472.2	-59.8	-374.7
14.9	13.4	18.5	EBIT/Interest	8.1	18.5	18.0	23.5	23.3	77.9
(168) 5.2	(190) 3.5	(201) 4.3		(33) 2.9	(44) 4.1	(31) 3.5	(26) 5.9	(31) 4.8	(36) 7.5
1.5	1.2	1.2		-2.7	1.4	1.3	1.8	.9	2.1
10.5	5.6	13.9	Net Profit + Depr., Dep., Amort./Cur. Mat. L/T/D						
(19) 2.3	(23) 1.3	(21) 3.2							
.9	.7	1.2							
.1	.1	.1	Fixed/Worth	.0	.2	.1	.2	.1	.2
.6	.9	.6		.8	.6	.5	.7	.5	.8
UND	-4.2	44.8		-2.1	-8.6	UND	1.5	2.4	17.6
1.0	1.4	.8	Debt/Worth	.8	.9	.5	.9	.7	.7
4.0	5.5	3.8		21.6	4.9	4.9	2.5	3.1	2.7
UND	-11.8	UND		-4.9	-41.9	UND	7.9	14.0	519.1
107.3	92.3	102.9	% Profit Before Taxes/Tangible Net Worth	88.5	144.3	75.1	82.5	116.6	158.2
(150) 45.9	(160) 29.3	(190) 31.2		(27) 23.2	(39) 30.3	(29) 37.7	(25) 31.0	(34) 31.0	(36) 41.5
18.6	5.7	9.5		.5	7.7	19.5	13.9	7.0	9.8
29.7	23.6	28.1	% Profit Before Taxes/Total Assets	38.2	32.1	20.1	28.3	20.9	33.5
11.5	7.2	9.4		6.2	9.3	7.9	14.6	10.2	11.8
2.2	.1	.9		-7.2	.8	1.7	.2	.6	4.0
126.1	109.2	115.5	Sales/Net Fixed Assets	UND	108.5	118.6	103.7	149.4	84.1
38.4	31.6	33.3		35.1	37.1	40.3	40.4	37.2	25.5
14.2	12.5	11.6		7.2	11.7	12.2	13.7	19.2	11.1
5.1	5.2	5.5	Sales/Total Assets	5.7	5.2	4.3	5.5	7.5	5.6
3.2	3.2	3.1		2.4	3.0	3.1	3.3	3.7	3.3
2.0	2.0	2.0		1.7	1.9	1.7	2.1	2.2	2.3
.4	.5	.4	% Depr., Dep., Amort./Sales	1.2	.4	.2	.4	.3	.5
(140) .9	(145) 1.1	(162) 1.3		(22) 2.7	(35) 1.2	(21) 1.4	(20) 1.0	(34) 1.1	(30) 1.1
1.8	2.3	2.4		4.3	2.1	2.1	2.5	2.0	2.2
2.4	1.6	1.8	% Officers', Directors' Owners' Comp/Sales	5.2	2.6	1.4	1.6	1.9	
(98) 4.5	(94) 3.3	(103) 3.7		(25) 7.5	(25) 3.9	(18) 2.9	(13) 2.4	(15) 2.6	
7.9	7.4	7.5		10.6	7.1	10.8	3.9	6.4	
6204997M	9205659M	11173401M	Net Sales ($)	22853M	97489M	151614M	208489M	644991M	10047965M
2412357M	3162562M	4100067M	Total Assets ($)	10749M	36945M	82531M	77748M	235367M	3656727M

M = $ thousand   MM = $ million
See Pages 9 through 22 for Explanation of Ratios and Data

TRANSPORTATION AND WAREHOUSING

Current Data Sorted by Assets   Comparative Historical Data

0-500M	500M-2MM	2-10MM	10-50MM	50-100MM	100-250MM	Type of Statement	4/1/05-3/31/06 ALL	4/1/06-3/31/07 ALL
		2	7	2	2	Unqualified	9	11
		3	3			Reviewed	2	4
			1			Compiled	4	3
7	5	3				Tax Returns	8	6
2	3	12	11	2	1	Other	31	34
	9 (4/1-9/30/09)		57 (10/1/09-3/31/10)					
9	**8**	**20**	**22**	**4**	**3**	**NUMBER OF STATEMENTS**	**54**	**58**
%	%	%	%	%	%		%	%
						ASSETS		
		14.8	13.2			Cash & Equivalents	13.1	14.0
		26.3	13.8			Trade Receivables (net)	14.7	16.3
		7.4	7.6			Inventory	4.6	4.9
		2.3	4.9			All Other Current	5.1	5.1
		50.8	39.5			Total Current	37.4	40.4
		36.6	40.8			Fixed Assets (net)	50.2	44.4
		1.3	5.7			Intangibles (net)	2.6	5.0
		11.3	13.9			All Other Non-Current	9.8	10.3
		100.0	100.0			Total	100.0	100.0
						LIABILITIES		
		7.5	2.5			Notes Payable-Short Term	12.2	4.1
		5.0	5.8			Cur. Mat.-L.T.D.	6.3	4.8
		15.8	14.7			Trade Payables	13.1	14.1
		.1	.1			Income Taxes Payable	.2	.2
		15.1	12.6			All Other Current	17.5	16.3
		43.6	35.7			Total Current	49.3	39.5
		31.1	14.2			Long-Term Debt	39.7	39.7
		.2	1.5			Deferred Taxes	.3	.1
		2.4	4.8			All Other Non-Current	6.8	5.0
		22.6	43.7			Net Worth	3.9	15.8
		100.0	100.0			Total Liabilities & Net Worth	100.0	100.0
						INCOME DATA		
		100.0	100.0			Net Sales	100.0	100.0
						Gross Profit		
		94.1	99.1			Operating Expenses	91.2	95.3
		5.9	.9			Operating Profit	8.8	4.7
		2.6	-.7			All Other Expenses (net)	4.2	3.3
		3.2	1.5			Profit Before Taxes	4.6	1.4
						RATIOS		
		2.4	2.1				1.5	1.5
		1.2	1.1			Current	.9	1.0
		.9	.7				.6	.7
		1.5	1.4				1.4	1.0
		.9	.7			Quick	.6	.7
		.7	.4				.3	.5
		21 17.7	10 35.1				1 352.6	12 30.3
		32 11.2	18 20.0			Sales/Receivables	17 22.0	21 17.5
		54 6.8	34 10.9				30 12.0	34 10.6
						Cost of Sales/Inventory		
						Cost of Sales/Payables		
		6.3	7.4				12.5	15.8
		45.5	167.4			Sales/Working Capital	-76.5	-571.5
		-54.7	-17.1				-8.6	-14.9
		5.8	8.9				7.7	5.0
		(17) 3.3	(18) 4.1			EBIT/Interest	(47) 1.7	(48) 2.3
		.3	.3				-.6	.8
								3.4
						Net Profit + Depr., Dep., Amort./Cur. Mat. L/T/D	(14) .5
								-2.1
		.4	.7				1.1	.9
		1.7	1.1			Fixed/Worth	10.5	2.5
		6.2	1.6				-4.3	-14.1
		1.6	.6				2.1	1.7
		4.2	1.6			Debt/Worth	23.4	4.4
		14.2	4.8				-8.3	-29.2
		33.1	42.3				61.5	60.9
		(17) 22.9	(20) 18.6			% Profit Before Taxes/Tangible Net Worth	(29) 34.4	(40) 32.5
		-28.8	4.8				-3.2	1.3
		12.1	13.6				15.1	14.6
		4.0	5.4			% Profit Before Taxes/Total Assets	3.1	4.8
		-2.3	-.2				-3.7	-.9
		23.5	25.4				15.7	16.6
		5.9	3.4			Sales/Net Fixed Assets	3.5	3.9
		2.9	1.6				1.2	1.7
		3.6	2.8				3.6	3.3
		2.4	1.7			Sales/Total Assets	2.0	1.9
		1.6	.8				.8	1.1
		.6	1.3				1.4	1.6
		(18) 3.7	(20) 5.1			% Depr., Dep., Amort./Sales	(41) 3.3	(50) 4.2
		6.9	13.0				11.0	6.8
							1.3	2.2
						% Officers', Directors' Owners' Comp/Sales	(14) 2.2	(15) 3.0
							12.8	7.5
3745M	15708M	253814M	989975M	527490M	631318M	Net Sales ($)	2914524M	4674435M
2421M	7723M	109255M	534342M	316625M	473009M	Total Assets ($)	1538019M	2092881M

M = $ thousand   MM = $ million
See Pages 9 through 22 for Explanation of Ratios and Data

Comparative Historical Data   **Current Data Sorted by Sales**

4/1/07-3/31/08 ALL	4/1/08-3/31/09 ALL	4/1/09-3/31/10 ALL	Type of Statement	0-1MM	1-3MM	3-5MM	5-10MM	10-25MM	25MM & OVER
12	11	13	Unqualified				1	7	6
2	2	6	Reviewed					2	3
1	5	1	Compiled					1	
8	5	15	Tax Returns	7	4	1		1	2
28	30	31	Other	3	3	2	4	9	10
				9 (4/1-9/30/09)			**57 (10/1/09-3/31/10)**		
51	53	66	**NUMBER OF STATEMENTS**	10	7	3	5	20	21
%	%	%	**ASSETS**	%	%	%	%	%	%
17.6	13.1	12.5	Cash & Equivalents	15.0				16.8	10.1
16.4	18.2	16.7	Trade Receivables (net)	11.1				17.4	20.2
6.5	6.1	6.4	Inventory	1.4				8.4	6.0
3.3	5.6	4.6	All Other Current	7.8				2.3	5.5
43.8	43.0	40.3	Total Current	35.3				44.9	41.8
42.9	40.2	41.4	Fixed Assets (net)	50.4				45.3	32.9
4.1	3.7	5.0	Intangibles (net)	6.1				3.6	8.5
9.2	13.0	13.2	All Other Non-Current	-7.8				6.1	16.8
100.0	100.0	100.0	Total	100.0				100.0	100.0
			LIABILITIES						
7.0	8.0	7.9	Notes Payable-Short Term	4.3				4.7	2.4
5.6	3.8	4.9	Cur. Mat.-L.T.D.	6.1				6.3	4.0
13.7	11.1	12.4	Trade Payables	3.5				12.9	16.7
.1	.2	.1	Income Taxes Payable	.0				.2	.1
15.0	20.3	14.5	All Other Current	14.9				10.5	21.2
41.4	43.3	39.8	Total Current	28.7				34.6	44.4
31.2	37.9	27.7	Long-Term Debt	39.3				25.6	16.4
.5	.1	.9	Deferred Taxes	1.2				.6	1.4
13.8	4.6	5.3	All Other Non-Current	3.5				3.6	4.8
13.2	14.1	26.4	Net Worth	27.3				35.7	32.9
100.0	100.0	100.0	Total Liabilities & Net Worth	100.0				100.0	100.0
			INCOME DATA						
100.0	100.0	100.0	Net Sales	100.0				100.0	100.0
			Gross Profit						
92.3	95.6	94.6	Operating Expenses	86.4				95.9	95.2
7.7	4.4	5.4	Operating Profit	13.6				4.1	4.8
1.6	3.2	1.8	All Other Expenses (net)	6.4				.7	.7
6.1	1.3	3.6	Profit Before Taxes	7.2				3.4	4.1
			RATIOS						
2.0	1.9	2.5		6.5				2.7	1.6
1.3	1.1	1.3	Current	2.7				1.3	1.1
.8	.7	.7		.8				.9	.6
1.5	1.4	1.7		5.1				2.3	.9
.8	.7	.8	Quick	2.4				.8	.6
.5	.5	.5		.3				.6	.5
10 36.9	8 45.2	10 35.7		0 UND				21 17.7	12 31.6
23 15.9	24 15.5	23 15.7	Sales/Receivables	21 17.7				30 12.2	21 17.7
39 9.3	34 10.8	44 8.2		86 4.3				48 7.6	38 9.6
			Cost of Sales/Inventory						
			Cost of Sales/Payables						
10.2	9.8	6.0		1.3				4.7	13.2
27.9	46.1	22.0	Sales/Working Capital	3.5				17.6	83.6
-19.0	-20.2	-17.1		UND				-27.6	-16.7
5.1	7.2	8.0						8.0	11.1
(43) 3.1	(44) 1.8	(56) 3.3	EBIT/Interest				(19) 2.6	(16) 5.5
1.4	.1	.4						.5	.4
6.3		4.3	Net Profit + Depr., Dep.,						
(13) 1.7		(13) 2.0	Amort./Cur. Mat. L/T/D						
.6		.9							
1.1	.7	.9		.9				.9	.7
2.5	1.6	1.4	Fixed/Worth	3.7				1.4	1.3
30.3	NM	6.0		UND				6.2	2.0
1.4	1.4	.9		.7				.7	1.0
4.3	4.0	3.1	Debt/Worth	4.1				2.3	2.5
47.7	-42.8	9.4		UND				14.0	5.7
56.2	48.5	45.1	% Profit Before Taxes/Tangible					26.6	65.7
(40) 31.2	(39) 22.4	(54) 23.7	Net Worth				(16) 14.4	(18) 33.6
8.7	-3.0	5.0						5.7	8.5
18.8	11.9	13.3	% Profit Before Taxes/Total	11.1				12.7	16.7
7.5	2.7	5.2	Assets	6.2				4.3	9.7
1.7	-3.8	-1.2		-1.2				-1.2	-1.3
16.3	45.1	19.7		79.9				8.7	35.6
5.6	6.0	4.2	Sales/Net Fixed Assets	1.2				3.0	11.4
2.4	1.9	1.8		.3				1.7	2.6
3.4	4.3	2.8		1.7				2.7	3.8
2.5	2.2	1.8	Sales/Total Assets	.7				1.6	2.4
1.4	1.0	1.0		.2				.8	1.6
1.5	1.1	1.2						1.5	.8
(46) 3.7	(44) 4.0	(58) 4.1	% Depr., Dep., Amort./Sales				(19) 6.2	(17) 1.8
6.6	7.7	9.0						9.3	5.7
1.0	1.2	1.5	% Officers', Directors'						
(15) 1.4	(15) 1.6	(12) 3.7	Owners' Comp/Sales						
11.6	6.5	9.3							
3787906M	5109112M	2422050M	Net Sales ($)	3656M	12216M	11526M	36882M	312350M	2045420M
1701582M	2144300M	1443375M	Total Assets ($)	8425M	5106M	50033M	19659M	330468M	1029684M

© RMA 2010

M = $ thousand   MM = $ million
See Pages 9 through 22 for Explanation of Ratios and Data

Current Data Sorted by Assets   Comparative Historical Data

						Type of Statement		
		5	8		3	Unqualified	16	18
	1	4	7			Reviewed	6	11
	2	8				Compiled	13	13
1	4	1		2		Tax Returns	8	12
4	2	17	15	3	4	Other	50	54
	14 (4/1-9/30/09)		77 (10/1/09-3/31/10)				4/1/05-3/31/06	4/1/06-3/31/07
0-500M	500M-2MM	2-10MM	10-50MM	50-100MM	100-250MM		ALL	ALL
5	9	35	30	5	7	NUMBER OF STATEMENTS	93	108
%	%	%	%	%	%		%	%
		9.0	6.4			Cash & Equivalents	8.3	11.3
		13.9	13.8			Trade Receivables (net)	20.4	17.2
		11.9	7.0			Inventory	9.1	9.7
		4.4	5.3			All Other Current	3.4	4.8
		39.2	32.5			Total Current	41.3	43.0
		45.3	54.9			Fixed Assets (net)	45.7	42.7
		3.1	4.3			Intangibles (net)	1.9	3.7
		12.5	8.4			All Other Non-Current	11.2	10.6
		100.0	100.0			Total	100.0	100.0
						LIABILITIES		
		17.6	5.0			Notes Payable-Short Term	7.0	8.6
		7.7	6.8			Cur. Mat.-L.T.D.	7.2	6.7
		10.5	8.3			Trade Payables	12.8	11.0
		.2	.1			Income Taxes Payable	.1	.4
		11.3	10.6			All Other Current	8.3	8.3
		47.3	30.9			Total Current	35.5	34.9
		40.6	34.8			Long-Term Debt	41.6	40.5
		.6	1.7			Deferred Taxes	.8	.7
		10.5	4.1			All Other Non-Current	4.5	6.3
		1.1	28.5			Net Worth	17.6	17.6
		100.0	100.0			Total Liabilties & Net Worth	100.0	100.0
						INCOME DATA		
		100.0	100.0			Net Sales	100.0	100.0
						Gross Profit		
		100.3	97.5			Operating Expenses	93.9	94.0
		-.3	2.5			Operating Profit	6.1	6.0
		3.5	2.1			All Other Expenses (net)	3.0	2.8
		-3.8	.4			Profit Before Taxes	3.0	3.2
						RATIOS		
		1.7	1.7				2.2	2.3
		.9	1.0			Current	1.4	1.2
		.5	.6				.8	.8
		1.1	1.1				1.7	1.5
		.6	.5			Quick	.8	.8
		.2	.3				.4	.4
	13	28.6 18	20.7				17 20.9 12	30.0
	21	17.1 28	13.0			Sales/Receivables	28 13.3 28	12.9
	33	11.0 43	8.4				44 8.2 43	8.6
						Cost of Sales/Inventory		
						Cost of Sales/Payables		
		7.5	10.7				6.3	8.2
		-99.3	NM			Sales/Working Capital	29.8	36.7
		-7.4	-7.7				-27.3	-25.3
		2.9	6.9				6.2	5.6
	(32)	.5 (26)	1.7			EBIT/Interest	(86) 2.3 (93)	2.8
		-.6	.3				1.0	.6
			2.5				5.0	3.6
		(11)	1.5			Net Profit + Depr., Dep., Amort./Cur. Mat. L/T/D	(17) 3.6 (15)	1.7
			.6				1.9	1.1
		.7	1.3				.8	.7
		8.6	2.5			Fixed/Worth	1.6	1.7
		-1.9	7.8				7.7	26.5
		2.1	1.3				1.3	1.2
		22.2	2.8			Debt/Worth	3.1	3.0
		-5.4	10.0				56.3	40.6
		9.0	28.9				59.1	45.4
	(18)	-1.8 (25)	15.3			% Profit Before Taxes/Tangible Net Worth	(72) 17.2 (83)	22.6
		-9.4	-6.9				2.8	1.2
		1.3	9.7				12.8	14.2
		-1.4	3.4			% Profit Before Taxes/Total Assets	5.1	6.1
		-5.9	-2.6				.0	-1.3
		11.8	5.2				15.0	19.4
		3.1	2.5			Sales/Net Fixed Assets	3.6	4.6
		1.6	1.3				1.6	1.8
		2.3	1.9				3.3	3.1
		1.7	1.3			Sales/Total Assets	1.6	1.8
		.9	.9				.8	1.0
		1.2	3.0				1.3	1.2
	(27)	5.3 (27)	6.2			% Depr., Dep., Amort./Sales	(73) 5.4 (78)	3.8
		12.0	9.4				12.5	10.4
							1.2	2.0
						% Officers', Directors' Owners' Comp/Sales	(18) 2.7 (26)	3.7
							6.4	5.2
7333M	20935M	284504M	934504M	319267M	1101410M	Net Sales ($)	4592461M	2462377M
1218M	9804M	164726M	630806M	343558M	1159265M	Total Assets ($)	2392497M	1623201M

M = $ thousand   MM = $ million
See Pages 9 through 22 for Explanation of Ratios and Data

Comparative Historical Data — Current Data Sorted by Sales

			Type of Statement	0-1MM	1-3MM	3-5MM	5-10MM	10-25MM	25MM & OVER
22	11	16	Unqualified		1		1	7	7
6	6	12	Reviewed		2		2	5	4
12	12	11	Compiled	1	4	2	3	1	
12	9	7	Tax Returns	2	1	1	1		2
50	46	45	Other	4	7		14	6	14
4/1/07-3/31/08 ALL	4/1/08-3/31/09 ALL	4/1/09-3/31/10 ALL			14 (4/1-9/30/09)		77 (10/1/09-3/31/10)		
102	84	91	**NUMBER OF STATEMENTS**	8	12	4	21	19	27
%	%	%	**ASSETS**	%	%	%	%	%	%
9.7	11.0	9.9	Cash & Equivalents		14.8		8.6	8.8	9.4
22.3	15.0	15.1	Trade Receivables (net)		9.9		17.2	13.0	15.7
7.6	8.2	8.5	Inventory		14.7		8.0	8.0	7.3
5.3	5.2	5.1	All Other Current		7.8		5.4	3.1	5.8
44.9	39.4	38.6	Total Current		47.3		39.2	32.9	38.2
43.7	46.0	45.7	Fixed Assets (net)		39.4		45.4	51.9	44.7
2.4	4.4	4.6	Intangibles (net)		1.8		1.5	4.9	9.1
9.0	10.2	11.1	All Other Non-Current		11.5		13.9	10.3	8.1
100.0	100.0	100.0	Total		100.0		100.0	100.0	100.0
			LIABILITIES						
7.6	11.1	11.4	Notes Payable-Short Term		16.7		9.1	8.4	4.1
4.7	5.4	6.2	Cur. Mat.-L.T.D.		6.6		5.2	7.4	6.5
16.0	10.0	13.6	Trade Payables		20.5		9.6	11.4	11.6
.7	.5	.2	Income Taxes Payable		.1		.3	.0	.3
11.8	10.5	12.5	All Other Current		17.3		10.0	8.5	16.1
40.8	37.5	43.9	Total Current		61.2		34.2	35.7	38.6
44.3	44.6	38.5	Long-Term Debt		34.2		42.7	34.8	29.0
.4	.7	.9	Deferred Taxes		.7		.5	1.0	1.5
6.4	5.7	7.1	All Other Non-Current		5.4		8.4	8.9	7.3
8.1	11.5	9.5	Net Worth		-1.5		14.3	19.5	23.6
100.0	100.0	100.0	Total Liabilties & Net Worth		100.0		100.0	100.0	100.0
			INCOME DATA						
100.0	100.0	100.0	Net Sales		100.0		100.0	100.0	100.0
			Gross Profit						
95.2	98.3	98.7	Operating Expenses		93.7		100.3	99.2	96.6
4.8	1.7	1.3	Operating Profit		6.3		-.3	.8	3.4
3.3	2.9	2.8	All Other Expenses (net)		1.9		2.1	.7	3.2
1.5	-1.2	-1.5	Profit Before Taxes		4.4		-2.4	.1	.2
			RATIOS						
1.9	1.8	1.7			1.6		2.6	2.0	1.5
1.1	1.1	1.0	Current		1.0		.9	1.1	1.0
.8	.7	.5			.3		.7	.5	.6
1.3	1.4	1.1			1.1		1.4	1.1	1.1
.7	.6	.6	Quick		.2		.6	.6	.6
.3	.3	.2			.1		.2	.4	.3
16 22.3	5 69.7	13 27.4		5 77.6		18 20.8	13 28.6	18 19.7	
27 13.4	19 19.5	25 14.4	Sales/Receivables	8 48.2		29 12.5	27 13.7	30 12.2	
48 7.6	37 9.9	43 8.5		22 16.5		45 8.0	35 10.5	50 7.3	
			Cost of Sales/Inventory						
			Cost of Sales/Payables						
10.8	12.1	10.8			6.1		12.2	6.3	11.3
58.4	83.9	256.1	Sales/Working Capital		NM		-83.7	51.7	85.1
-13.5	-18.1	-7.4			-5.9		-11.1	-9.7	-9.1
7.5	4.6	4.5			4.2		4.2	2.4	8.6
(90) 3.1	(75) 1.4	(79) .7	EBIT/Interest	(11) 1.7		(18) .4	(18) .6	(23) 3.3	
.5	-1.2	-.1			.8		-.3	-.7	.2
3.8	8.8	2.6							
(18) 1.4	(22) 2.7	(22) 1.2	Net Profit + Depr., Dep., Amort./Cur. Mat. L/T/D						
.9	.9	.4							
.6	.9	.9			.5		.6	1.6	1.3
2.5	3.1	3.3	Fixed/Worth		2.2		4.6	3.8	2.8
-4.8	-4.5	-3.8			NM		-13.1	-8.2	-3.8
1.7	1.2	1.3			.8		1.2	1.2	1.4
4.9	4.4	6.4	Debt/Worth		4.8		6.4	4.5	5.0
-11.7	-9.6	-9.2			NM		-18.1	-11.3	-9.2
55.6	42.9	30.3					31.7	18.0	33.8
(71) 30.1	(58) 15.1	(59) 5.3	% Profit Before Taxes/Tangible Net Worth				(12) -.2	(12) -2.1	(20) 16.2
10.1	-3.9	-8.3					-12.2	-4.5	5.6
12.7	9.7	7.2			16.4		4.1	5.5	10.7
6.0	1.7	-.9	% Profit Before Taxes/Total Assets		.7		-2.5	-1.1	4.2
-2.2	-7.5	-5.8			-2.9		-5.2	-2.4	-5.8
15.9	17.6	9.1			11.1		19.3	6.7	7.1
4.2	4.3	3.1	Sales/Net Fixed Assets		2.9		3.2	2.7	3.2
1.7	1.8	1.5			1.6		1.3	1.5	1.7
3.1	3.6	2.2			3.9		2.3	2.9	2.2
1.7	2.0	1.4	Sales/Total Assets		1.0		1.8	1.4	1.4
1.0	1.0	.9			.7		.9	1.0	1.0
1.2	1.8	2.1					1.1	2.8	2.1
(80) 3.9	(69) 3.9	(68) 5.2	% Depr., Dep., Amort./Sales				(19) 4.5	(17) 9.3	(19) 3.2
9.0	9.4	10.3					11.5	11.5	6.2
1.5	1.6	1.8							
(19) 3.4	(16) 3.8	(16) 2.9	% Officers', Directors' Owners' Comp/Sales						
6.6	7.6	5.8							
3023799M	2609380M	2667953M	Net Sales ($)	6254M	24908M	17325M	148727M	321821M	2148918M
2430649M	1932324M	2309377M	Total Assets ($)	9333M	27201M	20717M	121988M	308991M	1821147M

M = $ thousand   MM = $ million
See Pages 9 through 22 for Explanation of Ratios and Data

Current Data Sorted by Assets   Comparative Historical Data

0-500M	500M-2MM	2-10MM	10-50MM	50-100MM	100-250MM	Type of Statement	4/1/05-3/31/06 ALL	4/1/06-3/31/07 ALL
		4	4	4		Unqualified	10	12
		2	3			Reviewed	9	12
	2	2	1			Compiled	3	7
3	1					Tax Returns	2	5
1	6	7	9	1	1	Other	18	20
	9 (4/1-9/30/09)		42 (10/1/09-3/31/10)					
4	9	15	17	5	1	**NUMBER OF STATEMENTS**	42	56
%	%	%	%	%	%		%	%
						ASSETS		
		8.2	6.5			Cash & Equivalents	6.4	6.4
		22.6	7.4			Trade Receivables (net)	12.9	14.5
		5.2	4.7			Inventory	5.8	10.5
		7.8	2.5			All Other Current	2.4	4.5
		43.7	21.1			Total Current	27.5	35.9
		43.5	57.0			Fixed Assets (net)	56.6	52.1
		1.7	4.3			Intangibles (net)	2.7	2.1
		11.1	17.6			All Other Non-Current	13.3	9.9
		100.0	100.0			Total	100.0	100.0
						LIABILITIES		
		4.8	6.0			Notes Payable-Short Term	4.7	7.4
		2.1	3.9			Cur. Mat.-L.T.D.	2.6	4.4
		9.5	6.8			Trade Payables	10.2	13.8
		.4	.4			Income Taxes Payable	.2	.2
		21.2	15.4			All Other Current	8.3	15.5
		38.0	32.4			Total Current	26.0	41.3
		28.8	34.8			Long-Term Debt	33.9	36.1
		.5	1.2			Deferred Taxes	1.3	.3
		1.8	9.4			All Other Non-Current	4.8	9.9
		31.0	22.2			Net Worth	34.0	12.4
		100.0	100.0			Total Liabilties & Net Worth	100.0	100.0
						INCOME DATA		
		100.0	100.0			Net Sales	100.0	100.0
						Gross Profit		
		84.2	93.8			Operating Expenses	93.5	97.2
		15.8	6.2			Operating Profit	6.5	2.8
		4.8	9.1			All Other Expenses (net)	2.9	4.2
		11.0	-2.9			Profit Before Taxes	3.5	-1.4
						RATIOS		
		3.0	1.3			Current	2.0	1.8
		1.3	.9				1.0	.9
		.7	.4				.5	.5
		1.3	.8			Quick	1.5	.9
		.8	.5				.6	.5
		.3	.4				.3	.2
		0 UND	10 38.1			Sales/Receivables	8 47.6	6 62.8
		24 15.4	29 12.7				20 18.2	19 19.5
		37 10.0	44 8.3				48 7.6	38 9.6
						Cost of Sales/Inventory		
						Cost of Sales/Payables		
		7.5	17.3			Sales/Working Capital	10.5	12.9
		29.0	-11.7				NM	-60.1
		-21.7	-3.5				-12.9	-6.6
			4.3			EBIT/Interest	4.4	6.2
		(14)	1.2				(35) 1.5	(51) .7
			-1.7				.7	-1.0
						Net Profit + Depr., Dep., Amort./Cur. Mat. L/T/D		7.9
							(13) 1.0	
								-1.2
		.3	1.2			Fixed/Worth	1.1	.7
		1.4	2.4				1.8	2.5
		3.1	-3.8				7.4	20.0
		.5	.8			Debt/Worth	.9	1.2
		2.0	2.9				1.9	3.1
		6.7	-6.8				13.0	UND
		30.9	16.2			% Profit Before Taxes/Tangible Net Worth	30.5	32.2
		(14) 8.2	(11) 3.1				(35) 4.9	(43) 8.2
		-9.2	-6.6				-7.0	-6.8
		7.5	7.0			% Profit Before Taxes/Total Assets	9.4	8.5
		3.1	-1.0				1.4	-1.2
		-5.6	-3.1				-2.1	-8.6
		57.9	10.0			Sales/Net Fixed Assets	5.0	13.4
		1.4	1.5				1.5	2.6
		.8	.7				.7	.9
		2.8	1.2			Sales/Total Assets	2.2	2.6
		.9	.8				.8	1.4
		.2	.4				.5	.6
		.6	3.8			% Depr., Dep., Amort./Sales	2.2	1.5
		(14) 6.5	(14) 9.0				(37) 8.0	(47) 5.5
		11.1	11.2				10.1	12.1
						% Officers', Directors' Owners' Comp/Sales		1.7
							(13)	3.4
								8.1
824M	12344M	190357M	250971M	598997M	140522M	Net Sales ($)	1010524M	1182014M
705M	7564M	82341M	290327M	345245M	209856M	Total Assets ($)	975905M	767397M

Comparative Historical Data   Current Data Sorted by Sales

			Type of Statement						
12	10	12	Unqualified		2	1	2	3	4
11	3	5	Reviewed			1		3	1
4	5	5	Compiled		3		1	1	
7	5	4	Tax Returns	3	1				
21	27	25	Other	7	6	2		6	4
4/1/07-3/31/08 ALL	4/1/08-3/31/09 ALL	4/1/09-3/31/10 ALL		9 (4/1-9/30/09)			42 (10/1/09-3/31/10)		
				0-1MM	1-3MM	3-5MM	5-10MM	10-25MM	25MM & OVER
55	50	51	NUMBER OF STATEMENTS	10	12	4	3	13	9
%	%	%	ASSETS	%	%	%	%	%	%
7.8	10.3	8.3	Cash & Equivalents	12.6	5.9			6.7	
17.6	17.9	13.2	Trade Receivables (net)	6.7	7.6			10.8	
8.3	5.2	6.3	Inventory	.1	13.0			9.1	
1.6	3.4	3.6	All Other Current	4.8	1.0			3.8	
35.3	36.7	31.4	Total Current	24.1	27.4			30.4	
47.7	47.9	51.1	Fixed Assets (net)	60.9	47.1			56.2	
1.9	5.7	5.9	Intangibles (net)	14.0	.3			4.6	
15.1	9.7	11.6	All Other Non-Current	.9	25.2			8.8	
100.0	100.0	100.0	Total	100.0	100.0			100.0	
			LIABILITIES						
8.8	7.0	8.3	Notes Payable-Short Term	16.2	10.1			6.1	
5.5	7.8	4.7	Cur. Mat.-L.T.D.	4.1	3.9			6.7	
10.5	9.3	12.4	Trade Payables	28.4	6.3			6.5	
.2	.1	.2	Income Taxes Payable	.0	.0			.5	
17.3	11.4	14.1	All Other Current	3.3	7.6			18.7	
42.3	35.6	39.7	Total Current	52.0	27.8			38.5	
39.4	43.4	40.1	Long-Term Debt	74.8	36.3			30.5	
.2	.6	.8	Deferred Taxes	.0	.0			1.6	
16.2	6.1	5.2	All Other Non-Current	4.9	10.8			4.1	
2.0	14.3	14.2	Net Worth	-31.7	25.1			25.4	
100.0	100.0	100.0	Total Liabilities & Net Worth	100.0	100.0			100.0	
			INCOME DATA						
100.0	100.0	100.0	Net Sales	100.0	100.0			100.0	
			Gross Profit						
89.1	88.9	87.8	Operating Expenses	80.3	82.1			89.7	
10.9	11.1	12.2	Operating Profit	19.7	17.9			10.3	
3.1	7.4	7.1	All Other Expenses (net)	18.5	6.5			4.9	
7.8	3.8	5.1	Profit Before Taxes	1.2	11.4			5.4	
			RATIOS						
1.6	2.2	1.6		3.9	1.8			1.4	
1.0	1.1	.9	Current	.8	.9			1.0	
.4	.5	.5		.1	.2			.5	
1.1	1.7	1.0		1.3	1.5			.7	
.5	.7	.6	Quick	.6	.4			.5	
.2	.3	.3		.1	.1			.2	
9 42.6	7 49.7	0 999.8		0 UND	0 UND			17 20.9	
22 16.6	26 13.9	25 14.7	Sales/Receivables	0 UND	4 94.4			29 12.7	
35 10.5	43 8.6	44 8.3		59 6.1	36 10.3			42 8.7	
			Cost of Sales/Inventory						
			Cost of Sales/Payables						
16.1	9.8	12.6		9.4	7.3			11.7	
-298.1	133.0	-56.8	Sales/Working Capital	-16.2	-79.0			-108.9	
-7.6	-7.4	-6.6		-2.1	-7.3			-7.7	
8.8	9.2	4.7						5.3	
(46) 2.2	(37) 2.7	(39) 2.0	EBIT/Interest					(12) 2.1	
.1	.5	-.3						-1.4	
	2.6	12.5							
	(11) 1.6	(10) 2.7	Net Profit + Depr., Dep., Amort./Cur. Mat. L/T/D						
	.1	.4							
.5	.5	.8		.4	.6			1.1	
2.1	1.9	2.3	Fixed/Worth	16.0	1.4			1.5	
-224.1	-6.4	-6.5		-.4	-5.6			-24.4	
1.1	1.0	1.3		5.7	.5			.8	
4.6	4.3	3.6	Debt/Worth	NM	1.4			2.9	
-311.0	-9.7	-7.3		-1.6	-7.0			-26.8	
40.8	75.5	26.1							
(41) 21.8	(35) 24.7	(35) 8.9	% Profit Before Taxes/Tangible Net Worth						
7.8	-3.0	-4.8							
13.5	15.2	7.8		6.1	13.1			10.9	
6.5	5.6	3.3	% Profit Before Taxes/Total Assets	1.8	3.2			4.0	
-.6	-1.5	-3.0		-6.2	-2.5			-4.8	
15.4	28.8	12.4		112.3	10.4			8.4	
3.2	3.4	1.6	Sales/Net Fixed Assets	.8	4.4			1.5	
1.7	1.0	.9		.2	1.4			.9	
2.6	2.7	1.9		1.3	2.5			1.7	
1.4	1.4	1.0	Sales/Total Assets	.7	1.1			1.0	
1.1	.8	.5		.2	.2			.7	
2.1	1.1	3.2			3.4			5.0	
(44) 4.7	(43) 6.5	(42) 7.1	% Depr., Dep., Amort./Sales		(11) 5.6			(12) 9.6	
10.3	14.4	12.3			8.8			22.5	
1.9									
(13) 4.5			% Officers', Directors' Owners' Comp/Sales						
8.2									
1494790M	1627505M	1194015M	Net Sales ($)	5128M	23064M	15649M	19208M	240502M	890464M
811656M	1056612M	936038M	Total Assets ($)	29282M	51173M	27045M	34302M	334379M	459857M

© RMA 2010   M = $ thousand   MM = $ million
See Pages 9 through 22 for Explanation of Ratios and Data

TRANSPORTATION—Line-Haul Railroads NAICS 482111

| Current Data Sorted by Assets | | | | | | | Comparative Historical Data | |

Type of Statement

						Type of Statement		
		2	11	1	8	Unqualified	23	20
	1	3	4			Reviewed	5	4
2		2	2			Compiled	4	6
3	1	4				Tax Returns	6	2
2	7	8	12		4	Other	24	29
	17 (4/1-9/30/09)		60 (10/1/09-3/31/10)				4/1/05-3/31/06	4/1/06-3/31/07
0-500M	500M-2MM	2-10MM	10-50MM	50-100MM	100-250MM		ALL	ALL
7	9	19	29	1	12	NUMBER OF STATEMENTS	62	61
%	%	%	%	%	%		%	%
		5.9	9.8		7.9	Cash & Equivalents	8.8	9.0
		21.3	12.8		5.7	Trade Receivables (net)	17.2	17.8
		4.2	2.0		.6	Inventory	4.4	1.3
		.9	2.8		2.2	All Other Current	4.2	5.3
		32.3	27.4		16.4	Total Current	34.6	33.4
		50.6	54.7		72.3	Fixed Assets (net)	53.2	54.5
		2.0	3.7		5.8	Intangibles (net)	2.7	3.6
		15.1	14.2		5.4	All Other Non-Current	9.5	8.5
		100.0	100.0		100.0	Total	100.0	100.0

LIABILITIES

						LIABILITIES		
		2.6	1.7		.6	Notes Payable-Short Term	5.6	5.8
		8.9	6.2		2.3	Cur. Mat.-L.T.D.	3.3	3.4
		7.8	7.0		2.4	Trade Payables	11.4	10.6
		.6	.6		.0	Income Taxes Payable	.4	.5
		15.6	10.6		5.4	All Other Current	9.6	9.2
		35.5	26.1		10.8	Total Current	30.3	29.5
		26.1	25.5		33.3	Long-Term Debt	23.4	28.4
		.0	2.2		9.2	Deferred Taxes	3.9	2.6
		3.4	2.9		8.2	All Other Non-Current	6.3	6.2
		35.1	43.2		38.5	Net Worth	36.2	33.3
		100.0	100.0		100.0	Total Liabilties & Net Worth	100.0	100.0

INCOME DATA

						INCOME DATA		
		100.0	100.0		100.0	Net Sales	100.0	100.0
						Gross Profit		
		93.5	89.5		81.9	Operating Expenses	85.6	84.8
		6.5	10.5		18.1	Operating Profit	14.4	15.2
		2.9	-.2		2.8	All Other Expenses (net)	1.3	1.2
		3.6	10.7		15.3	Profit Before Taxes	13.0	14.0

RATIOS

						RATIOS		
		3.0	2.3		2.5		2.2	1.7
		1.1	1.1		1.8	Current	1.1	1.0
		.5	.6		.8		.7	.7
		2.8	1.9		2.0		1.6	1.4
		1.1	.8		1.7	Quick	.8	.9
		.5	.4		.6		.5	.5
	24	15.0	12 30.8	36	10.2		19 19.0	31 11.6
	36	10.0	48 7.6	49	7.5	Sales/Receivables	56 6.5	45 8.2
	56	6.5	65 5.6	57	6.4		75 4.9	64 5.7
						Cost of Sales/Inventory		
						Cost of Sales/Payables		
		6.3	6.6		2.8		5.1	10.6
		75.4	47.0		6.8	Sales/Working Capital	45.7	486.8
		-10.1	-8.1		-19.4		-9.5	-12.2
		4.8	10.4		7.7		23.4	12.9
	(18)	2.5	(28) 4.7	(11)	4.1	EBIT/Interest	(55) 5.9	(55) 3.8
		.4	1.3		1.8		1.5	2.1
			4.5				10.1	8.8
			(14) 1.9			Net Profit + Depr., Dep., Amort./Cur. Mat. L/T/D	(19) 3.9	(24)* 2.4
			1.0				2.2	1.4
		.8	.9		1.7		.9	.8
		1.1	1.4		2.3	Fixed/Worth	1.8	1.9
		9.5	3.4		3.7		4.0	5.5
		.5	.5		1.1		.9	.7
		1.8	1.7		1.8	Debt/Worth	1.9	3.0
		9.9	6.4		3.6		6.6	6.3
		31.1	27.6		36.8		54.7	51.9
	(15)	8.4	(28) 15.2		17.2	% Profit Before Taxes/Tangible Net Worth	(56) 22.5	(56) 27.2
		-5.8	4.8		8.2		10.3	8.5
		10.9	11.7		9.9		15.6	15.8
		3.0	7.1		4.9	% Profit Before Taxes/Total Assets	9.0	8.8
		-1.6	.8		2.1		2.0	3.1
		12.3	2.7		.9		5.1	4.4
		4.3	1.5		.6	Sales/Net Fixed Assets	1.5	1.4
		.7	.7		.4		.6	.7
		3.2	1.2		.5		1.6	1.8
		2.1	.9		.4	Sales/Total Assets	.8	.8
		.5	.5		.3		.4	.4
		1.3	5.0				3.4	3.7
		8.0	10.0			% Depr., Dep., Amort./Sales	(56) 6.9	(57) 7.3
		15.6	11.5				10.2	11.1
						% Officers', Directors' Owners' Comp/Sales		
6894M	33648M	223820M	849221M	200684M	858349M	Net Sales ($)	1316210M	1945841M
1544M	10950M	110061M	709087M	79971M	1854707M	Total Assets ($)	1568645M	2097061M

M = $ thousand   MM = $ million
See Pages 9 through 22 for Explanation of Ratios and Data

Comparative Historical Data / Current Data Sorted by Sales

	4/1/07-3/31/08 ALL	4/1/08-3/31/09 ALL	4/1/09-3/31/10 ALL	Type of Statement	0-1MM	1-3MM	3-5MM	5-10MM	10-25MM	25MM & OVER
	20	19	22	Unqualified		1		4	4	13
	14	12	8	Reviewed		1	1	1	2	3
	4	9	6	Compiled	1	1		1	3	
	5	5	8	Tax Returns	2		2	2	2	2
	28	33	33	Other	6	4	2	6	8	7
						17 (4/1-9/30/09)			60 (10/1/09-3/31/10)	
NUMBER OF STATEMENTS	71	78	77		9	7	5	14	19	23
	%	%	%	**ASSETS**	%	%	%	%	%	%
	9.6	7.2	9.5	Cash & Equivalents				10.7	5.3	11.4
	15.8	16.4	16.0	Trade Receivables (net)				27.4	15.9	15.4
	3.9	2.1	2.0	Inventory				1.5	3.3	2.7
	4.9	3.5	3.5	All Other Current				1.3	2.4	2.2
	34.2	29.2	30.9	Total Current				41.0	26.8	31.8
	54.2	56.2	52.3	Fixed Assets (net)				45.1	57.9	54.8
	1.6	2.2	2.9	Intangibles (net)				2.6	5.7	3.3
	10.0	12.4	13.9	All Other Non-Current				11.3	9.6	10.2
	100.0	100.0	100.0	Total				100.0	100.0	100.0
				LIABILITIES						
	3.2	5.7	2.6	Notes Payable-Short Term				2.3	2.1	2.4
	3.6	4.8	6.0	Cur. Mat.-L.T.D.				5.4	10.9	3.2
	11.1	8.6	9.0	Trade Payables				11.6	7.8	7.0
	.2	1.0	.4	Income Taxes Payable				.9	.0	.5
	7.8	12.4	27.1	All Other Current				48.8	7.4	12.1
	25.9	32.5	45.0	Total Current				69.0	28.4	25.2
	26.3	27.4	29.4	Long-Term Debt				16.2	32.6	24.6
	1.7	1.9	2.3	Deferred Taxes				1.1	1.5	5.7
	4.1	4.1	3.2	All Other Non-Current				5.1	2.8	5.3
	42.2	34.1	20.2	Net Worth				8.7	34.7	39.2
	100.0	100.0	100.0	Total Liabilities & Net Worth				100.0	100.0	100.0
				INCOME DATA						
	100.0	100.0	100.0	Net Sales				100.0	100.0	100.0
				Gross Profit						
	80.9	82.9	88.9	Operating Expenses				93.3	93.0	89.7
	19.1	17.1	11.1	Operating Profit				6.7	7.0	10.3
	1.5	1.7	2.0	All Other Expenses (net)				1.4	-.5	1.4
	17.6	15.4	9.1	Profit Before Taxes				5.4	7.5	8.9
				RATIOS						
	2.4	1.9	2.3					1.7	2.4	2.2
	1.4	1.1	1.1	Current				1.1	1.1	1.1
	.9	.6	.6					.5	.6	.8
	1.7	1.7	1.8					1.6	1.8	1.8
	1.0	.7	.8	Quick				.9	.7	.9
	.5	.4	.4					.3	.4	.7
	26 14.3	18 20.7	15 24.9					30 12.3	24 15.1	35 10.4
	44 8.3	36 10.2	38 9.5	Sales/Receivables				51 7.1	33 11.1	52 7.0
	58 6.3	55 6.6	57 6.4					70 5.2	48 7.6	59 6.2
				Cost of Sales/Inventory						
				Cost of Sales/Payables						
	5.1	7.6	6.2					9.5	6.6	5.2
	12.4	67.1	74.0	Sales/Working Capital				47.6	205.7	47.0
	-30.4	-10.9	-8.4					-3.0	-7.8	-18.1
	17.2	10.1	8.7					12.1	8.7	8.3
	(60) 7.5	(68) 3.8	(69) 2.8	EBIT/Interest				4.5	(18) 3.7	(21) 2.0
	3.8	2.1	1.2					.2	1.1	1.3
	14.7	9.2	5.6							8.0
	(23) 2.4	(24) 3.9	(28) 1.9	Net Profit + Depr., Dep., Amort./Cur. Mat. L/T/D						(13) 2.0
	1.7	1.3	1.4							1.6
	.8	.9	.8					.6	1.0	1.1
	1.3	1.7	1.5	Fixed/Worth				1.2	2.4	1.7
	3.2	3.9	4.7					4.5	999.8	3.0
	.6	.7	.6					.6	.9	1.0
	1.4	2.1	1.8	Debt/Worth				1.7	2.6	1.8
	3.3	6.2	7.2					7.2	999.8	3.7
	56.7	64.3	32.0					24.7	59.5	26.2
	(66) 30.3	(71) 30.3	(66) 15.2	% Profit Before Taxes/Tangible Net Worth			(12) 14.6	(15) 26.4	13.1
	13.0	10.1	3.6					-3.6	9.5	2.1
	19.4	14.6	12.8					9.4	13.9	11.8
	11.3	7.6	6.3	% Profit Before Taxes/Total Assets				5.3	7.8	4.2
	5.5	2.9	.8					-2.1	1.0	.6
	5.1	7.3	7.1					64.2	4.3	6.3
	1.5	1.7	1.7	Sales/Net Fixed Assets				2.3	1.8	1.1
	.7	.6	.7					.5	1.2	.5
	1.8	2.3	2.4					4.0	2.7	1.4
	.8	.9	.9	Sales/Total Assets				1.2	1.1	.8
	.5	.5	.4					.3	.6	.4
	2.9	2.2	3.8					.9	7.6	2.2
	(63) 6.2	(69) 6.7	(70) 8.8	% Depr., Dep., Amort./Sales			(13) 7.3	10.0	(19) 7.5
	9.6	9.1	11.6					11.7	11.5	9.8
				% Officers', Directors' Owners' Comp/Sales						
	2088264M	2528706M	2172616M	Net Sales ($)	3534M	12829M	18803M	116331M	329670M	1691449M
	2039450M	2882789M	2766320M	Total Assets ($)	14602M	30106M	20439M	180777M	332093M	2188303M

M = $ thousand   MM = $ million
See Pages 9 through 22 for Explanation of Ratios and Data

Current Data Sorted by Assets   Comparative Historical Data

	0-500M	500M-2MM	2-10MM	10-50MM	50-100MM	100-250MM		4/1/05-3/31/06 ALL	4/1/06-3/31/07 ALL
		1 (4/1-9/30/09)		30 (10/1/09-3/31/10)			**Type of Statement**		
		1	1	3	3	6	Unqualified	7	7
		1	1	2			Reviewed	2	2
		1	1				Compiled	2	1
		1	1	1			Tax Returns	1	
		4	4	5	2	1	Other	5	5
			8	11	5	7	**NUMBER OF STATEMENTS**	17	15
	%	%	%	%	%	%	**ASSETS**	%	%
				22.9			Cash & Equivalents	9.3	11.5
	D	D		15.3			Trade Receivables (net)	11.6	13.7
	A	A		.4			Inventory	.7	.5
	T	T		2.0			All Other Current	4.5	4.1
	A	A		40.6			Total Current	26.1	29.8
				51.5			Fixed Assets (net)	62.6	57.9
	N	N		1.8			Intangibles (net)	2.1	2.3
	O	O		6.1			All Other Non-Current	9.2	10.0
	T	T		100.0			Total	100.0	100.0
							LIABILITIES		
	A	A		9.2			Notes Payable-Short Term	2.0	1.3
	V	V		6.2			Cur. Mat.-L.T.D.	3.2	4.0
	A	A		12.0			Trade Payables	5.9	4.4
	I	I		.0			Income Taxes Payable	.2	.7
	L	L		3.9			All Other Current	7.6	9.9
	A	A		31.2			Total Current	18.9	20.3
	B	B		22.9			Long-Term Debt	40.1	33.8
	L	L		1.1			Deferred Taxes	2.6	1.6
	E	E		10.0			All Other Non-Current	10.2	7.8
				34.9			Net Worth	28.2	36.4
				100.0			Total Liabilties & Net Worth	100.0	100.0
							INCOME DATA		
				100.0			Net Sales	100.0	100.0
							Gross Profit		
				83.0			Operating Expenses	89.7	81.6
				17.0			Operating Profit	10.3	18.4
				4.4			All Other Expenses (net)	3.3	7.7
				12.6			Profit Before Taxes	7.0	10.8
							RATIOS		
				2.7			Current	2.8	2.4
				1.3				1.5	1.6
				.7				.2	.6
				2.7			Quick	2.1	2.0
				1.1				1.4	1.1
				.5				.2	.5
			0	UND			Sales/Receivables	0 / UND 20 / 18.7	
			55	6.7				29 / 12.5 36 / 10.2	
			64	5.7				72 / 5.1 79 / 4.6	
							Cost of Sales/Inventory		
							Cost of Sales/Payables		
				2.7			Sales/Working Capital	3.5	7.2
				8.8				17.0	12.3
				-6.6				-7.6	-16.9
							EBIT/Interest	7.9	7.5
								(15) 5.2 (13) 4.0	
								1.0	2.5
							Net Profit + Depr., Dep., Amort./Cur. Mat. L/T/D		
				1.2			Fixed/Worth	1.0	.4
				1.8				1.8	1.9
				3.3				-20.8	2.9
				1.3			Debt/Worth	1.1	.9
				3.3				1.7	1.9
				5.6				-36.1	3.7
				46.4			% Profit Before Taxes/Tangible Net Worth	33.9	43.6
				12.8				(12) 21.6 (13) 28.2	
				1.6				7.3	8.6
				9.1			% Profit Before Taxes/Total Assets	12.6	18.3
				2.2				6.2	9.2
				.9				.2	2.8
				10.5			Sales/Net Fixed Assets	3.4	6.5
				.9				1.7	1.3
				.4				.6	.5
				.9			Sales/Total Assets	1.8	2.0
				.4				1.2	.8
				.2				.4	.4
				4.6			% Depr., Dep., Amort./Sales	5.9	3.3
				8.8				(15) 8.0 (14) 5.8	
				30.7				15.3	8.0
							% Officers', Directors' Owners' Comp/Sales		
			113379M	207689M	451930M	696652M	Net Sales ($)	670229M	618380M
			46418M	266926M	453792M	1226212M	Total Assets ($)	749441M	898421M

M = $ thousand   MM = $ million
See Pages 9 through 22 for Explanation of Ratios and Data

Comparative Historical Data   Current Data Sorted by Sales

Type of Statement	4/1/07-3/31/08 ALL	4/1/08-3/31/09 ALL	4/1/09-3/31/10 ALL	0-1MM	1-3MM	3-5MM	5-10MM	10-25MM	25MM & OVER
Unqualified	5	7	13				1	1	11
Reviewed	1		3				1	2	
Compiled	1	1	1					1	
Tax Returns	1		2					1	
Other	5	5	12	1	1	1	1	2	6
					1 (4/1-9/30/09)		30 (10/1/09-3/31/10)		
NUMBER OF STATEMENTS	13	13	31	2	1	1	3	7	17
	%	%	%	%	%	%	%	%	%
ASSETS									
Cash & Equivalents	12.2	6.6	12.6						6.4
Trade Receivables (net)	12.6	10.7	12.9						15.9
Inventory	.2	.2	1.9						3.0
All Other Current	4.8	5.9	5.6						6.9
Total Current	29.8	23.4	33.0						32.2
Fixed Assets (net)	58.5	63.5	55.0						59.8
Intangibles (net)	5.0	3.5	2.5						4.0
All Other Non-Current	6.7	9.7	9.5						4.0
Total	100.0	100.0	100.0						100.0
LIABILITIES									
Notes Payable-Short Term	2.2	1.1	5.8						5.0
Cur. Mat.-L.T.D.	3.8	2.7	6.3						7.9
Trade Payables	6.6	3.7	7.4						6.5
Income Taxes Payable	.7	.0	.1						.1
All Other Current	10.0	7.0	7.4						8.7
Total Current	23.3	14.6	27.0						28.2
Long-Term Debt	37.3	30.5	28.2						34.2
Deferred Taxes	2.2	1.1	2.3						4.2
All Other Non-Current	1.9	10.1	5.2						2.5
Net Worth	35.3	43.7	37.3						31.0
Total Liabilties & Net Worth	100.0	100.0	100.0						100.0
INCOME DATA									
Net Sales	100.0	100.0	100.0						100.0
Gross Profit									
Operating Expenses	82.5	79.3	86.8						94.2
Operating Profit	17.5	20.7	13.2						5.8
All Other Expenses (net)	2.9	6.2	1.9						2.2
Profit Before Taxes	14.6	14.5	11.3						3.6
RATIOS									
Current	3.5	3.3	2.2						1.7
	1.1	1.1	1.2						1.1
	.4	.9	.7						.6
Quick	2.3	1.9	1.8						1.3
	1.0	1.0	1.0						1.0
	.3	.9	.2						.3
Sales/Receivables	14 26.6	23 16.1	14 25.6						22 16.8
	30 12.3	30 12.0	38 9.7						44 8.4
	61 6.0	81 4.5	55 6.7						53 6.8
Cost of Sales/Inventory									
Cost of Sales/Payables									
Sales/Working Capital	5.1	4.3	7.0						8.6
	39.8	29.0	38.2						40.4
	-4.5	-91.3	-9.2						-9.8
EBIT/Interest	12.0	6.4	5.1						4.5
	3.8 (11)	4.0 (27)	1.8						2.1
	2.3	2.6	1.2						1.3
Net Profit + Depr., Dep., Amort./Cur. Mat. L/T/D									
Fixed/Worth	.6	.7	1.1						1.3
	1.4	2.0	1.6						1.7
	NM	2.6	4.4						24.9
Debt/Worth	.8	.5	.7						1.3
	1.1	1.6	2.1						2.1
	NM	2.1	6.2						26.5
% Profit Before Taxes/Tangible Net Worth	36.8	32.2	47.3						53.1
	(10) 26.5	(12) 21.8	(29) 15.3					(15)	18.0
	10.5	9.1	2.1						5.1
% Profit Before Taxes/Total Assets	15.6	12.8	9.1						8.7
	9.4	9.5	3.4						2.4
	5.5	4.9	1.6						1.9
Sales/Net Fixed Assets	3.9	2.2	10.5						10.7
	1.1	.9	1.1						1.3
	.6	.6	.5						.5
Sales/Total Assets	1.6	1.1	2.5						3.0
	.6	.6	.5						.9
	.4	.4	.3						.4
% Depr., Dep., Amort./Sales	3.6	3.2	2.2						2.9
	(11) 4.7	(10) 4.4	(24) 5.5					(13)	4.6
	8.3	6.7	11.5						6.9
% Officers', Directors' Owners' Comp/Sales									
Net Sales ($)	826546M	904061M	1469650M	1251M	2685M	3491M	24145M	89199M	1348879M
Total Assets ($)	1170225M	1439483M	1993348M	20510M	23330M	7185M	77883M	142682M	1721758M

© RMA 2010

M = $ thousand   MM = $ million
See Pages 9 through 22 for Explanation of Ratios and Data

Current Data Sorted by Assets — **Comparative Historical Data**

0-500M	500M-2MM	2-10MM	10-50MM	50-100MM	100-250MM	Type of Statement	4/1/05-3/31/06 ALL	4/1/06-3/31/07 ALL
	1	7	6	7	10	Unqualified	22	30
1	3	6	2	1		Reviewed	8	7
4	5	2	1			Compiled	9	9
				1		Tax Returns	1	5
2	10	20	25	4	9	Other	38	43
	10 (4/1-9/30/09)		117 (10/1/09-3/31/10)					
7	19	35	34	13	19	**NUMBER OF STATEMENTS**	78	94
%	%	%	%	%	%	**ASSETS**	%	%
	18.3	8.6	11.1	3.1	9.0	Cash & Equivalents	9.0	8.2
	19.2	13.2	12.4	4.9	6.3	Trade Receivables (net)	19.2	14.8
	1.5	.1	.4	.5	2.2	Inventory	1.6	1.5
	6.1	2.4	4.3	5.5	3.2	All Other Current	3.4	2.5
	45.2	24.2	28.2	14.1	20.8	Total Current	33.3	27.0
	46.3	61.4	66.2	69.9	72.9	Fixed Assets (net)	56.3	62.9
	1.4	2.2	2.0	4.4	3.5	Intangibles (net)	2.2	2.4
	7.0	12.2	3.5	11.6	2.8	All Other Non-Current	8.3	7.7
	100.0	100.0	100.0	100.0	100.0	Total	100.0	100.0
						LIABILITIES		
	3.3	2.2	4.6	4.5	.8	Notes Payable-Short Term	4.6	5.1
	11.6	7.7	3.9	2.8	3.8	Cur. Mat.-L.T.D.	4.8	4.5
	9.3	8.6	4.8	2.6	4.2	Trade Payables	8.7	7.4
	.1	.1	.3	.0	.2	Income Taxes Payable	.6	.3
	18.6	9.9	5.2	7.6	7.4	All Other Current	7.5	6.3
	43.0	28.5	18.8	17.6	16.4	Total Current	26.2	23.7
	25.6	43.6	35.1	41.5	40.2	Long-Term Debt	30.3	34.4
	.0	.4	.7	1.9	5.5	Deferred Taxes	2.8	2.5
	10.4	5.7	2.3	3.8	2.3	All Other Non-Current	6.3	2.8
	21.0	21.8	43.0	35.3	35.6	Net Worth	34.5	36.6
	100.0	100.0	100.0	100.0	100.0	Total Liabilities & Net Worth	100.0	100.0
						INCOME DATA		
	100.0	100.0	100.0	100.0	100.0	Net Sales	100.0	100.0
						Gross Profit		
	100.3	87.0	85.0	87.8	86.9	Operating Expenses	84.5	80.8
	-.3	13.0	15.0	12.2	13.1	Operating Profit	15.5	19.2
	2.0	6.7	6.2	4.9	4.0	All Other Expenses (net)	1.7	4.2
	-2.2	6.3	8.7	7.3	9.1	Profit Before Taxes	13.8	15.0
						RATIOS		
	2.5	4.1	2.9	2.4	2.1	Current	2.5	2.1
	1.4	1.0	1.7	1.7	1.2		1.3	1.1
	.3	.4	.6	.5	.8		.8	.5
	2.5	1.8	2.4	2.1	1.7	Quick	2.1	1.8
	.8	.8	1.2	1.0	1.0		1.0	.9
	.2	.4	.4	.3	.4		.6	.5
	0 UND	0 UND	28 12.8	15 24.2	14 26.8	Sales/Receivables	31 11.9	18 20.5
	18 20.8	27 13.7	41 8.8	27 13.7	33 11.1		44 8.2	39 9.2
	28 13.2	49 7.4	60 6.0	42 8.8	52 7.1		83 4.4	63 5.8
						Cost of Sales/Inventory		
						Cost of Sales/Payables		
	7.3	5.5	5.3	6.0	5.3	Sales/Working Capital	4.4	7.2
	33.2	-999.8	10.8	21.9	30.1		17.6	38.1
	-5.4	-5.9	-8.8	-9.3	-23.0		-26.0	-11.3
	3.9	7.5	11.7	4.6	3.5	EBIT/Interest	9.8	16.7
	(14) -1.6	(27) 3.6	(27) 3.5	(12) 2.3	(18) 2.8		(70) 4.9	(83) 5.1
	-8.7	-.1	.5	-.1	1.9		2.8	2.3
						Net Profit + Depr., Dep., Amort./Cur. Mat. L/T/D	4.0	4.5
							(26) 1.9	(23) 2.2
							1.2	1.2
	.7	1.2	.8	1.3	1.4	Fixed/Worth	1.0	1.0
	1.7	3.2	2.2	1.4	2.8		1.7	1.9
	7.2	-8.1	7.6	23.5	5.9		3.7	5.1
	.7	.8	.3	.7	1.0	Debt/Worth	.9	.9
	3.9	3.6	1.9	1.7	2.1		1.9	2.0
	9.2	-18.6	8.2	25.4	6.1		4.1	5.0
	45.3	72.9	36.8	23.4	28.0	% Profit Before Taxes/Tangible Net Worth	44.2	51.8
	(16) -2.3	(24) 22.0	(30) 20.0	(11) 9.7	(18) 19.3		(70) 28.5	(85) 33.7
	-31.0	1.9	3.1	-2.9	3.0		17.0	16.9
	6.4	12.2	15.6	7.6	7.1	% Profit Before Taxes/Total Assets	17.3	20.6
	-1.6	3.9	7.9	4.2	5.7		11.1	9.8
	-17.9	-6.1	-2.1	-1.0	1.7		5.3	4.4
	39.3	6.1	2.0	2.1	1.6	Sales/Net Fixed Assets	3.7	3.3
	5.1	1.5	1.1	.7	.7		1.7	1.6
	1.2	.3	.6	.5	.6		.9	.8
	4.3	1.9	1.3	.8	.9	Sales/Total Assets	1.8	1.5
	2.1	.9	.7	.6	.6		1.1	.9
	1.0	.3	.4	.3	.5		.6	.6
	2.2	3.1	5.6	6.1		% Depr., Dep., Amort./Sales	3.2	2.7
	(13) 5.4	(31) 8.4	(31) 9.1	(11) 7.0			(63) 5.8	(81) 5.4
	12.5	29.0	15.3	11.1			9.0	10.3
						% Officers', Directors' Owners' Comp/Sales	.7	.8
							(12) 3.8	(23) 2.8
							5.1	10.0
36216M	66511M	245705M	603929M	750056M	2699793M	Net Sales ($)	3294626M	4013975M
2478M	22627M	165750M	739484M	1046889M	3404577M	Total Assets ($)	3442710M	4505600M

Comparative Historical Data | Current Data Sorted by Sales

4/1/07-3/31/08 ALL	4/1/08-3/31/09 ALL	4/1/09-3/31/10 ALL	Type of Statement	0-1MM	1-3MM	3-5MM	5-10MM	10-25MM	25MM & OVER
26	23	23	Unqualified			1	1	4	17
3	9	11	Reviewed		2	1	1	5	2
8	8	11	Compiled		5	3	2	1	
7	11	12	Tax Returns	5	1	2	3	1	
39	59	70	Other	6	11	12	8	9	24
				10 (4/1-9/30/09)		117 (10/1/09-3/31/10)			
83	110	127	**NUMBER OF STATEMENTS**	11	19	19	15	20	43
%	%	%	**ASSETS**	%	%	%	%	%	%
10.5	10.1	12.3	Cash & Equivalents	21.2	7.1	13.5	16.2	11.5	10.8
12.1	12.8	12.1	Trade Receivables (net)	5.0	6.9	15.0	16.5	19.7	10.0
1.2	4.0	.9	Inventory	1.6	1.5	.5	.1	.2	1.3
4.5	4.2	3.8	All Other Current	.5	2.7	5.1	9.8	.3	4.1
28.3	31.2	29.1	Total Current	28.3	18.1	34.1	42.5	31.7	26.1
64.9	58.1	61.4	Fixed Assets (net)	61.4	75.9	51.7	49.3	60.7	63.9
1.6	3.7	2.5	Intangibles (net)	.7	2.4	2.3	1.6	3.5	2.9
5.3	7.0	7.0	All Other Non-Current	9.6	3.6	11.9	6.6	4.0	7.2
100.0	100.0	100.0	Total	100.0	100.0	100.0	100.0	100.0	100.0
			LIABILITIES						
3.5	3.1	3.0	Notes Payable-Short Term	1.8	2.8	5.6	1.5	4.3	2.2
4.0	4.5	6.2	Cur. Mat.-L.T.D.	8.5	5.9	4.6	17.7	4.4	3.2
4.7	7.8	6.0	Trade Payables	.8	1.7	4.1	18.1	7.4	5.1
.4	.2	.2	Income Taxes Payable	.0	.2	.1	.0	.5	.1
6.6	7.9	10.3	All Other Current	11.3	6.2	6.5	23.8	6.8	10.4
19.1	23.6	25.6	Total Current	22.4	16.8	20.9	61.1	23.4	21.0
37.3	36.0	37.3	Long-Term Debt	41.5	53.0	35.9	36.0	29.5	34.0
2.5	1.7	1.3	Deferred Taxes	.0	.7	.2	.0	.1	3.4
2.6	3.3	4.5	All Other Non-Current	13.3	7.1	8.3	.6	1.2	2.3
38.4	35.3	31.3	Net Worth	22.8	22.4	34.7	2.2	45.8	39.4
100.0	100.0	100.0	Total Liabilities & Net Worth	100.0	100.0	100.0	100.0	100.0	100.0
			INCOME DATA						
100.0	100.0	100.0	Net Sales	100.0	100.0	100.0	100.0	100.0	100.0
			Gross Profit						
80.0	84.2	87.8	Operating Expenses	67.5	87.0	96.6	92.8	87.2	88.1
20.0	15.8	12.2	Operating Profit	32.5	13.0	3.4	7.2	12.8	11.9
5.5	3.4	5.1	All Other Expenses (net)	10.7	10.9	4.1	3.5	3.5	3.0
14.5	12.4	7.0	Profit Before Taxes	21.8	2.1	-.7	3.7	9.4	8.9
			RATIOS						
3.2	2.3	2.5	Current	2.9	1.8	5.2	4.7	2.7	2.4
1.3	1.5	1.4		1.3	.7	1.9	.7	1.5	1.5
.8	.9	.6		.2	.1	.8	.4	.7	.8
2.8	1.8	2.1	Quick	2.1	1.7	4.6	1.4	2.6	2.0
1.1	1.2	1.0		1.3	.6	1.3	.6	1.5	1.2
.6	.4	.4		.2	.1	.4	.2	.7	.4
23 16.2	16 23.1	5 66.7	Sales/Receivables	0 UND	0 UND	0 UND	0 UND	28 13.1	15 24.6
38 9.5	34 10.9	30 12.2		0 UND	22 16.5	34 10.7	21 17.0	41 9.0	34 10.9
55 6.6	47 7.8	47 7.7		25 14.8	35 10.4	49 7.4	33 11.0	60 6.1	51 7.2
			Cost of Sales/Inventory						
			Cost of Sales/Payables						
4.0	5.8	5.6	Sales/Working Capital	1.9	7.0	5.2	6.8	6.1	5.3
20.7	14.9	24.2		6.3	-15.5	11.7	-24.6	18.6	16.7
-28.7	-165.4	-9.5		-2.7	-5.4	-19.5	-4.9	-38.8	-23.0
13.9	11.1	7.9	EBIT/Interest		4.1	4.4	8.8	22.1	11.7
(67) 4.6	(94) 4.6	(102) 2.9		(15) 1.4	(14) 1.1	(11) 2.1	(16) 4.9	(40) 3.1	
2.4	2.0	.4			-2.5	-9.0	-2.0	.5	1.9
3.3	11.8	4.6	Net Profit + Depr., Dep., Amort./Cur. Mat. L/T/D						4.6
(18) 2.3	(25) 3.9	(16) 3.3						(10) 3.4	
1.5	2.4	1.1							1.2
.9	.9	1.0	Fixed/Worth	1.4	1.6	.7	.5	.7	1.2
1.9	2.0	2.4		3.2	4.9	1.9	5.3	2.0	1.7
4.7	5.0	10.6		-19.2	50.3	-75.3	-3.1	5.7	3.6
.7	.8	.8	Debt/Worth	1.4	1.7	.2	2.7	.4	.8
2.0	2.1	2.1		2.3	4.2	1.9	8.5	1.6	1.7
4.9	6.0	12.9		-33.8	50.4	-78.2	-5.3	6.0	3.8
46.9	49.4	49.0	% Profit Before Taxes/Tangible Net Worth		60.6	29.5	200.8	40.5	31.4
(78) 27.3	(95) 28.5	(105) 16.4		(15) 5.9	(14) -2.7	(10) 41.0	(18) 21.4	(40) 19.1	
15.8	10.2	-1.6			-33.8	-21.6	7.2	-8.8	7.6
18.4	16.9	11.1	% Profit Before Taxes/Total Assets	19.0	7.7	5.0	9.5	26.3	10.4
9.5	8.7	4.8		7.9	2.0	-2.1	3.5	7.3	6.2
4.5	3.2	-2.2		-4.2	-10.2	-21.7	-23.4	-2.0	2.4
2.6	3.7	3.6	Sales/Net Fixed Assets	1.5	1.5	6.0	11.0	6.0	2.7
1.0	1.4	1.2		.3	.9	2.7	2.7	1.5	1.0
.6	.7	.6		.3	.3	.7	1.0	.6	.6
1.5	1.8	1.6	Sales/Total Assets	.9	1.0	2.6	3.3	2.9	1.5
.7	.9	.9		.3	.7	1.3	1.2	1.1	.7
.5	.5	.5		.2	.3	.4	.6	.5	.5
3.1	2.9	4.0	% Depr., Dep., Amort./Sales		5.2	3.1	4.1	3.8	2.7
(69) 6.0	(86) 5.9	(97) 8.7		(17) 17.7	(17) 8.4	(10) 9.0	(19) 8.1	(26) 6.6	
10.4	8.9	18.4			30.6	21.0	22.3	11.1	9.6
.6	.9	1.3	% Officers', Directors' Owners' Comp/Sales						
(17) 2.2	(23) 1.3	(17) 2.3							
8.4	3.2	12.2							
3859157M	5518590M	4402210M	Net Sales ($)	5686M	34453M	75603M	108505M	311579M	3866384M
4651107M	5969113M	5381805M	Total Assets ($)	19378M	91541M	122147M	145516M	348434M	4654789M

M = $ thousand   MM = $ million
See Pages 9 through 22 for Explanation of Ratios and Data

	Current Data Sorted by Assets							Comparative Historical Data	

Type of Statement

						Type of Statement		
2	2	11	28	7	13	Unqualified	74	81
7	33	87	43	2	1	Reviewed	208	191
37	65	81	8			Compiled	245	237
124	94	50	4	1	1	Tax Returns	211	214
62	95	106	54	19	13	Other	363	337

146 (4/1-9/30/09)			904 (10/1/09-3/31/10)				4/1/05-3/31/06 ALL	4/1/06-3/31/07 ALL
0-500M	500M-2MM	2-10MM	10-50MM	50-100MM	100-250MM			
232	289	335	137	29	28	NUMBER OF STATEMENTS	1101	1060
%	%	%	%	%	%	ASSETS	%	%
15.9	10.9	10.2	7.9	6.6	3.4	Cash & Equivalents	9.9	10.4
20.6	29.5	27.7	20.8	18.8	19.1	Trade Receivables (net)	28.0	26.8
1.4	1.6	2.6	3.2	3.0	.5	Inventory	1.8	1.6
3.6	5.2	4.3	3.6	3.9	6.7	All Other Current	4.5	3.9
41.6	47.2	44.9	35.5	32.4	29.6	Total Current	44.2	42.7
43.7	40.5	41.7	51.6	47.6	50.8	Fixed Assets (net)	45.1	45.6
4.1	3.2	3.1	5.1	9.1	11.9	Intangibles (net)	2.8	2.8
10.6	9.2	10.2	7.8	10.9	7.7	All Other Non-Current	7.8	8.9
100.0	100.0	100.0	100.0	100.0	100.0	Total	100.0	100.0
						LIABILITIES		
19.7	10.6	9.0	5.0	6.6	2.5	Notes Payable-Short Term	9.1	8.9
12.3	9.1	8.3	9.1	7.7	8.4	Cur. Mat.-L.T.D.	8.8	8.5
11.5	12.8	9.2	8.6	6.7	9.3	Trade Payables	11.9	11.2
.1	.1	.2	.2	.2	.2	Income Taxes Payable	.3	.3
16.1	11.5	7.8	7.4	6.0	7.9	All Other Current	10.3	11.0
59.7	44.1	34.5	30.3	27.2	28.3	Total Current	40.4	39.9
40.2	31.7	23.0	26.8	29.0	34.7	Long-Term Debt	29.8	30.8
.0	.4	1.0	2.1	3.3	2.0	Deferred Taxes	1.0	.9
15.7	5.5	4.6	3.5	1.9	4.1	All Other Non-Current	3.9	4.5
-15.6	18.2	36.9	37.3	38.6	30.9	Net Worth	25.0	23.8
100.0	100.0	100.0	100.0	100.0	100.0	Total Liabilities & Net Worth	100.0	100.0
						INCOME DATA		
100.0	100.0	100.0	100.0	100.0	100.0	Net Sales	100.0	100.0
						Gross Profit		
97.4	97.0	96.3	96.5	95.7	94.9	Operating Expenses	95.2	95.0
2.6	3.0	3.7	3.5	4.3	5.1	Operating Profit	4.8	5.0
1.0	1.8	1.8	1.6	3.0	2.3	All Other Expenses (net)	1.1	1.1
1.5	1.2	1.9	1.8	1.3	2.8	Profit Before Taxes	3.7	3.8
						RATIOS		
2.2	2.2	2.3	1.8	1.6	1.4	Current	2.0	2.1
.7	1.2	1.3	1.1	1.2	1.1		1.2	1.1
.2	.5	.8	.7	.8	.8		.7	.7
2.1	1.9	2.0	1.5	1.2	1.1	Quick	1.7	1.9
.5	1.0	1.0	.9	1.0	.8		1.0 (1058)	1.0
.2	.4	.6	.5	.7	.5		.6	.6
0 UND	13 28.8	22 16.5	29 12.8	24 15.1	36 10.0	Sales/Receivables	17 22.1	16 23.5
2 149.7	30 12.1	36 10.1	38 9.6	39 9.5	40 9.1		33 11.1	31 11.7
28 13.0	42 8.8	50 7.3	48 7.6	51 7.2	48 7.5		46 8.0	43 8.4
						Cost of Sales/Inventory		
						Cost of Sales/Payables		
24.4	12.8	9.1	11.6	15.6	13.0	Sales/Working Capital	13.3	13.2
-52.5	50.8	30.7	55.0	30.8	113.3		60.8	75.6
-9.6	-16.4	-26.2	-19.4	-27.3	-38.3		-29.0	-22.0
8.0	6.6	5.9	5.2	4.7	5.6	EBIT/Interest	8.3	7.5
(183) 1.8	(255) 1.6	(307) 2.0	(128) 1.9	(26) 1.9	2.2		(1009) 3.4	(936) 3.0
-1.7	-1.4	-.6	.5	.5	.8		1.2	1.1
	2.1	2.5	2.3			Net Profit + Depr., Dep., Amort./Cur. Mat. L/T/D	3.1	3.2
(30) 1.1	(91) 1.3	(49) 1.3					(251) 1.6	(217) 1.7
.4	.6	.9					1.0	1.1
.6	.5	.5	1.0	.7	1.4	Fixed/Worth	.7	.7
14.7	1.8	1.2	1.6	1.8	2.2		1.6	1.8
-1.0	-13.8	3.2	3.1	3.4	NM		6.4	6.6
1.7	.9	.8	1.0	1.1	1.7	Debt/Worth	1.1	1.0
UND	3.3	1.9	2.0	2.1	2.4		2.6	2.7
-2.7	-24.5	4.6	4.3	4.6	NM		12.4	13.7
160.8	36.6	25.5	23.5	24.8	19.9	% Profit Before Taxes/Tangible Net Worth	54.6	53.6
(117) 34.0	(207) 11.8	(295) 7.4	(124) 9.1	(26) 8.7	(21) 11.4		(904) 23.8	(855) 23.5
.0	-4.7	-12.1	-1.0	-8.9	2.7		7.5	5.3
29.5	11.6	9.1	7.8	5.6	6.3	% Profit Before Taxes/Total Assets	16.5	16.2
4.4	2.3	2.6	2.6	2.5	3.6		6.7	6.6
-14.1	-8.3	-5.0	-1.2	-2.1	-1.2		.8	.6
58.9	36.7	16.3	6.7	8.9	5.0	Sales/Net Fixed Assets	18.9	18.2
13.4	11.1	6.1	3.2	2.9	2.7		6.9	6.6
5.7	4.2	3.2	2.0	2.3	2.0		3.1	3.2
8.4	5.1	3.5	2.4	2.5	1.9	Sales/Total Assets	4.7	4.6
5.4	3.5	2.4	1.9	1.6	1.5		2.9	2.8
2.6	2.1	1.5	1.2	1.2	1.2		1.9	1.8
1.7	1.2	1.9	2.8	3.4		% Depr., Dep., Amort./Sales	1.8	2.0
(143) 4.6	(215) 4.6	(294) 5.0	(127) 6.2	(18) 6.4			(940) 4.2	(907) 4.4
9.6	9.1	8.2	9.5	9.5			7.8	7.7
2.7	2.0	1.1	1.1			% Officers', Directors' Owners' Comp/Sales	1.5	1.6
(87) 5.0	(138) 3.9	(129) 2.4	(28) 1.9				(428) 3.2	(411) 3.0
7.8	6.0	4.6	4.5				6.3	6.2
347621M	1181159M	3970761M	6500053M	5643193M	6672200M	Net Sales ($)	24261087M	26170393M
54484M	322095M	1491863M	3119644M	2007668M	4177815M	Total Assets ($)	9146205M	9074639M

M = $ thousand   MM = $ million
See Pages 9 through 22 for Explanation of Ratios and Data

Comparative Historical Data / Current Data Sorted by Sales

Hist 4/1/07-3/31/08 ALL	Hist 4/1/08-3/31/09 ALL	Hist 4/1/09-3/31/10 ALL	Type of Statement	0-1MM	1-3MM	3-5MM	5-10MM	10-25MM	25MM & OVER
63	56	63	Unqualified	2	2	1	4	5	49
195	180	173	Reviewed	5	24	18	35	55	36
231	195	191	Compiled	25	40	29	45	44	8
245	233	274	Tax Returns	75	82	50	44	17	6
347	331	349	Other	43	62	37	71	61	75
				146 (4/1-9/30/09)			904 (10/1/09-3/31/10)		
1081	995	1050	**NUMBER OF STATEMENTS**	150	210	135	199	182	174
%	%	%	**ASSETS**	%	%	%	%	%	%
10.6	11.5	11.1	Cash & Equivalents	13.9	12.3	12.3	9.5	11.6	7.5
26.7	25.4	25.3	Trade Receivables (net)	16.4	20.7	27.0	30.1	31.2	25.3
1.4	1.8	2.1	Inventory	1.4	1.3	2.3	2.8	2.0	3.0
4.0	4.0	4.4	All Other Current	3.8	4.6	3.8	4.1	5.1	4.6
42.7	42.6	42.8	Total Current	35.5	38.8	45.4	46.4	50.0	40.3
45.9	44.9	43.5	Fixed Assets (net)	53.2	47.0	38.4	37.1	40.6	45.3
3.2	3.0	4.0	Intangibles (net)	3.3	2.5	4.2	5.8	2.6	5.7
8.2	9.4	9.7	All Other Non-Current	8.0	11.7	12.0	10.7	6.8	8.6
100.0	100.0	100.0	Total	100.0	100.0	100.0	100.0	100.0	100.0
			LIABILITIES						
8.8	10.8	11.0	Notes Payable-Short Term	17.6	11.1	11.9	12.3	8.8	5.7
9.2	9.0	9.5	Cur. Mat.-L.T.D.	8.6	13.8	8.6	8.5	8.4	8.2
11.1	10.5	10.5	Trade Payables	7.4	11.4	10.5	10.6	12.2	10.5
.3	.3	.2	Income Taxes Payable	.1	.2	.1	.2	.1	.2
9.5	11.0	10.6	All Other Current	12.5	13.9	10.6	8.7	8.4	9.2
38.9	41.6	41.8	Total Current	46.2	50.4	41.6	40.2	37.9	33.7
31.8	31.1	30.2	Long-Term Debt	38.7	40.7	26.3	27.7	23.0	23.5
.8	.7	.9	Deferred Taxes	.0	.2	.6	.8	1.3	2.1
5.1	5.9	7.1	All Other Non-Current	12.1	10.6	5.1	7.7	3.8	2.7
23.4	20.6	20.1	Net Worth	2.9	-1.9	26.4	23.6	34.0	38.1
100.0	100.0	100.0	Total Liabilities & Net Worth	100.0	100.0	100.0	100.0	100.0	100.0
			INCOME DATA						
100.0	100.0	100.0	Net Sales	100.0	100.0	100.0	100.0	100.0	100.0
			Gross Profit						
95.5	95.7	96.7	Operating Expenses	91.2	97.6	97.6	98.3	98.0	96.7
4.5	4.3	3.3	Operating Profit	8.8	2.4	2.4	1.7	2.0	3.3
1.2	1.5	1.6	All Other Expenses (net)	5.8	1.2	.8	1.0	.6	1.1
3.2	2.9	1.6	Profit Before Taxes	3.0	1.2	1.6	.7	1.4	2.3
			RATIOS						
2.0	2.0	2.1	Current	3.1	2.0	2.3	2.3	2.2	1.7
1.1	1.1	1.1		.7	.9	1.2	1.2	1.4	1.1
.7	.6	.6		.2	.4	.6	.6	.9	.8
1.7	1.7	1.8	Quick	2.9	1.7	2.1	1.9	2.0	1.4
(1080) 1.0	1.0	.9		.5	.7	.9	1.0	1.2	1.0
.6	.5	.5		.2	.3	.5	.5	.7	.6
14 25.3	9 41.7	11 31.8	Sales/Receivables	0 UND	0 UND	9 40.2	18 19.8	27 13.5	28 13.2
31 11.7	27 13.3	32 11.6		7 56.1	22 16.9	32 11.4	34 10.7	37 10.0	38 9.6
45 8.1	42 8.7	46 8.0		33 10.9	36 10.2	46 8.0	50 7.3	49 7.5	46 7.9
			Cost of Sales/Inventory						
			Cost of Sales/Payables						
13.3	13.7	11.3	Sales/Working Capital	11.3	17.8	10.5	10.3	10.4	13.1
76.2	92.0	82.4		-21.5	-149.8	69.7	44.0	24.3	56.5
-24.9	-17.8	-16.6		-4.4	-10.1	-22.9	-19.5	-72.6	-36.2
5.7	6.6	6.3	EBIT/Interest	6.9	4.9	6.5	5.8	6.6	6.4
(961) 2.1	(877) 2.3	(927) 1.9		(100) 2.0	(183) 1.3	(121) 1.9	(185) 1.9	(171) 2.0	(167) 2.6
.7	.5	-.4		-.9	-1.2	-.8	-.9	-.2	.7
2.6	2.4	2.3	Net Profit + Depr., Dep., Amort./Cur. Mat. L/T/D		1.6	2.5	2.7	2.3	2.7
(212) 1.5	(199) 1.5	(188) 1.2		(25) 1.0	(14) .9	(40) 1.2	(51) 1.2	(55) 1.5	
1.0	1.0	.7			.5	.3	.3	.8	.9
.7	.6	.6	Fixed/Worth	.5	.9	.4	.4	.5	.8
1.8	1.7	1.7		5.2	3.7	1.3	1.4	1.3	1.5
11.3	13.8	25.5		-4.0	-1.4	5.4	47.7	3.0	2.6
1.1	1.0	.9	Debt/Worth	.8	1.1	.7	.9	1.0	1.0
2.9	2.8	2.7		10.2	6.8	2.5	2.9	2.0	2.0
23.9	28.8	UND		-5.6	-3.7	23.2	-173.7	4.3	4.1
47.6	47.1	33.8	% Profit Before Taxes/Tangible Net Worth	74.1	43.9	38.0	31.6	29.8	24.9
(855) 17.5	(778) 19.4	(790) 10.6		(90) 14.8	(125) 11.8	(106) 10.1	(149) 7.3	(159) 10.4	(161) 11.3
1.6	2.7	-5.5		.0	-15.0	-11.0	-12.2	-5.6	-.4
14.0	14.1	11.4	% Profit Before Taxes/Total Assets	16.2	14.6	13.7	10.4	9.6	8.0
4.6	4.7	2.7		2.7	1.6	2.4	2.6	3.2	4.0
-1.0	-1.4	-5.8		-6.7	-10.5	-5.7	-6.8	-3.3	-.8
20.0	21.5	22.3	Sales/Net Fixed Assets	20.0	20.0	37.6	30.6	22.2	13.0
6.4	7.2	7.7		3.7	9.0	12.1	9.7	7.5	4.5
3.1	3.3	3.0		1.5	3.3	4.0	4.1	3.5	2.7
4.5	5.0	4.8	Sales/Total Assets	3.7	6.0	5.5	4.9	4.4	3.3
2.8	3.0	2.7		1.8	3.5	3.4	3.2	2.7	2.2
1.7	1.8	1.6		.7	1.9	1.8	1.8	1.9	1.5
1.9	1.9	1.8	% Depr., Dep., Amort./Sales	6.0	2.3	1.1	1.6	1.7	1.8
(910) 4.6	(811) 4.6	(804) 5.0		(93) 11.7	(152) 5.5	(104) 3.2	(164) 4.4	(162) 4.3	(129) 3.4
8.7	7.9	8.9		20.8	10.0	6.8	7.5	7.3	7.7
1.3	1.5	1.6	% Officers', Directors', Owners' Comp/Sales	5.0	3.4	1.9	1.5	1.1	.9
(396) 2.8	(338) 2.7	(389) 3.4		(35) 6.4	(98) 4.5	(69) 3.3	(89) 2.2	(68) 2.2	(30) 1.6
5.9	5.7	6.2		19.6	7.5	6.2	4.5	4.2	4.2
22125752M	20491156M	24314987M	Net Sales ($)	72593M	403932M	531643M	1399937M	2868185M	19038697M
9801992M	8263007M	11173569M	Total Assets ($)	70258M	189057M	256222M	714616M	1235549M	8707867M

© RMA 2010

M = $ thousand   MM = $ million
See Pages 9 through 22 for Explanation of Ratios and Data

Current Data Sorted by Assets   **Comparative Historical Data**

						Type of Statement		
2	4	18	56	29	31	Unqualified	197	176
2	25	101	99	3	1	Reviewed	257	281
29	58	103	19	4	1	Compiled	286	303
60	55	42	2	1	1	Tax Returns	171	170
38	77	162	115	40	31	Other	525	464
	171 (4/1-9/30/09)		1,038 (10/1/09-3/31/10)				4/1/05-3/31/06	4/1/06-3/31/07
0-500M	500M-2MM	2-10MM	10-50MM	50-100MM	100-250MM		ALL	ALL
131	219	426	291	77	65	NUMBER OF STATEMENTS	1436	1394
%	%	%	%	%	%	ASSETS	%	%
19.5	10.4	9.3	7.5	5.3	3.9	Cash & Equivalents	8.5	8.6
25.5	32.4	29.8	23.1	17.9	17.1	Trade Receivables (net)	29.5	27.6
2.1	1.0	1.2	1.9	1.0	1.2	Inventory	1.2	1.2
7.3	5.1	6.1	4.7	3.5	4.7	All Other Current	4.0	4.3
54.4	48.9	46.5	37.2	27.7	26.9	Total Current	43.2	41.7
35.3	40.1	42.4	53.2	59.4	56.7	Fixed Assets (net)	47.0	48.1
2.8	1.7	2.3	3.2	4.1	6.5	Intangibles (net)	1.9	1.8
7.6	9.3	8.7	6.4	8.9	9.9	All Other Non-Current	7.9	8.4
100.0	100.0	100.0	100.0	100.0	100.0	Total	100.0	100.0
						LIABILITIES		
23.4	11.7	10.0	7.7	4.3	3.5	Notes Payable-Short Term	7.6	8.0
10.5	8.9	9.9	11.8	10.8	8.6	Cur. Mat.-L.T.D.	9.9	9.8
15.5	12.2	9.0	8.0	6.8	6.1	Trade Payables	10.4	9.5
.1	.1	.2	.2	.1	.1	Income Taxes Payable	.3	.3
26.0	12.4	9.3	7.4	8.2	10.5	All Other Current	10.2	10.5
75.5	45.4	38.2	35.1	30.2	28.6	Total Current	38.4	38.1
40.2	24.6	22.8	25.0	32.7	34.1	Long-Term Debt	29.8	31.2
.0	.5	1.2	2.4	3.4	4.1	Deferred Taxes	1.4	1.4
8.9	8.4	3.8	2.8	5.0	4.9	All Other Non-Current	4.0	3.8
-24.7	21.2	34.0	34.7	28.6	28.3	Net Worth	26.4	25.6
100.0	100.0	100.0	100.0	100.0	100.0	Total Liabilities & Net Worth	100.0	100.0
						INCOME DATA		
100.0	100.0	100.0	100.0	100.0	100.0	Net Sales	100.0	100.0
						Gross Profit		
97.4	96.7	95.9	97.1	95.3	97.7	Operating Expenses	95.0	95.1
2.6	3.3	4.1	2.9	4.7	2.3	Operating Profit	5.0	4.9
1.4	1.3	1.3	1.4	3.5	2.5	All Other Expenses (net)	1.0	1.2
1.2	2.1	2.7	1.5	1.2	-.2	Profit Before Taxes	4.0	3.7
						RATIOS		
2.6	2.2	2.1	1.5	1.4	1.6	Current	1.7	1.7
1.1	1.0	1.2	1.1	1.0	1.0		1.1	1.1
.3	.6	.8	.7	.6	.7		.8	.7
2.0	1.8	1.8	1.3	1.1	1.3	Quick	1.5	1.5
.8	(218) .9	1.0	(290) .8	.8	.9		1.0	.9
.2	.5	.6	.5	.5	.5		.6	.6
0 UND	12 31.5	25 14.6	30 12.2	29 12.6	35 10.5	Sales/Receivables	23 15.6	23 16.1
7 52.3	27 13.6	35 10.5	36 10.0	36 10.0	40 9.0		34 10.6	32 11.2
28 13.0	40 9.1	46 8.0	45 8.2	43 8.5	46 8.0		44 8.2	42 8.7
						Cost of Sales/Inventory		
						Cost of Sales/Payables		
19.4	13.5	10.7	15.9	21.8	18.6	Sales/Working Capital	15.9	18.1
248.0	143.2	40.4	117.2	-342.6	120.9		84.4	124.0
-16.6	-14.4	-23.9	-16.9	-9.2	-11.9		-28.4	-24.5
5.1	7.5	5.4	4.2	4.2	2.0	EBIT/Interest	7.7	6.0
(91) 1.5	(182) 2.1	(386) 1.8	(281) 1.6	(73) 1.5	1.2		(1315) 3.5	(1285) 2.6
-2.7	-1.6	-.4	.5	.3	.2		1.7	1.3
	2.1	2.2	2.0	1.5	7.0	Net Profit + Depr., Dep., Amort./Cur. Mat. L/T/D	2.9	2.3
	(25) 1.2	(100) 1.4	(117) 1.1	(20) 1.2	(10) 1.2		(393) 1.5	(379) 1.5
	.1	.9	.8	.9	.9		1.1	1.0
.0	.4	.6	1.1	1.3	1.2	Fixed/Worth	.8	.8
3.0	1.6	1.4	1.8	2.1	2.6		1.8	1.9
-1.1	28.0	3.5	3.3	4.4	7.0		4.5	4.8
1.3	.9	.9	1.1	1.3	1.3	Debt/Worth	1.2	1.3
15.2	2.9	2.0	2.2	2.5	3.1		2.8	2.8
-2.6	-266.7	5.5	4.6	6.6	15.2		7.6	7.8
112.1	39.9	32.2	20.2	22.3	14.3	% Profit Before Taxes/Tangible Net Worth	56.0	46.5
(70) 26.6	(163) 13.2	(376) 8.9	(272) 7.0	(70) 6.9	(53) 4.5		(1249) 28.1	(1210) 22.5
-33.9	-15.1	-6.7	-3.9	-3.1	-4.4		10.4	7.2
30.0	14.9	9.8	5.8	6.0	2.4	% Profit Before Taxes/Total Assets	14.8	13.4
3.7	3.2	2.5	2.0	1.5	.5		7.0	5.5
-20.4	-10.9	-4.1	-1.6	-2.0	-2.0		2.4	1.1
999.8	43.9	21.2	6.0	4.2	4.6	Sales/Net Fixed Assets	17.3	16.2
37.6	9.9	6.5	3.6	2.6	2.5		5.8	5.3
7.5	4.9	3.3	2.4	2.0	1.8		3.0	2.7
10.3	5.5	4.1	2.8	2.1	1.9	Sales/Total Assets	4.4	4.4
6.6	3.8	2.8	2.0	1.6	1.4		2.8	2.7
3.7	2.4	1.7	1.5	1.2	1.2		1.8	1.7
.6	1.1	2.0	3.8	4.2	.9	% Depr., Dep., Amort./Sales	1.9	1.9
(66) 3.3	(169) 4.1	(364) 5.2	(276) 7.0	(50) 7.2	(17) 2.4		(1191) 4.6	(1157) 4.9
8.9	9.0	9.9	10.6	9.2	5.4		7.7	8.2
3.5	2.0	1.1	1.0	1.3		% Officers', Directors' Owners' Comp/Sales	1.1	1.1
(52) 4.9	(95) 3.0	(136) 1.8	(54) 2.6	(11) 4.9			(465) 2.2	(468) 2.3
7.6	5.9	4.0	10.2	17.2			5.0	4.8
238424M	1052012M	6133420M	15331902M	10264656M	16368653M	Net Sales ($)	61743652M	59769526M
31327M	251262M	2114278M	6910993M	5226662M	9793627M	Total Assets ($)	25270395M	25756691M

© RMA 2010

M = $ thousand   MM = $ million
See Pages 9 through 22 for Explanation of Ratios and Data

Comparative Historical Data   Current Data Sorted by Sales

			Type of Statement						
137	142	140	Unqualified	1	2	4	5	17	111
251	237	231	Reviewed	3	8	15	35	73	97
268	255	214	Compiled	18	28	25	48	63	32
147	166	161	Tax Returns	39	46	21	31	18	6
477	490	463	Other	27	48	48	62	98	180
4/1/07-3/31/08 ALL	4/1/08-3/31/09 ALL	4/1/09-3/31/10 ALL		171 (4/1-9/30/09)			1,038 (10/1/09-3/31/10)		
				0-1MM	1-3MM	3-5MM	5-10MM	10-25MM	25MM & OVER
1280	1290	1209	**NUMBER OF STATEMENTS**	88	132	113	181	269	426
%	%	%	**ASSETS**	%	%	%	%	%	%
8.1	9.7	9.6	Cash & Equivalents	17.8	12.3	12.4	7.4	10.4	6.8
28.1	26.8	26.8	Trade Receivables (net)	14.3	24.9	27.4	29.4	30.3	26.4
1.5	1.4	1.4	Inventory	1.1	1.1	2.1	1.5	1.2	1.6
4.7	5.0	5.5	All Other Current	6.4	4.6	5.9	5.8	6.2	4.9
42.3	42.9	43.3	Total Current	39.7	42.8	47.7	44.1	48.1	39.7
46.7	46.0	45.7	Fixed Assets (net)	52.2	45.9	41.0	43.0	41.8	49.1
2.3	2.2	2.8	Intangibles (net)	1.7	2.7	1.6	2.5	2.2	3.8
8.6	8.9	8.2	All Other Non-Current	6.4	8.6	9.7	10.3	7.9	7.4
100.0	100.0	100.0	Total	100.0	100.0	100.0	100.0	100.0	100.0
			LIABILITIES						
8.4	8.4	10.5	Notes Payable-Short Term	8.7	16.0	13.4	12.5	10.4	7.6
9.8	10.2	10.2	Cur. Mat.-L.T.D.	7.9	10.1	11.6	10.1	10.7	10.1
9.5	9.6	9.7	Trade Payables	11.1	8.3	11.1	10.7	10.5	8.6
.2	.2	.1	Income Taxes Payable	.1	.0	.3	.2	.1	.1
9.7	10.7	11.2	All Other Current	15.0	20.2	11.4	8.6	9.2	9.9
37.6	39.1	41.8	Total Current	42.8	54.6	47.9	42.2	40.9	36.4
30.2	28.6	26.8	Long-Term Debt	46.2	31.0	30.1	24.3	21.8	24.8
1.4	1.3	1.5	Deferred Taxes	.0	.4	.7	.8	1.3	2.8
3.7	4.6	5.1	All Other Non-Current	8.4	6.4	7.4	5.9	4.1	3.7
27.1	26.3	24.9	Net Worth	2.7	7.5	13.9	26.8	32.0	32.4
100.0	100.0	100.0	Total Liabilities & Net Worth	100.0	100.0	100.0	100.0	100.0	100.0
			INCOME DATA						
100.0	100.0	100.0	Net Sales	100.0	100.0	100.0	100.0	100.0	100.0
			Gross Profit						
96.2	95.9	96.6	Operating Expenses	83.9	94.9	95.6	98.5	98.5	97.9
3.8	4.1	3.4	Operating Profit	16.1	5.1	4.4	1.5	1.5	2.1
1.1	1.3	1.5	All Other Expenses (net)	6.6	2.4	1.3	.5	.9	1.1
2.7	2.8	1.9	Profit Before Taxes	9.5	2.7	3.1	.9	.6	1.0
			RATIOS						
1.7	1.8	1.9		3.4	2.7	2.5	1.8	1.9	1.6
1.1	1.1	1.1	Current	.9	1.0	1.3	1.1	1.2	1.1
.7	.7	.7		.2	.4	.6	.6	.7	.8
1.5	1.5	1.6		2.2	2.1	2.2	1.5	1.7	1.4
.9	.9 (1207)	.9	Quick	(87) .8	.8	(112) .9	.9	.9	.9
.6	.6	.5		.1	.3	.5	.5	.6	.6
23 16.0	18 19.8	21 17.4		0 UND	0 UND	9 39.0	22 16.3	25 14.4	31 11.8
33 11.0	28 13.0	34 10.8	Sales/Receivables	0 UND	22 16.5	28 12.9	33 11.1	34 10.9	38 9.7
44 8.4	38 9.7	44 8.4		22 16.5	42 8.7	40 9.0	46 7.9	43 8.5	45 8.2
			Cost of Sales/Inventory						
			Cost of Sales/Payables						
16.4	16.0	13.5		7.1	12.3	12.6	14.7	12.8	15.9
70.1	72.4	82.4	Sales/Working Capital	-266.8	-296.8	63.3	108.4	48.9	83.4
-23.1	-26.7	-17.4		-7.7	-8.7	-18.7	-17.8	-22.1	-23.8
4.5	4.9	4.9		9.2	5.5	6.8	5.0	4.3	4.8
(1173) 2.0	(1173) 2.0 (1078)	1.7	EBIT/Interest	(53) 3.0	(108) 1.2	(95) 2.7	(166) 1.4	(244) 1.6	(412) 1.7
.7	.7	-.3		.6	-2.7	-.8	-1.2	-.3	.3
2.3	2.2	2.0				2.8	1.9	2.2	2.1
(336) 1.3	(302) 1.3 (273)	1.2	Net Profit + Depr., Dep., Amort./Cur. Mat. L/T/D		(16) 1.4	(34) 1.2	(66) 1.3	(148) 1.1	
.9	.9	.8				.5	.7	.9	.8
.7	.7	.7		.2	.4	.4	.7	.6	1.0
1.8	1.8	1.7	Fixed/Worth	3.6	1.8	1.6	1.5	1.6	1.8
4.3	4.8	4.6		-2.6	77.1	-114.0	4.0	3.6	3.4
1.2	1.1	1.0		.5	.9	.8	1.0	.9	1.1
2.7	2.5	2.5	Debt/Worth	7.2	3.2	2.9	2.3	2.4	2.3
7.4	7.6	8.8		-4.9	-12.7	-49.1	9.7	6.2	5.4
33.3	32.9	28.7		78.1	34.7	44.5	22.0	29.9	21.1
(1108) 12.9	(1088) 13.4 (1004)	8.5	% Profit Before Taxes/Tangible Net Worth	(58) 29.8	(92) 9.8	(82) 15.4	(149) 5.7	(237) 6.4	(386) 7.6
.0	1.3	-6.3		6.3	-31.9	-2.2	-11.6	-8.3	-3.5
10.3	10.1	8.7		22.0	12.9	16.8	9.2	7.3	6.0
3.5	3.5	2.2	% Profit Before Taxes/Total Assets	4.4	2.1	4.1	1.7	2.1	2.0
-1.0	-.8	-4.1		-12.2	-13.3	-7.0	-6.2	-4.7	-1.7
17.5	20.2	19.8		134.2	39.9	32.5	21.0	25.4	9.3
5.7	5.9	5.7	Sales/Net Fixed Assets	4.4	7.4	8.1	7.3	6.7	4.1
2.8	3.1	2.7		.4	3.3	3.6	3.4	3.3	2.5
4.4	4.6	4.3		5.0	5.7	5.9	4.5	4.7	3.3
2.7	2.8	2.6	Sales/Total Assets	2.2	3.1	3.3	2.9	2.9	2.1
1.7	1.8	1.6		.3	1.5	1.8	1.9	1.8	1.6
1.9	2.0	2.1		5.2	1.9	1.7	2.0	1.9	2.2
(1069) 4.9	(1009) 5.0 (942)	5.7	% Depr., Dep., Amort./Sales	(53) 12.0	(94) 7.7	(85) 5.5	(149) 4.9	(230) 5.5	(331) 5.3
8.3	8.1	9.8		25.0	14.1	10.2	8.8	9.0	8.5
1.2	1.2	1.5		5.5	2.1	1.7	1.6	1.3	.9
(392) 2.5	(395) 2.6 (353)	2.8	% Officers', Directors', Owners' Comp/Sales	(21) 7.6	(54) 4.0	(46) 2.8	(72) 2.5	(93) 2.0	(67) 2.6
5.4	5.4	6.0		16.5	7.7	5.1	4.1	4.4	11.8
55675103M	65282580M	49389067M	Net Sales ($)	45602M	277092M	448165M	1330621M	4443210M	42844377M
25058200M	27427207M	24328149M	Total Assets ($)	74263M	275291M	325267M	606562M	1885982M	21160784M

M = $ thousand   MM = $ million
See Pages 9 through 22 for Explanation of Ratios and Data

Current Data Sorted by Assets   **Comparative Historical Data**

Type of Statement

0-500M	500M-2MM	2-10MM	10-50MM	50-100MM	100-250MM	Type of Statement	4/1/05-3/31/06 ALL	4/1/06-3/31/07 ALL
	1	3	4	4	7	Unqualified	30	26
	1	10	4		1	Reviewed	14	21
1	2	8	5			Compiled	17	26
5	1	6	1			Tax Returns	7	11
2	6	12	9	5	2	Other	26	44
	10 (4/1-9/30/09)		90 (10/1/09-3/31/10)					
8	11	39	23	9	10	**NUMBER OF STATEMENTS**	94	128

0-500M %	500M-2MM %	2-10MM %	10-50MM %	50-100MM %	100-250MM %		4/1/05-3/31/06 ALL %	4/1/06-3/31/07 ALL %
						ASSETS		
	6.2	7.8	8.0		3.4	Cash & Equivalents	7.7	8.3
	43.6	32.1	21.3		18.4	Trade Receivables (net)	28.4	27.5
	.1	2.3	1.5		3.4	Inventory	1.1	1.7
	2.9	2.4	6.2		4.9	All Other Current	5.1	3.1
	52.8	44.5	37.0		30.1	Total Current	42.2	40.6
	35.2	47.0	52.4		63.6	Fixed Assets (net)	50.6	47.8
	3.9	1.3	2.0		2.8	Intangibles (net)	1.7	4.2
	8.0	7.2	8.5		3.5	All Other Non-Current	5.5	7.5
	100.0	100.0	100.0		100.0	Total	100.0	100.0
						LIABILITIES		
	4.5	6.8	5.9		4.9	Notes Payable-Short Term	4.4	5.6
	3.5	9.6	8.2		10.1	Cur. Mat.-L.T.D.	9.1	10.1
	16.4	7.6	7.6		3.6	Trade Payables	9.3	8.9
	.0	.1	.1		.1	Income Taxes Payable	.5	.1
	18.4	8.6	7.9		11.4	All Other Current	10.4	10.9
	42.7	32.7	29.6		30.2	Total Current	33.7	35.5
	33.8	24.7	26.9		28.5	Long-Term Debt	31.3	30.8
	.0	.6	4.1		1.1	Deferred Taxes	1.7	1.8
	2.6	2.6	1.3		8.5	All Other Non-Current	2.5	2.0
	20.9	39.4	38.1		31.7	Net Worth	30.8	29.9
	100.0	100.0	100.0		100.0	Total Liabilities & Net Worth	100.0	100.0
						INCOME DATA		
	100.0	100.0	100.0		100.0	Net Sales	100.0	100.0
						Gross Profit		
	88.9	96.2	96.4		97.6	Operating Expenses	95.3	95.7
	11.1	3.8	3.6		2.4	Operating Profit	4.7	4.3
	5.0	2.9	2.8		2.2	All Other Expenses (net)	1.2	1.3
	6.1	1.0	.8		.2	Profit Before Taxes	3.5	3.1
						RATIOS		
	3.1	2.2	1.7		1.4	Current	1.7	1.7
	1.4	1.3	1.4		1.0		1.1	1.2
	1.1	.8	.9		.6		.9	.8
	3.1	2.0	1.5		1.2	Quick	1.6	1.6
	1.1	1.1	1.1		.8		1.0	1.0
	.5	.6	.7		.4		.7	.7
	26 13.9	25 14.5	33 11.2		37 9.8	Sales/Receivables	24 14.9	26 14.3
	32 11.3	37 9.9	36 10.2		39 9.3		35 10.4	35 10.4
	50 7.3	53 6.9	44 8.2		47 7.8		43 8.6	42 8.7
						Cost of Sales/Inventory		
						Cost of Sales/Payables		
	14.4	12.1	11.0		21.1	Sales/Working Capital	17.8	15.9
	20.4	26.3	23.9		NM		62.4	48.1
	147.8	-32.2	-51.7		-11.0		-62.5	-48.8
		3.4	3.0		3.1	EBIT/Interest	6.8	5.6
	(33) 1.4	1.2			1.3		(79) 3.6	(111) 3.0
		.2	-.9		.0		2.2	1.7
		2.6	2.4			Net Profit + Depr., Dep., Amort./Cur. Mat. L/T/D	2.6	2.1
	(11) 1.3		(15) 1.4				(28) 1.4	(45) 1.4
		.9	.6				1.0	.9
	.2	.5	.9		1.2	Fixed/Worth	1.0	.9
	1.1	1.2	1.5		2.0		2.0	1.9
	6.9	2.4	2.6		NM		3.6	-4.5
	1.2	1.0	.7		1.2	Debt/Worth	1.1	1.1
	3.6	1.3	1.8		1.7		2.4	2.4
	-16.1	3.5	3.0		NM		4.7	8.8
		19.3	14.1			% Profit Before Taxes/Tangible Net Worth	49.4	43.7
	(36) 5.0	(21) 5.7					(87) 28.2	(107) 23.6
		-4.5	-3.3				12.5	10.1
	17.1	7.1	5.0		4.1	% Profit Before Taxes/Total Assets	13.9	13.1
	3.9	.9	.5				7.4	6.0
	-4.4	-2.7	-2.2		-5.6		3.8	2.9
	131.9	15.8	6.2		4.7	Sales/Net Fixed Assets	10.6	16.3
	23.0	6.4	3.5		2.3		5.1	5.1
	5.7	2.4	2.3		1.6		2.7	2.6
	7.2	4.1	2.8		2.0	Sales/Total Assets	3.8	4.1
	4.7	2.8	2.0		1.6		2.7	2.6
	2.9	1.5	1.3		1.3		1.8	1.6
		2.7	3.3			% Depr., Dep., Amort./Sales	2.5	1.7
	(35) 4.9	(22) 5.8					(70) 4.5	(98) 4.6
		9.1	8.8				7.1	7.0
		1.2				% Officers', Directors' Owners' Comp/Sales	1.0	1.5
	(15) 1.9						(24) 2.0	(36) 3.6
		3.2					4.0	5.3
14045M	57628M	548482M	1241738M	1182747M	2578954M	Net Sales ($)	7101392M	9800860M
2510M	13140M	191716M	614587M	615572M	1536526M	Total Assets ($)	3477605M	4670421M

Comparative Historical Data · **Current Data Sorted by Sales**

	4/1/07-3/31/08 ALL	4/1/08-3/31/09 ALL	4/1/09-3/31/10 ALL	10 (4/1-9/30/09) 0-1MM	1-3MM	3-5MM	90 (10/1/09-3/31/10) 5-10MM	10-25MM	25MM & OVE
Type of Statement									
Unqualified	22	25	19	1				2	16
Reviewed	20	19	16			2		9	5
Compiled	27	19	16			1	3	4	5
Tax Returns	11	7	13	3	1	1	6	2	
Other	44	49	36	3	1	2	6	6	18
NUMBER OF STATEMENTS	124	119	100	10	2	6	15	23	44
	%	%	%	%	%	%	%	%	%
ASSETS									
Cash & Equivalents	7.4	8.0	8.2	13.9			9.0	6.2	7.6
Trade Receivables (net)	26.4	27.5	28.9	21.4			37.1	39.0	22.0
Inventory	2.1	2.1	1.6	.1			2.5	1.9	1.8
All Other Current	5.7	4.3	3.5	1.5			.7	2.9	5.3
Total Current	41.5	42.0	42.2	36.9			49.3	50.1	36.7
Fixed Assets (net)	47.8	45.6	47.6	52.3			39.8	40.1	53.9
Intangibles (net)	2.9	3.6	2.4	1.1			2.0	1.4	3.0
All Other Non-Current	7.8	8.7	7.8	9.7			8.9	8.4	6.3
Total	100.0	100.0	100.0	100.0			100.0	100.0	100.0
LIABILITIES									
Notes Payable-Short Term	7.0	5.2	6.1	3.3			8.2	7.0	5.7
Cur. Mat.-L.T.D.	10.1	8.8	9.3	10.3			7.4	8.4	10.2
Trade Payables	11.5	8.8	8.4	10.3			11.1	8.0	7.8
Income Taxes Payable	.2	.2	.1	.1			.0	.2	.1
All Other Current	10.8	11.5	11.9	24.9			5.4	10.0	10.2
Total Current	39.6	34.4	35.8	48.9			32.1	33.7	33.9
Long-Term Debt	30.4	28.0	26.6	31.8			25.3	22.2	27.2
Deferred Taxes	1.0	1.3	1.5	.0			.0	1.4	2.6
All Other Non-Current	4.3	3.5	3.4	2.3			.5	4.2	4.8
Net Worth	24.7	32.8	32.7	17.0			42.1	38.6	31.4
Total Liabilties & Net Worth	100.0	100.0	100.0	100.0			100.0	100.0	100.0
INCOME DATA									
Net Sales	100.0	100.0	100.0	100.0			100.0	100.0	100.0
Gross Profit									
Operating Expenses	94.8	93.0	96.0	80.9			94.6	98.0	98.9
Operating Profit	5.2	7.0	4.0	19.1			5.4	2.0	1.1
All Other Expenses (net)	2.0	2.8	2.8	14.6			.8	.5	2.1
Profit Before Taxes	3.3	4.2	1.2	4.5			4.6	1.5	-1.0
RATIOS									
Current	1.5	1.7	1.9	1.8			3.1	2.2	1.7
	1.0	1.2	1.2	1.2			1.1	1.5	1.1
	.7	.7	.8	.4			.5	1.0	.8
Quick	1.2	1.5	1.7	1.7			3.1	2.2	1.3
	(123) .9	1.0	1.0	.8			1.1	1.1	.9
	.6	.6	.6	.4			.5	.9	.5
Sales/Receivables	24 15.4	22 16.6	31 11.7	0 UND			12 30.3	34 10.6	33 11.2
	34 10.7	30 12.3	37 9.9	33 11.1			39 9.4	37 9.8	38 9.7
	43 8.6	39 9.3	47 7.7	84 4.3			53 6.9	51 7.2	42 8.8
Cost of Sales/Inventory									
Cost of Sales/Payables									
Sales/Working Capital	21.8	16.9	14.2	12.0			16.3	12.0	18.6
	512.1	49.6	37.1	82.9			45.6	16.9	87.3
	-20.9	-23.1	-25.1	-2.7			-17.1	689.9	-21.1
EBIT/Interest	6.4	6.8	3.6				8.6	3.7	2.9
	(112) 2.0	(100) 2.7	(89) 1.4				(14) 1.7	(20) 1.5	(43) 1.2
	.6	.9	-.2				.9	.3	-.4
Net Profit + Depr., Dep., Amort./Cur. Mat. L/T/D	2.1	2.7	2.2						2.4
	(31) 1.3	(33) 1.2	(29) 1.3					(19) 1.3
	.9	.9	.8						.8
Fixed/Worth	.9	.6	.6	.4			.1	.5	1.1
	1.9	1.8	1.6	4.0			1.5	1.1	1.9
	5.3	8.3	3.1	-194.1			2.1	2.6	5.2
Debt/Worth	1.2	1.1	1.0	.5			.8	1.0	1.1
	2.7	2.0	1.9	4.2			1.4	1.3	2.1
	8.3	18.7	5.4	-198.5			3.6	3.3	7.1
% Profit Before Taxes/Tangible Net Worth	43.0	41.2	19.7				35.8	19.0	15.6
	(105) 15.6	(98) 16.7	(86) 6.4				(21) 8.5	(37) 6.1	5.5
	.7	3.1	-3.3				-1.5	-3.4	-3.3
% Profit Before Taxes/Total Assets	9.8	11.0	6.7	28.3			8.0	8.7	4.2
	3.8	4.8	1.1	.7			2.5	1.5	.5
	-1.1	-.3	-2.7	-8.8			-.3	-1.0	-6.0
Sales/Net Fixed Assets	13.3	22.3	14.5	42.7			73.3	25.4	6.1
	5.0	5.3	5.5	3.4			8.4	7.1	3.9
	2.7	2.6	2.4	.2			2.4	2.7	2.5
Sales/Total Assets	3.5	4.5	3.9	3.5			5.6	5.3	2.9
	2.6	2.5	2.2	1.3			2.8	3.6	2.0
	1.7	1.7	1.5	.2			1.5	2.0	1.6
% Depr., Dep., Amort./Sales	2.2	1.8	2.5				1.0	2.9	
	(99) 5.3	(91) 4.4	(73) 5.0				(12) 3.8	(18) 4.9	(31) 5.2
	8.3	7.5	8.3				9.8	7.0	8.2
% Officers', Directors' Owners' Comp/Sales	1.4	1.4	1.2						.8
	(32) 2.6	(29) 2.2	(30) 2.5						(10) 4.1
	4.9	2.9	6.2						8.9
Net Sales ($)	8216990M	8616177M	5623594M	6088M	4532M	21408M	103693M	362995M	5124878M
Total Assets ($)	3550159M	3827601M	2974051M	13091M	7016M	8354M	77399M	129827M	2738364M

M = $ thousand   MM = $ million
See Pages 9 through 22 for Explanation of Ratios and Data

| | Current Data Sorted by Assets | | | | | | | Comparative Historical Data | |

Type of Statement	0-500M	500M-2MM	2-10MM	10-50MM	50-100MM	100-250MM		4/1/05-3/31/06 ALL	4/1/06-3/31/07 ALL
Unqualified			1	7				7	10
Reviewed	2	14	16	11				24	33
Compiled	4	21	12	2				21	24
Tax Returns	14	18	2					13	27
Other	15	17	24	5	1	2		40	47
		16 (4/1-9/30/09)		172 (10/1/09-3/31/10)					
NUMBER OF STATEMENTS	35	70	55	25	1	2		105	141
	%	%	%	%	%	%	ASSETS	%	%
Cash & Equivalents	16.8	11.0	14.2	7.7				9.0	9.0
Trade Receivables (net)	29.8	28.3	31.0	31.6				33.1	29.5
Inventory	.9	.4	.3	.8				.8	.7
All Other Current	2.1	7.6	4.2	6.9				3.5	5.6
Total Current	49.6	47.2	49.7	47.0				46.3	44.9
Fixed Assets (net)	34.5	34.6	32.8	34.0				39.6	38.9
Intangibles (net)	7.7	2.1	3.1	7.8				2.5	2.9
All Other Non-Current	8.2	16.1	14.4	11.2				11.6	13.3
Total	100.0	100.0	100.0	100.0				100.0	100.0
							LIABILITIES		
Notes Payable-Short Term	19.4	4.3	5.9	9.3				8.8	8.1
Cur. Mat.-L.T.D.	10.4	11.8	5.4	3.8				5.8	6.7
Trade Payables	9.9	9.9	9.9	12.4				11.5	9.7
Income Taxes Payable	.3	.3	.5	.3				.4	.3
All Other Current	27.2	18.1	11.3	10.8				11.0	9.2
Total Current	67.1	44.3	32.9	36.7				37.5	33.9
Long-Term Debt	40.4	26.1	19.5	21.2				25.4	27.7
Deferred Taxes	.0	.3	.4	.7				.8	.8
All Other Non-Current	7.8	12.4	4.7	4.6				3.9	8.9
Net Worth	-15.4	16.9	42.4	36.8				32.4	28.7
Total Liabilities & Net Worth	100.0	100.0	100.0	100.0				100.0	100.0
							INCOME DATA		
Net Sales	100.0	100.0	100.0	100.0				100.0	100.0
Gross Profit									
Operating Expenses	98.4	96.5	97.6	96.8				94.1	95.6
Operating Profit	1.6	3.5	2.4	3.2				5.9	4.4
All Other Expenses (net)	2.6	2.5	1.5	1.3				.6	1.8
Profit Before Taxes	-1.0	1.0	1.0	1.9				5.3	2.6
							RATIOS		
Current	3.5	2.9	3.7	1.7				1.7	2.2
	1.1	1.2	1.5	1.4				1.3	1.3
	.4	.6	.9	1.1				1.0	1.0
Quick	3.5	2.4	3.4	1.5				1.6	1.9
	1.1	1.0	1.4	1.2				1.1	1.1
	.4	.5	.9	1.1				.8	.8
Sales/Receivables	0 UND	8 46.8	31 11.7	39 9.3				23 16.2	20 18.2
	25 14.7	26 14.2	43 8.4	46 8.0				41 9.0	34 10.6
	41 8.9	55 6.7	68 5.4	69 5.3				55 6.6	55 6.6
Cost of Sales/Inventory									
Cost of Sales/Payables									
Sales/Working Capital	15.5	8.3	5.1	11.1				12.6	11.1
	242.5	60.3	16.4	15.7				32.6	34.6
	-8.8	-17.0	-56.5	43.5				-199.7	-339.2
EBIT/Interest	16.1	12.9	6.9	3.2				7.6	5.8
	(32) 1.4	(53) 1.1	(48) 2.2	(22) 2.2				(92) 3.6	(125) 2.4
	-2.4	-3.3	-1.0	.5				2.1	1.2
Net Profit + Depr., Dep., Amort./Cur. Mat. L/T/D		2.1	2.4	4.9				3.4	3.3
		(11) 1.4	(14) 1.3	(16) 2.8				(34) 2.2	(36) 1.6
		-.1	-1.9	1.2				1.3	1.1
Fixed/Worth	.3	.3	.3	.7				.6	.5
	3.1	.8	.9	1.1				1.4	1.2
	-.5	NM	2.0	1.9				3.9	3.7
Debt/Worth	.5	.6	.6	1.4				1.2	1.0
	7.9	1.5	1.3	1.9				2.7	2.1
	-2.1	NM	3.4	4.2				7.1	7.2
% Profit Before Taxes/Tangible Net Worth	162.2	36.9	21.5	34.7				62.0	42.8
	(21) 16.7	(53) 8.8	(50) 2.9	(24) 8.9				(91) 24.8	(122) 15.4
	-3.6	-15.9	-7.1	-3.8				7.7	2.5
% Profit Before Taxes/Total Assets	26.9	12.5	9.2	5.6				15.7	11.9
	.5	1.9	.9	3.4				7.3	4.7
	-17.6	-7.0	-4.6	-1.1				2.6	.7
Sales/Net Fixed Assets	48.0	27.6	21.3	16.0				19.4	21.2
	24.2	15.2	6.7	7.0				9.6	8.5
	8.2	4.2	3.3	2.4				4.1	4.3
Sales/Total Assets	9.9	4.7	3.2	3.2				4.5	3.8
	4.3	3.5	2.2	2.0				2.8	2.7
	2.7	1.9	1.5	1.0				1.7	1.9
% Depr., Dep., Amort./Sales	1.2	1.5	1.6	1.8				1.7	1.7
	(24) 2.6	(55) 2.5	(44) 3.1	3.4				(90) 2.6	(118) 3.2
	4.6	7.2	5.0	4.3				5.6	5.4
% Officers', Directors' Owners' Comp/Sales	4.2	3.2	1.9					1.9	2.3
	(16) 6.6	(23) 6.0	(19) 2.8					(30) 2.7	(54) 4.4
	11.2	9.5	7.7					5.6	8.8
Net Sales ($)	50045M	300099M	600189M	1230234M	75397M	754318M		1954156M	2657587M
Total Assets ($)	9857M	77558M	253018M	534653M	62666M	320616M		922417M	1217296M

M = $ thousand　　MM = $ million
See Pages 9 through 22 for Explanation of Ratios and Data

Comparative Historical Data | Current Data Sorted by Sales

Type of Statement	4/1/07-3/31/08 ALL	4/1/08-3/31/09 ALL	4/1/09-3/31/10 ALL	0-1MM	1-3MM	3-5MM	5-10MM	10-25MM	25MM & OVER
Unqualified	7	9	8					2	6
Reviewed	32	29	43		9	3	16	8	7
Compiled	18	31	39	4	8	11	8	7	1
Tax Returns	15	34	34	12	10	7	4	1	
Other	36	43	64	10	16	7	12	11	8
				16 (4/1-9/30/09)			172 (10/1/09-3/31/10)		
NUMBER OF STATEMENTS	108	146	188	26	43	28	40	29	22
ASSETS	%	%	%	%	%	%	%	%	%
Cash & Equivalents	9.8	12.4	12.5	12.0	14.9	12.2	11.9	12.2	10.3
Trade Receivables (net)	28.0	31.1	30.0	10.5	34.9	25.8	29.1	38.5	39.3
Inventory	1.7	1.0	.5	1.0	.4	.3	.3	.5	.9
All Other Current	6.7	5.4	5.5	2.0	5.6	4.8	9.6	3.5	4.9
Total Current	46.1	50.0	48.5	25.5	55.8	43.1	50.9	54.7	55.4
Fixed Assets (net)	38.4	31.5	33.9	56.1	31.8	25.9	32.5	29.6	30.1
Intangibles (net)	3.6	3.5	4.3	7.2	3.4	4.0	1.4	5.7	6.1
All Other Non-Current	11.9	15.0	13.4	11.2	8.9	27.0	15.2	10.0	8.4
Total	100.0	100.0	100.0	100.0	100.0	100.0	100.0	100.0	100.0
LIABILITIES									
Notes Payable-Short Term	8.5	8.1	8.4	16.5	5.3	7.9	8.8	6.3	7.4
Cur. Mat.-L.T.D.	8.3	8.7	8.4	8.0	11.4	12.2	7.1	6.5	3.3
Trade Payables	9.6	10.2	10.3	3.7	8.4	9.7	10.0	13.5	18.8
Income Taxes Payable	.1	.1	.3	.0	.4	.4	.7	.4	.0
All Other Current	11.2	12.5	16.7	19.2	19.6	22.1	13.6	8.6	17.3
Total Current	37.7	39.6	44.1	47.5	45.1	52.2	40.2	35.3	46.8
Long-Term Debt	27.7	26.1	26.0	53.5	29.0	23.1	21.0	15.9	13.6
Deferred Taxes	.9	.9	.3	.0	.4	.0	.3	1.0	.4
All Other Non-Current	10.1	13.9	8.1	3.1	20.6	6.1	4.6	2.9	5.6
Net Worth	23.6	19.4	21.4	-4.1	4.9	18.6	33.9	44.9	33.6
Total Liabilities & Net Worth	100.0	100.0	100.0	100.0	100.0	100.0	100.0	100.0	100.0
INCOME DATA									
Net Sales	100.0	100.0	100.0	100.0	100.0	100.0	100.0	100.0	100.0
Gross Profit									
Operating Expenses	98.1	97.7	97.2	87.3	98.7	101.9	98.7	97.8	97.0
Operating Profit	1.9	2.3	2.8	12.7	1.3	-1.9	1.3	2.2	3.0
All Other Expenses (net)	.9	1.3	2.0	11.9	.8	-.3	.4	.8	.5
Profit Before Taxes	1.0	1.0	.7	.8	.6	-1.5	1.0	1.4	2.5
RATIOS									
Current	2.0 / 1.3 / .8	2.3 / 1.3 / 1.0	2.9 / 1.4 / .7	3.4 / .8 / .1	4.1 / 1.9 / .8	2.0 / .9 / .5	2.8 / 1.5 / .7	3.5 / 1.4 / .9	1.7 / 1.4 / 1.2
Quick	1.6 / 1.1 / .6	2.0 / 1.1 / .7	2.4 / 1.2 / .6	3.1 / .8 / .1	3.8 / 1.8 / .8	1.7 / .8 / .4	2.3 / 1.3 / .6	3.4 / 1.3 / .9	1.6 / 1.3 / 1.1
Sales/Receivables (days / ratio)	21 / 17.3, 38 / 9.6, 52 / 7.1	16 / 23.1, 33 / 11.1, 49 / 7.5	19 / 19.7, 38 / 9.7, 57 / 6.4	0 / UND, 7 / 49.2, 37 / 9.8	15 / 24.2, 41 / 8.9, 61 / 5.9	8 / 43.7, 25 / 14.8, 52 / 7.0	24 / 15.1, 38 / 9.7, 62 / 5.9	30 / 12.1, 39 / 9.3, 62 / 5.9	40 / 9.2, 46 / 8.0, 63 / 5.8
Cost of Sales/Inventory									
Cost of Sales/Payables									
Sales/Working Capital	10.7 / 26.7 / -40.4	11.9 / 31.0 / -434.9	9.0 / 26.1 / -23.3	10.4 / NM / -2.6	5.5 / 15.5 / -31.0	19.0 / -107.9 / -14.4	8.1 / 16.7 / -31.6	5.4 / 19.7 / -143.5	10.9 / 15.9 / 34.1
EBIT/Interest	(98) 4.0 / 2.1 / .4	(129) 4.5 / 2.1 / -.4	(158) 7.8 / 1.8 / -2.0	(20) 3.5 / .7 / -3.3	(35) 10.7 / 1.5 / -2.8	(24) 7.9 / 1.2 / -4.9	(35) 7.8 / 1.6 / -2.6	(25) 16.3 / 3.8 / -.7	(19) 4.1 / 2.4 / -.1
Net Profit + Depr., Dep., Amort./Cur. Mat. L/T/D	(27) 4.1 / 1.8 / .9	(44) 3.5 / 1.6 / .6	(44) 3.7 / 1.7 / .1				(11) 2.7 / 1.5 / .3		(13) 4.2 / 2.8 / 1.5
Fixed/Worth	.6 / 1.2 / 5.1	.5 / 1.0 / 3.1	.4 / .9 / 4.0	.9 / 8.7 / -2.2	.2 / .9 / 4.9	.3 / .6 / 4.2	.4 / 1.0 / 2.2	.1 / .7 / 1.8	.6 / .9 / 1.6
Debt/Worth	1.0 / 2.2 / 10.0	.8 / 2.0 / 6.8	.7 / 1.7 / 10.1	1.5 / 49.3 / -3.5	.4 / 1.0 / 6.2	.6 / 1.5 / 21.5	.9 / 1.6 / 6.8	.5 / 1.2 / 3.1	1.3 / 1.9 / 4.1
% Profit Before Taxes/Tangible Net Worth	(89) 36.0 / 9.1 / -1.6	(121) 34.7 / 8.5 / -1.2	(151) 30.3 / 7.0 / -6.4	(14) 17.9 / / -19.1	(34) 51.1 / 11.5 / -7.8	(23) 52.9 / 5.4 / -4.7	(34) 24.3 / 5.1 / -4.9	(25) 31.0 / 5.0 / -9.2	(21) 33.0 / 12.2 / .1
% Profit Before Taxes/Total Assets	9.8 / 3.6 / -3.0	9.8 / 2.6 / -2.0	10.1 / 1.7 / -5.3	8.1 / 1.1 / -13.1	24.8 / 1.2 / -9.9	9.0 / .6 / -15.8	9.6 / .6 / -3.4	12.7 / 1.8 / -4.4	8.2 / 4.0 / .8
Sales/Net Fixed Assets	16.7 / 8.3 / 3.6	31.7 / 14.4 / 5.3	28.2 / 12.0 / 4.1	10.2 / 3.4 / 1.2	32.4 / 15.3 / 5.5	37.3 / 19.7 / 10.6	21.0 / 8.4 / 3.2	28.6 / 10.5 / 4.5	34.6 / 12.4 / 6.8
Sales/Total Assets	3.7 / 2.6 / 1.7	5.0 / 3.4 / 2.1	4.3 / 2.8 / 1.7	3.0 / 1.5 / .9	4.9 / 3.1 / 2.3	5.3 / 3.8 / 2.2	3.9 / 2.2 / 1.5	4.0 / 2.7 / 1.6	4.2 / 2.7 / 2.1
% Depr., Dep., Amort./Sales	(94) 1.6 / 2.8 / 4.4	(123) 1.1 / 2.5 / 4.0	(151) 1.6 / 2.9 / 4.8	(20) 2.9 / 8.6 / 24.9	(34) 1.5 / 3.0 / 5.3	(21) 1.5 / 2.0 / 3.1	(33) 2.1 / 3.6 / 4.6	(24) 1.0 / 2.0 / 3.4	(19) 1.3 / 2.4 / 4.3
% Officers', Directors', Owners' Comp/Sales	(32) 1.5 / 4.3 / 9.3	(52) 2.3 / 3.2 / 6.8	(62) 2.2 / 4.9 / 9.0	(11) 6.1 / 11.1 / 16.7	(16) 2.7 / 6.0 / 7.3	(10) 2.1 / 5.3 / 9.6	(13) 1.9 / 3.2 / 8.7	(10) 1.5 / 2.2 / 5.0	
Net Sales ($)	2639031M	4316329M	3010282M	13954M	88512M	110750M	283756M	431922M	2081388M
Total Assets ($)	1289952M	1633344M	1258368M	16491M	37068M	38903M	165488M	210286M	790132M

M = $ thousand   MM = $ million
See Pages 9 through 22 for Explanation of Ratios and Data

TRANSPORTATION—Specialized Freight (except Used Goods) Trucking, Local   NAICS 484220

Current Data Sorted by Assets   **Comparative Historical Data**

Type of Statement

						Type of Statement		
	1			1		Unqualified	11	11
1	6	23	19			Reviewed	28	32
8	16	14	1			Compiled	30	30
32	22	6				Tax Returns	33	45
16	29	27	19	2	1	Other	52	53
	32 (4/1-9/30/09)		217 (10/1/09-3/31/10)				4/1/05-3/31/06 ALL	4/1/06-3/31/07 ALL

0-500M	500M-2MM	2-10MM	10-50MM	50-100MM	100-250MM		ALL	ALL
57	74	72	42	3	1	**NUMBER OF STATEMENTS**	154	171
%	%	%	%	%	%	**ASSETS**	%	%
18.6	12.2	9.2	6.9			Cash & Equivalents	11.3	12.1
19.7	26.1	22.2	24.5			Trade Receivables (net)	23.7	22.1
.2	2.6	1.9	2.6			Inventory	1.4	2.6
2.9	5.0	5.2	4.4			All Other Current	3.9	5.2
41.3	45.9	38.5	38.4			Total Current	40.4	42.0
41.0	43.1	49.7	50.8			Fixed Assets (net)	47.9	47.9
3.5	1.4	2.5	3.2			Intangibles (net)	1.6	2.6
14.1	9.5	9.3	7.6			All Other Non-Current	10.2	7.5
100.0	100.0	100.0	100.0			Total	100.0	100.0
						LIABILITIES		
6.9	8.9	5.9	4.5			Notes Payable-Short Term	7.7	8.7
11.9	7.7	9.7	10.4			Cur. Mat.-L.T.D.	7.6	7.8
13.3	11.9	9.5	8.1			Trade Payables	11.2	10.3
.0	.3	.6	.3			Income Taxes Payable	.3	.4
5.8	9.8	6.1	9.6			All Other Current	7.0	7.4
38.0	38.7	31.8	33.0			Total Current	33.9	34.6
55.1	27.4	30.4	23.2			Long-Term Debt	34.8	29.2
.0	.2	.7	1.1			Deferred Taxes	.9	.5
9.2	3.1	4.1	2.2			All Other Non-Current	6.5	4.0
-2.4	30.6	33.1	40.5			Net Worth	23.9	31.6
100.0	100.0	100.0	100.0			Total Liabilities & Net Worth	100.0	100.0
						INCOME DATA		
100.0	100.0	100.0	100.0			Net Sales	100.0	100.0
						Gross Profit		
93.6	96.5	96.1	97.4			Operating Expenses	95.1	94.0
6.4	3.5	3.9	2.6			Operating Profit	4.9	6.0
.7	.4	2.8	.5			All Other Expenses (net)	.8	1.0
5.7	3.2	1.2	2.1			Profit Before Taxes	4.1	5.0
						RATIOS		
3.0	2.8	1.9	2.1				2.3	2.2
.9	1.3	1.2	1.2			Current	1.2	1.3
.3	.7	.7	.8				.7	.7
2.8	2.4	1.7	1.6				2.1	1.7
.8	1.1	.9	1.0			Quick (153)	1.0	1.1
.2	.5	.6	.6				.5	.6
0 UND	6 61.3	18 20.8	24 15.2				9 41.3	11 34.1
8 43.1	22 16.6	31 11.9	36 10.1			Sales/Receivables	24 15.2	27 13.3
33 11.2	40 9.1	53 6.9	48 7.6				40 9.1	41 8.9
						Cost of Sales/Inventory		
						Cost of Sales/Payables		
16.9	13.8	10.8	9.4				15.2	12.4
-72.8	67.7	44.0	58.7			Sales/Working Capital	51.7	39.0
-15.7	-23.0	-25.4	-24.8				-21.5	-25.1
8.1	14.8	5.5	7.8				8.6	8.3
(44) 2.9	(66) 3.5	(64) 2.3	(41) 3.0			EBIT/Interest (135) 4.0 (153)	4.0	3.3
.8	.0	-.9	.6				1.0	1.5
		2.0	2.4			Net Profit + Depr., Dep.,	2.9	3.4
	(22)	(22) 1.5	(20) 1.7			Amort./Cur. Mat. L/T/D (34) 1.5 (41)	1.5	2.0
		.5	1.1				1.2	1.2
.3	.5	.8	.9				.7	.7
3.2	1.1	1.6	1.4			Fixed/Worth	1.7	1.6
-1.9	11.4	6.2	2.2				5.8	5.1
2.1	.5	1.0	.8				1.0	.9
6.7	1.7	1.9	1.8			Debt/Worth	2.4	2.3
-3.9	30.7	9.7	3.8				10.6	7.8
218.7	46.4	30.5	29.7			% Profit Before Taxes/Tangible	70.0	67.7
(35) 77.1	(57) 21.9	(61) 14.4	(39) 12.0			Net Worth (127) 30.8 (146)	30.8	29.2
3.6	-.5	-5.1	2.7				10.9	9.6
32.0	21.6	11.0	10.1			% Profit Before Taxes/Total	19.3	20.2
9.3	5.8	4.3	5.0			Assets	8.6	7.4
-.9	-2.5	-3.0	-1.0				.4	1.8
105.4	23.0	10.1	9.2				15.5	13.7
12.9	9.3	4.0	3.9			Sales/Net Fixed Assets	6.4	6.0
4.4	4.2	2.2	2.7				3.0	2.7
7.0	5.4	3.0	3.0				4.1	4.2
4.1	3.1	2.0	2.3			Sales/Total Assets	2.8	2.6
2.1	1.9	1.3	1.6				1.8	1.7
2.5	1.7	2.1	2.9				3.0	2.3
(28) 5.8	(59) 4.8	(67) 5.4	(39) 4.3			% Depr., Dep., Amort./Sales (127) 5.2 (138)	5.2	5.7
12.0	9.0	10.8	9.7				9.1	9.0
3.6	1.6	.8					1.3	1.1
(21) 5.3	(25) 2.7	(30) 2.4				% Officers', Directors' Owners' Comp/Sales (57) 2.6 (69)	2.6	3.0
8.2	6.8	5.9					4.7	5.4
60457M	311681M	852528M	2063971M	276148M	231731M	Net Sales ($)	2038114M	2700331M
12551M	83625M	355495M	830642M	160885M	202826M	Total Assets ($)	844023M	1166443M

M = $ thousand   MM = $ million
See Pages 9 through 22 for Explanation of Ratios and Data

Comparative Historical Data   Current Data Sorted by Sales

4/1/07-3/31/08 ALL	4/1/08-3/31/09 ALL	4/1/09-3/31/10 ALL		0-1MM	1-3MM	3-5MM	5-10MM	10-25MM	25MM & OVE
			Type of Statement		32 (4/1-9/30/09)		217 (10/1/09-3/31/10)		
12	11	7	Unqualified		1		1	1	4
28	48	49	Reviewed	1	6	5	4	16	17
36	46	39	Compiled	4	11	11	5	7	1
54	45	60	Tax Returns	18	21	9	8	4	
73	86	94	Other	15	22	11	11	19	16
203	236	249	**NUMBER OF STATEMENTS**	38	61	36	29	47	38
%	%	%	**ASSETS**	%	%	%	%	%	%
9.9	10.8	12.0	Cash & Equivalents	14.0	15.1	9.2	10.7	12.8	7.8
26.2	23.7	23.1	Trade Receivables (net)	11.1	23.8	21.8	24.6	27.5	28.3
2.4	1.7	1.8	Inventory	1.0	.9	4.1	.7	1.8	2.7
5.9	6.0	4.5	All Other Current	3.9	2.7	3.7	6.6	6.3	4.8
44.4	42.2	41.3	Total Current	30.1	42.5	38.8	42.7	48.3	43.6
43.2	46.1	45.8	Fixed Assets (net)	52.9	44.0	45.6	46.5	42.9	45.2
2.7	2.1	2.7	Intangibles (net)	4.6	1.8	2.6	.7	2.5	4.4
9.7	9.6	10.0	All Other Non-Current	12.4	11.7	13.0	10.2	6.3	6.8
100.0	100.0	100.0	Total	100.0	100.0	100.0	100.0	100.0	100.0
			LIABILITIES						
11.1	11.7	6.9	Notes Payable-Short Term	6.1	6.2	7.7	8.4	7.3	6.1
6.8	9.0	9.6	Cur. Mat.-L.T.D.	14.3	8.4	9.7	6.1	8.5	11.1
14.1	11.0	10.7	Trade Payables	8.8	9.5	13.3	12.3	12.9	8.5
.2	.3	.3	Income Taxes Payable	.1	.3	.7	.1	.5	.3
8.5	10.2	7.7	All Other Current	6.8	7.0	5.9	8.6	8.8	9.7
40.7	42.3	35.3	Total Current	36.0	31.5	37.3	35.4	38.0	35.9
28.8	29.2	33.8	Long-Term Debt	47.7	41.7	39.8	22.9	24.1	22.1
.6	.9	.5	Deferred Taxes	.1	.3	.6	.7	.5	.8
3.2	5.5	4.7	All Other Non-Current	11.3	2.5	8.3	2.8	2.2	2.7
26.7	22.2	25.7	Net Worth	4.9	24.1	14.0	38.2	35.3	38.6
100.0	100.0	100.0	Total Liabilities & Net Worth	100.0	100.0	100.0	100.0	100.0	100.0
			INCOME DATA						
100.0	100.0	100.0	Net Sales	100.0	100.0	100.0	100.0	100.0	100.0
			Gross Profit						
96.2	95.3	95.8	Operating Expenses	89.2	95.5	99.5	96.6	97.2	97.0
3.8	4.7	4.2	Operating Profit	10.8	4.5	.5	3.4	2.8	3.0
.5	1.3	1.2	All Other Expenses (net)	4.7	.5	.5	.5	.6	.7
3.3	3.4	3.0	Profit Before Taxes	6.1	4.0	.0	2.9	2.2	2.3
			RATIOS						
2.0	2.0	2.3	Current	2.7	3.6	2.9	2.4	2.3	1.9
1.2	1.2	1.2		.7	1.4	1.3	1.2	1.4	1.2
.6	.7	.6		.3	.6	.5	.8	.8	.8
1.6	1.7	2.0	Quick	1.6	2.8	2.2	2.2	1.9	1.6
.9	.9	1.0		.6	1.2	1.0	1.1	1.2	1.0
.4	.5	.5		.1	.6	.4	.4	.6	.6
10 36.2	10 37.8	11 32.5	Sales/Receivables	0 UND	5 66.5	12 30.8	1 529.5	18 20.3	28 13.0
28 13.2	25 14.5	26 13.9		5 74.9	25 14.5	22 16.6	21 17.8	29 12.6	36 10.1
42 8.7	39 9.4	43 8.5		34 10.9	50 7.3	39 9.3	51 7.2	47 7.8	46 8.0
			Cost of Sales/Inventory						
			Cost of Sales/Payables						
12.7	13.7	12.4	Sales/Working Capital	18.2	12.3	11.2	20.8	10.7	14.7
48.9	65.2	82.4		-24.0	62.9	58.6	63.9	26.6	72.3
-22.7	-21.6	-21.9		-7.6	-16.2	-19.1	-74.5	-35.0	-34.3
7.7	7.8	7.8	EBIT/Interest	9.8	8.6	3.9	16.3	7.3	8.1
(179) 2.7	(207) 2.8	(218) 2.8		(28) 2.8	(54) 2.5	(32) 2.2	(24) 5.3	(43) 2.7	(37) 3.0
1.1	.9	.1		-.8	.3	-.7	1.0	-.3	1.0
6.0	5.3	2.4	Net Profit + Depr., Dep.,					2.2	3.9
(46) 1.7	(51) 1.9	(52) 1.6	Amort./Cur. Mat. L/T/D					(13) 1.6	(22) 1.8
1.1	1.0	.8						.7	1.1
.6	.6	.6	Fixed/Worth	.5	.3	1.1	.6	.6	.7
1.5	1.5	1.4		3.8	1.7	1.5	.9	1.3	1.5
6.0	6.1	8.0		-2.7	20.8	-4.6	4.3	3.0	2.5
1.0	.8	.8	Debt/Worth	1.9	.6	.9	.6	1.0	.8
3.0	2.4	2.3		18.7	2.6	2.0	1.6	1.5	2.0
11.3	9.5	20.8		-4.2	82.5	-7.2	16.9	4.8	4.2
59.0	51.8	45.0	% Profit Before Taxes/Tangible	143.6	49.1	40.5	51.4	30.5	42.1
(167) 21.8	(195) 20.1	(195) 15.9	Net Worth	(23) 32.9	(47) 16.8	(26) 5.7	(24) 24.1	(40) 14.4	(35) 14.5
7.4	4.6	.0		5.0	-3.2	-15.1	6.4	-.5	2.9
15.5	15.6	17.6	% Profit Before Taxes/Total	27.0	25.9	16.4	16.0	14.8	10.4
7.5	5.8	5.6	Assets	5.8	5.9	2.3	6.7	6.1	5.0
.4	-.7	-2.3		-3.9	-1.7	-4.9	1.7	-3.0	.3
20.8	18.4	18.1	Sales/Net Fixed Assets	22.5	30.1	24.9	15.1	23.9	15.1
7.6	6.3	6.1		4.4	6.1	7.6	8.2	5.3	5.7
3.7	3.3	2.8		1.7	2.2	2.3	3.6	2.7	3.6
4.6	4.6	4.5	Sales/Total Assets	3.9	4.8	5.8	5.5	4.3	3.7
2.9	2.6	2.5		2.0	2.6	2.7	3.2	2.4	2.5
2.0	1.9	1.7		1.0	1.4	1.6	2.1	1.7	2.1
1.8	1.6	2.1	% Depr., Dep., Amort./Sales	5.5	3.0	1.7	1.7	1.6	1.8
(168) 4.9	(199) 4.3	(196) 5.1		(22) 12.4	(45) 6.6	(27) 4.5	(26) 4.5	(41) 5.0	(35) 3.8
8.4	8.5	10.3		19.5	10.6	11.5	6.9	9.5	8.5
1.1	1.3	1.3	% Officers', Directors'		2.3	1.2		.9	
(81) 2.8	(89) 3.3	(85) 3.1	Owners' Comp/Sales		(24) 4.9	(15) 3.1		(25) 1.9	
6.4	6.9	6.3			7.1	5.4		3.5	
7040280M	5836992M	3796516M	Net Sales ($)	17179M	113191M	142989M	205979M	782143M	2535035M
1289395M	2303670M	1646024M	Total Assets ($)	19634M	69708M	84394M	72644M	362778M	1036866M

© RMA 2010   M = $ thousand   MM = $ million
See Pages 9 through 22 for Explanation of Ratios and Data

TRANSPORTATION—Specialized Freight (except Used Goods) Trucking, Long-Distance NAICS 484230

Current Data Sorted by Assets							Comparative Historical Data	

Type of Statement

0-500M	500M-2MM	2-10MM	10-50MM	50-100MM	100-250MM		4/1/05-3/31/06 ALL	4/1/06-3/31/07 ALL
1	4	5	20	4	14	Unqualified	32	29
3	13	22	16	1	1	Reviewed	26	38
8	11	8	3	1		Compiled	20	24
5	12	3	25		6	Tax Returns	10	9
		25	27	10		Other	43	56
	27 (4/1-9/30/09)		195 (10/1/09-3/31/10)					
17	40	63	66	16	20	NUMBER OF STATEMENTS	131	156

ASSETS

%	%	%	%	%	%		%	%
15.9	14.3	10.4	8.9	7.1	4.2	Cash & Equivalents	7.7	9.3
9.6	27.0	27.7	23.6	20.4	17.1	Trade Receivables (net)	25.1	25.4
2.3	2.5	1.2	2.3	2.1	.8	Inventory	1.0	1.1
1.7	4.9	5.8	4.6	2.9	3.9	All Other Current	4.6	3.7
29.4	48.7	45.2	39.3	32.6	26.0	Total Current	38.4	39.5
53.2	38.2	42.8	49.7	59.9	55.8	Fixed Assets (net)	51.0	50.1
2.4	2.1	3.8	3.2	3.6	14.3	Intangibles (net)	3.0	2.0
14.5	11.0	8.2	7.8	3.9	4.0	All Other Non-Current	7.6	8.5
100.0	100.0	100.0	100.0	100.0	100.0	Total	100.0	100.0

LIABILITIES

45.9	14.6	10.6	8.5	1.8	1.6	Notes Payable-Short Term	7.6	6.3
11.1	11.4	7.9	10.7	11.7	7.6	Cur. Mat.-L.T.D.	11.3	11.0
3.4	6.1	11.2	8.8	7.2	6.3	Trade Payables	7.7	8.1
.0	.0	.5	.5	.0	.0	Income Taxes Payable	.2	.2
27.8	15.6	7.8	7.5	10.0	8.5	All Other Current	8.4	9.3
88.3	47.6	38.0	35.9	30.7	24.2	Total Current	35.2	35.0
53.0	27.0	22.0	22.2	31.1	34.5	Long-Term Debt	28.6	27.9
.0	.9	.6	2.3	3.3	6.3	Deferred Taxes	2.6	2.4
4.8	6.2	2.7	3.7	10.7	5.0	All Other Non-Current	2.7	4.1
-46.1	18.3	36.7	35.8	24.1	30.0	Net Worth	30.9	30.6
100.0	100.0	100.0	100.0	100.0	100.0	Total Liabilities & Net Worth	100.0	100.0

INCOME DATA

100.0	100.0	100.0	100.0	100.0	100.0	Net Sales	100.0	100.0
						Gross Profit		
96.8	99.0	96.5	97.2	98.5	98.7	Operating Expenses	94.8	95.0
3.2	1.0	3.5	2.8	1.5	1.3	Operating Profit	5.2	5.0
.4	.0	1.4	.8	1.4	2.4	All Other Expenses (net)	.8	.5
2.8	1.0	2.1	2.0	.2	-1.2	Profit Before Taxes	4.5	4.5

RATIOS

2.1	2.3	2.2	1.6	1.6	1.5		1.4	1.7
.3	1.0	1.2	1.1	1.0	1.1	Current	1.0	1.1
.1	.6	.7	.7	.7	.8		.7	.8
2.1	2.0	1.9	1.4	1.5	1.2		1.3	1.4
.3	1.0	1.0	.9	.8	.9	Quick	.9	.9
.0	.3	.5	.5	.6	.7		.6	.6
0 UND	0 885.6	24 15.4	28 13.2	30 12.1	34 10.7		23 15.7	23 15.7
0 UND	24 15.3	35 10.4	37 9.9	41 8.9	40 9.1	Sales/Receivables	34 10.8	34 10.8
1 374.5	36 10.1	45 8.0	45 8.1	47 7.8	46 8.0		44 8.4	43 8.6
						Cost of Sales/Inventory		
						Cost of Sales/Payables		
34.0	17.5	13.4	13.0	12.5	17.0		20.9	17.2
-34.8	114.0	31.2	80.4	NM	NM	Sales/Working Capital	115.9	93.4
-9.1	-23.1	-17.3	-18.6	-16.8	-24.8		-22.6	-37.5
7.6	7.1	8.9	5.9	4.3	2.0		6.6	7.5
(13) 1.1	(37) 1.8	(57) 3.6	(65) 2.5	(14) 1.5	(19) 1.2	EBIT/Interest	(123) 3.7	(143) 3.1
-1.3	.3	.7	1.0	-1.1	-.3		2.2	1.7
		2.6	3.4				1.9	2.2
		(19) 1.5	(40) 1.3			Net Profit + Depr., Dep., Amort./Cur. Mat. L/T/D	(54) 1.3	(50) 1.4
		1.1	.9				.8	1.0
.3	.4	.6	.9	1.4	1.5		1.1	1.0
5.6	1.4	1.5	1.5	2.3	3.3	Fixed/Worth	1.9	1.9
-2.4	14.4	2.9	3.1	3.4	55.4		4.1	3.5
.8	.9	.9	1.2	1.3	1.6		1.2	1.2
8.4	2.5	2.1	2.2	2.7	3.6	Debt/Worth	2.6	2.6
-1.8	38.9	6.5	4.0	3.3	108.6		5.3	5.1
593.8	47.8	31.8	25.3	32.5	16.7		52.2	50.6
(10) 84.9	(32) 14.8	(55) 20.7	(61) 10.4	(15) 6.9	(16) 10.4	% Profit Before Taxes/Tangible Net Worth	(117) 26.7	(146) 26.4
17.8	-14.9	.1	3.7	-30.4	-15.5		13.5	11.2
60.4	16.8	10.3	8.0	9.7	5.5		14.2	15.5
2.2	5.8	4.4	3.3	2.5	1.0	% Profit Before Taxes/Total Assets	7.2	6.7
-16.7	-6.0	.1	.1	-7.1	-4.1		3.4	2.5
242.9	39.4	16.9	8.0	5.2	5.3		10.2	9.0
11.8	14.0	5.8	3.9	2.2	2.5	Sales/Net Fixed Assets	4.6	4.3
6.2	6.1	3.3	2.5	1.4	1.5		2.4	2.5
11.1	5.6	3.8	2.6	2.3	1.9		3.6	3.4
8.0	4.6	2.6	2.0	1.5	1.3	Sales/Total Assets	2.3	2.3
4.6	3.0	1.8	1.5	1.1	1.0		1.6	1.6
	2.1	1.8	2.9	3.3			2.5	2.7
	(33) 4.2	(57) 4.9	(64) 5.7	(13) 7.0		% Depr., Dep., Amort./Sales	(113) 5.1	(133) 5.1
	9.4	8.2	9.8	10.5			7.7	8.2
	1.0	.6	1.0				1.3	1.1
	(22) 2.0	(23) 1.9	(15) 2.1			% Officers', Directors' Owners' Comp/Sales	(36) 2.6	(43) 3.0
		4.4	6.9				5.7	4.5
24243M	257169M	909020M	3868558M	3558637M	4866683M	Net Sales ($)	6787084M	6529744M
2858M	52152M	302506M	1562711M	1102718M	3100958M	Total Assets ($)	3321642M	3302879M

M = $ thousand   MM = $ million
See Pages 9 through 22 for Explanation of Ratios and Data

Comparative Historical Data

Current Data Sorted by Sales

			Type of Statement						
38	48	43	Unqualified				1	5	37
38	45	44	Reviewed	2	1	2	7	13	19
21	26	28	Compiled		4	6	9	6	3
13	20	22	Tax Returns	6	4	7	3	2	
53	75	85	Other	3	3	6	17	16	40
4/1/07-3/31/08 ALL	4/1/08-3/31/09 ALL	4/1/09-3/31/10 ALL		27 (4/1-9/30/09)			195 (10/1/09-3/31/10)		
				0-1MM	1-3MM	3-5MM	5-10MM	10-25MM	25MM & OVE
163	214	222	NUMBER OF STATEMENTS	11	12	21	37	42	99
%	%	%	ASSETS	%	%	%	%	%	%
8.0	9.7	10.3	Cash & Equivalents	5.1	25.1	14.6	12.3	9.3	7.8
29.0	27.4	23.5	Trade Receivables (net)	9.0	7.6	13.9	27.6	28.4	25.4
1.3	1.4	1.9	Inventory	1.9	1.3	1.9	2.1	.9	2.3
3.9	4.2	4.6	All Other Current	2.7	1.9	3.0	5.4	5.4	4.8
42.2	42.7	40.2	Total Current	18.7	35.9	33.5	47.4	44.0	40.3
47.8	45.7	47.2	Fixed Assets (net)	62.4	43.0	56.4	36.6	48.2	47.6
2.5	3.8	4.1	Intangibles (net)	.3	3.8	.2	6.6	2.0	5.4
7.6	7.8	8.4	All Other Non-Current	17.9	17.4	9.9	9.4	5.8	6.7
100.0	100.0	100.0	Total	100.0	100.0	100.0	100.0	100.0	100.0
			LIABILITIES						
7.8	8.1	12.0	Notes Payable-Short Term	66.7	3.0	11.0	13.1	10.9	7.2
9.4	8.7	9.8	Cur. Mat.-L.T.D.	10.4	16.6	10.2	9.1	9.9	9.1
9.9	9.5	8.2	Trade Payables	1.3	5.0	5.3	9.3	9.5	9.1
.3	.1	.3	Income Taxes Payable	.0	.0	.0	.7	.2	.3
9.2	10.6	10.9	All Other Current	33.0	10.7	16.8	6.0	9.5	9.6
36.7	37.0	41.2	Total Current	111.4	35.3	43.3	38.2	39.9	35.4
27.9	28.3	27.1	Long-Term Debt	63.1	48.0	32.4	18.8	25.3	23.3
1.7	1.8	1.8	Deferred Taxes	.0	.0	1.4	.6	1.1	3.1
2.5	4.6	4.6	All Other Non-Current	7.8	.9	1.7	6.0	3.8	5.1
31.2	28.3	25.3	Net Worth	-82.3	15.8	21.2	36.4	29.9	33.1
100.0	100.0	100.0	Total Liabilities & Net Worth	100.0	100.0	100.0	100.0	100.0	100.0
			INCOME DATA						
100.0	100.0	100.0	Net Sales	100.0	100.0	100.0	100.0	100.0	100.0
			Gross Profit						
95.8	95.4	97.5	Operating Expenses	88.5	95.1	100.2	98.9	97.4	97.7
4.2	4.6	2.5	Operating Profit	11.5	4.9	-.2	1.1	2.6	2.3
1.0	.8	1.0	All Other Expenses (net)	5.9	.3	-.1	.3	1.1	1.0
3.3	3.8	1.5	Profit Before Taxes	5.6	4.6	-.2	.8	1.4	1.3
			RATIOS						
1.7	1.8	1.8		.4	3.1	1.5	2.5	1.8	1.6
1.1	1.1	1.1	Current	.1	1.2	.9	1.3	1.2	1.1
.8	.8	.7		.1	.3	.2	.7	.8	.8
1.5	1.6	1.6		.4	3.1	1.3	2.3	1.6	1.4
1.0	1.0	.9	Quick	.1	1.1	.6	1.1	1.0	.9
.6	.6	.5		.0	.3	.2	.5	.6	.6
26 14.0	20 17.9	20 18.6		0 UND	0 UND	1 340.0	14 25.7	23 15.8	30 12.2
34 10.7	30 12.0	34 10.7	Sales/Receivables	0 UND	0 UND	20 18.7	35 10.4	33 11.1	40 9.2
45 8.1	40 9.2	44 8.4		0 UND	29 12.4	32 11.6	43 8.4	46 7.9	45 8.1
			Cost of Sales/Inventory						
			Cost of Sales/Payables						
14.4	15.7	15.9		-34.8	21.4	30.9	10.4	16.2	13.9
82.5	74.6	98.7	Sales/Working Capital	-6.5	82.1	-68.1	31.2	35.9	95.1
-26.2	-37.1	-16.9		-3.1	-16.7	-7.1	-52.4	-20.7	-21.0
5.6	6.8	5.9				5.8	7.2	5.0	6.6
(156) 2.6	(199) 2.6	(205) 2.3	EBIT/Interest		(20) 1.2	(32) 2.4	3.6	(95) 2.1
1.0	1.3	.4				-1.1	1.0	.6	.5
2.0	3.0	2.5						2.0	3.9
(60) 1.4	(68) 1.5	(74) 1.3	Net Profit + Depr., Dep., Amort./Cur. Mat. L/T/D				(14) 1.3	(47) 1.5
.9	1.0	.9						.7	.9
.7	.7	.7		1.7	.3	1.1	.5	.7	.8
1.8	1.7	1.8	Fixed/Worth	UND	3.5	2.5	1.5	1.4	1.8
3.6	3.9	3.9		-.6	-8.5	13.3	7.9	2.4	3.4
1.1	1.1	1.1		4.4	.5	1.8	.7	.8	1.2
2.6	2.6	2.6	Debt/Worth	-999.8	4.7	3.0	1.8	1.7	2.6
4.8	8.4	7.4		-1.5	-19.3	17.1	10.9	2.9	5.4
38.4	37.6	34.2				87.0	31.4	29.8	32.8
(152) 17.4	(182) 20.4	(189) 13.5	% Profit Before Taxes/Tangible Net Worth		(17) 22.1	(29) 14.4	(40) 17.3	(90) 10.2
2.4	4.7	-.4				-24.9	1.6	-4.6	1.7
14.7	12.7	10.1		14.0	52.3	15.5	16.6	9.9	8.0
5.0	5.0	3.6	% Profit Before Taxes/Total Assets	.8	4.6	2.4	5.8	6.1	2.7
.4	1.2	-1.9		-24.4	-7.8	-8.1	.0	-3.3	-1.5
12.7	17.5	15.3		11.8	28.0	17.6	24.5	15.6	9.6
4.7	6.1	5.5	Sales/Net Fixed Assets	7.1	8.6	6.0	11.8	5.1	4.0
2.6	3.1	2.6		1.2	4.0	2.4	5.0	2.4	2.3
3.8	4.6	4.1		8.9	8.8	5.1	4.8	3.9	3.0
2.5	2.6	2.5	Sales/Total Assets	5.2	3.5	3.0	3.4	2.6	2.0
1.6	1.8	1.5		1.2	1.2	2.1	2.5	1.7	1.4
2.4	2.2	2.3				3.8	1.7	2.3	1.9
(132) 5.2	(163) 4.7	(180) 5.2	% Depr., Dep., Amort./Sales		(18) 8.0	(30) 3.6	(40) 5.2	(78) 4.7
7.8	7.1	8.7				10.1	7.6	9.0	8.3
1.1	1.0	1.0					1.0	.5	.8
(52) 2.5	(63) 2.2	(68) 2.2	% Officers', Directors' Owners' Comp/Sales			(21) 1.9	(13) 1.8	(15) 1.6
5.8	5.1	5.0					4.0	3.9	6.9
7476195M	12059235M	13484310M	Net Sales ($)	6035M	22276M	85437M	272680M	671625M	12426257M
3783342M	5474850M	6123903M	Total Assets ($)	6625M	11920M	38092M	101593M	291069M	5674604M

M = $ thousand   MM = $ million
See Pages 9 through 22 for Explanation of Ratios and Data

TRANSPORTATION—Taxi Service   NAICS 485310

Current Data Sorted by Assets							Comparative Historical Data	

						Type of Statement		
		1	6		1	Unqualified		4
		3	2	1		Reviewed	5	8
4	1	2				Compiled	13	10
4	2	3				Tax Returns	15	7
7	4	5	4	1	1	Other	14	20
	12 (4/1-9/30/09)		40 (10/1/09-3/31/10)				4/1/05-3/31/06	4/1/06-3/31/07
0-500M	500M-2MM	2-10MM	10-50MM	50-100MM	100-250MM		ALL	ALL
15	7	14	12	2	2	NUMBER OF STATEMENTS	47	49
%	%	%	%	%	%	ASSETS	%	%
32.9		17.1	18.0			Cash & Equivalents	12.7	9.4
14.8		17.0	12.9			Trade Receivables (net)	15.6	16.9
.4		1.1	.5			Inventory	2.1	.6
12.6		7.3	13.3			All Other Current	8.7	2.0
60.7		42.5	44.8			Total Current	39.1	29.0
17.9		35.4	38.2			Fixed Assets (net)	31.7	39.0
8.6		.7	13.4			Intangibles (net)	10.9	12.3
12.8		21.4	3.7			All Other Non-Current	18.3	19.7
100.0		100.0	100.0			Total	100.0	100.0
						LIABILITIES		
13.7		13.9	3.8			Notes Payable-Short Term	3.3	15.7
7.2		5.6	5.6			Cur. Mat.-L.T.D.	14.4	5.0
25.3		7.1	6.4			Trade Payables	9.2	7.7
.1		.0	.2			Income Taxes Payable	.2	.5
25.0		19.3	21.1			All Other Current	13.7	13.2
71.3		46.0	37.1			Total Current	40.9	42.0
31.5		14.9	9.8			Long-Term Debt	23.5	26.3
.0		.4	4.5			Deferred Taxes	.3	1.0
11.4		7.9	4.6			All Other Non-Current	4.8	3.9
-14.2		30.9	44.1			Net Worth	30.6	26.8
100.0		100.0	100.0			Total Liabilities & Net Worth	100.0	100.0
						INCOME DATA		
100.0		100.0	100.0			Net Sales	100.0	100.0
						Gross Profit		
93.1		93.7	84.8			Operating Expenses	87.9	91.3
6.9		6.3	15.2			Operating Profit	12.1	8.7
3.9		1.5	3.9			All Other Expenses (net)	4.2	3.8
3.0		4.8	11.3			Profit Before Taxes	7.9	4.9
						RATIOS		
2.0		2.4	1.7				2.1	1.4
1.2		.7	1.5			Current	1.1	.9
.3		.3	.8				.5	.3
1.8		1.8	1.5				1.8	1.3
1.0		.4	.7			Quick	.8	.7
.2		.3	.5				.3	.3
0 UND		0 UND	3 129.1				0 UND	1 505.1
9 40.6		21 17.3	14 26.4			Sales/Receivables	8 44.6	26 13.9
31 11.8		46 7.9	21 17.1				33 11.0	51 7.2
						Cost of Sales/Inventory		
						Cost of Sales/Payables		
21.7		11.4	7.8				13.5	15.6
34.5		-31.3	22.2			Sales/Working Capital	51.7	-33.3
-9.0		-2.6	-62.1				-16.8	-9.7
		21.8					10.3	9.5
		(12) 3.6				EBIT/Interest	(35) 3.8	(41) 3.1
		.6					2.0	.6
						Net Profit + Depr., Dep.,	2.2	2.8
		(12) 1.6				Amort./Cur. Mat. L/T/D	(12) 1.6	(14) 1.7
		1.0					1.0	.7
.0		.1	.5				.2	.7
-1.7		1.5	1.2			Fixed/Worth	1.1	2.1
-.3		UND	4.0				3.3	-5.4
1.5		.6	1.0				1.0	1.0
-8.3		3.1	1.5			Debt/Worth	3.4	2.8
-3.8		UND	6.7				19.0	-9.5
		59.3	70.0			% Profit Before Taxes/Tangible	67.0	57.3
		(12) 37.7	(10) 55.0			Net Worth	(36) 34.0	(34) 19.4
		7.5	14.6				21.6	3.2
45.2		17.3	31.3			% Profit Before Taxes/Total	20.9	15.9
7.4		4.9	25.2			Assets	9.7	5.1
-1.3		.1	10.3				2.9	-1.8
UND		32.2	13.2				104.0	17.9
68.5		9.2	6.7			Sales/Net Fixed Assets	16.6	4.9
11.7		4.9	3.6				3.4	2.9
9.4		4.7	3.2				6.6	3.5
4.3		2.3	2.1			Sales/Total Assets	2.4	1.8
2.6		1.4	1.7				1.2	1.1
		.5					1.9	2.2
		(11) 3.8				% Depr., Dep., Amort./Sales	(33) 3.9	(37) 5.4
		6.9					8.3	10.2
						% Officers', Directors'	3.5	2.3
						Owners' Comp/Sales	(24) 5.1	(15) 4.2
							8.5	13.0
21589M	43377M	169717M	518273M	103651M	395065M	Net Sales ($)	620523M	821639M
3553M	7945M	68422M	227089M	188190M	390794M	Total Assets ($)	340979M	543953M

M = $ thousand   MM = $ million
See Pages 9 through 22 for Explanation of Ratios and Data

Comparative Historical Data

Current Data Sorted by Sales

			Type of Statement						
2	10	8	Unqualified		2		1	2	6
3	4	6	Reviewed		3			3	
13	10	7	Compiled	2	4	1			1
9	10	9	Tax Returns	1	4		2	2	
21	19	22	Other	3	5	1	4	4	5
4/1/07-3/31/08 ALL	4/1/08-3/31/09 ALL	4/1/09-3/31/10 ALL			12 (4/1-9/30/09)			40 (10/1/09-3/31/10)	
				0-1MM	1-3MM	3-5MM	5-10MM	10-25MM	25MM & OVE
48	53	52	NUMBER OF STATEMENTS	6	14	2	7	11	12
%	%	%	ASSETS	%	%	%	%	%	%
13.4	15.3	20.9	Cash & Equivalents		26.2			16.0	20.9
17.8	13.5	16.3	Trade Receivables (net)		14.9			25.0	14.4
.5	1.0	.6	Inventory		.1			.4	.4
5.2	4.9	11.3	All Other Current		17.1			4.3	6.9
36.9	34.7	49.2	Total Current		58.3			45.8	42.6
34.7	35.9	31.3	Fixed Assets (net)		19.9			39.2	36.5
16.3	13.1	8.0	Intangibles (net)		11.0			4.3	15.0
12.0	16.4	11.5	All Other Non-Current		10.8			10.8	5.8
100.0	100.0	100.0	Total		100.0			100.0	100.0
			LIABILITIES						
6.9	6.3	10.0	Notes Payable-Short Term		11.1			3.2	3.1
4.2	6.3	6.2	Cur. Mat.-L.T.D.		3.1			4.6	4.7
6.1	8.1	12.2	Trade Payables		20.1			4.5	8.1
.2	.0	.1	Income Taxes Payable		.1			.1	.2
12.3	15.0	23.2	All Other Current		27.0			25.1	18.1
29.6	35.7	51.6	Total Current		61.4			37.4	34.3
35.5	27.7	19.4	Long-Term Debt		16.6			25.2	12.6
.4	1.0	1.1	Deferred Taxes		.0			.2	4.5
9.5	14.8	9.0	All Other Non-Current		17.6			3.1	5.2
25.0	20.8	18.8	Net Worth		4.4			34.1	43.5
100.0	100.0	100.0	Total Liabilities & Net Worth		100.0			100.0	100.0
			INCOME DATA						
100.0	100.0	100.0	Net Sales		100.0			100.0	100.0
			Gross Profit						
89.0	93.5	88.8	Operating Expenses		84.8			82.1	90.4
11.0	6.5	11.2	Operating Profit		15.2			17.9	9.6
3.7	1.1	3.9	All Other Expenses (net)		9.5			6.8	-.8
7.3	5.4	7.3	Profit Before Taxes		5.6			11.2	10.3
			RATIOS						
3.0	2.5	1.9			2.2			7.9	1.7
.9	1.2	1.1	Current		1.4			1.1	1.4
.5	.3	.5			.5			.3	.8
2.2	2.2	1.6			1.4			7.8	1.5
.9	(52) .9	.7	Quick		.7			.7	1.1
.4	.3	.3			.3			.3	.6
2 237.4	0 999.8	0 744.1		0 UND			0 UND	3 127.1	
16 22.7	10 36.1	14 26.7	Sales/Receivables	10 36.3			14 26.9	14 25.9	
50 7.3	31 11.8	32 11.3		52 7.0			32 11.5	27 13.6	
			Cost of Sales/Inventory						
			Cost of Sales/Payables						
8.1	16.7	11.3			17.3			5.0	11.3
-109.1	129.0	76.4	Sales/Working Capital		31.7			70.7	22.2
-16.4	-12.1	-13.0			-8.3			-13.1	-62.1
12.8	10.1	18.3						29.5	
(36) 6.1	(38) 5.1	(37) 5.9	EBIT/Interest				(10) 17.9		
.6	1.0	.8						3.2	
6.3	16.2	6.9	Net Profit + Depr., Dep.,						
(10) 2.4	(10) 2.5	(10) 3.4	Amort./Cur. Mat. L/T/D						
1.6	1.3	1.8							
.2	.2	.2			.0			.0	.5
1.7	1.7	1.5	Fixed/Worth		1.3			.8	1.4
-4.7	-2.0	-6.2			-1.7			63.7	NM
.6	.6	1.3			2.2			.6	1.0
2.0	2.2	4.8	Debt/Worth		7.8			10.6	1.5
-4.4	-5.4	-14.7			-7.8			70.5	NM
60.4	68.7	86.8	% Profit Before Taxes/Tangible					423.6	
(31) 31.9	(37) 26.9	(36) 50.4	Net Worth					60.5	
1.6	3.1	15.5						15.5	
31.8	21.4	30.0	% Profit Before Taxes/Total		9.2			31.6	31.3
10.7	6.9	9.0	Assets		5.0			9.3	26.1
-1.2	.7	1.4			.0			1.1	12.6
84.9	42.2	78.5			UND			121.6	13.2
8.1	7.7	11.1	Sales/Net Fixed Assets		217.1			6.8	6.8
3.6	4.0	5.3			7.7			2.4	3.6
3.9	4.2	4.5			7.5			5.4	3.5
2.3	2.6	2.5	Sales/Total Assets		3.6			2.7	2.1
1.2	1.4	1.7			1.6			.8	1.8
2.7	2.4	3.1							
(27) 4.8	(36) 6.3	(29) 5.9	% Depr., Dep., Amort./Sales						
7.8	10.0	7.8							
2.6	1.7	1.0	% Officers', Directors'						
(12) 4.5	(17) 4.3	(12) 4.0	Owners' Comp/Sales						
9.1	9.3	8.6							
1886509M	840527M	1251672M	Net Sales ($)	3476M	23252M	7744M	58590M	188252M	970358M
786526M	529154M	885993M	Total Assets ($)	1200M	25820M	6304M	23628M	333017M	496024M

M = $ thousand   MM = $ million
See Pages 9 through 22 for Explanation of Ratios and Data

Current Data Sorted by Assets

		2	1		
	1	6			
1	3	3			
7	4	7	1		
3	3		40 (10/1/09-3/31/10)		
	2 (4/1-9/30/09)				
0-500M	500M-2MM	2-10MM	10-50MM	50-100MM	100-250MM
11	11	18	2		

%	%	%	%	%	%
14.5	11.5	7.0			
5.5	13.3	15.7			
.0	5.0	1.0	D	D	
.2	1.0	3.0	A	A	
20.2	30.9	26.8	T	T	
66.3	45.3	40.1	A	A	
7.2	11.1	18.2	N	N	
6.3	12.8	14.9	O	O	
100.0	100.0	100.0	T	T	
10.2	7.6	4.6	A	A	
16.7	6.9	8.2	V	V	
5.1	14.1	6.6	A	A	
.0	.0	.0	I	I	
6.5	20.0	4.3	L	L	
38.4	48.5	23.7	A	A	
56.7	48.6	28.5	B	B	
.0	.0	.7	L	L	
9.2	8.3	9.1	E	E	
-4.3	-5.4	38.0			
100.0	100.0	100.0			
100.0	100.0	100.0			
99.6	99.1	94.8			
.4	.9	5.2			
3.1	.2	1.4			
-2.6	.7	3.8			

2.7	1.4	2.6			
.7	.8	.9			
.3	.3	.4			
2.7	1.2	2.1			
.7	.5	.7			
.3	.2	.2			

0	UND	0	UND	7	54.0
0	UND	5	78.5	15	24.7
14	26.4	19	19.6	41	8.8

23.5	33.8	10.6			
-95.0	-36.2	-146.0			
-6.4	-9.7	-10.6			
(10) 3.9	(10) 3.5	(15) 5.7			
.9	1.0	3.5			
-1.7	-1.9	1.3			

2.9	.9	.5			
-5.5	-20.2	2.6			
-1.6	-.9	-709.7			
12.4	4.1	1.0			
-11.6	-38.6	3.2			
-3.1	-2.8	-750.8			
		67.0			
	(13)	17.4			
		-.1			
14.0	12.2	12.6			
-2.3	.5	4.5			
-20.7	-3.2	.3			
17.8	28.2	17.8			
4.9	6.2	6.0			
1.8	3.0	2.6			
4.7	6.1	2.7			
3.8	2.5	1.9			
1.3	1.3	1.1			
		3.3			
	(16)	9.6			
		11.3			

10966M	47780M	143077M	188095M		
3034M	12441M	75824M	72627M		

Comparative Historical Data

<table>
<tr><th>Type of Statement</th><th></th><th></th></tr>
<tr><td>Unqualified</td><td>7</td><td>4</td></tr>
<tr><td>Reviewed</td><td>2</td><td>2</td></tr>
<tr><td>Compiled</td><td>5</td><td>2</td></tr>
<tr><td>Tax Returns</td><td>5</td><td>8</td></tr>
<tr><td>Other</td><td>10</td><td>16</td></tr>
<tr><td></td><td>4/1/05-
3/31/06</td><td>4/1/06-
3/31/07</td></tr>
<tr><td>NUMBER OF STATEMENTS</td><td>ALL
29</td><td>ALL
32</td></tr>
</table>

	%	%
ASSETS		
Cash & Equivalents	12.5	10.1
Trade Receivables (net)	13.1	18.7
Inventory	2.3	1.8
All Other Current	2.4	2.9
Total Current	30.3	33.4
Fixed Assets (net)	52.1	53.2
Intangibles (net)	10.5	6.0
All Other Non-Current	7.1	7.3
Total	100.0	100.0
LIABILITIES		
Notes Payable-Short Term	6.4	9.3
Cur. Mat.-L.T.D.	12.1	11.5
Trade Payables	3.8	6.9
Income Taxes Payable	.0	.3
All Other Current	7.5	8.8
Total Current	29.8	36.8
Long-Term Debt	35.0	64.2
Deferred Taxes	.7	1.2
All Other Non-Current	8.7	4.1
Net Worth	25.9	-6.2
Total Liabilities & Net Worth	100.0	100.0
INCOME DATA		
Net Sales	100.0	100.0
Gross Profit		
Operating Expenses	95.2	94.8
Operating Profit	4.8	5.2
All Other Expenses (net)	.9	1.7
Profit Before Taxes	4.0	3.5
RATIOS		
Current	2.6	1.7
	1.0	1.1
	.6	.4
Quick	2.2	1.6
	.8	.8
	.4	.4

	0	UND	0	UND
Sales/Receivables	18	20.3	21	17.7
	50	7.4	35	10.3

Cost of Sales/Inventory				
Cost of Sales/Payables				

Sales/Working Capital	7.8		15.6	
	-278.6		NM	
	-11.1		-12.5	
EBIT/Interest	(27) 6.9		(30) 6.4	
	3.2		2.5	
	.7		1.8	
Net Profit + Depr., Dep., Amort./Cur. Mat. L/T/D				
Fixed/Worth	1.0		1.1	
	2.8		5.5	
	-2.7		-2.2	
Debt/Worth	1.1		1.4	
	2.1		7.5	
	-5.6		-5.9	
% Profit Before Taxes/Tangible Net Worth	(21) 65.1		(21) 80.4	
	22.1		37.2	
	7.5		15.3	
% Profit Before Taxes/Total Assets	15.3		15.7	
	6.5		8.8	
	-1.9		2.6	
Sales/Net Fixed Assets	9.7		18.3	
	5.4		4.3	
	1.9		2.1	
Sales/Total Assets	3.7		5.1	
	2.1		2.2	
	1.1		1.5	
% Depr., Dep., Amort./Sales	(22) 1.3		(27) 2.3	
	6.2		7.3	
	15.9		10.8	
% Officers', Directors' Owners' Comp/Sales	(11) 3.9		(15) 2.1	
	6.4		4.4	
	10.2		13.3	

Net Sales ($)	554242M	617259M
Total Assets ($)	387833M	282448M

M = $ thousand   MM = $ million
See Pages 9 through 22 for Explanation of Ratios and Data

Comparative Historical Data   Current Data Sorted by Sales

Type of Statement	4/1/07-3/31/08 ALL	4/1/08-3/31/09 ALL	4/1/09-3/31/10 ALL		0-1MM	1-3MM	3-5MM	5-10MM	10-25MM	25MM & OVER
Unqualified	5	3	3					1	1	1
Reviewed	1	4	1					1		
Compiled	6	5	10					5	1	
Tax Returns	20	13	14		4	3	1	2	4	1
Other	22	17	14		4	8	2	2		
					2 (4/1-9/30/09)		**40 (10/1/09-3/31/10)**			
NUMBER OF STATEMENTS	54	42	42		8	12	5	9	6	2
ASSETS	%	%	%		%	%	%	%	%	%
Cash & Equivalents	10.0	13.0	9.9			15.6				
Trade Receivables (net)	15.8	11.9	13.3			7.7				
Inventory	1.3	.8	1.8			.5				
All Other Current	5.5	4.5	1.8			.9				
Total Current	32.7	30.1	26.7			24.7				
Fixed Assets (net)	54.4	52.4	47.3			54.2				
Intangibles (net)	5.9	8.0	14.1			7.1				
All Other Non-Current	7.0	9.5	12.0			14.1				
Total	100.0	100.0	100.0			100.0				
LIABILITIES										
Notes Payable-Short Term	7.9	15.6	6.6			13.4				
Cur. Mat.-L.T.D.	8.2	9.9	10.1			14.4				
Trade Payables	6.8	4.8	8.7			4.0				
Income Taxes Payable	.0	.0	.0			.0				
All Other Current	13.8	22.7	9.1			6.2				
Total Current	36.7	52.9	34.6			38.0				
Long-Term Debt	39.9	44.7	42.3			38.1				
Deferred Taxes	.5	.4	.3			.0				
All Other Non-Current	6.0	5.5	8.7			15.4				
Net Worth	16.9	-3.4	14.2			8.5				
Total Liabilties & Net Worth	100.0	100.0	100.0			100.0				
INCOME DATA										
Net Sales	100.0	100.0	100.0			100.0				
Gross Profit										
Operating Expenses	94.4	96.9	97.3			99.8				
Operating Profit	5.6	3.1	2.7			.2				
All Other Expenses (net)	2.3	1.9	1.7			.7				
Profit Before Taxes	3.2	1.2	1.0			-.6				
RATIOS										
Current	1.7	1.8	2.2			2.6				
	1.0	1.0	.8			.8				
	.6	.5	.3			.3				
Quick	1.2	1.3	2.2			2.6				
	.8	.9	.7			.7				
	.4	.5	.2			.0				
Sales/Receivables	0 UND	0 UND	0 UND		0 UND					
	13 27.3	4 97.0	12 31.1		0 UND					
	37 9.9	29 12.4	36 10.2		19 18.8					
Cost of Sales/Inventory										
Cost of Sales/Payables										
Sales/Working Capital	22.9	20.0	23.8			9.2				
	412.7	452.3	-65.6			-65.6				
	-27.8	-18.0	-9.7			-9.6				
EBIT/Interest	4.7	5.5	4.8			5.0				
	(46) 2.1	(35) 1.6	(37) 1.5		(11) .9					
	.6	-.3	.0			.3				
Net Profit + Depr., Dep., Amort./Cur. Mat. L/T/D										
Fixed/Worth	1.1	1.1	1.3			3.0				
	3.9	2.4	UND			NM				
	-117.5	-2.8	-1.6			-2.3				
Debt/Worth	1.5	1.0	1.8			5.0				
	5.2	4.6	UND			NM				
	-131.7	-2.9	-3.3			-5.4				
% Profit Before Taxes/Tangible Net Worth	79.5	63.4	66.8							
	(40) 28.2	(25) 43.3	(22) 13.8							
	-.3	-3.3	-4.3							
% Profit Before Taxes/Total Assets	18.8	17.1	10.9			10.8				
	6.9	5.0	1.5			-.6				
	-1.0	-7.7	-3.8			-4.8				
Sales/Net Fixed Assets	9.9	9.3	18.1			17.9				
	5.6	5.2	5.8			5.1				
	3.1	3.2	2.7			2.6				
Sales/Total Assets	4.6	4.5	3.9			4.5				
	2.8	2.4	2.1			2.5				
	1.8	1.7	1.3			1.2				
% Depr., Dep., Amort./Sales	3.4	3.6	2.3							
	(51) 7.1	(29) 9.6	(36) 7.6							
	10.3	12.9	13.0							
% Officers', Directors' Owners' Comp/Sales	2.9	2.5	3.1							
	(24) 4.3	(14) 3.4	(20) 5.5							
	8.6	4.7	7.3							
Net Sales ($)	845007M	1076300M	389918M		3736M	21352M	19409M	64392M	92934M	188095M
Total Assets ($)	407383M	506764M	163926M		6243M	12221M	14039M	20930M	37866M	72627M

M = $ thousand   MM = $ million
See Pages 9 through 22 for Explanation of Ratios and Data

TRANSPORTATION—School and Employee Bus Transportation NAICS 485410

Current Data Sorted by Assets   **Comparative Historical Data**

0-500M	500M-2MM	2-10MM	10-50MM	50-100MM	100-250MM	Type of Statement	4/1/05-3/31/06 ALL	4/1/06-3/31/07 ALL
	1	3	8	3		Unqualified	18	16
	5	26	8	1		Reviewed	50	50
1	14	10	6			Compiled	24	36
6	13	11			1	Tax Returns	13	8
2	13	13	11	3		Other	31	31
	63 (4/1-9/30/09)		85 (10/1/09-3/31/10)					
9	35	63	33	7	1	**NUMBER OF STATEMENTS**	136	141
%	%	%	%	%	%	**ASSETS**	%	%
	15.5	13.7	11.9			Cash & Equivalents	11.6	12.7
	7.4	12.2	11.5			Trade Receivables (net)	12.2	11.2
	1.2	1.4	2.5			Inventory	2.4	2.7
	2.2	1.6	2.8			All Other Current	3.4	4.0
	26.3	28.9	28.8			Total Current	29.5	30.6
	57.7	59.3	61.1			Fixed Assets (net)	59.3	58.2
	6.5	4.3	2.5			Intangibles (net)	1.9	1.9
	9.6	7.4	7.6			All Other Non-Current	9.4	9.3
	100.0	100.0	100.0			Total	100.0	100.0
						LIABILITIES		
	6.7	2.9	8.4			Notes Payable-Short Term	5.6	5.0
	10.3	15.0	10.5			Cur. Mat.-L.T.D.	13.3	12.2
	2.9	2.8	3.2			Trade Payables	5.2	3.8
	.1	.5	.5			Income Taxes Payable	.5	.3
	7.6	5.9	3.7			All Other Current	8.2	7.0
	27.6	27.2	26.3			Total Current	32.9	28.3
	39.7	31.0	28.1			Long-Term Debt	28.2	29.7
	.3	2.3	2.7			Deferred Taxes	1.8	1.4
	6.2	3.6	2.9			All Other Non-Current	6.0	4.5
	26.2	35.9	40.0			Net Worth	31.1	36.0
	100.0	100.0	100.0			Total Liabilties & Net Worth	100.0	100.0
						INCOME DATA		
	100.0	100.0	100.0			Net Sales	100.0	100.0
						Gross Profit		
	92.8	90.0	93.4			Operating Expenses	93.8	93.1
	7.2	10.0	6.6			Operating Profit	6.2	6.9
	1.9	1.7	1.3			All Other Expenses (net)	2.0	1.6
	5.3	8.3	5.4			Profit Before Taxes	4.3	5.3
						RATIOS		
	2.4	1.8	2.0			Current	1.8	1.7
	.8	.9	1.4				.9	1.0
	.3	.5	.7				.4	.5
	2.4	1.6	1.8			Quick	1.5	1.4
	.8	.8	1.2				.8	.8
	.2	.4	.5				.3	.4
	0 UND	7 48.9	16 23.4			Sales/Receivables	7 51.3	6 63.5
	5 70.3	20 18.4	26 14.3				20 17.9	18 20.1
	19 19.2	37 9.7	40 9.2				36 10.0	32 11.4
						Cost of Sales/Inventory		
						Cost of Sales/Payables		
	9.9	10.6	9.1			Sales/Working Capital	12.1	12.1
	-76.6	-157.6	13.3				-108.1	-339.4
	-9.0	-8.4	-20.1				-8.1	-10.8
	7.7	11.2	7.2			EBIT/Interest	5.7	6.6
	(34) 3.7	(60) 3.7	(31) 4.1				(125) 2.2	(135) 2.9
	1.2	2.3	2.6				1.0	1.5
		2.1	2.4			Net Profit + Depr., Dep., Amort./Cur. Mat. L/T/D	1.5	2.1
		(28) 1.5	(15) 1.9				(48) 1.1	(50) 1.5
		1.0	.9				.8	1.2
	.9	1.1	1.1			Fixed/Worth	1.1	1.0
	2.2	2.2	1.7				1.9	1.7
	-8.4	5.0	2.9				4.3	3.2
	1.0	1.0	.8			Debt/Worth	1.2	.8
	2.3	2.1	1.8				2.1	1.7
	-10.3	5.1	3.2				5.6	4.1
	64.3	52.2	37.3			% Profit Before Taxes/Tangible Net Worth	40.3	41.2
	(24) 34.2	(56) 28.3	(32) 21.1				(118) 11.4	(129) 17.7
	5.6	13.8	13.3				.9	5.5
	20.1	16.9	10.4			% Profit Before Taxes/Total Assets	11.2	12.3
	4.7	8.8	8.4				2.9	6.0
	.3	4.0	5.1				-.2	1.7
	6.3	4.5	4.0			Sales/Net Fixed Assets	5.3	4.7
	4.0	2.5	2.1				2.7	2.9
	2.1	1.6	1.3				1.6	1.6
	3.3	2.0	2.0			Sales/Total Assets	2.4	2.2
	1.9	1.5	1.2				1.6	1.7
	1.2	1.1	1.0				1.1	1.2
	7.6	6.9	4.9			% Depr., Dep., Amort./Sales	7.4	7.2
	(29) 8.6	(61) 10.6	(30) 8.9				(128) 10.0	(132) 9.9
	14.1	13.6	12.3				14.5	14.0
	2.5	2.3	.5			% Officers', Directors' Owners' Comp/Sales	1.4	1.2
	(18) 5.0	(37) 4.0	(13) 1.3				(68) 3.2	(71) 3.3
	6.3	7.0	3.2				6.6	7.0
8801M	92422M	522674M	1185232M	646233M	528242M	Net Sales ($)	1700915M	1770317M
2720M	38640M	315810M	784026M	550222M	181037M	Total Assets ($)	1147153M	1103233M

M = $ thousand   MM = $ million
See Pages 9 through 22 for Explanation of Ratios and Data

Comparative Historical Data

Current Data Sorted by Sales

Type of Statement	4/1/07-3/31/08 ALL	4/1/08-3/31/09 ALL	4/1/09-3/31/10 ALL		0-1MM	1-3MM	3-5MM	5-10MM	10-25MM	25MM & OVER
Unqualified	22	14	15			1		1	7	6
Reviewed	48	36	40			6	5	13	12	4
Compiled	32	32	31		2	14	4	4	3	4
Tax Returns	16	28	31		8	10	4	4	4	4
Other	29	31	31		3	2	3	4	4	1 12
						63 (4/1-9/30/09)		85 (10/1/09-3/31/10)		
NUMBER OF STATEMENTS	147	141	148		13	33	16	26	33	27
	%	%	%		%	%	%	%	%	%
ASSETS										
Cash & Equivalents	12.0	13.8	14.1		16.7	16.7	17.5	8.2	15.9	10.9
Trade Receivables (net)	11.0	10.5	10.4		3.7	5.3	11.3	11.3	12.6	15.8
Inventory	2.3	2.2	1.7		.0	.5	2.9	1.3	1.4	3.8
All Other Current	3.7	3.8	2.1		.4	2.9	1.3	1.4	2.6	2.7
Total Current	29.0	30.3	28.3		20.9	25.5	33.1	22.2	32.5	33.1
Fixed Assets (net)	59.3	56.4	59.5		70.8	59.7	54.5	62.5	58.4	54.9
Intangibles (net)	2.8	3.5	4.3		4.1	4.3	4.9	5.6	5.0	1.9
All Other Non-Current	8.9	9.8	8.0		4.2	10.5	7.5	9.6	4.1	10.1
Total	100.0	100.0	100.0		100.0	100.0	100.0	100.0	100.0	100.0
LIABILITIES										
Notes Payable-Short Term	5.9	7.5	5.7		9.2	6.9	3.1	2.9	3.8	9.0
Cur. Mat.-L.T.D.	12.7	10.7	12.1		5.5	13.0	12.3	14.7	12.9	10.7
Trade Payables	3.4	3.5	2.9		1.8	1.8	1.5	2.9	3.6	4.9
Income Taxes Payable	.3	.3	.4		.0	.1	.2	.5	1.1	.1
All Other Current	5.9	6.8	6.1		6.2	7.0	9.7	5.8	3.9	5.6
Total Current	28.2	28.8	27.1		22.7	28.7	26.8	26.6	25.3	30.3
Long-Term Debt	35.0	33.4	33.9		63.0	34.8	36.8	30.9	28.8	26.4
Deferred Taxes	1.4	1.1	1.7		.5	.7	1.0	3.2	2.3	1.7
All Other Non-Current	3.8	4.6	4.3		1.8	3.4	4.2	7.6	2.1	5.9
Net Worth	31.5	32.1	32.9		11.9	32.3	31.1	31.6	41.5	35.7
Total Liabilties & Net Worth	100.0	100.0	100.0		100.0	100.0	100.0	100.0	100.0	100.0
INCOME DATA										
Net Sales	100.0	100.0	100.0		100.0	100.0	100.0	100.0	100.0	100.0
Gross Profit										
Operating Expenses	91.7	91.8	91.8		92.3	88.3	93.9	92.0	93.4	92.4
Operating Profit	8.3	8.2	8.2		7.7	11.7	6.1	8.0	6.6	7.6
All Other Expenses (net)	2.3	1.6	1.7		2.9	2.4	.6	1.6	1.3	1.5
Profit Before Taxes	6.0	6.6	6.5		4.7	9.3	5.4	6.4	5.3	6.2
RATIOS										
Current	1.9	2.1	2.1		3.4	2.4	2.3	1.5	2.4	2.0
	1.1	1.1	1.0		.7	.8	1.4	.7	1.5	1.3
	.5	.5	.5		.3	.3	.7	.4	.7	.8
Quick	1.7	1.8	1.9		3.4	2.4	2.3	1.3	2.1	1.7
	(146) .9	.8	.9		.7	.7	1.1	.6	1.3	1.2
	.3	.4	.4		.3	.2	.6	.3	.5	.5
Sales/Receivables	3 138.6	1 255.6	3 106.1		0 UND	0 UND	6 57.7	5 69.0	10 37.7	20 18.3
	20 18.7	16 22.2	18 20.1		0 UND	4 81.3	18 20.7	18 19.9	18 20.1	34 10.8
	33 11.1	31 11.8	34 10.8		2 206.0	29 12.4	31 11.7	37 9.8	28 13.2	45 8.0
Cost of Sales/Inventory										
Cost of Sales/Payables										
Sales/Working Capital	9.9	10.2	10.0		17.8	7.2	11.2	15.7	8.0	9.5
	90.4	183.2	853.4		-22.3	-18.9	584.5	-32.8	13.1	27.6
	-11.0	-12.6	-10.1		-7.1	-5.8	-13.3	-7.8	-16.3	-30.2
EBIT/Interest	(144) 6.3	(132) 7.6	(141) 7.6		(11) 5.0	7.6	(15) 12.7	(25) 9.6	(31) 7.2	(26) 8.7
	3.0	2.8	3.7		2.0	3.7	3.7	3.4	3.7	3.5
	1.3	1.3	2.0		.0	1.5	2.1	2.1	2.4	2.4
Net Profit + Depr., Dep., Amort./Cur. Mat. L/T/D	(53) 1.9	(40) 2.3	(57) 2.5					(16) 2.1	(15) 3.8	(13) 2.2
	1.5	1.6	1.9					1.7	2.1	1.9
	1.0	1.2	1.2					1.2	1.1	1.1
Fixed/Worth	.9	1.1	1.1		1.2	1.1	.8	1.1	1.1	1.0
	1.9	1.8	2.0		348.5	2.2	2.2	2.8	1.8	1.7
	4.9	6.6	5.7		-3.0	-17.3	NM	5.4	3.3	2.2
Debt/Worth	.9	.9	1.0		.9	1.0	.9	1.1	.8	1.0
	1.9	1.8	2.1		355.5	2.3	2.6	2.7	1.8	2.0
	5.2	8.2	7.2		-4.7	-24.8	NM	6.7	3.2	5.9
% Profit Before Taxes/Tangible Net Worth	(130) 43.4	(118) 43.3	(123) 50.4			57.5	57.8	63.3	41.9	35.0
	22.5	22.3	26.8			(24) 32.4	(12) 29.6	(24) 26.9	(30) 22.6	(26) 22.9
	7.2	5.4	13.0			5.6	14.6	11.5	12.3	14.0
% Profit Before Taxes/Total Assets	13.7	15.7	13.9		23.6	20.1	16.9	16.9	14.4	11.0
	7.4	6.7	8.1		3.2	8.7	7.6	7.6	8.8	8.9
	1.2	1.3	2.7		-5.1	.9	3.4	2.7	4.1	5.9
Sales/Net Fixed Assets	4.8	5.5	4.9		5.3	4.8	6.6	4.2	4.9	5.3
	2.7	3.0	2.7		4.0	2.7	4.3	2.4	2.6	3.1
	1.6	1.8	1.6		1.1	1.5	1.4	1.6	1.8	1.6
Sales/Total Assets	2.3	2.5	2.4		3.0	2.5	2.4	2.0	2.4	2.4
	1.6	1.8	1.6		2.1	1.5	1.5	1.5	1.5	1.7
	1.1	1.2	1.1		1.0	.8	1.0	1.3	1.1	1.2
% Depr., Dep., Amort./Sales	6.5	6.1	6.3		9.4	8.2	7.2	6.1	6.4	4.0
	(141) 9.9	(126) 9.4	(134) 9.8		(10) 10.4	(29) 12.5	(14) 10.4	10.1	(30) 9.0	(25) 6.2
	13.4	13.5	13.3		16.3	18.3	13.7	13.1	13.3	10.2
% Officers', Directors' Owners' Comp/Sales	2.1	1.2	2.1			2.4		3.3	1.9	.5
	(71) 3.7	(77) 3.5	(76) 3.9			(20) 5.1		(14) 4.0	(14) 2.9	(13) 1.3
	7.5	5.9	6.3						4.8	2.8
Net Sales ($)	1834974M	2046608M	2983604M		9217M	69578M	65622M	195115M	485157M	2158915M
Total Assets ($)	1196549M	1471929M	1872455M		5672M	60608M	47572M	123728M	343359M	1291516M

M = $ thousand   MM = $ million
See Pages 9 through 22 for Explanation of Ratios and Data

Current Data Sorted by Assets   Comparative Historical Data

Type of Statement			
		9	7
Unqualified		25	24
Reviewed		17	21
Compiled		11	21
Tax Returns		43	45
Other			

				4	1				
	3	14	4						
1	10	9	4						
1	15	6							
3	6	28	10	2	1				
	17 (4/1-9/30/09)		105 (10/1/09-3/31/10)				4/1/05-3/31/06	4/1/06-3/31/07	
0-500M	500M-2MM	2-10MM	10-50MM	50-100MM	100-250MM		ALL	ALL	
5	34	57	22	3	1	NUMBER OF STATEMENTS	105	118	

%	%	%	%	%	%	ASSETS	%	%
	11.8	8.3	12.2			Cash & Equivalents	7.8	6.9
	8.3	9.0	6.4			Trade Receivables (net)	10.8	9.4
	2.2	2.0	1.7			Inventory	2.3	1.9
	1.7	4.7	3.7			All Other Current	3.2	3.4
	24.1	24.0	23.9			Total Current	24.1	21.7
	64.8	65.6	67.9			Fixed Assets (net)	65.2	69.1
	4.4	1.4	2.6			Intangibles (net)	3.1	1.5
	6.8	8.9	5.6			All Other Non-Current	7.6	7.8
	100.0	100.0	100.0			Total	100.0	100.0
						LIABILITIES		
	5.3	5.0	1.1			Notes Payable-Short Term	6.1	3.6
	13.6	12.8	9.5			Cur. Mat.-L.T.D.	10.2	11.8
	6.0	5.0	3.5			Trade Payables	7.3	4.8
	.4	.2	.4			Income Taxes Payable	.3	.5
	6.8	10.5	4.1			All Other Current	8.3	8.5
	32.0	33.5	18.6			Total Current	32.2	29.2
	75.2	44.2	32.9			Long-Term Debt	50.3	55.7
	.0	1.6	3.5			Deferred Taxes	1.6	1.6
	7.6	4.1	7.7			All Other Non-Current	5.5	4.1
	-14.9	16.5	37.2			Net Worth	10.5	9.4
	100.0	100.0	100.0			Total Liabilities & Net Worth	100.0	100.0
						INCOME DATA		
	100.0	100.0	100.0			Net Sales	100.0	100.0
						Gross Profit		
	96.2	94.3	91.1			Operating Expenses	93.6	93.6
	3.8	5.7	8.9			Operating Profit	6.4	6.4
	2.4	1.8	2.2			All Other Expenses (net)	2.5	3.0
	1.4	3.9	6.7			Profit Before Taxes	3.8	3.4
						RATIOS		
	1.8	1.2	2.4				1.3	1.4
	.7	.7	1.5			Current	.7	.7
	.3	.4	.8				.4	.4
	1.5	.8	2.0				.9	1.1
	.7	.5	1.0			Quick	.5 (114)	.6
	.2	.3	.5				.3	.3
	0 UND	6 61.8	13 29.1				8 46.9 / 7 53.0	
	6 62.5	19 18.8	15 24.5			Sales/Receivables	16 23.1 / 13 27.6	
	18 20.2	29 12.5	30 12.2				27 13.5 / 33 11.2	
						Cost of Sales/Inventory		
						Cost of Sales/Payables		
	19.5	48.4	5.8				35.5	24.2
	-44.9	-18.3	15.1			Sales/Working Capital	-29.3	-27.1
	-9.5	-6.8	-32.0				-8.0	-7.5
	3.6	3.4	5.9				4.1	4.7
(33)	2.2	(52) 2.4	(21) 2.5			EBIT/Interest	(99) 2.4 / (105) 2.2	
	.6	1.4	1.6				1.3	1.1
		1.7	2.6			Net Profit + Depr., Dep.,	1.7	2.0
		(17) 1.4	(11) 1.6			Amort./Cur. Mat. L/T/D	(36) 1.3 / (34) 1.3	
		.9	1.3				.9	1.1
	2.4	1.6	1.3				1.7	1.8
	-88.8	3.4	1.9			Fixed/Worth	3.7	4.0
	-1.1	NM	4.9				-12.1	-11.2
	3.0	1.4	.9				1.7	1.8
	-117.5	4.1	1.7			Debt/Worth	3.6	5.6
	-2.3	NM	5.4				-20.5	-13.5
	54.2	38.7	27.2			% Profit Before Taxes/Tangible	56.4	35.5
(16)	17.9	(43) 19.2	(19) 16.0			Net Worth	(74) 22.7 / (84) 16.8	
	.8	6.4	5.2				4.9	5.8
	12.8	10.6	7.8			% Profit Before Taxes/Total	11.0	9.9
	2.9	5.0	5.1			Assets	4.0	5.1
	-3.1	1.7	1.2				.3	.6
	7.1	3.9	1.9				4.5	3.1
	3.3	2.1	1.5			Sales/Net Fixed Assets	2.1	1.9
	2.0	1.2	1.0				1.3	1.2
	3.2	1.9	1.3				2.4	2.2
	2.6	1.4	1.0			Sales/Total Assets	1.4	1.3
	1.6	.9	.7				1.0	.8
	5.6	6.5	7.0				4.8	6.1
(30)	11.6	(49) 11.1	(21) 9.0			% Depr., Dep., Amort./Sales	(100) 7.7 / (108) 9.5	
	15.1	15.3	16.4				12.5	14.9
	1.4	1.5				% Officers', Directors'	1.5	1.4
(18)	3.1	(22) 3.4				Owners' Comp/Sales	(41) 2.9 / (45) 3.0	
	4.5	5.7					5.3	6.8
8698M	100906M	451472M	424000M	274300M	123696M	Net Sales ($)	1733376M	1285015M
1329M	43355M	302728M	443362M	246910M	119862M	Total Assets ($)	1280996M	1094715M

M = $ thousand   MM = $ million
See Pages 9 through 22 for Explanation of Ratios and Data

© RMA 2010

Comparative Historical Data   Current Data Sorted by Sales

			Type of Statement						
8	7	5	Unqualified						
25	20	21	Reviewed		2	2	1	2	2
29	26	24	Compiled		5	8	7	8	2
34	16	22	Tax Returns		12	5	5	4	1
42	45	50	Other	1	9	11	14	10	6
4/1/07- 3/31/08	4/1/08- 3/31/09	4/1/09- 3/31/10			17 (4/1-9/30/09)		105 (10/1/09-3/31/10)		
ALL	ALL	ALL		0-1MM	1-3MM	3-5MM	5-10MM	10-25MM	25MM & OVER
138	114	122	NUMBER OF STATEMENTS	1	28	26	31	25	11
%	%	%	ASSETS	%	%	%	%	%	%
10.2	8.9	10.7	Cash & Equivalents		10.4	11.7	9.9	10.7	12.0
7.8	9.4	8.4	Trade Receivables (net)		4.4	12.1	8.5	8.3	9.9
1.8	1.8	2.0	Inventory		1.1	3.2	2.4	1.5	1.7
3.3	3.6	4.3	All Other Current		3.7	2.7	6.0	2.6	8.8
23.2	23.8	25.4	Total Current		19.7	29.7	26.8	23.1	32.3
68.5	64.9	64.7	Fixed Assets (net)		70.1	63.7	61.7	64.4	59.8
1.2	2.6	2.4	Intangibles (net)		3.4	2.6	2.2	2.2	.8
7.1	8.8	7.5	All Other Non-Current		6.8	4.0	9.2	10.2	7.0
100.0	100.0	100.0	Total		100.0	100.0	100.0	100.0	100.0
			LIABILITIES						
3.1	4.1	4.9	Notes Payable-Short Term		5.8	5.6	4.0	4.8	4.4
12.1	12.1	12.4	Cur. Mat.-L.T.D.		12.6	13.6	13.8	12.3	6.4
5.3	4.5	5.1	Trade Payables		3.4	6.1	5.0	6.4	5.2
.6	.3	.2	Income Taxes Payable		.2	.5	.0	.2	.5
6.9	11.0	8.5	All Other Current		6.2	10.9	9.6	8.6	6.6
28.0	31.9	31.3	Total Current		28.3	36.6	32.5	32.2	23.1
51.7	45.4	49.2	Long-Term Debt		68.8	54.3	44.9	39.5	18.6
1.7	1.1	1.4	Deferred Taxes		.1	.9	2.5	2.2	1.4
8.0	4.9	7.1	All Other Non-Current		12.4	2.7	6.6	4.4	11.3
10.5	16.6	11.0	Net Worth		-9.5	5.6	13.5	21.7	45.5
100.0	100.0	100.0	Total Liabilities & Net Worth		100.0	100.0	100.0	100.0	100.0
			INCOME DATA						
100.0	100.0	100.0	Net Sales		100.0	100.0	100.0	100.0	100.0
			Gross Profit						
93.0	93.2	94.4	Operating Expenses		94.8	95.4	93.8	93.6	95.3
7.0	6.8	5.6	Operating Profit		5.2	4.6	6.2	6.4	4.7
2.9	2.3	1.9	All Other Expenses (net)		3.8	2.4	.5	1.4	.2
4.1	4.5	3.7	Profit Before Taxes		1.4	2.2	5.6	5.0	4.5
			RATIOS						
1.3	1.3	1.6			1.7	1.3	1.6	1.5	2.4
.8	.7	.8	Current		.6	.8	.8	.9	1.3
.5	.4	.4			.2	.4	.6	.5	1.0
1.0	.9	1.2			1.4	1.2	1.4	1.2	1.7
(137) .6	.5	.6	Quick		.4	.5	.7	.6	.8
.3	.3	.3			.2	.3	.4	.3	.6
5 79.1	5 74.0	5 75.8		0 UND	5 70.7	6 65.0	8 43.5	13 27.1	
12 29.8	13 27.3	13 27.7	Sales/Receivables	4 95.8	18 20.8	23 15.7	14 26.7	27 13.4	
30 12.2	24 15.5	27 13.4		12 30.9	33 11.1	30 12.0	23 15.8	35 10.4	
			Cost of Sales/Inventory						
			Cost of Sales/Payables						
40.4	30.7	15.8			16.0	40.7	11.4	16.6	6.7
-39.1	-25.0	-41.0	Sales/Working Capital		-16.0	-35.8	-51.1	-37.5	27.8
-10.3	-10.5	-9.1			-7.9	-8.1	-8.4	-7.0	538.0
3.1	4.3	4.1			3.3	3.3	4.5	4.7	7.4
(128) 1.9	(105) 2.5	(114) 2.5	EBIT/Interest	(27) 2.1	(25) 1.8	(28) 2.6	(22) 2.5	6.3	
1.0	1.2	1.1			.4	.7	1.7	1.6	1.9
1.9	2.0	2.2	Net Profit + Depr., Dep.,					2.5	
(35) 1.5	(39) 1.5	(34) 1.5	Amort./Cur. Mat. L/T/D				(13)	1.4	
1.0	1.0	1.3						1.3	
1.7	1.6	1.5			2.3	1.5	1.4	1.7	1.1
5.4	3.0	3.2	Fixed/Worth		NM	6.5	2.4	2.7	1.5
-11.1	UND	-5.0			-1.3	-2.5	-8.0	NM	1.8
1.8	1.5	1.5			2.5	2.2	1.1	1.3	.9
5.9	3.4	4.4	Debt/Worth		NM	10.9	3.0	4.3	1.5
-14.9	UND	-7.2			-2.9	-5.4	-11.4	NM	1.8
33.2	37.6	34.3	% Profit Before Taxes/Tangible		47.6	91.3	27.2	35.0	21.1
(94) 16.5	(86) 18.9	(84) 18.6	Net Worth	(14) 18.1	(16) 17.0	(23) 16.8	(19) 19.2	16.5	
5.3	7.3	5.7			-8.7	6.7	5.5	11.2	1.7
9.8	10.8	10.6	% Profit Before Taxes/Total		15.2	10.0	10.6	11.0	9.2
4.2	5.3	5.0	Assets		4.8	2.9	5.3	5.6	6.5
.1	.7	.7			-5.2	-2.6	2.6	2.2	.7
4.3	5.1	4.3			6.4	6.8	4.0	3.4	2.4
2.2	2.3	2.2	Sales/Net Fixed Assets		2.3	2.8	2.2	1.9	1.8
1.1	1.2	1.3			1.1	1.2	1.5	1.2	1.7
2.5	2.7	2.4			3.1	3.2	2.1	1.9	1.4
1.5	1.5	1.4	Sales/Total Assets		1.6	1.9	1.5	1.4	1.3
.9	1.0	1.0			.9	1.0	.9	1.0	1.0
6.8	6.4	5.7			6.5	5.5	5.8	6.8	4.3
(125) 10.5	(101) 9.2	(108) 10.3	% Depr., Dep., Amort./Sales	(25) 12.6	(21) 10.6	(29) 10.3	(21) 9.3	6.7	
14.5	13.5	15.1			20.8	14.8	15.3	18.1	10.2
2.0	1.3	1.5			1.6			.5	
(49) 3.2	(40) 2.5	(48) 2.8	% Officers', Directors' Owners' Comp/Sales	(19) 3.0		(10)	1.5		
5.7	4.9	4.8			4.7			3.6	
1391293M	2040455M	1383072M	Net Sales ($)	746M	56106M	100646M	231797M	369425M	624352M
1124561M	1235336M	1157546M	Total Assets ($)	1342M	37729M	70230M	209991M	318089M	520165M

© RMA 2010   M = $ thousand   MM = $ million

See Pages 9 through 22 for Explanation of Ratios and Data

Current Data Sorted by Assets

Comparative Historical Data

							Type of Statement		
	3	5	7	2	2		Unqualified	21	24
	3	12	3				Reviewed	7	14
2	9	11	1				Compiled	19	13
4	7	3					Tax Returns	22	22
3	10	9	9	2	3		Other	35	31
	22 (4/1-9/30/09)		88 (10/1/09-3/31/10)					4/1/05-3/31/06 ALL	4/1/06-3/31/07 ALL
0-500M	500M-2MM	2-10MM	10-50MM	50-100MM	100-250MM		NUMBER OF STATEMENTS	104	104
9	32	40	20	4	5				
%	%	%	%	%	%		ASSETS	%	%
	15.7	9.0	11.1				Cash & Equivalents	12.3	13.8
	13.4	30.9	27.0				Trade Receivables (net)	23.1	23.4
	.3	.4	1.8				Inventory	2.3	.8
	4.0	2.5	3.9				All Other Current	3.6	5.2
	33.3	42.8	43.8				Total Current	41.3	43.2
	46.7	38.0	41.5				Fixed Assets (net)	42.0	41.3
	3.4	6.6	6.8				Intangibles (net)	6.2	5.7
	16.5	12.5	7.9				All Other Non-Current	10.6	9.8
	100.0	100.0	100.0				Total	100.0	100.0
							LIABILITIES		
	10.0	6.6	6.5				Notes Payable-Short Term	11.2	7.8
	9.8	9.9	10.2				Cur. Mat.-L.T.D.	9.2	10.2
	6.6	11.5	9.3				Trade Payables	8.9	11.5
	.0	.2	.4				Income Taxes Payable	.4	.2
	12.3	6.5	7.1				All Other Current	9.9	13.0
	38.7	34.8	33.5				Total Current	39.6	42.7
	28.3	25.7	22.8				Long-Term Debt	29.5	23.6
	.0	.2	.9				Deferred Taxes	.3	.5
	4.3	2.2	2.7				All Other Non-Current	9.9	8.8
	28.6	37.1	40.2				Net Worth	20.6	24.4
	100.0	100.0	100.0				Total Liabilties & Net Worth	100.0	100.0
							INCOME DATA		
	100.0	100.0	100.0				Net Sales	100.0	100.0
							Gross Profit		
	92.6	96.1	94.3				Operating Expenses	97.1	94.8
	7.4	3.9	5.7				Operating Profit	2.9	5.2
	1.3	.8	1.5				All Other Expenses (net)	1.0	1.2
	6.1	3.1	4.2				Profit Before Taxes	1.9	3.9
							RATIOS		
	2.2	2.6	2.9					2.0	2.4
	.9	1.2	1.4				Current	1.2	1.2
	.4	.4	.7					.6	.6
	2.1	2.3	2.5					1.8	2.2
	.6	1.1	1.1				Quick	.9	1.0
	.4	.4	.6					.4	.5
0 UND	18 20.7	19 19.0						0 UND	6 65.2
6 64.8	37 9.9	52 7.0					Sales/Receivables	23 15.8	27 13.4
29 12.5	55 6.7	69 5.3						51 7.2	48 7.6
							Cost of Sales/Inventory		
							Cost of Sales/Payables		
	15.3	8.1	4.8					12.9	10.7
	-64.6	52.4	13.7				Sales/Working Capital	40.0	38.6
	-11.5	-12.0	-20.5					-21.7	-19.6
	24.0	8.4	8.9					5.8	11.8
	(30) 5.1	(37) 3.2	(17) 3.3				EBIT/Interest	(99) 2.1	(90) 4.2
	1.1	1.6	2.2					.2	1.2
		8.8					Net Profit + Depr., Dep.,	3.0	3.2
		(10) 1.7					Amort./Cur. Mat. L/T/D	(17) 1.7	(17) 2.1
		1.0						.6	.8
	.5	.3	.6					.7	.5
	1.4	1.0	1.9				Fixed/Worth	1.5	1.3
	-28.6	3.6	5.0					-8.1	74.5
	.4	.8	.5					.9	.6
	4.7	2.0	3.1				Debt/Worth	3.5	2.4
	-39.9	7.1	9.0					-16.9	173.2
	69.7	54.0	50.9				% Profit Before Taxes/Tangible	56.2	76.9
	(23) 22.2	(34) 25.0	(16) 15.2				Net Worth	(73) 19.2	(79) 31.0
	5.9	5.2	-1.7					3.1	7.7
	28.0	12.6	14.5				% Profit Before Taxes/Total	14.2	24.4
	8.7	6.7	7.3				Assets	5.1	8.7
	.0	1.8	.4					-2.0	.2
	11.2	30.2	10.6					20.1	18.5
	7.6	10.3	4.3				Sales/Net Fixed Assets	8.3	9.8
	3.5	3.4	1.5					3.9	3.8
	4.9	4.3	2.6					4.3	4.5
	2.9	2.7	1.7				Sales/Total Assets	2.8	2.9
	1.9	1.8	.8					1.8	1.9
	3.8	1.6	3.1					2.7	1.9
	(27) 5.8	(34) 3.6	(18) 4.9				% Depr., Dep., Amort./Sales	(83) 5.1	(86) 4.2
	9.1	7.6	10.0					8.4	6.6
	3.7	1.0					% Officers', Directors'	3.6	1.3
	(12) 7.8	(16) 2.0					Owners' Comp/Sales	(41) 6.1	(30) 3.8
	18.1	5.0						9.8	8.2
5727M	111868M	537487M	635270M	474256M	1398670M		Net Sales ($)	1451323M	2196328M
1954M	35689M	174226M	378813M	278729M	842763M		Total Assets ($)	804547M	1073857M

M = $ thousand   MM = $ million
See Pages 9 through 22 for Explanation of Ratios and Data

Comparative Historical Data | Current Data Sorted by Sales

Type of Statement	4/1/07-3/31/08 ALL	4/1/08-3/31/09 ALL	4/1/09-3/31/10 ALL	0-1MM	1-3MM	3-5MM	5-10MM	10-25MM	25MM & OVER
Unqualified	21	21	19		1	2	1	8	7
Reviewed	15	14	18		1	4	3	7	3
Compiled	9	12	23		4	3	7	6	1
Tax Returns	16	16	14	2	4	3	7	6	1
Other	26	41	36	3 / 4	5 / 4	4 / 4	6 / 7	2 / 2	11
				22 (4/1-9/30/09)			88 (10/1/09-3/31/10)		

NUMBER OF STATEMENTS	87	104	110	9	15	17	18	29	22
ASSETS	%	%	%	%	%	%	%	%	%
Cash & Equivalents	10.8	10.4	12.7		20.6	11.9	15.2	9.2	8.1
Trade Receivables (net)	22.7	22.2	21.7		10.4	13.6	25.3	31.6	27.8
Inventory	.6	.6	.7		.0	.5	.7	1.3	.9
All Other Current	4.7	4.2	4.0		7.1	1.6	1.3	2.2	5.5
Total Current	38.8	37.4	39.1		38.0	27.7	42.4	44.3	42.2
Fixed Assets (net)	43.3	44.3	40.7		43.1	48.6	42.2	38.4	33.3
Intangibles (net)	9.1	9.7	7.1		6.2	4.5	5.0	6.2	15.3
All Other Non-Current	8.9	8.7	13.1		12.7	19.2	10.5	11.1	9.2
Total	100.0	100.0	100.0		100.0	100.0	100.0	100.0	100.0
LIABILITIES									
Notes Payable-Short Term	9.2	8.8	7.6		3.6	12.7	8.4	6.6	8.6
Cur. Mat.-L.T.D.	11.3	7.3	9.0		7.5	11.6	13.0	6.5	9.3
Trade Payables	10.9	6.3	8.5		2.2	8.1	7.1	5.9	21.1
Income Taxes Payable	.1	.3	.2		.0	.1	.3	.2	.4
All Other Current	10.6	12.5	10.6		12.9	8.0	9.6	8.7	9.1
Total Current	42.1	35.2	35.9		26.2	40.5	38.4	27.9	48.6
Long-Term Debt	30.0	25.9	26.8		29.8	32.9	30.7	24.3	20.6
Deferred Taxes	.4	.7	.5		.0	.1	.3	.5	1.5
All Other Non-Current	6.6	7.1	4.2		1.8	6.7	3.6	1.6	3.7
Net Worth	20.9	31.1	32.6		42.2	19.8	27.0	45.8	25.6
Total Liabilities & Net Worth	100.0	100.0	100.0		100.0	100.0	100.0	100.0	100.0
INCOME DATA									
Net Sales	100.0	100.0	100.0		100.0	100.0	100.0	100.0	100.0
Gross Profit									
Operating Expenses	95.2	93.9	94.9		94.2	96.4	92.6	94.7	97.3
Operating Profit	4.8	6.1	5.1		5.8	3.6	7.4	5.3	2.7
All Other Expenses (net)	2.5	2.0	1.3		1.1	1.2	.6	1.7	1.9
Profit Before Taxes	2.3	4.1	3.8		4.8	2.4	6.8	3.6	.8
RATIOS									
Current	2.3	2.6	2.2		4.3	1.2	2.3	3.0	1.4
Current	.9	1.3	1.1		1.5	.4	.9	1.6	.9
Current	.5	.7	.5		.5	.2	.5	1.0	.6
Quick	1.9	2.3	2.1		2.3	1.0	2.3	2.8	1.2
Quick	.8	1.1	.9		.7	.4	.8	1.6	.7
Quick	.3	.7	.6		.4	.2	.4	.9	.5
Sales/Receivables	11 33.6	4 86.1	4 93.6		0 UND	2 180.3	9 40.0	19 19.0	23 15.9
Sales/Receivables	30 12.2	27 13.6	26 13.9		2 194.9	18 20.7	25 14.8	44 8.2	36 10.1
Sales/Receivables	57 6.4	57 6.4	52 7.0		21 17.8	34 10.6	55 6.6	61 6.0	55 6.7
Cost of Sales/Inventory									
Cost of Sales/Payables									
Sales/Working Capital	8.5	8.3	8.9		7.5	NM	11.9	5.6	20.8
Sales/Working Capital	-106.6	45.1	74.3		68.0	-18.4	-81.2	16.9	-141.6
Sales/Working Capital	-12.7	-20.6	-16.1		-16.1	-6.8	-9.8	NM	-15.0
EBIT/Interest	(74) 4.5	(91) 10.8	(99) 11.9		(14) 42.9	(16) 17.4	(17) 12.6	(26) 8.7	(21) 11.3
EBIT/Interest	2.0	3.6	3.4		1.9	3.3	3.5	3.2	2.8
EBIT/Interest	.7	.9	1.3		.2	1.2	1.0	2.0	.7
Net Profit + Depr., Dep., Amort./Cur. Mat. L/T/D	(20) 2.0	(19) 3.1	(24) 2.3					(10)	2.1
Net Profit + Depr., Dep., Amort./Cur. Mat. L/T/D	1.1	1.5	1.7						1.7
Net Profit + Depr., Dep., Amort./Cur. Mat. L/T/D	.4	.4	1.2						1.4
Fixed/Worth	.7	.7	.5		.2	.6	.3	.5	1.0
Fixed/Worth	3.4	1.7	1.7		1.2	7.2	2.3	.8	3.7
Fixed/Worth	-2.4	NM	12.4		204.3	-5.6	NM	2.7	-1.6
Debt/Worth	1.5	.8	.8		.3	1.0	.8	.5	1.3
Debt/Worth	4.9	2.2	2.6		.9	14.6	2.2	1.8	8.3
Debt/Worth	-5.7	NM	157.5		254.3	-7.6	NM	3.6	-5.0
% Profit Before Taxes/Tangible Net Worth	(58) 60.6	(78) 69.1	(84) 58.7		(12) 51.6	(11) 36.9	(14) 82.6	(26) 34.0	(14) 99.8
% Profit Before Taxes/Tangible Net Worth	20.8	30.7	27.0		24.5	14.9	44.6	19.4	49.9
% Profit Before Taxes/Tangible Net Worth	5.8	3.7	4.5		-2.8	4.1	15.0	3.6	-4.0
% Profit Before Taxes/Total Assets	12.2	20.5	19.0		37.3	16.8	27.9	12.4	18.6
% Profit Before Taxes/Total Assets	4.4	6.5	6.9		1.4	6.5	8.9	6.9	5.2
% Profit Before Taxes/Total Assets	-1.3	-.3	1.1		-2.4	.8	1.0	1.9	-1.2
Sales/Net Fixed Assets	15.5	16.1	16.8		87.2	10.8	32.4	15.6	29.4
Sales/Net Fixed Assets	6.3	6.9	8.4		4.3	7.0	9.5	8.4	10.4
Sales/Net Fixed Assets	2.9	2.9	3.1		3.0	3.7	3.6	2.3	3.0
Sales/Total Assets	3.2	3.6	3.5		3.1	5.1	4.6	3.2	3.5
Sales/Total Assets	2.2	2.3	2.4		2.3	2.1	3.0	1.9	2.5
Sales/Total Assets	1.4	1.5	1.6		1.7	1.6	1.8	1.3	1.6
% Depr., Dep., Amort./Sales	(77) 2.5	(80) 2.6	(90) 2.3		(11) .4	(16) 3.9	(15) 2.1	(25) 1.7	(16) 2.4
% Depr., Dep., Amort./Sales	4.3	4.2	4.7		5.6	7.2	5.5	3.4	3.6
% Depr., Dep., Amort./Sales	7.7	7.2	9.1		9.4	10.2	9.4	7.0	6.8
% Officers', Directors' Owners' Comp/Sales	(25) 2.1	(38) 1.6	(36) 1.7					(10) .9	
% Officers', Directors' Owners' Comp/Sales	3.6	3.5	4.8					1.3	
% Officers', Directors' Owners' Comp/Sales	12.7	8.7	12.4					2.9	
Net Sales ($)	1728676M	3340932M	3163278M	4342M	29788M	68362M	127587M	443769M	2489430M
Total Assets ($)	1193951M	1695713M	1712174M	3070M	13479M	32041M	47881M	287925M	1327778M

© RMA 2010

M = $ thousand   MM = $ million
See Pages 9 through 22 for Explanation of Ratios and Data

TRANSPORTATION—Other Airport Operations NAICS 488119

| | Current Data Sorted by Assets | | | | | | Comparative Historical Data | |

Type of Statement

0-500M	500M-2MM	2-10MM	10-50MM	50-100MM	100-250MM	Type of Statement	4/1/05-3/31/06 ALL	4/1/06-3/31/07 ALL
	1	3	10	8	6	Unqualified	21	16
	3	7	5	1		Reviewed	14	10
2	2	2	2		1	Compiled	20	10
5	5	5	2			Tax Returns	11	11
6	13	16	12	4	4	Other	47	43
20 (4/1-9/30/09)			98 (10/1/09-3/31/10)					
0-500M	500M-2MM	2-10MM	10-50MM	50-100MM	100-250MM		ALL	ALL
13	24	30	27	13	11	NUMBER OF STATEMENTS	113	90

ASSETS

0-500M %	500M-2MM %	2-10MM %	10-50MM %	50-100MM %	100-250MM %	ASSETS	%	%
32.0	9.3	9.3	8.1	6.5	6.5	Cash & Equivalents	9.8	14.4
7.0	16.9	13.2	19.7	15.5	14.4	Trade Receivables (net)	21.4	18.6
6.6	8.9	13.5	4.9	3.6	1.7	Inventory	13.6	12.4
5.3	6.0	2.3	3.6	5.3	8.5	All Other Current	3.4	3.9
50.9	41.2	38.3	36.3	30.9	31.1	Total Current	48.1	49.3
36.7	52.2	44.8	46.9	57.0	45.0	Fixed Assets (net)	40.7	36.3
7.4	1.7	8.9	7.9	10.4	6.6	Intangibles (net)	4.7	4.6
5.1	4.9	8.0	8.9	1.7	17.3	All Other Non-Current	6.5	9.8
100.0	100.0	100.0	100.0	100.0	100.0	Total	100.0	100.0

LIABILITIES

0-500M	500M-2MM	2-10MM	10-50MM	50-100MM	100-250MM	LIABILITIES		
58.8	4.5	7.5	4.7	1.4	1.7	Notes Payable-Short Term	7.8	5.9
1.9	3.8	1.9	4.8	4.4	4.3	Cur. Mat.-L.T.D.	4.2	3.6
5.1	11.3	9.1	11.7	7.8	8.4	Trade Payables	14.1	12.6
.0	.4	.3	.0	.2	.0	Income Taxes Payable	.3	.4
7.8	9.3	17.4	8.8	8.2	17.3	All Other Current	11.5	13.8
73.6	29.2	36.2	30.0	21.9	31.8	Total Current	37.9	36.4
53.4	40.6	23.5	36.8	17.8	27.3	Long-Term Debt	30.3	28.2
.0	1.1	.0	.5	.7	.2	Deferred Taxes	.5	.5
9.5	20.7	5.9	3.0	3.2	11.3	All Other Non-Current	7.2	6.9
-36.5	8.3	34.4	29.8	56.4	29.3	Net Worth	24.0	27.9
100.0	100.0	100.0	100.0	100.0	100.0	Total Liabilities & Net Worth	100.0	100.0

INCOME DATA

0-500M	500M-2MM	2-10MM	10-50MM	50-100MM	100-250MM	INCOME DATA		
100.0	100.0	100.0	100.0	100.0	100.0	Net Sales	100.0	100.0
						Gross Profit		
86.7	93.7	95.0	99.0	98.2	98.2	Operating Expenses	94.0	94.7
13.3	6.3	5.0	1.0	1.8	1.8	Operating Profit	6.0	5.3
2.4	4.2	3.6	4.1	2.6	.1	All Other Expenses (net)	2.5	1.7
10.8	2.1	1.4	-3.1	-.9	1.7	Profit Before Taxes	3.4	3.6

RATIOS

0-500M	500M-2MM	2-10MM	10-50MM	50-100MM	100-250MM	RATIOS		
15.2	2.2	2.1	1.6	2.3	1.5	Current	2.3	2.1
.8	1.3	1.1	1.2	1.9	.9		1.3	1.3
.4	.8	.5	.7	1.2	.6		1.0	.9
14.4	1.4	1.2	1.3	2.0	1.1	Quick	1.6	1.3
.8	.9	.5	.8	1.3	.7		.9	.9
.3	.4	.3	.5	.8	.3		.5	.5
0 UND	7 54.0	5 72.7	14 26.3	19 19.4	18 20.1	Sales/Receivables	16 23.4	10 37.7
0 UND	19 18.8	18 20.0	30 12.0	35 10.6	40 9.1		28 13.1	26 14.0
15 25.0	33 11.1	33 10.9	48 7.6	47 7.7	54 6.8		44 8.4	50 7.3
						Cost of Sales/Inventory		
						Cost of Sales/Payables		
6.9	7.1	9.0	10.4	4.0	12.7	Sales/Working Capital	8.6	8.9
-184.0	22.5	190.9	30.4	9.2	-48.4		19.6	23.2
-9.0	-34.8	-13.2	-16.7	50.3	-7.3		-139.9	-100.8
	11.4	5.2	6.9	8.0	17.7	EBIT/Interest	10.2	7.8
	(21) 3.1	(24) 1.1	(24) 1.0	2.1	(10) 3.1		(100) 3.4	(74) 2.4
	-2.0	-1.2	-.4	.7	-.3		.9	.7
						Net Profit + Depr., Dep., Amort./Cur. Mat. L/T/D	11.1	3.8
							(25) 3.4	(16) 2.0
							1.5	1.3
.0	.9	.5	1.0	1.0	.8	Fixed/Worth	.7	.4
45.0	2.9	1.2	1.8	1.1	1.3		1.5	1.4
-.4	-2.9	6.6	-62.2	NM	-4.0		-11.4	UND
.4	1.5	.9	1.1	.1	1.0	Debt/Worth	.9	.9
-5.8	6.3	2.3	9.0	.7	2.5		2.6	3.3
-1.8	-5.1	15.7	-72.2	NM	-9.3		-35.2	UND
	51.9	39.7	59.4	18.8		% Profit Before Taxes/Tangible Net Worth	49.4	55.5
(16) 16.8	(24) 14.1	(20) 5.3	(10) .4				(82) 20.4	(69) 22.7
	-16.9	-2.4	-2.8	-1.4			.5	4.3
35.9	18.1	14.0	8.8	10.3	8.6	% Profit Before Taxes/Total Assets	18.5	14.4
4.0	5.1	2.1	-.3	2.5	3.8		4.6	4.2
-26.3	-8.3	-4.4	-4.1	-.4	-1.4		-.4	-.1
UND	12.7	21.2	10.6	8.0	6.8	Sales/Net Fixed Assets	18.9	31.3
44.9	3.7	3.9	2.7	2.3	4.4		6.6	6.0
7.1	2.0	2.3	1.3	.1	.7		2.6	3.3
8.9	3.2	2.8	2.1	1.6	1.6	Sales/Total Assets	3.3	3.3
3.4	2.1	1.9	1.2	1.3	.9		2.3	2.3
.9	1.3	.8	.8	.1	.5		1.3	1.4
	1.4	1.3	1.0	4.8		% Depr., Dep., Amort./Sales	1.1	1.1
(21) 4.7	(25) 2.6	(26) 4.0	(11) 5.6				(100) 2.1	(71) 2.4
	12.6	4.7	6.5	41.2			6.5	5.3
						% Officers', Directors' Owners' Comp/Sales	2.1	1.5
							(27) 3.7	(21) 2.5
							9.0	5.7
12936M	85157M	397956M	998861M	1127712M	1921367M	Net Sales ($)	3495008M	2664869M
2455M	33554M	152226M	655043M	831135M	1867950M	Total Assets ($)	2002254M	2113459M

M = $ thousand   MM = $ million
See Pages 9 through 22 for Explanation of Ratios and Data

Comparative Historical Data | Current Data Sorted by Sales

			Type of Statement						
21	25	28	Unqualified		4	2	3	4	15
12	15	16	Reviewed		1	5	1		5
10	9	7	Compiled		1	1	1	1	4
11	13	12	Tax Returns	3	1	1	1		1
35	38	55	Other	6	2	1	1	2	1
4/1/07-3/31/08 ALL	4/1/08-3/31/09 ALL	4/1/09-3/31/10 ALL			20 (4/1-9/30/09)			98 (10/1/09-3/31/10)	
				0-1MM	1-3MM	3-5MM	5-10MM	10-25MM	25MM & OVER
89	100	118	NUMBER OF STATEMENTS	15	18	16	14	18	37
%	%	%	ASSETS	%	%	%	%	%	%
10.0	12.9	10.9	Cash & Equivalents	27.0	9.8	10.1	7.9	7.5	8.2
15.3	17.5	15.1	Trade Receivables (net)	1.9	11.9	8.8	14.1	16.0	24.8
10.2	9.5	7.7	Inventory	2.2	10.0	8.9	9.0	6.7	8.2
3.6	3.3	4.6	All Other Current	.6	7.1	4.4	3.7	2.0	6.6
39.1	43.1	38.3	Total Current	31.7	38.9	32.2	34.7	32.2	47.7
46.6	42.8	47.3	Fixed Assets (net)	63.3	54.9	52.3	49.1	51.7	32.1
4.4	5.6	7.0	Intangibles (net)	3.9	2.9	9.8	8.2	4.2	9.9
9.9	8.4	7.4	All Other Non-Current	1.1	3.3	5.7	8.1	11.9	10.3
100.0	100.0	100.0	Total	100.0	100.0	100.0	100.0	100.0	100.0
			LIABILITIES						
8.0	7.7	10.7	Notes Payable-Short Term	8.1	10.7	37.4	4.5	3.7	5.9
4.4	3.7	3.4	Cur. Mat.-L.T.D.	1.0	4.3	2.7	1.7	2.6	5.3
10.9	11.8	9.5	Trade Payables	1.5	5.9	6.8	8.3	15.5	13.2
.5	.1	.2	Income Taxes Payable	.0	.0	.6	.7	.0	.1
14.3	13.6	11.7	All Other Current	5.3	6.0	10.8	19.0	10.3	15.3
38.1	37.0	35.5	Total Current	16.0	27.0	58.3	34.2	32.1	39.8
30.7	31.8	33.0	Long-Term Debt	60.5	41.6	21.5	34.4	28.0	24.7
.3	.3	.4	Deferred Taxes	.0	.0	1.6	.2	.0	.6
5.5	7.7	8.9	All Other Non-Current	17.6	13.8	7.3	6.7	5.6	6.0
25.4	23.1	22.2	Net Worth	6.0	17.6	11.2	24.6	34.2	28.9
100.0	100.0	100.0	Total Liabilities & Net Worth	100.0	100.0	100.0	100.0	100.0	100.0
			INCOME DATA						
100.0	100.0	100.0	Net Sales	100.0	100.0	100.0	100.0	100.0	100.0
			Gross Profit						
91.4	95.1	95.4	Operating Expenses	77.6	102.3	99.0	94.9	97.7	96.7
8.6	4.9	4.6	Operating Profit	22.4	-2.3	1.0	5.1	2.3	3.3
4.0	2.3	3.3	All Other Expenses (net)	12.7	2.8	1.7	3.5	.7	1.6
4.6	2.6	1.3	Profit Before Taxes	9.7	-5.2	-.7	1.6	1.6	1.7
			RATIOS						
2.0	2.1	2.0	Current	5.4	4.1	1.8	2.2	2.3	1.7
1.2	1.2	1.2		.8	1.7	1.2	1.4	.9	1.2
.6	.7	.6		.5	1.3	.3	.7	.5	.7
1.3	1.3	1.3	Quick	4.2	2.8	1.1	1.8	1.6	1.1
.8	.9	.7		.8	1.2	.5	.6	.7	.7
.3	.4	.4		.4	.7	.1	.3	.3	.5
10 35.9	9 42.2	9 39.1	Sales/Receivables	0 UND	10 35.8	4 96.8	11 33.1	19 19.4	19 18.9
26 14.3	19 19.3	22 16.9		0 UND	17 21.0	8 47.6	21 17.5	25 14.8	39 9.4
42 8.6	44 8.4	39 9.3		11 34.4	32 11.5	33 11.1	30 12.0	38 9.6	51 7.1
			Cost of Sales/Inventory						
			Cost of Sales/Payables						
10.1	8.9	8.3	Sales/Working Capital	8.7	3.7	9.9	6.4	9.9	9.5
36.8	32.6	30.3		-184.0	8.3	44.3	82.8	-59.8	37.1
-15.0	-28.0	-16.1		-6.8	31.7	-6.3	-17.8	-10.0	-15.5
(70) 4.7	(86) 8.7	(101) 7.8	EBIT/Interest		(15) 9.3	(13) 4.9	(12) 9.5	33.1	(34) 8.3
2.1	2.5	2.1			1.7	-1.3	1.0	2.9	2.8
.9	.6	-.8			-5.9	-4.0	-.4	-.8	.4
(15) 7.7	(15) 25.6	(20) 8.7	Net Profit + Depr., Dep., Amort./Cur. Mat. L/T/D					(12) 9.9	
1.7	4.9	2.4						2.8	
1.1	1.3	.5						.4	
1.0	.8	.8	Fixed/Worth	.9	1.0	.9	.5	.7	.4
2.1	1.5	1.7		14.8	1.8	1.3	2.0	1.4	1.3
11.4	-18.4	-9.5		-1.7	-1.8	NM	-11.7	18.6	-4.2
1.0	.7	.9	Debt/Worth	.2	.4	.6	.4	.9	1.2
3.1	2.8	2.7		25.6	2.3	5.3	3.0	1.7	2.5
27.8	-28.0	-16.2		-3.0	-3.6	NM	-16.0	33.0	-13.8
(69) 50.4	(71) 55.2	(84) 46.8	% Profit Before Taxes/Tangible Net Worth		(12) 46.9	(12) 14.2		(16) 66.0	(26) 50.5
20.4	13.1	14.1			-.7	3.7		31.0	17.5
2.0	.0	-1.6			-7.8	-88.4		-2.5	2.9
11.6	12.0	10.3	% Profit Before Taxes/Total Assets	25.0	14.1	4.2	24.7	15.6	10.0
4.3	3.2	2.5		1.2	2.0	.0	.4	2.3	3.8
-.3	-1.0	-4.1		-12.5	-4.7	-8.3	-4.7	-3.8	-.9
19.2	45.0	13.1	Sales/Net Fixed Assets	15.2	21.2	11.3	12.8	7.2	47.8
4.3	5.3	3.7		1.2	3.0	3.7	5.7	3.5	4.4
1.2	1.6	1.3		.2	.2	.6	1.4	1.8	2.5
3.1	3.4	2.9	Sales/Total Assets	3.4	2.6	2.3	3.9	3.1	3.5
1.7	2.0	1.5		.7	1.6	1.1	2.2	2.0	1.6
.6	1.0	.7		.2	.1	.5	.9	.9	1.1
(77) 1.0	(82) .7	(99) 1.6	% Depr., Dep., Amort./Sales	(11) 3.7	(13) 2.1	(14) 1.1	1.2	(16) 2.6	(31) 1.0
3.3	1.9	3.9		10.1	8.9	4.9	2.5	3.4	2.9
8.0	5.8	7.3		21.8	25.3	8.5	5.5	4.5	5.5
(21) 1.9	(30) 1.7	(25) 1.6	% Officers', Directors' Owners' Comp/Sales						
3.2	2.9	2.7							
7.1	6.5	9.7							
3079264M	4574897M	4543989M	Net Sales ($)	5485M	37281M	65501M	93048M	302626M	4040048M
2465041M	2619653M	3542363M	Total Assets ($)	11638M	178323M	88053M	175822M	489076M	2599451M

M = $ thousand   MM = $ million
See Pages 9 through 22 for Explanation of Ratios and Data

Current Data Sorted by Assets   Comparative Historical Data

						Type of Statement		
		1	9	3	2	Unqualified	10	11
	2	5	4	1		Reviewed	2	7
	3	3	1			Compiled	2	11
1	3	5				Tax Returns	3	3
3	6	15	7	3	3	Other	9	20
3	10 (4/1-9/30/09)		73 (10/1/09-3/31/10)				4/1/05-3/31/06 ALL	4/1/06-3/31/07 ALL
0-500M	500M-2MM	2-10MM	10-50MM	50-100MM	100-250MM	NUMBER OF STATEMENTS		
7	14	29	21	7	5		26	52
%	%	%	%	%	%	ASSETS	%	%
	5.1	17.9	9.3			Cash & Equivalents	11.8	13.3
	21.1	23.7	11.4			Trade Receivables (net)	19.0	19.4
	18.7	21.4	12.7			Inventory	14.4	17.5
	2.7	1.3	8.8			All Other Current	2.6	4.1
	47.6	64.4	42.3			Total Current	47.8	54.3
	35.9	27.6	48.7			Fixed Assets (net)	40.5	35.3
	8.6	4.4	2.6			Intangibles (net)	5.4	3.4
	7.9	3.6	6.4			All Other Non-Current	6.2	7.0
	100.0	100.0	100.0			Total	100.0	100.0
						LIABILITIES		
	7.5	8.3	8.0			Notes Payable-Short Term	11.3	13.1
	3.4	4.4	5.0			Cur. Mat.-L.T.D.	3.9	6.1
	10.7	13.1	7.8			Trade Payables	14.7	16.4
	.0	.3	.2			Income Taxes Payable	.6	.3
	7.9	11.0	11.9			All Other Current	18.2	17.5
	29.4	37.2	32.8			Total Current	48.9	53.4
	26.1	21.7	31.9			Long-Term Debt	31.1	34.0
	.1	.0	.3			Deferred Taxes	.2	.4
	6.4	7.1	7.8			All Other Non-Current	8.0	7.3
	37.9	34.0	27.2			Net Worth	11.8	4.9
	100.0	100.0	100.0			Total Liabilities & Net Worth	100.0	100.0
						INCOME DATA		
	100.0	100.0	100.0			Net Sales	100.0	100.0
						Gross Profit		
	96.5	92.5	94.1			Operating Expenses	94.2	95.2
	3.5	7.5	5.9			Operating Profit	5.8	4.8
	.7	3.4	1.7			All Other Expenses (net)	1.7	2.4
	2.7	4.1	4.2			Profit Before Taxes	4.1	2.4
						RATIOS		
	3.1	2.5	2.9				1.6	1.7
	1.9	1.7	1.1			Current	1.3	1.1
	.6	1.3	.8				.8	.6
	1.6	2.1	1.3				1.3	1.5
	.8	1.1	.7			Quick	.8	.7
	.5	.6	.4				.4	.3
	7 49.4	6 56.4	14 26.3				8 45.1 11 33.5	
	25 14.7	26 13.8	26 14.3			Sales/Receivables	30 12.0 21 17.1	
	38 9.6	43 8.5	58 6.3				46 7.9 43 8.5	
						Cost of Sales/Inventory		
						Cost of Sales/Payables		
	5.5	6.1	4.6				9.7	8.2
	14.9	10.0	67.9			Sales/Working Capital	27.2	26.1
	-18.4	24.6	-28.8				-39.4	-15.0
	10.7	15.6	6.0				10.0	10.4
	(12) 2.7	(24) 5.9	(19) 3.1			EBIT/Interest	(25) 4.8 (46) 3.2	
	1.2	2.3	.5				2.2	1.0
								21.2
						Net Profit + Depr., Dep., Amort./Cur. Mat. L/T/D	(13) 5.4	
								1.8
	.6	.2	.6				1.0	.6
	1.0	.7	2.4			Fixed/Worth	1.6	1.4
	8.1	3.2	34.3				NM	-11.5
	.6	1.0	.6				1.4	1.4
	2.1	1.8	2.5			Debt/Worth	2.3	3.2
	33.2	4.3	79.3				NM	-21.3
	32.9	46.2	59.8			% Profit Before Taxes/Tangible Net Worth	52.5	43.4
	(12) 8.4	(26) 29.5	(18) 18.2				(20) 26.6 (38) 23.2	
	-61.9	7.0	1.5				12.2	9.2
	15.3	21.1	9.4			% Profit Before Taxes/Total Assets	14.0	12.7
	2.5	5.7	4.0				9.4	5.7
	-8.3	2.6	-.7				2.0	-1.1
	32.2	66.3	7.2			Sales/Net Fixed Assets	24.0	32.1
	12.2	16.4	2.4				5.2	10.3
	3.1	4.3	1.2				2.6	3.4
	4.0	3.4	1.7			Sales/Total Assets	3.5	3.5
	2.3	2.4	1.3				1.8	2.5
	1.6	1.6	.9				1.3	1.4
	.7	.7	1.8			% Depr., Dep., Amort./Sales	1.0	.9
	(10) 1.4	(22) 1.7	(20) 4.0				(24) 2.8 (44) 2.3	
	4.4	3.0	7.0				4.6	4.0
			2.5			% Officers', Directors' Owners' Comp/Sales		3.8
		(16) 4.1					(11) 5.7	
			11.1					20.6
25257M	43621M	312391M	652542M	903149M	1066811M	Net Sales ($)	1121762M	1463927M
2207M	14375M	137953M	503445M	481856M	894657M	Total Assets ($)	684902M	964805M

M = $ thousand   MM = $ million
See Pages 9 through 22 for Explanation of Ratios and Data

Comparative Historical Data   &   Current Data Sorted by Sales

	4/1/07-3/31/08 ALL	4/1/08-3/31/09 ALL	4/1/09-3/31/10 ALL		0-1MM	1-3MM	3-5MM	5-10MM	10-25MM	25MM & OVER
				Type of Statement	10 (4/1-9/30/09)			73 (10/1/09-3/31/10)		
Unqualified	19	20	15		2	2	3	2	5	10
Reviewed	8	16	12		2	3	1	1	3	4
Compiled	4	5	8				1	1	1	1
Tax Returns	7	6	11		2	3	2	1	3	
Other	28	32	37		3	5	2	5	13	9
NUMBER OF STATEMENTS	66	79	83		7	10	8	9	25	24
ASSETS	%	%	%		%	%	%	%	%	%
Cash & Equivalents	9.9	10.7	14.3		12.4				17.9	11.1
Trade Receivables (net)	19.7	17.2	18.0		10.0				22.1	14.6
Inventory	13.7	17.2	15.8		19.6				17.2	13.9
All Other Current	4.9	7.0	4.3		.5				2.7	8.6
Total Current	48.1	52.0	52.4		42.5				60.0	48.2
Fixed Assets (net)	36.4	35.4	36.6		49.8				35.1	35.5
Intangibles (net)	4.4	3.0	4.9		5.7				2.1	6.0
All Other Non-Current	11.1	9.6	6.0		2.0				2.7	10.3
Total	100.0	100.0	100.0		100.0				100.0	100.0
LIABILITIES										
Notes Payable-Short Term	7.4	9.3	7.3		5.5				7.8	6.0
Cur. Mat.-L.T.D.	6.1	4.3	4.1		.5				2.9	4.9
Trade Payables	12.6	10.8	9.3		4.2				13.0	7.3
Income Taxes Payable	.6	.2	.1		.0				.2	.0
All Other Current	11.5	12.7	11.3		13.0				14.6	12.6
Total Current	38.2	37.3	32.2		23.2				38.5	30.7
Long-Term Debt	27.3	22.9	31.1		54.9				25.7	27.7
Deferred Taxes	.3	.1	.1		.0				.1	.1
All Other Non-Current	10.8	8.0	7.1		8.8				6.6	8.4
Net Worth	23.5	31.7	29.4		13.1				29.2	33.0
Total Liabilities & Net Worth	100.0	100.0	100.0		100.0				100.0	100.0
INCOME DATA										
Net Sales	100.0	100.0	100.0		100.0				100.0	100.0
Gross Profit										
Operating Expenses	94.8	93.7	92.7		95.8				92.9	93.3
Operating Profit	5.2	6.3	7.3		4.2				7.1	6.7
All Other Expenses (net)	1.4	1.7	1.9		.8				1.2	1.0
Profit Before Taxes	3.8	4.6	5.3		3.4				5.8	5.7
RATIOS										
Current	2.2 / 1.3 / .8	2.5 / 1.4 / .8	2.6 / 1.7 / 1.0		3.8 / 2.2 / .7				2.1 / 1.4 / 1.2	2.3 / 1.5 / .9
Quick	1.5 / .7 / .4	1.6 / .7 / .4	1.6 / 1.0 / .6		1.6 / 1.0 / .5				1.6 / .9 / .6	1.6 / 1.0 / .6
Sales/Receivables	15 24.5 / 25 14.7 / 51 7.2	8 43.3 / 23 16.0 / 50 7.3	13 28.9 / 24 15.2 / 48 7.6		0 UND / 6 58.2 / 33 11.0				6 56.6 / 33 11.0 / 49 7.4	16 22.7 / 24 15.5 / 49 7.4
Cost of Sales/Inventory										
Cost of Sales/Payables										
Sales/Working Capital	6.1 / 28.1 / -23.1	7.0 / 23.4 / -29.4	6.1 / 13.8 / -297.7		5.5 / 36.1 / -11.4				7.0 / 18.4 / 39.6	4.4 / 16.0 / -80.8
EBIT/Interest	(60) 8.6 / 2.8 / 1.4	(71) 10.2 / 3.4 / 1.2	(73) 10.2 / 3.6 / 1.8						(23) 6.7 / 4.3 / 2.8	(22) 11.1 / 3.4 / 1.4
Net Profit + Depr., Dep., Amort./Cur. Mat. L/T/D	(20) 10.9 / 2.9 / 1.7	(19) 6.6 / 1.3 / -.2	(14) 12.2 / 3.2 / 2.0							
Fixed/Worth	.4 / 1.6 / NM	.3 / 1.2 / 8.0	.4 / 1.3 / 9.6		.7 / 1.6 / NM				.4 / .9 / 3.8	.4 / 1.5 / 691.7
Debt/Worth	1.2 / 2.4 / NM	.7 / 2.3 / 20.4	.8 / 2.4 / 32.9		.6 / 1.4 / NM				1.1 / 2.4 / 7.3	.7 / 2.3 / 909.0
% Profit Before Taxes/Tangible Net Worth	(50) 56.1 / 28.0 / 10.9	(63) 58.8 / 21.6 / 2.0	(69) 52.6 / 24.3 / 3.6						(23) 69.7 / 40.4 / 12.1	(19) 53.6 / 23.7 / 2.7
% Profit Before Taxes/Total Assets	21.1 / 6.5 / -.5	16.8 / 6.7 / .2	15.9 / 5.4 / 1.0		12.0 / 2.4 / .5				22.4 / 9.2 / 3.1	11.0 / 4.1 / 1.2
Sales/Net Fixed Assets	15.7 / 6.6 / 3.0	21.3 / 6.5 / 2.8	24.9 / 6.3 / 1.8		36.8 / 4.6 / 1.8				40.1 / 16.2 / 2.3	11.0 / 4.5 / 1.9
Sales/Total Assets	3.1 / 1.9 / 1.2	2.8 / 1.9 / 1.2	3.3 / 1.7 / 1.1		4.2 / 1.8 / 1.5				3.9 / 2.6 / 1.6	2.1 / 1.2 / .9
% Depr., Dep., Amort./Sales	(57) 1.4 / 2.8 / 3.9	(70) .9 / 1.9 / 4.1	(68) 1.2 / 2.3 / 5.0						(21) .9 / 1.8 / 5.9	(22) 1.7 / 2.5 / 4.1
% Officers', Directors' Owners' Comp/Sales	(13) 4.3 / 6.2 / 16.5	(17) .9 / 3.4 / 7.0	(26) 2.1 / 4.1 / 11.6							
Net Sales ($)	2809757M	3916291M	3003771M		4144M	17673M	31697M	65207M	403683M	2481367M
Total Assets ($)	2000009M	2533158M	2034493M		14386M	9677M	16384M	55396M	225530M	1713120M

© RMA 2010

M = $ thousand   MM = $ million

See Pages 9 through 22 for Explanation of Ratios and Data

Current Data Sorted by Assets   Comparative Historical Data

0-500M	500M-2MM	2-10MM	10-50MM	50-100MM	100-250MM	Type of Statement	4/1/05-3/31/06 ALL	4/1/06-3/31/07 ALL
	1	3	12	7	5	Unqualified	26	26
	1	2	6	2		Reviewed	10	13
		3	3			Compiled	6	8
2	3	4	1			Tax Returns	5	2
	3	13	17	8	4	Other	35	33
		16 (4/1-9/30/09)		84 (10/1/09-3/31/10)				
2	8	25	39	17	9	**NUMBER OF STATEMENTS**	82	82
%	%	%	%	%	%		%	%
						ASSETS		
		10.3	12.3	10.7		Cash & Equivalents	11.1	11.6
		26.3	19.5	13.7		Trade Receivables (net)	24.3	24.1
		.3	1.2	1.0		Inventory	2.2	2.0
		1.8	8.1	6.7		All Other Current	4.5	3.7
		38.7	41.1	32.2		Total Current	42.2	41.4
		44.3	45.3	59.7		Fixed Assets (net)	45.2	44.4
		2.9	6.6	.5		Intangibles (net)	3.3	2.7
		14.2	7.0	7.6		All Other Non-Current	9.3	11.5
		100.0	100.0	100.0		Total	100.0	100.0
						LIABILITIES		
		9.3	4.4	4.5		Notes Payable-Short Term	4.7	5.4
		5.0	5.0	5.9		Cur. Mat.-L.T.D.	4.9	4.8
		14.5	8.3	4.3		Trade Payables	11.7	10.4
		.0	.3	.1		Income Taxes Payable	.4	.4
		7.8	8.4	9.7		All Other Current	9.7	10.6
		36.6	26.4	24.5		Total Current	31.5	31.6
		22.8	29.6	43.4		Long-Term Debt	23.2	22.8
		.0	1.3	.9		Deferred Taxes	1.3	1.4
		15.1	8.4	8.1		All Other Non-Current	5.3	4.9
		25.6	34.2	23.0		Net Worth	38.7	39.2
		100.0	100.0	100.0		Total Liabilties & Net Worth	100.0	100.0
						INCOME DATA		
		100.0	100.0	100.0		Net Sales	100.0	100.0
						Gross Profit		
		88.3	87.8	85.8		Operating Expenses	87.2	85.7
		11.7	12.2	14.2		Operating Profit	12.8	14.3
		3.3	2.7	2.5		All Other Expenses (net)	1.9	2.1
		8.4	9.5	11.7		Profit Before Taxes	10.9	12.2
						RATIOS		
		1.7	2.3	3.3		Current	2.1	2.3
		.9	1.8	1.9			1.4	1.3
		.6	1.0	.7			.9	.9
		1.7	1.8	2.5		Quick	2.0	2.0
		.8	1.2	1.3			1.1	1.1
		.5	.8	.4			.6	.6
		28 13.2	24 15.0	23 16.0		Sales/Receivables	28 13.2	30 12.1
		47 7.8	41 8.9	36 10.2			45 8.1	39 9.3
		63 5.8	60 6.1	54 6.8			65 5.6	59 6.2
						Cost of Sales/Inventory		
						Cost of Sales/Payables		
		10.4	3.7	6.3		Sales/Working Capital	6.2	6.8
		-54.2	13.7	9.3			18.4	24.0
		-7.7	248.8	-7.5			-46.9	-68.0
		7.8	10.1	15.1		EBIT/Interest	15.4	11.0
		(20) 2.1	(35) 3.5	(16) 4.8			(72) 6.5	(68) 7.3
		-1.8	1.2	2.2			3.2	3.6
			5.6			Net Profit + Depr., Dep.,	8.1	7.9
			(13) 3.1			Amort./Cur. Mat. L/T/D	(20) 4.2	(21) 3.3
			2.3				2.2	2.6
		.7	.6	.9		Fixed/Worth	.5	.5
		1.7	1.4	1.2			1.2	1.1
		4.3	2.3	2.3			2.4	2.5
		.8	.9	.6		Debt/Worth	.8	.7
		3.1	2.1	1.0			1.6	1.5
		7.0	4.6	2.4			4.0	3.8
		89.0	36.6	39.6		% Profit Before Taxes/Tangible	69.4	63.5
		(21) 29.6	(34) 8.4	(15) 18.0		Net Worth	(74) 28.4	(73) 36.7
		-2.0	1.2	9.7			13.5	19.7
		25.6	11.9	18.6		% Profit Before Taxes/Total	21.1	22.3
		9.8	5.5	8.8		Assets	10.3	12.6
		-3.4	.7	3.0			3.1	7.8
		13.2	10.6	3.3		Sales/Net Fixed Assets	13.8	12.8
		3.6	2.5	1.8			3.7	3.4
		1.6	1.1	.9			1.0	1.3
		2.6	2.1	1.6		Sales/Total Assets	2.7	2.3
		1.7	1.3	.8			1.6	1.6
		.8	.5	.6			.7	.7
		1.8	3.1	4.0		% Depr., Dep., Amort./Sales	2.1	2.1
		(22) 5.8	5.0	(16) 6.4			(72) 4.6	(70) 4.3
		11.2	8.7	9.5			9.2	7.0
						% Officers', Directors'		2.6
						Owners' Comp/Sales	(11) 3.4	
							7.1	
3286M	11769M	248344M	1238753M	1594910M	1778414M	Net Sales ($)	4310832M	4641255M
607M	10032M	145127M	864715M	1331789M	1601769M	Total Assets ($)	3070004M	2695661M

M = $ thousand   MM = $ million
See Pages 9 through 22 for Explanation of Ratios and Data

Comparative Historical Data | Current Data Sorted by Sales

4/1/07-3/31/08 ALL	4/1/08-3/31/09 ALL	4/1/09-3/31/10 ALL	Type of Statement	0-1MM	1-3MM	3-5MM	5-10MM	10-25MM	25MM & OVER
34	37	28	Unqualified		2		3	3	17
9	10	11	Reviewed	1			1	4	5
8	3	6	Compiled				4	2	
2	2	10	Tax Returns	2	4		1	2	
30	33	45	Other	1	2	3	9	6	24
					16 (4/1-9/30/09)		84 (10/1/09-3/31/10)		
83	85	100	**NUMBER OF STATEMENTS**	4	8	7	18	17	46
%	%	%	**ASSETS**	%	%	%	%	%	%
11.0	10.7	10.9	Cash & Equivalents				10.7	12.6	9.9
22.6	21.9	18.9	Trade Receivables (net)				20.6	25.5	19.8
1.8	1.7	1.5	Inventory				.0	1.4	1.3
6.6	6.1	5.7	All Other Current				2.4	3.5	8.5
42.0	40.5	36.9	Total Current				33.6	43.0	39.5
44.6	46.2	47.1	Fixed Assets (net)				52.6	38.0	48.2
3.8	2.5	5.1	Intangibles (net)				2.8	7.7	4.2
9.7	10.9	10.9	All Other Non-Current				11.0	11.3	8.2
100.0	100.0	100.0	Total				100.0	100.0	100.0
			LIABILITIES						
4.5	7.2	4.9	Notes Payable-Short Term				8.8	7.4	4.4
4.8	5.5	8.0	Cur. Mat.-L.T.D.				7.6	3.6	4.3
11.0	11.0	9.7	Trade Payables				13.8	6.8	8.4
.7	.2	.2	Income Taxes Payable				.0	.5	.2
9.1	9.1	11.4	All Other Current				6.1	8.7	10.4
30.2	32.9	34.2	Total Current				36.3	27.0	27.7
31.9	33.3	30.5	Long-Term Debt				30.4	21.1	28.8
1.1	.8	.7	Deferred Taxes				.0	.6	1.2
5.0	5.9	10.2	All Other Non-Current				25.5	9.6	7.9
31.8	27.0	24.3	Net Worth				7.8	41.7	34.4
100.0	100.0	100.0	Total Liabilities & Net Worth				100.0	100.0	100.0
			INCOME DATA						
100.0	100.0	100.0	Net Sales				100.0	100.0	100.0
			Gross Profit						
90.0	87.9	88.0	Operating Expenses				85.0	89.8	91.7
10.0	12.1	12.0	Operating Profit				15.0	10.2	8.3
1.8	1.2	2.7	All Other Expenses (net)				3.5	1.1	1.8
8.3	10.9	9.3	Profit Before Taxes				11.5	9.1	6.5
			RATIOS						
2.3	2.5	2.2					1.9	3.4	2.2
1.4	1.4	1.2	Current				.7	1.7	1.5
.8	.9	.7					.5	.8	.9
2.0	2.1	1.8					1.7	3.1	1.8
1.0	1.0	.9	Quick				.7	1.3	1.0
.6	.6	.5					.5	.7	.7
28 13.1	24 15.2	25 14.9		23 15.9	45 8.2	26 14.0			
43 8.5	38 9.6	39 9.3	Sales/Receivables	53 6.9	64 5.7	37 9.9			
59 6.2	60 6.0	57 6.4		71 5.1	83 4.4	50 7.3			
			Cost of Sales/Inventory						
			Cost of Sales/Payables						
6.1	6.6	6.5					5.5	3.8	8.0
15.3	14.1	31.5	Sales/Working Capital				-12.8	7.5	14.9
-28.8	-52.1	-10.6					-7.0	-21.7	-59.5
15.2	10.3	11.2					9.1	11.4	12.7
(71) 4.1	(77) 4.9	(87) 3.7	EBIT/Interest	(13) 2.1	(16) 7.5	(41) 3.5			
2.0	2.3	.8		-7.7	1.9	1.5			
5.6	8.9	6.2	Net Profit + Depr., Dep.,						6.1
(22) 2.9	(25) 3.7	(27) 3.2	Amort./Cur. Mat. L/T/D			(18)			3.1
1.6	2.0	2.4							2.9
.6	.7	.8					.9	.4	.8
1.3	1.4	1.5	Fixed/Worth				2.2	1.5	1.2
2.6	2.8	2.7					-2.6	2.1	1.9
.8	.8	.7					.9	.9	.7
1.7	2.2	1.8	Debt/Worth				3.5	1.7	1.3
4.8	4.0	4.6					-6.4	4.0	3.0
46.9	55.2	47.4	% Profit Before Taxes/Tangible				67.8	80.2	36.0
(70) 29.1	(77) 28.7	(83) 17.1	Net Worth	(13) 24.8	(15) 31.1	(42) 16.3			
13.8	13.8	3.2		-20.2	1.6	4.2			
17.4	17.3	14.0	% Profit Before Taxes/Total				14.0	18.5	10.8
8.6	9.0	5.3	Assets				5.8	12.0	4.5
2.8	3.4	.2					-2.0	1.0	1.5
10.4	9.5	10.0					5.4	16.9	10.2
3.4	3.3	2.7	Sales/Net Fixed Assets				2.1	4.6	3.1
1.5	1.3	1.0					.9	1.3	1.3
2.2	2.4	2.0					1.8	2.0	2.5
1.3	1.6	1.3	Sales/Total Assets				1.0	1.3	1.5
.8	.8	.6					.7	.6	.8
2.1	2.0	3.1					4.5	.8	3.0
(71) 4.8	(72) 4.0	(85) 5.8	% Depr., Dep., Amort./Sales	(16) 8.1	4.0	(38) 5.0			
7.4	8.4	10.4		16.1	7.0	8.6			
.5			% Officers', Directors'						
(10) 3.6			Owners' Comp/Sales						
9.1									
5102525M	5756588M	4875476M	Net Sales ($)	3400M	13797M	26012M	137672M	271711M	4422884M
3113007M	3167574M	3954039M	Total Assets ($)	4515M	22563M	77070M	177381M	371732M	3300778M

M = $ thousand   MM = $ million
See Pages 9 through 22 for Explanation of Ratios and Data

TRANSPORTATION—Navigational Services to Shipping   NAICS 488330

Current Data Sorted by Assets							Comparative Historical Data	

0-500M	500M-2MM	2-10MM	10-50MM	50-100MM	100-250MM	Type of Statement	4/1/05-3/31/06 ALL	4/1/06-3/31/07 ALL
		1	3	1	7	Unqualified	16	10
	1	3	3			Reviewed	11	11
	5	5	3			Compiled	17	18
	2					Tax Returns	3	4
	1	10	10	1	8	Other	44	28
	5 (4/1-9/30/09)		59 (10/1/09-3/31/10)					
	9	19	19	2	15	**NUMBER OF STATEMENTS**	91	71
%	%	%	%	%	%	**ASSETS**	%	%
		19.7	9.6		8.2	Cash & Equivalents	11.4	14.8
		17.5	17.1		8.2	Trade Receivables (net)	17.1	18.0
D		1.9	2.1		1.4	Inventory	.7	1.9
A		1.7	.9		3.0	All Other Current	3.6	4.9
T		40.8	29.7		20.8	Total Current	32.8	39.6
A		37.9	60.0		72.7	Fixed Assets (net)	55.0	51.8
		.5	3.9		.5	Intangibles (net)	1.6	1.6
N		20.8	6.5		5.9	All Other Non-Current	10.7	6.9
O		100.0	100.0		100.0	Total	100.0	100.0
T						**LIABILITIES**		
		4.7	2.9		3.4	Notes Payable-Short Term	4.0	3.5
A		5.0	4.4		4.5	Cur. Mat.-L.T.D.	6.1	4.6
V		2.2	9.3		5.1	Trade Payables	9.2	8.4
A		.0	.2		.0	Income Taxes Payable	.3	.6
I		16.9	4.8		3.1	All Other Current	6.1	7.0
L		28.8	21.7		16.1	Total Current	25.8	24.1
A		28.1	40.6		34.9	Long-Term Debt	35.3	27.4
B		.1	1.7		2.5	Deferred Taxes	1.7	1.2
L		1.3	5.2		2.6	All Other Non-Current	2.7	5.8
E		41.7	30.8		44.0	Net Worth	34.5	41.5
		100.0	100.0		100.0	Total Liabilities & Net Worth	100.0	100.0
						INCOME DATA		
		100.0	100.0		100.0	Net Sales	100.0	100.0
						Gross Profit		
		80.1	85.6		92.7	Operating Expenses	84.4	83.2
		19.9	14.4		7.3	Operating Profit	15.6	16.8
		4.1	3.6		2.0	All Other Expenses (net)	2.9	2.1
		15.8	10.8		5.3	Profit Before Taxes	12.8	14.7
						RATIOS		
		6.7	2.5		1.8		2.5	2.4
		1.4	1.4		1.3	Current	1.4	1.7
		.6	1.0		.9		.8	1.0
		6.1	2.0		1.7		2.2	2.1
		1.4	1.3		.9	Quick	1.2	1.3
		.4	.9		.7		.5	.8
	12	31.4	30 12.0		31 11.9		25 14.8	20 18.1
	27	13.4	46 8.0		40 9.1	Sales/Receivables	40 9.1	41 8.9
	49	7.4	68 5.4		53 6.8		56 6.5	58 6.3
						Cost of Sales/Inventory		
						Cost of Sales/Payables		
		4.0	4.6		7.1		5.4	6.6
		24.9	19.1		21.9	Sales/Working Capital	18.4	13.0
		-32.6	-812.4		-49.8		-19.6	-846.0
		16.3	24.9		4.2		10.8	9.7
	(12)	3.2	3.7	(13)	3.4	EBIT/Interest	(82) 5.3	(65) 6.3
		1.0	1.4		1.7		2.3	2.9
							4.3	5.9
						Net Profit + Depr., Dep., Amort./Cur. Mat. L/T/D	(22) 2.2	(24) 3.1
							1.6	1.9
		.2	1.0		1.1		.8	.7
		.9	2.8		1.8	Fixed/Worth	1.6	1.3
		1.6	6.3		2.7		2.9	2.5
		.7	1.0		.9		1.0	.6
		1.4	3.2		1.4	Debt/Worth	1.7	1.6
		4.0	8.6		2.1		3.9	3.2
		206.4	51.4		19.8		46.0	63.8
	(18)	9.0	(16) 16.7		5.0	% Profit Before Taxes/Tangible Net Worth	(84) 27.2	(69) 34.4
		1.7	3.6		3.0		10.9	16.0
		23.6	15.2		7.1		16.3	23.3
		9.0	8.6		2.2	% Profit Before Taxes/Total Assets	8.4	11.1
		.5	1.1		1.6		3.5	4.8
		8.4	4.2		1.6		5.2	6.4
		3.3	1.3		1.0	Sales/Net Fixed Assets	2.3	2.3
		1.8	1.0		.6		1.3	1.2
		2.1	1.7		1.1		2.2	2.1
		1.1	1.0		.6	Sales/Total Assets	1.3	1.3
		.7	.7		.5		.8	.8
		1.0	3.2				2.9	2.5
	(15)	2.4	6.6			% Depr., Dep., Amort./Sales	(82) 7.2	(63) 5.7
		6.5	13.6				10.5	8.2
							1.8	1.4
						% Officers', Directors' Owners' Comp/Sales	(20) 4.4	(13) 4.6
							12.4	9.4
	27289M	147550M	477982M	124357M	1660748M	Net Sales ($)	2551927M	2053663M
	12398M	94382M	409868M	182135M	2225640M	Total Assets ($)	2630176M	2053737M

(Left-hand column 0-500M: DATA NOT AVAILABLE)

© RMA 2010

M = $ thousand   MM = $ million
See Pages 9 through 22 for Explanation of Ratios and Data

Comparative Historical Data | Current Data Sorted by Sales

07-08	08-09	09-10	Type of Statement	0-1MM	1-3MM	3-5MM	5-10MM	10-25MM	25MM & OVER
9	10	12	Unqualified	1	1			1	11
12	8	7	Reviewed	2	1	3		2	2
8	16	13	Compiled	1	1	3	3	3	1
6	5	2	Tax Returns						
21	22	30	Other	2	2		4	6	14
4/1/07-3/31/08 ALL	4/1/08-3/31/09 ALL	4/1/09-3/31/10 ALL				5 (4/1-9/30/09)		59 (10/1/09-3/31/10)	
56	61	64	NUMBER OF STATEMENTS	6	5	6	7	12	28
%	%	%	**ASSETS**	%	%	%	%	%	%
15.8	12.0	12.3	Cash & Equivalents					8.3	8.7
14.4	16.5	16.4	Trade Receivables (net)					20.3	15.3
3.5	1.4	1.9	Inventory					3.1	2.2
3.7	3.2	1.7	All Other Current					1.2	2.2
37.4	33.1	32.3	Total Current					33.0	28.4
46.7	56.1	54.1	Fixed Assets (net)					54.4	63.0
4.1	2.2	2.1	Intangibles (net)					.8	1.4
11.8	8.7	11.5	All Other Non-Current					11.8	7.1
100.0	100.0	100.0	Total					100.0	100.0
			LIABILITIES						
6.0	2.4	3.2	Notes Payable-Short Term					3.4	3.2
4.7	5.2	5.1	Cur. Mat.-L.T.D.					6.6	3.7
6.6	5.8	5.7	Trade Payables					6.3	7.0
.4	.3	.1	Income Taxes Payable					.2	.0
6.3	5.4	8.6	All Other Current					15.1	5.2
24.0	19.1	22.7	Total Current					31.7	19.1
28.4	31.5	37.0	Long-Term Debt					44.9	29.4
1.3	1.7	1.1	Deferred Taxes					.3	2.2
4.2	4.2	3.0	All Other Non-Current					.1	3.6
42.1	43.6	36.2	Net Worth					22.9	45.7
100.0	100.0	100.0	Total Liabilities & Net Worth					100.0	100.0
			INCOME DATA						
100.0	100.0	100.0	Net Sales					100.0	100.0
			Gross Profit						
81.5	81.7	84.4	Operating Expenses					79.9	88.0
18.5	18.3	15.6	Operating Profit					20.1	12.0
1.7	3.5	3.0	All Other Expenses (net)					2.8	2.0
16.8	14.8	12.6	Profit Before Taxes					17.3	10.0
			RATIOS						
3.4	2.4	2.8						3.7	2.1
1.7	1.4	1.4	Current					1.2	1.4
.7	.8	.9						.5	1.0
3.2	2.1	1.9						3.4	1.7
1.3	1.3	1.3	Quick					1.2	1.4
.5	.6	.8						.3	.8
5 74.0	15 24.8	21 17.5						26 14.0	31 11.8
37 10.0	36 10.2	38 9.5	Sales/Receivables					47 7.7	42 8.7
52 7.0	45 8.2	55 6.6						53 7.0	62 5.9
			Cost of Sales/Inventory						
			Cost of Sales/Payables						
5.2	7.6	6.3						4.1	7.0
15.6	20.5	22.0	Sales/Working Capital					29.0	12.1
-18.8	-33.4	-51.0						-79.1	146.8
16.8	18.6	9.8						9.8	17.0
(49) 6.0	(53) 5.9	(54) 3.7	EBIT/Interest					(10) 2.6	(25) 3.9
2.2	2.3	1.8						.2	1.9
9.4	8.4	3.9	Net Profit + Depr., Dep.,						
(16) 2.9	(17) 2.7	(12) 2.1	Amort./Cur. Mat. L/T/D						
1.6	1.3	1.8							
.6	.6	.7						.9	.9
1.3	1.5	1.5	Fixed/Worth					2.2	1.4
3.2	2.5	3.4						7.5	2.6
.7	.7	.8						.9	.7
1.9	1.5	1.6	Debt/Worth					2.5	1.3
4.5	2.8	4.8						3.6	2.0
64.3	50.5	55.1	% Profit Before Taxes/Tangible					150.9	31.6
(52) 34.2	(57) 28.2	(57) 12.8	Net Worth					(10) 23.3	15.1
17.8	10.0	3.1						-11.2	4.0
28.5	20.7	15.0	% Profit Before Taxes/Total					23.0	8.7
12.5	11.3	7.5	Assets					9.0	6.9
4.7	4.2	1.7						-1.6	1.9
8.9	7.8	6.4						6.4	2.6
2.8	2.0	1.6	Sales/Net Fixed Assets					1.8	1.3
1.1	.9	.9						1.1	.8
2.3	2.5	1.7						1.9	1.6
1.1	1.2	.9	Sales/Total Assets					1.1	.9
.7	.6	.6						.8	.6
1.7	2.7	2.2						3.2	2.0
(49) 6.0	(50) 6.4	(51) 5.8	% Depr., Dep., Amort./Sales					(11) 9.8	(20) 5.7
10.7	11.4	10.2						18.5	7.8
3.9		1.6							
(15) 11.3		(16) 8.1	% Officers', Directors' Owners' Comp/Sales						
15.2		17.8							
1611756M	2045891M	2437926M	Net Sales ($)	3741M	9976M	22341M	48420M	182305M	2171143M
1814615M	2175498M	2924423M	Total Assets ($)	12359M	11558M	18521M	47768M	159527M	2674690M

M = $ thousand   MM = $ million
See Pages 9 through 22 for Explanation of Ratios and Data

TRANSPORTATION—Other Support Activities for Water Transportation NAICS 488390

Current Data Sorted by Assets						Comparative Historical Data	

Type of Statement

0-500M	500M-2MM	2-10MM	10-50MM	50-100MM	100-250MM	Type of Statement	4/1/05-3/31/06 ALL	4/1/06-3/31/07 ALL
			6	1	1	Unqualified	9	11
		2	2			Reviewed	9	9
		3	3			Compiled	9	7
	2	1	1			Tax Returns	3	6
	5	6		2	5	Other	28	26
	4 (4/1-9/30/09)		45 (10/1/09-3/31/10)					
	7	12	21	3	6	**NUMBER OF STATEMENTS**	58	59

0-500M	500M-2MM	2-10MM	10-50MM	50-100MM	100-250MM		4/1/05-3/31/06	4/1/06-3/31/07
%	%	%	%	%	%	**ASSETS**	%	%
D		16.7	10.6			Cash & Equivalents	13.8	11.6
A		25.8	14.4			Trade Receivables (net)	18.0	22.7
T		9.3	.2			Inventory	1.9	3.8
A		5.6	4.5			All Other Current	3.9	5.0
		57.3	29.7			Total Current	37.6	43.1
N		32.5	52.7			Fixed Assets (net)	53.2	47.3
O		1.9	4.1			Intangibles (net)	2.6	3.1
T		8.2	13.5			All Other Non-Current	6.6	6.5
		100.0	100.0			Total	100.0	100.0
A						**LIABILITIES**		
V		.6	2.5			Notes Payable-Short Term	5.4	5.1
A		3.7	4.8			Cur. Mat.-L.T.D.	5.5	5.5
I		16.9	8.2			Trade Payables	8.0	12.2
L		.0	.5			Income Taxes Payable	.2	.2
A		5.9	11.4			All Other Current	7.5	14.2
B		27.1	27.4			Total Current	26.6	37.3
L		28.4	25.2			Long-Term Debt	34.9	25.9
E		.0	1.0			Deferred Taxes	1.0	1.2
		9.3	2.4			All Other Non-Current	3.3	1.7
		35.2	44.0			Net Worth	34.2	34.0
		100.0	100.0			Total Liabilties & Net Worth	100.0	100.0
						INCOME DATA		
		100.0	100.0			Net Sales	100.0	100.0
						Gross Profit		
		90.5	86.1			Operating Expenses	83.9	83.6
		9.5	13.9			Operating Profit	16.1	16.4
		4.3	4.4			All Other Expenses (net)	3.9	1.9
		5.1	9.5			Profit Before Taxes	12.2	14.5
						RATIOS		
		6.8	2.7				2.6	1.9
		1.8	1.5			Current	1.7	1.3
		1.0	.5				.9	.6
		2.7	2.0				2.3	1.6
		1.6	1.0			Quick	1.3	.9
		.9	.4				.7	.4
	15	24.0	24 15.1				4 99.3	8 45.9
	48	7.6	39 9.3			Sales/Receivables	47 7.7	45 8.2
	63	5.7	57 6.4				77 4.7	75 4.9
						Cost of Sales/Inventory		
						Cost of Sales/Payables		
		3.3	3.0				4.8	7.0
		8.5	18.3			Sales/Working Capital	8.8	27.3
		NM	-9.4				-30.1	-9.8
			26.3				10.2	18.4
		(14)	2.9			EBIT/Interest	(50) 5.3	(52) 4.4
			1.3				2.3	1.2
						Net Profit + Depr., Dep.,	3.5	3.5
						Amort./Cur. Mat. L/T/D	(15) 2.9	(11) 2.3
							1.8	1.6
		.0	.3				.8	.6
		.3	1.4			Fixed/Worth	1.6	1.5
		4.3	3.0				6.9	10.5
		.6	.7				.9	.8
		2.3	1.3			Debt/Worth	1.9	1.8
		7.2	5.0				10.4	13.4
		137.3	34.5				90.6	74.3
	(10)	46.1	(19) 18.4			% Profit Before Taxes/Tangible Net Worth	(49) 38.3	(50) 41.4
		13.3	-.4				14.5	16.3
		31.3	21.0				19.2	31.7
		18.0	7.3			% Profit Before Taxes/Total Assets	8.7	9.4
		.7	.1				4.0	1.6
		274.3	8.7				6.4	12.1
		10.4	1.4			Sales/Net Fixed Assets	2.2	3.2
		1.7	1.0				.9	1.3
		4.1	1.4				2.1	2.3
		1.5	.9			Sales/Total Assets	1.1	1.5
		.8	.4				.7	.9
			2.5				1.7	1.6
		(19)	8.9			% Depr., Dep., Amort./Sales	(55) 4.4	(55) 4.4
			19.8				11.8	7.3
							2.7	1.5
						% Officers', Directors' Owners' Comp/Sales	(11) 4.3	(13) 4.4
							12.3	8.2
	25824M	128603M	706783M	299768M	571703M	Net Sales ($)	1507424M	1995740M
	9151M	59777M	443231M	234215M	931065M	Total Assets ($)	1436346M	1540375M

M = $ thousand   MM = $ million
See Pages 9 through 22 for Explanation of Ratios and Data

Comparative Historical Data

Current Data Sorted by Sales

			Type of Statement	0-1MM	1-3MM	3-5MM	5-10MM	10-25MM	25MM & OVER
21	11	8	Unqualified		1			4	3
3	6	4	Reviewed					3	1
7	6	6	Compiled		1	1	1	3	
6	5	4	Tax Returns		2	1	1		
20	20	27	Other	1	3	3	3		11
4/1/07- 3/31/08 ALL	4/1/08- 3/31/09 ALL	4/1/09- 3/31/10 ALL			4 (4/1-9/30/09)			45 (10/1/09-3/31/10)	
57	48	49	NUMBER OF STATEMENTS	1	7	5	5	16	15
%	%	%	ASSETS	%	%	%	%	%	%
12.4	11.1	12.2	Cash & Equivalents					14.3	9.7
19.0	18.9	17.9	Trade Receivables (net)					14.6	25.0
5.0	3.9	2.4	Inventory					.2	.4
4.9	6.0	6.0	All Other Current					5.1	4.9
41.4	39.9	38.5	Total Current					34.2	40.0
49.7	50.3	48.9	Fixed Assets (net)					47.6	51.8
1.4	2.6	3.2	Intangibles (net)					5.8	3.5
7.5	7.2	9.4	All Other Non-Current					12.4	4.8
100.0	100.0	100.0	Total					100.0	100.0
			LIABILITIES						
6.9	5.0	4.6	Notes Payable-Short Term					4.8	.6
5.7	4.6	3.9	Cur. Mat.-L.T.D.					4.4	4.2
9.0	9.4	10.3	Trade Payables					11.5	11.8
.1	.0	.3	Income Taxes Payable					.6	.2
13.4	11.0	9.7	All Other Current					6.8	12.5
35.0	30.0	28.7	Total Current					28.2	29.3
29.7	30.0	27.2	Long-Term Debt					18.4	30.3
.9	1.1	1.4	Deferred Taxes					1.3	3.1
3.4	8.6	5.1	All Other Non-Current					2.9	6.6
31.0	30.3	37.6	Net Worth					49.3	30.7
100.0	100.0	100.0	Total Liabilities & Net Worth					100.0	100.0
			INCOME DATA						
100.0	100.0	100.0	Net Sales					100.0	100.0
			Gross Profit						
81.7	87.7	89.5	Operating Expenses					88.5	86.0
18.3	12.3	10.5	Operating Profit					11.5	14.0
4.2	4.1	4.7	All Other Expenses (net)					.5	3.4
14.1	8.2	5.9	Profit Before Taxes					11.0	10.6
			RATIOS						
2.6	2.4	2.8						3.1	2.2
1.4	1.4	1.4	Current					1.4	1.4
.9	.9	.8						.6	.8
2.3	1.5	2.3						2.1	2.0
1.0	1.0	1.0	Quick					1.0	1.2
.5	.5	.4						.4	.4
5 70.9	12 31.5	23 15.7						28 13.1	24 15.1
48 7.6	37 9.8	38 9.6	Sales/Receivables					39 9.3	33 11.1
65 5.6	58 6.3	63 5.8						64 5.7	62 5.9
			Cost of Sales/Inventory						
			Cost of Sales/Payables						
5.4	5.6	4.7						3.0	6.9
19.1	13.0	11.4	Sales/Working Capital					19.1	18.3
-50.2	-123.2	-26.2						-11.2	-26.6
13.2	13.7	25.6						32.2	47.6
(46) 4.2	(40) 4.3	(35) 2.9	EBIT/Interest					(12) 2.9	(12) 7.8
1.4	1.6	1.5						1.1	2.2
5.3	3.1	5.9							
(13) 2.6	(12) 1.9	(10) 3.6	Net Profit + Depr., Dep., Amort./Cur. Mat. L/T/D						
1.7	1.6	1.5							
.6	.6	.3						.3	.3
1.7	1.8	1.5	Fixed/Worth					1.4	3.5
4.2	5.5	5.3						2.3	23.6
1.0	1.1	.8						.4	1.2
2.1	2.2	1.9	Debt/Worth					1.2	3.0
5.4	8.9	9.9						3.1	24.2
64.1	63.0	42.4						35.1	50.1
(48) 29.0	(41) 27.3	(41) 21.5	% Profit Before Taxes/Tangible Net Worth					(15) 23.0	(12) 33.7
16.8	4.1	1.4						4.3	13.5
21.9	20.8	19.8						24.5	16.2
9.0	7.5	4.8	% Profit Before Taxes/Total Assets					12.5	7.3
1.0	.5	.1						1.7	3.8
10.4	13.1	13.3						10.4	62.3
2.8	3.1	2.4	Sales/Net Fixed Assets					1.7	2.3
.8	1.1	.9						1.1	.6
2.3	2.3	1.9						1.4	4.0
1.2	1.4	.9	Sales/Total Assets					1.0	1.3
.6	.7	.5						.7	.5
2.3	2.2	2.5						2.5	
(46) 4.6	(42) 5.7	(39) 5.5	% Depr., Dep., Amort./Sales					(15) 8.9	
9.3	10.8	16.0						16.0	
1.4	1.8	.9							
(17) 2.8	(11) 2.6	(12) 2.8	% Officers', Directors' Owners' Comp/Sales						
8.6	8.4	5.9							
2737819M	1968024M	1732681M	Net Sales ($)	370M	14539M	19160M	29008M	234655M	1434949M
2711292M	1510684M	1677439M	Total Assets ($)	790M	65712M	15738M	25761M	261140M	1308298M

© RMA 2010

M = $ thousand   MM = $ million
See Pages 9 through 22 for Explanation of Ratios and Data

TRANSPORTATION—Motor Vehicle Towing   NAICS 488410

	Current Data Sorted by Assets						Comparative Historical Data	

Type of Statement

							7	6
			3	2	1	Unqualified	7	6
	1	3	2			Reviewed	8	1
4	6	5				Compiled	31	23
37	21	2				Tax Returns	49	51
11	12	5				Other	63	52
	19 (4/1-9/30/09)		3				4/1/05-3/31/06	4/1/06-3/31/07
			99 (10/1/09-3/31/10)				ALL	ALL
0-500M	500M-2MM	2-10MM	10-50MM	50-100MM	100-250MM	**NUMBER OF STATEMENTS**	158	133
52	40	15	8	2	1			
%	%	%	%	%	%	**ASSETS**	%	%
15.2	10.7	14.1				Cash & Equivalents	12.3	13.1
9.5	10.0	15.4				Trade Receivables (net)	12.1	11.9
5.9	7.7	7.9				Inventory	12.8	11.0
3.9	1.5	2.3				All Other Current	3.1	3.7
34.5	30.0	39.7				Total Current	40.3	39.7
45.0	49.0	48.4				Fixed Assets (net)	43.0	46.5
13.4	8.4	7.5				Intangibles (net)	7.8	6.1
7.1	12.6	4.4				All Other Non-Current	8.8	7.8
100.0	100.0	100.0				Total	100.0	100.0
						LIABILITIES		
20.5	5.4	9.9				Notes Payable-Short Term	9.5	7.6
11.4	7.9	11.2				Cur. Mat.-L.T.D.	7.1	6.6
6.6	7.1	10.5				Trade Payables	10.5	9.0
.1	.8	.0				Income Taxes Payable	.2	.1
15.4	6.2	5.5				All Other Current	8.3	12.5
53.9	27.3	37.2				Total Current	35.6	35.8
65.4	41.7	35.8				Long-Term Debt	39.5	39.6
.2	.2	.4				Deferred Taxes	.1	.1
20.6	6.1	3.0				All Other Non-Current	9.5	7.0
-40.1	24.7	23.6				Net Worth	15.2	17.5
100.0	100.0	100.0				Total Liabilities & Net Worth	100.0	100.0
						INCOME DATA		
100.0	100.0	100.0				Net Sales	100.0	100.0
						Gross Profit		
94.8	88.8	97.2				Operating Expenses	92.2	93.7
5.2	11.2	2.8				Operating Profit	7.8	6.3
2.0	4.6	3.3				All Other Expenses (net)	2.8	1.5
3.2	6.6	-.5				Profit Before Taxes	5.0	4.8
						RATIOS		
1.5	3.1	1.7					2.2	2.6
.8	1.6	.8				Current	1.2	1.3
.2	.5	.7					.7	.6
1.1	1.9	1.2					1.5	1.8
.5	1.1	.6				Quick	.7	.7
.1	.3	.2					.4	.3
0 UND	0 UND	11 32.8					1 482.6	1 382.4
0 UND	13 29.2	23 15.7				Sales/Receivables	8 47.0	10 38.3
14 26.4	28 13.0	45 8.1					28 12.9	22 16.4
						Cost of Sales/Inventory		
						Cost of Sales/Payables		
26.5	9.0	7.6					15.2	11.6
-97.3	36.2	-46.6				Sales/Working Capital	41.2	76.4
-9.8	-9.1	-7.9					-22.1	-21.8
6.0	4.5	3.9					11.8	7.7
(48) 2.0	(31) 1.7	(13) 1.4				EBIT/Interest	(138) 4.4	(115) 3.5
-.7	.2	.5					1.4	1.3
							3.1	
						Net Profit + Depr., Dep., Amort./Cur. Mat. L/T/D	(14) 2.0	
							1.3	
1.5	.5	.5					.6	.6
-9.9	2.5	2.2				Fixed/Worth	-2.1	2.4
-.5	-1.8	15.8					-14.3	-9.4
2.5	.5	1.1					1.2	1.2
-4.5	3.1	3.5				Debt/Worth	3.8	3.6
-1.8	-4.8	18.3					-10.7	-11.0
145.5	56.6	38.6					112.1	74.9
(23) 93.4	(29) 8.8	(13) 5.6				% Profit Before Taxes/Tangible Net Worth	(112) 50.2	(90) 39.7
-1.9	-6.0	-7.3					13.5	13.9
29.5	18.6	7.7					24.6	21.2
7.3	3.9	2.2				% Profit Before Taxes/Total Assets	10.3	8.5
-9.8	-2.0	-.7					1.4	1.1
26.6	12.0	17.9					21.9	21.2
11.0	5.2	3.2				Sales/Net Fixed Assets	8.0	6.2
4.0	2.2	1.8					2.7	3.1
6.4	3.6	2.6					4.9	4.8
3.9	2.1	1.7				Sales/Total Assets	2.5	2.8
2.4	.9	1.2					1.3	1.6
2.4	3.5	3.3					1.3	1.7
(33) 5.2	(31) 6.5	(12) 5.5				% Depr., Dep., Amort./Sales	(123) 3.7	(100) 4.7
9.4	13.1	14.3					6.5	8.7
2.4	3.6						2.3	2.5
(31) 6.3	(21) 5.4					% Officers', Directors' Owners' Comp/Sales	(65) 4.7	(66) 3.9
9.6	9.3						10.3	7.7
55484M	98384M	94089M	267210M	166167M	198321M	Net Sales ($)	2663382M	1170065M
13138M	42634M	52819M	146437M	146612M	132778M	Total Assets ($)	949418M	770175M

© RMA 2010

M = $ thousand   MM = $ million
See Pages 9 through 22 for Explanation of Ratios and Data

Comparative Historical Data | Current Data Sorted by Sales

4/1/07-3/31/08 ALL	4/1/08-3/31/09 ALL	4/1/09-3/31/10 ALL	Type of Statement	0-1MM	1-3MM	3-5MM	5-10MM	10-25MM	25MM & OVER
				19 (4/1-9/30/09)		99 (10/1/09-3/31/10)			
4	3	6	Unqualified	4	4	2	2	1	6
5	1	6	Reviewed			3	3	1	1
22	11	15	Compiled	29	22	5	4		
45	48	60	Tax Returns	9	12	2	5	2	1
37	21	31	Other			2			
113	**84**	**118**	**NUMBER OF STATEMENTS**	**42**	**38**	**12**	**14**	**4**	**8**
%	%	%	**ASSETS**	%	%	%	%	%	%
14.9	13.2	12.6	Cash & Equivalents	11.9	15.7	14.8	5.9		
12.2	11.6	10.9	Trade Receivables (net)	8.6	9.3	7.3	22.9		
10.4	10.3	7.0	Inventory	2.2	9.0	9.2	12.2		
3.5	3.7	2.9	All Other Current	3.5	1.8	4.4	2.3		
41.0	38.7	33.4	Total Current	26.3	35.8	35.7	43.3		
44.3	49.3	47.5	Fixed Assets (net)	53.5	42.0	49.2	48.0		
7.7	4.2	10.7	Intangibles (net)	13.0	12.5	4.0	.4		
7.1	7.8	8.4	All Other Non-Current	7.1	9.7	11.1	8.3		
100.0	100.0	100.0	Total	100.0	100.0	100.0	100.0		
			LIABILITIES						
9.7	18.5	12.4	Notes Payable-Short Term	20.1	10.7	3.4	10.5		
8.6	11.2	9.7	Cur. Mat.-L.T.D.	8.9	9.3	13.1	14.4		
9.6	9.3	7.6	Trade Payables	5.4	8.0	5.8	12.4		
.5	.3	.3	Income Taxes Payable	.1	.0	.2	2.2		
6.8	7.9	10.4	All Other Current	16.5	4.9	9.3	9.0		
35.2	47.3	40.5	Total Current	50.9	32.9	31.9	48.6		
39.4	41.7	51.3	Long-Term Debt	66.5	51.0	29.9	38.6		
.2	.2	.3	Deferred Taxes	.3	.0	1.2	.0		
7.5	4.8	12.5	All Other Non-Current	13.7	17.0	5.7	4.1		
17.7	6.0	-4.6	Net Worth	-31.5	-.9	31.3	8.7		
100.0	100.0	100.0	Total Liabilties & Net Worth	100.0	100.0	100.0	100.0		
			INCOME DATA						
100.0	100.0	100.0	Net Sales	100.0	100.0	100.0	100.0		
			Gross Profit						
92.7	95.5	93.1	Operating Expenses	88.8	94.7	97.3	96.5		
7.3	4.5	6.9	Operating Profit	11.2	5.3	2.7	3.5		
2.4	1.4	3.1	All Other Expenses (net)	7.0	1.2	.1	.5		
5.0	3.1	3.8	Profit Before Taxes	4.2	4.0	2.6	3.0		
			RATIOS						
2.5	2.8	1.9		1.4	2.5	3.1	2.4		
1.2	1.1	1.0	Current	.3	1.3	1.3	1.0		
.7	.5	.3		.2	.6	.6	.6		
1.6	1.4	1.7		1.2	1.8	1.9	1.4		
.8	.7	.6	Quick	.2	.8	.7	.7		
.3	.2	.2		.1	.3	.4	.2		
0 999.8	0 UND	0 UND		0 UND	0 UND	0 UND	19 19.0		
11 32.4	8 42.9	8 48.3	Sales/Receivables	0 UND	9 38.8	7 51.1	22 16.4		
26 13.9	24 15.5	25 14.9		17 21.3	25 14.5	20 17.9	39 9.4		
			Cost of Sales/Inventory						
			Cost of Sales/Payables						
10.6	13.1	17.1		25.7	11.5	6.9	17.4		
77.5	110.4	-807.8	Sales/Working Capital	-10.3	47.9	103.8	NM		
-20.2	-12.4	-9.6		-4.7	-21.6	-17.1	-6.9		
5.8	7.1	5.6		5.6	6.2	3.9	33.4		
(100) 2.4	(72) 1.6	(103) 1.7	EBIT/Interest	(33) 1.6	(34) 2.1	(11) 1.5	(13) 1.5		
1.1	-.2	.3		-.4	.4	-6.7	.9		
14.2		16.7							
(15) 1.7	(13) 1.7		Net Profit + Depr., Dep., Amort./Cur. Mat. L/T/D						
1.0		1.0							
.6	.7	1.0		1.8	1.0	.5	.3		
2.5	3.2	4.8	Fixed/Worth	140.0	9.5	1.9	1.7		
-14.2	-5.8	-1.1		-.7	-.8	23.0	4.9		
1.1	1.4	1.7		2.3	1.6	.4	1.1		
4.5	5.0	9.9	Debt/Worth	NM	34.8	2.1	2.3		
-11.9	-10.2	-2.9		-1.9	-2.2	41.0	8.2		
82.6	63.7	100.0		131.4	107.3	101.6	34.1		
(78) 23.6	(52) 22.9	(71) 18.1	% Profit Before Taxes/Tangible Net Worth	(21) 51.4	(22) 39.0	(10) 3.5	(12) 11.6		
7.8	.1	-4.3		-6.1	-4.4	-14.5	-.6		
18.0	24.6	19.2		20.5	22.2	36.1	19.4		
6.4	5.1	4.6	% Profit Before Taxes/Total Assets	4.3	7.7	2.5	3.1		
1.9	-4.6	-2.4		-5.3	-1.7	-6.0	.3		
29.5	16.2	19.3		14.7	26.2	12.4	20.3		
6.6	6.3	6.0	Sales/Net Fixed Assets	4.4	8.5	9.2	5.6		
3.4	3.3	3.0		1.6	3.4	4.0	2.9		
3.8	4.5	4.2		4.2	5.5	4.6	3.9		
2.7	3.0	2.4	Sales/Total Assets	2.0	3.1	3.2	3.1		
1.7	1.8	1.5		.8	1.8	2.3	2.0		
1.9	2.1	2.9		4.0	2.4	2.7	2.9		
(93) 4.6	(69) 5.1	(87) 5.4	% Depr., Dep., Amort./Sales	(29) 6.9	(24) 6.1	(11) 5.2	(12) 4.3		
7.9	10.2	12.5		24.3	9.7	12.5	12.1		
2.4	2.5	2.6		4.0	2.7	2.0			
(59) 4.1	(43) 4.2	(57) 5.4	% Officers', Directors' Owners' Comp/Sales	(19) 8.2	(22) 5.7	(10) 3.7			
9.0	7.6	9.4		11.8	7.9	7.5			
1320074M	629495M	879655M	Net Sales ($)	19902M	68093M	45646M	89714M	76841M	579459M
626677M	339352M	534418M	Total Assets ($)	17589M	29717M	15540M	41705M	41487M	388380M

© RMA 2010

M = $ thousand   MM = $ million
See Pages 9 through 22 for Explanation of Ratios and Data

TRANSPORTATION—Other Support Activities for Road Transportation   NAICS 488490

| Current Data Sorted by Assets | | | | | | | Comparative Historical Data | |

Type of Statement

							Type of Statement		
1	3	2	1		2		Unqualified	6	10
2	3	6	5				Reviewed	9	15
11	8	7					Compiled	13	4
4	7	4					Tax Returns	16	15
	9 (4/1-9/30/09)	10	9	1	1		Other	17	22
			78 (10/1/09-3/31/10)					4/1/05- 3/31/06	4/1/06- 3/31/07
0-500M	500M-2MM	2-10MM	10-50MM	50-100MM	100-250MM			ALL	ALL
18	21	29	15	1	3		NUMBER OF STATEMENTS	61	66
%	%	%	%	%	%		ASSETS	%	%
37.3	12.5	13.5	11.1				Cash & Equivalents	11.7	9.6
11.7	29.1	17.9	12.9				Trade Receivables (net)	28.7	24.0
2.7	8.2	5.3	5.7				Inventory	9.2	8.7
4.6	8.3	3.2	5.5				All Other Current	2.8	3.9
56.4	58.0	39.9	35.2				Total Current	52.4	46.3
20.9	27.7	43.6	49.7				Fixed Assets (net)	35.0	42.0
11.6	6.0	7.8	6.0				Intangibles (net)	2.5	5.0
11.1	8.3	8.8	9.1				All Other Non-Current	10.1	6.7
100.0	100.0	100.0	100.0				Total	100.0	100.0
							LIABILITIES		
6.8	9.2	5.2	3.8				Notes Payable-Short Term	11.3	9.1
10.8	4.6	9.6	6.8				Cur. Mat.-L.T.D.	7.5	7.5
10.5	12.6	7.3	3.8				Trade Payables	13.3	15.5
.0	.0	.0	.0				Income Taxes Payable	.1	.1
16.6	7.0	6.2	8.9				All Other Current	8.9	10.0
44.8	33.4	28.3	23.3				Total Current	41.1	42.2
43.1	22.3	22.4	19.4				Long-Term Debt	26.2	23.0
.0	.0	.1	.1				Deferred Taxes	.1	.5
16.9	9.8	7.8	4.0				All Other Non-Current	4.9	4.7
-4.9	34.5	41.4	53.2				Net Worth	27.7	29.5
100.0	100.0	100.0	100.0				Total Liabilties & Net Worth	100.0	100.0
							INCOME DATA		
100.0	100.0	100.0	100.0				Net Sales	100.0	100.0
							Gross Profit		
88.7	92.1	86.0	81.8				Operating Expenses	89.7	91.0
11.3	7.9	14.0	18.2				Operating Profit	10.3	9.0
.8	2.5	3.4	6.6				All Other Expenses (net)	2.5	3.1
10.5	5.5	10.6	11.6				Profit Before Taxes	7.8	5.9
							RATIOS		
5.0	2.4	3.5	1.8					2.0	1.9
1.3	1.5	2.0	1.3				Current	1.3	1.1
.7	.9	.8	.5					.7	.7
3.0	2.1	3.3	1.5					1.6	1.5
1.3	1.3	1.1	.8				Quick	1.0	.8
.5	.7	.7	.3					.5	.4
0 UND	8 47.4	16 22.7	8 45.9					0 UND	0 UND
0 UND	33 10.9	33 11.1	27 13.5				Sales/Receivables	32 11.5	26 13.9
7 50.2	57 6.4	50 7.3	39 9.4					50 7.3	48 7.6
							Cost of Sales/Inventory		
							Cost of Sales/Payables		
18.6	6.5	4.8	6.0					11.8	11.0
65.7	29.2	10.0	33.9				Sales/Working Capital	27.3	96.5
-70.2	-34.7	-41.0	-7.5					-17.1	-17.8
20.4	11.0	19.4	12.6					11.7	9.0
(10) 2.8	(18) 2.7	(24) 3.7	(11) 6.4				EBIT/Interest	(54) 5.8	(51) 3.5
.8	-1.3	1.3	2.3					2.3	1.2
									6.3
							Net Profit + Depr., Dep., Amort./Cur. Mat. L/T/D		(14) 2.1
									1.2
.0	.1	.2	.4					.3	.4
.3	.3	1.6	1.6				Fixed/Worth	1.1	1.5
NM	NM	4.9	2.1					3.8	4.4
.7	.7	.5	.3					1.0	1.1
3.7	1.4	2.3	1.3				Debt/Worth	2.7	2.3
-1.9	NM	5.4	2.3					7.9	10.2
100.0	77.3	58.3	39.8					94.7	55.9
(11) 55.8	(16) 29.2	(25) 29.9	(14) 19.2				% Profit Before Taxes/Tangible Net Worth	(51) 32.6	(54) 25.2
-21.0	-.3	10.1	5.0					19.2	8.8
41.9	22.4	21.5	20.0					20.8	18.5
9.9	4.9	7.4	10.1				% Profit Before Taxes/Total Assets	11.1	6.0
-8.2	-6.6	2.2	3.1					3.2	1.5
UND	46.3	40.8	17.8					54.2	38.0
134.3	23.5	3.1	3.7				Sales/Net Fixed Assets	10.8	8.0
8.0	4.1	1.0	1.5					2.6	2.2
13.7	4.5	2.4	2.4					4.5	4.2
3.1	2.7	1.5	1.6				Sales/Total Assets	2.3	2.3
1.6	1.2	.7	.3					1.6	.9
	.9	.7	1.9					1.1	.7
	(14) 1.7	(24) 5.2	8.8				% Depr., Dep., Amort./Sales	(50) 3.1	(56) 3.3
	5.5	13.2	15.1					6.1	10.1
								2.0	1.6
							% Officers', Directors' Owners' Comp/Sales	(29) 4.3	(21) 3.5
								11.0	5.0
20586M	72362M	205128M	388033M	50439M	557047M		Net Sales ($)	1296516M	2453096M
3378M	22631M	127298M	259285M	82991M	346341M		Total Assets ($)	576277M	995234M

M = $ thousand   MM = $ million
See Pages 9 through 22 for Explanation of Ratios and Data

Comparative Historical Data

Current Data Sorted by Sales

			Type of Statement						
5	7	5	Unqualified		1		1		3
16	6	15	Reviewed	1		5	3	2	4
9	7	12	Compiled	1	6	1	2	2	
20	16	23	Tax Returns	10	5	3	5		
27	27	32	Other	6	8	3	3		7
4/1/07-3/31/08 ALL	4/1/08-3/31/09 ALL	4/1/09-3/31/10 ALL		0-1MM	9 (4/1-9/30/09) 1-3MM	3-5MM	78 (10/1/09-3/31/10) 5-10MM	10-25MM	25MM & OVER
77	63	87	NUMBER OF STATEMENTS	18	20	12	14	9	14
%	%	%	ASSETS	%	%	%	%	%	%
12.3	12.6	18.0	Cash & Equivalents	24.2	18.2	15.0	13.6		16.1
23.5	18.0	18.3	Trade Receivables (net)	4.3	18.0	13.0	33.6		17.1
7.4	5.6	5.5	Inventory	5.8	2.1	10.8	5.6		7.3
5.2	6.2	5.1	All Other Current	3.4	7.9	3.1	2.5		6.5
48.3	42.4	46.8	Total Current	37.7	46.1	41.8	55.4		46.9
39.2	43.3	36.0	Fixed Assets (net)	37.2	43.7	36.0	23.6		41.7
4.5	7.0	8.2	Intangibles (net)	10.6	2.9	5.5	14.1		8.0
8.1	7.3	8.9	All Other Non-Current	14.5	7.3	16.7	7.0		3.3
100.0	100.0	100.0	Total	100.0	100.0	100.0	100.0		100.0
			LIABILITIES						
9.9	9.9	6.0	Notes Payable-Short Term	2.3	7.2	8.6	6.7		4.1
7.7	7.0	7.9	Cur. Mat.-L.T.D.	10.6	10.2	5.6	2.4		6.8
8.8	8.4	8.5	Trade Payables	4.8	9.2	9.3	12.4		4.9
.2	.2	.0	Income Taxes Payable	.0	.0	.0	.1		.1
11.2	11.8	9.0	All Other Current	15.0	5.6	4.6	6.4		10.1
37.8	37.4	31.5	Total Current	32.7	32.3	28.2	27.9		26.1
26.0	27.5	26.1	Long-Term Debt	50.9	29.0	18.6	18.0		14.8
.6	.3	.1	Deferred Taxes	.0	.0	.2	.0		.2
12.0	4.9	9.3	All Other Non-Current	13.6	18.6	8.8	1.0		5.5
23.5	29.9	33.0	Net Worth	2.7	20.2	44.2	53.0		53.5
100.0	100.0	100.0	Total Liabilities & Net Worth	100.0	100.0	100.0	100.0		100.0
			INCOME DATA						
100.0	100.0	100.0	Net Sales	100.0	100.0	100.0	100.0		100.0
			Gross Profit						
89.3	91.7	87.8	Operating Expenses	73.2	89.0	90.9	95.8		93.0
10.7	8.3	12.2	Operating Profit	26.8	11.0	9.1	4.2		7.0
2.5	3.2	3.2	All Other Expenses (net)	8.1	2.9	2.5	.0		2.5
8.3	5.2	9.0	Profit Before Taxes	18.7	8.2	6.6	4.2		4.5
			RATIOS						
2.8	2.2	2.8		2.0	6.5	2.3	2.9		2.6
1.4	1.0	1.5	Current	1.1	1.8	1.2	1.9		1.6
.7	.5	.8		.5	.7	.9	1.4		1.0
1.8	2.0	2.4		2.0	6.4	1.5	2.8		1.9
1.0	.8	1.2	Quick	.8	1.3	.9	1.7		1.4
.4	.4	.6		.4	.5	.5	.8		.8
0 UND	7 55.7	1 293.0		0 UND	0 UND	9 40.3	24 15.0	17 21.2	
28 13.2	29 12.7	22 16.7	Sales/Receivables	0 UND	4 95.3	22 16.8	33 11.1	31 11.7	
48 7.5	41 8.9	41 8.9		13 28.2	59 6.2	41 9.0	40 9.0	48 7.7	
			Cost of Sales/Inventory						
			Cost of Sales/Payables						
6.9	8.7	5.9		2.3	4.7	6.1	5.9		3.8
26.0	243.9	24.4	Sales/Working Capital	NM	17.2	42.7	19.4		9.7
-15.5	-15.0	-37.4		-4.4	-16.8	-35.4	NM		NM
12.0	9.0	15.3		3.6	5.8	7.0	23.0		31.3
(60) 3.4	(48) 4.1	(67) 3.6	EBIT/Interest	(10) 2.2	(16) 2.4	(11) 4.9	(11) 5.5	(11) 6.6	
1.0	.0	1.2		.0	-2.4	-.3	2.4		-.6
12.0									
(11) 2.6			Net Profit + Depr., Dep., Amort./Cur. Mat. L/T/D						
1.8									
.2	.5	.1		.0	.2	.2	.1		.4
1.5	1.6	1.0	Fixed/Worth	.9	1.8	.6	.2		1.1
7.7	4.0	3.3		-2.4	7.6	2.7	1.7		1.8
.9	1.1	.5		1.1	.7	.4	.5		.3
2.4	2.2	1.6	Debt/Worth	3.0	2.4	1.4	1.2		1.1
15.1	8.7	8.8		-2.4	NM	5.5	3.2		2.5
65.9	43.4	58.3		80.1	83.5	37.4	50.4		37.0
(62) 26.1	(53) 17.0	(69) 27.0	% Profit Before Taxes/Tangible Net Worth	(11) 18.3	(15) 29.9	(10) 4.3	31.2	(12) 20.0	
2.9	-5.6	4.7		5.3	.6	-5.6	8.4		5.8
19.7	16.1	22.5		30.1	22.9	10.6	24.7		22.1
8.8	5.5	7.4	% Profit Before Taxes/Total Assets	4.8	6.6	3.2	9.1		10.4
-.2	-3.1	.5		-7.1	-8.2	-5.0	2.5		1.6
57.1	41.1	82.3		UND	76.2	45.7	161.1		10.2
11.1	5.9	8.7	Sales/Net Fixed Assets	13.3	4.0	11.0	35.4		4.0
2.2	1.1	2.0		1.0	.9	1.4	4.7		2.8
4.5	3.6	3.0		1.9	5.5	2.9	4.7		2.5
2.5	2.3	1.8	Sales/Total Assets	1.0	1.7	1.4	2.5		2.0
.9	.7	.9		.4	.6	.7	1.9		1.1
.8	1.2	1.0		2.4	1.2	1.3			1.9
(61) 3.8	(49) 3.7	(61) 4.1	% Depr., Dep., Amort./Sales	(10) 4.9	(13) 12.3	(10) 3.3		(11) 4.8	
10.9	11.0	12.4		19.8	17.8	12.3			10.3
2.0	2.5	1.7							
(26) 3.3	(17) 4.0	(25) 2.8	% Officers', Directors' Owners' Comp/Sales						
6.6	9.5	7.1							
856170M	1791648M	1293595M	Net Sales ($)	8120M	39212M	45743M	101318M	122963M	976239M
491334M	1264312M	841924M	Total Assets ($)	23733M	47391M	57802M	45604M	44185M	623209M

M = $ thousand   MM = $ million
See Pages 9 through 22 for Explanation of Ratios and Data

TRANSPORTATION—Freight Transportation Arrangement   NAICS 488510

Current Data Sorted by Assets   **Comparative Historical Data**

Type of Statement

	Current Data						Comparative Historical	
Unqualified		1	8	25	6	3	53	58
Reviewed	3	10	32	25			65	83
Compiled	7	17	22	3	1		58	66
Tax Returns	20	22	13			1	46	47
Other	15	53	61	46	7	12	139	131
		54 (4/1-9/30/09)		359 (10/1/09-3/31/10)			4/1/05-3/31/06	4/1/06-3/31/07
	0-500M	500M-2MM	2-10MM	10-50MM	50-100MM	100-250MM	ALL	ALL
NUMBER OF STATEMENTS	45	103	136	99	14	16	361	385
	%	%	%	%	%	%	%	%
ASSETS								
Cash & Equivalents	20.8	12.2	13.6	11.9	12.5	12.1	10.9	12.8
Trade Receivables (net)	46.3	50.5	52.4	44.3	38.3	34.5	50.6	49.2
Inventory	.0	.1	1.1	1.0	1.0	.3	1.5	1.4
All Other Current	6.9	7.1	5.4	8.5	8.8	11.0	6.2	6.1
Total Current	74.0	69.9	72.5	65.7	60.6	57.9	69.3	69.5
Fixed Assets (net)	11.4	17.3	15.8	21.0	15.6	28.8	19.5	18.6
Intangibles (net)	2.5	2.0	3.1	7.0	19.3	6.2	4.2	4.0
All Other Non-Current	12.1	10.8	8.6	6.4	4.5	7.1	7.0	7.8
Total	100.0	100.0	100.0	100.0	100.0	100.0	100.0	100.0
LIABILITIES								
Notes Payable-Short Term	17.7	14.5	11.1	9.9	2.8	6.7	10.4	11.0
Cur. Mat.-L.T.D.	1.0	6.8	2.0	2.5	1.4	3.3	2.9	3.0
Trade Payables	35.1	25.3	29.4	24.6	23.5	14.1	28.2	28.1
Income Taxes Payable	.0	.0	.3	.2	.2	.2	.3	.2
All Other Current	14.3	9.7	9.5	13.3	15.8	16.7	13.0	14.1
Total Current	68.1	56.4	52.2	50.4	43.6	41.1	54.8	56.4
Long-Term Debt	4.2	12.8	8.7	16.6	15.6	15.3	12.1	11.8
Deferred Taxes	.1	.1	.2	.8	.8	1.3	.5	.4
All Other Non-Current	8.7	3.1	5.0	3.0	4.0	1.2	4.8	3.7
Net Worth	19.0	27.6	33.9	29.2	35.9	41.0	27.8	27.7
Total Liabilities & Net Worth	100.0	100.0	100.0	100.0	100.0	100.0	100.0	100.0
INCOME DATA								
Net Sales	100.0	100.0	100.0	100.0	100.0	100.0	100.0	100.0
Gross Profit								
Operating Expenses	100.8	95.2	95.7	96.9	97.3	95.0	95.2	94.5
Operating Profit	-.8	4.8	4.3	3.1	2.7	5.0	4.8	5.5
All Other Expenses (net)	-.1	3.1	1.2	.7	2.2	1.1	.9	.7
Profit Before Taxes	-.7	1.8	3.1	2.5	.4	3.9	4.0	4.7
RATIOS								
Current	3.5	2.6	2.0	1.7	2.3	2.1	1.8	1.8
	1.2	1.4	1.4	1.3	1.3	1.5	1.2	1.2
	.7	.8	1.0	1.0	1.1	1.0	1.0	1.0
Quick	2.6	2.3	1.9	1.5	1.5	1.9	1.6	1.7
	1.2	1.2	1.3	1.2	1.1	1.2	1.1	1.2
	.7	.7	.9	.9	1.0	.7	.9	.9
Sales/Receivables	0 UND	24 15.2	31 11.6	33 11.1	37 9.8	28 12.9	26 14.1	27 13.3
	25 14.8	35 10.3	46 8.0	46 8.0	45 8.1	52 7.0	40 9.2	39 9.4
	53 6.9	54 6.8	63 5.8	62 5.9	60 6.1	84 4.3	54 6.7	56 6.5
Cost of Sales/Inventory								
Cost of Sales/Payables								
Sales/Working Capital	11.6	9.3	10.1	11.7	5.8	6.0	14.1	12.3
	76.3	29.4	23.1	22.3	25.3	9.2	33.3	32.3
	-48.7	-32.7	NM	239.9	304.3	NM	999.8	-409.6
EBIT/Interest	8.3	13.7	21.4	19.5	19.6	10.1	23.3	22.0
	(20) 1.8	(73) 2.6	(108) 4.9	(92) 4.0	(13) 7.5	(15) 7.1	(291) 5.9	(311) 6.0
	-18.6	-2.5	1.3	.7	.2	3.2	2.0	1.9
Net Profit + Depr., Dep., Amort./Cur. Mat. L/T/D			12.8	38.1			5.5	10.4
		(24) 2.2	(31) 3.5				(76) 2.8	(86) 3.7
		.8	.9				1.7	1.6
Fixed/Worth	.0	.0	.1	.1	.2	.1	.1	.1
	.2	.3	.2	.6	.9	.4	.5	.4
	2.7	2.0	1.4	2.3	NM	1.6	1.9	2.1
Debt/Worth	.8	.8	.9	1.1	1.3	.6	1.2	1.2
	5.8	1.9	2.1	3.0	3.0	1.9	3.2	3.1
	-44.1	11.0	5.6	7.2	NM	4.8	8.1	9.8
% Profit Before Taxes/Tangible Net Worth	80.1	39.1	52.1	52.3	65.0	49.2	71.7	75.1
	(30) 37.0	(85) 14.9	(118) 17.3	(88) 20.3	(11) 16.8	(15) 17.7	(314) 32.3	(329) 33.1
	-45.9	-11.5	3.9	3.1	-6.7	8.5	11.5	11.6
% Profit Before Taxes/Total Assets	30.1	17.9	17.6	13.6	10.0	13.2	18.6	18.6
	5.7	4.3	5.5	3.7	4.4	5.4	7.7	8.4
	-28.3	-3.3	.8	-.4	-2.3	3.5	1.9	2.2
Sales/Net Fixed Assets	UND	516.4	195.4	111.5	73.5	56.3	207.9	257.6
	299.9	65.0	45.1	26.9	39.2	11.9	55.1	52.3
	43.2	15.1	12.6	7.7	6.7	2.2	11.6	10.1
Sales/Total Assets	11.1	7.1	6.2	5.1	4.9	3.8	6.8	6.5
	7.1	4.5	4.0	3.1	2.5	1.8	4.5	4.3
	3.3	2.6	2.2	1.7	.9	1.0	2.2	1.9
% Depr., Dep., Amort./Sales	.2	.2	.2	.4	.3	.6	.2	.2
	(18) .6	(58) .8	(110) .6	(76) .8	(11) 1.0	(10) 2.1	(262) .6	(294) .5
	1.8	4.0	1.8	3.0	1.8	3.0	2.2	2.1
% Officers', Directors' Owners' Comp/Sales	3.9	2.0	1.0	.9			1.1	1.0
	(14) 5.6	(45) 4.9	(45) 2.0	(15) 1.2			(123) 2.1	(104) 2.0
	12.1	14.7	6.4				4.1	3.7
Net Sales ($)	84345M	617316M	2855494M	7251265M	2854173M	10028594M	17679755M	18386786M
Total Assets ($)	10923M	116520M	680694M	2189021M	995165M	2546549M	5420085M	6472929M

M = $ thousand   MM = $ million
See Pages 9 through 22 for Explanation of Ratios and Data

Comparative Historical Data | Current Data Sorted by Sales

Type of Statement

			Type of Statement	0-1MM	1-3MM	3-5MM	5-10MM	10-25MM	25MM & OVER
48	41	43	Unqualified		1		1	4	37
92	77	70	Reviewed	2	4	4	6	20	34
69	62	50	Compiled	9	6	4	9	11	11
73	67	56	Tax Returns	15	11	11	10	7	2
154	196	194	Other	6	24	17	26	47	74

4/1/07-3/31/08 ALL	4/1/08-3/31/09 ALL	4/1/09-3/31/10 ALL		54 (4/1-9/30/09)			359 (10/1/09-3/31/10)		
436	443	413	NUMBER OF STATEMENTS	32	46	36	52	89	158
%	%	%	ASSETS	%	%	%	%	%	%
12.4	13.8	13.5	Cash & Equivalents	16.4	13.7	9.8	18.0	13.0	12.5
51.0	48.2	48.1	Trade Receivables (net)	25.9	52.0	49.3	45.1	51.9	50.1
.7	.6	.7	Inventory	.0	.0	.4	.5	.5	1.3
5.5	5.9	7.1	All Other Current	5.6	5.6	6.1	7.7	7.1	7.8
69.6	68.6	69.4	Total Current	47.9	71.2	65.5	71.3	72.6	71.7
19.1	18.3	17.4	Fixed Assets (net)	36.7	14.9	16.5	13.9	17.2	15.7
4.0	4.5	4.4	Intangibles (net)	2.3	2.5	3.5	5.3	2.3	6.4
7.3	8.6	8.8	All Other Non-Current	13.0	11.4	14.5	9.5	7.9	6.1
100.0	100.0	100.0	Total	100.0	100.0	100.0	100.0	100.0	100.0
			LIABILITIES						
10.8	12.6	11.9	Notes Payable-Short Term	9.0	18.6	13.0	11.7	11.6	10.6
3.9	3.8	3.2	Cur. Mat.-L.T.D.	2.5	3.1	3.5	1.9	5.9	2.2
29.2	29.3	27.1	Trade Payables	15.6	30.3	24.5	27.9	27.4	28.6
.3	.2	.1	Income Taxes Payable	.0	.0	.0	.1	.2	.2
10.0	12.8	11.5	All Other Current	8.5	15.0	4.4	10.6	9.6	14.0
54.1	58.8	53.8	Total Current	35.5	67.1	45.4	52.3	54.7	55.6
14.2	10.7	11.6	Long-Term Debt	22.4	7.8	11.3	5.2	12.7	12.1
.3	.4	.4	Deferred Taxes	.0	.1	.1	.3	.2	.7
4.5	4.0	4.3	All Other Non-Current	10.2	3.4	9.7	4.1	3.3	2.7
26.9	26.1	29.9	Net Worth	31.9	21.6	33.6	38.1	29.2	28.9
100.0	100.0	100.0	Total Liabilities & Net Worth	100.0	100.0	100.0	100.0	100.0	100.0
			INCOME DATA						
100.0	100.0	100.0	Net Sales	100.0	100.0	100.0	100.0	100.0	100.0
			Gross Profit						
94.9	95.2	96.4	Operating Expenses	84.9	98.6	96.1	98.9	96.7	97.3
5.1	4.8	3.6	Operating Profit	15.1	1.4	3.9	1.1	3.3	2.7
1.1	.8	1.4	All Other Expenses (net)	14.5	-.4	.2	.2	.4	.6
4.0	4.0	2.1	Profit Before Taxes	.5	1.8	3.7	.9	2.8	2.2
			RATIOS						
1.8	1.7	2.1		2.4	2.1	4.0	2.8	2.3	1.7
1.3	1.3	1.3	Current	1.2	1.2	1.4	1.5	1.4	1.3
1.0	.9	1.0		.7	.7	.8	.8	1.0	1.0
1.6	1.6	1.8		2.3	2.0	3.3	2.3	1.8	1.5
1.2	1.1	1.2	Quick	1.2	1.2	1.3	1.3	1.3	1.2
.9	.8	.8		.7	.7	.7	.7	.9	.9

Sales/Receivables

28	12.9	23	16.2	28	12.8		0 UND	25	14.8	24	15.1	28	12.9	31	11.9	31	11.9
41	8.9	35	10.5	40	9.1	Sales/Receivables	6 57.9	36	10.2	39	9.5	37	9.8	42	8.8	44	8.3
57	6.4	52	7.0	61	6.0		100 3.7	82	4.4	63	5.8	58	6.3	61	6.0	58	6.3

Cost of Sales/Inventory (no data)

Cost of Sales/Payables (no data)

			Sales/Working Capital						
12.0	14.8	9.9		5.0	9.5	6.7	8.1	10.7	12.3
30.0	36.3	26.7	Sales/Working Capital	79.2	30.5	16.2	24.1	26.7	26.4
-459.8	-107.9	-261.6		-11.0	-20.5	-64.7	-62.0	171.2	334.2

15.8		19.0		17.0		EBIT/Interest	10.3		3.5		14.2		15.5		18.8		21.3
(348)	4.9	(360)	6.0	(321)	4.1	EBIT/Interest	(11)	3.9	(30)	.9	(27)	6.4	(40)	1.5	(71)	4.6	(142)	6.3
	1.5		1.6		.5			-18.0		-10.9		.9		-15.9		1.6		1.3

7.0		12.1		19.5		Net Profit + Depr., Dep., Amort./Cur. Mat. L/T/D										7.1		38.6
(79)	2.6	(89)	4.0	(65)	3.5									(12)	2.2	(45)	6.2
	.8		1.4		.9											1.3		1.4

.1	.1	.1	Fixed/Worth	.0	.0	.0	.1	.1	.1
.4	.4	.3		.7	.3	.4	.2	.2	.4
2.1	1.7	1.8		2.6	19.3	2.5	1.3	1.7	1.6

1.1	1.1	1.0	Debt/Worth	.7	1.0	.8	.7	.8	1.2
2.8	2.7	2.6		2.9	3.5	2.5	1.2	2.6	2.8
11.2	10.1	8.3		16.9	-64.5	6.4	8.3	5.9	7.3

69.6		68.0		52.4		% Profit Before Taxes/Tangible Net Worth	23.8		63.8		59.3		31.3		48.6		63.9
(371)	29.1	(376)	25.7	(347)	18.1	% Profit Before Taxes/Tangible Net Worth	(27)	6.0	(32)	24.7	(30)	16.2	(42)	9.7	(79)	19.7	(137)	22.4
	9.2		9.3		2.0			-30.5		-16.2		4.7		-27.2		8.0		4.9

18.5	17.3	15.8	% Profit Before Taxes/Total Assets	8.7	22.8	19.1	16.2	17.1	14.8
6.8	6.9	4.9		1.8	.7	5.8	4.1	6.4	5.2
1.5	1.9	-1.3		-13.4	-13.5	.2	-7.4	1.6	.7

299.4	287.3	253.9	Sales/Net Fixed Assets	UND	512.5	382.4	353.4	244.7	188.8
61.9	62.3	50.8		9.9	53.7	32.4	43.1	94.3	55.0
11.1	15.0	12.2		.5	13.1	11.8	17.4	13.1	14.2

6.5	7.5	6.3	Sales/Total Assets	3.2	7.5	5.8	6.4	6.9	6.0
4.3	4.9	3.9		1.2	3.7	4.0	3.8	4.3	4.2
2.3	2.6	2.0		.3	2.0	1.7	3.0	2.1	2.3

.2		.2		.3		% Depr., Dep., Amort./Sales	1.8		.7		.5		.2		.2		.3
(307)	.6	(314)	.6	(283)	.8	% Depr., Dep., Amort./Sales	(17)	9.5	(20)	1.5	(22)	1.2	(34)	1.1	(69)	.7	(121)	.6
	2.5		2.0		2.4			29.3		4.6		2.2		3.1		2.2		1.4

1.3		1.3		1.3		% Officers', Directors' Owners' Comp/Sales			8.0		3.1		1.0		1.2		.9
(146)	2.5	(133)	2.7	(125)	3.3	% Officers', Directors' Owners' Comp/Sales			(20)	13.0	(15)	4.6	(20)	2.4	(29)	2.0	(35)	1.3
	5.3		6.3		7.9					18.7		5.7		5.5		4.9		4.8

19105539M	21198825M	23691187M	Net Sales ($)	15896M	91430M	141185M	382168M	1455930M	21604578M
6186957M	6494826M	6538872M	Total Assets ($)	28756M	31692M	58824M	121682M	544632M	5753286M

Current Data Sorted by Assets   Comparative Historical Data

© RMA 2010

0-500M	500M-2MM	2-10MM	10-50MM	50-100MM	100-250MM	Type of Statement	4/1/05-3/31/06 ALL	4/1/06-3/31/07 ALL
		1	2		1	Unqualified	12	11
	3	5	6			Reviewed	10	7
1	6	4		1		Compiled	6	8
5	5	3				Tax Returns	7	6
3	12	12	5	1		Other	16	22
	12 (4/1-9/30/09)		64 (10/1/09-3/31/10)					
9	26	25	13	2	1	NUMBER OF STATEMENTS	51	54
%	%	%	%	%	%	ASSETS	%	%
	16.1	9.2	8.9			Cash & Equivalents	10.3	9.1
	34.2	22.3	28.6			Trade Receivables (net)	28.5	37.6
	8.9	6.4	23.6			Inventory	10.6	9.6
	3.4	1.6	4.3			All Other Current	5.5	4.6
	62.5	39.6	65.3			Total Current	54.9	60.9
	21.5	45.4	23.1			Fixed Assets (net)	33.6	24.1
	6.2	1.7	8.1			Intangibles (net)	2.5	3.9
	9.7	13.3	3.4			All Other Non-Current	9.1	11.1
	100.0	100.0	100.0			Total	100.0	100.0
						LIABILITIES		
	6.7	28.6	12.0			Notes Payable-Short Term	8.3	13.1
	6.6	4.8	2.6			Cur. Mat.-L.T.D.	4.4	5.6
	14.8	9.4	19.1			Trade Payables	14.7	24.2
	.1	.0	.2			Income Taxes Payable	.4	.4
	18.1	13.2	7.8			All Other Current	13.4	18.8
	46.3	56.0	41.7			Total Current	41.2	62.1
	13.0	24.8	10.4			Long-Term Debt	21.6	14.5
	.3	.1	.6			Deferred Taxes	.0	.1
	3.8	2.4	3.8			All Other Non-Current	9.4	7.7
	36.6	16.7	43.6			Net Worth	27.8	15.5
	100.0	100.0	100.0			Total Liabilties & Net Worth	100.0	100.0
						INCOME DATA		
	100.0	100.0	100.0			Net Sales	100.0	100.0
						Gross Profit		
	93.1	86.7	93.9			Operating Expenses	93.6	94.8
	6.9	13.3	6.1			Operating Profit	6.4	5.2
	.4	5.7	.6			All Other Expenses (net)	1.6	1.1
	6.4	7.6	5.5			Profit Before Taxes	4.8	4.1
						RATIOS		
	4.2	2.4	2.0				2.1	2.0
	1.4	1.4	1.5			Current	1.3	1.2
	1.0	.7	1.3				.9	.8
	3.4	2.0	1.6				1.4	1.4
	1.3	1.3	1.1			Quick	.8	.9
	.7	.5	.4				.5	.5
32	11.5	24 15.0	13 27.1			Sales/Receivables	25 14.5	33 11.0
48	7.6	41 8.9	47 7.7				44 8.4	52 7.1
59	6.2	62 5.9	70 5.2				57 6.4	68 5.4
						Cost of Sales/Inventory		
						Cost of Sales/Payables		
	5.6	8.0	4.2			Sales/Working Capital	8.0	7.8
	13.0	20.0	10.2				21.4	31.0
	NM	-15.0	25.9				-60.9	-41.0
	18.9	25.1	21.2			EBIT/Interest	31.4	10.0
(21)	7.5	(20) 4.4	(12) 7.7				(44) 2.6	(48) 4.5
	1.3	1.5	1.7				.4	1.3
						Net Profit + Depr., Dep., Amort./Cur. Mat. L/T/D	51.9	10.3
							(13) 1.4	(10) 3.4
							.5	2.1
	.3	.6	.2			Fixed/Worth	.3	.2
	.5	1.8	.9				1.1	.7
	2.1	5.7	1.5				9.3	2.4
	.5	.6	.9			Debt/Worth	.9	1.1
	1.7	2.4	1.9				2.5	2.9
	174.1	8.5	3.3				15.7	31.0
	55.1	50.1	52.9			% Profit Before Taxes/Tangible Net Worth	60.7	67.1
(21)	17.8	(21) 29.6	(11) 20.4				(41) 22.7	(42) 26.4
	.7	17.5	6.9				4.5	11.2
	19.4	18.4	20.1			% Profit Before Taxes/Total Assets	27.2	16.9
	5.2	9.6	8.6				3.9	8.7
	-.1	3.2	1.9				-1.6	1.6
	33.9	10.0	35.5			Sales/Net Fixed Assets	32.0	40.9
	15.7	3.9	14.3				11.7	16.1
	10.6	2.2	7.0				5.0	5.6
	3.7	2.9	3.0			Sales/Total Assets	3.6	3.4
	2.9	1.7	2.4				2.7	2.5
	2.1	1.1	1.6				1.6	1.7
	1.0	1.6	.8			% Depr., Dep., Amort./Sales	1.0	.8
(18)	2.0	(22) 3.3	1.3				(47) 1.9	(44) 1.8
	2.9	6.3	2.9				3.9	4.7
	3.6					% Officers', Directors' Owners' Comp/Sales	1.7	1.6
(11)	4.9						(20) 5.7	(20) 4.5
	8.1						10.2	11.7
10060M	97076M	219522M	856682M	334677M	59258M	Net Sales ($)	1327867M	1539815M
2532M	31749M	114148M	269575M	129985M	126633M	Total Assets ($)	537120M	749625M

Comparative Historical Data   Current Data Sorted by Sales

H1	H2	H3	Type of Statement	0-1MM	1-3MM	3-5MM	5-10MM	10-25MM	25MM & OVER
11	8	4	Unqualified				2		2
12	15	15	Reviewed	1	1	2	5	2	5
6	15	11	Compiled		2	2	4	2	
3	7	13	Tax Returns	5	4	3	1		
30	10	33	Other	4	6	7	5	4	7
4/1/07-3/31/08 ALL	4/1/08-3/31/09 ALL	4/1/09-3/31/10 ALL		12 (4/1-9/30/09)			64 (10/1/09-3/31/10)		
62	55	76	**NUMBER OF STATEMENTS**	10	13	14	17	8	14
%	%	%	**ASSETS**	%	%	%	%	%	%
7.9	14.1	12.4	Cash & Equivalents	4.7	17.3	14.5	11.1		14.3
37.6	31.3	29.7	Trade Receivables (net)	27.3	24.1	38.6	28.0		31.4
10.1	9.7	11.4	Inventory	13.7	6.6	7.8	2.5		22.3
4.4	5.0	2.6	All Other Current	1.5	4.4	1.8	1.9		3.2
59.9	60.0	56.1	Total Current	47.3	52.4	62.7	43.5		71.3
24.9	24.1	28.5	Fixed Assets (net)	26.8	35.8	17.3	38.0		19.7
6.3	3.9	4.8	Intangibles (net)	.1	6.1	9.0	4.5		5.9
8.8	11.9	10.6	All Other Non-Current	25.8	5.7	11.1	14.0		3.2
100.0	100.0	100.0	Total	100.0	100.0	100.0	100.0		100.0
			LIABILITIES						
9.1	9.6	16.9	Notes Payable-Short Term	16.7	48.0	11.7	5.6		10.4
2.9	2.1	4.3	Cur. Mat.-L.T.D.	8.0	4.2	4.9	3.9		1.5
21.5	20.1	14.8	Trade Payables	20.9	10.6	13.1	12.2		19.7
.3	.6	.1	Income Taxes Payable	.0	.1	.0	.1		.2
9.3	9.5	13.7	All Other Current	9.9	24.1	20.3	10.1		8.4
43.1	41.9	49.8	Total Current	55.5	87.0	50.0	31.9		40.3
18.2	14.1	14.9	Long-Term Debt	14.1	13.5	12.4	23.4		6.7
.2	.3	.3	Deferred Taxes	.0	.5	.1	.0		.7
4.5	3.5	2.9	All Other Non-Current	6.9	.8	1.7	2.9		3.5
33.9	40.1	32.2	Net Worth	23.4	-1.9	35.9	41.9		48.8
100.0	100.0	100.0	Total Liabilities & Net Worth	100.0	100.0	100.0	100.0		100.0
			INCOME DATA						
100.0	100.0	100.0	Net Sales	100.0	100.0	100.0	100.0		100.0
			Gross Profit						
92.9	92.7	90.6	Operating Expenses	81.6	86.9	94.0	92.7		92.8
7.1	7.3	9.4	Operating Profit	18.4	13.1	6.0	7.3		7.2
.8	.8	2.4	All Other Expenses (net)	9.0	3.6	.2	2.2		.2
6.2	6.5	7.0	Profit Before Taxes	9.4	9.6	5.8	5.2		7.0
			RATIOS						
2.3	2.6	2.6	Current	8.1	4.2	3.2	3.1		2.9
1.4	1.6	1.4		.8	1.3	1.5	1.7		1.6
1.0	1.1	.9		.4	.6	.8	1.2		1.3
1.9	2.1	2.4	Quick	3.0	3.6	2.8	2.8		1.9
1.0	1.3	1.3		.6	1.0	1.2	1.5		1.3
.7	.8	.6		.3	.5	.7	.9		.6
34 10.8	23 15.9	29 12.7	Sales/Receivables	0 UND	29 12.5	35 10.5	31 11.7	18 20.2	
50 7.4	38 9.6	45 8.0		59 6.2	38 9.6	49 7.5	44 8.4	45 8.0	
63 5.8	55 6.6	61 6.0		81 4.5	63 5.8	67 5.4	58 6.3	61 6.0	
			Cost of Sales/Inventory						
			Cost of Sales/Payables						
6.3	6.1	6.3	Sales/Working Capital	5.1	8.1	5.4	6.3		3.3
15.6	12.6	15.5		-20.4	20.4	23.6	15.6		8.4
NM	249.1	-51.0		-7.7	-6.6	-33.2	30.4		25.7
8.0	23.4	21.0	EBIT/Interest		17.1	23.7	15.1		35.9
(48) 5.5	(43) 5.6	(59) 5.0			(10) 10.4	(12) 3.7	(14) 3.4	(12) 15.6	
2.9	1.7	1.3			-.6	1.0	1.2		3.3
7.7	8.4	4.2	Net Profit + Depr., Dep., Amort./Cur. Mat. L/T/D						
(10) 4.2	(11) 3.9	(12) 1.9							
2.6	1.8	1.1							
.2	.1	.3	Fixed/Worth	.0	.4	.3	.4		.1
.7	.5	.8		2.4	.8	.5	1.8		.3
2.6	1.4	2.4		NM	2.2	-4.7	4.2		1.0
.7	.6	.7	Debt/Worth	.9	.5	.5	.6		.6
2.3	1.0	1.9		6.6	2.1	1.9	1.8		1.3
9.0	2.7	8.1		NM	NM	-17.6	5.8		2.3
77.0	66.4	56.6	% Profit Before Taxes/Tangible Net Worth		206.7	98.1	36.5		63.7
(53) 28.1	(48) 30.5	(64) 27.5		(10) 24.3	(10) 19.7	(15) 19.5	(13) 27.9		
17.1	4.7	7.8			2.7	-13.0	-1.3		10.5
20.9	30.8	19.4	% Profit Before Taxes/Total Assets	27.2	19.9	16.3	13.3		19.0
12.0	11.4	8.0		5.3	14.1	3.8	6.5		10.8
4.5	2.1	2.2		-3.8	2.2	-2.5	.8		3.2
65.4	72.8	31.7	Sales/Net Fixed Assets	UND	69.3	33.9	16.9		42.6
14.9	16.9	12.1		32.1	5.6	16.4	7.2		29.3
5.6	7.9	5.1		2.0	1.9	12.4	2.3		7.0
3.4	4.7	3.5	Sales/Total Assets	3.4	2.8	3.6	3.7		3.4
2.7	2.9	2.5		1.8	1.7	2.9	2.1		2.7
1.9	2.0	1.3		.2	1.0	2.3	1.2		1.8
.5	.6	.9	% Depr., Dep., Amort./Sales		1.2	1.1	1.2		.7
(52) 1.0	(44) 1.2	(58) 2.1		(10) 3.6	(10) 2.0	(13) 2.4	(12) .8		
2.8	2.6	3.8			17.9	2.7	4.7		2.6
1.5	1.9	1.8	% Officers', Directors' Owners' Comp/Sales						
(24) 2.8	(26) 4.3	(25) 4.6							
5.4	8.3	7.2							
3308363M	2140662M	1577275M	Net Sales ($)	4582M	26395M	55481M	128466M	121470M	1240881M
1367162M	1009503M	674622M	Total Assets ($)	5715M	19896M	20867M	76836M	53702M	497606M

M = $ thousand   MM = $ million
See Pages 9 through 22 for Explanation of Ratios and Data

Current Data Sorted by Assets

Comparative Historical Data

						Type of Statement		
	1	4	11	3	4	Unqualified	19	29
1	4	7	5			Reviewed	23	20
3	1	9	1	1		Compiled	18	22
9	17	1				Tax Returns	24	20
9	10	20	6	2	1	Other	63	43
	15 (4/1-9/30/09)		115 (10/1/09-3/31/10)				4/1/05-3/31/06	4/1/06-3/31/07
0-500M	500M-2MM	2-10MM	10-50MM	50-100MM	100-250MM		ALL	ALL
22	33	41	23	6	5	NUMBER OF STATEMENTS	147	134
%	%	%	%	%	%	ASSETS	%	%
23.2	24.4	9.5	13.0			Cash & Equivalents	10.7	11.5
29.4	27.5	34.5	28.2			Trade Receivables (net)	29.6	30.1
5.5	2.6	7.3	8.5			Inventory	5.2	5.7
5.3	3.2	6.6	5.6			All Other Current	3.9	4.3
63.4	57.8	57.9	55.3			Total Current	49.3	51.6
25.3	27.1	32.1	32.6			Fixed Assets (net)	38.3	37.3
4.0	6.1	3.4	6.2			Intangibles (net)	5.4	4.3
7.3	9.1	6.6	6.0			All Other Non-Current	7.0	6.8
100.0	100.0	100.0	100.0			Total	100.0	100.0
						LIABILITIES		
6.6	5.6	8.9	5.7			Notes Payable-Short Term	10.2	7.6
4.5	7.2	3.3	2.8			Cur. Mat.-L.T.D.	8.2	5.9
20.2	11.3	16.9	14.9			Trade Payables	12.3	11.4
.0	.0	.3	.2			Income Taxes Payable	.4	.2
6.9	17.1	8.7	19.4			All Other Current	13.0	15.4
38.2	41.3	38.0	42.9			Total Current	44.1	40.5
42.5	23.8	16.5	14.5			Long-Term Debt	26.6	20.5
.8	.0	.2	.9			Deferred Taxes	.9	.7
21.2	5.6	6.0	3.0			All Other Non-Current	6.1	5.5
-2.6	29.2	39.3	38.7			Net Worth	22.4	32.8
100.0	100.0	100.0	100.0			Total Liabilties & Net Worth	100.0	100.0
						INCOME DATA		
100.0	100.0	100.0	100.0			Net Sales	100.0	100.0
						Gross Profit		
97.2	92.5	88.0	93.3			Operating Expenses	92.2	91.7
2.8	7.5	12.0	6.7			Operating Profit	7.8	8.3
1.0	1.7	1.8	1.1			All Other Expenses (net)	2.1	1.6
1.9	5.7	10.1	5.6			Profit Before Taxes	5.7	6.7
						RATIOS		
5.1	3.4	2.5	2.8			Current	2.0	2.3
1.8	1.5	1.6	1.0				1.2	1.3
.9	.9	1.0	.9				.8	.8
4.2	3.3	2.3	2.6			Quick	1.6	1.7
1.7	1.4	1.2	.8				1.0	1.0
.9	.7	.6	.7				.6	.6
12 29.2	1 250.8	21 17.0	24 15.5			Sales/Receivables	20 18.7	14 26.7
27 13.4	28 13.0	33 10.9	35 10.4				39 9.3	32 11.3
50 7.3	47 7.8	70 5.2	43 8.4				54 6.8	53 6.9
						Cost of Sales/Inventory		
						Cost of Sales/Payables		
5.3	9.9	6.2	9.5			Sales/Working Capital	10.1	9.9
16.5	23.4	15.2	141.7				49.8	36.8
-194.6	-73.2	-999.8	-38.0				-21.9	-34.7
17.1	14.7	28.0	17.0			EBIT/Interest	8.3	12.5
(10) 3.3	(25) 5.6	(31) 5.1	(19) 9.1				(126) 4.1	(96) 3.7
-.6	.4	2.2	3.3				1.6	1.4
						Net Profit + Depr., Dep.,	4.2	4.5
						Amort./Cur. Mat. L/T/D	(23) 1.9	(25) 2.1
							1.0	1.0
.0	.2	.3	.4			Fixed/Worth	.5	.2
.9	.6	.7	.9				1.5	1.0
-.6	4.0	1.6	6.2				13.2	3.4
.5	.6	.6	.7			Debt/Worth	1.4	.9
2.0	1.8	1.3	2.4				3.8	2.2
-2.4	NM	4.6	311.7				64.2	7.2
27.3	63.7	93.6	74.3			% Profit Before Taxes/Tangible	71.3	62.0
(13) -7.7	(25) 32.5	(37) 41.5	(18) 24.4			Net Worth	(116) 31.0	(113) 29.7
-33.7	8.9	13.7	8.2				15.7	10.6
17.5	26.8	31.6	13.4			% Profit Before Taxes/Total	17.5	21.4
4.2	10.5	9.7	7.5			Assets	8.6	9.2
-13.0	3.8	3.2	2.1				2.5	2.2
UND	72.9	46.7	50.3			Sales/Net Fixed Assets	35.6	76.3
63.8	14.9	14.0	9.8				7.3	8.5
7.7	6.4	3.6	2.9				3.1	3.7
5.2	5.7	5.2	4.4			Sales/Total Assets	3.9	4.5
3.8	3.2	2.3	1.8				2.4	2.6
2.1	1.6	1.7	1.2				1.3	1.4
.6	.5	.6	.9			% Depr., Dep., Amort./Sales	1.1	.7
(10) 1.9	(21) 2.9	(34) 1.7	(19) 3.4				(119) 3.4	(101) 2.9
10.8	11.7	3.1	9.5				7.5	6.1
		2.2	1.0			% Officers', Directors'	1.5	1.5
	(17) 3.4	(14) 3.6				Owners' Comp/Sales	(39) 3.5	(32) 3.0
		7.0	6.2				7.0	9.7
26233M	161222M	724260M	1600867M	732359M	1283830M	Net Sales ($)	4431944M	7064537M
6542M	38784M	195427M	559349M	429615M	967006M	Total Assets ($)	2532607M	3130752M

M = $ thousand   MM = $ million
See Pages 9 through 22 for Explanation of Ratios and Data

Comparative Historical Data | | | Current Data Sorted by Sales

			Type of Statement						
14	28	23	Unqualified			1	2	2	18
15	20	17	Reviewed		2	1	4	5	5
11	16	15	Compiled	1	4	2	4	3	1
10	28	27	Tax Returns	7	10	4	5	1	
45	53	48	Other	8	6	7	5	8	14
4/1/07-3/31/08 ALL	4/1/08-3/31/09 ALL	4/1/09-3/31/10 ALL		0-1MM	1-3MM	3-5MM	5-10MM	10-25MM	25MM & OVER
				15 (4/1-9/30/09)			115 (10/1/09-3/31/10)		
95	145	130	NUMBER OF STATEMENTS	16	22	15	20	19	38
%	%	%	ASSETS	%	%	%	%	%	%
11.3	15.2	16.0	Cash & Equivalents	16.5	24.5	10.3	20.8	10.7	13.4
29.5	26.8	29.3	Trade Receivables (net)	14.7	26.4	44.2	29.4	35.3	28.0
7.2	5.2	5.6	Inventory	7.6	.5	1.8	10.6	8.5	5.1
3.6	3.5	5.0	All Other Current	3.2	3.0	4.6	2.9	7.1	7.3
51.5	50.7	56.0	Total Current	42.0	54.5	60.9	63.8	61.6	53.8
35.0	35.5	30.2	Fixed Assets (net)	44.4	32.8	26.2	27.4	25.9	27.8
6.7	6.8	6.4	Intangibles (net)	3.3	6.3	1.4	5.4	4.6	11.2
6.8	6.9	7.5	All Other Non-Current	10.3	6.4	11.5	3.4	7.8	7.2
100.0	100.0	100.0	Total	100.0	100.0	100.0	100.0	100.0	100.0
			LIABILITIES						
8.5	12.9	6.5	Notes Payable-Short Term	9.1	2.7	9.3	9.4	5.3	5.6
6.0	6.3	4.9	Cur. Mat.-L.T.D.	8.7	7.0	3.4	3.6	3.2	4.0
14.0	11.9	14.8	Trade Payables	14.7	10.1	13.6	15.0	17.1	16.7
.1	.4	.2	Income Taxes Payable	.0	.0	.0	.1	.2	.4
10.7	14.6	12.4	All Other Current	7.9	15.1	12.1	6.9	12.9	15.4
39.3	46.1	38.7	Total Current	40.4	34.9	38.5	35.0	38.7	42.1
21.3	25.7	23.1	Long-Term Debt	37.9	51.1	18.1	10.7	18.1	11.7
.9	.2	.4	Deferred Taxes	.0	.8	.1	.3	.2	.8
5.2	3.8	7.7	All Other Non-Current	15.3	14.7	8.3	5.9	2.7	3.7
33.4	24.1	30.1	Net Worth	6.3	-1.4	35.0	48.0	40.4	41.7
100.0	100.0	100.0	Total Liabilties & Net Worth	100.0	100.0	100.0	100.0	100.0	100.0
			INCOME DATA						
100.0	100.0	100.0	Net Sales	100.0	100.0	100.0	100.0	100.0	100.0
			Gross Profit						
91.7	94.6	92.0	Operating Expenses	88.2	93.2	88.8	91.4	94.8	93.2
8.3	5.4	8.0	Operating Profit	11.8	6.8	11.2	8.6	5.2	6.8
1.5	1.8	1.6	All Other Expenses (net)	6.0	1.6	1.9	.4	.4	.7
6.7	3.6	6.4	Profit Before Taxes	5.7	5.2	9.3	8.2	4.9	6.1
			RATIOS						
2.1	1.9	2.7		2.1	4.1	2.7	5.2	3.5	2.1
1.2	1.2	1.4	Current	.9	1.6	1.3	1.7	1.8	1.3
.9	.8	.9		.5	1.1	.8	1.2	1.0	.9
1.7	1.7	2.3		2.1	3.3	2.3	4.5	2.8	1.9
1.0	.9	1.2	Quick	.8	1.5	1.2	1.5	1.1	1.0
.6	.6	.7		.3	1.1	.7	.9	.6	.6
16 22.7	9 42.3	16 23.1		2 181.9	2 237.9	22 16.8	14 26.9	20 18.5	23 16.0
34 10.7	29 12.6	33 11.2	Sales/Receivables	36 10.1	24 15.1	39 9.4	31 11.8	48 7.5	32 11.5
48 7.5	47 7.8	53 6.9		60 6.1	51 7.1	79 4.6	52 7.0	63 5.8	42 8.7
			Cost of Sales/Inventory						
			Cost of Sales/Payables						
10.3	13.3	7.8		4.8	6.4	6.4	4.9	7.7	12.2
49.0	43.2	18.8	Sales/Working Capital	-137.8	16.0	17.0	13.0	15.2	28.7
-56.5	-41.2	-74.3		-2.8	101.6	-17.5	82.1	-999.8	-59.3
14.1	13.1	17.0			8.2	11.2	77.6	26.6	13.0
(79) 4.1	(114) 3.3	(94) 4.8	EBIT/Interest	(14) 3.8	(12) 5.3	(16) 27.5	(15) 5.8	(29) 4.3	
1.7	1.2	1.6		1.8	.1	3.4	2.3	1.3	
5.4	7.5	7.7							7.5
(22) 2.1	(21) 2.1	(18) 3.2	Net Profit + Depr., Dep., Amort./Cur. Mat. L/T/D					(11) 4.0	
1.5	1.4	1.4							1.6
.3	.4	.2		.6	.1	.1	.1	.1	.4
1.2	1.5	.9	Fixed/Worth	3.9	1.3	.9	.5	.7	.9
5.9	UND	3.6		-.7	-.6	-70.8	1.0	1.1	3.0
.8	1.1	.6		.8	.6	.5	.2	.6	.7
2.5	2.9	1.9	Debt/Worth	3.3	2.4	1.8	1.2	1.4	2.2
19.6	UND	42.1		-4.1	-2.3	-90.2	37.2	4.1	14.5
58.6	61.8	67.7		44.6	69.0	51.7	116.3	102.8	67.5
(76) 32.0	(109) 20.1	(101) 23.1	% Profit Before Taxes/Tangible Net Worth	(10) 12.5	(15) 14.9	(11) 16.5	(17) 43.3	(17) 52.0	(31) 21.8
10.9	5.1	7.1		-42.5	-7.7	10.0	17.9	14.8	8.6
19.4	14.4	17.9		12.6	26.7	24.6	37.4	30.5	13.8
9.0	5.9	8.7	% Profit Before Taxes/Total Assets	3.6	8.6	10.6	14.0	10.3	8.5
2.0	.7	1.7		-11.3	-2.2	2.2	4.1	1.4	2.1
72.3	77.3	66.5		76.4	118.8	108.6	108.9	64.3	43.1
8.5	12.3	13.9	Sales/Net Fixed Assets	5.4	9.8	14.0	39.4	14.0	22.8
3.6	3.4	3.7		.7	3.4	9.1	3.4	5.1	3.9
4.7	5.8	4.8		2.8	4.6	5.9	5.5	5.4	5.8
2.4	2.6	2.5	Sales/Total Assets	1.1	2.5	3.2	2.7	2.3	3.3
1.6	1.5	1.4		.5	1.4	1.4	1.7	1.9	1.5
.7	.9	.8			1.1		.1	.5	.7
(77) 2.9	(109) 2.7	(91) 2.2	% Depr., Dep., Amort./Sales	(13) 5.6		(14) 1.7	(16) 1.2	(30) 1.6	
6.1	7.4	5.9		12.0		3.3	3.2	5.6	
2.3	2.0	1.9			1.7				
(22) 3.4	(33) 3.9	(38) 4.0	% Officers', Directors' Owners' Comp/Sales		(13) 3.3				
5.8	7.2	6.7			6.1				
4052955M	5323990M	4528771M	Net Sales ($)	7175M	41171M	56945M	142675M	278591M	4002214M
1875802M	2327227M	2196723M	Total Assets ($)	12097M	22605M	57240M	74322M	126181M	1904278M

© RMA 2010   M = $ thousand   MM = $ million
See Pages 9 through 22 for Explanation of Ratios and Data

TRANSPORTATION—Couriers and Express Delivery Services NAICS 492110

Current Data Sorted by Assets   ## Comparative Historical Data

Type of Statement

0-500M	500M-2MM	2-10MM	10-50MM	50-100MM	100-250MM	Type of Statement	4/1/05-3/31/06 ALL	4/1/06-3/31/07 ALL
		2	6	2	2	Unqualified	12	9
	7	6	2			Reviewed	12	13
	5	8	1			Compiled	16	15
13	6	2				Tax Returns	13	19
7	15	17	10	2	2	Other	45	33
	8 (4/1-9/30/09)		107 (10/1/09-3/31/10)					
20	33	35	19	4	4	**NUMBER OF STATEMENTS**	98	89

ASSETS

0-500M %	500M-2MM %	2-10MM %	10-50MM %	50-100MM %	100-250MM %		4/1/05-3/31/06 ALL %	4/1/06-3/31/07 ALL %
23.7	10.2	7.8	11.8			Cash & Equivalents	9.2	11.2
23.1	39.2	40.5	27.4			Trade Receivables (net)	39.0	31.6
.8	.0	1.5	.5			Inventory	1.1	1.6
1.1	6.3	5.1	8.0			All Other Current	5.0	6.0
48.8	55.7	54.9	47.7			Total Current	54.3	50.4
24.3	24.1	30.3	29.3			Fixed Assets (net)	26.1	29.3
16.5	11.4	5.2	12.7			Intangibles (net)	9.5	9.5
10.6	8.8	9.6	10.2			All Other Non-Current	10.0	10.8
100.0	100.0	100.0	100.0			Total	100.0	100.0

LIABILITIES

0-500M	500M-2MM	2-10MM	10-50MM	50-100MM	100-250MM		ALL	ALL
20.8	18.4	16.8	5.9			Notes Payable-Short Term	14.8	14.8
8.0	5.1	4.5	4.7			Cur. Mat.-L.T.D.	5.3	11.9
10.1	14.5	10.7	7.7			Trade Payables	13.6	8.2
.0	.1	.4	.5			Income Taxes Payable	.2	.2
25.5	13.3	9.4	14.9			All Other Current	16.0	14.0
64.3	51.4	41.8	33.7			Total Current	49.9	49.1
32.6	20.1	19.4	15.8			Long-Term Debt	20.6	25.3
.0	.1	.5	1.8			Deferred Taxes	.9	.4
3.2	3.2	8.6	7.7			All Other Non-Current	5.3	8.3
-.2	25.3	29.7	40.9			Net Worth	23.3	16.9
100.0	100.0	100.0	100.0			Total Liabilities & Net Worth	100.0	100.0

INCOME DATA

0-500M	500M-2MM	2-10MM	10-50MM	50-100MM	100-250MM		ALL	ALL
100.0	100.0	100.0	100.0			Net Sales	100.0	100.0
						Gross Profit		
95.3	94.4	93.2	97.3			Operating Expenses	96.4	94.7
4.7	5.6	6.8	2.7			Operating Profit	3.6	5.3
.2	4.0	4.0	1.7			All Other Expenses (net)	.7	1.4
4.4	1.6	2.8	1.1			Profit Before Taxes	2.9	3.9

RATIOS

0-500M	500M-2MM	2-10MM	10-50MM	50-100MM	100-250MM		ALL	ALL
2.3	1.7	2.0	2.1			Current	1.9	2.2
1.0	1.0	1.3	1.4				1.2	1.2
.3	.7	.9	1.1				.9	.7
2.3	1.6	1.7	1.9			Quick	1.8	2.0
.9	.9	1.1	1.3				1.1	1.0
.3	.6	.7	.8				.6	.5
0 UND	16 22.7	23 16.0	30 12.3			Sales/Receivables	18 20.6	5 75.0
0 UND	28 13.1	37 10.0	37 10.0				33 11.1	27 13.5
27 13.7	36 10.3	46 8.0	48 7.6				44 8.3	38 9.5
						Cost of Sales/Inventory		
						Cost of Sales/Payables		
35.3	17.1	12.6	9.2			Sales/Working Capital	14.8	11.6
NM	299.3	47.3	25.9				81.7	67.3
-8.8	-32.4	-69.1	132.1				-88.0	-35.3
11.1	6.4	19.9	11.8			EBIT/Interest	9.6	14.5
(14) 4.7	(29) 2.8	(31) 8.4	(18) 3.5				(84) 3.4	(79) 5.0
.1	1.1	3.3	.4				.7	1.3
						Net Profit + Depr., Dep., Amort./Cur. Mat. L/T/D	9.1	6.5
							(18) 3.3	(14) 2.1
							1.1	.9
.3	.5	.1	.4			Fixed/Worth	.2	.3
2.0	1.8	.6	1.2				1.1	1.1
-.4	-5.3	5.4	2.5				16.5	-2.4
.6	1.6	1.2	1.1			Debt/Worth	1.2	1.0
NM	7.7	2.7	1.5				3.6	2.9
-1.9	-18.8	6.2	3.5				-50.2	-5.9
96.0	74.0	65.4	30.3			% Profit Before Taxes/Tangible Net Worth	74.2	78.7
(10) 43.9	(22) 28.8	(30) 35.6	(16) 10.7				(72) 32.2	(62) 36.2
-1.9	9.3	11.2	2.9				7.4	10.3
42.1	11.7	21.3	11.4			% Profit Before Taxes/Total Assets	21.5	27.8
12.5	4.3	14.2	2.5				7.0	9.1
-4.8	1.5	3.5	-1.2				-.5	-.4
460.0	112.9	137.9	31.0			Sales/Net Fixed Assets	88.0	89.7
47.9	28.5	29.9	19.5				31.2	27.8
20.2	11.0	4.3	3.0				11.6	5.8
14.2	7.1	5.9	3.6			Sales/Total Assets	6.5	6.9
8.1	5.8	4.2	2.4				4.6	4.5
4.7	3.3	2.1	1.4				2.4	2.4
	.9	.6	1.1			% Depr., Dep., Amort./Sales	.6	.7
	(21) 2.2	(27) 1.3	(16) 1.6				(77) 1.3	(69) 1.7
	5.3	3.6	7.8				3.5	4.8
7.4	2.7	1.9				% Officers', Directors' Owners' Comp/Sales	2.5	2.4
(12) 10.5	(15) 4.0	(13) 2.8					(40) 4.1	(40) 3.8
17.2	5.9	4.7					7.1	6.4
33370M	225480M	604306M	1277774M	790327M	2573368M	Net Sales ($)	3127542M	1773656M
4198M	42697M	149868M	453747M	242402M	461490M	Total Assets ($)	964124M	417481M

© RMA 2010

M = $ thousand   MM = $ million
See Pages 9 through 22 for Explanation of Ratios and Data

Comparative Historical Data | **Current Data Sorted by Sales**

4/1/07-3/31/08 ALL	4/1/08-3/31/09 ALL	4/1/09-3/31/10 ALL	Type of Statement	0-1MM	1-3MM	3-5MM	5-10MM	10-25MM	25MM & OVER
11	9	12	Unqualified				1	1	10
12	12	15	Reviewed			1	4	5	5
16	11	14	Compiled		1		7	4	2
16	16	21	Tax Returns	7	7	3	3	1	
35	20	53	Other	5	4	6	11	10	17
					8 (4/1-9/30/09)		107 (10/1/09-3/31/10)		
90	68	115	NUMBER OF STATEMENTS	12	12	10	26	21	34
%	%	%	**ASSETS**	%	%	%	%	%	%
9.9	8.7	12.9	Cash & Equivalents	17.3	18.8	15.2	7.9	17.2	9.7
32.5	33.3	34.3	Trade Receivables (net)	6.1	24.9	34.9	35.8	41.4	41.9
2.8	1.5	.7	Inventory	.1	1.2	.0	1.2	1.0	.3
4.6	6.3	5.1	All Other Current	2.4	1.0	4.5	8.1	3.8	6.2
49.8	49.9	53.0	Total Current	25.9	46.0	54.6	52.9	63.4	58.1
28.1	29.6	26.9	Fixed Assets (net)	39.5	30.7	28.2	30.6	18.4	23.2
11.5	9.9	11.0	Intangibles (net)	20.1	20.0	6.1	8.4	7.9	9.8
10.6	10.7	9.1	All Other Non-Current	14.4	3.4	11.1	8.0	10.3	8.9
100.0	100.0	100.0	Total	100.0	100.0	100.0	100.0	100.0	100.0
			LIABILITIES						
16.4	16.7	15.9	Notes Payable-Short Term	10.9	20.8	15.3	21.3	13.3	13.5
6.4	5.0	5.3	Cur. Mat.-L.T.D.	13.7	2.9	5.1	4.7	3.1	5.2
15.8	9.8	11.5	Trade Payables	4.4	9.9	10.3	10.5	15.6	13.2
.2	.1	.2	Income Taxes Payable	.0	.0	.0	.2	.9	.1
14.1	13.8	14.5	All Other Current	27.6	13.3	14.9	11.7	9.7	15.2
53.0	45.4	47.5	Total Current	56.6	46.9	45.6	48.5	42.7	47.2
20.3	18.2	21.2	Long-Term Debt	44.8	52.7	18.2	15.1	10.5	13.7
.8	.4	.6	Deferred Taxes	.0	.0	.0	.8		1.4
4.3	5.5	5.6	All Other Non-Current	.1	5.9	2.5	2.3	11.6	7.3
21.6	30.6	25.1	Net Worth	-1.7	-5.4	33.7	33.3	34.9	30.4
100.0	100.0	100.0	Total Liabilties & Net Worth	100.0	100.0	100.0	100.0	100.0	100.0
			INCOME DATA						
100.0	100.0	100.0	Net Sales	100.0	100.0	100.0	100.0	100.0	100.0
			Gross Profit						
95.6	95.2	94.7	Operating Expenses	81.0	89.9	96.5	97.8	97.0	96.8
4.4	4.8	5.3	Operating Profit	19.0	10.1	3.5	2.2	3.0	3.2
.7	1.8	2.8	All Other Expenses (net)	11.6	8.6	.7	.7	.9	1.0
3.8	3.0	2.6	Profit Before Taxes	7.4	1.5	2.8	1.5	2.0	2.3
			RATIOS						
1.7	1.8	2.0	Current	1.4	4.4	2.1	2.0	2.1	2.1
1.1	1.1	1.3		.6	1.1	1.1	1.1	1.4	1.3
.7	.8	.8		.3	.4	.9	.7	1.0	.9
1.4	1.5	1.7	Quick	1.4	4.3	1.5	1.6	1.9	1.8
.9	.9	1.0		.4	.9	1.0	.9	1.4	1.2
.5	.6	.7		.1	.3	.9	.5	.9	.9
14 25.9	14 25.7	14 25.8	Sales/Receivables	0 UND	0 UND	25 14.8	18 20.1	17 21.2	31 12.0
32 11.5	31 11.7	31 11.8		0 UND	0 UND	34 10.8	29 12.4	32 11.5	36 10.1
42 8.8	40 9.2	42 8.8		0 UND	30 12.2	44 8.3	45 8.1	44 8.3	46 8.0
			Cost of Sales/Inventory						
			Cost of Sales/Payables						
16.9	16.4	15.7	Sales/Working Capital	NM	30.9	14.5	11.0	14.8	12.5
196.2	264.1	51.8		-12.1	864.8	76.5	138.8	27.1	32.2
-27.6	-39.0	-47.8		-5.6	-44.6	-100.3	-32.6	-531.9	-153.0
12.7	10.0	11.4	EBIT/Interest				8.6	17.3	23.2
(84) 4.9	(57) 3.7	(99) 4.5					(24) 3.1	(17) 5.8	(32) 5.7
1.7	1.5	1.4					.8	1.7	2.9
5.1	3.9	7.1	Net Profit + Depr., Dep., Amort./Cur. Mat. L/T/D						7.3
(17) 2.7	(12) 2.5	(17) 2.8							(12) 2.6
.7	1.7	1.4							1.6
.3	.6	.3	Fixed/Worth	.3	1.8	.3	.4	.1	.4
1.4	1.4	1.2		4.2	-.8	1.3	1.2	.3	.9
22.8	UND	16.2		-.9	-.3	4.7	4.3	NM	5.0
1.2	.9	1.2	Debt/Worth	2.1	2.1	1.2	1.2	.7	1.1
3.5	3.1	3.3		NM	-4.1	3.0	3.2	2.6	2.1
NM	UND	-57.6		-1.6	-1.9	12.3	NM	NM	15.9
91.5	96.1	70.3	% Profit Before Taxes/Tangible Net Worth				40.0	69.9	68.8
(68) 40.2	(52) 31.0	(84) 28.7					(20) 18.3	(16) 28.6	(29) 31.2
15.8	3.0	5.3					4.1	6.8	5.4
21.7	19.3	17.4	% Profit Before Taxes/Total Assets	47.3	39.9	18.5	12.4	20.7	17.4
12.5	7.4	9.1		8.3	3.3	12.3	5.3	10.0	9.8
2.5	.0	1.4		-1.2	-9.6	4.9	-.4	1.8	1.8
103.8	84.9	110.2	Sales/Net Fixed Assets	284.6	405.9	101.4	130.7	124.3	64.9
39.4	22.8	28.5		18.2	31.7	24.8	21.6	51.3	29.9
6.3	5.3	7.5		1.1	18.6	4.8	7.1	14.4	7.2
7.1	6.6	7.0	Sales/Total Assets	5.4	14.2	7.3	6.5	7.1	6.1
4.7	4.7	4.5		3.4	8.1	2.9	4.4	5.6	3.9
2.2	2.5	2.2		.7	4.3	1.9	2.4	2.8	1.7
.6	.6	.7	% Depr., Dep., Amort./Sales				1.1	.4	.5
(65) 1.3	(48) 2.1	(78) 1.7					(19) 2.4	(14) 1.1	(26) 1.1
3.5	4.0	3.8					5.4	2.6	3.2
1.2	2.5	2.8	% Officers', Directors' Owners' Comp/Sales				2.3		
(35) 3.5	(23) 4.9	(44) 4.3					(12) 2.8		
7.4	12.1	9.2					5.1		
2387107M	2402521M	5504625M	Net Sales ($)	7109M	26085M	37875M	185299M	303937M	4944320M
678283M	638763M	1354402M	Total Assets ($)	8361M	5324M	13719M	63671M	109174M	1154153M

© RMA 2010   M = $ thousand   MM = $ million
See Pages 9 through 22 for Explanation of Ratios and Data

Current Data Sorted by Assets   Comparative Historical Data

Type of Statement	0-500M	500M-2MM	2-10MM	10-50MM	50-100MM	100-250MM	4/1/05-3/31/06 ALL	4/1/06-3/31/07 ALL
Unqualified		4	5	12	6	6	39	39
Reviewed	2	5	28	20	2	2	56	48
Compiled	3	17	21	4	2		59	67
Tax Returns	27	45	36	2		1	70	67
Other	10	32	57	26	5	2	108	108
		37 (4/1-9/30/09)		345 (10/1/09-3/31/10)				
NUMBER OF STATEMENTS	42	103	147	64	15	11	332	329
ASSETS	%	%	%	%	%	%	%	%
Cash & Equivalents	14.8	10.0	10.4	10.8	10.0	10.6	9.8	8.7
Trade Receivables (net)	19.2	22.3	17.1	13.0	18.4	16.2	21.3	20.6
Inventory	1.7	1.6	2.3	2.2	6.9	13.0	3.4	3.0
All Other Current	4.0	3.4	3.5	3.4	2.7	3.6	2.8	3.3
Total Current	39.7	37.3	33.4	29.4	38.0	43.4	37.3	35.6
Fixed Assets (net)	40.7	51.3	53.6	55.9	48.7	45.8	49.4	49.6
Intangibles (net)	5.7	3.3	4.2	5.7	3.2	6.8	3.1	4.4
All Other Non-Current	13.9	8.1	8.8	9.1	10.0	3.9	10.1	10.5
Total	100.0	100.0	100.0	100.0	100.0	100.0	100.0	100.0
LIABILITIES								
Notes Payable-Short Term	20.9	6.8	7.0	6.4	4.8	12.1	8.2	8.0
Cur. Mat.-L.T.D.	7.6	6.1	4.6	6.5	5.3	4.8	4.6	3.9
Trade Payables	5.8	10.9	6.7	4.7	8.8	5.4	10.6	10.0
Income Taxes Payable	.0	.1	.1	.6	.0	.4	.4	.2
All Other Current	19.3	10.5	7.0	5.3	6.4	9.3	9.8	9.2
Total Current	53.5	34.5	25.4	23.5	25.3	32.0	33.6	31.4
Long-Term Debt	26.3	41.2	40.9	36.9	37.5	34.7	34.9	33.0
Deferred Taxes	.0	.0	.2	.4	.5	.2	.4	.4
All Other Non-Current	26.3	3.7	4.7	4.4	7.3	1.6	4.6	4.5
Net Worth	-6.0	20.7	28.8	34.7	29.4	31.5	26.6	30.7
Total Liabilities & Net Worth	100.0	100.0	100.0	100.0	100.0	100.0	100.0	100.0
INCOME DATA								
Net Sales	100.0	100.0	100.0	100.0	100.0	100.0	100.0	100.0
Gross Profit								
Operating Expenses	89.5	83.8	83.5	86.5	87.8	89.8	83.5	84.8
Operating Profit	10.5	16.2	16.5	13.5	12.2	10.2	16.5	15.2
All Other Expenses (net)	2.5	7.2	9.2	8.5	8.0	4.9	6.3	6.1
Profit Before Taxes	8.0	9.0	7.3	5.0	4.2	5.4	10.3	9.1
RATIOS								
Current	3.9	2.1	2.3	2.5	2.4	1.8	2.2	2.2
	1.3	1.1	1.1	1.4	1.6	1.4	1.2	1.2
	.3	.5	.7	.9	.9	1.1	.7	.6
Quick	2.7	1.9	2.0	2.1	2.3	1.6	1.9	2.0
	1.2	.9	1.0	1.1	.9	1.2	(331) 1.0	.9
	.2	.5	.5	.6	.5	.8	.5	.4
Sales/Receivables	0 UND	0 UND	0 UND	18 20.1	18 20.0	40 9.1	0 UND	9 41.5
	1 600.8	23 15.7	31 11.7	39 9.3	36 10.1	53 6.9	33 11.0	31 11.9
	24 14.9	39 9.3	47 7.8	48 7.6	44 8.3	102 3.6	48 7.6	49 7.4
Cost of Sales/Inventory								
Cost of Sales/Payables								
Sales/Working Capital	13.7	12.7	6.4	4.8	5.7	8.9	8.1	7.9
	121.6	194.5	39.4	14.7	23.5	14.9	34.5	38.8
	-11.6	-9.2	-8.2	-26.4	-23.8	47.7	-16.1	-13.4
EBIT/Interest	20.3	11.2	7.8	7.4	9.1	5.5	12.4	10.8
	(23) 3.3	(73) 3.6	(113) 2.4	(53) 2.8	(13) 2.5	(10) 3.7	(249) 3.5	(252) 3.5
	.6	.8	1.0	1.1	1.7	1.5	1.9	1.5
Net Profit + Depr., Dep., Amort./Cur. Mat. L/T/D		4.9	3.4	5.0			4.2	4.9
		(11) 1.7	(24) 1.9	(24) 2.5			(56) 2.0	(64) 2.0
		.4	1.2	1.4			1.0	.9
Fixed/Worth	.1	.6	.7	.7	.7	1.2	.6	.5
	1.9	2.2	2.3	2.0	1.0	1.9	1.9	1.6
	-7.3	-223.0	-257.5	6.8	8.3	3.8	7.5	4.7
Debt/Worth	.6	.9	1.0	.8	1.4	1.2	1.0	.9
	6.5	2.9	2.9	1.9	5.0	2.1	2.7	2.3
	-3.9	-77.8	-309.1	13.1	9.8	13.4	14.4	7.3
% Profit Before Taxes/Tangible Net Worth	85.8	69.5	37.7	33.3	80.3	36.9	57.9	47.6
	(26) 14.9	(75) 21.5	(110) 15.1	(53) 14.1	(14) 15.9	(10) 21.8	(276) 26.6	(279) 19.0
	.0	7.3	3.5	6.1	6.6	11.6	9.3	5.3
% Profit Before Taxes/Total Assets	37.0	18.2	8.3	9.5	6.8	12.2	15.6	14.1
	4.6	6.6	4.6	3.4	6.2	5.9	7.0	6.2
	-3.9	-.4	.4	-.6	.1	2.2	1.8	.9
Sales/Net Fixed Assets	190.1	22.9	11.3	6.1	22.2	5.3	18.7	14.5
	18.8	5.6	1.5	1.7	1.6	2.3	4.4	3.8
	3.3	.4	.3	.5	.5	1.4	.5	.6
Sales/Total Assets	8.8	3.5	2.5	1.5	2.6	2.0	3.2	3.0
	2.6	2.0	.8	.9	.9	1.1	1.5	1.4
	1.1	.3	.3	.3	.3	.3	.4	.4
% Depr., Dep., Amort./Sales	1.9	1.4	2.0	2.8	2.2		1.7	2.0
	(26) 3.8	(86) 3.9	(128) 5.7	(59) 6.8	(12) 6.4		(292) 4.3	(284) 4.3
	13.7	11.4	15.0	11.3	9.4		10.3	9.8
% Officers', Directors' Owners' Comp/Sales	6.3	2.5	1.9	2.9			2.1	2.2
	(17) 12.4	(30) 5.1	(39) 3.7	(11) 5.0			(88) 4.5	(70) 4.8
	17.7	9.0	7.8	10.3			9.6	12.4
Net Sales ($)	49786M	289641M	1055333M	1629225M	1981952M	2693308M	5914032M	6522171M
Total Assets ($)	10456M	117686M	687058M	1328313M	1026254M	1759637M	3627011M	3955567M

M = $ thousand   MM = $ million
See Pages 9 through 22 for Explanation of Ratios and Data

Comparative Historical Data | Current Data Sorted by Sales

			Type of Statement						
31	32	33	Unqualified		3	1	5	8	16
45	62	59	Reviewed	5	11	4	10	18	11
67	56	47	Compiled	13	12	5	5	8	4
86	90	111	Tax Returns	64	26	9	7	4	1
117	133	132	Other	22	30	16	23	24	17
4/1/07-3/31/08 ALL	4/1/08-3/31/09 ALL	4/1/09-3/31/10 ALL		37 (4/1-9/30/09) 0-1MM	1-3MM	3-5MM	345 (10/1/09-3/31/10) 5-10MM	10-25MM	25MM & OVER
346	373	382	NUMBER OF STATEMENTS	104	82	35	50	62	49
%	%	%	ASSETS	%	%	%	%	%	%
12.1	10.1	10.8	Cash & Equivalents	5.9	11.3	12.4	9.1	17.6	12.6
18.4	16.8	18.1	Trade Receivables (net)	3.4	15.2	25.8	28.9	27.4	25.5
2.6	3.4	2.5	Inventory	.7	1.5	1.0	1.6	2.9	9.9
3.6	3.9	3.5	All Other Current	2.9	3.0	2.0	3.9	4.6	4.7
36.7	34.2	34.9	Total Current	12.9	31.1	41.2	43.5	52.5	52.7
49.5	52.6	51.5	Fixed Assets (net)	74.2	52.6	41.4	46.4	34.8	35.0
3.3	4.6	4.4	Intangibles (net)	4.6	5.0	4.8	2.2	3.7	5.8
10.4	8.5	9.1	All Other Non-Current	8.2	11.4	12.6	7.9	8.9	6.5
100.0	100.0	100.0	Total	100.0	100.0	100.0	100.0	100.0	100.0
			LIABILITIES						
7.6	6.3	8.4	Notes Payable-Short Term	10.0	8.3	5.8	8.8	6.6	9.2
4.4	4.2	5.7	Cur. Mat.-L.T.D.	3.8	10.3	4.6	3.9	4.9	5.4
8.5	6.7	7.4	Trade Payables	.8	5.9	9.9	13.2	12.3	10.1
.2	.1	.2	Income Taxes Payable	.0	.0	.3	.2	.2	.7
10.1	9.5	9.1	All Other Current	6.4	13.1	9.2	7.8	7.6	11.2
30.7	26.9	30.8	Total Current	21.1	37.6	29.8	33.9	31.7	36.6
35.4	43.5	38.4	Long-Term Debt	54.4	42.5	37.7	32.6	25.6	20.0
.3	.2	.2	Deferred Taxes	.1	.1	.1	.4	.4	.4
6.9	6.7	6.8	All Other Non-Current	10.8	3.3	1.9	10.0	4.4	7.0
26.7	22.7	23.9	Net Worth	13.6	16.6	30.5	23.1	38.0	36.0
100.0	100.0	100.0	Total Liabilites & Net Worth	100.0	100.0	100.0	100.0	100.0	100.0
			INCOME DATA						
100.0	100.0	100.0	Net Sales	100.0	100.0	100.0	100.0	100.0	100.0
			Gross Profit						
84.9	83.1	85.1	Operating Expenses	65.9	89.7	90.3	94.2	93.6	94.1
15.1	16.9	14.9	Operating Profit	34.1	10.3	9.7	5.8	6.4	5.9
6.8	8.0	7.7	All Other Expenses (net)	18.8	6.2	3.3	3.5	1.3	1.9
8.3	8.9	7.3	Profit Before Taxes	15.3	4.1	6.4	2.3	5.1	4.1
			RATIOS						
2.3	2.4	2.4		2.1	2.2	2.7	2.4	3.2	2.1
1.3	1.3	1.2	Current	.6	1.1	1.3	1.5	1.5	1.4
.7	.6	.6		.2	.4	.9	1.0	1.0	1.1
2.1	1.8	2.0		1.5	1.9	2.5	2.1	2.7	1.8
1.1	.9	1.0	Quick	.5	.8	1.2	1.2	1.3	1.1
.7	.4	.5		.2	.4	.8	.9	.9	.7
0 940.0	0 UND	0 UND		0 UND	6 60.2	16 23.2	25 14.8	27 13.4	33 11.0
29 12.4	27 13.7	28 13.0	Sales/Receivables	0 UND	27 13.8	37 9.9	39 9.4	39 9.4	42 8.8
51 7.1	42 8.7	45 8.1		2 160.6	44 8.3	52 7.0	46 7.9	54 6.7	52 7.0
			Cost of Sales/Inventory						
			Cost of Sales/Payables						
7.3	8.4	7.5		18.1	8.0	9.5	6.2	5.0	8.9
25.3	33.1	41.4	Sales/Working Capital	-13.8	56.2	25.5	31.8	13.0	22.3
-15.7	-13.3	-12.9		-3.1	-6.1	-46.9	NM	NM	56.9
8.9	9.4	8.3		4.3	10.6	12.8	9.7	11.0	9.9
(268) 2.7	(266) 3.2	(285) 2.9	EBIT/Interest	(45) 2.7	(68) 2.4	(30) 2.8	(41) 2.3	(54) 3.9	(47) 3.8
1.2	1.2	1.0		.8	.5	-.2	.9	2.0	2.1
5.0	4.7	3.5					4.0	3.3	5.2
(52) 2.0	(59) 2.4	(67) 2.0	Net Profit + Depr., Dep., Amort./Cur. Mat. L/T/D			(13) 2.3	(17) 2.1	(18) 2.6	
.8	1.0	1.2				1.0	1.3	1.7	
.6	.7	.7		1.8	.8	.4	.3	.4	.4
1.8	2.2	2.1	Fixed/Worth	4.4	5.1	1.2	1.2	.9	1.0
6.1	28.2	23.1		-11.4	-6.7	-9.4	3.9	2.8	2.4
1.1	1.0	1.0		1.4	1.0	.6	1.0	.5	1.1
2.6	3.2	2.9	Debt/Worth	5.2	7.9	1.7	1.8	1.7	2.1
10.8	43.4	278.2		-10.5	-8.6	-30.3	7.3	5.3	7.9
48.4	49.4	42.5		25.0	62.9	75.0	36.2	52.0	59.1
(288) 20.1	(286) 17.3	(288) 16.3	% Profit Before Taxes/Tangible Net Worth	(69) 12.6	(51) 21.6	(26) 20.2	(41) 14.2	(55) 17.9	(46) 19.4
4.6	4.1	5.3		2.4	1.1	9.0	.0	7.6	9.2
13.8	12.7	11.2		7.7	13.9	22.4	8.9	13.2	12.5
4.8	4.6	4.7	% Profit Before Taxes/Total Assets	3.5	4.4	6.3	3.6	6.1	6.2
.1	.4	-.1		-.4	-1.8	-3.0	-1.3	1.5	2.1
14.1	16.6	15.1		1.3	14.9	23.6	22.8	23.1	36.1
4.1	2.7	2.7	Sales/Net Fixed Assets	.3	2.5	8.6	4.9	6.5	8.1
.6	.5	.5		.2	.7	1.5	.9	2.5	1.8
3.0	3.3	2.8		.6	2.6	3.9	4.3	3.1	3.4
1.4	1.2	1.1	Sales/Total Assets	.2	1.2	2.0	2.1	2.1	2.1
.5	.3	.3		.1	.5	.7	.7	1.0	1.1
2.0	1.9	2.0		8.3	2.4	1.4	1.7	1.2	1.2
(299) 4.2	(328) 5.8	(319) 5.1	% Depr., Dep., Amort./Sales	(82) 13.3	(69) 6.1	(30) 2.8	(44) 3.5	(52) 3.4	(42) 2.5
10.5	14.1	12.2		22.5	13.8	10.4	6.5	6.1	5.2
2.5	2.0	2.6		6.4	3.8	1.4	2.3	1.3	
(92) 5.2	(91) 4.3	(99) 5.0	% Officers', Directors' Owners' Comp/Sales	(14) 11.7	(29) 6.9	(10) 2.3	(18) 3.8	(23) 3.3	
10.0	7.6	9.6		16.9	12.3	3.7	4.6	8.4	
8755211M	9295829M	7699245M	Net Sales ($)	42841M	167660M	139824M	371160M	986880M	5990880M
4760011M	4980000M	4929404M	Total Assets ($)	197247M	291214M	146093M	417722M	821254M	3055874M

M = $ thousand   MM = $ million
See Pages 9 through 22 for Explanation of Ratios and Data

Current Data Sorted by Assets   Comparative Historical Data

	0-500M	500M-2MM	2-10MM	10-50MM	50-100MM	100-250MM		4/1/05-3/31/06 ALL	4/1/06-3/31/07 ALL
Type of Statement									
Unqualified			8	14	1	6		22	21
Reviewed			5	4	1			15	13
Compiled	1	3	7	7		1		19	25
Tax Returns	4	3	4					4	4
Other	2	9	19	10	2	3		42	41
		17 (4/1-9/30/09)		97 (10/1/09-3/31/10)					
NUMBER OF STATEMENTS	7	15	43	35	4	10		102	104
ASSETS	%	%	%	%	%	%		%	%
Cash & Equivalents		5.9	6.7	9.2		6.7		8.3	10.6
Trade Receivables (net)		17.5	15.9	6.6		7.5		18.6	18.1
Inventory		11.2	3.8	1.8		7.1		3.7	2.8
All Other Current		.2	4.0	1.8		.6		3.0	2.7
Total Current		34.8	30.5	19.3		22.0		33.5	34.3
Fixed Assets (net)		62.8	55.7	74.4		51.2		57.2	57.2
Intangibles (net)		.6	4.2	.9		25.6		2.9	2.5
All Other Non-Current		1.8	9.6	5.3		1.2		6.4	6.0
Total		100.0	100.0	100.0		100.0		100.0	100.0
LIABILITIES									
Notes Payable-Short Term		6.0	11.1	2.6		4.1		5.9	5.8
Cur. Mat.-L.T.D.		4.4	7.8	5.2		1.4		5.5	4.7
Trade Payables		6.2	6.4	2.4		3.6		7.7	6.5
Income Taxes Payable		.2	.5	.0		.0		.3	.2
All Other Current		56.0	3.8	4.8		4.6		4.7	14.1
Total Current		72.8	29.6	15.0		13.7		24.1	31.2
Long-Term Debt		24.1	39.9	46.3		32.0		34.7	32.3
Deferred Taxes		.0	.8	1.0		2.4		1.0	.7
All Other Non-Current		18.7	3.5	6.6		6.8		5.4	4.4
Net Worth		-15.6	26.2	31.1		45.1		34.8	31.4
Total Liabilities & Net Worth		100.0	100.0	100.0		100.0		100.0	100.0
INCOME DATA									
Net Sales		100.0	100.0	100.0		100.0		100.0	100.0
Gross Profit									
Operating Expenses		93.4	84.2	83.8		92.7		86.4	87.0
Operating Profit		6.6	15.8	16.2		7.3		13.6	13.0
All Other Expenses (net)		3.8	4.5	7.3		5.7		5.1	5.7
Profit Before Taxes		2.8	11.3	8.8		1.5		8.4	7.3
RATIOS									
		2.2	3.4	2.1		1.4		2.2	2.2
Current		.6	1.3	1.1		1.2		1.4	1.4
		.1	.6	.5		1.1		.9	.9
		.8	2.5	1.9		1.4		2.1	2.0
Quick		.6	1.1	.8		1.0		1.2	1.1
		.1	.4	.4		.9		.7	.6
		6 58.7	14 25.7	22 16.7		32 11.2		23 15.6	23 15.6
Sales/Receivables		23 16.1	30 12.1	29 12.7		43 8.4		34 10.7	38 9.5
		30 12.0	42 8.8	39 9.4		49 7.4		49 7.4	52 7.1
Cost of Sales/Inventory									
Cost of Sales/Payables									
		17.5	6.6	9.2		13.1		6.8	7.3
Sales/Working Capital		-11.3	31.4	57.0		26.2		19.8	20.0
		-4.5	-19.4	-7.8		165.7		-77.1	-35.4
		32.2	7.1	4.6				6.4	8.2
EBIT/Interest		(12) 3.1	(40) 3.1	(26) 2.7				(87) 2.7	(88) 2.4
		1.0	1.5	1.7				1.3	1.1
			8.5	2.7				4.7	4.2
Net Profit + Depr., Dep., Amort./Cur. Mat. L/T/D			(12) 2.5	(16) 1.6				(24) 2.0	(20) 1.6
			1.4	1.1				1.2	1.0
		.5	1.0	1.3		1.8		.8	.8
Fixed/Worth		5.6	2.6	2.3		2.4		1.7	1.7
		-2.8	10.2	5.1		NM		4.7	4.0
		.7	.9	1.4		1.3		.9	1.0
Debt/Worth		4.6	3.8	2.6		2.0		2.2	1.8
		-3.8	25.2	4.7		NM		7.0	5.7
		66.8	60.0	23.2				34.8	30.8
% Profit Before Taxes/Tangible Net Worth		(10) 28.9	(37) 20.1	(33) 12.8				(90) 14.8	(96) 15.2
		4.5	9.0	7.0				5.8	4.9
		23.4	15.3	6.6		6.5		11.2	11.8
% Profit Before Taxes/Total Assets		2.9	8.4	5.2		.6		4.9	5.0
		-1.3	2.5	-.9		-3.1		.9	.5
		25.0	6.8	1.0		2.9		7.7	7.1
Sales/Net Fixed Assets		4.3	2.5	.6		1.0		1.7	1.3
		1.4	.9	.4		.7		.5	.6
		5.5	2.5	.9		.8		3.1	2.6
Sales/Total Assets		3.1	1.2	.5		.7		1.0	.8
		1.1	.7	.3		.4		.5	.4
		.9	3.3	8.1				2.6	3.0
% Depr., Dep., Amort./Sales		(14) 3.8	(39) 6.1	(34) 10.5				(94) 7.1	(90) 8.3
		9.8	7.9	12.8				12.1	11.8
								1.5	2.4
% Officers', Directors' Owners' Comp/Sales								(33) 4.7	(30) 5.4
								8.2	9.3
Net Sales ($)	6384M	64467M	397143M	599765M	343771M	1100953M		3756261M	3626877M
Total Assets ($)	1412M	18640M	214035M	868378M	302444M	1620079M		2717163M	2693867M

Comparative Historical Data

Current Data Sorted by Sales

					Type of Statement						
	25		18	29	Unqualified		3	5	5	5	11
	15		11	10	Reviewed			2	3	4	1
	17		20	19	Compiled	1	1	4	5	3	5
	9		18	11	Tax Returns	3	5	2	1		
	43		49	45	Other	5	8	4	11	9	8
	4/1/07-3/31/08 ALL		4/1/08-3/31/09 ALL	4/1/09-3/31/10 ALL			17 (4/1-9/30/09)			97 (10/1/09-3/31/10)	
						0-1MM	1-3MM	3-5MM	5-10MM	10-25MM	25MM & OVER
	109		116	114	NUMBER OF STATEMENTS	9	17	17	25	21	25
	%		%	%	ASSETS	%	%	%	%	%	%
	7.8		9.0	10.2	Cash & Equivalents		14.0	3.8	5.2	6.5	12.9
	15.1		13.2	12.2	Trade Receivables (net)		9.0	12.2	10.4	14.5	16.9
	5.4		4.7	4.3	Inventory		.4	.5	4.6	3.7	7.4
	2.9		3.4	2.2	All Other Current		2.0	1.5	2.1	1.6	4.0
	31.2		30.3	28.8	Total Current		25.4	18.1	22.3	26.2	41.1
	57.6		57.4	60.6	Fixed Assets (net)		64.6	64.1	70.9	63.8	45.2
	3.7		4.4	4.3	Intangibles (net)		2.5	.8	1.4	5.5	11.0
	7.4		7.9	6.3	All Other Non-Current		7.4	17.1	5.4	4.5	2.8
	100.0		100.0	100.0	Total		100.0	100.0	100.0	100.0	100.0
					LIABILITIES						
	13.6		10.6	6.6	Notes Payable-Short Term		5.8	5.6	2.8	5.2	9.7
	7.0		4.5	5.8	Cur. Mat.-L.T.D.		3.3	5.1	9.5	5.1	5.7
	5.5		5.8	4.6	Trade Payables		1.4	2.4	3.9	7.6	7.7
	.1		.1	.2	Income Taxes Payable		.2	.0	.1	.0	.7
	7.6		6.3	12.1	All Other Current		6.8	5.0	28.6	5.3	8.4
	33.8		27.3	29.4	Total Current		17.5	18.1	44.9	23.3	32.2
	32.4		32.4	36.9	Long-Term Debt		37.0	35.1	47.6	39.2	22.9
	.7		1.1	.8	Deferred Taxes		.2	1.4	.2	.3	2.2
	6.8		6.6	7.2	All Other Non-Current		6.2	5.6	4.9	7.4	6.5
	26.3		32.6	25.8	Net Worth		39.1	39.8	2.4	29.9	36.3
	100.0		100.0	100.0	Total Liabilties & Net Worth		100.0	100.0	100.0	100.0	100.0
					INCOME DATA						
	100.0		100.0	100.0	Net Sales		100.0	100.0	100.0	100.0	100.0
					Gross Profit						
	86.7		88.0	86.4	Operating Expenses		78.9	87.1	83.9	92.5	92.3
	13.3		12.0	13.6	Operating Profit		21.1	12.9	16.1	7.5	7.7
	6.0		4.2	5.3	All Other Expenses (net)		6.2	5.7	6.9	3.8	3.1
	7.3		7.9	8.3	Profit Before Taxes		14.9	7.2	9.2	3.8	4.7
					RATIOS						
	2.2		2.4	2.5			8.7	3.6	2.2	1.6	3.7
	1.2		1.2	1.1	Current		2.3	1.0	1.1	.9	1.4
	.7		.7	.5			.1	.5	.6	.4	1.0
	1.9		2.0	2.1			5.7	3.4	1.9	1.3	3.1
	.9		.9	.9	Quick		2.1	.9	.8	.8	1.0
	.5		.5	.4			.1	.4	.4	.4	.6
22	16.3	17	21.7	17	21.8	Sales/Receivables	0	UND	0	UND	22	16.6	22	16.9	29	12.7
36	10.0	32	11.3	29	12.5		9	39.9	29	12.5	30	12.1	25	14.4	33	11.2
48	7.6	43	8.5	41	9.0		26	13.9	73	5.0	43	8.6	38	9.5	43	8.4
					Cost of Sales/Inventory						
					Cost of Sales/Payables						
	9.0		8.0	9.1			5.8	7.0	13.9	17.3	4.9
	28.0		34.2	40.7	Sales/Working Capital		18.8	181.3	57.0	-66.2	17.1
	-16.2		-16.6	-9.6			-5.6	-13.0	-8.8	-6.1	NM
	4.8		7.0	7.1			11.5	4.6	8.2	19.2	18.5
(91)	2.5	(98)	2.9	(96)	2.9	EBIT/Interest	(15)	3.1	(15)	2.5	(21)	3.4	(18)	2.4	(21)	3.0
	1.2		1.2	1.2			1.2	.6	2.1	1.0	1.0
	7.8		5.7	6.3	Net Profit + Depr., Dep., Amort./Cur. Mat. L/T/D					29.1
(32)	3.4	(26)	1.9	(32)	2.1						(12)	4.2
	1.5		1.0	1.4							1.7
	.9		.9	1.0			.6	.8	1.4	1.1	.5
	2.1		2.1	2.3	Fixed/Worth		2.1	1.5	2.6	3.0	1.8
	7.0		4.6	8.1			6.8	7.6	42.2	5.2	4.8
	1.0		.8	.9			.4	.9	1.0	1.1	.8
	2.2		1.8	2.2	Debt/Worth		1.2	1.5	2.2	3.0	2.0
	11.5		7.2	11.0			7.2	7.7	47.0	5.8	8.8
	39.4		37.4	37.8	% Profit Before Taxes/Tangible Net Worth		60.0	29.6	20.1	36.7	30.2
(93)	17.5	(103)	19.7	(98)	16.7		(14)	31.8	15.6	(21)	17.2	(19)	11.7	(21)	15.8
	6.2		5.7	6.2			10.6	-1.4	11.8	.0	3.0
	11.5		14.6	12.6	% Profit Before Taxes/Total Assets		18.3	9.9	11.0	9.0	17.3
	5.2		6.2	5.9			8.7	5.9	6.1	4.4	6.0
	.9		1.1	.6			2.1	-.8	1.7	-1.1	.6
	6.7		5.0	6.0			18.8	4.1	4.4	8.7	12.8
	1.5		1.6	1.3	Sales/Net Fixed Assets		1.1	1.1	1.0	1.3	2.9
	.7		.7	.6			.4	.5	.4	.6	.8
	2.6		2.0	2.4			3.3	1.3	2.0	2.9	3.0
	1.0		1.0	.8	Sales/Total Assets		.7	.8	.8	1.2	.9
	.5		.5	.5			.3	.4	.3	.5	.5
	3.0		3.4	3.4	% Depr., Dep., Amort./Sales		3.5	6.4	3.5	2.7	2.2
(99)	7.5	(99)	7.4	(101)	7.9		(15)	9.6	(16)	7.9	8.4	(20)	7.5	(22)	5.3
	10.7		10.5	11.0			18.4	11.6	12.5	11.1	10.0
	1.8		1.5	2.2	% Officers', Directors' Owners' Comp/Sales						
(32)	4.9	(33)	4.8	(20)	4.8						
	8.2		11.0	7.0							
	4079182M		3142074M	2512483M	Net Sales ($)	4317M	31446M	65935M	178855M	319756M	1912174M
	3254726M		2686390M	3024988M	Total Assets ($)	13948M	51702M	138312M	341650M	373760M	2105616M

M = $ thousand   MM = $ million
See Pages 9 through 22 for Explanation of Ratios and Data

Current Data Sorted by Assets   Comparative Historical Data

Type of Statement									
Unqualified	3	8	11	2	1			29	32
Reviewed	9	17	12					26	33
Compiled	3	3						6	12
Tax Returns	4	5						4	8
Other	2	6	7					15	14
		53 (4/1-9/30/09)		40 (10/1/09-3/31/10)				4/1/05-3/31/06 ALL	4/1/06-3/31/07 ALL
	0-500M	500M-2MM	2-10MM	10-50MM	50-100MM	100-250MM	NUMBER OF STATEMENTS	80	99
	21	39	30	2	1				

	0-500M	500M-2MM	2-10MM	10-50MM	50-100MM	100-250MM		80 ALL	99 ALL
	%	%	%	%	%	%	**ASSETS**	%	%
		10.5	12.2	8.3			Cash & Equivalents	11.8	9.4
		16.8	10.3	14.8			Trade Receivables (net)	16.3	17.8
		18.1	28.0	19.3			Inventory	21.0	22.6
		4.5	3.9	10.5			All Other Current	5.8	5.8
		50.0	54.4	53.0			Total Current	54.9	55.7
D		41.2	38.0	35.5			Fixed Assets (net)	40.1	37.8
A		.1	1.4	.1			Intangibles (net)	.4	.4
T		8.8	6.2	11.4			All Other Non-Current	4.6	6.1
A		100.0	100.0	100.0			Total	100.0	100.0
N							**LIABILITIES**		
O		17.3	10.0	10.1			Notes Payable-Short Term	13.8	24.5
T		2.2	2.6	4.7			Cur. Mat.-L.T.D.	3.4	3.4
		9.9	12.3	9.9			Trade Payables	13.3	9.5
A		.0	.3	.7			Income Taxes Payable	.2	.2
V		7.2	11.4	10.6			All Other Current	10.3	10.9
A		36.6	36.7	36.0			Total Current	41.0	48.4
I		11.4	15.4	19.6			Long-Term Debt	14.9	15.4
L		.9	1.8	.6			Deferred Taxes	.9	1.1
A		2.0	.6	3.2			All Other Non-Current	2.1	2.0
B		49.1	45.5	40.6			Net Worth	41.1	33.1
L		100.0	100.0	100.0			Total Liabilties & Net Worth	100.0	100.0
E							**INCOME DATA**		
		100.0	100.0	100.0			Net Sales	100.0	100.0
							Gross Profit		
		92.1	90.4	90.7			Operating Expenses	89.7	91.0
		7.9	9.6	9.3			Operating Profit	10.3	9.0
		.9	1.1	1.4			All Other Expenses (net)	1.2	1.6
		7.0	8.5	7.9			Profit Before Taxes	9.1	7.4
							RATIOS		
		2.1	2.6	2.9			Current	1.9	1.9
		1.3	1.4	1.5				1.2	1.2
		.8	1.0	1.0				1.1	1.1
		1.0	1.0	1.2			Quick	1.2	1.1
		.7	.5	.6				.6	.5
		.3	.2	.3				.2	.2
	1	334.0	3 · 109.3	7 · 51.0			Sales/Receivables	8 · 46.3	9 · 39.7
	16	22.2	10 · 36.2	22 · 16.6				17 · 21.4	23 · 16.1
	40	9.1	20 · 18.5	58 · 6.3				40 · 9.2	45 · 8.0
							Cost of Sales/Inventory		
							Cost of Sales/Payables		
		11.0	8.3	4.0			Sales/Working Capital	9.4	8.5
		27.7	21.3	16.7				22.1	20.6
		-26.1	182.2	130.7				65.8	116.1
		8.4	42.5	10.9			EBIT/Interest	9.8	8.8
	(17)	2.2	(38) 6.5	(29) 5.3				(75) 4.5	(92) 2.9
		-.9	3.1	2.1				1.8	1.7
			38.4	22.9			Net Profit + Depr., Dep., Amort./Cur. Mat. L/T/D	6.3	12.0
			(10) 7.0	(16) 6.4				(26) 2.5	(36) 3.4
			3.8	3.1				1.7	1.7
		.4	.4	.4			Fixed/Worth	.5	.5
		.6	.8	.8				.9	1.0
		1.3	1.2	1.7				1.6	1.8
		.4	.5	.7			Debt/Worth	.5	.7
		.9	1.4	1.7				1.7	2.0
		4.3	2.9	4.7				4.1	4.5
		27.2	38.9	39.5			% Profit Before Taxes/Tangible Net Worth	40.6	35.1
		19.8	(38) 22.8	(29) 21.1				(76) 18.3	(92) 16.9
		-4.6	13.7	10.6				6.3	7.6
		16.3	16.1	14.3			% Profit Before Taxes/Total Assets	15.4	11.1
		4.1	9.5	6.3				5.5	5.0
		-1.7	5.1	2.0				1.7	2.2
		25.1	26.0	13.2			Sales/Net Fixed Assets	18.6	15.5
		13.5	10.8	6.5				7.3	7.6
		1.5	2.1	1.3				1.8	3.0
		3.8	4.5	3.0			Sales/Total Assets	3.8	3.7
		1.9	2.5	1.1				2.5	2.1
		.8	1.1	.7				1.0	1.0
		.7	.6	1.0			% Depr., Dep., Amort./Sales	.6	.8
	(19)	2.5	(34) 1.1	(29) 2.5				(77) 1.8	(94) 1.8
		8.7	3.8	4.3				3.6	3.4
							% Officers', Directors' Owners' Comp/Sales	.8	.9
								(11) 1.4	(19) 2.0
								3.7	4.9
		74567M	506432M	1377419M	242341M	25282M	Net Sales ($)	4896411M	3271539M
		27295M	183751M	671684M	136252M	149439M	Total Assets ($)	1376793M	1197133M

Comparative Historical Data

Current Data Sorted by Sales

						Type of Statement						
	35		32		25	Unqualified	1	1	2	3	5	13
	35		37		38	Reviewed	3	7	1	7	11	9
	14		4		6	Compiled	2	1	1	1	1	
	5		6		9	Tax Returns	1	2		5	1	
	18		15		15	Other		2	1	4	2	6
	4/1/07-3/31/08		4/1/08-3/31/09		4/1/09-3/31/10		53 (4/1-9/30/09)			40 (10/1/09-3/31/10)		
	ALL		ALL		ALL		0-1MM	1-3MM	3-5MM	5-10MM	10-25MM	25MM & OVER
	107		94		93	NUMBER OF STATEMENTS	7	13	5	20	20	28
	%		%		%	ASSETS	%	%	%	%	%	%
	9.0		10.7		10.2	Cash & Equivalents		8.4		5.3	13.2	12.9
	16.1		16.3		13.5	Trade Receivables (net)		10.1		20.1	12.7	15.1
	27.2		23.3		23.4	Inventory		16.0		24.2	29.6	27.1
	7.3		10.4		6.1	All Other Current		3.0		6.8	5.6	7.7
	59.5		60.8		53.3	Total Current		37.5		56.4	61.1	62.9
	34.0		32.9		37.2	Fixed Assets (net)		52.0		34.7	32.6	24.9
	.6		.8		.7	Intangibles (net)		.1		1.7	1.0	.2
	5.8		5.5		8.8	All Other Non-Current		10.4		7.2	5.3	11.9
	100.0		100.0		100.0	Total		100.0		100.0	100.0	100.0
						LIABILITIES						
	21.5		18.3		12.1	Notes Payable-Short Term		17.7		15.4	8.2	12.4
	3.7		3.7		3.1	Cur. Mat.-L.T.D.		1.2		1.8	4.8	4.1
	10.9		10.3		11.1	Trade Payables		6.2		15.6	11.6	13.6
	.4		.4		.4	Income Taxes Payable		.1		.9	.1	.5
	10.6		11.5		10.1	All Other Current		5.0		8.5	11.6	14.7
	47.1		44.2		36.8	Total Current		30.2		42.2	36.4	45.2
	15.4		13.1		15.4	Long-Term Debt		5.9		11.8	18.0	11.8
	.8		.7		1.1	Deferred Taxes		.0		.6	1.7	1.4
	1.8		1.5		1.8	All Other Non-Current		1.5		4.0	.2	1.5
	35.0		40.6		44.9	Net Worth		62.3		41.4	43.7	40.1
	100.0		100.0		100.0	Total Liabilities & Net Worth		100.0		100.0	100.0	100.0
						INCOME DATA						
	100.0		100.0		100.0	Net Sales		100.0		100.0	100.0	100.0
						Gross Profit						
	90.7		89.5		90.6	Operating Expenses		85.6		90.0	93.9	94.4
	9.3		10.5		9.4	Operating Profit		14.4		10.0	6.1	5.6
	2.5		1.5		1.2	All Other Expenses (net)		1.0		-.1	.9	.7
	6.8		9.0		8.3	Profit Before Taxes		13.4		10.2	5.1	4.9
						RATIOS						
	1.7		2.1		2.3			1.6		2.9	2.6	1.8
	1.2		1.3		1.4	Current		1.2		1.2	1.9	1.4
	1.0		1.0		1.0			.1		.9	1.3	1.1
	1.1		1.1		1.1			1.0		1.2	1.1	1.0
	.5		.5		.6	Quick		.4		.7	.8	.5
	.2		.2		.3			.0		.3	.3	.3
6	58.4	5	78.0	4	85.4		0 UND		6 64.6	9 39.0	3 139.1
18	19.8	14	26.5	17	22.0	Sales/Receivables	5 68.3		21 17.7	17 21.3	13 27.9
41	8.9	38	9.6	33	11.0		40 9.1		43 8.5	43 8.4	27 13.4
						Cost of Sales/Inventory						
						Cost of Sales/Payables						
	8.7		6.0		8.0			11.1		6.9	4.0	14.8
	26.4		20.2		18.7	Sales/Working Capital		86.6		28.1	12.0	21.1
	252.7		54.2		151.9			-7.2		-46.5	24.8	63.5
	6.1		13.5		11.4			13.3		68.7	10.4	11.1
(102)	2.3	(90)	3.4	(87)	5.0	EBIT/Interest	(11) 4.9		(18) 7.2	(19) 4.6	6.7
	1.4		2.0		2.5			2.2		1.5	2.8	3.1
	6.2		9.7		24.4							32.5
(31)	3.6	(31)	4.7	(29)	6.0	Net Profit + Depr., Dep., Amort./Cur. Mat. L/T/D					(13) 10.1
	1.2		2.2		3.1							2.8
	.5		.4		.4			.3		.4	.4	.3
	1.0		.7		.8	Fixed/Worth		.8		.9	.7	.6
	1.7		1.2		1.3			1.2		2.3	1.4	.8
	.9		.7		.6			.2		.4	.7	.7
	2.3		1.9		1.4	Debt/Worth		.3		2.2	1.5	1.6
	4.9		4.3		3.1			1.4		8.2	2.8	3.3
	34.5		40.4		34.7			28.4		41.6	38.1	37.8
(102)	17.1	(91)	22.8	(91)	21.1	% Profit Before Taxes/Tangible Net Worth		13.9		24.9	(19) 19.1	24.4
	7.5		9.2		10.2			3.5		6.1	12.8	13.6
	9.4		14.6		15.5			16.2		20.0	13.3	15.1
	5.1		7.1		6.8	% Profit Before Taxes/Total Assets		6.6		7.8	8.2	7.3
	1.7		3.4		2.9			2.5		1.2	5.1	3.8
	20.8		28.3		21.4			25.3		16.7	27.2	34.5
	8.2		11.6		9.6	Sales/Net Fixed Assets		3.6		10.3	8.7	13.0
	2.7		2.1		1.5			.7		2.2	1.6	7.7
	3.2		3.7		3.7			2.3		3.7	4.4	5.1
	2.1		2.0		1.8	Sales/Total Assets		1.3		1.9	2.1	3.0
	1.1		.9		.8			.7		.8	.9	1.8
	.8		.6		.7			.6		1.1	.7	.5
(96)	1.6	(87)	1.4	(85)	1.6	% Depr., Dep., Amort./Sales	(10) 4.0		(18) 3.1	(19) 1.2	(26) .8
	2.8		3.8		4.3			7.3		4.6	3.8	2.1
	.8		.3		.6							
(23)	2.1	(16)	1.2	(21)	2.0	% Officers', Directors' Owners' Comp/Sales						
	3.1		2.6		2.6							
	3484657M		4662486M		2226041M	Net Sales ($)	4594M	25963M	20227M	149645M	311788M	1713824M
	1809747M		1784822M		1168421M	Total Assets ($)	10851M	25310M	34673M	114290M	199816M	783481M

M = $ thousand   MM = $ million
See Pages 9 through 22 for Explanation of Ratios and Data

Current Data Sorted by Assets   Comparative Historical Data

0-500M	500M-2MM	2-10MM	10-50MM	50-100MM	100-250MM		4/1/05-3/31/06 ALL	4/1/06-3/31/07 ALL
						Type of Statement		
		1	3	2	1	Unqualified	10	8
2	3	15	4		1	Reviewed	21	14
4	5	3	1			Compiled	13	13
5	8	5				Tax Returns	17	14
2	7	16	11	4	4	Other	28	25
	10 (4/1-9/30/09)		97 (10/1/09-3/31/10)					
13	23	40	19	6	6	**NUMBER OF STATEMENTS**	89	74
%	%	%	%	%	%	**ASSETS**	%	%
14.9	9.1	10.8	9.5			Cash & Equivalents	9.9	10.3
4.6	18.3	23.3	18.9			Trade Receivables (net)	19.5	16.8
.0	3.1	2.7	3.3			Inventory	3.6	6.0
5.1	2.3	3.4	4.4			All Other Current	2.2	3.0
24.6	32.7	40.2	36.1			Total Current	35.2	36.1
56.5	55.9	43.4	50.2			Fixed Assets (net)	50.6	52.7
7.7	3.5	6.5	5.6			Intangibles (net)	6.8	4.6
11.2	7.9	9.9	8.0			All Other Non-Current	7.3	6.6
100.0	100.0	100.0	100.0			Total	100.0	100.0
						LIABILITIES		
7.2	7.6	4.2	4.9			Notes Payable-Short Term	6.8	9.6
6.6	3.2	4.7	3.6			Cur. Mat.-L.T.D.	4.2	3.5
1.2	3.2	7.0	10.4			Trade Payables	7.4	7.5
.0	.0	.0	.2			Income Taxes Payable	.5	.5
2.6	9.9	6.0	5.7			All Other Current	5.1	8.6
17.6	23.9	22.0	24.7			Total Current	24.0	29.8
81.5	41.8	35.5	34.3			Long-Term Debt	34.7	34.5
.0	.0	.2	.0			Deferred Taxes	.4	.6
.0	4.8	12.5	7.9			All Other Non-Current	4.0	3.6
1.0	29.5	29.8	33.1			Net Worth	37.0	31.6
100.0	100.0	100.0	100.0			Total Liabilities & Net Worth	100.0	100.0
						INCOME DATA		
100.0	100.0	100.0	100.0			Net Sales	100.0	100.0
						Gross Profit		
73.8	84.0	83.1	87.2			Operating Expenses	85.0	79.2
26.2	16.0	16.9	12.8			Operating Profit	15.0	20.8
7.8	8.6	7.4	5.7			All Other Expenses (net)	7.8	7.4
18.4	7.4	9.5	7.1			Profit Before Taxes	7.2	13.4
						RATIOS		
2.1	2.5	4.2	1.7				2.6	2.8
1.3	1.5	1.9	1.5			Current	1.4	1.3
.7	.9	.8	1.1				.7	.6
1.7	2.3	3.5	1.5				2.2	2.1
.8	1.2	1.3	1.1			Quick	1.0	1.1
.4	.7	.6	.6				.5	.4
0 UND	0 UND	20 18.0	25 14.6				3 123.3	0 UND
0 UND	24 15.4	35 10.4	41 8.9			Sales/Receivables	34 10.9	27 13.3
32 11.4	52 7.0	50 7.3	48 7.6				52 7.0	50 7.3
						Cost of Sales/Inventory		
						Cost of Sales/Payables		
8.8	6.9	5.5	8.8				6.6	8.6
358.6	18.0	11.9	17.6			Sales/Working Capital	22.7	18.6
-21.5	-33.7	-21.9	125.2				-15.7	-13.0
	5.5	19.5	19.8				8.4	24.8
	(15) 1.8	(29) 4.4	(18) 2.0			EBIT/Interest	(64) 2.9	(56) 6.0
	.9	1.5	1.1				1.3	2.3
		9.4					4.7	9.0
		(10) 7.0				Net Profit + Depr., Dep., Amort./Cur. Mat. L/T/D	(22) 3.0	(14) 4.6
		3.3					1.4	1.4
.2	.8	.4	.6				.8	.6
1.3	2.2	1.5	1.5			Fixed/Worth	1.5	1.5
-1.8	-38.7	7.7	6.2				15.4	NM
.4	.7	.9	1.0				.7	.7
1.1	3.6	2.4	1.6			Debt/Worth	1.7	1.9
-2.5	-41.7	15.5	11.7				23.4	NM
	39.6	90.1	71.6				37.9	53.1
	(16) 16.4	(31) 30.2	(17) 32.4			% Profit Before Taxes/Tangible Net Worth	(72) 20.3	(56) 25.6
	1.4	9.7	3.5				5.1	12.8
31.5	15.4	22.2	18.6				15.2	21.5
3.1	4.6	7.5	2.6			% Profit Before Taxes/Total Assets	4.5	8.6
-47.4	.2	.5	.5				.8	1.7
21.0	9.4	13.9	8.1				12.3	15.1
6.0	2.8	5.3	2.1			Sales/Net Fixed Assets	2.8	3.1
.5	.4	.7	1.1				.5	.5
7.3	3.5	2.9	2.0				2.8	3.1
.7	1.4	1.4	1.3			Sales/Total Assets	1.2	1.3
.4	.3	.5	.7				.4	.3
	3.4	2.0	2.0				1.8	1.9
	(19) 8.2	(39) 5.0	(18) 4.5			% Depr., Dep., Amort./Sales	(84) 4.6	(69) 4.2
	15.6	9.4	10.5				10.2	11.6
							1.4	3.2
						% Officers', Directors' Owners' Comp/Sales	(26) 5.1	(16) 6.4
							13.2	12.6
7838M	41303M	463920M	714310M	374197M	711327M	Net Sales ($)	1584104M	826148M
3321M	26743M	196831M	520082M	350044M	1021758M	Total Assets ($)	1215426M	653290M

M = $ thousand   MM = $ million
See Pages 9 through 22 for Explanation of Ratios and Data

Comparative Historical Data   ## Current Data Sorted by Sales

9	8	7	Type of Statement						
			Unqualified	2	1			2	4
20	22	25	Reviewed		3	2	5	9	4
12	10	13	Compiled	4	6			2	1
13	19	18	Tax Returns	13	4	1			
39	42	44	Other	6	8	3	3	7	17
4/1/07-3/31/08 ALL	4/1/08-3/31/09 ALL	4/1/09-3/31/10 ALL		0-1MM	10 (4/1-9/30/09) 1-3MM	3-5MM	5-10MM	97 (10/1/09-3/31/10) 10-25MM	25MM & OVER
93	101	107	**NUMBER OF STATEMENTS**	25	22	6	8	20	26
%	%	%	**ASSETS**	%	%	%	%	%	%
12.6	12.4	9.8	Cash & Equivalents	8.1	9.0			11.0	5.7
20.9	20.9	18.3	Trade Receivables (net)	2.3	18.2			27.5	27.2
3.2	3.5	3.7	Inventory	.0	.6			5.0	8.5
2.8	4.1	3.5	All Other Current	5.2	3.1			2.3	4.1
39.5	40.9	35.2	Total Current	15.6	30.9			45.8	45.5
45.7	47.2	49.3	Fixed Assets (net)	69.7	52.3			41.9	41.8
8.1	5.1	6.5	Intangibles (net)	5.4	7.3			7.7	4.6
6.8	6.7	8.9	All Other Non-Current	9.4	9.5			4.7	8.1
100.0	100.0	100.0	Total	100.0	100.0			100.0	100.0
			LIABILITIES						
6.7	11.9	6.1	Notes Payable-Short Term	3.1	5.5			6.9	8.9
4.3	6.6	4.5	Cur. Mat.-L.T.D.	4.3	4.8			4.3	4.6
14.2	8.2	6.1	Trade Payables	.6	2.5			7.8	14.0
.2	.2	.1	Income Taxes Payable	.0	.0			.1	.1
7.8	9.9	6.3	All Other Current	2.4	9.7			6.9	6.0
33.1	36.8	23.1	Total Current	10.3	22.5			26.1	33.7
33.9	33.5	41.6	Long-Term Debt	60.9	66.4			16.8	28.1
.2	.2	.2	Deferred Taxes	.0	.0			.0	.4
5.2	4.6	8.0	All Other Non-Current	.0	9.8			14.2	6.7
27.5	25.0	27.1	Net Worth	28.8	1.2			42.9	31.2
100.0	100.0	100.0	Total Liabilties & Net Worth	100.0	100.0			100.0	100.0
			INCOME DATA						
100.0	100.0	100.0	Net Sales	100.0	100.0			100.0	100.0
			Gross Profit						
83.3	86.1	83.4	Operating Expenses	62.5	91.7			92.7	89.9
16.7	13.9	16.6	Operating Profit	37.5	8.3			7.3	10.1
5.0	7.6	7.1	All Other Expenses (net)	20.0	5.0			2.8	3.1
11.7	6.2	9.5	Profit Before Taxes	17.5	3.4			4.5	7.0
			RATIOS						
3.1	3.5	2.3	Current	2.8	2.5			3.1	1.7
1.5	1.4	1.5		1.3	1.3			1.8	1.4
.9	.9	.8		.5	.7			1.0	1.0
2.5	2.8	2.1	Quick	2.4	2.1			2.9	1.5
1.2	1.2	1.1		.8	1.0			1.7	1.1
.7	.7	.6		.1	.6			.6	.7
7 55.4	10 38.3	5 76.6	Sales/Receivables	0 UND	0 UND			31 11.6	38 9.7
36 10.2	33 11.1	38 9.7		0 UND	33 10.9			46 8.0	47 7.8
54 6.7	45 8.1	52 7.1		18 20.2	51 7.1			53 6.8	59 6.2
			Cost of Sales/Inventory						
			Cost of Sales/Payables						
5.8	6.7	7.2	Sales/Working Capital	3.7	9.9			7.0	9.6
17.5	18.8	17.6		18.0	40.2			10.8	16.3
-68.6	-46.9	-33.0		-11.5	-25.8			NM	-220.9
9.3	8.1	15.2	EBIT/Interest		3.2			36.8	15.7
(73) 4.9	(76) 3.9	(79) 3.6			(16) 1.1			(18) 5.3	(24) 3.7
2.0	1.5	1.1			-2.2			.2	1.7
7.0	10.7	9.4	Net Profit + Depr., Dep., Amort./Cur. Mat. L/T/D						7.9
(21) 2.5	(15) 3.5	(27) 5.1							(12) 2.7
.8	1.2	1.6							1.6
.6	.5	.6	Fixed/Worth	1.1	.8			.5	.6
1.7	1.5	1.6		4.4	4.6			1.1	1.4
9.5	7.6	12.2		-43.1	-3.4			2.6	5.3
.7	.8	.8	Debt/Worth	.5	1.1			.5	1.1
2.3	3.2	2.4		7.2	NM			1.5	1.6
48.4	15.4	31.1		-46.9	-4.9			8.5	10.7
47.5	54.4	59.6	% Profit Before Taxes/Tangible Net Worth	44.1	37.0			58.7	86.4
(71) 29.1	(84) 22.5	(82) 25.5		(17) 20.0	(11) 13.0			(18) 25.5	(25) 19.2
10.9	1.7	8.0		3.6	-18.1			6.8	9.6
15.8	12.9	16.0	% Profit Before Taxes/Total Assets	9.3	13.8			15.4	18.9
7.9	5.1	5.1		3.1	.5			8.9	4.5
2.6	-.2	.4		-1.2	-9.0			-1.2	1.3
11.8	16.0	11.4	Sales/Net Fixed Assets	.8	11.5			13.9	14.7
4.3	4.7	3.3		.4	4.8			5.3	3.5
.8	.8	.5		.2	.8			1.7	2.0
2.7	3.3	2.7	Sales/Total Assets	.5	3.6			3.2	2.8
1.7	1.6	1.3		.3	1.3			1.9	1.5
.5	.5	.4		.2	.6			.9	1.0
1.9	2.1	2.6	% Depr., Dep., Amort./Sales	5.9	2.8			1.9	1.9
(78) 4.4	(84) 5.0	(96) 5.3		(20) 12.2	(20) 7.6			3.6	(24) 3.9
9.3	9.2	10.5		19.5	17.9			7.3	7.2
3.3	2.4	2.0	% Officers', Directors' Owners' Comp/Sales						
(20) 4.7	(25) 5.2	(18) 4.6							
13.4	8.0	9.0							
1923904M	1458707M	2312895M	Net Sales ($)	9288M	40999M	22508M	60454M	309463M	1870183M
1317907M	1001471M	2118779M	Total Assets ($)	39915M	47966M	12667M	54505M	293396M	1670330M

© RMA 2010

M = $ thousand   MM = $ million
See Pages 9 through 22 for Explanation of Ratios and Data

INFORMATION

Current Data Sorted by Assets | Comparative Historical Data

Type of Statement	0-500M	500M-2MM	2-10MM	10-50MM	50-100MM	100-250MM		4/1/05-3/31/06 ALL	4/1/06-3/31/07 ALL
Unqualified	1		1	8	6	4		26	23
Reviewed		2	3	1				20	20
Compiled	1							8	5
Tax Returns	8	3	5	1				12	13
Other		3	9	9	4	2		33	35
		14 (4/1-9/30/09)		57 (10/1/09-3/31/10)					
NUMBER OF STATEMENTS	10	8	18	19	10	6		99	96
ASSETS	%	%	%	%	%	%		%	%
Cash & Equivalents	14.4		12.4	9.0	9.0			10.2	14.5
Trade Receivables (net)	39.9		22.7	17.9	9.4			23.0	23.8
Inventory	.5		4.6	6.1	.9			4.4	3.9
All Other Current	5.5		1.0	3.1	2.5			2.7	2.6
Total Current	60.4		40.8	36.0	21.9			40.2	44.7
Fixed Assets (net)	9.7		36.9	37.3	22.3			26.9	26.4
Intangibles (net)	16.8		6.7	20.7	39.5			19.8	18.8
All Other Non-Current	13.2		15.6	5.9	16.4			13.1	10.1
Total	100.0		100.0	100.0	100.0			100.0	100.0
LIABILITIES									
Notes Payable-Short Term	18.6		6.8	4.2	.0			4.5	4.2
Cur. Mat.-L.T.D.	.0		1.7	8.0	6.6			4.8	4.0
Trade Payables	22.4		9.7	5.3	1.9			11.1	8.3
Income Taxes Payable	.0		.0	.4	.0			.1	.1
All Other Current	13.4		7.8	13.0	42.4			9.8	13.5
Total Current	54.4		26.0	31.0	51.0			30.3	30.1
Long-Term Debt	15.4		14.9	22.8	54.1			28.6	26.0
Deferred Taxes	.0		.1	.3	1.3			.5	.8
All Other Non-Current	64.5		3.4	17.2	10.9			9.5	13.0
Net Worth	-34.4		55.7	28.7	-17.3			31.0	30.2
Total Liabilties & Net Worth	100.0		100.0	100.0	100.0			100.0	100.0
INCOME DATA									
Net Sales	100.0		100.0	100.0	100.0			100.0	100.0
Gross Profit	53.3		51.0	43.5	39.8			48.4	51.5
Operating Expenses	60.5		46.4	38.8	37.3			41.8	44.3
Operating Profit	-7.2		4.6	4.7	2.6			6.5	7.2
All Other Expenses (net)	.2		.3	1.7	3.2			.7	1.6
Profit Before Taxes	-7.4		4.3	3.1	-.6			5.8	5.6
RATIOS									
Current	6.6		2.8	2.2	1.3			2.1	2.4
	3.1		1.8	1.1	.7			1.5	1.5
	.6		1.1	.7	.5			1.0	1.0
Quick	6.5		2.6	1.7	1.2			1.8	2.1
	2.9		1.6	.8	.6			1.1	1.2
	.6		.8	.6	.4			.7	.8
Sales/Receivables	0 UND		36 10.1	35 10.6	27 13.4			31 11.8	32 11.4
	34 10.7		42 8.8	40 9.0	35 10.4			38 9.7	37 9.8
	56 6.6		51 7.2	54 6.8	40 9.2			45 8.1	47 7.7
Cost of Sales/Inventory	0 UND		0 UND	6 57.5	0 UND			0 UND	0 796.7
	0 UND		6 60.7	13 27.3	4 82.8			10 36.9	9 42.3
	0 UND		15 23.7	48 7.7	8 46.8			21 17.3	22 16.7
Cost of Sales/Payables	0 UND		14 25.7	11 34.0	4 86.1			13 28.8	14 26.9
	17 21.1		21 17.5	15 24.5	8 43.7			23 15.9	22 16.3
	52 7.0		62 5.8	39 9.3	17 21.9			49 7.5	42 8.7
Sales/Working Capital	7.5		6.6	5.5	22.4			8.6	8.6
	52.8		10.1	54.7	-18.8			18.7	16.4
	-11.8		NM	-12.8	-5.6			-186.6	-300.0
EBIT/Interest			(14) 6.8	(17) 3.0				(88) 12.6	(81) 10.9
			1.7	1.0				3.8	3.8
			-9.1	.3				1.5	1.9
Net Profit + Depr., Dep., Amort./Cur. Mat. L/T/D								(24) 4.1	(25) 3.6
								2.0	1.8
								1.2	1.0
Fixed/Worth	.1		.3	.8	9.1			.6	.3
	NM		.6	2.9	-.5			1.5	1.3
	-.1		1.2	-1.3	-.1			-2.3	-4.5
Debt/Worth	278.9		.2	1.5	34.9			.9	.7
	-3.2		.5	6.8	-2.0			3.4	2.4
	-1.5		2.3	-3.1	-1.4			-13.7	-8.9
% Profit Before Taxes/Tangible Net Worth			(16) 25.6	(11) 10.5				(67) 57.9	(67) 46.6
			11.2	.4				24.6	20.4
			-6.0	-15.7				9.9	4.2
% Profit Before Taxes/Total Assets	3.4		10.1	4.8	9.6			16.0	17.2
	-13.0		5.2	1.0	-.3			7.2	7.3
	-57.1		-6.0	-2.6	-11.2			.9	2.1
Sales/Net Fixed Assets	UND		22.8	7.5	16.2			22.0	33.1
	70.9		6.6	3.3	6.6			7.0	8.7
	23.1		2.4	2.2	2.5			3.6	3.7
Sales/Total Assets	7.9		2.0	1.8	1.3			2.7	2.7
	4.3		1.8	1.4	1.1			1.8	1.9
	2.0		1.4	.9	.8			1.2	1.3
% Depr., Dep., Amort./Sales			1.1	3.2				(88) 1.6	(83) 1.5
			(17) 2.8	4.6				3.0	3.0
			4.4	6.9				4.9	4.8
% Officers', Directors' Owners' Comp/Sales								(21) 2.2	(22) 4.1
								3.3	7.7
								9.2	12.5
Net Sales ($)	10485M	28355M	156005M	515607M	721347M	804786M		2959460M	3986837M
Total Assets ($)	2325M	8185M	92256M	329250M	676105M	935841M		2503187M	3065974M

M = $ thousand   MM = $ million
See Pages 9 through 22 for Explanation of Ratios and Data

Comparative Historical Data | Current Data Sorted by Sales

4/1/07-3/31/08 ALL	4/1/08-3/31/09 ALL	4/1/09-3/31/10 ALL	Type of Statement	0-1MM	1-3MM	3-5MM	5-10MM	10-25MM	25MM & OVER
20	12	20	Unqualified	1			1	5	13
13	11	6	Reviewed		2		3	1	
4	3	1	Compiled		1				
13	12	17	Tax Returns	5	5	2	3	2	
31	36	27	Other	1	2		7	7	10
				14 (4/1-9/30/09)			57 (10/1/09-3/31/10)		
81	74	71	**NUMBER OF STATEMENTS**	6	9	4	14	15	23
%	%	%	**ASSETS**	%	%	%	%	%	%
10.9	11.5	11.6	Cash & Equivalents				16.5	9.0	9.1
24.8	26.6	23.0	Trade Receivables (net)				28.0	18.2	14.7
4.3	3.0	3.3	Inventory				4.3	4.2	3.6
3.9	2.4	2.8	All Other Current				2.2	1.0	2.8
43.9	43.4	40.7	Total Current				51.1	32.4	30.2
25.4	25.5	28.1	Fixed Assets (net)				25.5	42.7	29.6
19.7	19.2	19.8	Intangibles (net)				10.3	21.2	28.2
11.0	12.0	11.4	All Other Non-Current				13.0	3.7	12.0
100.0	100.0	100.0	Total				100.0	100.0	100.0
			LIABILITIES						
3.1	7.4	6.8	Notes Payable-Short Term				4.2	4.6	2.7
3.9	4.3	4.3	Cur. Mat.-L.T.D.				1.6	8.3	5.9
8.3	13.4	9.6	Trade Payables				8.9	6.5	5.9
.1	.3	.2	Income Taxes Payable				.6	.0	.2
12.7	11.5	15.1	All Other Current				8.9	9.4	27.1
28.1	37.0	36.0	Total Current				24.1	28.8	41.8
22.1	25.3	24.4	Long-Term Debt				9.5	15.5	40.1
.5	.6	.4	Deferred Taxes				.0	.1	1.1
13.9	12.0	17.6	All Other Non-Current				3.2	10.8	14.6
35.3	25.2	21.6	Net Worth				63.2	44.9	2.5
100.0	100.0	100.0	Total Liabilities & Net Worth				100.0	100.0	100.0
			INCOME DATA						
100.0	100.0	100.0	Net Sales				100.0	100.0	100.0
47.6	53.6	50.0	Gross Profit				50.3	47.7	45.9
39.9	49.7	46.9	Operating Expenses				45.1	43.9	42.4
7.7	3.9	3.1	Operating Profit				5.2	3.8	3.4
1.5	2.4	2.0	All Other Expenses (net)				-.1	1.0	4.2
6.2	1.5	1.1	Profit Before Taxes				5.4	2.8	-.8
			RATIOS						
2.6	2.6	2.5					3.8	2.3	1.3
1.8	1.3	1.4	Current				2.1	1.5	.9
1.1	.8	.8					1.3	.5	.6
2.2	2.3	1.9					3.5	1.8	1.1
1.4	1.1	1.1	Quick				1.7	.9	.7
.8	.7	.7					1.0	.4	.5
35 10.4	31 11.9	33 11.2					38 9.7	38 9.7	32 11.5
39 9.3	38 9.7	39 9.5	Sales/Receivables				46 7.9	43 8.5	36 10.0
49 7.5	47 7.7	50 7.2					61 6.0	54 6.8	43 8.6
0 UND	0 UND	0 UND					0 UND	5 75.5	4 100.2
6 63.0	7 53.2	6 66.3	Cost of Sales/Inventory				8 43.9	8 44.4	8 44.6
18 20.5	24 15.1	16 22.9					16 22.8	25 14.8	21 17.7
12 30.9	13 29.1	10 37.0					11 32.9	12 31.5	7 50.4
23 15.9	28 13.0	17 20.9	Cost of Sales/Payables				20 18.3	15 24.5	15 24.3
42 8.7	53 6.9	44 8.4					56 6.5	44 8.3	38 9.7
6.6	7.0	7.7					5.9	7.4	22.4
13.2	15.2	31.5	Sales/Working Capital				7.2	17.8	-40.9
67.4	-26.2	-24.2					33.6	-6.6	-7.4
12.5	7.7	4.4					7.6	5.0	3.7
(67) 4.5	(61) 1.6	(57) 1.0	EBIT/Interest				(10) 2.8	(13) .9	(20) .9
1.4	-.6	-.9					-66.1	-.3	-.4
8.3	3.3		Net Profit + Depr., Dep.,						
(12) 2.5	(15) 1.1		Amort./Cur. Mat. L/T/D						
1.0	.3								
.3	.3	.5					.1	.8	2.5
1.2	1.3	2.9	Fixed/Worth				.4	1.9	-2.5
-1.5	-2.2	-1.2					.8	-1.3	-.3
.7	.7	.6					.3	.5	8.3
2.6	3.5	8.3	Debt/Worth				.5	1.6	-4.2
-4.4	-4.4	-2.8					2.3	-3.1	-2.1
52.5	27.0	25.6	% Profit Before Taxes/Tangible				38.9	22.8	
(53) 20.9	(50) 7.8	(40) 9.3	Net Worth				(13) 10.1	(10) 6.8	
9.9	-5.5	-7.6					-9.6	-9.9	
14.9	10.9	8.1	% Profit Before Taxes/Total				13.4	9.5	6.4
7.8	3.6	1.9	Assets				3.4	1.0	.1
1.7	-4.2	-5.0					-6.5	-2.6	-5.0
36.6	30.3	30.8					32.0	9.4	10.5
8.3	8.2	7.4	Sales/Net Fixed Assets				7.4	3.1	3.6
3.5	4.1	2.9					3.1	1.7	2.6
2.7	2.5	2.6					2.9	1.9	1.4
1.6	1.6	1.4	Sales/Total Assets				1.8	1.3	1.1
1.1	1.1	1.0					1.3	.9	.8
1.2	1.0	1.0					1.0	2.6	3.2
(67) 2.7	(58) 2.7	(57) 3.2	% Depr., Dep., Amort./Sales				(13) 2.0	4.1	(13) 3.5
4.8	4.3	4.8					5.1	6.1	5.2
1.6	1.1	2.1	% Officers', Directors'						
(19) 3.8	(20) 3.3	(13) 3.3	Owners' Comp/Sales						
5.4	6.1	15.7							
2943685M	1826852M	2236585M	Net Sales ($)	2701M	18345M	15700M	106521M	241902M	1851416M
2751466M	1537891M	2043962M	Total Assets ($)	1582M	11067M	4881M	77950M	197672M	1750810M

© RMA 2010

M = $ thousand   MM = $ million
See Pages 9 through 22 for Explanation of Ratios and Data

Current Data Sorted by Assets							Comparative Historical Data	
						Type of Statement		
		8	6	1	2	Unqualified	26	25
1	2	4	4			Reviewed	17	19
1	5	2	1			Compiled	20	9
4	2	3	1			Tax Returns	8	13
7	9	15	13	4	10	Other	35	34
24 (4/1-9/30/09)		81 (10/1/09-3/31/10)					4/1/05-3/31/06	4/1/06-3/31/07
0-500M	500M-2MM	2-10MM	10-50MM	50-100MM	100-250MM		ALL	ALL
13	18	32	25	5	12	NUMBER OF STATEMENTS	106	100
%	%	%	%	%	%	**ASSETS**	%	%
17.1	16.5	15.7	12.2		6.7	Cash & Equivalents	15.0	15.7
34.8	33.2	32.2	18.4		8.9	Trade Receivables (net)	29.3	26.3
7.1	5.4	7.4	7.0		.8	Inventory	6.7	6.8
.9	6.5	4.7	5.6		4.5	All Other Current	4.1	4.5
60.0	61.6	60.0	43.3		21.0	Total Current	55.1	53.3
20.5	10.1	16.2	20.4		4.5	Fixed Assets (net)	13.9	13.7
14.6	13.1	13.3	28.0		70.4	Intangibles (net)	20.0	21.6
4.9	15.1	10.4	8.3		4.1	All Other Non-Current	11.0	11.4
100.0	100.0	100.0	100.0		100.0	Total	100.0	100.0
						LIABILITIES		
23.4	10.1	8.3	3.6		1.1	Notes Payable-Short Term	8.2	9.7
17.7	4.3	4.8	2.3		14.6	Cur. Mat.-L.T.D.	3.6	4.8
9.5	20.7	16.8	10.2		4.5	Trade Payables	15.2	13.1
.0	.3	.1	.5		.1	Income Taxes Payable	.4	.4
18.2	35.4	22.3	16.8		16.3	All Other Current	16.8	19.5
68.9	70.8	52.4	33.4		36.6	Total Current	44.1	47.5
67.2	13.1	11.6	23.9		44.9	Long-Term Debt	15.9	26.6
.0	.0	.4	.5		1.6	Deferred Taxes	.4	.4
30.5	11.9	23.1	21.1		8.1	All Other Non-Current	26.5	12.3
-66.7	4.2	12.5	21.1		8.9	Net Worth	13.1	13.2
100.0	100.0	100.0	100.0		100.0	Total Liabilties & Net Worth	100.0	100.0
						INCOME DATA		
100.0	100.0	100.0	100.0		100.0	Net Sales	100.0	100.0
46.4	45.0	44.4	49.9		58.9	Gross Profit	49.2	51.7
39.6	47.0	41.4	44.5		54.3	Operating Expenses	41.9	44.4
6.8	-2.0	3.0	5.4		4.6	Operating Profit	7.3	7.2
1.9	1.0	2.0	2.7		13.0	All Other Expenses (net)	1.6	2.2
5.0	-3.0	1.0	2.8		-8.4	Profit Before Taxes	5.7	5.0
						RATIOS		
2.3	1.7	2.1	2.9		.9		2.3	1.8
.9	1.3	1.2	1.4		.7	Current	1.3	1.2
.4	.5	.8	.7		.5		.9	.7
2.0	1.5	1.9	1.9		.7		1.7	1.3
.8	.7	.9	.9		.5	Quick	1.1	1.0
.3	.4	.6	.5		.4		.6	.6
0 UND	**19** 18.9	**28** 12.8	**30** 12.3		**31** 11.9		**26** 13.8	**30** 12.3
36 10.2	**40** 9.1	**41** 9.0	**39** 9.4		**38** 9.5	Sales/Receivables	**42** 8.7	**41** 8.9
61 6.0	**65** 5.6	**61** 6.0	**64** 5.7		**51** 7.2		**62** 5.9	**62** 5.9
0 UND	**0** UND	**0** UND	**0** UND		**2** 146.2		**0** UND	**0** UND
0 UND	**0** UND	**5** 75.3	**16** 22.6		**9** 40.4	Cost of Sales/Inventory	**7** 49.3	**8** 44.6
0 UND	**14** 26.5	**22** 16.5	**53** 6.8		**19** 19.3		**24** 15.1	**29** 12.7
0 UND	**14** 25.8	**20** 18.4	**15** 24.8		**20** 18.3		**18** 20.2	**15** 25.0
7 53.3	**39** 9.4	**28** 13.1	**33** 11.0		**58** 6.2	Cost of Sales/Payables	**37** 9.8	**30** 12.0
32 11.4	**121** 3.0	**92** 4.0	**82** 4.5		**188** 1.9		**63** 5.8	**69** 5.3
10.0	9.8	8.3	4.7		-91.7		7.2	8.7
-288.0	18.7	20.5	18.6		-11.6	Sales/Working Capital	21.5	24.7
-12.6	-5.7	-20.2	-7.8		-4.3		-24.9	-13.7
4.7	2.7	16.7	21.6				22.3	13.6
(10) 1.4	(13) 1.0	(31) 3.0	(23) 3.2			EBIT/Interest	(94) 4.4	(85) 4.4
-.6	-35.2	-2.7	.7				.6	.9
							10.7	15.5
						Net Profit + Depr., Dep., Amort./Cur. Mat. L/T/D	(28) 4.4	(24) 3.2
							1.2	1.1
.0	.1	.4	.5		-.2		.2	.2
.5	.4	4.5	-2.6		-.1	Fixed/Worth	1.4	1.4
-.7	-1.4	-.2	-.2		.0		-.2	-.1
10.0	1.0	1.4	1.1		-1.8		1.2	1.3
-2.6	4.3	37.5	-8.0		-1.3	Debt/Worth	9.2	8.2
-1.3	-3.4	-4.0	-1.9		-1.2		-2.6	-2.2
	47.3	64.3	43.6				86.2	78.5
	(12) -5.5	(18) 4.4	(11) 13.3			% Profit Before Taxes/Tangible Net Worth	(56) 45.8	(55) 35.6
	-29.1	-29.6	6.8				17.5	13.8
40.2	9.9	12.9	8.4		3.8		22.8	20.7
12.5	.0	2.8	3.3		-5.0	% Profit Before Taxes/Total Assets	8.6	8.0
-13.5	-12.8	-7.8	-2.5		-9.8		-1.2	-.1
UND	89.8	64.0	28.8		43.4		63.4	63.4
337.3	39.6	28.4	10.0		17.1	Sales/Net Fixed Assets	30.9	29.7
20.6	15.5	11.3	3.1		10.3		11.7	11.1
8.6	3.5	3.4	1.9		1.1		3.3	3.4
4.7	2.8	2.4	1.5		.6	Sales/Total Assets	2.2	2.0
2.6	1.7	1.7	1.0		.4		1.5	1.3
	.4	.6	1.2				.5	.7
	(14) 1.0	(23) 1.0	(16) 2.2			% Depr., Dep., Amort./Sales	(81) 1.1	(72) 1.4
	1.6	1.7	4.5				2.5	3.2
		3.3					3.6	3.0
		(10) 4.8				% Officers', Directors' Owners' Comp/Sales	(31) 5.2	(28) 4.3
		8.7					10.3	11.7
20051M	63778M	356732M	944100M	251469M	1364518M	Net Sales ($)	3030258M	2362486M
3623M	22833M	160214M	639287M	363211M	1818612M	Total Assets ($)	2636418M	2179697M

M = $ thousand MM = $ million

See Pages 9 through 22 for Explanation of Ratios and Data

Comparative Historical Data   Current Data Sorted by Sales

Type of Statement	4/1/07-3/31/08 ALL	4/1/08-3/31/09 ALL	4/1/09-3/31/10 ALL	0-1MM	1-3MM	3-5MM	5-10MM	10-25MM	25MM & OVER
					24 (4/1-9/30/09)		81 (10/1/09-3/31/10)		
Unqualified	25	24	17				2	9	6
Reviewed	15	10	11	1	1		2	6	1
Compiled	9	8	9	1	2	2	3		1
Tax Returns	13	13	10	1	2	3	3	1	
Other	37	53	58	4	6	7	8	10	23
NUMBER OF STATEMENTS	99	108	105	7	11	12	18	26	31
ASSETS	%	%	%	%	%	%	%	%	%
Cash & Equivalents	13.8	13.9	14.2		17.1	13.9	21.1	15.3	10.1
Trade Receivables (net)	27.2	26.8	25.6		43.7	28.7	28.0	31.3	12.6
Inventory	6.0	5.2	5.9		.1	11.4	3.4	8.6	3.4
All Other Current	4.4	4.7	4.6		1.9	1.5	9.0	6.2	3.6
Total Current	51.5	50.6	50.3		62.6	55.5	61.5	61.4	29.8
Fixed Assets (net)	18.5	14.0	14.8		8.0	15.9	17.5	16.1	12.9
Intangibles (net)	17.0	22.0	25.8		21.3	10.4	10.1	14.6	50.7
All Other Non-Current	13.0	13.4	9.1		8.1	18.2	10.8	7.8	6.7
Total	100.0	100.0	100.0		100.0	100.0	100.0	100.0	100.0
LIABILITIES									
Notes Payable-Short Term	7.7	6.7	8.2		19.2	15.0	6.0	6.8	1.1
Cur. Mat.-L.T.D.	4.2	3.6	6.8		11.8	11.4	2.9	4.8	7.3
Trade Payables	12.5	14.0	12.9		14.5	19.8	15.2	18.2	5.8
Income Taxes Payable	.2	.8	.3		.2	.2	.3	.2	.7
All Other Current	21.9	17.7	21.8		36.7	13.7	24.5	18.7	18.6
Total Current	46.5	42.8	50.0		82.3	60.1	48.9	48.7	33.4
Long-Term Debt	24.0	26.4	26.1		48.9	36.2	13.0	17.7	30.0
Deferred Taxes	.2	.2	.5		.0	.0	.7	.4	.8
All Other Non-Current	19.5	20.0	19.1		34.4	17.6	19.7	20.1	17.4
Net Worth	9.8	10.5	4.4		-65.6	-13.9	17.6	13.0	18.4
Total Liabilties & Net Worth	100.0	100.0	100.0		100.0	100.0	100.0	100.0	100.0
INCOME DATA									
Net Sales	100.0	100.0	100.0		100.0	100.0	100.0	100.0	100.0
Gross Profit	48.2	51.8	47.9		48.4	47.7	51.5	37.3	54.5
Operating Expenses	41.5	47.1	44.4		49.0	50.6	47.5	33.5	49.6
Operating Profit	6.8	4.7	3.5		-.6	-3.0	4.0	3.8	4.9
All Other Expenses (net)	1.5	2.1	3.4		2.2	2.1	1.5	2.1	7.1
Profit Before Taxes	5.2	2.6	.0		-2.8	-5.0	2.5	1.7	-2.2
RATIOS									
Current	2.1	2.3	2.0		2.6	1.5	2.1	2.4	1.5
	1.4	1.3	1.0		.8	1.2	1.3	1.3	.8
	.8	.7	.6		.3	.6	.9	.7	.5
Quick	1.6	2.0	1.5		2.6	1.2	2.0	2.0	1.1
	(98) 1.1	.9	.8		.8	.7	1.0	1.1	.6
	.6	.5	.4		.3	.5	.7	.6	.4
Sales/Receivables	30 12.0	23 15.9	28 13.2		34 10.8	5 71.7	22 16.8	31 11.9	28 13.0
	41 8.9	37 10.0	39 9.4		59 6.2	32 11.4	39 9.4	40 9.0	38 9.6
	61 6.0	56 6.5	60 6.0		71 5.1	53 6.9	62 5.9	73 5.0	52 7.0
Cost of Sales/Inventory	0 UND	0 UND	0 UND		0 UND	0 UND	0 UND	0 UND	4 81.3
	5 68.1	5 74.5	5 67.7		0 UND	0 UND	0 UND	7 51.6	10 35.3
	29 12.6	25 14.4	23 15.6		0 UND	69 5.3	21 17.4	25 14.5	26 14.0
Cost of Sales/Payables	18 20.8	15 23.8	15 24.6		8 44.9	10 35.0	17 21.7	19 19.2	17 21.2
	29 12.6	32 11.5	33 11.0		39 9.4	21 17.6	28 13.0	29 12.7	38 9.5
	58 6.3	66 5.6	84 4.3		48 7.6	105 3.5	91 4.0	78 4.7	91 4.0
Sales/Working Capital	7.0	6.6	8.3		8.7	14.7	9.0	5.2	8.1
	18.2	25.4	183.6		-17.0	20.3	22.5	9.7	-21.0
	-29.8	-15.0	-8.1		-3.8	-30.4	-24.9	-16.3	-4.4
EBIT/Interest	9.2	20.6	7.0		3.3		34.6	17.9	6.4
	(84) 3.4	(89) 3.0	(89) 1.6		(10) 1.8		(16) 2.9	1.3	(25) 1.5
	.8	.1	-.9		-20.6		-2.4	-2.0	.3
Net Profit + Depr., Dep., Amort./Cur. Mat. L/T/D	24.8	5.1	2.3						
	(22) 3.3	(23) 2.0	(18) .6						
	.4	.3	-3.8						
Fixed/Worth	.3	.3	.3		.0	.1	.4	.2	5.0
	1.8	-2.1	49.0		.5	.9	2.0	-14.3	-.2
	-.4	-.2	-.1		.0	-.6	-2.0	-.2	-.1
Debt/Worth	1.3	1.5	1.8		19.0	.9	1.6	1.0	15.7
	5.9	-14.2	-8.0		-1.9	4.3	9.2	-36.2	-2.1
	-3.5	-2.8	-1.8		-1.3	-2.7	-9.0	-2.8	-1.2
% Profit Before Taxes/Tangible Net Worth	65.3	77.2	55.7				85.7	52.7	
	(62) 29.7	(48) 33.3	(47) 10.1				(13) 19.5	(12) 7.4	
	1.2	2.5	-18.5				-31.4	-1.9	
% Profit Before Taxes/Total Assets	16.9	16.7	9.7		24.4	9.0	12.0	9.8	6.3
	7.8	4.7	2.0		.0	-5.1	7.6	.6	.4
	-.9	-3.6	-8.1		-19.2	-36.3	-5.1	-4.4	-7.4
Sales/Net Fixed Assets	45.5	60.8	66.0		UND	81.1	56.8	69.9	27.3
	18.4	28.2	20.8		70.6	29.9	24.2	28.6	11.7
	8.2	10.5	10.2		17.0	15.0	9.8	8.4	8.7
Sales/Total Assets	3.0	3.5	3.0		4.7	5.9	3.4	2.9	1.6
	2.0	2.0	2.0		2.5	3.0	2.8	2.0	1.0
	1.2	1.2	1.0		1.7	1.9	1.3	1.5	.6
% Depr., Dep., Amort./Sales	.6	.8	.8			.5	.4	.6	1.7
	(76) 1.4	(64) 1.5	(64) 1.4			(10) 1.3	(13) .9	(19) 1.0	(16) 3.7
	3.1	3.8	2.2			1.6	1.6	1.8	4.2
% Officers', Directors' Owners' Comp/Sales	2.8	2.5	2.6						
	(29) 4.3	(26) 4.3	(29) 5.2						
	6.4	7.0	10.5						
Net Sales ($)	2763068M	3011835M	3000648M	3647M	22509M	45379M	126946M	420847M	2381320M
Total Assets ($)	2196962M	2852811M	3007780M	2913M	10216M	19828M	74841M	225641M	2674341M

© RMA 2010

M = $ thousand   MM = $ million
See Pages 9 through 22 for Explanation of Ratios and Data

Current Data Sorted by Assets   Comparative Historical Data

Type of Statement

0-500M	500M-2MM	2-10MM	10-50MM	50-100MM	100-250MM	Type of Statement	4/1/05-3/31/06 ALL	4/1/06-3/31/07 ALL
	2	7	6	7	2	Unqualified	19	30
		15	3	1	1	Reviewed	23	25
1	1					Compiled	9	9
2	5	5				Tax Returns	8	10
1	4	8	18	9	1	Other	36	36
4 (4/1-9/30/09) → 31		68 ← (10/1/09-3/31/10)						
4	12	35	27	17	4	NUMBER OF STATEMENTS	95	110

Main Data

(Ratio rows show counts in parentheses where applicable. Size columns: 0-500M, 500M-2MM, 2-10MM, 10-50MM, 50-100MM, 100-250MM.)

0-500M	500M-2MM	2-10MM	10-50MM	50-100MM	100-250MM		ALL	ALL
%	%	%	%	%	%	**ASSETS**	%	%
	17.1	8.6	14.2	8.6		Cash & Equivalents	10.4	12.0
	15.3	26.7	20.5	19.2		Trade Receivables (net)	27.2	24.0
	43.1	31.6	19.0	18.7		Inventory	27.9	29.2
	.1	6.9	8.4	6.1		All Other Current	4.4	3.5
	75.6	73.9	62.1	52.6		Total Current	69.9	68.7
	9.4	11.4	15.2	10.9		Fixed Assets (net)	11.8	10.5
	7.2	7.7	15.9	29.1		Intangibles (net)	9.5	10.8
	7.8	7.0	6.8	7.4		All Other Non-Current	8.9	10.0
	100.0	100.0	100.0	100.0		Total	100.0	100.0
						LIABILITIES		
	10.5	9.1	9.0	6.0		Notes Payable-Short Term	7.9	10.3
	3.8	2.4	2.7	3.0		Cur. Mat.-L.T.D.	3.6	2.3
	8.7	10.3	11.4	7.9		Trade Payables	15.3	14.9
	.5	.1	.9	.4		Income Taxes Payable	.6	.3
	3.9	15.5	13.2	13.4		All Other Current	14.0	11.5
	27.3	37.5	37.1	30.6		Total Current	41.5	39.3
	14.3	21.6	9.9	16.1		Long-Term Debt	9.2	9.2
	.0	.1	.3	1.4		Deferred Taxes	.9	.5
	17.6	11.4	13.7	6.0		All Other Non-Current	8.1	6.2
	40.8	29.4	38.9	46.0		Net Worth	40.3	44.8
	100.0	100.0	100.0	100.0		Total Liabilities & Net Worth	100.0	100.0
						INCOME DATA		
	100.0	100.0	100.0	100.0		Net Sales	100.0	100.0
	57.5	51.6	49.8	56.6		Gross Profit	50.7	54.5
	56.9	51.1	46.5	48.5		Operating Expenses	45.0	49.0
	.6	.5	3.3	8.0		Operating Profit	5.7	5.5
	-.1	2.5	.8	3.7		All Other Expenses (net)	1.6	.9
	.7	-2.0	2.5	4.4		Profit Before Taxes	4.1	4.6
						RATIOS		
	10.0	3.6	2.9	2.6		Current	2.7	3.0
	3.1	2.0	2.1	2.1			1.8	1.9
	1.9	1.4	1.3	1.1			1.1	1.2
	7.2	2.0	1.6	1.5		Quick	1.5	1.8
	1.4	.9	.9	1.2			.9	1.0
	.4	.4	.5	.6			.5	.5
	(12) 31.7	(34) 10.6	(30) 12.3	(33) 11.0		Sales/Receivables	(37) 9.9	(31) 11.6
	(19) 19.7	(63) 5.8	(47) 7.7	(72) 5.1			(58) 6.3	(54) 6.8
	(47) 7.7	(89) 4.1	(67) 5.5	(128) 2.9			(83) 4.4	(74) 4.9
	(113) 3.2	(63) 5.8	(17) 21.8	(97) 3.8		Cost of Sales/Inventory	(61) 6.0	(75) 4.9
	(200) 1.8	(170) 2.1	(67) 5.4	(154) 2.4			(145) 2.5	(161) 2.3
	(377) 1.0	(313) 1.2	(152) 2.4	(187) 2.0			(236) 1.5	(266) 1.4
	(11) 34.4	(12) 30.4	(26) 14.1	(31) 11.8		Cost of Sales/Payables	(31) 11.9	(30) 12.3
	(32) 11.4	(32) 11.3	(53) 6.9	(48) 7.6			(56) 6.5	(55) 6.6
	(77) 4.7	(82) 4.4	(79) 4.6	(116) 3.1			(110) 3.3	(119) 3.1
	2.1	2.6	3.2	2.2		Sales/Working Capital	3.1	2.7
	4.6	4.2	5.2	3.7			5.7	5.8
	7.0	10.4	15.2	31.5			25.3	15.5
	6.6	9.3	9.0	7.1		EBIT/Interest	11.5	7.0
	(10) 2.5	(30) 2.5	(26) 4.0	(16) 2.0			(80) 3.9	(91) 3.2
	1.4	-3.7	-.4	.1			.6	1.4
			34.4			Net Profit + Depr., Dep., Amort./Cur. Mat. L/T/D	7.6	5.1
		(10) 3.2					(22) 1.9	(20) 2.5
			.1				.4	1.7
	.1	.1	.1	.2		Fixed/Worth	.1	.1
	.2	.2	.2	.4			.2	.2
	.6	.8	11.9	-.9			1.2	1.1
	.4	.5	.7	.8		Debt/Worth	.8	.6
	1.6	1.1	2.9	2.5			2.1	1.3
	4.6	11.3	34.6	-2.9			8.8	7.7
	34.3	19.4	27.2	23.5		% Profit Before Taxes/Tangible Net Worth	36.3	34.0
	(10) 4.9	(29) 1.5	(21) 21.7	(11) 14.1			(79) 12.4	(93) 13.5
	2.1	-36.5	-.7	-.1			1.2	2.2
	10.9	8.2	14.9	9.3		% Profit Before Taxes/Total Assets	12.5	12.1
	2.7	.1	4.4	3.8			5.2	5.0
	.8	-12.0	-2.8	-1.4			.0	1.2
	81.0	71.6	38.4	25.4		Sales/Net Fixed Assets	80.1	76.1
	28.6	33.9	23.1	18.8			25.5	26.4
	16.3	8.9	4.9	6.0			11.1	12.0
	2.8	2.1	1.8	1.2		Sales/Total Assets	2.0	2.0
	2.0	1.5	1.5	1.0			1.5	1.5
	1.5	1.2	1.1	.7			1.1	1.0
		.6	1.1	1.8		% Depr., Dep., Amort./Sales	.8	.7
		(29) 1.4	(19) 2.6	(12) 2.5			(66) 1.5	(75) 1.5
		2.6	4.5	3.1			3.1	2.8
						% Officers', Directors' Owners' Comp/Sales	3.3	2.1
							(27) 5.7	(29) 5.3
							14.4	13.1
1744M	30439M	298371M	1044234M	1173841M	482473M	Net Sales ($)	3564416M	3055349M
891M	15206M	184457M	699638M	1186234M	583720M	Total Assets ($)	2724927M	2594843M

© RMA 2010

M = $ thousand   MM = $ million
See Pages 9 through 22 for Explanation of Ratios and Data

Comparative Historical Data   Current Data Sorted by Sales

4/1/07-3/31/08 ALL	4/1/08-3/31/09 ALL	4/1/09-3/31/10 ALL	Type of Statement	0-1MM	1-3MM	3-5MM	5-10MM	10-25MM	25MM & OVER
25	23	22	Unqualified		4	3	5	3	14
26	21	22	Reviewed		1	1	6	6	3
5	3	2	Compiled						
7	11	12	Tax Returns	2	5	3	1	1	
40	34	41	Other	1	4	1	4	9	22
				31 (4/1-9/30/09)			68 (10/1/09-3/31/10)		
103	92	99	**NUMBER OF STATEMENTS**	3	14	8	16	19	39
%	%	%	**ASSETS**	%	%	%	%	%	%
9.9	11.0	12.5	Cash & Equivalents		15.5		10.7	5.4	14.9
27.7	22.9	22.2	Trade Receivables (net)		14.2		25.5	26.7	21.1
29.4	29.3	26.3	Inventory		41.0		32.7	23.6	18.1
3.6	4.9	6.5	All Other Current		.9		7.4	10.7	7.4
70.5	68.2	67.6	Total Current		71.5		76.3	66.4	61.4
12.1	12.4	11.6	Fixed Assets (net)		10.2		10.1	12.3	12.3
8.7	12.0	13.6	Intangibles (net)		7.5		7.7	17.2	18.8
8.7	7.4	7.2	All Other Non-Current		10.8		6.0	4.1	7.5
100.0	100.0	100.0	Total		100.0		100.0	100.0	100.0
			LIABILITIES						
8.4	9.2	8.2	Notes Payable-Short Term		8.7		8.0	9.4	7.2
2.6	1.7	2.6	Cur. Mat.-L.T.D.		6.7		1.6	1.6	2.6
13.5	11.4	10.6	Trade Payables		8.9		12.3	10.0	11.2
.3	.2	.4	Income Taxes Payable		.1		.2	.3	.7
15.1	11.8	13.4	All Other Current		4.4		13.1	15.8	14.8
40.0	34.3	35.1	Total Current		28.9		35.2	37.2	36.4
11.9	12.3	16.0	Long-Term Debt		44.4		4.7	12.1	12.5
.2	.3	.4	Deferred Taxes		.0		.0	.4	.9
9.5	14.8	12.6	All Other Non-Current		16.2		6.7	17.4	12.8
38.4	38.4	35.9	Net Worth		10.5		53.4	32.9	37.4
100.0	100.0	100.0	Total Liabilities & Net Worth		100.0		100.0	100.0	100.0
			INCOME DATA						
100.0	100.0	100.0	Net Sales		100.0		100.0	100.0	100.0
48.5	53.0	53.0	Gross Profit		62.6		45.0	57.3	50.5
42.3	49.4	50.2	Operating Expenses		64.2		43.6	52.8	46.4
6.2	3.6	2.8	Operating Profit		-1.6		1.4	4.5	4.1
1.6	2.0	2.1	All Other Expenses (net)		2.4		2.4	1.5	2.3
4.6	1.6	.7	Profit Before Taxes		-4.0		-1.0	3.0	1.9
			RATIOS						
2.9	3.5	3.2	Current		8.6		4.9	2.5	2.9
2.0	2.2	2.1			2.5		2.4	1.9	2.1
1.3	1.4	1.3			1.6		1.9	1.4	1.1
1.6	1.6	1.8	Quick		4.7		2.9	1.3	1.7
1.0	.9	.9			1.1		1.0	.9	1.2
.6	.5	.5			.4		.3	.6	.5
36 10.0	31 11.6	28 13.2	Sales/Receivables		12 30.1		35 10.5	38 9.6	30 12.3
57 6.4	51 7.1	49 7.4			24 15.5		59 6.2	56 6.5	57 6.4
91 4.0	71 5.2	83 4.4			75 4.8		102 3.6	90 4.0	83 4.4
62 5.9	50 7.3	63 5.8	Cost of Sales/Inventory		147 2.5		117 3.1	42 8.7	52 7.0
151 2.4	174 2.1	140 2.6			254 1.4		167 2.2	184 2.0	96 3.8
276 1.3	247 1.5	246 1.5			513 .7		304 1.2	304 1.2	154 2.4
24 15.1	24 15.1	23 15.6	Cost of Sales/Payables		29 12.8		11 33.5	19 19.1	29 12.7
48 7.7	51 7.2	47 7.7			62 5.9		34 10.9	32 11.3	53 6.9
98 3.7	75 4.8	87 4.2			88 4.2		87 4.2	87 4.2	85 4.3
2.6	2.7	2.6	Sales/Working Capital		1.8		2.1	2.8	2.6
4.0	5.2	4.3			3.3		3.3	5.0	4.9
13.4	10.2	11.6			8.2		4.8	8.3	30.0
10.2	6.3	8.1	EBIT/Interest		5.4		8.6	6.7	11.4
(84) 3.6	(78) 2.3	(86) 2.8			(12) 1.3		(12) 2.8	2.9	(35) 3.8
.7	.4	-1.0			-2.0		-11.4	-4.3	.0
8.9	6.7	15.3	Net Profit + Depr., Dep.,						22.5
(20) 2.5	(21) 1.7	(20) 1.8	Amort./Cur. Mat. L/T/D					(10) 3.7	3.7
1.2	.7	.6							-2.8
.1	.1	.1	Fixed/Worth		.1		.0	.1	.1
.2	.3	.3			.1		.2	.3	.4
1.1	1.0	1.6			.7		.4	1.7	-1.5
.6	.5	.5	Debt/Worth		.3		.4	.8	.5
1.4	1.5	1.7			2.7		.9	2.0	2.9
7.7	6.7	34.6			10.1		3.7	-10.3	-6.3
35.8	19.3	24.5	% Profit Before Taxes/Tangible Net Worth		27.6		26.5	29.7	24.6
(87) 12.3	(75) 5.1	(76) 6.2			(12) 3.2		(14) 1.8	(14) 8.3	(27) 17.1
1.9	-2.6	-3.7			.1		-25.3	-14.8	.4
12.7	7.7	9.4	% Profit Before Taxes/Total Assets		6.1		7.7	12.5	10.2
4.9	2.3	2.4			1.5		1.2	3.6	3.8
-.9	-2.2	-3.4			-9.2		-14.2	-8.7	-2.3
79.1	37.9	55.2	Sales/Net Fixed Assets		74.8		102.8	53.1	28.8
22.3	22.7	24.6			26.9		24.4	34.2	18.0
7.9	7.4	8.2			7.8		9.3	8.2	6.5
2.0	2.2	1.8	Sales/Total Assets		2.1		1.7	2.4	1.6
1.4	1.5	1.4			1.5		1.4	1.5	1.2
1.0	1.0	1.0			1.0		1.2	1.0	.9
.7	1.0	.6	% Depr., Dep., Amort./Sales		.2		1.1	.8	2.0
(69) 1.7	(67) 1.7	(71) 1.8			(11) .4		(13) 1.8	(14) 1.4	(27) 2.6
2.7	3.0	2.9			.6		3.2	3.4	4.1
2.0	3.2	3.8	% Officers', Directors' Owners' Comp/Sales						
(21) 3.6	(18) 6.3	(19) 5.0							
9.1	10.9	11.8							
3283561M	2874421M	3031102M	Net Sales ($)	732M	29792M	30186M	113781M	299734M	2556877M
3081407M	2702938M	2670146M	Total Assets ($)	418M	23994M	17966M	90809M	271762M	2265197M

M = $ thousand   MM = $ million
See Pages 9 through 22 for Explanation of Ratios and Data

Current Data Sorted by Assets   Comparative Historical Data

Type of Statement

0-500M	500M-2MM	2-10MM	10-50MM	50-100MM	100-250MM	Type of Statement	4/1/05-3/31/06 ALL	4/1/06-3/31/07 ALL
		2			2	Unqualified	5	4
	1	3	1			Reviewed	4	7
	1	1				Compiled	5	2
2		1				Tax Returns	3	5
1	1	5	1	1	2	Other	8	9
	2 (4/1-9/30/09)		23 (10/1/09-3/31/10)					
3	4	11	2	3	2	NUMBER OF STATEMENTS	25	27
%	%	%	%	%	%		%	%

ASSETS

0-500M	500M-2MM	2-10MM	10-50MM	50-100MM	100-250MM		4/1/05-3/31/06 ALL	4/1/06-3/31/07 ALL
		13.0				Cash & Equivalents	10.2	6.4
		38.8				Trade Receivables (net)	35.8	40.1
		6.5				Inventory	2.9	3.3
		3.1				All Other Current	3.6	5.2
		61.3				Total Current	52.6	54.9
		23.7				Fixed Assets (net)	23.1	31.5
		6.7				Intangibles (net)	11.8	6.9
		8.3				All Other Non-Current	12.5	6.8
		100.0				Total	100.0	100.0

LIABILITIES

0-500M	500M-2MM	2-10MM	10-50MM	50-100MM	100-250MM		4/1/05-3/31/06 ALL	4/1/06-3/31/07 ALL
		9.4				Notes Payable-Short Term	8.5	8.2
		4.5				Cur. Mat.-L.T.D.	4.1	2.2
		14.0				Trade Payables	24.1	15.4
		.0				Income Taxes Payable	.1	.0
		19.8				All Other Current	43.5	21.4
		47.9				Total Current	80.4	47.2
		10.4				Long-Term Debt	11.8	26.1
		.3				Deferred Taxes	.0	.1
		6.4				All Other Non-Current	11.7	10.8
		35.1				Net Worth	-3.8	15.7
		100.0				Total Liabilities & Net Worth	100.0	100.0

INCOME DATA

0-500M	500M-2MM	2-10MM	10-50MM	50-100MM	100-250MM		4/1/05-3/31/06 ALL	4/1/06-3/31/07 ALL
		100.0				Net Sales	100.0	100.0
						Gross Profit		
		97.6				Operating Expenses	92.1	98.6
		2.4				Operating Profit	7.9	1.4
		.7				All Other Expenses (net)	1.1	2.5
		1.6				Profit Before Taxes	6.8	-1.1

RATIOS

0-500M	500M-2MM	2-10MM	10-50MM	50-100MM	100-250MM		4/1/05-3/31/06 ALL	4/1/06-3/31/07 ALL
		2.4				Current	1.4	1.9
		1.5					1.0	1.4
		.7					.5	.7
		2.4				Quick	1.3	1.7
		1.1					.8	1.2
		.6					.4	.6
	28	13.1				Sales/Receivables	26 14.0	20 17.9
	46	7.9					44 8.2	53 6.9
	69	5.3					70 5.2	71 5.2
						Cost of Sales/Inventory		
						Cost of Sales/Payables		
		6.5				Sales/Working Capital	20.4	11.3
		11.4					-97.5	34.8
		-15.1					-9.2	-40.2
		19.4				EBIT/Interest	38.5	16.9
	(10)	2.8					(21) 12.0	(22) 4.5
		-2.0					1.9	-.2
						Net Profit + Depr., Dep., Amort./Cur. Mat. L/T/D		
		.1				Fixed/Worth	.7	.5
		1.7					1.5	1.5
		5.6					-1.0	-2.5
		1.2				Debt/Worth	1.2	.7
		2.3					9.4	4.5
		18.4					-4.3	-4.8
						% Profit Before Taxes/Tangible Net Worth	176.3	30.1
							(17) 36.8	(18) 19.0
							15.5	-1.2
		11.6				% Profit Before Taxes/Total Assets	28.8	17.0
		2.7					9.8	3.2
		-1.7					6.1	-13.7
		73.6				Sales/Net Fixed Assets	41.4	32.4
		17.3					18.4	15.4
		4.5					8.1	5.0
		4.4				Sales/Total Assets	5.7	5.9
		2.7					2.8	3.4
		1.5					2.0	1.9
		.9				% Depr., Dep., Amort./Sales	1.1	1.0
	(10)	1.8					(21) 2.1	(21) 1.8
		3.9					3.6	4.3
						% Officers', Directors' Owners' Comp/Sales	3.2	1.4
							(11) 5.3	(11) 8.5
							10.5	9.8
3664M	17499M	127675M	87338M	275215M	209874M	Net Sales ($)	643217M	1480752M
693M	5039M	49476M	58079M	238745M	304897M	Total Assets ($)	391988M	552469M

© RMA 2010

M = $ thousand   MM = $ million
See Pages 9 through 22 for Explanation of Ratios and Data

Comparative Historical Data | Current Data Sorted by Sales

			Type of Statement						
5	4	4	Unqualified				1	1	2
4	4	5	Reviewed		1		2	1	1
2	5	2	Compiled			1	1		
6	8	3	Tax Returns		2		1		
16	16	11	Other	1	2		1	4	4
4/1/07-3/31/08 ALL	4/1/08-3/31/09 ALL	4/1/09-3/31/10 ALL			2 (4/1-9/30/09)		23 (10/1/09-3/31/10)		
				0-1MM	1-3MM	3-5MM	5-10MM	10-25MM	25MM & OVER
33	37	25	NUMBER OF STATEMENTS	1	5	1	5	6	7
%	%	%	ASSETS	%	%	%	%	%	%
9.5	13.3	11.6	Cash & Equivalents						
33.4	29.3	31.6	Trade Receivables (net)						
7.1	6.4	6.6	Inventory						
6.1	2.8	2.5	All Other Current						
56.0	51.8	52.2	Total Current						
21.3	24.2	23.2	Fixed Assets (net)						
13.6	13.6	12.7	Intangibles (net)						
9.0	10.3	11.8	All Other Non-Current						
100.0	100.0	100.0	Total						
			LIABILITIES						
21.6	4.4	8.1	Notes Payable-Short Term						
3.1	4.2	5.6	Cur. Mat.-L.T.D.						
13.2	12.5	11.9	Trade Payables						
.0	.0	.0	Income Taxes Payable						
17.4	19.3	21.3	All Other Current						
55.5	40.4	46.9	Total Current						
25.9	20.9	21.9	Long-Term Debt						
.1	.1	.2	Deferred Taxes						
8.8	10.6	10.6	All Other Non-Current						
9.8	28.0	20.4	Net Worth						
100.0	100.0	100.0	Total Liabilties & Net Worth						
			INCOME DATA						
100.0	100.0	100.0	Net Sales						
			Gross Profit						
94.2	93.3	97.4	Operating Expenses						
5.8	6.7	2.6	Operating Profit						
1.5	2.0	1.6	All Other Expenses (net)						
4.3	4.7	.9	Profit Before Taxes						
			RATIOS						
1.8	2.0	1.9	Current						
1.1	1.4	1.1							
.7	.9	.7							
1.5	1.5	1.5	Quick						
.8	1.2	.9							
.5	.8	.6							
14 25.3	22 16.4	26 14.2	Sales/Receivables						
41 9.0	42 8.6	46 7.9							
63 5.8	57 6.4	85 4.3							
			Cost of Sales/Inventory						
			Cost of Sales/Payables						
9.3	8.8	8.1	Sales/Working Capital						
80.9	23.0	49.7							
-23.2	-65.1	-10.7							
13.1	9.4	16.0	EBIT/Interest						
(30) 4.7	(32) 2.1	(20) 3.5							
.4	-7.2	.1							
			Net Profit + Depr., Dep., Amort./Cur. Mat. L/T/D						
.3	.2	.5	Fixed/Worth						
1.6	1.2	4.4							
-.9	NM	-.8							
1.7	.8	1.0	Debt/Worth						
6.9	2.9	7.9							
-4.9	NM	-10.3							
67.9	112.1	79.5	% Profit Before Taxes/Tangible Net Worth						
(18) 47.6	(28) 20.7	(17) 25.2							
15.6	-10.7	-68.5							
24.3	28.4	13.1	% Profit Before Taxes/Total Assets						
12.2	3.5	5.2							
-1.3	-5.7	-2.6							
43.3	59.0	36.7	Sales/Net Fixed Assets						
17.6	14.9	14.6							
10.3	5.9	5.1							
5.4	4.1	4.2	Sales/Total Assets						
3.0	2.8	2.7							
1.5	1.4	1.2							
1.2	.7	.9	% Depr., Dep., Amort./Sales						
(24) 1.9	(24) 2.4	(18) 2.4							
3.9	4.6	5.3							
			% Officers', Directors' Owners' Comp/Sales						
1398945M	1129280M	721265M	Net Sales ($)	768M	9482M	4996M	35303M	83488M	587228M
871888M	717157M	656929M	Total Assets ($)	178M	4773M	4542M	15643M	61953M	569840M

M = $ thousand   MM = $ million
See Pages 9 through 22 for Explanation of Ratios and Data

Current Data Sorted by Assets   Comparative Historical Data

Type of Statement	0-500M	500M-2MM	2-10MM	10-50MM	50-100MM	100-250MM		4/1/05-3/31/06 ALL	4/1/06-3/31/07 ALL
Unqualified		1	3	8	3	2		16	20
Reviewed		3	5	1				16	15
Compiled			2					8	6
Tax Returns	2			1				6	7
Other	2	8	7	7	2	3		31	26
		12 (4/1-9/30/09)		48 (10/1/09-3/31/10)					
NUMBER OF STATEMENTS	4	12	18	16	5	5		77	74
	%	%	%	%	%	%		%	%
ASSETS									
Cash & Equivalents		10.1	14.5	16.4				14.6	13.5
Trade Receivables (net)		35.8	26.5	22.0				31.9	29.8
Inventory		18.6	14.1	8.9				11.4	13.0
All Other Current		3.9	3.7	7.6				7.4	4.2
Total Current		68.4	58.8	54.9				65.4	60.6
Fixed Assets (net)		13.0	15.7	14.9				20.9	18.6
Intangibles (net)		13.5	19.7	25.5				4.9	11.0
All Other Non-Current		5.1	5.7	4.7				8.8	9.8
Total		100.0	100.0	100.0				100.0	100.0
LIABILITIES									
Notes Payable-Short Term		18.9	5.3	3.2				8.9	10.8
Cur. Mat.-L.T.D.		1.8	3.0	2.9				2.0	4.9
Trade Payables		18.0	14.1	18.6				16.1	14.6
Income Taxes Payable		.0	.4	.1				.5	.2
All Other Current		8.0	13.7	19.2				14.5	18.9
Total Current		46.8	36.5	44.1				42.0	49.3
Long-Term Debt		17.1	5.3	18.7				13.4	17.3
Deferred Taxes		.0	1.0	.7				.4	.6
All Other Non-Current		23.6	12.0	21.0				11.0	12.6
Net Worth		12.5	45.2	15.5				33.2	20.2
Total Liabilties & Net Worth		100.0	100.0	100.0				100.0	100.0
INCOME DATA									
Net Sales		100.0	100.0	100.0				100.0	100.0
Gross Profit		56.0	48.2	54.5				47.8	52.1
Operating Expenses		55.8	40.6	50.3				41.5	45.7
Operating Profit		.3	7.6	4.3				6.2	6.4
All Other Expenses (net)		.9	2.0	-3.4				.5	1.4
Profit Before Taxes		-.6	5.5	.9				5.8	5.0
RATIOS									
Current		2.0	3.1	2.2				3.1	2.4
		1.4	1.4	1.4				1.6	1.5
		1.0	1.1	.8				1.2	.9
Quick		1.3	2.3	1.5				2.2	1.8
		.9	1.1	1.0				1.2	.9
		.4	.6	.4				.7	.6
Sales/Receivables		16 22.3	34 10.9	34 10.8				28 13.2	29 12.4
		38 9.7	44 8.2	46 8.0				52 7.0	47 7.7
		58 6.3	60 6.1	69 5.3				65 5.6	66 5.5
Cost of Sales/Inventory		0 UND	0 UND	0 UND				0 UND	3 134.1
		24 15.4	14 25.4	12 30.9				23 15.7	27 13.7
		120 3.0	65 5.6	76 4.8				68 5.3	72 5.0
Cost of Sales/Payables		19 19.7	12 30.6	46 8.0				19 18.9	21 17.7
		39 9.3	17 21.7	63 5.8				38 9.5	43 8.6
		96 3.8	76 4.8	166 2.2				77 4.7	75 4.9
Sales/Working Capital		8.6	4.6	5.1				5.2	5.1
		22.2	9.3	13.3				11.5	14.0
		-165.6	86.4	-27.0				47.7	-44.6
EBIT/Interest		4.5	19.6	8.5				13.4	7.3
	(11) 1.8		(16) 5.7	(14) 2.9				(59) 5.1	(61) 3.3
		-8.3	2.1	-.1				.9	1.1
Net Profit + Depr., Dep., Amort./Cur. Mat. L/T/D								14.0	14.3
								(15) 2.7	(14) 2.6
								1.7	1.4
Fixed/Worth		.1	.2	.3				.2	.2
		22.9	.5	NM				.7	.8
		-.2	-87.6	-.1				4.9	-1.9
Debt/Worth		1.4	.9	1.6				.6	1.0
		49.6	2.7	NM				1.9	3.1
		-2.3	-206.2	-2.1				30.3	-13.1
% Profit Before Taxes/Tangible Net Worth			89.9					58.8	79.1
		(13) 26.9						(59) 21.8	(51) 42.8
			3.6					7.4	8.3
% Profit Before Taxes/Total Assets		16.7	16.3	9.1				24.0	18.5
		.0	8.4	2.0				8.7	7.8
		-11.9	1.5	-8.5				.5	.4
Sales/Net Fixed Assets		101.5	74.3	32.1				52.0	91.2
		38.8	41.0	15.3				16.2	15.4
		16.9	8.3	5.6				7.2	7.7
Sales/Total Assets		4.6	2.5	2.0				2.9	2.8
		2.8	2.0	1.6				2.1	2.1
		2.5	1.2	.8				1.5	1.3
% Depr., Dep., Amort./Sales			.4	1.9				.8	1.3
		(14) 1.0		(11) 3.3				(61) 2.4	(48) 2.5
			2.8	5.3				4.1	4.6
% Officers', Directors' Owners' Comp/Sales								3.5	4.1
			(28) 6.5					(15) 6.2	
								7.7	12.7
Net Sales ($)	1953M	49395M	175053M	604130M	657865M	499984M		1858926M	2770868M
Total Assets ($)	563M	15052M	85052M	437035M	403572M	732336M		1310264M	1776051M

M = $ thousand   MM = $ million
See Pages 9 through 22 for Explanation of Ratios and Data

Comparative Historical Data · Current Data Sorted by Sales

4/1/07-3/31/08 ALL	4/1/08-3/31/09 ALL	4/1/09-3/31/10 ALL	Type of Statement	0-1MM	1-3MM	3-5MM	5-10MM	10-25MM	25MM & OVER
					12 (4/1-9/30/09)		48 (10/1/09-3/31/10)		
10	13	17	Unqualified			2	2	2	11
14	8	9	Reviewed			1	3	3	2
4	5	2	Compiled				1	1	
5	8	3	Tax Returns				1		
30	28	29	Other	4	2	4	5	4	10
63	62	60	NUMBER OF STATEMENTS	6	2	7	12	10	23
%	%	%	**ASSETS**	%	%	%	%	%	%
12.0	13.0	13.7	Cash & Equivalents				17.3	18.7	11.9
26.9	26.5	25.2	Trade Receivables (net)				33.1	24.9	21.4
15.3	14.6	12.1	Inventory				12.7	19.1	9.6
4.9	4.8	5.2	All Other Current				4.2	4.7	6.5
59.1	59.0	56.2	Total Current				67.4	67.4	49.3
16.3	16.8	16.4	Fixed Assets (net)				10.1	13.3	17.2
11.5	13.7	19.7	Intangibles (net)				20.0	12.8	24.7
13.1	10.6	7.7	All Other Non-Current				2.5	6.5	8.7
100.0	100.0	100.0	Total				100.0	100.0	100.0
			LIABILITIES						
10.3	9.7	7.2	Notes Payable-Short Term				8.1	3.7	2.5
2.7	3.9	2.7	Cur. Mat.-L.T.D.				2.9	3.4	3.6
11.2	14.5	15.0	Trade Payables				20.9	12.9	13.5
.6	.9	.2	Income Taxes Payable				.0	.2	.1
17.6	15.7	15.9	All Other Current				10.7	12.8	26.0
42.4	44.7	40.9	Total Current				42.5	33.0	45.8
17.0	16.8	13.7	Long-Term Debt				3.4	13.7	16.1
.5	.9	.8	Deferred Taxes				.7	.8	1.1
13.4	11.2	17.2	All Other Non-Current				5.6	15.5	19.7
26.7	26.4	27.5	Net Worth				47.8	37.1	17.3
100.0	100.0	100.0	Total Liabilities & Net Worth				100.0	100.0	100.0
			INCOME DATA						
100.0	100.0	100.0	Net Sales				100.0	100.0	100.0
49.2	50.9	52.0	Gross Profit				41.2	58.4	52.6
42.1	46.2	47.0	Operating Expenses				39.6	47.9	47.7
7.1	4.6	5.0	Operating Profit				1.6	10.5	4.9
1.1	1.8	3.0	All Other Expenses (net)				1.0	2.1	4.7
6.1	2.8	2.0	Profit Before Taxes				.6	8.4	.1
			RATIOS						
2.5	2.4	2.1	Current				3.0	4.2	1.6
1.3	1.4	1.4					1.7	1.8	1.0
1.1	.9	1.0					.9	1.2	.8
1.5	1.4	1.5	Quick				2.7	2.2	1.2
1.0	.9	1.0					1.2	1.1	.6
.6	.5	.6					.6	.9	.4
29 · 12.5	26 · 13.9	32 · 11.3	Sales/Receivables				30 · 12.3	32 · 11.3	38 · 9.6
46 · 8.0	48 · 7.5	44 · 8.2					43 · 8.6	44 · 8.4	47 · 7.8
62 · 5.8	65 · 5.6	64 · 5.7					62 · 5.9	56 · 6.5	76 · 4.8
2 · 169.1	0 · UND	0 · UND	Cost of Sales/Inventory				0 · UND	0 · UND	0 · UND
32 · 11.2	31 · 11.8	15 · 25.1					16 · 22.3	69 · 5.3	15 · 25.2
105 · 3.5	128 · 2.9	77 · 4.7					25 · 14.5	329 · 1.1	77 · 4.8
17 · 21.6	18 · 20.5	17 · 22.1	Cost of Sales/Payables				14 · 25.9	15 · 24.3	22 · 16.4
37 · 9.9	30 · 12.1	42 · 8.6					31 · 11.8	43 · 8.5	49 · 7.4
53 · 6.9	89 · 4.1	82 · 4.5					70 · 5.2	119 · 3.1	66 · 5.6
5.9	4.9	5.6	Sales/Working Capital				4.9	3.1	9.5
18.1	15.1	16.6					14.8	8.1	-216.3
110.4	-36.0	-78.4					NM	17.7	-26.5
12.5	6.1	8.9	EBIT/Interest				6.4		13.8
(51) 4.7	(48) 3.2	(53) 3.2					(11) 1.9		(21) 3.2
1.2	.3	.2					-10.2		.1
4.0	5.8	6.8	Net Profit + Depr., Dep., Amort./Cur. Mat. L/T/D						
(14) 2.3	(16) 1.0	(12) 4.1							
.6	.1	1.1							
.1	.2	.2	Fixed/Worth				.1	.1	.3
.6	1.1	1.6					.3	.4	2.8
-3.1	-1.0	-.7					NM	NM	-.4
.7	1.0	1.3	Debt/Worth				.6	.5	2.3
2.3	5.0	6.5					3.0	1.9	24.6
-69.0	-8.2	-4.0					NM	NM	-2.4
73.6	111.8	80.8	% Profit Before Taxes/Tangible Net Worth						120.0
(47) 35.2	(42) 23.9	(37) 18.0							(12) 51.7
7.9	1.3	-6.5							-23.6
27.1	15.9	15.2	% Profit Before Taxes/Total Assets				7.3	22.1	15.4
8.4	5.7	5.2					2.7	10.2	2.1
1.9	-2.3	-6.4					-8.3	5.1	-5.1
49.9	72.0	61.3	Sales/Net Fixed Assets				91.1	41.7	35.3
21.0	16.2	19.9					63.3	19.0	10.9
6.9	6.9	6.4					24.0	7.7	5.2
3.1	3.1	2.7	Sales/Total Assets				4.1	2.5	2.0
2.1	1.8	1.9					2.2	1.9	1.8
1.3	1.3	1.1					1.6	.9	.9
.7	.8	.7	% Depr., Dep., Amort./Sales				.5		1.6
(52) 1.7	(44) 2.3	(41) 1.9					(11) .7		(16) 3.1
3.4	3.5	3.5					3.1		5.4
2.0	2.6		% Officers', Directors' Owners' Comp/Sales						
(15) 5.2	(16) 3.8								
8.4	9.7								
2019283M	2466502M	1988380M	Net Sales ($)	2997M	4593M	27190M	85455M	131845M	1736300M
1452575M	1420493M	1673610M	Total Assets ($)	2757M	3595M	14948M	41109M	120658M	1490543M

M = $ thousand   MM = $ million
See Pages 9 through 22 for Explanation of Ratios and Data

Current Data Sorted by Assets

Comparative Historical Data

Type of Statement	0-500M	500M-2MM	2-10MM	10-50MM	50-100MM	100-250MM		ALL 4/1/05-3/31/06	ALL 4/1/06-3/31/07
Unqualified	2	1	13	23	14	33		46	46
Reviewed	2	3	10	1	1			14	12
Compiled	2	3	1					10	12
Tax Returns	3	8	4					10	9
Other	8	11	36	37	14	29		83	82
		45 (4/1-9/30/09)		214 (10/1/09-3/31/10)					
NUMBER OF STATEMENTS	17	26	64	61	29	62		163	161
ASSETS	%	%	%	%	%	%		%	%
Cash & Equivalents	40.7	21.2	22.7	28.7	27.8	24.6		26.5	22.2
Trade Receivables (net)	19.1	36.0	31.1	27.9	18.0	12.7		33.3	32.9
Inventory	2.6	5.7	1.2	1.5	1.0	.8		3.0	2.2
All Other Current	7.5	3.8	7.6	5.4	6.3	4.3		4.4	4.8
Total Current	69.9	66.8	62.6	63.5	53.2	42.3		67.3	62.1
Fixed Assets (net)	12.9	19.3	11.5	11.9	9.1	5.3		10.8	11.4
Intangibles (net)	7.1	6.5	11.7	15.5	30.7	45.9		14.4	19.7
All Other Non-Current	10.3	7.4	14.2	9.0	7.0	6.5		7.6	6.8
Total	100.0	100.0	100.0	100.0	100.0	100.0		100.0	100.0
LIABILITIES									
Notes Payable-Short Term	18.2	11.5	13.0	3.0	.6	.5		6.4	6.2
Cur. Mat.-L.T.D.	2.1	3.1	2.4	9.9	1.8	2.0		2.4	3.2
Trade Payables	6.8	8.5	7.5	7.8	2.7	2.7		10.3	10.6
Income Taxes Payable	.0	.7	.5	.8	.6	1.1		1.3	.7
All Other Current	29.7	19.1	34.5	41.5	32.2	25.3		25.6	26.5
Total Current	56.7	42.9	57.8	62.9	37.9	31.7		46.0	47.1
Long-Term Debt	17.8	18.3	15.1	16.4	14.8	18.9		9.9	9.3
Deferred Taxes	1.3	.0	.2	1.0	.6	2.8		.6	.3
All Other Non-Current	4.5	15.8	9.2	10.7	3.4	10.1		21.6	17.4
Net Worth	19.4	23.0	17.7	9.1	43.3	36.4		21.9	25.8
Total Liabilities & Net Worth	100.0	100.0	100.0	100.0	100.0	100.0		100.0	100.0
INCOME DATA									
Net Sales	100.0	100.0	100.0	100.0	100.0	100.0		100.0	100.0
Gross Profit									
Operating Expenses	95.4	87.4	96.1	91.5	92.7	92.6		93.5	95.7
Operating Profit	4.6	12.6	3.9	8.5	7.3	7.4		6.5	4.3
All Other Expenses (net)	.3	3.9	2.4	2.9	3.9	6.8		1.2	1.2
Profit Before Taxes	4.3	8.7	1.5	5.6	3.4	.6		5.3	3.2
RATIOS									
Current	10.4	3.4	2.5	2.1	2.0	2.0		3.2	2.9
	3.0	1.8	1.3	1.1	1.1	1.2		1.6	1.5
	.8	1.3	.9	.7	.9	.7		1.0	1.0
Quick	9.2	3.3	2.3	1.8	1.7	1.8		2.9	2.4
	2.0	1.4	1.0	1.0	1.0	1.0		1.4	1.3
	.6	1.0	.6	.6	.7	.6		.8	.8
Sales/Receivables	0 UND	19 19.2	31 11.7	45 8.0	41 8.9	48 7.5		40 9.2	42 8.6
	20 18.4	53 6.9	55 6.6	61 6.0	61 5.9	65 5.6		64 5.7	67 5.4
	42 8.7	75 4.8	71 5.1	96 3.8	95 3.8	79 4.6		89 4.1	86 4.3
Cost of Sales/Inventory									
Cost of Sales/Payables									
Sales/Working Capital	3.7	4.6	5.4	5.7	3.8	2.8		3.3	3.9
	15.7	8.8	11.2	21.1	26.4	15.6		8.5	8.6
	-34.1	29.1	-29.1	-5.8	-14.7	-7.1		177.0	-110.3
EBIT/Interest		15.5	12.4	21.2	5.9	11.6		45.0	15.8
		(21) 8.1	(46) 2.4	(46) 5.2	(19) 2.7	(51) 1.4		(121) 10.7	(112) 3.3
		.9	-4.9	-.3	-9.8	-.9		1.0	-1.8
Net Profit + Depr., Dep., Amort./Cur. Mat. L/T/D				25.1				22.6	7.8
				(13) 1.7				(27) 11.1	(23) .9
				-1.3				3.2	-2.4
Fixed/Worth	.0	.2	.1	.2	.1	.1		.1	.1
	.2	.7	.5	1.1	1.2	NM		.4	.4
	1.6	NM	-.4	-.2	-.2	.0		-.8	-.8
Debt/Worth	.3	.7	.7	.9	1.0	1.3		.9	.9
	1.7	2.5	4.4	9.4	5.0	NM		2.4	2.6
	-3.4	NM	-5.8	-2.7	-2.8	-1.5		-10.2	-6.0
% Profit Before Taxes/Tangible Net Worth	147.1	130.7	73.3	74.8	72.5	41.9		81.8	57.5
	(12) 64.7	(20) 57.6	(44) 16.6	(35) 29.9	(20) 19.1	(31) 16.5		(112) 23.6	(112) 21.9
	13.5	9.8	-15.5	10.9	-37.5	-.2		2.5	-2.3
% Profit Before Taxes/Total Assets	70.8	34.5	14.7	19.2	13.2	7.2		22.8	19.5
	23.0	10.8	5.3	10.6	2.4	1.1		8.3	5.5
	-4.4	2.2	-8.3	-.7	-6.7	-4.7		-1.8	-4.7
Sales/Net Fixed Assets	870.4	71.1	60.1	54.8	27.7	33.8		51.4	50.2
	142.7	18.8	26.0	16.5	17.7	18.1		25.4	25.4
	9.0	10.2	12.3	10.3	8.6	11.4		13.0	12.9
Sales/Total Assets	9.4	3.4	3.0	1.9	1.1	.9		2.9	2.8
	4.0	2.5	1.7	1.3	.9	.7		1.8	1.6
	2.2	1.8	1.2	1.0	.6	.4		1.0	.9
% Depr., Dep., Amort./Sales		.8	1.2	1.0	2.3	2.1		.8	.9
		(17) 1.3	(41) 2.2	(41) 2.4	(17) 4.4	(18) 2.8		(106) 1.7	(105) 2.0
		2.9	3.2	5.9	6.2	5.0		3.4	4.1
% Officers', Directors' Owners' Comp/Sales			6.0					2.8	3.5
			(14) 11.0					(28) 10.5	(22) 12.7
			17.3					15.4	24.2
Net Sales ($)	24867M	86059M	641750M	2222894M	2064291M	7342915M		6061833M	6142797M
Total Assets ($)	4517M	34947M	316905M	1409389M	2056034M	10230915M		5726262M	6005632M

M = $ thousand   MM = $ million
See Pages 9 through 22 for Explanation of Ratios and Data

Comparative Historical Data | | Current Data Sorted by Sales

71	76	86	Type of Statement						
71	76	86	Unqualified	2	1	6	18	59	
17	14	17	Reviewed	1	4	2	4	2	4
17	8	6	Compiled		1	2	3		
15	17	15	Tax Returns	6	3	1	5		
97	122	135	Other	1	14	11	15	29	65
4/1/07-3/31/08	4/1/08-3/31/09	4/1/09-3/31/10			45 (4/1-9/30/09)		214 (10/1/09-3/31/10)		
ALL	ALL	ALL		0-1MM	1-3MM	3-5MM	5-10MM	10-25MM	25MM & OVER
217	237	259	NUMBER OF STATEMENTS	10	22	17	33	49	128
%	%	%	ASSETS	%	%	%	%	%	%
24.9	25.9	26.2	Cash & Equivalents	33.9	21.9	34.0	25.9	24.7	25.9
28.7	25.7	24.2	Trade Receivables (net)	11.3	28.3	26.4	30.6	31.4	19.8
1.8	1.6	1.7	Inventory	1.3	5.4	1.8	1.5	1.0	1.4
4.3	5.2	5.8	All Other Current	5.7	6.4	4.7	6.3	6.3	5.5
59.7	58.4	57.8	Total Current	52.3	62.0	70.0	62.8	63.4	52.5
10.2	10.0	10.7	Fixed Assets (net)	29.7	13.5	12.0	11.5	11.0	8.3
22.5	23.8	22.1	Intangibles (net)	12.3	10.3	6.8	12.6	17.1	31.3
7.6	7.8	9.4	All Other Non-Current	6.2	14.1	11.3	13.2	8.6	7.9
100.0	100.0	100.0	Total	100.0	100.0	100.0	100.0	100.0	100.0
			LIABILITIES						
5.4	7.3	6.5	Notes Payable-Short Term	11.8	16.9	3.9	17.9	7.1	1.4
2.8	2.6	4.0	Cur. Mat.-L.T.D.	.4	2.2	2.6	3.8	10.1	2.6
9.2	7.2	5.9	Trade Payables	3.6	7.8	3.9	6.3	9.1	4.8
.7	.6	.7	Income Taxes Payable	.0	.8	.6	.2	.6	.9
25.0	27.2	31.8	All Other Current	5.8	26.3	16.7	35.9	39.2	32.9
43.0	44.8	49.0	Total Current	21.6	54.0	27.6	64.2	66.1	42.6
16.8	15.8	16.8	Long-Term Debt	58.0	11.6	10.4	7.9	14.3	18.5
.6	1.1	1.1	Deferred Taxes	.9	.5	.0	.0	.9	1.7
13.5	10.6	9.5	All Other Non-Current	4.4	8.7	11.7	12.7	8.5	9.2
26.1	27.7	23.7	Net Worth	14.5	25.2	50.3	15.2	10.1	27.9
100.0	100.0	100.0	Total Liabilties & Net Worth	100.0	100.0	100.0	100.0	100.0	100.0
			INCOME DATA						
100.0	100.0	100.0	Net Sales	100.0	100.0	100.0	100.0	100.0	100.0
			Gross Profit						
94.1	94.8	92.9	Operating Expenses	78.2	96.9	89.1	94.0	96.6	92.1
5.9	5.2	7.1	Operating Profit	21.8	3.1	10.9	6.0	3.4	7.9
2.1	2.7	3.8	All Other Expenses (net)	12.8	.7	1.1	1.4	2.9	4.9
3.8	2.5	3.4	Profit Before Taxes	9.0	2.3	9.8	4.6	.5	3.0
			RATIOS						
2.2	2.6	2.4		9.6	2.7	6.0	2.1	1.6	2.1
1.4	1.3	1.3	Current	2.5	1.5	3.3	1.2	1.0	1.2
.9	.9	.8		1.3	.8	1.5	.7	.7	.8
2.1	2.1	2.1		7.8	2.4	5.6	1.9	1.4	1.8
1.2	1.2	1.0	Quick	2.0	1.2	3.3	1.1	.9	1.0
.7	.7	.6		.8	.6	1.4	.6	.6	.6
41	9.0	40	9.0	39	9.5	Sales/Receivables	0 UND	17	21.4	12	30.6	27	13.6	44	8.3	46	8.0

Sales/Receivables:

41 9.0	40 9.0	39 9.5	Sales/Receivables	0 UND	17 21.4	12 30.6	27 13.6	44 8.3	46 8.0
68 5.4	61 6.0	59 6.2		0 UND	44 8.3	65 5.6	55 6.6	61 6.0	61 5.9
90 4.1	81 4.5	80 4.6		47 7.8	77 4.7	91 4.0	69 5.3	88 4.1	82 4.5
			Cost of Sales/Inventory						
			Cost of Sales/Payables						
3.4	4.0	4.5	Sales/Working Capital	2.6	4.8	2.9	6.1	7.4	3.1
9.3	12.5	15.1		5.7	10.5	5.0	27.0	59.6	17.7
-19.7	-15.5	-12.4		NM	-31.3	8.9	-11.8	-8.2	-8.2
13.5	15.6	12.3	EBIT/Interest		10.6	100.4	28.0	12.6	10.3
(153) 3.2	(165) 2.3	(190) 3.1		(17) 2.9	(12) 16.5	(23) 6.0	(40) 2.4	(96) 2.3	
-.9	-1.7	-1.6		-12.1	6.0	-1.1	-9.1	-.7	
10.1	44.4	8.0	Net Profit + Depr., Dep., Amort./Cur. Mat. L/T/D					8.9	
(37) 4.3	(30) 3.1	(35) 2.8						(21) 2.3	
1.0	1.6	-.3						.0	
.1	.2	.2	Fixed/Worth	.0	.1	.0	.1	.2	.2
.6	.9	.7		1.4	.4	.4	.5	1.1	1.5
-.4	-.1	-.2		-.5	2.2	.7	-.5	-.1	-.1
.9	.9	.9	Debt/Worth	.3	.5	.3	.8	1.3	1.0
4.6	5.7	5.2		NM	2.7	1.2	2.6	9.0	10.3
-3.9	-2.6	-2.7		-2.7	NM	5.8	-5.0	-2.7	-1.9
56.7	56.9	74.3	% Profit Before Taxes/Tangible Net Worth		66.9	146.2	97.9	118.8	56.3
(135) 26.5	(138) 22.1	(162) 21.2		(17) 10.7	(16) 57.5	(24) 38.9	(27) 17.5	(73) 18.4	
-1.1	-.2	.9		-6.9	5.9	15.0	-20.5	-4.2	
19.2	18.6	16.3	% Profit Before Taxes/Total Assets	68.8	22.3	45.9	18.0	18.5	11.7
6.2	4.1	4.7		3.3	5.8	18.8	8.8	4.1	2.9
-3.8	-3.2	-6.2		-3.1	-9.5	2.7	-6.4	-11.0	-3.8
47.5	42.2	48.2	Sales/Net Fixed Assets	UND	76.2	97.3	64.8	57.5	37.1
21.2	22.1	19.7		6.4	23.8	21.5	32.9	20.0	18.1
12.3	12.4	11.3		.2	11.6	8.5	11.9	12.7	11.3
2.3	2.4	2.2	Sales/Total Assets	3.0	4.2	2.6	3.2	2.7	1.5
1.4	1.3	1.2		.8	2.5	1.4	1.9	1.6	.9
.8	.8	.8		.2	1.2	1.0	1.3	1.0	.6
.8	.9	1.2	% Depr., Dep., Amort./Sales		1.2	.7	1.1	1.0	1.7
(124) 2.1	(124) 2.2	(142) 2.5		(12) 2.5	(11) 1.3	(19) 2.3	(30) 2.2	(63) 3.1	
4.4	4.1	4.7		3.3	2.5	3.0	4.6	5.2	
5.5	3.8	4.2	% Officers', Directors' Owners' Comp/Sales						
(30) 9.7	(29) 8.7	(28) 9.5							
18.9	18.9	15.1							
9940731M	11215388M	12382776M	Net Sales ($)	2421M	40768M	66922M	211773M	811526M	11249366M
10928344M	12148508M	14052707M	Total Assets ($)	6755M	25223M	50268M	127062M	669290M	13174109M

© RMA 2010

M = $ thousand   MM = $ million
See Pages 9 through 22 for Explanation of Ratios and Data

		Current Data Sorted by Assets					Comparative Historical Data	
	1	3	6	4	2	**Type of Statement** Unqualified	12	13
	4	14		1		Reviewed	12	23
	6	3	3			Compiled	17	25
17	8	6			1	Tax Returns	19	22
12	11	25	9	4	1	Other	52	54
	20 (4/1-9/30/09)		121 (10/1/09-3/31/10)				4/1/05-3/31/06 ALL	4/1/06-3/31/07 ALL
0-500M	500M-2MM	2-10MM	10-50MM	50-100MM	100-250MM			
29	30	51	18	9	4	**NUMBER OF STATEMENTS**	112	137
%	%	%	%	%	%	**ASSETS**	%	%
19.2	22.4	16.1	9.4			Cash & Equivalents	12.5	14.9
22.2	26.8	26.2	17.1			Trade Receivables (net)	28.2	26.2
3.1	1.8	3.8	6.3			Inventory	4.7	2.9
2.1	5.3	8.8	8.4			All Other Current	5.7	4.6
46.7	56.3	54.9	41.2			Total Current	51.2	48.6
37.5	36.7	34.3	40.7			Fixed Assets (net)	35.6	35.5
6.5	.7	3.0	5.9			Intangibles (net)	4.8	6.8
9.4	6.3	7.8	12.2			All Other Non-Current	8.5	9.1
100.0	100.0	100.0	100.0			Total	100.0	100.0
						LIABILITIES		
22.9	11.4	7.3	1.7			Notes Payable-Short Term	16.0	16.3
8.2	2.8	3.9	7.8			Cur. Mat.-L.T.D.	5.1	6.7
11.7	10.6	8.3	7.4			Trade Payables	13.3	11.5
.2	.2	.6	.4			Income Taxes Payable	.6	.6
18.8	24.0	10.5	21.4			All Other Current	12.7	16.8
61.9	48.9	30.6	38.7			Total Current	47.7	51.9
21.9	15.1	15.3	22.5			Long-Term Debt	21.2	22.0
.0	.2	.2	1.1			Deferred Taxes	.4	.7
8.4	2.4	3.0	10.6			All Other Non-Current	12.6	15.3
7.8	33.4	50.9	27.1			Net Worth	18.1	10.0
100.0	100.0	100.0	100.0			Total Liabilties & Net Worth	100.0	100.0
						INCOME DATA		
100.0	100.0	100.0	100.0			Net Sales	100.0	100.0
						Gross Profit		
92.9	91.6	90.6	89.3			Operating Expenses	91.9	92.0
7.1	8.4	9.4	10.7			Operating Profit	8.1	8.0
2.1	1.7	.9	3.7			All Other Expenses (net)	1.7	2.4
5.0	6.7	8.5	6.9			Profit Before Taxes	6.5	5.6
						RATIOS		
2.9	3.4	3.6	1.8			Current	2.4	1.9
.9	1.2	2.0	1.0				1.2	1.1
.1	.7	.9	.7				.8	.7
2.6	2.5	3.3	1.1			Quick	2.0	1.8
.8	1.1	1.5	.8				1.0	.9
.1	.5	.7	.5				.6	.5
0 UND	0 UND	22 16.7	10 37.1			Sales/Receivables	21 17.0	15 24.8
11 34.7	34 10.8	45 8.0	52 7.0				43 8.5	42 8.7
44 8.3	78 4.7	73 5.0	86 4.3				66 5.6	65 5.6
						Cost of Sales/Inventory		
						Cost of Sales/Payables		
10.2	6.7	3.9	7.7			Sales/Working Capital	7.6	8.1
-34.4	39.0	7.4	53.6				40.3	76.6
-5.9	-14.1	-70.6	-12.2				-25.7	-17.0
9.0	19.0	22.4	4.8			EBIT/Interest	18.4	10.3
(19) 4.3	(19) 1.6	(45) 6.2	(16) 2.6				(100) 4.2	(118) 2.9
-1.3	-2.4	1.9	-.4				.9	.7
		7.3				Net Profit + Depr., Dep.,	5.3	5.3
		(11) 2.0				Amort./Cur. Mat. L/T/D	(23) 2.1	(26) 2.1
		1.1					1.3	1.1
.1	.1	.3	.2			Fixed/Worth	.4	.4
.7	.9	.6	2.2				1.1	1.5
-3.5	3.0	1.5	6.1				6.5	28.2
.8	.4	.4	.8			Debt/Worth	.9	1.1
9.7	1.7	1.1	2.8				2.5	3.0
-3.8	6.6	2.5	20.0				140.1	-15.5
101.9	111.9	42.4	97.4			% Profit Before Taxes/Tangible	81.8	91.5
(18) 40.4	(26) 20.8	(49) 14.0	(15) 30.2			Net Worth	(85) 44.3	(101) 36.1
2.8	-20.7	3.3	3.4				13.3	3.9
35.1	25.9	14.8	17.5			% Profit Before Taxes/Total	30.4	26.1
15.6	6.8	7.2	6.5			Assets	9.1	8.4
-5.9	-9.7	1.0	-1.5				.4	-1.3
70.5	79.0	15.2	23.6			Sales/Net Fixed Assets	33.6	29.4
14.2	8.2	7.4	4.6				8.7	8.5
6.7	5.1	2.2	1.4				3.3	3.3
6.9	3.8	2.4	1.5			Sales/Total Assets	4.4	3.6
4.1	2.8	1.7	.9				2.3	2.3
2.7	1.9	1.1	.8				1.5	1.4
1.5	.7	2.8	2.0			% Depr., Dep., Amort./Sales	1.2	2.1
(14) 2.1	(19) 3.6	(38) 5.2	(14) 6.7				(76) 3.8	(95) 4.4
7.4	10.0	9.2	15.6				8.8	8.4
7.5	4.2	3.8				% Officers', Directors'	5.3	4.1
(16) 11.2	(15) 9.8	(17) 5.1				Owners' Comp/Sales	(50) 7.5	(53) 8.7
20.9	14.0	9.1					13.2	14.9
35788M	99898M	443190M	612374M	522129M	727069M	Net Sales ($)	1882579M	2681369M
8166M	33437M	252012M	552697M	623550M	529000M	Total Assets ($)	1623825M	1969125M

Comparative Historical Data | | | Current Data Sorted by Sales

			Type of Statement						
17	15	16	Unqualified		1	1		4	10
19	21	19	Reviewed		4	2	9	2	2
13	15	12	Compiled	1	3	3	3		2
26	23	32	Tax Returns	9	11	8	2	1	1
52	52	62	Other	7	13	9	13	12	8
4/1/07-3/31/08	4/1/08-3/31/09	4/1/09-3/31/10			20 (4/1-9/30/09)		121 (10/1/09-3/31/10)			
ALL	ALL	ALL		0-1MM	1-3MM	3-5MM	5-10MM	10-25MM	25MM & OVER
127	126	141	NUMBER OF STATEMENTS	17	32	23	27	19	23
%	%	%	ASSETS	%	%	%	%	%	%
14.6	16.9	16.9	Cash & Equivalents	11.5	20.0	19.3	20.0	17.5	9.9
26.3	21.5	23.0	Trade Receivables (net)	13.7	27.4	34.2	21.8	19.3	17.2
3.6	4.1	3.7	Inventory	4.4	2.6	1.1	5.6	.4	7.6
5.2	6.0	6.7	All Other Current	2.9	.9	6.2	9.0	15.0	8.5
49.7	48.4	50.3	Total Current	32.4	50.9	60.8	56.5	52.2	43.2
34.7	36.0	36.0	Fixed Assets (net)	58.0	33.9	32.6	27.6	39.4	33.2
5.4	4.7	4.8	Intangibles (net)	3.2	3.6	2.6	7.3	1.6	9.4
10.2	10.9	8.9	All Other Non-Current	6.3	11.5	4.0	8.7	6.8	14.3
100.0	100.0	100.0	Total	100.0	100.0	100.0	100.0	100.0	100.0
			LIABILITIES						
9.9	9.9	10.3	Notes Payable-Short Term	20.4	18.4	7.3	8.0	2.3	3.7
5.1	5.5	4.9	Cur. Mat.-L.T.D.	11.0	3.5	2.4	3.9	7.3	3.9
18.3	10.9	9.3	Trade Payables	5.8	12.3	7.5	9.4	7.8	10.9
.3	.2	.4	Income Taxes Payable	.0	.4	.0	.8	.6	.2
17.6	13.1	17.0	All Other Current	14.4	15.9	27.9	11.2	14.6	18.4
51.1	39.7	41.9	Total Current	51.6	50.6	45.1	33.3	32.7	37.0
23.8	24.8	21.6	Long-Term Debt	29.8	19.8	14.8	12.3	10.1	45.4
.7	.7	.4	Deferred Taxes	.0	.1	.0	.4	.7	1.4
13.8	8.9	8.0	All Other Non-Current	12.3	3.5	2.1	4.1	1.9	26.3
10.7	25.9	28.1	Net Worth	6.3	26.0	38.0	49.9	54.5	-10.2
100.0	100.0	100.0	Total Liabilities & Net Worth	100.0	100.0	100.0	100.0	100.0	100.0
			INCOME DATA						
100.0	100.0	100.0	Net Sales	100.0	100.0	100.0	100.0	100.0	100.0
			Gross Profit						
91.4	91.1	91.1	Operating Expenses	79.0	96.2	88.6	92.6	93.9	91.1
8.6	8.9	8.9	Operating Profit	21.0	3.8	11.4	7.4	6.1	8.9
1.5	3.5	2.2	All Other Expenses (net)	4.5	.8	4.5	1.2	.5	2.7
7.2	5.4	6.7	Profit Before Taxes	16.5	3.0	6.9	6.1	5.6	6.2
			RATIOS						
2.4	2.3	2.9	Current	2.2	3.4	5.0	3.1	2.4	2.1
1.3	1.3	1.3		.6	1.4	1.6	1.5	1.7	1.2
.8	.7	.8		.1	.7	.9	.8	1.0	.7
2.1	1.8	2.4	Quick	1.9	3.1	4.9	2.6	2.0	1.2
1.1	1.0	.9		.3	1.2	1.6	1.0	.8	.7
.6	.4	.5		.1	.5	.8	.7	.5	.5
17 21.9	8 44.8	7 50.4	Sales/Receivables	0 UND	0 868.8	25 14.3	17 21.5	16 22.8	11 34.5
47 7.7	36 10.2	37 9.8		0 UND	34 10.8	52 7.1	38 9.6	35 10.5	40 9.1
68 5.4	62 5.9	64 5.7		39 9.4	63 5.8	104 3.5	62 5.9	73 5.0	64 5.7
			Cost of Sales/Inventory						
			Cost of Sales/Payables						
7.5	5.9	5.9	Sales/Working Capital	13.8	5.3	4.1	5.5	3.8	8.1
22.6	22.1	25.1		-19.2	56.0	7.2	11.1	17.7	16.1
-30.5	-19.7	-16.7		-3.2	-13.0	-66.5	-30.9	146.1	-20.0
13.7	12.8	14.0	EBIT/Interest	5.6	8.0	24.5	21.4	33.8	5.1
(107) 5.1	(107) 4.2	(110) 4.3		(11) 4.3	(22) 2.8	(17) 6.2	(22) 8.0	(18) 4.6	(20) 3.2
1.4	.9	-.1		.0	-2.6	-.9	.2	1.2	.4
3.9	4.9	4.5	Net Profit + Depr., Dep., Amort./Cur. Mat. L/T/D						
(18) 2.3	(20) 2.9	(21) 2.0							
1.4	1.4	.9							
.4	.3	.3	Fixed/Worth	.9	.1	.1	.2	.3	.8
1.6	1.3	.9		4.4	.7	.5	.6	.5	5.7
8.3	17.2	5.7		-2.0	3.0	5.8	2.2	1.2	-.6
.9	.8	.6	Debt/Worth	.8	.5	.3	.3	.6	2.4
3.0	2.7	2.0		4.0	1.7	1.2	1.2	1.0	18.8
-115.2	NM	19.9		-3.3	NM	8.9	3.1	1.6	-2.1
94.1	99.9	67.9	% Profit Before Taxes/Tangible Net Worth	72.7	59.5	130.9	48.8	47.8	174.3
(94) 43.3	(95) 26.8	(113) 21.1		(11) 25.0	(24) 11.4	(20) 26.1	(25) 13.7	8.8	(14) 51.5
12.4	7.6	2.2		15.7	-9.3	1.6	-18.5	2.2	18.9
31.1	17.9	21.3	% Profit Before Taxes/Total Assets	25.9	25.3	24.5	14.8	21.5	18.9
10.9	6.3	6.7		5.8	6.9	11.3	6.4	4.2	5.2
.7	-2.7	-1.5		-3.0	-3.7	-9.5	-4.7	1.0	-1.7
19.5	25.2	23.8	Sales/Net Fixed Assets	14.2	78.7	48.5	22.9	11.3	43.9
9.0	7.9	7.2		4.1	11.2	11.9	7.9	6.1	4.1
3.4	2.8	2.6		.2	5.3	4.5	3.0	2.3	1.8
3.2	3.1	3.3	Sales/Total Assets	3.8	5.3	3.3	2.8	2.7	2.0
2.1	1.9	1.9		1.9	3.2	1.9	1.8	1.8	1.2
1.2	1.0	1.1		.2	1.8	1.3	1.1	.9	.8
1.8	1.7	2.1	% Depr., Dep., Amort./Sales		1.1	.7	2.7	2.8	1.8
(89) 3.7	(85) 3.7	(90) 4.7			(18) 2.1	(14) 2.6	(21) 4.9	(16) 5.9	(12) 4.8
7.5	8.5	10.1			5.2	9.2	11.9	11.9	9.0
4.4	5.1	5.0	% Officers', Directors' Owners' Comp/Sales		7.7	4.0	3.9		
(44) 7.0	(48) 6.5	(50) 8.3			(16) 10.9	(10) 8.4	(14) 5.1		
12.0	10.3	12.7			20.9	11.7	9.9		
2614474M	2641816M	2440448M	Net Sales ($)	8682M	63257M	90911M	203796M	287565M	1786237M
2079897M	2289836M	1998862M	Total Assets ($)	10742M	31023M	74009M	207249M	296723M	1379116M

M = $ thousand   MM = $ million
See Pages 9 through 22 for Explanation of Ratios and Data

Current Data Sorted by Assets

Comparative Historical Data

							Type of Statement		
		1	5	5	3		Unqualified	17	19
	1	6	6	1			Reviewed	10	12
1	8	8	1				Compiled	15	18
8	5	5	3				Tax Returns	11	18
1	6	18	20	8	1		Other	45	43
	8 (4/1-9/30/09)		113 (10/1/09-3/31/10)					4/1/05-3/31/06	4/1/06-3/31/07
0-500M	500M-2MM	2-10MM	10-50MM	50-100MM	100-250MM			ALL	ALL
10	20	38	35	14	4		NUMBER OF STATEMENTS	98	110
%	%	%	%	%	%		ASSETS	%	%
25.5	11.5	8.1	8.1	5.9			Cash & Equivalents	12.2	11.9
1.9	.2	1.0	.8	.9			Trade Receivables (net)	1.7	1.5
4.7	1.2	1.0	.6	.6			Inventory	1.0	.8
8.3	.3	1.2	1.5	1.0			All Other Current	2.3	1.5
40.4	13.2	11.4	11.0	8.4			Total Current	17.1	15.7
49.9	74.2	79.9	79.9	78.1			Fixed Assets (net)	74.3	69.7
8.8	6.3	2.5	2.8	9.9			Intangibles (net)	2.8	4.7
.8	6.3	6.2	6.4	3.6			All Other Non-Current	5.8	9.9
100.0	100.0	100.0	100.0	100.0			Total	100.0	100.0
							LIABILITIES		
1.3	3.2	1.2	5.0	.9			Notes Payable-Short Term	2.2	4.9
.9	6.3	9.5	7.1	3.5			Cur. Mat.-L.T.D.	4.6	3.7
19.1	10.9	7.2	5.3	4.7			Trade Payables	6.7	6.9
.0	.0	.0	.0	.9			Income Taxes Payable	.1	.1
37.4	9.5	5.5	7.6	9.3			All Other Current	12.7	10.5
58.6	29.9	23.4	25.0	19.3			Total Current	26.3	26.0
12.7	42.5	47.2	46.2	42.2			Long-Term Debt	42.3	44.6
.0	.1	.0	.2	.3			Deferred Taxes	.2	.1
.0	22.7	12.8	8.9	17.3			All Other Non-Current	7.2	12.5
28.6	4.7	16.5	19.7	21.0			Net Worth	24.0	16.9
100.0	100.0	100.0	100.0	100.0			Total Liabilities & Net Worth	100.0	100.0
							INCOME DATA		
100.0	100.0	100.0	100.0	100.0			Net Sales	100.0	100.0
							Gross Profit		
95.0	86.2	83.2	87.2	87.5			Operating Expenses	90.1	87.4
5.0	13.8	16.8	12.8	12.5			Operating Profit	9.9	12.6
-.2	2.5	9.5	9.9	6.4			All Other Expenses (net)	5.8	6.6
5.2	11.3	7.2	2.9	6.1			Profit Before Taxes	4.1	6.1
							RATIOS		
6.8	.8	1.4	.8	.7				1.5	1.3
1.4	.4	.6	.4	.6			Current	.6	.7
.6	.1	.2	.3	.2				.3	.2
6.3	.7	1.3	.7	.7				1.3	1.1
1.2	.4	.4	.4	.4			Quick	.5	.5
.0	.1	.1	.2	.1				.2	.2
0 UND	0 UND	0 UND	0 UND	2 204.3				0 UND	0 UND
0 UND	0 UND	0 UND	1 538.0	4 102.3			Sales/Receivables	0 UND	0 UND
0 999.8	0 UND	1 485.0	3 131.6	5 76.2				3 122.1	2 200.8
							Cost of Sales/Inventory		
							Cost of Sales/Payables		
14.4	-67.9	34.5	-42.5	-19.0				23.1	28.7
UND	-20.8	-18.8	-11.9	-14.2			Sales/Working Capital	-18.0	-29.1
-10.0	-7.0	-3.7	-3.5	-6.5				-5.4	-7.1
	16.0	3.4	2.0	2.4				3.8	3.1
(14) 7.1	(32) 1.9	(28) 2.0	(13) 2.0				EBIT/Interest	(77) 1.9	(84) 1.8
2.0	1.0	.8	1.6					.9	.9
							Net Profit + Depr., Dep.,	2.9	2.8
							Amort./Cur. Mat. L/T/D	(11) 1.4	(14) 1.9
								.7	1.2
.6	1.5	2.2	2.0	3.7				1.5	1.7
1.3	3.5	4.2	4.1	4.2			Fixed/Worth	3.4	3.8
-1.1	NM	-8.0	15.1	NM				14.5	-17.2
.1	1.4	1.4	1.5	3.2				1.1	1.6
1.7	3.6	4.3	3.3	3.7			Debt/Worth	3.4	3.8
-2.6	NM	-12.5	17.5	NM				19.6	-16.7
	155.0	28.9	29.0	51.8			% Profit Before Taxes/Tangible	35.5	40.7
(15) 58.2	(24) 19.1	(29) 10.1	(11) 15.6				Net Worth	(78) 10.7	(80) 12.3
33.0	7.0	-2.9	9.9					.8	-.9
46.9	32.4	7.7	6.6	5.3			% Profit Before Taxes/Total	7.4	8.5
10.2	13.2	3.3	3.1	3.9			Assets	2.8	3.1
-1.9	4.3	-.4	-.4	2.6				-.8	-.6
22.6	7.1	1.6	2.2	1.8				3.7	3.3
14.4	2.1	.8	.9	1.0			Sales/Net Fixed Assets	1.0	1.1
7.2	1.1	.5	.5	.8				.6	.6
10.2	2.5	1.4	1.4	1.3				1.7	2.0
4.9	1.6	.6	.7	.8			Sales/Total Assets	.8	.8
2.9	1.0	.5	.4	.7				.5	.5
	1.9	4.9	5.3	5.9				4.2	3.9
	3.7	(36) 7.4	8.7	6.3			% Depr., Dep., Amort./Sales	(88) 6.9	(96) 6.5
	6.0	14.5	11.9	6.8				10.2	10.6
							% Officers', Directors'	2.5	2.4
							Owners' Comp/Sales	(23) 4.7	(24) 3.6
								6.1	7.2
10065M	58692M	227482M	878437M	898929M	563494M		Net Sales ($)	1894652M	2422932M
2620M	25475M	187206M	830939M	936990M	596654M		Total Assets ($)	2355137M	2489647M

M = $ thousand   MM = $ million
See Pages 9 through 22 for Explanation of Ratios and Data

Comparative Historical Data

Current Data Sorted by Sales

			Type of Statement						
14	18	14	Unqualified	1			1	2	10
11	12	14	Reviewed		4	3	2	1	4
10	16	18	Compiled	3	6	7	2		
15	13	21	Tax Returns	5	12	2	2	1	1
37	50	54	Other	6	9	4	6	9	20
4/1/07-3/31/08 ALL	4/1/08-3/31/09 ALL	4/1/09-3/31/10 ALL			8 (4/1-9/30/09)		113 (10/1/09-3/31/10)		
				0-1MM	1-3MM	3-5MM	5-10MM	10-25MM	25MM & OVER
87	109	121	NUMBER OF STATEMENTS	15	31	14	13	13	35
%	%	%	ASSETS	%	%	%	%	%	%
11.2	7.4	9.8	Cash & Equivalents	10.8	8.4	6.6	12.9	12.3	10.0
.4	.9	.8	Trade Receivables (net)	.1	.6	.3	.2	2.7	1.1
.9	1.3	1.2	Inventory	2.7	.7	.5	1.1	2.1	.9
1.7	2.4	1.8	All Other Current	5.4	.3	.7	.6	4.6	1.3
14.3	12.0	13.6	Total Current	19.1	10.1	8.1	14.8	21.7	13.2
75.2	77.7	75.9	Fixed Assets (net)	72.5	81.7	81.6	72.5	69.1	73.8
3.0	5.1	4.9	Intangibles (net)	2.8	5.6	5.4	2.2	1.7	7.3
7.5	5.1	5.5	All Other Non-Current	5.6	2.7	5.0	10.5	7.5	5.6
100.0	100.0	100.0	Total	100.0	100.0	100.0	100.0	100.0	100.0
			LIABILITIES						
1.8	2.5	2.7	Notes Payable-Short Term	.7	3.1	1.3	4.9	1.0	3.6
3.7	6.3	6.6	Cur. Mat.-L.T.D.	8.2	8.6	11.0	3.1	8.0	3.2
7.0	5.5	8.0	Trade Payables	9.2	6.6	3.3	10.1	13.5	7.7
.1	.0	.2	Income Taxes Payable	.0	.1	.0	.0	.1	.5
8.9	8.8	9.9	All Other Current	26.8	3.8	6.8	5.3	11.7	10.3
21.4	23.1	27.3	Total Current	44.9	22.2	22.3	23.4	34.3	25.2
44.8	46.3	42.0	Long-Term Debt	35.4	47.5	46.4	53.4	37.6	35.7
.1	.2	.1	Deferred Taxes	.0	.0	.2	.3	.4	.1
17.4	11.6	12.6	All Other Non-Current	2.7	4.7	5.0	33.8	7.6	21.0
16.3	18.9	17.9	Net Worth	16.9	25.5	26.0	-10.8	20.0	18.1
100.0	100.0	100.0	Total Liabilities & Net Worth	100.0	100.0	100.0	100.0	100.0	100.0
			INCOME DATA						
100.0	100.0	100.0	Net Sales	100.0	100.0	100.0	100.0	100.0	100.0
			Gross Profit						
93.0	89.7	86.6	Operating Expenses	64.4	87.5	87.7	85.9	92.2	92.9
7.0	10.3	13.4	Operating Profit	35.6	12.5	12.3	14.1	7.8	7.1
6.8	7.5	7.2	All Other Expenses (net)	15.8	8.3	8.7	5.5	4.1	3.5
.2	2.8	6.3	Profit Before Taxes	19.8	4.2	3.5	8.6	3.7	3.5
			RATIOS						
1.3	1.0	1.0	Current	2.3	1.1	1.1	1.0	1.1	.8
.5	.3	.5		.4	.5	.4	.8	.7	.5
.3	.1	.2		.0	.2	.2	.4	.3	.3
.7	.8	.8	Quick	2.3	1.0	1.1	.9	.7	.7
.4	(108) .2	.4		.1	.4	.3	.7	.5	.4
.2	.1	.1		.0	.1	.1	.3	.2	.2
0 UND	0 UND	0 UND	Sales/Receivables	0 UND	0 UND	0 UND	0 UND	0 UND	0 999.8
0 UND	0 UND	0 UND		0 UND	0 UND	0 UND	0 999.8	2 155.9	2 181.1
2 182.4	1 380.8	3 129.9		0 UND	0 999.8	0 UND	3 117.4	4 87.0	4 95.1
			Cost of Sales/Inventory						
			Cost of Sales/Payables						
123.0	-207.4	UND	Sales/Working Capital	20.0	123.8	63.9	NM	NM	-48.4
-14.2	-13.7	-17.3		-7.0	-18.3	-7.8	-15.9	-20.2	-15.1
-6.4	-4.8	-5.6		-1.4	-6.8	-2.7	-9.0	-5.6	-6.7
2.4	3.3	4.0	EBIT/Interest		5.9	5.4	4.1	4.4	3.7
(69) 1.3	(83) 1.5	(93) 2.1		(20) 1.9	(12) 2.0	(11) 2.8	(12) 2.0	(32) 1.9	
.3	.4	1.4			.4	1.1	1.8	1.5	1.4
4.7	5.6	15.5	Net Profit + Depr., Dep., Amort./Cur. Mat. L/T/D						16.3
(14) 1.7	(12) 2.0	(17) 3.1						(10)	3.9
.7	.9	1.4							2.6
2.1	2.3	2.0	Fixed/Worth	.8	1.8	2.2	1.6	2.0	2.0
5.0	5.1	4.0		12.2	3.8	3.7	3.1	4.2	4.0
155.3	-13.3	-28.3		-11.4	-10.6	-6.4	11.6	-15.1	20.7
1.5	1.8	1.5	Debt/Worth	1.4	1.3	1.5	2.3	1.9	1.6
4.4	5.0	3.5		12.0	3.2	3.0	3.1	3.9	3.5
159.6	-17.9	-30.0		-13.3	-11.7	-7.8	11.7	-28.7	20.8
32.9	33.8	46.7	% Profit Before Taxes/Tangible Net Worth		51.3	30.9	77.0		31.2
(67) 5.2	(74) 10.8	(89) 18.5		(23) 18.5	(10) 13.3	(11) 25.4		(28)	15.6
-19.6	-2.5	6.8			-4.4	2.4	11.5		7.4
7.8	7.7	10.5	% Profit Before Taxes/Total Assets	15.3	13.6	7.7	9.9	11.3	7.5
1.4	1.5	3.6		6.8	3.2	3.3	6.6	3.4	3.6
-4.0	-3.5	1.2		2.3	-1.3	-1.8	4.0	-.5	1.5
2.8	2.8	2.8	Sales/Net Fixed Assets	16.6	2.2	1.7	2.5	5.9	3.1
.9	1.0	1.1		.8	1.1	.6	.9	1.2	1.8
.5	.6	.6		.1	.4	.6	.5	.8	.9
1.6	1.8	2.1	Sales/Total Assets	8.0	1.7	1.4	2.0	3.2	2.1
.8	.9	1.0		.7	1.0	.6	.7	1.0	1.3
.5	.5	.5		.1	.3	.5	.4	.6	.8
4.2	4.4	4.3	% Depr., Dep., Amort./Sales	1.0	3.0	5.8	4.4	1.9	4.8
(83) 6.7	(94) 7.0	(115) 6.5		(13) 9.3	(29) 7.3	7.0	5.4	6.8	(33) 6.1
10.5	11.2	10.1		24.2	13.8	14.1	9.1	9.1	7.9
1.8	1.9	1.4	% Officers', Directors' Owners' Comp/Sales		1.5				
(22) 3.7	(21) 4.9	(20) 2.9			(11) 2.8				
7.7	9.9	5.4			3.6				
1959478M	2143388M	2637099M	Net Sales ($)	7338M	60205M	51515M	93827M	187456M	2236758M
2124375M	2263197M	2579884M	Total Assets ($)	26076M	143659M	83092M	185720M	194657M	1946680M

© RMA 2010

M = $ thousand   MM = $ million
See Pages 9 through 22 for Explanation of Ratios and Data

Current Data Sorted by Assets   **Comparative Historical Data**

0-500M	500M-2MM	2-10MM	10-50MM	50-100MM	100-250MM	Type of Statement	4/1/05-3/31/06 ALL	4/1/06-3/31/07 ALL
		3		1		Unqualified	4	4
		2		1		Reviewed	6	3
	4	1				Compiled	4	3
2	2					Tax Returns	6	7
	2	4	4	1	1	Other	14	14
	4 (4/1-9/30/09)		24 (10/1/09-3/31/10)					
2	8	10	4	3	1	**NUMBER OF STATEMENTS**	34	31
%	%	%	%	%	%	**ASSETS**	%	%
		18.1				Cash & Equivalents	15.8	19.9
		23.7				Trade Receivables (net)	30.2	28.9
		3.8				Inventory	7.3	3.3
		1.8				All Other Current	5.2	2.0
		47.4				Total Current	58.6	54.1
		43.0				Fixed Assets (net)	32.7	31.7
		.5				Intangibles (net)	4.7	6.6
		9.1				All Other Non-Current	4.1	7.5
		100.0				Total	100.0	100.0
						LIABILITIES		
		8.9				Notes Payable-Short Term	7.6	12.4
		10.5				Cur. Mat.-L.T.D.	4.7	3.9
		13.9				Trade Payables	10.3	12.0
		.8				Income Taxes Payable	.5	.4
		9.7				All Other Current	8.6	9.6
		43.8				Total Current	31.6	38.3
		16.8				Long-Term Debt	13.6	8.2
		1.3				Deferred Taxes	.0	.0
		6.2				All Other Non-Current	10.3	13.1
		31.9				Net Worth	44.5	40.3
		100.0				Total Liabilities & Net Worth	100.0	100.0
						INCOME DATA		
		100.0				Net Sales	100.0	100.0
						Gross Profit		
		97.5				Operating Expenses	90.3	95.4
		2.5				Operating Profit	9.7	4.6
		1.3				All Other Expenses (net)	1.8	.4
		1.2				Profit Before Taxes	7.9	4.2
						RATIOS		
		2.0				Current	4.5	3.0
		.9					2.1	1.3
		.6					1.0	.8
		1.8				Quick	3.6	2.9
		.8					2.1	1.1
		.6					.8	.7
	27	13.3				Sales/Receivables	26 14.1	30 12.1
	31	11.9					42 8.7	43 8.4
	60	6.1					61 6.0	63 5.8
						Cost of Sales/Inventory		
						Cost of Sales/Payables		
		13.9				Sales/Working Capital	5.2	7.5
		-168.1					13.1	22.5
		-14.1					NM	-70.5
		14.5				EBIT/Interest	34.3	16.2
		4.2					(25) 3.7	(25) 8.1
		-.6					.4	1.3
						Net Profit + Depr., Dep., Amort./Cur. Mat. L/T/D		
		.9				Fixed/Worth	.2	.2
		1.8					.6	.7
		5.7					7.1	3.4
		1.4				Debt/Worth	.3	.6
		2.2					1.3	1.5
		9.5					8.7	6.6
						% Profit Before Taxes/Tangible Net Worth	69.5	60.5
							(30) 25.1	(27) 39.1
							.2	6.3
		17.2				% Profit Before Taxes/Total Assets	23.2	23.5
		5.7					8.4	13.9
		-5.4					.3	2.3
		13.1				Sales/Net Fixed Assets	31.0	38.6
		5.0					7.5	9.0
		2.5					4.3	4.6
		3.2				Sales/Total Assets	3.9	3.9
		2.2					2.6	2.6
		1.4					1.4	1.5
		2.9				% Depr., Dep., Amort./Sales	2.6	2.7
		6.8					(27) 6.2	(23) 5.6
		10.4					9.3	7.4
						% Officers', Directors' Owners' Comp/Sales		2.2
							(14)	5.9
								17.7
2421M	25490M	103390M	237159M	205140M	144048M	Net Sales ($)	509150M	430089M
593M	10076M	43322M	137426M	196002M	132593M	Total Assets ($)	454908M	445800M

M = $ thousand   MM = $ million
See Pages 9 through 22 for Explanation of Ratios and Data

Comparative Historical Data   **Current Data Sorted by Sales**

			Type of Statement						
3	2	1	Unqualified			1	2		1
4	1	4	Reviewed			1	1		1
2	5	6	Compiled				1	2	
7	1	5	Tax Returns	1	1		1	1	
17	16	12	Other	1	2	2	2	2	5
4/1/07-3/31/08	4/1/08-3/31/09	4/1/09-3/31/10				4 (4/1-9/30/09)		24 (10/1/09-3/31/10)	
ALL	ALL	ALL		0-1MM	1-3MM	3-5MM	5-10MM	10-25MM	25MM & OVER
33	25	28	NUMBER OF STATEMENTS	2	5	3	6	5	7
%	%	%	ASSETS	%	%	%	%	%	%
15.5	11.4	15.7	Cash & Equivalents						
26.1	21.4	25.5	Trade Receivables (net)						
2.6	3.4	5.8	Inventory						
1.9	2.4	4.3	All Other Current						
46.0	38.7	51.3	Total Current						
34.3	42.5	35.2	Fixed Assets (net)						
7.8	6.7	2.5	Intangibles (net)						
11.9	12.1	10.9	All Other Non-Current						
100.0	100.0	100.0	Total						
			LIABILITIES						
8.7	4.9	13.7	Notes Payable-Short Term						
3.8	9.9	6.3	Cur. Mat.-L.T.D.						
8.3	10.0	10.3	Trade Payables						
.8	.1	.4	Income Taxes Payable						
18.6	10.1	9.2	All Other Current						
40.1	35.1	40.0	Total Current						
15.7	32.9	18.4	Long-Term Debt						
.1	.3	.7	Deferred Taxes						
6.1	6.0	11.3	All Other Non-Current						
37.9	25.9	29.6	Net Worth						
100.0	100.0	100.0	Total Liabilities & Net Worth						
			INCOME DATA						
100.0	100.0	100.0	Net Sales						
			Gross Profit						
95.1	98.7	94.8	Operating Expenses						
4.9	1.3	5.2	Operating Profit						
1.0	1.2	1.2	All Other Expenses (net)						
3.9	.1	4.0	Profit Before Taxes						
			RATIOS						
2.6	2.9	3.2	Current						
1.6	1.5	1.3							
.5	.6	.8							
2.5	2.3	2.5	Quick						
1.4	1.2	1.2							
.5	.5	.6							
22 16.9	24 15.1	28 13.1	Sales/Receivables						
44 8.3	51 7.2	39 9.3							
63 5.8	66 5.5	60 6.1							
			Cost of Sales/Inventory						
			Cost of Sales/Payables						
6.0	5.4	7.1	Sales/Working Capital						
13.0	16.2	14.1							
-13.5	-28.0	-18.0							
38.3	18.6	8.3	EBIT/Interest						
(30) 2.3	(21) 2.2	(27) 2.8							
.4	-.9	.8							
			Net Profit + Depr., Dep., Amort./Cur. Mat. L/T/D						
.2	.5	.5	Fixed/Worth						
.8	2.0	1.3							
5.5	-179.0	3.7							
.4	.4	.5	Debt/Worth						
1.6	3.3	2.2							
NM	-262.8	17.3							
51.4	35.1	56.5	% Profit Before Taxes/Tangible Net Worth						
(25) 14.6	(18) 13.9	(24) 8.1							
-1.2	-26.2	-.7							
16.4	12.0	7.5	% Profit Before Taxes/Total Assets						
2.9	4.4	4.1							
-2.5	-10.7	-.4							
21.9	11.5	30.8	Sales/Net Fixed Assets						
6.3	5.3	5.6							
3.2	2.2	2.7							
4.1	2.8	3.0	Sales/Total Assets						
1.8	1.3	2.2							
1.0	1.0	1.2							
2.2	3.8	1.9	% Depr., Dep., Amort./Sales						
(27) 5.6	(20) 8.4	(21) 4.3							
9.4	10.5	10.9							
2.6	3.7	2.2	% Officers', Directors' Owners' Comp/Sales						
(13) 7.7	(12) 10.0	(13) 4.7							
14.9	16.8	12.5							
586661M	402404M	717648M	Net Sales ($)	866M	10398M	10770M	44201M	81313M	570100M
492300M	346614M	520012M	Total Assets ($)	625M	7465M	5463M	18195M	56437M	431827M

M = $ thousand   MM = $ million
See Pages 9 through 22 for Explanation of Ratios and Data

Current Data Sorted by Assets   **Comparative Historical Data**

0-500M	500M-2MM	2-10MM	10-50MM	50-100MM	100-250MM		4/1/05-3/31/06 ALL	4/1/06-3/31/07 ALL
		6	10	6	3	**Type of Statement**		
		2	2	1		Unqualified	30	35
		2				Reviewed	11	11
2	3	2			1	Compiled	13	12
3	7	2				Tax Returns	7	7
3	4	22	20	8	6	Other	40	33
	12 (4/1-9/30/09)		101 (10/1/09-3/31/10)					
8	14	34	32	15	10	**NUMBER OF STATEMENTS**	101	98
%	%	%	%	%	%	**ASSETS**	%	%
	8.4	8.7	8.2	2.1	7.1	Cash & Equivalents	11.2	16.4
	20.3	14.4	7.8	6.9	8.4	Trade Receivables (net)	14.6	12.9
	.5	.0	.0	.9	.0	Inventory	.3	.3
	1.8	4.1	1.2	1.8	7.2	All Other Current	3.2	2.8
	31.0	27.2	17.2	11.7	22.6	Total Current	29.3	32.4
	26.7	24.2	23.9	16.4	16.0	Fixed Assets (net)	23.5	23.6
	36.2	32.9	45.2	66.2	59.6	Intangibles (net)	33.4	32.4
	6.2	15.7	13.7	5.7	1.9	All Other Non-Current	13.8	11.7
	100.0	100.0	100.0	100.0	100.0	Total	100.0	100.0
						LIABILITIES		
	14.1	7.8	4.9	.8	.3	Notes Payable-Short Term	2.6	3.3
	8.9	5.7	4.5	2.3	25.2	Cur. Mat.-L.T.D.	3.9	3.9
	3.3	2.5	1.5	3.9	2.0	Trade Payables	3.1	3.5
	.0	.1	.0	.1	.0	Income Taxes Payable	.1	.1
	6.7	17.7	6.3	2.7	4.2	All Other Current	9.5	4.6
	33.0	33.9	17.3	9.8	31.8	Total Current	19.2	14.4
	54.8	34.2	34.8	47.1	43.3	Long-Term Debt	43.9	38.0
	.0	.2	.6	2.9	.2	Deferred Taxes	1.7	.8
	17.0	19.9	21.2	10.3	5.1	All Other Non-Current	12.1	8.9
	-4.8	11.9	26.1	29.9	19.5	Net Worth	23.1	37.9
	100.0	100.0	100.0	100.0	100.0	Total Liabilities & Net Worth	100.0	100.0
						INCOME DATA		
	100.0	100.0	100.0	100.0	100.0	Net Sales	100.0	100.0
						Gross Profit		
	96.4	94.2	88.2	91.1	82.5	Operating Expenses	89.0	86.2
	3.6	5.8	11.8	8.9	17.5	Operating Profit	11.0	13.8
	3.3	7.3	14.5	13.1	24.6	All Other Expenses (net)	5.0	4.8
	.2	-1.5	-2.6	-4.3	-7.1	Profit Before Taxes	6.0	9.0
						RATIOS		
	3.4	3.3	3.7	2.4	1.8		4.8	6.6
	1.4	1.0	1.4	1.9	1.3	Current	2.0	2.5
	.4	.5	.4	1.5	.7		1.1	1.2
	3.0	2.1	3.3	2.0	1.3		4.6	5.3
	1.4	1.0	1.3	1.5	1.0	Quick	1.8	2.1
	.4	.5	.3	1.1	.6		.9	1.1
0 UND	39 9.4	40 9.1	41 8.9	56 6.6			40 9.0	30 12.1
45 8.2	57 6.4	53 6.9	55 6.7	58 6.2		Sales/Receivables	52 7.0	48 7.5
70 5.2	74 4.9	65 5.6	61 6.0	83 4.4			66 5.5	64 5.7
						Cost of Sales/Inventory		
						Cost of Sales/Payables		
	4.6	6.1	5.7	4.8	5.3		3.9	3.0
	NM	64.8	16.9	11.5	14.5	Sales/Working Capital	7.6	6.5
	-6.9	-4.4	-3.1	15.9	-11.5		72.5	23.6
	2.8	2.6	4.5	2.7			5.3	7.0
	(12) .7	(29) -.2	(23) 1.7	(13) .7		EBIT/Interest	(77) 2.8	(73) 2.7
	-2.1	-.7	-.7	-.3			1.3	.5
							4.5	5.8
						Net Profit + Depr., Dep., Amort./Cur. Mat. L/T/D	(21) 2.0	(16) 2.4
							1.1	1.4
	4.8	1.0	.7	-9.0	-2.2		.5	.4
	-.9	-1.8	-3.5	-.4	-.2	Fixed/Worth	-7.5	2.4
	-.2	-.3	-.2	-.2	-.1		-.4	-.5
	5.4	2.3	1.1	-19.4	-4.4		.8	.6
	-4.7	-3.6	-7.3	-1.6	-1.8	Debt/Worth	-15.2	11.0
	-1.6	-1.8	-1.5	-1.3	-1.3		-1.9	-1.9
		110.7	11.2				58.5	93.2
	(14) 28.7	(13) 5.3				% Profit Before Taxes/Tangible Net Worth	(49) 26.5	(55) 29.3
		-13.3	-5.4				8.9	7.2
	11.5	4.3	3.9	2.1	2.3		13.4	17.8
	.7	-.8	.7	-1.8	-1.4	% Profit Before Taxes/Total Assets	5.9	6.0
	-8.7	-8.4	-6.6	-3.8	-8.1		.9	-1.9
	16.2	15.4	5.8	3.4	7.7		11.5	8.3
	7.2	3.6	2.6	2.7	2.3	Sales/Net Fixed Assets	4.2	4.3
	3.2	2.0	1.3	1.9	1.7		2.2	2.4
	1.9	1.1	.7	.4	.5		1.4	1.4
	1.1	.6	.4	.4	.4	Sales/Total Assets	.9	.8
	.6	.4	.3	.3	.2		.5	.5
	5.1	2.6	3.4	4.5			3.0	2.7
	(12) 7.1	(26) 5.5	(29) 7.0	6.1		% Depr., Dep., Amort./Sales	(91) 4.8	(82) 5.0
	12.9	8.2	11.5	9.6			8.2	8.7
							3.0	2.9
						% Officers', Directors' Owners' Comp/Sales	(17) 7.8	(16) 5.2
							15.5	7.7
6426M	20557M	154288M	378615M	630129M	662307M	Net Sales ($)	1193402M	1365714M
2024M	17159M	182743M	696028M	1023215M	1705379M	Total Assets ($)	2043083M	2087407M

M = $ thousand   MM = $ million
See Pages 9 through 22 for Explanation of Ratios and Data

Comparative Historical Data

Current Data Sorted by Sales

			Type of Statement						
39	26	25	Unqualified		2	3	5	7	8
5	9	5	Reviewed		1	1	2	1	1
8	10	8	Compiled		4		1		1
12	18	12	Tax Returns	2	3	2			
46	53	63	Other	7	17	9	9	11	13
4/1/07-3/31/08	4/1/08-3/31/09	4/1/09-3/31/10		4					
					12 (4/1-9/30/09)		101 (10/1/09-3/31/10)		
ALL	ALL	ALL		0-1MM	1-3MM	3-5MM	5-10MM	10-25MM	25MM & OVE
110	116	113	NUMBER OF STATEMENTS	13	27	15	17	18	23
%	%	%	ASSETS	%	%	%	%	%	%
10.9	10.3	7.8	Cash & Equivalents	7.1	8.2	4.1	4.9	10.0	10.4
10.5	10.2	12.4	Trade Receivables (net)	19.0	14.7	8.4	16.4	7.8	9.4
.4	.2	.2	Inventory	.0	.2	.0	.0	.0	.6
2.8	2.6	2.8	All Other Current	1.2	2.8	5.4	.8	2.0	4.0
24.6	23.4	23.1	Total Current	27.3	25.9	17.9	22.1	19.8	24.3
25.3	27.0	23.1	Fixed Assets (net)	26.4	27.7	23.5	16.3	24.3	19.6
38.3	37.4	42.4	Intangibles (net)	28.3	35.9	38.3	54.8	46.5	48.4
11.8	12.3	11.3	All Other Non-Current	17.9	10.5	20.2	6.8	9.5	7.7
100.0	100.0	100.0	Total	100.0	100.0	100.0	100.0	100.0	100.0
			LIABILITIES						
4.1	4.5	7.9	Notes Payable-Short Term	15.0	16.5	4.8	7.7	1.3	1.1
4.2	5.0	6.9	Cur. Mat.-L.T.D.	5.6	6.8	11.4	2.4	2.3	11.9
2.2	3.3	4.1	Trade Payables	9.3	6.0	1.3	1.7	1.8	4.1
.0	.2	.0	Income Taxes Payable	.0	.0	.1	.0	.0	.1
5.8	6.7	17.1	All Other Current	47.6	28.0	7.3	10.4	5.8	7.2
16.3	19.6	36.0	Total Current	77.4	57.3	24.9	22.2	11.2	24.4
40.5	44.9	40.0	Long-Term Debt	61.7	40.6	34.5	36.2	39.1	34.2
.7	.8	.6	Deferred Taxes	.0	.2	.1	1.2	.0	2.0
7.8	10.9	15.9	All Other Non-Current	17.2	14.2	12.4	36.8	6.4	11.4
34.7	23.9	7.4	Net Worth	-56.3	-12.3	28.0	3.6	43.3	27.9
100.0	100.0	100.0	Total Liabilities & Net Worth	100.0	100.0	100.0	100.0	100.0	100.0
			INCOME DATA						
100.0	100.0	100.0	Net Sales	100.0	100.0	100.0	100.0	100.0	100.0
			Gross Profit						
88.8	90.4	91.5	Operating Expenses	96.0	90.6	88.7	89.5	96.9	89.2
11.2	9.6	8.5	Operating Profit	4.0	9.4	11.3	10.5	3.1	10.8
7.9	9.4	10.9	All Other Expenses (net)	6.8	8.9	10.5	13.1	10.7	14.2
3.3	.2	-2.4	Profit Before Taxes	-2.9	.5	.8	-2.6	-7.6	-3.4
			RATIOS						
4.1	3.0	2.4		2.2	5.1	1.6	2.6	3.1	2.1
1.9	1.5	1.3	Current	.6	.8	.9	2.0	1.5	1.6
.9	.6	.5		.1	.2	.2	.3	1.0	.9
3.8	2.6	2.2		2.2	2.6	1.5	2.4	2.9	1.8
1.6	1.2	1.1	Quick	.6	.8	.6	1.7	1.3	1.3
.7	.5	.5		.1	.2	.2	.3	.9	.9
34 10.8	29 12.7	39 9.4		0 UND	21 17.0	43 8.6	53 6.9	41 9.0	31 11.6
51 7.2	48 7.6	55 6.6	Sales/Receivables	45 8.1	44 8.2	62 5.9	58 6.3	56 6.5	56 6.5
61 6.0	57 6.4	67 5.5		70 5.2	77 4.8	72 5.1	66 5.5	64 5.7	64 5.7
			Cost of Sales/Inventory						
			Cost of Sales/Payables						
4.3	4.5	5.6		6.0	4.6	8.9	4.6	4.3	6.3
8.7	13.0	15.9	Sales/Working Capital	-6.5	-71.9	-85.9	7.6	13.7	13.3
-55.4	-12.4	-5.3		-1.1	-1.9	-1.7	-2.4	143.1	-58.7
8.1	3.9	3.0		1.8	2.8	2.0	10.7	3.0	9.4
(85) 2.1	(85) 1.3	(88) 1.0	EBIT/Interest	(10) .0	(21) 1.1	(12) 1.1	(15) .7	(16) .6	(14) 1.9
.4	-.4	-.6		-2.8	-.5	-2.5	-.5	-3.2	.2
8.7	3.3	2.8	Net Profit + Depr., Dep.,						
(18) 1.7	(22) .8	(20) 1.0	Amort./Cur. Mat. L/T/D						
1.0	-.9	.1							
.7	.8	1.5		5.2	1.1	.9	NM	.7	1.4
NM	-3.1	-.8	Fixed/Worth	-.6	-.7	-1.5	-.4	-2.1	-.4
-.3	-.3	-.2		-.1	-.2	-.7	-.1	-.3	-.2
1.0	1.4	5.5		120.2	UND	4.7	NM	.5	1.5
NM	-5.5	-2.9	Debt/Worth	-2.5	-3.3	-6.0	-1.9	-5.7	-3.1
-1.8	-1.7	-1.5		-1.3	-1.6	-1.8	-1.3	-1.5	-1.4
80.8	43.2	45.5	% Profit Before Taxes/Tangible						
(55) 28.4	(51) 14.9	(37) 5.9	Net Worth						
8.7	-1.2	-1.0							
11.5	6.8	3.9	% Profit Before Taxes/Total	4.1	8.7	3.8	8.4	3.0	3.9
2.3	.7	-.3	Assets	-4.3	.0	.8	-1.1	-1.5	-1.0
-3.8	-4.7	-7.2		-10.1	-6.5	-10.2	-7.2	-8.2	-3.8
8.8	7.4	8.4		81.2	28.6	4.8	9.9	3.5	7.1
3.7	3.4	3.2	Sales/Net Fixed Assets	7.6	5.7	2.5	5.7	2.7	3.0
2.1	1.8	1.8		2.6	1.9	1.6	2.2	1.7	1.8
1.2	1.2	1.0		1.6	1.3	1.0	1.0	.7	1.0
.7	.6	.5	Sales/Total Assets	.8	.6	.4	.6	.5	.5
.4	.4	.4		.5	.4	.3	.4	.3	.4
3.0	3.1	3.4		1.0	2.9	4.0	2.6	4.8	2.7
(92) 5.8	(107) 5.6	(97) 6.3	% Depr., Dep., Amort./Sales	(10) 8.1	(21) 5.5	(13) 6.6	(15) 4.1*	8.6	(20) 5.3
8.5	10.3	10.0		11.7	10.2	15.5	8.1	10.6	7.6
2.9	4.3	3.3	% Officers', Directors'						
(21) 5.1	(19) 6.5	(20) 5.9	Owners' Comp/Sales						
7.7	10.7	8.4							
1740783M	2057681M	1852322M	Net Sales ($)	7972M	50852M	58160M	118830M	272715M	1343793M
3381785M	3651609M	3626548M	Total Assets ($)	11555M	106255M	155023M	259014M	621653M	2473048M

M = $ thousand   MM = $ million
See Pages 9 through 22 for Explanation of Ratios and Data

INFORMATION—Television Broadcasting NAICS 515120

Current Data Sorted by Assets | Comparative Historical Data

0-500M	500M-2MM	2-10MM	10-50MM	50-100MM	100-250MM		4/1/05-3/31/06 ALL	4/1/06-3/31/07 ALL
		12	22	3	3	Type of Statement — Unqualified	40	39
		2				Reviewed	3	7
	2	2	1			Compiled	3	5
		1	1			Tax Returns	3	5
	2	8	11	5	6	Other	27	33
	29 (4/1-9/30/09)		52 (10/1/09-3/31/10)				27 (4/1/05-3/31/06)	33 (4/1/06-3/31/07)
	4	25	35	8	9	NUMBER OF STATEMENTS	76	89

0-500M %	500M-2MM %	2-10MM %	10-50MM %	50-100MM %	100-250MM %		%	%
						ASSETS		
		8.8	9.7			Cash & Equivalents	11.0	10.8
		8.9	7.4			Trade Receivables (net)	11.6	11.4
		.0	.4			Inventory	2.2	.6
		3.8	6.4			All Other Current	5.4	3.0
		21.5	23.9			Total Current	30.3	25.8
		53.4	39.1			Fixed Assets (net)	36.5	45.9
		11.1	19.8			Intangibles (net)	16.4	12.1
		13.9	17.3			All Other Non-Current	16.8	16.2
		100.0	100.0			Total	100.0	100.0
						LIABILITIES		
		4.6	3.4			Notes Payable-Short Term	5.9	4.1
		8.9	4.1			Cur. Mat.-L.T.D.	2.3	2.4
		5.0	4.7			Trade Payables	6.2	4.0
		.2	.0			Income Taxes Payable	.0	.1
		4.7	7.3			All Other Current	14.6	11.8
		23.4	19.6			Total Current	29.1	22.4
		36.2	19.5			Long-Term Debt	31.1	24.4
		.0	1.0			Deferred Taxes	.4	.7
		22.9	6.8			All Other Non-Current	13.2	10.6
		17.6	53.0			Net Worth	26.2	41.9
		100.0	100.0			Total Liabilities & Net Worth	100.0	100.0
						INCOME DATA		
		100.0	100.0			Net Sales	100.0	100.0
						Gross Profit		
		102.4	98.3			Operating Expenses	94.9	91.1
		-2.4	1.7			Operating Profit	5.1	8.9
		1.1	6.8			All Other Expenses (net)	4.7	2.5
		-3.5	-5.1			Profit Before Taxes	.4	6.4

RATIOS

0-500M	500M-2MM	2-10MM	10-50MM	50-100MM	100-250MM		4/1/05-3/31/06 ALL	4/1/06-3/31/07 ALL
		4.2	2.4			Current	3.0	3.4
		1.2	1.4				1.6	1.6
		.5	.6				.8	.8
		3.6	2.2			Quick	2.8	2.6
		.8	.9				1.1	1.2
		.4	.4				.5	.6
		(6) 65.5	(19) 19.4			Sales/Receivables	(14) 25.4	(25) 14.4
		(29) 12.5	(37) 9.9				(49) 7.4	(47) 7.7
		(56) 6.6	(66) 5.5				(67) 5.5	(66) 5.5
						Cost of Sales/Inventory		
						Cost of Sales/Payables		
		6.7	3.5			Sales/Working Capital	4.0	3.5
		21.9	11.8				9.1	10.5
		-6.6	-8.7				-20.5	-29.9
		3.2	5.4			EBIT/Interest	4.9	9.2
		(18) 1.4	(28) .8				(56) 1.4	(72) 3.0
		-5.0	-26.0				-1.1	-.2
						Net Profit + Depr., Dep., Amort./Cur. Mat. L/T/D		23.3
							(14)	2.2
								.7
		.8	.4			Fixed/Worth	.7	.6
		1.7	.9				1.1	1.1
		-1.1	8.7				-.8	5.3
		.3	.2			Debt/Worth	.4	.2
		.9	.8				2.0	1.2
		-2.6	48.5				-2.9	18.0
		4.1	12.3			% Profit Before Taxes/Tangible Net Worth	15.5	28.0
		(16) -5.7	(27) -1.4				(51) 2.5	(69) 9.6
		-16.1	-18.0				-6.8	.3
		3.0	7.9			% Profit Before Taxes/Total Assets	6.1	10.1
		-.1	-.8				.9	4.1
		-8.0	-12.1				-4.1	-.7
		2.8	3.8			Sales/Net Fixed Assets	4.8	3.6
		1.5	1.7				2.3	1.6
		.8	1.1				1.2	.9
		1.2	.8			Sales/Total Assets	1.1	1.1
		.7	.6				.8	.7
		.6	.5				.4	.4
		8.2	5.7			% Depr., Dep., Amort./Sales	6.4	5.3
		(23) 14.8	(34) 8.6				(63) 9.8	(86) 9.4
		21.9	13.6				15.2	13.1
						% Officers', Directors' Owners' Comp/Sales		
	6352M	148730M	615676M	438830M	624460M	Net Sales ($)	1527201M	1886885M
	5204M	168781M	960855M	626249M	1457431M	Total Assets ($)	2492695M	2660652M

(0-500M column: DATA NOT AVAILABLE)

M = $ thousand   MM = $ million
See Pages 9 through 22 for Explanation of Ratios and Data

Comparative Historical Data

Current Data Sorted by Sales

4/1/07-3/31/08 ALL	4/1/08-3/31/09 ALL	4/1/09-3/31/10 ALL	Type of Statement	0-1MM	1-3MM	3-5MM	5-10MM	10-25MM	25MM & OVER
42	40	40	Unqualified		4	3	10	14	9
3	5	2	Reviewed				2		
3	8	5	Compiled		2	2		1	
3	1	2	Tax Returns		1		1		
34	42	32	Other	2	1	3	4	11	11
					29 (4/1-9/30/09)		52 (10/1/09-3/31/10)		
85	96	81	**NUMBER OF STATEMENTS**	2	8	8	17	26	20
%	%	%	**ASSETS**	%	%	%	%	%	%
9.7	10.3	8.4	Cash & Equivalents				10.1	9.2	6.1
12.4	12.0	8.8	Trade Receivables (net)				6.9	8.8	9.8
.3	.8	.2	Inventory				.3	.3	.2
5.6	5.9	5.1	All Other Current				6.8	5.7	6.0
27.9	29.0	22.6	Total Current				24.2	23.9	22.1
40.7	38.5	41.2	Fixed Assets (net)				51.4	34.1	32.4
17.3	19.2	20.7	Intangibles (net)				9.1	25.0	32.7
14.1	13.3	15.5	All Other Non-Current				15.3	17.0	12.8
100.0	100.0	100.0	Total				100.0	100.0	100.0
			LIABILITIES						
4.0	6.3	3.9	Notes Payable-Short Term				5.4	2.8	1.4
4.7	7.4	5.2	Cur. Mat.-L.T.D.				10.0	5.6	3.1
5.1	4.7	4.3	Trade Payables				4.6	4.2	4.5
.4	.2	.1	Income Taxes Payable				.0	.0	.0
12.7	7.6	7.1	All Other Current				3.9	7.9	6.2
26.8	26.1	20.5	Total Current				24.0	20.6	15.2
28.5	28.2	35.1	Long-Term Debt				14.7	32.7	60.9
.8	.8	.6	Deferred Taxes				.0	.8	.8
13.3	14.9	11.5	All Other Non-Current				3.2	23.8	5.8
30.6	30.1	32.3	Net Worth				58.2	22.2	17.3
100.0	100.0	100.0	Total Liabilities & Net Worth				100.0	100.0	100.0
			INCOME DATA						
100.0	100.0	100.0	Net Sales				100.0	100.0	100.0
			Gross Profit						
92.7	94.6	98.0	Operating Expenses				102.7	99.3	93.7
7.3	5.4	2.0	Operating Profit				-2.7	.7	6.3
4.3	6.3	4.6	All Other Expenses (net)				4.0	5.6	4.8
3.0	-.9	-2.6	Profit Before Taxes				-6.8	-4.8	1.4
			RATIOS						
2.6	3.0	2.7	Current				2.4	3.1	2.3
1.7	1.4	1.3					2.0	1.0	1.5
.9	.7	.5					.9	.5	1.0
2.0	2.0	2.2	Quick				2.1	2.6	1.9
1.4	.9	1.0					.9	.8	1.0
.7	.4	.4					.7	.3	.6
17 21.7	19 19.6	16 23.5	Sales/Receivables				4 84.0	16 22.2	31 11.6
46 7.9	41 9.0	42 8.7					40 9.1	36 10.1	50 7.3
72 5.1	56 6.6	61 6.0					69 5.3	58 6.3	63 5.8
			Cost of Sales/Inventory						
			Cost of Sales/Payables						
4.9	4.6	4.7	Sales/Working Capital				3.4	4.7	5.3
8.7	15.2	16.1					11.5	NM	15.7
-43.5	-12.3	-8.1					NM	-5.9	NM
8.9	5.4	3.9	EBIT/Interest				4.5	3.7	4.5
(68) 2.2	(79) .6	(63) 1.3					(12) .7	(21) 1.2	(17) 1.7
.1	-3.0	-4.1					-32.8	-20.5	.1
8.2			Net Profit + Depr., Dep., Amort./Cur. Mat. L/T/D						
(10) 3.9									
-1.0									
.7	.6	.7	Fixed/Worth				.5	.7	.7
1.8	1.1	1.3					.8	1.6	-13.4
-1.8	-1.6	-1.1					1.7	-.3	-.7
.3	.3	.3	Debt/Worth				.1	.4	.9
2.9	1.3	1.3					.2	2.0	-26.5
-4.0	-3.5	-2.6					1.5	-1.6	-2.3
26.5	32.0	10.7	% Profit Before Taxes/Tangible Net Worth				4.4	13.9	
(56) 8.0	(63) 2.5	(52) .8					(14) -1.7	(17) .7	
-1.9	-11.1	-16.1					-14.9	-22.1	
10.2	7.2	3.8	% Profit Before Taxes/Total Assets				3.0	4.8	4.3
2.5	-1.6	.1					-.8	.2	1.6
-2.3	-9.0	-8.3					-9.8	-12.3	-3.0
4.1	4.4	3.4	Sales/Net Fixed Assets				2.1	4.1	3.5
2.0	2.1	1.7					1.3	2.6	1.8
1.1	1.2	1.2					1.0	1.4	1.5
1.0	1.1	1.0	Sales/Total Assets				.9	1.1	.8
.7	.7	.6					.6	.7	.6
.5	.5	.4					.5	.3	.4
4.3	4.9	5.8	% Depr., Dep., Amort./Sales				8.0	5.1	4.0
(75) 6.6	(83) 9.3	(71) 10.0					12.1	(25) 7.7	(13) 7.5
11.4	15.1	16.2					16.1	15.3	12.5
		9.3	% Officers', Directors' Owners' Comp/Sales						
	(10)	14.4							
		32.8							
2301767M	2477685M	1834048M	Net Sales ($)	1393M	17453M	33412M	123911M	448472M	1209407M
3370153M	3547446M	3218520M	Total Assets ($)	8635M	28960M	56259M	229742M	835098M	2059826M

M = $ thousand   MM = $ million
See Pages 9 through 22 for Explanation of Ratios and Data

INFORMATION—Cable and Other Subscription Programming   NAICS 515210

	Current Data Sorted by Assets							Comparative Historical Data	

Type of Statement

Type of Statement	0-500M	500M-2MM	2-10MM	10-50MM	50-100MM	100-250MM	4/1/05-3/31/06 ALL	4/1/06-3/31/07 ALL
Unqualified		2	5	6	4	8	22	25
Reviewed			4	2			11	7
Compiled	1	2	1	1			1	7
Tax Returns	3	5	2				17	7
Other		4	8	2	5	2	26	26

11 (4/1-9/30/09) | 56 (10/1/09-3/31/10)

	0-500M	500M-2MM	2-10MM	10-50MM	50-100MM	100-250MM	4/1/05-3/31/06 ALL	4/1/06-3/31/07 ALL
NUMBER OF STATEMENTS	4	13	20	11	9	10	77	72
	%	%	%	%	%	%	%	%
ASSETS								
Cash & Equivalents		17.6	19.1	9.8		11.4	9.3	13.0
Trade Receivables (net)		26.1	20.7	15.4		8.3	20.5	15.9
Inventory		.8	6.4	3.3		.2	3.9	5.1
All Other Current		6.7	2.8	1.6		1.7	4.7	5.1
Total Current		51.1	48.9	30.0		21.7	38.4	39.1
Fixed Assets (net)		28.0	34.1	43.5		33.8	40.2	35.5
Intangibles (net)		10.8	10.0	20.4		34.2	13.8	17.8
All Other Non-Current		10.0	7.0	6.0		10.3	7.6	7.6
Total		100.0	100.0	100.0		100.0	100.0	100.0
LIABILITIES								
Notes Payable-Short Term		8.3	6.3	5.9		.0	7.0	8.9
Cur. Mat.-L.T.D.		4.6	5.5	5.5		3.3	3.2	2.5
Trade Payables		11.4	13.0	6.2		4.9	13.3	18.1
Income Taxes Payable		.2	.3	.0		.9	.6	.4
All Other Current		23.6	15.7	8.1		9.2	9.1	8.6
Total Current		48.0	40.9	25.6		18.4	33.3	38.5
Long-Term Debt		30.6	16.8	42.2		40.9	25.6	28.7
Deferred Taxes		.2	.3	.9		3.9	2.1	1.2
All Other Non-Current		24.4	.3	6.2		5.5	14.6	14.1
Net Worth		-3.2	41.6	25.1		31.3	24.5	17.5
Total Liabilities & Net Worth		100.0	100.0	100.0		100.0	100.0	100.0
INCOME DATA								
Net Sales		100.0	100.0	100.0		100.0	100.0	100.0
Gross Profit								
Operating Expenses		97.1	90.2	87.7		91.7	93.0	93.1
Operating Profit		2.9	9.8	12.3		8.3	7.0	6.9
All Other Expenses (net)		.4	2.7	4.9		5.9	2.9	5.1
Profit Before Taxes		2.5	7.1	7.5		2.4	4.1	1.8
RATIOS								
Current		1.5	2.2	1.4		1.5	1.7	1.4
		.8	1.0	.7		.7	1.1	1.0
		.4	.6	.4		.5	.6	.6
Quick		1.3	2.0	1.3		1.4	1.2	1.3
		.5	.9	.5		.6	.7	.7
		.3	.4	.3		.3	.4	.5
Sales/Receivables		3 112.4	5 73.6	15 24.3		18 20.7	11 32.3	7 51.2
		12 30.2	11 33.4	31 11.7		24 15.4	25 14.4	25 14.4
		41 9.0	62 5.9	54 6.7		33 11.0	48 7.6	47 7.8
Cost of Sales/Inventory								
Cost of Sales/Payables								
Sales/Working Capital		19.6	7.1	14.5		8.2	12.5	15.0
		-14.4	NM	-15.4		-21.2	120.3	-314.5
		-8.8	-13.3	-5.7		-8.5	-12.9	-11.3
EBIT/Interest		13.6	18.4	8.6		2.4	10.4	8.0
		(11) 4.3	(16) 6.6	2.8		1.8	(63) 1.9	(61) 2.6
		.2	3.8	1.5		.7	-.4	.4
Net Profit + Depr., Dep., Amort./Cur. Mat. L/T/D							19.6	7.2
							(16) 3.3	(11) 3.6
							1.9	2.1
Fixed/Worth		.0	.1	.5		.8	.7	.6
		1.8	.5	9.5		-6.4	2.9	5.7
		-.4	2.2	-4.1		-1.0	-5.6	-2.9
Debt/Worth		.9	.8	1.2		2.6	1.2	2.1
		1.7	1.4	11.3		-10.1	4.1	11.9
		-3.6	5.9	-6.2		-2.2	-9.0	-5.3
% Profit Before Taxes/Tangible Net Worth			80.5				57.6	98.0
			(18) 42.1				(53) 23.9	(40) 31.4
			14.0				-1.7	7.0
% Profit Before Taxes/Total Assets		15.2	27.0	14.2		4.3	20.2	20.6
		5.4	6.7	6.2		2.0	5.0	4.3
		-.9	3.6	.8		-2.0	-1.8	-3.2
Sales/Net Fixed Assets		464.0	45.3	4.5		20.9	30.2	23.2
		39.8	17.3	1.8		1.5	4.4	5.3
		2.5	1.4	1.1		1.2	.9	1.1
Sales/Total Assets		6.2	4.2	1.3		1.2	4.0	3.4
		1.9	2.4	1.0		.7	1.6	1.4
		1.4	.8	.7		.4	.5	.5
% Depr., Dep., Amort./Sales			1.0	5.9			1.3	1.3
			(19) 1.5	13.2			(58) 8.7	(59) 6.2
			17.2	18.8			21.7	17.5
% Officers', Directors' Owners' Comp/Sales							1.4	1.6
							(25) 3.1	(20) 3.1
							10.1	4.1
Net Sales ($)	7448M	57087M	265240M	358211M	551011M	1255966M	2139019M	2528815M
Total Assets ($)	1016M	14617M	110339M	287488M	692790M	1542476M	2208241M	2810700M

M = $ thousand   MM = $ million
See Pages 9 through 22 for Explanation of Ratios and Data

Comparative Historical Data | Current Data Sorted by Sales

	4/1/07-3/31/08 ALL	4/1/08-3/31/09 ALL	4/1/09-3/31/10 ALL	0-1MM	1-3MM	3-5MM	5-10MM	10-25MM	25MM & OVER
Type of Statement					11 (4/1-9/30/09)			56 (10/1/09-3/31/10)	
Unqualified	25	21	25	2	1	3	3	3	13
Reviewed	11	9	6		1		1	1	3
Compiled	4	4	5				2	2	1
Tax Returns	5	7	10					1	
Other	19	19	21	4	4	1	1	7	10
NUMBER OF STATEMENTS	64	60	67	6	8	5	7	14	27
ASSETS	%	%	%	%	%	%	%	%	%
Cash & Equivalents	14.0	11.7	15.3					12.1	12.5
Trade Receivables (net)	13.5	17.9	16.2					34.7	11.3
Inventory	2.7	2.7	2.6					8.2	1.8
All Other Current	4.0	2.3	3.7					3.0	2.1
Total Current	34.1	34.6	37.8					58.0	27.6
Fixed Assets (net)	41.5	36.1	35.6					23.3	39.5
Intangibles (net)	19.3	23.2	18.2					11.0	25.2
All Other Non-Current	5.1	6.0	8.4					7.8	7.7
Total	100.0	100.0	100.0					100.0	100.0
LIABILITIES									
Notes Payable-Short Term	4.6	4.4	5.8					13.0	3.1
Cur. Mat.-L.T.D.	5.2	4.4	6.5					4.3	8.4
Trade Payables	11.6	10.0	9.1					19.7	6.2
Income Taxes Payable	.3	.1	.3					.3	.4
All Other Current	10.7	11.6	15.3					11.0	10.3
Total Current	32.4	30.5	36.9					48.3	28.3
Long-Term Debt	38.8	29.7	35.2					17.2	48.3
Deferred Taxes	.9	.6	.9					.0	1.9
All Other Non-Current	7.2	3.8	8.5					18.4	7.9
Net Worth	20.6	35.4	18.5					16.0	13.6
Total Liabilties & Net Worth	100.0	100.0	100.0					100.0	100.0
INCOME DATA									
Net Sales	100.0	100.0	100.0					100.0	100.0
Gross Profit									
Operating Expenses	92.9	90.9	91.7					91.9	91.8
Operating Profit	7.1	9.1	8.3					8.1	8.2
All Other Expenses (net)	4.7	5.8	4.1					1.6	6.0
Profit Before Taxes	2.4	3.3	4.2					6.4	2.2
RATIOS									
Current	1.8	1.8	1.4					2.1	1.4
	.9	1.0	.8					1.0	.7
	.5	.6	.4					.6	.3
Quick	1.4	1.7	1.3					1.6	1.3
	.7	.8	.6					.8	.6
	.4	.4	.3					.3	.2
Sales/Receivables	6 58.6	9 40.7	8 46.9					9 42.0	10 36.4
	20 18.3	27 13.7	21 17.4					34 10.8	22 16.9
	46 7.9	47 7.7	38 9.5					66 5.6	38 9.6
Cost of Sales/Inventory									
Cost of Sales/Payables									
Sales/Working Capital	12.2	12.2	14.5					10.9	19.9
	-51.2	-203.1	-24.7					NM	-15.4
	-9.8	-11.9	-7.8					-14.0	-7.3
EBIT/Interest	6.6	7.5	11.5					17.2	7.2
	(55) 2.5	(47) 2.3	(60) 3.4					(13) 9.2	1.8
	.9	.2	.9					3.6	.5
Net Profit + Depr., Dep., Amort./Cur. Mat. L/T/D		30.9							
		(10) 8.3							
		2.1							
Fixed/Worth	.6	.4	.3					.1	.7
	2.7	2.8	2.3					.3	-8.0
	-2.4	-1.6	-1.3					2.5	-1.6
Debt/Worth	1.0	1.0	1.2					1.1	1.4
	3.6	6.1	4.9					1.7	-12.4
	-5.1	-3.7	-5.6					13.5	-3.5
% Profit Before Taxes/Tangible Net Worth	35.8	60.1	51.5					86.1	74.0
	(40) 23.1	(35) 20.6	(39) 21.5					(12) 46.0	(12) 23.6
	7.8	6.6	7.6					18.4	3.9
% Profit Before Taxes/Total Assets	13.5	15.1	16.0					29.2	12.4
	4.1	3.8	5.4					11.9	2.1
	-2.0	-2.2	.5					5.8	-3.8
Sales/Net Fixed Assets	16.0	23.4	36.2					134.1	12.4
	2.5	3.0	3.4					32.5	1.8
	1.2	1.4	1.3					3.7	.9
Sales/Total Assets	3.3	2.4	2.8					5.1	1.9
	1.1	1.2	1.3					2.7	.8
	.6	.4	.6					1.2	.5
% Depr., Dep., Amort./Sales	2.0	1.7	1.4					.5	1.4
	(48) 7.0	(46) 6.7	(52) 8.3					(13) 1.0	(17) 10.3
	16.1	15.0	17.7					9.6	18.0
% Officers', Directors' Owners' Comp/Sales	1.8	1.5	.6						
	(15) 2.8	(16) 2.5	(12) 3.1						
	9.3	7.4	9.3						
Net Sales ($)	2212336M	1815565M	2494963M	3566M	14913M	20044M	52283M	214065M	2190092M
Total Assets ($)	2471393M	2339127M	2648726M	9595M	10909M	19301M	68448M	151879M	2388594M

M = $ thousand   MM = $ million
See Pages 9 through 22 for Explanation of Ratios and Data

Current Data Sorted by Assets   Comparative Historical Data

	0-500M	500M-2MM	2-10MM	10-50MM	50-100MM	100-250MM		4/1/05-3/31/06 ALL	4/1/06-3/31/07 ALL
Type of Statement									
Unqualified		3	29	73	35	29		144	137
Reviewed		6	25	7	1			13	22
Compiled	3	1	10	2				17	13
Tax Returns	12	10	14					14	16
Other	6	10	41	40	18	18		78	63
	0-500M	38 (4/1-9/30/09) 500M-2MM	2-10MM	355 (10/1/09-3/31/10) 10-50MM	50-100MM	100-250MM			
NUMBER OF STATEMENTS	21	30	119	122	54	47		266	251
	%	%	%	%	%	%	**ASSETS**	%	%
Cash & Equivalents	25.3	18.9	14.3	13.1	11.7	10.0		11.8	12.0
Trade Receivables (net)	14.8	34.8	23.7	12.6	8.9	10.2		15.2	17.4
Inventory	15.3	5.3	4.9	2.0	2.1	1.9		4.5	4.4
All Other Current	2.4	2.5	5.5	3.9	3.4	4.0		4.1	2.3
Total Current	57.8	61.5	48.4	31.5	26.2	26.2		35.7	36.0
Fixed Assets (net)	27.4	22.3	35.3	48.3	50.8	44.2		46.1	44.4
Intangibles (net)	3.7	3.0	6.9	10.0	15.9	21.6		6.9	8.2
All Other Non-Current	11.1	13.2	9.4	10.1	7.1	8.0		11.4	11.4
Total	100.0	100.0	100.0	100.0	100.0	100.0		100.0	100.0
							LIABILITIES		
Notes Payable-Short Term	17.0	10.8	8.7	1.7	1.2	1.3		3.5	4.2
Cur. Mat.-L.T.D.	14.7	6.4	3.7	4.0	3.0	4.3		4.4	4.4
Trade Payables	14.5	15.4	15.0	7.8	6.0	5.6		10.9	11.7
Income Taxes Payable	.0	.1	.2	.2	.6	.2		.7	.6
All Other Current	17.4	14.9	14.6	7.8	8.3	12.5		9.8	8.9
Total Current	63.6	47.6	42.2	21.5	19.1	24.0		29.3	29.8
Long-Term Debt	33.1	9.0	17.0	26.1	28.7	27.3		27.2	25.6
Deferred Taxes	.0	.0	1.2	1.4	.7	2.3		1.0	1.3
All Other Non-Current	.1	16.5	6.4	7.7	8.3	7.4		6.4	6.0
Net Worth	3.3	26.9	33.3	43.2	43.1	38.9		36.2	37.3
Total Liabilities & Net Worth	100.0	100.0	100.0	100.0	100.0	100.0		100.0	100.0
							INCOME DATA		
Net Sales	100.0	100.0	100.0	100.0	100.0	100.0		100.0	100.0
Gross Profit									
Operating Expenses	89.5	95.8	93.1	91.1	90.9	87.9		87.5	89.1
Operating Profit	10.5	4.2	6.9	8.9	9.1	12.1		12.5	10.9
All Other Expenses (net)	1.2	1.6	1.5	1.5	3.1	2.2		3.3	2.2
Profit Before Taxes	9.2	2.6	5.4	7.4	6.0	9.8		9.2	8.7
							RATIOS		
Current	2.4	2.6	1.8	2.5	2.1	2.5		2.3	2.1
	1.3	1.3	1.1	1.4	1.2	1.4		1.3	1.3
	.6	.8	.7	1.0	.7	.8		.9	.8
Quick	1.7	2.2	1.5	2.1	1.8	1.7		1.7	1.7
	.8	1.2	.8	1.1	.8	.9		1.0	1.1
	.2	.7	.5	.7	.5	.6		.6	.6
Sales/Receivables	0 UND	11 32.3	16 22.6	21 17.8	21 17.8	23 16.1		17 21.5	27 13.7
	0 UND	29 12.5	34 10.7	35 10.5	36 10.3	31 11.9		31 11.6	40 9.2
	16 22.8	68 5.4	57 6.4	49 7.5	49 7.4	45 8.1		46 7.9	56 6.6
Cost of Sales/Inventory									
Cost of Sales/Payables									
Sales/Working Capital	19.5	7.3	8.6	4.8	4.7	5.1		4.5	5.3
	93.9	37.2	53.9	11.9	19.5	9.3		14.0	17.8
	-17.3	-23.0	-14.2	-117.7	-13.7	-19.9		-52.5	-25.6
EBIT/Interest	8.2	28.4	16.5	10.4	9.3	11.7		8.4	9.9
	(13) 2.2	(24) 5.6	(107) 4.9	(110) 3.6	(51) 3.0	(44) 4.2		(236) 3.5	(210) 4.0
	-5.6	2.6	1.5	1.6	.6	2.1		1.6	1.6
Net Profit + Depr., Dep., Amort./Cur. Mat. L/T/D			7.8	11.3	4.5	7.4		5.2	5.2
			(33) 3.5	(60) 3.5	(22) 2.8	(14) 3.7		(116) 3.3	(92) 2.6
			2.3	1.7	1.9	2.2		2.2	1.6
Fixed/Worth	.1	.1	.3	.8	.9	1.1		.7	.6
	2.5	.7	1.0	1.3	1.7	3.0		1.4	1.5
	-.4	NM	3.0	3.5	4.1	-1.1		3.5	4.4
Debt/Worth	.5	.8	.9	.6	.7	.8		.8	.7
	3.9	2.4	1.9	1.4	1.5	3.0		1.6	1.9
	-2.6	NM	10.3	4.9	4.6	-4.5		5.4	8.0
% Profit Before Taxes/Tangible Net Worth	201.3	111.7	78.2	23.7	25.9	36.8		37.7	45.2
	(13) 83.3	(23) 25.4	(98) 25.0	(101) 8.3	(45) 10.0	(30) 14.7		(221) 14.1	(206) 17.7
	-8.2	11.0	5.4	2.6	-.3	8.3		5.3	5.4
% Profit Before Taxes/Total Assets	61.9	18.4	18.5	10.0	9.1	8.7		12.4	12.9
	27.8	10.6	8.2	4.0	3.6	5.1		5.4	6.3
	-16.6	.8	1.3	1.1	-.1	2.9		1.4	1.3
Sales/Net Fixed Assets	852.2	109.3	30.1	7.7	6.6	4.0		12.5	16.9
	30.6	37.0	11.0	1.1	1.1	1.2		1.1	1.3
	9.7	6.7	1.8	.7	.6	.7		.7	.7
Sales/Total Assets	17.7	5.3	3.5	1.5	1.1	1.0		2.3	2.2
	7.2	2.8	2.1	.6	.6	.5		.6	.7
	2.5	2.0	.8	.4	.4	.3		.4	.4
% Depr., Dep., Amort./Sales	.4	.4	1.1	6.9	7.0	6.6		2.2	3.0
	(10) 2.5	(21) 1.1	(105) 3.2	(115) 16.6	(42) 18.9	(18) 21.2		(229) 15.3	(200) 14.8
	6.4	6.1	14.9	21.5	24.0	27.4		20.9	20.9
% Officers', Directors' Owners' Comp/Sales		2.8	2.4					3.4	1.4
		(13) 5.7	(33) 6.2					(35) 5.6	(38) 3.7
		13.0	9.1					10.6	7.4
Net Sales ($)	30916M	130138M	1411597M	3373461M	3352618M	6439234M		6029367M	7049742M
Total Assets ($)	4396M	37637M	629858M	2977460M	3937212M	7384977M		8835663M	8371095M

M = $ thousand   MM = $ million
See Pages 9 through 22 for Explanation of Ratios and Data

Comparative Historical Data   Current Data Sorted by Sales

4/1/07-3/31/08 ALL	4/1/08-3/31/09 ALL	4/1/09-3/31/10 ALL	Type of Statement	0-1MM	1-3MM	3-5MM	5-10MM	10-25MM	25MM & OVE
139	109	169	Unqualified	1	10	9	31	45	73
18	35	39	Reviewed		1	6	13	12	7
11	19	16	Compiled	1	3		4	7	1
31	35	36	Tax Returns	7	12	4	6	6	1
121	142	133	Other	5	11	9	17	26	65
					38 (4/1-9/30/09)			355 (10/1/09-3/31/10)	
320	340	393	**NUMBER OF STATEMENTS**	14	37	28	71	96	147
%	%	%	**ASSETS**	%	%	%	%	%	%
14.5	12.6	14.0	Cash & Equivalents	8.4	16.4	13.8	15.1	13.6	13.7
17.5	20.9	17.0	Trade Receivables (net)	8.7	12.3	19.4	15.9	20.0	17.0
4.0	3.9	3.8	Inventory	21.2	2.5	3.7	3.3	3.7	2.9
3.0	3.7	4.1	All Other Current	.3	3.2	5.7	3.1	4.5	4.7
39.1	41.1	39.0	Total Current	38.7	34.3	42.7	37.5	41.8	38.4
39.7	38.1	41.1	Fixed Assets (net)	40.2	44.8	37.1	45.9	40.5	39.2
11.3	10.4	10.4	Intangibles (net)	4.5	5.4	8.2	6.6	9.0	15.3
9.9	10.3	9.5	All Other Non-Current	16.6	15.6	12.1	9.9	8.7	7.2
100.0	100.0	100.0	Total	100.0	100.0	100.0	100.0	100.0	100.0
			LIABILITIES						
7.8	7.6	5.2	Notes Payable-Short Term	13.4	8.7	9.3	5.5	5.4	2.5
4.5	4.5	4.6	Cur. Mat.-L.T.D.	9.3	8.6	1.9	5.6	3.3	3.9
11.6	12.0	10.4	Trade Payables	12.5	10.3	10.2	8.2	11.2	10.9
.3	.3	.3	Income Taxes Payable	.0	.2	.1	.2	.2	.4
13.1	13.3	11.5	All Other Current	22.3	11.4	10.7	9.5	10.1	12.6
37.4	37.6	32.0	Total Current	57.5	39.2	32.2	29.0	30.2	30.3
25.2	26.1	22.9	Long-Term Debt	38.0	27.3	15.8	22.6	16.3	26.2
.8	.8	1.2	Deferred Taxes	.0	1.0	1.3	2.1	.5	1.2
9.3	8.3	7.6	All Other Non-Current	2.1	11.5	6.7	8.0	8.7	6.5
27.3	27.1	36.3	Net Worth	2.4	21.0	44.0	38.3	44.3	35.7
100.0	100.0	100.0	Total Liabilities & Net Worth	100.0	100.0	100.0	100.0	100.0	100.0
			INCOME DATA						
100.0	100.0	100.0	Net Sales	100.0	100.0	100.0	100.0	100.0	100.0
			Gross Profit						
91.7	92.0	91.6	Operating Expenses	85.2	94.2	89.5	92.8	92.1	90.9
8.3	8.0	8.4	Operating Profit	14.8	5.8	10.5	7.2	7.9	9.1
2.2	2.7	1.8	All Other Expenses (net)	2.6	2.7	2.7	.9	.5	2.6
6.1	5.3	6.6	Profit Before Taxes	12.3	3.1	7.7	6.2	7.3	6.5
			RATIOS						
2.1	2.1	2.1	Current	1.6	1.9	2.7	2.6	2.2	1.9
1.2	1.2	1.3		1.0	.9	1.1	1.3	1.3	1.3
.8	.8	.8		.3	.4	.7	1.0	.9	.8
1.6	1.6	1.8	Quick	1.3	1.5	2.6	2.2	2.1	1.6
1.0	1.0	.9		.4	.7	.9	1.1	1.0	.9
.6	.6	.6		.0	.4	.3	.7	.6	.6
17 20.9	19 19.4	17 21.9	Sales/Receivables	0 UND	7 53.9	17 21.1	16 23.0	19 19.0	22 16.8
34 10.9	35 10.5	32 11.3		0 UND	19 19.4	31 11.6	33 11.0	33 11.2	36 10.2
57 6.4	52 7.0	49 7.4		37 9.8	46 8.0	52 7.1	53 6.9	45 8.1	50 7.2
			Cost of Sales/Inventory						
			Cost of Sales/Payables						
5.8	6.1	6.2	Sales/Working Capital	47.3	9.0	9.6	4.5	5.5	6.1
21.3	23.6	21.0		NM	-30.3	25.0	17.0	18.5	19.0
-20.1	-21.3	-23.4		-3.9	-7.9	-9.8	-301.9	-111.4	-21.9
10.0	9.9	12.1	EBIT/Interest	15.1	6.6	23.9	16.2	12.9	12.8
(266) 3.2	(287) 3.3	(349) 4.1		(10) 1.2	(28) 4.1	(26) 3.9	(68) 4.0	(88) 5.2	(129) 3.9
1.0	.9	1.5		-6.8	.1	1.5	1.5	1.9	1.7
10.8	8.7	6.6	Net Profit + Depr., Dep., Amort./Cur. Mat. L/T/D		3.4		7.8	11.1	5.4
(111) 3.2	(106) 3.4	(131) 3.4			(11) 1.6		(32) 3.6	(34) 4.5	(47) 3.2
1.8	1.9	1.9			1.0		2.2	3.1	1.8
.6	.5	.6	Fixed/Worth	.6	.8	.2	.6	.6	.6
1.6	1.5	1.3		4.0	1.6	1.3	1.2	1.1	1.5
-6.9	NM	5.8		-.7	-6.5	3.2	2.7	2.8	-24.9
.8	.7	.7	Debt/Worth	.9	.7	.5	.9	.6	.8
2.4	2.6	1.8		9.6	2.2	1.5	1.4	1.3	2.2
-13.9	-48.4	10.9		-2.7	-10.3	4.6	4.0	4.3	-32.8
55.2	53.7	44.5	% Profit Before Taxes/Tangible Net Worth		74.0	91.8	32.7	55.2	38.0
(233) 14.7	(253) 16.8	(310) 15.4			(27) 12.9	(24) 16.3	(61) 9.9	(79) 17.6	(110) 15.9
4.1	1.8	4.0			-6.7	.9	3.6	5.2	4.3
13.9	14.7	15.0	% Profit Before Taxes/Total Assets	37.4	15.5	15.4	12.8	16.0	14.3
5.2	5.4	5.7		1.9	6.4	7.1	4.8	7.1	5.2
-.2	-.8	1.2		-16.8	-4.1	.4	1.2	1.8	1.2
17.6	22.9	18.1	Sales/Net Fixed Assets	78.0	24.7	68.0	13.7	27.9	15.7
3.6	5.0	3.2		5.4	3.3	8.2	1.8	4.9	2.5
.8	.9	.8		1.5	.6	.6	.6	.9	.9
2.8	3.0	2.6	Sales/Total Assets	3.2	3.7	2.7	2.6	2.9	2.3
1.1	1.5	1.1		1.6	.7	.8	.7	1.5	.9
.5	.5	.5		.8	.5	.4	.4	.6	.5
2.3	2.1	2.3	% Depr., Dep., Amort./Sales		5.1	1.0	2.5	2.0	2.2
(250) 9.8	(261) 7.0	(311) 9.3			(30) 15.1	(22) 16.9	(65) 15.1	(86) 8.3	(101) 7.5
19.4	18.5	20.3			20.1	24.8	21.4	21.1	19.5
3.0	1.9	2.3	% Officers', Directors' Owners' Comp/Sales		1.6		4.4	2.2	.5
(43) 5.6	(49) 4.5	(64) 6.1			(11) 7.7		(15) 6.2	(16) 5.2	(10) 2.1
10.5	8.0	11.3			16.7		8.1	6.8	7.4
11556539M	11859267M	14737964M	Net Sales ($)	7253M	74978M	111085M	535001M	1564875M	12444772M
12523005M	11964160M	14971540M	Total Assets ($)	10458M	104477M	167783M	800286M	1803099M	12085437M

M = $ thousand   MM = $ million
See Pages 9 through 22 for Explanation of Ratios and Data

INFORMATION—Wireless Telecommunications Carriers (except Satellite) NAICS 517210

Current Data Sorted by Assets | **Comparative Historical Data**

Time-period note: 14 (4/1-9/30/09) · 108 (10/1/09-3/31/10)

Type of Statement	0-500M	500M-2MM	2-10MM	10-50MM	50-100MM	100-250MM	4/1/05-3/31/06 ALL	4/1/06-3/31/07 ALL
Unqualified			7	13	5	11		
Reviewed		1	10	2				
Compiled	1	6	1			1		
Tax Returns	14	7	4					
Other	6	5	11	10	6	1		
NUMBER OF STATEMENTS	21	19	33	25	11	13		

	0-500M (%)	500M-2MM (%)	2-10MM (%)	10-50MM (%)	50-100MM (%)	100-250MM (%)	4/1/05-3/31/06 ALL (%)	4/1/06-3/31/07 ALL (%)
ASSETS								
Cash & Equivalents	14.5	18.5	14.9	14.4	16.8	5.7	DATA NOT AVAILABLE	DATA NOT AVAILABLE
Trade Receivables (net)	14.6	22.9	21.6	18.0	13.7	4.2		
Inventory	20.0	20.1	13.1	7.7	3.3	3.1		
All Other Current	4.1	2.9	6.6	3.5	1.1	7.5		
Total Current	53.2	64.4	56.2	43.6	34.9	20.5		
Fixed Assets (net)	35.6	21.6	26.6	36.1	47.1	45.3		
Intangibles (net)	9.4	6.6	10.0	10.3	6.9	27.6		
All Other Non-Current	1.9	7.3	7.1	10.0	11.1	6.6		
Total	100.0	100.0	100.0	100.0	100.0	100.0		
LIABILITIES								
Notes Payable-Short Term	23.3	15.2	9.2	3.6	.0	4.8		
Cur. Mat.-L.T.D.	5.9	3.0	4.1	3.3	5.2	9.7		
Trade Payables	14.6	16.0	22.3	16.5	9.1	5.9		
Income Taxes Payable	.0	.1	.4	.0	.0	.1		
All Other Current	10.2	8.3	12.9	8.7	12.5	21.9		
Total Current	54.2	42.5	48.9	32.1	26.9	42.3		
Long-Term Debt	39.3	4.4	19.2	15.4	18.3	19.0		
Deferred Taxes	.0	.0	.3	.4	.5	1.9		
All Other Non-Current	22.5	4.4	4.4	3.8	6.1	10.1		
Net Worth	-16.0	48.7	27.2	48.3	48.3	26.6		
Total Liabilities & Net Worth	100.0	100.0	100.0	100.0	100.0	100.0		
INCOME DATA								
Net Sales	100.0	100.0	100.0	100.0	100.0	100.0		
Gross Profit								
Operating Expenses	92.0	90.2	94.7	90.8	83.2	87.8		
Operating Profit	8.0	9.8	5.3	9.2	16.8	12.2		
All Other Expenses (net)	.5	-.2	1.6	1.8	.3	3.7		
Profit Before Taxes	7.6	10.0	3.7	7.4	16.4	8.5		
RATIOS								
Current	6.4	3.5	1.7	2.7	1.6	1.0		
	1.1	1.5	1.2	1.6	1.3	.8		
	.6	1.1	.9	.9	.9	.4		
Quick	2.6	2.6	1.1	2.5	1.3	.8		
	.3	.9	.7	1.0	1.2	.4		
	.2	.6	.6	.5				
Sales/Receivables	0 UND	7 54.6	16 22.7	14 25.5	20 17.8	3 118.9		
	1 379.3	17 21.7	26 14.2	38 9.6	36 10.2	23 15.9		
	24 15.1	42 8.8	48 7.5	46 7.9	73 5.0	41 8.9		
Cost of Sales/Inventory								
Cost of Sales/Payables								
Sales/Working Capital	7.7	9.3	10.8	4.7	6.3	NM		
	63.1	13.6	48.7	11.4	22.0	-12.4		
	-40.7	84.6	-120.7	-298.9	-31.8	-4.0		
EBIT/Interest	12.0	45.6	43.3	39.2		4.5		
	(15) 3.8	(15) 23.9	(32) 8.3	(21) 5.9		(12) 3.0		
	.4	6.5	1.2	.4		1.1		
Net Profit + Depr., Dep., Amort./Cur. Mat. L/T/D								
Fixed/Worth	.5	.2	.3	.5	.4	2.7		
	8.0	.4	.9	.9	.9	4.1		
	-.6	.7	45.4	3.4	3.1	-3.2		
Debt/Worth	3.7	.4	.9	.6	.3	2.4		
	-14.8	1.1	2.7	1.3	1.0	8.8		
	-2.6	1.8	109.7	10.5	4.0	-5.5		
% Profit Before Taxes/Tangible Net Worth	391.9	109.7	94.2	61.8	71.1			
	(10) 161.2	(17) 55.8	(26) 36.8	(22) 16.8	(10) 50.2			
	-2.3	11.1	4.1	4.3	27.0			
% Profit Before Taxes/Total Assets	97.3	31.6	24.9	13.7	25.8	9.3		
	12.8	26.3	10.5	6.0	12.0	5.6		
	-.5	6.9	.4	.3	9.4	-.1		
Sales/Net Fixed Assets	123.4	77.0	46.2	32.8	13.9	3.2		
	24.3	24.7	10.7	4.8	2.3	1.9		
	3.8	12.4	4.6	1.3	1.0	.8		
Sales/Total Assets	9.7	6.2	4.0	3.1	2.1	1.2		
	3.4	4.0	2.2	1.0	1.1	.6		
	1.4	2.5	1.4	.7	.7	.4		
% Depr., Dep., Amort./Sales	.8	.5	.7	1.2	3.7			
	(12) 1.4	(14) 1.4	(30) 2.6	(22) 6.8	(10) 6.3			
	12.6	3.2	5.6	13.6	17.3			
% Officers', Directors' Owners' Comp/Sales	2.3	1.2	1.9					
	(10) 5.2	(11) 1.8	(11) 2.8					
	9.1	3.3	9.0					
Net Sales ($)	37092M	81863M	455268M	1427304M	1059793M	2734529M		
Total Assets ($)	5307M	19219M	163855M	580393M	812288M	2447080M		

M = $ thousand MM = $ million
See Pages 9 through 22 for Explanation of Ratios and Data

Comparative Historical Data | Current Data Sorted by Sales

4/1/07-3/31/08 ALL	4/1/08-3/31/09 ALL	4/1/09-3/31/10 ALL		0-1MM	1-3MM	3-5MM	5-10MM	10-25MM	25MM & OVER
			Type of Statement		14 (4/1-9/30/09)			108 (10/1/09-3/31/10)	
26	32	36	Unqualified		1	3	3	5	24
15	11	13	Reviewed			2	5	4	2
10	13	9	Compiled	1	3	2	1	1	1
15	15	25	Tax Returns	4	3	2	1	4	5
31	40	39	Other	7	7	5	4	5	15
97	111	122	**NUMBER OF STATEMENTS**	12	14	15	17	22	42
%	%	%	**ASSETS**	%	%	%	%	%	%
11.7	12.0	14.5	Cash & Equivalents	10.7	13.2	13.8	22.0	16.2	12.3
21.3	19.4	17.3	Trade Receivables (net)	5.5	29.4	15.2	16.6	17.8	17.4
10.6	10.4	12.3	Inventory	14.7	15.7	17.4	13.8	12.6	7.9
5.0	4.8	4.6	All Other Current	7.7	1.6	1.8	5.2	5.0	5.1
48.5	46.5	48.7	Total Current	38.6	59.9	48.2	57.7	51.6	42.7
38.6	34.2	33.2	Fixed Assets (net)	49.7	24.2	44.8	24.0	23.1	36.3
7.3	9.4	11.0	Intangibles (net)	3.0	12.4	4.3	13.3	10.4	14.7
5.6	9.9	7.1	All Other Non-Current	8.7	3.5	2.8	5.0	14.9	6.2
100.0	100.0	100.0	Total	100.0	100.0	100.0	100.0	100.0	100.0
			LIABILITIES						
6.0	8.7	10.1	Notes Payable-Short Term	8.7	16.6	27.4	14.0	3.1	4.3
4.1	3.5	4.8	Cur. Mat.-L.T.D.	7.4	3.0	5.7	3.1	3.7	5.6
15.1	15.0	15.9	Trade Payables	13.2	17.3	13.4	10.2	16.4	19.0
.3	.1	.1	Income Taxes Payable	.0	.1	.1	.5	.1	.1
11.3	12.3	11.8	All Other Current	4.6	11.6	9.0	13.1	11.8	14.4
36.8	39.7	42.7	Total Current	33.9	48.6	55.5	40.9	35.2	43.3
24.7	19.1	19.5	Long-Term Debt	45.1	23.3	29.0	7.5	17.1	13.6
.3	.5	.4	Deferred Taxes	.0	.0	.0	.5	.1	.9
5.9	5.3	8.2	All Other Non-Current	12.5	1.6	22.8	8.3	3.7	6.2
32.2	35.5	29.3	Net Worth	8.5	26.5	-7.3	42.8	44.0	36.0
100.0	100.0	100.0	Total Liabilties & Net Worth	100.0	100.0	100.0	100.0	100.0	100.0
			INCOME DATA						
100.0	100.0	100.0	Net Sales	100.0	100.0	100.0	100.0	100.0	100.0
			Gross Profit						
93.1	91.0	91.0	Operating Expenses	86.2	92.8	92.2	95.4	92.7	88.6
6.9	9.0	9.0	Operating Profit	13.8	7.2	7.8	4.6	7.3	11.4
1.7	2.3	1.3	All Other Expenses (net)	1.6	.8	2.3	.2	.7	1.8
5.2	6.8	7.8	Profit Before Taxes	12.2	6.4	5.6	4.5	6.6	9.6
			RATIOS						
2.3	2.0	2.1		4.0	2.4	7.6	2.2	2.0	1.5
1.5	1.4	1.2	Current	1.1	1.4	1.2	1.3	1.7	1.0
1.0	.9	.8		.7	.8	.7	1.1	1.0	.8
1.6	1.5	1.4		2.3	1.8	5.0	2.0	1.6	1.1
1.0	1.0	.8	Quick	.5	.8	.8	.9	1.0	.7
.6	.5	.4		.3	.2	.2	.6	.7	.4
22 16.7	12 31.2	8 47.5		0 UND	13 27.8	1 379.3	10 35.7	13 27.3	9 40.4
35 10.5	28 13.0	25 14.7	Sales/Receivables	0 UND	24 14.9	16 22.8	23 16.2	36 10.0	31 12.0
57 6.4	50 7.2	46 8.0		39 9.3	45 8.1	42 8.6	44 8.4	48 7.6	46 7.9
			Cost of Sales/Inventory						
			Cost of Sales/Payables						
6.7	7.1	8.1		4.4	7.8	9.8	9.6	5.6	14.6
15.0	19.1	32.7	Sales/Working Capital	18.1	13.7	63.1	21.9	11.3	NM
-131.4	-71.9	-30.2		-9.0	-59.1	-20.7	64.7	NM	-16.7
13.1	13.9	28.7			44.6	38.5	72.5	41.0	26.4
(83) 3.9	(91) 5.4	(104) 6.4	EBIT/Interest	(12) 10.2	(11) 1.8	(15) 8.8	(20) 11.4	(37) 6.4	
1.5	1.7	1.6		-.3	.3	-.2	2.9	2.4	
9.8	17.1		Net Profit + Depr., Dep.,						
(12) 3.1	(13) 3.6		Amort./Cur. Mat. L/T/D						
1.8	1.6								
.5	.3	.4		.9	.1	.5	.3	.2	.6
1.4	1.1	.9	Fixed/Worth	5.1	.7	3.6	.7	.5	1.4
2.8	10.0	37.5		-3.7	-.8	-1.7	1.7	1.3	8.8
.8	.5	.7		.6	.4	.2	.6	.8	1.0
2.0	2.0	2.4	Debt/Worth	12.1	1.3	4.7	2.1	1.1	2.8
8.6	119.1	NM		-4.9	-3.4	-5.3	12.2	4.7	29.5
60.8	80.9	99.4	% Profit Before Taxes/Tangible			97.1	103.7	91.6	92.8
(80) 24.6	(84) 25.6	(92) 35.8	Net Worth		(10) 19.7	(14) 67.8	(19) 19.1	(33) 45.6	
6.8	6.8	7.8				6.6	11.9	5.0	15.4
17.1	23.1	26.8	% Profit Before Taxes/Total	22.0	61.5	26.3	46.9	28.4	20.5
7.0	9.3	10.5	Assets	6.9	16.6	9.2	12.2	10.2	10.5
1.0	1.2	1.9		-2.5	-.8	1.6	-1.3	3.9	4.6
21.1	42.6	41.9		16.1	180.1	81.3	56.1	48.8	34.6
6.7	8.8	9.0	Sales/Net Fixed Assets	3.2	25.8	10.1	10.7	14.5	4.1
1.5	1.8	2.0		.5	8.0	1.8	4.6	4.7	1.7
3.7	4.0	4.0		3.2	7.5	8.1	5.5	4.3	3.4
1.8	1.9	2.1	Sales/Total Assets	.9	3.6	2.4	2.2	2.3	1.5
.7	.9	.9		.3	2.2	.9	1.1	.8	.7
1.1	1.0	.7			.5	.6	2.1	.7	.6
(83) 2.4	(81) 3.0	(90) 2.9	% Depr., Dep., Amort./Sales		(10) 2.2	(13) 3.1	(13) 3.8	(19) 2.3	(27) 2.7
12.1	11.0	11.0			4.7	17.8	10.2	12.3	9.5
2.4	2.5	1.8	% Officers', Directors'						
(24) 6.8	(32) 5.0	(36) 3.1	Owners' Comp/Sales						
10.3	7.8	7.6							
3158379M	5120257M	5795849M	Net Sales ($)	4253M	27948M	60707M	124780M	339873M	5238288M
2671600M	3796638M	4028142M	Total Assets ($)	3495M	13056M	47744M	69954M	295669M	3598224M

M = $ thousand   MM = $ million
See Pages 9 through 22 for Explanation of Ratios and Data

Current Data Sorted by Assets   **Comparative Historical Data**

	0-500M	500M-2MM	2-10MM	10-50MM	50-100MM	100-250MM	Type of Statement	4/1/05-3/31/06 ALL	4/1/06-3/31/07 ALL
			2	2		2	Unqualified		
			5	2			Reviewed		
	1	1		1			Compiled		
	3	2		1			Tax Returns		
	1	1	5	4	2	2	Other		
		2 (4/1-9/30/09)		35 (10/1/09-3/31/10)					
	5	4	12	10	2	4	NUMBER OF STATEMENTS		
	%	%	%	%	%	%		%	%
			17.8	6.5			Cash & Equivalents		
			33.8	32.0			Trade Receivables (net)	D	D
			11.7	12.0			Inventory	A	A
			6.8	9.0			All Other Current	T	T
			70.1	59.5			Total Current	A	A
			11.1	17.7			Fixed Assets (net)		
			8.0	10.1			Intangibles (net)	N	N
			10.8	12.7			All Other Non-Current	O	O
			100.0	100.0			Total	T	T
							LIABILITIES	A	A
			6.9	14.8			Notes Payable-Short Term	V	V
			2.0	5.7			Cur. Mat.-L.T.D.	A	A
			31.9	25.0			Trade Payables	I	I
			.0	.6			Income Taxes Payable	L	L
			24.9	17.9			All Other Current	A	A
			65.8	64.0			Total Current	B	B
			1.4	20.7			Long-Term Debt	L	L
			.2	.0			Deferred Taxes	E	E
			11.0	5.8			All Other Non-Current		
			21.6	9.5			Net Worth		
			100.0	100.0			Total Liabilties & Net Worth		
							INCOME DATA		
			100.0	100.0			Net Sales		
							Gross Profit		
			95.9	87.3			Operating Expenses		
			4.1	12.7			Operating Profit		
			-.1	4.1			All Other Expenses (net)		
			4.2	8.6			Profit Before Taxes		
							RATIOS		
			1.7	1.4			Current		
			1.0	.8					
			.7	.6					
			1.2	.9			Quick		
			.8	.6					
			.5	.4					
			5 76.7	0 UND			Sales/Receivables		
			26 13.8	35 10.5					
			55 6.6	45 8.2					
							Cost of Sales/Inventory		
							Cost of Sales/Payables		
			11.0	18.9			Sales/Working Capital		
			NM	-78.2					
			-13.5	-10.2					
							EBIT/Interest		
							Net Profit + Depr., Dep., Amort./Cur. Mat. L/T/D		
			.2	.8			Fixed/Worth		
			1.0	-1.1					
			-2.0	-.3					
			.8	2.3			Debt/Worth		
			15.3	-7.4					
			-12.7	-4.4					
							% Profit Before Taxes/Tangible Net Worth		
			22.7	20.1			% Profit Before Taxes/Total Assets		
			11.4	10.4					
			3.5	2.4					
			217.3	103.2			Sales/Net Fixed Assets		
			80.2	38.0					
			23.9	20.8					
			7.7	4.7			Sales/Total Assets		
			3.3	3.6					
			2.7	2.6					
			.2				% Depr., Dep., Amort./Sales		
		(11)	.8						
			1.9						
							% Officers', Directors' Owners' Comp/Sales		
	3258M	31778M	327560M	884142M	95620M	1009199M	Net Sales ($)		
	963M	4741M	54540M	253004M	152455M	850955M	Total Assets ($)		

M = $ thousand   MM = $ million
See Pages 9 through 22 for Explanation of Ratios and Data

Comparative Historical Data | Current Data Sorted by Sales

	7 2 3 1 12	9 3 2 1 12	6 7 3 6 15	Type of Statement	0-1MM	1-3MM	3-5MM	5-10MM	10-25MM	25MM & OVER
Unqualified	7	9	6					1	1	4
Reviewed	2	3	7					2	1	4
Compiled	3	2	3		1			1		1
Tax Returns	1	1	6		3				2	
Other	12	12	15		1	1		3	4	7
	4/1/07-3/31/08 ALL	4/1/08-3/31/09 ALL	4/1/09-3/31/10 ALL			2 (4/1-9/30/09)			35 (10/1/09-3/31/10)	
NUMBER OF STATEMENTS	25	31	37		5	1		7	8	16

Right-side columns 0-1MM through 10-25MM for the following ASSETS / LIABILITIES / INCOME DATA / RATIOS sections are marked: **DATA NOT AVAILABLE**

ASSETS (%)

08	09	10		25MM & OVER
16.5	10.6	10.8	Cash & Equivalents	11.3
28.5	27.2	28.2	Trade Receivables (net)	31.2
14.6	11.9	14.5	Inventory	8.9
2.9	4.2	5.4	All Other Current	4.1
62.4	53.9	58.9	Total Current	55.5
21.8	17.8	16.9	Fixed Assets (net)	14.0
9.1	14.3	12.1	Intangibles (net)	19.9
6.7	14.0	12.0	All Other Non-Current	10.6
100.0	100.0	100.0	Total	100.0

LIABILITIES (%)

08	09	10		25MM & OVER
15.7	11.5	17.2	Notes Payable-Short Term	8.8
3.4	2.6	3.8	Cur. Mat.-L.T.D.	3.9
18.9	36.1	28.0	Trade Payables	30.6
.3	.5	.4	Income Taxes Payable	.9
12.6	12.2	16.3	All Other Current	19.2
50.9	62.9	65.6	Total Current	63.5
8.5	18.5	18.9	Long-Term Debt	25.0
.9	.7	.4	Deferred Taxes	.9
4.2	13.4	7.0	All Other Non-Current	6.9
35.5	4.5	8.1	Net Worth	3.8
100.0	100.0	100.0	Total Liabilities & Net Worth	100.0

INCOME DATA (%)

08	09	10		25MM & OVER
100.0	100.0	100.0	Net Sales	100.0
			Gross Profit	
92.2	92.8	93.6	Operating Expenses	95.5
7.8	7.2	6.4	Operating Profit	4.5
.5	3.0	2.8	All Other Expenses (net)	3.5
7.3	4.2	3.6	Profit Before Taxes	1.0

RATIOS

08	09	10		25MM & OVER
1.8	1.6	1.7	Current	1.3
1.3	1.2	1.0		.9
.9	.8	.6		.6
1.4	1.2	.9	Quick	1.1
1.0	.8	.6		.6
.6	.6	.4		.5
23 15.9	18 20.0	13 27.7	Sales/Receivables	20 17.9
38 9.7	31 11.7	31 11.9		36 10.2
51 7.2	55 6.7	51 7.1		49 7.5
			Cost of Sales/Inventory	
			Cost of Sales/Payables	
8.2	9.0	10.7	Sales/Working Capital	18.4
18.1	50.5	-152.5		-138.3
-65.3	-33.6	-9.8		-12.5
12.6	5.0	16.7	EBIT/Interest	10.3
(23) 4.4	(26) 1.9	(33) 5.3		(15) 3.1
1.3	-1.0	.6		1.6
			Net Profit + Depr., Dep., Amort./Cur. Mat. L/T/D	
.4	.5	.3	Fixed/Worth	1.3
.6	2.7	2.1		-1.5
NM	-.4	-.4		-.3
1.0	1.9	1.7	Debt/Worth	56.8
1.8	11.5	-17.0		-8.2
NM	-4.9	-2.9		-4.3
64.2	98.2	84.5	% Profit Before Taxes/Tangible Net Worth	
(19) 31.4	(19) 28.5	(18) 24.1		
16.2	11.7	11.2		
19.1	10.8	18.2	% Profit Before Taxes/Total Assets	14.9
9.9	4.2	6.5		6.5
2.8	-10.2	-.8		2.6
58.1	213.4	120.5	Sales/Net Fixed Assets	133.1
23.7	41.1	36.7		33.2
7.1	11.2	12.3		7.6
3.7	4.3	5.9	Sales/Total Assets	6.0
2.9	1.8	3.2		3.6
1.6	1.1	1.7		1.6
.4	.4	.5	% Depr., Dep., Amort./Sales	.1
(21) 1.3	(21) .9	(27) .9		(10) .6
6.7	3.4	2.8		1.8
			% Officers', Directors' Owners' Comp/Sales	

Dollar Totals

08	09	10		0-1MM	1-3MM	3-5MM	5-10MM	10-25MM	25MM & OVER
1389514M	1605716M	2351557M	Net Sales ($)	3258M	1781M		56079M	133739M	2156700M
917596M	1056762M	1316658M	Total Assets ($)	963M	965M		20248M	135871M	1158611M

M = $ thousand   MM = $ million
See Pages 9 through 22 for Explanation of Ratios and Data

Current Data Sorted by Assets

Comparative Historical Data

	1		3		10		17		5		4	Type of Statement	4/1/05-3/31/06 ALL	4/1/06-3/31/07 ALL
			2		8		4		1			Unqualified		
	2		4		5							Reviewed		
	6		8		3							Compiled		
	7		14		27		25		10		6	Tax Returns		
			21 (4/1-9/30/09)				151 (10/1/09-3/31/10)					Other		
	0-500M		500M-2MM		2-10MM		10-50MM		50-100MM		100-250MM			
	16		31		53		46		16		10	NUMBER OF STATEMENTS		
	%		%		%		%		%		%	ASSETS	%	%
	37.6		11.8		12.2		13.1		6.3		8.0	Cash & Equivalents	D	D
	14.8		24.9		34.4		23.5		12.1		18.4	Trade Receivables (net)	A	A
	1.2		10.1		8.5		5.6		2.4		5.0	Inventory	T	T
	5.0		7.2		4.8		6.2		4.4		2.7	All Other Current	A	A
	58.6		53.9		60.0		48.5		25.1		34.0	Total Current		
	24.2		30.0		24.2		29.5		42.8		34.3	Fixed Assets (net)	N	N
	9.7		7.0		7.4		12.7		24.1		25.4	Intangibles (net)	O	O
	7.5		9.1		8.5		9.3		8.1		6.2	All Other Non-Current	T	T
	100.0		100.0		100.0		100.0		100.0		100.0	Total		
												LIABILITIES	A	A
	16.1		15.7		11.1		5.0		1.8		2.0	Notes Payable-Short Term	V	V
	4.0		4.3		3.3		4.7		3.3		3.2	Cur. Mat.-L.T.D.	A	A
	6.6		11.6		19.5		19.9		8.2		6.4	Trade Payables	I	I
	.0		.1		.2		.2		.0		.0	Income Taxes Payable	L	L
	17.1		18.3		16.3		18.9		24.9		17.1	All Other Current	A	A
	43.9		50.0		50.4		48.7		38.2		28.7	Total Current	B	B
	29.1		27.3		17.5		18.8		27.5		33.0	Long-Term Debt	L	L
	.0		.1		.7		1.2		.1		2.4	Deferred Taxes	E	E
	3.3		4.9		7.2		6.8		13.5		7.9	All Other Non-Current		
	23.7		17.7		24.2		24.6		20.6		27.9	Net Worth		
	100.0		100.0		100.0		100.0		100.0		100.0	Total Liabilities & Net Worth		
												INCOME DATA		
	100.0		100.0		100.0		100.0		100.0		100.0	Net Sales		
												Gross Profit		
	88.6		90.6		96.5		96.1		91.7		87.6	Operating Expenses		
	11.4		9.4		3.5		3.9		8.3		12.4	Operating Profit		
	.4		3.4		1.0		1.0		4.5		4.8	All Other Expenses (net)		
	10.9		6.0		2.5		2.8		3.8		7.6	Profit Before Taxes		
												RATIOS		
	7.6		2.2		1.7		1.4		1.0		2.0			
	1.3		1.2		1.1		1.1		.8		1.2	Current		
	.5		.7		.9		.6		.4		.7			
	5.9		1.4		1.5		1.2		.8		1.5			
	1.3		.6		.9		.7		.6		.8	Quick		
	.5		.4		.6		.5		.4		.5			
0	UND	13	27.5	25	14.4	20	18.4	15	24.2	14	25.6			
6	59.6	32	11.5	45	8.1	47	7.8	43	8.4	39	9.4	Sales/Receivables		
11	31.8	51	7.1	63	5.8	65	5.6	60	6.0	85	4.3			
												Cost of Sales/Inventory		
												Cost of Sales/Payables		
	12.4		10.2		9.4		9.7		716.8		6.4			
	84.2		46.9		33.6		34.9		-47.4		20.2	Sales/Working Capital		
	-45.0		-14.0		-30.2		-9.7		-2.8		-17.3			
			11.4		13.2		17.9		21.1					
		(26)	4.2	(46)	5.2	(38)	3.0	(15)	1.7			EBIT/Interest		
			1.9		1.6		-.8		.6					
					4.6		13.4					Net Profit + Depr., Dep.,		
				(12)	2.1	(12)	2.4					Amort./Cur. Mat. L/T/D		
					.8		1.1							
	.0		.3		.3		.2		1.2		1.4			
	.7		.9		.7		2.4		5.2		-36.1	Fixed/Worth		
	-12.3		-.7		1.8		-.9		-.8		-.5			
	.1		1.3		1.1		1.5		2.3		1.5			
	23.9		3.7		2.1		4.9		12.4		-43.2	Debt/Worth		
	-4.9		-3.8		10.8		-4.8		-2.7		-2.9			
	460.4		81.6		44.0		66.7		123.1			% Profit Before Taxes/Tangible		
(10)	86.3	(22)	20.5	(43)	21.2	(30)	26.1	(10)	40.1			Net Worth		
	49.9		9.1		5.5		3.9		11.8					
	176.7		21.1		14.3		11.2		10.2		6.9	% Profit Before Taxes/Total		
	45.0		7.8		8.6		5.5		3.3		5.6	Assets		
	.8		1.8		1.7		-2.9		-1.2		.1			
	UND		37.5		45.8		37.2		20.2		25.3			
	155.2		15.2		17.7		12.1		2.4		5.8	Sales/Net Fixed Assets		
	22.2		7.9		4.3		2.7		1.0		.6			
	26.8		4.8		3.5		2.8		1.1		1.5			
	3.9		2.9		2.4		1.7		.9		.8	Sales/Total Assets		
	2.1		1.2		1.6		.7		.7		.4			
			1.1		1.0		1.5							
		(24)	2.5	(44)	2.0	(36)	4.6					% Depr., Dep., Amort./Sales		
			5.6		5.4		12.4							
												% Officers', Directors' Owners' Comp/Sales		
	62559M		116139M		734710M		2172116M		1349714M		1722065M	Net Sales ($)		
	4325M		35907M		264617M		1102043M		1100912M		1713804M	Total Assets ($)		

M = $ thousand   MM = $ million
See Pages 9 through 22 for Explanation of Ratios and Data

Comparative Historical Data   ## Current Data Sorted by Sales

Hist 1	Hist 2	Hist 3	Type of Statement	0-1MM	1-3MM	3-5MM	5-10MM	10-25MM	25MM & OVER
36	34	40	Unqualified		2	2	9	8	19
9	16	15	Reviewed			1	3	5	6
15	14	11	Compiled	1	1	3	4	1	1
12	14	17	Tax Returns	7	4	1	2	2	1
58	71	89	Other	5	11	5	16	18	34
4/1/07-3/31/08 ALL	4/1/08-3/31/09 ALL	4/1/09-3/31/10 ALL			21 (4/1-9/30/09)		151 (10/1/09-3/31/10)		
130	149	172	NUMBER OF STATEMENTS	13	18	12	34	34	61
%	%	%	ASSETS	%	%	%	%	%	%
14.5	15.1	14.0	Cash & Equivalents	22.0	12.9	8.2	18.6	12.1	12.1
31.5	31.9	24.9	Trade Receivables (net)	11.2	17.7	31.4	25.3	26.0	28.0
7.3	6.6	6.6	Inventory	2.2	6.0	9.4	7.2	8.4	5.7
4.8	4.8	5.5	All Other Current	4.5	4.8	9.6	5.9	5.1	5.0
58.1	58.4	50.9	Total Current	40.0	41.4	58.6	56.9	51.7	50.8
24.4	26.7	29.0	Fixed Assets (net)	42.0	32.4	27.2	25.8	31.7	25.8
7.9	6.6	11.6	Intangibles (net)	12.1	9.5	8.5	11.5	7.3	15.1
9.7	8.4	8.5	All Other Non-Current	6.0	16.7	5.7	5.7	9.4	8.3
100.0	100.0	100.0	Total	100.0	100.0	100.0	100.0	100.0	100.0
			LIABILITIES						
10.7	9.3	9.4	Notes Payable-Short Term	15.9	14.2	7.7	11.8	8.2	6.2
4.2	4.6	3.9	Cur. Mat.-L.T.D.	4.1	1.7	2.8	7.1	3.4	3.3
17.5	18.4	15.2	Trade Payables	3.2	10.1	13.3	13.4	15.2	20.6
.4	.3	.1	Income Taxes Payable	.0	.0	.1	.0	.2	.2
16.6	15.1	18.3	All Other Current	13.4	12.2	20.0	17.7	18.1	21.2
49.4	47.6	46.8	Total Current	36.5	38.1	44.0	50.0	45.0	51.4
19.5	18.3	22.5	Long-Term Debt	44.5	25.5	25.3	21.1	18.3	19.6
.4	.2	.7	Deferred Taxes	.0	.3	.0	1.2	1.7	.3
6.6	4.7	7.0	All Other Non-Current	8.3	7.3	.1	8.9	5.7	7.5
24.2	29.2	23.0	Net Worth	10.7	28.8	30.6	18.8	29.3	21.2
100.0	100.0	100.0	Total Liabilities & Net Worth	100.0	100.0	100.0	100.0	100.0	100.0
			INCOME DATA						
100.0	100.0	100.0	Net Sales	100.0	100.0	100.0	100.0	100.0	100.0
			Gross Profit						
91.4	92.8	93.7	Operating Expenses	77.5	99.5	94.3	96.1	93.8	93.8
8.6	7.2	6.3	Operating Profit	22.5	.5	5.7	3.9	6.2	6.2
2.4	2.7	1.9	All Other Expenses (net)	6.3	2.1	1.0	.8	1.9	1.8
6.2	4.6	4.4	Profit Before Taxes	16.2	-1.6	4.7	3.1	4.3	4.4
			RATIOS						
1.9	2.0	1.7		4.8	1.8	2.9	2.1	1.4	1.6
1.3	1.2	1.1	Current	1.0	1.0	1.1	1.2	1.1	1.1
.8	.8	.6		.4	.7	.8	.6	.7	.6
1.5	1.6	1.4		3.4	1.4	2.7	1.9	1.2	1.2
1.0	1.0	.8	Quick	1.0	.9	.7	.9	.8	.7
.5	.6	.5		.4	.3	.4	.5	.5	.5
24 · 15.5	22 · 16.4	17 · 21.4		0 UND	6 · 59.8	15 · 24.4	21 · 17.7	17 · 21.7	20 · 18.6
44 · 8.3	41 · 8.9	38 · 9.6	Sales/Receivables	8 · 45.8	34 · 10.7	52 · 7.0	32 · 11.3	37 · 9.8	44 · 8.2
71 · 5.1	64 · 5.7	60 · 6.1		27 · 13.4	54 · 6.8	62 · 5.9	60 · 6.1	64 · 5.7	65 · 5.6
			Cost of Sales/Inventory						
			Cost of Sales/Payables						
8.2	7.2	10.7		4.4	5.3	16.8	10.9	10.1	11.8
19.8	24.6	46.5	Sales/Working Capital	15.5	NM	49.0	42.3	46.5	35.7
-26.1	-43.4	-13.4		-10.0	-10.7	-21.9	-15.4	-34.1	-10.1
9.7	18.5	13.9			4.3	9.2	9.8	16.5	18.2
(100) 3.8	(114) 4.2	(141) 3.7	EBIT/Interest	(15) .3	(10) 2.6	(29) 5.4	(31) 5.2	(50) 3.8	
1.2	.8	1.0		-9.2	2.2	1.0	1.3	1.6	
4.9	9.4	8.1						6.3	12.2
(21) 2.4	(23) 1.9	(30) 3.3	Net Profit + Depr., Dep., Amort./Cur. Mat. L/T/D				(10) 1.8	(11) 6.9	
1.3	.7	1.1						1.2	2.2
.2	.3	.3		.0	.6	.3	.3	.4	.2
1.0	.8	1.4	Fixed/Worth	9.1	1.8	.9	.9	.9	1.9
17.1	7.4	-2.5		-6.3	-12.5	6.4	-.8	NM	-1.2
1.2	.8	1.3		2.1	.8	.8	1.2	1.1	1.5
3.1	3.0	4.1	Debt/Worth	41.7	3.0	3.6	3.5	3.3	4.7
69.6	53.2	-5.4		-2.1	-15.3	12.0	-3.3	NM	-4.6
86.8	69.3	66.0			21.1	114.8	54.6	72.8	70.4
(100) 33.1	(116) 35.2	(119) 26.0	% Profit Before Taxes/Tangible Net Worth	(12) -9.0	(10) 20.5	(22) 26.3	(26) 30.0	(42) 32.9	
10.1	3.8	8.3		-17.8	2.1	11.8	12.2	11.0	
23.0	21.3	14.4		45.0	12.0	23.1	17.9	12.6	14.5
7.0	6.7	6.4	% Profit Before Taxes/Total Assets	5.8	-1.5	7.1	9.1	4.4	5.8
.8	-.7	.9		1.0	-8.2	1.6	3.0	.5	2.4
49.1	47.4	48.5		UND	29.7	34.0	54.8	50.2	44.4
17.6	19.2	14.8	Sales/Net Fixed Assets	13.2	8.4	15.4	16.9	14.0	16.0
6.2	5.6	3.7		.3	1.3	6.9	4.3	1.6	3.9
3.8	3.7	3.3		2.5	3.2	4.0	4.8	3.5	3.2
2.6	2.7	2.0	Sales/Total Assets	1.7	1.2	2.7	2.4	1.9	1.9
1.3	1.3	1.0		.2	.6	2.0	1.5	.7	1.0
.8	.7	1.1			.7		1.3	.8	.8
(99) 1.9	(113) 1.8	(123) 2.3	% Depr., Dep., Amort./Sales	(15) 3.9		(26) 2.5	(27) 2.0	(40) 2.0	
5.3	6.8	8.1			7.6		7.8	14.6	5.7
2.2	1.4	1.1							
(33) 5.0	(36) 3.4	(32) 4.6	% Officers', Directors' Owners' Comp/Sales						
11.7	9.7	13.1							
5010857M	5524499M	6157303M	Net Sales ($)	5878M	34783M	47315M	254821M	542977M	5271529M
3283391M	3102250M	4221608M	Total Assets ($)	5867M	36496M	42123M	141562M	546556M	3449004M

M = $ thousand   MM = $ million
See Pages 9 through 22 for Explanation of Ratios and Data

Current Data Sorted by Assets   **Comparative Historical Data**

	0-500M	500M-2MM	2-10MM	10-50MM	50-100MM	100-250MM	Type of Statement	4/1/05-3/31/06 ALL	4/1/06-3/31/07 ALL
	2	1	20	38	13	19	Unqualified	49	63
	1	4	9	7			Reviewed	18	23
	6	6	6	1		1	Compiled	15	13
	11	12	9		1	1	Tax Returns	17	30
	20	28	51	32	9	9	Other	94	132
		42 (4/1-9/30/09)		275 (10/1/09-3/31/10)					
NUMBER OF STATEMENTS	40	51	95	78	23	30		193	261
	%	%	%	%	%	%	**ASSETS**	%	%
	33.4	20.6	18.6	16.8	15.7	13.0	Cash & Equivalents	16.6	16.7
	20.3	38.1	33.2	24.0	14.1	11.9	Trade Receivables (net)	32.1	31.6
	3.0	2.4	1.9	1.5	.3	1.1	Inventory	4.4	3.2
	6.0	3.1	4.7	6.2	4.8	5.6	All Other Current	5.1	5.3
	62.7	64.3	58.4	48.6	34.9	31.5	Total Current	58.3	56.7
	20.4	18.6	23.7	21.5	23.0	21.8	Fixed Assets (net)	19.7	21.1
	4.5	4.5	9.7	17.7	27.1	40.4	Intangibles (net)	12.3	12.5
	12.2	12.7	8.2	12.2	15.0	6.3	All Other Non-Current	9.6	9.7
	100.0	100.0	100.0	100.0	100.0	100.0	Total	100.0	100.0
							LIABILITIES		
	51.5	14.3	8.6	6.5	1.3	.2	Notes Payable-Short Term	8.7	10.0
	4.2	2.1	4.6	4.1	3.9	3.4	Cur. Mat.-L.T.D.	5.0	3.5
	9.0	12.8	14.7	9.0	7.6	4.3	Trade Payables	12.8	13.9
	.3	.3	.3	.7	.6	.1	Income Taxes Payable	.6	.8
	33.5	18.6	18.2	17.4	13.6	15.9	All Other Current	17.0	17.3
	98.6	47.9	46.4	37.7	27.0	23.9	Total Current	44.0	45.5
	25.5	17.3	12.1	14.6	19.5	38.2	Long-Term Debt	13.5	19.0
	.0	.3	.7	.7	1.3	1.8	Deferred Taxes	.4	.6
	21.6	17.0	6.1	9.4	8.1	5.1	All Other Non-Current	12.0	9.9
	-45.7	17.4	34.7	37.6	44.2	31.0	Net Worth	30.1	25.0
	100.0	100.0	100.0	100.0	100.0	100.0	Total Liabilities & Net Worth	100.0	100.0
							INCOME DATA		
	100.0	100.0	100.0	100.0	100.0	100.0	Net Sales	100.0	100.0
							Gross Profit		
	94.1	96.7	91.5	93.6	89.4	90.0	Operating Expenses	93.3	92.8
	5.9	3.3	8.5	6.4	10.6	10.0	Operating Profit	6.7	7.2
	1.6	.9	2.6	2.4	3.5	5.0	All Other Expenses (net)	1.4	2.1
	4.3	2.4	5.9	3.9	7.1	4.9	Profit Before Taxes	5.3	5.1
							RATIOS		
	1.8	3.8	2.1	2.2	2.1	2.0	Current	2.5	2.4
	1.0	1.7	1.2	1.3	1.2	1.3		1.4	1.3
	.4	1.0	.9	.9	.5	.8		.9	.9
	1.8	3.8	1.9	1.8	1.6	1.5	Quick	2.1	2.1
(39)	.9	1.5	1.0	1.0	1.1	1.1		1.1	1.1
	.3	.8	.7	.7	.5	.5		.7	.7
0	UND	20 18.1	30 12.2	29 12.7	22 16.6	19 19.3	Sales/Receivables	29 12.5	26 13.8
3	135.4	45 8.1	48 7.7	47 7.8	39 9.3	34 10.8		47 7.8	48 7.6
30	12.0	57 6.4	68 5.4	65 5.6	57 6.4	53 6.9		71 5.1	68 5.3
							Cost of Sales/Inventory		
							Cost of Sales/Payables		
	31.6	6.2	9.3	5.1	4.8	8.1	Sales/Working Capital	6.3	7.2
	UND	12.5	29.3	20.4	30.9	14.0		17.3	17.5
	-6.1	-196.0	-46.5	-51.4	-7.6	-32.8		-92.4	-39.2
	6.1	10.6	20.6	21.5	235.1	10.0	EBIT/Interest	18.3	14.5
(28)	1.3	(40) 2.2	(72) 5.2	(64) 4.2	(20) 11.5	(27) 3.3		(152) 5.6	(208) 3.6
	-4.5	-3.0	1.1	.7	1.5	.4		1.3	.4
			21.4	6.8			Net Profit + Depr., Dep., Amort./Cur. Mat. L/T/D	12.8	10.3
			(18) 3.1	(20) 1.5				(44) 4.1	(45) 3.3
			1.6	.4				1.7	1.2
	.3	.1	.2	.3	.1	1.4	Fixed/Worth	.2	.2
	3.8	.4	.8	.9	.6	-4.6		.7	.9
	-.3	57.6	3.4	-9.9	-3.3	-.3		4.6	-1.7
	2.0	1.3	.8	.8	.5	1.3	Debt/Worth	.8	.9
	UND	3.3	2.1	2.4	1.6	-18.2		2.4	2.8
	-1.7	-12.2	13.2	-30.3	-10.0	-2.2		30.5	-7.7
	360.3	82.9	64.8	51.8	51.0	120.3	% Profit Before Taxes/Tangible Net Worth	74.4	73.2
(21)	38.6	(37) 32.2	(73) 24.6	(58) 27.1	(15) 20.6	(11) 22.6		(149) 28.9	(182) 32.7
	-97.0	-18.2	8.7	8.8	15.1	10.2		8.7	6.0
	36.8	22.0	18.9	16.5	14.2	13.9	% Profit Before Taxes/Total Assets	23.5	22.3
	2.8	5.3	8.1	6.9	8.2	5.9		9.7	8.3
	-17.8	-7.0	.7	-1.6	1.4	-1.9		1.6	-.9
	155.7	115.2	50.2	24.0	35.6	12.6	Sales/Net Fixed Assets	49.9	63.5
	47.2	32.3	19.5	9.5	8.2	9.5		19.2	18.4
	19.2	8.2	7.5	5.3	5.5	1.5		7.8	6.4
	10.2	4.8	3.7	2.3	1.5	1.3	Sales/Total Assets	3.6	3.5
	5.8	3.1	2.3	1.5	1.2	.8		2.3	2.0
	3.4	1.5	1.4	.8	.9	.6		1.4	1.1
	.4	.7	.6	1.3	1.7		% Depr., Dep., Amort./Sales	.8	.9
(22)	1.2	(30) 2.4	(68) 2.1	(63) 4.0	(15) 4.3			(141) 2.1	(169) 2.6
	2.1	6.4	5.7	8.2	8.8			4.1	5.9
	4.4	2.2	2.3				% Officers', Directors' Owners' Comp/Sales	3.0	3.4
(18)	7.9	(18) 5.0	(22) 4.4					(41) 6.5	(59) 5.8
	14.8	13.3	15.7					13.0	11.3
	52935M	253822M	1332672M	2967492M	2007811M	4753630M	Net Sales ($)	5234794M	9257677M
	8609M	60927M	515361M	1750002M	1737733M	4842920M	Total Assets ($)	3564105M	6289266M

M = $ thousand   MM = $ million
See Pages 9 through 22 for Explanation of Ratios and Data

Comparative Historical Data | Current Data Sorted by Sales

	4/1/07-3/31/08 ALL	4/1/08-3/31/09 ALL	4/1/09-3/31/10 ALL	Type of Statement	0-1MM	1-3MM	3-5MM	5-10MM	10-25MM	25MM & OVER
	61	80	93	Unqualified	1	2	1	14	17	58
	17	27	21	Reviewed		3		6	7	5
	15	24	20	Compiled	4	6	3	1	2	4
	29	22	34	Tax Returns	6	9	8	2	6	3
	127	127	149	Other	16	20	10	27	38	38
					42 (4/1-9/30/09)			275 (10/1/09-3/31/10)		
NUMBER OF STATEMENTS	249	280	317		27	40	22	50	70	108
	%	%	%	ASSETS	%	%	%	%	%	%
	20.3	17.6	19.6	Cash & Equivalents	26.2	27.9	17.1	17.9	18.0	17.3
	32.7	30.2	26.7	Trade Receivables (net)	18.9	20.0	40.1	32.6	30.9	22.9
	2.7	2.3	1.8	Inventory	4.0	1.8	1.7	1.5	1.5	1.7
	4.5	5.5	5.1	All Other Current	3.9	4.1	3.0	4.7	6.5	5.5
	60.2	55.6	53.2	Total Current	53.0	53.8	61.9	56.8	56.9	47.3
	19.7	20.7	21.7	Fixed Assets (net)	29.6	21.6	11.9	25.4	19.4	21.5
	11.1	15.6	14.3	Intangibles (net)	6.2	11.2	13.5	6.2	14.4	21.4
	9.0	8.1	10.7	All Other Non-Current	11.3	13.3	12.7	11.6	9.3	9.8
	100.0	100.0	100.0	Total	100.0	100.0	100.0	100.0	100.0	100.0
				LIABILITIES						
	12.2	10.3	13.1	Notes Payable-Short Term	48.8	28.9	12.1	7.5	7.1	5.0
	3.4	6.3	3.9	Cur. Mat.-L.T.D.	2.2	4.7	2.4	3.6	5.3	3.5
	11.8	12.6	10.8	Trade Payables	9.7	5.8	20.3	11.6	11.4	10.1
	.6	.3	.4	Income Taxes Payable	.0	.6	.0	.4	.5	.4
	20.8	21.1	19.4	All Other Current	29.5	20.2	16.9	18.3	20.7	16.9
	48.8	50.6	47.6	Total Current	90.2	60.2	51.8	41.4	45.0	35.9
	16.3	19.3	18.3	Long-Term Debt	41.0	15.8	12.1	16.1	12.1	19.7
	.4	.6	.7	Deferred Taxes	.0	.4	.3	.9	.4	1.1
	10.7	8.1	10.7	All Other Non-Current	14.3	7.7	37.6	11.9	6.7	7.4
	23.8	21.4	22.8	Net Worth	-45.5	15.9	-1.8	29.7	35.8	36.0
	100.0	100.0	100.0	Total Liabilities & Net Worth	100.0	100.0	100.0	100.0	100.0	100.0
				INCOME DATA						
	100.0	100.0	100.0	Net Sales	100.0	100.0	100.0	100.0	100.0	100.0
				Gross Profit						
	91.8	94.0	92.9	Operating Expenses	87.6	97.4	97.9	91.2	93.3	92.1
	8.2	6.0	7.1	Operating Profit	12.4	2.6	2.1	8.8	6.7	7.9
	1.5	2.2	2.4	All Other Expenses (net)	8.0	1.3	1.3	1.2	1.3	3.0
	6.7	3.9	4.6	Profit Before Taxes	4.5	1.3	.9	7.6	5.4	4.9
				RATIOS						
	2.3	2.3	2.1		1.6	2.7	3.8	2.5	2.3	1.9
	1.4	1.3	1.2	Current	1.0	1.2	1.2	1.4	1.4	1.3
	.9	.8	.8		.4	.5	.8	1.0	.9	.9
	2.1	2.1	1.9		1.5	2.5	3.8	2.2	1.9	1.6
	1.3	1.1 (316)	1.0	Quick	(26) .8	1.1	1.1	1.0	1.1	1.1
	.7	.6	.7		.3	.4	.6	.8	.7	.7
	28 12.8	23 15.8	20 18.1		2 199.2	0 UND	25 14.6	28 12.9	30 12.2	22 16.6
	49 7.5	44 8.2	42 8.6	Sales/Receivables	22 16.2	21 17.3	39 9.4	45 8.1	57 6.4	40 9.2
	70 5.2	62 5.9	60 6.0		53 6.8	56 6.6	55 6.7	62 5.9	76 4.8	53 6.9
				Cost of Sales/Inventory						
				Cost of Sales/Payables						
	6.5	6.9	7.4		20.2	7.6	7.5	6.8	6.5	8.0
	21.1	20.5	27.1	Sales/Working Capital	-196.0	45.6	49.7	17.5	15.0	21.4
	-66.0	-34.9	-37.3		-4.3	-12.3	-23.6	-373.2	-46.9	-80.5
	16.4	14.8	17.6		7.0	5.5	8.6	12.0	29.9	25.8
	(190) 5.1	(223) 3.7	(251) 3.7	EBIT/Interest	(17) 1.6	(30) 1.2	(17) 3.5	(41) 3.7	(56) 5.1	(90) 5.5
	1.0	.4	.4		-6.3	-3.1	-1.6	.6	1.0	1.1
	13.4	5.0	12.7	Net Profit + Depr., Dep.,				20.4	7.0	20.1
	(36) 1.8	(46) 2.8	(50) 2.8	Amort./Cur. Mat. L/T/D			(10) 2.8	(16) 1.4	(21) 8.7
	.8	1.4	1.1					.9	.1	2.1
	.2	.2	.2		.3	.1	.1	.2	.2	.2
	.7	1.2	1.0	Fixed/Worth	3.0	1.0	.5	.5	.9	1.1
	-8.3	-1.0	-3.3		-.3	-2.0	-.1	2.2	-3.3	-2.6
	.9	1.0	.9		2.5	.9	2.1	.8	.9	.8
	2.6	4.4	3.1	Debt/Worth	52.0	9.8	15.2	2.0	2.9	2.5
	-20.3	-5.1	-10.2		-1.7	-5.4	-3.1	7.1	-13.5	-10.1
	90.6	74.4	67.1	% Profit Before Taxes/Tangible	183.3	40.6	73.4	67.3	70.1	61.2
	(181) 42.0	(186) 30.9	(215) 26.0	Net Worth	(16) 8.0	(22) 22.8	(13) 35.2	(42) 32.3	(51) 31.9	(71) 26.0
	13.4	9.7	8.4		-98.5	-38.3	-28.6	6.0	10.0	11.2
	27.9	19.3	18.1	% Profit Before Taxes/Total	16.7	24.8	19.9	19.4	18.8	15.5
	11.0	6.9	7.0	Assets	.3	3.4	4.7	8.6	7.7	7.5
	.8	-.8	-1.8		-11.3	-11.0	-9.7	.4	1.0	.6
	66.4	58.0	48.6		95.5	116.3	303.7	45.4	36.7	34.3
	19.2	17.0	14.4	Sales/Net Fixed Assets	23.4	32.3	44.9	13.5	12.8	11.7
	8.2	6.4	6.6		3.6	7.2	14.1	4.5	6.7	5.6
	3.9	3.7	3.8		7.5	5.2	5.0	3.4	3.3	2.8
	2.3	2.3	1.9	Sales/Total Assets	2.0	3.2	3.4	1.8	1.9	1.6
	1.5	1.2	1.1		.4	1.5	2.2	1.3	1.2	1.0
	.7	.7	.9		.7	.9	.3	.9	1.5	.8
	(175) 2.2	(177) 2.2	(204) 2.8	% Depr., Dep., Amort./Sales	(14) 2.6	(25) 1.7	(10) 1.8	(37) 3.1	(51) 3.1	(67) 3.1
	4.8	5.3	6.3		15.1	5.8	3.8	9.4	5.9	6.3
	2.7	2.3	2.4	% Officers', Directors'		4.1	1.8		1.8	
	(66) 6.8	(65) 5.9	(67) 4.8	Owners' Comp/Sales		(18) 9.7	(11) 4.9		(19) 2.7	
	10.5	11.7	12.6			14.9	9.3			
	7081062M	12580482M	11368362M	Net Sales ($)	13596M	72498M	87389M	368623M	1158234M	9668022M
	5058850M	8226720M	8915552M	Total Assets ($)	27300M	37845M	44371M	268161M	856059M	7681816M

M = $ thousand   MM = $ million
See Pages 9 through 22 for Explanation of Ratios and Data

Current Data Sorted by Assets

Comparative Historical Data

			4	2	1	Type of Statement		
	2	1				Unqualified		
3	2					Reviewed		
2	2		4	2	3	Compiled		
1	1	4	3	2		Tax Returns		
	3 (4/1-9/30/09)		27 (10/1/09-3/31/10)			Other	4/1/05- 3/31/06 ALL	4/1/06- 3/31/07 ALL
0-500M	500M-2MM	2-10MM	10-50MM	50-100MM	100-250MM			
5	5	5	7	4	4	NUMBER OF STATEMENTS		
%	%	%	%	%	%	ASSETS	%	%
						Cash & Equivalents	D	D
						Trade Receivables (net)	A	A
						Inventory	T	T
						All Other Current	A	A
						Total Current		
						Fixed Assets (net)	N	N
						Intangibles (net)	O	O
						All Other Non-Current	T	T
						Total		
						LIABILITIES	A	A
						Notes Payable-Short Term	V	V
						Cur. Mat.-L.T.D.	A	A
						Trade Payables	I	I
						Income Taxes Payable	L	L
						All Other Current	A	A
						Total Current	B	B
						Long-Term Debt	L	L
						Deferred Taxes	E	E
						All Other Non-Current		
						Net Worth		
						Total Liabilites & Net Worth		
						INCOME DATA		
						Net Sales		
						Gross Profit		
						Operating Expenses		
						Operating Profit		
						All Other Expenses (net)		
						Profit Before Taxes		
						RATIOS		
						Current		
						Quick		
						Sales/Receivables		
						Cost of Sales/Inventory		
						Cost of Sales/Payables		
						Sales/Working Capital		
						EBIT/Interest		
						Net Profit + Depr., Dep., Amort./Cur. Mat. L/T/D		
						Fixed/Worth		
						Debt/Worth		
						% Profit Before Taxes/Tangible Net Worth		
						% Profit Before Taxes/Total Assets		
						Sales/Net Fixed Assets		
						Sales/Total Assets		
						% Depr., Dep., Amort./Sales		
						% Officers', Directors' Owners' Comp/Sales		
7606M	30620M	235177M	354234M	516076M	488609M	Net Sales ($)		
1235M	6201M	21366M	172555M	294905M	634658M	Total Assets ($)		

© RMA 2010

M = $ thousand   MM = $ million
See Pages 9 through 22 for Explanation of Ratios and Data

Comparative Historical Data | Current Data Sorted by Sales

	4/1/07-3/31/08 ALL	4/1/08-3/31/09 ALL	4/1/09-3/31/10 ALL		0-1MM	1-3MM	3-5MM (3 (4/1-9/30/09))	5-10MM	10-25MM (27 (10/1/09-3/31/10))	25MM & OVER
Type of Statement										
Unqualified	2	4	7						2	5
Reviewed	1	2				1		1		1
Compiled	1	2	3			3				
Tax Returns	1	4	5					1	1	
Other	12	18	15		1		3		4	7
NUMBER OF STATEMENTS	17	30	30		1	4	3	2	7	13
	%	%	%		%	%	%	%	%	%
ASSETS										
Cash & Equivalents	13.9	17.6	28.5							27.4
Trade Receivables (net)	25.2	33.8	19.2							18.0
Inventory	3.8	1.5	3.3							4.4
All Other Current	3.7	6.9	7.6							4.7
Total Current	46.5	59.7	58.5							54.5
Fixed Assets (net)	14.0	19.3	11.7							12.5
Intangibles (net)	28.1	12.9	22.2							23.5
All Other Non-Current	11.4	8.1	7.6							9.6
Total	100.0	100.0	100.0							100.0
LIABILITIES										
Notes Payable-Short Term	7.6	13.5	26.0							2.0
Cur. Mat.-L.T.D.	2.7	4.4	2.6							1.3
Trade Payables	8.1	18.7	11.8							13.7
Income Taxes Payable	.0	2.8	.2							.4
All Other Current	22.2	18.7	22.5							21.7
Total Current	40.6	58.0	63.1							39.1
Long-Term Debt	6.8	23.8	24.0							16.6
Deferred Taxes	.1	.1	.2							.4
All Other Non-Current	7.9	11.6	8.7							5.8
Net Worth	44.5	6.5	4.1							38.0
Total Liabilities & Net Worth	100.0	100.0	100.0							100.0
INCOME DATA										
Net Sales	100.0	100.0	100.0							100.0
Gross Profit										
Operating Expenses	92.3	92.7	95.1							93.8
Operating Profit	7.7	7.3	4.9							6.2
All Other Expenses (net)	1.9	2.9	1.0							1.7
Profit Before Taxes	5.8	4.5	3.9							4.5
RATIOS										
Current	2.5	2.1	2.4							2.0
	1.6	1.3	1.4							1.4
	.7	.6	.9							.8
Quick	2.4	1.8	2.4							1.8
	1.1	1.1	1.1							1.2
	.5	.4	.7							.6
Sales/Receivables	15 24.0	9 38.8	3 139.8							3 123.6
	43 8.4	35 10.5	23 16.2							19 19.3
	54 6.7	59 6.2	62 5.9							67 5.5
Cost of Sales/Inventory										
Cost of Sales/Payables										
Sales/Working Capital	10.8	9.1	8.1							6.1
	28.1	23.4	15.9							28.4
	-9.3	-8.2	-25.6							-21.0
EBIT/Interest	147.6	12.8	12.4							
	(11) 5.8	(22) .9	(22) 3.5							
	.7	-2.5	-4.3							
Net Profit + Depr., Dep., Amort./Cur. Mat. L/T/D										
Fixed/Worth	.2	.2	.1							.1
	.7	1.8	1.5							1.1
	-.2	-.4	-.4							-.8
Debt/Worth	.6	1.4	1.8							.7
	1.5	4.9	13.3							2.0
	-3.3	-2.9	-1.9							-11.6
% Profit Before Taxes/Tangible Net Worth	62.5	102.9	90.4							
	(11) 47.0	(18) 42.4	(16) 45.1							
	13.8	-26.4	17.1							
% Profit Before Taxes/Total Assets	29.3	22.5	32.3							13.3
	6.8	2.8	9.0							9.2
	1.9	-11.3	-2.9							-1.6
Sales/Net Fixed Assets	101.9	89.8	116.7							81.4
	33.8	30.3	32.9							22.5
	11.9	13.3	19.3							17.8
Sales/Total Assets	6.1	5.1	6.0							2.3
	1.5	2.9	2.3							2.0
	.9	1.3	1.3							.8
% Depr., Dep., Amort./Sales		.6	.5							
	(16)	1.7	(17) 1.4							
		4.4	2.7							
% Officers', Directors' Owners' Comp/Sales										
Net Sales ($)	819731M	977983M	1632322M		887M	5142M	10684M	14252M	115207M	1486150M
Total Assets ($)	525773M	500831M	1130920M		143M	2146M	3081M	4138M	76134M	1045278M

M = $ thousand   MM = $ million
See Pages 9 through 22 for Explanation of Ratios and Data

Current Data Sorted by Assets | Comparative Historical Data

0-500M	500M-2MM	2-10MM	10-50MM	50-100MM	100-250MM	Type of Statement	4/1/05-3/31/06 ALL	4/1/06-3/31/07 ALL
		4	4	2	2	Unqualified	6	3
	5	3	1			Reviewed	1	2
	1					Compiled	1	1
7	6	3				Tax Returns	2	1
6	3	7		1	4	Other	7	11
	7 (4/1-9/30/09)		52 (10/1/09-3/31/10)					
13	15	17	5	3	6	**NUMBER OF STATEMENTS**	17	18
%	%	%	%	%	%	**ASSETS**	%	%
30.6	10.6	17.4				Cash & Equivalents	24.1	13.6
37.0	48.8	35.5				Trade Receivables (net)	32.5	35.0
5.1	9.4	8.9				Inventory	3.6	2.6
.5	2.5	3.2				All Other Current	6.5	7.6
73.2	71.3	65.0				Total Current	66.8	58.8
17.0	17.2	17.1				Fixed Assets (net)	15.8	15.6
.8	.0	7.7				Intangibles (net)	6.3	18.6
9.0	11.4	10.2				All Other Non-Current	11.2	7.0
100.0	100.0	100.0				Total	100.0	100.0
						LIABILITIES		
33.9	8.2	13.0				Notes Payable-Short Term	3.6	15.4
.1	.8	2.0				Cur. Mat.-L.T.D.	4.6	3.1
20.7	19.5	11.5				Trade Payables	33.6	8.0
.0	.7	.0				Income Taxes Payable	1.0	.8
23.9	13.5	26.8				All Other Current	23.8	19.9
78.7	42.6	53.4				Total Current	66.7	47.2
10.9	4.0	21.3				Long-Term Debt	14.6	21.0
.0	.0	.2				Deferred Taxes	.1	.5
10.8	5.6	8.9				All Other Non-Current	4.5	7.7
-.3	47.8	16.2				Net Worth	14.2	23.6
100.0	100.0	100.0				Total Liabilities & Net Worth	100.0	100.0
						INCOME DATA		
100.0	100.0	100.0				Net Sales	100.0	100.0
						Gross Profit		
96.6	95.2	91.1				Operating Expenses	96.1	93.4
3.4	4.8	8.9				Operating Profit	3.9	6.6
.5	-.5	2.4				All Other Expenses (net)	.8	2.5
2.9	5.3	6.4				Profit Before Taxes	3.1	4.2
						RATIOS		
2.1	2.6	3.6				Current	2.4	2.5
1.1	1.6	1.5					1.3	1.5
.4	1.3	.7					1.1	.8
2.0	2.1	3.3				Quick	2.2	1.7
1.0	1.3	1.2					1.2	1.0
.4	1.0	.4					1.0	.6
0 UND	21 17.4	32 11.6				Sales/Receivables	36 10.2	38 9.5
25 14.4	34 10.8	49 7.4					51 7.2	60 6.1
43 8.5	94 3.9	93 3.9					82 4.5	97 3.7
						Cost of Sales/Inventory		
						Cost of Sales/Payables		
20.0	8.1	3.5				Sales/Working Capital	3.8	5.5
72.1	30.5	11.4					11.9	13.9
-10.2	51.2	-163.2					72.1	-11.7
36.8	21.7	12.7				EBIT/Interest	179.0	27.2
(10) 2.5	(11) 5.8	(13) 5.0					(14) 7.8	(15) 9.2
-3.4	-2.0	1.4					3.4	3.4
						Net Profit + Depr., Dep., Amort./Cur. Mat. L/T/D		
.0	.1	.1				Fixed/Worth	.2	.4
.3	.4	.4					.7	4.0
-2.8	.7	.7					NM	-.2
1.3	.4	1.2				Debt/Worth	1.0	1.1
14.9	1.3	2.5					2.1	NM
-4.7	2.4	6.8					NM	-3.1
	41.4	54.4				% Profit Before Taxes/Tangible Net Worth	106.9	
	20.3	(14) 14.0					(13) 29.1	
	-2.5	-.3					5.2	
24.4	16.9	11.3				% Profit Before Taxes/Total Assets	21.5	26.7
9.0	8.6	6.5					11.6	14.6
-9.6	-2.5	1.5					1.8	5.1
UND	165.7	124.1				Sales/Net Fixed Assets	58.4	69.7
215.5	46.3	15.4					14.5	15.9
43.5	14.8	7.4					9.7	10.7
7.1	6.0	4.0				Sales/Total Assets	3.2	3.3
6.0	4.2	1.6					2.0	2.1
3.3	2.2	.8					1.4	1.0
	.1	1.0				% Depr., Dep., Amort./Sales	1.0	
	(13) 1.4	(10) 1.7					(11) 2.3	
	2.3	5.2					3.8	
						% Officers', Directors' Owners' Comp/Sales		
27181M	75170M	213880M	239798M	136323M	1045136M	Net Sales ($)	819027M	4246874M
4320M	16898M	90496M	92390M	203116M	1134160M	Total Assets ($)	505624M	791662M

© RMA 2010

M = $ thousand   MM = $ million
See Pages 9 through 22 for Explanation of Ratios and Data

Comparative Historical Data

Current Data Sorted by Sales

			Type of Statement	0-1MM	1-3MM	3-5MM	5-10MM	10-25MM	25MM & OVER
5	41	12	Unqualified				1	5	6
3	11	9	Reviewed		2	4	1		2
	16	1	Compiled					1	
3	18	16	Tax Returns	4	5	4	2	1	
8	67	21	Other		7	2	4	2	6
4/1/07-3/31/08 ALL	4/1/08-3/31/09 ALL	4/1/09-3/31/10 ALL			7 (4/1-9/30/09)		52 (10/1/09-3/31/10)		
19	153	59	NUMBER OF STATEMENTS	4	14	10	8	9	14

%	%	%	ASSETS	%	%	%	%	%	%
13.3	18.3	18.8	Cash & Equivalents		17.4	27.3			17.6
31.6	24.3	34.4	Trade Receivables (net)		44.2	27.0			26.9
4.1	7.9	7.1	Inventory		5.6	14.9			4.4
4.5	4.3	3.0	All Other Current		1.1	4.8			4.9
53.6	54.8	63.3	Total Current		68.3	74.0			53.8
15.1	25.6	17.3	Fixed Assets (net)		12.2	20.3			13.2
19.2	7.8	9.5	Intangibles (net)		2.5	.0			29.1
12.1	11.8	9.9	All Other Non-Current		17.1	5.7			3.9
100.0	100.0	100.0	Total		100.0	100.0			100.0
			LIABILITIES						
38.7	9.0	13.9	Notes Payable-Short Term		36.7	9.0			2.5
8.5	2.8	3.0	Cur. Mat.-L.T.D.		.0	.6			10.6
6.6	10.7	14.6	Trade Payables		7.3	12.7			10.5
.4	.4	.2	Income Taxes Payable		.0	.0			.1
18.4	16.1	20.1	All Other Current		22.4	9.2			22.9
72.6	38.9	51.9	Total Current		66.4	31.6			46.6
24.6	18.9	13.8	Long-Term Debt		7.8	8.3			18.7
.7	.5	.5	Deferred Taxes		.0	.4			1.7
7.6	7.9	8.6	All Other Non-Current		13.6	4.3			9.0
-5.5	33.8	25.2	Net Worth		12.2	55.4			24.0
100.0	100.0	100.0	Total Liabilties & Net Worth		100.0	100.0			100.0
			INCOME DATA						
100.0	100.0	100.0	Net Sales		100.0	100.0			100.0
			Gross Profit						
89.6	92.9	93.1	Operating Expenses		89.7	99.7			91.4
10.4	7.1	6.9	Operating Profit		10.3	.3			8.6
5.6	2.2	1.4	All Other Expenses (net)		.2	-.4			3.5
4.7	4.9	5.5	Profit Before Taxes		10.1	.6			5.1
			RATIOS						
2.4	3.2	2.4			2.8	6.0			1.7
.9	1.5	1.4	Current		1.1	2.0			1.3
.6	1.0	1.0			.5	1.4			1.0
2.3	2.5	2.0			1.7	4.7			1.4
.8	1.2	1.2	Quick		1.0	1.7			1.2
.3	.6	.5			.5	.8			.7
15 24.4	11 32.2	18 20.5		18 19.9	0 UND			28 12.9	
45 8.0	39 9.4	39 9.4	Sales/Receivables	43 8.5	28 13.1			42 8.7	
83 4.4	61 6.0	63 5.8		97 3.8	57 6.4			63 5.8	
			Cost of Sales/Inventory						
			Cost of Sales/Payables						
6.5	5.4	5.5			8.2	2.4			13.9
-60.7	13.9	19.7	Sales/Working Capital		73.0	13.3			18.7
-9.1	335.4	117.3			-10.5	44.7			NM
10.9	15.0	12.4			6.3				5.0
(18) 2.0	(120) 3.1	(45) 3.6	EBIT/Interest		(10) 1.2				(11) 3.4
.1	.5	.4			-2.1				1.7
	31.2		Net Profit + Depr., Dep.,						
	(18) 5.5		Amort./Cur. Mat. L/T/D						
	1.5								
.1	.2	.1			.0	.1			.2
1.6	.7	.5	Fixed/Worth		.4	.4			6.6
-.3	5.0	1.7			10.5	.6			-.2
1.2	.8	.9			.6	.4			2.1
10.2	2.0	2.3	Debt/Worth		9.2	.9			13.0
-2.0	16.8	19.5			NM	2.2			-2.4
51.9	51.9	54.4	% Profit Before Taxes/Tangible		159.0	36.0			
(10) 29.8	(120) 17.6	(46) 22.7	Net Worth		(11) 66.8	11.0			
8.4	3.7	.3			-34.1	-8.4			
15.6	16.8	12.3	% Profit Before Taxes/Total		30.0	21.0			11.8
6.5	5.3	6.7	Assets		9.4	3.5			7.8
-1.2	-.5	-.8			-7.3	-3.1			3.0
64.2	52.5	168.9			380.3	45.1			83.4
22.1	18.9	30.4	Sales/Net Fixed Assets		144.3	16.0			19.5
13.3	4.7	10.6			23.6	12.2			10.2
5.1	4.0	5.0			6.1	7.8			4.0
2.6	1.8	2.5	Sales/Total Assets		3.2	3.8			1.7
.9	.9	1.3			2.0	1.7			.9
.3	.8	.4							
(10) 1.0	(111) 1.8	(37) 1.6	% Depr., Dep., Amort./Sales						
3.7	4.5	3.1							
	2.2	2.8	% Officers', Directors'						
(38) 6.1	(19) 6.3		Owners' Comp/Sales						
9.1	22.6								
902002M	4616574M	1737488M	Net Sales ($)	1659M	28683M	42173M	51750M	138190M	1475033M
864962M	3786595M	1541380M	Total Assets ($)	3976M	12311M	19535M	22081M	181116M	1302361M

M = $ thousand   MM = $ million

See Pages 9 through 22 for Explanation of Ratios and Data

FINANCE AND INSURANCE

Current Data Sorted by Assets   Comparative Historical Data

0-500M	500M-2MM	2-10MM	10-50MM	50-100MM	100-250MM	Type of Statement		
		2	4		1	Unqualified	8	13
			1			Reviewed	1	4
			1			Compiled	2	4
2		1	2		2	Tax Returns	1	4
1	3	4	2			Other	4	15
	3 (4/1-9/30/09)		23 (10/1/09-3/31/10)				4/1/05-3/31/06 ALL	4/1/06-3/31/07 ALL
3	3	7	10		3	NUMBER OF STATEMENTS	16	40

10-50MM %		ASSETS	4/1/05-3/31/06 %	4/1/06-3/31/07 %
4.6		Cash & Equivalents	7.3	9.4
70.2	D	Trade Receivables (net)	59.2	53.6
.1	A	Inventory	.6	.4
.4	T	All Other Current	1.8	10.8
75.3	A	Total Current	68.8	74.2
.6		Fixed Assets (net)	8.1	7.2
5.3	N	Intangibles (net)	2.2	2.9
18.8	O	All Other Non-Current	20.9	15.6
100.0	T	Total	100.0	100.0
		LIABILITIES		
39.0	A	Notes Payable-Short Term	19.1	24.4
4.5	V	Cur. Mat.-L.T.D.	.6	1.2
6.4	A	Trade Payables	4.1	2.7
.3	I	Income Taxes Payable	.0	.1
3.5	L	All Other Current	13.0	11.0
53.7	A	Total Current	36.9	39.3
13.0	B	Long-Term Debt	13.7	12.7
1.1	L	Deferred Taxes	.9	.0
7.3	E	All Other Non-Current	10.6	9.1
25.0		Net Worth	38.0	38.9
100.0		Total Liabilities & Net Worth	100.0	100.0
		INCOME DATA		
100.0		Net Sales	100.0	100.0
		Gross Profit		
82.0		Operating Expenses	72.1	63.5
18.0		Operating Profit	27.9	36.5
9.2		All Other Expenses (net)	8.3	13.3
8.8		Profit Before Taxes	19.6	23.1

RATIOS

10-50MM		Ratio	4/1/05-3/31/06	4/1/06-3/31/07
4.5 / 1.2 / .9		Current	3.8 / 2.0 / 1.2	3.5 / 2.0 / 1.2
4.5 / 1.2 / .8		Quick	3.7 / 1.9 / 1.2	2.7 / 1.5 / .7
429 .9 / 1395 .3 / 1734 .2		Sales/Receivables	85 4.3 / 657 .6 / 1184 .3	0 UND / 523 .7 / 1306 .3
		Cost of Sales/Inventory		
		Cost of Sales/Payables		
.3 / 1.0 / -24.5		Sales/Working Capital	.6 / 1.0 / 4.7	.6 / 1.3 / 8.6
		EBIT/Interest	(24) 24.6 / 4.5 / 3.4	
		Net Profit + Depr., Dep., Amort./Cur. Mat. L/T/D		
.0 / .0 / NM		Fixed/Worth	.0 / .0 / .2	.0 / .0 / .4
2.1 / 5.2 / NM		Debt/Worth	.6 / 2.0 / 7.6	.6 / 1.8 / 5.7
		% Profit Before Taxes/Tangible Net Worth	(37) 36.0 / 19.8 / 6.5	45.7 / 20.0 / 5.6
4.9 / 3.0 / .8		% Profit Before Taxes/Total Assets	10.0 / 3.9 / .9	13.6 / 5.2 / 2.1
305.1 / 105.3 / 32.0		Sales/Net Fixed Assets	UND / 82.3 / 11.3	355.7 / 37.1 / 12.1
.2 / .2 / .2		Sales/Total Assets	.5 / .2 / .2	.9 / .3 / .1
		% Depr., Dep., Amort./Sales	(21)	.5 / .9 / 4.1
		% Officers', Directors' Owners' Comp/Sales		

0-500M	500M-2MM	2-10MM	10-50MM	50-100MM	100-250MM		4/1/05-3/31/06	4/1/06-3/31/07
11078M	38011M	34775M	130087M		130767M	Net Sales ($)	231436M	678667M
815M	3277M	23924M	261055M		516982M	Total Assets ($)	670581M	1489930M

M = $ thousand   MM = $ million
See Pages 9 through 22 for Explanation of Ratios and Data

Comparative Historical Data

Current Data Sorted by Sales

			Type of Statement						
8	16	7	Unqualified	1		1	4		1
2		1	Reviewed				1		
1		1	Compiled						1
2	3	5	Tax Returns		4		1		
17	15	12	Other	2	2	1	2	4	1
4/1/07-3/31/08 ALL	4/1/08-3/31/09 ALL	4/1/09-3/31/10 ALL		0-1MM	3 (4/1-9/30/09) 1-3MM	3-5MM	23 (10/1/09-3/31/10) 5-10MM	10-25MM	25MM & OVE
30	34	26	NUMBER OF STATEMENTS	3	6	2	8	4	3
%	%	%		%	%	%	%	%	%
			ASSETS						
13.4	22.7	17.6	Cash & Equivalents						
53.4	44.9	45.2	Trade Receivables (net)						
1.0	3.4	.4	Inventory						
5.9	5.5	3.5	All Other Current						
73.7	76.5	66.8	Total Current						
10.6	5.6	8.1	Fixed Assets (net)						
5.5	4.2	4.8	Intangibles (net)						
10.2	13.8	20.4	All Other Non-Current						
100.0	100.0	100.0	Total						
			LIABILITIES						
23.4	21.7	24.3	Notes Payable-Short Term						
2.0	2.9	2.6	Cur. Mat.-L.T.D.						
2.1	5.4	5.2	Trade Payables						
.1	.1	.2	Income Taxes Payable						
22.3	22.5	18.3	All Other Current						
49.8	52.6	50.6	Total Current						
15.2	13.6	15.3	Long-Term Debt						
.0	.6	.4	Deferred Taxes						
8.9	11.4	7.1	All Other Non-Current						
26.1	21.8	26.7	Net Worth						
100.0	100.0	100.0	Total Liabilties & Net Worth						
			INCOME DATA						
100.0	100.0	100.0	Net Sales						
			Gross Profit						
62.1	74.4	85.0	Operating Expenses						
37.9	25.6	15.0	Operating Profit						
19.5	14.0	5.3	All Other Expenses (net)						
18.5	11.7	9.7	Profit Before Taxes						
			RATIOS						
3.0	2.4	2.9							
1.3	1.4	1.2	Current						
1.1	1.1	.8							
2.3	2.4	2.8							
1.3	1.2	1.2	Quick						
1.0	.7	.8							
4 102.0	1 383.6	0 UND							
213 1.7	64 5.7	431 .8	Sales/Receivables						
1518 .2	1376 .3	1522 .2							
			Cost of Sales/Inventory						
			Cost of Sales/Payables						
.7	.8	.9							
1.7	3.6	5.3	Sales/Working Capital						
19.6	17.0	-28.4							
8.2	13.2	5.0							
(20) 4.4	(17) 3.8	(15) 3.4	EBIT/Interest						
2.0	1.2	2.3							
			Net Profit + Depr., Dep., Amort./Cur. Mat. L/T/D						
.0	.0	.0							
.0	.1	.1	Fixed/Worth						
2.4	.3	7.4							
1.7	1.6	1.5							
3.9	3.6	3.7	Debt/Worth						
NM	12.4	18.7							
42.9	56.7	103.9	% Profit Before Taxes/Tangible Net Worth						
(23) 25.3	(30) 22.6	(21) 13.6							
6.1	5.5	8.2							
15.6	13.8	17.8	% Profit Before Taxes/Total Assets						
9.0	4.2	4.8							
2.0	.6	1.1							
748.1	196.2	171.1	Sales/Net Fixed Assets						
35.4	38.7	95.0							
9.2	21.9	21.2							
1.7	2.2	3.2	Sales/Total Assets						
.4	.6	.3							
.1	.1	.2							
.4	.4	.7	% Depr., Dep., Amort./Sales						
(19) 1.1	(19) 1.0	(11) .9							
3.6	2.2	2.0							
			% Officers', Directors' Owners' Comp/Sales						
709441M	1451828M	344718M	Net Sales ($)	1093M	13877M	6643M	57494M	68769M	196842M
1342908M	1903519M	806053M	Total Assets ($)	8400M	32142M	55243M	167894M	164580M	377794M

M = $ thousand   MM = $ million
See Pages 9 through 22 for Explanation of Ratios and Data

FINANCE—Sales Financing NAICS 522220

| Current Data Sorted by Assets | | | | | | | Comparative Historical Data | |

						Type of Statement	48	79
		8	43	15	22	Unqualified	48	79
	5	15	16	1		Reviewed	29	35
4	6	12	3			Compiled	13	23
8	7	8	1			Tax Returns	14	22
5	8	21	33	10	11	Other	50	64
	29 (4/1-9/30/09)		233 (10/1/09-3/31/10)				4/1/05-3/31/06 ALL	4/1/06-3/31/07 ALL
0-500M	500M-2MM	2-10MM	10-50MM	50-100MM	100-250MM	NUMBER OF STATEMENTS	154	223
17	26	64	96	26	33			
%	%	%	%	%	%	**ASSETS**	%	%
16.3	6.8	6.2	5.5	4.4	3.2	Cash & Equivalents	7.2	7.2
24.5	40.8	50.3	45.7	51.5	49.1	Trade Receivables (net)	49.1	47.5
4.1	10.6	4.2	4.3	4.2	4.0	Inventory	4.6	3.8
16.3	13.9	5.8	4.8	10.4	6.6	All Other Current	8.0	7.6
61.3	72.0	66.5	60.3	70.5	62.9	Total Current	68.9	66.1
19.6	16.6	18.3	12.3	5.3	12.0	Fixed Assets (net)	12.7	17.3
2.2	3.4	1.1	1.0	2.8	1.4	Intangibles (net)	1.3	.8
17.0	8.0	14.1	26.5	21.3	23.7	All Other Non-Current	17.1	15.8
100.0	100.0	100.0	100.0	100.0	100.0	Total	100.0	100.0
						LIABILITIES		
30.8	23.5	21.2	29.4	37.8	17.0	Notes Payable-Short Term	30.3	29.0
9.3	5.2	8.9	3.9	2.4	9.8	Cur. Mat.-L.T.D.	5.2	5.5
10.1	6.6	1.7	2.6	4.4	5.7	Trade Payables	3.1	3.9
.0	.0	.1	.3	.0	.6	Income Taxes Payable	.1	.1
25.6	8.2	10.5	7.3	9.2	8.6	All Other Current	9.4	8.2
75.7	43.5	42.5	43.4	53.8	41.6	Total Current	48.1	46.6
10.1	42.1	17.1	24.0	11.7	29.8	Long-Term Debt	17.6	21.8
.0	.7	.5	.9	.9	1.2	Deferred Taxes	.4	.4
15.8	7.0	8.1	7.8	8.2	4.7	All Other Non-Current	8.0	7.9
-1.6	6.8	31.9	24.0	25.4	22.7	Net Worth	26.0	23.3
100.0	100.0	100.0	100.0	100.0	100.0	Total Liabilties & Net Worth	100.0	100.0
						INCOME DATA		
100.0	100.0	100.0	100.0	100.0	100.0	Net Sales	100.0	100.0
						Gross Profit		
72.9	66.5	78.5	74.3	74.0	71.8	Operating Expenses	72.0	67.9
27.1	33.5	21.5	25.7	26.0	28.2	Operating Profit	28.0	32.1
7.3	8.8	8.3	14.8	17.0	17.4	All Other Expenses (net)	12.1	15.7
19.7	24.8	13.2	10.9	9.0	10.8	Profit Before Taxes	15.9	16.5
						RATIOS		
1.6	3.3	2.6	2.0	1.8	2.8		2.3	2.3
1.1	1.5	1.6	1.4	1.4	1.4	Current	1.3	1.3
.3	.7	.6	1.0	1.1	1.1		1.0	1.1
1.2	2.9	2.4	1.9	1.6	2.7		1.9	2.1
.3	.8	1.4	1.3	1.2	1.3	Quick	(152) 1.2	1.2
.1	.3	.2	.5	.6	.2		.5	.4
0 UND	1 255.1	1 316.4	16 22.4	19 18.9	9 41.2		15 24.6	8 44.9
0 UND	31 11.7	183 2.0	340 1.1	542 .7	368 1.0	Sales/Receivables	386 .9	281 1.3
75 4.9	1481 .2	1144 .3	1251 .3	1139 .3	1839 .2		1212 .3	1217 .3
						Cost of Sales/Inventory		
						Cost of Sales/Payables		
2.8	.5	.6	.6	.8	.5		.7	.7
78.9	3.3	1.9	2.0	1.5	1.0	Sales/Working Capital	2.5	2.3
-2.0	-10.6	-4.4	29.6	6.7	30.2		203.9	24.2
2.3	12.2	8.7	4.5	4.2	2.6		5.4	4.4
(11) 1.5	(20) 4.5	(47) 3.3	(59) 2.3	(19) 2.2	(21) 1.6	EBIT/Interest	(96) 2.8	(122) 2.7
-.5	1.4	2.0	1.2	1.6	1.4		1.6	1.7
						Net Profit + Depr., Dep.,		8.0
						Amort./Cur. Mat. L/T/D	(19) .9	.9
								.1
.0	.0	.0	.0	.0	.0		.0	.0
.5	.5	.0	.1	.0	.1	Fixed/Worth	.1	.1
NM	NM	1.3	.6	.2	.2		.5	.8
.4	.7	.8	1.9	2.7	1.9		1.6	2.0
3.0	3.8	2.3	4.2	3.9	3.5	Debt/Worth	3.9	4.8
NM	-10.6	6.3	13.3	6.4	5.8		10.6	9.7
46.5	38.3	38.2	29.0	22.8	18.1	% Profit Before Taxes/Tangible	39.9	41.8
(13) 15.8	(19) 13.7	(58) 16.1	(91) 11.4	(25) 13.6	(31) 9.5	Net Worth	(143) 23.5	(208) 22.7
6.7	4.0	6.0	2.9	3.5	4.7		7.4	10.1
11.4	10.6	9.5	5.8	5.9	4.1	% Profit Before Taxes/Total	9.6	8.6
3.8	4.6	4.7	2.7	3.0	2.3	Assets	3.8	3.7
-2.9	1.1	1.1	.3	.3	1.0		1.3	1.4
UND	UND	882.4	111.2	106.8	133.3		291.5	185.8
36.9	138.8	40.4	32.2	47.4	26.2	Sales/Net Fixed Assets	38.4	39.5
5.4	19.8	4.2	8.5	14.9	5.5		7.0	5.7
4.4	1.4	.7	.5	.4	.4		.7	.6
.7	.3	.4	.3	.3	.2	Sales/Total Assets	.3	.3
.2	.2	.2	.2	.2	.1		.2	.2
	.3	.3	.5	.4	.4		.6	.5
	(13) .7	(37) .6	(63) 1.1	(17) .7	(18) 1.6	% Depr., Dep., Amort./Sales	(96) 1.4	(147) 1.3
	66.9	15.7	3.0	2.7	3.6		7.9	7.3
		1.5	4.3				6.3	3.8
	(15)	9.9	(14) 11.7			% Officers', Directors'	(34) 9.7	(59) 8.6
		16.9	27.1			Owners' Comp/Sales	19.6	15.7
7840M	38421M	247911M	1103252M	936638M	3118942M	Net Sales ($)	2000600M	3778614M
5143M	31831M	309439M	2401827M	1824065M	4687199M	Total Assets ($)	3760896M	7461224M

© RMA 2010

M = $ thousand   MM = $ million
See Pages 9 through 22 for Explanation of Ratios and Data

Comparative Historical Data   Current Data Sorted by Sales

	Comparative Historical Data			Type of Statement	0-1MM	1-3MM	3-5MM	5-10MM	10-25MM	25MM & OVER
	58	84	88	Unqualified	2	9	11	17	24	25
	33	36	37	Reviewed	10	9	9	5	2	2
	20	17	25	Compiled	12	8	1	1	2	1
	14	29	24	Tax Returns	14	8	1	1		
	100	99	88	Other	18	17	9	14	14	16
	4/1/07-3/31/08 ALL	4/1/08-3/31/09 ALL	4/1/09-3/31/10 ALL		29 (4/1-9/30/09)		233 (10/1/09-3/31/10)			
	225	265	262	**NUMBER OF STATEMENTS**	56	51	31	38	42	44
	%	%	%	**ASSETS**	%	%	%	%	%	%
	5.8	5.2	6.1	Cash & Equivalents	8.1	8.6	6.8	4.1	3.5	4.5
	46.1	46.8	46.0	Trade Receivables (net)	39.2	52.2	48.3	50.0	39.4	48.6
	5.1	4.0	4.8	Inventory	2.3	1.1	6.7	4.2	7.9	8.7
	11.9	8.0	7.5	All Other Current	12.7	4.3	3.9	9.4	8.5	4.2
	68.9	64.0	64.4	Total Current	62.4	66.2	65.7	67.7	59.3	65.9
	10.2	13.3	13.9	Fixed Assets (net)	16.7	17.3	12.2	8.7	11.8	14.3
	1.2	.9	1.6	Intangibles (net)	2.0	1.5	.5	.8	1.5	2.5
	19.7	21.8	20.1	All Other Non-Current	18.9	15.1	21.5	22.8	27.4	17.3
	100.0	100.0	100.0	Total	100.0	100.0	100.0	100.0	100.0	100.0
				LIABILITIES						
	27.8	29.3	26.2	Notes Payable-Short Term	22.9	25.7	20.8	32.2	32.8	23.2
	5.1	5.3	6.2	Cur. Mat.-L.T.D.	8.1	6.0	7.2	4.1	8.9	2.4
	4.1	3.2	3.8	Trade Payables	3.3	2.1	5.0	2.4	3.4	7.3
	.1	.1	.2	Income Taxes Payable	.0	.1	.1	.3	.3	.4
	8.1	8.5	9.7	All Other Current	16.6	6.6	6.2	10.3	4.5	11.3
	45.2	46.3	46.1	Total Current	51.0	40.4	39.3	49.4	49.9	44.7
	21.0	19.8	22.7	Long-Term Debt	18.0	25.3	18.4	29.9	24.1	21.1
	.6	.4	.7	Deferred Taxes	.4	.6	.8	1.0	.7	1.2
	9.3	7.8	7.9	All Other Non-Current	10.4	9.9	8.8	6.1	5.6	5.8
	23.9	25.7	22.5	Net Worth	20.2	23.8	32.8	13.7	19.6	27.3
	100.0	100.0	100.0	Total Liabilities & Net Worth	100.0	100.0	100.0	100.0	100.0	100.0
				INCOME DATA						
	100.0	100.0	100.0	Net Sales	100.0	100.0	100.0	100.0	100.0	100.0
				Gross Profit						
	66.8	69.1	74.1	Operating Expenses	63.0	67.9	79.6	78.9	79.2	82.4
	33.2	30.9	25.9	Operating Profit	37.0	32.1	20.4	21.1	20.8	17.6
	17.3	15.7	12.7	All Other Expenses (net)	11.3	15.4	9.9	14.2	16.8	7.9
	15.9	15.2	13.2	Profit Before Taxes	25.7	16.6	10.5	6.9	3.9	9.6
				RATIOS						
	2.9	2.4	2.4		2.4	5.4	3.1	2.3	1.6	2.6
	1.4	1.3	1.4	Current	1.2	1.6	1.7	1.3	1.3	1.5
	1.1	.9	1.0		.6	1.1	1.3	1.1	.8	1.2
	2.2	1.9	2.0		1.8	5.4	2.2	1.8	1.5	2.2
	1.2	1.2	1.3	Quick	1.0	1.5	1.5	1.2	.9	1.3
	.4	.3	.2		.1	.7	.3	.1	.1	.6
6	63.2 / 14	25.2 / 5	76.4		0 UND	2 234.5	28 12.9	13 28.2	13 27.3	19 19.2
281	1.3 / 340	1.1 / 252	1.4	Sales/Receivables	6 63.4	617 .6	539 .7	396 .9	53 6.8	101 3.6
1117	.3 / 1295	.3 / 1193	.3		1463 .2	1506 .2	1246 .3	1049 .3	825 .4	909 .4
				Cost of Sales/Inventory						
				Cost of Sales/Payables						
	.6	.7	.7		.5	.4	.7	.7	1.4	.7
	2.0	2.2	2.0	Sales/Working Capital	2.2	1.1	1.2	2.8	3.9	3.2
	20.5	-55.9	188.3		-2.3	14.8	7.1	17.2	-9.9	32.7
	6.5	4.8	5.8		10.6	7.4	7.4	4.1	2.9	4.0
(118)	2.5 / (145)	2.4 / (177)	2.4	EBIT/Interest	(36) 4.1	(28) 3.0	(19) 3.5	(25) 2.3	(30) 1.7	(39) 2.1
	1.4	1.4	1.4		1.3	2.0	2.0	1.1	.9	1.4
	22.9	39.6	2.0	Net Profit + Depr., Dep.,						
(15)	1.5 / (13)	2.8 / (15)	.5	Amort./Cur. Mat. L/T/D						
	.1	.2	.1							
	.0	.0	.0		.0	.0	.0	.0	.0	.0
	.0	.0	.1	Fixed/Worth	.0	.0	.0	.1	.1	.1
	.3	.5	.7		1.5	.6	.1	.4	1.4	.7
	1.9	1.6	1.6		1.0	1.5	1.4	1.1	2.8	1.8
	4.7	3.9	3.5	Debt/Worth	3.0	3.5	2.6	4.3	5.4	3.5
	10.9	10.7	7.7		7.5	13.1	8.5	14.0	14.5	5.1
	43.2	25.2	30.8	% Profit Before Taxes/Tangible	36.3	33.6	34.9	30.6	22.6	29.4
(213)	20.5 / (242)	14.0 / (237)	13.2	Net Worth	(48) 15.7	(45) 17.1	(28) 13.7	(36) 8.6	(38) 11.0	(42) 14.9
	8.6	4.2	4.0		3.6	3.9	4.8	.3	1.9	6.8
	7.7	6.9	7.1	% Profit Before Taxes/Total	10.4	7.4	6.8	5.3	5.9	7.5
	3.5	3.1	3.0	Assets	5.0	3.7	3.5	2.5	1.3	3.0
	1.1	.5	.6		.8	.6	.9	-.9	-1.5	1.8
	348.0	201.4	235.9		UND	999.8	92.5	533.5	93.0	84.1
	47.4	44.2	38.7	Sales/Net Fixed Assets	131.0	65.4	35.4	36.4	27.9	26.6
	12.4	5.8	7.0		4.2	2.7	16.1	15.7	3.3	6.5
	.5	.4	.6		.4	.5	.6	.6	.7	2.0
	.3	.3	.3	Sales/Total Assets	.2	.2	.3	.3	.4	.4
	.2	.2	.2		.1	.2	.2	.2	.2	.3
	.4	.4	.4		.4	.5	.4	.6	.4	.4
(142)	1.0 / (159)	1.1 / (157)	1.1	% Depr., Dep., Amort./Sales	(28) 1.8	(27) 1.1	(23) .8	(22) 1.1	(27) 1.2	(30) .6
	2.6	5.2	4.0		55.6	23.8	1.9	2.9	6.5	2.1
	2.2	2.4	3.8	% Officers', Directors'		3.8				
(45)	5.7 / (43)	7.6 / (43)	7.4	Owners' Comp/Sales		(16) 10.2				
	11.0	16.3	19.3			17.5				
	4310857M	4093600M	5453004M	Net Sales ($)	24258M	100652M	122884M	269921M	660508M	4274781M
	7877668M	9119247M	9259504M	Total Assets ($)	117374M	530204M	523621M	1190806M	2343577M	4553922M

© RMA 2010

M = $ thousand   MM = $ million
See Pages 9 through 22 for Explanation of Ratios and Data

FINANCE—Consumer Lending NAICS 522291

Current Data Sorted by Assets | Comparative Historical Data

Type of Statement

	0-500M	500M-2MM	2-10MM	10-50MM	50-100MM	100-250MM		4/1/05-3/31/06 ALL	4/1/06-3/31/07 ALL
Unqualified			15	30	13	18		62	81
Reviewed	5	18	13	10	3	3		28	27
Compiled	3	7	26	3	3	2		25	24
Tax Returns	3		6	3	2			19	25
Other	4	23	42	29	12	12		75	79
		39 (4/1-9/30/09)		258 (10/1/09-3/31/10)					
NUMBER OF STATEMENTS	12	48	102	75	30	30		209	236

ASSETS (%)

	0-500M	500M-2MM	2-10MM	10-50MM	50-100MM	100-250MM		4/1/05-3/31/06	4/1/06-3/31/07
Cash & Equivalents	21.7	6.8	6.9	5.9	6.8	9.9		10.9	8.3
Trade Receivables (net)	47.4	75.8	70.8	74.7	65.2	64.6		62.4	60.2
Inventory	.0	.8	2.8	.9	1.1	.1		.6	.9
All Other Current	8.9	5.7	3.5	3.6	9.5	5.4		7.4	10.4
Total Current	78.0	89.0	84.0	85.1	82.7	80.0		81.3	79.8
Fixed Assets (net)	2.5	3.4	4.1	4.0	6.2	6.5		6.4	7.1
Intangibles (net)	6.8	.9	1.0	4.4	4.1	1.3		1.4	2.1
All Other Non-Current	12.7	6.7	10.8	6.4	7.1	12.3		10.8	10.9
Total	100.0	100.0	100.0	100.0	100.0	100.0		100.0	100.0

LIABILITIES

	0-500M	500M-2MM	2-10MM	10-50MM	50-100MM	100-250MM		4/1/05-3/31/06	4/1/06-3/31/07
Notes Payable-Short Term	29.0	28.2	36.0	42.3	36.9	29.1		32.9	35.4
Cur. Mat.-L.T.D.	1.9	1.8	1.4	1.3	3.1	4.0		2.6	2.3
Trade Payables	7.4	1.5	1.5	1.8	1.3	3.4		2.7	2.3
Income Taxes Payable	.0	.0	.1	.1	.2	.3		.2	.2
All Other Current	11.3	15.1	9.0	7.2	12.4	11.5		11.0	8.8
Total Current	49.6	46.6	48.0	52.6	54.0	48.2		49.4	48.9
Long-Term Debt	14.1	14.3	11.9	6.4	9.7	18.2		11.4	12.5
Deferred Taxes	.0	.2	.0	.0	.0	.0		.1	.1
All Other Non-Current	17.3	17.0	14.7	12.1	12.3	8.6		10.1	10.4
Net Worth	19.1	21.9	25.4	28.9	24.0	25.0		28.9	28.2
Total Liabilities & Net Worth	100.0	100.0	100.0	100.0	100.0	100.0		100.0	100.0

INCOME DATA

	0-500M	500M-2MM	2-10MM	10-50MM	50-100MM	100-250MM		4/1/05-3/31/06	4/1/06-3/31/07
Net Sales	100.0	100.0	100.0	100.0	100.0	100.0		100.0	100.0
Gross Profit									
Operating Expenses	78.1	76.4	74.8	74.8	69.4	75.0		71.3	71.8
Operating Profit	21.9	23.6	25.2	25.2	30.6	25.0		28.7	28.2
All Other Expenses (net)	8.4	11.0	11.9	12.8	16.8	11.5		13.8	12.5
Profit Before Taxes	13.4	12.6	13.3	12.4	13.9	13.5		14.9	15.7

RATIOS

	0-500M	500M-2MM	2-10MM	10-50MM	50-100MM	100-250MM		4/1/05-3/31/06	4/1/06-3/31/07
Current	2.9	4.7	3.3	2.2	2.5	2.9		3.2	2.6
	1.7	2.1	1.7	1.4	1.4	1.5		1.5	1.5
	1.2	1.3	1.3	1.3	1.1	1.3		1.2	1.2
Quick	2.9	4.4	3.0	2.0	2.2	2.5		2.9	2.4
	1.7	2.0	1.5	1.4	1.3	1.4		1.4	1.4
	.7	1.2	1.2	1.2	1.1	1.2		1.1	1.1
Sales/Receivables	0 UND	295 1.2	333 1.1	432 .8	179 2.0	116 3.1		110 3.3	102 3.6
	78 4.7	635 .6	748 .5	972 .4	566 .6	742 .5		725 .5	556 .7
	616 .6	969 .4	1193 .3	1419 .3	1469 .2	1062 .3		1342 .3	1337 .3
Cost of Sales/Inventory									
Cost of Sales/Payables									
Sales/Working Capital	.8	.7	.6	.7	.6	.8		.7	.7
	4.5	1.3	1.3	1.3	1.3	2.1		1.5	1.4
	50.0	3.8	3.0	2.2	3.8	4.1		4.5	5.0
EBIT/Interest	10.6	3.5	6.0	4.4	5.4	5.9		7.5	5.8
	(10) 2.5	(40) 1.9	(82) 3.2	(59) 2.6	(16) 3.0	(27) 2.6		(133) 2.8	(139) 2.9
	1.1	1.3	1.7	1.5	1.9	1.6		1.3	1.6
Net Profit + Depr., Dep., Amort./Cur. Mat. L/T/D								2.2	7.0
								(14) .5	(15) 2.3
								.1	.3
Fixed/Worth	.0	.0	.0	.0	.0	.0		.0	.0
	.0	.0	.1	.1	.1	.2		.1	.1
	.1	.7	.3	.3	.2	.6		.3	.4
Debt/Worth	1.1	1.6	1.7	1.4	2.2	1.9		1.3	1.3
	2.6	5.4	4.0	3.4	4.7	3.7		3.6	3.6
	8.7	39.0	10.6	7.6	15.6	8.0		7.6	10.8
% Profit Before Taxes/Tangible Net Worth	218.9	61.9	47.1	33.2	60.0	54.4		43.9	44.0
	(10) 38.5	(38) 22.3	(93) 22.3	(68) 15.4	(27) 23.6	(29) 21.1		(194) 17.9	(216) 21.5
	-8.6	3.5	5.8	6.1	9.5	9.1		4.8	7.6
% Profit Before Taxes/Total Assets	68.1	10.0	9.4	7.1	7.8	12.6		11.3	9.4
	8.2	3.9	4.3	3.7	4.1	6.9		3.9	4.3
	3.1	.5	1.2	1.5	1.2	2.9		.6	1.5
Sales/Net Fixed Assets	UND	UND	306.7	86.3	88.0	43.0		98.1	97.6
	168.5	99.1	40.9	30.7	34.9	22.5		26.6	27.9
	43.3	24.1	15.3	9.3	21.9	9.4		11.8	10.8
Sales/Total Assets	3.6	.8	.7	.5	.6	1.1		.8	.9
	.5	.5	.3	.3	.3	.4		.3	.3
	.5	.3	.2	.2	.2	.3		.2	.2
% Depr., Dep., Amort./Sales		.3	.5	.3	.5	.9		.6	.6
		(25) .8	(65) 1.0	(50) 1.3	(24) .9	(22) 1.7		(141) 1.6	(161) 1.1
		2.3	1.9	2.4	1.4	2.3		2.6	2.3
% Officers', Directors' Owners' Comp/Sales		3.3	2.9	4.3				6.7	6.5
		(19) 7.5	(20) 7.6	(19) 8.6				(47) 12.6	(48) 12.3
		17.8	15.0	20.7				21.5	22.9
Net Sales ($)	9630M	40240M	289570M	1322592M	807064M	3474257M		4045526M	5171499M
Total Assets ($)	4142M	50409M	538310M	1709929M	2102520M	5123107M		7259289M	8136114M

Comparative Historical Data   **Current Data Sorted by Sales**

			Type of Statement						
75	82	76	Unqualified	1	13	11	12	14	25
28	28	23	Reviewed	4	5	7	5	2	
28	33	55	Compiled	30	17	2	3	1	2
25	19	21	Tax Returns	8	8	2			3
102	134	122	Other	29	31	11	17	16	18
4/1/07-3/31/08 ALL	4/1/08-3/31/09 ALL	4/1/09-3/31/10 ALL		39 (4/1-9/30/09)			258 (10/1/09-3/31/10)		
				0-1MM	1-3MM	3-5MM	5-10MM	10-25MM	25MM & OVER
258	296	297	**NUMBER OF STATEMENTS**	72	74	33	37	33	48
%	%	%	**ASSETS**	%	%	%	%	%	%
6.5	7.3	7.5	Cash & Equivalents	5.7	7.5	7.6	5.0	7.7	12.2
70.8	68.1	70.5	Trade Receivables (net)	71.4	74.4	73.3	74.2	73.1	56.4
1.5	1.4	1.4	Inventory	.2	2.9	1.1	.4	3.0	1.1
5.4	6.3	4.9	All Other Current	5.7	3.6	4.2	6.3	4.4	5.4
84.2	83.1	84.3	Total Current	82.9	88.3	86.2	86.0	88.2	75.0
5.8	4.9	4.4	Fixed Assets (net)	3.5	1.9	5.3	3.8	6.3	7.9
1.9	1.4	2.4	Intangibles (net)	1.1	1.4	.8	4.9	.9	6.3
8.1	10.6	8.9	All Other Non-Current	12.4	8.4	7.7	5.4	4.6	10.8
100.0	100.0	100.0	Total	100.0	100.0	100.0	100.0	100.0	100.0
			LIABILITIES						
41.1	38.2	35.4	Notes Payable-Short Term	34.5	34.6	36.9	39.4	45.3	27.5
2.8	3.4	1.9	Cur. Mat.-L.T.D.	2.6	.2	1.1	1.9	1.7	4.1
2.1	2.7	2.0	Trade Payables	1.9	2.3	.6	.7	2.4	3.2
.1	.1	.1	Income Taxes Payable	.0	.1	.1	.1	.0	.3
9.0	7.4	10.2	All Other Current	9.8	13.7	8.9	9.4	6.1	9.9
55.1	51.7	49.6	Total Current	48.8	50.9	47.5	51.4	55.4	45.0
9.6	11.2	11.4	Long-Term Debt	16.1	8.4	3.6	9.6	12.1	15.3
.0	.0	.0	Deferred Taxes	.0	.1	.0	.0	.0	.0
11.5	9.9	13.7	All Other Non-Current	16.2	14.7	13.8	9.5	10.3	13.6
23.7	27.2	25.3	Net Worth	18.9	26.0	35.1	29.5	22.2	26.0
100.0	100.0	100.0	Total Liabilities & Net Worth	100.0	100.0	100.0	100.0	100.0	100.0
			INCOME DATA						
100.0	100.0	100.0	Net Sales	100.0	100.0	100.0	100.0	100.0	100.0
			Gross Profit						
71.4	77.1	74.7	Operating Expenses	71.7	73.2	73.8	76.5	74.4	80.8
28.6	22.9	25.3	Operating Profit	28.3	26.8	26.2	23.5	25.6	19.2
15.9	13.0	12.3	All Other Expenses (net)	15.8	12.8	11.6	9.5	13.4	8.0
12.7	9.9	13.0	Profit Before Taxes	12.6	14.0	14.5	14.0	12.1	11.2
			RATIOS						
2.3	2.8	2.7	Current	3.9	3.1	2.3	2.5	2.1	2.7
1.4	1.5	1.6		1.9	1.6	1.6	1.7	1.4	1.5
1.2	1.2	1.3		1.2	1.2	1.3	1.3	1.2	1.2
2.1	2.5	2.6	Quick	3.8	2.8	2.3	2.1	1.7	2.6
1.3	1.4	1.4		1.7	1.4	1.5	1.6	1.3	1.3
1.1	1.1	1.2		1.2	1.1	1.3	1.3	1.2	1.1
176 2.1	125 2.9	276 1.3	Sales/Receivables	475 .8	363 1.0	339 1.1	340 1.1	212 1.7	84 4.3
871 .4	697 .5	716 .5		852 .4	799 .5	890 .4	585 .6	655 .6	303 1.2
1370 .3	1147 .3	1207 .3		1611 .2	1198 .3	1270 .3	1261 .3	1289 .3	794 .5
			Cost of Sales/Inventory						
			Cost of Sales/Payables						
.7	.7	.7	Sales/Working Capital	.4	.7	.5	.7	1.1	1.3
1.4	1.7	1.3		.9	1.2	.9	1.3	1.9	2.4
5.7	3.9	3.0		2.6	2.9	2.4	2.1	3.3	5.7
3.5	4.2	4.9	EBIT/Interest	3.6	4.1	6.9	5.6	5.2	7.0
(138) 2.0	(193) 2.2	(234) 2.7		(53) 1.9	(54) 2.7	(28) 3.2	(30) 3.4	(27) 2.9	(42) 2.8
1.3	1.3	1.5		1.3	1.4	2.1	1.9	1.5	1.6
4.7	12.3	36.0	Net Profit + Depr., Dep., Amort./Cur. Mat. L/T/D						
(12) .9	(24) 4.5	(21) 5.2							
.2	.1	1.5							
.0	.0	.0	Fixed/Worth	.0	.0	.0	.0	.0	.1
.1	.1	.1		.0	.0	.1	.1	.1	.2
.4	.4	.3		.4	.2	.3	.4	.3	.8
2.0	1.5	1.5	Debt/Worth	1.6	1.7	1.0	1.4	1.9	1.9
4.2	4.0	3.9		5.9	4.3	2.2	3.5	3.9	3.7
10.5	11.4	10.0		23.3	10.6	4.3	10.5	9.2	10.1
38.4	44.3	47.2	% Profit Before Taxes/Tangible Net Worth	42.2	48.4	36.9	46.4	38.0	58.9
(231) 16.7	(262) 17.2	(265) 20.6		(59) 14.4	(67) 18.5	18.1	(34) 23.4	(31) 29.7	(41) 31.8
5.3	4.6	6.4		2.0	7.7	5.7	7.2	9.9	12.9
6.8	7.5	9.6	% Profit Before Taxes/Total Assets	6.7	8.9	10.0	12.1	9.5	13.6
3.2	3.7	4.3		3.1	3.4	4.8	4.1	5.9	7.9
.9	.5	1.4		.2	1.5	2.0	2.1	1.3	3.0
120.4	121.4	138.5	Sales/Net Fixed Assets	UND	999.8	117.2	58.9	72.1	52.0
30.6	33.2	36.3		95.0	38.8	42.4	31.8	32.9	24.6
15.2	12.3	13.4		23.1	18.6	6.3	9.8	10.3	10.1
.6	.8	.7	Sales/Total Assets	.5	.6	.7	.8	.9	1.1
.3	.3	.4		.3	.3	.3	.4	.4	.7
.2	.2	.2		.2	.2	.3	.2	.3	.4
.6	.5	.5	% Depr., Dep., Amort./Sales	.4	.3	.4	.5	.4	.9
(169) 1.1	(188) 1.2	(190) 1.1		(37) .9	(42) 1.1	(24) 1.3	(23) .9	(27) .9	(37) 1.5
2.3	2.4	2.1		2.2	1.9	2.8	1.5	2.1	2.3
4.1	3.2	3.3	% Officers', Directors' Owners' Comp/Sales	2.3	2.7	4.3			
(51) 11.7	(50) 7.7	(68) 7.6		(15) 7.1	(26) 6.6	(11) 8.6			
23.1	18.8	15.8		15.5	9.9	19.8			
4326682M	5785172M	5943353M	Net Sales ($)	33098M	131998M	131642M	267015M	558231M	4821369M
7687990M	10274047M	9528417M	Total Assets ($)	154550M	431776M	475095M	1069040M	1431536M	5966420M

M = $ thousand   MM = $ million
See Pages 9 through 22 for Explanation of Ratios and Data

FINANCE—Real Estate Credit NAICS 522292

Current Data Sorted by Assets							Comparative Historical Data	

Type of Statement

						Type of Statement		
3	10	48	74	23	19	Unqualified	381	421
		1	5			Reviewed	17	23
		7	4		1	Compiled	21	27
6	11	9	1			Tax Returns	52	46
7	10	24	33	12	8	Other	139	146
	32 (4/1-9/30/09)		284 (10/1/09-3/31/10)				4/1/05-3/31/06	4/1/06-3/31/07
0-500M	500M-2MM	2-10MM	10-50MM	50-100MM	100-250MM		ALL	ALL
16	31	89	117	35	28	NUMBER OF STATEMENTS	610	663
%	%	%	%	%	%	ASSETS	%	%
37.6	24.7	14.9	10.4	8.3	9.4	Cash & Equivalents	17.5	17.2
9.4	13.3	26.5	25.7	29.9	34.9	Trade Receivables (net)	36.3	30.4
.0	2.1	8.1	18.4	20.8	21.1	Inventory	5.2	5.4
6.6	12.0	21.6	20.3	16.6	5.1	All Other Current	15.5	21.9
53.6	52.1	71.2	74.8	75.5	70.5	Total Current	74.4	74.9
20.0	24.2	6.2	4.9	1.1	4.7	Fixed Assets (net)	8.6	7.8
8.2	1.5	2.2	2.6	4.6	2.2	Intangibles (net)	1.7	1.7
18.2	22.2	20.4	17.7	18.8	22.6	All Other Non-Current	15.3	15.6
100.0	100.0	100.0	100.0	100.0	100.0	Total	100.0	100.0
						LIABILITIES		
16.8	21.7	39.0	50.8	41.8	48.2	Notes Payable-Short Term	29.3	33.2
.6	1.2	2.7	1.7	2.5	1.4	Cur. Mat.-L.T.D.	1.2	1.4
30.3	.9	3.8	1.7	7.9	2.1	Trade Payables	22.1	16.3
.0	.0	.2	.1	.1	.4	Income Taxes Payable	.2	.2
19.6	8.1	7.9	5.4	10.2	5.3	All Other Current	6.5	8.8
67.3	31.9	53.7	59.6	62.4	57.5	Total Current	59.3	59.8
4.7	23.7	7.2	9.5	8.0	17.2	Long-Term Debt	6.5	8.1
.0	.0	.2	.2	.4	.0	Deferred Taxes	.3	.2
1.4	4.8	4.3	5.0	4.7	2.3	All Other Non-Current	3.0	2.7
26.6	39.6	34.7	25.7	24.6	22.9	Net Worth	30.9	29.1
100.0	100.0	100.0	100.0	100.0	100.0	Total Liabilities & Net Worth	100.0	100.0
						INCOME DATA		
100.0	100.0	100.0	100.0	100.0	100.0	Net Sales	100.0	100.0
						Gross Profit		
81.6	76.8	75.1	73.9	66.2	75.9	Operating Expenses	78.4	78.4
18.4	23.2	24.9	26.1	33.8	24.1	Operating Profit	21.6	21.6
2.0	9.1	11.2	10.8	13.3	10.0	All Other Expenses (net)	8.8	11.7
16.4	14.1	13.7	15.4	20.5	14.1	Profit Before Taxes	12.8	9.9
						RATIOS		
6.8	3.4	2.5	1.6	1.5	1.4	Current	1.7	1.7
2.9	1.4	1.3	1.1	1.1	1.2		1.2	1.2
.6	.5	1.0	1.0	1.1	1.0		1.1	1.0
6.8	3.4	1.7	1.1	1.1	1.2	Quick	1.4	1.4
2.9	1.1	1.0	.5	.7	.8		1.1	1.0
.2	.2	.2	.1	.1	.2		.3	.1
0 UND	0 UND	0 UND	0 UND	12 30.0	3 123.5	Sales/Receivables	0 UND	0 UND
0 UND	0 UND	17 21.3	16 23.5	37 9.9	58 6.3		28 12.9	15 24.1
5 73.2	26 14.3	353 1.0	565 .6	563 .6	1121 .3		541 .7	429 .9
						Cost of Sales/Inventory		
						Cost of Sales/Payables		
8.2	2.3	1.8	1.0	1.9	1.5	Sales/Working Capital	2.2	2.0
12.8	7.9	4.0	5.0	4.1	3.3		6.4	6.4
-8.5	-5.9	23.3	13.9	7.1	12.7		23.7	33.6
	6.5	7.2	4.3	8.5	7.3	EBIT/Interest	4.6	3.7
(21)	1.7 (64)	3.0 (78)	2.8 (22)	3.9 (16)	3.9		(419) 2.1	(402) 1.4
	.9	1.7	1.4	2.7	3.0		1.1	.7
			10.4			Net Profit + Depr., Dep., Amort./Cur. Mat. L/T/D	17.6	11.9
		(11)	1.9				(56) 4.2	(66) 2.1
			1.0				.4	-1.4
.0	.0	.0	.0	.0	.0	Fixed/Worth	.0	.0
.1	.1	.1	.1	.0	.1		.1	.1
.6	2.3	.2	.2	.1	.2		.4	.4
.2	.6	1.3	2.5	2.1	2.4	Debt/Worth	1.2	1.4
.5	2.3	2.7	5.9	5.7	5.6		4.0	4.1
6.8	5.5	5.4	9.1	12.9	10.0		8.5	9.9
170.7	53.6	35.8	55.5	70.6	71.4	% Profit Before Taxes/Tangible Net Worth	46.3	33.0
(13) 72.1	(29) 14.8	(86) 13.2	(112) 22.0	(33) 36.8	(26) 31.2		(591) 18.7	(636) 10.4
15.3	.7	3.1	3.6	13.3	7.5		3.1	-4.0
71.8	10.8	8.9	8.3	8.7	9.0	% Profit Before Taxes/Total Assets	9.7	7.0
20.7	3.1	4.1	4.1	5.1	4.6		3.5	1.8
1.7	-.3	.6	.7	3.1	1.8		.5	-.7
UND	204.0	156.7	195.6	204.2	95.7	Sales/Net Fixed Assets	81.2	105.1
79.5	15.6	45.9	53.0	66.9	44.6		31.3	36.0
5.9	1.5	11.4	16.3	34.7	6.1		14.3	15.3
6.3	1.4	.7	.6	.5	.5	Sales/Total Assets	1.3	1.3
3.3	.6	.5	.3	.3	.3		.5	.5
1.1	.3	.1	.1	.1	.1		.2	.2
	.4	.5	.4	.3	.4	% Depr., Dep., Amort./Sales	.5	.5
(15)	1.3 (55)	1.0 (72)	.7 (22)	.6 (20)	1.0		(437) 1.0	(469) 1.1
	6.6	1.7	1.1	1.1	1.5		1.6	1.9
		3.0	1.7			% Officers', Directors' Owners' Comp/Sales	2.5	2.0
		(24) 6.7	(21) 4.7				(184) 6.3	(215) 5.2
		16.0	8.6				15.1	12.5
6732M	31195M	305576M	1234831M	796068M	1622175M	Net Sales ($)	10491280M	10406311M
2564M	36543M	516742M	2818152M	2388022M	4435313M	Total Assets ($)	16313259M	18828703M

M = $ thousand   MM = $ million

See Pages 9 through 22 for Explanation of Ratios and Data

Comparative Historical Data   Current Data Sorted by Sales

			Type of Statement						
247	182	177	Unqualified	12	33	26	39	36	31
13	15	6	Reviewed		3	1	2		3
12	12	12	Compiled	5	3	2		2	
28	40	27	Tax Returns	23	4				
109	99	94	Other	27	21	5	15	13	13
4/1/07-3/31/08 ALL	4/1/08-3/31/09 ALL	4/1/09-3/31/10 ALL		0-1MM	32 (4/1-9/30/09) 1-3MM	3-5MM	5-10MM	284 (10/1/09-3/31/10) 10-25MM	25MM & OVER
409	348	316	**NUMBER OF STATEMENTS**	67	64	34	56	51	44
%	%	%	**ASSETS**	%	%	%	%	%	%
15.8	13.2	14.1	Cash & Equivalents	18.2	16.3	12.3	11.1	12.2	12.3
25.2	27.3	25.2	Trade Receivables (net)	20.2	30.1	25.9	28.0	22.0	25.2
5.5	6.2	13.5	Inventory	1.3	6.0	15.1	11.9	26.0	29.2
25.6	21.1	17.4	All Other Current	11.8	15.8	22.4	26.7	16.3	13.9
72.2	67.7	70.2	Total Current	51.5	68.2	75.6	77.7	76.5	80.6
7.3	8.4	7.5	Fixed Assets (net)	15.5	10.1	3.5	5.1	1.7	4.1
2.0	2.7	2.9	Intangibles (net)	2.2	2.2	5.0	.8	3.6	4.9
18.5	21.3	19.5	All Other Non-Current	30.8	19.5	15.8	16.4	18.2	10.4
100.0	100.0	100.0	Total	100.0	100.0	100.0	100.0	100.0	100.0
			LIABILITIES						
43.0	38.8	41.6	Notes Payable-Short Term	22.3	31.7	47.7	56.0	51.3	51.3
1.8	2.0	2.0	Cur. Mat.-L.T.D.	.7	3.2	3.0	1.2	1.7	2.5
6.0	8.4	4.4	Trade Payables	7.3	4.6	3.9	1.4	2.1	6.6
.2	.1	.2	Income Taxes Payable	.1	.1	.2	.2	.1	.3
7.2	8.1	7.6	All Other Current	13.0	5.4	4.0	4.9	7.9	8.5
58.1	57.5	55.8	Total Current	43.4	45.0	58.8	63.8	63.0	69.2
8.4	9.2	10.5	Long-Term Debt	15.0	15.4	7.3	7.1	9.9	3.9
.3	.3	.2	Deferred Taxes	.0	.0	.0	.7	.1	.1
3.8	3.6	4.3	All Other Non-Current	6.2	6.6	2.6	2.6	4.1	1.9
29.4	29.3	29.3	Net Worth	35.4	33.0	31.3	25.8	22.9	24.8
100.0	100.0	100.0	Total Liabilities & Net Worth	100.0	100.0	100.0	100.0	100.0	100.0
			INCOME DATA						
100.0	100.0	100.0	Net Sales	100.0	100.0	100.0	100.0	100.0	100.0
			Gross Profit						
77.6	78.4	74.2	Operating Expenses	66.9	72.2	72.8	78.1	77.5	80.6
22.4	21.6	25.8	Operating Profit	33.1	27.8	27.2	21.9	22.5	19.4
13.2	12.7	10.5	All Other Expenses (net)	18.3	10.6	9.7	9.2	8.9	2.6
9.2	8.9	15.3	Profit Before Taxes	14.7	17.3	17.5	12.7	13.6	16.7
			RATIOS						
1.8	1.8	1.8	Current	7.3	3.5	1.4	1.6	1.5	1.2
1.2	1.1	1.2		1.3	1.5	1.3	1.1	1.1	1.1
1.0	1.0	1.0		.5	1.1	1.1	1.1	1.1	1.1
1.4	1.3	1.4	Quick	4.2	2.2	1.1	1.1	1.2	1.0
(408) .9	(347) .8	.8		1.1	1.1	.6	.6	.3	.4
.1	.1	.1		.1	.3	.2	.1	.1	.1
0 UND	0 UND	0 UND	Sales/Receivables	0 UND	0 UND	0 UND	0 UND	0 UND	3 123.5
9 41.6	19 18.8	15 23.7		0 UND	41 8.8	18 19.7	27 13.5	19 18.7	14 25.5
430 .8	662 .6	452 .8		449 .8	853 .4	517 .7	428 .9	463 .8	413 .9
			Cost of Sales/Inventory						
			Cost of Sales/Payables						
1.3	1.4	1.6	Sales/Working Capital	.4	.9	1.1	1.9	3.1	3.3
4.9	5.0	4.6		8.1	2.5	3.3	6.1	5.9	5.5
44.0	82.5	15.3		-3.9	10.5	10.5	13.6	11.9	15.0
3.7	3.4	6.5	EBIT/Interest	9.7	8.9	6.5	4.6	4.1	8.4
(240) 1.3	(219) 1.9	(207) 3.2		(30) 2.6	(36) 3.2	(26) 3.4	(46) 2.6	(34) 2.8	(35) 4.1
.5	1.1	1.7		.9	1.5	2.0	1.3	2.0	2.3
5.3	5.2	13.1	Net Profit + Depr., Dep., Amort./Cur. Mat. L/T/D						
(26) .1	(19) .5	(20) 1.9							
-12.9	.0	1.0							
.0	.0	.0	Fixed/Worth	.0	.0	.0	.0	.0	.0
.1	.1	.1		.0	.1	.0	.1	.1	.1
.3	.3	.2		.4	.5	.2	.3	.1	.2
1.4	1.4	1.4	Debt/Worth	.3	1.2	1.8	1.7	2.8	3.1
3.7	3.6	4.0		2.1	2.9	2.8	4.3	6.5	5.3
9.1	8.6	7.8		7.1	7.0	5.6	7.6	11.1	8.0
25.9	24.4	53.7	% Profit Before Taxes/Tangible Net Worth	21.7	38.3	46.5	47.1	74.1	76.2
(386) 6.9	(331) 8.9	(299) 21.1		(60) 5.3	(60) 15.2	(33) 16.3	21.0	(49) 41.1	(41) 65.5
-4.7	.6	4.3		1.0	2.4	8.0	4.1	15.7	25.6
5.9	5.1	9.2	% Profit Before Taxes/Total Assets	5.2	7.6	9.2	8.7	8.7	14.7
1.6	1.7	4.4		1.7	3.5	5.0	4.5	4.6	9.0
-1.3	.0	.8		-.2	.4	1.0	.5	2.3	4.8
132.3	172.4	152.5	Sales/Net Fixed Assets	UND	411.5	229.7	169.9	83.1	110.4
31.6	36.2	49.8		55.1	34.4	49.8	68.4	45.1	51.3
11.5	10.9	12.9		2.9	6.3	13.0	13.3	26.3	28.4
.8	.7	.7	Sales/Total Assets	.6	.6	.6	.7	.6	.8
.4	.3	.4		.1	.2	.4	.4	.4	.6
.1	.1	.1		.1	.1	.1	.3	.2	.4
.6	.7	.4	% Depr., Dep., Amort./Sales	.7	.3	.5	.3	.4	.4
(261) 1.2	(207) 1.3	(191) .8		(21) 1.7	(34) 1.2	(19) .9	(41) .6	(41) .7	(35) .8
2.1	2.1	1.5		4.8	2.8	1.7	1.2	1.1	1.2
3.0	3.3	3.2	% Officers', Directors' Owners' Comp/Sales	6.8	4.1		2.1		
(86) 5.8	(78) 7.3	(60) 6.5		(13) 9.7	(13) 7.4		(14) 4.7		
12.3	14.2	14.0		21.0	16.6		9.5		
6505606M	3770623M	3996577M	Net Sales ($)	30323M	119152M	127278M	388447M	850889M	2480488M
12346643M	9464493M	10197336M	Total Assets ($)	252138M	653231M	674879M	1245928M	3117105M	4254055M

© RMA 2010

M = $ thousand   MM = $ million
See Pages 9 through 22 for Explanation of Ratios and Data

FINANCE—Secondary Market Financing NAICS 522294

Current Data Sorted by Assets | **Comparative Historical Data**

0-500M	500M-2MM	2-10MM	10-50MM	50-100MM	100-250MM	Type of Statement	20	21
			6	2	3	Unqualified	20	21
		2	1			Reviewed	3	2
	3	1	1			Compiled	2	4
	1	4	1			Tax Returns	1	9
2	1	2	3	4		Other	8	6
	8 (4/1-9/30/09)		27 (10/1/09-3/31/10)				4/1/05-3/31/06 ALL	4/1/06-3/31/07 ALL
2	4	9	11	6	3	NUMBER OF STATEMENTS	34	42
%	%	%	%	%	%		%	%
						ASSETS		
			13.5			Cash & Equivalents	24.2	18.0
			47.4			Trade Receivables (net)	29.4	37.5
			.0			Inventory	8.4	.7
			7.6			All Other Current	5.3	8.3
			68.5			Total Current	67.3	64.4
			.8			Fixed Assets (net)	17.1	21.7
			1.3			Intangibles (net)	1.3	.5
			29.4			All Other Non-Current	14.3	13.4
			100.0			Total	100.0	100.0
						LIABILITIES		
			29.6			Notes Payable-Short Term	21.1	21.3
			7.7			Cur. Mat.-L.T.D.	4.2	1.4
			1.6			Trade Payables	5.8	4.7
			.0			Income Taxes Payable	.0	.1
			6.8			All Other Current	8.1	7.0
			45.7			Total Current	39.3	34.6
			11.9			Long-Term Debt	15.9	23.6
			.0			Deferred Taxes	.0	.0
			3.5			All Other Non-Current	5.6	5.4
			38.9			Net Worth	39.1	36.4
			100.0			Total Liabilities & Net Worth	100.0	100.0
						INCOME DATA		
			100.0			Net Sales	100.0	100.0
						Gross Profit		
			64.0			Operating Expenses	76.1	64.5
			36.0			Operating Profit	23.9	35.5
			15.4			All Other Expenses (net)	9.7	16.9
			20.6			Profit Before Taxes	14.2	18.6
						RATIOS		
			9.7			Current	3.9	4.0
			1.5				1.8	1.8
			1.2				1.1	1.2
			3.9			Quick	3.9	3.9
			1.5				1.1	1.8
			1.1				.4	1.1
		26	14.0			Sales/Receivables	2 161.6	0 UND
		871	.4				24 15.3	32 11.6
		2000	.2				446 .8	1139 .3
						Cost of Sales/Inventory		
						Cost of Sales/Payables		
			.4			Sales/Working Capital	.7	.5
			1.5				6.6	2.5
			7.8				116.6	32.2
						EBIT/Interest	(20) 9.1	(18) 8.2
							4.1	4.5
							1.8	1.4
						Net Profit + Depr., Dep., Amort./Cur. Mat. L/T/D		
			.0			Fixed/Worth	.0	.0
			.0				.1	.1
			.0				1.3	1.5
			.2			Debt/Worth	.5	.8
			1.5				1.4	2.1
			7.9				7.8	17.1
						% Profit Before Taxes/Tangible Net Worth	(32) 42.7	(40) 48.7
							18.7	15.5
							7.8	7.8
			6.3			% Profit Before Taxes/Total Assets	10.0	9.9
			3.4				5.6	4.2
			.5				1.0	1.3
			UND			Sales/Net Fixed Assets	UND	UND
			999.8				50.1	29.3
			52.6				4.2	3.0
			.4			Sales/Total Assets	2.1	.8
			.2				.8	.3
			.1				.2	.1
						% Depr., Dep., Amort./Sales	(16) .7	(22) .7
							1.9	1.6
							3.9	4.2
						% Officers', Directors' Owners' Comp/Sales		1.5
								(11) 4.5
								13.1
3253M	26274M	20517M	63186M	100512M	131229M	Net Sales ($)	1068881M	607890M
386M	4090M	38840M	231445M	353836M	428975M	Total Assets ($)	925355M	1022169M

M = $ thousand   MM = $ million

See Pages 9 through 22 for Explanation of Ratios and Data

Comparative Historical Data   Current Data Sorted by Sales

			Type of Statement						
18	11	11	Unqualified	1	1	2	4	2	1
3	3	2	Reviewed		2				
1		2	Compiled		1				
5	5	8	Tax Returns	1		2	1		
8	9	12	Other	5	1	2	2	3	2
4/1/07-3/31/08 ALL	4/1/08-3/31/09 ALL	4/1/09-3/31/10 ALL		0-1MM	1-3MM 8 (4/1-9/30/09)	3-5MM	5-10MM	10-25MM 27 (10/1/09-3/31/10)	25MM & OVER
35	28	35	NUMBER OF STATEMENTS	8	5	7	7	5	3
%	%	%		%	%	%	%	%	%
			ASSETS						
16.5	12.3	15.3	Cash & Equivalents						
34.6	36.9	38.6	Trade Receivables (net)						
.3	1.4	2.1	Inventory						
10.6	12.5	7.4	All Other Current						
62.0	63.2	63.4	Total Current						
20.0	11.7	9.9	Fixed Assets (net)						
.6	1.0	2.7	Intangibles (net)						
17.3	24.1	23.9	All Other Non-Current						
100.0	100.0	100.0	Total						
			LIABILITIES						
19.7	23.0	24.0	Notes Payable-Short Term						
5.8	4.7	8.4	Cur. Mat.-L.T.D.						
3.1	1.7	4.3	Trade Payables						
.0	.0	.0	Income Taxes Payable						
4.8	7.0	11.5	All Other Current						
33.3	36.5	48.2	Total Current						
22.0	24.3	17.5	Long-Term Debt						
.0	.1	.0	Deferred Taxes						
8.2	6.6	11.1	All Other Non-Current						
36.5	32.6	23.1	Net Worth						
100.0	100.0	100.0	Total Liabilties & Net Worth						
			INCOME DATA						
100.0	100.0	100.0	Net Sales						
			Gross Profit						
65.1	61.6	72.8	Operating Expenses						
34.9	38.4	27.2	Operating Profit						
17.2	19.9	17.5	All Other Expenses (net)						
17.8	18.5	9.7	Profit Before Taxes						
			RATIOS						
4.7	5.5	4.5	Current						
2.0	2.0	1.4							
1.2	.9	1.1							
3.3	4.0	2.9	Quick						
1.8	1.5	1.4							
1.2	.7	.9							
2 209.0	3 107.5	9 40.8	Sales/Receivables						
63 5.8	528 .7	173 2.1							
1325 .3	1497 .2	1579 .2							
			Cost of Sales/Inventory						
			Cost of Sales/Payables						
.7	.4	.7	Sales/Working Capital						
1.6	.8	2.1							
4.7	NM	14.8							
8.2	4.0	6.4	EBIT/Interest						
(14) 3.2	(13) 2.1	(19) 2.8							
1.3	1.1	1.5							
			Net Profit + Depr., Dep., Amort./Cur. Mat. L/T/D						
.0	.0	.0	Fixed/Worth						
.1	.0	.0							
.8	.9	.6							
.4	.8	.7	Debt/Worth						
3.1	2.9	5.4							
12.2	10.1	43.6							
44.5	16.7	31.1	% Profit Before Taxes/Tangible Net Worth						
(32) 14.8	(26) 9.7	(27) 8.5							
8.8	4.6	-1.1							
11.7	7.6	3.8	% Profit Before Taxes/Total Assets						
5.0	3.1	1.6							
.8	.4	-.6							
UND	UND	UND	Sales/Net Fixed Assets						
35.1	86.7	106.2							
2.8	7.9	10.3							
.8	.3	.7	Sales/Total Assets						
.3	.2	.3							
.1	.1	.1							
.9	.6	1.0	% Depr., Dep., Amort./Sales						
(16) 3.2	(14) 2.0	(17) 1.5							
5.5	4.9	7.5							
			% Officers', Directors' Owners' Comp/Sales						
517597M	211105M	344971M	Net Sales ($)	3750M	9132M	26864M	49072M	83618M	172535M
1133106M	1029680M	1057572M	Total Assets ($)	43819M	54633M	165977M	161864M	377351M	253928M

M = $ thousand   MM = $ million
See Pages 9 through 22 for Explanation of Ratios and Data

Current Data Sorted by Assets   Comparative Historical Data

Type of Statement

0-500M	500M-2MM	2-10MM	10-50MM	50-100MM	100-250MM	Type of Statement		
1	2	22	66	22	21	Unqualified	103	122
	1	17	9	1		Reviewed	26	33
1	3	8	1		1	Compiled	16	26
						Tax Returns	22	28
5	15	7	3	1		Other	116	89
5	12	36	44	12	13		4/1/05-3/31/06	4/1/06-3/31/07
	44 (4/1-9/30/09)		285 (10/1/09-3/31/10)				ALL	ALL
12	33	90	123	36	35	NUMBER OF STATEMENTS	283	298

ASSETS

0-500M %	500M-2MM %	2-10MM %	10-50MM %	50-100MM %	100-250MM %	ASSETS	ALL %	ALL %
26.0	18.6	11.8	8.9	6.1	5.9	Cash & Equivalents	8.4	9.6
35.0	32.0	48.5	53.0	65.5	46.3	Trade Receivables (net)	47.2	46.9
5.7	12.3	1.7	2.5	.8	3.0	Inventory	2.6	3.0
7.2	10.7	8.2	7.4	5.4	5.3	All Other Current	10.7	12.2
73.9	73.7	70.3	71.9	77.7	60.4	Total Current	68.9	71.7
8.4	10.1	10.7	8.7	3.8	5.1	Fixed Assets (net)	12.2	9.5
4.2	6.8	.5	2.6	3.0	5.8	Intangibles (net)	1.1	2.8
13.5	9.4	18.6	16.8	15.4	28.6	All Other Non-Current	17.7	16.1
100.0	100.0	100.0	100.0	100.0	100.0	Total	100.0	100.0

LIABILITIES

0-500M	500M-2MM	2-10MM	10-50MM	50-100MM	100-250MM	LIABILITIES	ALL	ALL
18.0	19.5	24.9	29.3	40.5	23.0	Notes Payable-Short Term	28.1	29.0
4.6	3.5	5.7	3.8	2.0	5.9	Cur. Mat.-L.T.D.	5.3	4.2
6.3	4.2	3.4	4.5	7.7	4.3	Trade Payables	3.9	4.3
.0	.0	.1	.3	.1	.2	Income Taxes Payable	.3	.2
27.8	8.5	9.6	8.7	5.6	5.5	All Other Current	8.7	11.2
56.7	35.8	43.8	46.6	55.9	38.9	Total Current	46.2	48.9
3.6	14.9	14.0	16.8	11.0	29.9	Long-Term Debt	20.3	17.7
.0	.2	.1	.2	.3	.9	Deferred Taxes	.3	.2
4.7	10.4	7.2	8.3	8.6	4.7	All Other Non-Current	8.2	8.8
35.0	38.7	34.9	28.0	24.4	25.7	Net Worth	25.0	24.5
100.0	100.0	100.0	100.0	100.0	100.0	Total Liabilities & Net Worth	100.0	100.0

INCOME DATA

0-500M	500M-2MM	2-10MM	10-50MM	50-100MM	100-250MM	INCOME DATA	ALL	ALL
100.0	100.0	100.0	100.0	100.0	100.0	Net Sales	100.0	100.0
						Gross Profit		
81.6	80.2	74.3	73.0	66.1	73.2	Operating Expenses	66.2	65.9
18.4	19.8	25.7	27.0	33.9	26.8	Operating Profit	33.8	34.1
5.1	3.4	10.8	10.2	13.9	9.5	All Other Expenses (net)	15.6	17.0
13.3	16.4	14.9	16.8	20.0	17.4	Profit Before Taxes	18.2	17.2

RATIOS

0-500M	500M-2MM	2-10MM	10-50MM	50-100MM	100-250MM	RATIOS	ALL	ALL
4.1	13.3	3.1	2.6	1.7	3.4	Current	2.9	2.6
1.6	3.2	1.4	1.4	1.4	1.5		1.4	1.4
.6	1.3	1.0	1.2	1.1	1.1		1.1	1.1
2.0	5.3	2.4	2.2	1.6	2.7	Quick	2.6	2.2
.9	2.1	1.3	1.4	1.3	1.3	(282)	1.3	1.2
.6	.7	.9	.8	1.0	.5		.5	.5
0 UND	0 UND	16 22.3	29 12.6	172 2.1	21 17.6	Sales/Receivables	8 45.6	5 77.8
23 15.9	33 10.9	494 .7	775 .5	1376 .3	406 .9		291 1.3	227 1.6
705 .5	188 1.9	1136 .3	1797 .2	2000 .2	1812 .2		1542 .2	1436 .3
						Cost of Sales/Inventory		
						Cost of Sales/Payables		
1.2	1.3	.6	.6	.5	.4	Sales/Working Capital	.5	.6
5.3	3.6	1.5	1.0	.8	2.5		1.4	1.8
-10.4	11.9	NM	6.4	2.7	14.1		16.9	12.2
	32.0	6.8	3.6	5.4	9.2	EBIT/Interest	5.4	6.0
(20)	5.5 (63)	2.4 (68)	2.2 (22)	2.9 (17)	3.2	(150)	2.9 (141)	2.5
	1.9	1.4	1.5	2.1	1.6		1.4	1.1
						Net Profit + Depr., Dep., Amort./Cur. Mat. L/T/D	4.1	3.1
						(26)	1.3 (22)	1.1
							.1	.3
.0	.0	.0	.0	.0	.0	Fixed/Worth	.0	.0
.0	.1	.0	.1	.0	.1		.0	.0
NM	1.4	.3	.4	.1	2.5		.5	.4
.5	.3	.9	1.7	2.3	1.9	Debt/Worth	1.8	1.7
1.5	2.5	2.4	3.3	3.8	3.8		3.7	4.0
-91.4	20.7	5.2	10.3	8.9	55.4		10.2	12.6
	104.6	28.0	30.3	43.0	36.2	% Profit Before Taxes/Tangible Net Worth	32.7	36.7
(28)	29.9 (83)	11.9 (115)	15.1 (35)	16.2 (28)	11.5	(263)	20.0 (261)	19.2
	10.5	3.0	5.3	8.1	3.0		7.7	7.2
18.1	26.8	7.7	5.2	7.0	6.0	% Profit Before Taxes/Total Assets	7.0	7.9
7.6	9.5	3.4	2.8	3.2	2.7		3.5	3.4
.3	2.5	.6	1.1	1.3			1.1	1.0
UND	UND	804.3	162.9	301.4	116.9	Sales/Net Fixed Assets	288.0	510.1
268.2	72.9	52.1	38.9	55.5	30.2		35.7	46.9
13.8	16.1	8.1	9.1	20.9	8.5		7.9	11.7
2.8	3.8	.7	.4	.3	.8	Sales/Total Assets	.5	.6
1.1	1.6	.3	.2	.2	.2		.2	.3
.3	.3	.2	.2	.1	.1		.1	.1
	.3	.9	.5	.5	.6	% Depr., Dep., Amort./Sales	.6	.7
(14)	1.4 (43)	1.2 (79)	1.4 (24)	1.4 (18)	1.3	(181)	1.4 (181)	1.3
	8.4	6.2	3.1	2.8	2.3		4.2	2.7
	3.2	8.7	2.8			% Officers', Directors' Owners' Comp/Sales	3.1	6.1
(15)	9.9 (24)	15.2 (18)	7.7			(44)	8.8 (54)	10.8
	20.1	23.0	22.9				17.7	25.2
7757M	102843M	271693M	1768057M	609702M	2491072M	Net Sales ($)	4405958M	3547200M
3675M	39467M	467204M	3103376M	2691864M	5244390M	Total Assets ($)	8214479M	8328532M

M = $ thousand   MM = $ million
See Pages 9 through 22 for Explanation of Ratios and Data

Comparative Historical Data

Current Data Sorted by Sales

				Type of Statement						
144		100	134	Unqualified	9	22	20	35	22	26
28		18	28	Reviewed	7	6	6	5	4	
15		19	14	Compiled	4	6	2	1	1	
27		20	31	Tax Returns	12	13	1	4	1	
107		84	122	Other	30	26	12	19	15	20
4/1/07-3/31/08 ALL		4/1/08-3/31/09 ALL	4/1/09-3/31/10 ALL		44 (4/1-9/30/09)			285 (10/1/09-3/31/10)		
					0-1MM	1-3MM	3-5MM	5-10MM	10-25MM	25MM & OVER
321		241	329	NUMBER OF STATEMENTS	62	73	41	64	43	46
%		%	%	ASSETS	%	%	%	%	%	%
8.8		8.6	10.7	Cash & Equivalents	12.7	9.4	12.9	8.4	9.6	12.2
53.7		50.6	49.7	Trade Receivables (net)	42.1	52.2	47.7	62.5	50.7	38.8
2.1		3.1	3.3	Inventory	3.9	4.2	2.8	1.2	1.4	5.9
10.1		9.0	7.5	All Other Current	10.1	5.8	6.8	6.1	9.8	7.1
74.7		71.3	71.1	Total Current	68.8	71.6	70.2	78.2	71.5	64.0
6.8		7.7	8.4	Fixed Assets (net)	9.0	7.5	6.5	10.3	8.3	8.5
1.7		2.9	2.9	Intangibles (net)	1.1	3.4	.4	2.0	1.0	9.8
16.8		18.0	17.5	All Other Non-Current	21.1	17.5	23.0	9.5	19.2	17.7
100.0		100.0	100.0	Total	100.0	100.0	100.0	100.0	100.0	100.0
				LIABILITIES						
32.5		30.7	27.3	Notes Payable-Short Term	26.5	27.2	28.9	28.3	30.4	22.5
3.6		3.3	4.3	Cur. Mat.-L.T.D.	4.2	5.3	2.2	4.3	7.6	2.0
5.1		4.2	4.6	Trade Payables	2.9	2.9	2.9	5.8	7.0	7.0
.1		.1	.2	Income Taxes Payable	.0	.1	.0	.1	.4	.5
7.5		8.5	9.0	All Other Current	8.6	8.0	8.8	8.8	7.8	12.4
48.7		46.8	45.3	Total Current	42.2	43.5	42.8	47.3	53.2	44.4
16.5		16.8	16.1	Long-Term Debt	12.6	16.1	18.3	14.6	14.4	22.8
.2		.1	.3	Deferred Taxes	.4	.1	.0	.3	.3	.7
9.0		7.3	7.7	All Other Non-Current	8.1	7.9	6.9	9.6	7.1	5.7
25.6		29.1	30.6	Net Worth	36.7	32.4	32.1	28.3	25.0	26.5
100.0		100.0	100.0	Total Liabilities & Net Worth	100.0	100.0	100.0	100.0	100.0	100.0
				INCOME DATA						
100.0		100.0	100.0	Net Sales	100.0	100.0	100.0	100.0	100.0	100.0
				Gross Profit						
65.8		72.4	73.7	Operating Expenses	63.8	74.0	74.0	77.2	71.4	83.5
34.2		27.6	26.3	Operating Profit	36.2	26.0	26.0	22.8	28.6	16.5
16.4		14.8	9.8	All Other Expenses (net)	13.0	10.5	8.9	7.9	11.8	5.9
17.8		12.9	16.5	Profit Before Taxes	23.2	15.6	17.0	14.9	16.8	10.7
				RATIOS						
2.5		3.1	3.1		3.4	3.7	3.3	3.8	1.6	2.6
1.5		1.5	1.5	Current	1.6	1.5	1.7	1.4	1.4	1.4
1.2		1.1	1.1		1.0	1.2	1.3	1.2	1.1	1.0
2.2		2.7	2.4		2.5	3.2	2.5	3.3	1.4	2.1
1.3		1.3	1.4	Quick	1.4	1.4	1.6	1.4	1.2	1.0
.8		.7	.8		.5	1.0	1.0	1.1	.5	.6
18 19.8	25 14.9	17 21.6		Sales/Receivables	0 UND	11 32.2	13 29.1	65 5.6	25 14.4	15 24.8
771 .5	502 .7	526 .7			695 .5	543 .7	351 1.0	1036 .4	514 .7	57 6.4
1725 .2	1526 .2	1439 .3			1414 .3	1559 .2	1600 .2	1806 .2	1806 .2	662 .6
				Cost of Sales/Inventory						
				Cost of Sales/Payables						
.5		.6	.6		.4	.6	.5	.5	.6	1.9
1.2		1.5	1.4	Sales/Working Capital	1.0	1.4	1.0	.9	1.5	7.5
7.0		16.6	10.8		-29.8	8.5	5.0	4.3	10.7	-33.5
6.2	6.0	5.7		EBIT/Interest	9.7	5.1	7.9	5.0	5.3	7.6
(133) 2.7	(110) 2.2	(196) 2.5			(30) 2.5	(48) 2.3	(23) 2.7	(40) 2.4	(24) 3.0	(31) 2.8
1.5	1.3	1.5			1.5	1.5	1.5	1.5	1.8	1.8
8.0	2.4	5.5		Net Profit + Depr., Dep., Amort./Cur. Mat. L/T/D						
(24) .9	(18) .3	(26) 2.1								
.4	.0	.1								
.0		.0	.0		.0	.0	.0	.0	.0	.1
.0		.0	.0	Fixed/Worth	.0	.0	.0	.0	.1	.3
.2		.4	.4		.4	.2	.1	.3	.5	NM
1.8		1.4	1.4		.5	1.1	.6	2.0	2.5	1.7
3.8		3.8	3.2	Debt/Worth	2.1	3.0	2.6	3.5	3.8	3.6
10.1		11.8	9.5		7.7	6.1	9.0	8.9	8.9	NM
34.4	27.7	33.0		% Profit Before Taxes/Tangible Net Worth	20.4	34.3	32.7	31.6	43.9	53.0
(294) 18.2	(213) 12.3	(297) 15.1			(54) 9.5	(68) 13.2	(37) 16.7	(61) 18.0	(42) 18.3	(35) 23.2
6.5	2.8	4.8			2.6	4.7	4.2	7.9	9.4	3.6
6.9		6.9	7.7	% Profit Before Taxes/Total Assets	5.6	7.0	6.9	5.6	9.8	11.9
3.3		2.3	3.2		3.2	3.0	2.8	3.2	4.2	4.6
1.2		.6	1.1		.7	.9	.7	1.3	1.1	.8
555.9		270.5	258.2	Sales/Net Fixed Assets	UND	396.0	459.0	186.8	113.4	75.1
54.1		43.1	45.0		90.8	59.9	48.8	50.2	33.8	27.9
13.9		14.4	11.3		7.3	13.2	18.4	16.3	11.4	10.6
.4		.7	.6	Sales/Total Assets	.4	.6	.5	.6	.5	1.9
.2		.3	.3		.2	.3	.2	.3	.2	.8
.1		.1	.2		.1	.2	.1	.2	.1	.4
.4	.5	.5		% Depr., Dep., Amort./Sales	1.0	.3	.6	.5	.7	.7
(180) 1.2	(139) 1.2	(185) 1.3			(25) 2.0	(38) 1.1	(21) 1.4	(41) 1.0	(32) 1.4	(28) 2.0
2.6	2.7	3.0			10.5	2.4	2.5	3.4	2.1	4.4
5.2	4.2	4.3		% Officers', Directors' Owners' Comp/Sales	8.6	4.9				
(63) 10.1	(41) 11.7	(64) 11.5			(20) 17.9	(20) 11.7				
19.9	17.9	20.0			27.6	18.0				
4687210M	4227075M	5251124M		Net Sales ($)	35783M	141794M	162315M	460334M	678114M	3772784M
12510136M	9168676M	11549976M		Total Assets ($)	290576M	662271M	1010460M	2006089M	3061808M	4518772M

M = $ thousand   MM = $ million
See Pages 9 through 22 for Explanation of Ratios and Data

Current Data Sorted by Assets   Comparative Historical Data

Column period annotations: **25 (4/1-9/30/09)** applies to the 500M-2MM range; **186 (10/1/09-3/31/10)** applies to the 10-50MM / 50-100MM range.

0-500M	500M-2MM	2-10MM	10-50MM	50-100MM	100-250MM	Type of Statement	4/1/05-3/31/06 ALL	4/1/06-3/31/07 ALL
5	7	32	37	13	11	Unqualified	86	105
	2	2	2	1		Reviewed	9	4
1	2	2	1			Compiled	13	16
9	7	5				Tax Returns	42	31
11	11	12	19	10	11	Other	62	81
26	27	53	59	24	22	NUMBER OF STATEMENTS	212	237
%	%	%	%	%	%	**ASSETS**	%	%
47.2	26.0	17.7	9.9	11.1	5.0	Cash & Equivalents	23.7	24.2
2.8	12.0	21.7	33.4	44.8	43.6	Trade Receivables (net)	19.0	22.8
.0	6.5	10.6	19.1	3.8	4.8	Inventory	4.7	5.5
11.6	13.2	18.0	18.1	17.3	9.2	All Other Current	19.7	15.6
61.6	57.7	68.0	80.5	77.0	62.5	Total Current	67.1	68.2
15.5	21.1	9.8	3.5	3.2	1.5	Fixed Assets (net)	15.0	14.0
2.9	.6	1.3	3.1	.6	1.0	Intangibles (net)	1.1	2.4
20.0	20.6	20.9	12.9	19.3	35.0	All Other Non-Current	16.7	15.3
100.0	100.0	100.0	100.0	100.0	100.0	Total	100.0	100.0
						LIABILITIES		
41.2	26.8	39.6	56.2	42.9	33.0	Notes Payable-Short Term	29.4	35.7
4.5	3.6	1.5	.4	3.9	2.4	Cur. Mat.-L.T.D.	2.4	1.9
6.5	3.4	2.0	5.4	3.3	2.1	Trade Payables	4.1	3.7
.0	.0	.2	.2	.2	.1	Income Taxes Payable	.2	.7
18.5	9.2	13.5	5.5	3.5	9.0	All Other Current	9.7	10.7
70.8	43.0	56.7	67.6	53.8	46.6	Total Current	45.6	52.7
7.2	16.3	8.9	6.9	6.9	21.7	Long-Term Debt	13.1	10.6
.0	.0	.1	.0	.1	.0	Deferred Taxes	.2	.1
2.5	.8	1.0	4.6	6.9	8.5	All Other Non-Current	4.4	3.2
19.5	39.9	33.2	20.9	32.2	23.3	Net Worth	36.7	33.3
100.0	100.0	100.0	100.0	100.0	100.0	Total Liabilities & Net Worth	100.0	100.0
						INCOME DATA		
100.0	100.0	100.0	100.0	100.0	100.0	Net Sales	100.0	100.0
						Gross Profit		
92.9	85.0	76.4	79.6	75.2	69.9	Operating Expenses	82.4	82.3
7.1	15.0	23.6	20.4	24.8	30.1	Operating Profit	17.6	17.7
1.3	6.1	10.4	8.0	6.8	16.1	All Other Expenses (net)	4.9	6.7
5.8	9.0	13.2	12.3	17.9	14.0	Profit Before Taxes	12.8	11.0
						RATIOS		
6.2	6.6	1.8	1.4	1.8	2.1	Current	3.1	2.6
1.3	1.2	1.2	1.1	1.4	1.4		1.4	1.2
.5	.5	1.0	1.0	1.2	1.1		1.0	1.0
4.5	5.3	1.4	1.1	1.5	1.6	Quick	2.7	2.4
1.1	.8	.8	.5	1.3	1.3		1.1	1.0
.4	.2	.1	.1	.5	.1		.2	.3
0 UND	0 UND	0 UND	3 108.7	4 98.4	5 79.1	Sales/Receivables	0 UND	0 UND
0 UND	2 240.8	13 27.9	25 14.4	333 1.1	259 1.4		6 60.5	8 44.8
2 200.9	23 15.6	82 4.5	835 .4	1245 .3	1010 .4		70 5.2	110 3.3
						Cost of Sales/Inventory		
						Cost of Sales/Payables		
6.4	2.3	2.4	1.5	.9	.8	Sales/Working Capital	2.4	3.1
38.8	10.4	5.1	6.4	1.8	2.2		8.3	11.0
-21.3	-11.6	-197.6	15.7	4.0	NM		71.8	-155.0
	59.1	13.2	5.7	3.6	6.4	EBIT/Interest	7.9	10.6
	(18) 6.9	(38) 3.7	(35) 2.9	(18) 2.8	(15) 2.7		(138) 2.8	(161) 1.8
	1.9	2.0	2.1	2.1	1.4		1.3	.7
						Net Profit + Depr., Dep., Amort./Cur. Mat. L/T/D	2.5	15.4
				(18) .5			.5	(14) 2.0
							-.1	-1.6
.0	.0	.0	.0	.0	.0	Fixed/Worth	.0	.0
.1	.2	.0	.1	.0	.0		.2	.2
UND	.7	.2	.5	.1	.3		.7	.9
.2	.3	1.0	2.9	1.3	1.8	Debt/Worth	.6	.7
.4	2.4	3.3	4.4	2.6	4.5		2.4	3.0
-8.2	5.2	8.7	8.8	5.2	9.9		7.0	8.1
171.7	57.7	62.3	67.3	35.7	32.0	% Profit Before Taxes/Tangible Net Worth	64.4	56.4
(19) 43.9	(25) 21.7	(49) 23.9	(55) 26.8	(21) 15.7	13.3		(201) 26.4	(222) 16.2
-21.2	.7	6.8	6.8	9.2	3.0		5.6	-2.1
78.3	33.5	12.3	8.9	8.5	8.6	% Profit Before Taxes/Total Assets	19.6	16.7
20.9	6.3	4.4	4.8	4.7	1.7		6.2	4.0
-24.5	.3	1.9	1.1	2.7	.5		1.2	-.6
UND	999.8	437.4	80.7	101.9	390.3	Sales/Net Fixed Assets	84.6	105.7
73.3	28.1	53.2	39.3	54.9	67.9		29.3	33.3
16.9	5.7	11.1	17.7	19.5	20.9		10.7	12.3
7.5	2.3	1.1	.6	.7	.4	Sales/Total Assets	3.7	3.6
4.0	1.2	.4	.4	.3	.3		1.1	.9
2.6	.6	.2	.2	.2	.1		.3	.4
.5	.4	.3	.5	.5	.5	% Depr., Dep., Amort./Sales	.5	.5
(13) 1.3	(16) 1.1	(38) .7	(43) 1.1	(17) .6	(11) .8		(152) 1.0	(156) 1.1
2.4	2.3	1.6	1.6	1.7	1.8		1.9	1.8
						% Officers', Directors' Owners' Comp/Sales	3.9	2.7
							(59) 7.7	(65) 9.5
							16.9	13.8
20959M	44261M	189794M	1026768M	963600M	1220017M	Net Sales ($)	5790103M	7974664M
4650M	30000M	298105M	1477085M	1698462M	3572063M	Total Assets ($)	3708835M	4290025M

M = $ thousand   MM = $ million
See Pages 9 through 22 for Explanation of Ratios and Data

Comparative Historical Data | Current Data Sorted by Sales

Type of Statement

4/1/07-3/31/08 ALL	4/1/08-3/31/09 ALL	4/1/09-3/31/10 ALL	Type of Statement	0-1MM	1-3MM	3-5MM	5-10MM	10-25MM	25MM & OVER
108	106	105	Unqualified	10	24	6	30	14	21
8	5	5	Reviewed		2	1		1	1
17	11	6	Compiled	2	2	1			1
22	21	21	Tax Returns	13	6	1	1		
53	68	74	Other	16	15	8	7	15	13
				25 (4/1-9/30/09)			186 (10/1/09-3/31/10)		
208	211	211	NUMBER OF STATEMENTS	41	49	17	38	30	36

ASSETS (%)

4/1/07-3/31/08	4/1/08-3/31/09	4/1/09-3/31/10	Item	0-1MM	1-3MM	3-5MM	5-10MM	10-25MM	25MM & OVER
15.5	15.7	18.1	Cash & Equivalents	31.2	25.3	14.0	9.6	4.2	16.1
22.7	20.1	26.3	Trade Receivables (net)	6.8	21.8	23.4	33.3	44.2	33.9
6.5	8.9	9.8	Inventory	1.6	8.0	13.2	14.1	12.2	13.2
22.7	18.1	15.6	All Other Current	11.8	18.6	10.7	16.9	17.2	15.5
67.5	62.8	69.8	Total Current	51.4	73.7	61.3	73.9	77.7	78.7
13.2	12.3	8.6	Fixed Assets (net)	20.0	7.0	15.8	3.7	3.0	4.2
2.0	2.5	1.8	Intangibles (net)	1.8	.6	.3	3.9	.3	3.1
17.4	22.3	19.8	All Other Non-Current	26.8	18.7	22.6	18.6	18.9	14.0
100.0	100.0	100.0	Total	100.0	100.0	100.0	100.0	100.0	100.0

LIABILITIES

4/1/07-3/31/08	4/1/08-3/31/09	4/1/09-3/31/10	Item	0-1MM	1-3MM	3-5MM	5-10MM	10-25MM	25MM & OVER
37.6	41.4	42.5	Notes Payable-Short Term	39.6	37.0	36.0	52.4	55.4	35.0
2.7	2.9	2.2	Cur. Mat.-L.T.D.	2.1	2.9	3.7	.5	2.6	2.0
3.3	3.3	3.9	Trade Payables	3.3	4.4	3.3	1.4	3.3	7.1
.1	.1	.1	Income Taxes Payable	.0	.1	.0	.2	.0	.3
10.4	8.8	9.7	All Other Current	10.1	17.4	3.8	3.8	5.4	11.5
54.1	56.5	58.4	Total Current	55.1	61.8	46.7	58.3	66.7	56.0
12.7	14.4	10.2	Long-Term Debt	14.9	7.0	17.6	11.3	9.3	5.3
.1	.1	.1	Deferred Taxes	.0	.0	.0	.2	.0	.1
3.8	3.0	3.6	All Other Non-Current	2.2	2.0	1.1	5.3	5.3	5.5
29.2	26.0	27.8	Net Worth	27.9	29.2	34.6	24.9	18.7	33.1
100.0	100.0	100.0	Total Liabilities & Net Worth	100.0	100.0	100.0	100.0	100.0	100.0

INCOME DATA

4/1/07-3/31/08	4/1/08-3/31/09	4/1/09-3/31/10	Item	0-1MM	1-3MM	3-5MM	5-10MM	10-25MM	25MM & OVER
100.0	100.0	100.0	Net Sales	100.0	100.0	100.0	100.0	100.0	100.0
			Gross Profit						
83.8	83.4	79.6	Operating Expenses	81.5	81.9	74.1	78.0	76.2	81.6
16.2	16.6	20.4	Operating Profit	18.5	18.1	25.9	22.0	23.8	18.4
8.0	7.9	8.3	All Other Expenses (net)	12.7	5.9	8.6	9.4	9.5	3.9
8.2	8.7	12.1	Profit Before Taxes	5.8	12.2	17.3	12.5	14.3	14.5

RATIOS

4/1/07-3/31/08	4/1/08-3/31/09	4/1/09-3/31/10	Item	0-1MM	1-3MM	3-5MM	5-10MM	10-25MM	25MM & OVER
1.7	2.0	2.0	Current	9.2	1.8	2.7	1.8	1.4	2.0
1.2	1.1	1.2		1.3	1.1	1.1	1.1	1.2	1.3
1.0	.9	1.0		.2	1.0	1.0	1.0	1.0	1.1
1.3	1.5	1.5	Quick	6.9	1.4	2.6	1.3	1.4	1.5
.8	.5	.9		1.0	1.0	.8	.8	.9	1.0
.1	.1	.1		.1	.2	.2	.1	.1	.2
0 UND	0 UND	0 UND	Sales/Receivables	0 UND	0 UND	0 UND	9 41.2	6 58.3	3 109.2
9 41.0	6 59.0	13 28.2		0 UND	3 128.6	2 160.2	35 10.4	344 1.1	35 10.5
206 1.8	132 2.8	403 .9		13 27.4	245 1.5	394 .9	807 .5	1205 .3	477 .8
			Cost of Sales/Inventory						
			Cost of Sales/Payables						
1.8	1.9	1.8	Sales/Working Capital	1.9	1.9	1.7	1.2	1.1	1.8
6.5	9.4	6.1		7.9	6.2	11.6	5.3	3.8	4.8
69.0	-15.2	269.0		-2.4	NM	NM	16.2	15.6	13.5
6.2	5.0	8.8	EBIT/Interest	13.1	10.3	16.5	7.5	5.5	8.1
(133) 1.8	(135) 2.0	(132) 3.3		(15) 3.7	(30) 2.8	(11) 5.7	(25) 2.9	(19) 2.9	(32) 3.4
.5	.8	2.0		1.3	1.8	3.5	2.0	2.0	2.1
14.2			Net Profit + Depr., Dep., Amort./Cur. Mat. L/T/D						
(13) 1.0									
-1.1									
.0	.0	.0	Fixed/Worth	.0	.0	.0	.0	.0	.0
.1	.1	.1		.1	.0	.1	.1	.1	.1
.5	.6	.4		5.1	.3	1.1	.3	.3	.3
1.4	1.2	1.3	Debt/Worth	.1	1.0	1.7	2.4	3.4	1.2
3.8	4.4	3.3		2.4	2.4	3.1	5.2	5.1	2.8
8.5	10.2	7.6		UND	6.7	4.3	8.8	9.1	7.1
38.0	37.5	57.7	% Profit Before Taxes/Tangible Net Worth	40.2	46.3	73.0	65.7	67.1	62.4
(199) 9.7	(192) 11.9	(193) 21.1		(32) 3.7	(45) 16.1	32.0	(36) 24.3	28.0	(33) 31.8
-4.6	.1	6.8		-5.6	6.7	8.5	8.6	10.7	9.4
7.4	6.9	11.6	% Profit Before Taxes/Total Assets	14.3	11.0	22.3	9.6	8.8	18.7
1.9	2.4	4.9		.9	4.4	8.1	4.0	5.0	7.5
-.8	-.2	1.1		-2.7	2.2	2.0	.9	1.5	3.1
98.1	163.6	257.2	Sales/Net Fixed Assets	UND	343.8	526.7	150.5	81.8	128.8
28.0	43.3	48.3		33.3	75.7	27.6	49.2	36.4	56.3
8.3	10.6	14.9		4.5	21.3	4.4	24.9	11.5	21.9
1.4	1.5	1.5	Sales/Total Assets	2.9	2.2	1.7	.6	.5	1.7
.5	.5	.5		.7	.7	.4	.4	.3	.7
.2	.2	.2		.1	.2	.2	.2	.2	.4
.6	.5	.5	% Depr., Dep., Amort./Sales	1.1	.2	.5	.4	.4	.5
(145) 1.3	(136) 1.1	(138) .9		(18) 2.3	(35) .5	(12) 1.3	(27) 1.2	(22) .8	(24) .8
2.1	2.2	1.7		4.7	1.0	1.7	1.6	1.2	2.3
4.1	5.8	6.6	% Officers', Directors' Owners' Comp/Sales		8.4				
(45) 10.4	(46) 9.0	(33) 14.9			(13) 13.7				
28.8	17.4	26.0			29.5				
2167591M	1552604M	3465399M	Net Sales ($)	20321M	93882M	64113M	268028M	443529M	2575526M
4444657M	4196594M	7080365M	Total Assets ($)	82361M	245557M	309765M	1058312M	1793514M	3590856M

M = $ thousand   MM = $ million
See Pages 9 through 22 for Explanation of Ratios and Data

Current Data Sorted by Assets   Comparative Historical Data

Type of Statement

Type of Statement	0-500M	500M-2MM	2-10MM	10-50MM	50-100MM	100-250MM	4/1/05-3/31/06 ALL	4/1/06-3/31/07 ALL
Unqualified	2	2	7	13	10	8	11	15
Reviewed		1	2				2	5
Compiled		1		1			1	2
Tax Returns	2	1					3	
Other	2	8	14	12	3	7	18	21

Period groupings: 10 (4/1-9/30/09)   88 (10/1/09-3/31/10)

	0-500M	500M-2MM	2-10MM	10-50MM	50-100MM	100-250MM	4/1/05-3/31/06 ALL	4/1/06-3/31/07 ALL
NUMBER OF STATEMENTS	6	13	25	26	13	15	35	43
	%	%	%	%	%	%	%	%
ASSETS								
Cash & Equivalents		36.9	31.1	33.0	16.7	15.1	32.9	36.1
Trade Receivables (net)		5.0	14.4	26.7	6.7	20.0	22.3	18.0
Inventory		5.3	.3	1.6	6.9	.2	.7	1.8
All Other Current		6.8	16.4	4.5	12.3	17.9	10.1	14.1
Total Current		54.1	62.1	65.9	42.6	53.2	66.0	70.0
Fixed Assets (net)		36.2	16.7	12.2	6.5	6.9	8.5	16.7
Intangibles (net)		7.5	8.9	12.8	46.1	27.5	11.3	3.7
All Other Non-Current		2.1	12.3	9.1	4.8	12.3	14.1	9.6
Total		100.0	100.0	100.0	100.0	100.0	100.0	100.0
LIABILITIES								
Notes Payable-Short Term		12.5	10.6	4.2	7.8	2.4	6.1	11.1
Cur. Mat.-L.T.D.		7.3	3.6	7.2	3.8	4.0	2.5	3.9
Trade Payables		9.0	11.2	18.7	14.1	20.7	11.7	10.8
Income Taxes Payable		.0	1.0	.3	.9	.1	.7	.9
All Other Current		16.3	19.4	19.7	17.5	22.8	20.4	24.4
Total Current		45.1	45.8	50.1	44.1	50.1	41.4	51.1
Long-Term Debt		47.2	14.1	16.3	20.5	14.8	24.2	22.5
Deferred Taxes		.0	.5	.3	.7	1.6	.4	.1
All Other Non-Current		3.5	11.4	2.6	6.5	3.7	5.6	3.3
Net Worth		4.2	28.2	30.8	28.2	29.9	28.5	23.0
Total Liabilities & Net Worth		100.0	100.0	100.0	100.0	100.0	100.0	100.0
INCOME DATA								
Net Sales		100.0	100.0	100.0	100.0	100.0	100.0	100.0
Gross Profit								
Operating Expenses		95.3	91.7	83.4	92.4	91.2	88.2	89.4
Operating Profit		4.7	8.3	16.6	7.6	8.8	11.8	10.6
All Other Expenses (net)		4.6	2.7	3.2	3.3	.7	2.6	4.4
Profit Before Taxes		.1	5.5	13.5	4.4	8.1	9.2	6.1
RATIOS								
Current		3.7	1.8	1.7	1.5	1.2	3.1	4.1
		2.6	1.3	1.2	.9	1.1	1.5	1.2
		.4	1.0	1.0	.7	.8	1.0	1.0
Quick		3.6	1.4	1.6	.9	1.1	2.8	1.7
		1.1	1.0	1.1	.5	.8	1.2	1.1
		.3	.5	.6	.3	.5	.9	.7
Sales/Receivables		0 UND	4 103.2	25 14.5	7 49.3	14 26.8	3 107.9	2 211.7
		4 91.8	16 23.2	51 7.2	11 32.0	31 11.8	41 8.9	30 12.1
		11 34.6	42 8.6	98 3.7	36 10.1	78 4.7	85 4.3	73 5.0
Cost of Sales/Inventory								
Cost of Sales/Payables								
Sales/Working Capital		2.8	8.3	2.4	3.6	7.4	3.2	3.1
		8.9	19.0	9.9	-75.6	17.0	6.0	9.0
		-4.5	NM	-41.5	-9.5	-27.1	72.8	-354.3
EBIT/Interest			84.3	23.4	15.4	11.4	34.0	13.0
			(21) 2.7	(14) 6.1	(11) 2.1	(11) 7.8	(29) 7.7	(27) 2.8
			-2.7	.9	-2.1	3.5	1.4	1.0
Net Profit + Depr., Dep., Amort./Cur. Mat. L/T/D								26.5
								(11) 16.9
								2.8
Fixed/Worth		.1	.1	.1	.2	.3	.1	.1
		1.7	.5	.4	-3.3	1.3	.2	.4
		-2.8	1.5	-5.1	-.2	-.5	.9	1.3
Debt/Worth		.9	.8	.9	4.3	4.1	.6	.7
		2.6	2.5	4.8	-10.4	15.0	2.7	2.9
		-4.9	5.6	-17.0	-1.5	-3.2	10.6	7.0
% Profit Before Taxes/Tangible Net Worth			123.4	49.5		120.9	84.3	49.5
			(21) 36.0	(19) 34.1		(10) 29.8	(29) 45.3	(35) 15.1
			-1.7	12.3		5.6	11.4	3.3
% Profit Before Taxes/Total Assets		22.2	24.7	32.0	12.1	14.7	23.4	14.1
		-.5	9.4	6.7	1.4	6.1	11.3	3.5
		-9.1	-3.0	.8	-19.2	1.8	2.7	.3
Sales/Net Fixed Assets		61.9	99.3	88.8	36.4	27.1	36.8	35.6
		11.0	22.2	17.8	15.6	16.1	22.2	13.1
		3.1	7.7	5.2	5.6	8.8	10.9	5.7
Sales/Total Assets		4.0	2.7	1.7	1.6	1.9	2.1	2.1
		2.0	2.1	1.0	.7	1.1	1.2	1.4
		.8	1.2	.5	.4	.5	.7	.6
% Depr., Dep., Amort./Sales			.6	.9		1.9	1.6	1.2
			(17) 2.1	(18) 2.5		(10) 2.7	(26) 2.5	(31) 2.2
			4.2	4.6		5.3	4.6	5.0
% Officers', Directors' Owners' Comp/Sales								1.6
								(16) 3.4
								12.9
Net Sales ($)	6675M	45287M	351149M	764249M	940450M	2429866M	2354444M	1337000M
Total Assets ($)	972M	15055M	135382M	593442M	992277M	2401779M	1609309M	1401507M

© RMA 2010

M = $ thousand   MM = $ million

See Pages 9 through 22 for Explanation of Ratios and Data

Comparative Historical Data | Current Data Sorted by Sales

Type of Statement	4/1/07-3/31/08 ALL	4/1/08-3/31/09 ALL	4/1/09-3/31/10 ALL	0-1MM	1-3MM	3-5MM	5-10MM	10-25MM	25MM & OVER
Unqualified	28	46	42	2	2	3	3	8	24
Reviewed	2	3	3	1	1			1	
Compiled	4	8	2					1	
Tax Returns	1	11	5					1	1
Other	36	49	46	2	1		1	1	14
				5	3	3	11	10	14
				\(\)10 (4/1-9/30/09)			88 (10/1/09-3/31/10)		
NUMBER OF STATEMENTS	71	117	98	10	7	6	15	21	39
	%	%	%	%	%	%	%	%	%
ASSETS									
Cash & Equivalents	29.2	32.3	27.6	32.0			32.0	32.9	20.0
Trade Receivables (net)	19.5	24.0	15.9	8.9			17.0	14.0	17.2
Inventory	2.4	1.7	2.2	.0			2.3	1.7	2.7
All Other Current	7.4	8.8	12.4	16.8			10.4	9.6	15.4
Total Current	58.5	66.8	58.0	57.6			61.7	58.1	55.3
Fixed Assets (net)	18.1	13.7	15.6	14.0			20.4	18.9	8.5
Intangibles (net)	10.7	9.8	17.6	5.8			12.7	13.2	28.2
All Other Non-Current	12.7	9.7	8.8	22.6			5.1	9.8	8.0
Total	100.0	100.0	100.0	100.0			100.0	100.0	100.0
LIABILITIES									
Notes Payable-Short Term	10.0	13.6	8.4	13.6			8.3	4.9	4.1
Cur. Mat.-L.T.D.	3.6	5.0	5.8	.2			5.2	2.8	7.1
Trade Payables	12.4	11.4	15.3	3.8			21.4	11.5	16.6
Income Taxes Payable	.3	.5	.5	.0			.0	.9	.7
All Other Current	18.2	22.9	18.9	15.9			20.2	18.5	21.8
Total Current	44.5	53.3	48.9	33.5			55.2	38.6	50.3
Long-Term Debt	24.0	16.7	19.6	16.2			26.6	9.5	18.2
Deferred Taxes	.3	.1	.5	.6			.6	.2	.8
All Other Non-Current	7.3	7.3	6.6	13.8			17.1	1.5	4.7
Net Worth	23.8	22.6	24.3	35.9			.6	50.2	26.0
Total Liabilities & Net Worth	100.0	100.0	100.0	100.0			100.0	100.0	100.0
INCOME DATA									
Net Sales	100.0	100.0	100.0	100.0			100.0	100.0	100.0
Gross Profit									
Operating Expenses	91.7	87.1	90.2	88.8			96.3	87.7	90.8
Operating Profit	8.3	12.9	9.8	11.2			3.7	12.3	9.2
All Other Expenses (net)	2.6	2.1	2.8	7.5			1.9	1.6	2.0
Profit Before Taxes	5.7	10.9	7.0	3.7			1.8	10.7	7.2
RATIOS									
Current	2.2	2.1	1.8	2.8			2.1	2.2	1.3
	1.2	1.3	1.2	1.6			1.1	1.4	1.0
	.9	1.0	.8	1.1			1.0	1.1	.8
Quick	1.9	1.9	1.5	2.6			1.5	1.9	1.1
	1.1	1.1	1.0	1.2			1.0	1.1	.6
	.7	.7	.5	.4			.6	.7	.4
Sales/Receivables	3 109.7	4 91.0	4 81.1	0 UND			4 85.6	5 80.4	10 35.8
	28 12.9	28 12.9	21 17.4	0 UND			31 11.6	16 22.2	29 12.5
	57 6.4	92 3.9	50 7.2	34 10.9			96 3.8	43 8.5	50 7.4
Cost of Sales/Inventory									
Cost of Sales/Payables									
Sales/Working Capital	4.7	2.7	5.3	2.4			5.9	3.9	13.2
	13.8	8.8	17.0	11.2			8.6	11.1	-999.8
	-104.7	-75.9	-29.0	NM			90.0	38.3	-15.6
EBIT/Interest	14.0	27.7	19.5					107.1	29.0
	(50) 2.7	(78) 4.9	(66) 3.3				(13) 3.4	(32) 6.1	
	.0	.9	-.7					-9.7	1.2
Net Profit + Depr., Dep., Amort./Cur. Mat. L/T/D	15.3	80.5	25.5						28.8
	(16) 6.7	(16) 13.9	(18) 4.7					(12) 5.0	
	1.6	2.0	1.7						1.6
Fixed/Worth	.2	.1	.1	.0			.2	.2	.2
	.6	.3	.6	.1			.9	.4	1.3
	23.5	NM	-1.0	.8			-4.6	1.1	-.3
Debt/Worth	.9	.9	1.1	.3			2.5	.4	2.7
	3.5	4.3	4.6	2.2			14.5	1.1	15.0
	-7.4	-12.1	-4.3	NM			-6.1	7.1	-2.7
% Profit Before Taxes/Tangible Net Worth	64.9	82.1	87.2					94.2	151.7
	(53) 22.0	(86) 25.4	(67) 34.0				(18) 33.5	(23) 44.7	
	-6.4	8.1	1.9					-5.4	11.0
% Profit Before Taxes/Total Assets	20.4	20.9	20.3	137.2			9.4	38.7	22.6
	8.1	5.8	5.4	6.7			1.5	5.9	9.6
	-2.4	1.1	-3.3	-4.0			-11.6	-5.8	1.4
Sales/Net Fixed Assets	45.9	82.0	57.7	UND			60.3	22.0	51.7
	15.4	25.9	15.9	75.8			9.4	10.2	19.8
	6.4	6.5	6.2	14.8			3.9	3.8	10.2
Sales/Total Assets	2.7	2.5	2.5	7.2			2.7	2.4	2.3
	1.7	1.4	1.3	.9			1.0	1.7	1.3
	.7	.5	.6	.2			.4	.8	.8
% Depr., Dep., Amort./Sales	1.4	.8	1.6					1.8	1.7
	(44) 2.1	(70) 2.4	(61) 3.1				(15) 2.4	(25) 3.9	
	5.5	4.3	5.1					4.9	5.1
% Officers', Directors' Owners' Comp/Sales	1.8	2.0	2.1						
	(17) 5.3	(24) 5.0	(22) 4.9						
	13.6	10.0	10.1						
Net Sales ($)	2924124M	4244305M	4537676M	5891M	13431M	25624M	112517M	324260M	4055953M
Total Assets ($)	2468796M	3939846M	4138907M	15030M	6006M	62168M	237604M	483487M	3334612M

M = $ thousand   MM = $ million
See Pages 9 through 22 for Explanation of Ratios and Data

Current Data Sorted by Assets   Comparative Historical Data

0-500M	500M-2MM	2-10MM	10-50MM	50-100MM	100-250MM	Type of Statement	4/1/05-3/31/06 ALL	4/1/06-3/31/07 ALL
22	50	24	17	1	10	Unqualified	27	33
	2	6	1			Reviewed	4	7
4	6		1			Compiled	6	14
8	10			1		Tax Returns	11	9
3	5	14	15	5	7	Other	43	32
	11 (4/1-9/30/09)		201 (10/1/09-3/31/10)					
37	73	44	34	7	17	NUMBER OF STATEMENTS	91	95
%	%	%	%	%	%	ASSETS	%	%
63.2	63.3	40.2	27.7		16.0	Cash & Equivalents	28.5	31.0
4.7	5.3	16.1	33.0		41.2	Trade Receivables (net)	23.4	26.9
.1	.3	2.2	1.0		5.5	Inventory	4.1	3.0
4.0	2.4	6.3	8.4		3.6	All Other Current	8.9	8.7
72.0	71.3	64.9	70.1		66.3	Total Current	64.9	69.6
16.4	16.6	13.3	8.4		9.3	Fixed Assets (net)	12.6	12.1
3.1	5.1	13.1	8.9		15.4	Intangibles (net)	7.2	4.0
8.4	7.1	8.7	12.6		9.0	All Other Non-Current	15.3	14.2
100.0	100.0	100.0	100.0		100.0	Total	100.0	100.0
						LIABILITIES		
19.6	14.0	18.9	21.3		11.2	Notes Payable-Short Term	15.9	23.8
5.5	3.9	2.7	1.9		3.9	Cur. Mat.-L.T.D.	3.6	1.2
11.8	11.7	9.6	9.1		9.6	Trade Payables	7.0	8.2
.2	.1	.3	.1		.3	Income Taxes Payable	.4	.1
7.9	8.5	14.9	15.1		10.5	All Other Current	15.3	13.3
45.0	38.1	46.4	47.5		35.5	Total Current	42.3	46.7
9.4	8.7	10.1	14.0		24.5	Long-Term Debt	18.8	16.7
.0	.1	.0	.0		.7	Deferred Taxes	.6	.2
8.4	7.8	9.6	5.2		9.1	All Other Non-Current	10.5	7.5
37.2	45.4	33.9	33.4		30.2	Net Worth	27.8	29.0
100.0	100.0	100.0	100.0		100.0	Total Liabilities & Net Worth	100.0	100.0
						INCOME DATA		
100.0	100.0	100.0	100.0		100.0	Net Sales	100.0	100.0
						Gross Profit		
88.3	83.2	86.9	79.6		75.9	Operating Expenses	85.0	77.8
11.7	16.8	13.1	20.4		24.1	Operating Profit	15.0	22.2
2.7	3.3	4.0	9.6		9.2	All Other Expenses (net)	4.6	8.7
9.0	13.5	9.1	10.9		14.9	Profit Before Taxes	10.4	13.4
						RATIOS		
3.5	4.7	2.8	3.1		3.5		4.0	3.1
2.7	1.7	1.4	1.4		2.1	Current	1.7	1.6
1.3	1.2	1.1	1.0		1.1		1.0	1.0
3.5	4.5	2.2	2.9		3.1		3.9	3.1
2.6	1.7	1.3	1.2		2.1	Quick	1.4	1.4
1.3	1.2	1.0	.9		1.0		.8	.9
0 UND	0 UND	1 545.4	8 45.1		51 7.1		0 UND	0 UND
0 UND	0 UND	6 57.7	63 5.8		117 3.1	Sales/Receivables	38 9.6	23 15.5
4 96.6	3 113.7	40 9.1	418 .9		276 1.3		126 2.9	155 2.4
						Cost of Sales/Inventory		
						Cost of Sales/Payables		
2.0	1.5	1.3	1.1		2.1		2.0	2.0
4.4	3.5	5.6	4.2		3.9	Sales/Working Capital	4.6	3.9
20.0	8.4	51.2	92.3		NM		47.7	50.2
12.2	28.0	11.1	103.3		10.9		13.1	11.5
(24) 5.3	(56) 6.1	(34) 3.4	(22) 4.8		(14) 5.0	EBIT/Interest	(59) 4.5	(62) 4.3
2.6	1.8	1.4	1.3		2.8		1.3	1.7
	5.5					Net Profit + Depr., Dep.,	5.1	
	(11) 3.5					Amort./Cur. Mat. L/T/D	(12) 2.0	
	.8						.7	
.1	.1	.1	.0		.1		.1	.0
.2	.4	.4	.2		.4	Fixed/Worth	.3	.2
.5	.7	1.9	1.6		NM		1.3	1.0
.4	.5	1.0	1.3		1.5		.8	1.0
1.3	1.4	2.3	6.3		5.1	Debt/Worth	2.9	3.1
4.1	3.2	6.8	14.2		NM		10.6	9.1
49.7	43.1	30.3	40.4		96.4	% Profit Before Taxes/Tangible	58.3	70.0
(33) 19.6	(67) 23.0	(37) 17.8	(28) 17.6		(13) 39.6	Net Worth	(78) 21.8	(84) 28.5
5.8	4.7	8.5	1.5		16.0		5.8	6.8
33.1	19.1	10.4	17.3		16.7	% Profit Before Taxes/Total	19.2	22.8
6.9	8.0	5.7	2.3		11.8	Assets	7.1	5.7
2.4	2.0	1.1	.4		4.6		.8	1.3
58.7	30.8	54.3	123.2		25.0		84.2	102.8
14.2	9.2	10.0	28.4		11.2	Sales/Net Fixed Assets	19.4	24.8
8.9	4.8	4.7	7.7		5.8		8.4	7.5
1.9	1.2	1.2	1.1		1.3		1.8	1.8
1.4	.9	.8	.7		.9	Sales/Total Assets	1.1	1.0
1.0	.7	.4	.2		.4		.4	.2
.6	.7	.8	.5		.6		.7	.9
(27) 1.3	(61) 1.9	(32) 1.8	(24) 2.2		(12) 2.9	% Depr., Dep., Amort./Sales	(68) 1.6	(65) 1.9
2.4	2.9	3.4	3.6		3.7		3.1	4.0
8.7	7.9	3.6				% Officers', Directors'	6.4	4.6
(26) 14.0	(40) 13.0	(16) 6.8				Owners' Comp/Sales	(27) 13.0	(28) 12.4
25.3	18.4	22.7					22.7	20.9
20810M	76289M	512554M	699553M	598897M	2516021M	Net Sales ($)	1937107M	3627367M
10347M	74415M	232840M	830999M	499680M	2894775M	Total Assets ($)	2412667M	2735710M

© RMA 2010

M = $ thousand   MM = $ million

See Pages 9 through 22 for Explanation of Ratios and Data

Comparative Historical Data   Current Data Sorted by Sales

87 / 4 / 18 / 13 / 30	98 / 6 / 19 / 11 / 42	124 / 9 / 11 / 19 / 49	Type of Statement	55 / 4 / 8 / 13 / 6	26 / 2 / 3 / 4 / 13	9 / 1 / / 1 / 4	10 / 2 / / / 2	9 / / / / 7	15 / / / 1 / 17
4/1/07-3/31/08 ALL	4/1/08-3/31/09 ALL	4/1/09-3/31/10 ALL	Unqualified / Reviewed / Compiled / Tax Returns / Other		11 (4/1-9/30/09)		201 (10/1/09-3/31/10)		
				0-1MM	1-3MM	3-5MM	5-10MM	10-25MM	25MM & OVER
152	176	212	NUMBER OF STATEMENTS	86	48	15	14	16	33
%	%	%	ASSETS	%	%	%	%	%	%
45.1	43.9	47.5	Cash & Equivalents	61.5	50.4	37.6	45.7	27.8	21.9
17.7	14.4	15.4	Trade Receivables (net)	6.6	16.0	18.1	15.2	26.1	31.4
1.1	1.5	1.2	Inventory	.1	2.2	.5	6.2	.6	1.4
5.7	5.8	4.8	All Other Current	2.7	5.6	8.9	3.9	9.2	5.7
69.6	65.6	69.0	Total Current	70.8	74.2	65.1	70.9	63.7	60.5
15.5	15.6	13.5	Fixed Assets (net)	16.6	10.3	11.7	13.0	14.5	10.5
4.9	7.4	8.4	Intangibles (net)	4.0	8.8	9.9	5.6	9.5	18.9
10.0	11.4	9.1	All Other Non-Current	8.5	6.7	13.3	10.4	12.3	10.2
100.0	100.0	100.0	Total	100.0	100.0	100.0	100.0	100.0	100.0
			LIABILITIES						
19.0	16.1	17.3	Notes Payable-Short Term	16.8	24.6	21.4	6.8	21.0	8.9
3.8	4.6	3.6	Cur. Mat.-L.T.D.	2.4	4.3	7.2	1.0	7.8	3.0
11.6	8.6	10.3	Trade Payables	11.6	7.7	11.2	14.1	6.5	10.7
.2	.2	.2	Income Taxes Payable	.1	.1	1.0	.0	.2	.1
14.7	14.6	11.0	All Other Current	8.8	8.3	13.9	19.0	18.7	12.2
49.3	44.1	42.4	Total Current	39.7	45.0	54.7	40.9	54.2	34.9
10.9	11.8	11.4	Long-Term Debt	8.0	10.2	10.5	6.3	14.5	23.3
.1	.1	.1	Deferred Taxes	.0	.1	.0	.0	.0	.6
9.9	12.4	7.7	All Other Non-Current	8.4	6.9	9.1	7.6	5.2	7.7
29.8	31.7	38.3	Net Worth	43.9	37.8	25.6	45.2	26.1	33.4
100.0	100.0	100.0	Total Liabilities & Net Worth	100.0	100.0	100.0	100.0	100.0	100.0
			INCOME DATA						
100.0	100.0	100.0	Net Sales	100.0	100.0	100.0	100.0	100.0	100.0
			Gross Profit						
82.6	83.8	83.1	Operating Expenses	82.2	82.1	85.2	85.4	84.3	84.1
17.4	16.2	16.9	Operating Profit	17.8	17.9	14.8	14.6	15.7	15.9
6.7	5.5	5.2	All Other Expenses (net)	5.5	4.6	6.6	2.8	7.5	4.5
10.7	10.7	11.7	Profit Before Taxes	12.3	13.3	8.2	11.8	8.2	11.3
			RATIOS						
3.1 / 1.6 / 1.1	3.2 / 1.5 / 1.0	3.4 / 1.6 / 1.1	Current	3.5 / 2.0 / 1.2	4.8 / 1.5 / 1.2	2.9 / 1.4 / .7	7.4 / 1.4 / 1.1	2.6 / 1.2 / 1.0	3.5 / 1.8 / 1.0
2.8 / 1.4 / 1.0	3.0 / 1.3 / .9	3.3 / 1.5 / 1.1	Quick	3.5 / 1.9 / 1.2	4.8 / 1.4 / 1.1	2.9 / 1.3 / .6	7.3 / 1.3 / .9	2.5 / 1.1 / .8	3.1 / 1.3 / .9
0 UND / 2 150.2 / 56 6.6	0 UND / 2 172.5 / 31 11.9	0 UND / 3 114.1 / 53 6.9	Sales/Receivables	0 UND / 0 UND / 3 124.0	0 UND / 3 132.1 / 43 8.4	1 610.4 / 8 46.9 / 116 3.1	5 73.1 / 19 19.2 / 248 1.5	3 123.8 / 4 82.3 / 153 2.4	34 10.7 / 58 6.3 / 127 2.9
			Cost of Sales/Inventory						
			Cost of Sales/Payables						
2.1 / 4.6 / 20.0	2.3 / 5.4 / 36.3	1.6 / 4.1 / 18.5	Sales/Working Capital	1.3 / 2.8 / 9.1	1.5 / 5.2 / 14.5	1.4 / 5.4 / -9.4	.8 / 1.7 / 11.6	2.1 / 18.4 / NM	2.5 / 4.4 / -65.1
(113) 13.4 / 5.0 / 1.3	(124) 15.9 / 3.7 / 1.7	(154) 16.6 / 5.2 / 1.7	EBIT/Interest	(60) 17.5 / 5.0 / 2.0	(33) 12.5 / 5.5 / 1.5	(10) / 5.4 / 2.4	115.0 / 5.4 / 2.4	(14) 151.3 / 1.7 / 1.3	(28) 18.1 / 5.8 / 2.4
(18) 16.1 / 2.1 / .7	(29) 9.3 / 2.6 / .5	(33) 9.9 / 2.8 / 1.0	Net Profit + Depr., Dep., Amort./Cur. Mat. L/T/D						
.1 / .3 / 1.2	.1 / .3 / 1.7	.1 / .3 / 1.1	Fixed/Worth	.0 / .3 / .6	.0 / .2 / .7	.0 / .4 / -6.2	.0 / .2 / 1.0	.1 / .6 / 6.7	.1 / .4 / -.5
1.1 / 2.7 / 7.9	1.0 / 3.0 / 12.8	.6 / 1.8 / 7.3	Debt/Worth	.5 / 1.4 / 3.5	.6 / 2.1 / 7.0	.6 / 7.2 / -29.0	.3 / 1.9 / 7.8	1.1 / 4.9 / 22.7	1.1 / 2.9 / -4.2
(132) 47.9 / 19.8 / 6.5	(146) 49.1 / 25.6 / 9.0	(182) 44.8 / 20.6 / 6.3	% Profit Before Taxes/Tangible Net Worth	(81) 44.8 / 22.9 / 5.8	(42) 59.0 / 13.2 / 3.3	(11) 32.1 / 17.8 / 9.1	25.3 / 17.2 / 3.4	(13) 72.9 / 17.2 / 4.5	(21) 100.0 / 39.6 / 17.9
16.5 / 5.9 / .8	15.9 / 6.5 / 2.1	16.9 / 6.8 / 1.7	% Profit Before Taxes/Total Assets	16.6 / 7.0 / 1.6	18.5 / 6.7 / 2.0	12.5 / 2.5 / .7	6.7 / 2.4 / 1.0	16.0 / 6.1 / .5	22.5 / 12.1 / 4.6
52.7 / 17.9 / 6.5	54.1 / 15.4 / 6.2	54.3 / 12.1 / 5.8	Sales/Net Fixed Assets	39.9 / 10.0 / 4.6	49.4 / 17.2 / 6.2	98.3 / 7.5 / 4.1	84.7 / 8.4 / 4.1	56.7 / 22.0 / 4.9	63.8 / 15.5 / 8.0
1.7 / 1.1 / .5	1.6 / 1.0 / .5	1.3 / .9 / .5	Sales/Total Assets	1.2 / .9 / .6	1.3 / 1.1 / .4	1.4 / .8 / .5	1.0 / .5 / .3	2.2 / 1.0 / .5	1.7 / 1.2 / .8
(123) .7 / 1.7 / 3.2	(136) .9 / 1.5 / 3.0	(160) .6 / 1.8 / 3.1	% Depr., Dep., Amort./Sales	(70) .8 / 1.7 / 2.9	(31) .6 / 1.8 / 2.7	(11) .5 / 1.8 / 4.9	(11) .4 / 1.2 / 4.3	(13) .5 / 2.2 / 4.0	(24) .5 / 2.6 / 3.5
(73) 6.1 / 11.1 / 19.6	(66) 6.8 / 12.6 / 26.4	(88) 7.0 / 12.2 / 22.5	% Officers', Directors' Owners' Comp/Sales	(50) 8.3 / 13.1 / 19.2	(22) 8.7 / 13.5 / 28.5				
2467847M	4024922M	4424124M	Net Sales ($)	45234M	90558M	56830M	101464M	258250M	3871788M
3150060M	3307047M	4543056M	Total Assets ($)	88468M	232222M	167834M	364880M	520811M	3168841M

M = $ thousand   MM = $ million
See Pages 9 through 22 for Explanation of Ratios and Data

FINANCE—Investment Banking and Securities Dealing NAICS 523110

Current Data Sorted by Assets

Comparative Historical Data

Type of Statement	0-500M	500M-2MM	2-10MM	10-50MM	50-100MM	100-250MM		4/1/05-3/31/06 ALL	4/1/06-3/31/07 ALL
Unqualified		3	4	12	4	8		22	42
Reviewed								1	4
Compiled			2	1					4
Tax Returns			2						3
Other	2	2	2		1			7	17
	4		4						

13 (4/1-9/30/09) 50 (10/1/09-3/31/10)

	0-500M	500M-2MM	2-10MM	10-50MM	50-100MM	100-250MM		4/1/05-3/31/06 ALL	4/1/06-3/31/07 ALL
NUMBER OF STATEMENTS	6	7	13	24	5	8		30	70
	%	%	%	%	%	%		%	%
ASSETS									
Cash & Equivalents			14.9	36.3				27.7	38.0
Trade Receivables (net)			11.8	13.2				14.6	17.6
Inventory			4.2	3.9				5.3	8.9
All Other Current			4.3	10.6				18.0	9.6
Total Current			35.1	64.0				65.6	74.1
Fixed Assets (net)			30.5	2.9				16.5	10.6
Intangibles (net)			14.4	7.6				6.1	3.8
All Other Non-Current			20.0	25.5				11.9	11.5
Total			100.0	100.0				100.0	100.0
LIABILITIES									
Notes Payable-Short Term			1.9	6.1				18.4	9.9
Cur. Mat.-L.T.D.			2.2	2.0				.7	1.1
Trade Payables			6.2	12.0				10.5	17.2
Income Taxes Payable			.0	.1				.1	.2
All Other Current			14.7	17.2				21.0	17.5
Total Current			25.1	37.3				50.8	45.9
Long-Term Debt			23.2	3.7				3.5	5.5
Deferred Taxes			2.8	.1				.0	.3
All Other Non-Current			1.3	4.0				4.7	3.0
Net Worth			47.6	54.9				40.9	45.4
Total Liabilties & Net Worth			100.0	100.0				100.0	100.0
INCOME DATA									
Net Sales			100.0	100.0				100.0	100.0
Gross Profit									
Operating Expenses			76.7	79.7				88.7	77.2
Operating Profit			23.3	20.3				11.3	22.8
All Other Expenses (net)			11.0	.0				-.2	3.0
Profit Before Taxes			12.3	20.3				11.5	19.8

RATIOS

Ratio	2-10MM	10-50MM	4/1/05-3/31/06 ALL	4/1/06-3/31/07 ALL
Current	2.9	2.7	2.5	2.9
	1.9	1.5	1.5	1.3
	.5	.8	1.1	1.1
Quick	2.5	2.1	2.4	2.0
	1.0	1.0	1.2	1.1
	.5	.2	.6	.6
Sales/Receivables	0 UND	0 UND	0 UND	0 UND
	2 198.6	8 46.1	13 29.2	12 30.5
	49 7.4	77 4.7	40 9.0	79 4.6
Cost of Sales/Inventory				
Cost of Sales/Payables				
Sales/Working Capital	2.8	2.1	3.2	2.8
	10.9	4.1	8.9	4.8
	-17.1	-23.6	80.0	28.9
EBIT/Interest		49.5	55.7	177.5
		(11) 5.9	(22) 13.9	(36) 6.4
		4.5	2.9	2.3
Net Profit + Depr., Dep., Amort./Cur. Mat. L/T/D				
Fixed/Worth	.0	.0	.1	.0
	1.0	.0	.2	.1
	3.1	.1	1.2	.3
Debt/Worth	.7	.2	.6	.4
	1.7	1.2	1.4	1.5
	4.2	3.7	7.2	4.7
% Profit Before Taxes/Tangible Net Worth	101.9	40.2	64.4	69.3
	9.5	(22) 19.0	(27) 29.3	(67) 26.5
	-.5	1.7	4.4	6.2
% Profit Before Taxes/Total Assets	28.8	24.9	19.5	35.5
	4.9	7.5	11.8	7.2
	-.1	.7	1.5	1.9
Sales/Net Fixed Assets	115.6	UND	85.4	157.3
	12.2	145.0	36.1	54.7
	.9	36.6	11.6	24.4
Sales/Total Assets	1.9	1.8	4.1	2.6
	.6	.7	1.4	1.0
	.1	.2	.6	.3
% Depr., Dep., Amort./Sales			.4	.4
			(22) .8	(51) .6
			1.8	1.5
% Officers', Directors' Owners' Comp/Sales				8.7
			(15) 16.6	
			33.6	

	0-500M	500M-2MM	2-10MM	10-50MM	50-100MM	100-250MM		4/1/05-3/31/06 ALL	4/1/06-3/31/07 ALL
Net Sales ($)	10295M	21127M	81814M	574088M	407358M	1983091M		891319M	2677648M
Total Assets ($)	1414M	8423M	68204M	558671M	377244M	1640371M		1326424M	2346093M

M = $ thousand   MM = $ million
See Pages 9 through 22 for Explanation of Ratios and Data

Comparative Historical Data | Current Data Sorted by Sales

Type of Statement

			Type of Statement						
45	32	31	Unqualified		4	2	3	5	17
1	3	1	Reviewed					1	
3	2	3	Compiled		1				
2	5	6	Tax Returns	1	2	1	1		
27	21	22	Other	2	8	1	5	4	2
4/1/07-3/31/08	4/1/08-3/31/09	4/1/09-3/31/10		3	13 (4/1-9/30/09)		50 (10/1/09-3/31/10)		
ALL	ALL	ALL		0-1MM	1-3MM	3-5MM	5-10MM	10-25MM	25MM & OVER
78	63	63	NUMBER OF STATEMENTS	6	15	4	9	10	19
%	%	%	ASSETS	%	%	%	%	%	%
28.8	32.6	30.7	Cash & Equivalents		40.5			29.3	37.6
17.5	17.2	16.5	Trade Receivables (net)		12.3			16.8	21.0
6.3	4.3	2.9	Inventory		1.2			.0	5.2
9.1	6.9	11.1	All Other Current		5.5			16.7	16.2
61.6	61.0	61.2	Total Current		59.5			62.8	80.0
9.8	17.4	13.6	Fixed Assets (net)		22.7			4.5	4.5
6.9	4.6	6.6	Intangibles (net)		.1			15.0	5.9
21.7	17.0	18.6	All Other Non-Current		17.7			17.7	9.6
100.0	100.0	100.0	Total		100.0			100.0	100.0
			LIABILITIES						
12.1	6.5	8.8	Notes Payable-Short Term		8.8			10.7	4.9
1.2	4.4	1.3	Cur. Mat.-L.T.D.		2.6			1.8	.1
13.7	13.0	11.3	Trade Payables		13.6			3.6	15.9
.3	.4	.1	Income Taxes Payable		.1			.0	.1
20.7	19.5	15.4	All Other Current		7.4			20.5	21.5
48.0	43.8	36.8	Total Current		32.4			36.6	42.5
10.4	13.4	8.1	Long-Term Debt		9.2			6.5	3.5
.3	.0	.6	Deferred Taxes		.0			1.6	.0
2.4	3.9	4.1	All Other Non-Current		3.9			2.3	3.0
38.8	38.9	50.4	Net Worth		54.5			52.9	50.9
100.0	100.0	100.0	Total Liabilties & Net Worth		100.0			100.0	100.0
			INCOME DATA						
100.0	100.0	100.0	Net Sales		100.0			100.0	100.0
			Gross Profit						
74.6	77.1	81.8	Operating Expenses		81.4			79.1	83.7
25.4	22.9	18.2	Operating Profit		18.6			20.9	16.3
4.0	8.7	3.3	All Other Expenses (net)		.2			5.0	.6
21.4	14.2	14.9	Profit Before Taxes		18.4			15.9	15.7
			RATIOS						
4.3	3.1	2.9			8.5			3.3	2.7
1.4	1.6	1.9	Current		2.0			1.8	2.0
1.0	1.0	1.1			.4			.7	1.4
3.1	2.4	2.1			8.2			2.3	2.0
1.1	1.2	1.4	Quick		1.4			.9	1.4
.5	.5	.5			.1			.5	1.1
0 UND	0 UND	0 UND		0 UND			0 UND	7 55.4	
14 25.8	12 31.2	8 44.5	Sales/Receivables	0 UND			10 35.4	44 8.3	
83 4.4	61 6.0	81 4.5		4 97.1			187 1.9	146 2.5	
			Cost of Sales/Inventory						
			Cost of Sales/Payables						
2.4	2.3	2.4			1.9			1.6	3.0
5.2	5.0	4.5	Sales/Working Capital		5.7			3.5	4.0
-137.1	93.3	241.0			-11.8			-19.8	5.3
21.7	59.5	57.6							60.2
(38) 3.2	(35) 13.0	(33) 15.6	EBIT/Interest					(10) 33.7	
.8	1.2	2.7							19.5
			Net Profit + Depr., Dep., Amort./Cur. Mat. L/T/D						
.0	.0	.0			.0			.0	.0
.1	.1	.1	Fixed/Worth		.1			.0	.1
.5	.7	.5			1.9			.4	.3
.5	.7	.5			.0			.7	.5
1.6	1.8	1.2	Debt/Worth		.7			1.6	1.1
6.1	6.0	3.1			4.1			2.2	1.7
49.0	48.1	80.9			95.8				84.0
(67) 19.9	(57) 20.8	(59) 19.3	% Profit Before Taxes/Tangible Net Worth	(14) 4.9			(18) 35.1		
5.5	2.4	2.0			1.2				12.6
25.5	18.6	31.9			34.6			14.3	39.3
6.2	5.7	6.5	% Profit Before Taxes/Total Assets		2.8			5.6	18.9
1.2	.4	.5			-.1			-5.3	5.6
324.3	83.7	356.2			UND			UND	91.9
74.2	32.8	39.3	Sales/Net Fixed Assets		39.3			150.5	39.9
26.7	6.2	17.5			17.5			27.3	18.8
2.4	2.0	2.0			5.6			1.3	1.9
.9	.7	1.0	Sales/Total Assets		1.0			.8	1.6
.3	.3	.3			.1			.4	.9
.3	.7	.6							.7
(48) .7	(42) 1.3	(35) .9	% Depr., Dep., Amort./Sales					(11) .8	
1.3	3.1	1.9							1.9
3.3	3.4	3.3							
(12) 18.4	(17) 13.2	(14) 7.3	% Officers', Directors' Owners' Comp/Sales						
35.0	20.5	29.7							
2351609M	2637569M	3077773M	Net Sales ($)	2299M	26099M	13644M	71809M	167967M	2795955M
2710295M	3112435M	2654327M	Total Assets ($)	14556M	124538M	20096M	105801M	440145M	1949191M

M = $ thousand   MM = $ million
See Pages 9 through 22 for Explanation of Ratios and Data

FINANCE—Securities Brokerage NAICS 523120

	Current Data Sorted by Assets							Comparative Historical Data	
							Type of Statement		
2	5	17	24	9	5		Unqualified	53	64
		2	1				Reviewed	4	1
1		2			1		Compiled	12	11
10	3	2					Tax Returns	16	14
4	1	12	8	3	4		Other	66	43
	18 (4/1-9/30/09)		98 (10/1/09-3/31/10)					4/1/05-3/31/06 ALL	4/1/06-3/31/07 ALL
0-500M	500M-2MM	2-10MM	10-50MM	50-100MM	100-250MM		NUMBER OF STATEMENTS	151	133
17	9	35	33	12	10				
%	%	%	%	%	%		**ASSETS**	%	%
42.3		33.1	33.9	36.3	15.0		Cash & Equivalents	37.3	39.3
10.1		17.0	15.2	24.1	26.6		Trade Receivables (net)	15.9	17.5
.0		3.1	2.6	1.8	5.4		Inventory	6.0	2.3
5.8		8.5	8.1	9.7	14.6		All Other Current	10.3	10.5
58.2		61.7	59.7	71.8	61.7		Total Current	69.6	69.5
23.5		9.2	8.7	4.3	2.8		Fixed Assets (net)	13.3	9.9
2.7		9.7	5.4	8.2	7.6		Intangibles (net)	5.3	4.2
15.6		19.4	26.2	15.6	27.9		All Other Non-Current	11.9	16.4
100.0		100.0	100.0	100.0	100.0		Total	100.0	100.0
							LIABILITIES		
32.9		6.1	3.6	7.4	16.1		Notes Payable-Short Term	10.3	9.5
5.0		2.7	.8	.0	4.6		Cur. Mat.-L.T.D.	1.5	1.4
8.1		14.1	9.8	16.3	16.3		Trade Payables	12.2	12.9
.0		.6	.4	.1	.1		Income Taxes Payable	.5	.9
27.6		15.3	16.4	22.7	14.2		All Other Current	21.6	25.7
73.6		38.9	31.1	46.5	51.3		Total Current	46.1	50.3
13.7		7.8	9.9	3.7	21.4		Long-Term Debt	7.3	5.8
.0		.3	.1	.3	2.0		Deferred Taxes	.2	.1
11.9		5.3	2.3	3.0	9.8		All Other Non-Current	5.3	4.5
.9		47.7	56.6	46.6	15.5		Net Worth	41.2	39.3
100.0		100.0	100.0	100.0	100.0		Total Liabilties & Net Worth	100.0	100.0
							INCOME DATA		
100.0		100.0	100.0	100.0	100.0		Net Sales	100.0	100.0
							Gross Profit		
89.5		86.9	78.0	84.7	73.0		Operating Expenses	82.9	83.9
10.5		13.1	22.0	15.3	27.0		Operating Profit	17.1	16.1
1.3		1.5	3.4	1.5	9.5		All Other Expenses (net)	1.5	2.6
9.2		11.6	18.5	13.8	17.5		Profit Before Taxes	15.5	13.4
							RATIOS		
2.9		4.3	4.4	2.3	5.7			3.3	2.7
.9		2.6	1.9	1.6	1.2		Current	1.7	1.6
.3		1.3	1.3	1.2	.8			1.1	1.1
2.4		4.1	3.2	1.9	1.2			2.8	2.3
.9		1.7	1.7	1.3	.9		Quick	1.3	1.4
.3		.6	.7	.7	.5			.6	.7
0 UND		0 UND	0 UND	10 37.9	6 60.4			0 UND	0 UND
0 UND		15 24.0	20 18.6	30 12.4	44 8.3		Sales/Receivables	13 28.4	11 33.7
2 214.4		37 10.0	52 7.0	115 3.2	450 .8			64 5.7	41 8.9
							Cost of Sales/Inventory		
							Cost of Sales/Payables		
8.1		2.0	2.3	1.9	1.8			2.3	2.9
-123.4		7.0	5.8	4.7	7.9		Sales/Working Capital	4.9	7.3
-12.8		19.3	26.0	10.9	NM			43.1	43.7
		66.6	45.8					32.9	38.6
	(21)	12.3	(20) 12.2				EBIT/Interest	(79) 7.4	(76) 9.0
		1.3	5.0					3.2	2.8
							Net Profit + Depr., Dep., Amort./Cur. Mat. L/T/D	16.3	
								(10) 3.4	
								.6	
.1		.0	.0	.0	.0			.0	.0
.4		.1	.1	.1	.0		Fixed/Worth	.1	.1
-1.4		.2	.2	.3	-.2			.4	.4
.6		.2	.3	.6	2.2			.4	.6
8.4		1.0	.6	1.6	9.7		Debt/Worth	1.3	1.4
-4.5		3.2	3.3	3.2	-21.0			7.3	6.2
486.8		33.1	74.7	59.3			% Profit Before Taxes/Tangible Net Worth	44.4	71.2
(11) 53.1		(29) 16.7	(30) 25.3	(10) 33.3				(131) 19.7	(119) 32.4
-2.4		3.2	3.5	22.1				5.7	9.6
61.1		22.8	43.1	23.4	14.0		% Profit Before Taxes/Total Assets	25.6	38.1
38.9		8.8	8.7	10.2	1.3			8.8	13.4
-3.0		.4	.5	2.5	-3.4			1.9	2.5
394.4		351.7	153.7	185.1	UND		Sales/Net Fixed Assets	206.6	162.2
56.1		100.3	61.8	30.6	552.0			53.7	40.8
10.4		26.2	19.8	21.2	26.5			18.1	21.4
12.2		4.2	2.7	1.5	2.1		Sales/Total Assets	3.1	4.5
4.1		1.7	1.2	1.2	.5			1.3	1.9
2.7		.6	.5	.6	.1			.6	.7
.3		.2	.6				% Depr., Dep., Amort./Sales	.4	.4
(10) 1.1		(26) .6	(19) 1.0					(98) .9	(90) .8
4.5		2.2	3.2					1.7	1.4
							% Officers', Directors' Owners' Comp/Sales	3.9	7.6
								(38) 19.7	(24) 17.8
								35.6	25.8
20647M	62273M	450016M	1144389M	1109424M	2352508M		Net Sales ($)	4344279M	5416807M
4070M	10754M	177495M	793741M	889807M	1812635M		Total Assets ($)	3942561M	4241264M

© RMA 2010

M = $ thousand   MM = $ million
See Pages 9 through 22 for Explanation of Ratios and Data

Comparative Historical Data				Current Data Sorted by Sales					
			Type of Statement						
59	66	62	Unqualified	1	6	7	5	14	29
3	1	3	Reviewed	2		1			
7	2	4	Compiled	1		1	1		1
12	15	15	Tax Returns	6	7	1	1		
36	19	32	Other	5	2	3	5	6	11
				18 (4/1-9/30/09)			98 (10/1/09-3/31/10)		
4/1/07-3/31/08 ALL	**4/1/08-3/31/09 ALL**	**4/1/09-3/31/10 ALL**		**0-1MM**	**1-3MM**	**3-5MM**	**5-10MM**	**10-25MM**	**25MM & OVER**
117	103	116	**NUMBER OF STATEMENTS**	15	15	13	12	20	41
%	%	%	**ASSETS**	%	%	%	%	%	%
35.5	37.4	33.2	Cash & Equivalents	28.7	48.4	24.1	27.0	33.7	33.9
13.2	15.6	17.2	Trade Receivables (net)	9.3	5.7	9.7	28.1	24.7	19.8
3.9	1.7	2.3	Inventory	.0	.0	7.0	1.6	.2	3.8
9.9	11.3	9.0	All Other Current	3.9	6.8	12.0	5.0	7.0	12.8
62.4	66.1	61.7	Total Current	41.9	60.8	52.8	61.6	65.6	70.3
11.0	9.5	10.8	Fixed Assets (net)	30.9	23.3	2.9	7.8	3.3	6.0
6.1	5.7	6.7	Intangibles (net)	9.5	.7	9.5	6.2	3.4	8.8
20.4	18.8	20.7	All Other Non-Current	17.6	15.2	34.8	24.4	27.7	14.9
100.0	100.0	100.0	Total	100.0	100.0	100.0	100.0	100.0	100.0
			LIABILITIES						
6.1	7.6	9.8	Notes Payable-Short Term	12.6	28.1	10.8	4.9	4.5	5.9
2.8	2.0	2.9	Cur. Mat.-L.T.D.	8.1	1.8	.9	2.8	1.5	2.6
8.9	9.9	12.8	Trade Payables	9.1	.7	5.6	16.3	21.2	15.8
.5	.4	.4	Income Taxes Payable	.0	.1	.1	.8	1.5	.1
24.9	19.9	17.4	All Other Current	16.0	22.0	9.6	6.1	14.7	23.4
43.2	39.7	43.3	Total Current	45.8	52.6	27.0	31.0	43.4	47.8
9.1	9.5	11.5	Long-Term Debt	34.1	13.1	6.9	7.4	9.4	6.4
.0	.0	.3	Deferred Taxes	.0	.1	.3	.0	.4	.6
4.0	2.2	5.2	All Other Non-Current	12.2	8.4	7.1	5.8	2.3	2.3
43.7	48.6	39.6	Net Worth	7.9	25.9	58.7	55.8	44.5	42.9
100.0	100.0	100.0	Total Liabilties & Net Worth	100.0	100.0	100.0	100.0	100.0	100.0
			INCOME DATA						
100.0	100.0	100.0	Net Sales	100.0	100.0	100.0	100.0	100.0	100.0
			Gross Profit						
82.0	87.5	83.4	Operating Expenses	73.6	87.6	78.4	93.4	73.5	89.0
18.0	12.5	16.6	Operating Profit	26.4	12.4	21.6	6.6	26.5	11.0
4.2	2.5	2.9	All Other Expenses (net)	10.8	1.0	3.8	1.2	5.0	.0
13.9	10.0	13.7	Profit Before Taxes	15.6	11.4	17.8	5.3	21.5	11.1
			RATIOS						
2.5	3.1	3.3		8.9	4.3	20.4	4.5	2.8	2.7
1.5	1.8	1.7	Current	.9	2.4	3.0	2.7	1.5	1.7
1.0	1.3	1.0		.5	.3	.3	1.0	1.2	1.3
2.2	2.7	2.9		8.4	4.3	12.1	4.0	2.8	2.6
1.3	1.6	1.4	Quick	.9	1.5	1.5	2.6	1.3	1.4
.5	.7	.6		.2	.3	.3	.7	.7	.7
0 UND	**0** UND	**0** UND		**0** UND	**0** UND	**0** UND	**11** 32.4	**0** UND	**3** 105.0
7 51.7	**8** 44.9	**15** 23.7	Sales/Receivables	**0** UND	**0** UND	**13** 28.0	**34** 10.9	**28** 12.9	**18** 20.1
41 8.8	**34** 10.7	**40** 9.1		**16** 22.4	**10** 36.9	**42** 8.7	**110** 3.3	**162** 2.3	**34** 10.7
			Cost of Sales/Inventory						
			Cost of Sales/Payables						
3.4	3.6	3.1		1.9	2.0	.7	2.5	1.5	3.6
12.1	9.9	7.9	Sales/Working Capital	-123.4	9.6	3.7	5.8	9.2	9.0
NM	29.7	NM		-8.4	-13.1	-21.6	NM	29.7	14.4
28.0	32.5	32.9						30.6	112.6
(62) 12.0	(52) 7.2	(68) 10.6	EBIT/Interest					(12) 10.2	(25) 10.3
2.0	1.1	1.2						1.7	1.0
			Net Profit + Depr., Dep., Amort./Cur. Mat. L/T/D						
.0	.0	.0		.0	.0	.0	.0	.0	.0
.1	.1	.1	Fixed/Worth	2.2	.1	.1	.0	.0	.1
.3	.2	.6		-3.1	999.8	.1	.3	.1	.3
.4	.4	.4		1.7	.1	.1	.2	.5	.5
1.2	1.0	1.2	Debt/Worth	-22.6	.8	1.0	.4	1.6	.9
3.6	2.3	10.2		-5.5	999.8	2.5	2.7	3.4	5.8
65.5	71.2	61.4			200.4	16.3	31.6	32.2	75.7
(105) 21.7	(92) 29.0	(93) 23.2	% Profit Before Taxes/Tangible Net Worth		(12) 25.3	(11) 11.3	(11) 10.9	(19) 28.3	(33) 34.8
5.0	2.6	4.0			-5.1	2.8	-9.0	8.1	6.9
28.5	31.8	28.2		38.9	56.8	13.0	24.3	18.0	44.4
9.3	13.6	8.6	% Profit Before Taxes/Total Assets	6.2	19.7	9.3	4.5	6.8	14.6
1.7	.6	.2		.3	-4.0	1.6	-7.3	2.1	.2
328.2	382.8	391.5		152.6	253.9	UND	351.3	UND	270.1
53.0	70.3	67.9	Sales/Net Fixed Assets	23.0	64.9	41.9	76.3	173.1	61.8
20.5	26.4	22.9		.4	12.2	13.1	35.8	33.9	27.8
4.2	4.6	3.9		4.1	4.1	2.2	3.2	3.2	4.5
1.8	2.1	1.5	Sales/Total Assets	.8	3.2	.6	1.9	.9	2.1
.8	.9	.6		.2	.7	.3	.8	.3	1.2
.4	.3	.3		.5	.3				.3
(75) .9	(70) .7	(73) .8	% Depr., Dep., Amort./Sales	(10) 3.4	(10) .8				(28) .8
1.5	1.7	2.3		16.5	1.8				1.6
4.7	6.7	4.1							
(19) 12.8	(15) 18.5	(22) 8.2	% Officers', Directors' Owners' Comp/Sales						
27.9	29.0	27.3							
6140279M	**6189125M**	**5139257M**	Net Sales ($)	**8331M**	**27089M**	**52701M**	**88401M**	**347059M**	**4615676M**
4423202M	**3241434M**	**3688502M**	Total Assets ($)	**32677M**	**46863M**	**290611M**	**90834M**	**796545M**	**2430972M**

M = $ thousand MM = $ million

See Pages 9 through 22 for Explanation of Ratios and Data

FINANCE—Commodity Contracts Dealing NAICS 523130

| Current Data Sorted by Assets | | | | | | | Comparative Historical Data | |

0-500M	500M-2MM	2-10MM	10-50MM	50-100MM	100-250MM	Type of Statement	4/1/05-3/31/06 ALL	4/1/06-3/31/07 ALL
	1	6	2	2	3	Unqualified	5	13
		2				Reviewed	1	3
		2				Compiled	2	5
		5				Tax Returns		6
1	3	8	4	2	1	Other	8	22
1	4 (4/1-9/30/09)		39 (10/1/09-3/31/10)				16	49
1	5	23	6	4	4	NUMBER OF STATEMENTS	16	49
%	%	%	%	%	%	**ASSETS**	%	%
		30.1				Cash & Equivalents	24.5	26.2
		17.8				Trade Receivables (net)	18.8	16.0
		12.2				Inventory	4.3	10.5
		7.8				All Other Current	3.3	9.4
		68.0				Total Current	50.9	62.0
		25.0				Fixed Assets (net)	15.6	15.9
		1.8				Intangibles (net)	1.0	1.2
		5.1				All Other Non-Current	32.5	21.0
		100.0				Total	100.0	100.0
						LIABILITIES		
		11.5				Notes Payable-Short Term	29.1	11.6
		1.7				Cur. Mat.-L.T.D.	.8	2.2
		5.9				Trade Payables	6.9	8.0
		.1				Income Taxes Payable	.1	.3
		11.3				All Other Current	7.4	11.1
		30.6				Total Current	44.4	33.2
		17.0				Long-Term Debt	10.9	21.5
		.0				Deferred Taxes	.0	.0
		4.7				All Other Non-Current	9.5	5.4
		47.8				Net Worth	35.2	39.9
		100.0				Total Liabilities & Net Worth	100.0	100.0
						INCOME DATA		
		100.0				Net Sales	100.0	100.0
						Gross Profit		
		72.9				Operating Expenses	68.6	61.7
		27.1				Operating Profit	31.4	38.3
		6.6				All Other Expenses (net)	10.8	8.9
		20.5				Profit Before Taxes	20.6	29.3
						RATIOS		
		6.8				Current	4.2	4.3
		2.1					1.2	2.0
		1.0					.7	1.1
		5.4				Quick	4.0	4.2
		1.2					.9	1.0
		.5					.7	.6
		0 UND				Sales/Receivables	0 UND	0 UND
		8 45.1					10 37.4	20 18.5
		37 9.7					26 14.0	47 7.7
						Cost of Sales/Inventory		
						Cost of Sales/Payables		
		1.7				Sales/Working Capital	3.6	1.2
		5.6					15.1	5.4
		999.8					-12.8	28.4
		13.2				EBIT/Interest		21.9
	(13)	4.3					(26)	7.2
		3.5						2.9
						Net Profit + Depr., Dep., Amort./Cur. Mat. L/T/D		
		.0				Fixed/Worth	.0	.0
		.1					.1	.0
		.9					.6	.6
		.3				Debt/Worth	.1	.5
		1.1					3.0	1.9
		3.7					NM	7.3
		49.3				% Profit Before Taxes/Tangible Net Worth	107.6	54.6
	(22)	30.6					(12) 23.7	(47) 26.6
		16.2					13.5	9.9
		21.6				% Profit Before Taxes/Total Assets	18.3	25.8
		10.3					6.7	6.5
		7.0					.6	2.3
		999.8				Sales/Net Fixed Assets	UND	UND
		53.2					485.4	69.9
		.9					15.3	2.2
		3.0				Sales/Total Assets	2.7	1.5
		1.8					.4	.3
		.3					.1	.2
		1.2				% Depr., Dep., Amort./Sales		.5
	(15)	1.7					(31)	1.6
		12.4						9.0
						% Officers', Directors' Owners' Comp/Sales		.9
							(11)	7.2
								23.5
57M	4813M	288210M	25843M	790503M	1301986M	Net Sales ($)	246980M	2730633M
354M	5449M	97542M	180890M	241127M	612410M	Total Assets ($)	331805M	1861392M

© RMA 2010

M = $ thousand   MM = $ million
See Pages 9 through 22 for Explanation of Ratios and Data

Comparative Historical Data   Current Data Sorted by Sales

7	10	14	Type of Statement	1	1	1	3	2	6
7	10	14	Unqualified	1	1	1	3	2	6
3	5	2	Reviewed	1			1		
5	4	2	Compiled				1	1	
6	3	6	Tax Returns	2			1		1
15	14	19	Other	7	3	1	1	3	3
4/1/07-3/31/08 ALL	4/1/08-3/31/09 ALL	4/1/09-3/31/10 ALL		0-1MM	1-3MM 4 (4/1-9/30/09)	3-5MM	5-10MM	10-25MM 39 (10/1/09-3/31/10)	25MM & OVER
36	36	43	NUMBER OF STATEMENTS	11	6	2	8	6	10
%	%	%	ASSETS	%	%	%	%	%	%
23.9	19.0	28.6	Cash & Equivalents	19.1					28.7
26.2	26.3	21.9	Trade Receivables (net)	12.7					33.4
9.8	13.4	8.9	Inventory	.0					18.9
5.3	9.2	9.1	All Other Current	9.5					6.1
65.2	68.0	68.5	Total Current	41.2					87.0
19.8	20.3	22.5	Fixed Assets (net)	49.0					7.4
1.2	1.2	1.7	Intangibles (net)	.4					.4
13.8	10.6	7.2	All Other Non-Current	9.4					5.1
100.0	100.0	100.0	Total	100.0					100.0
			LIABILITIES						
14.7	13.0	13.2	Notes Payable-Short Term	15.3					13.6
1.5	1.8	1.6	Cur. Mat.-L.T.D.	3.5					.0
24.6	9.6	8.5	Trade Payables	.0					23.9
.2	.2	.1	Income Taxes Payable	.0					.2
3.6	14.1	16.7	All Other Current	5.0					15.9
44.6	38.7	40.1	Total Current	23.9					53.7
23.1	25.5	17.2	Long-Term Debt	27.1					3.4
.0	.0	.0	Deferred Taxes	.0					.0
7.1	4.3	4.1	All Other Non-Current	1.7					2.7
25.2	31.5	38.6	Net Worth	47.4					40.2
100.0	100.0	100.0	Total Liabilities & Net Worth	100.0					100.0
			INCOME DATA						
100.0	100.0	100.0	Net Sales	100.0					100.0
			Gross Profit						
67.8	74.7	70.3	Operating Expenses	48.5					82.5
32.2	25.3	29.7	Operating Profit	51.5					17.5
7.4	8.3	8.6	All Other Expenses (net)	18.1					3.6
24.8	17.0	21.0	Profit Before Taxes	33.4					13.9
			RATIOS						
7.3	5.8	5.1	Current	1.7					5.0
2.6	2.5	1.4		.9					1.3
1.2	1.1	1.0		.2					1.2
5.0	4.2	3.4	Quick	1.6					4.4
2.2	1.5	1.0		.5					1.1
.9	.6	.5		.0					.8
1 581.2	0 UND	0 UND	Sales/Receivables	0 UND				6	61.6
16 22.5	12 30.6	22 16.9		0 UND				16	22.8
57 6.4	69 5.3	66 5.5		3 108.1				69	5.3
			Cost of Sales/Inventory						
			Cost of Sales/Payables						
1.5	1.0	1.4	Sales/Working Capital	.5					4.7
6.0	3.9	7.1		-8.1					23.2
27.9	42.2	999.8		-3.2					49.3
30.6	9.9	16.5	EBIT/Interest						
(21) 15.6	(25) 4.8	(24) 7.8							
2.5	1.7	3.7							
			Net Profit + Depr., Dep., Amort./Cur. Mat. L/T/D						
.0	.0	.0	Fixed/Worth	.0					.0
.2	.2	.2		.9					.1
1.3	1.1	1.0		3.3					.4
.6	.8	.5	Debt/Worth	.7					.5
1.4	2.6	2.4		1.4					3.3
6.8	9.0	6.2		2.4					4.1
79.8	47.6	50.2	% Profit Before Taxes/Tangible Net Worth	31.3					74.7
(31) 37.0	(32) 28.2	(40) 24.1		7.6					31.8
14.9	12.1	8.6		4.0					16.1
32.5	17.0	17.4	% Profit Before Taxes/Total Assets	10.5					18.1
10.2	6.7	9.5		7.3					11.0
2.7	2.4	2.2		1.2					9.1
999.8	855.0	590.4	Sales/Net Fixed Assets	UND					767.3
26.4	31.3	38.8		.6					328.9
2.6	1.7	.9		.2					24.0
4.2	4.1	2.9	Sales/Total Assets	.2					10.3
.7	.7	.5		.2					4.3
.2	.2	.1		.1					.5
.1	.1	.6	% Depr., Dep., Amort./Sales						
(24) 1.4	(23) 1.1	(29) 1.6							
4.6	5.5	8.8							
			% Officers', Directors' Owners' Comp/Sales						
2621812M	3820859M	2411412M	Net Sales ($)	5138M	11534M	6954M	59452M	86685M	2241649M
988991M	1389676M	1137772M	Total Assets ($)	27279M	75151M	53111M	88465M	80005M	813761M

M = $ thousand   MM = $ million
See Pages 9 through 22 for Explanation of Ratios and Data

Current Data Sorted by Assets

Comparative Historical Data

						Type of Statement		
		2	4		1	Unqualified	12	10
		1	1			Reviewed	2	2
			1			Compiled		2
3	2					Tax Returns	2	3
1	4					Other	16	9
	4 (4/1-9/30/09)	4	3	25 (10/1/09-3/31/10)	2		4/1/05- 3/31/06	4/1/06- 3/31/07
0-500M	500M-2MM	2-10MM	10-50MM	50-100MM	100-250MM		ALL	ALL
4	6	7	9	2	1	NUMBER OF STATEMENTS	32	26
%	%	%	%	%	%	ASSETS	%	%
						Cash & Equivalents	29.7	20.0
						Trade Receivables (net)	37.2	40.3
						Inventory	8.7	10.1
						All Other Current	5.1	10.5
						Total Current	80.6	80.9
						Fixed Assets (net)	8.0	10.6
						Intangibles (net)	1.5	.9
						All Other Non-Current	9.9	7.5
						Total	100.0	100.0
						LIABILITIES		
						Notes Payable-Short Term	8.9	20.0
						Cur. Mat.-L.T.D.	.3	1.0
						Trade Payables	27.8	22.4
						Income Taxes Payable	.0	.1
						All Other Current	11.4	9.6
						Total Current	48.4	53.0
						Long-Term Debt	3.5	5.7
						Deferred Taxes	.0	.0
						All Other Non-Current	5.9	5.9
						Net Worth	42.2	35.4
						Total Liabilities & Net Worth	100.0	100.0
						INCOME DATA		
						Net Sales	100.0	100.0
						Gross Profit		
						Operating Expenses	90.3	90.8
						Operating Profit	9.7	9.2
						All Other Expenses (net)	-.9	-.4
						Profit Before Taxes	10.5	9.6
						RATIOS		
							3.7	4.1
						Current	1.6	1.3
							1.1	1.0
							2.3	3.9
						Quick	1.4	1.0
							1.0	.6
							24 15.0	25 14.6
						Sales/Receivables	37 9.7	35 10.6
							45 8.0	62 5.9
						Cost of Sales/Inventory		
						Cost of Sales/Payables		
							3.9	3.4
						Sales/Working Capital	11.7	13.3
							34.0	214.6
							22.9	30.8
						EBIT/Interest	(25) 4.7	(23) 3.8
							2.6	2.3
						Net Profit + Depr., Dep., Amort./Cur. Mat. L/T/D		
							.0	.0
						Fixed/Worth	.0	.0
							.2	.7
							.4	.8
						Debt/Worth	1.8	3.7
							8.5	10.4
							54.1	81.3
						% Profit Before Taxes/Tangible Net Worth	(31) 22.3	(25) 46.5
							11.1	16.4
							19.5	23.4
						% Profit Before Taxes/Total Assets	5.1	6.8
							1.6	2.4
							999.8	UND
						Sales/Net Fixed Assets	332.0	360.1
							29.2	10.4
							6.1	5.2
						Sales/Total Assets	3.2	2.7
							1.4	1.0
							.0	.0
						% Depr., Dep., Amort./Sales	(19) .1	(16) .1
							1.4	2.0
							.7	
						% Officers', Directors' Owners' Comp/Sales	(10) 1.6	
							22.7	
6154M	79380M	114970M	1242747M	437893M	925129M	Net Sales ($)	2047308M	1689901M
262M	7663M	28866M	205925M	117063M	113940M	Total Assets ($)	768809M	459083M

M = $ thousand   MM = $ million
See Pages 9 through 22 for Explanation of Ratios and Data

Comparative Historical Data | Current Data Sorted by Sales

7 4 1 2 10	5 3 2 2 6	7 2 1 5 14	Type of Statement							
			Unqualified		1		1	1	4	
			Reviewed					1	1	
			Compiled						1	
			Tax Returns	1	1	1	4	1	1	
4/1/07-3/31/08 ALL	4/1/08-3/31/09 ALL	4/1/09-3/31/10 ALL	Other	2	4 (4/1-9/30/09)		25 (10/1/09-3/31/10)		5	
				0-1MM	1-3MM	3-5MM	5-10MM	10-25MM	25MM & OVER	
24	18	29	NUMBER OF STATEMENTS	3	2	1	5	6	12	
%	%	%	ASSETS	%	%	%	%	%	%	
16.7	15.1	19.7	Cash & Equivalents						27.4	
36.1	42.5	43.4	Trade Receivables (net)						58.2	
17.3	15.3	7.5	Inventory						6.3	
12.3	2.6	3.9	All Other Current						2.5	
82.4	75.4	74.4	Total Current						94.3	
8.3	11.2	9.6	Fixed Assets (net)						2.3	
.0	.4	1.6	Intangibles (net)						1.1	
9.3	12.9	14.4	All Other Non-Current						2.3	
100.0	100.0	100.0	Total						100.0	
			LIABILITIES							
16.0	16.3	16.2	Notes Payable-Short Term						11.3	
.3	2.2	1.5	Cur. Mat.-L.T.D.						.4	
24.3	26.4	24.3	Trade Payables						32.3	
.0	.1	.6	Income Taxes Payable						.4	
15.9	11.2	15.4	All Other Current						19.2	
56.6	56.3	57.9	Total Current						63.6	
6.3	6.5	7.0	Long-Term Debt						3.6	
.0	.0	.3	Deferred Taxes						.1	
4.5	2.9	.5	All Other Non-Current						.2	
32.6	34.3	34.2	Net Worth						32.5	
100.0	100.0	100.0	Total Liabilties & Net Worth						100.0	
			INCOME DATA							
100.0	100.0	100.0	Net Sales						100.0	
			Gross Profit							
89.8	90.9	88.4	Operating Expenses						92.1	
10.2	9.1	11.6	Operating Profit						7.9	
-.5	-1.8	.2	All Other Expenses (net)						.0	
10.7	10.9	11.4	Profit Before Taxes						7.9	
			RATIOS							
2.1	1.8	2.4							1.7	
1.3	1.4	1.4	Current						1.3	
1.1	1.1	1.1							1.2	
1.7	1.4	2.4							1.5	
1.0	1.0	1.2	Quick						1.2	
.4	.4	.6							1.1	
17 21.4	11 34.4	8 46.9						20	18.4	
33 11.0	22 16.4	28 13.0	Sales/Receivables					33	11.1	
60 6.0	49 7.5	50 7.2						47	7.8	
			Cost of Sales/Inventory							
			Cost of Sales/Payables							
4.2	14.5	9.5							14.9	
11.1	31.2	26.0	Sales/Working Capital						44.7	
28.3	160.6	105.7							89.3	
6.6	10.5	64.3							236.8	
(19) 4.3	(13) 2.7	(23) 12.4	EBIT/Interest					(10)	17.4	
2.3	1.6	2.2							9.1	
			Net Profit + Depr., Dep., Amort./Cur. Mat. L/T/D							
.0	.0	.0							.0	
.0	.2	.1	Fixed/Worth						.0	
.7	.7	.7							.1	
.8	1.4	.9							1.8	
3.5	2.6	2.8	Debt/Worth						3.9	
8.6	8.9	7.1							5.1	
81.3	96.2	73.0	% Profit Before Taxes/Tangible						63.8	
35.2	(17) 48.8	(26) 36.7	Net Worth						49.8	
15.7	9.5	8.8							34.6	
14.4	28.1	26.0	% Profit Before Taxes/Total						24.7	
6.5	7.1	7.8	Assets						7.8	
2.9	1.1	2.2							6.8	
999.8	999.8	999.8							999.8	
598.6	219.1	614.5	Sales/Net Fixed Assets						975.2	
17.2	7.0	40.6							607.1	
4.9	8.0	11.1							11.4	
3.2	4.6	6.3	Sales/Total Assets						7.4	
.9	1.1	2.5							5.6	
.0	.0	.0								
(15) .7	(11) 1.4	(17) .2	% Depr., Dep., Amort./Sales							
2.6	3.6	2.0								
		1.6	% Officers', Directors'							
	(11) 2.6		Owners' Comp/Sales							
		7.7								
1530871M	1853983M	2806273M	Net Sales ($)	1367M	2605M	3921M	32576M	92163M	2673641M	
879205M	323047M	473719M	Total Assets ($)	5030M	3752M	81M	24873M	35392M	404591M	

© RMA 2010

M = $ thousand   MM = $ million
See Pages 9 through 22 for Explanation of Ratios and Data

Current Data Sorted by Assets / Comparative Historical Data

0-500M	500M-2MM	2-10MM	10-50MM	50-100MM	100-250MM	Type of Statement	4/1/05-3/31/06 ALL	4/1/06-3/31/07 ALL
2	1	6	17	12	5	Unqualified	41	39
	1	4	6	1	1	Reviewed	15	17
2	2	4		1		Compiled	22	12
6	10	9	1			Tax Returns	50	23
9	11	27	14	6	7	Other	109	82
	15 (4/1-9/30/09)		150 (10/1/09-3/31/10)					
19	25	50	38	20	13	NUMBER OF STATEMENTS	237	173
%	%	%	%	%	%	ASSETS	%	%
25.7	11.0	14.4	14.7	12.0	10.2	Cash & Equivalents	15.0	14.1
12.3	11.1	12.6	16.7	5.7	23.9	Trade Receivables (net)	13.5	17.8
5.2	.5	2.6	4.9	5.0	.9	Inventory	6.5	5.5
9.8	13.9	7.4	11.3	5.5	8.0	All Other Current	6.3	6.7
53.1	36.5	36.9	47.7	28.2	43.0	Total Current	41.4	44.1
24.9	39.3	32.8	12.7	24.7	26.4	Fixed Assets (net)	30.6	25.0
1.9	5.2	2.4	1.0	.0	7.1	Intangibles (net)	3.4	4.2
20.1	19.0	27.9	38.6	47.1	23.6	All Other Non-Current	24.6	26.8
100.0	100.0	100.0	100.0	100.0	100.0	Total	100.0	100.0
						LIABILITIES		
19.3	23.2	12.9	13.7	4.4	17.9	Notes Payable-Short Term	16.0	17.2
2.6	3.3	2.9	.5	.8	.7	Cur. Mat.-L.T.D.	3.8	3.9
5.5	3.4	6.1	5.7	1.9	9.2	Trade Payables	5.0	5.8
.0	.3	.0	.3	.1	.1	Income Taxes Payable	.5	.1
13.3	12.6	6.6	6.0	6.5	12.6	All Other Current	13.5	10.9
40.7	42.8	28.5	26.2	13.9	40.4	Total Current	38.7	37.9
24.5	23.2	27.8	19.0	16.3	19.0	Long-Term Debt	22.9	22.0
.0	.0	.0	.0	.0	.5	Deferred Taxes	.2	.1
6.5	3.8	4.4	3.6	10.5	1.7	All Other Non-Current	8.6	6.1
28.3	30.2	39.4	51.2	59.3	38.3	Net Worth	29.5	33.9
100.0	100.0	100.0	100.0	100.0	100.0	Total Liabilities & Net Worth	100.0	100.0
						INCOME DATA		
100.0	100.0	100.0	100.0	100.0	100.0	Net Sales	100.0	100.0
						Gross Profit		
80.2	58.3	69.2	63.5	62.1	59.2	Operating Expenses	66.3	67.9
19.8	41.7	30.8	36.5	37.9	40.8	Operating Profit	33.7	32.1
10.0	20.8	16.0	10.8	5.6	17.0	All Other Expenses (net)	9.2	13.8
9.8	20.9	14.8	25.8	32.3	23.8	Profit Before Taxes	24.5	18.3
						RATIOS		
19.3	2.4	3.9	4.3	7.4	1.6		3.6	2.1
1.5	1.1	1.4	1.9	1.5	1.2	Current	1.2	1.2
.4	.2	.2	1.2	.8	.4		.4	.5
4.7	1.8	3.9	3.1	7.4	1.5		2.5	1.6
1.4	.4	.9	1.3	.8	1.1	Quick	.7	.7
.3	.1	.2	.7	.2	.2		.1	.2
0 UND	0 UND	0 UND	0 UND	0 UND	4 101.5		0 UND	0 UND
0 UND	0 UND	1 333.3	7 52.3	5 76.3	45 8.2	Sales/Receivables	3 128.4	9 42.7
6 62.0	13 27.4	36 10.2	49 7.5	44 8.4	149 2.4		36 10.2	66 5.5
						Cost of Sales/Inventory		
						Cost of Sales/Payables		
5.6	3.6	3.3	.5	2.9	1.2		2.1	2.6
24.6	39.9	11.0	3.0	15.9	12.0	Sales/Working Capital	23.8	13.4
-67.7	-3.1	-3.8	25.0	-8.9	-2.6		-6.1	-7.1
	29.3	8.3	30.0	22.2			15.6	14.2
	(11) 3.3	(27) 5.3	(18) 4.8	(13) 3.0		EBIT/Interest	(131) 5.9	(87) 4.4
	1.3	1.5	1.0	-.5			1.9	2.0
						Net Profit + Depr., Dep., Amort./Cur. Mat. L/T/D	6.9	4.7
							(20) 2.9	(18) 1.6
							1.0	1.1
.0	.0	.0	.0	.0	.0		.0	.0
.1	.9	.3	.0	.2	.2	Fixed/Worth	.4	.2
.9	-16.2	3.7	.3	.9	3.5		3.6	2.6
.1	.8	.5	.2	.0	.7		.5	.6
.5	2.7	2.1	1.3	.9	2.7	Debt/Worth	2.0	1.9
-7.5	-21.3	8.3	3.3	3.0	8.8		13.7	8.3
76.3	81.5	50.9	22.1	13.9	21.7		64.9	64.3
(14) 5.5	(17) 16.9	(45) 9.9	(37) 9.1	(19) 3.6	(11) 14.4	% Profit Before Taxes/Tangible Net Worth	(195) 22.9	(150) 14.1
-23.8	-.9	.6	1.3	2.0	6.8		7.5	3.2
68.6	19.6	11.9	9.7	5.1	8.5		18.8	21.6
4.4	7.1	3.8	3.2	2.6	3.9	% Profit Before Taxes/Total Assets	7.6	5.1
-14.8	.3	.6	.6	.6	1.6		1.6	.6
UND	526.2	UND	UND	UND	92.1		381.4	UND
112.9	14.0	24.5	132.7	19.1	11.8	Sales/Net Fixed Assets	16.3	21.3
3.1	.2	.2	8.4	.3	.2		.7	2.5
7.8	2.0	1.4	.8	.9	.6		2.0	1.9
2.7	.4	.2	.2	.1	.1	Sales/Total Assets	.4	.4
.6	.1	.1	.1	.0	.1		.2	.1
.3	5.6	.7	.3		.4		1.0	.9
(10) 1.5	(11) 17.2	(30) 3.8	(19) .8	(12) 1.8		% Depr., Dep., Amort./Sales	(139) 2.8	(102) 2.5
5.7	34.3	22.6	3.1	17.0			11.3	10.2
						% Officers', Directors' Owners' Comp/Sales	1.1	1.4
							(29) 12.2	(23) 8.1
							29.6	26.4
21839M	38438M	290254M	459737M	993818M	935193M	Net Sales ($)	3102242M	2879042M
4812M	27373M	263758M	1057923M	1319791M	2120422M	Total Assets ($)	5062352M	4221898M

M = $ thousand   MM = $ million
See Pages 9 through 22 for Explanation of Ratios and Data

Comparative Historical Data

Current Data Sorted by Sales

			Type of Statement						
25	53	43	Unqualified	4	11	4	6	10	8
11	11	13	Reviewed	11	4	3	3	1	2
14	11	9	Compiled	5	3		1		
26	25	26	Tax Returns	19	5	1		1	
68	92	74	Other	24	14	5	8	12	11
4/1/07-3/31/08 ALL	4/1/08-3/31/09 ALL	4/1/09-3/31/10 ALL		15 (4/1-9/30/09)			150 (10/1/09-3/31/10)		
				0-1MM	1-3MM	3-5MM	5-10MM	10-25MM	25MM & OVER
144	192	165	**NUMBER OF STATEMENTS**	52	37	13	18	24	21
%	%	%	**ASSETS**	%	%	%	%	%	%
13.7	13.1	14.6	Cash & Equivalents	9.8	15.1	10.0	19.9	18.1	20.2
12.4	21.2	13.3	Trade Receivables (net)	6.1	11.8	21.6	23.2	14.4	19.4
4.6	1.8	3.3	Inventory	3.7	2.3	.5	1.7	3.1	7.1
7.8	13.7	9.4	All Other Current	6.8	10.8	14.1	11.3	7.7	10.7
38.5	49.8	40.6	Total Current	26.3	40.0	46.2	56.1	43.3	57.4
32.9	23.1	26.7	Fixed Assets (net)	42.8	19.7	17.7	16.1	21.8	19.7
4.0	3.4	2.5	Intangibles (net)	2.2	2.5	.4	2.0	3.2	4.4
24.5	23.7	30.1	All Other Non-Current	28.6	37.8	35.7	25.8	31.7	18.6
100.0	100.0	100.0	Total	100.0	100.0	100.0	100.0	100.0	100.0
			LIABILITIES						
12.1	19.5	14.8	Notes Payable-Short Term	11.8	24.3	15.0	15.0	12.2	8.0
4.9	2.3	1.9	Cur. Mat.-L.T.D.	2.6	2.0	.7	.7	1.5	2.4
4.2	5.7	5.3	Trade Payables	.5	2.9	2.3	7.8	8.0	17.8
.1	.1	.1	Income Taxes Payable	.0	.3	.1	.0	.4	.1
10.0	12.7	8.6	All Other Current	4.5	6.6	4.4	14.7	17.7	9.1
31.3	40.3	30.7	Total Current	19.4	36.1	22.5	38.2	39.8	37.5
28.2	26.2	22.6	Long-Term Debt	36.8	16.8	20.5	15.7	13.2	15.7
.1	.1	.0	Deferred Taxes	.0	.0	.0	.0	.0	.3
3.7	6.2	4.9	All Other Non-Current	6.0	1.3	2.5	1.1	8.7	8.9
36.7	27.2	41.8	Net Worth	37.9	45.8	54.5	45.0	38.4	37.6
100.0	100.0	100.0	Total Liabilities & Net Worth	100.0	100.0	100.0	100.0	100.0	100.0
			INCOME DATA						
100.0	100.0	100.0	Net Sales	100.0	100.0	100.0	100.0	100.0	100.0
			Gross Profit						
59.3	67.1	65.9	Operating Expenses	54.2	63.4	65.8	68.6	77.7	83.2
40.7	32.9	34.1	Operating Profit	45.8	36.6	34.2	31.4	22.3	16.8
15.0	14.6	13.6	All Other Expenses (net)	24.9	9.5	7.9	10.5	9.3	4.4
25.8	18.3	20.5	Profit Before Taxes	21.0	27.1	26.3	20.8	13.0	12.4
			RATIOS						
3.2	2.6	3.8	Current	7.6	2.9	5.5	3.8	2.8	4.0
1.3	1.3	1.4		1.2	1.4	2.9	1.5	1.2	1.5
.4	.5	.5		.2	.7	1.7	.7	.4	1.1
2.0	1.9	2.9	Quick	4.1	2.7	3.6	3.1	2.7	2.7
(143) .6	.9	1.0		.5	1.0	2.4	1.4	.6	1.1
.1	.2	.2		.1	.3	.9	.3	.2	.6
0 UND	0 UND	0 UND	Sales/Receivables	0 UND	0 UND	2 196.4	0 UND	1 523.4	3 116.7
0 999.8	5 77.2	2 203.3		0 UND	0 UND	27 13.6	10 36.3	14 25.6	17 21.8
34 10.6	69 5.3	41 9.0		2 191.4	22 16.7	150 2.4	78 4.7	48 7.5	55 6.6
			Cost of Sales/Inventory						
			Cost of Sales/Payables						
2.1	1.3	2.0	Sales/Working Capital	1.5	2.9	.5	1.2	3.3	4.7
25.0	11.6	9.5		8.0	15.1	2.7	5.4	18.5	9.8
-4.6	-12.1	-7.8		-3.0	-11.5	14.6	-57.1	-3.3	45.8
10.4	7.3	25.3	EBIT/Interest	10.7	6.6		21.4	34.1	49.8
(71) 5.5	(101) 3.0	(84) 3.7		(15) 3.4	(21) 3.5		(10) 6.6	(16) 3.7	(16) 2.6
2.5	1.4	1.2		1.3	1.4		3.9	-.8	1.1
	17.8		Net Profit + Depr., Dep., Amort./Cur. Mat. L/T/D						
	(12) 10.3								
	2.0								
.0	.0	.0	Fixed/Worth	.0	.0	.0	.0	.0	.0
.5	.1	.1		.5	.0	.0	.1	.2	.2
6.6	3.1	2.1		4.3	1.8	.7	.6	3.5	3.0
.5	.8	.3	Debt/Worth	.3	.0	.2	.2	.3	.7
2.0	2.8	1.7		1.9	1.1	.7	1.6	2.4	2.7
18.1	14.3	8.1		11.6	4.5	2.3	3.9	9.6	14.2
68.2	49.5	37.9	% Profit Before Taxes/Tangible Net Worth	35.1	20.7	68.7	51.6	36.5	87.2
(116) 18.2	(156) 16.1	(143) 9.5		(44) 4.9	(30) 3.6	16.3	(17) 10.6	(21) 14.4	(18) 17.0
4.9	5.0	1.3		-.6	1.3	1.5	6.1	.2	6.3
21.7	15.4	11.1	% Profit Before Taxes/Total Assets	5.5	8.7	31.1	17.1	20.9	24.6
6.1	4.9	3.6		1.9	3.4	4.5	5.5	3.3	4.0
1.6	1.1	.6		-.1	.9	.6	2.6	.1	.5
337.6	549.2	UND	Sales/Net Fixed Assets	UND	UND	UND	312.5	124.9	102.5
13.4	27.4	30.7		5.4	331.8	544.9	45.8	22.6	33.6
.6	1.8	1.0		.2	3.1	12.1	3.1	1.8	11.6
1.7	1.7	1.5	Sales/Total Assets	.3	2.0	1.4	2.1	1.9	3.0
.4	.4	.2		.1	.2	.3	.7	.6	1.2
.1	.1	.1		.1	.1	.1	.1	.1	.5
1.2	.6	.7	% Depr., Dep., Amort./Sales	7.1	.2		.2	.7	.4
(86) 3.4	(112) 1.6	(89) 2.4		(25) 20.5	(11) .7		(12) .9	(17) 1.4	(17) 1.2
13.6	5.2	17.6		34.8	11.5		3.9	4.9	3.3
2.5	4.9	3.9	% Officers', Directors' Owners' Comp/Sales						
(23) 6.7	(28) 12.8	(18) 9.6							
15.3	20.6	22.9							
2383313M	3586580M	2739279M	Net Sales ($)	21555M	67896M	52809M	120733M	401124M	2075162M
4009584M	5064696M	4794079M	Total Assets ($)	233856M	610955M	254531M	486621M	1295914M	1912202M

M = $ thousand   MM = $ million
See Pages 9 through 22 for Explanation of Ratios and Data

Current Data Sorted by Assets   Comparative Historical Data

Type of Statement	0-500M	500M-2MM	2-10MM	10-50MM	50-100MM	100-250MM	4/1/05-3/31/06 ALL	4/1/06-3/31/07 ALL
Unqualified	2	2	7	15	6	4	24	38
Reviewed		2	3	1	1	1	5	5
Compiled	4				1		10	11
Tax Returns	17	8	3	1			16	25
Other	11	10	16	17	4	6	30	44
	13 (4/1-9/30/09)		2-10MM	128 (10/1/09-3/31/10)				
NUMBER OF STATEMENTS	34	22	29	34	12	10	85	123
	%	%	%	%	%	%	%	%
ASSETS								
Cash & Equivalents	23.3	21.5	31.9	20.7	31.2	36.7	19.5	29.2
Trade Receivables (net)	10.2	13.9	22.5	12.6	23.1	11.4	13.4	13.8
Inventory	.0	.0	.1	1.4	1.4	1.2	1.5	.5
All Other Current	15.0	10.4	6.8	7.9	5.3	11.1	6.0	6.7
Total Current	48.4	45.8	61.4	42.6	61.1	60.4	40.3	50.2
Fixed Assets (net)	24.6	23.4	18.7	19.6	6.1	10.6	25.6	18.1
Intangibles (net)	5.2	4.5	6.2	8.3	12.8	15.9	7.1	7.6
All Other Non-Current	21.8	26.3	13.7	29.4	20.0	13.2	26.9	24.0
Total	100.0	100.0	100.0	100.0	100.0	100.0	100.0	100.0
LIABILITIES								
Notes Payable-Short Term	37.0	15.1	3.4	7.0	14.4	9.9	18.3	16.8
Cur. Mat.-L.T.D.	6.6	2.9	6.3	3.2	1.5	2.6	4.7	2.5
Trade Payables	3.4	3.9	5.6	6.2	3.4	1.5	3.4	4.0
Income Taxes Payable	.6	.2	.0	.1	.0	.0	.2	.8
All Other Current	41.4	13.3	16.5	6.7	17.0	17.5	21.9	18.6
Total Current	89.0	35.3	31.8	23.2	36.3	31.5	48.4	42.8
Long-Term Debt	32.3	26.9	36.0	13.0	7.0	36.9	29.2	20.2
Deferred Taxes	.0	.9	.0	.2	.0	1.6	.2	.1
All Other Non-Current	10.0	11.5	3.6	3.2	3.4	33.3	8.3	7.1
Net Worth	-31.2	25.4	28.6	60.5	53.4	-3.3	13.9	29.8
Total Liabilities & Net Worth	100.0	100.0	100.0	100.0	100.0	100.0	100.0	100.0
INCOME DATA								
Net Sales	100.0	100.0	100.0	100.0	100.0	100.0	100.0	100.0
Gross Profit								
Operating Expenses	85.1	81.8	74.7	69.3	66.4	65.5	68.7	68.3
Operating Profit	14.9	18.2	25.3	30.7	33.6	34.5	31.3	31.7
All Other Expenses (net)	3.1	11.1	5.3	8.3	4.7	2.9	9.1	6.1
Profit Before Taxes	11.8	7.2	20.0	22.4	28.9	31.6	22.2	25.6
RATIOS								
Current	3.2	3.3	4.2	11.8	3.8	5.4	3.3	4.7
	1.1	2.0	2.3	2.3	1.4	1.9	1.6	1.8
	.3	.7	1.0	1.4	.9	1.0	.6	.7
Quick	2.6	2.8	4.0	8.8	3.0	5.3	2.9	4.7
	.8	1.0	1.9	1.9	1.4	1.3	1.2	1.4
	.1	.3	1.0	.8	.6	.7	.3	.5
Sales/Receivables	0 UND	0 UND	0 UND	0 UND	0 UND	0 UND	0 UND	0 UND
	0 UND	1 257.9	17 21.3	24 15.3	22 16.5	17 21.7	0 999.8	4 89.7
	0 824.4	21 17.7	61 6.0	80 4.6	103 3.6	45 8.1	32 11.5	39 9.4
Cost of Sales/Inventory								
Cost of Sales/Payables								
Sales/Working Capital	23.5	6.7	3.3	2.1	.6	1.1	4.0	1.8
	289.6	27.6	6.2	6.8	7.1	3.0	15.4	8.3
	-8.3	-16.7	NM	54.8	-13.4	NM	-13.6	-24.2
EBIT/Interest	76.0	23.7	105.6	56.6			24.5	23.6
	(20) 2.1	(12) 6.9	(19) 8.3	(12) 5.9			(51) 8.6	(67) 9.6
	.0	-13.6	1.8	1.8			2.1	2.8
Net Profit + Depr., Dep., Amort./Cur. Mat. L/T/D								
Fixed/Worth	.0	.1	.1	.0	.0	.0	.1	.0
	.7	1.7	.1	.2	.1	.3	.4	.2
	-.3	NM	NM	.9	2.8	-136.4	5.1	3.6
Debt/Worth	.2	1.0	.4	.1	.2	.3	.5	.4
	10.3	3.5	1.0	.6	3.0	4.8	1.8	1.5
	-1.8	NM	NM	4.5	26.4	-1.7	26.6	39.0
% Profit Before Taxes/Tangible Net Worth	460.0	49.9	69.9	65.3	371.9		80.7	108.8
	(19) 98.7	(17) 17.8	(22) 28.2	(30) 12.9	(11) 54.0		(68) 24.8	(97) 21.6
	.8	-5.5	7.3	.2	6.4		9.7	4.0
% Profit Before Taxes/Total Assets	108.9	34.0	38.6	29.3	32.6	37.6	30.0	33.0
	13.6	4.9	15.4	11.8	6.1	3.2	7.8	10.2
	-1.7	-1.5	3.6	.1	2.7	.4	1.9	1.9
Sales/Net Fixed Assets	UND	171.7	87.9	253.4	UND	UND	82.0	999.8
	69.8	35.4	29.0	17.8	60.9	23.9	33.7	48.8
	12.5	1.8	3.3	7.1	21.5	4.3	5.7	14.9
Sales/Total Assets	9.0	3.9	3.4	1.7	1.3	1.6	3.9	3.3
	4.8	1.5	1.8	1.0	.5	.6	1.7	1.3
	2.3	.2	.7	.2	.1	.1	.2	.2
% Depr., Dep., Amort./Sales	.4	.5	.6	.7			.6	.4
	(19) 1.2	(13) 1.6	(23) 1.4	(25) 2.5			(58) 1.6	(77) 1.2
	5.0	11.3	5.5	4.3			4.7	3.4
% Officers', Directors' Owners' Comp/Sales	16.3						9.2	10.5
	(15) 23.2						(20) 20.8	(25) 23.3
	31.0						34.3	34.5
Net Sales ($)	55020M	44030M	234822M	980682M	808050M	1359927M	4059594M	1620725M
Total Assets ($)	7004M	21405M	145827M	948988M	877492M	1518706M	1466326M	2644876M

© RMA 2010

M = $ thousand   MM = $ million
See Pages 9 through 22 for Explanation of Ratios and Data

Comparative Historical Data

Current Data Sorted by Sales

			Type of Statement						
36	42	36	Unqualified	3	3	3	4	9	14
4	10	7	Reviewed	2	1	1	1	1	1
10	4	5	Compiled	1	3	1			
19	18	29	Tax Returns	17	8	2	2		
58	62	64	Other	11	13	4	11	10	15
4/1/07- 3/31/08 ALL	4/1/08- 3/31/09 ALL	4/1/09- 3/31/10 ALL		13 (4/1-9/30/09)			128 (10/1/09-3/31/10)		
				0-1MM	1-3MM	3-5MM	5-10MM	10-25MM	25MM & OVER
127	136	141	NUMBER OF STATEMENTS	34	28	11	18	20	30
%	%	%	ASSETS	%	%	%	%	%	%
26.2	24.2	25.8	Cash & Equivalents	18.0	27.5	26.1	27.1	29.9	29.4
14.7	15.8	15.1	Trade Receivables (net)	6.4	15.6	7.7	13.0	19.4	25.4
1.2	.3	.6	Inventory	.0	.0	.4	1.1	1.3	1.0
9.5	8.5	9.8	All Other Current	6.3	9.5	9.2	14.9	13.1	8.8
51.6	48.8	51.2	Total Current	30.8	52.6	43.4	56.1	63.7	64.6
16.6	23.9	19.4	Fixed Assets (net)	32.9	23.9	13.0	10.8	8.1	15.1
5.7	6.5	7.4	Intangibles (net)	8.7	1.2	1.9	9.6	12.8	9.0
26.1	20.7	21.9	All Other Non-Current	27.6	22.3	41.7	23.5	15.5	11.2
100.0	100.0	100.0	Total	100.0	100.0	100.0	100.0	100.0	100.0
			LIABILITIES						
15.1	12.0	15.6	Notes Payable-Short Term	9.2	38.9	8.9	13.2	10.0	8.7
2.4	3.8	4.4	Cur. Mat.-L.T.D.	2.4	7.2	1.2	6.2	4.6	4.2
5.2	4.9	4.5	Trade Payables	1.1	4.9	2.5	5.8	4.7	7.6
.3	.3	.2	Income Taxes Payable	.3	.0	1.1	.0	.0	.1
18.4	15.9	19.8	All Other Current	14.3	39.3	10.2	17.6	10.9	18.3
41.4	36.9	44.4	Total Current	27.3	90.3	24.0	42.8	30.2	38.9
16.9	25.3	25.7	Long-Term Debt	36.5	29.4	14.4	26.5	16.9	19.6
.3	.3	.3	Deferred Taxes	.0	.0	1.8	.0	.2	.6
8.2	6.3	8.3	All Other Non-Current	12.4	5.9	6.7	4.0	1.5	13.7
33.2	31.1	21.2	Net Worth	23.8	-25.6	53.1	26.7	51.1	27.1
100.0	100.0	100.0	Total Liabilties & Net Worth	100.0	100.0	100.0	100.0	100.0	100.0
			INCOME DATA						
100.0	100.0	100.0	Net Sales	100.0	100.0	100.0	100.0	100.0	100.0
			Gross Profit						
69.4	70.7	75.6	Operating Expenses	69.5	82.8	83.8	80.8	76.9	69.1
30.6	29.3	24.4	Operating Profit	30.5	17.2	16.2	19.2	23.1	30.9
5.8	8.1	6.2	All Other Expenses (net)	18.8	4.4	3.1	1.2	1.3	1.0
24.8	21.2	18.2	Profit Before Taxes	11.7	12.8	13.1	18.1	21.9	30.0
			RATIOS						
5.0	5.5	4.2		4.4	4.2	4.2	4.9	7.3	3.0
1.9	1.9	1.9	Current	1.7	.8	2.5	2.2	2.4	1.8
.9	.6	.9		.6	.3	.9	.9	1.4	.9
3.8	4.2	3.6		3.6	3.9	3.7	4.3	4.5	2.2
1.3	1.4	1.3	Quick	1.0	.6	2.5	1.5	2.0	1.5
.4	.4	.5		.4	.2	.1	.4	1.1	.8
0 UND	0 UND	0 UND		0 UND	0 UND	0 UND	0 UND	0 UND	9 41.0
2 214.3	1 414.9	2 177.8	Sales/Receivables	0 UND	0 UND	2 223.7	4 91.8	27 13.7	35 10.4
41 9.0	41 8.9	38 9.6		1 270.9	17 22.0	18 20.3	55 6.6	58 6.3	80 4.6
			Cost of Sales/Inventory						
			Cost of Sales/Payables						
2.6	3.3	3.3		3.7	4.6	3.2	2.8	3.6	2.9
9.7	16.5	11.6	Sales/Working Capital	42.6	-36.3	15.1	8.6	8.1	6.5
-28.4	-11.7	-16.9		-11.0	-8.2	-19.3	-27.3	11.2	-39.0
41.5	36.2	47.4		7.3	20.1			191.4	61.5
(64) 10.5	(77) 7.2	(78) 7.4	EBIT/Interest	(10) 1.1	(21) 3.2		(12)	33.9	(17) 8.0
2.2	1.9	1.2		-.9	.3			7.5	3.4
		8.8	19.3	Net Profit + Depr., Dep.,						
	(11) 2.3	(10) 2.3	Amort./Cur. Mat. L/T/D						
		.7	.4							
.0	.0	.0		.0	.0	.0	.0	.0	.1
.1	.3	.4	Fixed/Worth	1.2	1.4	.1	.2	.1	.5
2.9	3.8	14.7		NM	-.3	1.6	-.2	.7	3.5
.4	.4	.3		.2	.4	.2	.2	.3	.3
1.6	1.9	1.5	Debt/Worth	4.3	3.3	.6	.7	.7	1.7
20.8	21.7	-154.2		-17.5	-2.6	1.9	-4.6	5.6	110.8
109.5	118.6	84.7	% Profit Before Taxes/Tangible	99.4	52.8	36.2	79.2	96.0	166.3
(105) 33.7	(111) 41.7	(105) 22.2	Net Worth	(25) 20.0	(18) 9.0	(10) 10.3	(12) 19.1	(16) 28.2	(24) 56.1
6.6	3.5	2.1		-1.6	.5	-23.1	4.2	10.6	12.5
36.7	40.8	42.1	% Profit Before Taxes/Total	11.0	50.8	25.4	43.3	35.3	66.1
10.2	13.1	9.8	Assets	2.1	5.1	5.0	9.7	19.7	27.2
2.1	1.0	.2		-.7	-.1	-10.7	2.0	5.5	6.6
999.8	410.0	208.1		UND	939.7	UND	294.6	178.7	55.6
51.0	32.8	35.0	Sales/Net Fixed Assets	9.4	64.3	40.7	67.8	56.4	18.2
12.1	7.3	8.6		.5	9.6	28.3	23.7	17.1	7.3
3.2	3.9	3.4		2.7	7.7	5.1	3.6	3.5	2.0
1.5	1.6	1.6	Sales/Total Assets	.6	3.0	2.0	1.6	1.7	1.6
.3	.3	.3		.1	.2	.3	.2	.8	.8
.5	.5	.6		1.5	.4		.2	.4	.7
(76) 1.2	(78) 1.8	(92) 1.5	% Depr., Dep., Amort./Sales	(20) 7.9	(15) 1.1	(10)	.5	(15) 1.2	(25) 1.7
3.2	4.3	5.0		14.2	11.5		1.9	2.1	3.3
7.6	10.3	9.4	% Officers', Directors'						
(29) 22.5	(23) 20.2	(24) 18.7	Owners' Comp/Sales						
35.5	38.2	27.2							
2301211M	4913207M	3482531M	Net Sales ($)	13422M	49923M	43564M	139526M	299358M	2936738M
2824370M	3000777M	3519422M	Total Assets ($)	109555M	225612M	113346M	551001M	376703M	2143205M

M = $ thousand   MM = $ million
See Pages 9 through 22 for Explanation of Ratios and Data

FINANCE—Investment Advice NAICS 523930

	Current Data Sorted by Assets							Comparative Historical Data	

Type of Statement

0-500M	500M-2MM	2-10MM	10-50MM	50-100MM	100-250MM		ALL 4/1/05-3/31/06	ALL 4/1/06-3/31/07
1	1	7	11	5	4	Unqualified	23	36
1	1	1	1			Reviewed	8	7
5	4	4				Compiled	10	10
18	13	4			1	Tax Returns	21	30
15	18	13	11	2	9	Other	54	54
	10 (4/1-9/30/09)		140 (10/1/09-3/31/10)					
40	37	29	23	7	14	NUMBER OF STATEMENTS	116	137

0-500M %	500M-2MM %	2-10MM %	10-50MM %	50-100MM %	100-250MM %	ASSETS	ALL %	ALL %
32.0	25.7	17.8	32.3		16.0	Cash & Equivalents	24.2	30.2
11.3	14.3	16.9	28.1		9.7	Trade Receivables (net)	23.6	18.9
.0	.8	1.4	2.9		.7	Inventory	2.2	.5
5.6	5.2	5.8	11.1		15.4	All Other Current	9.3	6.2
48.9	46.0	41.9	74.4		41.7	Total Current	59.2	55.7
30.2	25.5	26.0	8.4		8.1	Fixed Assets (net)	17.3	16.7
9.3	11.7	14.4	11.2		26.6	Intangibles (net)	10.9	7.0
11.6	16.8	17.7	5.9		23.6	All Other Non-Current	12.6	20.6
100.0	100.0	100.0	100.0		100.0	Total	100.0	100.0
						LIABILITIES		
52.7	20.7	5.4	2.6		21.3	Notes Payable-Short Term	20.0	11.9
1.6	8.6	3.8	4.0		6.1	Cur. Mat.-L.T.D.	6.5	4.2
3.8	5.6	3.6	9.1		2.1	Trade Payables	5.9	4.3
.8	.2	.0	.9		.0	Income Taxes Payable	.4	.2
32.4	9.0	9.4	21.4		17.8	All Other Current	15.4	17.2
91.4	44.1	22.2	37.9		47.4	Total Current	48.1	37.8
25.4	29.2	22.6	4.2		35.2	Long-Term Debt	22.5	17.5
.0	.0	1.0	.1		.2	Deferred Taxes	.6	.5
22.0	14.7	1.9	4.9		32.0	All Other Non-Current	8.4	8.2
-38.8	11.9	52.3	52.9		-14.9	Net Worth	20.4	36.1
100.0	100.0	100.0	100.0		100.0	Total Liabilties & Net Worth	100.0	100.0
						INCOME DATA		
100.0	100.0	100.0	100.0		100.0	Net Sales	100.0	100.0
						Gross Profit		
82.0	77.2	74.8	82.9		73.4	Operating Expenses	80.8	78.0
18.0	22.8	25.2	17.1		26.6	Operating Profit	19.2	22.0
6.3	5.6	6.9	.2		6.9	All Other Expenses (net)	2.5	3.4
11.7	17.2	18.3	17.0		19.7	Profit Before Taxes	16.7	18.6
						RATIOS		
2.6	3.5	4.9	4.1		2.7		3.0	4.6
.6	1.8	1.6	2.2		.8	Current	1.5	1.6
.3	.6	.9	1.3		.5		.8	.7
1.8	3.4	4.0	3.4		1.7		2.8	4.2
.6	1.3	1.6	1.9		.7	Quick	1.3	1.4
.3	.4	.6	1.1		.4		.5	.5
0 UND	0 UND	0 UND	23 16.2		0 UND		0 UND	0 UND
0 UND	0 UND	12 30.0	41 8.8		29 12.5	Sales/Receivables	17 21.7	10 35.2
10 35.5	23 16.0	76 4.8	85 4.3		64 5.7		64 5.7	41 8.9
						Cost of Sales/Inventory		
						Cost of Sales/Payables		
53.9	6.1	4.1	2.8		1.5		4.6	4.2
-42.0	41.4	7.7	4.8		-22.0	Sales/Working Capital	14.0	17.6
-13.5	-13.6	-308.9	23.4		-4.7		-46.0	-33.2
15.9	72.2	86.0	128.6		5.4		27.9	64.8
(18) 5.0	(23) 4.5	(19) 25.6	(12) 11.9		(12) 3.3	EBIT/Interest	(84) 12.1	(89) 14.3
-.2	1.2	3.0	-3.6		2.2		2.6	3.7
							11.7	7.9
						Net Profit + Depr., Dep., Amort./Cur. Mat. L/T/D	(10) 4.6	(12) 2.4
							1.5	1.0
.0	.1	.1	.0		.0		.1	.0
.7	.5	.2	.2		.7	Fixed/Worth	.4	.2
-.5	-.8	2.0	.5		-.1		3.7	2.2
.4	.5	.4	.3		4.9		.7	.3
24.1	4.2	1.1	1.1		-2.6	Debt/Worth	2.3	1.7
-1.7	-3.5	3.2	2.8		-1.7		-25.3	11.1
280.2	102.2	89.7	206.4				139.2	138.5
(22) 62.2	(22) 39.8	(25) 19.8	(20) 57.2			% Profit Before Taxes/Tangible Net Worth	(86) 37.4	(114) 62.5
17.0	3.4	6.3	24.7				13.3	13.3
74.7	55.8	43.2	62.5		17.7		55.4	86.6
25.6	11.0	7.6	31.1		5.8	% Profit Before Taxes/Total Assets	16.2	20.5
-3.3	1.3	2.5	6.5		2.7		4.1	4.7
UND	88.6	64.8	88.7		UND		105.6	171.9
49.3	44.2	27.2	50.8		32.8	Sales/Net Fixed Assets	42.7	42.4
16.8	13.7	3.9	15.8		16.0		15.9	14.7
17.4	4.8	2.7	3.0		1.3		5.3	5.5
6.7	2.5	1.8	2.0		.6	Sales/Total Assets	2.6	2.7
3.0	1.2	.3	1.1		.2		1.3	1.1
.6	.4	.7	.8				.6	.4
(21) 1.3	(21) .9	(24) 2.6	(15) 1.0			% Depr., Dep., Amort./Sales	(76) 1.1	(78) 1.1
3.5	3.3	4.4	2.2				2.4	2.3
9.1							10.6	9.1
(15) 21.2						% Officers', Directors' Owners' Comp/Sales	(27) 16.8	(45) 21.7
32.3							30.3	31.4
40658M	158323M	352838M	943876M	502933M	2280126M	Net Sales ($)	3459984M	2356077M
6115M	39055M	149359M	495470M	578624M	2356641M	Total Assets ($)	1699756M	2270579M

M = $ thousand   MM = $ million
See Pages 9 through 22 for Explanation of Ratios and Data

Comparative Historical Data — Current Data Sorted by Sales

Type of Statement

Type of Statement	4/1/07-3/31/08 ALL	4/1/08-3/31/09 ALL	4/1/09-3/31/10 ALL	0-1MM	1-3MM	3-5MM	5-10MM	10-25MM	25MM & OVER
Unqualified	41	29	29		2	1	3	9	14
Reviewed	6	6	4		1	1	1	1	
Compiled	10	13	13	5	3		4	1	
Tax Returns	29	30	36	17	8	4	3	2	2
Other	65	72	68	19	13	4	6	10	16
				10 (4/1-9/30/09)			140 (10/1/09-3/31/10)		
NUMBER OF STATEMENTS	151	150	150	41	27	10	17	23	32

ASSETS (%)

	07-08	08-09	09-10	0-1MM	1-3MM	3-5MM	5-10MM	10-25MM	25MM & OVER
Cash & Equivalents	28.8	28.2	25.1	18.2	32.1	30.6	20.5	28.9	26.0
Trade Receivables (net)	18.6	17.8	15.4	7.9	11.3	28.3	16.9	19.1	21.0
Inventory	1.4	1.0	1.0	.0	.0	3.0	.1	.0	3.6
All Other Current	4.9	6.5	7.1	5.3	3.8	12.6	7.4	6.3	11.1
Total Current	53.7	53.5	48.7	31.5	47.2	74.5	44.9	54.4	61.7
Fixed Assets (net)	16.6	20.7	22.5	42.7	25.5	10.2	14.3	12.2	9.6
Intangibles (net)	12.3	9.3	15.0	12.1	12.3	6.7	15.3	22.7	18.1
All Other Non-Current	17.5	16.5	13.8	13.8	15.1	8.6	25.5	10.7	10.6
Total	100.0	100.0	100.0	100.0	100.0	100.0	100.0	100.0	100.0

LIABILITIES

	07-08	08-09	09-10	0-1MM	1-3MM	3-5MM	5-10MM	10-25MM	25MM & OVER
Notes Payable-Short Term	10.7	15.2	22.6	37.5	31.3	9.3	36.2	.3	9.4
Cur. Mat.-L.T.D.	2.8	3.0	4.8	1.3	2.3	4.1	1.0	15.8	5.9
Trade Payables	3.6	5.1	4.7	3.5	2.9	7.8	5.5	4.7	6.4
Income Taxes Payable	.1	.4	.4	.8	.3	.0	.0	.5	.3
All Other Current	18.5	15.8	18.5	17.6	19.3	22.9	9.7	14.6	24.9
Total Current	35.8	39.4	51.1	60.7	56.1	44.2	52.4	35.8	46.8
Long-Term Debt	18.6	24.3	23.3	36.7	28.8	13.7	4.2	20.2	16.8
Deferred Taxes	.3	.4	.4	.0	.0	.0	1.5	.1	.9
All Other Non-Current	4.7	7.5	14.2	22.4	12.9	15.9	.8	4.8	18.1
Net Worth	40.6	28.4	11.1	-19.8	2.2	26.1	41.1	39.0	17.4
Total Liabilities & Net Worth	100.0	100.0	100.0	100.0	100.0	100.0	100.0	100.0	100.0

INCOME DATA

	07-08	08-09	09-10	0-1MM	1-3MM	3-5MM	5-10MM	10-25MM	25MM & OVER
Net Sales	100.0	100.0	100.0	100.0	100.0	100.0	100.0	100.0	100.0
Gross Profit									
Operating Expenses	75.9	80.1	79.1	64.5	85.8	92.1	87.9	83.7	79.9
Operating Profit	24.1	19.9	20.9	35.5	14.2	7.9	12.1	16.3	20.1
All Other Expenses (net)	3.2	4.4	5.3	13.9	3.0	-.1	1.6	.8	2.9
Profit Before Taxes	20.9	15.5	15.7	21.6	11.2	8.0	10.5	15.5	17.2

RATIOS

	07-08	08-09	09-10	0-1MM	1-3MM	3-5MM	5-10MM	10-25MM	25MM & OVER
Current	5.4	3.5	3.4	3.0	3.8	5.8	4.0	4.4	2.5
	1.8	1.5	1.4	.6	1.1	2.4	1.0	1.7	1.4
	.8	.9	.5	.3	.5	1.8	.3	1.3	.7
Quick	4.3	2.9	2.9	2.4	3.8	5.8	4.0	2.8	2.3
	1.5	1.3	1.1	.6	1.0	2.2	.9	1.6	1.0
	.6	.6	.4	.2	.3	1.3	.1	1.2	.5
Sales/Receivables	0 UND	0 UND	0 UND	0 UND	0 UND	0 UND	0 UND	5 69.6	4 89.1
	8 47.6	5 67.5	4 88.6	0 UND	0 UND	21 17.4	12 30.0	49 7.4	37 9.8
	51 7.2	52 7.0	50 7.3	3 119.2	25 14.7	80 4.5	46 8.0	88 4.2	72 5.1
Cost of Sales/Inventory									
Cost of Sales/Payables									
Sales/Working Capital	4.5	5.2	5.3	27.2	6.9	3.8	4.8	2.8	4.9
	17.1	21.4	39.2	-24.1	286.0	5.7	148.5	6.7	15.7
	-54.8	-66.1	-15.3	-8.1	-15.2	13.1	-15.0	41.4	-13.9
EBIT/Interest	91.7	64.7	37.8	9.6	15.9		129.9	57.1	53.2
	(93) 12.8	(97) 7.6	(89) 5.2	(19) 5.2	(14) 2.5	(14) 8.2	(14) 12.3	(21) 4.3	
	1.5	1.8	2.0	3.0	.1		1.6	2.6	2.2
Net Profit + Depr., Dep., Amort./Cur. Mat. L/T/D		6.6	13.2						
		(13) 1.7	(12) 1.2						
		.6	-.2						
Fixed/Worth	.1	.1	.1	.0	.1	.1	.0	.1	.1
	.3	.5	.5	2.1	.6	.1	.2	.3	.5
	1.8	8.3	-2.0	-2.5	-.5	-1.8	1.1	-2.2	-.4
Debt/Worth	.4	.4	.4	.7	.2	.3	.3	.3	.9
	1.2	1.6	2.3	10.9	11.2	1.3	.7	1.2	4.6
	7.3	NM	-3.0	-1.7	-2.7	-21.3	8.0	-3.4	-2.5
% Profit Before Taxes/Tangible Net Worth	225.5	138.6	112.8	222.7	116.6		82.0	62.7	215.6
	(126) 64.4	(113) 50.8	(98) 44.2	(24) 43.8	(15) 57.7	(14) 17.4	(17) 48.8	(21) 73.5	
	13.9	13.6	6.4	7.9	18.7		2.5	5.8	10.9
% Profit Before Taxes/Total Assets	83.6	66.3	52.1	66.3	42.3	60.4	43.2	44.8	61.4
	26.2	16.4	12.2	12.0	13.7	9.5	7.6	8.4	13.9
	4.0	2.8	1.5	1.2	.5	.5	.5	2.8	3.7
Sales/Net Fixed Assets	119.3	86.5	118.5	UND	373.8	193.0	596.0	85.2	66.5
	39.1	31.6	36.0	19.8	47.8	49.4	51.0	31.1	35.9
	14.6	12.2	12.8	.2	13.5	23.0	24.5	9.0	16.4
Sales/Total Assets	5.1	5.2	5.7	7.8	6.5	4.4	6.8	2.4	3.2
	2.6	2.5	2.1	1.3	3.0	3.2	3.4	1.5	2.1
	1.2	1.4	.7	.2	1.2	1.9	2.3	.5	.8
% Depr., Dep., Amort./Sales	.5	.5	.7	1.5	.5		.7	.4	.8
	(97) 1.1	(104) 1.1	(92) 1.3	(23) 5.0	(15) .8	(11) .9	(16) .9	(21) 1.1	
	2.3	2.5	3.3	22.7	1.7		2.8	3.6	2.1
% Officers', Directors' Owners' Comp/Sales	8.4	7.0	9.9	8.0					
	(51) 20.7	(43) 15.0	(32) 16.0	(12) 18.6					
	30.5	24.2	28.4	28.7					
Net Sales ($)	3958636M	3995016M	4278754M	14669M	50341M	38621M	125686M	407590M	3641847M
Total Assets ($)	1961048M	2177934M	3625264M	31048M	43736M	13500M	466207M	584914M	2485859M

M = $ thousand   MM = $ million
See Pages 9 through 22 for Explanation of Ratios and Data

FINANCE—Trust, Fiduciary, and Custody Activities   NAICS 523991

Current Data Sorted by Assets							Comparative Historical Data	

						Type of Statement		
1	1	4	3	1	2	Unqualified	8	16
		1				Reviewed	2	3
	3	2	1			Compiled	3	1
		2				Tax Returns	2	4
1	2	8	6	3		Other	24	21
	5 (4/1-9/30/09)		37 (10/1/09-3/31/10)				4/1/05-3/31/06	4/1/06-3/31/07
0-500M	500M-2MM	2-10MM	10-50MM	50-100MM	100-250MM		ALL	ALL
3	6	17	10	4	2	**NUMBER OF STATEMENTS**	39	45
%	%	%	%	%	%	**ASSETS**	%	%
		29.2	34.0			Cash & Equivalents	22.9	28.8
		18.8	11.9			Trade Receivables (net)	13.6	16.6
		.9	8.7			Inventory	2.3	.6
		3.5	7.5			All Other Current	6.0	4.8
		52.4	62.1			Total Current	44.8	50.8
		32.0	10.1			Fixed Assets (net)	25.1	24.5
		1.2	1.1			Intangibles (net)	6.5	6.9
		14.4	26.7			All Other Non-Current	23.6	17.8
		100.0	100.0			Total	100.0	100.0
						LIABILITIES		
		3.9	.7			Notes Payable-Short Term	16.0	3.5
		3.6	.3			Cur. Mat.-L.T.D.	1.1	3.1
		7.4	5.1			Trade Payables	3.9	6.3
		.0	4.3			Income Taxes Payable	.1	.1
		7.5	33.5			All Other Current	17.0	10.9
		22.4	44.0			Total Current	38.3	24.0
		41.2	14.3			Long-Term Debt	15.5	14.6
		.2	.5			Deferred Taxes	.7	.5
		5.5	13.0			All Other Non-Current	9.1	3.3
		30.7	28.3			Net Worth	36.5	57.7
		100.0	100.0			Total Liabilties & Net Worth	100.0	100.0
						INCOME DATA		
		100.0	100.0			Net Sales	100.0	100.0
						Gross Profit		
		76.2	79.0			Operating Expenses	71.1	65.6
		23.8	21.0			Operating Profit	28.9	34.4
		11.4	1.3			All Other Expenses (net)	8.1	7.9
		12.3	19.7			Profit Before Taxes	20.8	26.5
						RATIOS		
		3.3	33.5				8.5	14.6
		2.3	1.7			Current	3.5	2.3
		1.5	.9				1.2	1.1
		3.2	33.5				7.8	14.4
		1.9	1.4			Quick	2.0	2.2
		1.1	.4				.5	.7
		0 UND	0 UND				0 UND	0 UND
		32 11.5	38 9.7			Sales/Receivables	17 21.0	0 UND
		78 4.7	74 4.9				48 7.7	41 8.9
						Cost of Sales/Inventory		
						Cost of Sales/Payables		
		1.7	.6				1.1	1.9
		3.3	6.5			Sales/Working Capital	5.4	4.9
		23.6	NM				20.4	UND
							11.0	14.5
						EBIT/Interest	(19) 5.0	(15) 6.9
							1.0	3.6
						Net Profit + Depr., Dep., Amort./Cur. Mat. L/T/D		
		.0	.0				.0	.0
		.5	.3			Fixed/Worth	.2	.2
		10.2	.8				1.2	1.0
		.3	.9				.2	.1
		1.5	3.2			Debt/Worth	.5	.7
		9.5	19.2				6.0	3.4
		34.0					17.4	43.8
		(14) 8.1				% Profit Before Taxes/Tangible Net Worth	(32) 7.2	(40) 19.4
		1.0					1.3	6.8
		21.1	12.0				12.3	22.1
		2.7	2.5			% Profit Before Taxes/Total Assets	4.6	8.7
		-.6	-.8				.0	2.1
		39.3	UND				UND	UND
		16.6	31.5			Sales/Net Fixed Assets	27.1	37.0
		.2	9.1				1.3	1.0
		1.7	2.3				1.8	2.4
		.6	.5			Sales/Total Assets	.5	.9
		.1	.2				.1	.1
		1.2					.8	.6
		(11) 1.8				% Depr., Dep., Amort./Sales	(21) 3.7	(25) 2.0
		8.0					8.3	11.5
						% Officers', Directors' Owners' Comp/Sales		
4029M	8481M	116271M	211907M	213581M	457637M	Net Sales ($)	687746M	2203428M
148M	6309M	90226M	208175M	358185M	310468M	Total Assets ($)	1125745M	1609028M

M = $ thousand   MM = $ million
See Pages 9 through 22 for Explanation of Ratios and Data

Comparative Historical Data / Current Data Sorted by Sales

4/1/07-3/31/08 ALL	4/1/08-3/31/09 ALL	4/1/09-3/31/10 ALL	Type of Statement	0-1MM	1-3MM	3-5MM	5-10MM	10-25MM	25MM & OVER
12	13	12	Unqualified	1	2		3	3	3
1	1	1	Reviewed		1				
6	7	6	Compiled	3	2	1			
2	1	3	Tax Returns	2	1				
12	19	20	Other	6	1	4	1	2	6
						5 (4/1-9/30/09)		37 (10/1/09-3/31/10)	
33	**41**	**42**	**NUMBER OF STATEMENTS**	**12**	**7**	**5**	**4**	**5**	**9**
%	%	%	**ASSETS**	%	%	%	%	%	%
33.7	23.2	31.9	Cash & Equivalents	24.9					
10.0	14.6	13.3	Trade Receivables (net)	.7					
3.4	3.7	4.1	Inventory	.0					
4.0	7.3	5.7	All Other Current	10.7					
51.1	48.8	55.0	Total Current	36.3					
17.5	21.7	23.4	Fixed Assets (net)	35.2					
3.4	5.6	4.7	Intangibles (net)	7.1					
27.9	23.9	17.0	All Other Non-Current	21.4					
100.0	100.0	100.0	Total	100.0					
			LIABILITIES						
1.2	3.1	2.8	Notes Payable-Short Term	2.1					
1.4	3.3	2.0	Cur. Mat.-L.T.D.	.7					
6.9	4.5	5.7	Trade Payables	.7					
.1	.2	1.0	Income Taxes Payable	.0					
11.8	21.4	21.1	All Other Current	28.2					
21.4	32.5	32.7	Total Current	31.6					
12.7	16.4	26.4	Long-Term Debt	39.3					
.7	.3	.2	Deferred Taxes	.0					
3.7	7.2	5.6	All Other Non-Current	4.5					
61.6	43.7	35.1	Net Worth	24.5					
100.0	100.0	100.0	Total Liabilities & Net Worth	100.0					
			INCOME DATA						
100.0	100.0	100.0	Net Sales	100.0					
			Gross Profit						
68.1	73.8	76.0	Operating Expenses	51.2					
31.9	26.2	24.0	Operating Profit	48.8					
6.0	7.1	7.7	All Other Expenses (net)	21.7					
26.0	19.1	16.3	Profit Before Taxes	27.1					
			RATIOS						
8.1	2.4	4.2	Current	3.4					
2.7	1.6	1.8		1.2					
1.6	.9	1.0		.6					
6.8	2.2	4.2	Quick	3.4					
2.0	1.1	1.3		1.2					
1.3	.5	.8		.4					
0 UND	0 UND	0 UND	Sales/Receivables	0 UND					
10 36.0	23 15.8	30 12.1		0 UND					
34 10.7	46 7.9	52 7.0		0 UND					
			Cost of Sales/Inventory						
			Cost of Sales/Payables						
.7	1.6	2.0	Sales/Working Capital	.6					
3.0	9.7	7.6		75.0					
36.6	UND	-830.0		-62.8					
31.2	25.0	12.4	EBIT/Interest						
(12) 5.7	(21) 5.5	(18) 7.0							
.7	1.8	1.3							
			Net Profit + Depr., Dep., Amort./Cur. Mat. L/T/D						
.0	.0	.0	Fixed/Worth	.0					
.1	.2	.5		.8					
.6	2.7	1.7		10.6					
.2	.3	.5	Debt/Worth	.7					
.5	1.3	1.6		6.3					
1.5	24.8	9.2		UND					
24.5	41.8	31.2	% Profit Before Taxes/Tangible Net Worth						
(30) 11.1	(35) 14.4	(35) 8.9							
2.7	3.8	1.0							
14.1	13.3	13.2	% Profit Before Taxes/Total Assets	10.8					
6.6	6.5	3.6		1.4					
1.6	.9	.2		.2					
UND	999.8	857.8	Sales/Net Fixed Assets	UND					
37.2	23.8	23.0		.7					
4.9	.6	1.6		.2					
2.6	1.7	2.4	Sales/Total Assets	.6					
.6	.5	.7		.1					
.1	.1	.2		.0					
.8	.8	1.3	% Depr., Dep., Amort./Sales						
(18) 1.8	(21) 2.4	(24) 2.3							
4.6	11.5	9.3							
			% Officers', Directors' Owners' Comp/Sales						
912367M	988463M	1011906M	Net Sales ($)	5356M	14783M	19695M	33192M	76555M	862325M
1172343M	1124565M	973511M	Total Assets ($)	64985M	33241M	21198M	52577M	264983M	536527M

© RMA 2010

M = $ thousand   MM = $ million
See Pages 9 through 22 for Explanation of Ratios and Data

Current Data Sorted by Assets | Comparative Historical Data

Type of Statement	0-500M	500M-2MM	2-10MM	10-50MM	50-100MM	100-250MM		4/1/05-3/31/06 ALL	4/1/06-3/31/07 ALL
Unqualified		1	4	5	3	5		11	11
Reviewed		1	1					1	1
Compiled		1	1					2	6
Tax Returns	2	1	7	2	1			2	6
Other	6	4	14	13	21	7	5	20	26
		6 (4/1-9/30/09)		104 (10/1/09-3/31/10)					
NUMBER OF STATEMENTS	14	21	26	28	11	10		36	50
ASSETS	%	%	%	%	%	%		%	%
Cash & Equivalents	33.1	11.6	8.9	17.8	20.0	17.3		18.1	28.3
Trade Receivables (net)	2.2	4.7	27.5	26.9	8.2	30.5		18.4	13.8
Inventory	.0	1.0	2.1	.1	.0	1.1		4.5	2.1
All Other Current	13.8	21.1	3.0	4.7	4.5	7.1		4.0	5.2
Total Current	49.1	38.3	41.5	49.5	32.7	56.0		44.9	49.5
Fixed Assets (net)	22.2	36.0	41.1	17.9	13.6	23.6		23.3	20.5
Intangibles (net)	7.9	.6	.3	6.2	5.1	5.4		4.1	3.7
All Other Non-Current	20.8	25.0	17.1	26.5	48.5	15.0		27.8	26.3
Total	100.0	100.0	100.0	100.0	100.0	100.0		100.0	100.0
LIABILITIES									
Notes Payable-Short Term	52.3	19.4	11.6	11.7	19.9	24.3		10.0	15.1
Cur. Mat.-L.T.D.	20.4	.9	5.7	.7	3.4	.1		.6	2.4
Trade Payables	2.1	2.2	3.7	5.0	1.4	.8		3.2	3.7
Income Taxes Payable	.0	.0	.0	.1	.0	.1		.8	.1
All Other Current	23.9	10.9	9.2	10.2	.9	7.8		19.9	8.0
Total Current	98.7	33.4	30.2	27.8	25.5	33.0		34.4	29.3
Long-Term Debt	36.9	48.6	36.5	19.1	24.8	27.1		35.0	26.5
Deferred Taxes	.0	.8	.0	.0	.1	.0		.4	.4
All Other Non-Current	1.4	9.1	4.2	5.1	.8	11.1		7.5	.9
Net Worth	-37.0	8.2	29.1	48.0	48.8	28.7		22.7	42.8
Total Liabilities & Net Worth	100.0	100.0	100.0	100.0	100.0	100.0		100.0	100.0
INCOME DATA									
Net Sales	100.0	100.0	100.0	100.0	100.0	100.0		100.0	100.0
Gross Profit									
Operating Expenses	92.0	67.6	58.7	59.5	37.3	72.9		71.9	67.4
Operating Profit	8.0	32.4	41.3	40.5	62.7	27.1		28.1	32.6
All Other Expenses (net)	-.6	8.8	23.1	12.3	13.8	24.2		12.5	16.0
Profit Before Taxes	8.6	23.6	18.2	28.2	48.9	2.8		15.6	16.7
RATIOS									
Current	2.9	4.0	3.1	3.6	3.7	27.0		3.9	5.1
	1.7	1.2	1.1	1.5	1.5	1.8		1.6	1.9
	.1	.3	.4	.9	.5	1.1		.4	.8
Quick	2.9	2.2	2.7	3.4	3.7	5.2		2.8	3.9
	1.1	.4	.6	1.3	1.2	1.3		1.1	1.6
	.1	.4	.4	.9	.3	.9		.2	.4
Sales/Receivables	0 UND	0 UND	0 UND	0 UND	0 UND	9 40.0		0 UND	0 UND
	0 UND	0 UND	7 53.9	9 40.2	0 UND	32 11.5		21 17.8	1 276.7
	0 UND	7 48.7	568 .6	156 2.3	29 12.5	2000 .1		61 6.0	52 7.0
Cost of Sales/Inventory									
Cost of Sales/Payables									
Sales/Working Capital	13.9	4.1	.7	.8	.3	.4		1.5	.4
	77.3	38.9	27.4	3.3	1.3	.9		13.9	4.9
	-10.0	-3.2	-2.8	-12.5	-9.3	3.1		-10.9	-45.1
EBIT/Interest			51.1	39.7				28.1	33.3
		(12) 4.2		(12) 3.1				(16) 6.7	(20) 6.4
		1.5		.7				2.7	-.9
Net Profit + Depr., Dep., Amort./Cur. Mat. L/T/D									
Fixed/Worth	.0	.0	.0	.0	.0	.0		.0	.0
	.4	.5	.6	.0	.0	.4		.3	.1
	-.5	4.1	4.1	.8	2.3	2.9		4.5	1.1
Debt/Worth	.5	.6	.8	.4	.2	1.8		.5	.4
	1.3	2.6	2.8	1.3	1.8	4.4		2.2	1.4
	-1.5	5.7	19.4	3.2	67.1	53.7		15.7	4.8
% Profit Before Taxes/Tangible Net Worth		71.8	38.3	70.9	30.8			24.8	32.3
		(18) 21.1	(22) 13.5	(25) 10.4	(10) 7.4			(30) 13.9	(46) 12.3
		7.5	.8	1.5	6.0			5.3	1.8
% Profit Before Taxes/Total Assets	97.8	23.3	11.5	14.9	6.0	2.6		16.9	21.4
	46.8	6.2	2.5	3.8	4.1	.2		5.5	3.3
	5.2	1.4	.3	.6	1.6	-4.0		1.2	.3
Sales/Net Fixed Assets	UND	UND	UND	UND	UND	301.7		123.9	UND
	143.8	12.4	17.8	98.5	962.8	36.2		25.8	33.1
	18.9	.4	.2	6.1	.2	.2		4.0	1.1
Sales/Total Assets	11.5	1.4	.5	1.4	.2	.3		2.1	1.4
	7.9	.7	.2	.2	.1	.1		.9	.2
	4.0	.3	.1	.1	.0	.1		.1	.1
% Depr., Dep., Amort./Sales		.6	2.0	1.2				.6	1.1
		(12) 6.0	(15) 16.1	(13) 3.5				(20) 1.7	(29) 2.1
		27.5	23.1	19.2				9.7	10.4
% Officers', Directors' Owners' Comp/Sales									
Net Sales ($)	16370M	27199M	90664M	431829M	140223M	266859M		1174650M	422857M
Total Assets ($)	2624M	23087M	113509M	637052M	780845M	1486410M		1666040M	1534883M

M = $ thousand   MM = $ million
See Pages 9 through 22 for Explanation of Ratios and Data

Comparative Historical Data | Current Data Sorted by Sales

					0-1MM	1-3MM	3-5MM	5-10MM	10-25MM	25MM & OVER
Type of Statement										
14	30	18	Unqualified		3	3		3	5	4
		2	Reviewed		1	1				
13	12	4	Compiled		3	1				
6	12	20	Tax Returns		11	6		1	2	
31	46	66	Other		27	15	6	3	6	9
4/1/07- 3/31/08 ALL	4/1/08- 3/31/09 ALL	4/1/09- 3/31/10 ALL			6 (4/1-9/30/09)			104 (10/1/09-3/31/10)		
64	100	110	**NUMBER OF STATEMENTS**		45	26	6	7	13	13
%	%	%	**ASSETS**	%	%	%	%	%	%	%
18.7	20.8	16.6	Cash & Equivalents		12.8	17.2			15.9	21.9
18.9	19.0	18.1	Trade Receivables (net)		9.9	13.1			43.3	22.2
2.1	2.7	.8	Inventory		.2	.0			4.0	.7
12.9	8.8	8.8	All Other Current		10.8	9.1			8.8	8.5
52.6	51.3	44.4	Total Current		33.7	39.4			71.9	53.2
17.8	14.6	27.5	Fixed Assets (net)		40.7	21.5			21.0	9.9
5.2	3.0	3.8	Intangibles (net)		1.9	5.0			1.1	13.8
24.4	31.1	24.4	All Other Non-Current		23.7	34.1			6.0	23.1
100.0	100.0	100.0	Total		100.0	100.0			100.0	100.0
			LIABILITIES							
27.4	28.2	20.3	Notes Payable-Short Term		17.3	30.3			17.3	3.5
2.3	2.0	4.6	Cur. Mat.-L.T.D.		8.1	3.1			3.1	.9
2.6	3.3	3.0	Trade Payables		1.2	1.1			10.2	7.9
.0	.1	.1	Income Taxes Payable		.0	.0			.3	.1
7.9	8.7	10.7	All Other Current		10.2	15.0			12.7	10.4
40.2	42.3	38.7	Total Current		36.9	49.6			43.6	22.9
20.5	26.1	32.4	Long-Term Debt		39.9	43.3			18.5	16.0
.0	.1	.2	Deferred Taxes		.3	.1			.1	.0
4.4	11.7	5.3	All Other Non-Current		5.2	5.4			3.3	12.4
34.8	19.8	23.4	Net Worth		17.6	1.6			34.6	48.7
100.0	100.0	100.0	Total Liabilities & Net Worth		100.0	100.0			100.0	100.0
			INCOME DATA							
100.0	100.0	100.0	Net Sales		100.0	100.0			100.0	100.0
			Gross Profit							
51.7	58.8	64.0	Operating Expenses		59.0	70.8			74.2	68.4
48.3	41.2	36.0	Operating Profit		41.0	29.2			25.8	31.6
23.4	18.9	13.8	All Other Expenses (net)		18.2	13.4			9.0	10.7
24.9	22.3	22.2	Profit Before Taxes		22.8	15.8			16.9	20.9
			RATIOS							
4.4	4.3	3.6			2.6	4.2			2.9	5.0
1.7	1.5	1.5	Current		.9	1.5			1.5	2.2
.9	.6	.5			.3	.4			1.0	1.3
3.3	2.5	2.9			1.8	3.9			1.8	4.7
1.0	(99) 1.1	1.2	Quick		.5	1.4			1.2	1.3
.1	.3	.4			.2	.1			.7	.6
0 UND	0 UND	0 UND			0 UND	0 UND		14 26.0		1 524.2
2 197.9	0 904.7	0 UND	Sales/Receivables		0 UND	0 UND		62 5.9		25 14.8
86 4.3	71 5.1	52 7.0			8 48.6	12 29.6		986 .4		61 6.0
			Cost of Sales/Inventory							
			Cost of Sales/Payables							
.8	1.3	.9			1.8	1.0			1.0	1.8
4.9	6.2	10.3	Sales/Working Capital		-14.3	18.1			3.4	5.7
-36.5	-13.3	-6.9			-3.5	-9.0			NM	51.3
162.9	18.9	18.2			9.0	19.3				
(13) 16.1	(44) 5.4	(47) 4.2	EBIT/Interest		(13) 5.4	(15) 2.7				
2.0	1.8	1.2			1.2	2.1				
		25.0	Net Profit + Depr., Dep.,							
	(10) 1.7		Amort./Cur. Mat. L/T/D							
		.8								
.0	.0	.0			.0	.0			.0	.0
.0	.0	.1	Fixed/Worth		.8	.2			.2	.0
1.1	1.0	2.4			4.3	2.1			1.6	NM
.4	.6	.5			.7	1.1			1.0	.3
3.8	2.3	2.1	Debt/Worth		1.5	2.7			2.3	1.6
79.6	27.6	8.2			21.0	81.9			5.1	NM
43.7	60.2	58.2			43.2	42.9			81.7	220.5
(51) 21.6	(83) 18.0	(93) 12.5	% Profit Before Taxes/Tangible Net Worth		(38) 11.0	(21) 13.6			44.4	(10) 64.9
4.7	2.6	3.0			.8	6.3			5.6	.6
7.5	12.4	19.3			13.9	20.8			24.7	133.6
2.8	3.3	3.8	% Profit Before Taxes/Total Assets		2.4	3.6			5.8	13.4
1.0	.3	.5			.2	1.3			.8	-3.1
UND	UND	UND			UND	UND			981.3	702.2
281.2	173.6	40.3	Sales/Net Fixed Assets		18.4	67.5			43.1	47.8
10.0	9.1	.5			.2	2.8			3.1	11.3
.4	1.7	1.3			.7	1.7			1.7	2.9
.2	.2	.3	Sales/Total Assets		.2	.5			.5	1.0
.1	.1	.1			.1	.1			.1	.4
1.0	.7	1.0			7.5	1.0				
(22) 2.9	(38) 2.4	(55) 5.8	% Depr., Dep., Amort./Sales		(21) 16.1	(12) 3.3				
14.2	9.9	22.9			29.9	19.7				
		3.7	% Officers', Directors'							
	(13) 17.2		Owners' Comp/Sales							
		22.6								
670215M	1001419M	973144M	Net Sales ($)		23803M	44079M	21903M	49994M	225922M	607443M
2291084M	3374631M	3043527M	Total Assets ($)		206876M	399670M	261747M	392779M	817433M	965022M

M = $ thousand   MM = $ million
See Pages 9 through 22 for Explanation of Ratios and Data

FINANCE—Direct Life Insurance Carriers NAICS 524113

Current Data Sorted by Assets · **Comparative Historical Data**

Type of Statement	0-500M	500M-2MM	2-10MM	10-50MM	50-100MM	100-250MM		ALL 4/1/05-3/31/06	ALL 4/1/06-3/31/07
Unqualified			1	6	3	6		8	12
Reviewed			2	2					1
Compiled			1					1	
Tax Returns	2	1	1					4	1
Other	1	1	7	3	1	3		11	10
		7 (4/1-9/30/09)		33 (10/1/09-3/31/10)					
NUMBER OF STATEMENTS	3	2	11	11	4	9		24	24
ASSETS	%	%	%	%	%	%		%	%
Cash & Equivalents			33.7	52.4				28.8	58.5
Trade Receivables (net)			17.7	7.6				19.6	9.8
Inventory			4.6	3.2				7.3	.0
All Other Current			.8	11.9				5.1	4.3
Total Current			56.9	75.0				60.9	72.7
Fixed Assets (net)			8.1	4.5				10.4	3.9
Intangibles (net)			12.1	6.2				8.1	5.0
All Other Non-Current			23.0	14.2				20.7	18.4
Total			100.0	100.0				100.0	100.0
LIABILITIES									
Notes Payable-Short Term			8.9	2.8				13.7	7.5
Cur. Mat.-L.T.D.			5.8	1.0				1.5	1.7
Trade Payables			7.2	11.7				20.5	13.2
Income Taxes Payable			.0	.0				.1	.1
All Other Current			25.7	51.4				33.3	17.4
Total Current			47.6	67.0				69.0	39.9
Long-Term Debt			32.6	5.5				13.2	6.8
Deferred Taxes			.2	.1				.0	.2
All Other Non-Current			5.4	1.0				10.2	27.5
Net Worth			14.1	26.4				7.6	25.6
Total Liabilities & Net Worth			100.0	100.0				100.0	100.0
INCOME DATA									
Net Sales			100.0	100.0				100.0	100.0
Gross Profit									
Operating Expenses			82.4	95.9				88.6	87.3
Operating Profit			17.6	4.1				11.4	12.7
All Other Expenses (net)			7.4	-1.7				3.3	.7
Profit Before Taxes			10.1	5.8				8.2	12.0
RATIOS									
Current			3.3	1.5				1.2	18.3
			1.3	1.2				.9	1.8
			.7	.9				.7	1.1
Quick			3.3	1.2				1.0	18.3
			1.3	.9				.7	1.6
			.6	.6				.4	1.0
Sales/Receivables			1 431.8	0 UND				0 UND	0 UND
			16 23.1	28 13.1				20 18.5	10 37.2
			209 1.7	57 6.4				138 2.6	105 3.5
Cost of Sales/Inventory									
Cost of Sales/Payables									
Sales/Working Capital			1.2	.9				14.9	.4
			7.4	8.1				-21.7	3.5
			-7.3	-3.0				-3.8	29.5
EBIT/Interest								(20) 120.2	(12) 26.4
								8.1	15.9
								1.9	.3
Net Profit + Depr., Dep., Amort./Cur. Mat. L/T/D									
Fixed/Worth			.0	.0				.0	.0
			.1	.0				.6	.0
			-.7	.4				UND	.4
Debt/Worth			.6	.7				4.8	1.9
			5.5	3.6				11.4	4.8
			-3.8	18.2				UND	12.8
% Profit Before Taxes/Tangible Net Worth								557.0	32.5
								(18) 16.7	(22) 16.6
								.8	1.4
% Profit Before Taxes/Total Assets			16.3	8.2				15.1	7.3
			2.9	2.4				3.5	1.9
			.5	.8				.3	.3
Sales/Net Fixed Assets			UND	UND				UND	UND
			47.7	999.8				51.3	UND
			4.7	48.6				20.2	29.6
Sales/Total Assets			2.1	1.3				3.1	1.2
			1.2	.4				1.2	.3
			.3	.2				.2	.1
% Depr., Dep., Amort./Sales								.8	
								(13) 1.3	
								5.9	
% Officers', Directors' Owners' Comp/Sales									
Net Sales ($)	4557M	7945M	46085M	125672M	194472M	1463303M		2370785M	610975M
Total Assets ($)	764M	2536M	47766M	281566M	292696M	1557139M		1318441M	1186018M

M = $ thousand   MM = $ million
See Pages 9 through 22 for Explanation of Ratios and Data

Comparative Historical Data   ## Current Data Sorted by Sales

			Type of Statement						
12	12	15	Unqualified		1	1	2	5	6
	2	3	Reviewed		1		1	1	
1	2	2	Compiled		1		1		
2	6	4	Tax Returns		3	1			
9	11	16	Other	1	3	4	2	2	4
4/1/07-3/31/08	4/1/08-3/31/09	4/1/09-3/31/10			7 (4/1-9/30/09)		33 (10/1/09-3/31/10)		
ALL	ALL	ALL		0-1MM	1-3MM	3-5MM	5-10MM	10-25MM	25MM & OVER
24	33	40	NUMBER OF STATEMENTS	1	9	7	5	8	10
%	%	%	ASSETS	%	%	%	%	%	%
31.0	40.3	49.5	Cash & Equivalents						52.9
19.2	11.6	12.8	Trade Receivables (net)						9.9
1.9	.0	2.2	Inventory						.0
15.2	5.8	5.3	All Other Current						7.0
67.3	57.7	69.9	Total Current						69.7
11.8	13.5	5.6	Fixed Assets (net)						9.2
1.5	6.0	5.7	Intangibles (net)						1.4
19.4	22.8	18.8	All Other Non-Current						19.7
100.0	100.0	100.0	Total						100.0
			LIABILITIES						
10.9	12.1	6.7	Notes Payable-Short Term						.5
.8	.8	3.9	Cur. Mat.-L.T.D.						1.5
21.7	15.6	10.6	Trade Payables						4.6
1.1	.1	.1	Income Taxes Payable						.2
24.1	27.0	45.4	All Other Current						52.4
58.6	55.6	66.8	Total Current						59.2
14.2	14.8	11.6	Long-Term Debt						4.6
.4	.1	.1	Deferred Taxes						.0
14.3	3.7	6.9	All Other Non-Current						4.8
12.6	25.9	14.6	Net Worth						31.4
100.0	100.0	100.0	Total Liabilities & Net Worth						100.0
			INCOME DATA						
100.0	100.0	100.0	Net Sales						100.0
			Gross Profit						
85.4	84.6	90.0	Operating Expenses						92.0
14.6	15.4	10.0	Operating Profit						8.0
6.3	6.3	3.2	All Other Expenses (net)						2.8
8.3	9.1	6.8	Profit Before Taxes						5.2
			RATIOS						
1.6	1.7	2.2							2.0
1.2	1.1	1.2	Current						1.2
.9	.8	.9							1.0
1.5	1.7	2.1							2.0
1.0	.9	1.1	Quick						1.0
.5	.7	.7							.8
0 UND	0 UND	0 857.8						1	280.6
30 12.3	13 27.6	18 20.0	Sales/Receivables					33	10.9
132 2.8	91 4.0	66 5.5						44	8.3
			Cost of Sales/Inventory						
			Cost of Sales/Payables						
1.0	3.4	1.6							3.3
11.0	29.9	7.8	Sales/Working Capital						19.0
-22.9	-5.1	-5.5							NM
17.8	29.4	29.1							
(15) 8.2	(20) 7.3	(24) 6.7	EBIT/Interest						
3.2	1.8	2.6							
			Net Profit + Depr., Dep., Amort./Cur. Mat. L/T/D						
.0	.0	.0							.0
.1	.1	.0	Fixed/Worth						.1
2.1	1.7	.8							.6
2.2	1.5	1.3							1.1
6.7	5.2	4.8	Debt/Worth						3.0
43.1	16.2	16.2							8.4
46.3	33.9	42.6							49.9
(20) 20.5	(28) 9.8	(33) 14.4	% Profit Before Taxes/Tangible Net Worth						18.0
8.6	1.1	4.5							7.2
14.7	8.5	11.7							11.0
1.9	2.2	3.4	% Profit Before Taxes/Total Assets						8.0
.9	.3	.6							.6
UND	UND	UND							UND
63.6	51.2	114.6	Sales/Net Fixed Assets						53.1
14.6	16.9	31.9							9.5
2.5	1.6	2.2							2.6
.7	.4	.8	Sales/Total Assets						1.1
.1	.2	.2							.4
	.8	.5							
	(12) 2.0	(16) 1.6	% Depr., Dep., Amort./Sales						
	3.9	3.7							
			% Officers', Directors' Owners' Comp/Sales						
887816M	1824893M	1842034M	Net Sales ($)	221M	15906M	28655M	36745M	147461M	1613046M
1543109M	1654699M	2182467M	Total Assets ($)	5339M	76771M	33280M	129894M	586290M	1350893M

M = $ thousand   MM = $ million
See Pages 9 through 22 for Explanation of Ratios and Data

Current Data Sorted by Assets   Comparative Historical Data

0-500M	500M-2MM	2-10MM	10-50MM	50-100MM	100-250MM		4/1/05-3/31/06 ALL	4/1/06-3/31/07 ALL
						Type of Statement		
		3	24	14	10	Unqualified	32	48
						Reviewed		
1	1					Compiled	1	4
2	5	3			1	Tax Returns	2	8
3	6	8	6	3	7	Other	46	37
	18 (4/1-9/30/09)		79 (10/1/09-3/31/10)					
6	12	14	30	17	18	**NUMBER OF STATEMENTS**	81	97
%	%	%	%	%	%	**ASSETS**	%	%
	29.5	39.4	56.0	47.2	37.8	Cash & Equivalents	41.5	37.9
	29.0	16.4	14.3	16.1	12.8	Trade Receivables (net)	13.4	15.3
	.0	.0	.5	.3	.9	Inventory	1.9	1.0
	2.2	6.5	6.4	8.7	3.2	All Other Current	9.1	3.9
	60.7	62.3	77.2	72.2	54.8	Total Current	65.8	58.1
	17.4	30.7	11.4	11.2	12.1	Fixed Assets (net)	15.6	16.4
	15.9	.7	4.6	5.6	10.7	Intangibles (net)	6.3	9.4
	6.0	6.3	6.9	11.0	22.4	All Other Non-Current	12.2	16.0
	100.0	100.0	100.0	100.0	100.0	Total	100.0	100.0
						LIABILITIES		
	10.3	2.0	3.6	.8	2.8	Notes Payable-Short Term	2.2	5.6
	1.7	.9	1.0	1.6	1.5	Cur. Mat.-L.T.D.	1.8	1.9
	15.8	3.8	12.1	16.7	12.6	Trade Payables	12.3	10.8
	.0	.0	.2	.1	.2	Income Taxes Payable	.2	.2
	31.1	33.2	25.9	31.5	19.0	All Other Current	24.2	28.3
	59.0	39.9	42.8	50.6	36.0	Total Current	40.8	46.8
	8.2	23.6	7.4	5.6	10.4	Long-Term Debt	9.9	12.4
	.0	.5	.8	.3	.6	Deferred Taxes	.2	.3
	9.6	1.2	5.9	3.1	4.1	All Other Non-Current	8.7	7.9
	23.3	34.9	43.1	40.4	48.8	Net Worth	40.3	32.7
	100.0	100.0	100.0	100.0	100.0	Total Liabilties & Net Worth	100.0	100.0
						INCOME DATA		
	100.0	100.0	100.0	100.0	100.0	Net Sales	100.0	100.0
						Gross Profit		
	95.9	92.6	94.1	96.2	95.2	Operating Expenses	94.3	96.2
	4.1	7.4	5.9	3.8	4.8	Operating Profit	5.7	3.8
	1.0	3.3	-.7	-.4	-.2	All Other Expenses (net)	.0	-.1
	3.1	4.1	6.6	4.2	4.9	Profit Before Taxes	5.7	3.9
						RATIOS		
	2.9	3.8	3.9	3.2	3.0		3.2	2.2
	1.0	2.2	1.9	1.4	1.5	Current	1.7	1.3
	.5	1.0	1.3	1.0	1.1		1.2	.9
	2.7	3.7	3.4	3.2	2.9		2.4	2.0
	.9	1.7	1.9	1.2	1.4	Quick	1.4	1.2
	.5	.8	1.3	.8	.9		1.0	.8
	0 UND	0 UND	3 130.8	7 52.5	7 50.2		4 85.7	3 108.7
	18 20.1	18 20.1	19 18.8	17 21.3	19 19.1	Sales/Receivables	15 24.2	16 23.2
	67 5.5	47 7.7	32 11.4	31 11.8	31 11.7		41 8.9	39 9.4
						Cost of Sales/Inventory		
						Cost of Sales/Payables		
	11.8	4.0	4.2	4.4	5.2		3.2	6.6
	UND	9.0	8.0	16.2	16.0	Sales/Working Capital	9.0	19.8
	-9.1	NM	22.3	NM	NM		18.3	-55.5
			42.0	73.1	25.1		14.7	12.9
			(15) 9.7	(10) 16.7	(10) 5.6	EBIT/Interest	(38) 5.6	(52) 5.1
			1.1	2.2	2.1		1.5	1.5
								20.8
						Net Profit + Depr., Dep., Amort./Cur. Mat. L/T/D		(12) 6.3
								1.8
	.1	.0	.0	.0	.0		.0	.1
	1.0	.6	.3	.1	.1	Fixed/Worth	.2	.4
	-.5	22.2	.9	.6	.7		1.0	3.1
	.5	.6	.5	.6	.6		.6	.8
	2.8	1.5	1.2	1.9	1.2	Debt/Worth	1.7	2.0
	-2.6	64.2	8.9	5.3	3.6		6.3	14.6
		40.5	44.5	34.6	32.0	% Profit Before Taxes/Tangible Net Worth	51.0	71.0
	(12) ...	(25) 10.9	(16) 15.9	(16) 14.2	14.6		(77) 21.3	(81) 23.1
		1.8	1.4	-.2	3.5		3.2	6.2
	54.7	10.9	13.2	9.0	14.6	% Profit Before Taxes/Total Assets	13.8	18.9
	6.1	4.1	6.9	3.8	9.0		6.4	8.2
	-.2	.0	.2	.1	1.7		1.5	.6
	105.8	390.8	808.5	505.1	241.3	Sales/Net Fixed Assets	304.2	165.1
	56.0	28.3	47.2	43.6	47.6		33.7	38.9
	14.2	2.4	9.9	11.4	9.0		6.0	10.3
	5.4	5.9	3.7	4.7	3.5	Sales/Total Assets	4.0	4.1
	3.6	1.6	2.3	3.6	2.0		2.1	3.0
	1.7	.6	1.0	1.0	1.3		.9	1.5
			.2	.2	.3	% Depr., Dep., Amort./Sales	.4	.4
		(21)	.5 (12)	.7 (11)	1.3		(54) 1.8	(65) 1.0
			2.9	3.7	2.4		4.7	2.7
								6.9
						% Officers', Directors' Owners' Comp/Sales		(12) 17.3
								38.6
9230M	61284M	219547M	2236360M	4315400M	6141995M	Net Sales ($)	13067491M	13116850M
2232M	14618M	80802M	816874M	1223555M	2616245M	Total Assets ($)	5087041M	5289526M

Comparative Historical Data   ## Current Data Sorted by Sales

	07-08 ALL	08-09 ALL	09-10 ALL		0-1MM	1-3MM	3-5MM	5-10MM	10-25MM	25MM & OVER
Type of Statement										
Unqualified	40	46	51			2		2	3	44
Reviewed	2		1					1		
Compiled	3	5	11		2	3	1	1	2	2
Tax Returns	3	2	1		1					
Other	27	26	33		5	3	3	2	4	16
	4/1/07-3/31/08	4/1/08-3/31/09	4/1/09-3/31/10			18 (4/1-9/30/09)			79 (10/1/09-3/31/10)	
NUMBER OF STATEMENTS	75	79	97		8	8	4	6	9	62
	%	%	%		%	%	%	%	%	%
ASSETS										
Cash & Equivalents	35.1	43.5	43.0							47.0
Trade Receivables (net)	15.5	15.0	16.3							16.9
Inventory	.7	.5	.4							.5
All Other Current	4.6	4.7	5.4							5.3
Total Current	55.8	63.6	65.1							69.8
Fixed Assets (net)	18.1	12.8	15.6							11.8
Intangibles (net)	8.8	8.1	7.3							6.2
All Other Non-Current	17.3	15.5	12.0							12.2
Total	100.0	100.0	100.0							100.0
LIABILITIES										
Notes Payable-Short Term	3.5	9.5	3.7							2.7
Cur. Mat.-L.T.D.	2.1	1.2	1.2							1.3
Trade Payables	12.4	13.4	12.9							13.2
Income Taxes Payable	.2	.4	.2							.2
All Other Current	23.5	28.4	26.2							27.0
Total Current	41.6	52.8	44.2							44.4
Long-Term Debt	17.5	8.8	10.3							7.5
Deferred Taxes	.4	.3	.5							.3
All Other Non-Current	8.6	5.1	6.1							4.5
Net Worth	31.9	33.0	39.0							43.3
Total Liabilties & Net Worth	100.0	100.0	100.0							100.0
INCOME DATA										
Net Sales	100.0	100.0	100.0							100.0
Gross Profit										
Operating Expenses	95.9	93.4	93.8							95.6
Operating Profit	4.1	6.6	6.2							4.4
All Other Expenses (net)	-.7	.6	.4							-.1
Profit Before Taxes	4.9	6.0	5.7							4.5
RATIOS										
Current	2.3	2.3	3.3							3.1
	1.5	1.5	1.6							1.6
	1.0	1.0	1.0							1.2
Quick	2.1	2.0	3.0							2.9
	1.4	1.4	1.5							1.6
	.8	.9	.8							.9
Sales/Receivables	4 99.6	3 134.6	5 77.4							7 53.6
	18 19.8	18 20.3	18 20.4							18 19.9
	39 9.4	36 10.0	33 10.9							30 12.1
Cost of Sales/Inventory										
Cost of Sales/Payables										
Sales/Working Capital	6.1	7.3	5.2							5.2
	15.1	15.9	12.3							12.6
	163.1	-55.4	UND							39.6
EBIT/Interest	22.5	25.6	58.4							52.4
	(46) 6.0	(37) 9.7	(53) 6.6						(32)	7.9
	1.9	1.6	1.9							2.3
Net Profit + Depr., Dep., Amort./Cur. Mat. L/T/D		17.1	18.6							18.6
		(11) 12.0	(17) 4.0						(13)	2.2
		.4	1.1							1.1
Fixed/Worth	.1	.0	.0							.0
	.3	.2	.3							.2
	1.1	.8	1.4							.8
Debt/Worth	.7	.6	.6							.6
	1.3	1.3	1.5							1.2
	9.7	11.4	11.5							4.6
% Profit Before Taxes/Tangible Net Worth	44.3	41.8	38.3							34.3
	(65) 18.7	(65) 16.6	(81) 15.9						(53)	15.2
	5.7	2.5	1.1							3.1
% Profit Before Taxes/Total Assets	14.9	11.6	13.8							12.7
	8.2	5.0	6.1							6.2
	2.4	1.1	.4							1.2
Sales/Net Fixed Assets	154.6	295.7	362.1							364.0
	20.1	60.9	43.6							48.2
	8.4	13.0	10.9							11.6
Sales/Total Assets	3.9	4.0	4.2							4.3
	2.2	2.8	2.4							3.1
	1.2	1.2	1.0							1.6
% Depr., Dep., Amort./Sales	.3	.2	.2							.2
	(58) 1.5	(55) .7	(65) .8						(44)	.4
	2.9	2.4	2.8							2.5
% Officers', Directors' Owners' Comp/Sales			4.7							
		(11)	7.5							
			14.2							
Net Sales ($)	9971497M	12004306M	12983816M		4542M	17511M	16419M	45209M	132585M	12767550M
Total Assets ($)	4103183M	4268118M	4754326M		32335M	26834M	8427M	31523M	106462M	4548745M

© RMA 2010

M = $ thousand   MM = $ million
See Pages 9 through 22 for Explanation of Ratios and Data

Current Data Sorted by Assets   Comparative Historical Data

0-500M	500M-2MM	2-10MM	10-50MM	50-100MM	100-250MM	Type of Statement	4/1/05-3/31/06 ALL	4/1/06-3/31/07 ALL
	2	1	12	4	13	Unqualified	29	36
	1	1	1			Reviewed	5	2
2	1	2				Compiled	6	8
	2			1		Tax Returns	1	7
1	3	7	13	5	10	Other	26	29
		7 (4/1-9/30/09)		75 (10/1/09-3/31/10)				
3	9	11	26	10	23	**NUMBER OF STATEMENTS**	67	82
%	%	%	%	%	%	**ASSETS**	%	%
		35.6	52.1	18.5	54.0	Cash & Equivalents	45.9	45.8
		11.0	12.3	14.2	11.9	Trade Receivables (net)	15.6	11.1
		2.3	.0	.0	.0	Inventory	.0	.1
		6.5	7.7	20.3	8.2	All Other Current	7.3	8.7
		55.4	72.1	53.1	74.1	Total Current	68.9	65.8
		5.1	4.1	3.3	1.2	Fixed Assets (net)	6.1	5.8
		7.3	1.6	3.2	.8	Intangibles (net)	5.8	3.5
		32.2	22.2	40.4	23.8	All Other Non-Current	19.2	24.9
		100.0	100.0	100.0	100.0	Total	100.0	100.0
						LIABILITIES		
		8.1	1.1	5.7	.1	Notes Payable-Short Term	3.9	7.2
		5.8	.5	.1	.4	Cur. Mat.-L.T.D.	.9	1.3
		7.7	15.8	4.3	7.4	Trade Payables	15.3	14.5
		.0	.5	.0	.2	Income Taxes Payable	.4	.7
		28.0	35.2	45.6	38.4	All Other Current	28.2	25.9
		49.6	53.1	55.8	46.5	Total Current	48.7	49.7
		14.9	3.4	.9	1.8	Long-Term Debt	14.7	14.7
		.0	.1	.0	.0	Deferred Taxes	.3	.1
		1.7	5.2	10.2	18.9	All Other Non-Current	11.3	18.3
		33.9	38.2	33.1	32.9	Net Worth	25.0	17.3
		100.0	100.0	100.0	100.0	Total Liabilties & Net Worth	100.0	100.0
						INCOME DATA		
		100.0	100.0	100.0	100.0	Net Sales	100.0	100.0
						Gross Profit		
		74.2	94.0	93.2	91.6	Operating Expenses	87.6	85.9
		25.8	6.0	6.8	8.4	Operating Profit	12.4	14.1
		6.8	-2.2	-4.0	-2.6	All Other Expenses (net)	.2	-1.8
		19.0	8.2	10.7	11.0	Profit Before Taxes	12.1	15.8
						RATIOS		
		1.9	1.9	2.5	2.4		1.9	2.3
		1.2	1.5	1.1	1.6	Current	1.4	1.5
		.9	1.2	.3	1.3		1.1	.9
		1.5	1.7	1.7	2.3		1.8	2.2
		1.1	1.4	.6	1.5	Quick	1.3	1.3
		.7	1.0	.2	1.0		1.0	.8
		0 UND	0 UND	0 UND	31 11.7		5 77.4	0 UND
		19 18.8	30 12.4	51 7.2	74 5.0	Sales/Receivables	47 7.7	23 15.8
		43 8.6	90 4.1	127 2.9	165 2.2		103 3.5	64 5.7
						Cost of Sales/Inventory		
						Cost of Sales/Payables		
		2.8	1.3	1.3	.8		1.6	1.1
		10.1	3.8	NM	1.2	Sales/Working Capital	5.1	3.7
		-337.5	17.6	-1.9	7.4		34.6	-43.1
		8.6					36.9	73.3
		(10) 3.6				EBIT/Interest	(36) 14.7	(32) 12.9
		-2.2					1.4	2.9
						Net Profit + Depr., Dep., Amort./Cur. Mat. L/T/D		
		.0	.0	.0	.0		.0	.0
		.0	.0	.0	.0	Fixed/Worth	.1	.0
		.4	.2	.5	.1		.4	.4
		.5	.6	.9	1.4		1.5	1.1
		.8	1.8	1.8	2.0	Debt/Worth	2.4	2.3
		3.7	2.4	11.4	4.3		3.8	4.4
			29.2		16.8		42.5	44.7
			(24) 9.1		9.5	% Profit Before Taxes/Tangible Net Worth	(61) 18.4	(70) 22.0
			-4.7		4.8		7.1	12.5
		38.9	7.8	9.3	4.8		13.3	13.6
		14.3	4.3	2.5	3.1	% Profit Before Taxes/Total Assets	6.2	6.0
		3.7	-2.0	.3	.9		1.4	2.8
		UND	UND	UND	UND		UND	UND
		73.5	116.5	535.5	69.9	Sales/Net Fixed Assets	36.6	67.6
		21.1	11.4	29.3	26.3		11.6	22.1
		1.9	1.2	.8	.4		1.4	1.4
		1.3	.7	.5	.3	Sales/Total Assets	.6	.5
		.5	.4	.4	.2		.3	.4
			.3				.5	.6
			(10) .8			% Depr., Dep., Amort./Sales	(37) 1.4	(39) 1.2
			2.1				2.4	2.5
							9.1	4.2
						% Officers', Directors' Owners' Comp/Sales	(14) 16.0	(13) 10.9
							25.1	23.9
1430M	7220M	80221M	435094M	388049M	1527264M	Net Sales ($)	1693000M	1934552M
957M	10062M	45732M	513104M	661620M	4005357M	Total Assets ($)	3370705M	4027570M

M = $ thousand   MM = $ million
See Pages 9 through 22 for Explanation of Ratios and Data

Comparative Historical Data   ## Current Data Sorted by Sales

23	28	32	Type of Statement	2	3	1	2	5	19
	2	3	Unqualified		1	1			1
1		5	Reviewed	3	1			1	
3	5	3	Compiled	1	1				1
46	44	39	Tax Returns	4	2	1	9	7	16
4/1/07-3/31/08 ALL	4/1/08-3/31/09 ALL	4/1/09-3/31/10 ALL	Other	0-1MM	1-3MM	3-5MM	5-10MM	10-25MM	25MM & OVER
				7 (4/1-9/30/09)			75 (10/1/09-3/31/10)		
73	79	82	NUMBER OF STATEMENTS	10	8	3	11	13	37
%	%	%	ASSETS	%	%	%	%	%	%
41.6	47.7	44.8	Cash & Equivalents	49.5			41.8	48.8	43.2
10.8	12.9	13.8	Trade Receivables (net)	15.1			11.5	15.0	13.2
.6	.0	.3	Inventory	.0			2.3	.0	.0
9.8	9.4	8.3	All Other Current	1.7			5.7	8.9	11.4
62.8	70.0	67.2	Total Current	66.3			61.2	72.6	67.8
5.2	6.9	3.3	Fixed Assets (net)	3.3			3.6	1.9	4.0
4.1	5.8	2.5	Intangibles (net)	.4			1.2	1.4	1.8
27.9	17.3	27.0	All Other Non-Current	30.0			34.0	24.0	26.4
100.0	100.0	100.0	Total	100.0			100.0	100.0	100.0
			LIABILITIES						
6.2	1.3	4.2	Notes Payable-Short-Term	16.2			.1	.5	2.2
.5	1.4	1.1	Cur. Mat.-L.T.D.	.0			2.8	.0	.6
8.2	12.5	13.6	Trade Payables	22.0			11.6	19.7	7.4
.5	.6	.2	Income Taxes Payable	.1			.4	.6	.1
32.5	34.2	33.6	All Other Current	18.6			36.0	26.9	39.1
48.0	50.0	52.7	Total Current	56.9			50.8	47.7	49.4
11.8	8.9	4.0	Long-Term Debt	.9			1.0	1.1	2.9
.1	.2	.0	Deferred Taxes	.0			.0	.2	.0
9.1	13.1	9.0	All Other Non-Current	1.2			4.4	10.9	13.3
31.1	27.9	34.2	Net Worth	41.0			43.7	40.1	34.4
100.0	100.0	100.0	Total Liabilities & Net Worth	100.0			100.0	100.0	100.0
			INCOME DATA						
100.0	100.0	100.0	Net Sales	100.0			100.0	100.0	100.0
			Gross Profit						
83.6	90.4	90.6	Operating Expenses	92.7			83.0	92.7	95.6
16.4	9.6	9.4	Operating Profit	7.3			17.0	7.3	4.4
-.7	-1.2	-1.1	All Other Expenses (net)	-1.4			-3.4	-2.3	-2.4
17.1	10.8	10.6	Profit Before Taxes	8.8			20.4	9.5	6.8
			RATIOS						
1.9	2.6	1.9	Current	1.9			1.9	3.9	2.1
1.4	1.7	1.5		1.0			1.5	1.6	1.5
1.0	1.1	1.0		.6			1.1	1.3	1.0
1.7	2.5	1.7	Quick	1.9			1.7	3.5	1.9
1.2	1.3	1.3		1.0			1.3	1.5	1.4
.6	.8	.7		.6			.9	1.0	.6
0 UND	0 UND	2 188.6	Sales/Receivables	0 UND		0 UND	0 UND	0 UND	11 34.0
33 11.2	45 8.2	39 9.3		12 31.1		29 12.6	53 6.9	68 5.4
81 4.5	97 3.8	109 3.3		70 5.2		112 3.3	158 2.3	112 3.3
			Cost of Sales/Inventory						
			Cost of Sales/Payables						
1.3	1.0	1.0	Sales/Working Capital	.7			1.2	1.1	.9
4.0	3.6	3.9		NM			1.7	3.8	3.8
112.3	156.1	NM		-2.8			63.3	8.6	64.8
25.1	15.6	17.6	EBIT/Interest						47.2
(32) 7.1	(33) 4.9	(30) 3.6						(15) 8.8
3.4	-1.0	2.2							3.0
			Net Profit + Depr., Dep., Amort./Cur. Mat. L/T/D						
.0	.0	.0	Fixed/Worth	.0			.0	.0	.0
.0	.0	.0		.0			.0	.0	.1
.1	.3	.2		.1			.2	.1	.3
1.0	1.3	.8	Debt/Worth	.3			.7	.6	1.4
1.9	2.4	2.0		2.0			1.2	1.9	2.0
3.8	13.8	4.6		7.5			1.8	11.8	3.6
34.5	45.3	20.7	% Profit Before Taxes/Tangible Net Worth				58.8	41.0	16.8
(67) 19.9	(66) 12.6	(75) 9.8		(10) 21.9			21.9	12.3	(35) 8.3
10.8	1.0	2.5					6.5	4.4	3.1
12.5	12.2	7.0	% Profit Before Taxes/Total Assets	5.4			25.1	11.2	6.1
7.9	4.8	3.3		1.2			6.9	4.1	2.7
2.8	-.1	.4		-3.9			2.2	.3	.9
UND	UND	UND	Sales/Net Fixed Assets	UND			UND	UND	954.1
41.3	67.7	116.5		UND			73.5	488.2	36.3
18.7	20.4	21.7		25.3			11.4	116.5	15.7
1.0	1.0	1.2	Sales/Total Assets	1.6			.8	1.6	.8
.5	.5	.5		.9			.4	1.1	.4
.3	.3	.3		.2			.3	.3	.3
.6	.2	.5	% Depr., Dep., Amort./Sales						.5
(32) 1.1	(31) 1.2	(28) 1.0						(14) .7
1.8	2.4	1.7							1.7
		5.7	% Officers', Directors' Owners' Comp/Sales						
		(10) 9.9							
		22.1							
2119747M	3013461M	2439278M	Net Sales ($)	5169M	12385M	12110M	76352M	234740M	2098522M
4220942M	5325827M	5236832M	Total Assets ($)	10328M	62493M	19723M	170420M	581481M	4392387M

M = $ thousand   MM = $ million
See Pages 9 through 22 for Explanation of Ratios and Data

188 FINANCE—Direct Title Insurance Carriers NAICS 524127

| | Current Data Sorted by Assets | | | | | | Comparative Historical Data | |

0-500M	500M-2MM	2-10MM	10-50MM	50-100MM	100-250MM	Type of Statement	4/1/05-3/31/06 ALL	4/1/06-3/31/07 ALL
1	1	2	4		1	Unqualified	16	25
		2				Reviewed	4	5
1	1	1				Compiled	3	7
4	4					Tax Returns	16	13
1	5	5	2	2	2	Other	29	42
	3 (4/1-9/30/09)		36 (10/1/09-3/31/10)					
7	11	10	6	2	3	NUMBER OF STATEMENTS	68	92
%	%	%	%	%	%	ASSETS	%	%
	38.8	27.1				Cash & Equivalents	39.5	40.0
	1.1	10.1				Trade Receivables (net)	6.6	6.2
	.0	.1				Inventory	.0	1.1
	5.6	3.8				All Other Current	6.5	8.9
	45.5	41.2				Total Current	52.7	56.2
	33.0	21.2				Fixed Assets (net)	23.6	19.0
	7.0	22.9				Intangibles (net)	7.1	7.2
	14.5	14.7				All Other Non-Current	16.6	17.6
	100.0	100.0				Total	100.0	100.0
						LIABILITIES		
	21.8	9.4				Notes Payable-Short Term	5.5	6.5
	3.6	2.4				Cur. Mat.-L.T.D.	2.4	1.8
	8.5	6.8				Trade Payables	9.8	8.9
	.0	1.2				Income Taxes Payable	.3	.4
	5.8	10.0				All Other Current	25.5	20.7
	39.6	29.7				Total Current	43.5	38.3
	29.2	17.5				Long-Term Debt	17.8	10.7
	.1	1.8				Deferred Taxes	.5	.5
	3.9	7.3				All Other Non-Current	4.0	8.3
	27.2	43.7				Net Worth	34.2	42.2
	100.0	100.0				Total Liabilties & Net Worth	100.0	100.0
						INCOME DATA		
	100.0	100.0				Net Sales	100.0	100.0
						Gross Profit		
	91.5	95.3				Operating Expenses	88.7	94.4
	8.5	4.7				Operating Profit	11.3	5.6
	6.4	1.3				All Other Expenses (net)	1.2	-1.2
	2.1	3.4				Profit Before Taxes	10.1	6.8
						RATIOS		
	6.0	3.8				Current	2.1	2.6
	2.3	1.6					1.3	1.5
	1.0	1.1					.7	1.0
	3.5	3.8				Quick	2.0	2.4
	1.5	1.4					1.1 (91)	1.3
	1.0	.9					.6	.6
0 UND	0 UND					Sales/Receivables	0 999.8	0 968.5
0 UND	3 132.8						5 74.4	4 92.6
4 99.9	22 16.4						9 40.4	12 30.0
						Cost of Sales/Inventory		
						Cost of Sales/Payables		
	6.2	9.5				Sales/Working Capital	6.6	6.2
	9.5	22.5					25.5	19.1
	-254.4	59.4					-51.5	999.8
						EBIT/Interest	34.2	38.4
							(50) 11.9	(58) 9.2
							2.6	-.3
						Net Profit + Depr., Dep., Amort./Cur. Mat. L/T/D	13.9	28.9
							(11) 5.4	(16) 4.6
							2.7	.5
	.3	.3				Fixed/Worth	.3	.1
	.9	.8					.7	.4
	-.5	-.3					6.7	1.3
	.6	.7				Debt/Worth	.8	.5
	4.0	1.1					2.4	1.0
	-7.3	-3.9					17.7	7.4
						% Profit Before Taxes/Tangible Net Worth	115.4	88.9
							(54) 46.4	(80) 31.8
							11.1	-5.0
	26.4	35.9				% Profit Before Taxes/Total Assets	35.6	34.3
	7.9	13.2					15.4	9.3
	-3.6	-4.2					2.9	-4.2
	45.2	59.2				Sales/Net Fixed Assets	41.3	52.4
	9.1	26.8					15.2	18.8
	1.2	13.6					8.6	8.6
	3.3	5.5				Sales/Total Assets	4.0	4.0
	2.4	2.4					2.2	2.3
	.7	1.3					1.0	1.3
						% Depr., Dep., Amort./Sales	1.2	1.3
							(52) 1.6	(62) 2.0
							3.0	3.0
						% Officers', Directors' Owners' Comp/Sales	4.1	4.3
							(15) 9.1	(21) 9.0
							23.3	17.8
4841M	28559M	143550M	368079M	322134M	305225M	Net Sales ($)	3050891M	3700935M
1397M	15133M	45448M	144006M	149158M	524977M	Total Assets ($)	1513298M	1693159M

M = $ thousand   MM = $ million
See Pages 9 through 22 for Explanation of Ratios and Data

Comparative Historical Data

Current Data Sorted by Sales

4/1/07-3/31/08 ALL	4/1/08-3/31/09 ALL	4/1/09-3/31/10 ALL	Type of Statement	0-1MM	1-3MM	3-5MM	5-10MM	10-25MM	25MM & OVER
20	17	9	Unqualified	1	1		2	3	2
2	2	2	Reviewed		1		1		
2	3	3	Compiled	1	1	1			
11	8	8	Tax Returns	6	1		1		
37	21	17	Other	1	4	2	1		9
				3 (4/1-9/30/09)			36 (10/1/09-3/31/10)		
72	**51**	**39**	**NUMBER OF STATEMENTS**	9	8	3	5	3	11
%	%	%	**ASSETS**	%	%	%	%	%	%
32.8	33.3	31.6	Cash & Equivalents						34.1
6.7	7.0	5.3	Trade Receivables (net)						11.2
1.7	1.4	.3	Inventory						.0
10.7	11.3	5.5	All Other Current						8.4
51.8	53.1	42.8	Total Current						53.7
19.1	18.7	24.1	Fixed Assets (net)						19.5
9.8	6.6	13.9	Intangibles (net)						12.0
19.3	21.7	19.3	All Other Non-Current						14.8
100.0	100.0	100.0	Total						100.0
			LIABILITIES						
11.3	17.1	9.9	Notes Payable-Short Term						.5
1.6	1.7	2.1	Cur. Mat.-L.T.D.						.7
9.8	7.2	5.6	Trade Payables						4.9
.8	1.0	.6	Income Taxes Payable						.8
20.1	18.8	13.3	All Other Current						15.2
43.6	45.9	31.5	Total Current						22.2
13.3	13.6	24.1	Long-Term Debt						22.3
.5	.3	.7	Deferred Taxes						.5
13.0	10.7	13.3	All Other Non-Current						18.7
29.6	29.6	30.5	Net Worth						36.3
100.0	100.0	100.0	Total Liabilities & Net Worth						100.0
			INCOME DATA						
100.0	100.0	100.0	Net Sales						100.0
			Gross Profit						
101.7	102.2	92.6	Operating Expenses						90.0
-1.7	-2.2	7.4	Operating Profit						10.0
-2.6	1.4	2.9	All Other Expenses (net)						.6
.9	-3.6	4.5	Profit Before Taxes						9.4
			RATIOS						
3.0	2.9	4.3	Current						7.4
1.2	1.6	1.5							1.5
.7	.9	1.0							1.2
2.3	2.4	2.6	Quick						7.4
(71) 1.0	1.1	1.4							1.4
.5	.5	.9							1.1
0 UND	0 UND	0 UND	Sales/Receivables						0 999.8
5 69.5	8 45.4	3 110.5							13 27.1
15 24.5	21 17.7	14 27.0							31 11.8
			Cost of Sales/Inventory						
			Cost of Sales/Payables						
7.4	5.5	6.7	Sales/Working Capital						3.9
24.7	13.4	18.4							10.5
-21.9	-55.5	368.1							85.1
7.1	6.0	37.1	EBIT/Interest						
(39) 1.6	(28) -.5	(28) 5.3							
-6.1	-17.6	.4							
5.2			Net Profit + Depr., Dep., Amort./Cur. Mat. L/T/D						
(11) 1.2									
-2.3									
.1	.1	.2	Fixed/Worth						.1
.4	.3	.9							.3
NM	1.9	-.6							13.5
.6	.4	.6	Debt/Worth						.6
1.3	1.8	1.8							.8
-84.7	16.0	-7.3							82.4
48.9	33.3	90.0	% Profit Before Taxes/Tangible Net Worth						
(53) 3.2	(40) -4.4	(28) 22.7							
-29.1	-47.6	-1.5							
16.4	11.5	32.9	% Profit Before Taxes/Total Assets						47.7
1.0	-4.6	6.3							30.4
-19.0	-21.7	-1.5							1.0
60.1	49.1	56.0	Sales/Net Fixed Assets						37.5
17.2	19.8	21.8							18.9
8.9	11.4	7.0							10.8
4.2	3.7	3.5	Sales/Total Assets						5.5
2.3	1.9	2.3							2.4
1.3	1.0	.8							.7
1.2	1.0	.7	% Depr., Dep., Amort./Sales						
(51) 2.1	(36) 2.6	(27) 1.3							
3.3	3.5	3.5							
6.6			% Officers', Directors' Owners' Comp/Sales						
(17) 14.2									
22.9									
3359721M	1919185M	1172388M	Net Sales ($)	5415M	14188M	12452M	39617M	52982M	1047734M
1672663M	1162627M	880119M	Total Assets ($)	5782M	39026M	4727M	16411M	27023M	787150M

M = $ thousand   MM = $ million
See Pages 9 through 22 for Explanation of Ratios and Data

Current Data Sorted by Assets							Comparative Historical Data	

Type of Statement	0-500M	500M-2MM	2-10MM	10-50MM	50-100MM	100-250MM	4/1/05-3/31/06 ALL	4/1/06-3/31/07 ALL
Unqualified		3	4	6	6	6	16	32
Reviewed	1	1		1			1	3
Compiled	5	3	1	1			6	1
Tax Returns							4	2
Other			4	7	3	5	22	24
		8 (4/1-9/30/09)		49 (10/1/09-3/31/10)				
NUMBER OF STATEMENTS	6	7	9	15	9	11	49	62
	%	%	%	%	%	%	%	%
ASSETS								
Cash & Equivalents				69.6		48.5	43.9	47.9
Trade Receivables (net)				5.2		4.6	16.1	9.4
Inventory				.0		.2	.9	.1
All Other Current				3.6		1.0	4.4	5.7
Total Current				78.4		54.2	65.4	63.2
Fixed Assets (net)				2.2		3.2	10.9	7.9
Intangibles (net)				7.0		7.8	5.6	11.7
All Other Non-Current				12.4		34.9	18.1	17.2
Total				100.0		100.0	100.0	100.0
LIABILITIES								
Notes Payable-Short Term				4.1		.5	9.5	3.3
Cur. Mat.-L.T.D.				.1		.8	6.2	4.0
Trade Payables				11.5		11.0	18.7	13.4
Income Taxes Payable				1.1		.5	.8	.7
All Other Current				28.9		34.0	21.2	27.7
Total Current				45.7		46.9	56.4	49.1
Long-Term Debt				1.7		8.5	13.5	8.8
Deferred Taxes				1.0		.8	.2	.2
All Other Non-Current				7.9		18.5	10.1	10.1
Net Worth				43.7		25.4	19.8	31.7
Total Liabilities & Net Worth				100.0		100.0	100.0	100.0
INCOME DATA								
Net Sales				100.0		100.0	100.0	100.0
Gross Profit								
Operating Expenses				88.9		90.3	86.4	86.1
Operating Profit				11.1		9.7	13.6	13.9
All Other Expenses (net)				-2.5		-.3	.8	.0
Profit Before Taxes				13.6		10.1	12.8	13.8
RATIOS								
Current				2.8		2.4	2.4	2.4
				2.0		1.1	1.3	1.2
				1.1		.7	.8	.8
Quick				2.6		2.2	2.1	2.1
				1.9		1.1	1.3	1.1
				1.1		.7	.6	.7
Sales/Receivables				0 UND		5 70.8	0 UND	0 UND
				3 142.3		16 22.9	19 19.6	11 32.7
				110 3.3		59 6.1	75 4.9	63 5.8
Cost of Sales/Inventory								
Cost of Sales/Payables								
Sales/Working Capital				.6		1.0	1.7	2.4
				1.8		6.5	9.8	10.3
				5.4		-7.5	-23.1	-7.5
EBIT/Interest							11.3	34.5
							(24) 6.1	(35) 8.9
							2.3	4.2
Net Profit + Depr., Dep., Amort./Cur. Mat. L/T/D								
Fixed/Worth				.0		.0	.0	.0
				.0		.0	.1	.1
				.1		.3	2.6	2.2
Debt/Worth				.7		1.1	1.8	1.0
				2.0		3.8	3.4	3.0
				5.3		24.3	UND	26.7
% Profit Before Taxes/Tangible Net Worth				48.3			90.4	59.5
				(14) 10.5			(38) 23.7	(48) 36.7
				2.1			9.7	11.9
% Profit Before Taxes/Total Assets				6.8		7.0	20.2	19.1
				3.4		3.1	5.9	8.1
				-.6		-.3	2.1	1.9
Sales/Net Fixed Assets				UND		172.2	UND	UND
				UND		31.6	57.1	64.6
				26.9		21.1	17.2	21.7
Sales/Total Assets				1.1		.9	2.2	2.2
				.5		.3	.7	.7
				.2		.2	.3	.5
% Depr., Dep., Amort./Sales							.6	.5
							(21) 1.6	(26) 1.2
							2.7	1.6
% Officers', Directors' Owners' Comp/Sales							4.8	
							(10) 18.5	
							31.4	
Net Sales ($)	5514M	27207M	77369M	263095M	661396M	1363839M	1828411M	2489434M
Total Assets ($)	919M	6923M	37132M	422121M	657681M	2002526M	1816606M	3367493M

M = $ thousand   MM = $ million
See Pages 9 through 22 for Explanation of Ratios and Data

Comparative Historical Data | Current Data Sorted by Sales

			Type of Statement	0-1MM	1-3MM	3-5MM	5-10MM	10-25MM	25MM & OVER
29	33	25	Unqualified		3	1	5	3	13
3	3		Reviewed						
2	5	3	Compiled		2			1	
6	4	10	Tax Returns	5	2		3		
25	29	19	Other		1	3	4	2	9
4/1/07-3/31/08 ALL	4/1/08-3/31/09 ALL	4/1/09-3/31/10 ALL			8 (4/1-9/30/09)		49 (10/1/09-3/31/10)		
65	74	57	NUMBER OF STATEMENTS	5	8	4	12	6	22
%	%	%	ASSETS	%	%	%	%	%	%
49.0	52.1	48.5	Cash & Equivalents				63.8		47.2
11.0	9.7	8.7	Trade Receivables (net)				5.7		7.4
.0	.2	.8	Inventory				.0		.2
7.1	5.0	5.0	All Other Current				5.3		3.1
67.1	67.0	63.0	Total Current				74.8		58.0
7.6	5.4	3.8	Fixed Assets (net)				2.4		5.2
5.6	4.6	10.5	Intangibles (net)				3.5		14.8
19.7	23.0	22.7	All Other Non-Current				19.3		22.0
100.0	100.0	100.0	Total				100.0		100.0
			LIABILITIES						
8.2	4.7	10.6	Notes Payable-Short Term				3.5		1.8
2.5	.6	2.0	Cur. Mat.-L.T.D.				.3		.7
11.7	10.6	10.2	Trade Payables				4.6		16.4
.8	.6	.6	Income Taxes Payable				1.0		.6
26.0	31.1	28.2	All Other Current				41.6		27.2
49.3	47.6	51.5	Total Current				51.0		46.7
5.1	6.5	5.4	Long-Term Debt				4.0		6.7
.3	.4	.7	Deferred Taxes				.5		.4
13.5	15.0	13.0	All Other Non-Current				11.4		13.7
31.9	30.5	29.4	Net Worth				33.1		32.5
100.0	100.0	100.0	Total Liabilities & Net Worth				100.0		100.0
			INCOME DATA						
100.0	100.0	100.0	Net Sales				100.0		100.0
			Gross Profit						
88.8	88.9	89.3	Operating Expenses				80.7		92.3
11.2	11.1	10.7	Operating Profit				19.3		7.7
-.2	.4	.1	All Other Expenses (net)				-1.4		-.2
11.4	10.7	10.7	Profit Before Taxes				20.7		7.9
			RATIOS						
2.7	2.7	2.8					2.7		1.8
1.6	1.6	1.5	Current				1.9		1.0
1.0	1.0	.9					1.2		.8
2.6	2.7	2.7					2.6		1.8
1.4	1.4	1.4	Quick				1.7		1.0
.8	.8	.7					1.0		.7
0 UND	0 UND	0 UND					0 UND		6 57.1
8 46.2	7 48.9	7 50.6	Sales/Receivables				1 324.5		15 24.3
43 8.4	44 8.3	43 8.5					40 9.0		61 5.9
			Cost of Sales/Inventory						
			Cost of Sales/Payables						
1.8	1.4	1.7					.9		2.1
4.9	4.4	6.6	Sales/Working Capital				2.6		NM
UND	133.4	-20.7					10.9		-9.0
21.7	23.3	31.2							29.4
(28) 9.1	(31) 9.5	(26) 7.8	EBIT/Interest					(11)	5.9
1.4	1.7	.4							-2.7
			Net Profit + Depr., Dep., Amort./Cur. Mat. L/T/D						
.0	.0	.0					.0		.0
.0	.0	.0	Fixed/Worth				.0		.1
1.4	.4	.2					.1		NM
1.3	.9	.8					1.0		1.3
3.0	2.2	2.7	Debt/Worth				1.9		4.3
8.0	14.4	9.8					5.0		NM
61.5	57.9	53.1					212.8		48.4
(57) 31.1	(62) 16.9	(48) 13.8	% Profit Before Taxes/Tangible Net Worth		(11)		15.6	(17)	11.0
9.9	2.6	1.4					5.4		-4.5
14.9	15.2	18.5					29.1		8.6
5.6	4.8	4.3	% Profit Before Taxes/Total Assets				10.1		3.6
1.7	.5	.1					1.9		-.4
UND	UND	UND					UND		148.1
127.9	283.3	164.0	Sales/Net Fixed Assets				UND		32.0
23.6	40.4	26.6					712.5		19.6
2.4	2.4	2.3					2.9		1.8
.7	.7	.7	Sales/Total Assets				.8		.6
.4	.3	.4					.2		.4
.5	.3	.3							
(27) 1.1	(25) .7	(21) .9	% Depr., Dep., Amort./Sales						
2.2	1.3	1.8							
3.3	2.7								
(10) 9.0	(10) 15.6		% Officers', Directors' Owners' Comp/Sales						
15.2	25.9								
2824851M	2695775M	2398420M	Net Sales ($)	2121M	15648M	18436M	91844M	108718M	2161653M
2968794M	4184720M	3127302M	Total Assets ($)	870M	11389M	63250M	177048M	363436M	2511309M

© RMA 2010   M = $ thousand   MM = $ million
See Pages 9 through 22 for Explanation of Ratios and Data

Current Data Sorted by Assets   Comparative Historical Data

						Type of Statement		
	5	29	41	11	21	Unqualified	130	119
5	24	44	18	1		Reviewed	107	117
19	44	36	7			Compiled	101	114
127	104	29	1	1		Tax Returns	222	242
49	80	99	53	15	16	Other	280	247
	115 (4/1-9/30/09)		764 (10/1/09-3/31/10)				4/1/05-3/31/06	4/1/06-3/31/07
0-500M	500M-2MM	2-10MM	10-50MM	50-100MM	100-250MM		ALL	ALL
200	257	237	120	28	37	NUMBER OF STATEMENTS	840	839
%	%	%	%	%	%	ASSETS	%	%
35.2	23.6	29.0	31.1	35.7	37.8	Cash & Equivalents	31.0	30.1
10.3	14.5	22.6	21.6	23.2	12.7	Trade Receivables (net)	19.0	18.9
.1	.1	.0	.9	.0	.0	Inventory	.2	.2
5.5	4.9	7.1	5.9	9.8	14.9	All Other Current	6.0	5.5
51.1	43.1	58.7	59.5	68.6	65.4	Total Current	56.2	54.9
17.5	15.3	12.0	8.1	5.4	4.0	Fixed Assets (net)	13.1	14.3
16.5	23.9	12.8	15.1	14.0	21.0	Intangibles (net)	15.5	15.5
14.8	17.6	16.5	17.3	12.0	9.6	All Other Non-Current	15.2	15.3
100.0	100.0	100.0	100.0	100.0	100.0	Total	100.0	100.0
						LIABILITIES		
20.6	9.3	8.2	4.2	.7	4.2	Notes Payable-Short Term	12.7	11.1
9.8	5.4	2.4	2.1	1.4	.7	Cur. Mat.-L.T.D.	3.4	3.5
11.2	18.8	23.5	24.6	20.8	15.4	Trade Payables	21.5	21.8
.0	.1	.5	.7	.0	.5	Income Taxes Payable	.4	.4
22.0	16.1	18.7	21.0	34.8	30.8	All Other Current	18.8	19.8
63.6	49.6	53.2	52.6	57.8	51.6	Total Current	56.7	56.5
24.8	25.5	15.4	11.0	13.7	7.3	Long-Term Debt	17.7	18.2
.0	.1	.1	.2	.1	.9	Deferred Taxes	.2	.3
12.2	8.3	5.1	4.6	6.3	5.0	All Other Non-Current	5.7	6.7
-.6	16.4	26.2	31.6	22.2	35.2	Net Worth	19.6	18.3
100.0	100.0	100.0	100.0	100.0	100.0	Total Liabilities & Net Worth	100.0	100.0
						INCOME DATA		
100.0	100.0	100.0	100.0	100.0	100.0	Net Sales	100.0	100.0
						Gross Profit		
87.4	88.8	87.4	88.9	87.4	90.1	Operating Expenses	88.4	87.2
12.6	11.2	12.6	11.1	12.6	9.9	Operating Profit	11.6	12.8
1.7	2.7	2.6	1.9	2.6	2.4	All Other Expenses (net)	1.3	1.4
10.9	8.4	10.0	9.2	10.0	7.4	Profit Before Taxes	10.2	11.4
						RATIOS		
2.9	1.6	1.7	1.4	1.5	1.8		1.7	1.5
1.0	.9	1.1	1.1	1.1	1.3	Current	1.1	1.0
.4	.4	.7	.9	.9	1.0		.7	.6
2.5	1.4	1.6	1.3	1.3	1.5		1.5	1.4
.8	.8	1.0	1.0	1.0	1.0	Quick	(839) 1.0	(838) 1.0
.3	.3	.6	.7	.8	.7		.5	.5
0 UND	0 UND	8 47.5	17 21.9	41 9.0	1 293.8		0 UND	0 UND
0 UND	9 42.7	39 9.5	53 6.9	95 3.8	52 7.0	Sales/Receivables	22 16.4	19 19.5
8 48.6	34 10.7	106 3.4	92 4.0	181 2.0	114 3.2		74 4.9	75 4.9
						Cost of Sales/Inventory		
						Cost of Sales/Payables		
15.8	13.3	4.6	5.0	3.3	1.2		7.6	8.0
UND	-53.9	32.3	23.1	13.7	3.7	Sales/Working Capital	54.4	93.1
-9.9	-7.7	-12.0	-14.8	-10.1	68.1		-12.3	-12.0
31.8	14.4	26.2	35.1	46.3	92.5		24.3	21.6
(128) 7.6	(202) 5.4	(169) 5.2	(82) 6.6	(21) 15.0	(22) 4.7	EBIT/Interest	(612) 7.3	(611) 7.4
1.5	1.6	1.9	2.1	5.2	.9		2.6	2.5
		3.4	10.2	9.7		Net Profit + Depr., Dep.,	6.7	6.6
	(25) 1.4	(32) 2.0	(26) 2.8			Amort./Cur. Mat. L/T/D	(116) 2.9	(107) 2.7
	.7	.9	.6				1.1	1.4
.1	.1	.0	.1	.0	.0		.1	.1
.7	1.6	.3	.3	.3	.1	Fixed/Worth	.6	.6
-.6	-.2	-16.6	NM	-.7	-10.2		-1.1	-1.2
.8	1.6	1.3	1.8	3.5	1.3		1.6	1.6
11.7	8.5	4.9	4.6	7.9	5.6	Debt/Worth	5.3	6.8
-2.2	-2.4	-35.8	NM	-13.5	-115.9		-5.8	-6.6
295.1	129.9	81.2	55.7	87.1	38.5	% Profit Before Taxes/Tangible	116.0	119.2
(110) 87.9	(151) 38.5	(171) 21.9	(90) 23.9	(18) 47.9	(27) 18.4	Net Worth	(560) 38.5	(565) 39.7
8.7	4.8	6.1	9.6	3.0	3.9		11.7	12.0
89.5	22.6	17.4	11.7	12.0	6.7	% Profit Before Taxes/Total	24.7	25.4
22.2	8.9	6.1	4.8	6.5	2.2	Assets	8.9	10.0
.0	1.1	1.3	1.2	.9	-.6		2.3	2.5
486.5	112.2	107.6	63.4	77.2	UND		98.0	111.3
65.8	32.5	29.4	22.2	29.0	28.2	Sales/Net Fixed Assets	30.3	28.8
20.8	11.9	13.1	11.3	13.7	10.5		13.3	12.5
9.2	3.3	1.8	1.3	1.1	.6		3.4	3.1
4.7	2.0	1.2	.9	.8	.4	Sales/Total Assets	1.7	1.6
2.5	1.2	.7	.5	.4	.3		.9	.9
.5	.6	.8	1.0	.4	.7		.7	.7
(95) 1.0	(150) 1.5	(146) 1.4	(73) 2.0	(17) 1.8	(14) 1.2	% Depr., Dep., Amort./Sales	(520) 1.5	(533) 1.5
2.3	2.9	2.5	3.5	3.4	2.2		2.7	2.7
9.3	6.7	6.0	2.0			% Officers', Directors'	7.3	7.1
(138) 16.2	(144) 12.9	(86) 11.5	(15) 6.1			Owners' Comp/Sales	(372) 13.9	(382) 14.6
26.2	20.7	21.1	20.9				22.7	23.1
215168M	836429M	1741663M	2725738M	2340800M	2949638M	Net Sales ($)	13006005M	13221096M
42280M	298539M	1131041M	2819579M	2034582M	6179683M	Total Assets ($)	11528431M	10296333M

M = $ thousand   MM = $ million
See Pages 9 through 22 for Explanation of Ratios and Data

Comparative Historical Data | | Current Data Sorted by Sales

4/1/07-3/31/08 ALL	4/1/08-3/31/09 ALL	4/1/09-3/31/10 ALL	Type of Statement	0-1MM	1-3MM	3-5MM	5-10MM	10-25MM	25MM & OVE
100	101	107	Unqualified	3	9	5	14	27	49
111	98	92	Reviewed	5	22	24	22	11	8
100	98	106	Compiled	17	26	33	18	9	3
242	250	262	Tax Returns	118	85	31	19	7	2
297	309	312	Other	64	69	41	44	44	50
				115 (4/1-9/30/09)			764 (10/1/09-3/31/10)		
850	856	879	**NUMBER OF STATEMENTS**	207	211	134	117	98	112
%	%	%	**ASSETS**	%	%	%	%	%	%
30.6	29.6	29.7	Cash & Equivalents	25.5	27.6	30.8	32.7	32.1	34.7
17.9	18.3	16.9	Trade Receivables (net)	11.0	17.0	19.5	19.7	21.1	17.9
.2	.1	.2	Inventory	.1	.0	.1	.9	.1	.0
5.7	6.2	6.4	All Other Current	6.1	4.2	5.2	7.6	7.5	10.3
54.5	54.2	53.1	Total Current	42.7	48.8	55.6	61.0	60.8	63.0
13.6	14.1	13.1	Fixed Assets (net)	18.8	13.4	11.5	10.1	11.1	9.2
17.5	17.8	17.6	Intangibles (net)	20.6	21.5	15.7	13.3	11.4	16.7
14.4	13.9	16.1	All Other Non-Current	18.0	16.3	17.2	15.6	16.6	11.1
100.0	100.0	100.0	Total	100.0	100.0	100.0	100.0	100.0	100.0
			LIABILITIES						
9.6	10.5	10.4	Notes Payable-Short Term	18.0	10.7	9.4	8.8	5.8	2.4
4.1	3.3	4.8	Cur. Mat.-L.T.D.	8.4	5.2	2.9	3.8	3.6	1.9
20.6	20.0	19.1	Trade Payables	9.3	18.5	22.5	25.8	25.2	21.5
.7	.3	.3	Income Taxes Payable	.1	.2	.1	.6	.7	.5
18.5	20.5	20.0	All Other Current	18.8	16.6	13.8	22.3	27.9	26.8
53.5	54.6	54.5	Total Current	54.5	51.2	48.8	61.3	63.1	53.1
21.1	20.5	19.5	Long-Term Debt	30.3	20.7	17.2	16.0	11.7	10.7
.2	.2	.1	Deferred Taxes	.0	.1	.2	.0	.3	.4
6.0	6.9	7.6	All Other Non-Current	11.6	6.1	3.3	10.0	6.8	6.3
19.2	17.8	18.2	Net Worth	3.5	22.0	30.5	12.7	18.1	29.5
100.0	100.0	100.0	Total Liabilities & Net Worth	100.0	100.0	100.0	100.0	100.0	100.0
			INCOME DATA						
100.0	100.0	100.0	Net Sales	100.0	100.0	100.0	100.0	100.0	100.0
			Gross Profit						
87.3	89.3	88.1	Operating Expenses	81.8	88.3	89.2	92.9	90.5	91.3
12.7	10.7	11.9	Operating Profit	18.2	11.7	10.8	7.1	9.5	8.7
1.6	2.1	2.3	All Other Expenses (net)	5.7	2.5	.5	.5	1.3	.9
11.0	8.6	9.5	Profit Before Taxes	12.5	9.2	10.3	6.7	8.1	7.8
			RATIOS						
1.7	1.7	1.7	Current	2.1	1.9	2.1	1.4	1.5	1.6
1.1	1.1	1.0		.8	1.0	1.2	1.0	1.1	1.2
.7	.6	.6		.3	.5	.8	.7	.8	.9
1.5	1.5	1.6	Quick	1.8	1.8	1.7	1.3	1.3	1.3
(849) 1.0	1.0	.9		.6	.9	1.1	.9	1.0	1.0
.5	.5	.4		.2	.4	.7	.5	.6	.7
0 UND	0 UND	0 UND	Sales/Receivables	0 UND	0 UND	1 462.1	9 42.7	5 68.8	13 28.4
17 21.1	18 20.6	17 21.6		0 UND	11 31.7	22 16.3	28 12.9	32 11.3	45 8.1
64 5.7	66 5.5	59 6.2		21 17.2	59 6.2	63 5.8	66 5.5	70 5.2	96 3.8
			Cost of Sales/Inventory						
			Cost of Sales/Payables						
7.7	8.0	7.3	Sales/Working Capital	11.7	8.6	6.6	6.0	8.0	4.1
66.6	97.7	83.8		-32.9	-427.2	27.3	-723.5	33.5	17.5
-14.0	-10.8	-10.2		-6.5	-8.3	-13.9	-11.4	-20.5	-28.2
23.1	18.3	25.5	EBIT/Interest	16.4	13.5	38.2	30.5	31.3	53.2
(600) 5.9	(591) 5.0	(624) 6.0		(130) 4.6	(158) 5.4	(105) 6.8	(84) 5.0	(66) 7.5	(81) 12.0
1.6	1.3	1.8		1.4	1.7	1.8	1.2	2.5	3.0
9.3	6.9	8.0	Net Profit + Depr., Dep., Amort./Cur. Mat. L/T/D		3.4	3.6	4.5	16.0	15.0
(104) 3.2	(80) 2.1	(98) 1.9			(23) 1.3	(14) 1.7	(10) .8	(16) 3.1	(31) 4.5
1.3	.9	.8			.8	.5	.5	.7	1.5
.1	.1	.1	Fixed/Worth	.0	.0	.1	.1	.1	.1
.7	.6	.6		1.0	.9	.3	.7	.3	.5
-1.0	-.8	-.8		-.6	-.5	5.4	-.4	NM	-2.4
1.7	1.4	1.3	Debt/Worth	1.5	1.2	1.0	1.9	1.3	1.7
6.8	6.7	6.2		13.8	8.5	2.9	8.1	4.3	5.7
-5.5	-4.4	-4.4		-2.1	-2.8	-68.9	-5.9	-230.5	-13.9
146.5	112.6	119.7	% Profit Before Taxes/Tangible Net Worth	135.5	121.5	134.4	107.2	96.6	73.6
(559) 44.7	(552) 36.3	(567) 31.3		(114) 26.8	(127) 31.6	(100) 29.9	(77) 31.3	(73) 38.0	(76) 30.8
10.3	5.9	6.3		1.9	4.2	7.0	7.2	9.0	11.3
26.6	23.3	21.7	% Profit Before Taxes/Total Assets	42.5	25.1	23.5	18.5	18.7	13.5
9.6	6.7	7.1		9.3	6.9	8.5	6.4	6.5	6.0
1.4	.4	1.1		.0	1.0	1.3	.5	2.0	1.3
101.6	115.7	131.6	Sales/Net Fixed Assets	282.0	148.3	124.6	116.0	107.7	75.0
29.8	32.7	33.5		37.9	34.0	33.1	40.0	40.3	22.7
11.7	13.5	13.7		10.5	13.8	13.5	16.3	18.9	11.5
3.2	3.5	3.2	Sales/Total Assets	4.4	3.3	2.9	2.7	3.3	1.6
1.6	1.7	1.6		1.7	1.6	1.8	1.6	1.6	.9
.8	.8	.8		.6	1.0	1.0	.8	.9	.5
.8	.8	.7	% Depr., Dep., Amort./Sales	.9	.7	.6	.6	.6	.7
(519) 1.6	(487) 1.4	(495) 1.4		(84) 2.2	(126) 1.4	(85) 1.3	(64) 1.3	(69) 1.1	(67) 1.8
2.9	2.7	2.6		4.4	3.1	2.1	2.6	2.0	3.0
8.2	6.6	6.8	% Officers', Directors' Owners' Comp/Sales	8.9	8.6	6.7	5.8	2.1	.9
(365) 14.1	(371) 13.7	(389) 13.4		(114) 16.3	(127) 15.4	(66) 11.9	(41) 9.5	(24) 4.5	(17) 5.3
22.2	22.7	22.5		25.2	22.2	20.0	18.7	10.3	19.8
12287714M	11552528M	10809436M	Net Sales ($)	113203M	390994M	520795M	813996M	1524052M	7446396M
12645205M	11639528M	12505704M	Total Assets ($)	147276M	509992M	563204M	804394M	1454168M	9026670M

© RMA 2010

M = $ thousand   MM = $ million
See Pages 9 through 22 for Explanation of Ratios and Data

Current Data Sorted by Assets   **Comparative Historical Data**

0-500M	500M-2MM	2-10MM	10-50MM	50-100MM	100-250MM	Type of Statement	4/1/05-3/31/06 ALL	4/1/06-3/31/07 ALL
	2	10	17	6	5	Unqualified	11	18
2	1	1				Reviewed	4	1
3	5	3	1		1	Compiled	3	4
2	11	15	9	2	1	Tax Returns	3	2
						Other	10	21
	13 (4/1-9/30/09)		86 (10/1/09-3/31/10)					
7	19	31	27	8	7	NUMBER OF STATEMENTS	31	46
%	%	%	%	%	%	ASSETS	%	%
	25.0	25.9	31.1			Cash & Equivalents	25.1	28.6
	18.7	15.5	20.5			Trade Receivables (net)	24.2	19.9
	.4	.9	3.4			Inventory	1.3	.0
	5.7	11.4	8.7			All Other Current	7.1	9.1
	49.7	53.7	63.7			Total Current	57.7	57.6
	23.0	23.0	16.3			Fixed Assets (net)	11.8	17.0
	16.4	6.3	10.5			Intangibles (net)	14.2	12.9
	10.9	17.0	9.5			All Other Non-Current	16.2	12.5
	100.0	100.0	100.0			Total	100.0	100.0
						LIABILITIES		
	6.3	4.3	8.9			Notes Payable-Short Term	7.2	11.0
	5.2	3.0	1.0			Cur. Mat.-L.T.D.	2.7	2.5
	8.2	12.2	14.8			Trade Payables	10.2	12.4
	.3	1.0	.2			Income Taxes Payable	.0	.4
	13.3	34.4	29.2			All Other Current	26.2	33.7
	33.3	54.9	54.1			Total Current	46.4	59.9
	31.9	9.6	7.7			Long-Term Debt	11.4	17.3
	.0	.2	.4			Deferred Taxes	.5	.7
	7.3	7.9	16.0			All Other Non-Current	8.3	7.3
	27.5	27.4	21.8			Net Worth	33.4	14.7
	100.0	100.0	100.0			Total Liabilities & Net Worth	100.0	100.0
						INCOME DATA		
	100.0	100.0	100.0			Net Sales	100.0	100.0
						Gross Profit		
	82.5	88.0	90.3			Operating Expenses	91.7	93.9
	17.5	12.0	9.7			Operating Profit	8.3	6.1
	2.1	2.3	1.5			All Other Expenses (net)	.7	-.6
	15.4	9.7	8.2			Profit Before Taxes	7.6	6.8
						RATIOS		
	2.9	1.9	2.7				1.9	2.0
	1.2	1.1	1.3			Current	1.3	1.1
	.9	.7	.9				.9	.5
	2.9	1.6	1.8				1.7	1.6
	1.0	.8	1.1			Quick	1.1	.8
	.7	.4	.7				.6	.4
	0 UND	0 UND	1 583.8				14 26.3	8 46.5
	6 62.2	15 24.3	28 13.1			Sales/Receivables	33 11.0	28 13.3
	27 13.3	35 10.5	52 7.0				51 7.1	49 7.5
						Cost of Sales/Inventory		
						Cost of Sales/Payables		
	12.5	6.0	4.2				6.3	8.0
	63.9	55.6	8.8			Sales/Working Capital	26.0	93.2
	-35.7	-11.0	-34.8				-23.5	-7.2
	43.3	53.4	43.7				33.8	18.3
	(15) 25.7	(26) 8.4	(18) 12.3			EBIT/Interest	(20) 8.4	(31) 6.3
	4.4	1.6	1.8				2.6	1.3
						Net Profit + Depr., Dep., Amort./Cur. Mat. L/T/D		9.0
							(13) 2.9	
								.9
	.1	.2	.2				.1	.2
	1.4	1.0	.6			Fixed/Worth	.6	.8
	32.0	7.9	-4.0				-12.6	-1.1
	1.0	1.2	.8				1.1	1.2
	2.5	2.2	4.5			Debt/Worth	2.0	7.0
	254.3	46.2	-24.3				-48.5	-5.1
	427.0	100.9	88.6			% Profit Before Taxes/Tangible Net Worth	70.2	117.4
	(15) 104.6	(24) 19.8	(19) 33.1				(23) 43.3	(30) 34.2
	15.3	2.5	11.8				9.2	11.5
	73.6	31.8	16.6			% Profit Before Taxes/Total Assets	22.6	24.9
	25.7	8.4	7.0				10.1	8.0
	6.4	.9	3.0				2.7	.3
	101.7	44.3	253.3			Sales/Net Fixed Assets	43.6	52.7
	33.2	19.0	17.2				27.1	23.0
	16.1	5.7	10.3				10.6	8.6
	5.5	4.1	2.6			Sales/Total Assets	3.4	3.7
	3.7	1.7	1.4				1.9	2.0
	1.3	.7	.8				1.2	1.0
	.8	.7	1.4			% Depr., Dep., Amort./Sales	1.1	1.2
	(12) 1.6	(28) 1.9	(18) 2.0				(27) 1.6	(34) 2.0
	2.6	3.3	2.8				3.2	3.0
						% Officers', Directors' Owners' Comp/Sales		
12172M	82650M	337999M	774677M	1054580M	1405740M	Net Sales ($)	1664934M	2111236M
1758M	21832M	153026M	464513M	558141M	1086531M	Total Assets ($)	921167M	1299328M

M = $ thousand   MM = $ million
See Pages 9 through 22 for Explanation of Ratios and Data

Comparative Historical Data   Current Data Sorted by Sales

			Type of Statement						
20	33	40	Unqualified		8	2	11	19
3	6	2	Reviewed		1	1	1	
1	4	4	Compiled		1	1	1	
4	8	13	Tax Returns	3	1	1	4	1	3	1
30	25	40	Other	9	2	7	3	8	11
4/1/07-3/31/08 ALL	4/1/08-3/31/09 ALL	4/1/09-3/31/10 ALL			13 (4/1-9/30/09)		86 (10/1/09-3/31/10)		
				0-1MM	1-3MM	3-5MM	5-10MM	10-25MM	25MM & OVER
58	76	99	**NUMBER OF STATEMENTS**	12	4	20	8	24	31
%	%	%	**ASSETS**	%	%	%	%	%	%
26.6	32.1	27.5	Cash & Equivalents	31.5		24.3		40.5	19.1
21.8	22.0	17.3	Trade Receivables (net)	7.2		16.5		17.1	22.8
.2	.2	1.3	Inventory	.0		.0		.4	.1
7.8	7.0	8.2	All Other Current	4.6		13.8		4.7	9.3
56.5	61.3	54.2	Total Current	43.3		54.6		62.8	51.3
13.3	11.6	19.1	Fixed Assets (net)	36.5		15.4		16.7	16.9
11.7	12.1	14.6	Intangibles (net)	9.1		13.6		8.5	23.0
18.5	15.0	12.0	All Other Non-Current	11.1		16.3		12.1	8.8
100.0	100.0	100.0	Total	100.0		100.0		100.0	100.0
			LIABILITIES						
8.4	7.1	6.2	Notes Payable-Short Term	3.4		12.1		4.3	1.3
3.9	2.3	3.9	Cur. Mat.-L.T.D.	6.5		4.7		1.8	3.3
18.1	19.1	11.9	Trade Payables	3.9		6.5		19.9	10.7
.3	.3	.4	Income Taxes Payable	.1		.1		1.2	.2
25.9	22.9	26.5	All Other Current	13.1		35.5		30.6	25.6
56.6	51.7	48.9	Total Current	27.1		58.9		57.9	41.1
15.0	12.0	16.3	Long-Term Debt	21.2		18.3		8.4	14.1
.8	.4	.4	Deferred Taxes	.0		.1		.1	1.2
19.4	9.0	10.7	All Other Non-Current	10.2		3.7		3.1	21.9
8.1	27.0	23.7	Net Worth	41.4		19.0		30.6	21.7
100.0	100.0	100.0	Total Liabilties & Net Worth	100.0		100.0		100.0	100.0
			INCOME DATA						
100.0	100.0	100.0	Net Sales	100.0		100.0		100.0	100.0
			Gross Profit						
91.9	93.6	88.2	Operating Expenses	70.8		86.9		93.2	91.7
8.1	6.4	11.8	Operating Profit	29.2		13.1		6.8	8.3
1.2	.6	1.6	All Other Expenses (net)	8.3		.5		1.1	.5
6.9	5.8	10.2	Profit Before Taxes	20.9		12.6		5.7	7.8
			RATIOS						
2.1	2.1	2.2		2.6		1.8		2.9	2.1
.9	1.3	1.2	Current	1.0		1.1		1.1	1.4
.6	1.0	.7		.6		.5		.9	.8
1.9	1.9	1.8		2.2		1.5		2.5	1.7
.9	1.2	1.0	Quick	1.0		.8		1.1	1.2
.4	.7	.6		.4		.3		.7	.7
6 66.2	7 55.9	1 583.8		0 UND	0 UND		4 84.8	14 26.0
25 14.6	30 12.0	17 21.3	Sales/Receivables	0 UND	10 38.3		19 19.0	34 10.8
45 8.2	47 7.7	39 9.4		13 27.1	22 16.6		38 9.6	49 7.4
			Cost of Sales/Inventory						
			Cost of Sales/Payables						
8.1	6.0	5.9		2.7		5.4		5.9	6.0
-42.6	25.1	29.0	Sales/Working Capital	NM		71.6		41.4	23.0
-8.8	-63.5	-15.9		-4.6		-8.1		-27.5	-24.3
26.0	37.8	38.6				41.9		159.2	37.8
(42) 4.7	(52) 4.7	(77) 10.6	EBIT/Interest		(17) 25.7		(17) 17.0	(26) 4.3
1.7	.8	2.0				8.0		5.2	.0
22.0	5.0	12.7	Net Profit + Depr., Dep.,						
(12) 5.6	(11) 3.2	(17) 2.5	Amort./Cur. Mat. L/T/D						
1.8	1.4	1.6							
.1	.1	.2		.0		.1		.2	.3
.5	.5	1.0	Fixed/Worth	1.7		1.0		.6	1.0
-1.1	-6.5	-2.0		NM		NM		6.7	-.4
1.3	1.1	1.2		.4		1.5		1.0	1.2
10.6	5.1	4.4	Debt/Worth	1.0		8.9		4.7	5.5
-3.9	-17.4	-9.8		NM		-22.6		38.6	-2.3
83.9	98.5	115.3	% Profit Before Taxes/Tangible			254.5		173.9	74.5
(34) 43.7	(53) 38.2	(68) 35.5	Net Worth		(14) 81.2		(19) 64.7	(18) 27.8
14.9	9.7	7.9				8.6		20.1	10.0
27.3	22.0	27.9	% Profit Before Taxes/Total	10.3		36.9		37.2	20.2
13.1	6.7	8.4	Assets	3.9		14.1		13.1	6.3
1.6	-.6	2.2		2.1		4.2		4.2	1.1
138.6	170.8	50.5		387.4		153.4		60.9	26.0
25.2	31.0	19.3	Sales/Net Fixed Assets	66.4		25.2		23.7	17.0
13.3	13.3	9.4		.2		10.4		17.3	6.9
4.4	4.0	3.8		2.5		4.3		4.2	3.7
2.4	2.2	1.8	Sales/Total Assets	.2		2.0		1.9	1.8
1.2	.9	.8		.1		1.0		1.0	.9
.6	.6	.8				1.0		.5	1.8
(41) 1.8	(48) 1.3	(72) 1.9	% Depr., Dep., Amort./Sales		(12) 1.8		(21) 1.3	(22) 2.3
3.4	2.6	2.9				3.8		2.0	4.1
	3.8	3.7	% Officers', Directors'						
	(16) 6.5	(20) 7.0	Owners' Comp/Sales						
	11.6	10.2							
3009437M	2976965M	3667818M	Net Sales ($)	6201M	6574M	78525M	57951M	372101M	3146466M
1564872M	1710346M	2285801M	Total Assets ($)	23468M	5678M	61618M	54987M	223417M	1916633M

M = $ thousand   MM = $ million
See Pages 9 through 22 for Explanation of Ratios and Data

Current Data Sorted by Assets

Comparative Historical Data

	0-500M	500M-2MM	2-10MM	10-50MM	50-100MM	100-250MM	Type of Statement		4/1/05-3/31/06 ALL	4/1/06-3/31/07 ALL
			3	1	4	2	Unqualified		5	7
			1				Reviewed		2	1
	1	4	1			1	Compiled		4	1
	3	2					Tax Returns		2	5
	1	4	6	7	3	2	Other		6	11
		4 (4/1-9/30/09)		42 (10/1/09-3/31/10)						
NUMBER OF STATEMENTS	5	10	11	8	7	5			19	25
	%	%	%	%	%	%	**ASSETS**		%	%
		25.0	18.1				Cash & Equivalents		35.7	31.0
		20.9	42.4				Trade Receivables (net)		19.8	24.9
		.0	.0				Inventory		.0	.3
		4.1	4.1				All Other Current		12.1	9.2
		50.0	64.5				Total Current		67.6	65.5
		9.4	16.9				Fixed Assets (net)		22.7	18.9
		13.2	14.7				Intangibles (net)		4.4	10.4
		27.4	3.9				All Other Non-Current		5.4	5.2
		100.0	100.0				Total		100.0	100.0
							LIABILITIES			
		10.6	9.9				Notes Payable-Short Term		1.8	29.8
		1.4	1.5				Cur. Mat.-L.T.D.		2.6	3.2
		12.3	17.9				Trade Payables		21.7	16.5
		.0	1.1				Income Taxes Payable		1.5	.2
		17.6	15.7				All Other Current		15.3	18.1
		41.8	46.0				Total Current		42.8	67.9
		12.7	20.1				Long-Term Debt		18.2	15.5
		.1	.0				Deferred Taxes		.3	.2
		18.6	.0				All Other Non-Current		7.3	15.0
		26.7	33.9				Net Worth		31.3	1.5
		100.0	100.0				Total Liabilities & Net Worth		100.0	100.0
							INCOME DATA			
		100.0	100.0				Net Sales		100.0	100.0
							Gross Profit			
		77.9	94.0				Operating Expenses		77.8	90.6
		22.1	6.0				Operating Profit		22.2	9.4
		6.9	.3				All Other Expenses (net)		1.0	.6
		15.2	5.7				Profit Before Taxes		21.3	8.7
							RATIOS			
		9.8	1.7						2.3	2.2
		.9	1.3				Current		1.4	1.3
		.5	.7						1.0	1.1
		8.7	1.7						1.8	1.9
		.9	1.2				Quick		1.3	1.3
		.4	.6						.6	.8
	0 UND		10 38.2					0 UND		2 191.4
	17 21.1		39 9.3				Sales/Receivables	22 16.8		35 10.4
	55 6.6		49 7.4					114 3.2		69 5.3
							Cost of Sales/Inventory			
							Cost of Sales/Payables			
		8.2	5.8						2.6	5.5
		NM	16.6				Sales/Working Capital		6.4	9.5
		-6.7	-38.7						510.0	74.5
										9.4
							EBIT/Interest		(19)	4.7
										1.1
							Net Profit + Depr., Dep., Amort./Cur. Mat. L/T/D			
		.0	.1						.0	.4
		.4	.3				Fixed/Worth		.3	1.8
		-.4	2.8						4.1	-.5
		.7	.9						1.1	1.7
		2.7	1.8				Debt/Worth		2.5	6.2
		-5.1	5.5						42.0	-5.0
										86.4	124.9
							% Profit Before Taxes/Tangible Net Worth	(15) 36.7	(16) 66.6
										13.8	39.0
		43.7	21.7						48.5	25.2
		7.9	7.7				% Profit Before Taxes/Total Assets		13.8	14.2
		-5.5	1.7						6.2	1.9
		UND	374.3						107.0	62.2
		28.5	42.2				Sales/Net Fixed Assets		28.5	13.9
		19.4	8.4						2.1	6.7
		4.6	4.9						2.3	3.5
		2.1	4.3				Sales/Total Assets		1.0	1.6
		.6	1.4						.5	.8
										.9	.7
							% Depr., Dep., Amort./Sales	(14) 1.7	(14) 1.5
										6.2	3.0
							% Officers', Directors' Owners' Comp/Sales			
	1758M	31331M	211168M	222256M	502750M	903946M	Net Sales ($)		374810M	1157558M
	1059M	11087M	56081M	154471M	493993M	686471M	Total Assets ($)		472266M	901497M

M = $ thousand   MM = $ million
See Pages 9 through 22 for Explanation of Ratios and Data

Comparative Historical Data

Current Data Sorted by Sales

6	15	10	Type of Statement					2	8
		1	Unqualified	1					
2	2	7	Reviewed	1	2	1		2	1
4	4	5	Compiled	4		3	1		
15	12	23	Tax Returns	4	2	3	2	4	8
4/1/07-3/31/08 ALL	4/1/08-3/31/09 ALL	4/1/09-3/31/10 ALL	Other	0-1MM	1-3MM	4 (4/1-9/30/09) 3-5MM	5-10MM	42 (10/1/09-3/31/10) 10-25MM	25MM & OVER
27	33	46	**NUMBER OF STATEMENTS**	10	4	4	3	8	17
%	%	%	**ASSETS**	%	%	%	%	%	%
26.6	29.9	27.7	Cash & Equivalents	15.2					20.5
28.6	26.2	23.1	Trade Receivables (net)	19.3					28.1
.0	.3	.1	Inventory	.0					.3
11.1	7.3	8.6	All Other Current	17.2					7.6
66.4	63.8	59.5	Total Current	51.7					56.6
9.8	13.7	11.5	Fixed Assets (net)	7.0					20.2
5.7	10.3	16.5	Intangibles (net)	18.0					16.2
18.1	12.3	12.5	All Other Non-Current	23.4					7.0
100.0	100.0	100.0	Total	100.0					100.0
			LIABILITIES						
25.6	18.9	10.4	Notes Payable-Short Term	24.9					3.1
1.0	2.4	1.9	Cur. Mat.-L.T.D.	5.0					2.0
13.3	13.5	12.8	Trade Payables	2.6					16.4
.3	.5	.6	Income Taxes Payable	.0					1.0
23.7	24.4	20.9	All Other Current	16.1					22.0
63.9	59.8	46.7	Total Current	48.6					44.5
11.0	11.6	12.2	Long-Term Debt	11.5					12.0
.4	.5	.4	Deferred Taxes	.1					.9
9.8	11.8	10.4	All Other Non-Current	11.3					13.8
14.9	16.5	30.3	Net Worth	28.5					28.8
100.0	100.0	100.0	Total Liabilties & Net Worth	100.0					100.0
			INCOME DATA						
100.0	100.0	100.0	Net Sales	100.0					100.0
			Gross Profit						
79.8	87.4	85.0	Operating Expenses	67.4					94.6
20.2	12.6	15.0	Operating Profit	32.6					5.4
1.2	1.8	1.8	All Other Expenses (net)	7.3					.4
19.0	10.9	13.1	Profit Before Taxes	25.4					5.0
			RATIOS						
1.8	2.4	1.8	Current	13.9					1.6
1.4	1.4	1.3		.7					1.4
.9	1.1	.7		.3					1.0
1.6	2.3	1.7	Quick	10.8					1.5
1.3	1.2	1.2		.4					1.3
.8	.9	.5		.2					.8
11 33.3	4 81.7	8 43.7	Sales/Receivables	0 UND					33 11.2
36 10.0	29 12.7	35 10.3		13 28.3					39 9.3
91 4.0	48 7.6	49 7.5		46 7.9					49 7.5
			Cost of Sales/Inventory						
			Cost of Sales/Payables						
3.5	5.2	5.7	Sales/Working Capital	.8					10.0
11.6	16.1	16.9		-20.4					17.3
-93.2	127.2	-24.1		-1.8					399.4
31.9	71.9	54.4	EBIT/Interest						54.4
(17) 10.7	(22) 14.7	(29) 3.8							(13) 6.2
7.9	3.0	-5.1							-4.0
			Net Profit + Depr., Dep., Amort./Cur. Mat. L/T/D						
.1	.0	.0	Fixed/Worth	.0					.3
.4	.3	.3		.0					.9
2.1	NM	NM		-1.5					NM
1.3	.9	1.1	Debt/Worth	1.0					1.3
1.7	1.9	2.7		2.7					3.0
26.6	NM	-7.4		-5.5					NM
221.0	72.8	81.1	% Profit Before Taxes/Tangible Net Worth						92.5
(22) 75.7	(25) 54.3	(34) 35.6							(13) 42.2
27.3	15.1	6.8							6.8
32.6	31.3	20.4	% Profit Before Taxes/Total Assets	29.5					26.3
15.5	11.2	7.5		5.5					11.8
10.2	3.3	-.7		-3.6					-3.4
147.1	162.2	359.1	Sales/Net Fixed Assets	UND					33.8
36.1	41.8	33.9		UND					16.1
19.1	16.2	17.8		25.7					6.5
4.0	4.7	3.8	Sales/Total Assets	1.3					3.8
2.3	2.8	1.7		.7					2.5
.9	.9	.4		.3					1.2
.5	.4	.6	% Depr., Dep., Amort./Sales						.8
(17) 1.4	(24) 1.2	(24) 1.4							(13) 1.5
2.1	2.1	2.4							2.5
		5.3	% Officers', Directors' Owners' Comp/Sales						
	(13)	7.6							
		27.0							
877594M	2184549M	1873209M	Net Sales ($)	4001M	8778M	16545M	25971M	138277M	1679637M
696595M	1020893M	1403162M	Total Assets ($)	8335M	8467M	30936M	86317M	383235M	885872M

M = $ thousand   MM = $ million
See Pages 9 through 22 for Explanation of Ratios and Data

FINANCE—Open-End Investment Funds NAICS 525910

Current Data Sorted by Assets							Comparative Historical Data	

0-500M	500M-2MM	2-10MM	10-50MM	50-100MM	100-250MM	Type of Statement	4/1/05-3/31/06 ALL	4/1/06-3/31/07 ALL
	1	3	9	2	6	Unqualified	26	27
	1	1	1			Reviewed	2	3
		1	1			Compiled	5	3
2		3	1			Tax Returns	7	11
	3	6	10	5	2	Other	39	27
		9 (4/1-9/30/09)	49 (10/1/09-3/31/10)					
2	5	14	21	8	8	NUMBER OF STATEMENTS	79	71
%	%	%	%	%	%	**ASSETS**	%	%
		10.6	22.9			Cash & Equivalents	16.6	23.9
		17.3	18.8			Trade Receivables (net)	13.6	13.2
		.0	1.4			Inventory	3.1	2.6
		13.7	3.1			All Other Current	7.5	5.5
		41.6	46.3			Total Current	40.8	45.3
		18.6	9.4			Fixed Assets (net)	22.0	20.6
		.0	7.5			Intangibles (net)	6.8	6.8
		39.7	36.7			All Other Non-Current	30.4	27.3
		100.0	100.0			Total	100.0	100.0
						LIABILITIES		
		3.7	8.9			Notes Payable-Short Term	12.7	7.7
		1.6	4.3			Cur. Mat.-L.T.D.	3.5	2.8
		3.4	3.3			Trade Payables	2.8	5.2
		.0	.2			Income Taxes Payable	.2	.2
		10.6	11.0			All Other Current	7.2	16.0
		19.3	27.7			Total Current	26.5	31.9
		12.8	11.0			Long-Term Debt	21.9	15.9
		.4	.6			Deferred Taxes	.2	.0
		1.4	1.4			All Other Non-Current	8.3	6.6
		66.1	59.2			Net Worth	43.2	45.6
		100.0	100.0			Total Liabilities & Net Worth	100.0	100.0
						INCOME DATA		
		100.0	100.0			Net Sales	100.0	100.0
						Gross Profit		
		71.5	71.2			Operating Expenses	56.6	65.4
		28.5	28.8			Operating Profit	43.4	34.6
		5.8	8.1			All Other Expenses (net)	6.5	4.0
		22.7	20.7			Profit Before Taxes	36.9	30.6
						RATIOS		
		9.4	11.1				6.6	10.5
		4.1	1.5			Current	1.4	1.8
		.8	.6				.4	.5
		7.1	10.1				5.4	8.9
		1.8	1.3			Quick	.9	1.4
		.2	.4				.2	.3
		0 UND	0 UND				0 UND	0 UND
		0 UND	19 19.1			Sales/Receivables	1 256.3	4 86.3
		45 8.2	52 7.0				90 4.1	36 10.1
						Cost of Sales/Inventory		
						Cost of Sales/Payables		
		1.2	2.9				2.2	2.5
		8.6	12.8			Sales/Working Capital	11.2	19.2
		-16.9	-4.4				-5.9	-10.3
			89.6				187.7	37.7
			(12) 8.9			EBIT/Interest	(48) 9.3	(35) 6.7
			1.3				3.2	2.2
						Net Profit + Depr., Dep., Amort./Cur. Mat. L/T/D		
		.0	.0				.0	.0
		.1	.1			Fixed/Worth	.0	.2
		.6	NM				1.4	1.9
		.1	.1				.2	.1
		.3	.4			Debt/Worth	.9	1.1
		1.2	-228.6				5.4	8.3
		135.0	95.5			% Profit Before Taxes/Tangible Net Worth	79.6	114.2
		25.8	(15) 9.2				(71) 32.0	(60) 24.0
		5.0	1.6				11.0	5.2
		84.6	61.9			% Profit Before Taxes/Total Assets	31.5	33.9
		18.4	6.5				11.6	10.1
		4.5	.3				3.0	1.2
		86.1	UND			Sales/Net Fixed Assets	UND	UND
		35.6	48.8				53.4	32.0
		6.4	10.5				5.6	10.7
		2.9	2.2			Sales/Total Assets	1.7	2.6
		1.1	.8				.5	1.0
		.1	.1				.2	.2
			.7			% Depr., Dep., Amort./Sales	1.0	.6
			(12) 1.0				(35) 3.1	(37) 1.7
			1.8				10.2	6.6
						% Officers', Directors' Owners' Comp/Sales	5.9	3.7
							(14) 13.2	(10) 10.2
							34.9	38.3
1418M	10462M	94930M	752345M	170204M	253528M	Net Sales ($)	2402034M	8777750M
846M	5805M	52266M	540120M	560132M	1472411M	Total Assets ($)	2546462M	2097658M

RMA 2010

M = $ thousand   MM = $ million
See Pages 9 through 22 for Explanation of Ratios and Data

Comparative Historical Data | Current Data Sorted by Sales

			Type of Statement	0-1MM	1-3MM	3-5MM	5-10MM	10-25MM	25MM & OVER
15	26	21	Unqualified	1	3	1	3	4	9
2	3	3	Reviewed	2	1				
3	5	2	Compiled	1	1				
5	8	6	Tax Returns	4	1			1	
31	24	26	Other	2	4	4	2	8	6
4/1/07-3/31/08	4/1/08-3/31/09	4/1/09-3/31/10			9 (4/1-9/30/09)			49 (10/1/09-3/31/10)	
ALL	ALL	ALL							
56	66	58	**NUMBER OF STATEMENTS**	10	10	5	5	13	15
%	%	%	**ASSETS**	%	%	%	%	%	%
23.8	22.8	20.1	Cash & Equivalents	16.6	15.1			17.7	27.1
15.2	11.1	13.3	Trade Receivables (net)	11.5	3.8			22.0	18.2
2.0	2.0	1.8	Inventory	.0	.0			4.2	3.3
7.6	6.8	6.1	All Other Current	6.6	8.8			5.8	2.8
48.6	42.7	41.3	Total Current	34.8	27.7			49.8	51.5
18.8	17.5	14.0	Fixed Assets (net)	27.9	1.7			16.2	16.8
4.9	7.2	3.0	Intangibles (net)	.0	.2			1.0	6.6
27.7	32.6	41.7	All Other Non-Current	37.3	70.5			33.1	25.1
100.0	100.0	100.0	Total	100.0	100.0			100.0	100.0
			LIABILITIES						
11.6	9.0	7.6	Notes Payable-Short Term	15.1	3.7			4.1	5.7
4.5	4.2	2.7	Cur. Mat.-L.T.D.	1.4	.0			3.9	2.2
6.3	4.8	3.4	Trade Payables	3.2	.5			3.3	5.9
.2	.0	.1	Income Taxes Payable	.0	.0			.0	.2
12.3	13.2	11.7	All Other Current	1.0	17.7			16.3	16.8
34.9	31.1	25.5	Total Current	20.8	21.9			27.6	30.8
21.5	27.1	13.5	Long-Term Debt	38.4	4.7			8.5	8.8
.7	.4	.9	Deferred Taxes	.0	.0			.4	1.7
7.8	7.4	3.2	All Other Non-Current	2.4	.0			8.5	3.2
35.2	34.0	57.0	Net Worth	38.4	73.3			54.9	55.5
100.0	100.0	100.0	Total Liabilities & Net Worth	100.0	100.0			100.0	100.0
			INCOME DATA						
100.0	100.0	100.0	Net Sales	100.0	100.0			100.0	100.0
			Gross Profit						
63.1	64.8	66.8	Operating Expenses	50.6	68.0			82.7	67.6
36.9	35.2	33.2	Operating Profit	49.4	32.0			17.3	32.4
7.6	10.6	8.4	All Other Expenses (net)	26.9	4.1			1.0	2.7
29.3	24.5	24.8	Profit Before Taxes	22.6	27.9			16.3	29.7
			RATIOS						
9.2	5.0	6.8		18.5	29.4			5.0	4.6
1.6	1.7	1.7	Current	1.2	5.3			2.3	1.5
.7	.5	.6		.2	.7			1.3	1.3
7.6	4.3	4.9		18.1	26.3			4.9	4.2
1.0	1.1	1.5	Quick	.7	2.4			1.8	1.3
.4	.4	.4		.0	.5			.5	.7
0 UND	0 UND	0 UND		0 UND	0 UND			17 21.1	0 UND
1 680.0	0 730.3	5 73.3	Sales/Receivables	0 UND	0 UND			39 9.4	8 46.5
54 6.8	47 7.8	44 8.3		4 92.7	12 31.3			50 7.3	42 8.8
			Cost of Sales/Inventory						
			Cost of Sales/Payables						
2.8	3.5	1.7		.3	.7			1.7	2.9
8.7	14.0	8.6	Sales/Working Capital	NM	7.5			7.5	6.7
-19.1	-8.5	-6.1		-2.6	-40.0			29.7	19.2
55.9	176.7	127.3							205.9
(27) 4.6	(35) 5.7	(29) 9.5	EBIT/Interest					(10) 13.6	
2.0	3.0	2.4							6.6
			Net Profit + Depr., Dep., Amort./Cur. Mat. L/T/D						
.0	.0	.0		.0	.0			.0	.1
.1	.1	.1	Fixed/Worth	.4	.0			.2	.2
4.2	8.6	.7		NM	.0			.6	-2.5
.2	.1	.1		.3	.0			.3	.2
1.0	1.4	.6	Debt/Worth	2.6	.1			.8	.7
29.9	-72.4	2.6		-318.1	.4			1.8	-74.3
115.6	66.1	41.5	% Profit Before Taxes/Tangible Net Worth					135.3	123.1
(46) 38.7	(49) 20.2	(49) 13.5						27.0	(11) 27.9
5.8	3.8	1.7						.1	13.9
80.0	54.3	30.2	% Profit Before Taxes/Total Assets	5.6	34.3			93.4	88.8
9.5	5.5	7.4		1.8	4.4			15.2	21.7
2.9	1.4	1.2		-.1	1.2			.1	4.5
222.6	UND	UND		UND	UND			35.1	49.9
32.9	50.7	40.6	Sales/Net Fixed Assets	39.5	UND			12.0	23.4
7.4	10.8	7.4		.2	49.9			6.7	6.9
3.0	2.4	2.1		.2	2.3			3.2	3.4
.9	.8	.4	Sales/Total Assets	.1	.4			.8	1.8
.2	.1	.1		.0	.0			.3	.3
.6	.6	.7						.9	.7
(29) 2.0	(39) 1.2	(33) 1.2	% Depr., Dep., Amort./Sales				(10) 1.4	(12) 1.0	
7.3	7.6	6.6						2.9	7.0
			% Officers', Directors' Owners' Comp/Sales						
1354813M	1586311M	1282887M	Net Sales ($)	3843M	16351M	21119M	36533M	219064M	985977M
1494673M	2028657M	2631580M	Total Assets ($)	66508M	214976M	101078M	297349M	680258M	1271411M

© RMA 2010

M = $ thousand   MM = $ million
See Pages 9 through 22 for Explanation of Ratios and Data

Current Data Sorted by Assets							Comparative Historical Data	
2	1		5	8	7	Type of Statement	16	26
	1	3	1			Unqualified	3	5
1	6	3	3	1		Reviewed	6	9
7	25	16	1			Compiled	15	28
6	12	34	22	6	6	Tax Returns	30	39
	15 (4/1-9/30/09)			162 (10/1/09-3/31/10)		Other	4/1/05-3/31/06 ALL	4/1/06-3/31/07 ALL
0-500M	500M-2MM	2-10MM	10-50MM	50-100MM	100-250MM			
16	45	56	32	15	13	NUMBER OF STATEMENTS	70	107
%	%	%	%	%	%	ASSETS	%	%
26.7	17.3	13.3	17.2	8.7	16.8	Cash & Equivalents	26.7	26.0
6.3	9.7	11.8	21.6	15.9	16.1	Trade Receivables (net)	11.2	16.4
8.3	1.1	.2	.6	.4	5.1	Inventory	3.7	2.8
7.7	4.4	7.4	12.8	3.1	12.3	All Other Current	11.0	9.1
49.0	32.6	32.8	52.1	28.0	50.4	Total Current	52.6	54.4
34.7	51.5	49.7	23.4	24.3	22.9	Fixed Assets (net)	23.7	15.0
1.1	3.2	.8	6.5	9.2	2.7	Intangibles (net)	2.1	5.6
15.3	12.7	16.7	17.9	38.5	24.0	All Other Non-Current	21.7	25.1
100.0	100.0	100.0	100.0	100.0	100.0	Total	100.0	100.0
						LIABILITIES		
18.8	10.8	13.4	12.8	17.6	14.6	Notes Payable-Short Term	19.2	11.3
3.1	2.6	2.9	3.5	7.0	.3	Cur. Mat.-L.T.D.	.8	3.2
7.0	2.8	1.2	2.7	2.6	3.5	Trade Payables	6.2	4.2
.0	.0	.1	.1	1.4	.2	Income Taxes Payable	.5	.3
6.6	6.5	8.4	5.8	9.2	14.5	All Other Current	12.8	17.7
35.5	22.7	26.0	24.9	37.8	33.1	Total Current	39.4	36.6
29.9	44.7	40.8	36.6	28.9	18.8	Long-Term Debt	15.5	15.5
.0	.1	.2	.8	.6	.4	Deferred Taxes	.4	.2
38.9	3.1	5.2	2.6	8.1	6.3	All Other Non-Current	7.2	8.2
-4.3	29.4	27.8	35.1	24.6	41.4	Net Worth	37.6	39.6
100.0	100.0	100.0	100.0	100.0	100.0	Total Liabilities & Net Worth	100.0	100.0
						INCOME DATA		
100.0	100.0	100.0	100.0	100.0	100.0	Net Sales	100.0	100.0
						Gross Profit		
68.7	64.5	63.0	60.1	65.7	76.6	Operating Expenses	61.8	62.2
31.3	35.5	37.0	39.9	34.3	23.4	Operating Profit	38.2	37.8
16.2	18.9	21.3	14.3	20.6	8.9	All Other Expenses (net)	15.2	11.8
15.0	16.6	15.6	25.6	13.7	14.5	Profit Before Taxes	23.0	26.0
						RATIOS		
9.5	3.2	3.7	7.2	1.6	2.7		3.2	5.3
2.0	1.1	1.3	2.4	1.4	1.2	Current	1.2	1.5
.1	.2	.3	1.3	.4	.9		.8	.8
5.2	3.2	3.0	6.0	1.5	1.7		2.1	3.1
1.1	1.1	1.1	1.4	.8	1.1	Quick	1.0	1.1
.0	.1	.1	.4	.4	.3		.2	.3
0 UND	0 UND	0 UND	0 UND	0 UND	0 UND		0 UND	0 UND
0 UND	0 UND	0 UND	30 12.3	33 11.1	51 7.1	Sales/Receivables	0 UND	0 UND
0 UND	4 91.0	26 14.2	92 4.0	87 4.2	373 1.0		45 8.2	87 4.2
						Cost of Sales/Inventory		
						Cost of Sales/Payables		
4.1	5.0	2.4	.4	2.7	.6		2.3	1.3
17.7	187.4	17.2	1.1	12.6	2.8	Sales/Working Capital	6.4	5.1
-2.7	-5.5	-3.6	8.9	-4.2	-101.8		-11.3	-8.4
	24.0	25.4	11.5				19.4	28.4
	(18) 8.1	(28) 5.8	(18) 3.0			EBIT/Interest	(36) 5.4	(61) 7.9
	2.0	.8	1.3				.6	2.5
						Net Profit + Depr., Dep., Amort./Cur. Mat. L/T/D		
.0	.3	.1	.0	.0	.0		.0	.0
1.6	3.0	2.2	.1	.5	.2	Fixed/Worth	.2	.1
NM	22.4	13.0	2.0	3.8	.8		3.8	.9
.2	.7	.8	1.5	1.1	.6		.5	.2
7.0	3.2	3.1	3.3	6.6	1.0	Debt/Worth	1.8	1.8
NM	23.2	61.1	11.5	106.4	7.9		11.5	13.7
85.5	59.6	33.9	22.3	27.0	12.5		93.2	58.9
(12) 48.5	(36) 23.1	(44) 13.4	(27) 13.0	(13) 11.0	(12) 4.2	% Profit Before Taxes/Tangible Net Worth	(60) 23.3	(91) 15.6
17.1	1.0	.0	2.3	-.3	.2		2.0	3.2
36.7	32.9	12.6	5.9	4.0	5.8		19.3	18.8
6.9	3.1	1.5	3.1	.9	2.4	% Profit Before Taxes/Total Assets	4.0	5.6
.0	.1	-.4	1.1	-.4	.1		.7	1.3
UND	23.9	21.3	UND	UND	UND		UND	UND
22.8	1.5	.6	8.0	9.3	7.5	Sales/Net Fixed Assets	34.8	61.5
.5	.1	.2	.3	.4	.4		2.4	7.4
4.6	2.1	.9	.4	.7	.5		1.5	1.5
1.1	.5	.2	.1	.1	.1	Sales/Total Assets	.4	.4
.3	.1	.1	.1	.1	.1		.1	.1
	3.3	2.2	3.5				.9	.6
	(29) 16.6	(36) 9.8	(18) 10.8			% Depr., Dep., Amort./Sales	(39) 2.6	(47) 2.7
	27.5	23.0	22.6				11.7	8.7
								3.2
						% Officers', Directors' Owners' Comp/Sales		(13) 8.5
								19.2
13023M	55814M	167627M	282005M	403311M	640925M	Net Sales ($)	818645M	1576123M
4897M	48522M	265419M	783847M	1136521M	2108029M	Total Assets ($)	2051117M	3171297M

M = $ thousand   MM = $ million
See Pages 9 through 22 for Explanation of Ratios and Data

Comparative Historical Data   Current Data Sorted by Sales

	4/1/07-3/31/08 ALL	4/1/08-3/31/09 ALL	4/1/09-3/31/10 ALL	Type of Statement	0-1MM	1-3MM	3-5MM	5-10MM	10-25MM	25MM & OVER
	36	30	23	Unqualified	1	3	2	7	6	4
	9	10	5	Reviewed	2	1		2		
	13	13	14	Compiled	9	3	1	1	1	
	50	50	49	Tax Returns	33	10	3	2	1	
	60	77	86	Other	28	17	11	13	8	9
					15 (4/1-9/30/09)			162 (10/1/09-3/31/10)		
NUMBER OF STATEMENTS	168	180	177		73	34	16	25	16	13
	%	%	%	ASSETS	%	%	%	%	%	%
Cash & Equivalents	14.3	15.7	16.1		8.1	24.3	17.8	22.4	20.8	19.6
Trade Receivables (net)	10.7	10.2	13.2		4.8	9.6	28.7	28.5	18.1	15.2
Inventory	1.8	1.4	1.6		2.2	.6	.2	.4	4.1	1.9
All Other Current	5.7	5.1	7.6		4.3	8.2	15.6	11.6	7.9	7.1
Total Current	32.4	32.4	38.6		19.5	42.7	62.4	62.8	50.8	43.8
Fixed Assets (net)	44.2	42.8	39.9		59.6	37.7	22.1	18.7	20.2	22.5
Intangibles (net)	4.3	4.8	3.3		1.9	3.3	.2	2.3	6.3	13.8
All Other Non-Current	19.1	20.0	18.2		19.0	16.2	15.4	16.2	22.7	19.9
Total	100.0	100.0	100.0		100.0	100.0	100.0	100.0	100.0	100.0
				LIABILITIES						
Notes Payable-Short Term	11.3	10.9	13.6		14.3	9.5	16.8	23.5	6.4	6.4
Cur. Mat.-L.T.D.	3.1	3.6	3.1		3.2	3.1	1.1	5.5	1.0	2.7
Trade Payables	3.4	2.6	2.7		1.4	2.5	1.2	3.7	4.6	8.5
Income Taxes Payable	.0	.2	.2		.0	.0	.0	.8	.3	.4
All Other Current	9.1	9.1	7.8		4.0	7.8	2.4	10.6	17.9	17.6
Total Current	27.0	26.3	27.4		23.0	22.8	21.5	44.0	30.2	35.6
Long-Term Debt	34.8	36.4	37.4		50.7	35.6	39.1	15.9	37.0	7.2
Deferred Taxes	.3	.2	.3		.1	.9	.0	.0	.0	1.1
All Other Non-Current	7.4	6.6	7.6		12.9	.8	.6	4.1	5.5	13.3
Net Worth	30.5	30.5	27.4		13.3	39.9	38.8	36.1	27.3	42.8
Total Liabilities & Net Worth	100.0	100.0	100.0		100.0	100.0	100.0	100.0	100.0	100.0
				INCOME DATA						
Net Sales	100.0	100.0	100.0		100.0	100.0	100.0	100.0	100.0	100.0
Gross Profit										
Operating Expenses	60.5	59.0	64.6		53.9	60.9	76.6	73.7	75.5	88.9
Operating Profit	39.5	41.0	35.4		46.1	39.1	23.4	26.3	24.5	11.1
All Other Expenses (net)	20.2	19.8	18.0		30.1	14.9	8.2	8.5	7.4	1.4
Profit Before Taxes	19.3	21.2	17.4		15.9	24.2	15.2	17.8	17.1	9.8
				RATIOS						
Current	3.5	4.1	3.5		3.1	7.5	9.6	3.1	4.5	1.8
	1.1	1.2	1.4		1.0	2.5	3.2	1.4	1.4	1.1
	.3	.3	.4		.1	.3	1.5	.9	.8	.7
Quick	2.9	3.0	2.8		2.1	5.3	8.6	2.8	4.4	1.6
	.8	1.0	1.1		.6	1.9	2.5	1.1	1.2	.8
	.1	.2	.2		.0	.2	1.3	.4	.6	.4
Sales/Receivables	0 UND	0 UND	0 UND		0 UND	0 UND	0 UND	0 UND	0 UND	0 UND
	0 UND	0 UND	0 UND		0 UND	0 UND	37 9.9	20 18.2	26 14.0	51 7.2
	35 10.5	35 10.3	41 8.8		0 UND	17 20.9	169 2.2	438 .8	65 5.6	85 4.3
Cost of Sales/Inventory										
Cost of Sales/Payables										
Sales/Working Capital	2.4	1.8	1.9		4.1	2.2	.4	1.0	.8	4.8
	32.3	14.3	9.8		-197.5	7.8	2.1	4.8	9.7	45.7
	-2.3	-3.5	-5.7		-1.8	-6.6	4.4	-55.7	NM	-20.1
EBIT/Interest	12.5	8.7	15.7		7.5	50.5	5.9	16.6	22.7	12.9
	(77) 4.1	(75) 4.0	(88) 5.1		(22) 4.7	(17) 8.8	(10) 1.5	(15) 3.1	(13) 10.3	(11) 4.5
	1.3	1.5	1.3		1.6	3.3	-.1	1.5	1.3	.8
Net Profit + Depr., Dep., Amort./Cur. Mat. L/T/D										
Fixed/Worth	.0	.0	.0		.2	.1	.0	.0	.0	.2
	1.6	1.2	1.0		3.8	.4	.1	.2	.1	.3
	6.3	6.2	8.0		326.6	5.4	1.0	1.6	-6.1	1.2
Debt/Worth	.7	.7	.7		1.5	.5	.3	.6	1.1	.8
	3.1	2.9	3.2		7.0	2.5	2.4	1.9	6.8	1.1
	11.4	13.1	19.4		-305.8	11.1	4.1	9.1	-8.8	6.2
% Profit Before Taxes/Tangible Net Worth	33.0	32.8	35.4		33.8	73.0	20.9	42.1	17.9	28.4
	(135) 10.5	(150) 9.2	(144) 13.4		(54) 7.3	(30) 31.2	(15) 15.2	(22) 15.4	(11) 3.9	(12) 10.3
	1.5	.7	.9		.4	17.1	-1.6	1.9	-.6	.1
% Profit Before Taxes/Total Assets	10.9	8.1	9.0		4.0	45.4	6.4	21.6	17.1	7.7
	4.0	2.9	2.6		.9	8.7	3.5	3.9	1.8	4.0
	.0	.0	.0		-.2	2.4	-1.2	.5	.0	-1.2
Sales/Net Fixed Assets	100.9	173.5	72.4		8.4	74.6	UND	UND	160.7	26.6
	2.6	2.5	4.3		.3	9.3	32.4	26.7	17.1	7.5
	.2	.2	.2		.1	.2	2.7	1.2	4.6	2.6
Sales/Total Assets	.7	.6	.9		.3	2.3	.9	1.8	2.1	1.3
	.2	.1	.2		.1	.5	.2	.2	.6	.7
	.1	.1	.1		.1	.1	.1	.1	.1	.4
% Depr., Dep., Amort./Sales	2.0	2.9	2.7		6.5	1.4		1.1		1.9
	(105) 8.0	(106) 14.1	(105) 9.1		(46) 20.7	(19) 11.4		(13) 3.5		(10) 2.5
	20.0	25.4	22.2		30.1	23.3		11.9		6.9
% Officers', Directors' Owners' Comp/Sales	4.5	4.1	2.1							
	(19) 9.0	(18) 11.6	(23) 10.9							
	16.2	15.4	15.6							
Net Sales ($)	6088659M	2826103M	1562705M		26506M	60560M	57618M	174389M	236243M	1007389M
Total Assets ($)	4535727M	4787222M	4347235M		210251M	310222M	289012M	972662M	932920M	1632168M

© RMA 2010   M = $ thousand   MM = $ million
See Pages 9 through 22 for Explanation of Ratios and Data

REAL ESTATE AND RENTAL AND LEASING

REAL ESTATE—Lessors of Residential Buildings and Dwellings NAICS 531110

Current Data Sorted by Assets							Comparative Historical Data	

						Type of Statement		
8	68	130	68	18	16	Unqualified	204	249
2	10	28	24	1	5	Reviewed	56	45
20	68	102	38	1	1	Compiled	140	172
276	646	519	78	2	6	Tax Returns	686	859
90	226	332	107	19	14	Other	400	441
	176 (4/1-9/30/09)		2,746 (10/1/09-3/31/10)				4/1/05-3/31/06 ALL	4/1/06-3/31/07 ALL
0-500M	500M-2MM	2-10MM	10-50MM	50-100MM	100-250MM	NUMBER OF STATEMENTS		
396	1018	1111	315	41	41		1486	1766
%	%	%	%	%	%	ASSETS	%	%
14.3	5.4	4.7	5.9	10.6	8.2	Cash & Equivalents	7.2	6.9
3.5	1.1	1.7	2.8	8.1	3.4	Trade Receivables (net)	2.1	2.7
1.0	1.2	2.0	2.1	2.9	4.2	Inventory	3.0	3.5
2.0	1.1	1.5	1.8	4.0	1.1	All Other Current	2.7	2.6
20.9	8.8	9.9	12.6	25.6	16.9	Total Current	15.0	15.7
69.7	83.4	80.2	74.5	51.7	61.8	Fixed Assets (net)	75.6	75.2
1.7	1.2	1.7	1.6	4.2	1.8	Intangibles (net)	1.3	1.6
7.6	6.6	8.2	11.3	18.5	19.4	All Other Non-Current	8.1	7.6
100.0	100.0	100.0	100.0	100.0	100.0	Total	100.0	100.0
						LIABILITIES		
4.4	3.3	3.5	3.3	5.1	6.3	Notes Payable-Short Term	5.6	6.2
5.4	4.9	3.4	3.1	1.3	4.1	Cur. Mat.-L.T.D.	3.3	3.9
3.2	.8	.9	1.3	3.7	1.4	Trade Payables	1.9	1.9
.1	.0	.0	.0	.0	.0	Income Taxes Payable	.1	.0
15.0	7.5	5.5	5.0	6.6	6.6	All Other Current	5.4	6.4
28.1	16.5	13.3	12.6	16.8	18.5	Total Current	16.3	18.4
69.7	75.0	75.8	67.0	41.0	65.1	Long-Term Debt	71.0	66.7
.0	.1	.0	.2	.2	.1	Deferred Taxes	.0	.0
4.3	2.8	2.8	3.3	3.7	3.4	All Other Non-Current	3.8	3.5
-2.2	5.6	8.2	16.9	38.2	12.9	Net Worth	9.0	11.3
100.0	100.0	100.0	100.0	100.0	100.0	Total Liabilities & Net Worth	100.0	100.0
						INCOME DATA		
100.0	100.0	100.0	100.0	100.0	100.0	Net Sales	100.0	100.0
						Gross Profit		
67.5	65.6	66.7	73.1	83.3	75.7	Operating Expenses	71.5	70.4
32.5	34.4	33.3	26.9	16.7	24.3	Operating Profit	28.5	29.6
19.5	25.0	26.0	23.3	16.5	18.9	All Other Expenses (net)	21.8	21.5
13.0	9.4	7.3	3.6	.2	5.4	Profit Before Taxes	6.6	8.1
						RATIOS		
2.2	1.4	1.8	2.5	5.4	3.9		2.2	2.0
.8	.4	.6	.7	1.5	1.3	Current	.8	.7
.2	.1	.1	.2	.5	.3		.2	.2
1.9	1.2	1.4	1.7	3.4	2.9		(1483) 1.5	(1763) 1.4
.6	.3 (1110)	.4	.5	.8	.9	Quick	.5	.4
.1	.1	.1	.1	.3	.1		.1	.1
0 UND	0 UND	0 UND	0 UND	0 UND	0 UND		0 UND	0 UND
0 UND	0 UND	0 UND	1 281.6	5 75.4	3 142.6	Sales/Receivables	0 UND	0 UND
0 UND	0 UND	2 148.5	9 39.3	39 9.4	36 10.2		3 106.0	4 102.0
						Cost of Sales/Inventory		
						Cost of Sales/Payables		
9.1	24.5	9.0	4.7	.9	1.5		7.3	7.6
-34.0	-8.2	-10.0	-22.5	10.9	24.6	Sales/Working Capital	-36.1	-19.7
-3.6	-2.6	-2.3	-2.4	-5.0	-2.2		-3.4	-3.1
8.4	5.2	5.1	4.6	10.7	3.3		6.7	5.4
(156) 3.6	(372) 2.8	(377) 2.5	(113) 1.7	(17) 2.2	(19) 2.1	EBIT/Interest	(584) 2.8	(681) 2.5
1.3	1.3	1.1	.6	.2	.0		1.2	1.3
		4.6	3.4				3.4	3.2
	(18) 2.0	(14) .5				Net Profit + Depr., Dep., Amort./Cur. Mat. L/T/D	(32) 1.4	(41) 1.7
	.7	.1					.5	.8
1.3	2.5	2.3	1.7	.3	.8		1.8	1.7
5.9	8.0	7.6	4.8	1.6	3.2	Fixed/Worth	6.0	5.4
-5.7	-9.4	-10.7	-29.6	4.0	NM		-19.0	-26.7
1.1	2.1	2.0	1.5	.7	1.8		1.8	1.6
6.4	8.4	8.3	5.7	2.5	4.2	Debt/Worth	6.7	6.1
-7.6	-11.4	-13.3	-33.5	6.1	NM		-21.5	-27.5
81.9	30.2	25.5	14.4	9.7	15.2		31.6	28.8
(254) 18.1	(672) 8.8	(722) 6.3	(223) 2.2	(37) -.8	(31) 5.6	% Profit Before Taxes/Tangible Net Worth	(1035) 8.7	(1250) 8.8
.0	-1.5	-3.9	-5.7	-3.5	-7.5		-4.7	-2.8
17.5	6.2	5.1	3.1	3.4	3.0		6.7	6.6
4.4	1.7	1.1	.3	-.3	.3	% Profit Before Taxes/Total Assets	1.4	1.8
-1.9	-1.4	-1.5	-1.8	-1.7	-1.6		-1.4	-1.0
2.9	.4	.3	.4	13.3	1.8		.7	.7
.4	.2	.2	.2	.3	.2	Sales/Net Fixed Assets	.2	.2
.2	.1	.1	.1	.1	.2		.1	.1
1.2	.3	.3	.3	.5	.3		.4	.5
.3	.2	.2	.2	.1	.2	Sales/Total Assets	.2	.2
.2	.1	.1	.1	.1	.1		.1	.1
7.5	12.1	12.1	9.9	3.4	6.9		9.6	8.7
(316) 15.2	(917) 18.8	(949) 20.1	(268) 18.6	(32) 14.2	(30) 14.6	% Depr., Dep., Amort./Sales	(1288) 16.9	(1510) 16.7
23.9	26.2	29.1	29.0	31.3	20.7		26.4	25.2
4.9	2.2	2.7	2.0				2.9	2.8
(26) 7.4	(103) 5.8	(89) 4.8	(41) 4.5			% Officers', Directors' Owners' Comp/Sales	(174) 6.1	(203) 6.7
15.1	11.1	10.1	9.3				13.1	13.2
97263M	459612M	1500279M	2051544M	1766531M	3364991M	Net Sales ($)	4538349M	5622159M
103519M	1199618M	4929989M	6474811M	2647011M	6828207M	Total Assets ($)	10807055M	12357034M

M = $ thousand   MM = $ million
See Pages 9 through 22 for Explanation of Ratios and Data

Comparative Historical Data / Current Data Sorted by Sales

4/1/07-3/31/08 ALL	4/1/08-3/31/09 ALL	4/1/09-3/31/10 ALL	Type of Statement	0-1MM	1-3MM	3-5MM	5-10MM	10-25MM	25MM & OVER
251	264	308	Unqualified	154	69	19	25	20	21
57	68	70	Reviewed	23	14	8	12	9	4
199	182	229	Compiled	143	57	19	8	2	
961	1219	1527	Tax Returns	1244	207	33	30	4	9
467	690	788	Other	516	153	33	42	28	16
				176 (4/1-9/30/09)			2,746 (10/1/09-3/31/10)		
NUMBER OF STATEMENTS									
1935	2423	2922		2080	500	112	117	63	50
%	%	%	**ASSETS**	%	%	%	%	%	%
6.8	6.8	6.5	Cash & Equivalents	5.4	7.1	10.8	12.5	11.1	16.7
2.3	2.4	2.0	Trade Receivables (net)	1.2	1.8	3.6	6.7	9.9	10.9
3.2	2.1	1.6	Inventory	.9	2.4	4.7	4.1	6.8	5.6
2.4	2.1	1.5	All Other Current	1.1	2.0	2.3	3.0	5.0	3.2
14.7	13.3	11.6	Total Current	8.6	13.4	21.4	26.3	32.9	36.4
76.2	76.3	78.6	Fixed Assets (net)	83.7	74.4	62.0	53.1	49.2	43.6
1.7	1.6	1.6	Intangibles (net)	1.3	1.8	2.6	2.0	2.7	4.6
7.4	8.8	8.2	All Other Non-Current	6.4	10.5	14.1	18.6	15.2	15.4
100.0	100.0	100.0	Total	100.0	100.0	100.0	100.0	100.0	100.0
			LIABILITIES						
6.1	5.1	3.6	Notes Payable-Short Term	3.0	4.2	4.7	7.6	4.7	6.5
4.0	4.7	4.2	Cur. Mat.-L.T.D.	4.5	3.7	3.1	2.6	3.5	2.9
2.1	1.6	1.3	Trade Payables	.9	.9	1.6	3.8	4.7	7.9
.0	.1	.0	Income Taxes Payable	.0	.0	.0	.1	.0	.0
6.9	7.8	7.5	All Other Current	7.3	6.4	7.8	14.2	8.8	8.7
19.2	19.2	16.5	Total Current	15.7	15.2	17.3	28.2	21.7	26.0
68.9	69.8	73.1	Long-Term Debt	73.5	82.0	78.0	51.3	48.6	35.5
.0	.0	.1	Deferred Taxes	.0	.0	.5	.2	.0	.1
3.1	3.4	3.1	All Other Non-Current	3.0	3.0	3.2	1.9	5.8	6.5
8.9	7.5	7.3	Net Worth	7.7	-.2	1.0	18.4	23.9	31.9
100.0	100.0	100.0	Total Liabilties & Net Worth	100.0	100.0	100.0	100.0	100.0	100.0
			INCOME DATA						
100.0	100.0	100.0	Net Sales	100.0	100.0	100.0	100.0	100.0	100.0
			Gross Profit						
70.2	69.0	67.5	Operating Expenses	64.4	71.1	76.2	81.7	83.4	88.5
29.8	31.0	32.5	Operating Profit	35.6	28.9	23.8	18.3	16.6	11.5
23.0	23.9	24.2	All Other Expenses (net)	27.2	19.9	19.7	10.0	10.1	7.8
6.7	7.1	8.3	Profit Before Taxes	8.5	9.0	4.1	8.3	6.5	3.7
			RATIOS						
1.9	1.8	1.8	Current	1.5	2.0	3.8	2.5	3.5	3.9
.7	.6	.6		.4	.7	1.0	1.0	1.6	1.4
.2	.2	.1		.1	.2	.2	.5	.6	.8
1.3	1.3	1.4	Quick	1.2	1.7	2.7	1.5	2.3	2.6
.4 (2421)	.4 (2921)	.4		.3 (499)	.5	.7	.7	.9	1.1
.1	.1	.1		.1	.1	.1	.2	.4	.3
0 UND	0 UND	0 UND	Sales/Receivables	0 UND	0 UND	0 UND	0 UND	1 471.4	0 UND
0 UND	0 UND	0 UND		0 UND	0 UND	3 138.6	3 118.0	12 30.3	7 53.6
3 133.4	2 147.0	2 171.4		0 UND	3 129.9	11 31.9	27 13.4	43 8.4	34 10.6
			Cost of Sales/Inventory						
			Cost of Sales/Payables						
9.1	9.3	10.5	Sales/Working Capital	16.1	7.7	3.1	3.9	3.3	4.9
-15.8	-11.9	-11.1		-7.7	-24.1	374.4	280.8	9.8	12.1
-3.0	-2.6	-2.6		-2.2	-3.7	-3.3	-6.6	-14.4	-20.7
4.9	4.6	5.5	EBIT/Interest	5.1	5.5	10.4	8.9	8.5	12.5
(712) 2.4	(899) 2.2	(1054) 2.6		(623) 2.7	(231) 2.6	(47) 2.5	(72) 2.1	(45) 2.5	(36) 2.4
1.1	.9	1.1		1.1	1.3	.9	1.1	.4	.1
2.3	3.0	4.4	Net Profit + Depr., Dep., Amort./Cur. Mat. L/T/D	6.5	5.7				
(41) 1.1	(52) 1.2	(41) 2.1		(15) 2.1	(11) 2.8				
.7	.4	.5		.7	.6				
1.9	2.0	2.1	Fixed/Worth	2.5	2.3	1.0	.6	.5	.3
5.7	7.2	6.8		7.3	10.6	4.3	2.7	1.4	1.0
-19.7	-13.1	-11.2		-12.9	-4.6	-11.3	63.6	5.7	7.5
1.8	1.8	1.9	Debt/Worth	2.0	2.4	1.4	1.0	.7	.6
6.4	8.4	7.3		7.7	12.6	6.6	4.3	2.5	1.6
-21.4	-15.2	-13.4		-14.4	-6.7	-12.6	269.1	10.0	16.3
29.8	28.0	27.8	% Profit Before Taxes/Tangible Net Worth	26.9	30.4	20.5	67.0	24.2	33.5
(1329) 7.6	(1606) 7.4	(1939) 7.0		(1392) 6.9	(285) 7.1	(79) 4.5	(90) 11.1	(54) 6.9	(39) 13.3
-4.2	-4.2	-3.2		-3.5	-2.3	-6.6	-.6	-2.9	-10.1
6.4	6.1	6.0	% Profit Before Taxes/Total Assets	5.6	7.0	5.9	9.3	7.0	10.1
1.4	1.3	1.3		1.1	2.0	.8	2.9	2.0	1.8
-1.5	-1.6	-1.5		-1.7	-1.0	-1.8	-.3	-1.3	-2.7
.6	.6	.5	Sales/Net Fixed Assets	.3	.8	1.4	13.6	6.6	18.3
.3	.2	.2		.2	.3	.4	.7	1.3	3.9
.2	.1	.1		.1	.2	.2	.3	.4	.3
.4	.4	.3	Sales/Total Assets	.3	.5	.6	1.3	1.4	2.7
.2	.2	.2		.2	.3	.2	.3	.5	.9
.1	.1	.1		.1	.1	.1	.2	.2	.3
9.1	9.8	11.0	% Depr., Dep., Amort./Sales	13.4	8.3	5.0	3.1	1.6	1.2
(1696) 16.6	(2049) 17.7	(2512) 18.8		(1810) 20.4	(426) 16.8	(92) 12.0	(93) 8.3	(51) 5.0	(40) 2.5
25.0	26.7	27.1		29.1	23.9	24.0	17.2	13.2	13.7
3.3	3.5	2.7	% Officers', Directors' Owners' Comp/Sales	3.6	2.9	3.8	1.1		
(220) 6.0	(236) 6.0	(270) 5.3		(136) 5.9	(63) 5.5	(23) 6.3	(33) 2.5		
13.2	11.3	11.0		11.8	11.0	13.0	6.7		
8004279M	8263148M	9240220M	Net Sales ($)	693509M	829195M	431254M	797260M	964748M	5524254M
13712681M	18088802M	22183155M	Total Assets ($)	4313713M	3939410M	2209500M	2978325M	3377899M	5364308M

M = $ thousand   MM = $ million
See Pages 9 through 22 for Explanation of Ratios and Data

REAL ESTATE—Lessors of Nonresidential Buildings (except Miniwarehouses) NAICS 531120

Current Data Sorted by Assets | Comparative Historical Data

Type of Statement	0-500M	500M-2MM	2-10MM	10-50MM	50-100MM	100-250MM		4/1/05-3/31/06 ALL	4/1/06-3/31/07 ALL
Unqualified	3	26	64	84	22	23		198	241
Reviewed	11	46	131	55	12	8		232	282
Compiled	70	308	425	107	7	1		665	790
Tax Returns	671	2742	2095	267	8	6		2476	3479
Other	169	763	1157	319	59	31		1330	1494
	269 (4/1-9/30/09)			9,421 (10/1/09-3/31/10)					
NUMBER OF STATEMENTS	924	3885	3872	832	108	69		4901	6286
ASSETS	%	%	%	%	%	%		%	%
Cash & Equivalents	8.9	4.3	4.1	4.8	5.3	5.3		5.4	5.1
Trade Receivables (net)	2.1	1.0	1.1	2.2	3.9	2.1		2.0	1.9
Inventory	1.0	.6	.8	2.2	3.1	1.8		1.4	1.4
All Other Current	1.4	.9	1.4	2.1	1.9	4.0		1.7	1.7
Total Current	13.5	6.8	7.4	11.2	14.2	13.2		10.5	10.1
Fixed Assets (net)	79.2	87.4	84.9	78.1	69.2	69.3		81.3	82.3
Intangibles (net)	2.1	1.4	1.9	1.6	1.2	4.1		1.7	1.6
All Other Non-Current	5.2	4.5	5.8	9.0	15.4	13.4		6.4	5.9
Total	100.0	100.0	100.0	100.0	100.0	100.0		100.0	100.0
LIABILITIES									
Notes Payable-Short Term	6.1	2.9	2.9	3.9	5.3	3.4		4.8	4.5
Cur. Mat.-L.T.D.	6.7	4.6	4.0	4.3	3.5	4.1		3.9	4.4
Trade Payables	2.6	.7	.7	1.2	2.7	1.7		1.3	1.4
Income Taxes Payable	.0	.0	.0	.1	.1	.3		.0	.1
All Other Current	11.7	3.3	3.2	3.9	5.0	3.4		4.9	4.6
Total Current	27.1	11.5	10.8	13.4	16.6	12.8		15.0	15.0
Long-Term Debt	64.9	70.2	69.3	59.7	53.9	56.0		64.8	65.8
Deferred Taxes	.0	.0	.0	.2	.3	.2		.1	.1
All Other Non-Current	4.1	2.0	2.7	3.4	2.5	4.2		3.2	2.6
Net Worth	3.9	16.3	17.2	23.3	26.7	26.8		16.9	16.5
Total Liabilities & Net Worth	100.0	100.0	100.0	100.0	100.0	100.0		100.0	100.0
INCOME DATA									
Net Sales	100.0	100.0	100.0	100.0	100.0	100.0		100.0	100.0
Gross Profit									
Operating Expenses	50.5	46.0	49.7	57.2	65.4	66.9		51.1	49.5
Operating Profit	49.5	54.0	50.3	42.8	34.6	33.1		48.9	50.5
All Other Expenses (net)	23.4	30.8	31.2	26.5	21.2	20.7		25.3	28.7
Profit Before Taxes	26.1	23.2	19.1	16.4	13.3	12.4		23.6	21.7
RATIOS									
Current	1.6	1.6	1.8	2.4	2.0	2.1		1.9	1.8
	.5	.5	.6	.8	.8	1.0		.6	.6
	.1	.1	.1	.2	.3	.3		.2	.1
Quick	1.3	1.3	1.4	1.7	1.2	1.9		1.5	1.4
	(923) .4	(3883) .4	(3869) .4	.4	.5	.5	.7	(4897) .4	(6282) .4
	.1	.1	.1	.1	.2	.1		.1	.1
Sales/Receivables	0 UND	0 UND	0 UND	0 UND	0 UND	0 UND		0 UND	0 UND
	0 UND	0 UND	0 UND	0 UND	8 47.1	6 57.2		0 UND	0 UND
	0 UND	0 UND	0 UND	13 27.7	27 13.6	28 13.0		0 999.8	0 UND
Cost of Sales/Inventory									
Cost of Sales/Payables									
Sales/Working Capital	17.4	11.6	7.8	4.3	6.4	3.5		8.3	9.3
	-10.0	-8.3	-9.9	-19.9	-16.6	-203.9		-13.1	-10.7
	-3.0	-2.5	-2.5	-2.5	-2.7	-3.0		-2.6	-2.3
EBIT/Interest	8.9	7.4	6.5	6.1	4.5	6.1		7.7	7.5
	(347) 4.8	(1039) 4.3	(1025) 3.7	(296) 3.2	(45) 2.5	(27) 2.1		(1591) 4.0	(1763) 4.1
	3.0	2.5	2.1	1.7	1.4	.5		2.3	2.2
Net Profit + Depr., Dep., Amort./Cur. Mat. L/T/D		2.6	3.4	3.9	6.6	2.5		3.2	3.5
		(46) 1.6	(108) 1.6	(81) 1.7	(16) 1.3	(12) 1.5		(214) 1.6	(265) 1.7
		.9	.8	.7	.5	.4		1.0	1.0
Fixed/Worth	1.7	2.5	2.5	1.8	1.1	1.4		2.2	2.3
	4.8	5.7	6.1	4.1	3.0	3.1		5.1	5.2
	-14.2	120.7	122.9	23.5	9.8	16.4		57.1	53.4
Debt/Worth	1.2	1.9	2.0	1.6	1.1	1.1		1.8	1.8
	4.8	5.3	5.9	4.0	3.0	4.4		5.1	5.2
	-13.8	148.6	142.0	27.8	13.0	25.5		67.3	67.3
% Profit Before Taxes/Tangible Net Worth	49.9	35.5	31.8	21.2	14.0	25.4		43.8	37.9
	(648) 20.9	(2958) 16.0	(2952) 13.1	(671) 8.6	(92) 5.8	(57) 9.0		(3815) 19.0	(4873) 16.7
	6.3	4.6	2.4	1.8	1.2	-.8		6.6	5.2
% Profit Before Taxes/Total Assets	15.3	7.6	5.8	4.8	4.1	5.5		8.7	8.1
	6.1	3.4	2.5	2.1	1.8	1.7		3.9	3.5
	1.1	.6	.2	.0	.2	-1.0		.9	.7
Sales/Net Fixed Assets	.7	.3	.2	.3	.9	.5		.4	.3
	.3	.2	.2	.2	.2	.2		.2	.2
	.2	.1	.1	.1	.1	.1		.1	.1
Sales/Total Assets	.5	.2	.2	.2	.3	.3		.3	.3
	.2	.1	.1	.1	.1	.1		.2	.2
	.1	.1	.1	.1	.1	.1		.1	.1
% Depr., Dep., Amort./Sales	8.2	12.7	13.7	13.3	6.2	15.2		10.7	10.8
	(787) 13.8	(3606) 18.2	(3504) 19.4	(749) 20.2	(92) 15.3	(46) 18.5		(4465) 16.3	(5772) 16.5
	21.4	24.4	26.5	28.2	24.9	24.0		23.1	23.0
% Officers', Directors' Owners' Comp/Sales	4.7	2.5	2.0	2.4	.9			3.1	2.8
	(76) 9.6	(167) 4.9	(249) 5.2	(74) 4.1	(14) 5.2			(378) 6.5	(458) 6.4
	18.1	11.8	10.9	10.0	10.6			15.3	14.9
Net Sales ($)	221493M	1218399M	3835187M	5081624M	4834278M	4680422M		18004325M	16165689M
Total Assets ($)	292074M	4561945M	16582818M	16157631M	7460573M	11260083M		32625013M	38104097M

M = $ thousand   MM = $ million

See Pages 9 through 22 for Explanation of Ratios and Data

Comparative Historical Data | Current Data Sorted by Sales

	4/1/07-3/31/08 ALL	4/1/08-3/31/09 ALL	4/1/09-3/31/10 ALL	Type of Statement	0-1MM	1-3MM	3-5MM	5-10MM	10-25MM	25MM & OVER
	206	238	222	Unqualified	72	34	17	26	32	41
	248	291	263	Reviewed	124	64	17	26	23	9
	720	851	918	Compiled	672	175	36	22	9	4
	3887	5067	5789	Tax Returns	5098	549	71	40	18	13
	1668	2144	2498	Other	1819	407	97	81	60	34
					269 (4/1-9/30/09)			9,421 (10/1/09-3/31/10)		
NUMBER OF STATEMENTS	6729	8591	9690		7785	1229	238	195	142	101
	%	%	%	ASSETS	%	%	%	%	%	%
Cash & Equivalents	5.0	5.0	4.7		4.1	5.8	9.7	7.2	9.8	10.7
Trade Receivables (net)	1.6	1.5	1.3		.7	2.0	2.4	7.3	11.5	13.3
Inventory	1.1	1.0	.9		.3	1.5	3.4	4.0	9.4	15.8
All Other Current	1.8	1.5	1.3		1.1	1.7	2.9	3.0	3.3	3.6
Total Current	9.5	9.0	8.2		6.2	11.0	18.4	21.5	34.0	43.5
Fixed Assets (net)	83.2	83.2	84.5		87.5	78.8	70.0	63.2	52.3	43.0
Intangibles (net)	1.4	1.5	1.7		1.5	2.2	2.9	2.7	3.4	3.5
All Other Non-Current	5.9	6.3	5.7		4.9	8.1	8.6	12.5	10.3	10.1
Total	100.0	100.0	100.0		100.0	100.0	100.0	100.0	100.0	100.0
				LIABILITIES						
Notes Payable-Short Term	3.4	3.6	3.3		2.9	4.5	4.4	5.3	6.2	8.5
Cur. Mat.-L.T.D.	4.5	4.3	4.5		4.6	4.0	4.9	3.7	3.7	4.7
Trade Payables	1.2	1.1	1.0		.4	1.8	3.0	4.3	6.8	9.7
Income Taxes Payable	.0	.0	.0		.0	.0	.1	.0	.2	.2
All Other Current	4.3	4.1	4.1		3.6	4.7	11.2	6.4	7.0	9.3
Total Current	13.4	13.2	12.9		11.6	15.1	23.5	19.7	24.0	32.4
Long-Term Debt	67.3	68.1	68.1		69.5	69.6	58.3	52.1	43.4	31.3
Deferred Taxes	.1	.0	.0		.0	.1	.1	.2	.2	.6
All Other Non-Current	3.1	2.9	2.6		2.4	3.1	3.5	4.8	4.4	7.7
Net Worth	16.2	15.7	16.3		16.5	12.1	14.6	23.1	28.1	28.0
Total Liabilities & Net Worth	100.0	100.0	100.0		100.0	100.0	100.0	100.0	100.0	100.0
				INCOME DATA						
Net Sales	100.0	100.0	100.0		100.0	100.0	100.0	100.0	100.0	100.0
Gross Profit										
Operating Expenses	48.8	49.2	49.2		45.6	57.4	67.2	74.4	80.7	88.7
Operating Profit	51.2	50.8	50.8		54.4	42.6	32.8	25.6	19.3	11.3
All Other Expenses (net)	30.2	30.3	29.7		32.3	22.4	17.1	14.8	12.2	4.8
Profit Before Taxes	21.1	20.5	21.1		22.1	20.3	15.6	10.8	7.1	6.5
				RATIOS						
Current	1.8	1.8	1.7		1.6	2.2	2.5	2.0	2.9	2.0
	.5	.6	.5		.5	.7	.9	.9	1.4	1.2
	.2	.2	.1		.1	.2	.3	.3	.6	.8
Quick	1.3	1.3	1.4		1.3	1.7	1.7	1.3	2.1	1.3
	(6723) .4	(8587) .4	(9684) .4		(7781) .4	(1227) .5	.5	.6	.9	.7
	.1	.1	.1		.1	.1	.1	.2	.3	.3
Sales/Receivables	0 UND	0 UND	0 UND		0 UND	0 UND	0 UND	0 UND	2 220.2	5 67.5
	0 UND	0 UND	0 UND		0 UND	0 UND	1 475.9	7 51.6	11 31.9	22 16.7
	0 UND	0 UND	0 UND		0 UND	5 72.1	13 27.5	26 13.8	49 7.4	35 10.5
Cost of Sales/Inventory										
Cost of Sales/Payables										
Sales/Working Capital	9.7	9.6	9.1		10.7	6.1	7.2	6.7	3.7	6.6
	-10.0	-9.9	-9.5		-7.7	-20.7	-132.0	-77.9	13.4	24.4
	-2.6	-2.7	-2.6		-2.4	-3.2	-4.1	-4.0	-11.2	-28.5
EBIT/Interest	6.8	6.7	7.0		7.1	6.6	9.5	6.0	9.8	7.5
	(1764) 4.0	(2320) 3.9	(2779) 4.0		(1843) 4.3	(524) 3.5	(127) 3.2	(118) 2.6	(84) 2.5	(83) 2.3
	2.2	2.1	2.2		2.7	1.9	1.3	1.1	.7	1.1
Net Profit + Depr., Dep., Amort./Cur. Mat. L/T/D	4.3	3.7	3.3		2.4	3.9	5.2	4.2	2.2	7.7
	(257) 1.9	(278) 1.9	(267) 1.6		(112) 1.5	(54) 1.9	(33) 1.8	(18) 1.8	(23) 1.1	(27) 2.3
	.9	.8	.8		.8	1.0	.6	.5	.2	1.3
Fixed/Worth	2.3	2.3	2.3		2.5	2.2	1.8	1.3	.5	.4
	5.2	5.3	5.6		5.8	5.5	4.0	3.1	1.8	1.4
	66.5	128.5	118.2		105.0	-34.0	999.8	16.6	12.8	5.4
Debt/Worth	1.8	1.8	1.8		1.9	1.8	1.5	1.4	1.0	1.0
	5.0	5.2	5.3		5.5	5.5	4.5	4.0	3.0	2.1
	81.4	180.5	164.1		126.8	-34.3	-259.7	27.4	18.0	11.8
% Profit Before Taxes/Tangible Net Worth	35.2	33.9	33.3		32.7	38.2	48.8	31.0	22.0	43.0
	(5208) 15.9	(6552) 14.9	(7378) 14.2		(5959) 14.2	(881) 16.1	(178) 13.0	(153) 11.5	(117) 11.6	(90) 13.7
	4.5	3.5	3.1		3.1	4.1	3.2	1.3	.0	.7
% Profit Before Taxes/Total Assets	7.8	7.3	7.0		6.7	8.1	7.7	7.3	8.2	10.9
	3.4	3.1	3.0		2.9	3.6	3.3	2.1	2.1	2.8
	.6	.4	.3		.3	.7	.2	-.2	-.7	.1
Sales/Net Fixed Assets	.3	.3	.3		.2	.5	1.5	7.5	11.3	25.9
	.2	.2	.2		.2	.2	.3	.4	1.1	6.7
	.1	.1	.1		.1	.1	.2	.2	.2	1.0
Sales/Total Assets	.3	.2	.2		.2	.3	.8	1.6	2.0	3.1
	.2	.2	.1		.1	.2	.2	.3	.4	1.9
	.1	.1	.1		.1	.1	.1	.1	.2	.6
% Depr., Dep., Amort./Sales	11.1	11.7	12.6		13.5	10.4	7.2	2.3	1.5	1.1
	(6113) 16.6	(7807) 17.4	(8784) 18.5		(7086) 19.0	(1117) 17.0	(210) 14.6	(172) 11.6	(123) 8.9	(76) 2.9
	23.3	24.3	25.4		25.9	24.5	24.2	19.9	17.7	6.6
% Officers', Directors' Owners' Comp/Sales	2.7	2.1	2.4		3.1	2.6	2.0	1.8	.8	.5
	(429) 5.9	(540) 5.2	(584) 5.3		(265) 6.4	(173) 6.1	(47) 2.9	(53) 4.1	(31) 2.4	(15) 1.5
	13.0	11.6	11.8		13.5	11.5	9.2	9.7	4.8	5.1
Net Sales ($)	20406044M	20685589M	19871403M		2437806M	2003716M	909258M	1377168M	2216878M	10926577M
Total Assets ($)	39567965M	52875159M	56315124M		17618300M	11788461M	4366048M	6179240M	8441397M	7921678M

M = $ thousand   MM = $ million
See Pages 9 through 22 for Explanation of Ratios and Data

Current Data Sorted by Assets   Comparative Historical Data

						Type of Statement		
1	5	7	2	1	3	Unqualified	4	4
4	14	17	5	1		Reviewed	5	8
34	107	70	1	1		Compiled	17	26
22	49	66	4		1	Tax Returns	68	103
			21	1		Other	39	62
	11 (4/1-9/30/09)		426 (10/1/09-3/31/10)				4/1/05-3/31/06	4/1/06-3/31/07
0-500M	500M-2MM	2-10MM	10-50MM	50-100MM	100-250MM		ALL	ALL
61	175	160	33	4	4	NUMBER OF STATEMENTS	133	203
%	%	%	%	%	%	ASSETS	%	%
24.4	4.2	3.6	5.2			Cash & Equivalents	7.2	6.9
3.9	1.6	1.2	2.1			Trade Receivables (net)	3.2	1.6
3.2	.8	1.4	2.3			Inventory	.6	1.3
2.1	1.3	.9	2.1			All Other Current	1.0	2.3
33.6	7.9	7.0	11.7			Total Current	12.0	12.1
53.9	85.5	88.1	81.7			Fixed Assets (net)	78.3	80.4
1.6	2.1	1.6	1.5			Intangibles (net)	2.1	1.2
10.9	4.5	3.3	5.0			All Other Non-Current	7.5	6.2
100.0	100.0	100.0	100.0			Total	100.0	100.0
						LIABILITIES		
5.5	2.0	4.7	2.2			Notes Payable-Short Term	7.7	7.8
5.5	3.6	2.6	3.1			Cur. Mat.-L.T.D.	3.4	4.5
5.5	.3	.7	1.0			Trade Payables	1.9	1.1
.0	.0	.0	.1			Income Taxes Payable	.0	.0
16.8	5.2	3.7	5.9			All Other Current	4.7	8.4
33.3	11.2	11.6	12.4			Total Current	17.7	21.8
36.5	76.6	74.3	62.2			Long-Term Debt	66.0	67.2
.0	.0	.0	.3			Deferred Taxes	.0	.0
6.7	2.1	1.6	2.1			All Other Non-Current	5.2	3.9
23.6	10.1	12.4	23.1			Net Worth	11.1	7.0
100.0	100.0	100.0	100.0			Total Liabilties & Net Worth	100.0	100.0
						INCOME DATA		
100.0	100.0	100.0	100.0			Net Sales	100.0	100.0
						Gross Profit		
75.0	62.2	60.1	67.6			Operating Expenses	65.4	63.7
25.0	37.8	39.9	32.4			Operating Profit	34.6	36.3
7.8	23.7	28.7	28.1			All Other Expenses (net)	20.3	20.6
17.1	14.1	11.1	4.3			Profit Before Taxes	14.3	15.7
						RATIOS		
5.2	2.2	1.7	2.6				2.5	3.0
1.5	.6	.5	.9			Current	.8	.7
.4	.2	.2	.3				.2	.2
4.3	1.5	1.4	2.0				2.0	1.9
1.1	.4	.5	.6			Quick	.6	.5
.3	.1	.1	.2				.2	.1
0 UND	0 UND	0 UND	0 UND				0 UND	0 UND
0 UND	0 UND	0 UND	5 76.2			Sales/Receivables	0 UND	0 UND
2 223.1	0 UND	5 78.1	25 14.6				5 69.3	1 373.0
						Cost of Sales/Inventory		
						Cost of Sales/Payables		
9.6	17.2	11.1	2.8				10.6	12.2
65.8	-16.0	-11.5	-10.0			Sales/Working Capital	-40.0	-24.2
-6.9	-2.7	-2.5	-1.8				-4.1	-3.7
9.7	5.0	4.4	3.7				5.9	4.8
(27) 2.6	(77) 3.0	(45) 2.5	(12) 2.3			EBIT/Interest	(56) 3.0	(71) 3.1
.4	1.9	1.5	.4				1.6	1.7
						Net Profit + Depr., Dep., Amort./Cur. Mat. L/T/D		
.2	2.9	3.2	2.3				2.3	2.2
1.4	11.3	8.7	4.0			Fixed/Worth	8.6	6.7
UND	-14.2	-29.4	11.9				-9.7	-10.0
.2	2.3	2.7	1.7				2.1	1.8
2.1	11.1	9.8	4.7			Debt/Worth	8.3	6.9
-23.8	-15.5	-31.2	11.9				-11.3	-11.8
110.1	49.3	30.9	25.3				57.2	47.3
(45) 32.8	(109) 19.9	(106) 10.6	(28) 9.1			% Profit Before Taxes/Tangible Net Worth	(81) 20.8	(137) 16.1
9.0	3.0	-.9	-5.2				7.6	4.8
39.0	9.3	4.7	3.9				8.0	9.0
9.2	3.1	1.5	1.9			% Profit Before Taxes/Total Assets	3.8	3.9
-1.0	-.1	-.2	-1.9				.3	.9
56.8	.4	.3	.3				.6	.6
2.4	.3	.2	.2			Sales/Net Fixed Assets	.3	.3
.4	.2	.1	.1				.2	.2
5.8	.4	.2	.2				.4	.5
1.3	.2	.2	.2			Sales/Total Assets	.2	.2
.3	.2	.1	.1				.2	.2
2.8	10.2	12.8	7.9				9.0	7.8
(37) 8.9	(151) 13.8	(121) 17.4	(31) 17.1			% Depr., Dep., Amort./Sales	(116) 13.5	(180) 13.2
20.0	22.1	24.1	27.4				18.4	19.2
	4.8	3.8					3.4	2.9
	(22) 8.7	(24) 6.6				% Officers', Directors' Owners' Comp/Sales	(30) 9.1	(26) 7.9
	14.2	15.7					14.7	13.0
29768M	71425M	133852M	219035M	226587M	440867M	Net Sales ($)	263992M	344087M
13287M	217877M	675767M	740693M	311400M	703487M	Total Assets ($)	710041M	1213547M

M = $ thousand   MM = $ million
See Pages 9 through 22 for Explanation of Ratios and Data

Comparative Historical Data | Current Data Sorted by Sales

	7·11·23·185·93 4/1/07-3/31/08 ALL	13·8·28·193·164 4/1/08-3/31/09 ALL	6·19·37·216·159 4/1/09-3/31/10 ALL	Type of Statement	0-1MM	1-3MM 11 (4/1-9/30/09)	3-5MM	5-10MM	10-25MM 426 (10/1/09-3/31/10)	25MM & OVER
	7	13	6	Unqualified	10	4	3	1	1	4
	11	8	19	Reviewed	29	5	1	1	1	2
	23	28	37	Compiled						
	185	193	216	Tax Returns	194	18	1	1	1	1
	93	164	159	Other	115	31	5	4	2	2
	319	406	437	**NUMBER OF STATEMENTS**	348	58	10	7	5	9
	%	%	%	**ASSETS**	%	%	%	%	%	%
	7.0	6.6	7.0	Cash & Equivalents	6.5	7.2	5.9			
	2.0	2.1	1.8	Trade Receivables (net)	1.3	3.8	1.4			
	1.7	1.1	1.5	Inventory	1.1	1.8	.0			
	2.2	1.4	1.4	All Other Current	1.0	2.7	2.5			
	12.9	11.3	11.7	Total Current	10.0	15.5	9.8			
	80.3	81.1	81.2	Fixed Assets (net)	83.6	77.8	72.0			
	2.1	1.9	2.0	Intangibles (net)	1.6	2.6	1.7			
	4.7	5.8	5.2	All Other Non-Current	4.8	4.1	16.5			
	100.0	100.0	100.0	Total	100.0	100.0	100.0			
				LIABILITIES						
	3.6	4.7	3.5	Notes Payable-Short Term	3.5	3.7	5.6			
	4.3	4.2	3.5	Cur. Mat.-L.T.D.	3.5	3.1	5.3			
	1.3	1.5	1.3	Trade Payables	1.1	1.4	.2			
	.1	.1	.0	Income Taxes Payable	.0	.0	.0			
	10.0	6.0	6.3	All Other Current	6.2	7.0	4.3			
	19.3	16.5	14.6	Total Current	14.3	15.3	15.3			
	68.1	66.5	68.7	Long-Term Debt	68.7	68.5	106.2			
	.1	.0	.0	Deferred Taxes	.0	.0	.0			
	4.0	5.5	2.8	All Other Non-Current	2.3	3.9	5.9			
	8.5	11.5	13.9	Net Worth	14.7	12.4	-27.5			
	100.0	100.0	100.0	Total Liabilties & Net Worth	100.0	100.0	100.0			
				INCOME DATA						
	100.0	100.0	100.0	Net Sales	100.0	100.0	100.0			
				Gross Profit						
	62.2	64.5	64.0	Operating Expenses	62.3	68.0	61.0			
	37.8	35.5	36.0	Operating Profit	37.7	32.0	39.0			
	23.9	23.4	23.5	All Other Expenses (net)	24.4	21.8	28.5			
	13.9	12.0	12.6	Profit Before Taxes	13.3	10.2	10.5			
				RATIOS						
	2.2	2.0	2.2	Current	1.9	4.1	2.5			
	.8	.7	.6		.6	1.4	.4			
	.3	.2	.2		.2	.3	.1			
	1.8	1.6	1.7	Quick	1.5	2.9	1.7			
	.6	.6	.5		.4	.8	.4			
	.2	.1	.1		.1	.3	.1			
	0 UND	0 UND	0 UND	Sales/Receivables	0 UND	0 UND	0 UND			
	0 UND	0 UND	0 UND		0 UND	1 275.8	4 90.2			
	3 128.0	4 98.4	3 120.0		0 UND	19 19.3	17 20.9			
				Cost of Sales/Inventory						
				Cost of Sales/Payables						
	12.4	15.7	11.8	Sales/Working Capital	17.1	3.8	8.0			
	-34.3	-25.7	-19.7		-13.5	26.6	-14.6			
	-4.5	-3.2	-3.0		-2.6	-3.9	-1.5			
	8.8	4.7	5.0	EBIT/Interest	4.8	5.5				
	(117) 3.7	(142) 2.7	(166) 2.8		(122) 2.8	(27) 2.5				
	2.0	1.6	1.7		1.8	1.0				
	5.8	7.8	2.3	Net Profit + Depr., Dep.,						
	(13) 2.6	(14) 1.6	(13) 1.4	Amort./Cur. Mat. L/T/D						
	1.3	.6	.7							
	2.6	2.7	2.4	Fixed/Worth	2.5	2.0	5.4			
	9.2	7.4	6.6		7.4	5.7	NM			
	-8.8	-17.6	-24.0		-20.2	-43.4	-7.1			
	2.0	2.2	1.7	Debt/Worth	1.9	1.6	5.2			
	10.3	8.1	6.6		7.6	5.1	NM			
	-10.8	-19.3	-26.4		-25.3	-51.2	-12.3			
	51.9	40.9	40.4	% Profit Before Taxes/Tangible	41.7	29.9				
	(199) 21.9	(282) 14.8	(294) 15.6	Net Worth	(231) 17.6	(39) 9.8				
	3.8	1.0	1.2		.3	3.9				
	9.3	6.9	7.9	% Profit Before Taxes/Total	8.0	7.5	11.3			
	3.2	2.7	2.7	Assets	2.7	2.7	3.9			
	-.3	.0	-.2		-.4	.1	-.3			
	.6	.5	.4	Sales/Net Fixed Assets	.4	.7	6.3			
	.3	.3	.2		.2	.3	.3			
	.2	.2	.2		.1	.2	.2			
	.5	.4	.4	Sales/Total Assets	.3	.5	1.0			
	.2	.2	.2		.2	.2	.2			
	.2	.1	.1		.1	.1	.2			
	7.6	9.1	10.5	% Depr., Dep., Amort./Sales	11.3	10.6				
	(271) 12.7	(310) 14.2	(346) 15.4		(270) 15.5	(49) 15.9				
	18.5	20.5	22.9		23.7	19.8				
	4.9	3.5	3.7	% Officers', Directors'	4.8	2.0				
	(40) 10.5	(44) 7.0	(60) 7.1	Owners' Comp/Sales	(43) 8.9	(12) 4.6				
	13.8	12.3	14.0		16.2	13.9				
	1424935M	938197M	1121534M	Net Sales ($)	131211M	93334M	39007M	43612M	81155M	733215M
	1880863M	2388156M	2662511M	Total Assets ($)	685843M	452568M	200766M	140394M	336603M	846337M

M = $ thousand   MM = $ million

See Pages 9 through 22 for Explanation of Ratios and Data

Current Data Sorted by Assets   Comparative Historical Data

								Type of Statement				
	4		9		44	26	4	12	Unqualified		79	98
	6		27		38	22	4	3	Reviewed		90	125
	18		93		112	30	2	1	Compiled		262	290
	128		477		348	53	1	1	Tax Returns		679	831
	37		179		254	106	16	15	Other		536	531
		103 (4/1-9/30/09)				1,967 (10/1/09-3/31/10)					4/1/05-3/31/06	4/1/06-3/31/07
	0-500M		500M-2MM		2-10MM	10-50MM	50-100MM	100-250MM			ALL	ALL
	193		785		796	237	27	32	NUMBER OF STATEMENTS		1646	1875
	%		%		%	%	%	%	ASSETS		%	%
	11.5		5.2		4.8	5.6	5.5	4.7	Cash & Equivalents		6.2	6.2
	4.7		1.5		1.8	2.7	2.2	5.2	Trade Receivables (net)		3.2	2.5
	2.0		1.0		1.2	3.1	5.5	1.4	Inventory		2.6	3.0
	1.6		1.8		1.9	3.1	1.6	2.6	All Other Current		2.6	2.3
	19.8		9.5		9.7	14.5	14.8	13.8	Total Current		14.7	14.0
	72.4		82.7		81.5	71.3	69.3	75.2	Fixed Assets (net)		75.8	77.5
	2.4		1.6		2.2	1.9	2.9	2.3	Intangibles (net)		1.8	1.6
	5.4		6.2		6.6	12.2	13.0	8.7	All Other Non-Current		7.7	6.9
	100.0		100.0		100.0	100.0	100.0	100.0	Total		100.0	100.0
								LIABILITIES			
	6.2		4.2		2.6	5.2	5.0	6.4	Notes Payable-Short Term		6.0	4.8
	8.6		5.4		5.1	3.3	3.0	6.8	Cur. Mat.-L.T.D.		4.1	4.3
	4.1		.9		.8	1.5	2.6	4.9	Trade Payables		2.3	2.0
	.0		.0		.0	.1	.1	.1	Income Taxes Payable		.0	.0
	8.4		5.2		4.0	6.3	6.3	4.7	All Other Current		6.3	5.6
	27.4		15.7		12.5	16.4	16.9	22.9	Total Current		18.8	16.7
	69.6		68.7		63.3	54.0	56.6	54.3	Long-Term Debt		58.8	58.3
	.0		.0		.1	.2	.6	.3	Deferred Taxes		.1	.1
	3.3		3.4		4.0	3.7	7.1	5.3	All Other Non-Current		4.8	4.1
	-.3		12.2		20.1	25.7	18.7	17.1	Net Worth		17.5	20.8
	100.0		100.0		100.0	100.0	100.0	100.0	Total Liabilities & Net Worth		100.0	100.0
								INCOME DATA			
	100.0		100.0		100.0	100.0	100.0	100.0	Net Sales		100.0	100.0
									Gross Profit			
	52.1		50.4		52.9	62.7	68.0	74.4	Operating Expenses		56.0	54.3
	47.9		49.6		47.1	37.3	32.0	25.6	Operating Profit		44.0	45.7
	18.4		26.8		27.2	20.5	15.0	21.3	All Other Expenses (net)		22.2	24.7
	29.5		22.8		19.9	16.7	17.1	4.3	Profit Before Taxes		21.8	21.0
								RATIOS			
	2.0		1.6		2.7	3.8	3.1	1.1			2.1	2.0
	.6		.5		.7	.9	.9	.5	Current		.7	.7
	.2		.1		.1	.2	.4	.2			.2	.2
	1.3		1.3		1.9	2.5	2.2	1.0			1.5	1.3
	.5	(784)	.4		.4	(236) .5	.5	.4	Quick	(1644)	.4	(1872) .4
	.1		.1		.1	.1	.1	.1			.1	.1
0	UND	0	UND	0	UND	0 UND	0 UND	0 UND		0	UND	0 UND
0	UND	0	UND	0	UND	1 527.0	2 219.1	8 43.8	Sales/Receivables	0	UND	0 UND
0	UND	0	UND	2	177.3	16 22.5	15 24.1	47 7.8		3	131.4	2 163.0
								Cost of Sales/Inventory			
								Cost of Sales/Payables			
	17.2		13.5		4.5	2.4	2.2	18.5			7.2	6.9
	-17.5		-9.6		-13.5	-30.8	-59.0	-8.1	Sales/Working Capital		-15.5	-14.1
	-2.8		-2.5		-2.4	-2.3	-5.0	-1.3			-2.7	-3.0
	10.8		8.3		7.2	6.5	6.7	5.2			7.5	7.4
(83)	5.5	(275)	4.2	(263)	4.5	(103) 3.0	(17) 2.4	(15) 2.3	EBIT/Interest	(659)	3.7	(664) 4.0
	2.9		2.5		2.4	1.1	1.2	1.5			1.8	2.0
			3.2		2.9	4.0					4.2	5.1
		(14)	1.6	(35)	2.0	(20) 2.1			Net Profit + Depr., Dep., Amort./Cur. Mat. L/T/D	(91)	2.0	(99) 2.0
			.7		1.4	1.0					.9	.8
	1.2		2.2		1.9	1.3	2.0	1.6			1.8	1.7
	3.5		5.3		4.6	3.6	5.2	4.5	Fixed/Worth		4.5	3.9
	-10.9		-183.4		40.1	20.1	71.6	84.0			54.9	22.0
	1.0		1.6		1.4	1.2	1.7	1.7			1.6	1.3
	3.8		5.1		4.5	3.7	4.8	5.4	Debt/Worth		4.5	3.8
	-6.8		-155.9		41.5	27.1	72.6	86.4			65.7	31.5
	58.4		41.3		28.2	26.6	30.5	28.5	% Profit Before Taxes/Tangible Net Worth		42.2	38.7
(132)	20.9	(580)	16.1	(618)	12.7	(191) 11.8	(21) 11.4	(25) 7.2		(1275)	18.6	(1500) 15.8
	10.4		4.4		2.2	1.2	6.8	-1.4			6.2	4.0
	21.7		9.6		6.8	5.0	5.7	4.1			9.4	9.5
	8.2		4.0		3.0	2.3	2.1	1.6	% Profit Before Taxes/Total Assets		3.9	3.8
	1.7		.3		.1	-.2	-.5	-1.4			.8	.5
	1.8		.4		.3	.4	.7	.4			.6	.5
	.4		.2		.2	.2	.3	.3	Sales/Net Fixed Assets		.2	.2
	.2		.1		.1	.1	.2	.1			.1	.1
	1.1		.3		.2	.2	.3	.3			.4	.3
	.3		.2		.1	.1	.2	.2	Sales/Total Assets		.2	.2
	.2		.1		.1	.1	.1	.1			.1	.1
	5.9		10.3		12.1	9.0	4.2	10.7			8.5	8.3
(150)	12.5	(706)	16.7	(725)	19.0	(208) 17.1	(24) 15.9	(26) 17.8	% Depr., Dep., Amort./Sales	(1466)	15.7	(1673) 15.8
	20.0		24.6		26.5	26.1	22.4	22.0			23.8	23.5
	4.1		4.2		2.5	4.0					3.0	2.6
(17)	8.2	(66)	9.1	(60)	6.7	(20) 5.8			% Officers', Directors' Owners' Comp/Sales	(154)	6.2	(184) 6.3
	12.3		15.7		12.3	9.9					13.0	12.2
	69998M		332891M		980760M	1777045M	738543M	1926836M	Net Sales ($)		5282831M	11641641M
	59532M		909891M		3525728M	4858230M	1942449M	5658895M	Total Assets ($)		11422374M	15774566M

© RMA 2010

M = $ thousand   MM = $ million
See Pages 9 through 22 for Explanation of Ratios and Data

Comparative Historical Data   Current Data Sorted by Sales

07-08	08-09	09-10	Type of Statement	0-1MM	1-3MM	3-5MM	5-10MM	10-25MM	25MM & OVER
82	99	99	Unqualified	38	18	6	9	13	15
89	102	100	Reviewed	50	25	9	5	9	2
241	262	256	Compiled	166	62	9	13	4	2
902	1071	1008	Tax Returns	880	101	15	9	3	2
533	584	607	Other	365	133	38	26	23	22
4/1/07-3/31/08 ALL	4/1/08-3/31/09 ALL	4/1/09-3/31/10 ALL		103 (4/1-9/30/09)			1,967 (10/1/09-3/31/10)		
1847	2118	2070	NUMBER OF STATEMENTS	1499	339	77	62	52	41
%	%	%	ASSETS	%	%	%	%	%	%
6.2	6.0	5.7	Cash & Equivalents	4.8	6.7	10.6	11.8	8.7	7.4
2.2	2.2	2.1	Trade Receivables (net)	1.1	2.1	7.0	6.7	7.2	15.8
2.6	1.7	1.5	Inventory	.6	2.7	3.1	7.2	5.3	5.9
2.5	2.2	2.0	All Other Current	1.5	3.0	4.1	3.7	3.3	4.4
13.4	12.0	11.2	Total Current	8.0	14.5	24.8	29.4	24.4	33.5
78.2	79.5	79.7	Fixed Assets (net)	84.2	74.2	60.9	59.2	62.3	48.7
1.6	1.9	2.0	Intangibles (net)	1.6	2.7	4.3	2.0	1.2	7.4
6.7	6.5	7.1	All Other Non-Current	6.2	8.6	10.0	9.4	12.1	10.4
100.0	100.0	100.0	Total	100.0	100.0	100.0	100.0	100.0	100.0
			LIABILITIES						
3.9	4.4	3.9	Notes Payable-Short Term	3.4	5.5	4.3	9.5	4.3	2.8
4.5	4.8	5.3	Cur. Mat.-L.T.D.	5.6	5.3	2.6	4.5	3.6	5.4
1.5	1.4	1.3	Trade Payables	.6	1.7	4.2	3.3	4.2	10.4
.1	.1	.0	Income Taxes Payable	.0	.1	.1	.0	.1	.2
5.3	5.0	5.2	All Other Current	4.1	5.2	15.0	12.9	8.8	9.1
15.2	15.8	15.8	Total Current	13.7	17.7	26.1	30.2	21.0	28.0
59.5	64.2	64.7	Long-Term Debt	67.9	65.2	49.3	35.5	47.0	38.0
.1	.0	.1	Deferred Taxes	.0	.1	.4	.1	.6	.0
3.8	3.8	3.7	All Other Non-Current	3.3	3.8	8.1	3.8	5.8	8.7
21.5	16.2	15.8	Net Worth	15.1	13.3	16.2	30.4	25.6	25.3
100.0	100.0	100.0	Total Liabilities & Net Worth	100.0	100.0	100.0	100.0	100.0	100.0
			INCOME DATA						
100.0	100.0	100.0	Net Sales	100.0	100.0	100.0	100.0	100.0	100.0
			Gross Profit						
52.8	53.4	53.6	Operating Expenses	48.3	60.7	74.2	74.4	78.9	85.6
47.2	46.6	46.4	Operating Profit	51.7	39.3	25.8	25.6	21.1	14.4
25.9	27.1	25.2	All Other Expenses (net)	28.7	18.9	14.1	9.6	13.1	6.7
21.3	19.5	21.3	Profit Before Taxes	23.0	20.4	11.7	16.1	8.0	7.8
			RATIOS						
2.1	2.0	2.2	Current	1.9	3.5	4.0	2.7	2.8	1.6
.7	.7	.6		.5	.8	1.0	1.0	1.2	1.1
.2	.2	.2		.1	.2	.4	.3	.4	.5
1.4	1.5	1.6	Quick	1.4	1.8	2.6	2.4	2.5	1.4
(1845) .5	.4 (2068)	.4		.4 (337)	.5	.6	.5	.7	.8
.1	.1	.1		.1	.1	.1	.1	.1	.3
0 UND	0 UND	0 UND	Sales/Receivables	0 UND	0 UND	0 UND	0 UND	3 132.8	4 95.2
0 UND	0 UND	0 UND		0 UND	0 UND	4 85.9	3 143.5	13 27.1	29 12.6
1 331.0	1 446.6	2 214.3		0 UND	8 47.4	24 15.4	13 27.7	38 9.6	53 6.9
			Cost of Sales/Inventory						
			Cost of Sales/Payables						
6.4	7.4	6.5	Sales/Working Capital	8.5	3.9	4.3	5.0	5.0	7.1
-15.5	-13.4	-12.6		-9.1	-25.7	-89.9	NM	50.6	162.5
-2.9	-2.7	-2.4		-2.1	-3.2	-3.3	-4.8	-4.6	-9.1
6.9	7.0	7.6	EBIT/Interest	7.6	7.1	6.3	19.8	7.3	10.8
(624) 3.7	(668) 4.0	(756) 4.2		(435) 4.6	(167) 3.7	(44) 2.7	(44) 3.5	(34) 3.5	(32) 2.3
1.8	1.9	2.0		2.8	1.4	.8	1.4	1.7	1.2
3.7	3.0	2.8	Net Profit + Depr., Dep., Amort./Cur. Mat. L/T/D	2.6	3.7				
(82) 2.0	(91) 1.7	(77) 1.8		(30) 1.6	(19) 2.0				
1.0	.9	1.0		.8	1.0				
1.8	1.9	1.8	Fixed/Worth	2.1	1.7	1.2	.7	1.1	1.0
4.1	4.5	4.6		5.0	4.3	2.4	2.3	3.7	2.3
22.6	85.2	116.0		97.5	-26.2	48.4	11.0	38.2	13.4
1.4	1.5	1.5	Debt/Worth	1.6	1.4	1.0	.8	1.1	1.6
4.0	4.5	4.6		4.8	4.9	2.6	2.7	3.6	2.8
27.1	155.1	198.6		132.6	-26.5	80.4	13.0	56.4	18.1
37.5	33.5	33.3	% Profit Before Taxes/Tangible Net Worth	32.1	40.3	30.9	63.8	36.0	32.9
(1476) 16.6	(1610) 13.8	(1567) 14.6		(1142) 14.2	(238) 16.7	(59) 11.0	(54) 19.5	(41) 18.8	(33) 13.6
4.7	2.8	3.0		2.9	4.8	-1.0	8.6	3.1	2.3
8.7	8.2	8.2	% Profit Before Taxes/Total Assets	7.6	9.8	10.2	11.6	8.3	12.6
3.8	3.2	3.4		3.2	4.1	3.3	4.7	3.7	2.7
.6	.1	.2		.2	.3	-.6	1.1	-1.1	.4
.4	.4	.4	Sales/Net Fixed Assets	.3	.7	3.7	11.0	5.7	15.3
.2	.2	.2		.2	.3	.4	.8	.5	2.0
.1	.1	.1		.1	.2	.2	.3	.2	.4
.3	.3	.3	Sales/Total Assets	.2	.4	1.6	1.9	1.6	2.1
.2	.2	.2		.1	.2	.3	.4	.3	.8
.1	.1	.1		.1	.1	.2	.2	.2	.3
9.0	9.9	10.6	% Depr., Dep., Amort./Sales	12.2	8.2	4.9	1.7	1.9	2.0
(1621) 15.7	(1874) 17.1	(1839) 17.3		(1342) 18.5	(306) 15.2	(65) 10.5	(51) 6.8	(44) 11.2	(31) 5.0
22.7	25.0	25.0		26.6	23.4	23.0	17.0	21.9	10.8
2.2	3.1	4.0	% Officers', Directors', Owners' Comp/Sales	4.1	3.7	5.6	1.8	1.6	
(160) 5.4	(165) 6.3	(173) 7.1		(72) 9.0	(52) 7.2	(14) 9.3	(19) 4.2	(13) 4.5	
13.1	12.5	13.2		20.9	11.1	21.0	6.0	8.3	
8903227M	5639253M	5826073M	Net Sales ($)	494785M	563234M	288635M	436648M	881522M	3161249M
12889684M	14673104M	16954725M	Total Assets ($)	3412468M	3034400M	1235906M	1524427M	3468682M	4278842M

Current Data Sorted by Assets

Comparative Historical Data

0-500M	500M-2MM 78 (4/1-9/30/09)	2-10MM	10-50MM 756 (10/1/09-3/31/10)	50-100MM	100-250MM	Type of Statement	4/1/05-3/31/06 ALL	4/1/06-3/31/07 ALL
2	3	15	13	5	8	Unqualified	91	69
2	12	15	8	3		Reviewed	45	53
16	36	33	8	2	1	Compiled	117	112
141	116	88	14	1	3	Tax Returns	408	372
74	77	69	46	12	11	Other	412	342
235	244	220	89	23	23	NUMBER OF STATEMENTS	1073	948
%	%	%	%	%	%	ASSETS	%	%
35.4	14.8	11.6	15.6	23.6	10.3	Cash & Equivalents	20.0	19.3
5.2	6.2	6.4	6.4	6.3	8.1	Trade Receivables (net)	6.9	8.1
1.1	2.3	3.2	5.0	5.2	7.7	Inventory	6.4	5.5
4.9	5.2	4.4	6.9	5.6	12.0	All Other Current	4.8	7.2
46.6	28.5	25.6	33.9	40.7	38.0	Total Current	38.1	40.0
30.9	51.1	56.8	46.3	35.8	41.6	Fixed Assets (net)	43.1	41.4
7.9	5.7	4.7	4.8	11.5	8.8	Intangibles (net)	5.1	5.4
14.6	14.7	13.0	15.0	12.0	11.6	All Other Non-Current	13.6	13.1
100.0	100.0	100.0	100.0	100.0	100.0	Total	100.0	100.0
						LIABILITIES		
30.8	12.7	8.3	8.5	10.7	3.6	Notes Payable-Short Term	12.6	13.1
6.1	3.2	5.6	2.3	3.9	3.3	Cur. Mat.-L.T.D.	3.2	3.8
5.7	3.7	3.3	3.5	6.0	6.9	Trade Payables	4.0	5.2
.0	.1	.1	.1	.0	.2	Income Taxes Payable	.1	.1
28.5	11.7	9.0	10.1	13.1	10.4	All Other Current	16.0	17.1
71.2	31.3	26.2	24.4	33.7	24.5	Total Current	35.9	39.3
27.6	39.2	44.5	34.0	29.6	46.8	Long-Term Debt	33.9	31.7
.0	.0	.0	.1	.2	.1	Deferred Taxes	.2	.1
15.5	7.2	4.9	1.5	4.4	6.2	All Other Non-Current	4.8	7.6
-14.3	22.2	24.3	40.0	32.1	22.5	Net Worth	25.1	21.3
100.0	100.0	100.0	100.0	100.0	100.0	Total Liabilities & Net Worth	100.0	100.0
						INCOME DATA		
100.0	100.0	100.0	100.0	100.0	100.0	Net Sales	100.0	100.0
						Gross Profit		
91.4	75.9	71.4	77.7	86.0	85.9	Operating Expenses	75.6	79.0
8.6	24.1	28.6	22.3	14.0	14.1	Operating Profit	24.4	21.0
2.3	12.4	16.3	14.0	7.9	7.6	All Other Expenses (net)	8.9	8.9
6.3	11.7	12.3	8.3	6.1	6.5	Profit Before Taxes	15.5	12.1
						RATIOS		
3.1	2.3	2.5	3.8	2.1	2.9		3.1	2.5
.8	1.0	1.0	1.3	1.3	1.4	Current	1.2	1.1
.3	.3	.3	.5	.5	1.1		.4	.4
2.7	2.0	1.9	2.5	1.6	1.4		2.0	1.8
.6	.6	(218) .6	1.0	.7	.9	Quick	(1072) .8	(947) .7
.3	.2	.1	.2	.4			.2	.2
0 UND	0 UND	0 UND	0 UND	2 152.6	3 124.0		0 UND	0 UND
0 UND	0 UND	1 429.2	8 43.4	33 11.0	15 25.0	Sales/Receivables	0 UND	0 UND
1 449.0	5 78.9	13 28.2	26 14.0	56 6.5	38 9.6		7 54.7	10 36.0
						Cost of Sales/Inventory		
						Cost of Sales/Payables		
23.8	7.3	4.9	2.4	2.5	2.7		6.5	8.0
-133.0	257.1	UND	25.5	28.2	14.7	Sales/Working Capital	65.9	144.5
-8.6	-5.7	-3.8	-6.3	-3.7	39.9		-10.2	-11.1
8.9	11.4	9.7	5.4	17.6	4.4		26.7	16.7
(134) 1.9	(132) 2.6	(122) 3.5	(51) 2.6	(12) 3.7	(20) 2.1	EBIT/Interest	(625) 5.3	(563) 4.3
-4.2	-2.6	1.0	.0	1.3	.5		1.8	1.3
		3.5					6.3	4.6
		(15) 2.0				Net Profit + Depr., Dep.,	(55) 2.4	(56) 1.8
		.5				Amort./Cur. Mat. L/T/D	.5	.6
.1	.6	.7	.3	.1	.2		.2	.2
1.1	2.7	2.9	1.3	.8	1.6	Fixed/Worth	1.5	1.6
-1.0	-23.4	403.0	4.3	15.7	9.9		14.1	21.5
.4	.8	1.0	.6	1.0	1.4		.8	.9
4.9	3.6	3.3	1.6	5.2	3.2	Debt/Worth	2.8	3.1
-2.5	-23.3	NM	6.0	26.5	38.9		27.0	297.1
164.4	51.0	31.8	24.1	17.1	41.4		100.0	89.9
(138) 42.0	(174) 13.5	(165) 12.9	(75) 7.8	(19) 12.2	(18) 13.6	% Profit Before Taxes/Tangible Net Worth	(850) 37.3	(724) 31.7
2.3	-.7	1.8	-.9	1.9	-1.7		10.4	6.5
44.9	9.8	8.4	7.0	6.6	9.1		32.5	23.3
6.3	3.3	3.4	2.8	2.2	2.3	% Profit Before Taxes/Total Assets	8.2	6.9
-17.8	-2.2	.0	-.9	-2.1	-.9		1.6	.3
276.0	37.9	14.4	18.0	36.3	26.7		58.5	71.3
41.2	3.2	.5	.6	5.4	4.7	Sales/Net Fixed Assets	10.2	14.7
8.4	.2	.2	.2	.4	.7		.3	.4
13.6	3.4	1.6	1.4	1.8	1.6		4.5	5.2
6.3	.7	.3	.2	.4	.7	Sales/Total Assets	1.3	1.7
2.1	.2	.1	.1	.2	.3		.2	.3
.5	1.0	1.8	1.8	2.0	.9		.7	.7
(137) 1.2	(184) 6.2	(186) 12.2	(75) 7.5	(18) 5.9	(21) 2.1	% Depr., Dep., Amort./Sales	(765) 2.9	(676) 2.2
3.4	17.9	18.8	19.8	26.0	6.3		14.0	11.4
3.6	1.4	1.5	2.2				2.4	2.2
(92) 8.6	(60) 4.8	(50) 4.1	(12) 3.3			% Officers', Directors' Owners' Comp/Sales	(251) 5.9	(245) 5.7
18.0	10.4	11.1	9.7				12.7	14.0
304885M	655260M	1231202M	1901101M	1812006M	4995526M	Net Sales ($)	17951321M	16840523M
45116M	269381M	991895M	1913868M	1621631M	3487141M	Total Assets ($)	10533386M	7039898M

Comparative Historical Data | Current Data Sorted by Sales

			Type of Statement	0-1MM	1-3MM	3-5MM	5-10MM	10-25MM	25MM & OVER
63	44	46	Unqualified	7	6	4	9	4	16
53	47	40	Reviewed	10	8	4	7	7	4
97	94	96	Compiled	37	30	7	9	10	3
404	366	363	Tax Returns	218	81	25	16	14	9
296	314	289	Other	107	62	18	33	28	41
4/1/07-3/31/08 ALL	4/1/08-3/31/09 ALL	4/1/09-3/31/10 ALL		78 (4/1-9/30/09)			756 (10/1/09-3/31/10)		
913	865	834	NUMBER OF STATEMENTS	379	187	58	74	63	73
%	%	%	ASSETS	%	%	%	%	%	%
16.8	18.0	20.0	Cash & Equivalents	15.2	22.5	28.4	22.5	26.5	23.2
6.8	6.8	6.0	Trade Receivables (net)	3.1	4.0	12.5	12.7	10.9	10.8
4.9	3.5	2.7	Inventory	1.5	4.7	2.8	3.4	.2	5.4
7.5	6.3	5.3	All Other Current	3.2	6.5	5.3	7.8	6.2	9.7
36.0	34.6	34.0	Total Current	22.9	37.7	49.0	46.5	43.7	49.0
44.3	46.1	45.7	Fixed Assets (net)	61.6	38.9	28.0	30.1	29.5	24.7
6.4	6.3	6.2	Intangibles (net)	3.7	7.9	8.1	6.1	8.2	11.7
13.3	12.9	14.1	All Other Non-Current	11.8	15.4	15.0	17.4	18.6	14.5
100.0	100.0	100.0	Total	100.0	100.0	100.0	100.0	100.0	100.0
			LIABILITIES						
13.3	14.6	15.9	Notes Payable-Short Term	16.9	18.9	13.4	14.8	13.9	7.5
4.5	5.0	4.5	Cur. Mat.-L.T.D.	4.0	8.2	1.9	3.1	3.3	2.6
4.8	5.0	4.3	Trade Payables	2.1	4.3	5.1	8.6	8.1	7.3
.1	.2	.1	Income Taxes Payable	.0	.0	.2	.1	.2	.1
18.5	16.5	15.5	All Other Current	15.0	14.2	17.0	13.6	17.8	20.6
41.2	41.3	40.3	Total Current	38.1	45.7	37.6	40.3	43.3	38.1
34.6	35.0	36.7	Long-Term Debt	49.1	31.1	25.3	18.8	23.2	25.9
.1	.1	.0	Deferred Taxes	.0	.0	.2	.1	.0	.1
5.7	8.8	8.2	All Other Non-Current	7.9	9.4	10.5	7.9	7.0	6.8
18.4	14.9	14.7	Net Worth	4.9	13.9	26.5	33.0	26.5	29.2
100.0	100.0	100.0	Total Liabilities & Net Worth	100.0	100.0	100.0	100.0	100.0	100.0
			INCOME DATA						
100.0	100.0	100.0	Net Sales	100.0	100.0	100.0	100.0	100.0	100.0
			Gross Profit						
80.7	82.4	79.9	Operating Expenses	67.9	85.1	94.0	92.6	91.1	94.6
19.3	17.6	20.1	Operating Profit	32.1	14.9	6.0	7.4	8.9	5.4
9.8	10.8	10.5	All Other Expenses (net)	17.8	7.1	3.0	3.4	1.6	1.8
9.5	6.8	9.7	Profit Before Taxes	14.2	7.8	3.0	3.9	7.3	3.6
			RATIOS						
2.2	2.1	2.8	Current	2.2	2.9	5.8	3.6	2.3	2.8
1.0	1.0	1.1		.7	1.1	1.5	1.5	1.3	1.4
.3	.3	.3		.2	.4	.6	.8	.5	.9
1.6	1.6	2.1	Quick	1.8	2.2	5.4	2.7	2.2	1.6
.6 (863)	.6 (832)	.7		(377) .4	.6	1.1	1.1	1.1	1.1
.1	.2	.2		.1	.2	.4	.4	.3	.4
0 UND	0 UND	0 UND	Sales/Receivables	0 UND	0 UND	0 UND	0 UND	0 999.8	2 236.8
0 UND	0 UND	0 UND		0 UND	0 UND	3 104.3	4 92.0	3 111.2	10 36.1
8 46.7	9 42.8	9 41.6		1 299.0	6 64.2	17 21.7	38 9.6	20 18.5	35 10.3
			Cost of Sales/Inventory						
			Cost of Sales/Payables						
9.9	12.6	7.9	Sales/Working Capital	8.2	9.5	10.4	6.5	7.2	6.4
779.8	-999.8	177.3		-27.7	431.7	36.0	35.3	81.8	22.1
-7.8	-6.8	-6.1		-2.8	-10.2	-36.2	-23.9	-22.3	-135.3
10.2	7.6	9.0	EBIT/Interest	7.1	8.1	3.7	29.4	19.9	8.7
(512) 2.9	(482) 1.2	(471) 2.6		(154) 2.5	(120) 2.0	(38) .7	(55) 3.9	(45) 3.4	(59) 4.1
.1	-2.9	-.6		-.3	-2.4	-4.9	-.8	1.1	.5
4.5	2.6	2.6	Net Profit + Depr., Dep., Amort./Cur. Mat. L/T/D	2.5					9.0
(36) 1.6	(38) 1.7	(42) 1.3		(11) 1.2				(13)	1.4
.4	-1.6	.2		-.4					.3
.3	.4	.3	Fixed/Worth	1.0	.3	.2	.2	.2	.2
1.9	2.4	2.0		3.5	1.9	.6	.9	1.1	.7
UND	-30.9	-21.4		-35.4	-3.3	-142.1	8.6	-6.4	11.9
1.0	.9	.8	Debt/Worth	1.0	.7	.5	.5	.6	.9
3.5	4.3	3.4		4.5	4.0	1.9	1.5	3.0	2.5
-40.0	-22.2	-12.4		-16.2	-5.7	-30.6	19.5	-12.5	34.2
77.9	40.1	50.5	% Profit Before Taxes/Tangible Net Worth	42.8	66.9	74.4	52.5	71.1	60.2
(663) 22.0	(615) 10.9	(589) 14.8		(265) 14.8	(123) 12.4	(41) 12.3	(59) 16.5	(45) 19.2	(56) 15.5
2.2	-6.4	.9		1.1	.7	-8.3	-1.2	5.1	.7
17.7	9.8	12.6	% Profit Before Taxes/Total Assets	9.6	15.0	14.4	19.0	17.2	11.2
4.4	1.5	3.4		2.9	3.7	2.1	6.0	4.6	4.8
-1.8	-5.7	-2.0		-1.5	-3.8	-8.6	-2.1	.8	-.8
55.5	48.8	51.6	Sales/Net Fixed Assets	14.4	64.5	315.3	84.0	61.6	61.1
11.4	8.2	6.9		.4	13.9	40.3	24.9	19.8	18.5
.4	.3	.3		.1	.7	6.7	4.8	6.2	5.7
5.4	5.2	4.8	Sales/Total Assets	1.4	6.0	11.4	8.1	7.2	4.0
1.5	1.4	1.1		.2	1.9	5.1	2.7	2.6	2.1
.3	.2	.2		.1	.4	1.2	.5	1.4	1.0
.8	1.0	1.0	% Depr., Dep., Amort./Sales	4.9	.6	.4	.6	.4	.7
(671) 2.8	(641) 3.3	(621) 4.3		(284) 14.3	(135) 1.8	(39) 1.3	(53) 1.3	(48) 1.0	(62) 1.6
12.6	14.9	16.4		21.1	12.0	4.7	9.8	2.8	2.8
2.7	1.7	2.3	% Officers', Directors' Owners' Comp/Sales	5.3	2.4	2.0	1.3	1.2	2.7
(239) 5.4	(221) 4.9	(221) 6.1		(65) 11.9	(72) 5.9	(21) 3.9	(28) 2.8	(19) 1.5	(16) 6.3
15.7	11.8	12.9		20.4	12.6	7.6	8.0	3.6	12.9
11119705M	8892674M	10899980M	Net Sales ($)	145993M	334558M	218758M	550426M	988006M	8662239M
6749598M	5829371M	8329032M	Total Assets ($)	658073M	665620M	258022M	940645M	945955M	4860717M

M = $ thousand   MM = $ million
See Pages 9 through 22 for Explanation of Ratios and Data

Current Data Sorted by Assets   Comparative Historical Data

0-500M	500M-2MM	2-10MM	10-50MM	50-100MM	100-250MM	Type of Statement	4/1/05-3/31/06 ALL	4/1/06-3/31/07 ALL
8	17	19	12	1	6	Unqualified	25	23
	7	6	6		1	Reviewed	11	8
10	10	16	4	2		Compiled	20	15
73	85	65	8	1	2	Tax Returns	66	64
42	53	57	30	4	3	Other	59	64
	53 (4/1-9/30/09)		495 (10/1/09-3/31/10)					
133	172	163	60	8	12	NUMBER OF STATEMENTS	181	174
%	%	%	%	%	%	**ASSETS**	%	%
33.2	17.3	9.1	11.2		15.3	Cash & Equivalents	15.2	18.4
8.4	6.0	7.8	5.4		5.7	Trade Receivables (net)	6.7	6.4
2.2	1.7	3.3	4.0		9.4	Inventory	3.1	5.2
3.1	3.2	2.1	3.7		1.4	All Other Current	6.6	5.7
47.0	28.2	22.3	24.3		31.9	Total Current	31.6	35.8
33.0	55.4	60.6	51.7		40.7	Fixed Assets (net)	50.2	43.5
6.3	2.8	3.8	3.2		9.9	Intangibles (net)	4.4	3.2
13.8	13.5	13.3	20.7		17.5	All Other Non-Current	13.8	17.5
100.0	100.0	100.0	100.0		100.0	Total	100.0	100.0
						LIABILITIES		
16.3	7.0	7.1	3.4		11.7	Notes Payable-Short Term	10.7	10.1
3.4	3.9	2.6	2.4		2.2	Cur. Mat.-L.T.D.	3.3	4.2
6.8	3.4	3.3	5.3		8.0	Trade Payables	5.1	4.2
.0	.0	.1	.0		1.7	Income Taxes Payable	1.4	.0
43.3	11.9	13.9	13.8		4.5	All Other Current	11.8	12.3
69.8	26.3	27.1	24.9		28.1	Total Current	32.2	30.9
29.7	47.0	47.4	39.8		30.1	Long-Term Debt	53.1	33.9
.0	.1	.0	.2		.4	Deferred Taxes	.1	.0
3.5	3.1	3.0	2.3		4.5	All Other Non-Current	5.3	4.3
-3.0	23.5	22.4	32.8		36.9	Net Worth	9.2	30.9
100.0	100.0	100.0	100.0		100.0	Total Liabilities & Net Worth	100.0	100.0
						INCOME DATA		
100.0	100.0	100.0	100.0		100.0	Net Sales	100.0	100.0
						Gross Profit		
84.6	73.3	73.5	73.7		89.9	Operating Expenses	77.5	81.8
15.4	26.7	26.5	26.3		10.1	Operating Profit	22.5	18.2
5.0	17.1	17.7	17.9		3.4	All Other Expenses (net)	12.5	8.8
10.4	9.5	8.8	8.4		6.7	Profit Before Taxes	10.0	9.4
						RATIOS		
2.0	2.8	1.6	1.6		6.5		3.0	3.4
.9	.9	.6	.8		1.1	Current	1.0	1.1
.2	.2	.1	.2		.6		.3	.4
1.9	2.4	1.2	1.2		6.1		2.2	2.7
.7	.7	.4	.4		1.0	Quick	.5	.7
.1	.1	.1	.1		.2		.1	.1
0 UND	0 UND	0 UND	0 UND		0 UND		0 UND	0 UND
0 UND	0 UND	0 UND	4 94.1		14 25.4	Sales/Receivables	0 UND	0 UND
6 56.7	10 35.3	25 14.9	28 12.9		35 10.3		17 21.5	17 21.6
						Cost of Sales/Inventory		
						Cost of Sales/Payables		
8.8	7.0	11.9	8.3		3.1		5.0	5.1
-419.5	-117.9	-10.6	-22.3		144.0	Sales/Working Capital	-102.8	66.4
-6.8	-3.5	-2.3	-1.8		-3.9		-4.7	-6.1
16.9	6.7	8.4	14.7		15.3		16.0	9.5
(55) 6.8	(75) 2.9	(83) 2.9	(28) 4.1		(11) 4.0	EBIT/Interest	(95) 5.0	(85) 3.4
1.9	.7	1.0	-.4		2.1		1.4	.2
		16.6				Net Profit + Depr., Dep.,		
	(10) 2.7					Amort./Cur. Mat. L/T/D		
		.8						
.0	.4	1.0	.3		.4		.3	.2
1.0	3.4	3.7	1.7		1.1	Fixed/Worth	3.4	1.6
22.4	-19.6	-305.4	10.5		NM		-16.9	25.1
.9	1.0	1.3	.8		.7		1.1	.4
4.0	4.7	5.2	2.5		2.0	Debt/Worth	5.2	2.6
-6.9	-16.7	-71.7	20.8		NM		-12.1	176.1
151.1	41.4	35.3	15.3			% Profit Before Taxes/Tangible	70.2	67.1
(91) 35.1	(119) 16.2	(120) 11.4	(48) 4.2			Net Worth	(120) 25.7	(136) 14.0
10.8	-.9	1.0	-7.8				3.2	.0
36.1	10.4	7.9	5.6		11.6	% Profit Before Taxes/Total	18.7	15.1
9.7	3.1	2.0	1.6		2.1	Assets	3.6	3.9
-2.2	-.9	-.2	-1.4		.8		-.3	-1.4
UND	31.1	11.5	16.1		22.7		34.3	78.1
80.5	.6	.4	.9		2.2	Sales/Net Fixed Assets	2.3	4.7
2.7	.2	.1	.1		.3		.2	.3
6.4	1.5	.9	.9		3.6		2.3	2.4
2.5	.4	.2	.2		.9	Sales/Total Assets	.7	.6
.7	.1	.1	.1		.1		.2	.2
.6	2.2	2.4	1.6		1.6		1.4	1.4
(63) 2.1	(131) 11.0	(132) 12.6	(47) 8.6		(10) 8.0	% Depr., Dep., Amort./Sales	(121) 8.1	(118) 6.8
10.7	19.4	24.7	25.9		16.5		18.4	18.7
6.4	2.5	2.4				% Officers', Directors'	5.0	2.8
(33) 12.1	(37) 5.4	(22) 5.3				Owners' Comp/Sales	(40) 12.2	(31) 5.5
16.1	13.1	11.4					19.8	11.8
102399M	246137M	548396M	1160356M	207935M	3157608M	Net Sales ($)	1653078M	837634M
30113M	191715M	711130M	1189936M	512241M	1619186M	Total Assets ($)	1300951M	1316811M

M = $ thousand   MM = $ million
See Pages 9 through 22 for Explanation of Ratios and Data

Comparative Historical Data **Current Data Sorted by Sales**

			Type of Statement						
38	48	63	Unqualified	15	21	7	7	6	7
10	12	20	Reviewed	5	4	1	5	5	
17	21	42	Compiled	23	10	2	2	4	1
77	145	234	Tax Returns	170	36	14	5	7	2
83	170	189	Other	86	46	15	16	16	10
4/1/07-3/31/08 ALL	4/1/08-3/31/09 ALL	4/1/09-3/31/10 ALL		0-1MM	1-3MM	3-5MM	5-10MM	10-25MM	25MM & OVER
				53 (4/1-9/30/09)		495 (10/1/09-3/31/10)			
225	396	548	**NUMBER OF STATEMENTS**	299	117	39	35	38	20
%	%	%	**ASSETS**	%	%	%	%	%	%
20.0	19.1	17.9	Cash & Equivalents	15.6	19.6	26.4	24.5	13.0	24.5
7.0	7.2	7.0	Trade Receivables (net)	3.8	8.0	7.9	14.6	16.0	15.9
6.9	4.3	2.8	Inventory	1.9	2.6	5.8	.5	5.5	9.9
5.4	4.2	3.0	All Other Current	1.9	3.7	3.8	2.2	8.7	5.0
39.3	34.8	30.7	Total Current	23.3	33.8	43.9	41.8	43.3	55.3
42.4	46.5	50.6	Fixed Assets (net)	62.5	41.4	32.7	30.1	35.5	27.3
2.8	3.8	4.1	Intangibles (net)	2.4	6.6	4.1	6.2	7.1	6.8
15.4	14.9	14.5	All Other Non-Current	11.9	18.1	19.3	21.9	14.1	10.7
100.0	100.0	100.0	Total	100.0	100.0	100.0	100.0	100.0	100.0
			LIABILITIES						
9.2	8.0	8.9	Notes Payable-Short Term	9.7	7.9	12.0	10.6	4.4	3.0
7.9	4.3	3.2	Cur. Mat.-L.T.D.	3.7	2.4	3.8	2.3	2.2	2.3
5.8	4.2	4.5	Trade Payables	2.5	4.4	5.8	8.6	9.7	16.3
.0	.0	.1	Income Taxes Payable	.0	.0	.0	.6	.5	.0
14.8	20.4	20.3	All Other Current	19.6	19.6	19.6	22.2	25.9	22.6
37.7	36.8	37.0	Total Current	35.5	34.3	41.2	44.3	42.8	44.3
41.0	44.6	41.5	Long-Term Debt	51.1	35.2	32.4	20.9	24.5	21.4
.0	.0	.1	Deferred Taxes	.0	.0	.0	.4	.2	.2
2.9	3.5	3.1	All Other Non-Current	2.4	4.4	3.9	6.7	.9	2.9
18.4	15.1	18.3	Net Worth	11.0	26.1	22.6	27.7	31.6	31.2
100.0	100.0	100.0	Total Liabilities & Net Worth	100.0	100.0	100.0	100.0	100.0	100.0
			INCOME DATA						
100.0	100.0	100.0	Net Sales	100.0	100.0	100.0	100.0	100.0	100.0
			Gross Profit						
82.9	79.9	76.7	Operating Expenses	68.9	83.5	86.1	89.1	87.5	93.5
17.1	20.1	23.3	Operating Profit	31.1	16.5	13.9	10.9	12.5	6.5
9.6	12.5	14.0	All Other Expenses (net)	21.1	7.8	4.3	4.2	3.7	-.1
7.5	7.6	9.3	Profit Before Taxes	10.0	8.8	9.6	6.7	8.9	6.5
			RATIOS						
3.4	2.6	2.0		1.8	2.6	2.9	2.2	2.8	2.2
1.1	1.0	.8	Current	.4	.9	1.1	1.1	1.0	1.2
.4	.3	.2		.1	.2	.5	.5	.6	1.0
2.1	2.2	1.7		1.6	1.9	2.6	2.2	1.5	1.5
(224) .7	.5	.6	Quick	.3	.7	.9	1.0	.7	.9
.1	.1	.1		.1	.2	.2	.3	.3	.6
0 UND	0 UND	0 UND		0 UND	0 UND	0 UND	0 999.8	1 354.7	7 56.1
1 326.2	0 999.8	0 UND	Sales/Receivables	0 UND	1 337.8	1 325.6	12 30.7	21 17.4	16 23.1
18 20.5	14 26.1	14 25.6		5 72.0	16 23.2	13 27.7	38 9.7	41 8.8	31 11.8
			Cost of Sales/Inventory						
			Cost of Sales/Payables						
4.2	4.9	8.5		8.8	7.3	7.9	11.9	5.0	6.1
61.3	-94.4	-29.4	Sales/Working Capital	-9.0	-54.8	314.5	40.3	NM	17.6
-4.2	-3.7	-3.3		-1.9	-5.4	-10.8	-17.1	-15.5	741.7
8.9	9.5	10.7		6.0	11.8	23.0	34.0	26.9	15.1
(108) 3.3	(185) 2.6	(256) 3.3	EBIT/Interest	(92) 2.5	(70) 3.3	(27) 5.0	(23) 4.6	(28) 5.5	(16) 4.4
.7	.1	.9		.6	.7	2.9	1.0	2.0	2.1
		4.2							
	(19) 1.3	(23) 3.1	Net Profit + Depr., Dep., Amort./Cur. Mat. L/T/D						
	.0	1.3							
.1	.1	.2		.7	.1	.0	.2	.4	.3
1.6	1.9	2.3	Fixed/Worth	3.7	1.3	1.2	1.0	1.4	.8
124.0	21.1	275.7		UND	79.8	-13.5	-7.5	-8.5	3.8
.7	.9	1.0		1.5	.7	.7	.6	.6	.9
3.2	3.9	4.3	Debt/Worth	5.6	2.3	4.3	2.5	3.5	1.4
-120.4	-34.6	-39.7		-45.5	NM	-8.1	-9.5	-28.2	8.6
47.2	55.9	47.0		38.7	42.9	191.4	70.2	92.6	65.3
(166) 14.6	(292) 10.8	(394) 15.1	% Profit Before Taxes/Tangible Net Worth	(211) 15.0	(88) 10.9	(26) 29.9	(25) 29.3	(28) 12.9	(16) 20.1
-.4	-3.8	.2		-1.1	-.8	10.5	3.2	1.3	3.0
12.5	12.7	12.2		7.6	12.6	52.6	29.9	31.1	13.2
2.5	2.0	3.2	% Profit Before Taxes/Total Assets	2.0	3.9	8.6	8.7	5.0	7.0
-1.4	-2.0	-.8		-1.1	-1.4	4.0	.4	1.3	1.3
97.5	65.8	54.5		26.2	119.1	144.7	61.4	36.3	61.3
6.9	2.1	1.2	Sales/Net Fixed Assets	.3	6.7	24.9	14.6	15.7	14.7
.3	.2	.2		.1	.5	1.5	2.3	1.1	3.1
2.1	2.2	2.1		.8	2.6	5.2	5.7	4.3	3.7
.8	.5	.5	Sales/Total Assets	.2	.8	2.9	2.3	1.6	2.0
.2	.2	.1		.1	.3	.7	.6	.5	1.1
1.1	2.0	1.8		9.2	.8	.6	.8	.7	.6
(152) 5.9	(261) 8.9	(391) 9.6	% Depr., Dep., Amort./Sales	(212) 17.1	(83) 3.7	(25) 2.3	(23) 1.9	(32) 1.8	(16) 1.1
14.5	18.8	19.4		25.4	13.7	4.8	4.8	4.9	4.2
4.3	4.3	3.1		4.7	3.3	5.1			
(46) 8.3	(68) 9.0	(102) 7.0	% Officers', Directors' Owners' Comp/Sales	(39) 8.5	(28) 11.3	(14) 7.0			
14.5	19.4	14.2		19.2	14.7	12.2			
2209381M	3943306M	5422831M	Net Sales ($)	108154M	193154M	161352M	250395M	638186M	4071590M
1707626M	3121525M	4254321M	Total Assets ($)	570792M	562803M	189687M	395605M	1088929M	1446505M

M = $ thousand   MM = $ million
See Pages 9 through 22 for Explanation of Ratios and Data

REAL ESTATE—Nonresidential Property Managers · NAICS 531312

| | Current Data Sorted by Assets | | | | | | | Comparative Historical Data | |

Type of Statement

0-500M	500M-2MM	2-10MM	10-50MM	50-100MM	100-250MM	Type of Statement	4/1/05-3/31/06 ALL	4/1/06-3/31/07 ALL
1		5	9	2	3	Unqualified	2	14
	1	9	6	1		Reviewed	7	18
3	18	11	5			Compiled	12	30
24	48	33	2	1		Tax Returns	40	65
23	29	45	20	2	4	Other	42	61
	17 (4/1-9/30/09)		288 (10/1/09-3/31/10)					
51	96	103	42	6	7	NUMBER OF STATEMENTS	103	188
%	%	%	%	%	%	ASSETS	%	%
28.8	8.0	7.5	14.1			Cash & Equivalents	7.8	8.3
5.9	3.9	3.1	5.0			Trade Receivables (net)	5.9	5.8
.0	1.1	3.4	.1			Inventory	3.1	3.4
3.9	4.1	2.9	3.0			All Other Current	3.6	3.7
38.6	17.1	17.0	22.2			Total Current	20.4	21.2
44.8	72.1	69.7	62.7			Fixed Assets (net)	69.1	65.4
4.5	3.6	3.0	2.1			Intangibles (net)	2.2	3.3
12.1	7.1	10.3	13.0			All Other Non-Current	8.3	10.1
100.0	100.0	100.0	100.0			Total	100.0	100.0
						LIABILITIES		
17.6	6.8	3.0	4.8			Notes Payable-Short Term	7.1	5.5
3.7	3.7	5.5	7.6			Cur. Mat.-L.T.D.	4.3	3.7
4.2	2.1	1.5	2.4			Trade Payables	2.7	3.5
.0	.0	.0	.0			Income Taxes Payable	.1	.1
28.6	6.4	4.5	7.4			All Other Current	7.0	7.2
54.1	18.9	14.4	22.2			Total Current	21.2	19.9
43.6	52.6	49.9	43.4			Long-Term Debt	63.8	52.4
.0	.0	.0	.1			Deferred Taxes	.1	.0
2.3	4.0	7.3	6.3			All Other Non-Current	5.9	3.3
-.1	24.4	28.3	28.0			Net Worth	9.0	24.3
100.0	100.0	100.0	100.0			Total Liabilities & Net Worth	100.0	100.0
						INCOME DATA		
100.0	100.0	100.0	100.0			Net Sales	100.0	100.0
						Gross Profit		
76.0	58.2	63.4	72.2			Operating Expenses	62.8	59.6
24.0	41.8	36.6	27.8			Operating Profit	37.2	40.4
8.0	23.8	21.5	18.7			All Other Expenses (net)	22.4	20.8
16.0	18.0	15.1	9.1			Profit Before Taxes	14.8	19.6
						RATIOS		
4.0	2.2	3.2	2.6			Current	2.9	2.9
1.3	.7	.9	1.1				.6	.9
.2	.2	.3	.1				.2	.2
3.1	1.7	2.2	2.6			Quick	1.6	1.9
1.1	(95) .5	.7	.9				.5	.6
.2	.1	.2	.0				.1	.1
0 UND	0 UND	0 UND	0 UND			Sales/Receivables	0 UND	0 UND
0 UND	0 UND	0 UND	2 155.1				0 UND	0 UND
1 370.0	1 303.5	7 54.0	23 15.9				12 29.8	9 41.5
						Cost of Sales/Inventory		
						Cost of Sales/Payables		
10.8	6.3	3.7	3.1			Sales/Working Capital	4.2	5.1
90.5	-30.3	-96.6	24.0				-11.3	-40.4
-12.0	-3.4	-4.0	-.9				-3.5	-3.5
17.3	9.8	7.7	17.2			EBIT/Interest	7.2	9.2
(21) 5.8	(40) 4.7	(45) 3.0	(20) 3.5				(42) 3.7	(74) 4.0
3.7	1.8	1.0	1.6				1.5	1.9
						Net Profit + Depr., Dep., Amort./Cur. Mat. L/T/D		5.6
							(10)	1.5
								.0
.2	1.5	1.2	.5			Fixed/Worth	1.2	1.0
1.4	4.7	3.6	3.7				3.9	3.9
25.6	23.8	13.9	15.5				40.2	30.3
1.0	1.1	1.0	1.0			Debt/Worth	1.3	1.2
2.7	4.7	3.3	4.2				3.7	4.7
-3.1	27.4	13.4	21.4				77.7	45.2
161.7	42.6	26.7	30.6			% Profit Before Taxes/Tangible Net Worth	40.1	45.2
(36) 59.3	(80) 17.3	(84) 9.5	(35) 16.0				(79) 16.9	(151) 17.8
13.0	2.7	.9	-1.0				.0	1.7
113.0	11.0	7.9	5.8			% Profit Before Taxes/Total Assets	11.6	10.5
20.1	2.7	3.1	2.1				3.9	3.5
4.4	.2	-.3	-1.0				-.2	.3
107.8	2.5	.7	3.3			Sales/Net Fixed Assets	5.5	6.2
24.6	.2	.2	.2				.2	.3
1.0	.1	.1	.1				.1	.1
10.1	.6	.3	.5			Sales/Total Assets	.8	.8
3.5	.2	.2	.2				.2	.2
.6	.1	.1	.1				.1	.1
.7	5.4	7.7	5.6			% Depr., Dep., Amort./Sales	5.5	2.5
(28) 2.6	(82) 15.8	(87) 17.2	(37) 16.3				(80) 14.3	(159) 11.9
11.4	23.7	26.2	29.6				22.7	20.3
5.2	3.6	3.4				% Officers', Directors' Owners' Comp/Sales		3.0
(15) 9.3	(11) 9.0	(14) 13.8					(18) 9.7
20.5	23.6	20.4						17.0
44985M	76721M	246160M	408609M	506582M	371174M	Net Sales ($)	780246M	1022142M
12109M	103500M	458790M	819324M	418400M	1051392M	Total Assets ($)	797541M	1596163M

© RMA 2010

M = $ thousand   MM = $ million
See Pages 9 through 22 for Explanation of Ratios and Data

Comparative Historical Data / Current Data Sorted by Sales

Hist 1	Hist 2	Hist 3	Type of Statement	0-1MM	1-3MM	3-5MM	5-10MM	10-25MM	25MM & OVER
12	18	20	Unqualified	2	4	3	1	5	5
11	14	17	Reviewed	5	3	1	2	5	1
32	35	37	Compiled	24	9	2	2		
71	123	108	Tax Returns	86	17	2	2	1	1
106	144	123	Other	63	31	13	8	6	2
4/1/07-3/31/08 ALL	4/1/08-3/31/09 ALL	4/1/09-3/31/10 ALL		17 (4/1-9/30/09)			288 (10/1/09-3/31/10)		
232	334	305	NUMBER OF STATEMENTS	180	64	21	14	17	9
%	%	%	ASSETS	%	%	%	%	%	%
11.9	9.6	12.2	Cash & Equivalents	8.0	19.1	18.3	11.1	20.9	
4.8	5.1	4.3	Trade Receivables (net)	1.0	6.9	4.9	9.6	16.8	
1.3	1.3	1.6	Inventory	.4	3.0	4.2	.1	7.0	
3.6	3.1	3.7	All Other Current	2.0	5.6	7.9	2.4	3.7	
21.5	19.1	21.7	Total Current	11.3	34.6	35.3	23.1	48.4	
64.7	66.5	65.0	Fixed Assets (net)	78.0	50.9	48.2	44.2	37.9	
1.8	2.1	3.2	Intangibles (net)	3.1	3.2	1.7	7.2	3.0	
12.0	12.3	10.0	All Other Non-Current	7.6	11.3	14.8	25.4	10.7	
100.0	100.0	100.0	Total	100.0	100.0	100.0	100.0	100.0	
			LIABILITIES						
6.5	5.6	7.3	Notes Payable-Short Term	5.5	12.4	5.7	10.2	5.4	
2.8	3.4	4.7	Cur. Mat.-L.T.D.	4.5	7.2	3.3	2.6	2.5	
2.9	3.0	2.3	Trade Payables	1.1	2.8	4.8	3.9	6.2	
.1	.1	.0	Income Taxes Payable	.0	.0	.0	.3	.0	
9.4	6.0	10.0	All Other Current	5.3	21.0	11.9	9.8	14.7	
21.7	18.0	24.4	Total Current	16.3	43.4	25.8	26.9	28.9	
51.0	53.9	48.3	Long-Term Debt	61.7	30.9	29.8	26.5	22.7	
.0	.0	.1	Deferred Taxes	.0	.1	.7	.0	.1	
4.0	4.7	5.1	All Other Non-Current	4.1	5.6	3.2	14.5	6.8	
23.3	23.4	22.2	Net Worth	17.9	20.0	40.5	32.2	41.5	
100.0	100.0	100.0	Total Liabilities & Net Worth	100.0	100.0	100.0	100.0	100.0	
			INCOME DATA						
100.0	100.0	100.0	Net Sales	100.0	100.0	100.0	100.0	100.0	
			Gross Profit						
61.4	61.4	65.7	Operating Expenses	55.7	75.3	80.0	79.9	92.7	
38.6	38.6	34.3	Operating Profit	44.3	24.7	20.0	20.1	7.3	
19.7	20.7	18.9	All Other Expenses (net)	26.6	11.1	5.5	7.3	2.9	
18.9	18.0	15.4	Profit Before Taxes	17.8	13.6	14.5	12.8	4.4	
			RATIOS						
2.3	2.8	2.7	Current	2.5	2.2	6.0	3.5	3.6	
.8	.9	.9		.7	.8	.9	1.5	2.6	
.2	.3	.2		.2	.2	.1	.4	1.2	
1.9	2.3	2.2	Quick	2.1	1.6	3.2	3.1	2.8	
.6	.7 (304)	.7		(179) .5	.6	.6	1.3	1.6	
.2	.2	.2		.2	.1	.1	.2	.8	
0 UND	0 UND	0 UND	Sales/Receivables	0 UND	0 UND	0 UND	2 199.8	12 31.1	
0 UND	0 UND	0 UND		0 UND	0 UND	3 105.9	6 59.7	31 11.9	
13 27.2	12 30.7	8 44.6		0 UND	9 39.4	40 9.2	28 12.9	57 6.4	
			Cost of Sales/Inventory						
			Cost of Sales/Payables						
6.3	7.9	5.5	Sales/Working Capital	8.1	4.9	2.2	5.2	3.1	
-35.3	-115.4	-79.7		-28.4	-99.5	-49.3	19.1	5.5	
-3.2	-4.9	-3.4		-3.1	-4.3	-2.9	-5.7	48.0	
8.4	8.6	9.3	EBIT/Interest	6.9	9.4	14.9		22.3	
(93) 4.3	(142) 4.2	(135) 4.2		(56) 4.4	(37) 4.5	(13) 5.8	(12)	1.9	
1.6	1.5	1.7		2.2	2.0	1.1		-2.8	
4.9	5.4	3.5	Net Profit + Depr., Dep., Amort./Cur. Mat. L/T/D						
(10) 2.1	(17) 3.1	(15) 2.4							
1.4	1.7	.6							
.8	1.1	1.0	Fixed/Worth	1.8	.3	.1	.0	.2	
3.3	3.6	3.6		4.7	2.3	1.2	1.2	.9	
64.5	15.3	15.6		21.7	51.8	8.3	6.6	3.4	
.9	1.1	1.0	Debt/Worth	1.3	1.1	.5	.4	.5	
3.4	3.7	3.6		4.7	3.2	1.1	2.3	.9	
114.1	19.3	19.2		30.0	59.9	8.1	8.6	3.4	
47.1	46.6	43.7	% Profit Before Taxes/Tangible Net Worth	34.0	75.0	70.8	89.0	31.2	
(178) 16.7	(272) 14.3	(247) 14.7		(143) 12.7	(50) 22.9	(19) 19.9	(12) 21.5	(14) 6.0	
2.7	3.3	1.9		2.0	.5	4.4	1.5	-5.5	
12.1	9.8	10.9	% Profit Before Taxes/Total Assets	8.3	15.7	19.5	19.8	15.3	
4.1	3.5	3.4		2.7	6.6	5.2	4.0	4.7	
.3	.4	.0		.0	.2	.7	-6.5	-.9	
10.9	4.9	10.3	Sales/Net Fixed Assets	.3	34.6	46.3	299.2	22.5	
.3	.3	.2		.2	4.1	4.0	1.5	3.5	
.2	.2	.1		.1	.2	.2	.2	.4	
1.1	.8	1.0	Sales/Total Assets	.3	2.8	2.0	2.5	2.2	
.2	.2	.2		.2	.5	.4	.5	1.3	
.1	.1	.1		.1	.2	.2	.2	.3	
3.6	5.6	4.2	% Depr., Dep., Amort./Sales	10.9	1.4	.5	3.6	1.3	
(175) 12.2	(266) 14.5	(245) 15.6		(149) 18.6	(49) 7.7	(16) 15.1	(10) 14.2	(15) 5.2	
19.6	22.1	24.5		25.1	19.4	26.3	21.8	19.2	
3.0	4.8	4.1	% Officers', Directors' Owners' Comp/Sales	6.2	2.7				
(23) 5.7	(35) 8.8	(49) 9.8		(18) 15.9	(16) 9.2				
14.4	12.4	19.6		27.2	19.2				
1781986M	3039662M	1654231M	Net Sales ($)	60706M	113072M	78228M	104285M	291247M	1006693M
2403171M	3243923M	2863515M	Total Assets ($)	383945M	368253M	310590M	368926M	614238M	817563M

© RMA 2010

M = $ thousand   MM = $ million
See Pages 9 through 22 for Explanation of Ratios and Data

Current Data Sorted by Assets   Comparative Historical Data

						Type of Statement		
7	6	25	33	12	14	Unqualified	55	91
3	10	20	11	2	2	Reviewed	25	32
16	29	38	11	1		Compiled	52	83
177	291	303	37	4	5	Tax Returns	325	547
74	143	236	99	13	16	Other	227	369
	105 (4/1-9/30/09)		1,533 (10/1/09-3/31/10)				4/1/05-3/31/06 ALL	4/1/06-3/31/07 ALL
0-500M	500M-2MM	2-10MM	10-50MM	50-100MM	100-250MM	NUMBER OF STATEMENTS		
277	479	622	191	32	37		684	1122
%	%	%	%	%	%	ASSETS	%	%
25.5	6.4	5.1	7.1	9.6	6.9	Cash & Equivalents	12.0	10.9
6.1	4.2	3.4	6.6	10.8	7.9	Trade Receivables (net)	6.5	5.2
8.0	11.1	13.7	18.5	16.1	9.0	Inventory	16.3	20.0
3.6	2.4	2.2	4.7	3.8	2.2	All Other Current	4.1	5.1
43.2	24.1	24.4	36.9	40.3	25.9	Total Current	38.9	41.2
39.4	63.4	62.0	42.4	30.9	31.8	Fixed Assets (net)	43.2	41.1
3.1	1.7	2.2	1.7	4.7	7.6	Intangibles (net)	2.5	2.3
14.4	10.8	11.4	19.0	24.1	34.7	All Other Non-Current	15.4	15.4
100.0	100.0	100.0	100.0	100.0	100.0	Total	100.0	100.0
						LIABILITIES		
23.3	8.2	8.2	11.5	15.9	12.0	Notes Payable-Short Term	16.9	16.3
6.0	4.3	3.7	2.3	2.6	2.6	Cur. Mat.-L.T.D.	3.2	3.0
4.7	2.7	2.0	2.3	3.8	4.1	Trade Payables	4.0	3.4
.2	.0	.1	.1	.0	.0	Income Taxes Payable	.1	.1
28.5	7.6	7.2	9.0	9.9	7.8	All Other Current	10.0	11.0
62.7	22.8	21.1	25.2	32.2	26.5	Total Current	34.2	33.9
31.2	55.1	53.4	44.6	28.6	35.3	Long-Term Debt	36.5	36.6
.1	.1	.0	.3	.9	.6	Deferred Taxes	.1	.1
6.8	4.3	4.4	6.9	4.7	6.0	All Other Non-Current	5.2	4.7
-.7	17.8	21.0	23.0	33.5	31.5	Net Worth	23.9	24.8
100.0	100.0	100.0	100.0	100.0	100.0	Total Liabilties & Net Worth	100.0	100.0
						INCOME DATA		
100.0	100.0	100.0	100.0	100.0	100.0	Net Sales	100.0	100.0
						Gross Profit		
77.9	64.7	67.2	73.5	77.4	76.8	Operating Expenses	74.0	73.1
22.1	35.3	32.8	26.5	22.6	23.2	Operating Profit	26.0	26.9
8.8	23.3	24.7	15.8	11.7	13.7	All Other Expenses (net)	10.9	12.1
13.3	12.0	8.1	10.7	11.0	9.5	Profit Before Taxes	15.1	14.7
						RATIOS		
2.5	2.2	2.2	4.3	5.0	3.0	Current	3.9	3.1
.8	.8	.8	1.4	1.3	1.4		1.2	1.2
.2	.2	.2	.4	.7	.4		.3	.4
1.4	1.2	1.1	2.2	1.6	2.6	Quick	2.1	1.5
.4	.4	.3	(189) .4	.8	(36) .4		(682) .4	(1120) .3
.1	.1	.0	.1	.1	.1		.1	.1
0 UND	0 UND	0 UND	0 UND	0 UND	0 UND	Sales/Receivables	0 UND	0 UND
0 UND	0 UND	0 UND	1 638.0	9 38.7	7 49.4		0 UND	0 UND
0 891.9	0 UND	5 72.0	23 15.6	70 5.2	40 9.1		8 45.4	8 47.7
						Cost of Sales/Inventory		
						Cost of Sales/Payables		
8.7	6.2	3.5	1.4	1.6	1.9	Sales/Working Capital	3.4	2.7
-50.6	-21.2	-18.3	10.3	4.1	9.1		25.5	24.1
-4.0	-3.1	-2.1	-5.2	NM	-3.2		-5.5	-5.1
6.4	10.7	5.0	14.9	14.9	6.6	EBIT/Interest	23.9	10.9
(113) 2.2	(183) 3.3	(245) 2.0	(91) 3.4	(20) 4.4	(19) 3.2		(382) 5.3	(569) 3.8
-2.0	.5	.8	.9	.5	1.5		1.8	1.3
	3.8	5.2	14.5			Net Profit + Depr., Dep., Amort./Cur. Mat. L/T/D	12.5	2.9
	(10) 1.9	(11) 1.8	(12) 5.7				(17) 3.3	(21) 1.4
	.9	.1	1.9				1.9	.4
.0	.8	1.0	.0	.0	.0	Fixed/Worth	.1	.0
1.6	3.7	3.7	1.6	.8	.7		1.5	1.1
-98.3	193.4	21.8	7.7	4.1	4.8		9.5	6.5
.7	1.4	1.7	1.2	.8	.9	Debt/Worth	1.0	1.0
4.5	5.4	5.4	3.7	4.5	3.1		3.9	3.8
-6.2	-141.0	53.0	23.3	25.9	6.6		24.7	26.1
100.0	40.4	27.5	26.5	61.1	25.1	% Profit Before Taxes/Tangible Net Worth	79.5	71.8
(181) 22.1	(356) 10.3	(492) 7.4	(156) 8.3	(27) 14.8	(32) 5.8		(559) 30.5	(920) 22.0
.0	.0	-1.3	.0	1.8	-1.7		5.3	4.2
24.2	8.1	4.0	6.0	7.7	6.4	% Profit Before Taxes/Total Assets	16.4	13.5
5.5	2.0	1.2	1.8	2.9	2.4		5.0	4.1
-4.5	-1.0	-.9	-.2	-1.1	-1.2		.4	.2
UND	8.6	3.8	70.6	31.5	129.7	Sales/Net Fixed Assets	76.2	273.3
16.5	.2	.2	1.1	3.3	9.3		3.7	5.3
.3	.1	.1	.2	.4	.2		.3	.3
5.9	.6	.3	.6	.5	.7	Sales/Total Assets	1.6	1.4
1.6	.2	.1	.2	.2	.3		.5	.5
.2	.1	.1	.1	.1	.1		.2	.2
1.3	5.7	4.6	1.2	1.6	.4	% Depr., Dep., Amort./Sales	.8	.9
(147) 4.8	(338) 16.3	(444) 17.2	(120) 10.2	(20) 5.6	(25) 3.9		(420) 4.4	(635) 5.6
16.7	24.1	26.6	20.5	10.8	22.0		16.5	16.9
4.0	2.6	1.8	.4			% Officers', Directors' Owners' Comp/Sales	2.3	2.1
(57) 11.9	(60) 5.8	(76) 4.7	(18) 1.8				(139) 4.6	(184) 5.4
23.4	12.4	10.5	3.3				12.0	14.4
164361M	408525M	1289356M	2426786M	1270186M	4118641M	Net Sales ($)	6046473M	9758464M
65962M	567616M	2861394M	4181592M	2244981M	5830165M	Total Assets ($)	8234480M	12207747M

M = $ thousand   MM = $ million

See Pages 9 through 22 for Explanation of Ratios and Data

Comparative Historical Data | Current Data Sorted by Sales

			Type of Statement						
88	101	97	Unqualified	16	19	9	7	17	29
37	46	48	Reviewed	17	7	2	8	10	4
106	95	95	Compiled	48	27	8	6	6	
625	743	817	Tax Returns	634	118	27	24	7	7
471	571	581	Other	337	113	40	34	27	30
4/1/07-3/31/08 ALL	4/1/08-3/31/09 ALL	4/1/09-3/31/10 ALL		105 (4/1-9/30/09)			1,533 (10/1/09-3/31/10)		
				0-1MM	1-3MM	3-5MM	5-10MM	10-25MM	25MM & OVER
1327	1556	1638	NUMBER OF STATEMENTS	1052	284	86	79	67	70
%	%	%	ASSETS	%	%	%	%	%	%
8.9	9.7	9.3	Cash & Equivalents	7.7	12.7	11.8	9.0	14.5	12.2
5.0	4.6	4.7	Trade Receivables (net)	2.1	6.0	10.0	10.8	13.7	15.7
18.6	13.8	12.5	Inventory	9.9	16.1	17.1	21.5	14.9	18.1
4.8	3.4	2.8	All Other Current	2.0	3.0	7.4	5.0	4.0	6.2
37.3	31.5	29.3	Total Current	21.7	37.8	46.2	46.2	47.0	52.3
45.7	53.3	55.0	Fixed Assets (net)	65.6	40.8	36.0	32.4	31.5	24.0
2.0	1.5	2.3	Intangibles (net)	1.8	2.7	2.4	4.5	2.9	5.6
15.0	13.7	13.4	All Other Non-Current	10.9	18.6	15.3	16.9	18.6	18.2
100.0	100.0	100.0	Total	100.0	100.0	100.0	100.0	100.0	100.0
			LIABILITIES						
13.8	11.1	11.4	Notes Payable-Short Term	9.0	17.9	15.0	12.0	10.2	16.4
4.2	4.2	4.0	Cur. Mat.-L.T.D.	4.5	3.1	3.5	3.5	4.7	1.9
3.3	2.7	2.8	Trade Payables	1.2	3.5	6.3	8.0	6.2	10.2
.1	.0	.1	Income Taxes Payable	.0	.2	.1	.1	.0	.1
10.2	10.4	11.2	All Other Current	10.0	13.8	12.7	13.3	11.9	14.0
31.5	28.4	29.4	Total Current	24.7	38.5	37.7	36.9	33.0	42.6
42.5	48.3	48.2	Long-Term Debt	55.0	41.9	34.1	30.1	35.0	22.1
.1	.2	.1	Deferred Taxes	.0	.1	.1	.1	1.3	.3
5.0	5.1	5.1	All Other Non-Current	4.3	5.5	11.3	8.8	3.7	5.5
20.9	17.9	17.1	Net Worth	16.0	14.0	16.8	24.1	27.0	29.6
100.0	100.0	100.0	Total Liabilities & Net Worth	100.0	100.0	100.0	100.0	100.0	100.0
			INCOME DATA						
100.0	100.0	100.0	Net Sales	100.0	100.0	100.0	100.0	100.0	100.0
			Gross Profit						
70.9	70.8	69.4	Operating Expenses	61.9	80.3	80.5	90.2	84.0	86.7
29.1	29.2	30.6	Operating Profit	38.1	19.7	19.5	9.8	16.0	13.3
16.6	19.0	20.1	All Other Expenses (net)	26.8	10.3	8.5	4.9	6.6	3.6
12.5	10.2	10.5	Profit Before Taxes	11.3	9.5	11.0	4.9	9.4	9.6
			RATIOS						
2.6	2.7	2.5	Current	2.1	3.8	4.4	3.8	3.5	2.0
1.1	1.0	.9		.6	1.1	1.3	1.5	1.5	1.3
.3	.2	.2		.1	.2	.6	.7	.8	.8
1.3	1.5	1.3	Quick	1.0	1.8	1.3	1.7	2.6	1.3
(1326) .3	(1555) .4	(1635) .3		.3	.4	(84) .4	.6	.8	(69) .5
.1	.1	.1		.0	.1	.1	.2	.2	.2
0 UND	0 UND	0 UND	Sales/Receivables	0 UND	0 UND	0 UND	0 UND	0 999.8	0 UND
0 UND	0 UND	0 UND		0 UND	0 UND	1 266.5	5 73.1	11 33.3	8 43.0
8 45.1	7 50.9	5 69.6		0 UND	12 29.5	19 18.9	52 7.0	37 9.8	41 8.8
			Cost of Sales/Inventory						
			Cost of Sales/Payables						
2.7	3.0	3.8	Sales/Working Capital	4.9	2.3	2.0	2.1	2.5	4.7
45.7	UND	-50.6		-10.6	40.9	24.8	9.4	13.3	14.7
-4.5	-3.0	-2.8		-1.9	-4.6	-13.4	-29.4	-25.6	-65.3
8.8	8.0	7.2	EBIT/Interest	6.0	4.9	11.9	10.2	19.4	27.8
(598) 2.8	(632) 2.4	(671) 2.6		(299) 2.5	(166) 1.9	(49) 2.2	(61) 2.2	(45) 5.0	(51) 6.5
.8	.3	.6		.4	.3	.4	.2	1.5	1.7
6.7	5.8	6.6	Net Profit + Depr., Dep., Amort./Cur. Mat. L/T/D	2.2					51.5
(35) 2.2	(42) 2.5	(45) 2.4		(13) 1.4				(11) 8.0	
.9	.5	.8		.8					1.3
.0	.2	.3	Fixed/Worth	1.0	.0	.0	.1	.1	.0
1.8	2.8	2.8		4.1	1.7	1.4	.8	.8	.4
17.2	45.7	27.1		82.5	23.5	-18.7	13.3	3.3	3.4
1.3	1.4	1.3	Debt/Worth	1.5	1.1	1.0	1.0	.7	1.1
4.4	5.0	4.9		5.8	3.8	3.8	3.6	2.8	3.2
90.5	UND	942.6		-417.5	NM	-20.6	26.1	13.1	8.3
48.8	37.5	36.4	% Profit Before Taxes/Tangible Net Worth	28.4	51.5	42.7	34.0	68.5	102.0
(1030) 15.4	(1169) 10.9	(1244) 9.6		(786) 7.7	(213) 12.6	(61) 15.1	(65) 10.9	(57) 15.8	(62) 26.8
.8	-.9	-.7		-1.3	-.5	3.7	-1.5	1.9	13.0
10.3	6.8	7.0	% Profit Before Taxes/Total Assets	5.3	9.3	12.2	6.2	17.1	19.8
2.6	1.6	1.7		1.2	2.4	3.9	1.8	4.8	7.0
-.4	-1.1	-.9		-1.0	-1.1	3.7	-1.3	-.1	1.9
98.8	25.0	25.2	Sales/Net Fixed Assets	2.6	68.9	177.7	83.1	79.7	96.0
1.9	.6	.4		.2	4.2	6.3	10.6	11.4	23.8
.2	.1	.1		.1	.4	.6	1.1	.7	4.2
1.1	.7	.7	Sales/Total Assets	.3	1.5	2.0	2.2	2.3	3.4
.3	.2	.2		.1	.5	.7	.9	.7	1.4
.1	.1	.1		.1	.2	.2	.2	.3	.5
1.6	2.1	2.8	% Depr., Dep., Amort./Sales	10.3	.8	1.2	.8	.7	.4
(810) 8.9	(1023) 12.3	(1094) 13.9		(718) 18.2	(174) 4.0	(50) 4.4	(55) 2.3	(44) 2.2	(53) 1.2
18.4	21.4	23.4		26.9	18.3	15.7	7.3	8.1	3.5
2.2	1.9	2.1	% Officers', Directors' Owners' Comp/Sales	3.9	2.5	1.8	1.0	.8	
(195) 5.1	(212) 5.0	(218) 5.1		(94) 9.0	(64) 6.9	(20) 3.3	(19) 1.8	(12) 2.5	
14.3	12.1	12.6		18.9	12.5	10.2	3.7	4.8	
10404961M	8493209M	9677855M	Net Sales ($)	351885M	506445M	330914M	552821M	1050261M	6885529M
15187587M	14557198M	15751710M	Total Assets ($)	2667732M	1973597M	1001894M	1867747M	2854377M	5386363M

M = $ thousand   MM = $ million
See Pages 9 through 22 for Explanation of Ratios and Data

Current Data Sorted by Assets

Comparative Historical Data

	0-500M	500M-2MM	2-10MM	10-50MM	50-100MM	100-250MM	Type of Statement	4/1/05-3/31/06 ALL	4/1/06-3/31/07 ALL
		2	1	12	4	7	Unqualified	20	20
		2	8	7			Reviewed	24	13
	1	2	14	4			Compiled	29	24
	14	6	11				Tax Returns	15	20
	4	5	20	5	6	2	Other	39	35
		25 (4/1-9/30/09)		112 (10/1/09-3/31/10)					
NUMBER OF STATEMENTS	19	17	54	28	10	9		127	112
	%	%	%	%	%	%	**ASSETS**	%	%
	20.0	12.9	8.7	10.7	7.7		Cash & Equivalents	7.4	6.7
	8.3	3.3	8.7	5.6	12.7		Trade Receivables (net)	5.7	5.8
	3.1	16.4	9.2	22.0	25.6		Inventory	13.3	15.1
	2.3	5.5	4.8	4.0	1.8		All Other Current	8.9	8.8
	33.7	38.2	31.5	42.3	47.9		Total Current	35.3	36.5
	57.1	46.5	59.2	49.3	40.9		Fixed Assets (net)	53.4	53.7
	.0	1.3	1.4	2.6	6.0		Intangibles (net)	3.9	3.1
	9.2	14.0	7.9	5.8	5.3		All Other Non-Current	7.4	6.7
	100.0	100.0	100.0	100.0	100.0		Total	100.0	100.0
							LIABILITIES		
	36.2	24.8	21.7	30.6	16.9		Notes Payable-Short Term	32.2	32.2
	4.2	6.3	6.5	7.9	18.3		Cur. Mat.-L.T.D.	6.7	7.1
	14.0	3.6	4.3	3.6	3.1		Trade Payables	9.3	5.6
	.1	.2	.1	.3	.3		Income Taxes Payable	.2	.1
	21.2	9.5	6.5	8.1	14.5		All Other Current	6.3	9.5
	75.7	44.4	39.1	50.5	53.1		Total Current	54.7	54.5
	31.3	24.6	38.1	19.3	21.7		Long-Term Debt	26.1	31.8
	.0	.7	.4	.9	.4		Deferred Taxes	.7	.5
	3.6	.2	3.3	2.5	4.7		All Other Non-Current	4.3	2.7
	-10.5	30.2	19.0	26.8	20.0		Net Worth	14.2	10.4
	100.0	100.0	100.0	100.0	100.0		Total Liabilities & Net Worth	100.0	100.0
							INCOME DATA		
	100.0	100.0	100.0	100.0	100.0		Net Sales	100.0	100.0
							Gross Profit		
	85.1	83.6	90.0	91.8	94.0		Operating Expenses	93.1	92.8
	14.9	16.4	10.0	8.2	6.0		Operating Profit	6.9	7.2
	3.2	2.9	3.0	3.9	2.2		All Other Expenses (net)	2.9	4.4
	11.7	13.5	6.9	4.2	3.8		Profit Before Taxes	4.0	2.8
							RATIOS		
	1.2	2.0	1.8	1.5	2.6			1.3	1.3
	.5	.8	.8	.9	1.2		Current	.8	.6
	.2	.2	.3	.3	.2			.2	.2
	1.1	.9	1.1	.7	1.6			.6	.5
	.5	.3	.4	.3	.2		Quick	.2	.2
	.2	.1	.1	.1	.1			.1	.1
	0 UND	0 UND	5 81.1	8 48.5	9 39.0			4 90.9	3 121.3
	2 176.8	2 156.6	12 31.4	16 22.7	19 19.1		Sales/Receivables	12 31.3	10 37.9
	23 15.5	28 12.9	34 10.7	28 13.2	26 13.8			24 15.3	23 15.6
							Cost of Sales/Inventory		
							Cost of Sales/Payables		
	19.0	3.7	12.2	4.4	3.9			18.6	8.4
	-14.2	-19.2	-39.1	-61.9	11.1		Sales/Working Capital	-20.7	-12.7
	-2.6	-3.0	-3.6	-1.7	-1.8			-2.2	-2.2
	9.1	9.4	4.8	3.3				3.2	2.3
	(14) 5.8	(15) 3.6	(48) 1.9	(26) 1.5			EBIT/Interest	(113) 1.7	(101) 1.2
	.7	1.0	1.1	.7				1.1	.9
									20.0	3.6
							Net Profit + Depr., Dep., Amort./Cur. Mat. L/T/D	(11) 5.8	(11) 1.6
								1.1	.6
	.6	.6	1.1	.2	1.2			.7	.6
	1.5	2.3	2.8	3.4	2.5		Fixed/Worth	3.6	3.8
	-5.4	NM	10.3	9.0	6.5			14.4	15.0
	1.3	.9	2.0	2.2	4.4			2.0	2.2
	3.1	2.8	4.4	4.9	7.0		Debt/Worth	5.3	7.2
	-6.5	NM	15.3	24.7	10.5			32.5	38.9
	114.5	48.8	29.3	30.2	40.1		% Profit Before Taxes/Tangible Net Worth	36.1	25.7
	(14) 45.6	(13) 24.1	(46) 10.2	(26) 6.5	23.0			(104) 14.8	(91) 7.3
	13.0	1.2	3.3	-7.6	15.0			3.7	.0
	22.1	19.2	7.6	5.2	4.0		% Profit Before Taxes/Total Assets	6.9	7.4
	7.8	1.9	3.0	1.7	2.4			2.6	1.6
	-1.4	-.4	.4	-.7	1.2			-.5	-.5
	6.4	33.8	5.2	17.8	8.1		Sales/Net Fixed Assets	15.9	17.3
	2.2	2.1	1.3	1.6	2.4			2.0	2.0
	1.0	1.2	.8	.7	1.3			.8	.8
	2.7	1.5	1.5	1.1	1.1		Sales/Total Assets	1.7	1.8
	.9	.7	.8	.8	.9			.8	.8
	.5	.5	.6	.6	.5			.5	.5
	5.8	12.5	7.6	14.3			% Depr., Dep., Amort./Sales	5.1	9.7
	(13) 17.9	(13) 21.7	(43) 23.8	(19) 32.8				(88) 18.7	(79) 20.1
	54.3	44.6	32.7	42.3				35.0	39.0
			2.2				% Officers', Directors' Owners' Comp/Sales	1.9	1.7
			(20) 2.9					(50) 3.7	(41) 3.6
			7.1					7.2	6.8
	7635M	32467M	367789M	551938M	607334M	568756M	Net Sales ($)	2368035M	1968403M
	4795M	18408M	252803M	589217M	691266M	1137397M	Total Assets ($)	2300971M	1885448M

M = $ thousand   MM = $ million
See Pages 9 through 22 for Explanation of Ratios and Data

Comparative Historical Data   Current Data Sorted by Sales

4/1/07-3/31/08 ALL	4/1/08-3/31/09 ALL	4/1/09-3/31/10 ALL	Type of Statement	0-1MM	1-3MM	3-5MM	5-10MM	10-25MM	25MM & OVER
23	24	26	Unqualified	1	1		4	8	12
14	14	17	Reviewed		3	1	4	6	3
19	14	21	Compiled	2	9	4	5	1	
11	10	31	Tax Returns	20	6	2	1	2	
30	34	42	Other	8	11	4	3	7	9
				25 (4/1-9/30/09)		112 (10/1/09-3/31/10)			
97	96	137	**NUMBER OF STATEMENTS**	31	30	11	17	24	24
%	%	%	**ASSETS**	%	%	%	%	%	%
6.8	8.3	10.9	Cash & Equivalents	13.0	11.3	3.7	14.2	11.7	7.6
4.6	6.7	7.9	Trade Receivables (net)	5.3	7.0	3.4	5.4	3.8	20.1
17.8	16.0	12.5	Inventory	8.5	3.5	27.4	14.0	21.2	12.4
8.1	3.8	4.7	All Other Current	3.3	1.7	6.5	1.7	10.8	5.7
37.3	34.9	36.0	Total Current	30.1	23.4	41.0	35.3	47.6	45.8
53.5	52.4	53.2	Fixed Assets (net)	55.8	69.6	44.0	56.7	44.1	40.4
3.2	2.8	2.2	Intangibles (net)	.1	.6	1.9	2.9	3.3	5.6
5.9	9.9	8.6	All Other Non-Current	14.1	6.4	13.1	5.1	5.1	8.2
100.0	100.0	100.0	Total	100.0	100.0	100.0	100.0	100.0	100.0
			LIABILITIES						
34.9	27.6	27.4	Notes Payable-Short Term	26.2	20.6	36.7	23.8	32.6	30.5
6.1	7.6	7.2	Cur. Mat.-L.T.D.	3.1	8.1	2.8	10.6	7.2	10.8
3.9	4.5	5.2	Trade Payables	3.7	8.8	1.1	3.3	2.9	8.2
.2	.1	.2	Income Taxes Payable	.2	.0	.5	.5	.0	.5
5.9	6.6	9.8	All Other Current	13.7	9.1	3.2	5.6	9.8	11.4
51.1	46.4	49.7	Total Current	46.9	46.6	44.3	43.7	52.5	61.3
26.2	32.8	28.9	Long-Term Debt	35.3	35.5	45.5	22.3	22.2	15.8
.7	.7	.5	Deferred Taxes	.4	.0	.6	.5	1.2	.8
4.5	4.5	2.7	All Other Non-Current	2.5	3.5	10.0	.6	1.3	1.7
17.5	15.6	18.1	Net Worth	15.0	14.3	-.5	32.9	22.9	20.4
100.0	100.0	100.0	Total Liabilities & Net Worth	100.0	100.0	100.0	100.0	100.0	100.0
			INCOME DATA						
100.0	100.0	100.0	Net Sales	100.0	100.0	100.0	100.0	100.0	100.0
			Gross Profit						
91.9	94.6	89.0	Operating Expenses	75.0	92.9	95.6	92.4	93.7	92.5
8.1	5.4	11.0	Operating Profit	25.0	7.1	4.4	7.6	6.3	7.5
6.8	3.0	3.3	All Other Expenses (net)	7.3	1.1	2.2	.4	3.9	2.9
1.3	2.4	7.7	Profit Before Taxes	17.7	6.0	2.2	7.2	2.4	4.6
			RATIOS						
1.2	1.5	1.5	Current	2.0	1.5	1.5	3.1	1.9	1.2
.7	.9	.8		.8	.5	1.0	1.0	.9	.9
.2	.3	.2		.1	.2	.5	.3	.4	.2
.5	.9	.9	Quick	1.1	1.3	.5	1.9	.6	.8
.2	.3	.3		.3	.4	.4	.4	.3	.2
.1	.1	.1		.1	.2	.0	.1	.1	.1
4 90.4	3 131.9	3 107.1	Sales/Receivables	0 UND	2 161.6	7 49.1	6 65.8	4 82.5	17 22.1
13 28.9	12 31.1	13 28.3		0 UND	12 31.7	11 33.5	14 26.5	11 32.8	27 13.5
25 14.7	30 12.3	29 12.4		26 14.2	45 8.2	28 13.2	29 12.5	25 14.4	36 10.1
			Cost of Sales/Inventory						
			Cost of Sales/Payables						
10.3	11.0	10.7	Sales/Working Capital	6.3	26.4	2.6	6.0	5.2	11.7
-24.3	-79.8	-19.7		-9.2	-12.5	141.7	140.7	-58.0	-37.6
-2.4	-3.1	-2.2		-2.0	-3.0	-2.0	-2.7	-2.3	-1.5
1.8	2.6	5.8	EBIT/Interest	12.5	4.7	2.1	7.0	3.1	6.0
(84) 1.1	(89) 1.4	(120) 1.7		(22) 6.7	(29) 1.6	1.1	(15) 2.4	(21) 1.4	(22) 2.3
.7	.5	1.1		1.0	1.1	.6	.5	.9	1.5
19.3	12.0	6.5	Net Profit + Depr., Dep., Amort./Cur. Mat. L/T/D						
(10) 3.6	(10) 2.7	(14) 2.8							
1.6	1.4	.8							
.3	.4	.7	Fixed/Worth	.6	1.7	.4	.5	.2	.6
3.2	3.4	2.6		1.5	3.7	2.1	2.6	3.4	2.5
11.1	16.2	8.6		17.1	9.1	10.4	5.0	35.3	6.5
2.4	2.3	1.9	Debt/Worth	.8	2.3	2.1	1.3	3.1	4.2
6.1	7.3	4.3		1.9	3.3	12.8	3.1	5.6	6.7
17.3	33.8	15.6		19.0	9.3	66.5	6.0	41.4	14.9
22.6	32.1	39.6	% Profit Before Taxes/Tangible Net Worth	59.6	24.3		53.6	100.5	32.0
(85) 11.0	(76) 14.3	(117) 15.4		(25) 24.9	(24) 7.7		(16) 16.4	(21) 10.2	(22) 22.1
-4.1	.2	2.1		1.9	1.8		8.6	.6	10.0
3.7	5.5	7.6	% Profit Before Taxes/Total Assets	21.2	6.1	4.8	11.5	5.2	5.9
1.1	2.0	2.7		4.4	1.9	.4	4.2	2.1	2.7
-1.2	-2.3	.2		-1.1	.7	-.7	.4	.2	1.7
12.5	19.1	6.5	Sales/Net Fixed Assets	4.3	2.2	29.5	5.5	58.5	12.9
1.4	1.4	1.5		1.4	1.0	2.1	1.9	2.3	2.1
.8	.8	.8		.6	.7	.9	1.2	1.3	.8
1.1	1.2	1.2	Sales/Total Assets	.9	1.1	.9	1.6	1.4	1.2
.7	.7	.7		.6	.8	.6	1.2	1.0	.7
.5	.6	.5		.3	.6	.6	.6	.7	.5
11.4	14.7	7.9	% Depr., Dep., Amort./Sales	10.7	21.3		7.0	5.8	.2
(66) 21.5	(59) 31.6	(94) 22.7		(22) 28.1	(26) 30.8		(14) 13.8	(15) 21.4	(10) 4.6
37.1	43.9	38.4		51.7	47.7		25.9	40.4	25.0
2.1	1.0	1.5	% Officers', Directors' Owners' Comp/Sales						
(31) 4.0	(33) 2.8	(40) 2.9							
7.3	4.4	7.2							
1373745M	1820826M	2135919M	Net Sales ($)	10630M	64365M	41922M	130008M	360672M	1528322M
1865883M	2034269M	2693886M	Total Assets ($)	32012M	103896M	61576M	152729M	426651M	1917022M

M = $ thousand   MM = $ million
See Pages 9 through 22 for Explanation of Ratios and Data

Current Data Sorted by Assets   Comparative Historical Data

Type of Statement

	0-500M	500M-2MM	2-10MM	10-50MM	50-100MM	100-250MM	Type of Statement	4/1/05-3/31/06 ALL	4/1/06-3/31/07 ALL
	1		2	15	4	5	Unqualified	26	28
			8	14		2	Reviewed	40	29
	3	4	12	8			Compiled	29	24
	8	6	3	1			Tax Returns	15	11
	4	3	14	9	5	3	Other	36	41
	26 (4/1-9/30/09)		108 (10/1/09-3/31/10)						
NUMBER OF STATEMENTS	16	13	39	47	9	10		146	133

0-500M %	500M-2MM %	2-10MM %	10-50MM %	50-100MM %	100-250MM %		4/1/05-3/31/06 %	4/1/06-3/31/07 %
						ASSETS		
17.0	4.0	4.3	4.2		8.7	Cash & Equivalents	6.9	6.0
9.7	6.4	12.6	7.6		4.2	Trade Receivables (net)	10.2	8.9
4.0	.7	8.6	4.0		1.1	Inventory	7.8	7.9
.6	4.6	10.1	2.1		1.3	All Other Current	5.0	7.5
31.4	15.7	35.6	17.8		15.4	Total Current	29.9	30.3
60.6	78.8	46.2	50.4		46.2	Fixed Assets (net)	45.4	48.8
.0	.0	1.2	1.7		.4	Intangibles (net)	2.1	1.7
8.1	5.5	17.0	30.1		38.0	All Other Non-Current	22.6	19.1
100.0	100.0	100.0	100.0		100.0	Total	100.0	100.0
						LIABILITIES		
19.6	.9	8.7	12.7		14.4	Notes Payable-Short Term	16.3	16.6
15.0	21.4	9.6	5.8		4.2	Cur. Mat.-L.T.D.	8.6	8.4
.6	.5	6.1	1.8		1.5	Trade Payables	5.0	5.2
.9	.0	.1	.3		.0	Income Taxes Payable	.3	.3
24.2	5.0	5.7	3.5		4.4	All Other Current	3.9	6.7
60.3	27.8	30.3	24.2		24.6	Total Current	34.0	37.2
34.8	75.0	50.9	59.2		52.9	Long-Term Debt	46.7	40.7
.0	.4	.9	1.2		1.6	Deferred Taxes	.8	.8
2.1	2.5	12.0	3.3		1.8	All Other Non-Current	4.8	4.4
2.8	-5.6	6.0	12.2		19.2	Net Worth	13.7	16.9
100.0	100.0	100.0	100.0		100.0	Total Liabilties & Net Worth	100.0	100.0
						INCOME DATA		
100.0	100.0	100.0	100.0		100.0	Net Sales	100.0	100.0
						Gross Profit		
86.2	97.7	84.1	89.5		78.5	Operating Expenses	85.9	84.9
13.8	2.3	15.9	10.5		21.5	Operating Profit	14.1	15.1
9.6	2.8	13.4	9.7		13.9	All Other Expenses (net)	7.8	7.7
4.3	-.5	2.5	.8		7.6	Profit Before Taxes	6.3	7.4
						RATIOS		
1.0	1.7	7.8	3.5		4.1	Current	2.2	1.8
.5	.7	1.3	1.2		1.1		1.0	1.0
.2	.2	.2	.3		.2		.3	.2
1.0	1.4	7.1	1.5		2.1	Quick	1.6	1.1
.5	.3	.3	.8		.7		.4	.3
.1	.1	.2	.2		.2		.1	.1
0 UND	0 UND	7 52.8	10 38.0		9 42.4	Sales/Receivables	2 181.7	2 199.5
0 UND	6 61.8	30 12.1	15 23.8		23 15.9		12 29.9	12 31.1
11 32.1	22 16.4	59 6.2	27 13.3		29 12.4		43 8.4	36 10.3
						Cost of Sales/Inventory		
						Cost of Sales/Payables		
NM	14.6	1.9	5.0		2.9	Sales/Working Capital	5.4	4.0
-13.6	-4.7	10.9	166.1		73.3		59.0	-275.8
-1.5	-1.9	-2.2	-4.0		-6.8		-2.8	-1.9
		2.4	2.0			EBIT/Interest	3.2	3.2
	(29)	1.2	(39) 1.3				(111) 1.6	(101) 1.5
		.9	1.0				1.1	1.2
						Net Profit + Depr., Dep., Amort./Cur. Mat. L/T/D	1.4	1.6
							(15) 1.0	(13) .7
							.2	.3
1.7	2.1	1.7	.8		.0	Fixed/Worth	.1	.2
7.6	-100.5	10.7	5.5		2.9		2.8	2.6
-4.4	-2.1	-10.1	9.6		3.5		13.0	8.1
4.3	2.2	3.7	5.6		2.7	Debt/Worth	3.4	3.0
-17.7	-121.0	15.7	9.6		3.3		9.5	6.7
-5.8	-3.6	-22.4	21.3		14.5		33.4	17.3
		58.3	21.0			% Profit Before Taxes/Tangible Net Worth	34.0	38.8
	(26)	10.9	(45) 9.2				(122) 16.9	(119) 15.7
		.0	1.7				5.7	8.3
22.5	4.3	3.6	2.4		3.4	% Profit Before Taxes/Total Assets	4.1	5.1
5.4	1.8	.9	.9		3.0		1.7	2.0
-1.9	-5.2	.0	.1		.8		.5	.8
219.2	.9	18.7	8.2		36.7	Sales/Net Fixed Assets	92.3	29.9
.7	.6	1.5	.7		1.0		1.5	1.1
.5	.4	.5	.5		.4		.6	.5
3.6	.7	1.3	.6		.8	Sales/Total Assets	.8	.7
.4	.5	.4	.4		.5		.5	.5
.3	.3	.3	.3		.2		.3	.3
17.1	63.1	3.0	5.4			% Depr., Dep., Amort./Sales	2.2	8.0
(12) 53.3	77.2	(28) 32.6	(27) 24.4				(103) 26.8	(90) 39.9
84.4	88.4	66.4	39.9				57.1	63.7
		2.5	2.5			% Officers', Directors' Owners' Comp/Sales	1.0	1.1
	(15)	5.0	(16) 3.6				(36) 3.5	(29) 3.8
		10.4	4.9				5.9	6.4
18145M	8329M	195134M	704812M	243580M	562376M	Net Sales ($)	1602702M	1453113M
3571M	16067M	203640M	1253035M	637372M	1415944M	Total Assets ($)	3365730M	3132974M

© RMA 2010

M = $ thousand   MM = $ million

See Pages 9 through 22 for Explanation of Ratios and Data

Comparative Historical Data | Current Data Sorted by Sales

			Type of Statement						
22	23	27	Unqualified	1		3	3	15	5
23	27	24	Reviewed	1	4	4	9	5	1
30	18	27	Compiled	9	6	6	4	2	
13	21	18	Tax Returns	11	4		1	2	
59	60	38	Other	9	5	5	4	8	7
4/1/07-3/31/08 ALL	4/1/08-3/31/09 ALL	4/1/09-3/31/10 ALL			26 (4/1-9/30/09)			108 (10/1/09-3/31/10)	
				0-1MM	1-3MM	3-5MM	5-10MM	10-25MM	25MM & OVER
147	149	134	NUMBER OF STATEMENTS	31	19	18	21	32	13
%	%	%		%	%	%	%	%	%
5.8	5.5	6.0	Cash & Equivalents	9.7	5.2	5.2	2.9	6.5	3.7
9.8	13.2	9.0	Trade Receivables (net)	8.0	10.2	6.9	11.5	8.0	11.2
6.9	6.6	4.6	Inventory	.3	3.6	8.5	6.1	5.5	6.1
7.7	8.4	4.7	All Other Current	5.5	7.2	4.8	3.3	4.0	2.5
30.2	33.7	24.4	Total Current	23.6	26.3	25.4	23.8	24.1	23.7
45.8	46.4	53.3	Fixed Assets (net)	66.1	54.0	40.7	50.2	47.4	59.2
1.4	1.2	1.0	Intangibles (net)	.0	4.1	.5	.1	.2	2.7
22.6	18.7	21.3	All Other Non-Current	10.3	15.6	33.4	25.9	28.3	14.5
100.0	100.0	100.0	Total	100.0	100.0	100.0	100.0	100.0	100.0
			LIABILITIES						
18.5	16.9	10.8	Notes Payable-Short Term	9.1	11.6	3.8	4.3	15.1	23.2
7.0	8.1	9.8	Cur. Mat.-L.T.D.	13.7	6.0	15.1	7.1	11.0	.2
3.4	3.2	2.8	Trade Payables	.6	2.1	1.0	4.5	1.6	11.7
.2	.2	.2	Income Taxes Payable	.5	.0	.1	.2	.3	.0
3.9	6.2	7.1	All Other Current	13.7	5.7	1.4	6.1	5.8	6.5
33.1	34.6	30.8	Total Current	37.6	25.4	21.4	22.2	33.8	41.6
44.9	45.7	54.9	Long-Term Debt	58.7	46.1	64.2	70.9	47.0	39.0
.8	.8	.9	Deferred Taxes	.5	1.2	1.1	.2	1.5	.7
4.9	3.9	5.3	All Other Non-Current	6.2	10.6	5.0	4.3	3.8	.9
16.3	15.1	8.2	Net Worth	-2.9	16.7	8.3	2.4	13.9	17.8
100.0	100.0	100.0	Total Liabilties & Net Worth	100.0	100.0	100.0	100.0	100.0	100.0
			INCOME DATA						
100.0	100.0	100.0	Net Sales	100.0	100.0	100.0	100.0	100.0	100.0
			Gross Profit						
82.9	82.4	86.9	Operating Expenses	82.6	88.9	83.5	92.7	86.4	90.6
17.1	17.6	13.1	Operating Profit	17.4	11.1	16.5	7.3	13.6	9.4
11.1	12.3	10.6	All Other Expenses (net)	12.5	11.4	15.7	7.7	9.4	5.6
6.0	5.3	2.5	Profit Before Taxes	4.9	-.3	.8	-.3	4.3	3.8
			RATIOS						
2.9	2.1	2.6		1.7	4.3	19.6	2.7	2.9	1.2
1.1	1.1	1.0	Current	.5	1.3	1.4	1.2	1.1	.8
.3	.3	.3		.1	.2	.3	.4	.3	.2
1.7	1.6	1.5		1.5	2.2	13.5	1.3	1.3	.7
(146) .5	.5	.5	Quick	.3	.3	1.2	1.0	.6	.4
.1	.1	.2		.1	.2	.2	.2	.1	.1
3 114.5	2 161.7	4 88.2		0 UND	5 71.9	10 38.1	10 36.0	2 151.1	6 57.9
17 21.0	14 25.7	15 24.8	Sales/Receivables	3 129.2	19 19.6	32 11.5	22 16.4	20 18.5	11 34.2
51 7.1	54 6.7	38 9.7		48 7.5	42 8.7	58 6.3	36 10.0	37 9.9	23 15.9
			Cost of Sales/Inventory						
			Cost of Sales/Payables						
3.7	3.1	4.2		3.4	2.8	1.8	5.0	4.1	33.8
27.8	68.4	NM	Sales/Working Capital	-4.7	10.9	5.9	63.4	167.7	-62.0
-3.5	-2.2	-2.4		-1.5	-1.8	-3.7	-11.5	-4.5	-1.6
2.4	2.6	2.5		3.5	2.2	1.3	2.9	3.9	3.5
(106) 1.4	(106) 1.3	(99) 1.4	EBIT/Interest	(16) 1.9	(14) 1.3	(14) 1.1	(19) 1.3	(26) 1.6	(10) 2.2
1.1	1.0	1.0		.5	-.2	.8	1.0	1.2	1.8
		1.0	Net Profit + Depr., Dep.,						
	(10)	.8	Amort./Cur. Mat. L/T/D						
		-.1							
.2	.2	1.4		2.3	1.4	.1	1.8	.3	2.9
3.1	3.1	5.8	Fixed/Worth	8.1	8.7	3.5	13.0	3.7	3.7
11.0	8.1	86.3		-4.0	-14.0	14.4	192.2	9.4	NM
3.8	3.7	3.9		3.2	2.8	5.6	9.2	3.8	2.8
8.1	7.5	10.2	Debt/Worth	-23.4	12.2	8.8	22.1	7.6	3.2
20.5	21.8	600.3		-6.2	-15.8	28.1	211.2	12.9	NM
32.6	26.4	22.5	% Profit Before Taxes/Tangible	32.7	38.8	24.7	46.3	21.5	22.9
(126) 13.6	(129) 12.3	(102) 11.9	Net Worth	(14) 10.6	(14) 5.8	(16) 8.6	(18) 7.2	(30) 11.6	(10) 13.8
4.2	1.9	1.9		-1.1	-5.2	-7.2	-1.4	6.4	11.9
4.3	3.3	3.4	% Profit Before Taxes/Total	7.4	2.4	1.8	2.3	2.9	5.7
1.7	1.0	1.2	Assets	1.1	.9	.6	.5	1.6	3.4
.3	.0	.1		-2.2	-2.5	-.3	-.4	.7	1.8
36.7	29.8	12.2		1.1	4.6	19.3	22.7	26.4	32.1
1.3	1.1	.8	Sales/Net Fixed Assets	.6	.6	1.6	.9	.7	1.0
.5	.5	.5		.4	.4	.7	.6	.5	.6
.7	.6	.6		.6	.5	.6	1.3	.6	1.9
.5	.4	.4	Sales/Total Assets	.4	.3	.4	.5	.4	.8
.3	.2	.3		.3	.2	.3	.4	.3	.4
3.5	3.8	6.3		54.9	7.3	20.3	5.0	1.0	
(106) 25.1	(97) 27.5	(86) 36.9	% Depr., Dep., Amort./Sales	(23) 76.6	(14) 56.2	(12) 32.6	(18) 23.0	(16) 2.0	
58.9	60.7	70.6		88.1	72.8	63.5	43.0	36.0	
2.6	1.8	2.3						2.1	
(36) 5.2	(36) 3.7	(39) 3.4	% Officers', Directors' Owners' Comp/Sales					(11) 2.9	
7.7	7.4	5.7						5.0	
1777787M	2343406M	1732376M	Net Sales ($)	12420M	33718M	70951M	159447M	563522M	892318M
4074451M	4930160M	3529629M	Total Assets ($)	43518M	102572M	241778M	335793M	1619106M	1186862M

© RMA 2010

M = $ thousand   MM = $ million
See Pages 9 through 22 for Explanation of Ratios and Data

Current Data Sorted by Assets | Comparative Historical Data

Type of Statement

0-500M	500M-2MM	2-10MM	10-50MM	50-100MM	100-250MM	Type of Statement	4/1/05-3/31/06 ALL	4/1/06-3/31/07 ALL
		5	16	10	14	Unqualified	53	61
	2	23	35	1	1	Reviewed	48	55
5	11	25	6			Compiled	47	44
11	15	7				Tax Returns	41	39
6	16	32	40	9	14	Other	94	96
	44 (4/1-9/30/09)		260 (10/1/09-3/31/10)					

M = $ thousand MM = $ million

0-500M	500M-2MM	2-10MM	10-50MM	50-100MM	100-250MM		4/1/05-3/31/06 ALL	4/1/06-3/31/07 ALL
22	44	92	97	20	29	NUMBER OF STATEMENTS	283	295
%	%	%	%	%	%	**ASSETS**	%	%
19.1	12.1	6.5	6.4	3.8	3.3	Cash & Equivalents	7.6	8.4
6.4	10.6	10.5	11.9	4.5	12.5	Trade Receivables (net)	10.0	10.4
8.0	8.2	11.9	9.8	5.8	2.1	Inventory	9.1	9.0
9.5	2.8	3.0	5.1	6.0	4.6	All Other Current	3.2	4.2
43.0	33.8	32.0	33.2	20.2	22.4	Total Current	29.9	32.1
51.5	53.3	60.1	57.1	63.1	58.9	Fixed Assets (net)	59.5	58.2
1.1	.7	1.2	2.3	1.0	3.3	Intangibles (net)	1.5	1.3
4.3	12.2	6.8	7.4	15.8	15.4	All Other Non-Current	9.2	8.5
100.0	100.0	100.0	100.0	100.0	100.0	Total	100.0	100.0
						LIABILITIES		
14.5	13.0	14.2	11.4	11.2	8.0	Notes Payable-Short Term	11.4	11.0
11.2	12.9	13.0	10.9	9.1	13.8	Cur. Mat.-L.T.D.	11.7	10.1
11.3	3.8	5.1	5.4	2.9	2.0	Trade Payables	5.1	5.0
.1	.3	.2	.1	.0	.2	Income Taxes Payable	.2	.3
48.3	8.9	5.5	5.3	7.1	4.0	All Other Current	7.5	8.5
85.4	38.8	38.0	33.1	30.4	28.0	Total Current	36.0	34.8
47.2	35.2	35.8	30.6	39.0	41.6	Long-Term Debt	37.9	38.0
.0	.0	.8	2.2	4.7	6.8	Deferred Taxes	1.7	1.6
7.7	12.0	2.7	4.3	1.3	3.2	All Other Non-Current	4.1	4.3
-40.4	14.0	22.7	29.7	24.5	20.5	Net Worth	20.3	21.2
100.0	100.0	100.0	100.0	100.0	100.0	Total Liabilities & Net Worth	100.0	100.0
						INCOME DATA		
100.0	100.0	100.0	100.0	100.0	100.0	Net Sales	100.0	100.0
						Gross Profit		
92.5	89.2	88.8	94.0	92.6	85.5	Operating Expenses	85.8	85.7
7.5	10.8	11.2	6.0	7.4	14.5	Operating Profit	14.2	14.3
4.3	4.0	4.5	3.8	9.6	10.7	All Other Expenses (net)	4.1	3.6
3.2	6.8	6.7	2.3	-2.2	3.8	Profit Before Taxes	10.1	10.7
						RATIOS		
3.2	2.6	1.8	1.5	1.1	1.2	Current	1.3	1.5
1.0	1.0	.9	1.1	.5	.8		.8	.9
.2	.3	.4	.6	.4	.4		.4	.4
1.6	1.8	1.2	1.0	.7	.9	Quick	.9	1.0
.3	.7	.5	.5	.4	.4		.5	.5
.0	.1	.2	.3	.1	.2		.2	.2
0 UND	0 UND	1 602.1	21 17.7	7 55.2	30 12.3	Sales/Receivables	0 UND	0 UND
0 UND	10 37.0	22 16.6	34 10.6	35 10.4	39 9.4		24 15.2	22 16.5
8 47.9	41 8.9	35 10.3	48 7.6	45 8.1	49 7.5		41 8.8	42 8.8
						Cost of Sales/Inventory		
						Cost of Sales/Payables		
9.5	6.1	8.3	9.4	NM	4.7	Sales/Working Capital	14.3	11.3
UND	NM	-35.8	85.9	-5.1	-13.8		-25.7	-55.3
-1.7	-2.8	-4.1	-6.4	-3.8	-2.7		-4.0	-4.3
20.3	5.0	4.1	2.5	1.8	2.7	EBIT/Interest	4.6	4.5
(18) 1.9	(35) 1.2	(85) 1.8	(86) 1.3	(17) 1.3	(24) 1.6		(250) 2.7	(257) 2.3
-.4	-.4	.6	.1	.1	1.2		1.5	1.3
		2.9	2.9			Net Profit + Depr., Dep., Amort./Cur. Mat. L/T/D	2.0	1.8
		(11) 1.6	(39) 1.3				(67) 1.4	(52) 1.3
		.7	.9				1.0	.9
.8	.4	1.3	1.4	1.1	2.0	Fixed/Worth	1.2	1.1
4.5	1.7	2.6	2.0	2.3	3.3		2.6	2.6
-.7	-10.5	40.1	4.6	8.0	4.8		10.1	6.1
.9	1.0	1.2	1.1	1.5	3.0	Debt/Worth	1.8	1.8
NM	3.2	3.8	2.9	3.3	4.1		4.2	3.9
-1.8	-17.8	64.0	9.4	13.7	7.8		15.2	10.3
100.0	59.5	29.1	23.0	10.6	13.8	% Profit Before Taxes/Tangible Net Worth	51.2	38.7
(11) 48.6	(31) 12.2	(71) 14.7	(86) 7.7	(17) 4.2	(28) 8.8		(237) 22.8	(251) 17.7
7.7	-14.7	1.8	-2.3	-7.0	4.8		10.0	8.0
19.1	10.9	7.8	4.0	2.8	2.7	% Profit Before Taxes/Total Assets	10.8	11.0
4.2	4.1	3.0	1.2	.9	1.4		4.8	4.0
-8.5	-6.9	-1.8	-2.5	-5.1	.5		1.7	1.1
96.2	6.1	3.6	5.1	1.5	2.3	Sales/Net Fixed Assets	5.5	4.7
2.3	1.6	1.4	1.5	.8	.8		1.4	1.3
1.1	.7	.6	.7	.6	.6		.6	.6
6.9	1.5	1.6	1.6	.8	.7	Sales/Total Assets	1.9	1.6
1.4	.9	.9	.9	.6	.4		.8	.8
.8	.4	.4	.5	.5	.3		.5	.4
4.7	3.5	8.0	5.4	15.8		% Depr., Dep., Amort./Sales	5.3	6.5
(11) 16.4	(33) 24.8	(81) 30.0	(88) 14.2	(12) 21.9			(225) 18.1	(228) 17.2
69.1	45.3	49.7	29.1	27.6			38.1	42.5
	1.1	1.3	1.1			% Officers', Directors' Owners' Comp/Sales	1.7	1.3
	(10) 8.2	(18) 2.6	(21) 2.0				(51) 4.2	(55) 3.5
	13.1	6.0	4.3				8.6	8.3
23942M	72256M	551353M	2953468M	860507M	2004796M	Net Sales ($)	7106126M	6614891M
5784M	51704M	486473M	2300040M	1309237M	4144647M	Total Assets ($)	6837364M	7568739M

M = $ thousand MM = $ million
See Pages 9 through 22 for Explanation of Ratios and Data

Comparative Historical Data | Current Data Sorted by Sales

Type of Statement									
				1	2	1	1	13	27	Unqualified
				1	10	3	13	19	16	Reviewed
				13	13	8	5	6	2	Compiled
				17	9	5	2			Tax Returns
				17	16	8	18	21	37	Other

	50	58	45	Unqualified	1	2	1	1	13	27
	53	67	62	Reviewed	1	10	3	13	19	16
	37	45	47	Compiled	13	13	8	5	6	2
	34	39	33	Tax Returns	17	9	5	2		
	102	117	117	Other	17	16	8	18	21	37
	4/1/07-3/31/08 ALL	4/1/08-3/31/09 ALL	4/1/09-3/31/10 ALL		0-1MM	1-3MM	3-5MM	5-10MM	10-25MM	25MM & OVER
					44 (4/1-9/30/09)			260 (10/1/09-3/31/10)		
NUMBER OF STATEMENTS	276	326	304		49	50	25	39	59	82

	%	%	%	**ASSETS**	%	%	%	%	%	%
	7.5	6.5	7.7	Cash & Equivalents	13.4	9.6	7.3	5.4	5.3	6.1
	10.5	11.7	10.5	Trade Receivables (net)	2.9	12.2	7.9	8.9	12.8	13.8
	7.8	6.4	9.1	Inventory	5.0	2.9	10.9	15.3	12.3	9.5
	4.1	4.6	4.5	All Other Current	2.7	3.5	6.9	6.8	3.3	5.0
	30.0	29.3	31.7	Total Current	24.0	28.3	33.0	36.3	33.7	34.3
	61.8	60.5	57.6	Fixed Assets (net)	63.4	59.9	55.9	57.1	54.9	55.5
	1.7	1.5	1.7	Intangibles (net)	.7	1.3	.8	.9	2.4	2.6
	6.5	8.7	9.0	All Other Non-Current	12.0	10.4	10.3	5.7	9.0	7.6
	100.0	100.0	100.0	Total	100.0	100.0	100.0	100.0	100.0	100.0

				LIABILITIES						
	11.4	9.3	12.4	Notes Payable-Short Term	9.1	11.5	9.8	20.4	11.9	12.2
	11.7	12.8	12.0	Cur. Mat.-L.T.D.	12.1	14.3	12.0	11.3	12.1	10.9
	4.5	4.4	5.0	Trade Payables	3.1	3.0	6.7	5.8	6.1	5.6
	.3	.2	.2	Income Taxes Payable	.2	.0	.9	.0	.1	.1
	6.0	7.2	9.0	All Other Current	13.2	14.6	9.5	6.7	5.9	6.3
	33.9	33.9	38.5	Total Current	37.7	43.4	39.0	44.2	36.1	35.1
	38.0	40.5	35.6	Long-Term Debt	44.4	41.6	37.2	29.4	35.4	29.4
	2.0	1.8	1.9	Deferred Taxes	.0	.4	2.0	.9	2.0	4.4
	3.9	4.9	4.9	All Other Non-Current	9.0	3.5	9.8	3.1	4.4	3.0
	22.2	18.9	19.0	Net Worth	8.9	11.1	12.0	22.4	22.2	28.1
	100.0	100.0	100.0	Total Liabilities & Net Worth	100.0	100.0	100.0	100.0	100.0	100.0

				INCOME DATA						
	100.0	100.0	100.0	Net Sales	100.0	100.0	100.0	100.0	100.0	100.0
				Gross Profit						
	86.6	88.5	90.7	Operating Expenses	79.2	86.1	99.5	93.8	93.5	94.1
	13.4	11.5	9.3	Operating Profit	20.8	13.9	.5	6.2	6.5	5.9
	5.8	5.9	5.1	All Other Expenses (net)	7.4	6.1	2.3	4.0	5.6	4.1
	7.6	5.5	4.2	Profit Before Taxes	13.3	7.8	-1.8	2.2	.8	1.7

				RATIOS						
	1.6	1.8	1.6	Current	2.7	1.9	2.7	1.3	1.5	1.4
	.9	.9	.9		.8	1.0	1.0	.8	1.1	.9
	.4	.3	.4		.1	.3	.3	.5	.5	.5
	1.1	1.1	1.1	Quick	1.5	1.6	1.5	.7	1.0	.9
	.5	.5	.5		.6	.6	.3	.4	.5	.4
	.2	.2	.2		.1	.2	.1	.1	.3	.2
	2 183.2	1 324.7	4 99.3	Sales/Receivables	0 UND	0 UND	0 UND	13 29.0	22 16.3	19 19.1
	28 12.9	26 14.2	27 13.7		0 UND	18 20.0	16 22.7	31 11.7	33 11.0	34 10.8
	44 8.2	46 7.9	42 8.6		16 22.2	63 5.8	33 11.0	43 8.5	48 7.6	43 8.5
				Cost of Sales/Inventory						
				Cost of Sales/Payables						
	10.2	9.4	8.3	Sales/Working Capital	6.5	2.8	3.9	10.3	9.2	13.1
	-98.7	-36.4	-59.5		-10.7	NM	-999.8	-15.8	61.7	-98.6
	-4.2	-4.0	-3.9		-1.8	-2.3	-3.5	-6.4	-6.2	-4.1
	3.7	2.8	3.1	EBIT/Interest	6.7	4.1	4.6	2.5	3.2	2.7
	(243) 1.8	(266) 1.5	(265) 1.5		(38) 1.9	(39) 1.8	(24) 1.0	(37) 1.3	(49) 1.2	(78) 1.6
	1.2	.9	.3		.2	-.4	-.6	.5	-.6	.8
	2.5	2.6	2.9	Net Profit + Depr., Dep., Amort./Cur. Mat. L/T/D					2.6	2.9
	(56) 1.2	(60) 1.2	(59) 1.3					(20) 1.1	(23) 1.3	
	.9	.9	.9					.9	1.0	
	1.3	1.3	1.2	Fixed/Worth	1.0	1.1	.8	1.4	1.4	1.6
	2.7	2.6	2.3		2.5	2.2	3.1	2.0	2.4	2.3
	7.3	10.7	11.7		-10.7	-34.2	-20.4	6.3	39.8	4.0
	1.8	1.5	1.4	Debt/Worth	.9	1.3	1.3	1.1	1.6	1.8
	3.6	3.7	3.6		3.5	3.2	4.6	2.5	5.8	3.2
	10.2	20.6	26.5		-18.1	-28.0	-23.6	12.9	65.7	5.9
	30.2	25.4	25.4	% Profit Before Taxes/Tangible Net Worth	68.0	33.3	33.7	27.4	24.9	17.9
	(237) 14.2	(270) 9.5	(244) 9.6		(34) 12.6	(36) 12.2	(17) 11.9	(34) 11.6	(48) 8.7	(75) 7.9
	5.6	1.5	.1		1.0	-1.8	-12.7	-2.6	1.3	2.0
	8.0	5.7	5.9	% Profit Before Taxes/Total Assets	10.4	7.6	5.9	6.5	3.3	3.7
	3.3	2.1	1.7		4.7	2.0	-.1	1.5	.8	1.8
	.9	-.8	-2.0		-3.5	-3.9	-7.3	-2.1	-6.1	-.2
	3.8	4.5	4.9	Sales/Net Fixed Assets	2.3	2.0	8.9	12.2	5.3	7.0
	1.2	1.1	1.4		1.0	.8	1.5	1.4	1.9	1.7
	.6	.6	.7		.4	.5	.7	.7	.9	.8
	1.6	1.7	1.5	Sales/Total Assets	1.0	1.1	2.0	1.6	1.8	2.0
	.8	.7	.8		.5	.5	.7	.9	.9	1.0
	.4	.4	.4		.3	.3	.5	.5	.6	.6
	6.0	6.8	5.6	% Depr., Dep., Amort./Sales	16.4	26.6	4.7	5.0	5.4	2.8
	(210) 19.5	(247) 22.3	(232) 20.6		(35) 40.0	(42) 36.1	(23) 25.2	(31) 24.2	(50) 12.5	(51) 7.5
	42.5	42.5	38.8		61.8	56.3	50.4	39.0	24.9	14.5
	1.0	.8	1.4	% Officers', Directors' Owners' Comp/Sales					1.7	
	(48) 3.2	(52) 2.8	(56) 2.6					(12) 3.6	(15) 2.1	
	6.3	7.1	8.0					6.0	4.6	
	8551283M	7209273M	6466322M	Net Sales ($)	23929M	91469M	98280M	278697M	941197M	5032750M
	8665091M	8964143M	8297885M	Total Assets ($)	58599M	249211M	162062M	423159M	1773434M	5631420M

© RMA 2010

M = $ thousand   MM = $ million
See Pages 9 through 22 for Explanation of Ratios and Data

REAL ESTATE—Consumer Electronics and Appliances Rental   NAICS 532210

	Current Data Sorted by Assets						Type of Statement	Comparative Historical Data	
		3	6	2	3		Unqualified	7	15
1	4	4	4	1			Reviewed	15	14
3	4	3					Compiled	22	23
9	13	2	1				Tax Returns	14	15
3	13	6	4		1		Other	18	21
	10 (4/1-9/30/09)			80 (10/1/09-3/31/10)				4/1/05-3/31/06 ALL	4/1/06-3/31/07 ALL
0-500M	500M-2MM	2-10MM	10-50MM	50-100MM	100-250MM				
16	34	18	15	3	4		NUMBER OF STATEMENTS	76	88
%	%	%	%	%	%		ASSETS	%	%
16.2	10.3	6.0	4.9				Cash & Equivalents	7.0	7.6
14.8	9.3	9.5	12.5				Trade Receivables (net)	15.1	13.6
14.6	14.1	23.3	12.5				Inventory	10.4	12.3
.8	2.0	2.9	10.7				All Other Current	3.3	4.7
46.4	35.7	41.8	40.6				Total Current	35.9	38.2
44.9	49.1	46.9	30.1				Fixed Assets (net)	48.7	44.4
2.2	4.2	4.9	3.1				Intangibles (net)	3.7	5.3
6.5	11.0	6.4	26.2				All Other Non-Current	11.7	12.2
100.0	100.0	100.0	100.0				Total	100.0	100.0
							LIABILITIES		
24.4	10.2	16.6	12.8				Notes Payable-Short Term	15.0	18.5
15.1	5.7	6.4	7.4				Cur. Mat.-L.T.D.	9.4	7.7
11.7	6.7	6.6	5.6				Trade Payables	7.3	7.5
.0	.1	.7	.3				Income Taxes Payable	.2	.2
29.7	4.0	8.2	8.7				All Other Current	7.5	7.1
80.9	26.7	38.5	34.8				Total Current	39.3	41.0
40.1	48.9	21.7	36.3				Long-Term Debt	31.5	22.3
.0	.4	.6	.0				Deferred Taxes	.1	.7
23.1	21.4	4.5	2.9				All Other Non-Current	5.2	7.8
-43.8	2.6	34.6	26.0				Net Worth	23.9	28.2
100.0	100.0	100.0	100.0				Total Liabilities & Net Worth	100.0	100.0
							INCOME DATA		
100.0	100.0	100.0	100.0				Net Sales	100.0	100.0
							Gross Profit		
93.1	85.6	90.4	88.6				Operating Expenses	86.5	90.4
6.9	14.4	9.6	11.4				Operating Profit	13.5	9.6
7.5	6.3	6.2	6.9				All Other Expenses (net)	3.8	3.6
-.6	8.1	3.5	4.5				Profit Before Taxes	9.7	6.0
							RATIOS		
1.9	3.8	2.9	1.4					1.7	2.2
.8	1.1	.8	1.4				Current	1.1	1.0
.4	.4	.3	.9					.4	.5
1.6	2.0	.9	.9					1.4	1.3
.6	.5	.5	.5				Quick	.6	.5
.1	.2	.1	.3					.2	.1
0 UND	0 UND	0 UND	0 UND					0 UND	0 UND
1 261.4	7 51.6	0 795.1	19 19.1				Sales/Receivables	12 29.3	12 29.3
33 11.1	30 12.0	28 13.2	69 5.3					44 8.3	37 9.7
							Cost of Sales/Inventory		
							Cost of Sales/Payables		
21.3	4.5	6.4	5.4					12.5	6.7
-39.0	139.5	-17.2	13.4				Sales/Working Capital	96.7	111.0
-5.4	-8.7	-5.9	-64.2					-9.2	-7.1
2.0	4.7	10.9	11.7					9.8	7.4
(11) .1	(29) 2.6	(14) 2.8	(13) 4.0				EBIT/Interest	(67) 2.3	(77) 2.5
-1.4	-.1	1.7	1.1					1.2	.9
									3.5
							Net Profit + Depr., Dep., Amort./Cur. Mat. L/T/D		(16) 1.6
									.3
1.0	1.0	.3	.1					.6	.4
-1.6	5.0	4.1	1.1				Fixed/Worth	1.9	1.6
-.6	-6.5	46.0	2.9					12.2	10.6
1.5	1.0	.7	1.8					.9	.6
-5.2	6.0	4.0	3.1				Debt/Worth	2.8	2.8
-2.3	-11.5	49.4	5.2					72.4	21.3
	29.4	60.1	49.4				% Profit Before Taxes/Tangible Net Worth	54.9	45.2
	(23) 16.2	(15) 21.5	(14) 20.4					(59) 22.1	(70) 30.9
	-2.7	3.3	2.9					8.0	8.8
10.9	15.3	15.1	10.3				% Profit Before Taxes/Total Assets	19.7	13.9
4.3	3.7	2.2	6.6					5.3	6.1
-13.5	-2.2	.9	.5					.9	.5
22.5	10.3	20.1	18.1				Sales/Net Fixed Assets	10.3	15.2
6.6	3.8	5.6	6.0					3.5	4.3
3.3	1.4	1.5	3.1					1.8	1.8
5.5	2.6	2.9	1.8				Sales/Total Assets	2.6	2.4
2.9	1.8	1.9	1.2					1.6	1.8
1.6	.6	.9	.6					.8	.8
2.6	2.3	1.0	1.4				% Depr., Dep., Amort./Sales	6.4	3.4
(12) 6.3	(31) 9.5	(15) 15.2	(11) 5.5					(59) 10.3	(67) 11.3
18.0	21.9	32.2	16.2					27.1	28.9
	3.4						% Officers', Directors' Owners' Comp/Sales	2.2	2.1
	(15) 5.6							(34) 4.1	(26) 4.9
	8.2							9.2	8.1
16908M	57839M	147708M	440551M	172592M	373737M		Net Sales ($)	739293M	968375M
4447M	37307M	78150M	374577M	185473M	609460M		Total Assets ($)	538453M	859505M

© RMA 2010

M = $ thousand   MM = $ million
See Pages 9 through 22 for Explanation of Ratios and Data

Comparative Historical Data | Current Data Sorted by Sales

4/1/07-3/31/08 ALL	4/1/08-3/31/09 ALL	4/1/09-3/31/10 ALL	Type of Statement	10 (4/1-9/30/09)			80 (10/1/09-3/31/10)		
				0-1MM	1-3MM	3-5MM	5-10MM	10-25MM	25MM & OVER
11	10	14	Unqualified			1	2	4	7
10	14	14	Reviewed	2	5	1		1	4
22	28	10	Compiled	1	5		3		
12	23	25	Tax Returns	12	9	2	2	1	1
24	25	27	Other	6	10	2	2	3	4
79	**100**	**90**	**NUMBER OF STATEMENTS**	**21**	**29**	**6**	**9**	**9**	**16**
%	%	%	**ASSETS**	%	%	%	%	%	%
7.7	9.2	9.1	Cash & Equivalents	8.3	12.9				4.8
12.5	12.6	10.6	Trade Receivables (net)	6.2	11.2				12.4
15.9	15.9	15.6	Inventory	5.4	17.8				15.7
4.3	4.1	3.4	All Other Current	1.6	1.5				7.1
40.4	41.9	38.7	Total Current	21.6	43.5				40.1
46.1	44.8	44.6	Fixed Assets (net)	62.4	43.2				38.9
4.9	3.2	4.8	Intangibles (net)	5.4	2.2				10.2
8.6	10.1	12.0	All Other Non-Current	10.6	11.2				10.7
100.0	100.0	100.0	Total	100.0	100.0				100.0
			LIABILITIES						
17.1	21.9	14.9	Notes Payable-Short Term	8.9	18.4				18.5
8.2	8.6	7.5	Cur. Mat.-L.T.D.	8.4	7.2				2.7
9.0	7.2	7.3	Trade Payables	4.4	8.7				6.6
.1	.2	.3	Income Taxes Payable	.0	.1				.6
7.0	8.7	10.2	All Other Current	2.0	17.3				9.3
41.6	46.6	40.2	Total Current	23.8	51.6				37.7
30.5	28.9	37.9	Long-Term Debt	62.7	32.9				25.8
.5	.3	.6	Deferred Taxes	.2	.3				1.9
9.5	9.8	13.9	All Other Non-Current	10.7	30.3				2.3
18.0	14.4	7.5	Net Worth	2.8	-15.1				32.3
100.0	100.0	100.0	Total Liabilities & Net Worth	100.0	100.0				100.0
			INCOME DATA						
100.0	100.0	100.0	Net Sales	100.0	100.0				100.0
			Gross Profit						
89.3	89.8	88.8	Operating Expenses	71.9	95.8				92.1
10.7	10.2	11.2	Operating Profit	28.1	4.2				7.9
6.4	4.8	6.5	All Other Expenses (net)	17.5	3.4				3.0
4.2	5.5	4.6	Profit Before Taxes	10.5	.8				4.9
			RATIOS						
2.1	2.0	2.1		2.0	3.9				1.6
1.0	1.1	1.1	Current	.5	1.2				1.1
.3	.4	.4		.2	.5				.7
1.4	1.4	1.2		1.0	2.3				.9
.4	.5	.5	Quick	.4	.8				.6
.1	.1	.2		.1	.2				.2
0 UND	0 UND	0 UND		0 UND	0 UND				0 791.3
6 57.6	10 36.6	11 33.0	Sales/Receivables	0 UND	5 70.6				21 17.0
29 12.6	37 9.9	33 11.2		24 15.4	35 10.5				64 5.7
			Cost of Sales/Inventory						
			Cost of Sales/Payables						
6.7	5.2	7.1		22.9	4.6				7.3
103.6	47.7	118.9	Sales/Working Capital	-9.4	38.7				33.4
-5.1	-5.6	-7.4		-4.7	-11.0				-8.3
3.5	6.4	4.9		3.6	4.9				8.9
(65) 1.9	(85) 1.9	(73) 2.6	EBIT/Interest	(13) 1.5	(25) 1.6				(15) 4.0
1.0	.8	1.1		-.9	-.5				3.3
4.5	9.8	2.6	Net Profit + Depr., Dep.,						
(15) 2.9	(11) 2.5	(10) 1.8	Amort./Cur. Mat. L/T/D						
1.8	1.2	.6							
.5	.6	.6		3.0	.4				.3
4.1	1.8	3.0	Fixed/Worth	19.0	4.4				1.7
-16.0	-5.9	-4.7		-1.1	-22.2				11.7
1.5	.9	1.1		3.0	.6				1.1
6.2	3.1	4.7	Debt/Worth	18.3	5.9				2.1
-23.3	-10.2	-11.8		-4.8	-33.3				12.8
58.2	52.7	49.9		50.0	70.5				54.7
(55) 22.1	(72) 17.7	(64) 16.9	% Profit Before Taxes/Tangible Net Worth	(11) 20.6	(21) 4.0				(13) 28.2
4.6	4.5	2.3		6.0	-13.0				13.9
9.0	13.9	10.6		10.1	11.0				10.3
4.2	3.1	4.1	% Profit Before Taxes/Total Assets	4.2	1.0				8.0
.0	-.6	.3		-1.5	-7.2				2.3
15.7	12.2	13.8		3.8	14.1				14.0
3.0	5.1	4.9	Sales/Net Fixed Assets	1.5	7.5				3.8
1.4	1.6	1.9		.2	2.9				1.2
2.3	2.5	2.8		1.7	3.2				1.8
1.5	1.6	1.8	Sales/Total Assets	.6	2.2				1.3
.7	.8	.8		.2	1.3				.6
3.5	3.6	2.2		8.1	2.1				
(61) 15.1	(70) 9.3	(72) 8.1	% Depr., Dep., Amort./Sales	(20) 19.1	(25) 6.5				
31.2	30.1	22.3		24.9	11.5				
2.6	3.6	3.1			3.4				
(22) 4.5	(31) 7.1	(38) 5.5	% Officers', Directors' Owners' Comp/Sales	(15)	5.7				
10.8	10.8	10.1			9.6				
860370M	1338007M	1209335M	Net Sales ($)	8253M	55410M	21091M	62234M	139189M	923158M
792676M	1330760M	1289414M	Total Assets ($)	21545M	47801M	35267M	44652M	106720M	1033429M

M = $ thousand   MM = $ million
See Pages 9 through 22 for Explanation of Ratios and Data

Current Data Sorted by Assets							Comparative Historical Data	
						Type of Statement		
			4	1	3	Unqualified	6	8
1		8	2	1		Reviewed	14	12
2	1	3				Compiled	6	7
6	9	5				Tax Returns	5	8
2	9	12	4		2	Other	24	26
	3 (4/1-9/30/09)		72 (10/1/09-3/31/10)				4/1/05-3/31/06 ALL	4/1/06-3/31/07 ALL
0-500M	500M-2MM	2-10MM	10-50MM	50-100MM	100-250MM			
11	19	28	10	2	5	NUMBER OF STATEMENTS	55	61
%	%	%	%	%	%	**ASSETS**	%	%
16.0	10.6	4.5	7.4			Cash & Equivalents	7.4	8.1
11.8	19.5	27.5	22.0			Trade Receivables (net)	25.8	21.5
8.8	9.9	13.1	7.5			Inventory	8.4	9.1
.6	1.7	3.2	2.6			All Other Current	1.9	2.8
37.2	41.7	48.2	39.4			Total Current	43.5	41.5
49.1	50.2	42.9	45.7			Fixed Assets (net)	44.1	47.9
.6	2.0	4.5	3.7			Intangibles (net)	5.8	5.5
13.1	6.1	4.3	11.1			All Other Non-Current	6.5	5.0
100.0	100.0	100.0	100.0			Total	100.0	100.0
						LIABILITIES		
16.4	5.7	8.4	6.7			Notes Payable-Short Term	9.4	11.0
9.2	8.6	9.7	9.1			Cur. Mat.-L.T.D.	8.3	6.8
6.5	6.2	12.4	9.1			Trade Payables	10.6	10.0
.0	.8	.2	.0			Income Taxes Payable	.7	.2
15.7	5.6	6.3	6.9			All Other Current	6.3	6.4
47.8	27.0	37.0	31.8			Total Current	35.4	34.3
50.5	35.1	27.1	16.7			Long-Term Debt	24.8	32.1
.0	.0	.4	3.1			Deferred Taxes	.9	.4
15.8	2.0	5.9	4.7			All Other Non-Current	4.8	3.5
-14.1	35.9	29.7	43.7			Net Worth	34.1	29.7
100.0	100.0	100.0	100.0			Total Liabilties & Net Worth	100.0	100.0
						INCOME DATA		
100.0	100.0	100.0	100.0			Net Sales	100.0	100.0
						Gross Profit		
97.3	89.0	87.2	85.7			Operating Expenses	87.6	90.1
2.7	11.0	12.8	14.3			Operating Profit	12.4	9.9
1.8	1.7	6.1	2.0			All Other Expenses (net)	3.3	2.9
.8	9.4	6.7	12.3			Profit Before Taxes	9.1	7.0
						RATIOS		
2.5	3.2	1.8	1.8				2.0	1.9
.5	1.6	1.3	1.2			Current	1.2	1.2
.1	.8	1.0	.8				.8	.7
2.0	2.4	1.5	1.4				1.6	1.5
.1	1.3	.9	.9			Quick	1.0	.9
.1	.6	.4	.6				.5	.5
0 UND	**0** UND	**41** 9.0	**30** 12.2				**29** 12.4	**2** 182.2
0 UND	**39** 9.4	**54** 6.7	**61** 5.9			Sales/Receivables	**54** 6.7	**45** 8.1
32 11.4	**53** 6.9	**64** 5.7	**83** 4.4				**77** 4.7	**72** 5.1
						Cost of Sales/Inventory		
						Cost of Sales/Payables		
11.7	9.3	6.5	8.2				5.5	5.2
-27.4	24.2	15.1	57.0			Sales/Working Capital	16.1	53.8
-3.5	-11.9	NM	-13.7				-17.3	-17.5
10.2	29.8	8.0					8.8	7.4
.6	(17) 4.1	(23) 4.1				EBIT/Interest	(49) 3.7	(51) 2.7
-2.4	-.9	1.9					1.5	.5
							4.3	3.0
						Net Profit + Depr., Dep., Amort./Cur. Mat. L/T/D	(15) 2.6	(14) 1.6
							1.2	.8
1.6	.6	.6	.3				.7	.8
-34.0	1.3	1.5	.9			Fixed/Worth	1.3	1.5
-.6	11.3	7.3	2.6				4.3	4.9
1.6	.6	.9	.6				.9	1.0
-77.0	2.7	2.4	1.8			Debt/Worth	2.1	2.3
-3.5	12.5	10.3	2.7				5.6	7.0
	99.3	43.4	39.2				58.4	49.5
	(15) 24.7	(23) 30.5	18.3			% Profit Before Taxes/Tangible Net Worth	(48) 20.5	(51) 18.8
	-6.5	6.0	9.5				6.3	2.0
19.7	48.6	15.9	14.0				15.4	13.8
-5.7	12.7	6.7	8.3			% Profit Before Taxes/Total Assets	5.9	5.0
-20.0	-3.8	1.6	2.8				1.4	-1.6
19.6	14.3	8.9	16.9				7.6	7.7
7.9	3.3	6.0	4.1			Sales/Net Fixed Assets	4.6	4.2
2.2	2.2	3.0	.9				2.0	1.9
4.7	2.7	2.3	2.4				2.3	2.2
3.0	1.8	2.0	1.3			Sales/Total Assets	1.6	1.7
1.0	1.1	1.1	.6				1.0	1.0
	2.2	3.7	.9				4.8	3.9
	(13) 11.4	(22) 5.7	7.3			% Depr., Dep., Amort./Sales	(49) 7.3	(53) 6.9
	15.1	15.0	27.1				13.5	15.4
							5.0	3.9
						% Officers', Directors' Owners' Comp/Sales	(22) 7.4	(18) 8.7
							15.8	17.9
8553M	43651M	210549M	273249M	104889M	593420M	Net Sales ($)	674553M	847271M
3091M	19778M	114136M	227947M	151858M	715169M	Total Assets ($)	605191M	709573M

M = $ thousand MM = $ million

See Pages 9 through 22 for Explanation of Ratios and Data

Comparative Historical Data   Current Data Sorted by Sales

4/1/07-3/31/08 ALL	4/1/08-3/31/09 ALL	4/1/09-3/31/10 ALL	Type of Statement	0-1MM	1-3MM	3-5MM	5-10MM	10-25MM	25MM & OVER
6	5	8	Unqualified				1	3	4
12	8	12	Reviewed	1			4	4	2
7	5	6	Compiled	2		1	2	2	
12	18	20	Tax Returns	10	7	1	1	1	
34	30	29	Other	4	6	5	4	5	5
					3 (4/1-9/30/09)		72 (10/1/09-3/31/10)		
71	66	75	NUMBER OF STATEMENTS	17	13	7	12	15	11
%	%	%	**ASSETS**	%	%	%	%	%	%
13.0	10.1	8.2	Cash & Equivalents	11.1	7.8		6.8	5.6	6.8
22.2	27.5	20.8	Trade Receivables (net)	7.9	22.8		29.8	26.7	19.7
5.5	9.4	9.8	Inventory	5.7	11.1		8.4	11.1	7.8
2.9	3.6	2.2	All Other Current	1.2	1.9		2.2	4.1	1.6
43.5	50.7	41.0	Total Current	25.9	43.5		47.2	47.5	35.9
40.9	36.7	44.9	Fixed Assets (net)	65.0	53.2		46.4	35.9	30.0
7.6	6.0	5.8	Intangibles (net)	.5	1.6		1.7	4.1	23.7
8.0	6.6	8.3	All Other Non-Current	8.6	1.7		4.7	12.5	10.3
100.0	100.0	100.0	Total	100.0	100.0		100.0	100.0	100.0
			LIABILITIES						
9.8	11.3	7.9	Notes Payable-Short Term	12.6	4.4		7.0	9.6	3.1
9.6	8.7	8.7	Cur. Mat.-L.T.D.	6.4	12.8		14.8	8.5	4.3
8.5	12.0	8.9	Trade Payables	5.2	5.5		5.4	16.3	8.6
.1	.2	.3	Income Taxes Payable	.0	1.2		.3	.2	.0
10.4	8.6	7.7	All Other Current	8.8	4.7		7.6	6.0	8.7
38.4	40.8	33.6	Total Current	32.9	28.8		35.1	40.5	24.7
29.4	21.4	32.8	Long-Term Debt	50.0	51.9		22.9	22.3	22.9
.6	.5	.7	Deferred Taxes	.0	.0		.7	1.2	2.6
3.7	4.7	6.5	All Other Non-Current	7.2	7.5		5.5	2.9	10.2
27.9	32.6	26.4	Net Worth	9.8	11.8		35.8	33.0	39.6
100.0	100.0	100.0	Total Liabilities & Net Worth	100.0	100.0		100.0	100.0	100.0
			INCOME DATA						
100.0	100.0	100.0	Net Sales	100.0	100.0		100.0	100.0	100.0
			Gross Profit						
84.8	89.7	88.4	Operating Expenses	83.0	93.1		88.6	90.6	88.1
15.2	10.3	11.6	Operating Profit	17.0	6.9		11.4	9.4	11.9
3.5	2.6	4.0	All Other Expenses (net)	10.2	1.6		2.0	3.0	2.6
11.6	7.7	7.6	Profit Before Taxes	6.8	5.3		9.4	6.4	9.3
			RATIOS						
1.9	2.1	1.9	Current	2.5	14.1		2.1	1.7	2.3
1.1	1.3	1.2		.5	1.4		1.2	1.1	1.3
.6	.8	.9		.2	.7		.9	1.0	1.0
1.4	1.5	1.6	Quick	2.2	6.9		1.6	1.3	1.7
.9	.9	.9		.4	1.2		.8	.9	1.1
.5	.6	.5		.1	.6		.6	.5	.8
2 238.9	17 21.4	7 52.7	Sales/Receivables	0 UND	2 164.5		51 7.2	17 20.9	31 11.7
51 7.1	51 7.2	46 8.0		0 UND	39 9.3		61 6.0	53 6.9	52 7.1
75 4.9	80 4.6	64 5.7		39 9.4	62 5.9		96 3.8	64 5.7	75 4.9
			Cost of Sales/Inventory						
			Cost of Sales/Payables						
6.4	6.8	8.6	Sales/Working Capital	8.1	4.2		7.1	10.8	5.2
49.7	43.2	37.7		-27.4	42.3		37.8	35.3	10.6
-8.9	-19.9	-27.4		-2.6	-15.7		NM	-28.7	-156.0
8.7	9.7	8.0	EBIT/Interest	10.3	5.3		11.1	6.7	22.4
(60) 4.3	(61) 3.7	(66) 4.1		(14) .9	(12) -.1		(11) 8.0	(14) 4.1	(10) 4.7
2.2	1.5	1.1		-.1	-7.1		4.4	2.4	1.5
4.4	10.8	3.7	Net Profit + Depr., Dep.,						
(12) 1.8	(10) 1.7	(11) 1.9	Amort./Cur. Mat. L/T/D						
.9	.6	1.2							
.7	.4	.6	Fixed/Worth	2.0	1.0		.6	.6	.6
2.2	1.5	1.7		6.9	1.6		1.1	1.4	1.4
-21.8	-65.1	-99.1		-8.2	NM		2.6	2.8	-.4
.9	.8	.9	Debt/Worth	1.6	.7		.7	.7	1.0
2.8	1.8	2.6		6.2	3.0		1.2	2.6	3.0
-63.1	-73.4	-159.5		-14.7	NM		3.5	7.0	-6.8
88.7	76.1	69.3	% Profit Before Taxes/Tangible	58.0	91.5		47.0	36.9	
(52) 30.7	(49) 21.9	(56) 24.2	Net Worth	(10) 22.6	(10) 17.3		(11) 42.0	(13) 17.6	
14.4	11.3	6.7		-2.5	-15.6		2.1	8.8	
25.2	22.6	18.8	% Profit Before Taxes/Total	14.4	18.6		21.7	10.3	18.8
11.4	7.0	6.8	Assets	.3	2.1		12.4	4.6	9.4
1.7	1.9	.3		-5.9	-24.9		2.8	3.3	1.6
11.0	22.5	12.3	Sales/Net Fixed Assets	10.2	8.8		9.1	9.1	13.3
4.7	6.9	4.9		1.2	3.3		4.9	7.0	6.2
1.9	3.0	2.2		.3	2.3		2.7	3.1	2.9
2.4	3.2	2.6	Sales/Total Assets	2.7	2.7		2.8	2.7	2.4
1.6	1.9	1.8		1.0	1.8		1.8	2.0	1.2
1.0	1.2	.9		.3	1.4		1.1	1.5	.7
2.8	1.8	2.3	% Depr., Dep., Amort./Sales	10.8			4.3	1.4	
(56) 6.4	(48) 6.4	(55) 6.2		(12) 17.6			6.0	(11) 5.2	
17.9	12.9	17.6		43.8			13.9	17.8	
1.5	3.0	3.0	% Officers', Directors'						
(14) 9.8	(20) 4.5	(21) 5.7	Owners' Comp/Sales						
21.4	8.9	17.0							
1162678M	1367061M	1234311M	Net Sales ($)	9450M	22821M	24707M	90683M	194664M	891986M
1119888M	1266479M	1231979M	Total Assets ($)	16645M	13256M	12695M	70071M	282916M	836396M

© RMA 2010

M = $ thousand   MM = $ million
See Pages 9 through 22 for Explanation of Ratios and Data

REAL ESTATE—All Other Consumer Goods Rental NAICS 532299

Current Data Sorted by Assets

Comparative Historical Data

0-500M	500M-2MM	2-10MM	10-50MM	50-100MM	100-250MM		4/1/05-3/31/06 ALL	4/1/06-3/31/07 ALL
						Type of Statement		
		1	1	1	1	Unqualified	1	2
	2	9				Reviewed	4	2
3	6	7	2			Compiled	10	12
10	7	2				Tax Returns	8	6
4	12	6	4	2	2	Other	7	12
	10 (4/1-9/30/09)		72 (10/1/09-3/31/10)					
17	27	25	7	3	3	**NUMBER OF STATEMENTS**	30	34
%	%	%	%	%	%	**ASSETS**	%	%
13.6	11.7	9.7				Cash & Equivalents	9.2	9.7
6.7	7.3	15.7				Trade Receivables (net)	10.6	12.2
19.3	15.9	14.5				Inventory	8.6	16.0
2.1	3.2	1.7				All Other Current	1.2	3.4
41.7	38.1	41.6				Total Current	29.6	41.3
45.0	49.7	46.0				Fixed Assets (net)	62.4	50.3
12.1	4.1	6.5				Intangibles (net)	2.9	3.3
1.2	8.1	5.9				All Other Non-Current	5.1	5.2
100.0	100.0	100.0				Total	100.0	100.0
						LIABILITIES		
14.3	18.8	13.5				Notes Payable-Short Term	18.8	19.8
10.2	5.4	4.0				Cur. Mat.-L.T.D.	6.4	9.0
11.3	4.1	7.1				Trade Payables	6.8	8.9
.1	.0	.3				Income Taxes Payable	.1	.0
4.0	4.5	7.7				All Other Current	5.0	13.7
39.9	32.8	32.7				Total Current	37.0	51.4
42.3	41.7	22.3				Long-Term Debt	27.3	23.9
.0	.0	.9				Deferred Taxes	.5	.2
13.9	6.2	17.4				All Other Non-Current	11.8	11.2
4.0	19.4	26.7				Net Worth	23.5	13.3
100.0	100.0	100.0				Total Liabilties & Net Worth	100.0	100.0
						INCOME DATA		
100.0	100.0	100.0				Net Sales	100.0	100.0
						Gross Profit		
97.1	80.3	97.1				Operating Expenses	87.1	96.8
2.9	19.7	2.9				Operating Profit	12.9	3.2
1.1	8.5	3.1				All Other Expenses (net)	5.4	3.0
1.8	11.2	-.1				Profit Before Taxes	7.5	.3
						RATIOS		
1.5	4.5	2.6					1.4	1.3
1.0	1.2	1.2				Current	.7	.7
.6	.4	.6					.3	.4
1.1	2.8	1.8					1.1	.8
.4	.6	.6				Quick	.4 (33)	.4
.1	.2	.3					.2	.2
0 UND	0 UND	17 21.1					0 UND	0 UND
0 837.0	8 47.9	27 13.5				Sales/Receivables	17 21.4	10 37.3
6 64.1	32 11.4	46 8.0					33 11.0	35 10.4
						Cost of Sales/Inventory		
						Cost of Sales/Payables		
12.0	3.1	4.1					21.4	14.8
UND	31.1	30.9				Sales/Working Capital	-24.0	-25.6
-29.4	-9.7	-8.4					-2.6	-5.7
4.9	6.9	1.9					3.4	4.8
(11) 2.7	(22) 3.4	(22) .4				EBIT/Interest	(24) 2.0	(31) 2.0
-.7	.2	-3.6					-.5	.3
						Net Profit + Depr., Dep., Amort./Cur. Mat. L/T/D		
.7	.7	.7					1.0	1.5
2.0	2.9	3.1				Fixed/Worth	2.3	3.07
-1.2	50.5	NM					31.1	-9.6
1.0	1.4	1.0					.9	1.6
UND	3.3	5.0				Debt/Worth	1.8	4.9
-2.8	51.9	NM					49.1	-89.4
	70.9	14.3					36.1	37.6
(21)	29.3	(19) -3.5				% Profit Before Taxes/Tangible Net Worth	(24) 8.0	(24) 12.9
	-14.2	-31.9					-.5	-5.5
21.3	19.6	8.6					10.5	6.8
11.3	10.5	-.5				% Profit Before Taxes/Total Assets	3.6	2.3
-7.2	-2.5	-7.2					-5.5	-2.9
74.8	17.9	13.6					5.2	9.6
4.2	3.3	3.5				Sales/Net Fixed Assets	2.5	3.4
3.2	.9	1.7					.7	1.5
5.2	2.2	2.0					2.3	2.7
2.5	1.5	1.3				Sales/Total Assets	1.6	1.5
1.1	.7	1.0					.6	.9
3.5	4.9	9.2					5.1	4.9
(11) 8.2	(18) 10.2	(22) 15.5				% Depr., Dep., Amort./Sales	(25) 12.5	(26) 10.1
15.8	20.4	18.0					24.8	17.8
	2.6	3.3					3.9	2.7
	(12) 5.0	(10) 5.1				% Officers', Directors' Owners' Comp/Sales	(10) 6.6	(15) 7.6
	10.3	7.7					11.6	15.4
14818M	43330M	164076M	166127M	145500M	339051M	Net Sales ($)	215595M	323937M
3789M	30634M	98626M	171880M	206634M	614655M	Total Assets ($)	152819M	227965M

© RMA 2010

M = $ thousand   MM = $ million
See Pages 9 through 22 for Explanation of Ratios and Data

Comparative Historical Data

Current Data Sorted by Sales

			Type of Statement						
3	5	4	Unqualified			1	1	1	1
5	7	13	Reviewed	1	3	3	1	4	1
9	12	16	Compiled	4	7	3	2		
13	12	19	Tax Returns	13	3	2	1		
13	22	30	Other	7	11	1	3	4	4
4/1/07-3/31/08	4/1/08-3/31/09	4/1/09-3/31/10		10 (4/1-9/30/09)			72 (10/1/09-3/31/10)		
ALL	ALL	ALL		0-1MM	1-3MM	3-5MM	5-10MM	10-25MM	25MM & OVER
43	58	82	**NUMBER OF STATEMENTS**	25	24	10	8	9	6
%	%	%	**ASSETS**	%	%	%	%	%	%
6.9	11.4	9.9	Cash & Equivalents	10.3	10.7	21.6			
10.6	17.1	12.4	Trade Receivables (net)	5.4	11.8	19.5			
13.9	10.1	14.2	Inventory	13.1	22.7	2.7			
3.7	3.1	2.4	All Other Current	.6	2.3	6.4			
35.2	41.6	38.8	Total Current	29.4	47.6	50.3			
53.0	42.4	47.9	Fixed Assets (net)	56.1	41.6	39.3			
2.8	6.0	6.5	Intangibles (net)	8.2	6.6	1.0			
9.1	10.0	6.8	All Other Non-Current	6.3	4.3	9.4			
100.0	100.0	100.0	Total	100.0	100.0	100.0			
			LIABILITIES						
16.0	16.1	15.2	Notes Payable-Short Term	13.7	18.2	8.0			
13.8	6.1	6.2	Cur. Mat.-L.T.D.	7.3	4.6	10.6			
5.9	6.5	6.5	Trade Payables	7.7	5.5	.5			
.2	.2	.1	Income Taxes Payable	.1	.0	.0			
11.8	13.0	5.8	All Other Current	2.7	6.5	3.5			
47.8	41.9	34.0	Total Current	31.4	34.7	22.6			
32.8	32.6	34.3	Long-Term Debt	55.6	24.5	29.8			
.5	.5	.5	Deferred Taxes	.0	.7	.8			
10.2	11.2	11.5	All Other Non-Current	12.1	6.8	16.8			
8.7	13.9	19.8	Net Worth	.9	33.2	30.0			
100.0	100.0	100.0	Total Liabilties & Net Worth	100.0	100.0	100.0			
			INCOME DATA						
100.0	100.0	100.0	Net Sales	100.0	100.0	100.0			
			Gross Profit						
91.3	91.3	89.7	Operating Expenses	79.2	96.6	88.3			
8.7	8.7	10.3	Operating Profit	20.8	3.4	11.7			
5.5	5.0	5.9	All Other Expenses (net)	9.9	1.4	8.5			
3.2	3.7	4.4	Profit Before Taxes	10.9	2.0	3.2			
			RATIOS						
2.1	2.6	2.4		1.9	3.1	10.9			
.8	.9	1.0	Current	1.0	1.6	1.7			
.4	.4	.6		.4	.6	1.0			
.9	1.4	1.5		1.4	2.1	6.5			
.4	.5	.6	Quick	.5	.6	1.7			
.2	.2	.2		.1	.3	.8			
0 UND	0 UND	0 UND		0 UND	5 78.4	0 UND			
17 22.1	22 16.4	17 21.1	Sales/Receivables	0 837.0	16 22.8	25 14.4			
30 12.0	62 5.9	40 9.1		15 23.6	44 8.2	57 6.4			
			Cost of Sales/Inventory						
			Cost of Sales/Payables						
9.9	5.2	4.9		5.5	3.0	2.9			
-36.1	-86.7	268.5	Sales/Working Capital	-419.0	22.4	29.5			
-3.9	-6.2	-8.9		-8.4	-10.7	UND			
3.8	4.9	4.3		4.3	6.9				
(36) .9	(48) 1.5	(65) 1.7	EBIT/Interest	(15) 2.5	(22) 2.6				
-.1	-.5	-.7		-.7	-.8				
		2.6	Net Profit + Depr., Dep.,						
	(11) 1.9		Amort./Cur. Mat. L/T/D						
		1.2							
.9	.5	.7		1.0	.4	.2			
2.1	1.9	2.3	Fixed/Worth	16.6	1.8	.7			
-5.1	-151.6	UND		-1.8	7.3	NM			
1.3	1.4	1.4		2.4	.9	.6			
4.0	2.7	4.6	Debt/Worth	16.1	2.1	5.8			
-8.4	-203.6	-42.1		-3.6	NM	NM			
68.0	28.3	39.4	% Profit Before Taxes/Tangible	104.5	37.5				
(27) 13.7	(42) 8.3	(61) 12.3	Net Worth	(16) 37.5	(18) 11.8				
-3.7	-2.7	-6.8		-3.1	-18.7				
11.5	11.3	15.1	% Profit Before Taxes/Total	20.3	16.5	14.9			
1.1	1.8	3.0	Assets	6.3	4.2	2.4			
-4.3	-3.4	-3.7		-2.7	-7.3	.3			
5.9	17.7	13.7		7.2	18.5	34.4			
3.1	5.0	3.9	Sales/Net Fixed Assets	2.6	6.1	8.8			
1.9	2.0	1.7		.6	1.9	2.6			
2.4	2.5	2.3		2.4	2.4	2.8			
1.7	1.4	1.4	Sales/Total Assets	.8	1.5	1.7			
1.0	.8	.7		.4	1.0	.9			
5.5	2.9	5.0		6.4	4.5				
(32) 10.7	(49) 9.7	(61) 11.7	% Depr., Dep., Amort./Sales	(17) 15.6	(16) 11.5				
16.4	14.4	17.9		27.7	16.6				
2.5	3.4	3.1	% Officers', Directors'		3.7				
(20) 4.8	(21) 5.5	(29) 5.1	Owners' Comp/Sales		(13) 5.1				
7.7	7.4	9.9			9.1				
776385M	1590813M	872902M	Net Sales ($)	12532M	47636M	41651M	60557M	148759M	561767M
718472M	825935M	1126218M	Total Assets ($)	17605M	36316M	72314M	46682M	351787M	601514M

© RMA 2010

M = $ thousand   MM = $ million
See Pages 9 through 22 for Explanation of Ratios and Data

Current Data Sorted by Assets   Comparative Historical Data

	0-500M	500M-2MM	2-10MM	10-50MM	50-100MM	100-250MM		4/1/05-3/31/06 ALL	4/1/06-3/31/07 ALL
Type of Statement									
Unqualified			3	5	2	1		4	10
Reviewed	1	3	5	1	2			6	17
Compiled	10	10	2					14	20
Tax Returns	17	20	6	1				17	35
Other	5	12	16	6		2		15	61
	11 (4/1-9/30/09)			119 (10/1/09-3/31/10)					
NUMBER OF STATEMENTS	33	45	32	13	4	3		56	143
	%	%	%	%	%	%		%	%
ASSETS									
Cash & Equivalents	14.9	9.1	3.0	6.1				9.0	7.6
Trade Receivables (net)	5.2	7.7	6.2	5.5				5.7	8.4
Inventory	14.3	4.1	13.6	7.4				9.1	9.0
All Other Current	1.3	2.6	1.5	9.4				1.9	3.5
Total Current	35.8	23.5	24.3	28.4				25.8	28.5
Fixed Assets (net)	51.2	66.7	68.0	48.7				67.0	60.6
Intangibles (net)	5.9	1.3	1.7	7.9				1.6	3.3
All Other Non-Current	7.0	8.4	6.0	14.9				5.7	7.5
Total	100.0	100.0	100.0	100.0				100.0	100.0
LIABILITIES									
Notes Payable-Short Term	19.4	9.2	10.9	6.8				13.0	10.8
Cur. Mat.-L.T.D.	13.9	5.6	7.8	5.5				8.2	9.7
Trade Payables	4.3	4.4	5.1	4.0				5.3	4.6
Income Taxes Payable	.0	.1	.0	.5				.1	.2
All Other Current	7.4	3.3	7.3	6.5				6.5	7.2
Total Current	45.0	22.6	31.1	23.3				33.1	32.7
Long-Term Debt	47.5	41.7	47.0	53.1				39.1	34.7
Deferred Taxes	.0	.2	.3	.1				.4	.5
All Other Non-Current	23.9	5.5	8.8	9.4				6.2	9.7
Net Worth	-16.4	30.1	12.8	14.2				21.2	22.4
Total Liabilties & Net Worth	100.0	100.0	100.0	100.0				100.0	100.0
INCOME DATA									
Net Sales	100.0	100.0	100.0	100.0				100.0	100.0
Gross Profit									
Operating Expenses	92.9	84.9	90.1	84.9				84.8	84.4
Operating Profit	7.1	15.1	9.9	15.1				15.2	15.6
All Other Expenses (net)	3.6	7.4	10.6	8.0				6.4	5.5
Profit Before Taxes	3.5	7.7	-.6	7.1				8.8	10.1
RATIOS									
Current	1.8	2.6	1.5	6.6				1.9	1.8
	.8	.8	.7	1.3				1.0	1.0
	.3	.3	.3	.6				.3	.3
Quick	1.0	1.9	.7	5.1				1.4	1.1
	.3	.5	.4	.7				.7 (142)	.6
	.2	.2	.1	.2				.2	.1
Sales/Receivables	0 UND	0 UND	0 UND	0 UND				0 UND	0 UND
	4 84.4	12 31.3	25 14.8	28 13.2				4 98.9	14 26.9
	13 27.5	29 12.7	51 7.2	46 7.9				24 15.5	33 11.0
Cost of Sales/Inventory									
Cost of Sales/Payables									
Sales/Working Capital	14.9	8.8	10.1	2.7				8.7	8.9
	-22.8	-46.1	-20.8	7.4				UND	-302.6
	-7.9	-4.1	-2.0	-8.4				-6.4	-4.3
EBIT/Interest	4.2	4.6	2.6	5.8				8.1	5.3
	(28) .6	(34) .9	(26) 1.1	(11) 1.2				(45) 2.6	(122) 2.8
	-1.8	-1.3	-.5	-.2				-.5	1.0
Net Profit + Depr., Dep., Amort./Cur. Mat. L/T/D									5.5
								(14) 2.0	
									1.5
Fixed/Worth	1.0	1.2	1.7	.2				1.2	1.2
	12.0	3.3	2.7	2.4				4.4	2.8
	-.6	10.3	-8.3	-1.1				-105.0	-405.5
Debt/Worth	.7	.8	1.3	1.4				1.2	1.2
	13.6	2.9	2.4	5.3				4.5	4.0
	-2.2	10.0	-13.8	-2.9				-233.0	-852.0
% Profit Before Taxes/Tangible Net Worth	86.8	29.6	19.4					45.4	66.4
	(19) 7.1	(37) 10.1	(22) 4.7					(41) 16.6	(107) 22.3
	-24.5	-9.7	-4.6					.5	9.8
% Profit Before Taxes/Total Assets	17.0	10.1	4.5	8.8				13.7	15.5
	-1.4	1.7	.1	.8				3.8	6.9
	-12.2	-3.9	-6.0	-3.3				-2.3	1.1
Sales/Net Fixed Assets	12.7	3.5	2.7	23.1				4.5	5.7
	5.1	1.5	.9	2.5				2.3	2.4
	2.6	.6	.2	.2				1.3	1.1
Sales/Total Assets	3.7	2.1	1.5	1.4				2.3	2.2
	2.4	1.1	.6	.5				1.4	1.3
	1.7	.3	.2	.2				.7	.6
% Depr., Dep., Amort./Sales	4.8	10.6	19.6	13.0				7.7	7.5
	(23) 8.2	(40) 16.2	(27) 27.2	(11) 15.8				(47) 10.0	(121) 13.2
	13.8	27.0	45.7	32.2				17.3	25.6
% Officers', Directors' Owners' Comp/Sales	5.3	3.8						4.3	1.8
	(18) 8.3	(23) 8.0						(23) 7.8	(46) 4.5
	14.4	11.6						14.6	7.0
Net Sales ($)	21304M	76015M	117978M	261498M	238923M	432515M		708440M	1704924M
Total Assets ($)	8589M	52984M	146933M	303664M	251583M	546092M		426245M	1808597M

© RMA 2010

M = $ thousand   MM = $ million
See Pages 9 through 22 for Explanation of Ratios and Data

Comparative Historical Data   Current Data Sorted by Sales

	4/1/07-3/31/08 ALL	4/1/08-3/31/09 ALL	4/1/09-3/31/10 ALL	Type of Statement	0-1MM	1-3MM	3-5MM	5-10MM	10-25MM	25MM & OVER
	10	11	11	Unqualified	1	3		1	4	3
	10	12	12	Reviewed		3	2	1	2	3
	23	13	22	Compiled	13	7	1	1		
	34	39	44	Tax Returns	30	10	4			
	61	46	41	Other	14	9	6	6	2	4
						11 (4/1-9/30/09)		119 (10/1/09-3/31/10)		
	138	121	130	**NUMBER OF STATEMENTS**	58	32	13	9	8	10
	%	%	%	**ASSETS**	%	%	%	%	%	%
	6.4	9.7	8.8	Cash & Equivalents	7.8	13.7	5.9			6.5
	9.7	8.5	6.6	Trade Receivables (net)	3.8	7.8	11.5			10.0
	9.7	9.6	10.0	Inventory	7.5	5.2	19.6			15.8
	4.1	3.5	3.0	All Other Current	1.7	2.5	1.0			7.3
	29.9	31.3	28.5	Total Current	20.8	29.2	37.9			39.6
	60.0	60.6	60.4	Fixed Assets (net)	68.6	63.4	52.0			50.8
	3.7	2.8	3.3	Intangibles (net)	3.8	1.2	1.3			4.6
	6.4	5.2	7.8	All Other Non-Current	6.8	6.2	8.8			5.0
	100.0	100.0	100.0	Total	100.0	100.0	100.0			100.0
				LIABILITIES						
	10.1	12.5	12.4	Notes Payable-Short Term	12.3	9.5	23.6			11.7
	8.5	7.8	8.1	Cur. Mat.-L.T.D.	9.8	5.5	8.4			4.7
	5.4	5.3	4.5	Trade Payables	2.3	5.6	8.6			7.6
	.1	.2	.1	Income Taxes Payable	.0	.1	.0			.0
	5.5	6.2	6.0	All Other Current	4.4	7.2	4.3			8.4
	29.6	32.0	31.1	Total Current	28.8	27.9	45.0			32.5
	38.3	39.1	44.3	Long-Term Debt	50.4	38.7	43.3			29.7
	.6	.6	.5	Deferred Taxes	.0	.6	.0			.1
	6.6	7.0	11.3	All Other Non-Current	15.4	3.6	16.1			5.9
	25.0	21.3	12.8	Net Worth	5.3	29.1	-4.4			31.8
	100.0	100.0	100.0	Total Liabilities & Net Worth	100.0	100.0	100.0			100.0
				INCOME DATA						
	100.0	100.0	100.0	Net Sales	100.0	100.0	100.0			100.0
				Gross Profit						
	85.4	85.6	88.5	Operating Expenses	81.6	90.3	102.6			96.6
	14.6	14.4	11.5	Operating Profit	18.4	9.7	-2.6			3.4
	5.9	5.5	6.9	All Other Expenses (net)	11.8	3.1	2.2			.3
	8.7	8.9	4.6	Profit Before Taxes	6.5	6.5	-4.8			3.0
				RATIOS						
	1.8	2.3	2.1	Current	2.0	4.2	1.5			2.0
	1.0	1.0	.8		.5	1.2	.8			1.1
	.4	.4	.3		.2	.5	.4			.7
	1.1	1.8	1.1	Quick	.9	4.1	.9			1.0
(136)	.5	.6	.5		.3	1.0	.5			.8
	.4	.1	.2		.1	.3	.2			.2
	0 UND	0 UND	0 UND	Sales/Receivables	0 UND	6 64.2	4 83.0			7 53.7
	14 26.2	11 31.9	12 29.3		4 96.9	14 26.4	24 15.2			31 11.9
	39 9.5	35 10.4	36 10.1		19 19.5	40 9.1	34 10.8			40 9.2
				Cost of Sales/Inventory						
				Cost of Sales/Payables						
	10.3	7.5	9.5	Sales/Working Capital	13.3	7.2	12.7			10.5
	UND	UND	-32.5		-16.1	31.9	-29.6			74.0
	-5.3	-7.2	-4.7		-1.8	-10.4	-6.6			-10.1
	5.2	4.6	3.5	EBIT/Interest	4.7	2.9	3.0			6.1
	(120) 2.4	(101) 2.6	(106) 1.0		(38) .7	(29) 1.0	1.6			1.7
	.8	.3	-.9		-1.4	-.6	-.7			-.3
	4.9	4.5	4.6	Net Profit + Depr., Dep., Amort./Cur. Mat. L/T/D						
	(12) 2.2	(12) 2.5	(15) 1.6							
	1.6	1.1	1.0							
	1.0	.9	1.2	Fixed/Worth	1.5	1.0	1.1			.8
	2.3	2.3	2.9		4.0	2.3	25.3			6.1
	10.1	103.4	-7.5		-7.6	12.3	-.9			-5.3
	1.1	1.0	1.2	Debt/Worth	1.2	1.1	1.6			.2
	3.8	3.0	2.9		3.3	1.9	27.1			6.8
	20.3	133.4	-12.7		-12.7	13.6	-2.5			-13.7
	51.5	44.1	30.2	% Profit Before Taxes/Tangible Net Worth	25.2	39.3				
	(114) 23.8	(93) 19.5	(91) 7.1		(42) 7.7	(26) 2.5				
	7.8	2.2	-4.8		-5.5	-16.1				
	13.6	11.6	7.9	% Profit Before Taxes/Total Assets	8.4	9.5	4.9			8.6
	5.5	5.1	.4		.3	.6	.8			2.0
	-.8	-.6	-5.0		-4.9	-4.4	-16.7			-2.9
	5.2	7.8	5.4	Sales/Net Fixed Assets	4.5	5.3	8.1			4.6
	2.5	2.6	2.3		1.0	2.8	2.9			2.8
	1.1	.8	.6		.2	.7	2.5			1.1
	2.1	2.1	2.2	Sales/Total Assets	2.1	2.4	2.5			1.7
	1.4	1.4	1.3		.7	1.4	1.8			1.0
	.5	.5	.4		.1	.5	1.3			.9
	7.5	6.6	8.9	% Depr., Dep., Amort./Sales	10.4	10.5	4.4			
	(110) 13.3	(92) 13.3	(104) 16.2		(51) 20.0	(23) 15.5	(11) 11.7			
	21.2	28.2	28.7		32.4	30.9	19.6			
	2.3	3.2	2.9	% Officers', Directors' Owners' Comp/Sales	5.7	2.9				
	(47) 5.2	(35) 4.6	(51) 5.8		(19) 9.5	(17) 5.9				
	9.4	6.7	11.5		16.4					
	2202984M	1451582M	1148233M	Net Sales ($)	28496M	52743M	48340M	61845M	120056M	836753M
	1758507M	1526148M	1309845M	Total Assets ($)	72148M	100902M	30149M	99085M	169175M	838386M

© RMA 2010

M = $ thousand   MM = $ million
See Pages 9 through 22 for Explanation of Ratios and Data

Current Data Sorted by Assets   **Comparative Historical Data**

	0-500M	500M-2MM	2-10MM	10-50MM	50-100MM	100-250MM	Type of Statement	4/1/05-3/31/06 ALL	4/1/06-3/31/07 ALL
			2	5	4	4	Unqualified	8	11
		3	4	11	1		Reviewed	6	7
		3	8	5			Compiled	8	8
	20	18	10	1			Tax Returns	2	7
	14	17	16	10	1	5	Other	7	20
		14 (4/1-9/30/09)		148 (10/1/09-3/31/10)					
NUMBER OF STATEMENTS	34	41	40	32	6	9		31	53
	%	%	%	%	%	%	**ASSETS**	%	%
Cash & Equivalents	17.6	10.0	6.5	8.5				7.0	8.0
Trade Receivables (net)	3.5	9.1	11.6	19.3				15.7	14.6
Inventory	1.3	1.0	2.4	5.6				4.2	6.3
All Other Current	2.5	4.9	3.3	2.5				5.7	4.1
Total Current	24.8	25.0	23.8	35.9				32.5	33.1
Fixed Assets (net)	67.8	58.9	56.7	56.5				55.3	51.0
Intangibles (net)	.4	3.7	1.5	2.9				2.6	1.7
All Other Non-Current	6.9	12.5	18.0	4.6				9.6	14.2
Total	100.0	100.0	100.0	100.0				100.0	100.0
							LIABILITIES		
Notes Payable-Short Term	6.2	9.2	5.5	5.3				8.9	6.1
Cur. Mat.-L.T.D.	22.6	6.9	7.0	7.2				3.6	6.6
Trade Payables	4.5	3.4	5.5	10.0				8.3	7.4
Income Taxes Payable	.0	.0	.1	.1				.2	.1
All Other Current	12.9	7.8	9.7	6.3				9.3	7.5
Total Current	46.3	27.3	27.7	28.9				30.3	27.7
Long-Term Debt	89.0	50.5	48.2	25.9				32.0	38.8
Deferred Taxes	.0	.0	.6	1.4				2.2	.9
All Other Non-Current	9.6	3.8	7.3	1.4				5.5	7.7
Net Worth	-44.9	18.4	16.2	42.4				30.0	25.0
Total Liabilties & Net Worth	100.0	100.0	100.0	100.0				100.0	100.0
							INCOME DATA		
Net Sales	100.0	100.0	100.0	100.0				100.0	100.0
Gross Profit									
Operating Expenses	63.2	68.7	82.0	84.7				85.4	80.5
Operating Profit	36.8	31.3	18.0	15.3				14.6	19.5
All Other Expenses (net)	7.1	15.1	9.5	7.2				7.7	10.3
Profit Before Taxes	29.7	16.2	8.5	8.1				6.9	9.2
							RATIOS		
Current	2.0	2.3	1.5	2.0				2.6	1.7
	.5	.9	.7	1.1				1.1	1.1
	.1	.2	.3	.6				.4	.4
Quick	2.0	1.9	1.4	1.5				1.6	1.4
	.4	.5	.5	.8				.7	.7
	.1	.1	.2	.4				.1	.2
Sales/Receivables	0 UND	0 UND	0 UND	24 14.9				12 30.9	0 UND
	0 UND	0 UND	16 22.6	51 7.1				34 10.9	22 16.4
	0 UND	57 6.4	58 6.3	65 5.6				71 5.1	68 5.4
Cost of Sales/Inventory									
Cost of Sales/Payables									
Sales/Working Capital	6.7	5.1	10.1	5.3				6.0	4.6
	-37.7	-12.4	-13.2	59.6				116.2	38.3
	-2.3	-2.5	-3.9	-6.5				-4.7	-3.3
EBIT/Interest	8.6	6.7	6.0	9.1				10.0	9.9
	(24) 3.8	(28) 2.6	(34) 2.1	(28) 3.3				(26) 3.7	(34) 3.1
	.5	.2	.6	1.8				1.5	1.4
Net Profit + Depr., Dep., Amort./Cur. Mat. L/T/D									
Fixed/Worth	.8	.9	1.9	.8				1.1	.7
	10.6	2.9	4.0	1.4				1.9	1.8
	-.9	NM	-4.9	2.8				4.4	7.7
Debt/Worth	.4	1.3	1.3	.6				1.1	.9
	21.4	4.1	5.7	1.6				2.3	2.8
	-1.8	-44.8	-10.9	4.0				11.2	11.4
% Profit Before Taxes/Tangible Net Worth	147.6	61.8	25.4	37.5				27.2	41.7
	(21) 17.5	(30) 28.1	(25) 5.9	(30) 9.8				(27) 13.5	(44) 14.3
	-65.1	5.1	-11.2	4.2				2.7	4.0
% Profit Before Taxes/Total Assets	53.6	16.2	11.3	11.5				11.2	12.1
	20.0	4.3	3.1	4.0				4.4	3.5
	2.1	.0	-2.4	1.2				-.2	.2
Sales/Net Fixed Assets	3.4	1.9	5.9	6.4				4.8	10.0
	1.8	.8	1.7	1.1				1.0	1.2
	1.0	.3	.4	.6				.5	.4
Sales/Total Assets	2.1	.9	1.5	1.5				1.3	1.3
	1.5	.5	.9	.7				.6	.5
	.6	.2	.4	.4				.3	.2
% Depr., Dep., Amort./Sales	12.9	13.0	3.2	3.3				3.8	2.9
	(24) 26.7	(24) 31.7	(37) 17.6	(31) 12.9				(25) 15.3	(42) 16.9
	43.9	57.5	36.1	25.6				27.8	47.8
% Officers', Directors' Owners' Comp/Sales			2.5						
		(11)	6.0						
			8.8						
Net Sales ($)	11903M	47139M	182186M	702107M	109770M	528007M		736198M	1271816M
Total Assets ($)	7605M	47069M	184520M	666429M	436240M	1405459M		1234151M	1811629M

Comparative Historical Data / Current Data Sorted by Sales

Type of Statement	4/1/07-3/31/08 ALL	4/1/08-3/31/09 ALL	4/1/09-3/31/10 ALL	0-1MM	1-3MM	3-5MM	5-10MM	10-25MM	25MM & OVER
Unqualified	8	12	15	2			1	5	6
Reviewed	8	16	19	2		3	5	6	3
Compiled	15	11	16	4	1	1	7	2	1
Tax Returns	22	25	49	34	11	2	2		
Other	21	44	63	32	6	2	7	9	7
				14 (4/1-9/30/09)			148 (10/1/09-3/31/10)		
NUMBER OF STATEMENTS	74	108	162	74	18	9	22	22	17
ASSETS	%	%	%	%	%	%	%	%	%
Cash & Equivalents	10.0	8.0	9.9	11.3	6.8		9.9	7.0	10.1
Trade Receivables (net)	5.3	14.1	10.1	5.1	10.9		15.6	12.0	20.4
Inventory	3.6	4.5	2.4	.2	1.5		4.0	8.6	3.2
All Other Current	2.8	3.0	3.5	3.6	.2		4.5	6.5	2.0
Total Current	21.7	29.6	25.9	20.3	19.5		34.0	34.1	35.8
Fixed Assets (net)	67.8	60.6	60.8	66.5	66.4		50.6	57.8	49.8
Intangibles (net)	1.1	2.0	2.1	2.2	.1		6.1	1.1	1.0
All Other Non-Current	9.5	7.8	11.2	11.0	13.9		9.4	7.0	13.5
Total	100.0	100.0	100.0	100.0	100.0		100.0	100.0	100.0
LIABILITIES									
Notes Payable-Short Term	8.4	8.2	7.4	7.9	1.8		7.4	11.9	6.7
Cur. Mat.-L.T.D.	12.6	10.2	10.2	14.7	6.7		8.4	5.0	4.8
Trade Payables	2.7	6.6	5.7	1.9	6.5		6.9	10.7	14.2
Income Taxes Payable	.0	.0	.0	.0	.1		.0	.1	.1
All Other Current	5.0	8.1	8.6	8.0	11.4		8.7	10.0	9.2
Total Current	28.7	33.2	32.0	32.4	26.5		31.4	37.7	34.9
Long-Term Debt	48.1	47.8	51.8	65.1	72.8		49.4	21.3	27.4
Deferred Taxes	.4	.8	.8	.0	.0		1.4	2.7	1.6
All Other Non-Current	5.5	4.6	5.2	9.2	2.7		1.9	1.0	1.7
Net Worth	17.4	13.6	10.2	-6.8	-2.0		15.9	37.3	34.3
Total Liabilities & Net Worth	100.0	100.0	100.0	100.0	100.0		100.0	100.0	100.0
INCOME DATA									
Net Sales	100.0	100.0	100.0	100.0	100.0		100.0	100.0	100.0
Gross Profit									
Operating Expenses	77.1	77.7	74.2	60.8	81.2		94.6	84.7	83.0
Operating Profit	22.9	22.3	25.8	39.2	18.8		5.4	15.3	17.0
All Other Expenses (net)	9.2	7.2	10.1	14.5	12.2		4.5	4.5	5.0
Profit Before Taxes	13.7	15.2	15.7	24.7	6.6		.9	10.8	12.0
RATIOS									
Current	2.0	2.0	1.7	1.8	2.0		2.1	1.6	1.3
	.8	.8	.8	.7	.6		.9	.9	1.1
	.4	.3	.3	.1	.2		.5	.6	.5
Quick	1.8	1.4	1.5	1.6	2.0		1.5	1.1	1.2
	.6	.6	.5	.3	.6		.5	.4	1.0
	.2	.1	.2	.1	.2		.1	.2	.3
Sales/Receivables	0 UND	0 UND	0 UND	0 UND	0 UND		25 14.7	6 64.3	20 18.4
	12 29.7	24 15.1	10 35.7	0 UND	3 104.7		49 7.5	27 13.3	35 10.3
	35 10.5	55 6.6	52 7.0	4 96.7	80 4.6		65 5.6	58 6.3	60 6.1
Cost of Sales/Inventory									
Cost of Sales/Payables									
Sales/Working Capital	8.5	7.1	8.0	6.5	10.2		6.7	7.2	15.5
	-17.4	-23.3	-16.5	-7.9	-58.1		-28.1	-46.8	31.5
	-3.4	-3.2	-3.2	-2.2	-2.4		-4.0	-5.6	-6.2
EBIT/Interest	7.6	10.0	6.8	7.0	4.2		4.1	9.3	6.1
	(54) 2.4	(86) 3.5	(126) 2.9	(49) 3.7	(13) .0		1.4	(19) 4.0	(15) 2.7
	1.3	1.6	1.1	1.4	-1.0		-1.0	1.9	1.6
Net Profit + Depr., Dep., Amort./Cur. Mat. L/T/D		3.3	10.6						
		(17) 1.6	(16) 3.1						
		.7	1.0						
Fixed/Worth	1.2	1.0	1.0	1.0	1.4		1.0	1.0	.5
	2.6	1.9	2.4	2.7	NM		4.0	1.6	1.6
	-41.5	12.1	UND	-7.3	-6.6		-11.8	5.5	3.5
Debt/Worth	.9	.9	1.0	.8	1.7		1.7	.6	1.6
	2.8	3.3	3.4	3.8	NM		5.7	2.0	2.3
	-44.4	27.1	-51.0	-6.4	-7.9		-16.1	6.8	3.4
% Profit Before Taxes/Tangible Net Worth	61.2	52.3	47.5	55.4			20.1	48.0	41.6
	(55) 17.1	(84) 19.7	(120) 12.4	(52) 16.3		(15) 4.9	(19) 10.6	20.0	
	4.6	6.7	1.9	2.1			-64.2	3.9	5.2
% Profit Before Taxes/Total Assets	15.0	14.8	15.6	24.8	15.0		10.7	11.3	11.6
	4.6	5.9	5.4	7.4	.0		1.3	6.1	5.7
	.2	1.1	.4	.7	-10.2		-10.2	1.8	2.0
Sales/Net Fixed Assets	2.3	5.0	3.2	2.0	4.4		7.7	6.1	54.6
	.7	1.0	1.1	.8	1.5		2.0	1.0	2.1
	.4	.5	.5	.3	.5		.7	.4	.6
Sales/Total Assets	1.1	1.6	1.5	1.0	1.6		2.0	1.7	2.6
	.5	.8	.6	.4	.9		1.2	.7	1.1
	.3	.2	.3	.2	.3		.5	.3	.3
% Depr., Dep., Amort./Sales	10.9	3.8	8.2	19.3	12.1		3.6	6.5	.2
	(59) 24.9	(92) 21.6	(125) 21.7	(52) 34.8	(15) 18.5	(20) 15.2	(19) 11.6	(11) 2.9	
	51.9	48.4	39.5	55.6	39.0		26.1	31.0	7.2
% Officers', Directors' Owners' Comp/Sales	1.3	.9	2.6						
	(13) 3.0	(18) 3.0	(33) 4.0						
	7.0	7.3	9.5						
Net Sales ($)	974667M	2324748M	1581112M	26070M	36643M	33534M	159404M	359056M	966405M
Total Assets ($)	2059477M	2721026M	2747322M	90669M	81854M	54023M	204892M	824506M	1491378M

© RMA 2010

M = $ thousand   MM = $ million
See Pages 9 through 22 for Explanation of Ratios and Data

Current Data Sorted by Assets   Comparative Historical Data

0-500M	500M-2MM	2-10MM	10-50MM	50-100MM	100-250MM	Type of Statement	4/1/05-3/31/06 ALL	4/1/06-3/31/07 ALL
	1	6	19	13	18	Unqualified	48	66
3	9	39	39	5	3	Reviewed	63	95
12	11	26	10			Compiled	67	58
7	22	12	1			Tax Returns	41	57
7	21	44	42	13	14	Other	117	117
	68 (4/1-9/30/09)		329 (10/1/09-3/31/10)					
29	64	127	111	31	35	**NUMBER OF STATEMENTS**	336	393
%	%	%	%	%	%	**ASSETS**	%	%
16.2	13.3	7.7	6.5	6.1	5.6	Cash & Equivalents	8.1	6.8
12.9	10.1	17.7	11.6	10.9	10.6	Trade Receivables (net)	15.2	14.5
1.4	7.9	13.2	13.1	16.5	7.0	Inventory	11.3	10.2
1.0	1.9	4.4	2.0	1.7	6.3	All Other Current	1.8	3.1
31.4	33.2	43.0	33.4	35.2	29.4	Total Current	36.5	34.7
60.3	59.3	49.3	55.9	55.4	56.8	Fixed Assets (net)	56.3	58.6
2.9	2.1	2.5	2.3	3.5	7.9	Intangibles (net)	1.7	1.5
5.4	5.4	5.2	8.4	5.9	5.8	All Other Non-Current	5.5	5.2
100.0	100.0	100.0	100.0	100.0	100.0	Total	100.0	100.0
						LIABILITIES		
6.9	7.0	12.1	10.0	12.3	4.6	Notes Payable-Short Term	10.6	10.4
13.2	10.4	9.0	10.9	9.9	5.0	Cur. Mat.-L.T.D.	8.9	10.9
5.2	4.0	6.6	3.2	5.4	3.7	Trade Payables	6.7	6.0
.0	.5	.3	.2	.4	.2	Income Taxes Payable	.4	.3
12.5	3.5	6.3	3.9	3.6	6.6	All Other Current	5.2	5.5
37.9	25.6	34.4	28.2	31.7	20.1	Total Current	31.7	33.0
37.9	32.6	23.1	34.8	30.5	35.1	Long-Term Debt	34.4	34.0
.0	.6	1.4	1.0	1.1	2.6	Deferred Taxes	1.0	.9
6.9	4.3	4.5	3.6	3.7	7.2	All Other Non-Current	3.1	3.6
17.3	37.0	36.7	32.4	33.0	34.9	Net Worth	29.7	28.4
100.0	100.0	100.0	100.0	100.0	100.0	Total Liabilities & Net Worth	100.0	100.0
						INCOME DATA		
100.0	100.0	100.0	100.0	100.0	100.0	Net Sales	100.0	100.0
						Gross Profit		
88.0	83.4	94.1	94.6	94.8	86.2	Operating Expenses	84.4	84.4
12.0	16.6	5.9	5.4	5.2	13.8	Operating Profit	15.6	15.6
2.8	4.2	4.0	5.2	5.1	6.6	All Other Expenses (net)	3.1	3.4
9.2	12.4	1.9	.2	.1	7.2	Profit Before Taxes	12.5	12.2
						RATIOS		
2.1	3.6	2.3	1.6	1.8	2.6		2.0	1.8
.8	1.1	1.3	1.1	1.2	1.7	Current	1.3	1.1
.3	.6	.6	.5	.8	.9		.6	.6
2.1	3.3	1.5	1.2	1.4	1.6		1.5	1.4
.8	.8	.7	.6	.7	(34) .9	Quick	.8	.7
.3	.3	.3	.3	.2	.5		.3	.3
0 UND	0 UND	28 13.2	33 11.2	32 11.4	29 12.4		8 45.1	17 21.0
0 UND	11 33.0	44 8.3	52 7.0	46 8.0	41 8.8	Sales/Receivables	43 8.5	42 8.7
57 6.4	43 8.4	66 5.5	71 5.1	55 6.6	65 5.6		73 5.0	66 5.6
						Cost of Sales/Inventory		
						Cost of Sales/Payables		
14.2	5.4	4.0	6.8	5.0	3.9		6.1	7.0
-45.0	103.8	11.8	44.1	19.0	9.5	Sales/Working Capital	21.2	50.5
-3.6	-10.3	-6.9	-4.8	-15.4	-24.9		-7.5	-6.2
22.8	8.1	4.9	3.1	4.1	4.5		6.9	6.6
(22) 2.3	(55) 2.9	(117) 1.2	(100) 1.3	(28) 1.5	(31) 2.7	EBIT/Interest	(300) 3.4	(365) 3.3
-1.1	-.3	-.5	-.3	.5	.4		2.1	1.7
	5.3	2.3	3.3				2.6	3.5
	(10) 1.7	(32) 1.2	(40) 1.2			Net Profit + Depr., Dep., Amort./Cur. Mat. L/T/D	(69) 1.8	(89) 1.5
	.9	.5	.7				1.1	1.1
.8	1.0	.6	.7	.9	1.0		1.0	1.1
2.5	1.7	1.4	2.0	1.7	2.3	Fixed/Worth	1.9	2.1
-1.2	4.3	3.5	4.7	5.1	5.8		4.2	4.7
.5	.7	.8	1.1	1.1	1.4		1.2	1.3
1.7	1.8	2.0	2.7	2.0	2.0	Debt/Worth	2.3	2.6
-4.1	5.4	5.3	5.1	7.4	6.8		6.0	6.2
144.7	41.2	29.3	16.4	11.6	25.4		45.3	51.8
(17) 19.7	(55) 21.4	(115) 4.8	(102) 3.0	(30) 4.5	(29) 13.3	% Profit Before Taxes/Tangible Net Worth	(295) 26.2	(355) 27.2
5.4	-10.2	-7.9	-21.3	-24.5	-2.8		11.8	12.5
19.4	19.9	8.4	4.9	6.1	8.7		14.8	15.3
2.2	8.8	.7	.6	.9	4.8	% Profit Before Taxes/Total Assets	7.9	7.3
-14.7	-4.5	-4.7	-5.8	-4.0	-2.9		2.4	2.5
9.0	4.9	8.6	3.4	3.5	1.9		4.8	4.1
2.2	1.6	2.3	1.2	1.2	1.0	Sales/Net Fixed Assets	1.6	1.6
.9	.6	.8	.6	.6	.5		.8	.8
2.6	1.7	1.6	1.0	1.1	1.0		1.6	1.5
1.1	.9	1.0	.7	.7	.5	Sales/Total Assets	1.0	1.0
.6	.5	.6	.5	.4	.3		.5	.6
12.4	7.7	6.0	8.9		4.3		5.3	6.7
(20) 27.3	(49) 23.9	(112) 13.4	(97) 14.4	(24) 10.3	(15) 9.8	% Depr., Dep., Amort./Sales	(288) 12.7	(327) 13.5
76.3	47.2	31.0	25.5	19.0	14.0		28.5	28.0
	4.6	3.1	1.2				1.7	2.4
	(19) 7.6	(41) 4.3	(12) 2.4			% Officers', Directors' Owners' Comp/Sales	(80) 4.6	(99) 5.1
	10.5	6.8	3.3				7.9	8.7
14718M	83763M	686067M	2083983M	1607601M	4266314M	Net Sales ($)	5737614M	8119047M
7076M	71341M	600944M	2655104M	2121717M	5416601M	Total Assets ($)	5345099M	7714163M

M = $ thousand   MM = $ million
See Pages 9 through 22 for Explanation of Ratios and Data

Comparative Historical Data

Current Data Sorted by Sales

						Type of Statement						
	68		66		57	Unqualified	1	2	1	5	12	36
	113		98		98	Reviewed	6	13	12	24	29	14
	78		57		59	Compiled	21	10	11	11	4	2
	47		46		42	Tax Returns	22	11	3	3	3	
	156		161		141	Other	17	28	15	19	31	31
	4/1/07-		4/1/08-		4/1/09-			68 (4/1-9/30/09)			329 (10/1/09-3/31/10)	
	3/31/08		3/31/09		3/31/10							
	ALL		ALL		ALL		0-1MM	1-3MM	3-5MM	5-10MM	10-25MM	25MM & OVER
	462		428		397	NUMBER OF STATEMENTS	67	64	42	62	79	83
	%		%		%	ASSETS	%	%	%	%	%	%
	7.1		7.7		8.6	Cash & Equivalents	10.7	12.4	7.5	9.5	6.5	5.7
	13.4		12.8		13.3	Trade Receivables (net)	8.6	11.1	15.7	17.4	14.3	13.4
	10.1		12.8		11.2	Inventory	1.8	10.2	14.9	11.4	13.4	15.4
	3.2		2.5		3.0	All Other Current	.9	5.8	3.3	1.6	2.4	4.2
	33.9		35.8		36.0	Total Current	22.0	39.5	41.4	39.9	36.6	38.6
	59.7		56.8		54.7	Fixed Assets (net)	70.0	47.2	53.7	52.4	55.5	49.6
	1.7		2.1		3.0	Intangibles (net)	2.8	2.7	.8	2.0	2.4	5.6
	4.7		5.3		6.3	All Other Non-Current	5.2	10.5	4.1	5.7	5.4	6.1
	100.0		100.0		100.0	Total	100.0	100.0	100.0	100.0	100.0	100.0
						LIABILITIES						
	9.7		10.1		9.7	Notes Payable-Short Term	4.5	11.9	12.8	10.5	11.2	8.5
	10.3		9.6		9.8	Cur. Mat.-L.T.D.	11.6	10.5	11.0	9.2	10.4	7.0
	6.0		5.1		4.8	Trade Payables	1.9	4.8	5.3	5.2	6.3	5.1
	.4		.2		.3	Income Taxes Payable	.6	.2	.3	.2	.1	.3
	4.5		5.5		5.5	All Other Current	4.9	6.8	7.7	4.4	3.6	6.2
	30.8		30.5		30.0	Total Current	23.5	34.2	37.1	29.6	31.6	27.2
	37.0		34.0		30.6	Long-Term Debt	38.9	26.7	28.6	28.1	29.9	30.6
	.8		.8		1.1	Deferred Taxes	.7	.7	1.5	1.0	1.1	1.9
	3.5		3.3		4.6	All Other Non-Current	6.6	3.1	4.4	2.3	5.3	5.1
	27.9		31.4		33.7	Net Worth	30.3	35.4	28.4	39.0	32.1	35.3
	100.0		100.0		100.0	Total Liabilties & Net Worth	100.0	100.0	100.0	100.0	100.0	100.0
						INCOME DATA						
	100.0		100.0		100.0	Net Sales	100.0	100.0	100.0	100.0	100.0	100.0
						Gross Profit						
	84.6		85.9		91.4	Operating Expenses	77.2	91.8	98.7	96.1	93.5	93.4
	15.4		14.1		8.6	Operating Profit	22.8	8.2	1.3	3.9	6.5	6.6
	4.0		4.4		4.6	All Other Expenses (net)	7.7	4.3	3.5	3.9	4.0	3.8
	11.3		9.7		4.0	Profit Before Taxes	15.1	3.8	-2.2	.0	2.5	2.7
						RATIOS						
	2.0		2.2		2.2		2.7	2.7	2.0	2.4	1.6	2.6
	1.1		1.2		1.2	Current	1.0	1.0	1.2	1.2	1.0	1.5
	.5		.6		.6		.4	.6	.5	.5	.6	1.0
	1.4		1.5		1.5		2.7	1.5	1.6	1.9	1.2	1.5
	.6		.7	(396)	.7	Quick	.9	.6	.5	.7	.6	(82) .9
	.3		.3		.3		.2	.3	.2	.4	.4	.5
13	27.6	17	20.9	21	17.5		0 UND	0 UND	30 12.0	30 12.3	33 11.2	32 11.4
40	9.2	40	9.2	41	8.8	Sales/Receivables	0 UND	23 15.7	51 7.2	45 8.1	53 6.9	46 8.0
64	5.7	63	5.8	64	5.7		61 6.0	47 7.8	67 5.5	64 5.7	75 4.9	61 6.0
						Cost of Sales/Inventory						
						Cost of Sales/Payables						
	7.1		5.5		5.0		3.9	5.3	5.8	4.9	6.4	4.6
	30.2		18.7		24.4	Sales/Working Capital	UND	-26.1	12.6	26.4	-158.3	9.6
	-5.6		-8.6		-6.6		-3.6	-5.4	-2.9	-5.7	-5.5	196.9
	6.2		6.1		4.5		8.4	8.3	1.2	4.9	3.7	4.4
(420)	3.0	(395)	2.8	(353)	1.6	EBIT/Interest	(52) 2.5	(52) 1.6	-.4	(55) 1.6	(74) 1.7	(78) 1.9
	1.5		1.1		-.4		-.4	-1.5	-1.1	.7	.2	.3
	3.0		3.7		2.8			2.6	1.3	2.6	1.6	8.0
(95)	1.6	(91)	1.8	(100)	1.2	Net Profit + Depr., Dep., Amort./Cur. Mat. L/T/D	(12) .8	(11) .6	(18) 1.3	(24) 1.1	(28) 2.2	
	1.2		1.1		.5			.2	.4	.4	.7	.9
	1.0		.9		.8		1.0	.6	.9	.6	.8	.7
	2.3		1.9		1.8	Fixed/Worth	2.3	1.5	1.8	1.4	2.3	1.5
	5.8		4.5		4.5		10.7	4.7	4.3	3.4	4.7	3.9
	1.3		1.1		.9		.6	.6	1.0	.7	1.2	1.0
	2.9		2.5		2.1	Debt/Worth	1.8	2.1	2.8	1.5	2.7	2.0
	7.0		6.5		5.7		9.8	9.0	7.8	5.1	5.1	6.3
	51.1		41.1		24.6		43.9	33.5	8.6	19.8	25.4	15.0
(410)	27.5	(380)	21.6	(348)	6.7	% Profit Before Taxes/Tangible Net Worth	(53) 13.0	(54) 12.3	(37) -7.7	(56) 5.4	(74) 7.5	(74) 6.8
	12.0		4.7		-11.2		-4.0	-9.7	-27.8	-1.4	-11.2	-12.9
	13.8		13.1		8.5		18.3	13.0	.9	8.1	5.4	8.0
	6.7		6.2		1.4	% Profit Before Taxes/Total Assets	4.2	2.0	-5.0	1.7	2.1	1.1
	1.9		.4		-4.7		-3.9	-7.4	-8.2	-2.5	-4.0	-4.3
	4.1		4.6		4.9		1.9	6.5	7.9	9.8	5.3	4.0
	1.5		1.6		1.4	Sales/Net Fixed Assets	.6	1.8	1.6	2.1	1.3	1.9
	.7		.8		.7		.4	.9	.8	.8	.6	.9
	1.5		1.5		1.4		1.0	1.7	1.6	1.6	1.3	1.4
	.9		.9		.8	Sales/Total Assets	.5	.8	1.0	1.0	.8	.9
	.5		.5		.5		.3	.5	.6	.6	.5	.6
	6.2		6.3		6.8		22.3	6.2	8.1	6.0	7.9	4.8
(401)	14.4	(352)	13.8	(317)	14.4	% Depr., Dep., Amort./Sales	(53) 46.9	(51) 22.8	(35) 14.5	(55) 12.3	(68) 14.4	(55) 8.5
	29.7		27.3		30.3		72.2	52.7	24.3	28.1	22.5	12.8
	1.6		1.2		2.2		7.2	2.7	2.8	3.8	2.0	.9
(101)	3.2	(102)	3.7	(86)	4.2	% Officers', Directors' Owners' Comp/Sales	(12) 10.0	(21) 4.6	(16) 4.8	(13) 4.8	(12) 2.9	(12) 1.3
	7.1		7.5		7.4		12.3	7.3	9.8	6.6	3.9	2.4
9920573M		10394268M		8742446M		Net Sales ($)	29478M	112220M	168292M	438998M	1269115M	6724343M
10279818M		11236597M		10872783M		Total Assets ($)	77213M	206848M	224266M	680014M	2078068M	7606374M

M = $ thousand   MM = $ million
See Pages 9 through 22 for Explanation of Ratios and Data

Current Data Sorted by Assets

Comparative Historical Data

Type of Statement

	23	22
Unqualified	23	22
Reviewed	10	8
Compiled	8	18
Tax Returns	16	29
Other	30	40

							4/1/05-3/31/06 ALL	4/1/06-3/31/07 ALL

	1	4	6	3	4			
	1	3	4		1			
3	4	8	2					
9	7	6						
8	10	11	6	5	4			
	15 (4/1-9/30/09)		95 (10/1/09-3/31/10)					

0-500M	500M-2MM	2-10MM	10-50MM	50-100MM	100-250MM		ALL	ALL
21	22	32	18	8	9	NUMBER OF STATEMENTS	87	117
%	%	%	%	%	%	ASSETS	%	%
18.4	16.9	11.1	4.5			Cash & Equivalents	7.5	7.3
9.5	9.0	14.7	16.0			Trade Receivables (net)	19.0	18.8
7.6	8.4	11.0	5.1			Inventory	5.2	8.5
8.9	10.2	10.3	5.8			All Other Current	6.5	6.4
44.5	44.5	47.1	31.4			Total Current	38.3	41.1
45.0	50.9	43.4	43.5			Fixed Assets (net)	43.8	40.2
2.0	.4	1.9	3.8			Intangibles (net)	1.8	1.9
8.5	4.2	7.6	21.4			All Other Non-Current	16.1	16.8
100.0	100.0	100.0	100.0			Total	100.0	100.0
						LIABILITIES		
7.1	12.8	8.0	12.4			Notes Payable-Short Term	10.7	14.9
14.8	10.8	8.1	11.7			Cur. Mat.-L.T.D.	12.3	10.9
9.7	8.8	6.9	5.6			Trade Payables	6.7	9.5
.0	.2	.1	.1			Income Taxes Payable	.3	.3
30.9	5.1	10.8	7.6			All Other Current	8.8	6.6
62.5	37.7	33.8	37.5			Total Current	38.8	42.2
22.0	44.6	22.5	25.4			Long-Term Debt	31.5	34.4
.1	.0	.3	1.4			Deferred Taxes	.4	.3
5.5	3.2	5.9	9.4			All Other Non-Current	7.1	9.9
9.9	14.5	37.6	26.3			Net Worth	22.2	13.3
100.0	100.0	100.0	100.0			Total Liabilities & Net Worth	100.0	100.0
						INCOME DATA		
100.0	100.0	100.0	100.0			Net Sales	100.0	100.0
						Gross Profit		
88.5	96.7	79.1	81.5			Operating Expenses	76.0	76.3
11.5	3.3	20.9	18.5			Operating Profit	24.0	23.7
4.2	5.3	4.5	8.6			All Other Expenses (net)	7.8	11.6
7.2	-1.9	16.4	9.9			Profit Before Taxes	16.3	12.1
						RATIOS		
5.9	17.0	2.5	1.7				1.7	1.5
.6	1.3	1.1	1.2			Current	1.0	1.0
.2	.6	.9	.3				.4	.4
3.0	7.4	2.0	1.1				1.4	1.1
.4	.6	.8	.7			Quick	.5	.5
.1	.3	.4	.1				.2	.2
0 UND	0 UND	0 UND	10 35.1				3 112.2	0 UND
0 UND	0 UND	27 13.3	44 8.3			Sales/Receivables	32 11.4	28 13.0
19 19.0	22 17.0	53 6.9	61 6.0				73 5.0	55 6.6
						Cost of Sales/Inventory		
						Cost of Sales/Payables		
3.0	3.0	2.2	3.0				5.3	5.6
-12.2	11.9	21.8	14.0			Sales/Working Capital	438.7	-95.8
-1.3	-5.0	-54.9	-1.7				-3.1	-3.7
4.9	4.3	14.7	6.7				9.5	7.2
(17) 1.3	(20) 2.3	(27) 3.5	(14) 2.2			EBIT/Interest	(68) 2.9	(89) 2.4
-.2	-2.1	1.0	1.8				1.7	1.2
						Net Profit + Depr., Dep.,	2.3	5.0
						Amort./Cur. Mat. L/T/D	(12) 1.5	(15) 2.2
							1.0	.8
.2	.6	.2	.1				.1	.1
2.8	2.8	1.3	2.0			Fixed/Worth	1.6	1.2
-91.7	-2.3	3.0	5.0				4.0	10.7
2.2	1.7	.6	2.0				1.8	1.5
5.0	5.6	2.0	3.8			Debt/Worth	4.2	5.6
-114.3	-9.8	9.6	8.1				13.1	31.1
105.6	99.8	34.8	27.9			% Profit Before Taxes/Tangible	64.7	52.7
(15) 35.6	(15) 20.0	(27) 17.7	(16) 15.7			Net Worth	(77) 27.1	(97) 23.7
2.6	.0	-.3	13.5				12.6	10.7
19.4	14.5	13.3	6.1			% Profit Before Taxes/Total	12.2	11.7
2.8	3.2	6.7	3.5			Assets	5.2	4.4
-10.2	-16.3	.3	2.5				2.1	.9
35.3	8.0	39.5	64.0				35.1	43.3
3.7	1.2	2.2	2.2			Sales/Net Fixed Assets	3.4	6.8
.9	.8	.7	.7				.9	.9
3.1	2.0	2.3	1.2				1.7	1.9
1.0	.9	1.1	.6			Sales/Total Assets	.7	.7
.5	.4	.3	.2				.3	.3
11.0	14.3	2.2	1.3				2.5	1.6
(12) 38.3	(17) 66.5	(22) 13.9	(13) 7.7			% Depr., Dep., Amort./Sales	(63) 14.6	(84) 8.5
70.9	82.4	53.6	22.9				39.6	50.1
						% Officers', Directors'	1.7	2.4
						Owners' Comp/Sales	(22) 3.9	(28) 6.2
							11.0	14.5
12780M	33146M	247992M	428235M	234325M	655627M	Net Sales ($)	827702M	1099029M
5291M	25953M	165906M	438464M	585860M	1730656M	Total Assets ($)	1654118M	2108902M

M = $ thousand   MM = $ million
See Pages 9 through 22 for Explanation of Ratios and Data

Comparative Historical Data   Current Data Sorted by Sales

4/1/07-3/31/08 ALL	4/1/08-3/31/09 ALL	4/1/09-3/31/10 ALL	Type of Statement	0-1MM	1-3MM	3-5MM	5-10MM	10-25MM	25MM & OVER
24	21	18	Unqualified	1	1	1	3	6	6
17	18	9	Reviewed	2	2	1	1	1	1
17	12	17	Compiled	8	3	2	2	1	1
21	34	22	Tax Returns	14	5	1	1	1	1
44	56	44	Other	12	4	7	3	7	11
				15 (4/1-9/30/09)			95 (10/1/09-3/31/10)		
123	141	110	NUMBER OF STATEMENTS	37	15	13	10	16	19
%	%	%	ASSETS	%	%	%	%	%	%
7.6	7.5	11.1	Cash & Equivalents	17.6	14.2	13.9	4.6	5.1	2.5
13.5	15.5	14.5	Trade Receivables (net)	3.1	13.3	23.2	24.4	15.3	25.9
7.3	7.0	7.4	Inventory	4.6	5.8	10.5	6.6	12.5	8.0
6.7	7.3	8.4	All Other Current	13.6	7.8	4.6	7.1	1.7	7.4
35.1	37.3	41.4	Total Current	38.9	41.1	52.2	42.7	34.6	43.9
42.4	41.3	41.5	Fixed Assets (net)	52.1	40.0	34.7	50.2	41.3	22.5
1.9	2.2	2.0	Intangibles (net)	.1	3.1	2.5	2.5	3.7	2.8
20.5	19.2	15.1	All Other Non-Current	8.8	15.7	10.6	4.7	20.4	30.9
100.0	100.0	100.0	Total	100.0	100.0	100.0	100.0	100.0	100.0
			LIABILITIES						
16.2	15.8	10.4	Notes Payable-Short Term	6.8	3.8	12.4	18.0	16.2	12.3
10.4	10.0	9.3	Cur. Mat.-L.T.D.	11.7	18.4	9.8	7.0	5.5	1.2
5.7	6.8	6.9	Trade Payables	5.4	2.3	14.6	2.9	7.3	9.8
.3	.1	.2	Income Taxes Payable	.1	.0	.3	.0	.0	.6
7.2	7.1	12.9	All Other Current	18.8	12.9	5.7	9.3	9.4	11.1
39.8	39.8	39.6	Total Current	42.9	37.4	42.8	37.1	38.4	35.0
31.6	34.4	30.3	Long-Term Debt	34.2	38.9	20.3	12.8	37.4	25.9
.6	.4	.5	Deferred Taxes	.1	.0	1.2	.0	.4	1.3
6.4	5.6	6.4	All Other Non-Current	2.6	7.4	5.1	9.2	5.2	13.3
21.6	19.8	23.3	Net Worth	20.2	16.3	30.7	40.8	18.7	24.5
100.0	100.0	100.0	Total Liabilities & Net Worth	100.0	100.0	100.0	100.0	100.0	100.0
			INCOME DATA						
100.0	100.0	100.0	Net Sales	100.0	100.0	100.0	100.0	100.0	100.0
			Gross Profit						
74.0	78.5	84.8	Operating Expenses	82.2	79.7	87.4	91.8	85.5	88.0
26.0	21.5	15.2	Operating Profit	17.8	20.3	12.6	8.2	14.5	12.0
12.3	9.2	6.6	All Other Expenses (net)	5.6	8.6	5.9	4.5	12.3	3.7
13.8	12.3	8.6	Profit Before Taxes	12.2	11.7	6.7	3.7	2.2	8.3
			RATIOS						
1.4	1.9	2.4		15.1	2.1	1.5	1.9	2.0	1.8
.9	.9	1.2	Current	1.3	1.1	1.3	1.2	1.0	1.2
.4	.3	.5		.4	.3	.9	.7	.4	.5
1.1	1.4	1.8		6.3	2.0	1.3	1.0	1.7	1.1
.4	.5	.7	Quick	.5	.5	1.0	.7	.4	.8
.1	.1	.2		.1	.2	.4	.4	.3	.5
0 UND	0 UND	0 UND		0 UND	0 UND	0 UND	40 9.2	11 33.2	19 19.3
23 16.1	17 21.6	19 19.2	Sales/Receivables	0 UND	13 28.4	34 10.6	59 6.2	26 14.0	35 10.5
45 8.1	51 7.1	52 7.1		13 28.8	37 9.8	65 5.6	105 3.5	43 8.5	61 6.0
			Cost of Sales/Inventory						
			Cost of Sales/Payables						
6.6	4.5	2.7		1.2	3.1	3.9	4.7	5.9	9.9
-22.3	-66.2	17.4	Sales/Working Capital	5.2	12.5	35.5	22.0	NM	18.0
-2.2	-3.2	-5.6		-2.4	-1.7	-37.0	-9.3	-6.2	-15.5
5.7	7.9	7.1		3.5	7.3	21.5		3.7	13.3
(88) 2.2	(98) 2.6	(91) 2.3	EBIT/Interest	(29) 1.4	(10) 2.3	(12) 6.0		(12) 1.7	3.8
1.3	1.3	1.0		-.2	-5.0	1.0		.5	1.6
2.7	3.2		Net Profit + Depr., Dep., Amort./Cur. Mat. L/T/D						
(19) 1.3	(14) 1.3								
.9	.4								
.1	.1	.2		.5	.0	.3	.8	.4	.1
1.5	1.2	1.8	Fixed/Worth	2.7	2.1	1.1	1.8	2.6	.8
9.7	5.5	7.4		NM	-2.9	6.8	3.3	NM	3.0
1.8	1.5	1.5		.7	1.8	1.0	.7	3.0	1.8
5.7	4.3	3.8	Debt/Worth	2.6	9.1	3.6	2.2	6.3	4.6
30.1	18.3	26.3		NM	-6.2	15.8	3.6	NM	31.8
43.7	51.7	42.8		39.8	77.4	86.8	32.2	34.1	42.1
(99) 23.2	(115) 20.0	(87) 16.9	% Profit Before Taxes/Tangible Net Worth	(28) 16.6	(11) 20.0	(11) 34.8	5.7	(12) 15.1	(15) 15.8
9.1	7.5	2.6		.0	15.4	12.8	-4.2	3.8	9.6
11.8	14.9	12.1		13.0	18.1	19.5	6.4	6.9	11.9
4.4	4.8	4.5	% Profit Before Taxes/Total Assets	2.8	4.7	6.2	3.1	3.5	5.3
1.3	.8	.0		-6.9	.3	.9	-.9	-.8	2.2
36.5	30.7	37.6		7.8	80.0	41.4	10.8	26.0	101.2
3.9	4.3	2.6	Sales/Net Fixed Assets	1.0	15.0	5.6	1.9	3.9	8.5
.7	.9	.8		.5	.9	1.3	1.1	1.0	1.8
1.4	1.8	1.7		.9	2.1	2.5	1.5	2.0	2.8
.5	.7	.7	Sales/Total Assets	.5	.9	1.8	1.0	.9	.7
.3	.3	.4		.3	.2	.5	.4	.2	.4
2.8	2.2	2.4		12.6					
(89) 15.4	(93) 11.3	(70) 14.6	% Depr., Dep., Amort./Sales	(29) 62.8					
49.9	44.0	62.3		79.3					
4.7	2.9	4.2							
(25) 8.6	(35) 6.2	(19) 5.3	% Officers', Directors' Owners' Comp/Sales						
13.8	12.0	11.8							
1506604M	1288523M	1612105M	Net Sales ($)	16157M	28093M	49849M	75432M	260398M	1182176M
2685582M	2251517M	2952130M	Total Assets ($)	42293M	86859M	96213M	145433M	636003M	1945329M

© RMA 2010

M = $ thousand   MM = $ million
See Pages 9 through 22 for Explanation of Ratios and Data

Current Data Sorted by Assets

Comparative Historical Data

0-500M	500M-2MM	2-10MM	10-50MM	50-100MM	100-250MM	Type of Statement	4/1/05-3/31/06 ALL	4/1/06-3/31/07 ALL
	5	15	31	8	15	Unqualified	80	87
3	8	40	31	2	1	Reviewed	101	87
7	34	21	6		1	Compiled	110	105
50	40	21	1		2	Tax Returns	124	115
20	56	64	56	13	11	Other	227	192
69 (4/1-9/30/09)			493 (10/1/09-3/31/10)					
80	143	161	125	23	30	**NUMBER OF STATEMENTS**	642	586
%	%	%	%	%	%	**ASSETS**	%	%
17.0	10.8	7.1	5.8	6.9	7.7	Cash & Equivalents	9.4	8.5
9.6	11.1	16.1	17.0	10.0	19.8	Trade Receivables (net)	15.6	15.9
1.2	6.5	7.9	9.6	11.0	4.9	Inventory	7.5	7.2
4.3	2.7	4.3	5.7	4.4	10.5	All Other Current	4.8	3.9
32.2	31.1	35.4	38.2	32.3	42.9	Total Current	37.3	35.4
57.0	58.3	57.0	45.3	50.0	32.8	Fixed Assets (net)	50.7	52.2
.6	1.7	1.9	4.0	2.6	5.1	Intangibles (net)	2.6	2.6
10.2	8.8	5.7	12.5	15.1	19.3	All Other Non-Current	9.5	9.8
100.0	100.0	100.0	100.0	100.0	100.0	Total	100.0	100.0
						LIABILITIES		
13.8	9.0	11.1	10.3	9.4	13.2	Notes Payable-Short Term	11.0	10.3
18.5	9.8	8.5	9.0	7.4	7.1	Cur. Mat.-L.T.D.	9.5	8.9
3.2	5.5	6.5	4.8	5.6	5.3	Trade Payables	6.9	6.2
.0	.1	.3	.1	.0	.2	Income Taxes Payable	.3	.3
16.8	8.3	4.8	5.7	5.9	6.1	All Other Current	9.7	7.9
52.3	32.7	31.1	30.0	28.4	31.8	Total Current	37.4	33.7
36.9	34.7	29.6	28.6	31.9	38.6	Long-Term Debt	31.9	33.7
.0	.2	.6	1.1	2.4	1.0	Deferred Taxes	.7	.8
9.4	5.0	4.9	5.7	5.4	4.7	All Other Non-Current	4.8	4.8
1.4	27.4	33.9	34.6	32.0	23.8	Net Worth	25.1	27.0
100.0	100.0	100.0	100.0	100.0	100.0	Total Liabilities & Net Worth	100.0	100.0
						INCOME DATA		
100.0	100.0	100.0	100.0	100.0	100.0	Net Sales	100.0	100.0
						Gross Profit		
71.5	81.3	84.1	87.4	92.5	83.4	Operating Expenses	81.0	78.9
28.5	18.7	15.9	12.6	7.5	16.6	Operating Profit	19.0	21.1
8.0	5.4	6.5	8.0	3.8	9.5	All Other Expenses (net)	5.0	6.6
20.5	13.3	9.4	4.6	3.7	7.1	Profit Before Taxes	14.0	14.5
						RATIOS		
2.3	2.7	1.9	2.6	1.9	2.2	Current	1.9	2.3
.6	1.0	1.1	1.3	1.2	1.1		1.1	1.1
.2	.4	.6	.7	.7	.9		.5	.5
1.7	1.9	1.5	1.6	1.2	1.2	Quick	(640) 1.4	1.6
.5	.7	.7	.8	.7	.8		.7	.7
.1	.3	.3	.3	.2	.2		.3	.3
0 UND	0 UND	7 50.9	22 16.4	16 22.6	17 21.2	Sales/Receivables	0 UND	0 UND
0 UND	12 30.2	33 11.1	42 8.7	36 10.2	48 7.6		26 13.8	28 13.1
14 26.2	41 8.8	62 5.9	74 4.9	48 7.6	102 3.6		52 7.1	60 6.1
						Cost of Sales/Inventory		
						Cost of Sales/Payables		
11.1	6.5	5.8	3.7	3.5	3.0	Sales/Working Capital	6.7	6.0
-16.7	-83.8	36.2	11.1	54.4	15.1		58.2	55.9
-2.0	-4.6	-9.6	-11.0	-16.5	-47.6		-6.7	-6.1
8.0	5.5	6.9	4.5	5.3	4.6	EBIT/Interest	8.6	8.5
(55) 3.2	(118) 2.3	(132) 2.3	(106) 1.8	(22) 1.9	(21) 2.8		(535) 3.7	(477) 3.6
1.2	.6	.2	.5	.0	1.6		1.7	1.7
	11.5	2.7	5.8			Net Profit + Depr., Dep., Amort./Cur. Mat. L/T/D	4.3	4.5
	(11) 2.8	(27) 1.5	(30) 1.3				(96) 2.0	(91) 2.2
	1.3	.9	1.0				1.1	1.1
.9	.8	.9	.5	.4	.2	Fixed/Worth	.7	.7
4.6	2.1	1.6	1.4	1.5	2.7		1.7	1.7
-3.1	86.4	4.5	3.4	3.2	5.0		6.7	5.7
1.0	.8	.8	.9	1.1	2.0	Debt/Worth	1.2	1.0
12.8	2.6	2.0	2.6	2.0	5.8		2.8	2.7
-4.9	90.0	8.6	8.9	5.8	17.8		10.4	10.8
143.5	56.1	33.7	27.3	33.1	42.5	% Profit Before Taxes/Tangible Net Worth	57.6	62.2
(43) 52.7	(110) 21.1	(142) 14.3	(113) 13.0	(22) 14.1	(26) 15.7		(539) 27.0	(501) 29.7
12.5	1.6	-2.8	1.8	1.7	7.4		9.9	12.2
39.5	19.8	11.8	9.9	6.7	6.6	% Profit Before Taxes/Total Assets	18.2	16.5
12.9	4.1	3.3	2.6	3.0	2.9		7.0	7.2
.1	-1.4	-1.9	-.4	-.8	.9		2.0	2.1
13.1	4.3	4.3	10.2	11.5	16.8	Sales/Net Fixed Assets	9.1	7.1
2.0	1.5	1.7	2.1	1.5	2.5		2.5	2.4
.8	.7	.6	.8	.7	.7		.9	.8
2.8	2.0	1.6	1.4	1.2	1.1	Sales/Total Assets	2.1	1.8
1.0	.8	.8	.7	.7	.4		1.1	1.0
.6	.4	.3	.4	.5	.3		.5	.4
12.9	5.8	6.3	3.2	2.5	2.9	% Depr., Dep., Amort./Sales	4.0	4.6
(55) 32.7	(123) 19.9	(132) 17.2	(111) 11.9	(13) 6.8	(12) 8.2		(527) 11.8	(491) 12.1
63.7	46.1	34.8	21.9	20.8	15.4		31.9	32.1
2.0	3.1	2.1	.7			% Officers', Directors' Owners' Comp/Sales	2.6	2.6
(17) 11.7	(34) 3.7	(22) 3.0					(141) 5.1	(149) 5.3
17.7	10.6	8.1	7.4				8.6	8.9
59109M	219133M	914973M	2790925M	1742555M	4944344M	Net Sales ($)	8216844M	7263416M
19722M	166182M	812142M	2931132M	1610087M	4545194M	Total Assets ($)	9089430M	8708889M

M = $ thousand   MM = $ million
See Pages 9 through 22 for Explanation of Ratios and Data

Comparative Historical Data | Current Data Sorted by Sales

87	69	74	Type of Statement						
93	77	85	Unqualified	9	6	4	12	13	30
101	75	69	Reviewed	7	16	9	15	28	10
109	129	114	Compiled	23	22	11	8	4	1
226	225	220	Tax Returns	75	23	7	5	2	2
4/1/07-	4/1/08-	4/1/09-	Other	60	37	15	31	40	37
3/31/08	3/31/09	3/31/10		69 (4/1-9/30/09)			493 (10/1/09-3/31/10)		
ALL	ALL	ALL		0-1MM	1-3MM	3-5MM	5-10MM	10-25MM	25MM & OVER
616	575	562	NUMBER OF STATEMENTS	174	104	46	71	87	80
%	%	%	ASSETS	%	%	%	%	%	%
8.5	9.5	9.2	Cash & Equivalents	12.7	9.7	6.9	6.0	7.4	6.9
15.1	13.7	14.1	Trade Receivables (net)	6.5	16.4	22.0	14.5	19.2	17.1
7.6	6.7	6.9	Inventory	1.0	7.8	8.6	9.2	9.5	12.9
4.2	4.7	4.5	All Other Current	3.4	4.9	4.7	5.6	4.3	5.7
35.4	34.6	34.7	Total Current	23.6	38.8	42.2	35.3	40.4	42.7
53.9	53.3	53.2	Fixed Assets (net)	64.0	50.6	45.7	53.7	48.7	41.6
2.2	2.4	2.3	Intangibles (net)	1.7	1.3	1.4	3.1	2.5	4.8
8.6	9.7	9.8	All Other Non-Current	10.7	9.3	10.7	8.0	8.4	10.9
100.0	100.0	100.0	Total	100.0	100.0	100.0	100.0	100.0	100.0
			LIABILITIES						
11.0	9.7	10.8	Notes Payable-Short Term	9.0	12.8	9.3	11.9	10.2	12.8
9.9	10.1	10.3	Cur. Mat.-L.T.D.	13.2	10.6	9.3	8.9	9.5	6.0
6.1	5.2	5.3	Trade Payables	2.5	4.6	7.9	5.2	7.9	7.9
.2	.2	.1	Income Taxes Payable	.1	.1	.1	.3	.1	.2
8.0	6.9	7.7	All Other Current	9.6	6.5	10.6	4.2	6.6	7.7
35.2	32.1	34.2	Total Current	34.4	34.6	37.3	30.5	34.3	34.5
35.4	36.6	32.3	Long-Term Debt	40.7	30.8	28.2	33.9	25.7	24.0
.7	.6	.6	Deferred Taxes	.0	.5	.5	.7	.8	1.8
4.4	5.1	5.8	All Other Non-Current	5.9	8.1	3.5	6.9	3.5	5.1
24.3	25.6	27.2	Net Worth	18.9	26.1	30.5	28.0	35.8	34.6
100.0	100.0	100.0	Total Liabilities & Net Worth	100.0	100.0	100.0	100.0	100.0	100.0
			INCOME DATA						
100.0	100.0	100.0	Net Sales	100.0	100.0	100.0	100.0	100.0	100.0
			Gross Profit						
81.0	80.1	82.6	Operating Expenses	67.5	85.6	86.8	88.8	92.9	92.4
19.0	19.9	17.4	Operating Profit	32.5	14.4	13.2	11.2	7.1	7.6
6.4	7.1	6.8	All Other Expenses (net)	11.2	4.9	5.3	6.9	3.9	3.9
12.6	12.8	10.6	Profit Before Taxes	21.2	9.6	7.9	4.4	3.1	3.7
			RATIOS						
1.9	1.9	2.2		2.4	2.7	1.7	1.9	2.3	2.0
1.0	1.0	1.1	Current	.7	1.2	1.1	1.2	1.3	1.1
.5	.5	.5		.2	.6	.8	.5	.8	.8
1.3	1.4	1.5		2.0	1.8	1.2	1.5	1.7	1.2
.7	.7	.7	Quick	.7	.7	.8	.7	.8	.8
.3	.3	.3		.2	.3	.5	.3	.4	.3
0 UND	0 UND	0 UND		0 UND	0 UND	15 24.3	8 44.2	26 13.8	26 14.1
28 13.1	23 15.8	27 13.3	Sales/Receivables	0 UND	21 17.5	38 9.7	34 10.9	43 8.5	39 9.4
57 6.4	48 7.6	55 6.7		33 10.9	56 6.5	64 5.7	56 6.5	64 5.7	52 7.0
			Cost of Sales/Inventory						
			Cost of Sales/Payables						
6.2	6.6	5.5		4.3	5.4	6.8	6.2	4.8	7.0
129.1	154.6	40.9	Sales/Working Capital	-10.8	17.9	44.5	32.9	12.0	29.5
-6.4	-6.6	-6.3		-2.2	-7.5	-14.2	-7.3	-15.5	-20.5
6.5	6.7	6.0		6.7	6.8	5.1	3.3	6.7	7.6
(490) 2.9	(457) 2.6	(454) 2.2	EBIT/Interest	(117) 3.3	(84) 1.8	(40) 1.7	(65) 1.9	(77) 2.1	(71) 2.8
1.3	1.0	.5		1.1	.4	.0	.3	-.3	1.2
4.3	4.1	4.0	Net Profit + Depr., Dep.,				3.9	2.8	8.9
(98) 1.9	(79) 1.7	(76) 1.6	Amort./Cur. Mat. L/T/D			(11) 1.2	(25) 1.5	(18) 2.8	
1.3	1.1	1.0					.1	.9	1.0
.7	.8	.7		.9	.4	.5	.9	.8	.6
1.9	2.1	1.8	Fixed/Worth	2.9	1.7	1.4	1.5	1.4	1.5
7.5	8.2	9.5		-16.7	11.1	2.9	7.1	3.0	3.6
1.3	1.1	.9		.7	.8	1.1	1.0	.9	1.1
3.3	3.1	2.6	Debt/Worth	4.0	2.3	2.1	3.4	1.9	2.4
12.8	13.6	15.9		-20.1	26.3	4.6	13.4	6.3	6.2
54.8	54.6	40.0	% Profit Before Taxes/Tangible	77.5	39.7	37.7	29.2	36.8	34.9
(521) 26.2	(479) 21.2	(456) 16.4	Net Worth	(118) 24.4	(83) 16.1	(42) 12.1	(63) 13.0	(79) 13.2	(71) 15.1
9.0	3.4	1.8		6.0	.1	-3.8	-2.9	-2.4	3.0
15.6	15.5	13.6	% Profit Before Taxes/Total	23.5	13.8	12.8	6.5	11.8	10.9
6.2	4.9	3.4	Assets	6.1	3.6	2.9	2.3	3.3	3.6
1.1	.0	-1.0		.0	-1.6	-1.5	-2.2	-3.0	.5
7.3	7.0	6.3		2.0	8.4	18.7	5.0	6.0	15.2
2.1	2.0	1.8	Sales/Net Fixed Assets	.9	2.0	3.4	1.9	2.9	3.4
.7	.7	.7		.4	.9	1.0	1.0	1.2	1.3
1.9	1.8	1.5		.9	1.9	2.3	1.6	1.8	1.7
.9	.9	.8	Sales/Total Assets	.5	.8	1.3	.8	1.3	1.1
.4	.4	.4		.3	.4	.4	.4	.6	.7
4.6	5.5	5.3		18.8	4.5	4.6	6.7	3.9	2.2
(500) 13.2	(459) 15.2	(446) 16.6	% Depr., Dep., Amort./Sales	(136) 34.9	(84) 16.8	(36) 15.4	(62) 14.1	(78) 10.3	(50) 4.9
33.0	33.0	35.5		63.7	34.2	36.0	29.9	19.1	13.1
2.2	2.2	2.2	% Officers', Directors'	2.2	3.7	2.5	1.9	1.2	.3
(152) 4.5	(125) 5.5	(114) 4.5	Owners' Comp/Sales	(22) 12.8	(29) 6.4	(16) 4.0	(20) 3.1	(16) 3.2	(11) 3.7
8.5	10.3	10.2		21.4	13.2	7.8	5.0	6.6	8.8
8465540M	7865076M	10671039M	Net Sales ($)	69635M	195835M	184205M	474962M	1404280M	8342122M
10056888M	9468348M	10084459M	Total Assets ($)	201286M	345449M	388468M	848590M	2353518M	5947148M

M = $ thousand   MM = $ million
See Pages 9 through 22 for Explanation of Ratios and Data

REAL ESTATE—Lessors of Nonfinancial Intangible Assets (except Copyrighted Works) NAICS 533110

Current Data Sorted by Assets | Comparative Historical Data

						Type of Statement		
	2	6	9	4	1	Unqualified	18	18
			1			Reviewed	4	3
	2	1			1	Compiled	3	5
2	9	6				Tax Returns	4	13
1	2	12	2	5	2	Other	13	25
	7 (4/1-9/30/09)		61 (10/1/09-3/31/10)				4/1/05-3/31/06	4/1/06-3/31/07
0-500M	500M-2MM	2-10MM	10-50MM	50-100MM	100-250MM		ALL	ALL
3	15	25	12	9	4	NUMBER OF STATEMENTS	42	64
%	%	%	%	%	%	ASSETS	%	%
	25.2	7.2	12.0			Cash & Equivalents	14.5	13.4
	5.3	3.5	15.6			Trade Receivables (net)	14.3	12.2
	2.3	3.8	.5			Inventory	4.8	2.0
	6.9	7.0	6.3			All Other Current	5.8	5.9
	39.6	21.6	34.3			Total Current	39.4	33.5
	41.4	59.6	11.9			Fixed Assets (net)	41.3	45.6
	5.5	8.2	32.7			Intangibles (net)	8.8	9.0
	13.4	10.7	21.1			All Other Non-Current	10.6	11.9
	100.0	100.0	100.0			Total	100.0	100.0
						LIABILITIES		
	18.4	5.3	2.2			Notes Payable-Short Term	6.3	3.0
	1.0	2.2	3.2			Cur. Mat.-L.T.D.	5.3	5.4
	4.0	2.4	9.3			Trade Payables	10.3	8.4
	.1	.0	.1			Income Taxes Payable	.0	.5
	6.2	10.5	19.3			All Other Current	11.9	11.9
	29.7	20.4	34.0			Total Current	33.8	29.2
	29.0	50.3	15.0			Long-Term Debt	43.0	41.3
	.0	.0	.2			Deferred Taxes	.9	.5
	4.8	3.8	7.4			All Other Non-Current	6.1	6.3
	36.5	25.5	43.4			Net Worth	16.2	22.8
	100.0	100.0	100.0			Total Liabilities & Net Worth	100.0	100.0
						INCOME DATA		
	100.0	100.0	100.0			Net Sales	100.0	100.0
						Gross Profit		
	69.4	64.6	90.8			Operating Expenses	83.2	78.0
	30.6	35.4	9.2			Operating Profit	16.8	22.0
	14.8	21.7	7.5			All Other Expenses (net)	6.7	10.5
	15.9	13.6	1.6			Profit Before Taxes	10.1	11.4
						RATIOS		
	2.7	4.1	1.2				2.1	3.2
	1.1	1.0	1.0			Current	1.1	1.2
	.6	.3	.4				.6	.4
	2.2	2.1	1.1				1.4	2.1
	1.1	.2	.6			Quick	.7 (63)	1.0
	.3	.1	.3				.4	.3
0 UND	0 UND	9 42.9					0 UND	0 UND
0 UND	2 162.7	36 10.1				Sales/Receivables	18 20.0	11 33.7
4 99.3	14 25.3	51 7.2					34 10.7	35 10.3
						Cost of Sales/Inventory		
						Cost of Sales/Payables		
	6.5	4.9	13.4				7.3	4.8
	58.1	111.8	NM			Sales/Working Capital	52.0	25.5
	-8.1	-2.6	-4.8				-14.1	-7.5
		6.1	20.7				18.6	11.4
	(13)	2.0 (11)	2.3			EBIT/Interest	(28) 5.3 (43)	5.0
		-.9	-2.3				1.4	1.5
							15.3	21.2
						Net Profit + Depr., Dep., Amort./Cur. Mat. L/T/D	(12) 6.9 (11)	6.2
							2.1	1.7
	.1	1.3	.2				.6	.5
	1.5	3.1	1.8			Fixed/Worth	2.6	3.2
	-92.5	-6.5	-.7				-18.5	-8.2
	.4	.9	2.5				1.6	.9
	4.8	3.1	6.6			Debt/Worth	4.8	9.7
	-93.6	-8.9	-5.4				-43.0	-11.8
	364.6	29.8				% Profit Before Taxes/Tangible Net Worth	54.6	72.6
	(11) 49.2	(16) 12.2					(30) 28.3 (43)	36.9
	-5.9	2.0					5.0	2.0
	125.0	8.4	14.2			% Profit Before Taxes/Total Assets	10.4	17.7
	14.9	2.4	3.7				5.7	6.3
	-2.3	-1.0	-3.8				1.2	.1
	469.4	5.2	30.2				17.9	18.6
	40.9	.4	16.5			Sales/Net Fixed Assets	3.6	2.6
	.2	.2	5.4				.5	.3
	2.5	.9	1.3				2.5	2.0
	1.3	.2	1.0			Sales/Total Assets	1.3	.7
	.2	.1	.6				.4	.2
	1.1	1.4					1.4	.8
	(10) 9.2	(23) 9.4				% Depr., Dep., Amort./Sales	(36) 5.8 (50)	4.2
	31.1	22.0					12.1	13.4
								1.5
						% Officers', Directors' Owners' Comp/Sales	(10) 6.8	
								25.4
1000M	28724M	92039M	245432M	1579001M	538375M	Net Sales ($)	905100M	1084176M
671M	15111M	108808M	257576M	681406M	487720M	Total Assets ($)	722104M	1310707M

© RMA 2010

M = $ thousand   MM = $ million
See Pages 9 through 22 for Explanation of Ratios and Data

Comparative Historical Data | Current Data Sorted by Sales

			Type of Statement			3-5MM			
12	21	22	Unqualified	2	2		6	4	8
2	4	1	Reviewed				1		
6	3	4	Compiled		1		2		1
15	10	17	Tax Returns		4		1		
26	26	24	Other	12	8		1	2	7
4/1/07- 3/31/08 ALL	4/1/08- 3/31/09 ALL	4/1/09- 3/31/10 ALL		7 (4/1-9/30/09)			61 (10/1/09-3/31/10)		
				0-1MM	1-3MM	3-5MM	5-10MM	10-25MM	25MM & OVER
61	64	68	NUMBER OF STATEMENTS	21	15		10	6	16
%	%	%	ASSETS	%	%	%	%	%	%
10.9	9.2	14.4	Cash & Equivalents	7.7	20.5	D	12.2		19.1
11.7	14.3	8.2	Trade Receivables (net)	3.4	3.7	A	13.9		11.1
8.3	3.3	2.1	Inventory	.0	3.2	T	1.8		4.5
5.0	4.0	8.4	All Other Current	8.0	2.3	A	10.5		10.7
35.8	30.8	33.1	Total Current	19.1	29.7		38.4		45.4
46.6	43.6	39.6	Fixed Assets (net)	68.8	48.4	N	9.0		20.1
6.0	12.4	11.9	Intangibles (net)	3.6	6.0	O	28.0		15.7
11.6	13.2	15.3	All Other Non-Current	8.5	15.9	T	24.6		18.9
100.0	100.0	100.0	Total	100.0	100.0		100.0		100.0
			LIABILITIES			A			
7.0	14.1	7.5	Notes Payable-Short Term	9.2	11.5	V	9.3		2.2
3.7	2.8	11.6	Cur. Mat.-L.T.D.	21.7	.6	A	2.6		16.9
8.8	7.2	4.9	Trade Payables	.3	4.8	I	3.5		7.6
.0	.0	.1	Income Taxes Payable	.0	.1	L	.1		.1
13.6	11.8	11.9	All Other Current	5.2	9.2	A	15.8		17.3
33.1	35.9	36.0	Total Current	36.4	26.3	B	31.3		44.1
44.0	38.3	35.9	Long-Term Debt	63.5	33.1	L	13.5		23.1
.4	.5	.3	Deferred Taxes	.0	.0	E	.2		1.2
4.7	7.4	6.5	All Other Non-Current	2.3	6.1		7.6		14.0
17.9	17.8	21.3	Net Worth	-2.1	34.6		47.4		17.6
100.0	100.0	100.0	Total Liabilties & Net Worth	100.0	100.0		100.0		100.0
			INCOME DATA						
100.0	100.0	100.0	Net Sales	100.0	100.0		100.0		100.0
			Gross Profit						
72.7	70.2	74.6	Operating Expenses	51.6	84.0		87.3		85.4
27.3	29.8	25.4	Operating Profit	48.4	16.0		12.7		14.6
11.6	11.4	14.1	All Other Expenses (net)	34.1	5.8		3.8		4.4
15.7	18.4	11.3	Profit Before Taxes	14.3	10.2		8.8		10.2
			RATIOS						
1.5	2.3	2.9		3.1	4.2		2.4		1.5
.9	1.0	1.0	Current	.9	1.1		1.0		1.0
.5	.4	.5		.2	.5		.3		.7
1.3	1.4	1.4		2.1	2.2		2.2		1.0
.6	.7	.6	Quick	.2	.6		.6		.7
.1	.3	.2		.0	.0		.1		.5
0 UND	0 UND	0 UND		0 UND	0 UND		0 UND		7 51.7
3 126.8	14 25.6	5 68.1	Sales/Receivables	0 UND	4 89.0		20 17.9		22 16.7
30 12.1	44 8.3	29 12.7		0 UND	17 21.9		55 6.6		35 10.3
			Cost of Sales/Inventory						
			Cost of Sales/Payables						
11.4	8.6	6.4		1.6	5.1		6.5		6.9
-31.0	-816.0	208.0	Sales/Working Capital	-81.3	49.0		-768.1		-295.2
-5.9	-5.7	-4.8		-1.6	-3.6		-4.1		-14.8
11.4	13.0	16.3			32.3				8.7
(37) 4.5	(40) 4.8	(44) 4.1	EBIT/Interest	(12) 2.5				(13) 4.3
1.5	1.9	1.0			-.4				1.4
	8.8	8.9	Net Profit + Depr., Dep., Amort./Cur. Mat. L/T/D						
(10) 4.1	(10) 1.1								
2.0	.5								
.5	.5	.5		2.1	.1		.1		.7
3.5	3.1	2.7	Fixed/Worth	8.9	1.5		.8		3.5
-5.0	111.2	-1.6		-8.4	46.7		-1.0		-.7
1.3	1.4	1.2		1.8	.3		.3		1.6
4.3	5.2	5.9	Debt/Worth	13.3	2.2		4.6		15.6
-14.0	213.2	-8.7		-10.1	50.1		-3.4		-4.0
113.8	163.2	57.2		26.9	41.4				
(41) 34.2	(49) 44.1	(43) 18.1	% Profit Before Taxes/Tangible Net Worth	(11) 7.3	(12) 24.4				
6.6	20.3	.2		-5.9	-2.2				
19.9	24.2	14.9		3.7	16.6		153.6		15.5
8.0	7.7	3.7	% Profit Before Taxes/Total Assets	2.2	7.9		7.7		6.2
.9	1.3	-2.1		-2.0	-2.6		1.1		-3.7
30.7	23.5	33.8		.4	45.9		140.3		81.1
3.6	4.7	4.9	Sales/Net Fixed Assets	.2	1.6		29.2		17.0
.3	.3	.3		.1	.7		13.2		2.6
2.2	1.9	1.8		.2	2.0		5.3		2.4
.9	.9	.7	Sales/Total Assets	.1	.8		1.2		1.1
.2	.2	.2		.1	.4		.7		.5
1.7	1.2	1.5		10.2	2.3				1.0
(46) 5.3	(48) 3.8	(52) 3.9	% Depr., Dep., Amort./Sales	(17) 19.5	(11) 3.9			(12) 2.9
16.3	18.4	16.3		26.5	16.7				5.5
2.7		2.1	% Officers', Directors' Owners' Comp/Sales						
(11) 8.3		(11) 8.8							
31.4		16.8							
859047M	1026808M	2484571M	Net Sales ($)	8282M	27561M		74266M	104783M	2269679M
719907M	997162M	1551292M	Total Assets ($)	49483M	56206M		105854M	130237M	1209512M

M = $ thousand   MM = $ million
See Pages 9 through 22 for Explanation of Ratios and Data

PROFESSIONAL, SCIENTIFIC, AND TECHNICAL SERVICES

Current Data Sorted by Assets   **Comparative Historical Data**

Type of Statement	0-500M	500M-2MM	2-10MM	10-50MM	50-100MM	100-250MM	4/1/05-3/31/06 ALL	4/1/06-3/31/07 ALL
Unqualified	2	10	17	49	22	15	75	110
Reviewed	8	28	96	67	8	2	164	187
Compiled	73	97	87	16	2		234	240
Tax Returns	378	171	85	16	1	3	420	517
Other	252	265	253	124	19	25	763	747
		126 (4/1-9/30/09)		2,065 (10/1/09-3/31/10)				
NUMBER OF STATEMENTS	713	571	538	272	52	45	1656	1801

ASSETS (%)

	0-500M	500M-2MM	2-10MM	10-50MM	50-100MM	100-250MM	05-06 ALL	06-07 ALL
Cash & Equivalents	40.0	31.3	29.2	29.0	31.2	33.1	33.6	31.9
Trade Receivables (net)	7.3	15.6	24.2	23.9	18.2	13.8	15.1	15.3
Inventory	.6	.7	1.7	2.8	3.8	2.2	1.2	1.4
All Other Current	11.5	13.8	12.3	9.9	6.8	11.6	12.2	12.8
Total Current	59.4	61.3	67.4	65.5	60.1	60.7	62.1	61.4
Fixed Assets (net)	22.7	20.8	18.1	21.3	25.6	25.2	21.5	22.1
Intangibles (net)	3.1	3.4	2.3	1.3	4.2	6.0	2.1	2.8
All Other Non-Current	14.8	14.6	12.3	11.9	10.1	8.0	14.3	13.8
Total	100.0	100.0	100.0	100.0	100.0	100.0	100.0	100.0

LIABILITIES

	0-500M	500M-2MM	2-10MM	10-50MM	50-100MM	100-250MM	05-06 ALL	06-07 ALL
Notes Payable-Short Term	48.6	22.5	13.8	5.2	5.5	6.0	23.1	25.6
Cur. Mat.-L.T.D.	7.9	2.1	2.9	3.2	2.9	6.5	4.9	4.6
Trade Payables	2.4	2.3	3.6	3.7	2.9	2.6	3.1	3.0
Income Taxes Payable	.4	.2	1.0	1.1	.1	.0	.6	.5
All Other Current	41.4	29.5	25.0	21.0	14.8	18.1	29.6	32.3
Total Current	100.6	56.6	46.4	34.1	26.3	33.2	61.2	65.9
Long-Term Debt	17.8	15.2	12.1	11.0	12.6	10.3	14.4	14.8
Deferred Taxes	.1	.0	.2	.7	.1	.1	.4	.2
All Other Non-Current	8.9	6.3	5.3	6.5	4.9	5.6	5.5	7.1
Net Worth	-27.3	21.9	36.0	47.6	56.1	50.9	18.4	11.9
Total Liabilities & Net Worth	100.0	100.0	100.0	100.0	100.0	100.0	100.0	100.0

INCOME DATA

	0-500M	500M-2MM	2-10MM	10-50MM	50-100MM	100-250MM	05-06 ALL	06-07 ALL
Net Sales	100.0	100.0	100.0	100.0	100.0	100.0	100.0	100.0
Gross Profit								
Operating Expenses	85.2	82.2	79.6	73.8	66.2	63.4	80.4	79.7
Operating Profit	14.8	17.8	20.4	26.2	33.8	36.6	19.6	20.3
All Other Expenses (net)	.7	2.5	1.8	1.3	1.3	1.4	1.4	1.3
Profit Before Taxes	14.1	15.3	18.6	24.9	32.5	35.2	18.2	18.9

RATIOS

	0-500M	500M-2MM	2-10MM	10-50MM	50-100MM	100-250MM	05-06 ALL	06-07 ALL
Current	1.5	2.7	3.4	5.1	6.2	10.0	3.2	2.8
	.8	1.2	1.6	2.2	3.1	2.8	1.2	1.2
	.3	.6	1.0	1.1	1.4	.9	.7	.6
Quick	1.3	2.0	2.7	3.9	4.9	7.4	2.6	2.2
	(710) .6	.9	(537) 1.3	1.6	2.6	2.4	(1652) 1.0	(1798) .9
	.2	.3	.6	1.0	1.1	.7	.4	.3
Sales/Receivables	0 UND	0 UND	0 UND	1 633.9	0 UND	0 UND	0 UND	0 UND
	0 UND	0 UND	7 52.4	13 28.7	7 50.2	3 108.7	0 UND	0 UND
	0 UND	19 19.5	65 5.6	75 4.9	49 7.4	46 8.0	17 20.9	17 21.9
Cost of Sales/Inventory								
Cost of Sales/Payables								
Sales/Working Capital	46.2	9.2	4.8	4.0	5.3	5.6	8.7	9.1
	-76.4	51.1	15.6	8.7	8.2	7.5	69.1	92.1
	-14.7	-20.3	-201.0	51.3	25.8	-139.3	-34.1	-25.2
EBIT/Interest	53.0	62.4	150.8	221.2	266.8	267.2	110.9	94.1
	(513) 11.7	(458) 8.5	(432) 19.7	(228) 85.0	(45) 117.2	(39) 106.1	(1332) 19.8	(1426) 16.8
	.8	1.1	2.4	9.8	49.0	48.8	2.0	1.9
Net Profit + Depr., Dep., Amort./Cur. Mat. L/T/D	4.5	6.5	5.4	12.2			5.6	10.4
	(16) 1.0	(27) 1.7	(48) 1.7	(35) 2.5			(97) 1.8	(117) 2.1
	-.1	.5	.6	1.2			.9	1.0
Fixed/Worth	.1	.1	.1	.1	.2	.3	.1	.2
	2.0	.7	.3	.4	.4	.4	.6	.7
	-.5	-6.5	2.4	1.0	.9	1.0	7.0	-12.8
Debt/Worth	1.4	.7	.6	.4	.2	.2	.6	.6
	-160.0	3.2	1.8	1.1	.7	.7	2.3	2.9
	-2.5	-19.7	11.6	3.9	1.9	2.4	-327.7	-15.6
% Profit Before Taxes/Tangible Net Worth	805.5	309.0	241.5	255.5	312.1	306.1	368.6	402.5
	(356) 214.6	(396) 81.4	(443) 88.0	(258) 102.9	(48) 186.3	(40) 191.5	(1237) 134.2	(1275) 139.5
	33.6	7.3	12.2	27.4	98.6	143.6	20.4	20.1
% Profit Before Taxes/Total Assets	190.0	94.4	96.2	124.6	175.9	185.3	148.0	162.4
	44.6	17.4	22.4	52.8	111.4	110.3	39.5	40.5
	.0	.8	1.8	8.8	41.8	80.3	2.0	2.0
Sales/Net Fixed Assets	710.8	178.3	99.0	38.2	32.9	19.7	110.5	103.3
	93.2	48.4	38.1	22.1	14.6	15.2	38.0	37.9
	28.9	18.8	18.1	12.1	10.7	10.5	18.5	17.8
Sales/Total Assets	19.3	8.0	4.9	4.2	4.6	4.2	9.7	9.7
	9.3	4.0	2.8	2.6	3.7	3.2	4.8	4.6
	4.7	2.0	1.6	1.7	1.8	2.1	2.5	2.5
% Depr., Dep., Amort./Sales	.3	.4	.4	.8		1.1	.5	.5
	(327) .5	(339) .8	(391) .9	(230) 1.4	(40) 1.6	(27) 1.2	(1124) 1.0	(1211) .9
	1.2	1.5	1.6	1.9	2.3	1.8	1.6	1.5
% Officers', Directors' Owners' Comp/Sales	12.4	9.7	6.9	3.7	8.5	2.7	12.7	11.9
	(419) 22.6	(287) 22.6	(220) 21.9	(88) 14.9	(12) 20.9	(12) 17.3	(777) 25.2	(791) 23.9
	34.3	36.0	32.9	31.5	30.8	36.4	35.4	35.1
Net Sales ($)	1771133M	3509926M	9255413M	19537748M	12552244M	35927818M	66951783M	73783173M
Total Assets ($)	149556M	634859M	2446438M	5982209M	3521890M	7264056M	14414017M	17028079M

Comparative Historical Data

Current Data Sorted by Sales

				Type of Statement						
100		117	115	Unqualified	2	5	5	8	14	81
176		202	209	Reviewed	2	5	8	25	65	104
244		259	275	Compiled	23	64	45	65	53	25
469		566	654	Tax Returns	186	181	94	105	64	24
769		905	938	Other	112	203	114	165	149	195
4/1/07-3/31/08 ALL		4/1/08-3/31/09 ALL	4/1/09-3/31/10 ALL		126 (4/1-9/30/09)			2,065 (10/1/09-3/31/10)		
					0-1MM	1-3MM	3-5MM	5-10MM	10-25MM	25MM & OVER
1758		2049	2191	NUMBER OF STATEMENTS	325	458	266	368	345	429
%		%	%		%	%	%	%	%	%
				ASSETS						
31.9		30.7	33.4	Cash & Equivalents	32.2	36.5	35.1	31.2	33.1	31.9
16.0		16.9	16.1	Trade Receivables (net)	7.8	12.4	17.2	18.0	23.0	18.3
1.1		1.5	1.3	Inventory	.7	.9	1.3	1.0	1.9	1.7
13.2		13.7	12.0	All Other Current	10.0	13.2	12.6	14.5	11.4	10.1
62.3		62.8	62.7	Total Current	50.7	63.0	66.2	64.6	69.5	62.0
21.8		21.1	21.0	Fixed Assets (net)	31.0	19.8	15.9	17.5	15.9	25.1
2.4		3.1	2.8	Intangibles (net)	3.6	3.1	3.7	3.2	1.5	2.2
13.4		13.0	13.5	All Other Non-Current	14.8	14.2	14.2	14.7	13.2	10.8
100.0		100.0	100.0	Total	100.0	100.0	100.0	100.0	100.0	100.0
				LIABILITIES						
26.6		27.6	26.0	Notes Payable-Short Term	35.6	42.6	32.4	24.5	14.7	7.2
4.6		4.4	4.4	Cur. Mat.-L.T.D.	7.7	4.3	2.8	4.5	3.3	3.9
2.8		3.2	2.9	Trade Payables	2.0	3.3	2.7	2.1	3.6	3.3
.4		.5	.6	Income Taxes Payable	.1	.4	.6	.9	.7	.6
31.9		29.6	30.6	All Other Current	31.4	34.6	36.8	31.9	28.0	22.9
66.2		65.2	64.4	Total Current	76.7	85.1	75.4	63.9	50.3	38.0
13.3		13.6	14.6	Long-Term Debt	22.7	19.0	11.1	12.8	8.8	12.3
.2		.2	.2	Deferred Taxes	.1	.1	.1	.2	.3	.3
5.8		5.1	6.9	All Other Non-Current	10.2	7.1	8.1	6.2	5.4	5.1
14.5		15.9	13.9	Net Worth	-9.7	-11.2	5.3	16.9	35.3	44.3
100.0		100.0	100.0	Total Liabilities & Net Worth	100.0	100.0	100.0	100.0	100.0	100.0
				INCOME DATA						
100.0		100.0	100.0	Net Sales	100.0	100.0	100.0	100.0	100.0	100.0
				Gross Profit						
79.5		79.4	80.7	Operating Expenses	77.9	84.9	83.7	83.7	79.9	74.8
20.5		20.6	19.3	Operating Profit	22.1	15.1	16.3	16.3	20.1	25.2
1.5		1.4	1.5	All Other Expenses (net)	5.2	1.1	.7	.5	.6	1.4
19.1		19.2	17.7	Profit Before Taxes	16.9	14.1	15.6	15.8	19.5	23.8
				RATIOS						
2.9		2.9	2.9	Current	1.6	2.1	2.5	2.5	3.7	4.8
1.2		1.2	1.2		.8	1.0	1.2	1.2	1.6	1.8
.6		.6	.6		.3	.4	.6	.6	.9	1.0
2.2		2.2	2.3	Quick	1.4	1.6	1.9	2.0	3.0	3.6
(1753) 1.0		(2046) 1.0	(2187) 1.0		(324) .6	(457) .7	1.0	(367) 1.0	1.3	(428) 1.5
.3		.3	.4		.1	.3	.3	.3	.6	.7
0 UND		0 UND	0 UND	Sales/Receivables	0 UND	0 UND	0 UND	0 UND	0 UND	0 UND
0 UND		0 UND	0 UND		0 UND	0 UND	0 UND	0 UND	4 82.4	5 67.8
21 17.3		31 11.9	24 15.1		0 UND	7 49.6	30 12.2	37 9.8	56 6.5	42 8.6
				Cost of Sales/Inventory						
				Cost of Sales/Payables						
8.7		8.6	8.0	Sales/Working Capital	16.6	13.7	9.1	8.2	5.6	6.1
65.2		57.1	51.2		-47.4	-231.2	65.5	52.3	20.1	17.6
-29.1		-25.2	-29.2		-6.3	-13.4	-24.3	-43.9	-233.2	377.1
91.2		108.6	118.6	EBIT/Interest	23.0	51.5	76.3	95.4	187.7	222.0
(1464) 17.8		(1647) 19.3	(1715) 17.9		(186) 5.2	(371) 11.8	(197) 16.0	(305) 14.1	(287) 41.3	(369) 80.5
2.4		2.1	1.8		.7	1.0	.8	1.6	3.5	6.6
7.1		6.3	7.5	Net Profit + Depr., Dep., Amort./Cur. Mat. L/T/D		5.5		2.9	6.8	12.4
(120) 2.5		(139) 1.9	(136) 1.8			(17) 1.6		(16) 1.0	(34) 2.5	(59) 1.8
.8		.9	.6			-.3		-.2	.9	1.1
.2		.1	.1	Fixed/Worth	.1	.1	.1	.1	.1	.2
.7		.6	.6		1.9	1.1	.4	.4	.4	.5
UND		-38.0	-24.3		-2.0	-.7	-1.4	-4.7	1.9	1.4
.6		.6	.6	Debt/Worth	1.4	1.0	.7	.8	.5	.4
2.9		2.5	3.0		12.4	30.0	3.9	3.7	1.3	1.2
-26.5		-20.8	-17.0		-4.1	-4.2	-4.8	-19.0	9.5	3.9
388.0		355.1	340.1	% Profit Before Taxes/Tangible Net Worth	412.0	407.5	350.8	400.0	283.3	322.0
(1273) 147.8		(1465) 119.2	(1541) 118.2		(194) 90.0	(250) 109.6	(169) 83.1	(259) 132.5	(279) 103.4	(390) 147.7
24.4		20.7	17.7		12.3	10.7	15.1	17.7	21.9	33.4
163.2		154.2	129.0	% Profit Before Taxes/Total Assets	94.0	106.5	115.0	127.8	129.6	165.4
43.6		41.2	31.0		13.9	25.2	27.5	25.1	33.9	79.3
3.2		3.0	1.8		.0	.1	1.1	1.4	5.0	7.4
107.4		130.7	158.6	Sales/Net Fixed Assets	481.8	327.4	300.8	201.9	125.2	41.3
39.3		40.8	43.3		30.6	53.4	67.3	63.7	48.7	23.4
17.8		17.8	17.8		7.0	21.2	28.1	29.8	24.7	13.1
9.7		9.1	8.9	Sales/Total Assets	6.5	11.0	10.9	12.0	9.1	7.0
4.6		4.5	4.2		3.1	4.7	5.1	4.6	4.0	4.1
2.5		2.3	2.2		1.1	2.1	2.2	2.3	2.3	2.6
.5		.4	.4	% Depr., Dep., Amort./Sales	.7	.3	.3	.3	.4	.8
(1174) .9		(1292) .9	(1354) .9		(148) 1.9	(231) .6	(145) .6	(222) .6	(252) .8	(356) 1.2
1.5		1.6	1.6		12.4	1.3	1.4	1.3	1.3	1.8
11.7		11.1	9.6	% Officers', Directors' Owners' Comp/Sales	12.6	10.1	8.4	10.1	7.7	6.1
(777) 23.1		(877) 21.0	(1038) 22.0		(153) 18.5	(255) 22.1	(139) 21.2	(195) 25.5	(150) 22.0	(146) 19.5
33.7		34.2	34.1		30.5	34.6	34.2	35.4	36.4	33.9
68261416M		87407896M	82554282M	Net Sales ($)	170495M	867075M	1056403M	2650249M	5484853M	72325207M
16701460M		22186517M	19999008M	Total Assets ($)	153841M	314246M	371036M	861143M	1885717M	16413025M

© RMA 2010

M = $ thousand   MM = $ million
See Pages 9 through 22 for Explanation of Ratios and Data

Current Data Sorted by Assets   Comparative Historical Data

Type of Statement								4/1/05-3/31/06	4/1/06-3/31/07
Unqualified	1	1	3	4		1		5	11
Reviewed		2	2					1	3
Compiled	2	3	5	1				13	12
Tax Returns	18	10	4	1				23	29
Other	10	20	9	4				33	37
		5 (4/1-9/30/09)		96 (10/1/09-3/31/10)				ALL	ALL
	0-500M	500M-2MM	2-10MM	10-50MM	50-100MM	100-250MM			
NUMBER OF STATEMENTS	31	36	23	10		1		75	92
	%	%	%	%	%	%		%	%
ASSETS									
Cash & Equivalents	42.8	36.2	24.5	24.0				32.9	33.5
Trade Receivables (net)	6.7	11.3	11.5	13.4				9.6	10.1
Inventory	.0	1.5	.4	.0				.0	.1
All Other Current	2.9	5.5	10.3	23.5				6.4	6.5
Total Current	52.4	54.6	46.6	61.0				49.0	50.2
Fixed Assets (net)	27.9	21.4	24.4	15.1	D			21.3	21.4
Intangibles (net)	7.3	8.2	15.9	11.0	A			8.2	9.7
All Other Non-Current	12.5	15.9	13.1	12.9	T			21.5	18.7
Total	100.0	100.0	100.0	100.0	A			100.0	100.0
LIABILITIES					N				
Notes Payable-Short Term	13.8	17.3	8.2	3.5	O			17.1	16.7
Cur. Mat.-L.T.D.	.4	2.6	2.2	.5	T			2.5	1.7
Trade Payables	29.1	11.2	5.1	5.0				7.3	6.4
Income Taxes Payable	.5	.0	.0	.0	A			.5	.5
All Other Current	21.6	19.2	26.0	42.5	V			24.3	27.9
Total Current	65.4	50.3	41.5	51.5	A			51.6	53.2
Long-Term Debt	12.6	13.4	18.9	10.4	I			21.5	15.6
Deferred Taxes	.0	.0	.0	1.3	L			.8	.5
All Other Non-Current	17.4	5.2	1.7	1.2	A			11.2	3.3
Net Worth	4.6	31.1	37.9	35.6	B			14.8	27.4
Total Liabilities & Net Worth	100.0	100.0	100.0	100.0	L			100.0	100.0
INCOME DATA					E				
Net Sales	100.0	100.0	100.0	100.0				100.0	100.0
Gross Profit									
Operating Expenses	90.4	89.8	97.2	93.3				88.3	90.2
Operating Profit	9.6	10.2	2.8	6.7				11.7	9.8
All Other Expenses (net)	.2	2.2	.0	-.7				1.7	-.1
Profit Before Taxes	9.4	8.0	2.8	7.4				10.0	10.0
RATIOS									
	5.0	2.1	1.9	2.4				2.8	2.2
Current	1.1	1.0	1.1	1.5				1.0	1.2
	.5	.4	.7	1.0				.5	.6
	3.7	1.9	1.5	1.8				2.8	2.2
Quick	1.1	.9	.9	1.4				.9	1.1
	.4	.2	.6	.5				.4	.4
	0 UND	0 UND	0 UND	1 349.5				0 UND	0 UND
Sales/Receivables	0 UND	1 294.6	4 85.3	11 33.3				0 UND	2 189.6
	4 99.4	30 12.3	37 9.9	28 12.9				14 26.7	17 21.4
Cost of Sales/Inventory									
Cost of Sales/Payables									
	16.7	7.9	9.7	6.5				9.8	8.6
Sales/Working Capital	683.0	578.7	293.6	12.9				668.6	33.2
	-22.7	-8.7	-32.8	NM				-16.4	-19.6
	27.6	40.0	18.1					17.3	17.0
EBIT/Interest	(17) 14.9	(23) 4.0	(21) 7.1					(47) 6.3	(63) 5.8
	7.6	-3.1	.2					.6	.6
Net Profit + Depr., Dep., Amort./Cur. Mat. L/T/D									
	.2	.2	.3	.3				.1	.1
Fixed/Worth	1.0	.6	1.2	.5				.5	.5
	-.7	-2.7	-1.5	1.6				10.6	3.7
	.4	.5	.9	1.0				.8	.6
Debt/Worth	1.7	3.0	1.7	1.6				2.6	2.3
	-4.0	-10.1	-27.4	124.6				-102.4	24.9
	414.1	204.2	139.1					139.9	118.5
% Profit Before Taxes/Tangible Net Worth	(22) 77.4	(25) 66.7	(17) 69.8					(56) 57.1	(74) 51.9
	32.0	10.3	-6.3					11.2	3.1
	76.9	44.6	20.5	30.9				35.0	45.3
% Profit Before Taxes/Total Assets	49.0	13.1	10.5	2.1				12.2	12.8
	15.8	-1.1	-3.6	-.2				.9	.6
	290.0	55.7	34.6	54.2				99.3	75.4
Sales/Net Fixed Assets	36.3	21.4	13.5	26.0				21.8	23.7
	15.2	10.3	7.7	4.7				11.0	8.4
	14.7	4.4	3.4	2.0				5.2	4.2
Sales/Total Assets	6.1	2.6	1.9	1.2				2.8	2.3
	2.9	1.1	1.3	.7				1.0	1.0
	.4	1.2	1.0					.8	.7
% Depr., Dep., Amort./Sales	(15) 1.0	(24) 1.7	(20) 2.2					(47) 1.3	(60) 1.7
	1.6	2.8	3.9					2.7	3.7
	6.5	5.2						6.2	3.6
% Officers', Directors' Owners' Comp/Sales	(15) 23.3	(16) 9.6						(29) 8.8	(31) 7.7
	35.1	16.9						20.9	16.4
Net Sales ($)	36197M	130784M	238621M	443743M		48585M		1211631M	1100597M
Total Assets ($)	5619M	39605M	99567M	201282M		118088M		467011M	712440M

© RMA 2010

M = $ thousand   MM = $ million
See Pages 9 through 22 for Explanation of Ratios and Data

Comparative Historical Data   Current Data Sorted by Sales

			Type of Statement						
3	5	10	Unqualified		2	1	3	1	3
2	4	4	Reviewed		1	1	1	1	
3	14	11	Compiled		2	1	3	2	1
20	23	33	Tax Returns	2	11	4	4	1	
41	44	43	Other	13	14	5	9	6	2
4/1/07-3/31/08	4/1/08-3/31/09	4/1/09-3/31/10		7	5 (4/1-9/30/09)		96 (10/1/09-3/31/10)		
ALL	ALL	ALL		0-1MM	1-3MM	3-5MM	5-10MM	10-25MM	25MM & OVER
69	90	101	**NUMBER OF STATEMENTS**	22	30	12	20	11	6
%	%	%	**ASSETS**	%	%	%	%	%	%
27.6	32.6	34.0	Cash & Equivalents	36.5	38.8	28.6	35.4	31.3	
12.0	9.0	10.1	Trade Receivables (net)	6.2	7.1	17.9	8.8	13.9	
.4	1.4	.7	Inventory	.0	.0	3.6	.6	.9	
8.4	6.0	7.6	All Other Current	1.9	6.9	1.6	5.8	22.0	
48.4	49.1	52.4	Total Current	44.7	52.8	51.7	50.6	68.2	
23.5	21.5	23.4	Fixed Assets (net)	35.3	23.1	16.9	18.5	19.6	
11.5	14.5	10.5	Intangibles (net)	4.7	7.7	20.0	15.8	9.9	
16.6	14.9	13.7	All Other Non-Current	15.4	16.4	11.3	15.1	2.3	
100.0	100.0	100.0	Total	100.0	100.0	100.0	100.0	100.0	
			LIABILITIES						
15.9	22.9	12.6	Notes Payable-Short Term	13.0	15.8	12.9	12.5	6.5	
1.9	4.2	1.6	Cur. Mat.-L.T.D.	1.0	2.2	.7	1.5	3.0	
8.4	7.9	14.6	Trade Payables	42.3	4.4	11.0	7.7	9.2	
.6	.2	.2	Income Taxes Payable	.7	.0	.0	.0	.0	
27.6	20.1	23.7	All Other Current	18.0	23.0	17.4	23.8	41.1	
54.3	55.2	52.7	Total Current	75.0	45.4	42.1	45.5	59.7	
16.8	14.0	14.3	Long-Term Debt	18.2	10.7	13.8	16.3	15.0	
.1	.3	.2	Deferred Taxes	.0	.0	.0	.1	.1	
4.7	3.9	7.7	All Other Non-Current	6.0	20.5	.0	.7	.5	
24.1	26.7	25.1	Net Worth	.8	23.5	44.1	37.3	24.7	
100.0	100.0	100.0	Total Liabilities & Net Worth	100.0	100.0	100.0	100.0	100.0	
			INCOME DATA						
100.0	100.0	100.0	Net Sales	100.0	100.0	100.0	100.0	100.0	
			Gross Profit						
96.1	93.7	92.1	Operating Expenses	87.4	92.1	95.2	96.1	94.3	
3.9	6.3	7.9	Operating Profit	12.6	7.9	4.8	3.9	5.7	
-.8	1.2	.9	All Other Expenses (net)	4.0	.6	-.8	-1.5	.6	
4.7	5.1	7.0	Profit Before Taxes	8.7	7.2	5.6	5.3	5.1	
			RATIOS						
2.8	2.6	2.3		1.9	5.5	2.2	2.8	1.8	
1.1	1.1	1.1	Current	.7	1.3	1.4	1.1	1.1	
.6	.5	.6		.2	.6	.9	.6	.9	
2.3	2.1	2.0		1.3	4.0	2.2	2.0	1.4	
1.0	1.0	1.0	Quick	.6	1.1	1.4	.9	.9	
.4	.3	.4		.2	.4	.7	.6	.3	
0 UND	0 UND	0 UND		0 UND	0 UND	0 UND	0 UND	0 999.8	
3 130.9	3 130.4	1 279.8	Sales/Receivables	0 UND	0 UND	10 37.5	3 129.2	9 40.9	
20 18.6	25 14.5	24 15.0		4 90.4	26 13.8	38 9.6	23 16.2	37 9.9	
			Cost of Sales/Inventory						
			Cost of Sales/Payables						
10.3	8.7	9.7		32.0	8.4	12.0	6.8	12.0	
75.9	107.6	114.5	Sales/Working Capital	-44.0	39.9	44.1	578.7	293.6	
-14.9	-8.8	-20.8		-6.1	-19.5	NM	-19.5	-61.6	
28.0	19.0	26.5		18.3	33.3		20.8	41.7	
(51) 3.3	(58) 1.8	(71) 10.5	EBIT/Interest	(10) 11.6	(25) 7.8		(11) 10.5	(10) 9.5	
-3.0	-6.1	.4		1.2	-1.8		-2.5	1.4	
			Net Profit + Depr., Dep., Amort./Cur. Mat. L/T/D						
.3	.2	.2		.3	.2	.2	.1	.3	
.9	.9	.9	Fixed/Worth	1.2	.6	.6	.7	1.4	
-2.5	-.8	-4.9		NM	-2.5	15.4	-1.6	3.4	
.5	.5	.6		.6	.4	.6	.3	1.2	
2.3	3.9	2.0	Debt/Worth	3.4	2.0	1.0	1.7	5.4	
-8.4	-4.4	-22.7		NM	-9.1	170.9	-5.0	125.1	
148.2	84.2	168.3		320.1	89.9	289.5	125.9		
(51) 31.1	(62) 27.4	(73) 71.0	% Profit Before Taxes/Tangible Net Worth	(17) 41.2	(20) 60.3	(10) 77.8	(13) 17.3		
-5.7	4.9	12.4		12.4	-.6	27.7	-1.5		
32.7	31.6	50.8		71.3	69.1	43.5	18.8	50.1	
5.0	4.7	16.2	% Profit Before Taxes/Total Assets	23.3	22.3	15.6	6.2	20.5	
-12.1	-3.5	.4		2.3	-1.8	8.4	-6.1	3.7	
38.9	75.9	53.5		51.9	98.3	55.2	60.8	49.6	
18.9	19.9	24.0	Sales/Net Fixed Assets	17.7	26.2	37.8	21.9	33.6	
8.9	8.3	10.6		10.9	10.9	9.7	10.6	11.7	
5.3	4.2	5.9		10.2	5.9	4.3	6.9	3.9	
2.9	2.3	2.7	Sales/Total Assets	2.5	2.9	2.6	2.8	2.7	
1.3	1.2	1.5		1.0	1.4	1.8	1.4	1.7	
.8	1.2	.9		.9	.9		1.1	.9	
(51) 1.9	(53) 2.3	(68) 1.6	% Depr., Dep., Amort./Sales	(12) 1.4	(19) 1.5		(16) 2.1	(10) 1.6	
4.0	3.9	3.2		3.7	1.9		4.2	3.0	
4.7	5.7	4.7		11.8	5.4				
(18) 9.5	(28) 11.4	(41) 9.3	% Officers', Directors' Owners' Comp/Sales	(11) 26.6	(15) 8.3				
27.6	27.6	26.7		35.1	11.1				
692954M	1185962M	897930M	Net Sales ($)	13351M	51473M	50176M	147103M	179013M	456814M
420367M	877575M	464161M	Total Assets ($)	7221M	36322M	20368M	88670M	71371M	240209M

Current Data Sorted by Assets

Comparative Historical Data

0-500M	500M-2MM	2-10MM	10-50MM	50-100MM	100-250MM	Type of Statement	4/1/05-3/31/06 ALL	4/1/06-3/31/07 ALL
2	4	14	7	2	8	Unqualified	21	22
		7	2			Reviewed	5	5
17	27	22	11	2	2	Compiled	109	105
155	51	15	2	2	2	Tax Returns	141	149
114	139	173	38	6	10	Other	444	482
	175 (4/1-9/30/09)		657 (10/1/09-3/31/10)					
288	221	231	60	10	22	**NUMBER OF STATEMENTS**	720	763
%	%	%	%	%	%	**ASSETS**	%	%
26.1	12.0	11.6	17.6	17.2	15.8	Cash & Equivalents	16.3	17.4
20.2	35.6	40.8	35.8	47.4	28.8	Trade Receivables (net)	33.4	31.6
.8	4.9	4.4	5.5	2.7	2.9	Inventory	3.9	4.1
4.4	4.2	6.8	7.5	6.8	5.7	All Other Current	6.3	7.0
51.6	56.8	63.6	66.4	74.2	53.2	Total Current	59.9	60.2
19.1	20.6	17.1	14.8	12.5	13.2	Fixed Assets (net)	17.9	18.4
14.0	12.4	9.9	8.6	6.7	18.6	Intangibles (net)	9.2	9.7
15.3	10.2	9.4	10.2	6.7	15.1	All Other Non-Current	13.0	11.7
100.0	100.0	100.0	100.0	100.0	100.0	Total	100.0	100.0
						LIABILITIES		
31.4	13.6	10.6	6.5	6.7	6.5	Notes Payable-Short Term	17.0	15.6
7.7	4.7	3.1	2.6	2.1	3.7	Cur. Mat.-L.T.D.	4.1	4.4
2.2	3.6	5.1	4.8	12.5	5.5	Trade Payables	3.8	4.2
.3	.1	.2	.2	.0	.3	Income Taxes Payable	.6	.5
30.1	11.6	15.1	14.5	8.8	16.1	All Other Current	18.2	17.9
71.7	33.6	34.1	28.6	30.2	32.0	Total Current	43.8	42.5
18.6	19.1	14.8	11.8	9.0	18.1	Long-Term Debt	18.5	16.9
.3	.3	.4	.0	.0	.5	Deferred Taxes	.3	.2
7.6	4.2	6.4	5.9	4.0	8.8	All Other Non-Current	8.8	7.7
1.8	42.7	44.4	53.7	56.8	40.7	Net Worth	28.7	32.6
100.0	100.0	100.0	100.0	100.0	100.0	Total Liabilties & Net Worth	100.0	100.0
						INCOME DATA		
100.0	100.0	100.0	100.0	100.0	100.0	Net Sales	100.0	100.0
						Gross Profit		
85.0	84.0	84.5	81.3	66.8	83.0	Operating Expenses	84.5	82.8
15.0	16.0	15.5	18.7	33.2	17.0	Operating Profit	15.5	17.2
1.2	4.4	3.0	2.0	2.4	2.7	All Other Expenses (net)	1.9	1.8
13.8	11.6	12.4	16.7	30.8	14.3	Profit Before Taxes	13.7	15.4
						RATIOS		
2.5	4.5	4.0	4.7	5.3	2.6		3.8	3.9
1.0	2.0	2.0	2.7	3.4	1.4	Current	1.7	1.8
.3	.9	1.2	1.6	1.7	.9		.9	1.0
2.4	3.6	3.1	4.3	4.3	2.0		3.0	3.1
.9	1.7	1.5	2.2	3.2	1.2	Quick	(719) 1.4	(761) 1.4
.2	.7	.9	1.1	1.5	.8		.7	.7
0 UND	0 756.1	36 10.2	38 9.6	44 8.3	18 20.0		0 UND	0 UND
0 UND	48 7.6	56 6.5	56 6.5	80 4.6	60 6.1	Sales/Receivables	42 8.6	45 8.1
35 10.5	73 5.0	77 4.7	77 4.7	211 1.7	72 5.0		72 5.1	71 5.1
						Cost of Sales/Inventory		
						Cost of Sales/Payables		
14.7	5.1	5.0	3.3	2.8	5.1		5.4	5.2
UND	10.3	8.7	5.2	4.2	11.6	Sales/Working Capital	12.2	11.5
-16.9	-36.7	36.5	13.6	5.9	-35.2		-116.4	-189.7
30.5	37.1	30.8	87.9		26.1		38.6	35.4
(210) 8.7	(179) 7.5	(197) 8.8	(46) 27.1		(17) 3.6	EBIT/Interest	(584) 10.2	(606) 8.9
2.1	1.6	1.7	7.0		1.1		2.3	2.4
	10.4	6.8					7.5	7.6
	(10) 4.6	(16) 2.2				Net Profit + Depr., Dep., Amort./Cur. Mat. L/T/D	(35) 2.4	(36) 2.4
	.4	.6					.7	1.1
.0	.1	.1	.1	.2	.2		.1	.1
.5	.3	.3	.2	.2	.7	Fixed/Worth	.3	.4
-5.6	4.3	1.9	.5	.4	-.4		4.6	3.1
.7	.4	.5	.3	.5	.4		.5	.5
7.1	1.4	1.7	1.0	.7	3.2	Debt/Worth	1.7	1.7
-2.4	29.4	8.4	2.8	1.7	-9.6		189.4	125.3
408.2	130.2	118.4	117.4	152.8	225.6		150.5	173.8
(179) 118.4	(174) 37.5	(196) 40.5	(55) 45.0	108.8	(15) 84.3	% Profit Before Taxes/Tangible Net Worth	(548) 62.8	(585) 77.6
19.1	4.6	4.6	17.9	83.1	51.5		13.7	14.0
114.6	44.4	49.9	64.5	74.2	64.5		67.2	75.7
35.4	12.1	13.5	19.7	61.8	25.0	% Profit Before Taxes/Total Assets	19.4	23.0
4.7	.8	1.5	4.7	9.5	2.2		3.5	4.2
UND	95.3	45.2	34.4	21.9	34.6		75.5	78.5
71.8	29.3	27.2	22.5	17.6	12.8	Sales/Net Fixed Assets	31.1	26.7
20.8	13.0	14.0	13.3	10.4	8.9		14.6	13.4
11.9	4.0	3.3	2.7	2.5	3.0		4.7	4.6
5.7	2.7	2.5	2.3	2.0	2.0	Sales/Total Assets	2.9	2.9
3.2	1.6	1.8	1.7	.8	1.0		1.9	1.9
.7	.8	1.1	1.2	1.1	1.1		1.0	1.0
(125) 1.2	(150) 1.6	(163) 1.6	(53) 1.6	1.7	(10) 2.4	% Depr., Dep., Amort./Sales	(460) 1.7	(493) 1.6
2.7	3.7	2.6	2.8	2.2	3.7		2.5	2.6
10.7	11.6	14.5	6.0				14.6	13.9
(192) 21.1	(102) 21.5	(88) 23.9	(19) 13.1			% Officers', Directors' Owners' Comp/Sales	(347) 23.2	(366) 24.6
31.7	31.4	34.5	31.8				33.3	32.7
397342M	770310M	2627041M	3061904M	1205087M	10677759M	Net Sales ($)	18628290M	20016925M
58855M	240621M	1028038M	1178583M	704931M	3670280M	Total Assets ($)	5241910M	6427869M

M = $ thousand   MM = $ million
See Pages 9 through 22 for Explanation of Ratios and Data

Comparative Historical Data   **Current Data Sorted by Sales**

Type of Statement									
Unqualified	19	36	37	4	1	2	4	10	16
Reviewed	7	15	9		1		2	4	2
Compiled	100	82	81	17	21	5	14	11	13
Tax Returns	165	167	225	99	70	26	16	11	3
Other	454	490	480	83	99	65	77	102	54
	4/1/07-3/31/08 ALL	4/1/08-3/31/09 ALL	4/1/09-3/31/10 ALL	175 (4/1-9/30/09)			657 (10/1/09-3/31/10)		
				0-1MM	1-3MM	3-5MM	5-10MM	10-25MM	25MM & OVER
NUMBER OF STATEMENTS	745	790	832	203	191	99	113	138	88
ASSETS	%	%	%	%	%	%	%	%	%
Cash & Equivalents	17.1	15.4	17.4	17.8	19.0	17.1	16.8	15.2	16.9
Trade Receivables (net)	31.3	33.0	31.7	15.9	34.3	30.9	36.3	43.0	40.0
Inventory	3.8	4.1	3.3	.8	3.9	3.8	4.2	4.4	4.5
All Other Current	7.6	6.8	5.3	4.7	3.3	5.4	5.3	7.9	7.1
Total Current	59.8	59.3	57.7	39.2	60.4	57.2	62.5	70.5	68.5
Fixed Assets (net)	18.0	19.0	18.4	29.8	13.6	17.2	17.5	13.3	12.9
Intangibles (net)	11.9	9.9	12.1	16.2	15.1	9.1	9.9	7.8	9.1
All Other Non-Current	10.3	11.8	11.8	14.8	10.9	16.5	10.1	8.4	9.5
Total	100.0	100.0	100.0	100.0	100.0	100.0	100.0	100.0	100.0
LIABILITIES									
Notes Payable-Short Term	17.2	17.6	18.2	30.9	22.7	12.4	9.8	11.4	6.7
Cur. Mat.-L.T.D.	5.6	4.5	5.1	8.3	5.4	4.3	4.2	2.5	2.9
Trade Payables	3.8	4.8	3.8	2.1	2.3	2.2	6.0	5.5	7.0
Income Taxes Payable	.3	.4	.2	.4	.0	.3	.2	.3	.2
All Other Current	19.8	18.8	19.2	24.0	16.1	26.5	15.5	16.8	15.7
Total Current	46.6	46.0	46.5	65.6	46.6	45.7	35.6	36.6	32.5
Long-Term Debt	17.8	16.6	17.0	28.9	15.8	14.9	12.0	10.9	11.0
Deferred Taxes	.1	.2	.3	.0	.5	.5	.4	.6	.1
All Other Non-Current	8.1	7.0	6.2	8.0	5.5	7.1	4.8	5.3	6.1
Net Worth	27.3	30.3	29.9	-2.5	31.7	31.8	47.3	46.8	50.3
Total Liabilities & Net Worth	100.0	100.0	100.0	100.0	100.0	100.0	100.0	100.0	100.0
INCOME DATA									
Net Sales	100.0	100.0	100.0	100.0	100.0	100.0	100.0	100.0	100.0
Gross Profit									
Operating Expenses	83.7	84.0	84.1	77.7	86.7	87.8	87.6	85.9	81.8
Operating Profit	16.3	16.0	15.9	22.3	13.3	12.2	12.4	14.1	18.2
All Other Expenses (net)	2.0	2.8	2.7	6.5	1.0	.9	1.2	2.4	1.6
Profit Before Taxes	14.3	13.2	13.3	15.9	12.3	11.3	11.2	11.8	16.6
RATIOS									
Current	3.6	3.5	3.8	2.2	4.9	4.0	4.5	4.2	4.0
	1.7	1.7	1.6	.7	1.6	1.8	2.0	2.3	2.2
	.8	.8	.8	.2	.7	.8	1.1	1.2	1.4
Quick	3.0	2.9	3.2	1.6	4.1	3.2	4.1	3.2	3.6
	(744) 1.3	1.4	1.3	.5	1.4	1.6	1.7	1.8	1.7
	.6	.6	.6	.1	.6	.7	.9	.9	1.1
Sales/Receivables	0 UND	0 UND	0 UND	0 UND	0 UND	0 UND	17 21.7	35 10.5	36 10.1
	42 8.7	45 8.2	41 8.9	0 UND	37 9.9	46 8.0	49 7.5	52 7.0	58 6.3
	70 5.2	74 4.9	68 5.3	40 9.1	73 5.0	69 5.3	73 5.0	69 5.3	74 4.9
Cost of Sales/Inventory									
Cost of Sales/Payables									
Sales/Working Capital	5.4	5.4	5.6	12.5	6.0	5.3	5.1	5.1	4.2
	12.0	12.3	15.5	-43.9	19.7	10.6	11.0	8.4	7.2
	-65.2	-78.3	-45.7	-6.6	-38.5	-119.9	171.0	26.7	15.5
EBIT/Interest	31.4	33.8	33.7	22.4	34.4	39.5	41.6	35.3	87.9
	(608) 8.9	(642) 8.5	(657) 9.6	(139) 6.4	(152) 8.9	(82) 7.8	(97) 9.9	(117) 12.5	(70) 23.5
	2.4	2.2	2.0	2.2	1.9	1.4	1.6	1.7	3.0
Net Profit + Depr., Dep., Amort./Cur. Mat. L/T/D	5.6	6.9	8.1				5.7		
	(46) 2.1	(50) 1.9	(34) 3.2				(11) 2.0		
	1.0	1.0	.7				.5		
Fixed/Worth	.1	.1	.1	.0	.0	.1	.1	.1	.1
	.4	.4	.3	1.4	.3	.3	.3	.3	.3
	22.1	5.3	4.3	-2.9	9.0	2.6	2.2	.9	.5
Debt/Worth	.5	.6	.5	1.0	.5	.4	.5	.4	.4
	1.8	1.9	1.9	17.6	2.2	1.8	1.0	1.0	1.1
	-27.9	63.1	UND	-2.3	-6.3	25.0	6.5	3.7	3.3
% Profit Before Taxes/Tangible Net Worth	153.5	143.1	151.6	293.7	285.7	131.0	130.0	130.1	143.1
	(540) 72.3	(605) 58.8	(629) 57.5	(118) 58.6	(134) 95.5	(79) 38.1	(96) 46.2	(123) 36.8	(79) 84.3
	16.4	13.9	8.8	12.0	18.7	3.0	5.2	3.0	25.2
% Profit Before Taxes/Total Assets	70.8	66.6	68.0	62.9	88.1	54.1	53.4	64.0	68.7
	22.0	18.2	18.7	19.5	28.1	10.7	13.7	17.2	31.1
	4.1	3.2	2.0	3.0	3.4	1.1	1.2	1.1	6.1
Sales/Net Fixed Assets	83.6	80.1	120.5	426.0	759.0	182.1	59.6	66.1	36.1
	29.3	29.9	31.4	22.6	55.8	32.5	31.8	31.1	21.9
	15.5	15.4	15.1	6.3	21.3	16.8	15.7	18.2	13.0
Sales/Total Assets	4.7	4.5	5.0	6.1	6.4	5.5	4.3	4.1	3.3
	2.8	2.9	3.0	2.6	3.8	3.1	2.8	3.0	2.5
	2.0	2.0	1.9	.9	2.3	1.9	2.0	2.3	2.0
% Depr., Dep., Amort./Sales	.9	.9	.9	1.2	.7	.8	.8	.8	1.1
	(477) 1.5	(538) 1.5	(511) 1.6	(108) 3.4	(102) 1.3	(55) 1.4	(79) 1.3	(101) 1.4	(66) 1.6
	2.5	2.5	2.8	12.2	2.4	2.3	2.5	2.2	2.7
% Officers', Directors' Owners' Comp/Sales	14.2	11.8	10.9	11.2	10.8	11.3	10.4	13.8	6.2
	(366) 22.8	(375) 21.4	(406) 21.9	(112) 19.0	(107) 20.0	(61) 23.3	(50) 22.4	(52) 23.0	(24) 20.7
	30.9	30.3	31.7	28.7	31.5	33.0	35.0	30.8	33.1
Net Sales ($)	16594587M	15157413M	18739443M	103217M	339254M	386495M	816216M	2011729M	15082532M
Total Assets ($)	5944918M	5826677M	6881308M	87330M	141028M	166964M	326240M	947040M	5212706M

M = $ thousand   MM = $ million
See Pages 9 through 22 for Explanation of Ratios and Data

Current Data Sorted by Assets   **Comparative Historical Data**

Type of Statement	0-500M	500M-2MM	2-10MM	10-50MM	50-100MM	100-250MM		4/1/05-3/31/06 ALL	4/1/06-3/31/07 ALL
Unqualified			4	1		7		5	8
Reviewed	2			2	1			1	2
Compiled	5	4	3	1				5	3
Tax Returns	4	3	3	4	1	2		3	5
Other								5	5
		7 (4/1-9/30/09)		40 (10/1/09-3/31/10)					
NUMBER OF STATEMENTS	11	7	10	8	2	9		19	23
	%	%	%	%	%	%		%	%
ASSETS									
Cash & Equivalents	50.1		31.6					38.6	34.5
Trade Receivables (net)	4.2		14.7					20.5	16.4
Inventory	.0		.0					.2	.4
All Other Current	21.9		28.3					6.1	15.2
Total Current	76.2		74.5					65.4	66.5
Fixed Assets (net)	13.3		13.9					16.9	9.4
Intangibles (net)	2.0		1.4					1.2	9.0
All Other Non-Current	8.4		10.2					16.4	15.1
Total	100.0		100.0					100.0	100.0
LIABILITIES									
Notes Payable-Short Term	47.4		6.2					6.3	15.8
Cur. Mat.-L.T.D.	.3		.9					1.2	.6
Trade Payables	4.3		2.1					4.6	3.6
Income Taxes Payable	.0		12.2					.0	1.2
All Other Current	34.9		54.9					45.3	31.0
Total Current	86.9		76.2					57.5	52.1
Long-Term Debt	1.2		8.7					25.5	17.1
Deferred Taxes	.0		.0					.2	.5
All Other Non-Current	10.7		.4					8.0	10.7
Net Worth	1.2		14.7					8.8	19.6
Total Liabilties & Net Worth	100.0		100.0					100.0	100.0
INCOME DATA									
Net Sales	100.0		100.0					100.0	100.0
Gross Profit									
Operating Expenses	88.0		92.3					93.9	101.9
Operating Profit	12.0		7.7					6.1	-1.9
All Other Expenses (net)	3.4		-.4					-.1	.6
Profit Before Taxes	8.7		8.0					6.2	-2.6
RATIOS									
Current	9.0		1.2					2.3	2.8
	1.8		1.0					1.1	1.2
	.7		1.0					.8	1.0
Quick	2.1		1.2					2.3	2.7
	1.5		.7					1.0	1.2
	.5		.1					.5	.3
Sales/Receivables	0 UND		0 UND					1 645.3	0 UND
	0 UND		3 111.2					1 276.2	14 26.0
	1 553.0		42 8.6					12 30.7	28 13.2
Cost of Sales/Inventory									
Cost of Sales/Payables									
Sales/Working Capital	19.4		15.1					26.9	5.8
	40.3		NM					422.1	28.5
	-26.2		-13.0					-17.7	-307.3
EBIT/Interest								43.7	18.2
								(11) 9.4	(16) 2.9
								3.6	-13.0
Net Profit + Depr., Dep., Amort./Cur. Mat. L/T/D									
Fixed/Worth	.0		.0					.0	.1
	.0		2.2					.7	1.4
	UND		NM					3.7	-1.2
Debt/Worth	.6		3.1					2.5	.8
	.9		6.1					6.1	12.6
	UND		NM					17.2	-30.3
% Profit Before Taxes/Tangible Net Worth								134.7	168.1
								(16) 50.3	(16) 29.2
								15.6	11.6
% Profit Before Taxes/Total Assets	113.5		12.2					19.7	23.5
	19.8		4.2					6.4	7.0
	1.2		2.2					2.2	-5.6
Sales/Net Fixed Assets	UND		296.2					999.8	447.7
	UND		29.9					253.8	24.7
	264.7		7.6					13.9	11.6
Sales/Total Assets	26.2		6.2					40.1	10.5
	17.2		1.0					8.6	1.3
	3.7		.3					.6	.3
% Depr., Dep., Amort./Sales									.5
								(15)	1.6
									3.5
% Officers', Directors' Owners' Comp/Sales									
Net Sales ($)	39046M	69758M	217396M	97822M	460192M	3657548M		8127029M	2747047M
Total Assets ($)	1538M	7866M	56141M	171707M	167036M	1515832M		455950M	1068767M

Comparative Historical Data   **Current Data Sorted by Sales**

			Type of Statement	0-1MM	1-3MM	3-5MM	5-10MM	10-25MM	25MM & OVER
8	7	8	Unqualified					2	6
2	2	7	Reviewed		1		1	3	2
4	3	2	Compiled		1	1			
2	5	13	Tax Returns	4	4	4	2	1	
10	19	17	Other	3	3	2		1	6
4/1/07-3/31/08 ALL	4/1/08-3/31/09 ALL	4/1/09-3/31/10 ALL			7 (4/1-9/30/09)		40 (10/1/09-3/31/10)		
26	36	47	**NUMBER OF STATEMENTS**	7	9	7	3	7	14
%	%	%	**ASSETS**	%	%	%	%	%	%
32.9	27.8	33.9	Cash & Equivalents						18.7
16.5	17.5	7.8	Trade Receivables (net)						11.3
.1	.3	.4	Inventory						.1
23.3	21.1	23.8	All Other Current						18.0
72.8	66.6	65.9	Total Current						48.1
11.7	10.1	13.4	Fixed Assets (net)						10.6
8.9	10.1	5.7	Intangibles (net)						15.8
6.6	13.2	14.9	All Other Non-Current						25.6
100.0	100.0	100.0	Total						100.0
			LIABILITIES						
9.5	11.6	14.7	Notes Payable-Short Term						4.3
.4	5.5	1.8	Cur. Mat.-L.T.D.						3.6
3.4	5.0	3.7	Trade Payables						6.7
.0	.1	2.6	Income Taxes Payable						1.7
45.5	47.6	45.8	All Other Current						42.0
58.8	69.9	68.6	Total Current						58.3
20.6	13.8	8.6	Long-Term Debt						12.6
.1	.1	.1	Deferred Taxes						.1
4.2	12.3	15.8	All Other Non-Current						12.8
16.3	3.9	6.9	Net Worth						16.2
100.0	100.0	100.0	Total Liabilities & Net Worth						100.0
			INCOME DATA						
100.0	100.0	100.0	Net Sales						100.0
			Gross Profit						
93.9	96.6	93.5	Operating Expenses						99.6
6.1	3.4	6.5	Operating Profit						.4
2.7	.9	1.4	All Other Expenses (net)						1.4
3.4	2.5	5.1	Profit Before Taxes						-1.0
			RATIOS						
1.7	1.8	1.8							1.5
1.1	1.3	1.0	Current						1.0
1.0	1.0	1.0							.3
1.5	1.5	1.7							1.5
1.0	1.0	1.0	Quick						.3
.1	.3	.1							.1
1 503.3	3 130.5	0 UND							1 327.1
9 38.5	9 42.4	1 325.4	Sales/Receivables						7 55.6
29 12.6	26 14.1	11 32.9							39 9.4
			Cost of Sales/Inventory						
			Cost of Sales/Payables						
3.2	9.5	8.8							8.2
20.5	77.9	47.4	Sales/Working Capital						65.0
-37.1	-26.4	-16.5							-12.1
20.6	19.5	15.0							15.2
(17) 3.2	(27) 1.3	(32) 5.8	EBIT/Interest					(12) -.8	
-3.8	-3.9	-1.7							-36.8
			Net Profit + Depr., Dep., Amort./Cur. Mat. L/T/D						
.1	.1	.0							.4
.7	2.0	.8	Fixed/Worth						.7
-.9	-.3	-.8							-.8
1.3	3.2	2.3							4.8
13.7	57.0	23.1	Debt/Worth						46.3
-7.9	-5.6	-30.4							-5.8
107.5	117.1	205.5							
(17) 20.2	(24) 51.9	(32) 42.7	% Profit Before Taxes/Tangible Net Worth						
5.3	-9.6	12.8							
9.4	18.7	16.6							12.9
2.9	2.9	5.3	% Profit Before Taxes/Total Assets						2.6
-4.0	-2.1	.2							-.8
87.1	598.5	303.0							153.9
12.8	26.0	30.9	Sales/Net Fixed Assets						21.6
7.6	9.9	8.5							11.0
3.0	14.9	9.5							11.5
.6	1.6	1.4	Sales/Total Assets						1.1
.3	.3	.3							.2
.9	.2	.5							
(14) 1.9	(24) 1.1	(24) 1.4	% Depr., Dep., Amort./Sales						
3.8	3.9	2.8							
		2.1							
	(13) 8.2		% Officers', Directors' Owners' Comp/Sales						
		12.7							
2899234M	4249877M	4541762M	Net Sales ($)	2138M	17818M	25561M	23170M	130179M	4342896M
1240071M	1621390M	1920120M	Total Assets ($)	6077M	45543M	40585M	48976M	166400M	1612539M

M = $ thousand   MM = $ million
See Pages 9 through 22 for Explanation of Ratios and Data

Current Data Sorted by Assets

Comparative Historical Data

0-500M	500M-2MM	2-10MM	10-50MM	50-100MM	100-250MM	Type of Statement	4/1/05-3/31/06 ALL	4/1/06-3/31/07 ALL
1		2	7	1	7	Unqualified	7	9
1	2	5	3			Reviewed	3	2
1	4	1	1			Compiled	6	8
45	13	3	2			Tax Returns	15	42
23	22	23	8	2	4	Other	37	75
	25 (4/1-9/30/09)		156 (10/1/09-3/31/10)					
71	41	34	21	3	11	NUMBER OF STATEMENTS	68	136
%	%	%	%	%	%	ASSETS	%	%
34.6	16.4	10.4	30.0		15.9	Cash & Equivalents	23.7	21.3
13.6	26.7	31.1	25.4		18.5	Trade Receivables (net)	29.6	25.5
.4	2.7	2.6	1.0		.1	Inventory	3.2	2.8
3.1	3.0	15.2	4.1		14.0	All Other Current	5.8	5.9
51.8	48.7	59.3	60.5		48.5	Total Current	62.3	55.4
20.2	29.6	16.6	6.2		6.1	Fixed Assets (net)	15.3	20.0
10.9	5.8	15.0	17.9		20.0	Intangibles (net)	11.4	9.9
17.0	15.8	9.1	15.5		25.5	All Other Non-Current	10.9	14.6
100.0	100.0	100.0	100.0		100.0	Total	100.0	100.0
						LIABILITIES		
17.8	10.8	12.7	8.1		.9	Notes Payable-Short Term	13.6	14.9
7.6	3.0	4.7	1.9		1.3	Cur. Mat.-L.T.D.	4.8	3.1
5.9	5.3	7.8	7.7		5.6	Trade Payables	7.5	6.0
.1	.2	1.1	.0		.5	Income Taxes Payable	.2	.6
26.9	16.9	24.2	35.4		29.4	All Other Current	19.4	22.3
58.3	36.3	50.6	53.1		37.7	Total Current	45.5	46.9
23.6	18.8	27.9	9.9		12.1	Long-Term Debt	10.3	15.0
.0	.0	.2	.5		.9	Deferred Taxes	.1	.2
29.3	7.6	2.8	10.2		23.0	All Other Non-Current	14.5	6.8
-11.2	37.3	18.6	26.3		26.2	Net Worth	29.6	31.1
100.0	100.0	100.0	100.0		100.0	Total Liabilities & Net Worth	100.0	100.0
						INCOME DATA		
100.0	100.0	100.0	100.0		100.0	Net Sales	100.0	100.0
						Gross Profit		
89.7	81.2	90.5	88.4		94.7	Operating Expenses	86.6	86.2
10.3	18.8	9.5	11.6		5.3	Operating Profit	13.4	13.8
.6	3.0	.2	1.4		2.4	All Other Expenses (net)	2.2	1.9
9.7	15.9	9.2	10.2		2.9	Profit Before Taxes	11.2	11.9
						RATIOS		
3.1	4.7	2.9	4.7		1.8	Current	3.8	2.9
1.0	1.6	1.2	1.1		1.3		1.4	1.4
.4	.8	.7	.7		1.0		1.0	.7
3.0	3.7	2.4	3.9		1.8	Quick	3.0	2.3
1.0	1.1	.8	1.0		1.0		1.2	1.1
.3	.6	.3	.6		.9		.8	.6
0 UND	0 UND	1 282.9	8 45.5		7 50.6	Sales/Receivables	0 UND	0 UND
0 UND	23 15.7	46 7.9	47 7.7		23 15.8		37 9.9	25 14.5
20 18.5	64 5.7	84 4.4	81 4.5		67 5.5		79 4.6	56 6.5
						Cost of Sales/Inventory		
						Cost of Sales/Payables		
15.1	6.5	5.5	3.5		6.0	Sales/Working Capital	5.3	7.3
999.8	24.7	18.6	51.0		10.6		15.9	32.0
-13.7	-40.4	-11.8	-8.1		41.6		-369.9	-23.1
26.0	22.1	23.2	12.7		14.2	EBIT/Interest	37.0	23.7
(39) 8.0	(28) 5.1	(26) 6.5	(15) 4.5		2.3		(47) 12.0	(92) 5.9
.7	.6	2.5	1.4		1.0		2.4	1.5
						Net Profit + Depr., Dep., Amort./Cur. Mat. L/T/D		3.8
							(10)	1.5
								-1.2
.0	.1	.2	.1		.6	Fixed/Worth	.1	.1
.7	.5	.6	.3		.9		.5	.4
UND	2.9	-2.3	-.4		-.2		UND	6.4
.8	.5	.7	.9		5.8	Debt/Worth	.6	.5
13.0	1.4	3.5	17.0		37.5		3.1	2.6
-2.7	7.4	-8.0	-17.6		-3.6		UND	-21.5
229.9	76.3	89.8	100.8			% Profit Before Taxes/Tangible Net Worth	157.9	109.7
(48) 82.9	(34) 27.0	(25) 55.0	(14) 31.1				(52) 91.6	(100) 62.1
3.1	10.4	23.3	24.4				29.4	11.9
76.5	33.9	25.9	20.1		14.4	% Profit Before Taxes/Total Assets	56.3	50.7
27.3	9.2	15.3	4.7		.9		18.9	14.3
.0	.5	4.6	1.3		.0		4.9	2.2
UND	82.6	48.2	50.8		31.9	Sales/Net Fixed Assets	88.9	92.1
43.2	17.6	22.2	23.5		12.7		34.3	28.3
12.4	4.4	7.3	11.4		6.3		12.8	10.9
11.9	4.0	3.4	2.2		1.6	Sales/Total Assets	5.9	5.0
4.6	2.3	2.1	.7		.6		2.4	2.8
2.2	.5	1.6	.3		.2		1.3	1.6
1.0	.9	.8	.6			% Depr., Dep., Amort./Sales	.8	.9
(29) 1.5	(26) 2.0	(25) 1.2	(14) 1.2				(44) 1.6	(79) 1.3
2.6	7.7	2.3	2.3				3.3	3.5
12.1	2.0	6.3				% Officers', Directors' Owners' Comp/Sales	9.4	5.2
(40) 19.5	(11) 16.7	(12) 13.2					(29) 16.0	(49) 9.0
32.2	31.5	23.6					31.7	18.9
76473M	158774M	335567M	694208M	283361M	4564225M	Net Sales ($)	3419110M	4109536M
12376M	44023M	131084M	487955M	216221M	1786495M	Total Assets ($)	1607894M	1413177M

M = $ thousand   MM = $ million
See Pages 9 through 22 for Explanation of Ratios and Data

Comparative Historical Data   Current Data Sorted by Sales

			Type of Statement						
9	20	18	Unqualified		1	1		4	12
9	8	11	Reviewed		4		5	1	1
18	16	7	Compiled		3	3		1	
30	40	63	Tax Returns	42	12	5	2	2	
66	81	82	Other	18	17	14	13	10	10
4/1/07-3/31/08 ALL	4/1/08-3/31/09 ALL	4/1/09-3/31/10 ALL		25 (4/1-9/30/09)			156 (10/1/09-3/31/10)		
				0-1MM	1-3MM	3-5MM	5-10MM	10-25MM	25MM & OVE
132	165	181	NUMBER OF STATEMENTS	60	37	23	20	18	23
%	%	%	ASSETS	%	%	%	%	%	%
22.2	22.1	23.9	Cash & Equivalents	30.4	27.2	17.3	15.7	20.4	17.9
22.6	24.8	21.8	Trade Receivables (net)	9.8	16.9	34.7	33.2	30.5	31.3
2.9	2.9	1.4	Inventory	.2	2.8	2.0	2.6	1.7	.1
8.1	7.0	6.2	All Other Current	2.2	7.3	6.3	10.6	4.2	12.3
55.8	56.8	53.2	Total Current	42.7	54.2	60.3	62.1	56.8	61.6
20.4	18.5	19.1	Fixed Assets (net)	28.0	20.8	15.3	9.4	15.5	7.9
9.6	12.3	12.3	Intangibles (net)	8.5	11.3	13.1	14.5	8.5	23.8
14.2	12.4	15.4	All Other Non-Current	20.7	13.7	11.2	14.0	19.1	6.7
100.0	100.0	100.0	Total	100.0	100.0	100.0	100.0	100.0	100.0
			LIABILITIES						
15.3	15.5	12.9	Notes Payable-Short Term	14.6	17.3	8.6	15.8	10.0	5.2
5.2	3.0	4.9	Cur. Mat.-L.T.D.	5.4	7.2	4.7	2.5	2.2	4.4
5.8	7.2	6.2	Trade Payables	6.7	2.0	5.2	5.4	6.4	13.5
.8	.3	.3	Income Taxes Payable	.1	.0	.4	1.9	.1	.2
22.3	22.8	25.0	All Other Current	26.8	28.8	11.5	28.5	18.5	29.6
49.4	49.0	49.3	Total Current	53.5	55.4	30.3	53.9	37.1	52.9
17.8	14.8	21.2	Long-Term Debt	26.7	18.2	16.7	31.8	9.5	15.9
.2	.2	.2	Deferred Taxes	.0	.0	.0	.0	.3	.9
11.7	8.9	16.4	All Other Non-Current	16.1	34.6	6.8	2.5	14.4	11.5
21.0	27.1	12.9	Net Worth	3.8	-8.3	46.2	11.8	38.6	18.7
100.0	100.0	100.0	Total Liabilities & Net Worth	100.0	100.0	100.0	100.0	100.0	100.0
			INCOME DATA						
100.0	100.0	100.0	Net Sales	100.0	100.0	100.0	100.0	100.0	100.0
			Gross Profit						
88.8	90.0	87.9	Operating Expenses	84.2	90.7	84.3	91.0	91.7	91.2
11.2	10.0	12.1	Operating Profit	15.8	9.3	15.7	9.0	8.3	8.8
.3	1.7	1.3	All Other Expenses (net)	1.8	.3	2.5	.3	.5	1.7
10.8	8.4	10.8	Profit Before Taxes	14.0	9.0	13.1	8.7	7.8	7.1
			RATIOS						
2.6	2.4	3.2	Current	3.6	2.8	6.8	3.9	3.8	2.6
1.3	1.3	1.2		.9	1.1	2.4	1.2	2.2	1.2
.6	.7	.6		.2	.8	1.0	.6	1.1	1.0
2.3	2.1	2.8	Quick	3.6	2.5	6.4	3.0	3.2	2.4
1.1	1.1	1.0		.8	1.0	2.1	1.1	2.1	1.0
.4	.5	.4		.2	.4	.5	.3	.9	.6
0 UND	0 UND	0 UND	Sales/Receivables	0 UND	0 UND	0 UND	0 783.5	11 32.4	23 15.8
25 14.8	21 17.0	13 27.1		0 UND	4 91.9	44 8.2	54 6.8	28 12.9	46 8.0
50 7.3	49 7.5	54 6.7		18 20.3	35 10.5	67 5.5	101 3.6	72 5.1	67 5.5
			Cost of Sales/Inventory						
			Cost of Sales/Payables						
7.6	8.3	6.2	Sales/Working Capital	8.4	23.3	5.4	4.8	4.3	6.0
20.1	29.5	38.5		-248.3	48.9	15.1	15.6	7.4	14.9
-25.6	-24.6	-16.1		-6.3	-80.5	199.5	-8.8	NM	-125.5
17.5	18.9	22.6	EBIT/Interest	25.0	21.1	24.2	31.5	53.8	11.4
(104) 4.5	(118) 4.9	(122) 5.6		(34) 6.9	(25) 5.0	(17) 15.9	(13) 6.3	(13) 5.8	(20) 4.7
1.3	1.3	1.2		.3	1.0	4.1	2.2	.6	1.7
	6.5	4.2	Net Profit + Depr., Dep., Amort./Cur. Mat. L/T/D						
	(14) 1.8	(12) 3.1							
	.9	1.1							
.2	.1	.1	Fixed/Worth	.0	.1	.1	.1	.1	.3
.6	.5	.7		.8	.9	.3	.4	.2	-3.4
19.2	37.7	UND		4.5	-.5	.8	NM	1.2	-.1
1.0	1.0	.7	Debt/Worth	.6	.9	.6	.9	.5	3.5
3.0	5.0	4.6		4.2	5.2	1.1	4.3	1.4	-168.2
-21.0	-21.6	-9.4		-8.5	-3.5	18.4	NM	14.6	-2.4
143.8	102.6	122.5	% Profit Before Taxes/Tangible Net Worth	128.7	172.7	98.5	121.8	94.8	87.0
(97) 61.0	(117) 48.7	(129) 49.2		(44) 46.9	(24) 54.5	(19) 64.2	(15) 59.1	(16) 38.8	(11) 36.3
10.6	5.4	13.6		5.3	1.8	29.3	29.9	1.0	14.7
48.0	42.4	38.8	% Profit Before Taxes/Total Assets	51.5	56.2	61.1	20.0	27.4	24.9
14.9	7.5	11.7		10.4	10.1	21.8	9.2	15.2	6.1
1.1	.5	.6		-.9	-.2	9.8	3.5	-.6	.5
90.7	84.2	86.6	Sales/Net Fixed Assets	UND	234.1	82.0	75.1	53.9	61.0
21.0	24.6	23.5		19.7	29.0	27.6	23.9	18.7	21.2
11.4	10.8	9.8		8.1	12.8	16.3	18.3	7.1	13.9
5.2	5.7	5.0	Sales/Total Assets	4.6	10.9	5.0	3.3	4.4	4.4
2.9	2.6	2.5		2.2	4.0	2.5	2.1	2.5	1.8
1.5	1.3	1.1		1.1	1.8	1.1	1.5	.7	.8
1.0	1.0	.9	% Depr., Dep., Amort./Sales	1.2	.8	.8	.6	.9	.9
(85) 1.6	(103) 1.7	(102) 1.4		(28) 2.2	(20) 1.4	(14) 1.1	(13) 1.2	(12) 1.5	(15) 1.2
2.7	2.6	2.8		7.3	2.7	2.3	4.4	2.5	2.2
4.5	3.6	8.9	% Officers', Directors' Owners' Comp/Sales	11.5	5.1				
(46) 13.0	(49) 11.2	(66) 17.8		(30) 18.8	(17) 17.1				
20.3	22.3	30.5		31.6	30.5				
1844282M	6529696M	6112608M	Net Sales ($)	26490M	67970M	89826M	141506M	296913M	5489903M
1215294M	2418742M	2678154M	Total Assets ($)	21135M	45947M	71302M	154509M	357609M	2027652M

M = $ thousand   MM = $ million
See Pages 9 through 22 for Explanation of Ratios and Data

Current Data Sorted by Assets   Comparative Historical Data

0-500M	500M-2MM	2-10MM	10-50MM	50-100MM	100-250MM	Type of Statement	4/1/05-3/31/06 ALL	4/1/06-3/31/07 ALL
1	1	13	22	3	2	Unqualified	40	36
1	17	56	37	1		Reviewed	74	102
21	33	40	5			Compiled	84	83
86	30	10	1			Tax Returns	83	91
54	60	72	27	6	3	Other	163	180
	55 (4/1-9/30/09)			547 (10/1/09-3/31/10)				
163	141	191	92	10	5	NUMBER OF STATEMENTS	444	492
%	%	%	%	%	%	ASSETS	%	%
26.8	16.5	10.1	11.4	15.1		Cash & Equivalents	14.1	14.4
18.2	40.5	53.9	51.5	45.4		Trade Receivables (net)	46.8	45.5
.5	2.0	2.4	1.0	.0		Inventory	2.2	2.1
4.9	5.6	6.5	11.7	6.7		All Other Current	6.2	7.0
50.5	64.7	72.9	75.6	67.3		Total Current	69.3	69.0
32.4	20.2	17.3	14.3	13.4		Fixed Assets (net)	18.5	18.8
3.3	3.4	2.9	2.3	5.1		Intangibles (net)	2.2	2.8
13.9	11.7	6.9	7.9	14.3		All Other Non-Current	10.1	9.4
100.0	100.0	100.0	100.0	100.0		Total	100.0	100.0
						LIABILITIES		
43.4	15.6	7.4	6.7	2.3		Notes Payable-Short Term	15.0	15.3
6.0	2.3	2.7	2.3	4.7		Cur. Mat.-L.T.D.	3.3	3.6
12.7	14.7	15.6	14.9	15.1		Trade Payables	15.9	14.2
.8	1.7	2.3	3.7	2.3		Income Taxes Payable	2.1	2.1
27.0	14.3	15.5	20.5	33.0		All Other Current	18.3	20.4
89.9	48.6	43.4	48.2	57.4		Total Current	54.6	55.6
17.5	10.6	8.9	5.4	6.2		Long-Term Debt	10.7	10.3
.0	.9	1.7	1.7	.7		Deferred Taxes	1.0	1.1
11.6	3.8	3.0	5.7	5.2		All Other Non-Current	5.9	4.6
-18.9	36.2	43.0	39.0	30.4		Net Worth	27.8	28.4
100.0	100.0	100.0	100.0	100.0		Total Liabilities & Net Worth	100.0	100.0
						INCOME DATA		
100.0	100.0	100.0	100.0	100.0		Net Sales	100.0	100.0
						Gross Profit		
96.0	96.8	98.5	97.4	98.9		Operating Expenses	92.6	92.1
4.0	3.2	1.5	2.6	1.1		Operating Profit	7.4	7.9
2.1	2.2	1.4	1.0	.7		All Other Expenses (net)	.8	.9
1.9	1.1	.1	1.7	.4		Profit Before Taxes	6.7	6.9
						RATIOS		
2.0	2.7	2.7	2.1	1.5		Current	2.3	2.3
.6	1.4	1.8	1.6	1.2			1.5	1.5
.2	.9	1.2	1.2	1.0			1.0	1.0
1.7	2.5	2.5	1.9	1.3		Quick	2.1	2.1
.6	1.3	(190) 1.5	1.3	1.1			(443) 1.3	1.3
.1	.7	1.0	.9	.9			.8	.8
0 UND	0 UND	59 6.2	63 5.8	55 6.7		Sales/Receivables	11 31.9	21 17.3
0 UND	58 6.3	84 4.4	86 4.3	76 4.8			73 5.0	70 5.2
36 10.1	88 4.1	125 2.9	124 2.9	114 3.2			105 3.5	98 3.7
						Cost of Sales/Inventory		
						Cost of Sales/Payables		
15.5	6.0	4.1	4.0	7.6		Sales/Working Capital	6.1	6.4
-44.3	16.7	7.6	8.3	24.8			14.0	13.1
-7.8	-58.5	19.7	17.3	NM			-212.9	999.8
29.0	10.2	15.7	26.4			EBIT/Interest	47.0	31.2
(115) 1.7	(109) 1.1	(156) 3.3	(80) 3.5				(371) 11.3	(392) 11.2
-8.0	-10.6	-13.7	-4.7				2.8	2.6
	12.7	4.9	6.8			Net Profit + Depr., Dep., Amort./Cur. Mat. L/T/D	6.8	6.5
	(21) 2.3	(54) 1.0	(38) 1.9				(90) 2.8	(96) 2.7
	-4.4	-1.9	.0				1.1	1.3
.2	.1	.1	.1	.4		Fixed/Worth	.1	.2
3.0	.4	.3	.3	.5			.4	.4
-.6	1.6	.7	.7	1.0			1.4	1.5
.8	.6	.6	.9	1.5		Debt/Worth	.8	.8
9.6	1.6	1.4	2.0	3.1			2.1	1.9
-3.0	8.1	3.2	3.4	5.8			7.0	6.0
159.5	42.4	31.3	29.6			% Profit Before Taxes/Tangible Net Worth	74.8	73.7
(92) 60.4	(118) -4.8	(181) 6.7	(91) 8.8				(372) 36.3	(413) 35.2
-20.1	-28.7	-23.8	-5.1				13.2	10.8
59.5	17.6	11.8	11.6	3.7		% Profit Before Taxes/Total Assets	31.1	31.5
9.6	1.4	2.3	2.4	1.2			11.7	12.4
-32.6	-11.9	-11.5	-2.1	-5.7			2.6	2.3
111.2	53.6	46.7	46.4	26.4		Sales/Net Fixed Assets	56.0	48.8
34.3	26.3	19.9	18.5	12.2			28.5	25.8
11.6	12.1	10.5	9.7	9.7			15.5	14.3
10.0	4.3	2.8	2.7	2.2		Sales/Total Assets	4.6	4.2
5.7	2.9	2.1	1.9	1.7			2.9	2.8
3.1	1.8	1.6	1.5	1.3			2.0	2.0
.5	.7	.9	.8			% Depr., Dep., Amort./Sales	.7	.8
(101) .9	(98) 1.3	(158) 1.6	(85) 1.7				(352) 1.2	(362) 1.3
2.1	2.9	2.6	2.7				1.9	1.9
10.8	6.2	4.5	2.9			% Officers', Directors' Owners' Comp/Sales	6.5	5.4
(108) 16.3	(56) 10.2	(60) 8.2	(22) 6.3				(205) 10.9	(223) 10.5
25.6	17.1	18.4	16.1				18.5	18.0
257151M	535545M	2002946M	4063028M	1315849M	1583336M	Net Sales ($)	6777216M	12853282M
36278M	162373M	902088M	1885594M	711190M	815887M	Total Assets ($)	3047333M	4734898M

Historical comparative column headers: 4/1/05-3/31/06 ALL, 4/1/06-3/31/07 ALL

M = $ thousand   MM = $ million
See Pages 9 through 22 for Explanation of Ratios and Data

Comparative Historical Data | Current Data Sorted by Sales

			Type of Statement						
28	39	42	Unqualified	1	1		2	13	25
104	127	112	Reviewed	1	5	14	32	33	27
74	96	99	Compiled	7	24	23	23	19	3
90	112	127	Tax Returns	62	33	13	14	4	1
190	221	222	Other	35	48	31	37	40	31
4/1/07-3/31/08 ALL	4/1/08-3/31/09 ALL	4/1/09-3/31/10 ALL		0-1MM	55 (4/1-9/30/09) 1-3MM	3-5MM	547 (10/1/09-3/31/10) 5-10MM	10-25MM	25MM & OVER
486	595	602	**NUMBER OF STATEMENTS**	106	111	81	108	109	87
%	%	%	**ASSETS**	%	%	%	%	%	%
14.3	15.2	16.4	Cash & Equivalents	19.9	21.9	17.0	15.3	11.4	12.5
45.2	45.2	40.5	Trade Receivables (net)	17.9	31.5	44.4	47.4	54.0	50.7
2.1	2.5	1.5	Inventory	.7	1.3	3.2	1.6	2.2	.2
5.9	6.1	6.7	All Other Current	5.5	4.4	4.5	7.1	7.9	11.2
67.5	69.1	65.2	Total Current	43.9	59.0	69.2	71.5	75.5	74.6
19.4	19.0	21.5	Fixed Assets (net)	38.1	24.6	18.8	17.0	15.1	13.6
2.9	2.2	3.1	Intangibles (net)	3.9	4.7	2.6	2.0	2.3	3.0
10.1	9.7	10.2	All Other Non-Current	14.2	11.7	9.4	9.6	7.0	8.8
100.0	100.0	100.0	Total	100.0	100.0	100.0	100.0	100.0	100.0
			LIABILITIES						
16.0	15.0	18.8	Notes Payable-Short Term	40.4	27.5	16.4	11.9	7.9	6.1
3.8	3.2	3.4	Cur. Mat.-L.T.D.	6.1	5.0	2.3	2.3	1.9	2.6
15.2	15.8	14.5	Trade Payables	12.6	11.4	15.0	15.1	17.8	15.4
1.7	1.6	1.9	Income Taxes Payable	.0	.7	3.4	1.5	3.1	3.5
19.3	19.6	19.5	All Other Current	25.1	18.3	14.1	16.2	18.3	25.1
56.0	55.3	58.2	Total Current	84.2	62.8	51.2	47.1	49.0	52.7
10.6	10.1	11.1	Long-Term Debt	30.4	9.8	4.9	7.5	5.8	5.7
1.1	1.2	1.0	Deferred Taxes	.0	.5	1.3	1.2	2.0	1.2
7.2	4.8	5.9	All Other Non-Current	8.7	7.9	5.7	4.2	3.5	5.4
25.1	28.6	23.7	Net Worth	-23.4	18.9	36.9	40.0	39.6	35.0
100.0	100.0	100.0	Total Liabilties & Net Worth	100.0	100.0	100.0	100.0	100.0	100.0
			INCOME DATA						
100.0	100.0	100.0	Net Sales	100.0	100.0	100.0	100.0	100.0	100.0
			Gross Profit						
91.7	93.8	97.2	Operating Expenses	91.3	96.9	100.8	99.3	99.1	96.5
8.3	6.2	2.8	Operating Profit	8.7	3.1	-.8	.7	.9	3.5
1.1	1.4	1.7	All Other Expenses (net)	6.3	1.2	.3	.5	.6	.8
7.2	4.8	1.1	Profit Before Taxes	2.4	1.9	-1.1	.2	.3	2.7
			RATIOS						
2.3	2.4	2.4		2.7	2.5	2.7	2.9	2.4	2.0
1.5	1.5	1.4	Current	.7	1.2	1.5	1.9	1.6	1.4
1.0	.9	.9		.2	.5	.9	1.2	1.1	1.1
2.2	2.1	2.2		1.9	2.3	2.6	2.7	2.1	1.8
1.3	1.3 (601)	1.2	Quick	.6	1.0 (80)	1.3	1.4	1.3	1.2
.8	.7	.7		.1	.4	.8	1.1	1.0	.9
7 52.5	14 26.5	0 UND		0 UND	0 UND	9 40.7	44 8.3	60 6.1	59 6.1
71 5.1	69 5.3	63 5.8	Sales/Receivables	0 UND	23 15.9	69 5.3	70 5.2	83 4.4	76 4.8
103 3.6	104 3.5	102 3.6		43 8.5	83 4.4	114 3.2	107 3.4	120 3.0	107 3.4
			Cost of Sales/Inventory						
			Cost of Sales/Payables						
5.9	5.8	5.6		8.7	6.3	4.9	4.6	4.5	6.4
13.2	13.2	13.7	Sales/Working Capital	-20.7	57.1	10.6	8.7	9.0	11.0
-207.7	-130.3	-54.0		-5.3	-14.1	-97.2	44.1	44.8	29.6
30.5	30.7	19.4		5.4	17.0	11.5	29.7	25.1	55.3
(388) 9.0	(475) 7.2	(473) 2.3	EBIT/Interest	(64) .7	(91) 1.7	(61) .2	(86) 4.5	(96) 2.3	(75) 6.7
2.5	1.1	-8.6		-5.2	-12.4	-19.7	-7.4	-13.7	1.3
7.5	9.8	5.9	Net Profit + Depr., Dep.,			8.0	4.0	6.1	6.6
(92) 3.5	(123) 3.3	(123) 1.6	Amort./Cur. Mat. L/T/D		(14) .2	(25) 1.1	(41) 1.6	(36) 2.6
1.2	1.3	-1.1				-6.3	-2.8	.1	.1
.1	.2	.1		.3	.1	.1	.1	.2	.2
.4	.4	.4	Fixed/Worth	4.3	.6	.3	.3	.4	.4
1.3	1.4	2.4		-.6	-6.3	1.2	.9	.7	.7
.7	.7	.7		.8	.8	.6	.5	.8	1.3
1.9	2.0	1.9	Debt/Worth	7.8	2.1	1.4	1.1	1.7	2.3
7.8	6.6	7.3		-3.5	-28.7	6.0	3.4	3.3	3.8
77.7	71.0	47.6	% Profit Before Taxes/Tangible	93.4	81.6	35.3	45.2	34.0	36.8
(411) 35.3	(504) 26.5	(496) 11.2	Net Worth	(60) 15.8	(81) 20.9	(69) -1.9	(99) 11.2	(103) 5.5	(84) 15.3
12.6	3.8	-20.6		-23.4	-23.5	-35.5	-20.6	-28.7	1.9
35.2	24.8	17.6	% Profit Before Taxes/Total	27.9	28.5	17.5	18.0	14.0	11.6
12.5	7.9	2.4	Assets	1.4	4.5	-1.1	3.8	2.2	3.2
3.1	.5	-11.8		-22.9	-24.2	-16.4	-7.7	-5.8	.3
65.7	61.1	54.6		64.1	88.4	57.0	51.6	49.6	40.9
27.6	25.9	23.4	Sales/Net Fixed Assets	16.8	32.2	23.4	25.5	21.8	21.0
13.5	14.1	10.9		4.1	11.6	12.0	13.1	12.6	11.3
4.3	4.3	4.3		7.2	5.8	4.6	4.4	3.2	3.1
2.7	2.7	2.6	Sales/Total Assets	2.9	3.1	2.5	2.8	2.3	2.2
2.1	2.0	1.7		1.3	2.0	1.7	1.9	1.7	1.7
.7	.8	.7		.7	.5	.7	.7	.8	.8
(372) 1.2	(427) 1.4	(453) 1.5	% Depr., Dep., Amort./Sales	(64) 2.1	(71) 1.0	(62) 1.3	(88) 1.4	(91) 1.5	(77) 1.8
1.9	2.2	2.5		10.1	2.7	2.4	2.1	2.4	2.3
6.2	4.9	6.4	% Officers', Directors'	11.5	8.1	7.5	4.9	3.1	1.4
(208) 11.6	(244) 10.7	(249) 12.4	Owners' Comp/Sales	(55) 17.3	(64) 14.5	(38) 12.0	(40) 8.2	(35) 8.1	(17) 6.5
19.2	18.2	19.5		28.3	20.8	18.2	16.8	18.1	18.4
7474408M	14120626M	9757855M	Net Sales ($)	55227M	203978M	309374M	765594M	1798368M	6625314M
3373499M	5633092M	4513410M	Total Assets ($)	49969M	85782M	134204M	299356M	836241M	3107858M

M = $ thousand   MM = $ million
See Pages 9 through 22 for Explanation of Ratios and Data

Current Data Sorted by Assets							Comparative Historical Data	
						Type of Statement		
			5	1		Unqualified	11	7
3	5	21	3	1		Reviewed	37	37
4	11	4				Compiled	41	39
31	23	6	1			Tax Returns	54	38
14	30	21	7			Other	63	61
	27 (4/1-9/30/09)		164 (10/1/09-3/31/10)				**4/1/05-3/31/06 ALL**	**4/1/06-3/31/07 ALL**
0-500M	**500M-2MM**	**2-10MM**	**10-50MM**	**50-100MM**	**100-250MM**			
52	69	52	16	2		**NUMBER OF STATEMENTS**	206	182
%	%	%	%	%	%	**ASSETS**	%	%
19.3	12.0	10.2	18.5		DATA NOT AVAILABLE	Cash & Equivalents	10.6	10.3
17.5	32.3	36.3	42.6			Trade Receivables (net)	29.5	33.3
4.8	8.6	4.6	5.5			Inventory	7.3	7.3
3.5	2.2	6.8	4.7			All Other Current	2.8	3.0
45.0	55.1	58.0	71.4			Total Current	50.2	54.0
39.2	31.5	32.7	19.3			Fixed Assets (net)	37.5	36.5
3.7	4.5	1.5	1.7			Intangibles (net)	3.7	3.0
12.1	8.8	7.8	7.7			All Other Non-Current	8.6	6.5
100.0	100.0	100.0	100.0			Total	100.0	100.0
						LIABILITIES		
28.3	14.3	10.2	4.6			Notes Payable-Short Term	13.7	14.7
12.7	3.9	5.2	1.9			Cur. Mat.-L.T.D.	5.1	6.2
15.2	13.1	11.8	11.4			Trade Payables	13.6	13.3
.0	.2	1.8	2.8			Income Taxes Payable	.5	.8
18.3	17.6	11.1	22.4			All Other Current	11.9	9.4
74.5	49.2	40.2	43.1			Total Current	45.0	44.4
29.7	21.8	13.1	9.9			Long-Term Debt	27.3	24.0
.0	.2	.5	1.2			Deferred Taxes	.4	.7
11.5	6.4	3.5	7.8			All Other Non-Current	4.4	5.7
-15.7	22.5	42.7	38.0			Net Worth	22.8	25.2
100.0	100.0	100.0	100.0			Total Liabilties & Net Worth	100.0	100.0
						INCOME DATA		
100.0	100.0	100.0	100.0			Net Sales	100.0	100.0
						Gross Profit		
97.3	96.8	94.7	96.6			Operating Expenses	93.2	94.4
2.7	3.2	5.3	3.4			Operating Profit	6.8	5.6
1.3	3.7	.3	.2			All Other Expenses (net)	1.7	1.3
1.4	-.6	5.0	3.2			Profit Before Taxes	5.1	4.3
						RATIOS		
1.8	3.7	2.2	2.3				2.2	2.2
.9	1.5	1.7	1.8			Current	1.2	1.3
.3	.7	1.1	1.1				.8	.9
1.6	2.8	1.8	2.3				1.7	1.8
.7	1.0	1.3	1.4			Quick	1.0	1.1
.2	.5	.8	.9				.5	.6
0 UND	**16** 22.9	**36** 10.1	**39** 9.4				**4** 96.5	**13** 27.6
6 64.8	**42** 8.6	**50** 7.4	**76** 4.8			Sales/Receivables	**34** 10.8	**40** 9.2
30 12.4	**69** 5.3	**78** 4.7	**110** 3.3				**62** 5.9	**63** 5.8
						Cost of Sales/Inventory		
						Cost of Sales/Payables		
18.6	5.4	5.8	5.3				9.9	7.9
-241.5	18.3	11.0	6.6			Sales/Working Capital	42.9	22.9
-9.4	-13.5	98.0	25.8				-36.6	-80.2
13.1	4.1	19.3	23.6				17.2	11.7
(38) 1.7	(54) 2.0	(47) 2.8	(13) 3.7			EBIT/Interest	(184) 4.8	(168) 4.1
-2.6	-2.2	.8	-1.1				1.3	1.4
		2.5					2.6	3.2
		(11) 1.0				Net Profit + Depr., Dep., Amort./Cur. Mat. L/T/D	(27) 1.6	(32) 1.7
		-.4					1.2	1.3
.5	.3	.4	.2				.6	.5
9.9	1.3	.7	.3			Fixed/Worth	1.4	1.2
-1.1	-25.8	1.5	.7				11.6	4.0
1.0	.8	.6	1.1				1.1	1.1
26.3	4.5	1.4	1.9			Debt/Worth	2.7	2.4
-2.9	-28.4	3.1	2.6				21.7	13.9
100.0	51.0	34.3	37.5				86.5	65.7
(30) 34.1	(48) 12.4	(49) 8.5	(15) 16.0			% Profit Before Taxes/Tangible Net Worth	(162) 34.5	(150) 26.0
-5.8	-13.2	1.8	-7.3				11.5	7.2
32.8	11.1	16.0	13.9				25.1	21.7
7.9	3.0	4.2	6.1			% Profit Before Taxes/Total Assets	9.3	8.3
-10.4	-6.5	.1	-3.3				.9	1.8
40.2	27.2	16.8	33.2				20.8	23.6
19.1	10.1	10.1	19.9			Sales/Net Fixed Assets	10.3	11.5
9.0	4.9	4.8	6.4				5.3	5.3
9.9	3.3	3.0	2.4				4.5	3.9
5.8	2.5	2.0	2.0			Sales/Total Assets	3.0	3.0
2.2	1.4	1.5	1.7				2.0	2.0
.8	1.7	2.3	1.5				1.8	1.4
(31) 2.3	(51) 3.6	(41) 3.5	(15) 1.9			% Depr., Dep., Amort./Sales	(167) 3.1	(147) 2.6
4.1	5.0	5.2	2.6				4.7	4.6
5.8	3.1	2.3					2.9	2.5
(31) 7.8	(40) 5.3	(16) 5.0				% Officers', Directors' Owners' Comp/Sales	(118) 5.7	(91) 5.7
13.5	10.6	9.1					9.3	9.6
68024M	**193206M**	**462192M**	**547448M**	**157007M**		Net Sales ($)	**3071016M**	**2101033M**
11373M	**72301M**	**199361M**	**303841M**	**129557M**		Total Assets ($)	**1326309M**	**933493M**

M = $ thousand MM = $ million

See Pages 9 through 22 for Explanation of Ratios and Data

Comparative Historical Data   Current Data Sorted by Sales

			Type of Statement						
7	6	6	Unqualified	2	5	3	9	2	4
26	35	33	Reviewed	5	7	5		10	4
25	25	19	Compiled					2	
33	57	61	Tax Returns	23	24	7	5	1	1
57	61	72	Other	13	16	19	8	10	6
4/1/07-	4/1/08-	4/1/09-		27 (4/1-9/30/09)		164 (10/1/09-3/31/10)			
3/31/08	3/31/09	3/31/10		0-1MM	1-3MM	3-5MM	5-10MM	10-25MM	25MM & OVER
ALL	ALL	ALL							
148	184	191	**NUMBER OF STATEMENTS**	43	52	34	22	25	15
%	%	%	**ASSETS**	%	%	%	%	%	%
11.9	11.7	14.1	Cash & Equivalents	12.7	15.1	14.6	13.5	13.2	16.3
30.9	31.0	30.0	Trade Receivables (net)	18.1	26.8	35.0	32.2	39.8	44.8
6.7	6.6	6.1	Inventory	6.7	7.5	5.0	4.3	6.6	4.4
4.0	3.9	4.0	All Other Current	2.5	3.2	4.1	5.7	6.9	3.4
53.6	53.2	54.3	Total Current	40.1	52.6	58.7	55.6	66.5	68.9
33.9	36.2	33.2	Fixed Assets (net)	46.7	32.1	30.3	28.5	28.8	19.0
4.2	2.2	3.2	Intangibles (net)	4.5	4.2	1.6	3.4	.4	3.9
8.4	8.3	9.3	All Other Non-Current	8.7	11.1	9.4	12.5	4.3	8.2
100.0	100.0	100.0	Total	100.0	100.0	100.0	100.0	100.0	100.0
			LIABILITIES						
11.4	14.0	16.1	Notes Payable-Short Term	20.3	17.3	16.6	16.6	11.7	4.8
7.2	4.7	6.5	Cur. Mat.-L.T.D.	12.1	6.7	4.6	4.0	4.0	1.6
13.4	9.3	13.1	Trade Payables	16.3	9.5	13.3	12.8	15.6	11.9
.5	.6	.8	Income Taxes Payable	.0	.1	1.1	.1	2.5	2.9
14.1	10.5	16.4	All Other Current	15.5	16.1	17.7	12.7	18.3	19.3
46.5	39.1	52.8	Total Current	64.1	49.7	53.3	46.2	52.1	40.6
22.6	26.9	20.5	Long-Term Debt	37.4	20.7	14.4	16.5	11.5	5.7
.5	.7	.3	Deferred Taxes	.1	.2	.4	.4	.2	1.2
3.0	4.9	7.0	All Other Non-Current	9.5	8.1	6.8	5.6	2.6	6.0
27.5	28.5	19.4	Net Worth	-11.2	21.3	25.0	31.4	33.6	46.5
100.0	100.0	100.0	Total Liabilities & Net Worth	100.0	100.0	100.0	100.0	100.0	100.0
			INCOME DATA						
100.0	100.0	100.0	Net Sales	100.0	100.0	100.0	100.0	100.0	100.0
			Gross Profit						
94.3	93.0	96.3	Operating Expenses	91.5	99.3	96.8	98.8	96.2	95.4
5.7	7.0	3.7	Operating Profit	8.5	.7	3.2	1.2	3.8	4.6
1.0	2.1	1.8	All Other Expenses (net)	6.7	.4	.6	.4	.1	.3
4.7	4.9	1.9	Profit Before Taxes	1.8	.3	2.5	.8	3.7	4.3
			RATIOS						
2.5	2.7	2.4		1.6	2.7	4.4	2.1	1.8	2.4
1.4	1.6	1.5	Current	.9	1.4	1.9	1.6	1.5	1.8
.8	.9	.7		.3	.7	.8	1.0	1.0	1.5
2.1	2.2	1.9		1.3	1.7	2.9	1.8	1.6	2.4
1.1	1.1	1.1	Quick	.7	1.0	1.4	1.2	1.2	1.7
.6	.6	.5		.1	.5	.7	.8	.7	1.4
15 25.0	12 29.4	8 45.7		0 UND	0 UND	27 13.7	14 26.6	28 13.1	39 9.3
39 9.3	37 9.8	39 9.4	Sales/Receivables	18 20.1	32 11.3	50 7.3	43 8.4	48 7.6	72 5.0
61 6.0	64 5.7	69 5.3		53 6.8	64 5.7	71 5.1	97 3.8	66 5.5	117 3.1
			Cost of Sales/Inventory						
			Cost of Sales/Payables						
7.0	5.7	6.5		6.4	5.9	4.6	6.2	9.5	5.3
20.8	17.1	18.1	Sales/Working Capital	-43.9	25.3	11.9	37.3	14.9	6.6
-38.6	-74.1	-25.7		-5.9	-21.5	-128.3	-776.4	NM	14.5
12.4	10.9	8.4		4.9	7.6	5.1	4.7	32.3	32.3
(134) 3.5	(155) 3.8	(154) 2.1	EBIT/Interest	(29) 1.2	(40) 2.9	(27) 1.9	(21) 2.0	(24) 5.7	(13) 6.0
1.0	1.4	-1.1		-3.8	-1.7	-.2	-2.5	1.6	-1.1
3.4	2.5	3.4	Net Profit + Depr., Dep.,						
(23) 2.4	(27) 1.5	(28) 1.4	Amort./Cur. Mat. L/T/D						
1.5	.7	-.3							
.4	.3	.3		.7	.4	.2	.3	.5	.1
.9	.9	.8	Fixed/Worth	190.0	1.0	.6	.8	.6	.4
4.1	3.5	86.7		-1.6	NM	4.4	4.7	1.4	.7
.8	.8	.8		1.6	.4	.4	.9	1.0	.9
2.1	2.1	2.1	Debt/Worth	UND	2.2	1.4	2.3	1.5	1.8
10.5	5.8	UND		-4.5	NM	12.0	7.6	3.2	2.2
61.2	57.7	52.0	% Profit Before Taxes/Tangible	77.9	46.5	48.1	20.9	79.5	37.5
(119) 27.4	(156) 20.0	(144) 15.0	Net Worth	(22) 23.7	(39) 14.9	(28) 11.4	(18) 4.8	(22) 18.7	16.0
8.5	3.9	-4.0		-4.2	-12.2	-24.2	-31.9	5.1	-7.3
21.0	20.6	16.6	% Profit Before Taxes/Total	18.1	18.6	19.2	11.1	19.3	19.7
8.0	6.1	4.1	Assets	1.3	4.3	6.1	1.8	7.8	6.5
.8	.6	-4.7		-7.0	-8.3	-5.1	-7.2	1.4	-1.9
24.9	23.6	28.9		20.5	36.5	24.5	69.6	23.6	34.7
11.2	10.4	11.5	Sales/Net Fixed Assets	9.0	13.1	10.3	12.6	11.9	25.9
5.9	4.7	5.2		2.1	5.0	6.4	5.9	7.1	8.4
4.1	4.0	4.1		6.2	4.8	3.8	6.6	4.0	2.8
2.9	2.8	2.6	Sales/Total Assets	1.8	2.7	2.7	2.6	3.0	2.0
2.0	1.7	1.6		.5	1.8	1.7	1.6	2.3	1.7
1.9	1.6	1.5		1.7	1.5	1.5	1.4	1.4	1.4
(120) 3.1	(140) 3.3	(140) 2.9	% Depr., Dep., Amort./Sales	(26) 3.7	(38) 2.9	(22) 3.6	(18) 2.7	(22) 3.3	(14) 1.8
4.7	5.3	4.8		8.4	4.8	4.8	4.5	4.3	2.8
3.3	2.9	3.9	% Officers', Directors'	5.3	5.3	2.7	2.7		
(70) 5.5	(93) 6.4	(88) 6.8	Owners' Comp/Sales	(22) 8.1	(33) 7.9	(16) 4.9	(10) 3.9		
8.7	12.1	11.5		16.2	12.5	8.6	7.0		
2752603M	1841212M	1427877M	Net Sales ($)	20068M	97818M	135835M	162940M	347555M	663661M
1006258M	807845M	716433M	Total Assets ($)	22018M	44534M	59266M	66197M	174246M	350172M

M = $ thousand   MM = $ million
See Pages 9 through 22 for Explanation of Ratios and Data

Current Data Sorted by Assets   Comparative Historical Data

© RMA 2010

							Type of Statement				
	2	10	70	92	23	25	Unqualified		220		251
	8	63	210	67	2	3	Reviewed		298		320
	29	93	83	14			Compiled		224		237
	143	100	37	4	1	1	Tax Returns		173		250
	84	166	220	126	23	15	Other		549		533
		216 (4/1-9/30/09)		1,498 (10/1/09-3/31/10)					4/1/05-3/31/06 ALL		4/1/06-3/31/07 ALL
	0-500M	500M-2MM	2-10MM	10-50MM	50-100MM	100-250MM					
	266	432	620	303	49	44	NUMBER OF STATEMENTS		1464		1591
	%	%	%	%	%	%	ASSETS		%		%
	26.2	16.2	13.3	12.0	13.2	12.9	Cash & Equivalents		13.2		13.3
	22.6	42.3	49.2	43.5	40.9	37.1	Trade Receivables (net)		47.1		46.2
	2.2	4.7	4.7	3.5	1.7	3.4	Inventory		4.0		4.0
	4.6	4.8	7.6	10.8	13.2	9.9	All Other Current		7.3		7.2
	55.6	68.0	74.7	69.8	69.0	63.4	Total Current		71.6		70.7
	27.9	20.8	15.0	16.4	10.6	14.1	Fixed Assets (net)		17.8		18.4
	3.7	4.0	3.1	5.8	15.9	15.8	Intangibles (net)		2.9		3.1
	12.9	7.2	7.2	8.0	4.5	6.7	All Other Non-Current		7.6		7.8
	100.0	100.0	100.0	100.0	100.0	100.0	Total		100.0		100.0
							LIABILITIES				
	45.6	12.9	9.9	6.1	2.9	4.1	Notes Payable-Short Term		13.9		13.3
	8.4	4.0	2.6	2.6	2.2	3.2	Cur. Mat.-L.T.D.		3.5		3.3
	8.1	8.7	10.8	11.3	13.4	11.5	Trade Payables		11.7		10.9
	.1	.6	2.0	3.7	2.5	2.6	Income Taxes Payable		1.9		2.0
	21.1	12.4	15.8	16.9	20.5	18.8	All Other Current		16.2		16.9
	83.5	38.6	41.1	40.7	41.5	40.1	Total Current		47.1		46.3
	22.7	16.4	7.5	8.7	9.1	16.2	Long-Term Debt		12.1		11.5
	.1	.5	1.2	1.3	.8	1.1	Deferred Taxes		1.1		1.0
	11.6	5.1	4.6	5.7	8.9	5.7	All Other Non-Current		5.7		5.0
	-17.9	39.4	45.6	43.6	39.7	36.9	Net Worth		34.0		36.2
	100.0	100.0	100.0	100.0	100.0	100.0	Total Liabilties & Net Worth		100.0		100.0
							INCOME DATA				
	100.0	100.0	100.0	100.0	100.0	100.0	Net Sales		100.0		100.0
							Gross Profit				
	96.3	94.4	95.0	94.3	95.9	95.3	Operating Expenses		93.2		92.4
	3.7	5.6	5.0	5.7	4.1	4.7	Operating Profit		6.8		7.6
	.9	2.3	1.0	1.1	.9	.5	All Other Expenses (net)		1.0		1.3
	2.8	3.3	4.0	4.6	3.2	4.2	Profit Before Taxes		5.8		6.3
							RATIOS				
	2.5	4.4	3.1	2.4	1.9	2.3			2.8		3.0
	.9	2.0	1.9	1.7	1.7	1.5	Current		1.7		1.7
	.3	1.1	1.3	1.3	1.4	1.3			1.2		1.2
	2.2	3.8	2.6	2.0	1.8	1.6			2.5		2.6
(265)	.8	1.8	(618) 1.6	1.4	1.3	1.2	Quick		1.4 (1590)		1.5
	.3	.9	1.0	.9	.9	.8			.9		.9
0	UND	26 13.9	46 7.9	54 6.7	53 6.9	55 6.7		43	8.6	41	8.8
0	UND	57 6.4	72 5.1	72 5.1	74 5.0	68 5.4	Sales/Receivables	70	5.2	66	5.5
39	9.4	88 4.1	101 3.6	100 3.6	91 4.0	85 4.3		93	3.9	93	3.9
							Cost of Sales/Inventory				
							Cost of Sales/Payables				
	13.3	4.7	4.3	5.0	5.1	5.9			5.2		5.3
	-309.0	8.8	7.4	7.2	8.3	8.6	Sales/Working Capital		9.7		9.4
	-13.1	46.5	18.8	15.8	13.5	16.5			28.8		30.5
	12.8	20.5	31.1	30.0	16.4	30.3			29.2		27.9
(193)	3.1	(341) 4.7	(529) 6.6	(261) 7.0	(40) 6.5	(39) 7.8	EBIT/Interest	(1241)	8.0	(1299)	8.1
	-4.3	-1.7	.6	1.5	2.2	1.6			2.4		2.2
		2.7	7.8	6.4	11.5	4.4			8.2		8.4
	(36)	1.3 (137)	3.0 (126)	2.7 (17)	3.6 (17)	1.8	Net Profit + Depr., Dep., Amort./Cur. Mat. L/T/D	(313)	2.7 (343)		3.4
		-1.8	.8	1.0	1.1	.6			1.3		1.5
	.2	.1	.1	.1	.2	.3			.1		.1
	1.8	.3	.3	.3	.4	.5	Fixed/Worth		.3		.3
	-.7	1.9	.6	.8	1.5	1.3			1.1		1.0
	1.0	.4	.5	.7	.9	1.2			.7		.6
	32.3	1.3	1.2	1.4	1.7	2.0	Debt/Worth		1.6		1.5
	-2.7	5.7	2.9	3.4	15.0	8.3			4.3		4.2
	162.9	59.8	42.6	37.8	40.5	60.4			65.8		64.6
(141)	58.6	(362) 20.8	(580) 17.8	(285) 18.5	(38) 14.6	(36) 30.1	% Profit Before Taxes/Tangible Net Worth	(1299)	30.7 (1408)		31.5
	-12.4	-3.1	.9	4.9	5.2	4.3			10.6		12.9
	51.8	25.7	18.9	16.2	9.8	12.5			26.2		27.3
	10.2	7.9	6.7	7.0	5.2	8.1	% Profit Before Taxes/Total Assets		11.2		11.5
	-18.7	-3.6	-.2	1.3	1.7	1.7			2.4		3.0
	165.1	71.3	58.5	49.5	46.3	62.9			59.1		56.8
	45.2	25.3	25.5	19.6	29.8	18.0	Sales/Net Fixed Assets		24.5		24.0
	14.7	10.3	11.8	8.3	12.2	7.1			12.3		12.5
	13.5	3.8	3.2	2.6	2.7	2.6			3.6		3.7
	6.2	2.8	2.4	2.0	1.9	1.9	Sales/Total Assets		2.6		2.6
	3.2	1.9	1.8	1.5	1.3	1.4			2.0		2.0
	.6	.8	.6	.7	1.0	.5			.8		.7
(149)	1.3	(308) 1.5	(531) 1.4	(272) 1.6	(37) 1.7	(30) 1.6	% Depr., Dep., Amort./Sales	(1178)	1.4 (1267)		1.4
	2.6	3.0	2.4	2.8	2.5	2.6			2.3		2.4
	9.3	4.9	2.2	1.0					3.9		3.6
(164)	14.3	(188) 8.7	(163) 5.2	(32) 2.5			% Officers', Directors' Owners' Comp/Sales	(454)	7.8 (516)		7.9
	21.3	13.7	10.5	8.4					14.0		15.1
	501943M	1543275M	7939160M	13610585M	7427513M	14105065M	Net Sales ($)		42299877M		50111380M
	62759M	501610M	3003912M	6448819M	3313185M	6642700M	Total Assets ($)		16675594M		19281735M

M = $ thousand   MM = $ million
See Pages 9 through 22 for Explanation of Ratios and Data

Comparative Historical Data | Current Data Sorted by Sales

			Type of Statement	0-1MM	1-3MM	3-5MM	5-10MM	10-25MM	25MM & OVER
224	249	222	Unqualified	2	7	4	13	49	147
313	324	353	Reviewed	6	21	38	106	125	57
199	218	219	Compiled	19	61	44	47	32	16
244	289	286	Tax Returns	66	110	42	40	22	6
589	657	634	Other	51	141	58	108	127	149
4/1/07-3/31/08 ALL	4/1/08-3/31/09 ALL	4/1/09-3/31/10 ALL		216 (4/1-9/30/09)			1,498 (10/1/09-3/31/10)		
1569	1737	1714	**NUMBER OF STATEMENTS**	144	340	186	314	355	375
%	%	%	**ASSETS**	%	%	%	%	%	%
14.2	14.2	15.8	Cash & Equivalents	16.2	20.6	17.1	15.6	13.8	12.6
46.4	44.4	41.8	Trade Receivables (net)	22.7	36.5	39.8	44.4	48.6	46.2
3.9	3.9	4.0	Inventory	2.8	3.4	4.6	4.9	4.5	3.2
7.0	6.7	7.2	All Other Current	3.9	4.8	5.2	6.7	7.7	11.6
71.6	69.2	68.7	Total Current	45.7	65.4	66.8	71.6	74.6	73.6
18.1	18.6	18.6	Fixed Assets (net)	37.0	21.8	20.4	16.6	14.9	12.8
2.9	3.6	4.6	Intangibles (net)	3.8	4.7	4.0	4.2	3.6	6.4
7.4	8.5	8.1	All Other Non-Current	13.5	8.2	8.8	7.6	6.9	7.3
100.0	100.0	100.0	Total	100.0	100.0	100.0	100.0	100.0	100.0
			LIABILITIES						
12.0	14.0	15.2	Notes Payable-Short Term	36.1	21.4	21.5	12.5	9.2	6.4
3.2	3.5	3.8	Cur. Mat.-L.T.D.	8.2	4.3	5.3	3.6	2.7	2.4
11.0	10.8	10.0	Trade Payables	8.2	8.7	7.4	8.1	11.3	13.5
1.7	1.7	1.7	Income Taxes Payable	.0	.5	.8	1.7	2.3	3.4
17.0	16.5	16.2	All Other Current	15.2	15.4	12.7	14.8	17.3	19.1
44.9	46.5	47.0	Total Current	67.7	50.3	47.7	40.7	42.8	44.7
11.9	12.8	12.6	Long-Term Debt	30.2	18.3	14.9	8.2	7.9	7.4
1.0	.9	.9	Deferred Taxes	.2	.3	.6	.8	1.6	1.1
4.5	6.3	6.2	All Other Non-Current	9.6	7.9	3.9	5.0	4.5	7.0
37.6	33.5	33.4	Net Worth	-7.8	23.1	32.8	45.3	43.2	39.8
100.0	100.0	100.0	Total Liabilities & Net Worth	100.0	100.0	100.0	100.0	100.0	100.0
			INCOME DATA						
100.0	100.0	100.0	Net Sales	100.0	100.0	100.0	100.0	100.0	100.0
			Gross Profit						
92.3	93.4	95.0	Operating Expenses	85.7	97.5	96.3	94.8	95.5	95.2
7.7	6.6	5.0	Operating Profit	14.3	2.5	3.7	5.2	4.5	4.8
1.5	1.5	1.3	All Other Expenses (net)	7.6	.8	.8	.6	.8	.7
6.2	5.1	3.7	Profit Before Taxes	6.7	1.8	3.0	4.5	3.7	4.1
			RATIOS						
2.9	2.9	3.0		2.4	4.1	3.9	3.9	2.7	2.4
1.7	1.7	1.8	Current	.9	1.9	1.8	2.0	1.8	1.7
1.2	1.1	1.1		.3	.9	1.1	1.2	1.3	1.3
2.5	2.5	2.6		2.0	3.7	3.3	3.0	2.4	1.9
(1567) 1.5	1.4 (1711)	1.4	Quick	(143) .8	(339) 1.6	(185) 1.6	1.6	1.5	1.3
.9	.9	.9		.2	.7	.9	1.0	1.0	1.0
42 8.7	37 9.8	33 11.0		0 UND	0 UND	23 15.7	41 8.9	46 7.9	50 7.3
69 5.3	64 5.7	62 5.9	Sales/Receivables	3 128.4	47 7.7	56 6.5	68 5.4	69 5.3	65 5.6
96 3.8	94 3.9	93 3.9		76 4.8	96 3.8	89 4.1	99 3.7	100 3.7	87 4.2
			Cost of Sales/Inventory						
			Cost of Sales/Payables						
5.1	5.2	5.0		6.7	4.8	4.5	4.1	5.0	5.4
9.0	9.7	9.2	Sales/Working Capital	-87.9	12.1	9.5	7.4	8.5	8.4
28.0	42.4	43.2		-4.9	-61.4	91.5	23.9	17.7	19.0
25.5	26.2	24.8		8.3	13.8	20.0	26.1	40.6	39.8
(1283) 7.5	(1444) 6.8	(1403) 5.5	EBIT/Interest	(87) 2.6	(269) 3.3	(155) 3.9	(265) 5.8	(311) 6.8	(316) 8.6
2.0	1.2	.2		-4.9	-3.6	-3.4	-.5	1.2	2.1
8.4	9.2	6.4			2.5	3.7	5.6	8.9	6.8
(339) 2.8	(393) 3.3	(342) 2.5	Net Profit + Depr., Dep., Amort./Cur. Mat. L/T/D		(19) .8	(22) 1.2	(62) 2.3	(92) 3.1	(143) 2.8
1.2	1.2	.8			-2.3	-.4	.0	.7	1.1
.1	.1	.1		.2	.1	.1	.1	.1	.1
.3	.4	.3	Fixed/Worth	3.1	.5	.4	.3	.3	.3
.9	1.2	1.2		-1.7	10.8	1.8	.9	.7	.7
.6	.6	.6		1.1	.5	.4	.4	.6	.8
1.4	1.5	1.5	Debt/Worth	9.2	1.5	1.3	1.1	1.4	1.5
4.3	4.7	5.6		-4.9	-36.2	6.1	3.2	3.3	3.9
66.0	59.7	50.4		72.2	62.1	55.8	50.5	45.2	49.0
(1408) 30.6	(1505) 26.1	(1442) 20.0	% Profit Before Taxes/Tangible Net Worth	(85) 17.6	(250) 17.2	(153) 20.1	(281) 19.3	(330) 17.1	(343) 24.5
9.0	5.0	.9		-14.3	-6.7	-8.4	.4	2.3	7.8
25.0	23.2	21.3		22.2	24.8	26.7	25.4	19.9	18.3
10.8	8.6	7.0	% Profit Before Taxes/Total Assets	2.8	6.0	7.8	7.4	6.6	8.3
2.5	.6	-1.0		-14.5	-9.8	-6.0	-1.7	.5	2.2
60.7	61.7	67.0		95.2	74.7	62.4	61.5	65.6	69.8
24.8	25.4	25.7	Sales/Net Fixed Assets	15.3	25.9	24.4	25.3	26.5	29.0
11.5	12.3	11.0		2.5	10.6	10.8	11.2	11.7	12.2
3.7	3.8	3.7		5.8	5.2	4.2	3.6	3.3	3.2
2.6	2.6	2.6	Sales/Total Assets	2.1	2.9	2.8	2.5	2.6	2.4
1.9	1.9	1.8		.7	1.7	2.0	1.8	1.9	1.9
.7	.7	.7		1.4	.8	.8	.8	.6	.5
(1250) 1.4	(1349) 1.5	(1327) 1.5	% Depr., Dep., Amort./Sales	(83) 3.3	(231) 1.5	(138) 1.6	(258) 1.5	(303) 1.4	(314) 1.3
2.3	2.5	2.6		14.2	3.0	2.9	2.6	2.5	2.1
3.7	3.4	4.2		12.4	6.2	5.3	3.2	2.0	.9
(511) 7.6	(537) 7.5	(551) 8.9	% Officers', Directors' Owners' Comp/Sales	(65) 18.5	(167) 11.1	(77) 8.1	(122) 5.9	(84) 4.5	(36) 2.9
14.7	13.7	15.4		27.1	16.5	13.6	10.9	10.1	11.4
48440781M	53653005M	45127541M	Net Sales ($)	77577M	661174M	735534M	2236972M	5672889M	35743395M
19812964M	21904315M	19972985M	Total Assets ($)	97563M	298761M	302397M	1027402M	2603332M	15643530M

M = $ thousand   MM = $ million
See Pages 9 through 22 for Explanation of Ratios and Data

Current Data Sorted by Assets

Comparative Historical Data

						Type of Statement				
		4	2	1	2	Unqualified		3		4
3	2	2				Reviewed		15		9
1	3	3				Compiled		18		8
19	4	3				Tax Returns		19		22
4	8	6	3	1	1	Other		34		27
	5 (4/1-9/30/09)		67 (10/1/09-3/31/10)					4/1/05-3/31/06		4/1/06-3/31/07
0-500M	500M-2MM	2-10MM	10-50MM	50-100MM	100-250MM			ALL		ALL
27	17	18	5	2	3	NUMBER OF STATEMENTS		89		70
%	%	%	%	%	%	ASSETS		%		%
22.3	14.1	7.3				Cash & Equivalents		13.9		16.5
19.4	37.6	38.9				Trade Receivables (net)		35.2		33.1
.0	2.9	3.5				Inventory		3.1		1.7
1.1	6.6	10.9				All Other Current		5.1		5.7
42.8	61.3	60.6				Total Current		57.2		57.0
31.7	16.4	27.9				Fixed Assets (net)		28.8		30.2
1.2	7.0	.1				Intangibles (net)		4.7		4.6
24.3	15.4	11.4				All Other Non-Current		9.3		8.2
100.0	100.0	100.0				Total		100.0		100.0
						LIABILITIES				
54.8	5.1	12.5				Notes Payable-Short Term		16.4		17.0
16.2	4.2	1.8				Cur. Mat.-L.T.D.		4.2		4.5
9.3	5.1	10.1				Trade Payables		5.2		8.2
.1	1.1	.0				Income Taxes Payable		1.4		.9
9.0	9.7	16.9				All Other Current		11.4		11.3
89.4	25.2	41.4				Total Current		38.6		41.8
44.2	18.5	15.4				Long-Term Debt		20.2		19.6
.0	.3	1.7				Deferred Taxes		.5		.5
30.0	7.0	2.5				All Other Non-Current		8.3		5.4
-63.7	48.9	39.0				Net Worth		32.4		32.7
100.0	100.0	100.0				Total Liabilities & Net Worth		100.0		100.0
						INCOME DATA				
100.0	100.0	100.0				Net Sales		100.0		100.0
						Gross Profit				
99.2	99.3	94.1				Operating Expenses		90.9		92.0
.8	.7	5.9				Operating Profit		9.1		8.0
1.0	1.4	3.8				All Other Expenses (net)		.9		1.6
-.2	-.7	2.1				Profit Before Taxes		8.2		6.4
						RATIOS				
2.0	7.9	5.4						4.2		2.6
.7	2.7	1.4				Current		1.7		1.5
.2	1.5	.9						1.0		.9
2.0	6.1	4.1						3.4		2.5
.6	1.8	1.1				Quick		1.6		1.2
.2	1.3	.5						.8		.8
0 UND	0 UND	31 11.8					0 UND		0 UND	
0 UND	86 4.2	73 5.0				Sales/Receivables	55 6.7		50 7.2	
35 10.3	115 3.2	114 3.2					98 3.7		93 3.9	
						Cost of Sales/Inventory				
						Cost of Sales/Payables				
34.6	2.9	5.1						5.4		6.8
-32.3	4.3	9.7				Sales/Working Capital		9.4		13.5
-11.1	18.1	-61.2						104.6		-51.7
5.4	11.1	14.1						23.3		30.2
(21) .2	(15) 6.8	(15) 4.4				EBIT/Interest	(81) 8.1		(64) 5.2	
-5.4	-7.1	-8.2						1.5		1.0
						Net Profit + Depr., Dep.,		2.1		21.4
						Amort./Cur. Mat. L/T/D	(17) 1.5		(14) 4.3	
								1.0		1.7
.1	.0	.1						.3		.3
-2.3	.2	.5				Fixed/Worth		.7		.6
-.4	1.0	NM						4.2		NM
.9	.3	.4						.5		.5
-5.4	.8	.9				Debt/Worth		1.7		1.3
-1.7	7.7	NM						7.4		NM
73.3	49.8	27.0				% Profit Before Taxes/Tangible		87.0		87.7
(11) 2.6	(15) 8.3	(14) 8.5				Net Worth	(72) 31.0		(53) 40.1	
-20.1	-52.7	-7.0						13.3		9.6
26.4	20.7	16.6				% Profit Before Taxes/Total		38.3		28.7
.0	4.6	2.6				Assets		12.2		11.0
-40.2	-27.0	-5.9						1.6		-.4
198.0	87.8	34.7						25.1		33.2
22.3	22.2	9.8				Sales/Net Fixed Assets		12.7		12.2
13.4	10.7	4.0						6.1		6.5
8.3	2.5	2.7						3.9		4.4
5.4	1.7	1.9				Sales/Total Assets		2.6		2.5
3.7	1.1	1.1						1.7		1.6
.6	1.4	.9						1.7		1.5
(21) 1.6	(11) 2.9	(16) 2.2				% Depr., Dep., Amort./Sales	(65) 2.7		(42) 2.5	
3.2	4.1	5.1						5.6		5.5
10.4						% Officers', Directors'		6.0		6.0
(20) 13.4						Owners' Comp/Sales	(32) 9.7		(32) 10.4	
19.3								15.8		16.1
27815M	32310M	151666M	126166M	143504M	571466M	Net Sales ($)		1597000M		1790185M
4461M	16486M	75438M	121019M	152373M	568916M	Total Assets ($)		664301M		729018M

M = $ thousand　　MM = $ million
See Pages 9 through 22 for Explanation of Ratios and Data

Comparative Historical Data | | | Current Data Sorted by Sales

			Type of Statement						
3	6	9	Unqualified				2	3	4
10	9	7	Reviewed	3	1	1	2		
11	8	7	Compiled	2	3	1	1	1	
24	20	26	Tax Returns	11	11	2	2		
36	32	23	Other	3	10	1	2	3	4
4/1/07-3/31/08	4/1/08-3/31/09	4/1/09-3/31/10		5 (4/1-9/30/09)			67 (10/1/09-3/31/10)		
ALL	ALL	ALL		0-1MM	1-3MM	3-5MM	5-10MM	10-25MM	25MM & OVER
84	75	72	**NUMBER OF STATEMENTS**	19	25	4	9	7	8
%	%	%	**ASSETS**	%	%	%	%	%	%
14.9	14.3	14.9	Cash & Equivalents	21.2	15.4				
35.6	34.9	28.8	Trade Receivables (net)	23.5	25.8				
2.9	1.8	1.7	Inventory	.0	2.0				
4.9	4.6	5.4	All Other Current	1.8	4.1				
58.4	55.6	50.8	Total Current	46.4	47.3				
27.6	25.9	24.2	Fixed Assets (net)	34.2	27.3				
6.6	7.8	8.6	Intangibles (net)	2.1	2.8				
7.5	10.8	16.4	All Other Non-Current	17.3	22.7				
100.0	100.0	100.0	Total	100.0	100.0				
			LIABILITIES						
12.2	17.8	25.8	Notes Payable-Short Term	44.9	26.6				
6.2	3.5	7.8	Cur. Mat.-L.T.D.	2.9	18.5				
6.0	6.3	8.0	Trade Payables	5.3	9.7				
2.0	1.7	.3	Income Taxes Payable	.0	.8				
10.3	10.7	11.4	All Other Current	6.2	11.9				
36.7	40.0	53.2	Total Current	59.4	67.4				
19.8	19.2	26.8	Long-Term Debt	43.1	33.6				
1.4	.9	1.0	Deferred Taxes	.0	.4				
6.1	6.7	15.5	All Other Non-Current	31.2	10.5				
35.9	33.3	3.5	Net Worth	-33.9	-11.9				
100.0	100.0	100.0	Total Liabilities & Net Worth	100.0	100.0				
			INCOME DATA						
100.0	100.0	100.0	Net Sales	100.0	100.0				
			Gross Profit						
94.1	97.6	96.2	Operating Expenses	93.0	101.9				
5.9	2.4	3.8	Operating Profit	7.0	-1.9				
1.2	1.3	2.4	All Other Expenses (net)	3.0	1.7				
4.8	1.0	1.4	Profit Before Taxes	4.0	-3.6				
			RATIOS						
4.4	4.2	4.1	Current	4.1	4.7				
1.6	1.6	1.3		.8	1.4				
1.1	1.0	.7		.3	.4				
3.4	4.1	3.3	Quick	3.9	3.7				
1.4	1.4	1.1		.7	1.3				
.9	.8	.5		.3	.4				
9 · 39.7	2 · 157.7	0 · UND	Sales/Receivables	0 · UND	0 · UND				
64 · 5.7	53 · 6.8	49 · 7.4		24 · 15.4	48 · 7.6				
87 · 4.2	84 · 4.4	93 · 3.9		59 · 6.2	97 · 3.7				
			Cost of Sales/Inventory						
			Cost of Sales/Payables						
4.5	5.9	5.0	Sales/Working Capital	6.7	3.8				
9.3	20.7	30.1		-47.5	32.6				
193.2	-293.0	-16.9		-11.8	-11.0				
23.2	8.3	10.1	EBIT/Interest	7.4	6.8				
(73) 3.4	(66) 3.1	(60) 3.3		(12) 1.6	(23) 1.2				
.6	-3.8	-4.8		-4.7	-10.1				
5.6			Net Profit + Depr., Dep., Amort./Cur. Mat. L/T/D						
(18) 1.6									
.8									
.3	.3	.1	Fixed/Worth	.0	.1				
.5	.9	.8		3.7	.6				
1.8	10.6	-.6		-.4	-.7				
.5	.5	.5	Debt/Worth	.4	.6				
1.3	2.1	3.0		-8.7	2.5				
4.3	72.7	-2.8		-1.8	-2.6				
71.4	62.1	48.5	% Profit Before Taxes/Tangible Net Worth		43.2				
(70) 17.2	(57) 13.5	(44) 9.1			(16) 4.0				
1.9	-21.4	-17.7			-49.7				
29.1	23.0	18.3	% Profit Before Taxes/Total Assets	21.5	19.6				
7.1	4.6	2.6		2.0	1.5				
-1.1	-12.9	-22.9		-34.3	-30.5				
25.0	31.5	47.3	Sales/Net Fixed Assets	198.0	106.9				
12.9	12.0	17.7		22.2	18.2				
6.8	8.8	8.6		8.6	10.1				
4.0	3.9	4.2	Sales/Total Assets	5.6	6.7				
2.5	2.4	2.5		4.0	2.9				
1.8	1.8	1.3		1.3	1.5				
1.5	2.0	1.0	% Depr., Dep., Amort./Sales	1.2	.8				
(66) 2.7	(56) 2.8	(54) 2.7		(12) 2.8	(20) 2.2				
5.2	5.2	4.0		3.8	3.5				
3.7	5.2	5.9	% Officers', Directors' Owners' Comp/Sales	10.6	7.1				
(44) 8.0	(30) 8.9	(35) 12.6		(10) 17.6	(16) 13.1				
14.7	15.1	19.6		24.7	18.0				
790824M	923992M	1052927M	Net Sales ($)	9246M	39835M	16530M	67597M	102539M	817180M
514482M	564291M	938693M	Total Assets ($)	5980M	18362M	12097M	46591M	62782M	792881M

M = $ thousand   MM = $ million
See Pages 9 through 22 for Explanation of Ratios and Data

Current Data Sorted by Assets   Comparative Historical Data

0-500M	500M-2MM	2-10MM	10-50MM	50-100MM	100-250MM	Type of Statement	4/1/05-3/31/06 ALL	4/1/06-3/31/07 ALL
	1	12	12	3	7	Unqualified	27	31
1	4	21	7			Reviewed	43	46
3	12	6	1			Compiled	29	31
12	21	9	1			Tax Returns	28	28
12	29	32	17	3	4	Other	89	65
35 (4/1-9/30/09)			195 (10/1/09-3/31/10)					
28	67	80	38	6	11	NUMBER OF STATEMENTS	216	201
%	%	%	%	%	%	**ASSETS**	%	%
23.1	10.9	13.4	11.9		14.0	Cash & Equivalents	11.0	11.6
24.6	35.0	29.4	26.3		19.5	Trade Receivables (net)	36.1	33.9
1.3	3.8	3.1	4.0		2.8	Inventory	4.4	3.5
6.9	4.1	4.5	4.3		3.6	All Other Current	4.0	3.7
55.9	53.8	50.4	46.4		40.0	Total Current	55.5	52.8
33.2	35.4	37.2	34.0		21.3	Fixed Assets (net)	35.2	35.2
2.1	3.5	5.2	12.5		29.2	Intangibles (net)	3.4	5.3
8.7	7.3	7.2	7.2		9.5	All Other Non-Current	5.9	6.7
100.0	100.0	100.0	100.0		100.0	Total	100.0	100.0
						LIABILITIES		
11.6	15.5	7.1	5.5		1.8	Notes Payable-Short Term	12.5	10.5
12.1	5.5	3.4	4.9		2.5	Cur. Mat.-L.T.D.	4.8	4.7
7.8	7.5	7.1	5.8		3.1	Trade Payables	11.6	9.4
.0	.1	.6	.4		.6	Income Taxes Payable	.5	.5
13.7	10.3	11.2	9.7		13.3	All Other Current	14.7	12.0
45.2	38.8	29.4	26.2		21.3	Total Current	44.2	37.1
14.2	20.5	17.8	18.2		31.4	Long-Term Debt	19.1	17.5
.0	.7	.8	.4		2.3	Deferred Taxes	.9	.6
5.6	4.9	4.5	6.3		6.9	All Other Non-Current	8.2	6.6
34.9	35.0	47.5	48.9		38.0	Net Worth	27.5	38.2
100.0	100.0	100.0	100.0		100.0	Total Liabilities & Net Worth	100.0	100.0
						INCOME DATA		
100.0	100.0	100.0	100.0		100.0	Net Sales	100.0	100.0
						Gross Profit		
91.0	90.4	90.4	92.4		89.4	Operating Expenses	91.2	90.4
9.0	9.6	9.6	7.6		10.6	Operating Profit	8.8	9.6
.5	2.3	2.4	2.1		3.5	All Other Expenses (net)	2.5	1.5
8.5	7.3	7.2	5.5		7.2	Profit Before Taxes	6.3	8.2
						RATIOS		
4.1	2.8	3.5	3.2		3.0		2.8	2.7
1.4	1.5	1.9	1.6		1.9	Current	1.5	1.5
.4	.8	1.0	1.1		1.4		1.1	1.0
3.5	2.8	2.9	2.6		2.9		2.4	2.5
1.2	1.4	1.6	1.3		1.6	Quick	1.3	1.4
.3	.7	.8	.9		1.2		.8	.8
0 UND	28 13.1	41 8.9	49 7.5		61 6.0		40 9.2	38 9.6
28 13.2	54 6.8	54 6.7	59 6.2		68 5.3	Sales/Receivables	62 5.9	63 5.8
53 6.9	71 5.1	74 4.9	84 4.3		83 4.4		85 4.3	83 4.4
						Cost of Sales/Inventory		
						Cost of Sales/Payables		
8.3	5.6	5.1	4.2		3.0		5.2	5.8
29.0	16.1	9.0	11.2		6.8	Sales/Working Capital	12.5	13.2
-25.1	-44.3	NM	NM		13.9		76.7	-175.5
19.0	9.3	30.3	20.3				15.5	18.6
(17) 6.4	(56) 4.6	(71) 5.8	(33) 5.8			EBIT/Interest	(183) 5.4	(176) 5.4
-.1	.5	1.6	.7				1.2	2.2
	5.3	7.7	8.7			Net Profit + Depr., Dep.,	7.2	5.5
	(12) 2.0	(22) 3.5	(14) 3.5			Amort./Cur. Mat. L/T/D	(60) 3.1	(53) 2.9
	.1	1.3	1.9				1.8	1.9
.3	.4	.4	.4		.5		.4	.5
1.3	1.0	.7	1.0		1.6	Fixed/Worth	.9	.9
10.2	4.7	1.9	3.1		-.4		2.7	2.0
.4	.7	.5	.5		1.0		.6	.6
1.4	1.6	.9	1.2		2.7	Debt/Worth	1.7	1.4
19.3	8.9	3.1	6.8		-2.0		6.5	3.8
133.3	68.0	62.5	44.3			% Profit Before Taxes/Tangible	56.9	61.1
(23) 54.0	(55) 21.7	(71) 21.8	(32) 17.0			Net Worth	(179) 27.3	(174) 30.9
14.3	1.0	6.5	2.7				7.6	11.4
52.7	20.6	23.1	15.3		9.0	% Profit Before Taxes/Total	23.5	26.7
26.0	9.4	9.3	6.1		6.8	Assets	9.6	11.3
2.1	.1	1.0	-1.0		-1.2		.6	3.7
55.2	20.5	10.6	7.6		6.2		14.4	12.2
14.9	9.2	4.7	4.8		3.9	Sales/Net Fixed Assets	6.8	6.8
4.5	4.5	3.2	2.9		3.2		3.8	4.0
6.6	3.3	2.4	1.8		1.4		2.9	2.8
3.5	2.3	1.8	1.3		.8	Sales/Total Assets	2.1	2.2
1.9	1.6	1.0	1.1		.5		1.5	1.4
1.1	1.8	2.4	2.8				1.8	1.9
(19) 3.5	(51) 3.1	(66) 4.0	(34) 4.6			% Depr., Dep., Amort./Sales	(188) 3.6	(179) 3.5
7.7	5.3	5.4	6.9				5.7	5.2
9.0	3.1	1.5				% Officers', Directors'	2.8	4.0
(12) 12.1	(29) 4.7	(18) 5.0				Owners' Comp/Sales	(69) 5.5	(63) 6.2
18.2	8.9	11.4					10.6	11.2
46269M	258258M	750653M	1155959M	631801M	1555249M	Net Sales ($)	2628896M	2600531M
7446M	73488M	397265M	792261M	364670M	1639970M	Total Assets ($)	1617157M	1779781M

M = $ thousand   MM = $ million
See Pages 9 through 22 for Explanation of Ratios and Data

Comparative Historical Data | | | Current Data Sorted by Sales

			Type of Statement						
27	38	35	Unqualified			2	4	14	15
32	29	33	Reviewed		4	6	8	10	5
35	31	22	Compiled	6	4	5	7		
32	44	43	Tax Returns	9	18	8	5	2	1
72	93	97	Other	17	16	10	16	19	19
4/1/07-	4/1/08-	4/1/09-				35 (4/1-9/30/09)		195 (10/1/09-3/31/10)	
3/31/08	3/31/09	3/31/10							
ALL	ALL	ALL		0-1MM	1-3MM	3-5MM	5-10MM	10-25MM	25MM & OVER
198	235	230	**NUMBER OF STATEMENTS**	32	42	31	40	45	40
%	%	%	**ASSETS**	%	%	%	%	%	%
10.7	11.8	13.6	Cash & Equivalents	18.9	11.3	14.4	8.6	12.7	17.3
32.5	32.4	29.6	Trade Receivables (net)	19.0	28.6	36.6	35.8	28.6	28.6
4.1	3.5	3.2	Inventory	1.0	3.3	6.9	2.1	3.0	3.3
3.7	4.4	4.6	All Other Current	4.2	5.1	2.8	5.2	5.5	4.2
50.9	52.2	51.0	Total Current	43.2	48.3	60.7	51.8	49.7	53.4
37.9	35.5	34.2	Fixed Assets (net)	47.5	38.0	26.9	34.9	34.8	24.0
4.4	5.4	7.3	Intangibles (net)	2.1	5.2	5.8	4.3	8.9	15.9
6.7	7.0	7.5	All Other Non-Current	7.2	8.5	6.6	9.1	6.6	6.7
100.0	100.0	100.0	Total	100.0	100.0	100.0	100.0	100.0	100.0
			LIABILITIES						
9.6	9.5	9.5	Notes Payable-Short Term	7.5	12.6	11.2	13.2	8.5	4.2
5.0	4.4	5.2	Cur. Mat.-L.T.D.	12.4	5.7	3.8	4.1	2.6	3.9
10.0	8.3	6.9	Trade Payables	6.3	6.4	10.0	5.9	7.6	5.9
.6	.6	.3	Income Taxes Payable	.0	.1	.2	.4	.9	.2
10.7	12.3	11.4	All Other Current	8.5	11.0	14.2	10.2	9.1	15.9
35.9	35.1	33.4	Total Current	34.8	35.8	39.4	33.8	28.7	30.1
21.6	19.8	18.4	Long-Term Debt	28.8	24.0	12.0	15.2	13.8	17.6
.8	.8	.7	Deferred Taxes	.0	.5	.5	1.7	.3	.9
5.4	5.8	5.1	All Other Non-Current	4.2	5.1	8.1	3.8	4.9	5.2
36.3	38.5	42.4	Net Worth	32.3	34.6	39.9	45.4	52.3	46.1
100.0	100.0	100.0	Total Liabilities & Net Worth	100.0	100.0	100.0	100.0	100.0	100.0
			INCOME DATA						
100.0	100.0	100.0	Net Sales	100.0	100.0	100.0	100.0	100.0	100.0
			Gross Profit						
90.0	91.5	90.9	Operating Expenses	77.7	92.8	94.9	94.6	91.7	91.9
10.0	8.5	9.1	Operating Profit	22.3	7.2	5.1	5.4	8.3	8.1
2.5	1.8	2.1	All Other Expenses (net)	5.8	1.4	.5	2.5	1.5	1.4
7.4	6.7	7.0	Profit Before Taxes	16.5	5.8	4.5	2.9	6.9	6.7
			RATIOS						
2.9	3.0	3.2		4.1	3.1	2.5	3.5	3.2	3.2
1.6	1.6	1.8	Current	1.2	2.0	1.4	1.6	2.2	1.8
1.0	1.0	1.0		.4	.8	1.0	1.0	1.2	1.3
2.2	2.4	2.8		3.5	2.8	2.1	3.1	2.8	2.9
(197) 1.3	1.3	1.5	Quick	1.1	1.5	1.2	1.3	2.0	1.5
.8	.8	.8		.4	.6	1.0	.8	.9	1.1
33 11.0	36 10.1	38 9.7		0 UND	27 13.4	40 9.1	48 7.6	34 10.8	52 7.1
55 6.6	56 6.5	55 6.6	Sales/Receivables	31 11.8	46 7.9	55 6.6	57 6.4	51 7.1	64 5.7
75 4.9	73 5.0	73 5.0		64 5.7	61 6.0	91 4.0	82 4.5	75 4.9	79 4.6
			Cost of Sales/Inventory						
			Cost of Sales/Payables						
5.4	5.0	5.2		7.1	5.1	6.1	5.0	5.0	4.3
11.5	12.2	11.4	Sales/Working Capital	27.4	10.5	19.0	12.4	9.0	10.1
-999.8	-107.4	-194.0		-6.1	-27.1	199.3	NM	23.2	20.0
14.5	13.4	17.9		11.3	9.7	7.5	17.5	59.4	20.3
(170) 5.2	(202) 4.6	(191) 5.2	EBIT/Interest	(21) 3.5	(33) 3.9	(27) 5.4	(36) 2.8	(39) 13.8	(35) 5.1
1.7	1.7	1.0		.4	.8	2.0	-.3	1.6	1.1
9.2	11.0	7.1					33.0		9.2
(49) 4.1	(61) 4.7	(52) 2.8	Net Profit + Depr., Dep., Amort./Cur. Mat. L/T/D			(14) 5.6		(14) 3.8	
2.1	2.2	1.3					.9		2.2
.4	.4	.4		.5	.4	.2	.4	.4	.3
1.0	.9	.9	Fixed/Worth	1.7	1.1	.9	.8	.6	.7
2.8	2.5	2.8		10.8	NM	1.8	2.1	2.1	2.3
.6	.6	.5		.3	.5	.8	.5	.4	.5
1.6	1.4	1.2	Debt/Worth	2.0	1.2	1.4	1.2	.8	1.9
6.4	4.8	6.7		12.2	NM	4.2	3.4	3.3	6.3
59.2	60.0	66.1	% Profit Before Taxes/Tangible Net Worth	112.0	77.3	36.7	38.0	74.9	60.5
(170) 32.8	(200) 27.4	(193) 22.8		(26) 33.0	(32) 13.2	(28) 21.7	(34) 9.4	(41) 42.1	(32) 25.2
11.8	7.8	6.5		14.3	-1.0	7.0	-1.2	3.3	12.1
21.3	22.8	21.1	% Profit Before Taxes/Total Assets	30.3	26.3	12.2	16.0	32.0	18.9
12.8	8.5	7.5		9.0	5.3	9.6	4.3	12.5	6.8
2.4	1.9	.3		1.5	-1.2	3.4	-2.2	.9	1.2
13.1	12.9	13.5		13.3	15.9	39.5	11.2	12.8	12.3
6.5	6.3	5.9	Sales/Net Fixed Assets	4.6	5.7	10.5	4.9	7.2	5.7
3.7	3.9	3.4		1.1	3.7	3.8	3.4	3.6	3.7
3.0	2.8	2.8		2.7	3.1	3.2	2.7	2.9	2.1
2.2	2.0	1.9	Sales/Total Assets	1.3	2.2	2.1	1.9	2.0	1.4
1.4	1.4	1.1		.7	1.1	1.6	1.2	1.2	1.1
1.9	2.0	2.1		1.5	2.6	1.5	2.4	2.1	1.8
(162) 3.5	(193) 3.9	(179) 3.8	% Depr., Dep., Amort./Sales	(21) 4.8	(34) 4.1	(25) 2.6	(35) 3.9	(35) 3.6	(29) 3.9
5.3	6.1	6.0		21.4	6.5	4.0	7.4	5.1	6.1
2.6	2.6	2.9		6.2	4.3	2.1			
(60) 5.6	(75) 4.9	(63) 6.2	% Officers', Directors' Owners' Comp/Sales	(10) 11.2	(21) 7.9	(12) 4.3			
9.4	8.1	11.0		15.0	11.7	8.9			
2998309M	4890000M	4398189M	Net Sales ($)	17507M	80970M	119401M	291265M	672521M	3216525M
1891566M	3485207M	3275100M	Total Assets ($)	29108M	54635M	68092M	189096M	422285M	2511884M

Current Data Sorted by Assets   Comparative Historical Data

Type of Statement	0-500M	500M-2MM	2-10MM	10-50MM	50-100MM	100-250MM		4/1/05-3/31/06 ALL	4/1/06-3/31/07 ALL
Unqualified		3	4	1				3	4
Reviewed	1	4	5		1			5	3
Compiled	15	7	6					6	10
Tax Returns	14	13	5	4	1	1		7	19
Other		10 (4/1-9/30/09)		75 (10/1/09-3/31/10)				13	23
NUMBER OF STATEMENTS	30	27	20	5	2	1		34	59
	%	%	%	%	%	%		%	%
ASSETS									
Cash & Equivalents	38.0	16.5	13.0					17.0	18.7
Trade Receivables (net)	12.4	28.0	42.3					27.8	25.4
Inventory	17.7	15.7	6.6					21.9	16.1
All Other Current	2.6	7.6	5.3					3.3	9.0
Total Current	70.7	67.8	67.1					70.1	69.2
Fixed Assets (net)	21.5	22.3	21.1					15.5	18.7
Intangibles (net)	2.7	3.2	.6					5.2	3.2
All Other Non-Current	5.0	6.7	11.1					9.2	8.9
Total	100.0	100.0	100.0					100.0	100.0
LIABILITIES									
Notes Payable-Short Term	28.1	18.2	6.5					10.8	9.7
Cur. Mat.-L.T.D.	.0	3.1	3.0					2.0	3.3
Trade Payables	30.2	21.6	15.1					15.8	13.2
Income Taxes Payable	3.1	.3	1.3					.3	.5
All Other Current	36.1	17.0	19.2					21.5	32.6
Total Current	97.5	60.2	45.1					50.4	59.2
Long-Term Debt	13.3	12.7	11.7					17.3	14.2
Deferred Taxes	.0	.0	1.1					.0	.7
All Other Non-Current	3.0	4.8	3.3					6.4	10.6
Net Worth	-13.9	22.3	38.8					26.0	15.3
Total Liabilties & Net Worth	100.0	100.0	100.0					100.0	100.0
INCOME DATA									
Net Sales	100.0	100.0	100.0					100.0	100.0
Gross Profit									
Operating Expenses	100.4	100.5	92.8					94.1	95.1
Operating Profit	-.4	-.5	7.2					5.9	4.9
All Other Expenses (net)	.7	.2	4.5					1.1	1.0
Profit Before Taxes	-1.1	-.7	2.7					4.8	3.9
RATIOS									
Current	2.8	1.8	3.5					2.5	2.2
	1.1	1.0	1.6					1.4	1.3
	.5	.8	.7					.9	.8
Quick	1.7	1.0	2.3					1.6	1.3
	.7	.6	1.1					.8	.8
	.3	.3	.7					.4	.3
Sales/Receivables	0 UND	9 38.8	26 14.2					9 39.2	3 126.3
	0 UND	27 13.8	54 6.8					31 11.9	22 16.8
	21 17.5	47 7.8	88 4.1					63 5.8	45 8.1
Cost of Sales/Inventory									
Cost of Sales/Payables									
Sales/Working Capital	9.8	8.6	5.0					7.6	8.0
	228.5	999.8	12.6					15.1	24.7
	-15.2	-26.8	-33.2					-34.3	-44.9
EBIT/Interest	11.6	37.7	21.4					16.1	35.6
	(20) 1.0	(20) 1.5	(16) 3.9					(28) 4.8	(46) 3.9
	-11.2	-3.2	.1					1.6	-.7
Net Profit + Depr., Dep., Amort./Cur. Mat. L/T/D									
Fixed/Worth	.0	.1	.1					.2	.2
	.6	.7	.2					.5	.6
	-.6	-11.0	1.3					NM	-3.9
Debt/Worth	.4	.8	.7					1.1	1.0
	9.4	7.0	1.5					3.8	5.5
	-2.4	-20.8	4.4					NM	-8.6
% Profit Before Taxes/Tangible Net Worth	158.8	99.1	56.6					117.0	94.3
	(18) 57.9	(20) 45.4	(19) 7.8					(26) 59.2	(40) 59.2
	-31.1	-9.8	1.4					4.6	8.2
% Profit Before Taxes/Total Assets	60.6	26.9	16.8					24.6	22.3
	1.6	.9	2.4					12.3	9.5
	-20.1	-9.8	-3.1					1.9	-3.5
Sales/Net Fixed Assets	UND	115.5	124.7					87.8	103.2
	91.3	20.5	31.3					29.8	27.6
	14.1	8.1	9.0					15.1	11.7
Sales/Total Assets	14.9	4.8	3.9					4.6	5.0
	6.6	2.9	2.9					3.0	3.5
	3.2	1.6	1.7					2.0	2.1
% Depr., Dep., Amort./Sales	.2	.4	.3					.5	.4
	(14) 1.0	(16) .6	(17) 1.4					(26) .9	(39) .9
	3.0	1.4	5.3					1.9	1.5
% Officers', Directors' Owners' Comp/Sales	9.9	3.3						2.8	2.9
	(19) 13.5	(14) 5.2						(20) 5.2	(30) 6.5
	17.1	7.4						6.7	9.6
Net Sales ($)	31360M	92044M	234602M	289411M	199858M	2034853M		1165476M	2902008M
Total Assets ($)	4906M	28196M	85307M	104930M	113757M	229020M		227238M	507252M

M = $ thousand   MM = $ million
See Pages 9 through 22 for Explanation of Ratios and Data

Comparative Historical Data | Current Data Sorted by Sales

4/1/07-3/31/08 ALL	4/1/08-3/31/09 ALL	4/1/09-3/31/10 ALL	Type of Statement	0-1MM	1-3MM	3-5MM	5-10MM	10-25MM	25MM & OVER
2	3	1	Unqualified		2	3	1		1
4	7	8	Reviewed			5	1	1	2
8	16	10	Compiled	1	2	5	1	3	1
20	33	28	Tax Returns	10	7	5	2	3	1
27	29	38	Other	13	10	3	2	4	6
				10 (4/1-9/30/09)			75 (10/1/09-3/31/10)		
61	**88**	**85**	**NUMBER OF STATEMENTS**	**24**	**19**	**15**	**8**	**9**	**10**
%	%	%	**ASSETS**	%	%	%	%	%	%
13.8	17.0	22.1	Cash & Equivalents	29.3	24.9	23.3			7.5
29.4	27.1	25.4	Trade Receivables (net)	10.7	26.2	28.2			31.0
21.0	19.3	14.1	Inventory	21.2	11.4	16.1			12.0
5.5	6.4	6.3	All Other Current	2.4	1.8	5.6			15.2
69.8	69.9	67.9	Total Current	63.6	64.3	73.3			65.7
17.3	19.8	22.1	Fixed Assets (net)	29.0	25.1	17.2			22.6
2.7	1.6	3.1	Intangibles (net)	4.5	3.1	.6			8.2
10.3	8.7	6.9	All Other Non-Current	2.8	7.5	8.9			3.5
100.0	100.0	100.0	Total	100.0	100.0	100.0			100.0
			LIABILITIES						
17.3	13.5	19.4	Notes Payable-Short Term	26.8	19.4	17.3			18.6
5.7	4.0	2.0	Cur. Mat.-L.T.D.	.6	3.1	1.3			4.1
18.0	13.6	22.7	Trade Payables	39.0	11.6	11.5			19.6
.1	.2	1.5	Income Taxes Payable	.0	4.9	.1			.0
24.5	24.6	24.6	All Other Current	30.5	26.2	17.9			18.1
65.6	56.0	70.3	Total Current	96.9	65.2	48.2			60.5
15.8	15.8	14.4	Long-Term Debt	25.6	7.7	10.6			25.4
.0	.1	.3	Deferred Taxes	.0	.0	1.5			.0
5.9	7.9	4.0	All Other Non-Current	3.8	5.0	5.4			5.0
12.7	20.2	11.2	Net Worth	-26.3	22.0	34.4			9.2
100.0	100.0	100.0	Total Liabilities & Net Worth	100.0	100.0	100.0			100.0
			INCOME DATA						
100.0	100.0	100.0	Net Sales	100.0	100.0	100.0			100.0
			Gross Profit						
93.7	94.8	98.4	Operating Expenses	99.6	98.0	96.5			97.4
6.3	5.2	1.6	Operating Profit	.4	2.0	3.5			2.6
1.1	.4	1.6	All Other Expenses (net)	4.3	.3	.2			2.1
5.2	4.9	.0	Profit Before Taxes	-3.9	1.7	3.3			.6
			RATIOS						
2.0 / 1.3 / .9	2.1 / 1.3 / 1.0	2.4 / 1.2 / .7	Current	2.0 / 1.0 / .4	2.6 / 1.0 / .8	4.0 / 1.6 / .7			2.1 / 1.6 / .8
1.6 / .7 / .3	1.4 / .8 / .3	1.6 / .8 / .4	Quick	1.4 / .6 / .3	2.4 / 1.0 / .4	3.7 / .9 / .4			1.7 / .8 / .3
8 43.7 / 27 13.6 / 49 7.4	3 111.0 / 25 14.9 / 54 6.7	0 UND / 24 15.1 / 47 7.8	Sales/Receivables	0 UND / 0 UND / 26 14.1	0 UND / 26 14.1 / 43 8.5	8 44.7 / 24 15.1 / 49 7.4			0 UND / 38 9.6 / 51 7.2
			Cost of Sales/Inventory						
			Cost of Sales/Payables						
6.7 / 22.6 / -43.2	8.1 / 20.0 / UND	8.2 / 46.7 / -15.6	Sales/Working Capital	6.2 / NM / -12.5	9.1 / 999.8 / -29.5	3.3 / 29.5 / -18.7			8.4 / 12.2 / -12.5
20.8 / (53) 6.0 / 1.9	17.3 / (73) 5.3 / 1.1	21.5 / (64) 1.7 / -1.5	EBIT/Interest	5.5 / (18) .0 / -15.4	61.5 / (11) .4 / -1.7	12.4 / (12) 2.0 / .1			52.6 / 1.4 / .1
		8.5 / (10) 1.7 / .1	Net Profit + Depr., Dep., Amort./Cur. Mat. L/T/D						
.2 / .6 / 6.7	.1 / .5 / -47.0	.1 / .6 / NM	Fixed/Worth	.0 / 3.9 / -.8	.0 / .6 / -5.3	.1 / .2 / 3.9			.2 / 1.0 / -3.2
1.1 / 3.5 / 44.5	.9 / 2.9 / -38.4	.7 / 2.8 / -13.2	Debt/Worth	1.8 / NM / -3.0	.4 / 2.8 / -10.2	.5 / 1.5 / 10.3			.9 / 1.8 / -9.8
86.5 / (48) 45.9 / 17.8	75.3 / (63) 30.0 / 9.1	93.0 / (61) 33.8 / -6.2	% Profit Before Taxes/Tangible Net Worth	193.7 / (12) 20.9 / -49.1	129.2 / (14) 48.5 / -25.8	98.2 / (13) 56.9 / 4.2			
24.6 / 9.1 / 1.5	25.9 / 9.5 / -.2	26.3 / 2.4 / -11.2	% Profit Before Taxes/Total Assets	19.5 / .0 / -34.4	39.0 / -1.9 / -18.6	45.1 / 3.4 / .9			28.8 / 1.6 / -3.8
78.5 / 37.9 / 14.1	86.8 / 29.7 / 11.8	217.2 / 26.7 / 9.6	Sales/Net Fixed Assets	418.6 / 20.0 / 5.3	371.6 / 18.3 / 8.1	157.1 / 26.7 / 14.1			55.3 / 13.5 / 7.8
4.8 / 3.4 / 1.8	4.9 / 3.2 / 2.1	5.4 / 3.3 / 2.0	Sales/Total Assets	9.3 / 3.5 / 1.1	6.5 / 3.2 / 1.9	6.3 / 3.3 / 1.8			4.3 / 2.8 / 2.0
.5 / (47) .9 / 1.8	.4 / (63) .9 / 1.8	.4 / (53) .9 / 3.0	% Depr., Dep., Amort./Sales	.4 / (11) 2.1 / 4.2		.4 / (12) .6 / 2.3			
2.4 / (30) 4.6 / 7.2	2.4 / (46) 5.2 / 8.8	3.5 / (44) 7.1 / 13.7	% Officers', Directors', Owners' Comp/Sales	11.6 / (11) 13.7 / 26.6	5.0 / (12) 9.2 / 13.6	3.3 / (12) 4.3 / 7.8			
1059035M	1284723M	2882128M	Net Sales ($)	12358M	33996M	59256M	59914M	131991M	2584613M
272260M	473650M	566116M	Total Assets ($)	11802M	11229M	23034M	18312M	40245M	461494M

M = $ thousand   MM = $ million
See Pages 9 through 22 for Explanation of Ratios and Data

Current Data Sorted by Assets | Comparative Historical Data

Type of Statement

Type of Statement	0-500M	500M-2MM	2-10MM	10-50MM	50-100MM	100-250MM	4/1/05-3/31/06 ALL	4/1/06-3/31/07 ALL
Unqualified	1	5	4	7	2		16	20
Reviewed	9	8	11	4			22	22
Compiled	20	12	2	4			35	40
Tax Returns	9	22	4	17		6	23	36
Other		16 (4/1-9/30/09)	17	127 (10/1/09-3/31/10)			58	86
NUMBER OF STATEMENTS	39	47	38	17	2		154	204

Main Data

(Columns 50-100MM and 100-250MM: DATA NOT AVAILABLE for Assets, Liabilities, and Income Data sections.)

	0-500M	500M-2MM	2-10MM	10-50MM	4/1/05-3/31/06 ALL	4/1/06-3/31/07 ALL
	%	%	%	%	%	%
ASSETS						
Cash & Equivalents	29.4	18.0	11.8	13.9	12.5	14.6
Trade Receivables (net)	21.2	34.3	33.7	22.3	34.3	29.0
Inventory	1.0	7.2	9.5	8.9	7.9	6.7
All Other Current	4.6	2.2	2.2	7.9	2.9	3.8
Total Current	56.3	61.6	57.2	53.0	57.6	54.2
Fixed Assets (net)	30.1	30.0	32.7	27.2	30.3	32.8
Intangibles (net)	3.7	4.2	3.0	6.1	4.8	4.8
All Other Non-Current	10.1	4.2	7.1	13.7	7.4	8.2
Total	100.0	100.0	100.0	100.0	100.0	100.0
LIABILITIES						
Notes Payable-Short Term	53.0	15.8	12.0	6.9	11.5	12.7
Cur. Mat.-L.T.D.	3.5	4.9	5.0	3.8	6.1	8.0
Trade Payables	12.0	13.4	11.5	11.6	14.3	11.8
Income Taxes Payable	.1	.4	.5	.1	.4	.4
All Other Current	23.2	7.9	8.9	13.1	13.7	15.3
Total Current	91.8	42.4	37.9	35.5	45.9	48.1
Long-Term Debt	12.6	17.2	14.5	15.9	21.2	23.4
Deferred Taxes	.0	.2	.4	.2	.3	.6
All Other Non-Current	13.3	7.4	9.0	2.0	8.7	6.3
Net Worth	-17.6	32.8	38.2	46.4	23.9	21.6
Total Liabilties & Net Worth	100.0	100.0	100.0	100.0	100.0	100.0
INCOME DATA						
Net Sales	100.0	100.0	100.0	100.0	100.0	100.0
Gross Profit						
Operating Expenses	96.7	97.9	95.9	90.7	94.4	94.9
Operating Profit	3.3	2.1	4.1	9.3	5.6	5.1
All Other Expenses (net)	1.2	1.5	.7	.1	1.6	1.4
Profit Before Taxes	2.1	.6	3.4	9.2	4.0	3.7
RATIOS						
Current	2.6	4.8	2.1	2.9	2.4	2.5
	.8	1.6	1.4	1.6	1.4	1.4
	.3	1.2	1.1	1.1	.9	.9
Quick	1.9	4.3	1.8	2.4	2.0	2.2
	.7	1.2	1.2	1.1	1.2	1.1
	.3	.7	.8	.5	.7	.6
Sales/Receivables	0 UND	23 16.0	42 8.7	35 10.5	28 12.8	19 18.8
	0 UND	36 10.2	58 6.3	50 7.3	46 7.9	45 8.1
	36 10.1	59 6.2	77 4.7	60 6.0	62 5.9	61 6.0
Cost of Sales/Inventory						
Cost of Sales/Payables						
Sales/Working Capital	14.5	5.4	7.4	3.9	7.6	7.0
	-72.0	14.3	12.3	8.3	15.9	19.5
	-13.1	122.4	122.7	46.3	-83.0	-53.9
EBIT/Interest	11.9	22.6	8.2	8.7	17.7	9.0
	(28) 1.2	(41) 3.1	(35) 2.4	(14) 3.9	(134) 3.5	(174) 3.4
	-7.1	-1.6	-.2	1.9	.9	.9
Net Profit + Depr., Dep., Amort./Cur. Mat. L/T/D			4.5		5.2	7.8
			(12) 1.3		(26) 1.9	(31) 2.3
			.3		.7	1.3
Fixed/Worth	.2	.3	.2	.3	.4	.4
	1.1	.6	.7	.6	1.0	1.2
	-.8	4.5	2.9	1.3	7.7	9.2
Debt/Worth	.6	.5	.7	.5	1.0	.8
	5.9	1.6	1.9	1.3	3.2	2.6
	-2.2	9.9	5.4	3.7	24.5	26.3
% Profit Before Taxes/Tangible Net Worth	52.6	63.6	39.9	17.6	90.1	52.6
	(23) 16.3	(40) 10.3	(34) 14.9	(15) 6.7	(119) 24.8	(162) 20.0
	-1.1	-36.1	2.1	2.9	6.1	1.7
% Profit Before Taxes/Total Assets	35.1	17.2	10.3	9.7	22.2	17.0
	4.4	6.3	4.0	4.2	6.5	6.2
	-20.7	-7.9	-1.4	1.4	.0	-.1
Sales/Net Fixed Assets	156.4	35.3	27.6	12.6	35.1	33.3
	28.7	12.7	6.3	9.7	11.2	9.9
	15.8	6.6	3.6	3.0	5.7	4.3
Sales/Total Assets	14.4	4.1	2.7	2.3	3.7	3.9
	5.7	2.8	2.1	1.9	2.5	2.5
	3.6	2.0	1.4	.9	2.0	1.6
% Depr., Dep., Amort./Sales	.6	.8	1.8	1.3	1.2	1.2
	(24) 1.2	(33) 2.2	(37) 4.2	2.0	(127) 2.6	(168) 2.5
	2.1	4.3	6.4	3.6	4.4	4.7
% Officers', Directors' Owners' Comp/Sales	10.1	2.8	1.2		4.0	3.7
	(28) 17.1	(26) 7.4	(10) 2.4		(72) 6.5	(81) 7.3
	23.7	13.9	6.7		9.9	13.8

	0-500M	500M-2MM	2-10MM	10-50MM	50-100MM	4/1/05-3/31/06 ALL	4/1/06-3/31/07 ALL
Net Sales ($)	63072M	155600M	388861M	571712M	193800M	2094622M	7341093M
Total Assets ($)	8523M	50631M	177892M	365172M	129817M	833215M	3074964M

© RMA 2010

M = $ thousand   MM = $ million
See Pages 9 through 22 for Explanation of Ratios and Data

Comparative Historical Data | Current Data Sorted by Sales

			Type of Statement						
18	13	13	Unqualified	1	1		2	2	7
21	22	21	Reviewed	1	4	2	4	7	3
30	26	19	Compiled	7	7	3	1	1	
25	35	36	Tax Returns	10	10	5	10	1	
62	72	54	Other	5	18	11	8	9	3
4/1/07-3/31/08 ALL	4/1/08-3/31/09 ALL	4/1/09-3/31/10 ALL		16 (4/1-9/30/09)			127 (10/1/09-3/31/10)		
				0-1MM	1-3MM	3-5MM	5-10MM	10-25MM	25MM & OVER
156	168	143	NUMBER OF STATEMENTS	24	40	21	25	20	13
%	%	%	ASSETS	%	%	%	%	%	%
14.3	14.2	18.8	Cash & Equivalents	20.0	26.9	17.8	15.3	9.8	14.0
30.4	30.5	28.9	Trade Receivables (net)	24.3	22.7	34.1	34.3	35.2	27.8
5.7	7.7	6.6	Inventory	1.2	3.7	6.3	6.9	14.0	13.6
3.7	4.8	3.5	All Other Current	3.9	3.9	2.4	1.2	3.9	7.3
54.0	57.3	57.8	Total Current	49.5	57.1	60.7	57.7	63.0	62.7
32.7	29.1	30.3	Fixed Assets (net)	38.3	30.3	31.1	30.8	26.8	18.6
4.3	5.4	4.2	Intangibles (net)	2.1	4.8	.6	5.7	2.8	11.4
9.0	8.2	7.7	All Other Non-Current	10.3	7.7	7.6	5.8	7.4	7.4
100.0	100.0	100.0	Total	100.0	100.0	100.0	100.0	100.0	100.0
			LIABILITIES						
18.1	14.9	23.7	Notes Payable-Short Term	30.3	39.0	22.0	13.9	10.2	6.4
4.0	6.5	4.4	Cur. Mat.-L.T.D.	2.5	3.9	7.9	5.4	4.2	2.2
11.7	11.6	12.2	Trade Payables	13.8	10.8	9.6	11.6	16.4	12.0
.5	.2	.3	Income Taxes Payable	.0	.1	.9	.6	.1	.1
14.0	13.5	13.0	All Other Current	15.2	12.0	9.7	14.7	12.5	15.0
48.3	46.7	53.5	Total Current	61.8	65.7	50.1	46.2	43.4	35.7
19.3	19.1	15.0	Long-Term Debt	25.5	13.0	18.6	9.5	12.1	10.9
.4	.2	.2	Deferred Taxes	.0	.3	.4	.0	.1	.3
5.5	6.0	8.7	All Other Non-Current	15.2	9.6	5.4	7.5	8.6	1.7
26.5	28.0	22.6	Net Worth	-2.6	11.5	25.4	36.7	35.7	51.5
100.0	100.0	100.0	Total Liabilities & Net Worth	100.0	100.0	100.0	100.0	100.0	100.0
			INCOME DATA						
100.0	100.0	100.0	Net Sales	100.0	100.0	100.0	100.0	100.0	100.0
			Gross Profit						
95.3	95.7	96.1	Operating Expenses	92.8	95.6	101.0	94.5	98.3	95.3
4.7	4.3	3.9	Operating Profit	7.2	4.4	-1.0	5.5	1.7	4.7
1.3	1.1	1.1	All Other Expenses (net)	3.3	1.0	.5	.7	-.3	.9
3.4	3.2	2.8	Profit Before Taxes	3.9	3.4	-1.6	4.9	2.0	3.8
			RATIOS						
2.4	2.9	2.8	Current	2.6	2.8	5.0	2.1	2.9	3.4
1.5	1.4	1.4		1.3	1.3	1.3	1.4	1.6	2.0
.9	1.0	.9		.4	.6	.6	.9	.9	1.2
2.1	2.3	2.2	Quick	2.6	2.6	4.0	1.8	1.7	2.9
1.1	1.1	1.2		1.1	1.1	1.1	1.2	1.2	1.0
.7	.6	.6		.3	.4	.6	.7	.8	.8
17 21.0	22 16.4	18 20.2	Sales/Receivables	5 78.0	0 UND	26 13.8	0 UND	47 7.8	32 11.6
43 8.5	40 9.2	38 9.5		32 11.5	25 14.7	54 6.8	48 7.6	51 7.1	51 7.1
63 5.8	59 6.2	60 6.0		48 7.7	47 7.8	66 5.5	73 5.0	67 5.4	61 6.0
			Cost of Sales/Inventory						
			Cost of Sales/Payables						
6.7	7.7	6.0	Sales/Working Capital	6.5	7.3	5.6	9.9	5.6	3.9
16.0	18.9	15.3		24.7	25.3	15.8	14.8	9.5	5.9
-62.9	183.8	-58.2		-22.5	-31.9	-12.3	NM	NM	44.4
9.9	13.5	11.0	EBIT/Interest	3.8	12.9	3.0	38.8	12.1	14.9
(133) 3.3	(150) 3.5	(120) 2.8		(16) .1	(33) 6.2	(17) 1.1	(23) 3.2	2.5	(11) 7.4
.8	-.1	-1.1		-2.8	-6.3	-6.1	1.7	1.2	3.5
3.3	3.4	4.7	Net Profit + Depr., Dep., Amort./Cur. Mat. L/T/D						
(23) 1.7	(24) 1.3	(24) 2.0							
.8	-.2	.3							
.4	.4	.3	Fixed/Worth	.5	.2	.2	.4	.2	.3
.8	.9	.7		2.3	.8	.9	.6	.7	.5
3.4	4.2	4.7		NM	4.5	3.8	9.1	3.1	.6
.6	.7	.6	Debt/Worth	.9	.5	.6	.6	.7	.5
1.8	2.2	2.0		4.2	1.6	1.7	2.1	2.0	1.1
10.2	11.6	19.8		NM	23.0	16.5	15.2	16.9	3.4
68.8	61.2	45.2	% Profit Before Taxes/Tangible Net Worth	43.7	88.6	13.3	72.7	35.7	18.8
(129) 24.0	(134) 19.1	(114) 12.1		(18) 5.7	(31) 16.3	(17) .8	(20) 20.0	(17) 16.3	(11) 12.0
3.8	1.6	-.3		-25.3	-8.5	-72.9	4.0	4.8	6.7
20.7	19.4	15.3	% Profit Before Taxes/Total Assets	19.0	32.7	6.4	29.8	10.7	10.7
6.6	5.7	4.5		1.3	9.0	.4	7.2	4.3	6.2
-.5	-3.7	-4.5		-19.2	-14.9	-27.1	2.4	.3	3.4
31.3	41.4	38.4	Sales/Net Fixed Assets	37.7	161.9	22.2	34.2	34.9	31.0
10.1	13.4	12.7		12.7	22.7	10.1	19.7	12.3	10.9
4.0	4.8	5.5		2.3	6.9	5.4	6.0	4.1	7.6
3.9	4.5	4.2	Sales/Total Assets	4.2	7.2	4.2	6.0	2.9	2.5
2.4	2.7	2.6		2.4	3.2	2.8	3.1	2.1	2.2
1.6	1.7	1.9		.8	2.0	1.9	2.2	1.6	1.8
1.3	1.1	.9	% Depr., Dep., Amort./Sales	.9	.9	1.1	.7	1.6	1.2
(119) 2.5	(125) 2.5	(113) 2.2		(16) 1.3	(25) 3.1	(17) 4.1	(23) 1.7	(19) 2.6	1.4
4.6	5.3	4.5		4.1	6.4	5.4	5.1	4.2	3.4
3.4	4.4	5.3	% Officers', Directors' Owners' Comp/Sales	15.5	7.8		2.3		
(65) 6.9	(77) 7.5	(65) 10.1		(12) 17.1	(25) 10.6		(14) 7.0		
13.6	14.0	19.0		23.4	19.0		24.7		
3828919M	2879799M	1373045M	Net Sales ($)	12744M	82719M	82981M	160659M	335649M	698293M
1993521M	1317493M	732035M	Total Assets ($)	27241M	34243M	49256M	60983M	174738M	385574M

M = $ thousand   MM = $ million
See Pages 9 through 22 for Explanation of Ratios and Data

Current Data Sorted by Assets

1	11	37	44	17	16
3	18	46	6	3	
7	25	28	3		1
41	44	16			
35	77	125	66	14	21

	82 (4/1-9/30/09)		620 (10/1/09-3/31/10)		
0-500M	500M-2MM	2-10MM	10-50MM	50-100MM	100-250MM

Comparative Historical Data

Type of Statement		
Unqualified	70	107
Reviewed	55	78
Compiled	28	51
Tax Returns	55	90
Other	208	248
	4/1/05-3/31/06	4/1/06-3/31/07
	ALL	ALL

Combined Table

0-500M	500M-2MM	2-10MM	10-50MM	50-100MM	100-250MM		NUMBER OF STATEMENTS		416	574
87	175	252	119	32	37					
%	%	%	%	%	%		ASSETS		%	%
37.4	19.1	20.8	21.5	25.4	34.0		Cash & Equivalents		20.9	20.0
23.8	44.5	44.8	37.9	19.7	17.8		Trade Receivables (net)		42.3	42.4
2.1	1.6	1.4	2.5	1.7	2.3		Inventory		2.7	2.2
5.4	6.0	5.8	5.4	6.4	9.9		All Other Current		5.1	4.7
68.7	71.2	72.8	67.3	53.3	64.0		Total Current		71.0	69.3
15.4	13.7	10.7	11.7	7.0	8.0		Fixed Assets (net)		12.4	12.4
5.5	4.9	8.3	15.1	28.2	20.9		Intangibles (net)		9.2	9.6
10.4	10.1	8.3	5.9	11.5	7.1		All Other Non-Current		7.3	8.6
100.0	100.0	100.0	100.0	100.0	100.0		Total		100.0	100.0
							LIABILITIES			
50.6	13.1	9.8	5.8	1.7	.2		Notes Payable-Short Term		13.9	13.8
10.3	2.5	2.2	2.7	1.4	.8		Cur. Mat.-L.T.D.		3.8	2.1
9.2	14.7	12.4	11.3	5.0	9.7		Trade Payables		12.7	11.0
.1	.5	.8	.7	.5	.3		Income Taxes Payable		1.2	.6
30.0	20.4	23.7	24.8	33.6	22.7		All Other Current		21.6	24.3
100.2	51.3	48.9	45.3	42.2	33.7		Total Current		53.2	51.8
16.7	8.5	10.1	6.2	6.1	7.9		Long-Term Debt		8.7	10.4
.0	.1	.6	.5	.5	1.2		Deferred Taxes		.5	.5
9.3	6.6	15.5	11.2	7.1	5.2		All Other Non-Current		10.7	11.8
-26.3	33.5	25.0	36.9	44.2	51.9		Net Worth		26.9	25.6
100.0	100.0	100.0	100.0	100.0	100.0		Total Liabilties & Net Worth		100.0	100.0
							INCOME DATA			
100.0	100.0	100.0	100.0	100.0	100.0		Net Sales		100.0	100.0
							Gross Profit			
94.4	93.7	93.6	93.3	91.7	91.4		Operating Expenses		93.9	94.4
5.6	6.3	6.4	6.7	8.3	8.6		Operating Profit		6.1	5.6
1.3	1.3	1.1	1.0	1.0	1.5		All Other Expenses (net)		.8	.8
4.3	5.0	5.3	5.7	7.3	7.0		Profit Before Taxes		5.3	4.8
							RATIOS			
3.2	3.7	2.6	2.5	2.3	3.7				2.8	2.9
1.3	1.5	1.6	1.6	1.2	1.9		Current		1.6	1.5
.5	1.0	1.0	1.1	1.0	1.1				1.0	1.0
3.1	2.8	2.3	2.3	2.2	3.0				2.6	2.6
(86) 1.3	1.4	1.5	1.4	1.0	1.5		Quick		1.4	1.4
.4	.9	.9	.9	.7	.9				.8	.8

Ratios with period counts

	0-500M		500M-2MM		2-10MM		10-50MM		50-100MM		100-250MM					
Sales/Receivables	0	UND	25	14.6	40	9.2	47	7.8	31	11.9	37	9.8	34	10.7	35	10.4
	1	378.2	45	8.1	57	6.4	69	5.3	58	6.3	58	6.3	56	6.6	58	6.3
	27	13.5	67	5.5	79	4.6	89	4.1	84	4.4	81	4.5	83	4.4	78	4.7

Cost of Sales/Inventory

Cost of Sales/Payables

0-500M	500M-2MM	2-10MM	10-50MM	50-100MM	100-250MM				ALL	ALL
14.6	6.7	5.4	3.6	3.8	1.5		Sales/Working Capital		5.4	5.9
58.4	17.0	11.7	8.8	18.7	3.6				10.8	13.9
-12.2	-230.3	161.0	47.3	75.9	15.2				UND	-220.9
14.7	26.6	26.4	31.6	66.2	58.4				37.9	29.5
(53) 2.2	(122) 7.4	(188) 9.2	(92) 9.1	(21) 5.9	(19) 5.6		EBIT/Interest		(312) 6.9	(451) 6.3
-2.2	-.2	1.9	1.8	.7	-.5				1.6	1.3
		13.4	11.0						20.1	26.1
		(34) 3.9	(21) 2.3				Net Profit + Depr., Dep., Amort./Cur. Mat. L/T/D		(62) 5.9	(70) 6.3
		1.2	-2.6						1.1	1.2
.0	.0	.1	.1	.2	.1				.1	.1
.5	.2	.3	.3	.4	.2		Fixed/Worth		.3	.3
-1.2	3.0	36.0	2.3	NM	.8				3.0	2.9
.7	.5	.7	.8	.9	.3				.7	.8
5.0	1.7	2.1	2.2	4.9	.9		Debt/Worth		2.2	2.2
-4.1	40.4	-57.1	21.4	-11.4	5.4				69.9	41.5
268.5	81.4	79.1	58.8	68.7	23.4		% Profit Before Taxes/Tangible Net Worth		74.0	78.6
(57) 44.1	(137) 33.8	(187) 33.9	(95) 26.7	(23) 28.7	(31) 15.4				(313) 37.3	(440) 39.1
10.5	9.4	15.0	3.2	7.6	3.1				12.8	11.5
51.5	29.5	21.6	19.5	19.0	12.2		% Profit Before Taxes/Total Assets		27.4	25.1
12.2	12.1	10.9	9.2	5.6	6.5				10.9	11.4
-10.5	1.1	2.6	.9	.4	-.3				1.9	1.3
429.4	360.4	141.8	74.6	40.0	27.4				103.2	113.5
123.4	56.5	49.5	30.4	23.4	16.1		Sales/Net Fixed Assets		37.3	42.1
31.6	22.6	18.1	13.6	11.7	10.9				16.4	16.1
15.6	4.9	3.9	2.7	1.5	1.2				4.2	4.3
6.8	3.7	2.7	1.7	1.1	.9		Sales/Total Assets		2.8	2.8
3.7	2.5	1.7	1.2	.8	.6				1.7	1.6
.3	.3	.3	.8	1.0	.9				.5	.4
(34) .6	(107) .8	(166) .8	(69) 1.6	(13) 1.9	(20) 3.2		% Depr., Dep., Amort./Sales		(279) 1.2	(359) 1.1
1.2	2.1	1.8	3.5	5.8	3.9				2.4	2.5
3.8	3.2	1.6	2.3						3.5	3.7
(44) 8.5	(68) 6.0	(59) 3.4	(17) 8.9				% Officers', Directors' Owners' Comp/Sales		(128) 8.1	(160) 7.2
17.9	11.2	8.9	19.0						13.6	12.8
174402M	823389M	3304071M	4824912M	2673438M	5738769M		Net Sales ($)		10859526M	14248138M
19651M	212835M	1162172M	2482168M	2221100M	5658303M		Total Assets ($)		6190434M	7607978M

M = $ thousand   MM = $ million
See Pages 9 through 22 for Explanation of Ratios and Data

Comparative Historical Data   **Current Data Sorted by Sales**

4/1/07-3/31/08 ALL	4/1/08-3/31/09 ALL	4/1/09-3/31/10 ALL	Type of Statement	0-1MM	1-3MM	3-5MM	5-10MM	10-25MM	25MM & OVER
86	112	126	Unqualified	2	1	8	17	29	69
57	68	73	Reviewed	1	4	8	19	28	13
38	57	64	Compiled	5	14	10	20	12	3
75	105	101	Tax Returns	19	27	17	23	15	
260	280	338	Other	24	37	46	65	77	89
				82 (4/1-9/30/09)			620 (10/1/09-3/31/10)		
516	622	702	**NUMBER OF STATEMENTS**	51	83	89	144	161	174
%	%	%	**ASSETS**	%	%	%	%	%	%
19.6	21.7	23.4	Cash & Equivalents	27.0	26.2	24.5	22.9	22.8	21.5
41.0	40.8	38.4	Trade Receivables (net)	23.7	29.6	39.3	41.1	44.0	39.0
2.4	2.1	1.8	Inventory	1.4	2.7	1.8	.9	1.2	2.7
5.3	5.1	6.0	All Other Current	4.8	6.7	3.9	7.4	5.7	6.2
68.2	69.7	69.6	Total Current	57.0	65.3	69.5	72.3	73.7	69.4
12.4	13.1	11.9	Fixed Assets (net)	27.7	14.8	11.8	12.4	8.8	8.4
10.1	8.8	9.8	Intangibles (net)	6.0	9.6	6.8	7.2	8.9	15.5
9.3	8.5	8.7	All Other Non-Current	9.4	10.4	11.8	8.1	8.5	6.6
100.0	100.0	100.0	Total	100.0	100.0	100.0	100.0	100.0	100.0
			LIABILITIES						
13.2	13.3	14.1	Notes Payable-Short Term	30.2	38.4	11.6	13.0	8.5	5.3
2.8	3.2	3.2	Cur. Mat.-L.T.D.	11.1	3.4	5.0	1.9	2.3	1.9
10.8	12.8	11.9	Trade Payables	10.7	10.1	11.2	10.9	13.0	13.4
.8	.6	.6	Income Taxes Payable	.0	.1	.9	.7	.8	.6
21.0	22.0	24.3	All Other Current	19.1	31.3	25.2	20.8	24.2	24.8
48.6	51.9	54.1	Total Current	71.0	83.3	53.9	47.3	48.8	46.0
10.0	12.3	9.5	Long-Term Debt	21.9	13.0	9.8	6.9	9.5	6.4
.5	.4	.4	Deferred Taxes	.0	.0	.1	.7	.6	.6
7.9	9.6	10.9	All Other Non-Current	5.5	13.4	11.3	9.9	15.7	7.3
33.1	25.8	25.1	Net Worth	1.6	-9.7	25.0	35.3	25.5	39.7
100.0	100.0	100.0	Total Liabilities & Net Worth	100.0	100.0	100.0	100.0	100.0	100.0
			INCOME DATA						
100.0	100.0	100.0	Net Sales	100.0	100.0	100.0	100.0	100.0	100.0
			Gross Profit						
94.5	94.0	93.5	Operating Expenses	84.7	93.8	95.7	93.9	94.8	93.2
5.5	6.0	6.5	Operating Profit	15.3	6.2	4.3	6.1	5.2	6.8
1.3	1.4	1.2	All Other Expenses (net)	6.7	.6	.5	1.0	.6	.9
4.2	4.5	5.3	Profit Before Taxes	8.6	5.6	3.8	5.1	4.6	5.9
			RATIOS						
2.8	2.8	2.8	Current	2.8	3.8	2.9	3.8	2.7	2.4
1.6	1.5	1.6		1.3	1.3	1.5	1.7	1.7	1.5
1.0	1.0	1.0		.5	.7	1.0	1.0	1.1	1.0
2.6	2.6	2.5	Quick	2.3	2.8	2.8	3.1	2.5	2.2
1.4 (621)	1.3 (701)	1.4		(50) 1.0	1.1	1.4	1.5	1.6	1.3
.9	.8	.8		.5	.5	.8	.8	.9	.8
35 10.6	31 11.6	29 12.7	Sales/Receivables	0 UND	4 82.9	22 16.9	33 11.0	35 10.3	42 8.6
58 6.3	52 7.0	52 7.0		12 29.3	38 9.5	44 8.4	52 7.0	55 6.7	61 6.0
78 4.7	74 4.9	75 4.9		43 8.5	71 5.2	67 5.5	71 5.1	79 4.6	80 4.5
			Cost of Sales/Inventory						
			Cost of Sales/Payables						
5.8	5.8	5.4	Sales/Working Capital	8.4	4.9	7.4	5.4	5.6	3.9
12.9	13.4	13.8		58.4	29.9	18.6	12.4	11.7	10.3
362.3	-130.4	-174.0		-7.6	-14.7	UND	171.5	71.1	58.0
19.9	29.7	27.2	EBIT/Interest	12.4	12.4	37.1	23.8	25.5	67.4
(373) 5.2	(469) 7.1	(495) 7.4		(24) 1.2	(62) 3.4	(68) 7.3	(97) 9.1	(122) 7.1	(122) 10.7
.9	.9	.7		-3.4	-1.7	-2.3	2.0	.1	2.2
30.0	10.8	14.1	Net Profit + Depr., Dep., Amort./Cur. Mat. L/T/D				13.1	20.9	13.1
(61) 3.8	(74) 4.0	(72) 3.4					(14) 5.6	(27) 2.5	(25) 3.4
.5	.8	.5					-2.3	1.2	.2
.1	.1	.1	Fixed/Worth	.1	.0	.1	.1	.0	.1
.3	.3	.3		.5	.9	.3	.3	.2	.2
1.9	5.1	6.0		57.8	-1.0	35.2	2.1	2.9	1.3
.6	.7	.7	Debt/Worth	.7	.7	.6	.6	.7	.7
1.8	2.1	2.0		3.4	8.9	1.8	1.8	1.7	1.9
13.3	69.1	182.1		-29.0	-5.0	UND	9.0	72.9	20.1
70.5	82.3	78.5	% Profit Before Taxes/Tangible Net Worth	91.9	82.9	103.9	77.7	91.7	57.5
(407) 34.6	(473) 34.0	(530) 30.5		(36) 29.9	(51) 36.9	(67) 33.6	(112) 34.8	(124) 32.6	(140) 26.4
9.3	6.9	9.8		1.5	7.4	9.5	15.1	13.3	6.2
24.1	26.2	24.4	% Profit Before Taxes/Total Assets	24.8	33.1	27.3	25.7	26.7	18.5
9.3	10.1	10.0		2.7	8.2	10.1	11.9	10.7	10.1
.2	.2	.9		-8.6	-2.0	-7.3	2.7	2.4	1.3
109.3	130.4	145.4	Sales/Net Fixed Assets	201.5	333.5	144.6	132.6	181.1	95.5
36.2	39.2	44.1		42.9	61.6	50.7	44.1	51.9	30.2
15.8	15.2	16.6		3.1	14.7	19.3	20.1	22.2	14.4
4.2	4.6	4.3	Sales/Total Assets	6.8	4.2	5.8	4.5	4.2	3.0
2.7	2.9	2.8		3.4	2.9	3.7	3.0	2.9	1.9
1.5	1.6	1.6		.4	1.8	2.1	1.9	1.8	1.1
.4	.4	.4	% Depr., Dep., Amort./Sales	.9	.3	.5	.3	.4	.5
(331) 1.1	(376) 1.0	(409) 1.0		(19) 2.4	(48) .7	(48) 1.1	(97) .8	(99) .9	(98) 1.2
2.7	2.6	2.2		18.5	2.4	2.5	1.9	1.7	3.4
3.1	3.0	2.7	% Officers', Directors' Owners' Comp/Sales	6.5	4.6	3.5	3.0	.8	1.6
(149) 6.6	(158) 5.9	(191) 6.0		(19) 12.6	(37) 8.1	(30) 6.8	(45) 10.8	(37) 2.2	(23) 3.7
13.5	13.1	11.9		22.9	13.0	10.2	10.8	6.3	11.5
12854996M	19137886M	17538981M	Net Sales ($)	27093M	165937M	348729M	1053527M	2467998M	13475697M
9278578M	10387008M	11756229M	Total Assets ($)	29566M	87568M	132875M	457285M	1242269M	9806666M

M = $ thousand   MM = $ million
See Pages 9 through 22 for Explanation of Ratios and Data

Current Data Sorted by Assets   Comparative Historical Data

0-500M	500M-2MM	2-10MM	10-50MM	50-100MM	100-250MM	Type of Statement	4/1/05-3/31/06 ALL	4/1/06-3/31/07 ALL
2	4	58	58	20	19	Unqualified	98	125
3	20	61	17		1	Reviewed	67	77
6	24	21	2			Compiled	50	58
41	33	17				Tax Returns	46	66
33	77	137	83	19	19	Other	186	234
	100 (4/1-9/30/09)		675 (10/1/09-3/31/10)					
85	158	294	160	39	39	NUMBER OF STATEMENTS	447	560
%	%	%	%	%	%	ASSETS	%	%
27.2	17.2	16.3	17.0	18.7	13.7	Cash & Equivalents	15.4	14.8
31.0	51.0	49.7	44.2	29.9	29.9	Trade Receivables (net)	48.8	47.0
5.5	4.1	5.8	4.0	2.1	3.9	Inventory	4.4	5.9
3.7	3.6	5.2	6.9	5.2	8.2	All Other Current	5.2	4.8
67.4	75.9	77.1	72.1	56.0	55.7	Total Current	73.8	72.4
13.9	14.0	10.4	9.7	8.5	6.8	Fixed Assets (net)	11.9	11.4
5.7	3.9	5.7	10.9	28.6	31.9	Intangibles (net)	6.9	7.7
13.0	6.2	6.8	7.2	6.9	5.6	All Other Non-Current	7.4	8.5
100.0	100.0	100.0	100.0	100.0	100.0	Total	100.0	100.0
						LIABILITIES		
37.2	17.8	10.7	10.0	7.5	3.3	Notes Payable-Short Term	15.5	13.8
8.4	2.0	2.5	1.7	4.4	2.6	Cur. Mat.-L.T.D.	2.3	3.7
16.4	17.5	19.0	17.3	11.1	15.8	Trade Payables	16.7	17.2
.1	.5	.6	.6	.2	1.2	Income Taxes Payable	.8	.6
22.4	17.5	19.2	19.1	19.2	17.2	All Other Current	17.7	18.2
84.6	55.3	52.1	48.7	42.4	40.2	Total Current	53.0	53.4
23.0	9.6	8.9	8.7	8.7	14.7	Long-Term Debt	8.2	9.9
.0	.2	.3	.5	1.1	1.2	Deferred Taxes	.4	.3
10.3	7.0	4.8	5.8	5.3	7.0	All Other Non-Current	8.2	7.5
-17.9	28.0	33.9	36.2	42.5	36.9	Net Worth	30.2	28.8
100.0	100.0	100.0	100.0	100.0	100.0	Total Liabilties & Net Worth	100.0	100.0
						INCOME DATA		
100.0	100.0	100.0	100.0	100.0	100.0	Net Sales	100.0	100.0
						Gross Profit		
94.6	94.3	94.1	94.9	93.8	93.5	Operating Expenses	94.3	94.3
5.4	5.7	5.9	5.1	6.2	6.5	Operating Profit	5.7	5.7
.9	1.1	1.2	1.4	1.5	3.3	All Other Expenses (net)	.9	1.0
4.5	4.6	4.7	3.7	4.7	3.1	Profit Before Taxes	4.8	4.7
						RATIOS		
2.4	2.7	2.2	2.1	2.1	2.0	Current	2.4	2.2
1.1	1.4	1.5	1.5	1.3	1.2		1.5	1.5
.5	1.0	1.1	1.1	1.0	1.0		1.1	1.0
1.7	2.2	1.9	2.0	2.1	1.6	Quick	2.1	2.0
1.0	1.4	1.3	1.2	1.1	1.0		1.3 (559)	1.2
.4	.9	.9	.9	.8	.6		.9	.8

Sales/Receivables

0	UND	33	11.2	41	8.9	46	8.0	38	9.6	51	7.2	41	8.9	38 9.7
18	20.4	48	7.6	57	6.4	66	5.6	58	6.3	69	5.3	62	5.9	59 6.2
48	7.6	66	5.5	72	5.0	84	4.3	72	5.1	91	4.0	82	4.5	79 4.6

Cost of Sales/Inventory

Cost of Sales/Payables

0-500M	500M-2MM	2-10MM	10-50MM	50-100MM	100-250MM		4/1/05-3/31/06	4/1/06-3/31/07
10.2	7.7	6.4	5.1	4.5	5.2	Sales/Working Capital	6.4	6.4
421.0	16.0	13.3	10.7	18.2	10.8		13.5	13.1
-11.5	-352.4	49.0	52.6	-250.6	-141.1		101.8	98.3
11.4	23.2	47.6	38.4	18.4	29.3	EBIT/Interest	21.7	22.4
(58) 3.7	(123) 8.9	(233) 9.3	(127) 6.4	(32) 4.1	(31) 2.8		(355) 5.9	(450) 5.7
-1.3	1.2	1.8	1.0	.9	.6		1.6	1.3
	5.1	33.8	9.2	19.6		Net Profit + Depr., Dep., Amort./Cur. Mat. L/T/D	21.9	15.8
(11) 2.7	(42) 3.2	(32) 4.2	(11) 7.3				(69) 5.8	(75) 3.2
-9.3	.3	1.4	1.8				2.1	.3
.0	.1	.1	.1	.1	.2	Fixed/Worth	.1	.1
.8	.2	.2	.3	.8	.6		.3	.3
-.3	1.4	1.5	1.6	-.2	-.1		1.6	1.9
1.1	.7	.8	.9	1.0	1.2	Debt/Worth	.9	.8
43.6	2.0	1.9	2.1	8.6	5.7		2.4	2.1
-2.7	15.7	7.6	12.5	-3.7	-2.3		14.6	15.8
214.2	68.9	57.2	45.9	79.5	58.0	% Profit Before Taxes/Tangible Net Worth	73.5	73.4
(45) 66.0	(131) 35.5	(248) 29.3	(128) 29.9	(23) 26.6	(27) 14.2		(367) 34.2	(445) 36.0
9.1	7.0	11.3	8.8	-8.1	-3.0		9.6	13.7
47.5	25.5	22.4	16.0	12.8	8.6	% Profit Before Taxes/Total Assets	22.2	22.2
15.6	7.6	10.5	6.8	5.7	4.2		9.4	9.5
-12.1	.9	2.6	.2	-1.3	-.2		1.3	1.6
477.8	268.6	156.8	124.6	133.0	82.0	Sales/Net Fixed Assets	115.3	121.4
96.0	58.2	62.3	56.9	43.7	29.6		39.5	50.4
32.6	20.5	24.4	17.4	17.0	10.6		18.4	20.6
9.7	5.6	4.1	3.2	2.7	2.1	Sales/Total Assets	4.2	4.3
5.7	4.0	3.1	2.4	1.4	1.2		3.1	3.0
3.3	2.5	2.1	1.5	1.0	.7		1.8	1.8
.4	.3	.3	.4	.2	.5	% Depr., Dep., Amort./Sales	.4	.4
(38) .7	(96) .7	(215) .6	(100) .7	(18) .7	(23) .9		(307) 1.1	(390) .9
1.4	2.0	1.6	1.4	3.5	2.8		2.0	2.0
5.4	2.7	2.1	1.2			% Officers', Directors' Owners' Comp/Sales	3.0	2.9
(45) 9.0	(60) 5.1	(59) 4.1	(17) 2.3				(116) 5.7	(135) 5.6
17.7	8.7	8.9	8.2				11.6	11.5
135409M	747752M	4664947M	7823433M	5224875M	9120876M	Net Sales ($)	12836455M	18214895M
19546M	190366M	1448033M	3342985M	2846926M	6219196M	Total Assets ($)	6765232M	8208790M

M = $ thousand   MM = $ million
See Pages 9 through 22 for Explanation of Ratios and Data

Comparative Historical Data

Current Data Sorted by Sales

			Type of Statement						
102	126	161	Unqualified	1	1	4	10	41	104
75	102	102	Reviewed	1	8	8	18	41	26
43	53	53	Compiled	2	13	10	14	11	3
63	82	91	Tax Returns	17	29	17	18	9	1
262	283	368	Other	26	34	32	68	95	113
4/1/07-3/31/08 ALL	4/1/08-3/31/09 ALL	4/1/09-3/31/10 ALL		100 (4/1-9/30/09)			675 (10/1/09-3/31/10)		
				0-1MM	1-3MM	3-5MM	5-10MM	10-25MM	25MM & OVER
545	646	775	NUMBER OF STATEMENTS	47	85	71	128	197	247
%	%	%	ASSETS	%	%	%	%	%	%
14.4	16.1	17.8	Cash & Equivalents	15.4	20.1	22.5	19.3	17.1	16.0
45.4	45.5	44.8	Trade Receivables (net)	30.4	36.2	41.3	48.2	50.0	45.6
5.4	4.7	4.8	Inventory	8.8	4.3	6.7	3.8	5.0	4.0
4.7	5.1	5.2	All Other Current	5.0	4.7	2.7	3.5	5.9	6.6
70.0	71.4	72.7	Total Current	59.5	65.2	73.2	74.8	78.0	72.2
13.4	11.5	11.1	Fixed Assets (net)	23.5	18.0	12.3	10.2	10.3	7.1
9.4	8.8	8.9	Intangibles (net)	4.1	5.7	5.2	7.2	6.6	14.6
7.3	8.3	7.4	All Other Non-Current	12.9	11.0	9.2	7.8	5.1	6.1
100.0	100.0	100.0	Total	100.0	100.0	100.0	100.0	100.0	100.0
			LIABILITIES						
13.1	15.5	14.4	Notes Payable-Short Term	16.1	26.7	29.9	13.7	10.4	8.9
2.8	2.4	3.0	Cur. Mat.-L.T.D.	4.3	6.7	2.3	2.6	2.8	2.1
17.5	18.0	17.5	Trade Payables	19.2	11.7	13.4	18.1	18.1	19.5
.7	.6	.5	Income Taxes Payable	.0	.3	.8	.3	.7	.6
17.4	17.9	19.1	All Other Current	24.7	14.8	17.8	21.0	19.5	18.6
51.6	54.4	54.5	Total Current	64.2	60.1	64.3	55.8	51.4	49.8
10.5	11.2	10.8	Long-Term Debt	29.7	15.9	11.1	7.1	9.7	8.2
.5	.3	.4	Deferred Taxes	.0	.0	.3	.2	.5	.5
7.7	7.5	6.2	All Other Non-Current	11.4	9.5	9.2	5.6	4.1	5.2
29.7	26.5	28.1	Net Worth	-5.3	14.5	15.1	31.2	34.3	36.3
100.0	100.0	100.0	Total Liabilties & Net Worth	100.0	100.0	100.0	100.0	100.0	100.0
			INCOME DATA						
100.0	100.0	100.0	Net Sales	100.0	100.0	100.0	100.0	100.0	100.0
			Gross Profit						
94.4	94.5	94.3	Operating Expenses	85.7	95.4	93.9	95.4	95.1	94.6
5.6	5.5	5.7	Operating Profit	14.3	4.6	6.1	4.6	4.9	5.4
.9	1.4	1.3	All Other Expenses (net)	5.9	1.4	.8	.6	.7	1.5
4.7	4.2	4.4	Profit Before Taxes	8.4	3.2	5.3	4.1	4.3	3.9
			RATIOS						
2.3	2.3	2.2		2.2	2.2	3.7	2.1	2.4	2.0
1.4	1.5	1.4	Current	1.1	1.4	1.4	1.3	1.6	1.5
1.0	1.0	1.0		.5	.7	.8	1.0	1.1	1.1
2.0	2.1	1.9		1.6	1.6	3.1	1.9	2.1	1.8
1.2	1.3	1.3	Quick	.9	1.2	1.3	1.2	1.4	1.2
.8	.8	.8		.3	.4	.6	.8	.9	.9
38 9.6	33 11.1	35 10.4		1 414.0	9 42.1	28 13.1	37 9.8	42 8.7	43 8.5
56 6.5	53 6.9	55 6.7	Sales/Receivables	36 10.0	37 9.9	46 7.9	50 7.3	58 6.3	62 5.9
77 4.7	72 5.1	73 5.0		75 4.9	65 5.6	60 6.0	73 5.0	73 5.0	79 4.6
			Cost of Sales/Inventory						
			Cost of Sales/Payables						
6.9	6.6	6.7		5.4	7.8	5.6	7.5	6.3	7.3
14.6	14.0	14.4	Sales/Working Capital	84.4	24.3	15.1	16.8	11.4	13.7
-999.8	299.8	793.9		-7.0	-26.0	-45.5	-427.7	41.2	50.4
25.3	26.5	32.6		11.8	22.0	20.3	33.6	43.4	38.4
(445) 5.7	(510) 7.0	(604) 7.6	EBIT/Interest	(28) 4.4	(68) 4.8	(54) 6.7	(97) 8.2	(158) 7.8	(199) 8.2
1.7	1.1	1.1		-.3	.2	.1	1.3	1.5	1.6
11.5	11.4	15.6					10.3	29.8	12.7
(74) 3.3	(83) 3.5	(103) 3.4	Net Profit + Depr., Dep., Amort./Cur. Mat. L/T/D			(17) 2.5	(32) 2.9	(49) 5.1
1.3	.7	.6				-1.1	.7	1.5
.1	.1	.1		.1	.0	.0	.1	.1	.1
.3	.3	.3	Fixed/Worth	1.2	.6	.2	.3	.2	.3
2.6	2.2	2.8		-.5	NM	UND	1.5	1.6	3.0
.9	.9	.9		.9	.9	.6	.8	.7	1.1
2.4	2.4	2.4	Debt/Worth	7.4	3.5	1.7	2.4	2.0	3.0
23.0	35.7	38.4		-4.4	-6.2	-13.1	16.0	7.8	23.6
76.7	66.7	64.5		76.4	80.3	77.4	69.6	58.1	55.9
(425) 38.8	(502) 35.7	(602) 30.1	% Profit Before Taxes/Tangible Net Worth	(28) 31.3	(60) 29.1	(52) 40.2	(107) 33.7	(162) 31.7	(193) 29.0
12.9	10.6	8.0		1.5	-2.0	7.3	7.0	12.8	7.9
24.1	22.4	21.8		30.1	34.0	29.2	24.0	22.5	15.7
10.4	9.6	8.0	% Profit Before Taxes/Total Assets	8.6	7.2	5.9	9.8	9.4	7.2
1.9	2.0	.3		-3.4	-1.9	.2	.6	2.3	1.0
122.9	144.5	157.9		173.8	278.8	256.9	155.0	169.5	129.4
43.3	50.9	58.0	Sales/Net Fixed Assets	43.5	42.2	67.3	58.2	64.9	59.6
17.4	22.1	20.9		3.7	16.8	24.5	25.2	22.1	23.3
4.3	4.4	4.3		4.0	6.4	5.5	5.3	4.1	3.8
2.9	3.3	3.0	Sales/Total Assets	2.2	3.6	3.6	3.3	3.2	2.7
1.8	2.0	1.9		.8	2.2	2.0	2.2	2.1	1.6
.4	.3	.3		.5	.6	.3	.3	.3	.3
(368) .9	(431) .7	(490) .7	% Depr., Dep., Amort./Sales	(26) 1.1	(42) 1.5	(41) .8	(87) .8	(138) .6	(156) .6
2.2	1.7	1.6		11.2	4.0	1.4	1.5	1.6	1.2
2.5	2.2	2.4		9.1	4.0	3.1	2.7	1.7	.8
(136) 5.1	(142) 4.7	(186) 5.2	% Officers', Directors' Owners' Comp/Sales	(21) 17.2	(40) 6.6	(24) 5.9	(45) 4.4	(33) 4.1	(23) 1.8
9.3	8.7	10.9		23.4	11.4	9.1	8.1	9.0	2.5
18391158M	23302122M	27717292M	Net Sales ($)	26320M	169568M	287953M	932148M	3112911M	23188392M
10003424M	11331466M	14067052M	Total Assets ($)	29147M	73618M	127728M	394182M	1308645M	12133732M

M = $ thousand   MM = $ million
See Pages 9 through 22 for Explanation of Ratios and Data

Current Data Sorted by Assets   Comparative Historical Data

						Type of Statement		
2	7	30	27	6	9	Unqualified	68	81
2	18	42	6			Reviewed	51	57
9	19	14	4		1	Compiled	37	41
60	50	17	1			Tax Returns	87	102
39	80	112	41	11	11	Other	185	196
	50 (4/1-9/30/09)		568 (10/1/09-3/31/10)				4/1/05-3/31/06 ALL	4/1/06-3/31/07 ALL
0-500M	500M-2MM	2-10MM	10-50MM	50-100MM	100-250MM			
112	174	215	79	17	21	**NUMBER OF STATEMENTS**	428	477
%	%	%	%	%	%	**ASSETS**	%	%
30.8	14.0	13.9	12.1	17.5	15.7	Cash & Equivalents	17.0	17.9
29.0	46.8	48.3	40.6	28.7	25.3	Trade Receivables (net)	43.9	42.5
3.2	4.6	4.4	5.5	1.0	.2	Inventory	4.9	5.5
3.5	3.9	3.9	7.2	4.6	6.1	All Other Current	4.3	4.4
66.5	69.3	70.5	65.4	51.8	47.4	Total Current	70.1	70.3
19.3	16.1	13.2	14.1	7.1	12.1	Fixed Assets (net)	14.0	15.4
3.6	5.4	8.8	10.9	35.6	34.1	Intangibles (net)	7.1	6.3
10.6	9.1	7.5	9.5	5.5	6.4	All Other Non-Current	8.9	8.0
100.0	100.0	100.0	100.0	100.0	100.0	Total	100.0	100.0
						LIABILITIES		
29.7	14.2	11.2	9.4	5.7	4.4	Notes Payable-Short Term	13.5	16.4
7.9	4.9	2.3	2.8	2.1	2.9	Cur. Mat.-L.T.D.	3.1	2.8
11.8	18.2	16.3	16.2	10.9	13.1	Trade Payables	16.2	15.8
.0	.3	.3	.4	.4	.2	Income Taxes Payable	.7	.6
25.8	17.5	16.0	18.4	15.5	12.7	All Other Current	19.2	18.4
75.2	55.2	46.0	47.3	34.5	33.3	Total Current	52.7	53.9
25.6	17.5	12.1	10.6	10.0	20.7	Long-Term Debt	13.7	11.8
.0	.0	.2	.3	2.7	1.0	Deferred Taxes	.3	.4
15.0	13.2	9.2	8.6	4.5	6.5	All Other Non-Current	11.1	11.1
-15.8	14.0	32.5	33.2	48.2	38.5	Net Worth	22.2	22.8
100.0	100.0	100.0	100.0	100.0	100.0	Total Liabilities & Net Worth	100.0	100.0
						INCOME DATA		
100.0	100.0	100.0	100.0	100.0	100.0	Net Sales	100.0	100.0
						Gross Profit		
93.8	94.8	94.4	95.2	94.7	92.6	Operating Expenses	93.7	93.6
6.2	5.2	5.6	4.8	5.3	7.4	Operating Profit	6.3	6.4
.8	1.8	1.1	1.1	1.5	4.3	All Other Expenses (net)	1.0	1.3
5.4	3.4	4.5	3.7	3.8	3.1	Profit Before Taxes	5.3	5.1
						RATIOS		
3.2	2.6	2.7	2.1	1.9	2.5		2.6	2.6
1.3	1.4	1.7	1.4	1.6	1.3	Current	1.4	1.5
.6	.9	1.1	1.1	1.2	.8		1.0	1.0
3.0	2.3	2.5	1.8	1.7	2.3		2.2	2.2
1.2	1.2	1.4	1.2	1.2	1.2	Quick	1.3 (476)	1.2
.4	.7	.9	.7	1.0	.6		.8	.8
0 UND	29 12.6	38 9.6	42 8.8	54 6.7	27 13.4		29 12.7	29 12.6
14 25.2	48 7.6	59 6.2	59 6.1	67 5.4	60 6.1	Sales/Receivables	54 6.8	52 7.0
36 10.3	66 5.5	76 4.8	76 4.8	81 4.5	86 4.2		74 5.0	76 4.8
						Cost of Sales/Inventory		
						Cost of Sales/Payables		
10.9	7.9	6.4	6.2	4.2	4.0		6.9	6.9
126.4	16.7	11.0	14.4	7.2	11.6	Sales/Working Capital	15.9	16.3
-31.6	-63.2	79.7	69.8	33.9	-20.7		-169.7	-241.5
17.5	17.3	39.6	29.0	7.2	29.7		29.1	17.7
(76) 6.4	(144) 2.9	(168) 7.1	(66) 6.6	(16) 4.7	(17) 4.0	EBIT/Interest	(350) 7.3	(360) 5.1
1.0	-1.4	1.3	1.9	1.0	.8		1.8	1.4
		16.1	11.9			Net Profit + Depr., Dep.,	18.1	19.4
	(16) 9.4	(15) 3.8				Amort./Cur. Mat. L/T/D	(41) 4.8	(46) 3.5
		2.9	2.6				.9	.8
.1	.1	.1	.1	.2	.2		.1	.1
.6	.4	.2	.3	.5	1.8	Fixed/Worth	.3	.4
-.4	-43.9	2.0	2.6	-1.2	-.2		13.3	22.2
.5	.8	.6	1.2	2.2	.8		.8	.9
4.8	3.6	1.9	2.7	3.2	5.5	Debt/Worth	2.5	2.9
-3.1	-11.5	8.7	12.8	-5.6	-2.6		UND	-125.4
155.9	81.1	60.9	72.1	47.7	26.8	% Profit Before Taxes/Tangible	82.0	75.4
(67) 75.5	(127) 26.0	(177) 30.1	(68) 31.8	(11) 29.3	(11) 12.8	Net Worth	(321) 40.5	(357) 37.4
30.5	1.3	9.3	7.3	-8.9	2.5		12.7	11.7
60.7	22.6	21.9	17.5	10.0	8.5	% Profit Before Taxes/Total	29.7	26.6
23.4	6.3	8.4	7.1	5.4	4.6	Assets	11.1	10.3
1.2	-2.4	1.2	.8	-1.6	.6		1.2	1.2
319.6	179.0	142.0	187.7	62.8	65.4		148.1	118.5
63.6	52.7	52.2	53.2	32.0	11.8	Sales/Net Fixed Assets	48.9	41.0
21.4	15.3	15.5	12.2	16.0	6.1		16.3	15.2
10.3	4.9	4.3	3.4	2.1	2.1		4.7	4.8
5.7	3.4	2.9	2.4	1.3	.9	Sales/Total Assets	3.3	3.2
4.0	2.4	1.7	1.3	.7	.6		2.1	2.0
.3	.3	.3	.3				.3	.4
(56) 1.0	(113) 1.0	(153) .7	(54) .7			% Depr., Dep., Amort./Sales	(291) .9	(330) 1.0
2.2	2.6	2.3	3.4				2.6	2.3
6.4	2.7	1.0				% Officers', Directors'	2.9	3.3
(58) 9.7	(78) 5.6	(57) 2.1				Owners' Comp/Sales	(129) 6.6	(152) 6.0
15.1	9.3	5.1					11.2	12.6
203699M	750327M	3033947M	4725591M	1681938M	4509071M	Net Sales ($)	9965407M	9139532M
25712M	200475M	992310M	1865549M	1147970M	3391508M	Total Assets ($)	5655571M	4666207M

M = $ thousand   MM = $ million
See Pages 9 through 22 for Explanation of Ratios and Data

Comparative Historical Data / Current Data Sorted by Sales

		Comparative Historical Data		Type of Statement		Current Data Sorted by Sales				
	59	81	81	Unqualified	1	3	6	13	16	42
	61	72	68	Reviewed	1	5	11	16	20	15
	40	53	47	Compiled	6	7	10	9	11	4
	93	125	128	Tax Returns	28	44	25	17	12	2
	216	205	294	Other	19	61	33	49	69	63
	4/1/07-3/31/08 ALL	4/1/08-3/31/09 ALL	4/1/09-3/31/10 ALL		0-1MM	50 (4/1-9/30/09) 1-3MM	3-5MM	568 (10/1/09-3/31/10) 5-10MM	10-25MM	25MM & OVER
NUMBER OF STATEMENTS	469	536	618		55	120	85	104	128	126
	%	%	%	ASSETS	%	%	%	%	%	%
	16.7	16.6	16.9	Cash & Equivalents	27.7	18.6	17.8	16.6	14.0	13.2
	42.3	40.5	42.1	Trade Receivables (net)	21.8	34.8	39.3	45.7	52.8	45.9
	5.8	5.3	4.2	Inventory	3.3	4.1	6.7	4.2	4.1	3.0
	4.1	4.4	4.3	All Other Current	4.5	2.7	3.9	3.9	5.2	5.7
	69.0	66.9	67.5	Total Current	57.3	60.2	67.6	70.4	76.1	67.7
	15.1	15.9	15.0	Fixed Assets (net)	27.7	20.7	13.8	14.0	10.5	10.4
	7.6	8.9	8.8	Intangibles (net)	6.0	6.9	8.6	7.8	7.4	14.2
	8.3	8.4	8.7	All Other Non-Current	9.0	12.2	10.0	7.8	6.0	7.7
	100.0	100.0	100.0	Total	100.0	100.0	100.0	100.0	100.0	100.0
				LIABILITIES						
	16.8	14.6	14.8	Notes Payable-Short Term	33.3	18.8	11.3	13.8	11.4	9.5
	3.2	3.9	4.1	Cur. Mat.-L.T.D.	9.0	7.2	4.3	2.7	1.7	2.7
	16.1	14.7	15.7	Trade Payables	7.8	12.3	16.1	17.4	17.9	18.6
	.4	.4	.2	Income Taxes Payable	.0	.0	.5	.1	.3	.4
	18.7	17.1	18.4	All Other Current	24.1	23.1	15.5	15.5	16.1	18.1
	55.2	50.7	53.3	Total Current	74.3	61.4	47.7	49.5	47.4	49.3
	13.0	15.9	16.1	Long-Term Debt	29.6	24.7	19.5	13.9	8.6	9.2
	.2	.2	.2	Deferred Taxes	.0	.1	.0	.1	.2	.8
	10.6	10.3	11.1	All Other Non-Current	10.8	18.1	7.6	17.6	7.3	5.3
	21.1	22.8	19.3	Net Worth	-14.6	-4.2	25.1	18.9	36.4	35.4
	100.0	100.0	100.0	Total Liabilities & Net Worth	100.0	100.0	100.0	100.0	100.0	100.0
				INCOME DATA						
	100.0	100.0	100.0	Net Sales	100.0	100.0	100.0	100.0	100.0	100.0
				Gross Profit						
	94.9	95.0	94.4	Operating Expenses	87.7	95.2	95.4	94.4	95.5	95.0
	5.1	5.0	5.6	Operating Profit	12.3	4.8	4.6	5.6	4.5	5.0
	.8	1.1	1.4	All Other Expenses (net)	4.1	1.6	1.0	1.0	.7	1.3
	4.3	3.9	4.2	Profit Before Taxes	8.2	3.2	3.6	4.6	3.8	3.7
				RATIOS						
	2.5	2.6	2.7	Current	2.9	3.2	2.7	2.6	2.8	2.0
	1.4	1.5	1.5		.8	1.4	1.7	1.5	1.8	1.4
	.9	1.0	.9		.3	.7	1.0	1.0	1.1	1.1
	2.2	2.3	2.3	Quick	2.3	3.0	2.3	2.4	2.6	1.8
(468)	1.2	1.3	1.2		.7	1.2	1.4	1.3	1.6	1.2
	.7	.8	.7		.3	.6	.7	.9	.9	1.2
30	12.0	26 14.1	26 14.1	Sales/Receivables	0 UND	17 20.9	18 20.4	34 10.6	40 9.2	41 8.8
48	7.5	47 7.7	49 7.5		14 26.4	39 9.2	45 8.2	55 6.6	56 6.5	60 6.1
69	5.3	69 5.3	70 5.2		32 11.4	63 5.8	68 5.4	73 5.0	68 5.4	76 4.8
				Cost of Sales/Inventory						
				Cost of Sales/Payables						
	7.6	6.9	7.1	Sales/Working Capital	9.6	7.4	6.8	6.6	7.3	6.9
	18.6	14.9	16.2		-66.2	22.8	15.3	14.4	11.3	15.4
	-74.3	-381.2	-98.8		-5.5	-24.5	164.3	NM	89.8	67.4
	17.0	21.4	24.4	EBIT/Interest	16.9	13.6	18.7	33.9	35.8	31.2
(369)	5.5	(428) 5.1	(487) 5.3		(32) 2.8	(96) 3.0	(70) 4.7	(79) 3.6	(100) 9.3	(110) 7.3
	1.2	1.2	1.0		-1.4	-.1	.5	-.9	1.3	2.8
	10.1	9.8	14.4	Net Profit + Depr., Dep., Amort./Cur. Mat. L/T/D						11.4
(47)	2.6	(53) 3.4	(42) 3.8						(20)	3.8
	.9	1.1	1.4							2.6
	.1	.1	.1	Fixed/Worth	.0	.1	.1	.1	.1	.1
	.4	.4	.3		3.6	1.3	.4	.3	.2	.3
	10.3	8.0	37.3		-.3	-.4	7.4	3.5	1.5	2.6
	.8	.8	.7	Debt/Worth	.8	.5	.7	.7	.6	1.2
	2.9	2.7	2.7		8.3	4.7	3.3	2.2	1.7	2.8
	-54.1	-72.3	-70.9		-2.9	-3.2	61.2	22.8	8.7	17.1
	96.4	75.2	77.7	% Profit Before Taxes/Tangible Net Worth	183.5	82.4	88.4	63.0	74.4	60.3
(347)	42.0	(399) 36.8	(461) 33.4		(29) 75.5	(77) 37.9	(66) 32.3	(82) 24.2	(106) 35.5	(101) 29.9
	12.0	11.6	7.4		15.9	3.4	3.7	2.5	10.7	10.2
	27.8	29.3	24.3	% Profit Before Taxes/Total Assets	73.5	27.4	25.1	20.7	25.3	17.4
	11.2	10.7	8.4		23.2	6.6	8.3	8.9	8.7	7.7
	1.5	.6	.5		.0	-3.4	.2	-.6	1.1	2.4
	167.4	165.9	172.4	Sales/Net Fixed Assets	229.0	117.8	197.9	178.0	181.1	188.0
	43.5	43.9	52.2		33.8	35.9	48.5	56.6	82.4	52.9
	15.8	14.8	15.9		12.3	10.7	18.5	16.8	26.6	16.1
	5.0	4.7	4.9	Sales/Total Assets	7.1	5.3	5.0	4.7	5.3	4.1
	3.3	3.4	3.2		3.7	3.3	3.1	3.2	3.6	2.7
	2.1	2.0	1.9		1.5	1.9	2.3	2.0	2.2	1.5
	.4	.4	.3	% Depr., Dep., Amort./Sales	.9	.6	.2	.3	.3	.2
(308)	1.0	(346) 1.0	(387) .8		(28) 2.2	(60) 1.9	(61) 1.0	(69) .8	(89) .6	(80) .6
	2.8	2.4	2.5		5.7	3.2	2.3	2.3	2.0	1.3
	2.9	2.9	2.2	% Officers', Directors' Owners' Comp/Sales	6.6	5.5	2.6	2.6	.9	.6
(157)	6.4	(177) 6.2	(201) 5.6		(18) 13.2	(63) 8.9	(33) 5.9	(34) 4.3	(38) 1.9	(15) 1.2
	11.7	10.8	10.2		20.7	13.8	7.9	7.3	4.1	2.7
	12201138M	13931296M	14904573M	Net Sales ($)	29560M	227994M	345381M	735708M	1992599M	11573331M
	5597101M	6459643M	7623524M	Total Assets ($)	18155M	104406M	142319M	338327M	783966M	6236351M

M = $ thousand   MM = $ million
See Pages 9 through 22 for Explanation of Ratios and Data

Current Data Sorted by Assets   Comparative Historical Data

	0-500M	500M-2MM	2-10MM	10-50MM	50-100MM	100-250MM	Type of Statement	4/1/05-3/31/06 ALL	4/1/06-3/31/07 ALL
	4	12	46	42	10	16	Unqualified	98	114
	2	10	58	6	1	1	Reviewed	75	70
	17	25	17	2			Compiled	59	52
	66	45	22	3		1	Tax Returns	74	91
	44	83	109	44	17	13	Other	212	224
		102 (4/1-9/30/09)		614 (10/1/09-3/31/10)					
NUMBER OF STATEMENTS	133	175	252	97	28	31		518	551
	%	%	%	%	%	%	ASSETS	%	%
	30.3	19.8	17.6	15.6	22.9	18.3	Cash & Equivalents	17.7	19.1
	21.7	38.9	40.5	38.2	25.1	18.9	Trade Receivables (net)	37.3	37.3
	1.5	3.4	1.6	2.7	2.0	3.1	Inventory	3.3	3.0
	6.3	5.4	7.3	8.2	9.4	9.8	All Other Current	4.9	6.8
	59.7	67.4	67.0	64.8	59.4	50.1	Total Current	63.1	66.1
	19.1	16.0	16.0	14.1	12.7	22.6	Fixed Assets (net)	17.1	15.6
	3.4	5.6	5.8	9.1	14.9	13.8	Intangibles (net)	6.7	7.4
	17.8	10.9	11.2	12.0	12.9	13.5	All Other Non-Current	13.1	10.8
	100.0	100.0	100.0	100.0	100.0	100.0	Total	100.0	100.0
							LIABILITIES		
	27.2	14.3	11.1	8.5	4.8	8.4	Notes Payable-Short Term	15.0	12.2
	6.7	2.9	2.7	1.8	3.5	2.7	Cur. Mat.-L.T.D.	3.6	2.9
	9.5	9.7	11.4	12.5	8.7	6.8	Trade Payables	11.1	10.9
	.2	.3	.4	.8	.4	1.3	Income Taxes Payable	.7	.8
	21.8	17.2	21.1	18.5	24.6	18.7	All Other Current	19.0	21.8
	65.3	44.4	46.8	42.1	42.1	37.9	Total Current	49.5	48.6
	14.1	11.2	11.6	11.3	11.5	13.3	Long-Term Debt	13.4	12.8
	.0	.1	.7	.6	1.0	1.8	Deferred Taxes	.5	.4
	10.5	9.0	6.7	6.7	6.6	10.2	All Other Non-Current	8.2	6.5
	10.1	35.3	34.2	39.2	38.9	36.8	Net Worth	28.4	31.6
	100.0	100.0	100.0	100.0	100.0	100.0	Total Liabilities & Net Worth	100.0	100.0
							INCOME DATA		
	100.0	100.0	100.0	100.0	100.0	100.0	Net Sales	100.0	100.0
							Gross Profit		
	88.5	89.8	91.3	89.6	91.9	90.6	Operating Expenses	90.4	90.0
	11.5	10.2	8.7	10.4	8.1	9.4	Operating Profit	9.6	10.0
	.8	1.8	1.9	2.5	3.0	1.1	All Other Expenses (net)	1.3	1.8
	10.7	8.4	6.8	7.9	5.1	8.3	Profit Before Taxes	8.2	8.3
							RATIOS		
	3.6	3.0	2.8	2.4	1.9	2.1	Current	3.0	3.1
	1.1	1.6	1.5	1.5	1.5	1.5		1.6	1.5
	.4	.9	1.0	1.1	1.1	1.0		.9	.9
	2.7	2.6	2.5	2.0	1.9	1.4	Quick	2.5	2.4
	1.0	1.5	1.4	1.4	1.2	1.0		1.3	1.2
	.3	.9	.8	.8	.6	.7		.7	.7
	0 UND	3 117.1	20 18.0	38 9.5	14 26.8	29 12.7	Sales/Receivables	10 36.0	11 34.4
	0 UND	42 8.7	48 7.6	60 6.1	54 6.8	49 7.5		47 7.7	45 8.0
	37 9.8	62 5.9	73 5.0	76 4.8	75 4.9	68 5.4		78 4.7	73 5.0
							Cost of Sales/Inventory		
							Cost of Sales/Payables		
	12.8	7.3	5.5	4.2	4.7	3.8	Sales/Working Capital	5.4	6.0
	157.2	15.6	12.6	9.7	8.6	10.3		15.8	16.2
	-17.2	-78.3	244.4	59.6	37.1	-286.8		-107.9	-147.9
	30.0	36.5	30.8	48.3	43.9	19.8	EBIT/Interest	30.2	34.4
	(77) 6.5	(121) 10.3	(197) 8.1	(71) 10.3	(22) 3.7	(27) 5.4		(390) 7.3	(416) 7.9
	1.0	1.3	1.3	3.2	.5	2.2		1.7	1.8
			13.8	7.1			Net Profit + Depr., Dep., Amort./Cur. Mat. L/T/D	12.1	9.0
		(34) 2.5		(16) 3.8				(64) 3.7	(70) 2.8
			.3	1.3				1.1	.5
	.0	.1	.1	.1	.2	.3	Fixed/Worth	.1	.1
	.4	.2	.3	.2	.3	.9		.3	.3
	-8.4	1.5	2.2	1.3	7.6	-3.4		2.0	2.6
	.3	.5	.7	.8	1.0	.8	Debt/Worth	.6	.7
	3.1	1.6	1.9	1.8	1.7	2.8		2.0	2.1
	-8.0	8.5	13.3	4.0	73.4	-42.6		25.3	17.9
	221.7	90.4	79.3	63.0	29.8	55.4	% Profit Before Taxes/Tangible Net Worth	84.9	83.4
	(93) 61.0	(142) 43.0	(206) 26.8	(82) 33.1	(22) 15.9	(23) 22.9		(407) 38.2	(441) 39.5
	9.2	9.0	8.5	12.4	3.0	6.5		12.3	10.8
	71.8	37.2	25.2	27.6	10.0	12.2	% Profit Before Taxes/Total Assets	30.6	34.4
	17.0	16.1	9.5	9.5	5.6	7.7		12.9	11.9
	.3	.7	1.2	3.3	-3.6	2.7		1.8	2.2
	UND	137.9	106.0	138.6	44.2	27.7	Sales/Net Fixed Assets	108.8	129.2
	81.9	51.7	39.9	44.7	21.2	10.2		38.3	42.4
	19.9	16.7	15.3	12.9	13.0	3.0		15.6	12.9
	10.8	5.0	3.9	3.2	2.2	1.8	Sales/Total Assets	4.5	4.4
	5.0	3.6	2.7	1.9	1.5	1.2		2.8	2.8
	2.9	1.8	1.6	1.3	.9	.8		1.7	1.7
	.5	.4	.5	.3	2.8	1.3	% Depr., Dep., Amort./Sales	.5	.5
	(62) 1.1	(108) 1.0	(185) 1.0	(77) .9	(13) 4.1	(22) 2.1		(363) 1.1	(373) 1.0
	2.1	2.4	2.1	2.2	5.3	3.5		2.4	2.1
	8.2	3.8	1.9	.9			% Officers', Directors' Owners' Comp/Sales	3.5	3.6
	(59) 14.0	(62) 9.2	(55) 4.5	(12) 3.3				(137) 7.8	(145) 8.4
	24.9	17.3	12.6	14.2				18.3	16.2
	186909M	741762M	3613861M	6248086M	3118444M	6622029M	Net Sales ($)	14969586M	14297679M
	28735M	206837M	1190680M	2016222M	1967114M	4976276M	Total Assets ($)	6683542M	7370251M

M = $ thousand   MM = $ million
See Pages 9 through 22 for Explanation of Ratios and Data

Comparative Historical Data | Current Data Sorted by Sales

			Type of Statement						
88	108	130	Unqualified	3	3	7	22	26	69
52	73	78	Reviewed	3	4	4	25	29	13
49	46	61	Compiled	8	17	11	14	11	
71	129	137	Tax Returns	47	44	17	20	7	2
210	248	310	Other	42	48	42	44	66	68
4/1/07-3/31/08 ALL	4/1/08-3/31/09 ALL	4/1/09-3/31/10 ALL		102 (4/1-9/30/09)			614 (10/1/09-3/31/10)		
				0-1MM	1-3MM	3-5MM	5-10MM	10-25MM	25MM & OVER
470	604	716	NUMBER OF STATEMENTS	103	116	81	125	139	152
%	%	%	ASSETS	%	%	%	%	%	%
19.6	19.6	20.4	Cash & Equivalents	18.2	29.1	23.1	18.6	18.1	17.7
37.3	36.2	34.8	Trade Receivables (net)	19.5	23.1	31.8	44.5	45.9	37.6
2.0	2.1	2.2	Inventory	2.0	1.9	3.7	1.7	2.5	2.0
5.8	6.6	7.0	All Other Current	6.2	7.5	5.6	5.4	7.0	8.9
64.8	64.4	64.4	Total Current	45.9	61.6	64.3	70.2	73.5	66.2
15.2	17.0	16.5	Fixed Assets (net)	25.5	19.4	15.0	15.3	12.5	13.4
7.4	6.6	6.5	Intangibles (net)	8.4	2.9	7.6	5.3	4.4	10.1
12.6	12.0	12.6	All Other Non-Current	20.2	16.1	13.0	9.2	9.5	10.3
100.0	100.0	100.0	Total	100.0	100.0	100.0	100.0	100.0	100.0
			LIABILITIES						
14.2	15.6	14.1	Notes Payable-Short Term	21.0	19.6	15.1	12.7	12.0	7.8
4.1	2.9	3.4	Cur. Mat.-L.T.D.	4.5	5.1	2.2	4.0	2.2	2.7
10.1	9.5	10.5	Trade Payables	12.2	5.5	8.9	10.6	13.1	11.5
.8	.7	.4	Income Taxes Payable	.0	.1	.4	.5	.6	.7
20.6	22.4	20.0	All Other Current	20.0	17.0	19.5	14.8	21.2	25.6
49.8	51.1	48.4	Total Current	57.8	47.3	46.1	42.7	49.1	48.3
11.7	11.7	12.0	Long-Term Debt	16.9	14.9	15.9	11.4	8.0	8.7
.5	.4	.5	Deferred Taxes	.1	.1	.0	.3	.6	1.2
8.2	5.8	8.1	All Other Non-Current	9.8	7.6	4.6	9.1	7.5	9.0
29.8	31.0	31.0	Net Worth	15.5	30.1	33.3	36.5	34.8	32.9
100.0	100.0	100.0	Total Liabilties & Net Worth	100.0	100.0	100.0	100.0	100.0	100.0
			INCOME DATA						
100.0	100.0	100.0	Net Sales	100.0	100.0	100.0	100.0	100.0	100.0
			Gross Profit						
90.1	89.6	90.2	Operating Expenses	80.5	89.9	90.6	91.7	92.8	93.1
9.9	10.4	9.8	Operating Profit	19.5	10.1	9.4	8.3	7.2	6.9
1.6	2.0	1.8	All Other Expenses (net)	5.1	2.3	.3	1.3	.8	1.2
8.3	8.4	8.0	Profit Before Taxes	14.4	7.8	9.1	7.0	6.3	5.7
			RATIOS						
3.0	2.6	2.8	Current	2.2	3.8	3.5	3.1	2.8	2.1
1.5	1.5	1.5		.9	1.6	1.5	1.9	1.5	1.5
1.0	1.0	.9		.3	.8	1.1	1.2	1.1	1.0
2.7	2.3	2.4	Quick	1.3	3.5	3.1	2.9	2.5	1.7
1.3	1.3	1.3		.6	1.4	1.4	1.7	1.4	1.2
.8	.8	.7		.2	.5	.7	1.0	.9	.8
7 50.5 / 6 57.9 / 8 47.1			Sales/Receivables	0 UND / 0 UND / 3 138.5			22 16.4 / 38 9.6 / 27 13.4		
48 7.5 / 45 8.1 / 42 8.6				1 281.7 / 8 47.0 / 36 10.1			48 7.6 / 52 7.1 / 50 7.3		
76 4.8 / 70 5.2 / 67 5.5				55 6.6 / 55 6.6 / 62 5.9			76 4.8 / 72 5.0 / 69 5.3		
			Cost of Sales/Inventory						
			Cost of Sales/Payables						
5.7	7.2	5.8	Sales/Working Capital	9.1	5.3	4.6	5.5	6.3	6.6
15.7	15.9	14.5		-72.0	17.2	13.2	9.4	13.2	12.5
-388.9	-304.4	-125.4		-4.5	-41.1	121.8	60.7	56.9	121.5
25.6	29.9	31.0	EBIT/Interest	28.3	24.8	35.2	34.2	28.7	49.8
(357) 6.7	(451) 8.0	(515) 8.4		(50) 6.1	(74) 5.3	(61) 6.6	(96) 12.3	(117) 9.7	(117) 10.0
2.0	2.1	1.4		.9	.1	.2	1.5	1.9	2.6
18.2	16.8	8.3	Net Profit + Depr., Dep., Amort./Cur. Mat. L/T/D				7.0	11.5	7.6
(52) 4.2	(74) 4.5	(73) 2.5				(12) 5.6	(26) 2.2	(29) 2.0	
1.5	1.1	.4					2.2	.2	.3
.1	.1	.1	Fixed/Worth	.0	.0	.1	.1	.1	.1
.3	.3	.3		.8	.3	.3	.2	.2	.3
2.0	2.3	2.8		UND	3.1	4.3	1.2	1.0	9.9
.7	.7	.6	Debt/Worth	.5	.5	.6	.6	.7	.8
2.3	2.0	1.9		4.5	1.8	1.8	1.5	1.9	1.9
12.7	12.4	16.0		-10.1	14.0	19.8	5.2	7.1	73.5
81.8	90.4	80.8	% Profit Before Taxes/Tangible Net Worth	119.2	97.8	85.9	76.9	79.5	66.1
(375) 37.9	(495) 38.7	(568) 33.7		(72) 29.1	(92) 34.1	(63) 40.5	(107) 34.1	(118) 32.1	(116) 32.3
11.0	10.8	9.1		5.1	6.7	1.7	8.2	11.0	15.4
30.5	35.1	31.9	% Profit Before Taxes/Total Assets	28.7	34.9	43.2	36.0	29.5	23.3
12.1	11.5	10.4		5.8	9.6	15.3	12.2	12.2	9.4
3.0	1.4	1.2		-.4	-.2	.4	.5	3.8	3.6
135.3	128.8	137.0	Sales/Net Fixed Assets	UND	208.0	126.5	125.3	128.7	105.1
44.1	46.0	43.0		30.2	49.8	48.5	54.7	42.9	36.6
14.6	14.0	15.0		4.5	13.6	17.9	15.1	19.7	15.7
4.3	4.6	4.7	Sales/Total Assets	3.7	5.8	4.8	4.8	4.5	4.3
2.8	2.9	2.8		1.4	3.2	2.8	3.1	2.9	2.3
1.6	1.8	1.5		.6	1.5	1.4	2.1	2.0	1.5
.4	.4	.5	% Depr., Dep., Amort./Sales	.8	.5	.3	.5	.5	.4
(315) 1.0	(407) 1.0	(467) 1.0		(48) 3.0	(72) 1.4	(51) .8	(88) 1.0	(103) .9	(105) .9
2.1	2.1	2.4		12.3	2.6	1.9	2.0	1.9	2.4
3.4	3.4	3.7	% Officers', Directors' Owners' Comp/Sales	10.4	7.5	5.7	2.3	1.6	.4
(119) 8.6	(166) 6.9	(191) 10.2		(35) 18.5	(52) 11.6	(27) 10.6	(37) 5.1	(29) 3.4	(11) 1.0
16.7	12.8	17.3		29.4	20.3	16.0	11.5	8.8	15.5
16782558M	22653996M	20531091M	Net Sales ($)	48416M	215190M	316869M	895999M	2280212M	16774405M
8546200M	9406455M	10385864M	Total Assets ($)	90108M	174953M	184641M	549577M	1132590M	8253995M

M = $ thousand   MM = $ million
See Pages 9 through 22 for Explanation of Ratios and Data

Current Data Sorted by Assets | Comparative Historical Data

Type of Statement

0-500M	500M-2MM	2-10MM	10-50MM	50-100MM	100-250MM	Type of Statement	4/1/05-3/31/06 ALL	4/1/06-3/31/07 ALL
	4	9	11	2	4	Unqualified	15	29
3	6	15	2			Reviewed	15	18
9	5	6				Compiled	21	17
13	4	2				Tax Returns	13	24
	16	24	7	1	4	Other	42	65
	18 (4/1-9/30/09)		129 (10/1/09-3/31/10)					
25	35	56	20	3	8	**NUMBER OF STATEMENTS**	106	153
%	%	%	%	%	%	**ASSETS**	%	%
38.1	21.8	19.0	16.4			Cash & Equivalents	16.7	20.2
15.7	38.7	40.1	31.5			Trade Receivables (net)	49.5	41.3
.0	.1	.9	1.2			Inventory	.4	.2
5.1	4.6	4.3	6.9			All Other Current	6.3	5.5
58.9	65.3	64.2	56.1			Total Current	72.9	67.2
14.7	16.7	16.8	14.7			Fixed Assets (net)	9.0	12.0
8.2	8.7	5.3	18.1			Intangibles (net)	7.9	8.4
18.2	9.3	13.7	11.1			All Other Non-Current	10.2	12.4
100.0	100.0	100.0	100.0			Total	100.0	100.0
						LIABILITIES		
39.6	19.5	10.9	7.2			Notes Payable-Short Term	26.9	16.1
1.7	6.0	1.5	4.1			Cur. Mat.-L.T.D.	2.9	3.1
24.1	6.5	8.3	4.3			Trade Payables	9.7	8.4
.0	.5	.6	.9			Income Taxes Payable	.5	.8
32.1	26.8	23.1	17.1			All Other Current	28.3	24.7
97.6	59.3	44.4	33.7			Total Current	68.3	53.1
7.1	25.6	10.9	11.5			Long-Term Debt	7.6	17.8
.0	.1	.7	1.0			Deferred Taxes	.3	.3
4.9	4.7	4.8	6.4			All Other Non-Current	9.3	6.1
-9.2	10.3	39.2	47.4			Net Worth	14.5	22.7
100.0	100.0	100.0	100.0			Total Liabilities & Net Worth	100.0	100.0
						INCOME DATA		
100.0	100.0	100.0	100.0			Net Sales	100.0	100.0
						Gross Profit		
91.3	94.3	95.6	96.4			Operating Expenses	93.2	95.0
8.7	5.7	4.4	3.6			Operating Profit	6.8	5.0
.8	3.1	.9	.8			All Other Expenses (net)	1.3	1.6
7.9	2.6	3.5	2.7			Profit Before Taxes	5.5	3.4
						RATIOS		
1.9	3.0	2.5	2.5			Current	2.0	2.1
.9	1.5	1.4	1.5				1.4	1.3
.5	.6	1.1	1.2				.9	.9
1.9	2.9	2.4	2.3			Quick	1.7	2.0
.7	1.4	1.2	1.2				1.3	1.2
.3	.5	1.0	1.0				.8	.7
0 UND	5 75.3	23 15.9	33 11.0			Sales/Receivables	17 21.2	5 68.6
0 UND	24 15.3	38 9.7	52 7.0				42 8.7	38 9.7
26 14.0	45 8.2	54 6.8	63 5.8				62 5.9	60 6.0
						Cost of Sales/Inventory		
						Cost of Sales/Payables		
17.9	9.2	7.5	5.2			Sales/Working Capital	10.5	10.8
-999.8	22.5	20.8	14.7				24.4	30.0
-16.6	-21.1	97.0	27.8				-49.9	-90.6
14.3	11.1	24.3	43.9			EBIT/Interest	21.5	11.5
(15) 4.0	(25) 3.4	(41) 5.2	(15) 11.3				(88) 7.5	(127) 4.0
-6.8	-4.2	.5	3.0				1.8	.9
						Net Profit + Depr., Dep., Amort./Cur. Mat. L/T/D	19.9	17.8
							(12) 5.5	(17) 3.5
							1.6	-1.6
.0	.0	.1	.2			Fixed/Worth	.0	.1
.5	.1	.2	.6				.2	.3
-.3	12.4	1.1	2.7				.8	UND
.5	.6	.6	.6			Debt/Worth	1.1	1.1
3.3	1.9	1.5	1.7				2.4	4.4
-3.3	208.7	3.8	9.5				-327.3	-44.9
231.8	79.7	75.8	47.1			% Profit Before Taxes/Tangible Net Worth	86.8	108.5
(13) 55.2	(27) 18.7	(50) 25.8	(16) 26.8				(79) 46.8	(112) 31.3
23.8	-3.3	7.4	3.6				12.9	8.3
109.6	24.4	24.7	16.7			% Profit Before Taxes/Total Assets	33.8	23.3
26.0	4.7	9.3	5.2				14.5	7.8
-16.3	-8.9	1.0	1.0				3.3	-.1
UND	999.8	188.1	101.5			Sales/Net Fixed Assets	441.4	283.6
227.6	111.4	59.8	19.0				83.9	78.9
45.2	26.8	9.7	6.3				33.5	30.8
17.0	8.5	5.3	3.4			Sales/Total Assets	7.4	8.6
7.0	4.6	3.9	1.9				4.8	4.6
3.0	2.6	1.7	1.2				2.6	2.3
.1	.4	.3	.5			% Depr., Dep., Amort./Sales	.2	.2
(11) .4	(17) .7	(40) .8	(15) 1.2				(71) .6	(102) .5
.7	2.8	3.8	1.8				1.4	1.2
4.1	3.2	1.1				% Officers', Directors' Owners' Comp/Sales	2.0	2.3
(13) 13.6	(11) 4.7	(12) 4.2					(30) 4.3	(34) 7.1
27.8	13.0	7.8					8.9	12.6
49806M	224170M	1421274M	1164552M	403285M	2805528M	Net Sales ($)	2377561M	6125637M
4909M	38719M	268114M	418563M	171981M	1332201M	Total Assets ($)	538347M	1351051M

M = $ thousand   MM = $ million
See Pages 9 through 22 for Explanation of Ratios and Data

Comparative Historical Data

Current Data Sorted by Sales

			Type of Statement						
20	27	30	Unqualified			1	4	7	18
23	15	23	Reviewed			2	7	11	3
15	19	14	Compiled	3	3	2	1	4	1
10	18	15	Tax Returns	3	3	3	4	2	
51	75	65	Other	12	8	7	6	16	16
4/1/07-3/31/08	4/1/08-3/31/09	4/1/09-3/31/10			18 (4/1-9/30/09)			129 (10/1/09-3/31/10)	
ALL	ALL	ALL		0-1MM	1-3MM	3-5MM	5-10MM	10-25MM	25MM & OVER
119	154	147	NUMBER OF STATEMENTS	18	14	15	22	40	38
%	%	%	ASSETS	%	%	%	%	%	%
16.3	20.7	22.3	Cash & Equivalents	38.8	24.5	17.2	27.8	17.3	17.9
44.7	41.7	33.9	Trade Receivables (net)	13.1	21.0	27.3	30.3	47.6	38.7
.8	.8	.5	Inventory	.0	.4	.2	1.2	.7	.5
4.8	6.6	5.3	All Other Current	6.4	1.7	.9	5.0	3.3	10.2
66.6	69.7	62.1	Total Current	58.4	47.6	45.6	64.4	68.9	67.3
13.5	13.6	15.3	Fixed Assets (net)	30.9	21.4	15.5	20.9	9.8	8.2
6.2	7.4	10.0	Intangibles (net)	5.7	8.0	14.6	7.1	8.0	14.7
13.6	9.3	12.6	All Other Non-Current	5.1	23.0	24.3	7.5	13.3	9.8
100.0	100.0	100.0	Total	100.0	100.0	100.0	100.0	100.0	100.0
			LIABILITIES						
21.3	15.8	16.9	Notes Payable-Short Term	27.2	25.4	10.9	21.5	16.0	9.3
3.2	2.0	3.5	Cur. Mat.-L.T.D.	1.1	1.2	6.3	7.5	2.2	3.4
10.4	8.7	10.2	Trade Payables	33.1	2.2	5.6	6.9	9.0	7.4
.7	.5	.6	Income Taxes Payable	.1	.0	.0	1.8	.3	1.1
27.5	23.2	25.3	All Other Current	40.7	11.7	38.3	13.1	23.0	27.6
63.2	50.2	56.6	Total Current	102.1	40.5	61.2	50.9	50.5	48.8
7.4	14.7	13.5	Long-Term Debt	23.4	13.8	26.8	22.1	6.1	6.2
.6	.4	.5	Deferred Taxes	.0	.0	.0	.5	1.1	.6
6.3	6.2	5.4	All Other Non-Current	3.3	11.9	7.9	6.8	3.2	4.7
22.7	28.5	24.0	Net Worth	-28.3	33.8	4.2	19.6	39.0	39.6
100.0	100.0	100.0	Total Liabilities & Net Worth	100.0	100.0	100.0	100.0	100.0	100.0
			INCOME DATA						
100.0	100.0	100.0	Net Sales	100.0	100.0	100.0	100.0	100.0	100.0
			Gross Profit						
95.7	95.4	94.8	Operating Expenses	82.6	90.7	96.5	98.7	97.7	96.0
4.3	4.6	5.2	Operating Profit	17.4	9.3	3.5	1.3	2.3	4.0
.8	1.0	1.5	All Other Expenses (net)	7.2	1.5	.9	-.1	.5	1.0
3.5	3.6	3.7	Profit Before Taxes	10.2	7.7	2.6	1.3	1.8	3.0
			RATIOS						
2.4	2.6	2.5		2.7	2.9	2.2	2.6	2.9	2.2
1.3	1.4	1.3	Current	.9	1.0	1.2	1.3	1.7	1.4
.8	1.0	.9		.3	.7	.2	.9	1.2	1.0
2.2	2.5	2.4		2.7	2.7	2.1	2.6	2.9	1.8
1.2	1.2	1.2	Quick	.7	1.0	1.2	1.2	1.5	1.1
.7	.8	.8		.3	.7	.1	.5	1.1	.8
12 30.5	9 42.1	9 39.0		0 UND	0 UND	5 75.3	0 UND	30 12.0	23 16.0
44 8.3	36 10.1	35 10.6	Sales/Receivables	0 UND	18 20.2	25 14.7	22 16.6	40 9.0	47 7.8
62 5.9	59 6.2	53 6.9		25 14.5	54 6.7	46 7.9	44 8.2	63 5.8	57 6.4
			Cost of Sales/Inventory						
			Cost of Sales/Payables						
9.0	8.4	8.7		12.9	12.2	9.2	7.5	7.1	11.4
25.2	22.0	22.5	Sales/Working Capital	UND	NM	97.9	17.6	19.8	23.1
-85.1	-977.9	-141.8		-10.4	-16.9	-7.3	NM	50.5	252.1
19.3	21.7	14.9		10.8	14.9	9.1	23.3	24.3	43.3
(97) 4.8	(123) 6.3	(106) 4.1	EBIT/Interest	(10) 5.3	(10) 3.5	(11) .7	(18) 4.4	(29) 4.0	(28) 9.9
1.0	1.3	-.1		-2.8	-1.6	-6.4	-5.4	.5	1.8
34.8	31.0	8.5							
(10) 16.9	(12) 12.2	(12) 2.1	Net Profit + Depr., Dep., Amort./Cur. Mat. L/T/D						
3.6	1.2	-.4							
.1	.1	.0		.0	.1	.0	.1	.0	.1
.3	.3	.3	Fixed/Worth	.4	.6	.7	.6	.2	.4
25.0	2.1	7.1		-19.7	-1.8	-.3	NM	1.1	NM
.7	.8	.6		.6	.4	.6	.6	.5	.7
2.7	1.8	1.7	Debt/Worth	6.0	4.6	1.0	1.5	1.5	1.7
-94.0	19.4	-808.2		-3.0	-10.7	-1.4	-5.0	3.7	NM
68.0	79.6	74.0		82.3	260.5	97.8	61.6	57.9	70.9
(89) 32.8	(125) 33.8	(110) 28.9	% Profit Before Taxes/Tangible Net Worth	(10) 37.1	(10) 94.4	(11) 56.8	(16) 7.9	(34) 22.7	(29) 36.3
4.6	5.3	4.5		5.8	17.1	-3.9	-5.2	3.3	6.9
22.8	28.5	26.0		50.6	41.8	36.4	15.8	24.2	25.6
8.9	10.1	7.0	% Profit Before Taxes/Total Assets	18.7	14.5	2.6	2.6	10.3	6.2
.6	.7	-1.2		-4.2	2.5	-26.4	-13.8	1.1	.2
290.0	383.8	364.0		UND	147.6	618.0	195.9	561.7	234.4
71.8	76.0	62.5	Sales/Net Fixed Assets	126.9	28.3	32.4	57.9	72.2	94.5
28.9	21.6	15.3		3.5	5.7	6.3	5.3	31.3	20.1
6.7	6.9	6.5		10.3	5.2	4.6	7.7	5.8	5.9
4.2	4.2	3.7	Sales/Total Assets	3.0	2.3	2.9	4.1	4.5	3.7
2.5	2.1	1.8		1.6	1.2	1.2	2.2	2.5	1.8
.2	.2	.3					.4	.2	.3
(82) .5	(106) .6	(89) .7	% Depr., Dep., Amort./Sales				(16) 1.0	(27) .5	(23) .6
1.0	1.7	1.9					4.0	1.2	1.5
1.4	1.9	2.9						1.5	
(22) 3.5	(45) 3.8	(40) 5.4	% Officers', Directors' Owners' Comp/Sales					(14) 4.2	
7.9	10.0	14.9						9.0	
3957832M	9053837M	6068615M	Net Sales ($)	8772M	24763M	56365M	160561M	624468M	5193686M
1188674M	2066991M	2234487M	Total Assets ($)	6298M	19348M	33255M	74845M	205381M	1895360M

M = $ thousand   MM = $ million
See Pages 9 through 22 for Explanation of Ratios and Data

PROFESSIONAL SERVICES—Marketing Consulting Services NAICS 541613

Current Data Sorted by Assets							Comparative Historical Data	

							Type of Statement		
	1	5	9		7		Unqualified	11	15
	3	14	4	2			Reviewed	6	8
5	8	8	2				Compiled	9	11
11	11	6	1				Tax Returns	10	10
17	18	21	12	5	3		Other	31	61
	18 (4/1-9/30/09)		155 (10/1/09-3/31/10)					4/1/05-	4/1/06-
								3/31/06	3/31/07
0-500M	500M-2MM	2-10MM	10-50MM	50-100MM	100-250MM			ALL	ALL
33	41	54	28	7	10		NUMBER OF STATEMENTS	67	105
%	%	%	%	%	%		ASSETS	%	%
31.5	17.8	19.1	18.7		8.4		Cash & Equivalents	15.6	16.7
22.3	38.5	37.8	29.6		24.5		Trade Receivables (net)	39.8	35.9
5.0	4.7	4.5	6.0		10.4		Inventory	8.1	4.2
3.8	4.5	5.5	8.0		8.9		All Other Current	3.9	6.1
62.5	65.5	66.9	62.3		52.1		Total Current	67.4	62.9
16.1	14.3	16.2	10.4		23.1		Fixed Assets (net)	15.4	13.1
2.4	7.6	5.4	19.8		19.8		Intangibles (net)	7.8	11.3
18.9	12.5	11.5	7.5		5.1		All Other Non-Current	9.5	12.7
100.0	100.0	100.0	100.0		100.0		Total	100.0	100.0
							LIABILITIES		
31.2	7.8	9.8	2.5		2.4		Notes Payable-Short Term	16.1	15.5
1.9	2.7	3.8	2.7		3.6		Cur. Mat.-L.T.D.	2.4	1.6
7.4	20.0	15.0	16.6		12.0		Trade Payables	21.6	17.7
1.1	.0	.2	.3		.2		Income Taxes Payable	.4	.6
14.7	13.6	25.0	26.0		17.9		All Other Current	15.7	18.6
56.3	44.1	53.8	48.1		36.2		Total Current	56.2	54.0
11.7	8.5	10.9	8.9		22.6		Long-Term Debt	10.6	12.2
.4	.0	.1	.7		.7		Deferred Taxes	.4	.2
10.1	12.6	8.1	3.3		8.3		All Other Non-Current	15.2	8.8
21.7	34.8	27.1	39.0		32.2		Net Worth	17.6	24.9
100.0	100.0	100.0	100.0		100.0		Total Liabilties & Net Worth	100.0	100.0
							INCOME DATA		
100.0	100.0	100.0	100.0		100.0		Net Sales	100.0	100.0
							Gross Profit		
90.0	94.8	92.5	91.8		94.0		Operating Expenses	93.6	92.0
10.0	5.2	7.5	8.2		6.0		Operating Profit	6.4	8.0
1.9	.0	1.5	1.5		2.5		All Other Expenses (net)	1.6	1.1
8.1	5.2	6.0	6.7		3.4		Profit Before Taxes	4.9	6.8
							RATIOS		
2.8	4.6	2.5	2.1		2.1			2.0	2.2
1.3	1.7	1.3	1.3		1.7		Current	1.2	1.4
.5	1.1	.8	1.0		1.0			.9	.8
2.8	2.4	2.0	1.3		1.6			1.7	1.9
1.2	1.3	1.1	1.0		1.2		Quick	1.0	1.1
.3	.8	.7	.7		.5			.7	.6
0 UND	19 19.5	20 17.9	29 12.8		39 9.4			22 16.6	29 12.8
2 196.0	44 8.3	49 7.4	52 7.0		52 7.1		Sales/Receivables	48 7.7	49 7.4
49 7.5	72 5.1	78 4.7	88 4.2		62 5.9			65 5.6	69 5.3
							Cost of Sales/Inventory		
							Cost of Sales/Payables		
11.8	8.1	7.6	6.5		5.5			6.9	6.7
32.7	19.6	19.9	16.6		7.2		Sales/Working Capital	30.9	21.7
-30.3	531.7	-14.8	NM		NM			-38.7	-33.4
12.4	34.9	35.0	28.6					34.0	16.2
(19) 1.5	(33) 3.1	(45) 4.7	(21) 3.8				EBIT/Interest	(56) 6.3	(82) 3.4
-6.8	-1.0	1.2	1.4					1.2	.0
							Net Profit + Depr., Dep.,		73.2
							Amort./Cur. Mat. L/T/D	(14)	18.6
									1.1
.0	.1	.1	.1		.3			.2	.1
.3	.3	.6	.5		2.2		Fixed/Worth	.7	.4
2.5	-7.4	-1.8	NM		-.8			-1.2	-1.1
.6	.4	.7	.9		1.3			.8	.9
1.5	1.8	4.5	4.2		55.1		Debt/Worth	5.8	3.3
NM	-66.3	-12.3	NM		-5.0			-6.6	-8.1
225.1	83.5	94.2	116.7				% Profit Before Taxes/Tangible	111.9	95.2
(25) 66.3	(30) 33.1	(38) 42.8	(21) 23.9				Net Worth	(47) 40.6	(71) 48.5
3.1	7.3	4.1	-.9					15.5	20.6
109.9	26.3	27.5	17.4		12.5		% Profit Before Taxes/Total	26.9	28.7
26.8	5.8	12.0	9.5		3.7		Assets	9.2	11.8
-6.2	-.9	.6	.5		.3			1.6	.7
UND	250.2	84.6	62.1		20.7			156.6	104.2
74.5	42.7	35.4	27.8		11.1		Sales/Net Fixed Assets	33.1	38.4
12.8	17.2	13.6	11.9		5.1			12.3	14.6
8.3	6.4	3.7	3.2		2.2			4.5	4.2
4.3	3.4	2.8	2.0		1.7		Sales/Total Assets	3.3	2.8
2.7	1.9	1.9	1.2		1.0			1.9	1.8
.6	.7	.5	.8					.5	.5
(12) 1.9	(26) 1.6	(45) 1.0	(20) 1.8				% Depr., Dep., Amort./Sales	(46) 1.2	(71) 1.1
3.7	2.3	2.1	2.5					2.7	2.6
5.2	2.5	3.9						4.3	2.7
(16) 9.0	(23) 6.6	(18) 6.0					% Officers', Directors'	(22) 8.1	(31) 4.7
24.3	16.8	8.8					Owners' Comp/Sales	16.2	10.2
70716M	251183M	787383M	1543112M	538217M	2905860M		Net Sales ($)	8719190M	3781817M
8605M	52451M	270478M	698007M	469617M	1632676M		Total Assets ($)	1780237M	2181947M

M = $ thousand   MM = $ million
See Pages 9 through 22 for Explanation of Ratios and Data

Comparative Historical Data   **Current Data Sorted by Sales**

19	22	24	Type of Statement						
12	13	21	Unqualified				1	7	16
15	21	23	Reviewed	2	2		5	8	6
24	28	29	Compiled		5	4	7	4	1
67	74	76	Tax Returns	3	10	5	6	4	1
4/1/07-	4/1/08-	4/1/09-	Other	11	14	5	8	17	21
3/31/08	3/31/09	3/31/10			18 (4/1-9/30/09)			155 (10/1/09-3/31/10)	
ALL	ALL	ALL		0-1MM	1-3MM	3-5MM	5-10MM	10-25MM	25MM & OVER
137	158	173	NUMBER OF STATEMENTS	16	31	14	27	40	45
%	%	%		%	%	%	%	%	%
			ASSETS						
18.8	17.6	20.0	Cash & Equivalents	22.7	18.5	20.4	22.8	24.7	14.1
30.7	31.5	32.2	Trade Receivables (net)	15.5	31.3	42.4	34.0	38.0	29.2
4.0	4.1	5.5	Inventory	5.1	6.3	6.0	2.2	4.0	8.2
7.8	7.3	5.3	All Other Current	4.6	2.7	2.9	6.6	4.9	7.8
61.3	60.5	63.0	Total Current	47.8	58.8	71.7	65.7	71.6	59.3
15.2	14.8	14.7	Fixed Assets (net)	22.3	16.1	18.2	16.2	10.1	13.3
10.1	11.8	10.5	Intangibles (net)	5.6	5.8	2.6	9.0	8.9	20.2
13.4	13.0	11.8	All Other Non-Current	24.3	19.3	7.4	9.1	9.4	7.2
100.0	100.0	100.0	Total	100.0	100.0	100.0	100.0	100.0	100.0
			LIABILITIES						
16.8	22.4	11.6	Notes Payable-Short Term	28.7	22.9	7.4	8.9	6.9	4.9
2.4	3.3	2.9	Cur. Mat.-L.T.D.	.9	2.7	2.6	2.2	4.7	2.8
13.5	13.9	14.8	Trade Payables	3.7	10.4	14.2	17.4	18.6	17.1
.6	.1	.4	Income Taxes Payable	2.3	.0	.0	.0	.3	.3
22.9	18.3	19.7	All Other Current	5.5	14.7	20.9	22.2	27.9	18.9
56.2	58.0	49.4	Total Current	41.0	50.8	45.1	50.7	58.5	43.9
10.8	11.0	11.0	Long-Term Debt	22.4	14.6	6.9	7.7	6.7	11.6
.2	.2	.3	Deferred Taxes	.9	.0	.1	.0	.3	.6
10.4	13.8	8.6	All Other Non-Current	17.3	4.9	16.0	8.4	9.1	5.3
22.5	17.0	30.7	Net Worth	18.4	29.9	31.9	33.2	25.3	38.6
100.0	100.0	100.0	Total Liabilities & Net Worth	100.0	100.0	100.0	100.0	100.0	100.0
			INCOME DATA						
100.0	100.0	100.0	Net Sales	100.0	100.0	100.0	100.0	100.0	100.0
			Gross Profit						
92.0	94.8	92.6	Operating Expenses	81.2	95.1	96.8	90.4	93.8	93.9
8.0	5.2	7.4	Operating Profit	18.8	4.9	3.2	9.6	6.2	6.1
1.3	1.5	1.3	All Other Expenses (net)	7.9	.2	-1.1	.4	1.0	1.4
6.7	3.7	6.1	Profit Before Taxes	10.8	4.8	4.3	9.2	5.2	4.7
			RATIOS						
2.2	2.2	2.5		2.9	3.3	3.4	2.5	2.5	1.9
1.3	1.3	1.3	Current	1.6	1.3	1.7	1.3	1.4	1.3
1.0	.8	.9		.4	.7	1.1	.9	.8	1.0
2.0	1.9	1.9		2.9	2.1	2.9	2.2	1.7	1.3
1.0	1.0	1.2	Quick	1.2	1.2	1.5	1.2	1.2	1.1
.6	.5	.7		.2	.5	.8	.7	.8	.7
13 28.8	17 22.0	18 20.1		0 UND	0 UND	21 17.7	21 17.7	20 17.9	26 14.0
47 7.8	41 8.9	43 8.5	Sales/Receivables	3 137.9	33 11.0	57 6.4	40 9.2	44 8.3	45 8.2
68 5.4	60 6.0	68 5.3		72 5.1	62 5.9	79 4.6	62 5.9	81 4.5	68 5.3
			Cost of Sales/Inventory						
			Cost of Sales/Payables						
8.0	7.4	7.7		7.0	10.4	5.6	8.0	8.0	7.2
24.2	25.8	19.6	Sales/Working Capital	25.8	23.9	11.5	24.7	23.1	18.8
-188.2	-29.2	-57.7		-3.2	-18.2	98.7	-55.0	-22.3	686.5
29.1	22.5	24.7			12.0	23.5	93.9	58.3	27.3
(102) 4.5	(123) 3.3	(134) 3.7	EBIT/Interest		(21) 2.9	(12) 11.4	(22) 3.2	(32) 12.1	(38) 3.5
1.3	-1.2	.7			-4.4	.9	.5	.1	1.2
16.4	6.9	4.3							
(17) 4.6	(21) 1.9	(15) 1.5	Net Profit + Depr., Dep., Amort./Cur. Mat. L/T/D						
2.0	-.4	.7							
.1	.1	.1		.1	.0	.1	.2	.1	.2
.4	.6	.5	Fixed/Worth	.6	.2	.5	.5	.5	.6
4.9	-1.2	-2.5		-5.3	1.7	-1.0	-2.0	-.8	-1.2
.9	1.0	.8		.5	.6	.4	.5	.9	1.2
3.7	3.8	3.4	Debt/Worth	5.5	1.8	1.2	2.9	6.0	5.0
176.3	-7.1	-12.2		-5.1	16.3	-5.4	-13.7	-11.0	-6.4
104.6	109.1	108.2		185.3	66.4	78.4	170.3	117.1	77.4
(105) 44.1	(107) 33.0	(122) 39.1	% Profit Before Taxes/Tangible Net Worth	(10) 91.4	(26) 33.3	(10) 41.7	(18) 12.7	(27) 68.1	(31) 22.7
3.1	7.2	4.7		-18.7	4.7	3.3	1.9	30.0	.3
29.2	22.2	25.9		80.6	30.4	27.5	23.3	31.3	17.5
10.6	8.0	7.5	% Profit Before Taxes/Total Assets	1.6	6.1	15.8	5.8	16.3	5.0
.4	-1.4	.2		-10.0	-.6	3.8	.4	.5	.3
135.9	134.3	111.6		UND	UND	80.9	115.8	112.5	62.6
36.5	31.4	35.2	Sales/Net Fixed Assets	19.9	71.8	36.2	41.4	38.9	26.7
11.1	13.8	12.8		5.9	12.5	11.1	12.5	22.8	11.5
4.2	4.3	4.6		2.8	5.6	5.3	4.7	5.6	3.4
2.7	3.0	2.7	Sales/Total Assets	1.8	3.2	2.5	3.4	3.1	2.1
1.6	1.8	1.7		1.1	1.9	1.9	2.0	2.2	1.4
.6	.6	.6			1.1	.4	.6	.5	.4
(98) 1.3	(96) 1.3	(109) 1.4	% Depr., Dep., Amort./Sales		(17) 1.9	(11) 1.6	(17) 1.0	(31) 1.0	(28) 1.6
2.5	3.0	2.2			3.3	2.9	2.8	1.9	2.5
4.2	2.9	2.9			5.0		2.3	1.7	
(38) 6.7	(47) 4.4	(60) 6.5	% Officers', Directors' Owners' Comp/Sales		(15) 10.8		(15) 5.8	(11) 6.5	
12.4	13.4	15.3			16.8		22.7	9.2	
4202060M	8142211M	6096471M	Net Sales ($)	6422M	62321M	52106M	195872M	650587M	5129163M
2907232M	3642460M	3131834M	Total Assets ($)	13017M	30728M	20155M	77394M	294083M	2696457M

© RMA 2010

M = $ thousand   MM = $ million
See Pages 9 through 22 for Explanation of Ratios and Data

Current Data Sorted by Assets

	1	11	11	4	5
1	4	8	4		1
2	3	9			
9		3			
4	15	23	11	3	3
	17 (4/1-9/30/09)		118 (10/1/09-3/31/10)		
0-500M	500M-2MM	2-10MM	10-50MM	50-100MM	100-250MM
16	23	54	26	7	9

%	%	%	%	%	%
23.3	15.9	8.2	6.6		
35.5	43.7	45.5	40.2		
2.6	4.5	5.4	6.2		
6.5	3.4	6.6	5.1		
67.9	67.5	65.8	58.1		
16.4	9.8	18.0	21.8		
1.4	3.8	5.4	12.8		
14.3	18.8	10.9	7.3		
100.0	100.0	100.0	100.0		
23.7	11.7	16.5	19.1		
5.2	.5	5.6	4.1		
19.5	17.3	17.9	19.8		
.0	.4	.3	.7		
15.4	12.6	11.7	11.4		
63.9	42.6	52.0	55.2		
1.4	4.1	9.3	8.3		
.0	.2	.2	.7		
5.8	6.5	6.9	1.1		
28.8	46.6	31.6	34.7		
100.0	100.0	100.0	100.0		
100.0	100.0	100.0	100.0		
94.6	90.9	98.5	97.0		
5.4	9.1	1.5	3.0		
.4	.5	.8	1.0		
5.0	8.6	.7	2.1		

Comparative Historical Data:

Comparative Historical Data

Type of Statement		
Unqualified	9	13
Reviewed	17	5
Compiled	11	12
Tax Returns	3	3
Other	32	35
	4/1/05-3/31/06 ALL	4/1/06-3/31/07 ALL
NUMBER OF STATEMENTS	72	68

ASSETS	%	%
Cash & Equivalents	9.6	10.2
Trade Receivables (net)	49.0	43.0
Inventory	4.7	5.4
All Other Current	4.3	6.3
Total Current	67.6	64.9
Fixed Assets (net)	17.1	17.7
Intangibles (net)	5.7	8.1
All Other Non-Current	9.6	9.4
Total	100.0	100.0

LIABILITIES		
Notes Payable-Short Term	12.6	12.6
Cur. Mat.-L.T.D.	7.0	5.4
Trade Payables	21.2	17.1
Income Taxes Payable	.3	.6
All Other Current	13.1	15.0
Total Current	54.3	50.8
Long-Term Debt	12.1	12.1
Deferred Taxes	1.0	.6
All Other Non-Current	6.4	3.6
Net Worth	26.3	33.0
Total Liabilities & Net Worth	100.0	100.0

INCOME DATA		
Net Sales	100.0	100.0
Gross Profit		
Operating Expenses	95.7	96.0
Operating Profit	4.3	4.0
All Other Expenses (net)	.8	.3
Profit Before Taxes	3.6	3.7

RATIOS

					Current		
2.5	3.2	2.1	1.3			2.1	2.3
1.2	1.6	1.3	1.0		Current	1.3	1.5
.4	.9	1.0	.9			1.0	.9
2.3	2.6	1.8	1.1			1.9	1.9
.8	1.6	1.1	.8		Quick	1.2	1.3
.3	.7	.7	.6			.8	.7

	Sales/Receivables		
0 UND	19 19.7	33 11.0	34 10.6	33 11.1	27 13.4
28 13.2	40 9.2	53 6.9	51 7.1	47 7.8	44 8.3
47 7.7	61 6.0	68 5.4	68 5.4	72 5.0	63 5.8

Cost of Sales/Inventory

Cost of Sales/Payables

				Sales/Working Capital		
8.5	7.1	7.9	16.2		8.6	8.5
NM	14.7	28.7	-483.1		29.4	19.9
-24.4	-125.8	-137.5	-33.4		895.6	-174.0

				EBIT/Interest		
	53.4	9.7	10.1		15.5	21.8
(18) 13.5	(49) 3.6	(22) 4.9		(62) 6.1	(53) 4.9
.5	.0	2.7		2.1	1.4

				Net Profit + Depr., Dep., Amort./Cur. Mat. L/T/D		
	7.1	3.7		7.1	38.0
(11) .4	(11) 2.6		(21) 2.9	(13) 3.0
.1	1.7		1.0	1.7

				Fixed/Worth		
.0	.0	.2	.2		.1	.1
.0	.1	.3	1.0		.3	.4
3.9	.4	1.7	NM		1.5	3.9

				Debt/Worth		
.5	.4	.7	1.5		.9	.9
2.7	1.1	2.2	4.0		2.3	2.9
NM	4.8	8.6	NM		6.7	16.0

				% Profit Before Taxes/Tangible Net Worth		
72.0	86.6	49.5	50.7		67.0	91.8
(12) 34.5	(20) 28.2	(46) 13.1	(20) 22.3	(59) 27.0	(56) 30.9
-.3	13.6	-.7	10.8		11.1	10.2

				% Profit Before Taxes/Total Assets		
73.5	45.7	17.6	11.9		18.8	20.9
10.0	16.3	3.6	6.1		9.1	8.8
-.2	-.9	-2.8	2.8		2.9	2.2

				Sales/Net Fixed Assets		
UND	999.8	78.3	90.7		201.4	157.3
UND	84.2	38.1	24.9		37.2	46.4
35.8	22.5	11.4	9.0		10.7	9.6

				Sales/Total Assets		
13.9	5.7	4.5	3.8		5.2	6.4
6.4	3.6	3.2	2.6		3.3	3.5
4.4	2.4	2.1	1.6		2.1	2.2

				% Depr., Dep., Amort./Sales		
		.3	.4		.3	.3
	(40) .7	(23) .8		(49) .9	(45) .6
		2.1	3.8		2.8	2.7

				% Officers', Directors' Owners' Comp/Sales		
		2.4			1.6	.8
	(14) 3.1			(21) 3.6	(16) 2.7
		5.9			6.2	4.8

						Net Sales ($)		
31155M	227867M	925108M	2026312M	871230M	4421881M	3217610M	7833080M
3627M	28028M	270881M	689212M	477671M	1567027M	1173345M	1476005M

Total Assets ($)

Comparative Historical Data | Current Data Sorted by Sales

Type of Statement											
14	27	32	Unqualified		1	1	2	8	20
7	13	18	Reviewed		2	1	4	4	7
14	8	14	Compiled		2	2	4	3	3
8	9	12	Tax Returns	4	3	2	1	1	1
42	51	59	Other	6	2	8	2	1	21
4/1/07-3/31/08 ALL	4/1/08-3/31/09 ALL	4/1/09-3/31/10 ALL			17 (4/1-9/30/09)		118 (10/1/09-3/31/10)		
				0-1MM	1-3MM	3-5MM	5-10MM	10-25MM	25MM & OVER
85	108	135	NUMBER OF STATEMENTS	10	10	13	22	28	52
%	%	%	ASSETS	%	%	%	%	%	%
13.3	12.7	11.8	Cash & Equivalents	17.5	16.5	12.4	12.0	6.3	12.4
39.2	43.7	41.4	Trade Receivables (net)	38.9	26.8	33.1	43.1	53.5	39.6
4.4	5.0	4.7	Inventory	13.3	.1	1.0	5.8	4.1	4.7
7.2	5.0	5.8	All Other Current	3.7	5.0	2.9	7.3	6.4	6.0
64.2	66.3	63.6	Total Current	73.4	48.3	49.4	68.2	70.2	62.8
15.6	15.6	17.7	Fixed Assets (net)	6.8	25.0	17.1	23.1	16.3	16.9
10.9	8.0	7.2	Intangibles (net)	.7	3.6	7.1	1.4	5.1	12.8
9.3	10.1	11.5	All Other Non-Current	19.1	23.1	26.4	7.3	8.4	7.5
100.0	100.0	100.0	Total	100.0	100.0	100.0	100.0	100.0	100.0
			LIABILITIES						
14.9	16.3	16.1	Notes Payable-Short Term	29.3	10.9	18.9	20.0	11.4	14.8
2.8	3.0	4.1	Cur. Mat.-L.T.D.	6.7	1.7	.6	3.0	5.9	4.4
16.0	22.5	18.4	Trade Payables	13.9	12.1	13.7	15.1	23.9	20.0
.5	.2	.4	Income Taxes Payable	.0	.0	.5	.2	.2	.6
19.1	17.1	12.3	All Other Current	11.7	10.7	5.3	13.5	9.2	15.7
53.3	59.1	51.3	Total Current	61.7	35.4	39.0	51.8	50.6	55.5
12.1	14.3	7.4	Long-Term Debt	.0	15.3	6.9	5.9	9.7	6.8
.2	.3	.4	Deferred Taxes	.0	.0	.9	.1	.0	.7
7.1	4.5	5.0	All Other Non-Current	.0	5.8	8.2	8.8	5.3	3.3
27.2	21.7	36.0	Net Worth	38.4	43.4	45.0	33.4	34.4	33.7
100.0	100.0	100.0	Total Liabilities & Net Worth	100.0	100.0	100.0	100.0	100.0	100.0
			INCOME DATA						
100.0	100.0	100.0	Net Sales	100.0	100.0	100.0	100.0	100.0	100.0
			Gross Profit						
94.4	95.2	95.9	Operating Expenses	90.0	91.7	97.4	97.7	95.6	96.8
5.6	4.8	4.1	Operating Profit	10.0	8.3	2.6	2.3	4.4	3.2
1.9	.5	.8	All Other Expenses (net)	1.2	1.7	1.5	.2	.8	.7
3.8	4.3	3.3	Profit Before Taxes	8.8	6.5	1.1	2.1	3.5	2.6
			RATIOS						
2.3	1.8	2.1		2.1	2.9	3.1	2.2	2.4	1.7
1.3	1.2	1.2	Current	1.4	1.1	1.8	1.5	1.4	1.1
.9	.9	.9		.4	.8	.7	.7	1.0	.9
1.8	1.6	1.8		2.1	2.4	2.2	2.0	1.9	1.5
1.0	1.0	1.0	Quick	.7	1.1	1.8	1.0	1.2	.9
.7	.7	.7		.3	.8	.6	.5	.8	.7
25 14.6	26 14.1	29 12.8		17 21.3	0 UND	19 18.7	22 16.6	41 8.8	32 11.3
38 9.6	39 9.3	45 8.1	Sales/Receivables	28 13.2	45 8.1	35 10.3	50 7.3	55 6.7	44 8.2
61 6.0	59 6.2	63 5.8		74 4.9	56 6.5	52 7.1	86 4.2	65 5.6	60 6.1
			Cost of Sales/Inventory						
			Cost of Sales/Payables						
9.4	11.8	9.1		6.1	9.2	6.4	6.9	7.0	15.1
24.9	38.6	33.9	Sales/Working Capital	12.9	29.6	10.0	13.0	19.6	145.9
-159.9	-82.4	-42.3		-9.8	-36.5	-71.2	-18.4	NM	-42.6
17.3	13.3	16.0				55.3	36.0	12.2	14.2
(72) 5.3	(91) 4.8	(112) 4.5	EBIT/Interest	(12) 12.7	(17) 3.6	(26) 4.1	(43) 5.0
1.7	1.3	.5				-6.3	-1.6	.2	2.3
32.5	8.4	6.0							8.3
(11) 6.4	(18) 3.2	(26) 2.3	Net Profit + Depr., Dep., Amort./Cur. Mat. L/T/D					(14) 2.6
1.4	1.2	.7							1.0
.1	.1	.1		.0	.0	.0	.1	.2	.2
.5	.4	.3	Fixed/Worth	.0	.6	.2	.3	.4	.5
4.0	2.4	1.8		.1	4.2	1.3	5.6	1.1	2.6
.8	1.0	.7		.4	.4	.4	.5	.7	1.2
2.8	3.2	2.3	Debt/Worth	1.6	2.4	.9	1.7	2.5	4.0
-50.1	86.5	7.3		NM	4.4	NM	10.0	5.1	10.3
79.0	85.4	55.9				48.9	50.2	34.0	64.4
(63) 44.0	(85) 35.0	(113) 20.2	% Profit Before Taxes/Tangible Net Worth	(10) 26.3	(18) 26.1	(25) 9.1	(43) 22.1
10.9	12.6	2.7				-11.5	-5.4	-2.2	7.6
27.3	19.4	16.8		31.4	46.1	47.1	26.6	10.1	12.9
9.0	7.0	5.9	% Profit Before Taxes/Total Assets	9.5	9.1	16.3	8.1	3.4	5.8
2.0	1.0	.0		-.9	.8	-6.8	-8.0	-2.2	2.0
210.9	251.1	124.4		UND	UND	375.9	82.8	83.1	99.1
38.7	50.9	39.4	Sales/Net Fixed Assets	UND	47.4	24.9	28.1	38.6	37.0
13.0	18.1	13.8		74.1	10.5	12.6	8.2	15.4	13.6
6.5	7.0	5.0		6.6	6.5	5.0	5.3	4.4	5.2
3.5	3.9	3.3	Sales/Total Assets	4.2	3.5	3.1	2.8	3.2	3.4
2.0	2.2	2.0		1.2	.6	1.8	2.1	2.7	1.9
.4	.4	.4					.8	.5	.4
(48) .9	(67) .9	(88) 1.0	% Depr., Dep., Amort./Sales	(14) 1.4	(22) .7	(39) .7
2.2	2.5	2.5					2.9	1.9	2.5
1.4	1.6	2.3							2.0
(17) 5.5	(17) 3.5	(27) 3.4	% Officers', Directors' Owners' Comp/Sales					(10) 2.3
7.7	11.0	6.9							2.5
5730996M	13110248M	8503553M	Net Sales ($)	5518M	18249M	50371M	148305M	505458M	7775652M
2000834M	2817040M	3036446M	Total Assets ($)	3833M	20225M	63824M	51307M	221865M	2675392M

© RMA 2010

M = $ thousand   MM = $ million
See Pages 9 through 22 for Explanation of Ratios and Data

Current Data Sorted by Assets — Comparative Historical Data

Type of Statement	0-500M	500M-2MM	2-10MM	10-50MM	50-100MM	100-250MM		4/1/05-3/31/06 ALL	4/1/06-3/31/07 ALL
Unqualified	1	6	37	27	10	9		60	86
Reviewed	1	9	34	6	4			58	62
Compiled	9	16	13	4	3			40	45
Tax Returns	32	31	8	3				38	48
Other	26	51	52	40	8	10		147	160
		57 (4/1-9/30/09)		386 (10/1/09-3/31/10)					
NUMBER OF STATEMENTS	69	113	144	80	18	19		343	401
	%	%	%	%	%	%		%	%
ASSETS									
Cash & Equivalents	30.0	18.5	15.2	16.6	20.1	10.4		15.6	17.1
Trade Receivables (net)	22.8	38.1	51.5	40.7	22.9	28.5		44.4	43.2
Inventory	2.3	4.6	2.4	1.7	1.2	1.0		3.0	2.3
All Other Current	6.0	6.4	6.9	9.8	6.7	10.8		6.5	7.7
Total Current	61.1	67.6	75.9	68.8	50.9	50.7		69.5	70.3
Fixed Assets (net)	19.4	17.4	12.3	12.4	20.4	17.4		16.4	15.3
Intangibles (net)	6.8	5.1	4.5	7.4	18.6	24.0		4.9	4.7
All Other Non-Current	12.7	10.0	7.3	11.4	10.1	7.9		9.2	9.7
Total	100.0	100.0	100.0	100.0	100.0	100.0		100.0	100.0
LIABILITIES									
Notes Payable-Short Term	39.9	14.2	11.5	10.5	13.4	6.1		14.8	14.7
Cur. Mat.-L.T.D.	5.1	2.9	2.7	3.9	1.4	2.5		3.8	3.4
Trade Payables	7.9	14.5	14.9	12.5	8.7	8.3		14.7	13.6
Income Taxes Payable	.1	.7	1.1	1.2	.2	1.6		.9	1.2
All Other Current	43.2	16.6	20.5	18.1	26.2	18.2		16.0	18.7
Total Current	96.2	48.9	50.7	46.2	49.9	36.7		50.1	51.6
Long-Term Debt	10.5	10.7	10.1	7.0	6.1	23.5		12.9	11.5
Deferred Taxes	.0	.1	.3	.3	.5	1.5		.7	.7
All Other Non-Current	11.7	6.6	5.3	7.1	10.9	10.3		6.3	6.9
Net Worth	-18.4	33.7	33.6	39.3	32.5	28.0		30.0	29.3
Total Liabilities & Net Worth	100.0	100.0	100.0	100.0	100.0	100.0		100.0	100.0
INCOME DATA									
Net Sales	100.0	100.0	100.0	100.0	100.0	100.0		100.0	100.0
Gross Profit									
Operating Expenses	90.4	91.8	93.3	91.7	93.2	92.8		91.3	91.3
Operating Profit	9.6	8.2	6.7	8.3	6.8	7.2		8.7	8.7
All Other Expenses (net)	.2	2.1	2.1	2.0	1.6	6.1		1.3	1.4
Profit Before Taxes	9.4	6.0	4.6	6.3	5.2	1.1		7.4	7.3
RATIOS									
Current	2.0	3.9	2.6	2.3	1.7	2.1		2.5	2.5
	.9	1.5	1.5	1.5	1.2	1.3		1.5	1.5
	.2	.9	1.1	1.1	.9	.8		1.1	1.0
Quick	1.8	3.0	2.2	2.1	1.6	1.5		2.2	2.2
	.7	1.4	1.3	1.2	1.1	.9		(342) 1.3	1.3
	.2	.6	.9	.9	.7	.5		.9	.8
Sales/Receivables	0 UND	12 30.4	39 9.3	45 8.2	25 14.8	26 14.1		22 16.7	27 13.5
	0 UND	40 9.2	64 5.7	66 5.5	38 9.6	57 6.4		58 6.3	57 6.5
	35 10.4	69 5.3	84 4.3	86 4.2	61 5.9	107 3.4		89 4.1	88 4.1
Cost of Sales/Inventory									
Cost of Sales/Payables									
Sales/Working Capital	16.1	6.7	5.3	4.5	11.2	4.7		5.7	5.7
	-194.5	14.8	10.5	8.7	39.8	14.6		12.7	12.6
	-10.8	-69.4	55.5	37.2	-12.5	-16.6		81.1	97.7
EBIT/Interest	15.3	37.5	43.2	87.7	108.9	9.3		24.0	27.4
	(36) 3.6	(86) 7.7	(115) 13.7	(66) 13.0	(16) 2.4	(16) 6.4		(274) 7.4	(312) 7.0
	-.8	1.9	1.6	2.4	.7	.0		1.7	1.8
Net Profit + Depr., Dep., Amort./Cur. Mat. L/T/D			8.9	61.8				5.4	11.3
			(24) 1.9	(17) 7.4				(57) 2.6	(65) 3.7
			.3	1.7				1.2	1.4
Fixed/Worth	.0	.1	.1	.1	.3	.1		.1	.1
	.3	.4	.2	.2	9.9	1.2		.3	.3
	UND	6.4	.8	.9	-.4	-.2		2.1	1.4
Debt/Worth	.6	.4	.7	.9	1.1	1.4		.7	.7
	6.7	1.7	2.0	1.7	18.9	4.8		2.0	1.9
	-2.6	524.8	5.5	4.6	-10.7	-1.9		12.2	10.8
% Profit Before Taxes/Tangible Net Worth	262.7	93.6	62.5	57.2	96.2	66.1		85.3	79.4
	(43) 63.1	(86) 38.6	(123) 28.9	(69) 29.7	(11) 30.4	(13) 23.6		(284) 36.8	(338) 38.3
	22.3	6.7	7.9	6.6	1.3	-16.6		8.9	12.4
% Profit Before Taxes/Total Assets	74.2	28.4	20.6	20.2	15.3	16.1		27.2	29.6
	22.4	9.2	9.1	9.3	4.0	4.0		9.4	10.7
	-4.8	.8	.9	1.7	-.2	-3.9		1.6	3.3
Sales/Net Fixed Assets	UND	170.4	107.3	129.5	50.8	46.4		98.7	107.5
	87.0	55.1	43.6	37.8	19.5	24.7		37.0	38.7
	17.9	12.7	18.7	22.4	7.9	11.8		15.2	14.8
Sales/Total Assets	11.9	4.9	3.8	3.2	2.7	2.4		4.2	4.1
	5.4	3.4	3.0	2.0	1.7	1.4		2.8	2.8
	3.5	2.0	1.9	1.2	1.1	.5		1.8	1.8
% Depr., Dep., Amort./Sales	.7	.2	.4	.4				.5	.4
	(28) 1.5	(74) .7	(111) .9	(57) .8				(258) 1.3	(295) 1.1
	3.4	2.2	1.9	1.8				2.3	2.2
% Officers', Directors' Owners' Comp/Sales	3.5	2.7	1.7					3.1	3.2
	(25) 8.2	(51) 6.0	(35) 2.7					(96) 6.5	(103) 6.8
	17.7	13.5	8.5					18.0	16.3
Net Sales ($)	108280M	511248M	2050079M	3851897M	2708530M	4384280M		11121142M	15242730M
Total Assets ($)	14623M	133768M	699331M	1742958M	1274094M	2892926M		4172270M	5357656M

© RMA 2010

M = $ thousand   MM = $ million
See Pages 9 through 22 for Explanation of Ratios and Data

Comparative Historical Data

Current Data Sorted by Sales

			Type of Statement						
80	78	90	Unqualified	1	4	5	12	22	46
42	53	50	Reviewed	1	3	4	14	17	11
41	43	42	Compiled	1	3	4	7	8	2
48	76	74	Tax Returns	5	12	8	7	8	2
154	165	187	Other	20	22	6	14	9	3
4/1/07-3/31/08 ALL	4/1/08-3/31/09 ALL	4/1/09-3/31/10 ALL		23	35	13	25	46	45
						57 (4/1-9/30/09)		386 (10/1/09-3/31/10)	
				0-1MM	1-3MM	3-5MM	5-10MM	10-25MM	25MM & OVER
365	415	443	NUMBER OF STATEMENTS	50	76	36	72	102	107
%	%	%	ASSETS	%	%	%	%	%	%
15.7	17.6	18.6	Cash & Equivalents	27.3	19.5	16.8	21.3	16.1	15.0
42.8	41.6	39.5	Trade Receivables (net)	15.8	29.3	38.5	49.2	47.5	44.0
2.5	3.0	2.7	Inventory	1.7	4.0	6.1	3.9	1.2	1.8
6.7	6.1	7.3	All Other Current	6.6	5.2	7.9	4.8	9.0	9.1
67.6	68.3	68.1	Total Current	51.3	58.0	69.2	79.2	73.7	70.0
16.1	14.9	15.3	Fixed Assets (net)	29.1	19.8	19.5	11.5	11.2	10.5
7.0	6.5	6.9	Intangibles (net)	5.8	7.8	1.5	4.0	5.8	11.7
9.2	10.3	9.7	All Other Non-Current	13.8	14.4	9.8	5.2	9.3	7.8
100.0	100.0	100.0	Total	100.0	100.0	100.0	100.0	100.0	100.0
			LIABILITIES						
12.7	17.7	16.2	Notes Payable-Short Term	35.3	23.2	18.0	8.4	12.4	10.8
3.1	4.3	3.3	Cur. Mat.-L.T.D.	2.1	4.5	1.2	2.0	4.9	3.0
14.5	12.0	12.8	Trade Payables	9.1	10.6	12.6	13.6	14.1	14.2
.8	.8	.9	Income Taxes Payable	.0	.7	1.1	.1	1.2	1.4
19.6	20.3	22.7	All Other Current	52.8	12.3	17.3	18.3	19.7	23.8
50.7	54.9	55.9	Total Current	99.3	51.3	50.2	42.4	52.3	53.2
14.1	15.2	10.2	Long-Term Debt	19.6	14.8	8.8	9.9	5.7	7.3
.3	.6	.3	Deferred Taxes	.0	.1	.0	.3	.2	.6
8.4	6.0	7.4	All Other Non-Current	12.6	11.8	6.1	3.3	5.6	6.9
26.5	23.3	26.3	Net Worth	-31.5	22.0	34.9	44.1	36.2	32.0
100.0	100.0	100.0	Total Liabilities & Net Worth	100.0	100.0	100.0	100.0	100.0	100.0
			INCOME DATA						
100.0	100.0	100.0	Net Sales	100.0	100.0	100.0	100.0	100.0	100.0
			Gross Profit						
90.2	90.8	92.1	Operating Expenses	82.0	92.8	93.3	94.4	94.7	92.2
9.8	9.2	7.9	Operating Profit	18.0	7.2	6.7	5.6	5.3	7.8
2.0	2.6	2.0	All Other Expenses (net)	5.8	1.5	1.5	1.2	1.3	1.9
7.9	6.6	5.9	Profit Before Taxes	12.2	5.8	5.2	4.5	4.1	6.0
			RATIOS						
2.6	2.4	2.5		2.2	3.5	2.6	4.6	2.2	2.1
1.5	1.5	1.4	Current	.9	1.5	1.7	1.9	1.3	1.4
1.0	1.0	1.0		.2	.6	1.0	1.3	1.0	1.0
2.3	2.1	2.1		1.8	3.4	1.9	3.5	2.1	1.7
(364) 1.3	(414) 1.3	1.2	Quick	.7	1.2	1.2	1.7	1.2	1.2
.8	.8	.7		.2	.4	.5	1.1	.9	.8
21 17.0	23 15.6	21 17.7		0 UND	0 UND	23 16.1	35 10.6	31 11.6	39 9.3
55 6.6	50 7.3	51 7.1	Sales/Receivables	0 UND	31 11.7	56 6.5	52 7.0	59 6.2	60 6.1
86 4.2	80 4.6	78 4.7		40 9.1	72 5.1	92 4.0	75 4.9	83 4.4	80 4.6
			Cost of Sales/Inventory						
			Cost of Sales/Payables						
5.6	6.0	6.2		9.5	6.3	4.7	4.7	6.8	7.1
13.6	14.6	14.7	Sales/Working Capital	-136.8	31.4	8.9	8.5	20.4	15.5
UND	-131.3	-140.7		-6.9	-18.7	762.2	25.0	-893.5	261.6
20.1	27.0	42.4		5.8	12.7	46.5	59.9	46.7	81.1
(271) 6.7	(322) 8.0	(335) 8.0	EBIT/Interest	(19) 2.8	(54) 3.6	(27) 7.8	(53) 16.9	(88) 12.3	(94) 9.1
1.8	2.0	1.6		1.5	.1	1.6	2.5	2.3	1.9
5.0	14.9	17.6						17.1	45.0
(43) 2.4	(61) 3.0	(60) 2.6	Net Profit + Depr., Dep., Amort./Cur. Mat. L/T/D				(19) 2.1	(24) 6.8	
1.3	1.0	.9						.3	1.6
.1	.1	.1		.0	.0	.0	.1	.1	.1
.3	.3	.3	Fixed/Worth	1.4	.4	.2	.1	.3	.3
7.1	3.4	2.0		-6.1	4.2	1.3	.7	.9	18.6
.7	.7	.7		.7	.6	.8	.3	.8	1.1
2.2	2.1	2.1	Debt/Worth	21.8	2.0	1.6	.9	2.4	3.0
50.4	47.4	22.5		-2.1	765.0	4.6	4.9	9.1	29.7
80.3	83.4	71.3		220.0	93.1	57.2	65.8	69.4	71.2
(281) 34.0	(320) 36.0	(345) 32.7	% Profit Before Taxes/Tangible Net Worth	(28) 39.1	(58) 21.1	(31) 38.3	(62) 26.7	(84) 40.6	(82) 34.1
11.3	8.4	8.3		7.9	1.4	9.8	7.8	11.9	13.8
27.2	28.6	25.7		41.2	32.1	27.2	26.1	23.7	20.8
11.0	11.5	9.8	% Profit Before Taxes/Total Assets	9.8	5.4	14.0	11.3	10.3	10.1
2.4	1.7	.8		-3.1	-.2	1.1	.9	1.8	2.4
115.2	151.9	143.9		UND	707.5	147.9	118.7	135.7	129.4
41.0	43.8	43.8	Sales/Net Fixed Assets	24.8	47.2	46.3	47.8	43.5	45.2
15.3	15.7	16.6		3.4	11.6	9.3	19.2	21.5	22.8
4.0	4.6	4.4		6.1	5.0	4.2	4.4	4.2	3.9
2.7	2.8	3.0	Sales/Total Assets	2.5	3.2	3.2	3.5	3.0	2.7
1.7	1.8	1.7		.7	1.7	1.9	2.2	1.9	1.5
.4	.5	.4		1.9	.6	.3	.4	.4	.3
(259) 1.0	(264) 1.2	(287) .9	% Depr., Dep., Amort./Sales	(23) 3.6	(45) 1.6	(24) .7	(57) .8	(68) .8	(70) .7
2.2	2.4	2.1		13.7	4.0	1.7	1.7	1.8	1.6
3.2	3.1	2.3		4.8	3.1	3.6	2.6	1.4	
(90) 6.3	(107) 8.2	(119) 5.0	% Officers', Directors' Owners' Comp/Sales	(15) 9.6	(31) 7.1	(14) 5.7	(30) 4.1	(20) 3.8	
15.6	17.0	9.8		17.2	16.7	8.1	8.3	9.1	
10382991M	15472197M	13614314M	Net Sales ($)	22686M	146338M	140856M	527494M	1675063M	11101877M
5551582M	7298284M	6757700M	Total Assets ($)	30532M	99636M	154421M	225114M	889991M	5358006M

M = $ thousand   MM = $ million
See Pages 9 through 22 for Explanation of Ratios and Data

PROFESSIONAL SERVICES—Environmental Consulting Services NAICS 541620

	Current Data Sorted by Assets						Type of Statement	Comparative Historical Data	
		2	8	9		1	Unqualified	6	15
	2	5	19	2			Reviewed	11	18
	3	6	6				Compiled	8	14
	13	9	2				Tax Returns	5	16
	9	14	26	8			Other	23	31
		12 (4/1-9/30/09)		132 (10/1/09-3/31/10)				4/1/05-3/31/06	4/1/06-3/31/07
	0-500M	500M-2MM	2-10MM	10-50MM	50-100MM	100-250MM		ALL	ALL
	27	36	61	19		1	NUMBER OF STATEMENTS	53	94
	%	%	%	%	%	%	ASSETS	%	%
	21.5	11.6	13.5	17.0			Cash & Equivalents	9.6	11.1
	28.3	39.9	52.3	50.0			Trade Receivables (net)	49.4	48.3
	2.3	3.4	1.5	1.0			Inventory	1.6	2.1
	3.1	4.8	6.4	6.9			All Other Current	7.8	5.3
	55.2	59.8	73.8	74.9			Total Current	68.4	66.9
	17.6	24.8	18.0	14.6			Fixed Assets (net)	23.1	22.9
	9.6	5.2	1.8	6.4			Intangibles (net)	3.2	4.4
	17.6	10.2	6.4	4.0			All Other Non-Current	5.4	5.8
	100.0	100.0	100.0	100.0			Total	100.0	100.0
							LIABILITIES		
	21.1	9.5	8.1	9.1			Notes Payable-Short Term	12.6	14.9
	4.8	4.1	3.3	3.4			Cur. Mat.-L.T.D.	2.8	3.3
	5.5	11.8	12.1	17.3			Trade Payables	11.3	13.3
	.0	.5	1.5	.9			Income Taxes Payable	1.5	1.1
	18.1	9.2	11.6	13.0			All Other Current	11.5	14.5
	49.5	35.1	36.7	43.7			Total Current	39.7	47.2
	29.7	12.0	9.0	7.5			Long-Term Debt	12.5	16.1
	.0	1.1	.6	1.4			Deferred Taxes	.5	.7
	4.7	3.7	2.9	3.0			All Other Non-Current	2.5	3.4
	16.0	48.1	50.8	44.4			Net Worth	44.9	32.6
	100.0	100.0	100.0	100.0			Total Liabilities & Net Worth	100.0	100.0
							INCOME DATA		
	100.0	100.0	100.0	100.0			Net Sales	100.0	100.0
							Gross Profit		
	92.2	96.6	94.0	94.9			Operating Expenses	93.1	92.7
	7.8	3.4	6.0	5.1			Operating Profit	6.9	7.3
	.2	1.1	.6	1.0			All Other Expenses (net)	.8	1.6
	7.6	2.3	5.4	4.1			Profit Before Taxes	6.1	5.6
							RATIOS		
	2.3	3.4	3.1	2.4				2.7	2.2
	1.1	1.5	2.1	1.9			Current	1.7	1.5
	.5	1.0	1.4	1.4				1.2	1.1
	1.8	2.9	2.8	2.2				2.4	1.8
	.8	1.3	2.0	1.6			Quick	1.6	1.3
	.3	.7	1.3	1.1				1.0	.9
	0 UND	21 17.1	57 6.4	65 5.6				48 7.6	46 7.9
	18 20.7	53 6.8	70 5.2	83 4.4			Sales/Receivables	74 4.9	75 4.9
	54 6.8	84 4.4	95 3.8	133 2.7				103 3.5	100 3.6
							Cost of Sales/Inventory		
							Cost of Sales/Payables		
	10.9	6.4	4.2	3.1				5.1	6.0
	250.5	17.7	6.5	5.5			Sales/Working Capital	9.8	13.9
	-11.3	NM	12.7	10.1				33.1	72.5
	34.3	39.5	34.9	30.7				26.0	23.6
	(18) 6.2	(31) 4.6	(50) 9.3	(15) 8.3			EBIT/Interest	(48) 7.3	(82) 6.2
	.2	-2.1	2.1	1.9				2.5	2.2
							Net Profit + Depr., Dep.,	8.1	11.8
							Amort./Cur. Mat. L/T/D	(13) 2.2	(18) 3.2
								1.4	1.0
	.0	.1	.1	.2				.3	.2
	1.4	.4	.3	.3			Fixed/Worth	.4	.5
	-3.4	2.0	.5	.5				.9	1.7
	.7	.3	.5	.6				.5	1.0
	5.2	1.0	.9	1.1			Debt/Worth	1.6	1.9
	-8.2	6.3	2.2	4.7				3.1	5.0
	554.5	54.3	39.2	30.1			% Profit Before Taxes/Tangible	49.7	61.9
	(19) 101.3	(30) 19.1	(59) 17.6	(17) 20.0			Net Worth	(51) 22.1	(81) 28.5
	11.4	-29.3	5.4	9.0				9.0	13.2
	56.1	31.1	19.5	12.1			% Profit Before Taxes/Total	21.6	24.8
	23.7	4.6	9.6	8.3			Assets	8.6	10.5
	.3	-11.1	2.7	1.2				3.5	3.1
	UND	55.2	45.0	58.0				30.3	48.2
	42.7	17.2	19.1	15.7			Sales/Net Fixed Assets	15.0	18.3
	16.9	6.5	8.9	8.0				7.3	10.4
	7.7	4.3	3.1	2.6				3.1	3.5
	5.1	2.8	2.5	1.6			Sales/Total Assets	2.5	2.6
	2.1	2.0	1.8	1.2				2.0	1.8
	.4	.8	.8	.5				1.1	.9
	(16) 1.1	(30) 1.6	(56) 1.5	(16) 1.8			% Depr., Dep., Amort./Sales	(43) 2.0	(73) 1.7
	3.5	4.1	2.7	3.6				2.8	3.2
	7.9	5.9	2.2				% Officers', Directors'	6.6	3.6
	(15) 11.9	(17) 8.7	(20) 4.5				Owners' Comp/Sales	(18) 13.1	(37) 9.2
	13.6	16.4	8.1					20.8	14.4
	28371M	148450M	699368M	714235M		490778M	Net Sales ($)	664285M	1609693M
	6075M	45561M	290587M	395638M		201243M	Total Assets ($)	269200M	605201M

M = $ thousand   MM = $ million

See Pages 9 through 22 for Explanation of Ratios and Data

Comparative Historical Data   Current Data Sorted by Sales

Current Data groupings: **12 (4/1-9/30/09)** and **132 (10/1/09-3/31/10)**

	14 / 4/1/07-3/31/08 ALL	14 / 4/1/08-3/31/09 ALL	20 / 4/1/09-3/31/10 ALL	0-1MM	1-3MM	3-5MM	5-10MM	10-25MM	25MM & OVER
Type of Statement									
Unqualified	14	14	20	1		2	1	8	8
Reviewed	13	20	28		4	2	10	10	1
Compiled	6	15	15	1	4	3	5	2	1
Tax Returns	13	20	24	7	12	1	3		
Other	36	57	57	6	13	5	13	15	5
NUMBER OF STATEMENTS	82	126	144	14	34	13	32	36	15
	%	%	%	%	%	%	%	%	%
ASSETS									
Cash & Equivalents	10.8	15.4	15.0	18.0	18.8	11.3	10.4	16.6	12.4
Trade Receivables (net)	43.8	38.7	44.2	36.0	24.6	60.9	49.7	51.6	52.6
Inventory	2.2	2.2	2.0	.2	4.1	.2	3.1	1.1	.9
All Other Current	5.7	6.3	5.6	4.9	1.6	3.1	8.6	6.1	9.7
Total Current	62.5	62.6	66.8	59.0	49.1	75.4	71.9	75.4	75.6
Fixed Assets (net)	25.5	22.3	19.2	19.6	25.1	18.3	19.7	14.6	16.0
Intangibles (net)	3.1	5.0	4.8	9.4	7.8	3.4	.8	4.6	4.1
All Other Non-Current	8.9	10.1	9.2	12.0	18.0	2.9	7.6	5.4	4.3
Total	100.0	100.0	100.0	100.0	100.0	100.0	100.0	100.0	100.0
LIABILITIES									
Notes Payable-Short Term	14.7	13.1	11.0	19.9	13.2	15.2	9.2	7.5	6.0
Cur. Mat.-L.T.D.	4.5	4.8	3.8	3.3	5.7	1.9	4.6	2.7	2.8
Trade Payables	14.1	13.0	11.5	5.8	7.1	13.2	11.8	15.6	15.0
Income Taxes Payable	1.3	.9	.9	.0	.1	.4	.3	2.4	1.2
All Other Current	11.9	12.7	12.5	18.5	9.7	9.9	9.7	14.4	17.1
Total Current	46.5	44.5	39.7	47.4	35.8	40.6	35.7	42.7	42.1
Long-Term Debt	20.8	15.9	13.4	33.7	21.9	5.1	10.3	5.7	7.4
Deferred Taxes	.5	.4	.7	.0	.5	.0	.9	.8	2.1
All Other Non-Current	3.8	4.6	3.5	9.1	4.2	2.4	2.1	3.1	1.8
Net Worth	28.4	34.7	42.6	9.6	37.6	51.9	51.1	47.7	46.7
Total Liabilities & Net Worth	100.0	100.0	100.0	100.0	100.0	100.0	100.0	100.0	100.0
INCOME DATA									
Net Sales	100.0	100.0	100.0	100.0	100.0	100.0	100.0	100.0	100.0
Gross Profit									
Operating Expenses	93.1	94.3	94.5	92.2	94.0	90.4	96.7	95.2	94.6
Operating Profit	6.9	5.7	5.5	7.8	6.0	9.6	3.3	4.8	5.4
All Other Expenses (net)	1.8	1.4	.7	.2	1.1	1.2	1.0	.1	.8
Profit Before Taxes	5.1	4.3	4.8	7.6	4.9	8.4	2.3	4.6	4.6
RATIOS									
Current	2.1	2.4	2.8	3.4	4.5	3.3	3.6	2.6	2.2
	1.4	1.6	1.8	1.2	1.4	2.3	2.4	2.0	1.7
	1.1	1.0	1.1	.6	.6	1.2	1.4	1.3	1.5
Quick	1.9	2.3	2.6	2.9	3.5	3.3	2.6	2.5	1.9
	1.2	1.3	1.5	1.0	1.2	2.1	1.8	1.7	1.6
	.8	.9	1.0	.4	.5	1.2	1.1	1.2	1.1
Sales/Receivables	53 7.0	33 11.0	35 10.5	0 UND	0 UND	55 6.6	55 6.6	52 7.0	55 6.7
	75 4.9	59 6.2	63 5.8	47 7.8	24 15.5	91 4.0	64 5.7	72 5.0	67 5.5
	98 3.7	83 4.4	91 4.0	81 4.5	59 6.2	174 2.1	87 4.2	93 3.9	87 4.2
Cost of Sales/Inventory									
Cost of Sales/Payables									
Sales/Working Capital	5.9	6.3	5.0	9.3	6.5	1.7	4.6	4.4	5.2
	12.6	13.3	8.8	35.8	22.5	4.9	7.3	6.9	9.0
	92.0	178.9	51.0	-9.8	-16.9	51.0	16.0	21.6	11.8
EBIT/Interest	21.3	23.8	34.5		40.2	36.3	13.7	52.0	38.8
	(67) 5.5	(105) 7.4	(115) 8.3	(29) 4.6	(10) 11.8	(26) 3.8	(31) 16.4	(11) 10.1	
	1.7	1.5	1.2		-.9	2.3	.0	2.1	6.6
Net Profit + Depr., Dep., Amort./Cur. Mat. L/T/D	8.1	16.5	10.1						
	(13) 1.6	(15) 7.0	(20) 3.1						
	1.3	1.4	.8						
Fixed/Worth	.2	.2	.1	.0	.1	.1	.2	.1	.2
	.6	.5	.4	1.2	1.0	.4	.4	.3	.3
	3.1	2.5	1.3	-1.4	NM	.8	.6	.5	.8
Debt/Worth	.9	.7	.5	.6	.2	.5	.4	.5	.6
	1.9	1.6	1.1	4.9	2.2	.7	.9	.9	1.1
	6.1	6.6	4.0	-5.5	NM	1.9	2.3	3.2	2.1
% Profit Before Taxes/Tangible Net Worth	52.2	56.0	47.3		138.4	42.6	23.8	47.3	37.6
	(69) 28.6	(106) 24.3	(126) 20.1	(26) 25.5	(12) 23.1	(31) 13.1	(34) 20.9	(14) 21.9	
	14.4	8.1	3.5		1.4	-33.5	-8.3	5.5	13.1
% Profit Before Taxes/Total Assets	23.5	21.0	23.8	62.0	45.2	25.8	11.9	21.1	23.2
	9.4	8.9	9.2	8.7	16.5	16.0	5.7	11.5	9.5
	2.7	.5	.2	-14.4	-4.0	-6.2	-3.7	2.2	4.8
Sales/Net Fixed Assets	40.0	49.1	56.5	UND	97.3	36.4	38.3	48.4	58.0
	17.3	21.2	20.8	39.6	26.9	15.3	20.0	22.4	26.5
	6.0	9.1	8.8	10.8	5.4	8.5	9.5	10.8	10.2
Sales/Total Assets	3.3	3.6	3.7	5.3	6.0	3.0	3.4	3.3	3.7
	2.2	2.6	2.6	2.5	2.8	2.0	2.6	2.4	2.6
	1.6	1.8	1.7	1.2	1.9	1.2	1.8	1.8	2.2
% Depr., Dep., Amort./Sales	1.0	1.0	.7		.6	.6	1.0	.6	.5
	(69) 2.1	(93) 1.9	(119) 1.4	(23) 1.3	(11) 1.6	(30) 1.9	(34) 1.4	(13) .9	
	3.9	3.5	3.4		7.7	2.8	3.4	2.3	2.5
% Officers', Directors' Owners' Comp/Sales	2.4	2.8	4.3		6.8		4.8	1.8	
	(25) 5.6	(40) 8.9	(54) 7.9	(17) 10.2		(12) 7.1	(10) 3.9		
	13.2	14.9	13.7		13.2		12.4	15.9	
Net Sales ($)	1509591M	2326648M	2081202M	6614M	67236M	50631M	232219M	550470M	1174032M
Total Assets ($)	755692M	1058086M	939104M	2557M	31942M	45966M	95046M	269503M	494090M

M = $ thousand   MM = $ million
See Pages 9 through 22 for Explanation of Ratios and Data

PROFESSIONAL SERVICES—Other Scientific and Technical Consulting Services NAICS 541690

Current Data Sorted by Assets							Comparative Historical Data	
1	1	19	24	4	3	Type of Statement		
1	8	16	6		1	Unqualified	8	21
2	6	6				Reviewed	8	10
12	12	4				Compiled	14	15
13	24	47	15	3	10	Tax Returns	12	18
	24 (4/1-9/30/09)		214 (10/1/09-3/31/10)			Other	29	55
							4/1/05-3/31/06	4/1/06-3/31/07
0-500M	500M-2MM	2-10MM	10-50MM	50-100MM	100-250MM		ALL	ALL
29	51	92	45	7	14	NUMBER OF STATEMENTS	71	119
%	%	%	%	%	%	ASSETS	%	%
27.3	16.1	19.0	12.3		10.2	Cash & Equivalents	14.5	14.3
29.2	44.7	49.9	36.6		32.7	Trade Receivables (net)	47.4	43.6
2.4	3.5	2.9	2.5		1.6	Inventory	5.5	3.0
4.8	2.9	6.0	5.9		13.3	All Other Current	4.3	5.6
63.6	67.2	77.8	57.3		57.8	Total Current	71.7	66.5
25.5	18.4	13.1	17.3		8.4	Fixed Assets (net)	14.0	17.2
1.7	3.2	3.1	15.3		31.1	Intangibles (net)	3.6	7.9
9.2	11.1	5.9	10.1		2.7	All Other Non-Current	10.7	8.4
100.0	100.0	100.0	100.0		100.0	Total	100.0	100.0
						LIABILITIES		
8.9	18.4	7.9	9.6		10.2	Notes Payable-Short Term	15.5	13.4
5.2	5.0	1.9	2.9		1.4	Cur. Mat.-L.T.D.	2.5	3.2
9.2	13.5	14.2	12.0		7.9	Trade Payables	13.5	14.1
.0	.0	.5	1.2		1.7	Income Taxes Payable	1.0	1.0
36.9	15.5	16.2	16.2		23.8	All Other Current	17.1	21.8
60.1	52.4	40.7	41.9		45.1	Total Current	49.5	53.6
53.2	13.8	4.3	12.8		10.5	Long-Term Debt	12.6	13.3
.0	.8	.6	.5		1.1	Deferred Taxes	.8	1.0
4.7	8.1	6.1	7.2		9.1	All Other Non-Current	4.1	7.0
-18.1	24.9	48.3	37.7		34.2	Net Worth	32.9	25.0
100.0	100.0	100.0	100.0		100.0	Total Liabilties & Net Worth	100.0	100.0
						INCOME DATA		
100.0	100.0	100.0	100.0		100.0	Net Sales	100.0	100.0
						Gross Profit		
93.4	90.2	93.7	95.4		91.1	Operating Expenses	94.0	90.4
6.6	9.8	6.3	4.6		8.9	Operating Profit	6.0	9.6
1.4	3.4	.1	1.3		3.0	All Other Expenses (net)	.7	1.0
5.2	6.3	6.3	3.3		5.9	Profit Before Taxes	5.3	8.6
						RATIOS		
3.7	2.3	3.7	2.0		1.8		3.4	2.3
1.3	1.3	2.1	1.4		1.3	Current	1.6	1.6
.7	1.0	1.2	1.0		.8		1.1	1.0
3.3	2.1	3.3	1.9		1.5		2.4	2.2
1.2	1.3	1.9	1.2		1.1	Quick	1.4	1.4
.4	.8	1.1	.8		.5		.8	.8
0 UND	1 519.6	39 9.3	34 10.6		40 9.1		33 11.1	24 15.1
23 16.2	44 8.3	61 6.0	63 5.8		61 5.9	Sales/Receivables	59 6.2	61 6.0
47 7.8	71 5.1	79 4.6	78 4.7		95 3.8		94 3.9	89 4.1
						Cost of Sales/Inventory		
						Cost of Sales/Payables		
11.4	7.4	4.6	6.9		5.2		5.4	5.8
39.9	23.1	7.7	14.0		14.2	Sales/Working Capital	11.1	13.4
-33.5	-126.4	30.0	NM		-44.9		70.4	800.0
32.3	26.8	73.0	19.8		43.9		35.3	31.6
(21) 10.8	(34) 10.7	(68) 9.5	(37) 5.1		(10) 8.9	EBIT/Interest	(54) 6.8	(93) 11.1
-.5	2.3	1.4	1.7		3.3		1.7	3.8
		7.4	41.8					4.7
	(13) 2.0	(13) 3.1				Net Profit + Depr., Dep., Amort./Cur. Mat. L/T/D		(11) 2.9
		1.2	2.0					1.0
.1	.2	.1	.1		.1		.1	.1
1.1	.4	.2	.3		1.2	Fixed/Worth	.2	.3
-6.3	7.5	.8	3.2		-.1		.9	2.8
.8	.9	.3	.9		2.4		.5	.9
3.2	2.7	1.1	3.1		5.1	Debt/Worth	1.6	2.1
-5.6	19.5	3.7	14.1		-2.0		3.7	UND
125.0	90.5	61.8	69.3				80.7	92.8
(19) 104.7	(40) 47.7	(84) 29.9	(39) 35.7			% Profit Before Taxes/Tangible Net Worth	(63) 37.7	(90) 44.3
-13.0	12.5	8.9	6.5				9.4	19.9
62.5	30.7	27.9	14.4		13.6		28.4	35.3
17.2	12.2	11.2	6.5		10.6	% Profit Before Taxes/Total Assets	12.7	18.8
-28.8	3.7	1.8	2.0		1.1		3.5	3.9
117.1	128.0	105.4	141.5		179.3		106.4	86.3
27.6	49.3	41.7	32.4		53.2	Sales/Net Fixed Assets	43.1	37.8
10.0	10.6	13.8	5.7		25.9		16.3	12.1
7.1	5.0	4.3	3.6		2.6		4.6	4.7
5.2	3.3	2.9	2.1		1.6	Sales/Total Assets	2.8	3.0
4.0	2.1	2.0	1.1		.9		1.7	1.9
.7	.2	.4	.5				.5	.5
(15) 1.1	(35) .6	(68) .9	(33) 1.7			% Depr., Dep., Amort./Sales	(42) 1.2	(87) 1.1
2.9	1.9	2.0	5.7				2.3	1.9
4.8	2.8	1.1					4.0	1.4
(11) 10.6	(16) 5.5	(23) 2.9				% Officers', Directors' Owners' Comp/Sales	(18) 9.1	(35) 5.0
11.7	10.8	9.7					14.5	9.0
37963M	221901M	1308034M	2319929M	934521M	3182155M	Net Sales ($)	2200426M	4323073M
6028M	57829M	413261M	929271M	507134M	1855854M	Total Assets ($)	1199106M	1974411M

M = $ thousand   MM = $ million
See Pages 9 through 22 for Explanation of Ratios and Data

Comparative Historical Data | | | | Current Data Sorted by Sales

24	35	52	Type of Statement						
12	20	32							
15	25	14							
14	20	28							
72	84	112							
24	35	52	Unqualified	1	1	1	6	19	24
12	20	32	Reviewed	1	1	4	10	9	7
15	25	14	Compiled	2	6		4	2	
14	20	28	Tax Returns	10	5	2	5	5	1
72	84	112	Other	11	18	12	13	30	28
4/1/07-3/31/08 ALL	4/1/08-3/31/09 ALL	4/1/09-3/31/10 ALL		24 (4/1-9/30/09)			214 (10/1/09-3/31/10)		
				0-1MM	1-3MM	3-5MM	5-10MM	10-25MM	25MM & OVER
137	184	238	NUMBER OF STATEMENTS	25	31	19	38	65	60
%	%	%	**ASSETS**	%	%	%	%	%	%
13.9	19.9	17.7	Cash & Equivalents	19.7	21.5	24.3	17.3	16.0	14.9
46.0	38.0	42.1	Trade Receivables (net)	21.8	37.3	43.8	48.9	45.5	44.4
3.3	2.6	2.9	Inventory	2.6	6.3	1.2	1.7	2.9	2.7
7.1	5.9	5.6	All Other Current	4.2	3.0	6.5	3.1	6.1	8.2
70.3	66.4	68.2	Total Current	48.3	68.1	75.8	70.9	70.4	70.2
16.0	19.3	16.4	Fixed Assets (net)	36.4	19.2	11.9	18.2	12.9	10.6
6.7	7.4	7.2	Intangibles (net)	1.7	5.0	2.1	3.2	8.7	13.2
6.9	6.9	8.1	All Other Non-Current	13.5	7.7	10.2	7.6	8.0	5.9
100.0	100.0	100.0	Total	100.0	100.0	100.0	100.0	100.0	100.0
			LIABILITIES						
13.3	12.6	10.7	Notes Payable-Short Term	8.4	10.9	19.7	14.0	6.4	11.2
2.5	3.0	3.1	Cur. Mat.-L.T.D.	3.6	3.8	7.5	3.2	2.3	1.9
15.9	12.8	12.6	Trade Payables	6.5	13.8	9.3	15.6	11.9	14.5
.7	.5	.6	Income Taxes Payable	.0	.1	.5	.2	.4	1.6
19.2	19.1	19.0	All Other Current	37.0	13.1	16.0	16.3	16.9	19.6
51.6	48.0	46.0	Total Current	55.4	41.7	53.0	49.3	38.0	48.8
10.0	13.2	14.4	Long-Term Debt	55.1	19.9	10.6	6.3	9.6	6.3
.6	.7	.6	Deferred Taxes	.0	.8	.1	1.0	.4	.8
5.2	11.7	7.0	All Other Non-Current	7.9	3.8	13.2	8.2	6.3	6.4
32.5	26.5	32.0	Net Worth	-18.4	33.7	23.1	35.2	45.8	37.7
100.0	100.0	100.0	Total Liabilities & Net Worth	100.0	100.0	100.0	100.0	100.0	100.0
			INCOME DATA						
100.0	100.0	100.0	Net Sales	100.0	100.0	100.0	100.0	100.0	100.0
			Gross Profit						
92.0	90.1	92.8	Operating Expenses	82.0	96.3	92.5	93.4	93.6	94.5
8.0	9.9	7.2	Operating Profit	18.0	3.7	7.5	6.6	6.4	5.5
.7	2.2	1.6	All Other Expenses (net)	7.6	-.3	.4	.4	1.8	1.0
7.3	7.6	5.6	Profit Before Taxes	10.3	4.1	7.1	6.2	4.6	4.5
			RATIOS						
2.2	2.5	3.1		2.3	3.6	3.6	3.2	3.7	2.1
1.5	1.5	1.6	Current	1.3	2.0	1.7	1.4	1.9	1.5
1.0	1.1	1.1		.4	1.0	1.3	1.0	1.2	1.1
2.0	2.3	2.7		2.2	3.2	3.1	2.6	3.0	1.9
1.2	1.3	1.4	Quick	1.0	1.6	1.7	1.3	1.6	1.2
.8	.8	.9		.3	.9	1.2	.8	1.1	.8
34 10.7	25 14.7	30 12.1		0 UND	26 14.2	38 9.5	34 10.6	40 9.1	32 11.4
58 6.3	49 7.5	54 6.7	Sales/Receivables	5 73.8	59 6.2	49 7.5	59 6.2	62 5.9	55 6.7
82 4.5	77 4.7	75 4.9		43 8.5	88 4.1	96 3.8	81 4.5	73 5.0	75 4.9
			Cost of Sales/Inventory						
			Cost of Sales/Payables						
6.9	5.7	5.3		11.4	4.0	3.7	6.2	5.2	5.9
14.7	15.4	13.0	Sales/Working Capital	49.0	10.4	6.1	14.3	11.4	13.0
982.7	89.7	79.3		-7.4	85.2	20.9	NM	34.5	67.9
27.1	28.4	38.3		26.4	28.6	72.3	34.3	51.8	73.6
(106) 5.8	(141) 8.4	(175) 8.0	EBIT/Interest	(15) 3.5	(22) 5.3	(14) 10.0	(27) 10.6	(50) 8.3	(47) 9.7
1.8	1.8	1.5		-2.3	-4.2	2.5	-.2	1.9	3.6
9.5	13.2	19.6						10.2	33.0
(17) 2.6	(28) 3.4	(34) 2.3	Net Profit + Depr., Dep., Amort./Cur. Mat. L/T/D				(13) 2.1	(14) 5.9	
.4	1.3	1.2						1.6	1.7
.1	.1	.1		.4	.1	.0	.1	.1	.1
.4	.5	.4	Fixed/Worth	7.5	.4	.2	.4	.2	.3
2.6	7.6	2.2		-1.1	1.0	21.3	3.3	1.3	1.6
.8	.7	.7		1.1	.5	.6	.7	.4	1.1
2.3	2.2	2.3	Debt/Worth	14.3	1.0	2.5	1.9	2.0	2.8
16.2	57.4	12.5		-5.4	3.3	30.4	58.4	5.2	13.4
99.0	83.2	77.9		153.1	53.0	69.3	121.8	63.5	69.8
(112) 50.3	(142) 38.6	(195) 36.6	% Profit Before Taxes/Tangible Net Worth	(15) 90.7	(27) 9.9	(15) 36.3	(30) 49.6	(58) 32.4	(50) 42.8
15.5	10.3	8.5		10.4	-13.0	6.1	14.6	10.2	11.2
36.6	28.9	26.6		43.0	25.4	27.5	43.7	25.3	19.0
13.4	14.8	10.0	% Profit Before Taxes/Total Assets	7.1	4.1	10.3	14.9	9.9	9.9
2.0	2.1	1.4		-9.5	-10.8	2.2	2.6	2.5	2.0
111.6	117.5	125.9		87.5	106.1	250.6	94.9	103.1	191.6
37.3	30.8	38.7	Sales/Net Fixed Assets	9.9	27.6	67.1	33.7	48.3	46.1
13.9	9.3	11.6		4.0	6.7	10.6	10.5	20.9	25.4
4.6	4.7	4.5		5.7	5.0	3.7	4.5	4.8	4.3
3.1	2.8	2.9	Sales/Total Assets	3.1	2.8	2.5	3.1	2.9	2.8
1.9	1.5	1.6		.9	1.3	1.5	2.3	1.9	1.7
.6	.4	.4		.6	.7	.5	.3	.4	.3
(83) 1.0	(127) 1.2	(164) 1.0	% Depr., Dep., Amort./Sales	(12) 2.0	(20) 1.6	(11) .7	(30) .9	(47) 1.0	(44) .7
1.8	2.7	2.2		6.3	2.8	2.7	2.4	1.7	1.8
2.8	2.7	2.3						2.8	.8
(28) 5.0	(41) 7.5	(54) 4.8	% Officers', Directors' Owners' Comp/Sales				(15) 4.3	(15) 2.5	
13.5	14.8	11.2						8.2	4.2
4850063M	5880581M	8004503M	Net Sales ($)	11814M	61210M	82873M	260283M	1017151M	6571172M
2465929M	2641159M	3769377M	Total Assets ($)	9443M	39678M	55000M	117448M	523253M	3024555M

M = $ thousand   MM = $ million
See Pages 9 through 22 for Explanation of Ratios and Data

Current Data Sorted by Assets   Comparative Historical Data

0-500M	500M-2MM	2-10MM	10-50MM	50-100MM	100-250MM	Type of Statement	4/1/05-3/31/06 ALL	4/1/06-3/31/07 ALL
	4	25	37	11	15	Unqualified		
	3	14	3	1		Reviewed		
2	4	2				Compiled		
5	8	6	1			Tax Returns		
6	19	27	32	6	11	Other		
	68 (4/1-9/30/09)		174 (10/1/09-3/31/10)					
13	38	74	73	18	26	NUMBER OF STATEMENTS		
%	%	%	%	%	%	ASSETS	%	%
37.8	20.6	20.0	21.0	19.0	22.1	Cash & Equivalents	D	D
27.5	31.8	32.6	25.6	21.9	16.7	Trade Receivables (net)	A	A
13.2	6.5	6.0	4.2	1.4	3.5	Inventory	T	T
2.1	7.1	6.7	6.8	8.4	4.7	All Other Current	A	A
80.7	65.9	65.3	57.6	50.8	47.0	Total Current		
12.7	18.6	22.4	23.2	36.3	24.3	Fixed Assets (net)	N	N
.0	4.5	2.5	7.2	3.8	11.1	Intangibles (net)	O	O
6.6	11.0	9.8	12.0	9.1	17.6	All Other Non-Current	T	T
100.0	100.0	100.0	100.0	100.0	100.0	Total		
						LIABILITIES	A	A
18.6	10.8	6.7	2.5	2.0	.7	Notes Payable-Short Term	V	V
.2	2.7	1.9	1.7	.8	1.7	Cur. Mat.-L.T.D.	A	A
14.6	11.7	11.9	10.1	9.6	5.5	Trade Payables	I	I
.0	.3	.5	.7	.2	.5	Income Taxes Payable	L	L
20.6	15.9	18.6	15.9	10.0	18.2	All Other Current	A	A
53.9	41.3	39.8	30.9	22.7	26.7	Total Current	B	B
17.6	10.5	9.6	9.8	13.7	7.4	Long-Term Debt	L	L
.0	.3	.4	.2	.6	1.7	Deferred Taxes	E	E
2.5	10.1	3.3	8.6	4.8	5.3	All Other Non-Current		
26.0	37.9	46.9	50.5	58.2	58.9	Net Worth		
100.0	100.0	100.0	100.0	100.0	100.0	Total Liabilties & Net Worth		
						INCOME DATA		
100.0	100.0	100.0	100.0	100.0	100.0	Net Sales		
						Gross Profit		
90.4	93.1	94.3	92.6	93.5	90.9	Operating Expenses		
9.6	6.9	5.7	7.4	6.5	9.1	Operating Profit		
-.4	.8	1.9	1.7	1.4	-.8	All Other Expenses (net)		
10.0	6.2	3.8	5.7	5.1	9.9	Profit Before Taxes		
						RATIOS		
6.0	3.9	3.9	3.1	6.0	3.3	Current		
2.4	2.0	1.8	1.9	2.4	1.8			
.7	1.2	1.2	1.2	1.4	1.3			
5.7	2.8	3.1	2.6	3.9	3.2	Quick		
1.0	1.6	1.5	1.5	1.4	1.4			
.6	.5	.9	.9	1.2	1.1			
0 UND	14 26.4	34 10.9	34 10.6	36 10.3	32 11.5	Sales/Receivables		
28 13.2	43 8.5	48 7.6	51 7.2	51 7.1	57 6.5			
41 8.9	63 5.8	68 5.4	74 4.9	103 3.5	69 5.3			
						Cost of Sales/Inventory		
						Cost of Sales/Payables		
3.5	4.7	3.8	3.3	2.0	2.4	Sales/Working Capital		
9.3	9.0	7.9	7.1	3.4	6.7			
-27.1	42.7	26.9	25.5	14.9	13.0			
	28.9	32.9	83.9	7.4	55.3	EBIT/Interest		
	(25) 3.2	(51) 10.1	(55) 8.0	(13) 3.3	(18) 16.0			
	1.7	2.2	-.2	-.8	1.0			
		19.9	6.3			Net Profit + Depr., Dep., Amort./Cur. Mat. L/T/D		
		(10) 5.0	(13) 1.9					
		1.0	.9					
.0	.1	.1	.1	.2	.3	Fixed/Worth		
.1	.3	.4	.3	.9	.5			
-17.9	1.0	1.1	1.3	1.2	.7			
.2	.3	.4	.5	.2	.2	Debt/Worth		
.7	1.2	1.0	1.0	.9	.8			
-100.5	4.9	4.3	2.3	1.8	2.7			
	65.1	49.4	47.0	28.6	37.2	% Profit Before Taxes/Tangible Net Worth		
	(33) 14.6	(68) 16.6	(65) 15.6	6.0	(23) 7.5			
	1.1	1.9	-.9	-.4				
96.7	26.9	24.2	18.6	9.7	12.5	% Profit Before Taxes/Total Assets		
35.1	5.6	9.3	7.5	3.3	5.9			
-8.2	.4	.9	.3	-.1	-.3			
UND	88.8	41.0	55.7	18.9	14.6	Sales/Net Fixed Assets		
43.8	22.9	17.0	12.3	3.1	6.9			
16.2	10.0	7.5	2.9	1.3	1.7			
6.0	3.8	3.0	2.5	1.6	1.6	Sales/Total Assets		
3.3	2.7	1.9	1.4	1.1	.7			
1.9	1.4	1.5	.8	.4	.5			
	.6	.9	1.2	1.7	1.4	% Depr., Dep., Amort./Sales		
	(27) 1.5	(60) 2.4	(59) 2.7	(15) 4.1	(21) 4.2			
	3.1	4.6	8.2	11.2	7.7			
	5.6	4.0				% Officers', Directors' Owners' Comp/Sales		
	(11) 9.9	(10) 6.6						
	14.8	11.5						
19857M	122062M	798970M	2999075M	1738421M	4303936M	Net Sales ($)		
3205M	46024M	372610M	1708781M	1190859M	4066431M	Total Assets ($)		

M = $ thousand   MM = $ million
See Pages 9 through 22 for Explanation of Ratios and Data

Comparative Historical Data — Current Data Sorted by Sales

Historical periods: 4/1/07-3/31/08 ALL | 4/1/08-3/31/09 ALL | 4/1/09-3/31/10 ALL
Current period split: 68 (4/1-9/30/09) · 174 (10/1/09-3/31/10)

	4/1/07-3/31/08 ALL	4/1/08-3/31/09 ALL	4/1/09-3/31/10 ALL	0-1MM	1-3MM	3-5MM	5-10MM	10-25MM	25MM & OVER
Type of Statement									
Unqualified	77	81	92	1	3	3	11	26	48
Reviewed	17	24	21			4	5	8	4
Compiled	15	9	8	1	1	3	2	1	
Tax Returns	19	22	20	6	7	3	2	2	
Other	89	101	101	4	17	8	13	23	36
NUMBER OF STATEMENTS	217	237	242	12	28	21	33	60	88
	%	%	%	%	%	%	%	%	%
ASSETS									
Cash & Equivalents	19.2	20.0	21.5	25.3	23.9	16.9	20.0	21.0	22.2
Trade Receivables (net)	28.4	30.4	27.6	19.7	19.3	36.2	25.3	31.0	27.7
Inventory	5.1	4.5	5.3	17.8	6.1	4.1	5.6	5.5	3.4
All Other Current	5.7	5.6	6.5	.5	6.4	3.3	8.8	4.9	8.2
Total Current	58.3	60.5	60.8	63.4	55.8	60.6	59.7	62.4	61.5
Fixed Assets (net)	23.5	23.9	22.8	16.9	30.1	25.5	24.0	22.1	20.6
Intangibles (net)	6.4	5.2	5.1	.1	4.3	2.6	2.1	6.4	6.9
All Other Non-Current	11.8	10.4	11.3	19.6	9.8	11.3	14.2	9.1	10.9
Total	100.0	100.0	100.0	100.0	100.0	100.0	100.0	100.0	100.0
LIABILITIES									
Notes Payable-Short Term	7.8	6.7	5.7	15.4	11.9	11.4	3.1	5.7	2.1
Cur. Mat.-L.T.D.	2.3	2.0	1.8	.4	2.4	3.7	1.5	1.3	1.7
Trade Payables	9.2	10.3	10.6	7.6	8.5	11.6	10.1	12.1	10.6
Income Taxes Payable	.4	.3	.5	.0	.0	.0	1.0	.2	.8
All Other Current	20.3	17.2	16.8	17.9	9.5	12.2	18.3	17.5	19.0
Total Current	39.9	36.5	35.4	41.3	32.4	38.8	34.0	36.9	34.3
Long-Term Debt	12.9	14.6	10.3	26.5	17.4	14.1	5.7	7.6	8.5
Deferred Taxes	.3	.4	.4	.0	.4	.1	.2	.4	.7
All Other Non-Current	7.6	4.7	6.3	2.4	6.2	13.0	3.6	2.9	8.4
Net Worth	39.3	43.8	47.6	29.8	43.6	33.9	56.4	52.2	48.1
Total Liabilties & Net Worth	100.0	100.0	100.0	100.0	100.0	100.0	100.0	100.0	100.0
INCOME DATA									
Net Sales	100.0	100.0	100.0	100.0	100.0	100.0	100.0	100.0	100.0
Gross Profit									
Operating Expenses	93.2	93.7	93.0	89.4	91.7	93.6	94.4	90.6	94.8
Operating Profit	6.8	6.3	7.0	10.6	8.3	6.4	5.6	9.4	5.2
All Other Expenses (net)	.7	2.1	1.2	3.4	2.3	2.4	1.1	1.9	-.2
Profit Before Taxes	6.2	4.3	5.8	7.2	6.0	3.9	4.5	7.5	5.4

RATIOS

	4/1/07-3/31/08	4/1/08-3/31/09	4/1/09-3/31/10	0-1MM	1-3MM	3-5MM	5-10MM	10-25MM	25MM & OVER
Current	3.7	3.3	3.5	6.9	6.8	3.7	3.7	3.7	2.9
	1.7	1.8	1.9	1.9	2.7	2.0	1.8	1.9	1.8
	1.1	1.2	1.2	.4	1.1	1.2	1.2	1.2	1.3
Quick	2.9	2.9	2.9	6.7	5.5	3.5	3.0	2.9	2.5
	1.4	1.5	1.5	.8	2.0	1.8	1.5	1.5	1.4
	.8	.9	.9	.2	.6	.9	.8	1.0	.9
Sales/Receivables	27 13.5	32 11.4	28 13.2	0 UND	3 123.7	30 12.3	19 19.5	35 10.5	39 9.4
	51 7.2	52 7.0	48 7.7	23 16.1	21 17.6	55 6.7	46 7.9	48 7.7	57 6.4
	80 4.6	76 4.8	68 5.3	58 6.3	60 6.1	88 4.1	67 5.4	66 5.5	74 4.9
Cost of Sales/Inventory									
Cost of Sales/Payables									
Sales/Working Capital	3.4	3.9	3.2	3.1	2.2	3.4	3.3	3.9	3.2
	9.2	7.8	7.6	5.1	7.5	9.9	7.3	6.4	7.7
	89.2	37.7	24.7	-4.5	174.5	22.5	43.6	19.5	18.2
EBIT/Interest	15.6	23.0	38.4		18.6	33.4	22.3	45.4	85.2
	(151) 5.7	(163) 3.6	(168) 8.8	(19) 3.1	(18) 5.2	(20) 8.3	(39) 10.4	(66) 11.0	
	1.6	-.5	1.4	-2.4	1.5	-.9	3.5	1.5	
Net Profit + Depr., Dep., Amort./Cur. Mat. L/T/D	8.9	15.3	9.4						7.1
	(41) 4.4	(37) 4.3	(34) 3.5					(20) 4.2	
	1.5	1.6	1.4						1.7
Fixed/Worth	.2	.1	.1	.0	.1	.1	.1	.1	.1
	.5	.4	.4	.1	.4	.3	.4	.4	.4
	1.8	1.1	1.1	NM	2.0	2.2	1.1	1.1	1.2
Debt/Worth	.4	.4	.4	.2	.3	.4	.2	.3	.5
	1.4	1.1	1.0	1.1	1.0	1.1	.7	1.0	1.1
	5.8	3.4	2.8	NM	22.0	3.8	2.3	2.9	2.5
% Profit Before Taxes/Tangible Net Worth	54.4	44.9	51.0		33.1	53.7	68.2	52.8	47.0
	(189) 20.7	(214) 18.6	(216) 14.7	(23) 10.8	(19) 14.6	7.0	(53) 21.6	(79) 15.1	
	1.9	-1.0	.7	-4.4	1.9	-6.3	5.9	2.9	
% Profit Before Taxes/Total Assets	19.0	18.3	19.7	38.4	21.7	29.2	27.6	24.1	16.9
	8.3	5.4	7.0	.8	4.2	5.5	3.9	10.7	8.2
	.5	-1.1	.2	.0	-3.9	1.3	-2.4	2.2	1.1
Sales/Net Fixed Assets	44.8	67.4	44.6	76.3	67.7	30.0	28.3	42.9	59.0
	14.5	16.5	14.6	37.4	15.3	11.4	11.2	18.2	11.0
	4.3	3.5	3.5	9.9	2.0	4.0	4.4	4.8	3.0
Sales/Total Assets	3.1	3.1	2.8	2.0	3.2	3.2	3.1	3.0	2.5
	1.8	1.9	1.7	1.6	1.4	2.3	1.8	1.9	1.5
	.9	1.0	1.0	.8	.7	1.3	.8	1.0	1.0
% Depr., Dep., Amort./Sales	1.0	.7	1.0		1.1	1.4	1.1	1.0	.6
	(174) 2.3	(176) 2.3	(187) 2.6	(17) 5.2	(18) 2.9	(30) 2.5	(45) 2.0	(69) 2.8	
	4.3	5.5	5.9	11.3	4.5	5.7	3.6	6.5	
% Officers', Directors' Owners' Comp/Sales	3.2	3.0	3.9						
	(31) 7.5	(34) 9.2	(33) 8.6						
	16.6	13.9	12.9						
Net Sales ($)	9239155M	11651357M	9982321M	6305M	48394M	83128M	239572M	932951M	8671971M
Total Assets ($)	6850277M	8568654M	7387910M	8116M	60535M	71439M	256360M	899864M	6091596M

Current Data Sorted by Assets   Comparative Historical Data

0-500M	500M-2MM	2-10MM	10-50MM	50-100MM	100-250MM		ALL	ALL
						Type of Statement		
1	3	9	11	6	5	Unqualified	17	17
	1		4			Reviewed	1	5
3	2	1				Compiled	3	5
3	1					Tax Returns		4
	4	3	5	2	4	Other	13	21
	30 (4/1-9/30/09)		38 (10/1/09-3/31/10)				4/1/05-3/31/06	4/1/06-3/31/07
7	11	13	20	8	9	**NUMBER OF STATEMENTS**	34	52
%	%	%	%	%	%	**ASSETS**	%	%
	25.2	25.7	22.2			Cash & Equivalents	20.1	23.6
	38.6	24.6	28.9			Trade Receivables (net)	32.5	30.2
	4.0	.2	.1			Inventory	.8	.5
	8.6	3.5	7.6			All Other Current	8.6	7.7
	76.4	54.1	58.8			Total Current	62.0	62.0
	15.8	23.1	15.7			Fixed Assets (net)	20.7	20.2
	.1	11.7	5.8			Intangibles (net)	7.5	8.1
	7.7	11.2	19.7			All Other Non-Current	9.8	9.7
	100.0	100.0	100.0			Total	100.0	100.0
						LIABILITIES		
	8.5	2.9	7.1			Notes Payable-Short Term	3.5	14.4
	2.1	4.9	.8			Cur. Mat.-L.T.D.	1.0	1.2
	10.0	11.9	9.9			Trade Payables	8.5	8.6
	.1	.0	.1			Income Taxes Payable	.0	.1
	17.1	14.0	16.4			All Other Current	17.8	25.3
	37.9	33.6	34.3			Total Current	30.9	49.6
	11.1	8.9	5.8			Long-Term Debt	11.7	11.7
	.0	.0	.3			Deferred Taxes	.0	.2
	5.7	8.1	4.9			All Other Non-Current	5.0	5.4
	45.3	49.4	54.7			Net Worth	52.3	33.1
	100.0	100.0	100.0			Total Liabilities & Net Worth	100.0	100.0
						INCOME DATA		
	100.0	100.0	100.0			Net Sales	100.0	100.0
						Gross Profit		
	102.4	101.2	97.6			Operating Expenses	96.2	92.4
	-2.4	-1.2	2.4			Operating Profit	3.8	7.6
	-1.7	1.4	.3			All Other Expenses (net)	-.1	.4
	-.8	-2.5	2.0			Profit Before Taxes	4.0	7.2
						RATIOS		
	3.3	3.7	2.7				3.6	2.6
	1.8	1.9	1.7			Current	1.9	1.8
	1.2	.9	1.2				1.4	1.0
	2.8	3.6	2.3				2.9	2.4
	1.8	1.8	1.6			Quick	1.6	1.3
	1.2	.5	.8				1.2	.9
5 72.1		2 204.6	4 82.3				22 16.4	18 20.2
51 7.1		44 8.4	45 8.2			Sales/Receivables	58 6.3	53 6.9
81 4.5		73 5.0	89 4.1				91 4.0	75 4.9
						Cost of Sales/Inventory		
						Cost of Sales/Payables		
	5.9	4.0	3.3				3.8	3.6
	9.9	8.4	10.3			Sales/Working Capital	6.7	8.3
	30.3	NM	146.9				20.0	-134.7
			36.9				52.4	26.7
		(15)	14.9			EBIT/Interest	(25) 10.8	(43) 6.8
			3.5				1.1	1.1
						Net Profit + Depr., Dep., Amort./Cur. Mat. L/T/D		
	.0	.1	.0				.1	.1
	.2	.3	.3			Fixed/Worth	.3	.4
	1.0	1.7	.6				.7	2.7
	.5	.4	.5				.5	.5
	1.5	.9	1.0			Debt/Worth	1.0	.9
	3.7	19.9	1.8				3.0	9.1
	23.7	19.4	34.6				100.0	49.5
	-4.9	(11) 2.3	(19) 13.3			% Profit Before Taxes/Tangible Net Worth	(31) 21.5	(42) 15.2
	-63.5	-12.9	-2.6				1.3	2.2
	15.6	9.4	18.5				27.4	19.3
	-3.3	-.2	4.7			% Profit Before Taxes/Total Assets	10.0	6.9
	-15.0	-6.0	-1.0				.2	.2
	140.9	63.0	178.3				47.5	102.6
	33.5	22.2	27.7			Sales/Net Fixed Assets	23.4	24.1
	11.2	4.7	2.8				3.4	4.2
	4.3	2.6	3.4				2.8	3.2
	3.6	2.1	2.0			Sales/Total Assets	1.7	1.7
	2.2	.7	1.0				1.0	1.1
		.8	.7				1.0	.6
		(10) 1.7	(14) 2.6			% Depr., Dep., Amort./Sales	(26) 1.5	(40) 2.3
		3.8	5.4				3.4	4.3
								3.8
						% Officers', Directors' Owners' Comp/Sales		(16) 8.7
								28.3
6363M	45793M	120643M	3404785M	979257M	1702796M	Net Sales ($)	1414289M	1995312M
1830M	12439M	68419M	427300M	584797M	1328466M	Total Assets ($)	1340232M	1811727M

M = $ thousand   MM = $ million
See Pages 9 through 22 for Explanation of Ratios and Data

Comparative Historical Data | Current Data Sorted by Sales

			Type of Statement						
20	31	35	Unqualified	2	3	2	7	6	15
5	8	5	Reviewed		1			3	1
7	3	6	Compiled	2	1	1	2		
2	7	4	Tax Returns	2	1		1		
26	21	18	Other		2	3	1	2	10
4/1/07-3/31/08 ALL	4/1/08-3/31/09 ALL	4/1/09-3/31/10 ALL		0-1MM	30 (4/1-9/30/09) 1-3MM	3-5MM	5-10MM	38 (10/1/09-3/31/10) 10-25MM	25MM & OVER
60	70	68	NUMBER OF STATEMENTS	6	8	6	11	11	26
%	%	%	ASSETS	%	%	%	%	%	%
24.4	26.6	23.0	Cash & Equivalents				33.3	17.7	23.3
27.5	31.0	30.0	Trade Receivables (net)				35.2	21.7	36.5
1.3	.8	1.0	Inventory				.3	.1	.8
6.4	4.3	6.6	All Other Current				1.0	6.9	6.8
59.6	62.7	60.6	Total Current				69.7	46.4	67.3
21.8	16.1	18.8	Fixed Assets (net)				11.9	23.2	13.4
12.8	7.2	6.8	Intangibles (net)				5.8	5.0	8.1
5.9	14.1	13.7	All Other Non-Current				12.6	25.3	11.2
100.0	100.0	100.0	Total				100.0	100.0	100.0
			LIABILITIES						
8.6	9.4	10.6	Notes Payable-Short Term				3.3	5.7	4.0
3.2	4.0	1.9	Cur. Mat.-L.T.D.				1.8	1.0	1.4
8.0	8.5	10.1	Trade Payables				8.7	6.9	12.3
1.5	.2	.1	Income Taxes Payable				.1	.2	.1
18.4	22.1	16.8	All Other Current				18.0	18.0	21.8
39.7	44.1	39.5	Total Current				31.8	31.7	39.6
14.2	11.7	10.2	Long-Term Debt				7.8	5.5	9.1
.2	.4	.1	Deferred Taxes				.0	.5	.0
8.3	6.3	5.9	All Other Non-Current				5.0	3.2	7.0
37.7	37.5	44.4	Net Worth				55.4	59.0	44.2
100.0	100.0	100.0	Total Liabilities & Net Worth				100.0	100.0	100.0
			INCOME DATA						
100.0	100.0	100.0	Net Sales				100.0	100.0	100.0
			Gross Profit						
91.8	94.0	99.2	Operating Expenses				97.8	98.7	97.4
8.2	6.0	.8	Operating Profit				2.2	1.3	2.6
1.5	2.6	.9	All Other Expenses (net)				-.4	1.4	.6
6.7	3.4	-.1	Profit Before Taxes				2.7	-.1	2.1
			RATIOS						
2.8	2.9	2.9					7.0	3.4	2.8
1.7	2.0	1.7	Current				1.8	2.0	1.7
1.1	1.1	1.1					1.2	1.1	1.2
2.4	2.7	2.6					7.0	2.9	2.2
1.4	1.5	1.5	Quick				1.8	1.2	1.4
.9	.9	.7					1.2	.4	1.1
32 11.3	17 21.9	6 63.5					10 37.6	2 225.8	35 10.3
61 6.0	57 6.4	53 6.8	Sales/Receivables				54 6.8	44 8.4	64 5.7
76 4.8	86 4.3	84 4.3					79 4.6	90 4.1	88 4.1
			Cost of Sales/Inventory						
			Cost of Sales/Payables						
3.8	3.9	3.4					2.7	3.1	3.9
6.1	7.5	10.1	Sales/Working Capital				6.8	14.1	10.3
62.4	45.2	73.3					47.6	109.5	51.9
32.6	11.8	25.1							26.4
(46) 9.4	(50) 1.8	(45) 6.0	EBIT/Interest					(19) 15.8	
1.3	-5.9	-3.8							1.8
17.9	17.1		Net Profit + Depr., Dep.,						
(13) 4.5	(12) 4.3		Amort./Cur. Mat. L/T/D						
2.5	1.9								
.1	.1	.1					.0	.1	.1
.7	.3	.3	Fixed/Worth				.1	.6	.3
NM	1.6	1.6					.7	1.3	1.7
.5	.5	.5					.3	.2	.6
2.1	1.1	1.3	Debt/Worth				.9	.5	1.5
-19.6	8.8	4.7					3.7	9.6	4.6
68.2	46.9	34.6	% Profit Before Taxes/Tangible				26.8	16.3	58.7
(44) 18.6	(59) 8.0	(59) 7.6	Net Worth				(10) 17.8	.7	(22) 13.1
6.2	-6.9	-5.0					-1.3	-18.5	6.3
25.4	12.8	12.9	% Profit Before Taxes/Total				10.2	11.8	16.5
8.1	1.5	2.4	Assets				3.8	.7	5.8
.3	-5.1	-4.5					-.2	-5.2	1.8
49.8	89.0	75.7					113.5	37.0	120.1
13.8	23.4	24.7	Sales/Net Fixed Assets				24.7	15.2	30.9
5.1	5.2	4.5					6.1	2.7	5.3
2.4	2.9	3.4					4.2	2.3	3.3
1.6	1.6	2.1	Sales/Total Assets				2.2	1.4	2.3
.8	.8	.9					.7	.9	1.0
.8	.7	.9					.6		.7
(44) 2.6	(54) 1.7	(48) 1.8	% Depr., Dep., Amort./Sales				(10) 1.0	(15)	2.2
4.8	3.2	3.6					2.6		3.2
	(15) 5.4	(16) 6.6	% Officers', Directors'						
	9.3	15.3	Owners' Comp/Sales						
	14.2	20.9							
2352509M	2515838M	6259637M	Net Sales ($)	3907M	14468M	22621M	79135M	212813M	5926693M
2079081M	2087681M	2423251M	Total Assets ($)	4084M	19521M	16129M	66382M	241192M	2075943M

M = $ thousand   MM = $ million
See Pages 9 through 22 for Explanation of Ratios and Data

PROFESSIONAL SERVICES—Advertising Agencies NAICS 541810

| Current Data Sorted by Assets | | | | | | | Comparative Historical Data | |

0-500M	500M-2MM	2-10MM	10-50MM	50-100MM	100-250MM	Type of Statement	4/1/05-3/31/06 ALL	4/1/06-3/31/07 ALL
	1	3	16	3	6	Unqualified	20	31
1	17	40	7	1	1	Reviewed	57	76
9	29	21	2			Compiled	58	70
58	28	9	1			Tax Returns	56	72
41	59	63	23	5	4	Other	159	159
	35 (4/1-9/30/09)		413 (10/1/09-3/31/10)					
109	134	136	49	9	11	**NUMBER OF STATEMENTS**	350	408
%	%	%	%	%	%	**ASSETS**	%	%
25.1	14.8	18.6	18.6		19.4	Cash & Equivalents	15.4	14.9
26.3	48.3	45.1	42.5		33.5	Trade Receivables (net)	45.9	47.2
1.8	3.0	3.3	6.2		.8	Inventory	4.1	3.6
4.3	4.8	5.8	5.8		3.6	All Other Current	4.5	4.5
57.5	71.0	72.8	73.1		57.4	Total Current	69.8	70.2
22.9	14.4	14.2	10.1		7.6	Fixed Assets (net)	16.1	15.8
5.4	3.1	3.5	10.6		33.2	Intangibles (net)	5.0	5.9
14.2	11.5	9.6	6.2		1.8	All Other Non-Current	9.0	8.1
100.0	100.0	100.0	100.0		100.0	Total	100.0	100.0
						LIABILITIES		
38.6	16.9	7.3	4.0		1.4	Notes Payable-Short Term	11.0	12.1
5.7	1.6	2.8	3.2		1.1	Cur. Mat.-L.T.D.	2.3	3.7
19.4	28.9	31.6	30.0		28.3	Trade Payables	29.2	30.3
.0	.0	.3	.9		.0	Income Taxes Payable	.6	.4
31.3	19.8	19.2	22.0		25.9	All Other Current	19.1	19.8
95.0	67.3	61.1	60.2		56.8	Total Current	62.1	66.3
20.5	8.2	6.4	7.9		9.5	Long-Term Debt	9.8	11.8
.1	.3	.1	.0		2.2	Deferred Taxes	.2	.3
12.7	5.1	8.3	4.9		4.9	All Other Non-Current	9.0	6.6
-28.2	19.2	24.1	27.0		26.6	Net Worth	18.8	15.0
100.0	100.0	100.0	100.0		100.0	Total Liabilties & Net Worth	100.0	100.0
						INCOME DATA		
100.0	100.0	100.0	100.0		100.0	Net Sales	100.0	100.0
						Gross Profit		
95.7	97.6	96.3	95.2		93.6	Operating Expenses	94.1	94.6
4.3	2.4	3.7	4.8		6.4	Operating Profit	5.9	5.4
1.1	1.2	.9	.9		3.1	All Other Expenses (net)	.9	1.3
3.2	1.1	2.8	3.9		3.3	Profit Before Taxes	5.0	4.0
						RATIOS		
1.7	1.9	1.7	1.7		1.5		1.8	1.7
.7	1.1	1.1	1.2		1.0	Current	1.1	1.1
.3	.7	.9	.9		.8		.8	.8
1.4	1.7	1.6	1.5		1.4		1.6	1.5
(108) .6	1.0	1.0	.9		.9	Quick	1.0 (407)	1.0
.2	.6	.7	.8		.8		.7	.7
0 UND	29 12.7	35 10.5	43 8.4	64	5.7		29 12.4	30 12.2
7 55.0	49 7.4	53 6.8	70 5.2	81	4.5	Sales/Receivables	48 7.6	48 7.6
43 8.5	71 5.2	83 4.4	108 3.4	229	1.6		74 5.0	73 5.0
						Cost of Sales/Inventory		
						Cost of Sales/Payables		
24.5	9.5	8.3	6.2		9.8		10.7	13.6
-51.2	43.7	32.1	21.2		-32.2	Sales/Working Capital	36.7	50.4
-7.3	-22.6	-44.1	-55.8		-5.5		-37.2	-31.5
20.9	15.6	26.6	23.5		17.5		34.6	23.4
(68) 3.9	(111) 2.9	(99) 4.3	(40) 8.8		(10) 1.6	EBIT/Interest	(272) 8.8	(323) 5.5
-2.5	-7.6	-2.7	2.2		1.1		1.6	1.3
		12.7					11.2	7.6
		(17) 2.1				Net Profit + Depr., Dep., Amort./Cur. Mat. L/T/D	(54) 3.5	(51) 2.6
		.1					1.3	1.1
.2	.1	.2	.2		.5		.2	.2
UND	.5	.5	.5		-1.1	Fixed/Worth	.6	.8
-.3	-1.2	4.4	-2.9		-.2		5.8	-47.3
1.5	1.0	1.2	1.4		3.2		1.6	1.5
-8.9	4.1	3.6	5.5		-5.0	Debt/Worth	4.4	5.7
-2.1	-10.7	14.6	-19.3		-2.6		71.3	-59.3
267.9	71.4	82.2	110.1				100.7	98.9
(51) 84.2	(90) 19.8	(109) 32.3	(36) 23.6			% Profit Before Taxes/Tangible Net Worth	(271) 51.9	(296) 45.0
16.7	-19.1	5.0	5.1				16.2	11.5
63.7	15.6	18.2	15.4		3.4		24.1	23.2
19.9	2.8	5.7	5.1		1.6	% Profit Before Taxes/Total Assets	9.2	7.3
-16.1	-12.3	-1.4	.5		.4		1.6	.8
209.0	107.2	75.0	99.2		21.9		87.2	93.4
46.8	43.4	30.9	40.1		14.0	Sales/Net Fixed Assets	37.7	36.7
21.5	15.9	14.8	13.4		10.2		15.1	17.8
12.6	5.0	4.0	3.6		1.3		4.9	5.1
6.0	3.7	3.0	2.0		1.2	Sales/Total Assets	3.4	3.5
3.4	2.3	1.7	1.2		.7		2.2	2.4
.3	.5	.5	.3				.5	.4
(57) 1.1	(92) 1.0	(104) 1.1	(40) .9			% Depr., Dep., Amort./Sales	(275) 1.0	(313) .9
2.3	1.8	1.8	1.8				1.9	1.8
5.4	3.9	2.6	.9				3.4	3.0
(58) 8.6	(59) 5.8	(51) 4.6	(12) 1.5			% Officers', Directors' Owners' Comp/Sales	(152) 6.6	(167) 6.1
12.9	10.0	8.6	6.3				11.6	11.4
181592M	597566M	1930967M	3254852M	874806M	1687296M	Net Sales ($)	6795109M	7352154M
21417M	156362M	628640M	1114986M	635395M	1714437M	Total Assets ($)	2400901M	3291179M

© RMA 2010

M = $ thousand   MM = $ million
See Pages 9 through 22 for Explanation of Ratios and Data

Comparative Historical Data — Current Data Sorted by Sales

	4/1/07-3/31/08 ALL	4/1/08-3/31/09 ALL	4/1/09-3/31/10 ALL	Type of Statement	0-1MM	1-3MM	3-5MM	5-10MM	10-25MM	25MM & OVER
	26	28	29	Unqualified	1	5	3	24	18	23
	52	55	67	Reviewed	1	21	11	11	13	16
	63	59	61	Compiled	2	11	11	9	3	3
	68	94	96	Tax Returns	29	24	17	15	9	2
	161	170	195	Other	26	47	21	26	45	30
	370	406	448	NUMBER OF STATEMENTS (35 (4/1-9/30/09) / 413 (10/1/09-3/31/10))	59	97	52	76	90	74
	%	%	%	**ASSETS**	%	%	%	%	%	%
	16.2	16.9	18.9	Cash & Equivalents	25.8	13.7	20.6	19.1	19.8	17.7
	46.7	44.6	40.7	Trade Receivables (net)	21.9	42.6	38.7	47.5	42.6	45.4
	3.1	2.9	3.3	Inventory	1.5	2.7	.9	4.7	5.7	2.6
	5.9	4.9	5.0	All Other Current	3.1	5.4	6.7	4.4	5.0	5.4
	71.9	69.4	67.9	Total Current	52.3	64.5	67.0	75.6	73.1	71.1
	13.4	15.1	15.7	Fixed Assets (net)	27.6	17.7	16.8	11.8	13.4	9.6
	6.0	6.2	5.9	Intangibles (net)	5.5	5.2	2.2	4.0	3.6	14.4
	8.7	9.4	10.6	All Other Non-Current	14.6	12.6	14.1	8.6	9.9	4.9
	100.0	100.0	100.0	Total	100.0	100.0	100.0	100.0	100.0	100.0
				LIABILITIES						
	12.6	15.9	17.2	Notes Payable-Short Term	29.5	26.7	21.0	15.9	9.2	3.2
	4.0	3.5	3.1	Cur. Mat.-L.T.D.	2.6	5.1	2.1	3.1	2.5	2.3
	28.2	29.9	27.5	Trade Payables	18.9	23.9	22.2	31.1	31.5	34.2
	.3	.2	.2	Income Taxes Payable	.0	.1	.0	.0	.3	.7
	20.0	19.1	22.9	All Other Current	30.4	25.6	19.6	20.1	21.9	20.0
	65.1	68.7	70.9	Total Current	81.4	81.3	64.9	70.3	65.4	60.3
	11.5	10.1	10.8	Long-Term Debt	26.7	14.6	7.7	5.0	4.8	8.6
	.2	.2	.2	Deferred Taxes	.1	.4	.0	.0	.2	.4
	9.5	8.5	7.9	All Other Non-Current	17.5	7.8	3.9	8.1	6.8	4.2
	13.7	12.5	10.2	Net Worth	-25.6	-4.1	23.4	16.5	22.9	26.5
	100.0	100.0	100.0	Total Liabilities & Net Worth	100.0	100.0	100.0	100.0	100.0	100.0
				INCOME DATA						
	100.0	100.0	100.0	Net Sales	100.0	100.0	100.0	100.0	100.0	100.0
				Gross Profit						
	94.5	95.0	96.3	Operating Expenses	91.8	97.7	98.3	97.5	96.1	95.5
	5.5	5.0	3.7	Operating Profit	8.2	2.3	1.7	2.5	3.9	4.5
	1.3	1.3	1.1	All Other Expenses (net)	4.4	1.2	.1	.4	.3	1.0
	4.2	3.7	2.6	Profit Before Taxes	3.8	1.1	1.6	2.1	3.6	3.5
				RATIOS						
	1.8	1.8	1.7	Current	2.2	1.6	2.4	1.7	1.7	1.6
	1.1	1.1	1.1		.6	1.1	1.2	1.1	1.1	1.1
	.8	.8	.7		.2	.5	.6	.8	.9	.9
	1.5	1.6	1.5	Quick	2.1	1.5	2.0	1.5	1.4	1.5
	(368) 1.0	(447) 1.0	.9		(58) .6	.9	1.1	.9	1.0	1.0
	.7	.7	.6		.3	.4	.5	.7	.6	.8
	26 14.0	28 13.3	24 15.4	Sales/Receivables	0 UND	17 21.4	0 UND	33 11.2	30 12.2	37 9.9
	49 7.5	45 8.1	46 7.9		10 37.7	49 7.5	50 7.4	50 7.4	51 7.1	52 7.0
	71 5.1	72 5.0	76 4.8		46 7.9	81 4.5	83 4.4	78 4.7	80 4.6	89 4.1
				Cost of Sales/Inventory						
				Cost of Sales/Payables						
	12.0	12.0	10.1	Sales/Working Capital	9.7	10.6	7.8	10.1	8.5	11.1
	46.1	51.9	65.2		-19.1	138.5	47.1	123.3	29.5	44.2
	-37.3	-27.0	-18.6		-4.7	-8.3	-30.3	-24.1	-46.5	-32.1
	24.9	24.5	20.9	EBIT/Interest	9.4	12.7	35.2	18.5	50.0	21.9
	(277) 6.0	(312) 5.9	(336) 3.7		(29) 3.0	(79) 2.1	(40) 6.3	(60) 1.9	(69) 12.6	(59) 5.7
	1.3	.7	-2.4		-2.3	-6.6	-5.5	-8.9	-1.3	1.4
	7.5	7.0	9.1	Net Profit + Depr., Dep., Amort./Cur. Mat. L/T/D						60.5
	(35) 2.4	(47) 2.1	(37) 2.1						(15) 5.2	
	1.3	.6	.5							1.7
	.2	.2	.2	Fixed/Worth	.1	.1	.1	.2	.2	.2
	.5	.6	.7		UND	.8	.5	.6	.6	.6
	-3.7	-3.4	-1.1		-.4	-.6	-7.3	-.8	4.8	-1.2
	1.4	1.2	1.3	Debt/Worth	.9	1.6	.6	1.4	1.3	1.6
	5.4	5.4	5.6		-9.7	7.3	3.0	5.3	4.6	7.7
	-15.3	-20.9	-6.5		-1.9	-4.2	-8.1	-15.0	34.4	-7.1
	95.0	100.0	99.7	% Profit Before Taxes/Tangible Net Worth	98.8	70.9	118.9	86.0	126.8	79.0
	(259) 43.0	(285) 36.3	(296) 31.1		(27) 31.7	(60) 26.9	(35) 32.0	(51) 18.8	(71) 44.6	(52) 23.8
	14.9	7.0	.7		-21.4	-7.7	-.1	-5.7	8.5	4.5
	24.4	23.4	22.1	% Profit Before Taxes/Total Assets	56.0	21.3	31.2	13.4	21.3	14.8
	7.2	7.4	5.1		8.0	2.9	6.3	3.5	8.1	3.3
	.9	-.1	-4.3		-13.9	-17.0	-12.3	-7.2	-.2	.4
	116.7	111.6	99.6	Sales/Net Fixed Assets	99.3	102.3	148.5	91.4	96.3	137.5
	46.0	40.3	37.5		31.6	34.4	39.7	43.4	36.1	43.8
	19.2	18.8	16.1		12.2	14.4	14.0	24.1	17.8	15.6
	5.3	5.5	5.1	Sales/Total Assets	7.1	5.3	7.7	5.0	4.7	4.6
	3.7	3.7	3.4		3.3	3.4	3.5	3.8	3.3	3.2
	2.3	2.3	1.8		1.8	1.9	1.9	2.4	2.0	1.3
	.4	.5	.5	% Depr., Dep., Amort./Sales	.7	.5	.8	.5	.5	.3
	(267) .8	(280) .9	(306) 1.1		(31) 1.4	(59) 1.4	(35) 1.2	(58) .9	(68) 1.2	(55) .6
	1.8	2.0	2.1		5.4	2.7	2.4	1.7	1.6	2.0
	2.7	2.5	3.2	% Officers', Directors' Owners' Comp/Sales	6.8	4.9	5.8	3.2	2.5	.6
	(160) 5.7	(168) 5.8	(182) 5.8		(22) 10.8	(47) 7.2	(23) 7.6	(33) 4.5	(34) 5.2	(23) 1.5
	12.0	11.3	11.1		18.0	13.7	12.6	6.5	11.7	3.9
	9144795M	9121021M	8527079M	Net Sales ($)	29490M	181005M	200816M	537269M	1339004M	6239495M
	3556690M	4319658M	4271237M	Total Assets ($)	20906M	74779M	72718M	207557M	600863M	3294414M

© RMA 2010

M = $ thousand   MM = $ million
See Pages 9 through 22 for Explanation of Ratios and Data

Current Data Sorted by Assets   Comparative Historical Data

0-500M	500M-2MM	2-10MM	10-50MM	50-100MM	100-250MM	Type of Statement	4/1/05-3/31/06 ALL	4/1/06-3/31/07 ALL
1	3	9	5	1	1	Unqualified	8	21
2	2	4	2			Reviewed	9	15
7	7	5				Compiled	18	12
7	6	6	4	2	1	Tax Returns	16	12
2						Other	33	33
	14 (4/1-9/30/09)		63 (10/1/09-3/31/10)					
0-500M	500M-2MM	2-10MM	10-50MM	50-100MM	100-250MM	NUMBER OF STATEMENTS	84	93
12	25	24	11	3	2			
%	%	%	%	%	%	ASSETS	%	%
40.5	19.9	24.9	12.8			Cash & Equivalents	20.8	18.8
23.3	49.5	37.6	43.3			Trade Receivables (net)	42.6	40.8
.3	.8	6.5	1.2			Inventory	1.3	2.5
4.1	2.4	3.4	5.9			All Other Current	3.4	4.8
68.1	72.6	72.4	63.3			Total Current	68.1	66.9
9.8	13.8	15.7	15.4			Fixed Assets (net)	19.9	17.4
2.4	4.1	2.2	14.0			Intangibles (net)	4.0	4.3
19.6	9.6	9.8	7.2			All Other Non-Current	7.9	11.5
100.0	100.0	100.0	100.0			Total	100.0	100.0
						LIABILITIES		
11.6	19.6	12.3	3.7			Notes Payable-Short Term	19.7	13.2
2.7	5.2	2.2	1.4			Cur. Mat.-L.T.D.	4.0	6.1
7.9	11.2	15.1	16.7			Trade Payables	11.0	13.9
.0	.8	.6	1.5			Income Taxes Payable	1.1	.7
35.2	15.8	24.7	21.0			All Other Current	20.4	19.1
57.5	52.5	54.9	44.3			Total Current	56.2	52.9
17.6	10.2	6.1	12.8			Long-Term Debt	9.9	12.8
.0	.4	1.3	.0			Deferred Taxes	.1	.6
8.1	9.2	12.9	5.5			All Other Non-Current	7.2	11.4
16.7	27.7	24.8	37.4			Net Worth	26.6	22.3
100.0	100.0	100.0	100.0			Total Liabilities & Net Worth	100.0	100.0
						INCOME DATA		
100.0	100.0	100.0	100.0			Net Sales	100.0	100.0
						Gross Profit		
90.8	93.3	95.4	86.6			Operating Expenses	93.0	93.2
9.2	6.7	4.6	13.4			Operating Profit	7.0	6.8
1.0	1.9	.9	3.8			All Other Expenses (net)	1.7	1.0
8.2	4.8	3.7	9.6			Profit Before Taxes	5.3	5.7
						RATIOS		
4.5	2.7	3.2	1.9				2.4	2.3
1.1	1.6	1.2	1.3			Current	1.5	1.5
.6	.8	.9	1.2				.9	.9
4.5	2.5	2.1	1.7				2.3	1.9
1.1	1.5	1.1	1.1			Quick	1.4	1.3
.5	.8	.8	1.1				.7	.8
0 UND	27 13.4	31 11.9	45 8.2				15 24.1	31 11.6
0 UND	54 6.7	45 8.1	72 5.1			Sales/Receivables	47 7.7	53 6.9
44 8.3	75 4.9	64 5.7	91 4.0				73 5.0	79 4.6
						Cost of Sales/Inventory		
						Cost of Sales/Payables		
24.1	5.9	5.3	7.0				7.5	6.8
NM	12.9	21.8	12.9			Sales/Working Capital	18.0	12.8
-23.4	-25.0	-35.9	22.9				-76.5	-158.6
	25.6	23.9	28.3				32.8	28.5
	(19) 5.1	(17) 6.9	(10) 14.6			EBIT/Interest	(63) 7.0	(75) 7.8
	1.2	.3	5.5				2.0	1.2
							18.2	28.1
						Net Profit + Depr., Dep., Amort./Cur. Mat. L/T/D	(11) 1.6	(17) 2.9
							1.1	.5
.0	.1	.2	.2				.1	.1
.2	.8	.5	.3			Fixed/Worth	.5	.4
-.6	-3.6	NM	1.7				3.4	2.6
.6	.4	1.1	1.3				.7	.8
2.0	1.9	2.5	2.3			Debt/Worth	1.9	2.0
-3.2	-21.7	NM	4.4				17.2	13.6
	66.0	68.5	46.8				99.6	88.8
(16) 17.9	(18) 37.9	(10) 23.2				% Profit Before Taxes/Tangible Net Worth	(70) 41.5	(73) 43.8
1.0	.0	14.9					1.1	9.3
185.5	29.5	20.1	13.0				34.4	39.3
51.7	7.6	8.3	7.2			% Profit Before Taxes/Total Assets	8.6	10.0
7.7	-1.3	-1.2	4.8				.1	.5
UND	208.3	84.7	65.6				78.0	80.4
233.6	45.2	32.2	42.4			Sales/Net Fixed Assets	33.2	36.4
28.4	24.9	17.3	16.3				15.7	16.2
24.0	5.4	3.9	3.0				5.4	4.6
11.4	4.1	2.9	2.3			Sales/Total Assets	3.5	2.7
5.0	2.7	2.2	1.2				2.3	1.8
	.4	.6	.4				.7	.5
(20) .9	(21) 1.1	(10) .6				% Depr., Dep., Amort./Sales	(66) 1.2	(75) 1.1
1.8	1.4	2.0					2.1	2.1
	6.0						6.3	6.0
(13) 8.7						% Officers', Directors' Owners' Comp/Sales	(40) 9.1	(28) 14.7
12.9							16.8	23.3
32481M	135823M	343115M	685322M	354337M	340403M	Net Sales ($)	3411858M	3028951M
2898M	29854M	117059M	320488M	234022M	337172M	Total Assets ($)	808127M	1493880M

Comparative Historical Data

Current Data Sorted by Sales

4/1/07-3/31/08 ALL	4/1/08-3/31/09 ALL	4/1/09-3/31/10 ALL	Type of Statement	0-1MM	1-3MM	3-5MM	5-10MM	10-25MM	25MM & OVER
15	15	19	Unqualified		2	2	3	3	9
13	14	9	Reviewed		2	1	2	3	1
11	10	14	Compiled		3	5	3	3	
10	13	13	Tax Returns		5	2	4	2	
16	21	22	Other		6	3	2	4	7
					14 (4/1-9/30/09)		63 (10/1/09-3/31/10)		
65	73	77	**NUMBER OF STATEMENTS**		18	13	14	15	17
%	%	%	**ASSETS**	%	%	%	%	%	%
23.6	22.7	23.9	Cash & Equivalents		24.2	30.0	25.1	27.9	14.2
41.3	38.2	39.0	Trade Receivables (net)		37.0	40.9	36.7	38.2	42.3
3.5	3.8	2.9	Inventory		.5	3.2	2.4	6.4	2.5
4.0	4.5	3.5	All Other Current		3.3	3.4	2.1	4.4	4.0
72.3	69.3	69.2	Total Current		65.0	77.6	66.4	76.9	62.9
16.7	17.2	14.6	Fixed Assets (net)		18.6	12.5	14.2	16.0	11.2
4.9	4.3	5.4	Intangibles (net)		3.0	1.1	4.9	1.0	15.7
6.1	9.2	10.7	All Other Non-Current		13.4	8.9	14.6	6.1	10.2
100.0	100.0	100.0	Total		100.0	100.0	100.0	100.0	100.0
			LIABILITIES						
13.9	14.1	12.7	Notes Payable-Short Term		19.7	8.2	21.3	7.5	6.3
6.3	10.5	3.0	Cur. Mat.-L.T.D.		2.1	1.9	5.6	3.9	2.0
10.5	11.3	12.3	Trade Payables		11.0	9.0	12.5	17.7	11.4
.7	.9	.7	Income Taxes Payable		.0	1.5	.8	.2	1.2
14.2	16.7	22.0	All Other Current		23.3	16.3	16.8	30.2	22.2
45.5	53.5	50.8	Total Current		56.0	37.0	57.1	59.4	43.1
6.7	8.2	11.5	Long-Term Debt		18.0	4.0	17.0	4.4	11.8
.5	.7	.7	Deferred Taxes		.5	.0	.0	1.8	1.2
10.6	7.3	9.3	All Other Non-Current		6.0	3.6	7.4	19.6	9.8
36.8	30.3	27.7	Net Worth		19.5	55.4	18.4	14.8	34.1
100.0	100.0	100.0	Total Liabilities & Net Worth		100.0	100.0	100.0	100.0	100.0
			INCOME DATA						
100.0	100.0	100.0	Net Sales		100.0	100.0	100.0	100.0	100.0
			Gross Profit						
92.0	93.4	93.0	Operating Expenses		87.2	92.7	94.8	96.3	94.8
8.0	6.6	7.0	Operating Profit		12.8	7.3	5.2	3.7	5.2
3.3	2.4	1.7	All Other Expenses (net)		2.9	2.8	.9	.6	1.3
4.6	4.2	5.4	Profit Before Taxes		9.9	4.5	4.3	3.2	3.9
			RATIOS						
3.4	3.2	2.7	Current		2.1	18.5	3.0	2.2	2.8
1.6	1.6	1.4			1.2	2.3	.8	1.3	1.5
1.1	1.0	.8			.6	1.5	.7	1.0	1.1
3.2	2.7	2.3	Quick		2.1	17.4	3.0	2.1	1.9
1.5	1.5	1.3			1.2	2.3	.8	1.1	1.2
.9	.9	.8			.5	1.5	.7	.8	1.1
23　15.9	13　27.2	25　14.5	Sales/Receivables	0　UND	0　UND	26　13.9	24　15.0	41　9.0	
51　7.1	44　8.2	45　8.1		46　8.0	37　9.8	46　8.0	35　10.4	57　6.4	
75　4.9	68　5.4	68　5.4		86　4.2	61　6.0	61　6.0	59　6.2	79　4.6	
			Cost of Sales/Inventory						
			Cost of Sales/Payables						
7.0	6.9	6.1	Sales/Working Capital		9.2	4.4	6.4	5.9	4.2
11.3	14.1	21.6			39.4	11.7	-28.9	15.1	12.9
131.0	-575.4	-47.1			-23.6	339.1	-18.0	753.2	88.6
18.7	20.4	23.9	EBIT/Interest		39.5		14.1	17.5	25.2
(50)　4.3	(51)　5.4	(58)　7.2			(14)　14.1		(10)　1.3	(11)　7.1	7.3
.9	-1.8	1.1			3.3		.5	.0	2.0
		14.8	Net Profit + Depr., Dep., Amort./Cur. Mat. L/T/D						
	(13)　2.7								
		.9							
.1	.1	.1	Fixed/Worth		.0	.1	.0	.2	.2
.3	.3	.4			.9	.2	NM	.4	.4
1.7	1.4	-8.0			-.4	1.1	-.7	2.8	NM
.5	.7	.9	Debt/Worth		.9	.1	.9	1.9	1.1
1.5	1.4	2.3			2.3	.6	NM	2.8	2.3
9.3	4.2	-30.9			-6.1	4.0	-9.9	13.5	NM
94.8	91.9	87.2	% Profit Before Taxes/Tangible Net Worth		134.5	76.2		80.1	69.1
(53)　20.8	(61)　30.7	(56)　25.7			(12)　28.2	(11)　12.9		(13)　37.9	(13)　25.6
-3.7	1.5	3.5			15.4	-3.5		-4.5	5.1
18.5	31.4	32.2	% Profit Before Taxes/Total Assets		58.7	43.9	33.0	20.7	14.0
7.4	10.4	7.7			21.1	4.4	6.8	9.3	7.7
-1.5	-2.3	-.1			1.2	-1.6	-2.1	-1.3	3.5
115.8	82.6	112.6	Sales/Net Fixed Assets		UND	560.5	338.4	36.0	67.0
29.4	43.0	36.0			42.7	50.4	48.2	31.2	46.5
15.1	18.7	19.3			19.4	27.0	13.4	19.0	19.1
5.1	5.4	4.9	Sales/Total Assets		6.5	6.2	4.8	4.3	4.1
3.4	3.2	3.3			3.7	4.4	3.7	3.3	2.4
2.0	2.4	2.2			1.9	2.7	2.2	2.8	1.2
.5	.5	.4	% Depr., Dep., Amort./Sales		.5		.2	.9	.4
(47)　1.1	(53)　1.0	(60)　1.0			(10)　1.3		(12)　.6	(13)　1.1	(16)　.7
2.1	2.0	1.6			2.4		2.1	1.3	2.0
4.8	4.8	6.0	% Officers', Directors' Owners' Comp/Sales						
(20)　8.0	(22)　7.2	(28)　10.5							
17.6	11.6	16.1							
3098599M	1424649M	1891481M	Net Sales ($)		35292M	51467M	104573M	228193M	1471956M
901622M	705769M	1041493M	Total Assets ($)		41825M	19699M	31853M	66546M	881570M

Current Data Sorted by Assets

Comparative Historical Data

						Type of Statement		
		1	1	2	2	Unqualified	3	4
1		1				Reviewed	1	1
	2					Compiled	6	5
4	3	1				Tax Returns	2	
1	4	4	5	2		Other	3	5
	5 (4/1-9/30/09)		29 (10/1/09-3/31/10)				4/1/05-3/31/06	4/1/06-3/31/07
0-500M	500M-2MM	2-10MM	10-50MM	50-100MM	100-250MM		ALL	ALL
6	9	7	6	4	2	NUMBER OF STATEMENTS	15	15
%	%	%	%	%	%	ASSETS	%	%
						Cash & Equivalents	21.3	19.5
						Trade Receivables (net)	32.1	26.6
						Inventory	4.0	5.6
						All Other Current	5.0	7.4
						Total Current	62.3	59.0
						Fixed Assets (net)	22.6	19.0
						Intangibles (net)	7.9	5.9
						All Other Non-Current	7.3	16.1
						Total	100.0	100.0
						LIABILITIES		
						Notes Payable-Short Term	6.7	12.6
						Cur. Mat.-L.T.D.	4.3	1.8
						Trade Payables	18.1	13.3
						Income Taxes Payable	.4	.2
						All Other Current	51.9	23.6
						Total Current	81.4	51.6
						Long-Term Debt	16.7	6.4
						Deferred Taxes	.1	.0
						All Other Non-Current	10.0	18.0
						Net Worth	-8.3	24.0
						Total Liabilties & Net Worth	100.0	100.0
						INCOME DATA		
						Net Sales	100.0	100.0
						Gross Profit		
						Operating Expenses	90.0	94.8
						Operating Profit	10.0	5.2
						All Other Expenses (net)	2.0	.6
						Profit Before Taxes	8.0	4.6
						RATIOS		
						Current	2.4 / 1.2 / 1.0	1.7 / 1.3 / .6
						Quick	1.7 / 1.2 / .8	1.5 / .8 / .5
						Sales/Receivables	4 85.4 / 42 8.7 / 75 4.9	3 108.2 / 42 8.7 / 80 4.6
						Cost of Sales/Inventory		
						Cost of Sales/Payables		
						Sales/Working Capital	6.7 / 22.8 / 368.5	9.9 / 32.0 / -7.4
						EBIT/Interest	30.8 / (10) 16.5 / 4.1	62.1 / (13) 9.7 / .4
						Net Profit + Depr., Dep., Amort./Cur. Mat. L/T/D		
						Fixed/Worth	.3 / .7 / -1.0	.1 / .8 / -3.8
						Debt/Worth	.7 / 3.8 / -3.0	.7 / 3.0 / -10.9
						% Profit Before Taxes/Tangible Net Worth	214.1 / (11) 68.2 / 12.3	175.4 / (11) 16.0 / 6.5
						% Profit Before Taxes/Total Assets	44.8 / 15.5 / 4.3	24.3 / 7.1 / .1
						Sales/Net Fixed Assets	152.7 / 27.8 / 8.8	98.2 / 21.0 / 6.4
						Sales/Total Assets	8.4 / 3.6 / 1.8	3.6 / 2.0 / 1.0
						% Depr., Dep., Amort./Sales	.4 / (10) 2.6 / 3.3	
						% Officers', Directors' Owners' Comp/Sales		
14710M	35097M	58354M	241284M	256334M	388456M	Net Sales ($)	651739M	7061967M
1529M	9074M	34106M	116348M	242065M	333406M	Total Assets ($)	384427M	461202M

M = $ thousand   MM = $ million
See Pages 9 through 22 for Explanation of Ratios and Data

Comparative Historical Data / Current Data Sorted by Sales

4/1/07-3/31/08 ALL	4/1/08-3/31/09 ALL	4/1/09-3/31/10 ALL	Type of Statement	0-1MM	1-3MM	3-5MM	5-10MM	10-25MM	25MM & OVER
4	6	6	Unqualified		1		1	1	5
3	4	2	Reviewed		1			1	
4	4	2	Compiled				1	1	
3	2	8	Tax Returns	2		2	3		
8	16	16	Other	1	3	3	2	2	5
				5 (4/1-9/30/09)			29 (10/1/09-3/31/10)		
22	32	34	**NUMBER OF STATEMENTS**	3	5	5	6	5	10
%	%	%		%	%	%	%	%	%
			ASSETS						
14.0	13.8	12.9	Cash & Equivalents						14.4
41.4	35.3	32.2	Trade Receivables (net)						26.8
1.0	3.1	2.4	Inventory						1.4
2.8	4.5	1.8	All Other Current						4.3
59.2	56.7	49.4	Total Current						46.8
21.9	20.6	21.4	Fixed Assets (net)						15.0
11.8	15.4	17.4	Intangibles (net)						35.1
7.1	7.2	11.8	All Other Non-Current						3.2
100.0	100.0	100.0	Total						100.0
			LIABILITIES						
7.4	12.4	17.2	Notes Payable-Short Term						9.9
3.0	3.5	2.2	Cur. Mat.-L.T.D.						3.7
27.5	25.3	16.3	Trade Payables						13.8
.2	.0	2.7	Income Taxes Payable						.2
13.3	11.3	14.9	All Other Current						21.1
51.4	52.6	53.2	Total Current						48.8
32.5	20.3	18.5	Long-Term Debt						12.1
.4	.8	.8	Deferred Taxes						2.5
3.8	5.3	7.0	All Other Non-Current						9.5
11.9	21.1	20.5	Net Worth						27.0
100.0	100.0	100.0	Total Liabilities & Net Worth						100.0
			INCOME DATA						
100.0	100.0	100.0	Net Sales						100.0
			Gross Profit						
92.1	96.1	99.3	Operating Expenses						96.5
7.9	3.9	.7	Operating Profit						3.5
4.3	4.2	1.9	All Other Expenses (net)						1.7
3.5	-.2	-1.1	Profit Before Taxes						1.8
			RATIOS						
2.6	1.6	1.5	Current						1.3
1.2	1.1	1.1							1.0
.7	.8	.7							.7
2.5	1.4	1.4	Quick						1.2
1.0	.9	.9							.8
.7	.6	.6							.6
25 14.3	29 12.6	12 31.0	Sales/Receivables					37	9.9
47 7.7	51 7.2	52 7.0						57	6.5
85 4.3	79 4.6	77 4.8						91	4.0
			Cost of Sales/Inventory						
			Cost of Sales/Payables						
8.0	9.1	9.2	Sales/Working Capital						9.2
39.8	57.3	323.3							NM
-16.2	-25.0	-14.2							-14.2
7.6	8.3	4.6	EBIT/Interest						28.5
(16) 1.8	(25) 1.4	(26) -.5							2.5
-.3	-.1	-7.7							-9.5
			Net Profit + Depr., Dep., Amort./Cur. Mat. L/T/D						
.3	.3	.4	Fixed/Worth						.6
2.8	1.1	2.3							NM
-2.0	-21.1	-1.0							-.8
1.5	2.2	1.2	Debt/Worth						4.0
12.7	13.8	15.4							NM
-6.8	-13.9	-4.2							-4.0
104.9	93.9	66.1	% Profit Before Taxes/Tangible Net Worth						
(13) 41.0	(21) 32.8	(20) 1.2							
11.7	-6.5	-102.5							
18.8	11.5	9.5	% Profit Before Taxes/Total Assets						16.0
4.1	1.9	-.9							3.2
-1.6	-3.7	-13.7							-3.4
80.9	71.3	87.5	Sales/Net Fixed Assets						56.0
31.6	17.4	21.6							15.1
8.4	5.8	7.6							6.6
4.4	4.4	4.7	Sales/Total Assets						1.9
2.8	2.0	2.3							1.4
1.4	.5	1.3							1.0
.6	.5	1.7	% Depr., Dep., Amort./Sales						
(20) 1.3	(24) 2.2	(18) 2.4							
4.3	4.6	4.3							
		4.0	% Officers', Directors', Owners' Comp/Sales						
	(13) 7.4								
		9.3							
786942M	970467M	994235M	Net Sales ($)	1782M	9268M	18402M	45845M	70050M	848888M
337030M	804828M	736528M	Total Assets ($)	1769M	8882M	3956M	19288M	35729M	666904M

M = $ thousand   MM = $ million
See Pages 9 through 22 for Explanation of Ratios and Data

Current Data Sorted by Assets   Comparative Historical Data

Type of Statement	0-500M	500M-2MM	2-10MM	10-50MM	50-100MM	100-250MM	4/1/05-3/31/06 ALL	4/1/06-3/31/07 ALL
Unqualified		1	2	4	1	1	4	10
Reviewed		2	6	5			11	8
Compiled	2	5	5		1		8	7
Tax Returns	5	5	4			3	12	14
Other	2	5	11	2	1		18	33
		7 (4/1-9/30/09)		65 (10/1/09-3/31/10)				
NUMBER OF STATEMENTS	9	18	28	11	2	4	53	72
	%	%	%	%	%	%	%	%
ASSETS								
Cash & Equivalents		6.9	15.8	5.2			8.6	7.0
Trade Receivables (net)		27.9	22.7	19.3			27.2	23.9
Inventory		11.0	6.2	5.1			8.6	8.9
All Other Current		4.9	4.3	2.4			2.5	3.0
Total Current		50.7	49.0	31.9			46.9	42.9
Fixed Assets (net)		36.4	38.5	44.2			37.6	40.7
Intangibles (net)		3.7	3.1	19.6			5.9	6.9
All Other Non-Current		9.2	9.3	4.3			9.6	9.6
Total		100.0	100.0	100.0			100.0	100.0
LIABILITIES								
Notes Payable-Short Term		16.0	5.4	7.3			20.0	11.2
Cur. Mat.-L.T.D.		6.3	2.9	9.5			4.4	6.7
Trade Payables		12.5	14.3	7.3			14.8	10.5
Income Taxes Payable		.0	.0	.0			.0	.0
All Other Current		6.4	10.0	11.5			13.2	10.3
Total Current		41.2	32.6	35.6			52.4	38.7
Long-Term Debt		33.6	39.1	27.1			24.1	31.6
Deferred Taxes		.0	.2	1.0			.2	.1
All Other Non-Current		3.1	2.9	3.0			9.1	6.9
Net Worth		22.1	25.2	33.2			14.2	22.6
Total Liabilities & Net Worth		100.0	100.0	100.0			100.0	100.0
INCOME DATA								
Net Sales		100.0	100.0	100.0			100.0	100.0
Gross Profit								
Operating Expenses		89.9	92.3	96.3			90.8	84.3
Operating Profit		10.1	7.7	3.7			9.2	15.7
All Other Expenses (net)		3.3	4.9	4.6			2.1	4.8
Profit Before Taxes		6.8	2.8	-.9			7.1	10.9
RATIOS								
Current		1.9	2.8	1.5			1.4	1.7
		1.0	1.5	1.0			1.0	1.2
		.8	1.0	.5			.5	.7
Quick		1.1	1.7	1.2			1.3	1.3
		.7	1.2	.9			.7	.9
		.5	.8	.3			.4	.4
Sales/Receivables		0 UND	20 18.6	30 12.1			20 18.2	17 22.0
		36 10.2	38 9.6	50 7.3			39 9.3	38 9.7
		60 6.1	57 6.4	81 4.5			69 5.3	62 5.9
Cost of Sales/Inventory								
Cost of Sales/Payables								
Sales/Working Capital		10.7	4.9	10.7			16.6	10.3
		247.5	8.4	93.6			199.5	37.0
		-39.8	99.5	-4.9			-7.8	-22.8
EBIT/Interest		31.5	5.5	4.1			15.4	12.2
		(17) 2.5	(22) 2.5	(10) 1.2			(48) 3.7	(61) 5.0
		.0	.7	-4.9			1.2	1.6
Net Profit + Depr., Dep., Amort./Cur. Mat. L/T/D								
Fixed/Worth		.5	.2	.9			.3	.5
		1.3	1.6	1.6			1.2	1.4
		NM	3.9	-1.5			NM	-38.7
Debt/Worth		.9	1.6	.7			1.5	1.0
		16.9	3.3	2.3			4.0	2.8
		-58.0	5.6	-4.8			-10.2	-61.8
% Profit Before Taxes/Tangible Net Worth		139.1	42.0				93.2	81.8
		(13) 12.1	(25) 10.8				(37) 33.9	(52) 41.3
		-10.2	-10.8				11.3	15.3
% Profit Before Taxes/Total Assets		21.8	9.7	6.0			17.6	24.7
		5.9	2.6	1.5			7.0	10.2
		-1.4	-1.9	-13.1			.4	2.5
Sales/Net Fixed Assets		53.0	72.7	16.4			39.9	43.9
		14.0	5.5	4.3			7.7	5.6
		2.7	.8	1.1			1.2	1.0
Sales/Total Assets		3.3	2.7	2.1			3.5	2.8
		2.0	1.4	1.0			1.6	1.7
		1.1	.6	.7			.7	.7
% Depr., Dep., Amort./Sales		.7	.6	4.2			1.0	.7
		(17) 2.8	(23) 3.1	(10) 7.5			(43) 3.7	(53) 4.6
		13.7	14.4	16.1			11.7	12.1
% Officers', Directors' Owners' Comp/Sales		3.1	2.4				3.5	2.7
		(11) 7.3	(13) 4.4				(21) 5.7	(21) 4.0
		9.2	8.2				8.8	6.3
Net Sales ($)	8287M	58809M	236447M	351555M	210202M	981435M	580102M	1491643M
Total Assets ($)	2576M	22384M	136930M	250610M	133111M	674466M	375265M	989234M

M = $ thousand   MM = $ million
See Pages 9 through 22 for Explanation of Ratios and Data

Comparative Historical Data   Current Data Sorted by Sales

	12 mo 4/1/07-3/31/08 ALL	9 mo 4/1/08-3/31/09 ALL	9 mo 4/1/09-3/31/10 ALL		0-1MM	1-3MM	3-5MM	5-10MM	10-25MM	25MM & OVER
				Type of Statement		7 (4/1-9/30/09)			65 (10/1/09-3/31/10)	
Unqualified	12	9	9					2	2	5
Reviewed	7	10	13			1		3	5	
Compiled	12	7	12		4	3		2	2	
Tax Returns	8	13	14			4	4	2		1
Other	45	39	24		5	4	2	5	5	4
NUMBER OF STATEMENTS	84	78	72		14	12	8	14	14	10
	%	%	%	**ASSETS**	%	%	%	%	%	%
Cash & Equivalents	11.0	10.4	12.3		9.7	5.2		14.4	16.7	19.2
Trade Receivables (net)	22.5	22.9	21.9		11.3	16.5		24.8	27.7	28.9
Inventory	6.2	7.2	7.3		2.1	7.2		7.0	8.3	10.7
All Other Current	3.2	2.1	5.5		9.4	5.8		3.3	6.5	4.0
Total Current	42.9	42.7	47.0		32.6	34.7		49.5	59.2	62.8
Fixed Assets (net)	43.1	40.3	39.0		62.2	49.2		36.0	21.2	20.4
Intangibles (net)	5.2	8.3	6.4		.3	5.5		3.8	14.2	14.0
All Other Non-Current	8.8	8.7	7.6		4.9	10.5		10.7	5.4	2.8
Total	100.0	100.0	100.0		100.0	100.0		100.0	100.0	100.0
				LIABILITIES						
Notes Payable-Short Term	12.9	11.7	10.2		15.1	11.0		13.3	5.8	5.1
Cur. Mat.-L.T.D.	5.0	4.4	4.9		6.2	5.4		3.7	2.5	3.1
Trade Payables	11.9	9.8	12.6		7.2	7.8		10.9	22.6	12.7
Income Taxes Payable	.0	.0	.0		.0	.0		.0	.0	.1
All Other Current	11.1	11.0	14.0		26.2	2.3		12.6	11.8	19.9
Total Current	40.9	37.0	41.7		54.7	26.4		40.4	42.8	40.9
Long-Term Debt	30.2	28.1	41.3		66.1	56.5		24.9	18.5	41.4
Deferred Taxes	.1	.2	.3		.0	.0		.1	.2	1.3
All Other Non-Current	12.9	4.4	4.3		5.9	4.4		2.2	2.5	6.7
Net Worth	15.9	30.4	12.5		-26.6	12.7		32.4	36.0	9.7
Total Liabilities & Net Worth	100.0	100.0	100.0		100.0	100.0		100.0	100.0	100.0
				INCOME DATA						
Net Sales	100.0	100.0	100.0		100.0	100.0		100.0	100.0	100.0
Gross Profit										
Operating Expenses	86.2	86.6	91.5		85.5	90.5		95.9	97.9	89.6
Operating Profit	13.8	13.4	8.5		14.5	9.5		4.1	2.1	10.4
All Other Expenses (net)	4.0	2.9	4.3		8.8	6.2		1.9	1.1	5.2
Profit Before Taxes	9.9	10.6	4.1		5.7	3.2		2.3	1.0	5.2
				RATIOS						
Current	2.5	2.4	2.0		1.2	5.2		1.9	1.9	3.2
	1.2	1.3	1.1		.7	1.4		1.1	1.2	1.7
	.7	.8	.9		.1	.7		.9	1.0	1.0
Quick	1.8	1.9	1.6		1.3	3.7		1.4	1.5	2.4
	.9 (77)	1.0 (71)	.9		(13) .4	.8		.8	1.0	1.5
	.4	.6	.4		.1	.4		.6	.9	.6
Sales/Receivables	12 29.4	16 22.3	17 20.9		0 UND	4 102.8		15 25.0	30 12.2	49 7.4
	38 9.7	35 10.5	39 9.3		18 20.4	32 11.5		32 11.3	40 9.0	56 6.6
	58 6.3	48 7.6	57 6.4		38 9.5	63 5.8		56 6.5	82 4.5	75 4.9
Cost of Sales/Inventory										
Cost of Sales/Payables										
Sales/Working Capital	6.5	8.4	6.9		18.0	3.3		7.4	6.0	3.4
	25.1	23.6	32.2		-13.5	9.5		94.1	25.0	8.9
	-16.2	-29.2	-45.7		-3.5	-31.3		-49.2	93.5	-772.6
EBIT/Interest	9.7	12.0	4.8		4.8	3.4		5.7	18.8	14.9
	(72) 3.1	(70) 3.6	(62) 1.8		(10) 1.6	(11) 1.1		(12) 2.4	(11) 1.3	1.7
	1.0	1.2	.2		-1.4	-3.5		.5	-.9	.6
Net Profit + Depr., Dep., Amort./Cur. Mat. L/T/D		(10) 10.3								
		3.2								
		.9								
Fixed/Worth	.6	.3	.6		2.1	1.3		.8	.1	.3
	1.4	1.1	1.7		NM	3.2		1.3	.6	-1.6
	20.8	3.4	-14.6		-.9	NM		3.3	1.6	-.7
Debt/Worth	.9	.9	1.5		7.2	1.8		1.4	.8	1.2
	2.3	2.2	5.0		-32.1	5.2		2.7	3.3	-7.0
	47.4	5.8	-16.4		-3.8	NM		6.9	12.6	-3.3
% Profit Before Taxes/Tangible Net Worth	64.1	81.6	46.6					94.0	35.7	
	(66) 32.4	(67) 31.4	(51) 10.8					(13) 12.5	(13) 7.1	
	6.2	7.1	-11.8					-9.6	-18.4	
% Profit Before Taxes/Total Assets	22.1	25.2	10.1		15.6	6.8		20.2	9.7	21.8
	9.3	8.8	1.4		-.1	.1		5.7	1.3	5.0
	-.9	.5	-2.7		-5.9	-6.6		-1.6	-4.8	-1.4
Sales/Net Fixed Assets	24.5	28.4	28.3		10.8	14.9		27.7	158.5	68.2
	5.6	6.3	9.7		.9	2.4		11.8	29.7	13.5
	1.2	1.2	1.0		.4	.6		2.2	4.2	4.7
Sales/Total Assets	2.8	3.4	2.7		2.0	2.0		3.7	3.3	2.5
	1.7	1.9	1.6		.8	1.0		2.3	1.9	1.6
	.8	.7	.7		.3	.5		1.3	.9	1.3
% Depr., Dep., Amort./Sales	1.3	1.0	1.1		4.2	.9		1.2	.4	
	(66) 4.6	(64) 3.9	(59) 3.9		(11) 18.7	(10) 8.8		(12) 3.0	(12)	
	12.4	11.9	14.4		36.4	15.2		5.9	8.5	
% Officers', Directors' Owners' Comp/Sales	3.0	3.4	3.2			3.3				
	(34) 4.7	(28) 5.1	(28) 5.2			(10) 7.8				
	8.2	13.5	8.5			11.7				
Net Sales ($)	1029640M	2158521M	1846735M		8060M	23892M	33154M	99936M	227714M	1453979M
Total Assets ($)	784367M	1344595M	1220077M		14717M	29486M	33004M	64653M	154635M	923582M

PROFESSIONAL SERVICES—Direct Mail Advertising NAICS 541860

Current Data Sorted by Assets | Comparative Historical Data

	0-500M	500M-2MM	2-10MM	10-50MM	50-100MM	100-250MM	Type of Statement		ALL	ALL
			1	7	3	1	Unqualified		9	17
		3	16	9			Reviewed		19	20
		6	8				Compiled		11	20
	2	13	3	1			Tax Returns		12	11
	4	11	14	14	6	2	Other		34	45
		20 (4/1-9/30/09)		104 (10/1/09-3/31/10)					4/1/05-3/31/06	4/1/06-3/31/07
	6	33	42	31	9	3	NUMBER OF STATEMENTS		85	113
	%	%	%	%	%	%	ASSETS		%	%
		20.5	19.1	10.7			Cash & Equivalents		13.5	11.7
		32.9	36.9	28.9			Trade Receivables (net)		37.2	39.0
		1.6	3.4	4.9			Inventory		5.2	3.7
		4.6	3.6	6.9			All Other Current		5.2	3.9
		59.6	62.9	51.3			Total Current		61.1	58.4
		24.7	26.4	27.5			Fixed Assets (net)		27.0	27.1
		7.9	4.8	14.1			Intangibles (net)		4.4	6.8
		7.7	5.9	7.1			All Other Non-Current		7.4	7.7
		100.0	100.0	100.0			Total		100.0	100.0
							LIABILITIES			
		5.2	8.9	6.3			Notes Payable-Short Term		10.1	8.5
		5.0	4.7	4.4			Cur. Mat.-L.T.D.		5.0	5.1
		15.8	19.7	12.8			Trade Payables		16.7	18.6
		.2	.6	.0			Income Taxes Payable		.2	.1
		17.4	20.9	16.8			All Other Current		19.1	19.2
		43.6	54.9	40.3			Total Current		51.0	51.5
		25.3	11.8	25.0			Long-Term Debt		15.4	18.6
		.2	.2	.4			Deferred Taxes		.4	.3
		5.8	12.0	6.6			All Other Non-Current		6.3	3.4
		25.1	21.1	27.7			Net Worth		27.0	26.3
		100.0	100.0	100.0			Total Liabilities & Net Worth		100.0	100.0
							INCOME DATA			
		100.0	100.0	100.0			Net Sales		100.0	100.0
							Gross Profit			
		93.7	98.5	93.3			Operating Expenses		92.8	94.0
		6.3	1.5	6.7			Operating Profit		7.2	6.0
		2.2	.7	2.0			All Other Expenses (net)		1.3	1.3
		4.2	.8	4.7			Profit Before Taxes		5.9	4.7
							RATIOS			
		2.7	1.8	1.8					1.9	1.5
		1.3	1.0	1.2			Current		1.2	1.1
		.8	.9	.9					.8	.9
		2.4	1.6	1.4					1.7	1.3
		1.3	1.0	.9			Quick		1.0	1.0
		.7	.8	.7					.6	.7
	13 28.2	33 11.2	36 10.1				Sales/Receivables	28 13.1	26 13.9	
	32 11.3	46 7.9	60 6.1					44 8.2	50 7.2	
	50 7.3	70 5.2	83 4.4					71 5.2	68 5.4	
							Cost of Sales/Inventory			
							Cost of Sales/Payables			
		8.4	7.0	6.4					10.7	13.7
		37.0	95.3	26.9			Sales/Working Capital		27.1	82.8
		-34.4	-51.0	-44.1					-35.2	-26.1
		28.6	18.2	10.9					17.2	16.3
	(25) 3.2	(37) 3.1	(30) 5.3				EBIT/Interest	(77) 6.6	(101) 4.6	
	-4.5	.7	1.6					2.7	1.1	
									6.1	8.2
							Net Profit + Depr., Dep., Amort./Cur. Mat. L/T/D	(20) 2.5	(27) 3.3	
									1.3	1.5
		.1	.5	.5					.3	.5
		.5	1.1	1.3			Fixed/Worth		1.3	1.1
		UND	NM	-1.6					8.3	8.1
		.9	1.1	1.3					1.4	1.2
		3.0	3.4	2.6			Debt/Worth		4.0	3.1
		-77.4	NM	-8.4					25.0	36.6
		177.0	61.1	44.1					104.7	83.8
	(24) 45.3	(32) 16.9	(23) 26.8				% Profit Before Taxes/Tangible Net Worth	(72) 50.9	(86) 42.7	
	-3.8	-7.8	4.2					18.1	3.7	
		24.3	11.6	12.7					27.8	27.2
		9.1	4.4	4.2			% Profit Before Taxes/Total Assets		11.6	8.4
		-3.2	-3.7	.8					4.4	.8
		105.6	31.7	13.2					37.3	31.5
		21.7	12.1	7.0			Sales/Net Fixed Assets		14.6	13.6
		11.0	6.0	4.6					6.4	6.2
		6.9	3.3	2.3					3.8	4.2
		3.2	2.6	1.7			Sales/Total Assets		2.9	3.0
		2.4	2.1	.9					2.1	1.8
		.6	1.2	1.5					.7	1.2
	(25) 1.7	(32) 2.9	(27) 3.7				% Depr., Dep., Amort./Sales	(72) 1.9	(97) 2.3	
	4.9	4.6	5.3					4.1	4.2	
		2.2	1.5						1.4	1.8
	(16) 4.8	(21) 3.8					% Officers', Directors' Owners' Comp/Sales	(34) 5.1	(43) 4.8	
	9.0	9.0						9.1	8.1	
	5695M	183497M	532618M	1334249M	795335M	559756M	Net Sales ($)		1539863M	2927185M
	998M	40844M	193547M	793281M	635261M	450719M	Total Assets ($)		737029M	1386235M

M = $ thousand   MM = $ million
See Pages 9 through 22 for Explanation of Ratios and Data

Comparative Historical Data / Current Data Sorted by Sales

Hist 1	Hist 2	Hist 3	Category	0-1MM	1-3MM	3-5MM	5-10MM	10-25MM	25MM & OVER
			Type of Statement						
14	15	12	Unqualified				1	1	10
15	17	28	Reviewed		1	2	9	13	4
18	23	14	Compiled		1	1	7	5	
13	19	19	Tax Returns	5	3	3	3	4	1
43	45	51	Other	2	8	2	8	12	19
4/1/07-3/31/08 ALL	4/1/08-3/31/09 ALL	4/1/09-3/31/10 ALL		20 (4/1-9/30/09)			104 (10/1/09-3/31/10)		
103	119	124	**NUMBER OF STATEMENTS**	7	12	8	28	35	34
%	%	%	**ASSETS**	%	%	%	%	%	%
14.1	14.2	16.3	Cash & Equivalents		24.5		15.9	17.7	10.5
36.0	33.9	31.6	Trade Receivables (net)		32.8		37.4	34.6	26.0
4.6	3.4	3.6	Inventory		.6		5.0	2.1	6.3
3.6	4.7	4.7	All Other Current		2.2		5.0	3.5	7.4
58.2	56.2	56.2	Total Current		60.1		63.4	58.0	50.3
24.8	25.7	24.8	Fixed Assets (net)		14.8		26.6	25.8	21.7
11.6	11.3	12.4	Intangibles (net)		19.7		2.1	8.2	24.1
5.4	6.8	6.5	All Other Non-Current		5.4		7.9	8.0	3.9
100.0	100.0	100.0	Total		100.0		100.0	100.0	100.0
			LIABILITIES						
7.9	12.0	7.0	Notes Payable-Short Term		7.6		10.4	7.4	5.5
5.4	5.7	7.8	Cur. Mat.-L.T.D.		2.6		4.9	4.4	3.5
18.9	16.7	15.3	Trade Payables		14.6		16.7	22.2	11.8
.1	.2	.3	Income Taxes Payable		.6		.0	.7	.0
17.5	18.0	17.7	All Other Current		15.4		20.8	18.5	17.4
49.7	52.8	48.1	Total Current		40.9		52.8	53.2	38.3
22.9	29.0	22.0	Long-Term Debt		25.9		16.9	12.9	28.0
.4	1.0	.3	Deferred Taxes		.0		.0	.2	.7
6.6	8.0	9.3	All Other Non-Current		6.2		4.3	13.7	11.2
20.4	9.2	20.4	Net Worth		27.0		26.1	20.1	21.8
100.0	100.0	100.0	Total Liabilities & Net Worth		100.0		100.0	100.0	100.0
			INCOME DATA						
100.0	100.0	100.0	Net Sales		100.0		100.0	100.0	100.0
			Gross Profit						
94.9	95.6	95.0	Operating Expenses		100.1		97.5	96.4	94.3
5.1	4.4	5.0	Operating Profit		-.1		2.5	3.6	5.7
1.4	2.1	1.8	All Other Expenses (net)		.9		1.9	.3	2.2
3.7	2.3	3.2	Profit Before Taxes		-1.0		.6	3.2	3.5
			RATIOS						
1.9	1.8	1.9	Current		4.0		1.9	1.5	1.8
1.1	1.1	1.3			1.8		1.2	1.0	1.3
.8	.7	.9			.7		.9	.9	.9
1.6	1.6	1.6	Quick		3.7		1.7	1.4	1.3
1.1	.9	1.0			1.7		1.0	1.0	.8
.7	.6	.7			.6		.8	.8	.7
31 11.9	22 16.3	28 13.2	Sales/Receivables		27 13.7		35 10.4	24 15.2	37 9.8
50 7.3	41 8.9	45 8.1			46 7.9		51 7.2	35 10.5	52 7.0
60 6.1	63 5.8	69 5.3			74 4.9		76 4.8	55 6.6	77 4.7
			Cost of Sales/Inventory						
			Cost of Sales/Payables						
10.6	12.4	7.4	Sales/Working Capital		4.0		7.2	14.5	7.2
74.7	43.5	34.5			15.5		28.1	266.6	24.0
-32.4	-23.3	-43.6			-29.3		-69.2	-43.5	-44.4
24.8	9.2	12.2	EBIT/Interest		5.7		31.8	28.8	10.9
(97) 3.9	(104) 1.9	(108) 3.2		(10) -1.9		(21) 3.0	(32) 5.1		4.1
1.2	.8	.9			-12.3		-1.4	1.3	1.1
7.3	2.5	3.5	Net Profit + Depr., Dep., Amort./Cur. Mat. L/T/D						3.9
(26) 3.3	(22) 1.4	(23) 1.4						(10) 2.7	
1.3	.6	.3							.9
.5	.5	.3	Fixed/Worth		.2		.3	.5	.7
1.7	2.0	1.4			UND		.8	1.1	2.2
-.9	-.7	-1.9			-1.6		4.9	5.0	-.3
1.4	1.7	1.2	Debt/Worth		.7		.7	1.6	1.6
4.1	6.1	3.6			UND		3.2	3.3	4.7
-6.2	-5.8	-6.7			-3.1		50.4	16.5	-2.2
93.2	57.0	70.8	% Profit Before Taxes/Tangible Net Worth				89.2	81.9	44.1
(69) 38.3	(76) 18.7	(84) 24.9				(22) 19.9	(27) 30.0	(19) 28.9	
10.2	.1	1.6					-6.4	4.2	9.6
21.4	14.8	15.9	% Profit Before Taxes/Total Assets		7.9		14.8	19.4	12.5
7.6	3.6	5.2			-3.9		3.8	7.4	6.4
.6	-1.0	-2.0			-19.7		-8.8	.5	.6
27.5	36.3	33.4	Sales/Net Fixed Assets		456.6		66.4	34.3	14.9
13.7	14.8	12.6			21.2		14.2	13.6	9.2
8.1	7.3	6.1			8.6		4.4	6.9	6.2
4.0	4.2	3.3	Sales/Total Assets		2.9		4.6	6.1	2.3
2.6	2.9	2.4			2.7		2.5	3.0	1.7
1.9	1.8	1.5			2.4		1.7	2.1	1.2
1.0	.8	1.2	% Depr., Dep., Amort./Sales				.8	1.2	1.3
(88) 2.3	(92) 2.6	(94) 2.8				(19) 3.6	(29) 2.7	(26) 3.2	
4.0	4.8	5.2					4.6	5.0	5.4
2.0	2.4	1.9	% Officers', Directors' Owners' Comp/Sales				4.0	.7	
(35) 3.7	(43) 5.0	(44) 4.9				(16) 5.6	(16) 1.5		
6.4	11.2	9.3					9.7	4.6	
2956738M	3097872M	3411150M	Net Sales ($)	4056M	25811M	30490M	205995M	604387M	2540411M
1654461M	1690755M	2114650M	Total Assets ($)	4233M	13174M	10576M	99711M	266167M	1720789M

© RMA 2010
M = $ thousand   MM = $ million
See Pages 9 through 22 for Explanation of Ratios and Data

PROFESSIONAL SERVICES—Advertising Material Distribution Services NAICS 541870

Current Data Sorted by Assets						Comparative Historical Data		

		2	9	1	2	Type of Statement		
	1	9	5			Unqualified	10	12
		2				Reviewed	8	11
1	2	3	1			Compiled	8	7
3	7	12	9	1		Tax Returns	12	4
						Other	32	19
	13 (4/1-9/30/09)		57 (10/1/09-3/31/10)				4/1/05-3/31/06 ALL	4/1/06-3/31/07 ALL
0-500M	500M-2MM	2-10MM	10-50MM	50-100MM	100-250MM	NUMBER OF STATEMENTS	70	53
4	10	28	24	2	2			
%	%	%	%	%	%	ASSETS	%	%
	3.6	17.0	16.5			Cash & Equivalents	13.2	15.9
	34.8	37.6	35.1			Trade Receivables (net)	43.7	31.1
	18.1	6.7	8.6			Inventory	5.9	10.2
	8.7	5.8	3.5			All Other Current	5.0	5.8
	65.2	67.1	63.8			Total Current	67.9	63.1
	23.9	24.3	16.7			Fixed Assets (net)	19.1	22.0
	9.5	6.0	14.6			Intangibles (net)	6.0	7.2
	1.4	2.6	5.0			All Other Non-Current	7.0	7.7
	100.0	100.0	100.0			Total	100.0	100.0
						LIABILITIES		
	33.3	9.5	4.3			Notes Payable-Short Term	9.4	8.0
	5.8	3.8	5.9			Cur. Mat.-L.T.D.	2.4	3.8
	19.3	19.0	22.0			Trade Payables	18.1	16.9
	.0	.4	.0			Income Taxes Payable	.2	.4
	30.4	19.4	16.2			All Other Current	17.2	19.0
	88.8	52.0	48.5			Total Current	47.4	48.1
	32.3	13.9	9.3			Long-Term Debt	16.1	14.4
	.0	.6	.8			Deferred Taxes	.3	.4
	7.9	4.0	8.0			All Other Non-Current	3.5	5.3
	-29.0	29.5	33.5			Net Worth	32.7	31.9
	100.0	100.0	100.0			Total Liabilities & Net Worth	100.0	100.0
						INCOME DATA		
	100.0	100.0	100.0			Net Sales	100.0	100.0
						Gross Profit		
	96.9	91.7	97.2			Operating Expenses	93.6	91.9
	3.1	8.3	2.8			Operating Profit	6.4	8.1
	.8	1.2	2.5			All Other Expenses (net)	1.4	1.4
	2.3	7.2	.3			Profit Before Taxes	4.9	6.8
						RATIOS		
	1.8	1.9	3.2				2.6	2.5
	.9	1.2	1.3			Current	1.4	1.3
	.4	.9	.9				1.0	.8
	1.0	1.6	3.0				2.4	2.1
	.6	1.0	1.2			Quick	1.1	.9
	.2	.5	.7				.8	.5
32	11.3	23 16.1	30 12.2				30 12.0	16 22.4
38	9.5	41 8.8	54 6.8			Sales/Receivables	53 6.9	36 10.3
52	7.0	68 5.4	70 5.2				73 5.0	58 6.3
						Cost of Sales/Inventory		
						Cost of Sales/Payables		
	9.2	7.2	4.4				6.5	6.9
	NM	21.9	12.4			Sales/Working Capital	14.8	34.5
	-2.9	-44.8	-46.0				UND	-24.7
		20.7	10.8				22.5	20.7
		(25) 4.8	(20) 2.2			EBIT/Interest	(56) 6.1	(41) 5.0
		2.1	-2.8				2.1	1.2
						Net Profit + Depr., Dep., Amort./Cur. Mat. L/T/D	6.1	
							(14) 3.7	
							1.2	
	.2	.1	.2				.2	.2
	NM	.8	.6			Fixed/Worth	.6	.7
	-.2	3.2	-2.3				2.0	NM
	2.8	1.0	.7				.9	.7
	NM	3.2	2.7			Debt/Worth	2.3	2.3
	-2.2	10.1	-68.0				13.6	NM
		102.7	32.2				63.8	82.9
		(23) 32.6	(17) 5.3			% Profit Before Taxes/Tangible Net Worth	(57) 30.6	(40) 27.9
		13.8	-6.7				6.1	12.4
	9.5	29.6	8.4				21.6	28.5
	1.9	5.7	1.8			% Profit Before Taxes/Total Assets	9.7	9.3
	-7.7	2.0	-6.6				1.6	1.3
	33.0	196.5	51.3				82.6	60.7
	23.4	24.2	24.6			Sales/Net Fixed Assets	24.5	22.2
	14.1	5.4	12.8				9.3	9.0
	4.7	4.5	3.6				3.9	4.3
	3.1	2.4	2.4			Sales/Total Assets	2.9	2.6
	1.5	1.7	1.5				2.2	1.8
		.2	1.1				.5	.5
		(25) .8	(19) 1.7			% Depr., Dep., Amort./Sales	(56) 1.3	(43) 1.3
		4.8	5.1				3.1	3.1
		.8					3.0	2.3
		(10) 2.6				% Officers', Directors' Owners' Comp/Sales	(23) 4.9	(14) 3.4
		7.0					8.1	6.3
10238M	50371M	438749M	1313340M	303930M	353763M	Net Sales ($)	1929407M	1251951M
1128M	13030M	151545M	525636M	142113M	383103M	Total Assets ($)	561008M	455788M

© RMA 2010

M = $ thousand   MM = $ million
See Pages 9 through 22 for Explanation of Ratios and Data

Comparative Historical Data | Current Data Sorted by Sales

	4/1/07-3/31/08 ALL	4/1/08-3/31/09 ALL	4/1/09-3/31/10 ALL	0-1MM	1-3MM	3-5MM	5-10MM	10-25MM	25MM & OVER
Type of Statement									
Unqualified	10	4	14				1	3	10
Reviewed	7	15	15	1		1	1	8	4
Compiled	5	2	2					2	
Tax Returns	7	6	7	2		2		3	
Other	26	12	32	2	2	1	10	6	11
				13 (4/1-9/30/09)			57 (10/1/09-3/31/10)		
NUMBER OF STATEMENTS	55	39	70	5	2	5	11	22	25
	%	%	%	%	%	%	%	%	%
ASSETS									
Cash & Equivalents	8.9	11.7	13.5				9.2	17.5	14.0
Trade Receivables (net)	41.7	39.2	35.0				44.9	35.0	36.1
Inventory	6.8	10.0	8.4				9.5	8.4	8.3
All Other Current	5.6	5.0	5.0				11.1	5.5	3.9
Total Current	63.0	66.0	61.8				74.6	66.5	62.3
Fixed Assets (net)	17.9	22.2	21.6				15.7	21.8	12.5
Intangibles (net)	11.6	4.5	12.7				4.1	7.8	21.5
All Other Non-Current	7.4	7.3	3.8				5.6	3.9	3.7
Total	100.0	100.0	100.0				100.0	100.0	100.0
LIABILITIES									
Notes Payable-Short Term	10.1	13.2	12.4				23.4	8.9	4.6
Cur. Mat.-L.T.D.	5.9	3.6	6.9				1.9	4.7	6.7
Trade Payables	18.9	18.4	20.2				15.8	19.0	23.3
Income Taxes Payable	.1	.0	.3				.0	.5	.4
All Other Current	13.5	12.2	19.9				30.6	20.2	19.0
Total Current	48.5	47.4	59.7				71.7	53.3	54.0
Long-Term Debt	12.2	14.1	16.1				8.1	19.1	10.4
Deferred Taxes	.1	.0	.7				.0	1.3	.6
All Other Non-Current	13.5	6.5	5.5				6.6	6.7	3.4
Net Worth	25.6	32.0	18.0				13.6	19.5	31.6
Total Liabilties & Net Worth	100.0	100.0	100.0				100.0	100.0	100.0
INCOME DATA									
Net Sales	100.0	100.0	100.0				100.0	100.0	100.0
Gross Profit									
Operating Expenses	93.5	91.4	94.8				94.0	93.1	97.5
Operating Profit	6.5	8.6	5.2				6.0	6.9	2.5
All Other Expenses (net)	1.8	1.7	1.9				.3	.9	2.9
Profit Before Taxes	4.7	6.9	3.4				5.7	6.0	-.4
RATIOS									
Current	2.4	2.7	2.3				1.6	2.3	2.7
	1.3	1.4	1.2				1.2	1.3	1.0
	.9	.9	.8				.9	1.1	.8
Quick	1.6	1.8	1.7				1.2	1.7	2.2
	1.1	1.2	.9				.8	1.2	.8
	.6	.7	.5				.6	.7	.5
Sales/Receivables	33 11.1	27 13.3	24 15.3				33 10.9	28 13.0	21 17.1
	47 7.7	50 7.3	42 8.6				39 9.4	52 7.1	43 8.5
	71 5.2	74 4.9	63 5.8				95 3.8	74 4.9	61 6.0
Cost of Sales/Inventory									
Cost of Sales/Payables									
Sales/Working Capital	8.6	7.1	7.0				9.7	5.4	8.5
	24.0	12.6	31.8				29.4	15.4	-999.8
	-58.1	-49.6	-27.1				-19.0	NM	-26.9
EBIT/Interest	12.1	11.9	13.5				114.3	15.3	17.4
	(45) 5.6	(30) 4.2	(62) 2.6				(10) 4.2	(20) 3.9	(22) 2.3
	1.4	1.2	.6				1.9	2.1	-3.1
Net Profit + Depr., Dep., Amort./Cur. Mat. L/T/D	5.7		2.2						
	(13) 2.0		(11) .3						
	1.1		-.4						
Fixed/Worth	.2	.1	.2				.0	.3	.2
	.6	.6	1.2				.3	.7	1.3
	5.9	1.7	-1.0				3.6	2.4	-.3
Debt/Worth	1.0	.8	1.1				1.3	1.2	.8
	3.3	2.2	3.4				3.4	2.9	6.8
	31.2	6.7	-4.6				11.0	5.3	-3.4
% Profit Before Taxes/Tangible Net Worth	88.4	60.7	64.9					60.9	77.9
	(42) 43.5	(32) 27.5	(48) 17.4					(18) 21.0	(15) 15.6
	4.0	11.7	2.9					10.7	-11.3
% Profit Before Taxes/Total Assets	28.2	21.0	12.9				30.6	19.6	11.1
	10.4	6.7	3.6				3.8	8.1	2.0
	-1.4	2.0	-.7				.8	2.9	-6.7
Sales/Net Fixed Assets	80.5	54.0	82.9				107.5	45.3	143.5
	25.3	22.7	23.2				27.0	16.9	37.0
	11.7	5.5	7.3				8.5	7.3	13.4
Sales/Total Assets	3.8	4.0	4.2				4.6	3.7	4.5
	2.8	2.2	2.6				3.0	2.2	2.8
	1.8	1.6	1.7				2.0	1.8	1.8
% Depr., Dep., Amort./Sales	.8	.6	.6				.1	.8	.4
	(39) 1.7	(30) 1.5	(56) 1.4				(10) .8	(20) 2.5	(18) 1.1
	3.5	3.3	3.9				3.5	5.2	2.0
% Officers', Directors', Owners' Comp/Sales	2.6	2.5	1.0						
	(15) 6.0	(10) 5.6	(19) 4.8						
	10.7	14.0	10.2						
Net Sales ($)	1550293M	1447504M	2470391M	2202M	3689M	20056M	81239M	401434M	1961771M
Total Assets ($)	695112M	565455M	1216555M	7348M	4044M	9540M	33330M	215783M	946510M

M = $ thousand   MM = $ million
See Pages 9 through 22 for Explanation of Ratios and Data

PROFESSIONAL SERVICES—Other Services Related to Advertising NAICS 541890

| Current Data Sorted by Assets | | | | | | Comparative Historical Data | |

						Type of Statement	4/1/05-3/31/06 ALL	4/1/06-3/31/07 ALL
	1	5	9	3	3	Unqualified	7	9
	4	8	5			Reviewed	10	9
	6	3		1		Compiled	14	15
3	14	6				Tax Returns	8	19
13	15	23	15	3	3	Other	24	51
12	22 (4/1-9/30/09)		133 (10/1/09-3/31/10)					
0-500M	500M-2MM	2-10MM	10-50MM	50-100MM	100-250MM	NUMBER OF STATEMENTS	63	103
28	40	45	29	7	6			
%	%	%	%	%	%	ASSETS	%	%
34.6	16.6	18.2	15.5			Cash & Equivalents	10.7	16.9
35.3	34.3	32.6	32.8			Trade Receivables (net)	38.1	37.0
2.0	9.8	7.5	8.6			Inventory	16.4	12.0
4.2	3.1	10.1	4.3			All Other Current	3.1	4.6
76.1	63.9	68.4	61.3			Total Current	68.4	70.6
14.4	15.9	14.1	20.4			Fixed Assets (net)	19.2	16.4
4.9	7.8	9.8	11.1			Intangibles (net)	6.3	6.7
4.6	12.5	7.7	7.2			All Other Non-Current	6.1	6.3
100.0	100.0	100.0	100.0			Total	100.0	100.0
						LIABILITIES		
29.9	16.1	12.7	4.2			Notes Payable-Short Term	17.8	15.3
4.7	6.1	3.3	4.8			Cur. Mat.-L.T.D.	3.4	5.0
32.5	19.8	19.1	16.6			Trade Payables	19.4	20.3
.1	.3	.3	.3			Income Taxes Payable	.5	.4
15.4	23.2	18.3	18.5			All Other Current	14.6	18.2
82.6	65.6	53.7	44.5			Total Current	55.6	59.3
14.3	15.4	10.8	17.4			Long-Term Debt	14.6	18.3
.0	.0	.3	.8			Deferred Taxes	.3	.3
12.0	7.3	3.4	8.4			All Other Non-Current	7.3	5.3
-8.8	11.7	31.8	28.9			Net Worth	22.1	16.9
100.0	100.0	100.0	100.0			Total Liabilities & Net Worth	100.0	100.0
						INCOME DATA		
100.0	100.0	100.0	100.0			Net Sales	100.0	100.0
						Gross Profit		
97.3	95.0	95.8	95.6			Operating Expenses	95.6	91.6
2.7	5.0	4.2	4.4			Operating Profit	4.4	8.4
1.5	2.8	1.4	2.0			All Other Expenses (net)	1.7	1.6
1.2	2.2	2.9	2.3			Profit Before Taxes	2.7	6.8
						RATIOS		
3.6	1.8	1.7	2.3			Current	2.1	2.2
1.4	1.0	1.2	1.6				1.3	1.4
.6	.7	.9	.9				.9	.9
3.6	1.3	1.5	2.0			Quick	1.4	1.5
1.3	.8	1.0	1.1				.9	1.0
.5	.4	.6	.6				.5	.6
0 UND	16 23.4	29 12.4	39 9.3			Sales/Receivables	32 11.3	23 16.2
12 29.8	35 10.5	41 8.8	53 6.9				42 8.6	46 8.0
38 9.5	54 6.7	62 5.9	86 4.2				65 5.6	68 5.4
						Cost of Sales/Inventory		
						Cost of Sales/Payables		
16.9	9.6	6.3	4.2			Sales/Working Capital	7.9	7.4
52.7	-501.6	15.8	9.0				25.2	23.8
-26.0	-9.5	-127.5	-181.7				-55.7	-63.6
26.0	7.0	14.0	14.9			EBIT/Interest	13.3	23.0
(19) 3.5	(35) 2.5	(39) 2.4	(26) 1.8				(56) 3.9	(87) 4.1
1.0	-.1	.5	-.1				1.0	1.5
						Net Profit + Depr., Dep., Amort./Cur. Mat. L/T/D	9.2	6.1
							(15) 4.8	(18) 3.3
							1.6	1.2
.0	.1	.1	.1			Fixed/Worth	.1	.1
2.0	1.1	.5	.8				.5	.5
-.7	-.7	-3.7	NM				18.9	4.7
.6	1.3	.9	1.0			Debt/Worth	1.1	1.1
9.7	7.4	2.2	2.1				3.8	3.0
-3.5	-5.5	-59.7	NM				-29.9	47.2
158.1	49.9	64.7	36.2			% Profit Before Taxes/Tangible Net Worth	66.2	87.6
(15) 60.0	(24) 13.1	(33) 11.7	(22) 8.8				(45) 23.8	(79) 30.3
6.9	.8	-7.5	-8.4				3.3	12.2
50.5	9.8	12.3	15.6			% Profit Before Taxes/Total Assets	21.1	25.4
5.7	2.6	3.6	3.9				5.6	7.5
-15.5	-6.1	-3.9	-3.3				.5	1.9
999.8	110.8	146.0	39.2			Sales/Net Fixed Assets	78.6	97.8
88.0	45.7	28.7	15.4				29.5	46.6
29.2	13.7	11.9	6.6				13.0	14.7
14.9	4.3	3.6	2.5			Sales/Total Assets	4.4	4.1
6.8	3.1	2.3	1.8				2.9	2.9
5.1	1.7	1.5	1.1				1.9	2.1
.7	.4	.5	1.0			% Depr., Dep., Amort./Sales	.6	.6
(14) 1.1	(31) 1.1	(32) 1.2	(26) 2.0				(47) 1.1	(74) 1.1
2.4	2.9	2.6	3.8				2.2	2.2
4.6	3.7	1.5				% Officers', Directors' Owners' Comp/Sales	3.2	3.0
(18) 10.6	(24) 5.2	(17) 4.3					(28) 6.3	(41) 4.7
26.5	10.8	10.4					12.9	8.5
59060M	141016M	545713M	1340319M	1100380M	1027405M	Net Sales ($)	1512420M	2698826M
6183M	43898M	197885M	678007M	493661M	852089M	Total Assets ($)	475983M	1116998M

M = $ thousand   MM = $ million
See Pages 9 through 22 for Explanation of Ratios and Data

Comparative Historical Data | Current Data Sorted by Sales

			Type of Statement						
14	18	21	Unqualified	1	1	1	1	3	16
8	17	17	Reviewed	1	1	1	2	9	1
14	22	13	Compiled		6	3	4		
13	27	33	Tax Returns	7	10	9	6	1	1
45	61	71	Other	8	10	10	7	19	17
4/1/07-3/31/08 ALL	4/1/08-3/31/09 ALL	4/1/09-3/31/10 ALL		0-1MM	1-3MM	3-5MM	5-10MM	10-25MM	25MM & OVER
				22 (4/1-9/30/09)			**133 (10/1/09-3/31/10)**		
94	145	155	**NUMBER OF STATEMENTS**	16	28	24	20	32	35
%	%	%	**ASSETS**	%	%	%	%	%	%
16.6	15.2	19.8	Cash & Equivalents	42.9	16.0	18.7	17.2	18.7	15.7
41.2	36.2	33.6	Trade Receivables (net)	17.9	37.1	32.8	33.7	34.3	37.9
11.0	9.3	7.1	Inventory	2.3	5.0	9.8	11.5	7.4	6.3
3.6	4.7	5.6	All Other Current	.5	2.7	13.2	3.6	6.3	5.6
72.4	65.4	66.1	Total Current	63.7	60.7	74.5	65.9	66.7	65.5
14.4	17.6	15.7	Fixed Assets (net)	18.1	14.8	16.5	12.3	16.8	15.6
5.4	9.0	10.2	Intangibles (net)	.4	16.4	5.4	8.3	10.3	14.2
7.8	8.1	8.0	All Other Non-Current	17.8	8.1	3.5	13.6	6.2	4.7
100.0	100.0	100.0	Total	100.0	100.0	100.0	100.0	100.0	100.0
			LIABILITIES						
13.3	14.2	14.2	Notes Payable-Short Term	40.7	18.7	13.5	15.0	8.1	4.1
4.6	5.8	4.4	Cur. Mat.-L.T.D.	7.4	4.9	4.7	2.3	4.5	3.7
18.9	17.5	20.6	Trade Payables	36.8	12.5	23.0	19.7	21.5	17.7
.3	.7	.4	Income Taxes Payable	.0	.0	.3	.7	.3	.8
18.5	18.1	19.1	All Other Current	9.5	20.1	20.6	17.4	19.5	22.2
55.6	56.4	58.7	Total Current	94.3	56.2	62.1	55.0	53.9	48.4
19.8	17.8	14.9	Long-Term Debt	14.0	18.8	19.1	7.0	12.3	16.1
.1	.3	.4	Deferred Taxes	.0	.0	.0	.5	.8	.9
5.2	6.5	6.7	All Other Non-Current	8.5	9.0	10.0	3.0	4.1	6.3
19.2	19.1	19.3	Net Worth	-16.8	16.0	8.8	34.5	29.0	28.3
100.0	100.0	100.0	Total Liabilities & Net Worth	100.0	100.0	100.0	100.0	100.0	100.0
			INCOME DATA						
100.0	100.0	100.0	Net Sales	100.0	100.0	100.0	100.0	100.0	100.0
			Gross Profit						
93.9	96.1	95.8	Operating Expenses	85.3	99.7	98.4	94.0	95.9	96.6
6.1	3.9	4.2	Operating Profit	14.7	.3	1.6	6.0	4.1	3.4
1.2	1.4	2.0	All Other Expenses (net)	5.0	2.4	1.1	1.5	1.8	1.4
4.9	2.5	2.2	Profit Before Taxes	9.7	-2.1	.6	4.5	2.3	2.0
			RATIOS						
2.2	2.1	2.1		3.1	2.0	2.6	2.2	2.3	2.1
1.4	1.3	1.2	Current	.9	1.1	1.3	1.3	1.2	1.3
1.0	.9	.8		.2	.7	.7	.9	1.0	.9
1.7	1.5	1.8		3.1	1.7	2.0	1.6	1.6	1.9
1.1	1.0	1.0	Quick	.9	1.0	.9	1.0	1.0	1.1
.7	.6	.5		.2	.5	.4	.7	.7	.7
29 12.6	21 17.1	23 15.6		0 UND	23 16.0	7 50.8	33 11.1	34 10.7	40 9.2
49 7.5	38 9.5	41 8.8	Sales/Receivables	0 UND	32 11.3	41 8.8	42 8.6	42 8.7	55 6.7
64 5.7	58 6.3	62 5.9		23 15.8	52 7.0	54 6.7	68 5.4	68 5.3	85 4.3
			Cost of Sales/Inventory						
			Cost of Sales/Payables						
6.9	7.3	6.5		8.0	9.7	9.5	6.1	6.3	5.9
16.1	25.9	24.8	Sales/Working Capital	-118.5	71.3	20.4	16.0	25.7	11.6
390.6	-43.0	-27.6		-5.4	-16.1	-24.4	-145.7	-241.0	-108.9
14.2	12.3	12.1			4.2	26.1	35.3	9.9	20.6
(79) 4.1	(124) 4.1	(132) 2.6	EBIT/Interest	(23) 2.3	(22) 2.2	(19) 4.2	(26) 1.8	(33) 4.4	
.9	.7	.6			-.9	-2.8	.6	-.1	1.0
13.1	8.3	6.5	Net Profit + Depr., Dep.,						
(21) 4.7	(31) 2.1	(21) 1.7	Amort./Cur. Mat. L/T/D						
.5	1.1	.8							
.1	.2	.1		.0	.2	.0	.1	.1	.1
.4	1.0	.8	Fixed/Worth	.2	1.0	2.4	.5	.7	.8
1.8	-2.4	-1.3		-5.0	-.5	-.5	-5.9	NM	-1.2
1.0	1.2	1.1		.3	.9	1.4	1.2	1.2	1.2
2.8	3.6	4.2	Debt/Worth	4.3	17.3	8.9	2.7	2.6	3.1
26.5	-10.1	-6.6		-7.5	-3.2	-3.8	-33.4	NM	-6.3
68.0	73.7	52.7	% Profit Before Taxes/Tangible	234.5	40.1	62.3	113.3	45.4	41.1
(72) 21.5	(104) 23.6	(102) 12.4	Net Worth	(10) 37.8	(15) 6.9	(15) 12.8	(14) 34.1	(24) 10.4	(24) 12.5
5.0	.9	-4.3		-10.1	.9	-36.9	-.4	-6.1	-6.0
19.0	20.0	16.8	% Profit Before Taxes/Total	81.8	6.4	22.3	29.7	10.9	16.8
7.7	5.3	3.2	Assets	9.6	1.1	2.3	4.0	2.2	4.4
.1	-.7	-3.3		.1	-14.2	-10.8	-.1	-3.1	.4
133.7	73.7	120.4		UND	123.0	117.7	85.5	181.5	50.3
41.0	27.9	30.7	Sales/Net Fixed Assets	90.1	33.8	40.4	28.3	22.3	25.5
13.0	11.2	12.2		8.7	13.7	17.3	15.8	10.8	11.1
5.0	4.9	4.6		13.3	5.4	6.0	4.4	4.6	2.9
2.9	3.0	2.5	Sales/Total Assets	3.2	3.1	3.6	2.4	2.6	2.2
2.1	2.0	1.6		.5	1.7	1.8	1.4	1.2	1.6
.4	.6	.6			.7	.3	.4	1.2	.7
(71) 1.0	(117) 1.5	(112) 1.4	% Depr., Dep., Amort./Sales	(22) 1.3	(14) .6	(16) .9	(22) 2.2	(30) 1.6	
2.2	2.9	3.3			3.7	1.9	1.3	3.7	3.5
2.8	2.4	2.6	% Officers', Directors'		2.3	4.2		1.4	
(38) 4.8	(58) 4.9	(63) 5.5	Owners' Comp/Sales	(19) 5.2	(13) 7.7		(13) 2.6		
9.1	9.1	11.6			11.2	14.3		4.5	
4477065M	6228423M	4213893M	Net Sales ($)	7182M	53136M	91164M	139894M	513816M	3408701M
1868305M	2622109M	2271723M	Total Assets ($)	6992M	22976M	38212M	191476M	285712M	1726355M

M = $ thousand   MM = $ million
See Pages 9 through 22 for Explanation of Ratios and Data

Current Data Sorted by Assets | Comparative Historical Data

0-500M	500M-2MM	2-10MM	10-50MM	50-100MM	100-250MM	Type of Statement	ALL 4/1/05-3/31/06	ALL 4/1/06-3/31/07
		9	7	5	4	Unqualified	18	21
	2	11	1			Reviewed	12	9
2	8	6			1	Compiled	21	25
9	3	4			1	Tax Returns	11	16
7	16	27	11	4	1	Other	30	32
21 (4/1-9/30/09)			117 (10/1/09-3/31/10)					
18	29	57	19	9	6	NUMBER OF STATEMENTS	92	103
%	%	%	%	%	%	ASSETS	%	%
25.2	12.2	14.3	17.9			Cash & Equivalents	14.6	18.7
20.8	50.8	41.2	37.5			Trade Receivables (net)	41.3	36.3
.4	3.0	3.4	1.3			Inventory	2.5	1.8
4.7	2.6	6.4	11.6			All Other Current	3.8	4.1
51.0	68.6	65.3	68.2			Total Current	62.2	60.9
24.5	22.9	17.0	17.2			Fixed Assets (net)	18.8	21.6
6.8	4.8	6.6	6.5			Intangibles (net)	7.0	5.4
17.6	3.8	11.1	8.1			All Other Non-Current	12.0	12.1
100.0	100.0	100.0	100.0			Total	100.0	100.0
						LIABILITIES		
44.3	10.9	8.9	2.3			Notes Payable-Short Term	14.4	12.9
22.1	3.0	6.0	2.1			Cur. Mat.-L.T.D.	2.8	4.2
15.8	18.7	15.3	11.9			Trade Payables	11.2	12.1
.0	.1	.3	.0			Income Taxes Payable	.4	.5
12.6	13.3	23.3	27.9			All Other Current	21.7	20.6
94.8	45.9	53.9	44.2			Total Current	50.5	50.2
23.2	15.1	13.6	7.7			Long-Term Debt	16.0	10.8
.0	.3	.1	1.5			Deferred Taxes	.3	.4
5.9	5.6	9.8	6.1			All Other Non-Current	7.9	5.9
-23.9	33.1	22.7	40.4			Net Worth	25.3	32.6
100.0	100.0	100.0	100.0			Total Liabilities & Net Worth	100.0	100.0
						INCOME DATA		
100.0	100.0	100.0	100.0			Net Sales	100.0	100.0
						Gross Profit		
97.7	95.9	92.1	92.9			Operating Expenses	93.8	89.9
2.3	4.1	7.9	7.1			Operating Profit	6.2	10.1
2.6	.7	2.5	.9			All Other Expenses (net)	1.0	1.5
-.3	3.5	5.4	6.2			Profit Before Taxes	5.2	8.6
						RATIOS		
2.2	4.0	2.0	2.1				2.0	2.8
1.1	1.6	1.2	1.3			Current	1.2	1.5
.2	1.1	.8	1.1				.8	.9
2.2	4.0	1.8	2.0				1.6	2.3
1.1	1.6	1.1	1.3			Quick	1.0	1.3
.1	1.0	.7	.7				.7	.8
0 UND	42 8.6	37 9.8	43 8.6				25 14.7	10 38.0
0 UND	58 6.3	61 6.0	49 7.4			Sales/Receivables	51 7.2	45 8.0
33 11.0	81 4.5	85 4.3	74 4.9				78 4.7	68 5.3
						Cost of Sales/Inventory		
						Cost of Sales/Payables		
19.5	5.1	6.0	5.5				7.5	7.2
303.3	18.2	18.3	14.3			Sales/Working Capital	28.3	22.4
-6.1	82.0	-38.9	40.3				-53.6	-61.1
5.6	25.0	19.2	59.9				19.2	19.7
(14) 2.4	(21) 6.3	(43) 7.2	(15) 15.1			EBIT/Interest	(76) 5.5	(73) 7.2
-4.0	.8	1.5	-2.5				.7	2.2
						Net Profit + Depr., Dep.,	9.3	9.1
						Amort./Cur. Mat. L/T/D	(14) 4.1	(15) 2.8
							1.7	1.8
.0	.1	.1	.2				.2	.2
.7	.6	.4	.5			Fixed/Worth	.4	.5
-1.3	1.5	2.5	1.2				2.4	3.2
.5	.3	1.1	.8				.9	.7
7.1	2.7	2.6	1.9			Debt/Worth	2.7	1.7
-2.2	11.6	7.8	4.3				37.7	18.5
367.1	65.8	65.2	39.2			% Profit Before Taxes/Tangible	67.1	129.4
(10) 29.5	(23) 15.5	(46) 24.4	18.4			Net Worth	(71) 36.0	(84) 50.6
15.3	2.3	5.0	-3.7				.0	14.9
39.6	25.9	19.3	12.8			% Profit Before Taxes/Total	25.6	35.7
6.6	4.5	7.0	6.7			Assets	9.1	12.2
-22.4	-2.3	.0	-1.4				-1.4	4.4
UND	143.8	68.2	64.8				70.1	62.5
57.4	29.3	27.7	16.8			Sales/Net Fixed Assets	30.7	24.2
12.5	5.1	10.2	10.0				11.8	11.0
12.8	4.4	3.4	3.0				4.2	5.1
6.3	2.7	2.4	2.2			Sales/Total Assets	3.1	3.1
4.6	1.6	1.8	1.7				2.1	2.2
.5	.7	.7	.5				.7	.8
(10) .8	(21) 1.3	(46) 1.7	(16) 1.3			% Depr., Dep., Amort./Sales	(70) 1.4	(78) 1.3
1.8	2.6	2.7	1.8				3.0	2.5
5.7	3.5	2.2				% Officers', Directors'	3.2	3.6
(10) 11.0	(11) 5.9	(12) 8.4				Owners' Comp/Sales	(34) 9.2	(35) 9.9
24.5	19.4	13.7					16.5	24.3
32949M	129252M	731123M	985704M	775082M	1111001M	Net Sales ($)	2212489M	2489991M
4105M	38617M	262670M	449537M	602822M	956753M	Total Assets ($)	821844M	1044180M

© RMA 2010

M = $ thousand   MM = $ million
See Pages 9 through 22 for Explanation of Ratios and Data

Comparative Historical Data | Current Data Sorted by Sales

			Type of Statement						
16	22	25	Unqualified	1			2	7	15
9	14	14	Reviewed		1	1	4	6	2
11	13	16	Compiled		5	4	3	3	
19	20	17	Tax Returns	1	6	2		2	2
34	43	66	Other	5	10	5	16	13	16
4/1/07-	4/1/08-	4/1/09-		6					
3/31/08	3/31/09	3/31/10			21 (4/1-9/30/09)		117 (10/1/09-3/31/10)		
ALL	ALL	ALL		0-1MM	1-3MM	3-5MM	5-10MM	10-25MM	25MM & OVER
89	112	138	NUMBER OF STATEMENTS	13	22	12	25	31	35
%	%	%	ASSETS	%	%	%	%	%	%
16.6	19.2	16.7	Cash & Equivalents	9.2	15.3	21.6	16.1	13.8	21.6
38.3	35.4	37.6	Trade Receivables (net)	9.3	41.8	33.9	46.0	48.4	31.4
1.2	2.4	2.3	Inventory	.5	.3	4.6	3.3	2.8	2.3
6.5	5.4	5.9	All Other Current	8.1	1.8	3.2	6.1	5.2	8.9
62.8	62.4	62.5	Total Current	27.1	59.1	63.3	71.5	70.1	64.2
20.2	20.6	19.2	Fixed Assets (net)	36.2	27.2	21.5	11.6	16.0	15.5
7.8	8.0	8.7	Intangibles (net)	7.1	8.8	10.7	5.0	5.2	14.1
9.3	9.0	9.6	All Other Non-Current	29.6	4.9	4.5	11.9	8.7	6.2
100.0	100.0	100.0	Total	100.0	100.0	100.0	100.0	100.0	100.0
			LIABILITIES						
15.6	14.6	12.4	Notes Payable-Short Term	44.2	10.9	27.2	8.7	9.2	2.2
5.9	3.7	6.5	Cur. Mat.-L.T.D.	28.2	6.8	5.0	2.2	4.6	3.5
13.9	13.2	14.6	Trade Payables	13.4	13.2	9.0	9.3	24.8	12.4
.4	.4	.2	Income Taxes Payable	.0	.2	.0	.5	.1	.1
21.6	19.6	19.3	All Other Current	11.4	13.9	9.9	22.4	21.7	24.6
57.5	51.4	53.0	Total Current	97.1	45.0	51.2	43.1	60.4	42.8
15.8	12.5	16.3	Long-Term Debt	26.8	18.9	25.2	12.7	12.2	13.8
.2	.3	.5	Deferred Taxes	.0	.1	.6	.1	.0	1.7
6.4	8.3	7.9	All Other Non-Current	5.8	5.8	9.1	2.2	14.4	7.9
20.1	27.4	22.3	Net Worth	-29.7	30.2	14.0	41.9	13.1	33.8
100.0	100.0	100.0	Total Liabilties & Net Worth	100.0	100.0	100.0	100.0	100.0	100.0
			INCOME DATA						
100.0	100.0	100.0	Net Sales	100.0	100.0	100.0	100.0	100.0	100.0
			Gross Profit						
94.6	95.7	93.7	Operating Expenses	83.0	94.7	95.2	95.7	93.8	95.0
5.4	4.3	6.3	Operating Profit	17.0	5.3	4.8	4.3	6.2	5.0
1.7	1.7	2.6	All Other Expenses (net)	11.0	.9	.3	.8	2.3	2.8
3.7	2.7	3.7	Profit Before Taxes	6.0	4.4	4.5	3.6	3.9	2.2
			RATIOS						
2.4	2.5	2.3		1.4	3.6	3.7	3.3	1.5	2.8
1.3	1.3	1.4	Current	.4	1.6	1.5	1.7	1.2	1.7
.9	.9	1.0		.2	1.0	.7	1.2	.8	1.1
2.1	2.2	2.1		1.3	3.6	3.7	3.0	1.5	2.7
1.1	(111) 1.2	1.2	Quick	.3	1.5	1.4	1.5	1.1	1.6
.7	.8	.8		.1	1.0	.6	.9	.8	.8
28 13.2	23 15.6	30 12.0		0 UND	29 12.6	0 UND	38 9.6	41 9.0	36 10.2
51 7.2	47 7.7	50 7.3	Sales/Receivables	0 UND	50 7.3	50 7.3	67 5.4	59 6.2	48 7.6
68 5.3	64 5.7	77 4.7		39 9.3	86 4.3	85 4.3	80 4.6	85 4.3	66 5.6
			Cost of Sales/Inventory						
			Cost of Sales/Payables						
8.6	7.2	6.0		7.3	6.5	4.6	4.6	9.8	4.8
22.8	28.5	18.3	Sales/Working Capital	-118.0	21.9	18.0	7.8	29.2	13.1
-37.3	-49.9	-195.5		-2.6	-176.7	NM	34.4	-21.9	44.6
17.3	23.5	19.5			10.5		44.1	24.8	20.5
(69) 2.9	(93) 4.1	(103) 5.4	EBIT/Interest	(16) 4.8		(18) 7.2	(27) 6.4	(26) 6.1	
1.1	.9	.9			1.0		2.0	1.5	-2.9
7.6	20.7	8.6							
(13) 3.7	(19) 2.7	(21) 4.4	Net Profit + Depr., Dep., Amort./Cur. Mat. L/T/D						
2.0	1.3	2.1							
.2	.2	.1		.0	.2	.0	.1	.2	.1
.6	.6	.5	Fixed/Worth	2.1	.8	.4	.3	.6	.5
-1.8	UND	4.1		-1.8	3.2	-.9	.4	7.6	-19.2
.8	.9	.8		1.9	.6	.5	.6	2.1	.8
3.3	2.7	2.7	Debt/Worth	6.6	3.7	2.9	1.0	4.6	2.5
-10.2	UND	36.7		-2.4	NM	-2.6	2.4	22.8	-159.2
91.4	82.6	64.3			51.2		61.9	76.3	58.3
(61) 26.5	(85) 20.2	(106) 21.6	% Profit Before Taxes/Tangible Net Worth	(17) 4.6		(24) 16.3	(24) 39.5	(26) 19.5	
8.4	2.7	2.1			-5.5		3.6	12.7	-6.0
23.0	23.2	19.5		14.0	23.5	42.0	19.3	18.6	20.8
6.2	5.8	6.7	% Profit Before Taxes/Total Assets	1.3	3.8	11.9	7.9	8.9	7.1
.6	-.1	-1.1		-10.6	-.2	-4.6	.7	-.6	-1.5
54.7	56.8	70.8		UND	58.9	368.2	58.1	79.0	71.8
28.4	24.4	27.0	Sales/Net Fixed Assets	9.5	16.7	40.2	27.7	33.4	26.9
11.3	11.4	9.8		.4	5.0	9.8	16.0	10.0	12.1
4.5	4.9	4.0		5.3	4.8	9.1	4.3	3.7	3.5
3.0	3.0	2.5	Sales/Total Assets	2.9	2.2	3.1	2.5	2.6	2.1
2.1	2.1	1.6		.2	1.1	2.4	2.0	1.9	1.0
.7	.9	.7			.9		1.3	.6	.5
(68) 1.3	(79) 1.5	(100) 1.5	% Depr., Dep., Amort./Sales	(16) 2.0		(18) 1.8	(26) 1.1	(24) 1.3	
2.1	2.5	2.6			4.4		3.1	1.9	1.9
2.8	4.3	3.3							
(27) 8.0	(42) 9.8	(33) 8.2	% Officers', Directors' Owners' Comp/Sales						
16.8	21.4	16.3							
4874062M	3465487M	3765111M	Net Sales ($)	7019M	48246M	47443M	177765M	491769M	2992869M
1558431M	1921247M	2314504M	Total Assets ($)	17290M	25550M	15362M	71476M	298743M	1886083M

M = $ thousand   MM = $ million
See Pages 9 through 22 for Explanation of Ratios and Data

Current Data Sorted by Assets							Comparative Historical Data	
							Type of Statement	
			1				Unqualified	4	4
	1		1	2	1		Reviewed	6	6
	3	1	1				Compiled	13	10
2	3	2	1				Tax Returns	14	20
16	3	2					Other	24	19
6	3	2	2	1				4/1/05-	4/1/06-
	8 (4/1-9/30/09)		42 (10/1/09-3/31/10)					3/31/06	3/31/07
0-500M	500M-2MM	2-10MM	10-50MM	50-100MM	100-250MM			ALL	ALL
24	10	7	5	3	1		NUMBER OF STATEMENTS	61	59
%	%	%	%	%	%		ASSETS	%	%
23.9	13.6						Cash & Equivalents	21.1	20.9
5.7	8.2						Trade Receivables (net)	9.6	9.4
9.6	5.5						Inventory	4.8	4.7
2.0	3.2						All Other Current	1.9	9.0
41.2	30.5						Total Current	37.4	44.0
42.2	40.0						Fixed Assets (net)	43.5	38.9
5.5	19.7						Intangibles (net)	9.6	4.4
11.3	9.8						All Other Non-Current	9.5	12.7
100.0	100.0						Total	100.0	100.0
							LIABILITIES		
41.9	10.7						Notes Payable-Short Term	11.6	11.3
4.0	6.3						Cur. Mat.-L.T.D.	11.0	4.8
7.9	12.2						Trade Payables	7.4	7.0
.0	.0						Income Taxes Payable	.4	.3
21.6	13.3						All Other Current	15.0	19.1
75.4	42.5						Total Current	45.4	42.4
31.1	48.5						Long-Term Debt	28.4	20.6
.0	.0						Deferred Taxes	.4	.4
6.7	9.9						All Other Non-Current	8.1	12.9
-13.1	-.9						Net Worth	17.8	23.8
100.0	100.0						Total Liabilities & Net Worth	100.0	100.0
							INCOME DATA		
100.0	100.0						Net Sales	100.0	100.0
							Gross Profit		
97.0	99.8						Operating Expenses	91.6	91.2
3.0	.2						Operating Profit	8.4	8.8
1.8	2.1						All Other Expenses (net)	1.6	1.5
1.3	-2.0						Profit Before Taxes	6.8	7.3
							RATIOS		
2.5	2.1							1.8	3.2
.6	.6						Current	.9	1.0
.2	.4							.4	.4
2.0	1.0							1.6	2.5
.4	.5						Quick	.6 (58)	.6
.1	.2							.2	.2
0 UND	0 UND							0 UND	0 UND
0 UND	4 103.4						Sales/Receivables	3 130.7	2 217.0
3 111.3	35 10.5							19 19.6	25 14.6
							Cost of Sales/Inventory		
							Cost of Sales/Payables		
13.0	12.0							16.6	5.6
-34.0	-65.9						Sales/Working Capital	-67.3	569.7
-6.9	-12.3							-17.5	-16.4
4.4								10.4	8.8
(15) -.1							EBIT/Interest	(51) 4.3	(46) 3.2
-7.6								1.8	-.3
							Net Profit + Depr., Dep.,	4.1	
							Amort./Cur. Mat. L/T/D	(12) 3.1	
								1.5	
.3	.9							.9	.3
1.7	-2.6						Fixed/Worth	1.9	1.4
-.8	-.5							-3.9	18.0
.7	3.7							1.0	.8
3.9	-5.3						Debt/Worth	2.5	2.7
-2.7	-2.0							-6.0	41.0
195.3							% Profit Before Taxes/Tangible	88.8	82.8
(14) 45.3							Net Worth	(43) 31.4	(45) 31.4
-16.3								6.4	2.1
32.6	6.1						% Profit Before Taxes/Total	28.2	29.5
-1.2	-2.2						Assets	8.8	7.3
-39.5	-13.9							2.7	-1.0
25.9	69.1							21.3	20.1
14.4	10.7						Sales/Net Fixed Assets	7.6	8.4
7.2	5.7							4.3	3.9
7.5	5.5							5.9	4.3
4.3	3.4						Sales/Total Assets	3.1	2.7
2.4	1.5							1.8	1.5
.7								1.8	1.7
(18) 1.9							% Depr., Dep., Amort./Sales	(43) 2.8	(44) 3.1
6.2								5.7	5.0
7.8	2.6						% Officers', Directors'	4.2	5.0
12.5	5.8						Owners' Comp/Sales	(29) 9.5	(29) 9.8
20.3	17.9							11.6	16.4
26564M	40798M	116626M	302869M	197048M	422000M		Net Sales ($)	1522454M	1134450M
4052M	11244M	27778M	165331M	175586M	167000M		Total Assets ($)	738968M	467766M

M = $ thousand   MM = $ million
See Pages 9 through 22 for Explanation of Ratios and Data

Comparative Historical Data   Current Data Sorted by Sales

	4/1/07-3/31/08 ALL	4/1/08-3/31/09 ALL	4/1/09-3/31/10 ALL	Type of Statement	0-1MM	1-3MM	3-5MM	5-10MM	10-25MM	25MM & OVER
	1	4	4	Unqualified						4
	7	7	3	Reviewed	2			1		2
	4	6	8	Compiled	14	4	2	5	1	1
	6	17	21	Tax Returns		3		1		4
	15	19	14	Other	4		1	1	1	
						8 (4/1-9/30/09)		42 (10/1/09-3/31/10)		
NUMBER OF STATEMENTS	33	53	50		20	7	3	7	1	11
ASSETS	%	%	%		%	%	%	%	%	%
Cash & Equivalents	18.5	15.5	17.9		14.4					13.1
Trade Receivables (net)	10.9	10.2	5.3		6.2					3.2
Inventory	4.9	5.9	7.3		11.5					6.6
All Other Current	4.2	2.5	3.1		.2					3.3
Total Current	38.4	34.1	33.5		32.3					26.2
Fixed Assets (net)	47.1	40.8	38.9		48.1					32.1
Intangibles (net)	10.5	14.0	16.6		3.2					36.2
All Other Non-Current	3.9	11.1	11.1		16.5					5.5
Total	100.0	100.0	100.0		100.0					100.0
LIABILITIES										
Notes Payable-Short Term	7.3	13.5	24.0		33.9					5.4
Cur. Mat.-L.T.D.	3.9	5.2	4.6		4.1					5.0
Trade Payables	10.8	6.7	11.0		2.4					11.8
Income Taxes Payable	.7	.6	.1		.0					.3
All Other Current	13.0	18.4	15.9		17.5					12.0
Total Current	35.7	44.4	55.7		57.9					34.5
Long-Term Debt	28.7	27.8	33.2		34.9					18.9
Deferred Taxes	.7	.5	.2		.0					.8
All Other Non-Current	8.9	16.8	9.2		8.0					18.1
Net Worth	26.0	10.4	1.8		-.7					27.7
Total Liabilities & Net Worth	100.0	100.0	100.0		100.0					100.0
INCOME DATA										
Net Sales	100.0	100.0	100.0		100.0					100.0
Gross Profit										
Operating Expenses	95.4	95.8	96.9		91.8					97.3
Operating Profit	4.6	4.2	3.1		8.2					2.7
All Other Expenses (net)	1.8	1.5	3.0		4.5					4.1
Profit Before Taxes	2.9	2.7	.1		3.7					-1.4
RATIOS										
Current	1.7	1.9	2.1		2.5					1.4
	1.2	.7	.6		.7					.6
	.6	.3	.3		.2					.4
Quick	1.4	1.4	1.3		1.9					1.1
	(32) .9	.5	.4		.4					.3
	.3	.2	.2		.2					.2
Sales/Receivables	1 384.9	0 UND	0 UND		0 UND					1 425.3
	5 72.2	4 96.5	1 364.3		0 UND					4 101.1
	20 18.1	15 24.2	8 44.9		7 54.5					8 45.5
Cost of Sales/Inventory										
Cost of Sales/Payables										
Sales/Working Capital	7.5	12.1	13.1		11.1					11.3
	75.1	-31.7	-32.9		UND					-17.3
	-22.7	-9.2	-7.3		-6.7					-11.3
EBIT/Interest	7.9	6.1	4.4		3.5					7.0
	(32) 2.7	(44) 1.6	(38) .0		(13) .5					.9
	.2	-.9	-4.0		-.2					-3.1
Net Profit + Depr., Dep., Amort./Cur. Mat. L/T/D										
Fixed/Worth	.8	.8	.7		.3					1.8
	2.0	4.3	NM		1.3					-1.1
	-3.7	-.8	-.6		-1.8					-.4
Debt/Worth	1.0	1.3	.9		.7					1.2
	2.4	8.2	NM		2.3					-3.7
	-6.9	-2.8	-2.1		-3.9					-2.0
% Profit Before Taxes/Tangible Net Worth	58.8	42.0	121.0		144.7					
	(22) 30.0	(30) 15.6	(25) 8.9		(14) 23.5					
	4.9	-10.2	-9.4		-4.8					
% Profit Before Taxes/Total Assets	16.3	14.3	12.8		32.6					12.0
	5.3	2.2	-1.1		-.3					-.2
	-5.4	-8.6	-15.5		-36.8					-11.1
Sales/Net Fixed Assets	8.7	18.1	20.2		15.1					17.8
	6.2	8.2	12.4		11.6					8.9
	3.0	4.4	5.9		4.9					3.8
Sales/Total Assets	3.0	3.9	6.2		5.8					3.0
	2.4	2.6	3.1		2.7					2.0
	1.8	1.8	1.7		1.1					1.0
% Depr., Dep., Amort./Sales	2.4	1.8	1.6		.8					
	(29) 3.2	(40) 3.5	(37) 3.0		(16) 2.8					
	6.2	5.7	5.8		7.6					
% Officers', Directors' Owners' Comp/Sales	2.5	4.0	3.5		11.1					
	(19) 8.8	(21) 9.8	(25) 8.7		(10) 18.4					
	12.2	15.9	18.4		22.2					
Net Sales ($)	1060655M	2160688M	1105905M		8367M	11148M	10554M	46009M	29215M	1000612M
Total Assets ($)	573752M	1059621M	550991M		6166M	2989M	4893M	9169M	6830M	520944M

M = $ thousand   MM = $ million
See Pages 9 through 22 for Explanation of Ratios and Data

Current Data Sorted by Assets   Comparative Historical Data

Type of Statement	3	4
Unqualified	3	4
Reviewed	11	2
Compiled	7	6
Tax Returns	5	9
Other	6	7
	4/1/05-3/31/06 ALL	4/1/06-3/31/07 ALL

0-500M	500M-2MM	2-10MM	10-50MM	50-100MM	100-250MM		4/1/05-3/31/06 ALL	4/1/06-3/31/07 ALL
		5						
	1	1						
1	1	2			1			
4	2	2						
3	4	2	17 (10/1/09-3/31/10)					
	10 (4/1-9/30/09)							
8	8	10		1		NUMBER OF STATEMENTS	32	28
%	%	%	%	%	%	ASSETS	%	%
		18.1	D		D	Cash & Equivalents	11.6	12.1
		14.3	A		A	Trade Receivables (net)	27.5	26.9
		7.5	T		T	Inventory	8.5	4.8
		2.5	A		A	All Other Current	5.8	7.1
		42.4				Total Current	53.3	50.9
		39.1	N		N	Fixed Assets (net)	35.0	36.8
		3.1	O		O	Intangibles (net)	4.2	5.0
		15.5	T		T	All Other Non-Current	7.5	7.3
		100.0				Total	100.0	100.0
			A		A	LIABILITIES		
		10.2	V		V	Notes Payable-Short Term	8.2	8.8
		6.4	A		A	Cur. Mat.-L.T.D.	4.8	5.1
		8.2	I		I	Trade Payables	10.1	6.9
		.0	L		L	Income Taxes Payable	.2	.9
		13.0	A		A	All Other Current	12.4	11.7
		37.8	B		B	Total Current	35.7	33.5
		37.6	L		L	Long-Term Debt	15.2	20.7
		1.3	E		E	Deferred Taxes	1.0	.3
		.7				All Other Non-Current	10.1	13.6
		22.6				Net Worth	37.9	31.9
		100.0				Total Liabilities & Net Worth	100.0	100.0
						INCOME DATA		
		100.0				Net Sales	100.0	100.0
						Gross Profit		
		92.2				Operating Expenses	97.1	88.1
		7.8				Operating Profit	2.9	11.9
		1.6				All Other Expenses (net)	1.1	3.5
		6.1				Profit Before Taxes	1.8	8.4
						RATIOS		
		1.7					2.5	3.9
		1.4				Current	1.7	1.7
		.9					1.0	.9
		1.5					1.8	3.0
		1.0				Quick	1.2	1.4
		.6					.7	.4
	4	100.1					19 18.9	4 95.6
	33	11.2				Sales/Receivables	38 9.7	47 7.8
	64	5.7					61 6.0	76 4.8
						Cost of Sales/Inventory		
						Cost of Sales/Payables		
		9.1					4.8	5.6
		14.2				Sales/Working Capital	14.3	9.7
		NM					UND	-94.3
							9.6	18.7
						EBIT/Interest	(27) 2.5	(23) 4.5
							-.1	1.8
						Net Profit + Depr., Dep., Amort./Cur. Mat. L/T/D		
		.9					.4	.3
		1.5				Fixed/Worth	1.0	.9
		NM					1.7	2.3
		.9					.8	.6
		4.0				Debt/Worth	1.4	1.4
		NM					4.5	5.4
							34.6	76.1
						% Profit Before Taxes/Tangible Net Worth	(30) 5.9	(25) 44.1
							-9.5	11.4
		20.5					12.9	37.3
		3.3				% Profit Before Taxes/Total Assets	2.4	10.5
		-2.2					-4.4	2.4
		12.5					15.6	20.5
		5.9				Sales/Net Fixed Assets	6.4	6.9
		2.7					3.5	3.8
		4.0					3.4	3.1
		1.7				Sales/Total Assets	2.2	2.4
		1.2					1.3	1.5
							1.7	1.7
						% Depr., Dep., Amort./Sales	(30) 4.0	(24) 3.5
							6.6	6.7
							5.2	6.0
						% Officers', Directors' Owners' Comp/Sales	(16) 9.1	(10) 12.0
							14.8	17.7
9512M	35465M	115487M		35852M		Net Sales ($)	230949M	551738M
1804M	10526M	49029M		66049M		Total Assets ($)	133548M	306073M

M = $ thousand   MM = $ million
See Pages 9 through 22 for Explanation of Ratios and Data

Comparative Historical Data / Current Data Sorted by Sales

4/1/07-3/31/08 ALL	4/1/08-3/31/09 ALL	4/1/09-3/31/10 ALL	Type of Statement	0-1MM	1-3MM	3-5MM	5-10MM	10-25MM	25MM & OVER
2	1	1	Unqualified		1		4	1	1
2	4	6	Reviewed						
4	3	2	Compiled		1	1	1	1	
5	6	8	Tax Returns	3	2	1	1	1	
14	11	10	Other	2	4		1	2	1
				10 (4/1-9/30/09)			17 (10/1/09-3/31/10)		
27	25	27	NUMBER OF STATEMENTS	5	8	2	6	4	2
%	%	%	**ASSETS**	%	%	%	%	%	%
13.0	12.1	12.1	Cash & Equivalents						
20.2	24.7	18.4	Trade Receivables (net)						
7.8	8.1	5.6	Inventory						
4.2	5.5	7.0	All Other Current						
45.2	50.3	43.1	Total Current						
40.5	38.8	41.3	Fixed Assets (net)						
4.7	2.6	7.3	Intangibles (net)						
9.6	8.4	8.3	All Other Non-Current						
100.0	100.0	100.0	Total						
			LIABILITIES						
16.7	15.0	13.3	Notes Payable-Short Term						
13.7	11.4	7.0	Cur. Mat.-L.T.D.						
16.7	20.1	12.1	Trade Payables						
.3	.9	.1	Income Taxes Payable						
11.2	11.7	26.5	All Other Current						
58.6	59.2	58.9	Total Current						
26.1	39.0	29.9	Long-Term Debt						
.4	.9	.9	Deferred Taxes						
4.0	4.8	7.3	All Other Non-Current						
10.8	-3.9	3.0	Net Worth						
100.0	100.0	100.0	Total Liabilities & Net Worth						
			INCOME DATA						
100.0	100.0	100.0	Net Sales						
			Gross Profit						
90.1	88.2	95.3	Operating Expenses						
9.9	11.8	4.7	Operating Profit						
3.1	4.2	3.2	All Other Expenses (net)						
6.8	7.6	1.5	Profit Before Taxes						
			RATIOS						
3.2	2.7	1.5	Current						
1.0	1.1	.9							
.6	.4	.4							
2.4	2.0	1.0	Quick						
.7	.7	.7							
.3	.3	.2							
(4) 100.8	(19) 19.6	(2) 222.7	Sales/Receivables						
(32) 11.6	(48) 7.6	(23) 15.9							
(63) 5.8	(68) 5.4	(61) 6.0							
			Cost of Sales/Inventory						
			Cost of Sales/Payables						
7.1	6.2	9.7	Sales/Working Capital						
-162.0	18.8	-75.0							
-10.0	-6.9	-11.7							
8.6	9.2	3.5	EBIT/Interest						
(20) 2.2	(21) 1.8	(22) 1.0							
.1	.1	-.5							
			Net Profit + Depr., Dep., Amort./Cur. Mat. L/T/D						
.5	.7	.9	Fixed/Worth						
1.3	1.4	5.4							
-2.7	-31.5	-2.1							
.7	1.1	1.3	Debt/Worth						
2.0	3.5	7.9							
-7.2	-44.3	-6.5							
82.3	51.9	36.0	% Profit Before Taxes/Tangible Net Worth						
(20) 44.9	(18) 19.7	(18) 7.7							
5.3	1.2	-25.5							
33.0	21.3	8.0	% Profit Before Taxes/Total Assets						
8.8	9.7	.0							
.6	-.5	-7.4							
22.2	17.8	19.3	Sales/Net Fixed Assets						
8.9	5.9	12.0							
3.3	3.0	3.1							
4.5	3.9	5.8	Sales/Total Assets						
2.5	2.4	1.9							
1.4	.9	1.2							
.9	2.1	3.3	% Depr., Dep., Amort./Sales						
(18) 3.1	(19) 3.8	(19) 4.6							
3.8	7.7	6.1							
5.9		4.5	% Officers', Directors' Owners' Comp/Sales						
(11) 8.6		(12) 6.4							
15.8		18.7							
439095M	304448M	196316M	Net Sales ($)	1589M	17307M	8385M	46361M	48106M	74568M
236851M	140088M	127408M	Total Assets ($)	1002M	10806M	4326M	24174M	14393M	72707M

M = $ thousand   MM = $ million
See Pages 9 through 22 for Explanation of Ratios and Data

PROFESSIONAL SERVICES—Veterinary Services NAICS 541940

Current Data Sorted by Assets							Comparative Historical Data	

						Type of Statement		
		2	4	2		Unqualified	9	7
2	4	6	1			Reviewed	13	8
42	26	5	1			Compiled	58	70
168	82	24	2	2	2	Tax Returns	174	171
66	43	19	3	1		Other	100	105
	27 (4/1-9/30/09)		480 (10/1/09-3/31/10)				4/1/05-3/31/06	4/1/06-3/31/07
0-500M	500M-2MM	2-10MM	10-50MM	50-100MM	100-250MM		ALL	ALL
278	155	56	11	5	2	NUMBER OF STATEMENTS	354	361
%	%	%	%	%	%	ASSETS	%	%
23.5	12.9	10.5	10.0			Cash & Equivalents	20.3	21.0
4.7	3.1	6.5	9.4			Trade Receivables (net)	6.2	6.0
11.3	3.6	6.4	8.4			Inventory	10.0	9.5
1.1	2.5	1.2	1.0			All Other Current	2.4	3.6
40.7	22.0	24.6	28.8			Total Current	38.9	40.1
34.4	47.2	55.0	27.7			Fixed Assets (net)	38.3	39.1
14.0	22.4	11.0	33.0			Intangibles (net)	14.4	11.1
10.9	8.5	9.4	10.5			All Other Non-Current	8.4	9.6
100.0	100.0	100.0	100.0			Total	100.0	100.0
						LIABILITIES		
17.4	5.4	4.8	6.3			Notes Payable-Short Term	9.9	8.5
6.6	5.2	4.5	2.6			Cur. Mat.-L.T.D.	4.6	5.2
9.9	4.9	8.2	10.3			Trade Payables	8.8	9.7
.0	.0	.0	.0			Income Taxes Payable	.2	.4
20.5	9.2	13.6	17.6			All Other Current	13.5	12.1
54.5	24.7	31.1	36.8			Total Current	37.0	36.0
43.6	51.1	45.8	22.8			Long-Term Debt	36.4	36.3
.1	.0	.0	.0			Deferred Taxes	.1	.1
6.3	2.1	3.5	1.8			All Other Non-Current	7.3	7.6
-4.5	22.1	19.6	38.7			Net Worth	19.2	20.1
100.0	100.0	100.0	100.0			Total Liabilities & Net Worth	100.0	100.0
						INCOME DATA		
100.0	100.0	100.0	100.0			Net Sales	100.0	100.0
						Gross Profit		
92.3	87.8	86.7	92.7			Operating Expenses	90.6	89.8
7.7	12.2	13.3	7.3			Operating Profit	9.4	10.2
1.1	5.6	8.4	7.6			All Other Expenses (net)	1.8	2.7
6.6	6.6	4.9	-.2			Profit Before Taxes	7.6	7.5
						RATIOS		
2.6	2.6	1.8	1.4				2.8	3.4
.8	1.0	.9	.6			Current	1.2	1.3
.4	.3	.4	.2				.5	.5
1.8	2.1	1.5	.7				1.9	2.3
.5 (154)	.7	.5	.3			Quick	.8 (359)	.8
.2	.1	.3	.1				.3	.3
0 UND	0 UND	0 UND	1 445.9				0 UND	0 UND
0 UND	0 UND	1 286.2	2 166.1			Sales/Receivables	0 UND	0 UND
3 128.4	3 105.0	6 58.1	21 17.4				5 77.0	5 75.9
						Cost of Sales/Inventory		
						Cost of Sales/Payables		
25.8	14.7	14.1	13.9				18.0	14.1
-156.4	-876.5	-56.9	-25.5			Sales/Working Capital	107.3	63.0
-17.3	-13.0	-9.4	-3.7				-28.9	-26.6
14.5	8.6	7.1					16.8	17.7
(208) 4.5	(125) 2.8	(43) 2.0				EBIT/Interest	(270) 5.2	(272) 5.7
.9	1.3	.9					2.0	1.6
							3.0	2.9
						Net Profit + Depr., Dep., Amort./Cur. Mat. L/T/D	(11) 1.7	(12) 1.7
							.8	1.0
.5	1.1	.9	.4				.5	.5
20.6	67.7	3.6	20.5			Fixed/Worth	3.0	2.1
-.5	-.9	-9.4	-.5				-1.5	-1.9
1.2	1.0	1.2	2.6				.8	.8
-84.7	81.1	6.7	20.8			Debt/Worth	5.2	3.1
-2.4	-2.5	-10.7	-1.9				-3.7	-4.3
278.7	158.8	74.1					191.6	172.3
(138) 97.1	(79) 54.9	(37) 23.1				% Profit Before Taxes/Tangible Net Worth	(219) 60.6	(236) 57.9
28.4	10.6	3.5					17.5	18.9
71.8	26.3	14.5	23.3				50.1	52.0
27.4	9.1	3.1	13.6			% Profit Before Taxes/Total Assets	18.2	19.3
.5	1.3	-1.2	-9.0				2.4	2.4
77.1	24.0	11.1	31.1				48.3	43.9
24.1	7.1	2.3	9.9			Sales/Net Fixed Assets	18.8	15.4
10.4	2.1	.7	2.3				6.4	5.5
10.7	3.8	3.0	3.6				8.4	7.5
6.4	2.0	1.5	1.4			Sales/Total Assets	4.7	4.3
3.7	1.1	.6	1.0				2.1	2.3
.8	1.5	2.5					1.0	.8
(178) 1.8	(112) 3.3	(45) 3.9				% Depr., Dep., Amort./Sales	(238) 1.8	(246) 2.2
3.6	6.2	9.2					3.3	3.8
6.8	4.3	3.6					7.1	6.6
(195) 10.1	(92) 8.1	(29) 7.2				% Officers', Directors' Owners' Comp/Sales	(215) 11.1	(222) 10.8
15.8	12.9	12.5					18.1	17.5
415346M	419683M	503681M	1305571M	2723703M	1895167M	Net Sales ($)	12218389M	4192249M
64330M	161242M	233252M	357483M	363817M	329905M	Total Assets ($)	2114018M	1212145M

© RMA 2010

M = $ thousand   MM = $ million
See Pages 9 through 22 for Explanation of Ratios and Data

Comparative Historical Data

Current Data Sorted by Sales

			Type of Statement						
6	6	8	Unqualified			1	2		5
12	11	13	Reviewed		3	2	3	2	3
72	78	74	Compiled	21	31	13	7	1	1
158	194	280	Tax Returns	85	142	29	13	2	9
103	107	132	Other	43	56	10	10	8	5
4/1/07-3/31/08	4/1/08-3/31/09	4/1/09-3/31/10		27 (4/1-9/30/09)		480 (10/1/09-3/31/10)			
ALL	ALL	ALL		0-1MM	1-3MM	3-5MM	5-10MM	10-25MM	25MM & OVER
351	396	507	NUMBER OF STATEMENTS	149	232	55	35	13	23
%	%	%	ASSETS	%	%	%	%	%	%
19.3	19.0	18.4	Cash & Equivalents	12.2	22.0	22.7	17.7	18.7	13.9
6.7	4.6	4.6	Trade Receivables (net)	4.7	3.7	3.2	5.2	9.0	13.5
10.1	11.0	8.4	Inventory	10.6	7.1	6.1	7.4	11.3	13.9
2.8	2.7	1.6	All Other Current	1.8	1.3	.5	2.4	5.3	2.3
38.9	37.3	33.1	Total Current	29.3	34.0	32.6	32.6	44.3	43.6
37.8	36.7	40.5	Fixed Assets (net)	47.2	37.2	41.7	44.3	34.4	26.5
12.7	15.7	16.4	Intangibles (net)	14.9	18.9	13.6	10.9	9.1	21.1
10.6	10.4	10.0	All Other Non-Current	8.7	9.9	12.0	12.2	12.2	8.8
100.0	100.0	100.0	Total	100.0	100.0	100.0	100.0	100.0	100.0
			LIABILITIES						
10.0	10.2	12.2	Notes Payable-Short Term	12.8	13.0	11.7	7.8	5.9	11.0
5.2	5.4	5.8	Cur. Mat.-L.T.D.	4.9	6.1	7.7	5.8	3.3	4.5
8.3	9.2	8.2	Trade Payables	9.2	5.7	10.6	10.3	15.0	13.2
.1	.1	.0	Income Taxes Payable	.0	.0	.1	.0	.0	.1
13.1	15.6	16.0	All Other Current	12.8	18.1	20.0	13.6	15.2	10.5
36.6	40.4	42.1	Total Current	39.7	42.9	50.1	37.6	39.4	39.3
36.5	38.9	45.4	Long-Term Debt	58.3	43.8	39.1	29.3	35.6	22.2
.1	.1	.1	Deferred Taxes	.1	.1	.0	.0	.0	.0
7.8	5.7	4.5	All Other Non-Current	7.7	3.5	2.1	2.9	4.4	1.7
19.0	14.9	7.9	Net Worth	-5.9	9.7	8.7	30.2	20.6	36.9
100.0	100.0	100.0	Total Liabilities & Net Worth	100.0	100.0	100.0	100.0	100.0	100.0
			INCOME DATA						
100.0	100.0	100.0	Net Sales	100.0	100.0	100.0	100.0	100.0	100.0
			Gross Profit						
89.8	90.0	90.4	Operating Expenses	86.3	91.0	93.9	95.1	91.6	95.9
10.2	10.0	9.6	Operating Profit	13.7	9.0	6.1	4.9	8.4	4.1
2.0	3.1	3.4	All Other Expenses (net)	7.5	1.9	1.2	1.0	.3	2.8
8.2	6.9	6.2	Profit Before Taxes	6.2	7.2	5.0	3.9	8.0	1.3
			RATIOS						
3.0	2.9	2.5		2.3	2.7	2.6	2.3	2.6	2.8
1.2	1.1	.9	Current	.8	1.0	.8	.9	1.3	1.4
.5	.4	.4		.3	.4	.4	.4	.5	.5
2.1	1.8	1.8		1.3	2.1	2.4	2.0	2.3	1.9
(350) .7	.6	(506) .5	Quick	.4	(231) .7	.5	.6	.4	.7
.2	.2	.2		.1	.2	.2	.2	.2	.2
0 UND	0 UND	0 UND		0 UND	0 UND	0 UND	0 UND	0 UND	0 UND
0 UND	0 UND	0 UND	Sales/Receivables	0 UND	0 UND	0 UND	1 285.0	3 109.8	2 166.1
4 81.8	3 132.2	3 108.7		3 108.2	3 139.1	4 103.0	3 109.8	8 44.5	37 9.9
			Cost of Sales/Inventory						
			Cost of Sales/Payables						
17.3	19.2	20.4		21.2	23.8	34.7	20.4	12.8	12.9
85.4	400.0	-202.0	Sales/Working Capital	-56.3	UND	-202.0	-162.3	52.8	19.6
-30.1	-16.2	-15.1		-7.1	-18.4	-16.2	-25.5	-22.0	-19.5
16.4	12.7	12.2		6.5	12.7	15.6	14.8	30.1	48.3
(279) 4.9	(301) 3.4	(391) 3.6	EBIT/Interest	(105) 2.6	(177) 4.0	(47) 2.9	(29) 1.7	(12) 10.5	(21) 6.0
1.5	1.0	.9		.7	1.3	.9	.7	4.0	.8
7.1	5.2	7.0							
(14) 3.5	(16) 4.1	(19) 4.8	Net Profit + Depr., Dep., Amort./Cur. Mat. L/T/D						
2.1	.7	1.1							
.5	.5	.7		1.1	.7	.5	.6	.5	.2
2.2	4.4	15.1	Fixed/Worth	-11.5	10.7	3.6	2.1	1.7	.8
-2.0	-1.1	-.8		-.7	-.5	-1.5	-4.9	-1.8	-1.0
.8	1.1	1.2		1.7	1.2	.8	.7	.8	1.2
3.8	15.0	69.0	Debt/Worth	-10.5	29.8	6.9	3.6	2.8	2.6
-5.2	-3.2	-2.7		-2.5	-2.3	-3.3	-7.2	-5.4	-3.3
227.0	180.8	201.1		125.6	251.7	175.0	203.0		215.4
(232) 83.6	(220) 62.8	(265) 61.4	% Profit Before Taxes/Tangible Net Worth	(61) 42.9	(125) 81.7	(30) 58.5	(26) 37.2		(14) 68.2
31.2	20.7	13.1		13.4	18.9	-1.0	1.2		22.4
58.3	46.8	46.5		28.2	60.6	48.8	43.8	73.7	30.7
21.1	14.9	13.6	% Profit Before Taxes/Total Assets	7.4	21.2	11.1	9.2	23.6	13.6
3.9	.7	.0		-1.1	1.9	-.8	-1.0	9.5	-.6
63.9	62.9	45.3		24.3	75.8	57.5	29.2	36.1	78.8
15.5	20.5	15.6	Sales/Net Fixed Assets	7.8	19.5	18.9	12.8	16.1	15.4
5.6	6.7	4.6		1.8	7.1	5.4	5.7	10.5	7.4
8.1	9.3	7.6		5.2	8.5	9.6	10.0	7.2	7.7
3.8	4.4	3.8	Sales/Total Assets	2.3	4.6	4.2	5.4	4.8	3.2
2.1	2.0	1.8		1.1	2.2	2.0	2.3	3.4	1.5
.9	1.0	1.1		1.5	.9	1.5	1.2	1.1	.5
(242) 2.0	(246) 2.0	(347) 2.5	% Depr., Dep., Amort./Sales	(102) 3.6	(157) 2.3	(35) 2.2	(27) 2.3	(10) 2.3	(16) 1.1
3.8	4.2	4.9		8.6	4.1	4.4	3.4	3.4	2.8
5.5	5.3	5.8		7.7	5.8	4.3	3.9		
(218) 9.4	(243) 9.0	(321) 9.6	% Officers', Directors' Owners' Comp/Sales	(85) 10.6	(158) 8.8	(35) 7.2	(26) 8.6		
15.3	15.1	14.0		14.6	13.6	13.3	13.5		
6697572M	3343372M	7263151M	Net Sales ($)	90775M	394900M	209483M	235728M	197511M	6134754M
1671296M	1013487M	1510029M	Total Assets ($)	79480M	147252M	75120M	100557M	49664M	1057956M

M = $ thousand   MM = $ million
See Pages 9 through 22 for Explanation of Ratios and Data

Current Data Sorted by Assets   **Comparative Historical Data**

						Type of Statement		
2	17	39	41	7	13	Unqualified	101	133
2	25	61	15			Reviewed	77	88
46	45	33	3		1	Compiled	132	133
171	113	47	3			Tax Returns	209	236
82	110	119	48	5	9	Other	319	336
	127 (4/1-9/30/09)		930 (10/1/09-3/31/10)				4/1/05-3/31/06	4/1/06-3/31/07
0-500M	500M-2MM	2-10MM	10-50MM	50-100MM	100-250MM		ALL	ALL
303	310	299	110	12	23	NUMBER OF STATEMENTS	838	926
%	%	%	%	%	%	ASSETS	%	%
30.6	18.4	15.1	16.7	17.0	12.3	Cash & Equivalents	17.7	16.6
16.1	29.6	37.0	26.4	26.2	20.6	Trade Receivables (net)	28.6	28.9
4.0	6.4	6.3	5.7	3.8	1.7	Inventory	6.6	6.6
3.6	3.2	5.2	7.5	4.2	5.7	All Other Current	4.3	4.8
54.3	57.6	63.7	56.3	51.2	40.3	Total Current	57.3	56.9
26.8	25.3	21.3	22.9	29.9	24.0	Fixed Assets (net)	28.4	27.0
4.8	5.4	5.2	8.5	15.6	28.9	Intangibles (net)	5.2	5.5
14.2	11.8	9.7	12.3	3.3	6.9	All Other Non-Current	9.1	10.7
100.0	100.0	100.0	100.0	100.0	100.0	Total	100.0	100.0
						LIABILITIES		
28.1	-12.2	11.8	8.3	7.9	5.3	Notes Payable-Short Term	14.8	13.0
5.3	3.0	3.5	2.1	8.7	2.0	Cur. Mat.-L.T.D.	4.9	4.3
7.7	11.7	12.0	13.4	9.0	5.0	Trade Payables	12.0	12.5
.1	.1	.3	.5	.2	.1	Income Taxes Payable	.4	.4
22.7	12.6	14.5	13.5	9.4	11.7	All Other Current	18.6	18.1
63.9	39.6	42.1	37.9	35.3	24.0	Total Current	50.7	48.3
22.5	17.4	12.2	11.5	25.6	26.4	Long-Term Debt	21.2	20.5
.0	.1	.3	.3	.1	2.1	Deferred Taxes	.4	.3
11.3	5.3	5.5	6.7	5.1	5.0	All Other Non-Current	9.1	6.2
2.2	37.5	39.9	43.6	34.0	42.6	Net Worth	18.7	24.8
100.0	100.0	100.0	100.0	100.0	100.0	Total Liabilties & Net Worth	100.0	100.0
						INCOME DATA		
100.0	100.0	100.0	100.0	100.0	100.0	Net Sales	100.0	100.0
						Gross Profit		
92.7	91.6	92.0	89.6	87.3	91.3	Operating Expenses	91.0	90.8
7.3	8.4	8.0	10.4	12.7	8.7	Operating Profit	9.0	9.2
1.4	1.9	1.4	2.2	2.0	10.3	All Other Expenses (net)	1.9	2.1
5.9	6.4	6.6	8.2	10.7	-1.5	Profit Before Taxes	7.1	7.1
						RATIOS		
4.2	3.2	3.3	2.8	2.6	3.3		2.7	2.5
1.3	1.5	1.6	1.4	2.0	1.4	Current	1.4	1.4
.4	.8	1.0	1.0	1.1	1.1		.8	.8
3.3	2.9	2.6	2.1	2.1	1.9		2.2	2.1
1.0	1.2	1.3	1.1	1.4	1.2	Quick	(837) 1.1 (925) 1.1	
.3	.7	.8	.6	1.0	.6		.6	.5
0 UND	1 396.2	24 15.0	19 19.6	15 24.5	35 10.5		1 402.3	1 673.4
0 UND	30 12.2	49 7.4	46 7.9	52 7.0	55 6.6	Sales/Receivables	32 11.4	33 11.0
25 14.7	56 6.6	75 4.9	69 5.3	88 4.1	84 4.4		58 6.3	62 5.9
						Cost of Sales/Inventory		
						Cost of Sales/Payables		
13.3	7.7	5.2	3.9	2.6	2.2		7.0	7.8
104.8	23.7	11.6	14.1	5.3	12.9	Sales/Working Capital	24.4	22.3
-17.5	-40.8	161.6	202.4	49.3	42.9		-48.1	-46.8
20.3	20.9	38.9	23.6	33.6	11.3		18.8	17.0
(192) 3.6	(238) 5.0	(257) 7.3	(82) 7.1	5.0	(19) 1.0	EBIT/Interest	(668) 5.2 (715) 4.3	
-1.6	.7	1.3	1.6	1.6	-.5		1.4	1.1
	6.2	13.0	14.0				5.8	6.5
	(18) 1.8	(33) 4.0	(12) 2.4			Net Profit + Depr., Dep., Amort./Cur. Mat. L/T/D	(79) 2.2 (99) 2.4	
	.2	1.4	.8				1.0	1.0
.1	.1	.1	.1	.4	.3		.2	.1
1.0	.6	.4	.4	1.3	2.2	Fixed/Worth	.9	.6
-.9	4.1	1.6	1.4	-1.8	-.3		11.4	4.3
.6	.5	.6	.5	1.4	.5		.9	.7
4.5	1.6	1.6	1.7	3.1	3.9	Debt/Worth	2.9	2.5
-3.4	17.6	4.2	5.0	-7.5	-2.0		UND	28.8
167.4	82.2	67.7	51.7		26.2		98.4	86.5
(185) 54.4	(250) 33.6	(263) 29.5	(96) 30.4		(15) 11.2	% Profit Before Taxes/Tangible Net Worth	(633) 38.3 (730) 37.1	
8.3	2.0	4.4	6.3		-.1		9.7	7.9
66.3	34.1	24.3	15.2	24.8	8.6		28.6	29.4
17.1	9.0	8.6	8.0	12.0	.1	% Profit Before Taxes/Total Assets	9.6	9.6
-7.1	-.3	.5	1.2	2.4	-5.1		1.2	.7
357.1	120.7	81.9	70.1	54.1	17.8		70.0	80.0
41.8	29.2	25.7	15.4	5.3	11.8	Sales/Net Fixed Assets	18.0	22.1
12.4	7.1	6.7	2.8	1.5	1.7		6.2	6.7
11.4	4.9	3.6	2.7	1.4	1.1		4.7	4.8
5.4	3.0	2.4	1.3	1.1	.5	Sales/Total Assets	2.9	3.0
3.0	1.8	1.4	.8	.8	.3		1.6	1.6
.5	.4	.6	.5		2.7		.7	.6
(157) 1.5	(219) 1.3	(229) 1.3	(88) 1.9		(14) 4.9	% Depr., Dep., Amort./Sales	(607) 1.7 (672) 1.6	
3.3	4.3	3.2	5.6		9.8		4.1	3.6
5.8	3.8	2.0	1.4				3.1	2.8
(176) 10.9	(160) 6.5	(101) 5.1	(17) 2.6			% Officers', Directors' Owners' Comp/Sales	(327) 6.8 (359) 6.1	
21.2	10.1	10.1	6.3				12.3	11.9
440913M	1395895M	3504940M	4512880M	1324128M	2899667M	Net Sales ($)	12260241M	12902099M
66401M	332858M	1293108M	2328804M	912848M	3590613M	Total Assets ($)	6841423M	8076763M

© RMA 2010

Comparative Historical Data   Current Data Sorted by Sales

			Type of Statement						
99	83	119	Unqualified	7	8	9	21	30	44
76	71	103	Reviewed	4	14	18	21	32	14
105	90	128	Compiled	24	40	17	28	16	3
242	314	334	Tax Returns	114	112	38	43	25	2
331	283	373	Other	56	92	51	56	63	55
4/1/07-3/31/08 ALL	4/1/08-3/31/09 ALL	4/1/09-3/31/10 ALL		127 (4/1-9/30/09)			930 (10/1/09-3/31/10)		
				0-1MM	1-3MM	3-5MM	5-10MM	10-25MM	25MM & OVER
853	841	1057	NUMBER OF STATEMENTS	205	266	133	169	166	118
%	%	%	ASSETS	%	%	%	%	%	%
19.3	20.6	20.6	Cash & Equivalents	24.7	23.1	17.2	20.5	17.8	16.1
28.3	28.1	27.3	Trade Receivables (net)	11.7	22.4	31.7	33.4	37.6	36.9
6.8	5.5	5.5	Inventory	2.6	6.0	7.3	5.7	6.6	5.3
4.9	4.1	4.4	All Other Current	2.6	3.5	4.9	4.9	6.6	5.4
59.3	58.3	57.8	Total Current	41.7	54.9	61.2	64.5	68.6	63.7
25.2	24.1	24.4	Fixed Assets (net)	37.4	25.3	22.4	21.3	17.9	15.3
4.9	5.6	6.1	Intangibles (net)	5.6	6.4	5.2	4.7	3.6	12.9
10.5	11.9	11.7	All Other Non-Current	15.4	13.3	11.2	9.5	9.9	8.2
100.0	100.0	100.0	Total	100.0	100.0	100.0	100.0	100.0	100.0
			LIABILITIES						
14.5	15.5	16.1	Notes Payable-Short Term	21.0	21.6	12.7	12.9	12.1	8.7
3.5	4.4	3.8	Cur. Mat.-L.T.D.	3.5	5.5	4.4	3.3	2.2	2.5
13.1	11.4	10.6	Trade Payables	4.7	8.9	12.5	13.0	14.6	13.9
.4	.2	.2	Income Taxes Payable	.0	.1	.1	.2	.3	.5
17.6	17.5	16.1	All Other Current	20.9	13.0	15.7	15.9	15.6	15.9
49.1	49.1	46.7	Total Current	50.2	49.1	45.4	45.3	44.8	41.5
18.2	17.3	17.1	Long-Term Debt	29.1	18.3	14.4	14.6	9.8	10.3
.2	.2	.2	Deferred Taxes	.0	.1	.1	.4	.3	.6
6.3	7.4	7.2	All Other Non-Current	9.8	6.6	5.2	9.2	5.9	5.3
26.1	26.0	28.8	Net Worth	10.9	26.0	34.8	30.5	39.2	42.3
100.0	100.0	100.0	Total Liabilties & Net Worth	100.0	100.0	100.0	100.0	100.0	100.0
			INCOME DATA						
100.0	100.0	100.0	Net Sales	100.0	100.0	100.0	100.0	100.0	100.0
			Gross Profit						
89.8	90.6	91.8	Operating Expenses	85.0	93.4	94.7	92.6	92.0	95.0
10.2	9.4	8.2	Operating Profit	15.0	6.6	5.3	7.4	8.0	5.0
2.1	2.0	1.8	All Other Expenses (net)	5.5	.8	.5	.9	1.0	1.9
8.2	7.4	6.4	Profit Before Taxes	9.5	5.8	4.8	6.5	7.0	3.1
			RATIOS						
2.9	3.0	3.3		3.6	3.6	2.9	4.0	2.9	2.5
1.4	1.4	1.5	Current	1.2	1.3	1.5	1.8	1.7	1.4
.8	.8	.8		.3	.6	.9	1.0	1.1	1.1
2.4	2.5	2.7		3.3	2.9	2.5	3.6	2.4	2.0
1.1	1.2	1.2	Quick	1.0	1.1	1.1	1.4	1.3	1.2
.6	.5	.6		.2	.4	.7	.8	.8	.9
0 UND	0 UND	0 UND		0 UND	0 UND	9 41.5	12 29.6	15 23.9	27 13.7
29 12.8	29 12.8	31 11.9	Sales/Receivables	0 UND	21 17.5	40 9.1	39 9.3	45 8.2	49 7.5
62 5.9	57 6.4	58 6.3		28 13.2	52 7.0	63 5.8	65 5.6	69 5.3	71 5.2
			Cost of Sales/Inventory						
			Cost of Sales/Payables						
6.6	7.1	6.8		10.5	7.6	6.9	5.7	6.3	6.0
20.8	23.8	22.8	Sales/Working Capital	165.0	35.8	19.0	14.2	12.4	17.8
-54.3	-42.1	-40.2		-6.0	-21.6	-51.9	449.7	161.5	59.4
16.9	26.6	25.0		10.6	13.1	14.4	73.8	37.2	43.5
(644) 5.1	(621) 6.5	(800) 5.3	EBIT/Interest	(115) 1.9	(197) 3.0	(109) 4.1	(145) 12.6	(136) 9.1	(98) 8.9
1.5	1.4	.7		-1.1	-.2	-.3	1.8	1.9	2.0
7.2	7.1	6.8			2.8		14.2	15.1	5.1
(71) 3.1	(58) 3.5	(77) 2.7	Net Profit + Depr., Dep., Amort./Cur. Mat. L/T/D		(12) 1.7		(16) 4.2	(21) 6.7	(17) 1.6
.9	1.5	.8			.9		1.6	2.2	.7
.1	.1	.1		.1	.1	.1	.1	.1	.1
.6	.7	.6	Fixed/Worth	1.5	.9	.6	.5	.3	.3
4.7	6.8	6.3		-11.8	-14.6	2.6	1.8	1.0	1.5
.6	.6	.6		.5	.6	.6	.4	.6	.7
2.3	2.7	1.9	Debt/Worth	3.8	2.2	1.6	1.1	1.7	2.0
66.2	342.5	64.7		-5.9	-13.7	23.4	7.8	4.9	5.3
93.6	101.3	81.5		109.0	86.6	70.0	98.7	65.3	67.6
(657) 40.6	(643) 43.8	(817) 32.6	% Profit Before Taxes/Tangible Net Worth	(136) 31.1	(193) 29.2	(106) 21.7	(140) 44.8	(145) 34.6	(97) 32.7
11.3	9.3	4.8		1.4	.1	-1.8	13.9	5.2	10.9
34.0	36.8	31.0		44.7	30.7	26.5	42.6	27.9	21.3
12.0	13.2	9.5	% Profit Before Taxes/Total Assets	6.2	7.2	7.9	16.0	11.4	10.0
1.4	.9	-.1		-2.6	-3.8	-2.1	2.9	1.5	1.8
86.4	124.7	120.7		135.5	176.1	105.5	106.3	99.9	128.1
24.5	31.9	28.1	Sales/Net Fixed Assets	11.6	28.3	30.2	33.9	34.4	33.7
7.1	7.5	7.8		1.9	8.0	8.8	11.9	12.4	8.8
4.8	5.8	5.1		5.4	5.6	5.2	5.8	4.6	4.4
2.8	3.0	2.9	Sales/Total Assets	2.3	3.2	2.8	3.2	3.0	2.6
1.6	1.6	1.5		.7	1.8	1.6	2.2	1.9	1.1
.6	.5	.5		1.5	.5	.5	.5	.3	.3
(584) 1.5	(525) 1.5	(716) 1.5	% Depr., Dep., Amort./Sales	(118) 4.3	(167) 1.4	(91) 1.2	(120) 1.4	(134) 1.1	(86) 1.1
3.9	4.1	3.9		12.2	3.2	3.5	3.3	2.2	3.4
3.3	2.8	3.4		7.0	4.5	3.1	2.9	1.8	.6
(327) 6.2	(341) 6.1	(455) 7.2	% Officers', Directors' Owners' Comp/Sales	(97) 13.1	(142) 8.5	(70) 7.0	(74) 5.8	(58) 3.6	(14) 1.4
13.0	12.0	14.7		26.0	14.4	10.7	11.4	8.2	4.2
12909839M	16366600M	14078423M	Net Sales ($)	102860M	486080M	524806M	1189562M	2542758M	9232357M
7953824M	6377385M	8524632M	Total Assets ($)	130771M	490542M	335575M	565367M	1453226M	5549151M

M = $ thousand   MM = $ million
See Pages 9 through 22 for Explanation of Ratios and Data

MANAGEMENT OF COMPANIES AND ENTERPRISES

Current Data Sorted by Assets   **Comparative Historical Data**

0-500M	500M-2MM	2-10MM	10-50MM	50-100MM	100-250MM	Type of Statement	ALL 4/1/05-3/31/06	ALL 4/1/06-3/31/07
		1	1		3	Unqualified	3	7
		2	1			Reviewed	1	1
		2	2	1		Compiled	8	4
1	2	1	1			Tax Returns	3	3
1	5	4	4	1	1	Other	15	7
	5 (4/1-9/30/09)		29 (10/1/09-3/31/10)					
2	7	10	9	2	4	NUMBER OF STATEMENTS	30	22
%	%	%	%	%	%	**ASSETS**	%	%
		4.9				Cash & Equivalents	14.7	15.2
		20.8				Trade Receivables (net)	11.0	7.0
		5.8				Inventory	4.2	2.5
		5.3				All Other Current	4.1	5.9
		36.9				Total Current	34.0	30.6
		23.6				Fixed Assets (net)	27.4	29.9
		11.0				Intangibles (net)	3.7	5.2
		28.5				All Other Non-Current	34.9	34.3
		100.0				Total	100.0	100.0
						LIABILITIES		
		10.2				Notes Payable-Short Term	10.3	8.4
		1.1				Cur. Mat.-L.T.D.	1.9	2.7
		11.5				Trade Payables	1.8	1.8
		.0				Income Taxes Payable	.3	.1
		4.4				All Other Current	17.4	14.6
		27.2				Total Current	31.6	27.6
		29.8				Long-Term Debt	32.2	28.3
		.2				Deferred Taxes	.2	.5
		1.2				All Other Non-Current	2.0	3.3
		41.6				Net Worth	34.1	40.3
		100.0				Total Liabilities & Net Worth	100.0	100.0
						INCOME DATA		
		100.0				Net Sales	100.0	100.0
						Gross Profit		
		78.4				Operating Expenses	50.8	57.8
		21.6				Operating Profit	49.2	42.2
		6.7				All Other Expenses (net)	9.6	9.5
		14.8				Profit Before Taxes	39.6	32.7
						RATIOS		
		2.5				Current	2.4	2.4
		1.4					.9	.8
		.2					.1	.1
		2.3				Quick	2.0	2.2
		.4					.5	.4
		.0					.1	.1
	0	UND				Sales/Receivables	0 UND	0 UND
	28	13.2					2 182.7	0 UND
	72	5.1					45 8.2	16 22.3
						Cost of Sales/Inventory		
						Cost of Sales/Payables		
		3.8				Sales/Working Capital	1.5	1.6
		21.7					NM	NM
		-6.4					-1.4	-3.2
						EBIT/Interest	22.1	11.9
							(15) 11.7	(15) 6.2
							6.6	1.8
						Net Profit + Depr., Dep., Amort./Cur. Mat. L/T/D		
		.0				Fixed/Worth	.0	.0
		.5					.3	.2
		NM					2.0	6.7
		.1				Debt/Worth	.3	.2
		3.6					2.2	3.2
		NM					7.3	15.6
						% Profit Before Taxes/Tangible Net Worth	35.2	68.8
							(28) 17.2	(20) 17.2
							6.8	7.6
		9.3				% Profit Before Taxes/Total Assets	10.9	9.8
		4.0					7.4	4.2
		-1.3					1.1	1.8
		UND				Sales/Net Fixed Assets	UND	UND
		114.1					3.2	6.7
		4.5					.2	.5
		2.4				Sales/Total Assets	.3	.8
		.4					.1	.2
		.2					.1	.1
						% Depr., Dep., Amort./Sales	1.3	4.1
							(20) 6.3	(11) 14.6
							15.2	16.3
						% Officers', Directors' Owners' Comp/Sales		
775M	23697M	39425M	114778M	6865M	303214M	Net Sales ($)	255865M	412167M
856M	7778M	43618M	160791M	105662M	656198M	Total Assets ($)	1147575M	972300M

M = $ thousand   MM = $ million
See Pages 9 through 22 for Explanation of Ratios and Data

Comparative Historical Data   Current Data Sorted by Sales

			Type of Statement	0-1MM	1-3MM	3-5MM	5-10MM	10-25MM	25MM & OVER
9	3	5	Unqualified		1		2	2	1
	1	3	Reviewed	1			1		
6	5	5	Compiled	2		3			
2	3	5	Tax Returns	2	1		1		1
9	13	16	Other	5	4	2	1	2	2
4/1/07-3/31/08 ALL	4/1/08-3/31/09 ALL	4/1/09-3/31/10 ALL		5 (4/1-9/30/09)			29 (10/1/09-3/31/10)		
26	25	34	NUMBER OF STATEMENTS	10	6	5	5	4	4
%	%	%	ASSETS	%	%	%	%	%	%
7.5	8.7	7.8	Cash & Equivalents	9.6					
14.4	19.6	18.1	Trade Receivables (net)	8.2					
3.2	6.1	6.6	Inventory	.0					
11.4	4.3	6.0	All Other Current	1.6					
36.5	38.8	38.4	Total Current	19.4					
17.0	30.6	23.8	Fixed Assets (net)	31.5					
3.3	7.9	7.2	Intangibles (net)	4.5					
43.2	22.8	30.6	All Other Non-Current	44.7					
100.0	100.0	100.0	Total	100.0					
			LIABILITIES						
10.0	10.2	14.0	Notes Payable-Short Term	14.0					
1.4	1.3	1.5	Cur. Mat.-L.T.D.	1.8					
9.0	7.9	12.5	Trade Payables	.3					
.1	.3	.2	Income Taxes Payable	.7					
10.6	11.6	5.8	All Other Current	4.5					
31.0	31.3	34.0	Total Current	21.4					
28.4	25.5	17.5	Long-Term Debt	16.8					
.5	.4	.4	Deferred Taxes	.2					
3.4	2.3	2.6	All Other Non-Current	.0					
36.7	40.5	45.5	Net Worth	61.6					
100.0	100.0	100.0	Total Liabilities & Net Worth	100.0					
			INCOME DATA						
100.0	100.0	100.0	Net Sales	100.0					
			Gross Profit						
55.9	61.4	67.2	Operating Expenses	41.2					
44.1	38.6	32.8	Operating Profit	58.8					
9.6	16.6	12.2	All Other Expenses (net)	17.2					
34.5	22.0	20.6	Profit Before Taxes	41.6					
			RATIOS						
1.8	1.9	1.9	Current	1.8					
1.1	1.1	1.2		.6					
.2	.7	.3		.0					
1.3	1.5	1.3	Quick	1.4					
.6	.8	.7		.1					
.1	.4	.1		.0					
0 UND	0 UND	0 UND	Sales/Receivables	0 UND					
0 UND	26 13.8	1 667.7		0 UND					
50 7.3	69 5.3	42 8.6		0 UND					
			Cost of Sales/Inventory						
			Cost of Sales/Payables						
1.8	1.9	4.6	Sales/Working Capital	6.6					
10.8	18.0	21.7		NM					
-2.8	-5.7	-4.2		-.6					
14.3	24.4	6.3	EBIT/Interest						
(18) 5.3	(17) 4.9	(17) 3.5							
2.5	1.9	.9							
			Net Profit + Depr., Dep., Amort./Cur. Mat. L/T/D						
.0	.0	.0	Fixed/Worth	.0					
.3	.8	.3		.0					
.7	3.1	2.1		13.5					
.2	.5	.3	Debt/Worth	.1					
2.5	2.1	1.3		.3					
11.9	8.5	7.7		12.5					
20.0	27.3	28.1	% Profit Before Taxes/Tangible Net Worth						
(23) 11.5	(21) 14.2	(30) 7.0							
4.8	1.3	2.8							
9.8	12.6	7.5	% Profit Before Taxes/Total Assets	7.8					
5.7	4.8	3.6		5.4					
1.0	.9	.4		2.4					
UND	114.3	UND	Sales/Net Fixed Assets	UND					
35.0	8.2	44.6		59.1					
1.4	.4	2.6		.3					
.6	1.0	1.9	Sales/Total Assets	.4					
.2	.3	.4		.2					
.1	.1	.1		.1					
3.1	1.4	1.3	% Depr., Dep., Amort./Sales						
(14) 4.9	(18) 4.5	(17) 5.2							
10.2	13.4	11.7							
			% Officers', Directors' Owners' Comp/Sales						
395807M	273688M	488754M	Net Sales ($)	4383M	9547M	17670M	41204M	47920M	368030M
1580016M	880307M	974903M	Total Assets ($)	46373M	91182M	114632M	358322M	23971M	340423M

M = $ thousand   MM = $ million
See Pages 9 through 22 for Explanation of Ratios and Data

Current Data Sorted by Assets   **Comparative Historical Data**

						Type of Statement		
5	6	19	28	18	13	Unqualified	81	100
2	11	28	14	4	3	Reviewed	83	67
5	21	48	17	1		Compiled	164	130
49	113	84	11	2		Tax Returns	260	221
32	59	68	59	20	15	Other	312	275
	68 (4/1-9/30/09)			687 (10/1/09-3/31/10)			4/1/05-3/31/06	4/1/06-3/31/07
0-500M	500M-2MM	2-10MM	10-50MM	50-100MM	100-250MM		ALL	ALL
93	210	247	129	45	31	NUMBER OF STATEMENTS	900	793
%	%	%	%	%	%	**ASSETS**	%	%
17.3	6.3	6.7	11.3	8.6	14.2	Cash & Equivalents	7.4	8.2
5.3	3.6	8.5	11.1	15.2	12.3	Trade Receivables (net)	7.0	7.0
2.9	1.7	4.2	7.8	13.2	5.1	Inventory	6.0	5.5
5.4	2.3	2.1	5.0	4.6	3.9	All Other Current	3.0	3.7
30.9	14.0	21.5	35.2	41.6	35.4	Total Current	23.3	24.4
49.7	72.7	58.2	44.9	34.0	38.1	Fixed Assets (net)	63.6	60.9
2.8	2.6	5.5	4.8	8.5	12.5	Intangibles (net)	2.8	3.5
16.6	10.7	14.7	15.1	15.9	13.9	All Other Non-Current	10.2	11.2
100.0	100.0	100.0	100.0	100.0	100.0	Total	100.0	100.0
						LIABILITIES		
15.0	5.2	5.5	7.0	6.7	3.3	Notes Payable-Short Term	6.2	6.1
3.8	4.9	4.6	3.9	5.9	4.3	Cur. Mat.-L.T.D.	3.9	4.4
4.4	2.4	4.4	5.7	9.6	4.7	Trade Payables	4.1	3.7
1.1	.2	.0	.4	.2	.1	Income Taxes Payable	.1	.1
11.0	8.6	10.2	11.2	10.1	9.5	All Other Current	6.6	8.2
35.3	21.3	24.7	28.2	32.4	21.8	Total Current	21.0	22.6
42.5	55.8	42.3	30.5	26.0	31.3	Long-Term Debt	47.6	44.6
.0	.0	.1	.7	.4	1.8	Deferred Taxes	.2	.3
10.9	6.6	4.5	5.1	4.8	12.6	All Other Non-Current	4.5	5.1
11.3	16.2	28.5	35.6	36.4	32.5	Net Worth	26.6	27.5
100.0	100.0	100.0	100.0	100.0	100.0	Total Liabilties & Net Worth	100.0	100.0
						INCOME DATA		
100.0	100.0	100.0	100.0	100.0	100.0	Net Sales	100.0	100.0
						Gross Profit		
70.8	54.3	64.2	73.7	90.5	91.7	Operating Expenses	61.0	61.8
29.2	45.7	35.8	26.3	9.5	8.3	Operating Profit	39.0	38.2
11.2	23.0	16.8	11.0	5.1	4.1	All Other Expenses (net)	17.4	17.5
18.1	22.7	19.0	15.3	4.4	4.2	Profit Before Taxes	21.6	20.8
						RATIOS		
3.2	1.9	1.9	2.0	2.0	2.6		2.1	2.1
.9	.6	.8	1.2	1.2	1.4	Current	1.0	1.0
.3	.2	.2	.4	.9	.8		.3	.3
2.1	1.4	1.3	1.3	1.0	2.1		1.5	1.4
.7	.4	.5	.6	.6	.9	Quick	(790) .6	.6
.2	.1	.2	.2	.4	.5		.1	.2
0 UND	0 UND	0 UND	0 UND	5 78.4	17 21.7		0 UND	0 UND
0 UND	0 UND	0 809.6	13 28.0	33 11.1	34 10.6	Sales/Receivables	0 UND	0 UND
2 193.8	2 216.8	36 10.0	43 8.5	56 6.5	44 8.3		23 16.0	27 13.5
						Cost of Sales/Inventory		
						Cost of Sales/Payables		
12.8	11.7	8.0	5.4	7.8	1.9		5.9	6.3
-130.0	-9.4	-19.4	23.0	16.0	12.8	Sales/Working Capital	-212.8	UND
-5.6	-2.2	-2.9	-3.4	-27.3	-15.8		-3.6	-3.7
6.3	9.1	7.6	11.3	5.2	6.3		9.8	10.3
(42) 2.9	(84) 4.3	(133) 3.9	(92) 3.8	(37) 2.5	(27) 2.5	EBIT/Interest	(433) 4.4	(397) 3.7
.8	1.5	1.3	1.5	.6	.4		2.0	1.6
		4.2	4.6	3.0	15.6	Net Profit + Depr., Dep.,	4.0	6.4
	(27) 2.0	(26) 2.0	(14) 1.9	(11) 1.8	4.4	Amort./Cur. Mat. L/T/D	(96) 2.1	(94) 2.4
		1.1	.8	.3	1.2		1.1	1.0
.2	1.5	.8	.4	.4	.3		.9	.9
2.3	3.9	3.0	1.4	1.1	1.4	Fixed/Worth	2.8	2.6
-19.0	58.7	14.0	5.6	3.3	-5.6		11.3	11.0
1.0	1.6	1.0	.9	.8	.8		1.1	1.1
3.5	4.7	3.6	2.1	2.8	2.3	Debt/Worth	3.3	3.0
-20.0	-32.5	26.1	9.4	5.7	-9.9		14.2	15.0
101.1	35.8	36.1	32.4	31.7	32.5	% Profit Before Taxes/Tangible	41.4	41.7
(66) 25.3	(155) 13.7	(198) 15.3	(113) 15.5	(38) 11.1	(23) 11.3	Net Worth	(745) 19.8	(648) 18.9
3.6	2.6	3.6	3.2	.2	-1.3		6.9	6.4
23.5	9.4	8.8	7.8	7.0	7.6	% Profit Before Taxes/Total	10.7	11.9
6.9	4.3	4.0	4.3	3.4	2.2	Assets	4.8	4.8
.1	.8	.3	.5	-.5	-2.0		1.2	1.1
172.8	.7	8.1	18.6	15.5	7.9		6.2	8.7
3.7	.2	.3	1.8	5.5	3.0	Sales/Net Fixed Assets	.3	.4
.3	.1	.2	.2	1.8	.6		.2	.2
4.7	.4	1.2	1.6	1.8	1.3		1.2	1.4
.9	.2	.2	.5	1.2	.8	Sales/Total Assets	.2	.2
.2	.1	.1	.1	.3	.2		.1	.1
3.2	10.1	3.2	1.5	1.1	2.3		3.6	3.2
(57) 11.1	(175) 17.0	(215) 15.6	(109) 5.4	(40) 2.9	(24) 4.8	% Depr., Dep., Amort./Sales	(787) 13.1	(658) 12.6
19.2	24.8	22.1	18.8	9.0	12.0		21.0	20.8
2.5	2.0	2.3					1.7	2.5
(21) 6.1	(24) 8.5	(37) 5.1				% Officers', Directors' Owners' Comp/Sales	(106) 4.9	(102) 6.7
30.1	22.4	9.9					13.5	16.4
61889M	145997M	1013903M	3285241M	4813724M	3752418M	Net Sales ($)	13669694M	13250110M
25184M	251856M	1148751M	3052928M	3153768M	4782461M	Total Assets ($)	12361076M	11006164M

M = $ thousand   MM = $ million
See Pages 9 through 22 for Explanation of Ratios and Data

Comparative Historical Data | Current Data Sorted by Sales

			Type of Statement			68 (4/1-9/30/09)	687 (10/1/09-3/31/10)		
86	82	89	Unqualified	14	10	4	7	10	44
59	52	62	Reviewed	17	8	5	12	9	11
121	112	92	Compiled	56	12	4	9	8	3
244	227	259	Tax Returns	191	37	8	16	4	3
252	261	253	Other	107	37	17	21	25	46
4/1/07-3/31/08 ALL	4/1/08-3/31/09 ALL	4/1/09-3/31/10 ALL		0-1MM	1-3MM	3-5MM	5-10MM	10-25MM	25MM & OVER
762	734	755	**NUMBER OF STATEMENTS**	385	104	38	65	56	107
%	%	%	**ASSETS**	%	%	%	%	%	%
9.2	8.3	9.1	Cash & Equivalents	6.8	7.6	7.4	12.3	18.4	12.6
8.0	8.2	7.7	Trade Receivables (net)	2.3	4.0	5.8	15.6	18.7	21.1
4.9	5.5	4.5	Inventory	.5	4.0	7.2	9.9	8.1	13.5
3.3	3.6	3.3	All Other Current	2.6	3.2	2.3	2.3	4.5	6.2
25.5	25.6	24.7	Total Current	12.2	18.8	22.7	40.1	49.8	53.4
59.3	57.1	56.7	Fixed Assets (net)	73.8	54.0	49.9	38.9	26.7	26.4
3.3	5.0	4.7	Intangibles (net)	2.0	5.3	10.8	5.9	7.3	9.9
12.0	12.3	13.9	All Other Non-Current	12.0	21.9	16.6	15.1	16.3	10.3
100.0	100.0	100.0	Total	100.0	100.0	100.0	100.0	100.0	100.0
			LIABILITIES						
5.3	5.9	6.8	Notes Payable-Short Term	6.8	5.2	3.3	7.1	9.8	8.0
4.1	5.4	4.5	Cur. Mat.-L.T.D.	4.5	5.8	4.4	3.9	3.3	4.2
4.7	5.1	4.4	Trade Payables	1.0	3.5	4.7	10.4	9.5	11.1
.1	.1	.3	Income Taxes Payable	.3	.4	.0	.0	.6	.3
8.1	8.0	10.0	All Other Current	6.0	13.3	17.3	15.5	10.2	15.0
22.3	24.6	26.0	Total Current	18.6	28.2	29.7	37.0	33.4	38.7
44.0	42.1	42.6	Long-Term Debt	58.0	34.8	41.5	24.2	19.8	18.5
.4	.2	.3	Deferred Taxes	.0	.1	.3	.2	.8	1.1
4.3	5.2	6.3	All Other Non-Current	5.6	8.1	5.7	6.9	4.8	7.7
29.0	27.9	24.8	Net Worth	17.8	28.9	22.9	31.7	41.2	34.1
100.0	100.0	100.0	Total Liabilties & Net Worth	100.0	100.0	100.0	100.0	100.0	100.0
			INCOME DATA						
100.0	100.0	100.0	Net Sales	100.0	100.0	100.0	100.0	100.0	100.0
			Gross Profit						
62.8	66.8	66.6	Operating Expenses	50.4	68.1	69.5	90.0	89.5	96.0
37.2	33.2	33.4	Operating Profit	49.6	31.9	30.5	10.0	10.5	4.0
16.9	16.1	15.6	All Other Expenses (net)	24.7	12.7	9.6	2.9	4.5	1.4
20.3	17.2	17.8	Profit Before Taxes	24.9	19.2	21.0	7.1	6.0	2.6
			RATIOS						
2.4	2.0	2.0	Current	2.0	1.3	1.5	2.0	2.3	2.0
1.1	1.0	.9		.6	.5	1.0	1.2	1.3	1.3
.3	.3	.3		.1	.1	.4	.9	1.0	1.0
1.7	1.3	1.4	Quick	1.5	.8	1.2	1.4	2.1	1.3
.7	(733) .6	.6		.4	.3	.4	.8	1.1	.8
.2	.2	.2		.1	.1	.2	.3	.4	.5
0 UND	0 UND	0 UND	Sales/Receivables	0 UND	0 UND	0 UND	2 152.1	4 88.2	17 21.8
0 UND	0 UND	0 999.8		0 UND	0 848.7	6 64.3	31 11.9	31 11.8	40 9.2
32 11.3	34 10.7	29 12.5		0 UND	12 29.9	38 9.7	50 7.3	53 6.8	58 6.3
			Cost of Sales/Inventory						
			Cost of Sales/Payables						
5.6	7.5	8.0	Sales/Working Capital	10.1	93.7	9.0	7.9	4.5	6.8
136.5	-173.9	-71.0		-8.7	-9.3	133.2	38.8	10.7	13.7
-3.7	-3.5	-3.3		-2.2	-2.0	-3.0	-46.1	NM	-391.3
8.9	8.9	8.4	EBIT/Interest	7.8	8.5	3.5	8.2	18.5	10.8
(388) 4.1	(398) 3.6	(415) 3.5		(141) 4.3	(54) 3.8	(25) 2.2	(47) 3.5	(49) 3.0	(99) 3.0
1.6	1.3	1.3		1.9	1.1	1.1	1.0	1.0	1.1
5.1	8.7	4.3	Net Profit + Depr., Dep., Amort./Cur. Mat. L/T/D	2.6				4.7	6.9
(84) 2.2	(97) 2.8	(88) 1.8		(16) 1.3			(13) 3.1	(41) 2.9	
1.0	1.0	.8		.6				.9	1.2
.8	.7	.7	Fixed/Worth	1.5	.6	.9	.4	.2	.3
2.3	2.5	2.6		4.0	1.8	5.3	1.4	.7	.9
7.9	13.4	21.8		33.8	39.0	-4.8	6.6	1.3	2.9
.9	1.1	1.0	Debt/Worth	1.3	.7	1.6	.7	.6	1.0
2.6	3.2	3.4		3.8	3.8	6.5	2.5	1.5	2.4
11.3	20.6	40.4		47.2	120.9	-13.4	11.0	6.7	7.8
36.5	41.2	38.6	% Profit Before Taxes/Tangible Net Worth	36.1	33.4	48.3	46.3	46.8	38.6
(631) 17.0	(594) 16.3	(593) 14.8		(298) 14.3	(79) 9.8	(25) 17.6	(53) 15.0	(49) 15.2	(89) 15.4
5.2	3.1	3.1		4.3	-1.2	5.4	-.2	-3.0	4.4
11.5	10.5	9.3	% Profit Before Taxes/Total Assets	8.6	8.4	9.6	12.2	12.4	9.4
4.9	4.3	4.2		4.2	2.6	5.2	4.5	4.0	4.3
.9	.3	.3		.6	-.6	.5	-.4	-1.1	1.0
8.7	10.4	10.0	Sales/Net Fixed Assets	.5	14.9	25.2	41.1	56.6	27.2
.4	.5	.5		.2	.8	1.4	4.8	11.6	8.5
.2	.2	.2		.1	.2	.2	1.3	1.9	3.6
1.5	1.6	1.3	Sales/Total Assets	.3	1.3	1.3	2.4	2.2	2.8
.2	.3	.3		.2	.3	.4	1.3	1.4	1.6
.1	.1	.1		.1	.1	.2	.6	.5	1.0
2.8	2.1	3.4	% Depr., Dep., Amort./Sales	12.9	3.1	2.3	1.3	.8	1.0
(654) 12.0	(603) 11.2	(620) 13.3		(319) 18.7	(80) 13.5	(31) 10.5	(54) 4.5	(47) 2.2	(89) 2.5
19.7	20.0	21.6		25.6	23.0	18.3	12.7	5.0	4.8
1.5	1.4	2.1	% Officers', Directors' Owners' Comp/Sales	4.9	2.1		.9	1.2	.6
(97) 3.8	(90) 3.0	(95) 5.2		(29) 12.9	(20) 6.5		(15) 3.5	(13) 4.0	(11) 1.4
10.3	11.9	13.4		31.3	9.5		6.1	15.7	2.7
17092827M	18547998M	13073172M	Net Sales ($)	130660M	178763M	151319M	470973M	943463M	11197994M
12427990M	14695221M	12414948M	Total Assets ($)	771200M	773552M	540799M	1046624M	1448799M	7833974M

ADMINISTRATIVE AND SUPPORT AND WASTE MANAGEMENT AND REMEDIATION SERVICES

Current Data Sorted by Assets   Comparative Historical Data

						Type of Statement		
1	3	11	19	4	9	Unqualified	48	64
3	8	19	10			Reviewed	34	28
5	5	4	2			Compiled	31	23
35	18	12	2			Tax Returns	44	54
26	35	37	33	4	7	Other	116	87
	36 (4/1-9/30/09)		276 (10/1/09-3/31/10)				4/1/05-3/31/06	4/1/06-3/31/07
0-500M	500M-2MM	2-10MM	10-50MM	50-100MM	100-250MM		ALL	ALL
70	69	83	66	8	16	NUMBER OF STATEMENTS	273	256
%	%	%	%	%	%		%	%
						ASSETS		
28.4	16.6	21.7	15.3		16.9	Cash & Equivalents	18.5	21.2
16.6	24.0	27.1	25.5		14.6	Trade Receivables (net)	27.4	23.4
3.3	1.1	2.4	3.3		.0	Inventory	3.4	2.8
3.4	7.8	7.2	8.2		9.8	All Other Current	7.0	6.8
51.8	49.6	58.4	52.3		41.3	Total Current	56.2	54.1
24.3	27.0	24.2	23.1		16.7	Fixed Assets (net)	20.9	24.8
5.7	6.7	7.1	14.7		24.6	Intangibles (net)	5.8	6.2
18.2	16.6	10.4	10.0		17.5	All Other Non-Current	17.1	14.8
100.0	100.0	100.0	100.0		100.0	Total	100.0	100.0
						LIABILITIES		
26.8	11.2	5.8	7.9		7.5	Notes Payable-Short Term	9.4	10.2
2.7	2.3	3.1	2.9		6.4	Cur. Mat.-L.T.D.	3.4	3.3
8.1	10.4	15.7	7.1		14.5	Trade Payables	12.1	9.6
.0	.3	.4	1.2		.0	Income Taxes Payable	.6	.8
27.9	15.5	18.0	16.4		17.8	All Other Current	22.0	26.4
65.6	39.7	43.1	35.6		46.3	Total Current	47.5	50.3
24.3	31.6	16.5	19.1		25.3	Long-Term Debt	15.6	20.1
.0	.1	.1	.4		2.0	Deferred Taxes	.3	.3
15.5	5.3	9.5	6.6		11.1	All Other Non-Current	10.9	5.8
-5.4	23.3	30.8	38.4		15.3	Net Worth	25.7	23.6
100.0	100.0	100.0	100.0		100.0	Total Liabilties & Net Worth	100.0	100.0
						INCOME DATA		
100.0	100.0	100.0	100.0		100.0	Net Sales	100.0	100.0
						Gross Profit		
90.9	88.6	90.6	88.7		96.9	Operating Expenses	90.4	88.4
9.1	11.4	9.4	11.3		3.1	Operating Profit	9.6	11.6
.6	6.7	.9	3.7		3.7	All Other Expenses (net)	1.7	2.2
8.5	4.7	8.5	7.6		-.6	Profit Before Taxes	7.9	9.3
						RATIOS		
3.4	3.3	2.5	2.6		1.5		2.5	2.9
1.2	1.4	1.3	1.5		1.0	Current	1.2	1.3
.4	.5	.9	1.0		.5		.9	.7
2.9	2.7	2.1	2.2		1.4		2.0	2.1
1.0	1.1	1.1	1.2		.9	Quick (272)	1.0	1.0
.2	.3	.6	.6		.4		.6	.5
0 UND	0 UND	1 301.8	16 23.2		11 32.0		0 999.8	0 UND
0 UND	13 27.7	29 12.7	36 10.0		26 14.2	Sales/Receivables	29 12.4	24 15.4
7 54.7	49 7.4	64 5.7	65 5.7		61 6.0		57 6.4	56 6.5
						Cost of Sales/Inventory		
						Cost of Sales/Payables		
15.0	5.9	4.9	4.4		9.2		7.5	6.2
221.0	17.1	17.5	14.1		-729.0	Sales/Working Capital	30.7	28.4
-22.4	-22.8	-158.9	84.0		-7.7		-58.0	-29.7
13.2	39.3	23.4	36.5		23.6		18.8	16.2
(36) 4.8	(52) 7.3	(64) 5.6	(54) 8.7		(14) 1.8	EBIT/Interest (197)(188)	5.7 3.9	
-2.3	1.4	1.0	3.1		-.2		1.3	1.1
		5.5	11.4			Net Profit + Depr., Dep.,	6.2	12.8
		(13) 2.2	(11) 3.0			Amort./Cur. Mat. L/T/D (39)(27)	1.8 3.1	
		1.0	1.5				.2	.8
.0	.1	.1	.1		.1		.1	.1
.4	.7	.9	.6		1.5	Fixed/Worth	.5	.9
UND	22.3	3.7	7.2		-.5		3.3	-12.9
.5	.6	.7	.9		1.3		.8	.8
3.6	2.1	2.8	2.8		47.2	Debt/Worth	2.3	3.2
-3.1	-23.0	127.0	26.1		-1.9		29.9	-17.6
196.2	71.7	69.0	65.5			% Profit Before Taxes/Tangible	88.2	90.3
(48) 48.4	(50) 36.8	(65) 43.0	(53) 38.3			Net Worth (216)(185)	35.3 38.2	
11.8	6.9	1.6	18.0				4.6	8.2
47.8	28.8	19.0	20.8		7.1	% Profit Before Taxes/Total	26.8	27.9
17.0	9.2	8.7	12.2		1.7	Assets	8.9	8.9
-4.2	.8	.0	3.5		-5.8		.1	.7
UND	81.0	105.1	89.2		84.7		111.2	84.7
62.2	26.0	20.2	15.5		13.7	Sales/Net Fixed Assets	24.6	25.2
18.0	8.1	5.7	4.4		4.2		10.1	6.9
12.8	4.8	3.2	3.3		2.4		4.9	4.4
5.6	2.4	2.2	1.9		1.5	Sales/Total Assets	3.1	2.6
2.8	1.2	1.3	.8		.8		1.7	1.2
.4	.9	.4	.4				.6	.6
(32) 1.6	(48) 1.8	(64) 1.2	(53) 2.1			% Depr., Dep., Amort./Sales (193)(185)	1.5 1.8	
3.7	7.1	3.7	4.6				2.6	4.0
3.5	4.4	2.4	4.1			% Officers', Directors'	3.5	3.5
(25) 8.2	(19) 8.5	(23) 5.2	(10) 10.7			Owners' Comp/Sales (67)(57)	8.3 8.4	
29.7	18.1	12.2	21.2				17.3	22.3
98828M	260697M	1392299M	3513965M	1297768M	4413519M	Net Sales ($)	10090361M	7361079M
13878M	80426M	416967M	1537620M	668886M	2465902M	Total Assets ($)	4728722M	4481105M

M = $ thousand   MM = $ million
See Pages 9 through 22 for Explanation of Ratios and Data

Comparative Historical Data   Current Data Sorted by Sales

Type of Statement	4/1/07-3/31/08 ALL	4/1/08-3/31/09 ALL	4/1/09-3/31/10 ALL			0-1MM	1-3MM	3-5MM	5-10MM	10-25MM	25MM & OVER
Unqualified	48	54	47			2		2	4	8	31
Reviewed	21	21	40			2	4	5	10	8	11
Compiled	15	19	16			6	4	2	1	1	2
Tax Returns	48	84	67			29	18	8	9	3	
Other	109	140	142			30	22	14	16	25	35
							36 (4/1-9/30/09)			276 (10/1/09-3/31/10)	
NUMBER OF STATEMENTS	241	318	312			69	48	31	40	45	79
ASSETS	%	%	%			%	%	%	%	%	%
Cash & Equivalents	19.2	19.7	20.1			23.3	17.1	25.7	20.9	19.7	16.9
Trade Receivables (net)	25.9	20.4	22.8			9.4	22.4	30.1	23.9	28.4	28.3
Inventory	3.3	2.5	2.5			2.4	2.6	1.6	1.5	1.0	4.3
All Other Current	8.9	7.1	6.7			4.8	4.7	6.6	9.5	7.6	7.8
Total Current	57.3	49.7	52.2			39.9	46.8	63.9	55.9	56.7	57.3
Fixed Assets (net)	23.9	27.3	24.5			29.4	31.6	19.4	22.5	24.9	18.7
Intangibles (net)	5.6	7.4	9.6			8.8	5.9	5.8	4.9	9.2	16.6
All Other Non-Current	13.2	15.6	13.7			22.0	15.9	10.9	16.7	9.2	7.4
Total	100.0	100.0	100.0			100.0	100.0	100.0	100.0	100.0	100.0
LIABILITIES											
Notes Payable-Short Term	11.6	9.7	12.2			11.9	30.4	9.7	10.4	4.6	7.4
Cur. Mat.-L.T.D.	4.4	3.8	3.0			2.6	2.7	1.8	2.8	3.4	3.8
Trade Payables	9.6	9.9	10.8			6.0	7.9	13.5	13.9	13.8	12.4
Income Taxes Payable	.3	.3	.5			.2	.1	.3	.0	1.3	.7
All Other Current	19.8	22.0	19.1			19.1	14.3	20.4	24.6	18.2	19.2
Total Current	45.7	45.8	45.5			39.8	55.4	45.8	51.6	41.3	43.6
Long-Term Debt	15.7	22.1	22.8			27.1	34.8	29.9	19.5	14.1	15.6
Deferred Taxes	.1	.1	.2			.1	.0	.0	.1	.3	.6
All Other Non-Current	6.5	7.1	9.4			13.5	11.5	2.9	13.4	4.3	8.2
Net Worth	32.0	24.9	22.0			19.5	-1.7	21.4	15.4	40.1	32.0
Total Liabilities & Net Worth	100.0	100.0	100.0			100.0	100.0	100.0	100.0	100.0	100.0
INCOME DATA											
Net Sales	100.0	100.0	100.0			100.0	100.0	100.0	100.0	100.0	100.0
Gross Profit											
Operating Expenses	89.4	87.5	90.2			83.0	89.7	93.8	89.7	92.8	94.0
Operating Profit	10.6	12.5	9.8			17.0	10.3	6.2	10.3	7.2	6.0
All Other Expenses (net)	1.8	3.4	2.9			6.6	4.8	1.5	.6	.2	1.8
Profit Before Taxes	8.8	9.2	6.9			10.3	5.4	4.7	9.7	7.0	4.2
RATIOS											
Current	2.5	2.3	2.7			3.7	4.4	3.4	2.8	2.7	2.1
	1.3	1.3	1.4			1.2	1.3	1.4	1.4	1.5	1.3
	.8	.6	.7			.2	.3	1.0	.9	1.0	1.0
Quick	1.9	2.0	2.3			3.1	4.0	3.1	2.2	2.3	1.5
	(240) 1.1	(317) 1.0	1.1			1.0	1.1	1.3	1.2	1.1	1.1
	.6	.4	.4			.2	.2	.7	.5	.6	.6
Sales/Receivables	0 UND	0 UND	0 UND			0 UND	0 UND	9 41.9	0 UND	1 271.4	14 26.3
	26 14.1	18 20.8	19 19.1			0 UND	3 105.7	42 8.7	20 18.6	36 10.0	33 10.9
	56 6.5	50 7.3	54 6.8			6 64.9	38 9.5	75 4.9	58 6.3	56 6.6	59 6.2
Cost of Sales/Inventory											
Cost of Sales/Payables											
Sales/Working Capital	5.8	7.4	6.3			6.0	5.7	5.8	4.6	6.3	8.1
	27.6	38.5	22.9			38.4	46.9	17.1	22.4	17.2	22.9
	-62.9	-17.8	-49.3			-7.7	-24.0	-101.3	-89.7	-999.8	-637.2
EBIT/Interest	21.9	16.6	26.0			13.3	18.4	40.3	45.2	35.6	26.8
	(178) 6.5	(228) 5.5	(228) 6.7			(35) 4.8	(30) 2.6	(24) 8.1	(33) 8.5	(35) 8.5	(71) 7.6
	1.4	1.4	1.1			1.3	-7.6	2.0	.7	1.0	2.3
Net Profit + Depr., Dep., Amort./Cur. Mat. L/T/D	12.3	7.3	7.5								5.7
	(31) 5.5	(30) 2.7	(32) 2.5							(14) 1.9	
	1.6	1.3	1.0								1.1
Fixed/Worth	.1	.1	.1			.0	.1	.2	.0	.1	.2
	.5	.9	.7			.7	.7	.7	.5	.7	.7
	4.8	19.5	26.7			25.7	-12.3	30.9	3.8	6.7	-376.0
Debt/Worth	.8	.8	.7			.7	.6	.8	.9	.5	1.5
	2.3	2.8	2.8			5.6	3.0	2.8	1.8	1.9	2.9
	15.4	UND	-41.7			-9.5	-20.2	146.8	108.5	NM	-223.1
% Profit Before Taxes/Tangible Net Worth	83.5	111.6	74.7			93.3	164.9	109.3	107.9	53.8	66.9
	(194) 36.4	(240) 38.7	(229) 40.0			(48) 24.8	(34) 36.7	(24) 49.8	(31) 50.1	(34) 38.6	(58) 42.9
	9.0	9.4	8.7			5.0	-6.4	17.0	11.3	5.4	17.2
% Profit Before Taxes/Total Assets	26.6	32.6	26.1			23.9	47.0	19.1	41.3	27.9	19.5
	10.5	8.8	9.3			4.5	10.2	11.5	9.8	11.5	10.9
	1.4	1.2	.1			-.2	-10.7	2.4	.9	.1	2.9
Sales/Net Fixed Assets	216.4	123.2	112.8			406.1	189.7	70.8	151.6	76.3	101.1
	32.6	21.4	26.0			27.1	32.5	25.3	34.4	14.8	27.1
	6.5	5.0	6.1			1.7	9.5	11.4	10.3	4.9	6.8
Sales/Total Assets	4.9	4.7	4.5			3.8	10.0	3.9	4.9	4.4	4.3
	2.6	2.4	2.5			1.2	3.3	2.6	2.4	2.4	2.9
	1.3	1.0	1.2			.3	1.4	1.3	1.6	1.3	1.8
% Depr., Dep., Amort./Sales	.4	.6	.5			2.1	.5	.8	.5	.7	.2
	(154) 1.3	(205) 2.0	(210) 1.8			(39) 8.3	(32) 1.3	(20) 2.0	(28) 1.1	(35) 2.7	(56) 1.2
	4.1	5.5	4.1			15.9	3.9	3.9	5.2	3.6	2.3
% Officers', Directors' Owners' Comp/Sales	2.0	3.2	3.9			5.0	6.6	4.5	4.3	1.2	
	(55) 7.8	(73) 9.1	(79) 7.9			(19) 10.0	(17) 16.0	(13) 7.8	(13) 8.2	(10) 2.0	
	14.2	17.9	20.1			26.1	29.7	21.1	11.4	4.0	
Net Sales ($)	8221137M	9473596M	10977076M			36637M	91892M	122107M	281655M	673972M	9770813M
Total Assets ($)	3937202M	5596866M	5183679M			88912M	112235M	83749M	186979M	373309M	4338495M

M = $ thousand   MM = $ million
See Pages 9 through 22 for Explanation of Ratios and Data

Current Data Sorted by Assets — Comparative Historical Data

0-500M	500M-2MM	2-10MM	10-50MM	50-100MM	100-250MM	Type of Statement	4/1/05-3/31/06 ALL	4/1/06-3/31/07 ALL
	3	11	9	4	3	Unqualified	32	31
	6	11	2			Reviewed	10	14
4	8	3				Compiled	3	4
4		2	2			Tax Returns	10	7
5	16	15	7	1	3	Other	25	28
	15 (4/1-9/30/09)		104 (10/1/09-3/31/10)					
13	33	42	20	5	6	NUMBER OF STATEMENTS	80	84
%	%	%	%	%	%	ASSETS	%	%
31.3	18.0	18.0	7.5			Cash & Equivalents	12.9	11.0
29.3	37.1	38.2	39.6			Trade Receivables (net)	40.3	43.5
1.3	3.7	2.2	.8			Inventory	2.0	1.8
8.6	3.7	4.7	8.4			All Other Current	7.0	8.5
70.6	62.4	63.1	56.3			Total Current	62.2	64.7
18.4	25.9	27.6	31.6			Fixed Assets (net)	25.9	22.2
2.7	5.4	3.1	4.1			Intangibles (net)	4.4	3.8
8.3	6.3	6.2	8.0			All Other Non-Current	7.4	9.3
100.0	100.0	100.0	100.0			Total	100.0	100.0
						LIABILITIES		
12.4	11.2	10.7	7.7			Notes Payable-Short Term	10.9	9.5
3.6	3.0	4.4	5.2			Cur. Mat.-L.T.D.	4.9	5.1
7.5	10.4	11.5	9.0			Trade Payables	13.6	14.2
.2	.0	.4	.8			Income Taxes Payable	.9	1.0
18.8	10.3	16.8	17.0			All Other Current	14.8	16.1
42.6	34.8	43.8	39.5			Total Current	45.1	45.8
20.2	20.0	16.4	21.5			Long-Term Debt	15.4	14.6
.0	.0	.1	.6			Deferred Taxes	.1	.2
3.0	3.3	7.8	2.0			All Other Non-Current	3.5	4.2
34.2	41.9	31.9	36.3			Net Worth	35.9	35.1
100.0	100.0	100.0	100.0			Total Liabilities & Net Worth	100.0	100.0
						INCOME DATA		
100.0	100.0	100.0	100.0			Net Sales	100.0	100.0
						Gross Profit		
89.7	88.7	90.5	91.3			Operating Expenses	92.6	91.8
10.3	11.3	9.5	8.7			Operating Profit	7.4	8.2
.2	3.4	3.3	2.0			All Other Expenses (net)	2.2	1.2
10.1	8.0	6.1	6.8			Profit Before Taxes	5.3	7.0
						RATIOS		
17.1	2.8	2.6	2.1			Current	2.3	2.6
2.8	1.9	1.5	1.5				1.4	1.6
.8	1.2	.9	1.2				1.0	1.2
8.3	2.5	2.4	1.8			Quick	1.9	2.5
1.1	1.5	1.3	1.2				1.3 (83)	1.3
.8	1.0	.9	.8				.9	.9
1 349.1	1 539.4	26 13.9	35 10.3			Sales/Receivables	27 13.6	23 15.6
21 17.5	31 11.8	46 7.9	51 7.2				46 7.9	50 7.3
31 11.8	56 6.5	67 5.5	79 4.6				79 4.6	69 5.3
						Cost of Sales/Inventory		
						Cost of Sales/Payables		
6.1	7.4	5.7	7.6			Sales/Working Capital	5.9	7.6
10.1	16.0	13.9	12.5				14.9	14.9
-38.8	89.8	-124.9	41.1				169.0	38.2
	20.0	47.6	59.0			EBIT/Interest	17.6	23.0
	(26) 5.6	(34) 6.1	(15) 8.4				(68) 6.2	(67) 8.7
	1.9	-.4	1.1				1.4	2.6
						Net Profit + Depr., Dep., Amort./Cur. Mat. L/T/D	8.3	10.3
							(12) 3.4	(20) 5.3
							1.2	1.6
.0	.1	.1	.1			Fixed/Worth	.2	.1
.3	.3	.5	.5				.6	.5
4.6	3.0	2.9	1.8				2.9	2.1
.1	.5	1.1	.8			Debt/Worth	.8	.8
2.8	1.5	2.6	1.4				2.5	2.1
NM	3.8	4.7	6.4				6.5	7.1
96.8	64.1	49.6	58.5			% Profit Before Taxes/Tangible Net Worth	85.2	64.2
(10) 61.0	(28) 36.3	(38) 27.6	(17) 22.7				(68) 30.6	(73) 36.4
-4.4	13.0	.1	3.9				2.4	17.9
77.9	29.1	23.5	18.2			% Profit Before Taxes/Total Assets	24.4	20.4
19.0	11.1	7.5	12.7				8.0	11.2
9.3	.4	-2.0	.7				-.5	4.4
UND	87.0	173.5	84.0			Sales/Net Fixed Assets	70.6	137.4
91.3	23.4	36.6	14.6				24.9	32.1
20.8	8.8	4.0	1.3				6.2	6.5
7.0	5.9	4.7	3.9			Sales/Total Assets	4.9	4.7
4.8	3.4	2.4	2.1				2.8	3.0
3.8	1.7	1.2	.8				1.5	1.7
	.5	.4	.2			% Depr., Dep., Amort./Sales	.6	.5
	(24) 1.5	(30) 2.2	(13) 2.6				(66) 1.4	(67) 1.3
	2.8	8.9	4.2				4.4	3.7
	1.0					% Officers', Directors' Owners' Comp/Sales	3.8	1.0
	(10) 2.1						(19) 6.6	(17) 3.5
	4.7						17.3	8.8
25517M	163953M	600328M	1006912M	808024M	1790223M	Net Sales ($)	2105045M	3114873M
3599M	37978M	215356M	422054M	326255M	1048272M	Total Assets ($)	970408M	1177206M

© RMA 2010

M = $ thousand   MM = $ million
See Pages 9 through 22 for Explanation of Ratios and Data

Comparative Historical Data | | | | Current Data Sorted by Sales

			Type of Statement	0-1MM	1-3MM	3-5MM	5-10MM	10-25MM	25MM & OVER
30	33	30	Unqualified	2	3	3	3	5	14
9	16	19	Reviewed	1	1	2	4	7	4
6	5	7	Compiled	1	3		2	1	
9	12	16	Tax Returns	6	1	1	5	2	1
30	41	47	Other	6	7	4	10	7	13
4/1/07-3/31/08 ALL	4/1/08-3/31/09 ALL	4/1/09-3/31/10 ALL			15 (4/1-9/30/09)		104 (10/1/09-3/31/10)		
84	107	119	**NUMBER OF STATEMENTS**	16	15	10	24	22	32
%	%	%	**ASSETS**	%	%	%	%	%	%
14.3	15.6	17.2	Cash & Equivalents	12.3	28.4	20.5	18.5	19.4	11.0
43.3	39.3	36.3	Trade Receivables (net)	19.4	27.5	34.1	34.2	39.2	49.0
2.3	2.0	2.6	Inventory	.0	2.0	3.5	6.7	.1	2.4
6.5	6.1	5.5	All Other Current	4.5	1.5	2.9	3.9	7.3	8.6
66.5	63.0	61.6	Total Current	36.3	59.4	61.0	63.3	66.0	71.0
23.3	22.8	25.8	Fixed Assets (net)	51.6	25.2	32.5	24.1	21.2	15.7
2.3	2.8	4.9	Intangibles (net)	4.5	8.8	.9	4.8	3.8	5.5
7.9	11.4	7.7	All Other Non-Current	7.7	6.6	5.5	7.8	8.9	7.9
100.0	100.0	100.0	Total	100.0	100.0	100.0	100.0	100.0	100.0
			LIABILITIES						
9.9	7.9	9.9	Notes Payable-Short Term	11.8	8.7	3.2	8.5	15.8	8.7
4.5	3.9	3.9	Cur. Mat.-L.T.D.	3.5	4.3	6.5	2.4	2.5	5.1
13.2	14.8	10.3	Trade Payables	4.9	4.5	13.8	11.4	9.4	14.4
.2	.6	.3	Income Taxes Payable	.0	.0	.0	.4	.2	.8
17.5	15.9	16.1	All Other Current	12.5	7.4	11.6	14.4	17.5	23.8
45.4	43.0	40.5	Total Current	32.7	24.9	35.0	37.1	45.3	52.7
13.1	14.5	18.6	Long-Term Debt	39.7	16.2	25.2	18.7	13.7	10.4
.3	.3	.2	Deferred Taxes	.0	.0	.0	.3	.0	.6
2.7	2.2	4.7	All Other Non-Current	7.8	1.8	1.6	8.7	4.9	2.3
38.5	40.0	36.0	Net Worth	19.8	57.1	38.2	35.1	36.1	33.9
100.0	100.0	100.0	Total Liabilities & Net Worth	100.0	100.0	100.0	100.0	100.0	100.0
			INCOME DATA						
100.0	100.0	100.0	Net Sales	100.0	100.0	100.0	100.0	100.0	100.0
			Gross Profit						
90.6	91.6	90.5	Operating Expenses	71.8	86.1	93.8	94.7	93.3	95.6
9.4	8.4	9.5	Operating Profit	28.2	13.9	6.2	5.3	6.7	4.4
2.0	.8	2.6	All Other Expenses (net)	12.6	1.7	.8	1.3	1.2	.7
7.4	7.6	6.9	Profit Before Taxes	15.6	12.2	5.4	4.0	5.4	3.7
			RATIOS						
2.5	2.4	2.6		2.7	25.1	2.6	3.0	2.4	1.7
1.6	1.5	1.5	Current	1.0	3.6	2.3	1.8	1.6	1.3
1.1	1.0	1.0		.6	.9	1.2	1.2	1.1	1.1
2.4	1.9	2.4		2.2	18.8	2.3	2.6	2.3	1.5
1.5	1.3	1.3	Quick	.9	3.4	1.8	1.4	1.4	1.2
.9	.9	.9		.5	.9	1.2	.8	1.0	.9
27 13.3	27 13.7	20 18.5		0 UND	13 27.8	10 37.1	28 13.2	16 22.4	37 9.9
52 7.1	48 7.6	43 8.5	Sales/Receivables	22 16.7	30 12.1	49 7.5	52 7.0	34 10.9	51 7.2
71 5.1	66 5.6	62 5.9		55 6.7	62 5.9	62 5.9	66 5.5	49 7.5	68 5.4
			Cost of Sales/Inventory						
			Cost of Sales/Payables						
6.5	7.0	6.8		6.1	4.0	5.2	5.4	10.2	9.7
14.0	16.6	14.1	Sales/Working Capital	NM	7.5	8.8	12.8	25.5	15.4
58.4	350.0	964.0		-13.7	-50.5	NM	63.8	100.4	208.6
31.3	29.5	31.8			39.4		20.2	26.8	66.1
(66) 9.1	(87) 11.4	(94) 6.9	EBIT/Interest		(12) 10.0		(20) 4.4	(17) 3.5	(28) 9.3
3.2	2.6	1.2			3.5		.3	1.3	1.7
24.4	22.0	6.2							
(23) 5.6	(19) 8.6	(15) 2.0	Net Profit + Depr., Dep., Amort./Cur. Mat. L/T/D						
2.0	5.4	.3							
.1	.1	.1		.6	.1	.1	.1	.1	.1
.4	.4	.4	Fixed/Worth	3.8	.3	.4	.5	.2	.2
1.5	1.1	2.6		NM	2.8	2.3	2.9	1.3	1.0
.6	.7	.7		1.0	.0	.5	.5	1.0	1.2
1.5	1.5	1.9	Debt/Worth	3.4	.5	1.6	2.6	1.4	2.1
7.7	4.6	4.8		-10.3	3.2	3.6	8.6	3.4	6.3
72.2	74.3	60.1		57.3	81.1		92.2	78.6	46.4
(76) 38.6	(99) 38.8	(102) 29.4	% Profit Before Taxes/Tangible Net Worth	(11) 29.1	(13) 35.9	(21) 22.5	(19) 28.3	(29) 31.1	
20.0	12.3	5.8		-1.3	6.0		2.0	4.2	10.4
24.4	25.5	23.2		23.8	35.6	28.9	19.9	28.3	20.0
13.2	12.1	10.0	% Profit Before Taxes/Total Assets	6.0	18.6	9.2	4.2	14.6	8.0
3.4	3.3	.5		-1.0	9.3	4.7	-5.0	1.8	1.2
126.2	157.4	138.2		76.1	37.9	75.9	80.9	252.3	178.9
20.3	29.4	27.4	Sales/Net Fixed Assets	3.9	20.6	18.9	28.6	81.4	52.1
5.3	5.8	4.5		.1	3.7	3.6	4.5	5.0	15.6
4.3	4.1	4.7		3.1	5.1	3.5	4.2	8.2	4.6
3.0	3.2	2.8	Sales/Total Assets	.9	2.5	2.8	2.2	4.7	3.7
1.4	1.7	1.4		.1	1.6	1.7	1.2	1.4	2.1
.3	.4	.4		2.0	.3		.6	.4	.2
(64) 1.0	(70) 1.5	(82) 1.8	% Depr., Dep., Amort./Sales	(12) 10.2	(10) 1.4		(17) 2.2	(16) .5	(22) .8
3.4	3.8	3.1		22.4	3.7		5.0	3.0	2.2
.8	1.4	1.1							
(19) 1.9	(22) 2.8	(24) 3.2	% Officers', Directors' Owners' Comp/Sales						
	5.5	5.4							
3755832M	4988406M	4394957M	Net Sales ($)	8620M	31907M	41069M	175187M	347496M	3790678M
1899437M	2530255M	2053514M	Total Assets ($)	31572M	24275M	20193M	116831M	163270M	1697373M

© RMA 2010

M = $ thousand   MM = $ million
See Pages 9 through 22 for Explanation of Ratios and Data

Current Data Sorted by Assets **Comparative Historical Data**

0-500M	500M-2MM	2-10MM	10-50MM	50-100MM	100-250MM	Type of Statement	4/1/05-3/31/06 ALL	4/1/06-3/31/07 ALL
	6	21	14	2	2	Unqualified		
1	15	42	3			Reviewed		
9	24	10				Compiled		
25	17	8				Tax Returns		
22	42	62	19	5	5	Other		
	27 (4/1-9/30/09)		327 (10/1/09-3/31/10)					
57	104	143	36	7	7	**NUMBER OF STATEMENTS**		
%	%	%	%	%	%	**ASSETS**	%	%
26.8	9.7	13.4	12.0			Cash & Equivalents	D	D
35.8	54.3	56.0	53.6			Trade Receivables (net)	A	A
1.2	1.0	.2	.1			Inventory	T	T
9.9	6.0	6.1	7.1			All Other Current	A	A
73.7	71.1	75.7	72.7			Total Current		
12.0	11.6	9.2	7.2			Fixed Assets (net)	N	N
2.7	4.3	4.0	11.7			Intangibles (net)	O	O
11.6	13.1	11.2	8.4			All Other Non-Current	T	T
100.0	100.0	100.0	100.0			Total		
						LIABILITIES	A	A
30.4	17.6	20.7	14.5			Notes Payable-Short Term	V	V
6.1	3.3	1.7	4.0			Cur. Mat.-L.T.D.	A	A
4.2	8.2	7.8	7.4			Trade Payables	I	I
.1	.2	1.1	.3			Income Taxes Payable	L	L
41.9	17.3	19.5	19.9			All Other Current	A	A
82.7	46.6	50.7	46.1			Total Current	B	B
8.0	11.2	6.6	13.0			Long-Term Debt	L	L
.0	.0	.2	.1			Deferred Taxes	E	E
9.7	3.7	4.0	13.4			All Other Non-Current		
-.4	38.5	38.5	27.3			Net Worth		
100.0	100.0	100.0	100.0			Total Liabilities & Net Worth		
						INCOME DATA		
100.0	100.0	100.0	100.0			Net Sales		
						Gross Profit		
99.2	98.1	98.7	96.7			Operating Expenses		
.8	1.9	1.3	3.3			Operating Profit		
.4	1.8	.4	1.1			All Other Expenses (net)		
.5	.1	.9	2.2			Profit Before Taxes		
						RATIOS		
3.3	3.5	2.5	2.5			Current		
1.7	1.6	1.5	1.5					
.6	1.0	1.0	1.1					
3.1	3.3	2.4	2.4			Quick		
1.1	1.6	1.4	1.4					
.5	.9	.9	.9					
0 UND	26 14.3	32 11.5	40 9.2			Sales/Receivables		
22 16.5	40 9.2	47 7.8	53 6.9					
47 7.8	56 6.5	66 5.5	67 5.4					
						Cost of Sales/Inventory		
						Cost of Sales/Payables		
10.3	9.9	9.2	7.5			Sales/Working Capital		
85.5	18.4	17.0	16.2					
-17.1	444.5	186.9	80.8					
16.7	9.0	19.2	24.4			EBIT/Interest		
(34) 1.9	(82) 1.2	(119) 5.0	(34) 5.5					
-4.5	-8.1	.9	1.0					
		10.9				Net Profit + Depr., Dep., Amort./Cur. Mat. L/T/D		
		(17) 3.3						
		1.0						
.0	.0	.0	.1			Fixed/Worth		
.2	.1	.1	.3					
-5.4	.6	.6	14.3					
.3	.5	.6	1.0			Debt/Worth		
2.4	1.3	1.7	2.8					
-13.6	7.1	4.6	751.8					
161.3	36.5	56.0	63.3			% Profit Before Taxes/Tangible Net Worth		
(36) 24.5	(90) 8.9	(126) 16.3	(28) 23.2					
-9.7	-18.2	.4	2.4					
51.5	14.0	13.0	17.2			% Profit Before Taxes/Total Assets		
13.3	2.0	6.0	6.4					
-22.7	-11.5	-1.3	-2.3					
UND	741.0	327.9	196.9			Sales/Net Fixed Assets		
212.2	150.0	106.0	112.9					
46.8	39.3	36.2	39.2					
11.7	6.5	6.4	5.1			Sales/Total Assets		
6.3	4.9	4.2	3.8					
4.8	3.5	3.0	2.4					
.1	.1	.1	.2			% Depr., Dep., Amort./Sales		
(25) .5	(75) .4	(111) .3	(30) .4					
.8	.8	.7	.6					
2.2	1.8	.9				% Officers', Directors' Owners' Comp/Sales		
(24) 5.4	(38) 4.6	(39) 1.6						
9.3	7.5	4.0						
140517M	730875M	3430479M	2743934M	1424238M	4796704M	Net Sales ($)		
15470M	121845M	631802M	690248M	522272M	1077658M	Total Assets ($)		

M = $ thousand   MM = $ million
See Pages 9 through 22 for Explanation of Ratios and Data

Comparative Historical Data — **Current Data Sorted by Sales**

			Type of Statement						
52	52	45	Unqualified		2	4	2	11	26
62	57	61	Reviewed		4	8	6	26	17
41	59	43	Compiled	4	12	11	9	6	1
50	63	50	Tax Returns	4	16	5	17	7	1
130	141	155	Other	15	12	17	25	40	46
4/1/07-3/31/08 ALL	4/1/08-3/31/09 ALL	4/1/09-3/31/10 ALL		27 (4/1-9/30/09)			327 (10/1/09-3/31/10)		
				0-1MM	1-3MM	3-5MM	5-10MM	10-25MM	25MM & OVER
335	372	354	NUMBER OF STATEMENTS	23	46	45	59	90	91
%	%	%	ASSETS	%	%	%	%	%	%
13.8	16.4	14.4	Cash & Equivalents	16.6	19.1	14.0	15.4	11.5	13.7
53.8	46.6	51.5	Trade Receivables (net)	24.2	41.5	54.8	48.5	61.1	54.2
.1	.5	.6	Inventory	2.7	.1	2.3	.0	.3	.1
7.1	7.5	6.8	All Other Current	5.4	9.5	7.8	5.9	5.7	6.9
74.9	71.0	73.2	Total Current	48.9	70.2	78.9	69.9	78.7	74.9
9.0	10.1	10.0	Fixed Assets (net)	30.1	12.5	8.7	8.3	7.4	7.9
5.4	7.6	5.5	Intangibles (net)	7.1	4.3	1.5	5.7	3.4	9.7
10.7	11.3	11.3	All Other Non-Current	13.9	13.0	10.9	16.2	10.5	7.5
100.0	100.0	100.0	Total	100.0	100.0	100.0	100.0	100.0	100.0
			LIABILITIES						
21.8	21.6	20.3	Notes Payable-Short Term	7.7	24.1	23.3	23.8	19.1	18.9
3.0	3.0	3.1	Cur. Mat.-L.T.D.	8.0	5.9	3.5	2.3	1.6	2.2
7.4	6.8	7.4	Trade Payables	5.3	3.3	5.1	8.6	8.2	9.6
.7	.4	.5	Income Taxes Payable	.1	.1	.1	1.2	.3	.8
21.7	19.9	22.7	All Other Current	32.7	34.0	14.0	26.7	18.1	20.9
54.5	51.8	54.0	Total Current	53.7	67.4	46.0	62.5	47.2	52.4
8.6	14.1	9.1	Long-Term Debt	23.1	9.2	6.2	13.2	4.4	8.9
.2	.1	.2	Deferred Taxes	.0	.0	.1	.0	.2	.4
6.6	7.6	5.8	All Other Non-Current	18.7	3.6	4.0	4.4	3.2	8.1
30.1	26.4	30.9	Net Worth	4.6	19.8	43.8	19.9	44.9	30.2
100.0	100.0	100.0	Total Liabilties & Net Worth	100.0	100.0	100.0	100.0	100.0	100.0
			INCOME DATA						
100.0	100.0	100.0	Net Sales	100.0	100.0	100.0	100.0	100.0	100.0
			Gross Profit						
95.9	95.9	98.5	Operating Expenses	94.8	99.5	99.9	99.9	97.7	97.9
4.1	4.1	1.5	Operating Profit	5.2	.5	.1	.1	2.3	2.1
1.3	1.3	.9	All Other Expenses (net)	6.8	.7	.2	.1	.5	.7
2.8	2.7	.7	Profit Before Taxes	-1.6	-.1	-.2	-.1	1.8	1.4
			RATIOS						
2.3	2.8	2.8		2.4	2.7	6.7	3.4	2.8	2.1
1.4	1.6	1.5	Current	.9	1.3	2.3	1.4	1.7	1.4
1.0	1.0	1.0		.5	.7	1.2	.9	1.2	1.0
2.2	2.5	2.5		2.4	2.5	4.2	3.4	2.7	1.7
1.3	1.4	1.4	Quick	.7	1.1	2.0	1.3	1.6	1.3
.9	.8	.9		.5	.6	1.0	.8	1.1	.9
23 15.9	13 28.2	27 13.7		0 UND	0 UND	31 11.8	25 14.5	35 10.5	27 13.3
39 9.4	35 10.5	43 8.4	Sales/Receivables	9 42.5	36 10.1	42 8.6	39 9.3	49 7.5	48 7.7
56 6.5	51 7.1	63 5.8		71 5.1	62 5.9	77 4.7	53 6.8	66 5.5	64 5.7
			Cost of Sales/Inventory						
			Cost of Sales/Payables						
11.1	10.1	9.4		5.9	12.2	6.7	10.9	8.4	12.5
25.2	22.4	18.4	Sales/Working Capital	-247.5	43.5	10.5	22.7	15.8	22.1
433.2	UND	NM		-5.5	-18.3	59.2	-31.0	36.3	999.8
12.5	13.6	14.4		32.0	6.3	7.5	7.9	29.9	17.8
(275) 4.2	(292) 3.5	(283) 2.9	EBIT/Interest	(12) .5	(33) .9	(36) .0	(43) 2.1	(78) 6.5	(81) 5.3
1.1	.3	-2.2		-7.8	-4.8	-13.4	-3.2	-.7	.9
14.1	9.3	10.4	Net Profit + Depr., Dep.,					10.0	12.6
(34) 2.8	(38) 2.1	(34) 2.4	Amort./Cur. Mat. L/T/D					(15) 2.8	(17) 2.2
-.1	-1.5	.0						.0	.3
.0	.0	.0		.0	.0	.0	.0	.0	.0
.2	.2	.2	Fixed/Worth	1.8	.3	.1	.1	.1	.3
1.0	1.3	1.1		-4.4	-19.2	.5	1.1	.3	2.0
.8	.7	.6		.9	.5	.3	.5	.5	1.4
2.0	1.9	1.8	Debt/Worth	8.8	2.1	.8	2.0	1.1	2.9
7.3	26.9	11.1		-5.5	-42.4	4.8	14.9	3.1	22.8
73.6	73.4	57.4	% Profit Before Taxes/Tangible	33.8	81.7	31.6	89.8	56.9	60.9
(277) 31.5	(287) 24.8	(288) 15.1	Net Worth	(13) 14.6	(32) 11.7	(39) 9.1	(48) 11.5	(83) 17.4	(73) 22.5
5.5	2.0	-4.2		-48.8	-26.3	-14.8	-11.7	.2	2.8
24.5	24.3	16.3	% Profit Before Taxes/Total	15.4	25.1	16.1	14.7	17.4	14.2
10.0	7.7	5.1	Assets	1.0	2.4	2.4	3.9	6.8	6.0
.8	-.7	-5.7		-29.9	-12.6	-11.8	-9.1	-1.9	-.3
435.5	507.8	438.7		255.0	664.8	842.0	791.0	347.7	265.4
131.8	148.5	124.8	Sales/Net Fixed Assets	19.5	121.8	147.2	125.3	106.3	138.1
54.8	48.7	37.8		6.1	28.8	35.3	37.4	40.7	48.7
7.8	8.3	6.7		3.7	7.3	5.9	6.8	6.5	7.2
5.6	5.5	4.7	Sales/Total Assets	1.5	5.0	4.1	5.3	4.7	5.2
4.1	3.5	3.0		.8	2.8	2.7	3.2	3.3	3.4
.1	.1	.1		2.6	.2	.2	.1	.1	.1
(216) .3	(250) .3	(248) .4	% Depr., Dep., Amort./Sales	(10) 7.9	(33) .6	(25) .5	(42) .3	(68) .3	(70) .3
.6	.6	.7		18.2	1.5	1.1	.6	.8	.5
1.4	1.7	1.5	% Officers', Directors'		3.5	2.5	1.6	.9	1.0
(109) 3.2	(132) 3.5	(105) 2.8	Owners' Comp/Sales	(18) 6.5	(15) 2.8	(25) 4.6	(28) 1.6	(15) 1.6	
8.7	8.3	7.2			11.2	7.1		2.6	
14600806M	16493689M	13266747M	Net Sales ($)	12614M	92046M	178154M	432524M	1470271M	11081138M
3069114M	3874510M	3059295M	Total Assets ($)	13499M	29822M	59333M	95077M	368420M	2493144M

M = $ thousand   MM = $ million
See Pages 9 through 22 for Explanation of Ratios and Data

ADMIN & WASTE MANAGEMENT SERVICES—Temporary Help Services NAICS 561320

Current Data Sorted by Assets							Comparative Historical Data	

Type of Statement

	0-500M	500M-2MM	2-10MM	10-50MM	50-100MM	100-250MM		4/1/05-3/31/06 ALL	4/1/06-3/31/07 ALL
Unqualified		2	19	22	6	6		46	67
Reviewed		22	39	6				51	49
Compiled	4	18	20		1	1		48	46
Tax Returns	15	17	3		1	1		27	24
Other	14	50	56	42	7	9		123	140
		32 (4/1-9/30/09)		347 (10/1/09-3/31/10)					
NUMBER OF STATEMENTS	33	109	137	70	13	17		295	326
	%	%	%	%	%	%		%	%
ASSETS									
Cash & Equivalents	20.1	15.5	12.6	11.9	15.4	12.4		14.5	13.5
Trade Receivables (net)	46.1	51.7	56.9	50.5	49.5	45.2		52.5	56.7
Inventory	.0	.1	.1	.0	.2	.1		.2	.4
All Other Current	5.5	5.6	8.7	8.9	15.4	3.9		5.5	6.1
Total Current	71.7	72.8	78.3	71.3	80.5	61.6		72.7	76.7
Fixed Assets (net)	14.1	9.9	7.2	6.0	7.6	8.3		9.0	8.2
Intangibles (net)	3.4	2.4	4.8	14.1	4.9	24.5		7.8	6.0
All Other Non-Current	10.9	14.8	9.7	8.6	7.0	5.6		10.4	9.1
Total	100.0	100.0	100.0	100.0	100.0	100.0		100.0	100.0
LIABILITIES									
Notes Payable-Short Term	32.5	20.4	19.7	16.1	7.3	6.8		18.6	19.9
Cur. Mat.-L.T.D.	11.1	1.6	1.9	1.3	10.0	1.3		2.9	1.2
Trade Payables	4.3	6.3	7.5	8.4	23.1	7.7		8.8	6.5
Income Taxes Payable	1.3	.3	.4	.1	.6	.9		.4	.5
All Other Current	22.1	21.4	21.5	23.3	18.5	25.9		24.5	24.9
Total Current	71.2	50.0	51.0	49.2	59.4	42.6		55.3	52.5
Long-Term Debt	16.7	5.6	3.6	4.7	10.6	33.8		6.1	6.4
Deferred Taxes	.0	.1	.1	.4	.1	1.9		.3	.3
All Other Non-Current	26.0	6.6	7.1	8.1	4.5	5.3		7.0	6.9
Net Worth	-13.9	37.8	38.1	37.6	25.3	16.5		31.2	33.5
Total Liabilties & Net Worth	100.0	100.0	100.0	100.0	100.0	100.0		100.0	100.0
INCOME DATA									
Net Sales	100.0	100.0	100.0	100.0	100.0	100.0		100.0	100.0
Gross Profit									
Operating Expenses	100.8	98.9	98.5	98.3	94.8	97.3		96.6	96.6
Operating Profit	-.8	1.1	1.5	1.7	5.2	2.7		3.4	3.4
All Other Expenses (net)	2.0	.0	.5	.8	1.6	2.0		.3	.5
Profit Before Taxes	-2.8	1.1	1.1	1.0	3.6	.7		3.1	2.9
RATIOS									
	6.9	3.1	2.6	1.9	2.4	2.4		2.1	2.6
Current	1.2	1.7	1.5	1.4	1.6	1.6		1.4	1.5
	.6	1.0	1.1	1.0	1.0	1.0		1.0	1.1
	5.2	2.6	2.3	1.8	2.3	2.1		2.0	2.4
Quick	1.0	1.4	1.4	1.2	1.2	1.3		1.3	1.4
	.5	.9	1.0	1.0	.8	.9		.9	1.0
	0 UND	21 17.3	28 12.9	34 10.6	49 7.4	48 7.6		24 15.3	26 13.9
Sales/Receivables	25 14.5	37 10.0	41 8.8	47 7.8	57 6.4	55 6.7		38 9.6	42 8.8
	49 7.5	49 7.4	55 6.7	59 6.1	88 4.2	78 4.7		51 7.1	54 6.8
Cost of Sales/Inventory									
Cost of Sales/Payables									
	14.1	10.6	9.8	9.6	6.7	8.3		12.2	10.8
Sales/Working Capital	66.6	20.8	20.3	20.2	10.1	24.2		30.6	22.9
	-33.9	428.4	118.8	190.0	NM	NM		321.2	131.4
	(26) 7.8	(92) 22.1	(111) 15.4	(62) 13.1	49.0	4.3		(257) 21.6	(272) 18.1
EBIT/Interest	2.3	4.0	3.8	3.2	23.0	1.4		7.1	5.9
	-5.9	-1.8	-3.0	-.3	2.8	-3.1		2.6	1.9
Net Profit + Depr., Dep.,			11.8	18.3				20.0	40.4
Amort./Cur. Mat. L/T/D		(15)	3.6	(18) 4.4				(43) 5.6	(39) 4.6
			-.3	-3.1				.9	1.1
	.0	.0	.0	.1	.1	.5		.1	.1
Fixed/Worth	.3	.1	.1	.2	.3	-.2		.2	.2
	-.7	.7	.4	1.0	1.2	-.1		.8	.6
	.5	.6	.6	1.3	.8	2.1		.9	.7
Debt/Worth	9.2	1.2	1.5	2.5	4.5	-5.8		2.3	2.0
	-2.3	5.5	3.8	10.0	62.5	-2.6		13.7	5.9
	80.3	64.8	41.7	36.8	140.1			79.8	73.2
% Profit Before Taxes/Tangible Net Worth	(17) 17.6	(93) 15.2	(121) 17.4	(59) 8.5	(11) 72.5			(242) 41.5	(282) 41.8
	-17.3	-4.3	-2.1	-2.1	7.3			20.4	12.8
	15.8	17.5	14.8	13.1	38.7	16.5		25.3	24.1
% Profit Before Taxes/Total Assets	1.5	5.1	6.0	2.9	5.0	3.0		12.5	11.8
	-21.5	-4.5	-2.6	-1.8	1.3	-9.6		4.5	3.0
	UND	470.9	362.8	242.4	390.6	173.3		370.1	384.5
Sales/Net Fixed Assets	133.1	134.5	137.2	136.6	140.8	52.0		138.7	138.4
	40.3	41.1	64.2	60.6	18.4	32.3		46.5	55.5
	14.4	7.1	6.8	5.5	4.1	3.9		8.2	7.9
Sales/Total Assets	7.1	5.4	5.2	4.3	3.4	2.5		5.7	5.6
	5.6	4.0	3.7	3.2	1.6	2.0		3.7	3.9
	.2	.2	.1	.2	.3			.1	.1
% Depr., Dep., Amort./Sales	(17) .3	(81) .3	(103) .2	(53) .3	(10) .9			(220) .3	(240) .3
	.6	.8	.6	.6	1.9			.7	.6
	1.7	1.5	1.0					1.6	1.5
% Officers', Directors' Owners' Comp/Sales	(17) 4.7	(56) 3.3	(47) 1.8					(92) 2.6	(100) 2.9
	7.7	7.3	3.0					4.4	6.8
Net Sales ($)	81965M	964320M	4416392M	6806258M	3043927M	14020720M		21582727M	21763530M
Total Assets ($)	7802M	137390M	652651M	1450678M	983938M	2814015M		4124747M	4203209M

M = $ thousand   MM = $ million
See Pages 9 through 22 for Explanation of Ratios and Data

Comparative Historical Data / Current Data Sorted by Sales

			Type of Statement	0-1MM	1-3MM	3-5MM	5-10MM	10-25MM	25MM & OVER
53	60	55	Unqualified		1		1	10	43
42	57	67	Reviewed			5	15	24	23
45	49	43	Compiled	1	5	3	17	8	9
39	36	36	Tax Returns	7	9	7	6	6	1
136	167	178	Other	6	13	6	31	37	85
4/1/07-3/31/08	4/1/08-3/31/09	4/1/09-3/31/10		32 (4/1-9/30/09)			347 (10/1/09-3/31/10)		
ALL	ALL	ALL							
315	369	379	**NUMBER OF STATEMENTS**	14	28	21	70	85	161
%	%	%	**ASSETS**	%	%	%	%	%	%
13.3	14.6	14.0	Cash & Equivalents	20.5	14.5	9.6	12.8	14.9	14.0
53.9	51.7	52.5	Trade Receivables (net)	34.6	40.5	61.6	52.3	59.0	51.6
.4	.4	.1	Inventory	.0	.0	.0	.2	.1	.0
5.9	6.6	7.6	All Other Current	.2	15.2	2.6	5.3	5.9	9.4
73.4	73.2	74.2	Total Current	55.3	70.2	73.8	70.6	79.8	75.1
9.4	8.8	8.4	Fixed Assets (net)	27.4	15.1	10.6	8.1	6.1	6.7
7.3	7.8	6.6	Intangibles (net)	7.3	.4	1.2	5.1	5.4	9.6
10.0	10.2	10.8	All Other Non-Current	10.0	14.3	14.4	16.2	8.6	8.6
100.0	100.0	100.0	Total	100.0	100.0	100.0	100.0	100.0	100.0
			LIABILITIES						
22.6	21.6	19.4	Notes Payable-Short Term	30.7	25.7	24.9	22.2	17.7	16.3
1.8	2.8	2.8	Cur. Mat.-L.T.D.	.7	12.7	.8	1.8	2.5	2.0
7.6	7.7	7.6	Trade Payables	1.4	6.1	1.7	5.6	8.1	9.8
.5	.6	.4	Income Taxes Payable	.0	1.5	.0	.2	.1	.5
23.6	19.8	22.0	All Other Current	42.9	19.2	11.9	16.7	19.9	25.3
56.1	52.5	52.1	Total Current	75.6	65.2	39.3	46.4	48.3	53.8
9.4	9.1	7.1	Long-Term Debt	21.6	13.3	7.9	5.6	3.8	7.1
.1	.3	.2	Deferred Taxes	.0	.0	.3	.0	.1	.4
7.0	6.9	8.6	All Other Non-Current	32.5	13.1	2.0	8.3	4.7	8.8
27.5	31.1	32.0	Net Worth	-29.8	8.4	50.6	39.7	43.1	29.8
100.0	100.0	100.0	Total Liabilities & Net Worth	100.0	100.0	100.0	100.0	100.0	100.0
			INCOME DATA						
100.0	100.0	100.0	Net Sales	100.0	100.0	100.0	100.0	100.0	100.0
			Gross Profit						
96.1	97.1	98.6	Operating Expenses	97.1	100.7	96.9	99.7	97.9	98.4
3.9	2.9	1.4	Operating Profit	2.9	-.7	3.1	.3	2.1	1.6
.8	.7	.6	All Other Expenses (net)	5.4	.0	.2	-.1	.3	.8
3.0	2.1	.8	Profit Before Taxes	-2.5	-.6	2.9	.4	1.8	.7
			RATIOS						
2.3	2.5	2.5		1.3	7.2	6.8	3.1	2.8	2.3
1.4	1.5	1.5	Current	.8	2.0	1.9	1.7	1.7	1.4
1.0	1.1	1.0		.5	.9	1.2	1.0	1.2	1.1
2.2	2.2	2.3		1.3	4.2	6.5	3.1	2.5	2.0
1.3	1.3	1.4	Quick	.8	1.1	1.9	1.6	1.5	1.2
1.0	.9	.9		.5	.2	1.2	.9	1.1	1.0
24 15.0	21 17.2	26 14.1		0 UND	10 36.5	32 11.4	25 14.4	29 12.4	28 13.1
39 9.3	35 10.5	42 8.7	Sales/Receivables	0 UND	31 11.7	42 8.6	39 9.3	45 8.1	43 8.5
55 6.6	49 7.4	56 6.5		71 5.1	50 7.2	71 5.1	50 7.3	58 6.3	56 6.5
			Cost of Sales/Inventory						
			Cost of Sales/Payables						
10.9	11.3	10.2		54.3	6.9	10.2	10.1	9.3	10.5
25.7	23.4	20.8	Sales/Working Capital	-33.9	18.5	15.0	23.6	16.4	24.2
275.7	233.0	209.4		-7.7	-65.6	43.2	NM	54.4	204.4
13.1	15.4	15.6		5.5	6.4	16.1	21.0	19.3	14.4
(265) 5.3	(313) 3.8	(321) 3.3	EBIT/Interest	(11) .0	(21) 1.9	(18) 3.7	(61) 3.2	(74) 5.6	(136) 3.2
1.6	1.0	-2.1		-17.9	-7.2	2.0	-3.1	-.5	-1.6
30.8	11.8	13.0						14.2	15.6
(36) 4.2	(49) 1.9	(45) 3.2	Net Profit + Depr., Dep., Amort./Cur. Mat. L/T/D					(11) 6.0	(29) 3.2
-.2	.0	-.3						-.3	-.6
.1	.1	.0		.0	.1	.0	.0	.0	.1
.2	.2	.2	Fixed/Worth	2.4	.4	.2	.1	.1	.2
.9	.9	1.1		-.2	-4.1	.4	.5	.4	1.3
.9	.7	.6		1.9	.6	.2	.6	.6	1.1
2.5	2.1	1.8	Debt/Worth	-8.1	3.8	1.1	1.1	1.2	2.4
8.7	9.6	9.3		-2.0	-10.3	3.5	5.6	3.4	16.1
74.1	62.3	51.9			62.9	74.1	30.4	59.9	44.6
(260) 38.9	(303) 22.9	(308) 15.3	% Profit Before Taxes/Tangible Net Worth		(16) 14.1	(20) 32.8	(61) 8.7	(77) 20.9	(128) 15.3
11.2	4.8	-2.9			-20.6	2.9	-15.9	.6	.2
20.7	18.1	15.2		9.0	11.7	30.4	13.1	19.0	14.7
11.5	7.6	3.7	% Profit Before Taxes/Total Assets	-3.0	3.2	6.4	3.2	7.5	3.4
2.0	.2	-4.6		-72.6	-16.2	2.9	-7.6	-1.4	-2.4
347.1	341.9	353.1		UND	419.0	999.8	383.6	283.1	332.0
127.9	128.9	135.3	Sales/Net Fixed Assets	39.1	86.8	77.3	150.1	143.3	138.1
62.5	57.7	48.8		2.6	23.8	32.2	60.4	72.9	52.2
8.2	8.0	6.9		7.7	7.9	6.5	6.5	7.4	7.2
5.6	5.6	4.9	Sales/Total Assets	2.4	6.2	4.6	4.9	5.2	4.7
3.7	3.7	3.6		.4	2.0	3.7	3.9	3.5	3.6
.1	.1	.1			.2	.2	.2	.1	.1
(226) .3	(252) .3	(272) .3	% Depr., Dep., Amort./Sales	(18) .4	(15) .4	(52) .3	(64) .2	(117) .3	
.5	.5	.6			1.0	.9	.6	.5	.6
1.3	1.1	1.1			2.9	1.5	3.2	.9	.6
(101) 2.7	(115) 2.1	(131) 2.5	% Officers', Directors' Owners' Comp/Sales	(16) 5.6	(13) 3.1	(30) 4.3	(37) 1.4	(31) 1.4	
6.7	5.2	4.9			10.6	7.6	7.6	2.4	2.3
22896790M	21760986M	29333582M	Net Sales ($)	6048M	58708M	83119M	510267M	1389671M	27285769M
4762416M	5077454M	6046474M	Total Assets ($)	6673M	18593M	18348M	106787M	382320M	5513753M

M = $ thousand   MM = $ million
See Pages 9 through 22 for Explanation of Ratios and Data

ADMIN & WASTE MANAGEMENT SERVICES—Professional Employer Organizations   NAICS 561330

| Current Data Sorted by Assets | | | | | | | Comparative Historical Data | |

Type of Statement

0-500M	500M-2MM	2-10MM	10-50MM	50-100MM	100-250MM	Type of Statement	4/1/05-3/31/06 ALL	4/1/06-3/31/07 ALL
	2	5	7	3	2	Unqualified	8	5
	2	5				Reviewed	1	4
7						Compiled	3	
4	1	1				Tax Returns	2	3
4	9	11	5	1	2	Other	7	12
	3 (4/1-9/30/09)		68 (10/1/09-3/31/10)					
15	14	22	12	4	4	NUMBER OF STATEMENTS	21	24

0-500M	500M-2MM	2-10MM	10-50MM	50-100MM	100-250MM		4/1/05-3/31/06 ALL	4/1/06-3/31/07 ALL
%	%	%	%	%	%	**ASSETS**	%	%
67.2	33.6	20.3	12.7			Cash & Equivalents	20.9	26.6
.0	37.7	36.9	24.2			Trade Receivables (net)	41.6	35.4
.0	.0	.0	.0			Inventory	1.2	.1
7.4	18.4	16.5	19.6			All Other Current	10.5	14.7
74.6	89.7	73.7	56.5			Total Current	74.2	76.8
10.7	5.8	13.5	6.7			Fixed Assets (net)	6.9	8.8
.2	1.9	3.7	29.8			Intangibles (net)	8.0	7.5
14.6	2.6	9.0	7.0			All Other Non-Current	10.9	6.9
100.0	100.0	100.0	100.0			Total	100.0	100.0
						LIABILITIES		
13.3	14.2	11.3	1.5			Notes Payable-Short Term	13.8	9.4
.6	.9	2.0	1.1			Cur. Mat.-L.T.D.	7.0	.8
.0	4.1	6.1	7.0			Trade Payables	7.6	7.2
.0	5.6	1.3	.6			Income Taxes Payable	.3	1.0
57.6	49.9	31.9	40.9			All Other Current	33.6	39.5
71.5	74.8	52.6	51.1			Total Current	62.3	57.9
.7	8.9	12.1	16.4			Long-Term Debt	7.4	10.8
.0	.0	.0	1.1			Deferred Taxes	.0	.4
.0	4.5	1.6	4.1			All Other Non-Current	4.5	2.7
27.8	11.7	33.7	27.4			Net Worth	25.8	28.2
100.0	100.0	100.0	100.0			Total Liabilities & Net Worth	100.0	100.0
						INCOME DATA		
100.0	100.0	100.0	100.0			Net Sales	100.0	100.0
						Gross Profit		
99.7	99.2	93.8	97.0			Operating Expenses	95.5	96.3
.3	.8	6.2	3.0			Operating Profit	4.5	3.7
.2	.1	5.3	1.3			All Other Expenses (net)	.5	.8
.1	.7	.9	1.8			Profit Before Taxes	4.0	2.9
						RATIOS		
2.1	2.5	2.8	1.5				1.6	2.3
1.2	1.5	1.2	1.2			Current	1.1	1.3
.6	1.0	1.0	.8				.9	.9
1.7	1.8	2.2	1.3				1.3	1.7
1.1	1.3	1.1	.7			Quick	1.1	1.2
.6	.7	.4	.4				.7	.9
0 UND	0 999.8	0 999.8	0 761.9				3 144.9	1 526.5
0 UND	3 144.1	25 14.5	11 33.0			Sales/Receivables	43 8.5	9 40.1
0 UND	41 8.9	41 8.9	66 5.5				64 5.7	53 6.9
						Cost of Sales/Inventory		
						Cost of Sales/Payables		
115.1	12.3	9.9	9.4				12.4	23.2
219.4	90.3	51.8	101.5			Sales/Working Capital	62.3	78.5
-80.1	NM	-831.0	-156.7				-538.4	-489.5
	30.8	41.5	19.3				30.1	20.0
	(10) 2.3	(15) 1.4	(11) 5.2			EBIT/Interest	(18) 6.7	(18) 6.4
	-.3	.6	.3				2.3	3.8
						Net Profit + Depr., Dep., Amort./Cur. Mat. L/T/D		
.0	.0	.1	.1				.2	.1
.0	.1	.2	1.7			Fixed/Worth	.5	.2
.7	.5	.6	-.1				UND	1.8
.9	1.8	.7	1.9				1.8	1.8
1.3	2.5	4.3	20.3			Debt/Worth	4.9	4.2
11.8	NM	10.9	-2.6				UND	16.1
106.7	134.8	45.6					125.3	114.0
(12) 31.6	(11) 49.3	11.3				% Profit Before Taxes/Tangible Net Worth	(16) 61.0	(20) 80.4
8.9	4.1	-2.8					16.8	47.7
18.5	39.1	16.9	8.2				19.0	24.8
9.6	3.7	1.0	1.9			% Profit Before Taxes/Total Assets	9.1	13.9
-4.0	-.4	-.6	-5.6				1.8	4.2
UND	UND	786.5	670.7				389.0	943.3
UND	723.4	186.3	233.8			Sales/Net Fixed Assets	126.5	390.7
193.2	191.8	55.4	49.8				37.1	62.2
91.5	51.5	15.8	15.3				10.9	20.4
24.5	27.7	5.1	8.0			Sales/Total Assets	5.4	8.9
11.6	5.7	2.8	1.9				2.7	4.3
		.1					.1	.1
	(16) .2					% Depr., Dep., Amort./Sales	(15) .3	(17) .1
		1.4					.9	.5
								.2
						% Officers', Directors' Owners' Comp/Sales		(10) 4.2
								8.5
112656M	420515M	1014335M	2206137M	1417069M	2720779M	Net Sales ($)	1711163M	3020762M
2635M	14571M	105944M	283205M	241344M	679917M	Total Assets ($)	407871M	366107M

© RMA 2010

M = $ thousand   MM = $ million
See Pages 9 through 22 for Explanation of Ratios and Data

Comparative Historical Data   Current Data Sorted by Sales

9 3 4 5 11	15 8 2 5 25	19 7 7 6 32	Type of Statement				3 (4/1-9/30/09)		68 (10/1/09-3/31/10)		
				0-1MM	1-3MM	3-5MM	5-10MM	10-25MM	25MM & OVER	

4/1/07-3/31/08 ALL	4/1/08-3/31/09 ALL	4/1/09-3/31/10 ALL		0-1MM	1-3MM	3-5MM	5-10MM	10-25MM	25MM & OVER
			Type of Statement						
9	15	19	Unqualified			1	1	2	16
3	8	7	Reviewed		3		1	2	3
4	2	7	Compiled			1	1		
5	5	6	Tax Returns	2	3		2	2	1
11	25	32	Other	2	1	2	1	1	19
32	55	71	**NUMBER OF STATEMENTS**	5	6	3	7	12	38
%	%	%	**ASSETS**	%	%	%	%	%	%
14.6	27.7	31.8	Cash & Equivalents					21.1	25.4
37.7	29.9	26.4	Trade Receivables (net)					42.5	28.8
.0	.0	.1	Inventory					.0	.1
14.8	12.0	14.7	All Other Current					20.6	15.9
67.1	69.6	73.0	Total Current					84.2	70.2
6.3	9.9	9.3	Fixed Assets (net)					5.5	6.8
8.9	7.3	8.9	Intangibles (net)					5.2	14.0
17.7	13.2	8.8	All Other Non-Current					5.0	9.0
100.0	100.0	100.0	Total					100.0	100.0
			LIABILITIES						
17.1	10.3	9.5	Notes Payable-Short Term					11.7	7.4
4.6	2.0	1.2	Cur. Mat.-L.T.D.					.4	1.2
6.4	7.0	4.2	Trade Payables					4.3	5.5
1.0	1.3	1.8	Income Taxes Payable					.1	1.3
29.0	43.5	42.8	All Other Current					30.8	48.5
58.1	64.1	59.5	Total Current					47.3	63.8
9.4	15.7	9.0	Long-Term Debt					4.4	7.1
.1	.2	.3	Deferred Taxes					.0	.6
7.2	9.2	3.1	All Other Non-Current					.4	4.1
25.1	10.8	28.0	Net Worth					47.9	24.3
100.0	100.0	100.0	Total Liabilties & Net Worth					100.0	100.0
			INCOME DATA						
100.0	100.0	100.0	Net Sales					100.0	100.0
			Gross Profit						
92.9	95.2	97.1	Operating Expenses					97.4	98.2
7.1	4.8	2.9	Operating Profit					2.6	1.8
1.6	.6	1.9	All Other Expenses (net)					.3	.4
5.5	4.2	1.0	Profit Before Taxes					2.4	1.4
			RATIOS						
1.4	1.9	2.1						3.0	1.7
1.1	1.1	1.2	Current					1.7	1.1
.9	.9	.9						1.3	.9
1.4	1.7	1.8						2.3	1.5
1.0	1.0	1.0	Quick					1.6	1.0
.4	.6	.6						.5	.7
1 494.2	0 897.1	0 UND						0 UND	1 534.5
33 11.0	9 42.5	5 67.8	Sales/Receivables					39 9.2	9 41.9
63 5.8	44 8.4	42 8.7						64 5.7	42 8.7
			Cost of Sales/Inventory						
			Cost of Sales/Payables						
16.2	16.6	11.4						9.0	12.6
147.7	119.3	115.1	Sales/Working Capital					12.4	301.7
-84.1	-280.8	-497.4						165.0	-309.2
26.7	45.6	27.7							22.6
(24) 4.5	(42) 8.6	(46) 3.7	EBIT/Interest						(31) 3.9
1.6	2.9	.5							.8
		12.7	Net Profit + Depr., Dep.,						
	(11) 3.5		Amort./Cur. Mat. L/T/D						
		.8							
.0	.0	.0						.0	.1
.2	.3	.2	Fixed/Worth					.0	.4
2.0	14.8	.9						.5	1.6
1.8	1.5	1.2						.6	1.7
5.4	6.8	3.3	Debt/Worth					1.1	5.3
24.8	-107.5	14.3						2.3	54.1
91.3	166.7	64.2	% Profit Before Taxes/Tangible					66.7	66.0
(26) 37.5	(40) 68.3	(59) 20.4	Net Worth					(11) 35.6	(30) 21.3
20.9	12.5	.6						16.9	.2
17.9	27.8	16.7	% Profit Before Taxes/Total					35.9	10.3
10.4	9.7	2.7	Assets					17.7	2.5
3.4	3.1	-.7						3.6	-.6
999.8	999.8	999.8						999.8	759.9
431.1	168.8	419.6	Sales/Net Fixed Assets					840.0	295.7
47.4	44.9	66.6						86.6	78.3
15.1	21.6	23.6						29.2	24.5
5.7	6.9	9.8	Sales/Total Assets					6.1	13.5
2.5	3.1	4.1						3.3	4.8
.1	.1	.1							.1
(16) .4	(35) .2	(37) .2	% Depr., Dep., Amort./Sales					(26)	.1
2.0	.8	1.1							.7
1.2	3.2	.8							
(10) 1.9	(11) 7.0	(16) 1.6	% Officers', Directors' Owners' Comp/Sales						
4.6	9.8	5.8							
2943922M	4113094M	7891491M	Net Sales ($)	1427M	10020M	12741M	46624M	224596M	7596083M
696302M	1025196M	1327616M	Total Assets ($)	5762M	3374M	1822M	10206M	61400M	1245052M

M = $ thousand   MM = $ million
See Pages 9 through 22 for Explanation of Ratios and Data

Current Data Sorted by Assets   **Comparative Historical Data**

0-500M	500M-2MM	2-10MM	10-50MM	50-100MM	100-250MM	Type of Statement	4/1/05-3/31/06 ALL	4/1/06-3/31/07 ALL
		4	4	2	2	Unqualified	4	10
	6	8	1			Reviewed	14	11
3	6	1	1			Compiled	15	16
8	6	1				Tax Returns	21	19
10	3	9				Other	35	30
	10 (4/1-9/30/09)		62 (10/1/09-3/31/10)					
21	15	23	8	3	2	NUMBER OF STATEMENTS	89	86
%	%	%	%	%	%	**ASSETS**	%	%
18.4	12.2	10.1				Cash & Equivalents	11.6	11.7
26.0	31.7	39.6				Trade Receivables (net)	30.0	28.9
9.7	13.2	7.9				Inventory	8.1	9.0
1.3	2.1	1.4				All Other Current	2.9	2.8
55.3	59.1	59.0				Total Current	52.6	52.5
31.5	27.1	24.4				Fixed Assets (net)	36.2	29.3
7.4	1.1	10.1				Intangibles (net)	5.7	10.5
5.7	12.6	6.5				All Other Non-Current	5.6	7.7
100.0	100.0	100.0				Total	100.0	100.0
						LIABILITIES		
21.3	13.6	12.4				Notes Payable-Short Term	11.9	13.2
4.6	4.1	6.4				Cur. Mat.-L.T.D.	5.7	9.2
17.9	23.6	11.7				Trade Payables	12.1	12.0
.0	1.9	1.4				Income Taxes Payable	.6	.1
19.5	16.0	11.4				All Other Current	14.6	11.7
63.3	59.2	43.3				Total Current	44.9	46.2
24.5	13.8	18.6				Long-Term Debt	28.4	26.9
.0	.6	.5				Deferred Taxes	.4	.2
4.9	4.8	10.2				All Other Non-Current	6.0	5.7
7.2	21.6	27.4				Net Worth	20.3	21.1
100.0	100.0	100.0				Total Liabilities & Net Worth	100.0	100.0
						INCOME DATA		
100.0	100.0	100.0				Net Sales	100.0	100.0
						Gross Profit		
99.6	97.3	96.8				Operating Expenses	94.2	92.0
.4	2.7	3.2				Operating Profit	5.8	8.0
-.2	.5	1.7				All Other Expenses (net)	1.1	2.2
.6	2.2	1.6				Profit Before Taxes	4.7	5.8
						RATIOS		
2.2	1.8	1.9					2.3	2.1
1.5	1.3	1.5				Current	1.3	1.3
.4	.7	.7					.9	.9
1.5	1.5	1.9					2.1	1.6
.5	.8	1.0				Quick	1.0	.9
.3	.4	.7					.7	.6
(4) 90.8	(15) 23.6	(29) 12.4					(32) 11.4	(27) 13.8
(22) 16.7	(31) 11.7	(51) 7.2				Sales/Receivables	(41) 8.9	(40) 9.0
(39) 9.3	(47) 7.8	(80) 4.6					(54) 6.8	(52) 7.1
						Cost of Sales/Inventory		
						Cost of Sales/Payables		
11.3	17.1	5.4					8.3	9.3
25.5	29.5	11.9				Sales/Working Capital	23.3	25.5
-6.5	-20.0	-21.2					-59.6	-64.9
20.0	13.7	8.7					7.4	7.8
(15) 2.5	(12) 4.0	(22) 2.6				EBIT/Interest	(81) 4.0	(74) 3.6
-1.7	-.3	1.0					1.4	1.5
							4.7	4.5
						Net Profit + Depr., Dep., Amort./Cur. Mat. L/T/D	(15) 2.3	(19) 2.4
							1.4	1.5
.3	.6	.2					.5	.5
1.2	1.0	1.9				Fixed/Worth	1.7	1.6
-1.0	-2.9	-7.0					12.3	12.2
.8	1.3	1.1					.8	1.1
4.3	2.4	2.5				Debt/Worth	3.0	2.7
-3.9	-14.3	-44.6					19.8	182.8
94.0	36.7	46.4					74.2	91.5
(12) 16.0	(10) 21.5	(17) 17.0				% Profit Before Taxes/Tangible Net Worth	(69) 27.4	(66) 31.0
-75.0	-50.6	-.1					8.0	12.4
23.7	20.0	13.5					23.8	21.0
-2.0	8.3	8.5				% Profit Before Taxes/Total Assets	7.8	7.2
-34.6	-8.8	.0					1.3	1.4
93.6	27.9	42.1					20.1	42.1
11.7	18.8	16.4				Sales/Net Fixed Assets	8.6	9.8
5.9	12.8	4.5					4.3	5.6
5.4	5.1	3.0					3.7	4.0
3.3	4.3	2.4				Sales/Total Assets	2.7	2.6
2.7	3.2	1.6					1.9	1.7
1.1	.9	.9					1.4	1.4
(11) 3.4	(14) 2.0	(19) 2.0				% Depr., Dep., Amort./Sales	(73) 3.5	(68) 3.0
4.7	3.3	5.4					6.2	5.2
4.3	3.8						3.0	3.3
(11) 9.9	(10) 9.7					% Officers', Directors' Owners' Comp/Sales	(43) 5.9	(36) 5.8
15.1	15.9						11.3	8.9
17025M	74713M	274224M	301471M	408077M	186623M	Net Sales ($)	1288021M	1098249M
4409M	17036M	111332M	207143M	203894M	315735M	Total Assets ($)	649456M	726468M

M = $ thousand   MM = $ million

See Pages 9 through 22 for Explanation of Ratios and Data

Comparative Historical Data   Current Data Sorted by Sales

Type of Statement	4/1/07-3/31/08 ALL	4/1/08-3/31/09 ALL	4/1/09-3/31/10 ALL	0-1MM	1-3MM	3-5MM	5-10MM	10-25MM	25MM & OVER
Unqualified	10	7	12					3	8
Reviewed	10	12	9					6	1
Compiled	15	17	10	2	2	3	3		
Tax Returns	20	27	15	4	7	3	4		
Other	36	35	26	8	3	3	2	7	3
				10 (4/1-9/30/09)			62 (10/1/09-3/31/10)		
NUMBER OF STATEMENTS	91	98	72	14	12	9	9	16	12
	%	%	%	%	%	%	%	%	%
ASSETS									
Cash & Equivalents	14.4	14.9	13.3	11.8	24.7			9.1	13.5
Trade Receivables (net)	22.9	28.0	31.0	23.8	28.1			46.3	21.5
Inventory	8.1	9.5	8.6	10.8	7.2			6.0	1.9
All Other Current	2.2	2.5	1.8	.6	1.7			3.0	2.7
Total Current	47.6	54.9	54.7	47.0	61.7			64.3	39.6
Fixed Assets (net)	32.2	31.9	27.1	39.4	29.1			19.2	27.1
Intangibles (net)	11.9	6.6	10.9	7.6	4.1			9.1	28.0
All Other Non-Current	8.3	6.6	7.3	5.9	5.0			7.3	5.3
Total	100.0	100.0	100.0	100.0	100.0			100.0	100.0
LIABILITIES									
Notes Payable-Short Term	8.4	12.9	13.3	13.7	21.5			14.0	1.1
Cur. Mat.-L.T.D.	5.9	5.9	5.3	4.5	5.4			5.2	6.9
Trade Payables	10.9	11.8	15.8	13.9	24.6			13.9	10.2
Income Taxes Payable	.5	.1	1.2	.0	.1			2.1	2.1
All Other Current	10.6	13.6	14.5	19.2	12.2			14.9	12.1
Total Current	36.2	44.2	50.1	51.3	63.8			50.1	32.4
Long-Term Debt	26.8	25.6	19.5	22.9	32.9			12.4	18.2
Deferred Taxes	.4	.3	.7	.0	.6			.7	2.4
All Other Non-Current	5.7	6.4	7.3	4.6	8.2			9.5	8.1
Net Worth	31.0	23.4	22.5	21.2	-5.5			27.2	38.9
Total Liabilities & Net Worth	100.0	100.0	100.0	100.0	100.0			100.0	100.0
INCOME DATA									
Net Sales	100.0	100.0	100.0	100.0	100.0			100.0	100.0
Gross Profit									
Operating Expenses	92.3	94.2	98.3	98.3	102.6			95.7	98.8
Operating Profit	7.7	5.8	1.7	1.7	-2.6			4.3	1.2
All Other Expenses (net)	1.6	1.3	1.1	-.5	1.1			.7	3.2
Profit Before Taxes	6.1	4.5	.6	2.1	-3.6			3.6	-2.0
RATIOS									
Current	2.4	2.5	2.0	2.5	1.8			2.4	1.7
	1.5	1.3	1.4	1.6	1.4			1.6	1.2
	.8	.9	.7	.3	.7			.8	.8
Quick	2.0	2.1	1.6	1.7	1.5			2.1	1.7
	1.1	1.0	.9	.5	1.1			1.3	1.0
	.5	.6	.5	.2	.5			.7	.7
Sales/Receivables	21 17.0	22 16.5	21 17.6	4 90.4	17 21.9			23 15.7	33 10.9
	36 10.3	35 10.5	40 9.2	21 17.5	42 8.7			53 6.9	44 8.4
	54 6.7	48 7.6	66 5.5	34 10.7	65 5.6			88 4.1	67 5.5
Cost of Sales/Inventory									
Cost of Sales/Payables									
Sales/Working Capital	8.2	7.8	9.4	9.0	13.6			8.8	8.1
	18.9	24.4	24.0	20.2	27.5			11.6	54.7
	-21.8	-30.9	-15.7	-5.7	-12.2			-21.7	-22.0
EBIT/Interest	9.8	10.7	8.7	21.6	26.7			8.7	6.3
	(78) 3.7	(88) 2.7	(61) 2.3	(10) 5.9	(10) -1.0		(15)	7.0	(11) .8
	1.6	.9	-.6	1.5	-9.6			1.3	-3.3
Net Profit + Depr., Dep., Amort./Cur. Mat. L/T/D	3.6	2.0	3.2						
	(15) 2.1	(16) 1.7	(17) 1.9						
	1.4	.6	.7						
Fixed/Worth	.5	.4	.4	.3	.5			.3	.7
	1.4	1.5	1.6	1.4	.9			.8	NM
	-2.4	-2.2	-2.1	-1.9	-.6			-3.9	-1.1
Debt/Worth	1.1	.9	1.1	.6	2.1			1.2	1.0
	2.8	2.5	2.8	1.5	5.0			2.5	NM
	-8.7	-6.8	-6.5	-5.8	-2.6			-17.0	-3.0
% Profit Before Taxes/Tangible Net Worth	70.8	77.1	42.4					46.9	
	(64) 38.0	(67) 33.2	(45) 15.1				(11)	27.7	
	8.4	7.1	-15.0					.2	
% Profit Before Taxes/Total Assets	19.1	30.4	15.4	34.7	19.0			19.9	12.5
	9.0	7.7	2.2	5.9	-16.9			11.4	-1.7
	1.7	-.9	-8.2	-17.3	-45.1			1.0	-7.2
Sales/Net Fixed Assets	18.9	28.9	30.0	33.3	118.0			39.5	10.7
	8.7	11.7	14.7	8.1	15.9			19.2	6.3
	4.3	5.4	5.4	5.4	3.5			14.6	4.2
Sales/Total Assets	3.8	4.6	4.3	5.2	4.7			4.3	2.4
	2.3	2.9	2.8	3.0	3.9			3.0	1.8
	1.5	1.9	2.1	2.6	1.6			2.3	.7
% Depr., Dep., Amort./Sales	2.5	1.4	1.1					.7	1.9
	(75) 3.8	(75) 3.0	(55) 2.7				(14)	1.5	(10) 5.1
	6.3	6.6	5.4					2.8	10.0
% Officers', Directors' Owners' Comp/Sales	3.0	3.6	3.6						
	(42) 6.1	(42) 6.1	(25) 8.8						
	9.4	9.9	14.8						
Net Sales ($)	1070455M	1545097M	1262133M	6912M	20647M	35802M	55651M	255864M	887257M
Total Assets ($)	725758M	891013M	859549M	2324M	10053M	21576M	15702M	107613M	702281M

© RMA 2010

M = $ thousand   MM = $ million

See Pages 9 through 22 for Explanation of Ratios and Data

Current Data Sorted by Assets

Comparative Historical Data

0-500M	500M-2MM	2-10MM	10-50MM	50-100MM	100-250MM	Type of Statement	4/1/05-3/31/06 ALL	4/1/06-3/31/07 ALL
1	8	31	24	2	6	Unqualified	30	41
1	6	16	2			Reviewed	22	22
3	12	11				Compiled	18	18
10	10	7	1			Tax Returns	12	23
5	15	21	27	3	6	Other	45	37
	20 (4/1-9/30/09)		208 (10/1/09-3/31/10)					
20	51	86	54	5	12	NUMBER OF STATEMENTS	127	141
%	%	%	%	%	%	ASSETS	%	%
43.5	36.4	24.6	17.2		8.3	Cash & Equivalents	21.7	21.4
17.1	22.3	28.5	24.6		24.2	Trade Receivables (net)	24.8	22.8
.0	1.4	.6	3.5		.0	Inventory	1.0	1.5
7.0	8.9	10.7	14.2		5.8	All Other Current	10.7	6.7
67.6	69.0	64.5	59.5		38.3	Total Current	58.2	52.5
24.1	16.0	19.6	17.4		12.2	Fixed Assets (net)	20.9	23.5
1.8	2.9	6.8	16.2		45.6	Intangibles (net)	6.4	11.5
6.5	12.1	9.0	7.0		3.9	All Other Non-Current	14.5	12.6
100.0	100.0	100.0	100.0		100.0	Total	100.0	100.0
						LIABILITIES		
12.1	13.0	7.1	9.2		5.6	Notes Payable-Short Term	15.3	11.8
8.4	2.0	3.7	5.6		4.4	Cur. Mat.-L.T.D.	4.9	7.9
2.1	15.1	12.3	8.1		5.3	Trade Payables	11.4	10.2
.2	.4	.2	.2		.4	Income Taxes Payable	.3	.2
14.7	20.0	23.4	16.8		11.6	All Other Current	17.1	16.5
37.4	50.6	46.7	40.0		27.3	Total Current	48.9	46.6
35.2	12.1	13.7	14.1		29.8	Long-Term Debt	15.9	17.0
.5	.0	.1	1.0		2.5	Deferred Taxes	.0	.2
2.9	10.9	6.7	5.3		8.0	All Other Non-Current	8.2	4.8
24.0	26.3	32.7	39.6		32.3	Net Worth	26.9	31.3
100.0	100.0	100.0	100.0		100.0	Total Liabilities & Net Worth	100.0	100.0
						INCOME DATA		
100.0	100.0	100.0	100.0		100.0	Net Sales	100.0	100.0
						Gross Profit		
86.6	93.8	91.3	88.7		84.9	Operating Expenses	87.7	90.2
13.4	6.2	8.7	11.3		15.1	Operating Profit	12.3	9.8
.9	1.1	.9	1.8		4.5	All Other Expenses (net)	2.3	2.3
12.5	5.1	7.8	9.5		10.6	Profit Before Taxes	10.0	7.5
						RATIOS		
4.0	3.9	2.5	2.4		2.0		1.8	1.9
1.8	1.7	1.3	1.3		1.5	Current	1.2	1.2
.9	1.0	1.0	1.0		.9		.8	.7
3.9	3.3	1.7	2.2		1.6		1.6	1.7
1.7	1.7	1.1	1.0		1.3	Quick	1.0	1.0
.7	1.0	.7	.5		.8		.6	.5
0 UND	1 322.5	17 22.1	18 20.4		45 8.1		9 41.1	9 40.1
0 UND	18 19.7	28 13.2	33 11.0		47 7.8	Sales/Receivables	27 13.5	26 13.8
19 19.7	32 11.4	42 8.6	50 7.3		54 6.8		43 8.5	46 8.0
						Cost of Sales/Inventory		
						Cost of Sales/Payables		
8.6	7.2	7.8	5.3		5.2		7.7	8.8
42.8	17.6	22.2	15.3		10.9	Sales/Working Capital	36.1	45.4
NM	166.1	-199.0	400.1		-91.7		-70.4	-25.2
37.2	21.0	43.1	44.6		7.7		23.6	20.3
(10) 7.1	(36) 3.0	(70) 12.8	(43) 11.5		(11) 2.4	EBIT/Interest	(106) 7.9	(122) 6.3
1.0	.9	3.3	2.0		.8		2.5	1.0
			6.3				9.6	19.7
			(12) 3.1			Net Profit + Depr., Dep., Amort./Cur. Mat. L/T/D	(17) 4.8	(18) 2.6
			.5				2.1	1.1
.0	.1	.2	.2		.4		.3	.3
.5	.4	.4	.6		-1.0	Fixed/Worth	.9	1.1
1.6	4.1	1.1	2.7		-.1		4.4	10.8
.3	.5	1.0	.7		1.8		.9	.9
1.4	3.1	2.2	2.0		-3.5	Debt/Worth	2.6	2.8
6.9	14.6	5.2	26.2		-1.5		20.8	30.7
318.9	80.2	101.0	79.7			% Profit Before Taxes/Tangible Net Worth	110.5	89.6
(18) 90.7	(41) 42.3	(75) 56.6	(43) 45.4				(101) 56.6	(109) 47.4
33.0	5.0	25.8	17.0				17.0	8.6
169.1	32.4	34.9	32.5		11.1	% Profit Before Taxes/Total Assets	30.8	30.7
61.3	15.3	16.3	15.6		6.3		15.8	11.4
10.3	.9	6.1	2.2		.7		3.9	.5
999.8	99.8	44.3	41.5		18.6	Sales/Net Fixed Assets	40.8	38.1
60.0	45.9	21.9	19.8		12.8		20.1	16.5
21.8	19.4	12.3	8.9		7.3		10.6	8.7
24.8	6.7	4.2	3.1		1.6	Sales/Total Assets	4.7	4.0
7.0	4.3	3.3	2.1		1.2		2.8	2.6
2.7	2.8	2.1	1.1		.7		1.5	1.4
	.4	.9	1.4			% Depr., Dep., Amort./Sales	1.2	1.4
	(36) .9	(65) 1.7	(41) 2.0				(91) 1.9	(107) 2.1
	1.6	2.7	3.5				3.1	3.3
6.5	3.0	1.9				% Officers', Directors' Owners' Comp/Sales	3.2	2.7
(11) 10.1	(18) 4.0	(15) 3.8					(36) 6.5	(32) 6.2
18.7	6.1	9.5					13.6	13.4
53329M	295155M	1327776M	2422870M	363250M	2506911M	Net Sales ($)	6294036M	3259006M
5406M	61016M	434851M	1130360M	336379M	2080176M	Total Assets ($)	2534757M	1880043M

M = $ thousand   MM = $ million
See Pages 9 through 22 for Explanation of Ratios and Data

Comparative Historical Data

Current Data Sorted by Sales

			Type of Statement						
40	56	72	Unqualified		2		9	30	29
16	22	25	Reviewed			3	7	12	3
21	16	26	Compiled	2	7	3	6	6	2
26	25	28	Tax Returns	4	6	5	11	2	
45	75	77	Other	5	5	5	11	23	28
4/1/07- 3/31/08 ALL	4/1/08- 3/31/09 ALL	4/1/09- 3/31/10 ALL		**20 (4/1-9/30/09)**			**208 (10/1/09-3/31/10)**		
				0-1MM	1-3MM	3-5MM	5-10MM	10-25MM	25MM & OVER
148	194	228	NUMBER OF STATEMENTS	11	20	18	44	73	62
%	%	%	**ASSETS**	%	%	%	%	%	%
26.8	24.0	26.0	Cash & Equivalents	23.5	33.1	33.8	37.8	21.5	19.0
24.8	25.8	24.6	Trade Receivables (net)	20.1	14.5	26.4	17.1	31.3	25.6
1.6	1.0	1.4	Inventory	6.4	.0	.0	2.2	1.7	.4
6.4	9.4	10.4	All Other Current	1.0	14.1	7.1	11.1	10.4	11.2
59.6	60.2	62.4	Total Current	51.0	61.7	67.3	68.1	64.9	56.2
18.5	17.8	18.0	Fixed Assets (net)	38.1	20.9	20.1	13.4	15.6	19.0
9.7	11.7	11.0	Intangibles (net)	.5	3.6	2.6	7.4	11.6	19.5
12.2	10.4	8.6	All Other Non-Current	10.4	13.8	10.0	11.1	7.8	5.4
100.0	100.0	100.0	Total	100.0	100.0	100.0	100.0	100.0	100.0
			LIABILITIES						
10.9	12.7	9.2	Notes Payable-Short Term	14.8	6.3	10.2	14.1	8.0	6.5
4.6	5.1	4.2	Cur. Mat.-L.T.D.	5.3	3.1	1.7	5.9	2.6	5.6
10.3	9.4	10.5	Trade Payables	2.8	5.3	19.6	10.1	12.9	8.3
.2	.4	.3	Income Taxes Payable	.3	.7	.0	.4	.1	.3
17.7	21.4	19.4	All Other Current	17.7	17.6	25.8	16.3	21.4	18.2
43.8	49.0	43.4	Total Current	41.0	33.0	57.2	46.9	45.1	38.9
16.5	16.8	16.4	Long-Term Debt	73.9	13.3	7.9	14.9	9.4	19.1
.2	.3	.5	Deferred Taxes	.0	.5	.0	.1	.2	1.3
8.5	5.1	6.9	All Other Non-Current	5.3	3.2	12.6	9.8	7.1	4.4
31.1	28.9	32.7	Net Worth	-20.1	50.0	22.3	28.3	38.2	36.3
100.0	100.0	100.0	Total Liabilties & Net Worth	100.0	100.0	100.0	100.0	100.0	100.0
			INCOME DATA						
100.0	100.0	100.0	Net Sales	100.0	100.0	100.0	100.0	100.0	100.0
			Gross Profit						
89.9	91.5	90.4	Operating Expenses	77.3	86.5	94.4	92.5	92.1	89.2
10.1	8.5	9.6	Operating Profit	22.7	13.5	5.6	7.5	7.9	10.8
2.8	2.6	1.4	All Other Expenses (net)	6.2	2.3	.2	.7	1.1	1.4
7.3	5.9	8.2	Profit Before Taxes	16.5	11.2	5.5	6.8	6.8	9.4
			RATIOS						
2.8	2.3	2.8		3.1	5.7	3.8	3.8	2.0	2.3
1.5	1.3	1.4	Current	2.0	2.1	1.5	1.6	1.3	1.4
.8	.9	1.0		.0	.9	.6	1.0	1.0	1.0
2.6	1.8	2.2		3.1	3.2	3.0	2.9	1.7	1.9
1.3	1.1	1.2	Quick	2.0	1.5	1.4	1.3	1.1	1.3
.7	.7	.7		.0	.7	.6	.7	.8	.7
9 39.3	8 44.6	8 46.7		0 UND	0 UND	0 UND	0 UND	20 18.1	24 15.1
24 15.0	27 13.7	27 13.6	Sales/Receivables	3 137.0	9 41.3	20 18.2	17 21.9	31 11.8	35 10.5
46 7.9	50 7.3	45 8.2		54 6.7	32 11.2	44 8.3	33 11.2	49 7.4	48 7.7
			Cost of Sales/Inventory						
			Cost of Sales/Payables						
5.7	6.2	7.0		1.2	3.0	8.2	7.2	8.7	5.8
17.4	29.2	19.7	Sales/Working Capital	7.4	17.7	18.5	29.1	21.6	17.1
-45.1	-39.7	653.0		-2.1	NM	-13.9	543.9	120.4	-206.0
14.9	19.4	36.6			25.4	52.1	18.9	34.3	63.8
(114) 5.5	(150) 5.4	(174) 7.9	EBIT/Interest	(12) 4.0	(14) 9.3	(31) 4.3	(57) 13.6	(53) 11.5	
1.8	1.2	1.9			-4.9	1.9	1.1	2.2	2.1
6.7	7.9	4.8							3.6
(21) 2.3	(29) 2.5	(30) 2.7	Net Profit + Depr., Dep., Amort./Cur. Mat. L/T/D					(12)	2.2
-.9	.8	.6							.5
.2	.2	.2		.0	.1	.0	.1	.2	.3
.5	.7	.5	Fixed/Worth	2.2	.4	.4	.4	.4	.8
2.6	7.2	2.8		-128.4	1.4	NM	3.0	1.0	-1.0
.7	1.0	.7		1.8	.2	1.2	.7	.7	.8
2.7	3.1	2.3	Debt/Worth	8.3	.9	2.2	3.0	2.1	2.9
23.7	NM	13.3		-130.5	8.4	NM	13.5	5.4	-3.5
90.6	73.1	89.4	% Profit Before Taxes/Tangible Net Worth		108.6	132.0	81.5	100.7	87.8
(118) 41.9	(146) 38.4	(183) 49.5		(17) 37.5	(14) 35.2	(36) 46.6	(64) 55.7	(44) 53.9	
10.7	8.8	22.7			-11.0	10.7	22.1	17.4	26.8
29.7	24.6	34.1	% Profit Before Taxes/Total Assets	17.0	37.1	31.5	45.4	34.3	32.5
9.7	9.7	15.4		6.4	16.4	15.7	18.6	15.3	15.6
2.1	1.0	3.8		4.2	-5.8	5.6	1.5	3.4	6.4
50.4	54.7	62.4	Sales/Net Fixed Assets	136.3	69.6	184.7	100.6	47.3	31.6
21.5	20.0	25.3		25.5	24.5	29.8	45.2	26.4	15.8
10.9	11.3	11.6		1.4	11.7	9.0	19.5	15.4	9.0
4.6	4.2	4.7	Sales/Total Assets	3.1	5.3	5.5	5.8	4.8	3.5
2.8	2.7	3.1		.9	2.5	3.3	4.1	3.4	2.6
1.5	1.4	1.5		.4	1.3	1.8	2.6	1.8	1.4
1.1	1.0	.8	% Depr., Dep., Amort./Sales		.9	1.2	.6	.6	1.8
(119) 1.9	(139) 2.0	(156) 1.7		(13) 1.1	(12) 1.7	(26) 1.0	(60) 1.4	(41) 2.4	
3.0	3.1	2.8			2.5	3.8	1.9	2.4	3.5
4.4	2.9	2.5	% Officers', Directors' Owners' Comp/Sales					2.5	
(35) 5.6	(41) 4.3	(51) 4.6						(18) 3.6	
9.8	8.5	9.8						6.7	
3585516M	6585775M	6969291M	Net Sales ($)	5102M	40248M	72362M	316940M	1197949M	5336690M
2309209M	4058734M	4048188M	Total Assets ($)	9092M	40697M	33518M	125261M	573632M	3265988M

M = $ thousand   MM = $ million
See Pages 9 through 22 for Explanation of Ratios and Data

Current Data Sorted by Assets | Comparative Historical Data

Type of Statement

0-500M	500M-2MM	2-10MM	10-50MM	50-100MM	100-250MM	Type of Statement	4/1/05-3/31/06 ALL	4/1/06-3/31/07 ALL
2	9	33	34	18	19	Unqualified	134	115
1	26	61	14			Reviewed	111	102
10	31	47	5			Compiled	85	83
63	72	33	3		3	Tax Returns	150	126
47	98	125	53	23	13	Other	376	248
131 (4/1-9/30/09)		712 (10/1/09-3/31/10)						
123	236	299	109	41	35	NUMBER OF STATEMENTS	856	674
%	%	%	%	%	%		%	%

ASSETS

0-500M	500M-2MM	2-10MM	10-50MM	50-100MM	100-250MM		ALL	ALL
24.5	15.5	17.5	19.7	13.6	20.8	Cash & Equivalents	15.4	18.5
18.2	31.9	30.6	29.7	22.4	19.1	Trade Receivables (net)	31.8	29.3
3.7	7.6	8.8	7.5	4.7	5.2	Inventory	7.5	7.3
5.4	5.0	6.2	7.4	5.7	11.1	All Other Current	4.7	5.2
51.9	60.0	63.1	64.3	46.5	56.3	Total Current	59.3	60.3
28.4	26.7	24.4	18.8	16.9	14.2	Fixed Assets (net)	23.8	23.6
5.7	6.4	5.0	9.0	26.9	18.9	Intangibles (net)	7.0	7.0
14.1	6.9	7.5	8.0	9.7	10.6	All Other Non-Current	9.9	9.0
100.0	100.0	100.0	100.0	100.0	100.0	Total	100.0	100.0

LIABILITIES

0-500M	500M-2MM	2-10MM	10-50MM	50-100MM	100-250MM		ALL	ALL
31.8	11.4	7.6	7.8	8.5	4.1	Notes Payable-Short Term	13.5	11.6
7.0	2.8	3.9	3.7	4.4	1.6	Cur. Mat.-L.T.D.	3.6	3.3
8.9	14.5	12.2	12.0	6.4	6.6	Trade Payables	13.8	13.7
.6	.4	.5	.7	.2	1.4	Income Taxes Payable	.5	.5
30.1	17.3	16.5	19.1	20.9	21.0	All Other Current	17.4	17.1
78.5	46.4	40.8	43.3	40.4	34.8	Total Current	48.9	46.3
22.8	21.6	15.3	9.8	19.1	18.0	Long-Term Debt	16.0	16.5
.1	.3	.2	.5	1.0	1.3	Deferred Taxes	.3	.3
7.8	8.4	8.5	7.9	7.3	11.0	All Other Non-Current	8.9	7.8
-9.2	23.4	35.2	38.6	32.2	34.9	Net Worth	26.0	29.1
100.0	100.0	100.0	100.0	100.0	100.0	Total Liabilities & Net Worth	100.0	100.0

INCOME DATA

0-500M	500M-2MM	2-10MM	10-50MM	50-100MM	100-250MM		ALL	ALL
100.0	100.0	100.0	100.0	100.0	100.0	Net Sales	100.0	100.0
						Gross Profit		
90.9	89.7	93.4	90.6	92.6	94.6	Operating Expenses	91.8	89.9
9.1	10.3	6.6	9.4	7.4	5.4	Operating Profit	8.2	10.1
2.7	3.3	2.4	2.5	4.2	5.3	All Other Expenses (net)	2.0	1.9
6.4	7.0	4.2	6.9	3.2	.1	Profit Before Taxes	6.2	8.2

RATIOS

0-500M	500M-2MM	2-10MM	10-50MM	50-100MM	100-250MM		ALL	ALL
2.7	3.0	2.9	2.6	2.4	3.0	Current	2.2	2.4
.9	1.4	1.6	1.4	1.1	1.7		1.4	1.3
.3	.8	1.0	1.0	.9	1.1		.9	.9
2.1	2.2	2.2	2.0	1.5	2.4	Quick	1.8	2.0
(122) .8	1.1	1.2	1.1	1.0	1.2		1.1	1.1
.2	.4	.6	.7	.6	.6		.6	.6
0 UND	2 183.7	20 17.9	24 15.4	30 12.3	34 10.7	Sales/Receivables	13 28.3	7 53.3
0 UND	30 12.1	41 9.0	46 8.0	49 7.5	61 6.0		42 8.7	36 10.1
29 12.4	54 6.7	63 5.8	76 4.8	62 5.9	74 4.9		63 5.8	59 6.2
						Cost of Sales/Inventory		
						Cost of Sales/Payables		
9.9	6.9	5.5	4.5	4.9	3.8	Sales/Working Capital	7.2	7.1
-412.0	25.3	11.4	10.3	29.8	6.3		19.6	20.8
-10.9	-30.3	140.6	60.3	-47.1	19.3		-52.3	-113.8
10.9	17.7	18.9	25.3	11.2	18.4	EBIT/Interest	18.9	18.2
(76) 2.9	(173) 4.0	(243) 4.4	(82) 4.5	(34) 2.6	(29) 3.7		(694) 5.2	(503) 4.7
-1.9	.7	.6	1.6	.4	-.4		1.5	1.4
		10.8	6.5	7.7		Net Profit + Depr., Dep., Amort./Cur. Mat. L/T/D	5.9	10.4
	(36) 2.8	(14) 1.5	(13) 3.5	1.5			(113) 2.7	(99) 4.5
	.9	.3	1.4				.8	1.9
.2	.1	.2	.1	.4	.3	Fixed/Worth	.2	.1
2.0	.9	.6	.5	1.2	.5		.7	.7
-.8	344.4	2.7	1.8	-1.2	-.5		5.2	3.4
.8	.8	.7	.8	2.0	.5	Debt/Worth	1.0	.9
11.5	2.5	1.7	2.2	9.4	4.1		2.7	2.5
-3.4	-28.4	8.9	6.7	-3.0	-3.6		21.2	25.4
88.0	92.5	49.4	50.3	67.7	31.4	% Profit Before Taxes/Tangible Net Worth	84.8	81.1
(72) 29.8	(176) 34.4	(250) 20.9	(92) 24.9	(27) 11.6	(23) 10.4		(675) 32.5	(536) 38.2
-.4	4.0	1.7	6.1	-4.0	-9.9		7.9	10.3
32.3	28.4	19.2	15.5	8.6	9.9	% Profit Before Taxes/Total Assets	24.4	26.5
11.0	6.7	6.5	6.6	4.0	1.5		8.6	9.2
-8.6	-.3	-.2	1.7	-1.3	-3.3		1.3	2.0
149.9	143.0	60.2	55.5	28.6	29.5	Sales/Net Fixed Assets	70.2	85.6
34.9	32.0	21.1	22.5	14.0	9.4		22.5	21.1
8.4	6.5	5.7	6.7	6.1	5.0		6.8	7.2
8.2	4.7	3.6	3.0	2.4	1.9	Sales/Total Assets	4.3	4.4
4.5	2.9	2.4	2.4	1.7	1.0		2.7	2.6
2.6	1.2	1.5	1.0	.5	.4		1.5	1.5
.6	.5	.6	.6	1.7	1.7	% Depr., Dep., Amort./Sales	.7	.6
(68) 1.6	(147) 1.6	(238) 1.6	(79) 1.6	(28) 2.6	(14) 3.1		(641) 1.8	(495) 1.6
3.7	6.9	4.0	4.7	7.1	6.2		3.6	3.6
4.2	2.3	1.9	1.5			% Officers', Directors' Owners' Comp/Sales	2.6	2.3
(59) 9.9	(79) 5.8	(75) 4.0	(18) 3.3				(269) 5.6	(223) 5.8
18.2	10.8	5.9	14.0				11.4	10.9
182438M	996000M	4276365M	4440795M	4447423M	8809575M	Net Sales ($)	28721801M	22026656M
29816M	269981M	1427112M	2232156M	2916559M	6053376M	Total Assets ($)	12460481M	10071860M

Comparative Historical Data / Current Data Sorted by Sales

				Type of Statement	131 (4/1-9/30/09)			712 (10/1/09-3/31/10)		
					0-1MM	1-3MM	3-5MM	5-10MM	10-25MM	25MM & OVER
	101	116	115	Unqualified	4	5	4	12	28	62
	99	88	102	Reviewed	1	8	13	31	36	13
	78	100	93	Compiled	9	21	17	19	21	6
	116	124	174	Tax Returns	52	47	27	24	18	6
	247	273	359	Other	57	63	34	51	18	81
	4/1/07-3/31/08 ALL	4/1/08-3/31/09 ALL	4/1/09-3/31/10 ALL							
NUMBER OF STATEMENTS	641	701	843		123	144	95	137	176	168
	%	%	%	**ASSETS**	%	%	%	%	%	%
Cash & Equivalents	16.6	15.7	18.2		14.7	18.7	17.9	19.6	17.5	20.1
Trade Receivables (net)	29.7	29.0	28.2		12.0	23.9	34.7	32.7	34.7	29.5
Inventory	6.7	7.1	7.2		3.6	7.0	9.2	7.0	9.2	6.9
All Other Current	6.1	6.4	6.1		4.0	7.7	4.5	3.7	8.2	6.9
Total Current	59.2	58.2	59.7		34.3	57.3	66.3	63.0	69.6	63.3
Fixed Assets (net)	24.9	25.2	24.1		47.2	27.9	21.0	21.5	17.1	15.0
Intangibles (net)	7.1	7.5	7.7		9.2	5.2	3.1	6.1	6.6	13.6
All Other Non-Current	8.8	9.1	8.6		9.2	9.6	9.6	9.4	6.7	8.0
Total	100.0	100.0	100.0		100.0	100.0	100.0	100.0	100.0	100.0
				LIABILITIES						
Notes Payable-Short Term	11.1	12.5	12.1		15.5	20.2	16.5	10.3	8.4	5.7
Cur. Mat.-L.T.D.	4.1	4.0	4.0		3.7	3.2	7.2	4.9	3.0	3.2
Trade Payables	11.2	12.5	11.9		4.9	12.5	12.0	13.8	13.4	13.1
Income Taxes Payable	.3	.4	.5		.2	.3	.6	.4	.6	.8
All Other Current	19.0	16.3	19.5		20.8	20.8	14.8	18.9	19.4	20.5
Total Current	45.8	45.6	47.9		45.1	57.0	51.1	48.4	44.8	43.4
Long-Term Debt	17.3	17.3	17.7		39.1	23.7	12.2	13.7	8.8	12.7
Deferred Taxes	.3	.3	.3		.1	.2	.3	.3	.4	.6
All Other Non-Current	6.4	6.7	8.3		5.9	10.3	8.1	7.9	8.0	9.2
Net Worth	30.2	30.1	25.7		9.8	8.8	28.4	29.7	38.1	34.0
Total Liabilties & Net Worth	100.0	100.0	100.0		100.0	100.0	100.0	100.0	100.0	100.0
				INCOME DATA						
Net Sales	100.0	100.0	100.0		100.0	100.0	100.0	100.0	100.0	100.0
Gross Profit										
Operating Expenses	89.9	91.9	91.6		78.1	91.0	95.2	96.1	93.6	94.5
Operating Profit	10.1	8.1	8.4		21.9	9.0	4.8	3.9	6.4	5.5
All Other Expenses (net)	2.5	2.9	2.9		10.9	2.9	.6	.9	1.1	2.0
Profit Before Taxes	7.7	5.1	5.4		11.0	6.1	4.2	3.0	5.3	3.5
				RATIOS						
	2.6	2.4	2.8		2.7	4.0	2.7	2.3	2.9	2.7
Current	1.4	1.3	1.4		.9	1.3	1.5	1.4	1.7	1.4
	.9	.9	.9		.2	.6	1.0	.9	1.1	1.0
	2.2	1.9	2.1		1.9	3.3	2.1	2.0	2.1	2.0
Quick	(640) 1.1	1.1	(842) 1.1		.7 (143)	1.0	1.2	1.2	1.2	1.1
	.6	.5	.5		.2	.3	.7	.7	.7	.7
	7 49.1	9 39.7	8 46.1		0 UND	0 UND	15 23.8	20 18.3	25 14.9	19 19.2
Sales/Receivables	38 9.5	37 9.9	36 10.2		0 UND	29 12.4	35 10.5	41 9.0	40 9.1	43 8.4
	63 5.8	61 6.0	60 6.1		44 8.4	62 5.8	57 6.4	61 6.0	59 6.1	65 5.6
				Cost of Sales/Inventory						
				Cost of Sales/Payables						
	6.6	6.7	5.7		4.8	5.2	4.7	7.9	5.5	5.7
Sales/Working Capital	19.8	23.7	15.8		-48.7	18.3	14.7	15.5	10.9	16.9
	-59.6	-48.1	-54.6		-3.5	-11.5	-185.4	-92.0	48.6	169.9
	20.7	16.8	16.4		5.1	12.6	17.6	13.7	32.8	30.6
EBIT/Interest	(498) 5.4	(562) 4.6	(637) 3.9		(60) 1.5	(106) 3.1	(80) 4.0	(110) 3.1	(141) 6.1	(140) 5.9
	1.3	1.0	.5		-1.4	-.1	-.2	-.2	1.9	.8
	10.6	11.9	8.3					9.3	8.7	10.3
Net Profit + Depr., Dep., Amort./Cur. Mat. L/T/D	(92) 3.5	(89) 3.3	(79) 2.8				(12) 2.5	(22) 1.2	(31) 3.5	
	1.1	.8	.9				1.1	.6	1.6	
	.1	.2	.1		.4	.2	.1	.2	.1	.2
Fixed/Worth	.7	.8	.7		2.5	1.5	.5	.8	.3	.5
	3.3	6.0	11.4		-65.6	-2.4	2.9	18.5	1.4	9.8
	.8	.9	.8		1.1	.6	.6	.8	.7	.8
Debt/Worth	2.4	2.5	2.5		4.5	4.2	2.0	2.2	1.9	2.6
	14.3	32.7	378.0		-8.0	-5.6	20.4	-91.1	7.3	150.2
	87.0	70.3	64.1		43.7	76.3	70.1	77.8	64.6	55.0
% Profit Before Taxes/Tangible Net Worth	(515) 38.9	(539) 27.9	(640) 22.9		(85) 15.5	(99) 27.7	(77) 21.8	(101) 28.2	(151) 27.6	(127) 22.1
	8.7	3.6	2.7		-.9	3.0	-2.2	1.8	7.1	5.4
	25.8	19.6	20.6		12.3	26.2	27.1	23.9	21.2	18.7
% Profit Before Taxes/Total Assets	9.5	7.0	6.1		2.5	8.3	5.5	5.4	9.9	6.4
	1.0	-.1	-.5		-1.2	-.9	-2.0	-1.2	1.7	-.3
	72.6	66.1	75.0		43.5	73.1	109.4	90.0	70.1	58.6
Sales/Net Fixed Assets	20.0	18.5	23.8		3.2	23.8	27.9	28.5	32.9	23.7
	6.4	6.0	6.4		.2	4.4	9.9	8.0	9.5	8.9
	4.3	4.2	4.1		2.3	4.5	4.7	4.7	4.4	3.9
Sales/Total Assets	2.5	2.5	2.5		.6	2.4	3.2	2.7	2.7	2.4
	1.4	1.4	1.2		.2	1.1	1.8	1.9	1.7	1.2
	.6	.7	.6		3.1	.8	.5	.6	.5	.5
% Depr., Dep., Amort./Sales	(476) 1.6	(500) 1.7	(574) 1.7		(69) 11.5	(87) 2.9	(74) 1.6	(96) 1.4	(137) 1.1	(111) 1.7
	3.8	4.5	4.6		19.2	7.8	3.3	3.4	2.5	3.6
	2.4	2.2	2.4		5.3	4.2	4.2	1.8	1.3	.8
% Officers', Directors' Owners' Comp/Sales	(212) 5.5	(228) 5.0	(236) 4.9		(26) 12.0	(54) 8.4	(38) 7.4	(48) 3.0	(51) 3.9	(19) 2.0
	10.9	10.4	11.1		18.8	15.4	11.2	4.9	7.4	3.6
Net Sales ($)	18954331M	22642162M	23152596M		47955M	276219M	371666M	974863M	2769000M	18712893M
Total Assets ($)	9302770M	11600157M	12929000M		120474M	375950M	235789M	423670M	1719355M	10053762M

Current Data Sorted by Assets   Comparative Historical Data

0-500M	500M-2MM	2-10MM	10-50MM	50-100MM	100-250MM	Type of Statement	4/1/05-3/31/06 ALL	4/1/06-3/31/07 ALL
	1	5	6	2		Unqualified	15	16
	1	7	2			Reviewed	11	11
5	10	7	1			Compiled	14	16
8	8	4	2		1	Tax Returns	22	22
8	8	20	16	5	2	Other	30	30
	28 (4/1-9/30/09)		101 (10/1/09-3/31/10)					
0-500M	**500M-2MM**	**2-10MM**	**10-50MM**	**50-100MM**	**100-250MM**	**NUMBER OF STATEMENTS**	**92**	**95**
21	28	43	27	7	3			
%	%	%	%	%	%	**ASSETS**	%	%
45.8	42.8	28.3	40.5			Cash & Equivalents	35.2	29.3
13.1	15.2	14.6	21.9			Trade Receivables (net)	16.4	18.7
.9	.7	.2	.1			Inventory	.6	1.6
1.7	5.4	12.7	7.8			All Other Current	7.5	8.7
61.4	64.2	55.8	70.3			Total Current	59.7	58.2
21.4	13.1	15.5	6.6			Fixed Assets (net)	15.7	18.5
7.0	6.8	12.5	9.9			Intangibles (net)	10.0	10.1
10.1	15.9	16.2	13.3			All Other Non-Current	14.5	13.2
100.0	100.0	100.0	100.0			Total	100.0	100.0
						LIABILITIES		
17.4	11.6	5.7	4.8			Notes Payable-Short Term	10.1	15.6
4.2	2.5	1.0	.7			Cur. Mat.-L.T.D.	2.8	1.2
22.9	19.5	18.3	10.4			Trade Payables	18.1	20.4
.3	.1	.2	.1			Income Taxes Payable	.5	.2
37.1	38.1	33.8	43.8			All Other Current	40.9	29.9
82.0	71.7	59.1	59.8			Total Current	72.4	67.4
50.5	7.1	10.6	.7			Long-Term Debt	9.9	9.9
.0	.0	.1	.1			Deferred Taxes	.1	.1
15.5	5.7	6.6	8.9			All Other Non-Current	11.7	7.8
-48.0	15.4	23.6	30.5			Net Worth	5.8	14.8
100.0	100.0	100.0	100.0			Total Liabilities & Net Worth	100.0	100.0
						INCOME DATA		
100.0	100.0	100.0	100.0			Net Sales	100.0	100.0
						Gross Profit		
96.0	97.8	96.8	97.4			Operating Expenses	95.2	96.2
4.0	2.2	3.2	2.6			Operating Profit	4.8	3.8
1.2	.4	.7	.5			All Other Expenses (net)	.3	1.1
2.8	1.9	2.5	2.1			Profit Before Taxes	4.5	2.7
						RATIOS		
3.6	1.6	1.5	1.7				1.9	1.7
.9	1.0	.9	1.0			Current	1.0	1.0
.5	.5	.5	.7				.6	.6
3.5	1.5	1.1	1.6				1.6	1.6
.9	1.0	.6	.9			Quick	.9	.8
.4	.4	.3	.6				.4	.4
0 UND	0 999.8	1 599.9	1 257.0				0 816.9	1 402.9
1 270.3	3 110.2	17 21.7	12 29.6			Sales/Receivables	7 53.5	7 53.1
8 43.5	9 40.8	34 10.7	49 7.4				24 15.2	42 8.8
						Cost of Sales/Inventory		
						Cost of Sales/Payables		
18.5	32.6	8.1	5.8				14.7	23.2
-337.1	410.0	-98.8	779.3			Sales/Working Capital	NM	-721.0
-24.3	-14.3	-8.6	-12.0				-14.5	-15.6
16.7	17.7	20.2	166.2				28.5	22.1
(12) 1.1	(13) 3.7	(25) 3.2	(19) 12.7			EBIT/Interest	(57) 7.3	(59) 4.8
-1.2	1.5	-10.8	.2				1.5	1.0
							29.4	
						Net Profit + Depr., Dep., Amort./Cur. Mat. L/T/D	(11) 5.8	
							2.5	
.0	.1	.1	.1				.2	.2
2.2	.6	.9	.3			Fixed/Worth	.6	.8
-.4	NM	-1.6	3.3				-1.0	-26.9
.4	1.3	1.0	1.1				1.2	1.4
6.5	5.2	13.5	5.5			Debt/Worth	4.8	5.6
-2.2	-15.8	-20.5	41.4				-8.1	-49.8
133.3	106.7	50.6	38.6				59.8	72.4
(11) 17.6	(20) 42.2	(29) 18.1	(21) 12.9			% Profit Before Taxes/Tangible Net Worth	(61) 29.0	(70) 35.1
3.7	6.4	8.8	1.1				14.8	15.3
26.6	27.3	9.7	6.6				17.7	14.8
9.0	9.2	4.0	3.2			% Profit Before Taxes/Total Assets	6.9	5.4
-.9	1.0	-3.0	.3				1.2	.4
845.8	931.0	84.8	121.1				190.6	147.6
89.7	238.1	31.2	40.1			Sales/Net Fixed Assets	60.6	59.5
18.9	25.7	14.4	14.4				16.5	13.0
21.4	21.0	4.5	2.9				8.4	8.2
8.9	5.6	1.9	1.8			Sales/Total Assets	4.2	3.3
4.8	2.3	1.1	.9				1.4	1.6
.2	.1	.4	.3				.2	.3
(11) .4	(17) .3	(34) 1.2	(23) .8			% Depr., Dep., Amort./Sales	(60) .7	(68) .8
.8	1.4	2.9	2.2				2.0	1.7
1.8	1.0	2.7					.7	1.3
(13) 2.7	(12) 3.4	(11) 6.5				% Officers', Directors' Owners' Comp/Sales	(34) 2.3	(30) 4.4
12.5	5.7	18.7					8.6	10.1
65925M	505849M	711877M	1224862M	711949M	11257349M	Net Sales ($)	3279153M	3181812M
4766M	32811M	237664M	549781M	484592M	627232M	Total Assets ($)	1136526M	1338204M

M = $ thousand   MM = $ million
See Pages 9 through 22 for Explanation of Ratios and Data

Comparative Historical Data | | | Current Data Sorted by Sales

12	8	14	Type of Statement						
12	8	14	Unqualified		2		2	3	7
16	15	10	Reviewed				3	4	3
12	14	23	Compiled	3	9	1	4	3	3
21	21	23	Tax Returns	4	4	3	2	2	8
32	38	59	Other	4	3	6	16	10	20
4/1/07-3/31/08 ALL	4/1/08-3/31/09 ALL	4/1/09-3/31/10 ALL		28 (4/1-9/30/09)			101 (10/1/09-3/31/10)		
				0-1MM	1-3MM	3-5MM	5-10MM	10-25MM	25MM & OVER
93	96	129	**NUMBER OF STATEMENTS**	11	18	10	27	22	41
%	%	%	**ASSETS**	%	%	%	%	%	%
33.0	35.1	37.1	Cash & Equivalents	49.0	46.5	52.6	32.3	33.0	31.5
14.8	16.2	15.5	Trade Receivables (net)	10.5	9.5	11.5	14.6	21.2	17.9
.8	.1	.4	Inventory	.5	1.3	.1	.3	.4	.1
7.7	9.7	8.8	All Other Current	1.4	2.3	13.6	7.5	9.8	12.9
56.4	61.0	61.8	Total Current	61.5	59.6	77.8	54.6	64.3	62.4
20.2	15.7	14.1	Fixed Assets (net)	27.3	21.2	3.6	13.3	8.5	13.5
10.4	6.8	10.3	Intangibles (net)	5.0	3.5	5.5	11.9	13.9	12.8
13.0	16.5	13.8	All Other Non-Current	6.2	15.6	13.1	20.1	13.3	11.2
100.0	100.0	100.0	Total	100.0	100.0	100.0	100.0	100.0	100.0
			LIABILITIES						
10.4	12.0	8.8	Notes Payable-Short Term	22.9	12.0	1.0	10.6	2.9	7.5
2.2	1.6	1.9	Cur. Mat.-L.T.D.	.5	7.1	.2	.4	.9	1.9
19.7	14.6	17.3	Trade Payables	10.9	15.6	24.8	20.3	17.8	15.7
.8	.2	.2	Income Taxes Payable	.0	.6	.0	.1	.1	.1
37.2	26.4	37.1	All Other Current	63.6	22.7	17.9	39.8	40.1	37.6
70.3	54.7	65.3	Total Current	97.9	58.0	43.9	71.1	61.8	62.9
11.5	8.0	14.8	Long-Term Debt	31.0	30.5	30.0	14.1	1.9	7.2
.1	.1	.1	Deferred Taxes	.0	.0	.0	.1	.2	.2
9.1	8.7	8.4	All Other Non-Current	2.7	20.5	25.0	5.4	1.8	6.0
9.0	28.5	11.4	Net Worth	-31.6	-9.0	1.1	9.3	34.2	23.7
100.0	100.0	100.0	Total Liabilities & Net Worth	100.0	100.0	100.0	100.0	100.0	100.0
			INCOME DATA						
100.0	100.0	100.0	Net Sales	100.0	100.0	100.0	100.0	100.0	100.0
			Gross Profit						
95.0	95.4	96.3	Operating Expenses	91.2	95.2	100.5	97.9	96.8	95.9
5.0	4.6	3.7	Operating Profit	8.8	4.8	-.5	2.1	3.2	4.1
1.1	.1	.9	All Other Expenses (net)	1.9	.7	-.5	.2	1.5	1.2
3.9	4.5	2.8	Profit Before Taxes	6.9	4.1	.0	1.8	1.7	2.9
			RATIOS						
1.6	3.2	1.6	Current	3.3	2.9	13.1	1.2	1.5	1.5
.8	1.3	1.0		1.3	.9	3.0	.9	1.0	1.0
.5	.8	.6		.3	.5	.7	.5	.6	.6
1.3	2.3	1.5	Quick	3.3	2.6	11.3	1.1	1.4	1.3
.7	1.1	.8		1.3	.9	1.6	.6	.8	.8
.3	.5	.4		.3	.4	.5	.4	.4	.4
0 UND	0 742.1	0 999.8	Sales/Receivables	0 UND	0 UND	0 UND	1 702.6	4 97.6	0 963.5
5 79.8	7 54.4	6 64.8		2 238.0	3 140.8	0 UND	15 24.4	15 24.4	4 86.8
29 12.4	26 14.0	25 14.7		17 20.9	18 20.3	7 55.5	53 6.8	33 10.9	19 19.5
			Cost of Sales/Inventory						
			Cost of Sales/Payables						
20.9	9.5	10.4	Sales/Working Capital	7.1	6.2	1.2	12.8	8.1	22.4
-118.5	49.4	-947.2		61.0	-73.1	21.5	-43.3	-743.4	-602.5
-9.1	-34.0	-12.0		-4.4	-7.9	-256.3	-4.6	-6.7	-18.1
20.4	36.0	21.6	EBIT/Interest		14.0		23.6	54.2	75.0
(60) 6.1	(53) 6.5	(75) 3.7		(10) 3.3		(14) 4.6	(14) 7.1	(28) 3.0	
.8	1.8	-.4			1.1		-2.5	-.8	.3
22.0			Net Profit + Depr., Dep., Amort./Cur. Mat. L/T/D						
(12) 3.8									
1.1									
.2	.1	.1	Fixed/Worth	.0	.1	.0	.1	.1	.1
1.1	.4	.7		2.4	1.1	.1	.7	.7	.9
-.6	2.4	-1.6		-.6	-.5	NM	-.8	-34.6	-1.6
1.1	.6	1.1	Debt/Worth	.4	.9	.3	1.1	.9	1.3
7.5	1.9	6.5		14.0	3.0	6.6	13.5	4.8	6.4
-5.1	15.3	-7.0		-2.6	-10.6	NM	-2.4	-756.1	-7.2
60.4	51.5	58.6	% Profit Before Taxes/Tangible Net Worth		152.5		90.3	57.5	52.4
(60) 25.4	(77) 16.4	(87) 17.6		(12) 20.5		(19) 20.4	(16) 14.5	(26) 17.9	
12.4	4.7	3.7			-2.5		8.0	7.4	-5.2
14.8	18.2	12.4	% Profit Before Taxes/Total Assets	9.0	27.8	12.8	16.1	10.3	10.4
5.0	5.7	4.6		2.6	11.7	6.6	6.6	3.6	4.7
-1.2	.6	-.6		-20.0	-.1	-2.7	-.7	1.3	-1.3
153.6	301.5	240.2	Sales/Net Fixed Assets	UND	241.0	UND	108.2	142.3	269.4
41.9	58.3	48.6		89.7	22.2	999.8	31.8	28.4	57.0
10.4	18.2	14.9		8.5	6.9	26.9	12.8	14.4	18.3
10.3	13.4	6.7	Sales/Total Assets	7.9	6.9	15.0	5.4	4.6	10.3
3.0	3.3	2.6		4.8	2.4	3.9	2.4	2.0	3.2
1.5	1.7	1.4		1.1	1.4	.5	1.1	1.1	1.8
.2	.3	.3	% Depr., Dep., Amort./Sales		.2		.3	.3	.2
(70) .6	(58) .8	(90) .7		(12) .8		(20) 1.8	(17) 1.3	(31) .4	
2.1	2.5	2.4		2.2		3.3	2.5		
.9	1.3	1.6	% Officers', Directors' Owners' Comp/Sales						.6
(26) 3.0	(35) 3.0	(43) 3.3						(10) 1.3	
7.0	13.1	6.7							5.4
3431306M	1945610M	14477811M	Net Sales ($)	6540M	36880M	40181M	204635M	395503M	13794072M
1403468M	664155M	1936846M	Total Assets ($)	10329M	16876M	39688M	129899M	217025M	1523029M

M = $ thousand   MM = $ million
See Pages 9 through 22 for Explanation of Ratios and Data

ADMIN & WASTE MANAGEMENT SERVICES—Tour Operators NAICS 561520

Current Data Sorted by Assets | Comparative Historical Data

Type of Statement	0-500M	500M-2MM	2-10MM	10-50MM	50-100MM	100-250MM		4/1/05-3/31/06 ALL	4/1/06-3/31/07 ALL
Unqualified		1	1	4	2	5		5	8
Reviewed		2	5	1				5	2
Compiled	4	3	2					6	6
Tax Returns	4	10	3					5	11
Other	1	4	5	2	5	2		14	15
		13 (4/1-9/30/09)		53 (10/1/09-3/31/10)					
NUMBER OF STATEMENTS	9	20	16	7	7	7		35	42
	%	%	%	%	%	%		%	%
ASSETS									
Cash & Equivalents		25.3	22.1					28.0	24.2
Trade Receivables (net)		6.8	9.6					12.3	10.1
Inventory		.7	.5					.9	1.5
All Other Current		6.4	6.5					9.8	9.3
Total Current		39.2	38.8					51.1	45.2
Fixed Assets (net)		47.2	45.2					29.4	39.5
Intangibles (net)		.2	4.5					2.0	3.9
All Other Non-Current		13.4	11.5					17.5	11.5
Total		100.0	100.0					100.0	100.0
LIABILITIES									
Notes Payable-Short Term		7.6	3.2					5.9	5.4
Cur. Mat.-L.T.D.		10.5	8.4					7.2	4.7
Trade Payables		4.0	5.7					16.9	11.1
Income Taxes Payable		.0	.5					.1	.9
All Other Current		29.6	24.2					28.3	28.1
Total Current		51.8	42.0					58.4	50.2
Long-Term Debt		41.1	24.9					21.3	30.1
Deferred Taxes		.0	.4					.2	.0
All Other Non-Current		12.6	8.7					3.2	9.8
Net Worth		-5.5	24.0					16.9	9.9
Total Liabilities & Net Worth		100.0	100.0					100.0	100.0
INCOME DATA									
Net Sales		100.0	100.0					100.0	100.0
Gross Profit									
Operating Expenses		97.3	94.1					95.6	94.0
Operating Profit		2.7	5.9					4.4	6.0
All Other Expenses (net)		1.3	2.0					1.4	.8
Profit Before Taxes		1.4	3.9					3.0	5.2
RATIOS									
Current		1.2	1.9					1.7	1.6
		.7	.8					.9	.8
		.2	.3					.5	.4
Quick		.9	1.5					1.6	1.4
		.5	.6					.8	.6
		.1	.2					.3	.3
Sales/Receivables	0 UND	0 936.8						0 UND	0 UND
	0 UND	3 106.2						7 51.5	6 60.7
	5 72.6	24 15.1						25 14.6	21 17.1
Cost of Sales/Inventory									
Cost of Sales/Payables									
Sales/Working Capital		39.1	11.9					22.6	14.7
		-43.0	-16.9					-83.6	-32.3
		-4.9	-6.2					-17.1	-8.0
EBIT/Interest		7.0	10.8					16.5	8.1
		(12) 1.8	(10) 1.7					(24) 3.5	(32) 2.5
		.4	1.2					-.4	.2
Net Profit + Depr., Dep., Amort./Cur. Mat. L/T/D									
Fixed/Worth		1.0	.7					.2	.8
		NM	2.1					1.4	2.9
		-1.4	-7.5					-9.1	-3.8
Debt/Worth		3.0	.9					1.0	2.0
		NM	4.2					3.5	3.7
		-4.8	-53.2					-18.9	-30.1
% Profit Before Taxes/Tangible Net Worth		179.2	41.1					85.7	110.1
		(10) 86.0	(11) 17.2					(25) 31.4	(28) 30.0
		26.5	9.9					7.9	-.9
% Profit Before Taxes/Total Assets		19.1	14.3					22.7	21.3
		4.3	5.6					5.0	3.6
		-5.0	1.5					-1.4	-2.6
Sales/Net Fixed Assets		51.5	67.0					112.8	88.4
		9.2	2.9					15.7	10.0
		1.8	1.4					4.1	2.7
Sales/Total Assets		4.4	2.8					7.5	4.0
		2.2	1.6					3.2	2.6
		1.4	1.0					1.9	1.6
% Depr., Dep., Amort./Sales		.5	1.9					.3	.4
		(15) 6.8	(15) 4.9					(28) 1.5	(32) 3.5
		16.7	8.1					5.4	6.2
% Officers', Directors' Owners' Comp/Sales								3.2	
								(10) 4.7	
								7.4	
Net Sales ($)	17187M	127111M	160724M	511046M	723118M	2445442M		1840307M	2439170M
Total Assets ($)	2594M	23780M	85089M	136275M	482248M	1300507M		733234M	982052M

M = $ thousand   MM = $ million
See Pages 9 through 22 for Explanation of Ratios and Data

Comparative Historical Data | Current Data Sorted by Sales

Type of Statement

4/1/07-3/31/08 ALL	4/1/08-3/31/09 ALL	4/1/09-3/31/10 ALL	Type of Statement	0-1MM	1-3MM	3-5MM	5-10MM	10-25MM	25MM & OVER
12	11	13	Unqualified		1			2	10
3	6	7	Reviewed		1		1	2	1
9	7	10	Compiled	2	4	1	3		1
11	12	17	Tax Returns	1	5	5	1	4	1
29	21	19	Other		5	2	2		9
					13 (4/1-9/30/09)		53 (10/1/09-3/31/10)		
64	57	66	NUMBER OF STATEMENTS	3	16	8	8	9	22

ASSETS

%	%	%		%	%	%	%	%	%
30.3	30.2	28.0	Cash & Equivalents		23.4				39.8
7.3	9.2	7.6	Trade Receivables (net)		3.0				7.2
2.0	1.5	.5	Inventory		.2				.4
8.2	10.8	6.3	All Other Current		1.8				8.1
47.8	51.7	42.4	Total Current		28.4				55.5
34.6	30.1	36.1	Fixed Assets (net)		42.9				17.1
3.4	7.2	3.5	Intangibles (net)		.3				7.1
14.1	11.0	18.0	All Other Non-Current		28.4				20.3
100.0	100.0	100.0	Total		100.0				100.0

LIABILITIES

7.2	5.3	5.2	Notes Payable-Short Term		8.3				1.3
4.6	3.7	6.6	Cur. Mat.-L.T.D.		12.3				.5
14.5	13.2	8.0	Trade Payables		3.0				14.2
.1	.1	.2	Income Taxes Payable		.1				.3
31.6	29.8	30.8	All Other Current		32.4				37.8
57.9	52.1	50.8	Total Current		56.1				54.2
23.4	15.1	24.0	Long-Term Debt		28.2				6.2
.4	.4	.2	Deferred Taxes		.0				.0
11.5	7.5	9.2	All Other Non-Current		16.8				7.7
6.7	24.9	15.9	Net Worth		-1.1				31.9
100.0	100.0	100.0	Total Liabilities & Net Worth		100.0				100.0

INCOME DATA

100.0	100.0	100.0	Net Sales		100.0				100.0
			Gross Profit						
95.7	97.1	96.2	Operating Expenses		95.5				95.7
4.3	2.9	3.8	Operating Profit		4.5				4.3
.3	.7	1.3	All Other Expenses (net)		1.8				.9
4.0	2.3	2.6	Profit Before Taxes		2.8				3.4

RATIOS

4/1/07-3/31/08	4/1/08-3/31/09	4/1/09-3/31/10		0-1MM	1-3MM	3-5MM	5-10MM	10-25MM	25MM & OVER
1.3	1.6	1.4	Current		1.1				1.9
.8	1.0	.8			.4				1.1
.5	.5	.4			.1				.5
1.1	1.4	1.1	Quick		.9				1.4
.6	.9	.6			.4				.8
.3	.4	.3			.1				.4
0 UND	0 UND	0 UND	Sales/Receivables		0 UND				0 999.8
3 116.8	6 65.5	2 156.2			0 UND				5 69.1
12 30.2	17 21.8	10 37.0			6 61.8				10 37.0
			Cost of Sales/Inventory						
			Cost of Sales/Payables						
27.5	12.6	29.5	Sales/Working Capital		NM				8.0
-50.9	170.9	-40.5			-19.5				176.3
-9.0	-12.4	-6.6			-4.9				-7.7
8.5	11.5	9.7	EBIT/Interest						102.8
(43) 2.1	(36) 2.8	(34) 1.7							(10) 7.1
.9	.5	.4							-6.1
			Net Profit + Depr., Dep., Amort./Cur. Mat. L/T/D						
.3	.2	.3	Fixed/Worth		.5				.1
2.7	1.3	2.1			NM				.4
-6.0	-4.5	-6.4			-1.8				NM
2.7	1.5	1.2	Debt/Worth		1.8				.9
8.2	4.6	5.1			NM				2.1
-7.2	-10.5	-11.5			-6.4				NM
92.7	51.1	86.4	% Profit Before Taxes/Tangible Net Worth						67.7
(43) 46.0	(42) 19.7	(44) 24.4							(17) 15.0
6.1	.9	9.2							-2.9
16.8	12.4	13.4	% Profit Before Taxes/Total Assets		19.7				9.7
4.8	4.0	5.3			4.1				6.1
.1	-.2	.1			-5.0				-1.3
91.3	83.2	57.0	Sales/Net Fixed Assets		57.2				87.4
13.7	15.5	17.0			11.8				33.2
2.7	3.4	2.6			2.3				10.1
4.9	5.1	4.2	Sales/Total Assets		5.1				3.5
2.6	2.8	2.0			2.1				2.0
1.2	1.5	1.4			1.4				1.4
.4	.4	.6	% Depr., Dep., Amort./Sales		.5				.7
(47) 1.4	(42) 2.1	(53) 2.4			(13) 6.2				(14) 1.3
7.3	5.6	8.2			13.3				2.9
1.1	1.1	.7	% Officers', Directors' Owners' Comp/Sales						
(13) 1.8	(15) 1.8	(19) 1.7							
7.8	4.8	4.0							
3791407M	4837804M	3984628M	Net Sales ($)	1146M	28299M	31229M	55507M	140183M	3728264M
1550061M	1719057M	2030493M	Total Assets ($)	1356M	12420M	23110M	31175M	46210M	1916222M

M = $ thousand   MM = $ million
See Pages 9 through 22 for Explanation of Ratios and Data

Current Data Sorted by Assets   Comparative Historical Data

Type of Statement								4/1/05-3/31/06 ALL		4/1/06-3/31/07 ALL
Unqualified	1		2	6	2	2		11		17
Reviewed	1		2	1						1
Compiled			2					5		5
Tax Returns	2	1	2					4		4
Other	1	2	6	5	3	4		15		13

	0-500M	500M-2MM	2-10MM 5 (4/1-9/30/09)	10-50MM 40 (10/1/09-3/31/10)	50-100MM	100-250MM				
NUMBER OF STATEMENTS	5	3	14	12	5	6		35		40
ASSETS	%	%	%	%	%	%		%		%
Cash & Equivalents			23.8	28.4				24.5		36.0
Trade Receivables (net)			17.4	18.2				9.2		11.9
Inventory			3.2	.5				1.8		3.2
All Other Current			8.8	22.3				4.6		9.4
Total Current			53.3	69.4				40.1		60.5
Fixed Assets (net)			30.6	9.4				41.6		21.4
Intangibles (net)			4.5	13.6				1.8		3.4
All Other Non-Current			11.6	7.6				16.5		14.7
Total			100.0	100.0				100.0		100.0
LIABILITIES										
Notes Payable-Short Term			6.7	3.9				7.6		5.6
Cur. Mat.-L.T.D.			1.7	.2				2.5		2.6
Trade Payables			11.6	14.6				7.9		11.3
Income Taxes Payable			.7	4.1				1.1		.6
All Other Current			12.9	26.1				14.9		17.7
Total Current			33.7	48.9				34.0		37.7
Long-Term Debt			17.7	2.9				21.4		8.6
Deferred Taxes			.0	.3				.3		.6
All Other Non-Current			5.2	11.6				7.1		7.6
Net Worth			43.5	36.4				37.2		45.4
Total Liabilities & Net Worth			100.0	100.0				100.0		100.0
INCOME DATA										
Net Sales			100.0	100.0				100.0		100.0
Gross Profit										
Operating Expenses			94.4	89.5				86.7		89.9
Operating Profit			5.6	10.5				13.3		10.1
All Other Expenses (net)			3.5	7.3				3.2		1.1
Profit Before Taxes			2.1	3.2				10.1		9.0
RATIOS										
Current			2.7	2.6				2.8		4.1
			1.4	1.4				1.4		1.7
			.8	.8				1.0		1.1
Quick			2.2	2.4				2.5		2.5
			1.1	.9				1.3		1.5
			.5	.4				.7		.8
Sales/Receivables		4	88.9	5 79.5			0	UND	0	UND
		23	16.1	25 14.8			1	249.6	5	80.6
		45	8.2	48 7.5			20	18.5	17	21.6
Cost of Sales/Inventory										
Cost of Sales/Payables										
Sales/Working Capital			4.8	1.7				3.3		2.3
			16.9	17.2				16.9		10.8
			-40.0	-27.1				-403.6		125.6
EBIT/Interest								29.3		51.2
							(25)	6.6	(27)	19.7
								1.9		4.0
Net Profit + Depr., Dep., Amort./Cur. Mat. L/T/D										
Fixed/Worth			.1	.1				.3		.0
			.3	.4				1.0		.3
			1.9	-.2				2.5		1.0
Debt/Worth			.8	.8				.4		.4
			1.0	2.1				1.4		1.1
			2.2	-5.8				4.1		3.3
% Profit Before Taxes/Tangible Net Worth			38.1					51.2		45.5
		(13)	4.5				(31)	16.1	(35)	15.0
			-2.9					5.2		7.0
% Profit Before Taxes/Total Assets			18.0	10.0				28.0		29.4
			5.0	7.1				9.7		8.1
			-1.0	-2.2				2.3		2.7
Sales/Net Fixed Assets			70.7	192.3				29.1		244.1
			25.4	45.3				5.5		16.5
			1.1	7.1				1.1		4.2
Sales/Total Assets			5.2	3.0				3.1		4.5
			2.2	1.2				1.5		1.5
			.9	.8				.7		.8
% Depr., Dep., Amort./Sales			.5					1.7		.7
		(11)	2.1				(24)	2.5	(22)	2.5
			5.4					6.8		6.8
% Officers', Directors' Owners' Comp/Sales										
Net Sales ($)	4925M	6298M	202756M	748682M	317249M	736898M		659306M		1147014M
Total Assets ($)	805M	2888M	62868M	363147M	386035M	950193M		381974M		979907M

M = $ thousand   MM = $ million
See Pages 9 through 22 for Explanation of Ratios and Data

Comparative Historical Data | Current Data Sorted by Sales

Type of Statement

07-08	08-09	09-10	Type of Statement	0-1MM	1-3MM	3-5MM	5-10MM	10-25MM	25MM & OVER
13	17	13	Unqualified	2	1	1		5	6
2	6	4	Reviewed		1				1
3	6	2	Compiled			1	1		
3	6	5	Tax Returns	2	3				
19	17	21	Other	2		1	2	3	13
4/1/07-3/31/08 ALL	4/1/08-3/31/09 ALL	4/1/09-3/31/10 ALL		5 (4/1-9/30/09)			40 (10/1/09-3/31/10)		
40	52	45	**NUMBER OF STATEMENTS**	6	5	3	3	8	20

07-08 %	08-09 %	09-10 %		0-1MM %	1-3MM %	3-5MM %	5-10MM %	10-25MM %	25MM & OVER %
			ASSETS						
32.8	28.3	27.7	Cash & Equivalents						29.7
11.8	14.2	16.9	Trade Receivables (net)						17.4
1.1	2.4	1.5	Inventory						2.9
13.5	7.9	11.6	All Other Current						11.7
59.2	52.8	57.7	Total Current						61.6
22.8	24.8	22.4	Fixed Assets (net)						13.4
6.9	8.0	8.5	Intangibles (net)						13.4
11.1	14.4	11.2	All Other Non-Current						11.6
100.0	100.0	100.0	Total						100.0
			LIABILITIES						
3.8	4.7	5.7	Notes Payable-Short Term						2.2
5.4	1.9	.8	Cur. Mat.-L.T.D.						.6
13.5	10.4	14.7	Trade Payables						16.9
.8	2.2	1.6	Income Taxes Payable						.9
21.3	19.9	19.6	All Other Current						25.8
44.8	39.1	42.3	Total Current						46.3
8.5	13.2	9.4	Long-Term Debt						2.5
.1	.3	.3	Deferred Taxes						.5
5.7	9.2	14.2	All Other Non-Current						7.5
40.8	38.1	34.0	Net Worth						43.3
100.0	100.0	100.0	Total Liabilities & Net Worth						100.0
			INCOME DATA						
100.0	100.0	100.0	Net Sales						100.0
			Gross Profit						
88.6	93.1	93.4	Operating Expenses						94.5
11.4	6.9	6.6	Operating Profit						5.5
1.9	3.2	2.8	All Other Expenses (net)						-.2
9.5	3.7	3.8	Profit Before Taxes						5.6
			RATIOS						
2.5	2.1	2.9							1.9
1.6	1.2	1.4	Current						1.4
.9	1.0	.7							.8
2.1	2.0	2.8							1.5
1.0	1.0	1.0	Quick						1.0
.7	.6	.5							.6
0 UND	4 97.2	5 72.8						14	26.4
7 54.4	11 32.2	21 17.1	Sales/Receivables					25	14.8
46 7.9	40 9.2	44 8.4						44	8.3
			Cost of Sales/Inventory						
			Cost of Sales/Payables						
3.3	4.4	2.1							3.1
9.2	18.3	12.5	Sales/Working Capital						22.4
-145.4	-585.8	-23.5							-27.1
22.2	11.6	25.0							48.0
(23) 6.1	(32) 3.2	(26) 3.8	EBIT/Interest					(12)	16.7
1.1	.8	-.3							-6.9
			Net Profit + Depr., Dep., Amort./Cur. Mat. L/T/D						
.2	.1	.2							.2
.6	.6	.5	Fixed/Worth						.4
2.1	2.8	NM							NM
.5	.8	.8							.9
1.7	1.8	1.2	Debt/Worth						1.3
7.1	4.4	NM							NM
67.6	45.8	32.0	% Profit Before Taxes/Tangible Net Worth						32.4
(36) 19.2	(43) 10.7	(34) 13.2						(15)	15.7
6.2	.0	-.7							12.8
19.6	16.1	11.1	% Profit Before Taxes/Total Assets						11.7
8.0	4.5	6.9							8.0
.8	-1.1	-1.6							-1.4
116.1	97.4	64.8	Sales/Net Fixed Assets						86.9
16.2	12.2	13.1							10.9
4.6	3.4	4.1							4.6
3.4	2.8	3.3	Sales/Total Assets						4.1
1.4	1.4	1.2							1.2
.7	.9	.7							.7
.4	.5	.3	% Depr., Dep., Amort./Sales						.1
(27) 2.6	(36) 1.9	(28) 1.9						(14)	.7
3.9	3.5	3.5							2.9
	.8		% Officers', Directors' Owners' Comp/Sales						
	(11) 6.7								
	22.3								
1227038M	3040687M	2016808M	Net Sales ($)	3050M	10150M	12876M	24772M	145095M	1820865M
1013801M	1994172M	1765936M	Total Assets ($)	8047M	6011M	21400M	10616M	169705M	1550157M

© RMA 2010

M = $ thousand   MM = $ million
See Pages 9 through 22 for Explanation of Ratios and Data

Current Data Sorted by Assets | Comparative Historical Data

Type of Statement	0-500M	500M-2MM	2-10MM	10-50MM	50-100MM	100-250MM	4/1/05-3/31/06 ALL	4/1/06-3/31/07 ALL
Unqualified		2	11	11	4	2	15	18
Reviewed		5	14	5		1	18	19
Compiled	1	6	8	2			10	13
Tax Returns	11	3	2				5	9
Other	6	10	18	13	2	3	49	30
	21 (4/1-9/30/09)			119 (10/1/09-3/31/10)				
NUMBER OF STATEMENTS	18	26	53	31	6	6	97	89
	%	%	%	%	%	%	%	%
ASSETS								
Cash & Equivalents	39.6	16.1	11.8	4.9			9.5	10.6
Trade Receivables (net)	20.0	48.0	51.5	62.1			50.1	50.9
Inventory	.1	.9	1.7	1.2			1.1	1.3
All Other Current	3.8	6.1	5.4	7.1			4.4	3.4
Total Current	63.4	71.1	70.4	75.2			65.1	66.1
Fixed Assets (net)	22.7	18.0	11.3	9.9			16.7	16.0
Intangibles (net)	.7	3.7	6.2	7.5			6.3	7.9
All Other Non-Current	13.2	7.2	12.1	7.3			11.9	9.9
Total	100.0	100.0	100.0	100.0			100.0	100.0
LIABILITIES								
Notes Payable-Short Term	15.8	16.6	21.5	20.9			17.6	16.5
Cur. Mat.-L.T.D.	2.0	4.1	2.3	3.4			3.9	3.9
Trade Payables	5.5	6.0	7.2	10.9			6.1	7.3
Income Taxes Payable	.0	1.0	.7	.5			.3	4.5
All Other Current	32.1	15.4	17.4	22.0			22.2	21.6
Total Current	55.3	43.1	49.1	57.7			50.2	53.8
Long-Term Debt	24.8	11.8	11.6	7.8			16.5	14.3
Deferred Taxes	.0	.0	.2	.1			.6	.2
All Other Non-Current	16.2	2.8	6.6	7.0			10.2	4.2
Net Worth	3.8	42.4	32.6	27.4			22.5	27.5
Total Liabilities & Net Worth	100.0	100.0	100.0	100.0			100.0	100.0
INCOME DATA								
Net Sales	100.0	100.0	100.0	100.0			100.0	100.0
Gross Profit								
Operating Expenses	94.4	95.2	95.7	97.3			94.7	95.8
Operating Profit	5.6	4.8	4.3	2.7			5.3	4.2
All Other Expenses (net)	.1	.6	.7	.8			1.0	.8
Profit Before Taxes	5.5	4.2	3.6	1.8			4.3	3.4
RATIOS								
Current	3.3	3.1	2.2	2.0			2.4	2.0
	2.1	1.7	1.4	1.3			1.4	1.2
	.6	1.2	1.0	1.0			1.0	.9
Quick	3.3	2.9	2.0	1.7			2.2	1.9
	2.0	1.5	1.2	1.2			1.3	1.2
	.6	.9	.8	.8			1.0	.9
Sales/Receivables	0 UND	31 11.6	36 10.1	43 8.6			36 10.2	35 10.4
	0 UND	39 9.4	41 9.0	51 7.1			47 7.7	47 7.8
	20 18.1	44 8.3	56 6.5	64 5.7			57 6.4	59 6.2
Cost of Sales/Inventory								
Cost of Sales/Payables								
Sales/Working Capital	21.1	8.7	8.6	11.8			10.7	11.8
	78.5	17.2	22.7	25.0			22.5	32.1
	-21.7	NM	-168.7	276.2			290.9	-161.6
EBIT/Interest	18.8	19.2	19.7	12.6			16.0	16.0
	(11) 5.5	(23) 4.9	(50) 7.5	(30) 5.3			(83) 5.5	(79) 4.1
	-1.3	1.5	2.8	1.5			2.4	2.2
Net Profit + Depr., Dep., Amort./Cur. Mat. L/T/D			9.7	10.6			6.9	10.0
		(14) 4.5	(14) 4.2				(27) 2.4	(24) 2.8
			.9	.7			1.3	1.2
Fixed/Worth	.0	.1	.1	.1			.2	.2
	.5	.4	.3	.3			.5	.4
	-.5	1.8	1.2	1.5			3.3	4.2
Debt/Worth	.6	.6	.7	1.4			.9	1.0
	1.6	1.5	1.7	2.5			2.6	2.8
	-5.7	3.3	9.2	10.7			9.5	20.2
% Profit Before Taxes/Tangible Net Worth	366.5	72.1	57.9	53.6			75.1	68.5
	(12) 106.7	(23) 32.8	(45) 29.6	(24) 23.0			(80) 32.3	(72) 38.1
	70.2	2.0	11.3	10.0			17.6	15.7
% Profit Before Taxes/Total Assets	95.4	26.1	14.7	12.1			20.4	19.9
	39.6	11.7	9.7	7.5			9.7	8.5
	13.4	1.1	4.0	1.9			4.1	3.5
Sales/Net Fixed Assets	416.4	242.7	114.2	132.1			104.7	85.2
	143.2	33.7	57.2	64.4			50.3	45.4
	34.2	10.8	29.7	36.3			23.4	29.2
Sales/Total Assets	16.6	5.6	5.3	5.3			5.5	5.6
	9.5	4.5	4.4	4.4			4.2	4.5
	6.7	3.6	3.2	3.8			3.0	2.7
% Depr., Dep., Amort./Sales		.2	.3	.4			.4	.4
		(19) 1.1	(43) .7	(23) .5			(75) .8	(78) .7
		1.9	1.2	1.0			1.6	1.3
% Officers', Directors' Owners' Comp/Sales	1.5	3.0	1.5				1.1	.9
	(11) 4.1	(11) 6.3	(14) 2.6				(32) 3.3	(27) 2.4
	8.5	12.2	6.5				6.7	4.9
Net Sales ($)	37456M	136621M	1123102M	3138839M	1417197M	3806336M	3692458M	6960345M
Total Assets ($)	3271M	26675M	264887M	719728M	438215M	742981M	1101068M	1974700M

M = $ thousand   MM = $ million
See Pages 9 through 22 for Explanation of Ratios and Data

Comparative Historical Data

Current Data Sorted by Sales

4/1/07-3/31/08 ALL	4/1/08-3/31/09 ALL	4/1/09-3/31/10 ALL	Type of Statement	0-1MM	1-3MM	3-5MM	5-10MM	10-25MM	25MM & OVER
							21 (4/1-9/30/09)	119 (10/1/09-3/31/10)	
14	22	30	Unqualified		1		2	4	23
16	17	25	Reviewed		1		2	10	10
12	12	17	Compiled		4	2	4	5	2
12	12	16	Tax Returns	4	5	1	4	2	
28	45	52	Other	2	8	2	7	12	23
82	108	140	NUMBER OF STATEMENTS	6	19	5	19	33	58
%	%	%	ASSETS	%	%	%	%	%	%
13.9	7.9	14.0	Cash & Equivalents		21.2		24.0	14.3	5.2
53.9	50.8	49.3	Trade Receivables (net)		32.3		41.2	46.5	63.0
1.1	1.3	1.3	Inventory		.8		2.2	2.0	1.1
5.2	6.0	6.0	All Other Current		5.7		1.5	6.3	7.4
74.1	66.0	70.6	Total Current		59.9		68.9	69.1	76.6
13.1	16.3	14.0	Fixed Assets (net)		20.2		14.9	11.8	9.6
5.2	6.7	5.5	Intangibles (net)		2.9		4.6	7.4	6.4
7.6	11.0	9.9	All Other Non-Current		17.0		11.5	11.7	7.4
100.0	100.0	100.0	Total		100.0		100.0	100.0	100.0
			LIABILITIES						
18.0	21.0	18.8	Notes Payable-Short Term		17.3		13.0	21.5	20.6
2.6	2.7	2.9	Cur. Mat.-L.T.D.		3.0		3.3	2.2	2.9
7.4	7.8	7.7	Trade Payables		7.3		5.2	5.9	9.8
.8	.9	.6	Income Taxes Payable		1.2		.1	.9	.5
18.6	18.5	21.2	All Other Current		18.9		13.6	19.4	23.4
47.4	51.0	51.2	Total Current		47.8		35.3	49.8	57.2
11.1	13.9	12.0	Long-Term Debt		15.6		22.6	14.0	5.4
.4	.3	.1	Deferred Taxes		.0		.4	.0	.1
5.5	8.3	7.6	All Other Non-Current		12.0		3.8	10.6	5.4
35.7	26.6	29.1	Net Worth		24.6		38.0	25.6	31.9
100.0	100.0	100.0	Total Liabilities & Net Worth		100.0		100.0	100.0	100.0
			INCOME DATA						
100.0	100.0	100.0	Net Sales		100.0		100.0	100.0	100.0
			Gross Profit						
94.8	95.7	95.8	Operating Expenses		94.9		95.5	95.8	96.9
5.2	4.3	4.2	Operating Profit		5.1		4.5	4.2	3.1
.8	1.0	.7	All Other Expenses (net)		.6		-.2	1.0	.7
4.4	3.3	3.5	Profit Before Taxes		4.6		4.6	3.2	2.5
			RATIOS						
2.6	1.8	2.1	Current		2.1		3.9	2.2	1.8
1.4	1.3	1.5			1.4		1.8	1.4	1.4
1.1	1.0	1.0			.7		1.4	.9	1.1
2.6	1.7	2.1	Quick		2.1		3.8	2.0	1.7
1.3	1.2	1.3			1.2		1.8	1.2	1.2
1.0	.8	.8			.6		.8	.8	1.0
39 9.3	34 10.6	34 10.7	Sales/Receivables	0 UND			32 11.4	34 10.7	40 9.2
45 8.1	43 8.4	41 8.9		30 12.2			38 9.6	39 9.4	47 7.8
59 6.2	59 6.2	54 6.7		54 6.8			43 8.5	48 7.5	66 5.5
			Cost of Sales/Inventory						
			Cost of Sales/Payables						
11.1	12.6	10.6	Sales/Working Capital		10.0		7.8	9.8	11.7
23.6	28.1	23.1			62.0		14.1	28.3	22.4
106.8	-259.2	UND			-18.4		85.7	-82.7	70.0
13.9	13.0	17.0	EBIT/Interest		16.9		26.1	19.8	13.8
(69) 4.4	(98) 3.6	(126) 5.5			(17) 8.6		(15) 13.7	(31) 8.5	(56) 5.3
1.9	1.2	2.2			3.9		1.5	2.7	2.3
9.8	7.4	6.7	Net Profit + Depr., Dep., Amort./Cur. Mat. L/T/D						9.3
(16) 3.1	(27) 2.1	(37) 2.9						(24)	4.1
1.6	.8	.9							.9
.1	.2	.1	Fixed/Worth		.0		.1	.1	.1
.4	.5	.3			.8		.3	.2	.3
2.1	2.0	2.0			16.8		1.2	10.7	.7
.6	1.2	.9	Debt/Worth		.8		.3	.7	1.2
2.5	2.2	1.9			2.5		.9	1.4	2.4
13.1	10.9	10.6			36.3		2.9	NM	8.4
75.3	101.6	79.2	% Profit Before Taxes/Tangible Net Worth		102.6		141.6	47.2	65.4
(67) 36.6	(87) 29.5	(113) 32.6			(15) 72.1		(16) 15.8	(25) 29.6	(48) 30.2
15.9	6.0	11.1			32.6		2.8	10.5	11.6
20.2	18.3	22.0	% Profit Before Taxes/Total Assets		40.1		44.9	18.2	15.2
9.0	6.9	10.1			20.0		11.2	11.1	7.5
3.2	.7	3.2			2.5		1.2	-3.2	3.3
84.0	90.8	140.0	Sales/Net Fixed Assets		645.5		124.4	129.7	120.4
48.4	44.8	59.1			38.2		45.6	57.2	68.8
28.0	19.9	22.9			10.9		15.6	23.0	39.5
5.6	5.9	5.9	Sales/Total Assets		9.2		6.1	5.1	5.6
4.5	4.5	4.4			4.7		4.4	4.2	4.5
3.2	3.1	3.4			2.8		2.7	3.3	3.8
.4	.4	.3	% Depr., Dep., Amort./Sales				.4	.3	.3
(58) .9	(81) .8	(102) .7					(15) .8	(27) .8	(45) .6
1.2	1.3	1.4					1.5	1.5	.9
1.1	1.3	1.6	% Officers', Directors' Owners' Comp/Sales					1.3	
(30) 2.0	(33) 2.2	(40) 3.8						(11) 2.4	
4.6	5.6	8.2						4.9	
4143862M	8089752M	9659551M	Net Sales ($)	4361M	39533M	18405M	123702M	563038M	8910512M
1189858M	2226184M	2195757M	Total Assets ($)	922M	16468M	5755M	32562M	149045M	1991005M

M = $ thousand   MM = $ million
See Pages 9 through 22 for Explanation of Ratios and Data

ADMIN & WASTE MANAGEMENT SERVICES—Security Systems Services (except Locksmiths)   NAICS 561621

Current Data Sorted by Assets						Comparative Historical Data		

Type of Statement

	3	11	20	4	6	Unqualified	25	19
8	8 / 13	33 / 7	2			Reviewed	43	49
16	13 / 21	5				Compiled	35	25
13	26	33	17	2	2	Tax Returns	24	21
	34 (4/1-9/30/09)	216 (10/1/09-3/31/10)				Other	51	64

0-500M	500M-2MM	2-10MM	10-50MM	50-100MM	100-250MM		4/1/05-3/31/06 ALL	4/1/06-3/31/07 ALL
37	71	89	39	6	8	**NUMBER OF STATEMENTS**	178	178
%	%	%	%	%	%	**ASSETS**	%	%
13.2	11.7	10.1	6.7			Cash & Equivalents	9.9	9.9
29.1	36.9	32.1	24.6			Trade Receivables (net)	37.5	36.2
8.2	12.6	10.7	8.4			Inventory	10.0	11.3
1.2	3.4	6.0	6.5			All Other Current	4.2	4.5
51.8	64.6	58.8	46.2			Total Current	61.6	62.1
27.6	20.6	16.9	11.2			Fixed Assets (net)	18.0	16.8
10.6	6.3	13.8	36.4			Intangibles (net)	11.0	12.1
10.1	8.6	10.4	6.2			All Other Non-Current	9.5	9.0
100.0	100.0	100.0	100.0			Total	100.0	100.0
						LIABILITIES		
21.7	14.8	11.8	6.1			Notes Payable-Short Term	12.4	11.4
6.0	4.7	3.0	5.8			Cur. Mat.-L.T.D.	4.5	4.7
27.1	18.4	12.5	11.2			Trade Payables	15.3	15.5
.0	.3	.4	.1			Income Taxes Payable	.2	.4
30.7	13.7	18.9	17.7			All Other Current	17.5	18.3
85.5	51.9	46.6	41.0			Total Current	49.9	50.3
17.8	22.6	24.1	37.6			Long-Term Debt	26.2	22.9
.0	.0	.2	.4			Deferred Taxes	.2	.3
10.5	8.9	9.5	9.5			All Other Non-Current	12.1	12.7
-13.7	16.6	19.7	11.5			Net Worth	11.6	13.8
100.0	100.0	100.0	100.0			Total Liabilities & Net Worth	100.0	100.0
						INCOME DATA		
100.0	100.0	100.0	100.0			Net Sales	100.0	100.0
						Gross Profit		
97.2	96.7	95.3	93.6			Operating Expenses	94.7	94.6
2.8	3.3	4.7	6.4			Operating Profit	5.3	5.4
1.5	1.4	2.2	3.4			All Other Expenses (net)	2.0	2.3
1.3	1.9	2.5	3.0			Profit Before Taxes	3.2	3.0
						RATIOS		
1.8	2.2	2.0	1.7				2.1	2.1
.8	1.3	1.4	1.0			Current	1.4	1.3
.4	.8	.8	.6				.9	.9
1.5	1.6	1.4	1.1				1.7	1.5
.7	1.0	1.0	.7			Quick	1.1	1.0
.3	.5	.5	.5				.6	.6
0 UND	25 14.4	27 13.5	21 17.1				30 12.2	27 13.7
20 18.7	40 9.1	45 8.0	43 8.4			Sales/Receivables	46 8.0	46 7.9
36 10.2	57 6.4	69 5.3	55 6.6				71 5.1	67 5.5
						Cost of Sales/Inventory		
						Cost of Sales/Payables		
35.2	8.8	6.5	9.7				7.7	7.6
-24.1	21.5	16.8	-646.2			Sales/Working Capital	20.8	18.7
-7.2	-43.5	-39.5	-11.3				-37.6	-57.8
5.6	15.3	16.3	21.8				11.2	9.0
(34) 1.1	(64) 4.4	(78) 4.5	(35) 2.5			EBIT/Interest	(163) 3.4	(158) 3.6
-1.8	.9	1.0	1.1				1.3	.8
		6.1					5.3	7.4
	(19) 2.6					Net Profit + Depr., Dep., Amort./Cur. Mat. L/T/D	(43) 1.8	(47) 3.2
		1.6					1.1	1.2
.5	.3	.2	.2				.2	.3
6.7	.7	.8	-1.9			Fixed/Worth	1.0	1.0
-.6	-5.6	-1.6	-.1				-1.2	-.8
2.8	.9	1.1	1.5				1.3	1.4
-256.0	3.0	3.2	-9.5			Debt/Worth	5.2	3.8
-2.9	-18.2	-8.6	-1.7				-4.8	-5.1
97.8	56.6	61.0	53.5				88.2	71.4
(18) 18.9	(52) 26.3	(62) 28.5	(17) 24.8			% Profit Before Taxes/Tangible Net Worth	(113) 29.8	(118) 29.0
-6.0	4.2	7.2	5.5				8.3	6.8
15.7	19.1	16.5	16.1				18.6	19.2
1.6	5.5	5.2	5.4			% Profit Before Taxes/Total Assets	5.5	7.2
-11.5	-1.5	-.4	.6				.9	-.4
68.0	44.8	46.1	63.9				53.6	48.7
28.5	22.2	21.3	26.8			Sales/Net Fixed Assets	27.2	21.6
9.9	10.8	11.0	14.0				11.7	11.7
6.5	4.3	2.9	3.4				4.1	3.9
4.4	3.1	2.2	1.6			Sales/Total Assets	2.7	2.6
3.2	2.1	1.6	1.1				1.7	1.6
.5	.9	.8	.6				.5	.8
(25) 1.3	(54) 1.6	(66) 1.4	(21) 1.9			% Depr., Dep., Amort./Sales	(139) 1.4	(129) 1.7
3.8	2.4	3.0	6.2				2.9	3.5
5.4	3.4	2.7					3.7	3.0
(20) 10.7	(42) 5.1	(33) 3.6				% Officers', Directors' Owners' Comp/Sales	(63) 6.6	(60) 5.2
16.1	8.9	7.2					11.6	9.2
52545M	279844M	994366M	1865128M	700618M	1284642M	Net Sales ($)	3821909M	4128241M
10672M	84505M	427164M	890673M	455713M	1167512M	Total Assets ($)	2102979M	2314457M

© RMA 2010

M = $ thousand   MM = $ million
See Pages 9 through 22 for Explanation of Ratios and Data

Comparative Historical Data | Current Data Sorted by Sales

			Type of Statement						
20	36	44	Unqualified			4	6	9	25
50	58	43	Reviewed		2	6	14	20	1
16	27	28	Compiled	5	10	4	7	1	1
34	27	42	Tax Returns	8	17	6	9	2	1
65	83	93	Other	6	21	12	22	13	19
4/1/07-3/31/08 ALL	4/1/08-3/31/09 ALL	4/1/09-3/31/10 ALL		34 (4/1-9/30/09)			216 (10/1/09-3/31/10)		
				0-1MM	1-3MM	3-5MM	5-10MM	10-25MM	25MM & OVER
185	231	250	NUMBER OF STATEMENTS	19	50	32	58	45	46
%	%	%	ASSETS	%	%	%	%	%	%
9.1	8.9	10.6	Cash & Equivalents	11.4	11.9	11.1	11.5	8.0	10.1
35.4	33.8	30.9	Trade Receivables (net)	23.3	33.0	31.4	34.9	32.1	25.4
10.7	10.3	10.1	Inventory	5.8	12.7	8.0	12.3	10.0	7.5
6.0	5.9	4.6	All Other Current	.2	2.5	5.3	5.2	4.6	7.4
61.2	58.9	56.2	Total Current	40.6	60.1	55.8	63.9	54.7	50.4
18.4	16.7	18.3	Fixed Assets (net)	33.9	20.2	21.6	15.3	20.2	9.6
12.9	14.8	15.9	Intangibles (net)	11.3	10.1	10.3	14.4	17.7	28.2
7.5	9.6	9.6	All Other Non-Current	14.2	9.6	12.3	6.4	7.4	11.8
100.0	100.0	100.0	Total	100.0	100.0	100.0	100.0	100.0	100.0
			LIABILITIES						
10.9	11.9	12.7	Notes Payable-Short Term	28.0	14.1	11.9	14.1	9.6	6.5
6.0	5.4	4.3	Cur. Mat.-L.T.D.	7.3	4.0	4.9	4.0	3.6	3.7
13.6	14.2	15.7	Trade Payables	16.5	22.8	20.1	13.8	12.2	10.7
.5	.7	.3	Income Taxes Payable	.0	.1	.5	.5	.1	.5
18.0	22.8	18.7	All Other Current	25.1	22.0	12.1	18.7	17.2	18.7
49.0	54.9	51.7	Total Current	76.8	62.9	49.6	51.1	42.7	40.1
24.3	26.1	26.3	Long-Term Debt	29.5	16.3	18.4	28.6	29.0	35.6
.3	.4	.1	Deferred Taxes	.0	.0	.1	.2	.1	.1
6.1	5.6	9.4	All Other Non-Current	17.6	4.5	10.7	7.4	13.8	8.5
20.3	13.0	12.5	Net Worth	-23.9	16.2	21.2	12.7	14.0	15.7
100.0	100.0	100.0	Total Liabilities & Net Worth	100.0	100.0	100.0	100.0	100.0	100.0
			INCOME DATA						
100.0	100.0	100.0	Net Sales	100.0	100.0	100.0	100.0	100.0	100.0
			Gross Profit						
93.7	94.4	95.6	Operating Expenses	94.7	96.7	96.6	95.6	96.4	93.3
6.3	5.6	4.4	Operating Profit	5.3	3.3	3.4	4.4	3.6	6.7
1.9	2.8	2.2	All Other Expenses (net)	3.4	1.9	1.3	2.0	2.5	2.5
4.5	2.8	2.2	Profit Before Taxes	1.8	1.5	2.1	2.4	1.1	4.2
			RATIOS						
1.9	1.8	2.0	Current	1.1	2.3	1.9	2.0	1.8	1.9
1.4	1.2	1.2		.7	1.1	1.2	1.3	1.3	1.2
1.0	.8	.7		.1	.7	.7	.9	.9	.7
1.5	1.3	1.4	Quick	.9	1.7	1.3	1.5	1.4	1.3
1.0	.9	.9		.4	.8	.9	1.0	1.0	.8
.6	.4	.5		.1	.4	.5	.5	.6	.5
25 14.5	26 14.0	23 16.2	Sales/Receivables	0 UND	19 19.3	23 15.6	25 14.5	28 13.0	22 16.2
41 8.8	42 8.6	38 9.7		20 18.7	33 11.1	40 9.2	40 9.2	47 7.7	36 10.1
61 6.0	63 5.8	58 6.3		45 8.2	56 6.6	56 6.5	66 5.5	73 5.0	53 6.8
			Cost of Sales/Inventory						
			Cost of Sales/Payables						
8.9	8.7	8.4	Sales/Working Capital	105.8	10.5	7.7	7.2	7.5	8.4
17.9	29.2	29.3		-18.4	58.8	27.3	20.6	24.4	26.7
-170.4	-22.1	-20.1		-3.1	-12.0	-22.4	-129.5	-57.5	-20.4
10.8	13.0	12.5	EBIT/Interest	5.4	6.0	18.3	15.2	17.3	27.7
(169) 3.7	(201) 3.4	(225) 3.0		(16) .2	(48) 2.4	(25) 4.7	(53) 3.3	(41) 4.8	(42) 2.9
1.3	.6	.7		-5.4	-.5	.9	1.2	1.2	1.2
6.4	7.3	7.4	Net Profit + Depr., Dep., Amort./Cur. Mat. L/T/D					4.6	
(41) 3.7	(52) 3.0	(34) 2.5						(12) 2.1	
1.9	1.2	1.5						1.5	
.2	.2	.2	Fixed/Worth	.5	.4	.2	.2	.2	.2
.7	1.3	1.0		6.7	1.0	1.0	.6	1.1	.6
-1.7	-.5	-.6		-.5	-.5	NM	-.7	-.4	-.2
1.2	1.4	1.2	Debt/Worth	3.6	.7	1.6	.9	1.2	1.3
3.3	5.4	4.2		-5.9	3.9	4.0	5.0	2.9	3.6
-6.3	-2.8	-3.8		-3.2	-4.9	NM	-6.6	-3.2	-2.1
79.8	65.3	56.6	% Profit Before Taxes/Tangible Net Worth		31.2	108.5	54.2	59.6	65.4
(126) 28.8	(136) 35.0	(156) 27.1		(32) 12.9	(24) 31.3	(37) 28.8	(29) 30.4	(26) 38.6	
9.3	9.4	4.3			-2.4	-1.1	5.2	7.7	8.0
20.0	20.0	16.7	% Profit Before Taxes/Total Assets	12.9	8.7	23.9	19.4	17.2	19.4
7.5	6.1	5.1		.5	2.5	8.2	5.5	5.2	7.8
1.6	-1.2	-2.4		-30.9	-3.8	-1.5	.2	.4	1.3
52.1	53.2	53.5	Sales/Net Fixed Assets	42.1	49.4	50.3	45.5	53.4	72.7
22.0	22.0	22.8		12.2	20.0	19.2	28.3	19.3	30.6
11.1	11.0	10.5		1.9	10.4	6.8	16.0	8.2	11.7
4.1	3.8	3.8	Sales/Total Assets	4.4	4.5	3.9	3.9	3.2	3.5
2.8	2.6	2.5		2.8	3.0	2.2	2.7	2.2	2.3
1.7	1.5	1.6		.9	1.8	1.5	2.0	1.6	1.1
.9	.7	.8	% Depr., Dep., Amort./Sales	1.1	1.0	1.1	.6	.8	.6
(136) 1.8	(160) 1.5	(173) 1.6		(13) 3.8	(34) 1.7	(22) 1.9	(44) 1.4	(34) 1.4	(26) 1.6
3.3	2.9	3.1		5.2	2.6	3.1	2.4	3.5	3.8
2.7	3.1	3.0	% Officers', Directors' Owners' Comp/Sales	7.4	3.7	2.2	3.0	2.6	
(73) 4.4	(67) 4.8	(98) 4.6		(10) 10.4	(30) 6.8	(16) 3.8	(24) 4.0	(14) 4.4	
9.1	9.2	10.4		18.9	11.9	10.0	8.5	6.9	
3689240M	5849488M	5177143M	Net Sales ($)	9882M	101770M	122570M	423359M	710576M	3808986M
1995579M	3568706M	3036239M	Total Assets ($)	6044M	46367M	67647M	212597M	377652M	2325932M

© RMA 2010   M = $ thousand   MM = $ million
See Pages 9 through 22 for Explanation of Ratios and Data

Current Data Sorted by Assets   **Comparative Historical Data**

Type of Statement	0-500M	500M-2MM	2-10MM	10-50MM	50-100MM	100-250MM		1 4/1/05-3/31/06 ALL	2 4/1/06-3/31/07 ALL
Unqualified			1	1				1	2
Reviewed			8	1				12	12
Compiled	2	4	4	1				19	19
Tax Returns	11	11	2	1	2			17	18
Other	7	19	10	7				20	27
	9 (4/1-9/30/09)		83 (10/1/09-3/31/10)						
NUMBER OF STATEMENTS	20	34	25	11	2			69	78
ASSETS	%	%	%	%	%	%		%	%
Cash & Equivalents	26.0	14.4	11.4	19.1				18.9	18.7
Trade Receivables (net)	12.7	17.3	21.4	19.1				20.4	23.4
Inventory	5.5	1.4	2.8	8.0				3.4	3.2
All Other Current	8.4	7.5	2.7	5.9				3.6	5.4
Total Current	52.7	40.7	38.2	52.1				46.2	50.7
Fixed Assets (net)	30.3	28.4	32.5	27.9				33.3	31.8
Intangibles (net)	8.9	18.4	20.9	14.9				11.8	10.4
All Other Non-Current	8.1	12.4	8.4	5.1				8.6	7.1
Total	100.0	100.0	100.0	100.0				100.0	100.0
LIABILITIES									
Notes Payable-Short Term	13.3	12.2	6.8	1.2				8.3	4.9
Cur. Mat.-L.T.D.	11.0	2.4	5.8	4.3				7.6	7.1
Trade Payables	6.9	6.4	9.8	11.6				10.5	9.8
Income Taxes Payable	.2	.0	.1	2.0				.4	.3
All Other Current	35.0	13.1	15.0	15.7				13.7	16.5
Total Current	66.3	34.1	37.6	34.8				40.6	38.6
Long-Term Debt	70.5	34.1	23.2	12.3				17.5	37.3
Deferred Taxes	.0	.0	.0	.0				.2	.1
All Other Non-Current	12.0	1.4	5.0	2.7				9.6	5.9
Net Worth	-48.9	30.4	34.1	50.2				32.1	18.2
Total Liabilities & Net Worth	100.0	100.0	100.0	100.0				100.0	100.0
INCOME DATA									
Net Sales	100.0	100.0	100.0	100.0				100.0	100.0
Gross Profit									
Operating Expenses	89.8	86.8	92.6	92.0				94.6	93.3
Operating Profit	10.2	13.2	7.4	8.0				5.4	6.7
All Other Expenses (net)	1.3	3.1	2.1	.1				.9	1.6
Profit Before Taxes	8.9	10.1	5.3	8.0				4.5	5.2
RATIOS									
Current	6.9	4.0	1.8	3.2				2.0	2.6
	1.0	1.3	1.2	2.0				1.2	1.5
	.5	.7	.8	.9				.7	.8
Quick	3.1	3.7	1.7	2.7				1.7	2.2
	.6	1.1	1.0	1.1				1.0	1.2
	.3	.4	.7	.6				.6	.7
Sales/Receivables	0 UND	0 UND	4 85.9	11 33.7				12 29.8	6 63.7
	0 UND	17 22.1	23 16.2	23 16.1				20 18.6	22 16.3
	19 18.7	33 11.2	49 7.4	31 11.9				28 12.9	33 11.1
Cost of Sales/Inventory									
Cost of Sales/Payables									
Sales/Working Capital	9.5	10.8	14.7	6.5				16.0	11.5
	NM	46.2	70.0	10.5				84.5	24.3
	-12.1	-16.8	-48.0	-99.4				-36.4	-49.0
EBIT/Interest	28.0	17.3	15.4	97.3				25.8	33.6
	(16) 5.5	(30) 4.7	(20) 5.9	(10) 13.9				(60) 8.1	(66) 5.1
	.5	1.6	1.1	3.2				2.8	2.4
Net Profit + Depr., Dep., Amort./Cur. Mat. L/T/D								14.3	5.4
								(13) 2.4	(20) 2.6
								2.0	1.3
Fixed/Worth	.2	.3	.8	.3				.6	.5
	-5.8	24.9	2.3	.6				1.3	1.1
	-.2	-1.4	-2.2	2.7				7.6	19.1
Debt/Worth	.7	1.0	1.5	.5				.7	1.1
	-4.0	32.8	5.8	2.1				2.6	2.2
	-1.7	-8.5	-7.6	3.4				21.6	-11.5
% Profit Before Taxes/Tangible Net Worth		94.4	69.8					97.7	109.5
		(19) 29.6	(16) 33.3					(56) 32.2	(58) 42.1
		12.9	1.1					9.5	17.6
% Profit Before Taxes/Total Assets	70.3	24.9	20.0	20.8				26.2	41.6
	20.8	11.1	10.6	17.8				11.8	13.8
	5.7	2.7	.7	3.9				1.8	4.7
Sales/Net Fixed Assets	92.3	42.9	26.6	16.1				23.3	34.8
	30.3	14.9	11.0	13.5				12.3	12.6
	10.4	7.9	5.5	4.8				7.0	7.7
Sales/Total Assets	8.6	3.8	4.0	3.1				4.8	5.1
	5.7	2.4	2.4	2.4				3.7	3.7
	3.5	1.3	1.7	1.4				2.5	2.6
% Depr., Dep., Amort./Sales	1.2	1.2	1.9	1.0				1.6	1.5
	(10) 2.3	(17) 2.8	(19) 3.3	(10) 2.8				(58) 3.0	(60) 2.4
	5.2	7.5	5.9	3.4				4.1	3.9
% Officers', Directors' Owners' Comp/Sales	4.0	3.5	3.2					4.0	3.2
	(15) 8.5	(19) 5.1	(12) 4.7					(43) 6.6	(49) 5.6
	12.1	7.8	8.1					13.8	9.3
Net Sales ($)	31293M	132596M	270875M	642269M	169419M			1054367M	1611998M
Total Assets ($)	5113M	39652M	97357M	250272M	131225M			358681M	506482M

M = $ thousand   MM = $ million
See Pages 9 through 22 for Explanation of Ratios and Data

Comparative Historical Data / Current Data Sorted by Sales

3	2	4	Type of Statement						
11	18	9	Unqualified				1		3
20	10	11	Reviewed				5		
27	24	25	Compiled	1	5	2	2	4	1
18	24	43	Tax Returns	6	12	2	2	3	
			Other	9	8	8	6	6	8
4/1/07-3/31/08 ALL	4/1/08-3/31/09 ALL	4/1/09-3/31/10 ALL		9 (4/1-9/30/09)			83 (10/1/09-3/31/10)		
				0-1MM	1-3MM	3-5MM	5-10MM	10-25MM	25MM & OVER
79	78	92	NUMBER OF STATEMENTS	16	25	10	16	13	12
%	%	%	ASSETS	%	%	%	%	%	%
14.6	16.4	16.5	Cash & Equivalents	14.5	18.7	19.1	13.9	17.9	14.1
20.6	19.5	17.6	Trade Receivables (net)	3.4	14.6	18.1	25.5	27.3	21.6
3.6	4.6	3.6	Inventory	.7	4.8	1.0	1.7	5.2	7.7
6.4	3.8	6.2	All Other Current	12.6	3.4	7.5	2.2	6.9	6.8
45.2	44.4	43.8	Total Current	31.2	41.5	45.7	43.4	57.3	50.2
35.3	32.1	29.8	Fixed Assets (net)	45.5	33.3	25.2	18.5	19.9	31.1
10.6	12.5	16.9	Intangibles (net)	11.1	14.9	23.4	28.6	12.6	12.2
9.0	11.0	9.5	All Other Non-Current	12.1	10.3	5.7	9.6	10.2	6.6
100.0	100.0	100.0	Total	100.0	100.0	100.0	100.0	100.0	100.0
			LIABILITIES						
8.6	14.4	9.5	Notes Payable-Short Term	11.4	8.6	25.9	6.0	7.6	1.6
7.7	10.6	5.6	Cur. Mat.-L.T.D.	3.1	10.4	2.0	3.9	4.2	5.5
8.9	8.9	8.0	Trade Payables	2.0	6.8	6.8	8.1	14.8	12.3
.2	.1	.3	Income Taxes Payable	.0	.2	.0	.0	.2	1.8
14.1	14.8	18.7	All Other Current	6.8	29.6	10.2	16.7	20.0	20.1
39.5	48.8	42.1	Total Current	23.2	55.6	44.9	34.7	46.7	41.3
26.5	32.3	36.8	Long-Term Debt	46.1	63.6	25.0	22.1	18.3	17.7
.2	.1	.0	Deferred Taxes	.0	.0	.0	.0	.1	.0
5.0	16.6	4.9	All Other Non-Current	.9	11.3	.7	1.5	6.5	3.4
28.8	2.2	16.2	Net Worth	29.8	-30.5	29.4	41.7	28.4	37.5
100.0	100.0	100.0	Total Liabilities & Net Worth	100.0	100.0	100.0	100.0	100.0	100.0
			INCOME DATA						
100.0	100.0	100.0	Net Sales	100.0	100.0	100.0	100.0	100.0	100.0
			Gross Profit						
94.2	94.2	89.9	Operating Expenses	71.7	92.5	95.0	94.1	94.5	93.7
5.8	5.8	10.1	Operating Profit	28.3	7.5	5.0	5.9	5.5	6.3
1.7	1.3	2.1	All Other Expenses (net)	8.5	.8	.8	1.0	.3	.2
4.1	4.5	8.1	Profit Before Taxes	19.8	6.7	4.1	4.8	5.2	6.1
			RATIOS						
2.7	2.4	2.5	Current	15.4	2.5	3.8	1.8	1.9	2.2
1.3	1.2	1.2		2.5	1.1	1.0	1.3	1.2	1.1
.8	.6	.6		.2	.5	.5	1.0	.8	.8
1.9	1.9	2.2	Quick	13.1	2.5	3.6	1.8	1.7	1.6
.9	.9	1.0		1.2	.6	.9	1.2	1.1	.8
.5	.5	.5		.2	.3	.4	.9	.7	.5
0 UND	3 138.2	0 UND	Sales/Receivables	0 UND	0 UND	0 UND	12 31.5	11 33.2	17 21.5
21 17.3	20 18.3	19 19.7		0 UND	9 41.0	25 14.6	28 13.0	19 19.5	25 14.7
31 11.7	30 12.2	32 11.6		7 52.6	30 12.0	33 10.9	49 7.4	31 11.7	40 9.1
			Cost of Sales/Inventory						
			Cost of Sales/Payables						
11.5	11.1	10.0	Sales/Working Capital	4.4	14.4	23.9	12.4	12.2	7.7
40.4	82.7	64.9		14.5	140.4	NM	23.5	28.6	120.7
-32.6	-18.9	-18.0		-7.6	-14.1	-10.8	NM	-62.8	-19.4
26.2	8.1	19.0	EBIT/Interest	12.1	26.3		19.6	30.1	81.7
(66) 4.1	(70) 3.5	(78) 5.5		(11) 4.8	(22) 5.6	(14) 5.9	(12) 10.8	(10) 11.5	
.9	1.5	1.5		.7	1.9		2.2	1.1	3.2
19.3	17.1	17.6	Net Profit + Depr., Dep., Amort./Cur. Mat. L/T/D						
(13) 6.7	(17) 2.5	(15) 7.6							
1.1	.6	.4							
.5	.7	.4	Fixed/Worth	.3	.6	.4	.2	.4	.4
1.3	3.1	2.5		1.5	-2.1	-6.6	1.1	2.0	1.3
-4.6	-1.6	-1.5		-8.6	-.3	-1.1	-5.4	-2.5	2.8
.7	1.2	1.0	Debt/Worth	.3	.9	1.6	1.1	1.4	1.4
2.6	6.6	7.5		7.4	-5.1	-17.5	2.9	7.8	2.8
-8.6	-4.3	-5.2		-5.3	-1.6	-4.7	-17.0	-11.4	5.2
129.2	81.8	72.3	% Profit Before Taxes/Tangible Net Worth	44.9			72.4		128.5
(56) 50.3	(47) 25.5	(52) 31.4		(10) 12.4		(11) 29.6		(10) 51.2	
17.7	10.5	13.9		3.4			21.4		18.9
24.4	18.7	24.1	% Profit Before Taxes/Total Assets	29.1	43.5	17.3	22.0	36.3	22.4
8.6	9.1	12.0		3.2	16.7	7.7	11.2	20.8	14.1
-.3	2.4	2.6		.1	6.2	-1.0	3.0	1.1	4.6
29.7	34.4	37.9	Sales/Net Fixed Assets	21.4	47.5	29.6	53.3	45.9	15.7
12.6	14.1	14.6		7.9	17.7	12.8	16.9	23.1	10.8
7.5	8.8	7.7		.2	7.6	8.4	10.7	13.0	4.6
5.6	5.0	4.4	Sales/Total Assets	3.1	7.8	3.7	4.0	7.0	3.6
3.5	3.2	2.9		1.0	3.5	2.8	2.6	4.3	2.6
2.2	2.2	1.7		.2	2.1	1.8	2.0	3.2	2.0
1.5	1.6	1.5	% Depr., Dep., Amort./Sales			1.2	.8		1.9
(71) 2.5	(57) 2.9	(58) 2.9			(14) 2.3		(10) 2.0		3.0
4.0	4.4	5.1			8.3		4.3		4.0
3.2	3.6	3.1	% Officers', Directors' Owners' Comp/Sales		3.4			3.1	
(52) 5.5	(47) 5.4	(53) 5.1		(20) 5.8			(11) 4.0		
12.5	8.6	8.4		10.0			5.1		
1011716M	1727773M	1246452M	Net Sales ($)	8247M	48370M	39439M	122635M	204178M	823583M
364440M	612459M	523619M	Total Assets ($)	13312M	17452M	15693M	50103M	60873M	366186M

© RMA 2010

M = $ thousand   MM = $ million
See Pages 9 through 22 for Explanation of Ratios and Data

Current Data Sorted by Assets

Comparative Historical Data

						Type of Statement		
1	4	10	12	8	1	Unqualified	46	29
1	11	33	10			Reviewed	47	49
8	12	7	2			Compiled	25	39
47	25	3	1		1	Tax Returns	45	63
31	39	28	13	6	2	Other	85	75
	37 (4/1-9/30/09)		279 (10/1/09-3/31/10)				4/1/05-3/31/06	4/1/06-3/31/07
0-500M	500M-2MM	2-10MM	10-50MM	50-100MM	100-250MM		ALL	ALL
88	91	81	38	14	4	NUMBER OF STATEMENTS	248	255
%	%	%	%	%	%	ASSETS	%	%
19.2	13.2	8.9	11.5	7.5		Cash & Equivalents	11.2	12.5
28.3	40.7	47.6	37.9	29.7		Trade Receivables (net)	41.7	37.4
2.5	5.2	1.9	2.4	1.5		Inventory	3.0	4.0
4.6	5.1	4.8	6.2	5.2		All Other Current	4.0	5.6
54.6	64.2	63.2	58.0	43.9		Total Current	59.9	59.5
25.1	18.4	18.2	21.3	14.2		Fixed Assets (net)	20.5	22.4
10.7	7.6	9.9	10.0	32.9		Intangibles (net)	7.8	8.0
9.6	9.8	8.6	10.7	9.0		All Other Non-Current	11.7	10.0
100.0	100.0	100.0	100.0	100.0		Total	100.0	100.0
						LIABILITIES		
21.2	11.2	16.7	8.8	2.3		Notes Payable-Short Term	12.9	15.4
11.2	5.4	2.4	3.1	2.3		Cur. Mat.-L.T.D.	4.1	4.0
11.4	13.5	15.2	10.2	10.1		Trade Payables	11.9	11.6
.7	.4	.5	.1	.1		Income Taxes Payable	.4	.3
16.0	16.1	17.5	14.6	15.7		All Other Current	14.9	17.9
60.5	46.6	52.4	36.7	30.5		Total Current	44.2	49.3
20.1	22.3	9.4	15.7	21.1		Long-Term Debt	17.8	19.5
.0	.4	.1	.7	1.4		Deferred Taxes	.3	.4
14.0	4.8	4.3	10.5	14.6		All Other Non-Current	7.1	6.0
5.4	25.8	33.8	36.4	32.4		Net Worth	30.5	24.9
100.0	100.0	100.0	100.0	100.0		Total Liabilties & Net Worth	100.0	100.0
						INCOME DATA		
100.0	100.0	100.0	100.0	100.0		Net Sales	100.0	100.0
						Gross Profit		
94.1	95.6	96.7	94.7	92.7		Operating Expenses	94.8	95.2
5.9	4.4	3.3	5.3	7.3		Operating Profit	5.2	4.8
.8	.7	.3	1.3	1.0		All Other Expenses (net)	.5	.6
5.1	3.7	3.0	4.0	6.3		Profit Before Taxes	4.7	4.2
						RATIOS		
1.8	2.2	1.8	2.5	1.7		Current	2.3	2.1
1.0	1.3	1.2	1.3	1.4			1.3	1.4
.6	1.0	.9	1.1	1.0			1.0	.9
1.7	1.9	1.5	2.1	1.6		Quick	2.2	1.9
.9	1.1	1.1	1.1	1.3			1.2 (254)	1.2
.4	.8	.7	.9	.8			.6	.6
0 UND	23 15.8	25 14.8	26 13.9	24 15.3		Sales/Receivables	23 15.7	17 20.9
16 22.8	32 11.5	36 10.2	36 10.1	47 7.8			38 9.6	32 11.3
34 10.6	54 6.8	52 7.0	49 7.5	60 6.1			55 6.7	51 7.1
						Cost of Sales/Inventory		
						Cost of Sales/Payables		
20.7	10.8	15.3	11.6	12.0		Sales/Working Capital	11.0	11.9
-715.4	32.0	49.0	20.2	20.7			22.9	31.8
-30.3	-220.3	-69.3	145.3	-294.1			-461.9	-52.1
25.5	19.0	42.8	20.4	45.8		EBIT/Interest	21.8	15.8
(68) 7.4	(84) 5.9	(78) 8.1	(34) 7.2	10.0			(216) 5.4	(232) 5.6
1.8	1.0	3.2	1.8	4.1			2.1	1.7
		4.7	10.1	22.4		Net Profit + Depr., Dep., Amort./Cur. Mat. L/T/D	6.7	13.1
	(12) 1.3	(21) 3.9	(10) 2.6				(61) 3.5	(48) 3.3
	.7	1.4	1.5				1.6	1.2
.3	.2	.3	.2	.3		Fixed/Worth	.2	.3
1.5	.7	.6	.6	1.5			.6	.9
-1.7	3.8	2.1	6.6	-.2			3.4	-22.9
1.4	1.2	1.1	.7	1.6		Debt/Worth	.8	1.0
6.8	2.5	2.4	3.1	NM			2.2	2.5
-4.1	13.7	8.6	14.9	-1.8			10.7	-38.3
353.8	82.4	75.0	87.2			% Profit Before Taxes/Tangible Net Worth	73.0	74.6
(55) 100.0	(71) 35.6	(69) 33.1	(31) 40.9				(197) 35.8	(184) 40.2
30.2	4.3	9.6	14.4				11.8	17.1
72.7	26.0	18.8	16.6	16.6		% Profit Before Taxes/Total Assets	24.5	25.6
29.8	9.4	9.4	10.8	10.0			11.5	12.2
6.7	.3	4.6	4.5	6.2			3.6	3.2
116.8	81.6	63.1	115.4	107.0		Sales/Net Fixed Assets	62.7	63.7
34.9	42.7	38.2	38.5	25.2			28.7	29.6
17.9	13.1	22.4	13.5	12.8			14.1	12.3
9.9	6.2	5.8	5.2	3.9		Sales/Total Assets	5.9	6.1
6.8	4.6	4.4	3.3	2.8			4.0	4.1
3.9	2.9	3.1	2.2	1.3			2.6	2.7
.6	.5	.5	.3			% Depr., Dep., Amort./Sales	.6	.7
(44) 1.4	(59) 1.1	(72) .8	(34) .7				(209) 1.2	(198) 1.2
3.2	2.2	1.5	2.5				2.3	2.7
3.6	2.6	1.8	.7			% Officers', Directors' Owners' Comp/Sales	2.3	2.4
(51) 5.8	(41) 5.0	(35) 3.0	(10) 2.7				(105) 4.4	(121) 4.7
10.1	8.6	5.9	5.2				7.0	7.4
192825M	482609M	1839851M	5013062M	2392282M	2656507M	Net Sales ($)	6952700M	10563876M
20846M	101299M	397971M	844193M	1031344M	615103M	Total Assets ($)	2059043M	2376111M

M = $ thousand   MM = $ million
See Pages 9 through 22 for Explanation of Ratios and Data

Comparative Historical Data

Current Data Sorted by Sales

			Type of Statement						
34	39	36	Unqualified		1	1	3	5	26
57	50	55	Reviewed			4	12	17	22
34	32	29	Compiled	1	11	2	9	4	2
60	63	77	Tax Returns	27	27	9	8	4	2
87	105	119	Other	12	23	12	18	28	26
4/1/07-3/31/08 ALL	4/1/08-3/31/09 ALL	4/1/09-3/31/10 ALL			37 (4/1-9/30/09)		279 (10/1/09-3/31/10)		
				0-1MM	1-3MM	3-5MM	5-10MM	10-25MM	25MM & OVER
272	289	316	NUMBER OF STATEMENTS	40	62	28	50	58	78
%	%	%	**ASSETS**	%	%	%	%	%	%
13.3	14.1	13.3	Cash & Equivalents	15.7	16.5	12.4	12.4	12.3	11.2
38.6	38.8	38.0	Trade Receivables (net)	16.3	35.4	36.3	42.0	43.6	45.2
3.6	2.8	3.0	Inventory	1.1	4.5	5.2	5.9	1.3	1.5
5.9	4.3	5.0	All Other Current	4.9	3.3	6.9	4.5	6.2	5.2
61.5	60.0	59.4	Total Current	38.0	59.7	60.9	64.9	63.4	63.1
20.3	20.8	20.2	Fixed Assets (net)	25.4	24.9	21.0	21.5	18.1	14.4
8.2	9.1	10.9	Intangibles (net)	23.3	7.6	4.6	5.1	9.8	14.1
10.0	10.1	9.5	All Other Non-Current	13.5	7.8	13.6	8.4	8.7	8.5
100.0	100.0	100.0	Total	100.0	100.0	100.0	100.0	100.0	100.0
			LIABILITIES						
14.7	12.8	14.6	Notes Payable-Short Term	13.3	22.5	14.9	12.3	13.5	10.9
4.6	5.2	5.9	Cur. Mat.-L.T.D.	10.2	5.5	12.0	8.5	2.7	2.4
12.0	13.7	12.7	Trade Payables	7.8	11.5	16.6	12.4	15.2	13.1
.4	.2	.5	Income Taxes Payable	.0	.7	1.3	.4	.6	.2
16.8	18.0	16.2	All Other Current	12.7	18.0	14.0	13.3	17.9	17.8
48.5	49.9	49.8	Total Current	44.0	58.2	58.7	46.9	49.9	44.5
18.4	22.1	17.8	Long-Term Debt	29.9	23.2	13.7	20.0	12.1	11.5
.4	.2	.3	Deferred Taxes	.0	.1	.2	.7	.2	.5
6.2	8.5	8.4	All Other Non-Current	11.7	5.8	23.5	5.0	2.9	9.7
26.5	19.2	23.7	Net Worth	14.1	12.7	3.9	27.3	35.0	33.7
100.0	100.0	100.0	Total Liabilities & Net Worth	100.0	100.0	100.0	100.0	100.0	100.0
			INCOME DATA						
100.0	100.0	100.0	Net Sales	100.0	100.0	100.0	100.0	100.0	100.0
			Gross Profit						
93.9	94.9	95.2	Operating Expenses	96.8	92.0	97.0	95.1	96.5	95.4
6.1	5.1	4.8	Operating Profit	3.2	8.0	3.0	4.9	3.5	4.6
1.1	1.2	.7	All Other Expenses (net)	2.2	.3	.5	.7	.4	.7
5.0	3.9	4.0	Profit Before Taxes	.9	7.7	2.5	4.2	3.1	3.9
			RATIOS						
2.2	1.8	2.0		1.4	2.2	2.0	2.6	1.8	2.0
1.4	1.3	1.2	Current	.9	1.3	1.2	1.4	1.2	1.3
1.0	.9	.9		.4	.8	.8	1.0	.9	1.0
1.8	1.7	1.8		1.3	1.9	1.2	2.4	1.8	1.9
1.2	1.2	1.1	Quick	.8	1.1	.9	1.0	1.1	1.2
.7	.7	.7		.3	.6	.6	.8	.7	.9
17 21.1	19 19.7	18 20.2		0 UND	13 28.9	9 38.5	17 22.0	22 16.5	26 13.9
35 10.6	32 11.5	31 11.7	Sales/Receivables	25 14.5	29 12.4	21 17.1	28 13.0	32 11.2	37 9.9
51 7.1	46 7.9	49 7.5		66 5.6	49 7.5	38 9.5	50 7.4	50 7.3	49 7.5
			Cost of Sales/Inventory						
			Cost of Sales/Payables						
11.8	14.1	13.5		24.5	12.2	20.7	10.5	14.9	13.8
29.0	35.3	42.3	Sales/Working Capital	-65.5	35.5	113.3	23.0	38.2	31.5
-208.5	-137.8	-67.6		-17.5	-36.5	-40.3	-857.6	-68.4	786.5
16.6	15.8	22.5		7.5	27.0	15.4	27.3	13.2	43.0
(230) 6.8	(251) 3.9	(282) 7.2	EBIT/Interest	(32) 2.0	(54) 8.4	(22) 6.4	(45) 7.5	(56) 6.8	(73) 10.7
2.1	1.3	1.9		.3	2.2	1.0	1.4	3.3	2.0
13.4	14.0	11.8	Net Profit + Depr., Dep., Amort./Cur. Mat. L/T/D				4.4	6.9	20.1
(55) 3.6	(56) 4.6	(51) 3.7				(10) 1.1	(11) 3.9	(24) 4.7	
1.8	1.9	1.2					-2.7	2.1	2.1
.2	.2	.2		.4	.2	.2	.2	.3	.2
.7	.7	.8	Fixed/Worth	3.7	1.1	1.1	.7	.6	.5
3.8	-19.2	20.8		-.4	-9.0	-13.0	2.0	2.2	3.9
.9	1.1	1.2		1.6	1.2	1.1	1.2	1.3	1.1
2.4	2.8	3.2	Debt/Worth	31.5	4.8	3.5	2.3	2.9	3.0
13.1	-32.4	-72.2		-2.1	-9.5	-38.7	6.6	8.5	49.8
93.0	91.5	103.7	% Profit Before Taxes/Tangible Net Worth	441.5	230.8	81.0	109.6	73.7	90.4
(215) 43.8	(213) 38.6	(234) 46.0		(21) 61.1	(42) 72.0	(19) 26.0	(44) 38.0	(48) 26.6	(60) 52.2
15.7	13.1	10.4		-50.5	16.5	4.3	6.9	10.1	12.7
28.7	26.1	28.6	% Profit Before Taxes/Total Assets	30.2	54.6	38.9	29.1	18.7	19.6
12.8	10.8	11.7		8.6	26.8	13.9	11.5	11.0	10.6
3.2	1.4	3.5		-8.1	6.3	.7	2.4	4.4	4.8
75.8	104.5	90.7	Sales/Net Fixed Assets	50.4	104.1	195.8	80.1	76.5	109.9
32.8	35.2	38.4		20.4	31.7	41.6	43.5	40.7	49.9
14.9	15.8	15.5		11.9	11.4	20.8	17.8	20.1	22.9
5.8	6.3	6.8	Sales/Total Assets	6.5	7.3	9.6	6.9	6.6	6.1
4.2	4.5	4.6		2.2	4.7	5.2	4.6	4.4	4.4
2.9	2.9	2.8		1.1	2.8	4.6	3.6	2.9	2.9
.5	.4	.5	% Depr., Dep., Amort./Sales	1.6	.6	.4	.5	.5	.3
(207) 1.0	(215) .9	(218) .9		(17) 3.2	(37) 1.6	(19) .8	(38) 1.0	(44) 1.0	(63) .6
1.8	1.9	2.0		5.4	3.2	2.0	1.8	1.6	1.2
2.0	2.1	2.6	% Officers', Directors' Owners' Comp/Sales	5.8	3.3	3.6	2.4	1.4	1.1
(112) 3.8	(124) 4.2	(137) 5.0		(18) 10.1	(34) 5.4	(15) 5.1	(26) 4.3	(27) 2.8	(17) 2.3
6.5	7.1	7.4		14.2	8.7	13.6	7.1	5.5	5.2
8843258M	11348126M	12577136M	Net Sales ($)	19575M	117601M	112128M	335076M	936203M	11056553M
2364077M	2906522M	3010756M	Total Assets ($)	11568M	34534M	21062M	93557M	275286M	2574749M

M = $ thousand   MM = $ million
See Pages 9 through 22 for Explanation of Ratios and Data

Current Data Sorted by Assets   **Comparative Historical Data**

0-500M	500M-2MM	2-10MM	10-50MM	50-100MM	100-250MM	Type of Statement	4/1/05-3/31/06 ALL	4/1/06-3/31/07 ALL
3	1	10	7	7	1	Unqualified	30	26
	25	38	6			Reviewed	68	87
24	37	15				Compiled	92	83
116	63	8	2		4	Tax Returns	131	149
37	71	56	14	4	2	Other	150	159
	42 (4/1-9/30/09)		509 (10/1/09-3/31/10)					
180	197	127	29	11	7	**NUMBER OF STATEMENTS**	471	504
%	%	%	%	%	%	**ASSETS**	%	%
15.8	10.8	11.9	10.2	6.3		Cash & Equivalents	9.4	10.7
15.3	25.4	30.6	21.8	21.1		Trade Receivables (net)	27.4	26.4
4.8	6.4	7.2	10.5	15.9		Inventory	6.6	5.8
2.4	3.4	4.9	5.1	5.0		All Other Current	2.5	3.5
38.3	46.0	54.6	47.7	48.3		Total Current	45.9	46.4
47.0	41.0	34.3	35.9	38.9		Fixed Assets (net)	42.5	43.4
4.1	4.3	4.0	7.1	6.9		Intangibles (net)	3.2	3.0
10.6	8.7	7.1	9.2	5.8		All Other Non-Current	8.4	7.1
100.0	100.0	100.0	100.0	100.0		Total	100.0	100.0
						LIABILITIES		
22.5	13.9	9.6	6.2	6.4		Notes Payable-Short Term	11.6	11.1
8.5	5.6	5.4	8.5	5.8		Cur. Mat.-L.T.D.	7.5	6.8
8.0	10.7	12.0	8.5	15.3		Trade Payables	10.8	11.6
.0	.2	.3	.8	.9		Income Taxes Payable	.3	.3
14.1	8.4	9.6	13.7	10.5		All Other Current	11.0	12.6
53.2	38.8	36.9	37.7	39.0		Total Current	41.2	42.4
49.0	28.1	16.2	15.9	21.9		Long-Term Debt	32.8	32.1
.0	.4	.5	.3	.9		Deferred Taxes	.4	.5
10.9	3.4	3.9	3.0	8.5		All Other Non-Current	5.7	4.9
-13.2	29.3	42.5	43.2	29.8		Net Worth	19.9	20.0
100.0	100.0	100.0	100.0	100.0		Total Liabilities & Net Worth	100.0	100.0
						INCOME DATA		
100.0	100.0	100.0	100.0	100.0		Net Sales	100.0	100.0
						Gross Profit		
94.5	95.1	95.1	96.9	95.2		Operating Expenses	94.3	93.5
5.5	4.9	4.9	3.1	4.8		Operating Profit	5.7	6.5
2.0	2.3	1.7	1.5	2.1		All Other Expenses (net)	1.2	1.5
3.5	2.6	3.2	1.6	2.7		Profit Before Taxes	4.5	5.0
						RATIOS		
2.2	2.4	2.3	2.2	1.4		Current	2.0	2.2
1.0	1.3	1.4	1.3	1.2			1.2	1.2
.3	.7	1.0	1.0	1.0			.6	.7
1.8	2.0	1.8	1.9	1.2		Quick	1.6	1.8
.6	1.1	1.2	.9	.8			(470) 1.0	(503) 1.0
.2	.5	.6	.4	.4			.5	.5
0 UND	12 29.6	28 12.9	22 16.6	33 11.0		Sales/Receivables	8 44.5	7 53.2
5 78.5	32 11.3	45 8.2	40 9.2	47 7.8			34 10.9	30 12.2
22 16.3	54 6.8	66 5.5	52 7.0	54 6.7			58 6.3	52 7.0
						Cost of Sales/Inventory		
						Cost of Sales/Payables		
17.4	9.1	7.5	7.9	7.1		Sales/Working Capital	10.7	11.0
-378.0	38.8	15.5	14.8	46.4			34.1	38.7
-13.7	-24.2	999.8	NM	-631.6			-32.6	-30.1
10.2	9.0	14.9	9.7	3.8		EBIT/Interest	9.9	11.4
(149) 2.4	(177) 2.4	(117) 5.5	(28) 4.7	2.8			(438) 3.9	(465) 4.6
.0	.2	.0	1.3	1.2			1.4	1.4
		4.2	8.0	4.6		Net Profit + Depr., Dep.,	3.2	3.7
	(27) 1.4	(28) 2.6	(11) 1.5			Amort./Cur. Mat. L/T/D	(91) 1.8	(83) 2.2
	.8	.4	.8				1.0	1.1
.8	.6	.4	.5	1.2		Fixed/Worth	.7	.6
9.4	1.6	.8	1.1	2.3			1.5	1.6
-1.1	15.4	1.5	2.1	3.6			32.3	7.2
1.2	.7	.6	.8	1.6		Debt/Worth	1.1	1.2
15.8	2.9	1.6	1.7	2.9			2.8	2.8
-3.2	39.1	3.4	3.3	5.1			98.3	17.6
166.6	57.7	43.3	35.7			% Profit Before Taxes/Tangible	74.5	82.7
(102) 55.1	(151) 18.9	(118) 16.9	(27) 19.4			Net Worth	(366) 33.3	(406) 35.0
.0	-1.4	.7	3.7				8.8	11.0
38.1	19.7	17.3	16.4	9.6		% Profit Before Taxes/Total	23.8	27.0
9.7	3.7	7.0	4.9	3.5		Assets	9.4	10.3
-4.6	-2.6	-.8	.8	.4			1.7	1.7
28.9	15.4	16.5	10.1	11.9		Sales/Net Fixed Assets	15.5	17.4
12.2	7.4	8.0	5.4	4.5			8.1	8.3
5.1	4.3	4.1	3.2	4.0			4.6	4.7
7.1	3.6	3.4	2.6	2.7		Sales/Total Assets	4.4	4.6
4.4	2.7	2.3	1.9	2.5			2.9	3.1
2.9	1.9	1.6	1.5	1.2			2.1	2.1
1.7	2.4	2.3	2.7			% Depr., Dep., Amort./Sales	2.1	2.1
(128) 3.6	(159) 4.2	(102) 3.7	(25) 3.9				(400) 3.6	(416) 3.6
6.5	6.8	5.4	5.2				6.0	5.7
4.8	2.2	1.8				% Officers', Directors'	2.9	2.7
(123) 7.7	(109) 4.5	(41) 2.9				Owners' Comp/Sales	(259) 4.6	(251) 4.7
12.7	6.7	4.2					7.3	7.6
196426M	603056M	1351617M	1242739M	1561461M	3622447M	Net Sales ($)	7560142M	10609644M
40744M	214418M	568564M	588515M	744670M	943077M	Total Assets ($)	2450201M	3131952M

Comparative Historical Data   Current Data Sorted by Sales

4/1/07-3/31/08 ALL	4/1/08-3/31/09 ALL	4/1/09-3/31/10 ALL	Type of Statement	0-1MM	1-3MM	3-5MM	5-10MM	10-25MM	25MM & OVER
26	30	26	Unqualified	3	16	11	5	7	14
79	80	72	Reviewed	19	31	14	16	20	6
73	71	76	Compiled	81	63	24	6	6	
182	173	193	Tax Returns	26	57	26	15	5	5
190	162	184	Other				31	27	17
				42 (4/1-9/30/09)			509 (10/1/09-3/31/10)		
550	516	551	**NUMBER OF STATEMENTS**	129	167	75	73	65	42
%	%	%	**ASSETS**	%	%	%	%	%	%
10.1	11.2	12.6	Cash & Equivalents	12.8	13.8	9.6	12.2	14.7	9.6
26.7	26.1	22.8	Trade Receivables (net)	11.4	22.2	29.1	27.9	33.7	23.6
6.4	6.5	6.5	Inventory	3.6	7.2	7.1	8.9	4.8	9.4
4.1	4.2	3.5	All Other Current	2.3	3.3	3.6	3.7	5.0	5.6
47.4	48.1	45.4	Total Current	30.2	46.6	49.4	52.6	58.2	48.3
42.3	39.2	41.2	Fixed Assets (net)	53.3	41.8	35.9	33.4	32.8	37.4
3.1	4.1	4.4	Intangibles (net)	5.5	3.5	4.1	4.5	3.9	6.4
7.2	8.6	9.0	All Other Non-Current	11.0	8.2	10.6	9.5	5.2	8.0
100.0	100.0	100.0	Total	100.0	100.0	100.0	100.0	100.0	100.0
			LIABILITIES						
12.5	14.7	15.2	Notes Payable-Short Term	21.8	14.8	16.6	12.5	8.3	9.1
8.2	7.2	6.6	Cur. Mat.-L.T.D.	7.5	7.2	5.6	6.4	5.1	6.3
11.7	10.7	10.1	Trade Payables	6.4	9.8	12.3	10.5	14.3	11.3
.3	.3	.2	Income Taxes Payable	.0	.1	.3	.3	.6	.5
10.8	10.6	10.9	All Other Current	13.5	8.9	9.9	9.3	11.9	13.5
43.4	43.5	43.0	Total Current	49.3	40.8	44.7	39.0	40.1	40.8
31.6	30.9	31.7	Long-Term Debt	55.2	33.3	23.1	18.8	11.4	22.5
.4	.3	.3	Deferred Taxes	.0	.3	.4	.6	.4	.5
4.8	6.4	6.1	All Other Non-Current	14.2	3.8	2.7	3.6	3.1	5.8
19.8	18.9	18.8	Net Worth	-18.7	21.9	29.1	37.9	45.0	30.4
100.0	100.0	100.0	Total Liabilties & Net Worth	100.0	100.0	100.0	100.0	100.0	100.0
			INCOME DATA						
100.0	100.0	100.0	Net Sales	100.0	100.0	100.0	100.0	100.0	100.0
			Gross Profit						
94.0	94.2	95.0	Operating Expenses	91.5	96.2	96.0	96.7	95.3	95.6
6.0	5.8	5.0	Operating Profit	8.5	3.8	4.0	3.3	4.7	4.4
1.7	1.6	2.0	All Other Expenses (net)	5.3	1.2	1.1	.7	.7	1.2
4.4	4.2	3.0	Profit Before Taxes	3.2	2.6	2.9	2.6	4.0	3.3
			RATIOS						
2.0	2.2	2.2		2.1	2.6	1.9	2.6	2.2	2.2
1.3	1.3	1.2	Current	.7	1.4	1.2	1.3	1.4	1.2
.7	.8	.7		.2	.7	.7	.9	1.1	1.0
1.7	1.8	1.8		1.6	2.3	1.6	2.1	1.7	1.8
.9 (514)	1.0	.9	Quick	.5	1.0	.9	1.1	1.2	.9
.4	.4	.4		.1	.5	.5	.5	.8	.4
7 54.8	6 57.4	6 61.2		0 UND	6 56.2	17 21.6	18 20.2	24 15.4	23 16.0
32 11.4	30 12.4	27 13.7	Sales/Receivables	0 UND	23 16.0	38 9.5	35 10.3	45 8.2	38 9.5
55 6.6	53 6.9	50 7.4		27 13.6	50 7.3	56 6.5	52 7.0	65 5.6	50 7.3
			Cost of Sales/Inventory						
			Cost of Sales/Payables						
10.4	10.1	10.2		17.2	9.8	10.9	8.1	7.9	9.1
33.7	29.0	36.8	Sales/Working Capital	-75.0	28.1	48.7	24.6	16.7	36.1
-27.3	-36.9	-24.6		-7.3	-19.6	-24.6	-52.2	183.4	-632.7
9.5	9.8	11.3		6.9	12.2	9.0	15.3	34.1	8.7
(510) 3.4	(456) 3.2	(487) 2.9	EBIT/Interest	(101) 1.6	(150) 2.4	(70) 2.8	(67) 4.2	(60) 8.6	(39) 3.3
1.2	1.0	.3		-.4	-.4	.8	.1	2.2	1.1
4.2	4.7	4.4			2.7	3.5	8.0	8.6	8.9
(76) 2.2	(71) 2.2	(76) 1.8	Net Profit + Depr., Dep., Amort./Cur. Mat. L/T/D		(13) 1.3	(15) 1.5	(11) 1.3	(21) 3.1	(12) 2.6
1.4	.6	.7			.1	.1	.3	1.3	1.0
.6	.6	.6		1.3	.6	.6	.4	.4	.8
1.7	1.5	1.5	Fixed/Worth	31.3	1.6	1.3	1.0	.7	1.5
11.2	33.0	172.0		-1.1	-29.1	3.7	2.7	1.2	3.5
1.1	1.1	.8		1.9	.8	.8	.7	.6	1.3
2.9	2.8	2.8	Debt/Worth	UND	3.3	2.8	1.9	1.5	2.4
32.7	64.7	-639.0		-2.9	-36.6	8.5	5.2	2.8	5.0
77.0	71.5	65.7		100.5	81.5	57.2	62.5	57.9	36.6
(436) 34.1	(397) 27.2	(413) 20.9	% Profit Before Taxes/Tangible Net Worth	(66) 20.6	(124) 19.4	(60) 21.0	(64) 20.4	(63) 22.7	(36) 19.0
10.0	4.5	.0		-.2	-4.9	.5	.0	8.6	3.9
23.5	21.0	22.4		30.1	25.3	21.1	21.5	22.0	15.9
9.3	7.6	6.1	% Profit Before Taxes/Total Assets	2.9	6.1	3.9	8.1	10.1	4.1
.7	.0	-2.4		-6.5	-3.7	-.8	-1.6	2.9	.4
17.0	19.6	18.5		19.1	19.2	15.8	19.0	20.2	14.5
8.9	10.5	8.6	Sales/Net Fixed Assets	7.6	7.5	8.7	11.2	9.9	6.3
4.4	4.6	4.3		2.5	4.2	6.3	5.9	5.5	4.0
4.6	4.7	4.3		5.3	4.8	4.0	4.6	3.7	3.1
3.0	3.0	2.8	Sales/Total Assets	3.2	2.9	2.7	3.1	2.7	2.5
2.0	2.0	1.9		1.4	1.9	2.2	1.8	2.0	1.8
2.0	1.8	2.1		2.2	2.4	1.9	1.9	2.3	2.0
(467) 3.7	(410) 3.6	(427) 3.9	% Depr., Dep., Amort./Sales	(100) 4.4	(120) 4.5	(62) 3.3	(60) 3.4	(52) 3.5	(33) 3.6
6.1	5.3	6.1		9.5	7.0	5.6	5.2	4.5	4.9
2.7	2.5	2.6		5.9	3.2	2.2	1.8	1.2	1.3
(279) 4.3	(258) 4.5	(285) 5.3	% Officers', Directors' Owners' Comp/Sales	(71) 9.0	(103) 5.5	(47) 3.7	(32) 3.2	(20) 2.7	(12) 4.2
7.3	8.4	8.8		17.2	7.0	5.6	5.1	4.5	10.4
12720660M	8583123M	8577746M	Net Sales ($)	65116M	310576M	297870M	517849M	991095M	6395240M
3383236M	2879797M	3099988M	Total Assets ($)	40908M	136417M	114504M	236489M	416457M	2155213M

M = $ thousand   MM = $ million
See Pages 9 through 22 for Explanation of Ratios and Data

Current Data Sorted by Assets   Comparative Historical Data

						Type of Statement		
			1			Unqualified	1	1
	1	6				Reviewed	3	5
2	5	2				Compiled	8	5
18	6	4	1			Tax Returns	8	13
12	10	2				Other	13	12
	8 (4/1-9/30/09)		62 (10/1/09-3/31/10)				4/1/05-3/31/06	4/1/06-3/31/07
0-500M	500M-2MM	2-10MM	10-50MM	50-100MM	100-250MM		ALL	ALL
33	22	14	1			NUMBER OF STATEMENTS	33	36
%	%	%	%	%	%	**ASSETS**	%	%
19.7	9.4	15.5				Cash & Equivalents	13.6	16.6
19.5	29.0	32.9				Trade Receivables (net)	22.3	25.0
5.4	4.0	3.4		D	D	Inventory	7.7	5.2
5.0	2.5	3.1		A	A	All Other Current	1.9	3.3
49.6	44.9	54.9		T	T	Total Current	45.5	50.1
28.0	27.5	28.7		A	A	Fixed Assets (net)	38.6	30.2
14.3	14.8	2.6				Intangibles (net)	6.2	8.5
8.1	12.7	13.8		N	N	All Other Non-Current	9.6	11.2
100.0	100.0	100.0		O	O	Total	100.0	100.0
				T	T	**LIABILITIES**		
32.0	17.1	10.6				Notes Payable-Short Term	10.4	16.7
2.9	4.9	8.2		A	A	Cur. Mat.-L.T.D.	4.8	3.3
8.4	9.5	9.8		V	V	Trade Payables	7.6	9.4
.0	.0	.0		A	A	Income Taxes Payable	.1	.0
16.5	4.5	5.5		I	I	All Other Current	10.4	6.6
59.8	36.1	34.2		L	L	Total Current	33.2	36.1
42.4	30.0	10.3		A	A	Long-Term Debt	29.3	26.8
.0	.1	.4		B	B	Deferred Taxes	.3	.3
9.3	2.9	4.2		L	L	All Other Non-Current	4.3	3.7
-11.5	30.9	50.8		E	E	Net Worth	33.0	33.1
100.0	100.0	100.0				Total Liabilities & Net Worth	100.0	100.0
						INCOME DATA		
100.0	100.0	100.0				Net Sales	100.0	100.0
						Gross Profit		
93.6	92.7	98.5				Operating Expenses	88.8	91.3
6.4	7.3	1.5				Operating Profit	11.2	8.7
.8	2.4	-.4				All Other Expenses (net)	1.5	.8
5.6	4.9	1.9				Profit Before Taxes	9.7	7.8
						RATIOS		
3.5	3.2	3.1					3.2	2.3
1.3	1.6	1.9				Current	1.7	1.3
.4	.7	.9					.6	.8
3.1	2.5	2.9					3.0	2.1
(32) 1.0	1.3	1.6				Quick	1.2	1.0
.3	.6	.8					.3	.5
0 UND	10 36.9	9 39.3					0 UND	0 UND
8 43.7	35 10.4	45 8.1				Sales/Receivables	8 43.9	19 19.0
30 12.3	59 6.2	95 3.8					38 9.6	47 7.8
						Cost of Sales/Inventory		
						Cost of Sales/Payables		
13.8	8.3	5.9					6.7	8.4
58.7	17.6	9.8				Sales/Working Capital	27.4	37.7
-14.7	-19.2	-115.4					-94.0	-63.2
28.0	10.1	39.5					23.9	25.4
(31) 3.8	(20) 3.3	8.8				EBIT/Interest	(30) 7.6	6.2
-.4	1.4	3.9					3.4	1.3
						Net Profit + Depr., Dep., Amort./Cur. Mat. L/T/D		
.4	.4	.2					.5	.3
1.2	2.0	.4				Fixed/Worth	1.6	1.4
-.4	-1.1	.8					18.0	121.8
1.0	1.0	.5					.6	.7
4.0	2.1	.8				Debt/Worth	1.5	2.9
-1.8	-6.5	1.3					255.0	228.2
251.4	82.1	31.1					153.9	183.1
(20) 88.2	(15) 41.3	(13) 23.8				% Profit Before Taxes/Tangible Net Worth	(26) 62.2	(28) 61.5
-12.3	7.5	11.5					18.9	9.1
95.8	23.4	19.0					48.7	31.4
12.6	8.0	9.3				% Profit Before Taxes/Total Assets	14.3	12.6
-9.6	1.3	2.5					5.3	1.9
86.7	50.5	46.9					21.4	46.4
25.0	12.8	12.1				Sales/Net Fixed Assets	15.6	15.9
12.4	6.4	7.1					8.4	7.2
8.2	3.7	3.7					6.8	5.8
5.0	2.5	2.7				Sales/Total Assets	3.6	4.3
3.5	1.7	1.6					2.4	2.8
.8	.8	.9					1.3	.8
(15) 3.3	(11) 2.9	(11) 2.5				% Depr., Dep., Amort./Sales	(21) 2.1	(27) 1.9
5.1	5.3	3.5					3.7	4.3
4.8	3.9						4.2	3.5
(25) 6.8	(12) 6.4					% Officers', Directors' Owners' Comp/Sales	(18) 9.4	(21) 5.0
11.4	9.2						14.4	7.5
44671M	54435M	133027M	28672M			Net Sales ($)	273615M	1147552M
7575M	21586M	51378M	22591M			Total Assets ($)	90391M	289299M

(Columns 50-100MM and 100-250MM: DATA NOT AVAILABLE)

Comparative Historical Data | | | Current Data Sorted by Sales

3	4	2	Type of Statement						
3	4	2	Unqualified	1					1
4	4	7	Reviewed		1	1	1	4	
3	9	9	Compiled		5	2	1	1	
12	26	28	Tax Returns	7	14	4	2	1	
19	20	24	Other	8			3	1	
4/1/07-3/31/08 ALL	4/1/08-3/31/09 ALL	4/1/09-3/31/10 ALL		0-1MM	8 (4/1-9/30/09) 1-3MM	3-5MM	62 (10/1/09-3/31/10) 5-10MM	10-25MM	25MM & OVER
41	63	70	**NUMBER OF STATEMENTS**	16	29	10	7	7	1
%	%	%	**ASSETS**	%	%	%	%	%	%
13.2	15.1	16.0	Cash & Equivalents	9.2	15.4	14.8			
22.9	23.6	25.1	Trade Receivables (net)	15.2	24.8	34.3			
1.8	3.5	4.6	Inventory	1.2	7.0	3.5			
1.5	3.5	3.8	All Other Current	8.1	2.5	.5			
39.4	45.7	49.5	Total Current	33.7	49.7	53.1			
37.4	34.0	28.0	Fixed Assets (net)	35.5	26.0	24.4			
13.0	11.2	11.9	Intangibles (net)	22.8	13.6	4.0			
10.2	9.2	10.6	All Other Non-Current	8.1	10.6	18.5			
100.0	100.0	100.0	Total	100.0	100.0	100.0			
			LIABILITIES						
20.1	18.7	22.6	Notes Payable-Short Term	39.0	26.6	6.6			
6.7	5.8	4.6	Cur. Mat.-L.T.D.	1.5	5.2	6.6			
9.2	8.5	9.0	Trade Payables	6.8	9.9	9.3			
.1	.1	.0	Income Taxes Payable	.0	.0	.0			
6.4	10.5	10.3	All Other Current	26.1	4.9	4.4			
42.5	43.7	46.5	Total Current	73.5	46.7	27.0			
38.5	31.5	31.7	Long-Term Debt	49.3	40.3	15.4			
.0	.0	.1	Deferred Taxes	.0	.0	.0			
4.4	4.4	6.2	All Other Non-Current	9.1	8.4	.2			
14.6	20.4	15.5	Net Worth	-31.9	4.7	57.5			
100.0	100.0	100.0	Total Liabilties & Net Worth	100.0	100.0	100.0			
			INCOME DATA						
100.0	100.0	100.0	Net Sales	100.0	100.0	100.0			
			Gross Profit						
93.7	90.9	94.3	Operating Expenses	87.1	96.7	94.3			
6.3	9.1	5.7	Operating Profit	12.9	3.3	5.7			
1.5	1.9	1.0	All Other Expenses (net)	4.0	.5	-1.1			
4.8	7.2	4.7	Profit Before Taxes	8.9	2.7	6.8			
			RATIOS						
2.6	3.0	3.2		2.1	2.6	6.5			
1.0	1.4	1.5	Current	.9	1.5	1.6			
.5	.6	.7		.2	.7	1.1			
1.9	2.7	2.9		1.3	2.7	6.5			
1.0	1.1 (69)	1.2	Quick	.8 (28)	1.2	1.3			
.3	.5	.6		.1	.5	.9			
1 543.3	2 201.4	3 118.2		0 UND	5 69.4	0 UND			
15 24.5	17 21.4	24 15.0	Sales/Receivables	8 46.4	31 11.7	28 13.2			
51 7.2	38 9.5	48 7.6		29 12.8	50 7.3	95 3.8			
			Cost of Sales/Inventory						
			Cost of Sales/Payables						
11.6	9.6	9.1		13.6	9.7	8.3			
UND	36.9	25.0	Sales/Working Capital	NM	21.6	23.0			
-14.3	-19.0	-21.5		-10.6	-17.4	NM			
8.1	17.9	19.6		9.8	11.5	26.2			
(38) 4.0	(58) 6.3	(66) 4.6	EBIT/Interest	(15) 1.5	(28) 3.5	14.6			
1.2	2.8	1.1		-.4	-1.9	7.3			
			Net Profit + Depr., Dep., Amort./Cur. Mat. L/T/D						
.6	.3	.3		.5	.5	.1			
2.2	1.0	.9	Fixed/Worth	NM	2.0	.2			
-2.1	-2.4	-1.6		-.2	-.8	1.0			
1.4	.6	.8		1.7	1.3	.4			
14.2	2.9	1.6	Debt/Worth	NM	5.7	1.0			
-4.8	-7.6	-4.6		-1.4	-3.1	1.4			
68.1	100.8	111.4	% Profit Before Taxes/Tangible Net Worth		355.2	74.5			
(22) 33.6	(43) 54.2	(49) 30.8			(17) 63.9	41.7			
6.6	21.8	8.4			15.6	26.3			
24.9	46.5	27.1	% Profit Before Taxes/Total Assets	83.0	25.6	34.4			
9.8	19.2	9.3		3.2	9.8	23.6			
.9	5.9	-1.2		-8.7	-10.1	8.5			
19.5	36.7	56.6	Sales/Net Fixed Assets	73.3	53.1	61.0			
10.3	13.6	16.7		24.8	13.8	42.9			
6.3	7.7	8.2		9.9	7.1	8.1			
4.8	5.5	5.5	Sales/Total Assets	6.2	5.6	4.9			
3.3	3.7	3.5		4.1	3.2	3.8			
2.0	2.4	2.3		1.8	2.3	2.4			
1.6	1.6	.9	% Depr., Dep., Amort./Sales		1.5				
(30) 2.5	(44) 2.9	(38) 2.6		(14)	3.6				
4.2	4.6	5.2			5.4				
2.3	3.2	3.1	% Officers', Directors' Owners' Comp/Sales	6.3	3.7				
(17) 7.3	(32) 6.6	(46) 6.4		(11) 7.4	(21) 6.2				
10.4	9.5	9.4		13.6	11.4				
182068M	452793M	260805M	Net Sales ($)	8651M	44436M	38195M	46668M	94183M	28672M
70672M	161748M	103130M	Total Assets ($)	4508M	16825M	12549M	19438M	27219M	22591M

M = $ thousand   MM = $ million
See Pages 9 through 22 for Explanation of Ratios and Data

Current Data Sorted by Assets | Comparative Historical Data

0-500M	500M-2MM	2-10MM	10-50MM	50-100MM	100-250MM		4/1/05-3/31/06 ALL	4/1/06-3/31/07 ALL
	2	2	3	1	1	Type of Statement		
						Unqualified	3	7
1	11	13	3			Reviewed	10	12
2	11	3				Compiled	14	19
18	16	3			1	Tax Returns	22	35
12	16	12	3			Other	11	37
	15 (4/1-9/30/09)		119 (10/1/09-3/31/10)					
33	56	33	9	1	2	NUMBER OF STATEMENTS	60	110
%	%	%	%	%	%	ASSETS	%	%
20.1	11.5	11.8				Cash & Equivalents	14.2	13.4
16.5	40.9	37.9				Trade Receivables (net)	36.1	36.7
10.5	7.7	3.8				Inventory	7.8	7.4
3.5	4.1	5.4				All Other Current	3.1	3.6
50.6	64.2	58.9				Total Current	61.1	61.1
26.2	24.7	26.6				Fixed Assets (net)	25.6	25.4
6.9	3.4	5.8				Intangibles (net)	6.8	6.1
16.3	7.7	8.7				All Other Non-Current	6.5	7.4
100.0	100.0	100.0				Total	100.0	100.0
						LIABILITIES		
24.9	11.2	9.8				Notes Payable-Short Term	17.2	12.3
4.8	4.2	4.1				Cur. Mat.-L.T.D.	4.4	4.6
7.4	14.3	14.1				Trade Payables	9.7	13.9
.1	.2	.6				Income Taxes Payable	.1	.2
14.1	14.6	8.6				All Other Current	9.4	13.8
51.3	44.4	37.2				Total Current	40.9	44.7
37.9	18.3	15.2				Long-Term Debt	23.1	22.3
.0	.6	.1				Deferred Taxes	.5	.3
9.6	8.9	5.5				All Other Non-Current	11.2	7.0
1.2	27.9	42.0				Net Worth	24.3	25.6
100.0	100.0	100.0				Total Liabilities & Net Worth	100.0	100.0
						INCOME DATA		
100.0	100.0	100.0				Net Sales	100.0	100.0
						Gross Profit		
93.8	93.3	92.1				Operating Expenses	91.9	91.3
6.2	6.7	7.9				Operating Profit	8.1	8.7
1.1	1.0	1.8				All Other Expenses (net)	1.6	1.7
5.1	5.7	6.1				Profit Before Taxes	6.5	7.0
						RATIOS		
2.9	2.8	3.0					4.0	2.8
1.2	1.6	1.6				Current	1.6	1.4
.7	.9	1.1					1.0	.9
2.4	2.8	2.4					3.0	2.3
.9	1.3	1.2				Quick	1.4	1.1
.4	.7	.9					.7	.7
0 UND	27 13.8	36 10.2					2 165.5	23 16.0
1 292.1	39 9.4	59 6.2				Sales/Receivables	40 9.0	42 8.8
30 12.0	68 5.4	75 4.9					73 5.0	67 5.4
						Cost of Sales/Inventory		
						Cost of Sales/Payables		
9.8	7.4	5.1					6.3	8.1
70.1	13.5	8.9				Sales/Working Capital	16.7	16.6
-59.5	-116.7	47.6					253.4	-164.5
16.4	20.8	10.5					12.1	20.0
(26) 3.4	(49) 8.1	(28) 2.6				EBIT/Interest	(50) 3.8	(95) 5.3
.2	2.8	1.2					1.3	2.1
		3.8						10.1
	(12)	2.1				Net Profit + Depr., Dep., Amort./Cur. Mat. L/T/D	(11)	6.6
		-.3						3.1
.1	.1	.2					.2	.3
3.4	.7	.6				Fixed/Worth	.7	1.0
-.9	4.3	1.9					6.9	6.7
.8	.7	.8					.8	.7
19.2	1.9	1.9				Debt/Worth	3.0	2.8
-2.8	38.3	3.9					45.3	35.7
231.3	58.7	62.2				% Profit Before Taxes/Tangible Net Worth	69.6	138.7
(19) 93.5	(44) 35.4	(31) 12.7					(47) 28.0	(87) 47.8
32.9	4.2	.2					4.2	17.0
54.8	27.4	16.1				% Profit Before Taxes/Total Assets	22.9	35.4
18.5	11.8	6.6					7.0	13.5
-2.4	1.8	.2					1.0	4.1
280.6	81.0	50.4					38.1	38.3
36.4	23.6	14.1				Sales/Net Fixed Assets	20.5	17.2
12.5	10.6	4.1					7.9	7.3
8.4	5.0	3.1					4.8	4.5
5.2	3.4	2.3				Sales/Total Assets	3.0	2.9
3.4	2.3	1.1					2.3	2.0
1.1	.7	.8					.8	.7
(13) 3.1	(39) 1.5	(28) 1.5				% Depr., Dep., Amort./Sales	(48) 1.6	(81) 1.7
4.9	3.1	5.6					4.7	4.0
6.8	3.6	1.2					4.2	2.0
(19) 8.5	(37) 6.5	(10) 3.9				% Officers', Directors' Owners' Comp/Sales	(30) 8.7	(53) 4.3
14.0	10.5	5.6					15.0	8.8
47297M	230618M	316839M	437334M	110227M	2051527M	Net Sales ($)	353092M	1137677M
7137M	59377M	137253M	191359M	87322M	424021M	Total Assets ($)	162412M	433228M

M = $ thousand   MM = $ million
See Pages 9 through 22 for Explanation of Ratios and Data

Comparative Historical Data | Current Data Sorted by Sales

4/1/07-3/31/08	4/1/08-3/31/09	4/1/09-3/31/10	Type of Statement	0-1MM	1-3MM	3-5MM	5-10MM	10-25MM	25MM & OVER
5	7	9	Unqualified		2			4	3
16	19	28	Reviewed		8	3	6	8	3
18	20	16	Compiled	1	7	3	3	2	
41	43	38	Tax Returns	13	14	5	4	1	1
28	49	43	Other	6	14	5	11	4	3
ALL	ALL	ALL		15 (4/1-9/30/09)			119 (10/1/09-3/31/10)		
108	138	134	**NUMBER OF STATEMENTS**	20	45	16	24	19	10
%	%	%	**ASSETS**	%	%	%	%	%	%
16.2	13.0	14.3	Cash & Equivalents	16.5	16.4	7.8	8.4	16.4	20.6
32.2	32.0	33.0	Trade Receivables (net)	7.8	29.9	44.0	47.2	36.2	39.8
5.8	5.7	7.2	Inventory	10.7	7.2	.8	8.7	10.0	1.6
5.7	4.9	4.2	All Other Current	.6	5.5	1.7	6.5	4.3	3.5
60.0	55.7	58.7	Total Current	35.6	59.1	54.4	70.8	67.0	65.5
29.6	31.0	25.6	Fixed Assets (net)	39.0	27.1	30.7	14.0	20.8	21.0
3.3	3.8	6.0	Intangibles (net)	8.8	3.6	4.9	7.3	6.2	9.8
7.2	9.5	9.6	All Other Non-Current	16.7	10.1	10.1	7.9	6.1	3.6
100.0	100.0	100.0	Total	100.0	100.0	100.0	100.0	100.0	100.0
			LIABILITIES						
17.5	13.7	13.4	Notes Payable-Short Term	16.4	17.1	10.3	11.8	12.1	1.6
4.8	5.5	4.2	Cur. Mat.-L.T.D.	4.9	4.2	4.9	3.5	4.4	2.9
11.6	11.9	12.1	Trade Payables	2.9	9.3	8.7	21.4	19.4	12.3
.1	.1	.3	Income Taxes Payable	.0	.2	.1	.6	.3	.4
16.4	12.6	13.1	All Other Current	5.4	13.3	19.2	13.0	11.1	21.3
50.4	43.8	43.0	Total Current	29.5	44.1	43.3	50.3	47.3	38.5
21.1	22.0	22.1	Long-Term Debt	42.0	22.9	25.4	8.9	20.0	9.4
.2	.1	.3	Deferred Taxes	.0	.6	.1	.2	.2	.2
6.7	4.8	8.0	All Other Non-Current	15.3	5.6	.7	7.4	13.1	7.1
21.6	29.3	26.6	Net Worth	13.0	26.8	30.5	33.2	19.4	44.8
100.0	100.0	100.0	Total Liabilities & Net Worth	100.0	100.0	100.0	100.0	100.0	100.0
			INCOME DATA						
100.0	100.0	100.0	Net Sales	100.0	100.0	100.0	100.0	100.0	100.0
			Gross Profit						
92.9	91.8	92.7	Operating Expenses	87.5	92.9	92.3	96.6	95.5	88.5
7.1	8.2	7.3	Operating Profit	12.5	7.1	7.7	3.4	4.5	11.5
2.3	2.4	1.1	All Other Expenses (net)	5.2	.5	1.6	.0	-.3	.5
4.8	5.8	6.1	Profit Before Taxes	7.3	6.6	6.0	3.4	4.8	11.0
			RATIOS						
2.4	2.3	2.9		4.9	4.0	3.1	2.5	2.5	2.8
1.4	1.4	1.6	Current	1.3	1.7	1.5	1.7	1.5	1.5
.8	.8	.9		.6	.8	.9	1.1	1.0	1.2
1.9	2.0	2.5		4.5	4.0	2.8	2.4	2.0	2.4
1.0	1.0	1.3	Quick	.9	1.4	1.5	1.3	1.2	1.3
.5	.5	.7		.5	.7	.9	.7	.8	1.1
8 47.4	9 41.0	9 41.7		0 UND	12 30.9	30 12.2	26 13.8	32 11.4	14 27.0
37 9.9	34 10.7	37 10.0	Sales/Receivables	0 UND	34 10.7	53 6.9	45 8.2	38 9.5	63 5.8
54 6.7	61 5.9	66 5.5		32 11.3	68 5.3	95 3.8	64 5.7	61 6.0	75 4.9
			Cost of Sales/Inventory						
			Cost of Sales/Payables						
7.7	7.7	6.9		4.0	7.0	5.9	7.6	6.4	8.6
27.4	23.0	14.8	Sales/Working Capital	109.8	14.6	13.9	15.8	12.8	18.2
-41.6	-26.3	-244.0		-26.7	-95.7	-111.1	76.4	-999.8	33.5
15.9	19.8	18.7		10.4	16.0	16.2	39.8	10.8	
(93) 5.5	(119) 5.6	(113) 5.6	EBIT/Interest	(13) 1.6	(37) 5.2	(14) 6.9	(23) 6.5	(17) 2.7	
1.7	1.6	1.4		-2.2	1.2	-.5	1.7	.8	
6.0	13.2	7.7	Net Profit + Depr., Dep.,						
(14) 3.1	(20) 2.5	(21) 2.5	Amort./Cur. Mat. L/T/D						
.5	.8	.5							
.3	.3	.2		.5	.1	.3	.1	.3	.2
.7	1.0	.7	Fixed/Worth	3.7	.6	1.1	.3	.5	.5
2.8	6.6	5.8		-1.9	3.7	-7.7	UND	1.4	NM
.7	.8	.7		1.3	.5	.6	.7	.8	.6
1.9	2.5	2.0	Debt/Worth	15.2	1.7	2.1	1.9	2.0	1.6
9.4	33.5	48.2		-2.9	4.9	-24.7	UND	9.1	NM
71.2	83.3	87.7	% Profit Before Taxes/Tangible	178.6	83.5	46.0	131.2	58.3	
(85) 35.1	(106) 32.1	(104) 36.8	Net Worth	(12) 33.2	(37) 44.9	(11) 31.5	(18) 39.5	(18) 15.1	
11.2	10.6	5.4		5.4	1.5	.2	14.9	-.9	
30.3	25.3	27.9	% Profit Before Taxes/Total	28.5	29.3	27.7	50.8	15.0	60.2
13.1	12.8	11.7	Assets	4.6	11.8	19.3	11.3	6.8	12.6
2.0	1.6	.8		-2.9	.4	-2.3	3.7	.2	7.7
49.6	45.5	72.3		100.8	46.8	57.1	266.7	59.3	80.9
15.1	17.0	22.1	Sales/Net Fixed Assets	13.8	20.3	10.8	39.3	21.5	29.8
6.7	6.1	8.7		2.2	8.3	6.2	18.4	8.3	10.5
5.4	5.1	5.2		4.4	5.1	6.2	7.3	3.6	5.6
3.3	3.1	3.1	Sales/Total Assets	2.8	3.1	3.2	4.2	2.9	3.4
2.1	1.9	1.9		.6	1.8	1.7	2.8	2.2	1.5
.9	1.0	.8		3.1	.9	1.1	.2	.8	
(79) 2.2	(103) 2.3	(87) 1.6	% Depr., Dep., Amort./Sales	(10) 7.8	(26) 1.7	(13) 3.1	(17) 1.4	(16) 1.4	
5.3	5.2	4.0		20.9	4.3	4.7	1.6	4.6	
2.8	2.3	3.4	% Officers', Directors'	4.2	6.6		2.8		
(67) 6.1	(66) 4.7	(68) 6.8	Owners' Comp/Sales	(11) 8.6	(28) 7.3		(10) 4.8		
10.9	10.2	11.0		21.3	11.0		8.6		
1473264M	1859301M	3193842M	Net Sales ($)	8187M	93739M	65019M	175898M	280481M	2570518M
467105M	708136M	906469M	Total Assets ($)	9475M	39685M	27116M	49851M	134526M	645816M

M = $ thousand   MM = $ million
See Pages 9 through 22 for Explanation of Ratios and Data

Current Data Sorted by Assets | Comparative Historical Data

						Type of Statement		
		4	3	1	1	Unqualified	4	3
	2	5	2			Reviewed	10	11
2	6	4				Compiled	3	5
6	9	1				Tax Returns	4	7
5	12	15	8	1	1	Other	12	24
	15 (4/1-9/30/09)		73 (10/1/09-3/31/10)				4/1/05-3/31/06	4/1/06-3/31/07
0-500M	500M-2MM	2-10MM	10-50MM	50-100MM	100-250MM		ALL	ALL
13	29	29	13	2	2	NUMBER OF STATEMENTS	33	50
%	%	%	%	%	%	ASSETS	%	%
21.3	10.6	5.8	3.5			Cash & Equivalents	8.1	10.8
18.8	26.5	26.8	26.5			Trade Receivables (net)	29.1	28.7
3.0	14.3	14.8	15.8			Inventory	16.1	13.4
2.0	3.2	2.4	2.2			All Other Current	1.0	3.2
45.2	54.6	49.7	47.9			Total Current	54.3	56.2
32.2	34.1	34.3	36.6			Fixed Assets (net)	33.1	33.0
6.7	3.5	11.8	9.1			Intangibles (net)	6.5	6.6
16.0	7.8	4.2	6.3			All Other Non-Current	6.1	4.1
100.0	100.0	100.0	100.0			Total	100.0	100.0
						LIABILITIES		
37.2	13.6	10.2	12.4			Notes Payable-Short Term	13.9	15.0
3.9	2.3	4.5	6.6			Cur. Mat.-L.T.D.	3.9	3.5
34.0	12.5	14.2	14.8			Trade Payables	22.2	20.7
.0	.1	.0	.6			Income Taxes Payable	.2	.1
54.4	6.4	13.0	6.2			All Other Current	7.6	12.8
129.4	34.9	41.9	40.7			Total Current	47.8	52.1
37.2	27.8	22.3	24.8			Long-Term Debt	23.3	21.7
.0	.0	.1	.0			Deferred Taxes	.2	.1
17.1	4.4	6.7	6.4			All Other Non-Current	3.2	7.1
-83.6	32.9	29.0	28.1			Net Worth	25.5	18.9
100.0	100.0	100.0	100.0			Total Liabilties & Net Worth	100.0	100.0
						INCOME DATA		
100.0	100.0	100.0	100.0			Net Sales	100.0	100.0
						Gross Profit		
89.7	93.0	91.2	92.3			Operating Expenses	94.0	92.7
10.3	7.0	8.8	7.7			Operating Profit	6.0	7.3
.8	2.6	6.4	1.9			All Other Expenses (net)	2.2	4.2
9.5	4.5	2.3	5.8			Profit Before Taxes	3.8	3.0
						RATIOS		
1.1	4.9	2.2	1.6				1.5	1.5
.4	1.6	1.4	1.3			Current	1.1	1.1
.2	1.0	.8	1.1				.9	.8
.6	2.5	1.5	1.2				1.4	1.3
.4	1.1	.9	.7			Quick	.7	.8
.2	.5	.4	.6				.5	.4
0 UND	24 15.3	33 11.0	38 9.5				27 13.4	22 16.5
1 347.0	32 11.3	41 8.9	54 6.8			Sales/Receivables	38 9.6	43 8.4
21 17.3	53 6.8	50 7.2	64 5.7				50 7.3	63 5.8
						Cost of Sales/Inventory		
						Cost of Sales/Payables		
NM	6.0	7.7	8.0				13.7	10.7
-14.4	8.9	13.3	16.6			Sales/Working Capital	62.5	50.2
-4.0	NM	-14.6	NM				-45.1	-55.7
	7.6	8.6	6.5				10.7	9.9
(21) 2.0	(23) 2.8	5.5			EBIT/Interest	(27) 4.5	(41) 2.9
	-.5	.6	1.0				1.6	.8
						Net Profit + Depr., Dep., Amort./Cur. Mat. L/T/D		
.4	.3	.4	.9				.7	.4
-17.4	1.4	1.0	1.3			Fixed/Worth	1.7	1.6
-.3	8.7	NM	4.8				5.4	15.6
1.3	.5	1.0	1.3				1.0	2.5
-9.5	2.2	1.9	5.4			Debt/Worth	5.5	5.1
-1.4	10.9	NM	12.5				224.4	NM
	31.5	61.2	123.8				126.3	98.8
(23) 16.1	(22) 20.4	(12) 51.2			% Profit Before Taxes/Tangible Net Worth	(26) 42.1	(38) 37.4
	3.2	6.4	3.4				8.3	2.8
55.7	16.3	13.9	19.0				18.8	14.2
29.7	4.2	5.9	10.3			% Profit Before Taxes/Total Assets	6.7	5.1
-2.9	-1.6	-.1	-.8				2.7	.6
182.7	28.7	25.4	15.7				22.9	33.6
16.7	9.7	7.9	4.2			Sales/Net Fixed Assets	10.0	9.5
6.6	5.1	2.9	2.7				4.6	3.8
9.2	4.1	3.3	2.6				4.4	4.0
5.6	2.7	2.0	1.9			Sales/Total Assets	2.6	2.2
3.7	1.3	1.2	1.4				1.8	1.5
	1.4	1.1	1.4				1.3	1.1
(23) 4.1	(24) 3.0	3.0			% Depr., Dep., Amort./Sales	(28) 2.1	(39) 1.7
	9.5	6.5	4.2				4.6	4.0
	3.6						2.3	1.7
(14) 8.9					% Officers', Directors' Owners' Comp/Sales	(11) 3.3	(13) 3.6
	16.2						5.6	6.0
13066M	92233M	313581M	444807M	173934M	960412M	Net Sales ($)	766431M	1740996M
2019M	35340M	154462M	219780M	145200M	268412M	Total Assets ($)	380924M	688436M

© RMA 2010

M = $ thousand   MM = $ million
See Pages 9 through 22 for Explanation of Ratios and Data

Comparative Historical Data

Current Data Sorted by Sales

			Type of Statement						
5	10	9	Unqualified				1	3	4
5	12	9	Reviewed			1	1	6	1
5	10	12	Compiled	3	3	2	1	2	1
9	12	16	Tax Returns	6	6	3	1		
21	19	42	Other	8	6	7	5	10	6
4/1/07-3/31/08	4/1/08-3/31/09	4/1/09-3/31/10			15 (4/1-9/30/09)		73 (10/1/09-3/31/10)		
ALL	ALL	ALL		0-1MM	1-3MM	3-5MM	5-10MM	10-25MM	25MM & OVER
45	63	88	**NUMBER OF STATEMENTS**	17	15	14	9	21	12
%	%	%	**ASSETS**	%	%	%	%	%	%
7.5	8.3	9.4	Cash & Equivalents	12.0	15.0	9.6		7.0	3.7
25.6	29.3	25.0	Trade Receivables (net)	9.6	24.8	27.4		31.7	27.8
14.6	16.3	13.4	Inventory	5.4	12.9	8.8		17.7	22.7
3.0	4.7	2.5	All Other Current	1.0	3.5	2.1		2.4	1.9
50.7	58.7	50.4	Total Current	28.0	56.2	48.0		58.8	56.1
34.1	30.9	34.2	Fixed Assets (net)	50.5	30.2	35.3		32.0	27.6
9.2	4.4	8.0	Intangibles (net)	3.0	10.2	9.6		5.4	11.4
6.0	6.0	7.4	All Other Non-Current	18.5	3.4	7.1		3.8	4.9
100.0	100.0	100.0	Total	100.0	100.0	100.0		100.0	100.0
			LIABILITIES						
12.7	14.9	15.4	Notes Payable-Short Term	28.0	5.2	21.3		11.8	12.0
3.7	5.7	4.1	Cur. Mat.-L.T.D.	3.4	2.9	2.4		4.8	7.4
15.3	21.2	16.6	Trade Payables	25.4	11.6	12.6		17.7	16.9
.0	.1	.1	Income Taxes Payable	.0	.0	.0		.4	.1
13.4	15.0	15.6	All Other Current	32.9	14.0	5.0		8.5	6.0
45.2	56.9	51.8	Total Current	89.8	33.7	41.3		43.1	42.3
31.8	19.7	27.0	Long-Term Debt	43.3	39.2	17.9		17.8	17.3
.1	.2	.1	Deferred Taxes	.0	.0	.0		.2	.1
10.3	4.7	7.5	All Other Non-Current	13.1	5.8	6.1		6.6	8.1
12.7	18.6	13.7	Net Worth	-46.2	21.3	34.7		32.3	32.2
100.0	100.0	100.0	Total Liabilities & Net Worth	100.0	100.0	100.0		100.0	100.0
			INCOME DATA						
100.0	100.0	100.0	Net Sales	100.0	100.0	100.0		100.0	100.0
			Gross Profit						
86.4	95.0	91.8	Operating Expenses	75.4	94.9	96.9		94.5	92.8
13.6	5.0	8.2	Operating Profit	24.6	5.1	3.1		5.5	7.2
6.1	2.9	3.5	All Other Expenses (net)	14.1	.3	.2		1.0	1.9
7.5	2.1	4.8	Profit Before Taxes	10.4	4.8	2.9		4.4	5.3
			RATIOS						
1.5	1.9	2.2		1.5	3.6	4.3		2.2	1.9
1.1	1.2	1.3	Current	.5	2.0	1.2		1.4	1.3
.8	.8	.8		.2	1.3	.8		1.0	1.0
1.1	1.2	1.5		.9	2.3	4.2		1.5	1.4
.7	.7	.8	Quick	.5	1.4	.8		.9	.6
.5	.4	.5		.2	.6	.4		.6	.5
26 14.0	25 14.4	24 15.0		0 UND	27 13.4	26 14.2		36 10.1	33 11.2
43 8.5	36 10.1	36 10.1	Sales/Receivables	0 UND	36 10.2	42 8.6		42 8.7	39 9.4
64 5.7	59 6.2	51 7.1		21 17.3	56 6.5	57 6.5		60 6.1	54 6.8
			Cost of Sales/Inventory						
			Cost of Sales/Payables						
10.8	10.9	7.7		31.1	5.6	7.8		7.9	8.3
28.0	36.0	20.3	Sales/Working Capital	-14.3	6.7	42.9		13.3	18.5
-21.0	-14.8	-19.5		-4.0	19.8	-10.6		NM	NM
10.2	10.7	7.9			6.5	28.6		6.3	13.1
(34) 1.9	(54) 3.0	(69) 2.8	EBIT/Interest		(13) 2.0	(13) 6.7	(18) 3.0		(11) 5.9
.4	-.1	.8			-.2	-.4		1.6	2.6
		9.1	Net Profit + Depr., Dep.,						
		(14) 4.8	Amort./Cur. Mat. L/T/D						
		1.2							
.4	.4	.5		.8	.5	.5		.3	.5
2.0	1.3	1.4	Fixed/Worth	6.4	1.4	1.4		.8	2.1
-20.6	-13.2	NM		-10.9	-.6	NM		6.0	5.8
2.0	1.0	.9		1.3	.6	.7		1.0	1.9
4.1	3.3	3.6	Debt/Worth	9.4	2.2	2.2		1.9	8.2
-7.1	-36.5	-48.4		-6.1	-2.5	NM		10.1	12.6
87.8	54.6	62.7		193.0	38.8	43.8		62.6	137.4
(32) 32.5	(45) 27.3	(65) 23.2	% Profit Before Taxes/Tangible Net Worth	(10) 4.9	(11) 18.9	(11) 28.9	(18) 26.4		(11) 59.1
1.4	3.5	3.8		-2.4	.2	-38.3		11.1	20.6
17.1	16.1	16.3		35.4	14.5	26.8		15.0	15.3
7.0	4.9	8.0	% Profit Before Taxes/Total Assets	4.2	2.1	14.2		9.0	10.4
.2	-3.1	.2		.3	-3.4	-4.9		3.0	5.6
36.7	26.4	21.4		20.6	27.2	26.5		25.4	31.4
8.5	11.3	8.8	Sales/Net Fixed Assets	6.5	11.9	8.8		7.9	13.6
3.2	4.7	4.1		.3	3.0	5.8		4.1	4.0
2.7	3.5	4.1		5.4	4.3	4.7		3.4	3.9
2.1	2.6	2.4	Sales/Total Assets	2.9	2.3	2.7		2.1	2.4
1.4	1.9	1.4		.2	1.2	1.7		1.6	1.5
.8	1.3	1.3		2.1	1.7			.9	.6
(37) 2.0	(51) 2.7	(70) 2.8	% Depr., Dep., Amort./Sales	(11) 8.3	(14) 4.4		(19) 1.8		1.5
6.3	3.7	6.2		21.0	8.8			3.5	4.0
1.7	2.9	2.3							
(11) 3.7	(17) 4.1	(28) 5.4	% Officers', Directors' Owners' Comp/Sales						
8.6	8.9	11.7							
1161827M	1829259M	1998033M	Net Sales ($)	9117M	30330M	56622M	62455M	333023M	1506486M
635369M	568382M	825213M	Total Assets ($)	20100M	17523M	29457M	30586M	170882M	556665M

M = $ thousand   MM = $ million
See Pages 9 through 22 for Explanation of Ratios and Data

Current Data Sorted by Assets   Comparative Historical Data

						Type of Statement		
1	2	12	7	2	6	Unqualified	24	24
	6	20	3			Reviewed	8	11
8	8	11	1		1	Compiled	9	12
27	21	16	1			Tax Returns	17	24
24	23	29	13	9	4	Other	24	54
	35 (4/1-9/30/09)		220 (10/1/09-3/31/10)				4/1/05-3/31/06	4/1/06-3/31/07
0-500M	500M-2MM	2-10MM	10-50MM	50-100MM	100-250MM		ALL	ALL
60	60	88	25	11	11	**NUMBER OF STATEMENTS**	82	125
%	%	%	%	%	%	**ASSETS**	%	%
19.4	16.5	15.3	15.0	7.2	14.4	Cash & Equivalents	15.7	15.3
21.2	23.6	26.4	24.5	21.1	18.9	Trade Receivables (net)	31.4	28.9
9.5	6.1	11.8	1.7	2.9	2.6	Inventory	8.6	8.3
2.3	3.0	4.9	5.5	6.3	16.8	All Other Current	5.4	4.3
52.4	49.0	58.4	46.7	37.6	52.8	Total Current	61.2	56.8
28.6	33.8	30.6	21.9	16.2	9.9	Fixed Assets (net)	24.8	28.2
6.5	8.0	2.7	23.3	42.7	26.5	Intangibles (net)	7.5	6.8
12.4	9.1	8.3	8.1	3.5	10.9	All Other Non-Current	6.6	8.3
100.0	100.0	100.0	100.0	100.0	100.0	Total	100.0	100.0
						LIABILITIES		
31.6	13.4	8.2	4.8	2.5	1.9	Notes Payable-Short Term	9.6	10.5
5.1	1.7	3.9	5.4	1.3	.9	Cur. Mat.-L.T.D.	2.7	4.2
11.0	8.8	13.8	10.5	6.7	9.1	Trade Payables	15.1	13.3
.2	.0	.4	.6	2.0	1.6	Income Taxes Payable	1.2	.5
19.0	14.5	14.7	13.1	14.6	20.2	All Other Current	12.4	14.6
66.8	38.4	41.0	34.4	27.1	33.7	Total Current	41.0	43.2
23.0	18.2	19.9	20.3	24.2	15.7	Long-Term Debt	14.6	17.6
.0	.2	.5	1.0	.5	1.6	Deferred Taxes	.8	.7
11.5	9.3	5.6	2.6	6.8	15.4	All Other Non-Current	4.9	7.0
-1.4	33.9	32.9	41.7	41.4	33.7	Net Worth	38.7	31.6
100.0	100.0	100.0	100.0	100.0	100.0	Total Liabilities & Net Worth	100.0	100.0
						INCOME DATA		
100.0	100.0	100.0	100.0	100.0	100.0	Net Sales	100.0	100.0
						Gross Profit		
92.3	94.9	90.2	92.3	95.5	88.1	Operating Expenses	91.7	92.3
7.7	5.1	9.8	7.7	4.5	11.9	Operating Profit	8.3	7.7
.8	2.4	3.0	2.9	1.4	.3	All Other Expenses (net)	1.1	1.0
7.0	2.6	6.8	4.8	3.0	11.6	Profit Before Taxes	7.3	6.7
						RATIOS		
2.1	3.0	2.8	2.4	2.6	2.3	Current	2.4	2.4
.9	1.3	1.3	1.4	1.9	1.4		1.4	1.2
.5	.6	.9	.9	.9	1.0		1.0	.9
1.3	2.7	2.1	2.3	1.9	2.2	Quick	1.9	1.8
.7	1.0	.9	1.1	1.1	1.1		(81) 1.1	1.0
.4	.4	.5	.7	.7	.4		.7	.6
0 UND	0 UND	9 41.9	21 17.4	44 8.3	15 24.0	Sales/Receivables	17 21.9	11 32.2
14 26.0	19 18.7	31 11.9	43 8.4	51 7.1	37 9.8		38 9.6	37 10.0
36 10.2	40 9.0	50 7.3	62 5.9	73 5.0	64 5.7		63 5.8	62 5.8
						Cost of Sales/Inventory		
						Cost of Sales/Payables		
14.5	8.2	7.5	6.6	6.0	3.8	Sales/Working Capital	7.2	7.7
-121.8	30.2	17.9	13.0	23.3	11.0		15.7	33.9
-9.9	-16.0	-47.3	-81.5	-23.1	-620.2		-128.9	-91.1
18.5	8.4	23.0	33.4		16.7	EBIT/Interest	29.1	16.0
(44) 3.2	(40) 2.6	(73) 4.6	(23) 4.3		(10) 3.6		(68) 7.1	(106) 3.1
-1.9	-.2	1.4	.6		.8		1.9	1.1
		8.0				Net Profit + Depr., Dep., Amort./Cur. Mat. L/T/D	43.5	9.1
		(15) 3.0					(15) 6.6	(18) 2.1
		1.6					2.0	1.6
.1	.2	.2	.3	.5	.4	Fixed/Worth	.1	.1
.9	.9	.8	1.2	3.5	.9		.7	.8
-.9	34.1	4.0	-.6	-.3	-.2		2.5	3.5
.9	.7	.8	.9	3.2	2.3	Debt/Worth	.8	.8
11.1	2.3	2.4	3.8	35.7	6.3		1.8	2.8
-2.8	-271.8	8.3	-4.7	-1.7	-5.3		9.9	22.3
98.5	45.0	58.6	61.7			% Profit Before Taxes/Tangible Net Worth	91.7	89.4
(32) 47.8	(44) 13.0	(76) 24.7	(17) 22.8				(67) 38.6	(102) 40.6
-9.3	.0	5.3	2.2				11.1	10.8
53.7	13.5	20.3	17.7	14.3	9.2	% Profit Before Taxes/Total Assets	24.5	25.8
6.2	1.9	8.1	8.5	4.8	6.8		13.3	9.0
-8.5	-5.0	1.0	-.6	-2.0	-.6		2.4	.8
121.4	87.2	46.9	53.2	52.7	124.1	Sales/Net Fixed Assets	116.9	91.8
22.6	14.0	14.1	23.9	8.3	19.9		18.2	14.6
8.2	3.9	4.0	5.7	3.5	4.0		5.0	4.9
7.6	5.1	4.0	2.7	1.6	2.9	Sales/Total Assets	4.3	4.4
4.2	2.4	2.3	1.3	1.1	.8		2.5	2.6
2.4	1.2	1.3	.7	.8	.6		1.5	1.5
.5	.6	.5	.5			% Depr., Dep., Amort./Sales	.6	1.1
(30) 1.9	(40) 2.4	(68) 2.2	(22) 1.8				(63) 2.1	(93) 2.5
3.7	6.6	4.9	5.1				4.8	6.6
2.9	2.2	2.4				% Officers', Directors' Owners' Comp/Sales	3.9	2.8
(27) 9.2	(26) 4.5	(29) 4.1					(29) 7.9	(47) 6.9
13.3	7.0	7.6					11.1	11.2
76169M	282582M	1232844M	965076M	1067865M	3567905M	Net Sales ($)	2885423M	4040409M
14101M	67795M	398381M	498804M	750881M	1925116M	Total Assets ($)	1677487M	2392592M

M = $ thousand   MM = $ million
See Pages 9 through 22 for Explanation of Ratios and Data

Comparative Historical Data | Current Data Sorted by Sales

			Type of Statement						
			Unqualified	2	3	2	1	7	15
			Reviewed		2	2	4	18	3
			Compiled	8	9	1	3	5	3
			Tax Returns	26	16	6	9	7	1
			Other	18	26	7	14	12	25
24	38	30							
12	26	29							
14	23	29							
24	48	65							
45	61	102							
4/1/07-3/31/08 ALL	4/1/08-3/31/09 ALL	4/1/09-3/31/10 ALL			35 (4/1-9/30/09)		220 (10/1/09-3/31/10)		
				0-1MM	1-3MM	3-5MM	5-10MM	10-25MM	25MM & OVER
119	196	255	NUMBER OF STATEMENTS	54	56	18	31	49	47
%	%	%	ASSETS	%	%	%	%	%	%
13.8	17.3	16.1	Cash & Equivalents	14.0	16.8	24.4	12.6	14.8	18.2
29.7	26.3	23.8	Trade Receivables (net)	15.0	21.1	13.2	30.1	33.1	27.3
7.8	7.8	8.1	Inventory	6.1	10.2	8.5	10.2	10.3	4.2
5.4	5.5	4.5	All Other Current	1.7	4.1	7.7	1.9	3.9	9.2
56.7	56.9	52.5	Total Current	36.8	52.2	53.7	54.9	62.1	58.9
27.3	25.6	28.5	Fixed Assets (net)	47.7	28.3	24.7	31.0	19.9	15.7
7.4	8.5	9.6	Intangibles (net)	2.8	9.3	10.2	5.6	11.2	18.6
8.6	9.0	9.4	All Other Non-Current	12.7	10.3	11.3	8.6	6.8	6.8
100.0	100.0	100.0	Total	100.0	100.0	100.0	100.0	100.0	100.0
			LIABILITIES						
9.5	8.9	14.1	Notes Payable-Short Term	23.0	17.5	12.5	17.2	7.3	5.4
3.5	3.9	3.6	Cur. Mat.-L.T.D.	5.3	2.1	4.1	4.7	4.5	1.3
14.9	13.5	11.1	Trade Payables	7.8	11.4	6.9	10.0	12.1	16.0
.4	.4	.4	Income Taxes Payable	.0	.0	.8	.1	.6	1.2
16.4	16.0	15.8	All Other Current	16.5	12.1	17.6	13.7	16.7	19.0
44.7	42.7	44.9	Total Current	52.5	43.2	41.8	45.6	41.2	42.9
22.1	19.8	20.3	Long-Term Debt	38.2	20.7	7.6	16.9	13.8	13.1
.7	.6	.4	Deferred Taxes	.0	.3	.5	.3	.4	1.1
4.2	9.5	8.1	All Other Non-Current	9.8	14.0	1.3	3.4	4.7	8.2
28.4	27.5	26.3	Net Worth	-.5	21.8	48.8	33.9	40.0	34.8
100.0	100.0	100.0	Total Liabilties & Net Worth	100.0	100.0	100.0	100.0	100.0	100.0
			INCOME DATA						
100.0	100.0	100.0	Net Sales	100.0	100.0	100.0	100.0	100.0	100.0
			Gross Profit						
88.3	91.2	92.2	Operating Expenses	83.7	95.4	96.9	96.5	91.4	94.2
11.7	8.8	7.8	Operating Profit	16.3	4.6	3.1	3.5	8.6	5.8
2.9	1.9	2.1	All Other Expenses (net)	6.5	.7	.2	1.1	2.1	.2
8.9	6.9	5.7	Profit Before Taxes	9.8	3.8	2.9	2.4	6.5	5.7
			RATIOS						
2.5	2.4	2.6		2.0	2.9	4.2	2.1	2.7	2.5
1.3	1.3	1.3	Current	.8	1.2	1.3	1.3	1.5	1.3
.8	.8	.8		.4	.7	.7	.8	.9	1.0
2.3	1.9	2.0		1.7	1.8	3.0	2.1	2.0	2.0
1.0	1.1	.9	Quick	.5	.9	1.1	1.0	1.0	1.1
.5	.5	.4		.2	.4	.3	.5	.7	.7
12 31.6	9 41.4	3 119.5		0 UND	1 324.9	0 UND	11 32.6	17 21.8	14 26.1
45 8.2	33 11.1	27 13.7	Sales/Receivables	12 31.1	23 15.9	21 17.6	36 10.2	31 11.6	32 11.4
70 5.2	55 6.7	48 7.5		44 8.3	45 8.0	41 8.9	52 7.0	48 7.7	60 6.1
			Cost of Sales/Inventory						
			Cost of Sales/Payables						
6.3	7.8	8.8		9.0	8.3	4.3	9.0	8.2	9.0
18.9	25.2	27.9	Sales/Working Capital	-28.4	35.9	44.8	38.8	15.9	23.3
-26.4	-52.1	-22.1		-5.2	-17.8	-22.2	-19.9	-81.5	-365.5
11.4	21.9	18.1		19.3	3.9	14.3	10.9	31.6	30.4
(87) 4.4	(161) 3.8	(198) 3.7	EBIT/Interest	(39) 3.7	(36) 1.8	(12) 1.2	(30) 3.3	(43) 8.2	(38) 3.8
1.1	1.2	.4		.9	-.7	-29.2	-1.0	2.4	.4
12.7	5.6	11.1						7.3	67.7
(17) 5.5	(31) 1.6	(29) 3.2	Net Profit + Depr., Dep., Amort./Cur. Mat. L/T/D					(12) 2.6	(11) 3.2
1.5	.4	1.7						1.3	1.7
.2	.2	.2		.3	.1	.2	.3	.2	.3
.9	.8	.9	Fixed/Worth	1.7	1.0	.9	1.1	.5	.8
8.3	7.1	-6.0		-3.6	-1.3	4.8	2.9	8.7	-.9
1.0	.9	.8		.9	.8	.2	.9	.7	1.5
3.6	3.1	3.2	Debt/Worth	5.9	6.4	1.1	2.4	2.3	3.8
15.7	42.7	-8.8		-4.7	-5.0	10.2	6.4	16.4	-10.0
78.9	89.1	60.0		73.6	55.8	24.2	47.6	66.7	73.1
(95) 34.3	(151) 32.0	(181) 23.3	% Profit Before Taxes/Tangible Net Worth	(34) 10.9	(31) 16.1	(15) 18.6	(29) 22.6	(39) 32.9	(33) 33.6
11.0	5.3	2.5		-.2	-1.0	-30.3	-14.8	14.1	13.0
24.1	21.1	20.3		29.4	14.8	15.6	21.9	32.6	14.4
9.1	8.2	6.4	% Profit Before Taxes/Total Assets	5.0	1.9	4.4	2.6	10.8	7.2
.9	.7	-1.7		-4.2	-5.2	-13.6	-5.7	4.2	-.6
41.5	99.0	74.6		31.9	75.1	87.8	40.3	93.8	88.7
15.1	17.1	15.1	Sales/Net Fixed Assets	5.7	17.2	14.4	12.2	22.9	31.7
4.5	5.8	5.2		.4	5.2	6.9	4.1	9.9	8.3
3.8	4.3	4.7		3.0	5.1	5.6	5.0	6.5	5.3
2.2	2.6	2.4	Sales/Total Assets	1.5	2.4	2.6	2.6	2.9	2.9
1.3	1.2	1.1		.2	1.1	.7	1.8	2.0	1.0
.8	.6	.5		1.9	.9	.2	1.1	.4	.3
(84) 2.0	(143) 2.1	(176) 2.3	% Depr., Dep., Amort./Sales	(33) 6.0	(32) 2.5	(11) .8	(21) 2.4	(41) 1.3	(38) 1.7
4.9	5.1	5.0		20.0	5.7	2.8	4.2	3.9	4.1
2.6	2.5	2.5		4.6	2.9		2.2	.9	
(37) 4.0	(64) 5.1	(85) 5.1	% Officers', Directors' Owners' Comp/Sales	(18) 9.2	(23) 5.5		(15) 3.4	(16) 3.2	
9.3	8.2	9.8		16.7	9.9		5.1	6.8	
4199439M	7100369M	7192441M	Net Sales ($)	24827M	113676M	65618M	216694M	773736M	5997890M
3189911M	4090868M	3655078M	Total Assets ($)	50207M	81451M	59116M	112562M	331993M	3019749M

M = $ thousand   MM = $ million
See Pages 9 through 22 for Explanation of Ratios and Data

Current Data Sorted by Assets   Comparative Historical Data

							Type of Statement		
	1	8	15	7	6		Unqualified	22	21
1	8	18	16				Reviewed	28	31
6	20	21	3				Compiled	18	21
21	34	17					Tax Returns	37	39
11	17	35	19	10	2		Other	55	80
	37 (4/1-9/30/09)		259 (10/1/09-3/31/10)					4/1/05-3/31/06	4/1/06-3/31/07
0-500M	500M-2MM	2-10MM	10-50MM	50-100MM	100-250MM			ALL	ALL
39	80	99	53	17	8	NUMBER OF STATEMENTS		160	192
%	%	%	%	%	%	ASSETS		%	%
16.9	13.7	10.0	11.1	5.6		Cash & Equivalents		11.4	8.3
23.8	16.8	16.4	14.9	12.1		Trade Receivables (net)		18.5	17.8
3.1	.2	2.2	.9	1.5		Inventory		.7	2.1
.6	4.1	3.2	3.6	3.9		All Other Current		2.4	2.8
44.4	34.8	31.8	30.5	23.1		Total Current		33.0	31.1
41.0	50.2	50.4	55.9	42.4		Fixed Assets (net)		51.3	54.9
6.9	6.0	9.0	6.8	24.6		Intangibles (net)		8.3	6.1
7.7	9.0	8.7	6.8	9.8		All Other Non-Current		7.4	7.9
100.0	100.0	100.0	100.0	100.0		Total		100.0	100.0
						LIABILITIES			
12.0	4.5	5.0	1.4	3.6		Notes Payable-Short Term		9.2	5.8
8.2	7.4	8.0	7.4	5.5		Cur. Mat.-L.T.D.		8.4	8.5
11.8	11.9	9.0	7.2	5.1		Trade Payables		10.8	11.0
.2	.1	.4	.2	.1		Income Taxes Payable		.1	.2
32.8	8.0	9.4	6.8	6.5		All Other Current		7.1	9.5
65.0	31.9	31.8	23.1	20.9		Total Current		35.7	35.0
47.6	42.2	34.3	29.6	37.7		Long-Term Debt		36.8	38.0
.0	.5	.6	1.7	.6		Deferred Taxes		1.0	.8
9.1	10.9	5.7	7.8	4.2		All Other Non-Current		6.9	10.1
-21.8	14.5	27.5	37.8	36.6		Net Worth		19.6	16.1
100.0	100.0	100.0	100.0	100.0		Total Liabilties & Net Worth		100.0	100.0
						INCOME DATA			
100.0	100.0	100.0	100.0	100.0		Net Sales		100.0	100.0
						Gross Profit			
95.9	94.1	92.7	91.5	90.4		Operating Expenses		94.1	92.3
4.1	5.9	7.3	8.5	9.6		Operating Profit		5.9	7.7
1.0	2.6	2.7	1.9	1.2		All Other Expenses (net)		1.8	2.5
3.1	3.3	4.6	6.6	8.4		Profit Before Taxes		4.1	5.3
						RATIOS			
3.2	2.3	1.8	2.4	1.3				1.6	1.5
.8	1.1	.9	1.2	1.1		Current		.9	.9
.3	.5	.6	.9	.7				.5	.5
3.3	2.1	1.5	2.2	1.1				1.5	1.3
.7 (38)	1.0	.7	1.0	.8		Quick		.8	.8
.3	.4	.4	.8	.6				.5	.5

0	UND	0	UND	20	18.3	28	12.8	33	11.0		16	22.3	15	24.0
23	15.8	26	14.2	32	11.3	38	9.7	41	8.9	Sales/Receivables	33	11.2	34	10.8
46	8.0	41	9.0	45	8.2	46	8.0	49	7.5		47	7.8	46	7.9

Cost of Sales/Inventory

Cost of Sales/Payables

16.8	11.9	11.9	6.2	13.2		Sales/Working Capital	18.2	19.3
-84.4	70.9	-50.6	30.0	181.5			-145.7	-78.3
-8.3	-15.5	-11.6	-35.1	-17.9			-10.3	-9.4

	8.8		7.4		6.5		9.6	9.0		5.7	5.5
(27)	2.5	(76)	2.4	(92)	2.9	(52)	4.5	4.8	EBIT/Interest (146)	2.6 (180)	2.5
	-.1		.4		1.1		2.2	3.0		1.1	1.1

				3.0	3.2	3.9		2.5	3.0
		(18)	1.8	(19) 1.6	(11) 2.5	Net Profit + Depr., Dep., Amort./Cur. Mat. L/T/D (35)	1.6 (43)	1.9
			1.4	1.3	1.7		1.0	1.2

.8	1.1	.9	1.2	1.1		Fixed/Worth	1.3	1.5
11.6	3.1	2.6	1.9	4.6			3.2	3.8
-.6	-2.8	19.8	5.0	-2.4			-7.8	-19.9

1.5	1.1	1.5	1.4	1.5		Debt/Worth	1.7	1.9
25.8	4.9	3.0	2.5	4.7			5.0	4.8
-2.2	-6.7	27.3	5.9	-4.7			-10.1	-37.1

	215.0		63.8		43.2	39.4	44.0	% Profit Before Taxes/Tangible Net Worth	73.4	55.9
(21)	50.0	(51)	23.5	(78) 19.5	(48) 26.4	(10) 24.9	(111) 29.9	(137) 25.5
	-8.4		9.3		3.6	10.7	7.0		8.4	9.9

38.1	13.0	12.6	12.9	10.6		% Profit Before Taxes/Total Assets	16.0	13.4
13.5	5.7	4.8	8.6	7.9			5.8	6.5
-8.1	-1.5	.5	2.7	3.0			.4	1.2

28.1	9.5	8.3	3.8	3.7		Sales/Net Fixed Assets	9.5	6.0
15.3	4.8	3.7	2.2	2.7			3.6	3.3
4.3	2.3	1.9	1.6	1.6			2.0	2.0

6.4	3.4	2.5	1.6	1.1		Sales/Total Assets	3.1	2.6
3.6	2.3	1.7	1.3	1.0			1.8	1.7
2.4	1.4	1.2	1.0	.8			1.2	1.2

	2.0		3.3		4.5	5.8	4.9	% Depr., Dep., Amort./Sales	3.4	4.7
(23)	6.3	(66)	7.3	(89) 7.7	8.9	(16) 7.1	(137) 6.4	(172) 7.7
	10.2		11.9		10.3	11.9	9.1		10.1	11.1

	5.1		2.7		1.3	.6		% Officers', Directors' Owners' Comp/Sales	2.6	2.4
(13)	6.2	(40)	4.9	(40) 4.0	(13) 3.2		(69) 4.0	(73) 5.7
	14.3		7.9		5.8	5.4			6.1	7.8

43002M	223050M	831380M	1459181M	1224029M	2153352M	Net Sales ($)	4879683M	3438786M
10168M	92840M	460716M	1115656M	1230736M	1221620M	Total Assets ($)	2950323M	2283259M

M = $ thousand   MM = $ million
See Pages 9 through 22 for Explanation of Ratios and Data

Comparative Historical Data

Current Data Sorted by Sales

H1	H2	H3	Type of Statement	0-1MM	1-3MM	3-5MM	5-10MM	10-25MM	25MM & OVER
31	28	37	Unqualified	3	1	4	13	17	22
24	32	43	Reviewed						
26	30	50	Compiled	9	9	13	11	7	5
52	72	72	Tax Returns	11	38	7	11	5	1
59	91	94	Other	10	18	14	14	14	24
4/1/07-3/31/08 ALL	4/1/08-3/31/09 ALL	4/1/09-3/31/10 ALL		37 (4/1-9/30/09)			259 (10/1/09-3/31/10)		
192	253	296	NUMBER OF STATEMENTS	33	66	40	52	53	52
%	%	%	**ASSETS**	%	%	%	%	%	%
9.4	10.9	11.8	Cash & Equivalents	15.9	11.8	12.8	12.3	9.8	9.9
16.4	18.0	17.0	Trade Receivables (net)	10.2	17.8	19.6	19.0	17.5	15.8
2.1	1.1	1.4	Inventory	.0	1.9	1.8	1.9	1.2	1.3
2.2	3.3	3.2	All Other Current	2.2	3.6	1.4	4.2	3.4	3.6
30.1	33.3	33.4	Total Current	28.3	35.1	35.6	37.3	31.8	30.6
53.6	51.1	49.4	Fixed Assets (net)	55.0	49.7	51.7	45.5	51.3	45.9
8.4	8.3	8.9	Intangibles (net)	12.7	4.2	7.0	9.5	6.5	15.7
7.9	7.3	8.3	All Other Non-Current	4.0	11.0	5.7	7.7	10.4	7.8
100.0	100.0	100.0	Total	100.0	100.0	100.0	100.0	100.0	100.0
			LIABILITIES						
5.8	5.6	5.0	Notes Payable-Short Term	4.5	6.5	5.3	7.1	3.9	2.1
8.1	9.1	7.5	Cur. Mat.-L.T.D.	6.2	8.9	6.3	7.2	9.2	6.3
9.2	9.7	9.7	Trade Payables	6.5	8.5	13.0	11.5	10.3	8.4
.1	.2	.3	Income Taxes Payable	.3	.0	.0	.1	.8	.4
8.7	6.9	11.4	All Other Current	17.5	18.9	8.8	6.8	8.7	7.3
31.8	31.4	33.9	Total Current	34.9	42.8	33.5	32.7	33.0	24.5
41.3	43.0	37.5	Long-Term Debt	53.9	45.8	33.3	33.1	30.5	31.4
.7	.9	.8	Deferred Taxes	.0	.3	.4	.9	.4	1.9
9.0	7.5	8.0	All Other Non-Current	5.0	12.8	10.6	8.4	4.2	5.3
17.1	17.2	19.8	Net Worth	6.2	-1.7	22.3	24.9	31.5	36.9
100.0	100.0	100.0	Total Liabilities & Net Worth	100.0	100.0	100.0	100.0	100.0	100.0
			INCOME DATA						
100.0	100.0	100.0	Net Sales	100.0	100.0	100.0	100.0	100.0	100.0
			Gross Profit						
93.0	93.5	93.1	Operating Expenses	84.0	94.7	94.7	96.3	94.6	91.2
7.0	6.5	6.9	Operating Profit	16.0	5.3	5.3	3.7	5.4	8.8
2.4	2.9	2.3	All Other Expenses (net)	6.5	2.7	1.5	1.4	1.3	1.5
4.6	3.7	4.6	Profit Before Taxes	9.5	2.6	3.8	2.3	4.1	7.2
			RATIOS						
1.6	1.8	2.0		3.3	2.9	1.8	2.4	1.7	1.5
1.0	1.1	1.0	Current	1.0	1.0	.9	1.1	1.0	1.1
.6	.6	.6		.3	.4	.6	.7	.6	.7
1.4	1.6	1.7		2.6	2.4	1.3	2.1	1.5	1.2
.8	.9	(295) .8	Quick	1.0	(65) .7	.9	1.0	.8	.9
.5	.5	.5		.3	.3	.5	.5	.8	.5
13 27.1	15 24.8	17 21.6		0 UND	0 UND	17 21.3	14 25.8	21 17.5	30 12.2
33 11.0	31 11.7	31 11.6	Sales/Receivables	15 25.1	28 12.9	31 11.9	33 10.9	30 12.3	39 9.3
44 8.3	41 8.8	45 8.2		39 9.4	44 8.4	52 7.0	45 8.1	42 8.7	45 8.0
			Cost of Sales/Inventory						
			Cost of Sales/Payables						
15.4	16.2	11.2		9.8	9.4	18.8	8.3	14.1	10.5
-158.2	196.5	UND	Sales/Working Capital	-207.7	UND	-92.2	32.4	-333.8	52.0
-12.9	-14.2	-14.3		-5.2	-11.2	-14.6	-16.0	-13.7	-19.8
5.4	5.8	7.5		7.6	7.8	12.5	5.7	6.2	10.5
(175) 2.6	(232) 2.9	(272) 3.2	EBIT/Interest	(23) 2.1	(59) 1.8	(37) 3.7	(49) 2.4	(52) 3.6	5.6
1.1	1.0	1.1		.8	-.1	1.0	1.0	2.0	2.7
2.8	2.9	3.4						2.7	3.5
(44) 1.8	(54) 1.6	(57) 1.9	Net Profit + Depr., Dep., Amort./Cur. Mat. L/T/D				(16) 1.8	(22) 2.0	
1.3	1.0	1.4						1.5	1.6
1.3	1.0	1.1		1.7	1.1	.9	1.1	.9	1.1
3.8	3.3	2.8	Fixed/Worth	11.6	4.7	2.7	2.5	2.4	2.0
-5.0	-6.0	-7.2		-1.4	-1.1	35.6	-10.0	7.2	-10.8
1.5	1.6	1.4		1.6	1.0	1.4	1.4	1.4	1.4
4.8	4.2	3.3	Debt/Worth	12.8	6.4	2.9	3.1	2.9	3.0
-7.3	-11.6	-12.2		-2.7	-4.2	49.6	-43.7	11.5	-17.8
66.6	59.2	50.2		75.3	60.1	65.2	46.6	50.2	39.2
(133) 32.3	(178) 29.3	(212) 25.7	% Profit Before Taxes/Tangible Net Worth	(19) 33.2	(39) 14.3	(31) 23.5	(38) 18.7	(47) 25.9	(38) 29.4
10.6	7.1	6.4		1.0	-.9	4.2	3.0	8.0	20.1
14.3	15.6	13.6		21.8	16.6	14.7	11.2	13.5	11.6
6.5	5.5	6.3	% Profit Before Taxes/Total Assets	4.3	3.3	6.9	4.9	8.4	8.2
.7	.0	.4		-.4	-5.3	-.9	.0	2.5	5.0
6.2	8.7	8.1		8.9	17.3	7.5	9.8	7.4	4.0
3.5	3.9	3.8	Sales/Net Fixed Assets	3.5	4.5	4.5	4.7	3.9	2.7
1.9	2.0	1.9		1.1	2.1	1.9	2.2	2.1	1.8
2.8	3.4	2.8		2.5	3.5	3.3	2.9	2.6	1.6
1.7	1.9	1.7	Sales/Total Assets	1.2	2.1	1.9	2.3	1.7	1.2
1.2	1.2	1.1		.8	1.3	1.2	1.4	1.4	1.0
4.6	5.0	4.5		6.3	3.3	5.4	4.1	5.1	4.8
(162) 7.6	(202) 7.5	(250) 7.6	% Depr., Dep., Amort./Sales	(23) 13.4	(51) 7.3	(36) 7.9	(44) 6.6	(50) 7.8	(46) 7.1
11.2	10.6	10.8		22.6	10.2	10.3	9.4	10.1	10.9
1.6	1.9	2.3			2.9	2.3	1.4	.6	.9
(83) 4.1	(104) 4.0	(110) 4.5	% Officers', Directors' Owners' Comp/Sales		(31) 5.8	(16) 3.8	(22) 4.2	(20) 2.5	(12) 3.9
6.6	7.7	6.9			7.6	6.6	6.1	5.5	5.6
4167555M	6402782M	5933994M	Net Sales ($)	17627M	120185M	156077M	371651M	863880M	4404574M
3680464M	4526778M	4131736M	Total Assets ($)	35082M	75847M	93733M	239519M	539490M	3148065M

Current Data Sorted by Assets							Comparative Historical Data	
						Type of Statement		
		1	1	1		Unqualified	6	3
		3	1			Reviewed	3	
	3	4				Compiled	9	5
5	5					Tax Returns	2	5
2	7	10	6	1		Other	5	10
	3 (4/1-9/30/09)		47 (10/1/09-3/31/10)				4/1/05-3/31/06	4/1/06-3/31/07
0-500M	500M-2MM	2-10MM	10-50MM	50-100MM	100-250MM		ALL	ALL
7	15	18	8	2		**NUMBER OF STATEMENTS**	25	23
%	%	%	%	%	%	**ASSETS**	%	%
	10.5	3.0			DATA NOT AVAILABLE	Cash & Equivalents	6.1	7.7
	20.8	18.2				Trade Receivables (net)	19.1	17.5
	2.5	2.7				Inventory	2.6	1.1
	1.5	5.5				All Other Current	2.7	1.5
	35.3	29.3				Total Current	30.6	27.8
	44.7	50.9				Fixed Assets (net)	52.2	51.4
	5.9	5.1				Intangibles (net)	9.9	15.0
	14.2	14.6				All Other Non-Current	7.3	5.9
	100.0	100.0				Total	100.0	100.0
						LIABILITIES		
	10.4	7.5				Notes Payable-Short Term	6.7	3.7
	14.5	7.0				Cur. Mat.-L.T.D.	7.6	10.8
	15.5	11.1				Trade Payables	6.5	8.3
	.0	.0				Income Taxes Payable	.3	.7
	5.8	6.7				All Other Current	7.7	4.9
	46.2	32.3				Total Current	28.8	28.5
	35.6	28.3				Long-Term Debt	50.8	48.8
	.0	1.1				Deferred Taxes	1.6	.8
	4.1	1.8				All Other Non-Current	8.1	9.0
	14.0	36.6				Net Worth	10.8	12.8
	100.0	100.0				Total Liabilties & Net Worth	100.0	100.0
						INCOME DATA		
	100.0	100.0				Net Sales	100.0	100.0
						Gross Profit		
	90.1	91.2				Operating Expenses	93.0	92.9
	9.9	8.8				Operating Profit	7.0	7.1
	4.5	1.5				All Other Expenses (net)	2.9	1.7
	5.4	7.3				Profit Before Taxes	4.1	5.4
						RATIOS		
	1.4	1.9					1.6	1.3
	.6	.9				Current	1.0	.8
	.2	.5					.7	.5
	1.1	1.8					1.5	1.1
	.5	.7				Quick	.8	.7
	.2	.4					.4	.5
	1 350.1	18 20.0					22 16.5	11 32.1
	30 12.1	43 8.5				Sales/Receivables	42 8.8	32 11.3
	52 7.1	71 5.2					51 7.1	45 8.1
						Cost of Sales/Inventory		
						Cost of Sales/Payables		
	14.6	13.5					12.4	44.4
	-25.3	-56.4				Sales/Working Capital	UND	-57.5
	-7.3	-10.6					-13.0	-13.2
	29.5	4.5					4.5	6.4
	(14) 3.2	(16) 1.7				EBIT/Interest	2.6	(21) 4.0
	.2	.7					1.2	1.6
						Net Profit + Depr., Dep., Amort./Cur. Mat. L/T/D		
	.5	1.1					1.7	1.4
	3.0	2.1				Fixed/Worth	5.3	4.7
	-1.5	NM					-2.9	-1.6
	1.9	.9					2.5	1.6
	11.8	2.7				Debt/Worth	10.9	5.3
	-6.1	NM					-5.3	-3.8
	210.7	47.7					57.1	133.3
	(10) 46.2	(14) 20.7				% Profit Before Taxes/Tangible Net Worth	(14) 37.5	(15) 45.7
	19.8	.5					21.7	36.4
	18.2	12.4					11.8	18.0
	7.8	5.7				% Profit Before Taxes/Total Assets	7.3	11.8
	-.3	-.3					.6	2.8
	57.9	4.8					6.0	9.1
	6.8	3.7				Sales/Net Fixed Assets	2.1	4.5
	2.3	1.8					1.3	1.5
	4.5	2.1					2.2	3.2
	2.5	1.4				Sales/Total Assets	1.3	1.9
	1.5	1.0					.8	1.0
		1.8					5.5	3.8
		(16) 6.3				% Depr., Dep., Amort./Sales	(21) 11.3	(22) 6.2
		12.5					15.0	13.4
								1.9
						% Officers', Directors' Owners' Comp/Sales		(10) 3.1
								8.8
18706M	45467M	114229M	275992M	162394M		Net Sales ($)	761259M	413653M
1921M	16328M	73577M	231125M	138250M		Total Assets ($)	594091M	245764M

M = $ thousand MM = $ million

See Pages 9 through 22 for Explanation of Ratios and Data

Comparative Historical Data   Current Data Sorted by Sales

4/1/07-3/31/08 ALL	4/1/08-3/31/09 ALL	4/1/09-3/31/10 ALL	Type of Statement	0-1MM	1-3MM	3-5MM	5-10MM	10-25MM	25MM & OVER
4	4	3	Unqualified		1				2
1	4	4	Reviewed		2	3	2	2	
5	4	7	Compiled		2	2	2	1	
6	6	10	Tax Returns	4	2	2	1	1	
14	6	26	Other	1	7	7	3	2	6
					3 (4/1-9/30/09)		47 (10/1/09-3/31/10)		
30	24	50	**NUMBER OF STATEMENTS**	5	12	12	8	5	8
%	%	%		%	%	%	%	%	%
			ASSETS						
9.8	9.7	7.3	Cash & Equivalents		11.6	5.0			
17.6	19.1	16.2	Trade Receivables (net)		13.4	19.8			
1.5	1.8	3.3	Inventory		.1	4.4			
3.0	1.7	3.4	All Other Current		1.5	5.4			
32.0	32.3	30.2	Total Current		26.5	34.5			
52.2	53.9	52.3	Fixed Assets (net)		60.1	31.0			
10.6	8.7	6.9	Intangibles (net)		6.6	12.0			
5.2	5.2	10.6	All Other Non-Current		6.8	22.5			
100.0	100.0	100.0	Total		100.0	100.0			
			LIABILITIES						
15.1	5.5	6.5	Notes Payable-Short Term		5.3	11.4			
7.6	10.2	9.6	Cur. Mat.-L.T.D.		13.0	6.5			
8.7	7.1	10.6	Trade Payables		5.9	16.1			
.0	.0	.0	Income Taxes Payable		.0	.0			
5.3	5.8	10.9	All Other Current		3.4	10.6			
36.7	28.7	37.7	Total Current		27.5	44.5			
39.8	36.9	41.5	Long-Term Debt		62.2	19.9			
.4	.7	.8	Deferred Taxes		.0	1.4			
8.3	13.5	2.5	All Other Non-Current		6.3	.2			
14.7	20.2	17.5	Net Worth		4.0	34.1			
100.0	100.0	100.0	Total Liabilities & Net Worth		100.0	100.0			
			INCOME DATA						
100.0	100.0	100.0	Net Sales		100.0	100.0			
			Gross Profit						
93.4	93.9	91.3	Operating Expenses		90.0	92.2			
6.6	6.1	8.7	Operating Profit		10.0	7.8			
3.3	2.3	2.3	All Other Expenses (net)		1.7	1.1			
3.3	3.8	6.4	Profit Before Taxes		8.3	6.7			
			RATIOS						
1.9	2.6	1.5	Current		1.8	1.8			
.9	.9	.8			.6	.8			
.3	.6	.4			.4	.4			
1.6	1.5	1.1	Quick		1.7	1.5			
.6	.9	.6			.6	.6			
.3	.6	.3			.3	.3			
17 21.1	28 12.9	7 52.2	Sales/Receivables		1 275.0	5 80.9			
35 10.4	40 9.2	31 11.8			23 15.8	45 8.1			
46 7.9	57 6.4	51 7.1			51 7.2	73 5.0			
			Cost of Sales/Inventory						
			Cost of Sales/Payables						
13.2	11.8	19.8	Sales/Working Capital		15.9	11.0			
-49.0	-102.5	-37.4			-128.2	-37.4			
-5.9	-12.5	-8.3			-14.6	-8.4			
6.0	6.4	8.0	EBIT/Interest	5.0		40.2			
(26) 2.2	3.6	(46) 2.5		(11) 3.3	(11) 1.9				
.7	1.1	1.1			1.5	.6			
			Net Profit + Depr., Dep., Amort./Cur. Mat. L/T/D						
1.4	1.1	1.1	Fixed/Worth		1.5	.5			
33.2	2.6	2.5			3.3	1.2			
-4.8	NM	-16.0			NM	-10.4			
1.5	1.0	1.6	Debt/Worth		1.8	1.1			
NM	3.5	4.0			2.9	9.6			
-10.4	NM	-29.7			NM	-17.6			
59.0	103.2	53.1	% Profit Before Taxes/Tangible Net Worth						
(15) 34.9	(18) 32.0	(35) 29.2							
7.9	10.0	9.7							
18.5	15.1	20.6	% Profit Before Taxes/Total Assets		15.6	35.9			
7.9	7.4	7.3			9.6	6.2			
-2.1	.5	.4			3.3	-.3			
10.4	6.2	9.4	Sales/Net Fixed Assets		19.0	40.5			
3.0	2.0	3.8			2.9	5.3			
1.3	1.7	1.6			1.1	3.1			
3.4	1.9	2.9	Sales/Total Assets		4.4	4.0			
1.7	1.4	1.7			1.6	1.7			
.9	1.1	1.0			.9	1.3			
4.9	5.8	2.6	% Depr., Dep., Amort./Sales						
(23) 10.7	(21) 10.1	(40) 7.4							
13.6	12.8	12.6							
2.3	1.5	2.1	% Officers', Directors' Owners' Comp/Sales						
(16) 4.5	(13) 3.9	(20) 3.4							
9.6	4.8	6.5							
594042M	490659M	616788M	Net Sales ($)	2059M	22762M	47453M	64040M	67346M	413128M
592580M	473366M	461201M	Total Assets ($)	1561M	21793M	26028M	51861M	29412M	330546M

Current Data Sorted by Assets   Comparative Historical Data

0-500M	500M-2MM	2-10MM	10-50MM	50-100MM	100-250MM	Type of Statement	4/1/05-3/31/06 ALL	4/1/06-3/31/07 ALL
		2	4	1	1	Unqualified	3	7
	2	10	2			Reviewed	12	16
	1	7				Compiled	5	8
3	1	1				Tax Returns	4	3
3	4	3	7	3	3	Other	8	15
	6 (4/1-9/30/09)		52 (10/1/09-3/31/10)					
6	8	23	13	4	4	**NUMBER OF STATEMENTS**	32	49
%	%	%	%	%	%	**ASSETS**	%	%
		7.0	10.6			Cash & Equivalents	10.4	9.7
		21.7	22.6			Trade Receivables (net)	23.3	25.9
		1.4	3.2			Inventory	2.6	1.5
		3.1	8.0			All Other Current	3.1	3.0
		33.2	44.4			Total Current	39.4	40.1
		48.5	36.4			Fixed Assets (net)	44.4	45.7
		11.0	12.8			Intangibles (net)	5.9	5.6
		7.3	6.5			All Other Non-Current	10.3	8.6
		100.0	100.0			Total	100.0	100.0
						LIABILITIES		
		5.1	3.7			Notes Payable-Short Term	6.8	4.8
		10.3	5.7			Cur. Mat.-L.T.D.	7.3	5.8
		10.1	12.8			Trade Payables	13.1	11.3
		.1	.4			Income Taxes Payable	.0	.1
		5.7	6.7			All Other Current	8.2	9.2
		31.3	29.3			Total Current	35.4	31.1
		22.5	17.3			Long-Term Debt	25.7	22.0
		.7	1.4			Deferred Taxes	.5	.3
		6.2	3.8			All Other Non-Current	11.4	5.9
		39.3	48.1			Net Worth	27.0	40.6
		100.0	100.0			Total Liabilties & Net Worth	100.0	100.0
						INCOME DATA		
		100.0	100.0			Net Sales	100.0	100.0
						Gross Profit		
		99.0	94.4			Operating Expenses	93.3	89.6
		1.0	5.6			Operating Profit	6.7	10.4
		2.1	1.5			All Other Expenses (net)	1.5	1.3
		-1.1	4.1			Profit Before Taxes	5.2	9.1
						RATIOS		
		1.4	2.1			Current	1.8	1.9
		1.2	1.4				1.1	1.3
		.8	1.0				.8	1.0
		1.3	1.8			Quick	1.6	1.7
		1.0	1.2				(31) .9	1.1
		.6	.8				.6	.8
		27 13.7	39 9.2			Sales/Receivables	27 13.7	26 14.0
		43 8.5	47 7.8				38 9.5	40 9.0
		60 6.1	65 5.6				58 6.3	64 5.7
						Cost of Sales/Inventory		
						Cost of Sales/Payables		
		13.4	5.2			Sales/Working Capital	16.9	9.8
		32.2	13.3				60.0	23.2
		-35.9	NM				-27.8	-136.2
		9.5	48.2			EBIT/Interest	12.5	18.6
		1.8	5.3				(30) 3.0	(44) 6.4
		-1.5	.1				1.6	2.8
						Net Profit + Depr., Dep., Amort./Cur. Mat. L/T/D		3.9
							(14) 2.4	
								1.4
		1.0	.5			Fixed/Worth	.8	.7
		1.4	.7				1.8	1.3
		3.4	3.3				4.6	3.2
		1.0	.5			Debt/Worth	1.5	.6
		1.9	1.6				3.0	2.0
		4.5	3.4				8.8	5.8
		35.6	32.1			% Profit Before Taxes/Tangible Net Worth	46.1	80.4
	(19)	3.4	(11) 12.4				(30) 16.5	(44) 39.4
		-37.9	-20.8				8.6	11.2
		13.3	16.7			% Profit Before Taxes/Total Assets	20.9	25.3
		2.5	6.3				4.8	14.1
		-8.0	-2.5				2.0	5.6
		6.3	11.1			Sales/Net Fixed Assets	11.8	6.8
		3.3	6.2				4.4	4.4
		2.1	2.7				3.0	2.9
		2.0	2.4			Sales/Total Assets	3.1	2.8
		1.5	1.5				2.2	1.9
		1.2	1.1				1.4	1.2
		4.7	3.1			% Depr., Dep., Amort./Sales	2.8	2.7
	(21)	7.8	(12) 5.4				(28) 5.4	(46) 4.7
		11.9	10.0				6.8	6.9
						% Officers', Directors' Owners' Comp/Sales	2.6	1.8
							(13) 3.9	(18) 3.6
							7.1	8.1
8945M	20554M	207270M	369571M	380423M	504930M	Net Sales ($)	515355M	1078237M
1177M	7761M	131850M	225739M	274982M	488042M	Total Assets ($)	363973M	831073M

M = $ thousand   MM = $ million
See Pages 9 through 22 for Explanation of Ratios and Data

Comparative Historical Data

Current Data Sorted by Sales

4/1/07-3/31/08 ALL	4/1/08-3/31/09 ALL	4/1/09-3/31/10 ALL	Type of Statement	0-1MM	1-3MM	3-5MM	5-10MM	10-25MM	25MM & OVER
							6 (4/1-9/30/09)	52 (10/1/09-3/31/10)	
9	7	8	Unqualified				2	1	5
16	9	14	Reviewed		1	1	7	5	
7	11	8	Compiled		1	2	4	1	
9	7	5	Tax Returns		1	2	3		
24	31	23	Other	3	4	1	2	3	10
65	65	58	**NUMBER OF STATEMENTS**	3	8	7	15	10	15
%	%	%	**ASSETS**	%	%	%	%	%	%
8.2	8.1	8.2	Cash & Equivalents				5.3	14.0	8.0
25.6	27.7	25.2	Trade Receivables (net)				22.3	24.9	23.7
1.6	2.0	1.7	Inventory				1.9	2.1	1.8
2.7	3.5	5.1	All Other Current				4.0	5.8	9.6
38.1	41.4	40.2	Total Current				33.5	46.8	43.2
47.3	42.3	39.6	Fixed Assets (net)				49.8	39.4	32.0
7.3	8.5	11.1	Intangibles (net)				10.4	8.2	16.6
7.2	7.8	9.1	All Other Non-Current				6.2	5.5	8.2
100.0	100.0	100.0	Total				100.0	100.0	100.0
			LIABILITIES						
6.7	12.8	7.5	Notes Payable-Short Term				7.0	3.4	2.6
9.0	8.1	8.3	Cur. Mat.-L.T.D.				9.9	10.0	5.6
13.4	13.1	13.1	Trade Payables				12.2	11.2	8.8
.3	.5	.2	Income Taxes Payable				.0	.1	.5
9.2	12.9	11.0	All Other Current				6.1	8.0	21.4
38.7	47.4	40.1	Total Current				35.3	32.7	39.0
30.8	21.7	22.7	Long-Term Debt				23.2	14.4	18.7
.3	.5	.9	Deferred Taxes				.6	1.1	.6
4.7	3.6	4.7	All Other Non-Current				3.1	6.3	7.4
25.6	26.8	31.7	Net Worth				37.8	45.5	34.4
100.0	100.0	100.0	Total Liabilites & Net Worth				100.0	100.0	100.0
			INCOME DATA						
100.0	100.0	100.0	Net Sales				100.0	100.0	100.0
			Gross Profit						
89.7	91.1	96.5	Operating Expenses				98.0	96.5	93.5
10.3	8.9	3.5	Operating Profit				2.0	3.5	6.5
2.2	2.1	1.4	All Other Expenses (net)				2.1	-.3	.8
8.1	6.8	2.1	Profit Before Taxes				-.1	3.8	5.8
			RATIOS						
1.7	1.7	1.8	Current				1.4	2.2	2.4
1.2	1.1	1.2					1.1	1.4	1.4
.8	.7	.7					.8	1.1	.9
1.5	1.5	1.4	Quick				1.2	2.0	1.6
1.1	(64) 1.0	1.0					.9	1.3	1.3
.6	.6	.6					.4	.8	.6
25 14.3	26 14.1	36 10.1	Sales/Receivables				29 12.5	33 11.1	44 8.4
42 8.7	51 7.2	47 7.7					53 6.9	42 8.6	48 7.7
67 5.4	75 4.8	62 5.9					79 4.6	60 6.1	72 5.0
			Cost of Sales/Inventory						
			Cost of Sales/Payables						
11.0	10.5	8.6	Sales/Working Capital				12.3	5.1	6.0
38.7	45.3	31.5					32.2	18.5	13.3
-24.3	-12.7	-25.9					-29.0	NM	-31.5
10.6	12.2	11.1	EBIT/Interest				6.1	21.6	12.9
(61) 5.2	(64) 5.2	(55) 3.6					2.1	7.3	6.1
2.2	.9	-.3					-1.3	1.1	1.3
6.2	12.1	4.4	Net Profit + Depr., Dep., Amort./Cur. Mat. L/T/D						
(13) 3.0	(16) 3.6	(17) 1.2							
1.8	2.2	.9							
.8	.9	.7	Fixed/Worth				1.1	.5	.6
1.7	1.6	1.1					1.9	1.1	.9
NM	8.9	3.5					3.4	1.9	1.7
.9	1.0	1.0	Debt/Worth				1.0	.6	.8
2.4	2.2	1.8					2.2	1.4	1.6
NM	17.0	18.7					4.5	4.0	11.9
69.8	59.8	36.2	% Profit Before Taxes/Tangible Net Worth				24.0		31.9
(49) 35.3	(50) 27.4	(45) 14.8					(13) 2.1		(12) 19.6
21.4	10.4	-7.9					-24.0		8.3
22.2	18.0	14.3	% Profit Before Taxes/Total Assets				13.7	14.2	14.3
9.1	7.0	6.0					1.3	7.1	6.7
2.5	-.2	-3.2					-4.1	1.8	1.7
7.9	11.6	14.3	Sales/Net Fixed Assets				6.7	8.4	10.7
4.1	3.8	5.0					2.8	4.1	6.2
2.3	2.0	2.5					1.7	3.2	2.2
2.5	2.6	2.5	Sales/Total Assets				2.2	2.0	2.4
1.8	1.7	1.6					1.5	1.7	1.5
1.2	1.1	1.2					.8	1.5	1.0
2.5	2.2	3.9	% Depr., Dep., Amort./Sales				3.6		3.1
(56) 4.7	(58) 4.6	(45) 5.3					(14) 5.2		(11) 4.7
7.7	7.5	9.1					10.5		6.1
1.2	1.9		% Officers', Directors' Owners' Comp/Sales						
(21) 3.0	(16) 4.0								
4.8	7.7								
1600044M	1978251M	1491693M	Net Sales ($)	1548M	16366M	27288M	115255M	166217M	1165019M
1452324M	1629671M	1129551M	Total Assets ($)	1058M	4948M	19465M	93498M	99257M	911325M

M = $ thousand   MM = $ million
See Pages 9 through 22 for Explanation of Ratios and Data

ADMIN & WASTE MANAGEMENT SERVICES—Solid Waste Landfill NAICS 562212

Current Data Sorted by Assets							Comparative Historical Data	

0-500M	500M-2MM	2-10MM	10-50MM	50-100MM	100-250MM	Type of Statement	ALL 4/1/05-3/31/06	ALL 4/1/06-3/31/07
	2	5	15	4	5	Unqualified	37	37
	2	11	5		1	Reviewed	36	24
3	6	3		1		Compiled	10	16
4	4	3				Tax Returns	23	13
	6	16	9	3	1	Other	63	41
	19 (4/1-9/30/09)		90 (10/1/09-3/31/10)					
7	20	38	29	9	6	NUMBER OF STATEMENTS	169	131
%	%	%	%	%	%	ASSETS	%	%
	18.4	12.0	8.0			Cash & Equivalents	8.6	11.7
	21.1	15.3	12.1			Trade Receivables (net)	18.1	20.5
	2.6	.5	2.4			Inventory	1.9	2.4
	4.8	4.9	1.1			All Other Current	3.2	2.2
	46.9	32.6	23.6			Total Current	31.9	36.8
	38.8	52.2	62.6			Fixed Assets (net)	53.7	48.2
	3.3	4.7	3.0			Intangibles (net)	4.5	5.1
	11.0	10.6	10.8			All Other Non-Current	9.9	9.9
	100.0	100.0	100.0			Total	100.0	100.0
						LIABILITIES		
	9.7	4.5	2.2			Notes Payable-Short Term	4.4	4.7
	3.7	4.6	6.0			Cur. Mat.-L.T.D.	6.9	5.4
	21.8	8.7	5.2			Trade Payables	9.5	10.3
	.0	.1	.1			Income Taxes Payable	.1	.3
	6.1	10.0	6.1			All Other Current	8.4	8.9
	41.3	28.1	19.6			Total Current	29.3	29.6
	18.5	36.6	27.0			Long-Term Debt	33.2	25.9
	.7	.8	.4			Deferred Taxes	.7	.7
	10.9	4.9	11.2			All Other Non-Current	5.6	4.8
	28.6	29.6	41.8			Net Worth	31.2	38.9
	100.0	100.0	100.0			Total Liabilities & Net Worth	100.0	100.0
						INCOME DATA		
	100.0	100.0	100.0			Net Sales	100.0	100.0
						Gross Profit		
	94.3	91.7	87.0			Operating Expenses	89.4	89.7
	5.7	8.3	13.0			Operating Profit	10.6	10.3
	.4	3.3	4.8			All Other Expenses (net)	2.4	1.4
	5.3	5.1	8.2			Profit Before Taxes	8.3	8.9
						RATIOS		
	3.1	2.4	3.7			Current	1.8	2.1
	1.4	1.3	1.0				1.1	1.1
	.6	.6	.6				.7	.8
	2.8	2.0	2.8			Quick	1.6	1.9
	1.3	1.1	1.0				.9	1.0
	.6	.3	.5				.6	.7
	7 49.4	20 17.9	32 11.5			Sales/Receivables	23 15.7	25 14.7
	27 13.6	34 10.7	43 8.4				38 9.7	38 9.7
	44 8.2	44 8.3	57 6.5				53 6.9	57 6.5
						Cost of Sales/Inventory		
						Cost of Sales/Payables		
	6.2	4.7	5.5			Sales/Working Capital	10.3	8.4
	32.1	24.4	143.3				80.1	64.1
	-21.5	-13.6	-7.4				-16.0	-32.2
	16.3	8.4	11.1			EBIT/Interest	9.3	13.0
	(15) 6.7	(33) 2.0	(24) 2.5				(156) 3.9	(118) 5.0
	4.4	.3	1.0				1.7	2.0
		1.8	3.1			Net Profit + Depr., Dep., Amort./Cur. Mat. L/T/D	3.5	4.7
		(11) 1.4	(11) 2.7				(41) 2.0	(39) 1.9
		.9	1.8				1.4	1.4
	.8	.9	.9			Fixed/Worth	1.0	.7
	1.8	2.1	1.6				1.9	1.4
	4.3	10.6	4.4				6.7	3.5
	.7	.8	.7			Debt/Worth	1.0	.8
	2.3	3.0	1.2				2.4	1.9
	19.2	17.1	4.5				9.2	4.8
	81.5	27.9	42.4			% Profit Before Taxes/Tangible Net Worth	60.4	67.4
	(17) 31.9	(32) 8.6	(27) 14.9				(142) 30.5	(119) 32.5
	8.3	-6.5	2.2				7.1	10.2
	22.1	12.5	9.0			% Profit Before Taxes/Total Assets	13.4	18.0
	12.8	2.8	2.0				6.5	8.3
	-.2	-1.7	.5				1.6	3.1
	34.5	5.0	2.6			Sales/Net Fixed Assets	5.1	7.3
	7.7	2.5	1.5				2.8	3.5
	3.5	.8	.6				1.4	1.7
	3.3	2.2	1.5			Sales/Total Assets	2.3	2.6
	2.7	1.2	1.0				1.5	1.6
	2.1	.5	.4				.8	1.0
	2.5	4.1	6.1			% Depr., Dep., Amort./Sales	3.7	3.3
	(13) 4.1	(36) 7.7	9.6				(154) 6.7	(117) 6.1
	6.5	14.2	16.2				10.4	9.7
	1.8	1.8				% Officers', Directors' Owners' Comp/Sales	1.6	1.2
	(10) 3.5	(10) 3.1					(46) 3.2	(36) 2.3
	5.0	5.7					5.8	5.0
6044M	72358M	261809M	725973M	388188M	654107M	Net Sales ($)	3697022M	2685406M
1581M	25184M	184922M	727766M	621167M	1115200M	Total Assets ($)	2796016M	2037750M

M = $ thousand   MM = $ million
See Pages 9 through 22 for Explanation of Ratios and Data

Comparative Historical Data | | Current Data Sorted by Sales

			Type of Statement						
30	39	31	Unqualified	1	3	2	5	3	17
25	24	19	Reviewed		1	6	4	6	2
15	14	13	Compiled	3	3	3	2	1	1
10	16	11	Tax Returns	4	2	2	2	1	
41	41	35	Other	4	7	4	5	7	8
4/1/07- 3/31/08 ALL	4/1/08- 3/31/09 ALL	4/1/09- 3/31/10 ALL		0-1MM	19 (4/1-9/30/09) 1-3MM	3-5MM	90 (10/1/09-3/31/10) 5-10MM	10-25MM	25MM & OVER
121	134	109	NUMBER OF STATEMENTS	12	16	17	18	18	28
%	%	%	ASSETS	%	%	%	%	%	%
13.6	12.2	13.1	Cash & Equivalents	18.5	13.9	14.8	13.6	11.0	10.2
18.7	14.7	14.5	Trade Receivables (net)	9.7	7.0	17.6	16.3	21.6	13.4
2.2	1.3	1.4	Inventory	.1	.2	1.3	1.7	3.0	1.4
3.0	3.7	4.6	All Other Current	8.8	7.4	8.4	1.8	3.2	1.5
37.5	31.9	33.5	Total Current	37.1	28.4	42.2	33.4	38.8	26.5
46.9	51.3	50.3	Fixed Assets (net)	50.6	57.6	44.2	44.2	54.2	51.2
6.5	6.7	5.2	Intangibles (net)	4.1	1.2	1.5	8.7	1.2	10.5
9.1	10.1	10.9	All Other Non-Current	8.2	12.8	12.1	13.7	5.8	11.9
100.0	100.0	100.0	Total	100.0	100.0	100.0	100.0	100.0	100.0
			LIABILITIES						
3.8	3.3	5.5	Notes Payable-Short Term	15.8	7.4	3.1	3.5	5.6	2.8
5.8	6.0	4.7	Cur. Mat.-L.T.D.	.6	6.1	3.7	4.8	6.6	4.9
10.3	6.8	9.8	Trade Payables	5.4	5.9	19.5	8.8	13.7	6.2
.4	.1	.1	Income Taxes Payable	.1	.0	.0	.2	.2	.1
6.7	8.5	12.0	All Other Current	45.6	5.7	10.3	8.4	7.9	7.2
27.0	24.8	32.1	Total Current	67.5	25.2	36.5	25.7	33.9	21.2
29.3	33.2	29.0	Long-Term Debt	44.3	33.2	25.0	29.3	21.1	27.6
.6	.7	.8	Deferred Taxes	.1	.0	.9	1.2	.8	1.1
7.3	7.9	8.8	All Other Non-Current	5.4	7.3	5.6	13.4	9.2	9.8
35.8	33.5	29.3	Net Worth	-17.3	34.4	32.0	30.4	35.0	40.4
100.0	100.0	100.0	Total Liabilities & Net Worth	100.0	100.0	100.0	100.0	100.0	100.0
			INCOME DATA						
100.0	100.0	100.0	Net Sales	100.0	100.0	100.0	100.0	100.0	100.0
			Gross Profit						
86.2	90.7	91.2	Operating Expenses	82.7	86.2	97.0	92.6	91.6	93.1
13.8	9.3	8.8	Operating Profit	17.3	13.8	3.0	7.4	8.4	6.9
1.8	3.4	3.1	All Other Expenses (net)	13.0	4.8	.5	1.2	2.1	1.5
12.1	5.9	5.6	Profit Before Taxes	4.3	9.0	2.5	6.2	6.2	5.4
			RATIOS						
2.1	2.2	2.8		2.4	1.9	5.9	3.7	2.2	1.6
1.2	1.3	1.3	Current	.8	1.2	2.3	1.6	1.3	1.3
.9	.7	.6		.3	.3	.5	.9	.5	.8
1.8	1.8	2.3		2.3	1.8	5.5	3.7	1.6	1.6
1.1	1.0	1.1	Quick	.8	.8	1.0	1.3	1.2	1.2
.7	.5	.5		.2	.2	.3	.6	.3	.7
21	17.3	16	22.9	24	15.4		0	UND	0	UND	25	14.7	24	15.0	17	21.5	32	11.3

| 37 | 9.8 | 34 | 10.9 | 37 | 10.0 | Sales/Receivables | 23 | 15.6 | 27 | 13.5 | 42 | 8.7 | 34 | 10.7 | 34 | 10.6 | 41 | 8.9 |
| 54 | 6.7 | 49 | 7.5 | 50 | 7.3 | | 34 | 10.7 | 51 | 7.1 | 48 | 7.6 | 47 | 7.8 | 59 | 6.2 | 55 | 6.7 |

			Cost of Sales/Inventory						

| | | | Cost of Sales/Payables | | | | | | |

6.6	6.8	5.5		11.3	5.0	3.4	3.6	6.1	6.3
26.1	29.5	24.3	Sales/Working Capital	-75.8	54.1	9.5	17.9	62.0	14.4
-50.8	-17.4	-13.6		-9.4	-6.6	-5.9	-79.1	-7.7	-29.0
	10.8		7.3		9.2			16.5	34.5	3.2	7.2	10.9
(108)	4.1	(117)	3.2	(91)	3.2	EBIT/Interest	(13) 6.7	(12) 6.4	(15) 2.0	(16) 3.3	(27) 2.6
	2.1		1.3		.8			5.3	-1.9	.9	-.1	1.3
	3.9		4.2		3.4	Net Profit + Depr., Dep.,					2.7
(41)	2.6	(51)	2.2	(30)	2.0	Amort./Cur. Mat. L/T/D				(12)	2.3
	1.6		1.2		1.4						1.6
.9	1.0	.8		.3	1.0	.6	1.2	.6	.8
1.7	1.9	1.8	Fixed/Worth	2.9	1.9	1.4	1.8	1.8	1.3
4.3	7.4	8.8		126.4	16.4	3.3	NM	3.4	23.5
.9	.9	.7		.8	.6	.5	.8	.9	.6
2.1	2.4	2.1	Debt/Worth	5.7	1.8	2.2	3.6	2.2	1.4
10.8	11.5	19.0		NM	21.3	14.2	NM	3.7	31.5
	82.3		63.3		38.6	% Profit Before Taxes/Tangible		53.8	31.9	43.8	55.8	43.3
(105)	39.3	(116)	21.0	(90)	15.8	Net Worth	(14) 16.2	(15) 15.8	(14) 6.5	(16) 22.3	(22) 12.9
	13.0		3.9		-.1			2.7	-26.3	1.6	-6.3	6.2
26.4	13.8	13.6	% Profit Before Taxes/Total	13.2	21.9	15.4	5.5	18.7	9.0
9.0	5.4	4.6	Assets	.5	9.2	6.8	2.6	8.2	4.6
4.3	.6	-.6		-6.8	1.8	-7.9	-.4	-1.7	1.1
7.0	6.2	6.7		45.4	7.1	14.1	9.3	7.1	3.3
3.4	2.5	2.2	Sales/Net Fixed Assets	2.0	2.0	3.1	2.5	3.5	1.8
1.6	1.1	1.0		.4	.7	1.1	1.4	1.6	1.4
2.5	2.2	2.4		4.9	2.8	2.6	2.9	3.0	1.5
1.5	1.2	1.2	Sales/Total Assets	1.1	1.3	1.2	1.3	2.1	.9
.8	.7	.6		.3	.4	.7	.5	1.0	.7
	3.5		4.3		4.3			3.0	4.1	4.3	2.6	6.9
(103)	6.7	(121)	7.4	(92)	7.8	% Depr., Dep., Amort./Sales	(12) 7.5	(14) 10.8	(17) 7.7	5.6	(23) 9.6
	10.6		12.1		14.0			19.0	20.1	13.6	10.1	12.8
	2.0		1.5		1.9	% Officers', Directors'					
(36)	3.4	(33)	2.8	(30)	3.3	Owners' Comp/Sales					
	5.8		5.0		5.0						
3029878M	3143469M	2108479M	Net Sales ($)	8142M	32795M	70873M	130031M	269236M	1597402M
2692913M	3260098M	2675820M	Total Assets ($)	22247M	50985M	87115M	194018M	238601M	2082854M

M = $ thousand   MM = $ million
See Pages 9 through 22 for Explanation of Ratios and Data

Current Data Sorted by Assets   Comparative Historical Data

0-500M	500M-2MM	2-10MM	10-50MM	50-100MM	100-250MM	Type of Statement	4/1/05-3/31/06 ALL	4/1/06-3/31/07 ALL
			6	2	2	Unqualified	5	3
		4	1			Reviewed	2	3
	1	1	2			Compiled	3	10
1	1	1	5			Tax Returns	1	
1	2	9				Other	3	6
	6 (4/1-9/30/09)		37 (10/1/09-3/31/10)					
3	4	19	11	2	4	NUMBER OF STATEMENTS	14	22
%	%	%	%	%	%	**ASSETS**	%	%
		6.7	11.2			Cash & Equivalents	6.6	6.7
		14.3	16.5			Trade Receivables (net)	14.5	21.5
		1.1	2.1			Inventory	4.9	.7
		4.1	1.3			All Other Current	1.6	2.5
		26.1	31.2			Total Current	27.7	31.3
		57.9	59.3			Fixed Assets (net)	51.0	54.1
		4.6	2.5			Intangibles (net)	13.5	6.8
		11.4	7.0			All Other Non-Current	7.9	7.8
		100.0	100.0			Total	100.0	100.0
						LIABILITIES		
		7.5	2.8			Notes Payable-Short Term	1.9	4.3
		6.6	4.3			Cur. Mat.-L.T.D.	7.9	8.3
		9.5	7.3			Trade Payables	9.4	13.1
		.0	.0			Income Taxes Payable	.0	.3
		6.2	5.2			All Other Current	7.4	9.7
		29.8	19.6			Total Current	26.6	35.7
		25.5	30.8			Long-Term Debt	31.9	35.3
		.4	2.3			Deferred Taxes	1.7	2.0
		12.8	5.9			All Other Non-Current	37.0	3.7
		31.5	41.4			Net Worth	2.8	23.3
		100.0	100.0			Total Liabilities & Net Worth	100.0	100.0
						INCOME DATA		
		100.0	100.0			Net Sales	100.0	100.0
						Gross Profit		
		88.8	91.8			Operating Expenses	91.9	92.0
		11.2	8.2			Operating Profit	8.1	8.0
		6.7	.3			All Other Expenses (net)	1.8	1.5
		4.5	7.9			Profit Before Taxes	6.3	6.4
						RATIOS		
		2.5	2.5				2.1	2.2
		1.0	1.4			Current	1.0	1.0
		.4	1.2				.8	.6
		2.5	2.3				2.0	1.8
		.5	1.3			Quick	1.0	.9
		.3	.8				.7	.5
	24	15.2	38 9.7				26 13.9	26 14.0
	34	10.6	57 6.5			Sales/Receivables	40 9.2	32 11.3
	43	8.6	68 5.4				47 7.8	41 8.9
						Cost of Sales/Inventory		
						Cost of Sales/Payables		
		7.3	9.0				7.2	18.4
		-99.6	12.4			Sales/Working Capital	NM	NM
		-6.4	16.0				-20.4	-14.3
		14.2	19.8				7.3	19.3
		(17) 1.0	1.8			EBIT/Interest	2.4	(21) 4.3
		-4.9	.6				.8	1.9
						Net Profit + Depr., Dep., Amort./Cur. Mat. L/T/D		
		.7	.8				2.7	1.0
		1.4	1.3			Fixed/Worth	4.5	2.1
		-6.5	5.9				-1.0	-9.4
		.6	.7				2.3	.8
		1.3	.9			Debt/Worth	5.6	2.6
		-10.4	-10.5				-3.3	-17.5
		55.2	49.4					81.7
		(14) 10.8	(10) 8.4			% Profit Before Taxes/Tangible Net Worth		(16) 63.9
		-14.0	-1.4					24.0
		16.8	17.4				18.0	30.9
		.0	1.9			% Profit Before Taxes/Total Assets	5.9	13.5
		-5.2	-.7				-.5	4.0
		5.5	2.5				4.6	7.0
		2.7	1.4			Sales/Net Fixed Assets	2.6	3.5
		.9	.8				1.6	2.3
		2.0	1.3				2.0	3.2
		1.6	1.0			Sales/Total Assets	1.2	2.1
		.8	.7				.6	1.4
		5.3	5.7				4.5	2.5
		(16) 7.1	(10) 8.1			% Depr., Dep., Amort./Sales	(13) 6.5	(19) 5.8
		15.4	19.7				9.8	10.3
						% Officers', Directors' Owners' Comp/Sales		
2125M	11624M	122731M	341817M	109777M	588849M	Net Sales ($)	466667M	1005001M
805M	3993M	88163M	340103M	113064M	619245M	Total Assets ($)	391245M	467739M

M = $ thousand   MM = $ million
See Pages 9 through 22 for Explanation of Ratios and Data

Comparative Historical Data

Current Data Sorted by Sales

4/1/07-3/31/08 ALL	4/1/08-3/31/09 ALL	4/1/09-3/31/10 ALL	Type of Statement	0-1MM	1-3MM	3-5MM	5-10MM	10-25MM	25MM & OVER
7	8	10	Unqualified				1	1	8
5	13	5	Reviewed				2	2	1
	3	5	Compiled	1		2		1	1
3	5	7	Tax Returns	2	2	1	2		
8	10	16	Other	2	4		6	2	2
					6 (4/1-9/30/09)		37 (10/1/09-3/31/10)		
23	39	43	**NUMBER OF STATEMENTS**	5	6	4	10	6	12
%	%	%	**ASSETS**	%	%	%	%	%	%
4.2	7.6	10.0	Cash & Equivalents				5.0		5.6
19.4	20.8	16.0	Trade Receivables (net)				17.3		17.4
1.7	2.8	2.2	Inventory				3.6		1.9
3.4	4.6	2.8	All Other Current				1.0		1.0
28.7	35.8	31.1	Total Current				27.0		25.8
56.9	52.7	54.6	Fixed Assets (net)				48.1		55.3
8.1	6.3	6.2	Intangibles (net)				6.6		12.9
6.3	5.2	8.1	All Other Non-Current				18.3		6.0
100.0	100.0	100.0	Total				100.0		100.0
			LIABILITIES						
2.2	9.3	4.8	Notes Payable-Short Term				3.0		1.4
6.5	7.4	5.0	Cur. Mat.-L.T.D.				6.9		2.1
10.9	11.1	10.7	Trade Payables				17.5		7.3
.5	.0	.1	Income Taxes Payable				.0		.2
5.4	6.4	10.2	All Other Current				7.9		7.2
25.6	34.2	30.8	Total Current				35.4		18.1
38.0	29.3	27.7	Long-Term Debt				29.9		31.0
.9	1.1	1.3	Deferred Taxes				.7		4.1
11.3	12.7	9.4	All Other Non-Current				14.0		10.6
24.2	22.7	30.8	Net Worth				20.1		36.2
100.0	100.0	100.0	Total Liabilities & Net Worth				100.0		100.0
			INCOME DATA						
100.0	100.0	100.0	Net Sales				100.0		100.0
			Gross Profit						
88.0	93.5	90.3	Operating Expenses				104.4		86.9
12.0	6.5	9.7	Operating Profit				-4.4		13.1
1.8	1.3	3.7	All Other Expenses (net)				-.2		2.6
10.2	5.2	6.0	Profit Before Taxes				-4.2		10.4
			RATIOS						
1.7	2.5	2.3	Current				2.7		1.8
1.0	1.2	1.3					.8		1.4
.6	.8	.8					.3		1.1
1.2	1.5	1.6	Quick				2.5		1.6
.9	.9	1.1					.5		1.4
.5	.6	.5					.3		.9
25 14.4	20 17.9	26 14.2	Sales/Receivables				26 13.8		35 10.3
37 9.8	37 9.8	37 10.0					36 10.2		61 6.0
61 5.9	46 7.9	60 6.1					44 8.3		71 5.1
			Cost of Sales/Inventory						
			Cost of Sales/Payables						
11.0	8.9	11.3	Sales/Working Capital				10.3		9.6
-320.3	30.6	26.2					-122.2		13.0
-10.9	-33.6	-26.7					-6.0		740.2
8.3	12.7	12.0	EBIT/Interest				3.4		18.1
(20) 5.9	(38) 3.3	(38) 1.4					-3.3		2.9
1.4	.6	-.9					-16.0		1.0
			Net Profit + Depr., Dep., Amort./Cur. Mat. L/T/D						
1.2	.8	.8	Fixed/Worth				.6		1.2
3.0	3.0	1.5					1.5		2.2
11.6	-17.2	10.3					-5.5		NM
1.2	1.0	.7	Debt/Worth				.8		.9
2.7	3.7	2.5					4.0		4.9
12.6	-27.5	13.1					-8.9		NM
71.2	50.7	54.0	% Profit Before Taxes/Tangible Net Worth						
(19) 41.0	(28) 27.6	(33) 11.8							
23.8	6.2	-3.9							
23.2	16.3	17.4	% Profit Before Taxes/Total Assets				4.0		17.3
10.1	5.8	1.9					-9.3		5.8
2.7	-2.0	-4.8					-15.9		.3
6.1	6.6	3.9	Sales/Net Fixed Assets				8.3		3.1
3.3	3.7	2.3					3.0		1.5
1.8	2.1	1.2					2.1		1.3
3.0	3.3	1.9	Sales/Total Assets				2.0		1.2
1.6	1.9	1.2					1.7		1.0
1.1	1.1	.8					1.1		.8
3.1	2.1	4.6	% Depr., Dep., Amort./Sales						
(19) 5.6	(34) 4.7	(33) 7.1							
9.3	8.0	13.1							
		1.3	% Officers', Directors' Owners' Comp/Sales						
	(11)	2.4							
		4.2							
785963M	1200090M	1176923M	Net Sales ($)	3035M	10090M	17821M	68173M	102314M	975490M
670117M	982419M	1165373M	Total Assets ($)	4674M	24410M	35333M	48119M	80480M	972357M

M = $ thousand   MM = $ million
See Pages 9 through 22 for Explanation of Ratios and Data

Current Data Sorted by Assets   Comparative Historical Data

Type of Statement	0-500M	500M-2MM	2-10MM	10-50MM	50-100MM	100-250MM		4/1/05-3/31/06 ALL	4/1/06-3/31/07 ALL
Unqualified		1	9	6	1	4		11	7
Reviewed	1	6	21	6				13	24
Compiled	1	8	2					4	10
Tax Returns	9	7	2					4	6
Other	3	11	14	8	1	1		7	9
	16 (4/1-9/30/09)			106 (10/1/09-3/31/10)					
NUMBER OF STATEMENTS	14	33	48	20	2	5		39	56

ASSETS	%	%	%	%	%	%		%	%
Cash & Equivalents	28.0	9.7	9.6	10.3				6.9	9.5
Trade Receivables (net)	28.9	40.3	44.0	26.6				48.8	43.4
Inventory	.3	3.2	4.3	1.1				2.8	3.1
All Other Current	2.4	4.3	5.0	9.4				11.6	10.9
Total Current	59.6	57.5	62.8	47.4				70.1	66.9
Fixed Assets (net)	27.1	34.6	24.5	38.2				21.0	21.9
Intangibles (net)	4.9	.2	3.1	6.2				3.5	6.1
All Other Non-Current	8.3	7.6	9.5	8.3				5.4	5.1
Total	100.0	100.0	100.0	100.0				100.0	100.0

LIABILITIES									
Notes Payable-Short Term	37.2	14.4	6.8	5.0				10.8	16.1
Cur. Mat.-L.T.D.	10.8	4.7	7.2	4.9				4.3	3.8
Trade Payables	14.2	15.4	14.2	13.1				17.0	16.5
Income Taxes Payable	1.6	.1	.8	.1				.4	1.3
All Other Current	5.1	9.2	11.3	11.7				11.9	14.9
Total Current	69.0	43.7	40.3	34.8				44.4	52.5
Long-Term Debt	30.1	28.8	16.8	17.5				16.7	15.2
Deferred Taxes	.0	.7	.2	2.8				1.0	.6
All Other Non-Current	17.0	4.5	2.3	5.1				2.2	3.6
Net Worth	-15.8	22.3	40.3	39.8				35.7	28.0
Total Liabilities & Net Worth	100.0	100.0	100.0	100.0				100.0	100.0

INCOME DATA									
Net Sales	100.0	100.0	100.0	100.0				100.0	100.0
Gross Profit									
Operating Expenses	93.6	101.0	94.9	91.6				96.7	95.4
Operating Profit	6.4	-1.0	5.1	8.4				3.3	4.6
All Other Expenses (net)	1.9	1.1	.2	1.5				1.1	1.0
Profit Before Taxes	4.5	-2.1	4.9	6.8				2.2	3.6

RATIOS									
Current	5.1	2.5	2.8	2.2				2.3	1.9
	1.5	1.5	1.5	1.4				1.5	1.3
	.5	1.0	1.2	1.2				1.2	1.0
Quick	4.5	2.3	2.4	2.0				1.9	1.5
	1.4	1.4	1.3	1.0				1.2	1.1
	.5	.7	1.0	.8				.7	.7
Sales/Receivables	0 UND	41 8.9	48 7.6	36 10.2				46 7.9	40 9.2
	12 29.9	57 6.4	76 4.8	62 5.9				70 5.2	74 5.0
	39 9.4	77 4.8	96 3.8	70 5.2				91 4.0	96 3.8
Cost of Sales/Inventory									
Cost of Sales/Payables									
Sales/Working Capital	11.0	6.3	5.0	6.2				6.7	8.2
	56.9	13.7	9.6	14.8				9.4	17.1
	-9.5	-105.1	57.4	37.5				22.3	233.0
EBIT/Interest	5.2	8.8	22.2	14.6				12.1	9.9
	(10) 1.4	(32) 1.7	(42) 5.7	(17) 2.6				(34) 3.4	(50) 4.1
	-1.4	-2.6	1.5	-.5				.6	1.8
Net Profit + Depr., Dep., Amort./Cur. Mat. L/T/D			13.1	4.4				13.6	5.9
			(16) 3.2	(11) 2.2				(11) 2.7	(16) 3.0
			.5	.3				.8	1.0
Fixed/Worth	.1	.4	.1	.4				.2	.2
	NM	1.1	.5	1.2				.4	.7
	-.7	4.4	1.1	2.1				1.4	4.7
Debt/Worth	1.4	.9	.5	.7				.8	1.3
	NM	1.6	1.3	2.1				2.3	2.4
	-2.3	11.4	2.7	4.4				6.0	15.3
% Profit Before Taxes/Tangible Net Worth		49.5	37.3	48.3				53.6	63.9
		(26) 10.2	(42) 23.8	(19) 16.3				(34) 23.1	(45) 32.1
		-23.2	9.2	-6.8				2.9	11.6
% Profit Before Taxes/Total Assets	37.4	17.7	18.4	21.3				13.3	17.9
	3.6	1.6	8.9	4.9				6.3	9.0
	-16.2	-18.2	3.1	-1.8				-1.3	3.6
Sales/Net Fixed Assets	205.3	18.8	38.0	13.2				35.6	37.5
	36.6	8.9	11.7	4.6				19.0	12.6
	21.3	3.2	5.0	2.3				8.4	6.6
Sales/Total Assets	9.8	3.0	3.1	2.3				3.6	3.7
	5.5	2.5	2.0	1.9				2.5	2.6
	2.7	1.6	1.6	1.0				1.8	1.9
% Depr., Dep., Amort./Sales	.4	2.1	.9	2.2				.9	1.0
	(10) 1.1	(26) 3.4	(44) 2.7	(18) 3.9				(31) 1.5	(49) 1.7
	3.7	5.4	5.5	7.4				2.9	3.6
% Officers', Directors' Owners' Comp/Sales		4.7	2.4					1.7	2.2
		(15) 8.1	(25) 3.8					(17) 3.5	(25) 4.6
		10.3	9.2					5.4	7.5
Net Sales ($)	24677M	93409M	495276M	853841M	210400M	535928M		945641M	895279M
Total Assets ($)	3297M	36850M	222958M	449851M	129152M	842025M		464052M	724704M

M = $ thousand   MM = $ million
See Pages 9 through 22 for Explanation of Ratios and Data

Comparative Historical Data   ## Current Data Sorted by Sales

			Type of Statement						
9	12	21	Unqualified	1	3	4	2	8	11
23	36	34	Reviewed	2	6	2	13	12	1
11	4	11	Compiled	4	9	1		1	
8	8	18	Tax Returns	2	10	6	2	2	
21	28	38	Other				9	5	6
4/1/07-3/31/08 ALL	4/1/08-3/31/09 ALL	4/1/09-3/31/10 ALL			16 (4/1-9/30/09)		106 (10/1/09-3/31/10)		
				0-1MM	1-3MM	3-5MM	5-10MM	10-25MM	25MM & OVER
72	88	122	NUMBER OF STATEMENTS	9	28	13	26	28	18
%	%	%	ASSETS	%	%	%	%	%	%
9.2	11.5	11.5	Cash & Equivalents		11.6	10.4	9.1	12.0	9.3
42.7	39.7	37.0	Trade Receivables (net)		35.5	42.9	39.7	43.2	28.5
2.7	4.2	2.8	Inventory		3.2	3.2	3.8	3.4	.7
8.8	5.5	5.3	All Other Current		4.1	3.1	4.5	5.2	12.0
63.5	60.9	56.7	Total Current		54.4	59.6	57.0	63.7	50.6
26.5	25.5	30.0	Fixed Assets (net)		35.9	28.6	30.4	25.3	25.8
3.5	5.4	4.8	Intangibles (net)		2.8	.4	3.9	2.0	16.9
6.5	8.2	8.6	All Other Non-Current		6.9	11.5	8.7	9.0	6.7
100.0	100.0	100.0	Total		100.0	100.0	100.0	100.0	100.0
			LIABILITIES						
9.3	12.1	11.7	Notes Payable-Short Term		19.8	9.4	11.9	6.8	2.9
4.0	5.5	6.2	Cur. Mat.-L.T.D.		6.5	4.8	6.9	7.1	3.0
12.5	13.1	14.1	Trade Payables		17.3	6.8	11.9	18.7	14.1
.8	.4	.6	Income Taxes Payable		.1	.0	.5	.9	.0
11.4	10.7	9.7	All Other Current		9.4	3.9	10.0	11.6	13.5
38.0	41.8	42.2	Total Current		53.1	24.9	41.3	45.1	33.6
19.4	20.0	21.7	Long-Term Debt		34.0	18.1	18.9	16.3	9.9
.2	.4	.9	Deferred Taxes		.9	.0	.1	1.1	3.2
1.6	4.5	5.7	All Other Non-Current		8.3	.1	4.2	2.3	7.5
40.8	33.3	29.4	Net Worth		3.8	56.8	35.5	35.2	45.9
100.0	100.0	100.0	Total Liabilties & Net Worth		100.0	100.0	100.0	100.0	100.0
			INCOME DATA						
100.0	100.0	100.0	Net Sales		100.0	100.0	100.0	100.0	100.0
			Gross Profit						
90.3	93.6	95.9	Operating Expenses		102.4	91.5	94.7	95.2	93.0
9.7	6.4	4.1	Operating Profit		-2.4	8.5	5.3	4.8	7.0
2.3	1.3	1.1	All Other Expenses (net)		1.2	-.4	1.0	.6	2.0
7.4	5.1	3.0	Profit Before Taxes		-3.6	9.0	4.3	4.3	5.0
			RATIOS						
2.7	2.3	2.5			2.4	6.8	2.7	1.9	2.3
1.7	1.5	1.5	Current		1.4	2.3	1.5	1.4	1.4
1.2	1.1	1.1			.8	1.4	1.0	1.2	1.2
2.4	1.9	2.2			2.0	5.4	2.5	1.9	2.1
1.3	1.3	1.3	Quick		1.1	2.2	1.3	1.3	1.1
1.0	1.0	.8			.4	1.3	.8	1.0	.7
33 10.9	35 10.3	35 10.3		4 82.1	49 7.5	48 7.7	38 9.6	31 11.6	
68 5.4	64 5.7	60 6.1	Sales/Receivables	54 6.8	77 4.7	70 5.2	64 5.7	57 6.4	
93 3.9	79 4.6	85 4.3		103 3.5	98 3.7	89 4.1	85 4.3	79 4.6	
			Cost of Sales/Inventory						
			Cost of Sales/Payables						
5.6	6.2	6.3			5.3	4.0	4.8	8.2	5.2
8.7	12.8	13.4	Sales/Working Capital		20.6	9.3	11.8	13.0	14.3
29.0	45.5	84.8			-21.1	18.2	NM	39.1	23.2
22.3	17.6	10.5			6.5	23.3	10.4	16.7	17.9
(63) 8.4	(82) 4.8	(107) 3.2	EBIT/Interest	(26) -.4	(12) 9.6	(23) 4.8	(25) 4.8	(15) 1.6	
2.5	1.0	-.6			-7.6	3.0	1.4	.5	-1.0
11.7	3.9	5.1						13.1	
(21) 5.1	(16) 1.2	(32) 2.1	Net Profit + Depr., Dep., Amort./Cur. Mat. L/T/D					(12) 3.3	
1.5	.3	.5						.5	
.2	.2	.3			.5	.2	.4	.1	.4
.6	.6	.7	Fixed/Worth		2.9	.4	.6	.4	.8
1.2	1.5	3.2			-1.3	.8	2.6	1.9	1.5
.6	.8	.7			1.2	.4	1.0	.8	.7
1.6	1.7	1.6	Debt/Worth		6.1	.5	1.3	1.6	1.9
3.3	6.2	6.5			-3.8	1.4	5.5	3.4	6.1
60.9	56.8	47.6			47.9	51.6	37.7	48.3	48.3
(65) 33.3	(74) 26.3	(98) 19.3	% Profit Before Taxes/Tangible Net Worth	(17) 5.6	(12) 27.8	(21) 26.5	(27) 17.2	(15) 10.4	
16.5	3.2	-4.9			-39.3	13.6	8.3	7.0	-6.2
23.9	25.8	18.0			11.5	27.1	13.6	17.6	15.4
11.3	8.9	5.8	% Profit Before Taxes/Total Assets		-2.5	22.0	9.4	6.3	3.3
4.0	-.4	-2.6			-23.6	5.1	2.6	.1	-1.7
32.9	28.6	28.1			28.3	17.1	20.5	71.0	17.4
15.0	13.2	9.6	Sales/Net Fixed Assets		6.0	8.4	9.0	16.9	10.7
6.4	4.9	3.9			2.9	4.8	3.5	4.6	4.3
3.3	3.1	3.2			3.1	3.0	2.7	4.0	2.4
2.4	2.3	2.1	Sales/Total Assets		2.2	2.4	1.9	2.5	2.1
1.8	1.8	1.5			1.5	1.7	1.5	1.6	.7
.9	1.0	1.4			1.7	2.3	2.3	.6	1.8
(59) 2.1	(70) 2.2	(103) 2.9	% Depr., Dep., Amort./Sales	(20) 3.4	(11) 4.3	(25) 3.1	(25) 2.5	(15) 2.2	
4.2	4.9	5.8			7.0	5.2	5.9	4.7	6.3
2.1	2.5	2.8			3.7		2.4	1.0	
(30) 4.1	(36) 4.2	(51) 5.8	% Officers', Directors' Owners' Comp/Sales	(14) 6.8		(12) 3.8	(13) 3.7		
8.8	7.5	10.1			10.4		10.9	8.3	
1475890M	1517527M	2213531M	Net Sales ($)	3634M	53780M	53854M	197906M	449344M	1455013M
702751M	1196402M	1684133M	Total Assets ($)	1709M	34114M	29644M	119174M	238569M	1260923M

M = $ thousand   MM = $ million
See Pages 9 through 22 for Explanation of Ratios and Data

Current Data Sorted by Assets | Comparative Historical Data

Type of Statement

Type of Statement	0-500M	500M-2MM	2-10MM	10-50MM	50-100MM	100-250MM		4/1/05-3/31/06 ALL	4/1/06-3/31/07 ALL
Unqualified			4	8	2			7	6
Reviewed	1	4	11	4	1			10	17
Compiled	1	10	3	2				7	7
Tax Returns	4	1	7	1				10	7
Other	1	4	12	12		1	1	8	19
	11 (4/1-9/30/09)			84 (10/1/09-3/31/10)					
NUMBER OF STATEMENTS	7	19	37	27	4	1		42	56

Data

0-500M	500M-2MM	2-10MM	10-50MM	50-100MM	100-250MM		4/1/05-3/31/06 ALL	4/1/06-3/31/07 ALL
%	%	%	%	%	%	**ASSETS**	%	%
	15.0	9.9	6.8			Cash & Equivalents	10.1	9.7
	16.1	19.6	17.8			Trade Receivables (net)	23.1	22.7
	7.4	6.2	11.6			Inventory	3.9	8.0
	8.8	3.2	2.8			All Other Current	4.8	4.2
	47.2	39.0	39.0			Total Current	42.0	44.5
	41.7	47.1	51.9			Fixed Assets (net)	44.5	40.0
	3.7	4.6	2.4			Intangibles (net)	3.5	4.8
	7.4	9.3	6.7			All Other Non-Current	10.1	10.6
	100.0	100.0	100.0			Total	100.0	100.0
						LIABILITIES		
	13.3	5.0	8.6			Notes Payable-Short Term	7.7	9.2
	5.9	5.9	4.4			Cur. Mat.-L.T.D.	5.9	4.8
	11.5	11.6	11.3			Trade Payables	17.4	13.6
	.0	.5	.1			Income Taxes Payable	.1	.8
	9.5	8.5	5.4			All Other Current	10.6	9.3
	40.2	31.4	29.7			Total Current	41.8	37.6
	22.9	30.3	25.9			Long-Term Debt	25.0	27.8
	.1	.3	.2			Deferred Taxes	.6	.4
	16.8	3.8	7.1			All Other Non-Current	13.9	4.6
	20.0	34.1	37.1			Net Worth	18.8	29.6
	100.0	100.0	100.0			Total Liabilities & Net Worth	100.0	100.0
						INCOME DATA		
	100.0	100.0	100.0			Net Sales	100.0	100.0
						Gross Profit		
	100.9	91.7	95.5			Operating Expenses	93.7	92.1
	-.9	8.3	4.5			Operating Profit	6.3	7.9
	1.3	3.9	.8			All Other Expenses (net)	3.3	3.7
	-2.2	4.4	3.6			Profit Before Taxes	3.0	4.2
						RATIOS		
	2.4	1.6	1.7				1.6	2.1
	1.1	1.0	1.2			Current	1.0	1.2
	.7	.7	.9				.6	.7
	2.2	1.3	1.1				1.4	1.6
	.8	.8	.8			Quick	.9	1.0
	.3	.4	.5				.5	.4
	1 281.6	23 16.0	30 12.0				20 18.0	16 22.4
	21 17.0	40 9.2	37 10.0			Sales/Receivables	32 11.5	30 12.3
	45 8.1	48 7.6	48 7.6				47 7.8	48 7.6
						Cost of Sales/Inventory		
						Cost of Sales/Payables		
	8.6	16.9	7.9				18.6	11.3
	84.9	-898.5	33.6			Sales/Working Capital	596.9	36.2
	-12.1	-11.6	-30.0				-11.4	-24.6
	4.0	10.9	6.7				11.7	8.9
	(18) 1.3	(34) 4.2	(26) 2.5			EBIT/Interest	(37) 3.5	(48) 2.5
	-3.3	1.0	-.7				1.0	1.5
			4.5					
		(10) 1.6				Net Profit + Depr., Dep., Amort./Cur. Mat. L/T/D		
		1.2						
	.6	.7	.9				.6	.4
	1.7	2.2	1.5			Fixed/Worth	1.7	2.0
	-1.6	4.0	3.1				17.0	8.4
	1.2	1.2	.6				.9	.9
	1.9	2.7	2.2			Debt/Worth	4.0	3.1
	-7.5	5.2	4.5				30.4	14.6
	29.7	34.2	31.9				44.6	49.5
	(14) 15.5	(33) 19.5	(25) 9.8			% Profit Before Taxes/Tangible Net Worth	(33) 21.1	(46) 20.5
	-7.5	2.2	-.6				10.6	7.6
	8.2	10.5	8.9				14.5	16.6
	.9	6.2	3.4			% Profit Before Taxes/Total Assets	4.4	4.7
	-10.4	.5	-1.8				.7	1.2
	14.7	9.8	6.5				15.3	21.9
	4.9	3.3	2.5			Sales/Net Fixed Assets	6.0	5.7
	2.9	1.9	1.5				2.1	2.9
	3.6	2.7	2.4				3.9	4.0
	2.1	1.5	1.3			Sales/Total Assets	2.4	2.6
	1.8	1.0	.9				1.1	1.1
	1.9	2.0	2.2				2.2	1.5
	(13) 4.8	(33) 5.0	(26) 4.5			% Depr., Dep., Amort./Sales	(37) 5.3	(51) 3.6
	8.8	8.5	7.8				8.9	9.2
		.3					1.7	1.0
		(10) 2.6				% Officers', Directors' Owners' Comp/Sales	(16) 3.4	(15) 2.1
		5.4					6.1	6.6
12926M	54305M	348280M	1080506M	381204M	419976M	Net Sales ($)	1196021M	1276855M
2197M	22264M	189615M	619125M	238316M	138382M	Total Assets ($)	536600M	542462M

M = $ thousand   MM = $ million
See Pages 9 through 22 for Explanation of Ratios and Data

Comparative Historical Data   Current Data Sorted by Sales

4/1/07-3/31/08 ALL	4/1/08-3/31/09 ALL	4/1/09-3/31/10 ALL	Type of Statement	0-1MM	11 (4/1-9/30/09) 1-3MM	3-5MM	84 (10/1/09-3/31/10) 5-10MM	10-25MM	25MM & OVER
9	12	14	Unqualified			2	1	2	9
13	18	21	Reviewed	3	2	2	2	9	3
11	15	16	Compiled	2	6	4	2		2
9	11	13	Tax Returns	1	2	2	7	1	
21	31	31	Other	2	6	2	6	5	10
63	87	95	**NUMBER OF STATEMENTS**	8	16	12	18	17	24
%	%	%	**ASSETS**	%	%	%	%	%	%
9.1	11.9	10.3	Cash & Equivalents		15.1	7.1	14.0	9.0	7.4
22.2	19.6	18.1	Trade Receivables (net)		16.7	14.6	11.9	20.9	26.0
6.5	5.2	8.4	Inventory		6.9	.5	10.1	10.0	13.2
5.1	3.5	4.0	All Other Current		4.7	1.2	7.4	2.9	3.9
43.0	40.1	40.8	Total Current		43.4	23.4	43.5	42.8	50.5
44.4	44.1	47.6	Fixed Assets (net)		44.0	65.5	38.9	46.8	41.2
5.7	6.4	3.7	Intangibles (net)		5.3	1.2	3.3	6.3	3.4
6.9	9.4	8.0	All Other Non-Current		7.3	10.0	14.4	4.2	5.0
100.0	100.0	100.0	Total		100.0	100.0	100.0	100.0	100.0
			LIABILITIES						
11.7	8.1	7.6	Notes Payable-Short Term		14.7	5.3	3.1	7.4	10.2
8.2	5.6	6.0	Cur. Mat.-L.T.D.		4.4	11.0	8.4	4.9	3.6
10.2	11.7	11.8	Trade Payables		11.2	8.3	9.7	11.7	15.2
.5	.1	.2	Income Taxes Payable		.0	.0	.1	.1	.7
7.8	9.3	9.8	All Other Current		7.2	4.8	17.2	8.0	6.6
38.4	34.8	35.4	Total Current		37.5	29.4	38.5	32.1	36.3
33.1	28.7	29.1	Long-Term Debt		31.3	39.4	31.6	20.0	20.1
.7	.2	.2	Deferred Taxes		.0	.1	.4	.3	.2
5.1	5.8	7.2	All Other Non-Current		15.5	6.0	7.4	8.6	3.5
22.8	30.5	28.0	Net Worth		15.7	25.1	22.2	39.0	39.8
100.0	100.0	100.0	Total Liabilties & Net Worth		100.0	100.0	100.0	100.0	100.0
			INCOME DATA						
100.0	100.0	100.0	Net Sales		100.0	100.0	100.0	100.0	100.0
			Gross Profit						
93.9	91.3	95.3	Operating Expenses		105.4	91.1	95.9	97.3	97.7
6.1	8.7	4.7	Operating Profit		-5.4	8.9	4.1	2.7	2.3
2.0	2.9	2.1	All Other Expenses (net)		1.4	5.6	.4	.8	.6
4.2	5.8	2.6	Profit Before Taxes		-6.9	3.2	3.7	1.8	1.7
			RATIOS						
2.0	2.2	1.8	Current		2.1	1.7	3.1	1.6	1.8
1.2	1.3	1.1			1.0	.8	1.0	1.2	1.5
.7	.7	.7			.8	.6	.5	.8	.9
1.5	1.7	1.3	Quick		2.0	1.7	2.0	1.2	1.2
.9	1.0	.8			.8	.8	.7	.8	.8
.5	.4	.4			.3	.5	.4	.5	.6
17 21.2	9 41.2	19 19.0	Sales/Receivables	14 27.0	21 17.1	2 159.6	26 14.1	34 10.7	
32 11.5	28 13.2	36 10.1		23 16.0	32 11.4	31 11.7	39 9.4	41 8.9	
46 8.0	49 7.5	47 7.8		38 9.6	55 6.6	50 7.4	50 7.3	47 7.8	
			Cost of Sales/Inventory						
			Cost of Sales/Payables						
11.8	12.3	11.2	Sales/Working Capital		9.2	91.8	6.5	12.5	8.7
39.8	35.1	84.9			NM	-23.8	NM	31.6	22.7
-21.0	-19.7	-14.3			-19.9	-9.8	-11.1	-15.8	NM
21.2	14.2	7.3	EBIT/Interest		4.2	7.2	6.7	12.6	19.2
(60) 3.9	(74) 3.6	(90) 2.6			.4	(11) 1.8	(16) 3.8	2.8	3.4
1.1	1.5	-.2			-3.6	-.5	.1	-.3	.7
17.2	11.9	7.1	Net Profit + Depr., Dep., Amort./Cur. Mat. L/T/D						
(17) 3.3	(13) 2.3	(18) 2.0							
1.9	.6	1.2							
.6	.5	.7	Fixed/Worth		.7	1.4	.1	.9	.4
1.9	1.8	1.7			5.1	1.8	1.2	1.5	1.1
-26.9	9.5	4.1			-4.6	3.4	7.4	3.0	2.2
1.2	.9	1.0	Debt/Worth		1.1	1.2	.4	.8	.7
2.3	2.9	2.2			5.6	2.0	1.5	2.0	1.9
-33.6	18.0	5.5			-10.4	4.4	8.4	4.9	3.7
79.3	72.7	33.3	% Profit Before Taxes/Tangible Net Worth		37.0	45.3	31.6	23.5	31.3
(47) 35.8	(69) 38.0	(82) 15.2		(11) 14.3	(10) 17.3	(16) 18.7	(16) 10.5	(22) 9.1	
6.2	13.6	1.3			-85.8	2.7	2.8	-5.3	2.1
21.1	27.7	9.7	% Profit Before Taxes/Total Assets		9.4	14.8	9.1	10.0	8.9
8.5	7.7	4.1			-1.8	5.1	6.3	3.5	3.8
.4	2.1	-1.8			-20.6	-8.9	-.5	-1.4	-.6
17.9	14.3	10.9	Sales/Net Fixed Assets		14.6	3.4	38.3	9.8	22.5
6.2	5.6	3.6			5.0	2.6	4.3	4.1	4.7
2.1	2.2	2.0			2.4	1.9	2.3	2.0	2.4
3.9	4.0	3.0	Sales/Total Assets		3.2	1.9	3.8	3.0	3.3
1.9	2.1	1.6			2.2	1.7	1.4	1.5	2.2
1.1	1.3	1.1			1.1	1.1	1.0	1.0	1.2
1.4	1.3	2.2	% Depr., Dep., Amort./Sales		3.2	4.4	.4	2.3	1.3
(58) 3.1	(72) 2.8	(81) 4.8		(10) 7.2	(10) 7.1	(17) 3.0	4.7	(21) 3.6	
7.1	7.6	8.5			13.3	10.2	8.3	9.1	5.4
.9	.9	.7	% Officers', Directors' Owners' Comp/Sales						
(22) 2.8	(31) 2.5	(26) 2.6							
4.7	6.3	4.8							
1934700M	3479947M	2297197M	Net Sales ($)	4919M	32913M	46741M	134174M	257122M	1821328M
973837M	1430503M	1209899M	Total Assets ($)	13087M	25546M	44236M	100019M	206387M	820624M

M = $ thousand   MM = $ million
See Pages 9 through 22 for Explanation of Ratios and Data

Current Data Sorted by Assets

Comparative Historical Data

						Type of Statement		
		6	8	1	1	Unqualified	18	20
1	6	15	3			Reviewed	31	20
4	7	7	4			Compiled	14	22
10	11	2				Tax Returns	20	33
4	6	11	16	2		Other	61	40
	19 (4/1-9/30/09)		106 (10/1/09-3/31/10)				4/1/05-3/31/06	4/1/06-3/31/07
0-500M	500M-2MM	2-10MM	10-50MM	50-100MM	100-250MM		ALL	ALL
19	30	41	31	3	1	NUMBER OF STATEMENTS	144	135
%	%	%	%	%	%	ASSETS	%	%
21.6	10.3	10.5	9.6			Cash & Equivalents	10.8	11.6
21.7	26.5	28.3	18.6			Trade Receivables (net)	27.2	26.6
6.6	2.7	3.7	3.4			Inventory	2.8	2.8
5.8	3.3	3.0	4.5			All Other Current	3.3	3.5
55.7	42.8	45.4	36.1			Total Current	44.1	44.6
32.4	42.6	39.6	47.6			Fixed Assets (net)	42.5	42.4
4.0	4.7	7.1	10.8			Intangibles (net)	5.0	5.5
7.9	10.0	7.9	5.5			All Other Non-Current	8.5	7.5
100.0	100.0	100.0	100.0			Total	100.0	100.0
						LIABILITIES		
19.7	7.5	9.1	5.2			Notes Payable-Short Term	6.9	7.8
5.9	7.4	7.0	7.3			Cur. Mat.-L.T.D.	7.2	6.7
12.8	12.5	12.7	11.6			Trade Payables	12.1	11.2
.0	.0	.7	.0			Income Taxes Payable	.5	1.0
11.2	4.8	4.5	4.1			All Other Current	10.3	8.4
49.7	32.2	33.9	28.3			Total Current	36.9	35.1
16.3	22.5	19.3	38.5			Long-Term Debt	28.5	27.9
.1	1.0	.8	1.0			Deferred Taxes	.6	.3
16.6	10.5	3.2	8.1			All Other Non-Current	5.9	2.7
17.2	33.7	42.8	24.1			Net Worth	28.1	34.0
100.0	100.0	100.0	100.0			Total Liabilties & Net Worth	100.0	100.0
						INCOME DATA		
100.0	100.0	100.0	100.0			Net Sales	100.0	100.0
						Gross Profit		
94.1	96.9	95.1	90.9			Operating Expenses	89.4	93.0
5.9	3.1	4.9	9.1			Operating Profit	10.6	7.0
1.1	1.3	1.8	2.9			All Other Expenses (net)	2.9	1.8
4.8	1.8	3.2	6.1			Profit Before Taxes	7.6	5.1
						RATIOS		
3.5	2.2	3.0	1.8				1.9	2.1
1.6	1.4	1.1	1.3			Current	1.3	1.4
.5	.9	.7	.9				.8	.8
3.4	2.0	2.5	1.4				1.8	1.9
.7	1.4	1.0	.9			Quick	1.1	1.1
.3	.7	.6	.7				.6	.6
0 UND	11 33.8	31 11.7	34 10.9				27 13.7	16 22.6
25 14.5	31 11.7	46 7.9	46 7.9			Sales/Receivables	46 7.9	38 9.5
47 7.8	66 5.6	84 4.4	57 6.4				72 5.1	65 5.6
						Cost of Sales/Inventory		
						Cost of Sales/Payables		
10.2	9.4	4.9	8.3				7.7	7.7
29.7	26.0	41.0	23.4			Sales/Working Capital	23.9	22.9
-18.0	-45.6	-19.6	-62.5				-31.7	-28.3
12.9	8.9	9.6	8.0				10.4	15.0
(14) 2.5	(25) 3.0	(39) 2.1	2.8			EBIT/Interest	(133) 3.9	(123) 4.1
.8	.5	.4	1.5				1.3	1.0
			4.6			Net Profit + Depr., Dep.,	3.4	5.7
		(12) 1.7				Amort./Cur. Mat. L/T/D	(31) 2.0	(28) 2.2
		1.4					1.4	.8
.5	.4	.4	1.2				.6	.6
6.3	1.3	1.3	3.1			Fixed/Worth	1.4	1.3
-.6	6.8	4.0	194.5				7.2	6.8
.5	.4	.7	1.7				1.0	.8
9.9	2.0	1.8	4.9			Debt/Worth	2.5	2.1
-4.7	8.8	5.2	440.8				24.2	8.3
131.9	56.9	37.3	55.7			% Profit Before Taxes/Tangible	67.0	72.6
(11) 28.6	(25) 20.8	(35) 16.9	(24) 27.1			Net Worth	(111) 32.7	(109) 24.8
17.8	7.8	.4	4.5				7.1	.6
42.1	13.9	14.1	16.3			% Profit Before Taxes/Total	20.3	22.7
7.6	7.6	5.2	4.6			Assets	9.1	7.5
-3.3	-.9	-1.2	1.1				1.9	-.1
55.3	23.1	12.8	4.5				13.4	13.5
20.0	5.1	4.1	2.6			Sales/Net Fixed Assets	5.5	6.2
8.0	3.1	2.4	1.6				2.5	3.0
10.1	3.6	2.3	1.7				2.8	3.5
6.2	2.2	1.7	1.1			Sales/Total Assets	1.9	2.1
2.2	1.8	1.2	.8				1.1	1.4
.2	2.2	2.3	5.4				2.1	2.7
(15) 2.1	(24) 5.4	(36) 4.2	(29) 9.3			% Depr., Dep., Amort./Sales	(120) 4.6	(113) 4.8
5.9	9.9	8.0	13.5				8.4	8.2
4.0	2.2					% Officers', Directors'	2.5	2.5
(10) 6.5	(15) 3.9					Owners' Comp/Sales	(51) 4.1	(53) 3.8
10.7	8.4						8.0	6.9
21672M	87114M	337821M	889288M	249270M	6630M	Net Sales ($)	2149817M	1919544M
3945M	35601M	177089M	705304M	201706M	116089M	Total Assets ($)	1873594M	1411431M

M = $ thousand　　MM = $ million
See Pages 9 through 22 for Explanation of Ratios and Data

Comparative Historical Data

Current Data Sorted by Sales

			Type of Statement						
18	18	16	Unqualified		1	3	3	2	7
33	36	25	Reviewed	2	1	6	6	7	3
18	17	22	Compiled	1	7	9	1	3	1
28	27	23	Tax Returns	7	7	8	1		
48	46	39	Other	3	10	6	2	10	8
4/1/07-3/31/08 ALL	4/1/08-3/31/09 ALL	4/1/09-3/31/10 ALL			19 (4/1-9/30/09)		106 (10/1/09-3/31/10)		
145	144	125	**NUMBER OF STATEMENTS**	0-1MM 13	1-3MM 26	3-5MM 32	5-10MM 13	10-25MM 22	25MM & OVER 19
%	%	%	**ASSETS**	%	%	%	%	%	%
9.4	12.1	12.0	Cash & Equivalents	14.1	12.7	14.6	7.3	10.1	10.5
25.4	25.4	24.2	Trade Receivables (net)	22.8	18.7	25.7	24.6	21.9	32.2
2.4	2.7	4.2	Inventory	5.1	4.6	2.6	2.4	6.0	4.8
3.7	3.4	4.1	All Other Current	3.2	5.6	2.3	4.5	4.5	5.1
40.9	43.5	44.5	Total Current	45.3	41.6	45.2	38.8	42.6	52.7
44.9	39.6	41.0	Fixed Assets (net)	40.9	44.1	40.0	48.8	38.0	36.5
5.6	7.1	6.8	Intangibles (net)	7.1	4.1	4.3	4.2	15.1	6.3
8.6	9.8	7.8	All Other Non-Current	6.7	10.1	10.5	8.1	4.3	4.6
100.0	100.0	100.0	Total	100.0	100.0	100.0	100.0	100.0	100.0
			LIABILITIES						
5.0	7.6	9.3	Notes Payable-Short Term	2.7	19.0	7.0	7.0	6.2	9.6
7.2	6.8	6.9	Cur. Mat.-L.T.D.	6.1	6.7	8.0	6.5	7.0	5.7
12.0	9.8	12.5	Trade Payables	6.0	13.5	12.7	10.3	13.1	16.1
.7	.7	.3	Income Taxes Payable	.1	.0	.3	1.1	.2	.2
6.7	6.2	5.8	All Other Current	11.8	3.7	5.3	4.2	2.8	10.1
31.6	31.0	34.7	Total Current	26.6	42.8	33.3	29.0	29.4	41.6
29.8	25.9	24.4	Long-Term Debt	21.6	23.0	23.3	23.6	24.0	30.7
.6	.4	.8	Deferred Taxes	.2	.3	1.5	.2	1.2	.6
9.3	5.3	8.2	All Other Non-Current	10.7	12.4	8.5	2.5	5.7	6.9
28.7	37.3	31.9	Net Worth	40.9	21.4	33.3	44.8	39.7	20.2
100.0	100.0	100.0	Total Liabilties & Net Worth	100.0	100.0	100.0	100.0	100.0	100.0
			INCOME DATA						
100.0	100.0	100.0	Net Sales	100.0	100.0	100.0	100.0	100.0	100.0
			Gross Profit						
93.8	92.0	94.2	Operating Expenses	93.8	93.5	96.6	88.2	92.7	96.9
6.2	8.0	5.8	Operating Profit	6.2	6.5	3.4	11.8	7.3	3.1
1.8	1.6	1.8	All Other Expenses (net)	2.8	1.3	1.6	2.6	2.5	1.1
4.5	6.4	4.0	Profit Before Taxes	3.5	5.2	1.8	9.2	4.8	2.0
			RATIOS						
2.2	2.7	2.4		4.5	2.6	2.5	2.3	2.5	1.9
1.3	1.4	1.3	Current	1.6	1.4	1.3	1.2	1.4	1.1
.8	.8	.8		.7	.6	.7	.6	.9	1.0
2.0	2.4	2.0		4.5	2.0	2.5	1.8	2.1	1.5
(144) 1.1	1.2	1.0	Quick	1.6	1.1	1.2	1.0	.9	1.0
.6	.6	.6		.6	.3	.6	.5	.6	.7
20 18.4	24 15.5	25 14.6		0 UND	0 UND	16 22.2	27 13.5	30 12.3	37 9.9
39 9.4	37 9.8	41 9.0	Sales/Receivables	29 12.7	30 12.1	41 8.9	38 9.7	43 8.5	54 6.7
60 6.1	65 5.7	67 5.4		87 4.2	51 7.2	77 4.7	80 4.6	61 5.9	69 5.3
			Cost of Sales/Inventory						
			Cost of Sales/Payables						
8.6	6.5	7.4		4.8	8.4	6.2	9.2	5.3	8.3
36.5	25.0	24.6	Sales/Working Capital	12.1	30.6	23.5	55.2	19.9	23.4
-24.7	-32.5	-24.6		-44.1	-11.2	-20.4	-16.3	-76.9	-169.9
7.5	11.3	8.5		4.7	9.9	13.2	9.6	9.7	7.9
(127) 3.3	(134) 4.3	(112) 2.9	EBIT/Interest	(10) 2.3	(21) 2.4	(30) 2.7	(11) 2.8	(21) 2.2	4.1
1.3	1.8	1.0		.6	1.1	.3	.6	.9	1.5
9.8	4.1	4.7	Net Profit + Depr., Dep.,						
(31) 2.3	(30) 2.0	(24) 2.0	Amort./Cur. Mat. L/T/D						
1.0	1.1	1.4							
.5	.5	.5		.6	.7	.5	.4	.4	.6
1.9	1.5	1.8	Fixed/Worth	1.2	3.0	1.9	1.5	2.8	1.5
7.2	5.0	11.1		-2.5	NM	5.3	3.0	62.8	-49.4
.8	.7	.8		.2	.7	.9	.6	.8	1.7
2.7	1.9	2.7	Debt/Worth	1.3	3.4	2.5	1.7	3.6	3.2
11.5	6.3	20.1		-13.0	NM	9.6	3.0	127.0	-161.5
58.1	52.9	49.6	% Profit Before Taxes/Tangible		104.8	32.9	74.6	65.6	31.5
(119) 27.8	(120) 25.1	(99) 20.8	Net Worth		(20) 36.0	(26) 15.6	21.0	(18) 22.6	(14) 21.6
10.7	12.3	3.9			12.4	-2.0	-1.1	8.5	2.2
16.1	22.2	15.0	% Profit Before Taxes/Total	15.2	24.1	11.7	17.0	15.7	12.2
7.4	9.8	5.3	Assets	2.3	8.3	4.7	7.4	4.3	4.9
.7	2.7	.0		-8.0	1.7	-3.3	-.3	-.4	1.6
11.3	14.1	15.2		81.5	24.8	19.4	22.5	7.5	16.6
5.5	6.3	4.5	Sales/Net Fixed Assets	7.5	6.7	4.2	4.7	3.4	4.6
2.4	2.8	2.4		2.0	2.4	3.1	.5	2.0	3.2
3.0	3.0	2.7		5.6	5.2	2.3	3.5	2.4	2.4
2.0	2.1	1.8	Sales/Total Assets	1.8	2.1	1.9	1.9	1.5	1.9
1.3	1.4	1.2		.8	1.4	1.4	.5	.9	1.3
2.2	2.5	2.0		.9	1.6	3.5	3.0	3.4	1.1
(127) 4.9	(124) 4.9	(108) 5.4	% Depr., Dep., Amort./Sales	(12) 4.8	(19) 3.7	(28) 6.0	(11) 9.3	(20) 6.9	(18) 4.6
9.3	8.9	10.1		13.2	9.5	10.1	15.5	10.8	8.7
2.4	2.2	2.1	% Officers', Directors'		3.6	2.2			
(62) 5.1	(60) 4.4	(40) 4.3	Owners' Comp/Sales	(11) 5.4	(12) 4.9				
7.9	9.7	8.3			8.4	8.8			
2284023M	1988890M	1591795M	Net Sales ($)	6708M	49438M	129566M	92328M	352078M	961677M
1539606M	1363086M	1239734M	Total Assets ($)	13130M	28931M	97931M	213657M	332901M	553184M

M = $ thousand   MM = $ million
See Pages 9 through 22 for Explanation of Ratios and Data

EDUCATIONAL SERVICES

EDUCATION—Elementary and Secondary Schools NAICS 611110

| Current Data Sorted by Assets | | | | | | Comparative Historical Data | |

						Type of Statement		
47	94	313	575	167	107	Unqualified	730	1037
4	9	40	18	2		Reviewed	57	85
7	17	24	8	1	1	Compiled	36	52
25	30	16	3	1		Tax Returns	36	59
35	47	105	114	26	14	Other	313	247
	1,699 (4/1-9/30/09)		151 (10/1/09-3/31/10)				4/1/05-3/31/06 ALL	4/1/06-3/31/07 ALL
0-500M	500M-2MM	2-10MM	10-50MM	50-100MM	100-250MM			
118	197	498	718	197	122	NUMBER OF STATEMENTS	1172	1480
%	%	%	%	%	%	ASSETS	%	%
38.9	30.8	19.4	18.4	18.5	20.7	Cash & Equivalents	22.5	22.6
14.4	11.5	6.9	4.4	3.4	3.1	Trade Receivables (net)	6.1	6.5
.8	.2	.2	.1	.2	.2	Inventory	.2	.2
3.3	3.7	2.2	2.8	2.9	3.1	All Other Current	4.2	4.2
57.4	46.2	28.6	25.7	24.9	27.1	Total Current	33.1	33.4
31.2	45.3	64.2	63.3	59.8	59.9	Fixed Assets (net)	53.6	54.3
1.4	1.3	.5	.6	.8	2.4	Intangibles (net)	.9	1.0
9.9	7.2	6.7	10.4	14.5	10.6	All Other Non-Current	12.4	11.3
100.0	100.0	100.0	100.0	100.0	100.0	Total	100.0	100.0
						LIABILITIES		
12.8	5.0	2.5	1.5	1.0	.8	Notes Payable-Short Term	3.1	2.8
4.2	2.2	2.7	2.0	1.7	2.1	Cur. Mat.-L.T.D.	1.7	2.2
11.5	5.0	3.4	2.2	1.7	1.9	Trade Payables	4.2	3.7
.0	.2	.2	.0	.0	.1	Income Taxes Payable	.2	.1
38.3	17.1	8.8	7.8	6.4	5.8	All Other Current	10.7	11.3
66.8	29.6	17.6	13.5	10.7	10.6	Total Current	19.9	20.2
27.2	23.4	33.2	30.8	34.0	40.0	Long-Term Debt	25.5	28.4
.0	.0	.0	.0	.0	.2	Deferred Taxes	.0	.0
10.9	6.3	5.1	5.1	6.0	3.2	All Other Non-Current	6.0	5.4
-4.9	40.7	44.0	50.5	49.3	46.0	Net Worth	48.7	46.0
100.0	100.0	100.0	100.0	100.0	100.0	Total Liabilties & Net Worth	100.0	100.0
						INCOME DATA		
100.0	100.0	100.0	100.0	100.0	100.0	Net Sales	100.0	100.0
						Gross Profit		
96.4	95.8	95.4	96.0	96.1	97.0	Operating Expenses	93.5	92.9
3.6	4.2	4.6	4.0	3.9	3.0	Operating Profit	6.5	7.1
.9	1.9	3.4	5.1	7.5	6.9	All Other Expenses (net)	1.0	1.2
2.8	2.3	1.2	-1.1	-3.5	-3.9	Profit Before Taxes	5.5	5.9
						RATIOS		
3.9	4.3	3.4	3.8	4.8	4.3		4.8	4.3
1.1	1.7	1.7	1.9	1.9	2.5	Current	1.9	1.9
.5	.7	.8	1.1	1.2	1.3		.9	.9
3.9	4.1	3.3	3.4	4.5	3.5		4.3	3.9
1.0	1.5	1.5	(717) 1.7	1.7	2.1	Quick	(1171) 1.6	1.6
.4	.6	.7	.8	.9	1.1		.7	.7
0 UND	0 UND	1 408.4	1 255.2	2 152.5	2 219.3		1 300.3	1 316.8
1 251.0	6 58.3	6 59.4	7 50.4	9 41.8	9 40.8	Sales/Receivables	7 54.1	7 53.6
14 26.9	20 18.7	23 15.8	26 13.9	26 13.8	26 13.8		25 14.5	28 13.0
						Cost of Sales/Inventory		
						Cost of Sales/Payables		
9.6	6.2	4.2	2.9	2.0	2.3		3.0	2.8
109.9	14.1	11.7	6.8	5.7	5.0	Sales/Working Capital	8.8	8.3
-23.9	-28.6	-27.8	80.2	35.5	16.8		-68.3	-88.6
12.0	12.0	4.0	3.1	2.8	1.8		7.8	6.7
(51) 2.2	(118) 2.7	(393) 1.4	(607) 1.1	(167) 1.0	(111) 1.1	EBIT/Interest	(821) 2.5	(1109) 2.6
-3.1	-.1	-.1	-1.1	-2.3	-.9		.8	.9
						Net Profit + Depr., Dep.,	6.7	12.0
						Amort./Cur. Mat. L/T/D	(13) 4.8 (14) 3.4	
							2.3	1.7
.2	.3	.8	.9	.7	.8		.6	.6
1.0	.8	1.5	1.2	1.1	1.7	Fixed/Worth	1.1	1.1
-6.0	2.6	3.3	2.1	2.2	2.8		2.1	2.3
.5	.3	.5	.4	.4	.5		.4	.4
2.4	.9	1.3	.9	1.0	1.5	Debt/Worth	.9	1.0
-6.7	5.0	3.2	2.0	2.3	3.0		2.3	2.7
100.0	34.1	14.2	7.3	9.1	5.0		16.1	16.8
(84) 20.8	(169) 10.7	(466) 2.6	(694) .3	(195) -.6	(118) -.1	% Profit Before Taxes/Tangible Net Worth	(1099) 5.9	(1383) 6.5
-2.1	-3.7	-6.6	-6.5	-7.5	-6.3		.0	.4
34.6	16.7	5.5	3.3	2.8	1.8		7.3	7.6
4.3	4.7	.9	.2	-.2	.1	% Profit Before Taxes/Total Assets	2.8	3.1
-10.1	-4.5	-2.8	-3.2	-3.5	-2.4		-.2	-.1
117.7	29.2	2.5	1.3	1.1	1.3		3.3	3.1
23.9	7.0	1.1	.8	.7	.8	Sales/Net Fixed Assets	1.1	1.1
11.0	1.6	.7	.6	.5	.6		.7	.7
9.2	3.7	1.3	.8	.7	.8		1.4	1.2
5.1	2.2	.7	.5	.4	.5	Sales/Total Assets	.6	.7
3.0	1.1	.5	.4	.3	.3		.4	.4
.8	1.0	2.6	3.7	3.7	2.7		2.9	2.7
(79) 1.6	(154) 2.1	(426) 4.5	(644) 5.6	(166) 6.1	(96) 4.3	% Depr., Dep., Amort./Sales	(934) 4.7	(1192) 4.6
2.6	3.8	6.6	7.8	8.6	7.6		6.9	6.5
4.0	2.4	3.7	4.1	1.9	4.0		3.3	4.1
(30) 7.2	(39) 6.4	(55) 7.4	(72) 7.7	(10) 7.0	(10) 4.8	% Officers', Directors' Owners' Comp/Sales	(142) 6.6	(177) 7.6
13.2	13.9	14.4	18.5	11.1	10.9		12.9	16.1
169686M	580033M	3019675M	12723566M	8371932M	11641768M	Net Sales ($)	17160586M	24700690M
29849M	230521M	2748409M	17236997M	13962398M	17713411M	Total Assets ($)	25161838M	36506894M

M = $ thousand   MM = $ million
See Pages 9 through 22 for Explanation of Ratios and Data

Comparative Historical Data / Current Data Sorted by Sales

Hist 1	Hist 2	Hist 3	Type of Statement	0-1MM	1-3MM	3-5MM	5-10MM	10-25MM	25MM & OVER
1004	1234	1303	Unqualified	20	150	156	290	395	292
68	78	73	Reviewed	7	27	15	18	6	
47	54	58	Compiled	13	21	12	6	4	2
51	65	75	Tax Returns	28	29	6	8	2	2
277	314	341	Other	33	82	57	52	71	46
4/1/07-3/31/08 ALL	4/1/08-3/31/09 ALL	4/1/09-3/31/10 ALL		1,699 (4/1-9/30/09)			151 (10/1/09-3/31/10)		
1447	1745	1850	NUMBER OF STATEMENTS	101	309	246	374	478	342
%	%	%	**ASSETS**	%	%	%	%	%	%
22.6	23.2	21.5	Cash & Equivalents	23.4	22.5	24.5	19.5	18.3	24.3
6.6	7.1	6.3	Trade Receivables (net)	7.4	8.6	5.5	5.5	5.9	5.7
.3	.3	.2	Inventory	.4	.2	.1	.2	.2	.2
4.0	3.6	2.8	All Other Current	1.6	2.1	3.0	2.3	2.9	4.0
33.4	34.3	30.7	Total Current	32.8	33.4	33.1	27.5	27.3	34.2
54.9	52.9	59.0	Fixed Assets (net)	58.5	59.4	57.0	61.8	59.0	57.0
.7	.9	.9	Intangibles (net)	1.2	1.0	.8	.5	.7	1.3
10.9	11.9	9.5	All Other Non-Current	7.4	6.1	9.1	10.2	13.0	7.5
100.0	100.0	100.0	Total	100.0	100.0	100.0	100.0	100.0	100.0
			LIABILITIES						
2.6	2.9	2.8	Notes Payable-Short Term	8.0	4.9	2.7	2.1	2.2	1.1
2.1	1.9	2.3	Cur. Mat.-L.T.D.	3.1	2.8	2.9	2.0	1.7	2.6
4.1	3.9	3.3	Trade Payables	3.0	4.6	3.5	2.8	3.0	3.2
.1	.1	.1	Income Taxes Payable	.0	.1	.1	.1	.0	.1
10.8	10.7	10.7	All Other Current	18.6	16.4	11.7	9.1	7.8	8.4
19.7	19.6	19.2	Total Current	32.7	28.8	20.9	16.0	14.6	15.3
28.2	28.3	31.4	Long-Term Debt	29.0	37.2	30.7	28.3	28.2	35.0
.0	.0	.0	Deferred Taxes	.0	.0	.0	.0	.0	.1
5.6	5.1	5.6	All Other Non-Current	5.2	5.6	6.2	5.8	5.3	5.5
46.6	47.0	43.8	Net Worth	33.1	28.4	42.1	49.9	51.8	44.1
100.0	100.0	100.0	Total Liabilties & Net Worth	100.0	100.0	100.0	100.0	100.0	100.0
			INCOME DATA						
100.0	100.0	100.0	Net Sales	100.0	100.0	100.0	100.0	100.0	100.0
			Gross Profit						
91.5	94.1	95.9	Operating Expenses	90.3	95.8	96.2	96.3	96.9	95.6
8.5	5.9	4.1	Operating Profit	9.7	4.2	3.8	3.7	3.1	4.4
1.1	2.9	4.4	All Other Expenses (net)	6.0	2.5	4.5	4.3	5.8	3.8
7.4	3.0	-.3	Profit Before Taxes	3.6	1.7	-.7	-.6	-2.7	.6
			RATIOS						
4.4	4.4	3.9	Current	6.3	3.5	4.3	3.7	4.0	3.8
1.9	2.0	1.8		1.2	1.6	1.6	1.8	2.0	2.1
1.0	1.0	.9		.4	.6	.7	1.0	1.1	1.3
3.9	3.9	3.5	Quick	6.3	3.3	4.0	3.5	3.5	3.4
(1445) 1.7	(1849) 1.8	1.6		1.0	1.5	1.4	1.7	(341) 1.7	1.8
.8	.8	.8		.4	.5	.6	.8	.8	1.1
1 368.2	1 370.2	1 339.4	Sales/Receivables	0 UND	0 UND	1 250.4	1 267.8	2 225.4	1 455.4
7 52.2	7 51.8	7 54.6		1 245.3	5 71.1	5 66.4	7 54.5	9 41.7	8 46.4
26 14.1	28 13.1	24 15.5		18 20.2	18 20.7	19 19.3	26 14.0	32 11.5	26 13.9
			Cost of Sales/Inventory						
			Cost of Sales/Payables						
3.0	3.0	3.2	Sales/Working Capital	4.1	5.3	3.2	3.1	2.7	3.5
8.2	7.9	9.0		48.1	12.4	11.1	8.5	6.6	7.5
529.4	178.8	-163.3		-7.0	-17.3	-26.9	-171.0	70.3	27.0
7.9	4.9	3.7	EBIT/Interest	2.9	5.1	4.6	4.1	3.1	3.4
(1092) 2.9	(1321) 1.8	(1447) 1.2		(57) .4	(214) 1.3	(184) 1.1	(304) 1.3	(392) .9	(296) 1.5
1.1	.3	-.7		-1.1	.0	-.6	-.6	-2.4	.5
7.5	7.9	10.2	Net Profit + Depr., Dep., Amort./Cur. Mat. L/T/D						
(19) 3.8	(16) 3.9	(17) 2.7							
.1	1.5	1.8							
.6	.6	.7	Fixed/Worth	.7	.7	.7	.8	.8	.7
1.1	1.1	1.2		1.8	1.5	1.4	1.1	1.1	1.5
2.3	2.3	2.5		9.7	4.4	2.8	2.2	1.8	2.6
.4	.4	.4	Debt/Worth	.4	.5	.4	.4	.4	.6
1.0	.9	1.1		1.9	1.5	1.2	.8	.9	1.3
2.6	2.7	2.6		13.2	4.8	3.3	2.2	1.9	2.6
19.3	14.9	11.8	% Profit Before Taxes/Tangible Net Worth	20.2	20.7	14.4	11.0	7.4	11.0
(1373) 8.6	(1631) 4.2	(1726) 1.5		(83) 2.3	(268) 3.7	(227) 1.3	(353) 1.3	(468) .1	(327) 2.3
1.0	-2.5	-6.5		-10.4	-6.1	-8.3	-4.9	-7.8	-4.7
8.8	6.2	5.0	% Profit Before Taxes/Total Assets	6.0	7.9	6.0	4.4	3.5	4.0
3.9	1.8	.6		.0	1.3	.5	.4	.1	1.0
.3	-1.3	-3.3		-6.5	-3.1	-3.4	-3.0	-4.2	-1.5
3.2	3.6	2.6	Sales/Net Fixed Assets	18.5	11.5	5.7	1.6	1.4	2.7
1.1	1.1	1.0		1.4	1.3	1.1	.9	.8	1.3
.7	.7	.6		.5	.6	.6	.6	.5	.8
1.4	1.4	1.3	Sales/Total Assets	2.2	3.1	1.8	1.0	.9	1.4
.7	.7	.6		.7	.9	.7	.6	.5	.8
.4	.4	.4		.4	.5	.4	.4	.3	.5
2.6	2.6	2.6	% Depr., Dep., Amort./Sales	2.1	1.7	2.7	3.4	3.4	2.3
(1160) 4.5	(1402) 4.7	(1565) 4.7		(73) 3.7	(242) 4.1	(212) 4.8	(347) 5.3	(427) 5.5	(264) 3.5
6.4	6.7	7.1		6.8	7.0	6.8	7.5	7.7	5.1
3.7	3.6	3.7	% Officers', Directors' Owners' Comp/Sales	4.0	2.7	2.6	3.5	3.6	4.1
(153) 7.1	(179) 7.6	(216) 7.1		(23) 9.7	(43) 7.2	(21) 4.9	(41) 7.4	(55) 7.7	(33) 6.6
13.3	13.8	14.4		13.9	14.9	11.7	14.3	15.0	10.9
29106068M	38437550M	36506660M	Net Sales ($)	63816M	608699M	970423M	2712202M	7337175M	24814345M
35983798M	53819064M	51921585M	Total Assets ($)	159066M	903581M	1616323M	5118636M	16479129M	27644850M

M = $ thousand   MM = $ million
See Pages 9 through 22 for Explanation of Ratios and Data

EDUCATION—Junior Colleges NAICS 611210

Current Data Sorted by Assets							Comparative Historical Data	

0-500M	500M-2MM	2-10MM	10-50MM	50-100MM	100-250MM	Type of Statement		
	3	6	18	10	11	Unqualified	32	37
						Reviewed		
1	2			1		Compiled	4	2
1						Tax Returns	2	1
1		3	3	6		Other	11	13
	50 (4/1-9/30/09)		16 (10/1/09-3/31/10)				4/1/05-3/31/06 ALL	4/1/06-3/31/07 ALL
2	6	9	21	17	11	NUMBER OF STATEMENTS	49	53
%	%	%	%	%	%	ASSETS	%	%
			16.9	18.3	21.0	Cash & Equivalents	19.6	19.2
			6.6	4.4	10.4	Trade Receivables (net)	14.8	12.6
			.7	1.0	.5	Inventory	.9	1.0
			4.7	3.9	3.2	All Other Current	4.1	3.2
			28.8	27.6	35.1	Total Current	39.4	36.0
			53.8	52.7	52.7	Fixed Assets (net)	46.2	46.2
			.9	5.5	6.9	Intangibles (net)	.8	1.6
			16.5	14.2	5.3	All Other Non-Current	13.5	16.2
			100.0	100.0	100.0	Total	100.0	100.0
						LIABILITIES		
			2.6	.5	1.1	Notes Payable-Short Term	1.3	.7
			1.7	2.6	1.7	Cur. Mat.-L.T.D.	1.7	2.5
			5.1	3.5	3.6	Trade Payables	4.8	4.5
			.0	.2	.0	Income Taxes Payable	.3	.3
			10.8	6.2	12.8	All Other Current	11.6	11.4
			20.3	13.1	19.3	Total Current	19.6	19.3
			21.3	31.4	23.4	Long-Term Debt	26.9	29.8
			.0	.0	.0	Deferred Taxes	.1	.3
			4.1	3.2	2.9	All Other Non-Current	5.2	3.8
			54.4	52.3	54.4	Net Worth	48.1	46.7
			100.0	100.0	100.0	Total Liabilities & Net Worth	100.0	100.0
						INCOME DATA		
			100.0	100.0	100.0	Net Sales	100.0	100.0
						Gross Profit		
			97.4	94.5	91.2	Operating Expenses	90.9	93.0
			2.6	5.5	8.8	Operating Profit	9.1	7.0
			4.5	.4	4.2	All Other Expenses (net)	1.7	.1
			-1.9	5.1	4.6	Profit Before Taxes	7.4	6.9
						RATIOS		
			2.8	2.9	2.7		4.0	4.1
			1.4	2.2	1.6	Current	2.1	1.8
			.7	1.6	1.2		1.3	1.1
			2.6	2.7	2.6		3.3	3.7
			1.2	2.0	1.4	Quick	1.9	1.7
			.6	1.1	1.2		1.0	.9
			8 43.5	6 59.7	18 19.9	Sales/Receivables	10 38.2	12 31.0
			15 24.2	23 15.9	64 5.7		27 13.7	23 16.2
			38 9.5	35 10.4	126 2.9		85 4.3	75 4.9
						Cost of Sales/Inventory		
						Cost of Sales/Payables		
			3.3	2.5	1.3		2.7	3.5
			16.2	4.6	4.6	Sales/Working Capital	5.7	7.8
			-52.1	14.2	15.4		23.6	34.1
			26.7	5.4	38.9		16.4	10.0
			(20) 4.8	(15) 2.6	5.0	EBIT/Interest	(38) 4.9	(43) 4.0
			-3.3	1.6	1.8		3.1	2.0
						Net Profit + Depr., Dep., Amort./Cur. Mat. L/T/D		
			.8	.7	.8		.6	.7
			.9	.9	1.0	Fixed/Worth	.8	.9
			1.3	1.2	1.8		1.4	1.3
			.5	.4	.3		.5	.4
			.8	.6	1.0	Debt/Worth	1.1	1.1
			1.8	1.1	2.1		2.6	2.1
			44.1	9.0	33.4	% Profit Before Taxes/Tangible Net Worth	29.0	38.1
			10.8	(16) 2.2	5.5		(48) 10.5	(52) 9.0
			-8.9	-.6	1.5		3.3	3.5
			16.3	6.7	10.6	% Profit Before Taxes/Total Assets	12.5	13.5
			4.2	1.8	2.7		5.4	4.3
			-5.3	-.2	.7		1.3	2.0
			3.5	1.9	1.5		6.2	5.4
			1.1	1.1	1.0	Sales/Net Fixed Assets	2.1	2.2
			.6	1.0	.6		1.0	.9
			1.4	.8	.9		1.8	1.8
			.6	.7	.5	Sales/Total Assets	1.0	.9
			.4	.6	.4		.5	.5
			1.9	2.6	3.0		2.0	2.0
			5.3	(15) 3.7	3.7	% Depr., Dep., Amort./Sales	(43) 3.9	(49) 3.7
			7.4	5.3	4.7		5.3	5.6
						% Officers', Directors' Owners' Comp/Sales		
1336M	17291M	86832M	512954M	982657M	1273850M	Net Sales ($)	1365997M	2155121M
393M	5590M	50023M	553584M	1187658M	1886306M	Total Assets ($)	1553238M	2711356M

© RMA 2010

M = $ thousand   MM = $ million
See Pages 9 through 22 for Explanation of Ratios and Data

Comparative Historical Data   Current Data Sorted by Sales

			Type of Statement						
41	57	48	Unqualified	1	3	3	6	10	25
	1	4	Reviewed		1				1
1			Compiled			2			
			Tax Returns	1					
10	13	13	Other	1			4	1	7
4/1/07-3/31/08	4/1/08-3/31/09	4/1/09-3/31/10			50 (4/1-9/30/09)			16 (10/1/09-3/31/10)	
ALL	ALL	ALL		0-1MM	1-3MM	3-5MM	5-10MM	10-25MM	25MM & OVER
52	72	66	NUMBER OF STATEMENTS	3	4	5	10	11	33
%	%	%	ASSETS	%	%	%	%	%	%
20.7	19.7	21.4	Cash & Equivalents				12.9	18.2	21.2
10.0	8.2	9.1	Trade Receivables (net)				4.9	11.1	7.6
1.2	.8	.8	Inventory				1.0	1.3	.7
2.7	3.1	4.4	All Other Current				3.7	1.7	5.0
34.6	31.8	35.7	Total Current				22.5	32.3	34.5
46.9	51.8	46.4	Fixed Assets (net)				61.0	43.9	50.9
4.5	1.7	3.3	Intangibles (net)				2.2	.8	5.3
14.0	14.7	14.6	All Other Non-Current				14.3	23.1	9.2
100.0	100.0	100.0	Total				100.0	100.0	100.0
			LIABILITIES						
1.0	1.2	1.2	Notes Payable-Short Term				3.9	2.4	.5
1.9	3.2	2.8	Cur. Mat.-L.T.D.				.8	3.1	2.2
4.6	3.9	6.1	Trade Payables				1.9	4.8	5.1
.3	.2	.1	Income Taxes Payable				.0	.1	.1
7.0	9.3	12.2	All Other Current				6.2	12.4	11.2
14.8	17.8	22.4	Total Current				12.8	22.7	19.1
22.8	26.1	20.9	Long-Term Debt				19.6	19.3	25.2
.5	.2	.2	Deferred Taxes				.0	1.1	.0
4.3	5.0	4.8	All Other Non-Current				3.9	4.8	4.2
57.7	50.9	51.7	Net Worth				63.7	52.1	51.6
100.0	100.0	100.0	Total Liabilties & Net Worth				100.0	100.0	100.0
			INCOME DATA						
100.0	100.0	100.0	Net Sales				100.0	100.0	100.0
			Gross Profit						
91.1	92.9	94.3	Operating Expenses				106.0	92.6	92.2
8.9	7.1	5.7	Operating Profit				-6.0	7.4	7.8
-1.0	1.3	2.6	All Other Expenses (net)				4.7	3.3	1.3
9.9	5.8	3.1	Profit Before Taxes				-10.7	4.1	6.5
			RATIOS						
5.2	3.2	2.7					6.0	2.0	2.7
2.6	1.8	1.7	Current				2.5	1.7	1.7
1.4	1.1	1.2					.4	.9	1.3
4.9	3.1	2.4					4.8	2.0	2.5
2.2	1.7	1.5	Quick				2.0	1.4	1.5
1.0	.9	.9					.2	.7	1.1
11 34.6	6 57.6	10 37.2					10 35.5	15 24.2	9 42.3
25 14.7	17 22.0	23 15.8	Sales/Receivables				22 16.4	28 13.3	23 15.9
46 7.9	41 8.8	45 8.1					32 11.4	51 7.1	49 7.4
			Cost of Sales/Inventory						
			Cost of Sales/Payables						
2.4	3.2	3.3					3.8	4.3	2.5
4.5	6.9	7.8	Sales/Working Capital				16.9	12.3	7.4
13.8	69.4	36.9					-3.0	-49.8	18.0
13.0	9.8	27.4						20.0	32.4
(43) 6.3	(59) 4.4	(55) 3.2	EBIT/Interest				(10) 7.2	(31) 5.0
2.8	1.8	.1						.1	1.8
			Net Profit + Depr., Dep., Amort./Cur. Mat. L/T/D						
.6	.6	.7					.7	.7	.8
.9	.9	.9	Fixed/Worth				.9	.9	.9
1.2	1.5	1.3					1.3	1.0	1.4
.4	.4	.5					.4	.5	.5
.7	.8	.8	Debt/Worth				.6	.9	.8
1.5	1.6	1.5					.8	2.3	1.6
30.9	25.1	39.0	% Profit Before Taxes/Tangible Net Worth				8.2	55.4	38.5
(50) 10.4	(68) 5.8	(64) 7.1					-5.7	10.8	(32) 6.6
5.2	1.8	-1.0					-13.5	1.0	1.1
12.8	8.3	16.0	% Profit Before Taxes/Total Assets				4.2	15.6	14.8
6.4	2.9	3.5					-4.3	6.2	3.1
2.4	1.1	-.9					-8.1	.6	.7
5.9	4.6	6.1					1.5	8.5	4.7
1.4	1.2	1.2	Sales/Net Fixed Assets				.7	1.2	1.2
.8	.8	.8					.5	.8	1.0
1.2	1.5	2.0					1.0	2.3	1.5
.8	.7	.7	Sales/Total Assets				.4	.6	.7
.5	.5	.5					.3	.5	.5
2.4	2.5	2.3	% Depr., Dep., Amort./Sales				4.3	2.0	2.3
(46) 4.6	(69) 4.4	(60) 3.7					6.8	4.1	(31) 3.6
6.4	7.0	6.3					7.7	6.6	4.7
			% Officers', Directors' Owners' Comp/Sales						
2399822M	2885334M	2874920M	Net Sales ($)	1202M	7561M	19906M	74254M	205403M	2566594M
3425107M	4194995M	3683554M	Total Assets ($)	4759M	28571M	8249M	164351M	283621M	3194003M

M = $ thousand   MM = $ million
See Pages 9 through 22 for Explanation of Ratios and Data

EDUCATION—Colleges, Universities, and Professional Schools NAICS 611310

Current Data Sorted by Assets　　　　　　　　　　　**Comparative Historical Data**

	0-500M	500M-2MM	2-10MM	10-50MM	50-100MM	100-250MM	4/1/05-3/31/06 ALL	4/1/06-3/31/07 ALL
Type of Statement								
Unqualified	1	7	39	199	166	204	503	597
Reviewed		1	2	2		1	4	6
Compiled	1	1		1			5	2
Tax Returns	1					1	5	1
Other	3	3	14	27	33	32	150	97
		655 (4/1-9/30/09)		86 (10/1/09-3/31/10)				
NUMBER OF STATEMENTS	6	14	55	229	199	238	667	703
	%	%	%	%	%	%	%	%
ASSETS								
Cash & Equivalents		34.2	20.4	15.4	14.5	15.1	15.8	15.9
Trade Receivables (net)		29.0	9.4	6.2	4.1	4.1	5.3	5.8
Inventory		2.5	.9	.6	.2	.4	.6	.5
All Other Current		.8	2.7	3.1	3.0	3.5	3.8	3.3
Total Current		66.5	33.5	25.3	21.8	23.1	25.5	25.6
Fixed Assets (net)		29.9	50.1	55.0	52.7	50.8	47.7	47.0
Intangibles (net)		.5	2.6	1.6	2.2	1.2	.8	1.5
All Other Non-Current		3.0	13.8	18.1	23.3	24.9	26.1	25.9
Total		100.0	100.0	100.0	100.0	100.0	100.0	100.0
LIABILITIES								
Notes Payable-Short Term		2.5	4.1	2.0	1.9	.6	2.1	1.7
Cur. Mat.-L.T.D.		9.1	3.2	1.9	1.4	1.2	1.2	1.5
Trade Payables		15.3	5.0	3.0	2.5	2.8	3.0	3.1
Income Taxes Payable		.1	.0	.0	.0	.1	.1	.1
All Other Current		12.4	20.2	7.3	5.6	5.7	6.6	7.4
Total Current		39.4	32.5	14.2	11.4	10.4	13.0	13.7
Long-Term Debt		19.0	17.2	30.7	26.0	28.0	24.6	24.4
Deferred Taxes		.6	.1	.0	.1	.1	.0	.1
All Other Non-Current		6.0	2.2	5.6	4.4	4.9	4.1	4.4
Net Worth		35.0	48.0	49.5	58.1	56.7	58.2	57.5
Total Liabilities & Net Worth		100.0	100.0	100.0	100.0	100.0	100.0	100.0
INCOME DATA								
Net Sales		100.0	100.0	100.0	100.0	100.0	100.0	100.0
Gross Profit								
Operating Expenses		82.6	92.6	93.7	94.6	94.3	92.2	90.7
Operating Profit		17.4	7.4	6.3	5.4	5.7	7.8	9.3
All Other Expenses (net)		2.4	4.8	7.7	9.9	12.6	.0	-.4
Profit Before Taxes		15.1	2.6	-1.4	-4.5	-7.0	7.8	9.7
RATIOS								
Current		4.6	2.8	3.1	3.6	3.7	4.1	3.9
		1.5	1.3	1.5	1.6	1.9	1.9	1.8
		1.0	.6	.9	.9	1.1	1.0	1.0
Quick		4.6	2.4	2.7	2.8	3.1	3.1	3.2
		1.3	1.2	1.2	1.4	1.6	1.5	1.4
		1.0	.5	.7	.7	.8	.7	.7
Sales/Receivables		0 UND	4 88.6	6 57.7	8 46.1	6 56.7	8 44.5	7 51.1
		19 19.4	11 33.0	14 25.3	20 18.4	18 20.1	17 20.9	17 21.2
		64 5.7	28 12.9	38 9.6	33 11.0	36 10.2	38 9.7	36 10.2
Cost of Sales/Inventory								
Cost of Sales/Payables								
Sales/Working Capital		5.7	5.1	3.4	2.9	2.3	2.6	2.7
		11.9	17.3	11.1	9.3	6.8	7.1	8.0
		NM	-11.3	-48.6	-38.2	65.6	-157.8	-171.2
EBIT/Interest			24.0	4.3	3.2	2.9	8.1	9.1
			(42) 2.8	(192) .8	(163) .2	(203) .0	(514) 3.9	(548) 4.3
			-.4	-2.4	-4.8	-4.9	1.4	1.9
Net Profit + Depr., Dep., Amort./Cur. Mat. L/T/D				30.4	7.6		7.9	8.1
				(14) 7.9	(10) 4.2		(18) 3.6	(25) 2.4
				2.7	2.8		1.9	1.1
Fixed/Worth		.0	.5	.7	.7	.7	.6	.5
		.4	.8	1.1	.9	.9	.8	.8
		1.8	2.4	1.8	1.4	1.2	1.2	1.2
Debt/Worth		.5	.3	.5	.4	.4	.3	.3
		1.1	1.0	.9	.7	.7	.6	.6
		NM	2.4	1.9	1.3	1.3	1.2	1.2
% Profit Before Taxes/Tangible Net Worth		89.4	34.2	10.4	3.6	4.0	10.6	13.1
		(11) 42.7	(49) 6.2	(221) .1	(194) -3.5	(235) -2.5	(648) 5.2	(677) 6.9
		15.6	-3.6	-9.6	-10.3	-11.1	1.1	2.4
% Profit Before Taxes/Total Assets		39.1	12.0	4.8	2.3	2.0	6.0	7.8
		18.6	3.8	-.2	-1.8	-1.3	3.2	4.1
		5.0	-1.6	-4.9	-6.3	-6.3	.6	1.3
Sales/Net Fixed Assets		332.7	8.8	1.6	1.2	1.0	1.5	1.7
		18.1	1.7	1.0	.9	.8	1.0	1.0
		1.5	.8	.7	.7	.6	.7	.8
Sales/Total Assets		5.3	1.8	.8	.6	.5	.7	.7
		2.5	.8	.6	.5	.4	.5	.5
		1.0	.5	.4	.4	.3	.3	.4
% Depr., Dep., Amort./Sales			2.3	3.8	4.5	5.0	4.3	4.1
			(46) 3.6	(219) 5.6	(181) 6.0	(221) 6.7	(599) 5.7	(639) 5.4
			6.5	7.5	7.7	8.5	7.5	6.9
% Officers', Directors' Owners' Comp/Sales				4.4	3.8	1.8	5.1	5.1
				(25) 12.3	(25) 9.6	(31) 9.3	(83) 10.9	(79) 8.8
				31.0	14.9	18.4	25.3	20.7
Net Sales ($)	5839M	78457M	379770M	4586386M	7909238M	18657805M	22732129M	26167377M
Total Assets ($)	1573M	15357M	276838M	6679532M	14824261M	38142013M	47955587M	52483450M

M = $ thousand　　　MM = $ million
See Pages 9 through 22 for Explanation of Ratios and Data

Comparative Historical Data | | | | Current Data Sorted by Sales

4/1/07-3/31/08 ALL	4/1/08-3/31/09 ALL	4/1/09-3/31/10 ALL	Type of Statement	0-1MM	1-3MM	3-5MM	5-10MM	10-25MM	25MM & OVER
505	613	616	Unqualified	3	23	21	49	155	365
10	3	6	Reviewed		1	1	2	2	
3	6	3	Compiled	1	1	1			
5	6	4	Tax Returns	1	1				
98	113	112	Other	4	5	5	9	25	64
					655 (4/1-9/30/09)		86 (10/1/09-3/31/10)		
621	741	741	NUMBER OF STATEMENTS	9	31	28	60	182	431
%	%	%	**ASSETS**	%	%	%	%	%	%
16.4	15.5	16.0	Cash & Equivalents		18.9	18.9	16.3	16.1	15.5
5.4	5.1	5.7	Trade Receivables (net)		10.7	10.7	6.3	5.2	5.1
.5	.6	.5	Inventory		1.2	.6	.5	.5	.5
3.4	3.3	3.1	All Other Current		2.8	1.7	3.3	2.8	3.4
25.8	24.6	25.3	Total Current		33.6	31.9	26.4	24.5	24.5
47.4	48.0	51.9	Fixed Assets (net)		51.1	47.2	58.5	52.0	51.1
1.1	1.1	1.7	Intangibles (net)		2.1	2.0	.6	1.4	2.0
25.8	26.3	21.0	All Other Non-Current		13.2	18.9	14.5	22.2	22.4
100.0	100.0	100.0	Total		100.0	100.0	100.0	100.0	100.0
			LIABILITIES						
1.6	1.9	1.7	Notes Payable-Short Term		1.9	2.1	2.1	2.3	1.1
1.4	1.5	1.8	Cur. Mat.-L.T.D.		5.3	1.4	2.7	1.7	1.4
3.4	2.9	3.2	Trade Payables		3.4	2.1	3.4	2.9	3.3
.2	.1	.0	Income Taxes Payable		.0	.0	.1	.0	.0
5.9	7.0	7.5	All Other Current		11.3	11.8	5.5	7.7	6.7
12.5	13.3	14.2	Total Current		21.8	17.4	13.8	14.7	12.6
26.7	26.3	27.2	Long-Term Debt		27.9	25.8	37.3	27.1	26.1
.1	.0	.1	Deferred Taxes		.0	.2	.0	.0	.1
4.6	4.3	4.8	All Other Non-Current		.6	4.8	3.9	3.8	5.7
56.1	56.1	53.7	Net Worth		49.6	51.7	45.0	54.3	55.5
100.0	100.0	100.0	Total Liabilties & Net Worth		100.0	100.0	100.0	100.0	100.0
			INCOME DATA						
100.0	100.0	100.0	Net Sales		100.0	100.0	100.0	100.0	100.0
			Gross Profit						
88.7	93.3	93.9	Operating Expenses		81.6	85.4	95.4	95.1	94.7
11.3	6.7	6.1	Operating Profit		18.4	14.6	4.6	4.9	5.3
-.1	5.6	9.5	All Other Expenses (net)		8.3	10.4	9.4	9.2	9.7
11.4	1.1	-3.4	Profit Before Taxes		10.1	4.2	-4.8	-4.3	-4.4
			RATIOS						
4.1	3.9	3.5	Current		4.4	2.8	4.3	3.5	3.5
1.9	1.8	1.7			2.1	2.0	1.4	1.6	1.7
1.0	1.0	.9			1.1	.9	.9	.7	1.0
3.5	3.4	2.9	Quick		3.7	2.7	4.1	3.0	2.8
1.5	1.4	1.4			1.5	1.9	1.3	1.2	1.4
.8	.6	.7			.9	.6	.6	.5	.8
7 55.0	7 50.8	6 57.1	Sales/Receivables	0 UND	1 289.8	5 70.3	6 60.7	8 45.2	
15 24.5	16 23.2	16 22.8		16 23.3	8 43.7	12 29.8	16 22.7	18 20.2	
34 10.7	36 10.3	35 10.4		58 6.3	21 17.4	31 11.7	41 8.9	34 10.8	
			Cost of Sales/Inventory						
			Cost of Sales/Payables						
2.6	2.5	3.2	Sales/Working Capital		3.3	3.6	2.6	2.6	3.2
7.3	8.0	8.8			6.6	11.8	10.7	8.9	8.5
206.6	-140.4	-103.7			27.6	-57.0	-92.5	-17.4	227.0
9.2	4.7	3.7	EBIT/Interest		25.6	49.6	2.9	3.5	3.6
(474) 5.0	(590) 1.5	(612) .6		(20) 2.6	(17) 1.5	(45) .8	(156) .5	(369) .5	
2.2	-1.1	-3.6			.3	-1.6	-2.6	-4.1	-3.6
8.3	11.0	16.5	Net Profit + Depr., Dep., Amort./Cur. Mat. L/T/D						19.4
(24) 2.4	(30) 3.4	(37) 6.6						(28)	6.9
.8	1.7	2.8							2.9
.6	.5	.7	Fixed/Worth		.3	.4	.7	.6	.7
.8	.8	.9			.8	.7	1.3	1.0	.9
1.2	1.2	1.5			1.9	2.1	2.5	1.6	1.3
.4	.3	.4	Debt/Worth		.4	.4	.5	.4	.4
.7	.6	.8			.9	1.0	1.0	.8	.7
1.2	1.2	1.5			2.2	2.4	2.6	1.7	1.3
14.9	7.3	7.2	% Profit Before Taxes/Tangible Net Worth		53.3	17.6	11.5	5.7	5.7
(595) 8.7	(708) 1.3	(715) -1.1		(28) 12.7	(27) 4.4	(54) .4	(178) -2.3	(422) -2.2	
3.8	-3.3	-10.1			-.3	-7.2	-9.3	-12.1	-10.3
8.7	4.2	4.1	% Profit Before Taxes/Total Assets		21.3	10.2	5.2	3.1	3.1
4.7	.7	-.7			3.9	2.2	-.3	-.9	-1.1
2.0	-2.1	-5.8			-1.4	-3.0	-4.9	-6.0	-5.9
1.7	1.5	1.5	Sales/Net Fixed Assets		15.5	10.0	1.4	1.4	1.4
1.0	.9	.9			1.0	1.0	.7	.9	.9
.7	.7	.6			.5	.5	.5	.6	.7
.7	.7	.7	Sales/Total Assets		1.1	1.3	.8	.7	.7
.5	.5	.5			.5	.6	.4	.5	.5
.4	.3	.3			.2	.2	.3	.3	.4
3.9	4.2	4.3	% Depr., Dep., Amort./Sales		2.0	2.3	3.5	4.3	4.3
(554) 5.3	(681) 5.6	(679) 6.0		(26) 5.2	(23) 5.2	(55) 6.1	(172) 6.3	(398) 5.9	
7.1	7.6	7.8			9.6	9.5	9.6	8.0	7.5
3.7	3.7	3.6	% Officers', Directors' Owners' Comp/Sales					5.3	2.4
(65) 7.7	(83) 8.7	(93) 10.3					(25)	12.3 (54)	9.5
16.3	18.5	19.7						30.1	18.1
24067575M	29513898M	31617495M	Net Sales ($)	4404M	60388M	107058M	473300M	3160073M	27812272M
47438602M	63226488M	59939574M	Total Assets ($)	21486M	241029M	408765M	1415177M	7729501M	50123616M

M = $ thousand   MM = $ million
See Pages 9 through 22 for Explanation of Ratios and Data

Current Data Sorted by Assets   Comparative Historical Data

0-500M	500M-2MM	2-10MM	10-50MM	50-100MM	100-250MM	Type of Statement	4/1/05-3/31/06 ALL	4/1/06-3/31/07 ALL
		10	8	1	3	Unqualified	11	24
		1				Reviewed		1
	3					Compiled	1	2
6	1	2	3		1	Tax Returns	3	4
3	10	3	6		1	Other	6	11
	22 (4/1-9/30/09)		37 (10/1/09-3/31/10)					
9	14	16	15	1	4	NUMBER OF STATEMENTS	21	42
%	%	%	%	%	%	ASSETS	%	%
	22.7	21.3	17.8			Cash & Equivalents	20.7	17.0
	20.6	24.5	6.6			Trade Receivables (net)	14.4	14.2
	2.4	.1	.4			Inventory	2.9	2.9
	8.9	4.5	5.6			All Other Current	4.0	7.7
	54.6	50.4	30.4			Total Current	42.1	41.8
	26.0	41.1	42.3			Fixed Assets (net)	43.4	41.1
	6.7	4.0	13.7			Intangibles (net)	.2	6.3
	12.6	4.5	13.6			All Other Non-Current	14.3	10.8
	100.0	100.0	100.0			Total	100.0	100.0
						LIABILITIES		
	16.4	2.4	2.2			Notes Payable-Short Term	6.2	8.3
	4.2	1.8	.9			Cur. Mat.-L.T.D.	5.1	2.8
	7.5	7.9	4.6			Trade Payables	6.8	5.9
	.7	.2	.0			Income Taxes Payable	.0	.1
	14.8	17.6	16.3			All Other Current	12.7	14.8
	43.7	30.0	24.0			Total Current	30.8	31.8
	12.4	16.2	27.8			Long-Term Debt	20.6	19.1
	.0	.3	.5			Deferred Taxes	1.7	.1
	17.8	2.8	4.7			All Other Non-Current	33.2	5.8
	26.1	50.8	42.9			Net Worth	13.8	43.2
	100.0	100.0	100.0			Total Liabilities & Net Worth	100.0	100.0
						INCOME DATA		
	100.0	100.0	100.0			Net Sales	100.0	100.0
						Gross Profit		
	96.0	96.5	89.2			Operating Expenses	92.2	97.9
	4.0	3.5	10.8			Operating Profit	7.8	2.1
	.7	.9	5.9			All Other Expenses (net)	2.7	1.3
	3.3	2.6	4.9			Profit Before Taxes	5.1	.8
						RATIOS		
	7.2	3.5	3.1				6.3	2.9
	1.5	2.3	1.4			Current	1.4	1.2
	.7	.8	.4				.8	.7
	7.0	3.5	1.9				3.6	2.3
	1.3	1.6	1.1			Quick	1.2	1.0
	.1	.6	.3				.5	.4
	0 UND	6 59.5	6 59.3				0 UND	1 356.6
	17 21.0	37 9.9	18 20.1			Sales/Receivables	3 143.7	14 26.0
	58 6.3	63 5.8	31 11.9				40 9.1	53 6.9
						Cost of Sales/Inventory		
						Cost of Sales/Payables		
	4.8	3.6	6.0				6.0	6.0
	21.0	5.8	12.7			Sales/Working Capital	12.9	22.3
	-21.4	-37.5	-5.0				-41.9	-37.2
		57.3	15.9				5.5	11.7
		(11) 2.3	(10) 2.4			EBIT/Interest	(17) 3.4	(34) 1.8
		-.4	-.3				1.4	-2.4
						Net Profit + Depr., Dep., Amort./Cur. Mat. L/T/D		
	.2	.2	.6				.3	.2
	3.6	.8	1.0			Fixed/Worth	1.2	1.0
	-1.5	2.5	6.1				2.2	2.4
	.1	.4	.5				.5	.5
	4.9	.8	1.3			Debt/Worth	1.4	1.2
	-8.4	2.6	18.1				4.8	6.1
		17.1	32.3				44.3	35.3
		(14) 5.3	(12) 10.3			% Profit Before Taxes/Tangible Net Worth	(19) 8.3	(36) 6.6
		-2.4	-2.8				1.6	-.5
	30.9	11.4	7.8				9.1	12.5
	6.1	3.4	4.3			% Profit Before Taxes/Total Assets	2.1	1.6
	-16.2	-.8	-3.4				.5	-1.6
	66.4	42.7	14.7				40.3	33.7
	23.1	5.0	2.3			Sales/Net Fixed Assets	7.2	5.4
	3.7	1.7	1.3				1.4	1.7
	4.5	2.8	1.3				4.5	2.4
	3.1	1.9	.8			Sales/Total Assets	1.7	1.3
	1.2	.9	.4				.9	.8
		1.3	2.0				1.1	1.3
		(14) 2.3	(12) 4.3			% Depr., Dep., Amort./Sales	(14) 2.5	(29) 2.6
		4.5	9.2				6.9	4.6
						% Officers', Directors' Owners' Comp/Sales		
11125M	48616M	148764M	332553M	57398M	860346M	Net Sales ($)	93348M	1694493M
2394M	16286M	87257M	287422M	71002M	657959M	Total Assets ($)	72412M	826122M

M = $ thousand   MM = $ million
See Pages 9 through 22 for Explanation of Ratios and Data

Comparative Historical Data / Current Data Sorted by Sales

4/1/07-3/31/08 ALL	4/1/08-3/31/09 ALL	4/1/09-3/31/10 ALL	Type of Statement	0-1MM	22 (4/1-9/30/09) 1-3MM	3-5MM	37 (10/1/09-3/31/10) 5-10MM	10-25MM	25MM & OVER
23	18	22	Unqualified		1	2	5	8	6
1	2	1	Reviewed					1	
1	1	3	Compiled		1		1	1	
7	3	10	Tax Returns	3	5		2		
10	20	23	Other	3	7	3	3	4	3
42	44	59	NUMBER OF STATEMENTS	6	14	6	11	13	9
%	%	%	**ASSETS**	%	%	%	%	%	%
21.2	24.3	21.3	Cash & Equivalents		22.7		27.8	24.8	
13.1	13.7	18.1	Trade Receivables (net)		12.3		21.7	18.2	
4.3	2.4	1.2	Inventory		2.0		.0	.6	
4.3	5.4	7.5	All Other Current		15.1		3.4	3.4	
43.0	45.7	48.1	Total Current		52.1		52.9	47.0	
36.4	31.4	31.8	Fixed Assets (net)		37.2		33.7	32.5	
8.2	10.3	10.0	Intangibles (net)		4.5		.1	14.0	
12.4	12.6	10.1	All Other Non-Current		6.2		13.3	6.5	
100.0	100.0	100.0	Total		100.0		100.0	100.0	
			LIABILITIES						
7.6	2.5	6.5	Notes Payable-Short Term		9.4		10.7	2.0	
4.0	2.2	2.9	Cur. Mat.-L.T.D.		6.2		.4	1.2	
5.0	6.4	7.1	Trade Payables		7.3		6.9	6.1	
.1	.2	.3	Income Taxes Payable		.6		.2	.1	
19.1	19.5	20.8	All Other Current		29.0		9.5	24.3	
35.8	30.7	37.5	Total Current		52.6		27.8	33.6	
16.3	20.1	18.2	Long-Term Debt		24.0		12.0	20.0	
.2	.1	.3	Deferred Taxes		.0		.0	.9	
6.8	10.2	9.1	All Other Non-Current		10.9		.6	5.6	
40.8	38.9	34.9	Net Worth		12.5		59.6	39.9	
100.0	100.0	100.0	Total Liabilities & Net Worth		100.0		100.0	100.0	
			INCOME DATA						
100.0	100.0	100.0	Net Sales		100.0		100.0	100.0	
			Gross Profit						
95.2	97.3	93.2	Operating Expenses		88.0		98.0	92.9	
4.8	2.7	6.8	Operating Profit		12.0		2.0	7.1	
1.4	1.2	2.0	All Other Expenses (net)		4.8		-.2	2.1	
3.4	1.5	4.8	Profit Before Taxes		7.2		2.2	4.9	
			RATIOS						
2.6	3.9	3.6	Current		3.2		12.5	3.2	
1.3	1.6	1.6			1.0		1.4	2.6	
.8	.7	.6			.4		.4	.8	
1.8	3.5	3.1	Quick		2.2		12.5	3.1	
1.1	1.5	1.3			.5		1.3	1.9	
.4	.6	.4			.2		.3	.6	
1 520.8	2 164.4	2 174.3	Sales/Receivables		0 UND		0 UND	18 20.6	
16 22.7	24 15.5	27 13.4			3 110.6		23 15.6	31 11.9	
46 8.0	46 7.9	49 7.5			36 10.2		62 5.9	58 6.3	
			Cost of Sales/Inventory						
			Cost of Sales/Payables						
4.7	4.6	5.0	Sales/Working Capital		5.5		5.6	3.6	
27.9	13.3	10.7			NM		7.1	6.6	
-26.9	-20.7	-10.2			-6.1		-16.7	-85.5	
12.7	14.3	13.4	EBIT/Interest					133.6	
(31) 2.1	(32) 3.6	(40) 3.8						(10) 4.8	
-.7	-.8	-.3						1.5	
			Net Profit + Depr., Dep., Amort./Cur. Mat. L/T/D						
.5	.3	.4	Fixed/Worth		.4		.1	.5	
1.0	.8	1.0			2.6		.5	.8	
3.8	7.6	-4.6			-.5		1.3	-.7	
.4	.7	.4	Debt/Worth		.2		.1	.6	
1.5	1.9	1.4			2.3		.9	1.3	
19.4	9.3	-14.2			-11.1		1.6	-4.5	
29.8	45.3	44.3	% Profit Before Taxes/Tangible Net Worth				27.6		
(34) 10.9	(35) 11.9	(43) 10.8					5.9		
-3.6	3.1	1.7					-4.5		
11.3	12.1	18.1	% Profit Before Taxes/Total Assets		37.1		27.4	17.9	
5.0	2.7	4.7			4.8		3.1	4.6	
-3.1	-3.2	-.9			-10.2		-1.8	.0	
31.2	37.5	35.3	Sales/Net Fixed Assets		87.5		61.6	16.0	
5.9	7.6	12.3			16.2		26.2	5.1	
2.3	2.5	2.3			.8		1.7	3.0	
2.9	3.3	3.6	Sales/Total Assets		5.4		4.2	2.3	
1.5	1.5	1.9			2.2		2.8	1.5	
.9	.8	.8			.6		.4	1.0	
1.0	1.4	1.1	% Depr., Dep., Amort./Sales					1.5	
(34) 2.3	(31) 3.1	(39) 2.0					(11)	2.0	
3.9	5.7	4.6						4.2	
	1.8	4.8	% Officers', Directors' Owners' Comp/Sales						
(10)	7.9	(14) 8.6							
	18.4	12.7							
1285924M	1386758M	1458802M	Net Sales ($)	3205M	28860M	22587M	78844M	192767M	1132539M
1066058M	1046362M	1122320M	Total Assets ($)	2741M	43283M	19336M	87802M	146006M	823152M

M = $ thousand   MM = $ million
See Pages 9 through 22 for Explanation of Ratios and Data

Current Data Sorted by Assets   Comparative Historical Data

0-500M	500M-2MM	2-10MM	10-50MM	50-100MM	100-250MM	Type of Statement	4/1/05-3/31/06 ALL	4/1/06-3/31/07 ALL
2	3	28	19	7	6	Unqualified	46	66
		1				Reviewed	6	5
2	2	4		1		Compiled	6	6
4	1	5	1			Tax Returns	7	12
4	15	17	9	3	3	Other	30	34
	56 (4/1-9/30/09)		81 (10/1/09-3/31/10)					
12	21	55	30	10	9	**NUMBER OF STATEMENTS**	95	123
%	%	%	%	%	%	**ASSETS**	%	%
26.3	17.5	21.3	16.9	20.3		Cash & Equivalents	18.8	22.1
18.1	21.9	18.9	17.1	8.8		Trade Receivables (net)	24.4	23.4
1.0	5.7	.6	1.7	.7		Inventory	1.1	1.4
5.7	4.3	2.7	3.7	8.7		All Other Current	2.7	3.5
51.1	49.4	43.4	39.4	38.5		Total Current	47.0	50.5
27.2	27.2	40.9	36.1	26.1		Fixed Assets (net)	36.0	35.0
5.9	9.1	6.5	13.4	16.5		Intangibles (net)	5.0	6.3
15.9	14.3	9.2	11.1	18.9		All Other Non-Current	12.0	8.3
100.0	100.0	100.0	100.0	100.0		Total	100.0	100.0
						LIABILITIES		
1.1	8.8	2.1	2.9	.0		Notes Payable-Short Term	4.5	6.1
4.7	6.0	4.1	2.1	1.6		Cur. Mat.-L.T.D.	2.9	2.5
18.1	5.8	6.6	4.5	3.6		Trade Payables	6.4	6.8
.0	1.0	.5	.6	.2		Income Taxes Payable	.7	.5
22.2	19.6	19.3	20.6	15.3		All Other Current	24.6	23.2
46.1	41.3	32.6	30.7	20.7		Total Current	39.1	39.2
21.2	16.2	13.1	20.0	14.0		Long-Term Debt	17.3	15.1
.0	.2	.2	.1	.0		Deferred Taxes	.2	.3
15.5	7.8	7.7	5.9	4.5		All Other Non-Current	9.1	5.3
17.1	34.5	46.4	43.3	60.7		Net Worth	34.2	40.2
100.0	100.0	100.0	100.0	100.0		Total Liabilties & Net Worth	100.0	100.0
						INCOME DATA		
100.0	100.0	100.0	100.0	100.0		Net Sales	100.0	100.0
						Gross Profit		
95.7	84.0	89.0	87.5	86.0		Operating Expenses	94.1	92.0
4.3	16.0	11.0	12.5	14.0		Operating Profit	5.9	8.0
-.3	3.0	2.1	3.1	2.5		All Other Expenses (net)	.8	.9
4.5	13.1	8.9	9.4	11.5		Profit Before Taxes	5.1	7.1
						RATIOS		
4.2	2.7	2.6	1.9	2.8		Current	2.8	2.3
1.2	1.2	1.3	1.3	1.7			1.5	1.2
.3	.8	.9	.9	1.2			.8	.8
4.0	1.9	2.5	1.8			Quick	2.3	2.2
.8	1.0	1.3	1.2				1.4	1.1
.2	.4	.8	.8				.8	.7
0 UND	5 70.8	8 46.0	16 22.5	11 32.9		Sales/Receivables	11 34.7	6 58.1
1 539.4	34 10.7	26 13.9	37 9.9	21 17.0			31 11.6	35 10.5
107 3.4	71 5.2	51 7.1	77 4.7	73 5.0			73 5.0	78 4.7
						Cost of Sales/Inventory		
						Cost of Sales/Payables		
4.9	5.2	4.6	5.8	1.7		Sales/Working Capital	5.3	4.9
28.3	11.4	12.2	11.7	4.6			15.0	19.0
-20.7	-18.2	-113.1	-31.8	NM			-19.9	-15.4
	16.5	29.0	21.1			EBIT/Interest	16.3	14.9
(18) 4.6	(39) 8.4	(26) 7.9					(73) 4.9	(83) 4.5
2.2	1.4	2.0					.8	1.5
		24.9				Net Profit + Depr., Dep., Amort./Cur. Mat. L/T/D	37.6	3.4
	(10) 6.2						(16) 2.2	(22) 1.8
		.8					-.9	.4
.1	.1	.6	.5	.2		Fixed/Worth	.4	.4
.4	.6	.9	.9	.5			.7	.8
-2.0	142.1	2.1	2.6	1.6			2.5	2.4
.8	.4	.5	1.0	.5		Debt/Worth	.5	.6
3.5	1.4	1.5	1.7	.9			1.6	1.7
-5.0	NM	2.8	5.1	2.2			5.0	5.6
	32.1	46.6	67.6			% Profit Before Taxes/Tangible Net Worth	42.8	45.9
(16) 19.6	(52) 18.4	(26) 25.1					(82) 14.3	(103) 17.6
8.9	4.3	4.0					.4	3.8
15.9	17.0	18.7	17.6	34.3		% Profit Before Taxes/Total Assets	14.3	17.5
6.7	8.7	7.1	8.0	5.7			4.2	5.2
-.8	3.1	1.4	1.5	1.1			-.1	1.2
66.6	49.7	11.5	13.9	14.2		Sales/Net Fixed Assets	18.2	18.7
10.5	7.1	4.2	4.5	3.0			6.2	6.9
5.5	3.6	1.7	1.5	.9			1.7	2.0
4.0	2.4	1.8	1.4	1.7		Sales/Total Assets	2.4	2.3
2.9	1.2	1.4	1.1	.4			1.5	1.6
.7	.9	.6	.6	.3			.8	.7
.4	1.9	1.2	1.7			% Depr., Dep., Amort./Sales	1.3	1.7
(11) 2.1	(14) 2.6	(51) 2.8	(28) 3.4				(83) 2.5	(99) 3.2
3.2	6.8	6.2	4.8				5.3	5.1
						% Officers', Directors' Owners' Comp/Sales	4.5	2.2
							(16) 11.0	(24) 4.0
							21.4	14.7
15222M	40134M	412405M	701705M	628310M	2746113M	Net Sales ($)	2245161M	3464217M
3446M	25020M	289149M	667262M	694966M	1379147M	Total Assets ($)	1608672M	2766346M

M = $ thousand   MM = $ million
See Pages 9 through 22 for Explanation of Ratios and Data

Comparative Historical Data

Current Data Sorted by Sales

	4/1/07-3/31/08 ALL	4/1/08-3/31/09 ALL	4/1/09-3/31/10 ALL	Type of Statement	0-1MM	1-3MM	3-5MM	5-10MM	10-25MM	25MM & OVER
	52	74	65	Unqualified	3	5	7	15	18	17
	6	2	1	Reviewed					1	
	8	15	9	Compiled	3	1		2	2	1
	12	14	11	Tax Returns	5	4		1	2	1
	25	33	51	Other	7	13	8	6	9	8
						56 (4/1-9/30/09)			81 (10/1/09-3/31/10)	
	103	138	137	**NUMBER OF STATEMENTS**	18	23	15	24	30	27
	%	%	%	**ASSETS**	%	%	%	%	%	%
	20.9	19.8	20.8	Cash & Equivalents	22.0	16.6	19.1	17.2	19.3	29.3
	25.7	17.3	17.9	Trade Receivables (net)	16.0	18.9	9.8	25.1	18.6	15.5
	1.6	1.4	1.7	Inventory	.8	4.9	1.4	.4	1.6	.9
	3.6	5.0	4.1	All Other Current	7.3	2.3	1.3	1.3	5.3	6.2
	51.8	43.5	44.4	Total Current	46.0	42.7	31.6	44.0	44.8	51.8
	33.5	38.2	34.8	Fixed Assets (net)	39.4	33.9	40.0	32.9	37.0	29.0
	7.1	9.6	9.2	Intangibles (net)	4.3	11.4	10.1	15.1	4.8	9.7
	7.6	8.7	11.5	All Other Non-Current	10.3	11.9	18.2	8.0	13.4	9.4
	100.0	100.0	100.0	Total	100.0	100.0	100.0	100.0	100.0	100.0
				LIABILITIES						
	4.6	4.8	3.1	Notes Payable-Short Term	1.3	5.2	5.4	1.9	2.2	3.5
	3.2	2.4	3.7	Cur. Mat.-L.T.D.	7.7	2.9	3.3	4.5	3.1	1.7
	9.1	4.8	6.9	Trade Payables	12.4	4.1	6.2	5.9	5.9	8.1
	.3	.4	.5	Income Taxes Payable	.0	1.1	.2	.5	.3	.9
	22.9	18.5	20.3	All Other Current	20.4	14.8	17.0	19.0	21.7	26.7
	40.1	30.9	34.6	Total Current	41.8	28.1	32.1	31.8	33.2	40.8
	13.4	18.2	16.1	Long-Term Debt	27.9	20.1	9.0	10.0	15.2	15.4
	.1	.3	.2	Deferred Taxes	.1	.1	.3	.3	.2	.4
	5.6	7.1	7.6	All Other Non-Current	12.5	7.9	3.6	9.4	6.5	6.0
	40.8	43.5	41.4	Net Worth	17.7	43.8	55.1	48.6	44.9	37.4
	100.0	100.0	100.0	Total Liabilties & Net Worth	100.0	100.0	100.0	100.0	100.0	100.0
				INCOME DATA						
	100.0	100.0	100.0	Net Sales	100.0	100.0	100.0	100.0	100.0	100.0
				Gross Profit						
	92.2	92.9	88.4	Operating Expenses	79.9	90.9	93.5	88.1	90.5	87.2
	7.8	7.1	11.6	Operating Profit	20.1	9.1	6.5	11.9	9.5	12.8
	.8	1.5	2.2	All Other Expenses (net)	5.4	2.5	1.0	.7	2.7	1.1
	7.0	5.6	9.4	Profit Before Taxes	14.7	6.6	5.5	11.2	6.8	11.7
				RATIOS						
	2.6	2.8	2.1	Current	5.7	3.0	2.1	2.4	2.7	1.9
	1.3	1.3	1.3		1.3	1.3	1.2	1.3	1.4	1.4
	.9	.9	.9		.4	1.1	.4	.8	1.0	1.0
	2.3	2.3	1.9	Quick	5.5	2.4	1.8	2.3	2.7	1.8
	1.2	1.2 (136)	1.2		1.1	1.1	1.1	1.3 (29)	1.2	1.2
	.9	.7	.7		.2	.6	.4	.8	.8	.9
	14 25.3	5 79.5	8 43.2	Sales/Receivables	0 UND	6 61.9	6 62.7	14 25.7	15 23.7	13 27.2
	36 10.0	28 13.2	28 13.2		0 UND	31 11.8	22 16.6	33 11.0	32 11.6	19 19.3
	98 3.7	74 4.9	68 5.3		124 2.9	89 4.1	37 9.7	97 3.7	62 5.9	55 6.7
				Cost of Sales/Inventory						
				Cost of Sales/Payables						
	5.4	5.0	4.7	Sales/Working Capital	2.2	3.3	6.4	4.6	4.7	5.2
	12.5	16.0	11.5		11.7	9.2	13.2	14.9	10.5	10.3
	-136.4	-56.3	-100.2		-12.5	127.2	-10.0	-42.5	NM	-474.3
	23.8	25.3	23.9	EBIT/Interest		35.9		23.4	30.2	73.7
	(77) 8.8	(98) 5.3	(100) 7.3			(20) 4.5		(16) 9.9	(24) 6.8	(22) 11.1
	1.1	1.5	2.0			1.9		1.8	2.1	6.3
	12.3	7.9	17.1	Net Profit + Depr., Dep., Amort./Cur. Mat. L/T/D						
	(13) 3.1	(26) 1.9	(22) 5.4							
	2.1	.5	2.8							
	.4	.4	.4	Fixed/Worth	.2	.3	.4	.6	.5	.3
	.8	.9	.8		1.0	.7	.7	.8	.9	.8
	1.8	2.3	2.1		-4.0	2.8	2.1	1.2	1.8	2.6
	.6	.8	.7	Debt/Worth	.7	.6	.3	.5	.7	1.1
	1.5	1.5	1.6		2.6	1.6	1.0	1.2	1.5	1.6
	4.4	3.9	4.1		-5.5	8.2	2.8	5.9	2.6	4.3
	54.7	43.8	55.7	% Profit Before Taxes/Tangible Net Worth	39.4	23.4	38.9	60.2	65.9	75.0
	(91) 25.4	(115) 17.4	(118) 19.4		(12) 9.0	(20) 14.6	(14) 5.0	(20) 26.0	(29) 32.6	(23) 40.9
	4.3	2.5	5.1		4.3	6.8	-.1	5.3	3.4	16.3
	20.4	17.7	17.7	% Profit Before Taxes/Total Assets	16.1	14.2	7.6	18.8	18.5	34.2
	8.4	7.1	7.3		6.4	6.8	1.1	8.2	9.6	8.8
	.3	.2	1.8		1.2	1.7	-.7	3.3	.8	5.5
	16.4	12.6	15.1	Sales/Net Fixed Assets	17.7	24.4	11.5	23.0	9.2	16.0
	7.8	4.8	5.4		3.8	5.8	2.9	8.1	4.5	7.6
	2.5	2.0	1.8		.6	2.0	1.0	2.0	1.7	3.0
	2.4	2.0	1.9	Sales/Total Assets	1.8	1.6	1.8	2.0	1.7	2.3
	1.5	1.3	1.3		.7	1.1	1.3	1.3	1.4	1.4
	.8	.7	.7		.3	.6	.6	.9	1.0	1.0
	1.6	1.8	1.5	% Depr., Dep., Amort./Sales	1.3	2.0	2.2	1.2	1.5	1.4
	(82) 3.0	(113) 3.0	(119) 3.0		(14) 4.6	(18) 4.9	(21) 3.5	(29) 1.9	(22) 4.0	2.8
	4.8	5.4	5.3		18.5	8.5	4.6	3.1	6.4	4.2
	3.2	3.9	4.2	% Officers', Directors' Owners' Comp/Sales						
	(21) 6.5	(24) 8.9	(16) 10.4							
	11.9	19.0	25.0							
	2092588M	2394547M	4543889M	Net Sales ($)	9126M	41954M	56937M	191834M	495254M	3748784M
	1726497M	2247452M	3058990M	Total Assets ($)	20728M	53444M	114413M	213716M	557656M	2099033M

M = $ thousand   MM = $ million
See Pages 9 through 22 for Explanation of Ratios and Data

Current Data Sorted by Assets   Comparative Historical Data

Type of Statement	0-500M	500M-2MM	2-10MM	10-50MM	50-100MM	100-250MM		4/1/05-3/31/06 ALL	4/1/06-3/31/07 ALL
Unqualified		5	10	11	1	1		30	20
Reviewed			1						1
Compiled	2							1	3
Tax Returns	10							6	3
Other	6	6	3					17	5
		33 (4/1-9/30/09)		23 (10/1/09-3/31/10)					
NUMBER OF STATEMENTS	18	11	14	11	1	1		54	32
ASSETS	%	%	%	%	%	%		%	%
Cash & Equivalents	38.5	15.2	15.5	14.8				19.4	19.3
Trade Receivables (net)	3.1	17.5	8.9	8.0				8.3	6.2
Inventory	7.9	.4	.3	.9				2.3	2.6
All Other Current	2.2	.7	3.0	4.1				6.5	1.5
Total Current	51.6	33.8	27.6	27.7				36.5	29.6
Fixed Assets (net)	33.8	38.6	54.8	46.0				46.1	50.3
Intangibles (net)	2.7	.2	3.5	1.8				4.0	3.2
All Other Non-Current	11.8	27.4	14.2	24.6				13.5	16.9
Total	100.0	100.0	100.0	100.0				100.0	100.0
LIABILITIES									
Notes Payable-Short Term	10.2	6.1	2.3	1.5				3.6	5.3
Cur. Mat.-L.T.D.	.6	1.4	1.5	1.1				1.4	.9
Trade Payables	10.5	5.9	3.1	1.8				4.4	2.8
Income Taxes Payable	.0	.0	3.4	.1				.0	.0
All Other Current	19.8	9.9	7.0	9.4				7.9	12.7
Total Current	41.1	23.3	17.4	13.9				17.3	21.7
Long-Term Debt	10.5	17.8	19.3	23.7				21.4	24.1
Deferred Taxes	.0	.0	.0	.0				.2	.0
All Other Non-Current	8.4	7.8	1.3	2.1				1.6	1.7
Net Worth	40.2	51.1	62.1	60.4				59.5	52.5
Total Liabilities & Net Worth	100.0	100.0	100.0	100.0				100.0	100.0
INCOME DATA									
Net Sales	100.0	100.0	100.0	100.0				100.0	100.0
Gross Profit									
Operating Expenses	91.5	95.3	96.5	96.4				88.9	91.2
Operating Profit	8.5	4.7	3.5	3.6				11.1	8.8
All Other Expenses (net)	.0	-.6	2.0	3.9				.7	.0
Profit Before Taxes	8.4	5.2	1.5	-.3				10.4	8.8
RATIOS									
Current	8.7	1.5	9.8	9.5				7.0	4.6
	1.3	1.2	1.5	3.9				2.8	1.8
	.5	1.0	1.1	1.0				1.1	.7
Quick	7.7	1.5	8.2	8.0				4.6	3.5
	.8	1.2	1.4	1.4				(53) 2.3	1.3
	.2	.5	.9	1.0				.6	.5
Sales/Receivables	0 UND	0 UND	1 413.9	10 36.4				0 UND	3 134.6
	0 UND	18 20.9	6 63.0	27 13.7				8 47.8	11 32.0
	0 UND	42 8.8	40 9.1	47 7.8				23 16.2	20 18.7
Cost of Sales/Inventory									
Cost of Sales/Payables									
Sales/Working Capital	9.8	5.0	4.8	1.7				3.7	5.4
	111.2	116.7	18.2	7.6				8.9	11.9
	-26.4	-999.8	NM	168.6				NM	-23.1
EBIT/Interest			25.4					13.4	16.9
		(10) 1.6						(34) 3.7	(19) 3.5
		-7.3						1.8	1.5
Net Profit + Depr., Dep., Amort./Cur. Mat. L/T/D									
Fixed/Worth	.2	.1	.6	.4				.4	.6
	.4	.8	.9	.8				.8	.9
	1.9	1.1	1.5	2.7				1.7	2.1
Debt/Worth	.1	.4	.1	.1				.2	.2
	.5	.5	.7	.3				.5	.6
	3.2	2.0	2.2	3.0				1.3	3.0
% Profit Before Taxes/Tangible Net Worth	156.1	43.8	23.7	11.6				33.3	40.1
	(16) 30.4	(10) 17.8	5.8	(10) 1.7				(48) 7.9	(27) 7.5
	7.7	-12.5	-7.8	-3.0				-1.5	-1.5
% Profit Before Taxes/Total Assets	68.7	16.5	11.5	1.8				19.2	24.3
	24.3	7.3	1.5	1.3				6.2	3.4
	5.0	-8.5	-5.6	-3.4				.7	-.3
Sales/Net Fixed Assets	62.7	21.0	5.4	5.2				15.0	8.8
	22.0	5.8	1.0	1.2				1.9	1.6
	7.9	1.6	.7	.5				.7	.9
Sales/Total Assets	10.9	2.9	1.5	1.3				3.0	2.4
	4.1	1.4	.7	.7				.8	.9
	2.7	.9	.4	.4				.4	.4
% Depr., Dep., Amort./Sales	.6		1.7	3.2				2.3	3.6
	(11) 1.3		(13) 4.5	4.4				(37) 4.8	(24) 5.2
	2.2		5.8	6.7				6.4	7.0
% Officers', Directors' Owners' Comp/Sales								4.0	
								(11) 10.4	
								14.9	
Net Sales ($)	12831M	19719M	60011M	134493M	250204M	39944M		495373M	146078M
Total Assets ($)	2473M	10723M	71555M	205588M	65731M	141426M		1067648M	272050M

M = $ thousand   MM = $ million
See Pages 9 through 22 for Explanation of Ratios and Data

Comparative Historical Data | Current Data Sorted by Sales

			Type of Statement						
27	32	28	Unqualified	1	6	4	6	8	3
1	1	1	Reviewed		1				
1	1	2	Compiled	2					
7	8	10	Tax Returns	5	5				
13	13	15	Other	9	5	1			
4/1/07-3/31/08 ALL	4/1/08-3/31/09 ALL	4/1/09-3/31/10 ALL		33 (4/1-9/30/09)			23 (10/1/09-3/31/10)		
				0-1MM	1-3MM	3-5MM	5-10MM	10-25MM	25MM & OVER
49	55	56	**NUMBER OF STATEMENTS**	17	17	5	6	8	3
%	%	%	**ASSETS**	%	%	%	%	%	%
20.8	20.4	22.2	Cash & Equivalents	35.1	18.5				
6.0	4.9	8.4	Trade Receivables (net)	7.1	6.3				
1.4	.8	2.8	Inventory	3.6	5.0				
2.5	3.2	2.5	All Other Current	.8	2.2				
30.6	29.4	36.0	Total Current	46.6	32.0				
49.5	53.1	42.6	Fixed Assets (net)	30.6	48.9				
2.8	2.7	2.1	Intangibles (net)	.2	2.9				
17.1	14.8	19.2	All Other Non-Current	22.6	16.1				
100.0	100.0	100.0	Total	100.0	100.0				
			LIABILITIES						
3.6	8.1	5.4	Notes Payable-Short Term	8.4	6.7				
.9	1.8	1.1	Cur. Mat.-L.T.D.	.1	1.6				
6.9	2.7	6.0	Trade Payables	10.4	4.7				
.0	.2	.9	Income Taxes Payable	.0	.0				
7.4	14.5	12.7	All Other Current	17.2	10.5				
18.9	27.3	26.0	Total Current	36.1	23.5				
25.3	19.2	16.9	Long-Term Debt	17.3	11.9				
.0	.0	.0	Deferred Taxes	.0	.0				
6.5	5.4	4.9	All Other Non-Current	10.2	4.0				
49.3	48.1	52.2	Net Worth	36.6	60.6				
100.0	100.0	100.0	Total Liabilities & Net Worth	100.0	100.0				
			INCOME DATA						
100.0	100.0	100.0	Net Sales	100.0	100.0				
			Gross Profit						
91.2	93.8	94.7	Operating Expenses	90.0	95.8				
8.8	6.2	5.3	Operating Profit	10.0	4.2				
1.9	3.1	1.3	All Other Expenses (net)	.8	1.0				
6.9	3.1	4.0	Profit Before Taxes	9.2	3.3				
			RATIOS						
5.0 / 1.7 / .6	4.1 / .9 / .6	6.7 / 1.3 / .9	Current	7.3 / 1.5 / .5	5.2 / 1.2 / .7				
4.3 / 1.6 / .5	2.7 / .8 / .5	5.3 / 1.1 / .5	Quick	7.3 / 1.0 / .3	4.1 / 1.1 / .5				
0 UND / 5 76.1 / 28 13.3	0 UND / 4 84.9 / 29 12.7	0 UND / 4 93.3 / 31 11.9	Sales/Receivables	0 UND / 0 UND / 4 95.2	0 UND / 0 999.8 / 21 17.1				
			Cost of Sales/Inventory						
			Cost of Sales/Payables						
4.1 / 24.6 / -18.7	4.8 / -58.2 / -11.1	5.0 / 28.7 / -96.9	Sales/Working Capital	3.0 / 43.1 / -24.5	20.5 / 46.5 / -105.7				
(29) 14.6 / 4.4 / 1.0	(41) 12.1 / 2.6 / -1.6	(35) 14.0 / 3.9 / -.4	EBIT/Interest		(12) 9.0 / 2.5 / -8.9				
			Net Profit + Depr., Dep., Amort./Cur. Mat. L/T/D						
.4 / .8 / 2.0	.4 / 1.1 / 2.0	.3 / .8 / 1.7	Fixed/Worth	.1 / .5 / 1.9	.3 / .9 / 1.4				
.2 / .5 / 2.9	.2 / .8 / 3.5	.2 / .6 / 2.3	Debt/Worth	.3 / .5 / 3.2	.2 / .5 / 1.5				
(43) 39.8 / 8.3 / .3	(51) 39.5 / 4.9 / -3.2	(52) 47.5 / 10.0 / -5.4	% Profit Before Taxes/Tangible Net Worth	(15) 83.8 / 21.6 / -5.4	(16) 77.9 / 12.9 / -9.5				
17.8 / 6.5 / .1	13.8 / 1.4 / -2.8	21.9 / 5.6 / -3.0	% Profit Before Taxes/Total Assets	35.5 / 14.3 / .0	26.3 / 7.3 / -5.5				
11.7 / 1.7 / .9	5.1 / 1.3 / .7	21.7 / 5.8 / 1.2	Sales/Net Fixed Assets	42.3 / 10.4 / 7.0	32.9 / 5.6 / .9				
2.2 / 1.0 / .5	1.8 / .9 / .4	3.3 / 1.4 / .7	Sales/Total Assets	6.8 / 2.5 / 1.0	4.0 / 2.2 / .6				
(38) 2.1 / 4.0 / 6.2	(46) 2.3 / 4.6 / 6.7	(43) 1.5 / 3.0 / 5.1	% Depr., Dep., Amort./Sales		(13) .9 / 2.1 / 4.8				
	(10) 4.7 / 6.6 / 12.0		% Officers', Directors' Owners' Comp/Sales						
253299M	535418M	517202M	Net Sales ($)	7442M	30568M	21506M	38413M	102665M	316608M
585768M	744299M	497496M	Total Assets ($)	6659M	33808M	40987M	51364M	140668M	224010M

M = $ thousand   MM = $ million
See Pages 9 through 22 for Explanation of Ratios and Data

Current Data Sorted by Assets   **Comparative Historical Data**

0-500M	500M-2MM	2-10MM	10-50MM	50-100MM	100-250MM	Type of Statement	4/1/05-3/31/06 ALL	4/1/06-3/31/07 ALL
7	11	30	39	11	7	Unqualified	46	76
		3	4			Reviewed	2	2
1	2	1	3			Compiled	2	10
13	10	3				Tax Returns	14	19
18	20	22	12	2	1	Other	18	33
	136 (4/1-9/30/09)		84 (10/1/09-3/31/10)					
39	43	59	58	13	8	**NUMBER OF STATEMENTS**	82	140
%	%	%	%	%	%	**ASSETS**	%	%
40.2	21.2	18.8	17.4	25.2		Cash & Equivalents	25.8	26.9
12.4	21.6	15.0	8.7	2.4		Trade Receivables (net)	13.8	12.0
1.3	2.2	1.6	.7	1.0		Inventory	1.6	2.3
2.2	5.0	4.2	4.8	3.3		All Other Current	5.1	3.8
56.1	50.1	39.6	31.6	31.9		Total Current	46.3	45.0
23.1	38.6	53.0	51.4	45.7		Fixed Assets (net)	41.0	38.1
8.2	5.1	1.7	6.8	6.9		Intangibles (net)	3.1	3.9
12.6	6.2	5.7	10.2	15.6		All Other Non-Current	9.6	13.0
100.0	100.0	100.0	100.0	100.0		Total	100.0	100.0
						LIABILITIES		
17.3	6.2	4.5	4.9	.3		Notes Payable-Short Term	7.6	7.6
4.1	2.7	2.3	1.6	2.1		Cur. Mat.-L.T.D.	3.8	3.2
8.9	4.2	5.3	3.6	2.3		Trade Payables	4.6	5.9
.1	.1	.1	.0	.1		Income Taxes Payable	.1	.3
29.2	17.6	10.8	12.6	10.1		All Other Current	14.9	14.5
59.5	30.9	23.0	22.7	15.0		Total Current	31.0	31.5
20.2	24.0	24.1	20.9	19.1		Long-Term Debt	17.9	15.9
.0	.0	.0	.3	.4		Deferred Taxes	.0	.0
32.4	7.5	4.1	4.6	5.2		All Other Non-Current	5.6	9.8
-12.1	37.5	48.7	51.6	60.3		Net Worth	45.4	42.8
100.0	100.0	100.0	100.0	100.0		Total Liabilties & Net Worth	100.0	100.0
						INCOME DATA		
100.0	100.0	100.0	100.0	100.0		Net Sales	100.0	100.0
						Gross Profit		
91.4	93.7	93.3	92.9	93.1		Operating Expenses	93.4	94.1
8.6	6.3	6.7	7.1	6.9		Operating Profit	6.6	5.9
1.3	4.1	3.4	6.3	6.8		All Other Expenses (net)	1.5	1.2
7.3	2.2	3.3	.8	.1		Profit Before Taxes	5.1	4.7
						RATIOS		
3.9	6.4	4.2	2.8	5.2		Current	4.6	4.8
1.6	2.2	1.8	1.6	1.7			1.7	1.5
.3	.8	.9	.9	1.1			.9	.8
3.5	6.4	3.8	2.7	4.7		Quick	3.8	3.9
1.5	1.6	1.4	1.3	1.5			1.4	1.3
.3	.5	.7	.7	.9			.7	.7
0 UND	0 UND	5 76.1	4 87.9	0 UND		Sales/Receivables	0 UND	1 513.2
0 UND	12 31.7	21 17.1	26 13.9	7 53.3			13 27.5	14 26.0
18 20.5	53 6.9	39 9.5	51 7.2	20 18.4			36 10.1	34 10.6
						Cost of Sales/Inventory		
						Cost of Sales/Payables		
10.6	3.3	3.3	3.4	3.0		Sales/Working Capital	3.5	4.3
45.9	8.9	8.9	12.2	8.5			13.6	12.7
-17.2	-23.7	-34.0	-17.1	NM			-72.1	-32.2
19.8	8.5	16.8	8.8			EBIT/Interest	13.3	11.4
(14) 4.9	(26) 2.5	(40) 2.6	(42) 1.8				(56) 3.1	(91) 3.2
1.2	1.0	.3	-.7				1.4	.6
						Net Profit + Depr., Dep., Amort./Cur. Mat. L/T/D		
.1	.1	.7	.7	.4		Fixed/Worth	.4	.4
.6	1.0	1.1	1.2	1.1			1.0	.7
-.2	3.9	2.5	2.0	1.4			2.1	2.3
.4	.5	.4	.5	.3		Debt/Worth	.3	.3
2.4	2.1	1.2	1.2	.7			1.1	1.0
-1.8	15.1	2.9	2.4	1.6			3.3	5.8
293.0	59.7	21.8	13.9	10.0		% Profit Before Taxes/Tangible Net Worth	37.3	32.9
(26) 72.0	(34) 15.9	(56) 7.0	(54) 2.7	(12) 2.1			(71) 14.2	(119) 10.8
28.6	-3.6	-.9	-6.7	-6.8			2.9	.0
91.3	15.1	10.4	6.2	8.0		% Profit Before Taxes/Total Assets	15.0	14.3
47.6	2.5	4.0	1.4	2.2			5.3	5.0
14.0	-3.2	-.6	-3.9	-3.6			1.0	-.4
264.0	95.0	10.7	5.0	4.7		Sales/Net Fixed Assets	22.9	19.1
66.7	5.6	2.0	1.4	1.7			4.9	5.3
17.3	1.7	.8	.5	.8			1.5	1.5
8.3	3.4	2.1	1.4	1.2		Sales/Total Assets	3.8	3.3
5.8	1.7	1.0	.7	.7			1.6	1.5
3.3	1.0	.6	.4	.5			.8	.6
.4	.4	1.8	2.1	2.6		% Depr., Dep., Amort./Sales	1.0	1.1
(14) .8	(30) 2.2	(52) 3.3	(50) 4.3	(10) 4.2			(62) 2.4	(109) 2.5
1.6	5.0	6.1	6.9	8.1			4.7	4.9
4.2	2.0					% Officers', Directors' Owners' Comp/Sales	2.2	3.3
(12) 6.3	(15) 3.3						(18) 5.4	(29) 6.8
14.1	7.0						7.6	11.2
50015M	121831M	444564M	1030378M	798335M	1179737M	Net Sales ($)	1580658M	1782658M
8314M	49808M	274086M	1152836M	956798M	1209583M	Total Assets ($)	869619M	1628906M

© RMA 2010   M = $ thousand   MM = $ million
See Pages 9 through 22 for Explanation of Ratios and Data

Comparative Historical Data | Current Data Sorted by Sales

	4/1/07-3/31/08 ALL	4/1/08-3/31/09 ALL	4/1/09-3/31/10 ALL	Type of Statement	0-1MM	1-3MM	3-5MM	5-10MM	10-25MM	25MM & OVER
						136 (4/1-9/30/09)		84 (10/1/09-3/31/10)		
Unqualified	83	204	105		4	19	14	22	19	27
Reviewed	4	15	7			1	1	3	1	1
Compiled	9	11	7			1	1	1	1	
Tax Returns	24	47	26		3	1	1	1	1	
Other	42	68	75		9	12	3	1	1	
					21	25	4	7	13	5
NUMBER OF STATEMENTS	162	345	220		37	58	23	34	35	33

ASSETS (%)

Hist 08	Hist 09	Hist 10		0-1MM	1-3MM	3-5MM	5-10MM	10-25MM	25MM & OVER
22.6	21.9	22.9	Cash & Equivalents	27.6	23.6	19.1	21.2	20.2	23.4
12.5	9.9	13.0	Trade Receivables (net)	11.0	11.7	19.9	13.4	18.4	6.5
1.6	1.8	1.4	Inventory	1.4	1.1	2.3	.3	2.3	1.3
5.6	4.0	4.0	All Other Current	1.4	4.9	1.6	3.9	5.9	5.4
42.3	37.6	41.3	Total Current	41.3	41.3	42.9	38.8	46.9	36.6
46.5	44.9	44.2	Fixed Assets (net)	44.6	44.3	50.4	50.0	33.7	44.4
2.2	3.5	5.5	Intangibles (net)	8.2	4.8	.6	.2	12.8	5.0
9.0	13.9	9.0	All Other Non-Current	5.9	9.6	6.1	11.0	6.5	14.0
100.0	100.0	100.0	Total	100.0	100.0	100.0	100.0	100.0	100.0

LIABILITIES

Hist 08	Hist 09	Hist 10		0-1MM	1-3MM	3-5MM	5-10MM	10-25MM	25MM & OVER
6.1	4.9	6.9	Notes Payable-Short Term	14.6	7.8	8.5	5.5	2.7	1.5
4.0	2.6	2.5	Cur. Mat.-L.T.D.	1.8	4.4	1.9	1.4	2.1	2.1
6.2	5.0	5.1	Trade Payables	4.0	5.9	4.1	5.4	5.2	5.1
.1	.2	.1	Income Taxes Payable	.0	.2	.0	.0	.0	.1
14.6	14.8	15.8	All Other Current	18.8	16.0	3.9	15.3	15.4	21.1
31.0	27.5	30.3	Total Current	39.2	34.2	18.5	27.6	25.5	29.8
19.3	23.3	22.3	Long-Term Debt	32.1	25.3	24.8	16.5	16.7	16.3
.0	.1	.1	Deferred Taxes	.0	.0	.0	.0	.6	.0
6.4	8.6	10.3	All Other Non-Current	14.0	19.4	10.4	2.7	3.3	5.0
43.3	40.5	37.0	Net Worth	14.8	21.0	46.4	53.2	53.8	48.9
100.0	100.0	100.0	Total Liabilities & Net Worth	100.0	100.0	100.0	100.0	100.0	100.0

INCOME DATA

Hist 08	Hist 09	Hist 10		0-1MM	1-3MM	3-5MM	5-10MM	10-25MM	25MM & OVER
100.0	100.0	100.0	Net Sales	100.0	100.0	100.0	100.0	100.0	100.0
			Gross Profit						
89.8	92.4	93.0	Operating Expenses	85.7	91.9	98.1	97.2	93.7	94.4
10.2	7.6	7.0	Operating Profit	14.3	8.1	1.9	2.8	6.3	5.6
1.5	3.4	4.2	All Other Expenses (net)	8.4	2.6	7.1	2.4	2.2	4.3
8.7	4.2	2.8	Profit Before Taxes	5.9	5.5	-5.2	.5	4.2	1.3

RATIOS

Hist 08	Hist 09	Hist 10		0-1MM	1-3MM	3-5MM	5-10MM	10-25MM	25MM & OVER
3.3	4.1	3.9	Current	6.2	4.3	8.5	4.4	2.8	2.6
1.7	1.9	1.7		1.8	1.9	2.2	2.0	1.8	1.2
.9	.9	.8		.4	.7	.6	.9	1.3	.7
2.8	3.6	3.6	Quick	5.7	3.8	8.4	3.7	2.6	1.9
1.4	1.5	1.4		1.8	1.4	2.0	1.7	1.5	.9
.6	.7	.6		.2	.4	.5	.8	1.0	.4
0 UND	0 958.0	1 636.2	Sales/Receivables	0 UND	0 UND	6 58.8	4 83.7	12 31.2	2 162.3
10 36.7	10 35.7	13 27.9		0 UND	4 85.8	36 10.1	19 18.8	31 11.9	9 42.2
35 10.6	35 10.5	38 9.6		37 9.8	23 15.8	78 4.7	44 8.2	49 7.4	18 19.7
			Cost of Sales/Inventory						
			Cost of Sales/Payables						
4.5	3.4	4.5	Sales/Working Capital	4.0	4.9	2.5	3.2	5.4	6.9
11.7	11.1	12.7		19.3	12.2	7.2	9.5	11.4	37.3
-68.9	-115.4	-21.1		-11.6	-17.7	-13.7	-17.1	21.8	-21.6
(122) 13.2	(246) 6.6	(137) 10.1	EBIT/Interest	(20) 11.3	(29) 11.2	(18) 4.6	(25) 8.5	(24) 26.6	18.2
3.7	2.1	2.5		2.5	2.5	1.2	1.9	4.2	3.9
1.6	.3	.4		.2	.3	-3.3	.0	1.5	-.2
			Net Profit + Depr., Dep., Amort./Cur. Mat. L/T/D						
.5	.4	.4	Fixed/Worth	.3	.3	.5	.4	.3	.6
1.0	1.0	1.1		2.0	1.4	1.1	1.0	.9	1.1
2.2	2.5	2.9		-2.9	4.2	2.2	1.5	2.4	2.6
.5	.4	.5	Debt/Worth	.6	.4	.5	.3	.5	.4
1.0	1.2	1.3		2.4	2.0	1.0	.7	1.1	1.2
3.4	3.5	4.8		-4.7	13.6	4.1	2.0	4.0	4.6
(146) 44.7	(306) 24.1	(189) 32.5	% Profit Before Taxes/Tangible Net Worth	(25) 93.2	(47) 30.7	(22) 12.2	(33) 14.5	(31) 53.6	(31) 27.8
18.3	8.1	7.3		32.6	20.1	1.9	2.8	9.1	3.6
3.8	-1.2	-3.4		2.8	2.2	-12.2	-8.9	.8	-8.1
20.5	10.5	15.0	% Profit Before Taxes/Total Assets	40.9	21.8	6.0	6.5	16.4	14.3
8.1	2.2	3.3		6.0	5.3	.1	1.8	6.5	2.8
1.6	-1.4	-1.5		.8	.3	-7.7	-5.3	.6	-3.6
15.9	14.1	21.9	Sales/Net Fixed Assets	150.9	44.5	24.7	9.8	17.1	6.9
4.0	2.4	4.3		10.1	5.0	.9	1.7	6.4	3.7
1.1	.8	.9		.4	1.4	.4	.8	1.5	1.3
2.9	2.4	3.1	Sales/Total Assets	5.2	4.2	2.1	2.4	2.2	2.2
1.6	1.0	1.4		1.5	1.7	.6	.9	1.2	1.4
.7	.5	.6		.3	.9	.3	.6	.7	.7
(123) 1.2	(274) 1.5	(161) 1.5	% Depr., Dep., Amort./Sales	(17) 1.9	(41) 1.3	(19) .9	(31) 1.8	(28) 1.2	(25) 2.0
2.6	3.3	3.0		4.7	2.4	5.1	3.3	2.1	3.4
5.1	6.1	6.1		19.3	6.1	8.7	5.7	4.7	4.4
(36) 3.0	(68) 3.4	(38) 3.2	% Officers', Directors' Owners' Comp/Sales	(13) 1.5	(13) 3.6				
6.4	6.5	6.3		6.7	5.4				
12.4	10.4	11.2		21.4	8.8				
2352552M	5325230M	3624860M	Net Sales ($)	20091M	106221M	90267M	252393M	594165M	2561723M
2053192M	6605063M	3651425M	Total Assets ($)	49251M	116555M	234703M	313226M	619875M	2317815M

© RMA 2010

M = $ thousand   MM = $ million
See Pages 9 through 22 for Explanation of Ratios and Data

Current Data Sorted by Assets   Comparative Historical Data

0-500M	500M-2MM	2-10MM	10-50MM	50-100MM	100-250MM	Type of Statement	4/1/05-3/31/06 ALL	4/1/06-3/31/07 ALL
9	17	64	92	29	13	Unqualified	173	208
1	2	13	6			Reviewed	15	19
		10	4			Compiled	26	19
17	6	2				Tax Returns	31	25
9	14	19	16	5	5	Other	111	68
	247 (4/1-9/30/09)		106 (10/1/09-3/31/10)					
36	49	102	114	34	18	**NUMBER OF STATEMENTS**	356	339
%	%	%	%	%	%		%	%
						ASSETS		
39.1	28.3	21.1	22.1	21.9	23.6	Cash & Equivalents	23.6	22.8
14.5	20.4	15.4	10.2	5.7	8.7	Trade Receivables (net)	12.3	14.3
2.7	2.4	2.2	1.7	2.2	1.1	Inventory	1.9	1.8
1.7	3.6	4.2	2.8	5.7	7.3	All Other Current	3.7	3.7
57.9	54.8	42.8	36.8	35.4	40.8	Total Current	41.6	42.7
28.2	26.1	43.9	45.7	46.8	36.7	Fixed Assets (net)	43.5	41.1
6.8	7.0	2.5	3.7	1.1	11.6	Intangibles (net)	3.3	2.5
6.9	12.1	10.8	13.8	16.7	11.0	All Other Non-Current	11.6	13.7
100.0	100.0	100.0	100.0	100.0	100.0	Total	100.0	100.0
						LIABILITIES		
51.4	7.3	2.8	2.1	1.7	1.4	Notes Payable-Short Term	4.6	5.1
9.3	8.5	2.9	2.0	1.4	2.8	Cur. Mat.-L.T.D.	3.0	1.8
15.2	7.6	5.1	4.8	2.8	2.3	Trade Payables	5.0	6.2
.0	.7	.0	.4	.0	.1	Income Taxes Payable	.2	.3
30.0	16.0	13.9	12.2	10.6	11.9	All Other Current	11.2	15.1
105.8	40.1	24.7	21.5	16.5	18.4	Total Current	24.0	28.5
19.7	13.1	22.9	25.1	27.0	18.7	Long-Term Debt	23.4	21.9
.0	.0	.1	.0	.0	.3	Deferred Taxes	.1	.0
18.9	2.8	7.0	5.6	3.6	5.0	All Other Non-Current	6.8	6.2
-44.5	44.0	45.3	47.8	52.9	57.7	Net Worth	45.7	43.4
100.0	100.0	100.0	100.0	100.0	100.0	Total Liabilties & Net Worth	100.0	100.0
						INCOME DATA		
100.0	100.0	100.0	100.0	100.0	100.0	Net Sales	100.0	100.0
						Gross Profit		
90.7	94.5	96.8	95.1	92.1	95.2	Operating Expenses	93.1	92.0
9.3	5.5	3.2	4.9	7.9	4.8	Operating Profit	6.9	8.0
1.2	1.5	3.2	5.1	11.7	4.1	All Other Expenses (net)	1.7	1.5
8.1	4.0	.0	-.2	-3.8	.7	Profit Before Taxes	5.2	6.5
						RATIOS		
2.1	5.6	4.0	4.2	4.1	4.6		5.0	3.8
.7	1.9	1.9	1.7	2.3	1.9	Current	2.0	1.6
.3	.8	1.2	1.0	1.1	1.0		.9	.9
1.7	5.4	3.4	3.8	3.4	3.3		4.1	3.3
.6	1.5	1.7	1.5	1.6	1.6	Quick	1.6	1.3
.3	.6	.9	.9	.8	.9		.8	.7
0 UND	0 UND	5 74.0	2 148.7	1 296.6	2 193.0		1 469.6	2 177.0
0 UND	16 22.4	17 21.2	21 17.5	12 30.3	16 23.4	Sales/Receivables	16 23.4	19 19.0
20 18.2	39 9.4	48 7.5	50 7.3	46 8.0	63 5.8		41 8.9	49 7.4
						Cost of Sales/Inventory		
						Cost of Sales/Payables		
13.1	3.7	3.3	2.5	2.5	2.6		3.3	3.7
-64.8	11.2	9.0	6.9	4.8	6.4	Sales/Working Capital	8.7	13.0
-7.8	-21.9	50.9	-176.3	168.7	-153.6		-92.5	-72.8
16.2	15.3	5.6	13.6	4.8	39.6		8.8	6.9
(25) 8.0	(35) 3.3	(73) 2.1	(87) 2.1	(26) 1.7	(17) 1.4	EBIT/Interest	(255) 2.4	(223) 2.6
.7	-2.7	.2	-.5	-7.3	-1.5		.6	1.1
						Net Profit + Depr., Dep., Amort./Cur. Mat. L/T/D	5.6	12.5
							(20) 2.5	(10) 8.7
							.6	1.2
.1	.1	.3	.3	.5	.5		.3	.3
3.0	.4	1.0	1.0	.9	.8	Fixed/Worth	.9	.9
-.2	1.7	1.9	2.1	1.4	18.7		2.4	2.3
2.2	.2	.5	.4	.4	.2		.4	.4
-4.2	.8	1.3	1.1	.7	1.3	Debt/Worth	1.0	1.2
-1.7	3.8	3.4	2.5	1.4	23.1		3.4	3.3
157.8	34.7	17.6	11.2	9.2	11.6		23.2	24.8
(15) 99.4	(42) 8.1	(96) 6.2	(106) 1.5	(31) 1.4	(15) .0	% Profit Before Taxes/Tangible Net Worth	(321) 7.2	(304) 9.7
12.5	-5.9	-5.9	-5.7	-11.3	-13.8		-1.3	1.1
84.1	20.2	6.7	5.2	4.8	5.1		10.6	11.0
20.1	5.1	1.6	.8	.6	.3	% Profit Before Taxes/Total Assets	3.2	3.5
-.9	-4.0	-3.6	-2.0	-4.5	-2.7		-.8	.0
93.1	87.1	28.2	8.8	4.8	10.3		17.3	23.1
43.4	30.3	3.8	1.7	1.1	2.5	Sales/Net Fixed Assets	3.0	3.1
12.0	4.5	.8	.6	.7	.8		.9	.9
10.7	3.5	2.3	1.3	1.0	1.3		2.1	2.3
5.3	2.7	1.1	.7	.6	.8	Sales/Total Assets	1.1	1.0
2.6	1.1	.5	.4	.4	.4		.5	.5
.4	.5	1.1	1.9	2.2	1.7		1.6	1.4
(20) 1.3	(32) 1.7	(79) 3.1	(102) 4.2	(30) 4.3	(11) 2.8	% Depr., Dep., Amort./Sales	(269) 3.8	(245) 3.3
3.3	3.7	5.3	7.7	6.1	4.7		6.2	5.9
5.5	4.1	2.0					4.2	2.4
(14) 9.9	(11) 8.3	(14) 6.3				% Officers', Directors' Owners' Comp/Sales	(58) 7.3	(51) 5.1
24.0	12.7	11.5					14.1	11.5
62299M	159372M	909241M	2651306M	1782564M	2495554M	Net Sales ($)	7270552M	7213686M
7595M	56507M	533379M	2946184M	2392054M	2936234M	Total Assets ($)	6393919M	6522010M

M = $ thousand   MM = $ million
See Pages 9 through 22 for Explanation of Ratios and Data

Comparative Historical Data

Current Data Sorted by Sales

			Type of Statement						
182	128	224	Unqualified	9	28	21	45	52	69
13	10	22	Reviewed	1	7	1	4	7	2
12	3	14	Compiled	1	8	1	4		
26	21	25	Tax Returns	10	12	1	1	1	
79	46	68	Other	14	11	7	10	12	14
4/1/07-3/31/08 ALL	4/1/08-3/31/09 ALL	4/1/09-3/31/10 ALL		247 (4/1-9/30/09)			106 (10/1/09-3/31/10)		
				0-1MM	1-3MM	3-5MM	5-10MM	10-25MM	25MM & OVER
312	208	353	**NUMBER OF STATEMENTS**	35	66	31	64	72	85
%	%	%	**ASSETS**	%	%	%	%	%	%
24.0	28.5	24.5	Cash & Equivalents	28.5	22.5	30.4	19.6	27.5	23.2
16.0	15.5	13.0	Trade Receivables (net)	10.9	8.5	11.1	17.0	14.6	13.8
2.0	3.2	2.1	Inventory	2.7	1.8	1.0	1.1	2.8	2.4
4.2	4.4	3.7	All Other Current	1.6	1.7	2.7	2.5	4.7	6.4
46.1	51.6	43.3	Total Current	43.7	34.6	45.3	40.2	49.7	45.9
38.1	30.6	40.3	Fixed Assets (net)	39.6	48.9	41.7	41.6	37.8	34.6
2.8	2.9	4.3	Intangibles (net)	8.3	3.7	3.2	3.7	1.6	6.3
12.9	14.8	12.1	All Other Non-Current	8.3	12.8	9.8	14.6	11.0	13.2
100.0	100.0	100.0	Total	100.0	100.0	100.0	100.0	100.0	100.0
			LIABILITIES						
3.4	5.6	8.0	Notes Payable-Short Term	41.6	10.1	3.7	3.6	2.7	1.8
2.3	1.5	3.9	Cur. Mat.-L.T.D.	9.9	1.9	2.9	7.2	2.6	2.0
5.9	7.6	6.0	Trade Payables	6.9	6.5	4.8	4.5	7.7	5.4
.1	.2	.2	Income Taxes Payable	.0	.2	.0	.3	.2	.4
16.9	18.1	14.9	All Other Current	7.7	13.2	12.1	18.9	15.8	16.3
28.6	33.0	33.0	Total Current	66.1	31.8	23.6	34.5	28.9	25.9
22.6	17.9	22.1	Long-Term Debt	28.2	27.9	23.8	21.8	19.1	17.2
.1	.1	.0	Deferred Taxes	.0	.0	.0	.1	.0	.1
9.5	8.1	6.7	All Other Non-Current	16.6	3.5	6.2	5.1	9.0	4.8
39.3	40.9	38.1	Net Worth	-10.9	36.7	46.4	38.4	43.0	52.0
100.0	100.0	100.0	Total Liabilities & Net Worth	100.0	100.0	100.0	100.0	100.0	100.0
			INCOME DATA						
100.0	100.0	100.0	Net Sales	100.0	100.0	100.0	100.0	100.0	100.0
			Gross Profit						
91.3	93.4	94.8	Operating Expenses	86.2	96.8	95.8	95.7	98.3	92.8
8.7	6.6	5.2	Operating Profit	13.8	3.2	4.2	4.3	1.7	7.2
1.3	4.0	4.2	All Other Expenses (net)	2.5	5.7	6.3	5.0	2.7	3.8
7.4	2.6	1.0	Profit Before Taxes	11.3	-2.5	-2.1	-.7	-1.0	3.4
			RATIOS						
4.4	5.0	4.1	Current	6.5	4.2	4.8	3.0	4.6	3.4
1.9	2.1	1.8		1.4	1.7	1.8	1.8	1.8	1.8
1.0	1.0	1.0		.3	.5	1.1	.7	1.1	1.2
3.5	4.3	3.5	Quick	6.5	3.4	4.0	2.9	4.1	3.2
1.5	1.7	1.5		1.4	1.3	1.7	1.4	1.5	1.5
.8	.8	.7		.3	.5	1.0	.7	.7	.9
2 223.2	3 116.1	1 333.9	Sales/Receivables	0 UND	0 UND	2 159.1	4 98.3	4 89.8	2 161.9
21 17.0	23 16.1	16 22.4		1 564.0	8 45.0	12 29.9	29 12.5	17 21.9	22 16.4
55 6.6	49 7.4	44 8.3		24 15.1	32 11.3	45 8.1	56 6.6	44 8.3	55 6.7
			Cost of Sales/Inventory						
			Cost of Sales/Payables						
3.3	2.9	3.1	Sales/Working Capital	3.1	3.4	2.3	3.4	2.7	3.1
10.9	7.8	8.6		13.5	18.3	5.4	13.0	8.1	6.7
NM	UND	-82.7		-9.3	-14.8	59.7	-16.8	178.7	25.8
11.0	9.0	10.5	EBIT/Interest	11.8	3.7	7.8	5.0	16.1	22.2
(212) 3.1	(129) 2.5	(263) 2.2		(25) 5.4	(44) 1.0	(21) 1.4	(46) 1.7	(54) 2.4	(73) 4.4
1.2	.3	-.4		1.2	-2.3	-4.9	-.8	-1.9	.9
15.0	13.7	7.6	Net Profit + Depr., Dep., Amort./Cur. Mat. L/T/D						
(11) 3.8	(12) 5.7	(13) 3.6							
1.5	1.6	1.6							
.2	.1	.2	Fixed/Worth	.2	.3	.5	.3	.2	.3
.8	.6	1.0		1.4	1.4	.9	1.1	.8	.7
2.0	1.7	2.1		-.5	4.2	1.9	2.0	1.4	1.4
.4	.3	.4	Debt/Worth	.4	.3	.4	.5	.5	.4
1.2	1.1	1.3		2.4	1.4	1.1	1.3	1.2	1.0
3.6	3.5	3.5		-2.6	6.7	3.3	3.2	3.3	2.0
27.9	28.4	17.5	% Profit Before Taxes/Tangible Net Worth	40.7	12.5	26.2	13.2	14.7	21.7
(273) 10.3	(183) 6.0	(305) 4.0		(22) 9.7	(54) -.7	(27) 5.0	(55) 4.4	(70) 1.1	(77) 4.8
2.0	-3.3	-5.3		4.4	-13.8	-4.7	-8.2	-12.8	-1.7
12.4	13.4	8.7	% Profit Before Taxes/Total Assets	29.8	7.7	14.3	5.2	6.6	9.7
4.2	1.8	1.3		5.8	-.3	.3	2.0	.6	1.6
.3	-1.9	-2.9		1.1	-5.7	-6.1	-4.0	-3.4	-.6
28.8	40.8	30.2	Sales/Net Fixed Assets	68.7	50.7	24.9	30.3	20.4	17.3
5.3	9.8	3.3		9.5	1.3	3.8	3.0	3.5	4.4
1.1	1.8	.9		1.0	.5	.7	.6	.9	1.4
2.5	2.9	2.3	Sales/Total Assets	3.6	2.8	2.6	2.5	2.1	1.8
1.2	1.4	1.1		1.9	.8	.8	1.0	1.2	1.2
.6	.7	.5		.5	.3	.5	.4	.5	.6
1.1	.8	1.3	% Depr., Dep., Amort./Sales	.9	1.1	1.6	1.5	1.3	1.3
(235) 3.0	(168) 2.0	(274) 3.4		(21) 4.2	(48) 4.5	(28) 3.5	(50) 4.1	(59) 3.4	(68) 2.3
5.2	4.6	5.6		5.3	8.0	5.7	8.6	5.9	4.1
1.5	4.3	4.1	% Officers', Directors' Owners' Comp/Sales		4.1			2.4	
(47) 6.8	(35) 8.0	(51) 8.2			(15) 8.3			(10) 7.5	
12.5	18.6	12.7			11.2			11.7	
9154602M	5552332M	8060336M	Net Sales ($)	20388M	132997M	120401M	476576M	1153287M	6156687M
7711899M	6658056M	8871953M	Total Assets ($)	28939M	293467M	268426M	873873M	1681669M	5725579M

M = $ thousand   MM = $ million
See Pages 9 through 22 for Explanation of Ratios and Data

HEALTH CARE AND SOCIAL ASSISTANCE

Current Data Sorted by Assets | Comparative Historical Data

0-500M	500M-2MM	2-10MM	10-50MM	50-100MM	100-250MM	Type of Statement	4/1/05-3/31/06 ALL	4/1/06-3/31/07 ALL
10	10	61	91	26	24	Unqualified	191	199
7	30	94	30	1		Reviewed	114	141
294	247	142	14		1	Compiled	611	657
947	457	198	27	2	3	Tax Returns	1080	1224
427	438	337	108	28	18	Other	992	987
409 (4/1-9/30/09)			3,663 (10/1/09-3/31/10)					
1685	1182	832	270	57	46	NUMBER OF STATEMENTS	2988	3208
%	%	%	%	%	%	ASSETS	%	%
39.0	24.2	15.0	14.2	15.6	11.6	Cash & Equivalents	26.6	25.8
3.4	8.2	18.9	20.9	19.1	14.0	Trade Receivables (net)	11.1	11.1
.9	1.0	1.2	1.3	1.6	.9	Inventory	.9	1.1
4.1	4.1	3.8	5.8	6.3	3.2	All Other Current	3.7	4.0
47.4	37.6	38.9	42.2	42.7	29.7	Total Current	42.4	41.9
34.6	45.7	47.5	41.7	38.2	40.9	Fixed Assets (net)	41.5	42.0
4.4	4.4	3.9	5.0	7.2	13.0	Intangibles (net)	3.9	4.1
13.6	12.4	9.6	11.0	11.9	16.4	All Other Non-Current	12.3	12.1
100.0	100.0	100.0	100.0	100.0	100.0	Total	100.0	100.0
						LIABILITIES		
29.6	14.4	8.3	3.9	3.2	6.9	Notes Payable-Short Term	19.8	20.7
9.9	7.2	6.2	5.2	4.6	3.2	Cur. Mat.-L.T.D.	8.3	8.0
2.3	2.7	4.5	6.0	5.3	4.0	Trade Payables	3.1	3.5
.2	.2	.5	1.0	1.2	.3	Income Taxes Payable	.5	.5
38.0	22.8	16.7	16.7	15.9	18.1	All Other Current	28.1	27.9
80.1	47.4	36.2	32.8	30.3	32.4	Total Current	59.9	60.7
30.4	33.8	36.8	28.5	30.7	35.5	Long-Term Debt	33.1	32.5
.1	.2	.2	.2	.7	.4	Deferred Taxes	.3	.1
5.7	4.2	3.9	3.0	6.4	8.1	All Other Non-Current	5.2	4.5
-16.2	14.3	22.9	35.5	31.9	23.6	Net Worth	1.5	2.2
100.0	100.0	100.0	100.0	100.0	100.0	Total Liabilities & Net Worth	100.0	100.0
						INCOME DATA		
100.0	100.0	100.0	100.0	100.0	100.0	Net Sales	100.0	100.0
						Gross Profit		
90.6	86.3	84.2	86.7	91.4	93.3	Operating Expenses	88.9	89.0
9.4	13.7	15.8	13.3	8.6	6.7	Operating Profit	11.1	11.0
.6	2.5	5.5	5.0	3.2	4.4	All Other Expenses (net)	1.9	2.1
8.8	11.1	10.3	8.3	5.4	2.3	Profit Before Taxes	9.2	8.9
						RATIOS		
2.0	2.0	2.3	2.1	2.2	2.4	Current	2.0	1.9
.7	.8	1.0	1.3	1.4	1.2		.8	.9
.2	.3	.4	.8	1.0	.7		.3	.3
1.7	1.8	2.0	1.7	2.0	2.1	Quick	1.8	1.6
(1682) .6	(1181) .7	(830) 1.0	1.0	1.1	(45) 1.2		(2982) .7	(3200) .7
.2	.2	.4	.6	.7	.7		.2	.2
0 UND	0 UND	0 UND	0 999.8	11 34.4	19 18.9	Sales/Receivables	0 UND	0 UND
0 UND	0 UND	1 607.2	27 13.4	35 10.5	41 8.8		0 UND	0 UND
0 UND	0 UND	38 9.6	45 8.1	52 7.0	52 7.1		8 45.2	13 28.2
						Cost of Sales/Inventory		
						Cost of Sales/Payables		
52.4	31.4	10.9	10.1	6.9	6.4	Sales/Working Capital	24.0	24.2
-101.9	-119.3	190.3	26.2	18.1	66.6		-137.6	-132.6
-20.8	-19.1	-19.0	-42.1	-551.7	-27.8		-21.6	-20.9
25.7	25.0	16.5	19.0	25.4	8.2	EBIT/Interest	20.6	17.7
(1169) 5.7	(948) 5.4	(647) 5.3	(216) 5.1	(52) 2.9	(41) 3.6		(2337) 4.5	(2496) 3.8
1.0	1.0	1.3	1.6	.7	1.0		1.0	.8
2.7	5.5	4.3	4.5	4.3	5.1	Net Profit + Depr., Dep., Amort./Cur. Mat. L/T/D	3.4	3.3
(33) 1.1	(55) 2.3	(79) 1.7	(44) 1.8	(21) 1.9	(13) 2.4		(167) 1.6	(206) 1.7
.1	.9	.7	1.0	.9	.8		.9	.9
.2	.6	.6	.5	.4	.6	Fixed/Worth	.6	.6
3.3	3.7	2.7	1.2	1.6	2.4		3.4	3.5
-.8	-4.7	-45.7	5.1	4.5	-7.4		-2.6	-3.3
1.1	1.2	1.2	.8	1.0	.8	Debt/Worth	1.2	1.3
51.1	7.4	4.3	2.0	2.3	3.1		8.8	9.2
-2.9	-9.5	-50.9	8.9	6.2	-10.4		-5.7	-6.7
476.6	229.8	109.2	55.0	42.1	21.7	% Profit Before Taxes/Tangible Net Worth	226.9	222.2
(896) 120.7	(739) 73.7	(606) 33.3	(233) 16.9	(46) 18.1	(29) 9.8		(1840) 52.5	(1999) 56.3
19.6	14.2	6.9	5.1	2.3	3.3		8.7	6.0
103.2	57.1	27.0	17.4	17.5	7.0	% Profit Before Taxes/Total Assets	55.3	54.4
24.8	13.2	7.0	5.8	5.0	3.5		10.6	10.2
.0	.3	.8	.9	-.8	-.6		.0	-.4
212.1	48.8	24.1	16.3	23.1	13.1	Sales/Net Fixed Assets	70.5	69.2
52.4	18.1	10.8	6.7	5.3	4.3		23.1	21.2
19.9	7.7	2.5	2.9	3.2	2.1		8.5	7.7
22.8	11.5	6.1	3.9	2.8	2.5	Sales/Total Assets	14.5	14.0
12.1	6.2	3.1	2.4	1.9	1.6		6.7	6.6
6.1	2.7	1.2	1.3	1.3	.9		2.9	2.8
.4	.9	1.4	1.6	1.8	1.3	% Depr., Dep., Amort./Sales	.8	.8
(935) 1.0	(876) 1.9	(718) 2.5	(246) 2.7	(51) 2.9	(34) 2.8		(2239) 1.7	(2367) 1.8
2.2	3.9	7.1	4.5	4.3	4.8		3.3	3.5
14.9	10.8	6.7	8.5	3.5		% Officers', Directors' Owners' Comp/Sales	14.9	15.1
(1131) 24.7	(652) 22.8	(318) 20.1	(69) 24.9	(14) 23.7			(1593) 25.8	(1720) 25.8
34.2	33.9	33.2	35.5	36.8			36.4	35.8
5356625M	9990393M	14814742M	18977824M	10692744M	37554090M	Net Sales ($)	69881505M	110263769M
366679M	1214587M	3675549M	5600450M	3852797M	7364352M	Total Assets ($)	14899872M	18600243M

M = $ thousand   MM = $ million
See Pages 9 through 22 for Explanation of Ratios and Data

Comparative Historical Data | Current Data Sorted by Sales

Hist 1	Hist 2	Hist 3	Type of Statement	0-1MM	1-3MM	3-5MM	5-10MM	10-25MM	25MM & OVER
201	198	222	Unqualified	5	12	8	25	44	128
132	140	162	Reviewed	5	6	13	19	52	67
579	646	698	Compiled	86	168	121	153	129	41
1107	1324	1634	Tax Returns	399	460	230	264	205	76
1015	1263	1356	Other	182	272	176	226	251	249
4/1/07- 3/31/08 ALL	4/1/08- 3/31/09 ALL	4/1/09- 3/31/10 ALL		409 (4/1-9/30/09)			3,663 (10/1/09-3/31/10)		
3034	3571	4072	NUMBER OF STATEMENTS	677	918	548	687	681	561
%	%	%	**ASSETS**	%	%	%	%	%	%
27.1	27.0	27.5	Cash & Equivalents	22.9	31.9	33.0	29.7	25.2	20.8
10.2	9.7	9.5	Trade Receivables (net)	4.0	5.9	6.8	10.8	13.4	18.2
1.0	1.0	1.0	Inventory	.7	.8	.8	1.5	1.0	1.4
4.6	4.4	4.2	All Other Current	3.1	4.4	3.5	4.2	4.1	5.8
42.9	42.0	42.2	Total Current	30.8	43.0	44.1	46.2	43.7	46.1
42.1	41.6	41.1	Fixed Assets (net)	52.8	36.6	37.9	39.6	41.6	38.4
3.7	4.1	4.5	Intangibles (net)	3.1	5.2	6.0	4.3	3.8	4.4
11.3	12.3	12.3	All Other Non-Current	13.2	15.2	11.9	9.9	10.9	11.2
100.0	100.0	100.0	Total	100.0	100.0	100.0	100.0	100.0	100.0
			LIABILITIES						
18.6	20.0	18.5	Notes Payable-Short Term	21.1	21.7	22.1	20.3	15.1	8.5
8.5	8.5	7.9	Cur. Mat.-L.T.D.	6.8	9.6	10.0	7.4	7.5	5.8
3.1	3.1	3.2	Trade Payables	1.7	2.7	2.3	2.8	4.5	5.5
.4	.5	.4	Income Taxes Payable	.2	.1	.4	.3	.5	.9
27.6	26.1	27.3	All Other Current	22.5	25.1	30.0	29.9	29.2	28.7
58.3	58.2	57.2	Total Current	52.2	59.1	64.7	60.7	56.7	49.4
31.8	31.9	32.6	Long-Term Debt	44.9	32.8	34.7	28.5	28.1	26.1
.2	.2	.1	Deferred Taxes	.0	.0	.1	.3	.2	.3
5.5	4.9	4.8	All Other Non-Current	6.5	5.8	4.1	4.5	3.6	3.4
4.3	4.9	5.2	Net Worth	-3.6	2.2	-3.6	5.9	11.4	20.8
100.0	100.0	100.0	Total Liabilities & Net Worth	100.0	100.0	100.0	100.0	100.0	100.0
			INCOME DATA						
100.0	100.0	100.0	Net Sales	100.0	100.0	100.0	100.0	100.0	100.0
			Gross Profit						
89.0	87.9	87.8	Operating Expenses	73.3	87.4	89.1	91.9	92.9	93.8
11.0	12.1	12.2	Operating Profit	26.7	12.6	10.9	8.1	7.1	6.2
2.4	2.6	2.6	All Other Expenses (net)	10.6	1.8	.7	.3	.5	1.3
8.6	9.5	9.6	Profit Before Taxes	16.1	10.8	10.2	7.9	6.6	4.9
			RATIOS						
2.0	2.0	2.1	Current	2.0	2.5	2.2	2.2	1.9	1.8
.9	.9	.9		.6	.9	.8	.9	.9	1.1
.3	.3	.3		.2	.3	.3	.4	.4	.6
1.7	1.8	1.8	Quick	1.9	2.2	1.8	2.0	1.7	1.5
(3027) .7	(3565) .7	(4065) .8		(675) .5	(916) .7	.7	.8	.8	(558) .9
.2	.2	.2		.1	.2	.2	.3	.3	.4
0 UND	0 UND	0 UND	Sales/Receivables	0 UND	0 UND	0 UND	0 UND	0 UND	0 UND
0 UND	0 UND	0 UND		0 UND	0 UND	0 UND	0 UND	0 UND	12 31.1
9 40.8	2 150.0	2 174.0		0 UND	0 UND	0 UND	10 36.0	24 15.4	36 10.2
			Cost of Sales/Inventory						
			Cost of Sales/Payables						
22.4	24.5	24.7	Sales/Working Capital	23.1	23.9	32.0	29.4	26.8	18.8
-205.2	-182.9	-207.7		-28.9	-147.9	-111.6	-234.3	-291.7	148.6
-22.5	-20.1	-20.9		-4.4	-16.4	-22.6	-28.4	-34.7	-36.1
16.7	22.5	22.7	EBIT/Interest	14.9	31.9	30.2	20.8	24.9	18.2
(2309) 3.8	(2701) 4.2	(3073) 5.4		(362) 4.5	(645) 7.1	(435) 7.5	(563) 4.5	(589) 5.3	(479) 4.2
.8	.8	1.0		1.0	1.4	1.2	.7	1.0	1.0
3.6	3.7	4.4	Net Profit + Depr., Dep., Amort./Cur. Mat. L/T/D		3.3	5.1	5.1	4.6	4.4
(184) 1.6	(204) 1.5	(245) 1.8		(20) 1.3	(16) 1.5	(34) 1.8	(58) 2.1	(111) 1.8	
.9	.7	.8		.4	.7	.7	.9	.9	
.5	.5	.5	Fixed/Worth	.6	.2	.4	.6	.6	.5
2.9	2.8	2.7		4.3	2.2	3.2	3.6	2.5	1.5
-3.9	-3.8	-3.4		-3.7	-1.8	-2.1	-2.3	-5.5	59.0
1.2	1.1	1.1	Debt/Worth	1.2	.8	1.4	1.2	1.1	1.1
7.4	6.5	6.8		7.1	7.8	16.8	11.0	5.4	3.7
-6.8	-6.9	-6.6		-5.8	-4.0	-3.9	-6.6	-10.6	-108.3
226.1	233.4	225.1	% Profit Before Taxes/Tangible Net Worth	172.1	315.9	456.1	257.7	209.1	100.3
(1916) 59.5	(2264) 60.2	(2549) 59.3		(416) 45.8	(560) 92.6	(310) 109.8	(410) 68.9	(439) 50.2	(414) 22.8
7.1	6.5	9.7		10.5	19.7	31.5	6.7	6.4	3.5
54.8	63.5	58.4	% Profit Before Taxes/Total Assets	50.5	86.1	83.2	54.1	47.3	24.6
9.8	11.3	12.0		8.8	26.8	23.8	11.1	8.6	5.1
-.3	-.3	.3		.5	1.2	1.4	-.3	.0	-.1
69.6	75.0	82.3	Sales/Net Fixed Assets	45.9	124.4	110.7	91.9	62.5	41.3
21.2	21.0	22.3		8.5	29.4	33.2	25.9	25.3	15.9
7.8	7.6	7.8		.3	8.9	11.2	10.9	11.8	7.0
14.0	13.4	13.5	Sales/Total Assets	7.1	12.9	17.0	17.1	17.1	10.3
6.5	6.5	6.4		2.3	6.2	8.8	9.0	8.8	4.9
2.7	2.7	2.6		.2	2.9	4.1	3.9	3.9	2.6
.8	.8	.8	% Depr., Dep., Amort./Sales	1.8	.6	.6	.7	.8	1.1
(2215) 1.9	(2468) 1.9	(2860) 1.8		(446) 8.5	(556) 1.6	(353) 1.4	(486) 1.5	(546) 1.6	(473) 1.8
3.4	4.0	3.7		19.8	4.1	2.9	2.8	2.7	2.9
13.7	12.3	12.3	% Officers', Directors' Owners' Comp/Sales	14.7	12.0	10.8	16.4	10.9	9.0
(1634) 24.9	(1898) 23.8	(2193) 23.8		(264) 23.5	(586) 20.0	(352) 22.8	(400) 27.3	(376) 25.6	(215) 25.7
35.3	33.8	34.0		33.3	31.3	33.2	36.1	36.4	36.9
104989116M	66197860M	97386418M	Net Sales ($)	364419M	1698772M	2115324M	4893325M	10580742M	77733836M
18078305M	18538944M	22074414M	Total Assets ($)	674307M	806717M	586050M	1151393M	2492085M	16363862M

M = $ thousand   MM = $ million
See Pages 9 through 22 for Explanation of Ratios and Data

HEALTH CARE—Offices of Physicians, Mental Health Specialists NAICS 621112

Current Data Sorted by Assets | Comparative Historical Data

Type of Statement

							Type of Statement	4/1/05-3/31/06 ALL	4/1/06-3/31/07 ALL
		3	3	2	1		Unqualified	8	13
		3	3	1			Reviewed	1	
	5	7	7				Compiled	13	15
	17	9	1				Tax Returns	25	18
	8	9	5			2	Other	12	19

	0-500M	500M-2MM	2-10MM	10-50MM	50-100MM	100-250MM		4/1/05-3/31/06 ALL	4/1/06-3/31/07 ALL
		14 (4/1-9/30/09)		74 (10/1/09-3/31/10)					
NUMBER OF STATEMENTS	30	28	19	8	1	2		59	65
	%	%	%	%	%	%		%	%
ASSETS									
Cash & Equivalents	33.1	14.0	10.1					33.0	24.7
Trade Receivables (net)	12.9	10.4	25.6					10.9	17.6
Inventory	.0	.2	1.5					.8	2.3
All Other Current	3.5	2.9	4.8					7.3	3.5
Total Current	49.5	27.5	41.8					51.9	48.1
Fixed Assets (net)	28.7	49.0	45.1					35.0	36.3
Intangibles (net)	4.9	9.2	4.9					3.0	4.8
All Other Non-Current	16.9	14.3	8.1					10.1	10.9
Total	100.0	100.0	100.0					100.0	100.0
LIABILITIES									
Notes Payable-Short Term	37.9	6.9	6.3					27.8	20.7
Cur. Mat.-L.T.D.	25.1	4.9	4.7					7.1	8.2
Trade Payables	7.8	5.8	5.7					3.1	3.3
Income Taxes Payable	.0	.0	.5					1.5	.2
All Other Current	40.1	23.9	8.9					33.3	29.4
Total Current	110.9	41.5	26.1					72.9	61.8
Long-Term Debt	13.7	41.2	35.5					31.7	22.5
Deferred Taxes	.0	.0	1.3					.0	.1
All Other Non-Current	2.9	8.6	.9					5.7	2.5
Net Worth	-27.4	8.7	36.3					-10.2	13.2
Total Liabilities & Net Worth	100.0	100.0	100.0					100.0	100.0
INCOME DATA									
Net Sales	100.0	100.0	100.0					100.0	100.0
Gross Profit									
Operating Expenses	86.0	87.0	82.9					90.6	86.2
Operating Profit	14.0	13.0	17.1					9.4	13.8
All Other Expenses (net)	.4	5.6	4.9					.1	2.2
Profit Before Taxes	13.6	7.4	12.1					9.3	11.6
RATIOS									
Current	2.2 / .6 / .2	2.1 / .8 / .2	3.1 / 1.6 / .7					2.5 / 1.1 / .4	2.8 / 1.1 / .4
Quick	1.3 / .6 / .2	1.6 / .6 / .2	2.6 / 1.4 / .7					2.1 / .8 / .3	2.3 / .9 / .3
Sales/Receivables	0 UND / 0 UND / 0 UND	0 UND / 0 UND / 24 15.1	23 16.1 / 42 8.6 / 53 6.9					0 UND / 0 UND / 8 48.2	0 UND / 1 470.2 / 47 7.8
Cost of Sales/Inventory									
Cost of Sales/Payables									
Sales/Working Capital	43.3 / -66.8 / -15.7	20.8 / -44.1 / -10.8	5.8 / 12.0 / -25.0					15.1 / 330.5 / -23.2	6.6 / 658.3 / -20.0
EBIT/Interest	114.8 / (20) 6.5 / .4	26.1 / (24) 2.0 / -1.4	14.7 / (14) 4.1 / .9					65.9 / (42) 9.7 / .5	28.1 / (41) 3.7 / .2
Net Profit + Depr., Dep., Amort./Cur. Mat. L/T/D									
Fixed/Worth	.1 / 1.7 / -.4	1.1 / 3.9 / -2.4	.3 / .9 / 3.6					.4 / 2.4 / -.8	.2 / 1.4 / 16.5
Debt/Worth	1.0 / NM / -2.1	1.1 / 6.2 / -6.0	.9 / 1.5 / 5.3					.7 / 6.6 / -3.1	.5 / 2.6 / UND
% Profit Before Taxes/Tangible Net Worth	441.6 / (15) 174.4 / 57.1	59.3 / (17) 6.6 / -8.9	89.1 / (18) 20.9 / -.3					173.8 / (35) 52.4 / 5.2	310.2 / (50) 24.6 / .0
% Profit Before Taxes/Total Assets	112.4 / 48.6 / 7.1	36.5 / 2.2 / -6.8	44.7 / 6.6 / -.1					106.1 / 16.2 / -.5	78.0 / 9.0 / -.5
Sales/Net Fixed Assets	373.8 / 79.2 / 28.1	32.0 / 7.4 / 2.2	20.0 / 5.7 / 1.4					78.2 / 33.2 / 10.2	74.5 / 18.7 / 4.7
Sales/Total Assets	23.2 / 10.8 / 4.2	9.4 / 2.9 / 1.0	3.2 / 2.1 / 1.1					15.9 / 7.9 / 3.8	11.5 / 4.4 / 1.4
% Depr., Dep., Amort./Sales	.1 / (15) .6 / 1.4	.9 / (24) 2.5 / 8.1	1.9 / (17) 2.9 / 9.7					.7 / (41) 1.3 / 2.6	.6 / (46) 1.3 / 3.8
% Officers', Directors' Owners' Comp/Sales	9.9 / (17) 14.0 / 30.2	4.9 / (10) 16.1 / 32.0						11.3 / (31) 22.5 / 31.9	9.1 / (24) 23.2 / 38.5
Net Sales ($)	76150M	149538M	211429M	422434M	61979M	514915M		1110168M	1667389M
Total Assets ($)	6470M	30472M	100229M	218869M	53890M	327671M		566361M	605090M

M = $ thousand   MM = $ million
See Pages 9 through 22 for Explanation of Ratios and Data

Comparative Historical Data   Current Data Sorted by Sales

			Type of Statement	0-1MM	1-3MM	3-5MM	5-10MM	10-25MM	25MM & OVER
9	14	9	Unqualified		3	1		3	2
	1	4	Reviewed		1	1		1	1
11	14	19	Compiled	7	4	1	1	5	1
25	27	27	Tax Returns	9	8	1	7	2	
13	26	29	Other	2	8	5	4	5	5
4/1/07-3/31/08 ALL	4/1/08-3/31/09 ALL	4/1/09-3/31/10 ALL		14 (4/1-9/30/09)			74 (10/1/09-3/31/10)		
58	82	88	**NUMBER OF STATEMENTS**	18	24	9	12	16	9
%	%	%	**ASSETS**	%	%	%	%	%	%
34.2	25.0	19.2	Cash & Equivalents	20.8	23.6		16.1	19.2	
7.2	14.3	14.8	Trade Receivables (net)	13.6	12.7		7.0	24.2	
.5	.7	.4	Inventory	.0	.1		1.0	.6	
6.1	5.9	3.8	All Other Current	1.0	3.7		6.0	3.8	
48.0	45.9	38.3	Total Current	35.3	40.0		30.0	47.8	
38.7	40.8	40.0	Fixed Assets (net)	50.2	36.5		34.3	33.4	
5.1	2.9	6.6	Intangibles (net)	5.1	3.4		11.8	4.0	
8.1	10.3	15.0	All Other Non-Current	9.4	20.1		23.8	14.7	
100.0	100.0	100.0	Total	100.0	100.0		100.0	100.0	
			LIABILITIES						
22.8	14.3	17.0	Notes Payable-Short Term	14.9	25.4		16.5	12.0	
9.3	4.2	11.7	Cur. Mat.-L.T.D.	5.9	24.5		13.4	3.3	
4.3	6.0	6.4	Trade Payables	.4	13.4		1.7	7.4	
.0	.0	.1	Income Taxes Payable	.0	.0		.0	.7	
30.3	24.9	24.9	All Other Current	15.9	27.9		35.3	23.4	
66.7	49.3	60.1	Total Current	37.1	91.2		67.0	46.8	
35.8	30.1	29.6	Long-Term Debt	33.8	15.9		41.6	27.5	
.4	.4	.3	Deferred Taxes	.0	.0		.0	.3	
3.6	4.7	4.3	All Other Non-Current	10.3	3.1		.8	1.5	
-6.7	15.6	5.7	Net Worth	18.8	-10.2		-9.3	23.8	
100.0	100.0	100.0	Total Liabilities & Net Worth	100.0	100.0		100.0	100.0	
			INCOME DATA						
100.0	100.0	100.0	Net Sales	100.0	100.0		100.0	100.0	
			Gross Profit						
88.4	90.8	86.8	Operating Expenses	70.6	87.0		89.3	96.0	
11.6	9.2	13.2	Operating Profit	29.4	13.0		10.7	4.0	
1.2	3.3	3.7	All Other Expenses (net)	13.7	.6		1.9	-.2	
10.4	5.9	9.5	Profit Before Taxes	15.7	12.4		8.8	4.2	
			RATIOS						
3.9	3.2	2.2		1.5	5.1		1.3	2.1	
1.2	1.1	.9	Current	.6	1.0		.7	1.6	
.4	.4	.4		.5	.2		.1	.8	
3.2	2.8	1.8		1.3	3.8		1.1	2.0	
.9	1.0	.8	Quick	.6	.8		.7	1.3	
.3	.3	.3		.4	.2		.1	.8	
0 UND	0 UND	0 UND		0 UND	0 UND		0 UND	0 UND	
0 UND	0 UND	1 428.1	Sales/Receivables	0 UND	0 UND		0 UND	22 16.5	
6 62.4	36 10.0	42 8.6		19 18.9	46 7.9		43 8.6	71 5.1	
			Cost of Sales/Inventory						
			Cost of Sales/Payables						
11.5	11.4	11.3		39.9	6.2		26.6	7.9	
95.0	211.3	-302.2	Sales/Working Capital	-10.6	NM		-249.5	36.2	
-36.7	-20.9	-13.1		-5.5	-17.0		-20.7	-76.3	
25.5	27.0	16.7			168.5		44.0	14.7	
(40) 5.1	(57) 3.3	(68) 3.0	EBIT/Interest	(19) 14.5	(10) 1.1	(15) 3.9			
1.5	.5	-.1			.5		-7.4	.8	
			Net Profit + Depr., Dep., Amort./Cur. Mat. L/T/D						
.3	.4	.5		.7	.3		.3	.3	
2.8	1.8	1.4	Fixed/Worth	3.2	.8		NM	.9	
-.9	-8.3	-2.7		21.9	-1.8		-.4	3.6	
.5	.6	1.0		1.4	.2		.4	1.1	
6.3	4.5	3.7	Debt/Worth	3.7	1.7		NM	2.1	
-3.7	-13.2	-5.7		25.1	-3.5		-2.3	7.8	
147.4	137.5	120.4		159.4	341.0			41.9	
(35) 27.8	(56) 30.5	(60) 26.6	% Profit Before Taxes/Tangible Net Worth	(15) 57.1	(15) 59.8			(13) 11.3	
8.6	5.3	-.2		3.2	-.5			-3.8	
82.7	25.7	50.8		73.7	106.1		47.8	13.2	
13.5	4.1	6.8	% Profit Before Taxes/Total Assets	11.9	46.2		8.5	5.5	
2.3	-.7	-1.7		.7	-2.9		-7.7	-3.5	
103.4	89.2	47.7		41.5	159.6		57.1	46.4	
25.0	16.4	18.9	Sales/Net Fixed Assets	4.5	35.0		29.7	20.2	
6.1	4.0	3.7		.2	3.2		6.7	6.8	
13.2	8.5	10.2		4.4	21.9		17.9	9.4	
4.5	4.0	3.3	Sales/Total Assets	1.1	4.0		12.6	3.3	
2.1	1.6	1.4		.2	1.7		1.6	1.9	
.5	.7	.9		.8	.5			.5	
(40) 1.9	(61) 2.0	(66) 2.2	% Depr., Dep., Amort./Sales	(14) 6.0	(16) 1.7		(15) 1.9		
3.9	4.7	4.9		14.9	4.8			2.5	
13.3	14.6	10.4			8.5				
(24) 25.6	(31) 27.1	(32) 16.0	% Officers', Directors' Owners' Comp/Sales	(12) 14.4					
33.6	35.2	31.2			23.3				
1928901M	1229216M	1436445M	Net Sales ($)	8900M	46874M	35269M	87836M	257026M	1000540M
295433M	547312M	737601M	Total Assets ($)	20320M	18779M	24638M	42653M	99678M	531533M

© RMA 2010

M = $ thousand   MM = $ million
See Pages 9 through 22 for Explanation of Ratios and Data

Current Data Sorted by Assets   Comparative Historical Data

	0-500M	500M-2MM	2-10MM	10-50MM	50-100MM	100-250MM	Type of Statement	4/1/05-3/31/06 ALL	4/1/06-3/31/07 ALL
	2	1	4	8	2	10	Unqualified	11	17
	1	1	4	2			Reviewed	12	12
	133	75	16	1		1	Compiled	148	173
	583	188	16		1	4	Tax Returns	389	465
	195	95	20	11	3	6	Other	203	208
	92 (4/1-9/30/09)			1,290 (10/1/09-3/31/10)					
	913	360	60	22	6	21	NUMBER OF STATEMENTS	763	875
	%	%	%	%	%	%	ASSETS	%	%
	25.7	14.6	14.2	16.5		14.0	Cash & Equivalents	23.0	20.7
	2.8	4.7	14.0	14.1		6.8	Trade Receivables (net)	5.7	5.6
	.3	.2	1.6	1.9		1.3	Inventory	.4	.5
	2.6	3.6	3.2	5.0		1.8	All Other Current	2.0	3.4
	31.5	23.0	33.0	37.6		23.9	Total Current	31.2	30.1
	42.4	44.4	47.8	34.1		35.7	Fixed Assets (net)	42.5	45.4
	15.3	21.3	10.2	14.2		35.1	Intangibles (net)	16.5	15.1
	10.8	11.2	9.0	14.2		5.3	All Other Non-Current	9.7	9.4
	100.0	100.0	100.0	100.0		100.0	Total	100.0	100.0
							LIABILITIES		
	16.6	8.4	6.6	11.5		13.0	Notes Payable-Short Term	16.4	13.4
	9.5	5.4	6.2	5.3		4.4	Cur. Mat.-L.T.D.	7.0	8.1
	1.9	1.2	2.8	6.5		2.4	Trade Payables	2.4	1.8
	.1	.1	1.4	.1		.3	Income Taxes Payable	.2	.2
	23.7	9.1	12.0	14.9		13.8	All Other Current	19.0	22.4
	51.8	24.2	29.1	38.3		33.8	Total Current	44.9	45.9
	48.4	55.5	36.2	18.5		49.9	Long-Term Debt	45.3	46.5
	.0	.0	.3	.1		2.7	Deferred Taxes	.1	.1
	6.9	4.3	5.2	11.5		9.1	All Other Non-Current	7.6	6.7
	-7.1	16.1	29.3	31.7		4.4	Net Worth	2.1	.8
	100.0	100.0	100.0	100.0		100.0	Total Liabilities & Net Worth	100.0	100.0
							INCOME DATA		
	100.0	100.0	100.0	100.0		100.0	Net Sales	100.0	100.0
							Gross Profit		
	88.5	83.3	85.1	95.3		87.9	Operating Expenses	87.7	87.7
	11.5	16.7	14.9	4.7		12.1	Operating Profit	12.3	12.3
	1.7	4.7	5.5	2.9		2.5	All Other Expenses (net)	1.9	2.1
	9.8	12.0	9.4	1.7		9.6	Profit Before Taxes	10.4	10.2
							RATIOS		
	2.3	3.0	1.7	2.1		1.4		2.2	2.0
	.7	.9	1.2	1.2		.9	Current	.9	.8
	.2	.3	.4	.6		.6		.3	.2
	2.1	2.4	1.5	1.6		1.2		2.0	1.8
	(912) .6	.7	.8	.9		.7	Quick	(759) .8	(870) .7
	.1	.2	.3	.4		.5		.2	.2
	0 UND	0 UND	0 UND	5 79.9		0 UND		0 UND	0 UND
	0 UND	0 UND	0 UND	18 19.8		20 18.4	Sales/Receivables	0 UND	0 UND
	0 UND	0 UND	31 11.9	27 13.3		30 12.3		0 UND	0 UND
							Cost of Sales/Inventory		
							Cost of Sales/Payables		
	40.6	14.8	11.6	11.1		34.4		26.9	33.1
	-78.1	-519.4	46.0	58.5		-74.7	Sales/Working Capital	-159.9	-110.5
	-15.0	-13.2	-19.1	-21.8		-22.0		-18.4	-17.1
	16.7	12.3	16.6	19.7		9.2		15.5	16.6
	(712) 4.4	(299) 4.3	(53) 4.7	(19) 9.7		(19) 3.6	EBIT/Interest	(601) 5.6	(684) 4.6
	1.1	1.5	1.0	5.4		1.5		1.4	1.1
	2.6							7.6	3.4
	(10) 1.0						Net Profit + Depr., Dep., Amort./Cur. Mat. L/T/D	(18) 1.8	(27) 2.0
	.4							.8	1.4
	.8	1.6	.8	.9		4.2		1.0	1.1
	-56.0	-30.8	3.0	2.7		-2.2	Fixed/Worth	29.1	36.8
	-.8	-.9	-7.9	-1.3		-.3		-1.0	-.9
	1.5	2.3	1.1	.9		5.1		1.6	1.7
	-14.4	-25.7	3.3	2.2		-4.2	Debt/Worth	-304.0	243.0
	-2.3	-2.7	-16.0	-4.3		-1.6		-2.6	-2.4
	414.0	188.9	140.6	80.3				307.8	370.0
	(426) 109.1	(168) 89.5	(42) 34.6	(14) 28.0			% Profit Before Taxes/Tangible Net Worth	(381) 110.0	(447) 119.0
	31.7	26.6	2.8	9.0				18.5	28.1
	80.7	41.5	29.8	19.7		32.1		67.9	71.6
	23.9	16.6	7.5	12.3		8.3	% Profit Before Taxes/Total Assets	25.6	21.0
	1.2	2.1	.0	1.6		1.3		1.6	1.3
	48.0	18.5	13.5	9.6		12.2		37.5	37.3
	18.6	7.3	5.5	6.9		7.9	Sales/Net Fixed Assets	14.4	14.2
	8.1	2.8	2.6	4.4		3.6		6.6	5.7
	10.4	3.5	3.5	3.1		4.9		9.2	9.2
	5.6	2.0	2.2	2.3		1.8	Sales/Total Assets	4.6	4.5
	3.2	1.3	1.1	1.5		1.2		2.4	2.3
	1.0	2.2	1.4	2.6				1.1	1.2
	(583) 2.3	(247) 4.3	(52) 2.7	(17) 3.5			% Depr., Dep., Amort./Sales	(510) 2.4	(594) 2.5
	4.7	8.6	5.2	5.2				4.8	5.2
	11.4	8.0	10.5					12.2	12.8
	(684) 18.6	(243) 14.6	(28) 17.0				% Officers', Directors' Owners' Comp/Sales	(554) 19.4	(614) 19.6
	27.0	23.7	25.6					27.3	26.8
	1234244M	868691M	740305M	1338878M	2472556M	12704256M	Net Sales ($)	23214943M	18559817M
	205997M	326042M	243829M	584966M	492657M	3392481M	Total Assets ($)	4063470M	3811253M

© RMA 2010

M = $ thousand   MM = $ million
See Pages 9 through 22 for Explanation of Ratios and Data

Comparative Historical Data | Current Data Sorted by Sales

Type of Statement

4/1/07-3/31/08 ALL	4/1/08-3/31/09 ALL	4/1/09-3/31/10 ALL	Type of Statement	0-1MM	1-3MM	3-5MM	5-10MM	10-25MM	25MM & OVER
19	18	27	Unqualified	1	2		1	3	20
19	6	7	Reviewed		1			2	4
158	187	226	Compiled	60	119	21	13	10	3
520	657	792	Tax Returns	353	340	53	31	9	6
243	297	330	Other	118	151	24	7	11	19
				92 (4/1-9/30/09)			1,290 (10/1/09-3/31/10)		
959	1165	1382	NUMBER OF STATEMENTS	532	613	98	52	35	52

ASSETS

4/1/07-3/31/08 ALL %	4/1/08-3/31/09 ALL %	4/1/09-3/31/10 ALL %	ASSETS	0-1MM %	1-3MM %	3-5MM %	5-10MM %	10-25MM %	25MM & OVER %
21.1	20.4	22.0	Cash & Equivalents	21.4	22.6	25.7	22.7	17.6	16.6
4.5	3.3	4.0	Trade Receivables (net)	2.3	3.8	4.4	6.2	17.2	12.8
.4	.5	.4	Inventory	.2	.3	.3	.9	1.2	2.0
3.1	3.6	2.9	All Other Current	2.5	3.1	3.6	2.5	4.5	3.2
29.0	27.7	29.3	Total Current	26.4	29.8	34.0	32.3	40.5	34.6
45.4	46.0	42.8	Fixed Assets (net)	44.5	41.2	46.7	50.4	35.8	34.6
14.8	16.7	17.0	Intangibles (net)	17.9	17.5	10.5	12.7	10.3	23.7
10.8	9.5	10.8	All Other Non-Current	11.2	11.4	8.8	4.5	13.4	7.1
100.0	100.0	100.0	Total	100.0	100.0	100.0	100.0	100.0	100.0

LIABILITIES

4/1/07-3/31/08 ALL	4/1/08-3/31/09 ALL	4/1/09-3/31/10 ALL	LIABILITIES	0-1MM	1-3MM	3-5MM	5-10MM	10-25MM	25MM & OVER
15.1	13.3	13.8	Notes Payable-Short Term	13.6	13.6	18.2	14.4	16.4	8.9
8.4	9.5	8.2	Cur. Mat.-L.T.D.	8.7	8.1	9.3	4.2	5.4	6.4
2.2	1.6	1.8	Trade Payables	1.3	1.6	1.9	4.8	4.8	5.1
.2	.1	.1	Income Taxes Payable	.1	.1	.2	.0	2.5	.2
19.4	16.6	19.0	All Other Current	21.4	16.2	18.6	29.0	21.1	17.9
45.1	41.1	43.0	Total Current	45.1	39.6	48.2	52.4	50.2	38.4
46.9	51.8	49.1	Long-Term Debt	53.9	48.8	38.7	53.3	34.0	30.7
.0	.1	.1	Deferred Taxes	.0	.0	.0	.0	.5	1.4
6.9	5.5	6.2	All Other Non-Current	7.2	5.3	6.8	3.7	7.8	7.6
1.0	1.6	1.5	Net Worth	-6.2	6.3	6.3	-9.4	7.5	21.9
100.0	100.0	100.0	Total Liabilities & Net Worth	100.0	100.0	100.0	100.0	100.0	100.0

INCOME DATA

4/1/07-3/31/08 ALL	4/1/08-3/31/09 ALL	4/1/09-3/31/10 ALL	INCOME DATA	0-1MM	1-3MM	3-5MM	5-10MM	10-25MM	25MM & OVER
100.0	100.0	100.0	Net Sales	100.0	100.0	100.0	100.0	100.0	100.0
			Gross Profit						
87.4	87.0	87.1	Operating Expenses	84.6	87.5	91.1	90.5	96.8	89.9
12.6	13.0	12.9	Operating Profit	15.4	12.5	8.9	9.5	3.2	10.1
2.6	3.2	2.7	All Other Expenses (net)	4.9	1.4	.9	1.0	1.4	1.4
10.0	9.9	10.2	Profit Before Taxes	10.5	11.1	8.0	8.5	1.8	8.6

RATIOS

(Each ratio cell lists the upper-quartile / median / lower-quartile values; figures in parentheses are the number of statements for that data set.)

4/1/07-3/31/08 ALL	4/1/08-3/31/09 ALL	4/1/09-3/31/10 ALL	RATIOS	0-1MM	1-3MM	3-5MM	5-10MM	10-25MM	25MM & OVER
1.8 / .7 / .2	2.0 / .7 / .2	2.3 / .8 / .2	Current	2.6 / .7 / .2	2.5 / .9 / .2	1.4 / .6 / .3	2.5 / .8 / .2	1.9 / 1.3 / .6	1.4 / 1.0 / .6
(957) 1.6 / .5 / .2	(1161) 1.8 / .6 / .2	(1381) 2.0 / .6 / .2	Quick	2.3 / .6 / .1	(612) 2.2 / .7 / .2	1.2 / .5 / .2	2.5 / .7 / .1	1.5 / 1.1 / .3	1.3 / .7 / .5
0 UND / 0 UND / 0 UND	0 UND / 0 UND / 0 UND	0 UND / 0 UND / 0 UND	Sales/Receivables	0 UND / 0 UND / 0 UND	0 UND / 0 UND / 0 UND	0 UND / 0 UND / 0 UND	0 UND / 0 UND / 0 UND	0 UND / 16 22.8 / 31 11.7	0 UND / 19 19.4 / 30 12.2
			Cost of Sales/Inventory						
			Cost of Sales/Payables						
36.8 / -64.0 / -15.9	34.1 / -75.2 / -14.1	25.8 / -111.7 / -14.9	Sales/Working Capital	26.4 / -74.0 / -8.7	23.3 / -166.0 / -16.8	100.7 / -55.1 / -23.2	25.8 / -126.8 / -33.6	11.9 / 489.0 / -20.3	23.8 / -542.7 / -25.4
(752) 12.4 / 4.0 / 1.1	(939) 14.2 / 4.1 / 1.2	(1107) 15.6 / 4.4 / 1.3	EBIT/Interest	(387) 9.7 / 3.7 / 1.1	(508) 19.6 / 5.0 / 1.5	(85) 20.7 / 5.5 / 1.0	(47) 32.0 / 3.6 / 1.0	(33) 15.2 / 3.3 / -.7	(47) 18.5 / 7.2 / 2.3
(26) 4.8 / 1.6 / .6	(34) 4.8 / 1.2 / .5	(30) 7.9 / 2.5 / 1.0	Net Profit + Depr., Dep., Amort./Cur. Mat. L/T/D						(13) 16.2 / 7.9 / 2.3
1.1 / 188.0 / -1.0	1.2 / -54.1 / -.9	.9 / UND / -.9	Fixed/Worth	1.0 / -9.2 / -.7	.9 / 53.0 / -.8	.9 / 34.9 / -1.6	2.0 / -5.0 / -1.3	.5 / 13.3 / -1.1	1.0 / 4.6 / -1.0
2.0 / -58.8 / -2.5	1.9 / -30.2 / -2.4	1.6 / -24.0 / -2.4	Debt/Worth	1.7 / -10.6 / -2.1	1.6 / UND / -2.4	1.9 / -37.6 / -3.7	1.8 / -12.1 / -3.5	1.3 / 27.6 / -4.7	1.5 / 9.5 / -3.7
(465) 356.4 / 123.3 / 33.7	(547) 339.4 / 117.8 / 29.4	(660) 283.5 / 96.3 / 24.2	% Profit Before Taxes/Tangible Net Worth	(233) 204.4 / 71.9 / 20.3	(308) 376.7 / 121.1 / 39.7	(48) 332.3 / 67.9 / 1.2	(23) 235.4 / 98.9 / 20.5	(19) 144.3 / 17.4 / -2.8	(29) 300.5 / 44.1 / 20.2
66.5 / 19.2 / .8	63.0 / 19.0 / 1.4	61.0 / 19.7 / 1.4	% Profit Before Taxes/Total Assets	49.4 / 17.2 / .3	72.5 / 26.3 / 3.7	83.0 / 16.5 / .3	88.0 / 11.1 / -.2	38.4 / 5.7 / -2.1	34.4 / 12.3 / 3.4
38.2 / 12.4 / 5.2	35.3 / 12.1 / 4.5	36.5 / 13.1 / 5.5	Sales/Net Fixed Assets	33.5 / 11.5 / 3.6	38.1 / 14.4 / 6.9	47.7 / 18.5 / 8.4	40.8 / 15.6 / 8.6	67.2 / 15.7 / 6.1	16.1 / 8.9 / 4.9
8.7 / 4.2 / 2.2	8.5 / 3.8 / 2.0	7.8 / 4.0 / 2.1	Sales/Total Assets	6.7 / 3.1 / 1.5	8.0 / 4.5 / 2.5	12.4 / 7.8 / 3.8	14.6 / 6.7 / 4.0	10.1 / 3.1 / 2.3	5.6 / 3.1 / 1.6
(649) 1.2 / 2.7 / 5.5	(781) 1.4 / 3.4 / 6.5	(910) 1.3 / 2.9 / 5.8	% Depr., Dep., Amort./Sales	(344) 1.6 / 4.1 / 7.8	(391) 1.3 / 2.8 / 5.0	(69) 1.0 / 1.7 / 3.0	(45) 1.1 / 2.5 / 3.2	(28) 1.1 / 2.2 / 3.3	(33) 1.7 / 3.1 / 5.1
(664) 11.9 / 19.1 / 28.8	(802) 10.4 / 18.1 / 25.8	(965) 10.6 / 17.7 / 26.4	% Officers', Directors', Owners' Comp/Sales	(353) 10.7 / 18.1 / 25.9	(472) 10.4 / 16.6 / 27.3	(69) 10.2 / 18.3 / 25.2	(38) 12.5 / 25.7 / 32.2	(19) 2.9 / 19.3 / 30.5	(14) 17.7 / 25.6 / 38.4
14421648M	11970487M	19358930M	Net Sales ($)	334207M	1019476M	374807M	347450M	523307M	16759683M
3250423M	2956731M	5245972M	Total Assets ($)	182809M	298075M	68933M	95124M	208623M	4392408M

M = $ thousand   MM = $ million
See Pages 9 through 22 for Explanation of Ratios and Data

HEALTH CARE—Offices of Chiropractors NAICS 621310

Current Data Sorted by Assets							Comparative Historical Data	

0-500M	500M-2MM	2-10MM	10-50MM	50-100MM	100-250MM	Type of Statement	4/1/05-3/31/06 ALL	4/1/06-3/31/07 ALL
		1	1	1		Unqualified	1	1
						Reviewed		
15	5					Compiled	14	14
70	5	2	1		1	Tax Returns	53	64
31	15	4	1			Other	27	42
	6 (4/1-9/30/09)		147 (10/1/09-3/31/10)					
116	25	7	3	1	1	NUMBER OF STATEMENTS	95	121
%	%	%	%	%	%	ASSETS	%	%
31.7	11.5					Cash & Equivalents	22.3	23.8
8.7	15.4					Trade Receivables (net)	8.5	10.5
.1	.2					Inventory	.4	.7
2.9	2.0					All Other Current	4.7	4.5
43.4	29.1					Total Current	35.9	39.6
35.5	47.0					Fixed Assets (net)	42.4	36.3
9.1	7.0					Intangibles (net)	11.6	8.8
12.0	16.9					All Other Non-Current	10.1	15.3
100.0	100.0					Total	100.0	100.0
						LIABILITIES		
22.9	7.1					Notes Payable-Short Term	24.0	23.2
3.8	5.1					Cur. Mat.-L.T.D.	5.4	4.9
1.8	1.7					Trade Payables	1.2	2.8
.1	.0					Income Taxes Payable	.1	.6
14.3	7.7					All Other Current	20.2	16.6
42.8	21.6					Total Current	50.8	48.1
32.4	40.6					Long-Term Debt	31.6	22.9
.4	.0					Deferred Taxes	.0	.0
2.8	2.2					All Other Non-Current	9.4	7.0
21.4	35.7					Net Worth	8.2	22.0
100.0	100.0					Total Liabilities & Net Worth	100.0	100.0
						INCOME DATA		
100.0	100.0					Net Sales	100.0	100.0
						Gross Profit		
82.7	78.9					Operating Expenses	82.8	85.7
17.3	21.1					Operating Profit	17.2	14.3
1.5	5.5					All Other Expenses (net)	3.2	2.1
15.8	15.6					Profit Before Taxes	14.0	12.3
						RATIOS		
3.6	13.5					Current	3.5	4.4
1.2	1.3						1.2	1.6
.4	.1						.3	.4
3.5	13.4					Quick	3.5	3.6
1.1	1.2						(94) 1.0	1.3
.3	.1						.2	.2
0 UND	0 UND					Sales/Receivables	0 UND	0 UND
0 UND	0 UND						0 UND	0 UND
0 UND	15 24.5						0 UND	5 76.4
						Cost of Sales/Inventory		
						Cost of Sales/Payables		
16.4	3.7					Sales/Working Capital	10.8	10.4
86.8	23.1						207.0	88.8
-25.1	-11.2						-20.4	-16.9
39.6	37.7					EBIT/Interest	28.6	17.1
(79) 13.0	(15) 4.7						(68) 6.7	(80) 4.5
3.5	2.3						1.2	1.8
						Net Profit + Depr., Dep., Amort./Cur. Mat. L/T/D		
.4	.4					Fixed/Worth	.6	.2
1.1	2.0						2.5	1.1
UND	-79.6						-1.5	-7.8
.3	.3					Debt/Worth	.6	.4
2.8	4.1						4.5	2.4
-28.8	-92.3						-3.3	-11.8
527.8	199.7					% Profit Before Taxes/Tangible Net Worth	435.1	247.6
(85) 155.6	(18) 47.3						(57) 116.4	(86) 82.2
50.6	15.5						26.5	31.1
137.8	39.6					% Profit Before Taxes/Total Assets	85.5	80.5
55.1	18.0						25.8	27.9
20.3	5.0						1.4	3.3
83.0	14.1					Sales/Net Fixed Assets	36.0	52.8
17.9	6.1						13.4	16.1
8.6	.8						6.9	5.9
8.7	2.6					Sales/Total Assets	7.5	7.8
5.1	1.3						3.3	3.6
2.7	.4						1.8	1.9
.7	.8					% Depr., Dep., Amort./Sales	.7	.8
(69) 2.0	(13) 1.3						(64) 2.4	(59) 1.8
3.9	6.0						4.0	3.7
11.3	3.0					% Officers', Directors' Owners' Comp/Sales	10.9	10.5
(77) 16.5	(11) 8.7						(60) 16.6	(73) 15.4
26.5	19.2						26.0	24.0
82472M	39367M	276984M	367353M	65100M	928814M	Net Sales ($)	1734242M	2772957M
16620M	25734M	31173M	84606M	78788M	184328M	Total Assets ($)	264611M	947739M

© RMA 2010

M = $ thousand   MM = $ million
See Pages 9 through 22 for Explanation of Ratios and Data

Comparative Historical Data | Current Data Sorted by Sales

Comparative Historical Data			Type of Statement	Current Data Sorted by Sales					
		1 3	Unqualified					1	2
		1	Reviewed						
19	12	20	Compiled	13	5	1	1		
77	64	79	Tax Returns	56	18	2		1	3
34	26	51	Other	34	11	3	2	1	
4/1/07- 3/31/08 ALL	4/1/08- 3/31/09 ALL	4/1/09- 3/31/10 ALL		6 (4/1-9/30/09)		147 (10/1/09-3/31/10)			
130	104	153	**NUMBER OF STATEMENTS**	0-1MM 103	1-3MM 34	3-5MM 6	5-10MM 3	10-25MM 2	25MM & OVER 5
%	%	%	**ASSETS**	%	%	%	%	%	%
23.4	27.8	27.7	Cash & Equivalents	29.1	25.0				
8.6	9.3	11.0	Trade Receivables (net)	8.9	8.2				
.5	.5	.2	Inventory	.2	.2				
4.8	3.3	2.6	All Other Current	2.6	1.3				
37.1	40.8	41.6	Total Current	40.7	34.8				
35.7	38.3	37.9	Fixed Assets (net)	36.4	47.3				
13.4	6.0	8.1	Intangibles (net)	10.1	4.1				
13.8	14.8	12.3	All Other Non-Current	12.7	13.9				
100.0	100.0	100.0	Total	100.0	100.0				
			LIABILITIES						
22.6	26.9	18.6	Notes Payable-Short Term	18.4	24.3				
7.0	4.3	3.8	Cur. Mat.-L.T.D.	4.6	2.9				
5.5	1.8	1.9	Trade Payables	1.6	2.2				
.5	.3	.1	Income Taxes Payable	.1	.0				
12.4	10.1	12.9	All Other Current	12.1	8.7				
47.9	43.4	37.3	Total Current	36.9	38.0				
34.7	31.1	33.2	Long-Term Debt	37.0	26.6				
.0	.0	.3	Deferred Taxes	.3	.6				
10.0	8.6	2.7	All Other Non-Current	2.6	4.1				
7.4	16.8	26.5	Net Worth	23.2	30.7				
100.0	100.0	100.0	Total Liabilities & Net Worth	100.0	100.0				
			INCOME DATA						
100.0	100.0	100.0	Net Sales	100.0	100.0				
			Gross Profit						
83.7	80.5	81.1	Operating Expenses	79.1	86.4				
16.3	19.5	18.9	Operating Profit	20.9	13.6				
3.1	2.7	2.2	All Other Expenses (net)	3.1	.9				
13.2	16.7	16.7	Profit Before Taxes	17.8	12.7				
			RATIOS						
2.7	3.3	4.0	Current	3.7	7.1				
1.0	1.4	1.3		1.3	1.2				
.3	.4	.4		.4	.2				
2.4	3.2	4.0	Quick	3.5	7.0				
(129) .8	1.2	1.2		1.1	1.1				
.2	.3	.3		.4	.2				
0 UND	0 UND	0 UND	Sales/Receivables	0 UND	0 UND				
0 UND	0 UND	0 UND		0 UND	0 UND				
0 UND	0 UND	0 UND		0 UND	0 UND				
			Cost of Sales/Inventory						
			Cost of Sales/Payables						
20.8	15.1	12.1	Sales/Working Capital	12.1	13.6				
-270.8	75.9	68.2		81.8	106.0				
-12.5	-25.1	-23.9		-16.3	-25.0				
12.9	38.9	38.6	EBIT/Interest	34.4	39.1				
(93) 5.8	(70) 12.4	(101) 12.0		(64) 12.7	(28) 10.2				
2.0	1.8	3.5		3.5	1.7				
			Net Profit + Depr., Dep., Amort./Cur. Mat. L/T/D						
.3	.3	.3	Fixed/Worth	.4	.4				
3.5	1.1	1.1		1.1	1.3				
-.9	UND	UND		-6.6	33.9				
.5	.4	.3	Debt/Worth	.3	.4				
34.2	2.0	2.5		3.0	1.5				
-2.9	-85.7	-165.1		-11.0	61.7				
412.5	496.7	415.3	% Profit Before Taxes/Tangible Net Worth	513.9	310.5				
(71) 155.3	(77) 145.8	(114) 99.8		(74) 154.7	(27) 72.7				
45.8	70.0	40.5		42.5	36.8				
109.5	135.1	99.3	% Profit Before Taxes/Total Assets	119.0	59.0				
31.1	53.2	43.3		49.5	30.7				
4.6	15.9	12.1		17.4	6.3				
52.5	51.2	59.9	Sales/Net Fixed Assets	77.3	34.8				
20.3	15.2	15.2		17.4	10.9				
7.4	6.0	6.2		6.2	6.9				
11.0	8.6	7.4	Sales/Total Assets	7.3	7.5				
4.5	4.5	3.9		3.9	4.1				
1.9	2.2	2.0		2.0	2.6				
.9	.6	.8	% Depr., Dep., Amort./Sales	.6	.8				
(77) 2.3	(68) 2.0	(89) 2.0		(55) 2.1	(26) 1.6				
4.5	4.2	3.9		4.1	5.4				
12.7	10.9	8.6	% Officers', Directors' Owners' Comp/Sales	12.3	5.2				
(81) 19.9	(68) 15.7	(93) 15.6		(61) 17.6	(25) 8.7				
27.4	21.7	25.7		27.0	21.2				
901972M	1205613M	1760090M	Net Sales ($)	45269M	53265M	21756M	18020M	24972M	1596808M
328176M	337105M	421249M	Total Assets ($)	25363M	17002M	6242M	12412M	19547M	340683M

MA 2010

M = $ thousand   MM = $ million

See Pages 9 through 22 for Explanation of Ratios and Data

HEALTH CARE—Offices of Optometrists NAICS 621320

Current Data Sorted by Assets | **Comparative Historical Data**

Type of Statement	0-500M	500M-2MM	2-10MM	10-50MM	50-100MM	100-250MM		4/1/05-3/31/06 ALL	4/1/06-3/31/07 ALL
Unqualified			2	1		1		1	6
Reviewed	2	5	6					6	5
Compiled	28	12	5	5		1		36	50
Tax Returns	109	22	15		1			75	93
Other	46	23	12	2		2		55	42
	17 (4/1-9/30/09)			283 (10/1/09-3/31/10)					
NUMBER OF STATEMENTS	185	62	40	8	1	4		173	196

	0-500M %	500M-2MM %	2-10MM %	10-50MM %	50-100MM %	100-250MM %		%	%
ASSETS									
Cash & Equivalents	26.6	13.1	14.5					15.7	17.7
Trade Receivables (net)	6.9	11.5	13.3					10.3	10.6
Inventory	16.3	6.8	4.9					12.3	13.3
All Other Current	1.4	.9	1.4					2.1	2.8
Total Current	51.3	32.4	34.0					40.4	44.5
Fixed Assets (net)	30.8	45.7	52.2					39.9	36.5
Intangibles (net)	10.5	12.6	5.6					10.4	11.7
All Other Non-Current	7.4	9.3	8.1					9.3	7.4
Total	100.0	100.0	100.0					100.0	100.0
LIABILITIES									
Notes Payable-Short Term	12.9	8.6	4.9					10.7	8.3
Cur. Mat.-L.T.D.	10.7	5.8	6.9					6.7	8.9
Trade Payables	6.0	4.8	4.8					6.1	5.5
Income Taxes Payable	.0	.2	.4					.4	.4
All Other Current	17.9	13.0	16.3					15.0	16.5
Total Current	47.5	32.4	33.3					38.9	39.6
Long-Term Debt	38.3	40.3	38.9					38.8	36.5
Deferred Taxes	.1	.0	.0					.0	.1
All Other Non-Current	7.7	3.9	3.5					10.0	9.4
Net Worth	6.6	23.4	24.3					12.2	14.5
Total Liabilities & Net Worth	100.0	100.0	100.0					100.0	100.0
INCOME DATA									
Net Sales	100.0	100.0	100.0					100.0	100.0
Gross Profit									
Operating Expenses	90.3	86.3	76.6					91.2	89.1
Operating Profit	9.7	13.7	23.4					8.8	10.9
All Other Expenses (net)	1.0	3.5	10.0					1.4	1.9
Profit Before Taxes	8.8	10.3	13.4					7.4	8.9

RATIOS

Ratio	0-500M	500M-2MM	2-10MM		4/1/05-3/31/06	4/1/06-3/31/07
Current	4.6	2.0	1.6		2.6	2.6
	1.3	1.2	.8		1.1	1.3
	.6	.6	.3		.5	.6
Quick	2.8	1.8	1.3		1.6	1.9
	.8	.8	.7		(172) .7	(195) .7
	.2	.3	.3		.2	.3
Sales/Receivables	0 UND	0 UND	0 UND		0 UND	0 UND
	0 UND	0 UND	6 61.4		0 UND	0 UND
	1 622.4	30 12.3	30 12.2		21 17.5	20 18.4
Cost of Sales/Inventory						
Cost of Sales/Payables						
Sales/Working Capital	14.8	18.7	20.6		15.2	15.7
	47.9	144.6	-126.9		133.1	94.9
	-43.2	-20.8	-12.8		-23.0	-30.1
EBIT/Interest	27.7	17.3	31.4		23.8	16.4
	(131) 5.5	(56) 5.5	(33) 6.2		(144) 3.3	(166) 4.1
	1.0	1.6	2.3		.8	.9
Net Profit + Depr., Dep., Amort./Cur. Mat. L/T/D						
Fixed/Worth	.4	1.0	.9		.8	.7
	1.8	2.9	3.5		5.8	3.0
	-.7	-3.9	216.4		-1.9	-2.6
Debt/Worth	.8	1.3	1.0		1.1	1.4
	7.4	3.8	4.2		10.4	7.4
	-2.6	-7.5	NM		-5.0	-4.7
% Profit Before Taxes/Tangible Net Worth	276.1	111.2	78.5		150.0	190.1
	(105) 93.7	(43) 57.5	(30) 30.5		(103) 50.0	(119) 58.6
	22.0	7.9	6.6		9.5	7.1
% Profit Before Taxes/Total Assets	83.2	36.1	35.9		47.0	57.0
	28.1	14.6	8.4		10.1	13.4
	.5	2.6	2.1		-.5	.0
Sales/Net Fixed Assets	95.5	21.5	18.5		30.9	55.8
	27.4	10.0	7.4		15.3	18.1
	11.6	3.7	.7		8.5	7.4
Sales/Total Assets	10.5	5.4	5.1		8.6	9.1
	6.6	2.9	2.7		4.8	4.5
	3.7	2.0	.7		2.6	2.7
% Depr., Dep., Amort./Sales	.8	1.8	2.5		1.3	1.4
	(111) 2.1	(44) 3.0	(30) 3.4		(133) 2.2	(137) 2.6
	3.9	5.7	13.4		4.5	4.2
% Officers', Directors', Owners' Comp/Sales	8.4	6.1	9.9		8.0	7.8
	(132) 14.0	(35) 13.2	(13) 17.8		(110) 16.0	(138) 13.5
	22.9	31.4	21.8		25.2	22.9

	0-500M	500M-2MM	2-10MM	10-50MM	50-100MM	100-250MM		Hist 1	Hist 2
Net Sales ($)	295061M	242439M	817017M	503245M	311369M	1016143M		2702809M	2869707M
Total Assets ($)	40154M	65099M	181387M	170246M	75460M	618203M		558921M	821270M

M = $ thousand   MM = $ million
See Pages 9 through 22 for Explanation of Ratios and Data

Comparative Historical Data

Current Data Sorted by Sales

	4/1/07-3/31/08 ALL	4/1/08-3/31/09 ALL	4/1/09-3/31/10 ALL	Type of Statement	0-1MM	1-3MM	3-5MM	5-10MM	10-25MM	25MM & OVER
	7	5	4	Unqualified	4	1		2	7	3
	5	3	18	Reviewed	13	12	8	7	4	4
	43	47	45	Compiled	57	54	17	12	5	1
	87	118	148	Tax Returns	30	26	11	6	7	3
	44	80	85	Other						5
					17 (4/1-9/30/09)			283 (10/1/09-3/31/10)		
NUMBER OF STATEMENTS	186	253	300		104	93	36	28	23	16
	%	%	%	**ASSETS**	%	%	%	%	%	%
Cash & Equivalents	18.7	16.6	21.5		18.6	23.4	23.9	29.7	13.1	22.4
Trade Receivables (net)	9.8	8.5	9.2		6.7	9.1	9.5	9.7	12.7	19.3
Inventory	11.6	10.8	12.5		16.2	13.3	9.5	7.7	5.8	7.9
All Other Current	2.8	4.0	1.6		1.4	1.0	.6	2.5	4.0	4.2
Total Current	42.8	40.0	44.8		43.0	46.8	43.5	49.5	35.6	53.8
Fixed Assets (net)	39.1	38.3	36.7		42.8	30.6	35.6	34.6	47.0	23.5
Intangibles (net)	8.2	10.2	10.5		9.5	12.6	12.9	6.0	6.8	12.0
All Other Non-Current	9.9	11.5	8.0		4.7	10.0	8.0	9.8	10.6	10.7
Total	100.0	100.0	100.0		100.0	100.0	100.0	100.0	100.0	100.0
				LIABILITIES						
Notes Payable-Short Term	12.2	11.0	10.5		10.0	12.9	12.4	10.8	4.5	3.5
Cur. Mat.-L.T.D.	7.1	7.9	9.1		11.3	8.9	5.9	8.2	4.8	11.3
Trade Payables	8.6	5.3	5.8		6.4	5.1	5.0	4.7	5.5	8.8
Income Taxes Payable	.3	.4	.1		.0	.1	.0	.0	.6	.0
All Other Current	16.0	16.6	16.3		12.1	14.9	26.4	16.5	18.7	25.5
Total Current	44.2	41.2	41.8		39.8	42.0	49.8	40.3	34.0	49.3
Long-Term Debt	39.3	40.9	38.6		42.9	43.4	29.8	33.1	23.5	34.2
Deferred Taxes	.1	.0	.1		.0	.1	.0	.0	.0	.4
All Other Non-Current	7.7	7.1	6.2		8.5	4.0	5.1	6.0	7.6	4.9
Net Worth	8.6	10.8	13.4		8.8	10.5	15.4	20.6	34.9	11.2
Total Liabilities & Net Worth	100.0	100.0	100.0		100.0	100.0	100.0	100.0	100.0	100.0
				INCOME DATA						
Net Sales	100.0	100.0	100.0		100.0	100.0	100.0	100.0	100.0	100.0
Gross Profit										
Operating Expenses	91.4	90.1	87.8		83.9	88.7	92.0	90.0	91.3	90.2
Operating Profit	8.6	9.9	12.2		16.1	11.3	8.0	10.0	8.7	9.8
All Other Expenses (net)	1.4	1.7	2.7		4.7	1.3	1.3	3.3	2.3	.9
Profit Before Taxes	7.3	8.2	9.5		11.5	10.0	6.7	6.7	6.4	8.9
				RATIOS						
Current	2.8	2.6	3.2		4.6	3.2	2.8	1.9	2.2	2.2
	1.1	1.2	1.3		1.6	1.3	1.0	1.2	1.1	1.1
	.5	.6	.6		.5	.6	.6	.8	.6	.7
Quick	1.9	1.8	2.1		2.7	2.7	1.5	1.8	1.3	1.7
	.6 (251)	.7 (299)	.8		.8	.6	.7	1.0	.7 (15)	.9
	.2	.2	.3		.1	.3	.3	.5	.5	.7
Sales/Receivables	0 UND	0 UND	0 UND		0 UND	0 UND	0 UND	0 UND	0 UND	0 UND
	0 UND	0 UND	0 UND		0 UND	0 UND	0 UND	0 UND	4 97.1	23 16.2
	17 21.5	19 19.5	15 24.8		7 55.7	5 68.3	19 19.6	28 13.1	23 16.0	40 9.1
Cost of Sales/Inventory										
Cost of Sales/Payables										
Sales/Working Capital	15.5	15.8	15.3		11.8	16.2	24.2	26.2	29.1	14.4
	307.1	110.9	75.6		31.6	71.7	-656.3	126.2	-132.3	79.5
	-27.8	-31.0	-30.6		-10.5	-61.4	-22.0	-67.5	-33.4	-70.8
EBIT/Interest	11.9	15.0	21.1		13.8	33.1	25.6	17.7	65.5	14.4
	3.7 (148)	4.2 (209)	5.5 (233)		4.8 (65)	7.5 (75)	4.3 (30)	4.2 (25)	8.1 (22)	4.1
	1.0	.7	1.5		1.2	1.5	.5	.8	2.6	2.7
Net Profit + Depr., Dep., Amort./Cur. Mat. L/T/D		6.1	2.5							
		1.1 (12)	1.6 (13)							
		.5	.8							
Fixed/Worth	.6	.6	.5		.6	.3	.7	.4	.9	.5
	2.5	3.9	2.5		3.6	2.0	3.7	2.3	1.5	6.3
	-3.5	-1.6	-1.4		-1.0	-1.1	-1.5	NM	262.0	-.9
Debt/Worth	1.0	1.0	1.1		1.0	.9	1.1	1.3	1.0	2.1
	5.5	8.5	4.9		5.5	4.6	21.9	4.9	1.5	NM
	-6.7	-4.7	-3.8		-3.0	-2.9	-6.5	NM	669.8	-4.6
% Profit Before Taxes/Tangible Net Worth	150.0	211.2	172.5		160.9	218.9	257.1	123.5	87.2	
	43.1 (119)	78.6 (158)	70.1 (187)		59.5 (63)	100.0 (55)	53.5 (22)	55.1 (21)	43.5 (18)	
	9.9	18.5	14.0		20.8	4.5	4.7	6.7	12.2	
% Profit Before Taxes/Total Assets	47.8	50.1	55.3		49.1	70.3	58.2	37.3	41.3	54.3
	12.3	15.5	18.5		19.3	33.9	13.1	7.9	8.6	14.6
	.6	.0	1.9		2.7	3.0	-1.4	-1.2	3.3	2.1
Sales/Net Fixed Assets	43.8	37.5	51.1		42.5	81.5	63.9	70.8	18.5	27.3
	16.3	13.7	17.8		11.0	26.5	24.7	28.0	12.5	10.1
	7.6	6.6	6.5		4.0	12.0	11.7	14.6	4.7	8.2
Sales/Total Assets	9.3	8.0	8.3		6.1	9.6	12.1	15.8	6.3	5.1
	5.5	4.4	4.5		3.7	6.3	6.8	8.2	5.0	3.8
	2.6	2.3	2.7		2.0	2.9	3.1	2.9	2.8	2.3
% Depr., Dep., Amort./Sales	1.1	1.7	1.3		1.9	.6	.6	1.5	1.6	1.0
	2.1 (134)	2.9 (168)	2.5 (196)		3.9 (64)	2.1 (53)	1.9 (28)	1.9 (20)	2.9 (19)	2.2 (12)
	3.8	5.1	4.3		7.7	4.1	3.1	3.0	4.5	3.3
% Officers', Directors' Owners' Comp/Sales	8.3	7.9	8.1		7.4	7.8	8.5	12.8	9.8	
	14.2 (123)	14.2 (165)	13.6 (183)		12.5 (61)	12.5 (64)	17.9 (25)	24.1 (19)	16.8 (12)	
	24.5	22.1	23.0		19.3	21.9	31.9	31.9	22.6	
Net Sales ($)	4216963M	2528226M	3185274M		61534M	159545M	135912M	193194M	377549M	2257540M
Total Assets ($)	1160827M	1007665M	1150549M		47059M	55758M	32366M	45405M	106670M	863291M

RMA 2010

M = $ thousand   MM = $ million
See Pages 9 through 22 for Explanation of Ratios and Data

HEALTH CARE—Offices of Mental Health Practitioners (except Physicians)   NAICS 621330

Current Data Sorted by Assets   **Comparative Historical Data**

Type of Statement

0-500M	500M-2MM	2-10MM	10-50MM	50-100MM	100-250MM	Type of Statement	4/1/05-3/31/06 ALL	4/1/06-3/31/07 ALL
	3	7	6	1		Unqualified	11	18
	1	7	2			Reviewed		1
4	1	1				Compiled	4	6
16	5	1				Tax Returns	6	21
5	4	9	2			Other	8	21
	27 (4/1-9/30/09)			48 (10/1/09-3/31/10)				
25	14	25	10	1		**NUMBER OF STATEMENTS**	29	67

0-500M	500M-2MM	2-10MM	10-50MM	50-100MM	100-250MM		4/1/05-3/31/06 ALL	4/1/06-3/31/07 ALL
%	%	%	%	%	%	**ASSETS**	%	%
43.4	14.7	15.4	20.7			Cash & Equivalents	25.8	31.0
4.1	38.3	29.0	18.2			Trade Receivables (net)	28.1	15.4
.0	.0	.3	.7			Inventory	.1	.6
2.5	1.0	10.7	2.9			All Other Current	6.7	4.3
50.0	54.0	55.5	42.5			Total Current	60.8	51.2
28.5	39.5	34.1	46.0			Fixed Assets (net)	29.1	36.0
10.4	1.7	2.7	2.5			Intangibles (net)	.4	3.3
11.1	4.8	7.7	9.0			All Other Non-Current	9.7	9.5
100.0	100.0	100.0	100.0			Total	100.0	100.0
						LIABILITIES		
9.0	16.3	2.4	4.0			Notes Payable-Short Term	20.5	23.9
2.5	3.6	.9	1.0			Cur. Mat.-L.T.D.	2.6	3.8
7.6	11.5	3.8	6.8			Trade Payables	7.3	2.9
2.8	.1	.0	.0			Income Taxes Payable	.0	.3
16.3	11.2	23.9	12.4			All Other Current	19.8	21.8
38.2	42.7	30.9	24.1			Total Current	50.2	52.7
39.8	20.9	10.8	27.0			Long-Term Debt	30.2	32.0
.0	.0	.0	.0			Deferred Taxes	.0	.1
11.7	7.8	2.9	1.2			All Other Non-Current	6.4	3.2
10.3	28.6	55.4	47.7			Net Worth	13.2	12.0
100.0	100.0	100.0	100.0			Total Liabilities & Net Worth	100.0	100.0
						INCOME DATA		
100.0	100.0	100.0	100.0			Net Sales	100.0	100.0
						Gross Profit		
91.2	89.6	92.5	91.4			Operating Expenses	94.6	92.5
8.8	10.4	7.5	8.6			Operating Profit	5.4	7.5
.0	3.4	2.1	6.2			All Other Expenses (net)	.6	1.9
8.8	7.0	5.4	2.4			Profit Before Taxes	4.8	5.6
						RATIOS		
5.4	2.9	3.5	2.7			Current	3.3	3.0
2.0	1.1	2.1	1.6				1.5	1.6
.8	.5	1.4	1.2				.9	.9
5.4	2.8	3.3	2.6			Quick	3.1	2.3
2.0	1.1	2.0	1.3				1.4	1.2
.6	.5	1.1	1.1				.8	.8
0 UND	0 UND	29 12.4	9 38.7			Sales/Receivables	0 UND	0 UND
0 UND	37 9.8	44 8.3	39 9.4				33 11.0	6 58.0
0 UND	66 5.5	56 6.5	51 7.2				75 4.9	44 8.4
						Cost of Sales/Inventory		
						Cost of Sales/Payables		
29.1	12.5	5.6	7.0			Sales/Working Capital	7.5	8.0
77.0	521.8	10.0	15.3				24.0	37.7
-70.0	-23.9	26.8	26.3				-102.4	-104.2
21.9	21.7	19.2				EBIT/Interest	9.6	14.5
(14) 2.9	(13) 6.1	(15) 2.0					(23) 4.8	(50) 4.0
-2.8	2.0	-.7					2.2	.9
						Net Profit + Depr., Dep., Amort./Cur. Mat. L/T/D		
.4	.4	.2	.4			Fixed/Worth	.5	.3
1.0	1.2	.7	1.1				1.1	.9
-1.4	NM	1.3	2.6				UND	-999.8
.3	.8	.3	.5			Debt/Worth	.7	.7
2.5	3.4	.6	1.6				2.6	2.0
-7.9	NM	1.4	3.1				UND	-999.8
462.8	61.6	44.8	18.9			% Profit Before Taxes/Tangible Net Worth	75.4	174.4
(16) 140.9	(11) 25.0	(22) 6.7	3.2				(22) 21.1	(50) 33.4
39.4	15.2	-5.0	-2.8				7.5	4.6
144.7	27.4	30.9	3.0			% Profit Before Taxes/Total Assets	25.9	52.1
46.2	7.7	3.6	1.0				7.3	6.7
1.6	2.7	-4.2	-1.0				3.9	-3.8
255.2	86.8	42.0	16.3			Sales/Net Fixed Assets	145.7	93.3
50.7	21.1	9.6	6.2				8.8	20.8
19.4	2.0	2.7	1.5				3.8	4.0
18.1	5.9	3.5	2.8			Sales/Total Assets	5.5	11.2
12.5	3.7	2.5	1.9				2.4	3.7
4.5	1.6	1.5	1.1				1.7	1.8
.1	.4	.8	.9			% Depr., Dep., Amort./Sales	.9	.6
(16) .9	(13) 2.5	(24) 1.7	2.3				(19) 2.2	(53) 1.7
1.2	4.4	2.8	3.4				3.0	2.7
7.9						% Officers', Directors' Owners' Comp/Sales	2.9	5.6
(14) 14.0							(10) 7.5	(27) 15.8
21.2							22.0	22.7
42240M	65627M	322590M	506949M	32596M		Net Sales ($)	167800M	2898144M
4134M	15664M	140727M	246548M	93811M		Total Assets ($)	76604M	386259M

(Columns 50-100MM and 100-250MM: DATA NOT AVAILABLE)

M = $ thousand   MM = $ million
See Pages 9 through 22 for Explanation of Ratios and Data

Comparative Historical Data | Current Data Sorted by Sales

			Type of Statement						
15	18	17	Unqualified		1		5	6	5
2	1	10	Reviewed					8	2
5	9	6	Compiled	4	1		1	2	
14	23	22	Tax Returns	6	9	3	2	2	
19	19	20	Other	5		4	2	5	1
4/1/07-3/31/08 ALL	4/1/08-3/31/09 ALL	4/1/09-3/31/10 ALL		0-1MM	27 (4/1-9/30/09) 1-3MM	3-5MM	48 (10/1/09-3/31/10) 5-10MM	10-25MM	25MM & OVER
55	70	75	NUMBER OF STATEMENTS	15	15	7	9	21	8
%	%	%	ASSETS	%	%	%	%	%	%
26.7	22.4	25.1	Cash & Equivalents	34.9	29.0			18.0	
18.2	19.3	20.7	Trade Receivables (net)	3.9	9.5			29.7	
.4	.2	.2	Inventory	.0	.0			.4	
5.2	5.7	5.0	All Other Current	4.2	.2			12.9	
50.5	47.5	51.0	Total Current	43.0	38.8			61.0	
32.7	35.5	34.6	Fixed Assets (net)	34.6	47.6			29.3	
7.3	6.8	5.0	Intangibles (net)	6.7	10.2			2.0	
9.5	10.2	9.4	All Other Non-Current	15.7	3.4			7.8	
100.0	100.0	100.0	Total	100.0	100.0			100.0	
			LIABILITIES						
20.8	19.8	7.4	Notes Payable-Short Term	8.1	15.7			3.1	
3.9	2.6	2.0	Cur. Mat.-L.T.D.	.7	5.1			.7	
4.2	5.5	6.8	Trade Payables	12.6	3.6			4.5	
.2	.0	.9	Income Taxes Payable	4.6	.0			.0	
22.0	20.1	17.3	All Other Current	16.2	9.8			26.9	
51.1	47.9	34.4	Total Current	42.2	34.3			35.3	
15.9	27.0	24.5	Long-Term Debt	53.1	34.3			9.4	
.0	.0	.0	Deferred Taxes	.0	.0			.0	
8.0	7.2	6.5	All Other Non-Current	2.6	19.5			2.5	
24.9	18.0	34.6	Net Worth	2.1	12.0			52.8	
100.0	100.0	100.0	Total Liabilities & Net Worth	100.0	100.0			100.0	
			INCOME DATA						
100.0	100.0	100.0	Net Sales	100.0	100.0			100.0	
			Gross Profit						
91.9	93.9	91.5	Operating Expenses	76.4	94.1			93.9	
8.1	6.1	8.5	Operating Profit	23.6	5.9			6.1	
.1	1.8	2.4	All Other Expenses (net)	9.2	.1			.1	
8.0	4.3	6.1	Profit Before Taxes	14.4	5.8			6.0	
			RATIOS						
3.0	2.3	3.9		6.0	4.1			3.8	
1.5	1.3	1.9	Current	.9	1.2			2.1	
.8	.7	.9		.5	.5			1.4	
2.9	2.0	3.8		6.0	3.9			3.6	
1.3	1.1	1.8	Quick	.7	1.2			1.9	
.6	.6	.8		.4	.4			1.1	
0 UND	0 UND	0 UND		0 UND	0 UND			19 19.0	
15 24.3	17 21.1	20 18.7	Sales/Receivables	0 UND	0 UND			42 8.7	
39 9.3	43 8.5	48 7.6		0 UND	3 105.4			56 6.5	
			Cost of Sales/Inventory						
			Cost of Sales/Payables						
6.2	8.5	9.7		45.8	25.7			5.6	
18.3	28.9	22.6	Sales/Working Capital	-87.6	999.8			10.6	
-28.0	-86.4	-87.6		-15.4	-16.5			37.3	
11.0	14.3	16.0			5.6			27.3	
(42) 3.9	(55) 2.5	(49) 2.9	EBIT/Interest		(12) 2.6			(15) 4.6	
1.2	.4	-.5			1.3			-.7	
			Net Profit + Depr., Dep., Amort./Cur. Mat. L/T/D						
.3	.3	.3		.5	.7			.2	
.7	1.2	.7	Fixed/Worth	11.4	6.8			.6	
2.8	8.0	6.8		-.5	-9.7			1.3	
.5	.7	.3		.2	.5			.3	
1.5	2.4	1.2	Debt/Worth	10.8	6.8			.7	
27.0	82.6	7.9		-4.2	-11.7			1.8	
98.7	92.9	97.5	% Profit Before Taxes/Tangible Net Worth		341.2			69.9	
(44) 16.2	(56) 14.2	(60) 23.2			(10) 24.6			(19) 30.6	
1.9	2.8	.5			19.4			-.3	
38.5	20.3	46.2	% Profit Before Taxes/Total Assets	111.2	46.2			39.1	
7.3	3.4	5.1		5.1	7.3			5.5	
.8	-1.2	-.2		-8.4	3.2			-1.3	
45.2	108.5	71.9	Sales/Net Fixed Assets	108.3	201.6			43.8	
12.6	19.5	20.4		45.7	14.3			20.4	
3.8	2.8	4.4		9.9	4.4			4.4	
5.1	7.7	6.6	Sales/Total Assets	14.0	16.3			4.0	
2.9	3.4	3.5		4.3	4.5			2.7	
1.7	1.7	1.8		1.5	3.6			1.8	
.6	.5	.7	% Depr., Dep., Amort./Sales	.8	.4			.7	
(40) 1.7	(51) 1.5	(64) 1.3		(12) 1.1	(11) 1.4			(20) 1.2	
3.2	3.2	3.0		8.3	4.1			2.7	
3.2	6.2	4.6	% Officers', Directors' Owners' Comp/Sales						
(15) 10.4	(26) 11.6	(27) 10.2							
22.0	31.0	15.0							
688500M	698186M	970002M	Net Sales ($)	9100M	27167M	26663M	70203M	338071M	498798M
330852M	380080M	500884M	Total Assets ($)	20208M	7231M	12176M	27025M	142098M	292146M

M = $ thousand   MM = $ million
See Pages 9 through 22 for Explanation of Ratios and Data

HEALTH CARE—Offices of Physical, Occupational and Speech Therapists, and Audiologists   NAICS 621340

Current Data Sorted by Assets   Comparative Historical Data

Type of Statement	0-500M	500M-2MM	2-10MM	10-50MM	50-100MM	100-250MM	4/1/05-3/31/06 ALL	4/1/06-3/31/07 ALL
Unqualified	2	2	6	7		1	21	20
Reviewed	1	4	15	1	1		9	14
Compiled	21	9	6				30	38
Tax Returns	69	16	7	1	2	1	72	84
Other	31	22	18	10			73	56
		21 (4/1-9/30/09)		232 (10/1/09-3/31/10)				
NUMBER OF STATEMENTS	124	53	52	19	3	2	205	212
	%	%	%	%	%	%	%	%
ASSETS								
Cash & Equivalents	33.7	19.3	13.2	14.6			26.4	23.1
Trade Receivables (net)	7.8	27.4	29.6	32.4			17.1	18.5
Inventory	.4	.1	.8	.2			1.1	1.0
All Other Current	3.5	2.2	5.7	6.4			4.0	3.9
Total Current	45.4	49.0	49.3	53.6			48.5	46.5
Fixed Assets (net)	33.7	29.8	31.4	33.5			34.9	34.2
Intangibles (net)	7.2	6.0	7.0	8.9			2.9	5.8
All Other Non-Current	13.7	15.2	12.4	4.0			13.6	13.4
Total	100.0	100.0	100.0	100.0			100.0	100.0
LIABILITIES								
Notes Payable-Short Term	25.8	13.8	9.3	3.5			23.8	19.7
Cur. Mat.-L.T.D.	9.3	3.8	5.5	2.1			5.8	5.4
Trade Payables	3.7	3.5	4.0	8.0			3.8	4.5
Income Taxes Payable	.0	.1	.1	.4			.2	.1
All Other Current	18.5	12.2	15.8	14.1			21.4	23.4
Total Current	57.2	33.4	34.6	28.2			54.9	53.1
Long-Term Debt	30.4	25.0	26.9	23.9			23.0	20.9
Deferred Taxes	.0	.0	.3	.6			.1	.3
All Other Non-Current	6.7	3.6	9.0	2.8			6.9	3.3
Net Worth	5.7	38.0	29.3	44.5			15.0	22.3
Total Liabilities & Net Worth	100.0	100.0	100.0	100.0			100.0	100.0
INCOME DATA								
Net Sales	100.0	100.0	100.0	100.0			100.0	100.0
Gross Profit								
Operating Expenses	85.7	87.4	87.5	91.9			90.0	90.6
Operating Profit	14.3	12.6	12.5	8.1			10.0	9.4
All Other Expenses (net)	2.4	2.4	1.2	1.9			1.0	1.1
Profit Before Taxes	11.9	10.2	11.3	6.3			9.0	8.4
RATIOS								
Current	3.9	4.5	3.6	4.0			3.2	2.3
	1.0	1.5	1.4	2.3			1.2	1.2
	.3	.6	.7	1.3			.5	.4
Quick	3.1	4.5	3.2	4.0			2.8	2.2
	.9	1.4	1.2	2.2			1.0	(211) 1.1
	.2	.5	.5	1.2			.4	.3
Sales/Receivables	0 UND	0 UND	0 UND	36 10.3			0 UND	0 UND
	0 UND	12 31.1	37 10.0	52 7.0			0 UND	0 UND
	0 UND	64 5.7	57 6.4	74 4.9			42 8.8	46 7.9
Cost of Sales/Inventory								
Cost of Sales/Payables								
Sales/Working Capital	15.7	8.0	5.6	3.4			9.7	10.9
	NM	18.2	19.5	7.8			65.5	77.0
	-18.8	-29.2	-22.2	29.5			-24.0	-25.2
EBIT/Interest	22.4	19.0	21.8	21.7			25.0	21.4
	(84) 8.2	(39) 7.6	(44) 6.7	(17) 4.8			(155) 5.6	(153) 6.3
	.3	2.7	3.3	1.5			1.2	1.5
Net Profit + Depr., Dep., Amort./Cur. Mat. L/T/D								8.5
							(12) 1.6
								.8
Fixed/Worth	.1	.1	.2	.3			.3	.3
	1.1	.8	.7	.8			1.0	.9
	-2.8	5.3	3.4	1.1			NM	25.6
Debt/Worth	.7	.6	.5	.4			.6	.5
	3.6	1.6	1.5	.9			2.6	2.0
	-4.3	16.4	18.6	2.9			-41.4	UND
% Profit Before Taxes/Tangible Net Worth	451.6	106.8	89.2	98.3			149.1	194.1
	(76) 188.6	(44) 55.5	(43) 33.7	(18) 10.9			(149) 43.1	(159) 33.6
	77.1	16.5	10.3	5.5			3.2	6.3
% Profit Before Taxes/Total Assets	126.4	37.6	34.6	23.1			65.2	56.4
	50.6	20.4	12.5	6.0			15.7	13.5
	2.5	6.6	3.6	.6			.4	.8
Sales/Net Fixed Assets	136.1	54.2	44.1	57.5			69.6	106.6
	32.0	25.2	13.6	13.5			18.7	25.1
	15.1	8.2	4.4	2.4			5.5	7.9
Sales/Total Assets	12.8	4.8	3.7	3.9			9.8	9.6
	6.8	3.1	2.8	1.6			4.2	4.1
	3.7	2.0	1.4	1.1			2.1	2.0
% Depr., Dep., Amort./Sales	.5	.5	.9	.7			.7	.5
	(72) 1.4	(39) 1.1	(40) 2.0	(18) 1.9			(149) 1.6	(148) 1.6
	2.8	2.0	3.7	3.1			2.9	2.6
% Officers', Directors' Owners' Comp/Sales	7.3	5.6	3.3				5.3	6.7
	(75) 12.1	(18) 8.4	(13) 12.9				(98) 12.7	(93) 14.2
	21.4	19.4	16.7				21.3	26.8
Net Sales ($)	179656M	214695M	1558163M	989518M	2569624M	816700M	2784050M	4339649M
Total Assets ($)	22527M	56288M	246163M	323414M	213979M	317926M	1063279M	1345204M

M = $ thousand   MM = $ million
See Pages 9 through 22 for Explanation of Ratios and Data

Comparative Historical Data | Current Data Sorted by Sales

Type of Statement	4/1/07-3/31/08 ALL	4/1/08-3/31/09 ALL	4/1/09-3/31/10 ALL	0-1MM	1-3MM	3-5MM	5-10MM	10-25MM	25MM & OVER
Unqualified	17	11	18	1	2	1	1	9	4
Reviewed	21	10	22			5	7	7	3
Compiled	18	10	36			4	8	8	3
Tax Returns	81	69	96	12	9	4	7	3	5
Other	59	63	81	45	34	2	7	3	8

Current Data periods: 21 (4/1-9/30/09), 232 (10/1/09-3/31/10)

	07-08 ALL	08-09 ALL	09-10 ALL	0-1MM	1-3MM	3-5MM	5-10MM	10-25MM	25MM & OVER
NUMBER OF STATEMENTS	196	163	253	79	67	18	33	36	20
	%	%	%	%	%	%	%	%	%
ASSETS									
Cash & Equivalents	26.1	25.8	24.8	28.6	30.5	17.0	23.0	15.6	16.8
Trade Receivables (net)	16.3	18.5	18.6	6.0	15.5	34.6	21.9	31.8	35.3
Inventory	.9	.6	.4	.2	.5	.0	1.2	.1	.4
All Other Current	6.2	5.9	3.8	3.7	2.0	1.4	1.4	8.7	7.8
Total Current	49.5	50.7	47.6	38.5	48.5	53.0	47.6	56.3	60.3
Fixed Assets (net)	33.1	29.8	32.4	36.8	32.5	24.0	33.4	30.2	24.8
Intangibles (net)	5.4	10.1	7.1	8.1	4.6	13.6	7.5	4.1	10.4
All Other Non-Current	12.0	9.4	12.8	16.5	14.4	9.3	11.5	9.4	4.6
Total	100.0	100.0	100.0	100.0	100.0	100.0	100.0	100.0	100.0
LIABILITIES									
Notes Payable-Short Term	22.7	18.6	18.3	18.9	22.0	17.1	18.4	14.2	11.8
Cur. Mat.-L.T.D.	6.0	3.9	6.8	5.0	12.5	2.8	5.7	4.7	4.0
Trade Payables	5.2	3.1	4.0	2.3	4.2	5.4	4.1	4.6	7.6
Income Taxes Payable	.1	.2	.1	.0	.0	.3	.0	.2	.2
All Other Current	19.6	16.0	16.8	17.2	10.9	14.1	19.5	13.8	38.0
Total Current	53.5	41.8	46.0	43.5	49.6	39.7	47.7	37.5	61.6
Long-Term Debt	27.2	23.9	28.3	33.0	31.9	14.9	30.4	15.8	28.6
Deferred Taxes	.3	.1	.1	.0	.0	.0	.5	.0	.6
All Other Non-Current	4.4	6.4	6.1	4.2	8.0	1.0	4.8	2.6	20.3
Net Worth	14.6	27.8	19.5	19.3	10.4	44.3	16.7	44.1	-11.1
Total Liabilities & Net Worth	100.0	100.0	100.0	100.0	100.0	100.0	100.0	100.0	100.0
INCOME DATA									
Net Sales	100.0	100.0	100.0	100.0	100.0	100.0	100.0	100.0	100.0
Gross Profit									
Operating Expenses	91.1	90.4	87.0	80.4	90.1	88.7	89.0	90.2	91.8
Operating Profit	8.9	9.6	13.0	19.6	9.9	11.3	11.0	9.8	8.2
All Other Expenses (net)	1.6	1.5	2.1	4.5	1.0	2.3	.8	.7	.6
Profit Before Taxes	7.2	8.1	10.9	15.1	9.0	9.1	10.2	9.1	7.7
RATIOS									
Current	3.0	5.2	4.1	4.1	4.3	5.7	4.5	3.1	4.0
	1.2	1.6	1.3	1.1	1.3	1.4	1.3	1.7	1.3
	.5	.6	.5	.4	.3	.6	.4	.9	1.1
Quick	2.9	4.1	3.8	4.0	4.3	5.6	4.5	2.7	4.0
	1.1	1.3	1.2	.8	1.2	1.4	1.2	1.4	1.3
	.4	.4	.4	.3	.2	.6	.3	.8	.8
Sales/Receivables	0 UND	0 UND	0 UND	0 UND	0 UND	0 UND	0 UND	0 UND	0 UND
	0 UND	0 UND	0 UND	0 UND	0 UND	58 6.3	12 31.1	37 10.0	48 7.5
	38 9.5	49 7.5	44 8.3	0 UND	25 14.7	93 3.9	45 8.1	57 6.4	68 5.4
Cost of Sales/Inventory									
Cost of Sales/Payables									
Sales/Working Capital	10.5	7.5	9.3	10.7	11.3	5.1	10.6	5.2	6.1
	55.2	30.1	38.9	88.3	107.9	15.0	68.6	16.1	21.3
	-24.4	-24.3	-26.1	-11.7	-17.8	-74.9	-24.5	NM	63.9
EBIT/Interest	(144) 18.6	(113) 24.8	(189) 21.7	(50) 21.0	(46) 19.6	(13) 97.7	(28) 14.8	(33) 29.5	(19) 84.5
	4.9	6.7	7.1	3.9	8.8	4.5	5.7	12.1	11.3
	1.0	1.4	1.8	.9	2.7	-.1	.9	4.0	2.4
Net Profit + Depr., Dep., Amort./Cur. Mat. L/T/D	(15) 2.5	(16)	10.6						
	1.8		3.7						
	1.2		1.7						
Fixed/Worth	.2	.1	.1	.1	.1	.1	.1	.2	.2
	.9	.8	.8	1.1	1.1	.5	1.3	.5	.6
	UND	65.5	17.0	-11.0	-3.3	65.1	-5.6	1.3	1.5
Debt/Worth	.5	.4	.6	.7	.4	.2	1.0	.5	.8
	2.4	2.4	2.2	2.2	3.4	1.3	3.6	1.0	2.6
	-27.5	-26.3	-14.9	-5.7	-6.9	116.2	-5.5	3.6	3.7
% Profit Before Taxes/Tangible Net Worth	(143) 135.3	(118) 163.1	(185) 210.2	(54) 293.0	(46) 397.9	(15) 113.9	(21) 220.9	(32) 88.2	(17) 111.2
	44.0	68.3	66.7	94.6	131.9	17.8	65.6	36.4	46.1
	5.7	10.4	16.0	23.2	47.0	-4.8	17.0	11.4	8.5
% Profit Before Taxes/Total Assets	50.6	66.7	72.8	105.9	92.1	35.6	44.7	40.3	32.8
	12.8	18.5	22.5	43.4	28.6	7.3	21.3	15.7	17.1
	.0	2.7	3.2	.4	7.6	-3.4	2.9	7.2	2.6
Sales/Net Fixed Assets	84.1	143.0	88.9	101.4	81.1	87.2	148.0	59.5	86.1
	22.8	31.0	22.5	20.5	29.0	27.6	23.7	14.0	17.7
	6.8	9.8	8.0	4.4	13.6	10.1	6.5	5.7	10.6
Sales/Total Assets	9.1	8.0	7.9	8.7	10.2	5.5	8.5	5.1	5.9
	3.9	4.1	4.0	3.9	5.2	2.7	4.2	3.3	3.7
	2.0	2.1	2.2	1.8	3.1	1.3	3.2	1.8	1.8
% Depr., Dep., Amort./Sales	(150) .5	(108) .5	(173) .6	(49) .9	(43) .5	(11) .7	(22) .7	(31) .5	(17) .6
	1.2	1.5	1.5	2.4	1.1	.9	1.3	1.8	1.5
	2.7	3.2	2.9	7.5	2.3	1.5	3.4	2.8	2.4
% Officers', Directors', Owners' Comp/Sales	(99) 6.1	(79) 6.4	(108) 6.8	(40) 9.6	(40) 5.8		(13) 5.4		
	12.5	10.7	11.9	17.1	9.3		8.3		
	21.7	18.4	20.1	22.6	16.9		17.3		
Net Sales ($)	4883279M	4488495M	6328356M	40833M	124664M	74912M	230967M	546653M	5310327M
Total Assets ($)	1058195M	929657M	1180297M	22555M	34466M	41995M	78008M	216549M	786724M

Current Data Sorted by Assets   Comparative Historical Data

0-500M	500M-2MM	2-10MM	10-50MM	50-100MM	100-250MM		4/1/05-3/31/06 ALL	4/1/06-3/31/07 ALL
	4 (4/1-9/30/09)		57 (10/1/09-3/31/10)			**Type of Statement**		
						Unqualified		
						Reviewed		
10	2	1				Compiled	2	6
34	5					Tax Returns	14	18
8		1				Other	4	9
52	7	2				**NUMBER OF STATEMENTS**	20	33
%	%	%	%	%	%	**ASSETS**	%	%
28.8			D	D	D	Cash & Equivalents	20.8	29.0
2.6			A	A	A	Trade Receivables (net)	5.0	6.6
1.6			T	T	T	Inventory	.7	.1
5.4			A	A	A	All Other Current	4.3	.9
38.4						Total Current	30.8	36.6
30.4			N	N	N	Fixed Assets (net)	41.1	34.8
12.7			O	O	O	Intangibles (net)	6.4	10.1
18.5			T	T	T	All Other Non-Current	21.7	18.5
100.0						Total	100.0	100.0
			A	A	A	**LIABILITIES**		
29.2			V	V	V	Notes Payable-Short Term	8.4	19.3
7.1			A	A	A	Cur. Mat.-L.T.D.	4.9	13.6
4.7			I	I	I	Trade Payables	1.6	3.4
.0			L	L	L	Income Taxes Payable	2.4	.1
27.0			A	A	A	All Other Current	18.7	23.7
67.9			B	B	B	Total Current	35.9	60.1
45.3			L	L	L	Long-Term Debt	29.5	41.2
.0			E	E	E	Deferred Taxes	.0	.0
3.5						All Other Non-Current	.5	12.7
-16.7						Net Worth	34.1	-14.0
100.0						Total Liabilities & Net Worth	100.0	100.0
						INCOME DATA		
100.0						Net Sales	100.0	100.0
						Gross Profit		
92.0						Operating Expenses	81.4	87.2
8.0						Operating Profit	18.6	12.8
1.0						All Other Expenses (net)	4.6	2.8
7.0						Profit Before Taxes	14.0	10.1
						RATIOS		
4.0						Current	2.0	1.7
.6							.9	.6
.1							.7	.2
2.6						Quick	1.2	1.7
.4							.8	.6
.1							.3	.2
0 UND						Sales/Receivables	0 UND	0 UND
0 UND							0 UND	0 UND
0 UND							0 UND	0 UND
						Cost of Sales/Inventory		
						Cost of Sales/Payables		
66.2						Sales/Working Capital	19.6	61.8
-31.9							NM	-39.4
-14.1							-33.9	-21.5
13.9						EBIT/Interest	(14) 58.4	(25) 18.4
(37) 3.2							12.1	4.6
-.7							2.2	.7
						Net Profit + Depr., Dep., Amort./Cur. Mat. L/T/D		
.4						Fixed/Worth	.2	.1
-3.4							1.3	3.5
-.4							4.1	-.7
.5						Debt/Worth	.9	1.7
-7.1							2.6	5.6
-2.0							17.3	-2.3
191.9						% Profit Before Taxes/Tangible Net Worth	561.8	356.1
(21) 97.0							(17) 102.8	(18) 100.3
29.9							20.1	16.8
79.8						% Profit Before Taxes/Total Assets	82.1	86.1
31.9							41.0	21.3
-2.5							5.6	.5
71.4						Sales/Net Fixed Assets	123.0	173.5
30.3							13.1	30.3
16.6							3.3	7.9
13.5						Sales/Total Assets	10.5	12.9
5.8							3.8	5.0
3.5							1.8	2.3
.8						% Depr., Dep., Amort./Sales	.2	.5
(33) 1.8							(14) 1.3	(22) 1.5
3.1							6.9	3.4
11.8						% Officers', Directors' Owners' Comp/Sales	15.0	19.0
(45) 19.6							(15) 21.4	(22) 25.1
30.8							40.4	41.9
76968M	12756M	20631M				Net Sales ($)	33563M	47273M
9841M	5239M	9866M				Total Assets ($)	10429M	14563M

M = $ thousand   MM = $ million
See Pages 9 through 22 for Explanation of Ratios and Data

Comparative Historical Data

Current Data Sorted by Sales

			Type of Statement						
			Unqualified						
			Reviewed						
			Compiled						
4	5	13	Tax Returns	9	2	1	1		
21	22	39	Other	22	11	3	2	1	
6	5	9		2	4	1	1	1	
4/1/07- 3/31/08 ALL	4/1/08- 3/31/09 ALL	4/1/09- 3/31/10 ALL			4 (4/1-9/30/09)		57 (10/1/09-3/31/10)		
				0-1MM	1-3MM	3-5MM	5-10MM	10-25MM	25MM & OVER
31	32	61	NUMBER OF STATEMENTS	33	17	5	4	2	
%	%	%		%	%	%	%	%	%
			ASSETS						DATA NOT AVAILABLE
30.3	31.7	25.9	Cash & Equivalents	25.2	30.2				
.7	5.8	4.0	Trade Receivables (net)	4.8	.0				
.2	.0	1.4	Inventory	2.3	.4				
5.2	2.2	4.6	All Other Current	5.6	.9				
36.4	39.8	36.0	Total Current	37.9	31.5				
40.4	31.9	32.3	Fixed Assets (net)	34.4	26.6				
6.8	6.9	13.7	Intangibles (net)	12.6	21.8				
16.4	21.4	18.0	All Other Non-Current	15.1	20.0				
100.0	100.0	100.0	Total	100.0	100.0				
			LIABILITIES						
15.8	20.4	25.5	Notes Payable-Short Term	21.5	38.9				
17.5	11.5	6.2	Cur. Mat.-L.T.D.	6.2	8.5				
.4	2.4	4.0	Trade Payables	5.0	.2				
.0	.0	.0	Income Taxes Payable	.0	.0				
20.6	20.5	23.2	All Other Current	25.4	26.9				
54.4	54.8	58.9	Total Current	58.0	74.6				
41.0	40.9	45.7	Long-Term Debt	55.2	38.7				
.0	.4	.0	Deferred Taxes	.0	.0				
4.8	2.3	4.0	All Other Non-Current	3.3	2.9				
-.1	1.6	-8.5	Net Worth	-16.5	-16.2				
100.0	100.0	100.0	Total Liabilities & Net Worth	100.0	100.0				
			INCOME DATA						
100.0	100.0	100.0	Net Sales	100.0	100.0				
			Gross Profit						
89.0	86.6	88.9	Operating Expenses	87.2	91.3				
11.0	13.4	11.1	Operating Profit	12.8	8.7				
2.3	2.5	2.9	All Other Expenses (net)	4.0	1.9				
8.6	10.9	8.1	Profit Before Taxes	8.8	6.8				
			RATIOS						
1.7	4.1	5.7		6.9	1.1				
.8	1.2	.6	Current	.6	.3				
.3	.1	.1		.1	.1				
1.7	3.2	5.1		6.0	.9				
.8	1.2	.6	Quick	.6	.3				
.1	.1	.1		.1	.1				
0 UND	0 UND	0 UND		0 UND	0 UND				
0 UND	0 UND	0 UND	Sales/Receivables	0 UND	0 UND				
0 UND	0 UND	0 UND		0 UND	0 UND				
			Cost of Sales/Inventory						
			Cost of Sales/Payables						
46.1	23.5	37.3		11.2	NM				
-56.6	134.1	-46.3	Sales/Working Capital	-27.2	-26.5				
-13.4	-8.8	-13.5		-8.8	-11.4				
19.7	43.8	14.4		10.0	21.8				
(25) 4.8	(26) 12.7	(44) 3.4	EBIT/Interest	(22) 3.1	(14) 3.8				
1.4	.4	-.5		-1.2	-.8				
			Net Profit + Depr., Dep., Amort./Cur. Mat. L/T/D						
.6	.3	.4		.3	.3				
5.0	1.5	-40.5	Fixed/Worth	-2.5	-5.3				
-1.0	-1.4	-.4		-.3	-.5				
.6	.8	.8		.5	1.2				
-11.2	4.2	-7.8	Debt/Worth	-3.5	-6.6				
-2.7	-4.4	-2.1		-1.8	-1.4				
128.0	498.8	169.2	% Profit Before Taxes/Tangible Net Worth	116.7					
(14) 65.2	(21) 138.5	(27) 83.9		(13) 53.4					
24.7	68.2	18.6		10.2					
55.5	131.2	76.7	% Profit Before Taxes/Total Assets	79.0	62.2				
17.5	39.6	31.4		12.5	44.6				
1.1	-2.7	-.9		-.5	-7.5				
145.0	194.7	70.9		61.8	111.4				
23.5	38.5	25.8	Sales/Net Fixed Assets	23.2	30.5				
9.8	12.0	13.5		7.4	19.8				
13.2	10.4	10.5		6.5	17.4				
6.0	5.6	5.3	Sales/Total Assets	3.9	5.7				
2.9	2.9	2.9		2.2	3.6				
.8	.3	.9		.8	.8				
(16) 2.0	(21) 1.0	(39) 1.9	% Depr., Dep., Amort./Sales	(21) 2.9	(10) 1.6				
6.3	3.4	3.8		5.4	2.3				
15.3	14.2	11.6	% Officers', Directors' Owners' Comp/Sales	11.3	9.9				
(23) 20.9	(22) 20.9	(49) 19.3		(26) 19.3	(14) 14.9				
32.2	35.0	30.8		31.3	31.6				
57533M	49750M	110355M	Net Sales ($)	17725M	25586M	17085M	28427M	21532M	
10071M	10263M	24946M	Total Assets ($)	7431M	4199M	1812M	3724M	7780M	

M = $ thousand   MM = $ million
See Pages 9 through 22 for Explanation of Ratios and Data

HEALTH CARE—Offices of All Other Miscellaneous Health Practitioners   NAICS 621399

Current Data Sorted by Assets   Comparative Historical Data

Type of Statement	0-500M	500M-2MM	2-10MM	10-50MM	50-100MM	100-250MM		4/1/05-3/31/06 ALL	4/1/06-3/31/07 ALL
Unqualified	3	7	13	26	1	3		21	31
Reviewed	2	7	11	3				9	8
Compiled	16	13	7	1		1		24	41
Tax Returns	78	32	10	2		2		42	72
Other	28	23	22	14	4	1		34	76
		53 (4/1-9/30/09)		277 (10/1/09-3/31/10)					
NUMBER OF STATEMENTS	127	82	63	46	5	7		130	228
	%	%	%	%	%	%		%	%
ASSETS									
Cash & Equivalents	28.1	16.5	15.3	19.3				23.8	20.9
Trade Receivables (net)	8.2	21.5	26.6	17.7				19.4	17.0
Inventory	4.2	3.2	2.7	1.5				2.4	2.6
All Other Current	4.4	4.3	2.8	5.2				3.2	4.3
Total Current	44.9	45.4	47.4	43.8				48.7	44.6
Fixed Assets (net)	33.5	33.8	40.9	46.2				37.2	38.6
Intangibles (net)	6.8	7.3	2.9	2.4				4.2	5.2
All Other Non-Current	15.0	13.5	8.8	7.6				9.8	11.6
Total	100.0	100.0	100.0	100.0				100.0	100.0
LIABILITIES									
Notes Payable-Short Term	25.4	13.3	6.1	1.7				17.7	14.0
Cur. Mat.-L.T.D.	9.3	5.1	3.8	3.2				4.2	7.1
Trade Payables	2.8	9.6	6.8	5.6				5.4	6.0
Income Taxes Payable	.0	.2	.4	.0				.6	.6
All Other Current	29.1	15.5	13.8	13.9				20.7	22.7
Total Current	66.6	43.7	31.0	24.5				48.6	50.4
Long-Term Debt	35.8	26.9	26.8	32.0				27.8	31.5
Deferred Taxes	.0	.0	.3	.4				.3	.3
All Other Non-Current	10.7	10.5	5.6	4.0				5.2	5.1
Net Worth	-13.1	19.0	36.3	39.1				18.2	12.7
Total Liabilties & Net Worth	100.0	100.0	100.0	100.0				100.0	100.0
INCOME DATA									
Net Sales	100.0	100.0	100.0	100.0				100.0	100.0
Gross Profit									
Operating Expenses	90.0	91.1	87.1	92.0				89.3	87.8
Operating Profit	10.0	8.9	12.9	8.0				10.7	12.2
All Other Expenses (net)	.7	2.4	4.6	2.2				2.3	2.4
Profit Before Taxes	9.4	6.6	8.3	5.8				8.4	9.8
RATIOS									
Current	2.6	2.1	2.8	3.0				2.2	2.7
	.8	1.1	1.7	1.8				1.2	1.2
	.2	.3	.8	1.3				.6	.5
Quick	2.1	1.9	2.5	2.5				2.0	2.2
	.6	.8	1.5	1.7				(129) 1.0	(226) 1.0
	.2	.3	.7	.9				.5	.4
Sales/Receivables	0 UND	0 UND	9 38.5	14 26.3				0 UND	0 UND
	0 UND	4 84.4	37 10.0	26 14.3				2 162.1	1 596.8
	0 UND	38 9.6	55 6.7	46 7.9				50 7.3	42 8.7
Cost of Sales/Inventory									
Cost of Sales/Payables									
Sales/Working Capital	19.2	13.1	6.5	4.3				10.7	10.1
	-406.5	137.5	10.3	10.7				130.8	76.6
	-18.5	-11.3	-32.1	34.3				-22.9	-23.1
EBIT/Interest	20.0	30.3	24.1	15.1				14.7	13.7
	(85) 6.0	(65) 7.9	(50) 8.3	(38) 3.1				(96) 4.2	(164) 3.5
	1.3	1.5	1.1	.4				.9	1.0
Net Profit + Depr., Dep., Amort./Cur. Mat. L/T/D									5.3
								(12)	2.9
									1.3
Fixed/Worth	.3	.2	.4	.5				.2	.4
	2.5	1.4	1.1	.9				1.0	1.6
	-.4	-28.9	5.9	2.3				35.9	-3.0
Debt/Worth	.9	.8	.7	.7				.8	.8
	9.2	4.7	1.9	1.4				2.4	2.8
	-2.2	-17.8	6.9	4.7				-39.0	-9.3
% Profit Before Taxes/Tangible Net Worth	372.1	205.8	76.8	32.8				123.9	161.5
	(70) 106.3	(57) 55.9	(57) 30.4	(43) 10.5				(97) 28.5	(162) 46.7
	26.7	12.3	-.4	.3				4.0	6.7
% Profit Before Taxes/Total Assets	104.7	34.7	21.9	13.8				35.6	46.5
	25.5	14.4	11.3	4.5				11.2	10.0
	3.1	1.1	.2	-.6				.0	.3
Sales/Net Fixed Assets	130.0	72.0	26.0	10.0				75.0	62.0
	41.9	17.4	6.0	2.6				15.8	13.9
	11.5	5.9	2.4	1.8				3.4	3.9
Sales/Total Assets	15.5	6.4	3.8	2.9				8.6	7.4
	7.5	4.1	2.1	1.5				3.7	3.5
	3.8	2.1	1.2	1.1				1.5	1.9
% Depr., Dep., Amort./Sales	.6	1.0	.8	2.0				.9	.7
	(77) 1.3	(61) 2.0	(59) 2.3	(40) 3.1				(94) 2.2	(170) 2.3
	3.1	4.3	5.5	4.7				4.6	4.4
% Officers', Directors' Owners' Comp/Sales	7.5	2.7	2.3					8.0	5.4
	(84) 13.6	(37) 10.5	(17) 3.9					(57) 13.6	(83) 11.9
	22.8	24.6	11.9					28.3	22.5
Net Sales ($)	272275M	439269M	725709M	2661952M	533968M	4362907M		2660880M	2985775M
Total Assets ($)	25219M	90881M	281203M	841622M	354949M	1122358M		810441M	1319955M

M = $ thousand   MM = $ million
See Pages 9 through 22 for Explanation of Ratios and Data

Comparative Historical Data

Current Data Sorted by Sales

	4/1/07-3/31/08 ALL	4/1/08-3/31/09 ALL	4/1/09-3/31/10 ALL	Type of Statement	0-1MM	1-3MM	3-5MM	5-10MM	10-25MM	25MM & OVER
	38	45	53	Unqualified	1	7	2	7	21	15
	9	31	23	Reviewed	2	6	1	6	5	3
	29	34	38	Compiled	13	10	3	5	4	3
	79	87	124	Tax Returns	38	46	13	14	9	4
	68	99	92	Other	17	15	17	11	15	17
					53 (4/1-9/30/09)			277 (10/1/09-3/31/10)		
	223	296	330	NUMBER OF STATEMENTS	71	84	36	43	54	42
	%	%	%	ASSETS	%	%	%	%	%	%
	22.1	21.6	21.4	Cash & Equivalents	21.0	21.8	17.9	25.0	21.0	20.7
	15.8	18.6	16.5	Trade Receivables (net)	5.6	12.0	20.1	23.2	22.5	26.3
	3.0	2.9	3.2	Inventory	4.8	3.2	4.0	3.7	1.1	1.7
	4.9	3.3	4.3	All Other Current	4.7	2.4	3.8	4.0	5.3	7.0
	45.7	46.4	45.3	Total Current	36.2	39.3	45.8	55.9	49.9	55.6
	40.0	36.7	36.7	Fixed Assets (net)	47.8	36.9	33.3	25.9	38.3	29.1
	3.0	4.4	5.8	Intangibles (net)	6.7	8.1	7.3	3.1	1.7	6.5
	11.3	12.5	12.2	All Other Non-Current	9.3	15.7	13.6	15.1	10.2	8.7
	100.0	100.0	100.0	Total	100.0	100.0	100.0	100.0	100.0	100.0
				LIABILITIES						
	17.6	16.1	14.9	Notes Payable-Short Term	18.8	21.7	14.6	8.7	10.3	7.2
	6.7	5.8	6.1	Cur. Mat.-L.T.D.	9.9	6.7	6.7	4.7	3.0	3.6
	7.0	7.8	5.7	Trade Payables	1.7	4.4	7.9	7.8	7.8	8.4
	.4	.1	.1	Income Taxes Payable	.0	.0	.4	.3	.0	.5
	16.6	16.0	19.9	All Other Current	22.6	15.2	18.9	21.3	24.8	18.0
	48.3	45.7	46.8	Total Current	52.9	48.0	48.4	42.8	46.0	37.7
	28.2	26.9	30.8	Long-Term Debt	37.1	41.7	25.5	25.1	20.9	21.5
	.2	.2	.1	Deferred Taxes	.0	.2	.0	.0	.3	.2
	6.9	4.2	8.4	All Other Non-Current	7.1	10.4	7.5	18.6	2.9	4.4
	16.4	22.9	13.8	Net Worth	2.9	-.3	18.6	13.5	29.9	36.2
	100.0	100.0	100.0	Total Liabilities & Net Worth	100.0	100.0	100.0	100.0	100.0	100.0
				INCOME DATA						
	100.0	100.0	100.0	Net Sales	100.0	100.0	100.0	100.0	100.0	100.0
				Gross Profit						
	88.2	87.5	89.9	Operating Expenses	82.6	89.0	91.2	94.2	95.2	91.4
	11.8	12.5	10.1	Operating Profit	17.4	11.0	8.8	5.8	4.8	8.6
	1.9	3.6	2.1	All Other Expenses (net)	5.7	2.2	1.3	-.2	.0	1.2
	9.8	8.9	8.1	Profit Before Taxes	11.7	8.8	7.5	6.0	4.8	7.5
				RATIOS						
	2.5	2.8	2.5	Current	2.3	2.7	3.2	2.5	2.6	2.4
	1.3	1.4	1.3		.5	1.0	1.1	1.8	1.7	1.6
	.6	.6	.5		.2	.3	.3	1.0	1.0	1.1
	2.4	2.5	2.2	Quick	1.9	2.4	3.1	2.3	2.3	2.1
	(222) 1.1	(295) 1.2	1.0		.4	.7	.9	1.4	1.5	1.2
	.4	.4	.3		.1	.2	.3	.7	.9	.7
	0 UND	0 UND	0 UND	Sales/Receivables	0 UND	0 UND	0 UND	0 UND	1 724.4	17 21.4
	2 213.0	12 30.7	2 228.3		0 UND	0 UND	9 39.3	22 16.4	27 13.5	30 12.2
	40 9.2	43 8.4	36 10.1		0 UND	35 10.5	51 7.1	36 10.2	41 8.8	54 6.7
				Cost of Sales/Inventory						
				Cost of Sales/Payables						
	8.8	9.4	9.8	Sales/Working Capital	13.2	11.1	8.3	8.2	7.6	8.4
	51.3	43.3	50.3		-34.5	UND	521.0	23.6	17.9	16.9
	-22.8	-25.4	-23.7		-8.5	-13.6	-24.1	-999.8	NM	70.3
	24.0	25.8	22.4	EBIT/Interest	21.0	16.4	19.5	42.1	23.1	32.0
	(171) 4.3	(230) 5.8	(249) 6.0		(41) 5.1	(63) 5.2	(32) 5.2	(34) 10.6	(44) 6.7	(35) 6.5
	1.1	1.0	1.2		1.3	1.6	.4	1.4	.6	1.5
		8.8	23.6	Net Profit + Depr., Dep., Amort./Cur. Mat. L/T/D						
	(24) 3.5	(12) 3.5								
	.5	.7								
	.4	.4	.3	Fixed/Worth	.7	.6	.3	.2	.3	.3
	1.3	1.2	1.3		4.7	3.0	2.2	.5	.8	.7
	-69.3	-40.7	-45.0		-3.5	-.8	NM	2.7	1.8	2.7
	.7	.6	.7	Debt/Worth	.9	.9	.7	.6	.5	.8
	2.4	2.1	2.7		8.5	5.8	3.3	1.7	1.6	1.9
	-24.8	-30.5	-19.7		-7.9	-3.2	-11.5	20.1	4.7	8.0
	158.8	120.9	124.2	% Profit Before Taxes/Tangible Net Worth	284.7	138.3	231.5	93.5	91.6	78.6
	(163) 25.3	(210) 32.3	(237) 40.3		(45) 61.3	(49) 56.0	(26) 26.4	(33) 42.5	(46) 18.4	(38) 27.3
	3.0	6.5	6.8		11.6	11.8	12.3	6.1	1.1	2.3
	60.9	47.5	44.9	% Profit Before Taxes/Total Assets	95.2	60.8	21.5	44.8	36.9	25.5
	8.4	11.5	12.7		12.7	17.7	7.9	12.9	8.9	13.0
	-.1	-.1	.8		.8	2.4	-.7	.1	-.2	1.0
	46.1	42.1	65.4	Sales/Net Fixed Assets	63.6	62.6	62.1	106.0	118.1	64.5
	11.8	13.1	15.3		10.2	18.6	14.3	26.8	14.8	12.7
	3.8	3.7	4.2		3.2	4.6	6.0	7.7	2.5	4.8
	6.4	6.4	7.7	Sales/Total Assets	7.2	8.5	8.6	7.9	9.5	5.5
	3.3	3.2	3.8		3.8	3.8	4.6	5.1	2.5	3.5
	1.7	1.5	1.8		1.8	1.9	1.8	2.8	1.5	1.5
	.9	.8	.8	% Depr., Dep., Amort./Sales	1.0	1.1	.9	.5	.5	.8
	(155) 2.2	(227) 2.2	(244) 2.1		(48) 2.9	(62) 2.3	(28) 2.0	(32) 1.4	(43) 2.0	(31) 2.0
	5.6	4.2	4.3		9.7	5.4	4.9	2.8	3.4	3.6
	6.1	5.3	5.9	% Officers', Directors' Owners' Comp/Sales	8.1	5.5	6.9	3.3	3.3	2.0
	(96) 14.6	(106) 11.6	(147) 11.9		(39) 16.2	(46) 9.4	(16) 13.8	(19) 8.2	(17) 10.5	(10) 15.3
	23.5	23.6	22.9		25.6	16.1	39.3	19.9	36.8	25.7
	2573984M	4993551M	8996080M	Net Sales ($)	39817M	159450M	140431M	294664M	866858M	7494860M
	1678940M	2375716M	2716232M	Total Assets ($)	33938M	122658M	96186M	93653M	372827M	1996970M

RMA 2010

M = $ thousand   MM = $ million
See Pages 9 through 22 for Explanation of Ratios and Data

Current Data Sorted by Assets   Comparative Historical Data

Type of Statement	0-500M	500M-2MM	2-10MM	10-50MM	50-100MM	100-250MM		4/1/05-3/31/06 ALL	4/1/06-3/31/07 ALL
Unqualified	2	4	7	15	4	1		21	23
Reviewed			1						
Compiled	1	2	1					2	1
Tax Returns	1	4	6	4	1	1		4	2
Other								10	13
		23 (4/1-9/30/09)		32 (10/1/09-3/31/10)					
NUMBER OF STATEMENTS	4	10	15	19	5	2		37	39
ASSETS	%	%	%	%	%	%		%	%
Cash & Equivalents		19.3	10.7	18.4				19.1	18.0
Trade Receivables (net)		8.8	16.7	8.3				21.2	14.9
Inventory		1.2	1.3	2.3				2.0	2.3
All Other Current		.9	2.5	2.3				6.2	6.3
Total Current		30.2	31.2	31.2				48.6	41.5
Fixed Assets (net)		65.8	49.2	51.2				38.2	40.9
Intangibles (net)		3.3	3.0	5.8				1.9	1.8
All Other Non-Current		.8	16.5	11.7				11.3	15.9
Total		100.0	100.0	100.0				100.0	100.0
LIABILITIES									
Notes Payable-Short Term		1.2	3.7	1.3				4.0	2.7
Cur. Mat.-L.T.D.		1.2	2.3	1.8				4.0	1.5
Trade Payables		2.3	4.7	4.5				8.9	6.7
Income Taxes Payable		.0	.0	.1				.4	.3
All Other Current		2.3	7.5	4.0				10.5	9.4
Total Current		7.0	18.2	11.8				27.6	20.6
Long-Term Debt		34.8	28.6	18.2				23.9	18.1
Deferred Taxes		.0	.0	.0				.0	.0
All Other Non-Current		.4	2.1	4.3				.6	1.7
Net Worth		57.7	51.1	65.6				47.9	59.7
Total Liabilties & Net Worth		100.0	100.0	100.0				100.0	100.0
INCOME DATA									
Net Sales		100.0	100.0	100.0				100.0	100.0
Gross Profit									
Operating Expenses		90.9	91.8	93.2				91.1	93.1
Operating Profit		9.1	8.2	6.8				8.9	6.9
All Other Expenses (net)		8.4	-.5	1.0				.6	.2
Profit Before Taxes		.7	8.7	5.8				8.3	6.6
RATIOS									
Current		27.4	3.6	4.2				3.1	4.1
		5.5	1.7	2.9				1.7	2.7
		1.2	1.0	2.3				1.2	1.3
Quick		26.8	3.2	3.4				2.6	3.6
		5.0	1.3	2.7				1.4	2.0
		.5	.7	2.0				.9	1.0
Sales/Receivables		0 UND	15 24.7	8 45.9				10 37.9	7 49.5
		0 UND	31 11.7	22 16.6				36 10.2	24 15.5
		29 12.6	53 6.9	34 10.8				59 6.2	62 5.9
Cost of Sales/Inventory									
Cost of Sales/Payables									
Sales/Working Capital		2.5	4.8	3.3				4.6	3.7
		6.4	9.6	5.1				12.5	7.8
		NM	-155.7	9.0				35.3	17.5
EBIT/Interest			31.6	8.3				20.6	15.5
			(14) 4.7	(15) .7				(29) 9.1	(32) 4.8
			1.2	-6.3				-.9	.7
Net Profit + Depr., Dep., Amort./Cur. Mat. L/T/D									
Fixed/Worth		.5	.4	.6				.3	.2
		1.5	1.1	.9				.7	.6
		2.5	2.5	1.1				1.8	1.5
Debt/Worth		.1	.3	.2				.4	.2
		.8	.9	.6				1.0	.6
		2.3	4.2	.9				2.2	1.2
% Profit Before Taxes/Tangible Net Worth			15.6	23.0				22.3	26.6
			(13) 8.2	(18) 2.1				(33) 6.6	(38) 6.6
			.6	-6.4				-4.6	.2
% Profit Before Taxes/Total Assets		2.8	11.3	17.7				15.3	8.1
		-.7	5.7	3.2				3.3	2.5
		-10.0	.1	-3.3				-3.8	-.4
Sales/Net Fixed Assets		3.3	7.9	3.3				22.6	9.4
		1.9	3.3	1.9				5.9	3.5
		.4	1.4	1.4				3.0	2.0
Sales/Total Assets		1.7	1.6	1.6				3.6	2.7
		1.4	1.3	1.1				2.0	1.4
		.3	1.0	.8				1.0	.9
% Depr., Dep., Amort./Sales			2.0	2.8				1.0	1.7
			(13) 2.8	(17) 3.7				(32) 2.4	(36) 3.0
			3.6	4.9				3.7	3.6
% Officers', Directors' Owners' Comp/Sales									
Net Sales ($)	5744M	10739M	126709M	410717M	227162M	318672M		523904M	685567M
Total Assets ($)	1182M	9792M	82124M	359283M	312344M	259519M		374146M	542766M

M = $ thousand   MM = $ million
See Pages 9 through 22 for Explanation of Ratios and Data

Comparative Historical Data

Current Data Sorted by Sales

18	34	33	Type of Statement	1	6	2	6	10	8
1		1	Unqualified				1		
	1		Reviewed						
			Compiled						
2	2	4	Tax Returns	1	2		2		1
13	14	17	Other	4	2	1	2	4	4
4/1/07-3/31/08 ALL	4/1/08-3/31/09 ALL	4/1/09-3/31/10 ALL			23 (4/1-9/30/09)			32 (10/1/09-3/31/10)	
				0-1MM	1-3MM	3-5MM	5-10MM	10-25MM	25MM & OVER
34	51	55	NUMBER OF STATEMENTS	6	10	3	9	14	13
%	%	%	ASSETS	%	%	%	%	%	%
15.3	23.8	18.2	Cash & Equivalents		26.9			16.7	18.9
18.9	13.6	11.0	Trade Receivables (net)		15.4			16.7	7.3
1.1	2.0	1.5	Inventory		.8			2.6	1.5
5.8	6.2	2.3	All Other Current		1.3			2.5	3.4
41.2	45.6	33.0	Total Current		44.5			38.5	31.1
44.8	37.1	49.8	Fixed Assets (net)		48.0			44.0	41.4
2.6	2.7	4.5	Intangibles (net)		4.4			1.0	11.1
11.4	14.6	12.7	All Other Non-Current		3.1			16.5	16.3
100.0	100.0	100.0	Total		100.0			100.0	100.0
			LIABILITIES						
3.4	4.3	1.9	Notes Payable-Short Term		1.8			4.9	.8
3.2	2.3	1.8	Cur. Mat.-L.T.D.		1.7			1.6	1.4
7.6	7.7	4.6	Trade Payables		5.7			5.2	4.5
.3	.0	.1	Income Taxes Payable		.0			.2	.0
9.6	8.7	5.6	All Other Current		4.5			5.8	8.0
24.2	23.0	14.0	Total Current		13.8			17.6	14.7
23.3	13.0	26.2	Long-Term Debt		37.8			15.3	21.3
.0	.0	.0	Deferred Taxes		.0			.0	.1
1.8	1.4	3.7	All Other Non-Current		4.7			1.4	8.1
50.7	62.6	56.0	Net Worth		43.7			65.6	55.8
100.0	100.0	100.0	Total Liabilities & Net Worth		100.0			100.0	100.0
			INCOME DATA						
100.0	100.0	100.0	Net Sales		100.0			100.0	100.0
			Gross Profit						
91.9	91.4	92.3	Operating Expenses		98.0			91.6	91.9
8.1	8.6	7.7	Operating Profit		2.0			8.4	8.1
-.6	1.1	2.1	All Other Expenses (net)		.2			1.3	.3
8.7	7.5	5.7	Profit Before Taxes		1.8			7.0	7.8
			RATIOS						
3.5	4.2	4.5			8.4			3.8	4.8
2.0	2.3	2.5	Current		1.8			2.9	2.5
1.1	1.2	1.2			1.1			1.2	.9
3.2	3.8	3.7			7.7			3.5	4.0
1.7	1.9	2.2	Quick		1.8			2.5	2.4
1.0	.9	.9			1.0			1.0	.8
5 73.0	10 35.7	5 71.5		0 UND			22 16.4		0 UND
31 11.6	27 13.7	22 16.6	Sales/Receivables	11 31.7			30 12.0		13 27.7
58 6.3	44 8.3	38 9.6		32 11.5			62 5.9		41 8.8
			Cost of Sales/Inventory						
			Cost of Sales/Payables						
4.8	2.8	3.4			4.3			3.3	3.2
10.5	5.9	6.5	Sales/Working Capital		14.9			5.8	6.5
64.2	60.5	33.7			NM			26.0	-92.7
24.9	35.7	14.5						48.5	
(28) 6.0	(34) 3.1	(41) 2.7	EBIT/Interest					(12) 1.2	
2.3	-1.3	.2						-5.4	
			Net Profit + Depr., Dep., Amort./Cur. Mat. L/T/D						
.4	.3	.4			.4			.3	.4
.8	.5	1.0	Fixed/Worth		1.6			.6	1.0
1.9	.9	2.4			-2.8			1.2	NM
.3	.2	.2			.1			.2	.4
.8	.4	.7	Debt/Worth		1.3			.4	.7
2.5	1.7	2.2			-5.0			.9	NM
46.8	35.5	13.8						19.5	15.3
(32) 15.5	(48) 4.1	(48) 6.6	% Profit Before Taxes/Tangible Net Worth					(10) 3.7	9.8
2.4	-6.5	-5.9						-6.1	6.6
18.0	16.9	10.0			12.9			15.2	13.6
6.5	2.9	3.5	% Profit Before Taxes/Total Assets		-3.1			1.0	6.3
.8	-3.7	-3.1			-10.2			-4.7	3.7
10.7	13.9	5.8			46.5			6.6	13.8
3.4	4.5	2.5	Sales/Net Fixed Assets		3.6			2.2	2.7
2.0	2.2	1.4			2.1			1.7	2.2
2.6	2.3	1.7			3.6			1.6	1.7
1.7	1.4	1.2	Sales/Total Assets		1.8			1.2	1.2
1.0	.8	.7			1.4			.9	.9
1.4	1.5	1.9						1.8	1.8
(31) 2.7	(43) 2.5	(45) 2.9	% Depr., Dep., Amort./Sales					(13) 3.2	(11) 3.1
3.5	3.4	4.6						4.8	3.7
			% Officers', Directors' Owners' Comp/Sales						
517104M	1201654M	1099743M	Net Sales ($)	2477M	15408M	10710M	68643M	234264M	768241M
456982M	1008015M	1024244M	Total Assets ($)	10442M	9004M	17800M	75296M	228588M	683114M

RMA 2010

M = $ thousand   MM = $ million
See Pages 9 through 22 for Explanation of Ratios and Data

Current Data Sorted by Assets   Comparative Historical Data

0-500M	500M-2MM	2-10MM	10-50MM	50-100MM	100-250MM	Type of Statement	4/1/05-3/31/06 ALL	4/1/06-3/31/07 ALL
2	12	44	32		1	Unqualified	42	61
						Reviewed	4	1
	2		1			Compiled	4	3
7	4	1				Tax Returns	2	5
2	8	17	5		1	Other	13	27
	92 (4/1-9/30/09)		47 (10/1/09-3/31/10)					
11	26	62	38	2		NUMBER OF STATEMENTS	65	97
%	%	%	%	%	%	ASSETS	%	%
29.6	21.4	22.0	21.5			Cash & Equivalents	20.0	19.7
6.5	38.6	19.2	14.4			Trade Receivables (net)	19.8	19.6
.0	.1	.1	.1			Inventory	.2	.3
10.8	6.3	4.9	4.1			All Other Current	5.7	5.2
46.9	66.4	46.1	40.2			Total Current	45.8	44.8
40.5	19.9	42.9	51.0			Fixed Assets (net)	42.4	45.1
8.2	6.7	2.0	3.8			Intangibles (net)	1.2	1.5
5.0	7.0	9.0	5.1			All Other Non-Current	10.6	8.6
100.0	100.0	100.0	100.0			Total	100.0	100.0
						LIABILITIES		
24.1	8.0	4.4	.8			Notes Payable-Short Term	5.1	2.5
11.6	3.1	1.8	2.8			Cur. Mat.-L.T.D.	2.5	2.7
4.8	12.2	7.0	4.3			Trade Payables	7.1	5.9
.0	.0	.3	.0			Income Taxes Payable	.1	.3
22.7	18.2	16.7	11.9			All Other Current	14.6	12.7
63.2	41.6	30.3	19.9			Total Current	29.3	24.1
12.9	12.2	20.6	27.3			Long-Term Debt	22.1	23.8
.0	.0	.1	.0			Deferred Taxes	.0	.0
.5	4.2	3.7	1.8			All Other Non-Current	5.0	2.1
23.4	42.0	45.4	51.0			Net Worth	43.7	49.9
100.0	100.0	100.0	100.0			Total Liabilities & Net Worth	100.0	100.0
						INCOME DATA		
100.0	100.0	100.0	100.0			Net Sales	100.0	100.0
						Gross Profit		
88.3	97.2	97.5	95.6			Operating Expenses	94.6	94.7
11.7	2.8	2.5	4.4			Operating Profit	5.4	5.3
-.2	.1	.0	1.3			All Other Expenses (net)	1.0	1.5
11.9	2.7	2.5	3.2			Profit Before Taxes	4.4	3.8
						RATIOS		
2.0	3.0	2.7	3.5			Current	2.8	3.8
1.5	1.8	1.9	2.2				1.5	1.9
.1	1.0	1.1	1.5				1.0	1.3
2.0	2.7	2.3	3.0			Quick	2.4	3.3
1.2	1.4	1.7	2.0				1.4	1.8
.0	.9	1.0	1.4				.9	1.1
0 UND	6 59.6	18 20.3	23 15.7			Sales/Receivables	9 40.3 17 21.5	
0 UND	32 11.4	29 12.5	35 10.5				28 13.1 31 12.0	
0 UND	42 8.7	46 7.9	48 7.5				47 7.7 51 7.1	
						Cost of Sales/Inventory		
						Cost of Sales/Payables		
15.0	8.4	5.7	3.9			Sales/Working Capital	7.9	4.0
31.3	18.5	10.3	7.7				16.1	10.5
-10.3	NM	66.7	12.9				NM	39.4
	15.9	8.5	5.1			EBIT/Interest	8.7	9.2
	(20) 4.4	(45) 3.1	(35) 3.0				(51) 2.7	(79) 2.7
	.1	.3	1.4				1.0	.7
						Net Profit + Depr., Dep., Amort./Cur. Mat. L/T/D		
.1	.1	.5	.7			Fixed/Worth	.5	.5
1.2	.4	1.0	1.1				1.0	.8
-1.1	1.4	2.0	1.6				1.6	1.6
.4	.6	.5	.6			Debt/Worth	.5	.4
1.1	1.2	1.1	.9				1.1	.8
-5.5	7.3	3.1	1.8				3.3	1.8
	63.9	13.4	13.6			% Profit Before Taxes/Tangible Net Worth	26.9	13.6
	(23) 21.4	(57) 5.4	(35) 5.9				(60) 8.9	(89) 6.1
	-.6	-2.8	.9				.2	-1.1
263.1	17.7	6.7	7.2			% Profit Before Taxes/Total Assets	11.7	8.4
24.8	7.4	2.1	3.1				3.9	3.0
6.7	-1.8	-2.9	.6				-.1	-.7
113.6	236.6	14.6	3.8			Sales/Net Fixed Assets	12.4	9.2
39.3	64.8	3.7	2.4				4.1	3.3
6.4	8.4	2.2	1.8				2.2	2.0
14.5	6.8	3.1	1.9			Sales/Total Assets	3.6	2.7
7.0	4.2	1.7	1.2				2.1	1.5
3.7	2.7	1.4	.9				1.2	1.0
	.3	1.1	1.8			% Depr., Dep., Amort./Sales	1.0	1.5
	(21) .7	(58) 1.8	(36) 2.4				(56) 2.2	(91) 2.7
	1.9	2.5	3.2				3.0	3.8
	2.3					% Officers', Directors' Owners' Comp/Sales		1.6
	(10) 6.2							(12) 6.0
	17.7							14.2
12216M	166087M	695750M	1227943M	194465M		Net Sales ($)	1117411M	1777072M
1454M	31837M	342180M	827736M	130632M		Total Assets ($)	593617M	1082051M

(Columns 50-100MM and 100-250MM: DATA NOT AVAILABLE)

M = $ thousand   MM = $ million
See Pages 9 through 22 for Explanation of Ratios and Data

Comparative Historical Data

Current Data Sorted by Sales

Type of Statement

84	77	91	Type of Statement	2	6	7	21	38	17
84	77	91	Unqualified	2	6	7	21	38	17
	1		Reviewed			1			2
5	6	3	Compiled						
6	11	12	Tax Returns	6	2	1	3		
23	37	33	Other		4	5	11	10	3
4/1/07-3/31/08 ALL	4/1/08-3/31/09 ALL	4/1/09-3/31/10 ALL		92 (4/1-9/30/09)			47 (10/1/09-3/31/10)		
				0-1MM	1-3MM	3-5MM	5-10MM	10-25MM	25MM & OVER
118	132	139	NUMBER OF STATEMENTS	8	12	14	35	48	22
%	%	%		%	%	%	%	%	%

ASSETS

84	77	91		0-1MM	1-3MM	3-5MM	5-10MM	10-25MM	25MM & OVER
20.7	21.2	22.1	Cash & Equivalents		19.0	18.3	19.7	22.9	23.6
20.2	19.9	20.4	Trade Receivables (net)		12.8	24.2	23.6	21.7	21.3
.5	.2	.1	Inventory		.0	.0	.1	.1	.2
4.6	5.3	5.3	All Other Current		9.9	1.9	5.3	5.1	5.8
46.0	46.6	47.9	Total Current		41.7	44.4	48.7	49.8	50.9
40.5	41.8	40.4	Fixed Assets (net)		44.2	44.4	37.6	40.6	39.3
2.4	2.6	4.4	Intangibles (net)		7.2	1.1	4.7	2.3	6.6
11.2	9.0	7.3	All Other Non-Current		7.0	10.1	9.1	7.4	3.2
100.0	100.0	100.0	Total		100.0	100.0	100.0	100.0	100.0

LIABILITIES

84	77	91		0-1MM	1-3MM	3-5MM	5-10MM	10-25MM	25MM & OVER
3.2	3.1	5.6	Notes Payable-Short Term		13.4	2.7	6.8	4.0	1.3
2.2	2.6	3.1	Cur. Mat.-L.T.D.		10.0	3.3	1.1	2.2	3.3
8.9	6.2	7.1	Trade Payables		2.2	3.4	9.3	6.6	9.5
.1	.1	.1	Income Taxes Payable		.0	.0	.0	.2	.4
12.0	11.7	16.0	All Other Current		14.3	7.6	15.4	19.2	15.5
26.4	23.6	32.0	Total Current		39.9	16.9	32.7	32.2	30.0
22.9	21.6	21.0	Long-Term Debt		16.9	26.6	17.9	19.5	28.0
.1	.0	.0	Deferred Taxes		.0	.0	.0	.1	.0
3.0	2.3	3.0	All Other Non-Current		.6	.2	2.8	3.3	3.8
47.6	52.4	44.1	Net Worth		42.6	56.3	46.6	45.0	38.1
100.0	100.0	100.0	Total Liabilities & Net Worth		100.0	100.0	100.0	100.0	100.0

INCOME DATA

84	77	91		0-1MM	1-3MM	3-5MM	5-10MM	10-25MM	25MM & OVER
100.0	100.0	100.0	Net Sales		100.0	100.0	100.0	100.0	100.0
			Gross Profit						
94.5	94.8	95.9	Operating Expenses		96.1	92.6	97.4	98.0	93.6
5.5	5.2	4.1	Operating Profit		3.9	7.4	2.6	2.0	6.4
.3	.7	.4	All Other Expenses (net)		-1.0	.2	.3	.4	1.6
5.2	4.5	3.7	Profit Before Taxes		4.9	7.2	2.3	1.6	4.8

RATIOS

84	77	91		0-1MM	1-3MM	3-5MM	5-10MM	10-25MM	25MM & OVER
3.1	3.2	2.8	Current		6.5	7.0	3.2	2.4	2.8
2.0	2.1	1.9			2.0	2.8	1.9	1.9	1.6
1.2	1.3	1.2			.5	1.3	1.0	1.3	1.3
2.8	3.1	2.6	Quick		6.2	7.0	3.0	2.1	2.6
1.7	1.9	1.7			1.8	1.9	1.5	1.8	1.5
1.1	1.0	1.0			.1	1.0	.9	1.2	1.0

Sales/Receivables (days | times)

84	77	91		0-1MM	1-3MM	3-5MM	5-10MM	10-25MM	25MM & OVER
17 22.1	14 25.7	14 25.9	Sales/Receivables		0 UND	20 18.1	19 19.7	18 19.9	15 24.5
32 11.3	32 11.4	30 12.0			25 14.3	39 9.3	33 11.1	30 12.0	37 9.9
46 8.0	47 7.8	46 7.9			61 6.0	54 6.7	45 8.1	40 9.1	58 6.2

84	77	91		0-1MM	1-3MM	3-5MM	5-10MM	10-25MM	25MM & OVER
			Cost of Sales/Inventory						
			Cost of Sales/Payables						
5.4	5.1	5.8	Sales/Working Capital		2.7	4.8	5.7	6.6	6.6
9.8	9.4	10.9			8.9	12.4	9.9	10.9	11.4
33.2	28.5	39.1			-36.6	29.5	595.6	19.8	35.2
9.5	10.2	8.3	EBIT/Interest			17.9	6.9	7.6	6.2
(95) 2.9	(100) 3.0	(107) 3.4				(13) 5.4	(27) 2.0	(35) 3.0	(20) 3.9
1.0	.9	1.0				-.6	-1.1	1.4	2.0
			Net Profit + Depr., Dep., Amort./Cur. Mat. L/T/D						
.5	.4	.4	Fixed/Worth		.3	.1	.2	.5	.6
.9	.9	1.0			1.2	1.0	.8	.9	1.1
1.8	1.6	1.9			3.2	1.6	2.3	1.5	1.7
.5	.4	.5	Debt/Worth		.4	.4	.4	.6	.7
1.0	.9	1.1			1.3	.7	1.3	.9	1.3
2.3	1.8	2.9			3.2	1.6	7.6	2.2	2.8
25.7	24.2	21.4	% Profit Before Taxes/Tangible Net Worth		21.6	57.3	24.4	12.3	25.3
(108) 7.1	(125) 8.2	(123) 6.6			(10) 8.4	22.7	(30) 5.3	(45) 5.5	(19) 8.0
.1	.9	-.3			-1.0	-5.6	-1.6	-.5	2.9
12.3	14.0	9.7	% Profit Before Taxes/Total Assets		21.0	37.6	8.0	4.3	13.7
3.3	4.3	3.1			8.1	8.4	2.0	2.4	6.1
.1	.1	-.2			.4	-2.9	-.8	-.3	1.5
15.5	18.9	25.5	Sales/Net Fixed Assets		112.9	29.2	49.5	16.4	25.3
4.2	4.6	4.3			3.4	4.3	5.8	4.0	3.7
2.2	2.1	2.2			1.0	2.0	2.6	2.4	2.1
3.2	3.6	3.9	Sales/Total Assets		7.5	3.6	4.4	3.9	3.0
1.8	1.7	1.8			1.7	1.6	1.8	1.8	1.6
1.1	1.2	1.2			.7	1.0	1.4	1.3	1.2
1.3	1.1	.9	% Depr., Dep., Amort./Sales		1.6		.9	.6	1.7
(108) 2.3	(111) 2.1	(122) 1.8			(11) 2.0		(34) 1.8	(45) 1.6	(19) 2.0
3.3	3.2	2.5			6.1		2.6	2.2	3.1
	(17) 2.9	5.9	% Officers', Directors' Owners' Comp/Sales						
	8.9	(24) 11.6							
	14.6	25.0							

Net Sales ($) / Total Assets ($)

84	77	91		0-1MM	1-3MM	3-5MM	5-10MM	10-25MM	25MM & OVER
2658130M	2397367M	2296461M	Net Sales ($)	3627M	21904M	53491M	253831M	796278M	1167330M
1545424M	1413395M	1333839M	Total Assets ($)	4844M	32721M	37264M	169151M	446634M	643225M

M = $ thousand   MM = $ million
See Pages 9 through 22 for Explanation of Ratios and Data

HEALTH CARE—HMO Medical Centers NAICS 621491

	Current Data Sorted by Assets						Type of Statement	Comparative Historical Data	
		4	2 1	6	3		Unqualified	8	12
							Reviewed	1	
1							Compiled		1
3							Tax Returns		1
2	3	3		2	1		Other	6	5
	2 (4/1-9/30/09)		29 (10/1/09-3/31/10)					4/1/05- 3/31/06	4/1/06- 3/31/07
0-500M	500M-2MM	2-10MM	10-50MM	50-100MM	100-250MM			ALL	ALL
6	3	7	3	8	4		NUMBER OF STATEMENTS	15	19
%	%	%	%	%	%		ASSETS	%	%
							Cash & Equivalents	32.8	45.8
							Trade Receivables (net)	7.2	9.3
							Inventory	.2	.5
							All Other Current	7.7	5.8
							Total Current	47.9	61.3
							Fixed Assets (net)	31.1	16.3
							Intangibles (net)	12.9	12.2
							All Other Non-Current	8.1	10.2
							Total	100.0	100.0
							LIABILITIES		
							Notes Payable-Short Term	10.8	1.8
							Cur. Mat.-L.T.D.	2.3	3.1
							Trade Payables	8.2	11.8
							Income Taxes Payable	.4	.5
							All Other Current	21.4	27.9
							Total Current	43.2	45.1
							Long-Term Debt	22.5	16.6
							Deferred Taxes	.4	.1
							All Other Non-Current	6.7	13.0
							Net Worth	27.2	25.2
							Total Liabilities & Net Worth	100.0	100.0
							INCOME DATA		
							Net Sales	100.0	100.0
							Gross Profit		
							Operating Expenses	86.3	89.0
							Operating Profit	13.7	11.0
							All Other Expenses (net)	8.5	6.2
							Profit Before Taxes	5.2	4.8
							RATIOS		
							Current	2.1	1.8
								1.1	1.5
								.9	1.1
							Quick	1.9	1.6
								.8	1.3
								.6	.8
							Sales/Receivables	0 UND	0 UND
								4 86.1	3 127.7
								17 20.9	14 26.9
							Cost of Sales/Inventory		
							Cost of Sales/Payables		
							Sales/Working Capital	6.9	6.5
								35.8	19.8
								-37.5	89.4
							EBIT/Interest	14.7	19.4
								(11) 5.1	(13) 9.0
								2.3	1.5
							Net Profit + Depr., Dep., Amort./Cur. Mat. L/T/D		
							Fixed/Worth	.8	.1
								3.1	.4
								-.9	-14.4
							Debt/Worth	1.1	1.4
								11.9	2.1
								-5.3	-187.5
							% Profit Before Taxes/Tangible Net Worth		49.6
								(13) 24.6	
									12.9
							% Profit Before Taxes/Total Assets	10.5	14.1
								3.9	8.8
								.8	.9
							Sales/Net Fixed Assets	81.9	105.6
								19.7	48.4
								2.9	12.4
							Sales/Total Assets	3.5	3.9
								2.1	2.0
								1.0	1.1
							% Depr., Dep., Amort./Sales	.8	.5
								(12) 1.2	(13) .9
								9.4	5.0
							% Officers', Directors' Owners' Comp/Sales		
13834M	42204M	111435M	53315M	1943575M	1276573M		Net Sales ($)	1509141M	2525078M
1265M	3254M	38121M	37658M	595694M	530608M		Total Assets ($)	649560M	1146275M

M = $ thousand   MM = $ million
See Pages 9 through 22 for Explanation of Ratios and Data

Comparative Historical Data   ## Current Data Sorted by Sales

			Type of Statement						
11	12	15	Unqualified	1	1		1	1	11
	1	1	Reviewed					1	
	2	3	Compiled			1			
7	8	11	Tax Returns	1		2			
4/1/07-	4/1/08-	4/1/09-	Other	1	3	1		1	5
3/31/08	3/31/09	3/31/10		0-1MM	2 (4/1-9/30/09)		29 (10/1/09-3/31/10)		
ALL	ALL	ALL		0-1MM	1-3MM	3-5MM	5-10MM	10-25MM	25MM & OVER
18	23	31	NUMBER OF STATEMENTS	3	4	4	1	3	16
%	%	%	ASSETS	%	%	%	%	%	%
39.1	46.7	34.3	Cash & Equivalents						42.7
12.0	11.3	9.2	Trade Receivables (net)						11.1
1.1	.0	.1	Inventory						.1
4.1	3.5	5.2	All Other Current						5.9
56.2	61.5	48.7	Total Current						59.8
21.2	16.8	22.8	Fixed Assets (net)						8.3
11.4	7.2	6.3	Intangibles (net)						12.1
11.1	14.4	22.2	All Other Non-Current						19.8
100.0	100.0	100.0	Total						100.0
			LIABILITIES						
.3	2.5	17.7	Notes Payable-Short Term						.1
1.7	1.7	1.3	Cur. Mat.-L.T.D.						1.6
11.2	10.6	12.2	Trade Payables						8.2
.6	.1	1.0	Income Taxes Payable						.3
18.8	21.4	21.2	All Other Current						24.9
32.5	36.2	53.4	Total Current						35.0
19.5	14.2	14.3	Long-Term Debt						10.3
.1	.2	.5	Deferred Taxes						1.0
3.7	1.3	1.9	All Other Non-Current						1.8
44.2	48.1	29.9	Net Worth						51.9
100.0	100.0	100.0	Total Liabilities & Net Worth						100.0
			INCOME DATA						
100.0	100.0	100.0	Net Sales						100.0
			Gross Profit						
90.4	94.7	91.8	Operating Expenses						94.4
9.6	5.3	8.2	Operating Profit						5.6
3.0	2.7	1.5	All Other Expenses (net)						-.1
6.6	2.6	6.7	Profit Before Taxes						5.7
			RATIOS						
2.7	2.9	2.0							3.9
1.5	1.6	1.4	Current						1.7
1.3	1.2	.8							1.0
2.7	2.5	1.9							3.8
1.4	1.6	.9	Quick						1.6
1.2	1.1	.4							.9
0 UND	1 721.7	0 UND						2	212.6
4 82.2	9 39.5	7 53.0	Sales/Receivables					9	41.5
33 11.1	22 16.5	22 16.5						21	17.2
			Cost of Sales/Inventory						
			Cost of Sales/Payables						
3.8	4.6	10.8							9.3
8.5	13.6	61.2	Sales/Working Capital						18.4
22.2	36.5	-31.8							290.3
95.0	24.6	28.9							31.9
(13) 6.5	(15) 8.2	(21) 9.0	EBIT/Interest					(10)	12.8
1.5	1.9	.9							6.8
			Net Profit + Depr., Dep., Amort./Cur. Mat. L/T/D						
.1	.0	.0							.0
.4	.2	.5	Fixed/Worth						.1
1.8	1.0	2.6							NM
.8	.4	.6							.4
1.4	1.2	1.3	Debt/Worth						1.0
6.8	1.9	15.4							NM
44.1	63.1	98.7	% Profit Before Taxes/Tangible Net Worth						63.4
(16) 25.0	(21) 14.9	(24) 5.0						(12)	3.9
2.8	1.0	-19.2							-24.0
22.0	15.3	42.9	% Profit Before Taxes/Total Assets						28.0
14.3	8.6	3.3							7.3
.7	-.1	-2.4							-6.0
144.7	144.8	185.6							376.5
28.8	34.4	57.1	Sales/Net Fixed Assets						67.3
10.2	16.0	10.3							24.5
2.9	4.7	7.6							6.0
1.8	2.4	2.6	Sales/Total Assets						3.1
1.1	1.8	1.6							2.0
.9	.5	.5							.4
(14) 2.0	(17) 1.4	(22) 1.4	% Depr., Dep., Amort./Sales					(10)	.6
5.8	2.1	3.1							1.5
			% Officers', Directors' Owners' Comp/Sales						
3463481M	3573362M	3440936M	Net Sales ($)	1873M	6725M	15107M	8968M	44655M	3363608M
1547201M	1450823M	1206600M	Total Assets ($)	9208M	20014M	3544M	4645M	18964M	1150225M

M = $ thousand   MM = $ million
See Pages 9 through 22 for Explanation of Ratios and Data

Current Data Sorted by Assets / Comparative Historical Data

Type of Statement	0-500M	500M-2MM	2-10MM	10-50MM	50-100MM	100-250MM	4/1/05-3/31/06 ALL	4/1/06-3/31/07 ALL
Unqualified	1	2	2	3	2	1	6	4
Reviewed	1	1	4	1			6	2
Compiled			2				2	1
Tax Returns	3	3	2				7	10
Other	3	12	15	8	2	1	27	27
		13 (4/1-9/30/09)		56 (10/1/09-3/31/10)				
NUMBER OF STATEMENTS	8	18	25	12	4	2	48	44
ASSETS	%	%	%	%	%	%	%	%
Cash & Equivalents		12.4	8.9	17.7			17.0	19.5
Trade Receivables (net)		26.2	30.8	22.4			26.1	25.4
Inventory		1.9	2.0	4.4			3.5	2.7
All Other Current		5.0	7.4	3.4			2.0	3.2
Total Current		45.5	49.1	48.0			48.6	50.8
Fixed Assets (net)		39.6	37.6	26.0			33.5	39.0
Intangibles (net)		4.3	8.8	9.7			10.4	5.9
All Other Non-Current		10.6	4.5	16.3			7.5	4.3
Total		100.0	100.0	100.0			100.0	100.0
LIABILITIES								
Notes Payable-Short Term		2.0	2.1	.9			3.9	6.8
Cur. Mat.-L.T.D.		5.2	12.8	3.9			4.3	8.9
Trade Payables		7.3	14.0	10.2			8.8	5.8
Income Taxes Payable		.0	.6	.1			.1	.6
All Other Current		27.8	17.4	15.3			16.4	23.9
Total Current		42.3	46.9	30.4			33.4	46.0
Long-Term Debt		23.0	21.3	12.0			21.6	29.4
Deferred Taxes		.0	.1	.0			.0	.1
All Other Non-Current		16.0	5.4	5.6			5.6	6.4
Net Worth		18.7	26.3	51.9			39.4	18.1
Total Liabilties & Net Worth		100.0	100.0	100.0			100.0	100.0
INCOME DATA								
Net Sales		100.0	100.0	100.0			100.0	100.0
Gross Profit								
Operating Expenses		83.1	85.8	96.4			82.9	88.0
Operating Profit		16.9	14.2	3.6			17.1	12.0
All Other Expenses (net)		5.1	2.8	.6			3.1	3.5
Profit Before Taxes		11.8	11.4	3.0			13.9	8.5
RATIOS								
Current		4.1	2.8	3.7			3.8	3.6
		1.3	1.6	2.0			2.6	1.7
		.7	.6	1.4			1.5	.8
Quick		3.7	2.7	3.3			3.7	3.3
		1.1	1.0	1.8			2.2	1.4
		.5	.5	1.0			1.2	.6
Sales/Receivables		0 UND	45 8.1	41 8.9			32 11.5	0 UND
		28 13.3	57 6.4	48 7.5			49 7.5	53 6.8
		64 5.7	69 5.3	77 4.7			77 4.7	73 5.0
Cost of Sales/Inventory								
Cost of Sales/Payables								
Sales/Working Capital		5.4	4.6	4.1			5.0	5.6
		36.0	14.2	7.2			7.2	10.5
		-42.3	-13.8	11.8			23.0	-66.8
EBIT/Interest		84.4	44.5	53.7			51.3	24.0
	(11) 8.9		(20) 9.8	(10) 14.9			(38) 10.4	(33) 7.2
		1.2	1.5	-4.9			2.3	1.8
Net Profit + Depr., Dep., Amort./Cur. Mat. L/T/D							16.4	
							(11) 6.7	
							.9	
Fixed/Worth		.2	.7	.4			.3	.6
		2.5	1.6	.5			.7	2.4
		-1.5	NM	.7			2.2	-2.7
Debt/Worth		.5	1.3	.4			.3	.4
		1.6	2.4	.9			.8	5.8
		-3.5	NM	2.0			3.7	-7.3
% Profit Before Taxes/Tangible Net Worth		132.9	138.2	48.0			107.3	102.0
	(10) 20.0		(19) 41.0	(11) 21.7			(38) 49.8	(27) 50.1
		5.2	5.8	-5.3			8.4	13.5
% Profit Before Taxes/Total Assets		53.1	45.9	20.8			46.6	28.4
		14.4	10.6	7.5			24.2	11.5
		2.9	.5	-3.2			2.2	1.0
Sales/Net Fixed Assets		30.1	16.5	15.6			27.1	22.6
		14.2	11.2	5.0			7.6	7.1
		5.1	2.3	3.4			3.8	3.4
Sales/Total Assets		4.5	3.2	2.0			3.6	4.3
		3.0	1.7	1.7			2.2	2.0
		1.4	1.3	1.4			1.1	1.3
% Depr., Dep., Amort./Sales		.9	1.8	1.8			1.5	1.0
	(16) 2.0		(21) 2.4	2.6			(42) 2.7	(41) 2.2
		4.7	3.8	3.4			4.2	4.4
% Officers', Directors' Owners' Comp/Sales							4.1	4.9
							(19) 8.0	(19) 8.1
							9.7	18.7
Net Sales ($)	18127M	83711M	261397M	377262M	368629M	275089M	586061M	557086M
Total Assets ($)	2743M	22344M	111336M	237184M	298631M	251580M	412031M	363816M

M = $ thousand   MM = $ million
See Pages 9 through 22 for Explanation of Ratios and Data

Comparative Historical Data

Current Data Sorted by Sales

				Type of Statement						
8	10	11		Unqualified	1		1	2	4	3
3	4	7		Reviewed		2		3	1	1
3	3	2		Compiled	1			1		
11	9	8		Tax Returns		3	2	2	1	
24	31	41		Other	3	7	5	7	8	11
4/1/07-	4/1/08-	4/1/09-								
3/31/08	3/31/09	3/31/10				13 (4/1-9/30/09)		56 (10/1/09-3/31/10)		
ALL	ALL	ALL			0-1MM	1-3MM	3-5MM	5-10MM	10-25MM	25MM & OVER
49	57	69		**NUMBER OF STATEMENTS**	5	12	8	15	14	15
%	%	%			%	%	%	%	%	%
17.5	17.7	13.0		ASSETS Cash & Equivalents		15.8		12.1	12.3	14.2
26.0	25.0	25.9		Trade Receivables (net)		26.1		34.6	27.3	22.5
2.5	2.2	2.6		Inventory		3.6		1.5	2.9	3.6
5.5	3.9	6.0		All Other Current		7.5		12.1	6.1	3.0
51.6	48.9	47.5		Total Current		53.0		60.4	48.7	43.4
32.2	35.1	34.2		Fixed Assets (net)		35.8		31.2	30.9	27.8
7.0	10.6	8.8		Intangibles (net)		1.9		3.8	12.6	13.9
9.1	5.4	9.5		All Other Non-Current		9.4		4.6	7.8	14.9
100.0	100.0	100.0		Total		100.0		100.0	100.0	100.0
				LIABILITIES						
8.7	5.5	1.5		Notes Payable-Short Term		.0		4.6	.0	.7
5.1	4.4	7.2		Cur. Mat.-L.T.D.		3.8		10.1	7.2	4.7
7.4	8.0	11.4		Trade Payables		18.9		11.3	15.3	7.9
.1	.0	.3		Income Taxes Payable		.0		.0	1.2	.1
21.0	17.6	22.8		All Other Current		30.6		42.7	18.1	16.5
42.2	35.5	43.1		Total Current		53.3		68.8	41.8	29.9
23.8	30.0	21.1		Long-Term Debt		24.8		14.7	14.3	16.3
.0	.1	.1		Deferred Taxes		.0		.0	.2	.2
3.9	5.1	8.9		All Other Non-Current		25.9		.5	8.8	6.4
30.0	29.3	26.8		Net Worth		-3.9		16.0	34.9	47.2
100.0	100.0	100.0		Total Liabilities & Net Worth		100.0		100.0	100.0	100.0
				INCOME DATA						
100.0	100.0	100.0		Net Sales		100.0		100.0	100.0	100.0
				Gross Profit						
86.1	90.6	88.4		Operating Expenses		90.5		85.7	92.3	94.4
13.9	9.4	11.6		Operating Profit		9.5		14.3	7.7	5.6
3.0	1.9	2.7		All Other Expenses (net)		.5		.6	1.5	.6
10.9	7.5	9.0		Profit Before Taxes		9.0		13.7	6.2	5.0
				RATIOS						
3.2	2.9	3.5				3.4		4.2	3.6	3.6
1.5	1.8	1.8		Current		1.7		1.3	1.7	2.0
.9	.9	.7				.5		.9	.7	1.3
2.9	2.7	3.1				3.1		3.7	3.1	2.5
1.1	1.4	1.5		Quick		.9		1.0	1.4	1.8
.7	.7	.5				.1		.3	.6	.9
18 20.2	8 47.8	10 35.1			0 UND		26 13.9	26 13.8	6 58.9	
48 7.5	53 6.9	51 7.2		Sales/Receivables	35 10.5		59 6.2	45 8.1	62 5.9	
68 5.3	65 5.6	69 5.3			73 5.0		67 5.4	56 6.6	79 4.6	
				Cost of Sales/Inventory						
				Cost of Sales/Payables						
5.2	5.7	4.9				5.3		5.6	5.3	5.1
14.4	11.6	8.7		Sales/Working Capital		26.8		26.9	14.8	7.1
-265.5	-83.4	-35.3				-27.2		-140.0	-18.2	12.9
19.1	14.2	35.4						133.5	25.3	34.8
(38) 7.8	(51) 4.5	(50) 8.8		EBIT/Interest		(11) 33.0		(12) 5.1	(13) 13.4	
2.4	1.6	1.2						1.2	-3.6	1.0
		47.0		Net Profit + Depr., Dep.,						
	(13) 9.3			Amort./Cur. Mat. L/T/D						
		1.0								
.3	.5	.4				.1		.2	.5	.5
.9	1.1	1.0		Fixed/Worth		2.7		1.6	.9	.7
UND	-6.8	-6.0				-.9		-1.6	NM	3.2
.4	.7	.5				.4		.2	.7	.4
2.0	1.9	1.8		Debt/Worth		NM		2.6	1.7	1.6
-11.5	-16.2	-6.6				-2.3		-3.9	NM	6.2
127.5	115.5	96.9							134.5	51.1
(35) 47.3	(39) 32.7	(49) 30.3		% Profit Before Taxes/Tangible Net Worth				(11) 12.7	(13) 30.3	
7.4	4.7	6.0							-16.5	16.6
38.2	32.3	31.0				33.1		76.2	26.6	18.3
14.4	10.6	10.0		% Profit Before Taxes/Total Assets		18.3		27.4	6.3	9.2
3.4	1.3	.9				5.2		.3	-3.7	1.6
32.9	16.4	19.4				33.2		46.8	19.2	15.5
6.6	6.7	8.8		Sales/Net Fixed Assets		9.8		14.8	8.8	5.2
3.9	3.7	3.7				5.1		5.4	3.5	3.8
3.7	3.8	3.5				4.7		4.4	4.1	2.0
2.1	1.7	2.0		Sales/Total Assets		3.2		3.2	2.6	1.7
1.3	1.2	1.3				1.7		1.7	1.6	1.2
1.7	1.7	1.3						.8	1.4	1.7
(42) 2.9	(53) 3.1	(61) 2.4		% Depr., Dep., Amort./Sales				(14) 2.1	(10) 2.2	2.4
4.6	4.7	3.8						3.8	3.0	4.3
4.7	2.6	4.4		% Officers', Directors' Owners' Comp/Sales						
(10) 31.9	(12) 7.7	(17) 8.0								
41.3	34.1	33.2								
1195225M	1725392M	1384215M		Net Sales ($)	1820M	25080M	30669M	101576M	213755M	1011315M
843566M	1229370M	923818M		Total Assets ($)	6443M	10547M	23490M	42085M	125328M	715925M

M = $ thousand   MM = $ million
See Pages 9 through 22 for Explanation of Ratios and Data

Current Data Sorted by Assets   Comparative Historical Data

						Type of Statement	4/1/05-3/31/06 ALL	4/1/06-3/31/07 ALL
1	3	13	6	4	4	Unqualified	15	25
	5	11	5	1		Reviewed	13	6
13	9	20	2			Compiled	29	23
29	24	24	4			Tax Returns	29	46
9	29	72	14	1	2	Other	62	73
	18 (4/1-9/30/09)		287 (10/1/09-3/31/10)					
0-500M	**500M-2MM**	**2-10MM**	**10-50MM**	**50-100MM**	**100-250MM**			
52	70	140	31	6	6	**NUMBER OF STATEMENTS**	148	173
%	%	%	%	%	%	**ASSETS**	%	%
32.8	17.7	13.4	13.4			Cash & Equivalents	20.0	19.4
4.5	14.0	19.8	23.6			Trade Receivables (net)	15.6	15.8
.0	2.8	3.0	2.1			Inventory	2.0	2.5
4.0	3.9	1.7	2.5			All Other Current	3.1	3.6
41.3	38.4	38.0	41.6			Total Current	40.8	41.3
39.1	47.5	50.3	31.1			Fixed Assets (net)	43.8	45.4
9.3	2.9	6.8	18.0			Intangibles (net)	6.3	5.3
10.3	11.2	4.9	9.3			All Other Non-Current	9.1	8.0
100.0	100.0	100.0	100.0			Total	100.0	100.0
						LIABILITIES		
44.9	10.7	6.1	2.1			Notes Payable-Short Term	23.0	10.4
12.2	9.0	5.9	3.8			Cur. Mat.-L.T.D.	6.7	7.3
5.7	6.0	5.1	4.4			Trade Payables	4.5	4.6
1.2	.0	.0	1.0			Income Taxes Payable	.1	.0
38.3	10.5	7.7	12.5			All Other Current	18.8	17.6
102.4	36.2	24.8	23.9			Total Current	53.1	40.0
47.0	37.6	33.1	26.8			Long-Term Debt	32.2	31.3
.0	.0	.1	.0			Deferred Taxes	.2	.1
7.4	3.0	3.6	5.0			All Other Non-Current	5.6	2.1
-56.8	23.2	38.4	44.4			Net Worth	8.9	26.5
100.0	100.0	100.0	100.0			Total Liabilties & Net Worth	100.0	100.0
						INCOME DATA		
100.0	100.0	100.0	100.0			Net Sales	100.0	100.0
						Gross Profit		
90.4	79.1	77.6	74.8			Operating Expenses	87.0	81.5
9.6	20.9	22.4	25.2			Operating Profit	13.0	18.5
.1	3.2	4.5	5.0			All Other Expenses (net)	2.2	2.2
9.4	17.7	17.9	20.2			Profit Before Taxes	10.8	16.3
						RATIOS		
1.0	2.8	3.2	4.3				2.5	3.6
.5	1.2	1.6	2.2			Current	1.0	1.3
.1	.5	.9	1.5				.4	.6
1.0	2.3	2.8	3.9				2.1	3.0
.5	1.0	1.4	2.0			Quick	.9	1.2
.1	.3	.7	1.4				.3	.4
0 UND	0 UND	0 UND	32 11.4				0 UND	0 UND
0 UND	0 UND	34 10.8	45 8.0			Sales/Receivables	1 265.5	18 20.0
0 UND	35 10.5	56 6.5	64 5.7				49 7.4	51 7.2
						Cost of Sales/Inventory		
						Cost of Sales/Payables		
627.3	11.9	6.6	3.6				9.5	6.2
-41.2	59.6	12.5	9.5			Sales/Working Capital	UND	28.6
-18.4	-23.7	-63.3	17.3				-18.4	-29.0
41.4	36.8	47.3	41.0				18.0	34.9
(42) 5.7	(57) 8.9	(123) 13.1	(27) 19.0			EBIT/Interest	(119) 6.5	(141) 7.7
.8	2.1	3.3	3.4				2.2	1.8
						Net Profit + Depr., Dep.,	8.1	6.2
						Amort./Cur. Mat. L/T/D	(15) 3.1	(12) 2.4
							1.2	.7
.4	.7	.5	.4				.6	.5
2.0	2.0	1.4	1.1			Fixed/Worth	3.9	1.7
-.8	NM	5.4	5.4				-4.7	10.1
1.3	1.0	.6	.6				.9	.6
NM	3.2	1.7	1.5			Debt/Worth	5.6	2.4
-1.9	NM	5.7	5.9				-8.0	17.8
321.1	231.6	178.7	136.9			% Profit Before Taxes/Tangible	166.5	192.5
(26) 153.4	(53) 107.3	(121) 69.4	(26) 90.1			Net Worth	(100) 63.9	(134) 75.2
13.3	37.4	19.8	35.4				20.0	21.2
104.2	94.8	66.3	54.9			% Profit Before Taxes/Total	43.1	66.8
35.7	29.5	26.3	18.5			Assets	15.4	23.7
.0	5.0	4.6	6.5				2.7	3.8
86.5	40.9	11.0	24.4				34.1	21.5
33.6	8.0	4.2	5.9			Sales/Net Fixed Assets	11.0	7.8
19.6	3.2	1.8	2.9				3.5	2.7
22.2	5.8	2.7	2.0				8.7	5.4
10.4	3.4	1.8	1.5			Sales/Total Assets	3.4	2.4
6.7	1.7	.9	.6				1.5	1.4
1.1	2.0	2.8	1.9				1.3	1.8
(33) 1.5	(53) 3.2	(124) 4.7	(27) 3.9			% Depr., Dep., Amort./Sales	(119) 2.8	(144) 3.7
2.7	8.2	9.5	6.6				5.2	6.1
17.7	4.1	4.7					7.3	6.5
(28) 32.1	(15) 7.1	(30) 7.0				% Officers', Directors' Owners' Comp/Sales	(49) 21.6	(50) 16.9
38.5	27.2	18.7					30.1	29.2
169661M	385674M	1189419M	951286M	421068M	1169720M	Net Sales ($)	1488277M	1889902M
14116M	87989M	610209M	633887M	440741M	1121555M	Total Assets ($)	664767M	1201986M

M = $ thousand   MM = $ million
See Pages 9 through 22 for Explanation of Ratios and Data

© RMA 2010

Comparative Historical Data

Current Data Sorted by Sales

			Type of Statement						
25	27	30	Unqualified	1	2	1	5	8	13
12	22	23	Reviewed		6		6	6	5
41	59	44	Compiled	4	8	8	11	12	1
54	62	81	Tax Returns	14	19	20	18	9	1
97	104	127	Other	7	18	27	35	9	9
4/1/07-3/31/08 ALL	4/1/08-3/31/09 ALL	4/1/09-3/31/10 ALL		18 (4/1-9/30/09)			287 (10/1/09-3/31/10)		
				0-1MM	1-3MM	3-5MM	5-10MM	10-25MM	25MM & OVER
229	274	305	NUMBER OF STATEMENTS	26	47	62	75	66	29
%	%	%	ASSETS	%	%	%	%	%	%
19.0	19.0	17.3	Cash & Equivalents	8.2	20.9	19.4	18.1	18.2	11.4
14.1	14.7	16.0	Trade Receivables (net)	1.9	7.9	14.0	17.6	23.1	26.0
2.8	2.7	2.3	Inventory	.0	.7	2.1	3.5	3.4	1.9
1.9	2.8	2.7	All Other Current	4.5	1.4	1.6	3.4	3.3	2.7
37.7	39.2	38.4	Total Current	14.6	30.9	37.1	42.6	48.1	41.9
49.9	46.6	45.6	Fixed Assets (net)	64.7	54.7	51.8	40.4	35.7	36.5
4.9	6.1	8.3	Intangibles (net)	2.1	6.8	5.3	10.0	9.6	15.2
7.5	8.0	7.7	All Other Non-Current	18.5	7.5	5.8	7.0	6.6	6.5
100.0	100.0	100.0	Total	100.0	100.0	100.0	100.0	100.0	100.0
			LIABILITIES						
13.5	12.1	13.3	Notes Payable-Short Term	15.2	24.7	12.0	16.9	5.8	3.8
9.0	10.7	7.4	Cur. Mat.-L.T.D.	6.1	7.5	11.0	6.8	6.8	3.5
4.6	4.4	5.2	Trade Payables	.3	3.3	5.3	8.4	4.9	5.1
.0	.2	.4	Income Taxes Payable	.0	.0	.8	.2	.3	1.0
13.3	16.4	14.0	All Other Current	12.5	18.6	14.8	13.2	12.2	12.7
40.4	43.8	40.4	Total Current	34.1	54.1	43.9	45.4	30.0	26.2
36.8	34.1	35.7	Long-Term Debt	49.1	54.6	34.8	34.3	23.2	27.4
.0	.1	.1	Deferred Taxes	.0	.0	.0	.0	.2	.5
3.7	6.6	4.4	All Other Non-Current	2.7	8.2	5.7	3.3	1.2	6.8
19.0	15.4	19.4	Net Worth	14.0	-17.0	15.5	16.9	45.4	39.1
100.0	100.0	100.0	Total Liabilities & Net Worth	100.0	100.0	100.0	100.0	100.0	100.0
			INCOME DATA						
100.0	100.0	100.0	Net Sales	100.0	100.0	100.0	100.0	100.0	100.0
			Gross Profit						
78.8	80.6	80.1	Operating Expenses	54.0	88.3	87.4	81.3	75.4	82.2
21.2	19.4	19.9	Operating Profit	46.0	11.7	12.6	18.7	24.6	17.8
2.5	3.4	3.4	All Other Expenses (net)	19.0	4.1	1.9	.8	1.6	1.8
18.7	16.0	16.5	Profit Before Taxes	27.0	7.6	10.6	17.9	23.0	16.1
			RATIOS						
2.8	2.8	2.8		1.0	3.9	2.8	2.2	3.9	2.5
1.4	1.3	1.5	Current	.5	1.0	.8	1.5	2.3	1.6
.5	.5	.5		.1	.2	.4	.7	1.0	.9
2.5	2.5	2.4		1.0	3.6	2.5	2.0	3.4	2.1
1.2	1.1	1.1	Quick	.3	1.0	.8	1.3	2.0	1.5
.4	.3	.4		.0	.1	.3	.5	.9	.9
0 UND	0 UND	0 UND		0 UND	0 UND	0 UND	0 UND	0 UND	32 11.4
23 16.0	17 21.7	24 15.2	Sales/Receivables	0 UND	0 UND	12 29.7	27 13.7	35 10.4	44 8.4
46 8.0	45 8.2	47 7.7		0 UND	47 7.8	41 8.9	44 8.2	54 6.8	59 6.2
			Cost of Sales/Inventory						
			Cost of Sales/Payables						
8.4	8.7	7.8		UND	6.9	11.1	8.8	6.2	6.8
34.5	33.5	29.2	Sales/Working Capital	-9.6	545.5	-86.3	22.9	9.8	13.3
-22.0	-22.5	-25.6		-2.9	-16.9	-19.5	-52.7	NM	-537.8
37.9	34.1	39.8			22.7	26.1	40.8	75.5	21.0
(200) 10.2	(232) 8.8	(261) 11.0	EBIT/Interest	(40) 5.7	(57) 4.8	(67) 22.6	(61) 29.3	(27) 8.5	
1.9	1.8	2.7		-.3	.6	4.6	9.1	3.5	
18.3	7.7	6.6							
(13) 4.0	(15) 3.3	(19) 2.3	Net Profit + Depr., Dep., Amort./Cur. Mat. L/T/D						
.8	1.8	1.4							
.7	.7	.5		.2	1.0	1.0	.5	.3	.6
1.8	1.9	1.6	Fixed/Worth	4.0	2.1	2.0	1.3	.9	2.3
-16.3	-10.3	13.5		44.5	-24.9	-23.6	8.0	2.2	NM
.7	.7	.7		1.7	1.1	1.2	.6	.6	.7
2.7	2.6	2.6	Debt/Worth	4.8	5.0	3.7	2.2	1.1	5.0
-15.3	-16.9	64.1		45.9	-31.8	-6.4	-55.0	4.0	NM
279.1	192.9	183.3		103.8	166.0	209.0	187.5	209.5	142.1
(167) 95.1	(195) 75.4	(234) 79.2	% Profit Before Taxes/Tangible Net Worth	(22) 59.3	(33) 71.4	(43) 62.7	(56) 97.6	(58) 131.4	(22) 38.7
28.3	22.7	20.0		10.3	-9.3	13.6	28.8	56.8	15.7
70.6	65.0	69.1		10.5	73.8	60.6	74.1	85.5	39.5
27.0	20.7	24.6	% Profit Before Taxes/Total Assets	5.3	19.0	16.1	34.2	52.9	12.0
2.9	3.1	4.7		.2	-4.3	.0	13.0	12.6	7.0
19.3	22.2	24.5		22.4	22.0	22.1	42.5	28.8	21.5
5.2	6.9	6.6	Sales/Net Fixed Assets	.3	3.8	4.8	7.6	11.9	8.2
2.5	2.5	2.6		.2	1.8	2.3	3.8	4.9	3.0
4.7	5.8	5.1		1.2	6.8	6.3	5.1	4.2	3.2
2.2	2.3	2.2	Sales/Total Assets	.3	2.5	2.6	2.4	2.6	1.9
1.4	1.3	1.2		.2	.9	1.4	1.7	1.6	.9
2.1	2.1	2.2		12.7	1.9	2.7	2.0	1.9	1.8
(196) 4.1	(222) 4.0	(248) 3.8	% Depr., Dep., Amort./Sales	(21) 17.8	(38) 4.0	(48) 5.1	(60) 3.2	(55) 3.1	(26) 3.8
7.6	8.2	7.5		23.3	9.4	9.3	5.7	4.6	5.5
5.9	3.6	5.8			6.3	3.5	6.0	5.8	
(63) 14.3	(77) 8.2	(80) 14.6	% Officers', Directors' Owners' Comp/Sales	(11) 33.6	(20) 16.6	(21) 12.3	(18) 13.3		
26.2	26.7	33.0		40.3	31.1	22.7	31.4		
2565124M 1457460M	3585593M 1904892M	4286828M 2908497M	Net Sales ($) / Total Assets ($)	13464M 43746M	93417M 91869M	241671M 117165M	527232M 256818M	1000431M 544589M	2410613M 1854310M

M = $ thousand   MM = $ million
See Pages 9 through 22 for Explanation of Ratios and Data

Current Data Sorted by Assets   Comparative Historical Data

Type of Statement	0-500M	500M-2MM	2-10MM	10-50MM	50-100MM	100-250MM		4/1/05-3/31/06 ALL	4/1/06-3/31/07 ALL
Unqualified	2	5	43	52	4	4		100	111
Reviewed	1	2	14	2				19	19
Compiled	6	8	9	5		1		26	33
Tax Returns	24	21	14					27	35
Other	14	30	50	18	6	1		100	100
	111 (4/1-9/30/09)			225 (10/1/09-3/31/10)					
NUMBER OF STATEMENTS	47	66	130	77	10	6		272	298
	%	%	%	%	%	%		%	%
ASSETS									
Cash & Equivalents	34.2	18.8	16.6	19.3	16.2			19.2	21.1
Trade Receivables (net)	8.9	19.5	21.4	18.5	19.1			19.7	19.1
Inventory	2.5	2.4	1.8	1.4	2.5			1.4	1.2
All Other Current	4.1	4.1	5.0	4.6	6.3			3.4	4.0
Total Current	49.6	44.9	44.8	43.9	44.0			43.7	45.5
Fixed Assets (net)	33.1	41.7	43.0	44.3	21.6			42.8	42.8
Intangibles (net)	7.9	3.4	3.5	2.1	17.8			3.8	4.0
All Other Non-Current	9.2	10.0	8.7	9.8	16.6			9.7	7.7
Total	100.0	100.0	100.0	100.0	100.0			100.0	100.0
LIABILITIES									
Notes Payable-Short Term	16.5	8.4	3.8	2.9	2.5			6.4	7.7
Cur. Mat.-L.T.D.	3.9	8.5	4.3	2.9	9.0			6.2	5.3
Trade Payables	9.0	5.7	7.3	5.7	6.5			6.3	6.6
Income Taxes Payable	.0	.0	.2	.1	.2			.1	.2
All Other Current	26.2	8.9	12.4	12.7	9.1			12.6	13.3
Total Current	55.6	31.4	28.0	24.3	27.4			31.5	33.1
Long-Term Debt	23.7	35.2	26.1	26.4	30.9			29.6	27.1
Deferred Taxes	.6	.0	.3	.1	.1			.1	.4
All Other Non-Current	14.1	3.8	3.6	4.9	4.9			4.8	4.2
Net Worth	6.0	29.6	41.9	44.4	36.7			33.9	35.3
Total Liabilities & Net Worth	100.0	100.0	100.0	100.0	100.0			100.0	100.0
INCOME DATA									
Net Sales	100.0	100.0	100.0	100.0	100.0			100.0	100.0
Gross Profit									
Operating Expenses	91.9	77.2	87.1	94.9	90.8			89.2	89.1
Operating Profit	8.1	22.8	12.9	5.1	9.2			10.8	10.9
All Other Expenses (net)	.9	4.8	3.1	.9	2.6			2.3	2.7
Profit Before Taxes	7.2	18.0	9.8	4.2	6.5			8.5	8.2
RATIOS									
Current	2.2	5.8	3.3	3.7	2.8			3.4	3.2
	1.1	1.5	1.7	2.1	2.4			1.6	1.7
	.4	.7	.9	1.2	1.4			.9	.9
Quick	2.0	5.9	2.9	3.5	2.4			3.0	2.8
	1.0	(65) 1.0	1.5	1.9	1.7			1.4 (297)	1.5
	.3	.4	.7	.9	.8			.7	.7
Sales/Receivables	0 UND	0 UND	12 29.3	23 16.0	24 15.4			1 582.9	0 UND
	0 UND	0 UND	39 9.4	35 10.5	36 10.2			34 10.7	33 11.2
	0 975.0	49 7.4	53 6.9	54 6.7	76 4.8			56 6.6	54 6.8
Cost of Sales/Inventory									
Cost of Sales/Payables									
Sales/Working Capital	34.9	6.2	5.8	3.6	3.4			5.2	5.7
	259.4	30.2	11.7	7.7	8.4			15.8	15.3
	-19.7	-36.7	-86.8	26.3	NM			-87.7	-139.2
EBIT/Interest	30.6	124.0	19.7	11.2				19.6	22.6
	(28) 9.5	(50) 32.3	(102) 5.0	(64) 4.0				(220) 5.0	(226) 5.8
	3.1	3.3	1.1	.8				1.2	1.4
Net Profit + Depr., Dep., Amort./Cur. Mat. L/T/D			*					3.6	6.5
								(16) 1.6	(19) 1.5
								1.1	.6
Fixed/Worth	.1	.3	.4	.6	.5			.4	.4
	1.0	1.1	1.0	1.0	1.0			1.1	1.0
	-1.5	7.2	2.6	2.1	-.8			4.4	6.2
Debt/Worth	1.0	.5	.6	.5	.9			.5	.5
	4.2	1.3	1.2	1.2	1.9			1.8	1.4
	-2.7	14.9	4.8	2.8	-4.5			7.1	10.3
% Profit Before Taxes/Tangible Net Worth	432.4	145.9	79.5	24.5				68.1	68.4
	(29) 176.3	(53) 87.6	(114) 21.7	(70) 7.6				(223) 17.0	(240) 19.6
	76.4	23.9	2.3	-.3				1.8	2.7
% Profit Before Taxes/Total Assets	106.1	81.1	24.6	9.7	15.3			24.8	22.8
	34.4	42.8	7.3	3.0	7.2			5.5	7.0
	10.0	3.4	.2	-.7	-.9			.4	.2
Sales/Net Fixed Assets	177.9	23.2	13.3	5.4	36.9			17.6	18.6
	25.2	10.2	4.8	2.9	11.3			5.4	5.3
	12.5	3.3	1.7	1.8	3.2			2.5	2.3
Sales/Total Assets	15.0	4.2	2.9	2.1	3.1			3.5	3.4
	7.3	2.6	1.7	1.4	1.5			1.9	2.0
	4.3	1.3	1.0	.9	.8			1.1	1.0
% Depr., Dep., Amort./Sales	.8	2.0	1.5	1.8				1.5	1.3
	(25) 2.0	(47) 3.3	(113) 3.3	(72) 3.0				(234) 2.9	(259) 3.0
	3.4	7.4	8.2	4.3				6.3	6.2
% Officers', Directors' Owners' Comp/Sales	7.4	2.2	3.3	1.8				4.3	4.3
	(15) 18.5	(14) 8.2	(17) 6.9	(13) 5.9				(54) 9.2	(52) 9.0
	25.0	17.6	18.2	29.6				27.6	27.1
Net Sales ($)	115119M	230047M	1554125M	2644576M	1267722M	1326938M		7349342M	6782191M
Total Assets ($)	12033M	75327M	696711M	1566100M	677682M	951315M		3522708M	3666670M

© RMA 2010

M = $ thousand   MM = $ million

See Pages 9 through 22 for Explanation of Ratios and Data

Comparative Historical Data

Current Data Sorted by Sales

			Type of Statement						
95	115	110	Unqualified		7	5	20	41	37
14	12	19	Reviewed	1	4	4	2	6	2
29	22	29	Compiled	4	8	4	6	3	4
38	48	59	Tax Returns	16	19	12	5	6	1
101	106	119	Other	9	22	20	22	22	24
4/1/07-3/31/08	4/1/08-3/31/09	4/1/09-3/31/10			111 (4/1-9/30/09)			225 (10/1/09-3/31/10)	
ALL	ALL	ALL		0-1MM	1-3MM	3-5MM	5-10MM	10-25MM	25MM & OVER
277	303	336	NUMBER OF STATEMENTS	30	60	45	55	78	68
%	%	%	ASSETS	%	%	%	%	%	%
17.7	19.7	20.1	Cash & Equivalents	14.7	20.4	23.2	18.3	18.9	22.9
20.0	18.8	18.4	Trade Receivables (net)	11.5	16.6	15.1	18.7	20.8	22.0
1.5	1.6	1.9	Inventory	2.6	3.0	.8	1.4	1.9	1.9
5.0	5.3	4.7	All Other Current	2.7	4.7	2.3	5.5	4.3	7.0
44.2	45.4	45.1	Total Current	31.5	44.7	41.3	44.0	45.9	53.9
43.2	41.1	40.6	Fixed Assets (net)	53.3	40.9	43.4	45.1	38.6	31.7
3.9	5.2	4.8	Intangibles (net)	7.5	5.8	4.3	3.7	2.2	6.9
8.7	8.2	9.5	All Other Non-Current	7.3	8.6	11.0	7.3	13.3	7.5
100.0	100.0	100.0	Total	100.0	100.0	100.0	100.0	100.0	100.0
			LIABILITIES						
7.4	8.8	6.2	Notes Payable-Short Term	8.0	9.9	6.8	9.0	3.7	2.3
5.4	6.1	4.9	Cur. Mat.-L.T.D.	3.5	4.2	8.3	4.9	5.0	3.7
6.8	6.3	6.8	Trade Payables	10.0	6.1	3.7	6.7	6.6	8.3
.3	.2	.1	Income Taxes Payable	.0	.0	.0	.1	.2	.3
13.2	14.0	13.5	All Other Current	17.2	10.3	11.1	14.0	10.5	19.6
33.1	35.5	31.5	Total Current	38.7	30.4	29.9	34.7	25.9	34.2
28.7	27.4	27.6	Long-Term Debt	46.6	26.9	31.0	34.4	21.4	19.3
.2	.4	.3	Deferred Taxes	1.0	.0	.3	.1	.2	.0
3.9	6.3	5.5	All Other Non-Current	8.5	11.0	2.7	2.2	3.2	6.7
34.1	30.5	35.1	Net Worth	5.3	31.7	36.0	28.5	49.3	39.4
100.0	100.0	100.0	Total Liabilities & Net Worth	100.0	100.0	100.0	100.0	100.0	100.0
			INCOME DATA						
100.0	100.0	100.0	Net Sales	100.0	100.0	100.0	100.0	100.0	100.0
			Gross Profit						
87.8	90.5	87.8	Operating Expenses	78.1	81.1	86.1	88.8	91.7	93.8
12.2	9.5	12.2	Operating Profit	21.9	18.9	13.9	11.2	8.3	6.2
2.6	2.2	2.6	All Other Expenses (net)	12.1	4.2	1.9	1.4	.2	1.1
9.6	7.3	9.6	Profit Before Taxes	9.8	14.7	12.0	9.8	8.1	5.1
			RATIOS						
3.5	3.7	3.5		2.5	5.8	4.5	3.0	3.3	3.2
1.6	1.8	1.7	Current	.8	1.3	2.0	1.5	2.3	1.8
.8	.9	.9		.3	.7	.7	.9	1.3	1.2
2.8	2.8	3.1		1.5	6.0	4.4	2.9	3.0	2.9
1.3	1.5 (335) 1.4		Quick	.8 (59) 1.0	1.8		1.4	2.1	1.6
.6	.7	.7		.3	.3	.5	.7	1.0	.9
0 813.5	0 UND	0 UND		0 UND	0 UND	0 UND	0 UND	23 16.1	13 27.4
33 11.2	31 11.9	28 12.9	Sales/Receivables	0 UND	0 UND	20 18.1	41 8.8	38 9.6	30 12.2
56 6.5	52 7.1	50 7.3		46 8.0	42 8.7	46 7.9	55 6.6	53 6.9	49 7.5
			Cost of Sales/Inventory						
			Cost of Sales/Payables						
5.1	5.0	5.8		9.5	5.0	5.9	6.3	4.6	6.0
14.5	13.1	16.5	Sales/Working Capital	-22.5	51.6	33.7	20.2	7.5	12.3
-54.4	-84.0	-87.3		-4.4	-51.9	-18.3	-84.2	27.3	46.9
19.4	16.6	28.5		11.5	29.5	46.4	35.1	29.5	18.3
(217) 5.2	(230) 3.3	(257) 6.0	EBIT/Interest	(14) 4.9	(39) 8.1	(39) 6.9	(47) 4.9	(64) 4.3	(54) 6.9
1.2	.8	1.3		1.6	1.1	.7	.9	1.1	2.6
9.0	18.0	12.9							14.6
(14) 6.5	(14) 6.6	(27) 5.2	Net Profit + Depr., Dep., Amort./Cur. Mat. L/T/D					(11)	5.6
2.3	.5	1.1							1.1
.5	.4	.4		.5	.3	.4	.7	.4	.5
1.1	1.0	1.0	Fixed/Worth	3.6	1.1	1.2	1.2	.8	1.0
4.8	4.3	3.7		NM	NM	6.8	2.6	1.3	2.2
.6	.6	.6		2.1	.4	.3	.6	.4	.8
1.3	1.3	1.4	Debt/Worth	5.7	1.6	1.3	1.6	.9	1.4
7.2	9.9	7.1		-7.0	-14.3	11.4	7.6	2.0	6.0
80.7	60.2	100.8		89.5	174.3	156.1	100.1	48.1	77.3
(229) 19.7	(243) 12.6	(277) 24.3	% Profit Before Taxes/Tangible Net Worth	(20) 15.9	(44) 99.2	(38) 51.0	(46) 34.4	(71) 9.0	(58) 13.9
3.2	.8	3.4		6.4	23.4	18.8	-.6	2.1	1.5
30.2	26.1	37.0		22.8	58.7	69.7	42.5	19.1	23.7
7.5	5.5	9.3	% Profit Before Taxes/Total Assets	7.8	24.8	23.4	13.2	3.8	6.5
.5	-.1	.3		-1.8	1.8	.1	-.6	-.1	.9
16.9	16.2	17.4		11.5	35.5	20.0	16.5	10.8	18.7
4.6	5.6	6.3	Sales/Net Fixed Assets	2.9	10.0	5.7	5.4	4.0	8.9
2.1	2.6	2.4		.2	2.0	1.7	2.4	2.4	3.8
3.4	3.8	3.9		2.6	5.1	5.5	4.2	2.6	4.2
1.9	2.0	1.9	Sales/Total Assets	1.1	2.6	1.8	2.2	1.6	2.3
1.1	1.1	1.1		.2	1.2	1.0	1.2	1.2	1.5
1.3	1.6	1.6		4.2	1.5	2.1	1.6	1.6	1.1
(236) 2.7	(248) 3.0	(271) 3.0	% Depr., Dep., Amort./Sales	(20) 14.7	(43) 2.9	(35) 5.2	(45) 3.1	(71) 2.4	(57) 2.0
5.1	5.5	5.5		19.5	8.0	10.1	5.7	4.0	3.5
4.2	3.4	3.2			9.3	3.2			1.7
(52) 7.1	(48) 6.8	(60) 9.8	% Officers', Directors' Owners' Comp/Sales	(12) 16.1	(14) 6.2			(11)	14.1
18.2	17.3	20.8		20.5	15.5				35.6
5320406M	7537356M	7138527M	Net Sales ($)	15649M	118709M	174392M	400569M	1195033M	5234175M
3371779M	5170930M	3979168M	Total Assets ($)	31278M	107387M	167061M	238685M	872121M	2562636M

RMA 2010

M = $ thousand   MM = $ million
See Pages 9 through 22 for Explanation of Ratios and Data

Current Data Sorted by Assets | **Comparative Historical Data**

Type of Statement

Type of Statement	0-500M	500M-2MM	2-10MM	10-50MM	50-100MM	100-250MM	4/1/05-3/31/06 ALL	4/1/06-3/31/07 ALL
Unqualified		2	9	21	9	9	50	51
Reviewed		1	17	6	1		18	20
Compiled	5	10	7	2			20	29
Tax Returns	27	8	14		1	1	22	23
Other	18	28	33	30	7	8	95	85
		40 (4/1-9/30/09)		234 (10/1/09-3/31/10)				
NUMBER OF STATEMENTS	50	49	80	59	18	18	205	208

Main Data

	0-500M %	500M-2MM %	2-10MM %	10-50MM %	50-100MM %	100-250MM %	4/1/05-3/31/06 ALL %	4/1/06-3/31/07 ALL %
ASSETS								
Cash & Equivalents	29.5	16.0	13.5	13.1	16.0	9.2	15.4	15.3
Trade Receivables (net)	9.8	25.3	33.1	25.2	22.6	16.0	21.5	22.8
Inventory	1.1	1.6	2.4	2.4	3.3	4.0	3.0	2.5
All Other Current	1.9	2.9	2.7	3.1	4.0	5.8	4.0	3.4
Total Current	42.3	45.8	51.8	43.8	45.9	35.0	43.8	44.1
Fixed Assets (net)	40.2	40.2	33.1	43.2	25.2	22.1	40.8	41.0
Intangibles (net)	3.4	4.6	7.6	6.7	19.3	35.4	5.7	7.7
All Other Non-Current	14.1	9.4	7.6	6.3	9.6	7.6	9.6	7.2
Total	100.0	100.0	100.0	100.0	100.0	100.0	100.0	100.0
LIABILITIES								
Notes Payable-Short Term	18.2	6.5	5.1	3.6	1.8	5.6	8.6	9.1
Cur. Mat.-L.T.D.	9.9	9.7	8.2	6.3	3.9	1.9	8.4	6.9
Trade Payables	8.0	6.2	10.9	8.7	8.6	5.4	9.2	8.5
Income Taxes Payable	.1	.2	1.4	.2	1.3	.1	.7	.2
All Other Current	44.9	14.0	9.6	12.2	13.0	7.8	15.6	16.8
Total Current	81.0	36.6	35.2	31.0	28.7	20.8	42.5	41.5
Long-Term Debt	39.7	22.1	20.3	27.0	13.7	34.6	32.7	25.5
Deferred Taxes	.0	.0	.3	.2	.9	1.5	.3	.4
All Other Non-Current	20.4	2.5	4.8	4.1	2.6	21.3	7.5	5.1
Net Worth	-41.1	38.8	39.3	37.6	54.1	21.8	17.0	27.6
Total Liabilities & Net Worth	100.0	100.0	100.0	100.0	100.0	100.0	100.0	100.0
INCOME DATA								
Net Sales	100.0	100.0	100.0	100.0	100.0	100.0	100.0	100.0
Gross Profit								
Operating Expenses	91.8	83.8	87.3	92.3	87.6	84.2	91.2	88.7
Operating Profit	8.2	16.2	12.7	7.7	12.4	15.8	8.8	11.3
All Other Expenses (net)	.6	1.8	2.1	1.9	1.2	3.0	1.7	1.5
Profit Before Taxes	7.6	14.3	10.6	5.8	11.1	12.8	7.1	9.7
RATIOS								
Current	1.8	3.4	2.9	2.2	3.0	2.9	2.5	2.3
	.9	1.5	1.5	1.5	1.3	1.8	1.4	1.4
	.1	.8	.9	1.0	1.2	1.3	.7	.8
Quick	1.7	3.2	2.7	1.9	2.6	2.0	2.0	2.1
	.7	1.4	1.4	1.4	1.1	1.3	1.2	1.1
	.1	.6	.8	.8	1.0	.8	.5	.6
Sales/Receivables	0 UND	0 UND	31 11.6	35 10.4	44 8.3	36 10.1	0 UND	0 UND
	0 UND	28 13.0	43 8.5	48 7.5	55 6.6	54 6.8	41 8.9	41 9.0
	7 52.5	52 7.1	73 5.0	73 5.0	67 5.4	61 6.0	58 6.3	62 5.9
Cost of Sales/Inventory								
Cost of Sales/Payables								
Sales/Working Capital	47.6	9.7	5.8	5.8	5.7	2.8	6.2	7.1
	-833.4	20.2	12.4	11.1	9.8	7.5	19.9	25.7
	-14.5	-32.3	-54.5	865.5	23.1	14.8	-31.2	-39.9
EBIT/Interest	17.7	35.0	35.6	13.2	121.4	23.6	12.8	19.4
	(33) 6.2	(42) 9.7	(69) 6.3	(52) 5.3	(15) 21.3	(16) 12.6	(166) 3.7	(177) 6.0
	1.6	2.3	2.2	1.6	3.4	2.5	1.0	2.1
Net Profit + Depr., Dep., Amort./Cur. Mat. L/T/D			18.5	2.5			3.5	8.8
			(14) 2.6	(16) 1.6			(31) 1.7	(32) 3.7
			-4.0	1.1			.4	1.5
Fixed/Worth	.3	.3	.3	.7	.3	.5	.4	.5
	1.2	.8	1.0	1.2	.7	1.4	1.3	1.2
	-1.4	3.7	5.2	2.7	3.6	-.3	9.7	13.5
Debt/Worth	.7	.3	.6	.8	.4	.7	.7	.7
	3.2	1.4	1.7	1.6	1.9	7.3	1.8	1.8
	-3.0	4.8	9.6	7.9	7.3	-1.7	44.9	16.9
% Profit Before Taxes/Tangible Net Worth	260.4	124.8	113.1	54.3	101.1	99.1	82.9	92.1
	(29) 94.1	(40) 62.6	(70) 44.5	(49) 24.4	(15) 31.4	(10) 32.6	(160) 25.9	(162) 36.0
	24.2	19.8	10.0	5.1	11.0	7.2	6.0	11.2
% Profit Before Taxes/Total Assets	77.6	55.1	35.5	19.4	31.6	20.7	26.5	34.5
	26.7	20.2	12.3	10.4	7.8	6.5	8.6	10.3
	6.4	2.7	2.3	2.5	5.2	2.9	.1	2.1
Sales/Net Fixed Assets	110.6	31.0	31.4	9.0	11.0	11.5	18.7	20.1
	31.2	7.2	7.3	4.4	6.2	4.1	7.0	7.2
	9.2	4.0	2.9	2.6	4.6	2.9	2.9	2.7
Sales/Total Assets	20.1	4.0	3.1	2.3	2.2	1.3	4.0	3.7
	8.1	3.0	2.1	1.8	1.4	.7	2.1	2.2
	3.0	1.7	1.2	1.2	1.0	.5	1.1	1.2
% Depr., Dep., Amort./Sales	1.0	2.3	1.4	2.9	2.8		1.9	1.5
	(31) 2.4	(31) 5.4	(69) 3.2	(57) 4.2	(15) 3.4		(159) 3.9	(174) 3.0
	4.7	12.0	7.0	6.6	4.7		7.7	6.0
% Officers', Directors' Owners' Comp/Sales	6.2	3.0	2.2				3.5	4.8
	(24) 13.8	(11) 8.2	(19) 8.9				(53) 12.6	(60) 11.2
	17.9	13.4	21.3				29.1	25.8
Net Sales ($)	122573M	160194M	888175M	2130764M	2245401M	3066451M	5361606M	6203932M
Total Assets ($)	10737M	53726M	389362M	1170794M	1323482M	3245500M	3830099M	4565051M

M = $ thousand   MM = $ million
See Pages 9 through 22 for Explanation of Ratios and Data

Comparative Historical Data

Type of Statement	4/1/07-3/31/08 ALL	4/1/08-3/31/09 ALL	4/1/09-3/31/10 ALL
Unqualified	35	50	50
Reviewed	19	16	25
Compiled	21	23	24
Tax Returns	24	40	51
Other	107	108	124
NUMBER OF STATEMENTS	206	237	274
	%	%	%
ASSETS			
Cash & Equivalents	15.8	13.4	16.7
Trade Receivables (net)	21.8	24.0	23.9
Inventory	3.0	2.8	2.2
All Other Current	3.6	5.2	3.0
Total Current	44.2	45.3	45.8
Fixed Assets (net)	40.2	38.1	36.6
Intangibles (net)	8.4	9.3	8.7
All Other Non-Current	7.1	7.2	9.0
Total	100.0	100.0	100.0
LIABILITIES			
Notes Payable-Short Term	9.0	6.9	7.3
Cur. Mat.-L.T.D.	7.4	8.0	7.7
Trade Payables	7.9	9.5	8.5
Income Taxes Payable	.5	.8	.6
All Other Current	12.6	12.9	17.5
Total Current	37.4	38.1	41.5
Long-Term Debt	31.8	25.1	26.1
Deferred Taxes	1.0	.3	.3
All Other Non-Current	8.8	3.3	8.0
Net Worth	21.0	33.2	24.0
Total Liabilities & Net Worth	100.0	100.0	100.0
INCOME DATA			
Net Sales	100.0	100.0	100.0
Gross Profit			
Operating Expenses	89.7	89.7	88.4
Operating Profit	10.3	10.3	11.6
All Other Expenses (net)	2.1	1.7	1.7
Profit Before Taxes	8.2	8.6	9.9
RATIOS			
Current	2.5	2.6	2.6
	1.6	1.4	1.5
	.8	.9	.9
Quick	2.2	2.2	2.2
	1.3	(236) 1.2	1.2
	.6	.7	.7
Sales/Receivables	5 72.5	21 17.8	13 29.1
	41 8.8	44 8.3	39 9.4
	58 6.3	59 6.2	61 6.0
Cost of Sales/Inventory			
Cost of Sales/Payables			
Sales/Working Capital	6.7	6.2	7.0
	17.3	17.5	17.6
	-35.7	-46.3	-60.9
EBIT/Interest	13.6	21.4	28.3
	(171) 4.3	(208) 5.0	(227) 6.8
	1.2	1.4	2.3
Net Profit + Depr., Dep., Amort./Cur. Mat. L/T/D	9.0	7.6	9.9
	(30) 3.7	(44) 4.2	(46) 2.4
	1.3	1.5	1.3
Fixed/Worth	.5	.5	.4
	1.2	1.1	1.1
	UND	6.6	8.2
Debt/Worth	.8	.7	.6
	1.9	2.1	1.8
	-147.7	18.2	31.2
% Profit Before Taxes/Tangible Net Worth	71.8	97.2	101.3
	(153) 28.2	(187) 36.9	(213) 39.2
	7.5	7.3	10.4
% Profit Before Taxes/Total Assets	26.4	29.9	35.5
	8.0	11.1	12.7
	.7	1.2	2.9
Sales/Net Fixed Assets	21.7	20.0	24.7
	7.5	7.1	7.5
	2.6	2.9	3.2
Sales/Total Assets	3.8	3.5	3.9
	2.1	2.0	2.2
	1.1	1.2	1.3
% Depr., Dep., Amort./Sales	1.6	1.8	1.9
	(164) 3.7	(189) 3.8	(212) 3.8
	7.8	7.8	6.3
% Officers', Directors' Owners' Comp/Sales	2.7	2.9	2.8
	(53) 11.3	(53) 8.5	(65) 8.5
	20.3	15.2	16.7
Net Sales ($)	6480955M	7977926M	8613558M
Total Assets ($)	4658427M	5707933M	6193601M

Current Data Sorted by Sales

	40 (4/1-9/30/09)			234 (10/1/09-3/31/10)		
Type of Statement	0-1MM	1-3MM	3-5MM	5-10MM	10-25MM	25MM & OVER
Unqualified		1		6	8	35
Reviewed		2	1	4	15	3
Compiled	2	8	4	3	5	2
Tax Returns	14	14	12	1	7	3
Other	15	23	10	14	27	35
NUMBER OF STATEMENTS	31	48	27	28	62	78
	%	%	%	%	%	%
ASSETS						
Cash & Equivalents	22.0	17.9	18.2	17.4	15.4	14.1
Trade Receivables (net)	12.1	16.2	22.9	27.9	34.9	23.6
Inventory	1.7	1.4	1.0	.6	3.1	3.1
All Other Current	1.5	2.2	1.5	4.0	2.7	4.4
Total Current	37.3	37.7	43.5	50.0	56.1	45.2
Fixed Assets (net)	42.0	46.1	34.2	37.8	33.2	31.6
Intangibles (net)	5.4	5.4	6.9	8.6	5.6	15.2
All Other Non-Current	15.2	10.8	15.4	3.6	5.0	8.1
Total	100.0	100.0	100.0	100.0	100.0	100.0
LIABILITIES						
Notes Payable-Short Term	25.4	6.1	4.6	8.1	4.3	3.7
Cur. Mat.-L.T.D.	4.0	14.5	8.3	10.6	6.0	4.9
Trade Payables	7.6	7.5	4.0	10.7	9.6	9.5
Income Taxes Payable	.0	.1	.4	.2	1.8	.5
All Other Current	15.5	28.9	11.0	15.9	17.9	13.7
Total Current	52.5	57.1	28.3	45.6	39.5	32.3
Long-Term Debt	41.1	34.9	31.1	16.7	15.6	24.9
Deferred Taxes	.0	.0	.0	.3	.3	.7
All Other Non-Current	31.6	2.5	3.9	1.0	6.2	7.5
Net Worth	-25.2	5.4	36.7	36.5	38.4	34.7
Total Liabilities & Net Worth	100.0	100.0	100.0	100.0	100.0	100.0
INCOME DATA						
Net Sales	100.0	100.0	100.0	100.0	100.0	100.0
Gross Profit						
Operating Expenses	88.9	88.4	84.8	87.7	88.4	89.6
Operating Profit	11.1	11.6	15.2	12.3	11.6	10.4
All Other Expenses (net)	2.5	2.2	1.3	1.7	1.4	1.6
Profit Before Taxes	8.6	9.4	13.9	10.7	10.2	8.8
RATIOS						
Current	4.6	1.7	3.1	3.2	3.1	2.2
	1.0	1.0	1.4	1.6	1.8	1.5
	.3	.3	.9	.7	1.3	1.1
Quick	4.0	1.6	3.1	3.1	2.8	1.9
	.9	.9	1.4	1.5	1.7	1.2
	.3	.3	.8	.6	.9	.9
Sales/Receivables	0 UND	0 UND	0 UND	25 14.6	33 10.9	35 10.5
	0 UND	0 UND	23 15.8	42 8.8	46 8.0	47 7.8
	43 8.5	37 9.9	75 4.8	64 5.7	74 4.9	58 6.3
Cost of Sales/Inventory						
Cost of Sales/Payables						
Sales/Working Capital	8.7	18.1	6.7	7.3	5.7	5.8
	293.0	NM	18.3	21.3	9.8	11.0
	-6.6	-16.0	-84.0	-15.5	60.5	116.0
EBIT/Interest	13.0	35.0	13.3	29.9	46.1	28.3
	(23) 4.5	(38) 6.2	(24) 7.3	(22) 3.8	(54) 6.8	(66) 11.3
	1.0	.0	2.7	.3	2.8	2.9
Net Profit + Depr., Dep., Amort./Cur. Mat. L/T/D					6.0	26.7
				(14) 2.0	(22) 2.9
					1.3	1.9
Fixed/Worth	.2	.7	.4	.4	.3	.5
	2.5	1.0	1.2	.9	.8	1.3
	-1.5	-2.1	3.1	2.7	1.9	24.5
Debt/Worth	.8	.5	.6	.4	.4	.6
	3.9	3.1	1.4	1.5	1.1	2.1
	-3.0	-4.1	3.5	8.6	4.8	364.4
% Profit Before Taxes/Tangible Net Worth	111.1	187.5	97.4	142.5	92.6	96.4
	(19) 47.0	(31) 62.0	(25) 43.4	(23) 66.3	(55) 29.8	(60) 33.1
	19.6	2.6	11.7	9.8	14.7	7.8
% Profit Before Taxes/Total Assets	41.8	58.3	33.2	55.6	35.7	24.4
	20.0	14.4	17.8	17.4	12.4	9.8
	.0	-5.5	5.7	-1.6	5.2	3.1
Sales/Net Fixed Assets	98.9	31.4	36.2	28.2	32.8	11.8
	11.2	8.5	7.1	8.1	7.6	6.8
	2.7	4.0	2.5	3.1	3.2	3.6
Sales/Total Assets	5.2	6.7	4.4	3.5	4.0	2.8
	2.2	3.2	2.4	2.3	2.3	1.7
	1.4	1.7	1.0	1.6	1.5	1.0
% Depr., Dep., Amort./Sales	3.2	1.4	4.0	2.1	1.3	2.3
	(17) 7.5	(33) 2.8	(19) 5.8	(23) 3.6	(57) 2.7	(63) 3.3
	14.2	8.6	8.1	6.4	5.9	4.9
% Officers', Directors' Owners' Comp/Sales		3.3			2.7	.9
		(14) 9.4			(19) 7.7	(10) 2.0
		20.6			21.3	24.9
Net Sales ($)	17782M	102142M	105338M	195853M	973895M	7218548M
Total Assets ($)	17906M	54336M	70721M	114550M	535934M	5400154M

M = $ thousand   MM = $ million
See Pages 9 through 22 for Explanation of Ratios and Data

HEALTH CARE—Diagnostic Imaging Centers NAICS 621512

Current Data Sorted by Assets						Type of Statement	Comparative Historical Data			
1		8	7	1	1	Unqualified		11		25
1	2	15	5			Reviewed		12		16
5	13	16	1			Compiled		24		40
11	16	11	1			Tax Returns		13		30
9	33	46	29	3	2	Other		55		85
	18 (4/1-9/30/09)		219 (10/1/09-3/31/10)					4/1/05-3/31/06 ALL		4/1/06-3/31/07 ALL
0-500M	500M-2MM	2-10MM	10-50MM	50-100MM	100-250MM	NUMBER OF STATEMENTS		115		196
27	64	96	43	4	3					
%	%	%	%	%	%	ASSETS		%		%
25.1	16.9	12.4	10.9			Cash & Equivalents		13.9		14.6
18.4	15.6	16.1	19.3			Trade Receivables (net)		15.5		17.2
.0	1.3	.5	.1			Inventory		.3		.6
4.2	2.9	3.5	4.0			All Other Current		4.1		3.6
47.6	36.7	32.5	34.3			Total Current		33.8		36.1
40.7	50.0	52.9	49.9			Fixed Assets (net)		51.5		49.6
.8	5.5	8.7	7.3			Intangibles (net)		6.6		5.6
10.8	7.8	5.9	8.4			All Other Non-Current		8.1		8.7
100.0	100.0	100.0	100.0			Total		100.0		100.0
						LIABILITIES				
42.8	6.3	5.6	6.1			Notes Payable-Short Term		4.3		6.1
9.4	16.2	12.9	9.0			Cur. Mat.-L.T.D.		11.3		10.0
17.7	6.4	5.9	3.9			Trade Payables		3.7		5.1
.9	.0	.3	.3			Income Taxes Payable		.3		.2
22.3	11.5	10.6	7.8			All Other Current		16.2		14.9
93.2	40.4	35.3	27.1			Total Current		35.7		36.4
19.6	41.7	39.0	32.5			Long-Term Debt		43.2		36.1
.0	.0	.0	.1			Deferred Taxes		.5		.1
13.4	4.6	2.9	3.9			All Other Non-Current		3.2		5.7
-26.2	13.3	22.7	36.5			Net Worth		17.4		21.7
100.0	100.0	100.0	100.0			Total Liabilties & Net Worth		100.0		100.0
						INCOME DATA				
100.0	100.0	100.0	100.0			Net Sales		100.0		100.0
						Gross Profit				
93.1	86.8	87.1	85.9			Operating Expenses		84.9		84.5
6.9	13.2	12.9	14.1			Operating Profit		15.1		15.5
1.1	3.2	2.7	1.9			All Other Expenses (net)		2.8		3.0
5.8	10.0	10.2	12.3			Profit Before Taxes		12.3		12.5
						RATIOS				
1.6	3.2	1.6	2.1					2.0		2.5
.5	.9	.8	1.2			Current		1.0		1.1
.2	.3	.5	.8					.5		.6
1.5	2.7	1.4	1.9					1.9		2.0
.5	.7	.7	1.1			Quick	(114)	.9	(195)	1.0
.2	.2	.3	.6					.5		.4
0 UND	0 UND	0 UND	20 18.4				0 UND		0 UND	
0 UND	19 19.1	29 12.7	34 10.7			Sales/Receivables	32 11.3		38 9.7	
25 14.5	42 8.6	52 7.0	49 7.4				51 7.1		57 6.4	
						Cost of Sales/Inventory				
						Cost of Sales/Payables				
19.4	7.7	16.1	8.9					10.7		9.1
-73.6	-36.2	-53.0	33.0			Sales/Working Capital		-130.7		96.5
-5.4	-4.9	-11.3	-18.8					-15.8		-14.2
10.6	12.2	17.1	19.2					13.6		17.3
(17) 2.3	(53) 2.5	(91) 5.4	(40) 8.0			EBIT/Interest	(101) 4.4		(170) 5.3	
-1.5	.7	2.1	2.6					1.5		1.2
		4.4						3.4		4.1
		(10) 2.1				Net Profit + Depr., Dep., Amort./Cur. Mat. L/T/D	(17) 1.4		(12) 3.0	
		1.0						.8		.8
.2	.7	1.2	.8					1.1		.7
2.4	3.3	2.8	1.7			Fixed/Worth		2.9		1.9
-.9	-2.6	-10.1	9.2					-8.2		NM
1.4	.7	1.4	.6					1.1		.9
5.6	4.4	3.6	1.7			Debt/Worth		3.5		2.4
-2.2	-6.6	-14.7	12.1					-11.4		-24.2
143.8	104.7	142.8	97.5			% Profit Before Taxes/Tangible Net Worth		164.5		150.2
(15) 92.0	(43) 47.7	(68) 64.0	(36) 46.3				(75) 67.7		(144) 61.0	
33.3	6.2	20.5	14.3					24.6		21.3
60.1	49.8	46.7	26.8			% Profit Before Taxes/Total Assets		40.6		41.4
24.8	8.4	15.7	17.8					15.7		16.2
-12.4	-1.0	3.0	5.5					3.4		1.0
89.3	13.0	9.6	7.3					9.3		9.5
14.7	5.0	4.4	3.9			Sales/Net Fixed Assets		3.9		4.1
6.0	2.0	2.1	2.4					2.1		2.0
8.0	4.0	3.2	2.9					3.7		3.7
5.3	2.5	1.8	1.8			Sales/Total Assets		2.0		2.0
2.5	1.4	1.0	1.4					1.1		1.1
.6	3.0	3.9	5.2					3.5		3.6
(20) 3.9	(53) 6.4	(90) 8.5	(37) 6.8			% Depr., Dep., Amort./Sales	(94) 6.8		(167) 7.7	
10.7	13.3	13.1	10.4					13.9		12.8
	4.7	4.3	13.7					3.5		4.8
	(10) 9.4	(27) 11.8	(12) 18.8			% Officers', Directors' Owners' Comp/Sales	(26) 19.0		(47) 9.8	
	30.8	20.1	25.2					32.6		20.5
56415M	228671M	1198693M	1584605M	489830M	515232M	Net Sales ($)		3972185M		3352071M
7157M	73313M	444894M	767990M	303288M	553675M	Total Assets ($)		1686248M		2215494M

M = $ thousand   MM = $ million
See Pages 9 through 22 for Explanation of Ratios and Data

Comparative Historical Data | Current Data Sorted by Sales

4/1/07-3/31/08 ALL	4/1/08-3/31/09 ALL	4/1/09-3/31/10 ALL	Type of Statement	0-1MM	1-3MM	3-5MM	5-10MM	10-25MM	25MM & OVER
16	19	18	Unqualified	1	1		6	1	9
26	29	23	Reviewed		2	2	6	9	4
25	33	35	Compiled	5	9	5	8	4	4
31	36	39	Tax Returns	7	13	10	3	6	
107	113	122	Other	13	24	12	20	27	26
				18 (4/1-9/30/09)			219 (10/1/09-3/31/10)		
205	230	237	NUMBER OF STATEMENTS	26	49	29	43	47	43
%	%	%	ASSETS	%	%	%	%	%	%
12.4	13.2	14.9	Cash & Equivalents	15.3	14.1	14.9	18.8	12.7	14.2
17.7	14.2	16.8	Trade Receivables (net)	13.3	15.8	13.0	24.2	15.8	16.2
.4	.3	.6	Inventory	.0	1.5	.1	1.0	.1	.2
4.3	4.0	3.6	All Other Current	2.3	3.5	3.8	3.1	3.6	4.6
34.8	31.7	35.8	Total Current	31.0	34.9	31.8	47.1	32.2	35.1
49.6	54.6	49.8	Fixed Assets (net)	52.7	53.5	53.3	40.0	51.6	49.1
6.8	6.5	7.1	Intangibles (net)	7.7	3.4	10.1	6.0	8.4	8.5
8.8	7.1	7.3	All Other Non-Current	8.7	8.1	4.8	7.0	7.8	7.2
100.0	100.0	100.0	Total	100.0	100.0	100.0	100.0	100.0	100.0
			LIABILITIES						
7.8	7.5	9.9	Notes Payable-Short Term	23.0	6.9	25.0	2.8	3.2	9.9
10.7	12.6	12.5	Cur. Mat.-L.T.D.	13.7	15.7	12.9	11.7	12.1	8.9
5.3	5.8	7.0	Trade Payables	17.9	4.5	5.5	10.7	3.5	4.5
.4	.2	.3	Income Taxes Payable	1.0	.0	.0	.2	.2	.8
13.2	10.8	11.7	All Other Current	8.1	15.0	12.0	6.1	10.3	17.1
37.4	36.9	41.5	Total Current	63.6	42.2	55.4	31.5	29.3	41.2
36.5	44.7	36.5	Long-Term Debt	38.9	42.3	45.0	32.6	28.4	35.4
.1	.0	.1	Deferred Taxes	.0	.0	.0	.0	.1	.3
6.2	5.9	4.7	All Other Non-Current	2.8	6.3	8.8	2.2	3.2	5.6
19.8	12.5	17.2	Net Worth	-5.3	9.1	-9.3	33.7	38.9	17.6
100.0	100.0	100.0	Total Liabilities & Net Worth	100.0	100.0	100.0	100.0	100.0	100.0
			INCOME DATA						
100.0	100.0	100.0	Net Sales	100.0	100.0	100.0	100.0	100.0	100.0
			Gross Profit						
86.6	85.7	87.6	Operating Expenses	90.7	92.2	84.5	82.3	85.8	90.1
13.4	14.3	12.4	Operating Profit	9.3	7.8	15.5	17.7	14.2	9.9
2.6	3.5	2.5	All Other Expenses (net)	7.5	3.4	2.9	1.1	1.0	1.1
10.7	10.8	9.9	Profit Before Taxes	1.9	4.4	12.6	16.6	13.1	8.8
			RATIOS						
2.1	1.8	1.9	Current	1.2	3.0	1.5	3.3	1.9	1.6
1.0	.9	1.0		.4	.8	.5	1.4	1.1	1.0
.6	.4	.4		.3	.3	.2	.8	.8	.5
1.9	1.6	1.8	Quick	1.2	2.5	1.5	2.8	1.8	1.4
.9	(229) .8	.8		.4	.5	.5	1.2	1.0	.9
.4	.3	.3		.2	.2	.2	.7	.6	.3
0 UND	0 UND	0 UND	Sales/Receivables	0 UND	0 UND	0 UND	18 20.4	0 UND	0 UND
37 9.7	26 14.0	26 14.0		22 16.4	19 19.0	16 23.2	35 10.5	26 14.1	26 14.0
55 6.6	47 7.8	46 7.9		46 8.0	49 7.4	58 6.3	59 6.2	41 8.9	39 9.3
			Cost of Sales/Inventory						
			Cost of Sales/Payables						
9.7	12.8	12.2	Sales/Working Capital	18.7	7.0	13.8	6.6	18.2	14.7
999.8	-70.7	-327.6		-4.2	-26.4	-19.7	33.9	68.1	-732.4
-12.0	-10.8	-10.6		-2.3	-4.8	-6.1	-43.5	-24.6	-13.9
14.0	12.4	14.7	EBIT/Interest	2.4	7.4	14.9	17.9	26.8	12.9
(174) 4.1	(196) 4.1	(208) 4.6		(17) 1.1	(41) 2.3	(26) 5.0	(40) 7.3	(44) 11.7	(40) 4.8
1.0	.9	1.2		.0	-1.8	1.1	3.5	2.6	2.1
2.5	3.1	3.2	Net Profit + Depr., Dep., Amort./Cur. Mat. L/T/D						
(14) 1.4	(17) 1.2	(15) 2.0							
.5	.8	1.0							
.9	1.1	1.0	Fixed/Worth	1.2	.8	1.6	.4	1.0	1.7
2.5	3.7	2.6		5.4	2.9	-4.9	1.4	1.5	3.4
-15.0	-5.0	-6.8		-6.3	-1.8	-.9	4.8	4.2	-6.2
1.1	1.3	1.1	Debt/Worth	2.6	.7	1.7	1.1	.8	1.7
3.1	5.8	3.7		8.9	4.6	-6.5	2.4		4.2
-32.3	-9.6	-8.6		-2.5	-4.2	-2.2	5.8	17.4	-11.4
118.7	132.9	115.2	% Profit Before Taxes/Tangible Net Worth	84.4	95.1	175.0	161.7	137.2	115.6
(149) 46.5	(156) 60.0	(166) 53.9		(17) 8.7	(32) 54.7	(12) 64.0	(35) 49.9	(40) 68.6	(30) 37.1
9.4	8.1	15.6		-25.1	7.9	33.2	19.3	26.8	11.8
40.4	33.2	42.2	% Profit Before Taxes/Total Assets	4.1	39.8	87.3	52.3	43.5	26.8
10.8	11.0	14.0		1.0	9.3	12.3	22.4	19.6	18.9
-.2	-1.5	1.6		-8.2	-8.4	3.6	6.5	6.4	2.9
9.8	8.3	10.8	Sales/Net Fixed Assets	17.8	8.8	10.6	15.1	9.9	13.1
4.2	3.6	4.6		1.5	4.7	4.7	5.6	4.5	5.8
2.2	1.8	2.3		.6	1.6	2.7	2.5	2.8	3.6
3.5	3.7	3.7	Sales/Total Assets	1.8	3.7	4.5	3.8	3.8	5.0
1.9	1.9	2.0		.7	1.8	2.1	2.0	2.1	2.8
1.1	1.1	1.2		.3	1.0	1.2	1.3	1.5	1.8
4.4	4.7	3.8	% Depr., Dep., Amort./Sales	16.4	2.6	3.0	3.8	4.7	2.0
(174) 8.1	(191) 8.4	(202) 6.9		(19) 28.0	(44) 6.2	(26) 6.1	(36) 7.4	(43) 7.5	(34) 5.7
13.6	14.5	12.5		46.5	17.4	12.6	12.4	10.3	6.9
4.3	7.1	5.0	% Officers', Directors' Owners' Comp/Sales	6.0				4.9	7.8
(45) 10.9	(58) 13.6	(56) 13.7		(11) 13.4				(15) 10.2	(12) 19.4
25.8	23.5	23.5		18.7				20.1	25.8
3381016M	3659940M	4073446M	Net Sales ($)	13527M	95260M	110400M	303008M	722475M	2828776M
1886849M	2198651M	2150317M	Total Assets ($)	33544M	71067M	68483M	174927M	362524M	1439772M

M = $ thousand   MM = $ million
See Pages 9 through 22 for Explanation of Ratios and Data

Current Data Sorted by Assets

Comparative Historical Data

0-500M	500M-2MM	2-10MM	10-50MM	50-100MM	100-250MM	Type of Statement	4/1/05-3/31/06 ALL	4/1/06-3/31/07 ALL
4	12	45	48	13	6	Unqualified	79	108
1	7	21	6	1		Reviewed	22	25
9	21	7	3			Compiled	35	32
50	22	11				Tax Returns	38	58
41	57	76	29	7	6	Other	116	137
	91 (4/1-9/30/09)		412 (10/1/09-3/31/10)					
105	119	160	86	21	12	NUMBER OF STATEMENTS	290	360
%	%	%	%	%	%	**ASSETS**	%	%
33.2	16.2	19.0	22.1	12.3	14.8	Cash & Equivalents	18.0	20.1
25.7	44.8	38.1	26.4	22.6	17.8	Trade Receivables (net)	36.7	34.8
.4	1.6	1.5	.7	1.4	.9	Inventory	2.0	1.4
4.1	3.2	3.6	2.7	2.9	3.4	All Other Current	4.2	3.9
63.4	65.8	62.2	52.0	39.2	37.0	Total Current	61.0	60.3
14.8	15.3	23.0	24.2	10.6	13.3	Fixed Assets (net)	20.5	23.5
5.8	7.2	5.2	8.9	46.1	46.2	Intangibles (net)	4.8	4.9
15.9	11.7	9.7	14.9	4.2	3.5	All Other Non-Current	13.7	11.4
100.0	100.0	100.0	100.0	100.0	100.0	Total	100.0	100.0
						LIABILITIES		
19.7	12.1	6.7	5.0	1.9	.0	Notes Payable-Short Term	10.1	9.6
3.6	2.7	2.3	3.1	6.0	1.9	Cur. Mat.-L.T.D.	2.5	2.7
9.0	9.6	9.0	6.6	7.9	4.7	Trade Payables	8.8	8.2
.0	.6	.3	.2	.2	.0	Income Taxes Payable	.2	.2
35.0	19.5	19.8	12.6	12.8	10.6	All Other Current	21.2	20.1
67.4	44.4	38.0	27.5	28.8	17.3	Total Current	42.6	40.7
10.8	13.0	13.6	14.8	19.8	28.9	Long-Term Debt	16.4	15.1
.0	1.7	.2	.3	2.8	2.9	Deferred Taxes	.1	.1
13.0	6.4	4.3	2.6	11.8	3.1	All Other Non-Current	7.0	6.7
8.9	34.5	43.9	54.8	36.9	47.8	Net Worth	33.8	37.5
100.0	100.0	100.0	100.0	100.0	100.0	Total Liabilities & Net Worth	100.0	100.0
						INCOME DATA		
100.0	100.0	100.0	100.0	100.0	100.0	Net Sales	100.0	100.0
						Gross Profit		
92.8	94.0	93.7	93.3	87.4	89.6	Operating Expenses	94.1	93.8
7.2	6.0	6.3	6.7	12.6	10.4	Operating Profit	5.9	6.2
.6	.8	1.2	.6	2.1	6.3	All Other Expenses (net)	.9	.4
6.6	5.2	5.1	6.1	10.5	4.0	Profit Before Taxes	5.1	5.7
						RATIOS		
3.1	3.5	3.3	4.3	2.2	2.7		3.5	3.6
1.3	1.9	1.9	2.0	1.2	2.2	Current	1.8	1.8
.6	1.0	1.2	1.2	1.0	1.5		1.1	1.1
3.1	3.5	3.3	3.7	1.8	2.3		3.3	3.3
1.2	1.7	1.8	1.9	1.0	1.7	Quick	1.6	1.7
.5	.9	1.0	1.1	.8	1.2		.9	.9
0 UND	20 18.3	31 11.6	32 11.3	39 9.4	21 17.2		20 17.8	23 15.7
0 UND	37 9.9	45 8.2	40 9.2	53 6.9	44 8.3	Sales/Receivables	46 8.0	44 8.3
29 12.7	61 6.0	60 6.1	53 6.9	68 5.4	62 5.9		67 5.4	62 5.9
						Cost of Sales/Inventory		
						Cost of Sales/Payables		
17.2	7.5	5.8	3.9	7.3	5.0		5.3	6.0
78.3	17.6	9.9	8.3	31.6	8.7	Sales/Working Capital	13.3	12.3
-43.6	-285.5	37.4	46.8	NM	15.0		72.2	103.6
31.3	36.1	26.9	18.2	20.5			33.0	21.0
(58) 7.6	(89) 7.3	(120) 7.1	(65) 7.7	6.5		EBIT/Interest	(211) 9.7	(261) 5.7
1.3	1.1	2.0	.8	2.8			1.4	1.3
		36.5		3.5		Net Profit + Depr., Dep.,	8.5	14.1
		(12) 3.1		(10) 1.9		Amort./Cur. Mat. L/T/D	(28) 3.0	(19) 4.8
		1.6		1.5			1.0	1.2
.0	.1	.1	.1	1.0	.3		.1	.1
.2	.3	.4	.6	-.2	-1.3	Fixed/Worth	.3	.4
27.1	1.9	1.4	1.4	-.1	-.1		1.8	1.9
.6	.4	.4	.3	1.5	.9		.4	.4
3.0	1.6	1.1	.8	-3.3	-5.4	Debt/Worth	1.2	1.1
-21.5	16.8	3.5	3.0	-1.8	-2.0		7.7	6.4
418.7	95.3	59.5	28.2			% Profit Before Taxes/Tangible	71.1	76.2
(76) 93.3	(93) 46.5	(143) 21.5	(73) 12.1			Net Worth	(238) 23.1	(301) 27.2
17.6	14.2	3.5	.2				5.5	5.7
84.1	37.0	28.7	15.8	17.1	9.0	% Profit Before Taxes/Total	25.3	28.6
27.4	17.1	9.6	8.6	13.2	2.7	Assets	10.2	9.9
2.6	2.5	2.0	2.0	5.2	-3.6		1.1	1.4
UND	159.4	95.3	69.2	65.3	67.7		129.6	132.8
155.0	77.0	25.0	11.9	22.9	25.8	Sales/Net Fixed Assets	31.1	28.5
44.6	21.9	5.8	3.7	13.2	9.1		8.0	5.8
15.4	6.0	4.0	2.5	2.0	1.6		4.8	5.0
7.3	4.4	2.7	1.6	1.5	1.0	Sales/Total Assets	2.7	2.9
5.3	2.7	1.9	1.2	.9	.9		1.6	1.5
.3	.3	.5	.9	.6			.5	.5
(38) .6	(85) .5	(128) 1.2	(76) 1.4	(17) 1.4		% Depr., Dep., Amort./Sales	(225) 1.2	(262) 1.2
1.4	1.1	2.7	2.4	2.2			2.4	2.7
3.7	2.3	1.7					2.6	2.8
(43) 5.6	(36) 5.0	(32) 3.8				% Officers', Directors' Owners' Comp/Sales	(63) 4.8	(83) 6.8
13.2	7.8	12.7					10.7	13.0
245388M	606304M	2381153M	3469973M	2322340M	3558548M	Net Sales ($)	7435831M	13854009M
26504M	137641M	802660M	1903696M	1394829M	2107595M	Total Assets ($)	3066438M	4055659M

M = $ thousand   MM = $ million

See Pages 9 through 22 for Explanation of Ratios and Data

Comparative Historical Data   Current Data Sorted by Sales

4/1/07-3/31/08 ALL	4/1/08-3/31/09 ALL	4/1/09-3/31/10 ALL		0-1MM	1-3MM	3-5MM	5-10MM	10-25MM	25MM & OVER
			Type of Statement		91 (4/1-9/30/09)		412 (10/1/09-3/31/10)		
99	123	128	Unqualified	2	6	8	17	38	57
21	31	36	Reviewed	1	1	3	10	10	11
24	35	40	Compiled	6	7	5	15	5	2
85	85	83	Tax Returns	12	32	15	17	6	1
161	182	216	Other	11	40	34	42	38	51
390	456	503	**NUMBER OF STATEMENTS**	32	86	65	101	97	122
%	%	%	**ASSETS**	%	%	%	%	%	%
19.9	18.8	21.5	Cash & Equivalents	31.2	22.4	21.9	19.1	21.0	20.3
35.7	35.9	34.0	Trade Receivables (net)	25.6	30.0	35.4	35.8	38.6	33.1
1.5	1.3	1.1	Inventory	.1	1.7	1.1	.7	1.9	.8
4.9	4.5	3.4	All Other Current	2.1	4.8	2.2	3.6	2.6	3.9
61.9	60.5	60.0	Total Current	58.9	59.0	60.5	59.3	64.1	58.1
19.9	21.1	18.9	Fixed Assets (net)	22.8	20.9	15.8	21.6	18.0	16.7
6.5	7.4	9.1	Intangibles (net)	8.5	8.8	7.5	5.3	5.4	16.6
11.7	11.0	12.0	All Other Non-Current	9.8	11.4	16.3	13.9	12.6	8.6
100.0	100.0	100.0	Total	100.0	100.0	100.0	100.0	100.0	100.0
			LIABILITIES						
10.2	11.0	10.0	Notes Payable-Short Term	5.7	16.7	16.1	11.4	6.8	4.7
2.8	3.7	2.9	Cur. Mat.-L.T.D.	1.8	4.7	2.5	2.0	1.9	3.8
7.3	8.4	8.6	Trade Payables	4.3	10.2	9.3	5.7	11.2	8.4
.4	.4	.3	Income Taxes Payable	.0	.0	.0	.5	.5	.3
18.0	18.1	21.2	All Other Current	38.3	26.9	18.9	22.2	15.3	17.6
38.7	41.6	43.0	Total Current	50.2	58.5	46.8	41.7	35.8	34.8
15.4	15.9	13.7	Long-Term Debt	21.6	15.3	15.5	11.1	12.1	12.9
.1	.2	.7	Deferred Taxes	.0	.0	.1	.2	2.2	1.0
7.6	9.8	6.6	All Other Non-Current	23.2	9.7	4.0	4.0	3.6	6.0
38.1	32.5	36.0	Net Worth	5.0	16.4	33.6	43.0	46.2	45.3
100.0	100.0	100.0	Total Liabilties & Net Worth	100.0	100.0	100.0	100.0	100.0	100.0
			INCOME DATA						
100.0	100.0	100.0	Net Sales	100.0	100.0	100.0	100.0	100.0	100.0
			Gross Profit						
93.0	93.3	93.2	Operating Expenses	87.4	94.9	92.0	94.4	93.1	93.1
7.0	6.7	6.8	Operating Profit	12.6	5.1	8.0	5.6	6.9	6.9
.6	1.6	1.0	All Other Expenses (net)	2.6	1.1	1.0	1.4	.4	.7
6.4	5.1	5.8	Profit Before Taxes	10.0	4.0	7.0	4.2	6.5	6.2
			RATIOS						
3.5	3.5	3.3		4.8	3.4	3.3	3.5	3.5	2.9
1.8	1.9	1.8	Current	1.3	1.4	1.9	1.5	2.0	1.8
1.1	1.1	1.0		.8	.6	.9	.9	1.3	1.2
3.3	3.2	3.1		4.8	3.4	3.1	3.5	3.3	2.7
1.6	1.7	1.6	Quick	1.2	1.3	1.7	1.5	2.0	1.6
.9	.9	.9		.6	.5	.7	.9	1.2	1.0
21 17.5	24 15.5	19 18.9		0 UND	0 UND	0 UND	15 24.3	32 11.4	32 11.4
43 8.4	44 8.2	38 9.5	Sales/Receivables	0 UND	24 15.3	32 11.3	36 10.0	46 8.0	43 8.5
61 6.0	64 5.7	56 6.5		45 8.1	49 7.5	58 6.3	55 6.6	57 6.4	58 6.3
			Cost of Sales/Inventory						
			Cost of Sales/Payables						
6.2	5.7	6.3		9.2	7.9	7.2	7.7	5.0	5.4
12.7	12.6	15.4	Sales/Working Capital	98.9	31.5	20.1	21.8	10.1	10.8
104.2	89.8	-999.8		-26.2	-35.8	-99.1	-156.9	26.8	42.4
23.7	26.6	26.7		9.6	17.6	12.6	36.6	37.3	25.8
(289) 7.2	(331) 7.8	(362) 7.1	EBIT/Interest	(12) 4.1	(55) 3.1	(45) 3.8	(82) 8.2	(69) 8.7	(99) 8.4
1.8	1.3	1.7		1.7	-.9	1.5	.7	1.9	3.1
16.8	6.7	23.0							7.8
(28) 3.8	(35) 2.4	(39) 3.7	Net Profit + Depr., Dep., Amort./Cur. Mat. L/T/D					(21) 2.6	
1.7	1.1	1.8							1.7
.1	.1	.1		.0	.1	.1	.1	.1	.1
.4	.4	.4	Fixed/Worth	.1	.6	.2	.4	.3	.6
1.4	2.0	2.7		40.9	-3.5	2.4	1.5	.9	-14.9
.5	.5	.4		.5	.6	.4	.4	.4	.4
1.3	1.2	1.4	Debt/Worth	3.7	2.2	1.6	1.2	1.0	1.3
6.1	11.7	12.8		-18.7	-9.2	8.3	6.1	2.6	-86.8
84.3	75.5	91.7		146.1	105.4	122.9	112.9	55.3	84.3
(327) 28.5	(363) 25.4	(398) 29.7	% Profit Before Taxes/Tangible Net Worth	(22) 70.6	(59) 36.9	(53) 38.1	(87) 37.8	(86) 17.8	(91) 24.7
6.6	3.2	5.9		21.5	.4	6.1	.6	7.5	5.7
33.3	30.5	33.6		65.6	42.8	35.2	40.5	27.4	24.6
11.5	9.5	11.4	% Profit Before Taxes/Total Assets	17.2	9.9	12.2	11.1	11.1	11.9
2.4	.5	2.2		2.6	.2	2.3	-.8	2.9	4.0
155.6	139.6	159.4		UND	171.1	392.4	160.7	131.8	85.2
37.5	35.6	44.3	Sales/Net Fixed Assets	263.0	52.2	91.9	50.6	35.0	24.6
9.4	7.4	11.2		10.2	14.5	18.6	9.9	8.6	7.3
5.0	4.7	5.5		7.0	7.0	7.6	6.5	4.5	3.9
3.2	3.0	3.2	Sales/Total Assets	3.5	4.9	4.0	3.7	2.7	2.2
1.7	1.6	1.7		1.2	2.3	2.5	2.3	1.6	1.4
.4	.4	.4			.3	.3	.3	.4	.7
(282) 1.0	(337) 1.0	(350) 1.0	% Depr., Dep., Amort./Sales		(48) 1.0	(38) .6	(79) .7	(78) 1.0	(99) 1.2
2.2	2.2	2.2			2.7	1.8	1.6	2.2	2.1
3.1	2.3	2.3			3.6	3.7	2.2	1.4	.7
(100) 5.2	(108) 5.7	(125) 5.0	% Officers', Directors' Owners' Comp/Sales		(28) 5.0	(24) 5.6	(31) 4.2	(18) 3.0	(16) 2.1
8.9	10.2	10.2			13.4	10.3	7.4	6.1	8.4
8583959M	12201616M	12583706M	Net Sales ($)	18745M	171017M	250800M	719918M	1530822M	9892404M
4186073M	6648118M	6372925M	Total Assets ($)	19351M	72019M	95876M	295722M	882259M	5007698M

Current Data Sorted by Assets   Comparative Historical Data

	0-500M	500M-2MM	2-10MM	10-50MM	50-100MM	100-250MM	Type of Statement	4/1/05-3/31/06 ALL	4/1/06-3/31/07 ALL
		2	6	9		3	Unqualified	8	16
			6	5			Reviewed	7	9
	3	3	4	2	1		Compiled	7	12
	5	11	6	13	1	1	Tax Returns	4	10
	1	10	13			4	Other	14	18
		17 (4/1-9/30/09)		92 (10/1/09-3/31/10)					
NUMBER OF STATEMENTS	9	26	35	29	2	8		40	65
	%	%	%	%	%	%	**ASSETS**	%	%
		13.6	19.1	7.1			Cash & Equivalents	17.3	16.4
		19.8	27.1	38.2			Trade Receivables (net)	35.4	26.9
		.5	1.3	.7			Inventory	1.1	1.8
		5.7	6.3	5.9			All Other Current	2.1	4.0
		39.5	53.9	51.9			Total Current	55.9	49.2
		51.6	36.3	30.4			Fixed Assets (net)	36.5	42.1
		2.7	2.5	10.2			Intangibles (net)	4.2	3.0
		6.2	7.3	7.4			All Other Non-Current	3.5	5.7
		100.0	100.0	100.0			Total	100.0	100.0
							LIABILITIES		
		7.9	8.0	9.6			Notes Payable-Short Term	5.4	9.4
		8.5	5.2	4.3			Cur. Mat.-L.T.D.	5.5	6.0
		2.9	5.1	5.2			Trade Payables	5.6	4.9
		.0	.4	1.2			Income Taxes Payable	.6	.6
		5.1	9.7	9.6			All Other Current	5.9	9.0
		24.4	28.4	29.9			Total Current	23.1	29.9
		45.3	21.1	22.9			Long-Term Debt	17.3	34.9
		.0	1.1	.4			Deferred Taxes	1.0	.7
		4.4	3.1	5.5			All Other Non-Current	2.1	3.1
		25.9	46.4	41.3			Net Worth	56.5	31.3
		100.0	100.0	100.0			Total Liabilities & Net Worth	100.0	100.0
							INCOME DATA		
		100.0	100.0	100.0			Net Sales	100.0	100.0
							Gross Profit		
		91.3	91.8	89.5			Operating Expenses	93.3	90.2
		8.7	8.2	10.5			Operating Profit	6.7	9.8
		2.8	.6	.8			All Other Expenses (net)	1.7	1.1
		5.9	7.6	9.7			Profit Before Taxes	5.0	8.7
							RATIOS		
		18.3	3.8	3.1			Current	5.0	3.7
		2.0	2.3	1.6				2.6	1.9
		.6	1.0	1.1				1.7	1.0
		18.1	3.7	2.4			Quick	4.9	3.5
		1.4	2.2	1.4				2.5	1.6
		.6	.9	.9				1.6	.8
		0 UND	16 22.7	48 7.6			Sales/Receivables	33 11.1	0 UND
		0 UND	38 9.7	68 5.4				56 6.6	45 8.1
		36 10.0	57 6.4	93 3.9				72 5.1	78 4.7
							Cost of Sales/Inventory		
							Cost of Sales/Payables		
		6.7	5.7	4.8			Sales/Working Capital	4.2	5.2
		17.3	9.9	7.3				7.6	10.2
		-24.2	118.3	41.0				23.8	-999.8
		23.6	25.7	8.3			EBIT/Interest	16.1	16.4
		(23) 3.8	(31) 9.4	(23) 4.8				(36) 7.1	(56) 5.1
		2.1	3.0	2.8				2.3	1.6
				4.6			Net Profit + Depr., Dep., Amort./Cur. Mat. L/T/D		6.3
				(13) 2.6					(14) 3.3
				1.6					1.2
		.7	.4	.4			Fixed/Worth	.3	.4
		1.7	.9	1.0				.7	1.0
		NM	2.0	2.7				1.2	3.0
		.3	.3	.4			Debt/Worth	.3	.4
		2.1	1.2	1.7				.7	1.1
		NM	3.5	5.7				1.8	4.9
		82.5	87.9	57.4			% Profit Before Taxes/Tangible Net Worth	41.4	49.9
		(20) 44.9	(31) 41.7	(24) 27.2				(37) 15.4	(57) 19.9
		4.5	22.3	9.6				3.5	10.8
		29.3	34.8	15.5			% Profit Before Taxes/Total Assets	21.1	22.0
		10.7	17.3	11.2				8.3	8.9
		3.1	7.2	3.7				2.5	1.9
		11.9	12.7	13.8			Sales/Net Fixed Assets	18.1	11.7
		6.4	7.1	9.1				8.5	6.0
		2.5	5.0	3.2				4.1	3.7
		4.2	3.6	2.4			Sales/Total Assets	3.5	3.5
		2.6	2.5	1.8				2.4	2.2
		1.7	2.0	1.2				1.6	1.5
		2.4	2.1	1.7			% Depr., Dep., Amort./Sales	2.3	2.6
		(22) 4.9	(31) 3.6	(26) 2.8				(34) 3.9	(60) 3.9
		10.0	4.9	4.7				6.8	6.6
		3.3	1.0				% Officers', Directors' Owners' Comp/Sales	3.1	1.6
		(10) 4.1	(15) 1.9					(11) 4.1	(23) 3.8
		6.4	7.8					6.6	4.9
	20917M	95404M	469793M	1151679M	226034M	5928697M	Net Sales ($)	681344M	1079583M
	2921M	29641M	162963M	695864M	121351M	1330996M	Total Assets ($)	394122M	574222M

M = $ thousand   MM = $ million

See Pages 9 through 22 for Explanation of Ratios and Data

Comparative Historical Data   Current Data Sorted by Sales

Type of Statement

4/1/07-3/31/08 ALL	4/1/08-3/31/09 ALL	4/1/09-3/31/10 ALL	Type of Statement	0-1MM	1-3MM	3-5MM	5-10MM	10-25MM	25MM & OVER
14	21	20	Unqualified		2		2	6	10
9	17	11	Reviewed				1	4	6
10	11	13	Compiled	1	4	2	1	3	2
9	12	24	Tax Returns	4	5	6	6	1	2
30	35	41	Other	1	5	4	6	9	16

17 (4/1-9/30/09)   92 (10/1/09-3/31/10)

Data

4/1/07-3/31/08	4/1/08-3/31/09	4/1/09-3/31/10	Item	0-1MM	1-3MM	3-5MM	5-10MM	10-25MM	25MM & OVER
72	96	109	NUMBER OF STATEMENTS	6	16	12	16	23	36
%	%	%	ASSETS	%	%	%	%	%	%
18.7	15.6	16.1	Cash & Equivalents		13.4	25.7	14.2	17.6	13.7
29.3	31.7	26.3	Trade Receivables (net)		20.8	12.6	25.6	33.3	31.7
1.0	1.3	.8	Inventory		1.6	.2	.9	.8	.8
3.3	2.3	5.3	All Other Current		2.0	4.4	10.0	8.7	3.6
52.3	50.9	48.5	Total Current		37.8	43.0	50.7	60.3	49.8
35.9	36.6	37.9	Fixed Assets (net)		53.1	45.9	38.0	27.1	30.2
4.5	3.4	6.8	Intangibles (net)		2.6	9.1	1.7	4.0	13.1
7.4	9.1	6.8	All Other Non-Current		6.4	2.1	9.6	8.5	6.9
100.0	100.0	100.0	Total		100.0	100.0	100.0	100.0	100.0
			LIABILITIES						
8.7	10.7	9.6	Notes Payable-Short Term		20.6	9.6	7.8	5.1	8.2
5.7	8.2	5.8	Cur. Mat.-L.T.D.		4.5	7.1	9.5	5.1	4.8
4.3	5.8	4.5	Trade Payables		3.3	1.2	6.3	4.7	5.6
.4	.2	.5	Income Taxes Payable		.0	.4	.2	.4	.9
7.1	13.8	11.3	All Other Current		7.4	6.4	10.8	9.7	17.6
26.2	38.7	31.5	Total Current		35.9	24.8	34.6	25.0	37.1
29.0	22.7	28.3	Long-Term Debt		46.0	32.0	23.7	20.6	24.3
.0	.4	.6	Deferred Taxes		.0	.0	.6	1.2	.9
5.1	3.9	4.3	All Other Non-Current		2.0	.8	4.7	5.0	6.2
39.7	34.3	35.3	Net Worth		16.2	42.4	36.3	48.1	31.5
100.0	100.0	100.0	Total Liabilities & Net Worth		100.0	100.0	100.0	100.0	100.0
			INCOME DATA						
100.0	100.0	100.0	Net Sales		100.0	100.0	100.0	100.0	100.0
			Gross Profit						
91.7	94.0	91.2	Operating Expenses		95.7	89.9	94.7	88.6	92.8
8.3	6.0	8.8	Operating Profit		4.3	10.1	5.3	11.4	7.2
2.2	1.4	1.6	All Other Expenses (net)		2.2	1.2	.3	.6	1.5
6.1	4.6	7.3	Profit Before Taxes		2.1	8.9	5.0	10.7	5.8
			RATIOS						
3.8	3.4	3.8	Current		2.1	59.9	3.7	5.0	2.5
2.2	1.6	1.7			1.4	3.8	1.7	2.9	1.3
1.4	.9	.9			.8	.5	.7	1.1	1.1
3.4	3.3	3.3	Quick		2.0	59.4	3.6	4.1	2.3
2.1	1.5	1.4			1.3	1.7	1.0	2.2	1.2
1.3	.7	.8			.7	.5	.5	1.0	.8
21 17.1	26 14.0	0 UND	Sales/Receivables		0 UND	0 UND	0 UND	16 22.7	48 7.6
51 7.2	50 7.3	41 8.9			28 13.2	0 UND	26 14.1	38 9.7	61 6.0
78 4.7	81 4.5	66 5.5			59 6.2	40 9.1	55 6.7	68 5.4	88 4.1
			Cost of Sales/Inventory						
			Cost of Sales/Payables						
3.9	5.4	5.8	Sales/Working Capital		9.2	3.3	7.5	4.6	6.0
8.4	11.8	16.0			42.1	9.4	15.4	8.2	18.6
32.1	-46.5	-65.7			-31.4	-33.0	-268.2	102.1	86.3
14.1	13.9	17.0	EBIT/Interest		8.3		30.2	27.2	15.3
(63) 5.5	(84) 3.6	(93) 5.6			(14) 2.4		7.0	(19) 11.5	(30) 5.6
1.2	1.2	2.9			-2.8		2.3	3.4	3.3
5.0	4.4	4.7	Net Profit + Depr., Dep., Amort./Cur. Mat. L/T/D						5.1
(11) 2.5	(16) 2.8	(24) 2.8						(15)	3.4
1.8	2.0	1.9							1.8
.4	.4	.5	Fixed/Worth		.7	.5	.5	.2	.5
.8	1.0	1.1			2.0	.7	1.2	.7	1.3
2.7	2.5	5.1			18.7	NM	NM	2.1	3.2
.5	.6	.4	Debt/Worth		.4	.3	.4	.3	1.0
1.2	1.4	1.9			2.1	.6	1.4	1.2	3.3
4.2	5.7	7.7			23.8	NM	NM	3.5	8.2
50.3	58.3	68.6	% Profit Before Taxes/Tangible Net Worth		82.5		81.8	90.9	60.1
(61) 26.8	(79) 21.9	(87) 33.8			(13) 18.9	(12) 42.1	(20) 48.4	(28) 32.1	
7.7	4.3	9.4			-6.3		19.4	17.5	16.2
22.2	16.4	27.0	% Profit Before Taxes/Total Assets		15.9	44.4	36.7	44.9	17.0
9.9	8.8	11.5			3.9	10.7	15.2	20.2	11.2
1.1	.8	3.2			-11.6	1.7	6.0	10.7	3.5
14.8	16.7	13.8	Sales/Net Fixed Assets		15.6	14.3	16.1	29.8	12.4
6.8	7.2	7.3			3.0	8.2	6.3	12.6	7.4
3.7	4.0	4.3			2.0	5.4	4.9	7.1	3.4
2.9	4.0	3.5	Sales/Total Assets		3.7	7.8	5.6	5.0	2.6
2.0	2.4	2.2			1.9	3.6	2.6	2.8	1.9
1.4	1.3	1.6			1.6	1.8	2.2	1.6	1.1
2.4	2.9	2.1	% Depr., Dep., Amort./Sales		3.6	3.1	1.4	1.1	1.8
(62) 4.2	(78) 4.1	(90) 3.5			(12) 5.7	(11) 4.1	(14) 4.4	(18) 2.7	(30) 3.1
6.6	6.2	5.6			9.2	4.7	5.7	4.0	4.4
1.8	2.6	1.9	% Officers', Directors' Owners' Comp/Sales						
(21) 2.8	(23) 4.7	(33) 4.0							
6.9	7.2	7.8							
998848M	1809580M	7892524M	Net Sales ($)	2437M	33941M	47135M	115399M	369367M	7324245M
660008M	992716M	2343736M	Total Assets ($)	3691M	29136M	33362M	39843M	149671M	2088033M

M = $ thousand   MM = $ million
See Pages 9 through 22 for Explanation of Ratios and Data

Current Data Sorted by Assets   Comparative Historical Data

Row	0-500M	500M-2MM	2-10MM	10-50MM	50-100MM	100-250MM	Type of Statement	4/1/05-3/31/06 ALL	4/1/06-3/31/07 ALL
			6	23	7	2	Unqualified	17	28
			1				Reviewed		
							Compiled	1	1
							Tax Returns	2	1
		25 (4/1-9/30/09)		27 (10/1/09-3/31/10)			Other	11	18
	1		3	6	1	2			
	1		10	29	8	4	NUMBER OF STATEMENTS	31	48
	%	%	%	%	%	%	ASSETS	%	%
			20.5	15.3			Cash & Equivalents	18.2	20.4
D			27.4	19.6			Trade Receivables (net)	19.4	21.5
A			3.1	5.4			Inventory	3.9	5.3
T			2.8	1.3			All Other Current	7.7	4.6
A			53.9	41.6			Total Current	49.2	51.8
			30.1	43.8			Fixed Assets (net)	32.1	32.5
N			7.5	.3			Intangibles (net)	2.5	1.6
O			8.5	14.4			All Other Non-Current	16.2	14.1
T			100.0	100.0			Total	100.0	100.0
							LIABILITIES		
A			.3	2.5			Notes Payable-Short Term	5.1	4.2
V			.8	1.7			Cur. Mat.-L.T.D.	1.4	1.2
A			13.1	8.7			Trade Payables	10.2	9.8
I			.0	.3			Income Taxes Payable	.0	.1
L			8.8	8.5			All Other Current	10.6	7.9
A			22.9	21.7			Total Current	27.3	23.2
B			13.2	17.2			Long-Term Debt	13.4	14.1
L			.0	.0			Deferred Taxes	.0	.0
E			.6	4.0			All Other Non-Current	5.7	3.2
			63.3	57.1			Net Worth	53.7	59.5
			100.0	100.0			Total Liabilities & Net Worth	100.0	100.0
							INCOME DATA		
			100.0	100.0			Net Sales	100.0	100.0
							Gross Profit		
			91.2	95.0			Operating Expenses	92.7	92.4
			8.8	5.0			Operating Profit	7.3	7.6
			.6	.5			All Other Expenses (net)	.1	-.4
			8.3	4.5			Profit Before Taxes	7.2	8.0
							RATIOS		
			4.6	4.2				3.9	4.3
			3.2	1.8			Current	2.4	2.8
			1.7	1.4				1.3	1.6
			4.2	3.9				3.2	3.5
			3.0	1.3			Quick	2.0	2.3
			1.4	1.0				1.0	1.4
			31 11.8	36 10.2				25 14.7	27 13.5
			40 9.1	42 8.6			Sales/Receivables	37 9.9	42 8.6
			54 6.8	55 6.6				50 7.3	52 7.0
							Cost of Sales/Inventory		
							Cost of Sales/Payables		
			4.2	4.0				4.1	3.6
			5.4	9.1			Sales/Working Capital	8.9	5.3
			29.7	18.3				38.1	12.0
				22.9				35.8	23.4
				(25) 8.3			EBIT/Interest	(23) 6.7	(31) 6.5
				.9				2.1	3.3
							Net Profit + Depr., Dep., Amort./Cur. Mat. L/T/D		
			.2	.5				.4	.2
			.4	.8			Fixed/Worth	.7	.6
			1.2	1.1				1.5	1.3
			.2	.3				.3	.2
			.4	.7			Debt/Worth	.8	.7
			2.6	1.4				1.7	1.4
				22.5				31.7	36.4
				12.7			% Profit Before Taxes/Tangible Net Worth	(30) 13.9	(47) 12.4
				.8				8.5	6.2
			19.9	10.7				17.6	16.5
			5.5	8.7			% Profit Before Taxes/Total Assets	9.4	7.2
			-2.9	.1				4.1	3.2
			26.9	6.5				18.3	23.2
			8.7	3.1			Sales/Net Fixed Assets	6.1	4.7
			4.6	2.3				3.4	2.7
			2.8	2.1				2.7	2.4
			1.9	1.4			Sales/Total Assets	2.1	1.6
			1.3	1.0				1.1	1.0
				1.8				1.2	.7
				2.5			% Depr., Dep., Amort./Sales	(28) 2.3	(40) 2.5
				3.6				2.9	3.1
							% Officers', Directors' Owners' Comp/Sales		
		3335M	124132M	1043995M	857880M	981337M	Net Sales ($)	899478M	1895536M
		512M	61478M	694635M	643739M	596207M	Total Assets ($)	607113M	1117544M

M = $ thousand   MM = $ million
See Pages 9 through 22 for Explanation of Ratios and Data

Comparative Historical Data

Current Data Sorted by Sales

			Type of Statement						
22	31	38	Unqualified			1	3	12	22
	1	1	Reviewed					1	
1	1		Compiled						
	3		Tax Returns						
16	13	13	Other		1			3	9
4/1/07-	4/1/08-	4/1/09-			25 (4/1-9/30/09)			27 (10/1/09-3/31/10)	
3/31/08	3/31/09	3/31/10		0-1MM	1-3MM	3-5MM	5-10MM	10-25MM	25MM & OVER
ALL	ALL	ALL							
39	49	52	NUMBER OF STATEMENTS	2	3			16	31
%	%	%	ASSETS	%	%	%	%	%	%
19.4	18.1	15.8	Cash & Equivalents	D	D			21.6	13.6
23.6	17.3	20.8	Trade Receivables (net)	A	A			20.6	20.0
6.3	7.8	6.7	Inventory	T	T			3.2	8.5
3.0	2.6	2.1	All Other Current	A	A			1.3	2.3
52.3	45.9	45.3	Total Current					46.7	44.4
35.2	36.4	39.2	Fixed Assets (net)	N	N			41.9	38.3
.5	2.5	1.8	Intangibles (net)	O	O			.7	.4
12.2	15.2	13.7	All Other Non-Current	T	T			10.6	16.9
100.0	100.0	100.0	Total					100.0	100.0
			LIABILITIES	A	A				
5.5	1.5	2.1	Notes Payable-Short Term	V	V			2.7	1.3
1.6	1.8	1.5	Cur. Mat.-L.T.D.	A	A			1.0	1.8
12.3	8.5	10.0	Trade Payables	I	I			8.8	10.0
.1	.1	.1	Income Taxes Payable	L	L			.0	.2
8.5	8.1	9.3	All Other Current	A	A			8.1	9.9
28.0	20.0	23.1	Total Current	B	B			20.6	23.1
15.7	16.8	17.0	Long-Term Debt	L	L			14.1	17.1
.0	.0	.0	Deferred Taxes	E	E			.0	.0
1.2	.9	2.5	All Other Non-Current					.8	3.8
55.0	62.4	57.3	Net Worth					64.4	56.0
100.0	100.0	100.0	Total Liabilities & Net Worth					100.0	100.0
			INCOME DATA						
100.0	100.0	100.0	Net Sales					100.0	100.0
			Gross Profit						
96.1	95.1	94.5	Operating Expenses					95.3	96.2
3.9	4.9	5.5	Operating Profit					4.7	3.8
-1.5	.8	-.1	All Other Expenses (net)					.2	-.5
5.5	4.1	5.6	Profit Before Taxes					4.5	4.2
			RATIOS						
4.3	3.4	3.7						5.3	3.1
2.6	2.5	2.1	Current					3.4	2.1
1.8	1.8	1.4						1.4	1.5
3.8	2.8	3.3						4.9	2.4
2.2	2.1	1.5	Quick					3.0	1.3
1.1	1.1	.9						1.0	1.0
37 9.9	34 10.7	34 10.7						37 9.8	33 11.0
49 7.4	46 7.9	42 8.7	Sales/Receivables					41 9.0	44 8.3
60 6.0	57 6.4	51 7.1						58 6.3	52 7.1
			Cost of Sales/Inventory						
			Cost of Sales/Payables						
3.1	3.3	4.0						3.4	4.0
5.2	5.8	7.0	Sales/Working Capital					4.7	8.4
11.4	12.5	16.7						16.1	16.2
20.5	13.8	31.6						78.0	29.1
(28) 8.6	(36) 5.9	(42) 14.7	EBIT/Interest			(11) 6.2		(27) 20.8	
3.4	1.5	4.1						1.2	5.6
			Net Profit + Depr., Dep., Amort./Cur. Mat. L/T/D						
.3	.4	.5						.5	.5
.5	.6	.6	Fixed/Worth					.6	.7
1.1	.9	.9						.9	.9
.3	.4	.3						.2	.4
.6	.6	.6	Debt/Worth					.5	.7
1.1	1.0	1.3						1.1	1.0
17.3	17.7	18.4	% Profit Before Taxes/Tangible					15.0	20.8
(37) 10.5	(48) 7.4	(50) 12.2	Net Worth					12.0 (30)	12.2
6.2	.4	4.3						.3	4.1
9.8	10.8	10.0	% Profit Before Taxes/Total					10.7	9.8
6.4	4.7	7.7	Assets					8.7	7.3
2.8	.0	1.3						.0	2.2
13.0	9.3	8.2						7.6	8.1
4.4	3.4	3.5	Sales/Net Fixed Assets					2.5	3.6
2.2	2.6	2.3						1.6	2.6
2.1	1.9	2.2						2.0	2.3
1.4	1.3	1.5	Sales/Total Assets					1.2	1.6
1.1	1.0	1.0						.8	1.2
1.8	1.8	1.9						2.1	2.1
(35) 2.6	(48) 2.6	(49) 2.8	% Depr., Dep., Amort./Sales			(15) 3.2		(29) 2.5	
3.7	3.5	3.3						4.3	3.1
			% Officers', Directors' Owners' Comp/Sales						
1931827M	2586112M	3010679M	Net Sales ($)	7061M	24944M			312412M	2666262M
1336918M	1945086M	1996571M	Total Assets ($)	3168M	21517M			283999M	1687887M

M = $ thousand   MM = $ million
See Pages 9 through 22 for Explanation of Ratios and Data

HEALTH CARE—All Other Miscellaneous Ambulatory Health Care Services NAICS 621999

Current Data Sorted by Assets | **Comparative Historical Data**

	0-500M	500M-2MM	2-10MM	10-50MM	50-100MM	100-250MM	Type of Statement	4/1/05-3/31/06 ALL	4/1/06-3/31/07 ALL
	1	6	27	45	9	10	Unqualified	118	120
	8	2	10	2	1		Reviewed	14	19
	16	22	9	8	2		Compiled	42	26
	12	19	32	31	5	10	Tax Returns	41	29
		75 (4/1-9/30/09)		223 (10/1/09-3/31/10)			Other	166	94
	37	60	86	80	15	20	NUMBER OF STATEMENTS	381	288
	%	%	%	%	%	%	**ASSETS**	%	%
	27.6	19.3	16.1	22.0	19.2	8.7	Cash & Equivalents	19.0	16.6
	8.2	20.9	28.4	24.2	16.6	22.8	Trade Receivables (net)	22.6	26.3
	2.6	5.4	4.0	1.7	5.9	3.3	Inventory	3.4	3.0
	3.3	3.0	4.4	4.6	2.8	5.9	All Other Current	3.3	3.7
	41.6	48.5	52.9	52.5	44.6	40.7	Total Current	48.3	49.6
	36.1	38.4	32.8	33.6	35.2	17.5	Fixed Assets (net)	33.8	31.0
	7.8	5.5	5.1	5.1	13.1	24.6	Intangibles (net)	6.4	7.3
	14.5	7.6	9.2	8.7	7.2	17.2	All Other Non-Current	11.4	12.1
	100.0	100.0	100.0	100.0	100.0	100.0	Total	100.0	100.0
							LIABILITIES		
	21.4	8.2	8.7	2.7	4.0	.7	Notes Payable-Short Term	7.9	8.8
	4.1	6.0	4.2	3.1	3.0	1.5	Cur. Mat.-L.T.D.	3.5	3.8
	7.1	6.7	10.9	8.7	6.5	6.8	Trade Payables	7.8	9.1
	.0	.0	.1	.2	.4	.1	Income Taxes Payable	.2	.6
	21.6	11.0	11.6	14.3	15.7	10.2	All Other Current	16.2	15.9
	54.3	32.0	35.5	29.0	29.5	19.3	Total Current	35.6	38.1
	23.1	25.6	18.2	20.3	31.2	21.4	Long-Term Debt	23.6	23.9
	.0	.0	.0	.2	.8	2.1	Deferred Taxes	.2	.2
	24.2	4.6	7.1	3.8	2.9	5.1	All Other Non-Current	7.2	5.2
	-1.6	37.7	39.2	46.7	35.6	52.1	Net Worth	33.3	32.6
	100.0	100.0	100.0	100.0	100.0	100.0	Total Liabilities & Net Worth	100.0	100.0
							INCOME DATA		
	100.0	100.0	100.0	100.0	100.0	100.0	Net Sales	100.0	100.0
							Gross Profit		
	87.7	89.2	89.8	94.4	93.8	88.8	Operating Expenses	89.5	89.7
	12.3	10.8	10.2	5.6	6.2	11.2	Operating Profit	10.5	10.3
	3.5	4.6	2.3	2.1	2.8	1.2	All Other Expenses (net)	2.4	2.1
	8.8	6.3	8.0	3.6	3.4	10.0	Profit Before Taxes	8.1	8.2
							RATIOS		
	3.5	3.7	2.7	3.1	1.8	2.6		3.3	2.6
	1.4	1.5	1.6	1.7	1.3	2.0	Current	1.7	1.5
	.3	.6	1.0	1.3	1.0	1.5		1.0	1.0
	3.5	3.0	2.2	2.7	1.5	2.1		2.9	2.3
	1.0	1.2	1.4	1.5	1.1	1.6	Quick	1.4	1.4
	.2	.4	.8	.8	.7	1.3		.8	.8
	0 UND	0 UND	20 18.7	28 13.0	19 18.8	31 11.8		0 819.5	8 46.4
	0 UND	5 70.1	37 9.8	42 8.6	35 10.3	47 7.8	Sales/Receivables	36 10.1	39 9.3
	2 160.8	39 9.3	58 6.3	61 6.0	50 7.3	61 6.0		56 6.5	61 5.9
							Cost of Sales/Inventory		
							Cost of Sales/Payables		
	22.3	6.2	6.2	3.6	6.4	5.8		5.3	6.0
	352.7	19.2	16.0	8.1	17.4	9.2	Sales/Working Capital	13.0	14.3
	-23.9	-48.5	NM	16.4	114.4	13.9		UND	-619.1
	35.0	19.0	26.5	14.8	15.0	33.0		18.5	13.0
(21) 8.8	(40) 3.6	(67) 7.7	(59) 3.9	(14) 3.9	(18) 5.3		EBIT/Interest	(282) 5.3	(217) 3.9
	1.3	.9	1.6	1.4	.7	.4		1.4	1.1
				4.5				6.7	6.7
			(15) 2.2				Net Profit + Depr., Dep., Amort./Cur. Mat. L/T/D	(30) 1.6	(24) 3.1
				1.5				.4	1.9
	.0	.2	.2	.2	.5	.2		.3	.3
	1.8	1.2	.9	.6	1.5	.9	Fixed/Worth	.8	.8
	-2.8	3.9	3.2	2.2	-10.6	16.9		3.8	4.3
	.7	.7	.5	.6	.8	.6		.5	.5
	5.7	1.9	1.4	1.3	2.7	1.5	Debt/Worth	1.6	1.7
	-4.5	5.5	4.5	3.7	-18.6	144.2		10.1	10.8
	801.7	44.5	56.2	44.0	25.6	115.6		56.8	62.0
(25) 110.1	(49) 12.4	(74) 21.2	(76) 9.2	(11) 13.7	(16) 29.0		% Profit Before Taxes/Tangible Net Worth	(309) 21.3	(230) 17.9
	20.1	-12.4	1.2	4.3	4.9	-4.1		4.6	3.2
	71.1	27.3	25.7	10.4	13.9	16.9		20.2	22.3
	23.4	5.8	9.8	3.6	3.9	5.9	% Profit Before Taxes/Total Assets	8.0	7.0
	.1	-4.2	-.7	1.1	-1.5	-.6		.9	.8
	817.7	55.6	37.2	30.0	15.8	68.1		34.7	43.6
	63.4	15.5	9.5	4.8	6.9	6.8	Sales/Net Fixed Assets	9.7	9.8
	13.1	4.0	3.4	2.1	2.0	3.7		2.7	3.3
	18.0	5.2	3.6	2.1	2.4	2.4		4.1	3.6
	9.7	3.0	2.2	1.3	1.5	1.5	Sales/Total Assets	1.9	2.2
	3.7	1.5	1.1	.9	.7	.7		1.0	1.1
	.9	.8	1.0	1.3	1.7	1.1		1.1	1.3
(19) 2.0	(44) 2.1	(70) 2.1	(71) 2.3	(14) 3.5	(12) 1.9		% Depr., Dep., Amort./Sales	(312) 2.5	(233) 2.5
	4.6	8.3	4.0	3.9	5.9	4.0		4.5	4.6
	5.1	4.1	2.5					5.6	5.4
(20) 13.6	(18) 7.4	(12) 6.7					% Officers', Directors' Owners' Comp/Sales	(73) 11.8	(48) 11.5
	24.6	12.2	16.0					23.9	25.9
	115294M	222772M	1259409M	3534866M	1589705M	5971582M	Net Sales ($)	13216176M	12975800M
	8098M	62585M	434717M	1882080M	1040328M	3298792M	Total Assets ($)	7125882M	6772995M

© RMA 2010

M = $ thousand   MM = $ million
See Pages 9 through 22 for Explanation of Ratios and Data

Comparative Historical Data | Current Data Sorted by Sales

Comparative Historical Data			Type of Statement	0-1MM	1-3MM	3-5MM	5-10MM	10-25MM	25MM & OVER
113	108	98	Unqualified	3	5	4	15	23	48
20	18	15	Reviewed		2		3	6	4
17	21	30	Compiled	4	5	8	6	6	1
39	45	46	Tax Returns	16	16	7	4	2	1
109	124	109	Other	7	12	12	18	16	44
4/1/07-3/31/08 ALL	4/1/08-3/31/09 ALL	4/1/09-3/31/10 ALL		|——75 (4/1-9/30/09)——|			|——223 (10/1/09-3/31/10)——|		
298	316	298	NUMBER OF STATEMENTS	30	40	31	46	53	98
%	%	%	ASSETS	%	%	%	%	%	%
15.0	17.6	19.4	Cash & Equivalents	10.8	23.8	13.5	27.9	17.4	19.1
26.8	24.7	22.3	Trade Receivables (net)	3.4	18.7	28.7	23.0	22.6	27.0
3.1	2.8	3.5	Inventory	.2	5.4	9.6	2.3	2.2	3.1
3.9	4.1	4.1	All Other Current	1.3	3.7	4.1	2.6	5.5	5.0
48.8	49.2	49.3	Total Current	15.7	51.5	55.9	55.9	47.8	54.2
34.5	34.2	33.7	Fixed Assets (net)	68.2	24.2	27.6	34.9	36.4	26.8
7.6	6.8	7.3	Intangibles (net)	2.0	7.8	9.7	3.5	5.5	10.5
9.1	9.9	9.8	All Other Non-Current	14.0	16.4	6.7	5.8	10.2	8.5
100.0	100.0	100.0	Total	100.0	100.0	100.0	100.0	100.0	100.0
			LIABILITIES						
8.8	8.7	7.8	Notes Payable-Short Term	6.8	11.7	16.0	7.9	9.1	3.2
5.5	5.9	4.0	Cur. Mat.-L.T.D.	4.5	3.9	5.4	4.0	3.5	3.8
9.4	8.8	8.5	Trade Payables	4.7	6.7	7.5	6.7	10.7	10.4
.4	.1	.1	Income Taxes Payable	.0	.0	.0	.0	.2	.3
15.9	14.9	13.5	All Other Current	4.8	10.1	15.0	13.3	16.5	15.7
40.0	38.4	34.0	Total Current	20.8	32.4	44.0	31.9	40.0	33.3
23.6	25.8	21.7	Long-Term Debt	42.4	21.1	15.7	19.0	21.3	19.1
.2	.2	.3	Deferred Taxes	.0	.0	.1	.0	.2	.6
4.6	7.5	7.5	All Other Non-Current	18.2	11.7	10.6	2.6	5.5	7.5
31.6	28.1	36.5	Net Worth	18.5	34.8	29.7	46.6	33.0	42.1
100.0	100.0	100.0	Total Liabilities & Net Worth	100.0	100.0	100.0	100.0	100.0	100.0
			INCOME DATA						
100.0	100.0	100.0	Net Sales	100.0	100.0	100.0	100.0	100.0	100.0
			Gross Profit						
89.6	90.0	90.8	Operating Expenses	73.8	91.8	92.2	94.3	90.6	93.5
10.4	10.0	9.2	Operating Profit	26.2	8.2	7.8	5.7	9.4	6.5
2.4	3.0	2.8	All Other Expenses (net)	15.8	1.2	1.4	1.0	2.9	.6
7.9	7.0	6.5	Profit Before Taxes	10.4	6.9	6.4	4.6	6.5	5.9
			RATIOS						
2.7	2.8	2.9	Current	5.0	3.9	3.9	3.2	2.9	2.3
1.4	1.5	1.6		.8	1.6	1.8	1.6	1.5	1.6
.8	.9	1.0		.2	.9	.9	1.2	.8	1.3
2.3	2.6	2.3	Quick	5.0	2.9	2.6	2.9	2.8	2.0
1.2	1.4	1.4		.6	1.5	1.4	1.6	1.3	1.4
.7	.7	.8		.2	.7	.5	1.0	.7	1.1
11 32.0	5 69.3	3 105.3	Sales/Receivables	0 UND	0 UND	0 UND	1 499.1	21 17.6	27 13.4
39 9.3	35 10.6	33 11.0		0 UND	6 64.3	32 11.4	38 9.6	37 9.8	41 9.0
62 5.9	61 5.9	54 6.8		0 UND	46 8.0	71 5.2	56 6.5	57 6.5	55 6.7
			Cost of Sales/Inventory						
			Cost of Sales/Payables						
6.3	6.0	6.1	Sales/Working Capital	7.2	5.4	5.2	4.3	6.1	6.6
20.2	16.0	14.4		NM	19.9	9.6	14.8	15.4	12.0
-63.4	-107.4	680.1		-7.0	-173.8	-182.0	64.0	-50.9	38.4
17.1	17.6	21.2	EBIT/Interest	22.3	28.3	18.4	27.5	16.1	23.6
(233) 4.0	(244) 5.2	(219) 5.2		(11) 7.8	(27) 3.7	(25) 7.6	(33) 4.5	(40) 3.4	(83) 6.6
1.2	1.0	1.4		-10.8	-.2	2.1	.6	.8	2.2
5.7	8.7	10.1	Net Profit + Depr., Dep., Amort./Cur. Mat. L/T/D						12.4
(34) 1.2	(38) 2.1	(29) 2.6							(24) 2.3
.3	1.2	1.6							1.6
.4	.3	.2	Fixed/Worth	.9	.0	.2	.2	.4	.2
1.1	1.1	.9		2.8	.8	.7	.6	1.2	.7
10.7	5.0	3.3		UND	NM	3.6	1.6	3.2	2.8
.6	.6	.6	Debt/Worth	.7	.6	.5	.4	.6	.8
2.0	1.8	1.6		2.7	2.5	1.8	1.2	1.8	1.6
31.8	16.4	6.2		UND	-18.6	5.4	2.8	10.2	5.2
55.1	69.9	64.6	% Profit Before Taxes/Tangible Net Worth	71.8	63.6	119.1	41.4	35.9	82.8
(229) 21.7	(248) 20.2	(251) 14.4		(25) 12.5	(29) 17.1	(26) 31.2	(42) 6.5	(42) 8.6	(87) 20.4
5.3	3.2	2.1		-1.1	3.6	11.4	-10.4	-2.7	5.7
22.9	25.8	21.5	% Profit Before Taxes/Total Assets	21.9	33.3	31.2	18.7	16.6	16.1
7.6	7.2	6.4		2.8	11.6	11.6	3.7	4.1	5.8
1.5	.0	.3		-2.9	.5	5.2	-3.7	-.8	2.3
36.7	42.5	42.9	Sales/Net Fixed Assets	13.1	414.9	42.8	29.7	88.9	39.8
9.7	11.7	10.4		.3	25.1	13.3	13.2	6.2	9.9
3.3	2.8	3.0		.1	9.6	6.2	2.9	2.2	4.3
4.0	4.2	4.1	Sales/Total Assets	2.6	5.1	7.0	4.5	3.4	4.0
2.1	2.2	2.1		.3	2.7	2.9	2.3	1.7	2.1
1.2	1.1	1.1		.1	1.2	1.2	1.3	1.0	1.2
.9	1.1	1.1	% Depr., Dep., Amort./Sales	6.4	.8	.6	1.2	.9	1.0
(243) 2.4	(245) 2.6	(230) 2.3		(22) 12.9	(24) 2.3	(22) 2.0	(40) 2.2	(43) 2.2	(79) 1.9
4.4	4.8	4.1		24.0	4.8	3.4	3.4	3.4	3.7
4.3	5.3	4.2	% Officers', Directors' Owners' Comp/Sales		1.8	6.4			1.9
(45) 7.3	(50) 9.8	(60) 7.9			(18) 5.7	(11) 8.0			(14) 7.3
24.5	25.6	16.7			15.5	16.2			20.4
12419348M	11332833M	12693628M	Net Sales ($)	12836M	78675M	123043M	320211M	860831M	11298032M
6109414M	5820088M	6726600M	Total Assets ($)	50158M	76007M	65852M	272750M	609952M	5651881M

Current Data Sorted by Assets   Comparative Historical Data

Type of Statement	0-500M	500M-2MM	2-10MM	10-50MM	50-100MM	100-250MM	4/1/05-3/31/06 ALL	4/1/06-3/31/07 ALL
Unqualified	2	6	26	99	70	81	353	385
Reviewed	1	3	6	3			10	11
Compiled	4	5	6	5		1	21	21
Tax Returns	3	7	3				22	14
Other	6	7	39	82	48	55	248	248
		289 (4/1-9/30/09)			279 (10/1/09-3/31/10)			
NUMBER OF STATEMENTS	16	28	80	189	118	137	654	679
ASSETS	%	%	%	%	%	%	%	%
Cash & Equivalents	30.7	26.8	16.0	13.5	11.8	12.5	12.6	14.5
Trade Receivables (net)	10.7	17.7	27.5	19.6	14.8	12.2	16.8	17.7
Inventory	.7	2.3	2.6	2.4	2.2	1.7	2.1	2.2
All Other Current	8.0	6.0	2.5	2.5	4.6	3.6	3.6	3.7
Total Current	50.1	52.8	48.6	37.9	33.5	29.9	35.1	38.0
Fixed Assets (net)	31.1	32.8	44.4	45.7	45.2	47.1	44.0	43.1
Intangibles (net)	12.8	4.9	1.6	2.6	2.2	1.8	2.0	2.0
All Other Non-Current	6.0	9.6	5.4	13.8	19.2	21.2	18.9	16.8
Total	100.0	100.0	100.0	100.0	100.0	100.0	100.0	100.0
LIABILITIES								
Notes Payable-Short Term	47.4	9.8	2.1	1.7	1.9	.2	2.5	2.1
Cur. Mat.-L.T.D.	4.2	6.4	6.6	4.3	2.5	2.4	3.0	3.3
Trade Payables	5.6	2.5	6.9	7.4	5.9	4.4	6.0	6.3
Income Taxes Payable	.0	.2	.0	.1	.0	.0	.1	.1
All Other Current	26.7	18.3	13.5	11.8	10.1	8.7	11.1	11.2
Total Current	84.0	37.1	29.1	25.2	20.5	15.8	22.8	23.1
Long-Term Debt	36.5	29.7	26.0	28.7	30.8	29.8	27.8	28.5
Deferred Taxes	.0	.2	.1	.1	.0	.1	.0	.1
All Other Non-Current	4.8	7.2	4.4	4.5	5.5	5.5	5.1	4.8
Net Worth	-25.2	25.8	40.4	41.6	43.2	48.8	44.3	43.5
Total Liabilities & Net Worth	100.0	100.0	100.0	100.0	100.0	100.0	100.0	100.0
INCOME DATA								
Net Sales	100.0	100.0	100.0	100.0	100.0	100.0	100.0	100.0
Gross Profit								
Operating Expenses	91.3	83.7	85.7	93.6	96.9	96.5	94.7	94.0
Operating Profit	8.7	16.3	14.3	6.4	3.1	3.5	5.3	6.0
All Other Expenses (net)	1.0	4.1	3.3	1.2	1.1	.7	.8	.5
Profit Before Taxes	7.8	12.3	11.1	5.2	2.0	2.8	4.5	5.5
RATIOS								
Current	4.1	4.8	4.0	3.1	2.7	2.7	2.9	2.9
	2.0	2.0	2.1	1.8	1.8	2.0	1.9	1.9
	.8	.8	1.1	1.2	1.3	1.5	1.3	1.2
Quick	3.2	4.6	3.3	2.6	2.1	2.2	2.4	2.4
	1.7	1.7	1.9	1.6	1.5	1.6	1.6	1.6
	.8	.6	1.0	1.0	1.0	1.2	1.0	1.0
Sales/Receivables	0 UND	0 UND	27 13.6	38 9.5	39 9.5	37 9.8	37 9.8	37 10.0
	0 UND	0 UND	43 8.5	47 7.8	46 7.9	46 7.9	49 7.5	49 7.4
	28 13.2	40 9.1	61 6.0	59 6.2	52 7.0	53 6.9	60 6.1	60 6.0
Cost of Sales/Inventory								
Cost of Sales/Payables								
Sales/Working Capital	7.1	6.9	4.4	4.6	4.9	4.5	5.0	4.9
	23.4	30.7	8.1	9.6	9.2	7.0	8.5	8.3
	-299.2	-28.1	51.5	25.4	23.3	14.9	24.9	27.1
EBIT/Interest	12.1	80.4	23.7	8.2	5.4	5.1	8.9	8.3
	(10) 2.4	(21) 21.3	(68) 5.7	(172) 3.0	(116) 2.0	(130) 2.7	(597) 4.1	(600) 3.7
	-.1	4.2	1.3	.7	.0	1.0	1.4	1.3
Net Profit + Depr., Dep., Amort./Cur. Mat. L/T/D							9.9	8.0
							(28) 4.7	(30) 4.0
							1.8	1.8
Fixed/Worth	.3	.3	.5	.7	.7	.7	.6	.6
	1.6	.7	1.1	1.0	1.0	1.0	.9	.9
	-.2	-34.7	2.7	3.0	1.7	1.3	1.6	1.6
Debt/Worth	.3	.4	.5	.5	.6	.6	.5	.5
	1.7	1.4	1.3	1.1	1.1	1.1	1.0	1.0
	-1.4	-39.8	4.1	3.6	2.7	1.6	2.6	2.5
% Profit Before Taxes/Tangible Net Worth	614.9	139.3	86.3	18.6	8.6	10.0	14.4	18.0
	(10) 67.6	(19) 79.9	(72) 22.1	(163) 7.5	(104) 3.3	(132) 4.5	(596) 7.7	(617) 8.1
	-.6	20.7	3.6	-1.0	-2.9	.1	2.2	2.1
% Profit Before Taxes/Total Assets	81.5	61.5	23.3	8.2	4.9	5.5	7.1	8.6
	7.1	28.6	8.3	3.8	1.6	2.4	3.8	4.1
	-11.4	.7	.7	-.7	-1.3	.0	.7	.4
Sales/Net Fixed Assets	253.3	62.1	10.7	4.8	-3.2	2.6	4.0	5.2
	29.6	18.5	4.7	2.7	2.5	2.0	2.6	2.7
	7.1	5.0	2.2	1.8	1.8	1.5	1.8	1.8
Sales/Total Assets	18.8	6.7	3.0	1.8	1.4	1.1	1.6	1.8
	6.7	3.6	1.9	1.3	1.1	.9	1.1	1.2
	2.2	1.6	1.1	.9	.8	.8	.8	.9
% Depr., Dep., Amort./Sales		1.2	2.3	2.9	4.2	4.1	3.4	3.2
	(16)	2.9	(73) 3.4	(182) 4.5	(114) 5.1	(88) 5.1	(578) 4.6	(582) 4.4
		8.8	7.2	5.9	6.2	6.0	5.9	5.8
% Officers', Directors' Owners' Comp/Sales			8.4	2.1	3.4	9.5	5.1	7.0
		(11)	19.5	(15) 8.9	(10) 11.0	(18) 31.1	(74) 15.9	(71) 14.4
			29.8	36.0	23.5	42.4	37.6	37.8
Net Sales ($)	27464M	136233M	983555M	6776859M	9576384M	22388792M	46447006M	48064321M
Total Assets ($)	3284M	33316M	427270M	4953881M	8129357M	23407561M	44925945M	43606580M

M = $ thousand   MM = $ million
See Pages 9 through 22 for Explanation of Ratios and Data

Comparative Historical Data | Current Data Sorted by Sales

			Type of Statement						
317	321	284	Unqualified	7	2	4	14	46	211
8	10	13	Reviewed		2	1	3	2	5
20	22	21	Compiled	2	2	4	6	1	6
20	22	13	Tax Returns	2	4	4	6	3	
237	233	237	Other	3	12	6	14	40	162
4/1/07-3/31/08	4/1/08-3/31/09	4/1/09-3/31/10		289 (4/1-9/30/09)			279 (10/1/09-3/31/10)		
ALL	ALL	ALL		0-1MM	1-3MM	3-5MM	5-10MM	10-25MM	25MM & OVE
602	608	568	**NUMBER OF STATEMENTS**	14	22	19	37	92	384
%	%	%	**ASSETS**	%	%	%	%	%	%
11.8	11.9	14.4	Cash & Equivalents	12.2	19.5	20.6	23.6	15.2	12.8
18.3	17.0	17.6	Trade Receivables (net)	5.2	8.9	20.6	22.6	21.9	16.9
2.3	2.1	2.2	Inventory	.8	1.4	2.0	2.5	2.2	2.2
3.4	3.7	3.5	All Other Current	3.2	7.9	1.9	1.9	3.5	3.5
35.8	34.7	37.6	Total Current	21.5	37.7	45.1	50.5	42.8	35.4
44.0	46.2	44.7	Fixed Assets (net)	72.4	43.4	44.0	36.9	44.4	44.6
2.4	2.6	2.6	Intangibles (net)	2.1	9.1	3.8	4.6	1.9	2.1
17.8	16.5	15.1	All Other Non-Current	4.0	9.8	7.2	8.0	10.8	17.9
100.0	100.0	100.0	Total	100.0	100.0	100.0	100.0	100.0	100.0
			LIABILITIES						
2.5	2.6	3.1	Notes Payable-Short Term	53.3	10.2	1.7	1.5	2.4	1.3
3.4	3.4	3.9	Cur. Mat.-L.T.D.	3.4	5.1	7.3	4.4	4.3	3.5
7.4	5.5	6.0	Trade Payables	3.6	2.5	3.6	5.3	7.0	6.3
.1	.1	.0	Income Taxes Payable	.0	.0	.3	.1	.0	.0
10.4	10.6	11.7	All Other Current	29.8	7.0	12.3	13.5	10.0	11.5
23.8	22.2	24.7	Total Current	90.1	24.8	25.1	24.8	23.8	22.6
27.9	30.2	29.3	Long-Term Debt	35.3	49.7	23.2	22.7	31.3	28.4
.1	.0	.1	Deferred Taxes	.0	.3	.0	.1	.0	.1
4.7	5.4	5.1	All Other Non-Current	.8	3.0	2.6	6.7	5.6	5.2
43.6	42.1	40.8	Net Worth	-26.2	22.2	49.0	45.7	39.3	43.8
100.0	100.0	100.0	Total Liabilties & Net Worth	100.0	100.0	100.0	100.0	100.0	100.0
			INCOME DATA						
100.0	100.0	100.0	Net Sales	100.0	100.0	100.0	100.0	100.0	100.0
			Gross Profit						
94.1	94.2	93.3	Operating Expenses	77.8	77.2	86.0	87.1	93.7	95.7
5.9	5.8	6.7	Operating Profit	22.2	22.8	14.0	12.9	6.3	4.3
.5	2.0	1.5	All Other Expenses (net)	17.7	6.8	1.9	1.1	.6	.8
5.4	3.8	5.2	Profit Before Taxes	4.5	16.0	12.0	11.8	5.7	3.5
			RATIOS						
2.7	2.6	3.0		4.8	8.7	4.6	4.1	3.5	2.7
1.8	1.8	1.9	Current	.9	2.1	2.4	2.4	2.1	1.8
1.2	1.3	1.3		.1	.8	.9	1.6	1.2	1.3
2.3	2.3	2.4		2.8	7.1	4.2	3.6	3.1	2.2
(601) 1.5	1.5	1.6	Quick	.8	1.7	2.1	2.0	1.8	1.5
1.0	1.0	1.1		.1	.5	.9	1.3	.9	1.1
37 10.0	37 9.8	36 10.2		0 UND	0 UND	0 UND	10 35.7	35 10.4	38 9.6
48 7.5	48 7.5	45 8.1	Sales/Receivables	1 345.4	0 UND	38 9.5	43 8.5	46 8.0	46 7.9
61 6.0	60 6.1	55 6.7		31 11.7	36 10.0	58 6.3	62 5.9	65 5.6	54 6.8
			Cost of Sales/Inventory						
			Cost of Sales/Payables						
5.2	5.3	4.7		4.4	2.9	4.6	3.6	4.3	5.0
9.3	9.4	8.6	Sales/Working Capital	NM	17.5	7.8	7.5	8.0	8.9
40.1	24.9	24.0		-1.0	-33.0	-72.8	17.1	24.7	21.5
8.9	6.5	8.3			17.9	17.3	32.5	9.8	6.4
(542) 3.5	(549) 2.1	(517) 2.9	EBIT/Interest	(17) 5.6	(16) 8.8	(34) 5.5	(81) 2.8	(363) 2.7	
1.1	-.4	.9		2.6	1.5	1.5	.9	.7	
6.7	9.2	5.6							5.0
(38) 3.6	(31) 4.8	(23) 2.9	Net Profit + Depr., Dep., Amort./Cur. Mat. L/T/D					(17) 2.6	
1.6	1.8	1.6							1.6
.6	.7	.7		1.1	.5	.4	.4	.6	.7
.9	1.0	1.0	Fixed/Worth	3.3	1.3	.9	.7	1.1	1.0
1.9	1.9	2.0		-18.3	-5.3	2.9	2.1	2.4	1.6
.5	.6	.6		.6	.6	.3	.4	.5	.6
1.0	1.1	1.1	Debt/Worth	3.0	1.1	1.3	1.1	1.2	1.1
3.1	2.7	2.9		-21.2	-12.9	3.4	2.5	4.1	2.5
21.5	15.3	17.2			123.6	137.2	91.2	20.9	12.2
(542) 9.0	(543) 4.8	(500) 6.6	% Profit Before Taxes/Tangible Net Worth	(15) 30.9	(17) 39.1	(33) 28.4	(81) 8.8	(345) 5.3	
2.5	-4.2	.0		5.8	12.4	4.8	-.2	-.8	
8.3	7.2	9.0		3.0	44.5	38.0	43.7	8.4	7.2
4.1	2.2	3.1	% Profit Before Taxes/Total Assets	-.6	16.0	11.7	16.3	3.7	2.6
.2	-2.2	-.5		-10.5	1.9	.3	2.3	-1.0	-.5
5.3	4.5	4.7		3.3	44.4	17.7	14.1	6.7	4.1
2.6	2.4	2.6	Sales/Net Fixed Assets	.3	5.5	2.6	4.6	2.6	2.5
1.8	1.7	1.8		.1	1.0	2.1	2.4	1.7	1.8
1.9	1.7	1.7		1.7	5.0	3.7	2.9	2.0	1.5
1.2	1.1	1.2	Sales/Total Assets	.3	1.9	1.7	1.7	1.3	1.1
.8	.8	.8		.1	.5	1.0	.9	.9	.8
3.1	3.2	3.3		7.3	2.1	2.3	2.8	2.8	3.3
(530) 4.6	(540) 4.6	(481) 4.7	% Depr., Dep., Amort./Sales	(11) 28.3	(15) 4.9	(16) 4.5	(29) 3.7	(84) 4.2	(326) 4.7
6.1	6.1	6.1		30.7	22.0	11.1	6.7	5.9	5.9
6.7	5.1	6.2							6.9
(69) 17.6	(64) 13.5	(66) 13.8	% Officers', Directors' Owners' Comp/Sales					(42) 14.2	
37.4	37.0	36.5							37.9
44328410M	45792607M	39889287M	Net Sales ($)	5359M	42348M	69952M	268437M	1578552M	37924639M
39495844M	42589129M	36954669M	Total Assets ($)	30732M	54018M	91885M	219934M	1415131M	35142969M

M = $ thousand   MM = $ million
See Pages 9 through 22 for Explanation of Ratios and Data

Current Data Sorted by Assets / Comparative Historical Data

0-500M	500M-2MM	2-10MM	10-50MM	50-100MM	100-250MM		4/1/05-3/31/06 ALL	4/1/06-3/31/07 ALL
						Type of Statement		
		9	46	64	88	Unqualified	152	229
						Reviewed		3
						Compiled		3
						Tax Returns		1
1		7	35	28	45	Other	80	94
	182 (4/1-9/30/09)		141 (10/1/09-3/31/10)					
1		16	81	92	133	NUMBER OF STATEMENTS	232	330
%	%	%	%	%	%	**ASSETS**	%	%
	DATA NOT AVAILABLE	12.1	12.4	11.5	9.7	Cash & Equivalents	12.0	11.1
		18.6	17.0	15.5	12.2	Trade Receivables (net)	15.7	15.9
		4.8	2.4	2.0	1.6	Inventory	1.9	1.9
		3.7	2.7	2.8	3.0	All Other Current	3.6	3.4
		39.2	34.5	31.7	26.4	Total Current	33.2	32.3
		44.0	48.2	46.8	47.2	Fixed Assets (net)	44.3	44.5
		1.7	.4	.9	.8	Intangibles (net)	.8	.9
		15.1	17.0	20.5	25.6	All Other Non-Current	21.7	22.4
		100.0	100.0	100.0	100.0	Total	100.0	100.0
						LIABILITIES		
		1.2	.2	.7	.5	Notes Payable-Short Term	.8	1.0
		2.5	3.0	2.1	1.7	Cur. Mat.-L.T.D.	3.0	2.6
		8.7	6.8	5.6	5.1	Trade Payables	6.2	6.2
		.0	.0	.0	.0	Income Taxes Payable	.0	.0
		17.6	9.8	10.9	7.7	All Other Current	11.0	9.8
		30.0	19.9	19.3	15.0	Total Current	21.1	19.6
		20.7	26.2	25.4	27.5	Long-Term Debt	26.5	28.1
		.0	.0	.0	.1	Deferred Taxes	.0	.0
		4.8	3.9	5.9	7.7	All Other Non-Current	5.4	4.0
		44.5	50.0	49.4	49.7	Net Worth	47.0	48.2
		100.0	100.0	100.0	100.0	Total Liabilties & Net Worth	100.0	100.0
						INCOME DATA		
		100.0	100.0	100.0	100.0	Net Sales	100.0	100.0
						Gross Profit		
		97.9	97.9	98.1	96.9	Operating Expenses	96.1	96.3
		2.1	2.1	1.9	3.1	Operating Profit	3.9	3.7
		.4	.5	.5	1.3	All Other Expenses (net)	.1	.4
		1.7	1.6	1.5	1.8	Profit Before Taxes	3.8	3.3
						RATIOS		
		2.6	2.4	2.5	2.5		2.7	2.6
		1.6	1.9	1.8	1.8	Current	1.9	1.9
		.5	1.3	1.2	1.4		1.4	1.3
		2.1	2.0	2.1	2.1		2.2	2.2
		1.0	1.6	1.5	1.5	Quick	1.6	1.5
		.5	1.1	1.0	1.0		1.1	1.0
		21 17.4	**38** 9.6	**40** 9.2	**38** 9.5		**40** 9.2	**42** 8.7
		41 8.9	**46** 7.9	**49** 7.4	**45** 8.0	Sales/Receivables	**49** 7.5	**50** 7.4
		57 6.5	**57** 6.4	**58** 6.3	**51** 7.1		**58** 6.3	**58** 6.3
						Cost of Sales/Inventory		
						Cost of Sales/Payables		
		5.9	5.0	5.4	5.6		4.9	5.1
		16.3	8.5	7.9	9.6	Sales/Working Capital	7.6	8.7
		-19.0	20.6	38.2	17.5		16.0	21.5
		11.8	4.7	4.4	5.4		7.4	7.1
		(12) 2.5	(78) 2.2	(87) 2.2	(131) 3.2	EBIT/Interest	(220) 3.3	(312) 3.3
		-3.2	-.5	.3	1.1		1.8	1.1
						Net Profit + Depr., Dep., Amort./Cur. Mat. L/T/D		
		.4	.7	.7	.7		.6	.6
		.8	1.0	1.0	1.0	Fixed/Worth	.9	.9
		2.0	1.4	1.4	1.3		1.4	1.3
		.4	.6	.5	.6		.5	.5
		1.0	.9	1.1	.9	Debt/Worth	1.0	.9
		2.2	1.6	1.9	1.7		1.8	1.6
		17.5	10.8	7.3	9.2		12.2	11.0
		(14) 8.1	(78) 2.8	(91) 2.6	4.3	% Profit Before Taxes/Tangible Net Worth	(222) 7.1	(309) 6.2
		.2	-3.9	-1.1	.1		2.9	.9
		9.2	5.7	4.5	4.6		6.4	5.9
		2.1	1.9	1.4	2.2	% Profit Before Taxes/Total Assets	3.5	3.2
		-8.6	-1.7	-.7	.1		1.3	.1
		9.4	3.8	3.1	2.7		3.4	3.4
		3.7	2.8	2.3	2.0	Sales/Net Fixed Assets	2.5	2.4
		2.1	2.1	1.8	1.6		1.8	1.9
		2.1	1.6	1.4	1.2		1.4	1.4
		1.6	1.3	1.0	.9	Sales/Total Assets	1.0	1.1
		1.0	1.0	.9	.8		.8	.8
		2.1	3.5	3.6	4.5		3.9	3.8
		(14) 4.8	4.7	(91) 4.8	(87) 5.5	% Depr., Dep., Amort./Sales	(204) 4.8	(297) 4.9
		6.0	5.7	6.4	6.5		6.0	5.8
							1.8	1.6
						% Officers', Directors' Owners' Comp/Sales	(12) 10.0	(11) 20.3
							32.4	40.8
22M		173545M	3286050M	7442506M	22545468M	Net Sales ($)	21133289M	30914081M
13M		112384M	2432244M	6600485M	22441530M	Total Assets ($)	20819908M	29191942M

M = $ thousand MM = $ million

See Pages 9 through 22 for Explanation of Ratios and Data

Comparative Historical Data | **Current Data Sorted by Sales**

			Type of Statement	0-1MM	1-3MM	3-5MM	5-10MM	10-25MM	25MM & OVE
229	245	207	Unqualified		2	1	2	17	185
1			Reviewed						
2	1		Compiled						
1			Tax Returns						
113	134	116	Other	1	1		3	15	96
4/1/07-3/31/08 ALL	4/1/08-3/31/09 ALL	4/1/09-3/31/10 ALL			182 (4/1-9/30/09)		141 (10/1/09-3/31/10)		
346	380	323	**NUMBER OF STATEMENTS**	1	3	1	5	32	281
%	%	%	**ASSETS**	%	%	%	%	%	%
11.2	11.5	11.0	Cash & Equivalents					12.4	10.9
15.6	15.2	14.7	Trade Receivables (net)					16.7	14.5
1.8	1.8	2.1	Inventory					2.3	1.9
2.8	3.0	2.9	All Other Current					3.0	3.0
31.5	31.5	30.7	Total Current					34.3	30.3
43.6	46.2	47.1	Fixed Assets (net)					47.8	46.8
.9	.7	.8	Intangibles (net)					1.0	.8
23.9	21.5	21.4	All Other Non-Current					16.9	22.2
100.0	100.0	100.0	Total					100.0	100.0
			LIABILITIES						
.8	.7	.5	Notes Payable-Short Term					.3	.5
2.4	2.1	2.2	Cur. Mat.-L.T.D.					2.4	2.2
6.6	6.0	5.9	Trade Payables					5.9	5.8
.0	.0	.0	Income-Taxes Payable					.0	.0
9.4	10.6	9.6	All Other Current					11.6	9.4
19.1	19.4	18.2	Total Current					20.2	17.9
27.1	27.6	26.2	Long-Term Debt					23.6	26.4
.0	.0	.0	Deferred Taxes					.0	.1
4.5	6.9	6.1	All Other Non-Current					2.7	6.3
49.3	46.2	49.5	Net Worth					53.5	49.3
100.0	100.0	100.0	Total Liabilities & Net Worth					100.0	100.0
			INCOME DATA						
100.0	100.0	100.0	Net Sales					100.0	100.0
			Gross Profit						
96.7	97.5	97.5	Operating Expenses					97.9	97.5
3.3	2.5	2.5	Operating Profit					2.1	2.5
-.1	2.1	.8	All Other Expenses (net)					1.2	.7
3.5	.4	1.6	Profit Before Taxes					.8	1.8
			RATIOS						
2.5	2.5	2.5	Current					2.7	2.5
1.8	1.7	1.8						1.9	1.8
1.3	1.3	1.3						1.5	1.3
2.2	2.3	2.1	Quick					2.3	2.1
1.6	1.5	1.5						1.7	1.5
1.0	1.0	1.0						1.3	1.0
42 8.8	39 9.3	38 9.6	Sales/Receivables					40 9.1	38 9.5
50 7.3	49 7.5	46 7.9						52 7.0	46 7.9
58 6.2	57 6.4	54 6.7						62 5.8	53 6.8
			Cost of Sales/Inventory						
			Cost of Sales/Payables						
5.0	5.1	5.5	Sales/Working Capital					4.6	5.6
8.3	9.6	9.1						7.0	9.4
25.6	24.4	21.2						13.8	21.4
6.3	4.4	4.9	EBIT/Interest					5.5	4.8
(329) 3.0	(354) 1.8	(308) 2.6						(28) 1.0	(271) 2.7
1.2	-.5	.4						-.9	.7
			Net Profit + Depr., Dep., Amort./Cur. Mat. L/T/D						
.6	.7	.7	Fixed/Worth					.5	.7
.9	1.0	1.0						.9	1.0
1.2	1.5	1.4						1.4	1.3
.6	.6	.6	Debt/Worth					.4	.6
.9	1.1	.9						.7	.9
1.5	1.9	1.7						1.6	1.7
10.4	9.0	9.2	% Profit Before Taxes/Tangible Net Worth					9.4	9.0
(331) 6.4	(365) 2.4	(317) 3.6						(30) .9	(277) 3.8
.6	-6.6	-.9						-3.9	-.4
5.5	4.3	4.8	% Profit Before Taxes/Total Assets					5.6	4.7
2.7	1.0	1.8						.4	1.9
.1	-3.0	-.6						-3.1	-.3
3.4	3.0	3.1	Sales/Net Fixed Assets					3.4	3.1
2.4	2.3	2.3						2.2	2.3
1.9	1.8	1.7						1.5	1.8
1.4	1.3	1.4	Sales/Total Assets					1.5	1.4
1.1	1.0	1.0						1.2	1.0
.8	.8	.8						.8	.9
3.8	3.7	4.0	% Depr., Dep., Amort./Sales					4.4	4.0
(298) 4.6	(322) 4.9	(274) 5.0						(30) 5.5	(234) 4.9
5.7	5.9	6.0						7.0	6.0
2.0	4.0	10.1	% Officers', Directors' Owners' Comp/Sales						
(16) 10.6	(17) 11.2	(10) 21.1							
17.2	17.7	41.6							
34155607M	40264786M	33447591M	Net Sales ($)	22M	6323M	3760M	40705M	599651M	32797130M
33396848M	38525970M	31586656M	Total Assets ($)	13M	37396M	4830M	29742M	830973M	30683702M

© RMA 2010

M = $ thousand   MM = $ million
See Pages 9 through 22 for Explanation of Ratios and Data

Current Data Sorted by Assets   Comparative Historical Data

0-500M	500M-2MM	2-10MM	10-50MM	50-100MM	100-250MM	Type of Statement	4/1/05-3/31/06 ALL	4/1/06-3/31/07 ALL
1	2	17	21	3	2	Unqualified	38	54
1		2	2			Reviewed	1	
2						Compiled	4	4
1	1	3				Tax Returns	1	3
1		13	8	2	3	Other	35	23
	46 (4/1-9/30/09)		39 (10/1/09-3/31/10)					
6	3	35	31	5	5	NUMBER OF STATEMENTS	79	84
%	%	%	%	%	%	**ASSETS**	%	%
		16.0	17.1			Cash & Equivalents	15.7	20.0
		26.7	15.3			Trade Receivables (net)	21.9	17.1
		.3	.8			Inventory	.6	.4
		2.4	4.8			All Other Current	2.5	3.7
		45.5	38.0			Total Current	40.7	41.2
		45.9	43.9			Fixed Assets (net)	43.3	46.1
		2.2	8.3			Intangibles (net)	1.1	2.2
		6.5	9.9			All Other Non-Current	14.8	10.4
		100.0	100.0			Total	100.0	100.0
						LIABILITIES		
		5.9	2.4			Notes Payable-Short Term	3.2	3.9
		4.5	2.8			Cur. Mat.-L.T.D.	3.2	2.7
		10.7	5.4			Trade Payables	7.1	6.3
		.3	.0			Income Taxes Payable	.0	.1
		18.4	10.9			All Other Current	11.1	11.0
		39.9	21.6			Total Current	24.6	24.0
		30.2	25.5			Long-Term Debt	18.8	23.7
		.0	.0			Deferred Taxes	.0	.0
		5.4	1.8			All Other Non-Current	4.0	2.5
		24.5	51.2			Net Worth	52.6	49.7
		100.0	100.0			Total Liabilities & Net Worth	100.0	100.0
						INCOME DATA		
		100.0	100.0			Net Sales	100.0	100.0
						Gross Profit		
		91.6	94.4			Operating Expenses	95.4	93.1
		8.4	5.6			Operating Profit	4.6	6.9
		3.9	1.6			All Other Expenses (net)	1.1	1.8
		4.5	3.9			Profit Before Taxes	3.5	5.1
						RATIOS		
		2.5	3.1			Current	2.8	3.5
		1.8	1.9				1.8	1.8
		.8	1.2				1.2	1.1
		2.2	2.7			Quick	2.5	3.0
		1.5	1.7				1.5	1.6
		.8	.9				1.1	.9
		16 23.3	28 12.9			Sales/Receivables	24 15.0	17 21.9
		39 9.3	37 9.8				42 8.8	40 9.2
		55 6.6	47 7.7				58 6.3	52 7.0
						Cost of Sales/Inventory		
						Cost of Sales/Payables		
		6.1	4.2			Sales/Working Capital	5.4	4.9
		14.4	8.0				10.1	10.7
		-35.6	39.7				49.5	68.3
		12.3	8.8			EBIT/Interest	14.2	6.3
		(30) 3.6	(27) 2.6				(65) 5.5	(68) 3.4
		.8	.5				1.9	.2
						Net Profit + Depr., Dep., Amort./Cur. Mat. L/T/D		
		.8	.6			Fixed/Worth	.5	.5
		1.3	1.0				.8	.9
		-4.4	2.0				1.2	1.6
		.7	.6			Debt/Worth	.4	.4
		1.6	.9				.8	1.0
		-7.7	2.7				2.1	2.8
		30.1	24.4			% Profit Before Taxes/Tangible Net Worth	18.3	16.6
		(26) 8.7	(29) 5.6				(77) 7.7	(78) 6.1
		-3.8	-1.6				2.4	-.6
		17.1	7.2			% Profit Before Taxes/Total Assets	9.6	10.6
		6.1	3.3				4.2	3.4
		-1.5	-.6				1.1	-.6
		11.3	5.3			Sales/Net Fixed Assets	5.5	5.9
		4.4	2.8				3.8	3.1
		2.9	2.1				2.1	2.0
		3.0	1.8			Sales/Total Assets	2.3	2.2
		2.3	1.4				1.5	1.4
		1.4	1.0				1.0	1.0
		1.3	1.8			% Depr., Dep., Amort./Sales	1.7	1.7
		(33) 2.0	2.5				(72) 2.5	(75) 2.5
		3.0	3.7				3.4	3.6
						% Officers', Directors' Owners' Comp/Sales		8.4
							(10) 15.3	
								33.8
14361M	11352M	425050M	949540M	389702M	813118M	Net Sales ($)	1910340M	4562677M
1212M	2196M	180423M	697728M	314743M	741378M	Total Assets ($)	1451469M	1392979M

RMA 2010

M = $ thousand   MM = $ million
See Pages 9 through 22 for Explanation of Ratios and Data

Comparative Historical Data   Current Data Sorted by Sales

			Type of Statement						
57	56	46	Unqualified	1	2	3	3	20	17
1	3	5	Reviewed				1	1	3
2	4	2	Compiled		1		1		
	1	5	Tax Returns	1	1		1	2	
			Other	1	1	1	4	7	12
25	28	27			46 (4/1-9/30/09)		39 (10/1/09-3/31/10)		
4/1/07-3/31/08	4/1/08-3/31/09	4/1/09-3/31/10		0-1MM	1-3MM	3-5MM	5-10MM	10-25MM	25MM & OVE
ALL	ALL	ALL							
85	92	85	**NUMBER OF STATEMENTS**	3	6	4	10	30	32
%	%	%	**ASSETS**	%	%	%	%	%	%
18.6	19.1	17.9	Cash & Equivalents				13.9	16.8	17.9
19.0	18.0	18.9	Trade Receivables (net)				21.8	23.3	19.0
.5	.6	.5	Inventory				.0	.5	.8
4.9	3.5	4.0	All Other Current				1.0	2.7	4.3
43.0	41.2	41.3	Total Current				36.7	43.2	42.1
43.2	42.9	42.6	Fixed Assets (net)				40.0	39.5	43.4
3.1	4.7	5.3	Intangibles (net)				5.9	6.1	5.0
10.8	11.3	10.8	All Other Non-Current				17.5	11.1	9.5
100.0	100.0	100.0	Total				100.0	100.0	100.0
			LIABILITIES						
3.3	3.8	12.6	Notes Payable-Short Term				17.4	5.7	2.7
2.3	2.4	3.7	Cur. Mat.-L.T.D.				4.3	3.0	2.9
5.7	5.9	8.6	Trade Payables				17.3	10.1	7.5
.3	.1	.1	Income Taxes Payable				.0	.4	.0
14.2	13.3	13.5	All Other Current				10.6	12.6	18.2
25.8	25.6	38.4	Total Current				49.6	31.8	31.3
21.5	27.8	27.7	Long-Term Debt				29.0	24.1	26.5
.0	.1	.0	Deferred Taxes				.0	.0	.1
3.6	9.4	4.5	All Other Non-Current				6.8	7.4	2.8
49.1	37.1	29.4	Net Worth				14.6	36.7	39.4
100.0	100.0	100.0	Total Liabilties & Net Worth				100.0	100.0	100.0
			INCOME DATA						
100.0	100.0	100.0	Net Sales				100.0	100.0	100.0
			Gross Profit						
95.9	95.2	93.6	Operating Expenses				93.8	94.7	95.9
4.1	4.8	6.4	Operating Profit				6.2	5.3	4.1
.5	3.2	2.4	All Other Expenses (net)				3.6	1.3	1.2
3.7	1.6	4.0	Profit Before Taxes				2.6	4.0	2.9
			RATIOS						
2.8	3.1	2.8					1.9	2.8	2.9
1.9	2.0	1.8	Current				.8	1.9	1.9
1.1	1.2	1.0					.5	1.0	1.2
2.7	2.8	2.5					1.9	2.7	2.5
1.6	1.7	1.6	Quick				.8	1.6	1.7
1.0	.9	.8					.4	.9	.9
17 20.9	16 23.2	18 20.0		0 UND			27 13.5		29 12.8
37 9.9	39 9.3	37 9.8	Sales/Receivables	41 8.9			38 9.5		39 9.4
59 6.2	54 6.7	55 6.7		61 6.0			55 6.7		57 6.4
			Cost of Sales/Inventory						
			Cost of Sales/Payables						
4.7	5.1	4.6					8.9	5.5	4.2
10.5	8.9	11.4	Sales/Working Capital				-239.1	12.7	8.4
49.0	39.5	-365.2					-28.7	-562.9	42.3
12.2	10.5	8.8					7.0		7.7
(68) 3.0	(76) 2.0	(71) 3.1	EBIT/Interest				(25) 3.5	(30) 3.0
1.4	-.9	.4					.8		.9
		16.2	Net Profit + Depr., Dep.,						
	(10) 3.1	Amort./Cur. Mat. L/T/D							
		.2							
.5	.6	.7					.8	.6	.8
.9	1.0	1.1	Fixed/Worth				6.7	.9	1.1
1.4	2.4	3.1					-.9	2.9	2.3
.5	.5	.6					2.0	.5	.6
.9	1.0	1.3	Debt/Worth				11.7	.9	1.0
2.2	3.7	6.5					-4.0	4.8	3.3
22.4	18.4	28.3	% Profit Before Taxes/Tangible				11.5	29.2
(79) 6.6	(79) 6.0	(68) 6.6	Net Worth				(24) 5.5	(27) 7.5
1.6	-5.9	-1.7						-2.0	1.8
11.8	9.6	12.4	% Profit Before Taxes/Total				22.4	12.8	8.4
3.2	2.5	4.1	Assets				14.0	3.7	4.1
.6	-2.6	-1.3					-5.4	-.7	.3
7.6	8.6	10.0					94.7	9.8	7.1
3.3	3.4	3.5	Sales/Net Fixed Assets				7.3	4.0	3.0
1.9	2.0	2.2					3.2	2.6	2.1
2.5	2.3	2.7					10.7	2.7	2.0
1.5	1.5	1.8	Sales/Total Assets				2.7	1.9	1.5
1.1	1.0	1.1					1.7	1.3	1.0
1.5	1.5	1.5						1.3	1.8
(81) 2.7	(81) 2.5	(79) 2.4	% Depr., Dep., Amort./Sales				(28) 2.1	(31) 2.5
3.7	3.7	3.6						3.6	3.9
			% Officers', Directors' Owners' Comp/Sales						
2036852M	2987261M	2603123M	Net Sales ($)	831M	9575M	15535M	76542M	475614M	2025026M
1526606M	2272749M	1937680M	Total Assets ($)	5018M	5235M	15991M	31718M	361783M	1517935M

Current Data Sorted by Assets

Comparative Historical Data

						Type of Statement		
		16	29	10	13	Unqualified	61	64
6	1	2	3			Reviewed	4	1
3	1	3	1			Compiled	11	7
3	2	1	1	1		Tax Returns	6	6
3	10	26	19	7	10	Other	47	46
	51 (4/1-9/30/09)		120 (10/1/09-3/31/10)				4/1/05-3/31/06	4/1/06-3/31/07
0-500M	500M-2MM	2-10MM	10-50MM	50-100MM	100-250MM		ALL	ALL
15	14	48	53	18	23	NUMBER OF STATEMENTS	129	124
%	%	%	%	%	%	ASSETS	%	%
20.5	35.5	12.5	13.4	14.0	10.8	Cash & Equivalents	16.7	16.7
7.2	13.6	23.6	21.3	13.5	19.1	Trade Receivables (net)	21.3	22.5
4.2	1.4	2.0	1.6	1.6	1.0	Inventory	1.2	1.0
23.9	6.9	4.2	2.8	2.2	3.1	All Other Current	3.9	4.3
55.8	57.4	42.3	39.2	31.3	34.1	Total Current	43.1	44.4
25.4	29.5	48.5	40.4	42.1	39.9	Fixed Assets (net)	37.9	35.4
8.1	6.2	2.9	4.9	10.3	3.9	Intangibles (net)	2.9	2.9
10.7	7.0	6.2	15.4	16.3	22.2	All Other Non-Current	16.2	17.3
100.0	100.0	100.0	100.0	100.0	100.0	Total	100.0	100.0
						LIABILITIES		
15.1	6.4	2.0	2.0	.3	1.0	Notes Payable-Short Term	6.0	8.2
3.3	1.7	3.9	3.9	2.7	2.3	Cur. Mat.-L.T.D.	4.5	3.8
8.0	6.7	6.5	8.2	5.3	8.7	Trade Payables	9.4	9.4
.0	.0	.6	.0	.1	.0	Income Taxes Payable	.1	.2
55.5	30.1	17.9	10.3	6.9	13.0	All Other Current	13.6	20.3
82.0	44.9	30.8	24.3	15.3	25.0	Total Current	33.6	41.8
16.8	27.5	36.1	24.5	32.8	39.8	Long-Term Debt	19.4	22.4
.1	.0	.0	.2	.0	.0	Deferred Taxes	.2	.1
.0	.0	3.2	3.7	4.8	9.2	All Other Non-Current	4.2	2.9
1.1	27.6	29.8	47.2	47.0	26.1	Net Worth	42.7	32.8
100.0	100.0	100.0	100.0	100.0	100.0	Total Liabilties & Net Worth	100.0	100.0
						INCOME DATA		
100.0	100.0	100.0	100.0	100.0	100.0	Net Sales	100.0	100.0
						Gross Profit		
95.1	85.7	84.5	87.3	91.5	97.6	Operating Expenses	91.4	91.3
4.9	14.3	15.5	12.7	8.5	2.4	Operating Profit	8.6	8.7
.1	3.4	4.5	3.5	2.8	2.9	All Other Expenses (net)	1.7	2.5
4.8	10.9	11.0	9.1	5.7	-.5	Profit Before Taxes	6.9	6.2
						RATIOS		
2.0	4.5	2.9	2.7	3.7	2.6	Current	3.0	2.6
1.5	1.3	1.6	1.6	1.9	1.7		1.6	1.5
.3	.6	1.0	1.2	1.3	1.0		.9	.8
1.3	2.6	2.3	2.4	3.2	2.1	Quick	2.5	2.2
.3	1.2	1.5	1.5	1.6	1.4		1.4	1.2
.2	.6	.8	.9	1.3	.9		.6	.7
0 UND	0 UND	7 54.5	20 18.7	34 10.8	42 8.7	Sales/Receivables	19 19.2	14 25.2
0 UND	1 592.7	35 10.6	41 8.9	50 7.2	54 6.7		41 8.9	47 7.7
3 106.6	29 12.8	55 6.6	53 6.9	58 6.3	64 5.7		62 5.9	65 5.6
						Cost of Sales/Inventory		
						Cost of Sales/Payables		
19.0	6.0	7.0	6.2	2.8	5.1	Sales/Working Capital	5.3	4.8
22.4	91.1	14.1	12.7	6.7	10.5		11.8	13.7
-27.1	-25.5	NM	49.2	19.5	-141.4		-50.1	-33.8
		13.1	44.0	26.3	4.2	EBIT/Interest	14.6	10.9
	(36) 3.7	(37) 3.4	(17) 2.8	(21) 1.9			(105) 4.2	(94) 3.8
		1.5	1.2	.9	-.5		.6	.9
						Net Profit + Depr., Dep.,	8.2	
						Amort./Cur. Mat. L/T/D	(10) 4.6	
							2.0	
.4	.3	.3	.4	.5	.6	Fixed/Worth	.4	.4
.7	.8	1.4	.8	1.0	2.1		.8	.8
-.4	-2.0	9.6	2.7	11.3	13.1		1.9	2.9
.6	.6	.4	.4	.4	.5	Debt/Worth	.5	.5
1.1	2.9	2.4	1.1	1.2	4.1		1.0	1.2
-2.9	-13.7	11.9	4.3	14.1	25.7		3.8	8.4
		132.1	65.9	57.2	14.6	% Profit Before Taxes/Tangible	44.3	35.5
	(39) 56.8	(47) 20.6	(16) 4.8	(18) -2.2		Net Worth	(114) 10.1	(102) 11.2
		19.6	.5	.8	-18.7		1.0	3.7
40.4	52.9	27.2	22.3	13.0	5.2	% Profit Before Taxes/Total	14.4	13.6
16.4	16.8	11.9	6.7	1.9	3.9	Assets	5.2	5.1
8.3	-.4	2.7	.1	-.6	-4.7		-.8	.1
53.3	46.4	31.9	10.5	6.4	4.7	Sales/Net Fixed Assets	12.5	21.1
29.6	17.5	3.5	4.3	1.8	3.6		3.9	4.8
24.8	9.3	.9	1.9	1.0	1.9		2.1	2.3
10.8	6.4	3.6	2.4	1.4	2.1	Sales/Total Assets	2.8	2.7
6.8	4.7	1.3	1.4	.9	1.0		1.6	1.5
4.2	1.7	.6	.8	.5	.8		.8	.8
.3	.5	.6	1.7	2.6	2.0	% Depr., Dep., Amort./Sales	1.6	1.4
(12) .4	(13) 1.5	(44) 3.8	(48) 2.8	(17) 4.8	(21) 3.2		(113) 2.8	(108) 2.8
1.2	2.3	7.0	5.7	7.9	4.7		5.1	4.9
			1.1			% Officers', Directors'	8.1	11.2
		(10) 5.0				Owners' Comp/Sales	(24) 21.8	(18) 22.4
			23.1				34.2	29.6
23162M	86604M	665093M	2052548M	1254906M	4257522M	Net Sales ($)	5406867M	5763915M
3084M	15436M	264389M	1296848M	1290250M	3317644M	Total Assets ($)	5086906M	5389820M

M = $ thousand   MM = $ million
See Pages 9 through 22 for Explanation of Ratios and Data

Comparative Historical Data | **Current Data Sorted by Sales**

			Type of Statement						
58	54	68	Unqualified		6	4	6	12	40
4	2	12	Reviewed	1	7	1	1	1	1
7	9	8	Compiled	1	2	2	1	1	1
8	8	8	Tax Returns	2	1	2	1		2
50	51	75	Other	3	11	3	9	13	36
4/1/07-3/31/08 ALL	4/1/08-3/31/09 ALL	4/1/09-3/31/10 ALL		0-1MM	51 (4/1-9/30/09) 1-3MM	3-5MM	120 (10/1/09-3/31/10) 5-10MM	10-25MM	25MM & OVER
127	124	171	**NUMBER OF STATEMENTS**	7	27	12	18	27	80
%	%	%	**ASSETS**	%	%	%	%	%	%
18.7	15.6	15.3	Cash & Equivalents	17.0	19.8	12.3	14.5	14.1	
18.9	20.2	19.0	Trade Receivables (net)	6.6	8.1	16.9	30.7	22.9	
2.0	1.3	1.9	Inventory	.4	.6	.9	2.2	2.0	
5.6	6.0	5.4	All Other Current	11.1	2.2	5.4	3.8	2.9	
45.1	43.2	41.5	Total Current	35.1	30.7	35.5	51.3	42.0	
38.2	37.5	40.6	Fixed Assets (net)	54.7	51.1	44.7	31.8	38.2	
3.6	2.1	5.2	Intangibles (net)	1.8	1.7	2.3	7.9	5.8	
13.0	17.1	12.7	All Other Non-Current	8.5	16.6	17.5	9.0	13.9	
100.0	100.0	100.0	Total	100.0	100.0	100.0	100.0	100.0	
			LIABILITIES						
8.1	10.8	3.2	Notes Payable-Short Term	3.5	9.6	5.7	1.3	1.9	
4.8	3.6	3.3	Cur. Mat.-L.T.D.	2.9	2.1	6.6	5.4	2.1	
7.8	8.1	7.3	Trade Payables	4.5	3.8	5.7	9.6	8.8	
.0	.2	.2	Income Taxes Payable	.1	.0	1.4	.0	.1	
12.8	12.1	18.0	All Other Current	35.5	13.7	6.9	29.2	12.6	
33.5	34.8	32.0	Total Current	46.4	29.2	26.3	45.5	25.4	
26.9	23.4	30.3	Long-Term Debt	46.0	46.9	22.9	17.1	28.1	
.1	.1	.1	Deferred Taxes	.4	.0	.0	.0	.0	
4.2	4.6	3.8	All Other Non-Current	4.1	1.4	1.6	3.3	5.0	
35.3	37.0	33.8	Net Worth	3.1	22.5	49.2	34.2	41.3	
100.0	100.0	100.0	Total Liabilties & Net Worth	100.0	100.0	100.0	100.0	100.0	
			INCOME DATA						
100.0	100.0	100.0	Net Sales	100.0	100.0	100.0	100.0	100.0	
			Gross Profit						
90.9	91.9	88.9	Operating Expenses	83.6	82.5	87.6	90.9	92.1	
9.1	8.1	11.1	Operating Profit	16.4	17.5	12.4	9.1	7.9	
1.6	3.6	3.3	All Other Expenses (net)	9.1	6.2	2.0	.0	2.3	
7.5	4.5	7.8	Profit Before Taxes	7.3	11.3	10.4	9.1	5.7	
			RATIOS						
3.0	3.0	2.7	Current	2.0	1.5	3.5	4.0	2.7	
1.7	1.8	1.7		1.5	1.1	1.5	2.2	1.7	
.9	1.1	1.0		.5	.5	.7	1.0	1.4	
2.5	2.5	2.3	Quick	1.9	1.5	2.3	2.9	2.4	
1.4	1.5	1.4		.8	1.0	1.2	1.7	1.5	
.7	.8	.8		.2	.5	.6	.8	1.1	
11 33.3	14 26.0	8 48.5	Sales/Receivables	0 UND	0 UND	5 80.9	33 10.9	35 10.6	
46 8.0	47 7.7	38 9.5		2 163.2	7 53.2	26 14.3	43 8.6	50 7.4	
67 5.5	64 5.7	55 6.7		26 13.9	12 30.0	46 7.9	56 6.5	60 6.1	
			Cost of Sales/Inventory						
			Cost of Sales/Payables						
4.8	5.2	6.4	Sales/Working Capital	8.0	9.7	4.4	4.1	6.3	
11.0	11.4	13.4		22.5	46.4	29.4	11.6	10.1	
-148.5	175.6	155.5		-26.6	-15.1	-31.3	-128.2	27.7	
15.3	16.4	19.6	EBIT/Interest	13.2	21.8	8.6	12.9	32.1	
(100) 3.5	(100) 4.0	(128) 3.4		(13) 2.6	(11) 3.4	(13) 2.3	(21) 2.0	(67) 3.9	
1.3	.5	1.0		.5	1.9	.5	.9	1.2	
		4.3	Net Profit + Depr., Dep., Amort./Cur. Mat. L/T/D						
	(14) 2.5								
	-.9								
.4	.4	.4	Fixed/Worth	.7	.5	.3	.3	.5	
1.0	.8	.9		3.7	6.1	.7	.9	.8	
8.0	3.1	10.1		-6.3	-5.6	3.7	6.1	4.7	
.5	.4	.5	Debt/Worth	1.0	.8	.1	.3	.5	
1.6	1.0	1.5		4.4	6.7	.9	1.4	1.2	
17.5	7.2	14.8		-10.8	-11.3	5.4	11.7	12.7	
69.9	48.7	82.4	% Profit Before Taxes/Tangible Net Worth	85.7		56.1	114.5	74.1	
(101) 10.8	(101) 9.3	(138) 21.8		(18) 32.1	(16) 20.6	(22) 45.9	(70) 18.1		
3.5	.3	.9		.2		5.5	-1.3	.7	
26.4	15.4	24.0	% Profit Before Taxes/Total Assets	16.3	38.4	21.5	38.3	22.8	
5.4	3.8	6.7		6.5	11.7	9.2	9.1	4.7	
.8	-1.0	.0		-1.0	3.4	-.4	.0	.0	
16.8	15.9	21.4	Sales/Net Fixed Assets	24.8	22.3	17.6	40.2	10.2	
4.5	3.9	4.7		2.6	1.1	5.2	5.5	4.3	
2.1	1.8	1.6		.5	.6	1.2	2.3	2.0	
2.9	2.8	3.1	Sales/Total Assets	4.6	5.3	3.2	3.8	2.4	
1.6	1.5	1.5		1.0	.9	1.2	2.3	1.5	
.7	.7	.8		.4	.5	.6	.9	.9	
1.6	1.8	1.2	% Depr., Dep., Amort./Sales	.3	1.8	2.0	1.1	1.5	
(109) 3.2	(106) 3.7	(155) 2.7		(26) 1.4	5.7 (16)	4.2 (24)	2.5 (73)	2.7	
5.0	5.1	5.5		9.2	9.1	6.6	5.2	4.6	
4.6	3.5	5.0	% Officers', Directors' Owners' Comp/Sales						3.5
(18) 8.0	(19) 9.7	(29) 11.4						(13)	18.9
19.8	24.8	28.4							28.4
5234318M	5144051M	8339835M	Net Sales ($)	4441M	54000M	45581M	127540M	457849M	7650424M
5137682M	5074935M	6187651M	Total Assets ($)	2680M	108741M	103575M	153307M	357215M	5462133M

M = $ thousand   MM = $ million
See Pages 9 through 22 for Explanation of Ratios and Data

Current Data Sorted by Assets   **Comparative Historical Data**

						Type of Statement		
	31	163	229	47	43	Unqualified	449	549
2	36	103	30	3		Reviewed	144	123
9	31	61	12	4		Compiled	157	158
43	41	58	6		1	Tax Returns	124	128
52	182	274	108	42	27	Other	631	526
	394 (4/1-9/30/09)		1,244 (10/1/09-3/31/10)				4/1/05-3/31/06	4/1/06-3/31/07
0-500M	500M-2MM	2-10MM	10-50MM	50-100MM	100-250MM		ALL	ALL
106	321	659	385	96	71	NUMBER OF STATEMENTS	1505	1484
%	%	%	%	%	%	ASSETS	%	%
23.4	14.5	10.6	10.7	9.4	11.2	Cash & Equivalents	12.4	11.9
19.0	34.6	20.9	11.8	9.6	10.1	Trade Receivables (net)	20.2	21.2
.4	.6	.2	.2	.2	.5	Inventory	.4	.5
4.7	4.4	2.9	3.6	3.4	2.6	All Other Current	3.9	3.7
47.5	54.1	34.5	26.3	22.6	24.4	Total Current	36.9	37.2
33.5	30.1	50.2	53.4	54.1	50.5	Fixed Assets (net)	46.4	45.4
5.5	4.9	4.9	6.2	4.8	5.8	Intangibles (net)	4.0	4.1
13.5	10.9	10.4	14.1	18.5	19.2	All Other Non-Current	12.7	13.3
100.0	100.0	100.0	100.0	100.0	100.0	Total	100.0	100.0
						LIABILITIES		
12.4	5.9	3.1	1.8	1.2	1.3	Notes Payable-Short Term	5.6	4.5
5.0	3.1	4.3	3.0	2.6	3.3	Cur. Mat.-L.T.D.	3.1	2.9
16.5	14.5	9.3	5.9	5.1	4.6	Trade Payables	9.8	10.5
.0	.0	.0	.0	.0	.0	Income Taxes Payable	.1	.1
54.8	27.6	13.8	10.5	9.5	9.0	All Other Current	17.9	18.3
88.8	51.1	30.6	21.3	18.4	18.2	Total Current	36.5	36.3
15.2	25.5	47.8	47.7	48.1	49.4	Long-Term Debt	40.3	41.0
.0	.1	.2	.1	.2	.4	Deferred Taxes	.1	.1
15.2	8.4	5.2	7.9	10.6	13.7	All Other Non-Current	9.0	8.8
-19.1	14.8	16.3	23.1	22.8	18.4	Net Worth	14.1	13.8
100.0	100.0	100.0	100.0	100.0	100.0	Total Liabilties & Net Worth	100.0	100.0
						INCOME DATA		
100.0	100.0	100.0	100.0	100.0	100.0	Net Sales	100.0	100.0
						Gross Profit		
93.4	88.9	84.6	88.5	90.2	95.0	Operating Expenses	89.5	90.8
6.6	11.1	15.4	11.5	9.8	5.0	Operating Profit	10.5	9.2
1.9	2.8	6.9	4.8	5.5	4.4	All Other Expenses (net)	5.3	4.5
4.8	8.2	8.4	6.6	4.3	.6	Profit Before Taxes	5.2	4.6
						RATIOS		
1.9	2.0	2.1	2.4	2.0	2.1		2.2	2.1
.8	1.1	1.3	1.4	1.2	1.4	Current	1.2	1.2
.3	.6	.7	.8	.8	.9		.7	.8
1.6	1.9	2.0	2.1	1.6	2.0		1.9	2.0
.7	1.0	1.2	1.1	1.1	1.2	Quick	1.1	1.1
.2	.5	.6	.6	.6	.7		.6	.6
0 UND	8 46.3	15 24.1	20 18.1	19 19.6	24 15.0	Sales/Receivables	12 29.8	15 23.6
5 72.1	31 11.7	33 11.0	34 10.9	31 11.9	34 10.6		32 11.5	34 10.9
17 21.1	44 8.2	46 7.9	45 8.1	43 8.5	41 8.9		48 7.7	47 7.7
						Cost of Sales/Inventory		
						Cost of Sales/Payables		
32.7	12.8	9.0	6.2	7.9	6.2	Sales/Working Capital	8.3	8.4
-78.6	55.6	27.6	19.8	29.5	19.6		32.5	35.6
-9.2	-15.1	-19.4	-23.7	-21.4	-47.5		-17.1	-22.2
16.4	27.9	11.7	6.1	4.1	3.7		6.1	5.4
(52) 4.5	(218) 6.0	(510) 3.8	(336) 2.6	(84) 1.7	(68) 1.8	EBIT/Interest	(1189) 2.3	(1196) 2.3
-.2	1.2	1.4	1.2	.9	.5		.9	.9
		7.9	7.1	7.1	6.9	Net Profit + Depr., Dep.,	7.9	7.4
	(50) 3.0	(41) 4.1	(10) 3.3	(12) 4.1		Amort./Cur. Mat. L/T/D	(90) 3.1	(97) 2.8
	1.5	2.3	1.5	2.5			1.2	1.0
.2	.2	.8	1.1	1.2	1.4		.8	.8
2.0	1.0	3.7	3.4	3.7	3.9	Fixed/Worth	3.1	2.8
-.6	-8.9	-8.6	-12.4	-45.2	-33.4		-7.3	-8.4
.9	1.1	1.4	1.3	1.3	2.1		1.4	1.3
9.9	3.7	5.4	4.4	4.8	6.8	Debt/Worth	5.1	5.0
-2.6	-10.7	-12.6	-18.5	-51.6	-55.1		-12.8	-14.0
157.5	107.0	77.4	40.6	31.4	32.1	% Profit Before Taxes/Tangible	65.8	59.8
(60) 75.6	(228) 52.7	(450) 35.7	(272) 13.6	(70) 8.6	(48) 11.4	Net Worth	(1011) 19.9	(1019) 17.7
32.1	10.6	13.6	2.6	.2	-2.3		3.3	3.9
44.0	33.7	17.5	9.4	6.8	5.7	% Profit Before Taxes/Total	13.6	11.9
17.8	10.8	7.0	4.0	2.1	2.1	Assets	4.1	3.8
-5.0	.5	1.4	.6	-.1	-1.9		-.2	-.4
162.1	65.2	12.4	3.4	3.0	3.6	Sales/Net Fixed Assets	19.6	19.7
39.9	24.0	3.0	1.7	1.4	1.6		2.9	3.0
9.7	5.7	1.1	.9	.6	.7		1.0	1.1
12.5	5.3	2.8	1.4	1.4	1.6	Sales/Total Assets	3.0	3.0
6.8	3.9	1.5	.9	.7	.8		1.4	1.3
3.4	1.6	.7	.5	.3	.4		.6	.6
.3	.4	1.2	2.4	2.6	2.8	% Depr., Dep., Amort./Sales	1.1	1.1
(68) 1.1	(260) 1.1	(618) 2.7	(374) 4.1	(93) 5.3	(69) 4.2		(1389) 3.0	(1371) 2.9
3.1	3.0	5.7	7.0	10.3	10.2		6.6	6.3
2.6	1.2	1.8	2.3			% Officers', Directors'	2.5	2.2
(39) 5.8	(43) 2.5	(75) 3.7	(44) 5.1			Owners' Comp/Sales	(211) 5.3	(206) 4.5
8.3	6.5	5.8	14.9				8.4	8.5
167734M	1405867M	5813099M	10521222M	7662470M	10734047M	Net Sales ($)	27103021M	31501453M
24137M	390797M	3360005M	8831141M	6955879M	10662861M	Total Assets ($)	26872461M	31092073M

M = $ thousand   MM = $ million
See Pages 9 through 22 for Explanation of Ratios and Data

Comparative Historical Data   Current Data Sorted by Sales

4/1/07-3/31/08 ALL	4/1/08-3/31/09 ALL	4/1/09-3/31/10 ALL	Type of Statement	0-1MM	1-3MM	3-5MM	5-10MM	10-25MM	25MM & OVER
508	449	513	Unqualified	15	30	30	100	183	155
125	129	174	Reviewed	6	18	20	64	50	16
137	130	117	Compiled	13	22	21	34	18	9
120	155	149	Tax Returns	35	39	17	38	16	4
574	644	685	Other	96	120	73	157	136	103
				394 (4/1-9/30/09)		1,244 (10/1/09-3/31/10)			
1464	1507	1638	NUMBER OF STATEMENTS	165	229	161	393	403	287
%	%	%	ASSETS	%	%	%	%	%	%
11.7	11.5	12.2	Cash & Equivalents	10.6	12.5	14.0	12.4	11.7	12.2
21.4	21.7	20.2	Trade Receivables (net)	7.8	10.6	25.1	26.8	22.2	20.3
.4	.2	.3	Inventory	.2	.6	.3	.2	.2	.4
5.4	4.0	3.5	All Other Current	2.8	2.5	3.6	3.7	3.3	4.6
38.8	37.4	36.1	Total Current	21.4	26.1	43.0	43.0	37.5	37.5
44.4	44.9	46.2	Fixed Assets (net)	63.1	55.4	41.3	40.4	43.9	42.8
3.8	3.7	5.3	Intangibles (net)	6.5	6.2	4.1	5.0	4.9	5.5
13.0	14.0	12.4	All Other Non-Current	9.0	12.3	11.6	11.6	13.7	14.1
100.0	100.0	100.0	Total	100.0	100.0	100.0	100.0	100.0	100.0
			LIABILITIES						
5.8	4.7	3.8	Notes Payable-Short Term	4.9	6.6	4.0	3.4	3.0	2.3
3.2	3.1	3.7	Cur. Mat.-L.T.D.	5.3	5.4	2.9	2.7	3.7	3.1
10.8	10.4	9.5	Trade Payables	4.7	7.9	10.0	11.2	10.7	9.4
.1	.1	.0	Income Taxes Payable	.0	.0	.1	.0	.0	.1
17.3	19.6	17.9	All Other Current	19.4	22.2	18.8	19.0	15.4	15.4
37.1	37.9	34.9	Total Current	34.2	42.1	35.8	36.3	32.8	30.2
40.5	41.7	41.4	Long-Term Debt	58.2	54.4	32.1	35.2	36.7	41.5
.1	.1	.1	Deferred Taxes	.0	.0	.2	.3	.0	.1
8.5	7.4	7.8	All Other Non-Current	10.1	9.6	7.0	6.0	8.1	7.6
13.8	12.9	15.8	Net Worth	-2.5	-6.1	24.8	22.2	22.3	20.6
100.0	100.0	100.0	Total Liabilities & Net Worth	100.0	100.0	100.0	100.0	100.0	100.0
			INCOME DATA						
100.0	100.0	100.0	Net Sales	100.0	100.0	100.0	100.0	100.0	100.0
			Gross Profit						
89.4	88.6	87.7	Operating Expenses	59.6	81.2	90.5	92.3	93.2	93.6
10.6	11.4	12.3	Operating Profit	40.4	18.8	9.5	7.7	6.8	6.4
5.1	6.3	5.1	All Other Expenses (net)	17.6	11.0	3.4	2.2	1.9	2.7
5.5	5.1	7.2	Profit Before Taxes	22.7	7.8	6.0	5.5	4.9	3.7
			RATIOS						
2.2	2.1	2.1	Current	2.2	1.6	2.3	2.5	2.2	2.0
1.3	1.2	1.2		.9	.8	1.3	1.4	1.3	1.3
.8	.7	.7		.2	.2	.8	.8	.8	.8
1.9	1.9	2.0	Quick	1.9	1.4	2.2	2.3	2.0	1.8
1.1 (1506)	1.1	1.1		.7	.7	1.2	1.3	1.2	1.2
.6	.6	.6		.1	.2	.7	.8	.6	.7
13 27.5	14 26.8	11 32.2	Sales/Receivables	0 UND	0 UND	8 45.6	25 14.8	27 13.6	29 12.4
34 10.7	34 10.7	32 11.3		0 UND	5 70.9	32 11.5	34 10.8	36 10.2	37 10.0
47 7.8	48 7.6	44 8.3		17 21.2	27 13.7	48 7.6	46 7.9	46 8.0	46 8.0
			Cost of Sales/Inventory						
			Cost of Sales/Payables						
8.2	9.4	8.9	Sales/Working Capital	6.7	13.7	9.5	8.9	8.5	8.5
27.3	34.0	34.2		-26.0	-42.8	33.1	26.5	26.9	21.7
-22.8	-15.5	-19.5		-4.1	-6.9	-40.2	-41.2	-23.9	-43.3
4.9	6.3	9.5	EBIT/Interest	6.6	7.5	12.6	11.7	10.4	7.9
(1126) 2.2	(1173) 2.3	(1268) 3.1		(68) 3.6	(143) 1.9	(125) 4.3	(314) 3.6	(353) 3.1	(265) 2.6
.9	.7	1.3		1.3	.4	1.3	1.4	1.3	1.4
6.5	7.1	7.3	Net Profit + Depr., Dep., Amort./Cur. Mat. L/T/D				9.0	7.4	7.1
(103) 3.0	(94) 3.6	(118) 3.6					(28) 3.2	(29) 3.8	(47) 3.9
1.5	1.0	1.6					1.5	.8	2.5
.7	.7	.7	Fixed/Worth	2.5	1.2	.2	.5	.7	.8
2.5	3.0	3.0		11.2	34.7	1.4	2.3	2.3	2.8
-9.0	-6.4	-8.9		-6.1	-1.6	21.8	-30.4	-25.8	-46.0
1.2	1.3	1.3	Debt/Worth	2.7	1.9	1.1	1.0	1.1	1.6
4.3	5.2	4.9		16.0	126.1	3.1	3.9	3.4	5.1
-14.3	-11.8	-13.0		-7.0	-3.6	83.5	-54.3	-44.4	-61.0
54.3	71.7	74.8	% Profit Before Taxes/Tangible Net Worth	82.5	94.9	74.2	78.7	66.8	62.9
(1024) 18.2	(1011) 22.2	(1128) 28.7		(100) 35.0	(118) 35.2	(122) 23.7	(289) 37.2	(296) 22.1	(203) 22.6
3.9	2.2	6.1		13.1	3.0	6.1	8.6	4.5	6.0
12.8	13.7	16.7	% Profit Before Taxes/Total Assets	12.5	17.1	18.7	22.4	15.0	12.6
4.2	4.3	5.9		4.8	3.2	5.1	8.6	6.4	5.5
-.1	-.9	.6		.6	-1.3	.6	1.1	1.0	1.5
19.8	22.7	19.6	Sales/Net Fixed Assets	8.0	27.3	45.7	32.0	15.0	10.8
3.1	3.3	3.1		.4	1.7	7.3	5.8	3.0	3.2
1.2	1.1	1.1		.2	.5	1.5	1.8	1.4	1.6
3.1	3.4	3.3	Sales/Total Assets	.9	2.8	4.5	4.0	3.1	2.8
1.4	1.4	1.4		.3	.9	2.1	2.1	1.4	1.5
.7	.6	.7		.1	.4	.8	1.1	.8	.9
1.1	1.0	1.2	% Depr., Dep., Amort./Sales	4.2	2.1	.9	.7	1.1	1.4
(1307) 2.7	(1371) 2.8	(1482) 2.9		(136) 15.1	(187) 5.7	(139) 2.2	(355) 2.1	(387) 2.8	(278) 2.6
5.9	5.9	5.9		26.0	13.0	5.0	3.9	5.1	4.4
2.1	1.6	1.7	% Officers', Directors' Owners' Comp/Sales	3.2	1.2	1.7	1.7	1.4	1.5
(230) 4.3	(181) 3.5	(217) 3.9		(25) 6.1	(36) 3.6	(23) 3.2	(58) 3.9	(38) 3.9	(37) 5.0
9.5	7.2	7.8		8.7	5.9	9.6	7.9	7.2	12.3
32100782M	31076987M	36304439M	Net Sales ($)	88530M	425491M	654474M	2920316M	6059038M	26156590M
28882403M	27822741M	30224820M	Total Assets ($)	401548M	857872M	809529M	2493484M	6997916M	18664471M

M = $ thousand   MM = $ million
See Pages 9 through 22 for Explanation of Ratios and Data

Current Data Sorted by Assets

Comparative Historical Data

0-500M	500M-2MM	2-10MM	10-50MM	50-100MM	100-250MM	Type of Statement	4/1/05-3/31/06 ALL	4/1/06-3/31/07 ALL
1	13	39	41	8	6	Unqualified	52	78
1		2				Reviewed	2	
1		2				Compiled	3	2
1	1	2				Tax Returns	2	9
3	10	28	5	4	3	Other	11	18
	114 (4/1-9/30/09)		56 (10/1/09-3/31/10)					
6	24	73	46	12	9	NUMBER OF STATEMENTS	70	107
%	%	%	%	%	%	ASSETS	%	%
	21.8	15.9	13.9	14.1		Cash & Equivalents	20.9	18.8
	16.3	22.6	18.4	18.4		Trade Receivables (net)	19.6	16.9
	.0	.3	.2	.0		Inventory	.1	.1
	11.0	2.3	3.5	5.4		All Other Current	3.8	2.7
	49.1	41.2	36.0	37.9		Total Current	44.4	38.5
	43.6	49.3	51.4	52.6		Fixed Assets (net)	44.7	50.0
	.9	2.1	2.8	.9		Intangibles (net)	1.2	1.4
	6.3	7.4	9.7	8.6		All Other Non-Current	9.8	10.1
	100.0	100.0	100.0	100.0		Total	100.0	100.0
						LIABILITIES		
	3.2	2.9	5.4	6.2		Notes Payable-Short Term	4.8	3.9
	3.3	3.3	3.3	2.4		Cur. Mat.-L.T.D.	2.1	2.2
	4.7	7.1	6.1	8.8		Trade Payables	7.7	7.0
	.1	.2	.0	.3		Income Taxes Payable	.4	.2
	13.1	13.8	11.6	10.7		All Other Current	14.8	11.6
	24.4	27.2	26.5	28.5		Total Current	29.7	24.9
	31.0	26.3	31.0	41.3		Long-Term Debt	24.3	33.5
	.3	.1	.0	.0		Deferred Taxes	.0	.0
	4.7	3.7	3.4	6.5		All Other Non-Current	5.4	1.9
	39.6	42.6	39.0	23.7		Net Worth	40.5	39.7
	100.0	100.0	100.0	100.0		Total Liabilties & Net Worth	100.0	100.0
						INCOME DATA		
	100.0	100.0	100.0	100.0		Net Sales	100.0	100.0
						Gross Profit		
	90.3	95.4	95.8	92.8		Operating Expenses	95.9	93.6
	9.7	4.6	4.2	7.2		Operating Profit	4.1	6.4
	3.8	2.3	1.7	7.4		All Other Expenses (net)	.6	2.0
	6.0	2.3	2.5	-.2		Profit Before Taxes	3.5	4.4
						RATIOS		
	4.3	3.0	1.9	1.4		Current	2.7	2.6
	2.3	1.5	1.4	1.1			1.5	1.6
	1.3	1.0	1.0	.9			.9	.9
	3.8	2.9	1.7	1.1		Quick	2.5	2.5
	2.1	1.4	1.2	1.0			1.3	1.4
	.9	.9	.8	.8			.8	.8
	1 478.2	21 17.3	27 13.4	18 20.1		Sales/Receivables	23 15.8	14 25.6
	15 23.8	34 10.6	41 9.0	50 7.3			35 10.5	32 11.4
	30 12.2	49 7.5	52 7.0	61 6.0			49 7.5	51 7.1
						Cost of Sales/Inventory		
						Cost of Sales/Payables		
	3.1	6.1	7.3	8.8		Sales/Working Capital	5.7	5.2
	8.7	17.3	16.4	33.5			15.1	13.4
	49.3	NM	-163.8	-152.3			-47.9	-131.9
	16.6	7.0	3.9			EBIT/Interest	8.2	5.3
	(20) 4.2	(55) 2.4	(44) 2.4				(55) 2.8	(81) 2.1
	1.3	.0	1.4				1.3	1.0
						Net Profit + Depr., Dep., Amort./Cur. Mat. L/T/D		
	.3	.6	.9	1.6		Fixed/Worth	.5	.5
	1.0	1.1	1.4	3.1			1.2	1.3
	1.8	2.0	2.8	5.5			2.7	3.3
	.6	.6	.8	1.7		Debt/Worth	.7	.6
	1.2	1.3	1.9	5.1			1.5	1.5
	5.7	2.9	3.8	8.5			3.6	4.2
	43.0	20.9	20.2	14.6		% Profit Before Taxes/Tangible Net Worth	24.4	18.9
	(23) 13.8	(67) 7.5	9.9	4.6			(66) 7.8	(94) 6.8
	.8	-.4	2.0	-2.9			1.5	.6
	17.7	7.9	5.9	2.0		% Profit Before Taxes/Total Assets	9.3	7.7
	8.2	2.4	3.8	1.4			3.6	2.7
	.5	-1.2	.7	-.4			.6	.1
	18.3	8.9	4.2	4.2		Sales/Net Fixed Assets	6.7	6.0
	5.9	3.8	2.9	2.4			3.2	2.6
	2.0	2.4	1.9	2.0			2.2	1.6
	3.5	3.0	1.9	1.7		Sales/Total Assets	2.4	2.3
	2.4	1.9	1.6	1.4			1.6	1.5
	1.1	1.3	1.1	1.1			1.0	.9
	1.3	1.5	1.8	2.3		% Depr., Dep., Amort./Sales	1.4	1.5
	(19) 2.2	(68) 2.3	(45) 2.9	(11) 3.4			(62) 2.3	(103) 2.6
	3.4	3.1	3.8	4.0			3.3	4.0
						% Officers', Directors' Owners' Comp/Sales		3.5
							(16)	4.7
								16.0
7284M	80011M	846536M	1695088M	1099358M	1335999M	Net Sales ($)	1557869M	2511451M
1207M	28975M	415595M	1094099M	819321M	1128687M	Total Assets ($)	1109416M	2190039M

© RMA 2010

M = $ thousand   MM = $ million
See Pages 9 through 22 for Explanation of Ratios and Data

Comparative Historical Data | Current Data Sorted by Sales

Type of Statement

4/1/07-3/31/08 ALL	4/1/08-3/31/09 ALL	4/1/09-3/31/10 ALL	Type of Statement	0-1MM	1-3MM	3-5MM	5-10MM	10-25MM	25MM & OVER
86	85	108	Unqualified	6	6	5	18	29	44
1	2	2	Reviewed				1	1	
4	5	3	Compiled		1		2		
5	9	4	Tax Returns		3			1	
24	37	53	Other	3	7	6	12	13	12
				114 (4/1-9/30/09)			56 (10/1/09-3/31/10)		
120	138	170	NUMBER OF STATEMENTS	9	17	11	33	44	56

Data

H1 %	H2 %	H3 %	Item	0-1MM	1-3MM %	3-5MM %	5-10MM %	10-25MM %	25MM & OVER %
			ASSETS						
17.1	17.1	16.1	Cash & Equivalents		19.4	21.5	16.1	17.1	12.3
19.6	19.3	20.4	Trade Receivables (net)		13.6	17.5	18.6	22.3	23.3
.1	.2	.2	Inventory		.1	.0	.1	.5	.2
4.3	3.5	4.0	All Other Current		7.4	3.7	1.3	4.5	3.9
41.2	40.1	40.7	Total Current		40.5	42.8	36.1	44.4	39.7
47.7	47.6	48.1	Fixed Assets (net)		47.2	49.4	49.4	49.9	45.5
1.1	3.1	1.9	Intangibles (net)		1.0	3.9	2.2	.4	3.2
10.0	9.2	9.2	All Other Non-Current		11.3	4.0	12.4	5.3	11.6
100.0	100.0	100.0	Total		100.0	100.0	100.0	100.0	100.0
			LIABILITIES						
4.4	5.4	4.3	Notes Payable-Short Term		4.4	2.6	4.0	3.6	5.6
2.7	3.4	3.2	Cur. Mat.-L.T.D.		4.4	2.7	1.6	3.9	3.5
7.9	7.1	6.4	Trade Payables		3.2	6.1	5.6	6.3	8.7
.2	.2	.1	Income Taxes Payable		.0	.0	.2	.0	.2
13.4	13.6	13.3	All Other Current		10.3	9.7	10.6	17.4	13.0
28.7	29.6	27.3	Total Current		22.3	21.2	22.0	31.2	31.1
31.3	29.0	30.0	Long-Term Debt		44.4	27.3	29.1	26.5	28.7
.0	.0	.1	Deferred Taxes		.0	.7	.1	.1	.0
2.6	3.7	4.0	All Other Non-Current		5.7	2.9	1.9	1.4	5.5
37.5	37.6	38.7	Net Worth		27.6	47.9	46.9	40.7	34.7
100.0	100.0	100.0	Total Liabilities & Net Worth		100.0	100.0	100.0	100.0	100.0
			INCOME DATA						
100.0	100.0	100.0	Net Sales		100.0	100.0	100.0	100.0	100.0
			Gross Profit						
94.1	94.3	94.5	Operating Expenses		88.6	94.7	93.0	97.2	97.4
5.9	5.7	5.5	Operating Profit		11.4	5.3	7.0	2.8	2.6
1.4	2.4	2.8	All Other Expenses (net)		8.3	1.4	3.7	.4	1.3
4.5	3.2	2.7	Profit Before Taxes		3.0	3.9	3.3	2.4	1.3
			RATIOS						
3.0	2.2	2.7	Current		5.0	4.0	3.5	2.6	1.8
1.4	1.3	1.4			1.5	1.4	1.9	1.4	1.2
.9	.9	1.0			1.0	.7	1.2	1.1	.9
2.8	2.0	2.6	Quick		4.0	3.9	3.3	2.4	1.5
1.1	1.1	1.3			1.4	1.4	1.8	1.3	1.1
.7	.7	.8			.8	.4	1.0	.8	.8
23 15.6	17 22.0	20 18.4	Sales/Receivables		0 UND	13 28.3	22 16.5	21 17.0	35 10.5
34 10.7	33 11.1	34 10.6			2 159.0	17 21.3	33 11.1	33 10.9	47 7.8
48 7.5	46 8.0	51 7.2			30 12.0	31 11.9	47 7.8	51 7.1	55 6.6
			Cost of Sales/Inventory						
			Cost of Sales/Payables						
5.2	6.6	6.5	Sales/Working Capital		4.3	5.3	6.6	5.9	9.9
15.9	25.1	17.2			23.3	23.4	14.0	17.3	36.3
-89.2	-50.2	-401.7			NM	-38.8	30.3	102.1	-59.0
4.7	4.4	5.2	EBIT/Interest			12.4	5.1	8.3	3.6
(89) 2.5	(113) 2.0	(140) 2.3				(10) 3.1	(25) 2.4	(38) 2.1	(51) 2.0
1.1	.9	.8				-.5	.1	.4	.8
			Net Profit + Depr., Dep., Amort./Cur. Mat. L/T/D						
.7	.6	.7	Fixed/Worth		.3	.6	.5	.7	.8
1.4	1.4	1.2			.9	1.1	1.1	1.3	1.5
3.3	2.9	2.7			-94.2	4.3	1.8	2.1	3.5
.6	.7	.7	Debt/Worth		.3	.4	.5	.7	1.1
1.7	1.8	1.5			1.3	1.4	1.3	1.3	2.1
4.5	4.1	4.3			-97.6	4.6	2.4	3.0	5.2
20.9	19.1	21.2	% Profit Before Taxes/Tangible Net Worth		38.6	40.3	23.8	17.8	17.9
(106) 9.9	(129) 5.3	(161) 8.3			(12) 12.1	7.5	7.4	(42) 6.7	(55) 7.4
3.8	-.8	.7			9.5	-28.5	-.4	-1.3	.7
7.9	5.4	7.8	% Profit Before Taxes/Total Assets		19.4	18.8	8.5	8.1	4.6
3.6	1.5	2.6			7.8	4.9	2.3	2.6	2.2
.5	-.3	-.2			.7	-3.4	-.2	-1.9	.1
5.8	8.4	7.9	Sales/Net Fixed Assets		39.6	17.0	7.7	8.4	6.4
3.1	3.6	3.4			5.6	4.2	2.9	3.4	3.5
2.0	2.1	2.0			1.2	1.5	1.5	2.5	2.3
2.4	2.7	2.5	Sales/Total Assets		2.7	2.6	2.6	3.1	2.1
1.6	1.6	1.7			1.3	2.3	1.6	1.9	1.6
1.2	1.2	1.2			.5	.9	.9	1.6	1.4
1.5	1.5	1.6	% Depr., Dep., Amort./Sales		1.6	2.2	1.8	1.6	1.5
(108) 2.5	(122) 2.3	(156) 2.4			(12) 2.6	(10) 2.8	(30) 2.7	(43) 2.3	(53) 2.3
3.5	3.6	3.4			11.7	3.1	4.0	3.2	3.4
2.6	2.8	1.2	% Officers', Directors' Owners' Comp/Sales						1.8
(13) 4.4	(15) 6.0	(23) 2.7							(11) 3.6
24.7	12.5	4.6							14.6
3662286M	4121118M	5064276M	Net Sales ($)	4329M	29568M	41624M	249910M	676385M	4062460M
2800442M	2857567M	3487884M	Total Assets ($)	8969M	43693M	25999M	428658M	376148M	2604417M

Current Data Sorted by Assets | Comparative Historical Data

	0-500M	500M-2MM	2-10MM	10-50MM	50-100MM	100-250MM	Type of Statement	ALL	ALL
	3	17	63	61	3	3	Unqualified	170	189
		1			1		Reviewed	9	7
	1	1	1		1	1	Compiled	6	6
	8	1	3				Tax Returns	13	8
	5	13	33	27	6	3	Other	86	61
		140 (4/1-9/30/09)		115 (10/1/09-3/31/10)				4/1/05-3/31/06 ALL	4/1/06-3/31/07 ALL
NUMBER OF STATEMENTS	17	33	100	88	11	6		284	271
	%	%	%	%	%	%	ASSETS	%	%
	27.7	18.3	15.5	13.5	11.3		Cash & Equivalents	15.0	15.3
	9.8	15.6	18.0	15.7	7.7		Trade Receivables (net)	16.2	17.5
	.0	.1	.1	.2	.0		Inventory	.1	.2
	3.5	4.5	1.7	3.1	4.0		All Other Current	4.1	2.9
	41.0	38.5	35.3	32.4	23.0		Total Current	35.5	36.0
	53.3	54.9	51.2	54.4	54.6		Fixed Assets (net)	52.7	51.4
	3.9	1.4	2.5	1.2	1.7		Intangibles (net)	1.2	1.9
	1.7	5.2	11.0	12.0	20.6		All Other Non-Current	10.6	10.7
	100.0	100.0	100.0	100.0	100.0		Total	100.0	100.0
							LIABILITIES		
	10.0	1.4	2.2	2.7	1.3		Notes Payable-Short Term	5.4	4.3
	15.8	14.0	1.9	3.8	3.5		Cur. Mat.-L.T.D.	2.8	3.2
	5.7	5.8	4.5	5.5	4.7		Trade Payables	5.5	5.8
	.4	.0	.1	.0	.0		Income Taxes Payable	.1	.1
	5.6	23.3	14.5	11.2	4.5		All Other Current	11.8	12.8
	37.5	44.6	23.3	23.1	13.9		Total Current	25.6	26.2
	38.4	28.8	28.3	31.6	42.4		Long-Term Debt	31.7	32.0
	.0	.0	.0	.1	.0		Deferred Taxes	.0	.0
	17.2	7.5	3.8	4.9	6.9		All Other Non-Current	5.1	4.4
	7.0	19.1	44.6	40.4	36.8		Net Worth	37.5	37.4
	100.0	100.0	100.0	100.0	100.0		Total Liabilties & Net Worth	100.0	100.0
							INCOME DATA		
	100.0	100.0	100.0	100.0	100.0		Net Sales	100.0	100.0
							Gross Profit		
	93.4	90.2	96.2	96.7	94.6		Operating Expenses	95.0	94.8
	6.6	9.8	3.8	3.3	5.4		Operating Profit	5.0	5.2
	3.1	4.7	1.8	2.4	3.0		All Other Expenses (net)	2.3	2.4
	3.4	5.1	2.0	.9	2.4		Profit Before Taxes	2.7	2.8
							RATIOS		
	6.5	2.9	2.9	2.2	3.1			2.8	2.3
	1.4	1.3	1.8	1.4	1.9		Current	1.6	1.4
	.6	.3	1.1	1.1	.9			1.0	.9
	3.2	2.8	2.6	2.1	2.4			2.4	2.1
	1.1	1.1	1.6	1.3	1.5		Quick	1.4	1.3
	.5	.3	1.1	.9	.7			.8	.8
	0 UND	1 693.1	18 20.3	26 14.3	9 42.0			17 21.0	18 20.5
	0 999.8	26 13.8	33 11.0	41 9.0	31 11.7		Sales/Receivables	34 10.8	35 10.4
	11 34.3	41 9.0	51 7.2	50 7.2	60 6.1			51 7.2	50 7.3
							Cost of Sales/Inventory		
							Cost of Sales/Payables		
	11.4	5.2	6.4	7.3	2.3			5.6	6.6
	55.1	30.8	11.6	16.9	7.8		Sales/Working Capital	14.7	20.3
	-22.0	-4.6	104.5	103.3	-62.0			UND	-58.3
	15.7	7.2	6.2	3.4	6.2			5.7	5.1
	(11) 4.1	(19) 2.2	(81) 1.6	(78) 2.0	(10) 1.8		EBIT/Interest	(229) 2.3	(222) 2.2
	.2	-1.0	-.1	1.1	-2.0			1.2	1.0
							Net Profit + Depr., Dep.,	7.7	4.7
							Amort./Cur. Mat. L/T/D	(11) 2.6	(15) 1.4
								1.9	.7
	1.1	.6	.6	.9	.8			.6	.7
	1.9	1.2	1.3	1.5	1.3		Fixed/Worth	1.4	1.4
	-5.9	7.9	2.1	2.7	-49.8			3.3	3.2
	.7	.5	.7	.8	.4			.6	.8
	3.5	1.0	1.2	1.6	2.4		Debt/Worth	1.5	1.6
	-5.4	8.9	2.7	3.6	-69.8			4.1	4.2
	112.0	30.2	14.8	16.9			% Profit Before Taxes/Tangible	16.0	20.0
	(11) 43.7	(27) 7.6	(91) 5.8	(86) 6.2			Net Worth	(251) 6.5	(238) 6.9
	.0	-1.1	-3.6	.3				1.1	.2
	42.0	10.2	7.0	5.0	5.6		% Profit Before Taxes/Total	6.5	7.6
	11.1	2.6	1.9	2.0	.2		Assets	2.2	2.9
	-2.1	-2.1	-2.0	.1	-1.4			.2	-.1
	26.2	13.8	7.9	4.6	1.5			5.7	6.3
	6.5	3.5	3.0	2.2	1.3		Sales/Net Fixed Assets	2.5	2.8
	3.9	1.3	1.7	1.5	.7			1.3	1.5
	7.2	3.1	2.5	1.9	1.0			2.2	2.2
	4.3	1.7	1.5	1.3	.6		Sales/Total Assets	1.3	1.4
	2.1	.9	.8	.9	.3			.7	.8
	1.1	1.4	1.4	2.1	2.3			1.7	1.5
	(11) 2.5	(29) 2.5	(90) 2.2	(85) 3.1	5.8		% Depr., Dep., Amort./Sales	(264) 3.0	(254) 2.6
	3.1	4.3	3.9	4.1	8.1			5.3	4.6
							% Officers', Directors'	3.1	2.8
							Owners' Comp/Sales	(33) 5.8	(20) 6.3
								9.7	10.0
	16107M	77470M	934253M	2757996M	526434M	665087M	Net Sales ($)	4597753M	5963871M
	3938M	37348M	555310M	2060489M	792412M	926341M	Total Assets ($)	4188300M	4455449M

M = $ thousand   MM = $ million
See Pages 9 through 22 for Explanation of Ratios and Data

Comparative Historical Data / Current Data Sorted by Sales

			Type of Statement						
171	86	150	Unqualified	8	22	10	25	46	39
4	5	2	Reviewed		1				1
6	7	4	Compiled		2		1	1	
10	10	12	Tax Returns	3	7	1	1		
70	53	87	Other	9	12	3	22	15	26
4/1/07-3/31/08	4/1/08-3/31/09	4/1/09-3/31/10		140 (4/1-9/30/09)			115 (10/1/09-3/31/10)		
ALL	ALL	ALL		0-1MM	1-3MM	3-5MM	5-10MM	10-25MM	25MM & OVER
261	161	255	**NUMBER OF STATEMENTS**	20	44	14	49	62	66
%	%	%	**ASSETS**	%	%	%	%	%	%
14.7	16.1	15.7	Cash & Equivalents	13.5	20.6	14.4	14.7	15.8	14.0
16.3	19.9	15.7	Trade Receivables (net)	5.1	9.2	19.1	15.7	18.2	20.4
.2	.2	.1	Inventory	.0	.1	.0	.2	.1	.0
3.8	3.4	2.7	All Other Current	1.5	2.9	3.4	3.1	2.6	2.7
35.0	39.5	34.3	Total Current	20.2	32.7	36.9	33.6	36.7	37.4
52.5	49.3	53.2	Fixed Assets (net)	64.7	60.0	56.1	50.5	51.1	48.4
1.5	1.5	1.9	Intangibles (net)	4.0	.9	1.2	3.6	.5	2.2
11.0	9.7	10.6	All Other Non-Current	11.2	6.3	5.8	12.3	11.7	12.0
100.0	100.0	100.0	Total	100.0	100.0	100.0	100.0	100.0	100.0
			LIABILITIES						
4.2	4.2	2.8	Notes Payable-Short Term	4.3	2.8	4.9	1.7	2.0	3.3
2.9	2.7	5.1	Cur. Mat.-L.T.D.	2.0	16.3	1.3	2.3	3.5	3.1
5.3	6.3	5.1	Trade Payables	1.8	5.3	4.0	4.3	4.6	7.4
.0	.0	.1	Income Taxes Payable	.0	.2	.0	.0	.1	.0
12.8	13.4	13.3	All Other Current	9.7	13.6	11.9	16.8	13.4	11.6
25.3	26.6	26.4	Total Current	17.7	38.2	22.1	25.1	23.7	25.5
32.9	28.9	31.3	Long-Term Debt	56.0	31.5	15.4	26.5	28.1	33.6
.0	.1	.0	Deferred Taxes	.0	.0	.0	.1	.0	.0
4.7	1.9	5.9	All Other Non-Current	8.6	10.1	1.5	4.5	4.1	6.0
37.1	42.5	36.4	Net Worth	17.7	20.3	61.0	43.8	44.1	34.9
100.0	100.0	100.0	Total Liabilties & Net Worth	100.0	100.0	100.0	100.0	100.0	100.0
			INCOME DATA						
100.0	100.0	100.0	Net Sales	100.0	100.0	100.0	100.0	100.0	100.0
			Gross Profit						
94.8	97.2	95.3	Operating Expenses	77.0	97.5	95.1	96.0	98.0	96.4
5.2	2.8	4.7	Operating Profit	23.0	2.5	4.9	4.0	2.0	3.6
2.1	1.4	2.5	All Other Expenses (net)	9.2	4.0	.8	3.0	1.0	.9
3.1	1.3	2.2	Profit Before Taxes	13.8	-1.6	4.0	.9	1.0	2.7
			RATIOS						
2.5	2.7	2.8		2.0	3.3	6.0	3.1	2.2	2.5
1.6	1.7	1.6	Current	.5	1.7	2.2	1.6	1.6	1.4
1.0	1.0	1.0		.2	.7	1.5	.9	1.3	1.0
2.3	2.7	2.5		1.9	3.3	4.9	3.0	2.1	2.3
1.4	1.4	1.4	Quick	.5	1.6	2.2	1.3	1.4	1.3
.9	.9	.8		.2	.5	1.5	.7	1.2	.9
15 24.9	19 19.4	13 27.8		0 UND	0 999.8	28 13.1	17 21.0	20 18.0	31 11.9
34 10.8	37 9.9	33 10.9	Sales/Receivables	0 UND	9 42.2	43 8.5	32 11.5	35 10.3	46 7.9
48 7.6	52 7.0	50 7.3		16 23.4	32 11.5	51 7.2	46 8.0	50 7.3	56 6.5
			Cost of Sales/Inventory						
			Cost of Sales/Payables						
5.7	6.0	6.6		10.6	5.2	5.6	5.8	8.3	7.6
14.0	13.7	15.0	Sales/Working Capital	-12.3	12.9	7.7	15.3	13.1	16.5
196.5	351.5	999.8		-1.2	-42.6	35.9	NM	33.9	454.4
5.1	5.7	5.1			4.1	6.2	6.7	4.7	4.4
(213) 2.3	(130) 2.6	(205) 1.8	EBIT/Interest	(31) .7	(10) 2.5	(42) 1.4	(54) 2.0	(59) 2.3	
.9	.4	.2		-1.0	-.9	-.4	-.2	1.3	
			Net Profit + Depr., Dep., Amort./Cur. Mat. L/T/D						
.7	.6	.8		1.6	.7	.5	.9	.7	.8
1.5	1.2	1.4	Fixed/Worth	4.4	1.4	1.1	1.2	1.2	1.7
2.8	2.4	2.9		NM	4.3	1.6	2.1	1.8	3.0
.6	.6	.7		1.3	.6	.3	.5	.7	.9
1.6	1.1	1.4	Debt/Worth	4.2	1.0	.6	1.3	1.2	2.3
3.7	3.1	3.9		NM	6.6	1.1	2.9	2.6	4.4
19.3	19.7	18.8		75.9	23.1	16.8	23.6	11.1	22.8
(233) 7.8	(148) 7.6	(228) 6.7	% Profit Before Taxes/Tangible Net Worth	(15) 12.1	(35) -.8	10.7	(44) 5.8	(58) 5.3	(62) 9.4
.6	-4.1	-1.3		.0	-8.4	-2.0	-2.7	-2.1	2.6
6.9	8.9	6.6		9.9	8.3	11.3	9.9	5.0	5.6
2.5	3.2	2.0	% Profit Before Taxes/Total Assets	3.4	-.4	5.6	.8	1.8	2.5
-.7	-2.4	-.9		-1.0	-5.7	-1.1	-2.2	-1.3	.7
6.1	7.1	6.0		6.1	14.1	4.3	7.4	6.3	5.5
2.4	3.5	2.6	Sales/Net Fixed Assets	1.1	2.0	2.3	2.5	2.7	2.8
1.3	2.0	1.5		.3	.6	1.5	1.4	1.8	1.7
2.2	2.7	2.2		2.1	3.2	2.1	2.4	2.2	2.0
1.3	1.8	1.4	Sales/Total Assets	.3	1.3	1.4	1.4	1.6	1.5
.7	1.1	.9		.1	.5	1.1	.8	1.0	1.1
1.8	1.5	1.7		2.5	1.5	1.6	1.4	1.6	1.9
(242) 2.8	(151) 2.1	(232) 2.8	% Depr., Dep., Amort./Sales	(14) 7.8	(37) 3.6	2.2	(43) 2.8	(61) 2.4	(63) 2.7
5.1	3.4	4.3		39.0	7.9	4.0	3.9	3.3	4.5
4.1	4.2	3.9							
(22) 7.5	(23) 8.3	(27) 8.1	% Officers', Directors' Owners' Comp/Sales						
21.5	11.1	11.3							
4742171M	2506062M	4977347M	Net Sales ($)	8808M	83089M	57120M	371291M	1052926M	3404113M
4549380M	1780799M	4375838M	Total Assets ($)	37197M	122272M	43146M	375815M	914477M	2882931M

M = $ thousand   MM = $ million
See Pages 9 through 22 for Explanation of Ratios and Data

Current Data Sorted by Assets   Comparative Historical Data

						Type of Statement		
1	7	33	96	65	32	Unqualified	145	189
2	8	13	9			Reviewed	19	29
7	4	9	3		1	Compiled	30	30
15	5	10	1			Tax Returns	19	13
13	22	49	52	22	16	Other	145	114
	141 (4/1-9/30/09)		354 (10/1/09-3/31/10)				4/1/05-3/31/06 ALL	4/1/06-3/31/07 ALL
0-500M	500M-2MM	2-10MM	10-50MM	50-100MM	100-250MM			
38	46	114	161	87	49	**NUMBER OF STATEMENTS**	358	375
%	%	%	%	%	%	**ASSETS**	%	%
21.2	11.7	11.2	10.2	8.6	8.1	Cash & Equivalents	10.9	10.7
23.2	23.5	11.4	5.4	4.5	3.4	Trade Receivables (net)	11.7	9.1
.2	.8	.2	.2	.1	.0	Inventory	.4	.2
8.0	4.7	2.4	2.2	2.4	3.0	All Other Current	2.7	3.1
52.6	40.7	25.2	18.0	15.6	14.6	Total Current	25.7	23.1
27.1	42.5	58.3	64.1	64.1	63.6	Fixed Assets (net)	57.5	60.1
6.6	4.0	2.9	2.2	2.7	2.0	Intangibles (net)	2.2	3.0
13.7	12.8	13.5	15.7	17.7	19.7	All Other Non-Current	14.6	13.8
100.0	100.0	100.0	100.0	100.0	100.0	Total	100.0	100.0
						LIABILITIES		
36.0	1.6	2.0	1.8	1.1	.7	Notes Payable-Short Term	4.9	2.9
4.7	2.6	4.5	4.6	3.1	3.5	Cur. Mat.-L.T.D.	3.2	2.0
19.1	8.1	4.6	2.8	2.8	2.5	Trade Payables	6.2	5.0
.0	.6	.0	.0	.1	.0	Income Taxes Payable	.0	.1
50.8	29.5	10.6	6.9	5.5	4.7	All Other Current	11.1	12.1
110.6	42.4	21.7	16.1	12.5	11.5	Total Current	25.5	22.1
18.3	43.4	57.8	49.3	54.0	52.3	Long-Term Debt	47.4	50.5
.0	.0	.0	.9	1.0	.0	Deferred Taxes	.2	.1
28.9	8.9	4.6	17.4	28.8	33.1	All Other Non-Current	13.5	15.4
-57.8	5.3	15.9	16.3	3.7	3.1	Net Worth	13.4	11.9
100.0	100.0	100.0	100.0	100.0	100.0	Total Liabilities & Net Worth	100.0	100.0
						INCOME DATA		
100.0	100.0	100.0	100.0	100.0	100.0	Net Sales	100.0	100.0
						Gross Profit		
94.4	89.8	86.8	92.3	96.2	95.0	Operating Expenses	91.6	91.1
5.6	10.2	13.2	7.7	3.8	5.0	Operating Profit	8.4	8.9
2.1	3.4	7.6	5.0	7.9	6.5	All Other Expenses (net)	5.5	6.2
3.6	6.7	5.6	2.8	-4.1	-1.6	Profit Before Taxes	2.9	2.8
						RATIOS		
3.2	1.7	2.5	2.7	2.5	2.7		2.3	2.4
.9	.9	1.0	1.5	1.4	1.5	Current	1.3	1.3
.2	.3	.5	.7	.8	.8		.8	.7
2.3	1.4	2.0	2.2	2.2	1.9		2.1	2.0
.8	.8	.9	1.3	1.1	1.0	Quick	1.1	1.1
.1	.3	.4	.7	.5	.6		.6	.5
0 UND	0 UND	2 163.8	7 49.8	11 32.9	12 31.5		6 57.6	4 83.1
8 45.2	13 27.3	20 17.9	22 17.0	21 17.4	19 19.6	Sales/Receivables	23 16.0	22 16.4
20 18.5	35 10.5	34 10.6	35 10.5	35 10.4	34 10.7		37 10.0	41 9.0
						Cost of Sales/Inventory		
						Cost of Sales/Payables		
19.4	16.1	7.9	4.5	3.1	2.0		7.5	5.6
NM	-91.2	148.6	17.5	14.1	11.7	Sales/Working Capital	29.8	24.5
-6.9	-8.1	-9.2	-20.2	-24.5	-27.1		-22.3	-19.6
19.4	44.2	5.2	3.6	3.6	1.9		3.7	3.5
(18) 2.5	(28) 8.5	(81) 1.8	(139) 1.4	(73) 1.3	(44) 1.0	EBIT/Interest	(288) 1.9	(295) 1.8
-3.8	2.8	1.1	.5	.2	.2		.8	.9
							2.9	6.7
						Net Profit + Depr., Dep., Amort./Cur. Mat. L/T/D	(14) 2.0	(12) 2.7
							1.2	1.2
.4	.3	1.1	1.4	1.8	3.7		1.2	1.3
NM	3.0	4.1	4.6	15.3	36.7	Fixed/Worth	4.3	4.1
-.3	-1.8	-6.0	-7.7	-5.0	-5.8		-8.6	-8.0
1.4	.9	.8	1.5	2.3	5.0		1.5	1.6
NM	7.0	5.4	6.3	19.4	143.8	Debt/Worth	6.2	6.5
-1.6	-5.2	-7.5	-12.0	-7.9	-9.2		-14.3	-12.8
244.4	101.8	41.5	24.6	20.0	18.5		41.9	36.3
(19) 80.2	(25) 47.0	(74) 15.5	(108) 8.4	(50) 5.7	(26) -1.1	% Profit Before Taxes/Tangible Net Worth	(241) 11.7	(257) 9.5
21.1	15.0	-.7	-1.5	-5.0	-9.3		1.8	1.8
39.4	26.2	12.5	5.1	3.0	2.0		6.6	6.0
7.6	9.6	3.5	1.3	.3	-.2	% Profit Before Taxes/Total Assets	2.2	1.9
-10.1	-.7	-.6	-.8	-3.3	-1.6		-.8	-.5
134.1	31.4	6.2	1.6	.8	.6		4.5	2.3
41.5	12.4	1.3	.7	.5	.4	Sales/Net Fixed Assets	1.1	.8
18.8	.9	.6	.5	.3	.2		.5	.4
10.8	4.8	1.7	.8	.5	.3		1.8	1.2
6.9	2.9	.8	.5	.3	.3	Sales/Total Assets	.7	.5
4.1	.8	.5	.3	.2	.2		.3	.3
.6	.8	1.7	5.0	7.7	7.0		2.2	2.9
(27) 1.0	(42) 1.7	(109) 4.6	(155) 8.1	(85) 12.0	(48) 12.8	% Depr., Dep., Amort./Sales	(334) 5.9	(358) 7.0
1.6	5.5	7.8	11.5	15.9	16.5		11.0	12.3
		2.7	4.7				1.9	1.5
		(11) 4.7	(22) 6.4			% Officers', Directors' Owners' Comp/Sales	(58) 5.8	(45) 3.6
		13.8	14.4				12.8	15.6
61315M	162327M	644738M	2600626M	3038186M	2487734M	Net Sales ($)	7275730M	7580701M
9596M	54184M	550656M	3953704M	6280615M	6956600M	Total Assets ($)	10707679M	12477395M

Comparative Historical Data

Current Data Sorted by Sales

Hist 4/1/07-3/31/08 ALL	Hist 4/1/08-3/31/09 ALL	Hist 4/1/09-3/31/10 ALL	Type of Statement	0-1MM	1-3MM	3-5MM	5-10MM	10-25MM	25MM & OVER
174	232	234	Unqualified	6	13	18	41	106	50
26	33	32	Reviewed	4	9	4	8	5	2
34	26	24	Compiled	2	8	5	5	3	1
19	48	31	Tax Returns	6	16	5	5	4	1
125	166	174	Other	15	32	19	39	38	31
				141 (4/1-9/30/09)			354 (10/1/09-3/31/10)		
378	**505**	**495**	**NUMBER OF STATEMENTS**	**33**	**78**	**51**	**93**	**156**	**84**
%	%	%	**ASSETS**	%	%	%	%	%	%
10.1	11.1	10.9	Cash & Equivalents	5.6	12.5	13.4	9.5	11.1	11.4
9.9	11.3	9.5	Trade Receivables (net)	4.8	12.1	10.5	12.1	6.7	10.4
.2	.4	.2	Inventory	.9	.1	.4	.2	.2	.1
2.9	3.2	3.0	All Other Current	4.4	4.5	3.3	1.3	2.8	3.3
23.1	26.0	23.7	Total Current	15.6	29.1	27.6	23.2	20.8	25.2
59.5	56.2	57.9	Fixed Assets (net)	69.5	55.1	57.5	55.2	60.9	53.6
2.6	2.8	3.0	Intangibles (net)	2.4	4.9	2.8	2.4	2.1	3.7
14.8	15.0	15.5	All Other Non-Current	12.6	10.9	12.1	19.2	16.2	17.5
100.0	100.0	100.0	Total	100.0	100.0	100.0	100.0	100.0	100.0
			LIABILITIES						
2.7	2.7	4.2	Notes Payable-Short Term	14.7	12.7	3.4	1.1	.8	2.4
2.9	4.3	4.0	Cur. Mat.-L.T.D.	9.5	3.9	4.7	5.5	2.6	2.5
4.4	5.2	4.9	Trade Payables	7.0	8.6	3.9	4.5	3.1	5.2
.0	.0	.1	Income Taxes Payable	.0	.0	.4	.0	.1	.1
13.2	13.4	12.8	All Other Current	27.4	19.0	14.8	13.3	8.0	8.3
23.2	25.7	26.0	Total Current	58.6	44.3	27.2	24.4	14.5	18.6
49.2	46.5	49.5	Long-Term Debt	64.5	51.1	55.7	41.4	50.3	45.6
.4	.3	.5	Deferred Taxes	.0	.0	.0	.7	.3	1.3
13.5	14.8	18.1	All Other Non-Current	14.4	16.1	9.3	11.2	28.2	15.6
13.7	12.7	6.0	Net Worth	-37.4	-11.5	7.9	22.3	6.6	18.9
100.0	100.0	100.0	Total Liabilties & Net Worth	100.0	100.0	100.0	100.0	100.0	100.0
			INCOME DATA						
100.0	100.0	100.0	Net Sales	100.0	100.0	100.0	100.0	100.0	100.0
			Gross Profit						
91.1	92.6	91.9	Operating Expenses	80.3	86.3	88.6	96.2	94.4	94.4
8.9	7.4	8.1	Operating Profit	19.7	13.7	11.4	3.8	5.6	5.6
5.6	7.0	5.9	All Other Expenses (net)	16.7	7.1	5.9	5.7	4.5	3.2
3.2	.4	2.2	Profit Before Taxes	3.1	6.6	5.5	-1.9	1.1	2.4
			RATIOS						
2.4	2.4	2.5		1.3	2.1	2.1	2.6	3.4	2.1
1.3	1.3	1.3	Current	.3	.8	1.0	1.4	1.5	1.4
.7	.7	.6		.1	.3	.5	.7	.7	.9
2.1	2.1	2.0		1.1	2.0	1.9	2.1	2.7	1.9
1.0	1.0	1.1	Quick	.2	.7	.9	1.2	1.2	1.1
.5	.5	.5		.0	.2	.4	.6	.6	.7
3 108.3	4 82.4	5 74.0		0 UND	0 UND	1 517.5	16 23.4	12 30.9	19 19.5
20 18.2	22 17.0	19 18.9	Sales/Receivables	0 UND	4 90.8	8 48.5	28 13.2	21 17.5	30 12.0
38 9.7	38 9.5	34 10.7		7 52.7	16 22.6	28 12.9	42 8.6	33 11.1	44 8.2
			Cost of Sales/Inventory						
			Cost of Sales/Payables						
5.9	6.1	6.1		32.1	12.8	7.1	6.1	3.8	6.6
24.0	23.3	31.7	Sales/Working Capital	-7.2	-109.3	169.5	21.1	14.2	17.3
-15.6	-14.8	-11.7		-1.4	-6.4	-16.5	-11.8	-24.1	-103.5
3.7	3.8	3.9		3.9	5.8	4.4	3.2	3.7	4.6
(306) 1.9	(408) 1.3	(383) 1.5	EBIT/Interest	(17) .6	(49) 2.2	(40) 1.8	(67) 1.3	(133) 1.5	(77) 1.6
.9	.1	.5		-1.7	1.0	.9	.1	.6	.5
6.3	8.1	6.3							
(11) 2.0	(23) 2.9	(12) 2.7	Net Profit + Depr., Dep., Amort./Cur. Mat. L/T/D						
1.2	2.1	.8							
1.3	1.2	1.4		3.2	1.1	1.2	.9	2.0	1.2
3.8	3.9	5.7	Fixed/Worth	-5.6	13.7	6.7	4.1	6.4	2.6
-12.4	-6.4	-5.0		-.9	-2.3	-3.9	-10.5	-4.5	NM
1.5	1.3	1.7		3.6	1.7	1.9	.9	2.3	1.7
5.6	5.5	8.0	Debt/Worth	-12.8	15.3	10.7	6.1	8.7	3.8
-19.9	-11.0	-7.5		-2.6	-4.7	-7.1	-15.2	-7.5	NM
42.5	36.6	36.8		66.0	65.3	189.9	26.0	28.0	32.7
(260) 10.4	(341) 8.0	(302) 11.0	% Profit Before Taxes/Tangible Net Worth	(12) 7.3	(41) 21.0	(33) 17.8	(63) 6.7	(90) 10.9	(63) 8.3
1.2	-3.7	-1.8		-8.4	2.8	-4.3	-4.0	-.7	-1.5
7.1	7.5	7.8		7.8	16.3	16.1	9.1	5.1	7.3
1.9	1.1	1.7	% Profit Before Taxes/Total Assets	-1.4	5.0	3.1	1.2	1.3	1.8
-.6	-2.2	-1.5		-4.2	-1.4	-.6	-3.5	-1.2	-1.1
3.0	4.6	3.7		1.7	30.8	16.5	3.8	1.4	3.4
.9	1.0	.8	Sales/Net Fixed Assets	.7	1.3	1.0	1.0	.6	1.3
.4	.4	.4		.3	.4	.4	.5	.3	.6
1.4	1.7	1.5		1.0	5.7	2.9	1.5	.7	1.6
.6	.6	.5	Sales/Total Assets	.4	.8	.7	.6	.4	.7
.3	.3	.3		.2	.3	.4	.3	.2	.3
2.8	2.3	2.8		4.1	1.1	2.4	2.0	5.4	2.3
(359) 6.4	(463) 6.2	(466) 7.2	% Depr., Dep., Amort./Sales	(31) 9.6	(65) 6.5	(45) 6.1	(89) 5.6	(153) 9.8	(83) 5.2
11.8	11.7	13.0		21.1	14.0	14.9	11.0	13.7	10.9
2.7	2.5	2.6			4.3		2.5	3.3	
(49) 4.8	(64) 5.2	(54) 5.3	% Officers', Directors' Owners' Comp/Sales		(12) 5.7		(10) 5.2	(16) 6.9	
10.9	9.2	11.9			12.9		9.7	11.9	
7682723M	10028324M	8994926M	Net Sales ($)	17338M	149444M	197369M	719637M	2534004M	5377134M
13127485M	17241637M	17805355M	Total Assets ($)	59012M	281605M	389619M	1918153M	7855354M	7301612M

M = $ thousand   MM = $ million
See Pages 9 through 22 for Explanation of Ratios and Data

HEALTH CARE—Homes for the Elderly NAICS 623312

Current Data Sorted by Assets | **Comparative Historical Data**

Type of Statement

	0-500M	500M-2MM	2-10MM	10-50MM	50-100MM	100-250MM	Historical 4/1/05-3/31/06 ALL	Historical 4/1/06-3/31/07 ALL
Unqualified		6	21	24	5	5	30	47
Reviewed	1	2	4	3			3	5
Compiled	3	4	7	2			6	7
Tax Returns	19	11	14	20			10	12
Other	9	7	20	14	2	1	32	36

Period grouping: 40 (4/1-9/30/09); 144 (10/1/09-3/31/10); Historical periods 4/1/05-3/31/06 ALL, 4/1/06-3/31/07 ALL

Main Data

0-500M	500M-2MM	2-10MM	10-50MM	50-100MM	100-250MM		4/1/05-3/31/06 ALL	4/1/06-3/31/07 ALL
32	30	66	43	7	6	**NUMBER OF STATEMENTS**	81	107
%	%	%	%	%	%	**ASSETS**	%	%
33.8	18.3	8.6	11.5			Cash & Equivalents	9.7	10.7
12.6	6.7	4.5	5.1			Trade Receivables (net)	8.1	8.6
.1	.3	.2	.1			Inventory	.1	.1
7.1	2.6	2.7	1.6			All Other Current	2.7	2.8
53.6	27.9	16.0	18.3			Total Current	20.5	22.1
30.9	56.6	70.0	65.2			Fixed Assets (net)	64.3	62.4
4.6	1.0	2.5	3.0			Intangibles (net)	2.0	2.8
10.9	14.4	11.6	13.5			All Other Non-Current	13.2	12.7
100.0	100.0	100.0	100.0			Total	100.0	100.0
						LIABILITIES		
17.1	1.2	.4	3.0			Notes Payable-Short Term	3.4	2.3
2.7	3.1	7.4	1.1			Cur. Mat.-L.T.D.	2.2	4.5
21.0	8.1	4.2	2.6			Trade Payables	3.7	5.0
.1	.0	.0	.0			Income Taxes Payable	.0	.0
45.4	35.0	7.5	8.4			All Other Current	8.4	20.8
86.4	47.5	19.4	15.1			Total Current	17.6	32.6
15.9	40.6	70.3	52.6			Long-Term Debt	56.0	47.5
.0	.0	.0	.0			Deferred Taxes	.0	.0
5.0	1.8	9.2	15.0			All Other Non-Current	3.9	6.4
-7.3	10.1	1.0	17.2			Net Worth	22.5	13.5
100.0	100.0	100.0	100.0			Total Liabilities & Net Worth	100.0	100.0
						INCOME DATA		
100.0	100.0	100.0	100.0			Net Sales	100.0	100.0
						Gross Profit		
91.2	85.2	81.3	93.8			Operating Expenses	91.0	88.0
8.8	14.8	18.7	6.2			Operating Profit	9.0	12.0
3.6	9.2	14.2	9.1			All Other Expenses (net)	7.2	5.9
5.2	5.6	4.5	-2.9			Profit Before Taxes	1.8	6.2
						RATIOS		
1.6	1.7	1.7	2.8			Current	2.5	2.1
1.1	.6	.9	1.1				1.2	1.1
.3	.2	.4	.5				.4	.4
1.4	1.7	1.5	2.8			Quick	2.2	1.9
.8	.5	.6	1.1				.8	1.0
.2	.1	.2	.4				.3	.4
0 UND	0 UND	0 UND	1 272.2			Sales/Receivables	0 990.7	1 349.0
0 UND	3 130.0	3 109.3	9 40.4				10 37.7	13 27.1
9 39.5	11 32.1	21 17.3	28 13.0				33 11.1	32 11.3
						Cost of Sales/Inventory		
						Cost of Sales/Payables		
27.0	14.1	9.7	4.9			Sales/Working Capital	7.5	10.4
117.4	-29.4	-45.2	39.5				68.8	133.0
-6.2	-5.6	-6.0	-10.3				-10.1	-9.1
32.5	41.3	3.9	4.2			EBIT/Interest	4.9	5.8
(23) 10.4	(19) 1.8	(46) 1.6	(25) 1.6				(67) 1.8	(71) 1.9
1.5	.8	1.1	.8				.7	.9
						Net Profit + Depr., Dep., Amort./Cur. Mat. L/T/D		
.1	.6	3.0	1.3			Fixed/Worth	1.1	1.0
.9	2.7	57.9	5.4				2.8	5.2
-1.4	-4.2	-3.7	-4.8				-47.7	-17.3
1.4	.7	3.5	1.5			Debt/Worth	.9	.8
46.3	3.0	63.2	4.5				6.4	5.2
-2.5	-5.7	-5.5	-6.8				-71.8	-21.3
353.7	41.4	54.5	18.0			% Profit Before Taxes/Tangible Net Worth	41.3	33.7
(17) 116.0	(20) 18.0	(35) 8.6	(28) 7.2				(60) 9.6	(74) 13.4
63.6	-1.8	-1.2	-.9				-.6	-3.3
58.8	10.0	7.9	5.1			% Profit Before Taxes/Total Assets	10.5	8.9
20.0	3.7	2.8	1.0				2.0	3.4
.2	-.8	-.3	-4.1				-1.4	-1.0
181.5	22.8	1.5	2.0			Sales/Net Fixed Assets	2.4	5.0
48.6	1.9	.7	.6				.8	1.4
7.5	.5	.4	.2				.5	.5
10.4	4.1	.9	.8			Sales/Total Assets	1.4	1.8
6.4	1.2	.5	.4				.7	.9
3.5	.4	.3	.2				.4	.4
.4	1.1	4.5	4.2			% Depr., Dep., Amort./Sales	2.9	2.0
(20) 1.2	(27) 4.4	(59) 8.0	(40) 9.7				(77) 7.0	(101) 4.8
2.6	22.4	14.3	15.2				11.0	9.8
		4.4				% Officers', Directors' Owners' Comp/Sales	2.3	4.1
	(11) 6.1						(15) 5.2	(17) 8.7
		33.3					8.7	12.0
38357M	71277M	248367M	1034492M	308275M	303724M	Net Sales ($)	677424M	848676M
6732M	35519M	311246M	1010337M	620664M	858599M	Total Assets ($)	1368701M	1390269M

M = $ thousand   MM = $ million
See Pages 9 through 22 for Explanation of Ratios and Data

Comparative Historical Data   Current Data Sorted by Sales

			Type of Statement						
38	112	61	Unqualified	6	10	10	9	17	9
12	10	10	Reviewed	1	3	2	4		
8	10	16	Compiled	7	4	3	1		1
15	26	44	Tax Returns	24	14	3	3		
56	89	53	Other	7	21	7	7	5	6
4/1/07-3/31/08 ALL	4/1/08-3/31/09 ALL	4/1/09-3/31/10 ALL		40 (4/1-9/30/09)			144 (10/1/09-3/31/10)		
				0-1MM	1-3MM	3-5MM	5-10MM	10-25MM	25MM & OVER
129	247	184	**NUMBER OF STATEMENTS**	45	52	25	24	22	16
%	%	%	**ASSETS**	%	%	%	%	%	%
12.4	15.1	15.1	Cash & Equivalents	14.1	18.5	11.9	10.8	19.8	12.0
7.6	11.1	6.4	Trade Receivables (net)	2.5	7.0	4.6	7.6	7.1	15.0
.7	.2	.2	Inventory	.1	.1	.1	.2	.5	.1
5.0	2.6	3.1	All Other Current	4.1	2.7	2.6	1.8	3.8	3.5
25.8	29.0	24.7	Total Current	20.8	28.2	19.3	20.3	31.2	30.5
61.4	55.8	59.3	Fixed Assets (net)	63.7	56.8	72.1	59.5	47.9	49.7
2.1	2.4	2.7	Intangibles (net)	2.5	4.0	2.2	1.9	.6	4.2
10.6	12.9	13.3	All Other Non-Current	12.9	10.9	6.4	18.3	20.3	15.7
100.0	100.0	100.0	Total	100.0	100.0	100.0	100.0	100.0	100.0
			LIABILITIES						
3.4	4.8	4.0	Notes Payable-Short Term	9.1	3.3	.4	3.3	.0	4.6
4.4	4.8	4.1	Cur. Mat.-L.T.D.	3.5	5.4	6.6	3.4	1.5	2.7
5.3	5.5	7.3	Trade Payables	8.3	8.3	5.2	6.2	5.5	8.3
.1	.0	.0	Income Taxes Payable	.1	.0	.1	.0	.0	.1
19.5	19.8	18.6	All Other Current	24.7	16.6	19.8	17.1	10.2	19.6
32.7	34.9	34.0	Total Current	45.7	33.6	32.0	30.0	17.2	35.2
51.9	43.1	51.6	Long-Term Debt	59.5	45.8	58.8	51.4	47.4	42.9
.0	.0	.0	Deferred Taxes	.0	.0	.0	.0	.0	.0
10.1	7.1	9.0	All Other Non-Current	9.6	5.2	7.7	12.6	16.2	5.5
5.2	14.8	5.4	Net Worth	-14.9	15.4	1.5	5.9	19.2	16.3
100.0	100.0	100.0	Total Liabilties & Net Worth	100.0	100.0	100.0	100.0	100.0	100.0
			INCOME DATA						
100.0	100.0	100.0	Net Sales	100.0	100.0	100.0	100.0	100.0	100.0
			Gross Profit						
88.6	91.9	87.3	Operating Expenses	75.1	87.8	91.6	93.1	93.7	96.0
11.4	8.1	12.7	Operating Profit	24.9	12.2	8.4	6.9	6.3	4.0
9.1	6.5	9.9	All Other Expenses (net)	20.7	8.0	6.3	6.4	5.7	2.0
2.4	1.6	2.8	Profit Before Taxes	4.2	4.2	2.1	.6	.6	1.9
			RATIOS						
2.5	2.2	2.2		3.1	1.5	1.7	2.7	3.8	2.1
1.0	1.2	1.0	Current	.5	1.0	.6	1.0	2.5	1.1
.4	.6	.4		.1	.4	.4	.3	.9	.5
2.3	2.0	1.7		1.6	1.5	1.5	2.1	3.3	2.1
(128) .9	1.0	.8	Quick	.5	.8	.5	.9	1.8	1.0
.1	.5	.2		.1	.2	.3	.3	.3	.4
0 UND	2 173.6	0 UND		0 UND	0 UND	2 218.0	5 80.6	5 74.8	16 23.4
6 57.8	18 20.0	4 89.7	Sales/Receivables	0 UND	1 310.9	4 91.6	10 36.5	16 22.2	29 12.4
30 12.0	42 8.8	20 18.2		4 89.2	7 49.6	15 24.1	29 12.6	31 11.8	38 9.5
			Cost of Sales/Inventory						
			Cost of Sales/Payables						
7.4	6.8	9.0		9.2	26.7	12.6	11.1	3.4	8.8
171.7	39.2	NM	Sales/Working Capital	-13.1	NM	-14.6	NM	6.7	91.7
-8.5	-14.4	-6.8		-2.8	-9.9	-4.1	-7.2	-142.8	-12.6
3.6	4.7	6.7		7.2	18.3	5.5	6.4	3.6	5.4
(90) 1.3	(185) 1.6	(126) 1.8	EBIT/Interest	(22) 1.6	(35) 3.0	(21) 1.4	(18) 2.2	(16) 1.4	(14) 1.7
.6	.4	1.0		.5	1.5	1.0	.7	-.6	1.0
			Net Profit + Depr., Dep., Amort./Cur. Mat. L/T/D						
1.2	1.0	1.1		3.8	.5	1.9	1.0	.7	1.1
5.5	2.6	7.7	Fixed/Worth	-18.4	4.3	28.1	10.2	1.7	3.2
-8.6	-12.4	-4.3		-2.2	-7.0	-4.9	-4.1	NM	-5.1
1.5	1.1	1.7		4.8	1.2	1.6	1.2	1.2	1.9
10.7	3.6	12.4	Debt/Worth	-22.0	10.2	32.3	19.6	3.1	3.5
-10.7	-15.0	-5.9		-4.0	-7.6	-6.4	-6.0	NM	-7.3
45.4	22.7	68.9	% Profit Before Taxes/Tangible Net Worth	116.0	148.1	45.3	39.5	22.5	
(74) 10.2	(174) 7.4	(106) 11.7		(19) 14.1	(31) 41.0	(16) 8.9	(14) 11.6	(17) 6.9	
.5	-3.9	1.9		.0	5.9	-22.5	.0	.9	
9.3	6.8	8.1	% Profit Before Taxes/Total Assets	5.8	21.9	7.9	9.9	4.9	7.1
.8	1.2	2.2		.7	5.1	1.1	2.0	1.3	1.7
-1.2	-2.3	-.6		-3.0	.8	-.5	-4.3	-1.5	-2.5
5.9	5.8	8.7		8.2	44.0	2.0	17.0	6.8	8.9
1.0	1.7	.9	Sales/Net Fixed Assets	.4	1.0	.8	1.3	.7	1.8
.4	.6	.4		.2	.5	.4	.6	.4	1.3
2.0	2.1	2.5		3.0	4.7	1.5	2.8	1.8	3.2
.7	.9	.7	Sales/Total Assets	.3	.8	.7	.7	.5	1.0
.3	.4	.3		.1	.4	.4	.4	.2	.7
2.8	1.8	2.6		6.6	1.2	3.5	1.2	2.1	2.0
(117) 6.0	(220) 4.0	(159) 6.9	% Depr., Dep., Amort./Sales	(35) 22.4	(41) 6.2	(23) 6.6	(23) 4.2	8.2	(15) 3.1
12.6	10.3	14.3		31.6	12.0	11.1	9.6	13.1	4.8
6.0	5.1	5.0	% Officers', Directors' Owners' Comp/Sales		4.7				
(24) 9.1	(21) 6.4	(31) 6.5			(13) 6.4				
16.8	15.9	11.4			10.6				
1200256M	4537967M	2004492M	Net Sales ($)	22894M	103280M	94252M	167963M	350067M	1266036M
1979682M	5756804M	2843097M	Total Assets ($)	84365M	192217M	187144M	286361M	1083612M	1009398M

M = $ thousand   MM = $ million
See Pages 9 through 22 for Explanation of Ratios and Data

Current Data Sorted by Assets   Comparative Historical Data

	0-500M	500M-2MM	2-10MM	10-50MM	50-100MM	100-250MM	Type of Statement	4/1/05-3/31/06 ALL	4/1/06-3/31/07 ALL
		8	47	39	7	5	Unqualified	56	102
	3	1	2	2			Reviewed	1	7
	1		6	1			Compiled	4	5
	10	9	3				Tax Returns	3	9
	9	15	19	14	1	2	Other	30	57
		99 (4/1-9/30/09)		105 (10/1/09-3/31/10)					
	23	33	77	56	8	7	NUMBER OF STATEMENTS	94	180
	%	%	%	%	%	%	ASSETS	%	%
	18.9	12.3	15.6	15.4			Cash & Equivalents	14.5	15.9
	13.9	22.9	16.8	14.1			Trade Receivables (net)	13.9	14.3
	.0	.1	.8	.2			Inventory	.3	.2
	7.6	3.3	3.0	1.9			All Other Current	3.9	3.7
	40.4	38.6	36.2	31.6			Total Current	32.5	34.1
	39.1	49.4	54.2	52.2			Fixed Assets (net)	50.5	53.1
	6.6	3.1	2.3	1.5			Intangibles (net)	4.1	3.0
	13.9	9.0	7.3	14.7			All Other Non-Current	12.9	9.8
	100.0	100.0	100.0	100.0			Total	100.0	100.0
							LIABILITIES		
	16.8	9.6	3.5	4.8			Notes Payable-Short Term	6.1	4.3
	6.8	1.4	2.5	2.2			Cur. Mat.-L.T.D.	2.6	2.9
	7.8	5.4	4.8	4.8			Trade Payables	5.1	5.3
	.0	.0	.1	.0			Income Taxes Payable	.0	.0
	31.3	10.5	11.3	10.4			All Other Current	13.1	12.6
	62.7	27.0	22.2	22.2			Total Current	26.9	25.1
	25.3	39.9	34.3	34.2			Long-Term Debt	34.3	35.0
	.0	.0	.3	.0			Deferred Taxes	.0	.0
	21.2	4.2	4.2	4.7			All Other Non-Current	3.8	6.5
	-9.2	28.9	39.0	38.9			Net Worth	35.0	33.4
	100.0	100.0	100.0	100.0			Total Liabilities & Net Worth	100.0	100.0
							INCOME DATA		
	100.0	100.0	100.0	100.0			Net Sales	100.0	100.0
							Gross Profit		
	92.9	93.2	93.3	95.0			Operating Expenses	93.4	93.8
	7.1	6.8	6.7	5.0			Operating Profit	6.6	6.2
	.4	2.8	3.5	4.7			All Other Expenses (net)	2.0	2.5
	6.7	4.0	3.2	.4			Profit Before Taxes	4.6	3.7
							RATIOS		
	3.0	4.1	3.2	2.9			Current	2.5	2.8
	.8	1.9	1.7	1.4				1.4	1.6
	.2	.7	.9	.9				.7	.8
	2.1	3.5	2.8	2.6			Quick	2.3	2.5
	.4	1.8	1.6	1.3				1.2	1.3
	.2	.7	.8	.8				.6	.7
	0 UND	3 125.7	11 34.6	8 43.7			Sales/Receivables	4 104.2	4 85.9
	0 UND	31 11.9	31 11.6	31 11.9				33 11.0	29 12.8
	3 118.1	66 5.6	50 7.4	48 7.6				47 7.7	42 8.8
							Cost of Sales/Inventory		
							Cost of Sales/Payables		
	27.7	4.6	5.0	4.8			Sales/Working Capital	6.3	6.3
	-82.0	15.3	14.8	16.7				21.9	16.1
	-8.0	-37.5	-56.6	-50.6				-25.7	-46.6
	38.3	6.5	5.4	5.2			EBIT/Interest	7.4	8.4
	(12) 17.3	(27) 2.3	(61) 1.7	(46) 2.7				(75) 2.5	(145) 2.2
	1.9	1.0	.7	.4				.9	1.0
							Net Profit + Depr., Dep., Amort./Cur. Mat. L/T/D		
	.2	.3	.6	.6			Fixed/Worth	.7	.6
	1.1	1.7	1.2	1.3				1.4	1.5
	-1.6	16.8	4.0	4.8				7.7	6.1
	.4	.5	.5	.6			Debt/Worth	.6	.5
	7.3	1.4	1.3	1.4				1.8	1.7
	-2.8	17.8	6.7	5.7				11.7	8.3
	567.5	45.4	17.7	22.3			% Profit Before Taxes/Tangible Net Worth	18.9	22.4
	(14) 45.4	(28) 14.8	(64) 6.4	(49) 4.8				(77) 6.5	(153) 9.2
	23.1	6.6	-2.2	-3.5				.3	-.9
	57.7	16.2	6.8	5.5			% Profit Before Taxes/Total Assets	9.4	9.2
	20.5	5.3	2.9	1.6				2.6	3.7
	9.0	.5	-.4	-2.2				-.2	-.1
	59.6	22.1	6.3	4.6			Sales/Net Fixed Assets	6.7	5.7
	25.6	3.7	2.7	2.1				2.3	2.6
	13.0	1.6	.9	.8				1.3	1.2
	11.5	2.9	2.3	1.7			Sales/Total Assets	1.9	2.4
	5.6	1.9	1.3	.9				1.2	1.3
	3.2	1.1	.6	.6				.7	.7
	.5	.9	1.7	2.1			% Depr., Dep., Amort./Sales	1.7	1.9
	(14) 1.8	(29) 2.4	(69) 2.9	(53) 3.6				(82) 3.0	(163) 3.2
	2.8	4.1	6.2	6.9				4.7	5.2
							% Officers', Directors' Owners' Comp/Sales	2.8	2.9
								(20) 6.3	(27) 6.4
								17.0	8.9
	27051M	102504M	652600M	1692103M	703061M	549375M	Net Sales ($)	1543686M	2702658M
	5159M	45109M	425203M	1292232M	491112M	1002825M	Total Assets ($)	1394853M	2477101M

M = $ thousand   MM = $ million
See Pages 9 through 22 for Explanation of Ratios and Data

Comparative Historical Data | Current Data Sorted by Sales

				Type of Statement						
85		118	106	Unqualified	1	15	13	21	31	25
6		6	8	Reviewed	1	2	2		3	
7		11	8	Compiled	1	2		3	2	
14		14	22	Tax Returns	9	13				
46		58	60	Other	6	14	10	9	9	12
4/1/07-3/31/08 ALL		4/1/08-3/31/09 ALL	4/1/09-3/31/10 ALL			99 (4/1-9/30/09)			105 (10/1/09-3/31/10)	
					0-1MM	1-3MM	3-5MM	5-10MM	10-25MM	25MM & OVE
158		207	204	NUMBER OF STATEMENTS	18	46	25	33	45	37
%		%	%	ASSETS	%	%	%	%	%	%
16.6		16.5	15.4	Cash & Equivalents	15.7	11.0	15.1	16.2	16.8	18.5
15.5		15.3	16.3	Trade Receivables (net)	7.4	9.2	15.1	20.4	18.0	24.5
.3		.1	.4	Inventory	.0	.2	.1	1.5	.1	.3
2.4		2.6	3.1	All Other Current	.7	5.0	2.0	5.4	1.7	2.5
34.7		34.6	35.2	Total Current	23.8	25.4	32.4	43.4	36.6	45.7
51.9		49.1	50.8	Fixed Assets (net)	52.1	62.1	58.3	43.7	50.7	37.8
3.4		2.8	2.6	Intangibles (net)	8.2	3.5	1.8	1.6	1.3	1.7
10.1		13.5	11.4	All Other Non-Current	15.9	9.1	7.5	11.4	11.4	14.8
100.0		100.0	100.0	Total	100.0	100.0	100.0	100.0	100.0	100.0
				LIABILITIES						
6.0		5.1	6.1	Notes Payable-Short Term	7.4	10.4	7.3	3.4	3.7	4.8
2.4		3.5	2.7	Cur. Mat.-L.T.D.	3.4	4.4	2.1	1.7	2.0	2.4
5.3		5.0	5.4	Trade Payables	2.5	4.6	4.6	5.5	3.7	10.2
.0		.0	.0	Income Taxes Payable	.0	.0	.1	.0	.0	.0
11.0		11.6	13.1	All Other Current	20.5	12.9	7.4	15.7	8.6	16.6
24.6		25.2	27.3	Total Current	33.8	32.4	21.4	26.3	18.1	34.1
29.7		29.7	34.7	Long-Term Debt	36.2	50.0	35.5	29.3	32.0	22.8
.0		.1	.1	Deferred Taxes	.0	.0	.0	.8	.0	.0
5.8		7.3	6.5	All Other Non-Current	15.4	9.0	2.2	5.8	2.9	7.1
39.9		37.6	31.3	Net Worth	14.5	8.6	40.8	37.8	47.0	36.1
100.0		100.0	100.0	Total Liabilities & Net Worth	100.0	100.0	100.0	100.0	100.0	100.0
				INCOME DATA						
100.0		100.0	100.0	Net Sales	100.0	100.0	100.0	100.0	100.0	100.0
				Gross Profit						
93.1		93.2	93.8	Operating Expenses	92.5	86.2	94.4	100.2	95.4	95.6
6.9		6.8	6.2	Operating Profit	7.5	13.8	5.6	-.2	4.6	4.4
2.5		4.0	3.5	All Other Expenses (net)	2.2	8.0	3.1	1.3	3.0	1.2
4.4		2.8	2.8	Profit Before Taxes	5.3	5.9	2.5	-1.5	1.6	3.2
				RATIOS						
3.0		3.0	3.0		4.9	2.4	4.2	3.2	3.3	2.1
1.6		1.5	1.5	Current	1.3	1.1	1.3	1.7	1.8	1.2
.9		.8	.8		.1	.3	.7	1.0	1.0	1.0
2.6		2.8	2.7		4.8	2.1	4.0	2.7	3.2	1.9
1.5		1.4	1.4	Quick	1.3	.8	1.2	1.5	1.8	1.1
.9		.7	.7		.1	.3	.6	.9	.9	1.0

															Sales/Receivables												

5	79.7	4	89.6	3	108.8	Sales/Receivables	0	UND	0	UND	14	26.2	18	19.9	21	17.6	23	15.5
30	12.1	29	12.4	29	12.7		0	UND	3	121.5	28	12.9	35	10.3	35	10.4	43	8.6
48	7.6	46	7.9	48	7.6		3	140.9	32	11.6	45	8.1	54	6.8	44	8.4	56	6.5

					Cost of Sales/Inventory						

					Cost of Sales/Payables						

					Sales/Working Capital						
4.6		5.9	5.5		6.0	5.2	3.4	4.8	5.7	6.7
14.5		16.2	21.1		NM	63.8	26.4	8.8	11.7	26.5
-111.6		-45.0	-43.1		-6.1	-8.4	-33.8	NM	260.5	-147.9

						EBIT/Interest								
	9.7		6.1		6.1			13.0		6.5		3.2		5.0		3.9		12.0
(122)	2.8	(169)	1.8	(160)	2.1		(11)	2.1	(35)	2.7	(19)	1.4	(25)	1.2	(37)	1.7	(33)	3.2
	1.5		.3		.6			-1.0		1.3		-.4		-.2		.5		.7

					Net Profit + Depr., Dep., Amort./Cur. Mat. L/T/D						

					Fixed/Worth						
.6		.5	.6		.7	1.1	.5	.4	.4	.5
1.3		1.2	1.3		4.6	2.9	1.9	.8	1.2	.9
4.9		4.6	6.4		-1.4	-28.5	106.7	2.5	2.5	2.4

					Debt/Worth						
.5		.5	.5		.3	1.0	.2	.5	.5	.9
1.3		1.3	1.5		33.7	2.9	2.1	1.0	.8	2.1
6.3		6.6	10.7		-2.6	-32.0	170.5	5.3	3.4	5.7

						% Profit Before Taxes/Tangible Net Worth								
	24.4		26.0		28.4			30.3		49.4		28.3		13.9		21.1		35.1
(138)	11.3	(183)	6.0	(170)	8.0		(11)	14.3	(34)	17.0	(20)	7.8	(27)	1.2	(42)	5.0	(36)	9.6
	2.6		-2.3		-1.1			7.5		-.6		-6.2		-3.8		-2.6		1.0

					% Profit Before Taxes/Total Assets						
10.0		7.7	9.3		21.2	16.6	6.5	8.7	6.4	10.5
4.4		2.5	3.4		7.1	4.8	2.9	1.0	2.6	4.1
.8		-1.0	-.7		-.4	-.4	-3.2	-2.4	-1.1	.0

					Sales/Net Fixed Assets						
7.0		7.2	9.0		27.5	9.1	4.0	17.1	6.3	12.0
2.6		2.7	2.8		10.9	1.5	2.0	2.7	2.9	4.6
1.1		1.1	1.1		1.3	.5	.8	1.2	1.3	2.1

					Sales/Total Assets						
2.3		2.3	2.6		8.2	2.7	2.1	2.5	2.4	3.4
1.3		1.3	1.4		1.5	1.1	1.2	1.3	1.5	1.8
.7		.6	.6		.8	.4	.5	.8	.7	.8

						% Depr., Dep., Amort./Sales								
	1.8		2.0		1.8			2.0		2.8		2.4		1.2		1.9		1.3
(145)	2.8	(189)	2.9	(180)	3.0		(12)	2.8	(38)	5.0	(23)	3.3	(29)	2.5	(44)	3.0	(34)	2.2
	5.3		5.0		5.5			4.3		8.6		7.3		3.9		4.8		4.2

						% Officers', Directors' Owners' Comp/Sales								
	1.7		3.1		4.1					3.6								
(28)	5.4	(33)	5.9	(25)	6.4				(11)	6.1								
	9.6		10.9		12.1					10.2								

| 2361502M | | 4425843M | 3726694M | Net Sales ($) | 10000M | 86908M | 98137M | 232765M | 722744M | 2576140M |
| 2167072M | | 4101974M | 3261640M | Total Assets ($) | 10006M | 185989M | 152635M | 227772M | 782867M | 1902371M |

© RMA 2010

M = $ thousand   MM = $ million
See Pages 9 through 22 for Explanation of Ratios and Data

HEALTH CARE—Child and Youth Services NAICS 624110

	Current Data Sorted by Assets							Comparative Historical Data	
							Type of Statement		
9	41	105	91	11	5		Unqualified	136	223
3		2					Reviewed	5	5
1		2					Compiled	3	7
10	10	2	1				Tax Returns	8	12
14	22	35	19	2	2		Other	43	82
	294 (4/1-9/30/09)			93 (10/1/09-3/31/10)				4/1/05-3/31/06	4/1/06-3/31/07
0-500M	500M-2MM	2-10MM	10-50MM	50-100MM	100-250MM			ALL	ALL
37	73	146	111	13	7		**NUMBER OF STATEMENTS**	195	329
%	%	%	%	%	%		**ASSETS**	%	%
29.2	25.6	18.9	16.0	17.5			Cash & Equivalents	19.7	20.1
13.6	17.6	16.6	13.6	7.3			Trade Receivables (net)	18.2	17.6
.2	.6	.2	.8	.0			Inventory	.6	.7
6.5	2.5	3.3	3.0	7.3			All Other Current	4.6	3.6
49.5	46.2	39.0	33.5	32.1			Total Current	43.0	42.0
39.2	44.5	50.6	49.5	43.1			Fixed Assets (net)	41.2	42.2
2.0	1.5	.5	.2	.3			Intangibles (net)	1.3	1.5
9.3	7.7	9.8	16.7	24.5			All Other Non-Current	14.5	14.2
100.0	100.0	100.0	100.0	100.0			Total	100.0	100.0
							LIABILITIES		
9.2	5.4	4.5	2.3	1.8			Notes Payable-Short Term	6.9	4.5
3.2	1.0	1.7	.9	1.2			Cur. Mat.-L.T.D.	1.6	1.5
11.0	10.5	7.8	5.5	5.5			Trade Payables	8.0	7.4
.0	.0	.0	.0	.0			Income Taxes Payable	.0	.2
26.8	9.1	8.6	8.8	7.0			All Other Current	9.6	9.7
50.1	26.0	22.7	17.5	15.4			Total Current	26.1	23.4
15.0	27.1	18.6	20.0	25.3			Long-Term Debt	17.3	20.2
.0	.0	.0	.0	.0			Deferred Taxes	.0	.0
10.1	3.8	4.6	3.2	5.0			All Other Non-Current	5.2	4.2
24.9	43.0	54.2	59.3	54.2			Net Worth	51.3	52.2
100.0	100.0	100.0	100.0	100.0			Total Liabilties & Net Worth	100.0	100.0
							INCOME DATA		
100.0	100.0	100.0	100.0	100.0			Net Sales	100.0	100.0
							Gross Profit		
96.5	97.0	98.5	101.5	100.0			Operating Expenses	97.6	94.8
3.5	3.0	1.5	-1.5	.0			Operating Profit	2.4	5.2
.6	3.3	1.3	1.6	1.0			All Other Expenses (net)	.6	.2
2.9	-.4	.2	-3.1	-.9			Profit Before Taxes	1.8	5.1
							RATIOS		
8.3	5.4	3.2	3.4	3.1				3.3	4.3
1.5	2.8	1.9	1.9	1.8			Current	1.8	2.1
.3	1.0	1.1	1.1	1.2				1.1	1.3
6.0	5.2	3.1	3.1	3.0				3.0	3.8
1.3	2.8	1.7	1.7	1.8			Quick	1.5	1.9
.3	.9	1.0	1.0	.9				.9	1.4
0 UND	3 141.3	9 40.5	20 18.0	10 35.0				12 30.1	9 39.4
0 UND	20 17.9	28 12.9	35 10.3	29 12.7			Sales/Receivables	33 11.1	30 12.2
26 14.0	37 9.8	45 8.1	58 6.3	50 7.4				56 6.6	51 7.1
							Cost of Sales/Inventory		
							Cost of Sales/Payables		
5.6	4.2	5.3	3.2	3.7				4.7	4.0
71.8	8.5	11.1	10.4	9.6			Sales/Working Capital	12.6	9.1
-13.4	-123.4	106.4	48.4	21.4				171.3	35.1
18.9	3.8	4.6	3.4	4.0				10.1	9.7
(22) 7.3	(44) 1.0	(98) 1.2	(90) 1.2	(11) 1.1			EBIT/Interest	(130) 2.6	(220) 3.5
.4	-5.0	-1.5	-5.7	-2.3				.0	.8
							Net Profit + Depr., Dep., Amort./Cur. Mat. L/T/D		
.2	.4	.6	.5	.3				.3	.3
.8	.9	.9	.8	.9			Fixed/Worth	.8	.8
NM	1.9	1.7	1.3	1.7				1.4	1.4
.2	.3	.3	.3	.3				.3	.2
.9	.8	.6	.7	1.0			Debt/Worth	.7	.7
-12.0	3.0	1.7	1.5	1.4				2.1	1.9
37.9	14.4	8.7	6.6	5.8			% Profit Before Taxes/Tangible Net Worth	12.6	17.6
(27) 6.2	(65) .0	(142) .3	-.1	.7				(182) 3.8	(306) 7.1
-2.3	-12.8	-4.5	-6.1	-7.6				-3.7	.1
23.3	7.7	3.8	2.4	2.8			% Profit Before Taxes/Total Assets	7.1	9.6
6.1	.0	.1	-.1	.1				1.8	3.7
-4.8	-7.1	-3.0	-4.2	-3.8				-2.0	-.2
42.0	30.9	7.3	4.8	3.7				14.1	14.2
27.3	4.4	3.0	1.9	1.5			Sales/Net Fixed Assets	3.7	3.4
6.7	1.4	1.0	.9	1.0				1.6	1.5
8.5	3.6	3.0	1.6	1.5				2.7	2.6
4.4	1.5	1.4	1.0	.6			Sales/Total Assets	1.5	1.4
3.2	.9	.7	.5	.4				.7	.7
.6	.9	1.2	1.7	2.3				1.2	1.3
(26) 1.2	(62) 2.1	(129) 2.2	(103) 2.8	2.7			% Depr., Dep., Amort./Sales	(174) 2.3	(289) 2.4
1.8	4.0	4.9	4.8	4.8				4.0	4.0
2.4								1.1	2.8
(13) 7.7							% Officers', Directors' Owners' Comp/Sales	(23) 3.7	(38) 5.7
12.3								7.2	10.5
44053M	235950M	1598339M	2867596M	903815M	757151M		Net Sales ($)	3115810M	6708133M
9274M	88986M	796500M	2268948M	904112M	840299M		Total Assets ($)	2674392M	5060833M

© RMA 2010

M = $ thousand   MM = $ million
See Pages 9 through 22 for Explanation of Ratios and Data

Comparative Historical Data

Current Data Sorted by Sales

ALL	ALL	ALL	Type of Statement	0-1MM	1-3MM	3-5MM	5-10MM	10-25MM	25MM & OVE
243	246	262	Unqualified	13	46	18	52	76	57
7	6	5	Reviewed	3	1	1			
7	7	3	Compiled	1	1		1		
15	16	23	Tax Returns	8	7	5	2	1	
76	76	94	Other	18	26	8	13	18	11
4/1/07-3/31/08	4/1/08-3/31/09	4/1/09-3/31/10		294 (4/1-9/30/09)			93 (10/1/09-3/31/10)		
ALL	ALL	ALL		0-1MM	1-3MM	3-5MM	5-10MM	10-25MM	25MM & OVE
348	351	387	**NUMBER OF STATEMENTS**	43	81	32	68	95	68
%	%	%	**ASSETS**	%	%	%	%	%	%
22.2	20.6	20.5	Cash & Equivalents	20.7	19.8	20.5	16.8	20.2	25.6
15.7	18.1	15.1	Trade Receivables (net)	7.4	10.8	16.2	14.8	18.5	19.8
.5	.5	.4	Inventory	.0	.4	2.9	.2	.1	.3
4.2	3.4	3.5	All Other Current	2.8	3.0	2.1	2.9	3.9	5.3
42.7	42.6	39.5	Total Current	31.0	34.0	41.7	34.7	42.7	51.0
44.0	42.8	47.7	Fixed Assets (net)	62.0	51.0	48.1	53.6	42.6	35.8
.8	.8	.8	Intangibles (net)	3.2	.6	.3	.3	.7	.4
12.6	13.8	12.0	All Other Non-Current	3.8	14.4	10.0	11.4	14.0	12.8
100.0	100.0	100.0	Total	100.0	100.0	100.0	100.0	100.0	100.0
			LIABILITIES						
3.4	3.4	4.3	Notes Payable-Short Term	6.8	4.2	4.9	4.1	5.4	1.4
2.0	1.1	1.5	Cur. Mat.-L.T.D.	1.8	1.9	1.3	2.0	1.0	1.0
6.7	7.3	7.8	Trade Payables	4.4	5.7	7.3	5.4	8.6	14.2
.0	.0	.0	Income Taxes Payable	.0	.0	.0	.0	.0	.0
8.7	9.9	10.4	All Other Current	16.1	7.9	8.5	8.8	10.4	12.1
20.8	21.6	24.0	Total Current	29.1	19.8	22.0	20.2	25.5	28.8
18.6	17.2	20.5	Long-Term Debt	23.3	18.2	37.4	20.9	16.1	19.0
.0	.0	.0	Deferred Taxes	.0	.0	.0	.0	.0	.0
3.4	3.0	4.6	All Other Non-Current	9.3	3.2	1.2	2.8	4.2	7.2
57.2	58.1	50.9	Net Worth	38.4	58.8	39.3	56.1	54.2	44.9
100.0	100.0	100.0	Total Liabilities & Net Worth	100.0	100.0	100.0	100.0	100.0	100.0
			INCOME DATA						
100.0	100.0	100.0	Net Sales	100.0	100.0	100.0	100.0	100.0	100.0
			Gross Profit						
93.9	97.6	99.0	Operating Expenses	90.7	100.6	101.3	99.0	100.1	99.6
6.1	2.4	1.0	Operating Profit	9.3	-.6	-1.3	1.0	-.1	.4
.9	1.8	1.6	All Other Expenses (net)	7.6	1.4	.5	1.6	.6	.1
5.2	.6	-.6	Profit Before Taxes	1.7	-1.9	-1.8	-.7	-.8	.3
			RATIOS						
4.4	3.9	3.7	Current	5.5	6.3	3.5	3.7	2.8	2.7
2.3	2.1	2.0		1.5	3.1	2.3	1.6	1.9	1.8
1.3	1.3	1.0		.3	.9	1.2	1.0	1.1	1.2
4.0	3.6	3.5	Quick	4.5	5.7	3.5	3.3	2.7	2.4
2.0	1.8	1.8		1.5	2.8	2.1	1.5	1.6	1.7
1.0	1.0	.9		.3	.7	1.0	1.0	1.0	1.0
4 95.8	11 32.7	6 66.1	Sales/Receivables	0 UND	0 UND	6 65.6	15 24.1	16 22.7	5 70.2
29 12.8	33 11.0	26 14.0		0 UND	19 18.8	24 14.9	31 11.6	32 11.4	29 12.8
49 7.5	54 6.7	44 8.2		25 14.6	43 8.5	41 8.9	49 7.5	46 8.0	43 8.5
			Cost of Sales/Inventory						
			Cost of Sales/Payables						
3.6	3.8	4.5	Sales/Working Capital	3.2	3.3	3.5	4.8	6.1	7.1
7.8	9.0	10.5		32.0	6.8	8.8	15.7	12.1	11.4
36.8	37.4	754.0		-14.3	-71.7	36.1	NM	58.6	39.6
10.2	6.7	4.7	EBIT/Interest	6.0	7.5	3.7	3.6	3.7	6.1
(236) 3.0	(247) 1.4	(269) 1.2		(22) .9	(50) .4	(24) .8	(48) 1.0	(72) 1.6	(53) 2.1
.4	-1.9	-3.0		-1.1	-4.0	-5.8	-5.2	-2.4	-.9
			Net Profit + Depr., Dep., Amort./Cur. Mat. L/T/D						
.3	.3	.5	Fixed/Worth	.8	.4	.4	.6	.4	.4
.7	.7	.9		1.5	.8	.8	1.0	.7	.7
1.3	1.2	1.6		3.1	1.6	1.3	1.7	1.4	1.4
.2	.2	.3	Debt/Worth	.2	.2	.2	.2	.3	.5
.6	.6	.7		.7	.5	.6	.7	.7	1.1
1.6	1.3	1.9		3.8	1.6	1.7	1.7	1.4	2.7
14.2	11.5	8.6	% Profit Before Taxes/Tangible Net Worth	11.9	7.8	4.6	11.8	7.1	15.3
(335) 5.8	(338) 1.7	(365) .6		(37) 1.6	(76) -1.5	(29) -1.4	(67) .4	(89) 1.7	(67) 1.4
-1.5	-6.0	-5.9		-3.0	-9.0	-7.6	-5.8	-4.1	-5.5
9.3	5.8	4.2	% Profit Before Taxes/Total Assets	6.1	4.2	2.7	4.6	4.2	4.3
2.9	.6	.3		.6	-1.1	-.9	.1	.8	.5
-1.0	-3.2	-4.0		-2.7	-6.2	-4.3	-3.4	-2.6	-1.9
14.0	13.0	10.2	Sales/Net Fixed Assets	14.2	10.1	28.0	4.3	11.5	17.0
3.3	3.1	2.9		1.7	1.8	2.0	2.5	3.6	5.3
1.3	1.2	1.1		.3	.6	.8	1.0	1.8	2.3
2.3	2.5	2.9	Sales/Total Assets	3.6	2.0	2.6	2.1	3.5	3.4
1.3	1.3	1.3		1.0	1.0	1.0	1.2	1.7	1.7
.7	.7	.7		.3	.4	.5	.7	1.0	1.2
1.2	1.2	1.3	% Depr., Dep., Amort./Sales	1.5	1.3	1.2	1.7	1.0	1.0
(306) 2.3	(319) 2.2	(339) 2.3		(29) 6.4	(70) 2.9	(27) 3.2	(62) 2.6	(88) 1.9	(63) 1.7
3.9	4.0	4.5		15.6	6.4	6.8	4.7	3.2	2.7
2.9	2.5	2.2	% Officers', Directors' Owners' Comp/Sales		6.6				
(35) 6.4	(41) 5.5	(37) 6.2		(13) 11.9					
11.9	15.7	12.3			16.8				
6049248M	8469766M	6406904M	Net Sales ($)	23839M	145678M	125360M	471537M	1486452M	4154038M
5209319M	6040500M	4908119M	Total Assets ($)	51330M	308013M	166744M	507527M	1246698M	2627807M

M = $ thousand   MM = $ million
See Pages 9 through 22 for Explanation of Ratios and Data

Current Data Sorted by Assets   Comparative Historical Data

0-500M	500M-2MM	2-10MM	10-50MM	50-100MM	100-250MM	Type of Statement	4/1/05-3/31/06 ALL	4/1/06-3/31/07 ALL
5	17	72	41	7	2	Unqualified	66	101
	2	3		1		Reviewed	2	1
1	3					Compiled	2	4
2	5	2	1			Tax Returns	5	8
4	5	24	10	1		Other	19	34
	152 (4/1-9/30/09)		56 (10/1/09-3/31/10)					
12	32	101	52	9	2	NUMBER OF STATEMENTS	94	148
%	%	%	%	%	%	ASSETS	%	%
34.8	18.0	19.7	21.1			Cash & Equivalents	19.2	20.5
19.8	22.4	19.0	14.3			Trade Receivables (net)	18.6	19.0
.0	1.9	.2	.5			Inventory	.4	.9
4.2	5.4	3.9	4.7			All Other Current	4.7	4.7
58.8	47.7	42.7	40.6			Total Current	42.8	45.0
33.5	35.8	48.4	47.6			Fixed Assets (net)	45.8	44.9
.0	2.6	1.3	3.1			Intangibles (net)	2.1	1.8
7.7	13.9	7.6	8.7			All Other Non-Current	9.3	8.3
100.0	100.0	100.0	100.0			Total	100.0	100.0
						LIABILITIES		
22.5	6.9	2.5	3.5			Notes Payable-Short Term	5.3	3.2
1.0	2.9	2.3	2.4			Cur. Mat.-L.T.D.	2.4	2.0
10.0	6.7	4.8	5.9			Trade Payables	7.7	7.2
.0	.0	.0	.1			Income Taxes Payable	.0	.0
25.1	26.1	12.2	10.8			All Other Current	12.2	12.7
58.6	42.5	21.8	22.7			Total Current	27.6	25.1
13.5	29.7	21.8	26.1			Long-Term Debt	25.6	22.1
.0	.0	.0	.1			Deferred Taxes	.0	.1
35.3	.8	3.9	4.8			All Other Non-Current	5.0	3.7
-7.4	27.0	52.4	46.3			Net Worth	41.8	48.9
100.0	100.0	100.0	100.0			Total Liabilities & Net Worth	100.0	100.0
						INCOME DATA		
100.0	100.0	100.0	100.0			Net Sales	100.0	100.0
						Gross Profit		
104.3	93.2	95.7	97.2			Operating Expenses	96.5	94.4
-4.3	6.8	4.3	2.8			Operating Profit	3.5	5.6
-.2	3.1	2.1	1.2			All Other Expenses (net)	.9	.5
-4.1	3.7	2.2	1.6			Profit Before Taxes	2.6	5.1
						RATIOS		
7.0	3.6	4.7	3.4			Current	2.9	3.3
1.0	1.8	2.2	1.9				1.6	1.9
.6	.4	1.4	1.1				.9	1.1
7.0	3.2	4.1	2.8			Quick	2.6	2.8
1.0	1.2	2.0	1.8				1.4 (147)	1.7
.5	.3	1.2	1.0				.9	.9
2 146.8	0 UND	23 16.0	18 20.5			Sales/Receivables	10 36.3	13 27.5
23 15.7	26 14.1	33 11.2	30 12.1				32 11.5	31 11.7
48 7.7	48 7.7	47 7.7	42 8.8				45 8.1	48 7.6
						Cost of Sales/Inventory		
						Cost of Sales/Payables		
7.0	5.2	4.1	3.8			Sales/Working Capital	5.9	4.5
NM	28.0	7.6	8.0				16.2	10.2
-11.1	-10.2	20.5	64.6				-182.1	117.9
	17.3	5.8	8.4			EBIT/Interest	8.1	11.6
(20)	4.0	(86) 2.7	(46) 2.0				(70) 2.4	(110) 3.7
	.4	.2	-.1				1.1	1.3
						Net Profit + Depr., Dep., Amort./Cur. Mat. L/T/D		
.1	.4	.6	.6			Fixed/Worth	.5	.5
1.5	1.1	.9	1.1				1.1	1.0
NM	6.3	1.5	2.4				2.6	1.7
1.1	.6	.4	.6			Debt/Worth	.5	.4
2.7	2.0	.8	1.3				1.2	1.0
-3.2	10.1	1.5	3.2				3.8	2.9
	44.6	12.8	13.9			% Profit Before Taxes/Tangible Net Worth	19.2	22.7
(25)	17.5	(96) 5.0	(50) 6.9				(85) 8.9	(138) 10.7
	-1.9	-.4	-4.7				.8	3.0
10.2	11.7	7.4	6.8			% Profit Before Taxes/Total Assets	8.8	12.9
.2	5.6	3.1	2.2				3.5	4.2
-6.9	-1.5	-.2	-1.5				.3	.9
416.6	30.5	7.9	6.2			Sales/Net Fixed Assets	11.3	10.9
39.9	8.9	3.2	2.9				4.2	3.5
4.6	2.3	1.9	1.6				2.2	2.0
6.2	3.7	2.6	1.9			Sales/Total Assets	2.7	2.5
3.5	2.2	1.7	1.4				1.9	1.8
1.3	.9	1.1	.8				1.3	1.1
	.6	1.5	2.0			% Depr., Dep., Amort./Sales	1.7	1.3
(29)	1.4	(95) 2.4	(50) 3.1				(83) 2.7	(134) 2.5
	2.9	3.9	4.1				3.9	4.0
		1.0				% Officers', Directors' Owners' Comp/Sales	2.7	2.7
	(12)	3.6					(15) 4.7	(21) 5.8
		12.2					16.7	19.6
11195M	101529M	863206M	1698243M	639519M	374526M	Net Sales ($)	1619098M	2797770M
2773M	35961M	487881M	1077792M	554267M	244040M	Total Assets ($)	988306M	1941468M

M = $ thousand   MM = $ million
See Pages 9 through 22 for Explanation of Ratios and Data

Comparative Historical Data | Current Data Sorted by Sales

				Type of Statement	0-1MM	1-3MM	3-5MM	5-10MM	10-25MM	25MM & OVER
	109	122	144	Unqualified	12	16	9	39	41	27
	5	6	6	Reviewed		2		1	2	1
	5	5	4	Compiled	1	2	1			
	9	9	10	Tax Returns	2	4		1	3	
	43	58	44	Other	4	9	7	9	8	7
	4/1/07-3/31/08	4/1/08-3/31/09	4/1/09-3/31/10		152 (4/1-9/30/09)			56 (10/1/09-3/31/10)		
	ALL	ALL	ALL							
	171	200	208	NUMBER OF STATEMENTS	19	33	17	50	54	35
	%	%	%	ASSETS	%	%	%	%	%	%
	20.5	22.9	20.1	Cash & Equivalents	21.4	22.8	24.6	19.3	18.0	18.9
	18.3	19.9	18.3	Trade Receivables (net)	4.7	16.2	15.6	21.5	20.5	21.0
	.8	.6	.6	Inventory	.0	.5	3.0	.1	.5	.8
	3.0	4.4	4.4	All Other Current	3.0	3.5	2.1	3.5	6.9	4.7
	42.7	47.8	43.4	Total Current	29.1	43.1	45.2	44.3	45.9	45.4
	45.0	41.5	44.9	Fixed Assets (net)	53.4	42.2	50.9	48.7	42.7	37.7
	2.5	1.6	1.8	Intangibles (net)	.4	1.8	.9	.7	3.5	2.1
	9.8	9.2	9.9	All Other Non-Current	17.0	13.0	3.1	6.2	7.9	14.7
	100.0	100.0	100.0	Total	100.0	100.0	100.0	100.0	100.0	100.0
				LIABILITIES						
	3.2	6.5	4.6	Notes Payable-Short Term	4.0	11.8	1.2	3.5	3.2	3.4
	2.3	2.7	2.4	Cur. Mat.-L.T.D.	2.5	1.9	1.6	2.6	2.5	2.6
	8.0	7.7	5.9	Trade Payables	3.1	5.7	3.0	5.2	7.0	8.1
	.0	.0	.0	Income Taxes Payable	.0	.0	.1	.0	.1	.0
	14.8	15.6	14.9	All Other Current	27.1	6.9	8.6	19.2	13.0	15.5
	28.4	32.5	27.7	Total Current	36.8	26.3	14.4	30.4	25.9	29.7
	25.6	20.2	24.2	Long-Term Debt	24.2	31.2	22.5	23.4	20.6	25.0
	.1	.1	.0	Deferred Taxes	.0	.0	.0	.0	.1	.0
	3.6	5.2	5.6	All Other Non-Current	24.4	1.6	2.6	4.1	4.3	4.6
	42.3	42.0	42.5	Net Worth	14.6	40.9	60.4	42.0	49.1	40.8
	100.0	100.0	100.0	Total Liabilties & Net Worth	100.0	100.0	100.0	100.0	100.0	100.0
				INCOME DATA						
	100.0	100.0	100.0	Net Sales	100.0	100.0	100.0	100.0	100.0	100.0
				Gross Profit						
	95.8	96.2	96.3	Operating Expenses	91.3	96.4	96.0	96.6	97.5	96.5
	4.2	3.8	3.7	Operating Profit	8.7	3.6	4.0	3.4	2.5	3.5
	1.0	1.1	1.9	All Other Expenses (net)	10.7	1.5	1.3	.9	.7	1.0
	3.2	2.7	1.9	Profit Before Taxes	-2.0	2.1	2.7	2.5	1.8	2.5
				RATIOS						
	3.3	3.5	3.6		7.6	7.5	4.6	5.2	2.8	2.2
	1.7	2.1	2.0	Current	.7	2.3	3.2	2.1	2.1	1.3
	1.0	1.1	1.1		.4	.9	1.7	1.3	1.2	1.1
	3.0	3.2	3.4		5.4	7.3	4.2	4.1	2.7	1.8
	1.5	1.7	1.8	Quick	.6	2.2	2.2	2.0	1.9	1.2
	.9	.9	.9		.3	.8	1.7	1.2	.9	.9
8	46.2	14 25.4	18 20.8		0 UND	9 38.6	14 26.2	25 14.7	18 20.3	26 14.1
27	13.6	31 11.8	31 11.7	Sales/Receivables	22 16.6	25 14.4	28 13.1	33 11.2	32 11.3	32 11.5
45	8.2	47 7.8	47 7.8		47 7.8	48 7.6	45 8.0	47 7.8	45 8.1	51 7.2
				Cost of Sales/Inventory						
				Cost of Sales/Payables						
	5.3	4.4	4.6		2.9	2.9	3.5	4.4	5.7	7.4
	13.4	10.9	8.9	Sales/Working Capital	-20.7	6.5	6.2	8.6	8.7	24.8
	302.5	116.1	74.6		-1.5	-51.5	8.6	20.5	42.3	142.3
	7.1	7.2	7.1			6.7	7.1	7.4	11.5	8.0
(122)	2.7	(153) 2.7	(170) 2.3	EBIT/Interest	(26) 1.5	(13) 1.3	(43) 4.1	(47) 2.7	(32) 2.6
	.8	.3	.3			-.8	-1.8	1.7	-.7	.6
				Net Profit + Depr., Dep., Amort./Cur. Mat. L/T/D						
	.4	.3	.5		.6	.6	.6	.6	.5	.5
	1.0	.9	1.0	Fixed/Worth	1.8	1.0	1.0	1.0	.8	1.1
	2.2	1.9	2.1		2.9	2.4	1.3	1.8	1.8	2.4
	.4	.5	.5		.7	.4	.2	.5	.6	.5
	.9	1.0	1.2	Debt/Worth	2.0	1.8	.6	1.0	1.0	2.0
	3.2	2.8	2.8		-88.1	3.1	1.3	2.1	2.3	4.6
	19.6	23.3	14.3	% Profit Before Taxes/Tangible Net Worth	17.5	38.5	13.3	13.5	10.6	22.5
(152)	9.1	(182) 6.7	(189) 5.6		(14) 1.7	(27) 2.4	2.9	(45) 8.0	(52) 4.2	(34) 9.0
	2.3	-.9	-2.3		-2.2	-4.8	-8.4	3.3	-3.0	-4.2
	9.9	10.8	8.0	% Profit Before Taxes/Total Assets	2.7	13.3	5.9	8.7	6.3	8.2
	3.9	2.9	2.6		.0	1.5	1.8	4.3	1.7	3.4
	.0	-.7	-1.1		-5.5	-2.2	-4.0	1.5	-1.1	-.9
	13.0	26.9	9.9		8.4	21.7	4.9	8.3	12.1	11.2
	3.6	4.4	3.4	Sales/Net Fixed Assets	1.2	4.7	2.7	3.2	3.8	4.7
	1.9	1.8	1.8		.3	1.5	2.0	1.7	2.4	2.3
	2.9	3.3	2.6		1.0	3.1	2.0	2.7	2.8	2.7
	1.7	1.8	1.6	Sales/Total Assets	.3	1.7	1.6	1.7	1.9	1.7
	1.1	1.0	1.0		.2	.9	1.1	1.1	1.3	1.4
	1.4	1.1	1.3		2.0	.9	1.7	1.4	1.1	1.2
(152)	2.6	(179) 2.3	(191) 2.4	% Depr., Dep., Amort./Sales	(14) 11.9	(31) 1.7	(16) 2.8	(46) 2.6	(52) 2.3	(32) 2.1
	4.0	4.1	3.9		21.7	4.0	4.5	4.0	3.4	3.4
	1.3	5.1	1.2	% Officers', Directors' Owners' Comp/Sales						
(20)	4.7	(24) 6.7	(29) 4.3							
	6.3	11.0	7.3							
	3007958M	3922747M	3688218M	Net Sales ($)	9187M	69307M	69766M	357840M	886157M	2295961M
	1873149M	2353122M	2402714M	Total Assets ($)	33448M	68243M	58381M	273711M	542694M	1426237M

Current Data Sorted by Assets   Comparative Historical Data

0-500M	500M-2MM	2-10MM	10-50MM	50-100MM	100-250MM	Type of Statement	4/1/05-3/31/06 ALL	4/1/06-3/31/07 ALL
14	46	210	176	30	4	Unqualified	426	509
1	5	2				Reviewed	8	8
5	4	3	1	1		Compiled	6	17
14	10	3	1			Tax Returns	20	13
19	30	75	54	10	6	Other	242	144
	504 (4/1-9/30/09)		220 (10/1/09-3/31/10)					
53	95	293	232	41	10	NUMBER OF STATEMENTS	702	691
%	%	%	%	%	%	ASSETS	%	%
36.1	23.6	21.0	17.3	14.4	5.7	Cash & Equivalents	20.1	20.6
20.1	23.7	18.8	14.9	9.6	8.7	Trade Receivables (net)	16.9	16.9
.2	2.5	1.4	1.0	.9	8.8	Inventory	.9	1.4
11.8	5.4	4.8	3.2	3.1	3.0	All Other Current	5.3	5.3
68.2	55.2	45.9	36.5	27.9	26.1	Total Current	43.3	44.2
22.9	34.3	43.1	48.3	41.6	54.8	Fixed Assets (net)	43.0	42.3
3.1	1.5	.4	1.1	.8	.4	Intangibles (net)	.7	.9
5.7	9.0	10.6	14.1	29.8	18.6	All Other Non-Current	13.1	12.5
100.0	100.0	100.0	100.0	100.0	100.0	Total	100.0	100.0
						LIABILITIES		
6.6	5.5	4.1	2.6	2.0	1.5	Notes Payable-Short Term	4.5	4.1
.9	2.9	1.8	1.8	1.3	1.2	Cur. Mat.-L.T.D.	2.0	2.0
9.3	5.3	7.8	5.2	4.7	4.7	Trade Payables	7.2	7.0
.0	.0	.1	.0	.0	.3	Income Taxes Payable	.1	.1
22.8	14.6	12.3	10.1	9.3	14.9	All Other Current	9.1	11.6
39.8	28.3	26.2	19.8	17.4	22.6	Total Current	23.0	24.7
11.5	11.8	17.1	21.1	23.8	24.9	Long-Term Debt	20.0	18.2
.0	.1	.0	.0	.1	.0	Deferred Taxes	.0	.0
11.6	4.6	3.6	3.4	5.4	3.7	All Other Non-Current	3.7	2.5
37.1	55.2	53.1	55.7	53.3	48.8	Net Worth	53.2	54.5
100.0	100.0	100.0	100.0	100.0	100.0	Total Liabilties & Net Worth	100.0	100.0
						INCOME DATA		
100.0	100.0	100.0	100.0	100.0	100.0	Net Sales	100.0	100.0
						Gross Profit		
97.1	97.2	98.0	98.1	97.7	101.9	Operating Expenses	96.3	96.6
2.9	2.8	2.0	1.9	2.3	-1.9	Operating Profit	3.7	3.4
.6	.0	1.0	2.4	3.7	2.8	All Other Expenses (net)	.6	.2
2.3	2.8	1.0	-.5	-1.4	-4.7	Profit Before Taxes	3.1	3.2
						RATIOS		
6.8	5.2	3.4	3.4	2.7	1.4		4.0	3.6
2.6	2.5	1.8	2.0	1.6	1.1	Current	2.0	2.0
1.0	1.2	1.2	1.3	.9	.7		1.2	1.2
6.6	4.2	3.1	2.8	2.4	1.4		3.6	3.1
1.8	1.9	1.5	1.8	1.4	1.1	Quick	1.6	1.7
.7	1.1	1.0	1.0	.9	.6		1.0	1.0
0 UND	3 133.7	15 25.0	16 23.3	9 38.5	26 14.1		11 32.4	13 29.0
8 45.9	23 15.8	32 11.4	34 10.6	29 12.5	51 7.1	Sales/Receivables	32 11.5	32 11.6
37 9.9	49 7.4	49 7.4	52 7.1	59 6.1	73 5.0		50 7.3	50 7.4
						Cost of Sales/Inventory		
						Cost of Sales/Payables		
7.1	4.7	5.0	4.2	3.2	12.5		4.1	4.2
14.4	10.6	9.7	8.9	10.0	52.2	Sales/Working Capital	9.8	9.1
UND	58.7	40.6	29.1	-48.9	-14.4		44.9	36.7
8.8	19.8	6.8	5.8	4.3			8.3	7.7
(26) 2.4	(60) 2.2	(209) 1.6	(181) 1.7	(33) .2		EBIT/Interest	(496) 2.7	(476) 2.9
-8.5	-3.1	-1.2	-.8	-4.2			.2	.4
						Net Profit + Depr., Dep.,	11.9	
						Amort./Cur. Mat. L/T/D	(10) 6.9	
							2.1	
.1	.2	.4	.5	.4	.6		.4	.3
.3	.5	.8	.9	.7	1.1	Fixed/Worth	.8	.8
2.6	1.2	1.4	1.5	1.6	4.6		1.5	1.3
.4	.2	.3	.3	.4	.2		.3	.3
1.0	.6	.8	.8	.9	1.1	Debt/Worth	.7	.7
204.3	1.8	1.7	1.7	1.7	8.2		1.9	1.6
59.4	30.8	13.6	9.5	4.4	11.3	% Profit Before Taxes/Tangible	12.7	13.6
(42) 23.6	(90) 5.5	(285) 2.8	(226) 2.0	.2	-2.9	Net Worth	(669) 4.5	(659) 4.9
-4.8	-5.8	-4.3	-3.8	-10.2	-18.4		-1.9	-.8
25.8	16.5	6.5	5.3	2.6	3.5	% Profit Before Taxes/Total	7.1	7.6
4.3	3.1	1.4	1.2	.2	-.5	Assets	2.3	2.5
-15.0	-3.1	-3.0	-2.4	-4.4	-5.1		-1.2	-.6
584.5	40.7	11.2	5.1	4.5	13.2		10.8	11.9
70.5	12.5	4.9	2.5	1.9	1.1	Sales/Net Fixed Assets	3.7	3.7
7.2	3.4	1.8	1.2	1.0	.6		1.8	1.7
6.5	4.1	2.7	1.8	1.4	1.0		2.5	2.4
4.7	2.7	1.7	1.2	.8	.6	Sales/Total Assets	1.5	1.5
3.0	1.3	1.0	.7	.4	.5		.8	.8
.5	.7	.9	1.7	2.3			1.2	1.2
(25) 1.2	(76) 1.4	(264) 1.9	(215) 3.0	(37) 4.1		% Depr., Dep., Amort./Sales	(606) 2.3	(614) 2.2
3.9	2.1	3.4	4.1	6.5			3.7	3.8
3.3	1.5	2.7	1.6				3.9	3.0
(19) 8.2	(13) 2.6	(26) 7.8	(14) 4.8			% Officers', Directors' Owners' Comp/Sales	(67) 6.6	(66) 7.8
21.0	5.0	13.8	13.5				14.5	15.4
65502M	421949M	3124025M	6899575M	3128187M	2234868M	Net Sales ($)	12295573M	14851298M
12099M	111672M	1559913M	5144942M	2877034M	1768214M	Total Assets ($)	9047681M	9093666M

M = $ thousand   MM = $ million
See Pages 9 through 22 for Explanation of Ratios and Data

Comparative Historical Data | Current Data Sorted by Sales

			Type of Statement	0-1MM	1-3MM	3-5MM	5-10MM	10-25MM	25MM & OVER
526	577	480	Unqualified	21	50	36	95	159	119
3	6	8	Reviewed		3		3	2	
10	10	14	Compiled	3	3	1	4	1	2
23	26	28	Tax Returns	11	8	3	2	4	
168	192	194	Other	19	36	21	26	52	40
4/1/07-3/31/08 ALL	4/1/08-3/31/09 ALL	4/1/09-3/31/10 ALL		504 (4/1-9/30/09)			220 (10/1/09-3/31/10)		
730	811	724	NUMBER OF STATEMENTS	54	100	61	130	218	161
%	%	%	ASSETS	%	%	%	%	%	%
20.5	19.5	20.7	Cash & Equivalents	29.9	24.3	21.6	18.1	18.8	19.5
17.9	16.5	17.6	Trade Receivables (net)	8.4	19.4	12.9	18.0	19.1	19.2
1.3	1.2	1.4	Inventory	.6	1.0	1.4	.7	1.1	2.9
5.3	5.3	4.8	All Other Current	8.9	5.8	4.9	4.0	3.8	4.6
45.0	42.4	44.4	Total Current	47.7	50.5	40.8	40.8	42.7	46.2
41.9	43.7	42.2	Fixed Assets (net)	43.5	38.7	44.0	43.4	45.2	38.2
.8	1.0	1.0	Intangibles (net)	2.1	.7	1.4	1.3	.7	.8
12.2	12.8	12.3	All Other Non-Current	6.6	10.1	13.7	14.4	11.4	14.7
100.0	100.0	100.0	Total	100.0	100.0	100.0	100.0	100.0	100.0
			LIABILITIES						
4.2	3.8	3.9	Notes Payable-Short Term	4.3	6.1	3.9	4.1	3.1	3.2
1.7	1.8	1.8	Cur. Mat.-L.T.D.	2.2	1.3	1.5	2.3	1.9	1.8
7.3	6.6	6.5	Trade Payables	5.9	4.6	4.2	5.7	7.1	8.7
.1	.1	.1	Income Taxes Payable	.0	.0	.1	.0	.1	.1
11.1	10.3	12.6	All Other Current	15.6	10.3	9.3	11.4	12.7	14.9
24.4	22.6	24.9	Total Current	28.0	22.4	18.8	23.5	24.9	28.6
19.0	19.1	17.7	Long-Term Debt	15.2	14.8	15.2	20.5	18.9	17.5
.0	.0	.0	Deferred Taxes	.0	.0	.0	.0	.0	.0
3.5	3.0	4.4	All Other Non-Current	8.5	3.3	2.3	3.5	4.8	4.5
53.0	55.3	53.0	Net Worth	48.3	59.3	63.7	52.4	51.4	49.3
100.0	100.0	100.0	Total Liabilities & Net Worth	100.0	100.0	100.0	100.0	100.0	100.0
			INCOME DATA						
100.0	100.0	100.0	Net Sales	100.0	100.0	100.0	100.0	100.0	100.0
			Gross Profit						
96.3	96.9	97.9	Operating Expenses	96.4	95.7	96.8	99.5	98.8	97.7
3.7	3.1	2.1	Operating Profit	3.6	4.3	3.2	.5	1.2	2.3
.3	1.7	1.4	All Other Expenses (net)	1.7	1.3	1.9	1.3	1.6	1.2
3.4	1.4	.6	Profit Before Taxes	1.9	3.0	1.3	-.8	-.5	1.2
			RATIOS						
3.6 / 1.9 / 1.1	3.9 / 2.0 / 1.2	3.6 / 1.9 / 1.2	Current	9.2 / 2.8 / 1.2	6.2 / 3.1 / 1.2	5.6 / 2.3 / 1.1	3.2 / 1.9 / 1.3	3.0 / 1.9 / 1.2	2.5 / 1.6 / 1.1
3.1 / 1.6 / 1.0	3.2 / 1.7 / 1.0	3.2 / 1.7 / 1.0	Quick	7.8 / 2.6 / .7	5.4 / 2.8 / 1.0	5.0 / 1.9 / .8	2.8 / 1.7 / 1.0	2.7 / 1.7 / 1.0	2.2 / 1.4 / .9
13 28.7 / 33 10.9 / 55 6.7	12 31.5 / 31 11.9 / 51 7.2	13 29.2 / 31 11.6 / 49 7.4	Sales/Receivables	0 UND / 1 346.3 / 32 11.6	1 313.0 / 27 13.8 / 52 7.0	14 27.0 / 32 11.3 / 49 7.5	14 25.6 / 33 11.2 / 47 7.7	18 20.2 / 34 10.6 / 52 7.0	15 24.4 / 33 11.0 / 50 7.3
			Cost of Sales/Inventory						
			Cost of Sales/Payables						
4.3 / 9.5 / 51.0	4.3 / 9.3 / 45.7	4.7 / 9.9 / 44.3	Sales/Working Capital	3.3 / 7.7 / 37.2	3.6 / 7.3 / 73.7	3.1 / 7.5 / 53.8	5.3 / 10.4 / 29.0	5.1 / 9.6 / 42.0	6.7 / 14.6 / 91.9
(514) 8.9 / 2.6 / .8	(588) 6.4 / 1.6 / -1.3	(516) 6.7 / 1.6 / -1.6	EBIT/Interest	(28) 7.7 / 1.1 / -6.0	(57) 6.0 / 1.0 / -3.7	(38) 8.2 / 1.3 / -4.6	(99) 6.7 / 1.6 / -2.9	(170) 6.0 / 1.6 / -.6	(124) 8.6 / 2.4 / -.8
			Net Profit + Depr., Dep., Amort./Cur. Mat. L/T/D						
.3 / .7 / 1.4	.4 / .8 / 1.4	.4 / .8 / 1.4	Fixed/Worth	.2 / .9 / 1.6	.2 / .6 / 1.2	.3 / .8 / 1.2	.4 / .8 / 1.4	.5 / .9 / 1.5	.4 / .8 / 1.4
.3 / .7 / 1.8	.3 / .7 / 1.7	.3 / .8 / 1.8	Debt/Worth	.2 / .9 / 2.4	.2 / .4 / 1.5	.1 / .4 / 1.2	.4 / .8 / 1.6	.4 / .8 / 1.8	.4 / 1.0 / 2.0
(703) 12.6 / 4.9 / -.7	(784) 12.1 / 1.6 / -5.7	(694) 14.9 / 2.8 / -4.7	% Profit Before Taxes/Tangible Net Worth	(47) 16.4 / 5.4 / -6.5	(94) 18.9 / 2.0 / -4.3	(59) 19.9 / .5 / -10.2	(127) 15.4 / 2.0 / -5.7	(211) 10.5 / 2.8 / -3.9	(156) 15.4 / 3.6 / -3.6
7.3 / 2.7 / -.6	6.6 / .8 / -3.2	7.0 / 1.4 / -3.0	% Profit Before Taxes/Total Assets	10.6 / 1.6 / -8.5	12.9 / 1.1 / -2.5	10.9 / -.6 / -6.9	6.6 / .6 / -3.8	4.9 / 1.4 / -2.4	7.2 / 2.1 / -1.5
13.5 / 3.6 / 1.7	11.4 / 3.4 / 1.4	13.2 / 4.0 / 1.7	Sales/Net Fixed Assets	95.3 / 2.3 / .8	55.3 / 4.8 / 1.3	12.5 / 2.3 / 1.0	11.4 / 4.0 / 1.6	9.1 / 3.5 / 1.8	15.9 / 4.8 / 2.5
2.5 / 1.5 / .8	2.5 / 1.4 / .7	2.8 / 1.5 / .8	Sales/Total Assets	4.8 / 1.2 / .3	3.3 / 1.3 / .7	1.8 / 1.0 / .7	2.6 / 1.5 / .8	2.7 / 1.7 / .9	2.9 / 1.8 / 1.1
(644) 1.2 / 2.2 / 3.7	(731) 1.2 / 2.4 / 3.8	(625) 1.1 / 2.2 / 3.9	% Depr., Dep., Amort./Sales	(28) 1.2 / 4.6 / 7.9	(80) .9 / 2.0 / 4.3	(51) 1.3 / 2.7 / 4.7	(119) 1.1 / 2.5 / 3.9	(200) 1.1 / 2.1 / 3.6	(147) .9 / 2.0 / 3.4
(71) 2.7 / 6.6 / 13.7	(84) 2.9 / 6.6 / 14.3	(74) 2.5 / 6.1 / 13.8	% Officers', Directors' Owners' Comp/Sales	(11) 4.3 / 10.0 / 16.6	(16) 2.8 / 5.3 / 16.8		(13) 2.3 / 5.3 / 15.6	(20) 1.6 / 4.2 / 15.6	(10) 2.4 / 7.0 / 17.5
13826589M	15732387M	15874106M	Net Sales ($)	29717M	182778M	234596M	937202M	3572840M	10916973M
10743927M	12381963M	11473874M	Total Assets ($)	70305M	214407M	304203M	1042867M	3305964M	6536128M

M = $ thousand   MM = $ million
See Pages 9 through 22 for Explanation of Ratios and Data

Current Data Sorted by Assets							Comparative Historical Data	
						Type of Statement		
	3	7	10		1	Unqualified	8	13
		1				Reviewed		
1	1	1				Compiled		1
						Tax Returns	1	
	3	3	2			Other	3	1
	23 (4/1-9/30/09)		10 (10/1/09-3/31/10)				4/1/05-3/31/06 ALL	4/1/06-3/31/07 ALL
0-500M	500M-2MM	2-10MM	10-50MM	50-100MM	100-250MM			
1	7	12	12		1	NUMBER OF STATEMENTS	12	15
%	%	%	%	%	%	**ASSETS**	%	%
		22.5	18.9	DATA NOT AVAILABLE		Cash & Equivalents	18.8	23.9
		2.7	4.0			Trade Receivables (net)	3.0	9.0
		18.1	10.7			Inventory	15.9	19.1
		2.8	3.2			All Other Current	6.2	2.4
		46.1	36.7			Total Current	43.9	54.3
		47.7	46.4			Fixed Assets (net)	37.9	35.8
		.0	1.1			Intangibles (net)	.0	.0
		6.1	15.7			All Other Non-Current	18.2	9.8
		100.0	100.0			Total	100.0	100.0
						LIABILITIES		
		1.9	.9			Notes Payable-Short Term	4.9	2.1
		.4	1.6			Cur. Mat.-L.T.D.	.6	.8
		1.9	8.4			Trade Payables	4.8	3.0
		.0	.0			Income Taxes Payable	.0	.0
		2.1	.6			All Other Current	2.1	7.4
		6.4	11.6			Total Current	12.4	13.3
		6.3	12.6			Long-Term Debt	9.7	5.7
		.0	.0			Deferred Taxes	.0	.0
		1.1	.2			All Other Non-Current	.0	1.8
		86.2	75.5			Net Worth	78.0	79.2
		100.0	100.0			Total Liabilities & Net Worth	100.0	100.0
						INCOME DATA		
		100.0	100.0			Net Sales	100.0	100.0
						Gross Profit		
		90.0	90.3			Operating Expenses	96.4	91.6
		10.0	9.7			Operating Profit	3.6	8.4
		.7	.2			All Other Expenses (net)	.3	-1.2
		9.2	9.5			Profit Before Taxes	3.3	9.7
						RATIOS		
		22.6	18.0			Current	10.6	14.7
		10.3	7.7				5.5	8.8
		4.0	2.8				1.8	3.0
		9.7	6.0			Quick	4.7	12.6
		5.3	4.3				2.7	3.6
		2.0	1.6				1.8	1.6
		0 955.8	0 UND			Sales/Receivables	0 UND	2 183.6
		3 128.7	2 231.3				1 316.5	6 60.8
		11 33.7	6 61.3				15 23.7	21 17.1
						Cost of Sales/Inventory		
						Cost of Sales/Payables		
		4.5	5.2			Sales/Working Capital	3.4	2.9
		6.5	6.8				6.5	4.9
		9.1	11.1				15.2	9.6
						EBIT/Interest		
						Net Profit + Depr., Dep., Amort./Cur. Mat. L/T/D		
		.3	.4			Fixed/Worth	.2	.2
		.5	.6				.6	.5
		.9	.8				.7	.6
		.0	.1			Debt/Worth	.1	.1
		.1	.3				.2	.1
		.4	.5				.6	.4
		35.0	36.5			% Profit Before Taxes/Tangible Net Worth	12.7	19.6
		14.9	22.0				3.5	(14) 7.1
		-4.2	5.8				-14.5	4.4
		26.9	27.8			% Profit Before Taxes/Total Assets	8.9	14.0
		12.6	12.8				2.5	6.1
		-3.1	5.4				-9.2	2.5
		12.1	12.5			Sales/Net Fixed Assets	17.8	24.0
		5.2	4.4				3.8	5.1
		2.1	2.6				1.5	1.6
		3.6	4.1			Sales/Total Assets	3.2	4.1
		1.7	1.9				1.2	1.5
		1.2	1.1				.7	.8
		.9	.5			% Depr., Dep., Amort./Sales	.7	.6
		(11) 1.5	(11) 1.2				(10) 2.0	1.2
		3.3	1.7				4.0	3.2
						% Officers', Directors' Owners' Comp/Sales		
393M	28791M	134480M	1107779M		433794M	Net Sales ($)	107262M	245263M
14M	8822M	52664M	269617M		118832M	Total Assets ($)	56548M	143313M

M = $ thousand MM = $ million

See Pages 9 through 22 for Explanation of Ratios and Data

Comparative Historical Data | | Type of Statement | | Current Data Sorted by Sales

FY08	FY09	FY10	Type of Statement	0-1MM	1-3MM	3-5MM	5-10MM	10-25MM	25MM & OVER
9	10	21	Unqualified			5	3	4	9
		1	Reviewed					1	
1	2	3	Compiled	1	2		2	1	
7	8		Tax Returns						
1	3	8	Other		3		2		2
4/1/07-	4/1/08-	4/1/09-			23 (4/1-9/30/09)			10 (10/1/09-3/31/10)	
3/31/08	3/31/09	3/31/10							
ALL	ALL	ALL							
18	23	33	**NUMBER OF STATEMENTS**	1	5	5	5	6	11
%	%	%	**ASSETS**	%	%	%	%	%	%
16.3	17.6	21.6	Cash & Equivalents						16.0
10.1	8.0	5.9	Trade Receivables (net)						4.2
7.9	10.8	14.4	Inventory						22.6
11.5	14.5	2.2	All Other Current						3.5
45.8	50.9	44.1	Total Current						46.3
41.6	37.2	45.0	Fixed Assets (net)						36.7
2.3	2.0	.4	Intangibles (net)						1.2
10.3	9.9	10.4	All Other Non-Current						15.8
100.0	100.0	100.0	Total						100.0
			LIABILITIES						
.7	4.6	2.8	Notes Payable-Short Term						1.4
2.0	5.3	.9	Cur. Mat.-L.T.D.						1.7
4.0	3.8	6.1	Trade Payables						8.6
.0	.0	.0	Income Taxes Payable						.0
24.8	22.7	3.7	All Other Current						.7
31.4	36.5	13.5	Total Current						12.3
16.8	8.3	9.8	Long-Term Debt						13.0
.0	.0	.0	Deferred Taxes						.0
1.0	2.3	5.2	All Other Non-Current						.3
50.8	52.8	71.5	Net Worth						74.4
100.0	100.0	100.0	Total Liabilities & Net Worth						100.0
			INCOME DATA						
100.0	100.0	100.0	Net Sales						100.0
			Gross Profit						
98.9	96.8	91.7	Operating Expenses						91.4
1.1	3.2	8.3	Operating Profit						8.6
-.6	.4	.4	All Other Expenses (net)						-.3
1.6	2.8	7.9	Profit Before Taxes						8.9
			RATIOS						
8.6	9.7	14.1	Current						18.9
3.1	4.5	6.9							11.3
.9	1.0	1.8							2.7
4.8	6.0	6.1	Quick						6.0
2.7	2.4	3.5							3.8
.2	.2	1.3							1.0
0 UND	0 UND	0 999.8	Sales/Receivables						0 UND
2 160.4	2 148.4	3 118.9							1 457.5
19 19.4	15 24.8	10 37.2							8 48.6
			Cost of Sales/Inventory						
			Cost of Sales/Payables						
6.6	4.0	5.0	Sales/Working Capital						5.2
8.9	9.1	7.0							7.5
-125.7	-676.7	13.2							11.7
28.1	56.3	21.6	EBIT/Interest						
(14) 5.1	(16) 8.7	(17) 6.1							
-1.5	-1.1	-4.0							
			Net Profit + Depr., Dep., Amort./Cur. Mat. L/T/D						
.4	.1	.3	Fixed/Worth						.1
.6	.6	.6							.5
1.5	1.6	.9							.8
.1	.1	.1	Debt/Worth						.1
.8	.4	.3							.3
2.3	3.4	.5							.5
14.8	31.9	35.7	% Profit Before Taxes/Tangible Net Worth						39.6
(15) 5.3	(20) 14.1	(32) 16.9							27.0
-8.8	1.7	-1.9							16.6
11.9	17.4	22.8	% Profit Before Taxes/Total Assets						30.3
3.4	6.0	11.4							17.5
-6.2	-1.0	-2.7							10.6
15.5	23.1	14.9	Sales/Net Fixed Assets						31.4
8.0	7.3	5.7							11.3
2.0	2.5	2.4							3.5
4.7	3.4	3.8	Sales/Total Assets						4.8
2.5	2.5	2.2							3.0
1.1	1.3	1.3							1.7
.9	.6	.7	% Depr., Dep., Amort./Sales						.3
(16) 1.2	(22) 1.7	(28) 1.3						(10)	.7
2.7	3.1	2.1							1.2
			% Officers', Directors' Owners' Comp/Sales						
176941M	945922M	1705237M	Net Sales ($)	393M	10465M	19930M	39356M	106884M	1528209M
70381M	201839M	449949M	Total Assets ($)	14M	6446M	11608M	32890M	42105M	356886M

© RMA 2010

M = $ thousand   MM = $ million
See Pages 9 through 22 for Explanation of Ratios and Data

Current Data Sorted by Assets   Comparative Historical Data

						Type of Statement		
	1	13	7		2	Unqualified	8	14
1	1					Reviewed	1	1
	1					Compiled		
						Tax Returns		1
1	2	4	1		1	Other	1	2
	28 (4/1-9/30/09)		6 (10/1/09-3/31/10)				1 4/1/05- 3/31/06 ALL	2 4/1/06- 3/31/07 ALL
0-500M	500M-2MM	2-10MM	10-50MM	50-100MM	100-250MM			
2	4	17	8		3	**NUMBER OF STATEMENTS**	10	18
%	%	%	%	%	%	**ASSETS**	%	%
		20.0				Cash & Equivalents	24.3	19.5
		8.4		D		Trade Receivables (net)	9.2	5.1
		.1		A		Inventory	.0	.1
		4.7		T		All Other Current	5.0	5.7
		33.2		A		Total Current	38.5	30.4
		49.3				Fixed Assets (net)	55.9	63.5
		.0		N		Intangibles (net)	.0	.0
		17.4		O		All Other Non-Current	5.6	6.1
		100.0		T		Total	100.0	100.0
				A		**LIABILITIES**		
		1.2		V		Notes Payable-Short Term	.2	1.3
		.5		A		Cur. Mat.-L.T.D.	.8	1.0
		2.3		I		Trade Payables	3.3	2.9
		.0		L		Income Taxes Payable	.0	.0
		3.6		A		All Other Current	8.0	2.1
		7.6		B		Total Current	12.3	7.4
		17.8		L		Long-Term Debt	11.0	15.1
		.0		E		Deferred Taxes	.0	.0
		.2				All Other Non-Current	.0	.4
		74.4				Net Worth	76.7	77.1
		100.0				Total Liabilities & Net Worth	100.0	100.0
						INCOME DATA		
		100.0				Net Sales	100.0	100.0
						Gross Profit		
		99.7				Operating Expenses	88.5	89.9
		.3				Operating Profit	11.5	10.1
		3.1				All Other Expenses (net)	-.9	-.2
		-2.8				Profit Before Taxes	12.3	10.3
						RATIOS		
		11.1					5.1	12.6
		4.5				Current	3.2	4.9
		2.7					1.6	1.8
		8.6					4.6	12.0
		3.6				Quick	2.5	3.6
		2.0					1.4	.9
	0 UND						0 UND	1 463.8
	10 36.4					Sales/Receivables	19 18.9	12 30.3
	33 11.2						37 10.0	41 9.0
						Cost of Sales/Inventory		
						Cost of Sales/Payables		
		2.4					2.0	2.5
		4.1				Sales/Working Capital	6.1	4.2
		5.5					42.6	8.4
		5.9						
		(11) 4.0				EBIT/Interest		
		-2.2						
						Net Profit + Depr., Dep., Amort./Cur. Mat. L/T/D		
		.3					.3	.6
		.6				Fixed/Worth	.7	.8
		1.1					1.0	1.2
		.1					.1	.1
		.3				Debt/Worth	.3	.2
		.6					.5	.5
		5.3				% Profit Before Taxes/Tangible	30.1	11.8
		-.2				Net Worth	4.8	6.1
		-8.3					1.1	.1
		3.7				% Profit Before Taxes/Total	24.4	9.1
		-.2				Assets	2.7	5.1
		-5.8					.9	.1
		3.4					11.1	1.8
		1.3				Sales/Net Fixed Assets	1.1	1.1
		.7					.8	.8
		1.2					2.1	1.2
		.8				Sales/Total Assets	.8	.7
		.4					.5	.5
		1.7						2.8
		3.4				% Depr., Dep., Amort./Sales	(16)	3.9
		5.7						4.9
						% Officers', Directors' Owners' Comp/Sales		
2816M	4322M	91322M	71804M		627296M	Net Sales ($)	28699M	50819M
733M	3579M	106366M	130525M		442847M	Total Assets ($)	38588M	71056M

M = $ thousand   MM = $ million
See Pages 9 through 22 for Explanation of Ratios and Data

Comparative Historical Data / Current Data Sorted by Sales

Comparative Historical			Type of Statement	Current Data Sorted by Sales					
16	18	23	Unqualified		6	3	8	5	1
1	1	1	Reviewed	1					
1	1	1	Compiled	1					
			Tax Returns						
7	8	9	Other	2	3	2	1		1
4/1/07-3/31/08 ALL	4/1/08-3/31/09 ALL	4/1/09-3/31/10 ALL		0-1MM	28 (4/1-9/30/09) 1-3MM	3-5MM	5-10MM	6 (10/1/09-3/31/10) 10-25MM	25MM & OVER
25	28	34	NUMBER OF STATEMENTS	4	9	5	9	5	2
%	%	%	ASSETS	%	%	%	%	%	%
17.7	17.9	16.9	Cash & Equivalents						
4.5	11.3	8.9	Trade Receivables (net)						
.3	.3	.2	Inventory						
6.5	5.8	3.1	All Other Current						
29.0	35.2	29.1	Total Current						
55.3	51.6	56.6	Fixed Assets (net)						
.0	1.0	.0	Intangibles (net)						
15.7	12.2	14.2	All Other Non-Current						
100.0	100.0	100.0	Total						
			LIABILITIES						
1.0	3.5	4.0	Notes Payable-Short Term						
1.0	.4	1.1	Cur. Mat.-L.T.D.						
2.4	3.7	2.5	Trade Payables						
.0	.0	.0	Income Taxes Payable						
8.2	3.6	4.3	All Other Current						
12.5	11.3	11.8	Total Current						
14.6	11.3	21.1	Long-Term Debt						
.0	.0	.0	Deferred Taxes						
.5	1.0	1.2	All Other Non-Current						
72.4	76.5	65.8	Net Worth						
100.0	100.0	100.0	Total Liabilities & Net Worth						
			INCOME DATA						
100.0	100.0	100.0	Net Sales						
			Gross Profit						
92.4	96.3	98.8	Operating Expenses						
7.6	3.7	1.2	Operating Profit						
-.4	-.6	2.2	All Other Expenses (net)						
8.0	4.3	-1.0	Profit Before Taxes						
			RATIOS						
5.3	8.8	5.4							
3.1	3.7	3.1	Current						
1.5	1.1	1.4							
4.6	6.4	4.0							
1.6	2.7	2.3	Quick						
1.0	.8	1.3							
0 UND	1 469.3	2 204.1							
7 54.1	22 16.3	22 16.8	Sales/Receivables						
30 12.0	56 6.5	48 7.6							
			Cost of Sales/Inventory						
			Cost of Sales/Payables						
3.1	2.8	3.2							
7.6	4.7	4.8	Sales/Working Capital						
15.3	55.2	14.2							
13.7	29.8	14.8							
(15) 7.8	(19) 1.3	(23) 1.9	EBIT/Interest						
2.2	-3.2	-2.2							
			Net Profit + Depr., Dep., Amort./Cur. Mat. L/T/D						
.4	.4	.5							
.8	.7	.9	Fixed/Worth						
1.1	1.0	1.3							
.1	.1	.2							
.3	.2	.4	Debt/Worth						
.7	.6	1.2							
14.6	4.8	6.9							
6.2	.5	-.6	% Profit Before Taxes/Tangible Net Worth						
1.6	-3.6	-7.7							
11.6	3.9	4.0							
3.8	.4	-.4	% Profit Before Taxes/Total Assets						
1.3	-2.6	-5.0							
2.8	3.6	3.0							
1.2	1.7	1.3	Sales/Net Fixed Assets						
.7	.7	.7							
1.2	1.4	1.2							
.7	.8	.8	Sales/Total Assets						
.5	.4	.5							
2.2	2.0	1.9							
(21) 3.1	(24) 2.9	(29) 3.1	% Depr., Dep., Amort./Sales						
5.6	5.3	5.7							
			% Officers', Directors' Owners' Comp/Sales						
274588M	204468M	797560M	Net Sales ($)	2959M	18868M	19721M	68539M	77525M	609948M
329150M	298961M	684050M	Total Assets ($)	2861M	44606M	30972M	105428M	246380M	253803M

© RMA 2010

M = $ thousand   MM = $ million
See Pages 9 through 22 for Explanation of Ratios and Data

| Current Data Sorted by Assets | | | | | | | Comparative Historical Data | | |

© RMA 2010

M = $ thousand   MM = $ million
See Pages 9 through 22 for Explanation of Ratios and Data

						Type of Statement		
	8	28	21	5	2	Unqualified	24	32
		1				Reviewed	2	2
						Compiled		
1	1					Tax Returns	1	1
2	6	14	7		3	Other	7	13
	64 (4/1-9/30/09)		35 (10/1/09-3/31/10)				4/1/05- 3/31/06	4/1/06- 3/31/07
0-500M	500M-2MM	2-10MM	10-50MM	50-100MM	100-250MM		ALL	ALL
3	15	43	28	5	5	NUMBER OF STATEMENTS	34	48
%	%	%	%	%	%	ASSETS	%	%
	10.8	11.0	9.5			Cash & Equivalents	12.1	12.4
	2.6	9.4	10.2			Trade Receivables (net)	8.7	6.8
	2.3	6.1	2.5			Inventory	1.7	4.6
	7.4	3.3	5.6			All Other Current	4.3	5.2
	23.0	29.7	27.9			Total Current	26.8	29.0
	58.4	46.4	42.9			Fixed Assets (net)	44.5	47.3
	.4	1.1	.3			Intangibles (net)	.5	.8
	18.1	22.9	28.9			All Other Non-Current	28.2	22.9
	100.0	100.0	100.0			Total	100.0	100.0
						LIABILITIES		
	5.5	2.8	2.0			Notes Payable-Short Term	2.1	7.1
	2.4	1.7	3.3			Cur. Mat.-L.T.D.	2.3	4.9
	5.4	4.1	4.1			Trade Payables	4.5	4.4
	.0	.0	.1			Income Taxes Payable	.0	.0
	5.2	5.0	5.0			All Other Current	5.8	4.8
	18.6	13.6	14.3			Total Current	14.7	21.2
	51.7	26.7	32.6			Long-Term Debt	35.3	28.2
	.0	.0	.0			Deferred Taxes	.0	.0
	1.1	3.6	4.1			All Other Non-Current	2.1	2.7
	28.7	56.2	49.0			Net Worth	47.9	48.0
	100.0	100.0	100.0			Total Liabilties & Net Worth	100.0	100.0
						INCOME DATA		
	100.0	100.0	100.0			Net Sales	100.0	100.0
						Gross Profit		
	83.3	93.9	94.7			Operating Expenses	89.9	90.7
	16.7	6.1	5.3			Operating Profit	10.1	9.3
	11.0	4.3	2.8			All Other Expenses (net)	4.2	2.8
	5.7	1.7	2.4			Profit Before Taxes	5.8	6.6
						RATIOS		
	2.0	4.2	5.4				4.5	3.5
	1.0	2.5	2.2			Current	1.8	1.6
	.5	1.3	1.1				1.0	.9
	1.2	3.2	3.6				2.2	2.4
	.5	1.6	1.8			Quick	1.4	1.0
	.1	.8	1.0				.8	.5

	0	UND	2	169.0	19	19.0	Sales/Receivables	2	218.0	0	UND
	4	89.5	23	15.9	32	11.3		16	22.4	21	17.0
	10	35.4	42	8.8	70	5.2		45	8.1	58	6.3

						Cost of Sales/Inventory		
						Cost of Sales/Payables		
	8.2	2.3	1.6				2.0	2.0
	-119.6	5.3	4.9			Sales/Working Capital	5.3	7.9
	-13.8	24.9	39.4				-602.8	-21.8

						EBIT/Interest				
		18.7	10.9					3.7		7.5
	(32)	1.4	(18)	3.2			(21)	1.5	(31)	2.8
		-.3	.6					.7		1.0

						Net Profit + Depr., Dep., Amort./Cur. Mat. L/T/D		
	.4	.2	.4				.2	.3
	1.7	.8	.9			Fixed/Worth	1.0	.9
	-11.1	2.5	2.1				2.4	1.8
	.7	.3	.5				.5	.5
	1.2	.6	1.1			Debt/Worth	.9	1.0
	-12.8	2.3	2.3				3.3	2.9

						% Profit Before Taxes/Tangible Net Worth				
		17.3	13.4	7.1				14.6		15.9
	(11)	5.2	(41)	2.2	(27)	2.6	(31)	4.1	(43)	4.6
		-1.2	-3.7	-3.5				-.8		-.9

	6.7	5.8	4.8			% Profit Before Taxes/Total Assets	3.9	7.3
	2.8	1.2	1.5				1.4	1.6
	-.5	-1.8	-.7				-.5	-.5
	5.7	6.3	3.6			Sales/Net Fixed Assets	11.9	4.9
	1.0	1.6	1.3				1.2	1.5
	.4	.6	.5				.4	.4
	1.0	.9	1.2			Sales/Total Assets	1.0	.9
	.5	.6	.5				.4	.4
	.3	.3	.2				.2	.2

						% Depr., Dep., Amort./Sales				
		1.3	1.4	1.8				1.2		1.4
	(12)	8.8	(40)	3.3	(24)	4.6	(28)	5.0	(42)	3.9
		16.1	6.1	8.8				8.6		7.7

						% Officers', Directors' Owners' Comp/Sales		

1007M	13363M	194629M	585748M	61559M	159364M	Net Sales ($)	355761M	322818M
911M	17927M	238102M	731200M	341973M	637599M	Total Assets ($)	517787M	745910M

Comparative Historical Data | Current Data Sorted by Sales

Hist 1	Hist 2	Hist 3	Type of Statement	0-1MM	1-3MM	3-5MM	5-10MM	10-25MM	25MM & OVER
30	44	64	Unqualified	10	18	6	11	14	5
2	1	1	Reviewed		1				
	2	2	Compiled						
2	2	2	Tax Returns	2					
14	19	32	Other	8	4	6	4	4	6
4/1/07-3/31/08 ALL	4/1/08-3/31/09 ALL	4/1/09-3/31/10 ALL		64 (4/1-9/30/09)			35 (10/1/09-3/31/10)		
48	68	99	**NUMBER OF STATEMENTS**	20	23	12	15	18	11
%	%	%	**ASSETS**	%	%	%	%	%	%
18.5	9.7	11.1	Cash & Equivalents	8.4	9.4	12.7	17.9	12.1	6.8
7.7	8.2	9.0	Trade Receivables (net)	3.5	7.0	8.8	11.2	14.3	11.8
3.6	4.5	4.2	Inventory	1.7	3.3	9.6	4.7	3.9	4.4
6.6	3.5	4.8	All Other Current	6.7	1.7	6.4	2.7	4.1	10.3
36.4	25.9	29.1	Total Current	20.3	21.5	37.6	36.5	34.5	33.4
43.5	45.1	45.6	Fixed Assets (net)	62.6	55.9	28.4	41.1	33.2	38.7
1.5	2.6	.6	Intangibles (net)	.3	.1	2.3	1.3	.1	.5
18.7	26.4	24.6	All Other Non-Current	16.8	22.5	31.7	21.1	32.2	27.5
100.0	100.0	100.0	Total	100.0	100.0	100.0	100.0	100.0	100.0
			LIABILITIES						
2.8	2.7	3.2	Notes Payable-Short Term	4.7	4.9	1.4	2.2	2.5	1.3
2.0	2.7	2.3	Cur. Mat.-L.T.D.	1.9	1.5	5.5	1.9	1.3	3.3
2.6	4.4	4.0	Trade Payables	1.1	3.9	2.3	3.1	6.8	8.3
.0	.0	.0	Income Taxes Payable	.0	.0	.0	.0	.0	.2
4.0	4.2	5.5	All Other Current	9.4	2.7	5.9	2.8	4.6	8.8
11.5	14.0	15.0	Total Current	17.0	13.1	15.2	10.1	15.2	21.9
29.7	25.9	33.7	Long-Term Debt	50.6	27.1	21.4	40.2	26.1	33.5
.0	.0	.0	Deferred Taxes	.0	.0	.0	.0	.0	.0
3.4	3.8	3.1	All Other Non-Current	2.4	1.3	4.9	4.4	2.3	5.5
55.4	56.3	48.2	Net Worth	30.0	58.5	58.5	45.4	56.4	39.1
100.0	100.0	100.0	Total Liabilities & Net Worth	100.0	100.0	100.0	100.0	100.0	100.0
			INCOME DATA						
100.0	100.0	100.0	Net Sales	100.0	100.0	100.0	100.0	100.0	100.0
			Gross Profit						
92.2	89.3	90.2	Operating Expenses	85.9	92.3	92.9	86.7	93.8	89.4
7.8	10.7	9.8	Operating Profit	14.1	7.7	7.1	13.3	6.2	10.6
2.3	3.1	5.9	All Other Expenses (net)	11.4	5.6	7.0	7.8	-.5	2.8
5.6	7.6	4.0	Profit Before Taxes	2.7	2.1	.1	5.5	6.7	7.8
			RATIOS						
6.8	5.4	4.2		1.9	5.7	5.3	9.0	6.9	2.1
4.7	2.4	2.2	Current	1.3	2.6	3.6	2.8	2.7	1.2
1.5	1.0	1.1		.4	1.0	1.5	1.9	1.4	1.1
5.3	3.0	2.8		1.2	4.2	2.6	8.9	3.4	1.6
2.6	1.7	1.3	Quick	.5	2.1	1.3	2.3	2.2	.7
1.0	.7	.6		.3	.9	.9	1.2	1.2	.6
2 185.5	1 677.5	3 123.8		0 UND	0 999.8	23 15.6	1 485.3	21 17.6	20 18.2
22 16.9	21 17.8	21 17.0	Sales/Receivables	3 141.0	9 42.0	31 11.6	15 24.3	38 9.6	33 11.1
60 6.0	65 5.6	49 7.4		12 31.4	94 3.9	62 5.9	134 2.7	71 5.1	45 8.1
			Cost of Sales/Inventory						
			Cost of Sales/Payables						
1.5	1.7	1.9		4.8	1.6	1.4	1.6	1.6	6.0
3.0	6.0	6.3	Sales/Working Capital	12.5	5.1	3.0	3.3	7.0	48.3
12.1	116.9	56.9		-14.1	-83.2	10.3	5.3	13.6	100.5
13.4	8.1	14.9		4.7	4.3			26.6	
(33) 1.8	(41) 1.2	(62) 1.9	EBIT/Interest	(11) 2.2	(18) 1.4			(11) 1.8	
-.6	-1.1	.0		.2	-1.7			.9	
			Net Profit + Depr., Dep., Amort./Cur. Mat. L/T/D						
.2	.2	.3		.4	.4	.1	.3	.1	1.0
.7	.7	.9	Fixed/Worth	1.4	1.0	.3	.8	.5	1.1
1.3	1.4	2.1		NM	2.3	2.1	2.8	1.0	2.4
.2	.3	.3		.5	.3	.2	.4	.3	1.1
.6	.7	1.0	Debt/Worth	1.1	.5	.6	1.4	.7	1.8
1.7	1.8	2.4		-7.8	2.3	2.2	2.8	1.7	3.8
18.3	8.9	9.7		13.3	5.3	23.9	7.4	18.7	22.4
(44) 4.1	(65) 3.0	(91) 3.4	% Profit Before Taxes/Tangible Net Worth	(14) 1.9	1.9	3.7	(14) 4.2	4.6	(10) 6.6
-.3	-3.4	-1.6		-1.3	-4.2	-10.9	-.9	.2	-1.4
8.2	5.6	5.8		6.2	3.4	8.8	3.0	13.3	20.1
2.5	1.1	1.6	% Profit Before Taxes/Total Assets	1.2	1.0	2.9	1.6	2.5	3.5
-1.0	-2.0	-.8		-.9	-2.5	-2.6	-.7	.1	.1
3.5	5.4	4.4		2.0	1.6	20.5	2.6	12.5	7.1
1.4	1.5	1.4	Sales/Net Fixed Assets	.6	.9	2.1	1.9	2.8	2.1
.4	.5	.6		.2	.4	1.0	.4	.8	1.7
1.2	.7	.9		.6	.6	.8	.9	1.9	1.6
.6	.4	.5	Sales/Total Assets	.4	.4	.6	.6	.6	1.2
.2	.3	.2		.1	.2	.3	.1	.3	.5
1.7	1.4	1.4		3.3	2.3	.9	2.1	.7	
(40) 3.1	(52) 2.8	(84) 3.6	% Depr., Dep., Amort./Sales	(16) 12.2	(21) 4.5	(11) 1.9	(14) 3.6	(16) 1.8	
12.0	7.4	8.6		17.5	8.3	5.1	10.7	4.7	
			% Officers', Directors' Owners' Comp/Sales						
299894M	621131M	1015670M	Net Sales ($)	9913M	42781M	48744M	106874M	279677M	527681M
553679M	1288066M	1967712M	Total Assets ($)	33081M	121812M	110397M	381752M	723112M	597558M

M = $ thousand   MM = $ million
See Pages 9 through 22 for Explanation of Ratios and Data

HEALTH CARE—Vocational Rehabilitation Services NAICS 624310

| | Current Data Sorted by Assets | | | | | | Comparative Historical Data | |

0-500M	500M-2MM	2-10MM	10-50MM	50-100MM	100-250MM	Type of Statement	ALL 4/1/05-3/31/06	ALL 4/1/06-3/31/07
5	16	70	54	8	6	Unqualified	145	205
	1	1	1			Reviewed	7	5
1	3	4				Compiled	6	8
2	5	4				Tax Returns	8	9
5	18	27	28	1	1	Other	69	56
	143 (4/1-9/30/09)		118 (10/1/09-3/31/10)					
13	43	106	83	9	7	**NUMBER OF STATEMENTS**	235	283
%	%	%	%	%	%	**ASSETS**	%	%
23.5	22.5	19.4	17.0			Cash & Equivalents	16.8	17.8
32.2	20.0	21.8	17.0			Trade Receivables (net)	21.7	18.7
.5	8.1	3.2	3.8			Inventory	2.5	2.8
6.2	6.2	2.6	2.3			All Other Current	4.0	4.9
62.4	56.8	46.9	40.1			Total Current	45.0	44.3
35.1	33.8	41.8	48.1			Fixed Assets (net)	44.3	45.0
.0	1.6	.7	1.2			Intangibles (net)	1.6	1.1
2.5	7.8	10.6	10.6			All Other Non-Current	9.1	9.7
100.0	100.0	100.0	100.0			Total	100.0	100.0
						LIABILITIES		
10.8	10.3	5.2	3.7			Notes Payable-Short Term	5.3	3.6
1.1	2.8	2.1	2.2			Cur. Mat.-L.T.D.	2.7	2.1
4.7	9.3	7.9	7.0			Trade Payables	7.9	6.4
.1	.0	.2	.1			Income Taxes Payable	.0	.1
28.0	13.7	12.3	11.6			All Other Current	11.6	11.1
44.7	36.1	27.7	24.5			Total Current	27.6	23.2
5.7	18.4	15.0	21.5			Long-Term Debt	20.2	19.2
.0	.0	.0	.0			Deferred Taxes	.0	.1
2.9	3.3	4.8	2.6			All Other Non-Current	4.9	3.5
46.7	42.1	52.5	51.4			Net Worth	47.2	53.9
100.0	100.0	100.0	100.0			Total Liabilities & Net Worth	100.0	100.0
						INCOME DATA		
100.0	100.0	100.0	100.0			Net Sales	100.0	100.0
						Gross Profit		
94.1	97.5	96.0	96.9			Operating Expenses	97.0	95.8
5.9	2.5	4.0	3.1			Operating Profit	3.0	4.2
1.9	.6	1.5	.8			All Other Expenses (net)	.8	.7
4.0	1.9	2.5	2.3			Profit Before Taxes	2.2	3.5
						RATIOS		
2.6	3.6	3.5	3.3			Current	4.0	3.6
2.0	1.9	1.9	1.8				1.9	2.0
1.0	1.2	1.1	1.3				1.2	1.2
2.5	3.0	3.3	2.6			Quick	3.1	3.2
1.8	1.8	1.6	1.5				1.6	1.6
.7	.7	1.0	1.0				1.0	1.0
0 UND	12 30.8	10 35.7	14 25.4			Sales/Receivables	13 27.8	13 28.6
30 12.0	27 13.7	38 9.7	31 11.9				34 10.8	32 11.4
47 7.7	40 9.0	52 7.0	55 6.6				50 7.2	49 7.5
						Cost of Sales/Inventory		
						Cost of Sales/Payables		
8.4	5.1	5.8	4.7			Sales/Working Capital	4.8	4.7
20.2	9.5	11.7	9.6				10.2	9.8
UND	45.7	33.2	25.0				32.2	32.1
52.6	8.5	12.6	7.4			EBIT/Interest	9.5	7.5
(10) 17.1	(33) 2.6	(88) 3.2	(72) 3.7				(183) 2.8	(230) 3.4
.9	-2.0	-.7	.1				.2	.3
						Net Profit + Depr., Dep., Amort./Cur. Mat. L/T/D		
.1	.2	.3	.5			Fixed/Worth	.5	.4
.6	.6	.8	1.0				1.0	.9
1.5	3.0	1.4	1.4				1.6	1.4
.3	.3	.4	.4			Debt/Worth	.5	.4
.8	1.4	.8	.8				.9	.8
11.6	5.0	2.4	1.7				2.0	1.6
33.8	33.0	18.6	15.7			% Profit Before Taxes/Tangible Net Worth	16.6	14.4
(11) 11.1	(38) 7.2	(104) 4.7	(80) 6.0				(226) 6.8	(277) 6.2
-6.0	-7.4	-5.2	-2.5				-2.5	-1.8
34.8	14.5	9.2	7.8			% Profit Before Taxes/Total Assets	8.6	8.4
7.8	2.0	2.6	3.4				3.5	3.4
-4.1	-5.0	-2.6	-1.2				-1.6	-.8
53.1	66.8	21.4	5.1			Sales/Net Fixed Assets	10.7	9.9
20.1	14.6	3.6	2.9				3.7	3.3
3.4	2.8	1.9	1.6				1.9	1.9
6.2	3.1	2.8	2.0			Sales/Total Assets	2.8	2.6
2.6	2.1	1.6	1.4				1.7	1.6
1.4	1.3	1.2	.9				.9	1.0
	1.0	1.0	1.9			% Depr., Dep., Amort./Sales	1.5	1.5
	(31) 2.0	(97) 2.9	(78) 2.9				(216) 2.7	(259) 2.7
	3.3	4.0	4.2				4.0	4.1
		1.5	2.0			% Officers', Directors' Owners' Comp/Sales	2.1	3.1
		(12) 3.4	(11) 5.7				(20) 7.2	(30) 9.8
		7.6	31.2				28.6	37.9
17506M	140491M	1174374M	3456557M	670146M	2973938M	Net Sales ($)	5022812M	5967530M
4019M	50832M	594019M	2072766M	633692M	1049778M	Total Assets ($)	3008963M	3697314M

M = $ thousand   MM = $ million
See Pages 9 through 22 for Explanation of Ratios and Data

Comparative Historical Data | Current Data Sorted by Sales

			Type of Statement						
188	199	159	Unqualified	5	15	17	26	45	51
9	6	3	Reviewed		1				2
5	2	8	Compiled	1	4		3		
11	10	11	Tax Returns			1	2	3	1
50	81	80	Other	7	15	6	14	18	20
4/1/07-3/31/08 ALL	4/1/08-3/31/09 ALL	4/1/09-3/31/10 ALL		143 (4/1-9/30/09)			118 (10/1/09-3/31/10)		
				0-1MM	1-3MM	3-5MM	5-10MM	10-25MM	25MM & OVER
263	298	261	NUMBER OF STATEMENTS	13	39	24	45	66	74
%	%	%	ASSETS	%	%	%	%	%	%
18.1	19.1	19.0	Cash & Equivalents	20.5	25.7	16.7	20.7	16.4	17.2
19.3	18.6	20.3	Trade Receivables (net)	15.2	17.0	16.7	17.9	22.4	23.8
3.3	3.1	4.1	Inventory	.4	7.6	3.7	3.7	3.4	3.8
2.8	3.5	3.4	All Other Current	7.8	5.4	3.6	1.3	2.5	3.6
43.6	44.1	46.8	Total Current	43.9	55.7	40.8	43.5	44.7	48.4
45.1	44.8	42.1	Fixed Assets (net)	52.2	36.7	48.3	42.1	42.7	40.6
1.5	1.4	1.2	Intangibles (net)	.0	1.8	.7	.6	.6	2.1
9.8	9.7	9.9	All Other Non-Current	3.8	5.8	10.2	13.8	12.0	8.9
100.0	100.0	100.0	Total	100.0	100.0	100.0	100.0	100.0	100.0
			LIABILITIES						
4.2	4.8	5.6	Notes Payable-Short Term	1.1	13.6	5.5	4.9	3.0	4.9
2.3	1.8	2.2	Cur. Mat.-L.T.D.	3.6	2.4	1.8	2.3	1.9	2.1
6.6	6.5	7.8	Trade Payables	2.5	5.3	4.5	9.0	8.3	10.1
.1	.2	.1	Income Taxes Payable	.0	.0	.0	.4	.0	.1
12.5	12.8	13.0	All Other Current	16.5	12.8	7.3	10.5	14.2	14.8
25.7	26.1	28.7	Total Current	23.7	34.2	19.1	27.2	27.4	32.1
19.3	17.3	17.4	Long-Term Debt	14.6	18.8	18.3	14.2	17.0	19.2
.0	.1	.0	Deferred Taxes	.0	.0	.1	.0	.0	.0
3.4	3.2	3.7	All Other Non-Current	.2	3.3	5.4	7.7	1.3	3.5
51.5	53.4	50.2	Net Worth	61.6	43.6	57.1	50.9	54.3	45.2
100.0	100.0	100.0	Total Liabilties & Net Worth	100.0	100.0	100.0	100.0	100.0	100.0
			INCOME DATA						
100.0	100.0	100.0	Net Sales	100.0	100.0	100.0	100.0	100.0	100.0
			Gross Profit						
96.2	96.8	96.6	Operating Expenses	97.9	92.6	98.3	96.4	98.6	96.1
3.8	3.2	3.4	Operating Profit	2.1	7.4	1.7	3.6	1.4	3.9
.6	1.1	1.0	All Other Expenses (net)	2.1	2.6	.5	1.0	1.0	.2
3.2	2.1	2.4	Profit Before Taxes	-.1	4.8	1.2	2.6	.3	3.7
			RATIOS						
3.2	3.6	3.3		9.3	4.8	5.7	3.3	3.3	2.5
1.9	2.0	1.9	Current	2.0	2.0	2.1	1.9	1.9	1.5
1.1	1.3	1.2		1.0	1.0	1.4	1.2	1.2	1.2
2.7	3.1	2.7		9.0	3.7	5.2	2.9	2.7	2.0
1.6	1.6	1.5	Quick	1.8	1.8	2.0	1.6	1.6	1.4
1.0	1.0	1.0		.2	.7	1.3	1.0	1.0	1.0
15 24.1	15 24.2	14 26.2		0 UND	12 30.8	17 21.4	6 56.7	11 34.3	21 17.0
33 11.1	32 11.3	31 11.6	Sales/Receivables	31 11.9	26 14.0	31 11.9	31 11.7	37 9.8	33 11.0
47 7.7	45 8.1	53 6.9		62 5.9	40 9.0	53 6.8	54 6.8	45 8.1	57 6.4
			Cost of Sales/Inventory						
			Cost of Sales/Payables						
4.8	4.6	5.0		3.1	4.0	2.8	6.6	4.8	6.3
10.7	9.7	11.6	Sales/Working Capital	6.0	8.2	8.4	11.7	10.0	13.8
53.7	32.1	30.1		UND	-460.3	19.3	28.6	34.0	28.0
10.1	7.4	13.2			8.8	4.9	12.8	12.2	20.0
(208) 3.7	(244) 2.2	(216) 3.5	EBIT/Interest	(31) 3.1	(20) 1.2	(37) 2.6	(56) 3.1	(64) 4.2	
1.2	-.7	-.5		-.4	-4.1	-1.4	-2.5	1.8	
			Net Profit + Depr., Dep., Amort./Cur. Mat. L/T/D						
.5	.5	.4		.2	.2	.4	.4	.4	.4
.9	.9	.8	Fixed/Worth	.7	.7	.9	.8	.8	.9
1.5	1.3	1.4		1.6	3.4	1.4	1.4	1.2	1.6
.4	.4	.4		.1	.3	.3	.4	.4	.6
.9	.7	.9	Debt/Worth	.5	1.4	.7	.9	.7	1.2
1.7	1.5	2.4		2.7	3.6	1.8	2.5	1.6	2.4
14.7	12.6	17.9		11.2	34.3	9.8	16.5	14.5	20.5
(251) 6.5	(289) 3.7	(249) 6.6	% Profit Before Taxes/Tangible Net Worth	.0	(33) 11.3	(23) 3.2	(44) 4.7	(65) 4.5	(71) 10.9
.5	-3.2	-3.5		-10.1	-2.8	-7.8	-3.5	-7.4	2.7
7.6	7.4	9.4		8.8	20.2	4.9	9.6	8.3	9.7
3.2	1.8	3.1	% Profit Before Taxes/Total Assets	.0	6.1	2.4	2.3	3.2	4.9
.2	-2.0	-2.2		-5.0	-2.8	-3.0	-3.0	-2.8	.5
10.6	10.0	16.5		93.4	41.2	6.0	16.3	17.9	13.2
3.3	3.2	3.6	Sales/Net Fixed Assets	3.3	8.6	2.4	3.5	3.3	4.5
1.9	1.9	2.0		.5	2.1	1.0	1.7	1.8	2.9
2.5	2.5	2.6		1.4	2.6	1.6	2.7	2.6	3.3
1.6	1.6	1.6	Sales/Total Assets	.9	1.9	1.3	1.5	1.6	1.9
1.1	1.0	1.1		.4	1.1	.6	1.0	1.1	1.4
1.6	1.4	1.4			1.0	2.0	1.1	1.6	1.4
(242) 2.9	(270) 2.7	(228) 2.6	% Depr., Dep., Amort./Sales	(29)	2.2	(22) 3.4	(41) 2.6	(58) 3.2	(70) 2.3
4.2	4.1	4.0			4.4	5.5	4.0	4.1	3.1
3.9	5.3	2.2							1.6
(28) 9.1	(33) 7.7	(34) 3.8	% Officers', Directors' Owners' Comp/Sales					(11)	5.7
34.4	31.9	8.8							17.4
6328351M	6757440M	8433012M	Net Sales ($)	7019M	70795M	94898M	325550M	1078842M	6855908M
3845222M	4322266M	4405106M	Total Assets ($)	12290M	66015M	95889M	297492M	879613M	3053807M

RMA 2010

M = $ thousand   MM = $ million
See Pages 9 through 22 for Explanation of Ratios and Data

HEALTH CARE—Child Day Care Services NAICS 624410

Current Data Sorted by Assets

Comparative Historical Data

0-500M	500M-2MM	2-10MM	10-50MM	50-100MM	100-250MM	Type of Statement	4/1/05-3/31/06 ALL	4/1/06-3/31/07 ALL
4	19	46	19	3	1	Unqualified	56	75
6	8	9	4			Reviewed	13	11
29	15	10	1			Compiled	50	45
139	43	17		1	1	Tax Returns	135	176
83	40	38	5	3	2	Other	99	105
	140 (4/1-9/30/09)		406 (10/1/09-3/31/10)					
261	125	120	29	7	4	NUMBER OF STATEMENTS	353	412
%	%	%	%	%	%	**ASSETS**	%	%
27.4	14.9	14.6	16.8			Cash & Equivalents	18.3	21.5
6.8	8.1	9.6	13.0			Trade Receivables (net)	9.1	8.3
.5	.1	.3	.2			Inventory	.8	.3
3.3	1.4	2.3	1.7			All Other Current	4.5	4.2
38.0	24.5	26.8	31.6			Total Current	32.7	34.3
40.4	59.8	62.9	56.8			Fixed Assets (net)	52.7	49.7
8.2	8.4	2.3	4.5			Intangibles (net)	6.0	7.0
13.5	7.2	8.1	7.1			All Other Non-Current	8.6	9.0
100.0	100.0	100.0	100.0			Total	100.0	100.0
						LIABILITIES		
10.1	3.5	2.2	1.6			Notes Payable-Short Term	5.6	5.9
6.5	5.9	2.5	3.8			Cur. Mat.-L.T.D.	4.3	4.5
4.9	4.2	5.5	5.9			Trade Payables	4.9	5.0
.0	.1	.0	.1			Income Taxes Payable	.0	.0
35.0	11.5	11.3	9.5			All Other Current	14.5	20.4
56.5	25.2	21.4	20.8			Total Current	29.3	35.7
30.9	50.0	39.1	34.4			Long-Term Debt	36.0	37.3
.0	.0	.1	.4			Deferred Taxes	.1	.1
14.7	6.2	3.8	6.2			All Other Non-Current	9.8	9.5
-2.2	18.7	35.6	38.1			Net Worth	24.7	17.4
100.0	100.0	100.0	100.0			Total Liabilities & Net Worth	100.0	100.0
						INCOME DATA		
100.0	100.0	100.0	100.0			Net Sales	100.0	100.0
						Gross Profit		
94.7	86.8	85.1	94.3			Operating Expenses	91.8	90.1
5.3	13.2	14.9	5.7			Operating Profit	8.2	9.9
.9	6.5	10.1	3.4			All Other Expenses (net)	3.5	4.2
4.4	6.6	4.8	2.3			Profit Before Taxes	4.6	5.6
						RATIOS		
3.8	2.4	2.3	2.9			Current	3.3	2.9
.9	.9	1.1	1.3				1.3	1.1
.2	.3	.5	.9				.5	.4
3.5	2.4	2.2	2.6			Quick	2.6	2.4
.8	.9	1.1	1.3				(350) 1.1	(410) .9
.2	.3	.4	.8				.3	.3
0 UND	0 UND	0 UND	1 348.5			Sales/Receivables	0 UND	0 UND
0 UND	0 UND	5 73.4	16 22.2				1 379.6	0 UND
2 172.5	12 30.2	25 14.4	37 9.9				15 24.4	15 25.1
						Cost of Sales/Inventory		
						Cost of Sales/Payables		
23.2	13.4	9.0	4.6			Sales/Working Capital	12.5	15.3
-676.0	-179.4	66.2	23.7				60.5	228.6
-16.0	-12.0	-15.9	-98.7				-27.6	-20.3
14.3	7.5	3.8	3.9			EBIT/Interest	9.9	9.5
(149) 5.5	(100) 1.9	(79) 1.6	(24) 2.1				(256) 3.5	(281) 2.6
1.0	.2	.6	.0				1.0	.9
						Net Profit + Depr., Dep., Amort./Cur. Mat. L/T/D	15.6	8.3
							(22) 5.0	(19) 3.6
							2.3	1.8
.5	1.1	.8	1.1			Fixed/Worth	.6	.6
1.8	5.5	1.6	1.7				1.9	2.0
-.8	-7.0	9.1	4.1				-232.8	-8.1
.4	1.1	.7	.8			Debt/Worth	.6	.7
4.4	6.8	1.8	1.6				2.1	2.7
-2.6	-9.2	8.7	5.4				-411.2	-10.0
133.0	48.4	23.7	10.7			% Profit Before Taxes/Tangible Net Worth	73.1	88.3
(148) 56.2	(82) 18.9	(103) 5.7	(25) 2.6				(264) 28.6	(283) 29.6
16.3	-.9	-.5	-7.1				3.5	4.3
47.7	10.7	6.6	6.7			% Profit Before Taxes/Total Assets	25.4	28.6
19.2	2.4	2.0	1.5				7.4	8.3
.2	-1.5	-.2	-2.3				.2	.0
54.8	11.8	7.7	7.3			Sales/Net Fixed Assets	22.0	33.7
19.9	2.1	1.4	2.1				6.8	8.0
8.5	.8	.5	1.4				1.4	1.6
10.4	2.7	2.6	2.5			Sales/Total Assets	5.5	6.2
5.9	1.4	1.0	1.3				2.8	2.9
3.6	.6	.5	.9				1.0	1.0
.8	1.8	1.2	1.3			% Depr., Dep., Amort./Sales	1.2	1.2
(170) 1.5	(100) 3.3	(107) 3.4	(28) 2.9				(282) 2.3	(311) 2.4
2.9	7.6	7.9	4.1				4.2	4.6
2.8	3.5	1.6				% Officers', Directors' Owners' Comp/Sales	3.1	2.5
(112) 5.6	(30) 6.0	(26) 4.9					(132) 5.7	(146) 5.8
10.9	12.4	10.2					10.7	9.4
278389M	289307M	963475M	835136M	1549047M	1402242M	Net Sales ($)	2533261M	7739800M
49615M	135603M	497869M	485471M	559227M	568197M	Total Assets ($)	1197786M	1939757M

M = $ thousand   MM = $ million
See Pages 9 through 22 for Explanation of Ratios and Data

Comparative Historical Data | Current Data Sorted by Sales

Hist 1	Hist 2	Hist 3	Type of Statement	0-1MM	1-3MM	3-5MM	5-10MM	10-25MM	25MM & OVER
78	76	92	Unqualified	5	15	14	14	27	17
8	9	27	Reviewed	8	8	1	6	4	
44	42	55	Compiled	24	23	4	4		
177	173	201	Tax Returns	107	83	6	2	1	2
111	139	171	Other	78	54	10	11	11	7
4/1/07-3/31/08 ALL	4/1/08-3/31/09 ALL	4/1/09-3/31/10 ALL		140 (4/1-9/30/09)			406 (10/1/09-3/31/10)		
418	439	546	NUMBER OF STATEMENTS	222	183	35	37	43	26
%	%	%	ASSETS	%	%	%	%	%	%
19.5	22.8	20.9	Cash & Equivalents	18.1	23.9	15.1	23.1	26.9	19.9
8.8	7.9	8.0	Trade Receivables (net)	5.5	5.6	17.2	12.2	16.9	12.5
.5	.3	.3	Inventory	.4	.1	1.6	.1	.2	.1
3.8	3.4	2.5	All Other Current	2.9	1.8	1.6	1.8	2.6	6.3
32.6	34.3	31.7	Total Current	26.8	31.4	35.5	37.3	46.6	38.7
50.0	49.0	50.8	Fixed Assets (net)	57.1	47.5	53.6	46.8	37.7	45.5
7.4	6.7	7.0	Intangibles (net)	6.3	9.8	1.7	2.8	7.1	6.2
10.0	10.0	10.5	All Other Non-Current	9.9	11.4	9.2	13.1	8.7	9.6
100.0	100.0	100.0	Total	100.0	100.0	100.0	100.0	100.0	100.0
			LIABILITIES						
5.9	8.4	6.2	Notes Payable-Short Term	9.2	5.0	4.7	4.3	1.2	2.7
5.1	5.0	5.3	Cur. Mat.-L.T.D.	5.8	6.4	3.6	3.8	2.1	2.9
6.0	5.9	4.9	Trade Payables	3.3	3.5	6.9	5.1	13.4	11.1
.1	.2	.0	Income Taxes Payable	.0	.0	.3	.0	.0	.2
16.6	15.9	22.4	All Other Current	28.0	20.9	17.0	17.2	16.8	10.2
33.7	35.4	38.8	Total Current	46.2	35.8	32.5	30.3	33.6	27.0
40.1	37.9	37.4	Long-Term Debt	42.9	40.2	36.8	21.9	18.0	24.3
.1	.0	.1	Deferred Taxes	.0	.0	.1	.2	.1	.9
8.4	9.1	9.8	All Other Non-Current	13.2	9.3	1.5	5.0	4.9	9.7
17.8	17.6	14.0	Net Worth	-2.3	14.7	29.1	42.5	43.5	38.0
100.0	100.0	100.0	Total Liabilities & Net Worth	100.0	100.0	100.0	100.0	100.0	100.0
			INCOME DATA						
100.0	100.0	100.0	Net Sales	100.0	100.0	100.0	100.0	100.0	100.0
			Gross Profit						
89.4	90.7	90.5	Operating Expenses	86.7	91.9	91.4	94.9	97.8	93.6
10.6	9.3	9.5	Operating Profit	13.3	8.1	8.6	5.1	2.2	6.4
3.7	4.4	4.4	All Other Expenses (net)	8.0	2.1	2.6	1.4	1.5	2.2
7.0	4.9	5.1	Profit Before Taxes	5.3	6.0	6.0	3.7	.7	4.3
			RATIOS						
2.9	3.4	2.8	Current	2.3	3.7	2.4	2.9	2.3	2.5
1.2	1.3	1.0		.7	1.1	1.1	1.5	1.4	1.1
.5	.4	.3		.2	.3	.5	.7	1.0	.9
2.5	3.1	2.5	Quick	2.1	3.6	2.4	2.8	2.2	2.3
1.1	1.1	1.0		.5	1.0	1.0	1.3	1.3	1.0
.3	.3	.3		.1	.3	.4	.6	.9	.4
0 UND	0 UND	0 UND	Sales/Receivables	0 UND	0 UND	0 UND	0 UND	6 64.3	1 647.8
0 UND	0 UND	0 UND		0 UND	0 UND	13 29.1	7 55.9	16 23.2	10 35.7
16 22.5	10 35.5	11 32.2		3 110.1	4 84.5	32 11.5	29 12.6	32 11.5	21 17.1
			Cost of Sales/Inventory						
			Cost of Sales/Payables						
12.6	12.1	14.4	Sales/Working Capital	24.2	13.6	8.8	6.8	9.7	13.6
87.5	78.0	999.8		-44.6	135.0	85.8	25.9	25.5	251.1
-18.7	-25.6	-15.3		-6.7	-19.9	-25.5	-35.9	-948.3	-85.7
11.5	10.0	9.4	EBIT/Interest	6.4	11.5	9.7	18.4	5.3	23.3
(286) 3.7	(300) 3.1	(361) 2.7		(128) 1.8	(122) 3.6	(30) 2.7	(32) 4.7	(29) 1.6	(20) 3.2
1.2	1.0	.7		.3	1.0	-.2	1.3	-1.1	1.1
11.8	7.9	8.6	Net Profit + Depr., Dep., Amort./Cur. Mat. L/T/D						
(16) 4.5	(20) 1.9	(18) 2.4							
2.1	.5	1.3							
.6	.5	.7	Fixed/Worth	1.0	.7	.6	.4	.4	.6
1.6	1.7	2.0		7.2	2.3	1.3	.9	1.0	1.3
-10.3	-22.7	-6.2		-1.6	-2.8	9.2	2.3	1.7	3.7
.6	.7	.7	Debt/Worth	.9	.6	.7	.5	.8	.7
2.6	2.6	3.5		11.9	4.9	1.8	1.2	1.4	1.8
-11.9	-11.4	-8.7		-3.3	-5.5	21.4	3.0	5.5	8.6
108.0	93.4	73.8	% Profit Before Taxes/Tangible Net Worth	58.3	125.8	36.5	28.6	11.6	54.8
(296) 29.0	(314) 23.9	(366) 20.9		(127) 23.7	(118) 44.9	(29) 15.0	(31) 8.2	(40) 2.0	(21) 6.9
6.0	3.9	1.4		2.4	5.3	-2.6	.9	-5.9	1.3
37.0	26.7	26.5	% Profit Before Taxes/Total Assets	22.8	38.9	25.7	14.8	7.2	16.2
8.8	5.9	5.9		5.4	14.6	8.1	6.6	1.0	4.9
.9	-.3	-.4		-1.7	.0	.1	.8	-2.9	.8
28.1	34.3	28.1	Sales/Net Fixed Assets	21.9	40.3	16.5	20.0	33.9	22.6
8.7	9.0	8.2		6.4	13.2	6.3	7.4	9.8	7.5
1.7	1.7	1.6		.8	2.1	1.4	1.5	2.5	3.7
6.0	6.8	6.4	Sales/Total Assets	6.0	8.2	5.2	5.3	4.8	5.9
3.2	3.2	3.1		2.3	4.0	2.4	2.5	3.1	3.3
1.2	1.0	1.0		.6	1.4	1.0	1.1	1.5	1.7
1.0	1.1	1.0	% Depr., Dep., Amort./Sales	1.3	1.1	1.2	.9	.6	.5
(316) 2.2	(333) 2.2	(412) 2.3		(163) 3.7	(130) 2.4	(31) 1.9	(29) 1.9	(38) 1.3	(21) 1.3
4.1	4.5	4.7		9.1	4.0	3.8	3.5	2.7	3.7
2.6	2.7	2.7	% Officers', Directors' Owners' Comp/Sales	4.8	2.9	1.9			
(163) 5.9	(179) 4.8	(175) 5.5		(66) 8.6	(76) 4.8	(10) 4.1			
10.6	8.3	11.0		14.6	8.8	7.5			
2896137M	2981409M	5317596M	Net Sales ($)	119891M	300563M	126724M	258157M	733106M	3779155M
1401519M	1721672M	2295982M	Total Assets ($)	163906M	175885M	91935M	156837M	567416M	1140003M

M = $ thousand   MM = $ million
See Pages 9 through 22 for Explanation of Ratios and Data

ARTS, ENTERTAINMENT, AND RECREATION

Current Data Sorted by Assets | Comparative Historical Data

						Type of Statement		
1	4	15	32	11	8	Unqualified	72	74
2	2	7	1			Reviewed	17	12
3	7	7	1	1		Compiled	36	26
13	12	4	1			Tax Returns	28	35
6	9	13	8	1	5	Other	55	56
	79 (4/1-9/30/09)		87 (10/1/09-3/31/10)				4/1/05-3/31/06	4/1/06-3/31/07
0-500M	500M-2MM	2-10MM	10-50MM	50-100MM	100-250MM		ALL	ALL
25	32	41	43	12	13	NUMBER OF STATEMENTS	208	203
%	%	%	%	%	%	ASSETS	%	%
28.3	16.0	11.6	15.3	12.9	11.3	Cash & Equivalents	15.3	16.9
2.9	3.2	6.0	3.3	3.9	2.9	Trade Receivables (net)	5.2	5.2
3.9	1.8	2.4	.4	.7	.4	Inventory	2.9	2.8
3.5	4.0	3.3	5.1	3.7	6.3	All Other Current	5.4	4.1
38.6	25.1	23.4	24.1	21.1	20.8	Total Current	28.8	28.9
42.8	58.5	53.0	52.4	51.5	36.5	Fixed Assets (net)	50.6	48.7
10.2	6.7	6.0	1.3	9.0	13.1	Intangibles (net)	5.3	5.0
8.3	9.7	17.7	22.2	18.3	29.6	All Other Non-Current	15.2	17.5
100.0	100.0	100.0	100.0	100.0	100.0	Total	100.0	100.0
						LIABILITIES		
17.3	6.3	3.9	3.6	1.1	1.5	Notes Payable-Short Term	6.6	10.7
3.7	1.6	2.8	2.7	1.5	.9	Cur. Mat.-L.T.D.	3.3	3.0
17.5	4.8	5.4	4.2	2.8	3.1	Trade Payables	7.8	7.2
.0	.1	.1	.0	.0	.1	Income Taxes Payable	.5	.2
14.2	10.9	6.4	11.6	8.8	5.8	All Other Current	16.6	13.5
52.7	23.8	18.5	22.1	14.1	11.4	Total Current	34.9	34.7
33.6	31.8	23.7	20.2	22.6	21.2	Long-Term Debt	25.8	21.2
.0	.0	.0	.1	.0	.0	Deferred Taxes	.1	.0
8.5	7.7	13.0	2.8	10.3	5.9	All Other Non-Current	6.1	4.0
5.2	36.7	44.8	54.8	53.0	61.5	Net Worth	33.2	40.0
100.0	100.0	100.0	100.0	100.0	100.0	Total Liabilities & Net Worth	100.0	100.0
						INCOME DATA		
100.0	100.0	100.0	100.0	100.0	100.0	Net Sales	100.0	100.0
						Gross Profit		
99.7	95.5	98.6	102.2	100.7	98.8	Operating Expenses	94.2	94.9
.3	4.5	1.4	-2.2	-.7	1.2	Operating Profit	5.8	5.1
-.5	1.9	4.9	3.4	3.8	1.6	All Other Expenses (net)	1.5	1.3
.8	2.6	-3.5	-5.5	-4.5	-.4	Profit Before Taxes	4.3	3.8
						RATIOS		
6.0	2.1	2.3	2.2	2.1	5.9		2.1	2.1
.7	.9	1.1	1.0	1.1	2.5	Current	.9	.9
.2	.4	.6	.5	.8	.9		.5	.4
5.7	1.4	1.6	2.0	1.9	3.1		1.6	1.4
(24) .5	.9	.8	.8	.9	1.8	Quick	.6	.6
.1	.2	.4	.3	.6	.5		.2	.2
0 UND	0 UND	2 210.7	2 223.6	2 165.6	5 67.4		0 UND	0 UND
0 UND	0 975.4	10 36.2	6 56.3	6 62.5	17 21.2	Sales/Receivables	2 179.5	3 130.6
1 529.3	3 114.2	30 12.0	23 16.2	34 10.6	41 8.9		13 28.9	13 29.0
						Cost of Sales/Inventory		
						Cost of Sales/Payables		
13.1	16.1	6.6	3.7	4.7	1.8		8.0	10.0
-29.7	-148.1	180.0	87.3	NM	5.9	Sales/Working Capital	-165.4	-71.8
-11.0	-14.4	-10.4	-8.3	-21.0	-54.5		-11.5	-9.2
4.8	6.0	8.1	4.2				10.3	11.8
(14) .3	(23) .3	(27) 1.5	(34) 1.1			EBIT/Interest	(154) 2.3	(153) 2.4
-12.1	-1.2	-2.3	-18.0				.0	-.1
							6.7	31.2
						Net Profit + Depr., Dep., Amort./Cur. Mat. L/T/D	(18) 2.6	(13) 4.1
							1.3	1.3
.5	.8	.6	.5	.4	.3		.6	.4
3.1	1.5	1.0	.9	1.0	.8	Fixed/Worth	1.2	1.2
-.7	-2.4	2.5	2.6	6.0	NM		9.7	3.2
.1	.2	.3	.2	.3	.1		.4	.3
3.3	.8	1.0	.5	.7	.7	Debt/Worth	1.7	1.1
-2.2	-4.4	3.4	2.4	6.0	NM		11.8	4.2
102.3	23.8	9.2	13.4	.3	2.4	% Profit Before Taxes/Tangible Net Worth	51.6	48.3
(14) 11.1	(23) 1.7	(36) .1	(39) -1.6	(10) -4.0	(10) -.6		(166) 14.3	(170) 13.0
-.5	-7.0	-12.5	-16.1	-26.5	-2.9		-.6	-2.8
19.1	6.6	5.3	4.2	2.7	2.5	% Profit Before Taxes/Total Assets	14.3	22.4
1.1	.1	-.6	-.5	-.8	.1		3.6	3.3
-18.8	-5.6	-6.9	-11.5	-5.3	-1.5		-1.6	-2.2
45.3	8.0	7.1	3.4	3.4	6.0		14.1	13.5
16.0	4.1	2.5	1.4	.6	1.5	Sales/Net Fixed Assets	3.3	3.6
4.7	.3	.8	.7	.4	.3		1.2	1.3
6.1	3.3	1.9	1.2	1.2	.9		3.1	3.7
4.0	2.0	1.0	.6	.4	.3	Sales/Total Assets	1.6	1.5
2.4	.3	.5	.4	.2	.2		.6	.7
1.6	1.7	2.9	3.6	3.9	1.6		1.7	1.5
(17) 2.3	(25) 2.5	(36) 4.2	(41) 5.2	(11) 7.6	(12) 4.5	% Depr., Dep., Amort./Sales	(171) 3.5	(179) 3.1
3.7	9.8	10.0	7.7	15.3	8.4		6.1	5.3
3.2							2.3	2.8
(10) 5.2						% Officers', Directors' Owners' Comp/Sales	(53) 4.7	(55) 4.6
14.1							9.6	12.2
25742M	91281M	288248M	796370M	536489M	979685M	Net Sales ($)	2938841M	2867301M
5496M	35881M	211380M	930374M	868117M	2161429M	Total Assets ($)	3005590M	2707607M

M = $ thousand   MM = $ million
See Pages 9 through 22 for Explanation of Ratios and Data

Comparative Historical Data

Current Data Sorted by Sales

			Type of Statement						
58	85	71	Unqualified	1	8	8	18	17	19
9	8	5	Reviewed	2		1			2
6	11	18	Compiled	5	5	3	3		2
32	24	30	Tax Returns	14	9	4	1	2	
47	60	42	Other	10	8	3	1	11	6
4/1/07-3/31/08	4/1/08-3/31/09	4/1/09-3/31/10		79 (4/1-9/30/09)			87 (10/1/09-3/31/10)		
ALL	ALL	ALL		0-1MM	1-3MM	3-5MM	5-10MM	10-25MM	25MM & OVER
152	188	166	NUMBER OF STATEMENTS	32	30	18	27	30	29
%	%	%	**ASSETS**	%	%	%	%	%	%
18.5	17.1	16.0	Cash & Equivalents	17.1	17.1	22.4	10.3	17.3	13.6
6.2	7.0	3.9	Trade Receivables (net)	2.2	2.4	5.6	5.4	5.5	3.3
3.4	2.6	1.7	Inventory	1.3	3.2	2.4	1.3	.4	2.1
4.9	5.2	4.2	All Other Current	3.2	3.5	2.9	4.5	6.9	3.7
33.0	31.8	25.8	Total Current	23.8	26.3	33.3	21.5	30.0	22.6
46.2	45.5	51.0	Fixed Assets (net)	61.4	56.1	48.3	46.5	45.4	45.8
5.7	3.8	6.3	Intangibles (net)	6.6	10.2	.5	3.9	1.7	12.6
15.1	18.8	16.9	All Other Non-Current	8.1	7.4	17.9	28.1	22.9	19.0
100.0	100.0	100.0	Total	100.0	100.0	100.0	100.0	100.0	100.0
			LIABILITIES						
5.4	9.3	5.9	Notes Payable-Short Term	10.8	7.1	5.7	4.2	3.3	3.7
2.4	2.8	2.4	Cur. Mat.-L.T.D.	1.5	3.0	1.6	2.4	.7	5.2
7.0	7.3	6.4	Trade Payables	10.5	6.0	4.7	4.5	5.6	6.1
.1	.2	.1	Income Taxes Payable	.0	.0	.4	.0	.0	.0
11.6	12.1	9.9	All Other Current	7.3	10.4	13.0	7.2	10.0	12.7
26.4	31.8	24.7	Total Current	30.1	26.5	25.4	18.3	19.7	27.7
22.1	22.6	25.6	Long-Term Debt	23.4	42.4	23.9	16.3	21.6	24.3
.4	.4	.0	Deferred Taxes	.0	.0	.0	.0	.0	.1
12.4	9.9	7.9	All Other Non-Current	4.3	10.3	5.6	14.4	4.3	8.7
38.7	35.3	41.8	Net Worth	42.3	20.8	45.1	51.0	54.4	39.2
100.0	100.0	100.0	Total Liabilties & Net Worth	100.0	100.0	100.0	100.0	100.0	100.0
			INCOME DATA						
100.0	100.0	100.0	Net Sales	100.0	100.0	100.0	100.0	100.0	100.0
			Gross Profit						
92.7	96.6	99.3	Operating Expenses	94.5	99.5	95.3	105.3	104.2	96.0
7.3	3.4	.7	Operating Profit	5.5	.5	4.7	-5.3	-4.2	4.0
.9	2.0	2.8	All Other Expenses (net)	4.3	3.2	.4	3.3	1.9	2.6
6.5	1.4	-2.0	Profit Before Taxes	1.1	-2.7	4.3	-8.6	-6.1	1.4
			RATIOS						
3.4	2.9	2.5		2.8	3.2	2.6	2.1	2.7	1.4
1.3	1.2	1.0	Current	.9	.9	1.6	.9	1.4	.9
.6	.5	.6		.4	.4	.6	.6	.8	.5
2.6	2.2	2.0		1.7	2.8	2.1	1.3	2.1	1.1
1.0 (187)	.9 (165)	.8	Quick	.8 (29)	.9	1.2	.7	1.1	.6
.3	.3	.3		.2	.2	.5	.6	.6	.3
0 UND	0 999.8	0 UND		0 UND	0 UND	0 UND	3 119.5	2 150.8	2 170.9
3 128.1	5 74.5	3 106.4	Sales/Receivables	0 UND	1 631.2	6 66.1	11 33.9	9 40.1	5 70.2
14 25.7	24 15.3	20 18.2		3 114.2	4 104.0	35 10.5	29 12.6	26 14.1	19 18.7
			Cost of Sales/Inventory						
			Cost of Sales/Payables						
5.3	5.4	6.2		14.7	4.9	6.1	6.3	3.4	10.4
36.2	44.8	228.2	Sales/Working Capital	-62.1	-336.0	13.1	-115.2	7.9	-54.1
-18.1	-13.6	-12.9		-7.3	-15.8	-17.0	-7.8	-45.7	-13.4
17.5	9.8	4.7		2.8	1.6	12.5	2.1	3.7	11.7
3.5 (112)	1.9 (138)	1.0 (116)	EBIT/Interest	-.5 (18)	-.6 (22)	8.5 (13)	-4.0 (21)	.8 (17)	3.1 (25)
.5	-1.1	-4.5		-3.0	-5.5	1.5	-16.1	-11.6	-.3
	11.6	18.1	Net Profit + Depr., Dep.,						
	2.4 (12)	4.5 (13)	Amort./Cur. Mat. L/T/D						
	1.1	1.5							
.4	.4	.5		1.0	.9	.5	.4	.5	.5
1.2	1.0	1.1	Fixed/Worth	1.6	2.9	.8	.9	.8	2.0
5.6	3.6	5.9		UND	-1.7	NM	1.9	1.6	-4.4
.3	.3	.2		.1	.3	.2	.2	.2	.6
1.1	.8	.8	Debt/Worth	.7	2.7	.4	.4	.7	3.0
7.0	4.2	5.5		UND	-2.9	NM	2.8	1.7	-9.4
47.6	31.6	10.0		16.7	5.9	28.2	5.6	1.0	36.6
10.9 (124)	6.2 (158)	-.2 (132)	% Profit Before Taxes/Tangible Net Worth	1.8 (25)	-5.3 (20)	4.8 (14)	-2.5 (25)	-1.0 (27)	2.9 (21)
-3.8	-4.9	-10.2		-2.3	-18.2	-4.0	-17.0	-13.1	-3.1
18.8	12.8	5.3		7.8	5.4	9.3	1.3	1.8	13.6
5.3	1.7	.0	% Profit Before Taxes/Total Assets	.4	-2.9	2.6	-3.6	-.6	2.0
-1.8	-4.1	-6.5		-4.3	-9.4	-2.0	-13.8	-9.9	-1.6
11.7	10.4	7.7		16.5	9.7	10.3	4.8	4.8	6.0
4.0	3.4	2.8	Sales/Net Fixed Assets	1.6	3.6	5.5	2.3	1.4	3.4
1.3	1.2	.7		.3	1.2	.9	.8	.5	1.5
3.3	2.9	2.3		3.4	3.5	4.1	1.8	1.4	2.0
1.5	1.3	1.0	Sales/Total Assets	1.3	2.0	1.6	.6	.6	1.2
.6	.5	.4		.2	.6	.7	.5	.3	.5
1.5	1.9	2.2		2.9	1.7	1.7	3.6	3.9	1.6
3.0 (128)	3.5 (159)	4.1 (142)	% Depr., Dep., Amort./Sales	10.1 (21)	3.1 (28)	3.0 (15)	4.5	5.4 (23)	3.2 (28)
5.6	6.2	8.1		15.2	6.6	4.7	8.1	8.8	7.9
3.7	2.6	2.9	% Officers', Directors' Owners' Comp/Sales						
5.3 (39)	6.6 (33)	4.4 (27)							
12.8	11.3	12.5							
1377246M	2500801M	2717815M	Net Sales ($)	15113M	58039M	69774M	193687M	491774M	1889428M
1784877M	3800914M	4212677M	Total Assets ($)	33591M	69249M	74028M	338293M	1241960M	2455556M

M = $ thousand   MM = $ million
See Pages 9 through 22 for Explanation of Ratios and Data

ENTERTAINMENT—Musical Groups and Artists NAICS 711130

Current Data Sorted by Assets						Comparative Historical Data		

						Type of Statement		
1	3	9	6	1	2	Unqualified	22	34
1		2			1	Reviewed	2	2
			1			Compiled	4	5
					1	Tax Returns	3	3
1	1	1	3			Other	21	21
3	3	3	3		3		4/1/05-3/31/06	4/1/06-3/31/07
	28 (4/1-9/30/09)		14 (10/1/09-3/31/10)				ALL	ALL
0-500M	500M-2MM	2-10MM	10-50MM	50-100MM	100-250MM	NUMBER OF STATEMENTS		
6	7	15	10	1	3		52	65
%	%	%	%	%	%		%	%
						ASSETS		
		16.1	27.6			Cash & Equivalents	17.9	22.5
		5.8	5.7			Trade Receivables (net)	12.2	7.2
		1.7	.1			Inventory	2.1	1.4
		3.8	7.7			All Other Current	7.7	5.9
		27.4	41.1			Total Current	40.0	37.0
		37.2	16.6			Fixed Assets (net)	26.7	24.7
		9.0	.0			Intangibles (net)	1.2	1.2
		26.4	42.3			All Other Non-Current	32.1	37.0
		100.0	100.0			Total	100.0	100.0
						LIABILITIES		
		10.3	5.1			Notes Payable-Short Term	13.3	7.6
		.9	1.7			Cur. Mat.-L.T.D.	3.5	1.6
		6.5	3.1			Trade Payables	10.7	14.9
		.0	.0			Income Taxes Payable	.1	.8
		11.2	6.4			All Other Current	13.8	13.4
		29.0	16.3			Total Current	41.6	38.2
		10.7	23.9			Long-Term Debt	10.0	12.6
		.0	.0			Deferred Taxes	.0	.0
		7.0	15.9			All Other Non-Current	7.6	10.7
		53.3	43.9			Net Worth	40.8	38.5
		100.0	100.0			Total Liabilties & Net Worth	100.0	100.0
						INCOME DATA		
		100.0	100.0			Net Sales	100.0	100.0
						Gross Profit		
		105.4	87.3			Operating Expenses	95.2	93.3
		-5.4	12.7			Operating Profit	4.8	6.7
		3.1	9.2			All Other Expenses (net)	2.1	.8
		-8.5	3.6			Profit Before Taxes	2.7	5.9
						RATIOS		
		3.4	3.8				2.8	2.8
		.5	2.6			Current	1.3	1.2
		.2	1.2				.5	.6
		3.3	3.7				2.0	2.0
		.3	1.6			Quick	.8	.9
		.1	.1				.3	.3
		1 261.6	0 UND				3 141.5	1 454.9
		12 29.3	4 88.7			Sales/Receivables	18 20.4	9 40.6
		18 20.8	40 9.1				59 6.2	38 9.7
						Cost of Sales/Inventory		
						Cost of Sales/Payables		
		3.2	3.4				5.0	4.5
		-9.4	6.2			Sales/Working Capital	19.9	27.1
		-3.5	NM				-6.1	-8.7
		-.5					7.1	12.6
		(13) -10.6				EBIT/Interest	(29) 1.6	(43) 4.1
		-24.5					-3.9	-.7
						Net Profit + Depr., Dep., Amort./Cur. Mat. L/T/D		
		.1	.0				.0	.1
		.7	.1			Fixed/Worth	.4	.3
		1.9	.7				1.3	1.4
		.5	.1				.3	.2
		.8	.6			Debt/Worth	.7	.6
		1.9	3.0				5.0	2.7
		-3.9					22.2	14.0
		(13) -13.6				% Profit Before Taxes/Tangible Net Worth	(43) 2.3	(54) 2.5
		-37.5					-2.7	-6.5
		-1.9	35.5				6.9	8.2
		-8.2	-7.0			% Profit Before Taxes/Total Assets	.7	1.9
		-16.7	-18.8				-4.0	-4.0
		63.4	82.8				53.1	39.5
		7.8	24.0			Sales/Net Fixed Assets	13.4	16.0
		1.3	2.1				2.7	2.1
		2.3	1.2				3.2	2.0
		1.0	.7			Sales/Total Assets	1.2	1.0
		.7	.4				.4	.4
		1.2					.9	.8
		(11) 3.1				% Depr., Dep., Amort./Sales	(43) 1.5	(48) 1.3
		6.6					4.1	4.0
							7.6	
						% Officers', Directors' Owners' Comp/Sales	(11) 9.4	
							17.2	
5828M	8282M	127943M	263875M	23081M	143563M	Net Sales ($)	863197M	1074932M
1473M	6684M	88668M	235976M	64013M	562024M	Total Assets ($)	1386324M	1763094M

M = $ thousand   MM = $ million
See Pages 9 through 22 for Explanation of Ratios and Data

Comparative Historical Data   Current Data Sorted by Sales

			Type of Statement						
32	36	22	Unqualified	2	4	3	5	5	3
1	1	3	Reviewed	1	~1		1		
2	1	2	Compiled				1		1
5	3	3	Tax Returns				1		1
17	19	12	Other	4	3	1		2	1
4/1/07-3/31/08 ALL	4/1/08-3/31/09 ALL	4/1/09-3/31/10 ALL		28 (4/1-9/30/09)			14 (10/1/09-3/31/10)		
				0-1MM	1-3MM	3-5MM	5-10MM	10-25MM	25MM & OVER
57	60	42	NUMBER OF STATEMENTS	8	9	4	8	7	6
%	%	%	ASSETS	%	%	%	%	%	%
18.5	24.4	17.4	Cash & Equivalents						
11.0	8.3	8.3	Trade Receivables (net)						
2.3	.9	1.0	Inventory						
3.5	5.1	4.4	All Other Current						
35.3	38.6	31.1	Total Current						
25.8	23.1	30.0	Fixed Assets (net)						
1.6	1.0	5.5	Intangibles (net)						
37.3	37.2	33.5	All Other Non-Current						
100.0	100.0	100.0	Total						
			LIABILITIES						
10.0	8.3	8.9	Notes Payable-Short Term						
2.3	1.6	1.0	Cur. Mat.-L.T.D.						
8.7	5.5	6.2	Trade Payables						
.0	.2	.0	Income Taxes Payable						
8.5	9.4	6.8	All Other Current						
29.4	25.0	23.0	Total Current						
11.1	13.3	22.5	Long-Term Debt						
.0	.3	.3	Deferred Taxes						
11.7	15.8	11.3	All Other Non-Current						
47.7	45.6	42.9	Net Worth						
100.0	100.0	100.0	Total Liabilties & Net Worth						
			INCOME DATA						
100.0	100.0	100.0	Net Sales						
			Gross Profit						
92.3	96.5	97.8	Operating Expenses						
7.7	3.5	2.2	Operating Profit						
1.5	4.2	5.9	All Other Expenses (net)						
6.2	-.7	-3.7	Profit Before Taxes						
			RATIOS						
3.8	5.2	4.3							
1.1	1.5	1.8	Current						
.5	.5	.3							
3.5	4.6	4.0							
.8	1.1	1.3	Quick						
.2	.2	.1							
2 238.0	2 235.1	1 499.3							
11 33.3	11 34.5	10 36.5	Sales/Receivables						
57 6.4	39 9.3	40 9.2							
			Cost of Sales/Inventory						
			Cost of Sales/Payables						
4.4	2.8	4.6							
45.5	11.7	24.1	Sales/Working Capital						
-8.0	-7.8	-4.9							
30.7	8.3	3.3							
(42) 2.8	(43) .2	(32) -2.9	EBIT/Interest						
-1.7	-6.4	-25.7							
			Net Profit + Depr., Dep., Amort./Cur. Mat. L/T/D						
.0	.0	.1							
.2	.2	.5	Fixed/Worth						
1.3	1.2	1.3							
.2	.2	.3							
.5	.5	.8	Debt/Worth						
1.4	1.7	3.0							
19.2	9.1	9.2							
(51) 5.9	(53) -2.4	(36) -7.2	% Profit Before Taxes/Tangible Net Worth						
-6.3	-10.3	-42.4							
9.2	5.7	3.8							
3.0	-1.0	-4.3	% Profit Before Taxes/Total Assets						
-4.9	-5.8	-16.8							
35.9	54.6	45.2							
11.7	19.4	9.1	Sales/Net Fixed Assets						
2.3	2.1	1.8							
1.6	1.7	2.2							
.8	.8	1.0	Sales/Total Assets						
.4	.4	.4							
.6	.7	1.0							
(47) 1.3	(49) 1.0	(28) 1.9	% Depr., Dep., Amort./Sales						
3.4	4.2	4.1							
			% Officers', Directors' Owners' Comp/Sales						
746836M	1463696M	572572M	Net Sales ($)	4226M	16693M	16197M	62808M	122536M	350112M
1505080M	1793422M	958838M	Total Assets ($)	5564M	17797M	14580M	245920M	151856M	523121M

M = $ thousand   MM = $ million
See Pages 9 through 22 for Explanation of Ratios and Data

Current Data Sorted by Assets   Comparative Historical Data

Type of Statement	0-500M	500M-2MM	2-10MM	10-50MM	50-100MM	100-250MM	4/1/05-3/31/06 ALL	4/1/06-3/31/07 ALL
Unqualified	1		6	6	6	28	40	63
Reviewed			3	4			7	6
Compiled	1	1	2				6	5
Tax Returns	10	6	3				9	10
Other	3	8	12	13	8	17	41	40
	57 (4/1-9/30/09)		81 (10/1/09-3/31/10)					
NUMBER OF STATEMENTS	15	15	26	23	14	45	103	124
ASSETS	%	%	%	%	%	%	%	%
Cash & Equivalents	32.2	16.1	17.4	8.3	11.8	9.9	14.7	12.5
Trade Receivables (net)	8.5	7.6	7.2	5.8	17.2	8.0	9.2	10.7
Inventory	2.1	3.7	1.0	1.0	.8	.5	1.3	1.1
All Other Current	.3	4.8	4.6	4.0	4.1	7.6	4.0	4.9
Total Current	43.2	32.3	30.3	19.0	33.9	26.0	29.2	29.2
Fixed Assets (net)	38.2	37.7	39.0	45.5	17.9	21.7	35.2	30.8
Intangibles (net)	.5	8.4	21.9	30.0	30.5	23.4	21.9	23.3
All Other Non-Current	18.2	21.6	8.8	5.4	17.6	28.9	13.7	16.7
Total	100.0	100.0	100.0	100.0	100.0	100.0	100.0	100.0
LIABILITIES								
Notes Payable-Short Term	3.2	9.5	4.3	6.2	2.6	8.9	10.9	11.9
Cur. Mat.-L.T.D.	9.6	4.5	1.5	4.1	.6	4.6	3.0	3.5
Trade Payables	4.6	9.3	2.5	4.9	8.8	6.4	5.8	7.4
Income Taxes Payable	.0	.0	.3	.0	.0	.0	.2	.2
All Other Current	23.4	15.6	21.6	16.8	29.9	19.6	20.5	19.8
Total Current	40.8	38.9	30.2	32.0	41.9	39.6	40.4	42.7
Long-Term Debt	13.4	36.4	16.1	52.4	67.1	50.2	40.0	33.5
Deferred Taxes	.0	.0	.1	.0	.0	1.0	.3	.1
All Other Non-Current	59.4	10.0	13.7	14.1	19.1	27.4	22.2	21.4
Net Worth	-13.7	14.7	39.9	1.4	-28.1	-18.2	-2.8	2.3
Total Liabilities & Net Worth	100.0	100.0	100.0	100.0	100.0	100.0	100.0	100.0
INCOME DATA								
Net Sales	100.0	100.0	100.0	100.0	100.0	100.0	100.0	100.0
Gross Profit								
Operating Expenses	91.5	95.4	94.6	96.4	95.1	101.7	93.9	94.9
Operating Profit	8.5	4.6	5.4	3.6	4.9	-1.7	6.1	5.1
All Other Expenses (net)	2.1	4.1	3.6	8.4	4.9	4.9	4.6	4.2
Profit Before Taxes	6.3	.5	1.8	-4.8	.1	-6.6	1.6	.8
RATIOS								
Current	3.3	1.9	2.1	.9	1.2	1.1	1.7	1.7
	1.6	.8	1.2	.5	.7	.7	.9	.9
	.5	.4	.4	.3	.6	.5	.4	.4
Quick	3.2	1.6	2.1	.8	1.1	.8	1.6	1.4
	1.5	.6	1.0	.3	.6	.5	.7	.8
	.5	.2	.3	.2	.5	.3	.2	.3
Sales/Receivables	0 UND	0 UND	3 124.0	7 50.4	25 14.6	14 26.4	3 115.3	9 40.5
	0 UND	6 61.7	14 25.8	12 29.8	36 10.0	31 11.9	17 21.3	27 13.6
	13 28.3	20 18.1	29 12.7	29 12.4	75 4.9	70 5.2	40 9.2	51 7.2
Cost of Sales/Inventory								
Cost of Sales/Payables								
Sales/Working Capital	11.0	9.5	4.3	-53.5	NM	48.3	9.7	9.5
	100.0	-95.9	29.3	-8.8	-12.4	-12.7	-49.2	-40.6
	-12.6	-5.0	-6.1	-3.2	-5.0	-3.1	-5.9	-3.8
EBIT/Interest		6.0	5.7	2.5	6.8	1.4	4.6	4.9
		(10) 1.3	(15) 2.4	(19) -.2	(13) 1.0	(42) -.4	(78) 1.1	(96) 1.0
		-25.0	.2	-2.1	-4.0	-2.4	-2.9	-1.4
Net Profit + Depr., Dep., Amort./Cur. Mat. L/T/D								
Fixed/Worth	.2	.6	.3	2.0	.0	2.9	1.0	.9
	1.9	3.7	1.1	5.3	3.2	-.5	-5.5	NM
	-.2	-.8	-1.1	-1.2	-.3	-.2	-.1	-.2
Debt/Worth	.4	1.3	.3	1.4	3.1	-7.7	1.7	1.9
	1.6	3.3	2.2	11.2	-4.1	-2.8	-7.5	-11.4
	-5.2	-3.4	-4.2	-2.3	-1.4	-1.8	-2.1	-1.8
% Profit Before Taxes/Tangible Net Worth	103.4	23.2	15.4			2.4	40.4	39.4
	(10) 16.8	(16) 5.7	(13) -10.1			(10) -32.2	(48) 10.0	(59) 7.6
	-10.1	-1.6	-38.5			-116.2	-.6	-2.9
% Profit Before Taxes/Total Assets	32.4	12.3	15.6	3.6	8.9	2.3	11.6	10.7
	9.6	1.1	3.3	-4.3	1.3	-4.8	1.9	.1
	.0	-47.6	-1.0	-8.6	-17.1	-12.0	-6.9	-7.3
Sales/Net Fixed Assets	33.1	28.2	29.4	5.5	234.3	41.5	39.1	45.3
	19.0	11.5	4.5	1.5	11.1	6.1	8.7	8.5
	3.0	1.7	.5	.5	3.3	2.8	.9	1.7
Sales/Total Assets	6.5	3.2	1.4	.7	1.8	1.0	1.9	1.5
	2.6	1.9	.8	.5	1.2	.7	1.0	.9
	1.7	.8	.2	.3	.7	.5	.5	.5
% Depr., Dep., Amort./Sales		1.1	1.9	5.0	1.8	1.0	1.4	1.2
		(10) 2.0	(22) 4.3	(19) 9.2	(10) 4.0	(23) 2.6	(74) 3.4	(88) 3.7
		4.6	10.7	14.7	7.6	5.7	9.8	7.8
% Officers', Directors' Owners' Comp/Sales							8.6	3.3
							(16) 14.6	(19) 8.8
							27.3	16.3
Net Sales ($)	10493M	31267M	99157M	578298M	1142324M	6227808M	6577667M	8237650M
Total Assets ($)	3507M	15067M	113833M	564025M	1038137M	7963431M	6778385M	8462856M

© RMA 2010

M = $ thousand   MM = $ million
See Pages 9 through 22 for Explanation of Ratios and Data

ENTERTAINMENT—Sports Teams and Clubs NAICS 711211

1487

Comparative Historical Data

Current Data Sorted by Sales

Type of Statement									
Unqualified	51	56	47	1	1	4	4	1	36
Reviewed	10	9	7	1	3			3	
Compiled	5	2	4		3	1			
Tax Returns	13	9	19	13	4	1	1		
Other	54	54	61	7	9	3	10	5	27
	4/1/07-3/31/08 ALL	4/1/08-3/31/09 ALL	4/1/09-3/31/10 ALL	0-1MM	1-3MM	3-5MM	5-10MM	10-25MM	25MM & OVER
				57 (4/1-9/30/09)			81 (10/1/09-3/31/10)		
NUMBER OF STATEMENTS	133	130	138	22	20	9	15	9	63
ASSETS	%	%	%	%	%	%	%	%	%
Cash & Equivalents	15.4	15.4	14.3	19.7	11.4		19.3		10.7
Trade Receivables (net)	9.8	8.8	8.4	7.5	4.4		7.0		10.8
Inventory	1.3	1.0	1.2	1.4	2.4		1.5		.8
All Other Current	6.8	5.7	5.0	3.1	.7		2.6		7.0
Total Current	33.3	31.0	29.0	31.6	18.9		30.3		29.3
Fixed Assets (net)	29.2	31.0	32.1	51.4	43.9		32.9		21.5
Intangibles (net)	22.4	19.4	20.8	.8	24.0		29.8		24.2
All Other Non-Current	15.2	18.6	18.1	16.2	13.2		7.0		25.0
Total	100.0	100.0	100.0	100.0	100.0		100.0		100.0
LIABILITIES									
Notes Payable-Short Term	14.3	11.2	6.4	4.0	2.7		8.9		8.7
Cur. Mat.-L.T.D.	4.6	3.1	4.1	3.7	9.0		2.8		3.5
Trade Payables	6.9	7.2	5.8	2.6	6.7		4.0		7.7
Income Taxes Payable	.1	.0	.1	.0	.0		.1		.0
All Other Current	28.1	19.0	20.5	18.8	14.0		11.4		25.3
Total Current	54.0	40.5	36.8	29.1	32.5		27.2		45.2
Long-Term Debt	33.5	36.5	40.4	30.0	23.6		27.1		57.4
Deferred Taxes	.2	.2	.3	.0	.0		.1		.7
All Other Non-Current	19.5	18.2	23.4	40.6	5.2		16.0		28.0
Net Worth	-7.2	4.5	-.9	.4	38.7		29.6		-31.3
Total Liabilities & Net Worth	100.0	100.0	100.0	100.0	100.0		100.0		100.0
INCOME DATA									
Net Sales	100.0	100.0	100.0	100.0	100.0		100.0		100.0
Gross Profit									
Operating Expenses	93.1	95.8	97.0	88.0	105.7		90.7		101.3
Operating Profit	6.9	4.2	3.0	12.0	-5.7		9.3		-1.3
All Other Expenses (net)	3.8	5.4	4.8	6.3	5.1		2.6		4.9
Profit Before Taxes	3.0	-1.2	-1.8	5.7	-10.8		6.7		-6.2
RATIOS									
Current	1.6	1.6	1.7	2.4	1.6		5.1		1.1
	.8	.8	.8	1.2	.7		1.1		.7
	.3	.5	.4	.5	.1		.3		.4
Quick	1.3	1.2	1.2	2.0	1.5		4.1		.8
	.5	.6	.6	.9	.4		1.0		.5
	.2	.3	.3	.5	.1		.2		.3
Sales/Receivables	6 66.0	7 54.9	6 58.6	0 UND	1 268.0		7 50.4		14 25.7
	20 18.2	23 16.0	18 20.5	0 UND	8 45.5		13 28.2		34 10.8
	41 8.8	44 8.3	42 8.6	29 12.7	19 18.8		28 12.9		67 5.4
Cost of Sales/Inventory									
Cost of Sales/Payables									
Sales/Working Capital	9.3	13.0	10.6	4.4	32.5		4.3		55.1
	-17.8	-28.4	-16.4	74.3	-13.3		30.8		-9.1
	-3.5	-5.3	-4.4	-10.6	-2.6		-5.2		-3.7
EBIT/Interest	3.9	2.7	2.9	13.2	2.5		47.0		1.4
	(110) .7	(100) .7	(108) .4	(12) 2.8	(13) -.3		(12) 2.2	(58) -.3	
	-2.1	-2.2	-1.9	.4	-4.8		-14.9		-2.7
Net Profit + Depr., Dep., Amort./Cur. Mat. L/T/D									
Fixed/Worth	.9	.7	.8	1.0	.5		1.0		1.9
	-10.6	9.4	19.0	2.9	1.8		6.1		-.8
	-.1	-.3	-.3	-.9	-4.2		-.6		-.2
Debt/Worth	1.9	1.2	1.6	.2	.8		1.1		-9.3
	-12.8	-188.7	-7.5	3.0	2.1		5.4		-2.8
	-1.7	-2.3	-2.2	-7.3	-5.8		-3.3		-1.7
% Profit Before Taxes/Tangible Net Worth	57.8	21.0	26.8	66.7	16.4				12.4
	(62) 14.3	(64) 3.9	(64) 2.5	(15) .7	(13) -5.4			(15) -5.2	
	-5.4	-16.0	-27.6	-.8	-81.1				-59.4
% Profit Before Taxes/Total Assets	10.1	5.1	6.4	17.9	2.5		15.8		2.7
	-.4	.2	-.5	.9	-5.1		3.6		-5.8
	-13.7	-8.8	-9.0	-2.1	-25.7		-.6		-14.4
Sales/Net Fixed Assets	45.3	52.0	28.4	23.3	39.6		11.7		68.0
	11.2	8.7	5.7	4.2	4.9		4.2		9.8
	1.9	1.6	1.6	.2	.8		1.5		2.9
Sales/Total Assets	1.8	1.5	1.7	2.2	2.8		2.1		1.2
	1.0	.9	.9	1.2	.8		.9		.8
	.6	.5	.5	.2	.3		.4		.6
% Depr., Dep., Amort./Sales	1.2	1.0	1.7	1.7	1.1		2.7		1.2
	(100) 3.6	(88) 3.2	(93) 3.7	(14) 4.5	(15) 2.5		(13) 5.0	(34) 2.6	
	8.3	8.7	9.3	15.7	10.3		11.9		6.8
% Officers', Directors' Owners' Comp/Sales	3.6	5.1	5.0						
	(23) 8.3	(16) 9.6	(14) 6.6						
	17.7	14.9	13.9						
Net Sales ($)	7215850M	8185833M	8089347M	11397M	36669M	32805M	108293M	130347M	7769836M
Total Assets ($)	7445233M	10223798M	9698000M	25522M	78356M	41516M	184794M	287107M	9080705M

M = $ thousand   MM = $ million
See Pages 9 through 22 for Explanation of Ratios and Data

Current Data Sorted by Assets   Comparative Historical Data

Type of Statement							4/1/05-3/31/06	4/1/06-3/31/07
Unqualified			1	6	2	2	23	23
Reviewed			1	1			1	2
Compiled	1		1				3	5
Tax Returns	8	4	3				15	7
Other	1	5	8	10	4	3	23	16

0-500M	500M-2MM	2-10MM	10-50MM	50-100MM	100-250MM		
	12 (4/1-9/30/09)		49 (10/1/09-3/31/10)			4/1/05-3/31/06 ALL	4/1/06-3/31/07 ALL

0-500M	500M-2MM	2-10MM	10-50MM	50-100MM	100-250MM			
10	9	14	17	6	5	**NUMBER OF STATEMENTS**	65	53
%	%	%	%	%	%	**ASSETS**	%	%
22.4		14.1	11.3			Cash & Equivalents	12.5	12.8
9.7		5.3	6.1			Trade Receivables (net)	6.7	7.4
1.8		3.0	3.8			Inventory	2.9	2.8
.0		.8	3.8			All Other Current	3.7	3.4
34.0		23.2	24.9			Total Current	25.8	26.4
63.8		66.9	58.1			Fixed Assets (net)	61.4	61.1
.1		.2	3.6			Intangibles (net)	3.8	4.1
2.2		9.7	13.4			All Other Non-Current	9.0	8.4
100.0		100.0	100.0			Total	100.0	100.0
						LIABILITIES		
9.5		8.2	1.6			Notes Payable-Short Term	6.0	5.3
17.5		8.2	5.9			Cur. Mat.-L.T.D.	3.8	6.0
2.7		6.5	5.4			Trade Payables	8.0	13.9
.0		.1	.0			Income Taxes Payable	.0	.0
40.7		20.9	12.9			All Other Current	17.1	19.4
70.6		43.9	25.8			Total Current	34.9	44.6
64.5		61.8	22.2			Long-Term Debt	31.9	27.5
.3		.7	1.1			Deferred Taxes	.7	.2
4.1		6.9	8.9			All Other Non-Current	9.0	11.3
-39.4		-13.2	41.5			Net Worth	23.5	16.3
100.0		100.0	100.0			Total Liabilities & Net Worth	100.0	100.0
						INCOME DATA		
100.0		100.0	100.0			Net Sales	100.0	100.0
						Gross Profit		
97.4		87.9	99.6			Operating Expenses	91.8	94.0
2.6		12.1	.4			Operating Profit	8.2	6.0
3.9		7.0	5.4			All Other Expenses (net)	3.7	2.1
-1.3		5.1	-5.0			Profit Before Taxes	4.6	3.9
						RATIOS		
1.7		3.1	2.6			Current	1.6	1.5
.5		.3	.7				.8	.7
.2		.1	.3				.4	.4
1.7		3.1	2.3			Quick	1.3	1.3
.4		.2	.4				.6 (52)	.5
.1		.0	.2				.3	.2
0 UND		1 255.0	5 70.4			Sales/Receivables	3 143.4	3 125.6
0 UND		7 52.7	21 17.0				8 48.2	10 35.1
21 17.6		13 28.0	45 8.1				23 15.7	23 15.6
						Cost of Sales/Inventory		
						Cost of Sales/Payables		
58.6		3.0	4.2			Sales/Working Capital	15.9	17.3
-75.0		-5.6	-19.5				-60.4	-22.9
-6.0		-1.7	-4.9				-8.2	-6.6
		4.5	8.2			EBIT/Interest	15.0	16.0
		(10) .8	(14) .7				(55) 2.1	(47) 3.5
		-2.6	-31.1				-.1	-.3
						Net Profit + Depr., Dep., Amort./Cur. Mat. L/T/D		
1.1		.6	.5			Fixed/Worth	1.1	1.0
NM		13.4	1.2				2.3	2.1
-1.7		-1.5	5.5				NM	21.1
.6		.4	.5			Debt/Worth	.9	.9
NM		13.5	1.0				3.2	2.0
-3.5		-2.8	7.5				NM	27.0
			19.9			% Profit Before Taxes/Tangible Net Worth	64.1	39.9
		(14)	5.8				(49) 20.2	(41) 18.6
			-40.0				-6.3	-4.0
24.5		8.3	9.7			% Profit Before Taxes/Total Assets	15.4	16.8
2.4		-.8	1.1				3.9	2.7
-9.7		-5.7	-10.5				-3.8	-5.8
40.8		4.9	5.9			Sales/Net Fixed Assets	4.8	4.5
3.1		1.4	2.4				2.6	2.5
2.1		.6	.6				1.2	1.3
20.2		1.6	1.7			Sales/Total Assets	2.7	2.5
2.4		.9	.9				1.6	1.6
1.5		.4	.5				.8	.9
		4.8	2.6			% Depr., Dep., Amort./Sales	2.8	2.5
		7.6	(15) 3.6				(61) 4.1	(50) 4.3
		16.9	14.4				7.6	6.8
						% Officers', Directors' Owners' Comp/Sales	1.6	
							(17) 5.5	
							12.9	
6943M	19082M	66975M	478080M	460056M	684203M	Net Sales ($)	3694737M	2554045M
1667M	11886M	69216M	476160M	362135M	941321M	Total Assets ($)	2195518M	1963209M

M = $ thousand   MM = $ million
See Pages 9 through 22 for Explanation of Ratios and Data

Comparative Historical Data

Current Data Sorted by Sales

	4/1/07-3/31/08 ALL	4/1/08-3/31/09 ALL	4/1/09-3/31/10 ALL	0-1MM	1-3MM	3-5MM	5-10MM	10-25MM	25MM & OVER
Type of Statement					12 (4/1-9/30/09)			49 (10/1/09-3/31/10)	
Unqualified	13	8	11				1	2	8
Reviewed	7	7	2				2		
Compiled	5	3	2	1	1				
Tax Returns	9	3	15	7	5	1	2		
Other	14	23	31	3	5	4	5	2	12
NUMBER OF STATEMENTS	48	44	61	11	11	5	10	4	20
	%	%	%	%	%	%	%	%	%
ASSETS									
Cash & Equivalents	16.0	18.4	13.5	15.7	12.7		19.0		8.9
Trade Receivables (net)	5.2	7.2	6.5	9.0	3.5		8.4		6.4
Inventory	1.8	3.2	2.8	1.5	.4		4.0		5.3
All Other Current	2.1	1.9	2.0	.1	.2		1.1		4.4
Total Current	25.1	30.8	24.9	26.3	16.8		32.5		25.0
Fixed Assets (net)	65.6	55.1	61.6	64.3	64.8		59.7		58.6
Intangibles (net)	4.1	4.9	4.3	7.9	5.6		.2		4.5
All Other Non-Current	5.2	9.3	9.3	1.5	12.8		7.7		11.9
Total	100.0	100.0	100.0	100.0	100.0		100.0		100.0
LIABILITIES									
Notes Payable-Short Term	12.9	5.9	6.9	8.7	15.3		8.4		2.7
Cur. Mat.-L.T.D.	8.4	10.2	9.4	7.6	11.7		2.5		5.4
Trade Payables	8.6	6.3	5.1	2.9	2.5		10.1		4.8
Income Taxes Payable	.1	.0	.0	.0	.0		.1		.0
All Other Current	16.9	17.9	22.7	33.8	12.8		17.5		17.7
Total Current	46.9	40.2	44.2	53.0	42.3		38.6		30.5
Long-Term Debt	39.8	27.9	39.5	60.8	51.7		54.5		21.5
Deferred Taxes	.7	.0	1.0	.3	.0		.9		2.6
All Other Non-Current	10.1	5.2	6.5	4.0	.0		8.4		10.6
Net Worth	2.5	26.7	8.8	-18.0	6.0		-2.4		34.9
Total Liabilties & Net Worth	100.0	100.0	100.0	100.0	100.0		100.0		100.0
INCOME DATA									
Net Sales	100.0	100.0	100.0	100.0	100.0		100.0		100.0
Gross Profit									
Operating Expenses	90.3	95.5	94.1	79.6	98.4		99.4		94.0
Operating Profit	9.7	4.5	5.9	20.4	1.6		.6		6.0
All Other Expenses (net)	3.4	3.2	5.5	7.7	5.0		6.3		4.4
Profit Before Taxes	6.3	1.4	.4	12.6	-3.4		-5.7		1.6
RATIOS									
Current	1.5	2.3	2.0	2.0	3.4		2.9		1.8
	.7	.8	.6	1.5	.4		.7		.7
	.2	.3	.2	.4	.2		.2		.4
Quick	1.3	1.6	1.9	2.0	3.4		2.8		1.2
	.5	.6	.4	1.5	.3		.4		.4
	.2	.3	.1	.4	.0		.1		.4
Sales/Receivables	2 182.3	5 70.3	1 423.6	0 UND	0 UND		2 163.1		5 72.8
	7 49.3	12 31.1	10 36.4	0 UND	5 74.2		20 18.2		16 23.4
	23 15.8	31 11.7	24 15.1	18 20.2	29 12.8		46 7.9		22 16.5
Cost of Sales/Inventory									
Cost of Sales/Payables									
Sales/Working Capital	13.6	12.2	8.5	5.1	17.8		2.5		10.3
	-13.8	-21.9	-19.5	19.7	-65.4		-7.0		-18.6
	-5.4	-5.5	-3.8	-6.1	-.9		-4.6		-4.8
EBIT/Interest	10.8	11.0	7.0						12.8
	(43) 3.6	(36) 2.4	(47) 1.0						(19) 2.4
	.9	-.2	-1.3						-2.6
Net Profit + Depr., Dep., Amort./Cur. Mat. L/T/D									
Fixed/Worth	1.1	.8	.8	1.2	.7		.3		.7
	3.1	1.8	2.1	2.1	2.7		3.9		1.5
	NM	UND	-3.9	-2.9	-.6		NM		NM
Debt/Worth	.9	.4	.6	.4	.1		.7		.5
	3.4	2.3	1.4	1.5	1.7		3.1		1.1
	-9.0	UND	-5.4	-4.2	-1.9		NM		NM
% Profit Before Taxes/Tangible Net Worth	47.4	29.1	36.6						25.1
	(35) 16.0	(33) 10.9	(43) 12.4						(15) 14.5
	6.7	-2.7	-4.0						-.5
% Profit Before Taxes/Total Assets	19.1	15.1	11.5	16.8	13.9		8.3		13.5
	5.5	4.4	1.1	3.7	.0		-3.7		4.1
	-.4	-2.4	-5.9	-3.0	-20.4		-12.2		-5.2
Sales/Net Fixed Assets	3.4	4.5	5.0	3.3	11.9		14.2		4.1
	1.7	2.2	2.1	2.1	1.4		3.2		2.3
	1.0	1.1	.7	.7	.4		.7		1.2
Sales/Total Assets	2.1	2.0	2.0	2.2	11.3		1.7		1.8
	1.2	1.2	1.0	.6	.7		1.1		1.2
	.6	.8	.5	.5	.4		.6		.8
% Depr., Dep., Amort./Sales	3.0	2.9	3.4				3.6		3.2
	(45) 5.4	(40) 4.9	(53) 7.0				7.6		(19) 4.1
	7.9	7.2	13.8				14.5		7.4
% Officers', Directors' Owners' Comp/Sales			1.8						
			(10) 7.0						
			9.4						
Net Sales ($)	1393790M	1377109M	1715339M	4565M	18514M	21199M	74386M	67112M	1529563M
Total Assets ($)	1413981M	1295253M	1862385M	8811M	33880M	12994M	136244M	147936M	1522520M

M = $ thousand   MM = $ million
See Pages 9 through 22 for Explanation of Ratios and Data

Current Data Sorted by Assets

Comparative Historical Data

Type of Statement	0-500M	500M-2MM	2-10MM	10-50MM	50-100MM	100-250MM		4/1/05-3/31/06 ALL	4/1/06-3/31/07 ALL
Unqualified	2	1	15	20	4	19		18	41
Reviewed		2	5	2				3	11
Compiled	2	5	8					9	7
Tax Returns	16	14	3	1				18	16
Other	9	12	13	3	1	5		16	19
		51 (4/1-9/30/09)		111 (10/1/09-3/31/10)					
NUMBER OF STATEMENTS	29	34	44	26	5	24		64	94
	%	%	%	%	%	%		%	%
ASSETS									
Cash & Equivalents	19.0	16.7	20.1	13.4		9.2		11.4	18.0
Trade Receivables (net)	7.4	12.1	6.8	4.0		9.4		7.1	7.7
Inventory	3.5	.9	.5	.5		.1		.9	3.4
All Other Current	3.4	3.1	2.4	5.9		8.5		3.7	5.8
Total Current	33.2	32.9	29.9	23.8		27.0		23.1	35.0
Fixed Assets (net)	48.0	51.0	48.6	64.9		25.4		59.1	48.9
Intangibles (net)	3.2	6.0	4.8	4.6		26.5		5.7	4.0
All Other Non-Current	15.6	10.2	16.8	6.6		21.0		12.1	12.2
Total	100.0	100.0	100.0	100.0		100.0		100.0	100.0
LIABILITIES									
Notes Payable-Short Term	12.8	3.5	4.0	.4		1.1		8.8	9.9
Cur. Mat.-L.T.D.	8.4	8.5	2.1	4.7		5.7		7.6	5.9
Trade Payables	13.6	6.2	4.1	6.2		4.5		6.2	6.3
Income Taxes Payable	1.9	.0	.0	.0		.0		.1	.0
All Other Current	17.2	13.9	10.7	14.8		17.6		8.7	11.1
Total Current	53.8	32.0	21.0	26.1		28.9		31.4	33.2
Long-Term Debt	36.4	22.8	21.4	29.4		42.1		35.3	27.1
Deferred Taxes	.0	.0	.7	.2		.6		.1	.0
All Other Non-Current	25.6	6.1	1.7	5.9		18.4		6.4	16.9
Net Worth	-15.9	39.1	55.1	38.4		10.0		26.8	22.8
Total Liabilties & Net Worth	100.0	100.0	100.0	100.0		100.0		100.0	100.0
INCOME DATA									
Net Sales	100.0	100.0	100.0	100.0		100.0		100.0	100.0
Gross Profit									
Operating Expenses	86.8	87.4	91.6	93.3		93.3		77.9	85.3
Operating Profit	13.2	12.6	8.4	6.7		6.7		22.1	14.7
All Other Expenses (net)	3.9	7.3	3.6	5.3		4.8		9.7	5.6
Profit Before Taxes	9.2	5.3	4.8	1.5		1.9		12.4	9.2
RATIOS									
Current	1.7	4.0	4.6	2.9		2.1		2.2	3.5
	.7	2.3	1.7	1.1		.9		.9	1.1
	.2	.3	.6	.5		.6		.4	.5
Quick	1.7	3.4	4.6	1.9		1.3		1.7	2.7
	.6	1.5	1.3	1.0		.7		.6	.8
	.2	.2	.4	.2		.3		.3	.4
Sales/Receivables	0 UND	0 UND	0 UND	5 72.3		14 25.7		0 UND	0 UND
	0 UND	5 81.0	5 75.4	12 30.7		26 14.0		5 67.7	8 47.7
	0 UND	20 18.4	21 17.1	20 18.7		74 5.0		22 16.3	27 13.7
Cost of Sales/Inventory									
Cost of Sales/Payables									
Sales/Working Capital	26.5	6.7	3.5	3.7		5.3		8.9	6.1
	-62.7	16.3	18.9	34.1		-49.3		-51.9	269.1
	-17.6	-8.2	-10.0	-9.6		-5.2		-4.9	-8.3
EBIT/Interest	15.7	14.5	16.3	5.6		5.1		6.8	11.1
	(16) 3.8	(21) 2.3	(29) 3.1	(20) .3		(20) .5		(32) 3.1	(58) 3.8
	1.4	.1	-1.3	-6.0		-1.8		1.1	.8
Net Profit + Depr., Dep., Amort./Cur. Mat. L/T/D									
Fixed/Worth	.2	.6	.2	1.0		1.1		.8	.4
	3.0	1.7	1.1	1.7		-.6		2.0	1.4
	-2.1	-13.3	1.8	6.3		-.1		24.9	NM
Debt/Worth	.8	.3	.3	.3		1.5		.4	.3
	76.5	1.8	.7	1.4		-3.0		2.1	2.0
	-3.0	-19.9	3.4	6.3		-1.8		46.9	-221.4
% Profit Before Taxes/Tangible Net Worth	140.8	45.1	26.8	12.1		24.5		47.3	51.4
	(16) 24.3	(25) 12.4	(41) 3.1	(23) .0		(10) 1.1		(49) 16.6	(69) 13.6
	-2.4	-4.2	-14.7	-5.5		-1.1		-1.7	1.1
% Profit Before Taxes/Total Assets	27.0	27.0	7.0	5.0		5.2		14.4	19.3
	8.0	4.8	2.5	.2		.1		2.7	4.7
	-5.5	-1.8	-5.5	-3.7		-4.6		-1.0	-1.3
Sales/Net Fixed Assets	71.1	85.4	28.9	1.8		17.7		7.7	32.9
	14.7	2.6	1.7	.7		4.6		.8	2.1
	2.5	.4	.7	.3		1.4		.2	.6
Sales/Total Assets	8.0	4.4	1.3	.8		1.3		2.0	3.0
	4.5	1.2	.8	.4		.8		.5	1.1
	1.9	.3	.3	.2		.3		.2	.3
% Depr., Dep., Amort./Sales	1.2	1.8	2.1	3.6		1.2		3.2	1.4
	(19) 3.0	(25) 7.1	(34) 4.3	(24) 9.5		(15) 3.2		(54) 8.7	(73) 6.4
	9.2	12.7	10.0	18.9		12.6		16.2	12.3
% Officers', Directors' Owners' Comp/Sales		2.9						5.8	3.4
		(12) 5.3						(11) 7.5	(18) 5.5
		9.6						30.2	17.9
Net Sales ($)	41637M	128241M	237316M	498889M	129590M	3434040M		855197M	1150321M
Total Assets ($)	7409M	38207M	210246M	714108M	327308M	4095839M		1557085M	1721877M

M = $ thousand   MM = $ million
See Pages 9 through 22 for Explanation of Ratios and Data

Comparative Historical Data

Current Data Sorted by Sales

			Type of Statement	51 (4/1-9/30/09)			111 (10/1/09-3/31/10)		
38	58	61	Unqualified	3	6	7	10	11	24
8	10	9	Reviewed	2	2	3			2
10	21	15	Compiled	6	4	1	1	2	1
33	21	34	Tax Returns	21	7	1	2	3	
34	32	43	Other	7	16	6	4	4	6
4/1/07-3/31/08 ALL	4/1/08-3/31/09 ALL	4/1/09-3/31/10 ALL		0-1MM	1-3MM	3-5MM	5-10MM	10-25MM	25MM & OVER
123	142	162	**NUMBER OF STATEMENTS**	39	35	18	17	20	33
%	%	%	**ASSETS**	%	%	%	%	%	%
14.3	16.9	16.1	Cash & Equivalents	13.8	12.9	22.1	21.6	20.9	13.0
8.5	8.3	7.8	Trade Receivables (net)	7.0	6.4	8.8	6.0	9.3	9.7
2.4	1.7	1.1	Inventory	2.7	1.0	.4	.4	.1	.5
3.7	5.0	4.2	All Other Current	.4	4.6	4.7	4.3	3.2	8.9
29.0	31.8	29.2	Total Current	24.0	24.9	36.0	32.3	33.6	32.0
51.8	49.3	47.8	Fixed Assets (net)	62.0	57.1	42.8	46.9	45.6	25.4
3.6	6.2	8.9	Intangibles (net)	2.3	5.2	8.0	7.9	6.2	23.1
15.6	12.6	14.2	All Other Non-Current	11.8	12.8	13.2	12.9	14.6	19.5
100.0	100.0	100.0	Total	100.0	100.0	100.0	100.0	100.0	100.0
			LIABILITIES						
6.9	3.4	4.7	Notes Payable-Short Term	2.8	9.1	5.5	1.6	2.2	4.8
3.5	4.4	5.5	Cur. Mat.-L.T.D.	11.0	4.7	.7	2.4	4.4	4.6
5.2	6.1	6.6	Trade Payables	6.6	5.8	7.2	4.9	5.5	8.5
.8	.0	.3	Income Taxes Payable	1.4	.0	.0	.1	.0	.0
10.7	12.9	14.1	All Other Current	8.8	10.7	17.4	18.8	12.7	20.8
27.2	26.9	31.2	Total Current	30.6	30.3	30.8	27.8	24.8	38.7
23.5	29.2	29.7	Long-Term Debt	42.0	26.8	14.0	26.7	12.2	38.7
.1	.3	.3	Deferred Taxes	.0	.7	.1	.0	.4	.6
13.0	7.6	10.2	All Other Non-Current	.3	13.6	25.7	.3	2.5	19.6
36.3	36.1	28.6	Net Worth	27.1	28.6	29.4	45.3	60.1	2.4
100.0	100.0	100.0	Total Liabilties & Net Worth	100.0	100.0	100.0	100.0	100.0	100.0
			INCOME DATA						
100.0	100.0	100.0	Net Sales	100.0	100.0	100.0	100.0	100.0	100.0
			Gross Profit						
84.3	84.3	90.2	Operating Expenses	76.5	94.9	89.4	93.6	100.3	93.9
15.7	15.7	9.8	Operating Profit	23.5	5.1	10.6	6.4	-.3	6.1
5.3	6.1	5.7	All Other Expenses (net)	9.7	5.1	8.3	3.3	.6	4.3
10.4	9.7	4.2	Profit Before Taxes	13.8	.0	2.3	3.1	-.9	1.9
			RATIOS						
3.6	4.0	3.1		4.2	3.1	3.4	2.6	3.3	1.8
1.1	1.3	1.1	Current	1.5	1.5	1.0	1.1	2.0	.9
.4	.5	.4		.3	.2	.6	.3	.9	.6
2.6	2.9	2.7		3.6	2.8	3.3	1.7	2.8	1.3
.8	1.1	.9	Quick	1.2	.9	1.0	.9	1.3	.7
.3	.4	.3		.3	.1	.4	.1	.6	.3
0 UND	0 UND	0 UND		0 UND	0 UND	0 UND	1 460.0	2 163.8	7 53.4
6 59.1	7 49.2	9 40.8	Sales/Receivables	0 UND	4 99.1	9 41.6	10 36.6	14 26.4	18 20.0
34 10.6	26 14.2	23 15.6		15 23.7	19 19.4	15 24.3	23 15.8	27 13.7	45 8.1
			Cost of Sales/Inventory						
			Cost of Sales/Payables						
3.7	3.6	5.6		4.7	5.3	5.0	5.5	5.9	8.9
79.3	25.3	51.8	Sales/Working Capital	25.7	27.4	NM	551.5	15.9	-52.2
-10.0	-12.5	-9.7		-5.6	-6.1	-13.0	-6.7	-53.3	-5.5
18.6	6.7	12.7		6.6	11.9	39.8	46.5	14.7	10.7
(85) 4.1	(95) 3.1	(110) 2.2	EBIT/Interest	(20) 3.3	(24) 1.7	(11) -.8	(13) 3.2	(13) 3.1	(29) 1.5
1.2	.6	-1.4		1.4	-1.1	-17.3	-1.8	-1.4	-2.2
			Net Profit + Depr., Dep., Amort./Cur. Mat. L/T/D						
.5	.5	.7		.9	.7	.3	.3	.3	1.1
1.1	1.2	1.6	Fixed/Worth	1.7	1.5	1.0	1.8	.9	-.8
4.4	10.2	-17.0		10.1	-13.8	NM	4.1	1.4	-.1
.3	.3	.4		.3	.4	.3	.4	.3	1.3
1.1	1.2	2.1	Debt/Worth	2.5	1.0	1.3	2.3	.8	-3.8
5.3	28.4	-16.9		-26.0	-17.5	-16.4	6.1	1.7	-1.8
32.5	42.8	29.5		43.4	15.7	42.6	25.0	19.0	33.2
(100) 12.8	(114) 9.6	(117) 6.3	% Profit Before Taxes/Tangible Net Worth	(29) 12.4	(26) -3.7	(12) 2.0	(16) 6.5	.4	(14) 21.2
2.1	-.1	-5.6		1.1	-24.0	-9.9	-4.4	-7.2	-.3
15.3	13.8	9.8		9.6	15.1	36.8	8.1	9.0	10.4
4.9	2.7	2.1	% Profit Before Taxes/Total Assets	3.6	1.1	2.0	1.6	.4	1.7
-.7	-1.3	-4.2		-1.3	-10.6	-2.7	-4.0	-3.1	-5.0
22.0	17.9	22.1		13.4	32.1	63.8	12.1	27.1	23.8
1.8	1.7	2.6	Sales/Net Fixed Assets	.5	2.5	14.0	3.1	2.1	9.8
.3	.5	.6		.2	.7	.9	.3	.7	2.1
2.0	1.8	2.6		1.8	3.1	5.5	2.5	3.2	2.0
.7	.7	.8	Sales/Total Assets	.4	1.0	1.3	.8	1.0	1.0
.3	.3	.3		.2	.5	.3	.2	.4	.6
1.9	2.2	1.9		4.8	1.2		1.3	2.2	1.2
(101) 6.1	(115) 5.0	(119) 5.3	% Depr., Dep., Amort./Sales	(29) 11.6	(28) 4.8		(15) 4.3	(18) 3.7	(20) 2.5
12.3	10.9	11.6		15.0	9.6		9.9	9.4	10.0
3.7	3.6	3.9							
(19) 6.4	(22) 5.6	(24) 6.9	% Officers', Directors' Owners' Comp/Sales						
13.3	10.4	11.2							
2025691M	3201839M	4469713M	Net Sales ($)	16518M	63722M	69261M	117170M	291901M	3911141M
2386156M	4208974M	5393117M	Total Assets ($)	57324M	99468M	192855M	294055M	668571M	4080844M

M = $ thousand   MM = $ million
See Pages 9 through 22 for Explanation of Ratios and Data

Current Data Sorted by Assets   Comparative Historical Data

0-500M	500M-2MM	2-10MM	10-50MM	50-100MM	100-250MM	Type of Statement	4/1/05-3/31/06 ALL	4/1/06-3/31/07 ALL
1	5	24	43	24	23	Unqualified	110	139
	2		4			Reviewed	4	3
		5			1	Compiled	5	3
3	2	3	1			Tax Returns	4	7
4	5	15	11	5	3	Other	42	41
	116 (4/1-9/30/09)		68 (10/1/09-3/31/10)					
8	14	47	59	30	26	NUMBER OF STATEMENTS	165	193
%	%	%	%	%	%	**ASSETS**	%	%
	9.2	14.7	11.7	10.3	10.1	Cash & Equivalents	14.9	12.5
	5.2	4.2	5.7	2.4	2.0	Trade Receivables (net)	4.3	4.3
	7.5	6.2	1.0	2.9	2.4	Inventory	3.8	2.5
	2.2	1.9	3.6	3.3	4.2	All Other Current	2.9	3.4
	24.2	26.9	22.1	18.9	18.8	Total Current	26.0	22.8
	58.6	56.3	53.0	51.5	41.7	Fixed Assets (net)	48.3	50.4
	.0	.3	.4	.2	.4	Intangibles (net)	.8	.5
	17.2	16.4	24.5	29.4	39.1	All Other Non-Current	24.9	26.4
	100.0	100.0	100.0	100.0	100.0	Total	100.0	100.0
						LIABILITIES		
	9.7	3.9	2.2	1.7	2.5	Notes Payable-Short Term	5.6	3.6
	1.9	1.1	.7	.8	1.2	Cur. Mat.-L.T.D.	1.2	.8
	6.4	4.2	2.4	1.9	1.6	Trade Payables	5.0	3.9
	.0	.0	.0	.0	.0	Income Taxes Payable	.1	.1
	4.7	5.2	3.7	2.8	1.7	All Other Current	4.8	2.9
	22.7	14.4	9.0	7.2	7.1	Total Current	16.7	11.3
	13.0	10.5	15.0	14.1	14.4	Long-Term Debt	13.4	11.7
	.0	.0	.0	.0	.0	Deferred Taxes	.0	.0
	13.3	3.8	2.3	2.9	2.2	All Other Non-Current	2.2	2.0
	51.1	71.3	73.7	75.7	76.3	Net Worth	67.8	75.0
	100.0	100.0	100.0	100.0	100.0	Total Liabilties & Net Worth	100.0	100.0
						INCOME DATA		
	100.0	100.0	100.0	100.0	100.0	Net Sales	100.0	100.0
						Gross Profit		
	93.6	102.0	94.5	96.5	94.4	Operating Expenses	94.5	88.6
	6.4	-2.0	5.5	3.5	5.6	Operating Profit	5.5	11.4
	1.0	3.6	7.3	6.1	5.7	All Other Expenses (net)	.5	.9
	5.4	-5.6	-1.8	-2.7	.0	Profit Before Taxes	5.0	10.5
						RATIOS		
	4.8	8.8	9.7	7.7	5.9	Current	5.6	6.5
	1.5	2.5	3.1	2.2	2.3		2.3	2.5
	.3	1.0	1.1	1.5	1.3		1.0	1.3
	4.5	7.6	8.8	2.9	4.5	Quick	4.3	5.3
	.6	1.5	1.8	1.5	1.5		1.6	1.7
	.3	.6	.4	.6	.6		.5	.7
	0 UND	0 999.8	2 213.6	1 485.3	2 179.3	Sales/Receivables	1 367.2	2 216.2
	0 UND	4 86.0	14 26.4	11 33.4	18 20.3		8 43.0	12 31.7
	18 20.1	24 15.4	96 3.8	42 8.6	33 11.1		48 7.6	48 7.6
						Cost of Sales/Inventory		
						Cost of Sales/Payables		
	2.8	1.6	1.4	1.3	1.7	Sales/Working Capital	1.6	1.6
	31.4	6.9	3.2	3.5	3.2		4.5	4.4
	-8.8	114.2	25.7	16.0	10.4		428.3	18.6
	10.8	3.4	2.9	7.0	12.2	EBIT/Interest	16.2	9.9
	(10) 4.8	(27) -1.4	(33) -.5	(24) -2.4	(18) 1.4		(103) 2.3	(129) 1.8
	-3.5	-12.4	-6.8	-5.0	-4.9		-1.9	-.6
						Net Profit + Depr., Dep., Amort./Cur. Mat. L/T/D		
	.5	.4	.3	.3	.3	Fixed/Worth	.3	.3
	.9	.8	.8	.7	.6		.7	.7
	1.7	1.1	1.1	1.2	.8		1.0	.9
	.2	.1	.0	.1	.1	Debt/Worth	.1	.1
	.6	.3	.2	.2	.3		.2	.2
	1.6	.8	.6	.7	.6		.7	.5
	25.8	8.7	7.3	6.8	6.8	% Profit Before Taxes/Tangible Net Worth	9.8	10.2
	(12) 5.1	(46) -2.8	-1.7	-.7	-.6		(158) 1.7	(187) 2.5
	-7.6	-7.1	-4.6	-3.5	-5.2		-3.0	-1.1
	22.6	5.2	5.3	3.7	5.5	% Profit Before Taxes/Total Assets	6.7	6.8
	4.2	-2.1	-.7	-.7	-.5		1.0	1.5
	-4.9	-5.0	-3.8	-2.8	-4.3		-2.2	-1.1
	8.0	1.7	1.3	1.0	.8	Sales/Net Fixed Assets	1.6	1.3
	.8	.8	.5	.6	.4		.7	.7
	.4	.3	.3	.3	.3		.3	.4
	1.9	.8	.4	.3	.3	Sales/Total Assets	.6	.6
	.5	.5	.3	.2	.2		.3	.3
	.3	.2	.2	.2	.1		.2	.2
		3.0	5.3	4.5	3.9	% Depr., Dep., Amort./Sales	3.5	4.3
	(40)	7.7	(54) 9.6	(28) 10.5	(23) 9.8		(147) 8.7	(170) 8.7
		19.9	16.8	17.8	14.6		15.6	14.9
						% Officers', Directors' Owners' Comp/Sales	3.0	3.3
							(21) 6.0	(21) 7.4
							19.2	22.2
5331M	19976M	139222M	480344M	624790M	876322M	Net Sales ($)	1788903M	2192689M
2332M	18406M	243780M	1467418M	2098796M	3651534M	Total Assets ($)	6195582M	7469434M

M = $ thousand   MM = $ million
See Pages 9 through 22 for Explanation of Ratios and Data

Comparative Historical Data | Current Data Sorted by Sales

115	126	120	Type of Statement						
115	126	120	Unqualified	8	21	19	18	37	17
5	5	6	Reviewed	2	2			1	1
7	3	6	Compiled	2	1		2		1
3	9	9	Tax Returns	3	3	1	1	1	
45	52	43	Other	12	10	6	3	10	2
4/1/07- 3/31/08	4/1/08- 3/31/09	4/1/09- 3/31/10			116 (4/1-9/30/09)			68 (10/1/09-3/31/10)	
ALL	ALL	ALL		0-1MM	1-3MM	3-5MM	5-10MM	10-25MM	25MM & OVER
175	195	184	NUMBER OF STATEMENTS	27	37	26	24	49	21
%	%	%	ASSETS	%	%	%	%	%	%
13.8	13.3	12.0	Cash & Equivalents	10.1	12.3	11.6	14.2	12.0	12.0
5.4	3.7	4.3	Trade Receivables (net)	3.0	4.5	5.2	5.5	3.6	4.8
2.9	2.8	3.9	Inventory	4.5	3.9	1.1	5.4	2.7	7.6
3.8	3.4	3.1	All Other Current	1.0	3.8	2.6	3.4	3.3	4.5
25.8	23.2	23.3	Total Current	18.6	24.5	20.5	28.5	21.5	28.8
48.2	52.9	52.5	Fixed Assets (net)	66.3	55.2	53.4	45.1	53.1	36.0
.5	.6	.3	Intangibles (net)	.1	.4	.1	.5	.3	.4
25.5	23.3	23.9	All Other Non-Current	15.0	19.9	26.0	25.9	25.1	34.7
100.0	100.0	100.0	Total	100.0	100.0	100.0	100.0	100.0	100.0
			LIABILITIES						
3.6	4.2	5.5	Notes Payable-Short Term	19.9	3.4	6.6	.8	1.3	4.1
1.0	.8	1.0	Cur. Mat.-L.T.D.	1.3	.8	1.0	1.0	1.0	1.0
3.6	3.2	3.6	Trade Payables	2.8	4.5	4.1	4.5	2.3	4.8
.0	.0	.0	Income Taxes Payable	.3	.0	.0	.0	.0	.0
4.8	4.2	4.1	All Other Current	3.3	4.5	2.3	6.0	2.6	7.9
13.0	12.5	14.2	Total Current	27.6	13.2	14.1	12.3	7.2	17.7
16.3	12.9	14.3	Long-Term Debt	20.1	14.5	12.8	8.8	16.5	9.3
.0	.1	.0	Deferred Taxes	.0	.0	.0	.0	.0	.0
3.5	3.2	3.9	All Other Non-Current	1.6	4.6	6.3	.6	4.6	4.7
67.3	71.3	67.6	Net Worth	50.7	67.7	66.8	78.3	71.6	68.3
100.0	100.0	100.0	Total Liabilities & Net Worth	100.0	100.0	100.0	100.0	100.0	100.0
			INCOME DATA						
100.0	100.0	100.0	Net Sales	100.0	100.0	100.0	100.0	100.0	100.0
			Gross Profit						
83.9	93.6	97.2	Operating Expenses	97.8	98.7	103.4	93.2	96.9	91.5
16.1	6.4	2.8	Operating Profit	2.2	1.3	-3.4	6.8	3.1	8.5
2.6	5.0	5.4	All Other Expenses (net)	10.6	4.4	2.2	8.2	4.7	2.8
13.4	1.4	-2.6	Profit Before Taxes	-8.4	-3.2	-5.6	-1.5	-1.6	5.7
			RATIOS						
7.7	6.0	7.2		19.7	9.5	7.7	7.7	7.9	2.4
2.9	2.3	2.2	Current	1.7	4.1	2.1	2.5	2.0	1.8
1.1	1.0	1.0		.3	1.0	1.0	1.2	1.2	1.1
5.4	4.4	5.1		15.3	8.9	3.3	5.3	5.9	1.7
1.6	1.4	1.5	Quick	1.0	2.2	1.3	2.0	1.6	.8
.7	.5	.5		.3	.5	.4	.5	.7	.5
2 146.0	1 274.5	1 725.5		0 UND	0 992.9	2 198.5	0 835.0	3 113.4	2 197.8
18 20.0	11 34.8	11 33.4	Sales/Receivables	0 UND	5 69.2	19 19.3	7 52.8	16 22.8	12 30.6
54 6.8	41 9.0	50 7.3		60 6.1	26 14.3	80 4.6	113 3.2	45 8.1	29 12.5
			Cost of Sales/Inventory						
			Cost of Sales/Payables						
1.6	1.8	1.8		1.9	1.5	1.8	1.9	1.9	2.5
4.7	6.5	4.3	Sales/Working Capital	9.5	3.2	5.4	3.4	4.2	4.3
35.7	-126.0	NM		-2.3	NM	-82.4	11.4	28.2	26.8
14.5	8.9	6.7		5.9	1.7	6.9	19.8	8.8	11.0
(115) 3.6	(132) .8	(119) -.6	EBIT/Interest	(17) .2	(22) -1.4	(17) -2.6	(11) -.7	(36) -.4	(16) 4.8
-.2	-7.2	-7.5		-7.6	-20.4	-8.9	-5.2	-5.2	-10.8
			Net Profit + Depr., Dep., Amort./Cur. Mat. L/T/D						
.3	.4	.4		.6	.4	.4	.2	.4	.1
.7	.7	.8	Fixed/Worth	1.1	.9	.7	.6	.8	.4
1.0	1.1	1.1		1.6	1.1	1.2	.9	1.1	1.0
.1	.1	.1		.2	.1	.1	.0	.1	.2
.2	.2	.3	Debt/Worth	.3	.4	.3	.1	.3	.4
.8	.7	.8		1.2	1.2	.6	.4	.7	.8
16.2	9.6	7.8	% Profit Before Taxes/Tangible Net Worth	7.0	5.5	4.0	8.4	6.2	12.1
(165) 3.3	(189) -.5	(178) -1.5		(25) -1.9	(35) -2.1	(24) -2.7	.3	-1.9	7.8
-1.9	-6.5	-5.3		-9.4	-4.4	-7.4	-6.3	-7.4	-2.0
11.1	6.5	5.2	% Profit Before Taxes/Total Assets	3.6	4.8	4.7	7.5	5.0	7.1
2.4	-.5	-.9		-1.9	-1.8	-2.0	.3	-1.2	2.2
-1.2	-4.8	-4.5		-5.0	-4.0	-6.0	-5.9	-4.6	-1.7
2.3	1.6	1.4		1.1	1.9	1.3	2.9	1.2	19.7
.7	.6	.6	Sales/Net Fixed Assets	.5	.6	.6	.9	.4	.9
.4	.3	.3		.2	.2	.3	.3	.3	.6
.6	.6	.5		.5	.6	.6	.8	.4	.8
.3	.3	.3	Sales/Total Assets	.3	.3	.3	.3	.2	.3
.2	.2	.2		.1	.1	.2	.2	.1	.2
2.7	4.0	4.4		4.6	4.7	2.4	6.1	6.4	2.9
(147) 7.1	(163) 8.5	(160) 9.5	% Depr., Dep., Amort./Sales	(22) 15.6	(31) 7.6	(22) 8.3	(20) 10.9	(47) 12.1	(18) 7.3
13.2	14.3	17.2		29.5	19.7	16.6	16.7	16.1	10.1
4.4	1.6	2.9							
(22) 6.6	(20) 6.7	(23) 6.0	% Officers', Directors' Owners' Comp/Sales						
12.7	14.6	14.9							
2323268M	2391781M	2145985M	Net Sales ($)	14825M	69051M	106103M	180459M	737278M	1038269M
7220773M	7730159M	7482266M	Total Assets ($)	81303M	313926M	483836M	789505M	3399951M	2413745M

M = $ thousand   MM = $ million
See Pages 9 through 22 for Explanation of Ratios and Data

	Current Data Sorted by Assets							Comparative Historical Data	
Type of Statement	0-500M	500M-2MM	2-10MM	10-50MM	50-100MM	100-250MM		4/1/05-3/31/06 ALL	4/1/06-3/31/07 ALL
Unqualified	1	1		4				13	11
Reviewed			7	7				16	10
Compiled	2	7	13	2				16	10
Tax Returns	9	8	7	1				15	17
Other	7	8	7	10	3	5		24	25
	7 (4/1-9/30/09)			102 (10/1/09-3/31/10)					
NUMBER OF STATEMENTS	19	24	34	24	3	5		84	73
	%	%	%	%	%	%	**ASSETS**	%	%
	13.5	6.1	10.2	8.5			Cash & Equivalents	9.1	11.8
	3.0	1.0	.8	1.2			Trade Receivables (net)	1.4	.8
	7.6	8.8	3.3	.8			Inventory	2.0	1.6
	.2	.6	1.1	1.9			All Other Current	2.4	2.0
	24.2	16.5	15.4	12.4			Total Current	14.8	16.2
	68.9	71.8	68.4	80.5			Fixed Assets (net)	73.7	72.8
	3.7	2.5	1.0	.8			Intangibles (net)	2.3	2.8
	3.2	9.2	15.3	6.4			All Other Non-Current	9.2	8.2
	100.0	100.0	100.0	100.0			Total	100.0	100.0
							LIABILITIES		
	11.0	8.9	4.1	2.1			Notes Payable-Short Term	6.0	2.8
	14.4	4.6	3.9	8.3			Cur. Mat.-L.T.D.	4.3	3.8
	4.2	6.4	2.3	2.0			Trade Payables	5.7	2.9
	.1	.0	.0	.0			Income Taxes Payable	.0	.1
	23.3	16.5	11.2	5.4			All Other Current	14.2	11.9
	53.0	36.3	21.5	17.8			Total Current	30.2	21.6
	41.7	63.4	42.9	39.5			Long-Term Debt	44.9	34.5
	.0	.1	1.1	.5			Deferred Taxes	1.0	.7
	22.2	17.0	6.7	7.8			All Other Non-Current	8.4	8.8
	-16.8	-16.8	27.7	34.5			Net Worth	15.5	34.4
	100.0	100.0	100.0	100.0			Total Liabilities & Net Worth	100.0	100.0
							INCOME DATA		
	100.0	100.0	100.0	100.0			Net Sales	100.0	100.0
							Gross Profit		
	94.9	92.4	84.6	93.7			Operating Expenses	92.6	90.2
	5.1	7.6	15.4	6.3			Operating Profit	7.4	9.8
	1.6	6.6	4.1	5.2			All Other Expenses (net)	5.1	4.4
	3.6	1.0	11.3	1.1			Profit Before Taxes	2.3	5.4
							RATIOS		
	.6	1.4	1.6	1.8				1.7	1.6
	.4	.7	.9	.6			Current	.8	.7
	.3	.1	.2	.3				.2	.2
	.5	.8	1.3	1.5				1.2	1.5
	.2	.3	.8	.3			Quick	.3	.4
	.1	.0	.1	.1				.1	.1
	0 UND	0 UND	0 UND	0 999.8				0 UND	0 UND
	0 UND	0 UND	1 634.5	1 360.8			Sales/Receivables	0 907.1	0 999.8
	0 UND	0 UND	2 147.9	6 60.8				3 112.5	4 103.0
							Cost of Sales/Inventory		
							Cost of Sales/Payables		
	-54.9	54.6	21.6	9.5				17.9	10.8
	-17.6	-25.8	-71.1	-21.9			Sales/Working Capital	-31.2	-32.6
	-6.4	-3.0	-4.8	-3.8				-4.5	-5.7
	9.1	4.8	4.5	2.6				3.9	3.7
	(10) .9	(19) 1.2	(30) 1.5	(21) 1.8			EBIT/Interest	(75) 1.7	(67) 1.6
	-3.1	-.3	.3	.6				.1	.4
							Net Profit + Depr., Dep.,	4.6	3.1
							Amort./Cur. Mat. L/T/D	(17) 2.5	(13) 2.3
								1.0	1.1
	1.1	1.8	1.2	1.1				1.4	1.0
	-7.2	-8.8	2.5	3.3			Fixed/Worth	3.2	3.2
	-1.1	-2.8	-46.5	92.1				-7.2	-13.4
	.4	1.2	.7	.5				.8	.4
	-12.6	9.8	2.6	2.8			Debt/Worth	3.9	2.5
	-2.5	-5.3	-49.9	95.7				-9.2	17.8
		47.1	43.0	24.5			% Profit Before Taxes/Tangible	29.5	34.9
	(13) 11.0	(25) 13.5	(19) 12.7				Net Worth	(60) 10.4	(61) 7.7
		-9.0	.9	.6				-2.9	-1.2
	12.5	9.2	11.0	5.7			% Profit Before Taxes/Total	9.0	10.1
	.0	2.3	2.1	1.0			Assets	3.1	3.0
	-15.1	-3.9	-1.7	-1.8				-3.9	-1.8
	17.8	3.8	2.9	1.0				2.9	2.4
	5.1	2.1	1.4	.5			Sales/Net Fixed Assets	1.2	1.1
	1.8	.5	.6	.3				.6	.6
	7.4	2.6	1.4	.7				1.8	1.4
	4.6	1.3	.9	.5			Sales/Total Assets	.9	.8
	1.4	.5	.4	.3				.5	.5
	2.8	6.1	5.5	9.6				5.8	6.2
	(15) 3.9	(22) 10.3	(32) 9.7	13.0			% Depr., Dep., Amort./Sales	(79) 9.2	(68) 10.1
	9.4	15.3	12.6	16.0				15.5	17.0
	2.8						% Officers', Directors'	2.9	1.4
	(11) 4.9						Owners' Comp/Sales	(22) 5.1	(22) 5.0
	12.4							7.7	16.8
	16673M	37635M	159936M	274173M	229153M	343824M	Net Sales ($)	1136801M	1039375M
	3888M	23626M	191296M	478616M	213975M	808619M	Total Assets ($)	1327912M	1095069M

© RMA 2010

M = $ thousand   MM = $ million
See Pages 9 through 22 for Explanation of Ratios and Data

Comparative Historical Data   Current Data Sorted by Sales

Row	4/1/07-3/31/08 ALL	4/1/08-3/31/09 ALL	4/1/09-3/31/10 ALL	0-1MM	1-3MM	3-5MM	5-10MM	10-25MM	25MM & OVER
Type of Statement				7 (4/1-9/30/09)		102 (10/1/09-3/31/10)			
Unqualified	11	13	6		1		4		1
Reviewed	19	16	14		3	3	5	3	
Compiled	13	19	24	5	8	5	4	2	
Tax Returns	21	19	25	12	9	2	2		
Other	20	44	40	10	6	6	5	3	10
	4/1/07-3/31/08 ALL	4/1/08-3/31/09 ALL	4/1/09-3/31/10 ALL						
NUMBER OF STATEMENTS	84	111	109	27	27	16	20	8	11
	%	%	%	%	%	%	%	%	%
ASSETS									
Cash & Equivalents	12.6	11.0	8.9	9.6	8.3	10.1	7.7		2.4
Trade Receivables (net)	1.3	1.6	1.4	.2	2.7	1.3	1.2		1.9
Inventory	4.2	3.3	4.6	5.1	6.8	.8	4.1		1.7
All Other Current	1.5	3.6	1.2	.1	.8	1.1	.9		3.4
Total Current	19.6	19.6	16.1	14.9	18.5	13.3	13.9		9.4
Fixed Assets (net)	70.3	66.4	72.2	73.0	70.1	80.6	71.1		71.9
Intangibles (net)	1.8	2.8	2.0	2.4	2.9	.4	1.3		3.7
All Other Non-Current	8.2	11.2	9.7	9.7	8.5	5.7	13.7		15.0
Total	100.0	100.0	100.0	100.0	100.0	100.0	100.0		100.0
LIABILITIES									
Notes Payable-Short Term	6.5	4.0	5.9	5.0	9.2	4.1	5.0		4.3
Cur. Mat.-L.T.D.	4.6	6.3	6.7	7.3	7.6	4.2	9.1		4.4
Trade Payables	4.6	4.4	3.6	2.1	6.2	1.7	2.4		4.0
Income Taxes Payable	.1	.3	.1	.0	.0	.1	.0		.7
All Other Current	12.1	12.5	12.8	21.3	8.8	12.1	12.8		7.5
Total Current	27.9	27.5	29.1	35.8	31.8	22.2	29.3		20.8
Long-Term Debt	49.8	39.8	45.9	50.5	42.1	46.7	55.8		34.2
Deferred Taxes	.7	.7	.8	.0	.4	.8	1.3		3.0
All Other Non-Current	5.8	10.3	11.6	5.7	29.6	1.9	6.6		1.9
Net Worth	15.8	21.7	12.6	8.0	-3.8	28.5	7.0		40.1
Total Liabilities & Net Worth	100.0	100.0	100.0	100.0	100.0	100.0	100.0		100.0
INCOME DATA									
Net Sales	100.0	100.0	100.0	100.0	100.0	100.0	100.0		100.0
Gross Profit									
Operating Expenses	88.7	90.2	90.7	89.5	83.6	98.7	95.0		92.3
Operating Profit	11.3	9.8	9.3	10.5	16.4	1.3	5.0		7.7
All Other Expenses (net)	4.5	4.4	4.1	6.5	4.7	2.6	3.0		.7
Profit Before Taxes	6.7	5.4	5.2	3.9	11.7	-1.3	2.1		7.0
RATIOS									
Current	2.1	2.0	1.5	1.1	2.4	1.5	1.8		.7
	.9	.7	.6	.4	.8	.3	.9		.5
	.3	.2	.2	.2	.2	.2	.3		.2
Quick	1.8	1.6	1.2	.7	1.7	1.4	1.3		.6
	.4	(110) .5	.3	.2	.5	.3	.6		.2
	.1	.1	.1	.0	.1	.1	.0		.1
Sales/Receivables	0 UND	0 UND	0 UND	0 UND	0 UND	1 693.0	0 979.5		1 316.6
	0 999.8	1 714.0	0 999.8	0 UND	0 UND	1 353.9	1 279.4		5 77.9
	4 100.6	4 90.9	3 114.2	0 UND	0 UND	7 55.7	4 84.9		7 48.8
Cost of Sales/Inventory									
Cost of Sales/Payables									
Sales/Working Capital	11.9	12.6	24.0	126.5	15.4	13.5	17.2		-34.5
	-46.0	-33.2	-23.0	-19.1	-38.8	-15.4	-480.2		-12.0
	-6.1	-5.4	-4.5	-2.6	-6.3	-3.9	-5.3		-3.4
EBIT/Interest	4.6	3.9	4.6	4.9	5.7	4.4	2.6		7.5
	(71) 2.2	(88) 1.8	(88) 1.6	(17) .7	(20) 1.4	(15) 1.3	(18) 1.8		4.3
	1.2	.0	.2	-4.0	.9	.5	.3		2.2
Net Profit + Depr., Dep., Amort./Cur. Mat. L/T/D	16.6	4.6	3.4						
	(15) 2.6	(14) 2.9	(16) 2.3						
	1.3	1.5	1.5						
Fixed/Worth	1.2	1.0	1.3	1.9	1.4	1.2	1.1		1.0
	2.8	2.6	3.8	-512.0	4.6	3.3	2.6		3.4
	23.7	18.2	-10.0	-2.9	-1.1	-80.9	NM		4.6
Debt/Worth	.8	.6	.8	1.3	.6	.4	.7		.5
	2.6	2.6	3.7	-514.0	3.7	3.1	2.3		3.9
	24.2	575.3	-13.3	-9.4	-2.7	-87.5	NM		4.7
% Profit Before Taxes/Tangible Net Worth	34.4	37.4	40.7	53.1	42.5	28.5	18.7		40.1
	(64) 17.0	(86) 13.7	(72) 13.3	(13) 15.8	(16) 11.3	(11) 5.5	(15) 6.8	(10) 19.4	
	4.3	-.4	.8	-22.1	.6	-9.7	-2.1		11.0
% Profit Before Taxes/Total Assets	14.0	11.2	8.3	7.9	14.7	7.4	4.8		7.4
	4.5	4.0	1.9	.9	2.2	.0	1.6		5.5
	.5	-2.9	-2.9	-10.0	.0	-5.4	-2.6		3.6
Sales/Net Fixed Assets	2.8	3.7	3.5	3.9	12.1	2.4	2.2		1.6
	1.6	1.3	1.3	1.5	3.4	1.0	.8		.9
	.7	.6	.5	.5	.3	.3	.5		.5
Sales/Total Assets	2.1	1.9	2.1	2.3	3.8	1.4	1.3		1.0
	.9	.8	.8	.9	2.1	.8	.6		.7
	.6	.5	.4	.5	.3	.3	.4		.4
% Depr., Dep., Amort./Sales	4.1	4.6	5.4	3.5	3.5	8.7	8.7		
	(83) 8.5	(98) 9.6	(99) 10.0	(24) 9.4	(22) 8.1	12.0	12.2		
	12.4	13.8	14.3	17.9	12.2	19.8	14.6		
% Officers', Directors' Owners' Comp/Sales	2.7	1.5	3.8	3.8	2.8				
	(23) 6.9	(22) 5.2	(30) 5.5	(10) 6.4	(11) 5.6				
	13.6	8.6	10.9	13.8	10.4				
Net Sales ($)	999623M	1362861M	1061394M	13791M	54677M	67955M	140466M	113405M	671100M
Total Assets ($)	1158862M	2022629M	1720020M	18375M	87603M	129195M	248690M	138687M	1097470M

Current Data Sorted by Assets   Comparative Historical Data

Type of Statement

0-500M	500M-2MM	2-10MM	10-50MM	50-100MM	100-250MM	Type of Statement	4/1/05-3/31/06 ALL	4/1/06-3/31/07 ALL
		2	8	2	1	Unqualified	24	27
		2				Reviewed	8	5
	3	3				Compiled	6	5
2	2	4				Tax Returns	11	9
2	5	6	11	1	10	Other	30	32
	13 (4/1-9/30/09)		51 (10/1/09-3/31/10)					
4	10	17	19	3	11	NUMBER OF STATEMENTS	79	78
%	%	%	%	%	%		%	%

ASSETS

0-500M	500M-2MM	2-10MM	10-50MM	50-100MM	100-250MM		4/1/05-3/31/06	4/1/06-3/31/07
	12.9	14.8	13.3		19.9	Cash & Equivalents	17.2	18.8
	.8	3.6	2.0		1.4	Trade Receivables (net)	2.5	4.3
	8.3	11.0	4.4		.5	Inventory	3.6	4.3
	12.7	6.2	3.0		.5	All Other Current	3.4	2.4
	34.7	35.6	22.6		22.3	Total Current	26.7	29.8
	56.9	44.6	69.0		74.0	Fixed Assets (net)	61.3	60.2
	5.5	9.5	.5		1.0	Intangibles (net)	4.3	6.2
	3.0	10.3	8.0		2.7	All Other Non-Current	7.6	3.8
	100.0	100.0	100.0		100.0	Total	100.0	100.0

LIABILITIES

0-500M	500M-2MM	2-10MM	10-50MM	50-100MM	100-250MM		4/1/05-3/31/06	4/1/06-3/31/07
	9.8	4.8	1.7		.3	Notes Payable-Short Term	8.1	3.7
	13.1	9.4	3.2		3.9	Cur. Mat.-L.T.D.	5.6	8.0
	5.0	5.6	7.9		2.2	Trade Payables	5.6	8.5
	.0	.1	.0		.0	Income Taxes Payable	.3	.2
	9.8	6.3	12.2		6.4	All Other Current	9.0	10.2
	37.7	26.3	25.0		12.8	Total Current	28.6	30.5
	52.1	20.2	31.0		30.8	Long-Term Debt	29.9	32.7
	.1	.1	.0		.0	Deferred Taxes	.1	.1
	2.0	4.9	2.0		2.3	All Other Non-Current	6.6	6.3
	8.0	48.5	42.0		54.1	Net Worth	34.8	30.4
	100.0	100.0	100.0		100.0	Total Liabilities & Net Worth	100.0	100.0

INCOME DATA

0-500M	500M-2MM	2-10MM	10-50MM	50-100MM	100-250MM		4/1/05-3/31/06	4/1/06-3/31/07
	100.0	100.0	100.0		100.0	Net Sales	100.0	100.0
						Gross Profit		
	91.3	94.9	87.0		78.1	Operating Expenses	78.8	80.6
	8.7	5.1	13.0		21.9	Operating Profit	21.2	19.4
	2.0	1.8	2.2		3.9	All Other Expenses (net)	3.6	2.9
	6.7	3.3	10.8		18.0	Profit Before Taxes	17.6	16.6

RATIOS

0-500M	500M-2MM	2-10MM	10-50MM	50-100MM	100-250MM		4/1/05-3/31/06	4/1/06-3/31/07
	2.2	8.9	1.7		3.1	Current	2.6	2.2
	1.2	1.4	.7		1.4		1.3	1.2
	.2	.4	.4		1.0		.6	.5
	1.0	4.2	1.4		3.0	Quick	2.4	1.9
	.2	.4	.6		1.2		(78) .9	.9
	.1	.2	.2		.8		.4	.4
	0 UND	0 UND	1 711.7		1 257.8	Sales/Receivables	0 UND	1 560.6
	0 UND	1 361.0	2 184.3		3 104.7		1 438.9	2 198.5
	1 623.4	19 19.7	3 113.4		11 32.2		6 61.2	6 65.1
						Cost of Sales/Inventory		
						Cost of Sales/Payables		
	9.2	3.3	16.1		4.8	Sales/Working Capital	8.4	11.7
	NM	9.9	-17.4		19.9		38.3	68.9
	-10.1	-9.5	-4.8		-307.7		-11.3	-11.4
	16.7	3.3	23.1		17.8	EBIT/Interest	22.4	25.5
	3.0	(15) .5	(17) 7.6		(10) 11.9		(66) 6.3	(68) 3.8
	1.2	-3.1	1.0		-.2		1.3	.8
						Net Profit + Depr., Dep., Amort./Cur. Mat. L/T/D		
	.8	.3	.9		.9	Fixed/Worth	.9	.9
	3.5	.9	1.4		1.6		1.6	1.7
	-4.2	NM	4.8		1.8		3.6	NM
	1.1	.1	.3		.3	Debt/Worth	.6	.5
	4.4	.7	.8		.8		1.7	1.6
	-6.1	NM	4.3		1.9		4.1	-40.3
		43.5	48.8		59.8	% Profit Before Taxes/Tangible Net Worth	99.9	113.6
	(13) 1.1	(15) 11.0			(10) 41.8		(65) 38.2	(58) 39.6
	-15.9	2.0	8.5				11.7	10.6
	15.2	24.1	32.4		38.5	% Profit Before Taxes/Total Assets	40.0	62.5
	3.0	.0	6.7		17.9		14.1	14.8
	1.1	-17.5	1.6		-1.6		2.2	1.8
	8.3	13.2	2.5		1.6	Sales/Net Fixed Assets	4.2	5.8
	3.8	3.6	1.6		1.2		2.1	2.5
	2.1	1.9	1.3		.8		1.3	1.6
	3.5	2.4	1.6		1.0	Sales/Total Assets	1.9	2.5
	2.1	1.5	1.3		1.0		1.4	1.7
	1.3	.9	.8		.7		.8	.9
		5.0	5.1			% Depr., Dep., Amort./Sales	3.9	3.6
		(15) 7.3	6.6				(65) 8.4	(64) 7.3
		10.6	9.1				11.5	11.6
						% Officers', Directors' Owners' Comp/Sales	2.4	1.4
							(19) 4.8	(18) 2.7
							11.1	6.9
1471M	33151M	144762M	726353M	140288M	1510414M	Net Sales ($)	3275633M	5510845M
656M	10301M	74104M	494671M	177534M	1743804M	Total Assets ($)	2898339M	3404939M

M = $ thousand   MM = $ million
See Pages 9 through 22 for Explanation of Ratios and Data

Comparative Historical Data | Current Data Sorted by Sales

Type of Statement

Type of Statement	4/1/07-3/31/08	4/1/08-3/31/09	4/1/09-3/31/10	0-1MM	1-3MM	3-5MM	5-10MM	10-25MM	25MM & OVER
Unqualified	13	12	13			1		6	6
Reviewed	6	2	2				1	1	
Compiled	6	4	6		2	2	1	1	
Tax Returns	12	3	8	3	2			3	
Other	45	46	35	3	5	1	4	3	19
	ALL	ALL	ALL		13 (4/1-9/30/09)			51 (10/1/09-3/31/10)	
NUMBER OF STATEMENTS	82	67	64	6	9	4	6	14	25

	%	%	%	%	%	%	%	%	%
ASSETS									
Cash & Equivalents	20.2	14.6	14.5					11.9	17.5
Trade Receivables (net)	5.0	2.9	2.7					2.3	2.1
Inventory	3.5	4.9	5.7					5.9	3.5
All Other Current	2.0	2.3	4.8					7.4	1.4
Total Current	30.7	24.7	27.6					27.5	24.5
Fixed Assets (net)	59.3	63.3	61.7					57.9	69.9
Intangibles (net)	5.9	5.1	4.5					3.7	.7
All Other Non-Current	4.1	6.9	6.3					11.0	4.8
Total	100.0	100.0	100.0					100.0	100.0
LIABILITIES									
Notes Payable-Short Term	5.1	6.5	5.4					4.3	.2
Cur. Mat.-L.T.D.	5.3	8.0	6.3					3.1	3.5
Trade Payables	5.2	7.5	7.2					6.3	5.2
Income Taxes Payable	.0	.1	.0					.1	.0
All Other Current	12.2	9.2	10.5					12.2	10.3
Total Current	27.7	31.3	29.4					26.1	19.2
Long-Term Debt	31.6	26.6	36.1					22.7	29.7
Deferred Taxes	.1	.1	.1					.2	.0
All Other Non-Current	5.1	6.1	4.3					2.5	1.6
Net Worth	35.6	35.9	30.1					48.5	49.4
Total Liabilties & Net Worth	100.0	100.0	100.0					100.0	100.0
INCOME DATA									
Net Sales	100.0	100.0	100.0					100.0	100.0
Gross Profit									
Operating Expenses	79.8	83.6	88.5					92.2	78.7
Operating Profit	20.2	16.4	11.5					7.8	21.3
All Other Expenses (net)	3.9	3.5	2.4					2.6	2.6
Profit Before Taxes	16.3	12.9	9.0					5.2	18.7

RATIOS

	4/1/07-3/31/08	4/1/08-3/31/09	4/1/09-3/31/10	0-1MM	1-3MM	3-5MM	5-10MM	10-25MM	25MM & OVER
Current	3.4 / 1.6 / .8	1.6 / .9 / .5	2.3 / 1.0 / .4					2.0 / .9 / .4	2.2 / 1.2 / .6
Quick	3.0 / 1.2 / .5	1.0 / .7 / .3	1.6 / .6 / .1					1.1 / .4 / .1	2.1 / 1.0 / .5
Sales/Receivables	0 UND / 2 199.8 / 6 56.6	0 999.8 / 2 206.0 / 6 64.2	0 UND / 1 372.9 / 5 74.8					0 UND / 1 480.2 / 4 84.6	1 490.0 / 2 184.3 / 7 48.7
Cost of Sales/Inventory									
Cost of Sales/Payables									
Sales/Working Capital	6.8 / 26.3 / -24.9	15.5 / -40.4 / -7.6	8.4 / 646.5 / -7.8					10.6 / NM / -6.7	10.0 / 71.5 / -14.3
EBIT/Interest	29.5 / (67) 6.4 / .9	18.8 / (57) 5.5 / .4	17.8 / (58) 3.5 / -.3					29.3 / (13) 2.7 / .8	32.5 / (23) 13.5 / 7.0
Net Profit + Depr., Dep., Amort./Cur. Mat. L/T/D									
Fixed/Worth	.8 / 1.4 / 8.1	.9 / 1.6 / 7.7	.8 / 1.4 / NM					.6 / 1.3 / 2.6	.8 / 1.4 / 1.8
Debt/Worth	.4 / 1.4 / 7.9	.5 / 1.3 / 7.9	.5 / 1.0 / NM					.6 / 1.1 / 2.1	.3 / .6 / 1.5
% Profit Before Taxes/Tangible Net Worth	90.0 / (64) 47.8 / 14.6	84.7 / (54) 36.3 / 5.3	56.8 / (48) 17.9 / .2					37.3 / (12) 5.9 / -.1	63.0 / (21) 34.5 / 12.9
% Profit Before Taxes/Total Assets	42.7 / 15.3 / .2	36.9 / 14.7 / -1.1	23.1 / 4.9 / -1.6					14.0 / 2.1 / -.3	48.6 / 19.9 / 6.3
Sales/Net Fixed Assets	4.4 / 2.3 / 1.1	4.1 / 2.0 / 1.2	4.2 / 2.1 / 1.3					5.9 / 2.2 / 1.2	2.3 / 1.5 / .9
Sales/Total Assets	2.2 / 1.3 / .8	1.9 / 1.3 / .8	2.0 / 1.3 / .8					2.7 / 1.2 / .7	1.6 / 1.2 / .8
% Depr., Dep., Amort./Sales	3.7 / (66) 7.3 / 11.7	4.5 / (50) 7.2 / 9.9	5.6 / (52) 7.6 / 10.6					6.2 / (13) 7.3 / 11.1	3.8 / (18) 6.5 / 8.2
% Officers', Directors' Owners' Comp/Sales	1.9 / (15) 4.6 / 7.7	1.9 / (15) 4.2 / 10.9	2.3 / (18) 4.4 / 6.9						
Net Sales ($)	6218450M	4243140M	2556439M	2719M	18218M	14106M	47978M	232819M	2240599M
Total Assets ($)	4056349M	3748134M	2501070M	2228M	15299M	14096M	29904M	244846M	2194697M

M = $ thousand   MM = $ million
See Pages 9 through 22 for Explanation of Ratios and Data

Current Data Sorted by Assets

Comparative Historical Data

						Type of Statement		
	1	6	10	8	13	Unqualified	56	51
	1	1				Reviewed	1	
3	2	2			1	Compiled		3
7	3	2		2		Tax Returns	4	8
2	3	10	26	16	15	Other	44	56
	23 (4/1-9/30/09)		111 (10/1/09-3/31/10)				4/1/05-3/31/06	4/1/06-3/31/07
0-500M	500M-2MM	2-10MM	10-50MM	50-100MM	100-250MM		ALL	ALL
12	10	21	38	24	29	NUMBER OF STATEMENTS	105	118
%	%	%	%	%	%	ASSETS	%	%
27.8	23.6	16.2	20.2	18.1	15.0	Cash & Equivalents	21.3	22.1
1.8	5.6	7.2	.8	1.7	.5	Trade Receivables (net)	1.0	1.0
1.5	1.2	1.6	.7	.7	.4	Inventory	.7	.7
4.3	13.1	2.0	2.9	1.1	.9	All Other Current	2.4	4.5
35.3	43.5	27.1	24.5	21.6	16.8	Total Current	25.5	28.3
39.1	34.1	58.6	65.7	72.0	73.7	Fixed Assets (net)	68.1	63.5
10.8	20.9	3.3	2.5	4.1	6.4	Intangibles (net)	2.5	3.9
14.7	1.5	11.0	7.2	2.4	3.1	All Other Non-Current	3.9	4.3
100.0	100.0	100.0	100.0	100.0	100.0	Total	100.0	100.0
						LIABILITIES		
8.8	.6	3.9	3.6	.0	.3	Notes Payable-Short Term	3.0	5.0
12.4	3.7	24.6	7.8	4.2	3.6	Cur. Mat.-L.T.D.	4.6	4.4
5.3	3.0	7.1	2.8	3.2	2.4	Trade Payables	3.8	4.1
.0	.5	.0	.0	.1	.0	Income Taxes Payable	.1	.0
8.5	18.3	12.4	12.3	8.4	8.5	All Other Current	10.2	11.8
35.1	26.2	48.1	26.4	16.0	14.8	Total Current	21.7	25.4
38.7	40.8	29.9	29.0	28.8	44.4	Long-Term Debt	28.8	28.1
.0	.0	.0	.0	.0	.0	Deferred Taxes	.1	.3
25.7	9.4	3.3	5.7	6.8	3.3	All Other Non-Current	2.4	1.8
.4	23.6	18.8	38.9	48.4	37.5	Net Worth	47.1	44.4
100.0	100.0	100.0	100.0	100.0	100.0	Total Liabilities & Net Worth	100.0	100.0
						INCOME DATA		
100.0	100.0	100.0	100.0	100.0	100.0	Net Sales	100.0	100.0
						Gross Profit		
96.3	87.6	82.9	75.8	77.3	74.4	Operating Expenses	70.5	72.6
3.7	12.4	17.1	24.2	22.7	25.6	Operating Profit	29.5	27.4
1.1	4.5	4.8	4.0	4.6	6.2	All Other Expenses (net)	2.8	3.6
2.7	7.9	12.3	20.3	18.1	19.4	Profit Before Taxes	26.7	23.7
						RATIOS		
3.6	6.0	1.8	2.0	2.2	1.5		2.2	2.4
1.5	1.2	.9	1.3	1.1	1.0	Current	1.3	1.2
.3	.4	.2	.7	.6	.8		.7	.8
2.7	3.4	1.7	1.7	2.0	1.5		2.0	2.1
(11) 1.6	.7	(20) .7	1.0	1.0	1.0	Quick	1.1	1.0
.3	.1	.1	.4	.5	.7		.6	.6
0 UND	0 UND	0 UND	1 499.9	1 484.6	1 451.5		0 999.8	0 999.8
0 UND	0 UND	1 521.5	1 315.3	2 217.5	2 239.2	Sales/Receivables	1 403.7	1 438.8
0 UND	0 UND	8 45.5	2 155.4	4 85.6	3 124.5		3 140.5	3 126.0
						Cost of Sales/Inventory		
						Cost of Sales/Payables		
25.1	4.7	15.9	9.1	10.0	14.2		9.9	11.9
118.4	67.4	-78.0	39.3	43.5	289.6	Sales/Working Capital	39.4	57.7
-12.5	-33.0	-5.7	-15.3	-14.7	-24.5		-26.2	-29.4
		30.6	41.6	23.6	27.8		44.4	33.1
	(19) 2.3	(31) 10.8	(21) 5.7	(25) 12.6	EBIT/Interest	(86) 17.4	(89) 11.3
		-1.0	4.2	2.0	2.2		8.0	2.9
						Net Profit + Depr., Dep., Amort./Cur. Mat. L/T/D		
.3	.2	.6	.9	.9	1.2		1.0	.9
1.9	3.8	10.8	1.5	1.7	2.1	Fixed/Worth	1.3	1.4
-.3	-6.2	-5.5	5.5	3.4	-97.0		2.4	3.6
.3	.6	.4	.4	.5	.5		.3	.3
1.7	NM	21.3	1.1	.9	1.5	Debt/Worth	.9	.9
-1.8	-4.8	-8.0	5.7	2.8	-120.7		2.1	4.1
		148.1	102.0	91.1	97.6		151.2	124.1
	(13) 38.7	(32) 42.0	(22) 49.4	(21) 56.1	% Profit Before Taxes/Tangible Net Worth	(95) 78.1	(104) 78.1
		-42.3	20.6	9.8	39.7		39.3	31.9
114.3	22.0	34.5	54.9	31.9	32.9		70.4	68.5
17.9	-1.1	7.4	20.5	19.9	18.9	% Profit Before Taxes/Total Assets	39.7	32.5
-25.4	-9.0	-7.5	6.4	1.2	4.7		18.8	6.6
131.9	29.8	6.9	3.2	2.4	1.5		3.5	4.6
25.4	8.1	2.9	1.8	1.3	1.2	Sales/Net Fixed Assets	2.1	2.1
4.0	2.0	1.2	1.2	.9	.9		1.5	1.4
11.8	4.4	2.7	1.7	1.4	1.1		2.1	2.4
6.4	1.8	1.4	1.2	1.1	.9	Sales/Total Assets	1.5	1.5
2.6	.9	.9	.8	.7	.7		1.1	1.0
.6		4.7	5.4	5.9	6.4		4.1	3.6
(10) 1.8	(19) 6.2	(35) 7.0	(20) 8.6	(12) 8.0	% Depr., Dep., Amort./Sales	(86) 5.9	(103) 5.8
5.4		7.4	8.8	11.4	10.2		7.8	8.1
						% Officers', Directors' Owners' Comp/Sales		1.7
							(13) 4.3	
								16.4
19145M	50689M	205696M	1297221M	1987548M	4232301M	Net Sales ($)	8988011M	8194227M
2391M	9546M	110687M	972629M	1588254M	4729910M	Total Assets ($)	5974141M	5669045M

M = $ thousand   MM = $ million
See Pages 9 through 22 for Explanation of Ratios and Data

Comparative Historical Data · **Current Data Sorted by Sales**

4/1/07-3/31/08 ALL	4/1/08-3/31/09 ALL	4/1/09-3/31/10 ALL	Type of Statement	0-1MM	1-3MM	3-5MM	5-10MM	10-25MM	25MM & OVER
40	36	38	Unqualified			1	4	4	29
	1	2	Reviewed			1	1		
2	3	8	Compiled	4	1		1		2
11	7	14	Tax Returns	5	3	2	2	2	
51	62	72	Other	4	4	1	6	11	46
					23 (4/1-9/30/09)		111 (10/1/09-3/31/10)		
104	109	134	**NUMBER OF STATEMENTS**	13	8	5	14	17	77
%	%	%	**ASSETS**	%	%	%	%	%	%
20.4	19.7	19.0	Cash & Equivalents	14.5			24.3	16.4	18.7
1.3	1.9	2.3	Trade Receivables (net)	11.6			2.9	.8	1.3
.5	.6	.9	Inventory	1.7			1.2	1.0	.7
3.0	2.2	2.9	All Other Current	3.8			2.0	3.4	2.0
25.2	24.4	25.1	Total Current	31.6			30.4	21.5	22.7
66.4	65.6	62.7	Fixed Assets (net)	41.5			51.9	72.8	70.6
4.0	3.2	5.9	Intangibles (net)	17.9			4.7	2.9	4.1
4.4	6.8	6.3	All Other Non-Current	8.9			13.0	2.9	2.6
100.0	100.0	100.0	Total	100.0			100.0	100.0	100.0
			LIABILITIES						
3.2	2.3	2.5	Notes Payable-Short Term	5.9			1.2	.0	2.7
4.8	3.7	9.0	Cur. Mat.-L.T.D.	13.3			18.4	23.4	4.7
3.9	4.5	3.7	Trade Payables	4.1			3.9	3.2	4.0
.0	.1	.1	Income Taxes Payable	.0			.0	.0	.0
10.4	10.6	10.9	All Other Current	4.6			10.3	9.1	12.2
22.3	21.3	26.2	Total Current	27.9			33.8	35.7	23.6
34.9	32.7	34.2	Long-Term Debt	49.1			38.3	28.4	31.9
.1	.1	.0	Deferred Taxes	.0			.0	.0	.0
4.0	5.5	7.1	All Other Non-Current	23.5			.8	2.9	6.0
38.7	40.4	32.5	Net Worth	-.5			27.1	32.9	38.5
100.0	100.0	100.0	Total Liabilites & Net Worth	100.0			100.0	100.0	100.0
			INCOME DATA						
100.0	100.0	100.0	Net Sales	100.0			100.0	100.0	100.0
			Gross Profit						
74.2	78.6	79.6	Operating Expenses	84.7			91.6	80.6	75.2
25.8	21.4	20.4	Operating Profit	15.3			8.4	19.4	24.8
4.0	4.3	4.5	All Other Expenses (net)	7.9			1.6	6.5	4.0
21.8	17.2	15.9	Profit Before Taxes	7.4			6.8	12.9	20.8
			RATIOS						
2.2	2.1	2.1		5.9			3.8	2.3	1.7
1.2	1.3	1.1	Current	.6			.9	1.4	1.0
.7	.8	.5		.3			.3	.5	.7
2.0	1.9	1.8		4.7			3.6	1.9	1.6
1.1	1.1	(132) .9	Quick	(12) 1.3			.8	1.1	.9
.6	.6	.4		.1			.2	.4	.5
0 999.8	0 768.4	0 999.8		0 UND			0 UND	0 999.8	1 437.6
1 372.5	1 260.8	1 315.3	Sales/Receivables	0 UND			0 760.7	1 389.1	1 250.7
3 112.1	4 82.2	3 120.5		5 74.1			5 77.0	2 158.9	3 110.2
			Cost of Sales/Inventory						
			Cost of Sales/Payables						
11.4	10.6	12.0		4.9			11.6	8.6	14.2
69.8	39.0	116.2	Sales/Working Capital	-41.3			-107.5	19.7	289.6
-19.0	-23.3	-15.0		-8.0			-7.9	-12.3	-18.5
27.2	28.4	31.0					10.5	23.7	37.5
(78) 9.7	(82) 10.9	(109) 5.8	EBIT/Interest				(11) 2.3	(15) 3.5	(67) 12.3
3.0	2.5	1.7					.3	1.5	2.9
			Net Profit + Depr., Dep., Amort./Cur. Mat. L/T/D						
.9	.9	1.0		.8			.3	.9	1.0
1.6	1.4	1.9	Fixed/Worth	3.1			11.2	1.9	1.7
5.3	7.4	37.7		-.3			-6.3	5.7	5.9
.4	.4	.5		.7			.3	.5	.5
1.4	1.1	1.5	Debt/Worth	-58.6			12.0	1.5	1.3
6.9	7.8	-139.1		-1.7			-7.9	5.8	6.2
148.3	107.8	96.1					69.3	68.3	102.0
(84) 72.8	(91) 58.6	(100) 45.7	% Profit Before Taxes/Tangible Net Worth				(10) 30.3	(15) 25.7	(60) 57.7
29.2	19.9	16.9					-82.8	.6	33.1
59.8	49.2	38.9		67.8			34.5	31.9	44.1
31.2	20.3	13.9	% Profit Before Taxes/Total Assets	-2.2			8.7	6.9	22.7
5.7	5.0	.5		-23.0			-3.5	.4	6.5
4.0	3.4	4.0		45.9			25.5	2.5	2.4
1.9	1.6	1.7	Sales/Net Fixed Assets	4.3			3.1	1.2	1.5
1.1	1.0	1.1		2.4			1.3	.9	1.0
2.2	1.9	2.1		4.4			3.6	1.8	1.7
1.4	1.2	1.1	Sales/Total Assets	2.0			1.6	1.0	1.1
.8	.8	.8		.9			1.1	.7	.8
3.8	4.2	4.8					2.2	6.8	5.7
(83) 6.2	(86) 6.3	(103) 6.8	% Depr., Dep., Amort./Sales	(13) 4.8			4.8	7.4	(52) 7.2
8.9	8.7	9.8					8.8	10.5	9.9
2.1	2.4	1.7							
(14) 3.1	(11) 3.8	(19) 3.8	% Officers', Directors' Owners' Comp/Sales						
7.4	5.0	5.2							
9620075M	7904068M	7792600M	Net Sales ($)	6460M	16381M	18878M	97483M	311316M	7342082M
6691547M	7057498M	7413417M	Total Assets ($)	8040M	45717M	20827M	66484M	342041M	6930308M

© RMA 2010

M = $ thousand   MM = $ million
See Pages 9 through 22 for Explanation of Ratios and Data

Current Data Sorted by Assets   Comparative Historical Data

0-500M	500M-2MM	2-10MM	10-50MM	50-100MM	100-250MM	Type of Statement	4/1/05-3/31/06 ALL	4/1/06-3/31/07 ALL
1	4	103	133	13	3	Unqualified	236	261
3	21	62	26			Reviewed	94	99
16	44	50	3			Compiled	146	141
40	41	46	3			Tax Returns	79	100
15	48	134	74	6	3	Other	278	303
	172 (4/1-9/30/09)		720 (10/1/09-3/31/10)					
75	158	395	239	19	6	NUMBER OF STATEMENTS	833	904
%	%	%	%	%	%	ASSETS	%	%
22.3	9.5	5.8	5.9	8.0		Cash & Equivalents	7.7	7.4
5.5	4.1	4.4	4.0	6.4		Trade Receivables (net)	4.8	4.8
8.4	3.2	1.5	1.3	.7		Inventory	2.5	2.1
2.5	1.8	.8	1.6	.9		All Other Current	1.4	1.5
38.7	18.6	12.5	12.7	16.0		Total Current	16.4	15.9
47.9	70.6	80.8	80.8	76.0		Fixed Assets (net)	76.9	77.6
3.6	3.4	1.6	1.2	1.9		Intangibles (net)	2.0	1.8
9.7	7.3	5.1	5.3	6.2		All Other Non-Current	4.7	4.7
100.0	100.0	100.0	100.0	100.0		Total	100.0	100.0
						LIABILITIES		
10.3	5.1	3.4	1.5	1.9		Notes Payable-Short Term	4.1	4.9
5.6	8.1	3.8	2.3	6.9		Cur. Mat.-L.T.D.	3.8	4.0
11.4	5.0	2.7	1.8	3.3		Trade Payables	3.5	3.1
.1	.3	.0	.1	.0		Income Taxes Payable	.1	.2
56.4	20.3	7.6	6.5	8.3		All Other Current	9.2	9.3
83.8	38.9	17.5	12.2	20.4		Total Current	20.7	21.5
39.9	51.4	43.0	28.8	27.0		Long-Term Debt	38.3	40.1
.0	.0	.1	.1	.0		Deferred Taxes	.1	.1
26.3	15.6	6.4	8.4	8.8		All Other Non-Current	10.3	8.0
-50.0	-5.9	33.1	50.5	43.9		Net Worth	30.5	30.3
100.0	100.0	100.0	100.0	100.0		Total Liabilties & Net Worth	100.0	100.0
						INCOME DATA		
100.0	100.0	100.0	100.0	100.0		Net Sales	100.0	100.0
						Gross Profit		
96.9	99.5	99.3	101.7	99.4		Operating Expenses	98.1	96.6
3.1	.5	.7	-1.7	.6		Operating Profit	1.9	3.4
1.7	4.3	3.9	2.1	2.4		All Other Expenses (net)	3.5	4.1
1.4	-3.8	-3.2	-3.8	-1.8		Profit Before Taxes	-1.6	-.7
						RATIOS		
1.6	1.1	1.6	2.1	1.1		Current	1.8	1.7
.6	.6	.9	1.2	1.0			.9	.9
.2	.2	.4	.7	.5			.5	.5
1.2	.9	1.4	1.6	1.1		Quick	1.4	1.4
.3	(157) .4	(394) .7	1.0	.9			(832) .7	(901) .7
.1	.1	.3	.5	.3			.3	.3
0 UND	0 UND	2 164.4	16 22.3	18 20.3		Sales/Receivables	1 590.9	1 336.8
0 UND	2 233.6	20 18.2	27 13.5	40 9.1			18 20.7	18 20.2
2 197.6	12 31.7	36 10.3	40 9.0	76 4.8			35 10.5	37 9.8
						Cost of Sales/Inventory		
						Cost of Sales/Payables		
26.2	67.9	12.5	6.4	13.1		Sales/Working Capital	10.2	10.7
-18.6	-14.2	-53.0	19.7	153.9			-108.8	-80.5
-5.4	-4.7	-6.5	-18.2	-5.9			-9.5	-8.0
3.3	2.5	1.6	1.9	4.0		EBIT/Interest	2.1	2.3
(47) .9	(131) .7	(349) .5	(205) .3	(14) .6			(682) .7	(748) 1.0
-1.2	-1.4	-.9	-1.9	-4.5			-.8	-.2
	3.4	3.2	5.5			Net Profit + Depr., Dep., Amort./Cur. Mat. L/T/D	3.7	4.8
	(13) 1.7	(26) 1.2	(26) 2.9				(59) 1.7	(64) 3.0
	.7	.5	1.2				.8	1.1
1.1	2.0	1.3	1.1	1.1		Fixed/Worth	1.2	1.2
-20.5	8.0	2.4	1.4	1.4			2.1	2.1
-.5	-2.2	9.7	2.6	5.8			8.8	7.9
3.1	1.7	.6	.3	.4		Debt/Worth	.6	.5
-6.5	9.8	1.8	.8	.7			1.7	1.5
-2.0	-3.5	10.8	2.2	5.2			11.3	9.3
108.8	19.2	3.3	2.1	5.7		% Profit Before Taxes/Tangible Net Worth	6.5	8.3
(31) 31.3	(96) -1.9	(320) -2.3	(219) -1.4	(16) -.2			(668) -.6	(723) .9
-12.5	-22.1	-12.6	-7.3	-8.3			-7.1	-6.5
18.9	5.5	1.4	1.2	2.8		% Profit Before Taxes/Total Assets	3.0	3.6
.7	-1.2	-1.3	-1.2	-.2			-.7	.1
-13.7	-8.6	-4.7	-4.0	-3.9			-4.3	-3.8
55.6	3.2	1.0	.7	.8		Sales/Net Fixed Assets	1.3	1.3
6.1	1.4	.7	.5	.5			.8	.7
2.4	.8	.5	.4	.4			.5	.5
5.8	1.8	.8	.6	.5		Sales/Total Assets	1.0	.9
2.9	1.0	.6	.4	.4			.6	.6
1.6	.7	.4	.3	.3			.4	.4
2.1	4.0	7.5	9.4	6.5		% Depr., Dep., Amort./Sales	6.5	7.0
(53) 4.2	(150) 7.6	(370) 10.3	(226) 12.2	11.2			(762) 9.4	(815) 9.7
8.4	12.0	13.3	15.7	14.5			12.7	12.7
4.3	2.5	3.3	1.7			% Officers', Directors' Owners' Comp/Sales	3.4	3.1
(20) 9.3	(37) 5.6	(57) 6.4	(23) 6.4				(133) 7.5	(155) 7.7
12.6	14.8	19.2	21.0				18.5	17.0
66093M	262711M	1253984M	2106490M	589455M	530853M	Net Sales ($)	5198458M	5102614M
19415M	191591M	2022344M	4629733M	1224101M	793269M	Total Assets ($)	6861904M	7436957M

Comparative Historical Data | **Current Data Sorted by Sales**

			Type of Statement	0-1MM	1-3MM	3-5MM	5-10MM	10-25MM	25MM & OVER
268	249	257	Unqualified	1	26	65	112	41	12
106	103	112	Reviewed	10	48	32	15	6	1
141	98	113	Compiled	33	67	7	6		
87	107	130	Tax Returns	58	57	10	4	1	
306	283	280	Other	41	106	48	57	20	8
4/1/07-3/31/08 ALL	4/1/08-3/31/09 ALL	4/1/09-3/31/10 ALL		172 (4/1-9/30/09)			720 (10/1/09-3/31/10)		
908	840	892	NUMBER OF STATEMENTS	143	304	162	194	68	21
%	%	%	ASSETS	%	%	%	%	%	%
6.8	7.5	7.9	Cash & Equivalents	9.3	8.0	7.4	6.7	8.5	10.4
4.8	4.7	4.3	Trade Receivables (net)	2.8	3.9	5.5	4.7	5.0	6.1
2.0	2.6	2.3	Inventory	2.6	3.0	1.9	1.9	1.1	2.0
1.4	1.2	1.3	All Other Current	1.2	1.0	1.6	1.3	3.0	1.1
14.9	16.0	15.9	Total Current	15.9	15.9	16.4	14.6	17.6	19.6
78.8	77.3	76.1	Fixed Assets (net)	71.5	75.9	78.1	80.0	72.2	73.3
1.4	1.3	2.0	Intangibles (net)	4.3	2.4	.9	.5	1.8	2.8
4.9	5.5	6.0	All Other Non-Current	8.3	5.8	4.6	4.9	8.3	4.3
100.0	100.0	100.0	Total	100.0	100.0	100.0	100.0	100.0	100.0
			LIABILITIES						
4.1	4.2	3.7	Notes Payable-Short Term	5.4	4.7	3.3	2.3	1.4	3.2
4.4	3.8	4.3	Cur. Mat.-L.T.D.	5.3	5.8	2.8	3.3	1.5	7.0
3.0	3.4	3.6	Trade Payables	3.7	4.5	3.2	2.6	2.7	5.4
.1	.1	.1	Income Taxes Payable	.1	.0	.1	.0	.8	.0
10.4	11.0	13.7	All Other Current	31.5	12.4	10.9	7.0	8.5	10.9
22.0	22.4	25.5	Total Current	46.1	27.4	20.2	15.3	15.0	26.5
40.5	40.2	40.0	Long-Term Debt	51.6	47.7	33.7	30.3	21.0	50.0
.1	.1	.1	Deferred Taxes	.1	.0	.1	.0	.3	.0
9.7	10.0	10.3	All Other Non-Current	16.4	12.6	6.2	7.2	5.9	8.8
27.7	27.3	24.2	Net Worth	-14.1	12.3	39.8	47.2	57.7	14.6
100.0	100.0	100.0	Total Liabilties & Net Worth	100.0	100.0	100.0	100.0	100.0	100.0
			INCOME DATA						
100.0	100.0	100.0	Net Sales	100.0	100.0	100.0	100.0	100.0	100.0
			Gross Profit						
97.2	99.8	99.8	Operating Expenses	97.4	98.5	101.7	102.1	100.1	96.4
2.8	.2	.2	Operating Profit	2.6	1.5	-1.7	-2.1	-.1	3.6
4.3	3.6	3.3	All Other Expenses (net)	6.5	4.9	.8	1.1	1.3	2.0
-1.4	-3.3	-3.0	Profit Before Taxes	-4.0	-3.4	-2.6	-3.2	-1.4	1.6
			RATIOS						
1.7	1.7	1.7		.9	1.5	1.9	2.0	2.1	1.5
.9	1.0	.9	Current	.4	.7	1.1	1.1	1.2	1.0
.4	.5	.4		.1	.3	.6	.7	.7	.3
1.3	1.4	1.4		.8	1.2	1.5	1.7	1.6	1.3
(907) .7	(839) .7	(890) .7	Quick	(142) .2	(303) .5	.9	.9	1.0	.8
.3	.3	.2		.1	.1	.5	.5	.5	.2
1 257.5	2 186.5	1 391.6		0 UND	0 UND	12 31.4	16 22.3	17 21.6	10 37.5
19 18.9	19 19.0	17 21.1	Sales/Receivables	0 UND	6 63.6	29 12.7	27 13.3	25 14.4	22 16.7
37 9.9	35 10.4	35 10.4		5 67.6	29 12.6	41 9.0	40 9.0	40 9.1	43 8.5
			Cost of Sales/Inventory						
			Cost of Sales/Payables						
11.8	11.2	11.6		-321.0	16.6	9.2	6.9	5.9	12.5
-52.4	-160.8	-59.3	Sales/Working Capital	-9.5	-26.5	57.3	42.3	24.2	-59.4
-6.9	-7.4	-6.9		-3.5	-4.8	-11.2	-17.8	-19.6	-4.9
2.1	1.7	1.9		1.7	1.7	1.9	1.9	3.2	3.2
(763) .9	(700) .5	(752) .5	EBIT/Interest	(102) .3	(255) .6	(150) .5	(173) .5	(52) .1	(20) 1.7
-.4	-.9	-1.2		-1.2	-.7	-1.5	-1.8	-4.8	.3
3.9	3.9	3.5	Net Profit + Depr., Dep.,	3.8	3.0	3.1	3.3		
(67) 2.4	(66) 2.2	(69) 1.5	Amort./Cur. Mat. L/T/D	(10) 1.1	(19) 1.3	(11) 1.4	(17) 1.7		
.7	.4	.6		.3	.0	.7	.9		
1.3	1.2	1.2		1.9	1.7	1.1	1.1	1.0	1.3
2.1	2.1	2.2	Fixed/Worth	17.0	4.3	1.7	1.5	1.3	2.2
9.4	9.7	28.6		-1.6	-7.5	4.2	2.7	1.9	NM
.6	.6	.5		1.5	1.0	.4	.3	.2	.6
1.6	1.6	1.8	Debt/Worth	25.4	4.5	1.1	.8	.5	3.4
11.3	12.6	54.5		-3.0	-9.1	4.4	2.4	1.3	NM
6.6	4.8	4.5	% Profit Before Taxes/Tangible	18.0	6.3	2.0	2.2	5.0	20.1
(729) .0	(670) -1.4	(688) -1.5	Net Worth	(83) -1.8	(203) -2.7	(145) -2.2	(178) -1.1	(63) -1.1	(16) 4.8
-7.7	-10.5	-10.9		-15.8	-14.3	-9.6	-9.0	-6.9	-2.6
2.7	2.1	2.0	% Profit Before Taxes/Total	3.4	2.4	1.3	1.4	3.6	4.7
-.5	-1.2	-1.2	Assets	-1.4	-1.5	-1.2	-.8	-1.0	1.2
-4.1	-5.2	-4.9		-8.3	-5.7	-4.7	-4.2	-4.2	-2.1
1.2	1.2	1.3		2.9	1.6	1.1	.9	1.0	1.7
.7	.7	.7	Sales/Net Fixed Assets	1.0	.8	.7	.6	.6	.8
.5	.5	.5		.4	.5	.5	.5	.5	.6
.9	.9	.9		1.6	1.0	.8	.7	.7	1.2
.6	.6	.6	Sales/Total Assets	.7	.6	.6	.5	.5	.6
.4	.4	.4		.4	.4	.5	.4	.4	.4
6.9	6.6	6.9		5.0	6.4	6.9	8.8	8.5	5.3
(823) 9.6	(772) 9.6	(822) 10.3	% Depr., Dep., Amort./Sales	(120) 10.1	(282) 9.7	(154) 10.2	(183) 11.3	(64) 11.6	(19) 7.3
12.8	12.6	13.9		15.8	13.4	12.6	14.5	14.4	10.1
3.1	3.3	2.8	% Officers', Directors'	4.2	3.4	2.8	1.7		
(138) 6.7	(134) 7.4	(139) 6.7	Owners' Comp/Sales	(34) 9.0	(55) 6.4	(21) 7.5	(20) 2.8		
14.5	17.0	16.0		15.8	12.0	32.5	17.4		
5113414M	4689497M	4809586M	Net Sales ($)	89275M	568224M	643741M	1332941M	1018635M	1156770M
7928848M	8729475M	8880453M	Total Assets ($)	180988M	1098238M	1165791M	2782693M	2104015M	1548728M

M = $ thousand   MM = $ million

See Pages 9 through 22 for Explanation of Ratios and Data

Current Data Sorted by Assets   **Comparative Historical Data**

0-500M	500M-2MM	2-10MM	10-50MM	50-100MM	100-250MM	Type of Statement	4/1/05-3/31/06 ALL	4/1/06-3/31/07 ALL
		4	14	4		Unqualified	15	13
	2	4	5	1		Reviewed	7	8
1	2	4				Compiled	4	5
				4		Tax Returns	4	
	2	2	6	5	3	Other	10	13
	39 (4/1-9/30/09)		18 (10/1/09-3/31/10)					
1	4	14	25	10	3	**NUMBER OF STATEMENTS**	40	39
%	%	%	%	%	%	**ASSETS**	%	%
		14.0	7.6	6.5		Cash & Equivalents	8.6	7.5
		.6	1.6	2.5		Trade Receivables (net)	1.3	1.3
		2.1	1.8	1.3		Inventory	2.3	4.0
		5.5	2.2	1.9		All Other Current	2.8	3.4
		22.2	13.2	12.2		Total Current	15.1	16.3
		63.0	76.1	72.4		Fixed Assets (net)	72.4	74.2
		1.7	3.7	3.4		Intangibles (net)	2.4	1.5
		13.1	7.1	12.0		All Other Non-Current	10.1	8.0
		100.0	100.0	100.0		Total	100.0	100.0
						LIABILITIES		
		3.9	5.0	.5		Notes Payable-Short Term	5.3	8.1
		6.4	2.9	1.6		Cur. Mat.-L.T.D.	6.8	3.5
		3.9	3.2	2.6		Trade Payables	5.2	7.1
		.3	.1	.2		Income Taxes Payable	.2	.3
		12.9	13.4	23.6		All Other Current	7.9	9.2
		27.3	24.5	28.4		Total Current	25.4	28.3
		32.0	18.1	12.8		Long-Term Debt	31.9	25.7
		1.0	3.0	2.0		Deferred Taxes	2.9	2.2
		5.5	6.6	4.9		All Other Non-Current	9.4	8.6
		34.2	47.8	52.0		Net Worth	30.4	35.1
		100.0	100.0	100.0		Total Liabilities & Net Worth	100.0	100.0
						INCOME DATA		
		100.0	100.0	100.0		Net Sales	100.0	100.0
						Gross Profit		
		82.6	95.2	95.4		Operating Expenses	90.9	94.2
		17.4	4.8	4.6		Operating Profit	9.1	5.8
		3.1	2.0	2.3		All Other Expenses (net)	6.6	.5
		14.3	2.7	2.2		Profit Before Taxes	2.5	5.3
						RATIOS		
		1.4	1.1	1.5			1.2	.9
		.5	.6	.7		Current	.7	.4
		.2	.2	.2			.4	.2
		.7	.8	1.1			.8	.6
		.3	.3	.5		Quick	.4	.2
		.1	.1	.1			.1	.1
		0 UND	1 296.3	5 77.0			1 721.8	1 671.9
		0 915.5	3 112.7	7 49.5		Sales/Receivables	3 142.3	3 112.0
		4 83.9	8 44.1	21 17.7			10 34.8	7 48.7
						Cost of Sales/Inventory		
						Cost of Sales/Payables		
		36.5	112.4	21.7			44.7	-113.4
		-11.1	-9.4	-15.0		Sales/Working Capital	-15.4	-9.9
		-4.5	-3.6	-2.2			-6.4	-4.1
		29.1	10.8	38.6			6.5	12.7
		(13) 2.9	2.1	2.6		EBIT/Interest	(35) 2.5	(36) 4.3
		1.2	.7	-2.0			.0	.2
						Net Profit + Depr., Dep.,	11.0	14.7
						Amort./Cur. Mat. L/T/D	(17) 2.0	(10) 2.0
							.9	.7
		.8	1.1	1.0			1.5	1.1
		2.0	1.6	1.2		Fixed/Worth	1.9	1.9
		4.0	2.3	-265.4			8.9	3.5
		.8	.7	.2			.9	.3
		1.6	1.3	.7		Debt/Worth	1.7	1.5
		5.7	2.0	-308.8			13.4	6.6
		67.3	12.8			% Profit Before Taxes/Tangible	27.9	33.5
		(12) 18.9	(23) 3.6			Net Worth	(33) 5.8	(34) 9.9
		.4	-1.2				-5.0	-1.1
		23.3	7.8	9.1		% Profit Before Taxes/Total	10.4	13.2
		5.9	1.4	4.3		Assets	3.0	4.7
		.8	-.9	-2.8			-3.1	-3.4
		5.2	1.5	1.3			1.9	2.4
		1.5	1.0	1.2		Sales/Net Fixed Assets	1.0	1.2
		1.0	.7	.8			.7	.9
		1.6	1.1	1.0			1.2	1.4
		1.2	.8	.8		Sales/Total Assets	.7	.9
		.9	.6	.7			.6	.7
		6.1	6.9				6.2	5.7
		(13) 9.7	(24) 12.4			% Depr., Dep., Amort./Sales	(36) 9.6	(32) 9.0
		14.0	14.6				11.6	12.2
								1.6
						% Officers', Directors'		(11) 4.6
						Owners' Comp/Sales		9.5
1114M	11093M	102270M	547633M	544056M	209287M	Net Sales ($)	1067002M	1044269M
226M	4413M	73822M	667709M	685800M	463898M	Total Assets ($)	1499732M	1429106M

© RMA 2010

M = $ thousand   MM = $ million
See Pages 9 through 22 for Explanation of Ratios and Data

Comparative Historical Data / Current Data Sorted by Sales

4/1/07-3/31/08 ALL	4/1/08-3/31/09 ALL	4/1/09-3/31/10 ALL	Type of Statement	0-1MM	1-3MM	3-5MM	5-10MM	10-25MM	25MM & OVER
20	16	22	Unqualified			1	4	12	5
5	9	12	Reviewed		2	2	2	4	2
5	4	7	Compiled		4		2	1	
1	1		Tax Returns						
18	23	16	Other		1		1	4	10
					39 (4/1-9/30/09)		18 (10/1/09-3/31/10)		
49	53	57	NUMBER OF STATEMENTS		7	3	9	21	17
%	%	%	**ASSETS**	%	%	%	%	%	%
7.8	7.2	8.8	Cash & Equivalents	DATA NOT AVAILABLE				6.0	10.1
1.6	1.9	1.4	Trade Receivables (net)					1.7	2.0
2.9	4.1	1.7	Inventory					2.9	1.0
3.8	2.4	3.2	All Other Current					4.3	3.5
16.2	15.6	15.1	Total Current					15.0	16.6
69.7	73.4	72.1	Fixed Assets (net)					74.5	69.8
1.8	2.8	3.2	Intangibles (net)					2.3	4.7
12.3	8.2	9.6	All Other Non-Current					8.2	8.9
100.0	100.0	100.0	Total					100.0	100.0
			LIABILITIES						
4.3	3.1	4.8	Notes Payable-Short Term					5.5	.7
3.7	3.1	4.5	Cur. Mat.-L.T.D.					3.0	4.6
5.8	4.9	4.3	Trade Payables					3.7	3.2
.2	.4	.2	Income Taxes Payable					.2	.3
12.5	11.7	13.6	All Other Current					11.8	20.4
26.5	23.2	27.4	Total Current					24.2	29.2
25.0	26.0	20.6	Long-Term Debt					17.1	10.8
1.3	1.9	1.9	Deferred Taxes					2.2	3.0
9.1	8.0	7.1	All Other Non-Current					6.1	10.3
38.2	40.8	42.9	Net Worth					50.4	46.8
100.0	100.0	100.0	Total Liabilties & Net Worth					100.0	100.0
			INCOME DATA						
100.0	100.0	100.0	Net Sales					100.0	100.0
			Gross Profit						
91.9	89.2	92.1	Operating Expenses					95.3	92.5
8.1	10.8	7.9	Operating Profit					4.7	7.5
1.7	3.5	3.0	All Other Expenses (net)					1.8	4.1
6.3	7.3	4.9	Profit Before Taxes					2.9	3.3
			RATIOS						
1.0	1.0	1.2	Current					1.1	1.6
.4	.6	.6						.7	.6
.2	.2	.2						.2	.3
.5	.7	.8	Quick					.8	1.1
.2	.3	.3						.3	.4
.1	.1	.1						.1	.1
1 583.1	0 761.2	0 915.5	Sales/Receivables					1 570.5	3 136.4
4 103.4	5 71.4	4 87.6						6 65.6	6 64.0
11 33.3	10 36.3	8 44.0						10 38.1	17 20.9
			Cost of Sales/Inventory						
			Cost of Sales/Payables						
120.7	NM	50.1	Sales/Working Capital					58.9	19.3
-7.9	-9.7	-11.0						-11.0	-12.9
-4.3	-4.9	-3.8						-3.8	-3.2
5.8	22.8	11.2	EBIT/Interest					8.5	23.6
(47) 1.8	(50) 4.2	(54) 2.2						1.3	(16) 5.7
.1	1.0	.6						.1	2.1
6.3	6.4	9.1	Net Profit + Depr., Dep., Amort./Cur. Mat. L/T/D						
(21) 2.8	(18) 2.9	(19) 4.4							
1.4	1.5	2.0							
1.2	1.2	1.1	Fixed/Worth					1.0	1.1
1.8	1.8	1.7						1.5	1.6
3.4	3.1	3.8						2.3	NM
.6	.8	.6	Debt/Worth					.6	.6
1.4	1.3	1.3						1.3	.9
5.2	3.3	4.3						1.8	NM
22.1	31.8	22.1	% Profit Before Taxes/Tangible Net Worth					19.1	15.4
(43) 9.4	(46) 18.6	(47) 6.6						(20) .9	(13) 9.9
-1.5	4.9	-1.2						-3.4	4.1
10.6	14.8	9.3	% Profit Before Taxes/Total Assets					9.8	8.3
3.6	6.0	3.3						.7	5.3
-1.4	-.2	-1.1						-1.8	1.4
1.9	1.8	2.0	Sales/Net Fixed Assets					1.5	1.7
1.3	1.3	1.2						1.0	1.2
.9	.8	.8						.6	.9
1.3	1.3	1.3	Sales/Total Assets					1.1	1.1
.9	.9	.9						.8	.9
.7	.6	.7						.4	.8
5.5	6.3	6.7	% Depr., Dep., Amort./Sales					6.2	6.9
(46) 10.1	(48) 9.6	(53) 10.0						(19) 12.7	(15) 8.8
12.3	13.1	13.4						16.5	12.3
			% Officers', Directors' Owners' Comp/Sales						
1381878M	1762040M	1415453M	Net Sales ($)		13691M	12257M	64353M	365944M	959208M
1508627M	2187596M	1895868M	Total Assets ($)		12870M	21092M	72316M	567863M	1221727M

M = $ thousand MM = $ million

See Pages 9 through 22 for Explanation of Ratios and Data

Current Data Sorted by Assets   Comparative Historical Data

	0-500M	500M-2MM	2-10MM	10-50MM	50-100MM	100-250MM		4/1/05-3/31/06 ALL	4/1/06-3/31/07 ALL
Type of Statement									
Unqualified	1		2	7				5	9
Reviewed		7	18	6	1			17	26
Compiled		11	12	2				30	34
Tax Returns	5	18	15	1				29	35
Other	5	22	25	14	2	1		53	55
		12 (4/1-9/30/09)		163 (10/1/09-3/31/10)					
NUMBER OF STATEMENTS	11	58	72	30	3	1		134	159
	%	%	%	%	%	%		%	%
ASSETS									
Cash & Equivalents	18.3	10.8	8.3	3.7				7.3	9.0
Trade Receivables (net)	6.6	7.4	4.1	3.3				6.7	6.9
Inventory	24.7	14.6	13.4	3.9				17.2	12.8
All Other Current	2.3	4.6	1.5	1.0				2.6	1.7
Total Current	52.0	37.4	27.3	11.9				33.9	30.3
Fixed Assets (net)	27.8	54.6	60.2	63.9				54.3	56.8
Intangibles (net)	5.2	2.2	5.4	12.3				5.4	5.5
All Other Non-Current	14.8	5.7	7.1	11.9				6.4	7.4
Total	100.0	100.0	100.0	100.0				100.0	100.0
LIABILITIES									
Notes Payable-Short Term	8.9	6.3	8.2	2.7				8.8	7.4
Cur. Mat.-L.T.D.	2.8	4.2	5.2	5.0				3.6	5.3
Trade Payables	7.8	3.1	2.9	3.5				3.9	3.7
Income Taxes Payable	.1	.0	.1					.6	.1
All Other Current	43.9	9.0	10.8	4.7				9.3	9.3
Total Current	63.5	22.6	27.1	15.8				26.2	25.8
Long-Term Debt	35.7	56.6	45.5	61.0				52.1	47.3
Deferred Taxes	.0	.0	.3	.3				.1	.1
All Other Non-Current	55.1	16.4	14.1	3.9				8.8	7.4
Net Worth	-54.3	4.4	13.0	19.0				12.8	19.5
Total Liabilities & Net Worth	100.0	100.0	100.0	100.0				100.0	100.0
INCOME DATA									
Net Sales	100.0	100.0	100.0	100.0				100.0	100.0
Gross Profit									
Operating Expenses	101.0	86.3	87.7	92.3				88.1	86.6
Operating Profit	-1.0	13.7	12.3	7.7				11.9	13.4
All Other Expenses (net)	.2	6.4	8.7	11.6				7.1	7.7
Profit Before Taxes	-1.2	7.4	3.6	-3.9				4.9	5.8
RATIOS									
Current	1.7	4.9	1.9	1.9				3.1	2.8
	.9	1.8	1.1	.9				1.3	1.3
	.7	.8	.5	.4				.9	.7
Quick	1.2	2.8	1.4	1.4				1.9	2.1
	.6	.8	(71) .4	.5				.6	.7
	.1	.2	.1	.2				.2	.2
Sales/Receivables	0 UND	0 UND	4 81.9	10 35.7				3 130.5	4 99.0
	2 242.0	16 23.5	16 22.4	24 15.0				12 31.4	16 22.2
	11 33.1	29 12.6	36 10.2	34 10.8				34 10.7	40 9.1
Cost of Sales/Inventory									
Cost of Sales/Payables									
Sales/Working Capital	19.7	3.7	4.9	7.8				4.9	6.1
	-76.0	9.1	38.8	NM				14.2	26.7
	-18.6	-33.6	-4.7	-2.9				-47.5	-13.9
EBIT/Interest		4.2	3.3	2.2				4.0	4.3
		(48) 2.0	(55) 1.4	(21) 1.0				(111) 1.8	(126) 1.5
		1.0	.5	-1.5					.8
Net Profit + Depr., Dep., Amort./Cur. Mat. L/T/D								3.0	3.5
								(19) 1.4	(11) .9
								.6	.2
Fixed/Worth	1.6	1.0	.9	1.3				1.0	1.0
	-.5	8.2	3.2	4.7				4.5	3.4
	-.2	-4.3	-5.4	-2.7				-5.8	-6.4
Debt/Worth	1.9	2.3	.9	.6				1.6	1.2
	-3.4	9.9	5.3	5.5				6.0	4.6
	-1.7	-8.6	-7.2	-3.8				-8.1	-11.7
% Profit Before Taxes/Tangible Net Worth		55.4	15.8	12.9				46.1	36.4
		(36) 19.7	(46) 4.8	(18) -1.1				(87) 21.6	(111) 18.0
		1.0	-4.3	-17.1				1.3	.9
% Profit Before Taxes/Total Assets	18.9	10.8	5.4	3.2				8.9	9.2
	.9	4.3	1.8	.2				3.8	3.2
	-13.1	.3	-1.5	-3.8				-.1	-.6
Sales/Net Fixed Assets	63.8	5.2	2.2	1.3				5.6	4.3
	13.3	2.3	.8	.6				1.5	1.5
	8.9	.8	.5	.3				.6	.6
Sales/Total Assets	4.7	1.7	.9	.7				1.5	1.5
	3.2	.9	.5	.4				.9	.9
	1.8	.6	.4	.2				.5	.4
% Depr., Dep., Amort./Sales		2.3	5.1	7.5				2.1	3.3
		(49) 5.7	(60) 7.9	(29) 14.1				(127) 6.9	(145) 7.4
		10.2	13.9	20.6				13.7	12.1
% Officers', Directors', Owners' Comp/Sales		3.2	1.6					1.5	2.3
		(18) 5.1	(17) 3.0					(36) 3.5	(47) 3.9
		10.1	5.6					5.9	10.2
Net Sales ($)	7941M	72668M	242496M	227634M	83227M	130970M		406439M	830125M
Total Assets ($)	2423M	69206M	350521M	510519M	203410M	119767M		537772M	1026866M

© RMA 2010

M = $ thousand   MM = $ million
See Pages 9 through 22 for Explanation of Ratios and Data

Comparative Historical Data   Current Data Sorted by Sales

Type of Statement	4/1/07-3/31/08 ALL	4/1/08-3/31/09 ALL	4/1/09-3/31/10 ALL		0-1MM	1-3MM	3-5MM	5-10MM	10-25MM	25MM & OVER
Unqualified	13	10	9				2	5	2	
Reviewed	19	14	33		4	18	4	2	5	
Compiled	24	25	25		4	12	4	3	2	
Tax Returns	46	47	39		18	17	4			
Other	58	74	69		21	22	13	8	3	2
				12 (4/1-9/30/09)			163 (10/1/09-3/31/10)			
NUMBER OF STATEMENTS	160	170	175		47	69	27	18	12	2
ASSETS	%	%	%		%	%	%	%	%	%
Cash & Equivalents	9.4	8.8	8.9		9.9	7.8	12.3	-4.4	10.2	
Trade Receivables (net)	6.1	6.2	5.2		3.6	6.3	6.8	3.2	4.7	
Inventory	12.4	13.8	12.9		9.7	15.7	11.8	11.0	12.2	
All Other Current	2.1	2.4	2.5		4.2	2.2	.7	2.6	1.6	
Total Current	29.9	31.2	29.4		27.3	32.0	31.5	21.2	28.7	
Fixed Assets (net)	55.7	55.9	57.2		59.7	54.7	58.4	66.0	46.5	
Intangibles (net)	5.5	4.7	5.5		5.1	4.9	6.7	5.5	7.7	
All Other Non-Current	8.8	8.2	7.9		7.8	8.4	3.4	7.2	17.1	
Total	100.0	100.0	100.0		100.0	100.0	100.0	100.0	100.0	
LIABILITIES										
Notes Payable-Short Term	8.1	7.1	6.6		4.6	8.5	1.6	7.3	12.8	
Cur. Mat.-L.T.D.	5.8	5.3	4.9		2.5	6.5	1.1	5.7	13.1	
Trade Payables	3.3	3.3	3.4		3.5	3.4	1.5	4.3	5.5	
Income Taxes Payable	.1	.1	.1		.0	.0	.0	.4	.2	
All Other Current	10.6	8.6	11.2		12.4	14.1	6.7	7.3	5.6	
Total Current	27.9	24.4	26.2		23.1	32.6	11.0	25.0	37.2	
Long-Term Debt	50.4	50.3	51.4		63.8	45.1	39.7	55.8	59.4	
Deferred Taxes	.1	.1	.2		.0	.2	.0	.5	.7	
All Other Non-Current	7.0	8.6	15.4		22.6	18.7	10.4	.9	3.4	
Net Worth	14.6	16.6	6.8		-9.4	3.4	38.9	17.8	-.8	
Total Liabilities & Net Worth	100.0	100.0	100.0		100.0	100.0	100.0	100.0	100.0	
INCOME DATA										
Net Sales	100.0	100.0	100.0		100.0	100.0	100.0	100.0	100.0	
Gross Profit										
Operating Expenses	86.4	86.3	88.9		84.1	89.8	91.8	90.5	92.9	
Operating Profit	13.6	13.7	11.1		15.9	10.2	8.2	9.5	7.1	
All Other Expenses (net)	8.4	7.7	8.2		12.8	6.9	4.8	8.9	4.8	
Profit Before Taxes	5.3	6.0	3.0		3.2	3.3	3.5	.6	2.3	
RATIOS										
Current	2.4	3.7	2.8		3.9	1.8	5.4	1.7	2.2	
	1.1	1.4	1.2		1.3	1.1	3.2	1.1	.6	
	.6	.7	.5		.6	.4	1.4	.5	.3	
Quick	1.7	2.6	1.7		1.8	1.1	3.9	1.2	1.1	
	.6	.7 (174)	.5		(46) .5	.3	1.7	.3	.2	
	.2	.2	.2		.1	.1	.7	.1	.1	
Sales/Receivables	3 113.5	3 132.4	4 83.2		0 UND	7 53.7	12 30.1	8 46.5	4 91.9	
	13 28.7	19 19.2	16 22.8		4 82.8	19 19.6	29 12.7	15 23.7	15 24.1	
	28 12.9	33 11.1	32 11.3		24 14.9	34 10.8	41 8.9	20 18.6	32 11.4	
Cost of Sales/Inventory										
Cost of Sales/Payables										
Sales/Working Capital	6.2	4.8	5.4		5.2	7.7	2.4	13.4	8.6	
	38.6	16.8	28.5		32.1	42.2	5.5	117.1	-17.1	
	-9.3	-16.2	-6.9		-9.9	-3.1	11.7	-6.8	-2.7	
EBIT/Interest	5.3	3.7	3.6		2.6	4.2	14.1	2.3	3.1	
	(125) 1.7	(143) 1.8	(132) 1.5		(30) 1.6	(55) 1.5	(22) 1.1	(13) 1.4	(10) 2.2	
	1.0	.8	.5		.1	.8	.1	-.5	-.1	
Net Profit + Depr., Dep., Amort./Cur. Mat. L/T/D										
Fixed/Worth	1.2	.9	1.2		2.6	1.2	.9	1.2	.8	
	5.9	3.2	4.8		-66.4	11.5	1.6	2.7	3.0	
	-6.4	-5.4	-3.9		-1.5	-4.7	63.6	-6.9	-1.7	
Debt/Worth	1.4	1.0	.9		2.9	1.5	.5	.5	1.2	
	8.3	4.9	8.0		-73.7	14.4	1.6	5.2	3.9	
	-9.9	-10.2	-6.5		-3.6	-9.8	73.9	-8.7	-3.0	
% Profit Before Taxes/Tangible Net Worth	36.2	33.0	25.6		26.0	31.1	30.2	13.1		
	(105) 13.3	(119) 12.9	(106) 6.5		(23) 7.6	(40) 8.1	(21) .2	(12) 4.4		
	-2.3	1.9	-3.9		-1.0	1.0	-10.6	-4.5		
% Profit Before Taxes/Total Assets	8.8	7.6	6.2		6.2	5.8	15.0	3.7	6.6	
	2.2	2.7	1.8		1.1	2.0	1.3	1.9	2.6	
	-.8	-.7	-2.0		-2.8	-1.1	-3.6	-1.3	-4.4	
Sales/Net Fixed Assets	6.1	4.3	3.1		2.8	3.3	2.7	2.5	7.7	
	1.6	1.4	1.1		.8	1.3	1.0	.8	2.1	
	.5	.6	.5		.3	.6	.5	.4	1.3	
Sales/Total Assets	1.5	1.3	1.2		1.0	1.4	1.2	1.0	1.5	
	.8	.7	.7		.5	.7	.5	.6	1.2	
	.3	.4	.4		.2	.4	.4	.4	.7	
% Depr., Dep., Amort./Sales	2.7	3.1	3.8		3.8	3.0	5.2	5.1	2.6	
	(137) 6.3	(143) 6.3	(148) 7.7		(32) 10.2	(62) 6.7	(24) 8.2	(16) 15.2	5.4	
	12.2	11.3	14.9		19.8	10.8	14.5	27.3	12.0	
% Officers', Directors' Owners' Comp/Sales	2.0	2.4	2.2		4.2	1.7				
	(52) 3.6	(51) 4.9	(50) 5.2		(12) 10.3	(17) 3.5				
	8.2	8.9	9.2		13.7	7.0				
Net Sales ($)	1721111M	735460M	764936M		29023M	123306M	105951M	127992M	183799M	194865M
Total Assets ($)	1251357M	897491M	1255846M		81442M	246708M	212567M	279775M	228922M	206432M

M = $ thousand   MM = $ million
See Pages 9 through 22 for Explanation of Ratios and Data

Current Data Sorted by Assets   Comparative Historical Data

Type of Statement	0-500M	500M-2MM	2-10MM	10-50MM	50-100MM	100-250MM		4/1/05-3/31/06 ALL	4/1/06-3/31/07 ALL
Unqualified		2	24	30	13	6		68	70
Reviewed	1	7	26	13	2			21	46
Compiled	16	25	18	6				59	62
Tax Returns	61	49	24	2				75	103
Other	35	38	63	43	8	6		139	167
	72 (4/1-9/30/09)			446 (10/1/09-3/31/10)					
NUMBER OF STATEMENTS	113	121	155	94	23	12		362	448
ASSETS	%	%	%	%	%	%		%	%
Cash & Equivalents	20.2	11.3	8.0	5.9	7.2	6.8		12.9	10.8
Trade Receivables (net)	2.1	2.6	4.1	3.4	4.9	1.5		4.7	4.2
Inventory	4.1	1.2	1.6	.4	1.3	.2		2.1	1.7
All Other Current	6.0	2.4	2.2	2.0	3.6	2.0		3.0	2.0
Total Current	32.4	17.5	15.9	11.7	16.9	10.5		22.7	18.8
Fixed Assets (net)	52.8	68.5	71.3	76.2	61.4	59.8		63.5	66.3
Intangibles (net)	6.5	6.4	4.4	4.2	11.5	14.6		5.4	5.2
All Other Non-Current	8.3	7.6	8.5	7.9	10.2	15.0		8.5	9.8
Total	100.0	100.0	100.0	100.0	100.0	100.0		100.0	100.0
LIABILITIES									
Notes Payable-Short Term	17.6	5.7	2.8	2.7	2.4	.1		4.9	5.0
Cur. Mat.-L.T.D.	6.1	5.6	5.6	3.9	4.9	3.5		3.8	4.2
Trade Payables	5.8	5.3	3.1	2.6	4.5	1.5		4.4	3.7
Income Taxes Payable	.0	.2	.0	.1	.0	.0		.1	.0
All Other Current	19.9	7.2	8.4	5.5	8.3	6.4		11.4	12.3
Total Current	49.5	24.0	19.9	14.7	20.0	11.6		24.7	25.3
Long-Term Debt	35.4	46.2	44.5	45.2	34.8	34.6		38.2	40.8
Deferred Taxes	.0	.0	.0	.0	.6	.7		.1	.1
All Other Non-Current	15.9	16.0	6.9	8.2	9.5	9.1		7.3	9.9
Net Worth	-.7	13.8	28.6	31.8	35.0	44.1		29.8	23.8
Total Liabilities & Net Worth	100.0	100.0	100.0	100.0	100.0	100.0		100.0	100.0
INCOME DATA									
Net Sales	100.0	100.0	100.0	100.0	100.0	100.0		100.0	100.0
Gross Profit									
Operating Expenses	93.7	89.5	91.3	92.2	91.9	86.0		91.3	90.2
Operating Profit	6.3	10.5	8.7	7.8	8.1	14.0		8.7	9.8
All Other Expenses (net)	1.9	4.6	5.8	4.5	4.3	3.1		3.9	4.9
Profit Before Taxes	4.4	5.9	2.9	3.3	3.8	10.9		4.8	4.8
RATIOS									
Current	2.7	2.5	1.9	2.0	1.4	1.7		2.4	2.0
	.8	1.0	.8	.8	.6	.9		.9	.9
	.2	.2	.3	.3	.3	.3		.4	.3
Quick	2.5	2.0	1.5	1.7	1.1	1.3		2.0	1.7
	(110) .3	.8	.7	.6	.5	.8		(361) .7	(447) .7
	.1	.1	.2	.2	.2	.2		.3	.2
Sales/Receivables	0 UND	0 UND	0 999.8	1 598.9	2 240.6	1 267.2		0 UND	0 UND
	0 UND	0 UND	7 55.0	8 47.2	8 44.9	7 54.9		2 152.3	3 131.4
	0 UND	5 66.8	22 16.7	20 17.9	20 18.1	27 13.6		16 22.6	17 21.6
Cost of Sales/Inventory									
Cost of Sales/Payables									
Sales/Working Capital	23.7	11.4	11.4	10.6	19.1	8.0		11.3	12.6
	-57.7	UND	-39.3	-32.6	-12.0	NM		-221.3	-80.3
	-6.6	-8.2	-6.7	-6.5	-5.9	-10.4		-10.2	-8.5
EBIT/Interest	9.8	5.7	4.2	3.6	4.3	7.0		5.5	6.2
	(78) 1.5	(103) 2.0	(137) 1.5	(81) 1.9	(22) 2.1	(10) 2.9		(282) 2.4	(361) 2.1
	-2.1	.4	.4	.4	.2	-.1		.7	.7
Net Profit + Depr., Dep., Amort./Cur. Mat. L/T/D			6.1	6.8				6.8	10.3
		(15) 1.5		(11) 2.3				(27) 2.3	(35) 3.0
			.8	.1				1.3	1.1
Fixed/Worth	.6	1.5	1.3	1.4	1.4	.9		1.0	1.2
	3.0	5.1	2.9	2.4	3.0	1.9		2.1	2.6
	-1.4	-6.0	31.3	7.1	4.9	10.2		37.9	UND
Debt/Worth	.5	1.1	.8	.8	1.4	.7		.7	.8
	5.5	6.9	3.0	1.8	2.8	3.7		1.9	2.5
	-2.8	-9.1	44.3	6.7	6.6	11.0		146.5	-112.2
% Profit Before Taxes/Tangible Net Worth	97.4	110.8	29.6	17.3	31.6	31.8		50.8	42.5
	(63) 43.1	(77) 31.0	(124) 3.7	(80) 6.1	(18) 13.8	(10) 13.6		(278) 13.5	(331) 11.4
	13.9	6.5	-4.8	-1.1	-8.4	7.3		.1	.0
% Profit Before Taxes/Total Assets	35.1	18.8	7.8	5.5	9.7	6.6		12.6	11.9
	9.9	4.6	1.0	2.2	2.7	4.5		3.7	3.0
	-7.3	-2.8	-3.0	-1.4	-2.6	.7		-.8	-1.1
Sales/Net Fixed Assets	21.2	3.6	2.0	1.0	2.8	1.7		6.4	5.2
	7.6	1.9	.9	.7	1.2	.9		1.6	1.3
	2.9	1.0	.6	.5	.7	.6		.7	.6
Sales/Total Assets	5.5	2.1	1.3	.8	1.3	.8		2.6	2.1
	3.0	1.3	.7	.5	.7	.6		1.0	.9
	1.8	.7	.5	.4	.5	.3		.5	.5
% Depr., Dep., Amort./Sales	1.8	5.2	5.3	6.4	5.3			3.9	4.3
	(73) 3.7	(106) 8.0	(145) 8.1	(82) 7.9	(22) 7.5			(306) 6.2	(381) 7.1
	8.3	12.5	11.5	11.8	10.6			9.1	10.9
% Officers', Directors' Owners' Comp/Sales	4.4	3.5	3.0					3.6	3.4
	(44) 7.5	(38) 7.6	(46) 5.7					(105) 6.8	(105) 6.7
	11.9	13.7	11.4					13.7	11.1
Net Sales ($)	90278M	181609M	745968M	1388485M	1432972M	1051190M		3740938M	4736480M
Total Assets ($)	25669M	129069M	756667M	1841101M	1559296M	1649665M		4048797M	5047789M

M = $ thousand   MM = $ million
See Pages 9 through 22 for Explanation of Ratios and Data

Comparative Historical Data | Current Data Sorted by Sales

	4/1/07-3/31/08 ALL	4/1/08-3/31/09 ALL	4/1/09-3/31/10 ALL	0-1MM	1-3MM	3-5MM	5-10MM	10-25MM	25MM & OVER
Type of Statement									
Unqualified	70	75	75	4	7	15	16	11	22
Reviewed	43	39	49	5	12	11	8	9	4
Compiled	60	63	65	19	28	7	9	2	
Tax Returns	114	136	136	67	54	9	4	1	1
Other	159	193	193	46	56	22	28	22	19
				72 (4/1-9/30/09)		446 (10/1/09-3/31/10)			
NUMBER OF STATEMENTS	446	506	518	141	157	64	65	45	46
	%	%	%	%	%	%	%	%	%
ASSETS									
Cash & Equivalents	11.4	9.5	11.0	14.7	11.6	8.0	8.0	9.0	8.1
Trade Receivables (net)	3.6	4.2	3.2	1.4	3.1	4.5	3.1	4.8	5.2
Inventory	1.7	1.3	1.8	2.6	2.0	1.1	.7	1.9	1.0
All Other Current	2.8	3.2	3.1	3.6	3.6	1.6	1.6	4.2	2.8
Total Current	19.6	18.3	19.0	22.4	20.2	15.2	13.4	20.0	17.1
Fixed Assets (net)	66.4	67.6	66.8	65.4	66.8	70.8	72.0	62.6	62.5
Intangibles (net)	5.4	6.0	5.8	6.3	4.8	4.4	3.2	8.5	10.8
All Other Non-Current	8.7	8.2	8.4	5.9	8.2	9.6	11.4	8.9	9.6
Total	100.0	100.0	100.0	100.0	100.0	100.0	100.0	100.0	100.0
LIABILITIES									
Notes Payable-Short Term	5.3	6.3	6.6	15.6	3.3	4.0	2.3	5.1	1.3
Cur. Mat.-L.T.D.	5.3	5.4	5.3	5.6	5.2	4.3	4.6	7.6	5.1
Trade Payables	3.9	4.8	4.1	3.8	5.1	3.8	2.0	4.9	4.5
Income Taxes Payable	.0	.1	.1	.1	.1	.0	.0	.1	.0
All Other Current	12.6	13.4	10.0	15.3	7.6	8.1	7.3	10.1	9.0
Total Current	27.1	30.0	26.2	40.3	21.4	20.3	16.2	27.8	19.9
Long-Term Debt	38.3	42.2	42.4	46.7	43.9	38.4	43.8	35.7	33.9
Deferred Taxes	.1	.1	.1	.0	.0	.0	.0	.0	.5
All Other Non-Current	13.0	11.2	11.4	13.2	13.8	6.3	6.5	7.4	15.9
Net Worth	21.5	16.5	20.0	-.2	20.9	34.9	33.5	29.1	29.7
Total Liabilties & Net Worth	100.0	100.0	100.0	100.0	100.0	100.0	100.0	100.0	100.0
INCOME DATA									
Net Sales	100.0	100.0	100.0	100.0	100.0	100.0	100.0	100.0	100.0
Gross Profit									
Operating Expenses	90.4	92.9	91.5	91.5	89.5	94.4	92.4	92.4	91.7
Operating Profit	9.6	7.1	8.5	8.5	10.5	5.6	7.6	7.6	8.3
All Other Expenses (net)	5.2	5.1	4.3	5.7	4.4	3.5	3.7	2.9	2.7
Profit Before Taxes	4.5	1.9	4.2	2.8	6.0	2.1	3.9	4.7	5.5
RATIOS									
Current	2.4	2.0	2.0	2.4	2.3	2.0	2.0	1.3	1.5
	.9	.8	.8	.6	1.0	.8	.6	.7	.7
	.3	.3	.3	.2	.4	.4	.3	.3	.3
Quick	1.8	1.3	1.6	1.9	1.9	1.6	1.8	1.1	1.2
	(444) .7	.6	(515) .6	(140) .4	(155) .8	.7	.5	.5	.5
	.2	.2	.2	.1	.2	.3	.2	.2	.2
Sales/Receivables	0 UND	0 UND	0 UND	0 UND	0 UND	1 296.2	2 218.4	0 UND	1 263.4
	2 196.9	3 140.8	1 271.3	0 UND	1 521.0	8 46.6	8 44.2	7 50.8	7 53.1
	16 23.1	17 21.3	16 23.2	0 UND	13 27.8	37 9.9	18 20.8	23 15.8	19 19.1
Cost of Sales/Inventory									
Cost of Sales/Payables									
Sales/Working Capital	11.3	16.6	13.1	14.1	11.8	17.2	10.8	20.5	14.4
	-94.3	-36.5	-55.4	-39.3	877.0	-38.9	-17.2	-23.8	-33.2
	-8.7	-6.8	-6.8	-4.4	-9.4	-6.6	-7.8	-6.7	-8.5
EBIT/Interest	5.9	4.3	4.9	2.8	6.8	4.8	3.6	6.5	4.6
	(366) 1.6	(418) 1.4	(431) 1.8	(96) 1.1	(133) 2.0	(59) 1.6	(59) 1.9	(44) 2.2	(40) 2.5
	.4	-.4	.3	-.6	.4	.4	.1	1.1	1.1
Net Profit + Depr., Dep., Amort./Cur. Mat. L/T/D	5.5	3.8	4.9		3.0				4.9
	(37) 2.7	(46) 1.7	(39) 2.6		(10) 1.5				(12) 3.0
	1.1	.4	.8		.6				2.0
Fixed/Worth	1.2	1.3	1.2	1.2	1.1	1.2	1.4	1.4	1.0
	2.8	3.1	3.1	6.4	3.0	2.4	2.1	2.9	3.2
	-19.1	-14.9	-24.6	-2.0	-554.0	5.9	16.7	NM	10.9
Debt/Worth	.7	.9	.8	.8	.8	.5	.9	.9	1.2
	2.7	3.3	3.0	23.4	3.1	2.1	1.5	2.4	3.0
	-21.9	-17.3	-24.7	-3.1	-137.9	6.5	18.4	NM	11.8
% Profit Before Taxes/Tangible Net Worth	48.9	52.4	56.6	69.3	101.9	25.2	37.5	75.8	39.2
	(323) 12.2	(360) 7.9	(372) 14.0	(77) 16.3	(116) 23.2	(53) 4.4	(56) 9.8	(34) 13.9	(36) 18.0
	-1.2	-5.3	-1.3	-1.5	-2.7	-2.8	-3.9	.2	5.3
% Profit Before Taxes/Total Assets	13.8	10.2	12.2	12.0	20.4	6.3	5.8	8.9	10.4
	2.7	1.4	2.8	1.1	5.0	1.2	2.9	4.0	4.5
	-1.9	-4.0	-2.7	-4.7	-2.5	-2.5	-3.2	.1	.7
Sales/Net Fixed Assets	4.6	4.9	4.7	8.2	5.2	2.4	1.6	4.3	4.4
	1.5	1.4	1.4	2.0	1.9	.9	.8	1.6	1.6
	.7	.6	.7	.7	.8	.6	.5	.7	.7
Sales/Total Assets	2.2	2.1	2.1	2.9	2.3	1.3	1.2	2.1	1.5
	.9	.9	1.0	1.4	1.3	.7	.7	1.0	.9
	.6	.5	.5	.6	.6	.5	.5	.5	.6
% Depr., Dep., Amort./Sales	4.0	4.5	4.8	3.8	4.6	5.4	5.5	4.5	4.8
	(372) 6.7	(416) 7.1	(436) 7.6	(104) 8.4	(133) 7.2	(59) 8.6	(57) 7.1	(43) 6.5	(40) 6.5
	10.0	11.0	11.4	15.8	11.2	11.1	9.6	9.7	9.7
% Officers', Directors' Owners' Comp/Sales	3.2	3.2	3.3	4.5	3.6	2.4	3.0		
	(115) 5.5	(131) 6.3	(138) 6.3	(44) 9.7	(51) 6.8	(16) 3.8	(17) 3.9		
	10.8	13.2	12.2	14.3	12.4	10.6	6.4		
Net Sales ($)	4371789M	5113917M	4890502M	75386M	277999M	252294M	467986M	728739M	3088098M
Total Assets ($)	5993886M	5563009M	5961467M	123723M	375792M	396665M	743140M	970504M	3351643M

M = $ thousand   MM = $ million
See Pages 9 through 22 for Explanation of Ratios and Data

508 ENTERTAINMENT—Bowling Centers NAICS 713950

Current Data Sorted by Assets							Comparative Historical Data	

	2		1			Type of Statement		
1	6	7	1			Unqualified	4	4
15	24	9	1			Reviewed	15	12
32	27	16				Compiled	44	33
7	16	8				Tax Returns	62	61
			2	4		Other	27	22
	51 (4/1-9/30/09)		128 (10/1/09-3/31/10)				4/1/05-3/31/06	4/1/06-3/31/07
0-500M	500M-2MM	2-10MM	10-50MM	50-100MM	100-250MM		ALL	ALL
55	75	40	5	4		NUMBER OF STATEMENTS	152	132

%	%	%	%	%	%	ASSETS	%	%
20.0	9.6	5.7				Cash & Equivalents	12.1	13.1
.4	1.0	.3				Trade Receivables (net)	1.8	.6
10.4	2.4	1.5				Inventory	4.9	4.1
2.8	2.7	.8				All Other Current	2.6	2.2
33.6	15.6	8.4				Total Current	21.2	20.0
50.2	73.5	75.0		D A T A		Fixed Assets (net)	62.6	62.9
4.9	3.8	3.8		N O T		Intangibles (net)	5.9	5.0
11.3	7.1	12.9		A V A I L A B L E		All Other Non-Current	10.3	12.1
100.0	100.0	100.0				Total	100.0	100.0
						LIABILITIES		
6.7	5.3	2.5				Notes Payable-Short Term	4.5	7.7
4.9	6.2	6.7				Cur. Mat.-L.T.D.	4.7	5.7
7.8	4.6	2.4				Trade Payables	6.4	5.0
.0	.0	.0				Income Taxes Payable	.2	.1
32.5	10.9	8.1				All Other Current	12.5	13.9
51.8	26.9	19.7				Total Current	28.2	32.4
47.9	66.6	66.1				Long-Term Debt	62.9	57.9
.0	.1	.2				Deferred Taxes	.2	.2
26.3	15.5	7.6				All Other Non-Current	22.0	14.7
-26.0	-9.1	6.4				Net Worth	-13.3	-5.2
100.0	100.0	100.0				Total Liabilities & Net Worth	100.0	100.0
						INCOME DATA		
100.0	100.0	100.0				Net Sales	100.0	100.0
						Gross Profit		
99.0	96.3	92.4				Operating Expenses	94.2	92.6
1.0	3.7	7.6				Operating Profit	5.8	7.4
.7	3.4	9.2				All Other Expenses (net)	3.3	4.0
.3	.3	-1.6				Profit Before Taxes	2.5	3.4
						RATIOS		
1.7	1.1	1.2					2.0	1.7
.8	.6	.7				Current	.8	.8
.2	.3	.3					.4	.3
1.1	.8	.8					1.4	1.2
(54) .4	.3	.5				Quick	.4 (131)	.5
.1	.1	.2					.2	.1
0 UND	0 UND	0 UND					0 UND	0 UND
0 UND	0 UND	0 UND				Sales/Receivables	0 UND	0 UND
0 UND	2 241.0	1 591.8					1 293.4	1 422.8
						Cost of Sales/Inventory		
						Cost of Sales/Payables		
24.7	31.4	44.7					22.5	20.0
-79.4	-21.8	-19.1				Sales/Working Capital	-51.2	-49.0
-15.5	-6.1	-7.2					-10.6	-9.4
3.8	2.6	1.6					3.7	3.7
(34) .8	(71) 1.2	(37) .9				EBIT/Interest	(127) 1.5	(118) 1.6
-.5	.0	.1					.3	.8
							2.5	2.3
						Net Profit + Depr., Dep., Amort./Cur. Mat. L/T/D	(14) 1.6	(15) 1.8
							.9	.9
.8	1.9	4.4					1.6	2.2
-13.9	46.5	18.7				Fixed/Worth	NM	55.6
-.6	-2.0	-4.8					-1.8	-1.9
.9	1.7	3.7					2.2	2.7
-40.5	55.8	21.4				Debt/Worth	-64.1	87.1
-2.1	-3.5	-6.4					-3.0	-3.7
36.2	57.8	17.3					52.9	78.1
(26) 1.0	(38) 15.8	(23) 2.4				% Profit Before Taxes/Tangible Net Worth	(74) 14.3	(68) 22.6
-25.7	2.4	-18.2					.3	4.6
9.5	6.1	2.9					12.8	10.8
-1.6	1.3	-.6				% Profit Before Taxes/Total Assets	2.3	3.3
-13.4	-6.3	-4.2					-4.8	-1.2
22.1	2.7	2.2					5.9	5.9
6.7	1.6	.8				Sales/Net Fixed Assets	2.2	1.9
4.3	1.0	.5					1.4	1.3
5.7	1.7	1.1					2.8	2.8
3.3	1.1	.7				Sales/Total Assets	1.5	1.3
2.5	.8	.5					.9	.9
1.5	4.2	6.0					3.3	3.2
(49) 3.5	6.8 (38)	8.6				% Depr., Dep., Amort./Sales	(142) 6.6	(125) 6.6
5.6	10.4	13.1					9.6	9.6
3.2	3.5	1.5					4.2	3.5
(33) 6.5	(28) 7.9	(15) 5.9				% Officers', Directors' Owners' Comp/Sales	(65) 8.1	(74) 6.0
9.3	14.2	7.6					11.4	12.4
42631M	107263M	117433M	85727M	223207M		Net Sales ($)	1618052M	262276M
12229M	82589M	159220M	110371M	245924M		Total Assets ($)	570814M	219660M

© RMA 2010

M = $ thousand   MM = $ million
See Pages 9 through 22 for Explanation of Ratios and Data

Comparative Historical Data
Current Data Sorted by Sales

Hist 1	Hist 2	Hist 3	Type of Statement	0-1MM	1-3MM	3-5MM	5-10MM	10-25MM	25MM & OVER
5	6	3	Unqualified	1	1				1
13	11	15	Reviewed	2	5	4	4		
39	44	49	Compiled	21	23	3	2		
56	60	75	Tax Returns	40	31	2	2		
38	24	37	Other	9	17	4	1	1	5
4/1/07-3/31/08 ALL	4/1/08-3/31/09 ALL	4/1/09-3/31/10 ALL		51 (4/1-9/30/09)			128 (10/1/09-3/31/10)		
151	145	179	**NUMBER OF STATEMENTS**	73	77	13	9	1	6
%	%	%	**ASSETS**	%	%	%	%	%	%
15.1	13.6	12.2	Cash & Equivalents	14.0	10.0	12.8			
1.3	.6	.6	Trade Receivables (net)	.5	.8	.1			
3.9	3.8	4.6	Inventory	6.8	3.2	3.3			
3.1	2.4	2.6	All Other Current	2.7	2.1	2.0			
23.5	20.3	20.0	Total Current	23.9	16.0	18.3			
62.8	65.9	66.4	Fixed Assets (net)	61.3	72.5	64.2			
4.9	3.8	4.1	Intangibles (net)	4.2	3.9	6.5			
8.8	10.0	9.5	All Other Non-Current	10.6	7.5	11.0			
100.0	100.0	100.0	Total	100.0	100.0	100.0			
			LIABILITIES						
4.9	8.5	4.9	Notes Payable-Short Term	5.2	4.4	10.4			
7.3	5.1	5.7	Cur. Mat.-L.T.D.	3.8	6.6	10.3			
4.8	3.8	5.0	Trade Payables	4.6	5.7	3.9			
.0	.0	.0	Income Taxes Payable	.0	.0	.0			
18.9	11.5	17.4	All Other Current	21.1	15.2	12.5			
35.9	28.9	33.0	Total Current	34.8	31.8	37.2			
60.0	59.2	59.7	Long-Term Debt	55.4	64.6	73.3			
.2	.2	.1	Deferred Taxes	.0	.1	.7			
19.2	15.9	17.1	All Other Non-Current	22.2	14.4	10.7			
-15.2	-4.2	-9.9	Net Worth	-12.4	-10.9	-21.9			
100.0	100.0	100.0	Total Liabilities & Net Worth	100.0	100.0	100.0			
			INCOME DATA						
100.0	100.0	100.0	Net Sales	100.0	100.0	100.0			
			Gross Profit						
91.3	92.8	96.3	Operating Expenses	97.7	94.9	95.2			
8.7	7.2	3.7	Operating Profit	2.3	5.1	4.8			
5.7	5.7	3.9	All Other Expenses (net)	3.5	4.3	4.3			
2.9	1.5	-.3	Profit Before Taxes	-1.2	.8	.5			
			RATIOS						
1.7 / .8 / .3	1.9 / .7 / .3	1.3 / .7 / .3	Current	1.7 / .7 / .3	1.1 / .6 / .3	1.1 / .6 / .3			
1.1 / .5 / .1	1.1 / .4 / .2	.9 / .4 / .1	Quick	1.1 / .4 / .1	.8 / .3 / .1	.9 / .5 / .2			
0 UND / 0 UND / 2 229.3	0 UND / 0 UND / 0 999.8	0 UND / 0 UND / 1 435.2	Sales/Receivables	0 UND / 0 UND / 0 UND	0 UND / 0 UND / 1 415.0	0 UND / 0 UND / 0 999.8			
			Cost of Sales/Inventory						
			Cost of Sales/Payables						
22.8 / -36.7 / -8.8	19.4 / -34.5 / -7.4	34.5 / -28.8 / -7.5	Sales/Working Capital	18.7 / -64.0 / -6.9	101.9 / -19.4 / -7.3	NM / -24.0 / -10.2			
(120) 3.1 / 1.2 / .3	(119) 2.1 / 1.1 / .1	(150) 2.1 / 1.0 / -.1	EBIT/Interest	(52) 2.2 / .7 / -.4	(70) 2.2 / 1.1 / .3	1.8 / 1.1 / -.5			
(12) 2.0 / 1.3 / .5	(12) 3.0 / 1.2 / .7	(13) 3.1 / 1.1 / .1	Net Profit + Depr., Dep., Amort./Cur. Mat. L/T/D						
2.5 / -148.3 / -1.7	1.7 / 14.2 / -1.9	1.9 / 22.1 / -2.0	Fixed/Worth	.9 / 35.1 / -1.2	2.8 / 21.5 / -2.2	5.5 / -36.5 / -.4			
2.5 / -64.0 / -3.5	1.9 / 51.8 / -4.1	2.1 / 32.0 / -3.5	Debt/Worth	.8 / 55.8 / -2.9	2.8 / 31.0 / -3.8	5.5 / -72.9 / -2.1			
(73) 58.2 / 20.7 / .9	(75) 37.2 / 14.2 / -6.2	(93) 31.5 / 6.0 / -13.1	% Profit Before Taxes/Tangible Net Worth	(37) 18.2 / 2.5 / -22.4	(40) 53.0 / 16.9 / .3				
12.7 / 1.8 / -4.3	7.8 / 1.3 / -4.0	6.0 / .0 / -6.4	% Profit Before Taxes/Total Assets	5.2 / -1.7 / -9.9	7.0 / .8 / -4.4	7.3 / .4 / -4.5			
6.9 / 1.9 / 1.0	5.0 / 1.8 / 1.0	5.8 / 1.9 / 1.0	Sales/Net Fixed Assets	8.9 / 2.6 / .9	4.1 / 1.7 / 1.0	5.6 / 2.7 / .7			
3.2 / 1.1 / .8	2.4 / 1.2 / .7	2.6 / 1.2 / .8	Sales/Total Assets	3.2 / 1.6 / .7	2.2 / 1.2 / .8	2.8 / 1.1 / .6			
(136) 2.9 / 5.8 / 9.4	(134) 4.4 / 7.0 / 10.5	(170) 3.5 / 6.4 / 10.2	% Depr., Dep., Amort./Sales	(67) 4.1 / 6.8 / 12.0	(75) 3.1 / 6.1 / 9.2	4.8 / 6.8 / 9.0			
(66) 2.9 / 5.6 / 11.2	(65) 4.0 / 7.7 / 11.5	(78) 2.7 / 6.3 / 9.8	% Officers', Directors' Owners' Comp/Sales	(32) 3.5 / 8.9 / 13.4	(33) 3.5 / 6.1 / 7.7				
1324514M	398267M	576261M	Net Sales ($)	43140M	130978M	50298M	58505M	13993M	279347M
604673M	446536M	610333M	Total Assets ($)	44006M	129960M	50043M	59614M	15508M	311202M

M = $ thousand   MM = $ million
See Pages 9 through 22 for Explanation of Ratios and Data

Current Data Sorted by Assets

Comparative Historical Data

0-500M	500M-2MM	2-10MM	10-50MM	50-100MM	100-250MM	Type of Statement		4/1/05-3/31/06 ALL		4/1/06-3/31/07 ALL
3	1	16	21	2	5	Unqualified		62		60
1	5	13	3			Reviewed		27		29
10	15	10	2			Compiled		50		42
50	32	13			1	Tax Returns		73		81
20	39	42	17	2	5	Other		153		125
	60 (4/1-9/30/09)		268 (10/1/09-3/31/10)							
84	92	94	43	4	11	NUMBER OF STATEMENTS		365		337
%	%	%	%	%	%	ASSETS		%		%
23.1	13.4	11.9	10.1		14.1	Cash & Equivalents		14.9		16.6
3.7	3.3	6.1	3.2		2.9	Trade Receivables (net)		6.0		6.1
6.0	6.1	4.5	4.9		4.2	Inventory		5.1		6.0
6.5	5.7	2.0	5.2		2.1	All Other Current		2.9		4.5
39.3	28.5	24.5	23.4		23.3	Total Current		29.0		33.2
45.3	56.4	64.8	50.7		55.7	Fixed Assets (net)		56.8		54.5
8.2	7.3	5.0	11.2		7.8	Intangibles (net)		4.8		4.5
7.1	7.8	5.7	14.7		13.2	All Other Non-Current		9.5		7.8
100.0	100.0	100.0	100.0		100.0	Total		100.0		100.0
						LIABILITIES				
25.2	10.7	1.7	4.9		.0	Notes Payable-Short Term		6.5		8.0
4.6	3.4	3.2	2.8		4.0	Cur. Mat.-L.T.D.		4.5		5.9
11.7	5.4	4.5	3.5		5.2	Trade Payables		6.7		9.0
1.6	.0	.1	.1		.0	Income Taxes Payable		.2		.1
32.7	14.8	11.4	9.2		7.7	All Other Current		17.7		15.5
75.8	34.4	20.9	20.4		16.9	Total Current		35.6		38.5
33.5	40.8	31.8	22.4		50.8	Long-Term Debt		37.4		37.1
.1	.1	.1	.9		.0	Deferred Taxes		.4		.2
24.8	12.8	6.3	7.0		13.1	All Other Non-Current		9.1		9.2
-34.3	11.9	40.9	49.2		19.3	Net Worth		17.5		15.1
100.0	100.0	100.0	100.0		100.0	Total Liabilities & Net Worth		100.0		100.0
						INCOME DATA				
100.0	100.0	100.0	100.0		100.0	Net Sales		100.0		100.0
						Gross Profit				
95.0	88.8	92.5	95.4		89.0	Operating Expenses		89.9		90.2
5.0	11.2	7.5	4.6		11.0	Operating Profit		10.1		9.8
2.6	5.8	5.3	2.5		4.3	All Other Expenses (net)		3.8		4.0
2.4	5.5	2.2	2.1		6.7	Profit Before Taxes		6.4		5.8
						RATIOS				
2.8	3.2	2.5	2.4		2.7			2.0		2.4
.8	.9	1.2	1.2		1.2	Current		1.0		1.1
.3	.2	.5	.5		.9			.4		.4
1.7	1.8	2.1	2.0		2.3			1.5		1.7
.4	.4	.7	.6		1.1	Quick	(364)	.6	(336)	.6
.1	.1	.3	.3		.6			.2		.2
0 UND	0 UND	0 UND	1 259.5		1 433.2		0 UND		0 UND
0 UND	0 UND	4 96.3	8 44.2		4 94.9	Sales/Receivables	1 268.3		1 303.8
0 UND	3 125.2	24 15.3	18 20.4		12 29.7		15 25.1		13 27.4
						Cost of Sales/Inventory				
						Cost of Sales/Payables				
19.6	7.6	6.2	3.2		8.7			11.1		7.8
-86.8	-45.4	114.1	32.9		29.0	Sales/Working Capital		-187.8		84.4
-9.5	-6.3	-7.4	-9.2		-47.2			-7.8		-9.9
10.0	10.7	8.2	3.5		10.3			6.7		6.2
(57) 2.7	(70) 2.4	(75) 2.0	(38) 1.5		(10) 3.8	EBIT/Interest	(280) 2.2	(256) 2.4
.9	.0	.0	-.4		-.6			.1		.3
		7.1						5.2		4.8
	(14) 3.3				Net Profit + Depr., Dep., Amort./Cur. Mat. L/T/D	(30) 2.3	(19) 2.6
		1.0						1.1		1.3
.7	.8	.9	.7		.9			.9		.8
3.0	2.1	1.8	1.1		1.9	Fixed/Worth		2.0		2.0
-.8	-1.7	10.3	2.7		-1.9			-10.7		-122.0
.9	.5	.2	.4		.6			.5		.7
13.9	3.0	1.7	.9		2.1	Debt/Worth		2.5		2.7
-2.0	-3.6	12.8	3.8		-4.2			-14.7		-24.7
120.0	44.4	22.8	17.7					53.0		52.4
(45) 32.0	(58) 21.2	(75) 5.4	(37) 2.1			% Profit Before Taxes/Tangible Net Worth	(261) 15.6	(245) 18.6
.7	2.7	-5.0	-4.5					-.5		2.0
26.5	13.5	9.1	5.2		19.4			14.3		18.2
7.8	3.8	1.9	1.1		2.9	% Profit Before Taxes/Total Assets		3.8		5.1
-6.5	-3.3	-3.9	-2.2		-4.5			-2.8		-2.1
38.3	11.5	3.6	5.3		1.9			10.4		13.7
11.8	2.1	1.2	1.5		1.4	Sales/Net Fixed Assets		2.4		2.6
3.5	.9	.5	.5		1.1			.9		1.0
7.1	2.7	1.6	1.1		1.1			2.9		3.0
3.9	1.1	.8	.7		.9	Sales/Total Assets		1.3		1.5
2.1	.6	.4	.4		.6			.6		.7
1.3	2.1	3.4	3.8					2.9		2.4
(65) 2.6	(69) 4.3	(83) 6.2	(39) 6.7			% Depr., Dep., Amort./Sales	(285) 5.9	(261) 5.5
6.6	10.4	13.4	10.3					10.3		9.9
2.5	2.8	1.9						2.8		2.8
(36) 5.8	(31) 4.6	(23) 4.4				% Officers', Directors' Owners' Comp/Sales	(93) 5.7	(79) 6.4
10.7	8.8	6.8						11.8		12.0
79820M	186471M	526022M	980178M	176511M	2697321M	Net Sales ($)		8042799M		6801969M
17604M	106713M	416062M	1051787M	263009M	2096096M	Total Assets ($)		6496812M		5043077M

M = $ thousand   MM = $ million
See Pages 9 through 22 for Explanation of Ratios and Data

Comparative Historical Data

Current Data Sorted by Sales

			Type of Statement						
58	59	48	Unqualified	3	7	7	8	13	10
24	21	22	Reviewed	3	5	2	4	6	2
44	44	37	Compiled	14	10	3	6	3	1
70	71	96	Tax Returns	57	26	9	3		1
127	105	125	Other	37	35	11	16	9	17
4/1/07-3/31/08	4/1/08-3/31/09	4/1/09-3/31/10		60 (4/1-9/30/09)			268 (10/1/09-3/31/10)		
ALL	ALL	ALL		0-1MM	1-3MM	3-5MM	5-10MM	10-25MM	25MM & OVE
323	300	328	**NUMBER OF STATEMENTS**	114	83	32	37	31	31
%	%	%	**ASSETS**	%	%	%	%	%	%
16.3	16.4	15.0	Cash & Equivalents	14.3	15.5	13.0	22.1	13.6	10.8
4.2	4.8	4.2	Trade Receivables (net)	2.5	2.0	5.1	9.0	8.1	5.6
4.6	3.8	5.4	Inventory	4.2	4.9	8.8	4.3	6.4	7.7
4.3	3.0	4.6	All Other Current	4.5	5.8	2.9	3.4	4.9	4.2
29.5	28.0	29.1	Total Current	25.6	28.3	29.9	38.7	33.0	28.3
54.7	56.4	55.3	Fixed Assets (net)	62.6	55.3	56.9	47.8	49.9	40.7
5.7	6.2	7.3	Intangibles (net)	7.3	6.5	7.8	3.9	5.7	14.6
10.1	9.4	8.3	All Other Non-Current	4.5	9.9	5.4	9.5	11.3	16.4
100.0	100.0	100.0	Total	100.0	100.0	100.0	100.0	100.0	100.0
			LIABILITIES						
6.6	13.4	10.6	Notes Payable-Short Term	18.7	8.4	5.9	6.7	2.9	3.5
4.4	4.4	3.6	Cur. Mat.-L.T.D.	4.4	3.3	2.0	3.3	3.4	3.2
6.7	5.1	6.5	Trade Payables	5.4	6.4	6.7	7.9	8.1	7.2
.1	.3	.5	Income Taxes Payable	.1	.1	.1	3.6	.0	.2
16.9	12.3	17.3	All Other Current	20.3	20.0	9.7	15.3	13.6	12.8
34.8	35.5	38.4	Total Current	48.9	38.2	24.5	36.8	28.1	26.8
32.1	34.5	34.0	Long-Term Debt	38.3	40.1	30.1	26.4	19.3	29.2
.2	.2	.2	Deferred Taxes	.2	.0	.2	.2	.2	.9
9.4	7.2	13.2	All Other Non-Current	22.0	8.5	7.5	8.0	4.8	14.3
23.4	22.6	14.2	Net Worth	-9.3	13.1	37.7	28.6	47.6	28.8
100.0	100.0	100.0	Total Liabilties & Net Worth	100.0	100.0	100.0	100.0	100.0	100.0
			INCOME DATA						
100.0	100.0	100.0	Net Sales	100.0	100.0	100.0	100.0	100.0	100.0
			Gross Profit						
89.9	91.1	92.4	Operating Expenses	89.3	95.3	93.2	93.9	92.5	93.9
10.1	8.9	7.6	Operating Profit	10.7	4.7	6.8	6.1	7.5	6.1
4.2	4.1	4.3	All Other Expenses (net)	7.5	2.7	2.3	2.8	1.9	3.2
5.9	4.8	3.3	Profit Before Taxes	3.3	2.1	4.5	3.3	5.7	2.8
			RATIOS						
2.3	3.0	2.6		2.9	2.7	3.6	3.1	2.3	1.6
1.0	1.2	1.0	Current	.7	.9	1.2	1.7	1.4	1.0
.5	.5	.4		.2	.2	.5	.7	.6	.6
1.8	2.4	1.9		1.7	1.4	3.0	2.6	2.2	1.1
.7	.8	.6	Quick	.3	.6	.6	1.3	.7	.6
.2	.3	.2		.1	.1	.3	.5	.3	.3
0 UND	0 UND	0 UND		0 UND	0 UND	0 999.8	1 254.9	0 938.6	2 207.3
0 832.8	1 591.3	1 607.4	Sales/Receivables	0 UND	0 UND	2 197.4	6 60.1	6 63.6	11 34.4
8 48.5	12 29.7	9 41.8		0 UND	5 78.5	22 16.5	21 17.5	18 20.3	16 22.8
			Cost of Sales/Inventory						
			Cost of Sales/Payables						
10.3	6.5	8.3		10.1	8.6	5.9	3.8	6.4	14.5
-999.8	59.5	722.7	Sales/Working Capital	-35.2	-214.8	21.0	16.8	31.7	193.2
-11.1	-11.8	-7.6		-4.8	-6.2	-14.1	-35.0	-9.5	-12.0
8.9	8.5	7.0		5.8	8.0	10.8	4.3	16.5	8.4
(233) 2.5	(228) 2.7	(253) 2.3	EBIT/Interest	(76) 2.0	(68) 2.1	(22) 1.5	(31) 2.1	(27) 3.9	(29) 2.5
.6	.5	.3		.3	-.3	.9	.3	1.7	-.5
15.1	4.5	4.1	Net Profit + Depr., Dep.,						
(22) 2.8	(24) 3.0	(24) 2.9	Amort./Cur. Mat. L/T/D						
1.2	.8	1.0							
.8	.9	.8		1.1	.8	.8	.3	.6	.8
1.9	1.7	1.9	Fixed/Worth	3.3	1.8	1.7	1.0	1.0	1.5
-25.2	55.3	-6.5		-2.2	-5.2	-9.5	9.4	2.1	-1.9
.5	.5	.5		.6	.5	.2	.4	.4	.6
2.3	1.6	2.3	Debt/Worth	7.9	2.3	1.2	1.3	.9	3.0
-26.4	UND	-7.8		-3.2	-5.2	-17.1	19.5	2.7	-7.6
62.0	43.1	36.6	% Profit Before Taxes/Tangible	51.1	34.9	36.4	23.1	30.7	60.7
(238) 15.8	(227) 12.5	(226) 7.8	Net Worth	(66) 10.2	(58) 6.6	(23) 6.8	(29) 7.8	(28) 6.3	(22) 26.4
.7	-.2	-2.9		-1.7	-10.8	-1.9	-3.2	1.8	-.6
19.5	15.8	13.1	% Profit Before Taxes/Total	13.9	15.3	10.3	10.9	8.3	17.7
5.4	4.2	2.9	Assets	2.4	2.2	2.2	3.4	3.4	2.9
-1.2	-2.2	-3.8		-4.1	-5.5	-1.6	-1.8	1.1	-4.6
9.9	9.0	12.9		9.7	15.9	5.8	17.7	7.6	20.3
2.6	2.2	2.5	Sales/Net Fixed Assets	2.3	2.4	1.8	3.9	2.6	3.7
1.0	.8	.9		.5	1.0	1.0	1.0	.8	1.4
2.9	2.7	2.9		3.1	3.0	3.0	4.1	2.7	2.4
1.3	1.1	1.3	Sales/Total Assets	1.3	1.3	1.2	1.6	1.0	1.1
.7	.5	.6		.4	.7	.6	.7	.5	.8
2.5	3.1	2.1		2.2	2.1	2.7	3.3	1.8	1.6
(258) 5.8	(234) 6.1	(262) 5.3	% Depr., Dep., Amort./Sales	(92) 6.4	(64) 4.6	(26) 5.2	(29) 4.3	(30) 4.6	(21) 5.7
9.4	11.1	10.6		16.2	11.3	9.0	8.0	6.8	9.8
1.9	4.0	2.4	% Officers', Directors'	3.0	2.8	2.0	1.3		
(85) 4.9	(74) 6.1	(94) 5.1	Owners' Comp/Sales	(33) 5.9	(32) 5.0	(12) 4.5	(10) 2.2		
9.9	13.2	9.5		12.7	7.5	6.8	5.8		
7839425M	4029350M	4646323M	Net Sales ($)	62081M	144703M	121214M	262683M	448462M	3607180M
5157534M	4325135M	3951271M	Total Assets ($)	100427M	157719M	155895M	295872M	527798M	2713560M

M = $ thousand   MM = $ million
See Pages 9 through 22 for Explanation of Ratios and Data

ACCOMMODATION AND FOOD SERVICES

FOOD SERVICES

RESTAURANT/LODGING—Hotels (except Casino Hotels) and Motels NAICS 721110

Current Data Sorted by Assets						Type of Statement	Comparative Historical Data	
1	6	27	51	19	11	Unqualified	114	140
6	15	54	39	7	3	Reviewed	100	95
36	95	155	29	1	1	Compiled	246	289
139	329	477	58	5	1	Tax Returns	705	798
42	124	373	111	20	13	Other	521	485
	118 (4/1-9/30/09)		2,129 (10/1/09-3/31/10)				4/1/05-3/31/06	4/1/06-3/31/07
0-500M	500M-2MM	2-10MM	10-50MM	50-100MM	100-250MM		ALL	ALL
224	569	1086	288	52	28	NUMBER OF STATEMENTS	1686	1807
%	%	%	%	%	%	ASSETS	%	%
28.5	7.9	4.9	6.7	8.9	8.5	Cash & Equivalents	9.0	8.8
7.5	2.5	1.7	1.8	4.2	1.4	Trade Receivables (net)	2.6	2.4
2.2	.6	.4	1.0	1.7	.7	Inventory	.9	1.0
4.4	2.0	1.2	1.9	2.5	1.7	All Other Current	2.0	2.1
42.6	13.0	8.2	11.5	17.3	12.3	Total Current	14.6	14.2
40.0	75.3	81.3	78.0	68.7	77.7	Fixed Assets (net)	75.4	75.8
5.2	3.7	3.3	2.9	2.3	5.4	Intangibles (net)	3.5	3.4
12.2	8.0	7.2	7.7	11.6	4.5	All Other Non-Current	6.5	6.5
100.0	100.0	100.0	100.0	100.0	100.0	Total	100.0	100.0
						LIABILITIES		
8.2	2.3	1.6	3.5	3.1	2.2	Notes Payable-Short Term	2.8	2.9
4.7	3.7	3.6	4.3	7.5	3.7	Cur. Mat.-L.T.D.	3.1	3.0
12.6	3.1	1.4	2.0	3.2	1.9	Trade Payables	2.9	2.6
.6	.0	.0	.1	.0	.0	Income Taxes Payable	.1	.1
36.9	10.3	6.9	9.8	9.9	6.6	All Other Current	8.6	10.0
63.1	19.5	13.6	19.7	23.8	14.4	Total Current	17.5	18.5
25.6	67.1	76.3	62.5	55.0	58.2	Long-Term Debt	64.6	64.3
.1	.0	.0	.2	.2	.0	Deferred Taxes	.1	.1
21.6	5.1	5.0	5.2	5.3	7.0	All Other Non-Current	8.3	6.0
-10.4	8.2	5.0	12.4	15.7	20.3	Net Worth	9.5	11.1
100.0	100.0	100.0	100.0	100.0	100.0	Total Liabilities & Net Worth	100.0	100.0
						INCOME DATA		
100.0	100.0	100.0	100.0	100.0	100.0	Net Sales	100.0	100.0
						Gross Profit		
97.7	88.4	85.8	91.0	89.5	91.7	Operating Expenses	82.4	82.3
2.3	11.6	14.2	9.0	10.5	8.3	Operating Profit	17.6	17.7
2.9	10.6	15.2	13.2	12.0	9.8	All Other Expenses (net)	10.2	10.9
-.6	1.1	-.9	-4.2	-1.5	-1.5	Profit Before Taxes	7.3	6.8
						RATIOS		
3.2	1.6	1.8	1.4	1.9	1.4		2.4	2.3
.9	.6	.6	.6	.9	.6	Current	.9	.9
.3	.2	.2	.2	.2	.4		.3	.3
2.6	1.4	1.5	1.1	1.3	1.3		2.0	1.9
.8	.5 (1084)	.5	.4	.6	.4	Quick	(1680) .7	(1805) .7
.2	.1	.2	.2	.2	.2		.2	.2
0 UND	0 UND	0 UND	2 150.0	3 120.0	2 182.1		0 UND	0 UND
0 UND	0 UND	3 126.9	6 59.2	7 53.1	8 43.1	Sales/Receivables	4 98.5	3 116.8
4 92.3	5 72.5	8 44.3	11 32.5	15 24.2	17 21.9		10 34.9	9 41.5
						Cost of Sales/Inventory		
						Cost of Sales/Payables		
16.8	24.7	15.3	20.0	7.9	15.6		13.1	12.4
-207.3	-24.0	-18.5	-11.8	-28.8	-14.4	Sales/Working Capital	-128.2	-135.2
-10.5	-5.2	-4.7	-3.4	-3.5	-4.3		-8.1	-7.6
12.2	2.8	2.3	1.9	2.8	2.0		3.2	3.1
(81) 1.0	(428) 1.2	(755) 1.2	(227) .9	(40) 1.3	(24) .9	EBIT/Interest	(1305) 1.8	(1375) 1.8
-3.8	.3	.4	.1	-.3	.2		1.0	1.1
	2.0	3.7	2.3				5.2	5.2
	(11) 1.6	(18) 1.7	(32) 1.2			Net Profit + Depr., Dep., Amort./Cur. Mat. L/T/D	(76) 2.8	(78) 2.4
	-.2	.9	.6				1.6	1.5
.3	1.9	4.1	2.8	2.1	2.3		2.5	2.5
1.7	9.9	16.6	7.3	3.7	9.7	Fixed/Worth	8.0	7.2
-1.8	-7.0	-6.7	-12.7	64.0	-11.3		-13.5	-14.4
.5	1.6	3.9	2.5	1.8	1.5		2.3	2.2
6.8	12.9	17.9	7.8	5.2	10.3	Debt/Worth	9.0	7.7
-3.0	-8.5	-8.7	-16.4	NM	-14.0		-15.0	-15.8
68.2	26.2	32.1	15.3	17.3	6.4		64.0	60.6
(133) 4.4	(342) 5.9	(637) 6.6	(192) .2	(39) 2.9	(20) -3.2	% Profit Before Taxes/Tangible Net Worth	(1102) 22.1	(1195) 21.2
-28.9	-7.3	-12.3	-15.1	-10.3	-20.6		3.1	3.5
15.6	6.5	3.9	2.6	3.4	3.9		9.8	9.6
-2.2	.5	-.1	-.7	.0	-.4	% Profit Before Taxes/Total Assets	3.6	3.6
-27.2	-4.0	-3.6	-4.3	-3.4	-3.5		-.5	-.4
124.4	1.7	.7	.8	1.1	.9		1.3	1.3
16.3	.6	.4	.4	.6	.5	Sales/Net Fixed Assets	.6	.6
4.8	.4	.3	.3	.3	.3		.4	.4
8.9	1.0	.5	.6	.7	.6		.9	.9
4.3	.5	.4	.3	.4	.4	Sales/Total Assets	.5	.5
1.9	.3	.3	.2	.2	.3		.4	.4
1.0	5.9	8.5	8.8	7.6	9.9		5.5	5.8
(157) 2.4	(511) 9.5	(983) 12.4	(269) 12.6	(47) 12.1	(24) 12.0	% Depr., Dep., Amort./Sales	(1516) 8.7	(1637) 8.8
5.5	14.1	18.7	20.2	15.5	18.3		12.5	12.4
2.6	3.0	1.9	1.1				2.6	2.4
(89) 4.5	(199) 5.6	(233) 4.3	(49) 2.7			% Officers', Directors' Owners' Comp/Sales	(470) 4.7	(532) 4.3
8.7	9.0	6.8	4.5				8.2	7.5
241662M	636889M	2344524M	3364775M	3116306M	1824175M	Net Sales ($)	11128748M	12252255M
52734M	713484M	4900325M	5911386M	3725522M	4188205M	Total Assets ($)	13523906M	16158284M

© RMA 2010

M = $ thousand   MM = $ million
See Pages 9 through 22 for Explanation of Ratios and Data

Comparative Historical Data | Current Data Sorted by Sales

Historical 4/1/07-3/31/08 ALL	Historical 4/1/08-3/31/09 ALL	Historical 4/1/09-3/31/10 ALL	Type of Statement	0-1MM	1-3MM	3-5MM	5-10MM	10-25MM	25MM & OVER
139	135	115	Unqualified	6	15	15	23	20	36
94	110	124	Reviewed	15	36	20	27	18	8
275	268	316	Compiled	135	129	33	12	4	3
930	893	1009	Tax Returns	498	400	55	36	14	6
545	641	683	Other	195	266	77	73	39	33
				118 (4/1-9/30/09)		2,129 (10/1/09-3/31/10)			
1983	2047	2247	**NUMBER OF STATEMENTS**	849	846	200	171	95	86
%	%	%	**ASSETS**	%	%	%	%	%	%
9.5	8.7	8.4	Cash & Equivalents	7.0	8.3	10.7	11.2	9.3	10.9
2.3	2.4	2.5	Trade Receivables (net)	1.6	2.4	4.2	4.4	2.3	5.9
1.0	.9	.8	Inventory	.4	.5	1.2	2.0	2.2	2.2
2.2	2.0	1.8	All Other Current	1.6	1.7	2.4	2.0	2.9	2.7
15.0	14.1	13.5	Total Current	10.6	12.9	18.5	19.6	16.7	21.7
74.4	74.3	74.9	Fixed Assets (net)	77.9	76.3	69.8	65.6	71.1	66.6
3.4	3.8	3.5	Intangibles (net)	3.5	3.7	2.5	3.8	2.6	4.6
7.2	7.8	8.0	All Other Non-Current	8.0	7.1	9.2	11.0	9.6	7.1
100.0	100.0	100.0	Total	100.0	100.0	100.0	100.0	100.0	100.0
			LIABILITIES						
2.5	3.4	2.7	Notes Payable-Short Term	3.5	1.7	3.1	2.7	5.0	2.3
3.8	4.0	3.9	Cur. Mat.-L.T.D.	3.8	3.6	5.0	3.5	7.1	3.6
2.9	2.7	3.1	Trade Payables	2.3	2.9	4.5	5.4	3.5	4.2
.1	.1	.1	Income Taxes Payable	.0	.1	.0	.0	.1	.1
9.2	10.7	11.2	All Other Current	11.4	9.1	12.8	14.4	11.9	18.8
18.4	20.9	21.1	Total Current	21.0	17.5	25.4	26.0	27.7	29.0
64.4	65.4	66.5	Long-Term Debt	65.7	72.3	63.6	59.6	53.2	50.9
.1	.0	.0	Deferred Taxes	.0	.0	.1	.2	.2	.1
5.8	5.6	6.8	All Other Non-Current	8.0	5.4	4.9	9.5	5.4	8.2
11.3	8.0	5.7	Net Worth	5.3	4.7	6.0	4.6	13.5	11.7
100.0	100.0	100.0	Total Liabilties & Net Worth	100.0	100.0	100.0	100.0	100.0	100.0
			INCOME DATA						
100.0	100.0	100.0	Net Sales	100.0	100.0	100.0	100.0	100.0	100.0
			Gross Profit						
81.4	84.8	88.4	Operating Expenses	86.8	87.7	89.9	93.5	92.9	92.8
18.6	15.2	11.6	Operating Profit	13.2	12.3	10.1	6.5	7.1	7.2
11.4	11.0	12.4	All Other Expenses (net)	15.3	12.1	9.7	7.7	8.7	6.6
7.2	4.2	-.8	Profit Before Taxes	-2.1	.2	.4	-1.2	-1.6	.6
			RATIOS						
2.4	2.0	1.7	Current	1.6	2.1	2.0	1.5	1.3	1.6
1.0	.8	.6		.5	.7	.9	.7	.6	.8
.3	.3	.2		.1	.2	.3	.3	.3	.4
2.0	1.6	1.5	Quick	1.4	1.8	1.5	1.2	.9	1.2
(1976) .7	(2044) .6	(2245) .5		(847) .4	.6	.7	.5	.4	.6
.1	.2	.2		.1	.2	.2	.2	.1	.2
0 UND	0 UND	0 UND	Sales/Receivables	0 UND	0 UND	2 223.2	2 163.5	3 120.6	4 94.0
3 125.7	2 149.4	2 146.9		0 UND	3 111.7	5 79.8	6 56.8	7 55.9	9 41.9
9 40.1	8 45.4	8 45.7		4 98.7	8 48.1	10 36.8	11 31.8	11 31.9	19 19.3
			Cost of Sales/Inventory						
			Cost of Sales/Payables						
11.4	14.9	18.0	Sales/Working Capital	25.4	13.2	11.7	18.9	19.5	19.2
-283.5	-44.9	-22.4		-14.6	-31.9	-39.4	-22.4	-12.9	-25.6
-8.3	-6.2	-4.9		-3.7	-5.7	-6.6	-6.2	-3.4	-5.0
3.1	2.9	2.4	EBIT/Interest	2.1	2.5	2.8	2.5	2.2	3.3
(1486) 1.8	(1515) 1.6	(1555) 1.2		(498) 1.0	(606) 1.3	(154) 1.2	(143) 1.2	(81) 1.1	(73) 1.3
1.1	.7	.2		.1	.4	.2	.2	.0	.4
6.7	6.0	2.4	Net Profit + Depr., Dep., Amort./Cur. Mat. L/T/D	2.2	1.9	11.9	2.9	2.4	
(81) 3.2	(93) 2.8	(73) 1.5		(10) 1.4	(12) 1.1	(11) 2.0	(14) 1.2	(17) 1.5	
1.2	1.1	.6		.5	.0	.6	.3	.7	
2.4	2.6	2.7	Fixed/Worth	2.7	3.5	1.7	1.8	2.0	1.5
7.2	8.7	10.8		11.5	14.9	7.6	8.4	4.8	5.2
-12.9	-9.1	-7.0		-7.2	-7.5	-4.4	-5.5	-9.2	-7.6
2.1	2.5	2.5	Debt/Worth	2.5	3.4	1.9	2.1	1.9	1.7
7.7	10.3	13.0		13.5	17.1	11.9	12.6	5.6	6.9
-15.2	-10.7	-8.5		-8.3	-9.9	-5.9	-7.5	-17.4	-7.6
62.0	50.3	26.6	% Profit Before Taxes/Tangible Net Worth	17.8	38.8	37.9	24.4	26.3	28.0
(1315) 22.0	(1293) 15.3	(1363) 4.9		(512) 1.0	(506) 7.6	(121) 7.8	(99) 9.1	(67) 6.4	(58) 5.5
3.2	-1.4	-12.2		-12.9	-15.0	-13.7	-8.1	-9.4	-6.6
9.7	7.6	4.5	% Profit Before Taxes/Total Assets	3.1	5.2	7.1	5.5	4.2	5.4
3.5	2.2	.0		-.5	.2	.1	.5	.0	.9
-.5	-2.2	-4.2		-4.2	-3.9	-5.4	-4.7	-3.8	-3.2
1.2	1.3	1.2	Sales/Net Fixed Assets	.8	1.1	2.0	3.9	1.6	1.7
.6	.6	.5		.4	.5	.7	.9	.7	.9
.4	.4	.3		.3	.3	.4	.5	.4	.6
.8	.8	.8	Sales/Total Assets	.6	.8	1.1	1.4	.9	.9
.5	.5	.4		.3	.4	.5	.7	.5	.7
.4	.3	.3		.2	.3	.3	.4	.3	.4
5.7	6.2	6.9	% Depr., Dep., Amort./Sales	7.8	6.9	5.7	5.1	6.9	6.2
(1764) 8.7	(1791) 9.6	(1991) 11.2		(754) 12.2	(750) 11.2	(172) 9.1	(151) 9.0	(90) 10.3	(74) 8.8
12.6	14.7	16.8		17.7	17.4	15.8	13.3	14.1	12.4
2.2	2.2	2.3	% Officers', Directors' Owners' Comp/Sales	3.1	2.0	1.7	1.4	1.1	
(545) 4.2	(530) 4.4	(576) 4.4		(284) 5.5	(196) 4.1	(40) 3.4	(36) 2.6	(13) 1.9	
7.8	7.3	7.9		8.9	6.8	5.3	5.2	4.0	
12990211M	11054434M	11528331M	Net Sales ($)	482216M	1469275M	742034M	1220660M	1495240M	6118906M
18862413M	18413725M	19491656M	Total Assets ($)	1678069M	3665850M	1599679M	2210935M	3310412M	7026711M

© RMA 2010

M = $ thousand　　MM = $ million
See Pages 9 through 22 for Explanation of Ratios and Data

RESTAURANT/LODGING—Casino Hotels NAICS 721120

| Current Data Sorted by Assets | | | | | | Comparative Historical Data | | |

0-500M	500M-2MM	2-10MM	10-50MM	50-100MM	100-250MM	Type of Statement	4/1/05-3/31/06 ALL	4/1/06-3/31/07 ALL
		2	8	4	12	Unqualified	14	16
		1	1			Reviewed	1	2
		1	1			Compiled		1
		2				Tax Returns	1	2
1	1	7	5	11	18	Other	25	29
1	4	15 (4/1-9/30/09)		64 (10/1/09-3/31/10)				
2	5	12	15	15	30	NUMBER OF STATEMENTS	41	50
%	%	%	%	%	%	ASSETS	%	%
		14.8	15.8	16.2	13.9	Cash & Equivalents	13.0	16.2
		.2	2.0	.5	1.2	Trade Receivables (net)	.8	1.2
		1.1	.9	.5	.5	Inventory	.3	.7
		5.5	1.9	1.8	2.0	All Other Current	3.2	2.1
		21.7	20.6	19.0	17.6	Total Current	17.3	20.2
		65.5	68.3	75.0	71.6	Fixed Assets (net)	69.5	70.3
		4.9	3.3	4.4	4.2	Intangibles (net)	9.1	6.8
		7.9	7.9	1.6	6.5	All Other Non-Current	4.1	2.7
		100.0	100.0	100.0	100.0	Total	100.0	100.0
						LIABILITIES		
		1.9	.9	.0	3.1	Notes Payable-Short Term	.3	1.0
		54.3	3.1	4.5	19.5	Cur. Mat.-L.T.D.	6.1	4.3
		5.6	3.5	2.5	1.7	Trade Payables	1.7	3.4
		.3	.0	.0	.3	Income Taxes Payable	.1	.1
		13.1	14.5	8.8	9.1	All Other Current	9.2	10.2
		75.1	22.0	15.8	33.8	Total Current	17.4	19.0
		35.8	30.9	32.5	29.0	Long-Term Debt	35.3	35.3
		.0	.2	.2	.6	Deferred Taxes	.2	.5
		19.9	12.1	.5	2.2	All Other Non-Current	2.7	6.9
		-30.8	34.7	51.0	34.4	Net Worth	44.4	38.2
		100.0	100.0	100.0	100.0	Total Liabilities & Net Worth	100.0	100.0
						INCOME DATA		
		100.0	100.0	100.0	100.0	Net Sales	100.0	100.0
						Gross Profit		
		92.5	86.6	74.7	80.6	Operating Expenses	79.1	77.1
		7.5	13.4	25.3	19.4	Operating Profit	20.9	22.9
		5.9	3.5	4.1	8.1	All Other Expenses (net)	3.8	5.2
		1.6	9.9	21.3	11.3	Profit Before Taxes	17.1	17.7
						RATIOS		
		1.5	2.0	2.2	1.8	Current	2.0	1.8
		.8	1.1	1.0	1.1		1.2	1.2
		.2	.4	.5	.8		.8	.7
		1.4	1.7	2.1	1.7	Quick	1.7	1.5
		(11) .4	.7	.9	1.0		1.0	1.0
		.3	.4	.4	.6		.6	.6
		0 UND	1 357.4	1 350.8	1 256.8	Sales/Receivables	1 422.9	1 457.0
		0 UND	2 167.4	1 254.3	3 124.9		3 143.9	3 145.2
		1 309.9	5 69.2	2 190.0	6 58.0		5 73.6	5 78.8
						Cost of Sales/Inventory		
						Cost of Sales/Payables		
		16.0	8.5	11.7	12.9	Sales/Working Capital	8.9	10.4
		-21.0	267.9	999.8	57.3		34.4	52.8
		-7.6	-12.2	-17.6	-21.8		-46.2	-37.6
			20.0	33.0	14.7	EBIT/Interest	23.9	60.7
			(13) 2.1	(14) 13.4	(26) 8.4		(36) 7.0	(39) 6.3
			-.5	5.6	1.7		1.9	2.5
						Net Profit + Depr., Dep., Amort./Cur. Mat. L/T/D		
		.9	1.2	1.0	1.1	Fixed/Worth	1.2	1.0
		NM	2.3	1.2	1.7		1.6	1.9
		-.7	-7.5	3.8	7.2		4.0	7.2
		.6	.5	.4	.6	Debt/Worth	.5	.5
		NM	1.9	.7	1.5		1.3	1.4
		-2.3	-12.2	3.2	7.8		5.2	7.9
			67.5	69.9	72.4	% Profit Before Taxes/Tangible Net Worth	80.4	97.3
			(11) 13.4	(13) 47.8	(24) 48.4		(35) 40.7	(41) 48.1
			-12.3	30.4	12.7		17.9	22.5
		6.6	53.2	45.3	28.5	% Profit Before Taxes/Total Assets	34.5	46.2
		-2.5	4.2	15.8	11.8		14.1	18.1
		-10.0	-6.8	10.5	-.9		3.5	3.9
		5.4	4.0	1.9	1.5	Sales/Net Fixed Assets	2.1	2.5
		1.6	2.3	1.7	1.1		1.7	1.6
		.6	.9	1.1	.8		1.0	.9
		2.9	2.3	1.5	1.0	Sales/Total Assets	1.4	1.8
		1.0	1.3	1.2	.8		1.0	1.1
		.6	.8	.9	.6		.7	.7
		2.4	4.9	5.7	6.5	% Depr., Dep., Amort./Sales	5.8	4.4
		(11) 6.1	7.0	(12) 6.3	(10) 7.5		(33) 7.6	(40) 6.6
		11.1	7.4	9.4	10.6		8.9	9.5
						% Officers', Directors' Owners' Comp/Sales		
917M	11021M	107602M	713566M	1298142M	4364764M	Net Sales ($)	3798456M	5351793M
266M	4567M	55189M	444530M	1015499M	5105442M	Total Assets ($)	3472211M	4330275M

M = $ thousand   MM = $ million
See Pages 9 through 22 for Explanation of Ratios and Data

Comparative Historical Data   **Current Data Sorted by Sales**

Type of Statement

4/1/07-3/31/08 ALL	4/1/08-3/31/09 ALL	4/1/09-3/31/10 ALL	Type of Statement	0-1MM	1-3MM	3-5MM	5-10MM	10-25MM	25MM & OVER
26	13	24	Unqualified					3	21
2	1	3	Reviewed					2	1
2		2	Compiled				2		
		4	Tax Returns	2		2			
30	43	46	Other	2	6		1	4	33
					15 (4/1-9/30/09)			64 (10/1/09-3/31/10)	
60	60	79	NUMBER OF STATEMENTS	4	6	2	3	9	55

Main Data

4/1/07-3/31/08 ALL %	4/1/08-3/31/09 ALL %	4/1/09-3/31/10 ALL %		0-1MM %	1-3MM %	3-5MM %	5-10MM %	10-25MM %	25MM & OVER %
			ASSETS						
17.4	12.5	16.0	Cash & Equivalents						15.3
1.0	3.6	2.4	Trade Receivables (net)						1.3
.8	.7	.7	Inventory						.6
1.8	4.0	2.9	All Other Current						2.2
21.0	20.8	22.1	Total Current						19.4
73.5	71.8	68.0	Fixed Assets (net)						70.7
2.7	2.1	3.9	Intangibles (net)						4.8
2.8	5.3	6.1	All Other Non-Current						5.1
100.0	100.0	100.0	Total						100.0
			LIABILITIES						
1.2	1.3	1.8	Notes Payable-Short Term						1.9
3.6	14.9	17.3	Cur. Mat.-L.T.D.						12.3
3.7	4.7	3.3	Trade Payables						2.4
.0	.1	.2	Income Taxes Payable						.2
11.2	11.9	10.0	All Other Current						11.2
19.7	33.0	32.6	Total Current						28.2
36.3	30.2	34.6	Long-Term Debt						28.8
.1	.1	.3	Deferred Taxes						.4
3.3	5.9	9.1	All Other Non-Current						3.6
40.6	30.8	23.4	Net Worth						39.1
100.0	100.0	100.0	Total Liabilities & Net Worth						100.0
			INCOME DATA						
100.0	100.0	100.0	Net Sales						100.0
			Gross Profit						
74.2	82.2	83.6	Operating Expenses						78.9
25.8	17.8	16.4	Operating Profit						21.1
4.4	5.2	5.6	All Other Expenses (net)						5.7
21.4	12.6	10.8	Profit Before Taxes						15.3
			RATIOS						
1.8	1.6	2.1	Current						1.9
1.2	.8	1.1							1.1
.7	.5	.5							.7
1.7	1.5	1.8	Quick						1.7
1.1	.7	(77) 1.0							1.0
.5	.3	.4							.4
1 726.6	1 483.6	1 451.2	Sales/Receivables						1 308.7
2 217.5	2 182.2	2 217.2							2 201.4
4 82.7	5 74.0	4 91.7							4 86.8
			Cost of Sales/Inventory						
			Cost of Sales/Payables						
12.1	15.2	11.4	Sales/Working Capital						12.2
38.9	-50.3	83.4							267.9
-18.6	-10.0	-16.9							-18.4
37.9	14.4	14.6	EBIT/Interest						23.3
(51) 7.9	(52) 6.0	(67) 6.4							(48) 10.5
1.7	1.1	1.0							2.1
			Net Profit + Depr., Dep., Amort./Cur. Mat. L/T/D						
1.1	1.2	1.0	Fixed/Worth						1.0
1.6	1.9	1.8							1.6
4.3	8.7	-30.2							5.8
.5	.7	.5	Debt/Worth						.5
1.1	1.4	1.7							1.2
4.6	9.8	-50.6							5.2
134.1	89.2	70.3	% Profit Before Taxes/Tangible Net Worth						71.9
(49) 60.0	(48) 38.2	(57) 39.5							(44) 51.0
26.9	17.9	8.4							18.2
72.1	35.1	28.6	% Profit Before Taxes/Total Assets						41.6
22.5	13.0	9.4							15.8
3.5	-.4	-1.6							2.9
2.5	1.9	2.8	Sales/Net Fixed Assets						2.2
1.8	1.3	1.6							1.5
1.1	.9	.9							1.1
1.8	1.4	1.7	Sales/Total Assets						1.5
1.3	1.0	1.0							1.0
.8	.7	.7							.7
4.2	5.8	4.9	% Depr., Dep., Amort./Sales						5.7
(41) 6.5	(28) 7.5	(53) 6.6							(32) 6.7
9.8	11.2	9.1							8.2
		2.5	% Officers', Directors' Owners' Comp/Sales						
	(11) 6.7								
		13.8							
8495224M	6417783M	6496012M	Net Sales ($)	1657M	12688M	8075M	21288M	129931M	6322373M
6337226M	6611135M	6625493M	Total Assets ($)	3933M	14707M	6484M	16133M	160171M	6424065M

M = $ thousand   MM = $ million
See Pages 9 through 22 for Explanation of Ratios and Data

RESTAURANT/LODGING—RV (Recreational Vehicle) Parks and Campgrounds NAICS 721211

Current Data Sorted by Assets — **Comparative Historical Data**

Type of Statement	0-500M	500M-2MM	2-10MM	10-50MM	50-100MM	100-250MM		4/1/05-3/31/06 ALL	4/1/06-3/31/07 ALL
Unqualified			4	1				4	8
Reviewed	4	11	6					5	9
Compiled	15	22	8					16	18
Tax Returns	6	10	7	2	2	1		38	34
Other					1	4		19	15

Period of data (current): 6 (4/1-9/30/09) [500M-2MM]; 98 (10/1/09-3/31/10) [10-50MM]

	0-500M	500M-2MM	2-10MM	10-50MM	50-100MM	100-250MM		4/1/05-3/31/06 ALL	4/1/06-3/31/07 ALL
NUMBER OF STATEMENTS	25	43	25	3	3	5		82	84
	%	%	%	%	%	%		%	%
ASSETS									
Cash & Equivalents	10.6	6.9	6.4					11.0	10.4
Trade Receivables (net)	.1	1.4	1.2					2.9	2.2
Inventory	2.3	5.7	3.4					8.9	5.8
All Other Current	1.0	.4	.7					.9	1.4
Total Current	14.0	14.4	11.7					23.7	19.7
Fixed Assets (net)	77.8	71.2	71.9					62.9	64.4
Intangibles (net)	6.8	5.4	6.9					4.3	6.4
All Other Non-Current	1.4	9.0	9.5					9.1	9.5
Total	100.0	100.0	100.0					100.0	100.0
LIABILITIES									
Notes Payable-Short Term	1.4	1.9	6.3					14.7	5.4
Cur. Mat.-L.T.D.	5.0	4.2	4.0					3.1	3.5
Trade Payables	1.2	1.3	1.1					2.5	1.8
Income Taxes Payable	.0	.0	.0					.1	.0
All Other Current	16.6	4.2	7.9					8.8	13.1
Total Current	24.2	11.6	19.4					29.2	23.7
Long-Term Debt	60.9	74.1	45.3					60.0	50.7
Deferred Taxes	.0	.0	.1					.0	.0
All Other Non-Current	6.6	7.8	2.1					5.7	12.0
Net Worth	8.2	6.5	33.1					5.2	13.5
Total Liabilities & Net Worth	100.0	100.0	100.0					100.0	100.0
INCOME DATA									
Net Sales	100.0	100.0	100.0					100.0	100.0
Gross Profit									
Operating Expenses	84.9	78.4	78.6					85.3	84.3
Operating Profit	15.1	21.6	21.4					14.7	15.7
All Other Expenses (net)	6.7	13.1	10.1					5.1	7.6
Profit Before Taxes	8.3	8.5	11.4					9.6	8.0
RATIOS									
Current	2.3	3.4	2.7					2.1	2.6
	.8	1.0	1.0					.9	.8
	.2	.4	.2					.3	.3
Quick	1.5	2.3	2.5					1.4	1.7
	.5	.6	.7				(81)	.4	.4
	.1	.2	.1					.1	.2
Sales/Receivables	0 UND	0 UND	0 UND					0 UND	0 UND
	0 UND	0 UND	0 740.5					0 UND	0 UND
	0 UND	0 UND	4 85.2					2 182.7	4 83.3
Cost of Sales/Inventory									
Cost of Sales/Payables									
Sales/Working Capital	15.0	9.0	7.3					9.9	6.6
	-87.4	368.3	-124.5					-133.8	-41.8
	-9.4	-7.1	-3.6					-7.1	-6.3
EBIT/Interest	5.5	3.8	6.0					5.3	7.8
	(17) 2.0	(26) 1.7	(16) 3.0				(67)	2.7	(65) 1.9
	-.6	1.1	1.8					1.6	.9
Net Profit + Depr., Dep., Amort./Cur. Mat. L/T/D									
Fixed/Worth	2.0	1.8	1.2					1.0	1.2
	8.4	17.0	3.3					3.2	4.8
	-3.1	-3.0	18.5					-4.7	-4.0
Debt/Worth	1.2	2.4	.7					1.2	1.9
	8.0	146.4	3.7					3.6	6.0
	-4.6	-4.8	19.4					-5.9	-7.1
% Profit Before Taxes/Tangible Net Worth	183.2	32.2	149.6					53.6	31.5
	(16) 38.0	(23) 16.7	(20) 14.0				(55)	25.1	(55) 11.0
	-16.2	3.7	3.2					7.1	-1.3
% Profit Before Taxes/Total Assets	21.2	10.3	12.9					15.7	17.5
	6.7	2.9	3.4					6.1	3.2
	-2.2	.3	.7					1.3	-.8
Sales/Net Fixed Assets	3.1	2.1	1.8					4.9	4.3
	1.8	.7	.6					1.8	1.0
	.6	.3	.3					.7	.5
Sales/Total Assets	2.4	1.0	.9					2.1	1.7
	1.2	.5	.4					1.1	.8
	.6	.3	.3					.5	.4
% Depr., Dep., Amort./Sales	5.6	5.6	4.4					3.6	3.9
	(23) 10.5	(34) 12.9	(23) 9.9				(74)	7.1	(73) 7.5
	14.1	19.9	19.1					12.3	15.0
% Officers', Directors' Owners' Comp/Sales		3.5	1.5					3.0	3.8
	(16)	6.8	(10) 4.4				(32)	7.8	(28) 5.9
		10.8	10.0					12.6	12.5
Net Sales ($)	13216M	32121M	99661M	40906M	226019M	771885M		236296M	405826M
Total Assets ($)	7600M	45938M	126514M	80119M	230596M	542804M		303749M	639304M

© RMA 2010

M = $ thousand   MM = $ million
See Pages 9 through 22 for Explanation of Ratios and Data

Comparative Historical Data / Current Data Sorted by Sales

4/1/07-3/31/08 ALL	4/1/08-3/31/09 ALL	4/1/09-3/31/10 ALL	Type of Statement	0-1MM	1-3MM	3-5MM	5-10MM	10-25MM	25MM & OVER
4	2		Unqualified						
3	6	5	Reviewed		1			2	
18	13	21	Compiled	9	9	2	2		2
36	34	47	Tax Returns	35	8	1		1	
26	22	31	Other	18	3	1	2	3	5
				6 (4/1-9/30/09)		98 (10/1/09-3/31/10)			
87	77	104	**NUMBER OF STATEMENTS**	62	21	4	4	6	7
%	%	%	**ASSETS**	%	%	%	%	%	%
8.8	11.5	8.6	Cash & Equivalents	6.4	10.3				
2.0	2.3	1.2	Trade Receivables (net)	.3	2.2				
3.4	5.4	3.8	Inventory	4.1	2.5				
2.2	1.4	1.1	All Other Current	.5	.9				
16.4	20.5	14.7	Total Current	11.3	15.9				
70.0	69.1	72.1	Fixed Assets (net)	79.8	66.1				
5.7	3.4	5.7	Intangibles (net)	5.4	5.3				
7.9	7.0	7.5	All Other Non-Current	3.5	12.7				
100.0	100.0	100.0	Total	100.0	100.0				
			LIABILITIES						
5.1	4.0	2.9	Notes Payable-Short Term	2.0	1.8				
3.4	3.2	4.4	Cur. Mat.-L.T.D.	4.4	3.2				
1.9	1.5	1.5	Trade Payables	1.1	1.3				
.0	.0	1.0	Income Taxes Payable	.0	.0				
8.3	9.3	8.4	All Other Current	7.3	7.2				
18.8	18.0	18.2	Total Current	14.8	13.5				
59.3	52.1	63.0	Long-Term Debt	72.0	53.2				
.1	.0	.0	Deferred Taxes	.0	.2				
12.2	10.9	7.3	All Other Non-Current	7.3	3.7				
9.6	19.0	11.4	Net Worth	5.9	29.5				
100.0	100.0	100.0	Total Liabilities & Net Worth	100.0	100.0				
			INCOME DATA						
100.0	100.0	100.0	Net Sales	100.0	100.0				
			Gross Profit						
82.2	85.8	79.7	Operating Expenses	78.5	83.0				
17.8	14.2	20.3	Operating Profit	21.5	17.0				
10.1	7.9	10.1	All Other Expenses (net)	13.3	6.4				
7.8	6.3	10.1	Profit Before Taxes	8.2	10.6				
			RATIOS						
2.1	4.1	2.6	Current	2.9	3.3				
.7	1.3	.8		.7	1.8				
.3	.4	.3		.2	.7				
1.4	3.2	2.2	Quick	1.7	2.8				
.5	(76) .7	.6		.4	1.7				
.1	.2	.1		.1	.5				
0 UND	0 UND	0 UND	Sales/Receivables	0 UND	0 UND				
0 UND	0 UND	0 UND		0 UND	0 UND				
3 111.8	2 231.2	2 183.3		0 UND	3 132.9				
			Cost of Sales/Inventory						
			Cost of Sales/Payables						
14.5	6.6	9.3	Sales/Working Capital	10.7	7.0				
-19.9	90.5	-114.3		-35.7	22.2				
-7.0	-9.0	-7.0		-5.7	-72.4				
3.6	6.2	5.7	EBIT/Interest	3.7	11.3				
(59) 2.1	(55) 2.3	(66) 2.4		(36) 1.7	(16) 2.5				
.8	1.2	1.2		.8	1.3				
			Net Profit + Depr., Dep., Amort./Cur. Mat. L/T/D						
1.8	1.1	1.4	Fixed/Worth	1.9	1.1				
7.0	3.6	6.4		12.5	2.6				
-3.3	-5.0	-3.7		-3.3	NM				
1.7	.7	.9	Debt/Worth	1.6	.6				
6.8	3.9	7.7		14.8	2.5				
-5.8	-7.0	-6.2		-4.7	NM				
59.0	46.3	67.4	% Profit Before Taxes/Tangible Net Worth	54.6	121.1				
(55) 27.9	(51) 19.6	(66) 17.9		(35) 16.7	(16) 6.6				
3.5	.7	3.6		-2.5	3.3				
12.2	12.7	13.5	% Profit Before Taxes/Total Assets	10.5	18.6				
4.6	4.3	4.3		3.1	2.8				
-.7	-1.0	-.1		-1.2	.7				
3.1	2.8	2.3	Sales/Net Fixed Assets	1.7	2.8				
.9	1.0	.8		.6	1.4				
.5	.5	.4		.3	.5				
1.5	1.6	1.3	Sales/Total Assets	1.0	1.7				
.7	.8	.6		.4	1.0				
.4	.4	.3		.3	.4				
4.7	3.7	5.2	% Depr., Dep., Amort./Sales	7.5	4.0				
(71) 8.7	(69) 8.8	(87) 10.4		(51) 13.2	(19) 7.6				
13.1	15.3	18.1		20.3	15.7				
3.8	2.6	2.7	% Officers', Directors' Owners' Comp/Sales	4.3	2.9				
(36) 7.5	(28) 5.5	(35) 5.8		(17) 7.4	(11) 7.3				
11.0	9.2	10.8		12.1	11.5				
507058M	356328M	1183808M	Net Sales ($)	27109M	35699M	15577M	27144M	93773M	984506M
661868M	570055M	1033571M	Total Assets ($)	60000M	58792M	20652M	57445M	119551M	717131M

© RMA 2010

M = $ thousand   MM = $ million

See Pages 9 through 22 for Explanation of Ratios and Data

Current Data Sorted by Assets   **Comparative Historical Data**

Type of Statement	0-500M	500M-2MM	2-10MM	10-50MM	50-100MM	100-250MM		4/1/05-3/31/06 ALL	4/1/06-3/31/07 ALL
Unqualified			5	2				8	15
Reviewed	2	1	8					9	7
Compiled	3	3	2					12	7
Tax Returns	1	8	4					9	14
Other		7	3	3				16	14
		10 (4/1-9/30/09)		42 (10/1/09-3/31/10)					
NUMBER OF STATEMENTS	6	19	22	5				54	57
	%	%	%	%	%	%		%	%
ASSETS									
Cash & Equivalents		8.9	5.5					10.0	15.2
Trade Receivables (net)		.9	2.9		DATA	DATA		2.3	1.4
Inventory		4.0	.7		NOT	NOT		.8	1.1
All Other Current		.3	4.5		AVAILABLE	AVAILABLE		2.2	1.2
Total Current		14.1	13.5					15.3	18.9
Fixed Assets (net)		72.6	63.4					67.3	65.3
Intangibles (net)		6.3	4.8					5.2	5.2
All Other Non-Current		6.9	18.3					12.2	10.7
Total		100.0	100.0					100.0	100.0
LIABILITIES									
Notes Payable-Short Term		10.8	2.3					3.6	2.1
Cur. Mat.-L.T.D.		3.9	6.0					3.8	4.6
Trade Payables		2.5	2.2					3.2	3.1
Income Taxes Payable		.0	.0					.3	.0
All Other Current		10.1	6.5					7.2	13.5
Total Current		27.3	17.0					18.1	23.3
Long-Term Debt		41.8	37.3					30.7	40.5
Deferred Taxes		.0	.1					.4	.0
All Other Non-Current		8.3	19.7					9.6	11.6
Net Worth		22.6	26.0					41.3	24.6
Total Liabilities & Net Worth		100.0	100.0					100.0	100.0
INCOME DATA									
Net Sales		100.0	100.0					100.0	100.0
Gross Profit									
Operating Expenses		96.1	88.9					86.4	88.2
Operating Profit		3.9	11.1					13.6	11.8
All Other Expenses (net)		6.9	1.0					5.4	4.3
Profit Before Taxes		-3.0	10.1					8.2	7.5
RATIOS									
Current		1.4	1.6					1.7	3.7
		.4	.3					.9	.7
		.1	.1					.4	.3
Quick		.7	1.0					1.6	3.2
		.2	.2					.6	.6
		.1	.0					.3	.2
Sales/Receivables	0 UND		0 UND					0 UND	0 UND
	0 UND		1 428.3					0 UND	0 UND
	2 226.0		5 79.7					5 74.9	8 47.7
Cost of Sales/Inventory									
Cost of Sales/Payables									
Sales/Working Capital		40.6	10.7					26.4	8.6
		-16.2	-17.4					-60.0	-42.8
		-2.3	-9.2					-8.3	-10.0
EBIT/Interest		13.0	8.2					(47) 10.9	(46) 9.1
		(13) 2.9	(18) 2.5					2.5	1.5
		.6	1.2					1.4	.1
Net Profit + Depr., Dep., Amort./Cur. Mat. L/T/D								(11) 6.1	
								3.4	
								.9	
Fixed/Worth		1.7	.7					1.0	1.2
		3.5	2.7					1.7	2.5
		-15.3	-11.5					4.3	-6.5
Debt/Worth		1.5	.7					.6	.8
		3.9	5.6					1.6	2.8
		-19.2	-13.5					5.6	-10.7
% Profit Before Taxes/Tangible Net Worth		64.5	26.3					(46) 30.7	(40) 43.1
		(14) 5.2	(14) 13.7					6.7	7.4
		-7.1	5.8					.2	-1.2
% Profit Before Taxes/Total Assets		14.2	11.7					9.1	19.7
		.5	3.9					2.9	2.7
		-7.5	1.1					.2	-1.7
Sales/Net Fixed Assets		4.7	2.3					2.9	3.3
		1.9	1.1					1.2	1.3
		.5	.7					.7	.6
Sales/Total Assets		2.1	1.1					1.6	1.6
		1.1	.8					.7	.7
		.4	.6					.4	.4
% Depr., Dep., Amort./Sales		3.5	3.0					(48) 3.9	(46) 4.5
		(17) 6.9	(21) 4.8					6.0	6.2
		8.5	7.2					7.7	10.3
% Officers', Directors' Owners' Comp/Sales								(20) 4.1	(17) 3.3
								6.4	6.3
								12.1	12.7
Net Sales ($)	3574M	25700M	91565M	54631M				266388M	322552M
Total Assets ($)	1282M	21526M	100657M	83396M				522977M	586602M

M = $ thousand   MM = $ million
See Pages 9 through 22 for Explanation of Ratios and Data

Comparative Historical Data   Current Data Sorted by Sales

			Type of Statement						
7	8	7	Unqualified		1	3	2	1	
4	2	9	Reviewed		4	5			
5	8	7	Compiled	2	3		1	1	
22	13	15	Tax Returns	4	9	2			
17	9	14	Other	8	2		2	2	
4/1/07-	4/1/08-	4/1/09-			10 (4/1-9/30/09)			42 (10/1/09-3/31/10)	
3/31/08	3/31/09	3/31/10							
ALL	ALL	ALL		0-1MM	1-3MM	3-5MM	5-10MM	10-25MM	25MM & OVER
55	40	52	**NUMBER OF STATEMENTS**	14	19	10	5	4	
%	%	%	**ASSETS**	%	%	%	%	%	%
8.4	12.8	9.7	Cash & Equivalents	8.4	8.0	10.0			D
3.3	3.5	1.7	Trade Receivables (net)	.5	2.2	2.9			A
1.7	2.0	2.0	Inventory	3.7	2.0	.0			T
4.6	2.1	2.3	All Other Current	.1	.4	9.2			A
17.8	20.3	15.7	Total Current	12.6	12.6	22.1			
65.5	67.3	64.7	Fixed Assets (net)	70.7	73.5	58.4			N
4.4	2.3	4.8	Intangibles (net)	7.7	1.2	.7			O
12.2	10.1	14.8	All Other Non-Current	8.9	12.7	18.8			T
100.0	100.0	100.0	Total	100.0	100.0	100.0			
			LIABILITIES						A
5.1	5.6	7.7	Notes Payable-Short Term	20.5	2.6	5.1			V
4.0	4.8	4.3	Cur. Mat.-L.T.D.	4.8	2.8	9.4			A
3.4	1.6	2.5	Trade Payables	1.7	2.7	2.8			I
.0	.0	.0	Income Taxes Payable	.0	.0	.0			L
14.5	12.7	7.1	All Other Current	2.0	6.9	15.0			A
27.1	24.7	21.5	Total Current	29.0	15.0	32.3			B
41.8	37.6	34.2	Long-Term Debt	37.2	41.0	28.9			L
.1	.0	.0	Deferred Taxes	.0	.0	.0			E
13.2	6.0	19.1	All Other Non-Current	13.0	23.7	18.4			
17.8	31.7	25.1	Net Worth	20.8	20.2	20.5			
100.0	100.0	100.0	Total Liabilities & Net Worth	100.0	100.0	100.0			
			INCOME DATA						
100.0	100.0	100.0	Net Sales	100.0	100.0	100.0			
			Gross Profit						
87.4	93.0	91.9	Operating Expenses	93.0	95.7	87.3			
12.6	7.0	8.1	Operating Profit	7.0	4.3	12.7			
7.5	2.9	3.6	All Other Expenses (net)	9.9	1.7	-.2			
5.1	4.1	4.5	Profit Before Taxes	-3.0	2.6	13.0			
			RATIOS						
1.8	2.6	1.6		2.0	1.4	2.5			
.5	1.1	.5	Current	.1	.8	.3			
.2	.2	.1		.0	.2	.1			
1.2	1.4	1.2		.4	1.2	1.4			
.3	.8	.3	Quick	.1	.6	.3			
.0	.1	.1		.0	.2	.0			
0 UND	0 UND	0 UND		0 UND	0 UND	0 UND			
0 UND	1 293.0	0 UND	Sales/Receivables	0 UND	0 UND	0 UND			
3 112.4	9 41.8	3 104.5		1 251.8	4 86.4	9 40.7			
			Cost of Sales/Inventory						
			Cost of Sales/Payables						
9.0	9.3	12.9		525.5	40.6	3.5			
-11.5	91.1	-21.0	Sales/Working Capital	-6.4	-56.5	-13.1			
-4.6	-7.5	-8.0		-1.3	-11.1	-6.8			
6.9	6.5	9.1			5.6				
(41) 1.5	(34) 2.3	(39) 2.9	EBIT/Interest	(16)	(16) 2.2				
.1	.3	1.2			1.1				
			Net Profit + Depr., Dep., Amort./Cur. Mat. L/T/D						
1.2	.9	1.1		1.2	1.4	.7			
3.7	1.8	2.6	Fixed/Worth	4.5	2.7	2.6			
-5.9	NM	-12.8		-4.2	-15.3	-21.9			
.7	.4	.8		.7	1.3	.7			
3.6	1.4	2.9	Debt/Worth	4.4	2.2	6.9			
-6.9	NM	-15.1		-5.2	-19.2	-48.7			
51.8	23.3	25.2	% Profit Before Taxes/Tangible Net Worth		42.2				
(37) 12.8	(30) 7.7	(36) 10.8		(13)	(13) 6.7				
-2.6	-3.4	.0			-.3				
14.0	10.7	12.4	% Profit Before Taxes/Total Assets	11.4	13.5	16.4			
1.3	2.1	3.0		-.5	2.8	6.5			
-2.3	-3.7	-.6		-10.1	-.2	1.2			
4.1	2.6	4.3		4.9	2.3	5.6			
1.1	1.6	1.4	Sales/Net Fixed Assets	1.0	1.6	1.3			
.6	.7	.7		.3	.7	1.0			
1.5	1.7	1.4		1.6	1.9	1.5			
.7	.8	.9	Sales/Total Assets	.4	1.0	.9			
.4	.4	.5		.3	.6	.6			
4.5	4.3	3.4		3.1	3.3	3.2			
(50) 6.7	(35) 5.3	(47) 5.1	% Depr., Dep., Amort./Sales	(10) 8.2	(18) 5.3	4.4			
12.2	8.5	7.9		24.0	8.7	6.1			
5.1	1.7	2.7	% Officers', Directors' Owners' Comp/Sales						
(16) 8.0	(16) 4.5	(20) 7.7							
13.4	9.9	12.5							
357066M	155074M	175470M	Net Sales ($)	7051M	35391M	38781M	31377M	62870M	
386880M	303604M	206861M	Total Assets ($)	13881M	41655M	47511M	43412M	60402M	

© RMA 2010

M = $ thousand   MM = $ million
See Pages 9 through 22 for Explanation of Ratios and Data

Current Data Sorted by Assets   Comparative Historical Data

Type of Statement	0-500M	500M-2MM	2-10MM	10-50MM	50-100MM	100-250MM	4/1/05-3/31/06 ALL	4/1/06-3/31/07 ALL
Unqualified	9	10	16	49	26	25	149	157
Reviewed	11	28	72	59	2		139	162
Compiled	176	187	115	18		2	443	465
Tax Returns	749	395	138	16	2	9	967	1053
Other	291	302	279	135	31	35	901	902
	227 (4/1-9/30/09)			2,960 (10/1/09-3/31/10)				
NUMBER OF STATEMENTS	1236	922	620	277	61	71	2599	2739
ASSETS	%	%	%	%	%	%	%	%
Cash & Equivalents	19.6	13.8	10.4	9.1	7.8	6.9	14.0	14.5
Trade Receivables (net)	1.9	1.8	2.2	1.8	2.3	1.8	2.6	2.4
Inventory	9.8	4.6	3.6	3.0	3.3	2.9	6.1	6.0
All Other Current	2.8	2.7	2.8	2.7	2.7	2.6	2.9	3.2
Total Current	34.2	22.9	19.1	16.5	16.0	14.2	25.6	26.1
Fixed Assets (net)	44.4	54.7	60.9	62.1	62.5	56.5	53.0	53.5
Intangibles (net)	10.8	10.8	11.2	12.6	14.6	22.4	10.7	9.9
All Other Non-Current	10.6	11.5	8.8	8.8	7.0	6.9	10.7	10.5
Total	100.0	100.0	100.0	100.0	100.0	100.0	100.0	100.0
LIABILITIES								
Notes Payable-Short Term	8.8	3.6	3.0	2.9	1.0	2.8	5.0	5.2
Cur. Mat.-L.T.D.	4.8	4.2	5.7	6.3	8.0	2.9	4.4	4.3
Trade Payables	13.3	8.2	7.1	6.3	7.3	5.4	11.1	10.0
Income Taxes Payable	.1	.1	.1	.1	.2	.1	.3	.1
All Other Current	33.1	16.3	12.6	10.7	15.7	13.8	19.6	19.2
Total Current	60.1	32.4	28.5	26.4	32.1	25.0	40.3	38.8
Long-Term Debt	29.1	38.4	43.5	42.3	43.1	43.9	37.4	34.9
Deferred Taxes	.1	.0	.1	.3	.4	2.0	.1	.1
All Other Non-Current	21.0	9.6	5.4	7.5	13.6	14.1	11.5	11.3
Net Worth	-10.3	19.6	22.6	23.5	10.8	14.9	10.7	14.9
Total Liabilities & Net Worth	100.0	100.0	100.0	100.0	100.0	100.0	100.0	100.0
INCOME DATA								
Net Sales	100.0	100.0	100.0	100.0	100.0	100.0	100.0	100.0
Gross Profit	60.7	62.2	62.2	59.7	60.9	60.5	59.2	60.0
Operating Expenses	58.3	57.7	57.2	54.6	55.6	56.6	54.6	55.2
Operating Profit	2.4	4.4	5.0	5.1	5.3	3.8	4.5	4.8
All Other Expenses (net)	.5	1.3	2.2	2.2	2.6	3.7	1.2	1.4
Profit Before Taxes	1.9	3.2	2.9	2.9	2.7	.1	3.3	3.4
RATIOS								
Current	2.0	1.7	1.2	1.1	.9	.9	1.5	1.5
	.7	.8	.6	.6	.5	.6	.7	.7
	.3	.3	.3	.3	.4	.3	.3	.3
Quick	1.3	1.2	.9	.7	.7	.5	1.0	1.0
	(1220) .4	(914) .5	(618) .3	.4	(70) .3	.3	(2588) .4	(2712) .4
	.1	.1	.1	.1	.2	.1	.1	.1
Sales/Receivables	0 UND	0 UND	0 UND	0 UND	0 UND	0 UND	0 UND	0 UND
	0 UND	0 UND	0 UND	1 360.4	2 160.3	2 169.8	0 UND	0 UND
	0 UND	1 376.8	3 137.8	3 107.2	6 59.1	6 63.3	2 209.1	2 210.0
Cost of Sales/Inventory	5 80.4	6 61.7	7 50.3	6 61.3	6 58.4	8 44.2	5 69.4	5 66.5
	10 36.8	10 35.5	11 33.3	11 34.7	13 27.4	12 31.7	10 37.9	10 37.0
	18 20.2	18 19.8	18 20.7	16 23.4	24 15.4	18 20.0	17 21.3	17 21.4
Cost of Sales/Payables	0 UND	2 206.4	11 32.8	14 26.1	16 22.5	11 32.1	3 129.6	3 118.6
	7 50.0	16 22.4	23 16.0	26 14.1	34 10.6	28 13.0	19 19.3	18 19.8
	26 14.2	35 10.5	44 8.4	46 8.0	65 5.6	44 8.3	38 9.5	36 10.1
Sales/Working Capital	40.4	31.4	61.6	113.4	-98.9	-77.0	40.9	40.1
	-89.7	-79.0	-31.2	-23.2	-20.6	-19.2	-47.5	-56.2
	-15.5	-11.7	-10.4	-11.6	-9.5	-9.4	-13.1	-14.5
EBIT/Interest	13.5	10.4	7.8	4.9	5.4	3.8	8.7	9.1
	(704) 2.8	(742) 3.2	(567) 2.7	(269) 2.6	(59) 2.1	(66) 1.4	(2020) 2.9	(2138) 3.0
	-1.5	.3	.7	1.3	.4	.4	.9	1.0
Net Profit + Depr., Dep., Amort./Cur. Mat. L/T/D		7.2	4.6	4.9	3.1	9.8	5.3	5.3
		(37) 3.1	(68) 2.1	(69) 2.3	(24) 2.1	(12) 3.9	(190) 2.4	(200) 2.6
		1.4	.9	1.3	.8	1.3	1.3	1.4
Fixed/Worth	.7	1.1	1.5	1.7	2.5	3.1	1.1	1.0
	3.1	3.7	4.8	5.2	5.8	-7.8	4.5	3.4
	-1.0	-2.9	-7.0	-5.8	-3.5	-1.4	-2.9	-3.8
Debt/Worth	.7	.8	1.4	1.4	2.0	3.4	1.2	1.0
	8.4	4.7	5.3	6.3	6.8	-12.7	6.5	5.1
	-2.4	-5.4	-11.8	-9.4	-5.7	-2.8	-4.8	-6.1
% Profit Before Taxes/Tangible Net Worth	148.6	84.2	67.2	59.0	37.2	49.4	99.5	98.3
	(696) 51.4	(579) 40.1	(407) 28.5	(182) 24.6	(34) 16.4	(26) 12.2	(1584) 39.6	(1731) 37.5
	8.0	8.5	4.4	7.8	-1.2	-8.6	8.4	9.8
% Profit Before Taxes/Total Assets	41.0	24.8	16.4	10.1	9.0	6.0	24.6	25.8
	11.6	9.1	5.9	5.6	3.6	2.0	7.8	9.2
	-7.9	-1.6	-.8	1.6	-1.7	-4.0	-.3	.5
Sales/Net Fixed Assets	44.9	12.1	7.3	5.3	4.4	4.8	16.5	16.3
	16.4	5.8	3.6	3.0	2.9	3.4	6.9	6.8
	7.3	2.7	1.8	2.1	2.0	2.4	3.1	3.1
Sales/Total Assets	9.7	4.2	3.3	2.5	2.2	2.2	5.9	5.7
	5.9	2.7	2.1	1.9	1.7	1.8	3.3	3.3
	3.7	1.7	1.2	1.4	1.4	1.4	1.9	1.9
% Depr., Dep., Amort./Sales	.8	1.5	2.2	2.7	3.4	2.8	1.3	1.3
	(947) 1.7	(788) 2.7	(571) 3.5	(271) 3.6	(50) 4.5	(25) 3.6	(2237) 2.3	(2351) 2.4
	3.3	4.7	5.4	5.0	5.3	4.2	3.8	3.9
% Officers', Directors' Owners' Comp/Sales	2.8	2.0	1.3	1.1		.5	2.3	2.3
	(616) 4.9	(389) 3.7	(218) 2.7	(55) 2.4		(13) 3.3	(1097) 4.4	(1132) 4.3
	7.8	6.5	5.4	4.8		7.6	7.6	7.6
Net Sales ($)	1675671M	2941556M	6739247M	12290344M	9082955M	24261511M	53335888M	46931992M
Total Assets ($)	282468M	942104M	2757887M	6040413M	4395208M	10900095M	18934876M	19548771M

M = $ thousand   MM = $ million
See Pages 9 through 22 for Explanation of Ratios and Data

Comparative Historical Data   **Current Data Sorted by Sales**

			Type of Statement						
129	141	135	Unqualified	1	9	5	10	12	98
130	126	172	Reviewed	4	15	16	27	53	57
499	502	498	Compiled	80	192	87	60	57	22
1083	1102	1309	Tax Returns	438	584	143	80	39	25
951	1086	1073	Other	115	376	148	121	128	185
4/1/07-3/31/08 ALL	4/1/08-3/31/09 ALL	4/1/09-3/31/10 ALL		227 (4/1-9/30/09)		2,960 (10/1/09-3/31/10)			
				0-1MM	1-3MM	3-5MM	5-10MM	10-25MM	25MM & OVER
2792	2957	3187	**NUMBER OF STATEMENTS**	638	1176	399	298	289	387
%	%	%	**ASSETS**	%	%	%	%	%	%
13.7	13.9	14.7	Cash & Equivalents	14.2	17.0	15.7	14.0	12.9	9.5
2.6	2.1	2.0	Trade Receivables (net)	1.1	2.0	2.1	2.2	2.7	2.4
6.2	6.4	6.2	Inventory	9.0	6.5	5.9	4.7	4.3	3.8
3.2	3.2	2.8	All Other Current	2.0	2.8	3.6	3.1	2.5	2.9
25.6	25.6	25.7	Total Current	26.4	28.3	27.2	23.9	22.4	18.6
53.1	52.6	52.8	Fixed Assets (net)	52.5	50.0	51.9	53.3	57.3	58.8
11.4	10.9	11.4	Intangibles (net)	10.7	10.4	11.5	11.3	12.1	14.6
9.9	11.0	10.2	All Other Non-Current	10.4	11.3	9.5	11.5	8.2	8.0
100.0	100.0	100.0	Total	100.0	100.0	100.0	100.0	100.0	100.0
			LIABILITIES						
5.2	6.2	5.4	Notes Payable-Short Term	10.0	5.1	4.2	3.9	3.3	2.6
4.8	4.7	5.0	Cur. Mat.-L.T.D.	5.1	4.4	5.0	4.7	6.7	6.5
10.1	10.1	9.7	Trade Payables	8.0	11.5	9.7	9.0	9.5	7.8
.2	.2	.1	Income Taxes Payable	.1	.1	.1	.1	.2	.1
19.8	20.6	21.5	All Other Current	32.0	22.0	19.4	18.1	13.4	13.8
40.1	41.8	41.7	Total Current	55.1	42.8	38.4	35.8	33.0	30.8
36.5	35.9	36.3	Long-Term Debt	37.0	34.1	36.8	35.0	38.7	40.8
.1	.1	.1	Deferred Taxes	.0	.1	.0	.0	.1	.7
11.3	11.7	13.2	All Other Non-Current	24.5	12.9	9.6	6.5	5.2	10.3
12.0	10.6	8.7	Net Worth	-16.6	10.2	15.1	22.6	23.0	17.4
100.0	100.0	100.0	Total Liabilities & Net Worth	100.0	100.0	100.0	100.0	100.0	100.0
			INCOME DATA						
100.0	100.0	100.0	Net Sales	100.0	100.0	100.0	100.0	100.0	100.0
60.1	60.3	61.3	Gross Profit	60.6	61.7	62.5	62.9	60.9	59.5
56.0	56.9	57.5	Operating Expenses	59.4	57.6	57.4	57.7	56.4	55.0
4.1	3.3	3.8	Operating Profit	1.1	4.1	5.1	5.3	4.6	4.5
1.5	1.4	1.3	All Other Expenses (net)	1.4	1.1	1.1	1.0	1.4	2.1
2.6	1.9	2.5	Profit Before Taxes	-.3	3.0	4.0	4.2	3.2	2.4
			RATIOS						
1.5	1.5	1.6		2.1	1.9	1.6	1.4	1.1	.9
.7	.7	.7	Current	.7	.7	.7	.8	.7	.6
.3	.3	.3		.2	.3	.3	.3	.3	.3
1.0	1.0	1.0		1.2	1.4	1.0	1.1	.8	.7
(2769) .4	(2937) .4	(3160) .4	Quick	(629) .3	(1160) .4	(398) .4	.4	.5	(386) .4
.1	.1	.1		.1	.1	.1	.1	.2	.1
0 UND	0 UND	0 UND		0 UND	0 UND	0 UND	0 UND	0 UND	0 999.8
0 UND	0 UND	0 UND	Sales/Receivables	0 UND	0 UND	0 999.8	0 999.8	1 541.4	1 266.1
2 182.5	1 255.3	1 276.1		0 UND	0 802.8	2 166.0	2 199.2	3 123.0	4 84.2
6 64.4	6 62.8	6 64.4		5 71.9	5 75.3	6 60.4	7 53.1	7 51.9	6 57.3
10 36.8	10 36.4	10 35.1	Cost of Sales/Inventory	13 29.2	10 37.0	10 36.3	10 36.3	10 34.8	11 34.7
17 21.0	17 21.3	18 20.2		23 15.7	17 21.2	17 21.0	17 21.3	15 24.3	16 22.6
2 156.5	2 233.7	1 424.0		0 UND	0 UND	6 58.6	10 36.0	13 28.1	14 26.5
17 21.1	16 22.4	16 22.5	Cost of Sales/Payables	0 UND	14 25.9	19 19.4	22 16.4	23 15.9	27 13.4
37 9.8	35 10.4	36 10.2		22 17.0	33 11.2	37 9.8	41 8.9	43 8.5	45 8.1
49.1	49.7	42.6		37.6	34.3	37.6	39.6	104.4	-156.5
-49.6	-45.2	-51.2	Sales/Working Capital	-70.3	-75.9	-58.9	-58.2	-33.6	-23.1
-13.4	-12.3	-12.4		-9.7	-13.9	-11.6	-11.9	-14.9	-12.1
7.5	7.5	9.1		5.1	12.0	12.7	12.3	8.5	6.0
(2180) 2.5	(2277) 2.3	(2407) 2.8	EBIT/Interest	(383) 1.0	(811) 3.0	(314) 3.2	(256) 4.0	(271) 3.4	(372) 2.6
.5	.0	.4		-2.2	.1	.5	1.1	1.0	1.1
5.4	4.4	4.9			8.0	7.9	4.4	5.1	4.7
(183) 2.2	(188) 1.8	(218) 2.4	Net Profit + Depr., Dep., Amort./Cur. Mat. L/T/D	(26) 2.8	(16) 2.0	(22) 1.8	(47) 2.8	(105) 2.3	
1.0	.8	1.2			.7	1.3	.7	1.5	1.2
1.1	1.0	1.0		.9	.8	1.0	1.2	1.4	1.9
4.0	4.3	4.3	Fixed/Worth	12.5	3.1	3.4	3.6	4.8	7.0
-3.0	-2.5	-2.3		-.8	-2.7	-2.8	-6.3	-3.8	-3.2
1.1	1.1	1.0		.9	.8	.8	1.1	1.2	1.7
5.7	6.3	6.1	Debt/Worth	97.8	4.5	4.0	4.4	5.3	8.7
-4.6	-4.4	-4.3		-2.1	-4.4	-4.9	-9.9	-6.4	-5.2
99.2	99.1	94.1		74.2	111.1	99.8	84.1	80.2	70.0
(1724) 37.2	(1782) 34.1	(1924) 36.5	% Profit Before Taxes/Tangible Net Worth	(329) 21.8	(739) 44.2	(249) 42.8	(200) 36.1	(184) 31.7	(223) 30.5
7.5	4.3	7.2		-2.0	9.2	9.2	8.7	9.6	8.8
24.8	22.9	23.9		18.8	31.4	30.8	23.3	19.3	12.4
7.6	5.9	7.3	% Profit Before Taxes/Total Assets	2.5	10.8	10.4	8.8	8.1	5.3
-2.3	-3.7	-2.0		-12.8	-1.5	-1.0	1.5	.2	.5
16.6	18.4	17.6		23.1	26.4	18.3	11.9	10.4	6.5
6.8	6.8	6.7	Sales/Net Fixed Assets	8.1	8.7	7.1	5.9	5.2	3.8
3.0	3.1	3.0		2.9	3.9	2.9	2.8	2.7	2.6
5.7	5.9	5.7		7.0	7.1	5.5	4.6	4.3	3.2
3.2	3.3	3.2	Sales/Total Assets	3.5	3.9	3.2	2.8	2.8	2.2
1.9	1.9	1.8		1.7	2.2	1.9	1.7	1.8	1.6
1.3	1.3	1.3		1.2	1.0	1.2	1.7	2.1	2.6
(2357) 2.5	(2461) 2.6	(2652) 2.7	% Depr., Dep., Amort./Sales	(513) 2.6	(928) 2.3	(347) 2.4	(270) 2.9	(270) 3.2	(324) 3.5
4.2	4.3	4.5		5.2	4.2	4.1	4.5	4.5	4.5
2.2	2.0	2.0		3.2	2.4	1.8	1.5	1.0	1.1
(1158) 4.2	(1176) 3.8	(1297) 4.0	% Officers', Directors' Owners' Comp/Sales	(309) 5.9	(536) 4.0	(155) 3.6	(129) 3.0	(89) 1.8	(79) 2.6
7.4	7.1	7.0		5.9	6.5	7.2	5.0	3.9	5.2
46442489M	56407256M	56991284M	Net Sales ($)	407054M	2140888M	1535494M	2163829M	4531428M	46212591M
22147813M	21935029M	25318175M	Total Assets ($)	200932M	845901M	662564M	973881M	2058810M	20576087M

M = $ thousand   MM = $ million
See Pages 9 through 22 for Explanation of Ratios and Data

Current Data Sorted by Assets   Comparative Historical Data

						Type of Statement		
3	5	22	54	16	18	Unqualified	47	96
3	15	48	40	6		Reviewed	54	77
113	165	152	19	1	2	Compiled	141	203
326	178	78	7	1	1	Tax Returns	244	259
167	159	157	95	21	18	Other	249	327
	127 (4/1-9/30/09)		1,763 (10/1/09-3/31/10)				4/1/05-3/31/06	4/1/06-3/31/07
0-500M	500M-2MM	2-10MM	10-50MM	50-100MM	100-250MM		ALL	ALL
612	522	457	215	45	39	NUMBER OF STATEMENTS	735	962
%	%	%	%	%	%	**ASSETS**	%	%
16.7	12.8	13.6	9.1	8.0	6.9	Cash & Equivalents	14.6	14.8
2.1	1.3	1.5	1.3	1.1	1.9	Trade Receivables (net)	1.1	1.3
7.3	3.1	2.6	2.1	2.0	2.1	Inventory	3.9	3.7
3.3	2.9	2.6	3.1	2.2	3.0	All Other Current	3.3	3.2
29.4	20.1	20.4	15.6	13.3	13.8	Total Current	23.0	23.0
45.3	52.1	53.8	55.9	54.0	51.2	Fixed Assets (net)	52.6	53.8
14.2	18.9	19.0	20.9	24.5	29.5	Intangibles (net)	15.5	15.3
11.0	8.9	6.8	7.6	8.1	5.5	All Other Non-Current	8.9	7.9
100.0	100.0	100.0	100.0	100.0	100.0	Total	100.0	100.0
						LIABILITIES		
7.0	2.6	2.8	1.9	1.1	.4	Notes Payable-Short Term	3.7	4.6
6.9	7.2	8.3	6.6	6.8	3.8	Cur. Mat.-L.T.D.	4.9	5.5
10.5	6.8	5.8	5.2	4.4	4.8	Trade Payables	9.4	7.9
.1	.0	.1	.1	.1	.1	Income Taxes Payable	.2	.1
30.0	14.3	10.2	9.1	8.1	11.8	All Other Current	14.4	14.4
54.4	30.9	27.2	22.9	20.6	21.0	Total Current	32.6	32.6
42.1	50.4	50.9	43.5	44.3	64.6	Long-Term Debt	44.9	43.2
.0	.0	.1	.3	.3	3.1	Deferred Taxes	.1	.2
14.6	7.4	4.3	4.7	4.1	10.0	All Other Non-Current	11.1	8.8
-11.2	11.3	17.6	28.6	30.8	1.3	Net Worth	11.3	15.2
100.0	100.0	100.0	100.0	100.0	100.0	Total Liabilities & Net Worth	100.0	100.0
						INCOME DATA		
100.0	100.0	100.0	100.0	100.0	100.0	Net Sales	100.0	100.0
61.1	62.1	63.5	62.1	62.4	55.9	Gross Profit	62.0	59.8
57.2	57.7	58.4	56.1	54.7	50.4	Operating Expenses	57.4	54.8
3.9	4.5	5.1	6.0	7.7	5.6	Operating Profit	4.5	5.1
.6	1.3	1.2	1.3	2.7	3.8	All Other Expenses (net)	1.2	1.5
3.2	3.2	4.0	4.7	5.0	1.8	Profit Before Taxes	3.3	3.6
						RATIOS		
1.9	1.4	1.3	1.2	1.0	.9		1.5	1.5
.7	.6	.6	.7	.7	.5	Current	.7	.7
.3	.3	.3	.4	.4	.4		.3	.3
1.3	1.0	1.0	.9	.8	.5		1.0	1.1
(605) .4	(519) .4	(456) .4	(214) .4	(44) .5	.3	Quick	(724) .4	(956) .5
.1	.1	.2	.2	.2	.2		.1	.1
0 UND	0 UND	0 UND	0 UND	0 UND	1 677.8		0 UND	0 UND
0 UND	0 UND	0 999.8	1 922.3	2 287.9	2 170.6	Sales/Receivables	0 UND	0 UND
0 UND	0 999.8	1 308.5	2 191.0	3 112.7	6 58.9		1 483.5	1 400.3
5 78.6	5 69.1	6 66.0	6 56.8	6 64.9	6 63.7		5 66.5	5 78.3
8 44.7	8 43.3	9 40.3	9 42.4	10 37.7	9 40.2	Cost of Sales/Inventory	8 43.0	8 45.8
12 30.5	11 32.1	11 32.5	11 32.1	14 26.9	12 30.0		12 30.0	12 30.9
0 UND	4 83.1	9 42.8	12 29.6	13 27.1	12 29.2		3 104.3	6 65.4
6 64.4	16 22.2	17 21.5	20 17.9	24 15.2	24 15.3	Cost of Sales/Payables	16 22.5	17 22.0
21 17.5	30 12.2	29 12.6	36 10.0	39 9.4	42 8.7		36 10.2	32 11.4
51.0	68.6	58.7	63.3	-953.0	-70.9		55.3	54.7
-81.4	-40.6	-34.2	-31.0	-35.7	-19.3	Sales/Working Capital	-53.0	-52.7
-15.9	-13.1	-15.0	-14.9	-13.5	-12.9		-15.0	-14.3
12.0	9.0	8.2	7.8	4.7	5.5		7.8	7.6
(423) 3.8	(475) 3.3	(434) 3.3	(208) 3.8	(43) 2.6	1.6	EBIT/Interest	(607) 3.0	(812) 2.9
.7	1.0	1.6	2.0	1.6	.9		1.3	1.0
	7.5	3.5	6.5	8.9		Net Profit + Depr., Dep.,	2.9	4.3
	(19) 2.0	(51) 1.9	(49) 2.3	(17) 2.5		Amort./Cur. Mat. L/T/D	(57) 1.7	(97) 2.1
	1.3	1.0	1.2	1.8			1.0	1.4
.9	1.7	1.8	1.7	2.5	4.7		1.3	1.3
7.1	-60.2	36.7	5.4	5.1	-4.9	Fixed/Worth	11.6	6.5
-.8	-1.1	-2.1	-3.1	-4.0	-.6		-1.9	-2.0
1.3	2.0	2.0	1.5	2.7	4.1		1.6	1.2
25.9	-72.2	94.2	9.2	7.0	-6.9	Debt/Worth	20.0	9.0
-2.2	-2.6	-3.8	-4.6	-5.4	-2.0		-3.5	-4.0
227.2	117.7	112.1	73.0	96.6	40.8	% Profit Before Taxes/Tangible	115.4	98.0
(321) 75.7	(255) 48.4	(230) 52.2	(130) 36.9	(29) 34.3	(13) 28.8	Net Worth	(398) 42.7	(548) 38.8
20.6	12.6	16.9	16.2	13.3	6.7		12.6	13.4
45.3	21.2	17.0	13.8	11.0	8.3	% Profit Before Taxes/Total	23.5	22.9
17.1	8.6	8.3	8.7	6.1	2.4	Assets	8.7	8.9
-1.4	.0	2.2	3.3	2.4	-.8		.9	.4
38.3	14.2	9.3	6.0	5.4	5.3		14.1	12.4
12.8	6.0	5.6	3.9	3.2	3.4	Sales/Net Fixed Assets	6.4	6.1
6.0	3.1	3.3	2.3	1.9	2.2		3.1	2.9
9.2	4.4	3.9	2.7	2.1	2.0		5.2	5.0
5.4	2.8	2.8	2.0	1.6	1.5	Sales/Total Assets	3.0	3.0
3.1	1.6	1.7	1.5	1.2	1.2		1.8	1.8
1.0	1.7	2.5	2.7	2.4	2.9		1.7	1.8
(469) 2.2	(439) 3.0	(424) 3.6	(200) 3.6	(43) 3.5	(16) 3.5	% Depr., Dep., Amort./Sales	(648) 2.9	(845) 2.9
4.1	5.3	5.1	4.9	5.0	4.1		4.2	4.3
2.3	1.7	1.1	.6				2.1	1.9
(249) 4.5	(192) 3.3	(170) 1.9	(37) 1.9			% Officers', Directors' Owners' Comp/Sales	(278) 3.9	(358) 3.6
7.8	5.3	3.7	2.7				6.5	6.3
742488M	1845727M	5953323M	9836449M	5517861M	10130007M	Net Sales ($)	16201240M	29808506M
134153M	548990M	2122634M	4717347M	3271309M	6083760M	Total Assets ($)	6456397M	12012619M

M = $ thousand   MM = $ million
See Pages 9 through 22 for Explanation of Ratios and Data

Comparative Historical Data | Current Data Sorted by Sales

			Type of Statement						
82	95	118	Unqualified	2	6	2	6	14	88
64	78	112	Reviewed	4	2	6	26	28	46
260	373	452	Compiled	66	113	59	97	92	25
316	481	591	Tax Returns	215	233	45	52	39	7
374	474	617	Other	98	168	56	64	95	136
4/1/07-3/31/08 ALL	4/1/08-3/31/09 ALL	4/1/09-3/31/10 ALL		127 (4/1-9/30/09)			1,763 (10/1/09-3/31/10)		
				0-1MM	1-3MM	3-5MM	5-10MM	10-25MM	25MM & OVER
1096	1501	1890	NUMBER OF STATEMENTS	385	522	168	245	268	302
%	%	%	ASSETS	%	%	%	%	%	%
13.9	12.7	13.6	Cash & Equivalents	13.6	14.6	14.8	15.0	14.2	9.6
1.2	1.2	1.6	Trade Receivables (net)	1.3	2.2	1.2	1.9	1.0	1.5
3.9	4.0	4.2	Inventory	6.5	4.5	3.3	3.6	3.3	2.5
2.3	2.7	3.0	All Other Current	3.5	3.2	2.9	2.7	2.1	3.0
21.4	20.5	22.4	Total Current	24.9	24.4	22.2	23.2	20.6	16.7
52.7	51.5	50.8	Fixed Assets (net)	51.7	48.1	50.1	48.8	52.8	54.6
16.3	18.7	18.0	Intangibles (net)	14.4	16.6	20.0	19.7	19.3	21.3
9.6	9.3	8.8	All Other Non-Current	9.0	11.0	7.8	8.3	7.3	7.4
100.0	100.0	100.0	Total	100.0	100.0	100.0	100.0	100.0	100.0
			LIABILITIES						
4.3	5.3	3.9	Notes Payable-Short Term	6.1	4.9	3.3	2.7	2.4	1.9
6.9	6.3	7.2	Cur. Mat.-L.T.D.	5.8	6.5	8.9	8.0	8.5	7.3
7.8	7.7	7.5	Trade Payables	7.9	8.2	7.8	7.6	6.6	6.2
.1	.1	.1	Income Taxes Payable	.1	.0	.2	.1	.1	.1
19.4	15.9	17.6	All Other Current	24.1	22.0	13.8	15.7	11.1	11.1
38.5	35.3	36.3	Total Current	44.0	41.7	34.0	34.2	28.7	26.7
45.4	46.7	47.2	Long-Term Debt	46.8	43.1	56.9	50.5	46.5	47.2
.2	.1	.1	Deferred Taxes	.0	.0	.0	.1	.1	.6
10.5	9.5	8.7	All Other Non-Current	15.4	9.3	8.5	6.2	3.5	5.6
5.5	8.4	7.8	Net Worth	-6.1	5.9	.7	8.9	21.2	19.8
100.0	100.0	100.0	Total Liabilties & Net Worth	100.0	100.0	100.0	100.0	100.0	100.0
			INCOME DATA						
100.0	100.0	100.0	Net Sales	100.0	100.0	100.0	100.0	100.0	100.0
61.4	60.9	62.0	Gross Profit	60.7	62.2	63.8	62.1	62.8	61.7
56.8	57.3	57.3	Operating Expenses	57.7	57.1	58.6	56.7	58.2	56.0
4.6	3.6	4.7	Operating Profit	2.9	5.1	5.2	5.4	4.5	5.7
1.7	1.4	1.1	All Other Expenses (net)	1.4	.9	1.3	1.2	.6	1.5
2.9	2.2	3.6	Profit Before Taxes	1.6	4.1	3.9	4.2	3.9	4.1
			RATIOS						
1.2	1.2	1.4	Current	2.4	1.5	1.2	1.3	1.3	1.0
.6	.6	.7		.8	.7	.6	.7	.6	.6
.3	.3	.3		.2	.3	.3	.4	.4	.4
.9	.9	1.0	Quick	1.6	1.1	.7	1.0	1.0	.8
(1088) .4	(1495) .4	(1877) .4		(379) .4	(519) .4	(167) .4	.5	(267) .5	(300) .4
.1	.1	.1		.1	.1	.1	.2	.2	.2
0 UND	0 UND	0 UND	Sales/Receivables	0 UND	0 UND	0 UND	0 UND	0 UND	0 UND
0 UND	0 UND	0 UND		0 UND	0 UND	0 UND	0 999.8	0 999.8	1 710.0
1 414.3	1 450.8	1 453.8		0 UND	0 999.8	1 564.6	2 220.7	1 343.6	2 185.9
5 72.0	5 68.5	5 69.1	Cost of Sales/Inventory	5 72.2	5 78.8	5 66.8	5 71.4	6 58.5	6 -56.7
8 43.2	9 42.2	9 42.3		9 40.8	9 45.4	9 42.8	9 41.0	9 40.3	9 41.8
12 30.4	12 30.1	12 31.5		14 26.1	11 32.2	11 31.8	11 33.2	11 32.7	11 32.0
4 99.7	3 122.9	3 138.3	Cost of Sales/Payables	0 UND	0 UND	5 71.3	8 45.3	9 40.2	12 30.4
14 25.5	15 24.2	15 24.0		2 230.0	14 26.3	17 21.2	17 21.5	17 21.6	22 16.9
31 11.9	30 12.1	28 13.2		20 18.4	27 13.6	30 12.0	28 13.0	29 12.8	36 10.2
95.2	104.1	59.9	Sales/Working Capital	33.0	63.9	89.2	53.4	73.5	NM
-39.5	-36.0	-44.5		-83.0	-55.0	-33.1	-41.6	-35.4	-27.6
-13.1	-12.7	-14.7		-12.1	-13.6	-14.6	-15.8	-16.2	-14.9
7.4	6.6	9.1	EBIT/Interest	8.0	10.0	9.6	10.8	8.7	8.2
(965) 2.7	(1304) 2.3	(1622) 3.4		(276) 2.1	(410) 3.7	(157) 3.4	(234) 3.3	(255) 4.0	(290) 3.5
.8	.6	1.2		-.4	1.0	1.1	1.3	1.8	1.8
7.0	4.7	3.9	Net Profit + Depr., Dep., Amort./Cur. Mat. L/T/D				3.7	3.4	4.9
(95) 2.7	(107) 2.1	(151) 2.1					(23) 1.8	(36) 2.1	(74) 2.4
1.3	1.1	1.1					.9	1.1	1.2
1.7	1.8	1.5	Fixed/Worth	1.2	1.2	2.9	1.5	1.5	2.0
86.3	-102.3	22.5		64.6	7.4	-12.7	-16.7	9.4	12.0
-1.7	-1.3	-1.3		-1.1	-1.2	-.8	-1.1	-2.6	-2.0
1.9	2.2	1.8	Debt/Worth	1.2	1.7	3.7	1.5	1.6	2.1
-110.3	-47.8	42.1		-83.8	15.3	-15.0	-18.9	13.9	15.4
-3.3	-2.9	-2.8		-2.4	-2.8	-2.2	-2.7	-4.2	-3.6
114.8	103.1	130.6	% Profit Before Taxes/Tangible Net Worth	122.5	197.6	185.7	100.5	117.6	82.0
(542) 45.6	(731) 38.0	(978) 50.9		(190) 38.8	(288) 65.4	(75) 76.5	(110) 40.8	(150) 55.1	(165) 36.8
12.8	7.9	16.9		3.8	20.0	26.3	9.6	20.8	16.8
22.5	18.3	23.6	% Profit Before Taxes/Total Assets	28.4	33.7	22.1	21.7	18.7	16.2
7.7	6.1	9.4		6.7	13.5	10.6	8.8	9.2	8.2
-.9	-1.4	1.0		-7.7	.8	.6	1.1	4.9	2.9
13.2	13.6	14.4	Sales/Net Fixed Assets	19.5	24.2	17.3	14.2	11.1	7.1
6.7	6.3	6.4		7.1	8.3	7.0	7.0	6.2	4.6
3.2	3.1	3.4		2.8	4.0	3.4	4.2	3.9	2.9
5.1	4.7	5.0	Sales/Total Assets	6.2	6.7	5.4	4.7	4.6	3.3
3.2	2.9	3.0		3.0	3.6	3.2	3.1	3.2	2.2
1.9	1.7	1.8		1.6	2.0	1.9	1.9	2.0	1.6
1.8	1.9	1.8	% Depr., Dep., Amort./Sales	1.6	1.3	1.8	2.0	2.3	2.5
(956) 2.8	(1274) 3.2	(1591) 3.2		(311) 3.3	(415) 2.5	(136) 3.4	(219) 3.2	(248) 3.4	(262) 3.4
4.4	4.9	4.9		5.8	4.7	5.5	4.9	4.6	4.7
1.6	1.4	1.5	% Officers', Directors' Owners' Comp/Sales	3.0	2.3	1.5	1.1	1.0	.6
(424) 3.2	(562) 3.0	(660) 3.1		(139) 5.2	(214) 3.9	(61) 2.3	(93) 1.9	(102) 1.9	(51) 1.3
5.4	5.7	5.6		11.0	5.9	4.2	3.4	3.7	2.6
21518858M	30224552M	34025855M	Net Sales ($)	239522M	931145M	642750M	1770807M	4229794M	26211837M
10292280M	13390780M	16878193M	Total Assets ($)	114871M	388983M	282987M	743571M	1640423M	13707358M

M = $ thousand   MM = $ million
See Pages 9 through 22 for Explanation of Ratios and Data

Current Data Sorted by Assets | Comparative Historical Data

							Type of Statement		
1	2		3	1			Unqualified	5	7
	9	5	2				Reviewed	2	7
9	12	3					Compiled	14	10
35	16	1					Tax Returns	19	42
15	4	8					Other	11	38
	9 (4/1-9/30/09)		121 (10/1/09-3/31/10)					4/1/05-3/31/06	4/1/06-3/31/07
0-500M	500M-2MM	2-10MM	10-50MM	50-100MM	100-250MM			ALL	ALL
60	43	17	7	2	1		NUMBER OF STATEMENTS	51	104
%	%	%	%	%	%			%	%
							ASSETS		
16.4	8.6	10.6					Cash & Equivalents	10.8	11.8
3.2	2.2	1.9					Trade Receivables (net)	4.1	2.5
6.4	3.5	2.3					Inventory	4.3	4.8
3.0	2.0	3.2					All Other Current	3.0	1.2
28.9	16.3	18.1					Total Current	22.3	20.3
47.5	42.6	45.2					Fixed Assets (net)	53.5	48.4
14.9	27.0	23.6					Intangibles (net)	14.2	15.7
8.7	14.1	13.2					All Other Non-Current	10.0	15.6
100.0	100.0	100.0					Total	100.0	100.0
							LIABILITIES		
5.9	.7	2.5					Notes Payable-Short Term	3.5	10.4
7.2	5.0	6.3					Cur. Mat.-L.T.D.	7.4	6.5
4.7	2.8	4.7					Trade Payables	6.8	5.9
.0	.0	.0					Income Taxes Payable	.0	.2
11.9	8.3	5.5					All Other Current	11.5	15.3
29.7	16.8	19.1					Total Current	29.1	38.3
42.1	44.8	43.7					Long-Term Debt	41.2	36.1
.0	.0	.0					Deferred Taxes	.0	.1
13.4	9.8	17.4					All Other Non-Current	12.4	11.8
14.9	28.5	19.8					Net Worth	17.2	13.7
100.0	100.0	100.0					Total Liabilities & Net Worth	100.0	100.0
							INCOME DATA		
100.0	100.0	100.0					Net Sales	100.0	100.0
							Gross Profit		
94.8	92.1	95.3					Operating Expenses	93.8	92.5
5.2	7.9	4.7					Operating Profit	6.2	7.5
1.7	2.5	1.6					All Other Expenses (net)	2.3	1.9
3.5	5.4	3.1					Profit Before Taxes	3.9	5.6
							RATIOS		
2.3	2.1	1.6						1.7	1.6
1.0	.7	1.0					Current	.8	.7
.3	.3	.4						.3	.1
1.5	1.3	.9						1.1	1.3
(58) .7	.4	.6					Quick	(103) .4	.5
.2	.1	.3						.1	.1
0 UND	0 UND	0 UND						0 UND	0 UND
0 UND	0 UND	1 395.5					Sales/Receivables	0 UND	0 UND
0 UND	1 388.8	4 90.5						2 174.1	1 284.2
							Cost of Sales/Inventory		
							Cost of Sales/Payables		
32.5	18.9	25.5						26.7	45.8
UND	-108.1	-351.2					Sales/Working Capital	-67.9	-51.7
-29.3	-14.0	-17.8						-14.3	-9.3
9.0	5.3	8.0						9.6	8.4
(47) 4.5	(37) 2.9	2.1					EBIT/Interest	(44) 2.8	(83) 2.7
1.1	1.3	.1						.4	1.5
							Net Profit + Depr., Dep., Amort./Cur. Mat. L/T/D		
.8	1.3	1.9						1.2	1.0
UND	6.0	9.9					Fixed/Worth	13.4	6.0
-2.1	-.9	-1.0						-1.8	-1.2
.8	1.0	2.1						1.3	.9
UND	12.9	12.9					Debt/Worth	16.6	10.1
-4.3	-2.5	-2.4						-3.9	-3.2
158.7	105.2							60.8	139.8
(30) 48.7	(25) 27.1						% Profit Before Taxes/Tangible Net Worth	(27) 33.7	(61) 56.8
11.4	7.0							-1.9	17.7
28.6	18.5	18.4						23.5	24.9
15.2	7.3	3.6					% Profit Before Taxes/Total Assets	8.6	8.4
.2	1.1	-2.2						-2.8	1.7
18.7	13.9	7.5						11.0	12.0
7.3	4.4	4.7					Sales/Net Fixed Assets	5.4	6.3
3.7	2.1	1.7						2.3	2.9
5.0	2.7	2.4						3.5	4.0
3.2	1.5	1.5					Sales/Total Assets	2.4	2.6
1.8	.9	.9						1.6	1.6
2.0	2.5	4.0						2.6	2.2
(42) 3.6	(39) 6.6	(15) 4.6					% Depr., Dep., Amort./Sales	(42) 3.7	(85) 3.7
5.5	9.6	8.0						6.1	5.3
1.9	1.6							2.4	2.1
(20) 6.3	(10) 4.6						% Officers', Directors' Owners' Comp/Sales	(21) 5.1	(32) 4.4
10.6	6.8							7.2	8.7
42771M	84118M	122656M	387515M	305073M	301553M		Net Sales ($)	1019027M	3951314M
13965M	41744M	62709M	168753M	152548M	125818M		Total Assets ($)	539396M	1220721M

© RMA 2010

M = $ thousand   MM = $ million

See Pages 9 through 22 for Explanation of Ratios and Data

Comparative Historical Data   **Current Data Sorted by Sales**

Type of Statement	4/1/07-3/31/08	4/1/08-3/31/09	4/1/09-3/31/10	9 (4/1-9/30/09)			121 (10/1/09-3/31/10)		
Unqualified	5	4	7	1		1		1	4
Reviewed	9	2	16	2	7	2	2	2	1
Compiled	5	9	24	11	8	2	1	2	
Tax Returns	67	31	52	31	19	2			
Other	39	58	31	15	5	3	2	3	3
	ALL	ALL	ALL	0-1MM	1-3MM	3-5MM	5-10MM	10-25MM	25MM & OVER
NUMBER OF STATEMENTS	125	104	130	60	39	10	5	8	8
ASSETS	%	%	%	%	%	%	%	%	%
Cash & Equivalents	10.3	8.3	12.7	13.7	9.9	14.1			
Trade Receivables (net)	1.2	3.3	3.2	3.1	2.0	1.6			
Inventory	3.6	6.7	4.9	5.1	4.4	3.0			
All Other Current	1.3	2.9	2.9	1.4	4.4	3.3			
Total Current	16.4	21.2	23.6	23.3	20.7	22.1			
Fixed Assets (net)	55.4	50.0	45.7	48.8	43.1	41.9			
Intangibles (net)	15.8	19.3	20.1	19.7	20.9	24.4			
All Other Non-Current	12.5	9.5	10.6	8.2	15.4	11.6			
Total	100.0	100.0	100.0	100.0	100.0	100.0			
LIABILITIES									
Notes Payable-Short Term	6.1	4.7	3.7	4.4	3.0	4.2			
Cur. Mat.-L.T.D.	4.9	5.1	6.2	5.5	7.5	6.1			
Trade Payables	5.6	7.7	4.8	4.1	2.9	4.8			
Income Taxes Payable	.0	.1	.0	.0	.0	.0			
All Other Current	12.3	16.3	10.2	11.3	7.7	7.6			
Total Current	28.9	33.9	24.8	25.3	21.2	22.7			
Long-Term Debt	47.5	44.9	41.4	50.9	36.5	34.3			
Deferred Taxes	.0	.0	.0	.0	.0	.0			
All Other Non-Current	13.9	18.0	13.4	13.0	9.3	29.0			
Net Worth	9.7	3.1	20.4	10.7	32.9	13.9			
Total Liabilities & Net Worth	100.0	100.0	100.0	100.0	100.0	100.0			
INCOME DATA									
Net Sales	100.0	100.0	100.0	100.0	100.0	100.0			
Gross Profit									
Operating Expenses	94.9	99.4	94.4	93.9	93.8	95.0			
Operating Profit	5.1	.6	5.6	6.1	6.2	5.0			
All Other Expenses (net)	3.0	2.2	1.9	2.8	1.6	-.1			
Profit Before Taxes	2.1	-1.6	3.7	3.4	4.6	5.1			
RATIOS									
Current	1.4	1.1	2.0	2.3	2.1	1.5			
	.7	.6	.9	1.0	.8	1.0			
	.2	.2	.4	.3	.3	.5			
Quick	1.0	.7	1.2	1.6	1.3	1.0			
	.4 (102)	.4 (128)	.6	.7 (59)	.5 (38)	.7			
	.1	.1	.2	.2	.2	.2			
Sales/Receivables	0 UND	0 UND	0 UND	0 UND	0 UND	0 UND			
	0 UND	0 UND	0 UND	0 UND	0 UND	0 999.8			
	0 UND	4 89.6	1 366.1	0 UND	1 442.0	5 80.4			
Cost of Sales/Inventory									
Cost of Sales/Payables									
Sales/Working Capital	86.4	118.1	26.1	22.2	26.5	55.7			
	-37.5	-36.4	-153.3	UND	-73.1	NM			
	-11.4	-10.3	-18.9	-13.9	-20.8	-14.4			
EBIT/Interest	6.8	4.0	8.2	7.2	6.7				
	2.6 (103)	1.6 (82)	3.1 (110)	2.6 (50)	3.1 (32)				
	.3	-2.3	.9	.5	1.8				
Net Profit + Depr., Dep., Amort./Cur. Mat. L/T/D									
Fixed/Worth	1.3	1.7	1.1	1.6	.6	3.0			
	-129.3	-8.6	10.1	-93.3	3.5	NM			
	-1.4	-.8	-1.3	-1.4	-1.3	-.8			
Debt/Worth	1.3	2.5	1.2	1.9	.5	5.3			
	-92.8	-15.0	27.3	-19.9	5.4	NM			
	-2.8	-2.6	-3.3	-3.3	-2.6	-2.2			
% Profit Before Taxes/Tangible Net Worth	129.3	127.3	105.9	167.2	52.2				
	67.2 (60)	51.3 (46)	34.8 (70)	41.3 (28)	25.7 (24)				
	17.2	4.9	4.7	5.4	1.7				
% Profit Before Taxes/Total Assets	23.3	18.1	21.9	21.7	20.7	29.6			
	6.2	4.0	8.5	8.5	8.4	19.0			
	-1.3	-7.3	-.4	-1.0	3.6	1.3			
Sales/Net Fixed Assets	9.4	11.5	14.5	11.0	16.8	19.6			
	5.0	5.0	5.4	4.7	8.1	4.8			
	2.5	2.4	2.8	2.2	2.4	3.1			
Sales/Total Assets	3.8	3.8	3.7	3.4	4.2	3.6			
	2.4	2.3	2.1	1.8	2.5	2.7			
	1.4	1.4	1.2	1.1	1.2	1.0			
% Depr., Dep., Amort./Sales	2.4	2.1	2.5	3.1	2.0				
	4.1 (111)	3.8 (85)	4.5 (104)	5.2 (44)	4.0 (34)				
	6.6	7.0	7.3	9.0	6.9				
% Officers', Directors' Owners' Comp/Sales	2.9	2.6	1.9	2.7	1.4				
	4.6 (42)	5.2 (28)	5.1 (31)	9.1 (17)	1.9 (10)				
	8.0	8.9	9.4	18.3	6.5				
Net Sales ($)	2007215M	1543136M	1243686M	33768M	61457M	38261M	35052M	119982M	955166M
Total Assets ($)	694303M	721248M	565537M	22259M	34734M	22570M	16745M	49601M	419628M

M = $ thousand   MM = $ million
See Pages 9 through 22 for Explanation of Ratios and Data

RESTAURANT/LODGING—Food Service Contractors NAICS 722310

	Current Data Sorted by Assets							Comparative Historical Data	
	1	1	2	5	3		**Type of Statement**	9	9
		3	5	2			Unqualified / Reviewed	4	8
	4	9	3		1		Compiled	5	4
	14	6	9				Tax Returns	3	2
	3	9	7	11	3	3	Other	14	15
		13 (4/1-9/30/09)		91 (10/1/09-3/31/10)				4/1/05-3/31/06 ALL	4/1/06-3/31/07 ALL
	0-500M	500M-2MM	2-10MM	10-50MM	50-100MM	100-250MM	**NUMBER OF STATEMENTS**	35	38
	22	28	26	19	6	3			
	%	%	%	%	%	%	**ASSETS**	%	%
	17.8	10.2	12.8	13.0			Cash & Equivalents	10.3	13.3
	10.5	21.5	27.2	22.8			Trade Receivables (net)	25.9	25.3
	6.1	6.0	10.9	11.8			Inventory	10.3	8.0
	1.3	9.2	3.4	3.6			All Other Current	3.1	5.2
	35.7	46.9	54.2	51.2			Total Current	49.6	51.7
	45.4	38.7	30.7	29.7			Fixed Assets (net)	33.9	27.8
	8.1	2.6	3.0	11.7			Intangibles (net)	3.8	4.7
	10.8	11.8	12.1	7.4			All Other Non-Current	12.7	15.8
	100.0	100.0	100.0	100.0			Total	100.0	100.0
							LIABILITIES		
	23.2	13.1	8.4	8.0			Notes Payable-Short Term	9.2	8.1
	5.0	3.3	3.6	4.3			Cur. Mat.-L.T.D.	2.8	3.6
	15.0	12.2	20.0	13.4			Trade Payables	16.1	17.7
	.0	.0	.3	.1			Income Taxes Payable	.3	1.2
	28.3	17.0	17.8	13.7			All Other Current	16.9	17.5
	71.5	45.6	50.1	39.5			Total Current	45.2	48.1
	27.8	31.0	28.4	22.6			Long-Term Debt	22.3	18.3
	.0	.0	.0	.5			Deferred Taxes	.2	.1
	21.6	13.1	5.0	4.7			All Other Non-Current	5.6	11.2
	-21.0	10.3	16.5	32.8			Net Worth	26.6	22.3
	100.0	100.0	100.0	100.0			Total Liabilties & Net Worth	100.0	100.0
							INCOME DATA		
	100.0	100.0	100.0	100.0			Net Sales	100.0	100.0
							Gross Profit		
	95.1	93.0	92.8	92.7			Operating Expenses	91.9	95.0
	4.9	7.0	7.2	7.3			Operating Profit	8.1	5.0
	.3	3.0	3.7	1.2			All Other Expenses (net)	3.0	1.5
	4.6	4.0	3.5	6.1			Profit Before Taxes	5.1	3.5
							RATIOS		
	1.5	1.9	1.7	2.7			Current	1.7	1.8
	.7	1.1	1.1	1.6				1.1	1.1
	.2	.6	.7	.9				.6	.5
	1.1	1.2	1.2	1.7			Quick	1.2	1.4
	.6	.7	.8	1.2				.9	.8
	.0	.3	.5	.6				.4	.4
	0 UND	0 UND	3 124.4	13 27.7			Sales/Receivables	1 592.2	9 42.4
	0 UND	8 48.6	21 17.6	26 14.1				17 21.0	14 26.7
	12 30.5	34 10.9	34 10.8	33 11.1				35 10.4	40 9.1
							Cost of Sales/Inventory		
							Cost of Sales/Payables		
	37.2	23.1	18.7	9.6			Sales/Working Capital	17.7	15.6
	-67.2	207.7	78.8	21.4				73.6	93.8
	-9.7	-14.3	-14.8	-38.9				-24.6	-20.7
	13.8	25.2	14.3	18.8			EBIT/Interest	8.9	13.8
	(14) 4.3	(24) 2.9	(22) 4.5	5.5				(26) 3.2	(29) 4.1
	.0	-.3	-.4	1.1				1.9	.6
							Net Profit + Depr., Dep., Amort./Cur. Mat. L/T/D		5.5
								(10)	3.7
									1.9
	9.3	.2	.2	.4			Fixed/Worth	.2	.3
	-2.9	1.2	.6	1.2				.9	1.0
	-.7	NM	12.6	5.7				-54.5	NM
	30.7	.8	1.8	1.1			Debt/Worth	1.0	.7
	-5.3	5.7	3.3	4.1				2.5	3.4
	-2.3	-5.2	22.3	23.1				-58.6	NM
		82.9	79.8	106.5			% Profit Before Taxes/Tangible Net Worth	76.7	57.8
	(20)	39.3	(21) 24.7	(15) 37.5				(26) 23.8	(29) 33.5
		5.1	-2.8	8.3				9.2	11.1
	67.4	22.2	22.7	26.5			% Profit Before Taxes/Total Assets	13.6	14.2
	8.3	8.0	4.7	7.2				8.2	9.4
	-.6	-.6	-1.6	.7				1.9	-1.4
	32.5	35.9	79.0	31.3			Sales/Net Fixed Assets	72.1	36.4
	12.4	12.3	17.4	12.2				16.1	16.9
	5.7	3.6	6.4	3.8				4.2	7.4
	7.8	6.4	5.5	3.9			Sales/Total Assets	5.7	5.1
	5.6	3.4	3.2	2.6				3.4	3.2
	3.3	2.1	2.0	1.9				2.2	2.1
	1.3	.7	.5	1.0			% Depr., Dep., Amort./Sales	.5	.6
	(16) 2.3	(25) 1.7	(25) 1.7	(17) 2.2				(32) 1.7	(30) 1.8
	3.8	2.5	3.5	3.0				2.6	3.1
		2.3	1.6				% Officers', Directors' Owners' Comp/Sales		1.2
		(11) 4.3	(11) 2.1					(13)	2.5
		9.1							5.8
	24013M	124870M	459021M	1090946M	710616M	621246M	Net Sales ($)	1501026M	1474936M
	4156M	29717M	114436M	385138M	413308M	491458M	Total Assets ($)	444114M	461050M

© RMA 2010

M = $ thousand   MM = $ million
See Pages 9 through 22 for Explanation of Ratios and Data

Comparative Historical Data   **Current Data Sorted by Sales**

			Type of Statement						
13	18	12	Unqualified		1			1	10
5	10	10	Reviewed			1		5	4
10	18	16	Compiled	4	6	4	1	1	
17	22	30	Tax Returns	11	9	1	6		3
23	27	36	Other	2	4	3	3	7	17
4/1/07-3/31/08 ALL	4/1/08-3/31/09 ALL	4/1/09-3/31/10 ALL		0-1MM	13 (4/1-9/30/09) 1-3MM	3-5MM	5-10MM	91 (10/1/09-3/31/10) 10-25MM	25MM & OVER
68	95	104	NUMBER OF STATEMENTS	17	20	9	10	14	34
%	%	%	ASSETS	%	%	%	%	%	%
11.9	10.2	12.6	Cash & Equivalents	8.4	19.0		14.1	11.9	11.8
21.5	19.8	20.3	Trade Receivables (net)	3.5	12.3		26.6	34.9	24.2
7.9	10.5	8.1	Inventory	4.7	5.6		10.7	12.8	9.5
4.8	2.4	4.5	All Other Current	1.6	3.8		3.4	3.1	4.0
46.1	43.0	45.5	Total Current	18.2	40.6		54.8	62.7	49.5
33.4	34.8	35.7	Fixed Assets (net)	63.3	44.1		25.1	24.4	27.1
10.2	12.9	7.9	Intangibles (net)	9.3	4.2		3.0	3.2	14.9
10.3	9.4	10.9	All Other Non-Current	9.1	11.0		17.1	9.8	8.6
100.0	100.0	100.0	Total	100.0	100.0		100.0	100.0	100.0
			LIABILITIES						
6.3	10.4	12.3	Notes Payable-Short Term	21.1	11.7		11.8	16.1	5.5
4.0	3.3	3.9	Cur. Mat.-L.T.D.	2.0	5.9		3.6	4.2	3.7
15.2	17.7	14.5	Trade Payables	4.0	18.4		18.7	16.1	16.9
.1	.2	.1	Income Taxes Payable	.0	.0		.8	.0	.1
17.2	19.0	18.8	All Other Current	12.2	28.2		16.8	18.2	16.2
42.9	50.6	49.6	Total Current	39.4	64.2		51.7	54.6	42.3
27.2	29.0	28.9	Long-Term Debt	46.8	32.5		35.4	11.4	28.9
.2	.2	.3	Deferred Taxes	.0	.0		.0	.3	.7
7.0	6.1	11.0	All Other Non-Current	15.4	19.5		6.6	4.5	5.9
22.7	14.0	10.1	Net Worth	-1.6	-16.2		6.4	29.2	22.1
100.0	100.0	100.0	Total Liabilities & Net Worth	100.0	100.0		100.0	100.0	100.0
			INCOME DATA						
100.0	100.0	100.0	Net Sales	100.0	100.0		100.0	100.0	100.0
			Gross Profit						
91.8	94.9	92.8	Operating Expenses	84.2	97.6		92.1	92.6	93.8
8.2	5.1	7.2	Operating Profit	15.8	2.4		7.9	7.4	6.2
3.7	2.6	2.4	All Other Expenses (net)	7.3	.4		2.0	2.3	1.9
4.5	2.5	4.7	Profit Before Taxes	8.6	2.0		5.9	5.2	4.3
			RATIOS						
2.1	1.7	1.8		1.7	1.9		1.5	1.8	1.8
1.1	1.1	1.1	Current	.8	.9		.9	1.1	1.4
.4	.4	.6		.2	.3		.7	.8	.8
1.4	1.1	1.2		1.3	1.0		1.1	1.6	1.4
.8	.8	.8	Quick	.6	.7		.8	1.1	1.0
.3	.3	.4		.2	.2		.6	.5	.6
1 305.1	0 UND	0 999.8		0 UND	0 UND		2 157.7	14 25.5	12 30.5
16 22.5	14 25.2	16 22.4	Sales/Receivables	0 UND	1 616.7		26 14.2	27 13.7	26 14.1
37 10.0	32 11.4	32 11.5		1 422.9	24 15.1		33 11.1	41 8.9	38 9.7
			Cost of Sales/Inventory						
			Cost of Sales/Payables						
14.8	19.3	17.0		35.9	38.5		20.7	19.7	13.2
77.4	121.9	125.5	Sales/Working Capital	-81.4	-258.5		-242.0	78.8	25.1
-16.8	-21.6	-14.3		-8.9	-11.3		-13.4	-17.3	-30.8
20.0	10.9	15.8			13.4		14.9	25.0	13.9
(60) 5.6	(80) 3.1	(88) 3.7	EBIT/Interest	(17) 2.0			4.9	(13) 3.0	(33) 3.7
1.6	.7	.5			-4.5		4.1	-1.0	.7
7.6	7.0	7.0	Net Profit + Depr., Dep.,						7.0
(11) 3.3	(17) 3.1	(14) 2.8	Amort./Cur. Mat. L/T/D					(10) 3.5	
1.5	1.4	.3							1.6
.4	.5	.3		6.3	.5		.2	.2	.4
1.7	2.1	2.6	Fixed/Worth	-8.6	NM		1.0	.5	1.4
-7.4	-2.5	-2.0		-2.3	-.7		-2.7	4.3	-3.1
1.2	1.7	1.6		5.6	.9		1.1	1.7	1.4
3.9	6.7	7.0	Debt/Worth	-14.0	NM		2.8	4.3	4.2
-29.6	-4.1	-4.7		-4.0	-2.1		-4.5	13.3	-5.7
111.6	77.8	98.7	% Profit Before Taxes/Tangible		131.3			81.3	108.3
(49) 46.3	(63) 38.0	(67) 40.9	Net Worth		(10) 35.9			(13) 65.0	(24) 43.0
18.0	14.3	6.1			12.9			-9.6	1.4
20.4	17.9	22.3	% Profit Before Taxes/Total	67.9	19.6		27.6	31.5	21.5
10.1	5.5	6.9	Assets	4.2	4.5		16.1	6.5	4.6
1.6	-1.2	.3		2.8	-6.3		3.1	-4.8	-.2
45.4	41.3	36.4		12.9	37.8		65.7	155.2	48.9
11.4	12.6	12.4	Sales/Net Fixed Assets	4.9	11.0		21.0	28.7	15.5
5.6	4.6	4.5		1.5	3.6		10.0	3.8	7.1
5.4	5.4	5.9		5.6	7.4		4.3	7.1	5.5
3.3	3.2	3.2	Sales/Total Assets	3.2	3.5		3.0	3.5	3.0
2.1	2.0	2.0		1.4	2.1		2.3	1.9	1.6
1.0	.6	.8		2.4	.6			.5	.7
(54) 2.1	(79) 1.9	(88) 1.8	% Depr., Dep., Amort./Sales	(13) 3.9	(18) 1.4		(12) .7	(28) 1.4
4.0	3.9	3.2		12.5	2.7			3.0	3.1
1.7	1.9	1.8			2.1				
(26) 2.8	(31) 5.3	(33) 3.4	% Officers', Directors' Owners' Comp/Sales	(12) 4.2					
12.6	8.8	7.6			7.9				
3494590M	3341136M	3030712M	Net Sales ($)	8140M	41366M	34780M	67247M	218594M	2660585M
1086235M	1160919M	1438213M	Total Assets ($)	6896M	15265M	11532M	22506M	84034M	1297980M

M = $ thousand   MM = $ million
See Pages 9 through 22 for Explanation of Ratios and Data

Current Data Sorted by Assets   Comparative Historical Data

	0-500M	500M-2MM	2-10MM	10-50MM	50-100MM	100-250MM		4/1/05-3/31/06 ALL	4/1/06-3/31/07 ALL
Type of Statement									
Unqualified	1	3	7	2	3	2		4	5
Reviewed	7	11	9	2				4	5
Compiled	42	16	9	4				5	13
Tax Returns	11	10	13	2		1		17	29
Other				3				11	18
		18 (4/1-9/30/09)		140 (10/1/09-3/31/10)					
NUMBER OF STATEMENTS	61	40	38	13	3	3		41	70
	%	%	%	%	%	%		%	%
ASSETS									
Cash & Equivalents	22.1	12.4	10.0	9.5				19.0	18.0
Trade Receivables (net)	4.2	10.8	9.3	13.8				16.3	18.6
Inventory	8.4	5.2	3.3	6.8				6.6	4.0
All Other Current	3.5	3.3	1.2	.8				2.3	2.9
Total Current	38.1	31.8	23.8	31.0				44.1	43.4
Fixed Assets (net)	41.9	47.3	51.7	50.0				38.0	43.1
Intangibles (net)	7.3	8.9	9.6	10.2				4.8	5.6
All Other Non-Current	12.6	12.0	14.9	8.8				13.1	7.9
Total	100.0	100.0	100.0	100.0				100.0	100.0
LIABILITIES									
Notes Payable-Short Term	10.4	13.9	3.8	8.1				12.5	9.7
Cur. Mat.-L.T.D.	5.5	3.3	5.4	8.0				3.0	3.4
Trade Payables	11.1	13.1	7.4	9.8				16.7	14.5
Income Taxes Payable	.1	.1	.3	.0				.1	1.4
All Other Current	43.9	30.5	13.9	16.9				23.6	25.4
Total Current	70.9	60.9	30.8	42.9				55.8	54.3
Long-Term Debt	31.8	30.3	36.8	42.7				39.3	30.3
Deferred Taxes	.0	.0	.1	.0				.1	.1
All Other Non-Current	21.4	6.9	7.1	27.3				4.6	11.8
Net Worth	-24.2	1.8	25.2	-12.8				.3	3.5
Total Liabilties & Net Worth	100.0	100.0	100.0	100.0				100.0	100.0
INCOME DATA									
Net Sales	100.0	100.0	100.0	100.0				100.0	100.0
Gross Profit									
Operating Expenses	96.3	93.3	85.6	94.8				93.9	92.2
Operating Profit	3.7	6.7	14.4	5.2				6.1	7.8
All Other Expenses (net)	1.5	3.6	6.0	3.9				1.6	2.5
Profit Before Taxes	2.2	3.1	8.4	1.2				4.5	5.3
RATIOS									
Current	1.7	1.0	1.3	1.2				1.7	1.6
	.8	.6	.5	.4				1.0	.8
	.4	.2	.2	.2				.4	.3
Quick	1.1	.8	.9	.8				1.5	1.4
	.5	.4	.5	.3				.7	.7
	.1	.2	.1	.1				.3	.3
Sales/Receivables	0 UND	0 UND	0 UND	1 573.3				0 UND	0 UND
	0 UND	4 104.0	4 104.0	8 48.1				5 75.7	6 61.1
	4 89.5	19 18.8	20 18.3	28 13.2				20 18.2	25 14.9
Cost of Sales/Inventory									
Cost of Sales/Payables									
Sales/Working Capital	63.4	NM	54.3	37.5				25.1	23.8
	-226.8	-17.3	-16.4	-8.6				-257.2	-77.1
	-11.7	-5.5	-4.8	-3.9				-20.8	-11.3
EBIT/Interest	(40) 11.6	(30) 7.9	(29) 8.9	(11) 6.6				(28) 12.1	(54) 10.3
	2.6	2.3	2.4	2.7				7.5	3.7
	-3.6	-2.5	1.2	1.0				1.7	1.4
Net Profit + Depr., Dep., Amort./Cur. Mat. L/T/D									
Fixed/Worth	.9	.9	.7	1.6				.8	.5
	24.5	4.0	3.3	7.8				2.2	3.1
	-.9	-4.1	298.0	-3.1				UND	-2.5
Debt/Worth	1.5	1.3	1.9	2.0				1.5	1.3
	-441.0	5.7	4.2	10.3				3.1	6.2
	-2.5	-4.2	312.7	-5.0				UND	-5.7
% Profit Before Taxes/Tangible Net Worth	188.2	58.9	75.2					153.8	111.9
	(30) 55.3	(22) 21.7	(30) 27.5					(31) 50.9	(44) 42.0
	7.2	3.9	4.3					24.1	15.0
% Profit Before Taxes/Total Assets	30.7	19.3	14.6	14.0				47.4	28.4
	6.5	2.6	3.7	3.9				15.5	9.1
	-8.7	-3.1	.7	-.9				2.6	1.6
Sales/Net Fixed Assets	43.7	22.3	12.4	7.8				59.2	33.4
	22.3	4.3	2.6	3.8				18.5	15.3
	8.7	2.6	1.0	1.4				6.5	3.6
Sales/Total Assets	10.3	4.2	2.1	3.3				7.6	7.1
	6.9	2.3	1.5	1.5				4.8	3.8
	3.7	1.5	.7	1.0				2.5	1.6
% Depr., Dep., Amort./Sales	.6	1.9	1.6	1.7				.7	.8
	(44) 1.5	(33) 2.2	(36) 2.9	2.1				(27) 1.4	(48) 2.1
	3.6	4.8	6.7	4.4				3.1	3.5
% Officers', Directors' Owners' Comp/Sales	2.8	2.3	1.5					3.0	2.6
	(31) 5.8	(21) 3.7	(15) 3.1					(20) 6.1	(34) 4.7
	9.2	8.5	5.4					7.5	7.9
Net Sales ($)	70589M	103351M	274516M	452023M	364689M	2099274M		866114M	940310M
Total Assets ($)	11540M	37320M	164961M	187300M	225355M	494201M		230345M	306977M

© RMA 2010

M = $ thousand   MM = $ million
See Pages 9 through 22 for Explanation of Ratios and Data

Comparative Historical Data

Current Data Sorted by Sales

						18 (4/1-9/30/09)		140 (10/1/09-3/31/10)			
4/1/07-3/31/08 ALL	4/1/08-3/31/09 ALL	4/1/09-3/31/10 ALL		**Type of Statement**		0-1MM	1-3MM	3-5MM	5-10MM	10-25MM	25MM & OVER
5	3	7		Unqualified		2		2	4	3	7
3	7	13		Reviewed		6	10	5	4	5	2
14	25	31		Compiled		28	25	5	8	3	1
33	49	70		Tax Returns		11	10	7	4	1	1
31	36	37		Other						2	2
86	120	158		**NUMBER OF STATEMENTS**		47	45	19	20	14	13
%	%	%		**ASSETS**		%	%	%	%	%	%
18.4	15.1	15.1		Cash & Equivalents		16.7	15.6	18.9	14.3	7.8	10.7
17.3	13.4	8.5		Trade Receivables (net)		1.9	6.0	9.7	10.0	17.2	27.3
5.9	5.4	6.3		Inventory		5.7	5.7	5.2	8.0	4.4	11.9
2.7	4.2	2.6		All Other Current		3.6	3.6	1.0	.4	2.6	1.0
44.3	38.2	32.5		Total Current		27.9	31.0	34.9	32.8	32.1	50.8
37.6	44.0	46.2		Fixed Assets (net)		53.9	48.0	43.4	36.4	45.4	31.7
8.1	6.3	8.8		Intangibles (net)		9.4	6.2	9.6	12.3	7.9	10.2
10.0	11.5	12.5		All Other Non-Current		8.7	14.9	12.1	18.6	14.6	7.2
100.0	100.0	100.0		Total		100.0	100.0	100.0	100.0	100.0	100.0
				LIABILITIES							
6.8	7.9	9.3		Notes Payable-Short Term		14.1	9.8	4.5	3.3	3.2	13.2
2.9	5.3	5.0		Cur. Mat.-L.T.D.		5.5	3.5	4.5	7.4	4.5	6.6
11.9	12.8	10.6		Trade Payables		6.4	10.9	11.4	16.1	11.0	14.8
.2	.1	.1		Income Taxes Payable		.0	.2	.0	.1	.6	.0
19.9	26.4	29.9		All Other Current		39.1	22.5	51.6	23.0	14.8	17.4
41.7	52.5	55.0		Total Current		65.1	46.8	72.0	49.9	34.2	51.9
35.2	30.7	33.0		Long-Term Debt		44.3	29.1	26.5	29.2	41.4	12.4
.1	.0	.0		Deferred Taxes		.0	.0	.0	.2	.0	.0
15.7	7.2	14.2		All Other Non-Current		14.0	17.0	5.7	15.8	3.2	26.5
7.4	9.6	-2.2		Net Worth		-23.5	7.1	-4.2	4.9	21.3	9.3
100.0	100.0	100.0		Total Liabilties & Net Worth		100.0	100.0	100.0	100.0	100.0	100.0
				INCOME DATA							
100.0	100.0	100.0		Net Sales		100.0	100.0	100.0	100.0	100.0	100.0
				Gross Profit							
93.5	93.3	92.9		Operating Expenses		88.9	94.0	97.6	91.8	94.3	96.7
6.5	6.7	7.1		Operating Profit		11.1	6.0	2.4	8.2	5.7	3.3
1.9	2.6	3.3		All Other Expenses (net)		7.1	1.7	.8	1.6	2.6	2.0
4.6	4.1	3.8		Profit Before Taxes		4.0	4.3	1.6	6.6	3.1	1.3
				RATIOS							
1.9	1.6	1.3				1.2	1.7	1.0	1.2	1.3	1.5
1.2	1.0	.6		Current		.6	.7	.5	.4	.9	1.0
.5	.4	.2				.2	.4	.2	.2	.3	.9
1.7	1.3	.9				1.0	1.1	.7	.6	1.0	1.0
1.0	.6	.5		Quick		.4	.4	.5	.2	.7	.7
.3	.2	.1				.1	.2	.2	.1	.2	.9
0 UND	0 UND	0 UND				0 UND	0 UND	0 999.8	0 UND	3 135.3	10 38.2
11 34.6	6 66.2	2 225.5		Sales/Receivables		0 UND	0 999.8	4 81.6	3 119.6	19 19.1	28 13.2
27 13.5	22 16.8	15 24.3				4 89.5	8 44.1	20 18.4	12 30.2	32 11.6	59 6.2
				Cost of Sales/Inventory							
				Cost of Sales/Payables							
17.3	22.9	60.1				99.9	43.7	-288.2	NM	40.7	34.8
69.5	-458.3	-35.6		Sales/Working Capital		-51.8	-197.3	-16.3	-15.1	-216.2	226.8
-11.8	-10.4	-7.0				-4.5	-11.4	-5.1	-4.7	-8.4	-40.1
11.6	13.3	8.5				8.5	8.5	4.7	15.9	6.2	9.4
(61) 3.0	(96) 3.0	(115) 2.4		EBIT/Interest		(31) 2.0	(31) 2.2	(14) 1.2	(17) 4.9	(12) 2.6	(10) 3.3
-.1	.6	.1				-.5	-4.5	-2.5	1.0	1.1	2.0
7.0	12.9	4.5		Net Profit + Depr., Dep.,							
(10) 1.5	(11) 2.1	(16) 2.3		Amort./Cur. Mat. L/T/D							
-.1	1.1	1.3									
.3	.7	.9				1.4	1.0	.7	.3	.7	.7
2.0	2.5	3.5		Fixed/Worth		82.5	3.5	8.8	1.9	3.0	1.7
-8.3	-5.2	-3.4				-.8	-1.8	-10.8	NM	-5.0	4.0
1.2	1.6	1.8				2.1	.7	2.6	1.6	1.9	1.5
5.3	4.5	8.3		Debt/Worth		UND	5.2	28.4	8.3	7.0	3.0
-13.7	-9.7	-5.4				-2.4	-4.8	-3.6	-8.0	-10.0	13.3
98.6	105.8	92.2		% Profit Before Taxes/Tangible		328.7	91.6	72.1	239.0	146.0	63.5
(59) 46.3	(80) 42.2	(95) 34.4		Net Worth		(24) 32.9	(26) 36.5	(11) 8.9	(13) 45.9	(10) 53.8	(11) 20.4
17.5	8.3	5.1				.3	9.1	-24.9	9.2	25.0	10.5
23.8	25.0	19.5		% Profit Before Taxes/Total		19.5	21.5	7.4	24.7	15.1	12.1
10.2	7.7	3.9		Assets		1.9	4.0	2.3	11.6	6.6	3.9
-1.3	-1.0	-2.3				-5.9	-3.1	-5.5	1.1	.7	.7
38.7	38.4	30.2				23.3	43.7	30.6	56.9	26.8	18.4
14.3	11.1	7.9		Sales/Net Fixed Assets		7.0	12.4	12.2	7.9	6.3	7.4
3.5	3.1	2.5				1.5	2.9	3.4	2.3	2.0	5.5
5.3	6.4	6.3				8.9	8.5	5.2	4.2	4.0	3.7
3.6	3.5	2.8		Sales/Total Assets		3.2	4.6	3.0	2.0	1.8	3.1
1.6	1.7	1.4				.7	2.1	1.3	1.5	1.3	1.7
.7	.8	1.5				1.2	.7	2.0	1.5	1.6	1.5
(62) 2.0	(97) 1.9	(130) 2.1		% Depr., Dep., Amort./Sales		(34) 2.4	(38) 2.0	(17) 2.3	(16) 1.8	(11) 2.1	1.9
3.9	4.2	4.4				7.6	4.8	3.4	5.3	4.0	2.1
2.6	2.4	2.4		% Officers', Directors'		5.2	2.3	1.5	3.1		
(43) 4.0	(52) 4.4	(73) 4.8		Owners' Comp/Sales		(19) 8.2	(22) 3.1	(11) 4.1	(12) 3.7		
6.1	7.0	8.7				10.0	6.1	7.4	9.2		
1550099M	1990905M	3364442M		Net Sales ($)		26579M	75110M	77789M	127567M	213149M	2844248M
467131M	688297M	1120677M		Total Assets ($)		26569M	45993M	36206M	68141M	113870M	829898M

© RMA 2010

M = $ thousand   MM = $ million

See Pages 9 through 22 for Explanation of Ratios and Data

RESTAURANT/LODGING—Drinking Places (Alcoholic Beverages) NAICS 722410

Current Data Sorted by Assets | **Comparative Historical Data**

	0-500M	500M-2MM	2-10MM	10-50MM	50-100MM	100-250MM		2 4/1/05-3/31/06 ALL	4 4/1/06-3/31/07 ALL
Type of Statement									
Unqualified	1							2	4
Reviewed		1		1				3	5
Compiled	13	12	3					27	26
Tax Returns	82	29	4	2				117	111
Other	25	19	7	2	1	2		38	46
		16 (4/1-9/30/09)		188 (10/1/09-3/31/10)					
NUMBER OF STATEMENTS	121	61	14	5	1	2		187	192
	%	%	%	%	%	%		%	%
ASSETS									
Cash & Equivalents	20.4	11.5	5.9					15.9	14.0
Trade Receivables (net)	1.6	1.2	.3					1.9	1.5
Inventory	10.5	3.7	2.6					8.1	9.3
All Other Current	3.2	1.9	.7					3.3	4.0
Total Current	35.6	18.4	9.5					29.1	28.8
Fixed Assets (net)	39.5	55.4	70.4					44.2	47.5
Intangibles (net)	17.8	18.7	7.9					15.3	14.5
All Other Non-Current	7.1	7.5	12.1					11.4	9.1
Total	100.0	100.0	100.0					100.0	100.0
LIABILITIES									
Notes Payable-Short Term	8.1	3.3	1.5					5.1	5.5
Cur. Mat.-L.T.D.	2.4	1.5	2.8					4.3	3.1
Trade Payables	7.4	4.4	1.8					7.1	5.6
Income Taxes Payable	.0	.0	.3					.2	.2
All Other Current	20.0	15.6	14.6					20.4	19.9
Total Current	37.9	24.7	21.0					37.1	34.3
Long-Term Debt	21.5	43.2	32.8					27.9	32.5
Deferred Taxes	.0	.2	.0					.0	.0
All Other Non-Current	28.5	10.2	1.0					18.4	15.8
Net Worth	12.1	21.7	45.2					16.6	17.4
Total Liabilties & Net Worth	100.0	100.0	100.0					100.0	100.0
INCOME DATA									
Net Sales	100.0	100.0	100.0					100.0	100.0
Gross Profit	58.9	60.0	68.2					58.4	58.7
Operating Expenses	54.6	55.5	69.6					53.6	53.9
Operating Profit	4.3	4.5	-1.5					4.8	4.8
All Other Expenses (net)	.4	1.4	2.5					.8	1.2
Profit Before Taxes	3.9	3.1	-4.0					4.1	3.6
RATIOS									
Current	3.6	3.4	1.8					3.3	3.1
	1.1	.9	.7					1.3	1.1
	.5	.5	.3					.4	.3
Quick	2.3	2.2	1.1					2.1	2.0
	(119) .5	.5	.3				(186) .6	(188) .4
	.1	.1	.0					.2	.1
Sales/Receivables	0 UND	0 UND	0 UND					0 UND	0 UND
	0 UND	0 UND	0 UND					0 UND	0 UND
	0 UND	0 UND	4 99.0					1 596.8	1 490.7
Cost of Sales/Inventory	6 62.8	7 50.3	11 34.4					9 41.0	8 46.9
	15 24.3	12 29.4	26 13.9					17 21.4	16 22.5
	24 15.2	25 14.4	50 7.3					26 13.8	29 12.6
Cost of Sales/Payables	0 UND	0 UND	0 UND					0 UND	0 UND
	1 411.0	11 34.4	13 28.6					8 44.2	3 136.8
	22 16.2	31 11.8	40 9.1					26 14.0	26 14.2
Sales/Working Capital	20.7	14.4	21.8					16.5	17.4
	244.3	-93.1	-54.6					84.5	485.7
	-35.1	-12.5	-11.5					-22.4	-16.7
EBIT/Interest	10.8	6.3	8.4					12.5	12.5
	(68) 3.0	(52) 1.8	2.7				(127) 3.5	(133) 2.3
	.4	.6	-5.2					1.0	.7
Net Profit + Depr., Dep., Amort./Cur. Mat. L/T/D									
Fixed/Worth	.7	1.4	1.2					.7	.8
	2.1	14.8	1.8					2.4	3.7
	-1.6	-1.2	NM					-1.6	-1.5
Debt/Worth	.6	1.6	.5					.6	.8
	5.6	15.8	1.2					3.7	5.9
	-2.7	-3.5	NM					-3.5	-2.9
% Profit Before Taxes/Tangible Net Worth	141.7	87.7	49.8					73.6	94.6
	(75) 51.9	(36) 33.2	(11) 19.6				(115) 37.9	(109) 38.6
	9.1	-4.6	-5.2					4.6	12.6
% Profit Before Taxes/Total Assets	36.3	23.0	21.7					26.8	31.3
	13.1	3.3	5.7					11.0	8.0
	.4	-1.5	-5.6					-.3	-1.3
Sales/Net Fixed Assets	42.3	8.9	4.1					23.0	26.1
	17.0	3.9	2.3					9.5	7.9
	7.2	1.8	.9					4.4	3.7
Sales/Total Assets	7.8	2.8	2.1					5.4	5.0
	4.8	1.7	1.3					3.1	3.1
	3.0	1.2	.7					1.8	1.7
% Depr., Dep., Amort./Sales	.8	2.2	2.6					1.1	1.3
	(94) 2.1	(49) 3.4	(13) 4.6				(157) 1.9	(152) 2.3
	3.6	6.6	6.3					3.9	4.0
% Officers', Directors' Owners' Comp/Sales	2.8	2.6						2.8	2.3
	(74) 4.8	(21) 4.4					(96) 4.7	(87) 4.4
	9.5	7.9						8.3	7.2
Net Sales ($)	116230M	150606M	96456M	536476M	472267M	1035141M		3226777M	3356360M
Total Assets ($)	23948M	61437M	61443M	101551M	94816M	436996M		823190M	941646M

© RMA 2010

M = $ thousand   MM = $ million
See Pages 9 through 22 for Explanation of Ratios and Data

Comparative Historical Data

Current Data Sorted by Sales

			Type of Statement						
2	3	2	Unqualified	1					1
5	2	1	Reviewed		1				
25	33	28	Compiled	12	10	4	1	1	
102	128	118	Tax Returns	63	40	10	3		2
55	42	55	Other	24	22	2	1	3	3
4/1/07-3/31/08 ALL	4/1/08-3/31/09 ALL	4/1/09-3/31/10 ALL		16 (4/1-9/30/09)			188 (10/1/09-3/31/10)		
				0-1MM	1-3MM	3-5MM	5-10MM	10-25MM	25MM & OVER
189	208	204	**NUMBER OF STATEMENTS**	100	73	16	5	4	6
%	%	%	**ASSETS**	%	%	%	%	%	%
16.9	13.5	16.4	Cash & Equivalents	18.5	13.5	18.4			
1.2	1.2	1.4	Trade Receivables (net)	.3	1.9	6.2			
8.7	8.4	7.6	Inventory	8.1	8.6	3.5			
3.0	4.8	2.5	All Other Current	2.9	2.8	.2			
29.8	27.8	27.9	Total Current	29.8	26.9	28.4			
47.4	48.9	46.9	Fixed Assets (net)	44.3	49.1	45.3			
14.4	14.6	17.1	Intangibles (net)	20.8	13.8	14.2			
8.4	8.6	8.1	All Other Non-Current	5.2	10.2	12.1			
100.0	100.0	100.0	Total	100.0	100.0	100.0			
			LIABILITIES						
7.2	6.4	5.9	Notes Payable-Short Term	7.2	5.8	3.0			
3.8	3.1	2.0	Cur. Mat.-L.T.D.	1.8	2.5	1.3			
8.5	8.1	5.9	Trade Payables	5.1	7.7	4.7			
.1	.1	.1	Income Taxes Payable	.1	.0	.3			
17.4	19.9	17.8	All Other Current	19.5	16.8	14.8			
37.0	37.4	31.7	Total Current	33.7	32.8	24.1			
32.6	33.1	29.6	Long-Term Debt	29.0	32.4	12.5			
.1	.2	.1	Deferred Taxes	.0	.2	.0			
18.6	15.9	20.9	All Other Non-Current	22.7	22.8	9.3			
11.7	13.4	17.7	Net Worth	14.6	11.8	54.1			
100.0	100.0	100.0	Total Liabilties & Net Worth	100.0	100.0	100.0			
			INCOME DATA						
100.0	100.0	100.0	Net Sales	100.0	100.0	100.0			
60.3	59.7	60.0	Gross Profit	60.7	59.1	62.3			
56.5	55.1	56.1	Operating Expenses	59.2	52.5	54.1			
3.7	4.6	4.0	Operating Profit	1.6	6.6	8.2			
.9	1.1	.9	All Other Expenses (net)	1.4	.5	.9			
2.8	3.6	3.0	Profit Before Taxes	.1	6.1	7.3			
			RATIOS						
2.8	2.0	3.2		3.8	2.9	4.7			
1.3	.9	1.0	Current	1.0	1.0	1.1			
.4	.4	.4		.4	.5	.3			
1.7	1.2	2.2		2.5	1.8	4.7			
(186) .7	(205) .4	(202) .5	Quick	(98) .5	.5	.8			
.1	.1	.1		.1	.1	.1			
0 UND	0 UND	0 UND		0 UND	0 UND	0 UND			
0 UND	0 UND	0 UND	Sales/Receivables	0 UND	0 UND	0 UND			
0 999.8	0 UND	0 UND		0 UND	0 UND	1 388.3			
8 45.5	9 42.5	7 52.7		9 42.1	6 62.1	3 122.6			
15 25.0	15 24.0	15 24.5	Cost of Sales/Inventory	16 22.8	12 29.5	10 38.2			
25 14.9	29 12.6	26 14.2		28 13.2	23 15.7	25 14.4			
0 UND	0 UND	0 UND		0 UND	0 UND	0 UND			
8 46.4	9 42.4	4 90.2	Cost of Sales/Payables	0 UND	9 42.6	5 76.3			
27 13.5	30 12.3	24 15.0		23 16.1	29 12.5	21 17.1			
17.5	27.0	19.0		14.3	30.7	14.4			
68.5	-157.2	UND	Sales/Working Capital	UND	-999.8	NM			
-17.1	-15.0	-24.9		-25.5	-21.5	-21.3			
9.9	8.8	8.7		5.6	9.8	18.6			
(134) 2.1	(153) 2.7	(140) 2.3	EBIT/Interest	(64) 1.3	(51) 3.7	(12) 7.8			
.2	.2	.4		.0	1.7	1.0			
5.9			Net Profit + Depr., Dep.,						
(10) 2.1			Amort./Cur. Mat. L/T/D						
-.4									
.7	1.1	.8		.7	1.0	.3			
4.1	4.0	3.2	Fixed/Worth	4.2	4.7	1.2			
-1.2	-1.3	-1.8		-1.3	-1.4	3.8			
.8	1.0	.8		1.0	1.0	.2			
8.3	6.1	6.2	Debt/Worth	11.9	7.5	.8			
-2.8	-3.7	-3.4		-2.4	-3.7	6.7			
78.9	77.4	97.8	% Profit Before Taxes/Tangible	69.5	153.1	94.9			
(107) 40.5	(122) 38.2	(127) 40.6	Net Worth	(56) 20.0	(46) 73.9	(14) 57.4			
1.8	4.3	3.1		-12.3	19.8	1.3			
25.1	25.2	28.1	% Profit Before Taxes/Total	20.6	31.0	39.1			
5.7	6.7	7.7	Assets	3.7	14.4	27.2			
-5.3	-4.1	-1.6		-5.7	4.5	.6			
25.3	18.3	27.1		33.2	21.6	23.3			
7.6	7.7	8.6	Sales/Net Fixed Assets	9.8	9.0	7.5			
3.7	3.5	3.4		3.1	3.7	4.1			
5.6	5.5	5.8		5.7	7.1	5.4			
3.1	3.2	3.1	Sales/Total Assets	3.0	3.9	2.9			
1.8	1.8	1.6		1.4	1.7	1.4			
1.2	1.6	1.6		1.8	.9	1.1			
(160) 2.2	(170) 2.8	(162) 2.8	% Depr., Dep., Amort./Sales	(72) 3.1	(63) 2.2	(15) 2.6			
4.3	4.6	5.0		6.5	3.9	4.6			
2.6	2.2	2.4	% Officers', Directors'	3.8	1.9				
(88) 4.8	(88) 3.9	(104) 4.6	Owners' Comp/Sales	(56) 6.8	(36) 3.7				
8.9	7.3	9.1		10.4	5.9				
5080841M	3295620M	2407176M	Net Sales ($)	56571M	127572M	59308M	41040M	75288M	2047397M
838565M	989206M	780191M	Total Assets ($)	44018M	46136M	24649M	24944M	44112M	596332M

© RMA 2010

M = $ thousand   MM = $ million
See Pages 9 through 22 for Explanation of Ratios and Data

OTHER SERVICES (EXCEPT PUBLIC ADMINISTRATION)

Current Data Sorted by Assets | Comparative Historical Data

						Type of Statement		
1		2	1	2	1	Unqualified	8	6
2	4	9	1			Reviewed	24	23
25	18	11				Compiled	86	72
189	75	14	2	1	1	Tax Returns	196	203
65	57	24	9	1	2	Other	115	123
	54 (4/1-9/30/09)		463 (10/1/09-3/31/10)				4/1/05-3/31/06 ALL	4/1/06-3/31/07 ALL
0-500M	500M-2MM	2-10MM	10-50MM	50-100MM	100-250MM			
282	154	60	13	4	4	NUMBER OF STATEMENTS	429	427
%	%	%	%	%	%	ASSETS	%	%
20.2	11.6	8.3	7.8			Cash & Equivalents	15.6	14.3
9.0	15.1	13.1	8.4			Trade Receivables (net)	12.1	11.8
16.7	18.3	22.1	20.1			Inventory	21.0	19.8
3.5	1.7	3.9	5.8			All Other Current	2.4	2.3
49.4	46.7	47.4	42.0			Total Current	51.2	48.1
33.2	37.7	34.4	42.3			Fixed Assets (net)	34.9	36.5
6.4	7.2	9.6	6.3			Intangibles (net)	5.7	7.5
11.0	8.3	8.7	9.3			All Other Non-Current	8.3	7.9
100.0	100.0	100.0	100.0			Total	100.0	100.0
						LIABILITIES		
19.4	7.8	5.6	13.3			Notes Payable-Short Term	10.9	10.8
7.6	4.6	2.9	3.6			Cur. Mat.-L.T.D.	4.8	4.6
16.0	15.1	14.0	10.2			Trade Payables	15.5	14.5
.1	.1	.0	.1			Income Taxes Payable	.1	.1
23.6	10.2	12.1	12.0			All Other Current	15.3	14.0
66.6	37.8	34.7	39.2			Total Current	46.7	44.0
36.9	33.2	33.9	30.0			Long-Term Debt	30.0	32.2
.0	.0	.3	1.2			Deferred Taxes	.1	.1
13.2	4.3	3.7	9.7			All Other Non-Current	8.5	13.1
-16.7	24.6	27.4	19.8			Net Worth	14.7	10.6
100.0	100.0	100.0	100.0			Total Liabilities & Net Worth	100.0	100.0
						INCOME DATA		
100.0	100.0	100.0	100.0			Net Sales	100.0	100.0
						Gross Profit		
96.1	91.6	94.6	89.1			Operating Expenses	94.7	95.0
3.9	8.4	5.4	10.9			Operating Profit	5.3	5.0
1.0	4.8	1.2	7.7			All Other Expenses (net)	1.4	1.4
2.9	3.6	4.1	3.2			Profit Before Taxes	3.9	3.6
						RATIOS		
2.3	2.4	2.2	1.4				2.5	2.5
1.0	1.2	1.4	1.1			Current	1.4	1.3
.4	.6	.8	.8				.7	.7
1.5	1.4	.9	.8				1.5	1.3
.5 (153)	.6	.5	.6			Quick	(426) .7	(426) .6
.1	.2	.3	.2				.3	.3
0 UND	2 200.7	2 147.6	2 237.9				0 UND	0 UND
1 285.5	8 46.0	10 36.8	18 20.0			Sales/Receivables	6 56.2	6 61.8
9 42.5	24 15.4	34 10.7	29 12.4				18 19.8	17 21.6
						Cost of Sales/Inventory		
						Cost of Sales/Payables		
19.5	8.6	9.2	8.2				11.0	13.6
-537.0	31.8	24.1	204.9			Sales/Working Capital	37.3	51.4
-18.4	-20.0	-48.9	-22.8				-44.7	-31.5
11.5	7.5	12.2	12.0				8.1	7.9
(207) 2.5	(113) 2.4	(54) 4.0	(10) 1.3			EBIT/Interest	(342) 2.8	(339) 2.7
-.1	.9	1.5	.2				.8	.8
						Net Profit + Depr., Dep., Amort./Cur. Mat. L/T/D	4.3	2.7
							(29) 3.1	(24) 1.6
							1.1	.8
.4	.3	.5	.8				.4	.4
8.1	1.7	1.2	2.6			Fixed/Worth	1.7	2.2
-.7	-8.6	-10.8	-5.8				-5.6	-2.9
1.0	1.0	1.4	1.7				1.1	1.2
223.0	4.5	2.7	3.5			Debt/Worth	3.8	5.0
-2.3	-19.0	-15.0	-11.3				-14.8	-6.0
166.5	46.7	79.8				% Profit Before Taxes/Tangible Net Worth	86.4	84.0
(145) 66.7	(106) 16.7	(43) 22.2					(297) 30.9	(282) 30.7
12.0	1.6	5.2					6.8	5.5
41.9	14.0	14.8	13.0			% Profit Before Taxes/Total Assets	23.5	25.2
12.9	3.3	7.3	2.8				7.2	6.9
-3.4	-.2	1.4	-1.0				.0	-.8
74.0	33.2	27.5	15.1			Sales/Net Fixed Assets	47.4	42.5
25.8	12.7	13.0	4.8				17.5	15.7
9.8	2.8	3.7	.9				7.0	5.2
10.1	4.1	3.6	2.8			Sales/Total Assets	6.4	5.8
5.7	2.3	2.5	2.1				3.9	3.8
3.7	1.1	1.5	.4				2.4	2.2
.7	.9	.9	1.4			% Depr., Dep., Amort./Sales	.9	.7
(197) 1.7	(123) 1.9	(53) 1.7	(12) 2.4				(327) 1.8	(331) 1.8
2.7	5.1	3.0	7.0				3.3	3.8
4.0	2.1	2.1				% Officers', Directors' Owners' Comp/Sales	3.1	3.5
(200) 6.7	(95) 3.4	(26) 3.7					(258) 5.9	(256) 5.8
10.7	5.8	4.8					9.5	9.7
317486M	408303M	717583M	419754M	1557041M	2785521M	Net Sales ($)	9574659M	6858857M
53652M	157754M	264889M	226789M	298829M	684685M	Total Assets ($)	2482918M	1849518M

M = $ thousand   MM = $ million
See Pages 9 through 22 for Explanation of Ratios and Data

Comparative Historical Data | Current Data Sorted by Sales

Yr1	Yr2	Yr3	Type of Statement	0-1MM	1-3MM	3-5MM	5-10MM	10-25MM	25MM & OVER
5	8	7	Unqualified	1		1		2	3
28	20	16	Reviewed	1	3	1	3	6	2
77	64	54	Compiled	16	15	15	7		1
217	238	282	Tax Returns	143	88	24	17	7	3
116	139	158	Other	46	59	18	14	10	11
4/1/07- 3/31/08	4/1/08- 3/31/09	4/1/09- 3/31/10		54 (4/1-9/30/09)			463 (10/1/09-3/31/10)		
ALL	ALL	ALL		0-1MM	1-3MM	3-5MM	5-10MM	10-25MM	25MM & OVER
443	469	517	NUMBER OF STATEMENTS	207	165	59	41	25	20
%	%	%	ASSETS	%	%	%	%	%	%
14.3	15.4	15.8	Cash & Equivalents	17.3	15.7	17.9	10.4	11.2	11.6
11.7	12.0	11.3	Trade Receivables (net)	9.4	11.6	14.8	16.7	7.8	10.6
18.4	19.7	18.0	Inventory	14.3	18.4	20.9	25.5	25.8	18.8
3.1	2.7	3.2	All Other Current	2.8	3.1	.9	4.9	5.0	7.6
47.4	49.9	48.2	Total Current	43.8	48.8	54.6	57.5	49.8	48.6
36.2	33.5	35.0	Fixed Assets (net)	38.4	34.2	33.5	27.3	26.6	36.8
6.5	6.9	7.0	Intangibles (net)	6.8	7.0	4.0	7.1	14.1	7.6
9.9	9.6	9.9	All Other Non-Current	10.9	10.0	7.9	8.1	9.6	7.0
100.0	100.0	100.0	Total	100.0	100.0	100.0	100.0	100.0	100.0
			LIABILITIES						
9.9	13.9	14.0	Notes Payable-Short Term	19.3	11.1	12.2	8.6	6.7	8.7
5.1	6.4	6.0	Cur. Mat.-L.T.D.	6.0	7.1	5.3	5.0	3.8	4.8
15.9	15.5	15.4	Trade Payables	13.0	17.2	15.9	15.1	19.9	18.1
.1	.1	.1	Income Taxes Payable	.1	.1	.1	.0	.0	.0
14.9	17.7	17.9	All Other Current	21.7	15.6	15.8	14.7	14.8	13.5
45.9	53.6	53.3	Total Current	60.1	51.1	49.2	43.4	45.2	45.1
31.3	32.0	35.2	Long-Term Debt	43.7	34.3	20.1	28.0	29.5	22.3
.0	.1	.1	Deferred Taxes	.0	.0	.0	.2	.5	.6
10.2	13.7	9.2	All Other Non-Current	13.3	7.6	6.5	4.5	3.0	6.3
12.6	.8	2.1	Net Worth	-17.0	6.9	24.3	23.9	21.7	25.6
100.0	100.0	100.0	Total Liabilties & Net Worth	100.0	100.0	100.0	100.0	100.0	100.0
			INCOME DATA						
100.0	100.0	100.0	Net Sales	100.0	100.0	100.0	100.0	100.0	100.0
			Gross Profit						
94.2	95.7	94.5	Operating Expenses	92.2	95.7	96.3	94.9	96.7	98.8
5.8	4.3	5.5	Operating Profit	7.8	4.3	3.7	5.1	3.3	1.2
1.7	1.5	2.3	All Other Expenses (net)	4.4	1.2	.3	1.3	.4	.9
4.1	2.9	3.2	Profit Before Taxes	3.4	3.0	3.5	3.9	2.9	.3
			RATIOS						
2.4	2.3	2.3	Current	2.3	2.3	2.6	2.4	1.5	1.7
1.2	1.2	1.1		.9	1.1	1.5	1.4	1.2	1.1
.7	.6	.5		.3	.6	.7	.8	.7	.9
1.6	1.5	1.3	Quick	1.5	1.4	1.6	.9	.6	.8
(440) .6	(467) .6	(516) .5		.5	(164) .5	.9	.5	.4	.6
.2	.2	.2		.1	.1	.3	.2	.2	.1
0 UND	0 UND	0 UND	Sales/Receivables	0 UND	0 UND	3 126.4	3 130.2	2 165.5	1 450.1
5 72.6	5 70.3	4 91.0		1 540.0	4 81.3	11 33.7	8 45.1	7 50.7	7 55.3
18 19.9	17 21.0	15 24.9		10 36.0	15 24.1	25 14.4	32 11.4	17 21.8	35 10.4
			Cost of Sales/Inventory						
			Cost of Sales/Payables						
13.2	12.3	13.3	Sales/Working Capital	18.1	12.2	10.3	7.7	16.2	14.6
51.5	88.3	126.7		-141.0	71.4	27.9	29.1	25.1	234.2
-34.2	-24.6	-19.8		-11.6	-32.0	-24.7	-58.2	-22.1	-102.9
8.2	8.4	9.7	EBIT/Interest	5.0	8.7	30.5	10.8	16.6	15.9
(326) 3.0	(374) 2.9	(392) 2.5		(140) 1.6	(125) 2.5	(50) 5.9	(35) 4.1	(24) 3.9	(18) 6.2
1.2	.9	.6		-.5	.6	1.1	1.2	2.0	.6
6.3	4.6	5.8	Net Profit + Depr., Dep., Amort./Cur. Mat. L/T/D						
(36) 2.1	(29) 2.2	(23) 1.4							
1.2	.8	.7							
.4	.4	.4	Fixed/Worth	.5	.3	.3	.3	.6	.9
1.7	2.6	2.6		-88.6	1.7	.8	1.2	1.1	1.4
-5.4	-1.6	-1.4		-.7	-1.8	14.6	-20.3	-2.3	NM
.8	1.2	1.1	Debt/Worth	1.6	.8	.5	1.7	1.5	1.5
3.5	5.6	7.7		-18.9	4.8	2.2	5.0	3.5	2.1
-11.3	-4.2	-4.4		-2.3	-5.5	UND	-18.7	-7.7	NM
97.8	92.4	100.0	% Profit Before Taxes/Tangible Net Worth	162.5	79.9	61.5	89.3	78.8	117.6
(305) 38.0	(296) 30.1	(308) 30.8		(95) 50.0	(108) 24.6	(45) 29.6	(29) 17.3	(16) 34.1	(15) 40.7
10.1	6.7	4.5		.0	3.5	9.5	4.7	9.6	22.2
28.9	24.0	27.2	% Profit Before Taxes/Total Assets	29.0	28.4	25.6	22.8	13.1	32.6
9.1	7.3	7.5		3.8	8.0	11.7	5.5	9.4	10.7
1.3	-.9	-.4		-5.2	.6	1.0	1.3	1.9	.4
43.0	60.9	48.5	Sales/Net Fixed Assets	57.3	48.4	38.3	83.8	49.3	26.6
16.2	19.7	18.3		17.3	19.2	23.2	28.1	14.7	12.3
6.1	6.3	5.9		4.2	7.4	7.7	9.6	8.9	4.9
6.7	6.9	6.8	Sales/Total Assets	8.5	6.8	6.2	7.4	4.4	6.8
3.9	3.9	3.9		4.0	4.1	4.0	3.7	3.4	3.4
2.4	2.3	2.1		1.7	2.1	2.3	1.8	2.3	2.3
.8	.7	.8	% Depr., Dep., Amort./Sales	1.1	.7	.7	.6	.7	1.0
(335) 1.7	(347) 1.5	(390) 1.7		(148) 2.2	(124) 1.4	(46) 1.6	(34) 1.5	(22) 1.3	(16) 1.7
3.9	3.3	3.0		4.5	2.7	2.9	2.4	1.8	2.2
3.9	3.1	2.9	% Officers', Directors' Owners' Comp/Sales	3.9	3.0	2.4	1.4	1.5	
(260) 5.9	(290) 5.5	(326) 5.2		(127) 7.4	(124) 5.2	(34) 4.2	(26) 2.3	(10) 3.2	
9.7	9.1	9.1		12.1	8.4	5.1	3.8	5.0	
7841371M	6939033M	6205688M	Net Sales ($)	115517M	285527M	231359M	286095M	370749M	4916441M
2249921M	2328782M	1686598M	Total Assets ($)	68573M	109430M	81370M	130981M	143522M	1152722M

© RMA 2010

M = $ thousand   MM = $ million
See Pages 9 through 22 for Explanation of Ratios and Data

| Current Data Sorted by Assets | | | | | | | Comparative Historical Data | |

Type of Statement

							2	2
						Unqualified	2	2
						Reviewed	6	5
						Compiled	5	5
						Tax Returns	11	10
						Other	7	13
							4/1/05-3/31/06	4/1/06-3/31/07
0-500M	500M-2MM	2-10MM	10-50MM	50-100MM	100-250MM		ALL	ALL
2 (4/1-9/30/09)			24 (10/1/09-3/31/10)		1			
13	**7**	**4**	**1**	**1**	**1**	**NUMBER OF STATEMENTS**	**31**	**35**
%	%	%	%	%	%		%	%

0-500M	500M-2MM	2-10MM	10-50MM	50-100MM	100-250MM		ALL	ALL
						ASSETS		
9.5						Cash & Equivalents	11.4	11.5
5.8						Trade Receivables (net)	7.5	6.6
18.3						Inventory	21.0	18.1
2.1						All Other Current	1.1	2.0
35.8						Total Current	41.1	38.2
38.6		DATA				Fixed Assets (net)	35.0	33.7
9.8		NOT				Intangibles (net)	11.0	15.1
15.8		AVAILABLE				All Other Non-Current	12.9	13.1
100.0						Total	100.0	100.0
						LIABILITIES		
2.0						Notes Payable-Short Term	6.1	2.2
1.0						Cur. Mat.-L.T.D.	2.8	4.2
17.0						Trade Payables	11.4	10.1
.0						Income Taxes Payable	.0	.0
38.2						All Other Current	20.1	16.4
58.2						Total Current	40.5	32.9
38.0						Long-Term Debt	43.4	31.3
.0						Deferred Taxes	.3	.3
24.7						All Other Non-Current	9.2	17.3
-21.0						Net Worth	6.7	18.3
100.0						Total Liabilities & Net Worth	100.0	100.0
						INCOME DATA		
100.0						Net Sales	100.0	100.0
						Gross Profit		
100.9						Operating Expenses	95.0	93.0
-.9						Operating Profit	5.0	7.0
.6						All Other Expenses (net)	2.5	3.4
-1.5						Profit Before Taxes	2.5	3.6
						RATIOS		
2.4							2.3	2.7
.7						Current	1.3	1.4
.2							.8	.8
.6							1.5	1.2
.2						Quick	.5	.6
.1							.2	.2
0 748.0							1 447.5 / 1 335.7	
1 275.5						Sales/Receivables	3 123.8 / 3 133.5	
5 72.3							8 47.8 / 10 37.6	
						Cost of Sales/Inventory		
						Cost of Sales/Payables		
38.0							14.7	12.0
-56.6						Sales/Working Capital	30.8	22.6
-11.6							-42.9	-20.8
							8.0	6.2
						EBIT/Interest	(26) 1.8 / (25) 1.5	
							1.0	-.1
						Net Profit + Depr., Dep., Amort./Cur. Mat. L/T/D		
.8							.4	.5
18.6						Fixed/Worth	2.3	5.1
-.7							-3.0	-.9
1.2							1.2	.9
39.5						Debt/Worth	5.5	11.8
-1.7							-2.8	-3.1
							78.1	49.7
						% Profit Before Taxes/Tangible Net Worth	(22) 22.4 / (21) 13.6	
							5.7	-5.2
10.9							14.1	13.8
2.4						% Profit Before Taxes/Total Assets	6.4	2.9
-19.6							.1	-3.8
27.5							74.4	25.9
11.9						Sales/Net Fixed Assets	10.3	11.1
7.6							5.9	5.7
9.3							5.6	4.8
5.1						Sales/Total Assets	3.3	3.1
2.9							2.1	1.4
.8							1.1	1.1
(12) 1.1						% Depr., Dep., Amort./Sales	(25) 2.5 / (29) 1.9	
2.6							3.1	3.4
							2.5	1.8
						% Officers', Directors' Owners' Comp/Sales	(20) 4.8 / (18) 2.8	
							6.5	5.0
9957M	17080M	42317M	66333M		38920M	Net Sales ($)	485962M	295336M
2400M	7503M	16583M	46735M		116681M	Total Assets ($)	259577M	395643M

© RMA 2010

M = $ thousand   MM = $ million
See Pages 9 through 22 for Explanation of Ratios and Data

Comparative Historical Data   Current Data Sorted by Sales

Type of Statement	4/1/07-3/31/08 ALL	4/1/08-3/31/09 ALL	4/1/09-3/31/10 ALL	0-1MM	1-3MM	3-5MM	5-10MM	10-25MM	25MM & OVER
Unqualified	1	1	2						
Reviewed	2	2	3				1	1	
Compiled	1	4	12	1			2		
Tax Returns	8	10	9	9	1	1		1	1
Other	4	8		5	1	1			1
(period)				2 (4/1-9/30/09)			24 (10/1/09-3/31/10)		
NUMBER OF STATEMENTS	**16**	**25**	**26**	**15**	**2**	**2**	**3**	**2**	**2**
	%	%	%	%	%	%	%	%	%
ASSETS									
Cash & Equivalents	13.5	7.9	12.3	8.4					
Trade Receivables (net)	6.3	7.4	6.2	3.1					
Inventory	21.2	16.8	13.9	15.3					
All Other Current	3.4	4.8	2.6	2.1					
Total Current	44.4	36.9	35.0	28.9					
Fixed Assets (net)	34.8	39.4	36.6	42.9					
Intangibles (net)	15.9	13.2	11.7	12.9					
All Other Non-Current	4.9	10.6	16.6	15.3					
Total	100.0	100.0	100.0	100.0					
LIABILITIES									
Notes Payable-Short Term	4.7	11.6	3.4	2.8					
Cur. Mat.-L.T.D.	4.4	2.5	1.4	1.0					
Trade Payables	13.2	20.0	12.8	12.9					
Income Taxes Payable	.0	.0	.1	.0					
All Other Current	5.7	19.2	22.5	23.5					
Total Current	28.0	53.3	40.2	40.1					
Long-Term Debt	27.1	27.2	32.2	42.0					
Deferred Taxes	.9	.3	.1	.0					
All Other Non-Current	21.4	4.4	15.3	16.5					
Net Worth	22.6	14.8	12.1	1.4					
Total Liabilities & Net Worth	100.0	100.0	100.0	100.0					
INCOME DATA									
Net Sales	100.0	100.0	100.0	100.0					
Gross Profit									
Operating Expenses	96.0	93.5	95.9	96.2					
Operating Profit	4.0	6.5	4.1	3.8					
All Other Expenses (net)	.8	3.5	4.1	6.6					
Profit Before Taxes	3.1	2.9	.0	-2.8					
RATIOS									
Current	4.3	1.6	3.0	3.0					
	1.8	.8	1.0	.7					
	1.0	.3	.3	.3					
Quick	1.5	.7	1.5	.7					
	1.0	.2	.3	.2					
	.4	.1	.2	.1					
Sales/Receivables	0 UND	1 621.9	1 675.1	0 UND					
	3 104.7	4 97.7	2 190.2	1 452.5					
	10 35.3	8 46.8	8 46.8	4 94.5					
Cost of Sales/Inventory									
Cost of Sales/Payables									
Sales/Working Capital	8.6	38.8	14.6	33.9					
	23.5	-38.3	NM	-56.6					
	NM	-8.4	-13.7	-12.8					
EBIT/Interest	17.1	8.0	5.7						
	(13) 2.0	(17) 1.4	(18) 1.6						
	1.4	-5.4	-4.2						
Net Profit + Depr., Dep., Amort./Cur. Mat. L/T/D									
Fixed/Worth	.7	.6	.5	.7					
	8.4	2.2	3.0	9.5					
	-.6	-3.7	18.9	-1.8					
Debt/Worth	.9	1.1	1.1	1.3					
	13.3	4.0	6.2	21.6					
	-3.3	-8.1	NM	-2.9					
% Profit Before Taxes/Tangible Net Worth		82.2	45.2	32.9					
	(16) 17.9	(20) 17.5	(10) 17.5						
		-8.5	.9	-384.6					
% Profit Before Taxes/Total Assets	33.4	14.8	10.8	9.6					
	5.2	1.6	2.9	1.7					
	2.8	-9.5	-13.8	-20.6					
Sales/Net Fixed Assets	55.0	32.6	22.6	34.0					
	17.6	18.7	13.5	11.9					
	6.3	5.7	5.4	3.6					
Sales/Total Assets	4.9	9.2	5.2	8.6					
	3.6	5.0	3.2	3.4					
	3.1	1.6	1.6	1.4					
% Depr., Dep., Amort./Sales	1.1	.9	1.0	1.0					
	(12) 2.6	(22) 1.6	(22) 1.8	(13) 1.4					
	3.2	2.9	2.5	3.1					
% Officers', Directors' Owners' Comp/Sales	2.9		2.2						
	(12) 5.4	(10) 4.8							
	8.3		14.3						
Net Sales ($)	111430M	98377M	174607M	9550M	4103M	7591M	24989M	23121M	105253M
Total Assets ($)	122770M	50824M	189902M	4803M	1073M	2097M	7978M	10535M	163416M

Current Data Sorted by Assets | Comparative Historical Data

	0-500M	500M-2MM	2-10MM	10-50MM	50-100MM	100-250MM		4/1/05-3/31/06 ALL	4/1/06-3/31/07 ALL
Type of Statement									
Unqualified								1	2
Reviewed			3	1	1			8	2
Compiled	7	8	4			1		16	19
Tax Returns	12	9	1			1		19	23
Other	8	8	3	4				14	18
Period		8 (4/1-9/30/09)		63 (10/1/09-3/31/10)					
NUMBER OF STATEMENTS	27	25	11	5	1	2		58	64
	%	%	%	%	%	%		%	%
ASSETS									
Cash & Equivalents	16.4	14.6	7.3					10.7	11.3
Trade Receivables (net)	16.3	12.7	17.2					16.8	17.0
Inventory	18.9	18.6	22.3					26.5	18.8
All Other Current	3.8	1.5	8.8					5.6	3.4
Total Current	55.5	47.4	55.6					59.6	50.5
Fixed Assets (net)	34.1	38.8	34.4					29.2	35.2
Intangibles (net)	4.1	8.9	5.1					6.4	5.5
All Other Non-Current	6.3	4.9	4.9					4.8	8.8
Total	100.0	100.0	100.0					100.0	100.0
LIABILITIES									
Notes Payable-Short Term	19.7	8.6	7.0					10.0	8.0
Cur. Mat.-L.T.D.	1.8	2.7	5.0					4.2	4.1
Trade Payables	15.4	8.1	11.9					15.5	14.1
Income Taxes Payable	.0	.0	1.1					.1	.2
All Other Current	17.5	7.6	10.4					16.2	16.8
Total Current	54.3	27.0	35.3					45.9	43.2
Long-Term Debt	22.2	29.5	24.7					28.8	34.3
Deferred Taxes	.0	.0	1.8					.5	.0
All Other Non-Current	14.5	5.7	4.1					6.6	11.2
Net Worth	8.9	37.8	34.0					18.3	11.3
Total Liabilities & Net Worth	100.0	100.0	100.0					100.0	100.0
INCOME DATA									
Net Sales	100.0	100.0	100.0					100.0	100.0
Gross Profit									
Operating Expenses	93.0	93.7	93.0					94.7	95.2
Operating Profit	7.0	6.3	7.0					5.3	4.8
All Other Expenses (net)	2.1	2.3	3.1					1.9	1.9
Profit Before Taxes	4.9	4.0	3.9					3.4	2.9
RATIOS									
Current	3.6	5.6	2.1					2.4	2.5
	1.5	1.6	1.4					1.5	1.3
	.7	1.0	.9					1.0	.7
Quick	3.0	2.6	1.3					1.4	1.9
	.5	1.2	.5					.5	.6
	.2	.6	.2					.2	.2
Sales/Receivables	0 UND	4 83.1	2 210.3					2 197.6	2 222.8
	7 52.3	14 25.4	30 12.0					10 37.1	13 28.8
	27 13.8	37 9.8	43 8.6					38 9.7	28 12.9
Cost of Sales/Inventory									
Cost of Sales/Payables									
Sales/Working Capital	7.5	6.0	8.9					8.4	9.6
	21.6	17.3	21.6					22.7	32.6
	-156.9	NM	-68.4					NM	-69.6
EBIT/Interest	3.9	5.2						13.7	7.5
	(19) 1.0	(23) 2.1						(48) 3.8	(53) 2.9
	-2.0	1.0						.0	1.2
Net Profit + Depr., Dep., Amort./Cur. Mat. L/T/D									
Fixed/Worth	.3	.4	.2					.3	.4
	2.1	1.3	1.1					.8	1.4
	-.4	5.5	8.9					8.3	-10.4
Debt/Worth	.5	.8	.5					.9	.9
	3.1	2.0	1.9					2.5	2.7
	-2.6	13.0	12.0					-127.5	-11.4
% Profit Before Taxes/Tangible Net Worth	188.2	34.3	134.4					44.2	40.1
	(17) 11.9	(20) 3.5	(10) 21.4					(43) 17.2	(44) 22.0
	-16.8	-14.8	2.8					1.1	3.4
% Profit Before Taxes/Total Assets	34.9	10.7	24.1					17.1	18.9
	.9	3.4	7.7					5.8	7.4
	-6.7	-1.7	.9					-.9	.6
Sales/Net Fixed Assets	85.0	33.7	23.2					42.3	39.2
	19.9	7.8	17.4					18.1	15.1
	6.3	2.6	5.8					6.8	4.3
Sales/Total Assets	6.1	3.9	5.5					5.8	5.2
	3.5	2.4	2.6					3.5	3.3
	2.1	1.3	1.9					2.0	1.8
% Depr., Dep., Amort./Sales	.6	.9	1.7					.7	.8
	(21) 1.1	(18) 2.1	2.1					(43) 1.2	(55) 1.6
	2.9	3.4	3.0					2.4	3.8
% Officers', Directors' Owners' Comp/Sales	2.2	2.8						3.2	2.3
	(13) 7.6	(15)						(33) 5.4	(41) 5.9
	10.4	8.2						10.4	9.1
Net Sales ($)	28139M	65858M	200668M	312803M	164041M	997992M		2034715M	1744285M
Total Assets ($)	6767M	24709M	47920M	126035M	79537M	317929M		405719M	389604M

M = $ thousand   MM = $ million
See Pages 9 through 22 for Explanation of Ratios and Data

Comparative Historical Data   **Current Data Sorted by Sales**

2	1	2	Type of Statement						2
1	3	3	Unqualified						1
23	15	20	Reviewed				1	1	1
25	40	23	Compiled	4	7	4	3	1	1
17	24	23	Tax Returns	9	11		2		1
			Other	9	5	1	3		5
4/1/07-3/31/08 ALL	4/1/08-3/31/09 ALL	4/1/09-3/31/10 ALL		8 (4/1-9/30/09)			63 (10/1/09-3/31/10)		
				0-1MM	1-3MM	3-5MM	5-10MM	10-25MM	25MM & OVER
68	83	71	NUMBER OF STATEMENTS	22	23	5	9	2	10
%	%	%	**ASSETS**	%	%	%	%	%	%
12.8	15.7	13.9	Cash & Equivalents	11.4	16.3				10.9
18.0	15.5	14.8	Trade Receivables (net)	13.0	15.3				10.9
21.1	18.8	19.4	Inventory	15.8	21.9				18.5
1.9	3.1	4.5	All Other Current	2.5	3.3				12.2
53.8	53.1	52.6	Total Current	42.7	56.8				52.5
35.0	33.7	35.5	Fixed Assets (net)	40.9	34.7				32.3
4.2	4.6	6.8	Intangibles (net)	9.7	3.9				11.0
7.0	8.6	5.1	All Other Non-Current	6.7	4.6				4.2
100.0	100.0	100.0	Total	100.0	100.0				100.0
			LIABILITIES						
10.9	9.2	12.5	Notes Payable-Short Term	17.3	13.7				7.4
2.8	6.4	2.6	Cur. Mat.-L.T.D.	2.0	1.9				3.3
12.9	13.1	12.0	Trade Payables	9.3	13.0				14.2
.0	.1	.2	Income Taxes Payable	.0	.0				.0
14.2	12.5	13.1	All Other Current	3.4	24.1				18.2
40.9	41.3	40.4	Total Current	32.1	52.7				43.1
30.6	22.7	25.1	Long-Term Debt	28.9	28.3				20.5
.1	.1	.3	Deferred Taxes	.0	.0				.0
11.0	11.7	9.0	All Other Non-Current	19.2	3.6				5.7
17.5	24.2	25.2	Net Worth	19.8	15.4				30.6
100.0	100.0	100.0	Total Liabilties & Net Worth	100.0	100.0				100.0
			INCOME DATA						
100.0	100.0	100.0	Net Sales	100.0	100.0				100.0
			Gross Profit						
94.0	93.0	93.5	Operating Expenses	88.0	96.2				95.4
6.0	7.0	6.5	Operating Profit	12.0	3.8				4.6
2.6	2.1	2.2	All Other Expenses (net)	5.4	.7				.4
3.4	5.0	4.3	Profit Before Taxes	6.6	3.1				4.2
			RATIOS						
2.9	2.6	3.1		3.8	3.6				1.6
1.7	1.5	1.5	Current	1.4	1.6				1.0
1.1	.7	.9		.8	1.2				.8
2.0	1.5	2.5		3.3	2.6				.8
.8	(82) .7	.8	Quick	.5	1.2				.3
.3	.3	.3		.3	.3				.2
2 161.7	1 427.7	1 381.5		0 UND	0 UND				1 421.1
17 21.3	13 27.9	14 26.2	Sales/Receivables	17 21.3	9 41.4				10 37.2
31 11.7	33 11.2	37 9.8		31 11.6	29 12.4				26 14.2
			Cost of Sales/Inventory						
			Cost of Sales/Payables						
7.7	8.3	7.5		6.9	6.5				15.7
17.2	33.7	21.0	Sales/Working Capital	17.5	21.6				NM
148.0	-24.8	-156.9		-12.5	60.2				-142.2
7.5	6.4	6.1		2.5	5.3				
(55) 2.6	(67) 2.6	(58) 2.1	EBIT/Interest	(16) .9	(19) 2.0				
.4	1.0	.6		-.2	-.6				
	14.7		Net Profit + Depr., Dep.,						
	(10) 7.3		Amort./Cur. Mat. L/T/D						
	.6								
.3	.2	.3		.4	.3				.2
1.1	1.0	1.3	Fixed/Worth	6.4	1.1				1.2
5.4	40.7	12.5		-1.7	-1.8				2.3
.6	.5	.6		.7	.5				1.5
2.1	2.1	2.3	Debt/Worth	11.0	2.2				3.5
19.6	77.1	-55.3		-3.6	-11.7				NM
48.6	89.3	60.7	% Profit Before Taxes/Tangible	29.5	135.6				
(52) 23.4	(63) 26.8	(53) 12.5	Net Worth	(13) 12.5	(17) 1.5				
-1.4	.0	-1.4		-7.4	-35.9				
17.8	22.6	15.0	% Profit Before Taxes/Total	6.7	15.9				40.5
6.2	4.5	3.4	Assets	1.8	1.3				10.6
-2.0	.0	-1.1		-3.6	-13.8				2.5
41.0	34.1	35.5		29.3	68.6				35.5
16.9	16.6	19.1	Sales/Net Fixed Assets	6.8	21.7				19.2
6.0	7.7	4.6		.8	7.2				7.3
4.9	5.4	4.5		3.0	6.1				5.4
3.0	3.5	2.9	Sales/Total Assets	1.9	3.5				3.2
2.1	2.2	1.9		.5	2.1				2.0
.9	.8	.7		.7	.5				
(51) 1.6	(69) 1.4	(55) 1.9	% Depr., Dep., Amort./Sales	(15) 2.5	(17) 1.1				
2.6	2.4	3.0		5.5	2.2				
2.0	1.9	2.1	% Officers', Directors'		2.5				
(40) 4.9	(41) 5.2	(35) 4.8	Owners' Comp/Sales		(16) 7.0				
9.0	8.8	8.2			9.8				
577315M	701879M	1769501M	Net Sales ($)	12177M	42122M	20374M	61908M	29682M	1603238M
207040M	282945M	602897M	Total Assets ($)	12677M	13305M	6229M	21632M	7022M	542032M

M = $ thousand   MM = $ million
See Pages 9 through 22 for Explanation of Ratios and Data

Current Data Sorted by Assets

Comparative Historical Data

	0-500M	500M-2MM	2-10MM	10-50MM	50-100MM	100-250MM	Type of Statement	ALL 4/1/05-3/31/06	ALL 4/1/06-3/31/07
		1	3	2	1	1	Unqualified	4	2
	2	4	11	1			Reviewed	18	13
	16	17	9		1	1	Compiled	41	61
	101	54	7	1	1	1	Tax Returns	115	133
	41	33	23	6	1	1	Other	106	96
		44 (4/1-9/30/09)		295 (10/1/09-3/31/10)					
NUMBER OF STATEMENTS	160	109	53	10	3	4		284	305
	%	%	%	%	%	%	**ASSETS**	%	%
Cash & Equivalents	21.9	19.5	11.7	12.0				14.1	13.8
Trade Receivables (net)	14.6	11.0	15.9	9.1				16.0	14.5
Inventory	10.4	8.3	10.3	7.0				13.0	12.8
All Other Current	2.7	3.6	2.8	4.3				2.4	2.9
Total Current	49.6	42.4	40.7	32.3				45.6	44.0
Fixed Assets (net)	33.6	36.5	43.2	33.4				40.5	40.7
Intangibles (net)	6.3	9.8	7.5	13.2				5.9	5.4
All Other Non-Current	10.5	11.2	8.6	21.1				8.0	9.9
Total	100.0	100.0	100.0	100.0				100.0	100.0
							LIABILITIES		
Notes Payable-Short Term	13.3	6.1	7.9	8.5				13.2	11.8
Cur. Mat.-L.T.D.	4.4	3.0	3.5	4.1				4.4	4.2
Trade Payables	18.4	13.4	15.0	8.3				17.5	18.7
Income Taxes Payable	.2	.0	.2	.0				.2	.3
All Other Current	23.5	12.2	8.6	12.0				15.4	14.5
Total Current	59.8	34.8	35.4	33.0				50.8	49.4
Long-Term Debt	32.8	28.5	36.5	32.7				34.4	34.9
Deferred Taxes	.1	.1	.2	1.0				.1	.1
All Other Non-Current	10.1	7.9	5.2	24.7				11.7	8.4
Net Worth	-2.7	28.8	22.8	8.6				3.1	7.3
Total Liabilities & Net Worth	100.0	100.0	100.0	100.0				100.0	100.0
							INCOME DATA		
Net Sales	100.0	100.0	100.0	100.0				100.0	100.0
Gross Profit									
Operating Expenses	96.9	95.2	90.2	97.8				94.7	94.7
Operating Profit	3.1	4.8	9.8	2.2				5.3	5.3
All Other Expenses (net)	.6	2.4	5.8	.6				2.2	2.2
Profit Before Taxes	2.6	2.4	4.1	1.6				3.1	3.1
							RATIOS		
Current	2.0	2.2	1.9	1.4				1.8	1.8
	1.0	1.2	1.1	1.1				1.1	1.0
	.5	.6	.7	.8				.5	.5
Quick	1.5	1.9	1.2	1.2				1.3	1.4
	.7	.8	.7	1.0				(283) .6	(303) .6
	.3	.3	.4	.4				.3	.3
Sales/Receivables	0 UND	3 119.8	8 47.7	6 63.5				2 227.6	0 999.8
	5 73.4	7 50.2	13 28.6	12 31.4				11 34.4	9 39.6
	12 31.4	15 24.0	24 15.0	26 13.9				21 17.2	20 18.7
Cost of Sales/Inventory									
Cost of Sales/Payables									
Sales/Working Capital	22.1	11.4	10.5	22.6				15.6	18.3
	483.2	64.2	149.3	85.8				156.6	UND
	-25.8	-25.7	-27.5	-32.8				-16.2	-21.0
EBIT/Interest	9.3	10.5	12.6					8.7	9.2
	(112) 2.4	(86) 3.3	(45) 4.4					(241) 2.3	(265) 3.0
	-.2	.8	1.9					.3	1.0
Net Profit + Depr., Dep., Amort./Cur. Mat. L/T/D			8.6					6.2	4.2
		(10) 2.4						(20) 2.0	(26) 1.6
		.8						.2	.6
Fixed/Worth	.4	.4	.7	2.5				.7	.6
	1.8	1.9	2.3	12.0				3.7	2.5
	-1.0	-231.4	-129.3	-.2				-2.3	-4.4
Debt/Worth	1.0	.7	1.6	6.4				1.4	1.4
	5.4	4.4	4.1	26.7				8.0	5.1
	-3.3	-46.1	-138.9	-15.6				-6.0	-7.6
% Profit Before Taxes/Tangible Net Worth	132.2	73.0	61.7					76.7	110.7
	(101) 50.0	(80) 22.3	(39) 31.7					(176) 31.5	(209) 39.3
	6.4	3.1	9.2					4.5	9.1
% Profit Before Taxes/Total Assets	39.5	15.7	13.2	6.8				17.9	26.0
	10.4	6.5	5.9	2.0				5.2	8.8
	-5.8	.1	2.9	-1.0				-1.2	.2
Sales/Net Fixed Assets	59.6	36.0	25.3	26.6				32.8	34.9
	28.3	17.2	8.0	20.6				12.8	13.8
	13.4	5.2	2.5	2.0				5.9	5.8
Sales/Total Assets	10.4	5.1	4.3	3.6				6.1	7.0
	6.8	3.4	2.6	1.5				4.3	4.5
	4.4	2.2	1.3	1.1				2.4	2.6
% Depr., Dep., Amort./Sales	.5	.9	1.1					1.1	.9
	(121) 1.0	(88) 1.4	(43) 2.1					(230) 2.0	(246) 1.6
	2.2	2.4	4.1					3.3	3.0
% Officers', Directors' Owners' Comp/Sales	3.4	2.6	1.1					3.1	2.8
	(112) 5.8	(76) 4.5	(27) 2.1					(172) 5.2	(193) 4.5
	9.9	6.5	3.6					8.9	7.9
Net Sales ($)	225842M	405547M	568555M	405963M	3260757M	1163700M		2549525M	4668632M
Total Assets ($)	33755M	112011M	207261M	227388M	224771M	659110M		912493M	1001930M

Comparative Historical Data   Current Data Sorted by Sales

10	7	8	Type of Statement						
					0-1MM	1-3MM	3-5MM	5-10MM	10-25MM	25MM & OVER
10	7	8	Unqualified		1	1		2	4
16	20	18	Reviewed		4	3	4	6	1
41	45	43	Compiled	7	15	8	6	6	1
137	143	165	Tax Returns	51	69	24	13	5	3
95	85	105	Other	19	43	15	9	11	8
4/1/07-3/31/08 ALL	4/1/08-3/31/09 ALL	4/1/09-3/31/10 ALL		44 (4/1-9/30/09)		295 (10/1/09-3/31/10)			
299	300	339	**NUMBER OF STATEMENTS**	77	132	51	32	30	17
%	%	%	**ASSETS**	%	%	%	%	%	%
15.0	17.8	19.2	Cash & Equivalents	20.5	18.5	21.3	22.1	13.8	16.3
13.4	13.2	13.4	Trade Receivables (net)	8.4	15.5	14.4	14.1	16.8	8.9
11.9	11.3	9.5	Inventory	8.5	11.0	6.1	10.8	12.0	5.6
3.2	2.7	3.1	All Other Current	1.1	4.1	3.1	2.6	2.3	6.2
43.5	44.9	45.1	Total Current	38.5	49.0	44.8	49.6	44.9	37.0
39.5	37.3	36.0	Fixed Assets (net)	44.9	34.3	31.4	33.3	32.8	34.8
8.5	6.0	8.4	Intangibles (net)	6.1	7.3	9.8	5.9	12.2	20.0
8.6	11.8	10.5	All Other Non-Current	10.5	9.4	14.0	11.1	10.1	8.2
100.0	100.0	100.0	Total	100.0	100.0	100.0	100.0	100.0	100.0
			LIABILITIES						
14.7	11.1	9.8	Notes Payable-Short Term	16.7	8.4	7.3	7.5	7.2	6.7
4.4	5.0	3.8	Cur. Mat.-L.T.D.	2.5	4.9	2.8	3.6	3.9	4.4
16.2	17.6	15.9	Trade Payables	10.6	16.9	17.1	17.1	23.9	11.6
.1	.2	.1	Income Taxes Payable	.0	.2	.1	.0	.2	.4
12.1	19.7	16.9	All Other Current	21.1	18.0	12.4	16.7	11.8	12.5
47.4	53.6	46.6	Total Current	50.9	48.5	39.7	44.9	46.9	35.6
30.2	29.1	31.8	Long-Term Debt	37.6	36.8	20.6	19.8	29.6	26.3
.2	.2	.2	Deferred Taxes	.0	.1	.1	.2	.6	.8
12.8	12.8	9.0	All Other Non-Current	11.0	7.7	7.4	12.9	5.2	13.9
9.4	4.3	12.6	Net Worth	.6	7.0	32.2	22.2	17.7	23.4
100.0	100.0	100.0	Total Liabilties & Net Worth	100.0	100.0	100.0	100.0	100.0	100.0
			INCOME DATA						
100.0	100.0	100.0	Net Sales	100.0	100.0	100.0	100.0	100.0	100.0
			Gross Profit						
93.8	95.2	95.3	Operating Expenses	92.3	95.8	96.1	97.0	96.8	97.4
6.2	4.8	4.7	Operating Profit	7.7	4.2	3.9	3.0	3.2	2.6
1.4	2.0	2.0	All Other Expenses (net)	5.3	1.2	1.0	.2	.8	1.5
4.7	2.8	2.7	Profit Before Taxes	2.3	3.0	2.9	2.8	2.5	1.1
			RATIOS						
2.1	2.1	2.0	Current	1.7	2.4	2.4	2.2	1.5	1.3
1.0	1.0	1.1		.9	1.2	1.2	1.0	1.0	1.0
.6	.6	.6		.3	.7	.8	.7	.6	.6
1.5	1.5	1.6	Quick	1.4	1.8	2.0	2.1	.9	1.1
(298) .7	.7	.7		.5	.8	1.0	.6	.7	.6
.3	.3	.3		.1	.3	.5	.4	.3	.4
0 UND	0 UND	1 541.0	Sales/Receivables	0 UND	1 329.0	4 88.6	4 82.7	8 43.2	5 72.3
8 44.5	8 43.7	7 49.1		0 UND	7 53.3	9 41.2	7 51.3	12 30.3	11 32.5
19 18.8	15 24.0	14 25.7		10 37.1	13 28.3	19 19.7	18 19.8	16 23.2	14 26.8
			Cost of Sales/Inventory						
			Cost of Sales/Payables						
17.9	19.4	16.3	Sales/Working Capital	23.2	13.5	9.3	11.6	35.7	32.0
267.0	-999.8	149.3		-346.5	65.6	60.8	999.8	877.0	-382.1
-28.1	-18.5	-26.8		-14.2	-51.9	-41.5	-27.8	-27.5	-28.1
8.5	7.2	9.6	EBIT/Interest	5.6	11.8	12.3	20.6	12.9	11.7
(250) 2.6	(236) 2.3	(258) 3.0		(40) 1.9	(107) 2.5	(41) 4.1	(27) 2.7	(28) 4.8	(15) 1.7
.9	.4	.8		-.2	.7	.7	.6	2.6	.3
3.3	4.4	6.6	Net Profit + Depr., Dep., Amort./Cur. Mat. L/T/D						
(24) 2.4	(19) 1.4	(27) 2.3							
.8	.6	1.2							
.7	.6	.5	Fixed/Worth	.5	.4	.4	.5	.6	1.5
2.9	2.7	2.3		7.5	2.4	1.1	1.9	2.5	2.9
-2.1	-1.9	-2.4		-1.6	-1.2	21.1	NM	-4.9	-1.7
1.3	1.4	1.0	Debt/Worth	1.0	.7	.7	1.3	1.8	2.3
4.8	7.0	5.4		12.0	5.0	1.6	3.2	7.1	23.6
-6.7	-5.9	-6.3		-3.8	-4.7	55.7	NM	-10.9	-4.7
124.8	104.8	106.1	% Profit Before Taxes/Tangible Net Worth	117.4	103.6	122.0	59.5	95.6	183.3
(197) 42.0	(199) 30.8	(229) 39.7		(47) 19.2	(88) 44.4	(40) 28.7	(24) 31.3	(20) 46.0	(10) 41.4
6.4	6.3	5.0		-1.6	11.3	5.3	.8	16.5	7.8
24.1	19.1	22.0	% Profit Before Taxes/Total Assets	15.0	36.2	23.6	17.2	17.3	16.3
8.1	5.2	7.7		4.0	8.4	9.2	8.4	9.0	4.5
.0	-1.4	-.5		-4.3	-.8	.7	-.3	3.1	.1
35.5	41.2	43.9	Sales/Net Fixed Assets	41.6	58.9	39.3	40.2	36.7	22.4
14.5	18.0	19.5		13.6	23.9	19.4	19.7	22.7	12.6
5.5	7.1	8.0		3.9	9.8	9.6	7.9	8.5	5.2
7.2	7.6	7.4	Sales/Total Assets	8.0	9.1	5.9	6.4	6.0	3.9
4.3	4.5	4.5		3.5	5.6	4.3	4.5	4.5	2.9
2.5	2.5	2.6		1.6	3.0	2.2	2.7	2.7	1.4
.7	.8	.7	% Depr., Dep., Amort./Sales	.6	.6	.9	.8	1.0	1.2
(232) 1.5	(238) 1.7	(264) 1.4		(59) 1.7	(104) 1.2	(40) 1.5	(27) 1.2	(21) 1.6	(13) 2.1
2.6	3.0	2.6		4.4	2.3	2.4	2.1	2.4	3.0
2.4	3.0	2.6	% Officers', Directors' Owners' Comp/Sales	4.0	3.1	2.6	1.6	.8	
(188) 4.3	(179) 5.1	(219) 4.8		(45) 6.5	(92) 5.3	(39) 4.2	(23) 3.3	(16) 1.6	
8.1	7.8	7.7		12.8	8.5	6.7	5.4	3.3	
7658377M	2449796M	6030364M	Net Sales ($)	43520M	247399M	201153M	208242M	469131M	4860919M
1298484M	947951M	1464296M	Total Assets ($)	32579M	74713M	66668M	71553M	128370M	1090413M

M = $ thousand   MM = $ million
See Pages 9 through 22 for Explanation of Ratios and Data

Current Data Sorted by Assets | Comparative Historical Data

0-500M	500M-2MM	2-10MM	10-50MM	50-100MM	100-250MM	Type of Statement	4/1/05-3/31/06 ALL	4/1/06-3/31/07 ALL
		2	1			Unqualified	3	1
	2					Reviewed	10	9
1	2					Compiled	4	4
4	8	2				Tax Returns	11	10
2	2	2	1		2	Other	5	8
7 (4/1-9/30/09)			24 (10/1/09-3/31/10)					
7	14	6	2		2	NUMBER OF STATEMENTS	33	32
%	%	%	%	%	%	**ASSETS**	%	%
	6.8			D		Cash & Equivalents	12.7	13.0
	21.1			A		Trade Receivables (net)	28.8	22.9
	32.3			T		Inventory	16.9	15.2
	1.1			A		All Other Current	.9	2.6
	61.3					Total Current	59.3	53.7
	19.9			N		Fixed Assets (net)	28.7	29.6
	5.2			O		Intangibles (net)	2.4	8.5
	13.6			T		All Other Non-Current	9.7	8.1
	100.0					Total	100.0	100.0
				A		**LIABILITIES**		
	14.9			V		Notes Payable-Short Term	9.1	12.2
	2.8			A		Cur. Mat.-L.T.D.	9.5	4.2
	15.8			I		Trade Payables	18.3	14.2
	.0			L		Income Taxes Payable	.1	.0
	4.4			A		All Other Current	7.9	9.1
	37.8			B		Total Current	44.8	39.7
	16.2			L		Long-Term Debt	22.4	28.2
	.3			E		Deferred Taxes	.0	.1
	12.5					All Other Non-Current	5.6	9.4
	33.2					Net Worth	27.2	22.7
	100.0					Total Liabilities & Net Worth	100.0	100.0
						INCOME DATA		
	100.0					Net Sales	100.0	100.0
						Gross Profit		
	93.7					Operating Expenses	96.4	98.4
	6.3					Operating Profit	3.6	1.6
	2.3					All Other Expenses (net)	.9	.8
	4.0					Profit Before Taxes	2.6	.8
						RATIOS		
	3.0						2.5	3.1
	1.5					Current	1.4	1.3
	1.1						1.0	.8
	2.1						1.5	2.3
	.7					Quick	1.0	.7
	.2						.6	.5
0	UND						19 · 19.5	7 · 49.9
19	19.7					Sales/Receivables	26 · 14.1	17 · 21.3
28	13.1						41 · 8.9	35 · 10.4
						Cost of Sales/Inventory		
						Cost of Sales/Payables		
	7.1						7.2	9.0
	15.4					Sales/Working Capital	17.2	30.0
	154.1						-402.7	-34.0
	3.6						(27) 9.0	(27) 5.9
	(11) 1.4					EBIT/Interest	1.4	2.0
	-3.7						-.3	-3.1
						Net Profit + Depr., Dep., Amort./Cur. Mat. L/T/D		
	.2						.3	.4
	.6					Fixed/Worth	.9	1.1
	1.9						8.3	-4.3
	.9						.8	.7
	2.2					Debt/Worth	2.0	4.4
	8.6						85.1	-6.8
	22.5					% Profit Before Taxes/Tangible	(26) 26.4	(22) 75.9
	(12) 4.1					Net Worth	3.3	11.7
	-36.4						-1.7	-13.8
	5.5					% Profit Before Taxes/Total	10.3	14.7
	1.8					Assets	2.8	3.0
	-8.5						-2.6	-9.3
	84.9						41.9	40.6
	25.8					Sales/Net Fixed Assets	19.3	15.0
	11.1						7.3	9.1
	5.1						4.5	6.5
	3.3					Sales/Total Assets	3.4	3.0
	1.3						2.4	2.1
	.8						(29) 1.1	(26) 1.3
	(11) 1.0					% Depr., Dep., Amort./Sales	1.6	2.0
	2.0						2.7	2.6
	2.0					% Officers', Directors'	(18) 3.6	(15) 3.2
	(10) 3.0					Owners' Comp/Sales	5.0	6.4
	7.8						8.7	9.5
7356M	66267M	112281M	41715M		2053383M	Net Sales ($)	598179M	305645M
1979M	16950M	29523M	48244M		249984M	Total Assets ($)	277026M	152035M

M = $ thousand   MM = $ million
See Pages 9 through 22 for Explanation of Ratios and Data

Comparative Historical Data   Current Data Sorted by Sales

Type of Statement	4/1/07-3/31/08 ALL	4/1/08-3/31/09 ALL	4/1/09-3/31/10 ALL		0-1MM	1-3MM	3-5MM	5-10MM	10-25MM	25MM & OVER
Unqualified	4	2	3						2	1
Reviewed	6	3	2					2	1	
Compiled	3	4	3		1			2	1	
Tax Returns	16	14	16		6	4	1	2		2
Other	7	8	7		1	1	1	2	2	1
		7 (4/1-9/30/09)						24 (10/1/09-3/31/10)		
NUMBER OF STATEMENTS	36	31	31		8	5	2	7	5	4
	%	%	%		%	%	%	%	%	%
ASSETS										
Cash & Equivalents	11.6	9.0	12.5							
Trade Receivables (net)	19.5	26.8	26.3							
Inventory	12.8	13.0	24.0							
All Other Current	4.7	3.9	2.0							
Total Current	48.7	52.6	64.8							
Fixed Assets (net)	34.5	27.4	21.9							
Intangibles (net)	8.6	9.8	3.1							
All Other Non-Current	8.2	10.1	10.1							
Total	100.0	100.0	100.0							
LIABILITIES										
Notes Payable-Short Term	16.0	9.4	10.5							
Cur. Mat.-L.T.D.	5.8	13.5	7.6							
Trade Payables	13.6	14.9	17.8							
Income Taxes Payable	.1	.0	.0							
All Other Current	9.8	13.3	9.0							
Total Current	45.3	51.0	44.9							
Long-Term Debt	22.7	23.3	25.5							
Deferred Taxes	.0	.0	.9							
All Other Non-Current	6.5	2.6	9.3							
Net Worth	25.5	23.1	19.4							
Total Liabilties & Net Worth	100.0	100.0	100.0							
INCOME DATA										
Net Sales	100.0	100.0	100.0							
Gross Profit										
Operating Expenses	93.1	92.8	95.9							
Operating Profit	6.9	7.2	4.1							
All Other Expenses (net)	1.5	1.6	1.9							
Profit Before Taxes	5.4	5.6	2.2							
RATIOS										
Current	2.5	2.8	2.8							
	1.4	1.4	1.4							
	.5	1.0	.9							
Quick	1.4	1.5	2.0							
	.8	1.0	.8							
	.3	.3	.4							
Sales/Receivables	0 UND	10 35.8	14 25.5							
	20 18.7	20 18.4	18 19.7							
	39 9.4	44 8.3	31 11.7							
Cost of Sales/Inventory										
Cost of Sales/Payables										
Sales/Working Capital	9.3	11.8	10.3							
	27.0	31.4	18.3							
	-23.3	-823.3	-40.5							
EBIT/Interest	(33) 15.9	(25) 8.3	(24) 3.8							
	4.7	2.0	.3							
	.9	-.1	-3.5							
Net Profit + Depr., Dep., Amort./Cur. Mat. L/T/D										
Fixed/Worth	.3	.3	.2							
	.7	.7	.9							
	-13.3	-4.9	-7.4							
Debt/Worth	.6	.6	.7							
	2.5	2.5	2.8							
	-9.2	-15.2	-40.7							
% Profit Before Taxes/Tangible Net Worth	(25) 99.1	(21) 29.3	(22) 22.2							
	13.4	12.0	1.9							
	6.2	-.2	-40.5							
% Profit Before Taxes/Total Assets	18.8	14.8	8.1							
	4.6	4.9	.9							
	-.3	-2.6	-10.2							
Sales/Net Fixed Assets	43.2	50.2	84.9							
	12.2	16.0	29.3							
	3.6	6.1	6.5							
Sales/Total Assets	5.4	5.5	6.2							
	3.4	3.1	3.3							
	1.4	2.2	1.5							
% Depr., Dep., Amort./Sales	(28) 1.2	(20) .8	(24) .7							
	2.0	1.5	1.1							
	3.2	3.4	2.7							
% Officers', Directors' Owners' Comp/Sales	(19) 3.8	(18) 3.2	(18) 2.0							
	5.4	4.9	4.1							
	12.9	7.3	8.6							
Net Sales ($)	298823M	193173M	2281002M		4576M	10337M	6327M	49463M	84655M	2125644M
Total Assets ($)	309238M	62022M	346680M		3734M	3728M	1526M	13608M	61937M	262147M

Current Data Sorted by Assets   Comparative Historical Data

		3 (4/1-9/30/09)		51 (10/1/09-3/31/10)			Type of Statement	4/1/05-3/31/06	4/1/06-3/31/07
							Unqualified		1
		1	1				Reviewed	1	1
2	2	1	1				Compiled	5	4
11	7	5					Tax Returns	10	11
6	9	4	3				Other	8	6
0-500M	**500M-2MM**	**2-10MM**	**10-50MM**	**50-100MM**	**100-250MM**		**NUMBER OF STATEMENTS**	**ALL**	**ALL**
19	18	12	5					24	23
%	%	%	%	%	%		**ASSETS**	%	%
15.9	5.0	7.0		D	D		Cash & Equivalents	20.8	15.7
5.0	.6	1.8		A	A		Trade Receivables (net)	5.6	6.7
23.4	1.7	5.1		T	T		Inventory	13.8	17.9
4.5	.3	2.5		A	A		All Other Current	3.1	1.4
48.8	7.6	16.4					Total Current	43.3	41.7
44.3	71.7	64.9		N	N		Fixed Assets (net)	37.3	42.5
4.4	14.9	16.2		O	O		Intangibles (net)	14.5	8.8
2.4	5.8	2.5		T	T		All Other Non-Current	4.9	7.1
100.0	100.0	100.0					Total	100.0	100.0
				A	A		**LIABILITIES**		
6.4	4.5	1.8		V	V		Notes Payable-Short Term	2.6	10.4
3.9	3.6	4.2		A	A		Cur. Mat.-L.T.D.	2.1	3.1
21.6	3.5	6.5		I	I		Trade Payables	10.2	18.5
.0	.0	.0		L	L		Income Taxes Payable	.0	.0
25.9	3.9	3.9		A	A		All Other Current	16.2	13.4
57.7	15.5	16.5		B	B		Total Current	31.1	45.5
48.8	74.6	41.8		L	L		Long-Term Debt	27.4	32.4
.0	.0	.2		E	E		Deferred Taxes	.0	.4
53.9	.8	6.3					All Other Non-Current	6.1	7.1
-60.4	9.1	35.2					Net Worth	35.4	14.7
100.0	100.0	100.0					Total Liabilties & Net Worth	100.0	100.0
							INCOME DATA		
100.0	100.0	100.0					Net Sales	100.0	100.0
							Gross Profit		
92.6	89.8	87.4					Operating Expenses	90.3	92.2
7.4	10.2	12.6					Operating Profit	9.7	7.8
1.5	8.1	4.6					All Other Expenses (net)	1.9	2.2
5.9	2.1	8.1					Profit Before Taxes	7.7	5.6
							RATIOS		
2.0	1.4	1.8						4.2	3.2
1.1	.4	.9					Current	1.5	.9
.4	.2	.4						.6	.4
1.3	1.3	.8						2.6	2.7
.5	.3	.7					Quick	.8	.4
.1	.1	.3						.3	.2
0 UND	0 UND	0 UND						1 392.8	1 426.5
0 UND	0 UND	2 239.0					Sales/Receivables	3 112.8	4 100.9
4 87.0	2 185.8	5 69.0						6 56.5	8 45.2
							Cost of Sales/Inventory		
							Cost of Sales/Payables		
27.3	83.4	22.1						9.0	12.9
57.2	-15.5	NM					Sales/Working Capital	46.9	-65.0
-19.3	-3.6	-7.6						-24.6	-10.9
11.0	4.5							28.7	10.8
(13) 1.7	(16) 2.2						EBIT/Interest	(16) 3.5	(14) 2.0
1.1	1.3							-.1	-1.1
							Net Profit + Depr., Dep., Amort./Cur. Mat. L/T/D		
.6	2.9	1.0						.4	.2
-22.4	-33.4	13.0					Fixed/Worth	1.2	1.8
-.9	-2.4	-6.6						-3.6	-4.9
1.6	2.8	.7						.4	.6
-4.7	-37.2	12.7					Debt/Worth	1.8	10.5
-1.9	-3.6	-9.3						-2.8	-4.4
							% Profit Before Taxes/Tangible Net Worth	64.4	69.4
								(16) 37.1	(13) 27.4
								20.5	13.8
18.5	12.6	12.7					% Profit Before Taxes/Total Assets	26.9	34.7
6.3	5.6	7.8						12.8	7.8
.7	-2.9	-3.6						1.2	-.6
582.0	2.7	6.9					Sales/Net Fixed Assets	25.4	33.2
7.4	.9	1.4						11.2	14.9
2.8	.4	.3						4.4	1.6
7.3	1.7	2.8					Sales/Total Assets	5.2	10.0
4.0	.8	1.1						3.1	2.5
1.9	.3	.2						1.6	1.0
2.0	4.6	2.6					% Depr., Dep., Amort./Sales	1.2	1.0
(13) 2.6	(13) 8.2	(11) 3.2						(20) 1.8	(20) 1.8
3.6	20.7	13.9						3.1	6.0
							% Officers', Directors' Owners' Comp/Sales		1.8
									(11) 2.3
									5.1
15709M	23276M	83567M	90883M				Net Sales ($)	501292M	182316M
3991M	22641M	50218M	88475M				Total Assets ($)	255639M	144182M

M = $ thousand   MM = $ million
See Pages 9 through 22 for Explanation of Ratios and Data

Comparative Historical Data / Current Data Sorted by Sales

			Type of Statement						
1	1	2	Unqualified					1	1
4	3	1	Reviewed					1	
6	2	6	Compiled	2	1	2		1	
10	19	23	Tax Returns	12	7	2	1	1	
8	12	22	Other	13	4	2	1	2	
4/1/07-3/31/08 ALL	4/1/08-3/31/09 ALL	4/1/09-3/31/10 ALL		0-1MM	1-3MM 3 (4/1-9/30/09)	3-5MM	5-10MM	10-25MM 51 (10/1/09-3/31/10)	25MM & OVER
29	37	54	NUMBER OF STATEMENTS	27	12	6	2	6	1
%	%	%	**ASSETS**	%	%	%	%	%	%
18.1	11.6	8.9	Cash & Equivalents	9.2	12.1				
2.7	1.5	3.1	Trade Receivables (net)	1.3	5.9				
9.0	9.3	10.7	Inventory	12.3	11.2				
3.0	3.6	2.5	All Other Current	1.5	4.2				
32.8	25.9	25.3	Total Current	24.3	33.4				
50.9	55.2	58.8	Fixed Assets (net)	62.8	52.8				
8.6	12.8	12.0	Intangibles (net)	10.1	12.0				
7.7	6.1	3.9	All Other Non-Current	2.8	1.8				
100.0	100.0	100.0	Total	100.0	100.0				
			LIABILITIES						
1.2	2.2	4.6	Notes Payable-Short Term	4.6	5.5				
3.7	6.4	4.0	Cur. Mat.-L.T.D.	2.2	5.7				
8.0	8.6	11.0	Trade Payables	12.0	10.2				
.0	.0	.0	Income Taxes Payable	.0	.0				
7.1	21.9	11.7	All Other Current	15.6	11.3				
20.0	39.1	31.3	Total Current	34.5	32.8				
39.0	50.7	56.3	Long-Term Debt	64.8	48.3				
.0	.2	.1	Deferred Taxes	.0	.0				
30.3	17.4	23.6	All Other Non-Current	36.0	7.4				
10.7	-7.3	-11.4	Net Worth	-35.3	11.4				
100.0	100.0	100.0	Total Liabilities & Net Worth	100.0	100.0				
			INCOME DATA						
100.0	100.0	100.0	Net Sales	100.0	100.0				
			Gross Profit						
90.0	84.5	91.4	Operating Expenses	88.1	91.2				
10.0	15.5	8.6	Operating Profit	11.9	8.8				
4.4	7.2	4.5	All Other Expenses (net)	7.5	2.0				
5.7	8.2	4.1	Profit Before Taxes	4.3	6.8				
			RATIOS						
4.4	1.5	1.6	Current	1.8	1.8				
1.6	.9	.8		.7	1.3				
.8	.3	.3		.3	.4				
3.3	1.0	.9	Quick	.9	1.3				
1.1	(36) .3	.4		.3	.6				
.3	.2	.2		.1	.3				
0 UND	0 UND	0 UND	Sales/Receivables	0 UND	0 UND				
1 323.6	2 180.9	0 759.3		0 UND	1 646.8				
3 116.0	4 98.8	4 85.9		2 165.7	4 91.9				
			Cost of Sales/Inventory						
			Cost of Sales/Payables						
8.1	26.8	43.2	Sales/Working Capital	54.5	18.8				
28.0	-116.5	-44.4		-26.6	67.4				
-56.9	-7.4	-8.1		-3.6	-17.7				
11.6	4.9	5.3	EBIT/Interest	5.5	5.7				
(25) 2.4	(25) 2.0	(42) 2.3		(18) 1.5	(10) 2.6				
1.4	.0	1.3		.5	1.5				
			Net Profit + Depr., Dep., Amort./Cur. Mat. L/T/D						
.7	1.1	1.2	Fixed/Worth	1.3	1.2				
2.0	8.8	102.8		-10.3	NM				
-3.1	-1.0	-1.9		-.9	-2.0				
1.2	2.6	2.6	Debt/Worth	2.2	2.6				
5.4	11.9	-45.1		-7.6	-34.7				
-4.9	-2.6	-3.6		-2.8	-4.3				
67.4	68.7	56.8	% Profit Before Taxes/Tangible Net Worth	27.3					
(18) 34.0	(21) 26.2	(26) 25.5		(11) 6.0					
12.7	3.6	3.8		-11.5					
24.4	8.8	12.9	% Profit Before Taxes/Total Assets	12.4	15.4				
6.9	4.4	6.4		1.7	8.6				
-2.8	-3.2	-1.0		-7.5	3.9				
15.4	12.7	9.1	Sales/Net Fixed Assets	7.4	62.2				
5.5	5.7	2.5		.9	6.1				
1.4	.7	.8		.4	1.8				
4.4	3.6	3.7	Sales/Total Assets	3.2	5.0				
2.3	1.7	1.5		.8	2.8				
1.0	.6	.6		.3	1.4				
1.5	2.3	2.5	% Depr., Dep., Amort./Sales	2.5					
(27) 2.6	(30) 3.8	(42) 3.8		(20) 12.9					
6.4	12.9	13.4		19.8					
1.9	2.6	1.9	% Officers', Directors' Owners' Comp/Sales						
(10) 4.1	(12) 3.6	(18) 4.1							
7.9	8.5	8.4							
711304M	242826M	213435M	Net Sales ($)	15247M	19300M	23867M	14386M	115210M	25425M
578172M	186853M	165325M	Total Assets ($)	30245M	8337M	34949M	8020M	72049M	11725M

© RMA 2010

M = $ thousand   MM = $ million

See Pages 9 through 22 for Explanation of Ratios and Data

Current Data Sorted by Assets							Comparative Historical Data	
						Type of Statement		
		2	2		1	Unqualified	5	13
	3	7	6			Reviewed	8	12
24	21	11	3			Compiled	67	102
72	64	31	3			Tax Returns	115	135
24	38	41	7			Other	119	81
	38 (4/1-9/30/09)		322 (10/1/09-3/31/10)				4/1/05-3/31/06 ALL	4/1/06-3/31/07 ALL
0-500M	500M-2MM	2-10MM	10-50MM	50-100MM	100-250MM			
120	126	92	21		1	NUMBER OF STATEMENTS	314	343
%	%	%	%	%	%	**ASSETS**	%	%
18.9	6.6	6.3	8.6	DATA NOT AVAILABLE		Cash & Equivalents	9.8	9.5
1.3	1.9	1.8	2.6			Trade Receivables (net)	2.3	3.1
6.3	3.3	1.7	1.8			Inventory	3.7	3.5
4.8	2.4	1.1	2.1			All Other Current	1.7	1.3
31.3	14.2	10.9	15.1			Total Current	17.5	17.3
47.7	67.2	75.4	74.4			Fixed Assets (net)	66.4	67.4
10.7	10.4	7.9	7.0			Intangibles (net)	8.3	8.3
10.3	8.2	5.9	3.4			All Other Non-Current	7.8	6.9
100.0	100.0	100.0	100.0			Total	100.0	100.0
						LIABILITIES		
8.9	3.4	2.1	4.0			Notes Payable-Short Term	3.0	4.7
7.7	4.6	3.8	4.0			Cur. Mat.-L.T.D.	4.2	6.4
7.3	2.3	2.1	3.4			Trade Payables	5.8	5.0
.2	.0	.1	.0			Income Taxes Payable	.2	.2
31.6	9.2	7.5	3.5			All Other Current	11.1	9.5
55.6	19.6	15.6	14.9			Total Current	24.3	25.7
43.6	68.5	67.6	58.5			Long-Term Debt	69.5	60.8
.2	.0	.1	.3			Deferred Taxes	.0	.0
26.4	7.4	4.2	2.5			All Other Non-Current	11.3	11.1
-25.8	4.5	12.5	23.9			Net Worth	-5.1	2.3
100.0	100.0	100.0	100.0			Total Liabilities & Net Worth	100.0	100.0
						INCOME DATA		
100.0	100.0	100.0	100.0			Net Sales	100.0	100.0
						Gross Profit		
96.5	88.1	82.1	87.9			Operating Expenses	90.3	88.3
3.5	11.9	17.9	12.1			Operating Profit	9.7	11.7
3.4	11.8	14.1	8.5			All Other Expenses (net)	8.4	9.9
.2	.1	3.8	3.6			Profit Before Taxes	1.3	1.7
						RATIOS		
3.2	1.9	1.4	2.3				1.8	1.9
.9	.7	.6	.9			Current	.6	.6
.4	.2	.2	.2				.2	.2
1.3	1.3	1.0	2.0				1.2	1.3
.4	.4	.4	(20) .7			Quick	(311) .4	.4
.1	.1	.1	.2				.1	.1
0 UND	0 UND	0 UND	1 680.3				0 UND	0 UND
0 UND	0 UND	0 UND	2 204.8			Sales/Receivables	0 UND	0 UND
0 UND	1 269.7	2 204.4	6 57.8				3 145.2	2 164.0
						Cost of Sales/Inventory		
						Cost of Sales/Payables		
39.4	19.4	24.2	6.3				20.6	24.6
UND	-37.3	-18.9	-39.8			Sales/Working Capital	-26.3	-26.8
-8.2	-3.6	-5.2	-5.9				-5.9	-5.2
7.6	4.3	3.4	3.7				3.2	3.0
(71) 1.8	(81) 1.3	(65) 1.6	(20) 1.7			EBIT/Interest	(235) 1.4	(247) 1.4
-.1	.3	.7	.7				.3	.5
							3.5	7.9
						Net Profit + Depr., Dep., Amort./Cur. Mat. L/T/D	(19) 1.4	(15) 2.4
							.6	.9
.9	2.2	3.7	2.0				2.5	2.1
-6.6	-77.9	13.8	4.1			Fixed/Worth	102.1	35.1
-.5	-2.2	-8.6	-596.4				-1.6	-2.9
.9	2.6	3.7	1.7				2.8	2.2
-5.8	-26.0	16.1	4.1			Debt/Worth	168.0	79.0
-1.9	-3.5	-9.8	-607.4				-3.3	-4.2
63.1	36.5	37.8	37.6				84.1	60.0
(52) 17.8	(59) 14.5	(55) 9.5	(15) 18.9			% Profit Before Taxes/Tangible Net Worth	(161) 30.1	(180) 21.8
-1.8	.2	-4.0	.7				4.2	.0
23.6	9.1	5.9	9.6				8.3	8.6
2.3	1.1	1.7	3.6			% Profit Before Taxes/Total Assets	1.6	1.4
-13.8	-4.3	-1.7	-.7				-4.5	-4.3
31.6	3.6	1.2	1.9				5.3	6.9
9.0	.8	.6	.8			Sales/Net Fixed Assets	1.4	1.3
3.0	.4	.3	.4				.5	.4
6.8	1.1	.8	1.1				2.3	2.3
3.2	.6	.4	.6			Sales/Total Assets	.9	.9
1.6	.3	.3	.3				.4	.4
1.4	3.8	4.3	4.1				3.6	3.2
(93) 4.5	(107) 12.1	(78) 13.0	(20) 7.8			% Depr., Dep., Amort./Sales	(276) 8.4	(282) 8.6
12.5	26.2	25.2	15.5				17.9	19.5
2.5	4.2	2.7	1.2				2.5	3.1
(56) 6.3	(34) 5.8	(23) 3.9	(10) 1.9			% Officers', Directors' Owners' Comp/Sales	(101) 5.3	(112) 6.3
10.5	9.6	9.3	3.3				10.3	10.9
91615M	145728M	241786M	317382M		205331M	Net Sales ($)	1169169M	3844160M
25697M	137786M	314593M	384682M		170213M	Total Assets ($)	985594M	1910973M

M = $ thousand MM = $ million

See Pages 9 through 22 for Explanation of Ratios and Data

Comparative Historical Data   Current Data Sorted by Sales

Type of Statement	6 / 8 / 53 / 117 / 100	5 / 14 / 54 / 141 / 116	5 / 16 / 59 / 170 / 110	0-1MM	1-3MM	3-5MM	5-10MM	10-25MM	25MM & OVER
Unqualified	6	5	5	2	2		2	1	2
Reviewed	8	14	16	2	2	1	2	7	2
Compiled	53	54	59	41	14		3	1	
Tax Returns	117	141	170	108	55	5	2		
Other	100	116	110	54	36	6	10	3	1
Period	4/1/07-3/31/08 ALL	4/1/08-3/31/09 ALL	4/1/09-3/31/10 ALL	38 (4/1-9/30/09)		322 (10/1/09-3/31/10)			
NUMBER OF STATEMENTS	284	330	360	205	107	12	19	12	5
ASSETS	%	%	%	%	%	%	%	%	%
Cash & Equivalents	8.5	10.1	10.7	10.7	9.7	18.1	10.3	13.6	
Trade Receivables (net)	2.2	2.4	1.7	1.0	1.5	2.2	4.2	10.3	
Inventory	3.3	3.7	3.8	1.8	6.9	8.5	5.5	3.0	
All Other Current	2.8	2.9	2.9	2.6	3.2	1.9	1.2	6.2	
Total Current	16.8	19.0	19.1	16.1	21.2	30.6	21.3	33.0	
Fixed Assets (net)	67.5	63.2	63.3	67.7	57.5	55.0	60.5	53.6	
Intangibles (net)	9.1	8.5	9.6	8.7	12.4	11.0	9.6	1.1	
All Other Non-Current	6.6	9.2	8.0	7.5	8.9	3.3	8.6	12.3	
Total	100.0	100.0	100.0	100.0	100.0	100.0	100.0	100.0	
LIABILITIES									
Notes Payable-Short Term	6.0	6.1	4.9	5.4	4.9	.1	3.4	5.6	
Cur. Mat.-L.T.D.	4.0	4.6	5.4	6.6	4.0	2.7	4.6	2.9	
Trade Payables	5.5	4.3	4.0	2.5	6.1	2.9	5.3	6.7	
Income Taxes Payable	.2	.2	.1	.1	.0	.1	.2	.3	
All Other Current	10.9	15.8	15.9	17.3	13.3	26.9	11.2	12.8	
Total Current	26.7	30.9	30.3	31.9	28.3	32.8	24.7	28.2	
Long-Term Debt	63.5	57.2	59.2	64.0	55.9	56.7	51.5	31.7	
Deferred Taxes	.0	.0	.1	.0	.0	.0	.6	.0	
All Other Non-Current	11.1	10.7	12.7	15.6	10.1	6.9	3.4	9.1	
Net Worth	-1.3	1.2	-2.3	-11.6	5.7	3.7	19.9	30.9	
Total Liabilities & Net Worth	100.0	100.0	100.0	100.0	100.0	100.0	100.0	100.0	
INCOME DATA									
Net Sales	100.0	100.0	100.0	100.0	100.0	100.0	100.0	100.0	
Gross Profit									
Operating Expenses	87.3	90.7	89.3	88.0	89.6	96.9	91.3	94.5	
Operating Profit	12.7	9.3	10.7	12.0	10.4	3.1	8.7	5.5	
All Other Expenses (net)	9.7	8.7	9.4	13.3	4.6	5.0	3.1	1.5	
Profit Before Taxes	3.0	.7	1.3	-1.3	5.8	-1.9	5.5	4.0	
RATIOS									
Current	2.2	2.2	2.0	2.0	2.0	2.3	1.4	6.1	
	.8	.7	.7	.5	.8	1.0	.9	1.4	
	.2	.2	.2	.2	.4	.3	.6	.3	
Quick	1.4	1.6	1.2	1.4	1.1	1.9	1.1	5.5	
	(282) .5	.4	(359) .4	.3 (106)	.4	.4	.6	.9	
	.1	.1	.1	.1	.1	.2	.2	.2	
Sales/Receivables	0 UND	0 UND	0 UND	0 UND	0 UND	0 UND	1 342.5	1 646.6	
	0 UND	0 UND	0 UND	0 UND	0 UND	2 169.9	2 234.4	2 226.2	
	2 212.1	2 182.1	1 271.2	0 UND	2 217.1	3 131.6	6 60.6	7 54.3	
Cost of Sales/Inventory									
Cost of Sales/Payables									
Sales/Working Capital	20.7	19.6	25.5	34.0	40.0	11.2	21.9	7.9	
	-31.9	-48.8	-41.9	-12.2	-124.8	NM	-73.8	50.3	
	-4.8	-5.4	-5.1	-3.1	-11.7	-14.1	-11.5	-9.7	
EBIT/Interest	4.2	3.5	4.7	2.9	6.7	4.0	4.9	14.9	
	(202) 1.6	(219) 1.7	(238) 1.6	(108) 1.2	(84) 2.1	(11) 2.4	(18) 1.8	3.5	
	.9	.5	.6	-.1	.8	-1.3	1.1	1.6	
Net Profit + Depr., Dep., Amort./Cur. Mat. L/T/D	4.2	3.9	2.9						
	(14) 1.3	(22) 1.7	(21) 2.5						
	.5	1.0	1.7						
Fixed/Worth	2.2	1.8	2.0	2.2	2.1	3.9	2.0	.3	
	23.9	11.8	28.5	-104.8	11.9	-596.4	5.9	2.5	
	-2.3	-2.3	-1.9	-1.7	-1.4	-1.5	-3.7	8.9	
Debt/Worth	2.2	1.7	2.3	2.5	2.4	11.7	2.2	.8	
	40.7	23.3	120.3	-25.4	24.6	-607.4	6.8	3.9	
	-3.7	-3.7	-3.1	-2.7	-3.1	-4.7	-10.9	10.0	
% Profit Before Taxes/Tangible Net Worth	62.7	44.0	38.4	34.1	68.0		30.1	38.8	
	(154) 24.7	(179) 15.6	(182) 16.1	(95) 8.0	(55) 22.9		(12) 12.5	(11) 37.5	
	1.0	-1.5	-2.1	-12.4	6.1		-1.6	3.6	
% Profit Before Taxes/Total Assets	11.1	8.4	9.6	5.5	26.1	11.5	9.7	14.1	
	2.1	1.6	1.8	.3	5.0	1.2	3.0	7.4	
	-3.4	-5.1	-4.0	-6.7	-.9	-10.7	.1	2.9	
Sales/Net Fixed Assets	5.1	9.4	8.2	5.2	20.5	16.9	6.8	26.1	
	1.2	1.5	1.3	.7	2.0	3.9	3.0	4.1	
	.4	.5	.5	.3	.8	.7	.6	1.3	
Sales/Total Assets	2.2	2.8	2.6	1.8	4.8	4.1	2.6	4.2	
	.7	.9	.8	.5	1.2	1.3	1.8	2.3	
	.4	.4	.4	.3	.6	.5	.5	1.1	
% Depr., Dep., Amort./Sales	3.8	3.0	2.9	5.9	1.6	1.1	2.3	.7	
	(225) 9.7	(262) 8.4	(298) 8.0	(167) 14.2	(86) 4.5	4.7	(18) 4.5	(11) 2.5	
	20.9	18.9	22.3	28.6	11.9	10.6	11.5	4.2	
% Officers', Directors' Owners' Comp/Sales	2.8	2.4	2.7	3.2	3.0		1.2		
	(89) 6.2	(116) 5.1	(124) 5.3	(59) 8.1	(45) 5.7		(10) 2.6		
	11.7	9.2	9.2	11.6	9.1		4.1		
Net Sales ($)	1793632M	4436632M	1001842M	95174M	181829M	46205M	135342M	165452M	377840M
Total Assets ($)	1327240M	1585779M	1032971M	211572M	213044M	53855M	192719M	95245M	266536M

© RMA 2010

M = $ thousand   MM = $ million
See Pages 9 through 22 for Explanation of Ratios and Data

Current Data Sorted by Assets | Comparative Historical Data

						Type of Statement		
1	1				1	Unqualified	8	9
	3	2	2			Reviewed	8	7
4	6	5	1			Compiled	34	28
33	29	4	2			Tax Returns	52	51
19	18	10	5			Other	42	40
	17 (4/1-9/30/09)		129 (10/1/09-3/31/10)				4/1/05-3/31/06	4/1/06-3/31/07
0-500M	500M-2MM	2-10MM	10-50MM	50-100MM	100-250MM	NUMBER OF STATEMENTS	ALL	ALL
57	57	21	10		1		144	135
%	%	%	%	%	%	ASSETS	%	%
19.5	13.9	11.6	2.9			Cash & Equivalents	13.6	13.0
13.5	22.4	10.3	9.8			Trade Receivables (net)	13.8	14.1
16.3	16.7	15.3	17.2			Inventory	17.8	21.3
1.7	2.7	1.3	1.2			All Other Current	2.6	1.9
51.0	55.7	38.5	31.1			Total Current	47.8	50.3
34.9	28.5	43.8	40.4			Fixed Assets (net)	38.4	34.5
7.2	8.1	8.4	25.0			Intangibles (net)	5.1	7.1
7.0	7.8	9.3	3.5			All Other Non-Current	8.6	8.2
100.0	100.0	100.0	100.0			Total	100.0	100.0
						LIABILITIES		
9.9	4.8	6.2	6.0			Notes Payable-Short Term	12.4	9.2
3.7	4.2	1.8	4.0			Cur. Mat.-L.T.D.	3.1	3.6
22.5	22.1	10.0	17.1			Trade Payables	11.1	13.4
.0	.0	.0	.2			Income Taxes Payable	.2	.9
38.5	10.5	18.6	6.4			All Other Current	11.1	11.3
74.6	41.5	36.6	33.7			Total Current	37.9	38.3
35.0	27.1	30.5	50.2			Long-Term Debt	31.0	28.6
.0	.0	.0	.1			Deferred Taxes	.1	.1
9.7	7.4	8.6	6.6			All Other Non-Current	9.3	16.0
-19.3	23.9	24.3	9.5			Net Worth	21.7	16.9
100.0	100.0	100.0	100.0			Total Liabilities & Net Worth	100.0	100.0
						INCOME DATA		
100.0	100.0	100.0	100.0			Net Sales	100.0	100.0
						Gross Profit		
98.5	93.8	88.6	90.8			Operating Expenses	92.0	93.6
1.5	6.2	11.4	9.2			Operating Profit	8.0	6.4
.4	2.2	5.5	2.6			All Other Expenses (net)	2.9	2.1
1.0	4.0	5.9	6.6			Profit Before Taxes	5.2	4.3
						RATIOS		
2.1	3.3	2.4	1.3				2.2	2.5
1.1	1.4	1.0	.9			Current	1.4	1.4
.5	.7	.5	.5				.8	.9
1.4	1.8	1.3	.9				1.6	1.7
.6	.9	.6	.4			Quick	.7 (134)	.7
.2	.3	.2	.2				.3	.3
0 UND	1 256.3	1 581.7	3 137.5				1 528.4	0 UND
4 89.0	12 31.2	6 63.4	12 31.5			Sales/Receivables	9 42.0	10 35.0
14 25.7	34 10.8	40 9.1	24 15.2				28 12.9	30 12.2
						Cost of Sales/Inventory		
						Cost of Sales/Payables		
22.6	8.1	7.0	29.9				10.6	9.4
94.4	18.8	-810.5	NM			Sales/Working Capital	26.4	26.0
-16.4	-18.7	-8.5	-12.3				-44.5	-73.5
10.7	12.0	6.6	6.1				13.5	7.0
(42) 2.5	(40) 2.8	(15) 2.4	3.8			EBIT/Interest	(118) 3.4	(110) 2.5
-1.4	1.4	.7	.8				1.0	1.1
							3.6	4.8
						Net Profit + Depr., Dep., Amort./Cur. Mat. L/T/D	(14) 2.9	(11) 2.9
							1.3	1.0
.4	.1	.4	3.8				.4	.3
2.7	1.0	2.6	NM			Fixed/Worth	1.9	1.3
-.9	-1.8	140.6	-.4				-7.7	-4.0
.8	.7	.9	5.0				1.0	.7
7.3	3.0	2.3	NM			Debt/Worth	4.1	4.3
-3.5	-7.6	302.7	-2.2				-12.8	-5.1
156.8	78.4	56.1					76.9	62.8
(32) 31.8	(36) 29.0	(17) 14.3				% Profit Before Taxes/Tangible Net Worth	(100) 32.9	(89) 27.5
.0	9.7	5.0					4.0	5.1
29.2	16.6	8.4	16.8				22.8	20.1
6.4	5.3	2.1	10.7			% Profit Before Taxes/Total Assets	7.9	6.7
-4.8	-.3	-1.1	-.7				-.1	.4
137.6	93.0	62.4	36.3				35.0	55.8
22.3	26.8	5.5	10.9			Sales/Net Fixed Assets	12.7	13.1
6.0	5.8	.7	1.3				4.0	5.3
9.6	5.3	2.9	3.8				4.7	5.1
4.9	2.7	1.6	2.2			Sales/Total Assets	2.9	3.0
2.7	1.0	.4	1.0				1.4	1.9
.5	.6	.6	.7				1.2	1.0
(37) 1.5	(40) 1.8	(17) 2.3	2.2			% Depr., Dep., Amort./Sales	(113) 2.0	(97) 2.3
-3.3	3.6	9.9	5.5				4.2	4.2
2.9	1.7						2.7	2.9
(27) 6.0	(35) 3.2					% Officers', Directors' Owners' Comp/Sales	(68) 5.0	(68) 6.1
11.2	7.5						9.5	10.1
65923M	214168M	153964M	418033M		168500M	Net Sales ($)	3410685M	3202564M
11631M	62960M	97793M	184291M		168300M	Total Assets ($)	1193943M	991436M

(Columns 50-100MM and 100-250MM: DATA NOT AVAILABLE for most rows.)

M = $ thousand　　MM = $ million
See Pages 9 through 22 for Explanation of Ratios and Data

Comparative Historical Data | Current Data Sorted by Sales

Hist 1	Hist 2	Hist 3	Type of Statement	0-1MM	1-3MM	3-5MM	5-10MM	10-25MM	25MM & OVER
5	3	3	Unqualified	1		1			1
6	9	7	Reviewed			2			2
18	25	16	Compiled	4	3	4	3	1	1
34	63	68	Tax Returns	24	32	8	2	1	1
34	47	52	Other	13	16	4	8	7	4
4/1/07-3/31/08 ALL	4/1/08-3/31/09 ALL	4/1/09-3/31/10 ALL		17 (4/1-9/30/09)		129 (10/1/09-3/31/10)			
97	147	146	NUMBER OF STATEMENTS	42	51	19	14	11	9
%	%	%	**ASSETS**	%	%	%	%	%	%
13.9	12.0	15.2	Cash & Equivalents	13.6	13.6	26.0	19.2	11.2	
16.2	11.0	16.3	Trade Receivables (net)	15.1	13.1	27.2	18.2	19.1	
18.6	15.8	16.3	Inventory	11.7	17.1	21.5	16.7	16.8	
2.4	1.9	2.0	All Other Current	.4	2.9	.4	1.4	7.9	
51.1	40.7	49.9	Total Current	40.7	46.7	75.1	55.5	55.0	
35.5	43.7	33.8	Fixed Assets (net)	42.6	37.4	16.7	26.4	27.4	
5.9	8.8	9.0	Intangibles (net)	8.2	9.0	1.9	10.3	8.6	
7.5	6.9	7.4	All Other Non-Current	8.5	6.9	6.3	7.8	9.0	
100.0	100.0	100.0	Total	100.0	100.0	100.0	100.0	100.0	
			LIABILITIES						
8.0	9.5	7.0	Notes Payable-Short Term	9.3	5.2	8.2	5.6	6.9	
5.1	6.4	3.6	Cur. Mat.-L.T.D.	3.3	5.7	1.5	1.1	2.9	
14.2	9.6	20.1	Trade Payables	16.1	25.9	20.0	16.9	12.1	
.7	.2	.0	Income Taxes Payable	.0	.0	.0	.0	.2	
10.7	7.0	22.3	All Other Current	42.8	9.5	18.0	24.1	17.5	
38.8	32.8	53.1	Total Current	71.6	46.3	47.8	47.7	39.6	
24.0	37.1	32.1	Long-Term Debt	49.7	33.9	8.2	12.7	17.9	
.1	.1	.0	Deferred Taxes	.0	.0	.0	.0	.1	
11.3	10.4	8.4	All Other Non-Current	5.8	12.3	5.5	4.6	1.6	
25.7	19.5	6.5	Net Worth	-27.2	7.4	38.5	35.0	40.9	
100.0	100.0	100.0	Total Liabilities & Net Worth	100.0	100.0	100.0	100.0	100.0	
			INCOME DATA						
100.0	100.0	100.0	Net Sales	100.0	100.0	100.0	100.0	100.0	
			Gross Profit						
95.5	91.1	94.7	Operating Expenses	96.5	92.7	94.5	94.9	96.0	
4.5	8.9	5.3	Operating Profit	3.5	7.3	5.5	5.1	4.0	
1.1	4.2	2.0	All Other Expenses (net)	3.3	2.8	.4	.3	-.9	
3.4	4.7	3.3	Profit Before Taxes	.2	4.5	5.2	4.8	4.9	
			RATIOS						
2.6	2.0	2.3		2.0	2.0	5.0	3.3	2.2	
1.4	1.1	1.1	Current	.9	1.1	2.4	1.2	1.2	
.9	.6	.6		.4	.6	1.1	1.0	.8	
1.6	1.4	1.6		1.3	1.2	4.0	1.4	1.3	
.7	.6	.6	Quick	.4	.6	1.7	.9	.6	
.4	.2	.2		.1	.2	.9	.5	.2	
2 147.2	0 UND	1 628.0		0 UND	0 UND	10 36.9	2 185.3	1 282.0	
14 26.5	6 57.8	7 52.2	Sales/Receivables	5 78.8	5 73.4	28 12.8	9 41.0	13 28.8	
23 15.6	22 16.5	25 14.6		17 21.4	17 21.8	41 8.9	35 10.4	27 13.6	
			Cost of Sales/Inventory						
			Cost of Sales/Payables						
9.9	12.0	10.6		16.1	10.3	6.4	12.9	10.8	
31.5	88.6	64.5	Sales/Working Capital	-19.2	68.4	12.8	42.4	103.9	
-116.0	-18.6	-15.3		-8.0	-17.7	60.6	-624.6	-61.1	
10.5	6.4	10.5		4.0	10.8	31.1		11.6	
(81) 3.6	(118) 2.5	(107) 2.8	EBIT/Interest	(30) 1.3	(36) 2.4	(13) 4.2		6.1	
.8	.9	.9		-.8	1.1	1.9		2.5	
		5.5	Net Profit + Depr., Dep., Amort./Cur. Mat. L/T/D						
	(16) 1.8								
		1.0							
.4	.6	.3		.9	.4	.0	.2	.1	
1.2	2.8	2.1	Fixed/Worth	NM	2.8	.2	.6	1.2	
43.6	-2.6	-1.3		-.4	-1.2	.7	3.4	4.2	
.8	1.1	.9		1.9	.9	.2	.4	.7	
2.2	4.1	4.5	Debt/Worth	-96.9	8.7	.9	1.3	2.3	
74.2	-5.0	-4.9		-4.3	-3.9	8.3	4.3	4.1	
74.6	93.3	85.5		82.0	135.6	96.1	91.9		
(76) 32.1	(99) 35.2	(91) 23.7	% Profit Before Taxes/Tangible Net Worth	(20) 25.6	(30) 23.5	(16) 32.4	(12) 41.8		
9.1	10.1	8.1		.8	5.3	12.7	11.3		
21.8	19.3	19.6		9.7	24.2	47.6	41.1	25.0	
8.0	5.6	5.3	% Profit Before Taxes/Total Assets	.9	5.3	11.2	13.1	10.5	
1.1	-.1	-.5		-4.6	-.1	4.1	-1.8	1.9	
43.6	29.1	91.6		104.6	59.8	171.4	206.9	111.0	
12.0	8.0	21.0	Sales/Net Fixed Assets	6.9	17.4	49.0	33.2	32.5	
5.3	2.2	4.8		1.7	4.4	20.6	6.1	11.9	
5.8	4.4	5.5		4.3	5.4	6.3	6.2	11.5	
3.2	2.5	3.1	Sales/Total Assets	2.0	3.1	3.6	3.6	4.0	
2.0	1.3	1.3		.9	1.1	3.3	2.2	1.6	
.8	1.0	.6		1.3	.8	.3	.4		
(76) 2.0	(116) 2.1	(105) 1.9	% Depr., Dep., Amort./Sales	(27) 2.5	(37) 2.2	(13) .7	(10) 1.7		
3.8	6.4	3.9		9.2	5.2	1.2	2.7		
2.9	2.4	2.2		2.2	2.9	1.8			
(46) 6.7	(67) 4.5	(67) 4.5	% Officers', Directors' Owners' Comp/Sales	(19) 5.8	(25) 4.9	(12) 3.3			
13.8	10.8	8.8		10.9	9.5	9.7			
1433640M	2918220M	1020588M	Net Sales ($)	21406M	83919M	75169M	102807M	166406M	570881M
630974M	929883M	524975M	Total Assets ($)	20430M	60727M	23623M	45989M	54159M	320047M

Current Data Sorted by Assets

Comparative Historical Data

Type of Statement

						Type of Statement		
	1	2	3	1		Unqualified	6	3
	1	1	2			Reviewed	7	5
1	3	1				Compiled	5	3
5	7	3				Tax Returns	4	8
3	3	8	4	2		Other	18	12
0-500M	3 (4/1-9/30/09) 500M-2MM	2-10MM	48 (10/1/09-3/31/10) 10-50MM	50-100MM	100-250MM		4/1/05-3/31/06 ALL	4/1/06-3/31/07 ALL
9	15	15	9	3		NUMBER OF STATEMENTS	40	31

0-500M	500M-2MM	2-10MM	10-50MM	50-100MM	100-250MM		ALL	ALL
%	%	%	%	%	%	**ASSETS**	%	%
	16.5	6.9				Cash & Equivalents	14.4	20.7
	30.4	38.9				Trade Receivables (net)	38.0	33.8
	13.9	22.3				Inventory	11.8	9.1
	3.4	7.8				All Other Current	2.1	3.9
	64.2	75.9				Total Current	66.3	67.5
	24.4	7.9				Fixed Assets (net)	18.2	15.7
	8.1	14.5				Intangibles (net)	5.2	12.1
	3.3	1.7				All Other Non-Current	10.3	4.7
	100.0	100.0				Total	100.0	100.0
						LIABILITIES		
	12.9	13.1				Notes Payable-Short Term	14.8	10.1
	4.0	1.9				Cur. Mat.-L.T.D.	2.7	6.6
	15.4	23.7				Trade Payables	16.2	15.0
	.0	.7				Income Taxes Payable	.9	.1
	9.3	15.9				All Other Current	11.7	22.6
	41.7	55.3				Total Current	46.4	54.4
	27.3	16.9				Long-Term Debt	9.2	12.3
	.0	.0				Deferred Taxes	.1	.0
	12.2	10.7				All Other Non-Current	10.9	7.4
	18.9	17.1				Net Worth	33.5	25.9
	100.0	100.0				Total Liabilities & Net Worth	100.0	100.0
						INCOME DATA		
	100.0	100.0				Net Sales	100.0	100.0
						Gross Profit		
	96.4	96.6				Operating Expenses	92.2	93.1
	3.6	3.4				Operating Profit	7.8	6.9
	.1	.8				All Other Expenses (net)	.9	1.0
	3.5	2.6				Profit Before Taxes	6.9	5.9
						RATIOS		
	2.2	2.0					2.8	2.3
	1.4	1.6				Current	1.5	1.3
	1.2	1.0					1.0	1.1
	1.5	1.6					2.1	2.1
	1.0	.7				Quick	1.2	1.1
	.9	.5					.7	.7
	7 49.9	32 11.4					27 13.4	16 22.2
	32 11.5	48 7.5				Sales/Receivables	42 8.8	44 8.3
	39 9.4	58 6.3					69 5.3	52 7.1
						Cost of Sales/Inventory		
						Cost of Sales/Payables		
	10.7	7.4					6.2	7.9
	28.1	14.5				Sales/Working Capital	13.0	22.8
	60.8	-201.4					363.4	80.8
	28.2	-19.1					29.6	40.0
	(14) 4.5	(14) 4.5				EBIT/Interest	(33) 4.6	(27) 6.1
	1.5	1.4					1.7	1.7
							18.4	
						Net Profit + Depr., Dep., Amort./Cur. Mat. L/T/D	(10) 11.1	
							1.2	
	.2	.2					.1	.2
	.5	3.3				Fixed/Worth	.3	.5
	-6.2	-.1					1.5	-10.9
	.9	1.2					.7	.9
	2.5	12.5				Debt/Worth	1.7	3.7
	-8.0	-4.0					7.4	-8.9
	83.6						83.3	117.7
	(10) 22.2					% Profit Before Taxes/Tangible Net Worth	(34) 37.7	(22) 54.3
	-3.2						11.2	7.6
	26.3	10.6					26.9	38.1
	4.6	5.6				% Profit Before Taxes/Total Assets	9.6	13.3
	-.5	3.0					2.9	1.2
	42.8	94.7					133.4	131.2
	24.0	40.4				Sales/Net Fixed Assets	41.6	45.6
	10.1	33.9					8.2	20.5
	4.8	4.8					4.3	5.9
	3.9	3.2				Sales/Total Assets	3.2	3.5
	2.7	2.0					1.8	1.9
	.4	.5					.6	.4
	(13) 1.5	(10) 1.0				% Depr., Dep., Amort./Sales	(26) 1.0	(22) .6
	2.4	1.3					1.5	1.6
	3.5						2.0	3.3
	(10) 6.5					% Officers', Directors' Owners' Comp/Sales	(13) 6.2	(12) 5.0
	11.2						15.8	10.1
15941M	65160M	247306M	373566M	430545M		Net Sales ($)	538238M	417258M
2077M	16379M	75386M	167671M	170828M		Total Assets ($)	293037M	210641M

In data columns 10-50MM, 50-100MM, and 100-250MM: **DATA NOT AVAILABLE**

M = $ thousand   MM = $ million
See Pages 9 through 22 for Explanation of Ratios and Data

Comparative Historical Data | Current Data Sorted by Sales

Comp Hist 1	Comp Hist 2	Comp Hist 3	Type of Statement	0-1MM	1-3MM	3-5MM	5-10MM	10-25MM	25MM & OVER
5	3	7	Unqualified					2	5
8	5	4	Reviewed		1			1	2
7	8	5	Compiled	1	4		1	3	
11	9	15	Tax Returns	3	1	4	3	3	
12	19	20	Other	2		3	5	2	5
4/1/07-3/31/08 ALL	4/1/08-3/31/09 ALL	4/1/09-3/31/10 ALL			3 (4/1-9/30/09)		48 (10/1/09-3/31/10)		
43	44	51	NUMBER OF STATEMENTS	6	6	7	9	11	12
%	%	%	**ASSETS**	%	%	%	%	%	%
12.3	11.7	10.7	Cash & Equivalents					9.1	9.0
39.2	33.8	32.1	Trade Receivables (net)					30.7	40.6
13.2	22.1	16.8	Inventory					16.7	21.4
4.9	3.2	4.2	All Other Current					10.0	4.0
69.6	70.7	63.8	Total Current					66.6	74.9
22.8	21.3	21.2	Fixed Assets (net)					20.1	13.0
2.8	3.8	10.8	Intangibles (net)					10.9	9.7
4.8	4.1	4.2	All Other Non-Current					2.4	2.4
100.0	100.0	100.0	Total					100.0	100.0
			LIABILITIES						
17.9	16.0	13.6	Notes Payable-Short Term					10.5	11.0
6.8	4.0	6.2	Cur. Mat.-L.T.D.					6.5	10.7
16.8	18.7	19.9	Trade Payables					17.9	13.8
.3	.3	.4	Income Taxes Payable					1.0	.0
15.8	17.4	18.4	All Other Current					18.7	34.2
57.6	56.4	58.4	Total Current					54.6	69.7
24.4	21.5	31.5	Long-Term Debt					20.5	14.1
.0	.1	.5	Deferred Taxes					.0	.6
9.2	9.4	7.8	All Other Non-Current					20.4	4.7
8.8	12.6	1.8	Net Worth					4.6	10.9
100.0	100.0	100.0	Total Liabilties & Net Worth					100.0	100.0
			INCOME DATA						
100.0	100.0	100.0	Net Sales					100.0	100.0
			Gross Profit						
95.5	95.8	95.5	Operating Expenses					96.5	93.5
4.5	4.2	4.5	Operating Profit					3.5	6.5
1.0	1.2	.8	All Other Expenses (net)					1.1	1.2
3.6	3.0	3.6	Profit Before Taxes					2.4	5.3
			RATIOS						
2.0	3.1	1.6	Current					1.6	1.7
1.3	1.3	1.2						1.3	1.3
1.0	.9	.9						.8	1.0
1.8	1.7	1.4	Quick					1.2	1.4
(42) 1.0	.9	.8						.6	.8
.6	.5	.5						.4	.6
24 15.0	24 15.0	23 15.6	Sales/Receivables					25 14.5	38 9.6
43 8.5	36 10.2	37 10.0						34 10.9	52 7.1
60 6.1	56 6.6	58 6.3						58 6.3	64 5.7
			Cost of Sales/Inventory						
			Cost of Sales/Payables						
9.7	8.0	10.9	Sales/Working Capital					10.4	10.5
17.7	23.3	38.3						38.3	20.7
UND	-55.9	-53.4						-53.4	NM
9.2	13.2	12.7	EBIT/Interest						44.6
(35) 2.3	(35) 2.1	(46) 3.2						(10)	4.4
.0	-.7	.9							1.1
12.3		3.2	Net Profit + Depr., Dep., Amort./Cur. Mat. L/T/D						
(10) 4.7		(10) 1.3							
1.1		.3							
.2	.3	.4	Fixed/Worth					.3	.2
.8	1.1	1.7						3.3	.7
UND	-15.3	-.6						-.2	NM
1.0	1.4	1.4	Debt/Worth					2.2	1.3
3.1	3.5	4.5						12.5	3.1
-15.2	-91.2	-2.9						-6.9	NM
62.8	91.3	79.3	% Profit Before Taxes/Tangible Net Worth						
(32) 33.8	(32) 19.9	(30) 38.6							
12.7	.6	7.5							
22.5	17.9	18.3	% Profit Before Taxes/Total Assets					9.3	18.3
6.9	4.2	5.6						5.7	11.6
-2.2	-1.8	-.5						-2.1	1.7
69.5	45.9	60.8	Sales/Net Fixed Assets					78.6	39.8
32.3	25.9	25.6						33.9	26.9
9.8	10.9	13.1						16.6	13.9
5.3	4.2	4.5	Sales/Total Assets					5.0	3.2
3.5	3.1	3.2						2.4	2.8
2.6	2.4	2.1						2.0	2.3
.4	.4	.9	% Depr., Dep., Amort./Sales						
(36) .7	(31) .8	(39) 1.5							
1.7	2.2	2.5							
3.0	3.0	2.3	% Officers', Directors' Owners' Comp/Sales						
(17) 7.0	(17) 4.9	(20) 4.9							
10.4	9.6	9.3							
751406M	790059M	1132518M	Net Sales ($)	3080M	9625M	27766M	66760M	178529M	846758M
219863M	266755M	432341M	Total Assets ($)	906M	3947M	8850M	19261M	79844M	319533M

M = $ thousand   MM = $ million
See Pages 9 through 22 for Explanation of Ratios and Data

Current Data Sorted by Assets

Comparative Historical Data

						Type of Statement		
		4	4	2	2	Unqualified	16	16
1	6	14	3			Reviewed	35	29
5	9	10	2			Compiled	51	26
5	12	4	1			Tax Returns	33	39
3	12	20	9	1		Other	74	49
	20 (4/1-9/30/09)		109 (10/1/09-3/31/10)				4/1/05-3/31/06	4/1/06-3/31/07
0-500M	500M-2MM	2-10MM	10-50MM	50-100MM	100-250MM		ALL	ALL
14	39	52	19	3	2	**NUMBER OF STATEMENTS**	209	159
%	%	%	%	%	%	**ASSETS**	%	%
30.9	10.4	12.1	8.9			Cash & Equivalents	11.5	9.9
25.1	34.7	29.6	35.1			Trade Receivables (net)	30.2	30.8
8.1	16.2	20.8	15.7			Inventory	19.4	21.0
5.9	4.5	4.1	6.4			All Other Current	2.8	3.6
70.0	65.9	66.5	65.9			Total Current	63.9	65.3
17.9	27.0	23.4	25.5			Fixed Assets (net)	26.5	25.3
5.2	.5	3.7	4.7			Intangibles (net)	4.8	3.8
7.0	6.7	6.4	3.9			All Other Non-Current	4.8	5.7
100.0	100.0	100.0	100.0			Total	100.0	100.0
						LIABILITIES		
14.3	12.0	11.2	12.9			Notes Payable-Short Term	12.2	13.3
.7	4.1	4.2	4.2			Cur. Mat.-L.T.D.	4.6	4.3
8.0	14.2	11.2	12.6			Trade Payables	16.5	14.0
.0	1.0	.1	1.0			Income Taxes Payable	.4	.5
14.9	12.5	13.9	17.1			All Other Current	10.6	13.4
37.9	43.9	40.7	47.8			Total Current	44.4	45.5
10.2	20.2	15.6	21.9			Long-Term Debt	21.3	24.4
.3	.2	.7	.6			Deferred Taxes	.3	.3
3.0	1.8	3.3	6.3			All Other Non-Current	5.4	5.8
48.6	34.0	39.7	23.4			Net Worth	28.6	24.0
100.0	100.0	100.0	100.0			Total Liabilties & Net Worth	100.0	100.0
						INCOME DATA		
100.0	100.0	100.0	100.0			Net Sales	100.0	100.0
						Gross Profit		
91.4	95.0	94.4	93.4			Operating Expenses	93.7	93.3
8.6	5.0	5.6	6.6			Operating Profit	6.3	6.7
.1	2.5	1.0	1.7			All Other Expenses (net)	1.3	1.4
8.4	2.5	4.6	4.8			Profit Before Taxes	5.0	5.2
						RATIOS		
7.1	2.9	3.2	1.9				2.4	3.0
1.7	1.4	1.5	1.5			Current	1.6	1.7
1.0	1.0	1.2	1.0				1.1	1.2
7.1	2.1	2.5	1.5				1.6	2.0
1.5	1.2	1.0	.9			Quick	1.0	1.0
.7	.4	.5	.7				.6	.6
0 UND	27 13.5	29 12.6	41 8.9				30 12.3	32 11.4
8 44.8	42 8.8	40 9.1	60 6.1			Sales/Receivables	44 8.3	46 7.9
41 9.0	54 6.8	56 6.6	72 5.0				59 6.2	60 6.1
						Cost of Sales/Inventory		
						Cost of Sales/Payables		
8.6	5.9	5.2	6.0				6.5	5.4
29.1	14.9	8.6	11.6			Sales/Working Capital	11.6	11.4
NM	-270.0	39.0	70.5				105.6	33.8
	7.9	16.4	8.1				10.2	9.3
	(34) 2.7	(46) 4.7	3.7			EBIT/Interest	(189) 3.9	(146) 3.3
	-.2	1.2	.6				1.6	1.6
		3.5					6.9	7.0
	(11) 2.3					Net Profit + Depr., Dep.,	(45) 2.6	(37) 2.6
	1.2					Amort./Cur. Mat. L/T/D	1.0	1.5
.1	.2	.2	.4				.3	.3
.4	.8	.6	.8			Fixed/Worth	.9	.8
2.3	4.2	1.1	1.7				5.7	4.4
.2	.6	.7	1.2				1.0	.9
1.0	2.4	2.0	2.1			Debt/Worth	2.4	2.3
12.7	5.9	4.3	4.6				23.8	15.9
129.9	49.8	35.9	68.1			% Profit Before Taxes/Tangible	61.6	59.6
(13) 28.6	(32) 20.2	(49) 23.1	(17) 13.9			Net Worth	(164) 29.0	(128) 34.1
12.1	.3	3.6	1.7				10.1	9.7
56.3	15.9	14.0	16.4			% Profit Before Taxes/Total	18.4	19.3
20.1	4.7	7.3	5.2			Assets	7.9	9.3
.5	-3.1	.9	-.6				2.1	2.2
UND	52.7	29.1	111.6				30.3	35.1
32.9	16.9	14.3	8.4			Sales/Net Fixed Assets	14.3	13.9
10.8	6.2	6.0	5.1				5.5	7.1
10.1	4.2	3.4	2.8				3.5	3.7
5.4	2.8	2.2	2.0			Sales/Total Assets	2.5	2.5
2.3	1.9	1.7	1.4				1.7	1.8
.1	.9	.6	1.3				1.1	1.0
(10) .9	(32) 2.0	(43) 1.8	(16) 3.1			% Depr., Dep., Amort./Sales	(169) 2.0	(131) 1.9
2.0	3.9	2.9	6.3				3.5	3.4
	5.0	1.9					2.1	3.2
	(22) 7.1	(19) 5.1				% Officers', Directors'	(86) 4.3	(73) 6.8
	10.2	7.2				Owners' Comp/Sales	9.1	10.4
23769M	142278M	619432M	795539M	372241M	314220M	Net Sales ($)	4288362M	2698177M
3609M	44781M	245468M	366646M	205415M	309833M	Total Assets ($)	1724868M	1563843M

© RMA 2010

M = $ thousand   MM = $ million
See Pages 9 through 22 for Explanation of Ratios and Data

Comparative Historical Data   Current Data Sorted by Sales

			Type of Statement						
13	9	12	Unqualified	2	4	2	1	3	8
24	18	24	Reviewed	4	9	4	4	8	4
20	10	26	Compiled	4	9	4	6	2	1
26	20	22	Tax Returns	3	7	7	3	2	
47	27	45	Other	1	5	7	7	16	9
4/1/07- 3/31/08 ALL	4/1/08- 3/31/09 ALL	4/1/09- 3/31/10 ALL		20 (4/1-9/30/09)		109 (10/1/09-3/31/10)			
				0-1MM	1-3MM	3-5MM	5-10MM	10-25MM	25MM & OVER
130	84	129	NUMBER OF STATEMENTS	10	25	20	21	31	22
%	%	%	ASSETS	%	%	%	%	%	%
12.8	11.0	13.0	Cash & Equivalents	20.8	12.4	17.2	15.2	10.4	7.8
32.5	39.4	31.2	Trade Receivables (net)	13.3	33.2	29.1	34.1	30.0	37.9
19.6	17.1	17.4	Inventory	5.8	14.0	18.7	15.8	24.4	16.9
3.2	2.7	4.7	All Other Current	7.5	4.5	2.3	5.9	3.4	6.4
68.1	70.2	66.2	Total Current	47.4	64.0	67.4	71.0	68.2	69.0
21.0	21.1	23.7	Fixed Assets (net)	43.7	23.8	23.5	19.7	24.6	17.4
5.3	3.4	4.0	Intangibles (net)	6.4	3.9	1.4	2.5	2.5	8.9
5.6	5.4	6.1	All Other Non-Current	2.7	8.2	7.8	6.8	4.8	4.7
100.0	100.0	100.0	Total	100.0	100.0	100.0	100.0	100.0	100.0
			LIABILITIES						
11.3	10.7	12.3	Notes Payable-Short Term	2.8	16.0	14.2	10.5	9.9	15.5
5.3	4.9	3.7	Cur. Mat.-L.T.D.	1.4	3.6	3.1	3.6	5.0	3.5
14.5	15.2	11.9	Trade Payables	2.8	7.8	17.3	13.9	12.6	13.0
.3	.2	.5	Income Taxes Payable	.0	1.6	.1	.0	.1	1.0
11.0	11.7	13.9	All Other Current	14.1	12.6	9.6	14.9	14.3	17.5
42.4	42.7	42.3	Total Current	21.1	41.7	44.2	42.9	41.9	50.6
16.6	16.1	17.3	Long-Term Debt	24.9	18.2	14.6	19.7	15.1	15.9
.2	.2	.5	Deferred Taxes	.5	.3	.4	.0	1.1	.7
3.8	3.0	3.4	All Other Non-Current	.6	1.5	4.3	2.8	2.2	8.5
37.0	38.0	36.5	Net Worth	52.9	38.2	36.4	34.6	39.7	24.3
100.0	100.0	100.0	Total Liabilities & Net Worth	100.0	100.0	100.0	100.0	100.0	100.0
			INCOME DATA						
100.0	100.0	100.0	Net Sales	100.0	100.0	100.0	100.0	100.0	100.0
			Gross Profit						
91.5	91.0	94.0	Operating Expenses	76.0	93.9	97.8	94.1	96.9	94.6
8.5	9.0	6.0	Operating Profit	24.0	6.1	2.2	5.9	3.1	5.4
1.3	1.2	1.5	All Other Expenses (net)	8.9	1.6	.5	.5	.4	1.5
7.2	7.8	4.5	Profit Before Taxes	15.1	4.4	1.7	5.4	2.7	3.9
			RATIOS						
3.0	2.9	3.1	Current	7.2	3.2	3.4	3.1	2.5	2.2
1.8	1.7	1.5		1.7	1.7	1.3	1.5	1.7	1.4
1.1	1.1	1.1		.2	.9	1.0	1.2	1.2	1.1
2.1	2.2	2.1	Quick	7.2	3.1	2.4	2.6	1.8	1.5
(129) 1.1	1.2	1.0		1.5	1.2	1.0	1.4	1.0	.9
.7	.8	.6		.2	.5	.6	.7	.6	.7
27 13.3	33 11.0	29 12.8	Sales/Receivables	0 UND	28 13.1	27 13.4	33 10.9	30 12.2	40 9.1
43 8.5	46 8.0	42 8.8		0 UND	40 9.1	41 8.8	41 8.8	41 8.9	51 7.2
58 6.3	59 6.2	58 6.3		32 11.4	58 6.2	54 6.8	58 6.3	54 6.8	72 5.1
			Cost of Sales/Inventory						
			Cost of Sales/Payables						
5.1	6.7	5.9	Sales/Working Capital	5.2	5.0	3.4	6.2	5.3	7.3
10.5	10.0	11.7		15.3	11.7	29.6	8.0	10.0	12.0
86.1	34.8	67.0		-5.4	NM	NM	42.4	33.9	40.2
14.5	25.0	12.2	EBIT/Interest		12.4	9.8	31.7	12.0	13.7
(110) 5.6	(75) 6.9	(112) 4.1		(22) 3.1	(18) 2.9	(20) 4.4	(27) 4.1	5.1	
1.6	3.0	.9		.6	-.1	1.3	.3	1.4	
4.9	13.1	3.6	Net Profit + Depr., Dep., Amort./Cur. Mat. L/T/D						
(24) 2.8	(15) 4.1	(27) 2.6							
1.0	1.6	1.2							
.2	.2	.2	Fixed/Worth	.1	.2	.2	.2	.2	.4
.5	.5	.6		.5	.8	.5	.6	.6	.6
1.7	1.3	1.6		7.8	2.2	2.4	1.4	1.1	1.4
.7	.6	.7	Debt/Worth	.2	.6	.6	.5	.8	1.8
1.7	1.3	2.1		.9	2.2	2.1	2.4	1.8	3.0
8.6	3.4	4.7		7.0	4.9	9.9	16.3	4.3	4.8
75.5	67.5	45.9	% Profit Before Taxes/Tangible Net Worth	66.8	83.0	35.2	33.4	33.8	62.2
(112) 41.0	(76) 34.9	(114) 22.0		25.2	(22) 24.5	(17) 14.0	(17) 23.9	(29) 10.2	(19) 39.1
7.4	14.3	2.9		6.2	2.9	-4.5	5.2	-1.1	11.6
27.4	25.8	17.3	% Profit Before Taxes/Total Assets	22.7	21.5	14.0	16.8	13.5	16.9
13.1	11.6	6.9		8.5	7.2	2.7	7.0	6.2	7.3
1.6	5.4	.2		1.8	-1.2	-3.0	.2	-.5	1.8
48.2	48.3	44.0	Sales/Net Fixed Assets	UND	32.0	91.5	56.4	25.9	43.8
16.0	18.6	14.9		5.7	12.8	17.2	23.5	15.3	15.4
8.7	8.5	6.1		.2	5.7	5.9	10.5	7.2	6.8
3.7	4.0	3.7	Sales/Total Assets	4.0	3.4	5.5	3.8	3.4	3.7
2.5	2.8	2.4		1.6	2.5	2.2	3.0	2.5	2.4
1.8	2.0	1.7		.2	1.5	1.8	1.9	1.8	1.5
.8	.8	.8	% Depr., Dep., Amort./Sales		1.1	.4	.5	.8	.6
(100) 1.6	(61) 1.6	(106) 1.8		(21) 3.0	(14) 1.4	(18) 1.0	(28) 1.8	(18) 1.5	
2.9	3.3	3.8		4.2	5.9	2.8	3.0	4.8	
3.5	2.7	3.1	% Officers', Directors' Owners' Comp/Sales	6.1	5.0				
(57) 5.5	(33) 6.3	(49) 6.3		(14) 9.3	(14) 6.8				
9.0	10.3	9.7		22.4	9.7				
1952568M	1349720M	2267479M	Net Sales ($)	5061M	49810M	79917M	161636M	474804M	1496251M
997001M	722090M	1175752M	Total Assets ($)	6381M	25295M	33368M	84814M	201907M	823987M

M = $ thousand   MM = $ million
See Pages 9 through 22 for Explanation of Ratios and Data

Current Data Sorted by Assets						Comparative Historical Data	

Type of Statement

	0-500M	500M-2MM	2-10MM	10-50MM	50-100MM	100-250MM	4/1/05-3/31/06 ALL	4/1/06-3/31/07 ALL
Unqualified	1	1	4	8	2	2	23	25
Reviewed		12	37	8	1		37	38
Compiled	16	24	19	3			50	51
Tax Returns	43	64	22			1	62	89
Other	26	32	34	14	1	3	69	88
		64 (4/1-9/30/09)		314 (10/1/09-3/31/10)				
NUMBER OF STATEMENTS	86	133	116	33	4	6	241	291
ASSETS	%	%	%	%	%	%	%	%
Cash & Equivalents	12.2	10.0	9.3	5.8			9.9	10.5
Trade Receivables (net)	23.7	28.9	26.6	26.9			32.0	32.5
Inventory	17.3	18.8	21.5	15.4			17.9	18.5
All Other Current	2.2	2.3	3.9	5.3			2.7	3.7
Total Current	55.5	60.0	61.2	53.4			62.4	65.2
Fixed Assets (net)	33.5	29.2	29.6	32.9			26.9	25.6
Intangibles (net)	6.0	2.8	3.1	4.5			3.2	3.2
All Other Non-Current	5.1	7.9	6.1	9.2			7.4	6.0
Total	100.0	100.0	100.0	100.0			100.0	100.0
LIABILITIES								
Notes Payable-Short Term	13.0	10.4	11.7	5.9			13.9	13.3
Cur. Mat.-L.T.D.	7.6	4.0	3.9	2.9			5.2	4.7
Trade Payables	15.7	16.1	11.3	11.6			16.0	15.9
Income Taxes Payable	.1	.1	.3	.1			.2	.2
All Other Current	14.2	10.6	7.8	12.2			10.5	11.4
Total Current	50.5	41.3	35.1	32.7			45.8	45.6
Long-Term Debt	39.8	18.7	19.7	16.8			22.0	24.6
Deferred Taxes	.0	.4	.4	1.0			.3	.3
All Other Non-Current	4.7	5.4	5.1	5.8			4.6	5.4
Net Worth	5.1	34.1	39.7	43.7			27.3	24.1
Total Liabilties & Net Worth	100.0	100.0	100.0	100.0			100.0	100.0
INCOME DATA								
Net Sales	100.0	100.0	100.0	100.0			100.0	100.0
Gross Profit								
Operating Expenses	96.0	95.9	93.8	94.4			95.4	93.8
Operating Profit	4.0	4.1	6.2	5.6			4.6	6.2
All Other Expenses (net)	.9	1.8	1.2	2.8			.8	1.0
Profit Before Taxes	3.2	2.4	5.0	2.8			3.8	5.2
RATIOS								
Current	2.8	2.8	2.8	3.2			2.2	2.5
	1.3	1.5	1.7	1.7			1.4	1.5
	.7	1.0	1.2	1.2			1.0	1.1
Quick	2.1	1.9	2.0	1.7			1.6	1.6
	.7	(132) 1.0	1.0	1.2			1.0	1.0
	.3	.6	.5	.6			.6	.6
Sales/Receivables	0 UND	19 19.1	30 12.1	37 9.9			26 14.0	25 14.8
	23 16.2	37 9.8	45 8.1	47 7.7			44 8.2	41 8.9
	42 8.7	57 6.4	57 6.3	59 6.2			65 5.6	58 6.3
Cost of Sales/Inventory								
Cost of Sales/Payables								
Sales/Working Capital	11.4	5.8	4.8	4.7			7.3	6.7
	36.0	13.9	8.5	10.3			15.2	12.7
	-22.5	-122.8	19.7	22.3			276.5	90.2
EBIT/Interest	7.4	10.3	10.7	16.7			10.4	14.5
	(67) 1.2	(117) 1.8	(108) 3.6	(28) 5.4			(215) 3.7	(252) 4.5
	-5.0	-1.5	1.2	1.4			1.3	1.5
Net Profit + Depr., Dep., Amort./Cur. Mat. L/T/D		4.0	15.0				4.0	4.9
		(17) 1.5	(29) 2.2				(40) 1.6	(44) 2.2
		-.3	1.2				.8	1.4
Fixed/Worth	.4	.3	.2	.3			.3	.3
	2.5	.7	.6	.8			1.0	.9
	-2.0	2.6	1.8	1.5			4.0	3.1
Debt/Worth	1.0	.7	.7	.6			1.0	1.0
	10.7	1.9	1.5	1.7			3.0	2.3
	-4.1	7.3	5.1	3.4			11.2	10.3
% Profit Before Taxes/Tangible Net Worth	78.2	43.9	31.8	39.3			70.4	73.0
	(51) 19.5	(113) 9.0	(107) 16.2	(31) 16.5			(200) 29.2	(239) 33.6
	-19.9	-5.5	3.3	4.6			7.4	10.8
% Profit Before Taxes/Total Assets	26.4	15.6	13.7	15.5			20.1	22.1
	3.3	1.9	6.2	7.7			7.8	9.3
	-15.4	-3.6	.4	1.5			.7	2.2
Sales/Net Fixed Assets	45.2	37.5	26.0	20.9			30.3	37.1
	14.7	15.6	9.3	6.9			14.5	14.7
	6.7	4.3	3.6	3.7			6.3	7.3
Sales/Total Assets	5.8	3.6	2.9	2.6			4.0	4.1
	3.6	2.5	2.0	1.9			2.7	2.8
	2.3	1.7	1.3	1.1			1.7	2.0
% Depr., Dep., Amort./Sales	.9	.7	1.0	1.1			.8	.8
	(61) 2.3	(104) 2.0	(104) 1.9	(27) 2.6			(209) 1.8	(243) 1.5
	4.5	4.1	3.9	5.4			3.6	2.9
% Officers', Directors' Owners' Comp/Sales	5.9	3.0	1.9				3.1	3.2
	(47) 8.8	(73) 5.7	(55) 3.4				(123) 5.7	(142) 5.5
	13.8	8.8	5.7				9.6	10.3
Net Sales ($)	86324M	429466M	1150632M	1346262M	481896M	2105835M	4115173M	4114285M
Total Assets ($)	22903M	152184M	536640M	710836M	237906M	1102789M	1229886M	1894537M

M = $ thousand   MM = $ million
See Pages 9 through 22 for Explanation of Ratios and Data

Comparative Historical Data | Current Data Sorted by Sales

4/1/07-3/31/08 ALL	4/1/08-3/31/09 ALL	4/1/09-3/31/10 ALL	Type of Statement	0-1MM	1-3MM	3-5MM	5-10MM	10-25MM	25MM & OVER
28	21	17	Unqualified		1		1	2	13
49	42	59	Reviewed		9	4	17	22	7
56	57	62	Compiled	12	17	15	13	4	1
97	121	130	Tax Returns	40	43	22	17	7	1
99	115	110	Other	20	35	9	16	14	16

Current data period: 64 (4/1-9/30/09); 314 (10/1/09-3/31/10)

4/1/07-3/31/08 ALL	4/1/08-3/31/09 ALL	4/1/09-3/31/10 ALL		0-1MM	1-3MM	3-5MM	5-10MM	10-25MM	25MM & OVER
329	356	378	**NUMBER OF STATEMENTS**	72	105	50	64	49	38
%	%	%	**ASSETS**	%	%	%	%	%	%
10.1	12.4	9.9	Cash & Equivalents	10.5	9.6	9.5	12.5	8.6	7.1
31.4	27.9	26.8	Trade Receivables (net)	18.3	23.2	32.5	29.7	33.3	32.0
18.6	17.3	18.9	Inventory	14.3	18.1	21.4	23.6	19.9	17.7
3.2	2.9	3.1	All Other Current	1.2	3.2	1.6	3.3	4.9	5.4
63.2	60.5	58.7	Total Current	44.3	54.1	65.0	69.1	66.7	62.3
27.1	29.2	30.5	Fixed Assets (net)	41.2	36.2	25.0	22.3	25.1	22.2
3.8	3.7	4.1	Intangibles (net)	7.6	3.2	1.4	1.6	3.8	8.6
5.9	6.6	6.7	All Other Non-Current	6.9	6.5	8.6	7.1	4.4	6.9
100.0	100.0	100.0	Total	100.0	100.0	100.0	100.0	100.0	100.0
			LIABILITIES						
11.4	11.1	10.9	Notes Payable-Short Term	9.8	13.5	9.5	11.2	10.8	7.5
5.4	5.0	4.6	Cur. Mat.-L.T.D.	5.8	5.3	5.1	4.1	3.3	2.7
17.0	14.3	14.0	Trade Payables	8.3	15.9	15.9	16.0	15.7	11.2
.3	.2	.2	Income Taxes Payable	.0	.1	.1	.2	.5	.2
10.9	9.8	10.8	All Other Current	10.0	10.9	13.4	7.4	11.8	12.9
44.9	40.3	40.5	Total Current	33.8	45.7	44.1	38.9	42.2	34.4
22.6	23.9	23.8	Long-Term Debt	47.2	24.6	18.4	11.9	15.5	14.7
.3	1.0	.4	Deferred Taxes	.0	.2	.0	.9	.8	1.1
5.7	6.4	5.3	All Other Non-Current	5.4	5.5	2.6	8.1	3.6	5.9
26.6	28.4	30.1	Net Worth	13.6	24.1	35.0	40.2	38.0	43.9
100.0	100.0	100.0	Total Liabilities & Net Worth	100.0	100.0	100.0	100.0	100.0	100.0
			INCOME DATA						
100.0	100.0	100.0	Net Sales	100.0	100.0	100.0	100.0	100.0	100.0
			Gross Profit						
93.0	93.4	95.2	Operating Expenses	93.5	93.8	97.6	95.8	96.0	96.6
7.0	6.6	4.8	Operating Profit	6.5	6.2	2.4	4.2	4.0	3.4
1.2	1.6	1.5	All Other Expenses (net)	4.6	1.5	.2	.0	.7	.7
5.8	5.1	3.4	Profit Before Taxes	2.0	4.7	2.2	4.1	3.3	2.7
			RATIOS						
2.6	3.0	2.8	Current	3.0	2.7	3.0	3.5	2.3	3.0
1.5	1.7	1.6		1.6	1.4	1.5	1.7	1.6	1.7
1.0	1.1	1.0		.7	.8	1.0	1.3	1.2	1.4
1.7	1.9	1.9	Quick	2.2	1.9	2.2	2.2	1.7	1.9
1.0 (355)	1.1 (377)	1.0		(71) 1.0	.8	.9	1.1	.9	1.3
.6	.6	.5		.3	.4	.6	.7	.7	.7
26 14.1	17 21.9	22 16.8	Sales/Receivables	0 UND	10 35.1	32 11.4	31 11.9	28 12.9	39 9.3
41 8.9	37 9.8	39 9.3		28 13.1	32 11.4	42 8.8	44 8.4	49 7.4	47 7.8
59 6.2	56 6.6	56 6.5		48 7.6	53 6.9	61 6.0	56 6.5	59 6.2	60 6.1
			Cost of Sales/Inventory						
			Cost of Sales/Payables						
6.6	6.2	5.8	Sales/Working Capital	5.5	6.1	5.8	4.8	6.0	6.1
13.7	12.8	13.6		20.4	19.6	16.5	9.3	12.2	10.3
422.4	152.4	-874.3		-25.3	-21.6	NM	27.3	21.0	15.7
13.3	10.8	9.9	EBIT/Interest	6.0	11.7	6.1	15.3	7.2	13.5
(302) 4.0	(318) 4.2	(330) 2.5		(55) 1.2	(93) 2.5	(43) 1.8	(58) 2.8	(46) 3.1	(35) 4.9
1.5	1.2	.0		-2.7	-2.4	-1.0	.4	1.6	1.6
4.4	6.7	8.1	Net Profit + Depr., Dep., Amort./Cur. Mat. L/T/D				21.4	7.7	17.3
(48) 2.1	(56) 2.3	(59) 2.2				(16) 2.9	(18) 2.0	(13) 6.3	
1.0	.6	1.1				.2	1.2	3.7	
.3	.3	.3	Fixed/Worth	.4	.3	.2	.2	.3	.3
.9	.8	.8		1.6	1.1	.9	.5	.6	.5
3.5	3.3	4.2		-6.4	-94.7	6.1	.9	1.8	1.5
.9	.9	.7	Debt/Worth	.6	.8	.4	.7	.9	.7
2.5	2.2	2.1		6.2	2.3	2.7	1.5	1.5	1.8
11.9	10.1	16.1		-9.4	-84.7	20.7	4.2	3.1	4.2
73.8	68.4	40.4	% Profit Before Taxes/Tangible Net Worth	48.4	69.0	36.2	34.3	31.2	45.9
(271) 34.2	(291) 25.2	(309) 14.0		(48) 3.4	(77) 14.0	(43) 9.3	(62) 15.8	(45) 14.4	(34) 23.7
9.6	9.2	-1.1		-24.0	-2.7	-9.8	.0		6.2
24.5	21.2	16.4	% Profit Before Taxes/Total Assets	21.1	23.0	13.8	18.1	12.3	15.3
9.1	7.5	3.3		1.6	2.6	1.4	4.1	3.7	9.7
1.8		-2.7		-7.4	-6.1	-3.4	.0	1.3	1.7
31.1	31.5	32.8	Sales/Net Fixed Assets	20.7	28.9	42.3	51.7	27.5	34.8
14.4	14.9	12.6		7.8	9.8	19.2	18.0	12.0	11.6
6.7	5.3	4.7		2.5	3.3	6.0	5.5	5.7	5.5
3.9	3.9	3.6	Sales/Total Assets	3.7	3.7	3.7	3.4	3.6	3.1
2.8	2.6	2.4		2.3	2.3	2.8	2.6	2.6	2.3
1.9	1.7	1.6		1.3	1.5	1.6	1.5	1.9	1.8
.9	1.0	.9	% Depr., Dep., Amort./Sales	1.9	.9	.8	.7	1.0	.8
(264) 1.8	(273) 2.0	(302) 2.0		(53) 4.3	(78) 2.6	(41) 2.1	(57) 1.6	(45) 1.8	(28) 1.6
3.7	3.7	4.2		8.7	5.0	3.2	4.0	2.5	2.6
2.6	2.8	2.9	% Officers', Directors' Owners' Comp/Sales	5.9	3.2	3.1	1.8	1.8	
(172) 4.8	(182) 4.6	(182) 5.5		(35) 9.4	(54) 6.5	(30) 4.7	(36) 2.9	(21) 3.6	
7.6	7.7	9.0		16.5	8.8	8.3	5.9	8.5	
11022140M	5425792M	5600415M	Net Sales ($)	44207M	190558M	201431M	454954M	758502M	3950763M
3375811M	2913165M	2763258M	Total Assets ($)	36798M	133087M	92630M	217625M	363656M	1919462M

© RMA 2010

M = $ thousand   MM = $ million
See Pages 9 through 22 for Explanation of Ratios and Data

Current Data Sorted by Assets | Comparative Historical Data

						Type of Statement		
	2	9	1			Unqualified	4	1
1	3	3	1			Reviewed	5	4
6	2	4				Compiled	8	6
8	1	7	1			Tax Returns	5	9
			6			Other	14	12
	10 (4/1-9/30/09)		45 (10/1/09-3/31/10)				4/1/05-3/31/06	4/1/06-3/31/07
0-500M	500M-2MM	2-10MM	10-50MM	50-100MM	100-250MM		ALL	ALL
15	8	23	9			NUMBER OF STATEMENTS	36	32
%	%	%	%	%	%	ASSETS	%	%
28.2		7.4		D	D	Cash & Equivalents	15.3	12.2
12.1		37.5		A	A	Trade Receivables (net)	40.9	28.2
15.5		16.5		T	T	Inventory	9.8	13.1
5.4		8.9		A	A	All Other Current	8.5	6.1
61.2		70.3				Total Current	74.5	59.6
27.2		19.7		N	N	Fixed Assets (net)	17.7	27.1
.8		5.7		O	O	Intangibles (net)	5.1	3.9
10.6		4.3		T	T	All Other Non-Current	2.7	9.4
100.0		100.0				Total	100.0	100.0
				A	A	LIABILITIES		
67.5		7.1		V	V	Notes Payable-Short Term	14.3	18.3
11.8		3.4		A	A	Cur. Mat.-L.T.D.	4.2	3.4
26.2		16.0		I	I	Trade Payables	19.5	10.8
.0		.1		L	L	Income Taxes Payable	.4	.9
17.4		14.0		A	A	All Other Current	18.1	14.2
122.9		40.6		B	B	Total Current	56.5	47.5
32.3		14.0		L	L	Long-Term Debt	14.9	21.4
.3		1.1		E	E	Deferred Taxes	.4	.6
4.8		1.6				All Other Non-Current	3.3	4.3
-60.2		42.8				Net Worth	24.9	26.3
100.0		100.0				Total Liabilities & Net Worth	100.0	100.0
						INCOME DATA		
100.0		100.0				Net Sales	100.0	100.0
						Gross Profit		
97.0		95.4				Operating Expenses	95.1	93.9
3.0		4.6				Operating Profit	4.9	6.1
1.6		.7				All Other Expenses (net)	.6	1.4
1.4		4.0				Profit Before Taxes	4.3	4.7
						RATIOS		
3.7		2.6					2.5	3.0
1.2		1.8				Current	1.6	1.3
.3		1.3					1.0	.9
2.1		1.4					1.8	2.1
.7		1.0				Quick	1.1	1.0
.1		.7					.7	.5
0 UND		34 10.9					32 11.5	11 34.3
0 UND		47 7.8				Sales/Receivables	46 7.9	26 14.1
9 39.0		54 6.8					67 5.5	60 6.1
						Cost of Sales/Inventory		
						Cost of Sales/Payables		
6.8		4.8					6.5	9.6
808.5		13.6				Sales/Working Capital	11.5	23.2
-3.5		25.8					219.3	-33.4
6.9		52.2					13.2	9.4
(11) .4		(21) 6.4				EBIT/Interest	(33) 7.3	(28) 5.2
-12.5		.9					2.5	1.7
						Net Profit + Depr., Dep., Amort./Cur. Mat. L/T/D		
.1		.1					.3	.3
.4		.5				Fixed/Worth	.5	1.1
-.6		1.6					1.5	6.8
.7		.6					1.1	1.1
UND		1.6				Debt/Worth	2.2	2.9
-1.7		4.8					5.4	124.2
		67.9					72.6	66.7
	(22)	17.7				% Profit Before Taxes/Tangible Net Worth	(32) 41.6	(25) 46.0
		7.2					11.6	21.9
36.1		20.5					21.4	28.8
12.0		7.2				% Profit Before Taxes/Total Assets	11.3	15.0
-84.4		1.5					4.0	2.5
211.5		72.3					43.6	34.9
37.5		20.2				Sales/Net Fixed Assets	22.1	15.8
21.6		9.7					13.8	8.4
11.0		3.7					4.0	4.5
5.2		2.9				Sales/Total Assets	3.2	3.4
3.5		2.0					2.4	2.0
.2		.5					.7	.8
(10) .5		(18) 1.3				% Depr., Dep., Amort./Sales	(28) 1.4	(28) 2.0
1.1		2.1					2.3	3.4
		2.5					4.5	3.4
	(11)	4.4				% Officers', Directors' Owners' Comp/Sales	(13) 6.3	(17) 5.0
		6.2					18.9	9.3
18043M	27746M	322563M	343355M			Net Sales ($)	540181M	242447M
2939M	8335M	109934M	158827M			Total Assets ($)	234276M	94553M

© RMA 2010

M = $ thousand   MM = $ million
See Pages 9 through 22 for Explanation of Ratios and Data

Comparative Historical Data   Current Data Sorted by Sales

4/1/07-3/31/08 ALL	4/1/08-3/31/09 ALL	4/1/09-3/31/10 ALL	Type of Statement	0-1MM	1-3MM	3-5MM	5-10MM	10-25MM	25MM & OVER
1	2	1	Unqualified						
5	11	12	Reviewed		1	1	3	4	1
4	5	7	Compiled	2	1	1	2	1	3
10	12	13	Tax Returns	2	6	1	1	2	1
8	26	22	Other	5	4		3	6	4
				10 (4/1-9/30/09)			45 (10/1/09-3/31/10)		
28	56	55	**NUMBER OF STATEMENTS**	9	12	3	9	13	9
%	%	%	**ASSETS**	%	%	%	%	%	%
15.2	10.0	15.1	Cash & Equivalents		16.3			10.2	
31.1	24.9	26.2	Trade Receivables (net)		13.1			35.7	
20.9	16.6	19.2	Inventory		27.7			13.2	
1.8	3.7	5.8	All Other Current		6.6			3.7	
69.0	55.2	66.3	Total Current		63.7			62.7	
22.8	26.0	22.4	Fixed Assets (net)		22.3			23.6	
5.0	4.2	3.5	Intangibles (net)		1.0			8.2	
3.2	14.6	7.8	All Other Non-Current		12.9			5.4	
100.0	100.0	100.0	Total		100.0			100.0	
			LIABILITIES						
8.5	7.4	23.5	Notes Payable-Short Term		31.9			3.9	
5.6	3.5	10.1	Cur. Mat.-L.T.D.		3.2			2.9	
11.6	16.6	18.0	Trade Payables		26.5			17.0	
1.2	.3	.2	Income Taxes Payable		.0			.6	
10.5	21.7	18.0	All Other Current		11.2			18.4	
37.4	49.7	69.8	Total Current		72.8			42.9	
24.1	19.7	18.6	Long-Term Debt		25.6			14.0	
.5	.4	.6	Deferred Taxes		.3			1.4	
5.4	6.9	4.5	All Other Non-Current		8.1			1.5	
32.6	23.4	6.5	Net Worth		-6.9			40.2	
100.0	100.0	100.0	Total Liabilities & Net Worth		100.0			100.0	
			INCOME DATA						
100.0	100.0	100.0	Net Sales		100.0			100.0	
			Gross Profit						
94.7	92.7	95.8	Operating Expenses		98.5			96.1	
5.3	7.3	4.2	Operating Profit		1.5			3.9	
2.0	1.5	.8	All Other Expenses (net)		.2			.2	
3.4	5.8	3.4	Profit Before Taxes		1.4			3.7	
			RATIOS						
3.7	2.6	2.5			2.7			2.1	
1.7	1.4	1.6	Current		1.4			1.5	
1.1	.6	.9			.5			1.3	
2.4	1.7	1.4			1.3			1.6	
1.0	.7	.9	Quick		.3			1.1	
.5	.2	.4			.1			.8	
23 15.9	4 95.3	2 186.1		0 UND			26 13.9		
36 10.1	35 10.6	34 10.9	Sales/Receivables	0 UND			41 8.8		
61 5.9	58 6.3	51 7.1		33 11.1			64 5.7		
			Cost of Sales/Inventory						
			Cost of Sales/Payables						
6.4	7.8	5.9			6.3			7.9	
10.2	26.2	13.6	Sales/Working Capital		20.2			18.4	
73.1	-10.2	-48.1			-62.9			26.0	
18.1	17.1	24.2			10.3			45.0	
(24) 4.2	(44) 3.4	(47) 6.4	EBIT/Interest	(10) 6.6			(12) 8.0		
1.8	1.6	.4			-2.3			2.7	
			Net Profit + Depr., Dep., Amort./Cur. Mat. L/T/D						
.2	.3	.1			.2			.3	
.5	.8	.5	Fixed/Worth		.5			.8	
3.7	4.3	2.4			UND			1.5	
.9	1.1	.7			.9			1.3	
2.3	3.4	2.3	Debt/Worth		1.7			2.3	
38.9	9.9	24.6			UND			4.7	
81.2	103.8	70.3			UND			70.8	
(23) 44.9	(46) 34.6	(44) 25.7	% Profit Before Taxes/Tangible Net Worth	(10) 37.1				27.7	
23.0	12.5	10.0			22.2			9.4	
25.3	24.4	20.7			21.5			19.6	
12.1	8.4	6.9	% Profit Before Taxes/Total Assets		13.1			8.3	
1.7	3.4	.2			-.1			3.0	
63.3	42.4	66.0			108.5			22.5	
20.7	17.9	20.9	Sales/Net Fixed Assets		35.9			10.5	
11.3	6.5	9.4			21.7			6.4	
3.5	4.1	4.6			7.9			4.0	
2.9	2.6	3.3	Sales/Total Assets		4.9			2.6	
2.0	1.9	2.1			3.3			1.8	
1.2	.7	.4						.4	
(21) 1.8	(45) 1.9	(40) 1.3	% Depr., Dep., Amort./Sales					(11) 1.4	
3.2	4.2	2.1						2.5	
2.0	3.4	2.6							
(12) 4.5	(18) 4.3	(26) 4.7	% Officers', Directors' Owners' Comp/Sales						
11.0	6.5	8.4							
1393837M	898772M	711707M	Net Sales ($)	5361M	24208M	11454M	69609M	200116M	400959M
482737M	446292M	280035M	Total Assets ($)	13635M	6500M	4875M	33963M	91907M	129155M

M = $ thousand   MM = $ million
See Pages 9 through 22 for Explanation of Ratios and Data

| Current Data Sorted by Assets | | | | | | | Comparative Historical Data | |

Type of Statement	0-500M	500M-2MM	2-10MM	10-50MM	50-100MM	100-250MM	4/1/05-3/31/06 ALL	4/1/06-3/31/07 ALL
Unqualified		1					2	1
Reviewed	2		3	1		2	2	6
Compiled	2	7	3	1			2	10
Tax Returns	21	14	5	1	1		7	12
Other	10	8	3	1			7	9
		6 (4/1-9/30/09)		80 (10/1/09-3/31/10)				
NUMBER OF STATEMENTS	33	32	14	4	3		20	38
	%	%	%	%	%	%	%	%
ASSETS								
Cash & Equivalents	18.6	8.6	17.3				12.7	13.1
Trade Receivables (net)	10.3	31.7	17.6				24.9	32.8
Inventory	20.7	14.8	22.2				9.0	16.6
All Other Current	6.2	2.4	7.8				3.9	2.4
Total Current	55.8	57.5	64.8				50.6	65.0
Fixed Assets (net)	30.9	32.4	22.8				37.6	28.5
Intangibles (net)	5.9	3.0	4.5				5.8	2.8
All Other Non-Current	7.4	7.0	7.9				6.0	3.7
Total	100.0	100.0	100.0				100.0	100.0
LIABILITIES								
Notes Payable-Short Term	19.1	7.9	15.4				9.2	6.5
Cur. Mat.-L.T.D.	8.2	5.8	3.1				5.5	4.8
Trade Payables	9.2	13.8	11.2				17.8	13.6
Income Taxes Payable	.0	.1	.8				2.4	.6
All Other Current	17.5	12.1	13.2				10.5	10.8
Total Current	54.0	39.8	43.7				45.3	36.3
Long-Term Debt	34.1	33.8	8.6				25.9	28.6
Deferred Taxes	.0	.1	.0				.2	.1
All Other Non-Current	7.2	5.5	3.4				4.2	5.1
Net Worth	4.7	20.8	44.4				24.4	29.9
Total Liabilties & Net Worth	100.0	100.0	100.0				100.0	100.0
INCOME DATA								
Net Sales	100.0	100.0	100.0				100.0	100.0
Gross Profit								
Operating Expenses	93.5	91.3	94.7				91.7	89.1
Operating Profit	6.5	8.7	5.3				8.3	10.9
All Other Expenses (net)	.6	2.8	.0				2.9	1.6
Profit Before Taxes	6.0	5.8	5.2				5.5	9.3
RATIOS								
Current	5.2	2.8	3.0				2.4	2.8
	1.2	2.0	1.3				1.3	1.8
	.5	.6	1.0				.9	1.2
Quick	2.0	2.2	1.7				1.7	2.1
	.5	1.4	.7				1.1	1.2
	.1	.4	.4				.5	.9
Sales/Receivables	0 UND	12 29.9	0 UND				0 UND	12 30.6
	0 UND	36 10.1	39 9.4				24 15.4	39 9.4
	11 33.4	54 6.8	53 6.9				62 5.9	71 5.1
Cost of Sales/Inventory								
Cost of Sales/Payables								
Sales/Working Capital	11.0	6.4	3.6				11.7	6.1
	26.8	14.4	13.9				23.1	10.1
	-28.0	-14.0	NM				UND	31.0
EBIT/Interest	21.0	9.2	65.7				16.0	21.5
	(24) 3.0	(24) 2.9	(12) 3.4				(17) 5.8	(33) 6.1
	.1	.7	1.1				.5	2.1
Net Profit + Depr., Dep., Amort./Cur. Mat. L/T/D								
Fixed/Worth	.4	.2	.2				.5	.1
	UND	2.1	.4				1.3	.6
	-.4	NM	.8				17.1	3.8
Debt/Worth	1.3	.7	.6				.8	.9
	UND	2.5	1.5				2.7	1.8
	-4.2	NM	3.1				37.9	16.2
% Profit Before Taxes/Tangible Net Worth	116.9	40.4	50.1				64.0	90.6
	(17) 60.0	(24) 18.0	(13) 22.3				(16) 41.6	(30) 41.7
	-20.4	.2	1.8				6.2	16.9
% Profit Before Taxes/Total Assets	51.9	18.1	29.8				25.3	32.0
	17.4	7.9	4.7				6.8	12.8
	-4.8	-1.0	.7				-.3	5.0
Sales/Net Fixed Assets	141.9	53.3	45.6				23.9	62.5
	36.6	16.4	9.6				15.2	17.1
	8.4	3.2	5.9				7.1	6.3
Sales/Total Assets	8.7	3.9	2.6				6.7	4.1
	5.2	2.8	1.9				2.9	2.8
	2.9	1.4	1.0				2.4	2.1
% Depr., Dep., Amort./Sales	.7	.9	.8				1.1	.6
	(17) 1.5	(23) 1.6	(13) 3.6				(15) 2.1	(27) 1.6
	6.7	3.7	6.1				3.4	3.4
% Officers', Directors' Owners' Comp/Sales	3.7	4.0					1.9	1.9
	(19) 6.7	(17) 5.1					(11) 3.5	(25) 3.2
	12.9	8.2					4.5	6.2
Net Sales ($)	36657M	103382M	93008M	59076M	542516M		883156M	1266662M
Total Assets ($)	6272M	35208M	49870M	59094M	198793M		118331M	233042M

(Columns 10-50MM, 50-100MM, and 100-250MM: DATA NOT AVAILABLE)

M = $ thousand   MM = $ million
See Pages 9 through 22 for Explanation of Ratios and Data

Comparative Historical Data / Current Data Sorted by Sales

			Type of Statement						
2	12	3	Unqualified			1		2	2
4	14	6	Reviewed			2	2		
8	19	13	Compiled	2	5	3	3		
20	37	42	Tax Returns	14	11	7	8	1	
14	42	22	Other	9	6	4	2	1	1
4/1/07-3/31/08	4/1/08-3/31/09	4/1/09-3/31/10		6 (4/1-9/30/09)			80 (10/1/09-3/31/10)		
ALL	ALL	ALL		0-1MM	1-3MM	3-5MM	5-10MM	10-25MM	25MM & OVER
48	124	86	NUMBER OF STATEMENTS	25	22	17	15	4	3
%	%	%	ASSETS	%	%	%	%	%	%
15.3	12.7	13.9	Cash & Equivalents	15.8	12.3	9.9	15.7		
28.8	25.0	20.6	Trade Receivables (net)	8.8	20.1	26.4	32.6		
15.6	16.0	18.9	Inventory	18.3	19.2	20.3	16.3		
1.9	4.0	4.7	All Other Current	8.3	.7	5.2	3.4		
61.6	57.7	58.1	Total Current	51.3	52.3	61.9	68.0		
27.4	29.6	29.5	Fixed Assets (net)	37.5	41.2	23.3	15.0		
4.8	7.2	4.8	Intangibles (net)	6.2	3.0	4.1	4.4		
6.2	5.4	7.5	All Other Non-Current	5.1	3.6	10.8	12.6		
100.0	100.0	100.0	Total	100.0	100.0	100.0	100.0		
			LIABILITIES						
12.9	10.0	13.4	Notes Payable-Short Term	14.0	8.6	19.4	15.4		
3.0	6.0	6.1	Cur. Mat.-L.T.D.	5.8	5.0	11.6	3.2		
10.3	11.8	11.4	Trade Payables	4.4	13.5	16.4	13.9		
.1	.4	.2	Income Taxes Payable	.0	.2	.7	.0		
10.1	11.9	13.7	All Other Current	18.5	5.3	17.5	13.9		
36.4	40.0	44.8	Total Current	42.7	32.6	65.6	46.4		
27.0	26.2	27.8	Long-Term Debt	42.1	34.3	26.6	6.5		
.0	.5	.1	Deferred Taxes	.0	.0	.2	.0		
5.7	6.0	5.8	All Other Non-Current	4.8	10.5	1.4	5.8		
30.9	27.3	21.5	Net Worth	10.4	22.7	6.2	41.2		
100.0	100.0	100.0	Total Liabilties & Net Worth	100.0	100.0	100.0	100.0		
			INCOME DATA						
100.0	100.0	100.0	Net Sales	100.0	100.0	100.0	100.0		
			Gross Profit						
90.2	92.7	92.4	Operating Expenses	87.7	93.8	94.8	95.8		
9.8	7.3	7.6	Operating Profit	12.3	6.2	5.2	4.2		
.7	1.8	1.7	All Other Expenses (net)	3.3	1.5	.6	-.3		
9.1	5.5	5.9	Profit Before Taxes	9.0	4.7	4.6	4.5		
			RATIOS						
3.8	2.7	3.4	Current	5.2	4.6	2.2	2.9		
1.9	1.6	1.5		1.5	1.7	1.2	1.9		
1.1	1.1	.7		.5	.7	.6	.9		
2.9	2.0	2.1	Quick	2.1	2.2	1.6	2.3		
1.1	(123) 1.1	.8		.3	1.3	.7	1.0		
.6	.6	.3		.1	.3	.4	.4		
3 106.8	11 32.4	0 UND	Sales/Receivables	0 UND	0 UND	0 UND	26 14.1		
33 11.2	31 11.9	22 16.5		0 UND	26 14.2	29 12.4	41 8.8		
50 7.4	47 7.8	46 7.9		14 26.8	52 7.0	43 8.5	54 6.8		
			Cost of Sales/Inventory						
			Cost of Sales/Payables						
5.7	7.0	6.1	Sales/Working Capital	8.3	6.7	6.6	3.7		
13.1	16.5	17.7		23.5	13.8	19.8	11.4		
178.5	56.3	-28.5		-28.0	-51.5	-19.6	-23.9		
20.5	13.0	19.3	EBIT/Interest	19.1	7.5	33.2	15.6		
(40) 7.7	(103) 4.2	(67) 3.0		(16) 3.0	(17) 1.8	(16) 7.9	(11) 2.3		
2.7	1.2	.4		.1	.0	.6	1.1		
	10.1		Net Profit + Depr., Dep., Amort./Cur. Mat. L/T/D						
	(18) 2.8								
	1.3								
.2	.3	.2	Fixed/Worth	.4	.3	.3	.1		
.7	1.0	1.3		4.7	2.4	61.8	.2		
2.3	5.7	-2.1		-1.2	-26.1	-.4	.8		
.5	.7	.7	Debt/Worth	1.1	.6	.6	.6		
1.4	2.6	2.5		7.2	3.1	61.3	1.7		
5.6	43.0	-10.9		-5.4	-35.1	-6.0	3.8		
94.1	76.3	61.2	% Profit Before Taxes/Tangible Net Worth	119.1	32.8		40.3		
(40) 46.6	(98) 30.0	(61) 22.3		(16) 59.7	(16) 11.7	(13) 19.2			
20.4	5.7	-2.2		-14.9	-3.9		1.8		
42.6	26.2	29.3	% Profit Before Taxes/Total Assets	49.1	15.3	36.6	28.9		
19.9	9.5	8.3		17.4	3.0	18.5	5.8		
4.8	1.2	-2.0		-5.6	-2.0	-3.0	.8		
36.0	46.9	59.2	Sales/Net Fixed Assets	69.8	51.2	135.8	136.5		
19.6	15.7	17.1		14.6	9.1	23.1	41.7		
5.9	5.4	5.8		4.1	2.5	12.1	7.9		
4.8	4.5	5.3	Sales/Total Assets	6.1	4.3	7.1	5.4		
3.4	2.8	2.8		3.0	2.5	3.4	2.8		
2.5	1.8	1.8		1.6	1.4	2.7	2.0		
1.0	.9	.8	% Depr., Dep., Amort./Sales	.7	.9	1.6	.3		
(36) 1.7	(97) 1.9	(59) 1.7		(14) 4.1	(16) 1.6	(10) 2.8	(13) 1.3		
3.8	4.0	4.5		8.1	8.3	3.8	3.7		
3.4	3.2	2.8	% Officers', Directors' Owners' Comp/Sales	4.8	4.5		1.8		
(26) 5.7	(52) 5.3	(47) 5.1		(13) 7.9	(12) 6.4	(12) 3.4			
11.5	8.1	9.2		12.1	10.2		5.4		
2847364M	3154841M	834639M	Net Sales ($)	11752M	39909M	63632M	102537M	74293M	542516M
407570M	1380170M	349237M	Total Assets ($)	6276M	39183M	20173M	39858M	44954M	198793M

© RMA 2010

M = $ thousand   MM = $ million
See Pages 9 through 22 for Explanation of Ratios and Data

Current Data Sorted by Assets   **Comparative Historical Data**

Type of Statement

						Type of Statement		
	2					Unqualified	5	7
	1	1				Reviewed	7	10
5	10	4				Compiled	19	19
72	18	7	1	1		Tax Returns	59	88
25	19	10	2	1		Other	39	50
	11 (4/1-9/30/09)	13	2	2	1		4/1/05-3/31/06	4/1/06-3/31/07
		186 (10/1/09-3/31/10)					ALL	ALL
0-500M	**500M-2MM**	**2-10MM**	**10-50MM**	**50-100MM**	**100-250MM**	**NUMBER OF STATEMENTS**	**129**	**174**
102	50	35	5	4	1			
%	%	%	%	%	%	**ASSETS**	%	%
18.9	19.2	15.6				Cash & Equivalents	17.3	19.5
1.1	4.4	6.9				Trade Receivables (net)	2.7	2.1
14.0	4.7	7.2				Inventory	11.9	12.9
2.0	3.1	2.7				All Other Current	2.7	1.7
36.0	31.5	32.4				Total Current	34.7	36.2
45.6	53.3	44.9				Fixed Assets (net)	48.7	43.6
10.4	6.5	13.7				Intangibles (net)	6.8	9.7
8.1	8.7	9.0				All Other Non-Current	9.8	10.5
100.0	100.0	100.0				Total	100.0	100.0
						LIABILITIES		
11.5	7.2	4.7				Notes Payable-Short Term	9.3	12.9
3.9	3.6	3.9				Cur. Mat.-L.T.D.	5.3	3.2
8.0	5.4	7.4				Trade Payables	7.2	8.2
.1	.0	.1				Income Taxes Payable	.1	.1
30.4	22.7	17.0				All Other Current	20.3	25.4
53.9	38.9	33.1				Total Current	42.2	49.8
28.0	24.1	42.5				Long-Term Debt	29.3	31.0
.0	.0	.0				Deferred Taxes	.0	.1
20.2	11.0	4.6				All Other Non-Current	7.4	13.7
-2.1	25.9	19.7				Net Worth	21.2	5.4
100.0	100.0	100.0				Total Liabilities & Net Worth	100.0	100.0
						INCOME DATA		
100.0	100.0	100.0				Net Sales	100.0	100.0
						Gross Profit		
95.9	89.1	89.5				Operating Expenses	93.7	94.1
4.1	10.9	10.5				Operating Profit	6.3	5.9
1.6	1.3	4.1				All Other Expenses (net)	1.7	1.8
2.5	9.6	6.4				Profit Before Taxes	4.6	4.0
						RATIOS		
2.8	2.0	1.6					2.4	1.7
1.0	.9	.8				Current	.9	.8
.3	.2	.3					.4	.3
1.2	1.7	1.0					1.2	1.0
.4	.5	.4				Quick	(127) .5	(172) .4
.1	.1	.2					.2	.1
0 UND	0 UND	0 UND					0 UND	0 UND
0 UND	0 UND	0 999.8				Sales/Receivables	0 UND	0 UND
0 UND	0 999.8	9 41.7					0 760.3	0 UND
						Cost of Sales/Inventory		
						Cost of Sales/Payables		
26.9	16.9	17.7					23.5	26.4
-397.1	-53.4	-131.8				Sales/Working Capital	-204.7	-52.0
-15.4	-11.6	-7.6					-12.4	-13.0
11.5	33.4	6.5					10.6	11.0
(63) 3.5	(43) 6.6	(31) 2.0				EBIT/Interest	(102) 4.2	(130) 3.5
.0	2.0	1.1					.5	1.0
								6.3
						Net Profit + Depr., Dep., Amort./Cur. Mat. L/T/D	(11) 3.6	
								.5
.5	.9	.7					.9	.8
4.2	1.7	5.2				Fixed/Worth	2.4	2.5
-1.0	-15.1	-147.4					-3.9	-2.4
.5	.9	1.8					.7	1.3
10.8	2.6	7.0				Debt/Worth	3.6	6.0
-2.8	-29.3	-341.4					-7.3	-4.7
101.4	90.7	94.2					105.0	144.2
(56) 48.1	(36) 61.2	(26) 29.8				% Profit Before Taxes/Tangible Net Worth	(92) 49.7	(105) 52.6
10.3	32.1	3.3					9.8	13.5
32.3	29.6	14.9					32.1	28.3
18.0	16.1	3.4				% Profit Before Taxes/Total Assets	9.1	9.9
-2.4	4.7	.6					-1.0	-.4
42.7	12.4	15.2					17.5	26.6
13.0	7.9	7.4				Sales/Net Fixed Assets	8.9	11.7
6.0	2.5	2.1					4.7	5.5
8.7	4.8	3.5					6.1	7.0
5.0	3.0	2.3				Sales/Total Assets	3.6	4.1
2.7	1.3	1.6					2.2	2.2
.8	1.2	1.5					1.0	.9
(72) 1.7	(44) 1.4	(32) 3.3				% Depr., Dep., Amort./Sales	(108) 2.0	(123) 2.2
3.3	3.0	5.9					3.3	3.5
3.3	2.3	1.2					3.7	2.9
(50) 6.1	(19) 3.6	(13) 1.8				% Officers', Directors' Owners' Comp/Sales	(63) 6.4	(82) 5.1
-11.6	7.0	5.1					13.7	10.1
98479M	165025M	347375M	192932M	849099M	1135729M	Net Sales ($)	1603511M	1839278M
19221M	50959M	133940M	104784M	288250M	114253M	Total Assets ($)	576634M	761430M

M = $ thousand   MM = $ million
See Pages 9 through 22 for Explanation of Ratios and Data

Comparative Historical Data   Current Data Sorted by Sales

4/1/07-3/31/08 ALL	4/1/08-3/31/09 ALL	4/1/09-3/31/10 ALL	Type of Statement	0-1MM	1-3MM	3-5MM	5-10MM	10-25MM	25MM & OVER
7	8	5	Unqualified	1	1			1	2
2	4	5	Reviewed					4	
15	18	24	Compiled			1		2	2
61	106	102	Tax Returns	5	8	3	4	2	2
60	67	61	Other	48	39	6	5	2	2
				18	16	11	4	8	4
				11 (4/1-9/30/09)			186 (10/1/09-3/31/10)		
145	203	197	NUMBER OF STATEMENTS	72	64	21	13	17	10
%	%	%	ASSETS	%	%	%	%	%	%
17.8	17.4	18.3	Cash & Equivalents	17.3	18.3	25.4	10.3	17.4	21.7
1.9	3.4	3.7	Trade Receivables (net)	.6	4.0	4.0	5.4	8.1	13.3
13.9	12.2	10.4	Inventory	12.4	9.2	8.2	3.8	12.9	13.4
2.3	2.4	2.5	All Other Current	2.1	2.7	1.2	3.8	3.0	4.0
35.9	35.5	34.9	Total Current	32.4	34.3	38.8	23.2	41.3	52.4
46.7	48.3	46.5	Fixed Assets (net)	49.8	48.2	41.6	48.8	42.4	27.2
8.3	5.9	10.3	Intangibles (net)	8.7	10.6	10.5	17.0	6.6	16.4
9.0	10.3	8.3	All Other Non-Current	9.2	6.8	9.1	11.0	9.7	4.0
100.0	100.0	100.0	Total	100.0	100.0	100.0	100.0	100.0	100.0
			LIABILITIES						
10.7	13.7	8.8	Notes Payable-Short Term	11.1	9.6	5.2	3.9	7.5	2.9
3.2	4.5	3.9	Cur. Mat.-L.T.D.	3.8	3.8	2.9	3.3	5.7	4.9
6.6	7.0	7.5	Trade Payables	4.5	8.6	9.5	6.5	10.7	13.6
.2	.1	.1	Income Taxes Payable	.1	.0	.1	.0	.1	.5
21.5	24.2	25.6	All Other Current	21.7	22.5	52.7	18.8	28.9	20.6
42.3	49.4	45.9	Total Current	41.2	44.5	70.3	32.5	52.9	42.6
30.3	37.2	30.8	Long-Term Debt	31.1	29.6	21.4	32.6	32.6	50.7
.1	.0	.0	Deferred Taxes	.0	.0	.0	.0	.0	.0
14.0	14.8	15.2	All Other Non-Current	18.3	17.4	6.3	2.2	10.8	22.9
13.4	-1.4	8.1	Net Worth	9.4	8.5	2.0	32.7	3.7	-16.3
100.0	100.0	100.0	Total Liabilities & Net Worth	100.0	100.0	100.0	100.0	100.0	100.0
			INCOME DATA						
100.0	100.0	100.0	Net Sales	100.0	100.0	100.0	100.0	100.0	100.0
			Gross Profit						
94.8	96.0	92.7	Operating Expenses	91.7	93.0	92.7	94.7	96.3	89.0
5.2	4.0	7.3	Operating Profit	8.3	7.0	7.3	5.3	3.7	11.0
1.3	2.1	2.0	All Other Expenses (net)	3.0	1.7	.8	1.7	.6	2.8
3.9	1.9	5.3	Profit Before Taxes	5.3	5.3	6.5	3.6	3.2	8.2
			RATIOS						
2.1	1.7	2.0	Current	2.6	3.3	1.6	1.0	1.4	1.5
1.0	.8	.9		1.0	.9	.6	.6	.8	1.2
.5	.3	.3		.2	.3	.2	.4	.4	.7
1.2	1.0	1.1	Quick	1.3	2.1	1.0	.5	.6	
(144) .5	.4	(196) .4		.5	.5	.4	.3	.4	
.2	.1	.1		.1	.1	.1	.2	.2	
0 UND	0 UND	0 UND	Sales/Receivables	0 UND	0 UND	0 UND	0 UND	0 999.8	0 UND
0 UND	0 UND	0 UND		0 UND	0 UND	0 UND	0 UND	1 470.9	22 16.4
0 999.8	0 UND	0 UND		0 UND	0 UND	0 804.1	1 629.3	6 58.0	25 14.8
			Cost of Sales/Inventory						
			Cost of Sales/Payables						
22.8	32.3	21.6	Sales/Working Capital	19.8	18.0	20.2	NM	39.9	16.8
UND	-70.9	-195.5		UND	-203.0	-46.4	-43.4	-45.8	29.1
-16.1	-10.6	-14.5		-11.5	-17.3	-8.4	-9.6	-11.2	-67.6
11.3	6.1	12.1	EBIT/Interest	8.0	14.8	34.3	22.1	16.7	19.7
(107) 3.7	(153) 1.6	(147) 4.3		(35) 3.7	(54) 3.9	(18) 5.4	1.7	4.0	5.3
.8	-.3	1.3		.6	1.0	2.0	.9	1.5	3.0
			Net Profit + Depr., Dep., Amort./Cur. Mat. L/T/D						
.6	.8	.6	Fixed/Worth	.5	.6	.7	.9	1.3	.3
2.2	5.3	3.1		1.9	4.9	1.6	7.3	4.2	NM
-4.1	-2.1	-1.7		-2.2	-1.1	-2.5	-5.4	NM	-.6
.8	1.6	.8	Debt/Worth	.4	.8	1.0	1.3	2.2	1.8
3.2	8.9	5.0		4.2	6.6	2.8	7.0	6.8	NM
-6.4	-3.8	-3.6		-3.5	-3.1	-4.1	-7.7	NM	-2.4
116.1	95.7	92.7	% Profit Before Taxes/Tangible Net Worth	90.8	72.2	119.9		174.4	
(98) 47.8	(121) 46.6	(123) 50.4		(49) 51.4	(34) 39.1	(14) 71.6		(13) 65.3	
16.3	6.7	14.0		7.5	9.3	30.4		20.4	
28.2	23.2	30.1	% Profit Before Taxes/Total Assets	27.2	32.2	36.1	22.8	21.1	40.9
10.5	5.1	11.3		10.6	18.1	15.5	3.4	9.5	23.4
.0	-5.3	.5		-1.8	.5	5.1	-.5	1.3	3.1
23.7	22.4	25.3	Sales/Net Fixed Assets	23.6	31.8	38.6	13.5	17.9	34.1
9.9	9.3	10.1		9.1	10.9	10.7	8.1	9.0	17.1
4.6	3.8	4.7		2.4	4.1	6.8	3.3	7.3	7.4
6.8	6.8	6.0	Sales/Total Assets	5.5	8.0	6.8	3.3	5.6	5.2
4.0	3.9	3.6		2.8	4.2	4.3	2.7	4.5	3.0
1.9	2.2	1.7		1.1	2.0	1.8	1.8	3.5	1.5
1.1	.9	1.0	% Depr., Dep., Amort./Sales	1.4	.9	.4	1.3	1.3	1.0
(111) 2.2	(152) 2.1	(158) 1.8		(44) 2.6	(57) 1.8	(19) 1.2	(11) 2.8	1.7	1.7
3.6	3.8	3.5		5.4	3.5	1.7	5.0	3.3	2.5
2.7	3.8	2.3	% Officers', Directors' Owners' Comp/Sales	3.2	2.6				
(69) 4.6	(98) 6.0	(86) 4.6		(33) 8.0	(31) 5.1				
10.0	10.5	11.2		14.8	10.6				
2112820M	1604397M	2788639M	Net Sales ($)	28329M	115775M	84868M	96315M	248030M	2215322M
816099M	651221M	711407M	Total Assets ($)	20835M	49317M	29014M	54887M	59189M	498165M

M = $ thousand   MM = $ million
See Pages 9 through 22 for Explanation of Ratios and Data

Current Data Sorted by Assets   Comparative Historical Data

0-500M	500M-2MM	2-10MM	10-50MM	50-100MM	100-250MM	Type of Statement	ALL 4/1/05-3/31/06	ALL 4/1/06-3/31/07
4						Unqualified	5	9
4	6	15	2		2	Reviewed	23	25
15	32	25	5			Compiled	93	106
63	75	22		1	1	Tax Returns	88	108
14	29	28	5	3	1	Other	85	77
	68 (4/1-9/30/09)		294 (10/1/09-3/31/10)				294	325
100	142	95	17	4	4	**NUMBER OF STATEMENTS**	294	325
%	%	%	%	%	%	**ASSETS**	%	%
14.7	12.6	8.8	8.5			Cash & Equivalents	10.2	10.7
19.8	14.3	7.7	8.1			Trade Receivables (net)	15.3	15.3
7.1	3.7	3.2	7.6			Inventory	3.7	5.1
2.9	2.0	1.9	2.9			All Other Current	2.2	2.5
44.6	32.6	21.6	27.1			Total Current	31.4	33.6
36.2	44.6	47.7	35.1			Fixed Assets (net)	42.7	41.7
9.2	10.7	9.3	8.2			Intangibles (net)	9.9	9.7
10.0	12.1	21.4	29.6			All Other Non-Current	15.9	15.1
100.0	100.0	100.0	100.0			Total	100.0	100.0
						LIABILITIES		
13.4	2.7	1.6	.3			Notes Payable-Short Term	5.2	4.7
8.6	4.0	2.8	2.2			Cur. Mat.-L.T.D.	4.6	4.1
9.3	5.1	3.4	3.1			Trade Payables	6.7	6.3
.2	.1	.3	.1			Income Taxes Payable	.3	.2
9.3	8.0	5.7	6.0			All Other Current	7.5	9.5
40.8	19.9	13.7	11.7			Total Current	24.2	24.8
30.5	47.2	42.2	28.0			Long-Term Debt	39.2	42.6
.0	.0	.4	.1			Deferred Taxes	.2	.1
12.8	5.8	12.3	19.8			All Other Non-Current	13.9	10.9
15.9	27.1	31.3	40.3			Net Worth	22.6	21.6
100.0	100.0	100.0	100.0			Total Liabilities & Net Worth	100.0	100.0
						INCOME DATA		
100.0	100.0	100.0	100.0			Net Sales	100.0	100.0
						Gross Profit		
94.0	91.2	90.3	86.7			Operating Expenses	93.4	92.7
6.0	8.8	9.7	13.3			Operating Profit	6.6	7.3
1.5	2.4	3.9	3.1			All Other Expenses (net)	2.6	2.3
4.5	6.4	5.7	10.2			Profit Before Taxes	4.0	5.0
						RATIOS		
3.6	5.0	3.7	5.1			Current	3.3	3.5
1.4	2.1	1.5	2.0				1.5	1.6
.6	1.0	.6	.9				.7	.8
2.7	4.1	2.7	4.3			Quick	2.5	2.8
1.1	1.7	1.2	1.0				1.2	1.3
.4	.9	.4	.5				.5	.5
5 72.2	18 20.3	18 20.7	15 25.0			Sales/Receivables	17 20.9	14 26.2
21 17.0	29 12.8	32 11.5	35 10.5				34 10.8	31 11.9
38 9.6	46 8.0	41 8.8	55 6.6				48 7.6	46 7.9
						Cost of Sales/Inventory		
						Cost of Sales/Payables		
7.5	5.4	6.3	2.5			Sales/Working Capital	6.1	5.9
44.0	11.8	16.6	6.9				18.0	16.3
-21.4	143.1	-15.6	NM				-19.9	-27.2
9.0	7.5	4.3	314.2			EBIT/Interest	5.3	6.2
(72) 3.6	(124) 2.8	(86) 2.2	(10) 2.6				(249) 2.3	(269) 2.4
.9	1.3	1.3	1.9				.8	1.0
		3.0				Net Profit + Depr., Dep., Amort./Cur. Mat. L/T/D	4.0	3.9
	(20) 1.0						(44) 2.0	(40) 1.7
		.6					1.0	1.2
.4	.6	.8	.4			Fixed/Worth	.7	.6
1.5	1.9	2.4	.8				2.0	1.7
-1.2	-12.4	-33.5	3.5				-3.1	-5.5
.5	.7	1.0	.6			Debt/Worth	.9	.8
2.5	3.8	2.8	3.4				3.4	2.9
-4.5	-17.2	-76.9	6.0				-8.7	-13.0
78.0	45.6	24.9	26.2			% Profit Before Taxes/Tangible Net Worth	32.8	38.5
(63) 33.3	(103) 16.7	(69) 11.4	(15) 9.3				(198) 11.9	(231) 14.6
12.9	2.6	2.9	5.3				.0	1.1
25.0	13.5	8.1	5.3			% Profit Before Taxes/Total Assets	11.1	12.4
10.7	5.7	4.2	3.9				2.9	4.8
.2	.4	.4	1.9				-1.0	-.4
27.1	8.6	4.7	4.5			Sales/Net Fixed Assets	8.1	10.1
11.2	4.6	1.6	1.9				4.4	5.0
5.1	1.5	1.0	1.0				1.7	1.9
4.4	2.2	1.2	.9			Sales/Total Assets	2.3	2.6
3.1	1.5	.8	.4				1.5	1.5
1.7	.9	.5	.3				.7	.8
1.1	2.1	2.5	1.9			% Depr., Dep., Amort./Sales	2.3	2.0
(83) 1.9	(129) 3.9	(88) 4.2	(15) 5.7				(270) 3.9	(278) 3.3
3.8	7.0	6.5	6.9				6.3	6.0
5.6	6.6	5.9				% Officers', Directors' Owners' Comp/Sales	6.9	6.9
(62) 9.0	(102) 10.1	(44) 9.3					(191) 10.7	(197) 10.4
13.1	15.8	13.9					16.0	15.3
83242M	223888M	339480M	218135M	189397M	713642M	Net Sales ($)	606298M	919950M
26154M	142547M	382766M	340424M	251829M	447990M	Total Assets ($)	655378M	1089380M

M = $ thousand   MM = $ million
See Pages 9 through 22 for Explanation of Ratios and Data

Comparative Historical Data   Current Data Sorted by Sales

				Type of Statement						
5		11	14	Unqualified	5	3	1		3	2
26		32	29	Reviewed	3	11	6	5	2	2
77		85	77	Compiled	21	39	9	7	1	
123		133	162	Tax Returns	73	72	12	3		2
74		81	80	Other	22	33	12	8	3	2
	4/1/07-3/31/08 ALL	4/1/08-3/31/09 ALL	4/1/09-3/31/10 ALL		68 (4/1-9/30/09)		294 (10/1/09-3/31/10)			
					0-1MM	1-3MM	3-5MM	5-10MM	10-25MM	25MM & OVER
	305	342	362	NUMBER OF STATEMENTS	124	158	40	23	9	8
	%	%	%	ASSETS	%	%	%	%	%	%
	10.7	11.0	11.8	Cash & Equivalents	10.3	12.9	13.2	11.9		
	15.2	13.6	13.8	Trade Receivables (net)	12.8	15.1	13.2	10.9		
	4.9	5.4	4.7	Inventory	5.5	4.0	4.2	4.8		
	2.4	3.4	2.2	All Other Current	3.0	1.3	3.4	2.4		
	33.2	33.5	32.5	Total Current	31.7	33.3	34.0	30.0		
	41.3	43.6	42.2	Fixed Assets (net)	46.2	41.7	40.8	30.3		
	9.6	7.4	10.0	Intangibles (net)	9.1	10.9	8.6	9.8		
	15.9	15.5	15.3	All Other Non-Current	13.0	14.1	16.5	30.0		
	100.0	100.0	100.0	Total	100.0	100.0	100.0	100.0		
				LIABILITIES						
	5.8	6.1	5.2	Notes Payable-Short Term	8.2	3.5	6.3	1.3		
	4.0	4.8	4.9	Cur. Mat.-L.T.D.	7.9	3.3	3.2	3.8		
	7.3	6.5	5.7	Trade Payables	5.6	5.9	6.0	4.3		
	.2	.2	.2	Income Taxes Payable	.1	.1	.3	.6		
	11.4	10.7	7.7	All Other Current	8.6	7.7	6.0	5.2		
	28.7	28.3	23.7	Total Current	30.4	20.4	21.8	15.1		
	39.4	40.4	39.9	Long-Term Debt	43.5	39.3	38.7	36.1		
	.1	.1	.1	Deferred Taxes	.0	.2	.3	.4		
	12.6	12.3	10.9	All Other Non-Current	13.5	7.8	9.1	17.2		
	19.1	19.0	25.4	Net Worth	12.6	32.3	30.0	31.3		
	100.0	100.0	100.0	Total Liabilties & Net Worth	100.0	100.0	100.0	100.0		
				INCOME DATA						
	100.0	100.0	100.0	Net Sales	100.0	100.0	100.0	100.0		
				Gross Profit						
	92.4	91.5	91.5	Operating Expenses	89.2	92.2	96.1	91.8		
	7.6	8.5	8.5	Operating Profit	10.8	7.8	3.9	8.2		
	2.8	2.7	2.6	All Other Expenses (net)	4.4	2.0	1.3	.3		
	4.8	5.8	6.0	Profit Before Taxes	6.4	5.8	2.6	8.0		
				RATIOS						
	3.3	3.1	3.9		4.3	3.6	4.8	6.3		
	1.7	1.5	1.7	Current	1.4	1.9	2.3	1.2		
	.8	.7	.8		.6	1.0	1.2	.6		
	2.6	2.3	3.2		2.9	3.2	3.7	3.7		
(304)	1.2	1.1	1.4	Quick	1.2	1.6	1.2	1.1		
	.5	.5	.6		.3	.8	.8	.5		
12	29.6 10	37.5 15	24.3		7 49.5	17 21.9	19 19.2	20 18.0		
30	12.2 26	13.9 29	12.8	Sales/Receivables	28 13.0	27 13.4	30 12.2	35 10.5		
44	8.3 43	8.4 44	8.2		48 7.6	41 8.9	47 7.7	41 8.8		
				Cost of Sales/Inventory						
				Cost of Sales/Payables						
	5.9	6.2	5.8		6.1	5.9	5.2	4.1		
	16.8	20.3	15.7	Sales/Working Capital	25.0	16.0	7.8	35.0		
	-35.9	-20.5	-40.7		-16.2	213.2	39.6	-22.8		
	6.1	8.5	7.1		4.8	8.2	2.9	19.5		
(245)	2.2 (281)	2.6 (299)	2.7	EBIT/Interest	(92) 4.8... 2.2	(135) 3.5	(35) 2.1	(22) 3.7		
	1.0	1.3	1.3		.9	1.3	.9	1.8		
	3.5	2.5	2.9			2.6				
(43)	1.4 (45)	1.3 (33)	1.2	Net Profit + Depr., Dep., Amort./Cur. Mat. L/T/D		(15) 1.7				
	.7	.9	.7			.7				
	.6	.5	.6		.8	.6	.6	.4		
	1.8	1.8	1.9	Fixed/Worth	5.1	1.7	1.4	1.4		
	-8.7	-5.6	-6.4		-2.6	-151.2	-17.0	-57.0		
	.8	.7	.8		1.0	.7	.6	.8		
	2.8	2.6	3.4	Debt/Worth	6.4	1.8	2.5	2.3		
	-13.9	-16.0	-14.8		-5.4	-249.3	-30.2	-347.6		
	43.7	43.3	43.8		66.2	43.2	16.6	26.3		
(214)	13.8 (239)	15.9 (253)	17.6	% Profit Before Taxes/Tangible Net Worth	(77) 27.5	(118) 16.5	(29) 6.7	(17) 15.1		
	1.1	3.8	5.3		10.7	5.8	-1.4	8.7		
	13.1	14.4	12.9		13.7	14.2	7.1	15.6		
	4.7	5.3	5.4	% Profit Before Taxes/Total Assets	6.5	6.0	1.8	5.9		
	-.4	1.0	.7		-.1	1.0	-.9	3.1		
	10.8	10.3	11.0		11.3	11.5	10.4	11.9		
	5.2	4.5	4.6	Sales/Net Fixed Assets	4.3	5.0	4.7	4.2		
	1.8	1.6	1.5		1.2	1.6	1.6	2.3		
	2.7	2.7	2.4		2.8	2.8	2.3	2.0		
	1.6	1.6	1.4	Sales/Total Assets	1.3	1.7	1.5	1.2		
	.7	.7	.7		.6	.8	.9	.7		
	1.8	2.0	1.7		1.9	1.5	2.3	1.3		
(274)	3.2 (301)	3.3 (320)	3.4	% Depr., Dep., Amort./Sales	(105) 4.6	(147) 3.2	(33) 3.1	(21) 2.8		
	5.6	6.0	6.2		8.3	5.9	4.2	4.0		
	7.1	6.9	6.2		6.1	6.2	6.0	5.9		
(200)	10.5 (192)	9.5 (214)	9.6	% Officers', Directors' Owners' Comp/Sales	(68) 9.4	(105) 9.8	(26) 10.5	(11) 7.5		
	14.5	14.0	14.7		15.9	14.7	14.2	11.7		
	1738157M	1288233M	1767784M	Net Sales ($)	70892M	283419M	155742M	161239M	119363M	977129M
	1169469M	1332939M	1591710M	Total Assets ($)	78643M	284549M	190122M	211504M	223162M	603730M

M = $ thousand   MM = $ million
See Pages 9 through 22 for Explanation of Ratios and Data

Current Data Sorted by Assets							Comparative Historical Data	

Type of Statement

	0-500M	500M-2MM	2-10MM	10-50MM	50-100MM	100-250MM		
Unqualified			2	3	1	1	5	6
Reviewed	1		3	1		1	4	4
Compiled	2	2	5	1			10	10
Tax Returns	7	2					4	13
Other	2	4	8	5	2		7	18
		11 (4/1-9/30/09)		42 (10/1/09-3/31/10)			4/1/05-3/31/06 ALL	4/1/06-3/31/07 ALL
NUMBER OF STATEMENTS	12	8	18	10	3	2	30	51

ASSETS	%	%	%	%	%	%	%	%
Cash & Equivalents	14.6		9.7	8.7			8.1	10.3
Trade Receivables (net)	11.0		13.7	10.3			20.2	14.4
Inventory	6.2		7.1	8.4			9.2	12.8
All Other Current	.2		1.0	.9			1.9	2.6
Total Current	32.0		31.5	28.4			39.5	40.1
Fixed Assets (net)	52.8		40.3	32.7			39.7	32.3
Intangibles (net)	2.1		3.0	2.9			3.6	4.1
All Other Non-Current	13.2		25.3	36.0			17.2	23.5
Total	100.0		100.0	100.0			100.0	100.0

LIABILITIES								
Notes Payable-Short Term	12.5		2.1	3.7			7.0	8.4
Cur. Mat.-L.T.D.	2.2		2.5	3.5			3.8	4.7
Trade Payables	4.4		2.3	1.3			4.1	5.4
Income Taxes Payable	.0		.0	.0			.1	.2
All Other Current	41.6		12.8	11.6			9.0	6.2
Total Current	60.7		19.7	20.0			24.0	24.9
Long-Term Debt	28.3		22.7	12.6			21.4	24.5
Deferred Taxes	.0		.0	.0			.2	.1
All Other Non-Current	6.7		21.9	20.3			15.7	18.6
Net Worth	4.4		35.7	47.0			38.7	31.9
Total Liabilties & Net Worth	100.0		100.0	100.0			100.0	100.0

INCOME DATA								
Net Sales	100.0		100.0	100.0			100.0	100.0
Gross Profit								
Operating Expenses	90.8		90.4	87.7			93.6	87.9
Operating Profit	9.2		9.6	12.3			6.4	12.1
All Other Expenses (net)	-.3		1.1	8.8			.0	2.3
Profit Before Taxes	9.5		8.4	3.5			6.3	9.8

RATIOS								
Current	3.6 / 1.0 / .4		3.3 / 2.0 / .7	17.2 / 3.4 / .6			3.7 / 1.8 / .7	8.3 / 2.5 / 1.2
Quick	3.1 / .9 / .4		2.6 / 1.3 / .6	10.7 / 2.2 / .5			3.0 / 1.3 / .5	5.7 / 1.6 / .7
Sales/Receivables	0 UND / 18 19.8 / 47 7.8		29 12.4 / 54 6.7 / 234 1.6	53 6.8 / 125 2.9 / 204 1.8			17 21.2 / 53 6.9 / 134 2.7	21 17.2 / 58 6.3 / 118 3.1
Cost of Sales/Inventory								
Cost of Sales/Payables								
Sales/Working Capital	5.5 / NM / -4.7		2.9 / 7.7 / -2.3	1.0 / 4.3 / -2.0			1.9 / 7.4 / -26.3	1.2 / 4.3 / 23.6
EBIT/Interest			7.0 / (17) 3.4 / .9				14.6 / (25) 3.4 / .7	8.0 / (39) 3.4 / 1.7
Net Profit + Depr., Dep., Amort./Cur. Mat. L/T/D							6.9 / (11) 3.2 / 1.0	
Fixed/Worth	.5 / 3.4 / NM		.7 / 1.2 / 7.1	.3 / .8 / 1.7			.5 / .9 / 10.3	.4 / .9 / 4.7
Debt/Worth	.5 / 3.6 / NM		.4 / 3.6 / 47.4	.4 / 1.2 / 6.1			.5 / 1.1 / 13.2	.7 / 3.6 / 14.2
% Profit Before Taxes/Tangible Net Worth			26.6 / (15) 12.8 / -1.8				22.2 / (25) 10.5 / 1.2	51.2 / (44) 13.4 / 4.1
% Profit Before Taxes/Total Assets	26.8 / 7.3 / -.3		13.4 / 3.5 / .8	4.1 / 1.7 / -1.4			9.9 / 3.0 / -.4	8.5 / 4.4 / 1.4
Sales/Net Fixed Assets	6.6 / 4.0 / 1.0		3.5 / 1.1 / .7	1.9 / 1.2 / .3			5.8 / 2.4 / 1.3	6.1 / 2.4 / 1.1
Sales/Total Assets	2.6 / 1.4 / .6		1.0 / .4 / .2	.4 / .2 / .2			1.6 / .6 / .3	1.3 / .5 / .3
% Depr., Dep., Amort./Sales	3.4 / (10) 6.9 / 13.6		2.8 / (15) 4.4 / 8.1	3.9 / 5.8 / 8.5			1.9 / (26) 3.6 / 6.0	1.2 / (39) 2.8 / 4.1
% Officers', Directors' Owners' Comp/Sales								3.6 / (11) 7.6 / 16.1
Net Sales ($)	5462M	9219M	42261M	56031M	45518M	146924M	468739M	680762M
Total Assets ($)	3512M	9425M	93060M	192615M	208291M	302673M	461556M	846561M

Comparative Historical Data   Current Data Sorted by Sales

			Type of Statement						
7	7	7	Unqualified		4	1		1	1
7	10	6	Reviewed	1	1	2	1		1
9	8	10	Compiled	4	1	4	1		
11	10	9	Tax Returns	6	3				
20	18	21	Other	8	7	1	1	4	
4/1/07-3/31/08	4/1/08-3/31/09	4/1/09-3/31/10		11 (4/1-9/30/09)		42 (10/1/09-3/31/10)			
ALL	ALL	ALL		0-1MM	1-3MM	3-5MM	5-10MM	10-25MM	25MM & OVER
54	53	53	NUMBER OF STATEMENTS	19	16	8	3	5	2
%	%	%	ASSETS	%	%	%	%	%	%
10.6	9.5	9.4	Cash & Equivalents	10.7	9.8				
13.4	15.3	12.3	Trade Receivables (net)	11.6	12.8				
7.4	11.3	7.5	Inventory	5.9	7.2				
2.0	1.2	1.9	All Other Current	3.5	.5				
33.4	37.3	31.1	Total Current	31.7	30.4				
30.4	36.6	39.1	Fixed Assets (net)	46.3	41.3				
3.3	5.3	4.7	Intangibles (net)	5.1	5.3				
32.9	20.9	25.1	All Other Non-Current	17.0	23.1				
100.0	100.0	100.0	Total	100.0	100.0				
			LIABILITIES						
3.4	10.3	4.5	Notes Payable-Short Term	9.0	2.3				
1.6	2.2	2.6	Cur. Mat.-L.T.D.	1.9	3.1				
5.2	6.5	3.4	Trade Payables	4.1	3.7				
.1	.0	.0	Income Taxes Payable	.0	.0				
10.0	9.5	16.9	All Other Current	32.4	10.7				
20.2	28.5	27.3	Total Current	47.3	19.8				
26.3	23.7	21.3	Long-Term Debt	30.1	23.0				
.6	.7	.7	Deferred Taxes	1.8	.0				
25.3	18.1	20.0	All Other Non-Current	15.7	17.5				
27.6	29.1	30.7	Net Worth	5.0	39.6				
100.0	100.0	100.0	Total Liabilities & Net Worth	100.0	100.0				
			INCOME DATA						
100.0	100.0	100.0	Net Sales	100.0	100.0				
			Gross Profit						
90.7	95.0	90.3	Operating Expenses	93.1	88.2				
9.3	5.0	9.7	Operating Profit	6.9	11.8				
2.1	1.8	2.1	All Other Expenses (net)	.5	4.7				
7.2	3.2	7.6	Profit Before Taxes	6.4	7.2				
			RATIOS						
6.0	6.0	4.9		2.6	7.0				
2.7	2.4	2.4	Current	.8	1.9				
1.5	.9	.7		.4	.8				
4.9	3.1	3.3		1.6	3.7				
1.6	1.4	1.4	Quick	.6	1.4				
.8	.6	.6		.4	.7				
24 15.5	13 27.5	24 15.1		16 22.5	42 8.7				
58 6.3	55 6.7	59 6.2	Sales/Receivables	49 7.5	58 6.3				
127 2.9	164 2.2	133 2.8		111 3.3	175 2.1				
			Cost of Sales/Inventory						
			Cost of Sales/Payables						
1.6	1.7	1.9		2.1	2.3				
4.5	6.3	6.6	Sales/Working Capital	-58.4	8.0				
11.1	-76.0	-5.6		-4.2	-6.3				
6.0	4.9	5.7		4.1	14.8				
(46) 2.7	(43) 1.9	(44) 3.3	EBIT/Interest	(16) 1.6	(13) 3.6				
1.2	.3	.9		.3	1.4				
6.0			Net Profit + Depr., Dep.,						
(11) 4.9			Amort./Cur. Mat. L/T/D						
1.7									
.4	.6	.6		1.0	.8				
1.1	1.0	1.2	Fixed/Worth	4.0	1.2				
6.5	13.2	6.1		-2.2	6.8				
.5	.7	.4		1.5	.4				
3.7	4.4	2.9	Debt/Worth	6.0	1.8				
26.7	23.4	11.1		-5.3	9.7				
27.9	24.3	29.7	% Profit Before Taxes/Tangible	59.3	40.7				
(46) 12.7	(42) 4.4	(43) 13.1	Net Worth	(13) 12.0	(13) 29.7				
2.9	-2.2	1.1		-6.0	-.3				
7.0	5.8	11.4	% Profit Before Taxes/Total	7.4	18.0				
3.4	1.9	3.7	Assets	1.8	5.3				
1.1	-.9	.4		-1.3	-.2				
4.9	6.1	3.9		4.6	3.4				
2.5	2.4	1.8	Sales/Net Fixed Assets	3.1	.9				
1.0	1.2	.8		.7	.5				
1.3	1.7	1.1		1.2	1.4				
.4	.6	.5	Sales/Total Assets	.5	.4				
.3	.3	.3		.4	.2				
2.2	2.5	3.3		3.2	4.8				
(47) 3.3	(42) 4.6	(45) 4.7	% Depr., Dep., Amort./Sales	(16) 4.4	(12) 8.3				
7.8	7.5	8.3		9.0	11.5				
5.9	2.4	4.0	% Officers', Directors'						
(13) 13.4	(16) 5.6	(12) 11.1	Owners' Comp/Sales						
20.0	11.3	16.5							
616609M	381292M	305415M	Net Sales ($)	9369M	30073M	30663M	19361M	69025M	146924M
1179193M	914359M	809576M	Total Assets ($)	23798M	107212M	75980M	62146M	237767M	302673M

M = $ thousand   MM = $ million
See Pages 9 through 22 for Explanation of Ratios and Data

OTHER SERVICES—Coin-Operated Laundries and Drycleaners NAICS 812310

Current Data Sorted by Assets   **Comparative Historical Data**

Type of Statement	0-500M	500M-2MM	2-10MM	10-50MM	50-100MM	100-250MM		4/1/05-3/31/06 ALL	4/1/06-3/31/07 ALL
Unqualified		2	4	1	1			3	2
Reviewed		1	1	1				2	2
Compiled	3	11	2	1				14	15
Tax Returns	20	3	8	1		1		35	34
Other	7			3				30	17
		12 (4/1-9/30/09)		59 (10/1/09-3/31/10)					
NUMBER OF STATEMENTS	30	17	15	7	7	1		84	70
	%	%	%	%	%	%		%	%
ASSETS									
Cash & Equivalents	17.1	5.6	11.5					11.6	12.8
Trade Receivables (net)	1.3	5.9	7.7					2.7	1.6
Inventory	1.5	.6	3.0					5.3	1.8
All Other Current	2.2	7.6	2.0					1.2	1.8
Total Current	22.1	19.6	24.2					20.9	18.0
Fixed Assets (net)	62.9	61.8	57.0					65.5	66.8
Intangibles (net)	1.8	14.3	9.4					7.5	8.5
All Other Non-Current	13.2	4.3	9.4					6.1	6.6
Total	100.0	100.0	100.0					100.0	100.0
LIABILITIES									
Notes Payable-Short Term	9.1	5.6	7.2					5.7	5.8
Cur. Mat.-L.T.D.	4.2	11.8	5.3					6.3	10.7
Trade Payables	2.7	3.8	6.2					4.8	4.3
Income Taxes Payable	.3	.0	.4					.0	.0
All Other Current	6.1	6.6	5.1					6.8	7.4
Total Current	22.4	27.7	24.2					23.6	28.2
Long-Term Debt	73.2	71.8	39.2					48.8	47.8
Deferred Taxes	.0	.4	.2					.4	.0
All Other Non-Current	9.4	7.0	9.5					7.1	8.7
Net Worth	-5.0	-6.8	26.8					20.1	15.3
Total Liabilties & Net Worth	100.0	100.0	100.0					100.0	100.0
INCOME DATA									
Net Sales	100.0	100.0	100.0					100.0	100.0
Gross Profit									
Operating Expenses	93.3	92.5	94.0					90.5	91.1
Operating Profit	6.7	7.5	6.0					9.5	8.9
All Other Expenses (net)	3.5	6.4	2.9					3.9	4.6
Profit Before Taxes	3.1	1.1	3.1					5.6	4.3
RATIOS									
Current	4.5	2.0	7.4					2.9	1.7
	.8	.4	.9					1.0	.5
	.2	.2	.2					.3	.1
Quick	2.1	.5	5.5					1.7	1.3
	.5	.3	.7					(83) .7	.5
	.2	.1	.2					.2	.1
Sales/Receivables	0 UND	0 UND	0 UND					0 UND	0 UND
	0 UND	0 981.0	1 300.6					0 UND	0 UND
	0 UND	9 41.3	22 16.6					5 72.2	1 321.5
Cost of Sales/Inventory									
Cost of Sales/Payables									
Sales/Working Capital	11.0	12.5	6.0					17.7	27.4
	-57.8	-14.7	-75.0					UND	-28.5
	-10.8	-4.4	-6.1					-16.2	-5.9
EBIT/Interest	8.7	4.4	2.7					6.9	7.3
	(20) 1.7	(14) 1.7	(12) 1.1					(73) 3.2	(58) 2.6
	.6	-.6	-.4					1.0	.7
Net Profit + Depr., Dep., Amort./Cur. Mat. L/T/D									
Fixed/Worth	.7	5.0	.6					1.1	1.2
	3.5	-10.7	3.7					3.6	3.0
	-2.1	-1.2	-4.7					-3.3	-15.8
Debt/Worth	.3	6.0	.6					.9	1.0
	3.6	-13.8	3.2					3.1	3.9
	-3.8	-2.2	-6.0					-5.9	-15.5
% Profit Before Taxes/Tangible Net Worth	53.5		50.9					57.0	51.7
	(18) 11.9		(10) 15.4					(54) 18.4	(48) 19.0
	-15.7		-5.4					1.4	1.5
% Profit Before Taxes/Total Assets	24.5	12.6	7.1					22.1	17.9
	6.5	1.5	.7					6.4	4.6
	-3.6	-5.1	-3.3					-.6	-1.5
Sales/Net Fixed Assets	7.1	5.7	7.7					5.8	5.5
	2.5	2.7	2.3					2.0	2.5
	.9	1.1	.7					1.2	1.0
Sales/Total Assets	2.4	2.4	2.2					2.6	2.5
	1.4	1.1	1.7					1.5	1.5
	.8	.7	.6					.7	.8
% Depr., Dep., Amort./Sales	2.8	4.7	4.7					4.8	4.3
	(25) 5.8	(16) 7.6	(13) 8.1					(76) 8.7	(59) 10.4
	18.8	22.8	16.9					14.2	15.6
% Officers', Directors' Owners' Comp/Sales		1.5						2.0	2.6
		(11) 4.5						(34) 5.5	(31) 6.7
		6.7						8.2	10.3
Net Sales ($)	10754M	27300M	103228M	228796M	19774M	183078M		684110M	736431M
Total Assets ($)	6119M	18480M	61979M	147793M	63537M	203408M		408360M	446299M

M = $ thousand   MM = $ million
See Pages 9 through 22 for Explanation of Ratios and Data

Comparative Historical Data   Current Data Sorted by Sales

	3 4/1/07-3/31/08 ALL	1 4/1/08-3/31/09 ALL	2 4/1/09-3/31/10 ALL	Type of Statement	0-1MM	1-3MM	3-5MM	5-10MM	10-25MM	25MM & OVER
	3	1	2	Unqualified						
	4	4	7	Reviewed		2	1	1	2	
	13	18	6	Compiled	2	2			3	
	18	32	35	Tax Returns	27	4	1	1		2
	29	14	21	Other	8	3	4	1	3	2
					12 (4/1-9/30/09)		59 (10/1/09-3/31/10)			
NUMBER OF STATEMENTS	67	69	71		37	11	6	4	9	4
	%	%	%	**ASSETS**	%	%	%	%	%	%
	14.4	11.6	11.7	Cash & Equivalents	13.6	9.9				
	4.0	2.7	3.9	Trade Receivables (net)	2.1	1.2				
	2.9	3.3	1.7	Inventory	1.3	.4				
	1.0	2.4	3.9	All Other Current	1.9	8.9				
	22.3	19.9	21.2	Total Current	18.8	20.4				
	59.8	62.6	61.0	Fixed Assets (net)	67.9	50.3				
	10.2	7.5	8.0	Intangibles (net)	2.9	24.1				
	7.6	10.0	9.7	All Other Non-Current	10.4	5.2				
	100.0	100.0	100.0	Total	100.0	100.0				
				LIABILITIES						
	5.9	7.5	6.7	Notes Payable-Short Term	8.5	7.1				
	8.3	9.2	7.5	Cur. Mat.-L.T.D.	5.3	10.2				
	3.4	3.7	4.0	Trade Payables	2.4	2.9				
	.1	.1	.2	Income Taxes Payable	.2	.0				
	18.9	11.4	6.1	All Other Current	4.6	11.2				
	36.6	32.0	24.5	Total Current	21.0	31.4				
	51.1	45.5	60.2	Long-Term Debt	81.6	44.1				
	.1	.1	.2	Deferred Taxes	.0	.0				
	8.3	6.7	8.2	All Other Non-Current	7.9	19.7				
	3.9	15.8	6.9	Net Worth	-10.5	4.9				
	100.0	100.0	100.0	Total Liabilities & Net Worth	100.0	100.0				
				INCOME DATA						
	100.0	100.0	100.0	Net Sales	100.0	100.0				
				Gross Profit						
	92.0	90.4	93.4	Operating Expenses	91.8	94.9				
	8.0	9.6	6.6	Operating Profit	8.2	5.1				
	4.3	4.2	4.1	All Other Expenses (net)	5.5	3.2				
	3.6	5.3	2.5	Profit Before Taxes	2.7	1.9				
				RATIOS						
	2.2	2.3	2.8	Current	5.3	.9				
	.9	.6	.8		.7	.3				
	.3	.2	.2		.2	.2				
	1.9	1.8	1.5	Quick	3.8	.4				
	.6	.4	.4		.4	.3				
	.1	.1	.2		.2	.1				
	0 UND	0 UND	0 UND	Sales/Receivables	0 UND	0 UND				
	0 UND	0 UND	0 UND		0 UND	2 156.5				
	4 94.1	2 157.5	7 51.8		0 UND	8 45.8				
				Cost of Sales/Inventory						
				Cost of Sales/Payables						
	23.3	23.2	8.9	Sales/Working Capital	8.9	-130.8				
	-148.8	-22.6	-71.0		-71.0	-8.8				
	-7.0	-4.6	-6.7		-7.9	-3.9				
	5.2	5.9	4.6	EBIT/Interest	6.6	5.3				
	(60) 2.1	(55) 1.9	(53) 1.6		(25) 1.8	(10) 1.4				
	.7	1.0	.6		-.2	.6				
				Net Profit + Depr., Dep., Amort./Cur. Mat. L/T/D						
	1.4	.9	.8	Fixed/Worth	.8	2.4				
	6.1	10.4	6.3		13.7	-60.7				
	-4.8	-4.1	-2.5		-1.6	-.6				
	.9	.7	.7	Debt/Worth	.4	8.6				
	6.5	11.0	8.5		21.4	-77.2				
	-6.7	-6.0	-4.2		-2.7	-1.6				
	86.4	49.8	53.9	% Profit Before Taxes/Tangible Net Worth	53.2					
	(40) 19.2	(37) 17.4	(41) 19.6		(19) 15.9					
	6.4	2.5	-7.2		-8.3					
	22.5	16.0	12.8	% Profit Before Taxes/Total Assets	16.2	17.5				
	6.7	3.6	3.6		5.5	1.1				
	-1.9	-.8	-3.3		-4.0	-2.5				
	7.3	5.7	6.5	Sales/Net Fixed Assets	5.4	6.8				
	3.0	2.4	2.4		1.5	3.1				
	1.2	1.4	1.1		.8	1.6				
	3.9	2.4	2.2	Sales/Total Assets	1.9	2.6				
	1.7	1.4	1.4		1.2	1.5				
	.8	.8	.7		.7	.7				
	6.5	4.6	4.5	% Depr., Dep., Amort./Sales	3.4	4.9				
	(53) 10.5	(65) 9.1	(62) 8.0		(31) 8.3	(10) 6.8				
	18.0	16.6	15.8		25.6	13.1				
	2.7	3.1	2.6	% Officers', Directors' Owners' Comp/Sales	3.3					
	(34) 4.8	(22) 6.5	(29) 4.4		(11) 5.3					
	8.3	9.3	7.7		12.2					
	310700M	482924M	572930M	Net Sales ($)	13324M	20291M	22754M	27382M	141153M	348026M
	201196M	329551M	501316M	Total Assets ($)	15019M	14237M	19159M	15027M	149356M	288518M

Current Data Sorted by Assets

Comparative Historical Data

						Type of Statement		
		5	7			Unqualified	8	10
1		8	2			Reviewed	9	16
7	12	11	1			Compiled	33	30
26	22	7	3			Tax Returns	49	56
11	14	10	4			Other	53	37
	22 (4/1-9/30/09)		129 (10/1/09-3/31/10)				4/1/05-3/31/06	4/1/06-3/31/07
0-500M	500M-2MM	2-10MM	10-50MM	50-100MM	100-250MM		ALL	ALL
45	48	41	17			NUMBER OF STATEMENTS	152	149
%	%	%	%	%	%	ASSETS	%	%
14.9	5.5	8.8	15.6	D	D	Cash & Equivalents	11.3	12.8
8.9	10.7	12.5	9.9	A	A	Trade Receivables (net)	9.8	11.0
2.5	1.7	4.9	4.4	T	T	Inventory	3.7	2.9
2.8	2.4	2.5	1.0	A	A	All Other Current	2.4	2.7
29.0	20.2	28.7	30.9			Total Current	27.2	29.4
50.3	59.0	47.6	53.8	N	N	Fixed Assets (net)	47.9	49.0
11.7	12.7	10.8	4.9	O	O	Intangibles (net)	12.9	9.9
8.8	8.0	12.8	10.4	T	T	All Other Non-Current	11.9	11.8
100.0	100.0	100.0	100.0			Total	100.0	100.0
				A	A	LIABILITIES		
14.2	7.8	6.1	.6	V	V	Notes Payable-Short Term	8.5	5.4
10.3	10.5	7.5	3.3	A	A	Cur. Mat.-L.T.D.	6.4	7.8
3.7	5.3	4.6	5.8	I	I	Trade Payables	6.5	6.9
.0	.1	.0	.3	L	L	Income Taxes Payable	.2	.2
26.2	8.9	13.0	8.6	A	A	All Other Current	11.9	8.4
54.4	32.7	31.3	18.7	B	B	Total Current	33.5	28.8
48.3	56.0	32.1	24.3	L	L	Long-Term Debt	44.3	43.8
.0	.0	.2	.8	E	E	Deferred Taxes	.3	.3
17.1	9.5	5.0	11.6			All Other Non-Current	10.1	6.2
-19.9	1.9	31.4	44.6			Net Worth	11.9	20.9
100.0	100.0	100.0	100.0			Total Liabilities & Net Worth	100.0	100.0
						INCOME DATA		
100.0	100.0	100.0	100.0			Net Sales	100.0	100.0
						Gross Profit		
94.9	90.9	92.9	90.7			Operating Expenses	93.2	91.6
5.1	9.1	7.1	9.3			Operating Profit	6.8	8.4
1.1	6.2	1.7	2.7			All Other Expenses (net)	2.8	3.5
3.9	2.9	5.4	6.7			Profit Before Taxes	4.0	4.9
						RATIOS		
1.9	1.1	2.3	2.7				2.1	2.8
.9	.5	1.1	1.6			Current	1.0	1.2
.4	.2	.5	1.0				.3	.6
1.8	.9	2.1	2.1				1.6	2.1
.7	.5	.7	1.1			Quick	.8	1.0
.2	.2	.4	.9				.2	.4
0 UND	0 UND	8 44.3	13 28.2				0 UND	0 UND
0 UND	4 90.8	22 16.9	25 14.6			Sales/Receivables	7 52.6	8 45.9
14 25.4	31 11.7	36 10.2	39 9.4				26 13.9	26 14.3
						Cost of Sales/Inventory		
						Cost of Sales/Payables		
19.4	43.9	11.0	6.8				17.3	12.0
-481.0	-15.4	72.5	16.7			Sales/Working Capital	UND	80.1
-17.9	-6.6	-18.9	NM				-13.2	-24.4
8.7	2.6	6.9	11.2				7.0	9.0
(36) 2.5	(39) 1.5	(38) 3.2	(16) 3.8			EBIT/Interest	(128) 2.7	(122) 3.3
-.3	.5	.9	2.1				1.3	1.2
						Net Profit + Depr., Dep., Amort./Cur. Mat. L/T/D	9.4	4.0
							(10) 3.0	(13) 1.9
							1.9	1.3
1.0	1.9	.6	.7				.9	.7
-8.6	NM	2.7	1.5			Fixed/Worth	2.6	2.1
-.9	-.8	-16.5	2.9				-1.7	-8.5
.8	2.6	.7	.8				.9	.9
-10.1	NM	3.5	1.1			Debt/Worth	4.0	2.8
-2.2	-2.6	-59.1	3.1				-3.7	-13.0
76.1	60.9	66.2	24.6				78.6	86.0
(20) 30.7	(24) 12.1	(29) 29.0	(15) 15.1			% Profit Before Taxes/Tangible Net Worth	(91) 21.8	(106) 31.0
-11.2	-.8	1.4	6.1				8.7	12.7
32.6	8.5	17.0	11.5				17.1	23.1
11.1	2.3	6.9	7.8			% Profit Before Taxes/Total Assets	5.6	7.5
-5.7	-.5	-.7	3.2				.6	1.1
16.2	8.8	6.2	6.1				11.3	13.7
8.2	4.4	4.9	3.1			Sales/Net Fixed Assets	5.7	5.7
4.8	.8	2.2	1.3				3.0	2.2
5.7	3.6	2.5	1.7				3.7	3.7
3.7	1.7	1.9	1.4			Sales/Total Assets	2.4	2.4
1.9	.6	1.2	1.0				1.2	1.2
1.4	3.1	3.7	3.7				2.4	2.5
(38) 3.1	(44) 6.3	(36) 4.9	4.3			% Depr., Dep., Amort./Sales	(133) 4.3	(131) 4.6
8.7	9.9	8.4	6.5				7.2	7.3
4.6	1.6	.9					3.1	3.8
(29) 7.3	(25) 4.4	(15) 3.7				% Officers', Directors' Owners' Comp/Sales	(78) 5.6	(79) 5.7
11.6	8.2	5.1					10.3	9.4
37545M	112345M	314588M	515058M			Net Sales ($)	662954M	1008293M
10080M	52133M	179183M	319853M			Total Assets ($)	354234M	446613M

M = $ thousand   MM = $ million
See Pages 9 through 22 for Explanation of Ratios and Data

Comparative Historical Data — Current Data Sorted by Sales

7	13	12	Type of Statement						
							4	5	3
17	17	11	Unqualified / Reviewed	1	1	1	5	3	
22	28	31	Compiled	8	7	8	5	2	1
55	63	58	Tax Returns	27	19	4	4	2	2
35	37	39	Other	12	8	1	11	6	1
4/1/07-3/31/08 ALL	4/1/08-3/31/09 ALL	4/1/09-3/31/10 ALL		22 (4/1-9/30/09)			129 (10/1/09-3/31/10)		
				0-1MM	1-3MM	3-5MM	5-10MM	10-25MM	25MM & OV
136	158	151	NUMBER OF STATEMENTS	48	35	14	29	18	7
%	%	%	ASSETS	%	%	%	%	%	%
11.8	9.4	10.3	Cash & Equivalents	9.2	10.7	11.9	8.7	10.1	
10.2	10.1	10.6	Trade Receivables (net)	5.1	11.7	15.9	13.2	13.7	
2.4	3.1	3.1	Inventory	1.7	1.5	1.5	6.4	5.6	
2.3	2.0	2.4	All Other Current	2.6	1.8	4.4	2.4	2.0	
26.7	24.6	26.4	Total Current	18.5	25.7	33.7	30.7	31.2	
53.4	51.3	52.8	Fixed Assets (net)	58.1	53.4	50.2	48.1	52.7	
10.2	11.5	11.0	Intangibles (net)	15.0	12.1	4.6	10.6	4.5	
9.6	12.6	9.8	All Other Non-Current	8.3	8.7	11.5	10.6	11.5	
100.0	100.0	100.0	Total	100.0	100.0	100.0	100.0	100.0	
			LIABILITIES						
5.8	5.6	8.4	Notes Payable-Short Term	10.6	8.0	13.0	8.4	2.9	
9.4	8.1	8.8	Cur. Mat.-L.T.D.	8.2	10.9	10.5	9.8	5.7	
5.0	5.5	4.7	Trade Payables	2.2	3.8	10.0	6.6	5.1	
.2	.2	.1	Income Taxes Payable	.0	.1	.1	.0	.2	
9.8	9.8	15.2	All Other Current	23.3	10.3	23.2	8.9	8.5	
30.1	29.2	37.2	Total Current	44.3	33.2	56.9	33.6	22.3	
42.7	41.5	43.6	Long-Term Debt	55.0	51.7	41.2	34.6	22.4	
.2	.2	.2	Deferred Taxes	.0	.0	.0	.3	.7	
5.8	5.6	10.8	All Other Non-Current	16.3	9.8	2.3	5.4	10.5	
21.2	23.5	8.2	Net Worth	-15.7	5.2	-.4	26.0	44.0	
100.0	100.0	100.0	Total Liabilities & Net Worth	100.0	100.0	100.0	100.0	100.0	
			INCOME DATA						
100.0	100.0	100.0	Net Sales	100.0	100.0	100.0	100.0	100.0	
			Gross Profit						
91.1	92.5	92.6	Operating Expenses	89.3	94.4	92.0	95.4	93.8	
8.9	7.5	7.4	Operating Profit	10.7	5.6	8.0	4.6	6.2	
3.9	3.8	3.1	All Other Expenses (net)	6.1	2.4	1.7	1.5	.4	
5.1	3.7	4.3	Profit Before Taxes	4.6	3.2	6.2	3.1	5.8	
			RATIOS						
2.1	2.1	2.1		1.3	2.0	2.4	2.4	2.3	
1.0	1.0	.9	Current	.7	.6	.6	1.1	1.7	
.4	.4	.4		.2	.2	.3	.5	.9	
1.7	1.6	1.8		1.3	1.9	2.4	2.0	1.7	
.7	.8	.7	Quick	.5	.5	.5	.7	1.1	
.2	.3	.3		.1	.2	.3	.4	.8	
0 UND	0 UND	0 UND		0 UND	0 UND	7 48.8	7 55.5	15 24.0	
6 60.8	9 38.6	10 36.8	Sales/Receivables	0 UND	8 43.5	16 22.3	24 15.0	23 15.7	
29 12.4	32 11.5	29 12.5		8 43.3	26 14.1	32 11.2	40 9.1	34 10.9	
			Cost of Sales/Inventory						
			Cost of Sales/Payables						
14.3	17.5	15.9		49.0	23.4	6.8	9.9	11.5	
-301.3	-299.2	-151.7	Sales/Working Capital	-48.2	-76.8	-17.7	64.2	18.0	
-12.6	-11.6	-11.9		-5.8	-11.3	-8.4	-17.4	-131.8	
6.4	5.0	5.2		3.9	2.9	9.3	4.4	12.0	
(111) 2.8	(132) 2.3	(129) 2.3	EBIT/Interest	(34) 2.3	(31) 1.4	(12) 2.9	(28) 2.2	(17) 4.1	
.8	.7	.7		1.0	-.2	.2	.2	2.0	
3.5	3.2	4.8	Net Profit + Depr., Dep., Amort./Cur. Mat. L/T/D						
(20) 2.3	(20) 1.6	(12) 1.2							
1.2	1.0	.9							
.9	.9	1.1		1.5	1.1	1.9	.7	.7	
3.2	3.0	3.8	Fixed/Worth	-5.8	-153.6	5.0	2.0	1.2	
-9.1	-6.9	-1.6		-1.0	-.9	-.6	-38.4	2.8	
1.0	.9	1.0		1.2	1.5	1.4	1.0	.7	
4.7	4.4	5.2	Debt/Worth	-8.4	-207.1	7.1	3.1	1.0	
-11.5	-9.0	-3.5		-2.4	-2.1	-2.7	-56.8	3.2	
67.9	42.2	53.2	% Profit Before Taxes/Tangible Net Worth	67.4	57.2		29.0	39.8	
(93) 22.4	(101) 19.3	(88) 20.5		(21) 18.1	(17) 12.3		(21) 11.9	(16) 24.5	
6.6	3.8	-.1		-.5	-8.9		-3.0	7.6	
16.8	12.3	17.0	% Profit Before Taxes/Total Assets	18.2	25.7	31.4	8.0	18.0	
5.9	4.1	4.3		2.3	3.1	15.0	3.0	10.0	
-.4	-1.1	-1.2		-1.6	-5.2	-2.0	-2.0	3.3	
9.8	7.8	9.5		9.9	13.4	8.7	8.7	6.7	
5.1	4.3	5.2	Sales/Net Fixed Assets	4.7	7.8	4.3	5.4	4.4	
2.0	2.0	2.2		.8	3.3	3.5	2.4	2.5	
3.6	3.1	3.8		3.3	5.3	4.7	3.2	3.1	
2.2	1.8	1.9	Sales/Total Assets	1.3	2.6	2.4	1.9	2.1	
1.1	1.0	1.1		.6	1.5	1.4	1.2	1.4	
2.8	3.1	2.8		3.1	1.6	2.1	3.6	3.7	
(117) 4.3	(139) 5.0	(135) 4.8	% Depr., Dep., Amort./Sales	(41) 7.3	(34) 3.7	(13) 4.7	(24) 4.8	(16) 4.1	
8.2	8.0	8.6		11.1	7.7	8.8	6.0	5.7	
2.9	3.6	2.5		5.1	3.9		.5		
(63) 6.4	(73) 5.6	(77) 4.7	% Officers', Directors' Owners' Comp/Sales	(23) 8.4	(24) 5.6		(14) 1.7		
9.0	9.9	9.4		13.9	9.4		4.1		
1659676M	845715M	979536M	Net Sales ($)	23671M	61558M	59378M	196110M	270871M	367948M
557969M	571698M	561249M	Total Assets ($)	25684M	37683M	31645M	119017M	156062M	191158M

© RMA 2010

M = $ thousand   MM = $ million
See Pages 9 through 22 for Explanation of Ratios and Data

OTHER SERVICES—Linen Supply   NAICS 812331

Current Data Sorted by Assets							Comparative Historical Data	

0-500M	500M-2MM	2-10MM	10-50MM	50-100MM	100-250MM	Type of Statement		
	1	3	7			Unqualified	14	14
	1	8	4	1		Reviewed	20	13
	4	3	1			Compiled	9	11
1	4	4				Tax Returns	4	7
3	8	12	9	1		Other	32	25
	20 (4/1-9/30/09)		55 (10/1/09-3/31/10)				4/1/05-3/31/06	4/1/06-3/31/07
							ALL	ALL
4	18	30	21	2		NUMBER OF STATEMENTS	79	70
%	%	%	%	%	%	ASSETS	%	%
	9.1	12.6	9.9		D	Cash & Equivalents	8.8	9.4
	28.1	21.0	16.0		A	Trade Receivables (net)	21.3	19.7
	4.9	8.1	6.8		T	Inventory	10.7	8.5
	3.2	1.7	4.5		A	All Other Current	2.1	2.0
	45.4	43.3	37.2			Total Current	42.9	39.6
	46.9	45.0	48.5		N	Fixed Assets (net)	45.0	46.9
	3.5	6.8	7.9		O	Intangibles (net)	5.1	5.6
	4.3	4.8	6.4		T	All Other Non-Current	7.1	8.0
	100.0	100.0	100.0			Total	100.0	100.0
					A	LIABILITIES		
	11.3	6.5	9.4		V	Notes Payable-Short Term	6.9	6.9
	4.9	5.0	5.4		A	Cur. Mat.-L.T.D.	5.9	5.4
	9.5	8.2	9.6		I	Trade Payables	9.6	10.0
	.2	.1	.2		L	Income Taxes Payable	.3	.3
	14.6	8.1	6.5		A	All Other Current	7.7	8.5
	40.5	28.0	31.1		B	Total Current	30.3	31.0
	22.6	25.0	23.5		L	Long-Term Debt	20.7	27.6
	.8	.4	.2		E	Deferred Taxes	.8	.4
	2.2	6.1	6.2			All Other Non-Current	6.2	5.0
	33.8	40.6	39.0			Net Worth	41.9	36.1
	100.0	100.0	100.0			Total Liabilities & Net Worth	100.0	100.0
						INCOME DATA		
	100.0	100.0	100.0			Net Sales	100.0	100.0
						Gross Profit		
	92.0	95.1	94.0			Operating Expenses	95.6	94.9
	8.0	4.9	6.0			Operating Profit	4.4	5.1
	2.4	.8	2.4			All Other Expenses (net)	1.6	1.9
	5.7	4.1	3.6			Profit Before Taxes	2.8	3.2
						RATIOS		
	2.9	2.9	1.9				2.2	2.0
	2.0	2.0	1.4			Current	1.4	1.3
	.6	.9	.8				.9	.9
	2.6	2.2	1.6				1.6	1.4
	1.3	1.7	1.0			Quick	(78) .9	1.0
	.5	.5	.5				.6	.6
29	12.5 31	11.6 33	11.0				31 11.8 28	13.0
35	10.3 35	10.4 37	9.9			Sales/Receivables	37 9.8 36	10.2
42	8.7 40	9.1 42	8.7				45 8.1 42	8.8
						Cost of Sales/Inventory		
						Cost of Sales/Payables		
	6.6	6.5	8.2				7.3	9.1
	14.7	15.2	10.1			Sales/Working Capital	18.2	34.1
	-14.4	-60.3	-28.6				-42.2	-63.5
	10.1	16.8	12.6				9.1	10.8
	(13) 2.0	(26) 3.9	4.7			EBIT/Interest	(74) 3.1 (64)	2.9
	.9	1.6	1.4				1.0	1.1
							2.9	7.2
						Net Profit + Depr., Dep., Amort./Cur. Mat. L/T/D	(22) 1.9 (17)	2.5
							1.1	1.3
	.6	.7	.9				.8	.7
	.9	1.4	1.5			Fixed/Worth	1.1	1.3
	4.9	2.1	3.7				2.5	3.6
	.3	.6	.7				.6	.6
	2.2	2.0	2.4			Debt/Worth	1.2	1.7
	5.8	3.5	4.4				3.9	6.9
	32.0	46.9	40.0				31.9	31.6
	(15) 22.8	(27) 18.0	(18) 22.2			% Profit Before Taxes/Tangible Net Worth	(72) 14.6 (61)	13.1
	3.6	7.0	5.2				1.7	.7
	14.5	16.2	12.0				12.3	13.1
	6.5	7.9	5.9			% Profit Before Taxes/Total Assets	4.7	5.3
	-.5	1.0	.1				.0	-.1
	12.2	7.8	5.2				8.4	8.3
	6.1	4.6	3.2			Sales/Net Fixed Assets	4.5	4.9
	2.8	2.7	2.3				2.6	2.5
	4.0	2.6	1.8				2.6	2.7
	2.2	1.8	1.6			Sales/Total Assets	2.0	2.1
	1.7	1.4	1.2				1.5	1.4
	2.4	2.7	2.5				2.8	2.9
	(15) 2.7	(28) 4.5	(19) 4.4			% Depr., Dep., Amort./Sales	(70) 4.0 (64)	4.6
	5.9	6.8	7.9				6.5	7.1
		1.6					2.4	2.3
	(15)	5.6				% Officers', Directors' Owners' Comp/Sales	(29) 4.5 (25)	4.9
		11.0					9.2	14.6
2802M	61419M	344590M	801553M	297632M		Net Sales ($)	1637468M	1514358M
912M	19664M	163549M	514463M	149729M		Total Assets ($)	792296M	717948M

M = $ thousand   MM = $ million
See Pages 9 through 22 for Explanation of Ratios and Data

Comparative Historical Data | Current Data Sorted by Sales

4/1/07-3/31/08 ALL	4/1/08-3/31/09 ALL	4/1/09-3/31/10 ALL	Type of Statement	0-1MM	1-3MM	3-5MM	5-10MM	10-25MM	25MM & OV
16	13	11	Unqualified		1	1	2	3	4
15	15	14	Reviewed		1		3	4	6
14	11	8	Compiled		1	1	3	2	1
9	10	9	Tax Returns	2	2	1	3	1	
26	32	33	Other	2	7	2	8	7	7
	20 (4/1-9/30/09)						55 (10/1/09-3/31/10)		
80	81	75	NUMBER OF STATEMENTS	4	12	5	19	17	18
%	%	%	ASSETS	%	%	%	%	%	%
11.4	8.9	11.5	Cash & Equivalents		10.3		14.7	9.4	9.4
19.3	20.0	22.7	Trade Receivables (net)		22.2		21.1	22.8	19.5
6.9	10.5	6.7	Inventory		6.4		5.1	8.8	8.4
1.9	1.8	2.8	All Other Current		3.1		1.1	3.4	4.8
39.4	41.2	43.7	Total Current		42.0		42.1	44.4	42.0
48.2	47.5	45.3	Fixed Assets (net)		47.7		45.0	46.5	43.9
5.0	5.2	6.0	Intangibles (net)		4.0		9.1	4.9	7.2
7.4	6.1	5.0	All Other Non-Current		6.2		3.8	4.2	6.9
100.0	100.0	100.0	Total		100.0		100.0	100.0	100.0
			LIABILITIES						
5.8	10.5	8.0	Notes Payable-Short Term		3.7		5.7	7.9	8.8
6.1	3.9	4.9	Cur. Mat.-L.T.D.		.9		5.9	3.8	4.9
8.6	8.8	8.6	Trade Payables		6.4		5.1	12.4	11.1
.2	.1	.2	Income Taxes Payable		.0		.2	.2	.0
7.4	10.3	9.6	All Other Current		15.8		8.1	8.3	9.1
28.1	33.5	31.2	Total Current		26.8		25.0	32.7	33.9
28.3	27.0	22.4	Long-Term Debt		22.7		32.8	10.3	22.3
.5	.4	.4	Deferred Taxes		.9		.0	.8	.2
6.0	3.8	4.9	All Other Non-Current		3.3		5.6	7.7	4.8
37.1	35.3	41.1	Net Worth		46.3		36.6	48.5	38.8
100.0	100.0	100.0	Total Liabilties & Net Worth		100.0		100.0	100.0	100.0
			INCOME DATA						
100.0	100.0	100.0	Net Sales		100.0		100.0	100.0	100.0
			Gross Profit						
93.2	92.7	94.7	Operating Expenses		96.4		94.5	94.7	93.3
6.8	7.3	5.3	Operating Profit		3.6		5.5	5.3	6.7
1.7	2.8	1.6	All Other Expenses (net)		1.0		.8	.9	1.8
5.0	4.5	3.8	Profit Before Taxes		2.5		4.7	4.5	4.9
			RATIOS						
2.6	2.6	2.6			3.8		3.5	2.5	1.9
1.6	1.4	1.9	Current		2.2		2.3	1.4	1.6
.9	.8	.9			1.3		1.0	.8	1.1
2.1	1.8	2.2			3.7		3.0	1.9	1.6
1.1	.9	1.2	Quick		1.7		2.0	1.1	1.1
.7	.5	.5			.5		.6	.5	.5
29 12.5	27 13.4	30 12.0			31 11.6		33 11.0	29 12.6	32 11.4
34 10.8	35 10.6	36 10.2	Sales/Receivables		38 9.7		38 9.7	34 10.7	36 10.0
39 9.4	41 9.0	42 8.8			43 8.6		40 9.2	37 9.7	42 8.7
			Cost of Sales/Inventory						
			Cost of Sales/Payables						
7.6	7.5	7.1			5.9		6.1	7.4	8.3
15.5	22.2	12.2	Sales/Working Capital		9.1		9.2	17.8	10.0
-68.1	-25.6	-63.7			73.1		-129.7	-21.3	NM
12.1	9.0	12.8					15.9	47.2	15.2
(73) 4.1	(66) 3.9	(63) 3.8	EBIT/Interest				(16) 2.1	(16) 11.8	6.3
1.4	.7	1.1					1.0	3.7	2.0
8.4	5.8	9.3							
(22) 3.9	(17) 3.4	(15) 5.0	Net Profit + Depr., Dep., Amort./Cur. Mat. L/T/D						
1.4	1.8	1.0							
.7	.7	.7			.6		.8	.7	.8
1.4	1.4	1.2	Fixed/Worth		.8		1.4	1.0	1.3
4.3	4.6	2.6			4.8		3.0	1.9	3.0
.7	.6	.5			.2		.7	.4	.7
1.5	2.1	1.9	Debt/Worth		1.7		2.3	1.8	2.5
5.3	8.5	3.6			6.0		7.6	2.8	5.9
47.0	55.5	38.5			26.2		39.1	48.4	44.4
(71) 16.4	(75) 18.3	(66) 21.4	% Profit Before Taxes/Tangible Net Worth	(10) 13.8		(16) 15.7	(16) 27.3	(16) 22.7	
6.0	3.5	5.2			4.5		3.1	9.8	8.7
15.8	13.7	15.5			12.5		14.6	20.8	13.8
7.5	3.8	6.6	% Profit Before Taxes/Total Assets		4.4		3.5	11.8	6.5
1.9	.3	.5			-1.7		.5	4.0	2.1
7.7	8.5	7.7			9.2		8.9	6.7	5.4
4.3	4.3	4.3	Sales/Net Fixed Assets		4.7		4.3	4.8	3.5
2.4	2.5	2.6			2.2		2.6	2.6	2.7
2.7	2.6	2.6			2.9		2.2	3.0	1.9
2.0	2.0	1.8	Sales/Total Assets		1.9		1.8	1.9	1.7
1.5	1.3	1.4			1.6		1.3	1.6	1.4
3.0	2.2	2.5			2.4		2.6	3.1	2.1
(73) 4.2	(71) 4.4	(67) 4.4	% Depr., Dep., Amort./Sales	(11) 4.9		(18) 4.7	(15) 4.6	(17) 4.3	
7.0	7.1	6.9			8.3		6.7	8.7	4.5
2.8	1.8	1.7					1.5		
(33) 4.9	(29) 4.0	(24) 3.7	% Officers', Directors' Owners' Comp/Sales				(10) 4.8		
7.0	6.8	9.1					8.5		
1994170M	1814865M	1507996M	Net Sales ($)	1247M	21345M	19102M	145267M	259114M	1061921M
1027568M	950594M	848317M	Total Assets ($)	978M	10543M	13733M	87361M	135955M	599747M

M = $ thousand   MM = $ million
See Pages 9 through 22 for Explanation of Ratios and Data

OTHER SERVICES—Pet Care (except Veterinary) Services NAICS 812910

| | Current Data Sorted by Assets | | | | | | | Comparative Historical Data | |

Type of Statement									
		1	2	6	2		Unqualified	2	3
		2					Reviewed		
	1	1	3				Compiled	1	3
	11	4	4		1		Tax Returns	11	10
		7	5	7	1		Other	7	5

0-500M	500M-2MM	2-10MM	10-50MM	50-100MM	100-250MM		4/1/05-3/31/06 ALL	4/1/06-3/31/07 ALL
	12 (4/1-9/30/09)		46 (10/1/09-3/31/10)					
12	15	14	14	3		NUMBER OF STATEMENTS	21	21
%	%	%	%	%	%	ASSETS	%	%
35.6	18.3	11.9	9.8			Cash & Equivalents	17.3	12.7
.9	1.2	7.2	11.4			Trade Receivables (net)	1.9	6.5
3.1	3.3	1.1	6.3			Inventory	9.5	3.6
1.8	.7	1.9	.4			All Other Current	3.3	4.3
41.5	23.6	22.1	28.0	DATA		Total Current	32.1	27.1
49.0	65.4	64.7	55.6	NOT		Fixed Assets (net)	58.3	63.7
2.9	3.0	1.1	.9	AVAILABLE		Intangibles (net)	5.6	2.9
6.6	8.0	12.1	15.5			All Other Non-Current	4.1	6.3
100.0	100.0	100.0	100.0			Total	100.0	100.0
						LIABILITIES		
28.2	15.3	2.2	8.5			Notes Payable-Short Term	1.0	5.6
9.0	1.1	1.8	6.5			Cur. Mat.-L.T.D.	12.6	1.7
1.6	3.7	2.6	17.4			Trade Payables	4.2	3.5
4.2	.0	.0	.0			Income Taxes Payable	.1	.0
11.5	11.7	8.0	9.3			All Other Current	9.6	65.0
54.5	31.8	14.6	41.7			Total Current	27.5	75.9
6.3	50.5	48.6	17.7			Long-Term Debt	42.8	34.3
.3	.0	.0	.0			Deferred Taxes	.0	.0
.0	.6	2.1	13.5			All Other Non-Current	11.7	6.0
38.9	17.1	34.7	27.1			Net Worth	18.0	-16.1
100.0	100.0	100.0	100.0			Total Liabilties & Net Worth	100.0	100.0
						INCOME DATA		
100.0	100.0	100.0	100.0			Net Sales	100.0	100.0
						Gross Profit		
91.8	76.4	88.0	98.1			Operating Expenses	90.1	85.8
8.2	23.6	12.0	1.9			Operating Profit	9.9	14.2
.5	14.5	9.2	5.6			All Other Expenses (net)	6.4	3.9
7.8	9.1	2.8	-3.7			Profit Before Taxes	3.5	10.3
						RATIOS		
1.5	2.5	7.3	3.2				6.0	6.5
1.2	1.4	1.3	1.0			Current	1.8	.9
.3	.4	.3	.3				.2	.2
1.5	2.2	6.3	2.5				5.7	3.9
1.0	.6	1.2	1.0			Quick	1.2	.6
.2	.3	.3	.1				.1	.2
0 UND	0 UND	0 UND	4 98.2				0 UND	0 UND
0 UND	0 UND	4 98.6	20 17.8			Sales/Receivables	0 UND	0 999.8
0 UND	3 130.3	61 6.0	66 5.5				0 UND	15 25.2
						Cost of Sales/Inventory		
						Cost of Sales/Payables		
52.1	7.6	4.5	6.1				9.3	9.1
139.2	40.3	230.1	UND			Sales/Working Capital	17.0	-105.6
-53.0	-4.5	-3.7	-1.4				-15.6	-16.9
	5.9						6.6	6.2
	(11) 2.3					EBIT/Interest	(14) 5.0	(16) 1.9
	-.2						1.2	1.0
						Net Profit + Depr., Dep., Amort./Cur. Mat. L/T/D		
.5	1.2	.5	.2				.5	.6
.9	2.4	2.0	1.0			Fixed/Worth	6.2	3.2
4.4	-4.7	NM	2.1				-3.9	-2.9
.4	.7	1.1	.3				.8	.5
1.2	3.8	1.8	1.1			Debt/Worth	5.6	2.7
UND	-7.3	NM	2.8				-8.1	-4.9
650.0		36.0	6.5				102.6	79.8
(10) 24.5	(11) 9.3	(13) -3.2				% Profit Before Taxes/Tangible Net Worth	(14) 38.7	(15) 10.1
10.9		.2	-8.9				12.0	-4.0
242.1	15.8	7.4	2.6				34.1	17.4
15.1	5.9	1.4	-1.7			% Profit Before Taxes/Total Assets	8.6	4.4
2.8	-.9	-.7	-4.3				-1.1	-3.9
87.0	6.4	2.7	5.9				31.4	7.2
16.5	1.3	.7	.6			Sales/Net Fixed Assets	3.7	1.3
7.2	.5	.4	.2				.4	.8
14.5	2.3	.9	1.1				7.5	2.9
7.9	.9	.5	.3			Sales/Total Assets	1.9	.9
3.7	.5	.2	.2				.4	.5
1.1	1.4	5.1	1.8				2.1	2.4
(10) 1.6	(12) 3.3	(10) 7.8	3.9			% Depr., Dep., Amort./Sales	(16) 6.2	(16) 5.2
2.1	6.9	13.8	6.5				8.9	8.9
							2.0	
						% Officers', Directors' Owners' Comp/Sales	(10) 11.6	
							19.8	
14203M	21138M	51778M	365939M	80240M		Net Sales ($)	19340M	473337M
1393M	17765M	71994M	299183M	192322M		Total Assets ($)	35236M	223522M

© RMA 2010

M = $ thousand   MM = $ million
See Pages 9 through 22 for Explanation of Ratios and Data

Comparative Historical Data | Current Data Sorted by Sales

			Type of Statement						
1	2	11	Unqualified		1	3	2	3	2
1	1	2	Reviewed	1		1			
2	3	5	Compiled		4		1		
15	15	20	Tax Returns	10	6	1	2		1
4	9	20	Other	9	5	1	2	1	2
4/1/07-3/31/08	4/1/08-3/31/09	4/1/09-3/31/10		12 (4/1-9/30/09)			46 (10/1/09-3/31/10)		
ALL	ALL	ALL		0-1MM	1-3MM	3-5MM	5-10MM	10-25MM	25MM & OVER
23	30	58	NUMBER OF STATEMENTS	20	16	6	7	4	5
%	%	%	**ASSETS**	%	%	%	%	%	%
21.3	12.5	18.1	Cash & Equivalents	24.6	13.6				
3.3	4.2	5.4	Trade Receivables (net)	1.1	1.6				
4.0	5.6	3.3	Inventory	.8	4.4				
2.9	.8	1.2	All Other Current	1.1	.1				
31.5	23.1	28.0	Total Current	27.6	19.6				
62.2	60.5	59.5	Fixed Assets (net)	60.5	68.9				
3.4	4.6	2.0	Intangibles (net)	3.4	1.7				
2.8	11.8	10.6	All Other Non-Current	8.6	9.7				
100.0	100.0	100.0	Total	100.0	100.0				
			LIABILITIES						
12.6	16.9	12.4	Notes Payable-Short Term	13.5	16.8				
1.6	1.1	4.2	Cur. Mat.-L.T.D.	5.1	2.2				
2.1	4.7	6.2	Trade Payables	.2	3.9				
.0	.0	.9	Income Taxes Payable	2.5	.0				
28.7	6.0	9.8	All Other Current	10.7	10.4				
45.0	28.7	33.5	Total Current	32.0	33.3				
35.3	36.2	32.3	Long-Term Debt	37.3	42.8				
.0	.0	.1	Deferred Taxes	.2	.0				
29.8	9.4	5.0	All Other Non-Current	.3	1.4				
-10.1	25.7	29.1	Net Worth	30.2	22.5				
100.0	100.0	100.0	Total Liabilities & Net Worth	100.0	100.0				
			INCOME DATA						
100.0	100.0	100.0	Net Sales	100.0	100.0				
			Gross Profit						
85.9	89.7	88.3	Operating Expenses	79.5	90.5				
14.1	10.3	11.7	Operating Profit	20.5	9.5				
5.5	5.5	7.6	All Other Expenses (net)	13.1	7.8				
8.5	4.8	4.0	Profit Before Taxes	7.4	1.7				
			RATIOS						
4.5	4.3	2.6		1.9	1.9				
1.0	.9	1.3	Current	1.0	.8				
.4	.4	.3		.3	.3				
3.0	3.1	2.2		1.8	1.5				
.8	.7	1.1	Quick	.9	.6				
.3	.2	.3		.3	.2				
0 UND	0 UND	0 UND		0 UND	0 UND				
0 UND	0 UND	2 209.0	Sales/Receivables	0 UND	0 UND				
1 411.3	5 67.8	20 18.1		0 UND	9 41.4				
			Cost of Sales/Inventory						
			Cost of Sales/Payables						
9.9	11.8	7.2		27.5	10.2				
UND	-135.0	71.1	Sales/Working Capital	NM	UND				
-16.5	-14.2	-4.8		-2.8	-5.5				
13.8	25.4	9.6		47.3	3.6				
(15) 4.4	(24) 3.7	(39) 2.3	EBIT/Interest	(12) 5.7	(12) 1.9				
1.5	.2	.8		.9	1.0				
			Net Profit + Depr., Dep., Amort./Cur. Mat. L/T/D						
1.8	.6	.6		.8	1.3				
12.3	2.5	1.5	Fixed/Worth	1.2	2.2				
-1.8	-32.4	7.9		UND	-38.8				
1.4	.8	.5		.4	.9				
13.0	2.8	1.6	Debt/Worth	2.9	2.1				
-3.8	-43.4	21.7		-14.0	-42.4				
179.4	66.3	32.6		99.9	31.4				
(14) 57.7	(22) 23.2	(46) 10.3	% Profit Before Taxes/Tangible Net Worth	(14) 18.7	(11) 12.9				
17.2	-5.3	-1.0		.3	-.8				
50.1	20.3	14.1		17.6	7.1				
19.1	3.3	2.1	% Profit Before Taxes/Total Assets	4.0	1.4				
1.7	-4.8	-1.8		-2.1	-.6				
24.0	12.3	10.1		17.2	7.7				
4.7	1.8	1.4	Sales/Net Fixed Assets	2.7	1.1				
1.5	.8	.4		.2	.5				
7.3	4.6	3.2		5.5	2.4				
2.6	1.3	.7	Sales/Total Assets	.7	.9				
1.0	.5	.3		.1	.4				
1.4	2.3	1.7		1.7	1.2				
(14) 3.5	(27) 3.3	(50) 4.0	% Depr., Dep., Amort./Sales	(15) 5.7	(15) 3.3				
7.6	7.5	8.6		8.6	11.1				
2.7	4.8	3.1							
(12) 6.9	(13) 8.9	(19) 6.0	% Officers', Directors' Owners' Comp/Sales						
13.9	13.1	11.2							
30611M	97112M	533298M	Net Sales ($)	9496M	28490M	22893M	47461M	69886M	355072M
22673M	143290M	582657M	Total Assets ($)	41694M	50278M	81527M	94348M	120358M	194452M

M = $ thousand   MM = $ million
See Pages 9 through 22 for Explanation of Ratios and Data

Current Data Sorted by Assets | Comparative Historical Data

	0-500M	500M-2MM	2-10MM	10-50MM	50-100MM	100-250MM	Type of Statement	4/1/05-3/31/06 ALL	4/1/06-3/31/07 ALL
		2	3				Unqualified	3	1
		1	1				Reviewed	7	5
		1	2				Compiled	4	3
	4	3	1	1			Tax Returns	3	8
	2	6	3	4			Other	8	14
		5 (4/1-9/30/09)		29 (10/1/09-3/31/10)					
	0-500M	500M-2MM	2-10MM	10-50MM	50-100MM	100-250MM	NUMBER OF STATEMENTS	25	31
	6	13	10	5					
	%	%	%	%	%	%	**ASSETS**	%	%
		5.7	7.1				Cash & Equivalents	8.9	14.9
		13.4	23.1	D	D		Trade Receivables (net)	28.7	18.7
		6.2	11.0	A	A		Inventory	8.0	6.5
		4.5	2.6	T	T		All Other Current	4.8	3.6
		29.7	43.9	A	A		Total Current	50.4	43.7
		54.8	42.4				Fixed Assets (net)	41.1	44.1
		5.1	6.0	N	N		Intangibles (net)	1.5	5.1
		10.3	7.7	O	O		All Other Non-Current	7.0	7.0
		100.0	100.0	T	T		Total	100.0	100.0
							LIABILITIES		
		5.9	8.5	A	A		Notes Payable-Short Term	13.2	15.3
		10.0	4.7	V	V		Cur. Mat.-L.T.D.	7.2	6.1
		7.9	10.6	A	A		Trade Payables	9.3	13.2
		.0	.3	I	I		Income Taxes Payable	.3	.2
		14.3	6.4	L	L		All Other Current	11.1	14.3
		38.1	30.5	A	A		Total Current	41.1	49.2
		35.8	28.6	B	B		Long-Term Debt	19.4	28.8
		.9	.0	L	L		Deferred Taxes	1.1	.9
		1.2	4.7	E	E		All Other Non-Current	14.7	18.0
		24.1	36.2				Net Worth	23.6	3.0
		100.0	100.0				Total Liabilities & Net Worth	100.0	100.0
							INCOME DATA		
		100.0	100.0				Net Sales	100.0	100.0
							Gross Profit		
		80.6	97.8				Operating Expenses	96.1	96.6
		19.4	2.2				Operating Profit	3.9	3.4
		8.4	1.5				All Other Expenses (net)	2.3	2.8
		11.0	.7				Profit Before Taxes	1.6	.7
							RATIOS		
		1.5	2.2				Current	3.0	1.9
		.7	1.4					1.5	1.1
		.3	1.0					.6	.7
		1.0	1.3				Quick	1.8	1.8
		.4	.9					1.0	.9
		.2	.6					.4	.5
	0 UND	18 19.8					Sales/Receivables	18 20.8	10 35.6
	16 23.4	31 11.9						30 12.3	23 15.8
	26 13.8	40 9.1						54 6.7	46 8.0
							Cost of Sales/Inventory		
							Cost of Sales/Payables		
		16.0	8.2				Sales/Working Capital	7.0	9.1
		-16.4	39.3					20.2	74.8
		-6.9	NM					-11.4	-13.7
		6.9					EBIT/Interest	11.4	5.0
	(10)	.6						(23) 3.4	(26) 2.0
		-4.7						1.0	-.4
							Net Profit + Depr., Dep., Amort./Cur. Mat. L/T/D		
		.5	.5				Fixed/Worth	.7	.6
		2.0	1.2					1.2	1.8
		3.9	NM					NM	12.3
		1.0	1.0				Debt/Worth	1.2	1.1
		2.2	1.9					2.0	2.7
		4.2	NM					NM	28.9
		15.6					% Profit Before Taxes/Tangible Net Worth	50.5	53.7
	(11)	5.8						(19) 17.0	(24) 19.6
		-41.9						5.4	2.4
		7.8	4.9				% Profit Before Taxes/Total Assets	17.2	11.8
		1.9	.7					9.5	5.3
		-15.6	-3.8					-1.9	-5.3
		23.3	12.7				Sales/Net Fixed Assets	12.8	10.8
		3.1	7.9					5.6	4.3
		.2	3.3					3.7	3.7
		2.9	3.1				Sales/Total Assets	3.8	3.3
		2.2	2.4					2.5	2.3
		.2	1.5					2.0	1.6
		2.8					% Depr., Dep., Amort./Sales	2.9	3.4
	(11)	5.7						(21) 4.6	(29) 4.6
		21.2						6.4	7.1
							% Officers', Directors' Owners' Comp/Sales		5.1
								(16) 7.3	
									10.6
	5915M	26819M	144203M	151076M			Net Sales ($)	124936M	164370M
	934M	15972M	54712M	95047M			Total Assets ($)	54891M	71480M

M = $ thousand   MM = $ million
See Pages 9 through 22 for Explanation of Ratios and Data

Comparative Historical Data   Current Data Sorted by Sales

	4/1/07-3/31/08 ALL	4/1/08-3/31/09 ALL	4/1/09-3/31/10 ALL	0-1MM	1-3MM	3-5MM	5-10MM	10-25MM	25MM & OVER
					5 (4/1-9/30/09)		29 (10/1/09-3/31/10)		
Type of Statement									
Unqualified	3	4	5					2	3
Reviewed	5	3	2			2	1		1
Compiled	1	5	3		2			1	
Tax Returns	7	8	9	3	3	1		2	
Other	13	16	15	6	1	2		3	3
NUMBER OF STATEMENTS	29	36	34	9	6	6	1	7	5
	%	%	%	%	%	%	%	%	%
ASSETS									
Cash & Equivalents	14.1	10.2	13.6						
Trade Receivables (net)	21.5	21.6	14.8						
Inventory	13.6	9.6	8.2						
All Other Current	2.0	1.8	2.7						
Total Current	51.1	43.3	39.2						
Fixed Assets (net)	39.7	35.0	45.4						
Intangibles (net)	4.4	10.9	7.7						
All Other Non-Current	4.7	10.9	7.7						
Total	100.0	100.0	100.0						
LIABILITIES									
Notes Payable-Short Term	5.9	15.4	6.5						
Cur. Mat.-L.T.D.	7.8	11.3	7.7						
Trade Payables	10.9	10.9	8.3						
Income Taxes Payable	.2	.0	.1						
All Other Current	12.7	20.0	14.2						
Total Current	37.4	57.6	36.8						
Long-Term Debt	27.6	21.6	31.4						
Deferred Taxes	.4	.2	.3						
All Other Non-Current	4.4	4.4	2.1						
Net Worth	30.2	16.2	29.3						
Total Liabilities & Net Worth	100.0	100.0	100.0						
INCOME DATA									
Net Sales	100.0	100.0	100.0						
Gross Profit									
Operating Expenses	92.2	94.8	91.5						
Operating Profit	7.8	5.2	8.5						
All Other Expenses (net)	2.9	2.9	3.7						
Profit Before Taxes	4.8	2.3	4.8						
RATIOS									
Current	2.6 1.5 .8	1.8 1.1 .5	1.9 1.1 .5						
Quick	1.7 .9 .4	1.2 .8 .3	1.3 .9 .4						
Sales/Receivables	13 29.1 32 11.5 44 8.4	11 32.1 28 13.0 51 7.1	0 UND 21 17.4 34 10.8						
Cost of Sales/Inventory									
Cost of Sales/Payables									
Sales/Working Capital	7.1 27.4 -65.9	9.1 58.6 -10.2	10.3 54.5 -12.2						
EBIT/Interest	21.1 (26) 2.9 .3	6.0 (35) 1.8 -.3	2.3 (25) .7 -2.2						
Net Profit + Depr., Dep., Amort./Cur. Mat. L/T/D									
Fixed/Worth	.4 1.2 3.7	.3 1.4 -39.6	.5 1.4 3.7						
Debt/Worth	.9 1.9 6.0	1.0 2.6 -9.8	1.0 1.9 5.3						
% Profit Before Taxes/Tangible Net Worth	75.2 (25) 23.4 6.2	44.1 (25) 12.0 -8.4	15.3 (28) 6.0 -13.1						
% Profit Before Taxes/Total Assets	26.9 5.8 -1.0	10.2 2.5 -3.8	9.7 1.5 -7.6						
Sales/Net Fixed Assets	18.7 7.8 3.6	55.0 9.1 3.9	16.6 7.9 2.5						
Sales/Total Assets	4.2 2.7 1.8	4.1 2.4 1.0	3.6 2.2 1.4						
% Depr., Dep., Amort./Sales	2.2 (25) 3.9 6.9	1.3 (24) 2.9 7.4	1.2 (28) 3.7 7.2						
% Officers', Directors' Owners' Comp/Sales	5.3 (13) 7.0 10.4	2.1 (15) 4.7 9.5	4.2 (12) 5.5 7.7						
Net Sales ($)	563776M	285416M	328013M	4835M	12565M	21658M	8244M	106692M	174019M
Total Assets ($)	146564M	173421M	166665M	6912M	6314M	9388M	3131M	57471M	83449M

M = $ thousand   MM = $ million
See Pages 9 through 22 for Explanation of Ratios and Data

Current Data Sorted by Assets   Comparative Historical Data

Type of Statement	0-500M	500M-2MM	2-10MM	10-50MM	50-100MM	100-250MM	4/1/05-3/31/06 ALL	4/1/06-3/31/07 ALL
Unqualified	2		7	7	2	2	13	8
Reviewed	2	3	4	2			5	3
Compiled		4	2	3			5	4
Tax Returns	3	7	2	2			10	8
Other		7	8	12	3	3	20	22
		10 (4/1-9/30/09)		77 (10/1/09-3/31/10)				
NUMBER OF STATEMENTS	7	21	23	26	5	5	53	45
ASSETS	%	%	%	%	%	%	%	%
Cash & Equivalents		15.1	13.4	9.1			18.1	19.1
Trade Receivables (net)		10.0	21.9	8.6			9.4	14.6
Inventory		6.5	.6	.0			1.0	.1
All Other Current		2.9	4.5	4.5			4.0	2.1
Total Current		34.4	40.5	22.1			32.5	35.9
Fixed Assets (net)		51.4	49.1	63.9			48.5	48.2
Intangibles (net)		4.2	4.2	2.7			4.4	7.1
All Other Non-Current		9.9	6.1	11.3			14.6	8.7
Total		100.0	100.0	100.0			100.0	100.0
LIABILITIES								
Notes Payable-Short Term		12.0	5.0	4.5			6.9	4.3
Cur. Mat.-L.T.D.		7.0	9.4	2.8			4.2	2.3
Trade Payables		4.4	11.6	5.6			6.3	7.3
Income Taxes Payable		.0	.1	.1			.1	.0
All Other Current		16.8	14.7	9.9			10.4	14.1
Total Current		40.1	40.8	23.0			27.8	28.0
Long-Term Debt		43.3	25.8	58.4			31.7	38.1
Deferred Taxes		.0	.0	.0			.4	.4
All Other Non-Current		6.1	7.0	4.6			8.1	4.8
Net Worth		10.5	26.4	13.9			32.0	28.7
Total Liabilities & Net Worth		100.0	100.0	100.0			100.0	100.0
INCOME DATA								
Net Sales		100.0	100.0	100.0			100.0	100.0
Gross Profit								
Operating Expenses		81.4	85.2	79.7			80.7	77.9
Operating Profit		18.6	14.8	20.3			19.3	22.1
All Other Expenses (net)		9.3	9.7	14.3			8.2	7.8
Profit Before Taxes		9.3	5.2	6.0			11.1	14.3
RATIOS								
Current		1.6	1.9	2.9			2.8	3.1
		1.0	.9	1.2			1.3	1.2
		.5	.4	.4			.6	.6
Quick		1.3	1.3	1.9			2.3	2.5
		.7	.8	.8			1.2	1.1
		.4	.4	.3			.5	.5
Sales/Receivables	0 UND	2 207.8	0 999.8				0 UND	0 731.4
	0 UND	17 21.1	4 85.9				7 55.7	8 46.5
	29 12.6	40 9.0	36 10.3				28 13.2	27 13.5
Cost of Sales/Inventory								
Cost of Sales/Payables								
Sales/Working Capital		15.2	13.5	4.1			5.7	7.8
		999.8	-76.3	72.8			59.3	50.9
		-5.9	-4.2	-7.0			-13.8	-10.5
EBIT/Interest		14.8	38.1	7.0			11.6	14.5
	(14) 3.7	(15) 7.5	(16) 1.5				(35) 4.1	(34) 5.1
		2.2	1.9	.8			1.7	1.3
Net Profit + Depr., Dep., Amort./Cur. Mat. L/T/D							5.7	
							(11) 1.9	
							.5	
Fixed/Worth		1.2	.4	1.9			.5	.4
		3.8	3.6	3.0			1.6	1.7
		-16.5	10.7	NM			23.2	-18.0
Debt/Worth		1.8	1.5	1.7			.8	.9
		4.8	4.1	3.7			2.1	3.1
		-18.2	12.0	NM			44.1	-22.4
% Profit Before Taxes/Tangible Net Worth		189.7	49.4	54.5			57.5	69.7
	(15) 43.1	(20) 20.5	(20) 2.2				(43) 24.0	(28) 26.8
		27.7	1.7	-2.2			6.9	4.5
% Profit Before Taxes/Total Assets		13.7	19.8	7.1			16.8	20.4
		8.5	3.8	1.3			7.5	6.0
		1.6	.3	-.6			1.4	1.5
Sales/Net Fixed Assets		12.1	45.0	4.6			23.8	31.3
		5.6	1.5	.6			3.4	5.5
		.5	.3	.2			.3	.4
Sales/Total Assets		3.9	5.3	2.0			3.8	4.0
		1.5	1.4	.4			1.0	.9
		.3	.2	.2			.3	.3
% Depr., Dep., Amort./Sales		.9	.6	3.6			1.7	.5
	(18) 4.5	(21) 3.4	(25) 10.1				(48) 4.6	(36) 2.5
		7.5	19.5	18.4			14.0	6.8
% Officers', Directors' Owners' Comp/Sales							2.3	2.2
							(16) 5.4	(14) 6.4
							12.7	14.4
Net Sales ($)	13336M	42088M	255664M	880828M	434685M	699207M	1366270M	1294744M
Total Assets ($)	1557M	23727M	112305M	572754M	359096M	886393M	1153732M	835016M

Comparative Historical Data

Current Data Sorted by Sales

Type of Statement									
Unqualified	9	15	20	2	5		2	2	9
Reviewed	3	5	11	2	4		2	2	1
Compiled	7	2	9	2	4	2	1		
Tax Returns	9	15	14	5	4	2	3		
Other	27	27	33	7	5	2	5	5	9
	4/1/07-3/31/08 ALL	4/1/08-3/31/09 ALL	4/1/09-3/31/10 ALL	0-1MM	1-3MM	3-5MM	5-10MM	10-25MM	25MM & OVER
				10 (4/1-9/30/09)			77 (10/1/09-3/31/10)		
NUMBER OF STATEMENTS	55	64	87	18	22	6	13	9	19
ASSETS	%	%	%	%	%	%	%	%	%
Cash & Equivalents	11.9	15.6	13.3	10.7	15.2		14.0		14.2
Trade Receivables (net)	12.8	15.5	12.7	.3	13.1		13.6		20.2
Inventory	.0	.1	1.7	.0	3.0		.8		.2
All Other Current	4.2	3.3	4.1	1.8	2.5		4.9		3.9
Total Current	29.0	34.4	31.9	12.7	33.7		33.2		38.5
Fixed Assets (net)	47.9	40.0	51.7	77.5	58.1		47.3		26.6
Intangibles (net)	6.1	7.8	7.8	2.2	5.8		1.4		23.2
All Other Non-Current	17.0	17.7	8.6	7.7	2.4		18.1		11.7
Total	100.0	100.0	100.0	100.0	100.0		100.0		100.0
LIABILITIES									
Notes Payable-Short Term	4.7	6.5	8.4	5.4	9.0		13.4		7.0
Cur. Mat.-L.T.D.	3.5	5.7	6.9	18.2	6.1		1.7		3.0
Trade Payables	9.9	9.4	6.8	.9	6.6		6.6		13.5
Income Taxes Payable	.0	.1	.1	.0	.0		.1		.4
All Other Current	12.4	17.1	15.2	4.6	23.6		6.8		20.7
Total Current	30.5	38.8	37.4	29.1	45.4		28.5		44.5
Long-Term Debt	43.8	43.8	43.5	58.1	42.2		53.1		30.2
Deferred Taxes	.2	.6	.3	.0	.0				1.3
All Other Non-Current	10.2	5.6	5.5	.5	11.5		7.5		5.5
Net Worth	15.3	11.2	13.3	12.3	.9		10.8		18.4
Total Liabilities & Net Worth	100.0	100.0	100.0	100.0	100.0		100.0		100.0
INCOME DATA									
Net Sales	100.0	100.0	100.0	100.0	100.0		100.0		100.0
Gross Profit									
Operating Expenses	81.5	84.8	82.4	58.6	89.3		82.3		96.0
Operating Profit	18.5	15.2	17.6	41.4	10.7		17.7		4.0
All Other Expenses (net)	7.5	5.0	10.1	26.8	9.7		5.4		1.0
Profit Before Taxes	11.0	10.2	7.5	14.6	1.0		12.3		3.1
RATIOS									
Current	1.9	2.0	2.0	2.0	3.8		3.2		1.2
	1.0	1.0	.9	.4	1.1		1.4		.8
	.6	.6	.5	.1	.4		.3		.6
Quick	1.7	2.0	1.6	2.0	3.7		1.8		.9
	(54) .9	.9	.7	.4	.8		.7		.7
	.6	.5	.4	.1	.4		.1		.6
Sales/Receivables	0 999.8	0 999.8	0 UND	0 UND	0 UND		0 999.8		13 28.9
	4 100.9	12 29.2	8 45.7	0 UND	19 19.7		1 266.3		28 13.2
	20 18.2	30 12.4	37 10.0	6 60.2	44 8.2		50 7.3		38 9.6
Cost of Sales/Inventory									
Cost of Sales/Payables									
Sales/Working Capital	14.0	11.7	12.5	26.2	5.0		3.6		87.0
	-371.7	NM	-166.7	-5.4	360.5		15.5		-24.7
	-8.6	-15.5	-7.8	-1.6	-5.0		-11.3		-13.2
EBIT/Interest	15.8	7.3	10.2		5.3		13.4		6.2
	(39) 5.6	(48) 3.6	(58) 3.2	(14) 2.6			(11) 4.9		(17) 1.8
	2.0	1.3	1.4	-17.9			1.2		1.4
Net Profit + Depr., Dep., Amort./Cur. Mat. L/T/D			17.1						
		(10) 3.5							
			.1						
Fixed/Worth	1.0	.8	1.3	2.7	1.7		.3		1.3
	2.8	3.0	4.0	7.3	4.3		2.9		47.5
	-2.6	-18.5	-5.6	NM	-.5		NM		-.1
Debt/Worth	1.0	2.0	1.7	2.0	1.7		2.0		4.1
	6.9	7.9	5.6	9.0	4.7		4.3		123.4
	-6.4	-16.2	-9.2	NM	-2.7		NM		-2.1
% Profit Before Taxes/Tangible Net Worth	146.1	118.2	104.7	57.1	58.1		209.0		207.3
	(36) 42.0	(44) 37.2	(61) 31.1	(14) 10.0	(14) 5.8		(10) 46.7		(11) 33.3
	10.9	7.5	1.3	-.8	-2.9		30.7		3.5
% Profit Before Taxes/Total Assets	26.8	18.8	13.4	8.5	11.7		22.8		8.5
	10.0	6.0	4.1	1.7	1.6		10.3		4.1
	1.3	.0	-.2	-.2	-5.0		2.4		1.8
Sales/Net Fixed Assets	28.3	26.8	25.9	.6	11.8		51.9		44.4
	6.6	10.2	1.6	.2	3.0		1.5		20.4
	.5	.8	.3	.1	.3		.6		3.5
Sales/Total Assets	3.6	5.5	3.7	.5	2.8		3.2		6.1
	1.2	1.6	1.2	.1	1.2		.8		2.5
	.3	.4	.2	.1	.2		.4		1.2
% Depr., Dep., Amort./Sales	1.5	.8	.9	6.2	1.2		1.0		.4
	(42) 3.5	(47) 3.3	(74) 5.8	(13) 17.3	(21) 6.9		(11) 6.0	(15)	1.6
	9.2	8.6	13.0	28.2	21.2		11.5		4.9
% Officers', Directors' Owners' Comp/Sales	2.0	1.4	1.7		3.5				
	(12) 8.7	(15) 2.7	(21) 4.2		(10) 4.5				
	26.3	12.6	11.3		17.2				
Net Sales ($)	1762276M	2637924M	2325808M	8792M	46636M	21739M	97876M	158450M	1992315M
Total Assets ($)	1197352M	1736064M	1955832M	75082M	135965M	29625M	156294M	218377M	1340489M

© RMA 2010

M = $ thousand   MM = $ million

See Pages 9 through 22 for Explanation of Ratios and Data

	Current Data Sorted by Assets						Comparative Historical Data	
Type of Statement								
Unqualified	3	3	12	10	3	6	24	25
Reviewed	1	8	21	4			17	20
Compiled	22	38	36	7			37	48
Tax Returns	152	90	35	2		1	94	146
Other	53	80	60	22	3		93	110
		60 (4/1-9/30/09)		612 (10/1/09-3/31/10)			4/1/05-3/31/06	4/1/06-3/31/07
	0-500M	500M-2MM	2-10MM	10-50MM	50-100MM	100-250MM	ALL	ALL
NUMBER OF STATEMENTS	231	219	164	45	6	7	265	349
ASSETS	%	%	%	%	%	%	%	%
Cash & Equivalents	26.3	15.4	13.6	18.9			17.8	20.0
Trade Receivables (net)	9.6	20.0	20.0	14.4			17.3	17.1
Inventory	4.5	7.5	14.4	9.2			5.5	5.1
All Other Current	2.3	3.1	2.6	2.0			3.2	5.2
Total Current	42.7	46.1	50.6	44.5			43.8	47.4
Fixed Assets (net)	37.6	38.3	35.2	36.0			39.7	38.7
Intangibles (net)	7.2	5.6	3.1	6.5			6.4	5.7
All Other Non-Current	12.4	10.1	11.1	13.0			10.1	8.3
Total	100.0	100.0	100.0	100.0			100.0	100.0
LIABILITIES								
Notes Payable-Short Term	19.2	10.8	6.9	3.8			12.0	14.3
Cur. Mat.-L.T.D.	7.0	4.0	2.3	4.1			3.4	5.1
Trade Payables	7.8	10.1	9.4	10.3			8.7	7.4
Income Taxes Payable	.2	.1	.2	.0			.2	.2
All Other Current	25.0	14.7	11.4	20.7			19.1	19.3
Total Current	59.2	39.7	30.2	38.8			43.4	46.3
Long-Term Debt	29.6	33.4	24.8	18.5			24.5	28.1
Deferred Taxes	.0	.1	.1	.2			.2	.1
All Other Non-Current	16.8	7.7	4.3	1.7			15.7	7.4
Net Worth	-5.6	19.1	40.6	40.7			16.2	18.1
Total Liabilties & Net Worth	100.0	100.0	100.0	100.0			100.0	100.0
INCOME DATA								
Net Sales	100.0	100.0	100.0	100.0			100.0	100.0
Gross Profit								
Operating Expenses	93.1	92.0	89.1	92.9			91.9	90.5
Operating Profit	6.9	8.0	10.9	7.1			8.1	9.5
All Other Expenses (net)	2.3	3.6	3.9	1.0			2.2	2.4
Profit Before Taxes	4.6	4.4	7.1	6.1			5.9	7.1
RATIOS								
Current	4.1	3.7	3.7	2.4			2.7	2.9
	.9	1.3	1.8	1.2			1.2	1.2
	.3	.6	.8	.9			.5	.5
Quick	2.7	2.8	2.6	1.6			2.1	2.2
	(230) .8	1.0	1.0	1.0			.9	.9
	.8	.4	.4	.5			.3	.3
Sales/Receivables	0 UND	0 UND	0 999.8	2 169.7			0 UND	0 UND
	0 UND	13 27.9	21 17.2	31 11.9			4 98.8	3 130.8
	8 43.6	40 9.1	53 6.9	52 7.0			40 9.2	35 10.5
Cost of Sales/Inventory								
Cost of Sales/Payables								
Sales/Working Capital	14.4	7.2	4.5	7.0			8.5	9.0
	-245.5	29.9	11.2	22.7			68.0	45.8
	-8.7	-21.1	-26.5	-435.4			-19.1	-15.0
EBIT/Interest	9.7	11.7	30.5	25.2			20.6	12.5
	(139) 2.3	(183) 2.8	(128) 4.3	(38) 4.0			(197) 4.4	(273) 3.7
	-.5	-.3	1.6	.7			1.0	1.1
Net Profit + Depr., Dep., Amort./Cur. Mat. L/T/D			19.5				13.5	12.6
		(17) 2.6					(22) 4.1	(24) 2.6
			1.4				1.1	1.1
Fixed/Worth	.2	.4	.1	.1			.3	.3
	2.2	1.8	.6	.8			1.7	1.7
	-1.2	-15.9	4.4	2.4			-16.9	-18.8
Debt/Worth	.6	1.1	.6	.4			.8	.8
	11.3	3.7	1.6	1.4			3.0	3.3
	-2.7	-17.2	7.5	3.3			-15.6	-15.5
% Profit Before Taxes/Tangible Net Worth	120.8	71.0	53.7	40.3			98.1	101.1
	(132) 47.5	(155) 23.8	(147) 20.7	(42) 11.9			(190) 41.8	(245) 36.9
	.0	.0	4.5	.3			10.7	7.2
% Profit Before Taxes/Total Assets	38.0	20.5	15.3	11.5			30.3	33.2
	11.3	6.1	6.1	5.5			9.5	9.3
	-5.3	-3.2	1.8	.1			-.2	.0
Sales/Net Fixed Assets	121.8	40.8	66.7	36.6			41.2	47.7
	18.8	9.6	12.9	11.2			9.8	11.6
	5.3	3.0	2.0	2.4			3.0	3.0
Sales/Total Assets	8.0	4.1	2.8	2.7			4.8	5.0
	3.8	2.4	1.8	1.6			2.7	2.8
	2.1	1.4	1.1	1.0			1.4	1.4
% Depr., Dep., Amort./Sales	1.0	.8	.7	.4			.9	1.0
	(137) 2.7	(163) 2.8	(127) 1.8	(38) 1.4			(198) 2.7	(254) 2.5
	7.2	7.2	6.8	7.3			6.9	6.6
% Officers', Directors' Owners' Comp/Sales	3.6	2.6	2.0	1.8			3.5	3.4
	(116) 7.0	(101) 5.2	(57) 4.2	(10) 3.4			(103) 6.2	(134) 6.5
	13.3	8.9	8.9	5.4			13.0	12.2
Net Sales ($)	237093M	714859M	1567048M	2814881M	360555M	1888822M	4778126M	6710279M
Total Assets ($)	49860M	228829M	710242M	930826M	421422M	1179450M	1701921M	2086452M

Comparative Historical Data | Current Data Sorted by Sales

Type of Statement									
Unqualified	30	37	37	2	2	3	3	7	20
Reviewed	18	39	34	1	6	3	12	11	1
Compiled	30	53	103	25	18	19	21	13	7
Tax Returns	173	214	280	131	84	25	23	14	3
Other	123	151	218	66	54	22	36	22	18
	4/1/07-3/31/08 ALL	4/1/08-3/31/09 ALL	4/1/09-3/31/10 ALL	60 (4/1-9/30/09) 0-1MM	1-3MM	3-5MM	612 (10/1/09-3/31/10) 5-10MM	10-25MM	25MM & OVER
NUMBER OF STATEMENTS	374	494	672	225	164	72	95	67	49
ASSETS	%	%	%	%	%	%	%	%	%
Cash & Equivalents	18.6	18.1	19.0	18.5	19.6	21.7	18.5	17.3	18.9
Trade Receivables (net)	16.8	18.0	15.8	7.9	14.6	20.3	23.0	29.5	17.2
Inventory	6.5	7.6	8.2	4.9	5.8	11.0	15.4	11.2	9.8
All Other Current	4.4	4.1	2.8	2.0	2.3	3.0	2.9	4.6	5.1
Total Current	46.3	47.8	45.9	33.2	42.3	56.0	59.7	62.5	51.0
Fixed Assets (net)	38.5	36.8	37.0	49.1	38.1	31.5	25.8	23.6	25.2
Intangibles (net)	6.7	6.0	5.8	6.6	7.0	4.1	3.5	2.2	10.7
All Other Non-Current	8.4	9.4	11.3	11.1	12.6	8.4	10.9	11.7	13.1
Total	100.0	100.0	100.0	100.0	100.0	100.0	100.0	100.0	100.0
LIABILITIES									
Notes Payable-Short Term	10.8	9.9	12.1	13.4	12.1	18.6	10.1	8.6	5.0
Cur. Mat.-L.T.D.	4.0	4.6	4.6	6.2	4.7	4.5	3.3	1.6	3.4
Trade Payables	8.7	10.1	9.1	6.3	8.8	10.8	11.8	11.4	11.5
Income Taxes Payable	.1	.6	.2	.1	.2	.3	.0	.3	.3
All Other Current	17.6	17.0	17.7	23.7	12.4	17.4	12.1	15.5	22.6
Total Current	41.2	42.1	43.6	49.6	38.1	51.7	37.4	37.5	42.8
Long-Term Debt	29.6	30.0	29.0	43.0	30.5	23.8	13.1	12.7	20.9
Deferred Taxes	.2	.1	.1	.0	.0	.3	.1	.1	.4
All Other Non-Current	7.9	6.7	9.6	12.3	12.5	8.5	4.8	4.9	5.2
Net Worth	21.2	21.1	17.6	-5.0	18.8	15.8	44.6	44.8	30.7
Total Liabilities & Net Worth	100.0	100.0	100.0	100.0	100.0	100.0	100.0	100.0	100.0
INCOME DATA									
Net Sales	100.0	100.0	100.0	100.0	100.0	100.0	100.0	100.0	100.0
Gross Profit									
Operating Expenses	91.3	91.7	91.7	86.9	94.0	91.7	95.8	93.9	94.3
Operating Profit	8.7	8.3	8.3	13.1	6.0	8.3	4.2	6.1	5.7
All Other Expenses (net)	2.5	3.6	3.0	7.3	1.2	1.3	.1	.6	1.1
Profit Before Taxes	6.3	4.7	5.3	5.7	4.7	7.0	4.2	5.5	4.7
RATIOS									
Current	3.1	2.7	3.7	4.3	3.2	3.5	4.3	3.6	2.8
	1.2	1.2	1.3	.9	1.4	1.3	1.8	1.8	1.3
	.6	.6	.5	.2	.5	.6	1.0	1.0	.8
Quick	2.0	2.1	2.7	2.8	2.8	2.7	2.8	2.6	1.9
	.8	.9 (671)	1.0	(224) .7	.9	1.0	1.3	1.2	1.1
	.4	.3	.3	.2	.4	.4	1.0	.7	.6
Sales/Receivables	0 UND	0 UND	0 UND	0 UND	0 UND	0 UND	1 286.1	4 96.6	2 154.1
	5 78.9	6 58.0	5 77.0	0 UND	5 76.0	22 16.9	26 13.9	29 12.4	15 24.8
	34 10.9	34 10.7	37 9.9	6 59.4	38 9.7	48 7.7	49 7.4	53 6.8	49 7.5
Cost of Sales/Inventory									
Cost of Sales/Payables									
Sales/Working Capital	9.5	8.7	7.2	9.6	9.2	5.4	5.2	5.8	5.9
	65.1	47.2	38.2	-122.0	47.7	24.2	14.2	20.4	25.3
	-19.6	-20.7	-17.0	-5.7	-16.6	-32.1	-809.5	999.8	-84.9
EBIT/Interest	11.6	12.9	14.1	6.0	7.0	38.6	36.1	61.2	27.3
	(285) 3.5	(378) 3.3	(499) 3.0	(129) 2.0	(135) 2.2	(61) 5.4	(79) 4.0	(54) 9.7	(41) 5.1
	1.0	.6	.4	-.5	-.2	2.2	1.2	1.8	1.0
Net Profit + Depr., Dep., Amort./Cur. Mat. L/T/D	20.3	14.0	25.3						
	(22) 2.4	(33) 5.5	(40) 2.3						
	1.0	.8	.7						
Fixed/Worth	.2	.2	.2	.5	.4	.1	.1	.1	.2
	1.4	1.2	1.4	6.3	1.9	.9	.4	.3	.5
	-27.2	-38.6	-21.4	-1.9	-5.0	21.7	1.5	1.2	21.5
Debt/Worth	.8	.8	.7	1.0	.9	.7	.3	.4	.7
	3.2	3.5	3.1	15.2	4.3	1.9	1.2	1.2	1.6
	-26.2	-30.7	-17.6	-3.2	-7.8	NM	3.4	3.8	34.8
% Profit Before Taxes/Tangible Net Worth	108.2	84.0	71.2	76.8	85.1	63.8	40.1	93.6	61.0
	(268) 50.2	(358) 28.9	(485) 24.4	(128) 25.7	(116) 32.4	(54) 22.5	(87) 15.0	(61) 34.7	(39) 19.0
	14.8	1.8	2.6	-.6	-6.1	8.1	2.5	7.4	3.1
% Profit Before Taxes/Total Assets	33.5	24.0	22.6	22.3	24.0	18.2	19.5	32.2	16.4
	12.0	6.7	6.7	4.1	6.1	9.8	6.8	11.1	5.5
	.8	-1.2	-1.1	-4.2	-2.7	1.9	1.0	2.9	.8
Sales/Net Fixed Assets	51.3	60.1	59.9	41.5	27.0	88.7	91.4	77.1	47.7
	11.2	14.2	12.8	5.6	10.0	21.9	36.4	28.5	15.3
	2.7	3.2	3.2	.9	4.0	4.6	5.6	8.2	4.3
Sales/Total Assets	4.7	4.9	4.4	4.0	4.8	4.9	4.1	5.4	3.8
	2.7	2.6	2.5	1.6	2.7	2.7	2.5	2.9	2.3
	1.4	1.2	1.3	.6	1.7	1.7	1.5	2.1	1.3
% Depr., Dep., Amort./Sales	1.0	.9	.8	1.9	1.5	.8	.3	.4	.4
	(277) 2.4	(356) 2.1	(474) 2.6	(149) 6.6	(114) 3.2	(51) 1.7	(72) 1.1	(50) .9	(38) 1.1
	7.1	5.8	7.1	14.7	7.3	3.9	3.6	1.9	3.2
% Officers', Directors' Owners' Comp/Sales	3.1	2.8	3.0	4.5	3.1	2.7	1.8	1.9	
	(166) 6.4	(231) 5.1	(285) 5.7	(77) 9.1	(89) 5.7	(44) 5.2	(46) 4.0	(25) 3.1	
	12.4	9.7	10.8	15.2	9.3	9.3	7.7	5.6	
Net Sales ($)	5474001M	5045837M	7583258M	102053M	306272M	280741M	686547M	976787M	5230858M
Total Assets ($)	2283191M	2486263M	3520629M	124165M	167351M	165907M	353252M	357083M	2352871M

M = $ thousand   MM = $ million
See Pages 9 through 22 for Explanation of Ratios and Data

Current Data Sorted by Assets — Comparative Historical Data

						Type of Statement		
5	11	125	251	71	44	Unqualified	324	398
	20	172	66	3	3	Reviewed	92	122
10	66	186	29			Compiled	158	223
4	3	2	1			Tax Returns	7	8
100	245	694	252	22	11	Other	1057	1188
	840 (4/1-9/30/09)			1,556 (10/1/09-3/31/10)			4/1/05-3/31/06	4/1/06-3/31/07
0-500M	500M-2MM	2-10MM	10-50MM	50-100MM	100-250MM		ALL	ALL
119	345	1179	599	96	58	NUMBER OF STATEMENTS	1638	1939
%	%	%	%	%	%	ASSETS	%	%
61.9	17.2	8.5	11.0	19.7	26.9	Cash & Equivalents	16.7	16.3
2.8	.7	.9	1.9	5.8	3.4	Trade Receivables (net)	1.8	1.8
.8	.1	.3	.4	.4	.6	Inventory	.3	.3
1.9	.7	.6	1.2	2.4	6.6	All Other Current	1.5	1.6
67.4	18.8	10.2	14.4	28.3	37.4	Total Current	20.4	20.1
22.8	76.3	86.3	77.3	43.6	34.8	Fixed Assets (net)	71.7	72.4
.5	.1	.2	.3	.1	.3	Intangibles (net)	.3	.3
9.3	4.8	3.3	8.0	27.9	27.5	All Other Non-Current	7.7	7.3
100.0	100.0	100.0	100.0	100.0	100.0	Total	100.0	100.0
						LIABILITIES		
11.5	3.4	1.8	2.1	3.8	2.0	Notes Payable-Short Term	3.3	2.7
7.1	1.8	1.5	2.1	1.3	1.7	Cur. Mat.-L.T.D.	1.5	1.4
5.8	.8	.6	1.3	1.9	2.2	Trade Payables	1.3	1.3
.0	.0	.0	.0	.0	.0	Income Taxes Payable	.0	.0
20.8	2.9	1.6	2.5	8.5	12.0	All Other Current	3.8	4.1
45.3	9.0	5.6	8.1	15.5	17.9	Total Current	10.1	9.5
49.1	45.8	34.1	27.7	13.1	20.5	Long-Term Debt	29.8	28.7
.0	.0	.0	.0	.0	.1	Deferred Taxes	.0	.0
3.2	1.5	.7	2.4	9.8	9.2	All Other Non-Current	1.9	1.9
2.3	43.7	59.6	61.7	61.5	52.3	Net Worth	58.2	59.8
100.0	100.0	100.0	100.0	100.0	100.0	Total Liabilities & Net Worth	100.0	100.0
						INCOME DATA		
100.0	100.0	100.0	100.0	100.0	100.0	Net Sales	100.0	100.0
						Gross Profit		
93.3	85.7	87.3	91.0	92.7	96.8	Operating Expenses	86.8	86.1
6.7	14.3	12.7	9.0	7.3	3.2	Operating Profit	13.2	13.9
2.9	7.4	7.8	6.6	7.8	8.0	All Other Expenses (net)	4.9	5.1
3.8	7.0	4.8	2.5	-.5	-4.8	Profit Before Taxes	8.3	8.8
						RATIOS		
15.3	11.4	8.4	6.2	5.8	5.8	Current	10.0	10.2
2.7	2.2	2.8	2.5	2.5	1.9		2.7	3.0
1.0	.6	.9	.9	.9	1.0		1.0	1.0
14.6	10.7	7.7	5.8	5.6	3.7	Quick	9.0	9.5
2.1	2.0	2.6	2.4	1.9	1.4		2.5	2.7
1.0	.6	.8	.7	.8	.8		.9	.9
0 UND	0 UND	0 UND	0 UND	0 UND	1 322.7	Sales/Receivables	0 UND	0 UND
0 UND	0 UND	0 UND	0 UND	11 32.9	15 24.7		0 UND	0 UND
0 UND	0 UND	0 UND	6 59.7	59 6.2	53 6.9		1 246.5	2 188.3
						Cost of Sales/Inventory		
						Cost of Sales/Payables		
3.5	3.8	3.5	3.1	1.4	1.0	Sales/Working Capital	3.1	2.8
9.9	13.9	9.3	8.5	4.7	5.0		8.3	7.7
UND	-36.9	-117.6	-69.8	NM	-35.6		352.1	233.6
3.5	2.7	3.0	3.2	5.3	2.1	EBIT/Interest	5.3	4.9
(41) 1.6	(196) 1.5	(811) 1.4	(402) 1.4	(65) 1.4	(43) .6		(1030) 2.2	(1160) 2.2
.0	.9	.6	.1	-1.0	-10.8		1.0	1.1
						Net Profit + Depr., Dep., Amort./Cur. Mat. L/T/D		
.0	1.0	1.1	.9	.2	.3	Fixed/Worth	.8	.8
.1	1.6	1.4	1.3	.6	.6		1.2	1.2
2.7	2.5	2.2	1.9	1.1	1.2		1.9	1.8
.2	.3	.3	.2	.2	.3	Debt/Worth	.2	.2
1.9	.9	.6	.6	.6	.9		.6	.6
UND	2.1	1.4	1.3	1.1	2.6		1.4	1.3
59.8	-10.4	5.3	4.7	6.3	1.9	% Profit Before Taxes/Tangible Net Worth	10.7	10.6
(94) 14.5	(323) 2.9	(1170) 1.2	(594) .6	(95) .2	(57) -2.9		(1600) 3.2	(1896) 3.4
-1.7	-.9	-1.5	-3.1	-4.3	-12.6		.0	.1
25.6	5.1	2.9	2.8	4.0	1.0	% Profit Before Taxes/Total Assets	5.6	5.8
4.8	1.6	.7	.3	.1	-.7		1.8	2.0
-3.1	-.7	-.9	-1.6	-2.6	-5.2		.0	.0
UND	.9	.5	.6	3.2	4.2	Sales/Net Fixed Assets	.9	.9
UND	.4	.3	.3	.8	1.2		.4	.4
3.0	.3	.2	.2	.3	.7		.3	.3
5.9	.6	.4	.4	.5	.4	Sales/Total Assets	.6	.5
2.2	.4	.3	.3	.3	.3		.3	.3
1.0	.2	.2	.2	.2	.2		.2	.2
2.6	3.9	5.4	5.2	1.8	1.7	% Depr., Dep., Amort./Sales	3.2	3.1
(20) 6.2	(110) 6.6	(551) 8.5	(386) 9.0	(73) 5.1	(47) 3.6		(744) 6.6	(882) 6.3
9.5	11.7	13.0	12.7	8.7	7.3		10.4	9.9
5.3	9.7	5.3	3.9			% Officers', Directors' Owners' Comp/Sales	6.1	6.3
(16) 12.4	(54) 17.0	(158) 12.7	(72) 9.7				(285) 12.8	(303) 11.6
26.2	27.3	24.5	25.2				24.9	23.4
60494M	250737M	2161515M	4983052M	2509001M	4088887M	Net Sales ($)	9911240M	14027492M
26098M	437181M	6144755M	12159038M	6419280M	8738728M	Total Assets ($)	21736179M	25399799M

M = $ thousand   MM = $ million
See Pages 9 through 22 for Explanation of Ratios and Data

Comparative Historical Data | Current Data Sorted by Sales

Type of Statement	07-08	08-09	09-10	0-1MM	1-3MM	3-5MM	5-10MM	10-25MM	25MM & OVE
Unqualified	351	483	507	21	76	93	115	112	90
Reviewed	133	213	264	35	142	45	25	14	3
Compiled	208	259	291	141	119	21	10		
Tax Returns	17	16	10	7	2			1	
Other	1198	1422	1324	609	481	93	76	47	18
	4/1/07-3/31/08 ALL	4/1/08-3/31/09 ALL	4/1/09-3/31/10 ALL	\<-- 840 (4/1-9/30/09) -->			\<-- 1,556 (10/1/09-3/31/10) -->		
NUMBER OF STATEMENTS	1907	2393	2396	813	820	252	226	174	111
	%	%	%	%	%	%	%	%	%
ASSETS									
Cash & Equivalents	16.6	15.2	13.9	14.5	11.5	12.0	13.2	18.0	27.1
Trade Receivables (net)	1.8	1.5	1.4	.6	1.0	1.2	1.9	3.9	6.3
Inventory	.4	.4	.3	.1	.1	.5	.7	.7	.8
All Other Current	1.5	1.3	1.0	.7	.6	.7	1.4	2.1	5.0
Total Current	20.3	18.4	16.7	15.9	13.3	14.5	17.2	24.7	39.3
Fixed Assets (net)	72.6	74.6	76.5	80.8	81.8	80.5	72.5	57.7	34.5
Intangibles (net)	.2	.2	.2	.2	.2	.1	.4	.3	.3
All Other Non-Current	6.9	6.7	6.6	3.1	4.6	4.9	10.0	17.3	26.0
Total	100.0	100.0	100.0	100.0	100.0	100.0	100.0	100.0	100.0
LIABILITIES									
Notes Payable-Short Term	2.5	2.7	2.7	4.0	1.8	2.0	1.8	2.9	2.4
Cur. Mat.-L.T.D.	1.7	2.2	2.0	2.2	1.7	2.8	2.1	1.5	1.2
Trade Payables	1.4	1.2	1.1	.9	.7	1.0	1.2	2.4	4.4
Income Taxes Payable	.0	.0	.0	.0	.0	.0	.1	.1	.0
All Other Current	3.8	4.2	3.5	3.9	2.0	2.1	3.4	7.1	10.1
Total Current	9.5	10.3	9.4	11.0	6.2	8.0	8.6	14.1	18.1
Long-Term Debt	29.0	30.8	33.8	37.1	38.0	31.3	30.2	18.3	15.3
Deferred Taxes	.0	.0	.0	.0	.0	.0	.0	.0	.0
All Other Non-Current	2.1	2.2	2.0	.7	1.0	1.5	3.0	5.7	10.7
Net Worth	59.4	56.7	54.9	51.1	54.8	59.2	58.2	61.8	55.9
Total Liabilties & Net Worth	100.0	100.0	100.0	100.0	100.0	100.0	100.0	100.0	100.0
INCOME DATA									
Net Sales	100.0	100.0	100.0	100.0	100.0	100.0	100.0	100.0	100.0
Gross Profit									
Operating Expenses	85.9	89.1	88.7	84.5	88.5	91.9	92.2	93.8	99.4
Operating Profit	14.1	10.9	11.3	15.5	11.5	8.1	7.8	6.2	.6
All Other Expenses (net)	5.8	6.8	7.2	9.2	6.7	6.2	6.4	4.6	4.0
Profit Before Taxes	8.3	4.0	4.1	6.2	4.8	1.9	1.4	1.6	-3.4
RATIOS									
Current	9.9	8.4	8.0	11.9	7.8	7.1	6.8	5.5	4.5
	2.9	2.5	2.6	2.4	2.9	2.5	2.7	2.1	2.1
	1.0	.9	.9	.8	1.0	1.0	1.0	.9	1.1
Quick	9.0	7.8	7.4	11.0	7.4	6.3	6.5	4.4	3.8
	2.6	(2392) 2.2	2.3	2.3	2.7	2.3	2.6	1.8	1.7
	.8	.7	.8	.7	.9	.8	.9	.7	.8
Sales/Receivables	0 UND	0 UND	0 UND	0 UND	0 UND	0 UND	0 UND	0 UND	0 762.3
	0 UND	0 UND	0 UND	0 UND	0 UND	0 UND	0 999.8	4 95.2	12 31.6
	2 215.3	1 267.1	1 294.2	0 UND	0 999.8	2 188.6	8 45.0	33 11.1	44 8.4
Cost of Sales/Inventory									
Cost of Sales/Payables									
Sales/Working Capital	2.9	3.3	3.2	3.1	3.7	3.6	3.1	2.4	1.9
	7.8	9.6	9.2	10.8	9.2	8.8	8.0	8.9	7.0
	UND	-77.9	-81.0	-36.9	-604.4	-204.8	-179.2	-19.2	65.6
EBIT/Interest	4.5	3.2	3.1	2.7	3.0	2.4	4.3	4.5	6.2
	(1117) 2.1	(1502) 1.5	(1558) 1.4	(431) 1.5	(568) 1.4	(198) 1.1	(163) 1.2	(119) 1.2	(79) .9
	.9	.4	.5	.9	.5	.0	-.3	-.6	-7.8
Net Profit + Depr., Dep., Amort./Cur. Mat. L/T/D									
Fixed/Worth	.9	.9	1.0	1.1	1.0	1.1	.8	.5	.2
	1.3	1.3	1.4	1.5	1.4	1.4	1.2	1.0	.6
	1.8	2.0	2.1	2.4	2.2	2.0	1.9	1.5	1.0
Debt/Worth	.2	.2	.3	.3	.3	.3	.3	.2	.3
	.6	.6	.7	.7	.7	.6	.7	.6	.8
	1.3	1.4	1.5	1.7	1.4	1.5	1.3	1.2	1.6
% Profit Before Taxes/Tangible Net Worth	10.6	6.9	6.2	6.6	6.2	4.8	6.2	7.0	6.2
	(1857) 3.1	(2322) 1.1	(2333) 1.2	(785) 1.7	(794) 1.4	(250) .3	(224) .5	(172) 1.1	(108) -1.7
	-.3	-2.2	-2.1	-.3	-1.6	-4.1	-4.9	-4.8	-12.7
% Profit Before Taxes/Total Assets	5.9	3.8	3.5	3.5	3.7	2.9	3.3	4.4	3.6
	1.8	.6	.7	.9	.8	.2	.3	.6	-.4
	-.2	-1.3	-1.2	-.3	-1.0	-2.1	-2.3	-2.8	-6.4
Sales/Net Fixed Assets	.9	.8	.7	.4	.6	.6	.8	2.2	6.9
	.4	.4	.4	.3	.3	.4	.5	.8	2.4
	.2	.2	.2	.2	.2	.3	.3	.4	1.0
Sales/Total Assets	.5	.5	.5	.4	.4	.5	.5	.7	1.2
	.3	.3	.3	.2	.3	.3	.3	.4	.6
	.2	.2	.2	.1	.2	.3	.3	.3	.4
% Depr., Dep., Amort./Sales	3.4	3.9	4.5	6.0	5.3	6.4	5.1	2.4	1.4
	(817) 6.7	(1116) 7.2	(1187) 8.1	(228) 10.9	(371) 8.7	(183) 8.6	(164) 8.3	(146) 5.8	(95) 2.4
	10.6	10.7	12.3	16.0	13.0	11.5	11.7	9.7	5.7
% Officers', Directors' Owners' Comp/Sales	5.4	5.9	5.1	9.2	4.3	3.5	3.9	2.8	
	(309) 13.0	(318) 13.3	(312) 12.8	(141) 16.9	(100) 9.6	(23) 7.2	(24) 11.3	(17) 7.2	
	22.7	23.5	24.7	26.3	22.1	27.1	35.2	13.9	
Net Sales ($)	10126196M	14375459M	14053686M	426412M	1480099M	976353M	1553979M	2655230M	6961613M
Total Assets ($)	25694391M	34857681M	33925080M	2195469M	5561000M	3223260M	5007833M	7411215M	10526303M

© RMA 2010

M = $ thousand   MM = $ million
See Pages 9 through 22 for Explanation of Ratios and Data

	Current Data Sorted by Assets						Type of Statement		Comparative Historical Data	
3	3	11	23	2	10		Unqualified		19	23
	1	1					Reviewed			
							Compiled		1	
							Tax Returns			2
2		5	6	3	3		Other		4	9
	51 (4/1-9/30/09)		22 (10/1/09-3/31/10)						4/1/05-3/31/06	4/1/06-3/31/07
0-500M	500M-2MM	2-10MM	10-50MM	50-100MM	100-250MM				ALL	ALL
3	6	17	29	5	13		NUMBER OF STATEMENTS		24	34
%	%	%	%	%	%		ASSETS		%	%
		27.6	26.5		39.1		Cash & Equivalents		34.2	33.1
		16.3	8.4		2.0		Trade Receivables (net)		9.0	8.4
		2.0	.0		.1		Inventory		1.8	.4
		.8	2.7		1.5		All Other Current		1.5	4.5
		46.7	37.7		42.6		Total Current		46.5	46.4
		40.7	35.1		15.6		Fixed Assets (net)		25.6	25.7
		.7	.6		.1		Intangibles (net)		.2	.6
		12.0	26.7		41.8		All Other Non-Current		27.8	27.3
		100.0	100.0		100.0		Total		100.0	100.0
							LIABILITIES			
		3.2	4.3		.2		Notes Payable-Short Term		5.2	4.2
		.6	1.0		.2		Cur. Mat.-L.T.D.		1.0	.4
		2.5	6.2		1.8		Trade Payables		2.8	2.4
		.0	.0		.0		Income Taxes Payable		.0	.0
		13.6	11.5		4.9		All Other Current		4.9	5.3
		20.0	23.0		7.2		Total Current		13.8	12.3
		18.8	22.9		5.8		Long-Term Debt		11.0	14.7
		.0	.0		.0		Deferred Taxes		.0	.0
		.3	2.1		7.4		All Other Non-Current		4.8	1.1
		61.0	52.1		79.6		Net Worth		70.4	71.9
		100.0	100.0		100.0		Total Liabilities & Net Worth		100.0	100.0
							INCOME DATA			
		100.0	100.0		100.0		Net Sales		100.0	100.0
							Gross Profit			
		87.7	84.2		82.1		Operating Expenses		75.3	68.4
		12.3	15.8		17.9		Operating Profit		24.7	31.6
		2.2	18.2		15.1		All Other Expenses (net)		2.2	3.4
		10.1	-2.4		2.9		Profit Before Taxes		22.5	28.2
							RATIOS			
		12.3	11.0		35.2				16.3	14.2
		2.5	2.0		12.0		Current		4.5	6.9
		1.2	1.2		1.5				1.3	2.7
		11.8	10.7		34.6				16.3	13.8
		2.5	1.6		11.5		Quick		3.5	4.1
		1.2	1.0		.9				1.1	1.6
0 UND		0 UND		0 UND					0 UND	0 UND
		32 11.3	8 44.0		7 54.2		Sales/Receivables		11 34.4	2 236.5
		84 4.3	71 5.2		29 12.6				51 7.1	20 17.9
							Cost of Sales/Inventory			
							Cost of Sales/Payables			
		1.2	.8		.2				.5	.4
		4.8	3.5		.9		Sales/Working Capital		1.6	1.9
		12.2	22.9		7.3				6.6	5.8
			6.8						42.2	75.3
		(12)	2.3				EBIT/Interest		(12) 6.7	(14) 4.7
			-1.2						2.4	2.2
							Net Profit + Depr., Dep., Amort./Cur. Mat. L/T/D			
		.1	.1		.0				.0	.0
		.4	.5		.1		Fixed/Worth		.2	.2
		1.4	1.1		.6				.8	.9
		.1	.1		.0				.0	.0
		.6	1.0		.1		Debt/Worth		.3	.3
		1.9	4.2		.6				.7	.8
		11.3	7.4		6.0		% Profit Before Taxes/Tangible Net Worth		14.2	24.4
		(16) 4.6	(26) .5		1.8				3.9	6.1
		-.9	-9.7		-3.1				1.9	2.3
		7.4	2.0		2.6		% Profit Before Taxes/Total Assets		7.9	11.9
		1.5	-.3		1.2				2.9	4.8
		-1.0	-3.9		-3.0				.7	1.7
		8.8	26.7		450.2		Sales/Net Fixed Assets		26.6	455.8
		1.3	1.2		2.7				1.7	1.7
		.3	.3		.8				.7	.4
		1.5	.7		.4		Sales/Total Assets		.4	.9
		.3	.2		.1				.2	.3
		.2	.1		.1				.1	.1
		.8	.3				% Depr., Dep., Amort./Sales		.7	.6
		(16) 2.2	(24) 3.6						(19) 2.1	(25) 2.7
		5.4	15.8						4.1	8.8
							% Officers', Directors' Owners' Comp/Sales			
3054M	9909M	87969M	418179M	141871M	403524M		Net Sales ($)		372301M	268127M
1001M	6479M	92264M	787035M	393927M	1873777M		Total Assets ($)		1137085M	1244405M

© RMA 2010

M = $ thousand   MM = $ million
See Pages 9 through 22 for Explanation of Ratios and Data

Comparative Historical Data   Current Data Sorted by Sales

					51 (4/1-9/30/09)		22 (10/1/09-3/31/10)		
4/1/07-3/31/08	4/1/08-3/31/09	4/1/09-3/31/10	**Type of Statement**	0-1MM	1-3MM	3-5MM	5-10MM	10-25MM	25MM & OVE
33	47	52	Unqualified	7	7	5	14	10	9
		2	Reviewed	2					
1			Compiled						
			Tax Returns						
14	10	19	Other	3	4	2	3	4	3
ALL	ALL	ALL							
48	57	73	**NUMBER OF STATEMENTS**	12	11	7	17	14	12
%	%	%	**ASSETS**	%	%	%	%	%	%
34.0	32.1	32.6	Cash & Equivalents	51.7	14.3		24.3	33.7	46.6
5.2	7.2	8.4	Trade Receivables (net)	1.6	4.8		6.1	8.8	14.4
1.0	.7	.7	Inventory	.3	.9		.3	1.9	.3
3.2	4.4	2.7	All Other Current	.1	4.3		4.0	.7	5.4
43.3	44.4	44.3	Total Current	53.7	24.3		34.7	45.1	66.7
25.6	26.1	30.4	Fixed Assets (net)	25.6	52.8		37.2	22.1	15.2
1.4	1.6	.4	Intangibles (net)	1.0	.7		.5	.1	.1
29.6	27.9	24.9	All Other Non-Current	19.7	22.2		27.6	32.7	18.0
100.0	100.0	100.0	Total	100.0	100.0		100.0	100.0	100.0
			LIABILITIES						
3.3	1.2	2.8	Notes Payable-Short Term	1.3	.3		4.2	.9	1.0
.3	.4	.6	Cur. Mat.-L.T.D.	.4	1.3		.7	.4	.9
2.5	2.6	3.9	Trade Payables	1.2	4.2		1.5	4.1	11.0
.0	.0	.1	Income Taxes Payable	.0	.0		.3	.0	.0
5.2	8.3	10.7	All Other Current	7.1	6.9		6.0	13.9	20.0
11.3	12.6	18.2	Total Current	9.9	12.5		12.7	19.3	32.9
18.7	15.1	15.5	Long-Term Debt	6.8	33.8		24.4	6.8	3.1
.0	.0	.0	Deferred Taxes	.0	.0		.0	.0	.0
2.2	3.8	2.8	All Other Non-Current	.3	2.6		2.0	1.5	9.2
67.8	68.6	63.5	Net Worth	83.0	51.1		60.8	72.5	54.8
100.0	100.0	100.0	Total Liabilities & Net Worth	100.0	100.0		100.0	100.0	100.0
			INCOME DATA						
100.0	100.0	100.0	Net Sales	100.0	100.0		100.0	100.0	100.0
			Gross Profit						
71.4	89.5	83.0	Operating Expenses	77.8	83.6		86.1	79.4	89.3
28.6	10.5	17.0	Operating Profit	22.2	16.4		13.9	20.6	10.7
4.0	10.1	10.7	All Other Expenses (net)	3.5	18.4		16.6	14.8	-2.1
24.7	.3	6.3	Profit Before Taxes	18.7	-2.1		-2.7	5.8	12.8
			RATIOS						
26.4	23.5	12.9		29.6	33.6		15.2	12.6	12.5
6.5	4.6	2.5	Current	8.4	2.0		4.6	1.9	2.0
1.5	2.3	1.3		2.0	.7		1.5	1.2	1.2
24.5	23.5	11.9		29.4	33.6		15.0	8.5	11.3
4.6	4.6	2.3	Quick	8.4	1.7		2.6	1.7	1.6
1.4	1.6	1.1		1.6	.7		1.3	1.1	1.1
0 UND	0 UND	0 UND		0 UND	0 UND		0 UND	0 UND	1 485.2
1 271.8	9 42.5	8 44.0	Sales/Receivables	0 UND	13 29.1		6 61.3	5 69.7	25 14.5
19 18.9	39 9.4	61 6.0		0 UND	78 4.7		31 11.7	138 2.6	68 5.4
			Cost of Sales/Inventory						
			Cost of Sales/Payables						
.4	.4	.7		.3	1.8		.5	.4	.8
1.5	1.5	2.8	Sales/Working Capital	.8	4.8		1.9	4.5	3.7
11.3	5.5	13.6		1.9	-6.0		11.9	11.0	22.4
17.9	5.2	10.1							
(19) 3.8	(26) .2	(31) 2.8	EBIT/Interest						
1.2	-4.9	-1.2							
			Net Profit + Depr., Dep., Amort./Cur. Mat. L/T/D						
.0	.0	.0		.0	.2		.1	.1	.0
.2	.2	.3	Fixed/Worth	.2	.8		.5	.2	.1
.9	.8	.8		.5	2.8		1.1	.5	.6
.0	.0	.1		.0	.2		.1	.1	.1
.3	.3	.5	Debt/Worth	.1	.9		.6	.4	.9
1.4	1.0	1.5		.5	4.8		1.9	.6	2.9
17.3	4.4	11.1		10.9			6.5	12.9	18.5
(46) 5.9	(55) -1.1	(69) 2.5	% Profit Before Taxes/Tangible Net Worth	3.0			(15) 1.3	2.7	9.5
1.4	-5.4	-2.6		-.9			-10.9	-5.8	3.1
9.8	3.4	6.3		8.5	.4		3.3	11.4	12.6
3.6	-1.4	1.2	% Profit Before Taxes/Total Assets	3.0	-.9		-1.4	1.8	2.2
.3	-3.6	-2.0		-.8	-1.9		-7.9	-3.8	1.6
88.4	55.5	55.2		UND	56.8		37.7	14.9	144.2
2.7	3.7	2.5	Sales/Net Fixed Assets	4.2	.3		1.2	2.8	14.8
.5	.6	.4		.3	.1		.2	.8	2.8
.6	.6	.7		.4	.3		.5	1.0	1.6
.2	.3	.3	Sales/Total Assets	.3	.2		.2	.2	.7
.1	.1	.1		.1	.1		.1	.1	.4
.6	.7	.5					.3	.2	.1
(39) 2.8	(44) 2.8	(58) 2.0	% Depr., Dep., Amort./Sales				(14) 2.3	(11) 1.3	(11) .6
9.1	7.7	7.7					14.7	4.1	4.2
			% Officers', Directors' Owners' Comp/Sales						
602274M	1188089M	1064506M	Net Sales ($)	5616M	23626M	25598M	113869M	227418M	668379M
2655653M	3385999M	3154483M	Total Assets ($)	29781M	143281M	291732M	619351M	1021885M	1048453M

OTHER SERVICES—Voluntary Health Organizations   NAICS 813212

Current Data Sorted by Assets							Comparative Historical Data	

Type of Statement

0-500M	500M-2MM	2-10MM	10-50MM	50-100MM	100-250MM		4/1/05-3/31/06 ALL	4/1/06-3/31/07 ALL
2	10	23	28	7	3	Unqualified	64	75
		1				Reviewed		1
						Compiled	1	
		1				Tax Returns	1	1
4	1	6	1			Other	9	18
	66 (4/1-9/30/09)		21 (10/1/09-3/31/10)					
6	11	31	29	7	3	NUMBER OF STATEMENTS	75	95
%	%	%	%	%	%	ASSETS	%	%
	19.8	27.7	21.7			Cash & Equivalents	25.3	24.1
	26.9	13.5	18.3			Trade Receivables (net)	16.4	20.0
	.5	2.7	.9			Inventory	.8	.5
	10.0	2.8	2.7			All Other Current	5.1	6.7
	57.2	46.6	43.7			Total Current	47.6	51.3
	26.3	35.6	36.4			Fixed Assets (net)	38.1	34.1
	.0	1.4	.5			Intangibles (net)	.3	.4
	16.5	16.4	19.4			All Other Non-Current	14.0	14.3
	100.0	100.0	100.0			Total	100.0	100.0
						LIABILITIES		
	8.5	1.2	2.1			Notes Payable-Short Term	4.2	4.8
	.2	1.9	3.4			Cur. Mat.-L.T.D.	1.5	1.5
	15.6	7.9	10.0			Trade Payables	7.4	7.5
	.0	.4	.0			Income Taxes Payable	.1	.2
	11.7	10.1	11.9			All Other Current	8.6	10.2
	35.9	21.5	27.4			Total Current	21.9	24.2
	5.9	16.5	21.1			Long-Term Debt	13.8	15.3
	.0	.0	.0			Deferred Taxes	.0	.1
	.6	1.1	3.0			All Other Non-Current	3.8	3.2
	57.6	60.9	48.4			Net Worth	60.4	57.2
	100.0	100.0	100.0			Total Liabilties & Net Worth	100.0	100.0
						INCOME DATA		
	100.0	100.0	100.0			Net Sales	100.0	100.0
						Gross Profit		
	102.7	94.7	90.5			Operating Expenses	95.5	94.2
	-2.7	5.3	9.5			Operating Profit	4.5	5.8
	-.2	2.3	4.0			All Other Expenses (net)	1.0	.7
	-2.5	3.1	5.5			Profit Before Taxes	3.5	5.0
						RATIOS		
	6.2	6.0	3.0			Current	4.5	4.6
	2.0	2.3	1.6				2.4	2.2
	.8	1.5	1.1				1.1	1.2
	3.7	3.5	2.9			Quick	3.9	4.1
	1.8	2.3	1.3				2.0	1.9
	.7	1.1	.9				1.0	1.0
	4 97.7	24 15.2	2 164.2			Sales/Receivables	0 856.2	8 43.7
	30 12.3	38 9.7	31 11.7				23 15.9	34 10.8
	57 6.4	59 6.2	51 7.2				44 8.4	53 6.9
						Cost of Sales/Inventory		
						Cost of Sales/Payables		
	4.3	2.4	5.3			Sales/Working Capital	3.1	2.7
	11.2	4.7	13.2				7.3	8.2
	-51.3	15.5	NM				49.3	24.9
		13.6	5.5			EBIT/Interest	9.0	9.1
		(22) 3.6	(21) 2.0				(46) 4.2	(62) 3.4
		1.5	.9				1.0	1.2
						Net Profit + Depr., Dep., Amort./Cur. Mat. L/T/D		
	.1	.1	.2			Fixed/Worth	.2	.1
	.4	.5	.9				.6	.5
	1.5	1.1	2.1				.9	1.0
	.2	.2	.3			Debt/Worth	.3	.3
	.6	.5	1.3				.5	.6
	3.0	1.2	2.7				1.5	1.6
	15.5	11.7	19.1			% Profit Before Taxes/Tangible Net Worth	14.4	19.3
	(10) -5.2	2.3	7.8				(73) 3.1	8.4
	-41.0	-3.4	-1.3				-3.3	.7
	6.6	7.8	8.2			% Profit Before Taxes/Total Assets	7.9	11.7
	-1.7	1.0	2.0				1.5	3.7
	-15.8	-2.0	-.9				-2.1	.1
	58.1	73.4	35.6			Sales/Net Fixed Assets	15.1	29.8
	21.5	3.0	4.3				4.4	5.1
	2.2	2.3	2.4				1.9	2.2
	4.9	2.2	2.5			Sales/Total Assets	2.3	2.2
	1.8	1.0	1.5				1.4	1.4
	.6	.6	.8				.7	.9
	.9	.6	1.1			% Depr., Dep., Amort./Sales	1.2	1.2
	(10) 1.2	(28) 1.5	(26) 2.3				(65) 2.1	(82) 2.1
	3.2	3.5	3.4				3.5	3.5
						% Officers', Directors' Owners' Comp/Sales	1.2	4.7
							(10) 6.9	(13) 11.8
							16.6	18.4
9095M	46715M	290814M	1246236M	731505M	432392M	Net Sales ($)	2300667M	2094685M
2548M	14776M	172405M	607798M	506911M	523093M	Total Assets ($)	1962645M	1934357M

M = $ thousand   MM = $ million
See Pages 9 through 22 for Explanation of Ratios and Data

Comparative Historical Data

Current Data Sorted by Sales

Type of Statement	4/1/07-3/31/08 ALL	4/1/08-3/31/09 ALL	4/1/09-3/31/10 ALL	0-1MM	1-3MM 66 (4/1-9/30/09)	3-5MM	5-10MM 21 (10/1/09-3/31/10)	10-25MM	25MM & OVER
Unqualified	65	77	73	6	6	7	11	15	28
Reviewed		1	1				1		
Compiled	2								
Tax Returns	1	2	1			1			
Other	23	21	12	1	8	1		2	
NUMBER OF STATEMENTS	91	101	87	7	14	9	12	17	28
ASSETS	%	%	%	%	%	%	%	%	%
Cash & Equivalents	24.5	26.8	25.8		24.8		19.5	25.2	28.7
Trade Receivables (net)	16.8	16.6	17.9		19.3		16.7	15.0	22.1
Inventory	.8	.5	1.5		.7		.3	.3	3.8
All Other Current	5.2	3.3	4.2		4.3		3.8	3.8	2.8
Total Current	47.3	47.2	49.5		49.2		40.3	44.3	57.4
Fixed Assets (net)	34.9	35.1	32.4		37.7		49.5	37.1	29.0
Intangibles (net)	1.3	2.3	.8		.1		.1	1.2	.9
All Other Non-Current	16.5	15.4	17.3		13.1		10.1	17.3	12.7
Total	100.0	100.0	100.0		100.0		100.0	100.0	100.0
LIABILITIES									
Notes Payable-Short Term	5.4	2.5	2.8		8.5		.4	4.0	.9
Cur. Mat.-L.T.D.	1.3	1.0	1.9		.7		3.9	1.2	2.2
Trade Payables	6.2	9.1	10.2		10.4		5.5	12.2	14.6
Income Taxes Payable	.1	.1	.1		.0		1.1	.0	.0
All Other Current	11.5	11.1	14.6		29.4		7.1	12.0	15.1
Total Current	24.6	23.8	29.6		48.9		18.0	29.4	32.9
Long-Term Debt	18.3	18.2	15.6		16.6		20.9	18.6	13.9
Deferred Taxes	.1	.0	.0		.0		.0	.0	.0
All Other Non-Current	4.0	3.8	2.7		2.6		3.9	1.2	4.4
Net Worth	53.0	54.2	52.1		31.9		57.2	50.7	48.7
Total Liabilties & Net Worth	100.0	100.0	100.0		100.0		100.0	100.0	100.0
INCOME DATA									
Net Sales	100.0	100.0	100.0		100.0		100.0	100.0	100.0
Gross Profit									
Operating Expenses	94.3	95.0	94.9		90.5		93.1	93.1	97.5
Operating Profit	5.7	5.0	5.1		9.5		6.9	6.9	2.5
All Other Expenses (net)	1.0	3.4	2.2		6.8		3.2	.8	.5
Profit Before Taxes	4.7	1.6	2.8		2.7		3.7	6.0	2.0
RATIOS									
Current	5.4	4.5	4.3		9.4		3.6	2.4	4.0
	2.0	2.0	2.0		2.3		2.8	1.6	1.8
	1.2	1.2	1.3		.7		1.8	1.0	1.0
Quick	4.1	3.9	3.5		6.9		3.4	2.3	2.9
	1.8	1.8	1.8		2.1		2.7	1.5	1.7
	1.0	1.1	1.0		.7		1.8	.9	1.0
Sales/Receivables	7 55.8	4 85.3	4 85.3		0 UND		3 135.2	3 111.0	14 26.0
	28 13.0	30 12.1	35 10.5		38 9.5		36 10.1	30 12.3	34 10.7
	53 6.9	53 6.9	54 6.8		65 5.6		52 7.0	38 9.6	58 6.3
Cost of Sales/Inventory									
Cost of Sales/Payables									
Sales/Working Capital	2.2	2.5	3.1		2.6		3.1	5.2	4.6
	10.1	6.5	6.5		6.2		5.3	13.2	14.8
	29.6	30.8	29.7		-8.5		11.5	NM	400.8
EBIT/Interest	10.4	4.5	8.9				13.8	5.0	10.0
	(56) 3.4	(59) 1.2	(60) 2.3		(10) 4.9		(12) 2.1		(22) 2.3
	1.0	-2.0	.5				1.5	.8	.1
Net Profit + Depr., Dep., Amort./Cur. Mat. L/T/D									
Fixed/Worth	.2	.2	.1		.0		.4	.2	.2
	.6	.4	.5		.7		.6	.9	.6
	1.4	1.4	1.4		1.4		3.1	1.8	1.4
Debt/Worth	.3	.3	.3		.4		.2	.3	.3
	.8	.9	.7		.9		.6	1.3	1.1
	2.1	1.8	2.6		13.9		3.2	2.6	3.1
% Profit Before Taxes/Tangible Net Worth	19.0	13.3	13.7		8.5		13.5	20.2	16.3
	(86) 7.9	(98) 1.7	(84) 2.5		(12) .5		6.4	2.4	(27) 7.0
	.3	-9.1	-5.8		-11.2		1.1	-2.5	-6.6
% Profit Before Taxes/Total Assets	6.9	5.3	7.6		7.9		8.5	10.9	7.2
	3.4	.4	.9		.0		4.0	.6	1.9
	.0	-3.5	-2.8		-3.5		.3	-1.2	-2.5
Sales/Net Fixed Assets	33.4	18.8	58.1		UND		2.9	12.8	78.7
	4.2	4.5	5.3		6.8		2.3	5.7	5.4
	2.0	1.9	2.3		2.0		.9	2.6	2.5
Sales/Total Assets	2.0	2.1	2.6		3.7		1.6	3.3	3.6
	1.2	1.2	1.4		1.1		1.3	1.6	2.0
	.7	.7	.7		.4		.4	1.0	1.2
% Depr., Dep., Amort./Sales	1.2	1.0	.8				1.4	.6	.4
	(77) 2.3	(88) 2.0	(76) 1.9				2.6	(16) 1.9	(26) 1.4
	3.5	3.9	3.3				4.3	3.5	2.6
% Officers', Directors' Owners' Comp/Sales	3.2	2.6	2.3						
	(16) 9.0	(11) 8.1	(11) 4.8						
	22.1	13.5	7.6						
Net Sales ($)	2843963M	2660877M	2756757M	4116M	26216M	34380M	93804M	271469M	2326772M
Total Assets ($)	2428628M	2569269M	1827531M	21330M	51488M	32327M	131645M	196504M	1394237M

M = $ thousand   MM = $ million
See Pages 9 through 22 for Explanation of Ratios and Data

Current Data Sorted by Assets | **Comparative Historical Data**

Type of Statement	0-500M	500M-2MM	2-10MM	10-50MM	50-100MM	100-250MM	4/1/05-3/31/06 ALL	4/1/06-3/31/07 ALL
Unqualified		3	16	10		3	21	13
Reviewed			1					
Compiled								
Tax Returns		1	1					
Other		2	5	4			4	4
	33 (4/1-9/30/09)			13 (10/1/09-3/31/10)				
NUMBER OF STATEMENTS		6	23	14		3	25	17
ASSETS	%	%	%	%	%	%	%	%
Cash & Equivalents	DATA NOT AVAILABLE		26.2	27.9	DATA NOT AVAILABLE		23.1	23.8
Trade Receivables (net)			21.7	14.6			15.1	13.1
Inventory			1.6	4.4			5.2	.8
All Other Current			.5	4.0			6.4	2.1
Total Current			49.9	50.9			49.9	39.8
Fixed Assets (net)			43.3	21.4			24.3	40.3
Intangibles (net)			.1	7.0			.9	.4
All Other Non-Current			6.7	20.7			25.0	19.4
Total			100.0	100.0			100.0	100.0
LIABILITIES								
Notes Payable-Short Term			1.0	.2			2.8	.9
Cur. Mat.-L.T.D.			2.2	.4			.4	1.1
Trade Payables			5.5	8.5			7.4	6.3
Income Taxes Payable			.0	.0			.0	.0
All Other Current			11.4	19.5			9.0	10.4
Total Current			20.1	28.7			19.6	18.7
Long-Term Debt			18.2	8.5			12.0	13.9
Deferred Taxes			.0	.0			.0	.0
All Other Non-Current			3.5	4.3			3.4	2.9
Net Worth			58.2	58.5			65.0	64.5
Total Liabilties & Net Worth			100.0	100.0			100.0	100.0
INCOME DATA								
Net Sales			100.0	100.0			100.0	100.0
Gross Profit								
Operating Expenses			98.0	99.3			78.3	89.1
Operating Profit			2.0	.7			21.7	10.9
All Other Expenses (net)			.9	1.2			4.4	2.1
Profit Before Taxes			1.2	-.5			17.3	8.9
RATIOS								
Current			15.3	5.1			8.8	5.9
			3.3	1.9			3.5	2.6
			1.3	1.2			1.7	1.3
Quick			15.3	5.0			7.7	3.5
			3.3	1.7			2.6	2.2
			1.3	1.0			1.4	1.1
Sales/Receivables			5 80.2	1 335.3			0 UND	2 183.2
			27 13.4	16 23.5			6 66.2	27 13.7
			65 5.6	100 3.6			100 3.6	111 3.3
Cost of Sales/Inventory								
Cost of Sales/Payables								
Sales/Working Capital			2.4	2.8			1.1	2.0
			5.4	4.8			3.0	4.3
			23.8	21.3			8.0	79.3
EBIT/Interest								
Net Profit + Depr., Dep., Amort./Cur. Mat. L/T/D								
Fixed/Worth			.1	.1			.0	.1
			.8	.4			.2	.5
			2.1	.9			.6	1.1
Debt/Worth			.2	.2			.1	.2
			.6	.7			.6	.5
			2.1	6.0			1.6	1.4
% Profit Before Taxes/Tangible Net Worth			9.1	12.1			33.7	14.2
			.4	(13) 3.5			12.3	8.3
			-18.8	-23.3			-3.5	-5.8
% Profit Before Taxes/Total Assets			6.0	6.9			16.5	11.0
			.3	.5			1.8	2.5
			-7.3	-9.1			-2.5	-4.7
Sales/Net Fixed Assets			134.5	85.4			103.7	19.6
			3.2	13.4			5.0	2.4
			1.2	1.8			1.6	1.3
Sales/Total Assets			3.4	1.7			1.9	1.6
			1.3	.7			.7	.9
			.5	.6			.3	.5
% Depr., Dep., Amort./Sales			.3	.4			.8	1.5
			(20) 1.1	(11) 1.1			(20) 1.2	(12) 2.9
			3.5	2.9			3.2	6.7
% Officers', Directors' Owners' Comp/Sales								
Net Sales ($)		16202M	226638M	304215M		113978M	541991M	409495M
Total Assets ($)		7392M	108354M	229963M		406875M	820390M	420607M

M = $ thousand MM = $ million

See Pages 9 through 22 for Explanation of Ratios and Data

Comparative Historical Data				Current Data Sorted by Sales					
17	30	32	**Type of Statement** Unqualified	1	4	4	5	12	6
	1	1	Reviewed					1	
1	1	1	Compiled						
1	1	2	Tax Returns	1	1				
4	8	11	Other	2	2	3	2	1	1
4/1/07-3/31/08 ALL	4/1/08-3/31/09 ALL	4/1/09-3/31/10 ALL			33 (4/1-9/30/09)			13 (10/1/09-3/31/10)	
				0-1MM	1-3MM	3-5MM	5-10MM	10-25MM	25MM & OVER
23	41	46	**NUMBER OF STATEMENTS**	4	7	7	7	14	7
%	%	%	**ASSETS**	%	%	%	%	%	%
18.8	23.2	27.5	Cash & Equivalents					21.4	
14.8	9.4	17.1	Trade Receivables (net)					13.8	
6.9	8.9	2.3	Inventory					2.6	
6.5	3.3	1.6	All Other Current					3.9	
47.1	44.8	48.5	Total Current					41.7	
29.8	36.0	36.3	Fixed Assets (net)					36.4	
.5	1.2	2.4	Intangibles (net)					3.6	
22.6	18.1	12.8	All Other Non-Current					18.3	
100.0	100.0	100.0	Total					100.0	
			LIABILITIES						
6.5	2.7	2.7	Notes Payable-Short Term					.7	
1.0	.8	1.3	Cur. Mat.-L.T.D.					3.7	
4.2	3.0	5.8	Trade Payables					6.5	
.0	.0	.0	Income Taxes Payable					.0	
14.0	9.3	15.2	All Other Current					10.7	
25.8	15.7	25.0	Total Current					21.6	
10.4	17.6	16.3	Long-Term Debt					16.4	
.0	.0	.0	Deferred Taxes					.0	
3.1	1.5	4.1	All Other Non-Current					2.8	
60.7	65.2	54.7	Net Worth					59.3	
100.0	100.0	100.0	Total Liabilties & Net Worth					100.0	
			INCOME DATA						
100.0	100.0	100.0	Net Sales					100.0	
			Gross Profit						
95.4	96.6	96.9	Operating Expenses					99.3	
4.6	3.4	3.1	Operating Profit					.7	
-1.6	.2	1.8	All Other Expenses (net)					2.0	
6.1	3.1	1.3	Profit Before Taxes					-1.3	
			RATIOS						
3.3	9.0	8.5	Current					6.0	
2.0	3.7	2.5						2.0	
1.2	1.5	1.1						.7	
2.3	6.0	5.7	Quick					5.0	
1.4	2.8	2.4						1.7	
.7	1.1	1.0						.4	
0 UND	0 UND	1 287.6	Sales/Receivables					0 UND	
21 17.4	10 34.9	20 17.9						15 23.9	
62 5.9	61 6.0	59 6.2						41 9.0	
			Cost of Sales/Inventory						
			Cost of Sales/Payables						
4.5	1.8	3.0	Sales/Working Capital					3.8	
8.6	4.1	6.1						12.5	
39.8	13.5	41.1						-26.7	
14.2	9.8	5.0	EBIT/Interest						
(12) 3.9	(20) -1.0	(21) .7							
-.3	-1.0	-4.6							
			Net Profit + Depr., Dep., Amort./Cur. Mat. L/T/D						
.1	.0	.1	Fixed/Worth					.0	
.5	.4	.6						.7	
.7	.9	1.9						2.3	
.2	.1	.3	Debt/Worth					.2	
.7	.6	.7						.6	
1.6	1.0	2.6						1.8	
12.4	14.8	11.4	% Profit Before Taxes/Tangible Net Worth					10.6	
4.3 (40)	2.6 (45)	3.5						-1.3	
-2.2	-4.8	-13.9						-37.3	
10.5	6.6	5.9	% Profit Before Taxes/Total Assets					9.8	
3.2	1.6	.3						-.9	
-.6	-2.7	-5.3						-21.8	
65.3	27.3	94.2	Sales/Net Fixed Assets					85.4	
8.1	3.9	4.7						4.7	
2.1	1.4	1.2						2.7	
2.5	1.8	2.6	Sales/Total Assets					3.1	
1.5	.9	1.1						1.6	
.6	.4	.5						1.0	
.4	.7	.4	% Depr., Dep., Amort./Sales					.8	
(20) 1.7	(33) 2.4	(36) 1.3						(12) 1.3	
3.8	4.6	3.7						3.1	
			% Officers', Directors' Owners' Comp/Sales						
463137M	850400M	661033M	Net Sales ($)	2392M	13636M	25720M	56215M	210093M	352977M
395208M	693456M	752584M	Total Assets ($)	6243M	32749M	37534M	62468M	299450M	314140M

OTHER SERVICES—Other Social Advocacy Organizations   NAICS 813319

	Current Data Sorted by Assets						Comparative Historical Data	
Type of Statement								
Unqualified	10	49	121	135	20	12	262	311
Reviewed	1	3	4	1			4	6
Compiled	3	1	1				9	16
Tax Returns	1	4	3				6	14
Other	7	23	54	36	9	4	186	99
		351 (4/1-9/30/09)		150 (10/1/09-3/31/10)			4/1/05-3/31/06	4/1/06-3/31/07
	0-500M	500M-2MM	2-10MM	10-50MM	50-100MM	100-250MM	ALL	ALL
NUMBER OF STATEMENTS	22	80	183	171	29	16	467	446
	%	%	%	%	%	%	%	%
ASSETS								
Cash & Equivalents	25.5	28.0	22.1	19.3	22.7	24.4	21.6	20.7
Trade Receivables (net)	27.5	18.1	14.9	12.6	13.9	6.2	14.7	14.5
Inventory	1.5	.8	1.4	1.8	.1	1.0	1.9	2.4
All Other Current	4.9	4.3	4.8	5.0	4.5	5.6	6.0	4.8
Total Current	59.4	51.2	43.2	38.6	41.1	37.2	44.2	42.5
Fixed Assets (net)	26.1	36.7	42.3	41.4	30.4	29.0	38.6	41.4
Intangibles (net)	1.2	.3	.7	.7	.2	.5	1.3	1.1
All Other Non-Current	13.3	11.8	13.8	19.3	28.3	33.3	15.9	15.1
Total	100.0	100.0	100.0	100.0	100.0	100.0	100.0	100.0
LIABILITIES								
Notes Payable-Short Term	2.6	4.7	2.6	2.3	.6	2.6	3.7	3.2
Cur. Mat.-L.T.D.	1.2	2.7	1.0	2.0	1.3	3.2	2.0	2.1
Trade Payables	9.0	7.0	7.2	4.8	5.1	3.4	6.8	6.2
Income Taxes Payable	.0	.7	.0	.1	.0	.0	.0	.1
All Other Current	20.7	12.1	9.1	9.6	10.3	12.4	10.5	9.8
Total Current	33.6	27.4	20.0	18.8	17.3	21.6	23.0	21.4
Long-Term Debt	11.6	15.8	16.6	22.0	18.5	26.4	20.8	20.6
Deferred Taxes	.0	.0	.0	.0	.0	.0	.0	.0
All Other Non-Current	1.3	2.2	3.5	4.8	5.9	9.8	3.6	2.7
Net Worth	53.5	54.6	59.9	54.5	58.3	42.2	52.6	55.3
Total Liabilities & Net Worth	100.0	100.0	100.0	100.0	100.0	100.0	100.0	100.0
INCOME DATA								
Net Sales	100.0	100.0	100.0	100.0	100.0	100.0	100.0	100.0
Gross Profit								
Operating Expenses	99.0	98.4	97.4	96.9	92.8	91.4	93.4	93.4
Operating Profit	1.0	1.6	2.6	3.1	7.2	8.6	6.6	6.6
All Other Expenses (net)	.3	.6	1.6	2.9	6.4	4.3	1.7	1.3
Profit Before Taxes	.7	1.1	1.0	.2	.8	4.3	5.0	5.3
RATIOS								
Current	6.3	5.4	4.9	4.8	5.0	3.5	4.8	4.8
	2.4	2.0	2.3	2.2	3.1	1.6	2.2	2.0
	1.8	1.0	1.3	1.2	1.3	.8	1.2	1.2
Quick	3.9	4.8	3.6	4.2	4.1	2.4	3.9	3.6
	2.1	1.6	2.1	1.8	2.4	1.2	1.8	1.6
	1.3	.9	1.1	1.0	1.2	.7	.8	1.0
Sales/Receivables	1 247.3	0 UND	7 55.5	11 33.7	27 13.6	3 127.9	5 78.4	4 95.2
	22 16.9	20 17.9	23 15.8	29 12.7	47 7.7	30 12.1	25 14.8	24 15.2
	43 8.4	55 6.6	42 8.7	60 6.1	133 2.7	48 7.6	48 7.6	48 7.6
Cost of Sales/Inventory								
Cost of Sales/Payables								
Sales/Working Capital	5.3	3.2	3.0	2.5	1.1	1.2	3.2	3.1
	8.1	12.4	7.1	6.0	4.1	11.9	7.2	8.0
	25.3	81.6	25.0	32.7	18.8	-21.4	41.0	35.0
EBIT/Interest		8.0	7.6	9.5	8.0	7.5	9.0	7.8
		(39) 1.4	(119) 2.6	(124) 2.1	(21) 2.8	(12) 1.9	(286) 2.5	(281) 2.4
		-4.5	-1.1	-.7	-1.5	.2	.4	.8
Net Profit + Depr., Dep., Amort./Cur. Mat. L/T/D								
Fixed/Worth	.1	.1	.2	.3	.1	.2	.2	.2
	.6	.5	.7	.7	.4	.5	.7	.7
	1.3	1.4	1.2	1.4	1.0	1.0	1.5	1.4
Debt/Worth	.2	.2	.3	.3	.3	.4	.3	.2
	.5	.6	.6	.8	.7	1.6	.7	.8
	2.4	2.5	1.3	2.1	1.4	2.8	2.1	1.9
% Profit Before Taxes/Tangible Net Worth	35.5	19.1	11.5	11.0	11.7	9.9	14.1	15.1
	(20) 15.0	(73) 2.9	(180) 3.4	(166) 2.9	(15) 4.6	2.9	(446) 4.7	(430) 4.8
	-12.5	-8.6	-4.7	-4.2	-4.8	-.4	-2.2	-.9
% Profit Before Taxes/Total Assets	25.0	8.8	5.7	5.1	5.7	3.5	7.5	7.5
	2.6	.5	1.8	1.0	2.4	.9	2.3	2.4
	-19.7	-5.9	-3.1	-2.7	-1.7	-.5	-1.3	-.5
Sales/Net Fixed Assets	76.4	39.5	20.2	8.5	15.3	13.9	18.4	14.7
	28.0	10.3	3.8	2.3	3.1	3.5	4.0	3.6
	5.9	2.1	1.0	1.1	1.4	.8	1.4	1.1
Sales/Total Assets	4.4	3.8	2.6	1.4	1.1	1.1	2.4	2.4
	3.0	1.8	1.3	.9	.6	.4	1.1	1.1
	1.8	.8	.5	.4	.3	.2	.5	.5
% Depr., Dep., Amort./Sales	.6	.5	.9	1.1	1.1	1.0	.9	1.0
	(11) 1.9	(61) 1.3	(157) 1.8	(162) 2.9	(25) 2.7	(15) 3.6	(401) 2.0	(375) 2.1
	4.7	3.1	4.6	4.8	4.0	7.4	4.1	4.5
% Officers', Directors' Owners' Comp/Sales			4.4	1.3			2.4	6.4
			(20) 9.7	(12) 3.9			(27) 8.0	(39) 11.8
			16.6	16.1			13.7	16.5
Net Sales ($)	18357M	270865M	1561935M	4945406M	1886382M	1879331M	8662913M	10150563M
Total Assets ($)	5956M	105241M	971727M	3736638M	2040541M	2655500M	8032195M	8190704M

M = $ thousand   MM = $ million
See Pages 9 through 22 for Explanation of Ratios and Data

Comparative Historical Data / Current Data Sorted by Sales

				Type of Statement	0-1MM	1-3MM	3-5MM	5-10MM	10-25MM	25MM & OVER
	329		357	347	Unqualified	19	53	44	56	106	69
	5		7	8	Reviewed	2	1	4			1
	12		10	5	Compiled	4			1		
	7		9	8	Tax Returns	2	3	1	1	1	
	123		124	133	Other	16	30	17	18	26	26
	4/1/07-3/31/08		4/1/08-3/31/09	4/1/09-3/31/10		351 (4/1-9/30/09)			150 (10/1/09-3/31/10)		
	ALL		ALL	ALL							
	476		507	501	NUMBER OF STATEMENTS	43	87	66	76	133	96
	%		%	%	**ASSETS**	%	%	%	%	%	%
	22.3		20.0	22.3	Cash & Equivalents	22.9	18.0	23.9	19.5	24.3	24.4
	14.4		13.1	14.8	Trade Receivables (net)	11.8	11.7	14.4	12.9	17.5	17.2
	1.5		1.8	1.3	Inventory	1.7	.7	.6	1.5	.9	2.8
	5.1		4.8	4.8	All Other Current	3.2	4.4	4.1	4.9	4.7	6.3
	43.3		39.7	43.3	Total Current	39.5	34.8	42.9	38.9	47.5	50.7
	38.4		42.3	39.3	Fixed Assets (net)	49.5	45.0	41.1	41.1	35.0	32.7
	.8		.8	.6	Intangibles (net)	1.3	.3	1.4	.3	.4	.5
	17.5		17.2	16.8	All Other Non-Current	9.7	19.8	14.6	19.8	17.0	16.1
	100.0		100.0	100.0	Total	100.0	100.0	100.0	100.0	100.0	100.0
					LIABILITIES						
	2.9		2.6	2.7	Notes Payable-Short Term	3.1	3.0	4.3	2.5	2.1	2.2
	2.3		1.9	1.7	Cur. Mat.-L.T.D.	1.6	2.2	2.1	1.8	1.4	1.4
	6.0		6.7	6.2	Trade Payables	2.7	3.5	7.2	5.4	8.0	7.7
	.1		.0	.2	Income Taxes Payable	1.3	.0	.0	.0	.1	.0
	9.4		9.8	10.5	All Other Current	8.1	8.1	8.7	9.0	11.8	14.2
	20.6		21.1	21.2	Total Current	16.8	16.8	22.4	18.7	23.4	25.5
	18.4		20.6	18.5	Long-Term Debt	22.9	21.2	16.9	20.3	16.0	17.2
	.0		.0	.0	Deferred Taxes	.0	.0	.0	.0	.0	.0
	3.2		3.9	4.0	All Other Non-Current	2.1	1.3	2.9	4.9	4.4	6.7
	57.8		54.4	56.3	Net Worth	58.1	60.8	57.8	56.2	56.2	50.6
	100.0		100.0	100.0	Total Liabilties & Net Worth	100.0	100.0	100.0	100.0	100.0	100.0
					INCOME DATA						
	100.0		100.0	100.0	Net Sales	100.0	100.0	100.0	100.0	100.0	100.0
					Gross Profit						
	93.4		96.1	97.0	Operating Expenses	93.8	94.0	98.3	100.2	97.0	97.8
	6.6		3.9	3.0	Operating Profit	6.2	6.0	1.7	-.2	3.0	2.2
	1.1		2.2	2.2	All Other Expenses (net)	4.7	3.5	1.3	2.2	2.0	.8
	5.6		1.6	.8	Profit Before Taxes	1.5	2.5	.5	-2.3	1.0	1.3
					RATIOS						
	4.7		4.7	4.8		6.8	9.8	5.0	3.5	4.0	3.7
	2.1		2.1	2.3	Current	2.4	2.6	2.0	2.0	2.4	2.0
	1.2		1.1	1.2		1.0	1.2	.9	1.4	1.3	1.2
	4.0		4.0	3.7		4.0	7.7	4.2	3.0	3.5	3.0
1.8	(506)		1.8	1.9	Quick	1.9	2.5	1.9	1.9	2.0	1.6
	1.0		.9	1.0		.7	.9	.9	.9	1.1	1.0
5	77.3	4	93.0	7 55.1		0 UND	1 393.8	6 56.8	10 36.2	12 29.3	11 33.5
26	13.9	23	16.0	27 13.4	Sales/Receivables	19 19.6	22 16.6	19 18.9	34 10.7	33 11.2	27 13.4
48	7.5	47	7.8	54 6.8		61 6.0	45 8.1	57 6.4	58 6.3	56 6.6	47 7.8
					Cost of Sales/Inventory						
					Cost of Sales/Payables						
	3.4		2.9	2.8		2.0	1.7	2.7	3.2	3.4	3.6
	7.4		8.3	7.2	Sales/Working Capital	6.7	4.4	8.1	7.6	6.8	9.8
	28.4		69.6	30.8		UND	31.7	-261.8	23.2	20.5	37.0
	9.3		6.8	8.8		3.6	9.1	7.0	5.6	8.9	17.6
(297)	2.6	(326)	1.7	(322) 2.3	EBIT/Interest	(25) 1.1	(48) 1.2	(37) 1.8	(55) 2.3	(85) 2.5	(72) 3.4
	.5		-.8	-1.1		-3.0	-4.0	-5.9	-1.4	-.5	1.1
					Net Profit + Depr., Dep., Amort./Cur. Mat. L/T/D						
	.2		.3	.2		.1	.2	.1	.2	.2	.2
	.6		.7	.6	Fixed/Worth	.8	.8	.7	.7	.6	.5
	1.2		1.4	1.2		2.0	1.6	1.4	1.3	1.1	1.0
	.2		.3	.3		.1	.1	.2	.2	.4	.4
	.7		.7	.7	Debt/Worth	.5	.4	.6	.7	.7	1.0
	1.6		1.8	1.8		2.3	1.9	1.9	1.9	1.7	2.4
	17.0		11.0	11.7		18.5	12.1	8.3	11.4	12.9	12.1
(464)	6.4	(481)	1.8	(483) 3.4	% Profit Before Taxes/Tangible Net Worth	(41) .9	(80) 1.8	(62) -1.1	(74) .8	(132) 5.2	(94) 4.9
	-1.0		-5.5	-4.5		-6.5	-4.8	-9.5	-4.3	-4.6	-.2
	9.0		5.4	6.0		6.6	8.1	5.9	4.2	6.8	5.3
	3.2		.8	1.2	% Profit Before Taxes/Total Assets	.3	1.1	-.5	.2	2.1	2.0
	-.8		-3.4	-3.0		-3.3	-3.1	-6.5	-3.2	-2.7	-.1
	20.3		16.1	20.5		54.5	22.8	24.7	9.9	19.3	25.6
	4.0		3.1	3.8	Sales/Net Fixed Assets	1.0	1.9	2.5	2.2	5.9	5.7
	1.3		1.1	1.3		.3	.5	.8	1.2	2.3	2.3
	2.3		2.0	2.2		1.4	1.5	2.1	2.2	3.0	2.6
	1.1		1.1	1.1	Sales/Total Assets	.5	.7	.9	.9	1.4	1.4
	.5		.5	.5		.2	.3	.5	.5	.8	.9
	.9		1.0	.9		1.3	1.3	.9	1.0	.9	.8
(401)	2.0	(431)	2.2	(431) 2.2	% Depr., Dep., Amort./Sales	(28) 5.3	(67) 4.7	(56) 2.7	(68) 2.5	(118) 1.7	(94) 1.5
	3.9		4.6	4.4		11.3	9.0	7.6	4.8	3.3	3.5
	3.0		2.1	2.9			3.9			2.8	
(29)	9.9	(34)	8.5	(44) 5.5	% Officers', Directors' Owners' Comp/Sales		(13) 6.0			(13) 8.5	
	24.1		18.8	16.1			15.0			18.1	
	9052605M		10038971M	10562276M	Net Sales ($)	24407M	151330M	252487M	561411M	2173595M	7399046M
	8527616M		8473172M	9515603M	Total Assets ($)	78083M	413086M	449327M	819917M	2614980M	5140210M

M = $ thousand   MM = $ million
See Pages 9 through 22 for Explanation of Ratios and Data

OTHER SERVICES—Civic and Social Organizations NAICS 813410

Current Data Sorted by Assets							Comparative Historical Data	
						Type of Statement		
11	27	118	137	24	14	Unqualified	219	266
	4	15	2			Reviewed	5	14
5	14	14	4		1	Compiled	18	22
8	23	7	2			Tax Returns	26	28
27	33	80	62	9	5	Other	154	116
	371 (4/1-9/30/09)		275 (10/1/09-3/31/10)				4/1/05-3/31/06	4/1/06-3/31/07
0-500M	500M-2MM	2-10MM	10-50MM	50-100MM	100-250MM		ALL	ALL
51	101	234	207	33	20	**NUMBER OF STATEMENTS**	422	446
%	%	%	%	%	%	**ASSETS**	%	%
40.8	21.0	20.8	18.4	18.2	22.0	Cash & Equivalents	25.3	21.3
13.6	7.5	8.9	6.9	3.8	5.0	Trade Receivables (net)	7.5	7.2
2.6	1.3	1.4	.9	.4	.1	Inventory	1.0	1.5
3.2	2.5	2.3	3.8	2.8	5.6	All Other Current	4.8	3.5
60.2	32.3	33.4	30.0	25.2	32.7	Total Current	38.6	33.4
32.6	56.9	55.7	53.5	53.9	31.7	Fixed Assets (net)	45.7	51.3
.3	1.6	.5	.4	.8	.3	Intangibles (net)	.7	.5
6.9	9.2	10.4	16.2	20.0	35.3	All Other Non-Current	15.0	14.8
100.0	100.0	100.0	100.0	100.0	100.0	Total	100.0	100.0
						LIABILITIES		
10.4	3.7	2.6	1.3	1.1	2.9	Notes Payable-Short Term	3.0	3.7
4.2	2.8	2.0	2.0	1.3	.8	Cur. Mat.-L.T.D.	2.6	2.0
9.3	3.3	3.5	4.0	3.4	3.2	Trade Payables	4.9	4.0
.5	.0	.1	.1	.1	.0	Income Taxes Payable	.1	.0
21.0	6.7	8.1	6.5	8.4	9.7	All Other Current	7.6	7.7
45.4	16.6	16.3	13.9	14.2	16.6	Total Current	18.2	17.4
26.7	35.9	20.3	21.6	21.9	12.7	Long-Term Debt	24.4	21.4
.3	.0	.0	.0	.0	.0	Deferred Taxes	.0	.0
6.6	4.9	4.7	3.9	4.4	10.4	All Other Non-Current	4.3	4.0
21.0	42.6	58.7	60.5	59.5	60.3	Net Worth	53.1	57.2
100.0	100.0	100.0	100.0	100.0	100.0	Total Liabilities & Net Worth	100.0	100.0
						INCOME DATA		
100.0	100.0	100.0	100.0	100.0	100.0	Net Sales	100.0	100.0
						Gross Profit		
99.1	96.6	94.5	98.8	95.2	91.4	Operating Expenses	92.6	93.3
.9	3.4	5.5	1.2	4.8	8.6	Operating Profit	7.4	6.7
1.3	2.4	3.1	2.5	2.7	6.7	All Other Expenses (net)	1.7	1.2
-.4	1.0	2.4	-1.3	2.1	1.9	Profit Before Taxes	5.7	5.4
						RATIOS		
5.9	11.1	5.6	5.1	3.1	4.3		6.8	5.9
1.6	3.2	2.2	2.4	1.7	2.7	Current	2.7	2.3
.9	1.2	.9	1.1	1.0	.8		1.2	1.0
5.9	9.4	4.7	4.3	2.8	3.2		5.2	5.2
1.5	2.6	1.9	2.0	1.3	1.9	Quick	2.1 (445)	1.8
.7	.9	.8	.8	.7	.4		.9	.8
0 UND	0 UND	0 UND	2 164.4	0 UND	1 535.5		1 587.6	0 936.6
1 279.5	3 139.9	11 32.1	12 29.3	6 57.4	11 34.3	Sales/Receivables	9 41.0	11 33.3
25 14.6	18 20.2	40 9.1	44 8.4	22 16.4	72 5.1		36 10.1	33 11.1
						Cost of Sales/Inventory		
						Cost of Sales/Payables		
3.6	2.9	2.4	2.0	3.0	1.4		2.2	2.5
16.4	7.2	6.7	4.5	9.3	4.8	Sales/Working Capital	5.1	7.9
-61.4	126.5	-50.1	58.5	NM	NM		57.1	250.0
3.0	2.7	4.6	4.3	10.5	17.5		7.4	6.6
(20) -.4	(58) .7	(156) 1.1	(150) 1.3	(26) 1.7	(12) 2.6	EBIT/Interest	(252) 2.3	(281) 2.3
-10.8	-2.6	-2.4	-1.7	.0	-6.5		-.5	.4
						Net Profit + Depr., Dep., Amort./Cur. Mat. L/T/D	(10) 24.7 3.7 1.1	
.1	.4	.4	.5	.5	.0		.2	.4
.6	1.1	1.0	.9	1.0	.3	Fixed/Worth	.8	.9
2.3	2.1	1.6	1.5	1.6	1.1		1.4	1.5
.2	.2	.3	.2	.2	.4		.2	.2
1.0	.7	.6	.5	.8	.5	Debt/Worth	.5	.5
9.3	2.1	1.4	1.2	1.3	1.4		1.2	1.4
17.0	11.4	6.5	5.8	6.8	7.5		10.6	11.1
(40) 2.7	(89) .8	(223) .6	(203) .6	1.3	4.8	% Profit Before Taxes/Tangible Net Worth	(396) 3.0	(421) 3.2
-15.0	-6.6	-5.5	-4.5	-5.6	-1.9		-2.9	-1.5
5.5	6.1	3.8	3.8	4.3	3.7		6.9	7.2
.0	.4	.2	.2	.7	1.7	% Profit Before Taxes/Total Assets	2.0	1.9
-14.3	-4.2	-3.8	-3.0	-3.3	-1.6		-2.0	-1.3
299.5	11.1	3.9	2.6	4.4	20.4		13.2	5.2
21.4	1.2	1.2	1.0	.7	1.3	Sales/Net Fixed Assets	1.3	1.2
2.8	.6	.5	.5	.5	.6		.7	.6
5.5	1.4	1.2	1.0	.7	.5		1.3	1.3
2.1	.8	.6	.5	.5	.4	Sales/Total Assets	.6	.7
1.0	.5	.3	.3	.4	.2		.4	.3
.6	1.6	1.9	2.3	2.9	2.5		1.8	1.9
(21) 1.7	(71) 4.7	(185) 4.4	(184) 5.6	(32) 7.6	(17) 4.8	% Depr., Dep., Amort./Sales	(317) 4.5	(349) 4.7
3.0	8.6	8.7	9.3	11.0	9.1		8.2	7.7
							4.5	5.0
	(15) 1.6 4.5	(13) 2.2 7.0	(14) 3.4 8.8			% Officers', Directors' Owners' Comp/Sales	(38) 9.3	(42) 10.6
	7.0	16.9	18.2				26.6	32.4
38065M	224158M	1161019M	3413507M	1437047M	1265666M	Net Sales ($)	4998434M	4061897M
13080M	123137M	1265500M	4640171M	2357817M	2973758M	Total Assets ($)	7336199M	6921121M

© RMA 2010

M = $ thousand   MM = $ million
See Pages 9 through 22 for Explanation of Ratios and Data

Comparative Historical Data | Current Data Sorted by Sales

Hist 1	Hist 2	Hist 3	Type of Statement	0-1MM	1-3MM	3-5MM	5-10MM	10-25MM	25MM & OVR
280	304	331	Unqualified	21	52	54	70	82	52
8	10	21	Reviewed	3	10	5	3		
18	30	38	Compiled	21	11	3		1	2
41	40	40	Tax Returns	27	10	2	1		
118	151	216	Other	56	46	30	31	22	31
4/1/07-3/31/08 ALL	4/1/08-3/31/09 ALL	4/1/09-3/31/10 ALL		371 (4/1-9/30/09)			275 (10/1/09-3/31/10)		
465	535	646	**NUMBER OF STATEMENTS**	128	129	94	105	105	85
%	%	%	**ASSETS**	%	%	%	%	%	%
23.3	22.7	21.5	Cash & Equivalents	22.6	20.1	20.0	22.7	23.7	19.7
8.2	7.4	8.1	Trade Receivables (net)	5.0	7.8	6.5	8.6	9.7	12.1
1.1	1.0	1.2	Inventory	1.5	1.0	.8	1.2	1.2	1.6
3.0	3.4	3.0	All Other Current	1.3	3.3	3.2	2.7	4.2	4.0
35.6	34.5	33.8	Total Current	30.3	32.3	30.5	35.1	38.8	37.4
49.1	49.6	52.5	Fixed Assets (net)	62.7	55.9	54.4	47.6	47.7	41.7
.5	.7	.6	Intangibles (net)	.3	1.3	.5	.3	.8	.5
14.7	15.1	13.1	All Other Non-Current	6.6	10.6	14.6	17.0	12.8	20.4
100.0	100.0	100.0	Total	100.0	100.0	100.0	100.0	100.0	100.0
			LIABILITIES						
3.2	2.6	2.9	Notes Payable-Short Term	5.6	3.4	2.6	1.2	2.6	1.0
1.9	1.7	2.2	Cur. Mat.-L.T.D.	2.6	2.5	2.2	2.6	1.8	1.3
4.2	4.0	4.1	Trade Payables	2.3	3.6	3.4	3.6	5.3	7.3
.0	.0	.1	Income Taxes Payable	.2	.1	.0	.0	.1	.2
8.0	7.0	8.5	All Other Current	5.6	8.7	7.3	8.4	9.3	12.6
17.4	15.3	17.8	Total Current	16.3	18.4	15.5	15.8	19.1	22.3
20.2	20.6	23.5	Long-Term Debt	31.6	22.6	26.2	16.7	25.3	16.0
.0	.0	.0	Deferred Taxes	.0	.1	.0	.0	.0	.0
3.8	4.1	4.8	All Other Non-Current	2.4	4.6	5.2	5.5	5.3	6.7
58.6	60.0	53.9	Net Worth	49.7	54.3	53.1	62.0	50.2	55.0
100.0	100.0	100.0	Total Liabilties & Net Worth	100.0	100.0	100.0	100.0	100.0	100.0
			INCOME DATA						
100.0	100.0	100.0	Net Sales	100.0	100.0	100.0	100.0	100.0	100.0
			Gross Profit						
92.6	95.1	96.5	Operating Expenses	92.6	96.2	99.0	99.1	97.1	96.3
7.4	4.9	3.5	Operating Profit	7.4	3.8	1.0	.9	2.9	3.7
1.4	3.9	2.7	All Other Expenses (net)	4.9	2.5	3.1	1.0	2.4	2.0
6.1	1.0	.7	Profit Before Taxes	2.5	1.3	-2.1	-.1	.6	1.7
			RATIOS						
6.5	6.1	5.6		10.6	6.6	5.6	5.3	4.5	3.0
2.5	2.4	2.3	Current	2.2	2.7	2.5	2.4	2.3	1.8
1.1	1.1	1.0		.7	1.0	1.2	1.0	1.1	1.0
5.5	5.7	5.1		9.8	5.6	5.6	5.1	3.4	2.6
(464) 2.1	(534) 1.9	2.0	Quick	2.0	2.3	1.9	2.1	2.1	1.5
.8	.8	.8		.8	.8	.7	.9	.9	.7
1 557.4	1 658.9	0 UND		0 UND	0 UND	2 166.6	1 268.9	3 116.8	3 131.6
12 29.6	11 34.6	9 42.4	Sales/Receivables	0 UND	7 52.0	12 30.5	11 32.6	12 29.3	15 24.5
36 10.1	36 10.0	36 10.2		11 32.6	33 11.1	41 8.8	42 8.7	41 8.9	42 8.7
			Cost of Sales/Inventory						
			Cost of Sales/Payables						
2.2	2.3	2.4		2.1	2.0	1.9	2.6	2.5	4.3
6.8	6.5	6.4	Sales/Working Capital	8.2	6.3	5.4	5.9	5.9	8.9
66.7	103.7	436.0		-25.9	-103.0	37.2	NM	28.7	NM
7.9	4.2	4.3		2.0	3.9	2.7	3.8	4.7	10.8
(301) 2.3	(362) 1.1	(422) 1.1	EBIT/Interest	(58) .7	(91) 1.1	(65) .3	(73) 1.0	(70) 1.9	(65) 2.8
.6	-2.7	-2.4		-1.4	-2.5	-3.3	-4.4	-1.4	.1
			Net Profit + Depr., Dep., Amort./Cur. Mat. L/T/D						
.3	.3	.4		.5	.4	.5	.4	.4	.2
.8	.8	.9	Fixed/Worth	1.2	1.0	1.0	.7	.9	.8
1.4	1.4	1.6		2.0	1.6	1.6	1.2	1.5	1.6
.2	.2	.2		.1	.2	.3	.2	.3	.3
.5	.5	.6	Debt/Worth	.6	.5	.6	.4	.7	.7
1.2	1.2	1.5		1.5	1.7	1.4	1.3	1.7	1.5
13.5	7.7	7.0		5.4	10.5	2.9	5.6	9.0	9.7
(445) 4.7	(515) .8	(608) .8	% Profit Before Taxes/Tangible Net Worth	(116) .3	(118) .8	(90) -1.1	(102) .3	(100) 2.5	(82) 4.2
-1.1	-5.7	-5.3		-4.1	-6.5	-6.9	-5.6	-4.1	-4.8
8.3	4.8	4.1		3.3	5.0	2.4	3.7	4.5	5.8
2.3	.5	.3	% Profit Before Taxes/Total Assets	.1	.3	-.7	.2	1.5	1.5
-.9	-3.6	-3.6		-2.8	-4.3	-4.0	-3.8	-3.1	-2.8
6.8	5.4	5.9		4.5	5.0	3.6	5.8	10.2	11.0
1.5	1.2	1.2	Sales/Net Fixed Assets	.7	1.0	.9	1.3	1.7	4.1
.7	.6	.6		.2	.5	.4	.8	.7	.9
1.3	1.2	1.2		1.0	1.0	.9	1.2	1.5	1.9
.7	.6	.6	Sales/Total Assets	.5	.5	.5	.7	.7	1.0
.4	.4	.3		.2	.3	.3	.4	.5	.5
2.0	1.9	2.0		2.7	2.0	2.1	2.3	1.8	1.1
(359) 4.5	(418) 4.5	(510) 4.7	% Depr., Dep., Amort./Sales	(70) 8.1	(91) 5.9	(81) 7.1	(92) 4.5	(100) 4.0	(76) 3.0
7.8	8.4	8.9		14.7	10.2	9.8	8.0	7.1	7.0
4.5	3.5	2.6		1.3	2.0				
(50) 10.6	(49) 7.1	(54) 7.0	% Officers', Directors' Owners' Comp/Sales	(15) 10.8	(15) 5.1				
21.2	25.8	14.6		23.4	7.2				
4692191M	5749889M	7539462M	Net Sales ($)	61696M	239031M	358155M	763389M	1644942M	4472249M
8233753M	9980617M	11373463M	Total Assets ($)	216747M	576472M	1031271M	1465559M	2850689M	5232725M

M = $ thousand   MM = $ million
See Pages 9 through 22 for Explanation of Ratios and Data

OTHER SERVICES—Business Associations NAICS 813910

Current Data Sorted by Assets							Comparative Historical Data	
						Type of Statement		
9	20	62	54	4	11	Unqualified	121	144
2	6	4	2			Reviewed	10	13
5	4	4	1			Compiled	8	9
4	2	6				Tax Returns	6	17
19	29	36	11	5	3	Other	69	83
	128 (4/1-9/30/09)		175 (10/1/09-3/31/10)				4/1/05-3/31/06	4/1/06-3/31/07
0-500M	500M-2MM	2-10MM	10-50MM	50-100MM	100-250MM		ALL	ALL
39	61	112	68	9	14	NUMBER OF STATEMENTS	214	266
%	%	%	%	%	%	**ASSETS**	%	%
35.3	38.7	37.7	37.5		27.6	Cash & Equivalents	37.3	38.7
20.7	15.6	10.4	11.4		10.4	Trade Receivables (net)	11.1	13.9
1.5	2.2	1.5	3.4		.5	Inventory	1.9	2.2
.7	2.1	2.9	5.1		5.9	All Other Current	5.2	4.3
58.2	58.6	52.5	57.4		44.4	Total Current	55.4	59.2
31.9	31.1	32.0	20.9		18.2	Fixed Assets (net)	27.2	23.5
1.9	.9	1.0	2.8		.1	Intangibles (net)	2.1	1.5
8.0	9.5	14.6	18.9		37.4	All Other Non-Current	15.3	15.8
100.0	100.0	100.0	100.0		100.0	Total	100.0	100.0
						LIABILITIES		
8.1	2.5	4.8	2.3		5.5	Notes Payable-Short Term	2.4	3.9
10.8	1.5	2.5	.8		.4	Cur. Mat.-L.T.D.	2.5	1.5
24.3	9.6	8.2	10.2		4.6	Trade Payables	9.8	11.7
.0	.1	.1	.4		.0	Income Taxes Payable	.2	.3
24.9	15.5	14.8	12.9		19.5	All Other Current	15.2	15.3
68.2	29.3	30.4	26.6		29.9	Total Current	30.0	32.7
11.1	16.4	13.9	8.5		12.1	Long-Term Debt	13.0	14.0
.0	.1	.0	.2		.0	Deferred Taxes	.1	.1
3.1	7.2	10.7	12.6		10.3	All Other Non-Current	8.8	7.7
17.6	47.0	44.9	52.1		47.7	Net Worth	48.0	45.5
100.0	100.0	100.0	100.0		100.0	Total Liabilities & Net Worth	100.0	100.0
						INCOME DATA		
100.0	100.0	100.0	100.0		100.0	Net Sales	100.0	100.0
						Gross Profit		
98.7	99.4	95.5	95.0		94.0	Operating Expenses	92.4	92.3
1.3	.6	4.5	5.0		6.0	Operating Profit	7.6	7.7
.9	.4	3.3	2.3		2.7	All Other Expenses (net)	.8	.4
.4	.2	1.2	2.7		3.3	Profit Before Taxes	6.9	7.3
						RATIOS		
7.0	8.1	5.1	3.8		5.0		5.6	5.6
3.0	3.7	1.9	2.2		1.5	Current	2.2	2.0
.5	1.3	.9	1.5		.8		1.1	1.1
7.0	7.8	4.5	3.6		5.0		4.5	4.9
3.0	3.5	1.7	2.0		1.5	Quick	1.9	1.8
.5	1.2	.8	1.1		.4		.9	1.0
0 UND	3 117.3	2 196.0	5 76.3		1 271.1		4 87.9	5 69.8
17 21.2	14 26.7	12 29.8	15 23.6		11 33.3	Sales/Receivables	15 24.8	19 19.1
41 9.0	54 6.8	36 10.1	41 8.8		32 11.3		39 9.3	38 9.5
						Cost of Sales/Inventory		
						Cost of Sales/Payables		
3.7	1.9	2.1	1.5		1.4		2.1	2.2
6.7	3.0	5.9	3.6		4.8	Sales/Working Capital	5.9	5.2
-25.8	14.8	-48.8	15.1		-25.1		43.7	42.7
14.5	12.8	6.1	18.2				15.8	17.7
(18) 2.1	(25) -.2	(59) 1.3	(33) 7.1			EBIT/Interest	(121) 5.1	(148) 6.5
-2.4	-1.7	-2.9	1.9				1.2	1.1
						Net Profit + Depr., Dep.,	7.5	16.9
						Amort./Cur. Mat. L/T/D	(12) 2.6	(14) 8.5
							1.5	3.3
.0	.0	.1	.1		.1		.1	.1
.6	.5	.6	.3		.4	Fixed/Worth	.4	.3
1.9	1.2	1.6	.8		.6		1.2	.9
.1	.2	.4	.4		.8		.4	.4
.7	.9	1.1	.7		1.0	Debt/Worth	.9	1.0
5.6	2.1	2.5	2.1		1.6		2.2	3.0
15.3	11.1	14.4	15.5		11.4	% Profit Before Taxes/Tangible	25.8	24.7
(31) 2.9	(56) 3.0	(102) .5	(62) 4.8		8.2	Net Worth	(200) 9.8	(244) 12.1
-27.5	-12.1	-10.7	-1.6		1.3		1.2	3.1
10.8	5.3	7.2	8.6		7.6	% Profit Before Taxes/Total	9.3	12.7
-1.1	.3	.1	2.8		3.3	Assets	4.8	5.5
-12.8	-8.1	-5.9	-.6		.5		.4	.8
319.0	55.3	28.5	25.5		66.4		34.3	46.2
20.0	7.6	3.8	8.7		4.5	Sales/Net Fixed Assets	7.3	8.9
2.7	1.6	1.5	3.3		1.9		2.0	2.7
4.6	2.3	1.5	1.6		.9		1.9	2.1
2.3	1.2	.9	.9		.6	Sales/Total Assets	1.0	1.2
1.0	.8	.5	.6		.4		.6	.6
.5	.9	1.1	1.1		.8		1.1	.9
(25) 1.3	(36) 2.0	(101) 2.2	(61) 2.0		(11) 2.6	% Depr., Dep., Amort./Sales	(172) 1.9	(205) 1.9
2.1	3.8	4.6	3.3		3.8		3.3	3.0
		1.9					1.0	2.3
	(11) 4.5					% Officers', Directors'	(27) 6.5	(36) 9.5
		10.6				Owners' Comp/Sales	25.1	17.3
34342M	129903M	878469M	2796194M	605821M	2150474M	Net Sales ($)	3996407M	6315000M
9251M	71178M	581563M	1527882M	603050M	2461116M	Total Assets ($)	3257526M	4862534M

© RMA 2010

M = $ thousand   MM = $ million
See Pages 9 through 22 for Explanation of Ratios and Data

Comparative Historical Data | Current Data Sorted by Sales

	Hist 4/1/07-3/31/08 ALL	Hist 4/1/08-3/31/09 ALL	Hist 4/1/09-3/31/10 ALL	Type of Statement	0-1MM	1-3MM	3-5MM	5-10MM	10-25MM	25MM & OVER
	134	154	160	Unqualified	9	32	21	22	45	31
	10	16	14	Reviewed	6	4	1	1	2	
	11	9	14	Compiled	7	3	1	1	2	1
	14	14	12	Tax Returns	8	2	1		1	
	65	77	103	Other	35	24	11	8	13	12
						128 (4/1-9/30/09)			175 (10/1/09-3/31/10)	
	234	270	303	**NUMBER OF STATEMENTS**	65	65	33	32	62	46
	%	%	%	**ASSETS**	%	%	%	%	%	%
	39.4	36.6	37.7	Cash & Equivalents	33.2	40.5	36.1	35.0	43.5	35.3
	10.6	11.2	12.8	Trade Receivables (net)	13.2	10.7	10.6	12.6	13.3	16.4
	1.9	2.8	2.0	Inventory	.9	2.0	1.4	1.0	1.7	5.1
	4.0	3.8	3.1	All Other Current	.7	3.4	.9	5.2	4.9	3.7
	55.9	54.3	55.6	Total Current	48.0	56.6	49.0	53.8	63.3	60.4
	27.2	28.8	28.2	Fixed Assets (net)	42.2	30.7	34.2	21.3	20.1	16.5
	1.2	1.9	1.4	Intangibles (net)	2.1	.5	.7	1.2	.8	3.4
	15.7	14.9	14.8	All Other Non-Current	7.8	12.2	16.1	23.7	15.7	19.7
	100.0	100.0	100.0	Total	100.0	100.0	100.0	100.0	100.0	100.0
				LIABILITIES						
	3.3	3.8	4.1	Notes Payable-Short Term	5.6	3.2	2.9	4.7	5.0	2.6
	2.3	2.4	2.8	Cur. Mat.-L.T.D.	1.7	2.1	14.1	1.3	.9	1.0
	9.3	9.0	10.9	Trade Payables	5.1	16.4	7.0	6.2	11.9	16.0
	.1	.1	.2	Income Taxes Payable	.1	.0	.0	.5	.2	.5
	13.8	14.1	16.0	All Other Current	18.9	14.1	17.7	16.3	13.0	17.5
	28.9	29.4	34.1	Total Current	31.4	35.8	41.7	28.9	31.0	37.6
	12.5	10.9	12.7	Long-Term Debt	18.8	16.0	14.2	12.6	4.4	9.2
	.1	.2	.1	Deferred Taxes	.0	.0	.1	.0	.3	.0
	9.4	10.3	9.7	All Other Non-Current	4.5	6.2	7.1	15.2	15.2	12.6
	49.1	49.3	43.5	Net Worth	45.3	42.0	36.8	43.2	49.1	40.6
	100.0	100.0	100.0	Total Liabilities & Net Worth	100.0	100.0	100.0	100.0	100.0	100.0
				INCOME DATA						
	100.0	100.0	100.0	Net Sales	100.0	100.0	100.0	100.0	100.0	100.0
				Gross Profit						
	95.6	97.8	96.6	Operating Expenses	91.5	98.7	100.4	97.2	98.4	95.3
	4.4	2.2	3.4	Operating Profit	8.5	1.3	-.4	2.8	1.6	4.7
	.3	3.6	2.0	All Other Expenses (net)	4.5	1.7	1.2	.4	.8	2.0
	4.1	-1.3	1.4	Profit Before Taxes	4.0	-.4	-1.5	2.4	.8	2.7
				RATIOS						
	5.1	5.4	5.6	Current	10.2	8.4	4.6	3.7	4.1	3.3
	2.1	2.0	2.2		3.3	3.7	2.0	2.0	2.2	1.6
	1.3	1.2	1.1		1.1	1.1	.8	1.3	1.3	1.0
	5.0	4.7	5.1	Quick	10.2	8.0	4.4	3.5	3.8	3.3
	1.9	1.8	2.1		3.3	3.5	1.9	1.7	2.0	1.4
	1.1	.9	.9		1.1	1.0	.7	.8	1.2	.9
	5 78.1	5 75.2	3 114.5	Sales/Receivables	0 UND	1 268.3	6 64.6	1 348.2	5 76.2	6 57.0
	16 23.4	16 22.3	15 24.6		17 21.2	11 34.7	19 19.5	14 26.3	12 29.2	20 18.6
	36 10.2	35 10.4	39 9.3		44 8.3	38 9.6	39 9.3	34 10.9	42 8.7	40 9.2
				Cost of Sales/Inventory						
				Cost of Sales/Payables						
	2.2	2.3	2.0	Sales/Working Capital	1.6	1.7	2.3	2.2	2.1	2.2
	4.7	5.6	4.9		3.9	3.4	6.2	4.7	5.1	9.8
	22.7	27.5	61.9		63.5	NM	-16.3	12.9	17.4	NM
	12.6	4.6	9.2	EBIT/Interest	7.9	9.0	7.2	7.5	24.6	13.0
(113)	4.0	(131) .7	(145) 2.3		(28) 1.2	(35) .3	(16) 2.2	(16) .5	(24) 3.4	(26) 7.3
	1.2	-4.1	-1.1		-1.1	-3.8	-5.7	-.2	-5.4	3.8
	14.6	4.7	19.0	Net Profit + Depr., Dep., Amort./Cur. Mat. L/T/D						
(13)	8.6	(18) 2.3	(17) 3.2							
	2.3	-.3	.2							
	.1	.1	.1	Fixed/Worth	.0	.1	.1	.1	.1	.1
	.4	.5	.4		.7	.4	.6	.3	.3	.5
	1.0	1.2	1.3		1.6	1.5	1.6	1.1	.6	.9
	.4	.4	.4	Debt/Worth	.1	.2	.4	.5	.4	.8
	.9	1.0	.9		.9	.6	1.1	1.1	.8	1.4
	2.1	2.6	2.5		2.5	2.4	2.3	2.4	1.7	3.4
	20.8	13.4	15.1	% Profit Before Taxes/Tangible Net Worth	11.5	11.5	6.6	13.2	14.8	34.3
(219)	8.4	(257) -.4	(274) 2.9		(59) 1.5	(57) 1.6	(30) 2.3	(28) 2.4	(57) 1.9	(43) 11.0
	-.2	-14.6	-10.1		-13.3	-16.6	-10.4	-8.6	-15.7	2.1
	9.9	4.9	8.3	% Profit Before Taxes/Total Assets	6.6	7.7	2.8	8.3	10.5	10.3
	3.7	-.3	1.3		.7	-.8	.5	.3	1.3	3.9
	-.6	-7.5	-5.4		-5.5	-9.0	-6.9	-3.1	-7.8	1.1
	38.7	41.4	32.1	Sales/Net Fixed Assets	55.3	34.7	18.3	29.7	31.6	48.9
	7.0	6.7	6.8		2.7	4.9	3.0	13.9	11.5	10.4
	2.3	1.8	1.9		.6	1.3	1.5	2.8	4.2	4.3
	1.9	1.8	2.0	Sales/Total Assets	1.9	1.7	1.8	1.4	2.6	2.6
	1.1	1.1	1.0		.8	1.0	.8	1.1	1.4	1.2
	.6	.6	.6		.3	.6	.5	.8	.8	.8
	1.1	.9	1.1	% Depr., Dep., Amort./Sales	1.3	.9	1.3	.9	1.0	.8
(181)	1.9	(207) 2.2	(241) 2.0		(40) 4.0	(47) 2.1	(31) 2.2	(30) 1.7	(53) 2.0	(40) 1.7
	3.5	4.1	3.9		9.9	4.6	4.3	3.5	3.1	3.6
	4.9	4.4	2.7	% Officers', Directors' Owners' Comp/Sales						
(24)	10.0	(25) 8.7	(26) 6.0							
	27.9	19.9	10.8							
	6155217M	6481515M	6595203M	Net Sales ($)	35158M	118685M	129882M	236610M	1037386M	5037482M
	4518702M	4929000M	5254040M	Total Assets ($)	93047M	172511M	154605M	244938M	1059616M	3529323M

© RMA 2010

M = $ thousand   MM = $ million
See Pages 9 through 22 for Explanation of Ratios and Data

OTHER SERVICES—Professional Organizations NAICS 813920

	Current Data Sorted by Assets						Comparative Historical Data	
Type of Statement								
Unqualified	1	10	50	46	18	21	105	135
Reviewed	1	2		1			6	8
Compiled	1		5				6	5
Tax Returns	1	1		1			5	5
Other	2	6	1	1	2	4	50	49
	3	10 (129 (4/1-9/30/09))	23	17 (97 (10/1/09-3/31/10))	2	4	4/1/05-3/31/06 ALL	4/1/06-3/31/07 ALL
	0-500M	500M-2MM	2-10MM	10-50MM	50-100MM	100-250MM		
NUMBER OF STATEMENTS	8	27	81	65	20	25	172	202
	%	%	%	%	%	%	%	%
ASSETS								
Cash & Equivalents		30.9	43.4	42.9	32.5	25.0	39.2	37.5
Trade Receivables (net)		11.1	13.1	6.9	4.3	6.6	10.0	12.0
Inventory		1.8	1.4	1.7	1.2	.7	1.2	1.3
All Other Current		6.2	2.3	3.5	2.9	2.8	3.9	4.4
Total Current		50.0	60.3	55.0	40.9	35.2	54.4	55.1
Fixed Assets (net)		38.4	28.2	26.1	30.6	25.6	27.4	25.1
Intangibles (net)		1.1	.8	1.0	2.8	3.0	.7	1.8
All Other Non-Current		10.6	10.7	17.9	25.7	36.2	17.6	18.1
Total		100.0	100.0	100.0	100.0	100.0	100.0	100.0
LIABILITIES								
Notes Payable-Short Term		11.0	2.3	.7	.5	.2	3.2	2.2
Cur. Mat.-L.T.D.		1.2	1.9	1.4	1.2	1.1	1.0	.9
Trade Payables		10.5	7.3	6.6	11.0	3.5	8.1	9.0
Income Taxes Payable		.0	.9	.8	.1	.1	.4	.4
All Other Current		14.1	15.2	12.7	15.3	13.6	11.9	12.8
Total Current		36.8	27.6	22.2	28.1	18.4	24.6	25.3
Long-Term Debt		22.7	12.8	10.8	21.9	17.5	10.6	12.5
Deferred Taxes		.0	.4	.0	.7	.6	.1	.1
All Other Non-Current		11.8	8.3	13.5	6.8	16.5	10.6	9.7
Net Worth		28.7	50.9	53.4	42.6	47.0	54.1	52.4
Total Liabilities & Net Worth		100.0	100.0	100.0	100.0	100.0	100.0	100.0
INCOME DATA								
Net Sales		100.0	100.0	100.0	100.0	100.0	100.0	100.0
Gross Profit								
Operating Expenses		97.6	97.4	98.5	97.9	93.2	93.0	93.8
Operating Profit		2.4	2.6	1.5	2.1	6.8	7.0	6.2
All Other Expenses (net)		1.6	1.2	3.0	4.7	-.6	-.8	-.8
Profit Before Taxes		.7	1.4	-1.4	-2.6	7.4	7.8	7.0
RATIOS								
Current		8.2	5.4	5.4	2.9	4.0	4.9	5.0
		2.8	2.4	2.2	1.4	2.1	2.5	2.5
		1.6	1.4	1.3	.7	1.0	1.2	1.3
Quick		5.9	4.4	5.2	2.0	3.8	4.4	4.6
		2.2	2.2	1.9	1.2	1.7	2.1	2.2
		1.2	1.3	1.0	.5	.8	1.0	1.1
Sales/Receivables	0 UND	2 158.5	6 60.6	6 64.7	15 25.0		5 77.7	5 74.1
	9 41.1	12 29.9	13 27.3	10 37.9	24 15.5		16 22.8	16 23.0
	39 9.3	32 11.4	28 12.9	26 13.8	39 9.4		36 10.3	39 9.4
Cost of Sales/Inventory								
Cost of Sales/Payables								
Sales/Working Capital		2.2	1.8	1.3	4.1	2.4	2.1	2.2
		5.5	3.6	2.9	12.5	6.7	4.9	4.5
		21.7	10.7	19.6	-9.8	NM	18.8	17.8
EBIT/Interest		4.9	11.3	5.2	20.4	13.5	29.7	23.0
	(15)	1.7 (32)	2.3 (31)	1.2 (15)	1.9 (18)	5.1	(83) 6.1 (100)	5.8
		-.9	-1.6	-13.1	-5.1	2.2	1.8	2.3
Net Profit + Depr., Dep., Amort./Cur. Mat. L/T/D								10.8
							(11)	6.0
								4.5
Fixed/Worth		.1	.1	.2	.2	.2	.1	.1
		.8	.6	.4	.7	.4	.3	.3
		9.2	1.1	.9	1.9	2.5	.9	1.0
Debt/Worth		.2	.5	.3	.4	.4	.4	.4
		1.0	.9	1.0	1.9	1.1	.8	.8
		8.2	1.7	1.6	2.6	5.6	1.7	1.9
% Profit Before Taxes/Tangible Net Worth		14.3	11.1	8.3	14.4	32.4	18.6	24.1
	(21)	-1.0 (78)	-.4 (63)	1.3 (18)	7.8 (23)	10.8	(167) 10.1 (191)	9.6
		-8.9	-12.8	-10.4	-4.7	-.1	1.9	1.1
% Profit Before Taxes/Total Assets		5.1	5.0	4.1	5.6	9.4	9.9	11.8
		-1.4	-.4	.8	2.3	4.8	4.9	5.5
		-6.3	-7.6	-6.5	-1.2	-.1	.8	.4
Sales/Net Fixed Assets		38.3	30.7	16.1	7.3	12.8	22.5	30.4
		5.1	6.6	4.1	3.5	4.8	5.2	8.8
		1.8	1.8	2.0	.7	2.4	2.3	2.1
Sales/Total Assets		2.3	1.9	1.0	1.0	1.2	1.6	1.8
		1.4	1.0	.7	.7	.7	1.0	1.0
		.6	.6	.6	.4	.5	.6	.6
% Depr., Dep., Amort./Sales		.9	1.2	1.9	2.2	1.4	1.5	1.2
	(19)	2.4 (69)	2.0 (58)	2.7 (18)	3.6 (23)	2.5	(142) 2.4 (161)	2.2
		6.4	4.3	4.6	8.9	3.8	3.8	3.3
% Officers', Directors' Owners' Comp/Sales							5.3	3.1
							(20) 11.9 (24)	6.9
							23.7	22.4
Net Sales ($)	5253M	59256M	596841M	1269753M	1515198M	4060934M	4871226M	4853996M
Total Assets ($)	1874M	33638M	415730M	1356277M	1304194M	4064444M	4729540M	5434337M

M = $ thousand   MM = $ million
See Pages 9 through 22 for Explanation of Ratios and Data

Comparative Historical Data   Current Data Sorted by Sales

Comp. Hist. 1	Comp. Hist. 2	Comp. Hist. 3	Type of Statement	0-1MM	1-3MM	3-5MM	5-10MM	10-25MM	25MM & OVER
140	160	146	Unqualified	4	21	11	27	37	46
3	5	4	Reviewed	1	1			1	1
2	11	7	Compiled	1		3	1	1	
5	4	10	Tax Returns	6	1	2	1		
42	44	59	Other	5	11	8	10	13	12
4/1/07-3/31/08 ALL	4/1/08-3/31/09 ALL	4/1/09-3/31/10 ALL		129 (4/1-9/30/09)			97 (10/1/09-3/31/10)		
192	224	226	NUMBER OF STATEMENTS	17	35	24	39	52	59
%	%	%	**ASSETS**	%	%	%	%	%	%
39.4	37.9	38.3	Cash & Equivalents	31.5	35.3	44.2	51.0	33.6	35.5
10.3	10.3	9.8	Trade Receivables (net)	3.7	8.0	9.6	11.1	13.4	8.6
1.1	1.3	1.6	Inventory	1.4	1.2	1.3	1.8	1.2	2.1
3.9	4.2	3.2	All Other Current	2.1	5.5	2.1	2.5	2.1	4.0
54.7	53.7	52.9	Total Current	38.6	50.0	57.2	66.5	50.3	50.3
27.1	25.4	28.9	Fixed Assets (net)	52.7	39.4	28.4	19.8	28.6	22.2
.7	1.8	1.4	Intangibles (net)	.9	.8	1.0	.0	1.7	2.5
17.4	19.1	16.9	All Other Non-Current	7.7	9.8	13.4	13.7	19.4	25.0
100.0	100.0	100.0	Total	100.0	100.0	100.0	100.0	100.0	100.0
			LIABILITIES						
2.9	2.2	2.8	Notes Payable-Short Term	6.8	7.5	1.3	1.7	2.5	.3
1.0	.9	1.5	Cur. Mat.-L.T.D.	2.6	2.7	.9	.5	1.6	1.4
8.9	8.1	7.4	Trade Payables	3.7	5.1	7.9	6.4	9.7	8.0
.4	.7	.6	Income Taxes Payable	.0	.0	.1	.0	2.5	.1
12.9	14.2	14.6	All Other Current	14.3	10.7	11.7	15.1	15.6	16.8
26.1	26.0	26.8	Total Current	27.4	26.0	21.8	23.8	31.8	26.6
12.3	13.7	15.6	Long-Term Debt	36.3	18.5	13.5	8.0	14.3	14.8
.2	.1	.3	Deferred Taxes	.0	.0	1.3	.0	.3	.3
11.7	11.6	11.3	All Other Non-Current	3.0	14.2	8.4	12.1	9.5	14.1
49.8	48.6	46.1	Net Worth	33.3	41.2	55.0	56.0	44.1	44.3
100.0	100.0	100.0	Total Liabilties & Net Worth	100.0	100.0	100.0	100.0	100.0	100.0
			INCOME DATA						
100.0	100.0	100.0	Net Sales	100.0	100.0	100.0	100.0	100.0	100.0
			Gross Profit						
93.2	96.6	97.5	Operating Expenses	96.7	94.9	97.6	100.4	98.8	96.2
6.8	3.4	2.5	Operating Profit	3.3	5.1	2.4	-.4	1.2	3.8
-1.0	3.8	1.9	All Other Expenses (net)	5.5	1.1	-.3	2.4	1.9	1.8
7.8	-.4	.6	Profit Before Taxes	-2.2	4.0	2.7	-2.8	-.7	2.0
			RATIOS						
5.3	5.2	5.3	Current	8.1	8.2	8.6	7.2	2.5	4.3
2.6	2.3	2.2		2.4	3.1	2.7	2.8	1.6	2.1
1.3	1.3	1.3		.4	1.4	1.7	1.7	1.0	1.1
5.0	4.9	4.5	Quick	6.0	7.2	8.6	7.1	2.3	4.1
2.3	2.1	1.9		1.5	2.9	2.4	2.6	1.4	1.6
1.2	1.1	1.1		.3	1.4	1.4	1.7	.9	.8
5 75.3	6 57.9	3 106.6	Sales/Receivables	0 UND	1 566.3	2 183.3	3 118.6	7 54.3	8 48.3
15 24.4	16 23.3	14 26.2		0 UND	11 33.4	16 22.7	12 29.9	16 23.0	18 20.3
37 9.7	37 9.9	32 11.5		9 40.6	32 11.5	39 9.4	34 10.7	36 10.3	31 11.7
			Cost of Sales/Inventory						
			Cost of Sales/Payables						
2.0	1.8	1.8	Sales/Working Capital	2.0	1.7	1.5	1.1	2.7	1.8
4.0	4.3	4.6		4.3	3.6	2.9	3.3	7.2	6.7
14.3	14.4	20.1		-5.1	12.6	6.1	6.4	303.9	194.9
21.7	9.0	6.7	EBIT/Interest		3.3		17.7	6.2	7.7
(86) 6.1	(108) 1.8	(115) 2.1			(17) 2.1		(17) 2.4	(27) -.5	(37) 4.4
1.2	-2.8	-1.7			.2		-16.2	-4.3	-2.2
15.3	3.1	9.7	Net Profit + Depr., Dep., Amort./Cur. Mat. L/T/D						
(12) 11.7	(14) 1.3	(15) 2.7							
3.8	-17.0	1.1							
.1	.1	.2	Fixed/Worth	.1	.2	.1	.0	.2	.2
.4	.4	.5		.9	.8	.6	.3	.6	.4
1.1	1.2	1.2		6.0	2.3	1.3	.5	1.4	1.2
.4	.4	.4	Debt/Worth	.2	.4	.3	.4	.5	.4
.8	1.0	1.0		1.0	.9	.6	.8	1.2	1.2
2.0	1.7	2.5		9.2	3.6	2.4	1.1	1.9	3.5
17.9	11.6	11.4	% Profit Before Taxes/Tangible Net Worth	2.9	11.3	18.9	6.8	8.8	24.9
(182) 10.7	(208) .5	(210) .8		(15) -1.0	(31) .0	(23) 1.7	(38) -2.4	(49) -1.0	(54) 8.5
2.3	-14.8	-9.8		-14.7	-8.9	-7.5	-21.0	-12.3	-1.9
11.4	5.6	5.0	% Profit Before Taxes/Total Assets	.7	5.1	6.3	3.7	3.3	7.7
5.1	.1	.3		-1.9	1.1	.5	-1.4	-.6	2.5
.9	-7.2	-6.3		-9.5	-3.6	-5.6	-10.0	-8.1	-.8
21.5	23.1	18.4	Sales/Net Fixed Assets	58.3	15.3	13.3	33.4	27.3	15.3
5.9	6.5	5.0		.9	2.0	4.4	8.5	4.2	6.8
2.1	2.1	1.9		.4	.8	2.1	2.8	1.8	3.5
1.5	1.4	1.5	Sales/Total Assets	2.3	1.5	1.4	1.9	1.5	2.0
.9	.9	.9		.5	.8	1.0	.9	.9	.9
.6	.6	.5		.3	.5	.6	.7	.6	.6
1.3	1.3	1.5	% Depr., Dep., Amort./Sales	2.2	1.9	1.2	1.4	1.6	1.4
(166) 2.2	(193) 2.3	(191) 2.5		(12) 8.1	(28) 3.4	(19) 2.2	(33) 2.0	(48) 2.5	(51) 2.7
3.5	3.5	4.7		17.4	5.3	3.8	2.6	4.6	4.2
2.8	2.7	3.3	% Officers', Directors' Owners' Comp/Sales						
(11) 6.8	(14) 8.0	(17) 8.3							
27.9	25.8	29.9							
4651308M	6792129M	7507235M	Net Sales ($)	7805M	66566M	89605M	283956M	789043M	6270260M
5170141M	7229900M	7176157M	Total Assets ($)	18539M	117325M	115104M	326367M	1040101M	5558721M

© RMA 2010

M = $ thousand   MM = $ million
See Pages 9 through 22 for Explanation of Ratios and Data

OTHER SERVICES—Labor Unions and Similar Labor Organizations NAICS 813930

Current Data Sorted by Assets | Comparative Historical Data

	0-500M	500M-2MM	2-10MM	10-50MM	50-100MM	100-250MM		4/1/05-3/31/06 ALL	4/1/06-3/31/07 ALL
Type of Statement		56 (4/1-9/30/09)		50 (10/1/09-3/31/10)					
Unqualified	1	6	23	22	3	5		36	38
Reviewed		2	1					1	2
Compiled	1	2	1			1		4	1
Tax Returns	1	5	1					1	3
Other	2	5	10	7	3	4		14	16
NUMBER OF STATEMENTS	5	20	36	29	6	10		56	60
ASSETS	%	%	%	%	%	%		%	%
Cash & Equivalents		60.6	36.6	46.8		48.7		44.1	39.8
Trade Receivables (net)		2.9	3.0	4.9		6.2		4.4	5.1
Inventory		.3	.3	.1		.2		.1	.0
All Other Current		1.4	3.3	3.8		11.3		5.5	4.0
Total Current		65.2	43.1	55.6		66.4		54.1	48.9
Fixed Assets (net)		26.6	49.8	30.4		11.9		35.0	33.5
Intangibles (net)		.0	.1	.0		1.0		.2	.1
All Other Non-Current		8.3	7.0	14.0		20.7		10.7	17.5
Total		100.0	100.0	100.0		100.0		100.0	100.0
LIABILITIES									
Notes Payable-Short Term		5.7	2.0	.2		.0		1.4	.6
Cur. Mat.-L.T.D.		.4	2.3	.9		.5		2.3	2.2
Trade Payables		1.3	1.6	3.4		5.4		9.5	2.9
Income Taxes Payable		.0	.0	.0		.0		.0	.0
All Other Current		5.5	9.3	8.8		27.1		5.9	9.0
Total Current		12.9	15.1	13.3		33.1		19.1	14.9
Long-Term Debt		4.2	18.5	11.5		6.1		12.8	16.1
Deferred Taxes		.0	.0	.1		.0		.0	.1
All Other Non-Current		.6	1.2	6.9		5.1		3.8	4.0
Net Worth		82.3	65.2	68.2		55.7		64.2	65.0
Total Liabilities & Net Worth		100.0	100.0	100.0		100.0		100.0	100.0
INCOME DATA									
Net Sales		100.0	100.0	100.0		100.0		100.0	100.0
Gross Profit									
Operating Expenses		97.6	92.2	96.2		94.5		98.3	92.5
Operating Profit		2.4	7.8	3.8		5.5		1.7	7.5
All Other Expenses (net)		-.4	5.4	3.6		-.6		-1.6	-.1
Profit Before Taxes		2.8	2.3	.2		6.1		3.3	7.6
RATIOS									
Current		210.4	29.3	27.1		12.7		51.5	25.1
		68.0	5.5	4.6		2.6		8.9	5.9
		4.6	1.8	2.4		1.5		2.6	2.2
Quick		210.4	25.2	27.0		12.5		51.3	25.1
		67.6	5.5	4.4		2.2		8.4	5.3
		3.7	1.2	2.3		1.1		2.6	1.9
Sales/Receivables	0 UND	0 UND	0 UND	0 UND		0 UND		0 UND	0 UND
	0 UND	0 UND	12 30.6			17 21.7		0 999.8	8 44.7
	6 57.6	19 19.3	21 17.2			43 8.6		22 16.7	25 14.6
Cost of Sales/Inventory									
Cost of Sales/Payables									
Sales/Working Capital		1.1	1.8	1.3		1.6		1.4	1.5
		1.8	4.0	2.8		3.6		2.8	3.5
		3.2	10.4	8.1		4.7		7.0	6.6
EBIT/Interest			3.4	18.4				10.3	8.0
		(18) 1.1	(14) .6					(34) 2.0	(33) 2.5
		-.8	-4.7					-2.8	-.2
Net Profit + Depr., Dep., Amort./Cur. Mat. L/T/D									
Fixed/Worth		.0	.1	.1		.0		.1	.0
		.2	.8	.3		.3		.4	.5
		.8	1.4	.8		.6		1.0	1.3
Debt/Worth		.0	.0	.1		.0		.0	.2
		.0	.5	.3		1.1		.3	.5
		.4	1.3	.6		2.5		1.0	1.2
% Profit Before Taxes/Tangible Net Worth		16.8	12.2	9.4		9.4		13.5	12.5
		1.2	(34) 2.6	(28) -1.3		-7.7		(54) 6.0	(58) 6.2
		-15.3	-7.3	-8.3		-22.9		-5.1	-2.4
% Profit Before Taxes/Total Assets		13.0	7.6	7.5		5.5		10.5	9.3
		1.1	.7	-.6		-3.9		5.3	3.7
		-15.2	-4.5	-5.9		-7.0		-2.6	-1.9
Sales/Net Fixed Assets		36.8	8.6	26.5		97.4		23.2	47.9
		7.5	2.1	4.8		7.2		4.0	4.2
		1.9	.7	1.5		3.9		1.6	1.3
Sales/Total Assets		1.4	1.5	1.3		1.5		1.7	1.4
		1.0	.8	.9		.7		1.0	.9
		.6	.4	.5		.2		.6	.4
% Depr., Dep., Amort./Sales		1.1	1.3	.8				.9	1.6
		(13) 3.3	(29) 2.7	(21) 2.1				(46) 2.3	(46) 2.8
		6.1	5.5	3.8				3.6	4.6
% Officers', Directors' Owners' Comp/Sales									7.7
									(10) 15.7
									27.0
Net Sales ($)	962M	26836M	168235M	766829M	375870M	1230537M		1072813M	1128631M
Total Assets ($)	784M	24771M	165767M	742005M	427596M	1441834M		1114709M	1320742M

M = $ thousand   MM = $ million
See Pages 9 through 22 for Explanation of Ratios and Data

Comparative Historical Data				Current Data Sorted by Sales					
			Type of Statement						
49	54	60	Unqualified	5	12	6	9	13	15
3	3	3	Reviewed	1	2				
5	1	5	Compiled	2	1	1		1	
6	6	7	Tax Returns	4	3				
14	22	31	Other	8	4	2	2	8	7
4/1/07-3/31/08 ALL	4/1/08-3/31/09 ALL	4/1/09-3/31/10 ALL			56 (4/1-9/30/09)			50 (10/1/09-3/31/10)	
				0-1MM	1-3MM	3-5MM	5-10MM	10-25MM	25MM & OVER
78	86	106	**NUMBER OF STATEMENTS**	20	22	9	11	22	22
%	%	%	**ASSETS**	%	%	%	%	%	%
41.8	48.4	48.2	Cash & Equivalents	52.8	50.8		28.1	50.2	49.6
4.0	4.7	4.0	Trade Receivables (net)	.8	3.9		1.2	6.1	7.2
.4	.4	.2	Inventory	.0	.3		.0	.0	.3
5.9	3.5	3.5	All Other Current	.2	1.7		6.5	1.6	9.0
52.0	57.0	55.9	Total Current	53.8	56.7		35.8	57.8	66.1
35.8	30.9	33.7	Fixed Assets (net)	38.5	36.8		62.0	26.2	18.3
.1	.1	.1	Intangibles (net)	.0	.0		.0	.5	.1
12.1	12.1	10.3	All Other Non-Current	7.7	6.5		2.2	15.5	15.5
100.0	100.0	100.0	Total	100.0	100.0		100.0	100.0	100.0
			LIABILITIES						
1.3	.8	1.9	Notes Payable-Short Term	1.1	7.1		.1	.2	.5
.9	1.0	1.5	Cur. Mat.-L.T.D.	4.8	.6		2.3	.4	.4
4.1	4.4	2.5	Trade Payables	.5	1.5		1.9	2.1	6.4
.0	.0	.0	Income Taxes Payable	.0	.0		.0	.0	.0
7.1	6.8	10.4	All Other Current	9.3	5.6		13.5	8.0	19.3
13.5	13.0	16.3	Total Current	15.6	14.8		17.8	10.7	26.6
17.3	14.2	11.6	Long-Term Debt	7.0	10.5		30.9	11.0	7.3
.0	.0	.0	Deferred Taxes	.0	.0		.0	.0	.1
7.8	8.7	3.9	All Other Non-Current	.0	1.8		.2	.6	15.8
61.4	64.0	68.2	Net Worth	77.3	72.9		51.1	77.7	50.2
100.0	100.0	100.0	Total Liabilities & Net Worth	100.0	100.0		100.0	100.0	100.0
			INCOME DATA						
100.0	100.0	100.0	Net Sales	100.0	100.0		100.0	100.0	100.0
			Gross Profit						
93.4	93.7	95.0	Operating Expenses	89.6	94.5		102.7	92.9	101.3
6.6	6.3	5.0	Operating Profit	10.4	5.5		-2.7	7.1	-1.3
.6	1.9	2.9	All Other Expenses (net)	2.0	3.5		3.7	3.9	.4
6.0	4.3	2.0	Profit Before Taxes	8.3	2.0		-6.4	3.1	-1.7
			RATIOS						
40.5	42.5	64.5		186.8	64.5		11.1	175.3	13.3
5.6	6.1	6.8	Current	66.1	8.4		1.6	8.0	2.7
2.4	2.4	2.1		1.0	3.6		1.2	3.1	1.8
40.3	42.4	63.5		186.8	63.5		11.1	153.2	12.9
5.2	5.9	6.1	Quick	66.0	8.4		1.5	8.0	2.6
1.8	2.2	1.8		1.0	3.2		.7	3.0	1.1
0 UND	0 UND	0 UND		0 UND	0 UND		0 UND	0 UND	2 152.4
0 999.8	1 688.7	1 299.4	Sales/Receivables	0 UND	1 508.2		1 266.2	13 28.4	14 26.2
20 18.3	26 14.2	22 16.4		0 UND	33 11.0		14 26.3	32 11.6	36 10.2
			Cost of Sales/Inventory						
			Cost of Sales/Payables						
1.6	1.1	1.3		.8	1.1		1.8	1.1	1.9
3.0	2.5	2.9	Sales/Working Capital	1.7	2.1		8.9	2.5	3.5
7.7	6.5	7.8		69.3	3.3		23.8	6.6	6.6
15.2	14.6	6.6						7.3	30.5
(43) 2.5	(44) 2.2	(46) .5	EBIT/Interest					(10) .7	(10) -7.4
-2.0	-.1	-4.0						-4.0	-51.7
			Net Profit + Depr., Dep., Amort./Cur. Mat. L/T/D						
.0	.0	.1		.0	.1		.6	.0	.1
.5	.3	.4	Fixed/Worth	.3	.4		.8	.2	.3
1.3	.9	1.0		1.0	1.1		3.9	.7	1.1
.0	.0	.0		.0	.0		.3	.0	.2
.4	.3	.3	Debt/Worth	.0	.3		.6	.2	.8
1.3	.9	1.0		.7	.7		4.0	.4	4.5
17.7	15.1	12.9	% Profit Before Taxes/Tangible Net Worth	14.6	10.3		3.6	15.0	9.4
(72) 6.1	(83) 4.9	(102) .7		(19) 5.0	.7		-1.6	(21) 3.2	(20) -6.0
-4.3	-4.0	-8.5		-3.5	-7.6		-8.9	-6.7	-18.2
12.9	10.1	9.3	% Profit Before Taxes/Total Assets	13.4	10.1		.7	12.8	6.5
2.8	3.0	.1		3.6	.6		-.7	2.0	-3.9
-3.0	-2.8	-6.0		-3.4	-7.5		-7.1	-5.8	-7.0
33.5	60.6	28.2		35.4	12.2		1.7	256.3	35.5
4.1	4.4	4.4	Sales/Net Fixed Assets	8.6	2.6		1.1	4.6	11.8
1.1	1.5	1.3		.2	1.1		.6	2.2	4.4
1.6	1.5	1.4		.8	1.3		.9	1.6	1.7
.9	.8	.9	Sales/Total Assets	.5	.8		.6	1.0	1.3
.5	.5	.5		.2	.5		.4	.6	.7
.9	.9	1.0		2.9	.9			.3	.7
(63) 1.9	(69) 2.2	(80) 2.1	% Depr., Dep., Amort./Sales	(13) 6.7	(18) 2.7			(16) 1.5	(18) 1.6
4.6	4.3	4.4		16.6	5.0			2.3	2.4
7.1	5.2	6.3	% Officers', Directors' Owners' Comp/Sales						
(21) 13.6	(16) 11.1	(18) 16.1							
27.1	26.6	32.2							
1495172M	2042583M	2569269M	Net Sales ($)	10160M	40730M	37179M	82041M	366340M	2032819M
1527054M	1998866M	2802757M	Total Assets ($)	34563M	61073M	44227M	168877M	714338M	1779679M

© RMA 2010

M = $ thousand   MM = $ million
See Pages 9 through 22 for Explanation of Ratios and Data

Current Data Sorted by Assets   **Comparative Historical Data**

Type of Statement	0-500M	500M-2MM	2-10MM	10-50MM	50-100MM	100-250MM		4/1/05-3/31/06 ALL	4/1/06-3/31/07 ALL
Unqualified	19	36	47	53	8	11		140	171
Reviewed	3	5	2	1				11	11
Compiled	7	3	4		1			6	18
Tax Returns	5	8	3					8	14
Other	28	38	36	22	3	5		113	109
		146 (4/1-9/30/09)		202 (10/1/09-3/31/10)					
NUMBER OF STATEMENTS	62	90	92	76	12	16		278	323
	%	%	%	%	%	%		%	%
ASSETS									
Cash & Equivalents	51.1	44.9	25.9	24.6	22.7	30.7		32.7	33.7
Trade Receivables (net)	14.3	9.5	6.5	7.8	2.8	9.2		7.5	8.3
Inventory	.7	.8	1.0	2.4	.2	1.6		2.1	1.4
All Other Current	4.8	4.4	4.3	4.8	6.5	5.8		5.0	5.2
Total Current	71.0	59.6	37.7	39.6	32.2	47.2		47.3	48.6
Fixed Assets (net)	16.7	27.4	51.5	46.8	41.4	30.0		38.4	35.8
Intangibles (net)	.1	.5	1.7	.7	3.1	.9		1.7	.9
All Other Non-Current	12.4	12.5	9.1	12.8	23.3	21.9		12.7	14.6
Total	100.0	100.0	100.0	100.0	100.0	100.0		100.0	100.0
LIABILITIES									
Notes Payable-Short Term	10.5	6.6	2.3	2.1	.7	.4		5.6	4.8
Cur. Mat.-L.T.D.	3.1	3.2	1.9	1.0	11.6	5.4		3.1	2.0
Trade Payables	13.6	6.1	4.3	3.0	3.1	3.9		5.5	6.6
Income Taxes Payable	.0	.1	.0	.0	.0	.0		.1	.1
All Other Current	15.8	12.6	7.7	13.2	13.7	15.3		10.0	12.5
Total Current	43.1	28.5	16.3	19.4	29.1	25.0		24.1	26.2
Long-Term Debt	28.7	31.1	27.7	14.1	34.5	20.0		19.2	22.5
Deferred Taxes	.0	.0	.0	.1	.0	.0		.1	.1
All Other Non-Current	5.1	3.8	2.7	6.4	1.5	6.0		7.8	5.7
Net Worth	23.0	36.6	53.3	59.9	34.9	49.0		48.7	45.6
Total Liabilities & Net Worth	100.0	100.0	100.0	100.0	100.0	100.0		100.0	100.0
INCOME DATA									
Net Sales	100.0	100.0	100.0	100.0	100.0	100.0		100.0	100.0
Gross Profit									
Operating Expenses	95.2	88.5	92.0	93.0	97.0	87.4		92.9	91.1
Operating Profit	4.8	11.5	8.0	7.0	3.0	12.6		7.1	8.9
All Other Expenses (net)	2.1	3.5	5.6	4.3	6.6	12.3		1.4	2.2
Profit Before Taxes	2.7	8.0	2.4	2.7	-3.6	.3		5.8	6.7
RATIOS									
Current	11.4	7.5	5.7	4.7	3.0	3.4		6.0	5.6
	3.2	3.0	2.4	2.2	1.3	1.7		2.2	2.2
	1.0	1.2	1.4	1.2	.7	1.2		1.1	1.1
Quick	10.5	6.9	5.2	3.9	2.5	2.8		5.0	4.6
	3.0	2.7	2.1	(75) 2.0	1.0	1.2		1.8	1.8
	.8	1.1	1.2	1.2	.6	.8		.9	.8
Sales/Receivables	0 UND	0 UND	1 510.5	3 107.1	0 UND	18 20.7		2 191.5	0 841.1
	6 63.0	8 44.9	13 29.2	14 26.2	13 27.5	46 7.9		9 38.8	10 37.3
	28 13.2	24 15.3	37 9.9	42 8.6	35 10.4	81 4.5		35 10.5	35 10.5
Cost of Sales/Inventory									
Cost of Sales/Payables									
Sales/Working Capital	2.3	1.7	2.6	2.1	1.6	1.8		2.1	2.1
	7.1	3.9	4.9	5.0	17.4	5.7		5.7	6.0
	UND	38.7	17.1	18.9	-12.2	15.5		32.9	45.9
EBIT/Interest	15.0	15.9	4.3	12.7		16.2		9.6	11.7
	(26) 3.7	(46) 3.9	(61) 1.3	(54) 3.4		(10) 2.1		(148) 2.6	(189) 3.1
	-1.5	.7	-1.4	.4		-.5		-.4	.3
Net Profit + Depr., Dep., Amort./Cur. Mat. L/T/D									
Fixed/Worth	.0	.0	.2	.3	.2	.0		.1	.0
	.0	.1	.9	.9	1.1	.4		.7	.5
	.8	1.1	1.8	1.2	3.6	1.5		1.3	1.1
Debt/Worth	.1	.2	.2	.2	.5	.4		.2	.2
	1.0	1.1	.7	.5	1.1	1.4		.6	.7
	UND	3.1	2.4	1.5	24.8	2.2		1.8	2.6
% Profit Before Taxes/Tangible Net Worth	36.7	25.1	10.9	9.6	5.5	13.1		16.4	18.0
	(49) 9.3	(75) 6.9	(86) 3.5	(75) 2.9	(10) .5	2.8		(250) 4.8	(289) 6.1
	-9.4	-3.5	-5.8	-3.0	-16.6	-2.9		-1.6	-1.8
% Profit Before Taxes/Total Assets	18.4	19.3	6.0	5.3	3.0	5.1		8.9	10.8
	2.4	5.4	1.4	1.5	.4	.9		2.9	3.3
	-12.7	-.9	-3.3	-2.0	-8.4	-1.8		-1.5	-1.2
Sales/Net Fixed Assets	UND	UND	10.8	7.2	6.1	106.5		54.9	113.7
	UND	55.3	1.2	1.7	1.0	5.5		3.5	4.2
	26.9	1.7	.5	.6	.4	.5		.7	.9
Sales/Total Assets	4.3	1.8	1.1	1.1	.8	1.1		1.5	1.8
	2.0	1.2	.6	.7	.5	.5		.8	.8
	1.1	.6	.4	.4	.2	.3		.4	.4
% Depr., Dep., Amort./Sales	.4	.7	1.5	2.3	1.6	.7		1.8	1.5
	(14) 1.6	(40) 2.5	(73) 4.7	(70) 5.2	(10) 7.6	(13) 1.8		(193) 4.1	(205) 3.8
	5.1	4.7	10.0	10.0	13.7	10.5		8.9	8.1
% Officers', Directors', Owners' Comp/Sales	5.8	5.4	3.9					5.6	4.5
	(12) 8.0	(12) 6.6	(10) 13.5					(18) 11.6	(29) 12.9
	11.7	14.9	31.4					27.2	25.6
Net Sales ($)	41098M	130017M	397458M	1713835M	433779M	2180082M		3895129M	3623612M
Total Assets ($)	14726M	102380M	493858M	1621789M	777816M	2447575M		5772881M	5359557M

M = $ thousand   MM = $ million
See Pages 9 through 22 for Explanation of Ratios and Data

Comparative Historical Data | Current Data Sorted by Sales

			Type of Statement						
140	195	174	Unqualified	27	42	25	23	30	27
18	15	11	Reviewed	6	5				
16	23	15	Compiled	9	5				1
12	13	16	Tax Returns	11	5				
113	143	132	Other	47	33	15	17	12	8
4/1/07-3/31/08	4/1/08-3/31/09	4/1/09-3/31/10				146 (4/1-9/30/09)		202 (10/1/09-3/31/10)	
ALL	ALL	ALL		0-1MM	1-3MM	3-5MM	5-10MM	10-25MM	25MM & OVER
299	389	348	**NUMBER OF STATEMENTS**	100	90	40	40	42	36
%	%	%	**ASSETS**	%	%	%	%	%	%
37.5	35.8	35.2	Cash & Equivalents	41.8	38.5	30.2	26.3	28.5	31.3
8.4	8.8	9.0	Trade Receivables (net)	9.4	8.1	9.5	7.2	10.8	8.9
1.2	1.1	1.2	Inventory	.3	1.5	.7	.5	.9	4.6
4.5	4.7	4.7	All Other Current	3.9	5.2	3.6	3.6	5.0	7.5
51.5	50.4	50.0	Total Current	55.4	53.4	44.0	37.7	45.3	52.3
34.6	33.1	36.7	Fixed Assets (net)	30.5	37.3	38.3	52.4	39.5	29.8
1.1	.7	.9	Intangibles (net)	1.1	.4	1.0	.3	1.3	1.7
12.8	15.8	12.4	All Other Non-Current	13.0	8.9	16.7	9.7	13.9	16.1
100.0	100.0	100.0	Total	100.0	100.0	100.0	100.0	100.0	100.0
			LIABILITIES						
2.3	6.0	4.7	Notes Payable-Short Term	7.6	7.5	1.1	1.5	1.3	1.2
3.0	2.6	2.8	Cur. Mat.-L.T.D.	2.7	2.6	3.4	.8	3.5	3.8
6.6	7.2	6.1	Trade Payables	5.5	6.0	9.9	6.9	5.1	3.8
.2	.1	.1	Income Taxes Payable	.0	.1	.0	.0	.1	.0
11.9	12.3	12.2	All Other Current	11.8	9.2	7.1	11.8	13.7	24.6
24.0	28.1	25.8	Total Current	27.7	25.4	21.5	21.1	23.7	33.5
21.9	21.8	25.7	Long-Term Debt	30.4	31.2	29.4	14.4	15.4	19.0
.1	.0	.0	Deferred Taxes	.0	.0	.0	.0	.1	.1
4.5	6.3	4.3	All Other Non-Current	3.7	2.9	3.8	5.2	8.5	4.5
49.5	43.8	44.2	Net Worth	38.2	40.4	45.2	59.4	52.4	42.9
100.0	100.0	100.0	Total Liabilities & Net Worth	100.0	100.0	100.0	100.0	100.0	100.0
			INCOME DATA						
100.0	100.0	100.0	Net Sales	100.0	100.0	100.0	100.0	100.0	100.0
			Gross Profit						
89.7	92.7	91.8	Operating Expenses	87.8	91.7	96.7	96.9	94.9	88.8
10.3	7.3	8.2	Operating Profit	12.2	8.3	3.3	3.1	5.1	11.2
2.3	3.7	4.5	All Other Expenses (net)	5.8	5.6	1.4	.9	1.8	9.0
8.0	3.6	3.7	Profit Before Taxes	6.4	2.8	1.9	2.2	3.3	2.1
			RATIOS						
7.0	5.8	6.0	Current	9.8	8.2	5.6	4.9	5.0	3.1
2.7	2.5	2.4		3.2	2.6	2.7	2.7	2.2	1.4
1.1	1.0	1.2		1.2	1.2	1.1	1.7	1.3	1.0
6.7	5.4	5.7	Quick	8.7	7.0	4.1	4.1	4.0	2.8
2.2	2.1	(347) 2.1		2.7	2.5	2.7	2.1	1.8	(35) 1.1
.9	.8	1.0		.9	1.0	1.0	1.4	1.1	.7
1 711.0	2 163.6	1 473.4	Sales/Receivables	0 UND	0 854.8	2 199.4	2 216.8	8 47.3	7 52.3
8 43.4	11 32.5	10 35.0		5 78.3	9 42.0	13 29.1	9 39.9	36 10.1	21 17.1
26 14.3	32 11.3	36 10.2		24 15.1	35 10.4	31 11.6	33 11.2	68 5.4	41 9.0
			Cost of Sales/Inventory						
			Cost of Sales/Payables						
1.9	2.0	2.1	Sales/Working Capital	1.7	1.8	2.7	3.2	1.9	3.9
4.1	4.9	4.9		4.5	4.4	4.8	5.0	3.8	10.8
32.8	256.8	30.5		65.5	30.0	69.0	10.5	11.1	NM
10.2	7.6	9.6	EBIT/Interest	11.0	4.3	12.3	6.2	24.5	16.9
(155) 3.3	(225) 1.6	(204) 2.7		(47) 2.7	(55) 1.4	(26) 2.5	(23) 2.5	(30) 6.3	(23) 2.9
.8	-1.3	.2		.5	-.9	.4	-.6	1.1	1.0
6.8	6.5	45.8	Net Profit + Depr., Dep., Amort./Cur. Mat. L/T/D						
(13) 3.0	(16) 2.6	(14) 8.1							
1.3	.0	2.1							
.0	.0	.0	Fixed/Worth	.0	.0	.0	.3	.2	.1
.5	.5	.5		.0	.5	.5	.9	.9	.5
1.1	1.3	1.3		1.2	1.6	1.0	1.5	1.1	1.4
.2	.3	.2	Debt/Worth	.2	.2	.1	.2	.3	.5
.6	.8	.8		.6	.8	.7	.5	.8	1.3
2.0	3.6	2.7		4.9	3.1	4.3	1.4	2.3	2.5
20.7	16.1	17.3	% Profit Before Taxes/Tangible Net Worth	23.7	18.9	8.0	9.0	16.2	11.3
(272) 6.6	(348) 3.9	(311) 4.2		(86) 5.7	(79) 3.3	(34) 3.5	(39) 1.8	(39) 6.1	(34) 3.1
-1.1	-5.8	-4.4		-3.7	-7.2	-6.2	-4.5	-.9	-5.4
12.2	9.6	9.2	% Profit Before Taxes/Total Assets	15.8	10.7	6.0	5.8	8.1	6.1
3.3	1.6	2.0		1.7	2.2	3.2	1.0	2.9	1.3
-.6	-3.4	-2.8		-2.9	-3.4	-2.9	-3.6	-1.4	-2.2
547.3	335.6	351.2	Sales/Net Fixed Assets	UND	122.0	77.2	7.2	10.7	43.1
4.1	5.5	5.6		UND	8.7	2.3	1.2	2.2	6.6
.9	1.1	.8		.8	.7	.6	.7	.8	1.9
1.5	1.8	1.7	Sales/Total Assets	1.7	1.7	2.1	1.3	1.3	2.3
.9	1.0	.8		.9	.9	.7	.7	.8	1.1
.5	.5	.4		.4	.4	.4	.5	.5	.7
1.6	1.3	1.2	% Depr., Dep., Amort./Sales	1.8	.9	2.4	1.7	1.8	.5
(184) 3.9	(240) 3.3	(220) 4.0		(27) 5.1	(61) 3.5	(28) 4.7	(36) 6.5	(37) 3.2	(31) 1.6
7.9	7.8	9.4		15.6	10.5	10.3	9.6	7.9	6.5
1.9	4.6	5.3	% Officers', Directors' Owners' Comp/Sales	6.6	5.0				
(19) 6.2	(36) 9.0	(43) 8.1		(12) 7.6	(15) 11.5				
14.0	15.5	23.1		8.3	13.6				
3576179M	5037478M	4896269M	Net Sales ($)	45588M	163245M	156194M	293551M	678471M	3559220M
4899800M	6152411M	5458144M	Total Assets ($)	109400M	335142M	266391M	490827M	1297651M	2958733M

M = $ thousand   MM = $ million
See Pages 9 through 22 for Explanation of Ratios and Data

Current Data Sorted by Assets   Comparative Historical Data

						Type of Statement		
		5	5		2	Unqualified	13	14
	6	7	2			Reviewed	25	20
2	5	6	1			Compiled	19	7
9	2	4				Tax Returns	19	37
3	14	12	5	3	3	Other	56	46
	18 (4/1-9/30/09)		78 (10/1/09-3/31/10)				4/1/05-3/31/06	4/1/06-3/31/07
0-500M	500M-2MM	2-10MM	10-50MM	50-100MM	100-250MM		ALL	ALL
14	27	34	13	3	5	NUMBER OF STATEMENTS	132	124
%	%	%	%	%	%	ASSETS	%	%
16.3	13.9	11.1	18.3			Cash & Equivalents	11.3	13.9
11.2	27.3	13.4	9.4			Trade Receivables (net)	18.0	17.8
12.6	7.0	8.6	14.4			Inventory	10.6	12.8
.0	1.6	2.6	3.8			All Other Current	5.7	6.9
40.1	49.8	35.7	46.0			Total Current	45.5	51.4
43.8	35.5	44.6	41.7			Fixed Assets (net)	39.7	33.0
7.9	5.9	5.4	5.9			Intangibles (net)	4.6	4.8
8.2	8.8	14.4	6.5			All Other Non-Current	10.2	10.8
100.0	100.0	100.0	100.0			Total	100.0	100.0
						LIABILITIES		
9.6	9.6	10.5	11.2			Notes Payable-Short Term	10.4	11.8
6.0	2.8	2.1	2.3			Cur. Mat.-L.T.D.	3.7	3.2
5.2	5.8	6.1	10.4			Trade Payables	9.3	12.2
.5	.1	.0	.0			Income Taxes Payable	.3	.7
7.5	7.5	5.9	5.3			All Other Current	9.8	12.1
28.7	25.8	24.6	29.2			Total Current	33.5	40.0
75.7	22.1	25.5	29.0			Long-Term Debt	29.1	23.0
.0	.2	.6	.1			Deferred Taxes	.1	.3
16.2	1.7	5.1	1.8			All Other Non-Current	2.8	3.4
-20.6	50.2	44.1	39.9			Net Worth	34.5	33.2
100.0	100.0	100.0	100.0			Total Liabilties & Net Worth	100.0	100.0
						INCOME DATA		
100.0	100.0	100.0	100.0			Net Sales	100.0	100.0
						Gross Profit		
75.9	86.2	78.0	88.0			Operating Expenses	79.8	83.4
24.1	13.8	22.0	12.0			Operating Profit	20.2	16.6
6.8	3.2	7.3	6.4			All Other Expenses (net)	5.2	6.9
17.3	10.6	14.6	5.6			Profit Before Taxes	15.0	9.7
						RATIOS		
3.4	5.7	2.8	2.4			Current	3.3	2.7
2.0	2.2	1.2	1.2				1.4	1.4
.7	1.5	.6	.8				.8	.9
3.4	4.5	2.3	2.3			Quick	2.4	2.0
1.1	1.7	.8	.5				.8	.8
.6	.8	.2	.2				.4	.3
0 UND	0 UND	0 UND	2 154.2			Sales/Receivables	0 UND	0 UND
0 UND	26 14.2	5 75.4	8 43.7				20 18.5	11 33.9
5 67.7	73 5.0	44 8.2	27 13.5				63 5.8	44 8.4
						Cost of Sales/Inventory		
						Cost of Sales/Payables		
21.4	3.8	7.3	2.0			Sales/Working Capital	6.3	6.8
191.0	7.3	31.9	71.2				24.6	20.5
-42.2	23.8	-5.2	-34.3				-37.1	-55.7
	55.4	11.9	4.4			EBIT/Interest	16.1	10.5
	(18) 12.4	(25) 3.1	(11) 2.6				(104) 5.0	(84) 3.2
	-.5	.9	1.5				2.0	.5
						Net Profit + Depr., Dep., Amort./Cur. Mat. L/T/D	5.5	10.8
							(12) 3.3	(18) 4.6
							1.2	1.6
1.0	.2	.6	.3			Fixed/Worth	.3	.2
NM	.6	.9	1.3				1.2	.8
-.6	1.7	3.3	6.0				4.3	15.3
5.3	.4	.4	.7			Debt/Worth	.9	.6
-26.1	.7	1.7	2.2				2.3	2.2
-1.8	1.6	4.5	5.8				9.1	61.8
	46.6	43.1	16.1			% Profit Before Taxes/Tangible Net Worth	65.9	64.5
	(24) 16.4	(30) 8.3	(11) 2.4				(111) 27.4	(99) 22.3
	-4.7	.8	-7.9				10.1	5.8
60.7	18.9	20.4	7.2			% Profit Before Taxes/Total Assets	17.7	20.2
33.0	6.4	3.2	2.7				8.2	5.6
-7.8	-4.8	.5	-2.6				2.8	.0
55.4	29.6	23.0	31.9			Sales/Net Fixed Assets	31.9	42.2
11.4	6.8	2.2	1.0				7.3	12.3
1.6	1.7	.4	.4				1.0	2.1
5.3	3.4	2.6	2.9			Sales/Total Assets	3.6	4.3
3.2	2.1	1.4	.6				1.6	2.0
.9	1.3	.2	.3				.5	.6
.9	.9	.8				% Depr., Dep., Amort./Sales	1.2	.8
(10) 3.8	(20) 1.7	(29) 4.1					(112) 2.7	(96) 2.1
13.3	3.7	11.4					7.9	5.5
						% Officers', Directors' Owners' Comp/Sales	1.6	2.4
							(43) 3.9	(35) 3.3
							12.7	11.3
11469M	68255M	340119M	329199M	130175M	1823848M	Net Sales ($)	2955651M	4160941M
3856M	29745M	168380M	235058M	230492M	920756M	Total Assets ($)	1522251M	1712164M

M = $ thousand   MM = $ million
See Pages 9 through 22 for Explanation of Ratios and Data

Comparative Historical Data | Current Data Sorted by Sales

Type of Statement	4/1/07-3/31/08 ALL	4/1/08-3/31/09 ALL	4/1/09-3/31/10 ALL	0-1MM	1-3MM	3-5MM	5-10MM	10-25MM	25MM & OVER
					18 (4/1-9/30/09)			78 (10/1/09-3/31/10)	
Unqualified	12	11	12		1	2	1	4	4
Reviewed	11	16	15	1	3	2	1	6	2
Compiled	16	13	14	3	7		2	2	
Tax Returns	25	23	15	12	1	2			
Other	41	44	40	11	12	6	1	2	8
NUMBER OF STATEMENTS	**105**	**107**	**96**	**27**	**24**	**12**	**5**	**14**	**14**
ASSETS	%	%	%	%	%	%	%	%	%
Cash & Equivalents	15.4	16.8	13.4	11.2	12.5	12.8		20.9	13.2
Trade Receivables (net)	14.7	14.2	16.0	2.7	27.2	13.0		25.9	15.9
Inventory	10.4	15.3	10.7	4.9	7.7	12.0		10.1	26.9
All Other Current	3.0	5.4	2.9	3.4	2.6	2.2		1.0	5.1
Total Current	43.5	51.7	43.1	22.3	50.1	40.0		57.9	61.1
Fixed Assets (net)	42.0	34.7	39.4	57.0	34.9	37.5		29.8	20.3
Intangibles (net)	4.3	2.6	6.8	8.5	5.2	3.6		3.4	14.0
All Other Non-Current	10.2	11.0	10.7	12.2	9.8	18.8		8.9	4.6
Total	100.0	100.0	100.0	100.0	100.0	100.0		100.0	100.0
LIABILITIES									
Notes Payable-Short Term	13.2	13.1	10.2	10.0	9.4	2.7		14.1	11.0
Cur. Mat.-L.T.D.	5.5	3.6	3.2	3.5	3.7	1.7		2.2	4.9
Trade Payables	9.3	10.1	7.0	2.0	3.7	7.2		9.3	20.6
Income Taxes Payable	.3	.2	.2	.3	.1	.0		.0	.3
All Other Current	11.1	16.8	6.6	3.0	8.7	6.3		6.9	10.2
Total Current	39.4	43.8	27.2	18.8	25.5	17.9		32.5	47.0
Long-Term Debt	31.6	29.7	32.3	50.3	27.9	40.9		14.1	11.4
Deferred Taxes	.1	.1	.7	.8	.1	1.6		.3	1.6
All Other Non-Current	3.5	8.7	5.2	7.7	3.3	1.4		6.3	4.2
Net Worth	25.4	17.8	34.6	22.4	43.2	38.3		46.7	35.8
Total Liabilties & Net Worth	100.0	100.0	100.0	100.0	100.0	100.0		100.0	100.0
INCOME DATA									
Net Sales	100.0	100.0	100.0	100.0	100.0	100.0		100.0	100.0
Gross Profit									
Operating Expenses	82.0	85.8	81.4	56.6	87.4	81.2		97.1	97.1
Operating Profit	18.0	14.2	18.6	43.4	12.6	18.8		2.9	2.9
All Other Expenses (net)	7.2	5.2	5.8	13.8	2.5	5.6		1.4	.9
Profit Before Taxes	10.8	9.0	12.9	29.6	10.1	13.2		1.5	2.0
RATIOS									
Current	2.2	2.6	3.4	4.5	2.9	9.5		4.1	1.8
	1.2	1.5	1.8	1.0	2.1	3.1		2.0	1.4
	.6	.8	.8	.2	1.4	1.7		1.0	1.0
Quick	1.7	1.8	2.6	2.6	2.7	8.9		3.2	1.7
	.8	.7	1.0	.8	1.6	2.1		1.8	.6
	.2	.2	.4	.1	.6	.7		.7	.6
Sales/Receivables	0 UND	0 UND	0 UND	0 UND	0 UND	3 125.0		11 33.2	5 79.4
	5 80.3	7 49.4	9 42.8	0 UND	18 20.2	25 14.4		30 12.2	11 32.8
	39 9.3	33 10.9	47 7.8	0 UND	77 4.8	62 5.9		48 7.6	48 7.6
Cost of Sales/Inventory									
Cost of Sales/Payables									
Sales/Working Capital	8.4	6.0	4.6	2.6	3.9	3.5		7.3	8.6
	40.2	29.4	22.9	UND	10.0	5.5		15.7	37.5
	-22.0	-26.8	-45.4	-3.1	271.4	24.4		NM	-194.7
EBIT/Interest	(72) 9.1	(76) 14.7	(69) 14.2	(14) 12.8	(20) 70.5			(11) 26.6	(12) 13.7
	5.1	4.1	3.7	4.0	8.1			2.3	4.4
	1.1	.8	.5	2.9	-1.1			.7	1.6
Net Profit + Depr., Dep., Amort./Cur. Mat. L/T/D	(11) 5.1	(12) 5.7	(13) 5.3						
	2.5	3.9	1.4						
	1.1	.7	.9						
Fixed/Worth	.3	.2	.3	.9	.2	.1		.2	.4
	1.2	.9	.9	2.6	.7	.9		.6	.6
	5.6	9.6	5.5	-2.7	1.6	8.4		3.1	NM
Debt/Worth	.6	.8	.6	.6	.5	.2		.4	1.0
	2.1	1.9	1.6	2.7	.7	1.6		1.2	2.5
	12.9	84.5	8.9	-9.1	3.2	16.1		4.3	NM
% Profit Before Taxes/Tangible Net Worth	(83) 47.9	(81) 42.7	(77) 34.4	(19) 37.5	(21) 54.6	(10) 51.2		(13) 31.4	(11) 21.9
	21.0	15.9	14.0	15.5	11.4	12.5		7.2	15.6
	4.5	2.8	.7	2.4	-8.6	-10.7		-8.5	7.6
% Profit Before Taxes/Total Assets	17.2	18.9	19.0	22.6	33.7	27.5		19.3	13.1
	6.5	5.4	4.5	4.9	5.6	2.0		2.8	5.4
	.4	.0	-1.0	.6	-9.8	-3.5		-1.4	1.6
Sales/Net Fixed Assets	36.4	80.3	32.1	1.8	23.5	33.4		130.0	34.5
	7.2	14.1	5.8	.4	6.6	5.4		18.2	21.8
	1.1	1.7	.6	.1	3.1	1.4		4.5	7.0
Sales/Total Assets	4.7	6.2	3.2	1.0	3.4	2.6		3.8	5.4
	1.6	2.3	1.7	.2	2.0	1.6		2.5	3.2
	.5	.6	.4	.1	1.3	.8		1.5	1.9
% Depr., Dep., Amort./Sales	(84) 1.0	(82) .6	(72) .9	(20) 3.0	(17) .8	(11) 1.3		(11) .4	(10) .3
	2.3	1.5	3.0	14.5	1.8	3.9		.9	1.1
	7.2	6.4	8.2	25.7	4.4	9.5		4.4	3.1
% Officers', Directors' Owners' Comp/Sales	(30) 1.5	(31) 1.8	(18) 2.1						
	2.3	4.1	5.8						
	6.6	9.5	9.0						
Net Sales ($)	2427861M	5667577M	2703065M	12180M	46184M	47305M	38531M	202869M	2355996M
Total Assets ($)	1328845M	1874564M	1588287M	67682M	147410M	117491M	60477M	118971M	1076256M

M = $ thousand   MM = $ million
See Pages 9 through 22 for Explanation of Ratios and Data

PUBLIC ADMINISTRATION

Current Data Sorted by Assets   **Comparative Historical Data**

Date-range note (left): 107 (4/1-9/30/09)   27 (10/1/09-3/31/10)

0-500M	500M-2MM	2-10MM	10-50MM	50-100MM	100-250MM		4/1/05-3/31/06 ALL	4/1/06-3/31/07 ALL
						Type of Statement		
	4	14	36	23	26	Unqualified	37	53
						Reviewed	1	
	1	1	2		1	Compiled	4	1
3	1	1				Tax Returns		3
2	7	5	6		1	Other	6	8
5	13	21	44	23	28	**NUMBER OF STATEMENTS**	48	65
%	%	%	%	%	%	**ASSETS**	%	%
	33.9	13.9	18.8	27.3	17.3	Cash & Equivalents	31.6	21.2
	7.6	15.0	7.6	6.4	4.2	Trade Receivables (net)	8.0	11.3
	2.2	3.2	.3	.3	.5	Inventory	.2	2.3
	.1	2.8	6.0	6.2	1.6	All Other Current	6.9	3.4
	43.8	35.0	32.6	40.2	23.6	Total Current	46.7	38.2
	50.0	51.3	58.2	53.0	60.3	Fixed Assets (net)	44.2	53.9
	.1	.6	.1	.3	.1	Intangibles (net)	1.6	.3
	6.1	13.2	9.1	6.4	15.9	All Other Non-Current	7.5	7.6
	100.0	100.0	100.0	100.0	100.0	Total	100.0	100.0
						LIABILITIES		
	5.0	.6	1.4	2.5	.1	Notes Payable-Short Term	.7	1.8
	1.6	2.2	1.8	2.0	2.4	Cur. Mat.-L.T.D.	2.0	1.4
	6.7	3.8	5.7	2.9	1.8	Trade Payables	4.8	4.5
	.0	1.8	.1	.0	.0	Income Taxes Payable	.1	.0
	9.5	6.3	10.0	9.7	5.8	All Other Current	9.0	4.1
	22.9	14.7	18.9	17.1	10.2	Total Current	16.7	11.8
	25.5	25.8	20.0	19.2	36.6	Long-Term Debt	25.4	22.4
	.0	.7	.0	.0	.0	Deferred Taxes	.1	.1
	5.0	1.2	3.3	12.1	.8	All Other Non-Current	8.7	11.5
	46.6	57.5	57.7	51.6	52.4	Net Worth	49.1	54.3
	100.0	100.0	100.0	100.0	100.0	Total Liabilities & Net Worth	100.0	100.0
						INCOME DATA		
	100.0	100.0	100.0	100.0	100.0	Net Sales	100.0	100.0
						Gross Profit		
	77.0	87.8	93.2	91.7	93.3	Operating Expenses	88.1	84.2
	23.0	12.2	6.8	8.3	6.7	Operating Profit	11.9	15.8
	12.6	6.4	2.1	4.5	4.8	All Other Expenses (net)	6.0	2.3
	10.4	5.8	4.7	3.8	2.0	Profit Before Taxes	5.9	13.5
						RATIOS		
	10.7	6.7	5.1	5.0	4.2		7.9	8.1
	1.1	2.9	2.6	2.5	2.3	Current	3.3	3.2
	.7	1.5	1.2	1.5	1.2		1.4	1.6
	10.7	5.5	4.5	4.9	3.3		5.2	8.1
	1.1	2.6	2.2	2.5	2.2	Quick	3.2	2.8
	.6	.9	1.0	.8	1.1		1.3	1.4
	0 UND	14 26.7	13 27.3	7 53.4	8 46.4		9 39.6	0 999.8
	0 UND	32 11.3	28 13.2	25 14.8	21 17.8	Sales/Receivables	20 18.1	32 11.6
	1 511.3	82 4.5	51 7.1	58 6.3	44 8.3		53 6.9	69 5.3
						Cost of Sales/Inventory		
						Cost of Sales/Payables		
	1.9	1.7	1.8	1.5	1.4		1.3	1.4
	24.0	2.9	3.7	2.9	4.5	Sales/Working Capital	4.2	3.5
	-28.4	8.7	13.1	7.7	28.9		14.4	6.9
		10.4	12.0	5.1	2.7		6.0	14.2
		(14) 1.3	(35) 3.3	(20) 1.9	(22) .9	EBIT/Interest	(27) 2.3	(42) 6.2
		-3.0	-.5	-4.1	-.7		.5	3.0
						Net Profit + Depr., Dep., Amort./Cur. Mat. L/T/D		
	.0	.5	.7	.7	.9		.0	.2
	1.5	1.0	1.0	1.0	1.3	Fixed/Worth	1.0	1.0
	3.1	1.3	1.4	1.3	1.6		1.7	1.3
	.3	.3	.3	.3	.4		.3	.3
	1.3	.6	.5	.5	.8	Debt/Worth	.6	.6
	3.0	1.4	1.9	1.3	1.6		2.1	1.2
	23.2	14.9	7.0	4.9	4.3		12.4	17.4
	(11) 4.1	(20) 1.6	2.6	(21) .5	(27) 1.0	% Profit Before Taxes/Tangible Net Worth	(43) 5.3	(63) 8.8
	2.0	-3.8	-1.7	-9.3	-4.4		1.4	4.0
	13.4	8.9	3.8	3.6	2.0		6.8	8.2
	2.0	.9	1.5	.8	.4	% Profit Before Taxes/Total Assets	3.6	5.4
	-.4	-2.0	-1.4	-2.4	-1.0		.3	1.9
	UND	29.0	2.3	3.5	.9		UND	42.7
	3.9	.9	.6	.7	.5	Sales/Net Fixed Assets	1.1	.6
	.3	.2	.3	.4	.3		.4	.3
	3.5	1.1	1.2	1.0	.5		1.4	.9
	.8	.3	.4	.4	.4	Sales/Total Assets	.6	.4
	.2	.2	.3	.2	.2		.3	.3
		3.2	4.0	6.4	5.6		2.7	3.8
		(13) 14.4	(31) 6.3	(14) 10.0	(20) 8.1	% Depr., Dep., Amort./Sales	(20) 5.8	(37) 9.6
		18.8	15.1	11.5	14.4		11.7	15.6
						% Officers', Directors' Owners' Comp/Sales		
12521M	27828M	86749M	1021242M	1088663M	2394600M	Net Sales ($)	2226776M	1458201M
965M	16352M	106821M	1115957M	1538125M	5105931M	Total Assets ($)	2252755M	2224883M

M = $ thousand   MM = $ million
See Pages 9 through 22 for Explanation of Ratios and Data

Comparative Historical Data   Current Data Sorted by Sales

			Type of Statement						
63	72	103	Unqualified	7	8	10	10	22	46
1	1		Reviewed						
3	1	5	Compiled	1		1	1	1	1
5	3	5	Tax Returns	3		2			
8	17	21	Other	7	4	2	3	2	3
4/1/07-3/31/08	4/1/08-3/31/09	4/1/09-3/31/10			107 (4/1-9/30/09)		27 (10/1/09-3/31/10)		
ALL	ALL	ALL		0-1MM	1-3MM	3-5MM	5-10MM	10-25MM	25MM & OVER
80	94	134	**NUMBER OF STATEMENTS**	18	12	15	14	25	50
%	%	%	**ASSETS**	%	%	%	%	%	%
23.7	25.6	21.4	Cash & Equivalents	17.7	37.0	16.7	14.2	17.6	24.4
5.1	5.5	7.6	Trade Receivables (net)	.8	4.7	8.1	8.0	13.4	7.4
.7	.9	1.0	Inventory	2.0	.5	2.1	.4	1.0	.5
4.7	5.6	3.8	All Other Current	.3	.6	.9	2.4	3.6	7.2
34.2	37.6	33.8	Total Current	20.9	42.7	27.8	24.9	35.7	39.6
56.6	53.7	55.6	Fixed Assets (net)	72.1	46.2	61.3	65.3	57.7	46.4
.7	.3	.2	Intangibles (net)	.1	.0	.4	.0	.3	.2
8.5	8.4	10.4	All Other Non-Current	7.0	11.0	10.6	9.8	6.2	13.8
100.0	100.0	100.0	Total	100.0	100.0	100.0	100.0	100.0	100.0
			LIABILITIES						
2.0	3.5	1.7	Notes Payable-Short Term	.0	2.2	3.1	.8	1.2	2.2
1.6	1.6	2.2	Cur. Mat.-L.T.D.	2.1	3.3	2.4	3.3	2.1	1.7
3.0	4.1	4.0	Trade Payables	.3	3.3	3.5	1.2	4.7	6.0
.1	.5	.3	Income Taxes Payable	.4	.0	.3	2.2	.0	.0
5.8	6.3	9.1	All Other Current	10.0	8.1	9.5	1.2	9.4	11.0
12.5	16.0	17.3	Total Current	12.9	16.9	18.8	8.8	17.3	21.0
23.3	20.7	24.7	Long-Term Debt	33.8	20.8	29.6	24.6	19.2	23.7
.0	.0	.1	Deferred Taxes	.0	.0	.0	.0	.6	.0
4.3	6.9	4.0	All·Other Non-Current	3.3	.8	1.9	2.1	13.9	1.3
59.9	56.2	53.8	Net Worth	50.0	61.6	49.7	64.6	49.0	54.1
100.0	100.0	100.0	Total Liabilties & Net Worth	100.0	100.0	100.0	100.0	100.0	100.0
			INCOME DATA						
100.0	100.0	100.0	Net Sales	100.0	100.0	100.0	100.0	100.0	100.0
			Gross Profit						
80.4	86.9	90.0	Operating Expenses	70.9	93.6	85.2	90.4	93.4	95.6
19.6	13.1	10.0	Operating Profit	29.1	6.4	14.8	9.6	6.6	4.4
5.3	4.3	4.9	All Other Expenses (net)	16.5	3.5	7.2	1.0	2.3	2.7
14.3	8.8	5.2	Profit Before Taxes	12.7	2.9	7.6	8.6	4.3	1.7
			RATIOS						
7.2	6.2	5.1		6.4	9.7	2.6	13.7	5.3	4.2
3.3	3.0	2.5	Current	1.4	6.7	2.0	3.4	2.9	2.2
1.8	1.5	1.1		.3	1.2	.8	1.8	1.3	1.1
6.8	5.6	4.8		3.9	9.7	2.6	8.7	5.3	3.4
2.7	2.8	2.1	Quick	1.4	6.4	1.8	3.0	2.8	2.0
1.2	1.2	.9		.3	1.2	.8	1.7	1.0	.8
0 972.5	2 171.9	5 76.0		0 UND	0. UND	0 999.8	17 21.0	18 20.5	7 50.2
18 20.1	13 27.2	23 15.7	Sales/Receivables	0 UND	19 19.3	24 15.3	41 8.9	46 7.9	21 17.8
41 8.8	37 10.0	46 7.9		34 10.8	32 11.3	70 5.2	48 7.6	88 4.1	38 9.5
			Cost of Sales/Inventory						
			Cost of Sales/Payables						
1.5	1.4	1.8		1.9	1.3	2.5	1.1	1.6	2.1
2.7	3.3	3.9	Sales/Working Capital	7.6	2.0	3.7	3.0	2.2	6.1
9.0	13.2	99.6		-9.3	751.0	-88.4	6.4	10.5	175.1
17.0	8.6	5.9				16.9	39.5	8.1	2.7
(52) 5.9	(67) 3.7	(101) 2.0	EBIT/Interest		(12) 9.9	(13) 8.7	(21) 2.6	(39) 1.0	
2.0	.1	-1.1			-2.4	3.7	-1.1	-2.9	
			Net Profit + Depr., Dep., Amort./Cur. Mat. L/T/D						
.6	.5	.7		1.0	.3	.9	.7	.7	.1
1.0	1.0	1.0	Fixed/Worth	1.8	.8	1.1	1.0	1.0	1.0
1.5	1.5	1.5		3.8	1.8	2.3	1.4	1.4	1.4
.2	.2	.3		.4	.1	.3	.2	.3	.3
.6	.5	.7	Debt/Worth	1.2	.6	.5	.5	.8	.7
1.3	1.2	1.7		3.0	1.2	7.0	.9	2.2	1.4
14.2	15.3	8.6		17.2	7.3	21.5	13.4	5.5	5.0
(77) 5.5	(91) 5.2	(128) 2.1	% Profit Before Taxes/Tangible Net Worth	4.0	(11) 2.1	(14) 4.1	5.8	(23) .9	(48) 1.1
1.4	.8	-3.1		-1.1	-7.7	-1.7	1.5	-8.8	-5.3
7.6	8.1	4.2		6.8	9.3	3.7	7.6	4.0	2.2
3.3	2.8	1.1	% Profit Before Taxes/Total Assets	1.5	1.4	1.2	3.8	.8	.5
1.1	.0	-1.4		-.7	-3.4	-.5	1.4	-2.1	-2.4
1.5	8.9	3.9		9.6	43.9	3.5	1.4	2.1	UND
.6	.6	.6	Sales/Net Fixed Assets	.2	1.5	.4	.4	.5	1.0
.3	.4	.3		.1	.4	.3	.3	.3	.6
.6	.8	1.0		.3	1.2	1.4	.6	.6	1.8
.4	.4	.4	Sales/Total Assets	.2	.7	.3	.3	.3	.6
.2	.2	.2		.1	.3	.2	.2	.2	.4
4.7	4.5	5.0		15.5		4.9		5.4	4.3
(49) 8.9	(55) 10.2	(88) 8.9	% Depr., Dep., Amort./Sales	(11) 19.2	(13) 11.5		(17) 8.8	(30) 6.4	
14.9	16.7	15.7		24.9		17.1		12.6	9.6
4.5	1.3	3.0							
(10) 6.8	(14) 8.6	(15) 8.9	% Officers', Directors' Owners' Comp/Sales						
16.7	20.9	26.1							
2174528M	2897555M	4631603M	Net Sales ($)	7836M	25205M	60095M	99082M	415599M	4023786M
4021140M	4917901M	7884151M	Total Assets ($)	73162M	51603M	350923M	314124M	1361731M	5732608M

M = $ thousand   MM = $ million
See Pages 9 through 22 for Explanation of Ratios and Data

Current Data Sorted by Assets   **Comparative Historical Data**

0-500M	500M-2MM	2-10MM	10-50MM	50-100MM	100-250MM	Type of Statement	4/1/05-3/31/06 ALL	4/1/06-3/31/07 ALL
2	1	9	25	6	13	Unqualified	16	29
						Reviewed		
		1				Compiled	1	1
						Tax Returns		
1	2		2	1		Other	3	2
	46 (4/1-9/30/09)		17 (10/1/09-3/31/10)					
3	3	10	27	7	13	**NUMBER OF STATEMENTS**	20	32
%	%	%	%	%	%	**ASSETS**	%	%
		31.7	20.2		19.1	Cash & Equivalents	37.1	36.0
		7.1	3.6		6.0	Trade Receivables (net)	5.7	3.8
		.2	.1		.6	Inventory	1.2	.4
		7.2	3.5		6.2	All Other Current	3.4	3.4
		46.2	27.3		31.9	Total Current	47.5	43.6
		41.9	67.4		58.7	Fixed Assets (net)	48.0	48.4
		.0	.8		.3	Intangibles (net)	.1	1.2
		11.9	4.5		9.2	All Other Non-Current	4.4	6.8
		100.0	100.0		100.0	Total	100.0	100.0
						LIABILITIES		
		.6	1.0		.7	Notes Payable-Short Term	.2	2.7
		1.6	2.3		1.8	Cur. Mat.-L.T.D.	1.6	3.0
		3.5	1.4		3.8	Trade Payables	4.0	2.7
		.0	1.3		.0	Income Taxes Payable	.0	1.0
		10.1	3.4		5.9	All Other Current	9.5	6.7
		15.9	9.4		12.3	Total Current	15.3	16.1
		21.9	27.4		35.0	Long-Term Debt	20.8	27.1
		.0	.0		.0	Deferred Taxes	.0	.0
		1.2	2.5		3.3	All Other Non-Current	10.2	2.6
		61.0	60.6		49.4	Net Worth	53.7	54.2
		100.0	100.0		100.0	Total Liabilties & Net Worth	100.0	100.0
						INCOME DATA		
		100.0	100.0		100.0	Net Sales	100.0	100.0
						Gross Profit		
		91.4	89.0		84.7	Operating Expenses	81.4	88.7
		8.6	11.0		15.3	Operating Profit	18.6	11.3
		1.4	1.5		9.4	All Other Expenses (net)	6.1	-.5
		7.2	9.5		5.9	Profit Before Taxes	12.6	11.8
						RATIOS		
		5.7	5.1		3.7		9.3	6.1
		2.9	2.8		2.5	Current	5.3	3.5
		1.6	1.8		1.8		1.8	1.6
		5.5	4.6		3.5		8.0	5.5
		2.4	2.4		2.2	Quick	4.8	3.2
		.9	1.5		1.6		1.6	1.4
		2 193.6	8 47.3		21 17.1		4 89.6	0 UND
		29 12.7	24 15.0		35 10.4	Sales/Receivables	17 21.7	14 25.5
		52 7.0	50 7.4		57 6.4		38 9.5	44 8.3
						Cost of Sales/Inventory		
						Cost of Sales/Payables		
		1.4	1.4		1.6		.9	1.4
		3.7	2.6		3.0	Sales/Working Capital	1.3	2.5
		NM	6.0		6.2		3.9	7.3
			6.8		4.3		7.7	7.4
			(25) 2.3		(10) 1.6	EBIT/Interest	(13) 2.5	(23) 3.4
			.9		1.3		.6	1.8
						Net Profit + Depr., Dep., Amort./Cur. Mat. L/T/D		
		.0	.9		1.1		.1	.1
		.7	1.1		1.3	Fixed/Worth	.9	.9
		2.0	1.5		1.6		1.7	1.3
		.2	.3		.6		.1	.3
		.5	.7		1.0	Debt/Worth	.5	.6
		1.8	.9		1.5		1.4	1.2
		22.2	5.9		10.0		11.1	11.9
		-.4	2.0		1.2	% Profit Before Taxes/Tangible Net Worth	(18) 2.4	(30) 6.3
		-11.5	.2		-2.7		-.4	2.0
		7.4	3.7		3.0		10.1	6.2
		-.1	1.4		.6	% Profit Before Taxes/Total Assets	2.6	3.8
		-6.4	.1		-.4		-.2	1.0
		UND	.9		2.1		485.7	UND
		1.1	.4		.6	Sales/Net Fixed Assets	.9	.8
		.4	.3		.3		.3	.4
		1.6	.5		1.1		1.0	.8
		.5	.3		.4	Sales/Total Assets	.4	.4
		.2	.2		.2		.2	.2
			6.0		3.2		5.9	4.5
			(23) 11.4		(12) 6.7	% Depr., Dep., Amort./Sales	(10) 9.7	(20) 7.7
			20.2		13.7		20.3	14.0
						% Officers', Directors' Owners' Comp/Sales		
882M	8923M	39836M	277706M	215636M	1767122M	Net Sales ($)	948898M	412517M
798M	3964M	51242M	720953M	514419M	2017002M	Total Assets ($)	876030M	1169080M

M = $ thousand   MM = $ million
See Pages 9 through 22 for Explanation of Ratios and Data

Comparative Historical Data | | | Current Data Sorted by Sales

28	28	56	Type of Statement	6	6	4	13	12	15
		1	Unqualified						
			Reviewed						
			Compiled					1	
			Tax Returns						
			Other	1	1	1	2	1	
6 4/1/07-3/31/08 ALL	7 4/1/08-3/31/09 ALL	6 4/1/09-3/31/10 ALL			46 (4/1-9/30/09)		17 (10/1/09-3/31/10)		
				0-1MM	1-3MM	3-5MM	5-10MM	10-25MM	25MM & OVER
34	35	63	NUMBER OF STATEMENTS	7	7	5	15	14	15
%	%	%	ASSETS	%	%	%	%	%	%
24.4	26.6	22.3	Cash & Equivalents				20.4	17.5	21.7
4.8	10.0	4.9	Trade Receivables (net)				5.8	2.9	6.3
.1	.1	.2	Inventory				.0	.1	.7
2.1	2.4	5.0	All Other Current				8.6	2.3	9.2
31.4	39.2	32.5	Total Current				34.9	22.8	37.8
59.5	53.8	60.5	Fixed Assets (net)				59.2	68.9	54.6
.3	.4	.5	Intangibles (net)				.1	.1	.7
8.8	6.6	6.4	All Other Non-Current				5.8	8.3	6.9
100.0	100.0	100.0	Total				100.0	100.0	100.0
			LIABILITIES						
.8	.8	.7	Notes Payable-Short Term				1.3	1.1	.6
2.7	2.0	2.1	Cur. Mat.-L.T.D.				1.9	2.3	1.6
3.9	3.9	2.6	Trade Payables				3.1	1.3	4.0
.0	.9	.5	Income Taxes Payable				.0	.0	2.3
2.9	4.8	5.2	All Other Current				5.4	1.8	7.8
10.3	12.4	11.2	Total Current				11.7	6.6	16.4
26.9	20.5	29.1	Long-Term Debt				22.3	28.9	34.9
.0	.0	.0	Deferred Taxes				.0	.0	.0
2.8	2.4	2.7	All Other Non-Current				1.9	2.8	5.2
59.9	64.8	57.1	Net Worth				64.1	61.6	43.5
100.0	100.0	100.0	Total Liabilities & Net Worth				100.0	100.0	100.0
			INCOME DATA						
100.0	100.0	100.0	Net Sales				100.0	100.0	100.0
			Gross Profit						
88.3	89.8	89.0	Operating Expenses				90.8	96.4	88.9
11.7	10.2	11.0	Operating Profit				9.2	3.6	11.1
-1.5	3.3	3.4	All Other Expenses (net)				-.3	3.9	7.1
13.2	6.9	7.5	Profit Before Taxes				9.5	-.3	3.9
			RATIOS						
8.9	5.0	4.7					4.6	6.4	3.3
4.7	3.4	2.5	Current				2.2	4.4	2.4
2.3	1.5	1.7					1.7	2.1	1.7
7.4	4.9	4.6					4.6	5.7	3.1
4.6	3.4	2.3	Quick				1.8	4.1	1.7
1.5	1.3	1.5					1.2	1.6	1.6
5 68.0	9 40.2	10 36.6	Sales/Receivables	22 16.4	10 37.9	15 24.8			
19 19.7	38 9.6	28 13.1		39 9.4	27 13.8	27 13.5			
40 9.1	65 5.6	50 7.3		77 4.8	39 9.4	50 7.3			
			Cost of Sales/Inventory						
			Cost of Sales/Payables						
1.2	1.4	1.6					1.5	1.7	1.9
2.5	3.0	3.4	Sales/Working Capital				3.7	2.5	5.0
5.5	7.9	6.5					6.5	5.7	9.1
11.1	6.8	5.1					7.4	9.7	3.8
(26) 4.1	(30) 2.9	(52) 2.4	EBIT/Interest	(14) 3.0	(13) 1.8	(12) 1.5			
2.3	-.4	.8					1.6	-.2	.8
			Net Profit + Depr., Dep., Amort./Cur. Mat. L/T/D						
.8	.2	.9					.5	.9	.9
.9	1.0	1.1	Fixed/Worth				1.1	1.1	1.3
1.2	1.3	1.6					1.5	1.6	2.4
.3	.3	.3					.3	.2	.7
.4	.5	.7	Debt/Worth				.6	.6	1.0
1.4	.8	1.1					.9	1.0	2.4
10.5	9.0	7.6					10.4	4.9	9.5
(32) 4.8	(62) 3.3	1.9	% Profit Before Taxes/Tangible Net Worth				2.0	(14) 1.5	.7
1.1	-4.5	-3.8					.1	-7.8	-7.1
6.3	5.0	4.8					7.5	3.1	4.5
3.0	2.3	1.0	% Profit Before Taxes/Total Assets				1.5	.9	.4
.4	-3.5	-.8					.1	-3.6	-4.9
1.4	4.9	1.4					1.4	1.0	2.8
.5	.5	.5	Sales/Net Fixed Assets				.4	.4	1.1
.4	.3	.3					.3	.2	.4
.9	.8	.8					.8	.7	1.2
.4	.3	.4	Sales/Total Assets				.3	.3	.6
.2	.2	.2					.2	.2	.3
5.5	6.8	4.5					8.3	4.5	2.6
(25) 11.1	(21) 11.0	(48) 8.8	% Depr., Dep., Amort./Sales	(10) 14.2	(12) 9.7	(13) 4.1			
17.3	14.2	18.2					20.9	16.5	7.0
			% Officers', Directors' Owners' Comp/Sales						
768813M	772788M	2310105M	Net Sales ($)	3392M	13141M	21698M	103183M	218137M	1950554M
1662860M	1743110M	3308378M	Total Assets ($)	27737M	49838M	111601M	380527M	781197M	1957478M

M = $ thousand   MM = $ million
See Pages 9 through 22 for Explanation of Ratios and Data

Current Data Sorted by Assets | **Comparative Historical Data**

Type of Statement	0-500M	500M-2MM	2-10MM	10-50MM	50-100MM	100-250MM	8 4/1/05-3/31/06 ALL	10 4/1/06-3/31/07 ALL
Unqualified			12	25	14	18	22	22
Reviewed		1						
Compiled			6				2	
Tax Returns								
Other	1			4	1	3	8	10
		69 (4/1-9/30/09)		16 (10/1/09-3/31/10)				
NUMBER OF STATEMENTS	1	1	18	29	15	21	32	32
	%	%	%	%	%	%	%	%
ASSETS								
Cash & Equivalents			35.8	19.8	16.0	18.2	27.5	24.0
Trade Receivables (net)			10.0	3.9	10.0	10.2	4.1	10.7
Inventory			2.8	.7	.7	.2	.5	1.1
All Other Current			3.4	5.6	4.9	1.7	2.1	5.2
Total Current			52.0	30.0	31.7	30.4	34.2	41.0
Fixed Assets (net)			36.7	61.8	63.0	65.9	61.1	53.9
Intangibles (net)			.9	.5	.0	1.3	.6	.0
All Other Non-Current			10.4	7.7	5.3	2.4	4.1	5.0
Total			100.0	100.0	100.0	100.0	100.0	100.0
LIABILITIES								
Notes Payable-Short Term			1.4	1.0	3.8	.1	.5	1.8
Cur. Mat.-L.T.D.			1.2	2.3	1.9	2.0	2.7	2.6
Trade Payables			7.6	2.7	1.9	1.5	2.2	4.4
Income Taxes Payable			1.9	.0	.0	.0	.0	.9
All Other Current			7.2	6.3	9.7	4.8	6.3	4.6
Total Current			19.3	12.3	17.3	8.4	11.6	14.2
Long-Term Debt			14.3	24.3	25.4	24.2	31.5	24.8
Deferred Taxes			.0	.0	.0	.2	.0	1.4
All Other Non-Current			3.3	4.8	3.0	8.1	1.0	6.1
Net Worth			63.0	58.7	54.3	59.1	56.0	53.5
Total Liabilities & Net Worth			100.0	100.0	100.0	100.0	100.0	100.0
INCOME DATA								
Net Sales			100.0	100.0	100.0	100.0	100.0	100.0
Gross Profit								
Operating Expenses			93.3	93.0	91.3	90.3	82.0	80.2
Operating Profit			6.7	7.0	8.7	9.7	18.0	19.8
All Other Expenses (net)			.2	1.9	1.1	3.8	1.7	.2
Profit Before Taxes			6.5	5.1	7.7	5.9	16.2	19.6
RATIOS								
Current			8.0	6.5	4.7	7.4	6.3	6.6
			3.1	2.0	2.2	4.5	2.5	3.8
			1.8	1.0	1.4	2.0	1.1	1.8
Quick			7.8	6.4	4.5	7.2	4.3	5.8
			2.5	1.7	1.8	3.2	2.4	2.4
			1.6	.7	1.1	1.7	1.0	1.7
Sales/Receivables			2 198.3	8 47.2	14 25.5	18 20.1	1 697.7	10 38.2
			9 39.6	20 17.8	45 8.1	40 9.0	27 13.3	39 9.5
			33 11.0	40 9.2	78 4.7	84 4.3	45 8.2	77 4.7
Cost of Sales/Inventory								
Cost of Sales/Payables								
Sales/Working Capital			1.5	1.2	1.2	1.1	1.3	1.5
			3.2	2.5	2.2	1.8	3.3	2.2
			18.3	192.2	5.3	4.9	32.1	5.5
EBIT/Interest			29.0	3.2	8.1	7.0	16.8	12.5
			(12) 1.6	(26) 1.6	3.3	(18) 2.2	(25) 4.6	(23) 5.5
			-1.6	-1.2	-1.8	1.0	2.0	2.6
Net Profit + Depr., Dep., Amort./Cur. Mat. L/T/D								
Fixed/Worth			.0	.8	.9	.8	.8	.6
			.6	1.0	1.1	1.1	1.2	1.1
			1.0	1.5	1.7	1.6	1.7	1.4
Debt/Worth			.2	.2	.2	.4	.3	.5
			.6	.7	.8	.6	1.0	.8
			1.5	1.3	1.7	1.0	1.5	1.3
% Profit Before Taxes/Tangible Net Worth			19.5	5.0	11.0	4.9	36.0	23.5
			(28) 5.3	1.2	1.9	(20) 2.0	(31) 7.3	(31) 9.0
			-6.5	-2.3	-3.8	-.5	1.5	3.9
% Profit Before Taxes/Total Assets			14.3	4.4	5.3	3.1	13.6	10.4
			3.1	.7	1.6	1.4	4.1	4.5
			-2.9	-1.4	-1.8	-.5	1.0	2.1
Sales/Net Fixed Assets			UND	1.3	1.3	.7	3.1	4.5
			2.2	.6	.4	.5	.6	1.0
			.8	.3	.2	.3	.4	.3
Sales/Total Assets			3.1	.8	.4	.5	1.3	1.3
			.9	.4	.2	.3	.5	.5
			.5	.2	.2	.2	.3	.2
% Depr., Dep., Amort./Sales			6.6		1.9	3.1	3.4	4.6
			(20) 11.4		(13) 7.7	(12) 8.6	(20) 6.6	(21) 5.7
			15.6		12.9	25.0	10.6	16.7
% Officers', Directors' Owners' Comp/Sales								
Net Sales ($)	1367M	4439M	175958M	519043M	411217M	2034469M	929001M	1150894M
Total Assets ($)	323M	1112M	88877M	767429M	1007393M	3281098M	1528104M	1843430M

M = $ thousand   MM = $ million
See Pages 9 through 22 for Explanation of Ratios and Data

Comparative Historical Data

Current Data Sorted by Sales

30	52	70	Type of Statement	12	6	8	25	19
			Unqualified					
	1	1	Reviewed					
			Compiled			1		
			Tax Returns	2	2	1	6	3
			Other					
13 4/1/07-3/31/08 ALL	13 4/1/08-3/31/09 ALL	14 4/1/09-3/31/10 ALL		69 (4/1-9/30/09)			16 (10/1/09-3/31/10)		
				0-1MM	1-3MM	3-5MM	5-10MM	10-25MM	25MM & OVER
43	66	85	NUMBER OF STATEMENTS		14	9	9	31	22

07-08	08-09	09-10		0-1MM	1-3MM	3-5MM	5-10MM	10-25MM	25MM & OVER
%	%	%	**ASSETS**		%	%	%	%	%
31.8	30.9	22.9	Cash & Equivalents	D	31.0			22.6	23.5
11.6	7.9	8.3	Trade Receivables (net)	A	2.1			5.2	12.6
.3	.8	1.0	Inventory	T	.0			1.9	.7
2.8	3.6	3.9	All Other Current	A	1.0			3.9	6.8
46.5	43.2	36.1	Total Current		34.2			33.6	43.6
41.2	49.5	56.2	Fixed Assets (net)	N	63.0			59.4	52.1
.3	.2	.7	Intangibles (net)	O	.1			.7	1.2
12.1	7.1	7.0	All Other Non-Current	T	2.8			6.3	3.1
100.0	100.0	100.0	Total		100.0			100.0	100.0
			LIABILITIES	A					
1.0	1.9	1.6	Notes Payable-Short Term	V	.5			2.7	.1
1.2	1.3	1.9	Cur. Mat.-L.T.D.	A	1.3			2.1	1.9
4.0	3.9	3.2	Trade Payables	I	1.7			2.3	6.0
.6	.5	.4	Income Taxes Payable	L	.0			.0	.0
8.8	9.4	6.7	All Other Current	A	3.1			5.0	8.8
15.6	16.8	13.8	Total Current	B	6.6			12.1	16.9
19.5	19.3	21.8	Long-Term Debt	L	21.8			23.3	20.7
.0	.0	.0	Deferred Taxes	E	.0			.1	.0
4.0	2.7	5.4	All Other Non-Current		.7			4.6	10.2
60.8	61.2	59.1	Net Worth		70.9			59.9	52.2
100.0	100.0	100.0	Total Liabilities & Net Worth		100.0			100.0	100.0
			INCOME DATA						
100.0	100.0	100.0	Net Sales		100.0			100.0	100.0
			Gross Profit						
90.5	92.0	92.4	Operating Expenses		88.5			91.4	94.8
9.5	8.0	7.6	Operating Profit		11.5			8.6	5.2
2.6	-.4	1.8	All Other Expenses (net)		3.4			2.6	1.4
6.8	8.4	5.9	Profit Before Taxes		8.1			6.0	3.8
			RATIOS						
5.6	5.9	6.8	Current		11.2			8.1	5.9
3.3	3.8	2.6			6.6			3.4	2.2
2.0	1.9	1.6			2.4			1.6	1.8
4.9	5.6	6.5	Quick		11.1			8.1	5.7
3.1	3.4	2.3			6.4			2.6	2.0
1.9	1.7	1.3			2.1			.8	1.4
8 43.8	9 39.1	8 46.6	Sales/Receivables		2 198.3			8 48.2	10 36.9
27 13.3	27 13.3	25 14.7			20 18.2			23 15.6	25 14.5
62 5.9	55 6.6	55 6.7			47 7.8			65 5.6	75 4.9
			Cost of Sales/Inventory						
			Cost of Sales/Payables						
1.8	1.5	1.3	Sales/Working Capital		.7			1.2	1.9
2.8	3.0	2.3			1.4			1.8	3.7
5.4	6.2	10.3			4.0			11.6	11.0
17.9	10.6	6.5	EBIT/Interest		10.1			5.5	9.4
(29) 4.6	(54) 3.4	(72) 2.0			(10) 1.2		(29) 1.9	(18) 2.3
1.8	.6	-.2			-4.3			-.1	.9
			Net Profit + Depr., Dep., Amort./Cur. Mat. L/T/D						
.0	.0	.6	Fixed/Worth		.6			.6	.4
.8	.9	1.0			1.0			1.0	1.0
1.2	1.2	1.5			1.4			1.5	1.6
.2	.2	.3	Debt/Worth		.1			.2	.4
.5	.5	.7			.4			.6	.8
1.0	1.0	1.3			1.0			1.1	1.9
18.4	11.5	7.4	% Profit Before Taxes/Tangible Net Worth		4.3			9.7	7.3
(41) 4.7	(65) 5.2	(83) 1.9			.2		(30) 1.1	(21) 2.2
1.7	-.4	-2.3			-2.5			-2.3	-1.4
9.4	7.6	4.7	% Profit Before Taxes/Total Assets		3.7			5.5	3.7
2.8	3.3	.9			.2			1.0	1.5
.7	-.3	-1.4			-1.9			-1.2	-1.3
UND	UND	1.8	Sales/Net Fixed Assets		1.0			1.6	UND
1.0	.6	.7			.6			.6	.8
.4	.3	.3			.1			.3	.6
1.9	1.4	.9	Sales/Total Assets		.6			.8	1.4
.6	.4	.4			.4			.4	.5
.3	.2	.2			.1			.2	.4
2.9	4.0	4.4	% Depr., Dep., Amort./Sales					5.0	3.0
(19) 7.5	(41) 9.6	(51) 9.7					(20) 9.7	(12) 5.5
16.1	15.7	13.1						13.6	11.5
		3.7	% Officers', Directors' Owners' Comp/Sales						
	(12)	13.2							
		27.1							
1552865M	2414053M	3146493M	Net Sales ($)		26104M	35341M	69885M	525215M	2489948M
2159845M	3935444M	5146232M	Total Assets ($)		175836M	130808M	299630M	1783057M	2756901M

M = $ thousand   MM = $ million

See Pages 9 through 22 for Explanation of Ratios and Data

Current Data Sorted by Assets   **Comparative Historical Data**

0-500M	500M-2MM	2-10MM	10-50MM	50-100MM	100-250MM		4/1/05-3/31/06 ALL	4/1/06-3/31/07 ALL
	12 (4/1-9/30/09)		13 (10/1/09-3/31/10)			**Type of Statement**	18	17
			4	1	2	Unqualified		
						Reviewed		
1 2		2	2	1	10	Compiled	1.	
						Tax Returns		
						Other	8	20
3		2	6	2	12	**NUMBER OF STATEMENTS**	27	37
%	%	%	%	%	%	**ASSETS**	%	%
					13.4	Cash & Equivalents	24.4	19.7
					1.7	Trade Receivables (net)	2.9	4.0
	D				.2	Inventory	.3	1.2
	A				2.5	All Other Current	3.1	3.0
	T				17.8	Total Current	30.7	28.0
	A				79.8	Fixed Assets (net)	65.8	69.4
					.2	Intangibles (net)	1.4	.9
	N				2.2	All Other Non-Current	2.1	1.7
	O				100.0	Total	100.0	100.0
	T					**LIABILITIES**		
					.0	Notes Payable-Short Term	.7	1.0
	A				3.0	Cur. Mat.-L.T.D.	3.0	1.6
	V				1.0	Trade Payables	2.0	2.7
	A				.0	Income Taxes Payable	.0	.0
	I				8.7	All Other Current	16.9	12.6
	L				12.7	Total Current	22.6	18.0
	A				33.4	Long-Term Debt	23.4	22.1
	B				.0	Deferred Taxes	.0	.0
	L				1.8	All Other Non-Current	1.0	2.6
	E				52.1	Net Worth	52.9	57.2
					100.0	Total Liabilties & Net Worth	100.0	100.0
						INCOME DATA		
					100.0	Net Sales	100.0	100.0
						Gross Profit		
					77.3	Operating Expenses	61.3	70.0
					22.7	Operating Profit	38.7	30.0
					1.9	All Other Expenses (net)	2.1	3.8
					20.8	Profit Before Taxes	36.7	26.2
						RATIOS		
					1.9		2.3	2.8
					1.5	Current	1.6	1.7
					.9		.7	.9
					1.7		2.3	2.4
					1.3	Quick	1.0	1.4
					.7		.6	.9
					2 215.7		0 999.8	1 526.3
					3 116.3	Sales/Receivables	1 650.8	4 88.2
					7 52.0		5 67.1	9 41.0
						Cost of Sales/Inventory		
						Cost of Sales/Payables		
					11.4		7.6	7.1
					19.5	Sales/Working Capital	18.5	20.9
					NM		-52.9	-120.6
					25.3		136.8	388.3
			(11)	10.8		EBIT/Interest	(21) 32.4	(29) 39.6
					3.4		12.0	7.7
						Net Profit + Depr., Dep., Amort./Cur. Mat. L/T/D		
					1.1		.8	.9
					1.5	Fixed/Worth	1.2	1.1
					2.2		2.6	1.7
					.4		.1	.2
					.9	Debt/Worth	.6	.4
					1.5		2.6	1.5
					69.1		187.8	159.8
					39.9	% Profit Before Taxes/Tangible Net Worth	(25) 98.8	(35) 86.8
					17.6		68.5	16.7
					35.9		94.9	97.6
					21.9	% Profit Before Taxes/Total Assets	61.8	39.9
					5.8		26.1	5.5
					1.8		5.1	4.2
					1.2	Sales/Net Fixed Assets	2.2	2.3
					.8		1.4	1.3
					1.4		2.1	2.5
					1.0	Sales/Total Assets	1.6	1.8
					.6		1.0	.9
							4.0	2.6
						% Depr., Dep., Amort./Sales	(16) 5.6	(27) 5.4
							7.8	6.5
						% Officers', Directors' Owners' Comp/Sales		
3761M		3431M	281516M	137372M	2118656M	Net Sales ($)	3878651M	5154011M
973M		11848M	191144M	105135M	2068643M	Total Assets ($)	2381788M	2941349M

(Columns 500M-2MM and 2-10MM marked "DATA NOT AVAILABLE")

M = $ thousand   MM = $ million
See Pages 9 through 22 for Explanation of Ratios and Data

Comparative Historical Data   **Current Data Sorted by Sales**

15	16	7	Type of Statement						
			Unqualified						
			Reviewed			1	1	5
		1	Compiled					
			Tax Returns	1				
			Other	4				13
15 4/1/07- 3/31/08 ALL	16 4/1/08- 3/31/09 ALL	17 4/1/09- 3/31/10 ALL		12 (4/1-9/30/09)			13 (10/1/09-3/31/10)		
				0-1MM	1-3MM	3-5MM	5-10MM	10-25MM	25MM & OVER
30	32	25	NUMBER OF STATEMENTS		5		1	1	18
%	%	%	ASSETS	%	%	%	%	%	%
20.2	22.0	19.6	Cash & Equivalents	D		D			18.7
3.3	1.9	7.5	Trade Receivables (net)	A		A			1.4
1.3	.4	.3	Inventory	T		T			.4
2.2	2.8	3.0	All Other Current	A		A			2.3
27.0	27.2	30.4	Total Current						22.8
70.9	70.4	66.4	Fixed Assets (net)	N		N			75.6
.2	.1	.1	Intangibles (net)	O		O			.2
1.8	2.3	3.1	All Other Non-Current	T		T			1.5
100.0	100.0	100.0	Total						100.0
			LIABILITIES	A		A			
1.5	1.1	2.9	Notes Payable-Short Term	V		V			.3
8.5	4.0	2.6	Cur. Mat.-L.T.D.	A		A			2.8
2.1	3.6	2.0	Trade Payables	I		I			2.0
.0	.0	.0	Income Taxes Payable	L		L			.0
17.9	20.9	9.7	All Other Current	A		A			10.2
30.1	29.7	17.2	Total Current	B		B			15.3
18.6	21.7	26.3	Long-Term Debt	L		L			32.8
.0	.0	.0	Deferred Taxes	E		E			.0
.7	2.9	3.3	All Other Non-Current						3.7
50.6	45.7	53.3	Net Worth						48.2
100.0	100.0	100.0	Total Liabilties & Net Worth						100.0
			INCOME DATA						
100.0	100.0	100.0	Net Sales						100.0
			Gross Profit						
70.3	72.6	77.1	Operating Expenses						71.6
29.7	27.4	22.9	Operating Profit						28.4
.5	4.1	3.5	All Other Expenses (net)						5.4
29.2	23.3	19.4	Profit Before Taxes						23.0
			RATIOS						
2.4	2.1	2.3							2.0
1.2	1.5	1.6	Current						1.5
.6	.7	1.2							1.1
2.0	1.9	2.1							1.9
1.0	1.0	1.4	Quick						1.3
.5	.5	1.0							.9
1 288.0	1 307.8	1 381.7							1 345.2
3 134.8	2 179.1	3 122.6	Sales/Receivables						2 169.5
6 57.0	7 54.7	13 27.3							7 53.9
			Cost of Sales/Inventory						
			Cost of Sales/Payables						
9.7	10.6	9.4							11.2
38.3	26.0	11.9	Sales/Working Capital						19.5
-15.6	-22.0	37.0							61.8
53.1	38.4	69.9							74.8
(22) 22.8	(19) 9.9	(20) 11.1	EBIT/Interest					(15)	10.8
8.2	1.2	3.5							3.9
			Net Profit + Depr., Dep., Amort./Cur. Mat. L/T/D						
.9	.9	.8							.9
1.3	1.3	1.1	Fixed/Worth						1.2
3.0	3.0	1.9							2.5
.2	.2	.3							.3
.7	.8	.6	Debt/Worth						.7
3.0	2.8	1.3							2.0
168.9	114.4	90.7	% Profit Before Taxes/Tangible						104.1
(29) 87.5	(29) 58.6	(24) 34.2	Net Worth					(17)	50.9
15.7	6.2	7.6							20.2
96.9	62.1	53.5	% Profit Before Taxes/Total						54.2
44.1	38.6	19.7	Assets						26.0
13.6	4.3	4.8							6.4
3.1	3.2	3.1							2.8
2.3	2.1	1.3	Sales/Net Fixed Assets						1.5
1.2	1.2	.9							1.0
2.4	2.2	2.0							1.8
1.6	1.5	1.0	Sales/Total Assets						1.0
.9	.7	.6							.8
3.0	2.4	2.9							
(20) 4.9	(20) 4.4	(11) 6.8	% Depr., Dep., Amort./Sales						
8.2	5.7	8.3							
			% Officers', Directors' Owners' Comp/Sales						
4515377M	3400775M	2544736M	Net Sales ($)		7192M		8846M	16762M	2511936M
2905409M	2684449M	2377743M	Total Assets ($)		12821M		44051M	25788M	2295083M

© RMA 2010   M = $ thousand   MM = $ million
See Pages 9 through 22 for Explanation of Ratios and Data

Current Data Sorted by Assets							Comparative Historical Data	

						Type of Statement		
1	15	37	79	32	32	Unqualified	164	194
	1		3	1	2	Reviewed	3	5
	3	2	2		2	Compiled	4	4
1			1			Tax Returns	1	2
6	14	17	18	8	2	Other	42	41
	209 (4/1-9/30/09)		70 (10/1/09-3/31/10)				4/1/05-3/31/06	4/1/06-3/31/07
0-500M	500M-2MM	2-10MM	10-50MM	50-100MM	100-250MM		ALL	ALL
8	33	56	103	41	38	NUMBER OF STATEMENTS	214	246
%	%	%	%	%	%	ASSETS	%	%
	46.0	34.1	24.1	18.6	19.4	Cash & Equivalents	29.8	28.3
	16.9	9.8	6.8	5.9	3.9	Trade Receivables (net)	10.1	9.0
	.9	1.2	.6	.3	.3	Inventory	1.0	1.2
	5.5	5.1	4.0	4.0	4.9	All Other Current	5.4	5.3
	69.2	50.2	35.6	28.8	28.6	Total Current	46.2	43.8
	22.1	40.6	56.6	60.9	62.0	Fixed Assets (net)	46.2	47.8
	.1	.8	.3	3.4	.1	Intangibles (net)	.7	.4
	8.6	8.5	7.4	6.9	9.3	All Other Non-Current	6.9	8.0
	100.0	100.0	100.0	100.0	100.0	Total	100.0	100.0
						LIABILITIES		
	5.5	.6	1.7	1.5	.4	Notes Payable-Short Term	1.9	2.3
	2.4	1.6	2.2	1.9	2.1	Cur. Mat.-L.T.D.	1.9	1.8
	8.4	5.1	3.0	2.5	3.6	Trade Payables	5.1	5.2
	.0	.0	.4	1.1	.1	Income Taxes Payable	.4	.5
	13.1	8.2	7.9	3.0	3.6	All Other Current	6.6	7.1
	29.3	15.5	15.2	10.0	9.8	Total Current	16.0	16.9
	7.9	26.0	26.1	24.8	31.3	Long-Term Debt	19.8	21.8
	.0	.0	.0	.0	.2	Deferred Taxes	.0	.0
	3.7	6.2	3.0	2.4	4.8	All Other Non-Current	4.4	4.5
	59.1	52.4	55.7	62.9	53.9	Net Worth	59.8	56.8
	100.0	100.0	100.0	100.0	100.0	Total Liabilties & Net Worth	100.0	100.0
						INCOME DATA		
	100.0	100.0	100.0	100.0	100.0	Net Sales	100.0	100.0
						Gross Profit		
	96.3	93.9	91.1	92.1	88.5	Operating Expenses	88.2	88.7
	3.7	6.1	8.9	7.9	11.5	Operating Profit	11.8	11.3
	1.8	2.4	4.9	2.5	5.7	All Other Expenses (net)	4.0	1.8
	1.9	3.6	3.9	5.3	5.8	Profit Before Taxes	7.8	9.5
						RATIOS		
	9.1	8.5	6.9	6.7	5.9		7.0	7.1
	3.1	3.7	3.2	3.1	2.2	Current	3.5	3.3
	1.2	2.1	1.4	1.9	1.6		1.7	1.7
	8.2	7.0	5.7	6.3	5.1		6.4	6.1
	3.0	3.1	2.7	2.9	1.8	Quick	3.0	2.7
	1.1	1.5	1.4	1.7	1.2		1.3	1.4
0	UND	0	UND	5	69.6	13	27.3	7	54.5		5	74.9	4	82.6
3	123.3	3	108.8	26	13.9	33	11.0	23	15.7	Sales/Receivables	27	13.7	25	14.8
33	11.1	47	7.8	60	6.1	67	5.5	62	5.9		54	6.8	47	7.7

						Cost of Sales/Inventory		

						Cost of Sales/Payables		

	2.6	1.4	1.4	1.4	1.3		1.3	1.4
	5.9	4.0	2.8	2.0	2.1	Sales/Working Capital	2.7	3.2
	35.1	7.7	9.2	3.9	7.7		8.1	7.8

		24.9		8.3		9.4		6.6		6.4		9.7		8.4
(16)	1.8	(30)	1.9	(72)	2.8	(30)	1.6	(28)	2.4	EBIT/Interest	(138)	3.7	(168)	4.0
	-.5		.2		.2		-.9		.1		1.1		1.5

						Net Profit + Depr., Dep., Amort./Cur. Mat. L/T/D		

	.0	.0	.6	.8	.9		.0	.2
	.0	.7	.9	1.1	1.2	Fixed/Worth	.9	.9
	1.0	1.4	1.5	1.6	1.7		1.2	1.3
	.2	.4	.2	.2	.3		.2	.2
	.5	.8	.5	.5	.8	Debt/Worth	.5	.6
	1.6	2.0	1.4	1.2	1.8		1.3	1.4

	14.9		9.0		5.7		5.7		6.9			10.6		15.1
(32)	1.8	(53)	1.6	(99)	.4	(39)	2.7		1.4	% Profit Before Taxes/Tangible Net Worth	(207)	4.0	(240)	6.8
	-5.4		-3.4		-3.2		-3.2		-2.4			-.8		.7

	11.2	5.0	3.8	4.0	3.0		6.8	7.8
	1.0	.9	.6	1.5	.9	% Profit Before Taxes/Total Assets	2.5	3.3
	-3.6	-1.6	-1.7	-1.4	-1.7		-.8	.3
	UND	809.4	2.5	.7	.9		UND	19.0
	152.0	2.5	.6	.4	.5	Sales/Net Fixed Assets	.9	1.0
	3.0	.5	.3	.3	.3		.4	.4
	3.3	2.2	.9	.5	.6		1.2	1.4
	2.3	.7	.4	.3	.3	Sales/Total Assets	.5	.5
	.8	.3	.2	.2	.2		.3	.3

	2.3		1.9		3.8		5.8		4.1			3.3		1.8
(12)	5.9	(31)	7.1	(66)	8.1	(23)	11.5	(27)	6.4	% Depr., Dep., Amort./Sales	(106)	8.2	(151)	5.9
	12.4		14.0		16.9		20.4		12.1			16.4		12.6

				6.0				5.8			3.5
		(11)		8.6			% Officers', Directors' Owners' Comp/Sales	(19)	12.7	(28)	14.9
				18.0				16.6			31.5

10639M	89931M	494393M	1892719M	1097732M	2595048M	Net Sales ($)	8387098M	9080859M
2318M	35560M	294006M	2553612M	2764178M	6065357M	Total Assets ($)	9173572M	11612842M

M = $ thousand　　MM = $ million
See Pages 9 through 22 for Explanation of Ratios and Data

Comparative Historical Data — Current Data Sorted by Sales

			Type of Statement						
183	220	196	Unqualified	8	27	20	42	51	48
5	1	7	Reviewed			2		1	4
2	6	9	Compiled	1	3	1	2		2
2	3	2	Tax Returns	1	1				
40	47	65	Other	11	14	4	10	15	11
4/1/07-3/31/08	4/1/08-3/31/09	4/1/09-3/31/10		209 (4/1-9/30/09)			70 (10/1/09-3/31/10)		
ALL	ALL	ALL		0-1MM	1-3MM	3-5MM	5-10MM	10-25MM	25MM & OVER
232	277	279	**NUMBER OF STATEMENTS**	21	45	27	54	67	65
%	%	%	**ASSETS**	%	%	%	%	%	%
29.2	31.7	28.3	Cash & Equivalents	43.3	29.3	22.9	26.9	23.6	31.1
7.3	7.4	8.2	Trade Receivables (net)	.8	8.6	11.5	7.1	8.5	9.4
1.1	.6	.7	Inventory	.0	1.1	1.2	1.1	.2	.5
4.7	5.0	4.7	All Other Current	1.8	4.0	2.9	4.6	3.7	8.0
42.3	44.8	41.9	Total Current	46.0	43.0	38.5	39.8	36.0	48.9
51.0	46.7	49.5	Fixed Assets (net)	48.6	48.8	53.1	48.6	58.9	39.8
.2	.3	.9	Intangibles (net)	.4	.3	1.4	.1	.8	2.1
6.6	8.2	7.8	All Other Non-Current	5.0	7.9	6.9	11.6	4.4	9.2
100.0	100.0	100.0	Total	100.0	100.0	100.0	100.0	100.0	100.0
			LIABILITIES						
1.8	.9	2.4	Notes Payable-Short Term	4.8	4.7	1.8	2.3	.8	2.1
1.7	1.7	2.0	Cur. Mat.-L.T.D.	2.8	1.4	2.6	1.4	2.1	2.3
4.3	5.1	4.0	Trade Payables	1.1	3.4	3.0	3.7	4.4	5.6
.3	.1	.3	Income Taxes Payable	.0	.0	.0	.0	.0	1.3
6.7	8.6	7.3	All Other Current	4.5	7.0	4.9	6.2	6.3	11.3
14.8	16.3	16.0	Total Current	13.3	16.5	12.3	13.6	13.6	22.6
23.3	20.1	23.7	Long-Term Debt	31.3	22.2	22.4	20.2	30.4	19.0
.0	.0	.0	Deferred Taxes	.0	.0	.0	.0	.0	.1
3.8	3.6	4.2	All Other Non-Current	1.2	6.4	2.0	4.2	3.5	5.2
58.1	59.9	56.0	Net Worth	54.2	54.8	63.4	62.0	52.5	53.1
100.0	100.0	100.0	Total Liabilities & Net Worth	100.0	100.0	100.0	100.0	100.0	100.0
			INCOME DATA						
100.0	100.0	100.0	Net Sales	100.0	100.0	100.0	100.0	100.0	100.0
			Gross Profit						
87.8	88.2	92.4	Operating Expenses	93.0	90.2	97.1	89.0	92.6	94.3
12.2	11.8	7.6	Operating Profit	7.0	9.8	2.9	11.0	7.4	5.7
1.9	2.6	3.8	All Other Expenses (net)	6.2	4.4	1.3	3.2	3.5	4.4
10.3	9.2	3.8	Profit Before Taxes	.8	5.4	1.6	7.8	3.9	1.3
			RATIOS						
6.4	7.1	7.4		15.0	10.2	6.2	8.7	5.4	6.3
3.2	3.5	3.1	Current	5.8	3.6	3.4	4.1	3.0	2.1
1.8	1.9	1.6		1.8	1.2	1.9	1.7	1.7	1.6
6.0	6.7	6.4		15.0	8.3	5.1	7.4	5.2	5.8
2.8	3.1	2.9	Quick	5.2	2.9	3.4	3.1	2.5	1.9
1.4	1.4	1.3		1.7	1.1	1.9	1.3	1.5	1.1
6 65.4	2 148.8	0 999.8		0 UND	0 UND	1 520.6	3 124.2	13 27.6	4 82.1
20 17.9	17 21.4	19 19.2	Sales/Receivables	0 UND	3 107.4	23 16.2	27 13.5	23 15.7	23 15.7
41 9.0	42 8.7	52 7.1		8 45.4	55 6.7	67 5.5	58 6.3	48 7.7	59 6.2
			Cost of Sales/Inventory						
			Cost of Sales/Payables						
1.4	1.3	1.5		.7	1.0	1.5	1.3	1.7	1.7
2.8	3.0	2.8	Sales/Working Capital	1.7	3.3	3.3	2.4	4.1	4.0
7.4	7.3	8.9		4.8	19.2	7.2	8.0	8.0	9.3
10.2	10.6	8.0		2.2	9.1	9.6	19.0	8.1	5.8
(152) 4.2	(187) 4.0	(180) 2.2	EBIT/Interest	(12) .5	(32) 3.2	(13) 3.8	(34) 3.5	(46) 1.7	(43) 1.4
1.5	1.1	-.3		-.9	-.3	.5	.9	-1.0	-.8
			Net Profit + Depr., Dep., Amort./Cur. Mat. L/T/D						
.4	.1	.2		.2	.0	.1	.3	.8	.0
1.0	.9	.9	Fixed/Worth	1.1	.9	.9	.9	1.1	1.0
1.3	1.2	1.4		2.0	1.6	1.1	1.3	1.5	1.5
.3	.2	.2		.2	.3	.2	.2	.2	.4
.6	.5	.6	Debt/Worth	.7	.8	.4	.5	.5	.9
1.4	1.2	1.6		5.5	1.6	1.4	1.3	1.3	2.2
15.1	12.8	7.5	% Profit Before Taxes/Tangible Net Worth	11.5	8.2	3.9	8.9	6.8	7.8
(225) 5.9	(267) 5.0	(267) 1.1		(19) -.9	(43) 1.6	(25) .5	(53) 3.1	(64) 1.0	(63) 1.1
1.3	.0	-3.2		-4.7	-3.9	-2.7	-2.1	-2.4	-12.1
7.5	7.3	4.1	% Profit Before Taxes/Total Assets	4.5	4.3	3.0	5.2	3.9	4.6
3.2	2.9	.8		-.7	1.0	.7	1.9	.7	.8
.4	-.1	-1.8		-2.6	-2.4	-.9	-1.2	-1.6	-5.2
13.5	118.3	34.1		12.9	UND	18.8	12.0	2.5	UND
.8	.8	.8	Sales/Net Fixed Assets	.9	.6	.8	.9	.5	1.5
.4	.4	.3		.2	.2	.3	.3	.4	.6
1.2	1.4	1.5		.7	2.1	2.1	1.5	1.0	1.7
.5	.4	.5	Sales/Total Assets	.4	.4	.5	.4	.4	.8
.2	.3	.2		.1	.2	.2	.2	.3	.4
2.4	4.0	3.8		8.3	3.8	3.6	4.4	2.7	3.1
(135) 7.1	(166) 8.0	(160) 8.2	% Depr., Dep., Amort./Sales	(13) 20.8	(26) 13.3	(14) 7.6	(33) 7.6	(43) 9.1	(31) 5.5
11.0	13.4	15.9		31.2	22.8	15.9	16.1	14.0	6.7
2.3	3.9	5.3	% Officers', Directors', Owners' Comp/Sales						
(19) 8.5	(19) 11.0	(30) 8.9							
15.6	18.2	18.1							
6970509M	8477845M	6180462M	Net Sales ($)	11845M	84762M	103775M	388661M	1109518M	4481901M
10604440M	13993055M	11715031M	Total Assets ($)	61681M	363518M	344856M	1530883M	3396257M	6017836M

© RMA 2010

M = $ thousand   MM = $ million
See Pages 9 through 22 for Explanation of Ratios and Data

Current Data Sorted by Assets   Comparative Historical Data

						Type of Statement			
1	10	19	7	1		Unqualified		27	25
	3	3				Reviewed		6	9
	5	2				Compiled		10	8
1	2	4		1		Tax Returns		6	11
	10	11	4	2		Other		20	16
	50 (4/1-9/30/09)		36 (10/1/09-3/31/10)					4/1/05-3/31/06	4/1/06-3/31/07
0-500M	500M-2MM	2-10MM	10-50MM	50-100MM	100-250MM			ALL	ALL
2	30	39	11	4		NUMBER OF STATEMENTS		69	69
%	%	%	%	%	%	ASSETS		%	%
	26.5	20.2	26.4			Cash & Equivalents		24.1	22.2
	9.2	9.8	14.2			Trade Receivables (net)		8.4	10.9
	1.2	2.1	4.8			Inventory		2.4	2.2
	1.0	3.9	7.0			All Other Current		3.4	2.4
	37.8	36.0	52.3			Total Current		38.4	37.7
	56.8	60.9	30.3			Fixed Assets (net)		56.8	58.1
	.7	.3	6.0			Intangibles (net)		.3	.3
	4.7	2.7	11.3			All Other Non-Current		4.5	3.9
	100.0	100.0	100.0			Total		100.0	100.0
						LIABILITIES			
	2.0	3.2	4.3			Notes Payable-Short Term		3.8	2.9
	2.6	3.0	1.3			Cur. Mat.-L.T.D.		3.3	2.5
	2.0	3.9	9.7			Trade Payables		4.2	4.0
	.3	.1	.1			Income Taxes Payable		.0	.0
	3.8	3.6	10.1			All Other Current		3.5	4.8
	10.6	13.8	25.6			Total Current		14.9	14.2
	17.8	25.9	18.3			Long-Term Debt		22.6	21.2
	.6	.5	.0			Deferred Taxes		.0	.0
	1.1	2.0	5.2			All Other Non-Current		3.2	1.4
	69.9	57.8	50.9			Net Worth		59.3	63.3
	100.0	100.0	100.0			Total Liabilities & Net Worth		100.0	100.0
						INCOME DATA			
	100.0	100.0	100.0			Net Sales		100.0	100.0
						Gross Profit			
	86.7	93.6	96.9			Operating Expenses		85.6	86.2
	13.3	6.4	3.1			Operating Profit		14.4	13.8
	2.3	2.1	2.6			All Other Expenses (net)		2.9	4.1
	10.9	4.3	.5			Profit Before Taxes		11.5	9.7
						RATIOS			
	8.0	5.4	10.6					14.3	11.7
	3.8	3.5	1.7			Current		5.0	5.4
	2.2	1.6	1.0					1.6	1.5
	6.6	5.4	10.1					12.9	11.6
	3.7	3.0	1.5			Quick		4.8	5.4
	2.1	1.4	.7					1.4	1.2
0 UND	0 UND	0 UND					0 UND	0 UND	
2 171.9	1 247.8	14 26.9				Sales/Receivables	0 797.0	4 101.0	
24 15.4	31 11.8	46 7.9					14 25.8	34 10.7	
						Cost of Sales/Inventory			
						Cost of Sales/Payables			
	2.5	1.5	1.3					1.4	1.4
	5.4	3.5	4.2			Sales/Working Capital		2.9	2.6
	8.9	9.3	115.0					11.8	11.4
	13.7	8.4						8.7	7.8
(18)	3.9 (29)	2.7				EBIT/Interest	(46) 4.5	(49) 4.4	
	1.2	.6						2.1	1.5
						Net Profit + Depr., Dep., Amort./Cur. Mat. L/T/D			
	.3	.7	.2					.4	.5
	.9	1.1	.7			Fixed/Worth		1.0	1.0
	1.1	1.6	3.1					1.6	1.4
	.1	.3	.3					.2	.2
	.3	.6	.8			Debt/Worth		.5	.5
	.9	1.7	7.8					1.4	1.2
	26.2	11.5	10.1			% Profit Before Taxes/Tangible Net Worth		17.2	21.0
	12.0	4.7 (10)	3.5				(68) 8.7	(68) 7.2	
	2.2	-3.2	-2.2					2.1	1.4
	16.0	5.6	3.7			% Profit Before Taxes/Total Assets		10.6	10.4
	8.1	2.9	2.8					5.2	3.9
	1.4	-1.5	-1.7					.5	1.0
	12.5	3.1	65.3					7.5	3.8
	1.1	.7	1.9			Sales/Net Fixed Assets		.7	.8
	.5	.3	.8					.3	.4
	1.7	1.5	2.5					1.8	1.1
	.9	.6	.8			Sales/Total Assets		.5	.5
	.4	.2	.4					.2	.3
	5.2	3.8						4.2	2.8
(21)	9.1 (30)	8.8				% Depr., Dep., Amort./Sales	(46) 11.8	(45) 12.1	
	17.8	26.8						20.1	26.8
						% Officers', Directors' Owners' Comp/Sales		3.4	2.5
							(13) 8.0	(12) 4.1	
								12.0	9.3
876M	49156M	167662M	343242M	463897M		Net Sales ($)		299919M	242166M
676M	41184M	168089M	223357M	233429M		Total Assets ($)		266354M	276913M

M = $ thousand   MM = $ million
See Pages 9 through 22 for Explanation of Ratios and Data

Comparative Historical Data   **Current Data Sorted by Sales**

			Type of Statement						
36	44	38	Unqualified	7	16	4	5	4	2
13	15	6	Reviewed	4	1		1		
11	5	7	Compiled	3	4				
7	8	8	Tax Returns	3	2		1	1	1
10	22	27	Other	9	4	4		5	5
4/1/07-3/31/08	4/1/08-3/31/09	4/1/09-3/31/10		50 (4/1-9/30/09)			36 (10/1/09-3/31/10)		
ALL	ALL	ALL		0-1MM	1-3MM	3-5MM	5-10MM	10-25MM	25MM & OVE
77	94	86	**NUMBER OF STATEMENTS**	26	26	9	7	10	8
%	%	%	**ASSETS**	%	%	%		%	%
20.7	23.3	23.5	Cash & Equivalents	15.1	25.9			13.8	
12.6	11.6	10.8	Trade Receivables (net)	1.5	4.2			27.7	
2.2	1.7	2.0	Inventory	1.0	1.7			3.6	
2.8	3.7	3.1	All Other Current	.3	2.3			10.2	
38.2	40.3	39.3	Total Current	17.8	34.1			55.3	
56.6	52.7	52.7	Fixed Assets (net)	75.3	63.0			35.4	
.8	.8	2.2	Intangibles (net)	1.4	.0			1.2	
4.3	6.2	5.8	All Other Non-Current	5.5	2.9			8.0	
100.0	100.0	100.0	Total	100.0	100.0			100.0	
			LIABILITIES						
4.0	3.8	3.5	Notes Payable-Short Term	2.5	3.4			4.7	
2.9	3.2	3.3	Cur. Mat.-L.T.D.	3.0	3.2			1.9	
5.2	3.2	4.0	Trade Payables	1.0	.9			10.3	
.0	.0	.2	Income Taxes Payable	.0	.3			.4	
5.2	5.5	5.2	All Other Current	.7	4.0			11.1	
17.4	15.6	16.2	Total Current	7.2	11.9			28.5	
20.9	22.7	21.8	Long-Term Debt	23.3	29.2			10.9	
.2	.1	.4	Deferred Taxes	.3	.0			.0	
1.0	3.6	2.0	All Other Non-Current	.0	.3			10.7	
60.6	58.0	59.6	Net Worth	69.2	58.6			50.0	
100.0	100.0	100.0	Total Liabilities & Net Worth	100.0	100.0			100.0	
			INCOME DATA						
100.0	100.0	100.0	Net Sales	100.0	100.0			100.0	
			Gross Profit						
87.3	92.0	92.0	Operating Expenses	86.9	92.8			96.6	
12.7	8.0	8.0	Operating Profit	13.1	7.2			3.4	
4.1	2.2	2.2	All Other Expenses (net)	1.9	3.1			-.2	
8.6	5.8	5.9	Profit Before Taxes	11.3	4.1			3.6	
			RATIOS						
8.2	8.5	6.6		9.0	5.4			3.7	
3.3	3.1	3.5	Current	4.2	3.2			1.5	
1.5	1.5	1.5		2.6	1.6			1.2	
7.6	8.4	6.4		8.4	5.4			3.0	
3.0	2.8	3.1	Quick	4.0	2.7			1.3	
1.2	1.3	1.3		2.6	1.5			.9	
0 UND	0 UND	0 UND		0 UND	0 UND			6 61.5	
1 520.3	7 48.8	5 67.6	Sales/Receivables	0 UND	1 290.6			39 9.4	
37 9.8	29 12.7	29 12.7		15 24.5	20 18.2			82 4.5	
			Cost of Sales/Inventory						
			Cost of Sales/Payables						
1.5	1.8	1.9		1.1	1.9			3.8	
3.3	4.4	4.4	Sales/Working Capital	2.7	3.7			10.2	
14.6	13.6	10.4		8.2	10.3			34.3	
11.3	6.4	8.1		6.2	6.4				
(54) 4.0	(73) 3.5	(60) 2.9	EBIT/Interest	(17) 3.9	(18) 2.3				
.5	1.4	.7		.9	.4				
			Net Profit + Depr., Dep., Amort./Cur. Mat. L/T/D						
.5	.4	.5		.9	.7			.1	
.8	.9	.9	Fixed/Worth	1.0	1.0			.7	
1.4	1.4	1.7		1.7	1.9			2.4	
.2	.3	.2		.1	.2			.3	
.5	.6	.5	Debt/Worth	.3	.6			1.0	
1.8	1.5	1.9		1.1	1.8			4.5	
23.3	18.0	17.4		11.0	17.0			42.4	
(75) 7.7	(91) 6.9	(83) 5.6	% Profit Before Taxes/Tangible Net Worth	(25) 3.9	6.5			6.6	
.3	.1	-.5		-.7	-3.4			-.8	
9.8	9.6	9.1		6.8	9.1			14.0	
3.4	3.5	3.3	% Profit Before Taxes/Total Assets	2.6	3.2			4.5	
-.3	-.2	-.4		-.5	-1.5			-1.3	
7.8	8.8	10.6		.6	2.2			47.7	
.9	1.1	1.1	Sales/Net Fixed Assets	.3	1.0			5.6	
.3	.4	.4		.2	.5			1.7	
1.8	2.0	1.9		.5	1.0			2.8	
.5	.7	.7	Sales/Total Assets	.2	.8			2.1	
.2	.3	.3		.2	.3			.8	
1.6	2.3	3.9		10.6	5.8				
(59) 10.4	(67) 7.8	(61) 8.5	% Depr., Dep., Amort./Sales	(19) 19.2	(22) 8.8				
18.8	18.8	19.1		32.0	18.4				
2.1	2.4	2.5							
(12) 5.1	(15) 3.9	(13) 4.4	% Officers', Directors' Owners' Comp/Sales						
11.6	8.1	11.3							
375306M	746514M	1024833M	Net Sales ($)	14089M	48453M	36340M	52440M	136386M	737125M
329150M	893732M	666735M	Total Assets ($)	54343M	80258M	28693M	67757M	115449M	320235M

M = $ thousand   MM = $ million
See Pages 9 through 22 for Explanation of Ratios and Data

Current Data Sorted by Assets | Comparative Historical Data

Type of Statement	0-500M	500M-2MM	2-10MM	10-50MM	50-100MM	100-250MM		4/1/05-3/31/06 ALL	4/1/06-3/31/07 ALL
Unqualified	1	8	20	46	25	24		55	83
Reviewed	2							1	
Compiled		1			1			3	3
Tax Returns								1	1
Other	2	3	9	9	3	2		24	18
		142 (4/1-9/30/09)		14 (10/1/09-3/31/10)					
NUMBER OF STATEMENTS	5	12	29	55	29	26		84	105

ASSETS	%	%	%	%	%	%		%	%
Cash & Equivalents		26.5	32.1	22.7	19.3	21.8		25.9	25.8
Trade Receivables (net)		5.5	10.1	8.2	5.0	4.8		12.9	11.3
Inventory		1.7	.2	1.5	.2	.1		3.0	.6
All Other Current		.5	2.9	4.1	1.8	3.9		5.9	3.7
Total Current		34.1	45.2	36.5	26.3	30.7		47.7	41.5
Fixed Assets (net)		43.5	38.8	55.1	59.5	55.2		43.1	46.5
Intangibles (net)		.0	.1	.4	2.8	.0		1.6	.7
All Other Non-Current		22.4	15.9	8.0	11.4	13.9		7.6	11.2
Total		100.0	100.0	100.0	100.0	100.0		100.0	100.0

LIABILITIES	0-500M	500M-2MM	2-10MM	10-50MM	50-100MM	100-250MM		05-06	06-07
Notes Payable-Short Term		11.4	1.1	1.5	.1	.3		1.6	2.8
Cur. Mat.-L.T.D.		2.9	2.1	2.9	2.3	3.7		2.8	3.1
Trade Payables		15.5	7.7	3.3	1.3	3.4		6.5	6.2
Income Taxes Payable		.0	.0	.0	.0	.0		.0	.0
All Other Current		15.7	11.2	8.9	8.3	8.3		10.4	12.8
Total Current		45.4	22.1	16.6	12.1	15.7		21.4	25.0
Long-Term Debt		7.3	16.9	26.8	32.4	33.1		23.5	29.7
Deferred Taxes		.0	.2	.1	.0	.0		.1	.0
All Other Non-Current		11.6	8.8	3.3	1.2	6.9		4.4	5.2
Net Worth		35.8	52.0	53.2	54.3	44.4		50.7	40.1
Total Liabilities & Net Worth		100.0	100.0	100.0	100.0	100.0		100.0	100.0

INCOME DATA	0-500M	500M-2MM	2-10MM	10-50MM	50-100MM	100-250MM		05-06	06-07
Net Sales		100.0	100.0	100.0	100.0	100.0		100.0	100.0
Gross Profit									
Operating Expenses		105.3	96.4	98.3	93.7	93.1		94.1	94.4
Operating Profit		-5.3	3.6	1.7	6.3	6.9		5.9	5.6
All Other Expenses (net)		-1.3	4.1	1.6	3.6	3.9		.6	1.3
Profit Before Taxes		-4.0	-.5	.1	2.7	3.0		5.3	4.3

RATIOS	0-500M	500M-2MM	2-10MM	10-50MM	50-100MM	100-250MM		05-06	06-07
Current		2.7	3.6	5.2	2.8	4.2		5.9	5.1
		1.9	2.0	2.0	2.0	2.0		2.4	2.2
		.2	1.1	1.3	1.4	1.3		1.1	1.1
Quick		2.7	3.3	4.2	2.4	4.0		4.7	4.5
		1.9	1.9	1.8	1.8	1.6		1.7	2.0
		.2	1.0	1.1	1.3	1.2		.9	.9
Sales/Receivables		0 UND	1 610.3	1 476.9	3 116.1	5 77.3		1 372.3	1 508.5
		3 118.4	20 18.7	10 36.3	12 31.0	18 20.3		13 27.6	10 36.3
		18 20.5	36 10.2	33 11.0	39 9.4	24 15.4		48 7.7	45 8.1
Cost of Sales/Inventory									
Cost of Sales/Payables									
Sales/Working Capital		5.5	4.5	2.7	3.1	3.0		3.5	3.7
		7.6	10.1	7.4	7.5	4.7		8.1	9.8
		-5.3	34.4	24.8	18.6	14.5		103.6	116.1
EBIT/Interest			21.5	8.5	4.0	3.8		11.6	5.8
			(15) .9	(47) 1.0	(24) 1.2	(19) 1.3		(54) 3.8	(67) 2.1
			-4.6	-.7	-.4	.3		.9	.2
Net Profit + Depr., Dep., Amort./Cur. Mat. L/T/D									
Fixed/Worth		.3	.1	.5	.7	.9		.2	.5
		.7	.5	1.0	1.3	1.4		.9	1.0
		2.2	1.4	1.9	2.2	1.9		2.1	2.2
Debt/Worth		.4	.2	.3	.4	.6		.3	.5
		.7	.7	.9	1.0	1.2		1.1	1.4
		5.9	2.1	1.9	1.8	2.7		2.4	3.4
% Profit Before Taxes/Tangible Net Worth		13.2	4.4	9.1	8.9	5.8		29.0	16.2
		(11) 1.8	(27) .0	1.5	(27) .9	(25) 2.6		10.3	(100) 6.7
		-34.1	-8.8	-6.4	-4.1	-4.6		.6	-.1
% Profit Before Taxes/Total Assets		7.5	3.2	4.6	4.5	2.5		12.9	6.8
		-6.9	.0	.5	.9	.8		4.0	2.8
		-30.2	-2.9	-2.5	-3.0	-2.2		.4	-.5
Sales/Net Fixed Assets		25.8	24.4	4.1	2.0	1.6		20.7	10.4
		7.7	4.2	1.5	1.2	.9		3.8	2.2
		2.2	.8	1.0	.8	.6		1.4	1.2
Sales/Total Assets		4.0	2.3	1.5	1.0	.9		2.6	2.1
		1.7	.9	1.0	.7	.6		1.4	1.0
		.7	.4	.5	.5	.4		.8	.7
% Depr., Dep., Amort./Sales		1.2	1.2	2.1	2.2	2.3		.7	1.0
		(11) 2.5	(22) 3.4	(45) 3.2	(25) 4.1	(19) 3.8		(47) 1.9	(78) 2.6
		2.9	9.8	4.5	6.1	5.1		3.1	3.8
% Officers', Directors' Owners' Comp/Sales								2.4	1.6
								(17) 10.0	(18) 6.0
								19.3	14.3
Net Sales ($)	9013M	46686M	191958M	1558488M	1501703M	2790207M		2832107M	3952834M
Total Assets ($)	1261M	16497M	147390M	1348540M	2114325M	3901487M		2553986M	4174005M

M = $ thousand   MM = $ million
See Pages 9 through 22 for Explanation of Ratios and Data

Comparative Historical Data | Current Data Sorted by Sales

102	125	124	Type of Statement						
	3	2		0-1MM	1-3MM	3-5MM	5-10MM	10-25MM	25MM & OVER
102	125	124	Unqualified	3	15	5	10	25	66
	3	2	Reviewed	1	1				
2	1	2	Compiled	1					1
3	1	1	Tax Returns						
18	26	28	Other	2	3	2	6	9	6
4/1/07-3/31/08	4/1/08-3/31/09	4/1/09-3/31/10			142 (4/1-9/30/09)			14 (10/1/09-3/31/10)	
ALL	ALL	ALL							
125	156	156	NUMBER OF STATEMENTS	7	19	7	16	34	73
%	%	%	ASSETS	%	%	%	%	%	%
30.8	25.5	24.1	Cash & Equivalents		25.7		41.1	24.8	22.8
8.0	9.9	8.2	Trade Receivables (net)		8.8		7.6	10.1	7.3
.9	.5	.8	Inventory		.9		.3	.8	1.0
4.6	4.4	3.1	All Other Current		1.1		4.9	2.5	3.8
44.3	40.4	36.2	Total Current		36.5		53.9	38.2	34.9
45.9	47.3	51.0	Fixed Assets (net)		44.8		34.8	47.4	56.5
1.1	1.1	.7	Intangibles (net)		.1		.0	.4	1.3
8.7	11.2	12.2	All Other Non-Current		18.6		11.2	14.0	7.3
100.0	100.0	100.0	Total		100.0		100.0	100.0	100.0
			LIABILITIES						
1.4	2.1	1.7	Notes Payable-Short Term		3.7		2.8	1.8	.6
3.3	2.8	2.7	Cur. Mat.-L.T.D.		1.2		1.6	2.9	3.1
6.9	5.2	5.2	Trade Payables		8.3		6.9	5.2	3.4
.2	.0	.0	Income Taxes Payable		.0		.0	.0	.0
9.3	10.6	9.7	All Other Current		7.8		14.4	10.3	10.0
21.0	20.8	19.2	Total Current		21.1		25.6	20.2	17.2
28.8	26.0	25.4	Long-Term Debt		14.1		18.3	20.6	31.4
.1	.1	.1	Deferred Taxes		.0		.3	.0	.1
7.4	3.5	5.1	All Other Non-Current		1.0		4.9	10.3	4.7
42.6	49.5	50.2	Net Worth		63.8		50.8	48.9	46.7
100.0	100.0	100.0	Total Liabilities & Net Worth		100.0		100.0	100.0	100.0
			INCOME DATA						
100.0	100.0	100.0	Net Sales		100.0		100.0	100.0	100.0
			Gross Profit						
93.3	93.9	96.7	Operating Expenses		101.8		92.8	100.4	95.0
6.7	6.1	3.3	Operating Profit		-1.8		7.2	-.4	5.0
1.3	2.7	2.5	All Other Expenses (net)		-1.2		4.9	1.0	2.8
5.3	3.4	.8	Profit Before Taxes		-.6		2.2	-1.4	2.3
			RATIOS						
4.7	4.6	4.0	Current		5.3		4.7	7.6	3.5
2.5	2.2	2.0			2.3		2.4	2.4	1.9
1.5	1.2	1.3			1.1		1.3	1.3	1.3
4.1	4.4	3.9	Quick		5.1		4.1	6.4	3.1
2.2	1.7	1.8			2.3		2.4	2.1	1.7
1.2	1.0	1.1			1.1		1.2	1.1	1.2
0 UND	2 216.3	2 195.3	Sales/Receivables		1 675.8		2 194.3	1 493.9	4 99.5
7 50.7	14 26.4	14 25.9			9 38.9		17 21.5	18 20.7	13 27.8
33 11.1	42 8.7	33 11.2			32 11.2		28 13.2	42 8.6	31 11.7
			Cost of Sales/Inventory						
			Cost of Sales/Payables						
3.3	2.9	3.4	Sales/Working Capital		4.4		3.2	2.4	3.3
6.6	7.6	7.3			7.0		6.1	8.8	7.0
24.1	40.5	26.6			66.1		10.2	23.4	22.7
8.4	6.4	4.3	EBIT/Interest		16.0		24.3	7.6	4.3
(75) 4.0	(109) 2.1	(112) 1.2			(11) 3.8		(10) -1.8	(24) .3	(60) 1.3
1.5	.8	-.7			-4.6		-75.5	-1.3	.2
			Net Profit + Depr., Dep., Amort./Cur. Mat. L/T/D						
.4	.4	.5	Fixed/Worth		.3		.2	.3	.8
1.0	1.0	1.0			.5		.7	.9	1.4
2.0	1.9	1.9			1.1		1.6	1.9	2.2
.4	.4	.3	Debt/Worth		.2		.5	.2	.6
1.2	1.0	.8			.3		.7	.5	1.2
3.0	2.1	2.2			.8		2.3	2.3	2.5
21.0	14.7	7.6	% Profit Before Taxes/Tangible Net Worth		5.8		6.2	4.3	9.6
(114) 9.0	(148) 4.3	(149) 1.7			(18) .5		(15) 1.2	(32) .9	(70) 2.7
3.3	-.3	-5.8			-13.4		-13.9	-8.3	-4.9
8.5	6.5	4.6	% Profit Before Taxes/Total Assets		5.8		4.2	4.1	4.9
4.0	2.0	.8			1.1		.3	.4	.9
1.0	-.5	-2.8			-7.9		-7.3	-2.5	-2.2
12.2	8.3	5.6	Sales/Net Fixed Assets		8.0		14.9	12.5	3.2
2.2	2.0	1.5			2.1		3.9	2.3	1.4
1.1	1.0	.8			.6		1.2	1.0	.8
2.3	1.7	1.5	Sales/Total Assets		1.4		2.7	1.7	1.4
1.1	1.0	.8			.8		1.0	1.0	.8
.7	.6	.5			.4		.6	.5	.6
.9	1.6	2.0	% Depr., Dep., Amort./Sales		2.3		1.4	1.2	2.1
(86) 2.3	(120) 3.0	(123) 3.3			(16) 2.8		(12) 2.8	(29) 3.2	(58) 3.3
4.0	4.8	5.1			12.6		4.2	5.5	4.6
1.6	2.3	2.3	% Officers', Directors' Owners' Comp/Sales						2.3
(16) 5.9	(18) 7.7	(23) 7.3							(16) 6.9
15.1	19.2	14.3							11.3
6674942M	5605142M	6098055M	Net Sales ($)	3772M	40420M	26876M	115552M	559395M	5352040M
4918226M	5939363M	7529500M	Total Assets ($)	13264M	81250M	73963M	267372M	890973M	6202678M

M = $ thousand   MM = $ million
See Pages 9 through 22 for Explanation of Ratios and Data

Current Data Sorted by Assets							Comparative Historical Data	
2	4	11	7	2	2	**Type of Statement**		
	1					Unqualified	18	22
		1				Reviewed	2	3
		2				Compiled		
		1	2			Tax Returns		
3		1				Other		
	25 (4/1-9/30/09)		13 (10/1/09-3/31/10)				5 4/1/05-3/31/06	6 4/1/06-3/31/07
0-500M	500M-2MM	2-10MM	10-50MM	50-100MM	100-250MM		ALL	ALL
2	8	15	9	2	2	NUMBER OF STATEMENTS	25	31
%	%	%	%	%	%	**ASSETS**	%	%
		30.3				Cash & Equivalents	27.8	33.2
		22.8				Trade Receivables (net)	24.2	19.3
		.2				Inventory	1.4	.8
		8.9				All Other Current	12.1	2.3
		62.3				Total Current	65.5	55.6
		21.6				Fixed Assets (net)	28.4	23.5
		4.4				Intangibles (net)	.1	5.0
		11.7				All Other Non-Current	6.1	15.9
		100.0				Total	100.0	100.0
						LIABILITIES		
		10.3				Notes Payable-Short Term	1.2	2.8
		3.3				Cur. Mat.-L.T.D.	2.6	2.6
		8.1				Trade Payables	12.9	5.8
		.0				Income Taxes Payable	.2	.1
		12.5				All Other Current	21.5	15.3
		34.2				Total Current	38.4	26.7
		5.1				Long-Term Debt	9.4	16.8
		.0				Deferred Taxes	.2	.1
		9.2				All Other Non-Current	2.8	2.6
		51.5				Net Worth	49.1	53.9
		100.0				Total Liabilities & Net Worth	100.0	100.0
						INCOME DATA		
		100.0				Net Sales	100.0	100.0
						Gross Profit		
		97.0				Operating Expenses	94.6	91.5
		3.0				Operating Profit	5.4	8.5
		.9				All Other Expenses (net)	.2	-.2
		2.2				Profit Before Taxes	5.2	8.7
						RATIOS		
		5.0				Current	3.4	4.8
		1.6					1.8	2.1
		1.0					1.0	1.3
		4.0				Quick	3.1	4.5
		1.6					1.6	1.8
		.7					.7	1.2
	3	128.3				Sales/Receivables	2 173.0	8 45.7
	26	13.9					32 11.6	31 11.8
	46	7.9					50 7.3	53 6.9
						Cost of Sales/Inventory		
						Cost of Sales/Payables		
		3.8				Sales/Working Capital	3.9	3.0
		9.7					8.0	6.3
		-948.3					-366.3	12.9
						EBIT/Interest	25.3	9.2
							(12) 11.0	(22) 5.7
							.5	2.0
						Net Profit + Depr., Dep., Amort./Cur. Mat. L/T/D		
		.1				Fixed/Worth	.2	.2
		.3					.8	.5
		1.6					1.5	.8
		.3				Debt/Worth	.4	.4
		.9					.8	.9
		2.6					4.2	2.7
		21.9				% Profit Before Taxes/Tangible Net Worth	25.2	29.9
	(14)	2.6					(30) 15.0	13.3
		-7.1					-1.2	-.4
		13.2				% Profit Before Taxes/Total Assets	10.3	14.6
		.6					3.7	5.7
		-4.2					.0	-.1
		73.0				Sales/Net Fixed Assets	101.2	25.5
		25.2					7.7	8.3
		5.9					4.1	4.7
		3.1				Sales/Total Assets	3.5	2.9
		2.6					2.7	2.0
		1.2					1.5	.9
		.9				% Depr., Dep., Amort./Sales	.7	.6
	(12)	1.2					(17) 1.4	(28) 1.3
		2.4					2.4	2.7
						% Officers', Directors' Owners' Comp/Sales		
3223M	15000M	193393M	527902M	78286M	172406M	Net Sales ($)	1386215M	1904190M
563M	10998M	75508M	184778M	129029M	388099M	Total Assets ($)	541961M	1149461M

© RMA 2010

Comparative Historical Data | | | | Current Data Sorted by Sales

			Type of Statement						
20	18	28	Unqualified	1	6	1	4	9	8
1	1	1	Reviewed		1				
	1	1	Compiled		1				
	1	2	Tax Returns	1	1				
8	3	6	Other	2	2		1	1	2
4/1/07-3/31/08 ALL	4/1/08-3/31/09 ALL	4/1/09-3/31/10 ALL		\<-- 25 (4/1-9/30/09) --\>			\<-- 13 (10/1/09-3/31/10) --\>		
				0-1MM	1-3MM	3-5MM	5-10MM	10-25MM	25MM & OVER
29	23	38	**NUMBER OF STATEMENTS**	3	9	1	5	10	10
%	%	%	**ASSETS**	%	%	%	%	%	%
35.5	33.7	29.3	Cash & Equivalents					33.2	34.6
16.7	20.3	20.4	Trade Receivables (net)					20.3	15.9
1.5	1.1	1.9	Inventory					.5	.1
2.6	5.4	4.4	All Other Current					12.6	1.2
56.3	60.5	56.0	Total Current					66.6	51.8
29.4	25.8	30.8	Fixed Assets (net)					25.2	31.8
2.1	2.2	2.1	Intangibles (net)					.1	1.2
12.3	11.5	11.1	All Other Non-Current					8.1	15.2
100.0	100.0	100.0	Total					100.0	100.0
			LIABILITIES						
4.0	3.2	4.6	Notes Payable-Short Term					10.8	.0
1.0	1.1	2.2	Cur. Mat.-L.T.D.					.5	2.3
6.1	11.2	6.8	Trade Payables					12.9	6.4
.2	.0	.0	Income Taxes Payable					.0	.0
15.4	18.1	13.2	All Other Current					11.6	15.0
26.7	33.6	26.8	Total Current					35.7	23.6
15.3	8.7	8.5	Long-Term Debt					5.3	16.0
.0	.0	.0	Deferred Taxes					.0	.0
4.1	6.2	7.6	All Other Non-Current					5.5	6.1
53.9	51.5	57.1	Net Worth					53.5	54.3
100.0	100.0	100.0	Total Liabilities & Net Worth					100.0	100.0
			INCOME DATA						
100.0	100.0	100.0	Net Sales					100.0	100.0
			Gross Profit						
89.0	96.0	94.8	Operating Expenses					101.4	92.3
11.0	4.0	5.2	Operating Profit					-1.4	7.7
1.9	.4	.9	All Other Expenses (net)					-1.1	.5
9.1	3.6	4.3	Profit Before Taxes					-.3	7.2
			RATIOS						
4.9 / 2.5 / 1.2	3.1 / 1.9 / 1.3	5.1 / 2.1 / 1.2	Current					5.3 / 1.6 / .9	3.5 / 2.1 / 1.8
4.4 / 2.4 / 1.2	2.9 / 1.6 / .8	4.2 / 1.9 / 1.1	Quick					4.2 / 1.5 / .6	3.5 / 2.1 / 1.7
6 / 65.9 38 / 9.5 54 / 6.8	3 / 132.6 34 / 10.7 57 / 6.5	2 / 161.6 23 / 15.9 51 / 7.2	Sales/Receivables					2 / 161.6 27 / 13.6 54 / 6.7	7 / 51.2 25 / 14.4 42 / 8.7
			Cost of Sales/Inventory						
			Cost of Sales/Payables						
2.4 / 5.7 / 16.3	4.1 / 11.8 / 25.0	3.2 / 6.7 / 23.5	Sales/Working Capital					4.6 / 8.3 / -719.9	3.0 / 8.8 / 13.0
(17) 14.7 / 4.8 / 2.5	(12) 36.1 / 9.6 / -4.2	(16) 18.6 / 6.1 / -1.6	EBIT/Interest						
			Net Profit + Depr., Dep., Amort./Cur. Mat. L/T/D						
.0 / .5 / 1.4	.1 / .3 / .8	.1 / .5 / 1.1	Fixed/Worth					.0 / .2 / .8	.3 / .6 / 1.6
.3 / .9 / 2.2	.6 / .9 / 2.1	.2 / .6 / 2.2	Debt/Worth					.5 / 1.9	.4 / .6 / 2.2
(22) 22.6 / 9.6 / 3.5	47.8 / 6.8 / -2.5	(37) 19.8 / 7.0 / -3.6	% Profit Before Taxes/Tangible Net Worth					18.2 / 5.2 / -7.1	22.7 / 14.4 / 2.5
9.2 / 3.4 / 1.5	16.2 / 3.6 / -1.9	11.2 / 3.4 / -1.5	% Profit Before Taxes/Total Assets					10.7 / 1.4 / -3.1	11.5 / 8.4 / .5
63.3 / 6.3 / 3.9	70.3 / 10.4 / 5.5	35.2 / 9.6 / 2.6	Sales/Net Fixed Assets					279.2 / 26.8 / 3.4	15.2 / 6.7 / 3.9
3.1 / 1.8 / .5	4.4 / 3.0 / 1.1	3.2 / 1.6 / .9	Sales/Total Assets					3.9 / 2.7 / 1.8	3.4 / 2.5 / .9
(21) .5 / 1.7 / 3.6	(16) .4 / 1.0 / 1.4	(30) .9 / 1.9 / 3.3	% Depr., Dep., Amort./Sales						
			% Officers', Directors' Owners' Comp/Sales						
1904918M	870688M	990210M	Net Sales ($)	1479M	16470M	3153M	37828M	189150M	742130M
1130792M	678620M	788975M	Total Assets ($)	3863M	14341M	52208M	19521M	79464M	619578M

© RMA 2010

M = $ thousand   MM = $ million
See Pages 9 through 22 for Explanation of Ratios and Data

Current Data Sorted by Assets   **Comparative Historical Data**

Type of Statement

0-500M	500M-2MM	2-10MM	10-50MM	50-100MM	100-250MM	Type of Statement	4/1/05-3/31/06 ALL	4/1/06-3/31/07 ALL
1	4	11	22	14	9	Unqualified	43	39
	2	3	2			Reviewed	8	8
2	2		1	1		Compiled	4	5
	1					Tax Returns	4	3
1	51 (4/1-9/30/09)	5	8 (10/1/09-3/31/10)	2	3	Other	35	21
3	9	19	33	17	12	NUMBER OF STATEMENTS	94	76

Financial Data

0-500M	500M-2MM	2-10MM	10-50MM	50-100MM	100-250MM		4/1/05-3/31/06 ALL	4/1/06-3/31/07 ALL
%	%	%	%	%	%	**ASSETS**	%	%
		16.0	11.8	8.3	9.7	Cash & Equivalents	12.0	14.2
		3.6	7.4	4.5	5.9	Trade Receivables (net)	14.4	15.3
		1.0	.4	.2	1.0	Inventory	1.2	2.9
		1.3	1.2	5.0	2.7	All Other Current	2.1	2.5
		21.9	20.8	18.0	19.3	Total Current	29.6	34.8
		74.6	68.8	72.5	50.7	Fixed Assets (net)	59.9	55.1
		.2	2.6	4.2	5.2	Intangibles (net)	2.8	2.0
		3.3	7.7	5.2	24.8	All Other Non-Current	7.8	8.1
		100.0	100.0	100.0	100.0	Total	100.0	100.0
						LIABILITIES		
		2.4	4.5	.0	.0	Notes Payable-Short Term	3.9	3.4
		11.6	3.0	2.7	1.3	Cur. Mat.-L.T.D.	5.6	3.0
		4.2	1.9	3.6	2.2	Trade Payables	5.9	7.5
		.0	.1	.0	.0	Income Taxes Payable	.0	.1
		3.1	2.9	7.0	3.9	All Other Current	6.9	6.4
		21.2	12.4	13.4	7.5	Total Current	22.4	20.3
		17.0	35.4	37.1	29.4	Long-Term Debt	28.7	31.1
		.0	.0	.2	.0	Deferred Taxes	.1	.1
		.9	1.5	2.4	3.1	All Other Non-Current	3.3	1.7
		60.9	50.7	46.9	60.0	Net Worth	45.5	46.8
		100.0	100.0	100.0	100.0	Total Liabilties & Net Worth	100.0	100.0
						INCOME DATA		
		100.0	100.0	100.0	100.0	Net Sales	100.0	100.0
						Gross Profit		
		87.3	80.1	93.3	85.3	Operating Expenses	86.7	87.1
		12.7	19.9	6.7	14.7	Operating Profit	13.3	12.9
		3.8	10.8	7.3	4.9	All Other Expenses (net)	4.4	3.3
		8.9	9.1	-.5	9.8	Profit Before Taxes	8.9	9.5
						RATIOS		
		6.7	4.3	4.4	3.9	Current	3.9	4.2
		2.1	1.8	1.4	2.3		2.1	1.9
		.4	.8	.8	1.2		1.0	1.1
		6.5	4.2	2.7	3.6	Quick	3.6	4.2
		2.1	1.5	1.1	1.9		1.7	1.4
		.3	.6	.5	.8		.9	.9
		2 171.7	19 19.6	24 15.4	27 13.5	Sales/Receivables	18 20.6	21 17.5
		32 11.3	34 10.7	39 9.3	32 11.4		38 9.7	33 11.1
		51 7.1	54 6.8	55 6.7	48 7.7		56 6.6	58 6.3
						Cost of Sales/Inventory		
						Cost of Sales/Payables		
		1.1	1.1	1.4	1.8	Sales/Working Capital	1.3	2.3
		3.3	12.0	8.0	6.0		5.0	8.8
		-2.5	-10.2	-10.0	26.4		NM	101.7
		4.5	15.2	4.0	7.0	EBIT/Interest	5.9	8.3
		(15) 1.7	(22) 3.2	(14) 1.5	(10) 3.9		(76) 2.8	(63) 2.9
		.8	1.4	-.2	.1		1.2	1.1
						Net Profit + Depr., Dep., Amort./Cur. Mat. L/T/D		
		.8	.9	1.1	.6	Fixed/Worth	.8	.7
		1.1	1.3	1.6	1.2		1.3	1.2
		1.9	2.9	3.0	1.6		2.2	2.1
		.1	.3	.5	.4	Debt/Worth	.3	.4
		.6	.9	1.2	.7		1.0	1.0
		1.3	2.5	3.9	1.7		3.0	3.5
		8.4	10.3	5.1	4.9	% Profit Before Taxes/Tangible Net Worth	15.0	25.5
		(17) 1.6	(28) 1.5	(16) 1.4	(11) 2.8		(79) 5.4	(69) 5.7
		-.2	-.3	-2.5	-1.3		1.5	.9
		7.1	5.6	3.4	3.5	% Profit Before Taxes/Total Assets	6.0	10.5
		2.1	.5	.7	1.5		2.2	2.7
		.2	-.4	-.8	-.6		.0	.1
		.6	.5	.4	7.1	Sales/Net Fixed Assets	5.8	11.0
		.3	.2	.1	.6		.5	.7
		.2	.1	.1	.2		.2	.2
		.4	.3	.3	.7	Sales/Total Assets	1.9	2.4
		.2	.1	.1	.2		.3	.4
		.2	.1	.1	.1		.2	.1
		11.3	7.1	16.8	3.8	% Depr., Dep., Amort./Sales	3.3	2.8
		(17) 18.7	(31) 18.6	(16) 23.2	(10) 9.3		(78) 13.2	(66) 11.4
		27.0	27.0	35.4	35.5		22.9	21.6
						% Officers', Directors' Owners' Comp/Sales	2.7	3.3
							(19) 5.1	(18) 5.9
							14.7	10.1
322M	15265M	40094M	264996M	364048M	864610M	Net Sales ($)	1258040M	884482M
867M	8009M	98392M	734648M	1267621M	1803200M	Total Assets ($)	2865089M	1749781M

M = $ thousand   MM = $ million
See Pages 9 through 22 for Explanation of Ratios and Data

Comparative Historical Data / Current Data Sorted by Sales

			Type of Statement						
45	45	61	Unqualified	12	14	3	11	10	11
7	5	7	Reviewed	2	1	1	2	1	
5	6	6	Compiled	2	2		1	1	
5		9	Tax Returns						
18	31	19	Other	2	9	1	2	3	2
4/1/07-3/31/08 ALL	4/1/08-3/31/09 ALL	4/1/09-3/31/10 ALL		0-1MM	51 (4/1-9/30/09) 1-3MM	3-5MM	42 (10/1/09-3/31/10) 5-10MM	10-25MM	25MM & OVER
80	96	93	NUMBER OF STATEMENTS	18	26	5	16	15	13
%	%	%	ASSETS	%	%	%	%	%	%
13.7	11.4	12.9	Cash & Equivalents	11.3	16.8		15.7	9.0	11.2
9.3	10.1	6.6	Trade Receivables (net)	6.7	6.6		3.8	4.7	13.4
2.9	1.7	1.5	Inventory	.6	.9		3.8	.6	1.5
2.5	1.8	2.1	All Other Current	.6	1.4		.6	2.5	7.6
28.4	25.0	23.1	Total Current	19.2	25.7		23.9	16.8	33.5
59.2	63.8	66.1	Fixed Assets (net)	79.1	68.0		62.1	70.8	37.1
2.0	1.3	2.7	Intangibles (net)	.4	1.1		1.3	1.4	13.0
10.5	9.9	8.1	All Other Non-Current	1.3	5.2		12.6	11.0	16.5
100.0	100.0	100.0	Total	100.0	100.0		100.0	100.0	100.0
			LIABILITIES						
2.3	3.1	2.6	Notes Payable-Short Term	6.8	.3		4.4	.8	2.5
3.6	4.1	4.6	Cur. Mat.-L.T.D.	6.9	4.0		5.5	3.5	2.5
5.3	5.0	3.0	Trade Payables	.5	2.7		4.4	1.8	7.3
.0	.0	.0	Income Taxes Payable	.0	.0		.0	.0	.2
4.5	3.4	3.7	All Other Current	2.4	1.6		1.6	2.2	15.0
15.8	15.7	13.9	Total Current	16.6	8.6		15.8	8.3	27.5
29.4	31.2	30.1	Long-Term Debt	23.3	35.5		29.1	28.7	26.4
.3	.1	.1	Deferred Taxes	.0	.0		.0	.0	.4
2.5	2.9	1.6	All Other Non-Current	.5	.3		2.3	3.2	3.9
52.1	50.1	54.2	Net Worth	59.6	55.6		52.8	59.8	41.8
100.0	100.0	100.0	Total Liabilities & Net Worth	100.0	100.0		100.0	100.0	100.0
			INCOME DATA						
100.0	100.0	100.0	Net Sales	100.0	100.0		100.0	100.0	100.0
			Gross Profit						
83.7	86.1	85.2	Operating Expenses	80.4	84.3		89.3	81.1	92.9
16.3	13.9	14.8	Operating Profit	19.6	15.7		10.7	18.9	7.1
3.4	5.1	7.3	All Other Expenses (net)	9.3	11.5		4.7	6.2	.9
12.8	8.8	7.4	Profit Before Taxes	10.3	4.2		6.0	12.8	6.2
			RATIOS						
4.0	4.9	4.9		9.5	7.6		3.9	4.7	2.3
2.0	1.8	1.9	Current	3.5	2.9		2.1	3.4	1.2
1.1	.9	.9		.9	.9		1.5	1.1	.8
3.3	4.8	4.6		7.1	7.2		3.8	3.8	1.9
1.6	1.6	1.7	Quick	3.5	2.5		2.0	1.6	.8
.8	.8	.6		.9	.8		1.3	.9	.5
23 16.0	20 18.0	13 27.7	Sales/Receivables	0 UND	8 47.3	4 96.5	26 13.9	28 13.1	
36 10.2	38 9.5	33 11.1		32 11.6	25 14.3	31 11.7	36 10.2	40 9.2	
55 6.6	61 6.0	48 7.6		42 8.6	65 5.6	45 8.0	49 7.4	67 5.5	
			Cost of Sales/Inventory						
			Cost of Sales/Payables						
1.6	1.9	1.4	Sales/Working Capital	1.0	1.0		1.1	1.8	6.9
6.5	6.7	6.0		4.2	5.9		2.6	4.2	18.2
60.6	-36.6	-14.3		-6.8	-18.0		7.3	30.5	-13.6
6.2	9.3	6.6		4.8	6.9		4.4	9.5	26.0
(64) 3.6	(73) 3.1	(69) 2.6	EBIT/Interest	(12) 1.5	(16) 2.8	(11) .7	(12) 2.3	4.7	
2.2	1.3	.8		.3	1.0		-2.0	1.0	3.3
			Net Profit + Depr., Dep., Amort./Cur. Mat. L/T/D						
.8	.9	.9	Fixed/Worth	.9	.8		.9	.9	.9
1.3	1.2	1.2		1.2	1.2		1.2	1.1	1.3
2.0	2.2	2.2		2.6	2.1		9.0	1.8	NM
.4	.4	.3	Debt/Worth	.1	.2		.2	.4	.7
.8	1.0	.8		.4	.9		.5	.6	2.0
1.8	2.1	1.9		1.9	1.6		9.2	1.5	NM
11.8	8.1	7.8	% Profit Before Taxes/Tangible Net Worth	4.2	14.2		7.8	5.1	34.2
(74) 5.2	(87) 3.4	(83) 2.3		(15) 1.4	(24) 2.2	(14) 2.7	1.0	(10) 7.5	
1.9	.4	-.5		-.5	-.4		-2.9	-1.3	3.5
6.5	5.3	5.6	% Profit Before Taxes/Total Assets	3.4	6.3		5.5	3.6	6.5
3.3	2.0	1.3		.7	.6		1.1	.5	5.4
.9	.1	-.3		-.2	-.4		-1.8	-.5	1.9
4.0	2.6	1.1	Sales/Net Fixed Assets	.5	.6		1.9	.5	10.7
.5	.3	.3		.2	.2		.2	.2	2.2
.2	.1	.1		.1	.1		.1	.2	.7
1.6	1.0	.6	Sales/Total Assets	.3	.4		.3	.5	1.4
.2	.2	.2		.2	.2		.1	.2	1.0
.1	.1	.1		.1	.1		.1	.1	.4
4.5	3.6	7.1	% Depr., Dep., Amort./Sales	12.0	10.3		6.3	12.8	.8
(77) 11.5	(87) 14.9	(83) 18.2		(15) 18.9	(23) 18.7	(14) 20.8	19.5	(11) 2.9	
19.9	23.1	27.4		30.4	28.8		33.2	35.4	5.7
3.1	3.2		% Officers', Directors' Owners' Comp/Sales						
(17) 4.3	(20) 6.1								
8.5	7.8								
1233432M	1525014M	1549335M	Net Sales ($)	9181M	50223M	21389M	103381M	241059M	1124102M
3446738M	4556536M	3912737M	Total Assets ($)	88106M	289530M	181112M	735925M	1258833M	1359231M

© RMA 2010

M = $ thousand   MM = $ million
See Pages 9 through 22 for Explanation of Ratios and Data

Current Data Sorted by Assets | Comparative Historical Data

Type of Statement	0-500M	500M-2MM	2-10MM	10-50MM	50-100MM	100-250MM	4/1/05-3/31/06 ALL	4/1/06-3/31/07 ALL
Unqualified	3	5	23	35	10	8	69	83
Reviewed			1				1	3
Compiled			1				2	1
Tax Returns			1				3	3
Other	1		6	9	1	4	42	29
		67 (4/1-9/30/09)		42 (10/1/09-3/31/10)				
NUMBER OF STATEMENTS	4	6	32	44	11	12	117	119
ASSETS	%	%	%	%	%	%	%	%
Cash & Equivalents			13.9	19.0	9.2	9.5	15.4	17.5
Trade Receivables (net)			4.2	6.9	2.0	10.9	10.3	5.7
Inventory			4.2	3.1	.3	.7	2.7	2.9
All Other Current			4.1	1.9	5.2	1.3	2.7	4.8
Total Current			26.4	30.8	16.7	22.3	31.0	30.9
Fixed Assets (net)			52.6	49.7	64.0	57.4	47.8	51.5
Intangibles (net)			2.3	1.0	.4	.2	.5	.8
All Other Non-Current			18.6	18.5	19.0	20.1	20.7	16.8
Total			100.0	100.0	100.0	100.0	100.0	100.0
LIABILITIES								
Notes Payable-Short Term			2.3	3.7	.2	.5	5.9	3.8
Cur. Mat.-L.T.D.			2.9	2.5	3.9	3.6	2.1	2.2
Trade Payables			3.7	2.1	2.0	.8	2.9	3.4
Income Taxes Payable			.0	.0	.0	.0	.0	.1
All Other Current			3.7	6.2	2.2	2.3	7.1	4.9
Total Current			12.6	14.4	8.2	7.3	18.0	14.3
Long-Term Debt			31.4	24.4	35.3	51.0	33.7	33.5
Deferred Taxes			1.0	.0	.0	.0	.0	.0
All Other Non-Current			2.7	4.3	1.5	2.6	4.7	3.7
Net Worth			52.3	56.8	54.9	39.1	43.7	48.5
Total Liabilties & Net Worth			100.0	100.0	100.0	100.0	100.0	100.0
INCOME DATA								
Net Sales			100.0	100.0	100.0	100.0	100.0	100.0
Gross Profit								
Operating Expenses			94.1	94.7	101.5	84.6	87.5	90.7
Operating Profit			5.9	5.3	-1.5	15.4	12.5	9.3
All Other Expenses (net)			6.0	1.1	.9	17.7	6.5	3.4
Profit Before Taxes			-.2	4.2	-2.5	-2.3	6.0	5.9
RATIOS								
Current			4.3	6.0	2.5	6.4	4.2	5.7
			2.9	2.9	1.8	2.1	2.1	2.2
			1.0	1.1	1.4	1.0	1.1	1.2
Quick			3.8	5.3	2.3	5.8	3.9	4.3
			1.5	2.6	1.6	1.5	1.6	1.6
			.7	1.1	.8	.7	.8	.8
Sales/Receivables			0 766.7	3 140.6	8 44.6	3 114.3	1 541.6	1 527.1
			5 68.5	9 38.9	17 20.9	6 61.3	8 46.3	7 53.7
			29 12.8	37 9.8	30 12.0	56 6.5	53 6.9	35 10.4
Cost of Sales/Inventory								
Cost of Sales/Payables								
Sales/Working Capital			1.5	2.0	4.1	.8	2.1	2.3
			4.5	4.7	6.4	2.8	6.1	4.8
			205.8	30.7	12.0	NM	62.0	22.3
EBIT/Interest			19.5	6.5	3.8		8.1	8.9
			(18) 1.4	(31) 1.5	(10) 1.3		(74) 3.0	(84) 2.6
			.0	-1.1	-4.4		1.0	.7
Net Profit + Depr., Dep., Amort./Cur. Mat. L/T/D								
Fixed/Worth			.3	.4	1.0	.2	.2	.4
			.9	.8	1.3	1.0	1.0	1.0
			3.0	1.6	1.4	2.8	1.9	2.2
Debt/Worth			.3	.2	.5	.3	.4	.3
			.7	.7	.8	2.0	1.2	.9
			2.1	2.0	1.1	30.7	4.2	3.4
% Profit Before Taxes/Tangible Net Worth			8.2	11.8	4.2	6.8	15.7	13.2
			(29) .3	1.6	-3.3	(11) .2	(112) 5.4	(110) 5.0
			-8.2	-2.5	-7.1	-3.1	-.5	-1.0
% Profit Before Taxes/Total Assets			4.4	2.8	2.8	3.0	5.8	6.7
			-.5	1.0	-1.2	-.1	1.7	2.1
			-2.0	-1.7	-3.6	-1.4	-.5	-.8
Sales/Net Fixed Assets			4.3	3.9	.7	11.0	8.3	4.1
			1.2	1.0	.5	.4	1.3	.7
			.3	.5	.4	.2	.4	.5
Sales/Total Assets			.8	.9	.4	.3	.9	.9
			.4	.5	.3	.2	.4	.5
			.2	.2	.2	.1	.2	.2
% Depr., Dep., Amort./Sales			1.6	2.4	4.9	5.6	1.6	2.3
			(27) 3.8	(36) 6.5	(10) 6.5	(10) 12.9	(92) 4.7	(102) 6.0
			13.7	11.9	12.9	16.7	11.1	12.1
% Officers', Directors' Owners' Comp/Sales							4.0	4.4
							(11) 12.7	(11) 17.4
							20.9	24.9
Net Sales ($)	796M	8104M	152927M	648461M	266749M	363907M	1645408M	1101804M
Total Assets ($)	1189M	5511M	175473M	961418M	774618M	1900455M	3096345M	2234103M

RMA 2010

M = $ thousand   MM = $ million
See Pages 9 through 22 for Explanation of Ratios and Data

Comparative Historical Data / Current Data Sorted by Sales

			Type of Statement						
90	72	84	Unqualified	10	15	8	16	22	13
3	1	1	Reviewed		1				
	7	2	Compiled						
2	1	1	Tax Returns	2					
35	26	21	Other	1					
4/1/07-	4/1/08-	4/1/09-		3	3	1	3	6	5
3/31/08	3/31/09	3/31/10			67 (4/1-9/30/09)		42 (10/1/09-3/31/10)		
ALL	ALL	ALL		0-1MM	1-3MM	3-5MM	5-10MM	10-25MM	25MM & OVER
130	107	109	**NUMBER OF STATEMENTS**	16	19	9	19	28	18
%	%	%	**ASSETS**	%	%	%	%	%	%
16.1	15.1	15.7	Cash & Equivalents	14.5	7.9		16.4	17.8	19.0
7.7	5.9	6.1	Trade Receivables (net)	5.7	1.9		4.6	10.8	6.7
5.5	4.7	2.7	Inventory	.0	7.7		2.1	.3	.5
4.2	3.7	3.4	All Other Current	2.3	1.0		1.3	3.9	2.9
33.6	29.4	27.9	Total Current	22.6	18.5		24.3	32.8	29.1
44.3	46.9	52.7	Fixed Assets (net)	53.1	59.0		50.4	53.7	54.4
.3	1.0	1.2	Intangibles (net)	.0	.7		4.8	.2	1.3
21.8	22.7	18.2	All Other Non-Current	24.3	21.9		20.5	13.3	15.2
100.0	100.0	100.0	Total	100.0	100.0		100.0	100.0	100.0
			LIABILITIES						
4.1	3.4	2.4	Notes Payable-Short Term	9.0	2.1		2.5	.6	.6
2.6	2.4	2.8	Cur. Mat.-L.T.D.	1.3	3.5		1.5	3.0	3.6
3.0	3.5	3.3	Trade Payables	5.6	1.4		2.3	3.9	2.8
.4	.0	.0	Income Taxes Payable	.0	.0		.0	.0	.0
5.0	4.7	5.4	All Other Current	5.8	3.7		8.2	3.1	6.1
15.1	13.9	13.9	Total Current	21.7	10.7		14.4	10.8	13.2
33.7	33.0	34.6	Long-Term Debt	61.0	44.1		27.0	27.4	27.8
.0	.0	.3	Deferred Taxes	.0	.0		.0	.0	.0
3.4	3.7	3.2	All Other Non-Current	1.4	.9		6.4	2.6	6.0
47.8	49.4	48.0	Net Worth	15.9	44.3		52.1	59.3	53.0
100.0	100.0	100.0	Total Liabilities & Net Worth	100.0	100.0		100.0	100.0	100.0
			INCOME DATA						
100.0	100.0	100.0	Net Sales	100.0	100.0		100.0	100.0	100.0
			Gross Profit						
90.6	92.4	94.1	Operating Expenses	85.5	92.8		97.2	97.0	92.1
9.4	7.6	5.9	Operating Profit	14.5	7.2		2.8	3.0	7.9
4.4	4.2	4.8	All Other Expenses (net)	12.6	7.6		1.8	3.4	3.7
5.0	3.4	1.1	Profit Before Taxes	1.9	-.4		1.0	-.4	4.3
			RATIOS						
6.2	5.6	5.2		5.0	4.1		3.9	5.6	7.3
2.4	2.3	2.3	Current	1.8	1.6		2.0	2.8	2.3
1.3	1.0	1.1		.5	.9		.9	1.4	1.1
4.9	4.0	4.2		4.1	2.4		3.7	5.1	6.1
1.6	1.3	1.5	Quick	1.6	1.0		1.4	2.3	1.9
.6	.7	.7		.4	.4		.9	1.2	.8
1 336.0	1 510.0	2 157.9		0 UND	0 833.0	3 111.3	5 80.7	4 95.1	
8 44.4	9 42.0	8 44.6	Sales/Receivables	2 190.1	16 23.4	9 40.5	19 19.5	7 52.1	
36 10.1	31 11.6	32 11.5		64 5.7	32 11.3	34 10.6	36 10.2	20 18.4	
			Cost of Sales/Inventory						
			Cost of Sales/Payables						
1.5	2.2	1.6		1.5	1.6		2.5	2.1	3.6
3.6	5.9	4.8	Sales/Working Capital	3.2	5.5		4.4	6.1	6.4
24.7	-944.5	43.2		-7.3	-22.6		-50.1	14.9	71.3
10.5	12.4	6.7		22.3	15.0		11.0	2.9	8.1
(95) 2.3	(74) 2.4	(74) 1.3	EBIT/Interest	(10) 3.2	(11) 3.6	(12) 1.2	(19) 1.2	(16) 1.2	
.3	-.2	-.5		.5	-.2		-2.0	-4.4	-1.1
			Net Profit + Depr., Dep., Amort./Cur. Mat. L/T/D						
.2	.2	.5		.5	.7		.6	.5	.4
.8	.8	1.0	Fixed/Worth	2.4	1.8		.9	1.0	1.0
1.8	1.8	2.0		-9.3	3.4		2.1	1.4	2.1
.3	.2	.4		.7	.4		.2	.2	.2
1.0	.8	.8	Debt/Worth	9.1	1.6		.8	.7	.7
3.7	3.3	2.4		-12.2	2.9		2.3	1.1	2.4
10.6	12.2	9.2		11.9	13.0		13.1	5.5	8.9
(123) 3.7	(99) 4.5	(101) 1.5	% Profit Before Taxes/Tangible Net Worth	(11) 5.9	(18) .2		.8	.4	(16) 1.8
-1.7	-1.6	-3.9		-3.5	-13.7		-5.8	-3.3	-5.5
5.5	4.6	3.0		2.9	3.7		5.3	2.5	4.5
1.0	1.9	.3	% Profit Before Taxes/Total Assets	-.3	-.8		.6	.4	-.3
-1.1	-1.0	-2.0		-2.7	-4.6		-1.7	-1.5	-4.4
6.8	5.2	3.0		2.0	2.0		3.7	3.7	11.0
1.4	1.1	.9	Sales/Net Fixed Assets	1.0	.4		.9	1.3	.7
.6	.4	.4		.2	.2		.4	.6	.4
.7	.7	.8		.7	.4		.7	1.1	1.3
.4	.5	.4	Sales/Total Assets	.3	.3		.4	.5	.4
.2	.2	.2		.1	.2		.2	.3	.3
1.3	1.9	2.4		1.4	6.9		3.6	2.6	.5
(108) 4.4	(94) 5.4	(92) 6.6	% Depr., Dep., Amort./Sales	(12) 10.1	(15) 12.2	(16) 8.2	(25) 5.5	(16) 4.3	
10.5	12.7	13.0		14.1	23.3		17.9	8.8	11.7
	4.8	2.7							
	(11) 16.7	(12) 7.3	% Officers', Directors' Owners' Comp/Sales						
	23.0	18.8							
1651244M	2500828M	1440944M	Net Sales ($)	7691M	35763M	37817M	137064M	493810M	728799M
3837946M	3455466M	3818664M	Total Assets ($)	41569M	159560M	99270M	595581M	1181122M	1741562M

Current Data Sorted by Assets							Comparative Historical Data	

Type of Statement

0-500M	500M-2MM	2-10MM	10-50MM	50-100MM	100-250MM		45	74
1	4	11	22	14	5	Unqualified	45	74
2		1				Reviewed		
2	1	1	1			Compiled	4	8
		1				Tax Returns	1	3
	2	10	9	2	2	Other	36	17
	57 (4/1-9/30/09)		34 (10/1/09-3/31/10)				4/1/05-3/31/06 ALL	4/1/06-3/31/07 ALL
0-500M	500M-2MM	2-10MM	10-50MM	50-100MM	100-250MM			
5	7	24	32	16	7	NUMBER OF STATEMENTS	86	102
%	%	%	%	%	%		%	%

ASSETS

0-500M	500M-2MM	2-10MM	10-50MM	50-100MM	100-250MM		ALL	ALL
		19.5	19.5	15.4		Cash & Equivalents	14.6	17.7
		9.5	14.9	13.0		Trade Receivables (net)	8.8	12.7
		6.4	2.0	.0		Inventory	1.4	2.0
		1.1	3.4	3.3		All Other Current	4.8	4.8
		36.5	39.7	31.7		Total Current	29.6	37.2
		42.9	31.2	38.1		Fixed Assets (net)	45.5	37.1
		.1	.3	.4		Intangibles (net)	1.4	.4
		20.5	28.8	29.8		All Other Non-Current	23.5	25.2
		100.0	100.0	100.0		Total	100.0	100.0

LIABILITIES

0-500M	500M-2MM	2-10MM	10-50MM	50-100MM	100-250MM		ALL	ALL
		6.1	3.6	.6		Notes Payable-Short Term	5.4	3.9
		4.1	6.0	4.5		Cur. Mat.-L.T.D.	4.1	3.4
		5.2	2.6	2.4		Trade Payables	3.4	5.0
		.0	.0	.0		Income Taxes Payable	.0	.0
		10.0	4.5	1.8		All Other Current	7.0	7.0
		25.3	16.6	9.3		Total Current	20.0	19.4
		25.2	39.0	42.7		Long-Term Debt	30.5	36.7
		.0	.0	.0		Deferred Taxes	.0	.0
		6.4	2.0	4.2		All Other Non-Current	5.1	5.4
		43.1	42.3	43.8		Net Worth	44.4	38.5
		100.0	100.0	100.0		Total Liabilities & Net Worth	100.0	100.0

INCOME DATA

0-500M	500M-2MM	2-10MM	10-50MM	50-100MM	100-250MM		ALL	ALL
		100.0	100.0	100.0		Net Sales	100.0	100.0
						Gross Profit		
		84.0	74.5	86.6		Operating Expenses	82.8	78.0
		16.0	25.5	13.4		Operating Profit	17.2	22.0
		7.3	12.3	8.0		All Other Expenses (net)	8.5	9.4
		8.7	13.2	5.4		Profit Before Taxes	8.7	12.6

RATIOS

0-500M	500M-2MM	2-10MM	10-50MM	50-100MM	100-250MM		ALL	ALL
		4.8	7.6	6.7			3.7	5.5
		2.9	2.9	3.2	Current	1.8	1.9	
		1.0	1.3	1.8		.8	.9	
		3.9	6.7	5.8		2.9	4.3	
		2.1	2.0	3.2	Quick	1.1	1.3	
		.9	1.2	1.7		.5	.5	
	5	67.9	3 133.9	31 11.8			0 UND	0 UND
	45	8.2	39 9.4	127 2.9	Sales/Receivables	35 10.3	22 16.8	
	106	3.4	95 3.8	577 .6		70 5.2	81 4.5	
						Cost of Sales/Inventory		
						Cost of Sales/Payables		
		1.4	.4	.4			1.1	.8
		3.4	1.0	.6	Sales/Working Capital	4.4	5.4	
		NM	4.3	2.6		-16.7	-32.3	
		9.6	6.6	5.3			5.9	8.0
	(21)	4.7	(25) 1.8	(10) 2.1	EBIT/Interest	(48) 2.2	(62) 3.0	
		.5	.6	.9		.1	1.2	
						Net Profit + Depr., Dep., Amort./Cur. Mat. L/T/D		
		.1	.0	.0			.2	.0
		.8	.6	.7	Fixed/Worth	1.0	.7	
		1.9	1.3	1.4		1.7	1.6	
		.5	.6	.7			.6	.5
		.9	1.4	1.5	Debt/Worth	1.2	1.3	
		2.4	3.8	2.1		2.9	4.4	
		9.4	13.0	5.9			12.0	18.2
	(22)	2.7	(30) 3.0	1.1	% Profit Before Taxes/Tangible Net Worth	(83) 4.7	(92) 6.8	
		-3.3	-.5	-.5		-1.5	.1	
		6.3	5.3	2.7			3.8	6.6
		2.0	.7	.6	% Profit Before Taxes/Total Assets	1.7	2.6	
		-1.7	-.3	-.2		-1.0	.0	
		8.6	58.3	52.6			14.3	80.1
		1.6	2.1	1.1	Sales/Net Fixed Assets	.7	2.2	
		.2	.4	.1		.2	.4	
		1.0	.4	.2			.5	.6
		.3	.2	.1	Sales/Total Assets	.2	.3	
		.2	.1	.1		.1	.1	
		.5	.6	.7			.9	.8
	(17)	3.2	(25) 3.6	(14) 1.8	% Depr., Dep., Amort./Sales	(70) 3.8	(66) 2.8	
		7.0	10.7	12.8		9.6	8.1	
						% Officers', Directors' Owners' Comp/Sales		

0-500M	500M-2MM	2-10MM	10-50MM	50-100MM	100-250MM		ALL	ALL
5412M	11966M	77685M	256697M	215828M	148264M	Net Sales ($)	947081M	831537M
1469M	7489M	141559M	796769M	1222209M	920452M	Total Assets ($)	2191335M	2675693M

© RMA 2010

M = $ thousand   MM = $ million
See Pages 9 through 22 for Explanation of Ratios and Data

Comparative Historical Data				Type of Statement	Current Data Sorted by Sales					
				Unqualified	7	13	6	16	10	5
				Reviewed	3					
				Compiled	1	4				
				Tax Returns				1		
				Other	5	6	2	8	3	1
65	60	57				57 (4/1-9/30/09)			34 (10/1/09-3/31/10)	
1		3								
6	5	5								
2		1								
22	26	25								
4/1/07-3/31/08 ALL	4/1/08-3/31/09 ALL	4/1/09-3/31/10 ALL			0-1MM	1-3MM	3-5MM	5-10MM	10-25MM	25MM & OVER
96	91	91		**NUMBER OF STATEMENTS**	16	23	8	25	13	6
%	%	%		**ASSETS**	%	%	%	%	%	%
16.3	21.2	19.7		Cash & Equivalents	25.4	19.7		15.9	26.3	
16.1	15.1	14.9		Trade Receivables (net)	15.4	17.0		10.6	20.8	
3.0	1.9	2.7		Inventory	2.9	4.2		4.2	.0	
5.1	4.6	3.5		All Other Current	1.9	6.4		3.0	4.0	
40.6	42.8	40.9		Total Current	45.6	47.3		33.8	51.1	
35.9	30.6	33.1		Fixed Assets (net)	43.8	30.0		30.6	21.3	
.5	.7	.3		Intangibles (net)	.1	.2		.3	.6	
23.0	25.9	25.7		All Other Non-Current	10.5	22.4		35.2	27.0	
100.0	100.0	100.0		Total	100.0	100.0		100.0	100.0	
				LIABILITIES						
7.0	6.0	4.9		Notes Payable-Short Term	8.5	9.7		.4	3.5	
3.2	3.9	4.8		Cur. Mat.-L.T.D.	2.9	3.8		5.8	6.8	
3.5	3.1	4.0		Trade Payables	3.8	3.9		4.4	3.7	
.0	.0	.0		Income Taxes Payable	.0	.0		.0	.0	
8.8	6.5	9.6		All Other Current	6.8	16.1		10.9	4.2	
22.5	19.6	23.3		Total Current	21.9	33.5		21.5	18.2	
35.5	36.9	33.9		Long-Term Debt	20.2	25.8		39.4	46.7	
.0	.0	.0		Deferred Taxes	.0	.0		.0	.0	
3.4	4.1	4.1		All Other Non-Current	.8	8.7		4.9	.7	
38.6	39.4	38.8		Net Worth	57.1	32.0		34.1	34.4	
100.0	100.0	100.0		Total Liabilities & Net Worth	100.0	100.0		100.0	100.0	
				INCOME DATA						
100.0	100.0	100.0		Net Sales	100.0	100.0		100.0	100.0	
				Gross Profit						
78.3	75.1	81.2		Operating Expenses	76.0	78.7		81.1	84.3	
21.7	24.9	18.8		Operating Profit	24.0	21.3		18.9	15.7	
11.3	13.7	10.9		All Other Expenses (net)	13.2	13.7		7.3	10.6	
10.4	11.1	7.9		Profit Before Taxes	10.9	7.6		11.6	5.1	
				RATIOS						
5.3	7.4	5.4		Current	7.2	7.7		5.1	4.9	
2.0	3.4	2.5			2.9	3.1		2.5	2.9	
1.2	1.3	1.4			1.2	1.4		1.4	1.8	
4.2	5.0	4.6		Quick	7.2	5.3		3.4	4.9	
1.6	2.4	2.0			2.5	2.0		2.0	2.9	
.6	1.1	1.2			.8	.7		1.2	1.2	
0 UND	0 UND	5 66.8		Sales/Receivables	0 UND	2 146.8		9 39.9	1 313.3	
20 18.5	25 14.4	45 8.2			39 9.3	41 8.9		45 8.2	207 1.8	
128 2.9	194 1.9	123 3.0			189 1.9	130 2.8		108 3.4	684 .5	
				Cost of Sales/Inventory						
				Cost of Sales/Payables						
.6	.5	.6		Sales/Working Capital	.6	.4		.9	.4	
4.5	1.8	1.7			1.6	1.4		2.7	.6	
19.8	14.4	9.0			6.9	11.6		13.1	2.7	
6.6	6.5	7.5		EBIT/Interest	8.0	5.7		10.0	4.1	
(57) 1.7	(62) 2.7	(65) 2.4			(10) 2.5	(18) 1.9		(19) 3.3	(10) 1.6	
-.2	.5	.6			-.4	-.2		1.0	.9	
				Net Profit + Depr., Dep., Amort./Cur. Mat. L/T/D						
.0	.0	.0		Fixed/Worth	.0	.0		.1	.0	
.5	.4	.7			.8	.6		.8	.2	
1.5	1.7	1.6			1.5	2.2		1.7	1.2	
.5	.6	.6		Debt/Worth	.3	.7		.8	.8	
1.4	1.6	1.5			.5	1.5		1.6	1.7	
3.4	3.6	3.8			2.2	5.7		3.4	4.8	
16.1	10.7	8.4		% Profit Before Taxes/Tangible Net Worth	4.2	10.3		14.2	11.8	
(90) 4.8	(84) 3.6	(83) 2.1			(15) .8	(20) 2.2		(22) 7.5	(12) .3	
-2.0	-1.9	-2.6			-4.0	-.2		1.2	-5.7	
5.3	5.5	4.1		% Profit Before Taxes/Total Assets	3.7	4.0		10.3	5.4	
2.0	2.0	.9			.4	.5		2.1	.2	
-1.0	-.9	-.9			-2.1	-.9		.3	-1.1	
87.4	92.8	43.2		Sales/Net Fixed Assets	UND	43.2		41.9	50.0	
2.5	3.3	2.5			.3	8.3		2.1	8.8	
.5	.5	.4			.1	.2		.7	.7	
.8	.5	.8		Sales/Total Assets	.3	1.2		1.0	.3	
.3	.2	.2			.1	.2		.4	.2	
.1	.1	.1			.1	.1		.1	.1	
.6	.8	.6		% Depr., Dep., Amort./Sales		.4		.5	.8	
(65) 1.6	(63) 3.1	(68) 2.9				(19) 2.0		(20) 1.5	(11) 2.5	
6.2	6.6	9.8				6.4		8.1	10.1	
				% Officers', Directors' Owners' Comp/Sales						
808275M	839530M	715852M		Net Sales ($)	9031M	43794M	34236M	184034M	188797M	255960M
2932143M	3404604M	3089947M		Total Assets ($)	85351M	297243M	353319M	857768M	992689M	503577M

PUBLIC ADMINISTRATION—Administration of General Economic Programs   NAICS 926110

Current Data Sorted by Assets   **Comparative Historical Data**

0-500M	500M-2MM	2-10MM	10-50MM	50-100MM	100-250MM		4/1/05-3/31/06 ALL	4/1/06-3/31/07 ALL
						Type of Statement		
	5	23	28	4	2	Unqualified	66	100
		1	1	1		Reviewed	3	3
1		1	1			Compiled	7	5
		2			1	Tax Returns	2	1
4	12	5	9	2	1	Other	34	30
	67 (4/1-9/30/09)		37 (10/1/09-3/31/10)					
5	18	32	38	7	4	**NUMBER OF STATEMENTS**	112	139
%	%	%	%	%	%	**ASSETS**	%	%
	29.6	22.4	19.4			Cash & Equivalents	18.9	22.2
	8.1	10.3	8.4			Trade Receivables (net)	10.6	12.7
	2.7	.7	.6			Inventory	2.5	2.0
	4.1	5.1	4.4			All Other Current	4.8	6.0
	44.5	38.5	32.8			Total Current	36.7	42.9
	39.2	41.3	48.2			Fixed Assets (net)	41.0	35.2
	.0	.2	.9			Intangibles (net)	1.6	1.6
	16.2	20.1	18.2			All Other Non-Current	20.6	20.3
	100.0	100.0	100.0			Total	100.0	100.0
						LIABILITIES		
	4.6	3.0	1.7			Notes Payable-Short Term	3.9	4.0
	.6	2.3	2.7			Cur. Mat.-L.T.D.	2.7	1.9
	8.2	3.4	3.2			Trade Payables	4.9	6.8
	.0	.0	.0			Income Taxes Payable	.0	.0
	5.0	5.8	7.6			All Other Current	7.8	8.0
	18.4	14.3	15.3			Total Current	19.3	20.7
	33.6	27.1	34.3			Long-Term Debt	30.0	24.2
	.0	.0	.0			Deferred Taxes	.0	.1
	.7	5.1	6.1			All Other Non-Current	5.0	5.2
	47.4	53.5	44.3			Net Worth	45.6	49.9
	100.0	100.0	100.0			Total Liabilities & Net Worth	100.0	100.0
						INCOME DATA		
	100.0	100.0	100.0			Net Sales	100.0	100.0
						Gross Profit		
	91.2	86.2	84.1			Operating Expenses	77.9	81.8
	8.8	13.8	15.9			Operating Profit	22.1	18.2
	8.0	10.6	14.8			All Other Expenses (net)	9.7	5.8
	.8	3.2	1.1			Profit Before Taxes	12.4	12.4
						RATIOS		
	13.2	6.4	4.2				4.8	4.4
	2.9	2.1	1.9			Current	2.2	2.2
	1.5	.9	1.0				1.1	1.3
	8.5	5.7	3.8				4.1	3.2
	2.9	1.7	1.4			Quick	1.7	1.8
	1.1	.5	.8				.7	1.0
	0 UND	1 256.0	0 UND				0 UND	1 330.7
	6 58.9	10 37.5	18 20.4			Sales/Receivables	15 24.4	23 15.8
	25 14.4	27 13.5	43 8.4				42 8.7	62 5.9
						Cost of Sales/Inventory		
						Cost of Sales/Payables		
	2.2	1.2	1.1				1.2	1.7
	4.1	5.7	5.0			Sales/Working Capital	5.5	5.2
	11.6	UND	226.3				43.1	19.6
		23.0	4.4				8.3	10.4
		(17) 3.8	(23) 2.4			EBIT/Interest	(52) 2.9	(66) 4.1
		-.8	.2				1.3	1.1
						Net Profit + Depr., Dep., Amort./Cur. Mat. L/T/D		
	.0	.0	.4				.1	.1
	.7	.7	1.0			Fixed/Worth	.8	.7
	1.5	1.6	2.6				1.7	1.3
	.4	.4	.4				.4	.4
	1.0	.8	1.5			Debt/Worth	1.1	1.1
	3.3	1.7	3.6				3.4	2.6
	18.7	9.9	14.0				15.1	21.7
	(17) 6.0	(31) 1.9	(35) 2.9			% Profit Before Taxes/Tangible Net Worth	(103) 6.6	(134) 6.8
	-1.2	-4.1	-4.5				1.0	-.8
	5.2	3.9	3.8				6.1	8.0
	1.0	.8	.7			% Profit Before Taxes/Total Assets	2.4	3.0
	-2.3	-2.0	-1.6				.1	-.3
	63.5	49.5	12.2				21.1	22.6
	6.3	2.6	.5			Sales/Net Fixed Assets	.9	3.2
	1.0	.3	.2				.2	.4
	2.2	1.0	.6				1.5	1.9
	.6	.3	.2			Sales/Total Assets	.3	.4
	.4	.1	.1				.1	.1
	.2	1.7	1.7				1.2	.9
	(11) 1.2	(26) 2.5	(34) 9.1			% Depr., Dep., Amort./Sales	(83) 4.6	(96) 2.3
	2.8	19.8	15.2				12.3	10.7
		4.2					4.5	
		(10) 7.3				% Officers', Directors' Owners' Comp/Sales	(14) 6.4	
		14.7					21.8	
10560M	25168M	146076M	575798M	240579M	59735M	Net Sales ($)	1003407M	1513275M
1257M	22222M	196057M	888984M	508299M	541464M	Total Assets ($)	2312040M	3104435M

M = $ thousand   MM = $ million
See Pages 9 through 22 for Explanation of Ratios and Data

Comparative Historical Data | Current Data Sorted by Sales

4/1/07-3/31/08 ALL	4/1/08-3/31/09 ALL	4/1/09-3/31/10 ALL	Type of Statement	0-1MM	1-3MM	3-5MM	5-10MM	10-25MM	25MM & OVE
66	80	62	Unqualified	13	14	10	9	9	7
4	3	3	Reviewed	1			1		1
6	5	3	Compiled	1			1		
2	1	3	Tax Returns		1				
32	28	33	Other	11	9	5	1	3	4
					67 (4/1-9/30/09)		37 (10/1/09-3/31/10)		
110	117	104	**NUMBER OF STATEMENTS**	28	25	15	12	12	12
%	%	%	**ASSETS**	%	%	%	%	%	%
24.1	25.2	24.6	Cash & Equivalents	20.5	25.0	18.6	11.0	38.8	40.3
11.8	13.6	8.4	Trade Receivables (net)	6.3	5.3	11.0	6.7	4.3	22.6
1.4	2.1	.9	Inventory	.2	.7	3.2	.4	.1	1.6
5.4	5.0	4.4	All Other Current	3.9	4.9	1.3	5.2	6.2	5.5
42.6	46.0	38.3	Total Current	31.0	35.9	34.1	23.3	49.3	70.0
34.5	36.9	42.0	Fixed Assets (net)	46.6	42.3	52.0	45.3	35.8	21.3
1.2	.4	.4	Intangibles (net)	.1	.0	.8	1.8	.2	.0
21.7	16.7	19.2	All Other Non-Current	22.3	21.8	13.2	29.6	14.6	8.7
100.0	100.0	100.0	Total	100.0	100.0	100.0	100.0	100.0	100.0
			LIABILITIES						
5.8	4.6	3.4	Notes Payable-Short Term	3.0	4.4	1.5	7.7	2.4	1.3
1.7	1.6	1.9	Cur. Mat.-L.T.D.	2.4	2.5	1.3	1.8	.9	1.3
6.4	6.3	5.3	Trade Payables	.5	8.4	7.1	4.3	4.4	10.1
.4	.0	.0	Income Taxes Payable	.0	.0	.0	.0	.0	.0
8.5	10.7	9.4	All Other Current	2.2	14.6	4.3	1.8	16.6	22.4
22.8	23.1	20.0	Total Current	8.1	29.8	14.1	15.6	24.3	35.2
27.5	23.0	28.6	Long-Term Debt	41.2	22.1	39.1	33.0	13.7	10.1
.1	.0	.0	Deferred Taxes	.0	.0	.0	.0	.0	.0
4.2	4.5	4.1	All Other Non-Current	5.1	2.4	3.0	1.2	10.8	2.6
45.3	49.4	47.3	Net Worth	45.6	45.7	43.8	50.2	51.2	52.1
100.0	100.0	100.0	Total Liabilities & Net Worth	100.0	100.0	100.0	100.0	100.0	100.0
			INCOME DATA						
100.0	100.0	100.0	Net Sales	100.0	100.0	100.0	100.0	100.0	100.0
			Gross Profit						
81.0	88.5	86.1	Operating Expenses	83.7	87.6	79.3	89.0	91.0	89.0
19.0	11.5	13.9	Operating Profit	16.3	12.4	20.7	11.0	9.0	11.0
8.0	6.6	11.2	All Other Expenses (net)	19.1	8.9	15.2	12.9	1.6	.2
11.0	4.9	2.8	Profit Before Taxes	-2.8	3.5	5.4	-2.0	7.4	10.8
			RATIOS						
5.5	5.4	4.9		15.7	6.0	4.7	3.8	3.3	9.5
2.3	2.5	2.0	Current	2.3	2.1	4.1	2.2	1.5	1.9
1.1	1.0	1.2		.7	1.2	1.2	1.2	1.2	1.1
5.4	5.0	4.7		15.6	4.8	4.5	2.7	3.1	9.4
1.9	2.2	1.6	Quick	2.0	1.8	3.7	2.0	1.3	1.7
.8	.8	.8		.5	.5	.7	1.1	1.0	1.0
2 183.3	4 99.8	0 UND	Sales/Receivables	0 UND	0 UND	5 79.7	0 UND	1 261.2	1 288.8
18 20.3	19 19.1	9 41.2		2 210.6	5 73.3	20 18.2	24 15.1	23 16.0	36 10.1
55 6.7	49 7.4	43 8.5		18 20.5	18 20.8	49 7.4	40 9.1	44 8.4	53 6.9
			Cost of Sales/Inventory						
			Cost of Sales/Payables						
1.2	1.8	1.3		.5	1.5	1.2	2.0	2.2	3.8
4.7	4.4	5.1	Sales/Working Capital	3.1	5.4	2.9	4.4	8.1	6.5
62.7	225.0	23.7		-27.2	NM	21.7	22.9	22.0	131.7
5.5	11.8	11.8			11.5				
(59) 2.2	(65) 2.0	(54) 2.6	EBIT/Interest		(15) 2.7				
.5	-.8	-.1			.1				
			Net Profit + Depr., Dep., Amort./Cur. Mat. L/T/D						
.1	.1	.1		.0	.1	.4	.4	.1	.1
.7	.7	.8	Fixed/Worth	.9	.8	1.0	.8	.8	.3
1.3	1.7	1.5		2.2	1.5	3.9	1.5	1.4	.7
.5	.3	.4		.3	.2	.5	.5	.5	.2
1.2	1.0	.9	Debt/Worth	1.3	.4	1.3	1.1	.9	1.0
3.6	2.5	2.7		7.3	1.5	4.4	2.3	1.8	2.7
14.8	12.7	12.9	% Profit Before Taxes/Tangible Net Worth	6.9	13.2	20.1	5.6	15.7	25.1
(104) 4.8	(109) 2.8	(98) 2.7		(26) .7	(23) 2.6	(13) 5.5	2.4	-2.0	18.5
-1.1	-5.2	-4.2		-5.6	-5.6	.0	.7	-5.7	1.8
5.1	5.9	4.7	% Profit Before Taxes/Total Assets	2.0	9.5	4.5	3.1	5.7	17.0
2.2	.9	.8		.2	1.8	1.8	1.0	-1.2	7.5
-.7	-2.2	-1.6		-2.4	-1.7	-2.5	-.3	-2.4	.0
26.3	42.6	34.9	Sales/Net Fixed Assets	64.6	115.6	3.6	4.6	56.9	77.6
4.4	4.3	2.2		.5	2.1	.9	.7	4.2	13.6
.4	.5	.2		.1	.2	.2	.2	.6	6.8
1.6	1.8	1.4	Sales/Total Assets	.4	1.8	2.5	.9	2.0	3.1
.4	.6	.3		.1	.4	.3	.2	.5	1.6
.1	.2	.1		.1	.1	.1	.1	.3	1.1
1.3	1.0	.9	% Depr., Dep., Amort./Sales	1.2	.5	2.7	2.4	.5	.3
(79) 2.8	(87) 2.0	(82) 3.7		(18) 20.4	(20) 2.4	(12) 7.2	(11) 8.3	(11) 2.5	(10) .7
7.7	5.8	16.0		32.4	9.8	26.9	21.0	9.1	1.8
4.4		3.0	% Officers', Directors' Owners' Comp/Sales						
(11) 11.9	(17) 7.5								
27.5		17.8							
1202402M	2364355M	1057916M	Net Sales ($)	15040M	50911M	59630M	81526M	187275M	663534M
2570260M	2440742M	2158283M	Total Assets ($)	149015M	173804M	330235M	519077M	533502M	452650M

M = $ thousand   MM = $ million
See Pages 9 through 22 for Explanation of Ratios and Data

CONSTRUCTION— PERCENTAGE OF COMPLETION BASIS OF ACCOUNTING*

CONSTRUCTION-% OF COMPLETION—Support Activities for Oil and Gas Operations   NAICS 213112

Current Data Sorted by Revenue						Comparative Historical Data				

0-1MM	1-10MM	10-50MM	50 & OVER	ALL	Type of Statement	ALL	ALL	ALL	ALL	ALL
	2	2	16	18	Unqualified	12	26	26	25	18
2	12	1		3	Reviewed	1	3	3	6	3
7		5		19	Compiled	19	20	17	22	19
		2		9	Tax Returns	2	5	2	7	9
3	14	7	7	31	Other	19	40	28	24	31
		5 (4/1-9/30/09)	75 (10/1/09-3/31/10)			4/1/05-3/31/06	4/1/06-3/31/07	4/1/07-3/31/08	4/1/08-3/31/09	4/1/09-3/31/10
12	28	17	23	80	**NUMBER OF STATEMENTS**	53	94	76	84	80
%	%	%	%	%	**ASSETS**	%	%	%	%	%
17.7	13.7	14.7	8.9	13.1	Cash & Equivalents	8.3	11.8	9.9	11.7	13.1
4.0	31.4	32.5	14.5	22.6	A/R - Progress Billings	37.4	34.9	32.5	29.5	22.6
.0	.2	.0	.2	.1	A/R - Current Retention	1.0	.0	.0	.8	.1
1.5	8.5	2.3	7.0	5.7	Inventory	5.0	7.5	6.8	5.0	5.7
.0	.0	.2	.4	.2	Cost & Est. Earnings In Excess Billings	.3	.2	.1	.1	.2
2.7	3.7	2.4	3.3	3.2	All Other Current	4.5	4.4	3.0	1.6	3.2
25.9	57.4	52.1	34.4	44.9	Total Current	56.5	58.8	52.3	48.8	44.9
52.7	30.3	35.8	50.4	40.6	Fixed Assets (net)	32.1	30.1	33.6	37.5	40.6
2.6	.7	1.8	.6	1.2	Joint Ventures & Investments	1.2	1.4	.8	.9	1.2
4.0	.9	.9	9.9	4.0	Intangibles (net)	4.2	3.5	5.9	4.8	4.0
14.8	10.7	9.4	4.7	9.3	All Other Non-Current	6.0	6.2	7.4	8.0	9.3
100.0	100.0	100.0	100.0	100.0	Total	100.0	100.0	100.0	100.0	100.0
					LIABILITIES					
6.1	12.6	5.4	1.5	6.9	Notes Payable-Short Term	9.8	8.6	6.8	6.5	6.9
1.8	6.7	14.3	5.6	7.2	A/P - Trade	9.7	11.5	9.2	8.8	7.2
.0	.0	.0	.1	.0	A/P - Retention	.1	.3	.0	.1	.0
.0	.0	.5	.2	.2	Billings in Excess of Costs & Est. Earnings	.1	.4	.3	.1	.2
.0	.4	.4	.3	.3	Income Taxes Payable	.2	.5	.5	.1	.3
9.2	3.0	2.5	2.6	3.7	Cur. Mat.-L/T/D	2.0	2.0	3.8	2.5	3.7
1.8	7.3	4.1	5.3	5.2	All Other Current	7.2	8.7	6.5	6.3	5.2
18.9	29.9	27.2	15.6	23.6	Total Current	29.0	31.9	27.0	24.4	23.6
44.8	16.1	14.1	24.6	22.4	Long-Term Debt	16.3	15.4	16.8	20.6	22.4
.0	.3	1.1	4.8	1.7	Deferred Taxes	1.3	1.1	1.8	1.7	1.7
7.7	6.4	1.6	4.3	5.0	All Other Non-Current	2.9	3.6	5.5	5.0	5.0
28.6	47.3	56.0	50.8	47.3	Net Worth	50.5	48.0	48.9	48.3	47.3
100.0	100.0	100.0	100.0	100.0	Total Liabilities & Net Worth	100.0	100.0	100.0	100.0	100.0
					INCOME DATA					
100.0	100.0	100.0	100.0	100.0	Contract Revenues	100.0	100.0	100.0	100.0	100.0
					Gross Profit					
81.9	90.1	94.9	96.4	91.7	Operating Expenses	88.2	83.2	85.0	83.0	91.7
18.1	9.9	5.1	3.6	8.3	Operating Profit	11.8	16.8	15.0	17.0	8.3
3.7	1.7	.1	2.1	1.8	All Other Expenses (net)	1.7	2.4	1.7	2.2	1.8
14.4	8.2	5.1	1.6	6.6	Profit Before Taxes	10.1	14.4	13.4	14.8	6.6
					RATIOS					
5.8	4.1	4.8	3.3	3.5	Current	2.9	3.1	3.0	4.2	3.5
1.9	1.9	2.2	2.4	2.2		1.8	2.0	1.8	2.0	2.2
.3	.8	1.1	1.5	1.1		1.3	1.2	1.1	1.2	1.1
	26.0	9.6	5.4	10.0	Receivables/Payables	12.5	6.7	10.3	10.1	10.0
(27) 6.7	6.7	3.9	2.9	(72) 3.3		3.6	(90) 3.3	3.3	(81) 4.3	(72) 3.3
	2.2	1.2	1.7	1.7		2.0	1.7	1.9	2.4	1.7
0 UND	34 10.8	44 8.3	52 7.0	35 10.4	Revenues/Receivables	60 6.1	46 8.0	50 7.3	44 8.3	35 10.4
0 UND	52 7.0	55 6.7	66 5.6	53 6.8		86 4.2	66 5.6	70 5.2	70 5.2	53 6.8
0 UND	81 4.5	69 5.3	73 5.0	69 5.3		109 3.3	88 4.1	90 4.1	86 4.3	69 5.3
					Cost of Revenues/Payables					
4.6	4.4	4.0	2.6	3.4	Revenues/Working Capital	3.9	3.7	4.2	4.5	3.4
13.2	9.5	7.8	4.5	7.3		6.3	6.9	7.3	7.3	7.3
-6.3	-34.1	NM	7.4	45.4		19.1	16.5	40.5	19.8	45.4
	22.0	9.2	5.9	8.4	EBIT/Interest	18.4	23.7	18.2	24.9	8.4
(25) 3.5	3.5	(14) 3.5	.7	(70) 2.8		(50) 7.0	(88) 11.4	(66) 8.2	(81) 10.2	(70) 2.8
	-.1	.6	-2.9	-1.0		2.4	4.6	3.8	2.9	-1.0
					Net Profit + Depr., Dep., Amort./Cur. Mat. L/T/D		20.7	73.4		
							(11) 11.3	(11) 6.0		
							7.5	1.1		
.6	.2	.2	.8	.4	Fixed/Worth	.2	.2	.2	.3	.4
2.2	.4	.6	1.2	.9		.8	.6	.7	1.0	.9
-1.9	3.7	1.5	2.1	2.6		1.6	1.3	1.9	2.1	2.6
.1	.3	.3	.7	.3	Debt/Worth	.6	.4	.4	.4	.3
2.1	.6	.7	1.3	.9		1.0	1.0	1.2	1.2	.9
-4.7	5.8	1.9	2.6	3.6		2.1	2.7	3.6	3.6	3.6
	28.1	27.4	12.0	23.1	% Profit Before Taxes/Tangible Net Worth	50.1	64.4	54.6	75.9	23.1
(23) 9.8	9.8	(16) 7.9	-5.4	(70) 7.9		(51) 33.1	(90) 42.4	(70) 29.6	(77) 35.3	(70) 7.9
	2.0	-1.9	-55.4	-8.2		2.4	23.4	15.9	19.5	-8.2
22.9	16.6	14.6	6.1	12.7	% Profit Before Taxes/Total Assets	23.3	27.6	22.1	27.4	12.7
8.6	4.5	5.2	-1.2	4.2		12.1	17.6	13.4	14.5	4.2
2.8	-.8	-2.1	-7.5	-3.7		1.4	8.0	6.0	7.2	-3.7
2.9	2.5	1.1		2.3	% Depr., Dep., Amort./Revenues	.6	.9	1.4	2.0	2.3
(11) 9.9	(17) 4.7	(15) 4.6	(49) 4.7			(39) 2.6	(53) 2.9	(41) 3.7	(49) 4.2	(49) 4.7
18.0	6.7	11.5		11.4		6.9	5.8	7.4	9.7	11.4
	6.9			4.2	% Officers', Directors' Owners' Comp/Revenues	2.8	3.5	3.9	4.3	4.2
(11) 7.8			(22) 7.1			(21) 5.0	(24) 5.8	(18) 7.3	(26) 7.3	(22) 7.1
	20.1			9.6		11.0	10.8	10.0	13.0	9.6
6275M	143304M	368319M	20423901M	20941799M	Contract Revenues ($)	5998666M	28400657M	23858274M	31950373M	20941799M
7021M	138779M	282140M	33567714M	33995654M	Total Assets ($)	7334030M	40507716M	33013528M	39179109M	33995654M

M = $ thousand   MM = $ million
See Pages 9 through 22 for Explanation of Ratios and Data

Current Data Sorted by Revenue | **Comparative Historical Data**

0-1MM	1-10MM	10-50MM	50 & OVER	ALL	Type of Statement	24	27	28	8	9
		4	5	9	Unqualified	24	27	28	8	9
1	17	17	2	37	Reviewed	97	69	71	33	37
9	46	9	1	65	Compiled	116	95	84	61	65
40	74	7	7	128	Tax Returns	248	202	171	151	128
21	54	13	5	93	Other	157	165	145	102	93
42 (4/1-9/30/09)		290 (10/1/09-3/31/10)				4/1/05-3/31/06	4/1/06-3/31/07	4/1/07-3/31/08	4/1/08-3/31/09	4/1/09-3/31/10
0-1MM	1-10MM	10-50MM	50 & OVER	ALL		ALL	ALL	ALL	ALL	ALL
71	191	50	20	332	NUMBER OF STATEMENTS	642	558	499	355	332
%	%	%	%	%	**ASSETS**	%	%	%	%	%
9.1	8.2	13.3	9.7	9.2	Cash & Equivalents	8.9	8.0	7.4	7.0	9.2
4.6	8.1	6.9	3.1	6.9	A/R - Progress Billings	6.9	6.4	6.5	6.6	6.9
.0	.5	.3	2.1	.5	A/R - Current Retention	.2	.4	.2	.5	.5
45.8	51.6	54.0	54.1	50.9	Inventory	53.4	54.6	55.3	53.9	50.9
2.0	1.9	3.0	3.5	2.2	Cost & Est. Earnings In Excess Billings	2.8	2.2	2.5	1.9	2.2
8.6	5.1	5.8	6.7	6.1	All Other Current	5.7	5.5	6.7	6.3	6.1
70.0	75.4	83.2	79.1	75.7	Total Current	78.0	77.0	78.6	76.1	75.7
18.7	12.8	4.7	5.7	12.4	Fixed Assets (net)	12.5	11.8	11.0	13.3	12.4
1.1	2.9	3.2	4.9	2.7	Joint Ventures & Investments	1.9	2.3	2.6	2.2	2.7
1.8	.5	.4	.4	.7	Intangibles (net)	.6	.6	.7	.9	.7
8.3	8.3	8.5	10.4	8.4	All Other Non-Current	7.1	8.3	7.1	7.4	8.4
100.0	100.0	100.0	100.0	100.0	Total	100.0	100.0	100.0	100.0	100.0
					LIABILITIES					
33.4	35.7	35.6	39.1	35.4	Notes Payable-Short Term	34.4	34.5	37.6	38.4	35.4
4.8	8.7	10.4	5.8	8.0	A/P - Trade	8.5	8.6	7.8	8.2	8.0
.4	.1	.0	.7	.2	A/P - Retention	.4	.3	.3	.2	.2
.4	2.0	4.4	2.2	2.0	Billings in Excess of Costs & Est. Earnings	2.4	2.1	1.0	1.6	2.0
.0	.2	.0	.0	.1	Income Taxes Payable	.3	.0	.1	.2	.1
4.5	2.8	2.0	1.3	2.9	Cur. Mat.-L/T/D	3.7	4.1	4.9	3.8	2.9
10.8	9.3	5.3	7.3	8.9	All Other Current	10.4	9.9	8.2	6.9	8.9
54.3	58.6	57.7	56.5	57.4	Total Current	60.0	59.4	59.8	59.3	57.4
27.1	17.2	5.8	14.8	17.4	Long-Term Debt	15.0	15.2	15.7	16.5	17.4
.0	.1	.0	.0	.1	Deferred Taxes	.1	.2	.1	.1	.1
13.4	6.6	2.8	8.3	7.6	All Other Non-Current	6.3	7.6	7.7	7.4	7.6
5.3	17.5	33.7	20.5	17.5	Net Worth	18.6	17.5	16.6	16.7	17.5
100.0	100.0	100.0	100.0	100.0	Total Liabilities & Net Worth	100.0	100.0	100.0	100.0	100.0
					INCOME DATA					
100.0	100.0	100.0	100.0	100.0	Contract Revenues	100.0	100.0	100.0	100.0	100.0
26.3	17.3	14.2	10.4	18.3	Gross Profit	20.9	20.5	17.7	18.0	18.3
24.4	14.8	12.8	12.7	16.4	Operating Expenses	15.0	14.9	14.9	15.3	16.4
1.9	2.5	1.4	-2.2	1.9	Operating Profit	5.9	5.6	2.8	2.7	1.9
3.7	1.3	1.2	-.4	1.7	All Other Expenses (net)	.6	1.5	1.9	2.2	1.7
-1.8	1.2	.3	-1.8	.2	Profit Before Taxes	5.2	4.0	1.0	.5	.2
					RATIOS					
3.8	2.4	2.1	2.2	2.6	Current	2.0	2.0	2.2	2.2	2.6
1.3	1.2	1.4	1.4	1.3		1.2	1.3	1.2	1.3	1.3
.7	.9	1.1	.9	.9		1.0	1.0	1.0	1.0	.9
1.9	1.4	.7	1.5	1.2	Receivables/Payables	1.4	1.2	1.0	1.4	1.2
(34) .0	(147) .2	(48) .0	(16) .3	(245) .1		(488) .1	(424) .1	(394) .1	(260) .1	(245) .1
.0	.0	.0	.0	.0		.0	.0	.0	.0	.0
0 UND	0 UND	0 UND	0 UND	0 UND	Revenues/Receivables	0 UND	0 UND	0 UND	0 UND	0 UND
0 UND	0 UND	1 635.6	0 999.8	0 UND		0 UND	0 UND	0 UND	0 UND	0 UND
0 UND	11 34.2	12 29.5	11 32.8	8 43.3		5 66.8	6 57.0	7 54.0	8 47.0	8 43.3
0 UND	0 UND	5 69.3	0 UND	0 UND	Cost of Revenues/Payables	0 UND	0 UND	0 UND	0 UND	0 UND
0 UND	10 36.7	15 25.0	6 58.8	8 43.3		11 33.3	10 38.2	10 36.3	7 48.7	8 43.3
21 17.7	31 11.8	26 13.9	28 13.1	28 13.0		29 12.4	28 13.1	26 13.8	26 14.0	28 13.0
.8	2.9	3.0	2.0	2.4	Revenues/Working Capital	4.5	4.0	3.3	2.9	2.4
6.3	11.7	9.8	10.4	9.8		14.4	13.0	10.4	9.0	9.8
-13.3	-38.9	262.9	NM	-43.5		-410.2	UND	159.7	-428.5	-43.5
2.5	9.8	19.2	1.8	8.8	EBIT/Interest	18.0	13.4	8.1	6.0	8.8
(56) .3	(158) 1.6	(43) 2.1	(13) .1	(270) 1.3		(516) 5.6	(448) 3.5	(407) 2.0	(284) 1.4	(270) 1.3
-3.5	-.3	.7	-5.5	-.8		1.7	1.2	.4	-.4	-.8
	1.8			3.5	Net Profit + Depr., Dep., Amort./Cur. Mat. L/T/D	8.0	13.1	18.2	23.1	3.5
	(12) .6			(17) .5		(27) 2.8	(22) 3.7	(28) 3.9	(17) 1.9	(17) .5
	-2.4			-1.8		.9	1.2	1.1	.2	-1.8
.0	.0	.0	.0	.0	Fixed/Worth	.0	.0	.0	.0	.0
.1	.4	.0	.1	.2		.2	.2	.2	.2	.2
4.1	9.0	.1	3.2	3.4		1.7	2.3	2.1	2.6	3.4
1.4	1.8	.9	1.1	1.4	Debt/Worth	1.8	2.0	2.0	1.7	1.4
6.1	6.0	2.1	2.7	4.6		5.5	5.6	5.6	5.4	4.6
-10.4	60.9	5.0	NM	44.9		26.9	31.0	39.8	86.8	44.9
22.5	48.6	25.8	8.3	38.2	% Profit Before Taxes/Tangible Net Worth	84.6	74.4	52.4	38.2	38.2
(50) -.2	(150) 9.8	(48) 13.2	(15) 1.2	(263) 7.8		(540) 39.6	(463) 34.0	(404) 17.8	(279) 6.9	(263) 7.8
-13.5	-7.1	-3.3	-21.9	-7.9		14.2	8.7	.3	-10.2	-7.9
4.2	9.1	10.1	3.0	8.1	% Profit Before Taxes/Total Assets	17.4	13.5	9.0	6.2	8.1
-.5	1.3	2.8	-.3	.7		6.8	4.5	2.3	.7	.7
-9.3	-2.6	-1.4	-11.4	-3.4		1.3	.3	-1.4	-3.2	-3.4
.8	.3	.2		.3	% Depr., Dep., Amort./Revenues	.2	.2	.2	.2	.3
(30) 1.6	(124) .9	(34) .3		(197) .7		(368) .6	(325) .5	(309) .5	(217) .6	(197) .7
5.1	1.5	.7		1.6		1.3	1.2	1.2	1.2	1.6
4.1	1.8	.8		1.7	% Officers', Directors' Owners' Comp/Revenues	1.4	1.6	1.5	1.6	1.7
(25) 10.3	(108) 3.1	(24) 1.4		(164) 3.1		(351) 3.1	(288) 3.2	(253) 2.8	(173) 3.2	(164) 3.1
16.2		4.7				5.8	6.2	5.5	6.6	5.7
36782M	680547M	1085413M	78137534M	79940276M	Contract Revenues ($)	94368836M	138951848M	57759246M	28436314M	79940276M
92012M	773040M	1034601M	52093020M	53992673M	Total Assets ($)	57039347M	77391611M	50831635M	33542288M	53992673M

M = $ thousand   MM = $ million
See Pages 9 through 22 for Explanation of Ratios and Data

Current Data Sorted by Revenue   **Comparative Historical Data**

0-1MM	1-10MM	10-50MM	50 & OVER	ALL	Type of Statement	4/1/05-3/31/06 ALL	4/1/06-3/31/07 ALL	4/1/07-3/31/08 ALL	4/1/08-3/31/09 ALL	4/1/09-3/31/10 ALL
	1		2	3	Unqualified	11	3	1	3	3
1	5	2		8	Reviewed	19	10	12	6	8
1	4		1	6	Compiled	7	3	3	6	6
3	9		1	13	Tax Returns	21	9	16	6	13
4		4	2	10	Other	3	14	8	8	10

Left current period spans: **5 (4/1-9/30/09)** (0-1MM, 1-10MM) and **35 (10/1/09-3/31/10)** (10-50MM, 50 & OVER)

0-1MM	1-10MM	10-50MM	50 & OVER	ALL		4/1/05-3/31/06 ALL	4/1/06-3/31/07 ALL	4/1/07-3/31/08 ALL	4/1/08-3/31/09 ALL	4/1/09-3/31/10 ALL
9	19	6	6	40	**NUMBER OF STATEMENTS**	61	39	40	29	40
%	%	%	%	%	**ASSETS**	%	%	%	%	%
	12.1			14.9	Cash & Equivalents	13.1	12.0	11.9	10.5	14.9
	19.9			13.7	A/R - Progress Billings	22.4	28.9	18.9	11.9	13.7
	.5			1.3	A/R - Current Retention	1.4	1.0	.1	1.5	1.3
	24.5			25.8	Inventory	22.0	22.0	15.7	39.4	25.8
	3.9			2.2	Cost & Est. Earnings In Excess Billings	4.2	5.3	2.1	1.1	2.2
	8.8			11.3	All Other Current	12.6	9.4	8.1	12.6	11.3
	69.6			69.1	Total Current	75.8	78.6	56.8	76.9	69.1
	20.3			20.6	Fixed Assets (net)	14.0	13.1	25.5	16.0	20.6
	2.4			1.7	Joint Ventures & Investments	2.0	3.3	2.8	1.1	1.7
	.7			.4	Intangibles (net)	.3	.9	2.7	.0	.4
	6.9			8.2	All Other Non-Current	7.9	4.1	12.2	6.0	8.2
	100.0			100.0	Total	100.0	100.0	100.0	100.0	100.0
					LIABILITIES					
	17.4			21.5	Notes Payable-Short Term	24.0	20.2	14.1	17.1	21.5
	10.0			11.6	A/P - Trade	17.0	19.6	10.8	15.3	11.6
	.2			.4	A/P - Retention	2.1	.1	1.4	.9	.4
	.2			1.9	Billings in Excess of Costs & Est. Earnings	4.2	3.0	4.0	2.2	1.9
	.0			.1	Income Taxes Payable	.1	.0	.0	.1	.1
	18.2			10.8	Cur. Mat.-L/T/D	6.8	2.8	5.2	3.3	10.8
	6.4			6.9	All Other Current	10.2	6.4	12.4	7.5	6.9
	52.3			53.2	Total Current	64.5	52.2	47.9	46.3	53.2
	43.6			30.6	Long-Term Debt	12.0	15.2	26.0	26.0	30.6
	.5			.3	Deferred Taxes	.1	.3	.1	.1	.3
	4.6			4.7	All Other Non-Current	4.1	14.3	7.6	2.4	4.7
	-1.0			11.2	Net Worth	19.2	18.0	18.4	25.2	11.2
	100.0			100.0	Total Liabilities & Net Worth	100.0	100.0	100.0	100.0	100.0
					INCOME DATA					
	100.0			100.0	Contract Revenues	100.0	100.0	100.0	100.0	100.0
	26.7			23.4	Gross Profit	18.9	19.7	24.8	13.6	23.4
	28.1			23.3	Operating Expenses	13.2	14.7	21.0	14.9	23.3
	-1.4			.1	Operating Profit	5.8	5.0	3.7	-1.2	.1
	1.4			2.8	All Other Expenses (net)	.3	1.0	1.8	2.7	2.8
	-2.8			-2.7	Profit Before Taxes	5.5	3.9	1.9	-3.9	-2.7
					RATIOS					
	3.4			3.9	Current	1.8	2.8	3.0	3.1	3.9
	2.2			1.6		1.3	1.5	1.3	1.5	1.6
	1.2			1.1		1.0	1.1	.5	1.0	1.1
	3.9			2.3	Receivables/Payables	2.2	3.0	3.6	1.1	2.3
	(16) 1.4		(33) .6			(48) 1.1	(33) 1.8	(31) 1.3	(27) .3	(33) .6
	.0			.0		.2	.7	.0	.0	.0
0 UND			0 UND		Revenues/Receivables	0 UND	0 UND	0 UND	0 UND	0 UND
16 22.5		4 82.0				9 39.0	34 10.7	2 159.0	4 96.5	4 82.0
64 5.7		49 7.4				60 6.1	68 5.4	54 6.8	44 8.3	49 7.4
7 50.3		1 333.9			Cost of Revenues/Payables	1 619.3	5 67.3	0 UND	15 24.4	1 333.9
30 12.2		28 12.9				26 14.3	24 15.2	11 31.9	31 11.6	28 12.9
59 6.2		58 6.2				48 7.5	47 7.8	41 8.8	63 5.8	58 6.2
	1.5			1.4	Revenues/Working Capital	8.5	5.1	6.6	1.7	1.4
	6.1			6.4		19.4	9.5	18.4	11.2	6.4
	34.4			157.5		295.8	29.4	-7.9	37.8	157.5
	6.1			7.3	EBIT/Interest	43.4	12.0	21.2	21.0	7.3
	(17) 1.5		(29) 1.5			(58) 10.5	(31) 4.8	(33) 2.3	(20) 3.5	(29) 1.5
	-7.5			-2.9		2.7	1.0	.4	1.1	-2.9
					Net Profit + Depr., Dep., Amort./Cur. Mat. L/T/D	16.4				
						(10) 9.3				
						2.4				
	.1			.0	Fixed/Worth	.1	.0	.1	.0	.0
	.3			.3		.3	.3	.4	.2	.3
	3.3			7.7		1.1	.8	9.1	1.0	7.7
	.8			1.1	Debt/Worth	1.3	1.4	1.5	1.3	1.1
	1.8			2.4		2.7	3.1	5.1	4.3	2.4
	8.7			10.4		10.8	14.7	117.8	15.7	10.4
	15.4			28.6	% Profit Before Taxes/Tangible Net Worth	71.0	81.2	74.1	32.8	28.6
	(15) .8		(33) 1.5			(53) 35.1	(35) 34.8	(31) 21.4	(25) 9.5	(33) 1.5
	-32.0			-21.8		13.1	4.9	-.3	-5.2	-21.8
	8.0			9.7	% Profit Before Taxes/Total Assets	19.4	18.8	13.7	6.8	9.7
	.4			.7		9.4	7.9	3.4	3.2	.7
	-8.6			-6.0		1.3	.1	-.9	-2.5	-6.0
	.6			.4	% Depr., Dep., Amort./Revenues	.3	.2	.3	.2	.4
	(16) .8		(24) .7			(46) .6	(25) .6	(24) 1.5	(16) .8	(24) .7
	1.8			1.8		1.5	1.2	2.7	2.2	1.8
	1.3			1.4	% Officers', Directors' Owners' Comp/Revenues	1.2	.9	1.5	1.0	1.4
	(12) 4.2		(17) 4.1			(27) 2.5	(15) 2.9	(20) 2.1	(10) 2.7	(17) 4.1
	9.7			11.5		4.6	5.0	7.9	11.6	11.5
4864M	61145M	119359M	5404434M	5589802M	Contract Revenues ($)	174048525M	3312017M	10557982M	6008892M	5589802M
15757M	113109M	39449M	8175049M	8343364M	Total Assets ($)	61759724M	5192073M	14682719M	7603974M	8343364M

M = $ thousand   MM = $ million
See Pages 9 through 22 for Explanation of Ratios and Data

Current Data Sorted by Revenue   **Comparative Historical Data**

0-1MM	1-10MM	10-50MM	50 & OVER	ALL	Type of Statement	ALL 4/1/05-3/31/06	ALL 4/1/06-3/31/07	ALL 4/1/07-3/31/08	ALL 4/1/08-3/31/09	ALL 4/1/09-3/31/10
	1		1	2	Unqualified	6	8	13	3	2
1	3	2		6	Reviewed	9	7	19	2	6
1	6	3		10	Compiled	16	20	21	9	10
1	3	2		6	Tax Returns	29	29	31	19	6
1	9	3	2	15	Other	19	23	32	16	15
	3 (4/1-9/30/09)		36 (10/1/09-3/31/10)							
0-1MM	**1-10MM**	**10-50MM**	**50 & OVER**	**ALL**						
4	22	10	3	39	**NUMBER OF STATEMENTS**	79	87	116	49	39
%	%	%	%	%	**ASSETS**	%	%	%	%	%
	4.8	10.0		6.8	Cash & Equivalents	9.3	9.3	6.9	6.9	6.8
	7.1	2.3		4.7	A/R - Progress Billings	5.9	5.0	3.8	3.4	4.7
	1.7	.0		1.0	A/R - Current Retention	.2	.0	.1	.4	1.0
	49.6	59.3		53.6	Inventory	53.7	55.8	57.5	58.1	53.6
	1.1	.3		.7	Cost & Est. Earnings In Excess Billings	2.3	2.2	4.0	.6	.7
	11.3	7.5		8.5	All Other Current	11.1	5.8	5.5	4.6	8.5
	75.6	79.4		75.3	Total Current	82.6	78.1	77.8	73.9	75.3
	19.8	7.7		15.5	Fixed Assets (net)	9.6	13.0	13.6	15.1	15.5
	.5	1.0		2.9	Joint Ventures & Investments	.5	1.2	1.3	1.1	2.9
	.0	.0		.0	Intangibles (net)	.9	.8	.3	.0	.0
	4.0	11.9		6.3	All Other Non-Current	6.4	6.9	6.9	9.8	6.3
	100.0	100.0		100.0	Total	100.0	100.0	100.0	100.0	100.0
					LIABILITIES					
	18.5	19.5		20.0	Notes Payable-Short Term	37.8	38.5	39.5	31.2	20.0
	4.9	4.3		4.4	A/P - Trade	11.3	8.9	6.5	7.5	4.4
	.0	.0		.0	A/P - Retention	.1	.5	.3	.0	.0
	.7	.7		.6	Billings in Excess of Costs & Est. Earnings	.6	.5	.7	.3	.6
	.0	.0		.0	Income Taxes Payable	.0	.0	.0	.1	.0
	7.7	1.5		5.0	Cur. Mat.-L/T/D	3.4	4.0	2.6	3.6	5.0
	8.8	14.5		9.0	All Other Current	10.5	10.0	8.6	5.1	9.0
	40.6	40.5		39.0	Total Current	63.8	62.5	58.3	47.9	39.0
	20.2	18.7		17.6	Long-Term Debt	16.3	11.7	14.2	20.5	17.6
	.2	.1		.2	Deferred Taxes	.1	.1	.4	.2	.2
	12.7	13.4		12.5	All Other Non-Current	7.5	7.1	6.8	14.6	12.5
	26.3	27.3		30.7	Net Worth	12.3	18.5	20.2	16.7	30.7
	100.0	100.0		100.0	Total Liabilities & Net Worth	100.0	100.0	100.0	100.0	100.0
					INCOME DATA					
	100.0	100.0		100.0	Contract Revenues	100.0	100.0	100.0	100.0	100.0
	20.8	12.0		17.1	Gross Profit	16.6	18.4	18.1	17.4	17.1
	23.2	12.8		19.3	Operating Expenses	11.0	12.1	14.2	16.3	19.3
	-2.4	-.8		-2.2	Operating Profit	5.6	6.3	3.9	1.0	-2.2
	3.2	5.9		4.4	All Other Expenses (net)	1.1	1.3	3.1	3.7	4.4
	-5.6	-6.7		-6.6	Profit Before Taxes	4.5	5.0	.9	-2.7	-6.6
					RATIOS					
	6.0	3.2		4.3	Current	1.8	1.7	1.9	2.9	4.3
	1.5	2.1		1.7		1.2	1.3	1.2	1.5	1.7
	1.1	1.0		1.0		1.0	1.0	1.0	1.1	1.0
	3.3			2.0	Receivables/Payables	.9	.8	.9	.4	2.0
	(20) .1			(35) .1		(60) .0	(63) .1	(97) .1	(41) .0	(35) .1
	.0			.0		.0	.0	.0	.0	.0
0 UND	1 727.5	0 UND		1 479.0	Revenues/Receivables	0 UND	0 UND	0 UND	0 UND	1 479.0
	16 22.7	1 330.4		9 41.3		0 UND	0 UND	0 999.8	0 UND	9 41.3
		21 17.8				2 208.1	6 62.8	7 55.7	2 158.3	
0 847.7	12 29.7	0 UND		0 797.0	Cost of Revenues/Payables	0 UND	0 UND	1 422.7	1 258.2	0 797.0
	29 12.4	11 32.5	12	12 30.9		8 45.0	13 28.9	12 30.0	16 22.2	12 30.9
		16 23.4	29	29 12.8		24 15.4	28 13.0	34 10.7	51 7.1	29 12.8
	2.0	.6		.8	Revenues/Working Capital	6.3	3.3	3.4	1.6	.8
	7.5	2.9		6.1		11.8	15.8	9.2	4.3	6.1
	NM	-83.8		50.0		59.2	-47.8	-140.5	42.9	50.0
	2.0			2.2	EBIT/Interest	22.0	13.9	5.5	4.2	2.2
	(12) 1.1			(23) 1.1		(59) 6.1	(70) 4.0	(83) 1.8	(41) .8	(23) 1.1
	-5.3			-3.1		2.2	1.0	.9	-.8	-3.1
					Net Profit + Depr., Dep., Amort./Cur. Mat. L/T/D					
	.0	.0		.0	Fixed/Worth	.0	.0	.0	.0	.0
	.4	.4		.2		.2	.2	.1	.2	.2
	1.8	.5		.8		1.0	1.6	1.0	1.4	.8
	1.2	1.3		1.1	Debt/Worth	2.5	2.0	2.0	1.5	1.1
	3.4	2.2		2.4		5.1	4.9	5.7	2.9	2.4
	6.4	99.4		6.3		21.7	35.7	24.3	23.0	6.3
	9.0			9.0	% Profit Before Taxes/ Tangible Net Worth	101.2	59.5	60.2	30.2	9.0
	(18) -.7			(33) -2.5		(69) 50.9	(75) 32.5	(101) 16.4	(41) 5.3	(33) -2.5
	-27.0			-22.8		12.5	5.5	1.4	-6.6	-22.8
	4.7	7.8		3.2	% Profit Before Taxes/ Total Assets	16.8	16.7	7.6	3.0	3.2
	.4	-2.2		-2.0		6.3	6.7	1.7	.1	-2.0
	-4.6	-8.4		-8.1		1.9	.3	-1.3	-2.9	-8.1
	.2			.2	% Depr., Dep., Amort./ Revenues	.2	.2	.1	.3	.2
	(14) .5			(24) .5		(47) .5	(52) .4	(63) .4	(26) .5	(24) .5
	5.3			1.5		1.0	.9	1.3	1.4	1.5
				1.3	% Officers', Directors' Owners' Comp/Revenues	1.1	1.1	1.0	.8	1.3
				(10) 1.8		(40) 2.8	(39) 3.0	(44) 2.7	(20) 1.8	(10) 1.8
				5.2		4.1	4.8	5.3	4.0	5.2
1763M	65056M	202083M	245507M	514409M	Contract Revenues ($)	17168691M	46391476M	16442642M	1697106M	514409M
5839M	112713M	452215M	653564M	1224331M	Total Assets ($)	5588958M	42797135M	15806132M	2773168M	1224331M

M = $ thousand   MM = $ million
See Pages 9 through 22 for Explanation of Ratios and Data

Current Data Sorted by Revenue | **Comparative Historical Data**

0-1MM	1-10MM	10-50MM	50 & OVER	ALL	Type of Statement	4/1/05-3/31/06	4/1/06-3/31/07	4/1/07-3/31/08	4/1/08-3/31/09	4/1/09-3/31/10
					Unqualified	1		1		
	3			3	Reviewed	3	4	4	3	3
2	3	1		6	Compiled	10	6	3	4	6
6	8	1		14	Tax Returns	22	14	20	14	14
1	2			4	Other	11	12	9	8	4
						4/1/05-3/31/06	4/1/06-3/31/07	4/1/07-3/31/08	4/1/08-3/31/09	4/1/09-3/31/10
9	16	2		27	**NUMBER OF STATEMENTS**	47	36	37	29	27

Left-hand columns 0-1MM, 10-50MM and 50 & OVER: DATA NOT AVAILABLE for body rows (only 1-10MM and ALL displayed).

1-10MM %	ALL %	ASSETS	ALL %	ALL %	ALL %	ALL %	ALL %
17.1	24.1	Cash & Equivalents	14.3	16.6	15.3	21.3	24.1
12.9	12.5	A/R - Progress Billings	12.9	17.3	14.3	18.2	12.5
.0	.0	A/R - Current Retention	.4	1.1	1.0	.0	.0
8.6	11.6	Inventory	27.4	14.9	13.5	14.7	11.6
1.6	1.7	Cost & Est. Earnings In Excess Billings	2.0	1.3	3.3	1.0	1.7
1.1	2.4	All Other Current	6.2	12.9	10.3	7.4	2.4
41.3	52.3	Total Current	63.3	64.2	57.7	62.6	52.3
36.7	33.8	Fixed Assets (net)	24.0	22.9	27.2	22.1	33.8
2.1	2.0	Joint Ventures & Investments	3.2	1.2	.0	.4	2.0
.1	.0	Intangibles (net)	3.0	3.1	2.5	2.7	.0
19.8	11.8	All Other Non-Current	6.6	8.6	12.5	12.1	11.8
100.0	100.0	Total	100.0	100.0	100.0	100.0	100.0
		LIABILITIES					
19.9	15.0	Notes Payable-Short Term	25.6	10.4	25.6	21.2	15.0
16.3	17.9	A/P - Trade	8.2	12.0	20.1	10.2	17.9
.0	.0	A/P - Retention	1.1	3.0	.0	.0	.0
1.5	1.1	Billings in Excess of Costs & Est. Earnings	1.6	3.2	4.7	3.3	1.1
.0	.0	Income Taxes Payable	.2	.0	.0	.0	.0
13.1	8.2	Cur. Mat.-L/T/D	7.1	6.2	4.0	4.5	8.2
18.4	18.2	All Other Current	7.9	8.8	12.6	14.0	18.2
69.2	60.4	Total Current	51.8	43.7	67.1	53.1	60.4
17.0	27.1	Long-Term Debt	22.4	20.0	20.6	15.9	27.1
.0	.0	Deferred Taxes	.2	.0	.0	1.1	.0
11.8	10.6	All Other Non-Current	11.0	10.3	13.5	6.4	10.6
2.0	1.8	Net Worth	14.6	26.0	-1.2	23.6	1.8
100.0	100.0	Total Liabilities & Net Worth	100.0	100.0	100.0	100.0	100.0
		INCOME DATA					
100.0	100.0	Contract Revenues	100.0	100.0	100.0	100.0	100.0
32.0	33.1	Gross Profit	32.4	30.3	30.2	36.3	33.1
29.3	28.2	Operating Expenses	25.8	26.5	30.2	31.6	28.2
2.7	4.8	Operating Profit	6.6	3.8	.0	4.7	4.8
.1	.5	All Other Expenses (net)	.2	.4	.9	.7	.5
2.6	4.3	Profit Before Taxes	6.4	3.4	-.9	4.0	4.3
		RATIOS					
1.6	4.0	Current	3.6	3.9	1.7	3.8	4.0
.7	.9		1.3	1.6	.9	1.3	.9
.2	.5		.8	.9	.4	.6	.5
1.6	1.6	Receivables/Payables	4.0	5.1	3.6	8.8	1.6
(12) .7	(20) .8		(38) .4	(28) 1.4	(22) .6	(19) 2.7	(20) .8
.4	.2		.0	.3	.2	1.0	.2
0 UND	0 UND	Revenues/Receivables	0 UND	0 UND	0 UND	0 UND	0 UND
6 62.4	4 82.1		0 759.5	8 43.3	0 UND	6 58.3	4 82.1
14 26.0	14 25.3		22 17.0	32 11.5	18 20.0	40 9.2	14 25.3
0 UND	0 UND	Cost of Revenues/Payables	0 999.8	0 UND	0 UND	0 UND	0 UND
10 37.2	9 40.1		10 37.8	14 25.6	15 24.5	5 68.8	9 40.1
18 20.2	19 19.2		28 13.1	31 11.6	33 10.9	20 18.5	19 19.2
NM	5.5	Revenues/Working Capital	7.0	8.8	9.0	7.8	5.5
-50.7	-260.1		31.4	17.5	-259.2	28.6	-260.1
-12.3	-25.6		-72.1	-61.6	-11.2	-21.2	-25.6
25.0	37.0	EBIT/Interest	33.5	36.0	6.5	28.8	37.0
(15) 14.0	(23) 14.0		(40) 9.7	(30) 6.6	(26) 1.8	(22) 5.7	(23) 14.0
-6.8	-.6		1.9	.2	-1.6	1.3	-.6
		Net Profit + Depr., Dep., Amort./Cur. Mat. L/T/D					
.8	.3	Fixed/Worth	.3	.0	.2	.1	.3
1.6	1.5		1.3	.3	1.8	.4	1.5
UND	UND		33.4	6.3	-2.7	4.4	UND
1.0	.7	Debt/Worth	1.6	.8	1.3	1.2	.7
2.8	5.6		4.6	2.4	6.3	2.4	5.6
UND	UND		135.0	19.6	-7.9	15.0	UND
121.5	102.3	% Profit Before Taxes/Tangible Net Worth	223.3	85.2	99.1	115.3	102.3
(13) 57.4	(21) 53.3		(39) 77.1	(29) 41.7	(24) 28.5	(24) 64.2	(21) 53.3
13.8	2.1		14.2	17.5	3.3	15.5	2.1
44.3	44.3	% Profit Before Taxes/Total Assets	31.7	37.4	19.3	37.5	44.3
17.3	20.0		11.4	12.7	1.6	17.2	20.0
-13.0	-4.8		1.5	-.4	-9.2	.9	-4.8
.4	.4	% Depr., Dep., Amort./Revenues	.4	.3	.4	.5	.4
.7	(23) .9		(36) 1.2	(16) 1.2	(23) 1.1	(18) 1.0	(23) .9
1.7	2.2		2.4	2.3	1.9	2.1	2.2
3.6	3.5	% Officers', Directors' Owners' Comp/Revenues	2.7	2.3	2.3	3.4	3.5
(12) 5.0	(18) 5.1		(29) 4.2	(15) 4.6	(20) 5.3	(18) 5.6	(18) 5.1
5.6	7.8		7.5	8.7	9.5	11.3	7.8

0-1MM	1-10MM	10-50MM	ALL		P1	P2	P3	P4	P5
5055M	45849M	35794M	86698M	Contract Revenues ($)	680567M	5774697M	4824907M	289684M	86698M
4168M	9228M	9784M	23180M	Total Assets ($)	894192M	1537369M	1154223M	72207M	23180M

RMA 2010

M = $ thousand   MM = $ million
See Pages 9 through 22 for Explanation of Ratios and Data

Current Data Sorted by Revenue   **Comparative Historical Data**

0-1MM	1-10MM	10-50MM	50 & OVER	ALL	Type of Statement	4/1/05-3/31/06 ALL	4/1/06-3/31/07 ALL	4/1/07-3/31/08 ALL	4/1/08-3/31/09 ALL	4/1/0 3/31/ ALL
1	1	10	7	19	Unqualified	50	31	23	20	19
1	24	9	1	35	Reviewed	63	48	42	34	35
	4	4		8	Compiled	12	11	15	11	8
1	4	1		6	Tax Returns	13	16	18	10	6
1	7	4	8	20	Other	21	14	35	17	20
19 (4/1-9/30/09)		69 (10/1/09-3/31/10)								
4	40	28	16	88	**NUMBER OF STATEMENTS**	159	120	133	92	88
%	%	%	%	%	**ASSETS**	%	%	%	%	%
	23.7	23.9	18.7	23.0	Cash & Equivalents	17.4	17.4	18.6	21.2	23.0
	32.9	36.6	34.9	33.9	A/R - Progress Billings	40.0	37.2	38.1	35.6	33.9
	1.6	4.0	3.3	2.6	A/R - Current Retention	5.2	4.0	2.9	2.6	2.6
	2.7	2.3	1.4	2.4	Inventory	2.9	6.4	2.7	2.2	2.4
	4.9	2.7	4.7	4.1	Cost & Est. Earnings In Excess Billings	5.1	4.7	4.0	4.5	4.1
	5.1	5.6	12.3	6.4	All Other Current	6.5	5.6	6.3	6.5	6.4
	70.9	75.2	75.3	72.4	Total Current	77.0	75.4	72.6	72.6	72.4
	18.5	17.1	15.2	18.6	Fixed Assets (net)	15.6	17.6	18.2	19.0	18.6
	.1	1.2	1.1	.7	Joint Ventures & Investments	1.2	.8	.5	.4	.7
	2.6	1.2	1.5	1.8	Intangibles (net)	.5	.7	1.1	1.5	1.8
	7.8	5.2	6.9	6.5	All Other Non-Current	5.7	5.5	7.7	6.4	6.5
	100.0	100.0	100.0	100.0	Total	100.0	100.0	100.0	100.0	100.0
					LIABILITIES					
	6.4	3.9	3.1	5.3	Notes Payable-Short Term	5.3	7.0	7.6	3.6	5.3
	23.9	29.4	25.4	25.8	A/P - Trade	29.9	26.5	25.6	25.2	25.8
	1.2	2.0	.3	1.2	A/P - Retention	2.1	.9	1.7	1.7	1.2
	6.1	9.8	9.2	7.9	Billings in Excess of Costs & Est. Earnings	8.5	8.1	7.8	9.2	7.9
	.8	.3	.3	.5	Income Taxes Payable	.3	.6	.4	.3	.5
	1.9	3.3	2.1	2.3	Cur. Mat.-L/T/D	3.1	3.4	3.2	2.9	2.3
	6.3	7.0	12.5	7.7	All Other Current	7.2	9.2	6.8	6.4	7.7
	46.6	55.7	53.0	50.7	Total Current	56.4	55.8	52.9	49.3	50.7
	5.9	7.2	9.0	7.5	Long-Term Debt	9.1	10.7	10.7	9.1	7.5
	1.2	.3	.5	.7	Deferred Taxes	.5	.6	.7	.9	.7
	6.0	1.8	3.2	4.5	All Other Non-Current	2.6	3.4	3.8	5.0	4.5
	40.3	35.0	34.4	36.5	Net Worth	31.3	29.5	31.9	35.8	36.5
	100.0	100.0	100.0	100.0	Total Liabilities & Net Worth	100.0	100.0	100.0	100.0	100.0
					INCOME DATA					
	100.0	100.0	100.0	100.0	Contract Revenues	100.0	100.0	100.0	100.0	100.0
	23.5	14.9	12.3	19.2	Gross Profit	15.7	17.2	19.4	17.1	19.2
	20.8	11.9	8.5	16.6	Operating Expenses	12.9	13.9	14.7	12.8	16.6
	2.7	2.9	3.8	2.6	Operating Profit	2.8	3.3	4.7	4.3	2.6
	-.4	.0	.6	.5	All Other Expenses (net)	.1	-.1	.0	.1	.5
	3.1	2.9	3.2	2.2	Profit Before Taxes	2.7	3.4	4.7	4.2	2.2
					RATIOS					
	2.3	1.7	1.7	1.8	Current	1.8	1.7	1.9	2.0	1.8
	1.6	1.4	1.3	1.4		1.3	1.4	1.3	1.4	1.4
	1.0	1.2	1.3	1.2		1.1	1.1	1.1	1.2	1.2
	2.4	1.9	2.9	2.3	Receivables/Payables	2.4	3.2	2.8	2.6	2.3
	(39) 1.3	1.4	1.9	(86) 1.4		(152) 1.4	(113) 1.5	(122) 1.5	(88) 1.4	(86) 1.4
	1.0	1.0	.9	1.0		1.0	1.0	1.0	.9	1.0
31 11.9	38 9.7	35 10.6	30 12.1		Revenues/Receivables	31 11.7	23 15.7	33 11.2	23 15.9	30 12.1
46 7.9	55 6.6	50 7.3	50 7.3			50 7.2	48 7.6	48 7.6	39 9.4	50 7.3
68 5.4	73 5.0	58 6.3	67 5.4			72 5.0	74 4.9	73 5.0	60 6.0	67 5.4
19 19.3	23 16.2	14 25.5	18 19.8		Cost of Revenues/Payables	18 19.8	13 28.2	15 23.7	18 20.5	18 19.8
41 8.9	39 9.3	26 14.0	39 9.4			42 8.8	34 10.7	38 9.7	30 12.1	39 9.4
60 6.1	62 6.4	47 7.9	59 6.2			62 6.0	57 6.4	60 6.0	52 7.0	59 6.2
	5.7	7.7	10.7	7.1	Revenues/Working Capital	9.5	8.0	8.7	7.8	7.1
	8.6	15.0	13.6	12.8		18.1	16.2	16.7	14.8	12.8
	NM	34.6	20.8	32.5		39.6	37.6	49.6	38.3	32.5
	70.5	33.4	445.2	67.8	EBIT/Interest	32.2	39.0	32.2	69.6	67.8
	(30) 3.5	(24) 11.7	(10) 10.6	(66) 6.3		(121) 8.8	(109) 10.1	(112) 9.0	(74) 15.4	(66) 6.3
	-5.1	1.6	.6	-.4		2.4	2.9	3.6	2.2	-.4
				6.1	Net Profit + Depr., Dep., Amort./Cur. Mat. L/T/D	6.6	5.4	10.9	12.9	6.1
				(17) 3.2		(42) 3.5	(39) 3.5	(37) 3.4	(24) 5.4	(17) 3.2
				.2		1.9	1.0	1.5	2.3	.2
	.1	.2	.1	.1	Fixed/Worth	.1	.2	.2	.2	.1
	.3	.4	.4	.4		.3	.4	.4	.4	.4
	1.3	.9	.8	1.0		.9	1.1	.9	.4	1.0
	.5	1.1	.8	.8	Debt/Worth	1.1	1.2	1.0	.9	.8
	1.5	2.1	2.6	1.8		2.4	2.4	1.9	2.0	1.8
	2.7	3.9	3.2	3.2		5.2	6.2	4.4	3.6	3.2
	51.6	48.9	52.1	49.9	% Profit Before Taxes/Tangible Net Worth	46.4	62.6	52.2	51.9	49.9
	(37) 18.2	(27) 31.1	(15) 24.8	(82) 20.7		(147) 25.5	(109) 30.7	(123) 33.7	(90) 30.8	(82) 20.7
	-7.1	6.1	17.4	.6		5.9	11.5	12.3	14.4	.6
	17.1	16.4	17.4	16.4	% Profit Before Taxes/Total Assets	14.9	17.7	23.1	20.4	16.4
	4.0	5.6	8.3	5.3		6.1	7.7	9.8	9.9	5.3
	-6.0	.4	4.2	-1.2		1.9	2.6	3.9	2.7	-1.2
	.5	.3	.3	.4	% Depr., Dep., Amort./Revenues	.3	.3	.3	.3	.4
	(29) 1.2	(26) .6	(11) .9	(69) .8		(128) .6	(108) .8	(115) .8	(82) .9	(69) .8
	1.9	1.7	1.6	1.9		1.2	1.5	1.8	1.6	1.9
	1.6	.8		1.1	% Officers', Directors' Owners' Comp/Revenues	1.3	1.4	1.0	.9	1.1
	(19) 4.3	(12) 1.4		(36) 3.3		(72) 2.3	(56) 2.8	(57) 2.1	(37) 2.3	(36) 3.3
	6.9	2.7		6.9		4.3	4.5	4.3	4.1	6.9
2921M	190575M	708438M	9592838M	10494772M	Contract Revenues ($)	21101359M	47794599M	8516638M	31034859M	10494772M
11636M	82336M	267499M	5678866M	6040337M	Total Assets ($)	8905415M	16179798M	2949634M	9777481M	6040337M

M = $ thousand   MM = $ million
See Pages 9 through 22 for Explanation of Ratios and Data

CONSTRUCTION-% OF COMPLETION—Commercial and Institutional Building Construction NAICS 236220

Current Data Sorted by Revenue						Comparative Historical Data				
	12	28	26	66	**Type of Statement**	138	98	98	86	66
3	67	51	6	127	Unqualified / Reviewed	206	171	159	159	127
4	13	1		18	Compiled	22	26	26	23	18
7	10	1		18	Tax Returns	34	31	34	16	18
5	28	10	6	49	Other	57	76	57	46	49
57 (4/1-9/30/09)		221 (10/1/09-3/31/10)				4/1/05-3/31/06	4/1/06-3/31/07	4/1/07-3/31/08	4/1/08-3/31/09	4/1/09-3/31/10
0-1MM	1-10MM	10-50MM	50 & OVER	ALL		ALL	ALL	ALL	ALL	ALL
19	130	91	38	278	**NUMBER OF STATEMENTS**	457	402	374	330	278
%	%	%	%	%	**ASSETS**	%	%	%	%	%
26.7	26.1	30.0	33.9	28.5	Cash & Equivalents	21.1	21.3	21.8	24.6	28.5
24.3	32.9	33.9	31.6	32.5	A/R - Progress Billings	38.1	39.6	39.2	38.1	32.5
.0	2.2	3.9	5.2	3.0	A/R - Current Retention	4.3	2.8	3.0	3.1	3.0
3.6	2.5	1.6	2.8	2.3	Inventory	2.8	4.0	3.1	3.1	2.3
.9	3.8	4.8	1.9	3.7	Cost & Est. Earnings In Excess Billings	5.7	4.7	4.8	3.9	3.7
2.6	5.4	8.5	8.0	6.6	All Other Current	7.6	5.4	6.6	5.8	6.6
58.1	72.9	82.9	83.4	76.6	Total Current	79.6	77.8	78.5	78.6	76.6
23.8	18.2	10.3	11.3	15.1	Fixed Assets (net)	12.9	14.1	13.8	13.6	15.1
2.9	.9	1.3	.9	1.2	Joint Ventures & Investments	2.3	1.9	2.3	1.7	1.2
4.4	1.1	.6	.8	1.1	Intangibles (net)	.4	.8	.8	1.0	1.1
10.5	6.9	5.0	3.6	6.1	All Other Non-Current	4.8	5.4	4.6	5.0	6.1
100.0	100.0	100.0	100.0	100.0	Total	100.0	100.0	100.0	100.0	100.0
					LIABILITIES					
30.3	8.9	3.5	.1	7.4	Notes Payable-Short Term	6.0	6.8	6.8	4.7	7.4
11.5	23.3	30.1	34.8	26.3	A/P - Trade	31.4	30.2	31.1	29.2	26.3
.0	.9	3.8	3.1	2.1	A/P - Retention	2.8	1.8	1.8	2.4	2.1
3.3	5.9	7.9	9.9	6.9	Billings in Excess of Costs & Est. Earnings	8.8	7.6	7.5	8.8	6.9
.0	.3	.4	.2	.3	Income Taxes Payable	.4	.5	.3	.4	.3
8.5	2.0	1.2	.5	2.0	Cur. Mat.-L/T/D	1.8	2.0	2.1	2.0	2.0
9.3	6.6	13.0	10.3	9.4	All Other Current	7.5	8.9	8.5	7.4	9.4
62.9	47.8	60.0	59.0	54.4	Total Current	58.7	57.7	58.2	54.9	54.4
15.0	8.0	3.6	7.8	7.0	Long-Term Debt	6.5	7.5	7.3	6.6	7.0
.0	.8	.7	.1	.6	Deferred Taxes	.5	.5	.5	.5	.6
.8	4.6	1.3	2.3	2.9	All Other Non-Current	2.9	2.2	2.2	2.2	2.9
21.6	38.9	34.3	30.9	35.1	Net Worth	31.4	32.0	31.8	35.9	35.1
100.0	100.0	100.0	100.0	100.0	Total Liabilties & Net Worth	100.0	100.0	100.0	100.0	100.0
					INCOME DATA					
100.0	100.0	100.0	100.0	100.0	Contract Revenues	100.0	100.0	100.0	100.0	100.0
41.1	18.6	12.4	13.8	17.4	Gross Profit	14.6	17.2	16.4	15.4	17.4
34.0	19.1	9.5	10.5	15.8	Operating Expenses	12.1	12.9	12.8	12.2	15.8
7.1	-.5	2.8	3.3	1.6	Operating Profit	2.5	4.3	3.6	3.2	1.6
.6	.4	.0	.9	.4	All Other Expenses (net)	-.1	-.1	.3	.2	.4
6.6	-.9	2.8	2.4	1.3	Profit Before Taxes	2.6	4.4	3.3	3.0	1.3
					RATIOS					
5.3	2.4	1.8	1.7	2.1	Current	1.7	1.9	1.8	1.9	2.1
1.5	1.6	1.5	1.3	1.5		1.3	1.4	1.4	1.4	1.5
.5	1.1	1.3	1.2	1.2		1.1	1.2	1.2	1.2	1.2
4.4	2.4	1.6	1.2	1.9	Receivables/Payables	1.8	2.1	1.9	2.1	1.9
(14) 2.1	(127) 1.5	(89) 1.2	(36) 1.0	(266) 1.3		(437) 1.2	(381) 1.3	(356) 1.3	(319) 1.3	(266) 1.3
1.5	.9	.8	.7	.9		.9	.9	.9	.9	.9
0 UND	23 16.0	28 13.2	15 24.4	23 15.5	Revenues/Receivables	26 13.9	30 12.2	27 13.7	29 12.8	23 15.5
26 14.2	41 8.9	46 8.0	47 7.8	44 8.3		49 7.4	49 7.4	48 7.6	48 7.7	44 8.3
70 5.3	68 5.4	62 5.9	64 6.2	64 5.7		70 5.2	70 5.2	69 5.3	66 5.6	64 5.7
0 UND	14 25.4	29 12.7	27 13.5	20 18.4	Cost of Revenues/Payables	24 15.2	22 16.8	21 17.1	20 18.5	20 18.4
14 26.0	36 10.0	47 7.8	50 7.3	40 9.0		43 8.5	40 9.2	43 8.5	39 9.4	40 9.0
54 6.8	54 6.8	62 5.9	65 5.6	58 6.3		63 5.8	58 6.3	61 6.0	60 6.1	58 6.3
4.3	5.5	6.7	8.1	6.5	Revenues/Working Capital	8.4	8.3	8.2	8.0	6.5
16.0	10.5	12.6	17.3	12.0		15.7	14.8	14.7	13.6	12.0
-7.8	34.0	20.8	27.6	27.8		36.2	33.7	37.2	25.7	27.8
	14.3	57.0	265.8	35.6	EBIT/Interest	40.9	47.2	54.1	48.5	35.6
(100) .9	(68) 17.3	(25) 11.6	(202) 5.3			(353) 10.2	(312) 11.7	(297) 12.1	(248) 10.0	(202) 5.3
	-14.3	2.7	3.7	-4.9		2.4	3.2	2.5	2.5	-4.9
	5.3	13.6		13.0	Net Profit + Depr., Dep., Amort./Cur. Mat. L/T/D	13.4	16.5	10.8	11.9	13.0
(30) .5	(20) 6.8		(57) 4.6			(115) 3.7	(88) 5.5	(84) 4.5	(83) 3.8	(57) 4.6
	-1.1	2.3		.2		1.5	2.5	1.3	1.4	.2
.1	.1	.1	.1	.1	Fixed/Worth	.1	.1	.1	.1	.1
.3	.3	.2	.1	.2		.2	.2	.2	.2	.2
1.9	1.0	.5	.5	.6		.6	.6	.6	.5	.6
.4	.6	1.0	1.8	.8	Debt/Worth	1.2	1.1	1.1	1.0	.8
1.3	1.5	1.6	3.1	1.7		2.3	1.9	2.2	1.8	1.7
21.1	3.7	3.0	4.3	3.5		4.5	4.0	4.4	3.5	3.5
120.0	21.8	36.1	49.6	36.6	% Profit Before Taxes/Tangible Net Worth	42.7	54.2	50.1	48.1	36.6
(15) 42.9	(120) .5	(87) 14.2	25.3	(260) 11.9		(432) 21.8	(380) 30.5	(354) 26.1	(314) 22.4	(260) 11.9
4.0	-24.0	6.9	11.0	-6.4		5.8	12.0	9.0	5.6	-6.4
25.1	9.4	13.1	15.3	13.7	% Profit Before Taxes/Total Assets	12.9	18.6	16.3	15.2	13.7
16.6	-.2	5.8	7.1	4.0		5.6	9.5	7.6	7.0	4.0
-20.7	-9.4	2.0	2.9	-3.7		1.4	3.2	2.0	1.4	-3.7
	.4	.2	.1	.2	% Depr., Dep., Amort./Revenues	.2	.2	.3	.2	.2
(112) 1.0	(83) .4	(27) .2	(231) .6			(390) .5	(336) .5	(311) .5	(286) .5	(231) .6
2.4	.9	.5	1.7			1.1	1.1	1.2	1.2	1.7
	2.1	1.0		1.4	% Officers', Directors' Owners' Comp/Revenues	1.1	1.3	1.1	1.3	1.4
(77) 4.0	(39) 1.9		(133) 3.4			(227) 2.2	(211) 2.6	(187) 2.4	(148) 3.1	(133) 3.4
7.2	3.3	6.7				4.1	4.6	4.5	6.0	6.7
8762M	603843M	2124638M	104182290M	106919533M	Contract Revenues ($)	126575084M	68776588M	66762127M	74343772M	106919533M
4371M	276713M	791201M	49156276M	50228561M	Total Assets ($)	57249591M	37193126M	38690253M	36047329M	50228561M

M = $ thousand   MM = $ million
See Pages 9 through 22 for Explanation of Ratios and Data

Current Data Sorted by Revenue   Comparative Historical Data

Type of Statement

0-1MM	1-10MM	10-50MM	50 & OVER	ALL	Type of Statement	4/1/05-3/31/06 ALL	4/1/06-3/31/07 ALL	4/1/07-3/31/08 ALL	4/1/08-3/31/09 ALL	4/1/..-3/31/.. AL
	4	3	7	14	Unqualified	32	27	19	20	
	17	9		26	Reviewed	50	45	34	32	2
5	5	2		12	Compiled	21	12	11	15	1
2	1	1	1	5	Tax Returns	11	9	6	5	
	2	3		5	Other	16	15	18	12	

Date spans (current data): 14 (4/1-9/30/09) covers 0-1MM and 1-10MM; 48 (10/1/09-3/31/10) covers 10-50MM and 50 & OVER.

0-1MM	1-10MM	10-50MM	50 & OVER	ALL		4/1/05-3/31/06 ALL	4/1/06-3/31/07 ALL	4/1/07-3/31/08 ALL	4/1/08-3/31/09 ALL	4/1/..-3/31/.. AL
7	29	18	8	62	**NUMBER OF STATEMENTS**	130	108	88	84	6
%	%	%	%	%	**ASSETS**	%	%	%	%	%
	20.0	18.1		17.8	Cash & Equivalents	14.8	17.1	15.4	16.3	17
	30.3	36.2		29.2	A/R - Progress Billings	31.2	30.5	30.6	31.6	29
	1.3	.5		.9	A/R - Current Retention	2.6	2.7	1.9	2.1	
	4.0	4.8		4.3	Inventory	4.1	2.7	2.2	2.5	4
	4.3	4.5		4.0	Cost & Est. Earnings In Excess Billings	3.8	3.9	3.4	3.1	4
	4.5	3.6		4.2	All Other Current	4.0	6.0	6.4	5.4	4
	64.4	67.7		60.3	Total Current	60.6	63.0	59.9	60.9	60
	28.9	27.3		30.8	Fixed Assets (net)	32.5	31.5	33.3	32.2	30
	.5	.0		.4	Joint Ventures & Investments	1.4	.8	.7	.6	
	1.4	.0		2.4	Intangibles (net)	.5	.2	.9	1.2	2
	4.8	5.0		6.1	All Other Non-Current	5.0	4.6	5.3	5.0	6
	100.0	100.0		100.0	Total	100.0	100.0	100.0	100.0	100
					LIABILITIES					
	7.1	2.9		7.3	Notes Payable-Short Term	5.9	9.6	8.1	6.3	7
	15.6	21.9		16.4	A/P - Trade	16.9	16.6	15.0	14.1	16
	.0	.4		.2	A/P - Retention	.5	.8	.7	.9	
	1.9	4.9		3.1	Billings in Excess of Costs & Est. Earnings	3.7	5.1	4.4	4.3	3
	.2	.1		.1	Income Taxes Payable	.6	.3	.1	.2	
	3.8	4.5		4.6	Cur. Mat.-L/T/D	6.2	5.5	5.8	5.9	4
	6.7	6.0		6.5	All Other Current	6.7	6.9	6.7	6.0	6
	35.2	40.6		38.2	Total Current	40.5	44.8	40.9	37.7	38
	10.2	11.9		15.0	Long-Term Debt	14.4	13.3	16.5	15.0	15
	3.5	1.7		2.3	Deferred Taxes	1.3	.9	1.8	1.4	2
	2.2	.9		3.3	All Other Non-Current	5.9	4.7	3.2	3.9	2
	48.8	45.0		41.1	Net Worth	37.8	36.3	37.7	42.0	41
	100.0	100.0		100.0	Total Liabilties & Net Worth	100.0	100.0	100.0	100.0	100
					INCOME DATA					
	100.0	100.0		100.0	Contract Revenues	100.0	100.0	100.0	100.0	100
	22.9	16.7		23.7	Gross Profit	27.9	25.0	27.4	24.6	23
	22.1	14.8		22.5	Operating Expenses	22.7	19.8	22.2	22.3	22
	.7	1.9		1.2	Operating Profit	5.2	5.2	5.2	2.3	
	-.3	.3		.0	All Other Expenses (net)	.0	.2	.0	.4	
	1.0	1.6		1.2	Profit Before Taxes	5.2	5.0	5.1	1.9	1
					RATIOS					
	3.1	2.3		2.5	Current	2.5	2.1	2.1	2.3	2
	2.0	1.5		1.5		1.5	1.5	1.5	1.5	1
	1.1	1.3		1.1		1.2	1.1	1.1	1.3	1
	3.8	2.4		3.0	Receivables/Payables	4.1	4.4	5.5	3.7	3
	(28) 2.6	1.8	(60)	1.9		(122) 2.2	(101) 1.9	(85) 2.3	(83) 2.4	(60) 1
	1.6	1.3		1.2		1.3	1.2	1.2	1.6	1
	39 9.4	39 9.3	29	12.5	Revenues/Receivables	32 11.5	29 12.6	27 13.5	36 10.2	29 12
	49 7.4	55 6.7	48	7.6		56 6.5	54 6.8	57 6.5	52 7.0	48 7
	81 4.5	77 4.8	72	5.0		75 4.9	82 4.5	80 4.5	74 4.9	72
	13 27.4	22 16.5	15	23.8	Cost of Revenues/Payables	13 28.2	12 29.9	10 36.6	14 26.3	15 23
	29 12.4	36 10.1	31	11.8		30 12.0	33 11.0	26 13.9	30 12.2	31 11
	71 5.2	45 8.1	60	6.1		55 6.6	50 7.3	54 6.8	43 8.5	60 6
	4.3	6.1		5.3	Revenues/Working Capital	5.7	6.5	6.2	5.7	5
	7.6	10.9		10.9		12.0	12.3	11.4	9.6	10
	30.4	20.6		56.2		25.0	40.2	30.8	20.1	56
	9.4	11.0		10.2	EBIT/Interest	18.7	19.2	12.8	19.1	10
	(23) 2.6	(16) 2.7	(51)	2.6		(121) 6.1	(101) 6.5	(77) 4.4	(72) 4.0	(51)
	-3.2	-2.0		-3.0		3.0	2.1	1.3	-.1	-3
				6.3	Net Profit + Depr., Dep., Amort./Cur. Mat. L/T/D	4.4	3.9	4.6	4.9	6
			(18)	2.8		(47) 2.5	(38) 2.4	(27) 1.7	(18) 2.5	(18) 2
				1.5		1.4	1.5	1.2	1.0	1
	.1	.3		.3	Fixed/Worth	.4	.3	.3	.3	
	.6	.6		.6		.7	.8	.8	.7	
	1.2	1.0		1.4		1.3	1.5	1.3	1.4	1
	.5	.7		.6	Debt/Worth	.7	.8	.8	.7	
	1.0	1.1		1.1		1.5	1.7	1.5	1.5	1
	2.7	2.3		2.9		2.9	3.3	3.1	2.9	2
	31.6	35.9		34.1	% Profit Before Taxes/Tangible Net Worth	43.4	53.5	41.8	34.2	34
	(28) 7.1	(17) 6.2	(56)	8.8		(121) 24.6	(102) 23.8	(80) 15.7	(79) 11.5	(56) 8
	-3.6	1.2		.6		8.3	7.9	5.6	-3.5	
	11.5	17.8		14.2	% Profit Before Taxes/Total Assets	18.4	21.9	17.7	12.1	14
	3.5	3.1		3.3		9.4	9.7	5.7	4.4	3
	-2.0	-2.2		-1.7		3.6	2.0	1.1	-3.9	-1
	2.9	1.7		2.1	% Depr., Dep., Amort./Revenues	1.4	1.6	1.7	2.2	2
	(24) 4.5	2.6	(50)	3.6		(120) 2.9	(103) 3.0	(81) 3.5	(69) 4.1	(50) 3
	8.4	4.8		6.6		5.1	4.8	6.0	6.8	4
	1.6			1.3	% Officers', Directors' Owners' Comp/Revenues	1.5	1.0	1.5	1.9	
	(13) 2.6		(25)	2.5		(68) 3.4	(56) 2.3	(47) 3.2	(47) 3.4	(25)
	5.7			5.9		5.8	4.0	4.0	5.4	6
4539M	149132M	337705M	4006966M	4498342M	Contract Revenues ($)	1883988M	1539617M	2097834M	3604883M	449834
2445M	88152M	138990M	3034434M	3264021M	Total Assets ($)	829236M	702439M	1174683M	1983786M	326402

© RMA 2010

M = $ thousand   MM = $ million
See Pages 9 through 22 for Explanation of Ratios and Data

	Current Data Sorted by Revenue					Comparative Historical Data				
Type of Statement										
			2	2	4	4	19	8	3	4
Unqualified	1	12								
Reviewed	7	8	4		17	19	25	22	14	17
Compiled	30	10	1		16	23	22	26	18	16
Tax Returns	16	7	1	1	42	60	58	79	44	42
Other			9	1	33	34	45	52	39	33
	10 (4/1-9/30/09)		102 (10/1/09-3/31/10)			4/1/05-3/31/06	4/1/06-3/31/07	4/1/07-3/31/08	4/1/08-3/31/09	4/1/09-3/31/10
	0-1MM	1-10MM	10-50MM	50 & OVER	ALL	ALL	ALL	ALL	ALL	ALL
NUMBER OF STATEMENTS	54	37	17	4	112	140	169	187	118	112
	%	%	%	%	%	%	%	%	%	%
ASSETS										
Cash & Equivalents	1.7	7.6	6.2		4.4	7.8	6.3	5.4	3.8	4.4
A/R - Progress Billings	.8	8.7	5.6		4.2	2.7	3.5	4.6	4.5	4.2
A/R - Current Retention	.0	.1	.8		.2	.6	.8	.5	.0	.2
Inventory	30.9	28.3	31.1		29.4	47.8	38.2	38.8	34.4	29.4
Cost & Est. Earnings In Excess Billings	.2	2.1	.5		.9	.5	.7	1.1	.7	.9
All Other Current	8.9	6.8	5.5		7.6	6.3	5.3	6.4	5.6	7.6
Total Current	42.5	53.7	49.7		46.6	65.8	54.7	56.7	49.1	46.6
Fixed Assets (net)	40.9	35.4	38.6		39.4	21.1	30.5	27.6	33.3	39.4
Joint Ventures & Investments	4.5	2.8	2.6		3.6	3.4	3.3	3.4	4.4	3.6
Intangibles (net)	3.3	.5	.4		1.8	.3	.3	1.3	1.5	1.8
All Other Non-Current	8.8	7.7	8.7		8.7	9.5	11.2	11.0	11.7	8.7
Total	100.0	100.0	100.0		100.0	100.0	100.0	100.0	100.0	100.0
LIABILITIES										
Notes Payable-Short Term	16.6	11.6	8.1		13.7	22.8	23.1	20.4	17.1	13.7
A/P - Trade	1.6	4.2	4.0		2.9	4.1	4.2	3.3	3.7	2.9
A/P - Retention	.0	.1	.0		.0	.0	.8	.8	.1	.0
Billings in Excess of Costs & Est. Earnings	.7	.2	.7		.5	.3	.3	.6	1.1	.5
Income Taxes Payable	.0	.0	.0		.0	.0	.0	.0	.0	.0
Cur. Mat.-L/T/D	8.6	4.6	11.2		7.5	3.5	2.3	4.4	4.2	7.5
All Other Current	1.6	4.1	17.8		4.9	6.4	7.1	6.0	5.1	4.9
Total Current	29.1	24.8	41.8		29.5	37.0	38.0	35.6	31.2	29.5
Long-Term Debt	37.3	36.2	35.4		37.0	24.1	30.6	31.5	37.4	37.0
Deferred Taxes	.0	.5	.9		.3	.0	.4	.2	.0	.3
All Other Non-Current	8.7	6.2	5.6		7.2	8.2	11.7	11.0	8.5	7.2
Net Worth	24.9	32.4	16.4		25.9	30.6	19.3	21.7	22.8	25.9
Total Liabilities & Net Worth	100.0	100.0	100.0		100.0	100.0	100.0	100.0	100.0	100.0
INCOME DATA										
Contract Revenues	100.0	100.0	100.0		100.0	100.0	100.0	100.0	100.0	100.0
Gross Profit										
Operating Expenses	83.5	80.4	100.1		85.0	86.4	82.4	83.8	88.6	85.0
Operating Profit	16.5	19.6	-.1		15.0	13.6	17.6	16.2	11.4	15.0
All Other Expenses (net)	22.9	11.3	7.9		17.1	2.2	7.9	9.9	10.0	17.1
Profit Before Taxes	-6.4	8.3	-7.9		-2.2	11.4	9.7	6.3	1.4	-2.2
RATIOS										
Current	5.2	6.8	4.7		5.5	5.1	4.5	4.7	4.7	5.5
	1.2	2.1	1.1		1.4	1.7	1.5	1.6	1.3	1.4
	.3	1.0	.7		.6	1.1	.8	.8	.6	.6
	4.7	4.0	19.9		4.6	2.0	1.7	2.2	2.3	4.6
Receivables/Payables	.0	(29) 1.4	(16) .8		(68) .5	(99) .1	(124) .1	(129) .1	(84) .1	(68) .5
	.0	.0	.1		.0	.0	.0	.0	.0	.0
	0 UND	0 UND	0 999.8		0 UND	0 UND	0 UND	0 UND	0 UND	0 UND
Revenues/Receivables	0 UND	1 375.3	6 66.2		0 UND	0 UND	0 UND	0 UND	0 UND	0 UND
	0 UND	39 9.3	36 10.2		8 48.5	8 48.4	5 80.1	6 57.0	10 36.7	8 48.5
Cost of Revenues/Payables										
	.4	1.2	2.2		.7	1.4	1.4	.8	1.3	.7
Revenues/Working Capital	3.7	4.6	18.7		5.3	4.5	6.5	4.1	7.7	5.3
	-2.5	NM	-2.8		-5.8	38.9	-20.9	-13.9	-8.3	-5.8
	5.0	7.0	1.0		4.1	12.8	9.3	5.5	3.3	4.1
EBIT/Interest	2.0	(23) 2.5	(11) -.1		(51) 1.5	(106) 3.3	(115) 3.2	(111) 1.5	(77) 1.2	(51) 1.5
	.8	.5	-1.6		-.5	1.2	1.2	.5	-.4	-.5
Net Profit + Depr., Dep., Amort./Cur. Mat. L/T/D										
	.0	.1	.2		.0	.0	.0	.0	.0	.0
Fixed/Worth	1.1	.5	2.3		1.1	.2	.7	.5	.8	1.1
	NM	10.1	8.6		11.1	2.6	5.0	5.8	7.6	11.1
	.9	.6	3.0		1.2	1.1	1.8	1.4	1.5	1.2
Debt/Worth	4.0	2.3	3.9		3.4	3.0	4.7	6.5	4.8	3.4
	-36.7	11.3	23.1		26.4	8.9	33.4	70.9	34.8	26.4
	1.8	26.5	4.1		10.3	73.8	63.0	37.3	22.1	10.3
% Profit Before Taxes/Tangible Net Worth	-1.2	(34) 6.2	(15) -11.7		(91) .0	(123) 28.9	(139) 24.6	(147) 8.7	(96) 4.8	(91) .0
	-6.0	-1.5	-56.2		-7.5	5.1	5.9	-3.6	-10.4	-7.5
	1.3	11.0	.4		3.1	15.6	13.4	7.7	4.9	3.1
% Profit Before Taxes/Total Assets	-.4	2.1	-3.2		.0	5.7	4.8	1.4	.5	.0
	-2.4	-.2	-4.9		-2.7	.8	-.1	-1.1	-3.2	-2.7
	6.0	.8	.7		1.3	.3	.5	.8	.9	1.3
% Depr., Dep., Amort./Revenues	(27) 15.4	(25) 5.6	(14) 4.6		(68) 7.5	(73) .9	(99) 1.5	(102) 2.4	(71) 3.0	(68) 7.5
	20.9	21.9	16.4		19.9	4.3	9.7	11.8	16.9	19.9
		.4			.8	1.5	2.4	2.3	1.8	.8
% Officers', Directors' Owners' Comp/Revenues		(11) 1.2			(24) 3.3	(39) 4.2	(36) 4.5	(38) 4.8	(26) 3.2	(24) 3.3
		5.2			6.4	9.0	6.5	11.8	16.9	6.4
Contract Revenues ($)	19544M	116090M	303734M	410565M	849933M	4880850M	6864316M	1888207M	2259339M	849933M
Total Assets ($)	163202M	437676M	971198M	4252475M	5824551M	7348294M	17878891M	6105175M	4099390M	5824551M

M = $ thousand   MM = $ million
See Pages 9 through 22 for Explanation of Ratios and Data

Current Data Sorted by Revenue   Comparative Historical Data

0-1MM	1-10MM	10-50MM	50 & OVER	ALL	Type of Statement	4/1/05-3/31/06 ALL	4/1/06-3/31/07 ALL	4/1/07-3/31/08 ALL	4/1/08-3/31/09 ALL	4/1/... 3/31/.. ALL
2	12	19	14	47	Unqualified	96	68	85	49	47
2	21	13	1	37	Reviewed	50	53	54	40	37
	8			8	Compiled	5	9	10	5	8
1	8			9	Tax Returns	12	8	5	5	9
3	7	8	1	19	Other	19	33	28	21	19

Left column heads: 21 (4/1-9/30/09) [0-1MM, 1-10MM]; 99 (10/1/09-3/31/10) [10-50MM, 50 & OVER, ALL]

0-1MM	1-10MM	10-50MM	50 & OVER	ALL	NUMBER OF STATEMENTS	ALL	ALL	ALL	ALL	ALL
8	56	40	16	120	NUMBER OF STATEMENTS	182	171	182	120	12.
%	%	%	%	%	ASSETS	%	%	%	%	%
	18.0	17.4	20.6	17.9	Cash & Equivalents	14.1	16.1	15.1	15.7	17.5
	27.0	32.1	14.0	27.4	A/R - Progress Billings	28.6	27.8	28.7	26.2	27.
	1.3	2.2	5.7	2.1	A/R - Current Retention	3.5	2.9	3.4	2.8	3.2
	1.9	3.8	7.1	3.2	Inventory	3.5	4.3	3.0	3.9	3.2
	1.9	2.5	2.9	2.3	Cost & Est. Earnings In Excess Billings	4.3	3.9	3.5	2.5	2.3
	2.3	4.0	11.2	4.2	All Other Current	3.8	3.6	3.8	4.9	4.2
	52.4	62.0	61.4	57.1	Total Current	57.9	58.5	57.4	55.9	57.
	38.3	30.2	27.0	34.0	Fixed Assets (net)	33.3	33.0	34.9	36.0	34.
	.6	.7	1.9	.9	Joint Ventures & Investments	2.1	1.9	1.1	1.5	
	1.5	.6	3.4	1.4	Intangibles (net)	.4	.9	.8	.8	1.
	7.2	6.6	6.3	6.7	All Other Non-Current	6.3	5.7	5.8	5.7	6.
	100.0	100.0	100.0	100.0	Total	100.0	100.0	100.0	100.0	100.
					LIABILITIES					
	6.7	4.9	3.8	5.6	Notes Payable-Short Term	6.6	6.0	5.1	4.6	5.
	15.9	16.7	12.1	16.1	A/P - Trade	16.6	15.8	15.6	15.5	16.1
	.1	.3	3.0	.6	A/P - Retention	.6	.6	.8	.5	
	3.0	3.2	9.6	3.9	Billings in Excess of Costs & Est. Earnings	3.9	4.1	4.4	3.3	3.
	.3	.1	.2	.2	Income Taxes Payable	.5	.6	.4	.4	
	6.0	5.4	3.1	5.1	Cur. Mat.-L/T/D	5.7	4.8	5.5	6.5	5.
	6.6	6.4	7.9	6.5	All Other Current	6.3	7.7	8.7	5.7	6.
	38.6	37.1	39.8	37.9	Total Current	40.3	39.6	40.5	36.6	37.
	17.0	10.8	10.5	14.1	Long-Term Debt	14.9	14.6	15.1	14.9	14.
	1.0	1.3	1.9	1.1	Deferred Taxes	1.6	1.9	1.4	1.6	1.
	1.4	1.2	2.2	1.6	All Other Non-Current	2.5	3.3	3.2	5.3	1.
	42.1	49.7	45.6	45.4	Net Worth	40.9	40.6	39.8	41.7	45.4
	100.0	100.0	100.0	100.0	Total Liabilities & Net Worth	100.0	100.0	100.0	100.0	100.
					INCOME DATA					
	100.0	100.0	100.0	100.0	Contract Revenues	100.0	100.0	100.0	100.0	100.0
	25.3	18.0	15.2	21.3	Gross Profit	19.7	20.6	21.2	19.9	21.
	24.5	14.2	9.1	18.8	Operating Expenses	15.8	15.6	16.0	16.4	18.
	.8	3.8	6.1	2.5	Operating Profit	3.9	5.0	5.2	3.5	2.
	.9	.4	.2	.5	All Other Expenses (net)	.0	.1	.3	.4	
	-.2	3.5	5.9	2.0	Profit Before Taxes	3.9	5.0	4.9	3.1	
					RATIOS					
	2.1	2.2	1.8	2.2	Current	2.0	2.0	2.2	2.2	2.2
	1.4	1.8	1.6	1.6		1.5	1.6	1.5	1.6	1.
	1.0	1.3	1.3	1.1		1.2	1.1	1.2	1.2	1.1
	4.0	4.4	2.0	4.0	Receivables/Payables	3.2	3.5	3.7	3.8	4.0
(55)	2.0	2.4 (14)	1.4 (117)	1.8		(179) 1.8	(169) 2.0	(181) 2.0	(118) 2.0	(117) 1.8
	1.3	1.4	.8	1.3		1.2	1.3	1.3	1.3	1.
26 14.1	28 13.2	18 20.3	27 13.7		Revenues/Receivables	29 12.8	29 12.5	29 12.6	30 12.0	27 13.
44 8.3	44 8.3	29 12.8	45 8.1			46 7.9	48 7.5	47 7.7	49 7.5	45 8.1
72 5.1	74 4.9	51 7.1	67 5.4			71 5.2	70 5.2	67 5.2	66 5.5	67 5.4
13 28.4	13 29.2	11 34.3	13 29.1		Cost of Revenues/Payables	16 22.1	15 23.7	15 24.5	11 33.1	13 29.1
27 13.7	23 15.8	29 12.4	27 13.4			29 12.5	30 12.2	28 13.0	26 14.1	27 13.4
56 6.5	42 8.6	47 7.8	52 7.1			45 8.1	45 8.1	42 8.7	46 8.0	52 7.1
	5.9	6.2	6.0	6.0	Revenues/Working Capital	7.2	6.9	7.5	6.5	6.
	14.9	10.4	9.4	12.1		13.5	12.1	11.8	12.3	12.
	463.5	20.6	15.9	32.4		36.2	35.4	28.2	26.2	32.4
	6.0	22.2	66.0	15.1	EBIT/Interest	13.5	20.1	14.8	13.1	15.1
(53)	2.2 (38)	8.9 (14)	10.5 (108)	4.5		(167) 5.7	(155) 6.6	(165) 5.9	(106) 4.6	(108) 4.
	-3.5	1.6	2.0	-.8		2.2	3.1	2.4	1.5	-.
	6.7	4.3		4.6	Net Profit + Depr., Dep., Amort./Cur. Mat. L/T/D	4.5	4.9	4.2	3.1	4.
(11)	.9 (12)	2.7		(26) 2.1		(69) 2.1	(70) 2.4	(59) 2.1	(40) 2.0	(26) 2.1
	.5	1.9		.7		1.3	1.5	1.4	.9	
	.4	.4	.4	.4	Fixed/Worth	.4	.4	.5	.5	
	.9	.6	.6	.7		.8	.7	.8	.8	
	2.0	1.0	1.0	1.4		1.3	1.4	1.4	1.4	
	.8	.5	.9	.6	Debt/Worth	.8	.8	.8	.6	
	1.4	1.0	1.2	1.3		1.4	1.4	1.3	1.3	1.
	2.9	2.2	2.3	2.5		2.7	2.6	2.7	2.5	2.
	21.4	41.4	36.0	32.4	% Profit Before Taxes/Tangible Net Worth	30.5	41.6	47.6	31.4	32.
(51)	7.0 (39)	19.0	22.9	(114) 12.0		(176) 19.0	(164) 26.2	(174) 24.4	(114) 12.3	(114) 12.0
	-12.8	3.9	7.6	-1.8		5.9	11.2	9.0	3.3	-1.
	8.3	18.7	16.8	13.0	% Profit Before Taxes/Total Assets	12.8	17.5	17.0	13.0	13.0
	2.1	7.8	9.1	5.7		7.8	9.4	9.2	5.4	5.
	-8.3	1.4	1.6	-1.7		2.1	4.2	2.7	1.1	-1.
	2.9	1.6	1.1	1.7	% Depr., Dep., Amort./Revenues	1.6	1.8	2.1	2.4	1.
(51)	4.6 (39)	2.7 (11)	2.9 (108)	3.5		(159) 3.1	(158) 3.0	(166) 3.1	(110) 3.3	(108) 3.
	6.8	4.3	3.2	5.5		4.7	4.3	4.6	4.9	5.
	1.9	1.0		1.2	% Officers', Directors' Owners' Comp/Revenues	1.3	1.3	1.3	1.4	1.
(31)	3.7 (27)	1.6		(62) 2.2		(88) 2.6	(76) 2.3	(78) 2.7	(61) 2.2	(62) 2.2
	7.2	3.7		5.9		4.7	4.7	5.3	4.0	5.
2569M	284181M	970431M	23407021M	24664202M	Contract Revenues ($)	45851388M	14560141M	15109325M	13593931M	24664202
1985M	187585M	428917M	21941741M	22560228M	Total Assets ($)	18173517M	7648964M	8348429M	7028336M	2256022

© RMA 2010

M = $ thousand   MM = $ million
See Pages 9 through 22 for Explanation of Ratios and Data

Current Data Sorted by Revenue   Comparative Historical Data

Type of Statement	0-1MM	1-10MM	10-50MM	50 & OVER	ALL	4/1/05-3/31/06 ALL	4/1/06-3/31/07 ALL	4/1/07-3/31/08 ALL	4/1/08-3/31/09 ALL	4/1/09-3/31/10 ALL
Unqualified		2	5	5	12	12	18	16	11	12
Reviewed	1	11	8		20	17	14	24	16	20
Compiled	1	1			2	6	5	7	3	2
Tax Returns	4	2	1		7	1	7	3	2	7
Other	1	5	6	2	14	6	6	9	12	14
	8 (4/1-9/30/09)		47 (10/1/09-3/31/10)							
NUMBER OF STATEMENTS	7	21	20	7	55	42	50	59	44	55
	%	%	%	%	%	%	%	%	%	%
ASSETS										
Cash & Equivalents		23.7	18.3		19.2	14.2	13.0	16.3	20.7	19.2
A/R - Progress Billings		30.2	36.2		30.8	27.7	32.2	33.2	35.2	30.8
A/R - Current Retention		1.5	1.3		1.6	2.0	.9	1.4	1.0	1.6
Inventory		.7	.8		1.8	4.6	4.0	3.7	1.0	1.8
Cost & Est. Earnings In Excess Billings		1.6	5.9		3.3	4.9	3.3	3.1	3.6	3.3
All Other Current		1.3	5.8		3.7	5.4	5.6	6.2	4.8	3.7
Total Current		59.0	68.3		60.4	58.8	59.0	63.9	66.4	60.4
Fixed Assets (net)		34.9	24.1		32.6	32.5	32.1	27.4	26.7	32.6
Joint Ventures & Investments		.6	.2		1.1	.6	.2	.3	1.1	1.1
Intangibles (net)		.3	.5		.8	1.6	1.4	1.7	.5	.8
All Other Non-Current		5.2	7.0		5.1	6.6	7.3	6.8	5.3	5.1
Total		100.0	100.0		100.0	100.0	100.0	100.0	100.0	100.0
LIABILITIES										
Notes Payable-Short Term		9.0	5.3		7.0	11.5	7.3	5.3	9.9	7.0
A/P - Trade		11.4	22.4		15.8	14.8	14.8	17.5	20.8	15.8
A/P - Retention		.0	.5		.3	.3	.9	.3	.3	.3
Billings in Excess of Costs & Est. Earnings		2.7	5.8		4.7	5.6	4.5	5.5	4.8	4.7
Income Taxes Payable		.5	.1		.2	.3	.4	.3	.1	.2
Cur. Mat.-L/T/D		6.0	2.6		5.1	5.9	6.8	5.9	4.8	5.1
All Other Current		4.8	7.7		6.0	7.6	10.0	9.0	5.9	6.0
Total Current		34.5	44.4		39.1	46.1	44.7	43.7	46.6	39.1
Long-Term Debt		12.8	9.4		14.2	14.5	21.5	14.3	12.2	14.2
Deferred Taxes		1.0	.8		.9	1.0	.8	1.1	1.3	.9
All Other Non-Current		3.1	.9		4.6	3.8	4.7	4.4	4.4	4.6
Net Worth		48.6	44.5		41.0	34.5	28.3	36.4	35.5	41.0
Total Liabilities & Net Worth		100.0	100.0		100.0	100.0	100.0	100.0	100.0	100.0
INCOME DATA										
Contract Revenues		100.0	100.0		100.0	100.0	100.0	100.0	100.0	100.0
Gross Profit		32.4	17.9		26.9	24.6	30.6	25.7	21.2	26.9
Operating Expenses		28.6	13.8		22.7	18.8	22.8	19.4	18.5	22.7
Operating Profit		3.7	4.1		4.2	5.8	7.9	6.3	2.7	4.2
All Other Expenses (net)		.9	-.2		.8	.7	.9	.3	.5	.8
Profit Before Taxes		2.9	4.3		3.4	5.1	7.0	6.0	2.2	3.4
RATIOS										
Current		4.1	2.2		2.2	1.8	1.7	2.2	2.2	2.2
		2.2	1.5		1.6	1.5	1.4	1.5	1.5	1.6
		1.0	1.1		1.1	1.1	1.1	1.1	1.2	1.1
Receivables/Payables		9.0	4.9		5.3	3.6	5.9	4.1	3.9	5.3
		(20) 4.3	2.0		(52) 2.2	(39) 1.9	(47) 2.1	2.0	2.2	(52) 2.2
		1.2	1.1		1.2	.7	1.3	1.3	1.1	1.2
Revenues/Receivables		17 20.9	37 10.0		29 12.5	11 34.3	31 12.0	31 11.9	37 9.8	29 12.5
		55 6.7	47 7.8		55 6.6	39 9.3	55 6.7	55 6.7	54 6.8	55 6.6
		97 3.8	76 4.8		86 4.3	71 5.1	75 4.9	91 4.0	90 4.1	86 4.3
Cost of Revenues/Payables		5 74.9	12 30.8		7 54.4	9 39.6	8 44.3	18 20.1	19 19.4	7 54.4
		15 23.9	31 11.8		29 12.6	27 13.5	29 12.5	31 11.7	31 11.6	29 12.6
		41 9.0	67 5.5		52 7.0	52 7.0	49 7.4	60 6.0	53 6.8	52 7.0
Revenues/Working Capital		2.4	5.1		4.7	7.6	7.9	5.9	5.7	4.7
		8.1	11.6		9.8	13.9	13.9	12.6	11.1	9.8
		449.5	40.2		90.4	98.8	41.1	38.6	35.6	90.4
EBIT/Interest		16.0	33.0		24.1	29.2	20.6	17.2	29.5	24.1
		(19) 6.0	6.8		(52) 6.1	(38) 7.2	(48) 7.0	(56) 5.4	(39) 7.0	(52) 6.1
		-.9	1.5		-.3	3.3	2.5	2.6	1.1	-.3
Net Profit + Depr., Dep., Amort./Cur. Mat. L/T/D					8.9	13.3	16.9	14.9	18.6	8.9
					(13) 3.1	(10) 8.2	(17) 3.5	(25) 4.1	(16) 3.4	(13) 3.1
					.3	2.5	1.0	1.6	1.0	.3
Fixed/Worth		.2	.2		.3	.3	.3	.3	.2	.3
		.5	.5		.5	.7	.9	.8	.6	.5
		1.4			1.6	1.5	1.9	1.5	1.6	1.6
Debt/Worth		.4	.5		.6	.9	.9	.7	.7	.6
		.9	1.4		1.3	1.5	1.4	1.9	1.7	1.3
		1.9	2.7		2.8	3.0	5.5	4.0	5.1	2.8
% Profit Before Taxes/Tangible Net Worth		32.7	33.8		35.0	55.0	51.5	42.0	35.0	35.0
		(20) 15.9	10.2		(51) 16.3	(37) 30.9	(43) 30.9	(53) 22.3	(41) 17.1	(51) 16.3
		-8.9	2.3		.1	12.1	9.5	6.8	2.5	.1
% Profit Before Taxes/Total Assets		20.1	17.7		16.8	22.6	20.1	17.1	16.1	16.8
		7.9	6.1		5.3	10.3	8.4	8.0	6.8	5.3
		-2.5	.9		-.6	5.3	3.9	2.2	-.4	-.6
% Depr., Dep., Amort./Revenues		1.2	.8		1.0	.9	1.4	.9	.7	1.0
		(19) 3.7	(18) 1.7		(48) 2.7	(38) 2.7	(47) 3.5	(55) 2.5	(37) 2.0	(48) 2.7
		13.4	2.7		4.9	5.9	5.2	4.8	4.7	4.9
% Officers', Directors' Owners' Comp/Revenues		4.3			1.7	1.9	1.5	1.3	1.5	1.7
		(10) 5.6			(21) 4.7	(21) 3.2	(25) 4.0	(30) 3.0	(18) 2.6	(21) 4.7
		6.9			6.2	5.9	5.2	4.8	6.6	6.2
Contract Revenues ($)	3182M	110171M	376212M	1356909M	1846474M	589960M	2126436M	1045430M	6369802M	1846474M
Total Assets ($)	3226M	87897M	169105M	1417619M	1677847M	255438M	2291730M	538704M	5377672M	1677847M

Current Data Sorted by Revenue   Comparative Historical Data

0-1MM	1-10MM	10-50MM	50 & OVER	ALL	Type of Statement	4/1/05-3/31/06 ALL	4/1/06-3/31/07 ALL	4/1/07-3/31/08 ALL	4/1/08-3/31/09 ALL	4/1/.-3/31/. ALL
	1			3	Unqualified	16	4	8	7	3
	14	11	2	25	Reviewed	44	24	27	26	25
2	10	1	1	14	Compiled	17	17	13	9	14
3	5			8	Tax Returns	21	20	15	12	8
1	4	10		15	Other	15	22	21	9	15
	8 (4/1-9/30/09)	57 (10/1/09-3/31/10)								
6	34	22	3	65	NUMBER OF STATEMENTS	113	87	84	63	65

ASSETS

0-1MM %	1-10MM %	10-50MM %	50 & OVER %	ALL %		%	%	%	%	%
	13.4	13.3		12.7	Cash & Equivalents	12.3	13.7	13.9	13.3	12.?
	44.8	35.2		38.5	A/R - Progress Billings	37.8	33.6	34.3	33.8	38.?
	1.6	1.6		1.5	A/R - Current Retention	1.6	1.7	2.1	2.4	1.?
	1.2	2.5		2.6	Inventory	3.1	2.6	3.1	3.0	2.?
	1.3	3.2		1.8	Cost & Est. Earnings In Excess Billings	2.4	.8	1.4	1.8	1.8
	3.3	8.6		4.9	All Other Current	4.0	4.4	4.3	4.1	4.?
	65.7	64.3		62.0	Total Current	61.3	56.6	59.0	58.3	62.0
	26.0	25.8		27.5	Fixed Assets (net)	30.4	35.2	32.2	33.3	27.?
	.1	.1		.1	Joint Ventures & Investments	.9	.1	.3	.9	.?
	1.3	3.4		2.5	Intangibles (net)	1.0	1.4	2.3	2.6	2.?
	7.0	6.4		8.0	All Other Non-Current	6.5	6.7	6.1	5.0	8.0
	100.0	100.0		100.0	Total	100.0	100.0	100.0	100.0	100.0

LIABILITIES

0-1MM	1-10MM	10-50MM	50 & OVER	ALL						
	10.7	7.6		12.0	Notes Payable-Short Term	9.5	8.9	11.8	11.6	12.0
	16.8	16.7		16.3	A/P - Trade	16.7	16.5	17.5	14.5	16.3
	.0	.2		.1	A/P - Retention	.2	.4	.3	.0	.?
	2.0	5.5		3.1	Billings in Excess of Costs & Est. Earnings	2.5	2.3	2.4	2.7	3.1
	.8	.1		.5	Income Taxes Payable	.7	.7	.5	.3	.?
	4.5	3.6		4.4	Cur. Mat.-L/T/D	5.8	4.6	4.7	5.0	4.4
	4.2	9.7		6.6	All Other Current	6.3	6.3	6.9	6.6	6.6
	38.9	43.3		42.8	Total Current	41.6	39.7	44.2	40.7	42.8
	14.1	10.5		14.1	Long-Term Debt	18.9	23.3	18.8	18.0	14.1
	1.0	.5		.7	Deferred Taxes	1.3	.6	.8	.7	.7
	2.8	6.8		5.7	All Other Non-Current	9.2	3.8	2.0	8.3	5.7
	43.2	39.0		36.7	Net Worth	29.0	32.6	34.2	32.4	36.7
	100.0	100.0		100.0	Total Liabilities & Net Worth	100.0	100.0	100.0	100.0	100.0

INCOME DATA

0-1MM	1-10MM	10-50MM	50 & OVER	ALL						
	100.0	100.0		100.0	Contract Revenues	100.0	100.0	100.0	100.0	100.0
	25.6	19.9		25.0	Gross Profit	30.1	31.8	29.5	24.2	25.0
	25.8	17.2		24.6	Operating Expenses	25.2	26.6	25.1	21.6	24.6
	-.3	2.7		.4	Operating Profit	4.9	5.3	4.4	2.7	.?
	.2	.3		.3	All Other Expenses (net)	.7	.9	1.0	.6	.?
	-.4	2.3		.1	Profit Before Taxes	4.2	4.4	3.4	2.0	.?

RATIOS

0-1MM	1-10MM	10-50MM	50 & OVER	ALL						
	3.0	2.4		2.9	Current	2.4	2.8	2.4	2.4	2.9
	1.8	1.6		1.7		1.5	1.5	1.3	1.5	1.7
	1.0	1.1		1.0		1.1	.9	1.0	1.0	1.0
	11.7	5.1		7.8	Receivables/Payables	6.0	7.9	3.9	6.1	7.8
	3.5 (21)	2.5		(64) 3.2		(104) 2.7	(81) 2.9	(79) 2.4	(59) 3.3	(64) 3.2
	2.0	1.8		1.8		1.4	1.2	1.7	1.7	1.8
	(46) 8.0	(28) 12.9		(31) 11.7	Revenues/Receivables	(30) 12.2	(19) 19.2	(21) 17.4	(29) 12.7	(31) 11.7
	(65) 5.6	(57) 6.4		(60) 6.1		(49) 7.5	(52) 7.1	(49) 7.5	(52) 7.0	(60) 6.1
	(92) 4.0	(77) 4.7		(83) 4.4		(80) 4.6	(81) 4.5	(80) 4.6	(72) 5.1	(83) 4.4
	(6) 57.1	(14) 25.8		(10) 35.0	Cost of Revenues/Payables	(10) 37.1	(4) 96.1	(12) 31.2	(6) 62.9	(10) 35.0
	(26) 14.1	(21) 17.1		(24) 14.9		(25) 14.8	(22) 16.9	(23) 16.2	(20) 18.3	(24) 14.9
	(51) 7.1	(49) 7.5		(48) 7.6		(47) 7.7	(44) 8.3	(51) 7.2	(42) 8.6	(48) 7.6
	4.7	6.8		5.9	Revenues/Working Capital	6.8	6.9	8.3	6.8	5.9
	8.4	16.5		10.6		17.8	21.1	18.9	14.3	10.6
	172.3	70.7		237.7		71.5	-99.3	NM	125.2	237.7
	17.5	18.8		13.2	EBIT/Interest	15.9	13.4	10.9	15.9	13.2
	(29) 1.1	(20) 8.9		(57) 2.3		(106) 5.7	(81) 4.3	(82) 4.7	(60) 2.5	(57) 2.3
	-7.8	3.6		-5.6		1.9	1.2	.7	.6	-5.6
				4.6	Net Profit + Depr., Dep., Amort./Cur. Mat. L/T/D	5.1	9.8	10.7	7.1	4.6
				(16) 2.7		(31) 2.8	(20) 4.9	(23) 2.8	(11) 4.3	(16) 2.7
				.6		1.4	1.4	1.0	2.0	.6
	.2	.3		.3	Fixed/Worth	.3	.3	.3	.4	.3
	.5	.6		.6		.7	1.0	.8	.8	.6
	1.1	1.3		1.3		2.0	3.8	2.1	3.9	1.3
	.4	.8		.6	Debt/Worth	.9	.7	.8	.9	.6
	1.0	1.4		1.3		1.9	2.2	2.2	2.4	1.3
	2.2	2.8		3.3		4.4	5.9	5.2	7.6	3.3
	27.8	40.1		37.1	% Profit Before Taxes/Tangible Net Worth	53.9	62.6	69.3	54.3	37.1
	(30) .9	(20) 17.6		(57) 12.4		(97) 24.3	(74) 30.7	(75) 23.1	(53) 13.4	(57) 12.4
	-22.8	12.2		-17.6		10.2	6.4	5.0	2.3	-17.6
	20.3	14.4		16.8	% Profit Before Taxes/Total Assets	17.6	20.9	19.5	15.7	16.8
	.6	9.9		4.0		7.4	8.6	6.8	3.9	4.0
	-14.8	1.5		-8.5		2.5	1.0	-.1	-1.5	-8.5
	1.5	.6		1.4	% Depr., Dep., Amort./Revenues	1.3	1.3	.9	1.5	1.4
	(33) 3.0	(20) 2.1		(60) 2.8		(98) 2.4	(73) 2.5	(71) 2.4	(53) 2.6	(60) 2.8
	4.9	3.0		4.9		5.3	5.3	4.9	4.7	4.9
	1.9	1.1		1.9	% Officers', Directors' Owners' Comp/Revenues	2.2	2.1	1.8	1.9	1.9
	(23) 5.6	(11) 3.5		(38) 4.2		(65) 4.2	(48) 4.5	(48) 3.7	(35) 4.1	(38) 4.2
	8.6	4.0		8.4		6.8	7.5	8.1	9.2	8.4
4139M	149582M	516428M	24081613M	24751762M	Contract Revenues ($)	10302438M	1300679M	12336218M	5251846M	24751762M
2305M	65622M	226992M	22069182M	22364101M	Total Assets ($)	3498357M	645701M	7968552M	2859822M	22364101M

© RMA 2010

M = $ thousand   MM = $ million
See Pages 9 through 22 for Explanation of Ratios and Data

CONSTRUCTION-% OF COMPLETION—Structural Steel and Precast Concrete Contractors   NAICS 238120

	Current Data Sorted by Revenue						Comparative Historical Data				

Type of Statement

0-1MM	1-10MM	10-50MM	50 & OVER	ALL	Type of Statement	4/1/05-3/31/06 ALL	4/1/06-3/31/07 ALL	4/1/07-3/31/08 ALL	4/1/08-3/31/09 ALL	4/1/09-3/31/10 ALL
		2	4	6	Unqualified	8	5	6	6	6
1	12	2		15	Reviewed	25	20	16	15	15
1	3	2		4	Compiled	9	8	6	6	4
1	1	1		3	Tax Returns	6	2	6	2	3
1	3	1	3	8	Other	6	6	5	9	8
	8 (4/1-9/30/09)		28 (10/1/09-3/31/10)							
4	19	6	7	36	**NUMBER OF STATEMENTS**	54	41	39	38	36
%	%	%	%	%	**ASSETS**	%	%	%	%	%
	26.9			25.3	Cash & Equivalents	12.6	10.8	14.2	16.5	25.3
	39.5			35.8	A/R - Progress Billings	43.2	46.6	49.1	43.5	35.8
	.6			2.7	A/R - Current Retention	2.2	1.2	1.8	3.6	2.7
	1.1			1.7	Inventory	5.8	4.3	3.6	2.8	1.7
	3.1			2.4	Cost & Est. Earnings In Excess Billings	3.9	3.8	2.6	3.9	2.4
	2.8			4.6	All Other Current	3.2	5.4	3.1	5.1	4.6
	74.1			72.5	Total Current	70.8	72.0	74.4	75.5	72.5
	16.9			19.4	Fixed Assets (net)	22.5	22.1	21.0	19.9	19.4
	.4			.3	Joint Ventures & Investments	1.1	1.2	.0	.1	.3
	.2			.1	Intangibles (net)	.8	.3	.4	.2	.1
	8.4			7.7	All Other Non-Current	4.8	4.4	4.2	4.4	7.7
	100.0			100.0	Total	100.0	100.0	100.0	100.0	100.0
					LIABILITIES					
	13.4			10.3	Notes Payable-Short Term	7.2	10.0	16.6	5.7	10.3
	13.1			11.4	A/P - Trade	17.1	16.9	22.0	15.0	11.4
	.0			1.0	A/P - Retention	.0	.0	.0	1.3	1.0
	3.5			4.1	Billings in Excess of Costs & Est. Earnings	6.8	4.4	5.9	6.4	4.1
	.0			.0	Income Taxes Payable	.2	.7	.3	.6	.0
	2.4			3.0	Cur. Mat.-L/T/D	3.1	3.1	2.0	2.4	3.0
	5.1			5.9	All Other Current	7.7	7.3	7.2	8.8	5.9
	37.5			35.8	Total Current	42.1	42.4	53.9	40.1	35.8
	5.1			11.5	Long-Term Debt	8.0	9.1	9.9	10.3	11.5
	.5			1.1	Deferred Taxes	.6	.5	.6	.7	1.1
	4.2			3.8	All Other Non-Current	4.5	2.3	3.9	1.5	3.8
	52.7			47.7	Net Worth	44.8	45.7	31.7	47.4	47.7
	100.0			100.0	Total Liabilities & Net Worth	100.0	100.0	100.0	100.0	100.0
					INCOME DATA					
	100.0			100.0	Contract Revenues	100.0	100.0	100.0	100.0	100.0
	24.8			26.2	Gross Profit	26.5	24.2	23.5	24.0	26.2
	22.1			22.9	Operating Expenses	20.1	17.6	21.1	17.5	22.9
	2.7			3.2	Operating Profit	6.4	6.7	2.4	6.4	3.2
	.3			.1	All Other Expenses (net)	.5	.7	-.1	.1	.1
	2.3			3.1	Profit Before Taxes	5.9	6.0	2.4	6.3	3.1
					RATIOS					
	4.0			4.1		2.5	3.1	2.3	2.9	4.1
	2.2			2.3	Current	1.7	2.1	1.8	1.9	2.3
	1.3			1.4		1.3	1.2	1.0	1.3	1.4
	9.3			6.6		(51) 7.0	(39) 5.7	(36) 5.7	(35) 5.3	(34) 6.6
	(18) 4.6		(34) 4.1		Receivables/Payables	2.6	3.0	2.3	3.0	4.1
	1.7			1.7		2.0	1.5	1.5	2.2	1.7
31	11.8		32	11.6		37 10.0	32 11.4	41 8.9	47 7.7	32 11.6
52	7.1		57	6.4	Revenues/Receivables	58 6.3	57 6.4	66 5.5	56 6.5	57 6.4
64	5.7		73	5.0		81 4.5	72 5.1	85 4.3	75 4.4	73 5.0
6	59.4		10	38.1		11 31.9	12 30.6	8 47.5	9 39.2	10 38.1
15	25.2		21	17.5	Cost of Revenues/Payables	24 15.4	23 16.0	26 14.1	21 17.2	21 17.5
24	15.3		26	14.1		45 8.2	39 9.4	58 6.3	36 10.0	26 14.1
	4.7			3.8		6.2	5.3	6.4	4.9	3.8
	8.6			5.8	Revenues/Working Capital	9.8	7.9	10.8	7.6	5.8
	32.6			13.6		22.9	35.8	152.1	22.2	13.6
	7.0			35.4		(49) 28.5	(38) 57.6	(34) 21.1	(35) 63.2	(28) 35.4
	(15) 4.7		(28) 4.4		EBIT/Interest	7.7	8.4	5.6	10.8	4.4
	1.0			1.1		3.2	1.4	1.3	6.0	1.1
							8.9		53.2	
					Net Profit + Depr., Dep., Amort./Cur. Mat. L/T/D		(13) 3.7		(10) 14.5	
							1.8		2.5	
	.1			.1		.2	.2	.1	.1	.1
	.5			.5	Fixed/Worth	.5	.4	.5	.4	.5
	.7			.7		1.0	.8	2.2	.6	.7
	.4			.4		.6	.5	.8	.4	.4
	.7			.7	Debt/Worth	1.1	1.1	1.5	1.2	.7
	1.7			1.8		2.7	2.7	6.0	2.3	1.8
	32.8			42.2		(52) 62.8	(39) 62.6	(33) 50.8	(36) 62.6	(34) 42.2
	(18) 9.8		(34) 12.4		% Profit Before Taxes/ Tangible Net Worth	28.2	26.4	26.7	33.0	12.4
	1.7			.8		9.9	3.3	11.2	11.4	.8
	24.1			28.2		28.1	29.0	21.2	28.9	28.2
	7.0			5.0	% Profit Before Taxes/ Total Assets	12.4	10.1	8.0	14.5	5.0
	.9			.1		5.9	1.9	1.1	6.4	.1
	.5			.5		.6	.6	.5	.3	.5
	(16) 1.6		(28) 1.6		% Depr., Dep., Amort./ Revenues	(41) 1.3	(37) 1.1	(33) 1.0	(32) .9	(28) 1.6
	2.7			2.7		1.8	2.3	2.3	2.1	2.7
				1.0		1.8	1.8	1.5	.8	1.0
			(19) 4.2		% Officers', Directors' Owners' Comp/Revenues	(25) 4.6	(22) 3.8	(23) 5.7	(17) 3.9	(19) 4.2
				13.5		7.5	5.9	9.5	7.2	13.5
1588M	85479M	169670M	34965498M	35222235M	Contract Revenues ($)	6590392M	933909M	7791812M	761765M	35222235M
1155M	31116M	80848M	21759766M	21872885M	Total Assets ($)	3250279M	485758M	4430386M	295147M	21872885M

M = $ thousand   MM = $ million
See Pages 9 through 22 for Explanation of Ratios and Data

Current Data Sorted by Revenue   **Comparative Historical Data**

					Type of Statement					
1	11	1	1	14	Unqualified	3	3	2	3	14
1	6			7	Reviewed	36	30	20	15	7
2	4	1		7	Compiled	8	8	7	6	7
1	3			4	Tax Returns	18	8	12	10	4
					Other	9	4	7	3	4
	5 (4/1-9/30/09)		27 (10/1/09-3/31/10)			4/1/05-	4/1/06-	4/1/07-	4/1/08-	4/1/0
						3/31/06	3/31/07	3/31/08	3/31/09	3/31/
0-1MM	1-10MM	10-50MM	50 & OVER	ALL		ALL	ALL	ALL	ALL	ALL
5	24	2	1	32	NUMBER OF STATEMENTS	74	53	48	37	32
%	%	%	%	%	ASSETS	%	%	%	%	%
	13.4			15.0	Cash & Equivalents	11.6	11.1	12.9	12.9	15.0
	43.9			40.3	A/R - Progress Billings	39.7	41.4	42.1	36.0	40.3
	2.6			1.9	A/R - Current Retention	4.6	5.6	1.7	5.6	1.9
	.9			1.2	Inventory	2.8	1.0	4.9	2.5	1.2
	1.6			1.4	Cost & Est. Earnings In Excess Billings	2.6	3.5	2.7	2.4	1.4
	4.4			3.7	All Other Current	4.1	5.0	4.4	8.5	3.7
	66.7			63.5	Total Current	65.5	67.6	68.7	67.8	63.5
	20.8			25.6	Fixed Assets (net)	26.3	23.4	22.1	24.7	25.6
	3.0			2.3	Joint Ventures & Investments	.6	1.5	1.3	.5	2.3
	2.1			1.7	Intangibles (net)	2.0	.0	.7	1.2	1.7
	7.4			6.9	All Other Non-Current	5.7	7.5	7.2	5.8	6.9
	100.0			100.0	Total	100.0	100.0	100.0	100.0	100.0
					LIABILITIES					
	16.6			23.9	Notes Payable-Short Term	10.3	11.6	10.5	12.8	23.9
	13.8			12.3	A/P - Trade	16.3	15.5	20.7	15.1	12.3
	.0			.0	A/P - Retention	.2	.0	.1	.0	.0
	2.6			2.5	Billings in Excess of Costs & Est. Earnings	6.3	8.6	5.7	6.3	2.5
	.1			.1	Income Taxes Payable	.7	.4	.3	.2	.1
	2.8			2.8	Cur. Mat.-L/T/D	3.8	3.1	3.1	2.7	2.8
	6.4			6.9	All Other Current	7.7	8.7	8.1	9.0	6.9
	42.3			48.5	Total Current	45.3	47.9	48.4	46.2	48.5
	15.4			14.3	Long-Term Debt	13.9	9.9	15.3	16.0	14.3
	.4			.3	Deferred Taxes	.7	.5	.7	.5	.3
	.8			9.8	All Other Non-Current	3.4	3.4	5.0	7.2	9.8
	41.0			27.1	Net Worth	36.7	38.2	30.6	30.2	27.1
	100.0			100.0	Total Liabilities & Net Worth	100.0	100.0	100.0	100.0	100.0
					INCOME DATA					
	100.0			100.0	Contract Revenues	100.0	100.0	100.0	100.0	100.0
	20.6			25.2	Gross Profit	27.6	25.3	26.8	24.2	25.2
	21.4			24.4	Operating Expenses	23.2	20.8	24.8	20.7	24.4
	-.8			.8	Operating Profit	4.4	4.5	2.0	3.6	.8
	-.3			-.1	All Other Expenses (net)	.0	.2	.1	.4	-.1
	-.5			.8	Profit Before Taxes	4.4	4.4	1.9	3.1	.8
					RATIOS					
	4.1			3.7		2.4	2.0	1.9	2.2	3.7
	1.7			1.8	Current	1.6	1.6	1.6	1.5	1.8
	1.0			1.0		1.2	1.2	1.2	1.1	1.0
	9.0			7.7		6.0	8.1	4.5	6.0	7.7
(22)	5.5	(28)		5.5	Receivables/Payables	(70) 3.4	(50) 3.4	(46) 2.8	(32) 3.6	(28) 5.5
	3.0			3.2		1.7	2.2	1.7	2.2	3.2
44 8.3		33 11.2				31 11.7	35 10.6	36 10.2	13 29.0	33 11.2
60 6.1		57 6.5			Revenues/Receivables	58 6.3	63 5.8	57 6.4	48 7.6	57 6.5
87 4.2		85 4.3				83 4.4	84 4.3	83 4.4	84 4.3	85 4.3
5 70.2		4 88.0				11 31.9	6 62.5	10 38.1	4 87.6	4 88.0
15 25.2		15 25.2			Cost of Revenues/Payables	21 17.2	17 21.7	26 14.2	21 17.3	15 25.2
30 12.1		33 11.1				35 10.4	35 10.5	53 6.9	33 11.0	33 11.1
	4.6			4.9		7.1	7.9	6.7	7.3	4.9
	9.1			9.1	Revenues/Working Capital	11.6	10.5	12.2	14.6	9.1
	-450.9			-185.6		27.8	42.5	53.4	100.8	-185.6
	19.7			17.2		18.8	18.8	17.7	12.0	17.2
(22)	6.8	(28)		6.6	EBIT/Interest	(68) 5.4	(46) 6.7	(44) 3.4	(32) 2.9	(28) 6.6
	-10.3			-8.5		1.5	2.0	.6	-.6	-8.5
					Net Profit + Depr., Dep., Amort./Cur. Mat. L/T/D	6.7	9.2			
						(18) 4.0	(14) 3.1			
						2.1	1.4			
	.2			.2		.3	.3	.2	.2	.2
	.3			.4	Fixed/Worth	.5	.5	.4	.5	.4
	2.1			2.3		1.3	1.1	1.3	1.6	2.3
	.2			.3		.7	.9	.9	.7	.3
	.9			.9	Debt/Worth	1.2	1.7	1.8	1.5	.9
	3.1			3.7		4.4	2.9	10.3	5.4	3.7
	34.6			54.8		66.3	59.0	45.9	80.1	54.8
(19)	2.9	(25)		9.3	% Profit Before Taxes/ Tangible Net Worth	(65) 21.3	(50) 25.5	(42) 18.4	(33) 30.6	(25) 9.3
	-26.3			-19.8		5.7	4.0	5.1	-6.0	-19.8
	20.3			25.1		20.9	22.0	15.1	35.5	25.1
	2.3			3.0	% Profit Before Taxes/ Total Assets	7.0	7.9	4.2	5.9	3.0
	-15.2			-15.2		1.3	1.4	.3	-2.7	-15.2
	1.0			1.0		1.1	.8	.8	1.0	1.0
(22)	1.4	(27)		1.6	% Depr., Dep., Amort./ Revenues	(63) 2.0	(44) 1.4	(38) 1.7	(31) 1.3	(27) 1.6
	3.6			3.4		3.9	2.4	2.7	2.2	3.4
	2.9			2.7		1.9	2.5	2.8	1.9	2.7
(15)	3.4	(20)		3.1	% Officers', Directors' Owners' Comp/Revenues	(51) 4.1	(30) 4.0	(30) 4.6	(23) 3.3	(20) 3.1
	5.9			5.8		6.7	8.0	8.0	6.2	5.8
1765M	93431M	28530M	4472338M	4596064M	Contract Revenues ($)	414066M	298397M	11599329M	252020M	4596064M
724M	33940M	8681M	1607858M	1651203M	Total Assets ($)	171555M	110686M	3908385M	85772M	1651203M

M = $ thousand   MM = $ million
See Pages 9 through 22 for Explanation of Ratios and Data

Current Data Sorted by Revenue   Comparative Historical Data

	0-1MM	1-10MM	10-50MM	50 & OVER	ALL		4/1/05-3/31/06 ALL	4/1/06-3/31/07 ALL	4/1/07-3/31/08 ALL	4/1/08-3/31/09 ALL	4/1/09-3/31/10 ALL
	8 (4/1-9/30/09)		12 (10/1/09-3/31/10)			Type of Statement					
Unqualified				1	1		3	2	2	1	1
Reviewed		4	8		12		14	14	12	13	12
Compiled		2	1		3		4	9	7	7	3
Tax Returns	1		1		2		6	5	2	4	2
Other		1	1		2		7	10	3	3	2
NUMBER OF STATEMENTS	1	7	11	1	20		34	40	26	28	20
	%	%	%	%	%	**ASSETS**	%	%	%	%	%
Cash & Equivalents			23.1		25.7		15.4	12.4	9.8	20.5	25.7
A/R - Progress Billings			48.9		42.8		45.6	54.5	56.8	49.6	42.8
A/R - Current Retention			5.5		3.1		3.3	.9	1.8	1.1	3.1
Inventory			2.2		3.2		7.4	8.9	7.9	7.7	3.2
Cost & Est. Earnings In Excess Billings			4.3		4.3		3.5	2.8	2.8	2.4	4.3
All Other Current			7.7		7.9		3.4	2.9	3.4	2.9	7.9
Total Current			91.8		87.0		78.6	82.3	82.5	84.2	87.0
Fixed Assets (net)			5.5		6.9		15.8	10.8	13.4	11.9	6.9
Joint Ventures & Investments			.1		1.2		2.6	1.4	.1	.9	1.2
Intangibles (net)			.3		.2		.2	.3	1.0	.1	.2
All Other Non-Current			2.3		4.7		2.9	5.2	3.0	2.9	4.7
Total			100.0		100.0		100.0	100.0	100.0	100.0	100.0
						LIABILITIES					
Notes Payable-Short Term			10.2		7.6		10.3	9.9	15.5	18.0	7.6
A/P - Trade			15.0		13.3		18.2	30.1	25.0	23.1	13.3
A/P - Retention			.2		.1		.0	.3	.0	.7	.1
Billings in Excess of Costs & Est. Earnings			7.8		7.5		5.5	5.9	8.9	4.9	7.5
Income Taxes Payable			1.1		.7		.2	.2	.4	.4	.7
Cur. Mat.-L/T/D			.6		1.1		2.4	2.6	3.5	2.5	1.1
All Other Current			6.4		7.5		6.7	8.3	7.3	6.2	7.5
Total Current			41.4		37.9		43.2	57.3	60.6	55.8	37.9
Long-Term Debt			.5		3.1		14.3	8.1	8.6	6.5	3.1
Deferred Taxes			.3		.2		.1	.1	.3	.3	.2
All Other Non-Current			7.2		5.2		9.0	5.9	5.0	5.2	5.2
Net Worth			50.6		53.6		33.5	28.5	25.5	32.2	53.6
Total Liabilities & Net Worth			100.0		100.0		100.0	100.0	100.0	100.0	100.0
						INCOME DATA					
Contract Revenues			100.0		100.0		100.0	100.0	100.0	100.0	100.0
Gross Profit			25.6		30.0		30.7	28.0	27.0	33.7	30.0
Operating Expenses			20.2		22.7		27.3	25.1	24.0	29.7	22.7
Operating Profit			5.5		7.3		3.5	2.9	3.0	3.9	7.3
All Other Expenses (net)			-.2		.1		-.1	-.1	.8	.1	.1
Profit Before Taxes			5.7		7.3		3.5	3.0	2.2	3.8	7.3
						RATIOS					
Current			3.9		3.9		3.3	1.6	1.9	2.8	3.9
			2.1		2.2		2.1	1.5	1.5	1.8	2.2
			1.9		1.7		1.4	1.2	1.1	1.2	1.7
Receivables/Payables			5.2		4.3		4.6	3.2	4.3	4.4	4.3
			3.4		3.5		(30) 3.6	(39) 1.9	2.5	2.1	3.5
			2.5		2.0		1.9	1.2	1.8	1.4	2.0
Revenues/Receivables		52	7.0	31	11.7		35 10.4	45 8.2	53 6.9	38 9.6	31 11.7
		61	6.0	56	6.5		56 6.5	59 6.2	74 4.9	59 6.1	56 6.5
		82	4.4	74	4.9		102 3.6	84 4.3	101 3.6	90 4.1	74 4.9
Cost of Revenues/Payables		17	22.0	17	21.4		11 34.2	29 12.7	26 13.8	20 18.1	17 21.4
		24	15.4	24	15.3		30 12.2	46 8.0	41 8.9	39 9.4	24 15.3
		26	14.0	28	13.2		44 8.3	61 6.0	64 5.7	58 6.3	28 13.2
Revenues/Working Capital			5.4		4.2		5.3	7.6	7.4	6.2	4.2
			7.9		8.0		8.1	12.9	10.8	10.4	8.0
			9.8		9.9		17.2	28.4	30.6	29.4	9.9
EBIT/Interest					95.1		59.6	12.1	17.0	22.0	95.1
				(17)	25.2		(29) 7.9	(32) 3.9	(23) 4.8	(23) 9.8	(17) 25.2
					6.4		4.1	.8	1.6	2.8	6.4
Net Profit + Depr., Dep., Amort./Cur. Mat. L/T/D											
Fixed/Worth			.0		.0		.1	.1	.2	.0	.0
			.1		.1		.2	.3	.4	.3	.1
			.2		.2		.8	1.4	1.1	.6	.2
Debt/Worth			.7		.4		.4	1.5	1.3	.5	.4
			1.0		1.0		1.2	2.1	1.9	1.5	1.0
			1.1		1.1		3.6	7.5	4.4	2.7	1.1
% Profit Before Taxes/Tangible Net Worth			76.2		69.7		41.5	67.0	43.9	78.5	69.7
			33.1		30.4		(30) 12.3	(36) 19.0	(22) 26.3	(26) 29.7	30.4
			11.2		11.4		5.6	5.2	7.5	8.2	11.4
% Profit Before Taxes/Total Assets			30.4		28.9		14.4	23.2	18.0	38.5	28.9
			16.1		13.8		7.2	4.0	5.9	7.7	13.8
			5.7		5.8		2.6	-.9	1.3	4.1	5.8
% Depr., Dep., Amort./Revenues			.2		.4		.5	.2	.5	.3	.4
			(10) .5		(16) .6		(30) .7	(34) .5	(24) .9	(24) .6	(16) .6
			1.0		1.2		1.3	1.1	1.5	1.8	1.2
% Officers', Directors' Owners' Comp/Revenues					1.7		1.8	2.4	3.0	2.0	1.7
			(12)		5.0		(25) 4.8	(29) 3.7	(14) 7.5	(15) 5.4	(12) 5.0
					12.1		8.5	7.3	9.9	9.6	12.1
Contract Revenues ($)	647M	33232M	187036M	140533M	361448M		588311M	1438839M	814614M	938669M	361448M
Total Assets ($)	225M	11065M	60474M	122435M	194199M		197809M	371899M	274050M	347489M	194199M

© RMA 2010

M = $ thousand   MM = $ million
See Pages 9 through 22 for Explanation of Ratios and Data

Current Data Sorted by Revenue   ## Comparative Historical Data

Type of Statement / Number of Statements

Type of Statement	0-1MM	1-10MM	10-50MM	50 & OVER	ALL		4/1/05-3/31/06 ALL	4/1/06-3/31/07 ALL	4/1/07-3/31/08 ALL	4/1/08-3/31/09 ALL	4/1/0?-3/31/1? ALL
Unqualified		1	1		2		10	12	7	3	2
Reviewed	2	17	6	2	27		48	42	40	29	27
Compiled	1	7	1		9		21	12	16	8	9
Tax Returns	1	5	1		7		10	8	5	8	7
Other	1	8	2		11		20	17	10	8	11

Periods (current): 8 (4/1-9/30/09) — 48 (10/1/09-3/31/10)

	0-1MM	1-10MM	10-50MM	50 & OVER	ALL		'06	'07	'08	'09	'10
NUMBER OF STATEMENTS	5	38	11	2	56		109	91	78	56	56

ASSETS (%)

Assets	0-1MM	1-10MM	10-50MM	50 & OVER	ALL		'06	'07	'08	'09	'10
Cash & Equivalents		14.7	10.7		13.9		9.4	11.4	16.3	16.1	13.9
A/R - Progress Billings		42.5	41.2		41.4		46.0	46.5	40.0	42.6	41.4
A/R - Current Retention		1.2	4.5		1.7		1.8	2.7	1.8	1.8	1.7
Inventory		8.9	6.8		8.5		6.6	6.1	4.6	4.5	8.5
Cost & Est. Earnings In Excess Billings		3.0	5.2		3.2		5.4	4.4	4.6	4.3	3.2
All Other Current		3.8	4.0		3.5		4.9	3.6	5.9	4.0	3.5
Total Current		74.1	72.4		72.2		74.0	74.7	73.2	73.2	72.2
Fixed Assets (net)		19.6	17.8		20.7		18.7	17.7	18.2	18.9	20.7
Joint Ventures & Investments		.1	.2		.1		.3	.1	.4	.6	.1
Intangibles (net)		.9	4.5		1.7		1.0	1.7	1.5	1.2	1.7
All Other Non-Current		5.2	5.1		5.3		6.0	5.8	6.8	6.1	5.3
Total		100.0	100.0		100.0		100.0	100.0	100.0	100.0	100.0

LIABILITIES

Liabilities	0-1MM	1-10MM	10-50MM	50 & OVER	ALL		'06	'07	'08	'09	'10
Notes Payable-Short Term		11.3	10.1		10.1		9.4	8.7	6.5	10.2	10.1
A/P - Trade		21.2	14.6		19.1		22.3	20.6	20.4	20.2	19.1
A/P - Retention		.3	.0		.2		.6	.5	.3	.6	.2
Billings in Excess of Costs & Est. Earnings		2.8	9.4		4.0		4.8	6.7	4.7	4.1	4.0
Income Taxes Payable		.2	.0		.1		.2	.4	.5	.3	.1
Cur. Mat.-L/T/D		2.1	4.9		3.0		4.1	3.4	3.1	3.0	3.0
All Other Current		5.2	11.5		6.6		6.9	8.5	8.4	8.5	6.6
Total Current		43.0	50.5		43.0		48.4	48.8	43.7	46.7	43.0
Long-Term Debt		10.2	3.4		10.2		12.9	10.1	8.9	10.3	10.2
Deferred Taxes		2.0	.0		1.4		.8	.4	.7	.7	1.4
All Other Non-Current		3.2	1.6		4.0		5.3	4.3	2.2	3.4	4.0
Net Worth		41.6	44.5		41.5		32.6	36.5	44.5	38.8	41.5
Total Liabilties & Net Worth		100.0	100.0		100.0		100.0	100.0	100.0	100.0	100.0

INCOME DATA

Income Data	0-1MM	1-10MM	10-50MM	50 & OVER	ALL		'06	'07	'08	'09	'10
Contract Revenues		100.0	100.0		100.0		100.0	100.0	100.0	100.0	100.0
Gross Profit		27.1	24.3		26.9		27.0	29.6	29.3	29.6	26.9
Operating Expenses		27.9	19.1		25.3		23.5	23.7	23.3	24.4	25.3
Operating Profit		-.8	5.1		1.5		3.6	5.9	6.0	5.3	1.5
All Other Expenses (net)		.3	-1.2		.0		.3	.1	.4	.2	.0
Profit Before Taxes		-1.1	6.3		1.5		3.3	5.8	5.6	5.1	1.5

RATIOS

Ratio	0-1MM	1-10MM	10-50MM	50 & OVER	ALL		'06	'07	'08	'09	'10
Current		2.2	2.7		2.4		2.1	2.4	2.7	2.8	2.4
		1.7	2.1		1.7		1.5	1.6	1.7	1.6	1.7
		1.3	1.0		1.3		1.2	1.2	1.3	1.1	1.3
Receivables/Payables		4.6	12.2		4.6		4.0	4.5	4.5	6.0	4.6
		2.1	3.7	(55) 2.2			(104) 2.3	(90) 2.5	(76) 2.3	(53) 2.6	(55) 2.2
		1.3	2.0		1.4		1.3	1.6	1.4	1.4	1.4
Revenues/Receivables	31 / 11.9	40 / 9.2	33 / 11.1				36 / 10.2	43 / 8.6	32 / 11.5	27 / 13.3	33 / 11.1
	54 / 6.7	56 / 6.7	54 / 6.7				62 / 5.9	59 / 6.2	48 / 7.6	53 / 6.9	54 / 6.7
	69 / 5.3	87 / 4.2	77 / 4.8				77 / 4.7	76 / 4.8	71 / 5.1	73 / 5.0	77 / 4.8
Cost of Revenues/Payables	18 / 20.9	8 / 48.2	15 / 25.0				19 / 19.0	15 / 24.3	15 / 24.7	11 / 33.5	15 / 25.0
	34 / 10.8	20 / 18.3	29 / 12.6				33 / 11.0	28 / 13.3	32 / 11.6	26 / 14.3	29 / 12.6
	51 / 7.1	27 / 13.4	52 / 7.0				55 / 6.7	51 / 7.2	49 / 7.4	50 / 7.3	52 / 7.0
Revenues/Working Capital		7.1	7.8		7.1		7.3	6.7	5.5	6.9	7.1
		10.8	12.1		11.5		11.9	12.3	11.2	15.4	11.5
		18.1	-999.8		20.5		30.9	26.3	22.3	64.4	20.5
EBIT/Interest		12.2	318.8		18.3		14.7	22.7	30.8	34.8	18.3
	(33) 3.9	(10) 151.0	(48) 4.6				(106) 6.5	(82) 7.4	(67) 9.4	(47) 8.0	(48) 4.6
		-1.2	1.3		-.7		2.6	2.6	2.7	1.2	-.7
Net Profit + Depr., Dep., Amort./Cur. Mat. L/T/D		9.3			10.3		5.7	13.2	13.8		10.3
	(11) 2.7		(14) 2.4				(33) 2.6	(20) 4.5	(16) 5.3	(14) 2.4	
		1.7			.7		1.3	1.8	2.2		.7
Fixed/Worth		.2	.1		.2		.2	.2	.1	.1	.2
		.4	.5		.4		.4	.4	.3	.4	.4
		1.1	2.2		1.2		1.3	.9	.8	.9	1.2
Debt/Worth		.7	.4		.5		.9	.9	.6	.5	.5
		1.7	.5		1.6		1.6	1.8	1.2	1.5	1.6
		3.2	3.7		3.4		4.2	3.0	2.2	3.5	3.4
% Profit Before Taxes/Tangible Net Worth		28.6			37.6		45.7	53.7	70.7	67.6	37.6
	(37) 5.0		(53) 6.3				(96) 25.7	(83) 29.4	(73) 35.3	(49) 35.5	(53) 6.3
		-17.6			-11.0		7.6	11.3	10.8	5.8	-11.0
% Profit Before Taxes/Total Assets		15.6	26.2		22.8		17.8	30.5	28.5	28.5	22.8
		1.6	23.9		3.5		7.9	9.8	12.0	12.1	3.5
		-7.1	.8		-5.6		2.9	4.6	3.4	.8	-5.6
% Depr., Dep., Amort./Revenues		.5			.6		.9	.6	.8	1.0	.6
	(35) 1.6		(50) 1.6				(95) 1.2	(75) 1.0	(67) 1.3	(46) 1.5	(50) 1.6
		2.1			2.4		1.9	2.2	2.1	2.0	2.4
% Officers', Directors' Owners' Comp/Revenues		2.2			1.9		2.2	1.9	2.1	1.9	1.9
	(28) 4.0		(37) 3.6				(67) 3.2	(53) 3.1	(52) 4.7	(35) 3.1	(37) 3.6
		6.2			5.2		7.4	7.0	6.8	6.3	5.2
Contract Revenues ($)	2932M	187159M	198369M	243180M	631640M		5788234M	5381093M	596818M	446313M	631640M
Total Assets ($)	1990M	66828M	80291M	59091M	208200M		3225718M	3807916M	225859M	144742M	208200M

M = $ thousand   MM = $ million
See Pages 9 through 22 for Explanation of Ratios and Data

CONSTRUCTION-% OF COMPLETION—Electrical Contractors NAICS 238210

Current Data Sorted by Revenue						Comparative Historical Data				

Type of Statement

0-1MM	1-10MM	10-50MM	50 & OVER	ALL	Type of Statement	4/1/05-3/31/06	4/1/06-3/31/07	4/1/07-3/31/08	4/1/08-3/31/09	4/1/09-3/31/10
3	4	7	6	17	Unqualified	33	31	24	15	17
	48	25	4	80	Reviewed	140	115	100	80	80
1	27	1	1	29	Compiled	44	36	27	21	29
11	17	1	1	30	Tax Returns	49	43	41	34	30
5	19	8	3	35	Other	39	55	55	31	35
						ALL	ALL	ALL	ALL	ALL
43 (4/1-9/30/09)		148 (10/1/09-3/31/10)								
20	115	42	14	191	NUMBER OF STATEMENTS	305	280	247	181	191
%	%	%	%	%	**ASSETS**	%	%	%	%	%
13.5	15.7	22.0	21.0	17.3	Cash & Equivalents	11.6	12.4	14.0	14.6	17.3
32.9	41.7	42.0	32.8	40.2	A/R - Progress Billings	46.3	47.4	46.4	41.2	40.2
.0	1.1	2.4	1.6	1.3	A/R - Current Retention	2.3	1.8	1.9	2.5	1.3
4.1	6.9	4.9	1.3	5.8	Inventory	6.7	7.1	6.9	6.3	5.8
.6	4.6	6.9	6.1	4.8	Cost & Est. Earnings In Excess Billings	4.8	4.2	4.7	4.4	4.8
1.4	4.1	7.6	19.0	5.7	All Other Current	4.2	5.2	5.1	5.9	5.7
52.6	74.1	85.8	81.7	75.0	Total Current	76.0	78.0	79.0	74.9	75.0
33.1	17.3	10.2	14.7	17.2	Fixed Assets (net)	16.6	15.1	13.9	17.4	17.2
.0	.9	.6	.3	.7	Joint Ventures & Investments	1.0	.7	.7	.4	.7
.7	.8	.5	.2	.7	Intangibles (net)	1.4	1.2	1.5	1.4	.7
13.5	6.9	2.9	3.1	6.4	All Other Non-Current	5.0	5.0	5.2	5.9	6.4
100.0	100.0	100.0	100.0	100.0	Total	100.0	100.0	100.0	100.0	100.0
					LIABILITIES					
16.5	15.2	4.9	.9	12.0	Notes Payable-Short Term	11.4	12.0	9.9	10.4	12.0
19.4	18.3	15.8	12.9	17.5	A/P - Trade	20.4	20.5	20.0	16.5	17.5
.0	.0	.5	.1	.1	A/P - Retention	.2	.2	.2	.1	.1
.3	4.9	11.4	13.5	6.5	Billings in Excess of Costs & Est. Earnings	5.5	5.8	7.1	7.7	6.5
.1	.3	.2	.4	.3	Income Taxes Payable	.4	.2	.2	.5	.3
3.6	4.4	1.3	5.2	3.7	Cur. Mat.-L/T/D	3.3	2.4	2.7	3.3	3.7
4.1	8.1	11.7	14.7	8.9	All Other Current	9.0	9.4	8.2	8.8	8.9
44.0	51.1	45.7	47.7	48.9	Total Current	50.2	50.5	48.2	47.3	48.9
32.1	10.4	3.7	7.2	11.0	Long-Term Debt	9.9	11.4	11.7	10.2	11.0
.0	.8	.5	.5	.6	Deferred Taxes	.5	.6	.5	.7	.6
11.7	3.5	4.7	3.8	4.6	All Other Non-Current	4.2	3.9	3.9	4.0	4.6
12.2	34.2	45.3	40.8	34.8	Net Worth	35.2	33.7	35.6	37.7	34.8
100.0	100.0	100.0	100.0	100.0	Total Liabilties & Net Worth	100.0	100.0	100.0	100.0	100.0
					INCOME DATA					
100.0	100.0	100.0	100.0	100.0	Contract Revenues	100.0	100.0	100.0	100.0	100.0
54.3	29.6	21.3	26.4	30.1	Gross Profit	26.9	26.8	27.4	28.9	30.1
55.3	28.7	17.1	20.1	28.3	Operating Expenses	22.9	22.5	21.8	24.4	28.3
-1.0	.9	4.2	6.3	1.8	Operating Profit	4.0	4.3	5.5	4.4	1.8
1.0	.4	.1	.4	.4	All Other Expenses (net)	.1	.5	.4	.5	.4
-2.1	.5	4.2	5.9	1.4	Profit Before Taxes	3.9	3.8	5.1	3.9	1.4
					RATIOS					
2.8	2.6	2.6	3.0	2.6	Current	2.2	2.6	2.6	2.7	2.6
1.3	1.6	1.9	1.6	1.7		1.6	1.6	1.7	1.7	1.7
.6	1.1	1.5	1.1	1.1		1.2	1.2	1.2	1.3	1.1
11.3	3.8	5.6	UND	4.7	Receivables/Payables	4.3	4.5	4.8	5.3	4.7
(17) 1.9	(110) 2.6	3.6	2.4	(183) 2.7		(293) 2.6	(265) 2.5	(240) 2.6	(171) 3.0	(183) 2.7
1.3	1.7	1.8	1.4	1.7		1.8	1.7	1.5	1.7	1.7
10 36.3	35 10.3	40 9.0	0 UND	10.7	Revenues/Receivables	41 9.0	40 9.0	40 9.1	35 10.4	34 10.7
21 17.3	48 7.6	59 6.2	56 6.5	7.4		62 5.9	61 6.0	59 6.2	52 7.0	49 7.4
81 4.5	70 5.2	77 4.8	71 5.1	5.0		85 4.3	81 4.5	78 4.7	72 5.1	72 5.0
0 UND	13 27.8	11 32.5	0 UND	32.5	Cost of Revenues/Payables	17 21.9	15 23.8	15 25.0	11 33.2	11 32.5
30 12.0	26 14.2	23 15.8	18 20.7	14.7		31 11.7	30 12.3	28 12.9	23 16.1	25 14.7
94 3.9	45 8.1	30 12.3	40 9.1	8.8		46 8.0	49 7.4	48 7.7	41 9.0	42 8.8
5.9	5.2	5.0	5.7	5.2	Revenues/Working Capital	6.7	6.5	5.8	6.4	5.2
22.9	11.2	7.8	10.6	10.2		10.6	9.8	9.5	10.0	10.2
-54.3	75.1	9.7	22.2	48.5		25.9	22.7	22.0	21.2	48.5
13.8	8.3	38.7	45.7	13.6	EBIT/Interest	20.3	19.0	25.0	32.3	13.6
(16) .7	(103) 3.1	(35) 10.7	(11) 21.3	(165) 4.3		(258) 6.4	(249) 6.3	(217) 6.9	(160) 9.2	(165) 4.3
-3.1	-5.0	3.3	6.4	-1.2		1.8	1.7	2.2	1.6	-1.2
	6.3	13.0		9.6	Net Profit + Depr., Dep., Amort./Cur. Mat. L/T/D	10.3	13.2	10.9	9.8	9.6
(22)	2.4	(10) 6.4		(35) 2.9		(72) 3.7	(55) 5.0	(38) 4.2	(32) 3.9	(35) 2.9
	.0	2.4		1.4		1.9	1.5	.9	1.2	1.4
.6	.1	.1	.2	.1	Fixed/Worth	.2	.1	.1	.2	.1
1.0	.4	.2	.3	.4		.3	.3	.3	.3	.4
NM	1.3	.4	.7	1.1		.9	.8	.8	1.0	1.1
1.1	.7	.5	.8	.7	Debt/Worth	.9	.8	.8	.7	.7
3.6	1.7	1.4	1.4	1.6		1.7	1.8	1.7	1.6	1.6
NM	4.9	2.4	2.5	4.4		4.3	4.6	4.8	3.6	4.4
75.0	41.1	39.8	67.9	44.2	% Profit Before Taxes/Tangible Net Worth	54.1	57.4	63.8	54.8	44.2
(15) 52.4	(100) 9.0	(40) 22.4	(13) 30.8	(168) 18.2		(272) 24.2	(248) 29.9	(219) 31.2	(159) 27.8	(168) 18.2
-65.8	-8.7	12.6	15.8	-1.9		5.8	12.0	10.1	4.8	-1.9
24.8	15.0	19.6	23.7	17.2	% Profit Before Taxes/Total Assets	22.3	21.0	24.8	23.6	17.2
.6	3.1	7.7	11.4	5.0		8.5	9.7	11.0	7.9	5.0
-17.5	-6.5	3.2	5.6	-2.4		1.8	2.1	2.8	1.5	-2.4
1.2	.6	.5		.5	% Depr., Dep., Amort./Revenues	.6	.5	.4	.5	.5
(16) 2.5	(102) 1.2	(38) .7	(164)	1.1		(268) 1.1	(236) 1.0	(194) .9	(148) 1.0	(164) 1.1
4.2	2.1	1.4		2.0		1.8	1.6	1.5	2.1	2.0
6.9	3.4	2.3		3.4	% Officers', Directors' Owners' Comp/Revenues	2.6	2.1	2.3	2.4	3.4
(13) 10.8	(71) 5.5	(25) 3.7	(118)	5.4		(182) 4.5	(167) 4.2	(141) 4.1	(109) 4.8	(118) 5.4
18.0	7.5	6.9		9.1		8.4	7.3	7.8	8.4	9.1
13407M	504331M	883364M	25229670M	26630772M	Contract Revenues ($)	13065767M	6016563M	8309209M	48104221M	26630772M
5143M	267378M	337794M	9832148M	10442463M	Total Assets ($)	4378559M	1993266M	2438338M	24767710M	10442463M

M = $ thousand   MM = $ million
See Pages 9 through 22 for Explanation of Ratios and Data

Current Data Sorted by Revenue   **Comparative Historical Data**

0-1MM	1-10MM	10-50MM	50 & OVER	ALL	Type of Statement	4/1/05-3/31/06 ALL	4/1/06-3/31/07 ALL	4/1/07-3/31/08 ALL	4/1/08-3/31/09 ALL	4/1/09-3/31/10 ALL
	2	10	2	14	Unqualified	31	22	18	6	14
	50	26	5	81	Reviewed	124	108	101	76	81
	24	4	1	29	Compiled	47	41	51	37	29
14	27	3		44	Tax Returns	57	42	62	54	44
3	28	4	3	38	Other	61	48	35	36	38
49 (4/1-9/30/09)		157 (10/1/09-3/31/10)								
17	131	47	11	206	**NUMBER OF STATEMENTS**	320	261	267	209	206
%	%	%	%	%	**ASSETS**	%	%	%	%	%
12.9	17.4	20.5	15.1	17.6	Cash & Equivalents	12.9	11.4	14.7	14.5	17.6
22.8	36.9	44.0	40.3	37.5	A/R - Progress Billings	41.2	42.7	40.4	38.7	37.5
.0	1.4	1.6	2.6	1.4	A/R - Current Retention	1.9	2.6	1.5	1.9	1.4
10.3	10.7	3.4	5.2	8.7	Inventory	9.0	8.8	7.8	9.8	8.7
.0	2.2	4.4	2.8	2.6	Cost & Est. Earnings In Excess Billings	3.6	3.9	2.9	2.5	2.6
.8	4.3	6.9	10.9	5.0	All Other Current	4.9	4.4	5.5	5.1	5.0
46.8	72.9	80.8	76.7	72.8	Total Current	73.5	73.8	72.8	72.4	72.8
28.0	19.3	10.4	17.5	17.9	Fixed Assets (net)	18.2	17.5	17.3	18.8	17.9
4.1	.5	.5	.4	.8	Joint Ventures & Investments	.7	.5	.7	.9	.8
8.3	1.9	.8	.0	2.1	Intangibles (net)	1.7	1.5	2.2	2.0	2.1
12.9	5.4	7.4	5.4	6.5	All Other Non-Current	6.0	6.6	7.0	5.9	6.5
100.0	100.0	100.0	100.0	100.0	Total	100.0	100.0	100.0	100.0	100.0
					LIABILITIES					
15.5	14.9	5.7	12.7	12.7	Notes Payable-Short Term	11.3	9.8	8.9	12.9	12.7
27.1	22.4	22.9	20.8	22.8	A/P - Trade	22.5	23.1	21.5	21.9	22.8
.0	.3	.5	.7	.4	A/P - Retention	.4	.1	.2	.2	.4
.0	3.5	11.0	7.4	5.1	Billings in Excess of Costs & Est. Earnings	4.7	6.0	6.6	5.9	5.1
.0	.1	.4	.0	.2	Income Taxes Payable	.4	.3	.4	.3	.2
8.6	5.7	2.0	4.2	5.0	Cur. Mat.-L/T/D	4.6	3.6	4.2	3.7	5.0
8.0	11.1	9.1	12.2	10.5	All Other Current	8.7	9.6	11.1	10.0	10.5
59.3	58.0	51.6	58.0	56.7	Total Current	52.5	52.5	52.9	54.9	56.7
39.3	19.1	4.2	11.7	17.0	Long-Term Debt	14.3	12.9	12.5	17.0	17.0
.0	.3	.8	.3	.4	Deferred Taxes	.5	.5	.4	.3	.4
9.0	5.4	1.7	1.3	4.6	All Other Non-Current	5.1	5.3	5.7	6.5	4.6
-7.5	17.1	41.8	28.7	21.3	Net Worth	27.6	28.9	28.4	21.3	21.3
100.0	100.0	100.0	100.0	100.0	Total Liabilities & Net Worth	100.0	100.0	100.0	100.0	100.0
					INCOME DATA					
100.0	100.0	100.0	100.0	100.0	Contract Revenues	100.0	100.0	100.0	100.0	100.0
48.0	31.2	19.6	21.0	29.4	Gross Profit	28.6	27.5	30.7	30.0	29.4
46.4	28.6	15.3	18.7	26.5	Operating Expenses	24.9	23.2	26.1	26.7	26.5
1.6	2.6	4.3	2.2	2.9	Operating Profit	3.6	4.3	4.6	3.4	2.9
2.6	.4	.0	.5	.5	All Other Expenses (net)	.4	.4	.3	.8	.5
-1.0	2.2	4.2	1.7	2.4	Profit Before Taxes	3.2	4.0	4.3	2.6	2.4
					RATIOS					
2.4	2.7	2.0	1.6	2.3		2.2	2.0	2.0	2.4	2.3
.7	1.4	1.6	1.5	1.5	Current	1.4	1.4	1.4	1.5	1.5
.4	1.0	1.2	1.1	1.0		1.1	1.1	1.1	1.1	1.0
2.0	3.9	3.0	4.1	3.3		3.5	3.6	4.0	3.8	3.3
(15) .4	(125) 1.9	2.3	(10) 1.6	(197) 1.9	Receivables/Payables	(304) 2.1	(246) 2.2	(245) 2.1	(194) 1.9	(197) 1.9
.1	1.0	1.4	1.1	1.0		1.3	1.3	1.2	1.4	1.0
0 UND	23 16.1	32 11.4	15 25.0	20 18.6		29 12.8	30 12.3	24 15.5	18 20.0	20 18.6
13 28.8	39 9.3	55 6.7	44 8.3	40 9.0	Revenues/Receivables	49 7.5	56 6.6	47 7.8	47 7.7	40 9.0
32 11.4	67 5.4	67 5.0	59 6.2	67 5.4		73 5.0	76 4.8	70 5.2	71 5.1	67 5.4
18 20.7	16 22.6	21 17.0	10 36.2	18 20.7		19 18.9	18 20.8	15 24.7	15 25.2	18 20.7
29 12.7	25 14.4	31 11.9	19 19.5	27 13.3	Cost of Revenues/Payables	30 12.1	33 11.1	28 13.3	26 13.8	27 13.3
56 6.5	47 7.8	46 8.0	43 8.5	45 8.1		45 8.1	49 7.4	47 7.8	49 7.5	45 8.1
15.0	6.0	6.6	10.4	6.8		8.2	7.7	8.2	7.3	6.8
-55.4	18.7	10.4	14.8	15.3	Revenues/Working Capital	15.1	15.2	16.0	13.6	15.3
-7.4	-277.7	31.5	47.8	521.3		58.5	57.0	85.8	94.0	521.3
3.2	12.2	66.7		15.2		18.2	17.5	23.8	17.6	15.2
(12) .9	(117) 3.9	(40) 13.7		(177) 5.4	EBIT/Interest	(283) 5.2	(229) 6.1	(234) 5.5	(178) 4.5	(177) 5.4
-1.0	-1.0	4.0		.8		2.0	1.7	1.6	1.0	.8
	4.6	77.3		7.7		5.9	9.3	15.8	5.3	7.7
	(24) 2.2	(14) 5.1		(38) 2.6	Net Profit + Depr., Dep., Amort./Cur. Mat. L/T/D	(78) 2.2	(61) 2.7	(53) 3.2	(32) 2.6	(38) 2.6
	-.6	.3		-.1		.9	1.0	1.2	1.4	-.1
.2	.2	.1	.1	.1		.2	.2	.2	.2	.1
1.4	.5	.2	.4	.4	Fixed/Worth	.5	.5	.4	.5	.4
-.8	-25.5	.5	1.5	2.6		1.5	1.2	1.9	2.9	2.6
1.1	.8	1.0	1.6	.9		.9	.9	1.0	1.0	.9
9.1	2.3	1.4	1.9	2.0	Debt/Worth	2.1	2.2	2.3	2.4	2.0
-2.8	-29.2	2.5	3.9	10.5		6.7	5.2	9.2	18.2	10.5
264.8	45.0	46.3	70.2	46.6		47.4	58.2	69.3	66.7	46.6
(10) 21.3	(95) 10.1	33.6	(10) 47.7	(162) 20.0	% Profit Before Taxes/Tangible Net Worth	(271) 25.2	(224) 31.3	(222) 32.5	(164) 26.8	(162) 20.0
-5.6	-1.0	12.4	3.9	2.4		7.7	6.9	10.0	7.6	2.4
17.2	18.4	17.7	16.4	17.6		16.8	21.0	23.7	19.4	17.6
.0	3.2	11.8	5.6	6.5	% Profit Before Taxes/Total Assets	8.1	9.7	9.2	7.4	6.5
-9.7	-4.3	3.7	1.7	-.8		1.2	2.0	.6	.6	-.8
1.2	.8	.4		.7		.6	.6	.6	.5	.7
(10) 2.4	(112) 1.4	(44) .8		(171) 1.1	% Depr., Dep., Amort./Revenues	(270) 1.1	(221) 1.0	(217) 1.0	(170) 1.1	(171) 1.1
5.4	2.0	1.2		1.9		1.8	1.7	1.7	1.9	1.9
5.1	3.0	1.0		2.8		1.9	1.9	2.0	2.5	2.8
(13) 10.8	(83) 5.0	(24) 2.7		(125) 5.0	% Officers', Directors' Owners' Comp/Revenues	(206) 4.3	(162) 3.8	(169) 4.4	(125) 4.4	(125) 5.0
13.6	5.4	5.5		8.2		7.4	7.3	7.7	8.2	8.2
11915M	545356M	1029448M	57069589M	58656308M	Contract Revenues ($)	6604897M	14535238M	30337111M	24041075M	58656308M
4738M	188739M	356156M	13122797M	13672430M	Total Assets ($)	1717449M	5080035M	8293981M	6055177M	13672430M

M = $ thousand   MM = $ million
See Pages 9 through 22 for Explanation of Ratios and Data

CONSTRUCTION-% OF COMPLETION—Drywall and Insulation Contractors NAICS 238310

Current Data Sorted by Revenue | Comparative Historical Data

0-1MM	1-10MM	10-50MM	50 & OVER	ALL	Type of Statement	4/1/05-3/31/06	4/1/06-3/31/07	4/1/07-3/31/08	4/1/08-3/31/09	4/1/09-3/31/10
	1	4	3	8	Unqualified	13	11	9	8	8
	14	11		25	Reviewed	46	33	40	29	25
	7			7	Compiled	14	10	11	10	7
3	5			8	Tax Returns	17	14	13	9	8
2	8	3		13	Other	13	14	14	9	13
16 (4/1-9/30/09)		45 (10/1/09-3/31/10)								
0-1MM	1-10MM	10-50MM	50 & OVER	ALL		ALL	ALL	ALL	ALL	ALL
5	35	18	3	61	**NUMBER OF STATEMENTS**	103	82	87	65	61
%	%	%	%	%	**ASSETS**	%	%	%	%	%
	15.0	21.6		17.6	Cash & Equivalents	11.7	11.6	16.4	11.7	17.6
	48.1	47.0		47.5	A/R - Progress Billings	50.6	52.7	50.0	54.6	47.5
	.8	2.2		1.4	A/R - Current Retention	3.1	2.0	2.5	2.3	1.4
	5.3	5.1		4.9	Inventory	5.9	5.1	4.9	6.1	4.9
	2.7	1.5		2.2	Cost & Est. Earnings In Excess Billings	4.6	4.6	3.6	2.9	2.2
	3.4	8.8		4.9	All Other Current	4.9	3.9	3.6	6.3	4.9
	75.3	86.3		78.5	Total Current	80.8	80.0	81.0	83.9	78.5
	12.4	6.5		12.0	Fixed Assets (net)	12.2	12.5	11.2	10.7	12.0
	.0	1.0		.3	Joint Ventures & Investments	.7	.1	1.1	.1	.3
	.7	.4		.7	Intangibles (net)	.4	.6	.3	.5	.7
	11.5	5.8		8.5	All Other Non-Current	5.8	6.9	6.5	5.0	8.5
	100.0	100.0		100.0	Total	100.0	100.0	100.0	100.0	100.0
					LIABILITIES					
	10.5	12.8		9.9	Notes Payable-Short Term	11.7	10.1	11.9	12.6	9.9
	12.7	10.8		16.6	A/P - Trade	15.1	15.2	12.5	14.2	16.6
	.0	.0		.0	A/P - Retention	.3	.1	.3	.1	.0
	5.6	8.7		6.8	Billings in Excess of Costs & Est. Earnings	6.3	5.4	10.1	7.9	6.8
	.0	.0		.0	Income Taxes Payable	.4	.2	.1	.1	.0
	1.9	.8		1.4	Cur. Mat.-L/T/D	3.3	1.9	2.3	1.4	1.4
	7.8	10.5		10.8	All Other Current	9.5	11.7	10.3	9.8	10.8
	38.4	43.7		45.6	Total Current	46.7	44.6	47.5	46.1	45.6
	5.8	2.6		5.5	Long-Term Debt	8.4	6.4	9.3	7.3	5.5
	.9	.1		.5	Deferred Taxes	.6	.6	.4	.5	.5
	9.4	.8		8.8	All Other Non-Current	4.3	7.3	7.7	3.8	8.8
	45.5	52.8		39.5	Net Worth	40.1	41.1	35.1	42.4	39.5
	100.0	100.0		100.0	Total Liabilities & Net Worth	100.0	100.0	100.0	100.0	100.0
					INCOME DATA					
	100.0	100.0		100.0	Contract Revenues	100.0	100.0	100.0	100.0	100.0
	24.0	22.9		24.8	Gross Profit	22.7	23.7	24.3	25.4	24.8
	24.9	16.9		23.4	Operating Expenses	18.5	19.4	19.5	20.6	23.4
	-.9	5.9		1.4	Operating Profit	4.2	4.3	4.9	4.8	1.4
	.3	.3		.3	All Other Expenses (net)	.1	.2	.5	.1	.3
	-1.2	5.6		1.1	Profit Before Taxes	4.1	4.1	4.4	4.7	1.1
					RATIOS					
	3.5 / 2.0 / 1.4	3.8 / 2.4 / 1.3		3.6 / 2.0 / 1.3	Current	2.6 / 1.7 / 1.3	2.9 / 1.9 / 1.3	2.9 / 1.8 / 1.4	3.6 / 1.9 / 1.3	3.6 / 2.0 / 1.3
	11.0 / (34) 4.8 / 2.7	7.8 / 5.0 / 3.8	(60) 4.8	9.6 / 4.8 / 2.7	Receivables/Payables	(98) 7.4 / 4.2 / 2.4	(79) 7.8 / 4.7 / 2.9	(79) 7.3 / 4.8 / 3.3	(64) 7.7 / 4.9 / 2.9	(60) 9.6 / 4.8 / 2.7
	44 8.3 / 54 6.8 / 72 5.1	44 8.2 / 54 6.8 / 66 5.6		44 8.3 / 54 6.8 / 69 5.3	Revenues/Receivables	51 7.1 / 65 5.6 / 80 4.6	40 9.1 / 59 6.2 / 77 4.7	37 9.7 / 67 5.5 / 81 4.5	50 7.3 / 63 5.8 / 87 4.2	44 8.3 / 54 6.8 / 69 5.3
	7 53.2 / 15 24.9 / 26 14.1	9 39.4 / 13 28.9 / 20 17.9		8 46.1 / 15 24.9 / 28 13.1	Cost of Revenues/Payables	10 37.1 / 18 20.8 / 33 11.2	9 40.3 / 16 22.5 / 27 13.4	7 50.3 / 17 21.0 / 24 15.1	9 40.9 / 17 21.6 / 30 15.1	8 46.1 / 15 24.9 / 28 13.1
	4.5 / 8.6 / 13.5	4.9 / 8.0 / 19.0		4.7 / 8.5 / 18.6	Revenues/Working Capital	6.1 / 10.1 / 17.8	6.4 / 10.0 / 20.0	6.4 / 9.6 / 16.3	5.5 / 8.4 / 16.4	4.7 / 8.5 / 18.6
	8.5 / (31) .5 / -12.1	106.8 / (14) 17.7 / 2.2	(49) 3.8	24.2 / 3.8 / -6.7	EBIT/Interest	(91) 39.4 / 7.3 / 2.3	(72) 31.5 / 12.0 / 1.9	(72) 44.4 / 9.2 / 2.3	(55) 35.4 / 8.6 / 1.5	(49) 24.2 / 3.8 / -6.7
					Net Profit + Depr., Dep., Amort./Cur. Mat. L/T/D	(24) 23.2 / 5.3 / 1.4	(14) 31.1 / 8.2 / 3.7	(17) 12.8 / 4.3 / 2.7	(11) 42.3 / 4.6 / 2.1	
	.1 / .2 / .5	.1 / .1 / .2		.1 / .1 / .5	Fixed/Worth	.1 / .2 / .5	.1 / .2 / .6	.1 / .2 / .4	.1 / .2 / .4	.1 / .1 / .5
	.4 / 1.2 / 2.4	.4 / .8 / 2.8		.4 / 1.0 / 2.5	Debt/Worth	.6 / 1.5 / 3.1	.5 / 1.2 / 2.7	.6 / 1.5 / 2.6	.6 / 1.5 / 3.0	.4 / 1.0 / 2.5
	24.8 / (31) -.3 / -42.5	59.9 / 26.9 / 11.7	(55) 16.1	32.9 / 16.1 / -10.1	% Profit Before Taxes/Tangible Net Worth	(98) 63.9 / 22.4 / 4.3	(75) 54.3 / 32.6 / 6.7	(80) 58.0 / 33.3 / 9.3	(61) 53.9 / 33.3 / 8.9	(55) 32.9 / 16.1 / -10.1
	12.7 / -.2 / -16.7	28.9 / 10.0 / 3.9		16.9 / 4.7 / -6.8	% Profit Before Taxes/Total Assets	24.1 / 8.2 / 1.8	26.9 / 13.1 / 1.2	30.7 / 11.0 / 3.1	26.2 / 10.3 / 1.3	16.9 / 4.7 / -6.8
	.6 / (31) 1.1 / 1.7	.4 / (15) .6 / .7		.5 / (51) .7 / 1.6	% Depr., Dep., Amort./Revenues	(89) .4 / .8 / 1.2	(66) .3 / .6 / 1.0	(70) .3 / .6 / 1.0	(51) .3 / .6 / 1.1	(51) .5 / .7 / 1.6
	2.5 / (19) 5.5 / 12.6		(30) 4.0	2.0 / 4.0 / 11.1	% Officers', Directors' Owners' Comp/Revenues	(64) 1.5 / 2.8 / 6.8	(51) 2.2 / 4.1 / 7.1	(57) 1.7 / 2.6 / 7.6	(37) 1.8 / 3.3 / 6.8	(30) 2.0 / 4.0 / 11.1
870M	171082M	394785M	212683M	779420M	Contract Revenues ($)	1607305M	14564606M	11179995M	8423309M	779420M
338M	70111M	139598M	87708M	297755M	Total Assets ($)	569994M	2338829M	2968525M	2531323M	297755M

M = $ thousand   MM = $ million
See Pages 9 through 22 for Explanation of Ratios and Data

Current Data Sorted by Revenue | **Comparative Historical Data**

Type of Statement

0-1MM	1-10MM	10-50MM	50 & Over	ALL	Type of Statement	4/1/05-3/31/06	4/1/06-3/31/07	4/1/07-3/31/08	4/1/08-3/31/09	4/1/09-3/31/10
	1	2		2	Unqualified	6	2	2	1	2
1	12	5		18	Reviewed	34	25	20	14	18
	6			6	Compiled	6	9	15	9	6
3	2			5	Tax Returns	7	8	12	5	5
2	11	1		14	Other	7	10	5	5	14
						4/1/05-3/31/06	4/1/06-3/31/07	4/1/07-3/31/08	4/1/08-3/31/09	4/1/09-3/31/10
10 (4/1-9/30/09)		35 (10/1/09-3/31/10)				ALL	ALL	ALL	ALL	ALL
6	31	8		45	NUMBER OF STATEMENTS	60	54	56	34	45

(Columns 0-1MM, 10-50MM, and 50 & Over marked "DATA NOT AVAILABLE" for the sections below.)

ASSETS

1-10MM %	ALL %	ASSETS	%	%	%	%	%
13.0	17.2	Cash & Equivalents	13.8	12.4	19.4	19.2	17.2
48.2	44.4	A/R - Progress Billings	48.0	46.2	43.7	39.2	44.4
.4	.3	A/R - Current Retention	.8	1.9	2.0	.3	.3
2.8	2.3	Inventory	2.3	3.4	2.5	2.4	2.3
6.2	5.4	Cost & Est. Earnings In Excess Billings	4.9	5.0	2.8	3.2	5.4
4.6	5.2	All Other Current	3.4	4.0	4.7	3.4	5.2
75.4	74.8	Total Current	73.2	72.8	75.1	67.5	74.8
15.5	16.1	Fixed Assets (net)	17.5	17.8	16.4	17.3	16.1
.9	.6	Joint Ventures & Investments	1.8	.7	1.1	.8	.6
1.5	1.1	Intangibles (net)	.8	.3	1.3	2.2	1.1
6.7	7.4	All Other Non-Current	6.7	8.4	6.2	12.1	7.4
100.0	100.0	Total	100.0	100.0	100.0	100.0	100.0

LIABILITIES

1-10MM %	ALL %	LIABILITIES	%	%	%	%	%
12.8	13.4	Notes Payable-Short Term	15.9	15.5	13.2	12.4	13.4
14.9	13.4	A/P - Trade	13.5	19.6	15.5	15.7	13.4
.0	.0	A/P - Retention	.0	.0	.1	.0	.0
2.9	3.0	Billings in Excess of Costs & Est. Earnings	2.1	3.3	2.1	2.6	3.0
.1	.2	Income Taxes Payable	.4	.5	.2	.1	.2
2.6	2.2	Cur. Mat.-L/T/D	2.6	4.6	2.8	3.0	2.2
8.4	10.0	All Other Current	8.4	9.4	12.0	7.6	10.0
41.6	42.2	Total Current	42.9	52.9	45.9	41.4	42.2
10.3	10.1	Long-Term Debt	12.0	13.0	12.7	8.9	10.1
.7	.6	Deferred Taxes	.6	.4	.6	.9	.6
8.5	6.8	All Other Non-Current	5.7	2.7	6.9	7.5	6.8
38.9	40.4	Net Worth	38.8	31.0	33.8	41.3	40.4
100.0	100.0	Total Liabilties & Net Worth	100.0	100.0	100.0	100.0	100.0

INCOME DATA

1-10MM %	ALL %	INCOME DATA	%	%	%	%	%
100.0	100.0	Contract Revenues	100.0	100.0	100.0	100.0	100.0
28.6	28.6	Gross Profit	27.7	30.6	32.6	36.5	28.6
28.5	27.6	Operating Expenses	23.9	25.9	26.8	31.2	27.6
.1	1.0	Operating Profit	3.8	4.7	5.8	5.3	1.0
.2	.1	All Other Expenses (net)	.3	.1	.4	-.5	.1
-.1	.9	Profit Before Taxes	3.6	4.6	5.5	5.8	.9

RATIOS

1-10MM	ALL	RATIOS					
3.2	3.2	Current	2.7	2.5	3.3	4.7	3.2
1.9	2.0		1.8	1.7	1.9	1.8	2.0
1.3	1.3		1.3	1.1	1.1	1.1	1.3
12.7	9.4	Receivables/Payables	(56) 6.6	(50) 7.6	(50) 8.7	(30) 11.5	(43) 9.4
(30) 5.5	(43) 4.2		3.9	3.6	3.8	4.1	4.2
1.6	1.9		2.5	1.5	2.3	2.1	1.9
39 9.3	29 12.4	Revenues/Receivables	41 8.9	33 11.2	29 12.7	27 13.7	29 12.4
59 6.1	56 6.6		72 5.1	62 5.9	54 6.8	47 7.7	56 6.6
72 5.0	72 5.1		93 3.9	79 4.6	77 4.8	79 4.6	72 5.1
7 52.4	8 43.8	Cost of Revenues/Payables	10 37.1	7 53.3	6 57.7	0 UND	8 43.8
17 21.8	14 26.0		21 17.3	21 17.5	16 22.6	14 26.7	14 26.0
46 8.0	37 9.7		36 10.0	38 9.5	34 10.8	34 10.9	37 9.7
5.0	5.0	Revenues/Working Capital	5.4	5.2	6.1	7.0	5.0
8.5	8.7		8.9	11.9	12.3	9.9	8.7
25.3	22.6		21.4	225.6	42.7	152.8	22.6
19.6	21.7	EBIT/Interest	(53) 15.4	(46) 19.2	(46) 18.5	(28) 21.2	(38) 21.7
(29) 2.3	(38) 3.8		3.8	4.9	5.4	6.8	3.8
-3.6	-3.2		1.7	2.0	1.8	1.3	-3.2
		Net Profit + Depr., Dep., Amort./Cur. Mat. L/T/D	(15) 8.3	(12) 8.2	(14) 9.1		
			2.7	2.6	2.7		
			1.3	1.6	1.4		
.1	.1	Fixed/Worth	.1	.1	.1	.1	.1
.3	.3		.3	.3	.3	.3	.3
1.0	.8		.9	1.1	1.5	.9	.8
.5	.5	Debt/Worth	.7	.7	.5	.3	.5
1.1	1.0		1.3	1.3	1.3	1.0	1.0
3.1	3.0		2.7	3.5	5.8	3.2	3.0
22.7	26.0	% Profit Before Taxes/Tangible Net Worth	(55) 44.6	(45) 55.2	(47) 55.0	(31) 74.5	(39) 26.0
(27) 5.6	(39) 12.0		23.6	20.7	26.3	28.2	12.0
-37.7	-6.0		8.0	4.7	6.0	1.6	-6.0
10.6	14.5	% Profit Before Taxes/Total Assets	16.5	30.8	29.6	41.5	14.5
2.4	3.6		8.0	6.3	12.8	13.1	3.6
-11.8	-9.4		2.4	1.9	3.1	.4	-9.4
.6	.7	% Depr., Dep., Amort./Revenues	(51) .7	(45) .6	(43) .6	(28) .7	(37) .7
(26) 1.0	(37) 1.1		1.0	.9	1.0	1.4	1.1
1.8	2.0		2.3	1.8	2.0	2.1	2.0
2.3	2.1	% Officers', Directors' Owners' Comp/Revenues	(33) 2.6	(29) 1.9	(33) 2.2	(23) 2.6	(21) 2.1
(15) 3.5	(21) 3.5		4.0	4.7	5.4	5.5	3.5
6.2	6.3		7.2	9.1	8.8	8.1	6.3

0-1MM	1-10MM	10-50MM	ALL		4/1/05-3/31/06	4/1/06-3/31/07	4/1/07-3/31/08	4/1/08-3/31/09	4/1/09-3/31/10
3543M	126084M	152699M	282326M	Contract Revenues ($)	11386706M	5392101M	2049461M	522849M	282326M
921M	47269M	56619M	104809M	Total Assets ($)	3311040M	723616M	521621M	228821M	104809M

M = $ thousand   MM = $ million
See Pages 9 through 22 for Explanation of Ratios and Data

Current Data Sorted by Revenue   Comparative Historical Data

					Type of Statement					
	4	12	3	19	Unqualified	40	38	35	28	19
3	38	19	1	61	Reviewed	95	92	82	46	61
6	6			12	Compiled	37	35	26	25	12
10	7		1	18	Tax Returns	36	26	22	27	18
8	15	4	1	28	Other	46	30	33	34	28
23 (4/1-9/30/09)		115 (10/1/09-3/31/10)				4/1/05-3/31/06	4/1/06-3/31/07	4/1/07-3/31/08	4/1/08-3/31/09	4/1/09-3/31/10
0-1MM	1-10MM	10-50MM	50 & OVER	ALL		ALL	ALL	ALL	ALL	ALL
27	70	35	6	138	NUMBER OF STATEMENTS	254	221	198	160	138
%	%	%	%	%	**ASSETS**	%	%	%	%	%
8.0	12.8	10.3		11.3	Cash & Equivalents	9.6	8.5	9.4	9.7	11.3
17.4	27.2	26.5		24.8	A/R - Progress Billings	28.7	29.3	29.9	26.7	24.8
.0	1.1	3.7		1.5	A/R - Current Retention	1.7	1.5	1.4	2.1	1.5
2.4	3.0	2.1		2.8	Inventory	3.6	3.8	3.0	2.8	2.8
.0	2.6	5.5		3.0	Cost & Est. Earnings In Excess Billings	2.5	2.4	2.2	3.0	3.0
.5	3.5	7.3		4.1	All Other Current	4.0	4.5	4.3	5.4	4.1
28.3	50.3	55.5		47.5	Total Current	50.0	49.9	50.2	49.7	47.5
64.1	41.4	38.1		45.0	Fixed Assets (net)	43.2	44.3	41.8	43.0	45.0
.0	1.2	.8		.8	Joint Ventures & Investments	.5	.7	.7	.6	.8
1.9	.1	1.9		.9	Intangibles (net)	1.1	.8	1.4	1.2	.9
5.7	7.0	3.6		5.8	All Other Non-Current	5.2	4.3	5.8	5.6	5.8
100.0	100.0	100.0		100.0	Total	100.0	100.0	100.0	100.0	100.0
					LIABILITIES					
8.8	10.8	4.8		8.6	Notes Payable-Short Term	8.9	7.3	7.5	9.8	8.6
12.4	11.5	15.7		12.6	A/P - Trade	12.5	14.1	12.6	13.1	12.6
.0	.1	.2		.1	A/P - Retention	.4	.2	.2	.2	.1
.3	1.3	5.6		2.5	Billings in Excess of Costs & Est. Earnings	3.3	3.4	4.1	3.3	2.5
.1	.0	.0		.0	Income Taxes Payable	.3	.2	.2	.3	.0
10.6	9.3	7.6		8.9	Cur. Mat.-L/T/D	7.9	8.1	8.8	7.9	8.9
10.2	3.3	6.9		5.9	All Other Current	7.0	5.3	4.6	5.5	5.9
42.4	36.5	40.9		38.6	Total Current	40.3	38.6	38.1	40.0	38.6
49.0	21.0	14.9		24.6	Long-Term Debt	23.4	21.7	22.9	20.8	24.6
.3	1.5	2.0		1.3	Deferred Taxes	1.4	1.2	1.4	1.1	1.3
8.0	3.1	3.8		3.8	All Other Non-Current	2.7	2.9	5.8	3.0	3.8
.3	37.9	40.0		31.6	Net Worth	32.2	35.5	31.8	35.1	31.6
100.0	100.0	100.0		100.0	Total Liabilities & Net Worth	100.0	100.0	100.0	100.0	100.0
					INCOME DATA					
100.0	100.0	100.0		100.0	Contract Revenues	100.0	100.0	100.0	100.0	100.0
51.6	31.6	18.7		31.9	Gross Profit	32.0	30.3	29.7	30.6	31.9
47.7	32.8	18.7		31.4	Operating Expenses	26.4	24.7	24.7	28.7	31.4
3.9	-1.2	.0		.6	Operating Profit	5.6	5.6	5.0	2.0	.6
3.9	.9	.9		1.5	All Other Expenses (net)	.8	.8	1.1	.6	1.5
.0	-2.1	-.9		-.9	Profit Before Taxes	4.8	4.8	3.9	1.3	-.9
					RATIOS					
2.0	2.8	1.8		2.1	Current	1.9	1.8	2.0	2.1	2.1
.8	1.3	1.4		1.3		1.3	1.3	1.3	1.3	1.3
.5	.9	1.1		.8		1.0	1.0	1.0	.9	.8
31.8	7.5	3.2		7.2	Receivables/Payables	4.6	3.6	5.1	5.7	7.2
(20) 3.1	(66) 3.4	(34) 1.9	(125) 2.7			(237) 2.5	(207) 2.2	(182) 2.6	(149) 2.8	(125) 2.7
1.4	1.7	1.3		1.5		1.5	1.4	1.5	1.5	1.5
0 UND	35 10.5	36 10.1	28 13.2		Revenues/Receivables	32 11.2	31 11.6	31 11.8	31 11.9	28 13.2
22 16.5	50 7.2	60 6.1	49 7.5			53 6.9	53 7.0	56 6.5	48 7.6	49 7.5
62 5.9	82 4.5	71 5.1	72 5.1			76 4.8	77 4.7	81 4.5	72 5.1	72 5.1
0 UND	6 59.2	22 16.5	5 73.0		Cost of Revenues/Payables	13 27.1	16 22.3	10 35.0	9 38.8	5 73.0
6 61.5	21 17.4	32 11.5	24 15.4			29 12.4	31 11.8	28 13.0	26 14.0	24 15.4
38 9.6	54 6.8	54 6.7	52 7.0			47 7.8	50 7.4	47 7.8	47 7.8	52 7.0
13.8	5.1	6.7		6.7	Revenues/Working Capital	7.8	8.6	8.0	6.6	6.7
-75.8	17.0	12.2		19.2		20.8	18.7	18.2	18.0	19.2
-6.0	-41.3	52.4		-36.0		-122.3	-119.1	-158.5	-59.8	-36.0
2.3	4.1	5.0		4.3	EBIT/Interest	10.6	10.5	8.5	8.3	4.3
(20) .9	(64) .2	(34) 1.6	(123) 1.2			(239) 4.3	(209) 4.3	(188) 2.8	(143) 1.9	(123) 1.2
-1.2	-4.4	-4.7		-3.4		1.9	1.4	1.1	-1.2	-3.4
	2.5	2.4		2.9	Net Profit + Depr., Dep., Amort./Cur. Mat. L/T/D	2.4	4.0	2.4	2.9	2.9
	(13) 1.0	(14) 1.3	(34) 1.4			(76) 1.6	(63) 2.0	(61) 1.5	(36) 2.0	(34) 1.4
	-.1	.9		.7		1.0	.9	1.1	1.0	.7
1.2	.5	.6		.6	Fixed/Worth	.7	.7	.6	.6	.6
2.8	1.2	1.0		1.2		1.3	1.2	1.2	1.1	1.2
-1.8	2.8	2.1		2.8		2.3	2.3	2.0	2.6	2.8
1.0	.6	.8		.8	Debt/Worth	1.0	1.1	1.0	.8	.8
2.1	1.4	1.5		1.6		2.0	1.8	1.8	1.7	1.6
-3.1	4.6	3.5		4.6		4.3	3.3	4.3	4.3	4.6
18.7	22.7	16.1		20.9	% Profit Before Taxes/Tangible Net Worth	48.2	51.6	41.9	31.5	20.9
(16) -2.1	(59) 1.6	(33) 3.2	(114) 3.2			(229) 25.8	(209) 22.6	(180) 17.5	(142) 7.6	(114) 3.2
-21.1	-22.8	-17.5		-19.8		9.3	3.9	2.1	-7.3	-19.8
5.2	8.4	5.6		8.0	% Profit Before Taxes/Total Assets	16.5	17.4	14.3	14.6	8.0
.0	-1.2	.9		.8		8.1	8.2	5.5	3.1	.8
-6.6	-17.9	-8.4		-11.4		2.4	1.3	.5	-4.9	-11.4
7.7	4.1	3.7		4.2	% Depr., Dep., Amort./Revenues	2.8	3.0	3.1	4.0	4.2
(20) 12.5	(60) 7.4	(34) 5.9	(118) 7.4			(228) 5.3	(197) 5.4	(177) 5.6	(141) 6.5	(118) 7.4
18.9	11.1	9.2		11.7		8.6	8.3	8.4	9.1	11.7
8.3	2.3	1.7		2.2	% Officers', Directors' Owners' Comp/Revenues	1.8	2.2	2.0	2.4	2.2
(11) 9.7	(29) 4.7	(10) 2.1	(53) 4.8			(139) 3.7	(111) 3.2	(100) 4.1	(70) 4.6	(53) 4.8
12.5	9.5	4.2		9.5		7.6	6.2	6.2	7.8	9.5
14562M	262324M	674737M	3998389M	4950012M	Contract Revenues ($)	16894511M	38123492M	66001098M	42605534M	4950012M
14973M	170685M	432080M	3437948M	4055686M	Total Assets ($)	6504366M	16198292M	26833564M	17114825M	4055686M

M = $ thousand   MM = $ million
See Pages 9 through 22 for Explanation of Ratios and Data

Current Data Sorted by Revenue | | | | | | ## Comparative Historical Data

0-1MM	1-10MM	10-50MM	50 & OVER	ALL	Type of Statement	4/1/05-3/31/06 ALL	4/1/06-3/31/07 ALL	4/1/07-3/31/08 ALL	4/1/08-3/31/09 ALL	4/1/0..-3/31/ ALL
1	23	5	1	5	Unqualified	20	7	8	10	5
	17	11		36	Reviewed	49	47	37	31	36
11	22	3		20	Compiled	31	31	26	23	20
3	15			33	Tax Returns	31	28	36	36	33
		11		29	Other	22	33	26	23	29
14 (4/1-9/30/09)		**109 (10/1/09-3/31/10)**								
15	77	30	1	123	NUMBER OF STATEMENTS	153	146	133	123	123

ASSETS

0-1MM %	1-10MM %	10-50MM %	50 & OVER %	ALL %		%	%	%	%	%
15.6	14.1	15.9		14.8	Cash & Equivalents	12.0	13.5	14.0	11.3	14.8
14.1	33.3	46.1		34.1	A/R - Progress Billings	34.5	34.5	35.9	33.5	34.1
.6	1.0	.3		.8	A/R - Current Retention	1.7	1.0	1.6	1.1	.8
9.9	9.5	8.0		9.2	Inventory	8.0	9.4	8.0	8.8	9.2
3.3	2.2	4.5		2.9	Cost & Est. Earnings In Excess Billings	2.9	1.9	2.2	3.1	2.9
.3	3.2	3.7		2.9	All Other Current	4.2	4.7	4.4	6.3	2.9
43.8	63.3	78.5		64.7	Total Current	63.5	65.0	65.9	64.1	64.7
36.5	20.6	14.5		21.2	Fixed Assets (net)	27.0	26.3	24.5	25.7	21.2
.0	.4	1.1		.5	Joint Ventures & Investments	1.5	.4	.6	.1	.5
3.7	3.7	.5		2.9	Intangibles (net)	2.0	1.9	2.8	3.4	2.9
16.0	11.9	5.4		10.7	All Other Non-Current	6.1	6.5	6.2	6.7	10.7
100.0	100.0	100.0		100.0	Total	100.0	100.0	100.0	100.0	100.0

LIABILITIES

0-1MM	1-10MM	10-50MM	50 & OVER	ALL						
28.5	12.0	14.6		14.6	Notes Payable-Short Term	11.2	17.2	14.2	13.9	14.6
23.5	15.2	20.8		17.8	A/P - Trade	18.7	16.1	19.6	18.4	17.8
.0	.0	.5		.1	A/P - Retention	.2	.2	.2	.2	.1
.0	1.8	5.1		2.4	Billings in Excess of Costs & Est. Earnings	3.3	2.6	2.8	2.7	2.4
.1	.1	.0		.1	Income Taxes Payable	.2	.2	.2	.1	.1
15.0	4.5	2.5		5.3	Cur. Mat.-L/T/D	4.6	5.7	5.0	10.0	5.3
11.0	8.4	9.1		8.8	All Other Current	10.3	9.2	7.9	9.8	8.8
78.1	42.0	52.6		49.1	Total Current	48.5	51.1	50.0	55.1	49.1
59.2	23.3	7.6		23.8	Long-Term Debt	19.5	17.4	20.6	21.0	23.8
.0	.4	1.0		.5	Deferred Taxes	.6	.6	.1	1.4	.5
5.6	3.4	1.5		3.3	All Other Non-Current	6.5	2.9	3.4	4.6	3.3
-42.9	30.9	37.3		23.4	Net Worth	24.9	27.9	25.8	17.9	23.4
100.0	100.0	100.0		100.0	Total Liabilties & Net Worth	100.0	100.0	100.0	100.0	100.0

INCOME DATA

0-1MM	1-10MM	10-50MM	50 & OVER	ALL						
100.0	100.0	100.0		100.0	Contract Revenues	100.0	100.0	100.0	100.0	100.0
47.8	36.3	21.6		33.9	Gross Profit	31.4	33.1	32.6	31.9	33.9
40.8	32.4	17.3		29.5	Operating Expenses	27.3	28.2	27.3	29.6	29.5
7.0	3.9	4.3		4.4	Operating Profit	4.1	4.9	5.3	2.3	4.4
1.3	.6	.5		.7	All Other Expenses (net)	.6	.6	.7	.6	.7
5.7	3.3	3.9		3.7	Profit Before Taxes	3.5	4.3	4.7	1.6	3.7

RATIOS

0-1MM	1-10MM	10-50MM	50 & OVER	ALL						
1.9	3.0	2.1		2.5	Current	2.3	2.2	2.4	2.6	2.5
.3	1.5	1.4		1.4		1.3	1.4	1.5	1.5	1.4
.1	1.0	1.1		.9		1.0	1.0	1.0	.9	.9
	10.2	4.0		5.8	Receivables/Payables	4.2	5.0	4.7	5.6	5.8
	(68) 2.7	2.4		(108) 2.4		(141) 2.2	(135) 2.2	(126) 2.4	(114) 2.2	(108) 2.4
	1.2	1.6		1.2		1.3	1.2	1.1	1.0	1.2
0 UND	15 23.7	34 10.7		14 25.4	Revenues/Receivables	18 20.4	13 28.0	22 16.3	19 19.4	14 25.4
8 43.3	38 9.5	56 6.5		39 9.4		48 7.6	40 9.2	43 8.5	42 8.8	39 9.4
21 17.2	65 5.6	82 4.4		66 5.5		77 4.8	74 5.0	69 5.3	64 5.7	66 5.5
0 UND	4 93.2	15 24.8		8 48.6	Cost of Revenues/Payables	13 28.5	8 43.3	9 40.5	7 53.4	8 48.6
16 22.1	21 17.7	27 13.6		22 16.5		26 14.1	24 15.3	25 14.8	22 16.4	22 16.5
35 10.3	45 8.1	51 7.1		46 8.0		43 8.5	46 8.0	49 7.4	47 7.8	46 8.0
9.0	6.3	5.9		6.3	Revenues/Working Capital	7.6	8.2	8.3	6.8	6.3
-10.4	18.3	12.6		18.5		15.7	16.5	15.3	15.5	18.5
-5.0	-238.1	32.7		-65.7		NM	-666.6	UND	-74.3	-65.7
17.3	18.2	32.7		20.2	EBIT/Interest	24.0	14.6	14.8	12.3	20.2
(13) 4.3	(68) 4.5	(26) 8.5		(108) 5.6		(140) 4.8	(128) 5.3	(123) 5.2	(109) 2.8	(108) 5.6
1.8	.8	1.5		1.2		1.3	1.3	1.7	-.2	1.2
	6.5			8.8	Net Profit + Depr., Dep., Amort./Cur. Mat. L/T/D	7.4	7.2	14.8	5.2	8.8
	(12) 2.0			(18) 3.4		(35) 2.5	(33) 2.4	(21) 7.0	(19) 2.6	(18) 3.4
	-1.0			.3		1.7	.8	1.8	1.3	.3
.6	.2	.1		.1	Fixed/Worth	.3	.2	.3	.2	.1
-10.8	.7	.2		.7		.6	.7	.6	.6	.7
-.5	3.6	.9		2.8		3.0	2.0	2.7	8.1	2.8
1.0	.6	.8		.8	Debt/Worth	.8	.9	.9	.7	.8
-13.4	1.9	2.3		2.3		2.1	1.9	2.7	2.1	2.3
-2.5	26.5	4.1		18.4		7.0	5.5	10.6	38.5	18.4
	91.9	46.0		73.8	% Profit Before Taxes/Tangible Net Worth	54.2	79.1	79.1	49.1	73.8
	(63) 33.3	(29) 19.7		(99) 26.7		(124) 24.4	(129) 31.3	(110) 38.9	(96) 19.7	(99) 26.7
	1.8	5.6		3.5		5.6	7.9	9.1	3.8	3.5
36.1	27.0	20.6		25.6	% Profit Before Taxes/Total Assets	17.8	25.9	25.5	18.3	25.6
16.0	8.2	9.2		10.0		7.6	10.3	10.1	5.3	10.0
.0	-.7	.8		.0		.9	1.5	1.4	-2.2	.0
	.7	.5		.7	% Depr., Dep., Amort./Revenues	.8	1.2	.8	1.0	.7
	(60) 1.7	(24) 1.2		(94) 1.6		(129) 1.8	(112) 2.3	(108) 1.8	(92) 2.0	(94) 1.6
	3.2	2.5		3.2		3.4	3.3	3.3	3.7	3.2
4.4	3.6	.5		2.6	% Officers', Directors' Owners' Comp/Revenues	2.5	2.7	1.7	2.4	2.6
(11) 10.5	(53) 4.8	(12) 1.8		(76) 4.7		(95) 4.9	(95) 4.5	(84) 3.9	(78) 4.2	(76) 4.7
21.7	8.3	3.5		8.5		6.6	7.2	6.6	6.6	8.5
7734M	291765M	574710M	52452M	926661M	Contract Revenues ($)	23002610M	10670425M	25225136M	22991743M	926661M
3250M	106816M	218191M	18113M	346370M	Total Assets ($)	37988227M	3522291M	8639005M	8446341M	346370M

M = $ thousand   MM = $ million
See Pages 9 through 22 for Explanation of Ratios and Data

CONSTRUCTION
FINANCIAL MANAGEMENT
ASSOCIATION DATA

About the Construction Financial Management Association (CFMA) Data
Web site: www.cfma.org

Once again, we are delighted to include excerpts from *CFMA's 2010 Construction Industry Annual Financial Survey.* CFMA is **The Source and Resource for Construction Financial Professionals** and has more than 7,000 members in 88 chapters throughout the U.S. and Canada.

The data presented are based on a survey to which approximately 4,300 general members employed within U.S. and Canadian construction firms were invited to respond. Additionally, this data was augmented by several hundred firms outside of CFMA member ranks. Of the 632 companies submitting data for the survey, 623 provided detailed financial statement and other required information and were included in the final respondent population. The data submitted were compiled and analyzed by Moss Adams LLP in cooperation with CFMA. Moss Adams was not engaged to and did not audit or review this information and, accordingly, does not express an opinion or any other form of assurance on it.

Almost all companies (92%) included in the survey recognize contract revenue and profit in accordance with the percentage of completion method of accounting. Likewise, our Statement Studies contractor data primarily reflects only this method of accounting. It is entirely possible that some of the same contractor companies are included in both the CFMA and Statement Studies data presentations. The inclusion of the CFMA data has not affected our Statement Studies contractor composite data.

Fiscal year-end closing dates reflected in the CFMA survey range from 3/31/09 through 3/31/10. The CFMA data are most comparable to the RMA contractor data from 4/1/09 through 3/31/10 appearing in this edition.

The survey respondents were classified into three categories of construction based on the type of work performed. Classification was based on the level of contract volume reported for various NAICS codes. A contractor was included in a classification if at least one half of its annual contract revenue was attributable to that classification. CFMA categorized certain NAICS codes together. The classifications and NAICS codes included in each are as follows:

NAICS Codes
INDUSTRIAL AND NONRESIDENTIAL CONTRACTORS:
236210   Industrial Building Construction
236220   Commercial and Institutional Building Construction

HEAVY AND HIGHWAY CONTRACTORS:
237110   Water and Sewer Line and Related Structures Construction
237120   Oil and Gas Pipeline and Related Structures Construction
237130   Power and Communication Line and Related Structures Construction
237210   Land Subdivision
237310   Highway, Street, and Bridge Construction
237990   Other Heavy and Civil Engineering Construction

SPECIALTY TRADES CONTRACTORS:
238110   Poured Concrete Foundation and Structure Contractors
238120   Structural Steel and Precast Concrete Contractors
238130   Framing Contractors
238140   Masonry Contractors
238150   Glass and Glazing Contractors
238160   Roofing Contractors
238170   Siding Contractors
238190   Other Foundation, Structure, and Building Exterior Contractors
238210   Electrical Contractors
238220   Plumbing, Heating, and Air-Conditioning Contractors
238290   Other Building Equipment Contractors
238310   Drywall and Insulation Contractors
238320   Painting and Wall Covering Contractors
238330   Flooring Contractors
238340   Tile and Terrazzo Contractors
238350   Finish Carpentry Contractors
238390   Other Building Finishing Contractors
238910   Site Preparation Contractors
238990   All Other Specialty Trade Contractors
561621   Security Systems Services (except Locksmiths)
562910   Environmental Remediation Services

The CFMA financial data includes balance sheets, statements of earnings, and financial ratios. The balance sheets and statements of earning represent a weighted average of all companies included in each classification. Percentages are presented for each dollar amount in the financial statements. Due to rounding, the totals may not agree to the sum of various accounts. Such variations are few and insignificant.

The financial ratios are calculated from the composite balance sheets and statements of earning data. They are not averages of ratios for all companies included in the classification.

If you wish to purchase *CFMA's 2010 Construction Industry Annual Financial Survey* or have questions regarding the data, contact Brian Summers, COO; Construction Financial Management Association, 100 Village Blvd, Suite 200, Princeton, NJ 08540; Phone 609-452-8000; Fax 609-452-0474; E-mail bsummers@cfma.org.

Interpretation of the
Construction Financial Management Association (CFMA) Data

CFMA's data should only be regarded as general information. It cannot be used to establish industry norms for a number of reasons, including the following:

(1) The financial statements used in the composite are not selected by any random or statistically reliable method. CFMA members voluntarily submitted their financial data. Note that contractors' statements have no upper asset/sales limit.

(2) Many companies provide varied services; CFMA includes a contractor in a classification if at least one-half (1/2) of its annual contract revenue was completed within that classification.

(3) Some of the NAICS group samples may be rather small in relation to the total number of firms in a given industry category. A relatively small sample can increase the chances that some of our composites do not fully represent an industry group.

(4) There is the chance that an extreme statement can be present in a sample, causing a disproportionate influence on the industry composite. This is particularly true in a relatively small sample.

(5) Companies within the same industry may differ in their method of operations, which in turn can directly influence their financial statements. Since such differences affect financial data included in our sample, our composite calculations could be significantly affected.

(6) Other considerations that can result in variation among different companies engaged in the same general line of business are: different labor markets; geographical location; different accounting methods; quality of service rendered; sources and methods of financing; and terms of sale.

The use of CFMA data may be helpful when considered with other methods of financial analysis. Nevertheless, RMA and CFMA do not recommend the use of CFMA's data to establish norms or parameters for a given industry or grouping, or the industry as a whole. Although CFMA believes that its data is accurate and representative within the confines of the aforementioned reasons, RMA and CFMA specifically make no representations regarding the accuracy of representativeness of the figures printed in this supplement of the RMA Annual Statement Studies.

All Companies

Composite

Balance Sheet

	2010 Participants		2009 Participants	
	Amount	Percent	Amount	Percent
Current assets				
Cash and cash equivalents	$ 8,766,996	21.4 %	$ 6,075,644	18.2 %
Marketable securities and short-term investments	1,986,410	4.8	1,330,902	4.0
Receivables				
Contract receivables currently due	13,045,413	31.8	9,861,865	29.5
Retainages on contracts	3,615,830	8.8	3,027,154	9.0
Unbilled work	174,294	0.4	154,703	0.5
Other receivables	1,355,980	3.3	3,004,245	9.0
Less allowance for doubtful accounts	(128,389)	(0.3)	(163,598)	(0.5)
Total receivables, net	18,063,127	44.1	15,884,370	47.5
Inventories	860,268	2.1	587,349	1.8
Costs and recognized earnings in excess of billings on uncompleted contracts	1,564,898	3.8	1,248,492	3.7
Investments in and advances to construction joint ventures	385,004	0.9	161,899	0.5
Income taxes:				
Current / refundable	108,670	0.3	103,635	0.3
Deferred	72,017	0.2	117,907	0.4
Other current assets	1,114,023	2.7	940,340	2.8
Total current assets	32,921,414	80.3	26,450,539	79.1
Property, plant and equipment	13,034,502	31.8	10,554,099	31.5
Less accumulated depreciation	(7,403,240)	(18.1)	(6,105,883)	(18.2)
Property, plant and equipment, net	5,631,262	13.7	4,448,216	13.3
Noncurrent assets				
Long-term investments	598,193	1.5	627,188	1.9
Deferred income taxes	86,257	0.2	105,910	0.3
Other assets	1,739,115	4.2	1,826,103	5.5
Total noncurrent assets	2,423,565	5.9	2,559,200	7.6
Total assets	$ 40,976,241	100.0 %	$ 33,457,955	100.0 %

	2010 Participants		2009 Participants	
	Amount	Percent	Amount	Percent
Current liabilities:				
Current maturity on long-term debt	$ 577,865	1.4 %	$ 582,286	1.7 %
Notes payable and lines of credit	478,425	1.2	561,047	1.7
Accounts payable:				
Trade, including currently due to subcontractors	10,178,510	24.8	6,491,750	19.4
Subcontracts retainages	2,475,727	6.0	1,970,344	5.9
Other	376,304	0.9	2,276,002	6.8
Total accounts payable	13,030,541	31.8	10,738,095	32.1
Accrued expenses	2,636,468	6.4	1,849,263	5.5
Billings in excess of costs and recognized earnings on uncompleted contracts	5,346,141	13.0	4,666,371	14.0
Income taxes:				
Current	91,693	0.2	153,861	0.5
Deferred	20,862	0.1	93,183	0.3
Other current liabilities	540,454	1.3	336,041	1.0
Total current liabilities	22,722,448	55.5	19,000,147	56.8
Noncurrent liabilities				
Long-term debt, excluding current maturities	2,641,282	6.4	2,436,306	7.3
Deferred income taxes	147,056	0.4	197,378	0.6
Other	908,790	2.2	636,523	1.9
Total liabilities	26,419,486	64.5	22,270,354	66.6
Minority interests	136,620	0.3	79,187	0.2
Net worth				
Common stock, par value	3,404,987	8.3	2,565,621	7.7
Preferred stock, stated value	21,227	0.1	129,018	0.4
Additional paid-in capital	840,332	2.1	951,672	2.8
Retained earnings	10,444,684	25.5	7,232,502	21.6
Treasury stock	(724,705)	(1.8)	(562,754)	(1.7)
Excess value of marketable securities	10,478	0.0	42,066	0.1
Other equity	423,232	1.0	750,290	2.2
Total net worth	14,420,235	35.2	11,108,414	33.2
Total liabilities and net worth	$ 40,976,241	100.0 %	$ 33,457,955	100.0 %

All Companies

Composite

Statement of Earnings

	2010 Participants		2009 Participants	
	Amount	Percent	Amount	Percent
Contract revenue	$ 103,086,329	98.6 %	$ 86,370,519	98.1 %
Other revenue	1,459,634	1.4	1,644,341	1.9
Total revenue	104,545,963	100.0	88,014,860	100.0
Contract cost	(91,909,826)	(87.9)	(76,908,124)	(87.4)
Other cost	(1,054,837)	(1.0)	(1,585,484)	(1.8)
Total cost	(92,964,663)	(88.9)	(78,493,608)	(89.2)
Gross profit	11,581,300	11.1	9,521,252	10.8
Selling, general and administrative expenses				
Payroll	(2,781,097)	(2.7)	(2,393,866)	(2.7)
Professional fees	(193,097)	(0.2)	(241,972)	(0.3)
Sales and marketing costs	(225,596)	(0.2)	(226,943)	(0.3)
Tecmology costs	(147,422)	(0.1)	(179,153)	(0.2)
Administrative bonuses	(546,369)	(0.5)	(558,151)	(0.6)
Other	(4,047,246)	(3.9)	(3,068,116)	(3.5)
Total SG&A expenses	(7,940,827)	(7.6)	(6,668,201)	(7.6)
Income from operations	3,640,473	3.5	2,853,052	3.2
Interest income	111,746	0.1	208,273	0.2
Interest expense	(107,236)	(0.1)	(186,308)	(0.2)
Other income / (expense), net	58,257	0.1	113,471	0.1
Net earnings / (loss) before income taxes	3,703,240	3.5	2,988,487	3.4
Income tax (expense) / benefit	(317,405)	(0.3)	(307,098)	(0.3)
Net earnings	$ 3,385,835	3.2 %	$ 2,681,389	3.0 %
Average backlog	$ 52,824,730		$ 48,321,602	

Number of Participants

	Number
2010	623
2009	808

Financial Ratios

	2010 Participants		2009 Participants	
	Average	Median	Average	Median
Liquidity Ratios				
Current Ratio	1.4	1.7	1.4	1.5
Quick Ratio	1.3	1.4	1.2	1.3
Days of Cash	30.2	26.4	24.9	19.0
Working Capital Turnover	10.3	8.5	11.8	10.1
Profitability Ratios				
Return on Assets	9.0 %	7.1 %	8.9 %	10.3 %
Return on Equity	25.7 %	17.1 %	26.9 %	30.9 %
Times Interest Earned	35.5	14.8	17.0	14.1
Leverage Ratios				
Debt to Equity	1.8	1.3	2.0	1.6
Revenue to Equity	7.2	6.0	7.9	7.5
Asset Turnover	2.6	2.7	2.6	2.9
Fixed Asset Ratio	39.1 %	23.0 %	40.0 %	24.0 %
Equity to SG&A Expense	1.8	1.6	1.7	1.4
Underbillings to Equity	12.1 %	6.0 %	12.6 %	8.0 %
Backlog to Equity	3.7	1.3	4.4	2.5
Efficiency Ratios				
Backlog to Working Capital	5.2	1.7	6.5	3.3
Months in Backlog	6.1	3.2	6.6	4.8
Days in Accounts Receivable	49.1	46.1	52.0	49.4
Days in Inventory	3.3	0.0	2.7	0.0
Days in Accounts Payable	40.9	30.6	40.2	30.6
Operating Cycle	41.8	-44.6	39.3	41.5

Industrial & Nonresidential Contractors

Composite

Balance Sheet

	2010 Participants		2009 Participants	
	Amount	Percent	Amount	Percent
Current assets:		%		%
Cash and cash equivalents	$ 12,010,978	23.5	$ 8,990,212	23.8
Marketable securities and short-term investments	2,975,512	5.8	2,036,401	5.4
Receivables				
Contract receivables currently due	19,311,172	37.7	13,376,596	35.4
Retainages on contracts	6,088,446	11.9	4,080,364	10.8
Unbilled work	127,308	0.2	73,235	0.2
Other receivables	2,915,571	5.7	3,149,894	8.3
Less allowance for doubtful accounts	(104,705)	(0.2)	(29,280)	(0.1)
Total receivables, net	28,337,792	55.4	20,650,810	54.6
Inventories	73,951	0.1	80,960	0.2
Costs and recognized earnings in excess of billings on uncompleted contracts	1,835,954	3.6	1,043,908	2.8
Investments in and advances to construction joint ventures	468,167	0.9	92,075	0.2
Income taxes				
Current / refundable	262,653	0.5	60,924	0.2
Deferred	30,014	0.1	42,817	0.1
Other current assets	936,129	1.8	715,020	1.9
Total current assets	46,931,151	91.7	33,713,127	89.1
Property, plant and equipment	5,502,378	10.8	4,067,406	10.8
Less accumulated depreciation	(3,391,839)	(6.6)	(2,329,223)	(6.2)
Property, plant and equipment, net	2,110,539	4.1	1,738,184	4.6
Noncurrent assets				
Long-term investments	1,146,272	2.2	612,621	1.6
Deferred income taxes	78,537	0.2	29,271	0.1
Other assets	907,531	1.8	1,736,413	4.6
Total noncurrent assets	2,132,340	4.2	2,378,304	6.3
Total assets	$ 51,174,029	100.0	$ 37,829,615	100.0
Current liabilities:		%		%
Current maturity on long-term debt	$ 231,658	0.5	$ 196,214	0.5
Notes payable and lines of credit	189,884	0.4	203,738	0.5
Accounts payable				
Trade, including currently due to subcontractors	20,329,820	39.7	12,076,370	31.9
Subcontracts retainages	6,638,359	13.0	4,541,782	12.0
Other	616,994	1.2	3,178,726	8.4
Total accounts payable	27,585,173	53.9	19,796,878	52.3
Accrued expenses	2,992,177	5.8	1,545,038	4.1
Billings in excess of costs and recognized earnings on uncompleted contracts	5,548,926	10.8	4,766,065	12.6
Income taxes				
Current	89,152	0.2	34,547	0.1
Deferred	11,804	0.0	9,086	0.0
Other current liabilities	213,093	0.4	423,982	1.1
Total current liabilities	36,861,868	72.0	27,031,275	71.5
Noncurrent liabilities				
Long-term debt, excluding current maturities	1,082,389	2.1	1,802,050	4.8
Deferred income taxes	74,332	0.1	166,669	0.4
Other	683,860	1.3	281,862	0.7
Total liabilities	38,702,449	75.6	29,261,856	77.4
Minority interests	59,123	0.1	51,730	0.1
Net worth:				
Common stock, par value	2,421,976	4.7	2,072,665	5.5
Preferred stock, stated value	6,728	0.0	20,827	0.1
Additional paid-in capital	980,041	1.9	837,556	2.2
Retained earnings	8,608,485	16.8	5,616,352	14.8
Treasury stock	(322,214)	(0.6)	(385,266)	(1.0)
Excess value of marketable securities	11,654	0.0	(51,300)	(0.1)
Other equity	705,787	1.4	405,195	1.1
Total net worth	12,412,457	24.3	8,516,030	22.5
Total liabilities and net worth	$ 51,174,029	100.0	$ 37,829,615	100.0

Industrial & Nonresidential Contractors

Composite

Statement of Earnings

	2010 Participants		2009 Participants	
	Amount	Percent	Amount	Percent
Contract revenue	$ 161,430,978	99.7 %	$ 121,514,818	99.7 %
Other revenue	525,963	0.3	321,590	0.3
Total revenue	161,956,941	100.0	121,836,408	100.0
Contract cost	(151,091,829)	(93.3)	(112,589,921)	(92.4)
Other cost	(417,298)	(0.3)	(150,027)	(0.1)
Total cost	(151,509,127)	(93.5)	(112,739,947)	(92.5)
Gross profit	10,447,814	6.5	9,096,461	7.5
Selling, general and administrative expenses:				
Payroll	(2,896,816)	(1.8)	(2,087,124)	(1.7)
Professional fees	(197,776)	(0.1)	(153,630)	(0.1)
Sales and marketing costs	(256,952)	(0.2)	(202,843)	(0.2)
Technology costs	(156,345)	(0.1)	(111,914)	(0.1)
Administrative bonuses	(521,364)	(0.3)	(445,114)	(0.4)
Other	(3,198,835)	(2.0)	(2,316,072)	(1.9)
Total SG&A expenses	(7,228,088)	(4.5)	(5,316,696)	(4.4)
Income from operations	3,219,726	2.0	3,779,765	3.1
Interest income	193,990	0.1	231,975	0.2
Interest expense	(52,188)	(0.0)	(79,665)	(0.1)
Other income / (expense), net	(59,409)	(0.0)	(36,190)	(0.0)
Net earnings / (loss) before income taxes	3,302,119	2.0	3,895,885	3.2
Income tax (expense) / benefit	(200,375)	(0.1)	(194,463)	(0.2)
Net earnings	$ 3,101,743	1.9 %	$ 3,701,422	3.0 %
Average backlog	$ 101,323,289		$ 78,268,724	

Number of Participants

	Number
2010	191
2009	275

Financial Ratios

	2010 Participants		2009 Participants	
	Average	Median	Average	Median
Liquidity Ratios				
Current Ratio	1.3	1.4	1.2	1.3
Quick Ratio	1.2	1.3	1.2	1.2
Days of Cash	26.7	31.5	26.6	22.4
Working Capital Turnover	16.1	12.4	18.2	14.8
Profitability Ratios				
Return on Assets	6.5 %	5.8 %	10.3 %	8.1 %
Return on Equity	26.6 %	19.8 %	45.8 %	34.6 %
Times Interest Earned	64.3	22.2	49.9	28.5
Leverage Ratios				
Debt to Equity	3.1	2.0	3.4	2.5
Revenue to Equity	13.0	10.6	14.3	12.2
Asset Turnover	3.2	3.4	3.2	3.5
Fixed Asset Ratio	17.0 %	13.0 %	20.4 %	15.0 %
Equity to SG&A Expense	1.7	1.6	1.6	1.4
Underbillings to Equity	15.8 %	5.0 %	13.1 %	7.0 %
Backlog to Equity	8.2	3.7	9.2	4.7
Efficiency Ratios				
Backlog to Working Capital	10.1	4.7	11.7	7.0
Months in Backlog	7.5	4.5	7.7	5.9
Days in Accounts Receivable	49.2	38.5	48.7	44.9
Days in Inventory	0.2	0.0	0.3	0.0
Days in Accounts Payable	49.8	36.2	48.7	39.6
Operating Cycle	26.3	34.0	26.9	27.8

Heavy & Highway Contractors

Composite

Balance Sheet

	2010 Participants		2009 Participants	
	Amount	Percent	Amount	Percent
Current assets:				
Cash and cash equivalents	$ 13,836,711	23.8 %	$ 6,944,305	15.3 %
Marketable securities and short-term investments	2,736,059	4.7	1,700,329	3.7
Receivables:				
Contract receivables currently due	10,162,270	17.5	9,057,226	19.9
Retainages on contracts	3,499,791	6.0	3,026,404	6.7
Unbilled work	360,593	0.6	217,379	0.5
Other receivables	1,562,932	2.7	3,028,018	6.7
Less allowance for doubtful accounts	(131,025)	(0.2)	(166,950)	(0.4)
Total receivables, net	15,454,562	26.6	15,160,076	33.3
Inventories	2,098,409	3.6	1,641,056	3.6
Costs and recognized earnings in excess of billings on uncompleted contracts	2,097,462	3.6	1,372,546	3.0
Investments in and advances to construction joint ventures	1,128,434	1.9	312,263	0.7
Income taxes:				
Current / refundable	27,770	0.0	62,430	0.1
Deferred	213,694	0.4	100,841	0.2
Other current assets	1,894,247	3.3	1,313,891	2.9
Total current assets	39,487,348	67.9	28,607,737	62.9
Property, plant and equipment	36,940,016	63.5	32,237,356	70.9
Less accumulated depreciation	(22,063,524)	(37.9)	(19,458,273)	(42.8)
Property, plant and equipment, net	14,876,491	25.6	12,779,083	28.1
Noncurrent assets:				
Long-term investments	691,814	1.2	1,450,912	3.2
Deferred income taxes	269,497	0.5	63,362	0.1
Other assets	2,823,836	4.9	2,584,659	5.7
Total noncurrent assets	3,785,146	6.5	4,098,932	9.0
Total assets	$ 58,148,986	100.0 %	$ 45,485,752	100.0 %

	2010 Participants		2009 Participants	
	Amount	Percent	Amount	Percent
Current liabilities:				
Current maturity on long-term debt	$ 1,575,032	2.7 %	$ 1,381,420	3.0 %
Notes payable and lines of credit	436,864	0.8	816,295	1.8
Accounts payable:				
Trade, including currently due to subcontractors	8,940,265	15.4	5,676,190	12.5
Subcontracts retainages	1,432,155	2.5	1,010,883	2.2
Other	394,892	0.7	1,377,211	3.0
Total accounts payable	10,767,311	18.5	8,064,285	17.7
Accrued expenses	3,365,917	5.8	2,469,309	5.4
Billings in excess of costs and recognized earnings on uncompleted contracts	7,333,829	12.6	4,799,538	10.6
Income taxes:				
Current	272,755	0.5	214,664	0.5
Deferred	48,496	0.1	50,323	0.1
Other current liabilities	407,806	0.7	225,164	0.5
Total current liabilities	24,208,011	41.6	18,020,998	39.6
Noncurrent liabilities				
Long-term debt, excluding current maturities	6,229,081	10.7	4,327,846	9.5
Deferred income taxes	588,460	1.0	371,753	0.8
Other	1,805,508	3.1	2,005,664	4.4
Total liabilities	32,831,060	56.5	24,726,261	54.4
Minority interests	397,907	0.7	2,661	0.0
Net worth:				
Common stock, par value	4,410,466	7.6	3,868,665	8.5
Preferred stock, stated value	22,273	0.0	313,492	0.7
Additional paid-in capital	3,158,685	5.4	1,856,786	4.1
Retained earnings	18,395,337	31.6	15,028,717	33.0
Treasury stock	(1,338,491)	(2.3)	(779,294)	(1.7)
Excess value of marketable securities	10,696	0.0	(21,334)	(0.0)
Other equity	261,053	0.4	489,798	1.1
Total net worth	24,920,020	42.9	20,756,830	45.6
Total liabilities and net worth	$ 58,148,986	100.0 %	$ 45,485,752	100.0 %

Heavy & Highway Contractors
Composite

Statement of Earnings

	2010 Participants		2009 Participants	
	Amount	Percent	Amount	Percent
Contract revenue	$ 117,898,262	98.7 %	$ 97,257,900	97.4 %
Other revenue	1,609,197	1.3	2,586,446	2.6
Total revenue	119,507,459	100.0	99,844,345	100.0
Contract cost	(103,912,738)	(87.0)	(86,203,575)	(86.3)
Other cost	(1,004,964)	(0.8)	(2,226,151)	(2.2)
Total cost	(104,917,701)	(87.8)	(88,429,725)	(88.6)
Gross profit	14,589,758	12.2	11,414,620	11.4
Selling, general and administrative expenses:				
Payroll	(2,832,923)	(2.4)	(2,944,137)	(2.9)
Professional fees	(241,470)	(0.2)	(272,371)	(0.3)
Sales and marketing costs	(128,197)	(0.1)	(167,826)	(0.2)
Technology costs	(132,413)	(0.1)	(153,664)	(0.2)
Administrative bonuses	(576,984)	(0.5)	(426,733)	(0.4)
Other	(4,453,665)	(3.7)	(2,946,599)	(3.0)
Total SG&A expenses	(8,365,653)	(7.0)	(6,911,120)	(6.9)
Income from operations	6,224,105	5.2	4,503,500	4.5
Interest income	132,920	0.1	204,878	0.2
Interest expense	(289,358)	(0.2)	(267,762)	(0.3)
Other income / (expense), net	291,650	0.2	170,656	0.2
Net earnings / (loss) before income taxes	6,359,317	5.3	4,611,872	4.6
Income tax (expense) / benefit	(498,610)	(0.4)	(258,481)	(0.3)
Net earnings	$ 5,860,707	4.9 %	$ 4,353,391	4.4 %
Average backlog	$ 71,600,040		$ 55,283,652	

Number of Participants

	Number
2010	110
2009	126

Financial Ratios

	2010 Participants		2009 Participants	
	Average	Median	Average	Median
Liquidity Ratios				
Current Ratio	1.6	1.7	1.6	1.7
Quick Ratio	1.3	1.4	1.3	1.4
Days of Cash	41.7	25.0	25.0	25.0
Working Capital Turnover	7.8	8.1	9.4	8.1
Profitability Ratios				
Return on Assets	10.9 %	8.7 %	10.1 %	8.7 %
Return on Equity	25.5 %	17.3 %	22.2 %	17.3 %
Times Interest Earned	23.0	9.5	18.3	9.5
Leverage Ratios				
Debt to Equity	1.3	1.3	1.2	1.3
Revenue to Equity	4.8	5.1	4.8	5.1
Asset Turnover	2.1	2.3	2.2	2.3
Fixed Asset Ratio	59.7 %	58.0 %	61.6 %	58.0 %
Equity to SG&A Expense	3.0	2.3	3.0	2.3
Underbillings to Equity	9.9 %	7.0 %	7.7 %	7.0 %
Backlog to Equity	2.9	1.7	2.7	1.7
Efficiency Ratios				
Backlog to Working Capital	4.7	3.1	5.2	3.1
Months in Backlog	7.2	4.9	6.6	4.9
Days in Accounts Receivable	34.9	44.4	43.0	44.4
Days in Inventory	7.2	0.0	6.7	0.0
Days in Accounts Payable	32.0	28.3	28.7	28.3
Operating Cycle	51.8	43.4	46.0	43.4

Specialty Trade Contractors

Composite

Balance Sheet

	2010 Participants		2009 Participants	
	Amount	Percent	Amount	Percent
Current assets		%		%
Cash and cash equivalents	$ 4,632,598	17.0	$ 3,541,593	13.8
Marketable securities and short-term investments	804,169	3.0	760,421	3.0
Receivables				
Contract receivables currently due	9,669,365	35.5	7,847,530	30.7
Retainages on contracts	2,282,898	8.4	2,312,514	9.0
Unbilled work	128,279	0.5	212,997	0.8
Other receivables	379,730	1.4	2,389,097	9.3
Less allowance for doubtful accounts	(150,927)	(0.6)	(290,701)	(1.1)
Total receivables, net	12,309,345	45.2	12,451,437	48.7
Inventories	833,398	3.1	538,841	2.1
Costs and recognized earnings in excess of billings on uncompleted contracts	1,205,418	4.4	1,269,605	5.0
Investments in and advances to construction joint ventures	14,237	0.1	176,172	0.7
Income taxes				
Current / refundable	43,108	0.2	173,131	0.7
Deferred	51,594	0.2	208,027	0.8
Other current assets	813,350	3.0	888,254	3.5
Total current assets	20,707,217	76.0	20,007,481	78.2
Property, plant and equipment	8,683,990	31.9	6,980,631	27.3
Less accumulated depreciation	(4,468,067)	(16.4)	(3,874,200)	(15.1)
Property, plant and equipment, net	4,215,922	15.5	3,106,430	12.1
Noncurrent assets				
Long-term investments	263,346	1.0	430,653	1.7
Deferred income taxes	30,778	0.1	192,788	0.8
Other assets	2,031,611	7.5	1,853,115	7.2
Total noncurrent assets	2,325,735	8.5	2,476,556	9.7
Total assets	$ 27,248,874	100.0 %	$ 25,590,468	100.0 %

	2010 Participants		2009 Participants	
	Amount	Percent	Amount	Percent
Current liabilities		%		%
Current maturity on long-term debt	$ 447,317	1.6	$ 538,492	2.1
Notes payable and lines of credit	696,077	2.6	749,927	2.9
Accounts payable				
Trade, including currently due to subcontractors	3,998,842	14.7	2,774,324	10.8
Subcontracts retainages	257,391	0.9	400,836	1.6
Other	216,311	0.8	1,684,274	6.6
Total accounts payable	4,472,544	16.4	4,859,434	19.0
Accrued expenses	2,212,580	8.1	1,919,164	7.5
Billings in excess of costs and recognized earnings on uncompleted contracts	4,221,240	15.5	4,421,960	17.3
Income taxes				
Current	23,558	0.1	216,363	0.8
Deferred	13,397	0.0	185,108	0.7
Other current liabilities	869,100	3.2	334,504	1.3
Total current liabilities	12,955,812	47.5	13,224,952	51.7
Noncurrent liabilities				
Long-term debt, excluding current maturities	2,323,351	8.5	2,147,675	8.4
Deferred income taxes	37,227	0.1	189,461	0.7
Other	785,114	2.8	455,907	1.8
Total liabilities	16,081,504	59.0	16,017,994	62.6
Minority interests	77,098	0.3	120,054	0.5
Net worth				
Common stock, par value	3,173,461	11.6	2,246,062	8.8
Preferred stock, stated value	33,179	0.1	174,665	0.7
Additional paid-in capital	(260,839)	(1.0)	714,946	2.8
Retained earnings	8,670,385	31.8	5,764,363	22.5
Treasury stock	(784,749)	(2.9)	(659,433)	(2.6)
Excess value of marketable securities	9,570	0.0	153,487	0.6
Other equity	249,265	0.9	1,058,328	4.1
Total net worth	11,090,272	40.7	9,452,419	36.9
Total liabilities and net worth	$ 27,248,874	100.0 %	$ 25,590,468	100.0 %

Specialty Trade Contractors

Composite

Statement of Earnings

	2010 Participants		2009 Participants	
	Amount	Percent	Amount	Percent
Contract revenue	$ 60,390,290	97.5 %	$ 55,629,236	96.6 %
Other revenue	1,536,708	2.5	1,932,103	3.4
Total revenue	61,926,998	100.0	57,561,339	100.0
Contract cost	(50,090,133)	(80.9)	(46,803,828)	(81.3)
Other cost	(1,116,264)	(1.8)	(2,214,605)	(3.8)
Total cost	(51,206,397)	(82.7)	(49,018,433)	(85.2)
Gross profit	10,720,601	17.3	8,542,906	14.8
Selling, general and administrative expenses:				
Payroll	(2,835,048)	(4.6)	(2,614,876)	(4.5)
Professional fees	(182,179)	(0.3)	(331,747)	(0.6)
Sales and marketing costs	(250,315)	(0.4)	(302,582)	(0.5)
Technology costs	(159,327)	(0.3)	(270,674)	(0.5)
Administrative bonuses	(562,463)	(0.9)	(758,002)	(1.3)
Other	(3,960,202)	(6.4)	(3,193,667)	(5.5)
Total SG&A expenses	(7,949,534)	(12.8)	(7,471,547)	(13.0)
Income from operations	2,771,067	4.5	1,071,359	1.9
Interest income	44,213	0.1	211,534	0.4
Interest expense	(73,095)	(0.1)	(237,989)	(0.4)
Other income / (expense), net	22,560	0.0	199,250	0.3
Net earnings / (loss) before income taxes	2,764,745	4.5	1,244,164	2.2
Income tax (expense) / benefit	(274,846)	(0.4)	(376,433)	(0.7)
Net earnings	$ 2,489,900	4.0 %	$ 867,722	1.5 %
Average backlog	$ 15,697,953		$ 22,697,256	

Number of Participants

	Number
2010	286
2009	336

Financial Ratios

	2010 Participants		2009 Participants	
	Average	Median	Average	Median
Liquidity Ratios				
Current Ratio	1.6	1.8	1.5	1.7
Quick Ratio	1.4	1.6	1.3	1.4
Days of Cash	26.9	19.7	22.1	13.8
Working Capital Turnover	8.0	6.7	8.5	7.9
Profitability Ratios				
Return on Assets	10.2 %	7.4 %	4.9 %	12.8 %
Return on Equity	24.9 %	16.7 %	13.2 %	30.3 %
Times Interest Earned	38.8	17.6	6.2	15.3
Leverage Ratios				
Debt to Equity	1.5	1.0	1.7	1.3
Revenue to Equity	5.6	4.9	6.1	6.5
Asset Turnover	2.3	2.6	2.2	2.8
Fixed Asset Ratio	38.0 %	24.0 %	32.9 %	24.0 %
Equity to SG&A Expense	1.4	1.4	1.3	1.2
Underbillings to Equity	12.0 %	8.0 %	15.7 %	8.0 %
Backlog to Equity	1.4	0.5	2.4	1.7
Efficiency Ratios				
Backlog to Working Capital	2.0	0.8	3.3	2.6
Months in Backlog	3.0	1.9	4.7	3.6
Days in Accounts Receivable	57.5	54.3	62.1	57.3
Days in Inventory	5.9	0.7	4.0	0.8
Days in Accounts Payable	29.6	26.7	32.7	26.7
Operating Cycle	60.7	55.2	55.4	52.1

CFMA Comparative Financial Data

Balance Sheet
Most Recent Year-End

	All Companies		Industrial & Nonresidential		Heavy & Highway		Specialty Trade	
	Amount	Percent	Amount	Percent	Amount	Percent	Amount	Percent
Current assets:		%		%		%		%
Cash and cash equivalents	$ 8,766,996	21.4	$ 12,010,978	23.5	$ 13,836,711	23.8	$ 4,632,598	17.0
Marketable securities and short-term investments	1,986,410	4.8	2,975,512	5.8	2,736,059	4.7	804,169	3.0
Receivables:								
Contract receivables currently due	13,045,413	31.8	19,311,172	37.7	10,162,270	17.5	9,669,365	35.5
Retainages on contracts	3,615,830	8.8	6,088,446	11.9	3,499,791	6.0	2,282,898	8.4
Unbilled work	174,294	0.4	127,308	0.2	360,593	0.6	128,279	0.5
Other receivables	1,355,980	3.3	2,915,571	5.7	1,562,932	2.7	379,730	1.4
Less allowance for doubtful accounts	(128,389)	(0.3)	(104,705)	(0.2)	(131,025)	(0.2)	(150,927)	(0.6)
Total receivables, net	18,063,127	44.1	28,337,792	55.4	15,454,562	26.6	12,309,345	45.2
Inventories	860,268	2.1	73,951	0.1	2,098,409	3.6	833,398	3.1
Costs and recognized earnings in excess of billings on uncompleted contracts	1,564,898	3.8	1,835,954	3.6	2,097,462	3.6	1,205,418	4.4
Investments in and advances to construction joint ventures	385,004	0.9	468,167	0.9	1,128,434	1.9	14,237	0.1
Income taxes:								
Current / refundable	108,670	0.3	262,653	0.5	27,770	0.0	43,108	0.2
Deferred	72,017	0.2	30,014	0.1	213,694	0.4	51,594	0.2
Other current assets	1,114,023	2.7	936,129	1.8	1,894,247	3.3	813,350	3.0
Total current assets	32,921,414	80.3	46,931,151	91.7	39,487,348	67.9	20,707,217	76.0
Property, plant and equipment	13,034,502	31.8	5,502,378	10.8	36,940,016	63.5	8,683,990	31.9
Less accumulated depreciation	(7,403,240)	(18.1)	(3,391,839)	(6.6)	(22,063,524)	(37.9)	(4,468,067)	(16.4)
Property, plant and equipment, net	5,631,262	13.7	2,110,539	4.1	14,876,491	25.6	4,215,922	15.5
Noncurrent assets:								
Long-term investments	598,193	1.5	1,146,272	2.2	691,814	1.2	263,346	1.0
Deferred income taxes	86,257	0.2	78,537	0.2	269,497	0.5	30,778	0.1
Other assets	1,739,115	4.2	907,531	1.8	2,823,836	4.9	2,031,611	7.5
Total noncurrent assets	2,423,565	5.9	2,132,340	4.2	3,785,146	6.5	2,325,735	8.5
Total assets	$ 40,976,241	100.0 %	$ 51,174,029	100.0 %	$ 58,148,986	100.0 %	$ 27,248,874	100.0 %

CFMA Comparative Financial Data

	All Companies		Industrial & Nonresidential		Heavy & Highway		Specialty Trade	
	Amount	Percent	Amount	Percent	Amount	Percent	Amount	Percent
Current liabilities:								
Current maturity on long-term debt	$ 577,865	1.4 %	$ 231,658	0.5 %	$ 1,575,032	2.7 %	$ 447,317	1.6 %
Notes payable and lines of credit	478,425	1.2	189,884	0.4	436,864	0.8	696,077	2.6
Accounts payable								
Trade including currently due to subcontractors	10,178,510	24.8	20,329,820	39.7	8,940,265	15.4	3,998,842	14.7
Subcontracts retainages	2,475,727	6.0	6,638,359	13.0	1,432,155	2.5	257,391	0.9
Other	376,304	0.9	616,994	1.2	394,892	0.7	216,311	0.8
Total accounts payable	13,030,541	31.8	27,585,173	53.9	10,767,311	18.5	4,472,544	16.4
Accrued expenses	2,636,468	6.4	2,992,177	5.8	3,365,917	5.8	2,212,580	8.1
Billings in excess of costs and recognized earnings on uncompleted contracts	5,346,141	13.0	5,548,926	10.8	7,333,829	12.6	4,221,240	15.5
Income taxes:								
Current	91,693	0.2	89,152	0.2	272,755	0.5	23,558	0.1
Deferred	20,862	0.1	11,804	0.0	48,496	0.1	13,397	0.0
Other current liabilities	540,454	1.3	213,093	0.4	407,806	0.7	869,100	3.2
Total current liabilities	22,722,448	55.5	36,861,868	72.0	24,208,011	41.6	12,955,812	47.5
Noncurrent liabilities								
Long-term debt, excluding current maturities	2,641,282	6.4	1,082,389	2.1	6,229,081	10.7	2,323,351	8.5
Deferred income taxes	147,056	0.4	74,332	0.1	588,460	1.0	37,227	0.1
Other	908,700	2.2	683,860	1.3	1,805,508	3.1	765,114	2.8
Total liabilities	26,419,486	64.5	38,702,449	75.6	32,831,060	56.5	16,081,504	59.0
Minority interests	136,520	0.3	59,123	0.1	397,907	0.7	77,098	0.3
Net worth:								
Common stock, par value	3,404,987	8.3	2,421,976	4.7	4,410,466	7.6	3,173,461	11.6
Preferred stock, stated value	21,227	0.1	6,728	0.0	22,273	0.0	33,179	0.1
Additional paid-in capital	840,332	2.1	980,041	1.9	3,158,685	5.4	(260,839)	(1.0)
Retained earnings	10,444,684	25.5	8,608,485	16.8	18,395,337	31.6	8,670,385	31.8
Treasury stock	(724,705)	(1.8)	(322,214)	(0.6)	(1,338,491)	(2.3)	(784,749)	(2.9)
Excess value of marketable securities	10,478	0.0	11,654	0.0	10,696	0.0	9,570	0.0
Other equity	423,232	1.0	705,787	1.4	261,053	0.4	249,265	0.9
Total net worth	14,420,235	35.2	12,412,457	24.3	24,920,020	42.9	11,090,272	40.7
Total liabilities and net worth	$ 40,976,241	100.0 %	$ 51,174,029	100.0 %	$ 58,148,986	100.0 %	$ 27,248,874	100.0 %

CFMA Comparative Financial Data

Statement of Earnings
Most Recent Year-End

	All Companies		Industrial & Nonresidential		Heavy & Highway		Specialty Trade	
	Amount	Percent	Amount	Percent	Amount	Percent	Amount	Percent
Contract revenue	$ 103,086,329	98.6 %	$ 161,430,978	99.7 %	$ 117,898,262	98.7 %	$ 60,390,290	97.5 %
Other revenue	1,459,634	1.4	525,963	0.3	1,609,197	1.3	1,536,708	2.5
Total revenue	104,545,963	100.0	161,956,941	100.0	119,507,459	100.0	61,926,998	100.0
Contract cost	(91,909,826)	(87.9)	(151,091,829)	(93.3)	(103,912,736)	(87.0)	(50,090,133)	(80.9)
Other cost	(1,054,837)	(1.0)	(417,298)	(0.3)	(1,004,964)	(0.8)	(1,116,264)	(1.8)
Total cost	(92,964,663)	(88.9)	(151,509,127)	(93.5)	(104,917,701)	(87.8)	(51,206,397)	(82.7)
Gross profit	11,581,300	11.1	10,447,814	6.5	14,589,758	12.2	10,720,601	17.3
Selling, general and administrative expenses								
Payroll	(2,781,097)	(2.7)	(2,896,816)	(1.8)	(2,832,923)	(2.4)	(2,835,046)	(4.6)
Professional fees	(193,097)	(0.2)	(197,776)	(0.1)	(241,470)	(0.2)	(182,179)	(0.3)
Sales and marketing costs	(225,596)	(0.2)	(256,952)	(0.2)	(128,197)	(0.1)	(250,315)	(0.4)
Technology costs	(147,422)	(0.1)	(156,345)	(0.1)	(132,413)	(0.1)	(159,327)	(0.3)
Administrative bonuses	(546,369)	(0.5)	(521,364)	(0.3)	(576,984)	(0.5)	(562,463)	(0.9)
Other	(4,047,246)	(3.9)	(3,198,835)	(2.0)	(4,453,665)	(3.7)	(3,960,202)	(6.4)
Total SG&A expenses	(7,940,827)	(7.6)	(7,228,088)	(4.5)	(8,365,653)	(7.0)	(7,949,534)	(12.8)
Income from operations	3,640,473	3.5	3,219,726	2.0	6,224,105	5.2	2,771,067	4.5
Interest income	111,746	0.1	193,990	0.1	132,920	0.1	44,213	0.1
Interest expense	(107,236)	(0.1)	(52,188)	(0.0)	(289,358)	(0.2)	(73,095)	(0.1)
Other income / (expense), net	58,257	0.1	(59,409)	(0.0)	291,650	0.2	22,560	0.0
Net earnings / (loss) before income taxes	3,703,240	3.5	3,302,119	2.0	6,359,317	5.3	2,764,745	4.5
Income tax (expense) / benefit	(317,405)	(0.3)	(200,375)	(0.1)	(498,610)	(0.4)	(274,846)	(0.4)
Net earnings	$ 3,385,835	3.2 %	$ 3,101,743	1.9 %	$ 5,860,707	4.9 %	$ 2,489,900	4.0 %
Average backlog	$ 52,824,730		$ 101,323,289		$ 71,600,040		$ 15,697,953	

Number of Participants

	All Companies	Industrial & Nonresidential	Heavy & Highway	Specialty Trade
	Number	Number	Number	Number
2010	623	191	110	286
2009	808	275	126	336

CFMA Comparative Financial Data

Financial Ratios
Most Recent Year-End

	All Companies		Industrial & Nonresidential		Heavy & Highway		Specialty Trade	
	Average	Median	Average	Median	Average	Median	Average	Median
Liquidity Ratios								
Current Ratio	1.4	1.7	1.3	1.4	1.6	1.7	1.6	1.8
Quick Ratio	1.3	1.4	1.2	1.3	1.3	1.4	1.4	1.6
Days of Cash	30.2	26.4	26.7	31.5	41.7	25.0	26.9	19.7
Working Capital Turnover	10.3	8.5	16.1	12.4	7.8	8.1	8.0	6.7
Profitability Ratios								
Return on Assets	9.0 %	7.1 %	6.5 %	5.8 %	10.9 %	8.7 %	10.2 %	7.4 %
Return on Equity	25.7 %	17.1 %	26.6 %	19.8 %	25.5 %	17.3 %	24.9 %	16.7 %
Times Interest Earned	35.5	14.8	64.3	22.2	23.0	9.5	38.8	17.6
Leverage Ratios								
Debt to Equity	1.8	1.3	3.1	2.0	1.3	1.3	1.5	1.0
Revenue to Equity	7.2	6.0	13.0	10.6	4.8	5.1	5.6	4.9
Asset Turnover	2.6	2.7	3.2	3.4	2.1	2.3	2.3	2.6
Fixed Asset Ratio	39.1 %	23.0 %	17.0 %	13.0 %	59.7 %	58.0 %	38.0 %	24.0 %
Equity to SG&A Expense	1.8	1.6	1.7	1.6	3.0	2.3	1.4	1.4
Underbillings to Equity	12.1 %	6.0 %	15.8 %	5.0 %	9.9 %	7.0 %	12.0 %	8.0 %
Backlog to Equity	3.7	1.3	8.2	3.7	2.9	1.7	1.4	0.5
Efficiency Ratios								
Backlog to Working Capital	5.2	1.7	10.1	4.7	4.7	3.1	2.0	0.8
Months in Backlog	6.1	3.2	7.5	4.5	7.2	4.9	3.0	1.9
Days in Accounts Receivable	49.1	46.1	49.2	38.5	34.9	44.4	57.5	54.3
Days in Inventory	3.3	0.0	0.2	0.0	7.2	0.0	5.9	0.7
Days in Accounts Payable	40.9	30.6	49.8	36.2	32.0	28.3	29.6	26.7
Operating Cycle	41.8	44.6	26.3	34.0	51.8	43.4	60.7	55.2

TEXT—KEY WORD INDEX OF INDUSTRIES APPEARING IN THE STATEMENT STUDIES

STATEMENT STUDIES KEY WORD INDEX

A complete description of each industry category listed below begins on page 35.

A

rasive Product Manufacturing, 478-479, mfg

hesive Manufacturing, 424-425, mfg

ministration of Air and Water Resource and Solid Waste Management Programs, 1622-1623, pub admin

ministration of Education Programs, 1618-1619, pub admin

ministration of General Economic Programs, 1628-1629, pub admin

ministration of Housing Programs, 1624-1625, pub admin

ministration of Public Health Programs, 1620-1621, pub admin

ministration of Urban Planning and Community and Rural Development, 1626-1627, pub admin

ministrative Management and General Management Consulting Services, 1276-1277, prof serv

vertising Agencies, 1294-1295, prof serv

vertising Material Distribution Services, 1304-1305, prof serv

and Gas Compressor Manufacturing, 620-621, mfg

-Conditioning and Warm Air Heating Equipment and Commercial and Industrial Refrigeration Equipment Manufacturing, 600-601, mfg

craft Engine and Engine Parts Manufacturing, 706-707, mfg

Other Amusement and Recreation Industries, 1510-1511, ent

Other Automotive Repair and Maintenance, 1550-1551, other

Other Basic Inorganic Chemical Manufacturing, 404-405, mfg

Other Basic Organic Chemical Manufacturing, 408-409, mfg

Other Business Support Services, 1340-1341, Admin

Other Consumer Goods Rental, 1230-1231, R/E

Other Converted Paper Product Manufacturing, 376-377, mfg

Other Cut and Sew Apparel Manufacturing, 330-331, mfg

Other General Merchandise Stores, 1006-1007, rtl

Other Grain Farming, 104-105, ag

Other Health and Personal Care Stores, 976-977, rtl

Other Home Furnishings Stores, 932-933, rtl

Other Industrial Machinery Manufacturing, 588-589, mfg

Other Information Services, 1142-1143, info

Other Insurance Related Activities, 1196-1197, fin

Other Miscellaneous Ambulatory Health Care Services, 1442-1443, HC

Other Miscellaneous Chemical Product and Preparation Manufacturing, 436-437, mfg

Other Miscellaneous Crop Farming, 124-125, ag

Other Miscellaneous Electrical Equipment and Component Manufacturing, 690-691, mfg

Other Miscellaneous Fabricated Metal Product Manufacturing, 566-567, mfg

Other Miscellaneous Food Manufacturing, 292-293, mfg

Other Miscellaneous General Purpose Machinery Manufacturing, 634-635, mfg

Other Miscellaneous Manufacturing, 764-765, mfg

Other Miscellaneous Nonmetallic Mineral Product Manufacturing, 482-483, mfg

Other Miscellaneous Schools and Instruction, 1396-1397, edu

All Other Miscellaneous Store Retailers (except Tobacco Stores), 1024-1025, rtl

All Other Miscellaneous Textile Product Mills, 316-317, mfg

All Other Miscellaneous Waste Management Services, 1380-1381, Admin

All Other Miscellaneous Wood Product Manufacturing, 356-357, mfg

All Other Motor Vehicle Dealers, 922-923, rtl

All Other Motor Vehicle Parts Manufacturing, 704-705, mfg

All Other Nondepository Credit Intermediation, 1156-1157, fin

All Other Outpatient Care Centers, 1430-1431, HC

All Other Personal Services, 1580-1581, other

All Other Petroleum and Coal Products Manufacturing, 402-403, mfg

All Other Plastics Product Manufacturing, 456-457, mfg

All Other Professional, Scientific, and Technical Services, 1316-1317, prof serv

All Other Publishers, 1114-1115, info

All Other Rubber Product Manufacturing, 464-465, mfg

All Other Specialty Food Stores, 964-965, rtl

All Other Specialty Trade Contractors, 238-239, cons-g

All Other Specialty Trade Contractors, 1653, cons-%

All Other Support Activities for Transportation, 1092-1093, trans

All Other Support Services, 1364-1365, Admin

All Other Telecommunications, 1136-1137, info

All Other Transit and Ground Passenger Transportation, 1072-1073, trans

All Other Transportation Equipment Manufacturing, 718-719, mfg

All Other Travel Arrangement and Reservation Services, 1346-1347, Admin

Aluminum Die-Casting Foundries, 506-507, mfg

Aluminum Extruded Product Manufacturing, 494-495, mfg

Aluminum Foundries (except Die-Casting), 510-511, mfg

Ambulance Services, 1438-1439, HC

American Indian and Alaska Native Tribal Governments, 1612-1613, pub admin

Amusement and Theme Parks, 1494-1495, ent

Amusement Arcades, 1496-1497, ent

Analytical Laboratory Instrument Manufacturing, 670-671, mfg

Animal (except Poultry) Slaughtering, 262-263, mfg

Apple Orchards, 112-113, ag

Appliance Repair and Maintenance, 1558-1559, other

Architectural Services, 1256-1257, prof serv

Art Dealers, 1018-1019, rtl

Asphalt Paving Mixture and Block Manufacturing, 398-399, mfg

Audio and Video Equipment Manufacturing, 646-647, mfg

Automatic Environmental Control Manufacturing for Residential, Commercial, and Appliance Use, 662-663, mfg

Automobile and Other Motor Vehicle Merchant Wholesalers, 768-769, wsle

Automobile Manufacturing, 692-693, mfg

Automotive Body, Paint, and Interior Repair and Maintenance, 1542-1543, other

Automotive Exhaust System Repair, 1538-1539, other

Automotive Glass Replacement Shops, 1544-1545, other

Automotive Oil Change and Lubrication Shops, 1546-1547, other

Automotive Parts and Accessories Stores, 924-925, rtl

B

Baked Goods Stores, 960-961, rtl

Ball and Roller Bearing Manufacturing, 562-563, mfg

Bare Printed Circuit Board Manufacturing, 648-649, mfg

Beauty Salons, 1562-1563, other

Beef Cattle Ranching and Farming, 126-127, ag

Beer and Ale Merchant Wholesalers, 890-891, wsle

Beer, Wine, and Liquor Stores, 966-967, rtl

Bituminous Coal and Lignite Surface Mining, 158-159, mng

Blind and Shade Manufacturing, 736-737, mfg

Blood and Organ Banks, 1440-1441, HC

Boat Building, 714-715, mfg

Boat Dealers, 920-921, rtl

Bolt, Nut, Screw, Rivet, and Washer Manufacturing, 546-547, mfg

Book Publishers, 1110-1111, info

Book Stores, 1002-1003, rtl

Book, Periodical, and Newspaper Merchant Wholesalers, 896-897, wsle

Books Printing, 388-389, mfg

Bottled Water Manufacturing, 296-297, mfg

Bowling Centers, 1508-1509, ent

Breweries, 298-299, mfg

Brick and Structural Clay Tile Manufacturing, 466-467, mfg

Brick, Stone, and Related Construction Material Merchant Wholesalers, 782-783, wsle

Broadwoven Fabric Finishing Mills, 306-307, mfg

Broadwoven Fabric Mills, 304-305, mfg

Broom, Brush, and Mop Manufacturing, 762-763, mfg

Business Associations, 1594-1595, other

Business to Business Electronic Markets, 906-907, wsle

C

Cable and Other Subscription Programming, 1128-1129, info

Canvas and Related Product Mills, 314-315, mfg

Car Washes, 1548-1549, other

Carpet and Rug Mills, 310-311, mfg

Carpet and Upholstery Cleaning Services, 1358-1359, Admin

Casino Hotels, 1516-1517, rest/lodg

Casinos (except Casino Hotels), 1498-1499, ent

Caterers, 1530-1531, rest/lodg

Cattle Feedlots, 128-129, ag

Cemeteries and Crematories, 1566-1567, other

Charter Bus Industry, 1070-1071, trans

Cheese Manufacturing, 258-259, mfg

Chicken Egg Production, 134-135, ag

Child and Youth Services, 1464-1465, HC

Child Day Care Services, 1478-1479, HC

Civic and Social Organizations, 1592-1593, other

Clothing Accessories Stores, 988-989, rtl

Coal and Other Mineral and Ore Merchant Wholesalers, 804-805, wsle

Coastal and Great Lakes Freight Transportation, 1048-1049, trans

Coated and Laminated Packaging Paper Manufacturing, 366-367, mfg

Coated and Laminated Paper Manufacturing, 368-369, mfg

Coated Paper Bag and Pouch Manufacturing, 370-371, mfg

Coffee and Tea Manufacturing, 282-283, mfg

Coin-Operated Laundries and Drycleaners, 1568-1569, other

Collection Agencies, 1338-1339, Admin

Colleges, Universities, and Professional Schools, 1388-1389, edu

STATEMENT STUDIES KEY WORD INDEX

A complete description of each industry category listed below begins on page 35.

Commercial Air, Rail, and Water Transportation Equipment Rental and Leasing, 1234-1235, R/E

Commercial and Industrial Machinery and Equipment (except Automotive and Electronic) Repair and Maintenance, 1556-1557, other

Commercial and Institutional Building Construction, 190-191, cons-g

Commercial and Institutional Building Construction, 1638, cons-%

Commercial Bakeries, 274-275, mfg

Commercial Flexographic Printing, 380-381, mfg

Commercial Lithographic Printing, 378-379, mfg

Commercial Photography, 1312-1313, prof serv

Commercial Screen Printing, 382-383, mfg

Commercial, Industrial, and Institutional Electric Lighting Fixture Manufacturing, 676-677, mfg

Commodity Contracts Brokerage, 1170-1171, fin

Commodity Contracts Dealing, 1168-1169, fin

Community Food Services, 1470-1471, HC

Computer and Computer Peripheral Equipment and Software Merchant Wholesalers, 792-793, wsle

Computer and Office Machine Repair and Maintenance, 1552-1553, other

Computer and Software Stores, 938-939, rtl

Computer Systems Design Services, 1272-1273, prof serv

Concrete Block and Brick Manufacturing, 472-473, mfg

Concrete Pipe Manufacturing, 474-475, mfg

Confectionery and Nut Stores, 962-963, rtl

Confectionery Manufacturing from Purchased Chocolate, 246-247, mfg

Confectionery Merchant Wholesalers, 866-867, wsle

Construction and Mining (except Oil Well) Machinery and Equipment Merchant Wholesalers, 820-821, wsle

Construction Machinery Manufacturing, 572-573, mfg

Construction Sand and Gravel Mining, 164-165, mng

Construction, Mining, and Forestry Machinery and Equipment Rental and Leasing, 1236-1237, R/E

Consumer Electronics and Appliances Rental, 1226-1227, R/E

Consumer Lending, 1150-1151, fin

Continuing Care Retirement Communities, 1458-1459, HC

Convenience Stores, 954-955, rtl

Conveyor and Conveying Equipment Manufacturing, 622-623, mfg

Cookie and Cracker Manufacturing, 276-277, mfg

Copper Wire (except Mechanical) Drawing, 496-497, mfg

Corn Farming, 102-103, ag

Corrugated and Solid Fiber Box Manufacturing, 360-361, mfg

Cosmetics, Beauty Supplies, and Perfume Stores, 970-971, rtl

Costume Jewelry and Novelty Manufacturing, 750-751, mfg

Cotton Farming, 122-123, ag

Cotton Ginning, 146-147, ag

Couriers and Express Delivery Services, 1094-1095, trans

Credit Card Issuing, 1146-1147, fin

Crude Petroleum and Natural Gas Extraction, 156-157, mng

Crushed and Broken Limestone Mining and Quarrying, 160-161, mng

Current-Carrying Wiring Device Manufacturing, 688-689, mfg

Custom Compounding of Purchased Resins, 434-435, mfg

Custom Computer Programming Services, 1270-1271, prof serv

Cut Stock, Resawing Lumber, and Planing, 346-347, mfg

Cut Stone and Stone Product Manufacturing, 480-481, mfg

Cutting Tool and Machine Tool Accessory Manufacturing, 610-611, mfg

D

Dairy Cattle and Milk Production, 130-131, ag

Dairy Product (except Dried or Canned) Merchant Wholesalers, 862-863, wsle

Data Processing, Hosting, and Related Services, 1138-1139, info

Dental Equipment and Supplies Manufacturing, 742-743, mfg

Dental Laboratories, 746-747, mfg

Department Stores (except Discount Department Stores), 1004-1005, rtl

Diagnostic Imaging Centers, 1434-1435, HC

Direct Health and Medical Insurance Carriers, 1184-1185, fin

Direct Life Insurance Carriers, 1182-1183, fin

Direct Mail Advertising, 1302-1303, prof serv

Direct Property and Casualty Insurance Carriers, 1186-1187, fin

Direct Title Insurance Carriers, 1188-1189, fin

Directory and Mailing List Publishers, 1112-1113, info

Display Advertising, 1300-1301, prof serv

Dried and Dehydrated Food Manufacturing, 254-255, mfg

Drilling Oil and Gas Wells, 166-167, mng

Drinking Places (Alcoholic Beverages), 1532-1533, rest/lodg

Drugs and Druggists' Sundries Merchant Wholesalers, 848-849, wsle

Drycleaning and Laundry Services (except Coin-Operated), 1570-1571, other

Drywall and Insulation Contractors, 224-225, cons-g

Drywall and Insulation Contractors, 1650, cons-%

E

Educational Support Services, 1398-1399, edu

Electric Power Distribution, 172-173, util

Electrical and Electronic Appliance, Television, and Radio Set Merchant Wholesalers, 808-809, wsle

Electrical Apparatus and Equipment, Wiring Supplies, and Related Equipment Merchant Wholesalers, 806-807, wsle

Electrical Contractors, 1648, cons-%

Electrical Contractors and Other Wiring Installation Contractors, 218-219, cons-g

Electromedical and Electrotherapeutic Apparatus Manufacturing, 658-659, mfg

Electronic Coil, Transformer, and Other Inductor Manufacturing, 652-653, mfg

Electronic Computer Manufacturing, 636-637, mfg

Electronic Connector Manufacturing, 654-655, mfg

Electronic Shopping, 1026-1027, rtl

Electroplating, Plating, Polishing, Anodizing, and Coloring, 552-553, mfg

Elementary and Secondary Schools, 1384-1385, edu

Employment Placement Agencies, 1330-1331, Admin

Engineering Services, 1260-1261, prof serv

Envelope Manufacturing, 372-373, mfg

Environmental Consulting Services, 1286-1287, prof serv

Ethyl Alcohol Manufacturing, 406-407, mfg

Executive and Legislative Offices, Combined, 1610-1611, pub admin

Executive Offices, 1606-1607, pub admin

Exterminating and Pest Control Services, 1352-1353, Admin

F

Fabric Coating Mills, 308-309, mfg

Fabricated Pipe and Pipe Fitting Manufacturing, 564-565, mfg

Fabricated Structural Metal Manufacturing, 524-525, mfg

Facilities Support Services, 1328-1329, Admin

Family Clothing Stores, 986-987, rtl

Family Planning Centers, 1420-1421, HC

Farm and Garden Machinery and Equipment Merchant Wholesalers, 822-823, wsle

Farm Machinery and Equipment Manufacturing, 568-569, mfg

Farm Product Warehousing and Storage, 1100-1101, trans

Farm Supplies Merchant Wholesalers, 894-895, wsle

Fertilizer (Mixing Only) Manufacturing, 414-415, mfg

Financial Transactions Processing, Reserve, and Clearinghouse Activities, 1160-1161, fin

Fine Arts Schools, 1394-1395, edu

Finfish Fishing, 142-143, ag

Finish Carpentry Contractors, 232-233, cons-g

Fire Protection, 1616-1617, pub admin

Fish and Seafood Merchant Wholesalers, 868-869, wsle

Fitness and Recreational Sports Centers, 1506-1507, ent

Flavoring Syrup and Concentrate Manufacturing, 284-285, mfg

Floor Covering Stores, 930-931, rtl

Flooring Contractors, 228-229, cons-g

Florists, 1008-1009, rtl

Flour Milling, 244-245, mfg

Flower, Nursery Stock, and Florists' Supplies Merchant Wholesalers, 898-899, wsle

Fluid Milk Manufacturing, 256-257, mfg

Fluid Power Valve and Hose Fitting Manufacturing, 556-557, mfg

Folding Paperboard Box Manufacturing, 362-363, mfg

Food (Health) Supplement Stores, 974-975, rtl

Food Product Machinery Manufacturing, 586-587, mfg

Food Service Contractors, 1528-1529, rest/lodg

Footwear Merchant Wholesalers, 856-857, wsle

Framing Contractors, 208-209, cons-g

Freestanding Ambulatory Surgical and Emergency Centers, 1428-1429, HC

Freight Transportation Arrangement, 1088-1089, trans

Fresh and Frozen Seafood Processing, 270-271, mfg

Fresh Fruit and Vegetable Merchant Wholesalers, 872-873, wsle

Frozen Fruit, Juice, and Vegetable Manufacturing, 248-249, mfg

Frozen Specialty Food Manufacturing, 250-251, mfg

Fruit and Vegetable Canning, 252-253, mfg

Fruit and Vegetable Markets, 958-959, rtl

Full-Service Restaurants, 1522-1523, rest/lodg

Funeral Homes and Funeral Services, 1564-1565, other

Furniture Merchant Wholesalers, 776-777, wsle

Furniture Stores, 928-929, rtl

G

Game, Toy, and Children's Vehicle Manufacturing, 754-755, mfg

Gasket, Packing, and Sealing Device Manufacturing, 758-759, mfg

Gasoline Stations with Convenience Stores, 978-979, rtl

General Automotive Repair, 1536-1537, other

STATEMENT STUDIES KEY WORD INDEX

A complete description of each industry category listed below begins on page 35.

eneral Freight Trucking, Local, 1052-1053, trans

eneral Freight Trucking, Long-Distance, Less Than Truckload, 1056-1057, trans

eneral Freight Trucking, Long-Distance, Truckload, 1054-1055, trans

eneral Line Grocery Merchant Wholesalers, 858-859, wsle

eneral Medical and Surgical Hospitals, 1444-1445, HC

eneral Medical and Surgical Hospitals (Non-Profit), 1446-1447, HC

eneral Rental Centers, 1232-1233, R/E

eneral Warehousing and Storage, 1096-1097, trans

ift, Novelty, and Souvenir Stores, 1012-1013, rtl

lass and Glazing Contractors, 212-213, cons-g

lass and Glazing Contractors, 1646, cons-%

lass Product Manufacturing Made of Purchased Glass, 468-469, mfg

olf Courses and Country Clubs, 1500-1501, ent

rain and Field Bean Merchant Wholesalers, 876-877, wsle

rantmaking Foundations, 1584-1585, other

rape Vineyards, 114-115, ag

raphic Design Services, 1268-1269, prof serv

H

and and Edge Tool Manufacturing, 520-521, mfg

ardware Manufacturing, 536-537, mfg

ardware Merchant Wholesalers, 812-813, wsle

ardware Stores, 944-945, rtl

ardwood Veneer and Plywood Manufacturing, 340-341, mfg

azardous Waste Treatment and Disposal, 1370-1371, Admin

eating Equipment (except Warm Air Furnaces) Manufacturing, 598-599, mfg

eating Oil Dealers, 1032-1033, rtl

ighway, Street, and Bridge Construction, 200-201, cons-g

ighway, Street, and Bridge Construction, 1641, cons-%

MO Medical Centers, 1424-1425, HC

obby, Toy, and Game Stores, 998-999, rtl

og and Pig Farming, 132-133, ag

ome Centers, 940-941, rtl

ome Furnishing Merchant Wholesalers, 778-779, wsle

ome Health Care Services, 1436-1437, HC

ome Health Equipment Rental, 1228-1229, R/E

omes for the Elderly, 1460-1461, HC

orses and Other Equine Production, 136-137, ag

otels (except Casino Hotels) and Motels, 1514-1515, rest/lodg

ousehold Appliance Stores, 934-935, rtl

uman Resources Consulting Services, 1278-1279, prof serv

I

e Cream and Frozen Dessert Manufacturing, 260-261, mfg

dustrial and Commercial Fan and Blower Manufacturing, 596-597, mfg

dustrial and Personal Service Paper Merchant Wholesalers, 846-847, wsle

dustrial Building Construction, 188-189, cons-g

dustrial Building Construction, 1637, cons-%

dustrial Machinery and Equipment Merchant Wholesalers, 824-825, wsle

dustrial Mold Manufacturing, 602-603, mfg

dustrial Process Furnace and Oven Manufacturing, 632-633, mfg

dustrial Supplies Merchant Wholesalers, 826-827, wsle

Industrial Truck, Tractor, Trailer, and Stacker Machinery Manufacturing, 626-627, mfg

Industrial Valve Manufacturing, 554-555, mfg

Inland Water Freight Transportation, 1050-1051, trans

Institutional Furniture Manufacturing, 726-727, mfg

Instrument Manufacturing for Measuring and Testing Electricity and Electrical Signals, 668-669, mfg

Instruments and Related Products Manufacturing for Measuring, Displaying, and Controlling Industrial Process Variables, 664-665, mfg

Insurance Agencies and Brokerages, 1192-1193, fin

Interior Design Services, 1266-1267, prof serv

Internet Publishing and Broadcasting and Web Search Portals, 1140-1141, info

Investment Advice, 1176-1177, fin

Investment Banking and Securities Dealing, 1164-1165, fin

Iron and Steel Forging, 514-515, mfg

Iron and Steel Mills, 484-485, mfg

Iron and Steel Pipe and Tube Manufacturing from Purchased Steel, 486-487, mfg

Iron Foundries, 502-503, mfg

J

Janitorial Services, 1354-1355, Admin

Jewelry (except Costume) Manufacturing, 748-749, mfg

Jewelry Stores, 994-995, rtl

Jewelry, Watch, Precious Stone, and Precious Metal Merchant Wholesalers, 838-839, wsle

Junior Colleges, 1386-1387, edu

K

Kidney Dialysis Centers, 1426-1427, HC

L

Labor Unions and Similar Labor Organizations, 1598-1599, other

Laminated Plastics Plate, Sheet (except Packaging), and Shape Manufacturing, 448-449, mfg

Land Subdivision, 198-199, cons-g

Land Subdivision, 1640, cons-%

Landscape Architectural Services, 1258-1259, prof serv

Landscaping Services, 1356-1357, Admin

Lawn and Garden Tractor and Home Lawn and Garden Equipment Manufacturing, 570-571, mfg

Leather and Hide Tanning and Finishing, 334-335, mfg

Legislative Bodies, 1608-1609, pub admin

Lessors of Miniwarehouses and Self-Storage Units, 1208-1209, R/E

Lessors of Nonfinancial Intangible Assets (except Copyrighted Works), 1242-1243, R/E

Lessors of Nonresidential Buildings (except Miniwarehouses), 1206-1207, R/E

Lessors of Other Real Estate Property, 1210-1211, R/E

Lessors of Residential Buildings and Dwellings, 1204-1205, R/E

Limited-Service Restaurants, 1524-1525, rest/lodg

Limousine Service, 1066-1067, trans

Line-Haul Railroads, 1046-1047, trans

Linen Supply, 1572-1573, other

Liquefied Petroleum Gas (Bottled Gas) Dealers, 1034-1035, rtl

Livestock Merchant Wholesalers, 878-879, wsle

Logging, 140-141, ag

Lumber, Plywood, Millwork, and Wood Panel Merchant Wholesalers, 780-781, wsle

M

Machine Shops, 542-543, mfg

Machine Tool (Metal Cutting Types) Manufacturing, 604-605, mfg

Machine Tool (Metal Forming Types) Manufacturing, 606-607, mfg

Mail-Order Houses, 1028-1029, rtl

Manifold Business Forms Printing, 386-387, mfg

Manufactured (Mobile) Home Dealers, 1020-1021, rtl

Manufactured Home (Mobile Home) Manufacturing, 352-353, mfg

Marinas, 1504-1505, ent

Marine Cargo Handling, 1078-1079, trans

Marketing Consulting Services, 1280-1281, prof serv

Marketing Research and Public Opinion Polling, 1308-1309, prof serv

Masonry Contractors, 210-211, cons-g

Masonry Contractors, 1645, cons-%

Materials Recovery Facilities, 1378-1379, Admin

Mattress Manufacturing, 734-735, mfg

Mayonnaise, Dressing, and Other Prepared Sauce Manufacturing, 286-287, mfg

Meat and Meat Product Merchant Wholesalers, 870-871, wsle

Meat Markets, 956-957, rtl

Meat Processed from Carcasses, 264-265, mfg

Mechanical Power Transmission Equipment Manufacturing, 616-617, mfg

Media Representatives, 1298-1299, prof serv

Medical Laboratories, 1432-1433, HC

Medical, Dental, and Hospital Equipment and Supplies Merchant Wholesalers, 796-797, wsle

Medicinal and Botanical Manufacturing, 418-419, mfg

Men's and Boys' Clothing and Furnishings Merchant Wholesalers, 852-853, wsle

Men's and Boys' Cut and Sew Apparel Contractors, 318-319, mfg

Men's and Boys' Cut and Sew Other Outerwear Manufacturing, 324-325, mfg

Men's and Boys' Cut and Sew Suit, Coat, and Overcoat Manufacturing, 322-323, mfg

Men's Clothing Stores, 982-983, rtl

Metal Coating, Engraving (except Jewelry and Silverware), and Allied Services to Manufacturers, 550-551, mfg

Metal Heat Treating, 548-549, mfg

Metal Service Centers and Other Metal Merchant Wholesalers, 802-803, wsle

Metal Stamping, 516-517, mfg

Metal Window and Door Manufacturing, 528-529, mfg

Mining Machinery and Equipment Manufacturing, 574-575, mfg

Miscellaneous Financial Investment Activities, 1180-1181, fin

Miscellaneous Intermediation, 1172-1173, fin

Mortgage and Nonmortgage Loan Brokers, 1158-1159, fin

Motion Picture and Video Production, 1118-1119, info

Motion Picture Theaters (except Drive-Ins), 1120-1121, info

Motor and Generator Manufacturing, 682-683, mfg

Motor Vehicle Body Manufacturing, 694-695, mfg

Motor Vehicle Metal Stamping, 702-703, mfg

Motor Vehicle Parts (Used) Merchant Wholesalers, 774-775, wsle

Motor Vehicle Seating and Interior Trim Manufacturing, 700-701, mfg

Motor Vehicle Supplies and New Parts Merchant Wholesalers, 770-771, wsle

Motor Vehicle Towing, 1084-1085, trans

Motorcycle, ATV, and Personal Watercraft Dealers, 918-919, rtl

Motorcycle, Bicycle, and Parts Manufacturing, 716-717, mfg

Museums, 1492-1493, ent

STATEMENT STUDIES KEY WORD INDEX

A complete description of each industry category listed below begins on page 35.

Mushroom Production, 118-119, ag
Musical Groups and Artists, 1484-1485, ent
Musical Instrument and Supplies Stores, 1000-1001, rtl
Musical Instrument Manufacturing, 760-761, mfg

N

Natural Gas Distribution, 174-175, util
Navigational Services to Shipping, 1080-1081, trans
New Car Dealers, 912-913, rtl
New Housing Operative Builders, 184-185, cons-g
New Housing Operative Builders, 1635, cons-%
New Multifamily Housing Construction (except Operative Builders), 182-183, cons-g
New Multifamily Housing Construction (except Operative Builders), 1634, cons-%
New Single-Family Housing Construction (except Operative Builders), 180-181, cons-g
New Single-Family Housing Construction (except Operative Builders), 1633, cons-%
Newspaper Publishers, 1106-1107, info
Nitrogenous Fertilizer Manufacturing, 412-413, mfg
Nonferrous (except Aluminum) Die-Casting Foundries, 508-509, mfg
Nonferrous Metal (except Copper and Aluminum) Rolling, Drawing, and Extruding, 498-499, mfg
Nonresidential Property Managers, 1216-1217, R/E
Nonscheduled Chartered Passenger Air Transportation, 1042-1043, trans
Nonupholstered Wood Household Furniture Manufacturing, 724-725, mfg
Nursery and Tree Production, 120-121, ag
Nursery, Garden Center, and Farm Supply Stores, 950-951, rtl
Nursing Care Facilities, 1452-1453, HC

O

Office Administrative Services, 1326-1327, Admin
Office Equipment Merchant Wholesalers, 790-791, wsle
Office Furniture (except Wood) Manufacturing, 730-731, mfg
Office Machinery and Equipment Rental and Leasing, 1238-1239, R/E
Office Supplies and Stationery Stores, 1010-1011, rtl
Offices of All Other Miscellaneous Health Practitioners, 1418-1419, HC
Offices of Bank Holding Companies, 1320-1321, mgmt
Offices of Certified Public Accountants, 1250-1251, prof serv
Offices of Chiropractors, 1408-1409, HC
Offices of Dentists, 1406-1407, HC
Offices of Lawyers, 1246-1247, prof serv
Offices of Mental Health Practitioners (except Physicians), 1412-1413, HC
Offices of Optometrists, 1410-1411, HC
Offices of Other Holding Companies, 1322-1323, mgmt
Offices of Physical, Occupational and Speech Therapists, and Audiologists, 1414-1415, HC
Offices of Physicians (except Mental Health Specialists), 1402-1403, HC
Offices of Physicians, Mental Health Specialists, 1404-1405, HC
Offices of Podiatrists, 1416-1417, HC
Offices of Real Estate Agents and Brokers, 1212-1213, R/E
Oil and Gas Field Machinery and Equipment Manufacturing, 576-577, mfg
Oil and Gas Pipeline and Related Structures Construction, 194-195, cons-g
Open-End Investment Funds, 1198-1199, fin

Ophthalmic Goods Manufacturing, 744-745, mfg
Ophthalmic Goods Merchant Wholesalers, 798-799, wsle
Optical Goods Stores, 972-973, rtl
Optical Instrument and Lens Manufacturing, 590-591, mfg
Orange Groves, 110-111, ag
Ornamental and Architectural Metal Work Manufacturing, 532-533, mfg
Other Accounting Services, 1254-1255, prof serv
Other Activities Related to Credit Intermediation, 1162-1163, fin
Other Activities Related to Real Estate, 1218-1219, R/E
Other Aircraft Parts and Auxiliary Equipment Manufacturing, 708-709, mfg
Other Airport Operations, 1074-1075, trans
Other Animal Food Manufacturing, 242-243, mfg
Other Apparel Accessories and Other Apparel Manufacturing, 332-333, mfg
Other Automotive Mechanical and Electrical Repair and Maintenance, 1540-1541, other
Other Building Equipment Contractors, 222-223, cons-g
Other Building Finishing Contractors, 234-235, cons-g
Other Building Material Dealers, 946-947, rtl
Other Business Service Centers (including Copy Shops), 1336-1337, Admin
Other Chemical and Allied Products Merchant Wholesalers, 884-885, wsle
Other Clothing Stores, 990-991, rtl
Other Commercial and Industrial Machinery and Equipment Rental and Leasing, 1240-1241, R/E
Other Commercial and Service Industry Machinery Manufacturing, 594-595, mfg
Other Commercial Equipment Merchant Wholesalers, 794-795, wsle
Other Commercial Printing, 390-391, mfg
Other Communications Equipment Manufacturing, 644-645, mfg
Other Community Housing Services, 1474-1475, HC
Other Computer Peripheral Equipment Manufacturing, 638-639, mfg
Other Computer Related Services, 1274-1275, prof serv
Other Concrete Product Manufacturing, 476-477, mfg
Other Construction Material Merchant Wholesalers, 786-787, wsle
Other Crushed and Broken Stone Mining and Quarrying, 162-163, mng
Other Direct Insurance (except Life, Health, and Medical) Carriers, 1190-1191, fin
Other Direct Selling Establishments, 1036-1037, rtl
Other Electronic and Precision Equipment Repair and Maintenance, 1554-1555, other
Other Electronic Component Manufacturing, 656-657, mfg
Other Electronic Parts and Equipment Merchant Wholesalers, 810-811, wsle
Other Fabricated Wire Product Manufacturing, 540-541, mfg
Other Farm Product Raw Material Merchant Wholesalers, 880-881, wsle
Other Financial Vehicles, 1200-1201, fin
Other Foundation, Structure, and Building Exterior Contractors, 216-217, cons-g
Other Gasoline Stations, 980-981, rtl
Other General Government Support, 1614-1615, pub admin
Other Grantmaking and Giving Services, 1588-1589, other
Other Grocery and Related Products Merchant Wholesalers, 874-875, wsle

Other Heavy and Civil Engineering Construction, 202-203, cons-g
Other Heavy and Civil Engineering Construction, 1642, cons-%
Other Household Textile Product Mills, 312-313, mfg
Other Individual and Family Services, 1468-1469, HC
Other Lighting Equipment Manufacturing, 678-679, mfg
Other Management Consulting Services, 1284-1285, prof serv
Other Measuring and Controlling Device Manufacturing, 672-673, mfg
Other Metal Container Manufacturing, 534-535, mfg
Other Metal Valve and Pipe Fitting Manufacturing, 560-561, mfg
Other Metalworking Machinery Manufacturing, 612-613, mfg
Other Millwork (including Flooring), 348-349, mfg
Other Miscellaneous Durable Goods Merchant Wholesalers, 840-841, wsle
Other Miscellaneous Nondurable Goods Merchant Wholesalers, 904-905, wsle
Other Motion Picture and Video Industries, 1122-1123, info
Other Nonferrous Foundries (except Die-Casting), 512-513, mfg
Other Nonhazardous Waste Treatment and Disposal, 1374-1375, Admin
Other Nonscheduled Air Transportation, 1044-1045, trans
Other Personal and Household Goods Repair and Maintenance, 1560-1561, other
Other Professional Equipment and Supplies Merchant Wholesalers, 800-801, wsle
Other Residential Care Facilities, 1462-1463, HC
Other Scientific and Technical Consulting Services, 1288-1289, prof serv
Other Services Related to Advertising, 1306-1307, prof serv
Other Services to Buildings and Dwellings, 1360-1361, Admin
Other Similar Organizations (except Business, Professional, Labor, and Political Organizations), 1600-1601, other
Other Snack Food Manufacturing, 280-281, mfg
Other Social Advocacy Organizations, 1590-1591, other
Other Support Activities for Air Transportation, 1076-1077, trans
Other Support Activities for Road Transportation, 1086-1087, trans
Other Support Activities for Water Transportation, 1082-1083, trans
Other Technical and Trade Schools, 1392-1393, edu
Other Vegetable (except Potato) and Melon Farming, 108-109, ag
Other Warehousing and Storage, 1102-1103, trans
Other Waste Collection, 1368-1369, Admin
Outdoor Power Equipment Stores, 948-949, rtl
Outpatient Mental Health and Substance Abuse Centers, 1422-1423, HC
Overhead Traveling Crane, Hoist, and Monorail System Manufacturing, 624-625, mfg

P

Packaged Frozen Food Merchant Wholesalers, 860-861, wsle
Packaging and Labeling Services, 1362-1363, Admin
Packaging Machinery Manufacturing, 630-631, mfg
Packing and Crating, 1090-1091, trans
Paint and Coating Manufacturing, 422-423, mfg

STATEMENT STUDIES KEY WORD INDEX

A complete description of each industry category listed below begins on page 35.

nt and Wallpaper Stores, 942-943, rtl

nt, Varnish, and Supplies Merchant Wholesalers, 902-903, wsle

nting and Wall Covering Contractors, 226-227, cons-g

nting and Wall Covering Contractors, 1651, cons-%

er (except Newsprint) Mills, 358-359, mfg

er Industry Machinery Manufacturing, 580-581, mfg

king Lots and Garages, 1578-1579, other

ssenger Car Leasing, 1222-1223, R/E

ssenger Car Rental, 1220-1221, R/E.

roll Services, 1252-1253, prof serv

iodical Publishers, 1108-1109, info

ishable Prepared Food Manufacturing, 290-291, mfg

sticide and Other Agricultural Chemical Manufacturing, 416-417, mfg

and Pet Supplies Stores, 1016-1017, rtl

Care (except Veterinary) Services, 1574-1575, other

roleum and Petroleum Products Merchant Wholesalers (except Bulk Stations and Terminals), 888-889, wsle

roleum Bulk Stations and Terminals, 886-887, wsle

roleum Lubricating Oil and Grease Manufacturing, 400-401, mfg

roleum Refineries, 396-397, mfg

armaceutical Preparation Manufacturing, 420-421, mfg

armacies and Drug Stores, 968-969, rtl

otofinishing Laboratories (except One-Hour), 1576-1577, other

otographic and Photocopying Equipment Manufacturing, 592-593, mfg

otographic Equipment and Supplies Merchant Wholesalers, 788-789, wsle

otography Studios, Portrait, 1310-1311, prof serv

ce Goods, Notions, and Other Dry Goods Merchant Wholesalers, 850-851, wsle

stics and Rubber Industry Machinery Manufacturing, 578-579, mfg

stics Bag and Pouch Manufacturing, 438-439, mfg

stics Bottle Manufacturing, 452-453, mfg

stics Material and Resin Manufacturing, 410-411, mfg

stics Materials and Basic Forms and Shapes Merchant Wholesalers, 882-883, wsle

stics Packaging Film and Sheet (including Laminated) Manufacturing, 440-441, mfg

stics Pipe and Pipe Fitting Manufacturing, 446-447, mfg

stics Plumbing Fixture Manufacturing, 454-455, mfg

te Work Manufacturing, 526-527, mfg

mbing and Heating Equipment and Supplies (Hydronics) Merchant Wholesalers, 814-815, wsle

mbing Fixture Fitting and Trim Manufacturing, 558-559, mfg

mbing, Heating, and Air-Conditioning Contractors, 220-221, cons-g

mbing, Heating, and Air-Conditioning Contractors, 1649, cons-%

ish and Other Sanitation Good Manufacturing, 428-429, mfg

ystyrene Foam Product Manufacturing, 450-451, mfg

rtfolio Management, 1174-1175, fin

stharvest Crop Activities (except Cotton Ginning), 150-151, ag

tato Farming, 106-107, ag

ultry and Poultry Product Merchant Wholesalers, 864-865, wsle

ultry Processing, 268-269, mfg

ured Concrete Foundation and Structure Contractors, 204-205, cons-g

ured Concrete Foundation and Structure Contractors, 1643, cons-%

Powder Metallurgy Part Manufacturing, 518-519, mfg

Power and Communication Line and Related Structures Construction, 196-197, cons-g

Power, Distribution, and Specialty Transformer Manufacturing, 680-681, mfg

Precision Turned Product Manufacturing, 544-545, mfg

Prefabricated Metal Building and Component Manufacturing, 522-523, mfg

Prefabricated Wood Building Manufacturing, 354-355, mfg

Prepress Services, 394-395, mfg

Printing and Writing Paper Merchant Wholesalers, 842-843, wsle

Printing Ink Manufacturing, 432-433, mfg

Printing Machinery and Equipment Manufacturing, 584-585, mfg

Private Households, 1602-1603, other

Process, Physical Distribution, and Logistics Consulting Services, 1282-1283, prof serv

Professional and Management Development Training, 1390-1391, edu

Professional Employer Organizations, 1334-1335, Admin

Professional Organizations, 1596-1597, other

Promoters of Performing Arts, Sports, and Similar Events with Facilities, 1490-1491, ent

Psychiatric and Substance Abuse Hospitals, 1448-1449, HC

Public Relations Agencies, 1296-1297, prof serv

Pump and Pumping Equipment Manufacturing, 618-619, mfg

Q

Quick Printing, 384-385, mfg

R

Racetracks, 1488-1489, ent

Radio and Television Broadcasting and Wireless Communications Equipment Manufacturing, 642-643, mfg

Radio Stations, 1124-1125, info

Radio, Television, and Other Electronics Stores, 936-937, rtl

Railroad Rolling Stock Manufacturing, 710-711, mfg

Ready-Mix Concrete Manufacturing, 470-471, mfg

Real Estate Credit, 1152-1153, fin

Recreational and Vacation Camps (except Campgrounds), 1520-1521, rest/lodg

Recreational Vehicle Dealers, 916-917, rtl

Recyclable Material Merchant Wholesalers, 836-837, wsle

Refrigerated Warehousing and Storage, 1098-1099, trans

Refrigeration Equipment and Supplies Merchant Wholesalers, 818-819, wsle

Relay and Industrial Control Manufacturing, 686-687, mfg

Religious Organizations, 1582-1583, other

Remediation Services, 1376-1377, Admin

Rendering and Meat Byproduct Processing, 266-267, mfg

Reseach and Development in the Physical, Engineering, and Life Sciences (except Biotechnology), 1290-1291, prof serv

Research and Development in the Social Sciences and Humanities, 1292-1293, prof serv

Residential Electric Lighting Fixture Manufacturing, 674-675, mfg

Residential Mental Health and Substance Abuse Facilities, 1456-1457, HC

Residential Mental Retardation Facilities, 1454-1455, HC

Residential Property Managers, 1214-1215, R/E

Residential Remodelers, 186-187, cons-g

Residential Remodelers, 1636, cons-%

Retail Bakeries, 272-273, mfg

Roasted Nuts and Peanut Butter Manufacturing, 278-279, mfg

Rolled Steel Shape Manufacturing, 488-489, mfg

Roofing Contractors, 214-215, cons-g

Roofing Contractors, 1647, cons-%

Roofing, Siding, and Insulation Material Merchant Wholesalers, 784-785, wsle

Rubber and Plastics Hoses and Belting Manufacturing, 460-461, mfg

Rubber Product Manufacturing for Mechanical Use, 462-463, mfg

RV (Recreational Vehicle) Parks and Campgrounds, 1518-1519, rest/lodg

S

Sales Financing, 1148-1149, fin

Sanitary Paper Product Manufacturing, 374-375, mfg

Sawmills, 336-337, mfg

Scheduled Passenger Air Transportation, 1040-1041, trans

School and Employee Bus Transportation, 1068-1069, trans

Search, Detection, Navigation, Guidance, Aeronautical, and Nautical System and Instrument Manufacturing, 660-661, mfg

Secondary Market Financing, 1154-1155, fin

Secondary Smelting and Alloying of Aluminum, 492-493, mfg

Secondary Smelting, Refining, and Alloying of Nonferrous Metal (except Copper and Aluminum), 500-501, mfg

Securities Brokerage, 1166-1167, fin

Security Guards and Patrol Services, 1348-1349, Admin

Security Systems Services (except Locksmiths), 1350-1351, Admin

Semiconductor and Related Device Manufacturing, 650-651, mfg

Service Establishment Equipment and Supplies Merchant Wholesalers, 828-829, wsle

Services for the Elderly and Persons with Disabilities, 1466-1467, HC

Setup Paperboard Box Manufacturing, 364-365, mfg

Sheet Metal Work Manufacturing, 530-531, mfg

Shellfish Fishing, 144-145, ag

Ship Building and Repairing, 712-713, mfg

Shoe Stores, 992-993, rtl

Showcase, Partition, Shelving, and Locker Manufacturing, 732-733, mfg

Sign Manufacturing, 756-757, mfg

Site Preparation Contractors, 236-237, cons-g

Site Preparation Contractors, 1652, cons-%

Skiing Facilities, 1502-1503, ent

Snack and Nonalcoholic Beverage Bars, 1526-1527, rest/lodg

Soap and Other Detergent Manufacturing, 426-427, mfg

Soft Drink Manufacturing, 294-295, mfg

Software Publishers, 1116-1117, info

Soil Preparation, Planting, and Cultivating, 148-149, ag

Solid Waste Collection, 1366-1367, Admin

Solid Waste Landfill, 1372-1373, Admin

Soybean Farming, 98-99, ag

Special Die and Tool, Die Set, Jig, and Fixture Manufacturing, 608-609, mfg

Specialized Freight (except Used Goods) Trucking, Local, 1060-1061, trans

Specialized Freight (except Used Goods) Trucking, Long-Distance, 1062-1063, trans

Specialty (except Psychiatric and Substance Abuse) Hospitals, 1450-1451, HC

Speed Changer, Industrial High-Speed Drive, and Gear Manufacturing, 614-615, mfg

Spice and Extract Manufacturing, 288-289, mfg

Sporting and Athletic Goods Manufacturing, 752-753, mfg

STATEMENT STUDIES KEY WORD INDEX

A complete description of each industry category listed below begins on page 35.

Sporting and Recreational Goods and Supplies Merchant Wholesalers, 832-833, wsle
Sporting Goods Stores, 996-997, rtl
Sports Teams and Clubs, 1486-1487, ent
Spring (Light Gauge) Manufacturing, 538-539, mfg
Stationery and Office Supplies Merchant Wholesalers, 844-845, wsle
Steel Foundries (except Investment), 504-505, mfg
Steel Wire Drawing, 490-491, mfg
Structural Steel and Precast Concrete Contractors, 206-207, cons-g
Structural Steel and Precast Concrete Contractors, 1644, cons-%
Supermarkets and Other Grocery (except Convenience) Stores, 952-953, rtl
Support Activities for Animal Production, 152-153, ag
Support Activities for Oil and Gas Operations, 168-169, mng
Support Activities for Oil and Gas Operations, 1632, cons-%
Surgical and Medical Instrument Manufacturing, 738-739, mfg
Surgical Appliance and Supplies Manufacturing, 740-741, mfg
Surveying and Mapping (except Geophysical) Services, 1262-1263, prof serv
Switchgear and Switchboard Apparatus Manufacturing, 684-685, mfg

T

Taxi Service, 1064-1065, trans
Telecommunications Resellers, 1134-1135, info
Telephone Apparatus Manufacturing, 640-641, mfg
Television Broadcasting, 1126-1127, info
Temporary Help Services, 1332-1333, Admin
Temporary Shelters, 1472-1473, HC
Testing Laboratories, 1264-1265, prof serv
Textile Machinery Manufacturing, 582-583, mfg
Theater Companies and Dinner Theaters, 1482-1483, ent
Third Party Administration of Insurance and Pension Funds, 1194-1195, fin

Tile and Terrazzo Contractors, 230-231, cons-g
Timber Tract Operations, 138-139, ag
Tire and Tube Merchant Wholesalers, 772-773, wsle
Tire Dealers, 926-927, rtl
Tire Retreading, 458-459, mfg
Title Abstract and Settlement Offices, 1248-1249, prof serv
Tobacco and Tobacco Product Merchant Wholesalers, 900-901, wsle
Tobacco Stores, 1022-1023, rtl
Toilet Preparation Manufacturing, 430-431, mfg
Totalizing Fluid Meter and Counting Device Manufacturing, 666-667, mfg
Tour Operators, 1344-1345, Admin
Toy and Hobby Goods and Supplies Merchant Wholesalers, 834-835, wsle
Tradebinding and Related Work, 392-393, mfg
Transportation Equipment and Supplies (except Motor Vehicle) Merchant Wholesalers, 830-831, wsle
Travel Agencies, 1342-1343, Admin
Travel Trailer and Camper Manufacturing, 698-699, mfg
Tree Nut Farming, 116-117, ag
Truck Trailer Manufacturing, 696-697, mfg
Truck, Utility Trailer, and RV (Recreational Vehicle) Rental and Leasing, 1224-1225, R/E
Truss Manufacturing, 342-343, mfg
Trust, Fiduciary, and Custody Activities, 1178-1179, fin

U

Unlaminated Plastics Film and Sheet (except Packaging) Manufacturing, 442-443, mfg
Unlaminated Plastics Profile Shape Manufacturing, 444-445, mfg
Upholstered Household Furniture Manufacturing, 722-723, mfg
Used Car Dealers, 914-915, rtl
Used Household and Office Goods Moving, 1058-1059, trans
Used Merchandise Stores, 1014-1015, rtl

V

Vending Machine Operators, 1030-1031, rtl
Veterinary Services, 1314-1315, prof serv

Vocational Rehabilitation Services, 1476-1477, HC
Voluntary Health Organizations, 1586-1587, other

W

Warm Air Heating and Air-Conditioning Equipment and Supplies Merchant Wholesalers, 816-817, wsle
Water and Sewer Line and Related Structure Construction, 192-193, cons-g
Water and Sewer Line and Related Structure Construction, 1639, cons-%
Water Supply and Irrigation Systems, 176-177, util
Welding and Soldering Equipment Manufacturing, 628-629, mfg
Wheat Farming, 100-101, ag
Wholesale Trade Agents and Brokers, 908-909, wsle
Wine and Distilled Alcoholic Beverage Merchant Wholesalers, 892-893, wsle
Wineries, 300-301, mfg
Wired Telecommunications Carriers, 1130-1131, info
Wireless Telecommunications Carriers (except Satellite), 1132-1133, info
Women's and Girls' Cut and Sew Dress Manufacturing, 326-327, mfg
Women's and Girls' Cut and Sew Other Outerwear Manufacturing, 328-329, mfg
Women's Clothing Stores, 984-985, rtl
Women's, Children's, and Infants' Clothing and Accessories Merchant Wholesalers, 854-855, wsle
Women's, Girls', and Infants' Cut and Sew Apparel Contractors, 320-321, mfg
Wood Container and Pallet Manufacturing, 350-351, mfg
Wood Kitchen Cabinet and Countertop Manufacturing, 720-721, mfg
Wood Office Furniture Manufacturing, 728-729, mfg
Wood Preservation, 338-339, mfg
Wood Window and Door Manufacturing, 344-345, mfg

Y

Yarn Spinning Mills, 302-303, mfg

RMA'S CREDIT & LENDING DICTIONARY

A

Absentee Owner: landlord who does not reside in his or her rental property.

Abstract of Title: condensed history of title to land and real property, consisting of ownership transfers and any conveyances or liens that may affect future ownership.

Acceleration Clause: provision in note or contract that allows holder to declare remaining balance due and payable immediately upon default in an obligation. Usual causes of default are failure to pay interest or principal installments in a timely manner, an adverse change in financing conditions, or failure to meet loan covenants.

Acceptance: drawee's signed agreement to honor draft as presented, which consists of signature alone, but will frequently be evidenced by drawee writing word "accepted," date it is payable, and signature. Sometimes called Trade Acceptance or Banker's Acceptance, depending upon function of acceptor.

Accommodation: 1. lending or extending credit to borrower. 2. loan or commitment to lend money.

Accord and Satisfaction: agreement between two or more persons or entities that satisfies or discharges obligation or settles claim or lawsuit. Generally involves disputed matter in which one party agrees to give and other party agrees to accept something in satisfaction different from, and usually less than, that originally asked for.

Account: 1. statement showing balance along with detailed explanation covering debits and credits. 2. right of payment for goods sold or leased or for services rendered on open account basis. 3. summarized record of financial transaction. 4. customer.

Accountant: person in charge of and skilled in the recording of financial transactions and maintenance of financial records.

Accounting: 1. theory and system of classifying, recording, summarizing, and auditing books of firm. 2. art of analyzing, interpreting, and reporting financial position and operating results of business.

Account Manager: 1. sometimes called Relationship Manager or Account Officer. 2. person responsible for overseeing all matters relating to a specific client or group of customers.

Account Number: unique identification number used to designate specific customer.

Accounts Payable: short-term liability representing amounts due trade creditors.

Accounts Payable Department: section of business office responsible for processing open account balances and paying amounts owed for goods and services purchased.

Accounts Receivable: money due to a business by its customers for goods sold or services performed on open account (or credit). Usually refers to short-term receivables.

Accounts Receivable Aging Report: report by customer that lists age of accounts receivable generally by 30-day intervals from invoice or due date. See also Aging of Accounts Receivable.

Accounts Receivable Financing: form of secured lending in which borrowings are typically limited to percentage of receivables pledged as collateral.

Accrual Accounting: basis of accounting in which expenses are recorded when incurred and revenues are recognized when earned, regardless of when cash is actually paid or received.

Accrue: 1. something gained, added, or accumulated, such as profit from a business transaction. 2. right to sue has become exercisable.

Accrued Expenses: short-term liabilities that represent expenses for goods used but not yet paid.

Accrued Income: income earned but not yet collected.

Accrued Interest: interest accumulated since last interest payment due date.

Accrued Liabilities: expenses or obligations for goods or services incurred but not yet paid.

ACH: see *Automated Clearinghouse*.

Acid Test: ratio between company's most liquid assets (generally, cash and accounts receivable) and current liabilities that represents the degree to which current liabilities can be paid with those assets.

Acknowledgment: 1. declaration making known receipt of something done or to be done; confirmation of receipt of order or of terms of contract. 2. statement of notary or other competent officer certifying that signature on document was personally signed by individual whose signature is affixed to instrument.

Acquisition: merger or taking over of controlling interest of one business by another.

Acquisition and Development Loan: loan made for the purpose of purchasing a property and completing all on-site improvements such as street layout, utility installation, and community area grading necessary to bring the site to a buildable state.

Acquittal: 1. release from obligation or contract. 2. to have accusation of crime dismissed by some formal legal procedure.

Active Account: 1. customer who makes frequent purchases. 2. bank account in which regular deposits or withdrawals are made.

Activity Charge: service charge imposed for check or deposit activity or any other maintenance charge.

Act of God: event that could not be prevented by reasonable foresight, is caused exclusively by forces and violence of nature, and is uninfluenced by human power (storm, flood, earthquake, or lightning).

Additional Dating: means of extending credit beyond normal sales terms, granted to induce buyers to place orders in advance of season or for other special reasons. See also *Advance Dating and Dating*.

Adjudication: judgment rendered by court, primarily used in bankruptcy proceedings.

Adjustable Interest Rate: interest rate on loan that may be adjusted up or down at specific intervals. Index used in determining adjusted interest rate and potential frequency of adjustments must be stated in loan documents.

Adjustable Rate Mortgage: loan is pursuant to an agreement executed at inception of the loan that permits creditor to adjust interest rate from time to time based on a specific interest rate index.

Adjuster: person who deals with insured party to settle amount of loss, claim, or debt.

Adjustment: 1. settlement of disputed account. 2. change or concession in price or terms. 3. determining amount one is to receive in settlement of claim. 4. in accounting, entry made to correct or compensate for error or difference in account.

Adjustment Bureau: organization that supervises debt extensions and compromise arrangements or oversees orderly liquidation of troubled businesses for benefit of creditors.

Advance: 1. payment made before it is due. 2. disbursement of loan proceeds.

Advance Dating: additional time granted customers to pay for goods received and to earn available discounts. See also Additional Dating and Dating.

Advancement of Costs: prepayment of necessary legal expenses. Such charges, set by law, may be for commencement of suit and vary in different courts and states. Some items for which prepaid costs may be requested are filing fees, process serving, premiums on court bonds, trial fees, posting security for costs, entering judgment, recording abstract of judgment, issue execution and discovery actions after judgment.

Advertising Allowance: promotional discount in price or payment given to customers who share expense of advertising supplier's product.

Affidavit: voluntary written statement of facts pertaining to a transaction or event, signed under oath and witnessed by an authorized person.

Affiliate: business entity connected with another through common ownership or management, usually responsible for payment of its own obligations.

After-Acquired Property: security interest by which secured creditor automatically obtains interest in assets that debtor acquires after lien had been filed.

Agency: legal relationship between two parties in which one is authorized to act for another.

Agent: person legally authorized to act for another.

Agent Bank: formal designation that applies to a bank responsible for negotiating, structuring, and overseeing a loan or commitment to a borrower in which more than one bank is involved. See also Lead Bank.

Aggregate Balances: combined total of two or more demand deposit accounts, money markets, or time certificates of deposit. Term can also be applied to credit facility totals.

Aging of Accounts Receivable: accounting record of customer's receivables showing how long receivables have remained unpaid beyond regular terms of sale. Used as basis for advancing credit.

Agreement: a contract involving an offer and an acceptance between two or more parties, governing the terms of the contract and binding on the parties to the agreement (i.e., a loan agreement, security agreement, or guaranty).

AKA: see *Also Known As*.

Alert Action: a series of information services provided by credit reporting agencies; provides subscribers with listing of specific accounts on which unfavorable payment condition has recently been reported.

Allegation: statement of party to action, setting out what he or she intends to prove or contend.

ALLL: see *Allowance for Loan and Lease Losses*.

Allocation: sub-limit within a total credit facility that is to be used for a specific purpose.

Allonge: paper attached to a negotiable instrument for additional endorsements or other terms and conditions.

Allowance: accounting provision used to set aside amounts for depreciation, returns, or bad debts.

Allowance for Bad Debts: contra account against which uncollectible receivables are charged. See also Bad Debt Reserve.

Allowance for Loan and Lease Losses (ALLL): contra account, generally found on asset side of balance sheet as deduction from total loans outstanding. The amount is intended to cover future losses of loans currently in the financial institution's portfolio. The ALLL should be adjusted monthly, concurrent with the generation of current financial statements.

Also Known As (AKA): sometimes used to designate a fictitious trade style or name.

Policy: an extended coverage title insurance policy that protects the lender against losses resulting from any defects in the title or claims against the property. The policy's coverage includes encroachments, mechanic's liens, and other matters that a physical inspection or inquiry of the parties would disclose.

ed Check: check on which original entries have been changed (date, payee, or amount); financial institutions generally refuse to honor or pay checks that have been altered.

nd: to correct, add to, or alter legal document.

cus Curiae: friend of court; uninvolved third party who intervenes in lawsuit, with court's permission, to introduce information or arguments in respect to the issue or principle of law to be decided.

rtization: 1. reduction of loan by periodic principal payments. 2. decline in the book value of an intangible asset over the period owned.

rtization Tables: calculation charts showing amounts required periodically to discharge debts over various periods of time and at different interest rates.

rtize: 1. to write off the value of an intangible asset over the period owned. 2. to reduce or pay off debt or obligation by making periodic payments of principal.

al Percentage Rate (APR): annual cost of credit expressed as percentage; creditors are required under Federal Truth in Lending Act to disclose true annual interest on consumer loans, as well as the total dollar cost and other terms of loan.

al Report: yearly report detailing a company's comparative financial and organizational conditions.

ity: series of fixed periodic payments made at regular intervals.

cedent Credit Information: historical record of significant business information concerning individuals who are involved in ownership or management of business enterprise.

cipation: bridge loan made to a municipal or government borrower to cover expenses until revenue or tax proceeds are collected.

eal: complaint made to higher court by either plaintiff or defendant for court's review, correction, or reversal of lower court's decision.

earance: coming into court formally as plaintiff or defendant in lawsuit.

aisal: opinion of current value of real or personal property based upon cost of replacement, market, income, or fair value analysis.

eciation: increase in value of asset over its cost due to economic and other conditions. Property that increases in value as result of improvements or additions is not considered to have appreciated.

opriation: sum of money designated for a special purpose only.

: See *Annual Percentage Rate*.

tration: submission for settlement of disputed matter, by nonjudicial means, to one or more impartial or disinterested third persons selected by disputants.

's Length: business transaction between two or more parties that is open, sincere, and without personal influence, favoritism, or close relations.

ngement: plan for corporate reorganization for rescheduling or extension of time for payment of unsecured debts, such as an arrangement under Chapter 11 or 13 of the U. S. Bankruptcy Code.

ars: total or partial debt amounts that remain unpaid and past due.

les of Agreement: any written statement or contract, terms to which all parties consent.

les of Incorporation: formal papers that set forth pertinent data for formation of corporation and are filed with appropriate state agency.

ss: 1. to fix rate or amount. 2. to set value of real and personal property, as for tax purposes.

ssed Value: in the case of real property, value set by government agency for purpose of levying taxes.

t: 1. anything owned having monetary value. 2. item listed on left-hand side of balance sheet representing cash, or property, real or personal, belonging to an individual or company and convertible to cash.

gned Account: 1. account receivable pledged by borrower to factor or lender as security. 2. past-due customer whose account has been placed with collection agency.

gned Risk: insurance plan that provides coverage for risks rejected by regular markets and in which all licensed insurers are made to participate by various state laws.

gnee: person to whom some rights, authority, or property is assigned.

gnment: 1. written contract for transfer of one's title, legal rights, or property from one person to another. 2. in some states, form used to transfer claim to agency that undertakes collection of account for benefit of assigning creditor.

gnment for the Benefit of Creditors: A liquidation technique in which an insolvent debtor goes out of business and an assignee facilitates the transfer of the insolvent debtor's estate for administration and payment of debts. Property transferred to assignee places such assets beyond control of debtor or reach of creditors.

gnment of Claim: claim assigned to third party for collection.

gnor: 1. one who transfers claim, right, or property. 2. individual, partnership, or corporation making assignment.

Assumed Liability: acknowledgment of responsibility for payment of obligation by third party.

At Sight: words used in negotiable instrument directing that payment be made upon presentation or demand.

Attached Account: legally frozen account on which payments have been suspended; release or disbursement of funds can be made only after court order.

Attachment: 1. legal writ or process by which debtor's property (or any interest therein) is seized and placed in custody of law. 2. Supplemental data provided as clarifying information to a document.

Attorney-in-Fact: private attorney who has written authorization to act for another. This authority is given by an instrument called power of attorney.

Attorney of Record: lawyer whose name must appear in permanent court records as person acting on behalf of party in legal matter.

Auction: public sale of property that is sold to highest bidder.

Audit: to examine a firm's records, accounts, or procedures for purpose of substantiating or verifying individual transactions or to confirm if assets and liabilities are properly accounted for, including income and expense items.

Audited Financial Statements: financial statements that have been examined by an independent certified public accountant to determine if the financial statements present fairly the financial position, results of operations, and cash flows in conformity with generally accepted accounting principles.

Auditor: person who deals with examination and verification of financial accounts and with making financial reports.

Auditor's Report: part of complete set of financial statements that explains degree of responsibility that independent accountant assumed for expressing an opinion on management's financial statements and assurance that is provided by said opinion.

Automated Cash Application: computerized procedures enabling payments to be quickly and automatically applied to accounts receivable.

Automated Clearinghouse (ACH): computer-based clearing and settlement facility for interchange of electronic debits and credits among financial institutions. ACH entries can be substituted for checks in recurring payments such as mortgages or in direct deposit distribution of federal and corporate benefits payments. Federal Reserve Banks furnish data processing services for most ACHs, although some are privately operated. Final settlement, or net settlement, of ACH transfers is made against reserve accounts at Federal Reserve Banks.

Available Balance: checking account balance that the customer actually may use; that is, current balance less deposits not yet cleared through the account.

Average Collected Balances: average dollar amount on deposit in checking accounts defined as the difference between ledger balance and deposit float, or those deposits posted to the account but having not yet cleared the financial institution upon which they are drawn. See also Uncollected Funds.

Average Collection Period: average number of days required to convert accounts receivable to cash.

Average Daily Balance: average amount of money that depositor keeps on deposit when calculated on a daily basis.

B

Backdating: predating document prior to date on which it was drawn.

Backlog: amount of revenue expected to be realized from work to be performed on uncompleted contracts, including new contractual agreements on which work has not begun.

Bad Check Laws: laws enacted in various states to encourage and facilitate lawful use of checks; statutes differ in various jurisdictions and are generally enforced according to state laws as well as local custom and usage.

Bad Debt: account receivable that proves uncollectible in normal course of business; full payment is doubtful.

Bad Debt Ratio: ratio of bad debt expense to sales, used as measure of quality of accounts receivable.

Bad Debt Reserve: reserve or provision for accounts receivables to be charged off company's books based on historical levels of bad debts or industry averages.

Balance: amount owed or unpaid on loan or credit transaction. Also called outstanding or unpaid balance.

Balance Due: total amount owed after applying debits and credits of account.

Balance Sheet: A financial statement listing the assets, liabilities, and owner's equity of a business entity or individual as of a specific date.

Balloon Payment: lump-sum payment of principal and sometimes accrued interest, usually due at end of term of installment loan in which periodic installments of principal and interest did not fully amortize loan.

Bank: financial institution chartered by state or federal government to transact financial business that includes receiving deposits, lending money, exchanging currencies, providing safekeeping, and investing money.

Bank Draft: sight or demand draft (order to pay) drawn by a bank (drawer) on its account at another bank (drawee).

Banker's Acceptance: draft or order to pay specified amount at specified time not to exceed 270 days, drawn on individuals, business firms, or financial institutions; draft becomes accepted when a financial institution formally acknowledges its obligation to honor such draft, usually by writing or stamping "Accepted" on face of instrument. When accepted in this manner, draft becomes liability of bank. See also *Draft* and *Time Draft*.

Bank Overdraft: check presented for collection for which there are not sufficient funds on deposit to make normal payment. Financial institution may honor such check, considering payment as loan to depositor for which the institution will usually collect interest or service charge.

Bankrupt: debtor who is unable to meet debt obligations as they become due or is insolvent and whose assets are administered for benefit of creditors.

Bankruptcy: Legal action taken under the U.S. Bankruptcy Code by or against an insolvent debtor who is unable to meet obligations as they become due. The bankrupt, if given discharge, is released from further liability of most debts listed as of the date of the bankruptcy filing.

• *Voluntary Bankruptcy:* any individual, partnership, corporation, estate, trust, or governmental unit may be afforded protection of debtor under U.S. Bankruptcy Code by filing petition. Exceptions: railroads, insurance or banking corporations, building and loan associations.

• *Involuntary Bankruptcy:* involuntary petition can be filed in bankruptcy court by three or more creditors or, if there are fewer than 12 creditors, by any one creditor. Petitioning creditors' claims must aggregate at least $5,000 in excess of value of any collateral of debtor. Involuntary cases may be filed against individuals, partnerships, or corporations other than farmers and nonprofit corporations and may be instituted under either Chapter 7 or Chapter 11 of the U.S. Bankruptcy Code. Involuntary petition must allege one of two grounds for relief: either that the debtor is generally not paying debts as they become due, or that the non-bankruptcy custodian, other than one appointed to enforce lien on less than substantially all of debtor's property, was appointed for, or took possession of, substantially all of debtor's property within 120 days of filing.

• *Chapter 7 Cases:* liquidation proceedings, formerly referred to as "straight bankruptcy," wherein nonexempt assets of debtor are converted to cash and proceeds distributed pro rata among creditors.

• *Chapter 9 Cases:* reorganization proceedings wherein municipality that is insolvent or unable to meet debts as they mature effects plan to adjust such debts.

• *Chapter 11 Cases:* reorganization proceedings available to all business enterprises; may be instituted either by debtor or creditor(s). For plan to be confirmed by court under Chapter 11, each class of creditors, as set forth in such plan, must accept plan or each class must receive at least that which it would receive on liquidation. Class of creditors has accepted plan when majority in number and two-thirds in dollar amount of those creditors actually voting approve it.

• *Chapter 12 Cases:* reorganization proceedings for agricultural concerns and small family-owned farms having debts under $1.5 million.

• *Chapter 13 Cases:* reorganization cases that may be instituted only by individuals with regular income who owe unsecured debts of less than $100,000 and secured debts of less than $350,000, other than stockbroker or commodity broker. For plan to be confirmed, it must provide for submission to trustee of all or any portion of debtor's future earnings as necessary for execution of plan, payment in full of all priority claims, and equal treatment of each member of class of creditors. While consent of unsecured creditors is not required, value of what they receive under plan may not be less than if debtor were liquidated.

Bankruptcy Judge: presiding judge of court in which bankruptcy cases are heard. (Formerly called Referee in Bankruptcy.) Duties of judge include supervising administrative details of bankrupt estates and ruling on all matters involving debtor-creditor problems.

Basis: 1. number of days used in calculating interest earned in investment or interest payable on bank loan. Also called accrual base. 2. original cost of asset plus capital improvements from which any taxable gains (or losses) are determined after deducting depreciation expenses.

Basis Point: 1/100th of a percent; 100 basis points equal 1%.

Bearer: negotiable item (check, note, bill, or draft) in which no payee is indicated or payee is shown as "cash" or "bearer." Item is payable to person in possession of it or to person who presents it for payment.

Bearer Paper: instrument that is made "payable to bearer." When negotiable instrument is endorsed in blank, it becomes bearer paper and can be transferred by delivery since it does not require endorsement.

Beneficiary: 1. person or organization named in will to inherit or receive property. 2. person or organization to whom insurance policy is payable. 3. person or organization for whose benefit trust is created.

Bid Bond: bond issued by surety on behalf of contractor that provides assurance to recipient of contractor's bid that if bid is accepted, contractor will execute contract and provide performance bond. Under bond, surety is obligated to pay recipient difference between contractor's bid and bid of next lowest responsible bidder if bid is accepted and contractor fails to execute cont or to provide performance bond.

Billing Cycle: number of days between payment due dates.

Bill of Costs: certified itemization of costs associated with lawsuit.

Bill of Lading: written instrument signed by common carrier or agent identify freight and representing both receipt and contract for shipment. It must sl name of consignee, description of goods, terms of carrier's contract, directions for assigning to specific person at specific place. In form of ne tiable instrument, it is evidence of holding title to goods being shipped.

Bill of Sale: written instrument evidencing transfer of title of specific perso property to buyer.

Binder: 1. written agreement that provides temporary legal protection penc issuance of final contract or policy. 2. temporary insurance contract; may oral or written; also called cover note.

Blank Endorsement: endorser's writing on check, promissory note, or bil exchange without indicating party to whom it is payable. Endorser me signs his or her name, making the instrument "payable to bearer." Also ca endorsement in blank.

Blanket Coverage: property coverage applicable to group of exposures (bu ings, inventory, equipment, etc., combined or individually, at one or m locations), in single total amount of insurance; contrasts with Specific Co age.

Blanket Mortgage: mortgage secured by two or more parcels of real prope frequently used by developers who acquire large tract of land for subdivis and resale to individual homeowners. Also called blanket trust deed.

Bond: contract issued by insurance or bonding company in support of princip obligation to obligee. See also *Fidelity Bond* and *Surety Bond*.

Bonded Warehouse: federally approved warehouse under bond for strict ob vance of revenue laws; used for storing goods until duties are paid or pr erty is otherwise released. Bonded warehouse assures owner of property operators of warehouse are insured against loss by fraud and will keep pro inventory and accounting of goods in transit.

Bonding Company: company authorized to issue bid bonds, performance bor labor and materials bonds, or other types of surety bonds.

Book Value: 1. company's net worth calculated by adding total assets minus t liabilities. 2. value of asset (cost plus additions, less depreciation) shown books or financial report of an entity.

Borrower's Certificate: A document required under a loan or other agreemen be submitted by the borrower or another designated party to certify the va of collateral and compliance with the terms of the agreement.

Bottom Line: (colloq.) final price, net profit, or end results.

Branch Banking: multioffice banking. Branch is any banking facility away fr bank's main office that accepts deposits or makes loans. State laws str control opening of new banking offices by state-chartered banks, natio banks, and thrift institutions.

Breach of Contract: failure to fulfill terms of contract, in part or whole.

Breach of Warranty: 1. failure to fully disclose information about condition property or insured party. 2. failure to perform as promised.

Break-Even Analysis: A method of determining the number of units that mus sold at a given price to recover all fixed and variable costs.

Break-even Point: 1. point at which total sales are equal to total expenses. M be expressed in units or dollars. 2. amount received from sale that exa equals amount of expense or cost.

Bridge Loan: loan that provides liquidity until defined event occurs that will g erate cash, such as sale of noncurrent asset, replacement financing, or eq infusion.

Bulk Sales Acts: statutes designed to prevent defrauding of creditors thro secret sale in bulk of merchant's goods. Most states require notice of p posed sale to all creditors.

Burden of Proof: 1. duty of producing sufficient evidence to prove position ta in lawsuit. 2. necessity of proving fact or facts as to truth of claim.

Business: 1. commercial, industrial, or mercantile activity engaged in by indi ual, partnership, corporation, or other form of organization for purpose making, buying, or selling goods or services at profit. 2. occupation, pro sion, or trade.

Business Failure: 1. suspension of business resulting from insolvency or ba ruptcy. 2. inability to fulfill normal business obligations.

Business Interruption Insurance: property insurance written to cover loss profits and continuing expenses as result of shutdown by insured peril; ex sure is classified as consequential loss. Also called earnings insurance.

Buyer's Market: market condition in which supply exceeds demand, wl causes prices to decline.

Buy Out: to purchase at least a controlling percentage of a company's stock take over its assets.

Bylaws: set of rules or regulations adopted to control internal affairs of organ tion.

C

of Credit: the "Five C's" of credit. A longstanding means of evaluating a customer by investigating Character, Collateral, Capacity, Conditions, and Capital.

endar Year: 12-month accounting period ending December 31.

able Loan: loan payable on demand.

celed Check: check that has been paid by a financial institution and on which the financial institution has imprinted evidence of payment so that it cannot be presented again.

cellation Clause: provision in contract or agreement allowing parties to rescind agreement under certain conditions.

acity: one of the "Five C's" of credit; a customer's ability to successfully absorb merchandise and to pay for the merchandise. Refers to customer's ability to produce sufficient cash so as to meet obligations when due.

ital: 1. one of the "Five Cs" of credit; refers to financial resources the customer has at the time order is placed and those that he or she is likely to have when payment is due. 2. amount invested in business by owners or stockholders. 3. owner's equity in the business.

h: 1. money readily available for current expenditures; usually consists of cash on hand or money in a financial institution. 2. money equivalent, such as a check, paid at time of purchase. 3. any medium of exchange that the financial institution will accept at face value upon deposit.

h Basis Accounting: basis of accounting in which revenues and expenses are reported in the income statement when cash is received or paid out for the time period in which the revenues and expenses occur.

h Basis Loan: loan on which interest payments are recorded when collected from borrower. This is a loan in which the borrower has fallen behind on interest payments and is classified as a nonaccrual asset.

h Concentration and Disbursement (CCD): corporate electronic payment used in business-to-business and intracompany transfers of funds. Funds are cleared on overnight basis through nationwide automated clearinghouse network.

h Equivalents: accounting term for actual cash on hand and total of bank deposits.

h Flow: is based on an activity format, which classifies cash inflows and outflows in terms of operating, investing, and financing activities.

hier's Check: check drawn on financial institution's account, becoming direct obligation of the financial institution.

h Management Account: special type of deposit service that permits corporate customers to invest cash in demand deposit account until needed for operations.

h Surrender Value: in life insurance, amount payable under whole life policy when terminated by insured.

ualty Insurance: coverage for automobile, liability, crime, boiler and machinery, health, bonds, aviation, workers' compensation, and other miscellaneous lines; contrasts with Property Insurance.

ificate of Insurance: written statement issued by insurer indicating that insurance policy has been issued and showing details of coverage at time certificate was written; used as evidence of insurance.

tified Check: depositor's check confirmed on its face as good by a financial institution and stamped "certified." It is then dated and signed by an authorized officer of the institution. Such check becomes an obligation of the financial institution, which guarantees that it is holding sufficient funds to cover payment of check on demand.

tified Copy of Policy: document that provides evidence of insurance as of certain date; coverage may be terminated or changed after certification.

tified Public Accountant (CPA): one who has been trained to do accounting and who has passed state test and received title of CPA; title certifies holder's qualification to practice accounting, audit, prepare reports, and analyze accounting information.

.: see Comprehensive General Liability.

racter: one of the "Five Cs" of credit; refers to evaluating qualities that would impel debtor to meet his or her obligations. Generally identified as customer's reputation, responsibility, integrity, and honesty.

rge-Off: portion of principal balance of a loan or account receivable that an entity considers uncollectible; this amount may be partially or fully recovered in future. Also called a Write-Off.

rt of Accounts: listing of all financial accounts or categories (usually numbered) into which business transactions are classified and recorded.

ttel: item of tangible personal property, animate or inanimate, as distinguished from real property.

ttel Mortgage: instrument of sale in which debtor transfers title in property to creditor as security for debt. Failure by debtor to comply with terms of contract may cause creditor's title in property to become absolute.

ck: order on a financial institution for payment of funds from depositor's account and payable on demand.

im: 1. action to recover payment, reimbursement, or compensation from entity legally liable for damage or injury.

imant: one who makes claim or asserts right.

Cleanup: period during which particular loan or entire borrowing has been paid off; out-of-debt period required under line of credit.

Clearinghouse: association of financial institutions or security dealers created to permit daily settlement and exchange of checks or delivery of stocks and other items between members in local geographic area.

Closed-End Credit: consumer installment loan made for predetermined amount calling for periodic payments of principal and interest over specified period o term. Finance charge may be fixed or variable rate. Borrower does not have option of obtaining extra funds under original loan agreement. Contrasts with Open-End Credit.

Cloud on Title: outstanding claim or encumbrance on property that may impai owner's title.

Cognovit Note: form of promissory note or statement that allows creditor, in case of default by debtor, to enter judgment without trial. (Not recognized in al jurisdictions.)

Collateral: 1. one of the "Five C's" of credit; refers to real or personal property that may be available as security. 2. asset pledged by borrower in support o loan. See also Secured Loan.

Collateral Note: form of promissory note given for loan, pledging real or persona property as security for payment of debt.

Collectible: account capable of being collected.

Collection Agency: professional business service employed as agent to collec creditors' unpaid (past-due) accounts. Collection agency is usually compen sated by receiving agreed upon contingent percentage of amount collected.

Collection Agency Report: report from collection agency that informs client o results of collection efforts, investigations, or recommendations.

Collection Charges: 1. fees charged by bank for collecting drafts, notes coupons, or other instruments. 2. compensation paid to collection agency o attorney for collecting delinquent accounts.

Collection Item: 1. term for item received for collection that is to be credited t depositor's account after payment. Most financial institutions charge specia (collection) fees for handling such items. 2. past due account assigned fo collection.

Collection Period: number of days required for company's receivables to be col lected and converted to cash.

Comaker: person who signs (and guarantees) note of another and by so doing promises to pay in full. See also Cosigner.

Commensurate: describes deposit balances that are in acceptable proportion t size of loan or commitment.

Commercial Debt: loan or obligation incurred for business purposes.

Commercial Law League of America (C.L.L.A.): national membership organiza tion of commercial attorneys, commercial credit and collection agencies credit insurance companies, and law list publishers. Objectives include settin standards for honorable dealings among members, improving the practice o commercial law, and promoting uniformity of legislation affecting commercia law.

Commercial Paper: short-term securities such as notes, drafts, bills of exchange and other negotiable paper that arise out of commercial activity and becom due on a definite maturity date.

Commercial Property: real estate used for business purposes or managed so a to produce income from rents and leases.

Commitment: agreement between a financial institution and borrower to make funds available under certain conditions for a specified period of time.

Commitment Fee: lender's charge for holding credit available, usually replaced with interest when funds are advanced, as in revolving credit. In busines credit, a commitment fee is often charged for unused portion of line of credit.

Commitment Letter: letter from lender stating willingness to advance funds to named borrower, repayable at specified rate and time period, subject t escape clause(s) allowing lender to rescind agreement in event of materially adverse changes in borrower's financial condition.

Committee Approval: credit is approved by several people acting as group.

Common Law: body of law that was originated, developed, and administered in England.

Community Property: property shared by husband and wife, each having one-hal interest in earnings of other; form of joint property ownership in some states.

Community Reinvestment Act of 1977 (CRA): federal law that requires mortgag lenders to demonstrate their commitment to home mortgage financing in eco nomically disadvantaged areas. Prohibits redlining or credit allocation base on geographic region and requires lenders to file annual compliance state ments.

Compensating Balance: demand deposit balance that must be maintained by borrower to compensate financial institution for loan accommodations an other services.

Compound Interest: interest calculated by adding accumulated interest to date t original principal. New balance becomes principal for additional interest cal culations.

Comprehensive General Liability (CGL): policy form providing automatic coverage for all insured's business operations; may include auto exposures; newer form of CGL is called commercial general liability.

Concession: 1. granting of special privilege to digress from regular terms or previous conditions. 2. allowance or rebate from established price. 3. business enterprise operated under special permission.

Conditional Sales Contract: contract for sale of goods under which possession is delivered to buyer but title retained by seller until goods are paid for in full or until other conditions are met. In most states, conditional sales contracts have been replaced by security agreements having substantially the same definition under Uniform Commercial Code.

Conditions: one of the "Five C's" of credit; refers to general business environment and status of borrower's industry.

Confession of Judgment Note: note in which (after maturity) debtor permits attorney to appear in court and have judgment entered if payment is not made as agreed. Acceptance of note varies by state. See also *Cognovit Note.*

Confirmation: 1. supplier's written acknowledgment that he or she has accepted buyer's order. 2. customer's written verification of order previously placed. 3. proof verifying agreement or existence of assets and liabilities or claims against assets and liabilities.

Consent Judgment: judgment that debtor allows to be entered against him or her by motion filed with court.

Consideration: 1. element in contract without which contract is not binding. Contract is generally not valid without consideration. 2. reason for contracting parties to enter into contract. Act, promise, price, or motive for which agreement is entered into. 3. value given in exchange for benefit that is to be derived from contract. 4. compensation. Exchange of consideration is usually mutual, each party giving something up to other.

Consign: to send or forward goods to merchant, factor, or agent for sale with title retained by seller and with payment delayed, generally until sale is made.

Consignee: person or entity to which goods or property is consigned or shipped; ultimate recipient of shipment.

Consignment: arrangement under which consignor (seller) remains owner of property until such time as consignee (buyer) pays for goods; usually consignee pays consignor when goods are sold or holds proceeds of sale in trust for benefit of consignor.

Consignor: 1. one who delivers shipment or turns it over to carrier for transportation and delivery. 2. one who consigns goods to be sold without giving up title.

Consolidated Financial Statement: combined statement showing financial condition of parent corporation and its subsidiaries.

Consolidating Financial Statement: combined statement of subsidiary and parent companies that shows complete statement for each entity without netting intercompany transactions.

Construction Loan: interim financing for development and construction of real property, generally converted to long-term financing upon completion of construction.

Consumer Credit: debt incurred for personal, family, or household use.

Consumer Credit Protection Act (Truth in Lending Act of 1968): law that requires most lenders and those who extend consumer credit to disclose true credit costs. Act provides for limits on garnishment of wages, prohibits excessive interest, and makes available contents of consumer credit reports.

Consumer Sale Disclosure Statement: form required to be provided by creditor to customer, disclosing finance charge details as required under Consumer Credit Protection Act.

Contingent Fee: fee to be paid only in event of specific occurrence, usually successful results. Arrangement, for example, in which collection agency will receive stated percentage of any amounts recovered or in which lawyer will receive payment only if successful in prosecuting lawsuit.

Contingent Liability: liability in which a person(s) or business(es) is indirectly responsible for obligations of a third party. Such indirect liability is usually established by guaranty or endorsement, and the liability holder may turn to guarantors or endorsers for satisfaction of debt. See also Endorsement and Guaranty.

Contra Account: account that partially or wholly offsets another account or balance.

Contract: agreement between two or more entities or legally competent persons that creates, modifies, or destroys legal arrangement.

Controlled Disbursement: funds management technique in corporate cash management designed to maximize funds available for temporary investment in money market or for payment to trade creditors. Controls flow of checks through banking system to meet corporate investment and funds management requirements. Contrasts with delayed disbursement. See also *Federal Reserve Float* and *Treasury Workstation.*

Controller: person in business organization responsible for finances, internal auditing, and accounting systems in use in company's operations.

Conversion: process of consolidating or transferring data from one system to another.

Conveyance: 1. transfer of right, generally instrument transferring interest in estate in form of deed. 2. transfer of property ownership (sometimes inclu leases and mortgages) from one person or organization to another.

Copyright: intangible right granted to author or originator by federal governm to solely and exclusively reproduce or publish specific literary, musical, artistic work for certain number of years.

Corporate Reorganization: see *Bankruptcy.*

Corporate Veil: convention that corporate organization insulates organizatic owners from liability for corporate activities.

Corporation: artificial person or legal entity organized under and treated by s* laws, legally distinct from its shareholders and vested with capacity of con uous succession irrespective of changes in its ownership either in perpet or for limited term. It may be set up to contract, own, and discharge busin within boundaries of powers granted it by its corporate charter.

Correspondent: organization or individual that carries on business relations acts as agent with others in different cities or countries.

Cosigner: one of joint signers of loan documents. One who signs note of ano* as support for credit of the principal maker.

Cost of Funds: dollar cost of interest paid or accrued on funds acquired from v ous sources within bank and borrowed funds acquired from other finan institutions, including time deposits, advances at Federal Reserve disco window, federal funds purchased, and Eurodollar deposits. Financial inst tion may use internal cost of funds in pricing loans it makes.

Covenant: written agreement, convention, or promise between parties v pledge to do or not to do certain things or that stipulates truth of certain fac

CPA: see *Certified Public Accountant.*

CRA: see *Community Reinvestment Act of 1977.*

Crash: sudden sharp decrease in business activity that can negatively affect st* market volumes and prices.

Credit: 1. privilege of buying goods and services, or for borrowing money return for promise of future payment. 2. in bookkeeping, entry on ledger s nifying cash payment, merchandise returned, or allowance to reduce debt accounting entry on right side of ledger sheet.

Credit Advisory Board (CAB): agency established by Financial Institutio Reform, Recovery, and Enforcement Act of 1989 "to monitor the credit st dards and lending practices of insured depository institutions and the sup vision of such standards and practices by the federal financial regulators" well as to "ensure that insured depository institutions can meet the dema of a modern and globally competitive world." This board was granted perr nent authorization by the Federal Deposit Insurance Corporation Improvem Act of 1991. Formerly known as Credit Standards Advisory Commi* (CSAC).

Credit Analyst: person who evaluates the financial history and financial sta ments of credit applicants to assess creditworthiness. Analysts are traine evaluate applicant's financial strength and to opine on the probability of repayment, collateral adequacy, or whether a credit enhancement throug cosigner or guarantor is needed.

Credit Application: form completed by potential borrower and used by credito determine applicant's creditworthiness.

Credit Approval: decision to extend credit.

Credit Approval System: internal methods by which credit decisions are made.

Credit Bureau: agency that gathers information and provides its subscribers w credit reports on consumers.

Credit Checking: examining and analyzing creditworthiness of customer by c* tacting references, reviewing credit reports, etc.

Credit Department: department within a financial institution that performs ope tions and credit support functions for underwriting activities. May incl maintenance of credit files, credit investigations, financial statement analy and spreading, customers' accounts receivable audits, lender training, por lio reporting, facilitation of credit meetings, etc.

Credit Enhancement: enhancement to creditworthiness of loans underlying ass backed security or municipal bond, generally to get investment-grade ra* from bond rating agency and to improve marketability of debt securities investors. There are two general classifications of credit enhancements:
- third-party enhancement, in which third party pledges its own creditwor ness and guarantees repayment in form of standby letter of credit or co mercial letter of credit issued by a financial institution, surety bond fr insurance company, or special reserve fund managed by financial guara firm in exchange for fee.
- self-enhancement, which is generally done by issuer through over-collate ization—that is, pledging loans with book value greater than face value bonds offered for sale.

Credit File: creditor's file that compiles information about customer, includ correspondence, credit memorandums and analyses, credit ratings, a cre history, payment patterns, and credit inquiries.

Credit Granting: approval and extension of credit to a customer.

Credit Inquiry: request made by a financial institution or trade creditor conce ing the responding bank's own customer.

dit Insurance: life and health insurance issued in conjunction with borrowing by individuals; covers payments or unpaid balance when borrower is disabled or dies; in business, covers loss of receivables when debtor becomes insolvent.

dit Interchange: exchange of credit information between individuals or groups.

dit Interchange Bureau (CIB): 1. local bureaus offering members or subscribers credit reports usually based on recent ledger experiences. Generally refers to organized system of cooperating bureaus operated by regional credit associations. 2. credit agency that may limit its reporting to a particular trade.

dit Investigation: inquiry made by a financial institution or trade creditor concerning subject that is not the responding financial institution's customer.

dit Limit: maximum amount of credit made available to customer by specific creditor.

dit Line: commitment by a financial institution to lend funds to a borrower up to a given amount over a specified future period under certain pre-established conditions. Normally reviewed annually.

dit Management: function of planning, organizing, implementing, and supervising credit policies of a company.

ditor: 1. one to whom debt is owed by another as a result of a financial transaction. 2. one who extends credit and to whom money is due.

ditors' Committee: voluntary representative group of creditors that may examine affairs of insolvent debtor. Group will usually advise as to continuation of business, study accountant's and appraiser's reports, act as watchdog over operating business, make recommendations to appropriate groups or legal body so that creditors will realize largest settlement possible, and advise as to acceptability of settlement.

ditors' Remedies: legal rights enabling creditors to collect delinquent debts owed them.

dit Policy: company's written procedures for making credit decisions. Used to aid company in meeting its overall risk management objectives.

dit Process Review: assessment of entire credit-granting process concerning specific financial institution loan portfolio(s).

dit Rating: appraisal made by a financial institution or credit agency as to creditworthiness of a person or company. Such a report will include background on owners, estimate of financial strength and ability to pay when due, and company's payment record.

dit Record: written history of how well a customer has handled debt repayment.

dit Report: 1. report to aid management in reaching credit, sales, and financial decisions. 2. confidential report containing information obtained by mercantile agency that has investigated a company's background, credit history, financial strength, and payment record.

dit Reporting Agency: company or trade interchange group that confidentially supplies subscribers or members with credit information and other relevant data as to a company's ability or likelihood to pay for goods and services purchased on credit.

dit Research Foundation (CRF): education and research affiliate of National Association of Credit Management.

dit Review: follow-up monitoring of loan or extension of credit by credit review officer or department, senior loan committee, auditor, or regulatory agency intended to determine whether loan was made in accordance with lender's written credit standards and policies and in compliance with banking regulations. Errors, omissions, concentrations, etc., if detected by credit review process, can then be corrected by lending officers, thus preventing deterioration in credit quality and possible loan losses. Also called loan review.

dit Risk: 1. evaluation of a customer's ability or willingness to pay debts on time. 2. risk that a financial institution assumes when it makes an irrevocable payment on behalf of its customer against insufficient funds.

dit Scoring: statistical model used to predict the creditworthiness of credit applicants. Credit scoring estimates repayment probability based on information in credit application and credit bureau report. The two main types of credit scoring are application scoring for new accounts and behavior scoring for accounts that have been activated and are carrying balances.

dit Terms: stated and agreed on terms for debt repayment.

dit Union: nonprofit cooperative financial organization chartered by state or federal government to provide financial services such as deposit and loan activities to a specific and limited group of people.

ditworthy: term used to describe individual or entity deemed worthy of extension of credit.

SAC: see *Credit Advisory Board.*

urrent Assets: short-term assets of company, including cash, accounts receivable, temporary investments, and goods and materials in inventory.

urrent Liabilities: short-term obligations due within one year, including current maturities of long-term debts.

Current Open Account: sale of goods or services for which customer does no pay for each purchase but rather is required to settle in full periodically o within specified time period after each transaction.

Current Ratio: total of current assets divided by total current liabilities; used a indication of a company's liquidity and ability to service current obligations.

D

D&B: see *Dun & Bradstreet, Inc.*

Dating (Terms): extension of credit terms beyond normal terms because o industry's seasonality or unusual circumstance.

Days Sales Outstanding (DSO): a calculation that expresses the average time i days that receivables are outstanding.

DBA: see *Doing Business As.*

DDA: see *Demand Deposit Account.*

Dealer Loan: see *Floor Plan.*

Debenture: unsecured, long-term indebtedness or corporate obligation.

Debit: entry on left side of accounting ledger.

Debit Card: magnetized plastic card that permits customers to withdraw cas from automatic teller machines and make purchases with charges deducte from funds on deposit at a predesignated account.

Debt: 1. specified amount of money, goods, or services that is owed from one t another, including not only obligation of debtor to pay but also right of cred tor to receive and enforce payment. 2. financial obligation of debtor.

Debtor: person or entity indebted to or owing money to another.

Debtor in Possession (DIP): In a Chapter 11 bankruptcy, a debtor may continu to maintain possession of its assets and use them in normal business opera tions.

Debtor-in-Possession Financing: credit facilities extended to borrower who reorganizing under Chapter 11 bankruptcy.

Debt Ratio: measure of firm's leverage position derived by dividing total debts equity.

Debt Service: total interest and scheduled principal payments on debt due with given time frame.

Decision: judgment, decree, or verdict pronounced by court in determination case.

Declarations Page: policy form containing data regarding insured, policy term premium, type and amount of coverage, designation of forms and endors ments incorporated at time policy is issued, name of insurer, and countersi nature of agent.

Deductible: portion of loss that is not insured; may be stated amount deducte from loss or percentage of loss or of value of property at time of loss.

Deduction: partial amount of payment that is withheld.

Deed: legal, written document used to transfer ownership of real property fro one party to another.

Deed of Trust: legal document used in some states in lieu of mortgage. Title real property passes from seller to trustee, who holds mortgaged proper until mortgage has been fully paid and then releases title to borrower. Trust is authorized to sell property if borrower defaults, paying amount of mortga loan to lender and any remaining balance to former owner.

Defalcation: misappropriation of funds held in trust for another.

Defamation: injury to person's or entity's character, reputation, or good name false and malicious statements (includes both libel and slander).

Default: to fail to meet obligation or terms of loan agreement such as payment principal or interest.

Default Charge: legally agreed upon charge or penalty added to account wh payment of debt is late or another event of default occurs under a loan agre ment.

Defendant: person or entity defending or denying claim; party against which s or charge has been filed in court of law. See also Plaintiff.

Defer: to postpone or delay action.

Deferred Payment Sale: selling on installment plan with payments delayed postponed until future date.

Deficiency Judgment: decree requiring debtor to pay amount remaining d under defaulted contract after secured property has been liquidated.

Deficit: difference between receipts and expenses when expenses are greater.

Defraud: to deprive person of property by fraud, deceit, or artifice.

Defunct: business that has ceased to exist and is without assets; concern that h failed.

Delayed Disbursement: practice in cash management whereby a firm pays ve dors and other corporations by disbursing payments from a financial insti tion in a remote city. Also called remote disbursement. Contrasts with co trolled disbursement. See also Federal Reserve Float.

Delinquent: 1. past-due obligation; overdue and unpaid account. 2. to be arrears in payment of debts, loans, taxes. 3. to have failed in duty or respon bility.

Demand Deposit Account (DDA): funds on deposit in checking account that are payable by a financial institution upon demand of depositor. See also *Time Deposit.*

Demand Draft: written order directing that payment be made, on sight, to a third party.

Demand Letter: correspondence sent by creditor, collection agency, or lawyer to debtor requesting payment of obligation by specific date.

Demand Loan: loan with no fixed due date and payable on demand by maker of loan; loan that can be "called" by lender at any time.

Demurrage: charge that is fixed by contract and payable by recipient of goods for detaining freight car or ship longer than agreed in order to load or unload. Purpose is remuneration to owner of vessel for earnings he or she was improperly caused to lose.

Deposit: 1. amount of money given as down payment for goods or as consideration for contract. 2. funds retained in customer's bank account.

Depreciation: decline in value of fixed assets, allocating purchase cost of an asset plus additions to value over its useful economic life as outlined by the Federal Tax Code.

Derivatives: broad family of financial instruments with characteristics of forward or option contracts.

Derogatory Account Information: adverse information on customers who have not paid accounts with other creditors according to payment terms, as reported to a credit bureau.

Directors and Officers Liability Insurance: legal liability coverage for wrongful acts including breach of duty but not fraud or dishonesty. Often known as E & O, or Errors and Omissions Insurance.

Disbursement: full or partial advancement of funds.

Discharge: 1. to cancel or release obligation. 2. to release debtor from all or most debts in bankruptcy.

Disclaimer Statement: notice disclaiming responsibility for accuracy, completeness, or timeliness of credit information. Most disclaimer statements urge recipients of the information not to rely unduly on it and stress the confidential nature of information being disclosed.

Discontinued Operations: operations of a segment of a company, usually a subsidiary whose activities represent a separate line of business that, although still operating, is the subject of a formal plan of disposal approved by management.

Discount: 1. interest deducted from face amount of note at time loan is made. 2. trade term used for reduction of invoice amount when payment has been made within specified terms.

Discounted Note: 1. borrowing arrangement in which interest is deducted from face amount of note before proceeds are advanced (see also Note). 2. term used when customer endorses note received from another party and presents it to a financial institution to obtain funds.

Dishonor: to fail to make payment of negotiable instrument on its due date.

Disintermediation: withdrawal of funds from interest-bearing deposit accounts when rates on competing financial instruments, such as money market mutual funds, stocks, and bonds, offer better returns.

Dismissal: court order or judgment disposing action, suit, or motion without trial.

Dispossess: legal action taken by landlord to put individual or business tenant out of his or her property.

Dissolution of Corporation: termination of entity's existence by law, expiration of charter, loss of all members, or failure to meet statutory level of members.

Distribution: one or more payments made to creditors who have approved claims filed in a bankruptcy proceeding, assignment for the benefit of creditors, or receivership.

Distributor: business engaged in the distribution or marketing of manufacturer's goods to customers or dealers. See also Wholesaler.

Dividend: 1. periodic distribution of cash or property to shareholders of corporation as return on their investment.

Document: any written instrument that records letters with figures or marks that may be used as evidence.

Documentary Evidence: any written record or inanimate object, as distinguished from oral evidence.

Documents of Title: Include bill of lading, dock warrant, dock receipt, warehouse receipt, order for the delivery of goods, and any other document that in the regular course of business or financing is treated as adequately evidencing that the person in possession of it is entitled to receive, hold, and dispose of the document and the goods it covers. To be a document of title, a document must purport to be issued by, or addressed to, a bailee and purport to cover goods in the bailee's possession that are either identified or are fungible portions of an identified mass.

Doing Business As (DBA): reference term placed before trade name under which business operates. Sometimes used as fictitious trade style acknowledging that name is not part of corporation title or registered trademark.

Domestic Corporation: company doing business in state in which it is incorporated.

Dormant Account: inactive deposit account in which there have been no deposits or withdrawals for a long period of time.

Doubtful Assets: assets that have all weaknesses inherent in substandard assets with added characteristic that weaknesses make collection or liquidation in full, on basis of currently existing facts, conditions, and values, highly questionable and improbable. Possibility of loss is extremely high. Because of certain important and reasonably specific pending factors that may strengthen assets, classification as estimated loss is deferred until more exact status may be determined. Pending factors include proposed merger, acquisition, liquidation procedures, capital injection, perfecting liens on additional collateral, and refinancing plans.

Downgrading: 1. lowering of assessment of customer's creditworthiness. 2. worsening the internally assigned credit quality rating of a loan or relationship in order to appropriately report risk.

Down Payment: up-front partial payment made to secure right to purchase goods.

Downstream Funding: funds borrowed by holding company for a subsidiary's use, generally to obtain more favorable rate; contrasts with Upstream Funding.

Draft: written order by one party (drawer) directing second party (drawee) to pay sum of money to third party (payee). See also *Banker's Acceptance, Letter of Credit, Sight Draft,* and *Time Draft.*

Drawee: person or entity that is expected to pay check or draft when instrument is presented for payment.

Drawer: party instructing drawee to pay someone else by writing or drawing check or draft. Also called maker or writer.

Drop Shipment: shipment of goods delivered directly from manufacturer to customer.

DSO: see *Days Sales Outstanding.*

Dual Banking: banking system in U.S., consisting of state banks, chartered and supervised by state banking departments, and national banks, chartered and regulated by Office of the Comptroller of the Currency.

Due Date: stated maturity date for debt obligation.

Due Diligence: 1. responsibility of an entity's directors and officers to act in prudent manner in evaluating credit applications; in essence, using same degree of care that an ordinary person would use in making same analysis. 2. review that is made of a loan portfolio of a potential merger candidate by acquiring institution.

Due Process of Law: law in its regular course of administration through courts guaranteed by U.S. Constitution.

Dun: to repeatedly demand payment of debt; to be insistent in following debtor for payment.

Dun & Bradstreet, Inc. (D&B): international mercantile agency supplying information and credit ratings on all types of businesses.

Dun Letter: letter or notice sent by creditor requesting payment of past-due debt.

D-U-N-S Number: (Data Universal Numbering System) code developed by Dun & Bradstreet that identifies specific business name and location.

Durable Goods: goods that provide long-lasting qualities and continuing service.

Duress: unlawful constraint that forces person to do what he or she would not have done by choice.

Duty: 1. legal, moral, or ethical obligation. 2. tax collected on import or export goods.

E

Earnest Money: money that one contracting party gives to another at the time of entering into the contract in order to bind the contract in good faith, and which will be forfeited if the purchaser fails to carry out the contract.

Earnings Report: 1. income statement showing a business's or individual's revenues and expenses for stated period of time.

Easement: right of owner of one parcel of land to use land of another for special purpose. Usually easement rights pass with land when it is sold.

Edge Act: banking legislation, passed in 1919, that allows national banks to conduct foreign lending operations through federal or state-chartered subsidiaries called Edge Act corporations. Such corporations can be chartered in other states and are allowed to own banks in foreign countries and to invest in foreign commercial and industrial firms.

EFT: see *Electronic Funds Transfer.*

Electronic Funds Transfer (EFT): computerized system enabling funds to be debited, credited, or transferred between financial institution accounts and vendors.

Embezzlement: fraudulent appropriation of one's property by person to whom it was entrusted.

Encumbrance: any right or interest in real or other property that diminishes the property's value and alters control of disposition.

Endorsement: 1. act of writing one's name on back of note, bill, check, or similar written instrument for payment of money; required on negotiable instrument to pass title properly to another. By signing such instrument, endorser

becomes party to it and thereby liable, under certain conditions, for its payment. 2. change or addition to insurance policy, informally called rider.

repreneur: person who plans, organizes, and runs operation of new business.

M Terms: Shipments during a month are invoiced in a single statement dated as of the last day of that month or the first day of the following month.

al Credit Opportunity Act of 1974: Federal Reserve Regulation B that prohibits creditors from discriminating against credit applicants on basis of age, race, color, religion, national origin, sex, marital status, age, or receipt of public assistance.

itable Subordination: principles in section 510 (c) of U.S. Bankruptcy Code that permit bankruptcy court to subordinate, for purposes of distribution, all or part of creditor's claim against debtor's estate to claims of another creditor of that debtor after court has determined that first creditor has engaged in some form of wrongful conduct that has improved position relative to other creditors.

ity: value of ownership, calculated by subtracting total liabilities from total assets.

heat: right of state to claim property or money if there is no legal claim made to it.

row Account: deposit account to which access is restricted or limited by terms of written agreement entered into by three parties, including a financial institution.

ate: any right, title, or interest that a person may have in lands or other personal property.

mate: amount of labor, materials, and other costs that a contractor anticipates for a project, as summarized in contractor's bid proposal for project.

nt of Default: a breach of an agreement between parties to a contract; a violation of one or more of the loan covenants as set forth in either the loan agreement, commitment letter, or promissory note.

rgreen Revolving Credit: commitment to lend money that remains in effect unless lender takes specific action to terminate agreement; agreement may provide that, in event of termination, any outstanding amount will convert to term loan.

hange Rate: value of one country's currency to that of another country at a particular point in time.

lusive Sales Agreement: contractual arrangement, generally between a retailer and a manufacturer or wholesaler, giving retailer exclusive rights for sale of articles or services within a defined geographic area or through a defined distribution channel.

cute: to complete and give validity to a legal document by signing, sealing, and delivering it.

mpt: 1. to release, discharge, or waive from a liability to which others in the same general class are subject. 2. property not available for seizure.

mption: 1. immunity from general burden, tax, or charge. 2. legal right of debtor to hold portion of property free from claims or judgments.

ense: cost or outlay of money used in business operating cycle.

ort-Import Bank: also called Ex-Im Bank. Provides guarantees of working capital loans for U.S. exporters; guarantees the repayment of loans or makes loans to foreign purchasers of U.S. goods and services. Ex-Im Bank also provides credit insurance that protects U.S. exporters against the risks of nonpayment by foreign buyers for political or commercial reasons. Ex-Im Bank does not compete with commercial lenders, but assumes the risks they cannot accept.

F

e Amount: indicated value of a financial instrument, as shown on its front.

ility Fee: lender's charge for making a line of credit or other credit facility available to borrower (for example, a commitment fee).

simile: exact copy of an original.

tor: entity that purchases borrower's accounts receivable and may extend funds to borrower prior to collection of receivables.

toring: short-term financing from nonrecourse sale of accounts receivable to third party or factor. Factor assumes full risk of collection, including credit losses. Factoring is most common in the garment industry, but has been used in other industries as well. There are two basic types of factoring:

- discount factoring, in which factor pays discounted price for receivables before maturity date.
- maturity factoring, in which factor pays the client purchase price of factored accounts at maturity.

Credit Billing Act of 1974 (FCBA): Federal Reserve Regulation Z details the provisions of this act by prescribing uniform methods of computing the cost of consumer credit, disclosure of credit terms, and procedures for resolving billing errors on certain kinds of credit accounts.

Credit Reporting Act: federal legislation that regulates consumer credit reporting activities and gives consumer right to learn contents of his or her credit bureau file.

Fair Market Value: price that property would sell for between willing buyer an willing seller, neither of whom is obligated to effect transaction.

Fannie Mae: see *Federal National Mortgage Association.*

FASB: see *Financial Accounting Standards Board.*

FFB: see *Federal Financing Bank.*

FCBA: see *Fair Credit Billing Act of 1974.*

FDIC: see *Federal Deposit Insurance Corporation.*

FDICIA: see *Federal Deposit Insurance Corporation Improvement Act of 1991.*

Federal Deposit Insurance Corporation (FDIC): 1. federal agency that insure bank accounts for up to $100,000 at both commercial banks and thrift through Bank Insurance Fund and Savings Association Fund. 2. federa regulator for state-chartered banks that are not members of Federal Reserv System.

Federal Deposit Insurance Corporation Improvement Act of 1991 (FDICIA): leg islation that provides for recapitalization of Bank Insurance Fund and restruc turing of financial services industry through:

- emphasis on more capital.
- government standards for lending, operations, and asset growth.
- quicker government seizure of struggling institutions.
- reduced liquidity options for all but the strongest banks.
- incentives for uninsured depositors to use only the largest and strongest banks.
- sharply increased regulatory costs and fees.
- easier rules for acquiring banks and thrifts.

Federal Financial Institutions Examination Council (FFIEC): interagency grou of federal banking regulators formed in 1979 to maintain uniform standard for federal examination and supervision of federally insured depository insti tutions, bank holding companies, and savings and loan holding companies Also runs schools for examiners employed by banks, thrifts, and credit unio agencies. Council produces Uniform Bank Performance Report.

Federal Financing Bank (FFB): agency in U.S. Treasury established by Congres in 1973 to centralize borrowing by federal agencies. Instead of selling securi ties directly to financial markets, all but largest federal agencies raise capita by borrowing from U.S. Treasury through FFB. FFB makes loans at favorabl rates to agencies that do not have ready access to credit markets; its debt i direct obligation of U.S. Treasury.

Federal Funds: unsecured advances of immediately available funds from exces balances in reserve accounts held at Federal Reserve Banks. Technically these funds are not borrowings but purchases of immediately available funds Banks advancing federal funds sell excess reserves; banks receiving federa funds buy excess reserves from selling banks. Federal funds sold are credi transactions on account of selling banks. See also *Federal Funds Rate.*

Federal Funds Rate: rate charged in interbank market for purchases of exces reserve balances. Rate of interest is key money market interest rate and corre lates with rates on other short-term credit arrangements. Because the federa funds rate re-prices with each transaction, it is the most sensitive of mone market rates and is watched carefully by the Federal Reserve Board.

Federal Home Loan Bank Board (FHLBB): federal agency established by Federa Home Loan Bank Act of 1932 to supervise reserve credit system, Federa Home Loan Bank System, for savings institutions. Board also acted as char tering agency and primary regulator of federal savings and loan association under Home Owners Loan Act of 1933. Financial Institutions Reform, Recov ery, and Enforcement Act of 1989 abolished board, transferring its powers i examination and supervision of federally chartered savings institutions to new agency, Office of Thrift Supervision, bureau of U.S. Treasury Department Regulatory oversight of district Home Loan Banks was transferred to the five member Federal Housing Finance Board.

Federal Home Loan Bank System: system of 11 regional banks established by Federal Home Loan Bank Act of 1932, acting as central credit system for sav ings and loan institutions. District Home Loan Banks make short-term credi advances to savings institutions, much like Federal Reserve System acts a lender of last resort to commercial banks. Each Home Loan Bank operate independently and has its own board of directors.

Federal Home Loan Mortgage Corporation (FHLMC): corporation authorized by Congress in 1970 as secondary market conduit for residential mortgages Corporation purchases loans from mortgage originators and sells its ow obligations and mortgage-backed bonds issued by Government Nationa Mortgage Association to private investors, namely financial institution trus funds, insurance companies, pension funds, and thrift institutions. Also called Freddie Mac.

Federal Housing Administration (FHA): federal agency that insures residentia mortgages. Created by National Housing Act of 1934, FHA is now part o Department of Housing and Urban Development. Both FHA and Department o Veterans Affairs have single-family mortgage programs to assist homebuyers who are unable to obtain financing from conventional mortgage lenders (banks, savings and loans, and other financial institutions).

Federal Housing Finance Board (FHFB): independent federal agency regulating credit advance activities of 11 Federal Home Loan Banks. This board, estab

lished by Financial Institutions Reform, Recovery, and Enforcement Act of 1989, has five members, including secretary of Housing and Urban Development, and four directors appointed by the President with Senate confirmation to serve seven-year terms. At least one director must represent the interests of community groups.

Federal National Mortgage Association (FNMA): federally chartered, stockholder-owned corporation that purchases residential mortgages insured or guaranteed by federal agencies, as well as conventional mortgages, in secondary mortgage market. Corporation raises capital to support its operations through collection of insurance and commitment fees, issuance of stock, and sale of debentures and notes. Also called Fannie Mae.

Federal Open Market Committee (FOMC): policy committee in Federal Reserve System that sets short-term monetary policy objectives for Fed. Committee is made up of seven governors of Federal Reserve Board, plus the presidents of six Federal Reserve Banks. President of Federal Reserve Bank of New York is permanent FOMC member. The other five slots are filled on rotating basis by presidents of other 11 Federal Reserve Banks. Committee carries out monetary objectives by instructing Open Market Desk at Federal Reserve Bank of New York to buy or sell government securities from special account, called open market account, at New York Fed.

Federal Reserve Board (FRB): U.S.'s central bank responsible for conduct of monetary policy; also oversees state-chartered banks that are members of Federal Reserve System, bank holding companies, and Edge Act corporations.

Federal Reserve Float: total amount of funds that Federal Reserve Banks, in their role as clearing agents, have credited to depositing institutions but have not charged to paying institutions.

Federal Reserve System: central bank of U.S. created by Federal Reserve Act of 1913. System consists of Board of Governors, made up of seven members, and a network of 12 Federal Reserve Banks and 25 branches throughout U.S. Board of Governors is responsible for setting monetary policy and reserve requirements. Board and banks share responsibility for setting the discount rate, the interest rate that depository institutions are charged for borrowing from Federal Reserve Banks.

Federal Trade Commission (FTC): federal regulatory agency that administers and enforces rules to prevent unfair business practices.

Fee Simple: estate in which owner is entitled to entire property and has unconditional power over its disposition.

FFIEC: see *Federal Financial Institutions Examination Council.*

FHA: see *Federal Housing Administration.*

FHLBB: see *Federal Home Loan Bank Board.*

FHLMC: see *Federal Home Loan Mortgage Corporation.*

Fictitious Name: pretend name used by firm in business transactions. Company is usually required to register this name with local authorities, along with true names and addresses of company's owners.

Fidelity Bond: contract issued by insurer to employer to cover loss caused by dishonest acts of employees; form of suretyship. Also called dishonesty insurance.

Fiduciary: person or entity acting in capacity of trustee for another.

Field Warehousing: method of using company's inventory to secure business loan. In leased and separate storage area of borrower's facility, goods act as security for loan and are released by custodian only upon lender's order.

FIFO: see *First-In First-Out.*

File: 1. organized folder containing accumulation of information and items retained for preservation or reference. 2. to deposit legal document with proper authority.

File Revision: routine gathering of credit information by credit grantor to update files on borrowers.

Filing Claims: 1. depositing of formal papers with proper public office and in manner and time frame prescribed by law in order to preserve creditor's rights. 2. method used to perfect security interest accomplished by recording in proper public office.

Finance Charges: total costs to an individual or business of obtaining credit, including interest and any fees.

Financial Analysis: evaluation by credit analyst of customer's financial situation to determine whether customer has ability to meet his or her obligations as they become due. Factors such as general condition of customer's industry, organizational structure, available collateral or guarantors, and past financial performance are considered.

Financial Accounting Standards Board (FASB): independent board responsible for establishing and interpreting generally accepted accounting principles, formed in 1973 to succeed and continue activities of Accounting Principles Board.

Financial Institutions Reform, Recovery, and Enforcement Act of 1989 (FIRREA): act signed into law on August 9, 1989, to provide funding and regulatory structure necessary to close several hundred insolvent savings associations and liquidate their assets, to consolidate federal insurance of banks and savings associations under direction of the Federal Deposit Insurance Corporation, to provide regulatory agencies with sweeping new enforcement pow-

ers, and to increase substantially civil and criminal penalties for violation federal banking statutes and regulations. Act substantially alters relations between savings institutions and regulators and imposes new requireme that must be observed in day-to-day operations of institutions.

Financial Position: standing of company, combining assets and liabilities entered on balance sheet.

Financial Statements: reports consisting of individual's or company's bala sheet, income statement, and statement of cash flows, footnotes, and supplemental schedules.

Financing Statement: form required to be completed by creditor and filed w appropriate county and state authorities in order to perfect creditor's secu interest in collateral and to give public notice of such interest.

FIRREA: see *Financial Institutions Reform, Recovery, and Enforcement Ac 1989.*

First Deed of Trust: first recorded deed of trust that acts as first lien on prop it describes.

First-In First-Out (FIFO): method of valuing inventory in which the first go received are the first goods used or sold. Using this method, costs of inv tory used to determine cost of goods sold are related to costs that w incurred first.

First Mortgage: mortgage on property that is superior to any others by fac having been filed first.

Fiscal: anything involving financial matters or issues.

Fiscal Agent: person or organization serving as another's financial agent or re sentative.

Fiscal Year: fixed accounting year used as basis for annual financial reportin business or government.

Five C's of Credit: method of evaluating potential borrower's creditworthin based on five criteria: Capacity, Capital, Character, Collateral, and Condition

Fixed Assets: property used in normal course of business that is of a long-t nature, such as land, machinery, fixtures, and equipment.

Fixed-Rate Loan: loan with interest rate that does not vary over term of loan.

Fixture: that which is permanently attached or affixed to real property.

Flagging an Account: temporarily identifying an account for specific purpos reason; may involve suspending activity.

Float: uncollected funds represented by checks deposited in one bank but not cleared through bank on which they are drawn.

Floating Interest Rate: loan interest rate that changes whenever the stated in rate, or base rate, changes.

Floating Lien: loan or credit facility secured by inventory or receivables. This of security agreement gives lender interest in assets acquired by borro after agreement, as well as those owned when agreement was made. W agreement covers proceeds from sales, lender also has recourse against c collected from the payment of receivables.

Floor Plan: loan made to dealer for purchase of inventory acquired for resale secured by that inventory, such as automobiles or appliances.

FNMA: see *Federal National Mortgage Association.*

FOB: see *Free on Board.*

FOB Point: point at which responsibility for freight charges begins and passes. See also *Free on Board.*

FOMC: see *Federal Open Market Committee.*

Forbearance: Temporarily giving up the right to enforce a valid claim, in return a promise. It is sufficient consideration to make a promise binding (for ex ple, protracted payment arrangements or interest rate reduction in excha for additional collateral or guarantors).

Forced Sale: 1. court-ordered sale of property, usually without owner's appr 2. voluntary sale of goods or property to raise cash or to reduce inventory.

Foreclosure: legal termination of all of debtor's rights in property secured mortgage after debtor has defaulted on obligation supported by such m gage.

Foreign Corporation: corporation established under laws of a state other that in which it is doing business.

Foreign Exchange: conversion of money of one country into its equivalent in rency of another country.

Foreign Item: check drawn on any financial institution other than the finan institution where it is presented for payment. Also called transit item.

Foreign Judgment: judgment obtained in state or country other than the where the debtor now lives, is doing business, or has assets.

Forfeiture: penalty resulting in automatic loss of cash, property, or rights for complying with legal terms of agreement.

Forgery: false making or material altering of any writing with intent to defraud

Form 8K: report disclosing significant events potentially affecting corporati financial condition or market value of its shares, required by Securities Exchange Commission. Report is filed within 30 days after event (pen merger, amendment to corporate charter, charge to earnings for credit los took place and summarizes information that any reasonable investor w want to know before buying or selling securities.

m 10K: annual financial report filed with Securities and Exchange Commission. Issuers of registered securities are required to file 10K, as are corporations with 500 or more shareholders or assets of $2 million and exchange-listed corporations. Report, which becomes public information once filed, summarizes key financial information, including sources and uses of funds by type of business, net pretax operating income, provision for income taxes and credit losses, plus comparative financial statements for past two fiscal years. Summary of 10K report is included in annual report to stockholders.

m 10Q: quarterly financial report filed by companies with listed securities and those corporations required to file annual 10K report with Securities and Exchange Commission. 10Q report, which does not have to be audited, summarizes key financial data on earnings and expenses and compares current financial information with data reported in same quarter of previous year.

warding: referral or placement of out-of-town claims with attorney who then acts on behalf of creditor. In collection process, when authorized, agency may forward account to attorney for collection or suit.

nchise: business agreement whereby one company allows another the right to conduct business under its name and/or distribute its products in exchange for royalties or another agreed upon method of payment.

ud: any act of deceit, omission, or commission used to deprive someone of right or property. Elements of fraud consist of intentional misrepresentation of fact, relied on by another to his or her detriment, that results in damages.

udulent Conveyance: a transfer of property by a debtor, for the intent and purpose of defrauding creditors. Such property may be reached by the creditors through appropriate legal proceedings.

: see *Federal Reserve Board*.

ddie Mac: see *Federal Home Loan Mortgage Corporation*.

e and Clear: 1. property with an unencumbered title. 2. title that is free of defects.

e and Clear Delivery Receipt: delivery receipt signed by consignee completely absolving carrier from any claim for loss or damages.

e Astray: freight shipment that has been lost. If it is carrier's fault and shipment is located, it is carrier's obligation to make delivery to original destination at no additional cost to shipper or consignee.

e Demand Letter Service: pre-collection letter sent by collection agency to debtor, requesting that payment be made directly to creditor by given date. No charge is made for payments received within free demand period, but balances remaining unpaid are followed for collection by agency at its regular rates.

e on Board (FOB): term identifying shipping point from which buyer assumes all responsibilities and costs for transportation.

e Port: place where goods are imported or exported free of any duty.

ght Forwarder: business that receives goods for transportation; services include consolidation of small freight shipments of less than carload, truckload, or container lots assembled for lower shipping rates.

en Account: 1. account to which customer no longer has access. 2. account suspended by court order, violation of loan covenants, or checking account agreement, etc.

en Assets: any assets that cannot be used by owner because of pending legal action.

: see *Federal Trade Commission*.

d: cash or equivalents set aside for specific purpose.

d Accounting: fiscal and accounting entity with self-balancing set of accounts recording cash and other financial resources, together with all related liabilities and residual equities or balances, and changes therein, which are segregated for purpose of carrying on specific activities or obtaining certain objectives in accordance with special regulations, restrictions, or limitations.

ded Debt: mortgages, bonds, debentures, notes, or other obligations with maturity of more than one year from statement date.

G

P: see *Generally Accepted Accounting Principles*.

ishee: 1. person or entity that has possession of money or property belonging to defendant and is served with writ of garnishment to hold money or property for payment of defendant's debt to plaintiff. 2. one against whom garnishment has been served.

ishment: legal warning or procedure to one in possession of another's property not to allow owner access to such property as it will be used to satisfy judgment against owner.

eral Contractor: contractor who enters into a contract with an owner for construction of a project and who takes full responsibility for its completion. Contractor may enter into subcontracts with various subcontractors for performance of specific parts or phases of project.

eral Ledger: bookkeeping record comprising all assets, liabilities, proprietorship, revenue, and expense accounts. Entries for each account are posted, and balances are included for each entry.

Generally Accepted Accounting Principles (GAAP): conventions, rules, and procedures that define accepted accounting practices, including broad guidelines as well as detailed procedures. Financial Accounting Standards Board, an independent self-regulatory organization, is responsible for promulgating these principles.

General Obligation Debt: long-term debt or bond repaid from all otherwise unrestricted revenues, sales taxes, property taxes, license fees, property sales, rents, and so forth of municipality.

General Partner: participant in a business relationship who is personally liable, without limitation, for all partnership debts.

Ginnie Mae: see *Government National Mortgage Association*.

GNMA: see *Government National Mortgage Association*.

Going Concern: assumes that a business entity has a reasonable expectation of continuing in business and generating a profit for an indefinite period of time.

Goods on Approval: goods offered by seller to buyer with option of examining goods for specific period of time before deciding to purchase them.

Goodwill: 1. intangible assets of business consisting of its good reputation, valuable clientele, or desirable location that results in above normal earning power. 2. value or amount for which business could be sold above book value of its physical property and receivables.

Government National Mortgage Association (GNMA): corporation created by Congress that administers mortgage-backed securities program that channels new sources of funds into residential mortgages through sale of securities. Also called Ginnie Mae.

Grace Period: specified length of time beyond payment due date during which late fee will not be assessed.

Grantee: person to whom title in property is made.

Grantor: person who transfers title to property.

Gross Margin: gross profit as a percentage of sales.

Gross Profit: net sales less cost of sales.

Gross Sales: sales before returns and allowances; discounts are deducted to arrive at net sales.

Guarantor: person who agrees by execution of a contract to repay the debt of another if that person defaults.

Guaranty: separate agreement by which a party (or parties) other than debtor assumes responsibility for payment of obligation if principal debtor defaults or is subsequently unable to perform under the terms of the obligation.

Guardian: person who is legally responsible for the care and management of a minor or individual who is not mentally or legally competent (or of such person's property).

H

Hard Goods: durable consumer goods, usually including such items as major appliances and furniture, with relatively long, useful lives.

Heavy Industry: industry involved in manufacturing basic products such as metals, machinery, or other equipment.

Hidden Assets: assets not easily identified and either intentionally not disclosed or publicly reported at lower value than their true worth.

High Credit: largest amount of credit used by borrower during specified period of time.

Holder in Due Course: person who has taken negotiable instrument (check or note) for value, in good faith, and on assurance that it is complete and regular, not overdue or dishonored, and has no defect in ownership on part of previous holder or endorser.

Holding Company: company organized to hold and control stock in other companies.

Homestead Exemption: state's law allowing householder or head of family to exempt residence from attachment by creditors.

Housing and Urban Development, Department of: cabinet-level federal agency, founded in 1965, that promotes housing development in U.S. through direct loans, mortgage insurance, and guaranties. It houses Federal Housing Administration and Government National Mortgage Association.

HUD: see *Housing and Urban Development, Department of*.

Hypothecate: to pledge or assign property owned by one entity as security or collateral for loan to second entity.

Hypothecation: 1. offer of stocks, bonds, or other assets owned by party other than borrower as collateral for loan, without transferring title. Borrower retains possession but gives lender right to sell property in event of default by borrower. 2. pledging of negotiable securities to collateralize broker's margin loan. If broker pledges same securities to bank as collateral for broker's loan, process is referred to as re-hypothecation.

I

Immunity: condition of being exempt from duty that others are generally required to perform.

Import Letter of Credit: commercial letter of credit issued to finance import of goods.

Import Duty: government tax on imported items.

Impound: to seize or take into legal custody, usually at order of court. Cash, documents, or records may be impounded.

Inactive Account: account that has shown little or no activity over a substantial period of time.

Inactive Files: 1. accounts on which collection activity has been completed or suspended (claims either collected or found to be uncollectible) and on which no further work is being done. Also called closed or dead files. 2. stored records available for reference.

In Arrears: amounts due but not yet paid.

Income Property: real property acquired as investment and managed for profit.

Income Statement: summary of revenue and expenses covering a specified period.

Income Tax: tax levied by federal, state, or local governments on personal or business earnings.

Incorporation: formation of legal entity, with qualities of perpetual existence and succession.

Incumbrance: see Encumbrance.

Indebtedness: total amount of money or liabilities owed.

In Default: failing to abide by terms and conditions of note or loan agreement. This can include payments on interest or principal (or both) being past due.

Indemnity: 1. contract or assurance to reimburse another against anticipated loss, damage, or failure to fulfill obligation. 2. type of insurance that provides coverage for losses of this nature.

Indirect Liability: contingent liability such as a continuing guarantee.

Individual Signature: credit approved by one person on his or her own authority.

Indorsement: see Endorsement.

Industrial Consumer: purchaser who buys goods or services for business purposes.

Inquiry: request for credit information on a bank's customer.

Insider Loans: loans to directors and officers of bank, which must be reported to bank regulators under Financial Institutions Reform Act of 1978. Banking laws require that loans to insiders be made at substantially the same rate and credit terms as loans to other borrowers.

Insolvency: 1. inability to meet debts as they become due in ordinary course of business. 2. financial condition in which assets are not sufficient to satisfy liabilities.

Installment Sale: contract sale in which merchandise is purchased with down payment and balance is made in partial payments over agreed period of time.

Instrument: written formal or legal document.

In-Substance Foreclosure Assets: loans for which borrower is perceived to have little or no equity in the asset or project and the financial institution can reasonably anticipate proceeds for repayment only from the operation or sale of collateral.

Insufficient Funds: see Non-sufficient Funds.

Insurable Interest: interest such that loss or damage inflicts economic loss.

Insurable Value: maximum possible loss to which property is exposed; actual amount depends on basis of calculation per insurance policy.

Intangible Assets: nonmaterial assets of business that have no value in themselves but that represent value. Examples include trademarks, goodwill, patents, and copyrights.

Interchange: confidential exchange of credit information between individuals and trade groups.

Interchange Bureau: association organized to record and exchange or furnish confidential credit information about a member's payment experience and manner in which customers meet obligations.

Interchange Group: trade membership group within specific industry that meets regularly to exchange credit experiences and other confidential information.

Interchange Report: report usually obtained through credit interchange bureau showing recent credit experience as supplied by participating members.

Inter-creditor Agreement: document used when there is more than one lender involved in credit transaction to spell out each lender's rights and obligations.

Interest: 1. legally allowed or agreed upon compensation to lender for use of borrowed money. 2. any right in property but less than title to it.

Interest Bearing: term describing note or contract calling for payment of agreed interest.

Interest Only: loan term during which no principal repayments are made.

Interest Rate: cost of borrowing money expressed as an annualized percentage of the loan.

Internal Guidance Line of Credit: credit facility similar to a line of credit, but customer may or may not be advised of it; established for internal financial institution purposes, it provides financing for recurrent requests without referring each one to credit committee or other approval source.

International Consumer Credit Association: professional trade association of retail credit professionals. Association keeps members informed of latest developments in consumer credit and provides educational courses, seminars, textbooks, and other published material.

Intestate: dying without leaving valid will or any other specific instructions a disposition of property.

Inventory: current assets of business that represent goods for sale, including materials, work in process, and finished goods.

Investigation: 1. gathering of credit information on a person or entity. 2. systematic research for information necessary for a business decision.

Investment: use of money for purpose of earning profit or return.

Investor: person or entity that puts money to use for capital appreciation or pr or to receive regular dividends.

Invoice: seller's descriptive, itemized billing for goods or services sold, show date, terms, cost, purchase order number, method of shipment, and ot identifying information.

Involuntary Bankruptcy: see Bankruptcy.

Itemized Statement: detailed listing of activity on account for particular perio time.

J

Jobber: see Wholesaler.

Joint Account: financial institution account shared or owned in name of two more persons with full privileges available to each person.

Joint and Several: relative to liability, a term used when creditor has optio pursuing one or more signers of an agreement individually or all sig together.

Joint Tenancy with Rights of Survivorship: interest in property held by two more persons that includes right of survivorship in which deceased pers interest passes to survivors. See also Tenancy by Entirety.

Joint Venture: business or undertaking entered into on one-time basis by tw more parties in which profits, losses, and control are shared.

Journal: account book of original entry in which all money receipts and exper are chronologically recorded.

Judgment: court's determination of rights of parties to claim.

Judgment Creditor: one who has obtained judgment against debtor and enforce it.

Judgment Debtor: one against whom judgment has been recovered but not sa fied.

Judgment Note: see Cognovit Note.

Judgment Lien: claim or encumbrance on property, allowed by law, usu against real estate of judgment debtor.

Judgment-Proof: term to describe judgment debtor from whom collection ca be obtained or person who has no money or assets or has conceale removed property subject to execution.

Judicial Sale: see Forced Sale.

Junior Mortgage: any mortgage filed after and subject to satisfaction of mortgage.

Jurisdiction: 1. legal authority, power, capacity, and right of court to act. 2. graphic area within which court or government agency exercises power.

K

Keyperson Life Insurance: insurance policy written on owner or princ employee in which death benefits are payable to company.

Key Ratios: performance measures used to determine probable ability of b ness to operate profitably. Results are expressed in percentages that are weighed against average percentages in each industry.

L

Landlord's Waiver: the relinquishment of a right(s) contained in a lease ag ment by a lessor.

Last-In First-Out (LIFO): method of valuating inventory in which last g received are the first ones sold. Using this method, inventory costs use determine cost of goods sold are related to costs of inventory that w incurred last.

Late Charge: special legally agreed upon fee, charged by creditor, on any ment that is not made when due.

Lawful Money: legal tender for payment of all debts.

Law List: compiled publication of names and addresses of those in legal pro sion, often including court calendars, private investigators, and other infor tion of interest to legal profession.

Lawsuit: suit, action, or cause instituted by one person against another in a c of law.

Lead Bank: financial institution that has the primary deposit or lending relat ship in a multi-bank situation; usually in the context of shared credit sometimes defined within an inter-creditor agreement. See also Agent Ba

Leaseback: agreement by which one party sells property to another and, completing sale, the first party rents it from second party.

Lease Contract: written agreement for which equipment or facilities ca obtained on rental payment basis for specified period of time.

sed Department: section of department store not operated by store but by independent outside organization on contract or percentage-of-sales arrangement.

sehold: rights tenant holds in property as conferred by terms of lease.

sehold Improvement: permanent improvements made to rented property. Leasehold improvements are considered fixtures and depreciate over lease period.

sehold Interest: lessee's equity or ownership in leasehold improvements.

se-Purchase Agreement: contract providing for set amount of lease payments to be applied to purchase of property.

ger: in accounting, book of permanent records containing series of accounts to which debits and credits of transactions are posted from books of original entry.

ger Experience: trade experience reported by credit manager or interchange group. Such reports provide picture of account's paying habits, high credit, and terms of repayment.

al and Sovereign Risk: risk that government may intervene to affect bank's system or any participant of such system detrimentally.

al Composition: identification and description of lawful ownership or title to business entity.

al Entity: business organization that has capacity to make contract or agreement or assume obligation. Such organization may consist of individual proprietorship, partnership, corporation, or association.

al Right: natural right, right created by contract, and right created or recognized by law.

al Tender: any money that is recognized by law for payment of debt unless contract exists specifically calling for payment in another type of money.

al Title: document establishing right of ownership to property that is recognized and upheld by law.

der: one who extends funds to another with expectation of repayment with interest.

der's Loss Payable Endorsement: form attached to property insurance policies to cover lender's interest in what is insured; extends coverage to give lender protection beyond that in basic policy; language may be prescribed by banking industry, standard form prepared by insurance industry, or specified by lender. See also *Loss Payee Clause.*

see: one to whom lease is given and therefore has right to use property in exchange for rental payments.

sor: owner who grants lease for use of property in return for rent.

er of Agreement: letter stating terms of agreement between addressor and addressee, usually prepared for signature by addressee as indication of acceptance of those terms as legally binding.

er of Credit: letter or document issued by bank on behalf of customer that is evidence of financial background of bank and ensures that payment will be made when proper documents confirm completion of related transaction. Such letters authorize drawing of sight or time drafts when certain terms and conditions are fulfilled. See also *Banker's Acceptance, Draft, Sight Draft, Standby Letter of Credit,* and *Time Draft.*

er of Intent: letter signifying intention to enter into formal agreement and usually setting forth general terms of such agreement.

le: duty or obligation enforceable by law.

ilities: indebtedness of an individual or entity.

l: written or published false and malicious statements about another that tend to defame or harm another's reputation.

R: see *London Interbank Offered Rate.*

: legal right or encumbrance to secure payment performance on property pledged as collateral until the debt it secures is satisfied.

: see *Last-In First-Out.*

ted Liability Company: legal entity that offers shareholders the same limitations on personal liability available to corporate shareholders. The owners of a limited liability company (LLC) have limited liability. They are not liable for the debts, liabilities, acts, or omissions of the company. Only their investment is at risk.

ted Liability: legal exemption corporate stockholders or limited liability companies have from full financial responsibilities for debts of company.

ted Partnership: partnership of one or more general partners who are personally, jointly, and separately responsible, with one or more special partners whose liabilities are limited to amount of investment.

of Credit: see *Credit Line.*

id Assets: assets that can be readily converted into cash.

idate: 1. to pay off or settle current obligation. 2. to sell off or convert assets into cash. 3. to dissolve business in order to raise cash for payment of debts.

idation: process of dissolving a business, settling accounts, and paying off any claims or obligations; remaining cash is distributed to the owners of the business.

idation Value: cash that can be realized from sale of assets in dissolving business, as distinct from its value as ongoing entity.

Liquidity: measure of quality and adequacy of current assets to meet current obligations as they come due.

Liquidity Ratio: company's most liquid assets (generally cash and accounts receivable) divided by current liabilities. Also called quick ratio.

List Price: generally advertised or posted price. Sometimes subject to trade o cash discounts.

Litigation: lawsuit brought to court for purpose of enforcing a right.

LLC: see *Limited Liability Company.*

Loan: money advanced to a borrower with agreement of repayment usually with interest within a specified period of time.

Loan Agreement: legal contract between a financial institution and a borrower that governs the terms and conditions for the life of a loan. Elements usually include description of loan, representations, and warranties reaffirming known facts about the borrower such as legal structure, affirmative and negative covenants, conditions that must be met before the loan is granted, delinquent payment penalties, and statement of remedies that the financial institution may take in event of default.

Loan Participation: sharing of loan(s) by a group of financial institutions that join together to make said loan(s), affording an opportunity to share the risk of a very large transaction. Arranged through correspondent banking networks in which smaller financial institutions buy a portion of an overall financing package. Participations are a convenient way for smaller financial institutions to book loans that would otherwise exceed their legal lending limits. Also called participation financing.

Loan Policy: principles that reflect a financial institution's credit culture, under writing procedures, and overall approach to lending.

Loans Past Due: loans with interest or principal payments that are contractually past due a certain number of days.

Loan-to-Value Ratio (LTV): relationship, expressed as percent, between principal amount of loan and appraised value of the asset securing financing.

Loan Value: amount of money that can be borrowed against real or personal property.

Lockbox: regional financial institution depository used by corporations to obtain earlier receipt and collection of customer payments. Arrangement provides creditor with better control of accounts receivable and earlier availability of cash balances. Many large financial institutions offer lockbox processing as a cash management service to corporate customers. Lockboxes can be:
- retail, designed for remittance processing for consumer accounts.
- wholesale, in which payments from other entities are collected and submitted through depository transfer check or electronic debit into a concentration account for investment and disbursement as needed.

London Interbank Offered Rate (LIBOR): key rate index used in international lending. LIBOR is the rate at which major financial institutions in London are willing to lend Eurodollars to each other. This index is often used to determine interest rate charged to creditworthy borrowers.

Long-Arm Statutes: state statutes that allow state courts to exercise jurisdiction over nonresident persons or property outside their state's borders.

Long-Term Capital Gain (Loss): gain or loss realized from sale or exchange of capital asset held for longer than 12 months.

Long-Term Liabilities: all senior debt, including bonds, debentures, bank debt, mortgages, deferred portions of long term-debt, and capital lease obligations owed for longer than 12 months.

Loss: 1. circumstance in which expenses exceed revenues. 2. result if an asset is sold for less than its depreciated book value.

Loss Assets: assets considered uncollectible and of such little value that their continuance as realizable assets is not warranted.

Loss Leader: deliberate sale of product or service at or below cost in order to attract new customers.

Loss Payee Clause: provision in insurance policy or added by endorsement to cover lender/mortgagee's interest in property loss settlement. Provision is not as broad as lender's loss payable endorsement. Also called mortgagee clause and loss payable clause.

LTV: see *Loan-to-Value Ratio.*

Lump-sum Settlement: payment made in full with single, one-time payment.

M

Magnetic Ink Character Recognition (MICR): description of numbers and symbols that are printed in magnetic ink on documents for automated processing. Fully inscribed MICR line of information may include item's serial number, routing and transit number, check digit, account number, process control number, and amount.

Mail-Fraud Statute: federal law against using mails to defraud creditors by mailing false financial statements. Prosecution under mail-fraud statute must prove beyond reasonable doubt that:
- statement is false.
- statement was made with intention it should be relied on.
- it was made for the purpose of securing money or property.

- statement was delivered by mail.
- money or property was obtained by means of false statement.

Mailgram: telegraphic message transmitted electronically by Western Union and delivered by U.S. Postal Service.

Mail Teller: employee of a financial institution who receives mail deposits, checks them for accuracy, and returns stamped receipts for deposits to customers.

Majority Stockholder: person or entity that owns more than 50% of voting stock of a corporation, thereby having controlling interest.

Maker: one who signs or executes negotiable instrument.

Malpractice: professional misconduct with negligence.

Management: persons responsible for administrating and carrying out policy of business or other organization.

Management Information System (MIS): established flow of information developed to keep managers informed of what is happening within their organization and to do it within a time frame that permits effective reaction when required. Efficient MIS helps managers make better decisions.

Management Report: statement in unaudited financial statements that says financials are representations of firm's management.

Manifest: shipping document that lists freight's origin, contents, value, destination, carrier, and other pertinent information for use at terminals or custom house.

Manufacturers Representative (Agent): independent, commissioned sales agent who represents several noncompeting manufacturers for sale of their products to related businesses within agreed, exclusive sales territory.

Marginal Account: borderline credit risk that does not have sufficient operating capital and from which payment may be delayed.

Markdown: price reduction of goods below normal selling price.

Market: 1. customer base for a company's goods or services. 2. securities exchange and its associated institutions.

Marketability: ease and rapidity with which product, service, or other asset can be sold or converted to cash.

Marketing: 1. activities necessary to facilitate the sale of goods or services through planned research, manufacturing, promotion, advertising, and distribution. 2. business promotion devoted to getting the maximum purchases of products or services by consumers.

Market Value: price that goods or property would bring in current market of willing buyers and sellers.

Markup: amount or percentage added to cost of goods to arrive at selling price.

Maturity Date: date when financial obligation, note, draft, bond, or instrument becomes due for payment.

Mechanic's Lien: enforceable claim, permitted by law in most states, securing payment to contractors, subcontractors, and suppliers of materials for work performed in constructing or repairing buildings. Lien attaches to real property, plus buildings and improvements situated on land, and remains in effect until workers have been paid in full or, in event of liquidation, gives contractor priority of lien ahead of other creditors.

Medium of Exchange: money or commodity accepted in payment or settlement of debt.

Memorandum (Consignment) Sale: sale of goods for which seller is not paid until retailer has sold merchandise. Seller retains title to such goods until retailer has sold merchandise and payment is made to retailer.

Mercantile Agency: organization that compiles credit and financial information and supplies subscribers or members with reports on applicants for credit; can also perform other functions such as collection of accounts or compiling of statistical trade information.

Merchandise Shortage: goods purchased but not included in shipment.

Merger: combining of two or more businesses to form a single organization.

Mezzanine Financing: 1. in corporate finance, leveraged buyout or restructuring financed through subordinated debt, such as preferred stock or convertible debentures. Transaction is financed by expanding equity, as opposed to debt. 2. second- or third-level financing of companies financed by venture capital. Senior to venture capital but junior to financial institution financing, it adds creditworthiness to firm. Generally used as intermediate-stage financing, preceding a company's initial public offering, it is considered less risky than start-up financing.

MICR: see *Magnetic Ink Character Recognition*.

Middle-of-Month (M.O.M.) Billing Term: billing system in which all shipments are charged on one invoice issued twice a month. For first half of month, credit period runs to the 25th and, for the second half, to the tenth of the following month.

MIS: see *Management Information System*.

Modified Accrual Accounting: basis of accounting in which expenditures are recognized when liability is incurred. Revenues are recognized when measurable and available. Exception is in debt service funds in which expenditures are recorded only when due.

M.O.M.: see *Middle-of-Month Billing Term*.

Money Judgment: court decision that adjudges payment of money rather than requiring act to be performed or property transferred.

Monitoring: service available through many credit reporting or interchange bureaus enabling subscribers to request that certain listed accounts be automatically monitored and reviewed and that updated reports be issued periodically.

Moratorium: 1. temporary extension or delay of normal period for payment account. 2. Formal postponement during which debtor is permitted to delay payment of obligations.

Mortgage: debt instrument giving conditional ownership of asset to borrower secured by the asset being financed. The instrument by which real estate is hypothecated as security for the repayment of a loan. Borrower gives lender mortgage in exchange for the right to use property while mortgage is in effect and agrees to make regular payments of principal and interest. Mortgage is lender's security interest and is recorded in title documents in public records. Lien is removed when debt is paid in full. Mortgage normally involves real estate and is considered long-term debt.

Mortgagee: lender who arranges mortgage financing, collects loan payments and takes security interest in property financed.

Mortgagee Clause: provision in property policy, or added by endorsement, that extends protection, in limited manner, to mortgagee; not as broad as lender loss payable endorsement.

Mortgagee Waiver: the relinquishment of right(s) contained in a mortgage by mortgagee.

Mortgage Verification: request made by mortgagee to applicant's financial institution for information on applicant's accounts, as part of mortgagee's credit approval process.

Mortgagor: borrower in a mortgage contract who mortgages property in exchange for a loan.

Multinational Corporation: corporation whose operations are conducted on an international basis.

Multiple Signature Credit Approval: describes credit approval process in which credit is approved by two or more persons acting together.

Mutual Account Revision: routine exchange of credit information between two or more credit grantors that have extended credit to subject of inquiry.

N

NACM: see *National Association of Credit Management*.

National Association of Credit Management (NACM): national business organization of credit and financial professionals that promotes laws for sound credit, protects businesses against fraudulent debtors, improves the interchange of commercial credit information, develops credit practices, and provides education and certification programs for its members.

Negligence: failure to use reasonable care that an ordinarily prudent person would in like circumstances.

Negotiable: anything capable of being transferred by endorsement or delivery.

Negotiable Instrument: any written evidence of indebtedness, transferable by endorsement and delivery or by delivery only, that contains unconditional promise to pay specified sum on demand or at some fixed date.

Negotiate: to discuss, bargain, or work out plan of settlement, terms, or compromise in business transaction.

Net: amount left after necessary deductions have been made from gross amount.

Net Assets: sum of individual's or entity's total assets less total liabilities.

Net Earnings: total sales, less total operating, administrative, and overhead expenses, but before other expenses and income such as interest and dividends.

Net Income: amount of income remaining after deducting all expenses from revenues.

Net Lease: agreement in which tenant assumes payment of other property expenses, such as taxes, maintenance, and insurance, in addition to rent payments.

Net Price: actual price paid after all discounts, allowances, and other authorized deductions have been taken.

Net Profit: income earned by business over specific period of time. Profit per transaction or sale, after deducting all costs, expenses, and miscellaneous reserves and adjustments from gross receipts.

Net Sales: total sales less returns, allowances, and discounts.

Net Working Capital: current assets less current liabilities; used as measure of company's liquidity and indicates its ability to finance current operations.

Net Worth: total assets less total liabilities; reflects owners' net interest in company.

No Account: notation on rejected check when check writer does not have account at the financial institution on which check is drawn.

No Asset Case: insolvent or bankrupt estate with no assets available for payment of creditors' claims.

No Funds: notation on rejected check when check writer has account but no funds to cover check.

Nominal Balance: an account balance of less than $100.

minal Owner: person whose name appears on title to asset, but who has no interest in it.

accrual: loan on which a financial institution does not accrue interest; also known as a nonperforming loan.

borrowing Account: banking relationship in which no extension of credit is involved.

financial Information: facts used to evaluate a customer's creditworthiness; focuses on background and history rather than financial measures.

payment: failure or neglect to pay or discharge debt in accordance with terms of agreement.

performing Assets: total of earning assets listed as nonaccrual; formerly, earning assets acquired in foreclosure and through in-substance foreclosures.

performing Loans: amount of loans not meeting original terms of agreement, including renegotiated, restructured, and nonaccrual loans. Loans included in this total vary according to bank policy and regulation.

profit Corporation: organization specifically classified by the IRS as generally tax exempt and whose primary purpose for existence is to provide services of a charitable, fraternal, religious, social, or civic nature.

recourse: inability of holder in due course to demand payment from endorser of debt instrument if party(ies) primarily liable fail to make payment.

-sufficient Funds (NSF): term used when collected demand deposit balances are less than the amount of the check being presented for payment and check is returned to payee's financial institution. See also Overdraft.

Protest (N.P.): instructions given by one financial institution to another not to protest check or note when presented for payment. N.P. is usually stamped on instrument to avoid protest fee.

th American Industrial Classification System (NAICS): the Standard Industrial Classification (SIC) code is being replaced by the NAICS code. NAICS classifies establishments by their primary type of activity within a six-digit code. NAICS provides structural enhancements over SIC and identifies over 350 new industries. See also *SIC* and *Standard Industrial Classification*.

ary Public: public officer authorized to administer oaths, attest and certify certain types of documents, and to take acknowledgements of conveyances.

e: unconditional written promise by borrower to pay certain amount of money to lender on demand or at specified or determinable date. This instrument should meet all requirements of laws pertaining to negotiable instruments.

es Payable: liabilities represented by promissory notes, excluding trade debts, that are payable in future.

es Receivable: assets represented by promissory notes, excluding amounts due from customers for credit sales, to be collected in future.

ce of Protest: formal statement that a certain bill of exchange, check, or promissory note was presented for payment or acceptance and that such payment or acceptance was not made. Such notice will also state that because instrument has been dishonored, maker, endorsers, or other parties to document will be held responsible for payment.

ation: substitution of old contract for new one between same or different parties; substitution of new debtor or creditor for previous one, by mutual agreement.

: see *Non-sufficient Funds*.

a Bona: report made by sheriff when no assets are found within his or her jurisdiction on which to satisfy judgment against debtor.

O

gation: 1. law or duty binding parties to an agreement. 2. written promise to pay money or to do a specific thing.

gee: person or entity to which payment is due.

gor: person or entity required by contract to perform specific act.

olescence: decline in perceived value of asset, frequently because of technological innovations, changes in an industry's processes, or changes required by law.

: see *Office of the Comptroller of the Currency*.

r: proposal to make contract, usually presented by one party to another for acceptance.

ring Basis: customer's loan requests considered individually on merits of each proposal.

e of the Comptroller of the Currency (OCC): branch of the Treasury Department that regulates federally chartered banks.

e of Thrift Supervision (OTS): branch of the Treasury Department that regulates state and federally chartered thrifts as well as those institutions in conservatorship.

et: amount allowed to be netted against another.

Account: generally describes partial payment made toward settlement of unpaid balance.

ccount Payment: partial payment not intended as payment in full.

emand: debt instrument that is due and payable on presentation.

Open (Book) Account: credit extended without a formal written contract and represented on books and records of the seller as an unsecured account receivable for which payment is expected within a specified period after purchase.

Open-End Credit: consumer line of credit that may be added to, up to preset credit limit, or paid down at any time. Customer has option of paying off outstanding balance, without penalty, or making several installment payments. Contrasts with Closed-End Credit. Also called revolving credit or charge account credit.

Open Terms: selling on credit terms as opposed to having customer pay cash.

Operating Performance Ratios: financial measures designed to assist in evaluation of management performance.

Operating Statement: report of an individual's or entity's income and expenses for a specified period of time. See also Income Statement.

Operational Risk: risk concerning computer network failure due to system overload or other disruptions; also includes potential losses from fraud, malicious damage to data, and error.

Oral Contract: agreement that may or may not be written in whole or in part or signed but is legally enforceable.

Order: informal bill of exchange or letter or request identifying person to be paid.

Order for Relief: order issued by bankruptcy court judge upon filing of petition by debtor or filing of petition by creditors.

Order to Order: agreement for payment to be made for prior shipment before next delivery will be made.

OREO: see *Other Real Estate Owned*.

Other Real Estate Owned: real property usually taken as collateral and subsequently acquired through foreclosure, or by obtaining a deed in lieu of foreclosure, in satisfaction of the debts previously contracted. Real property formerly used as banking premises, or real property sold in a "covered transaction" as defined by banking regulations.

OTS: see *Office of Thrift Supervision*.

Outlet Store: retail operation where manufacturers' production overruns, discontinued merchandise, or irregular goods are sold at discount.

Out-of-Court Settlement: 1. settlement made by distressed debtor through direct negotiations with creditors or through creditors' committee; acceptance of such settlement is not obligatory to nonconsenting creditors. 2. agreement reached between opposing parties to settle pending lawsuit before matter has been decided by court.

Out-of-Pocket Expense: business expenses for which individual pays.

Out-of-Trust: an event occurring in floor plan financing where a borrower sells inventory securing the financial institution's loan and fails to promptly remit the proceeds to the financial institution in accordance with the loan agreement.

Outstanding: 1. amount of credit facility that is being used versus total amount made available. 2. unpaid or uncollected account.

Overdraft: negative account balance created when a check is paid when collected demand deposit balances are less than amount of check being presented for payment. See also Non-sufficient Funds.

Overdue: debt obligation on which payments are past due.

Overhead: selling and administrative business costs as contrasted with costs of goods sold.

Oversold: condition in which manufacturer or wholesaler finds itself after taking more orders than it can deliver within an agreed period of time.

Owed: debt that is due and payable.

Own: to have legal title to property.

Owner: person or entity that owns or has title to property.

Owner's Equity: mathematical difference between total assets and total liabilities that represents shareholders' equity or an individual's net worth.

Ownership: exclusive rights that one has to property, to exclusion of all others; having complete title to property.

Owner's Risk: term used in transportation contracts to exempt carrier from responsibility for loss or damage to goods.

P

Packing List: detailed listing of information on shipment's contents (enclosed for inspection with package).

Paid Direct: payment made by debtor directly to original creditor instead of to collection agency or attorney handling account for collection.

Paper Profit: unrealized income or gain on asset.

Paralegal: trained aide to attorney who handles various legal tasks.

Parent Company: an entity that holds controlling majority interest in subsidiaries.

Partial Payment: payment not in full for amount owed.

Participation: purchase or sale of a loan or credit facility among two or more financial institutions in which the acquiring institution(s) has no formal or direct role in establishing the terms and conditions binding the borrower. Participants do not participate in the document negotiation between the originating financial institution and the borrower.

Partnership: business arrangement in which two or more persons agree to engage, upon terms of mutual participation, in profits and losses.

Party: person concerned or taking part in a transaction or proceeding.

Past Due: payment or account that remains outstanding and unpaid after its agreed-upon payment or maturity date.

Pay: to satisfy, or make partial payments on, a debt obligation.

Payable: obligation that is due now or in future.

Payables: liabilities owed to trade creditors for purchase of supplies. Also called accounts payable.

Payee: person or entity named on a negotiable instrument as the one to whom the obligation is due.

Payer: party responsible for making payment as shown on check, note, or other type of negotiable instrument; also called maker or writer.

Payment: discharge, in whole or in part, of debt or performance of agreement.

Payment for Honor: payment of past-due obligation by someone else to save credit or reputation of person responsible for payment.

Payoff: receipt of payment in full on an obligation.

Penalty: 1. legal fine, forfeiture, or payment imposed for defaulting or violating terms of contract. 2. interest charge imposed for late payments that is permissible by law and imposed with customer's prior agreement or knowledge of seller's terms of sale.

Percentage Lease: lease of real property in which rental payments are based on percentage of retailer's sales.

Percentage of Completion: method of accounting commonly used by contractors and developers in which costs are related to percentage of job completion.

Perfection: with respect to security interests in personal property under Article 9 of the UCC, the action required to give the secured party rights in the collateral as against third parties with competing claims. In general, a security interest is not perfected until a properly executed financing statement has been recorded or the secured party is in the possession of the collateral, whichever applies as to that specific collateral type.

Performance: fulfillment of promise or agreement according to terms of contract or obligation.

Performance Bond: guaranty to project owner that the contractor will perform the work called for by the contract in accordance with the plans and specifications. Customarily issued by bonding and insurance companies, although financial institution letters of credit may be used.

Perjury: willfully and knowingly giving false testimony under oath.

Person: individual (natural person) or incorporated enterprise (artificial person) having certain legal rights and responsibilities.

Personal Check: check drawn by individual on his or her own bank account.

Personality: legal term for personal property or possessions that are not real estate.

Personally Liable: individual's responsibility for payment of obligation, generally used to refer to owner's or guarantor's responsibility.

Personal Property: movable or chattel property of any kind.

Petition: written application, made in contradiction to motion. Also used in some states in place of complaint.

Petition in Bankruptcy: document filed in court to declare bankruptcy. Petition can be either voluntary (filed by debtor) or involuntary (filed by creditors), depending on bankruptcy chapter rules.

Petty Cash: cash on hand or in designated bank account that is available for small, miscellaneous purchases.

Physical Inventory: inventory verification obtained by visual observation of items and itemization of quantities of goods on hand.

Piercing the Corporate Veil: legal action taken by creditor, when fraud or unjust enrichment may be involved, to hold principals of corporation (or other entities) liable for debts of corporation.

Plaintiff: person or entity that initiates legal action against another.

Plan of Arrangement: procedure in bankruptcy under Chapter 11 for debtor to restructure debts or rehabilitate by arriving at arrangement with creditors. See also Bankruptcy, Chapter 11 Cases.

Pledge: promise of personal property as security for performance of act, payment of debt, or satisfaction of obligation.

Points: 1. percentage fee charged to obtain a mortgage loan. 2. in shares of stock, one point equals $1.00.

Policy: 1. written statement by management that explains an organization's philosophy and approach to doing business. 2. written contract of insurance between insured and the insurance company.

Pooling Accounts: arrangement by a debtor listing all his or her debts with a debt management or pro-rating service with the understanding that the service will receive, as its fee, a portion of debtor's payments to his or her creditors and proportionately distribute the balance of payments to each creditor on a scheduled basis. Activities of such services may be covered by individual state statutes.

Postdated Check: check written for payment, effective at future date.

Power of Attorney: written document that authorizes one person to act as another's agent.

Preference: 1. right of a creditor to be paid before other creditors by virt[ue of] having lien or collateral. 2. improperly paying or securing of one or [more] creditors, in whole or part, by an insolvent debtor to the exclusion of [other] creditors.

Preference Period: in bankruptcy, the 90-day period immediately prece[ding] debtor entering into bankruptcy. If a creditor files new or additional [claims] against a debtor during this time, such claims may be disallowed by b[ank]ruptcy court.

Preferred Creditor: creditor whose account takes legal preference for pay[ment] over claims of others.

Prepaid Expenses: payment for goods or services not yet received.

Prepayment: payment of loan or debt before it actually becomes due.

Prime Contractor: contractor who enters into contract with the owner of the [pro]ject for completion of all or portion of the project and takes full respons[ibility] for its completion. See also General Contractor.

Prime Rate: an index or base rate published or publicly announced by a fina[ncial] institution from time to time as the rate it is generally willing to give its [most] creditworthy customers.

Principal: 1. amount of money loaned or borrowed. 2. key decision mak[er in] management of entity.

Priority: legal preferences that secured creditors have over general credito[rs in] bankruptcy.

Priority Lien: lien recorded before other secured claims and payable ahea[d of] other liens if liquidation of pledged collateral occurs. First mortgage has p[rior]ity over second and third mortgages, known as junior liens. Secured cre[ditor] holding perfected security interest has priority over liens filed afterward.

Private Enterprise: business established to take economic risks for purpo[se of] making profit.

Privilege: right that nature of debt gives to one debt holder over others.

Proceeds: actual amount of money given to or received from creditor afte[r] deductions are made.

Profit: 1. amount of net income made by an entity in course of doing busine[ss. 2.] increase in value of an asset over its depreciated book value at the tim[e of] sale.

Profit and Loss Statement (P & L): financial report of an individual's or en[tity's] revenue and expenses for a given period of time. See also Income State[ment] and Operating Statement.

Pro Forma: projected financial statements.

Progress Payments: partial payments made on a long-term contract as it [pro]gresses. Required when a manufacturer or contractor cannot afford, or [does] not wish, to finance a project.

Projection: borrower's estimate of future performance over designated [time] period.

Promissory Note: written promise to make unconditional payment of spe[cific] amount on designated date, signed by maker.

Proof of Claim: creditor's formal document filed with court against esta[te of] debtor if creditor is owed funds.

Proof of Loss: sworn statement filed by insured when making claim.

Property: something of value that is legally owned and in which person has e[xclu]sive and unrestricted right or interest.

Property Insurance: coverage that applies to loss caused by physical dama[ge to] property (buildings, contents, earnings, etc.) owned by insured.

Proposal: oral or written offer that, if accepted, constitutes a contract.

Proprietorship: single and exclusive ownership of a business by one person.

Pro Rata: share calculated in proportion to total amount.

Pro Rata Distribution: payment proportionate to uniform percentage of ob[liga]tions to all creditors.

Protest: formal, written, notarized notice stating credit instrument has not [been] honored and that makers or endorsers will be held responsible for payme[nt.]

Prox.: see Proximo.

Proximo (Prox.): sales term used in invoices to mean next month after mon[th of] invoice. This term is sometimes used instead of EOM terms.

Proxy: written statement or power of attorney, authorizing an individual to a[ct or] speak for another.

Public Credit: debt incurred by government, federal and local, for a use that [meets] the needs of its citizens.

Purchase Money Lien: manufacturer's legal right to goods and products unt[il] buyer makes payment. Under the Uniform Commercial Code, manufactu[rer's] rights can take priority over lender's lien rights if both claim interest in [same] inventory. Lender may receive such priority if funds were provided to [pur]chase asset, provided liens are filed within 20 days of borrower taking [pos]session of collateral and noticing requirements have been met.

Purchase Money Mortgage: mortgage given by buyer to seller in lieu of cas[h as] partial payment on property.

Purchasing Power: value of money and its ability to buy goods and services [in a] given period.

Q

ified Acceptance: agreement to terms of contract only if certain conditions
re meet. This constitutes counteroffer and rejection of original offer.

ified Endorsement: transfer of debt instrument to endorsee without recourse
r liability to endorser.

ified Financial Statement: audit report issued by independent accountants
nat indicates restrictions on scope of audit performed, uncertainties, or dis-
greements with management.

ified Prospect: potential customer whose background and credit have been
hecked and approved.

itity Discount: price reduction extended to purchaser of a large volume of
oods.

terly Accounts Receivable Survey: index, compiled by Credit Research
oundation in affiliation with the National Association of Credit Management
nd published quarterly, that shows average days' sales outstanding for man-
facturers and wholesalers.

k Assets: current assets that can be readily converted into cash (generally,
ccounts receivable).

k Assets Ratio: cash and cash equivalents plus trade receivables (net)
ivided by total current liabilities; used as measure of liquidity.

Pro Quo: 1. giving of one valuable thing for another. 2. mutual consideration
etween parties to contract.

laim: to release or relinquish claim or title.

R

Jobber: wholesale distributor who sells housewares and other convenience-
vpe merchandise through retail stores and assumes responsibility for stock-
g and maintaining store's inventory.

of Exchange: amount of one country's currency that can be bought with
nother country's currency at a particular point in time.

of Interest: cost of borrowing money, usually expressed as annual percent-
ge charge.

g: 1. assessment of borrower's financial strength and creditworthiness. 2.
ymbol used to denote borrower's creditworthiness.

s: mathematical relationship between two or more things, used as indication
f a company's financial strength relative to other companies of comparable
ze or in same industry.

Property: land and anything erected or growing on it or affixed to it.

ivables: money due or collectible for goods sold, services performed, or
noney loaned. Also called accounts receivable.

ivables Turnover: measurement of how effective a company is in collecting
n its trade receivables.

iver: person appointed by the court to receive, take charge, and hold in trust
property in litigation or bankruptcy until a legal decision is made as to its
sposition.

ivership: 1. court action whereby money or property is placed under control,
nd administration of receiver is to be preserved for benefit of persons or
reditors ultimately entitled to it. 2. procedure used to help a distressed
ebtor or to resolve a dispute.

mation: 1. legal action by titleholder to recover property from another's
ossession. 2. process used to restore land to usable state.

rd: written account of act, transaction, or instrument drawn by proper legal
uthority that remains as permanent evidence.

urse: right of holder in due course to demand payment from anyone who
ndorsed instrument if original signer fails to pay.

very: amount finally collected; amount of judgment.

ence Check: contacting and interviewing business or professional associ-
es of credit applicant to gain information about his or her creditworthiness.

ences: names of trade suppliers or creditors provided by a customer to be
sed as a source of information about that customer.

to Maker: term stamped by financial institution on a check to indicate its
jection.

ance: to reorganize existing debts by obtaining new debt that incorporates
pays off existing debts.

ter: book of factual public information, kept by a public official.

lation 9: regulation issued by the Comptroller of Currency allowing national
anks to operate trust departments and act as fiduciaries. Under Regulation 9,
national bank is permitted to act as trustee, administrator, and registrar of
ocks and bonds and engage in related activities, such as management of a
ollective investment fund, as long as these activities do not violate state leg-
lation.

lation A: Federal Reserve Board regulation governing advances by Federal
eserve Banks to depository institutions at a Federal Reserve discount win-
ow. Credit advances are available to any bank or savings institution main-
ining transaction accounts or non-personal time deposits. The Fed has two
fferent programs for handling discount window borrowings:

- adjustment credit to meet temporary needs for funds when other sources are
not available.
- extended credit, designed to assist financial institutions with longer-term
needs for funds. This includes seasonal credit privileges extended to smaller
financial institutions that do not have ready access to money market funds.
Federal Reserve Banks may also extend emergency credit to financial institutions other than depository institutions in which failure to obtain credit
would affect the economy adversely.

Regulation B: Federal Reserve regulation prohibiting discrimination against consumer credit applicants and establishing guidelines for collecting and evaluating credit information. Regulation B prohibits creditors from discriminating
on the basis of age, sex, race, color, religion, national origin, marital status, or
receipt of public assistance. Regulation B also requires creditors to give written notification of rejection, statement of applicant's rights under Equal Credit
Opportunity Act of 1974, and statement listing reasons for rejection, or applicant has right to request reasons. If applicant is denied credit because of
adverse information in credit bureau report, applicant is entitled to receive
copy of bureau report at no cost. Creditors who furnish credit information
when reporting information on married borrowers must report information in
name of each spouse.

Regulation C: Federal Reserve regulation implementing Home Mortgage Disclosure Act of 1975, requiring depository institutions to make annual disclosure
of location of certain residential loans to determine whether depository institutions are meeting credit needs of their local communities. Specifically
exempted are institutions with assets of $10 million or less. Regulation C
requires lenders of mortgages that are insured or guaranteed by a federal
agency to disclose number and total dollar amount of mortgage loans originated or purchased in recent calendar year, itemized by census tract where
property is located.

Regulation D: Federal Reserve regulation that sets uniform reserve requirements
for depository financial institutions holding transaction accounts or non-personal time deposits. Reserves are maintained in form of vault cash or non-
interest-bearing balance at a Federal Reserve Bank or at a correspondent
bank.

Regulation E: Federal Reserve regulation that sets rules, liabilities, and procedures for electronic funds transfers (EFT) and establishes consumer protec-
tions using EFT systems. This regulation prescribes rules for solicitation and
issuance of EFT debit cards, governs consumer liability for unauthorized
transfers, and requires financial institutions to disclose annually terms and
conditions of EFT services.

Regulation F: Federal Reserve regulation requiring state-chartered banks with
500 or more stockholders and at least $1 million in assets to file financial
statements with the Board of Governors of the Federal Reserve System. In
general, these state-chartered member banks must file registration statements, periodic financial statements, proxy statements, and various other dis-
closures of interest to investors. These regulations are substantially similar to
those issued by Securities and Exchange Commission.

Regulation G: Federal Reserve regulation governing credit secured by margin
securities extended or arranged by parties other than banks or broker/dealers.
It requires lenders to register credit extensions of $200,000, secured by mar-
gin stock, or $500,000 in total credit, within 30 days after end of quarter.

Regulation H: Federal Reserve regulation defining membership requirements for
state-chartered banks that become members of the Federal Reserve System.
The regulation sets forth procedures as well as privileges and requirements
for membership. The regulation also requires state-chartered banks acting as
securities transfer agents to register with board.

Regulation I: Federal Reserve regulation requiring each member bank joining the
Federal Reserve System to purchase stock in its Federal Reserve Bank equal
to 6% of its capital and surplus. Federal Reserve Bank stock, which pays
interest semiannually, is nontransferable and cannot be used as collateral.
When bank increases or decreases its capital base, it must adjust its ownership of Federal Reserve stock accordingly.

Regulation J: Federal Reserve regulation providing legal framework for collection
of checks and other cash items and net settlement of balances through Federal Reserve System. It specifies terms and conditions under which Federal
Reserve Banks will receive checks for collection from depository institutions,
presentment to paying banks, and return of unpaid items. It is supplemented
by operating circulars issued by Federal Reserve Banks.

Regulation K: Federal Reserve regulation governing international banking operations by bank holding companies and foreign banks in the U.S. The regulation
permits Edge Act corporations to engage in range of international banking and
financial activities. It also permits U.S. banks to own up to 100% of nonfinancial companies located outside the U.S. Regulation K also imposes
reserve requirements on Edge Act corporations, as specified in Regulation D,
and limits interstate activities of foreign banks in the U.S.

Regulation L: Federal Reserve regulation prohibiting interlocking director
arrangements in member banks or bank holding companies. Management
official of state member bank or bank holding company may not act simulta-

neously as management official of another depository institution if both are not affiliated, are very large banks, or are located in same local area. Regulation L provides 10-year grandfather period for certain interlocks and allows some on exception basis, such as organizations owned by women or minority groups, newly chartered organizations, and in situations in which implementing regulation would endanger safety and soundness.

Regulation M: Federal Reserve regulation implementing consumer leasing provisions of Truth in Lending Act of 1968. It covers leases on personal property for more than four months for family, personal, or household use. It requires leasing companies to disclose in writing the cost of lease, including security deposit and monthly payments, taxes, and other payments, and in case of an open-end lease, whether a balloon payment may be applied. It also requires written disclosure of terms of lease, including insurance, guaranties, responsibility for servicing property, and whether lessor has an option to buy property at lease termination.

Regulation N: Federal Reserve regulation governing transactions among Federal Reserve Banks and transactions involving Federal Reserve Banks and foreign banks and governments. This regulation gives the board responsibility for approving in advance negotiations or agreements by Federal Reserve Banks and foreign banks, bankers, and governments. The Federal Reserve Bank may, under direction of the Federal Open Market Committee, undertake negotiations, agreements, or facilitate open market transactions. Reserve Banks must report quarterly to the Board of Governors on accounts they maintain with foreign banks.

Regulation O: Federal Reserve regulation limiting amount of credit member banks may extend to their own executive officers. Regulation O also implements reporting requirements of Financial Institutions Regulatory and Interest Rate Control Act of 1978 and Garn-St. Germain Depository Institutions Act of 1982.

Regulation P: Federal Reserve regulation that sets minimum standards for security devices, such as bank vaults and currency handling equipment, including automated teller machines. Member bank must appoint security officer to develop and administer program to deter thefts and file the annual compliance statement with its Federal Reserve Bank.

Regulation Q: Federal Reserve regulation requiring depository institutions to state clearly terms for depositing and renewing time deposits and certificates of deposit and also any penalties for early withdrawal of savings accounts.

Regulation R: Federal Reserve regulation prohibiting individuals who are engaged in securities underwriting, sale, and distribution from serving as directors, officers, or employees of member banks. Regulation R specifically exempts those involved in government securities trading and general obligations of states and municipalities.

Regulation S: Federal Reserve regulation implementing section of Right to Financial Privacy Act of 1978 requiring government authorities to pay reasonable fees to financial institutions for financial records of individuals and small partnerships available to federal agencies in connection with government loan programs or Internal Revenue Service summons.

Regulation T: Federal Reserve regulation governing credit extensions by securities brokers and dealers, including all members of national securities exchanges. Brokers/dealers may not extend credit to their customers unless such loans are secured by margin securities—securities listed and traded on national securities exchange, mutual funds, and over-the-counter stock designated by Securities and Exchange Commission as eligible for trading in national market system. Generally, brokers/dealers may not extend credit on margin securities in excess of percentage of current market value permitted by board.

Regulation U: Federal Reserve regulation governing extensions of credit by banks for purchasing and carrying margin securities. Whenever lender makes loan secured by margin securities, bank must have customer execute purpose statement regardless of use of loan.

Regulation V: Federal Reserve regulation dealing with financing of contractors, subcontractors, and others involved in national defense work. The regulation spells out the authority granted to Federal Reserve Banks under the Defense Production Act of 1950 to assist federal departments and agencies in making and administering loan guaranties to defense-related contractors and sets maximum interest rates, guaranty fees, and commitment fees.

Regulation X: Federal Reserve regulation extending provisions of other securities-related regulations—Regulations G, T, and U—to foreign persons or organizations who obtain credit outside U.S. for purchase of U.S. Treasury securities.

Regulation Y: Federal Reserve regulation governing banking and nonbanking activities of bank holding companies and divestiture of impermissible nonbank activities. Regulation Y spells out procedures for forming bank holding company and procedures to be followed by bank holding companies acquiring voting shares in bank or nonbank companies. Regulation Y also lists those nonbank activities that are deemed closely related to banking and therefore permissible for bank holding companies.

Regulation Z: Federal Reserve regulation implementing consumer credit pr tions in the Truth in Lending Act of 1968. Major areas of regulation re lenders to:
- give borrowers written disclosure on essential credit terms, including of credit expressed as finance charge and annual percentage rate.
- respond to consumer complaints of billing errors on certain credit acco within specified period.
- identify credit transactions on periodic statements of open-end c accounts.
- provide certain rights regarding credit cards.
- inform customers of right of rescission in certain mortgage-related within specified period.
- comply with special requirements when advertising credit.

Regulation AA: Federal Reserve regulation establishing procedures for han consumer complaints about alleged unfair or deceptive practices by a member bank.

Regulation BB: Federal Reserve regulation implementing Community Rein ment Act of 1977 (CRA). Banks are required to make available to pub statement indicating communities served, type of credit the lender is pre to extend, and public comments to its CRA statement.

Regulation CC: Federal Reserve regulation implementing Expedited Funds ability Act of 1987, setting endorsement standards on checks collecte depository financial institutions. Endorsement standard is designed to tate identification of endorsing bank and prompt return of unpaid checks regulation specifies funds availability schedules that banks must comply and procedures for returning dishonored checks.

Release: to discharge debt or give up claim against party from whom it is d party to whom it is due.

Remedy: legal means by which right is enforced or violation of right is prev or compensated.

Rent: periodic payments made by tenant to owner in return for leasing building space, or equipment.

Reorganization: 1. voluntary or court-ordered change in capital structure of poration in which all assets of an old corporation are transferred to a formed corporation. 2. restructuring of business entity, whether in or c bankruptcy.

Replevin: legal action taken to recover possession of property unlawfully tak

Repossess: action taken by creditor in which he or she takes possessi goods purchased under credit agreement or pledged as collateral if d defaults on terms of contract.

Rescind: to void contract from its inception. Result is that parties are restor relative positions before contract was made.

Rescission: agreement by parties to contract that effects cancellation of con

Reserve: in accounting, funds set aside for specific purpose.

Reserve for Bad Debts: valuation account established for accounts rece that may prove uncollectible.

Residence: place where person legally lives part or full time.

Residual Value: the estimated recoverable amount of a depreciable asset the time of its removal from service.

Resolution Trust Corporation (RTC): federal agency established in 1989 to see the savings and loan bailout.

Restraint of Trade: any action, by agreement or by combination, that ter eliminate competition, artificially sets up prices, or results in monopoly.

Restrictive Endorsement: endorsement on negotiable instrument that limit further negotiability, for example, "for deposit only" written on back of ch

Restructured Loan: loan on which a bank, for economic or legal reasons re to debtor's financial difficulties, grants concession to debtor that would r considered otherwise.

Retailer: company that sells its product directly to end-user.

Retained Earnings: cumulative earnings and losses of company that re undistributed to shareholders.

Retentions: amounts withheld by customer from total billings until contracto satisfactorily completed project.

Retroactive: 1. effective as of past date. 2. having reference to prior time.

Return: rate of profit or earnings on sales or investment.

Return Items/Returned Checks: checks, drafts, or notes returned unpaid to nating bank by drawee bank so that originator can correct any errors or ularities and may present items for collection again.

Revenue: 1. income from sales, interest, or dividends. 2. income from inves or wages.

Reviewed Financial Statements: business financial statements that are rev by independent accountants through inquiries of management and p mance of analytical procedures on financials to provide limited assuranc no material modifications are necessary for statements to conform to g ally accepted accounting principles. Independent accountants do not ex opinion on review statements.

lving Charge: credit type that allows borrower to become indebted up to an pproved credit limit, with no fixed maturity date. Finance costs are assessed nonthly on unpaid balance, and periodic payments are required.

lving Credit: commitment under which funds can be borrowed, repaid, and e-borrowed during life of credit. Such credits have stated maturity date at hich time borrower may have option of converting outstanding balance into rm loan. See also Evergreen Revolving Credit.

: any schedule or amendment attached to a contract or document that ecomes part of it.

of Rescission: consumer's right as prescribed by Truth in Lending Act of 968 to rescind certain credit and mortgage contracts within three days with-ut penalty.

of Setoff: right of financial institution to apply borrower's funds on deposit debt owed to the financial institution in event that payment on the debt is ot made as agreed.

Based Capital: level of capital that bank is required to maintain; level is etermined by relating capital to risk by type of asset.

see Risk Management Association.

General Figure Ranges: dollar amount ranges established by RMA to nsure accuracy and consistency when exchanging credit information. There e four ranges: low, 1-1.9; moderate, 2-3.9; medium, 4-6.9; and high, 7-9.9. anges can be applied to any figure category. Sample figure categories are: ominal = under $100; 3 figures = from $100 to $999; 4 figures = from ,000 to $9,999; 5 figures = from $10,000 to $99,999;and 6 figures = from 00,000 to $999,999. Information is reported, using both range description nd figure category; for example, "average balances are in medium 4-figure nge."

Management Association (RMA): association of lending, credit, and risk anagement professionals. Originally, RMA was founded to facilitate the xchange of credit information. Today, RMA works continuously to improve actices of the financial services industry and to provide members with net-orking opportunities, training, research publications, and seminars.

son-Patman Act: federal legislation prohibiting firms engaged in interstate mmerce from charging different buyers different prices for the same goods nless there is difference in costs or the price does not restrict competition.

Dating: payment term that uses date customer is in receipt of goods as fective sale date.

ty: compensation made to another for use of his or her work.

see Resolution Trust Corporation.

of 72: method commonly used to approximate time required for sum of oney to double at given rate of interest. Rule of 72 is computed by dividing terest rate by 72.

of 78s: mathematical formula used in computing interest rebated when bor-wer pays off loan before maturity. Rule of 78s is applied mostly to con-mer loans in which finance charges were computed using add-on interest discounted interest method of interest calculation. Also called sum of digits ethod.

S

agreement or contract that transfers title of goods or property from one rson or entity to another for consideration.

nd Lease Back: arrangement whereby company sells goods with intent to se those same goods from buyer.

n Approval: purchase of goods conditioned on buyer approval of goods or tention of them beyond reasonable time.

ge Value: estimated worth of a depreciated asset at the end of its useful life.

action: paying debt in full.

action of Judgment: legal evidence that recorded judgment has been paid settled and entered in court records.

action Piece: legal evidence that debt has been paid in full or settled and t liens on collateral have been released.

ee Small Business Administration.

ule: listing by account name or number of total sales, current sales, monies ing or paid, chargebacks, or credits. Also called aging schedule or trial bal-ce.

uled Liability: 1. in property insurance, listing of property—items or loca-ns—covered. 2. in dishonesty insurance (fidelity bonding), listing of per-ns or positions covered.

uled Payment: partial payments made at dates specified in credit agree-nt.

ules: in bankruptcy, lists showing debtor's property—location, quantity, d money value; names and addresses of creditors and their class; or names addresses of stockholders of each class.

Value: worth of asset that is going to be destroyed or used for its compo-nts.

nal Loans: loans used to finance cyclical buildup of current (working capi-assets until those assets can be converted to cash.

Second Lien: lien that can be honored only after first lien is satisfied.

Second Mortgage: mortgage secured by equity in property but one that cannot enforce payment until claims of first mortgage are satisfied.

Secret Partner: partner in business whose interest in partnership is not publicly known.

Secured Creditor: lender or other person whose claim is supported by taking col-lateral.

Secured Loan: loan supported by borrower's pledge of an asset such as mar-ketable securities, accounts receivable, inventories, real estate, equipment, etc.

Secured Note: note that provides, upon default, certain pledged or mortgaged property that may be applied or sold in payment of debt.

Secured Party: 1. lender or other person to whom or in whose favor security interest has been given. Includes person to whom accounts or chattel paper have been sold. 2. trustee or agent representing holders of obligations issued under indenture of trust, equipment trust agreement, or the like.

Securities: 1. documents that evidence debt or property pledged in fulfillment of obligation. 2. evidence of indebtedness or right to participate in earnings and distribution of corporate, trust, and other property.

Security: guaranty or assets pledged that can be applied to loan or obligation.

Security Agreement: formally executed document that gives lender rights to property pledged by borrower in support of debt.

Security Interest: right that lender or lienholder obtains to debtor's goods as evi-denced by security agreement.

Seller's Market: economic condition in which demand is greater than supply, and that typically causes prices to increase.

Sequestered Account: account that has been attached by court order with dis-bursements subject to court approval.

Service Business: firm that performs functions for its customers rather than sells goods.

Setoff: 1. defendant's counterdemand against plaintiff. 2. right of parties to con-tract to reduce debt owed to one party by netting it against amount owed by other. See also Right of Setoff.

Settle: 1. to mutually reach agreement for adjustment or liquidation of debt. 2. to negotiate payment of obligation or lawsuit for less than amount claimed.

Settlement: 1. adjustment or liquidation of accounts. 2. full and final payment of debt. See also Out-of-Court Settlement.

Shared National Credit (SNC): any loan originally $20 million or more that is shared at its inception by two or more financial institutions under a formal intercreditor or participation agreement or sold in part to one or more finan-cial institutions with purchasing financial institution assuming its pro rata share of credit risk.

Shareholder: person or entity that legally owns stock in a corporation.

Sheriff's Sale: court-ordered sale of property to satisfy judgment, mortgage, lien, or other outstanding debt against debtor.

Sherman Antitrust Act: federal legislation aimed at prevention of business monopoly; act declares illegal every contract, combination, or conspiracy in restraint of normal trade.

Short-Term Liabilities: current debts that are due within one year.

Short-Term Loan: current debt obligation that matures within one year, evidenced by promissory note that spells out terms of agreement.

SIC: see Standard Industrial Classification.

Sight Draft: draft payable on demand when presented to drawee. See also Draft, Letter of Credit, and Time Draft.

Signal Action: notices that provide subscriber with list of accounts in which sub-scriber has interest and on which delinquent payments have been reported.

Signature Loan: unsecured loan backed only by borrower's signature on promis-sory note. No collateral is taken by lender. This loan is generally offered to individuals with good credit standing. Also called good faith loan or character loan.

Signature Verification: examination of signature on negotiable instrument to determine whether handwriting is genuine and whether person signing check is authorized to use account.

Simple Interest: interest calculated on outstanding principal amount of debt or investment only.

Single Proprietorship: ownership of company by one person.

Skip Tracing: process used to obtain information to locate debtor's whereabouts in order to collect payment on debts. Sources used include other creditors, friends, relatives, neighbors, directories, credit bureaus, court records, and other informants or references.

Slander: oral defamation of another's reputation.

Small Business Administration (SBA): federal agency whose function is to advise and assist small businesses; provides loan guaranties for small busi-nesses, minorities, and veterans plus financial assistance to small businesses that have suffered catastrophes.

SNC: see Shared National Credit.

Soft Goods: nondurable consumer goods such as clothing and linen, having a short-term useful life.

Soldier's and Sailor's Relief Act: federal act, also passed by various states, under which right to legally enforce an obligation against a person is suspended during the period that person is in military service or for period thereafter.

Sole Owner: one with title to proprietorship.

Solvency: ability to pay one's debts in usual and ordinary course of business as they mature.

Special Material: made-to-order material or work done to customer's specifications that has no value to seller if order is canceled.

Special Mention Assets: as it relates to risk assessment of bank assets, assets that deserve management's close attention. If left uncorrected, these potential weaknesses may result in deterioration of repayment prospects for asset or in institution's credit position at some future date. Special mention assets are not adversely classified and do not expose institution to sufficient risk to warrant adverse classification.

Specific Coverage: property coverage on designated property or item. Contrasts with Blanket Coverage.

Specific Performance: court order directing party guilty of breach of contract to undertake complete performance of contractual obligation in instances in which damages would inadequately compensate injured party.

Speculation: investment made with hope of achieving large financial gain.

Speculator: one who makes risky investments for quick financial gain rather than long-term investment.

Stale Check: negotiable draft that has been held too long to be honored for payment; time varies from state to state.

Standard Industrial Classification (SIC): statistical classification standard underlying all establishment-based federal economic statistics classified by industry. SIC is used to promote comparability of establishment data describing various facets of the U.S. economy. Classification covers entire field of economic activities and defines industries in accordance with composition and structure of economy. It is revised periodically to reflect economy's changing industrial organization. See also *North American Industrial Classification System* and *NAICS*.

Standby Letter of Credit: type of letter of credit issued by bank that may be drawn on by payee only if party that makes letter of credit (drawer) defaults or does not perform according to terms of specific contract or agreement. See also Letter of Credit.

Statement: 1. itemized summary and accounting of charges, payments, and balance outstanding at close of billing period. 2. financial report.

Statement of Cash Flows: financial statement that shows cash receipts and disbursements for given period.

Statement of Changes in Owner's Equity: financial statement that reconciles changes in capital accounts (capital stock, paid in surplus, and retained earnings).

Statute: written law.

Statute of Frauds: law prohibiting filing of actions or suits against certain types of contracts unless the contracts are in writing.

Statute of Limitations: law that sets time frame for bringing action against another. Time frame varies according to nature of claim and jurisdiction.

Stay: act of arresting judicial proceeding by court order.

Stipulation: agreement between opposing attorneys in lawsuit, usually required to be in writing.

Stock: 1. merchandise or inventory on hand and available for sale. 2. certificate that indicates number of shares of ownership in corporation.

Stock Power: document executed in form of power of attorney by which owner of stock authorizes another party to sell or transfer stock.

Stop Payment Order: instructions given by depositor to a financial institution to dishonor, or not make payment on, a certain check.

Subchapter S: business concern chartered as corporation that is taxed as partnership. An S corporation has 35 or fewer shareholders and can use cash basis of accounting. Corporate gains (or losses) from operations are taxed to shareholders as individuals.

Subcontract: contract between prime contractor and another contractor or supplier to perform specified work or to supply specified materials in accordance with plans and specifications for project.

Subject: party on which credit information is requested.

Sublimit: specified, partial amount of credit facility that is designated for special use.

Subordination: 1. signed agreement acknowledging that one's claim or interest is inferior to another's. 2. act of agreeing to take secondary position.

Subpoena: process to demand person to appear in court and give testimony.

Subrogation: substitution of one creditor for another so that substituted creditor succeeds to rights, remedies, or proceeds of claim.

Subsidiary: business entity owned or controlled by another organization.

Substandard Assets: as it relates to risk assessment of bank assets, assets that are inadequately protected by current sound worth and paying capacity of obligor or of collateral pledged, if any. Assets so classified must have well-defined weakness or weaknesses that jeopardize liquidation of debt. They are

characterized by distinct possibility that bank will sustain some loss if ciencies are not corrected.

Summons: formal notice served on defendant stating that action has been tuted against him or her and requiring defendant to appear in court to a it.

Supplementary Proceedings: statutory action requiring judgment debt appear in court to discover property against which action can be tak creditor to enforce collection of judgment.

Supplier: business that sells goods, materials, or services to customers called vendor.

Surety: one who agrees to be primarily liable with another and to fulfill and obligations under terms of agreement.

Surety Bond: guaranty that payment or performance of some specific act completed under penalty or forfeiture of bond usually issued by a bo company.

Suretyship: undertaking by person or entity to pay obligation of obligee in of principal when obligee defaults; such undertaking by individual is kno personal suretyship and by insurance company as corporate suretyship.

Suspense File: group of accounts, records, or other items held temporaril final disposition is determined.

Swap: A financial derivative contract between two parties to exchange fixe interest payments for floating-rate interest payments, or floating-rate in payments on different bases (e.g., prime rate versus LIBOR), calculat specific floating indices by reference to a notional principal amount specified term.

Sweep Account: type of cash management tool in which, when prearr amount of cash accumulates in account, amount is automatically investe

Swindle: 1. to obtain money or property by deceitful misrepresentation. cheat or fraudulently induce individual to give up his or her property will

Swing Loan: see *Bridge Loan*.

Syndicate: temporary association of persons or firms formed to carry out ness venture or project of mutual interest.

Syndication: project financing whereby commercial or investment bankers to advance portion of funding. Syndicator acts as investment manage lecting loan origination fee or commitment fee from borrower and arra for sale to other banks in group. Typically, syndicator keeps only a sma tion of total financing. A syndicated loan differs from loan partici because syndicate members are known at outset to borrower. Syndi also separates lead bank from group of financial institutions that ultir fund obligation.

T

Takeover: acquisition, seizure, control, or management of one busine another.

Tangible Assets: assets that can be weighed, measured, or counted, inc cash, property, machinery, and buildings.

Tax: payments imposed by legislative authority for support of government a functions.

Taxable Income: portion of individual's or entity's income that is subject tc tion.

Tax Avoidance: act of using legal deductions, exemptions, and tax code sions to reduce taxes payable.

Tax Evasion: failure to report taxable income to avoid proper payment of ta

Tax Foreclosure: legal seizure and sale of property by authorized public offi satisfy unpaid taxes.

Tax Levy: legislative action by which tax is imposed.

Tax Lien: statutory claim by state or municipality against property of owing taxes. Property may be sold to satisfy obligation or judgmen against it.

Tax Sale: sale of property seized by governmental taxing body for nonpaym taxes.

Tenancy by Entirety: ownership in property by husband and wife in which becomes whole owner of the entire estate upon the other's death. Se Joint Tenancy with Rights of Survivorship.

Tenancy in Common: two or more persons who hold title to land or other erty in undivided ownership.

Tender: 1. unconditional offer of money or performance to satisfy claim. 2 to buy stock to take control of company.

Term Loan: fixed-term business loan with a maturity of more than one ye with defined periodic payments, providing borrower with working cap acquire assets or inventory or to finance plant and equipment.

Terms: conditions and requirements as set forth in sales proposal, contra promissory note.

Terms of Sale: mutually agreed upon conditions for transfer of title or own of goods or property.

Testimony: written or oral evidence given in court under oath.

Party: one who is not directly related to action between two parties but who ay be affected by its outcome.

Party Claim: demand made by person who is not party to action for delivy or possession of personal property, title to which is claimed by third party.

Deposit: 1. interest-bearing funds deposited in a financial institution for a ecified period of time, such as certificates of deposit and savings accounts. under Regulation D, deposit in which depositor is not permitted to make thdrawals within six days after date of deposit unless deposit is subject to rly withdrawal penalty.

Draft: draft payable on fixed date or certain number of days after sight or te of draft. See also *Banker's Acceptance, Draft, Letter of Credit*, and *Sight aft*.

document that evidences legal ownership and possession of property.

Company: business that as contracted researches specific property's history rough real estate records and issues policy to purchaser or lienholder guarteeing that there are no known defects in title.

nsurance: a guarantee by a title insurance company that it will indemnify e insured, in a specific amount, against losses resulting from defects in the e to a property. The insured may be the owner of the property, that person's irs and devises, or the lender and future assignees.

Search: to review history of property's ownership and any judgments or ns filed against it.

g the Statute: act of debtor to freeze statute of limitations that extends riod for creditor to legally enforce payment of account. Individual state laws d statutes apply.

iolation of legal duty that results in injury or damage to another.

Acceptance: draft; accepted by buyer, sent with shipment of goods, requir- customer to pay amount involved at specific date and place.

Credit: accounts payable; credit extended from one company to another.

Debts: liabilities due from one business to another for purchase of sup- es, inventory, etc.

in: property accepted by seller as partial down payment on purchase of w item.

Information: confidential exchange of payment history and credit informa- n among suppliers.

nark: distinctive identifying mark, word, or logo of product or service; pro- ted when registered with U.S. Patent Office.

Name: name used by a company to identify itself in the course of business. so known as Trade Style or Fictitious Name.

Payment Record: summary of performance of company in meeting terms its credit obligations.

References: names of suppliers or business creditors with whom credit ormation on customer can be exchanged.

ry Workstation: microcomputer-based information management system t allows corporate treasurer to automate daily balance reporting of col- ted balances, to invest idle funds in short-term money market, and to dis- rse funds to trade creditors. Overall aim is improvement in productivity and ntual integration of funds management and corporate accounting systems, h as order entry and invoicing.

alance: listing of all account balances from general ledger used in prepar- financial statements.

Jobber: wholesale merchant who sells and delivers products from truck entory at time of sale. Also called *Wagon Distributor*.

ight to real or personal property that is held by one for benefit of another.

Company: business that acts as fiduciary and agent, handling trusts, ates, and guardianships for individuals and businesses.

e: one who holds or is entrusted with management of property or funds for efit of another.

e in Bankruptcy: person appointed by court or elected by creditors to man- bankrupt property and carry out responsibilities of trust in proceedings.

Receipt: trust agreement (in receipt form) between a financial institution borrower. It is temporarily substituted for possessory collateral securing ditor's loan so that creditor may release instruments, documents, or other perty without releasing title to property. Borrower agrees to keep property llateral), as well as any funds received from its sale, separate and distinct n borrower's own property and subject to repossession by the financial titution in event that he or she fails to comply with conditions specified in st agreement.

Lending Act of 1968: See *Regulation Z*.

y: something that is constructed, supplied, or installed and fully ready as nded.

U

ee *Uniform Commercial Code*.

ires: unauthorized acts taken by corporation beyond powers conferred on y corporate charter.

Umbrella Policy: in liability insurance, policy that applies excess coverage to pri- mary or underlying contract; provides large limits and broad coverage or may cover only primary basis risks not otherwise insured.

Unaudited Financial Statement: financial statement or report based on figures that have not been verified by a qualified accountant.

Uncollected Funds: deposits not yet collected by a financial institution, such as checks that have not yet cleared.

Uncollectible Accounts: receivables or debts not capable of being settled or recovered.

Underwriter: 1. person who reviews application for insurance and decides whether or not to accept risk. 2. one who agrees to purchase entire issue of bonds or securities at end of certain period.

Undue Influence: improper or illegal pressure used to wrongfully take advantage of person or to influence his or her actions or decisions.

Unearned Discount: A term used to reflect a reduced price (from the face value of an invoice) taken by a buyer without the consent of the seller.

Unearned Income: income received in advance of being earned.

Unencumbered Property: property that has no legal defects in its title; a property free and clear of any liens or debts.

Unenforceable Claim: debt on which all collection efforts have failed.

Unfair Competition: any fraudulent or dishonest practice intended to harm or unfairly attract competitor's customers.

Uniform Commercial Code (UCC): comprehensive set of statutes created to pro- vide uniformity in business laws in all states, as approved by National Confer- ence of Commissioners on Uniform State Laws. Statutes can vary from state to state.

Unit Banking: banking system in several states that prohibits branching or opera- tion of more than one full-service banking office by state-chartered or national banks. Limited branching laws encourage chartering of large numbers of small, independently owned state banks and large multi-bank holding compa- nies that own numerous unit banks.

Unjust Enrichment: doctrine whereby one is not allowed to profit inequitably at another's expense.

Unsatisfied Judgment: recorded judgment that has not been released or dis- charged.

Unsecured Creditor: one who grants credit without taking collateral in support of it.

Unsecured Loan: loan made on strength of borrower's general financial condi- tion. Contrasts with Secured Loan.

Upstream Funding: funds borrowed by a subsidiary of a holding company for holding company's use. Contrasts with Downstream Funding.

Usury: The rate of interest that exceeds the legal limit allowed to be charged for the use of another's money. Legal limit of interest for different types of loan transactions is established by state law.

V

Valuable Consideration: see *Consideration*.

Valuation: 1. the estimated or determined worth of something. 2. process of appraising or affixing value of something.

Value Received: phrase used in bill of exchange or promissory note to denote that lawful consideration has been given.

Variable Interest Rate: interest rate that fluctuates with changes in an identified base rate or index.

Vendor: trade supplier or service provider.

Venture Capital: capital invested or available for investment in the ownership ele- ment of a new enterprise.

Verdict: formal decision of judge or jury on matter submitted in trial.

Verification: 1. affidavit or statement under oath swearing to truth or accuracy of written document. 2. in accounting, confirmation of entries in books of account.

Verification of Deposit (VOD): formal request by creditor to debtor's bank for account balance information.

Vest: 1. to give immediate transfer of title to property. 2. to obtain absolute own- ership.

VOD: see *Verification of Deposit*.

Void: having no legal force.

Voidable Contract: contract that is nullified as to party who committed invalid act but not with respect to other party, unless he or she agrees to treat it as such.

Voluntary Bankruptcy: bankruptcy initiated by debtor petitioning court to be declared bankrupt.

Voucher: 1. statement itemizing payment or receipt of money. 2. detachable por- tion of check that describes purpose for which check was issued.

W

Wage Assignment: agreement by borrower that permits creditor to collect certain portion of borrower's wages from employer in the event of a default.

Wage Garnishment: court order requiring that percentage of debtor's earnings be withheld by employer and paid directly to creditor.

Waiver: intentional or voluntary relinquishing of known legal right.

Warehouse Loans: loans made against warehouse receipts that are evidence of collateral for material stored in public warehouse.

Warehouse Receipt: receipt issued by person engaged in business of storing goods for hire. It is document of title that gives evidence that person in possession of warehouse receipt is entitled to receive, hold, and dispose of document and goods it covers. Warehouse receipt in turn obligates warehouser to keep goods safely and to redeliver them upon surrender of receipt, properly endorsed, and payment of storage charges.

Wholesaler: company whose primary function is as intermediary between manufacturer of goods and retailer or other wholesalers.

Will: legal declaration by person making disposition of property, effective only after death.

Windfall Profit: large, unexpected return or income.

Wire Fate: instructions to financial institution requesting confirmation by wire that out-of-town check, sent for collection, has been paid.

Without Exception: see *Free and Clear.*

Without Prejudice: legal term used in offer, motion, or suit to indicate that parties' rights or privileges involved remain intact and to allow new suit to be brought on same cause of action.

Without Recourse: term used in endorsing negotiable instrument excluding endorser from responsibility should obligation not be paid.

With Prejudice: legal term used for dismissal of lawsuit that bars any future action and that, if prosecuted to final adjudication, would have been adverse to plaintiff.

With Recourse: endorsement of negotiable instrument on which endorser remains responsible should obligation not be paid.

Working Capital: 1. current assets less current liabilities, used as measure of firm's liquidity. 2. funds available to finance company's current operations.

Working Papers: information or schedules used by accountant in preparing financial reports.

Work in Process (WIP): goods in act of being manufactured, but not yet finished and ready for sale, representing a portion of inventory.

Workout: problem loan on which the financial institution is working closely with borrower for repayment, restructuring, or modification because of noncompliance with loan covenants.

Wrap-Around Mortgage: A second or junior mortgage with a face value of both the amount it secures and the balance due under the first mortgage. Covenant contained within second mortgage used to induce sellers of commercial properties to sell to buyer who has small down payment, normally when interest rates are high.

Writ of Execution: 1. writ issued by court ordering sheriff to attach debtor's property to enforce payment of judgment.

Write-down: partial reduction in book value of asset as result of obsolescence or depreciation.

Write-off: see *Charge-off.*

Writ of Attachment: court order directing sheriff to seize property of debtor held as security for satisfaction of judgment.

Y

Yield: rate of return on investment.

Z

Zero Balance Account: a checking account (subordinate account) used for disbursing or collecting funds in which no balances are maintained. At the end of the processing day, funds are transferred from a master account or concentration account to cover activity in the subordinate account.

Zoning Ordinance: municipal regulation dividing land into districts and prescribing structural, architectural, and nature of use of buildings within these districts.

NOTES

NOTES

NOTES

NOTES